## 1999

### JANUARY
| S | M | T | W | T | F | S |
|---|---|---|---|---|---|---|
| | | | | | 1 | 2 |
| 3 | 4 | 5 | 6 | 7 | 8 | 9 |
| 10 | 11 | 12 | 13 | 14 | 15 | 16 |
| 17 | 18 | 19 | 20 | 21 | 22 | 23 |
| 24 | 25 | 26 | 27 | 28 | 29 | 30 |
| 31 | | | | | | |

### FEBRUARY
| S | M | T | W | T | F | S |
|---|---|---|---|---|---|---|
| | 1 | 2 | 3 | 4 | 5 | 6 |
| 7 | 8 | 9 | 10 | 11 | 12 | 13 |
| 14 | 15 | 16 | 17 | 18 | 19 | 20 |
| 21 | 22 | 23 | 24 | 25 | 26 | 27 |
| 28 | | | | | | |

### MARCH
| S | M | T | W | T | F | S |
|---|---|---|---|---|---|---|
| | 1 | 2 | 3 | 4 | 5 | 6 |
| 7 | 8 | 9 | 10 | 11 | 12 | 13 |
| 14 | 15 | 16 | 17 | 18 | 19 | 20 |
| 21 | 22 | 23 | 24 | 25 | 26 | 27 |
| 28 | 29 | 30 | 31 | | | |

### APRIL
| S | M | T | W | T | F | S |
|---|---|---|---|---|---|---|
| | | | | 1 | 2 | 3 |
| 4 | 5 | 6 | 7 | 8 | 9 | 10 |
| 11 | 12 | 13 | 14 | 15 | 16 | 17 |
| 18 | 19 | 20 | 21 | 22 | 23 | 24 |
| 25 | 26 | 27 | 28 | 29 | 30 | |

### MAY
| S | M | T | W | T | F | S |
|---|---|---|---|---|---|---|
| | | | | | | 1 |
| 2 | 3 | 4 | 5 | 6 | 7 | 8 |
| 9 | 10 | 11 | 12 | 13 | 14 | 15 |
| 16 | 17 | 18 | 19 | 20 | 21 | 22 |
| 23 | 24 | 25 | 26 | 27 | 28 | 29 |
| 30 | 31 | | | | | |

### JUNE
| S | M | T | W | T | F | S |
|---|---|---|---|---|---|---|
| | | 1 | 2 | 3 | 4 | 5 |
| 6 | 7 | 8 | 9 | 10 | 11 | 12 |
| 13 | 14 | 15 | 16 | 17 | 18 | 19 |
| 20 | 21 | 22 | 23 | 24 | 25 | 26 |
| 27 | 28 | 29 | 30 | | | |

### JULY
| S | M | T | W | T | F | S |
|---|---|---|---|---|---|---|
| | | | | 1 | 2 | 3 |
| 4 | 5 | 6 | 7 | 8 | 9 | 10 |
| 11 | 12 | 13 | 14 | 15 | 16 | 17 |
| 18 | 19 | 20 | 21 | 22 | 23 | 24 |
| 25 | 26 | 27 | 28 | 29 | 30 | 31 |

### AUGUST
| S | M | T | W | T | F | S |
|---|---|---|---|---|---|---|
| 1 | 2 | 3 | 4 | 5 | 6 | 7 |
| 8 | 9 | 10 | 11 | 12 | 13 | 14 |
| 15 | 16 | 17 | 18 | 19 | 20 | 21 |
| 22 | 23 | 24 | 25 | 26 | 27 | 28 |
| 29 | 30 | 31 | | | | |

### SEPTEMBER
| S | M | T | W | T | F | S |
|---|---|---|---|---|---|---|
| | | | 1 | 2 | 3 | 4 |
| 5 | 6 | 7 | 8 | 9 | 10 | 11 |
| 12 | 13 | 14 | 15 | 16 | 17 | 18 |
| 19 | 20 | 21 | 22 | 23 | 24 | 25 |
| 26 | 27 | 28 | 29 | 30 | | |

### OCTOBER
| S | M | T | W | T | F | S |
|---|---|---|---|---|---|---|
| | | | | | 1 | 2 |
| 3 | 4 | 5 | 6 | 7 | 8 | 9 |
| 10 | 11 | 12 | 13 | 14 | 15 | 16 |
| 17 | 18 | 19 | 20 | 21 | 22 | 23 |
| 24 | 25 | 26 | 27 | 28 | 29 | 30 |
| 31 | | | | | | |

### NOVEMBER
| S | M | T | W | T | F | S |
|---|---|---|---|---|---|---|
| | 1 | 2 | 3 | 4 | 5 | 6 |
| 7 | 8 | 9 | 10 | 11 | 12 | 13 |
| 14 | 15 | 16 | 17 | 18 | 19 | 20 |
| 21 | 22 | 23 | 24 | 25 | 26 | 27 |
| 28 | 29 | 30 | | | | |

### DECEMBER
| S | M | T | W | T | F | S |
|---|---|---|---|---|---|---|
| | | | 1 | 2 | 3 | 4 |
| 5 | 6 | 7 | 8 | 9 | 10 | 11 |
| 12 | 13 | 14 | 15 | 16 | 17 | 18 |
| 19 | 20 | 21 | 22 | 23 | 24 | 25 |
| 26 | 27 | 28 | 29 | 30 | 31 | |

## 2000

### JANUARY
| S | M | T | W | T | F | S |
|---|---|---|---|---|---|---|
| | | | | | | 1 |
| 2 | 3 | 4 | 5 | 6 | 7 | 8 |
| 9 | 10 | 11 | 12 | 13 | 14 | 15 |
| 16 | 17 | 18 | 19 | 20 | 21 | 22 |
| 23 | 24 | 25 | 26 | 27 | 28 | 29 |
| 30 | 31 | | | | | |

### FEBRUARY
| S | M | T | W | T | F | S |
|---|---|---|---|---|---|---|
| | | 1 | 2 | 3 | 4 | 5 |
| 6 | 7 | 8 | 9 | 10 | 11 | 12 |
| 13 | 14 | 15 | 16 | 17 | 18 | 19 |
| 20 | 21 | 22 | 23 | 24 | 25 | 26 |
| 27 | 28 | 29 | | | | |

### MARCH
| S | M | T | W | T | F | S |
|---|---|---|---|---|---|---|
| | | | 1 | 2 | 3 | 4 |
| 5 | 6 | 7 | 8 | 9 | 10 | 11 |
| 12 | 13 | 14 | 15 | 16 | 17 | 18 |
| 19 | 20 | 21 | 22 | 23 | 24 | 25 |
| 26 | 27 | 28 | 29 | 30 | 31 | |

### APRIL
| S | M | T | W | T | F | S |
|---|---|---|---|---|---|---|
| | | | | | | 1 |
| 2 | 3 | 4 | 5 | 6 | 7 | 8 |
| 9 | 10 | 11 | 12 | 13 | 14 | 15 |
| 16 | 17 | 18 | 19 | 20 | 21 | 22 |
| 23 | 24 | 25 | 26 | 27 | 28 | 29 |
| 30 | | | | | | |

### MAY
| S | M | T | W | T | F | S |
|---|---|---|---|---|---|---|
| | 1 | 2 | 3 | 4 | 5 | 6 |
| 7 | 8 | 9 | 10 | 11 | 12 | 13 |
| 14 | 15 | 16 | 17 | 18 | 19 | 20 |
| 21 | 22 | 23 | 24 | 25 | 26 | 27 |
| 28 | 29 | 30 | 31 | | | |

### JUNE
| S | M | T | W | T | F | S |
|---|---|---|---|---|---|---|
| | | | | 1 | 2 | 3 |
| 4 | 5 | 6 | 7 | 8 | 9 | 10 |
| 11 | 12 | 13 | 14 | 15 | 16 | 17 |
| 18 | 19 | 20 | 21 | 22 | 23 | 24 |
| 25 | 26 | 27 | 28 | 29 | 30 | |

### JULY
| S | M | T | W | T | F | S |
|---|---|---|---|---|---|---|
| | | | | | | 1 |
| 2 | 3 | 4 | 5 | 6 | 7 | 8 |
| 9 | 10 | 11 | 12 | 13 | 14 | 15 |
| 16 | 17 | 18 | 19 | 20 | 21 | 22 |
| 23 | 24 | 25 | 26 | 27 | 28 | 29 |
| 30 | 31 | | | | | |

### AUGUST
| S | M | T | W | T | F | S |
|---|---|---|---|---|---|---|
| | | 1 | 2 | 3 | 4 | 5 |
| 6 | 7 | 8 | 9 | 10 | 11 | 12 |
| 13 | 14 | 15 | 16 | 17 | 18 | 19 |
| 20 | 21 | 22 | 23 | 24 | 25 | 26 |
| 27 | 28 | 29 | 30 | 31 | | |

### SEPTEMBER
| S | M | T | W | T | F | S |
|---|---|---|---|---|---|---|
| | | | | | 1 | 2 |
| 3 | 4 | 5 | 6 | 7 | 8 | 9 |
| 10 | 11 | 12 | 13 | 14 | 15 | 16 |
| 17 | 18 | 19 | 20 | 21 | 22 | 23 |
| 24 | 25 | 26 | 27 | 28 | 29 | 30 |

### OCTOBER
| S | M | T | W | T | F | S |
|---|---|---|---|---|---|---|
| 1 | 2 | 3 | 4 | 5 | 6 | 7 |
| 8 | 9 | 10 | 11 | 12 | 13 | 14 |
| 15 | 16 | 17 | 18 | 19 | 20 | 21 |
| 22 | 23 | 24 | 25 | 26 | 27 | 28 |
| 29 | 30 | 31 | | | | |

### NOVEMBER
| S | M | T | W | T | F | S |
|---|---|---|---|---|---|---|
| | | | 1 | 2 | 3 | 4 |
| 5 | 6 | 7 | 8 | 9 | 10 | 11 |
| 12 | 13 | 14 | 15 | 16 | 17 | 18 |
| 19 | 20 | 21 | 22 | 23 | 24 | 25 |
| 26 | 27 | 28 | 29 | 30 | | |

### DECEMBER
| S | M | T | W | T | F | S |
|---|---|---|---|---|---|---|
| | | | | | 1 | 2 |
| 3 | 4 | 5 | 6 | 7 | 8 | 9 |
| 10 | 11 | 12 | 13 | 14 | 15 | 16 |
| 17 | 18 | 19 | 20 | 21 | 22 | 23 |
| 24 | 25 | 26 | 27 | 28 | 29 | 30 |
| 31 | | | | | | |

# CANADIAN ALMANAC & DIRECTORY 1998

## Also Published by ...

## Copp Clark Professional

**ASSOCIATIONS CANADA 1997/98: An Encyclopedic Directory/ Un Répertoire encyclopédique**
1608 pages, 8 1/2 x 11, Hardcover
7th edition, April, 1997

ISBN 1 895021 28 6

Over 20,000 entries profile Canadian and international organizations active in Canada. Over 3,000 subject classifications index activities, professions and interests served by associations. Includes listings of NGO's, institutes, coalitions, social agencies, federations, foundations, trade unions, fraternal orders, political parties. Organizational profiles are included for major organizations. Entries typically include professional staff, elected officials, membership profiles, services provided, resource centres, publications and convention details. Subject, geographic, alphabetic, executive name, acronym, mailing list indexes are included for easy reference, as is an association events awareness calendar.

**CANADIAN ENVIRONMENTAL DIRECTORY 1997/98**
1584 pages, 8 1/2 X 11, Hardcover
7th edition, June, 1997

ISBN 1 895021 29 4

The complete network of government agencies, associations, law firms, consulting firms, research and educational establishments involved in environment-related activities. A variety of indexes assist in locating specific subjects and issues with links to government and association contacts at all levels. Information Services provide a select bibliography, journalists, conferences, trade shows, awards, funding programs. A Directory of Products & Services categorizes the country's major suppliers of environmental products and services.

**FINANCIAL SERVICES CANADA 1998**
768 pages, 8 1/2 x 11, Hardcover.
1st edition, November, 1997

ISBN 1 895021 34 0

This new directory of Canadian financial institutions and organizations includes banks, trust companies and other depository institutions, non-depository institutions, investment management firms, mutual funds, stock exchanges, financial planners, insurance companies, accountants, major law firms, government and regulatory agencies, associations. Indexed by company name, location, executive name, website/ Email.

**THE REGISTER OF CANADIAN HONOURS/ Registre des distinctions honorifiques canadiennes**
448 pages, 8 1/2 x 11, illustrated, Hardcover.
1991

ISBN 1 895021 01 4 - regular edition.
ISBN 1 895021 06 5 - deluxe leatherbound edition.

This authorized directory of Canada's honours system includes listings of all members of The Order of Canada with their citations; The Order of Military Merit; Decorations for Bravery with the record of deeds; Exemplary Service and all other medals. Colour inserts depict all medals and their order of precedence. All armorial bearings created by the Canadian Heraldic Authority are included.

# CANADIAN ALMANAC & DIRECTORY 1998

CANADIAN 151st YEAR ALMANAC

COPP CLARK PROFESSIONAL

*Toronto*

**Distribution**

**U.S.A. and its possessions:** Gale Research Company, Book Tower, Detroit, Michigan 48226

**U.K. and Europe:** William Snyder Publishing Associates, 5, Five Mile Dr., Oxford 0X2 8HT, England

**Australia and New Zealand:** D.W. Thorpe, 271-273 Lane Cove Road, North Ryde, 2113, Australia

| | |
|---|---|
| EDITORIAL DIRECTOR: | Ann Marie Aldighieri |
| ASSOC. EDITORIAL DIRECTOR: | Peter Asselstine |
| EDITORS: | Beata Kulesza<br>Ward McBurney<br>Alison McNeil<br>Patrick Mullin<br>Anthony Sraka<br>Susan Traer |
| EDITORIAL ASSISTANT: | Shie-Mee Yeh |
| SYSTEMS MANAGER: | Ruth Watkins |
| PROGRAMMER: | Evangeline Landry |
| PRODUCTION CO-ORDINATOR: | Dana Bailey |

Astronomical Calculations: John R. Percy, Ph.D.
British & Commonwealth Honours: Maj. (Ret.) Richard K. Malott, C.D., M.Sc., B.A., F.R.P.S.C.
Forms of Address: Michael Measures

Design by *Artplus*
Translations by *In Other Words...*

**Dedicated to Publisher Frederick D. Wardle, with thanks from the Canadian Almanac team for years of guidance and encouragement.**

Every effort has been made to ensure that the information contained in this book is accurate and complete on publication date. The publisher cannot be held liable for errors or omissions.

Users of the *Almanac* are invited to make suggestions concerning information that might be added to future editions or changes to the presentation of listings and information that might make the book more useful. Please contact the Editor. Thanks to all who respond to our annual requests for information, and to all contriubutors, editorial, systems & production teams.

ISBN 1-895021-35-9

Copp Clark Professional
200 Adelaide St. West, 3rd Fl., Toronto, ON M5H 1W7
(416) 597-1616; Fax (416) 597-1617; Email: info@mail.CanadaInfo.com;
URL: http://www.canadainfo.com

Printed and bound in Canada by Tri-Graphic Printing (Ottawa) Ltd.

Canadian Cataloguing in Publication Data
The National Library of Canada has catalogued this publication as follows:

Main entry under title:

Canadian almanac & directory

Annual.
101st- year; 1948-
Also available on microfiche from: Toronto: Micromedia.
ISSN 0068-8193
ISBN 1-895021-35-9 (1998)

1. Almanacs, Canadian. 2. Canada - Directories. I. Title: Canadian almanac & directory.
AY414.C2 971'.0025 C75-032392-2

# INTRODUCTION

The *Canadian Almanac & Directory* is the longest running publishing success in Canadian history. It has been a bestseller every year since 1847. We hope that you will solve many of your information needs with this edition.

1997 marked the 150$^{th}$ anniversary of this work. It was an important year in which we changed the organization of information and the format of the bound volume. We thank our loyal supporters for their acceptance of the changes and for making 1997 the best sales year in the history of the *Almanac*. The 150$^{th}$ edition won the prestigious Cowles-Simba Award for editorial excellence in directory publishing. Editorial Director, Ann Marie Aldighieri accepted the award on behalf of all her editors at the U.S. National Directory Conference in Boston last September. We hope that you will find this 151$^{st}$ edition a fitting further refinement in the quest for current, accurate information.

This edition will be my last as publisher giving me cause for reflection. I first discovered the *Canadian Almanac & Directory* on joining McGraw Hill Canada in 1962. That firm, like countless others today, relied on the *Almanac* for myriad editorial, administrative and sales promotion uses. I became addicted.

From a chance encounter in 1983 with Copp Clark's president, Steve Mills, I undertook to market the *Almanac* on behalf of Copp Clark and in 1989 established a company to further develop the work and to create new Canadian directories. I continued my involvement with the *Almanac* through a 1996 Copp Clark restructuring. I am privileged then, to have managed the evolution of the *Almanac* over the past 15 years from card-indexed data sets to a new series of relational databases that contain many times the information first cobbled together by Hugh Scobie. I am proud to have assisted in creating the *Almanac's* foundation for the electronic future that will witness new indexing and retrieval methods just being imagined.

Ann Marie Aldighieri continues as the editorial director of this important multivariate work. Her skills have refined and developed the *Almanac* through eight editions, five as editorial director. I know that her determined leadership will continue the tradition of editorial excellence that she has fostered. Look to the exceptional *Canadian Almanac* team for continued authority in Canadian information publishing

*Frederick David Wardle*
*December, 1997*

Le *Canadian Alamanac & Directory* est la publication à succès ayant la plus longue parution continue dans l'histoire de l'édition au Canada. C'est un "best-seller" depuis 1847. Nous espérons qu'avec cette édition, vous trouverez la solution à nombre de vos besoins de renseignements.

L'année 1997 marque le 150$^{eme}$ anniversaire de cet ouvrage. Ce fut une année marquante durant laquelle nous avons modifié l'organisation de l'information et le format du volume relié. Nous remercions nos fidèles supporteurs pour leur acceptation de ces changements et pour avoir fait de 1997 la meilleure année à date pour les ventes dans l'histoire de *l'Almanac*. Cette 150$^{eme}$ édition s'est vu décerner le prestigieux Cowles-Simba Award pour l'excellence de sa rédaction dans la catégorie des publications de répertoires. Notre Rédactrice en chef, Ann Marie Aldighieri, accepta le prix au nom de tous ses rédacteurs lors de la National Directory Conference tenue à Boston en septembre dernier. Nous espérons que cette 151$^{eme}$ édition sera un outil raffiné, approprié à votre recherche de renseignements courants et précis.

Comme cette édition sera la dernière à laquelle je participerai en tant qu'éditeur, j'y trouve une occasion de retour en arrière. J'ai découvert le *Canadian Almanac & Directory* lors de mon emploi chez McGraw Hill Canada en 1962. Cette entreprise, comme des milliers d'autres aujourd'hui, se basait su *l'Almanac* pour une myriade d'utilisations en rédaction, en administration et pour la promotion des ventes. C'est là que je suis devenu un "mordu".

Suivant une rencontre fortuite en 1983 avec le président de Copp Clark, Steve Mills, j'ai entrepris la mise en marchéde *l'Almanac* au nom de Copp Clark et, en 1989, j'ai fondéune compagnie qui voyait au développement de ce volume et à la création de nouveaux répertoires canadiens. Mon implication avec *l'Almanac* continua lors de la restructuration de Copp Clark en 1996. Je me sens privilégié d'avoir dirigé l'évolution de *l'Almanac* au cours des 15 dernières années, passant d'un système de données sur cartes indexées à une nouvelle série de banques de données relationnelles qui contiennent une quantité de renseignements plusieurs fois supérieurs à ceux amassés au tout début par Hugh Scobie. Je suis fier d'avoir participé à la création de la base de l'avenir électronique de *l'Almanac*, un avenir qui verra des méthodes d'indexation et de récupération qui sont encore aujourd'hui au stade de l'imaginaire.

Ann Marie Aldighieri continuera son travail comme rédactrice en chef de cet important ouvrage à facettes multiples. Ses connaissances ont contribuéau développement et au raffinement de *l'Almanac* au cours des huit dernières éditions, dont cinq comme rédactrice en chef. Je sais que son leadership précis verra à continuer la tradition d'excellence en rédaction qu'elle a favorisée. Soyez assurés que l'équipe exceptionnelle du *Canadian Alamanac & Directory* fera en sorte de demeurer au premier plan de la publication de renseignements sur la société canadienne.

*Frederick David Wardle*
*Décembre 1997*

# CONTENTS

See ADDENDA at the back of this book for late changes & additional information.

# TOPICAL TABLE OF CONTENTS

**For detailed references, *see* Index.**

**For late changes, *see* Addenda.**

# ALPHABETICAL FASTFINDER



**Page numbers in boldface refer to the illustrated section found in the centre of the book.**

# TABLE DES MATIÈRES PAR SUJETS

**Pour référence detailée *voir* l'Index.**

**Pour modifications de dernière heure *voir* l'Addenda.**

# RAPIDINDEX ALPHABÉTIQUE



**Les numéros de page en caractères gros font référence à la section illustrée au milieu du livre.**

# SECTION 1

## ALMANAC & MISCELLANY



**See ADDENDA at the back of this book for late changes & additional information.**

## ASTRONOMICAL CALCULATIONS

**Prepared for this publication by John R. Percy, Ph.D., of the David Dunlap Observatory and Erindale College, University of Toronto.**

### ASTRONOMY IN CANADA

Canada possesses a number of major observatories and research institutes devoted to various aspects of astronomy. Some of these are operated by the National Research Council of Canada, others by Canadian universities. There are also planetariums and other facilities for astronomy education.

Astronomical research in the National Research Council is carried out by the Herzberg Institute of Astrophysics, which operates the following observatories: The Dominion Astrophysical Observatory at Victoria, with optical telescopes of 1.8m and 1.2m aperture; and the Dominion Radio Astrophysical Observatory near Penticton, which has a 26m paraboloid and a 7-element array of 9m antennae. The National Research Council also maintains Canada's Time Service in its Institute of National Measurement Standards. The Canadian Astronomy Data Centre is located at the Dominion Astrophysical Observatory.

A number of Canadian universities offer graduate education in astronomy: Victoria, British Columbia (Vancouver), Alberta (Edmonton), Calgary, Western Ontario (London), Waterloo, McMaster (Hamilton), York (Toronto), Toronto, Queen's (Kingston), Montréal, Laval (Québec), and St. Mary's (Halifax). Most of these have some local facilities for observational and theoretical studies, and all of them have access to national facilities in Canada and elsewhere. Among the major observatories operated by Canadian universities are: an infrared telescope opened in 1987 by the University of Calgary; a 1.2m telescope at the University of Western Ontario; a 1.9m telescope at the University of Toronto's David Dunlap Observatory in Richmond Hill, and a 0.6m telescope at its Las Campanas Observatory in the Chilean Andes; and a 1.5m telescope at the Mont Mégantic Observatory operated by the University of Montréal, and Laval University. There is also a Canadian Institute for Theoretical Astrophysics located at the University of Toronto.

Through the National Research Council, Canadian astronomers also have access to several international facilities. One of these is the 3.6m Canada-France-Hawaii optical telescope atop Mauna Kea on the island of Hawaii, at an elevation of nearly 4200m. This telescope is shared, both as to cost and operation, by Canada, France, and the state of Hawaii. Canadian astronomers also share (with the Netherlands and the UK) in the operation of the James Clerk Maxwell telescope, a sophisticated millimetre-wave radio telescope at the same site. Canada also is a partner, along with several other countries, in the twin Gemini 8m telescopes, which are under construction in Hawaii and in Chile.

### OBSERVATORIES

Observatories are open to the public as follows:

**Burke-Gaffney Observatory**
St. Mary's University, Halifax NS B3H 3C3
902/420-5633, 5896. URL: http://apwww.stmarys.ca/bgo/bgo.html
Public tours are held on the 1st & 3rd Sat. of each month at 7:00 p.m. (Nov.-Mar.) or 9:00 p.m. (Apr.-Oct.), weather permitting. Tours are held every Saturday evening from June through September. Mon. evenings or daytime groups by arrangement.

**Canada-France-Hawaii Telescope**
Mauna Kea, Hawaii, USA
808/885-7288; Fax: 808/885-7288; URL: http://www.cfht.hawaii.edu
By appointment only.

**Climenhaga Observatory**
Dept. of Physics & Astronomy, University of Victoria, PO Box 3055, Victoria BC V8W 3P6
604/721-7747

**David Dunlap Observatory**
Richmond Hill ON L4C 4Y6
905/884-2112. URL: http://www.astro.utoronto.ca/ddo-home.html
Wed. mornings: 10:00 a.m.; Sat. evenings Apr.-Oct. by reservation.

**Dominion Astrophysical Observatory**
5071 West Saanich Road, Victoria BC V8X 4M6
250/363-0001; Fax: 250/363-0045; URL: http://www.dao.nrc.ca
May-Aug.: daily 9:15 a.m. - 4:30 p.m.; Sept.-Apr.: Mon.-Fri., 9:15 a.m. - 4:30 p.m.; public observing, Sat. evenings, Apr.-Oct. inclusive.

**Dominion Radio Astrophysical Observatory**
Penticton BC V2A 6K3
250/490-4355; Fax: 250/493-7767; URL: http://www.drao.nrc.ca
Conducted tours: Sun., July-Aug.: 2:00 - 5:00 p.m. Visitors' Centre open year round during daylight hours.

**Hume Cronyn Observatory**
Dept. of Physics & Astronomy, University of Western Ontario, London ON N6A 3K7
519/661-3183; Fax: 519/661-2033; URL: http://phobos.astro.uwo.ca/dept/observatories.html
Summer open houses (slide show, followed by viewing of the sky through the 25cm refractor, weather permitting) are held each Saturday evening from mid-May until the end of August, 8:30 - 11:00 p.m. A winter public night program is available to groups and individuals by appointment.

**National Museum of Science & Technology**
1867 St. Laurent Blvd., Ottawa ON K1G 5A3
613/991-9219
38cm refractor (from the former Dominion Observatory), Starlab planetarium. "Discover the Universe" by appointment only, rain or shine. Oct.-May: group tours, Mon.-Thu.; phone for dates and times of public visits throughout the year.

**Observatoire Astronomique Du Mont Mégantic**
Notre-Dame-des-Bois QC J0B 2E0

514/343-6718; URL: http://www.astro.umontreal.ca/omm/omm_eng.html
Summer programs.

**Rothney Astrophysical Observatory**
Dept. of Physics & Astronomy, University of Calgary, 2500 University Dr. NW, Calgary AB T2N 1N4
403/220-5410; URL: http://www.ucalgary.ca/~milone/rao.html
Monthly open house, late spring and summer.

**Science North Solar Observatory**
100 Ramsey Lake Rd., Sudbury ON P3E 5S9
705/522-3701
Open every day except Christmas Day, Boxing Day & New Year's Day.

**Gordon Macmillan Southam Observatory**
Pacific Space Centre, 1100 Chestnut St., Vancouver BC V6J 3J9
604/738-STAR; Fax: 604/736-5665; URL: http://pacific-space-centre.bc.ca
Open weekends, weather and volunteers permitting. Extended hours during school holidays.

**University of Alberta Observatory**
Dept. of Physics, University of Alberta, Edmonton AB T6G 2J1
403/492-5286; Email: observatory@phys.ualberta.ca
The observatory is usually open Thursday evenings during the academic year, except for holidays, and weeks during which exams are scheduled.

**University of British Columbia Observatory**
2219 Main Mall, Vancouver BC V6T 1Z4
604/822-6186; Tours by appointment: 604/822-2217; Fax: 604/822-6047; URL: http://www.physics.ubc.ca
Clear Saturday evenings, year round.

**University of Saskatchewan Observatory**
Dept. of Physics & Engineering Physics, University of Saskatchewan, 116 Science Place, Saskatoon SK S7N 5E2
306/966-6429; Fax: 306/966-6400; URL: http://www.usask.ca/cgi-bin/people/observatory/WebEvent/WebEvent
Saturday evening programs year round; times vary. School groups by appointment.

**York University Observatory**
4700 Keele St., North York ON M3J 1P3
416/736-2100, ext. 77773 (recorded message)
Public viewing most Wednesday evenings.

There are the following planetariums, mostly with daily shows:

**Calgary Science Centre**
Box 2100, Calgary AB T2P 2M5
403/221-3700; Fax: 403/237-0186; Email: discover@calgaryscience.ca
Interactive exhibitions, super 70mm films, and multi-media.

**Doran Planetarium**
Laurentian University, Ramsey Lake Rd., Sudbury ON P3E 2C6
705/675-1151, ext. 2227 (reservations); URL: http://www.laurentian.ca/www/physics/Planetarium/planetarium.html

**Edmonton Space & Science Centre**
Coronation Park, Edmonton AB T5M 4A1
403/451-3344 (program information); Fax: 403/455-5882; URL: http://www.ee.ualberta.ca/essc
The Edmonton Space & Science Centre, where science comes alive, provides opportunities for the community to explore the world and beyond, in an educational and entertaining manner.

**The Halifax Planetarium**
The Nova Scotia Museum of Natural History, 1747 Summer St., Halifax NS B3H 3A6
902/424-7353; Fax: 902/424-0560

**The Lockhart Planetarium**
394 University College, 220 Dysart Rd., Winnipeg MB R3T 2M8
204/474-9785

**Manitoba Planetarium**
190 Rupert Ave., Winnipeg MB R3B 0N2
204/943-3142 (recorded information); Fax: 204/942-3679; Email: info@museummannature.mb.ca

**W.J. McCallion Planetarium**
Dept. of Physics & Astronomy, McMaster University, 1280 Main St., Hamilton ON L8S 4M1
905/525-9140, ext. 27777; Fax: 905/546-1252

**Ontario Science Centre**
770 Don Mills Road, North York ON M3C 1T3.
416/696-3127; Fax: 416/696-3197; URL: http://www.osc.on.ca
Open daily except Christmas Day.

**Pacific Space Centre Planetarium**
1100 Chestnut St., Vancouver BC V6J 3J9.
604/738-STAR, Fax: 604/736-5665; URL: http://pacific-space-centre.bc.ca
Includes planetarium, motion simulator, and exhibit gallery.

**Planetarium de Montréal**
Montréal QC H3C 1G7
514/872-4530; Fax: 514/872-8102; URL: http://www.planetarium.montreal.qc.ca

Many of Canada's professional astronomers, and most of Canada's enthusiastic amateur astronomers are members of the Royal Astronomical Society of Canada (see index) which has 22 Centres across Canada. A complete list of astronomy clubs in Canada was published in the May/June 1997 issue of SkyNews (see Suggestions for Further Reading). Many of these clubs have programs for the general public.

Most of Canada's professional astronomers belong to the Canadian Astronomical Society (see index).

## THE CALENDAR

The calendar is a method of identifying the passage of time and thereby regulating our civil life and religious observances.

Days, months, and years are based on astronomical periods. The day is the time it takes the earth to make one revolution on its axis, the month is associated with the period of orbiting of the moon around the earth, while the year has to do with the orbiting of the earth around the sun.

Many religious ideas and observances have been connected with the changes of the moon, and in ancient times the calendar took account of the moon rather than the seasons. From new moon to new moon is 29.530 days, and from one spring equinox to the next is 365.24219 days. Since the two are incommensurable, the modern calendar disregards the moon, except insofar as our months are roughly equal to a lunation.

### The Week

The division of the week is found only among Aryan nations and in nations and in regions into which they have penetrated. The day is, for convenience, divided into 24 equal parts and is the period of a single rotation of the earth upon its own axis.

A solar or astronomical day commences at midnight, and is divided into two equal portions of 12 hours each — those before noon being termed (A.M.) those after noon (P.M.).

The Chinese week consists of 5 days, which are named after iron, wood, water, feathers and earth; they divide the day into 12 parts of 2 hours each.

The Anglo-Saxons named the days of the week after the following deities: Sunday, the Sun; Monday, the Moon; Tuesday, Tuesco (God of War); Wednesday, Woden (God of Storms); Thursday, Thor (God of Thunder); Friday, Freya (Goddess of Love); Saturday, Saturn (God of Time).

The word week is from Wikon (German); = change, succession.

### The Julian Calendar

When Julius Caesar came to power, the Roman Calendar was hopelessly confused. With the advice of the Alexandrian astronomer Sosigenes, Julius Caesar established the Julian Calendar. The length of the year was taken as 365 1/4 days, and in order to account for the 1/4 day, an extra day was added every fourth year. From 45 B.C. each month has had its present number of days. In the old Roman Calendar which was based on the moon an extra month was inserted to straighten out the difference between twelve lunations 354.37 days, and 355 days, which they called a year. This was inserted when necessary after February 23rd. In the Julian Calendar the extra day was added by repeating the sixth day before the Kalends (1st) of March, whence comes our word bissextile for leap year.

No very significant change was made till the reform by Pope Gregory XIII in A.D. 1582.

The Julian Calendar is known as the "Old Style" whereas the calendar as improved by Pope Gregory is known as the "New Style". The difference between the two is now 13 days.

### The Gregorian Calendar

In that the Solar Year is 11 minutes, 12 seconds less than the Julian Year of 365 1/4 days, it followed in course of years that the Julian Calendar became inaccurate by several days, and in 1582 this difference amounted to 10 days. Pope Gregory XIII, at the suggestion of Aloysius Lilus, an astronomer of Naples, determined to rectify this, and devised the Calendar now known as the Gregorian Calendar. He dropped or cancelled these 10 days — October 5th being called October 15th — and made centurial years leap years only once in 4 centuries; so that whilst 1700, 1800 and 1900 were to be ordinary years 2000, would be leap year. This modification brought the Gregorian year into such close exactitude with the solar year that there is only a difference of 26 seconds, which amounts to a day in 3,323 years. This is the "New Style". The Gregorian Calendar was adopted in Italy, France, Spain, Portugal and Poland in 1582, by most of the German Roman Catholic states, Holland and Flanders in 1583, Hungary in 1587. The adoption in Switzerland began in 1584 and was not completed till 1812. The German and Dutch Protestant states generally, along with Denmark adopted it in 1700, British dominions in 1752, Sweden in 1753, Japan in 1873, China in 1912, Bulgaria in 1915, Soviet Russia in 1918, Yugoslavia in 1919, Romania and Greece in 1924, Turkey in 1927. The rules for Easter have not, however, been adopted by those oriental churches that are not subject to the Papacy.

The difference between the two "Styles" will remain 13 days until A.D. 2100.

### The Jewish Calendar

The Jewish Calendar from the institution of the Mosaic Law downward was a lunar one, consisting of twelve months. The cycles of religious feasts commencing with the Passover depended not only on the month but on the moon; the 14th of the month of Abid or Nisan was coincident with the full moon; and the new

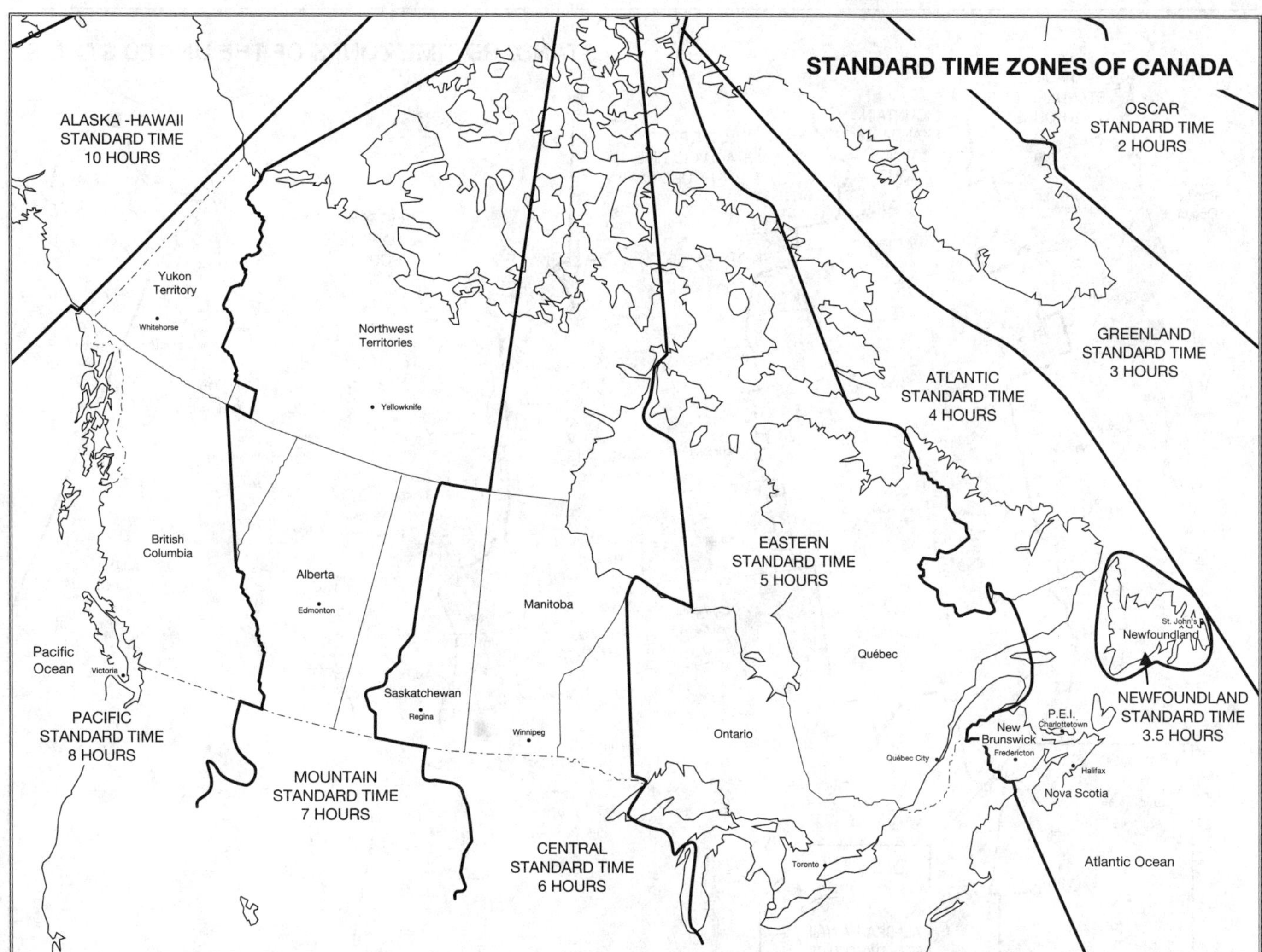


moons themselves were the occasions of regular festivals; the commencement of the month was generally determined by observations of the new moon, but twelve lunar months would make but 354 1/2 days, the years would be short twelve days of the true year and it was necessary that an additional month, Veader, be inserted about every third year.

The modern Jewish Calendar is based on fixed rules and not on observation. A common year may contain 353, 354 or 355 days and the leap year 383, 384 or 385 days. The intercalary month always contains 30 days and is inserted next before the month Adar which name and place it takes, Adar itself called second Adar or Veadar. Tishri 1 is the Jewish New Year and it cannot be a Sunday, Wednesday or Friday. Tishri 1 is not necessarily the day of new moon but is governed by a mean new moon which is calculated from the value of a mean lunation. It is complicated as compared with the Gregorian Calendar. The intercalary month is introduced seven times in every nineteen years.

The identification of the Jewish months with our own cannot be effected with precision on account of the variations existing between the lunar and solar month.

## The Muslim Calendar

The Muslim Calendar is called also the calendar of Hegira (i.e. Migration) and is attributed to the primary migration of Mohammed, the Prophet of Islam, on July 16th, 622 A.D. from Mecca, his native city in the land of Hejaz, Arabia, to the city of Medina in the north of the same land. In Medina the Prophet and Founder of the Islamic Faith died and was buried.

Each year consists of 12 lunar months and, since no intercalation is made, the months go round the seasons in between 32 and 33 years.

## Far Eastern Calendars

The ancient Chinese calendar is a lunar calendar, divided into 12 months of either 29 or 30 days. It is synchronized with the solar calendar by the addition of extra months as required. The four-day Chinese New Year (Hsin Nien) begins at the first new moon over China after the sun enters Aquarius, and may fall between January 21 and February 19. The calendar runs on a 60-year cycle, and each year has both a number and a name: 1997 (Ox), 1998 (Tiger), 1999 (Hare/Rabbit), 2000 (Dragon), 2001 (Snake). The three-day Vietnamese New Year (Tet) and the three-to-four-day Korean festival Suhl are set by the same new moon. The Japanese calendar uses the Gregorian date of new year, but with a different epoch.

## The Hindu Calendar

The Hindu calendar contains both lunar and solar elements, and is therefore complex. Furthermore, each lunar month is divided into two halves: the dark half (full moon to new moon) and the bright half (new moon to full moon). For some Hindus (primarily South Indian), the lunar month begins on the day following the new moon; for others (primarily North Indian), it begins on the day following the full moon. Likewise, the calculation of the date of New Year varies. There are some holidays which are set by the solar calendar, as well as several which are set by the lunar calendar.

## The Indian Calendar

Various religious groups in India have their own calendars (see The Muslim Calendar, and The Hindu Calendar, above). The Indian civil calendar sets the New Year on March 22 in a common year, and on March 21 in a leap year. The years are reckoned according to the native Saka historical era.

## The Zoroastrian Calendar

The Zoroastrian calendar is solar, and consists of 12 months of 30 days; five additional days called "gatha" bring the total days in a year to 365. The calculation of the date of the New Year varies among the various Zoroastrian groups.

## The Baha'i Calendar

The Baha'i calendar is astronomically fixed, commencing at the vernal equinox. The calendar is solar, and consists of 19 months of 19 days, with the addition of four or five days to bring the total to 365 or 366.

## US Civil Calendar 1998

New Year's Day .................... Thu. Jan. 1
Martin Luther King's Birthday ....... Mon. Jan. 19
Lincoln's Birthday .................. Thu. Feb. 12
Washington's Birthday ............ Mon. Feb. 16
Memorial Day .................... Mon. May 25
Independence Day .................... Sat. July 4
Labor Day ......................... Mon. Sept. 7
Columbus Day ....................Mon. Oct. 12
Election Day ...................... Tue. Nov. 3
Veterans Day .................... Wed. Nov. 11
Thanksgiving Day .................Thu. Nov. 26

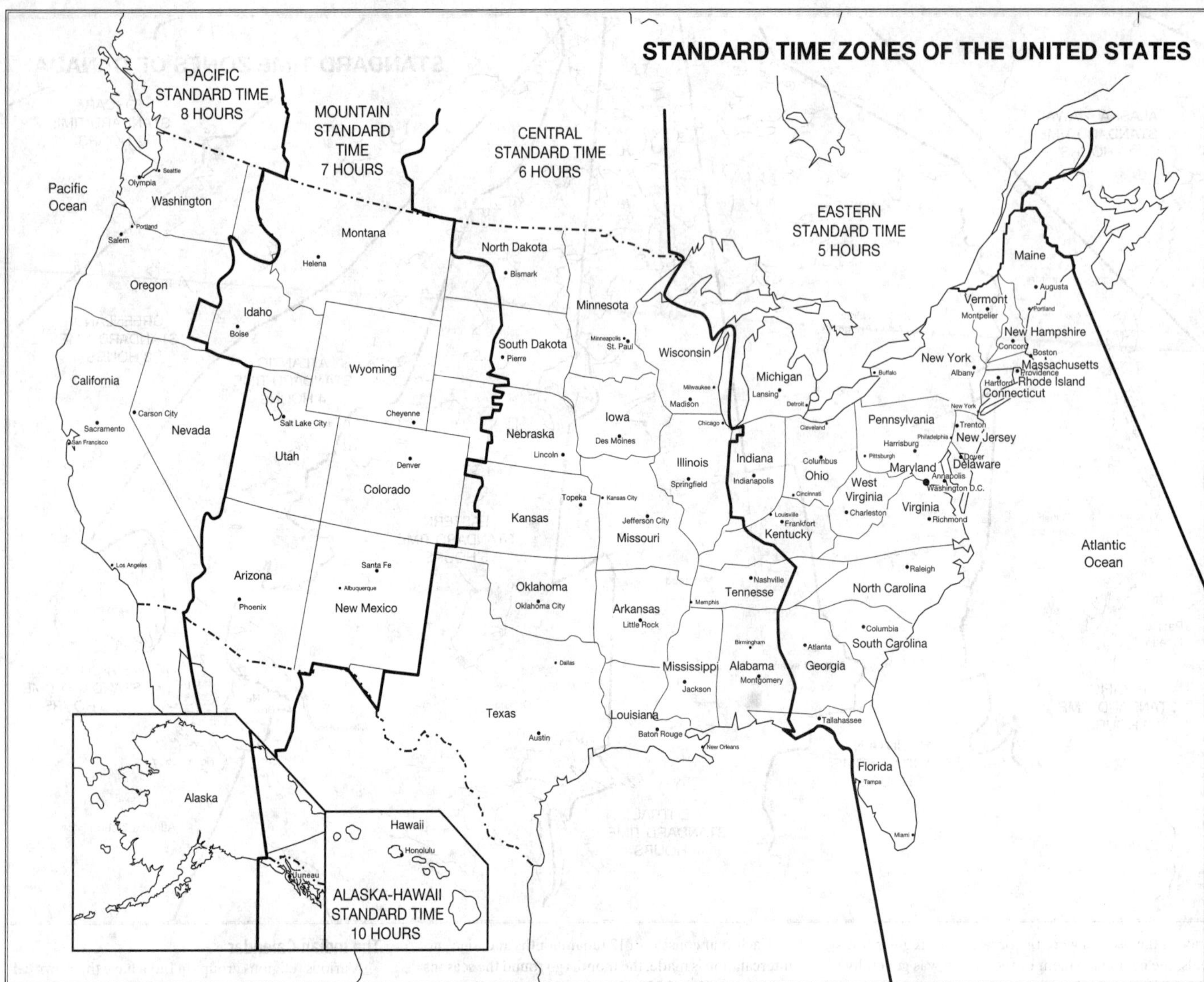


## United Kingdom Civil Calendar 1998

Accession of Queen Elizabeth II ....... Fri. Feb. 6
St. David (Wales)................... Sun. Mar. 1
Commonwealth Day ............... Mon. Mar. 9
St. Patrick (Ireland) ................Tue. Mar. 17
Birthday of Queen Elizabeth II ........Tue. Apr. 21
St. George (England) ...............Thu. Apr. 23
Coronation Day .................... Tue. June 2
Birthday of Prince Philip,
Duke of Edinburgh ............. Wed. June 10
The Queen's Official Birthday ........ Sat. June 13
Remembrance Sunday .............. Sun. Nov. 8
Birthday of the Prince of Wales ....... Sat. Nov. 14
St. Andrew (Scotland) ............. Mon. Nov. 30

## EPOCHS

The year 5759 of the Jewish era begins at sunset on Sept. 20, 1998, Gregorian Calendar.

The year 1419 of the Mohammedan era, or the era of the Hegira, begins at sunset on April 27, 1998, Gregorian Calendar.

The year 4635 of the Chinese era begins on Jan. 28, 1998.

The year 2658 of the Japanese era begins on Jan. 1, 1998.

The year 1920 of the Indian (Saka) era begins on Mar. 22, 1998.

January 1, 1998, Julian Calendar, corresponds to Jan. 14, 1998, Gregorian Calendar.

The 47th year of the reign of Queen Elizabeth II begins on Feb. 6, 1998.

The 132nd year of the Dominion of Canada begins July 1, 1998.

The 223rd year of the Independence of the United States of America begins July 4, 1998.

The Julian Day 2,450,815 begins at Greenwich mean noon Jan. 1, 1998, Gregorian Calendar.

## THE SEASONS 1998

Eastern Standard Time

Spring begins ........ March 20th..... 14 h 55 m
Summer begins....... June 21st ...... 09 h 03 m
Autumn begins....... Sept. 23rd...... 00 h 37 m
Winter begins ........ Dec. 21st....... 20 h 56 m

Eastern Standard time applies in Ontario and Québec. Newfoundland time is 1 1/2 hours later than Eastern Standard time; in the Maritime Provinces, on Atlantic time, time is 1 hour later; in Manitoba and the eastern half of Saskatchewan, on Central time, time is 1 hour earlier; in Alberta and the western half of Saskatchewan, on Mountain time, time is 2 hours earlier; in B.C., on Pacific time, time is 3 hours earlier.

## STANDARD TIME

Owing to the great breadth of Canada the difference in solar time in various parts of the country is adjusted by the creation of Standard Time Zones, one hour in width, fixed between arbitrary lines running approximately north and south, 15° of longitude apart, the time observed in each zone being an exact, except for Newfoundland, number of hours slow from Greenwich. Example: When it is 8 a.m. by Pacific Time it is 12 noon by Atlantic Time and 4 p.m. at Greenwich.

There are six zones divided as follows, reckoning from Greenwich:

Newfoundland Standard Time: Newfoundland, excluding Labrador, 3 1/2 hours slow.

Atlantic Standard Time/60th Meridian Time: Labrador, New Brunswick, Nova Scotia, Prince Edward Island, and those parts of Québec and Northwest Territories east of the 63rd Meridian, 4 hours slow.

Eastern Standard Time/75th Meridian Time: Québec west of the 63rd Meridian and Ontario as far west as the 90th Meridian; Northwest Territories between the 68th and 85th Meridian, 5 hours slow.

Central Standard Time/90th Meridian Time: Ontario west of the 90th Meridian, Manitoba, easterly part of Saskatchewan and Northwest Territories between the 85th and 102nd Meridian, 6 hours slow.

Mountain Standard Time/105th Meridian Time: Eastern Saskatchewan (in winter); throughout Alberta and in Northwest Territories west of the 102nd Meridian, 7 hours slow.

Pacific Standard Time/120th Meridian Time : Throughout most of British Columbia and in the Yukon, 8 hours slow.

Railways and airways make up their schedules according to Standard Time in winter and Daylight Saving Time in summer. Solar time around the globe varies four minutes with each degree of longitude.

## INTERNATIONAL TIME ZONES

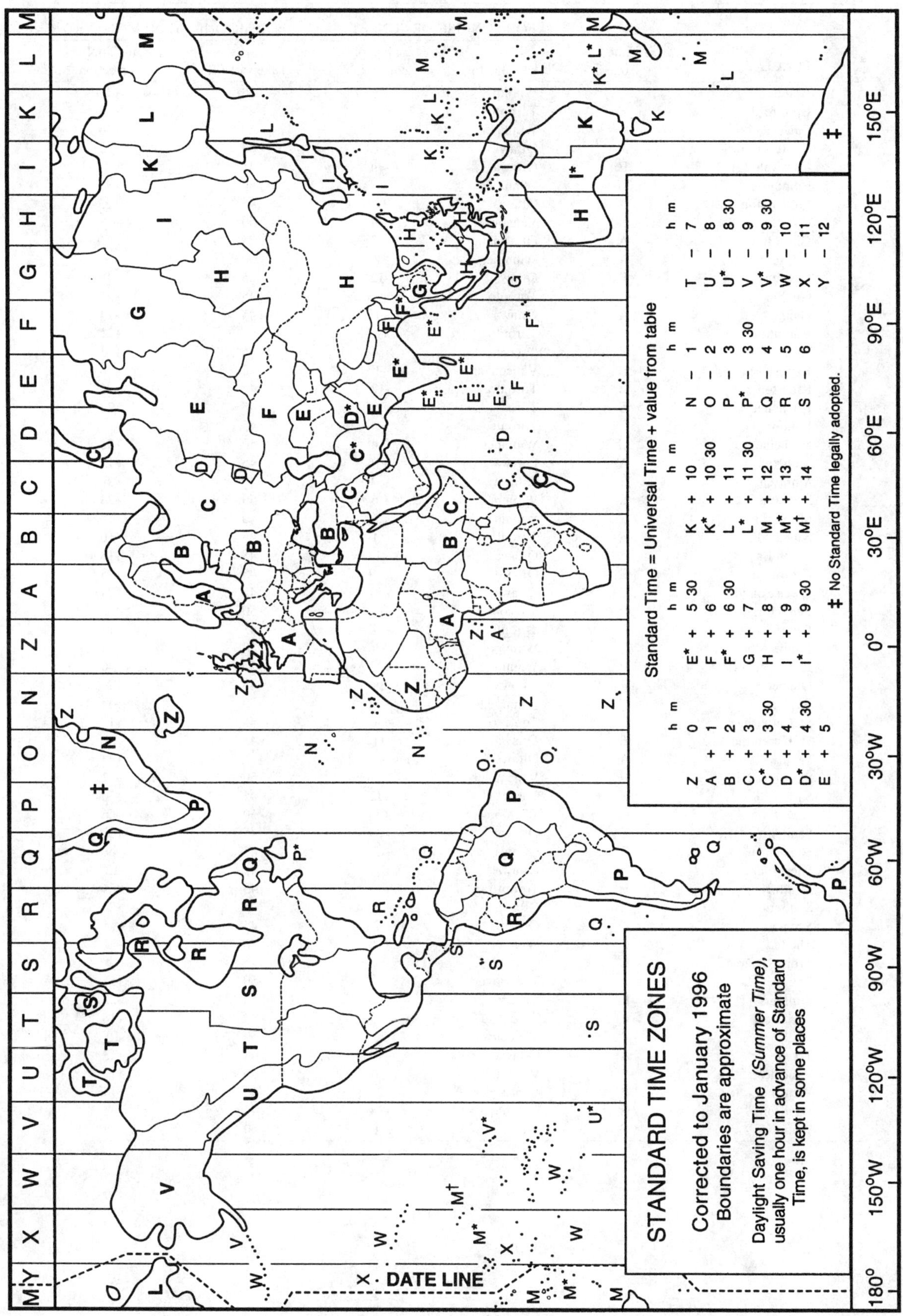


Reproduced, with permission, from data supplied by H.M. Nautical Almanac Office. © Particle Physics and Astronomy Research Council.

## TABLE FOR FINDING APPROXIMATE STANDARD TIME OF SUNRISE, SUNSET, MOONRISE, MOONSET, FOR CANADIAN CITIES AND TOWNS

| PLACE | Time Zone | FOR SUNRISE OR SUNSET Take value for | and apply correction | FOR MOONRISE OR MOONSET Take value for | and apply correction |
|---|---|---|---|---|---|
| Brandon | C | Winnipeg | +11*m* | 50° | +40*m* |
| Brantford | E | Toronto | + 4 | 45 | +21 |
| Calgary | M | Winnipeg | + 8 | 50 | +36 |
| Charlottetown | A | Ottawa | +10 | 45 | +13 |
| Cornwall | E | Ottawa | - 4 | 45 | - 1 |
| Edmonton | M | Winnipeg | + 6 | 50 | +34 |
| Fredericton | A | Ottawa | +24 | 45 | +27 |
| Gander | N | Vancouver | - 4 | 50 | + 8 |
| Glace Bay | A | Ottawa | - 3 | 45 | 0 |
| Goose Bay | A | Winnipeg | -26 | 50 | - 2 |
| Granby | E | Ottawa | -12 | 45 | - 9 |
| Guelph | E | Toronto | + 3 | 45 | +21 |
| Halifax | A | Ottawa | +11 | 45 | +14 |
| Hamilton | E | Toronto | + 2 | 45 | +21 |
| Hull | E | Ottawa | 0 | 45 | + 3 |
| Kapuskasing | E | Vancouver | +17 | 50 | +30 |
| Kingston | E | Toronto | -12 | 45 | + 6 |
| Kitchener | E | Toronto | + 4 | 45 | +22 |
| London | E | Toronto | + 8 | 45 | +25 |
| Medicine Hat | M | Winnipeg | - 4 | 50 | +22 |
| Moncton | A | Ottawa | +16 | 45 | +19 |
| Montréal | E | Ottawa | - 9 | 45 | - 6 |
| Moosonee | E | Winnipeg | - 6 | 50 | +23 |
| Moose Jaw | C | Winnipeg | +34 | 50 | +62 |
| Niagara Falls | E | Toronto | - 1 | 45 | +16 |
| North Bay | E | Ottawa | +14 | 45 | +18 |
| Ottawa | E | Ottawa | 0 | 45 | + 3 |
| Owen Sound | E | Ottawa | +21 | 45 | +24 |
| Penticton | P | Vancouver | -14 | 50 | - 2 |
| Peterborough | E | Toronto | - 4 | 45 | +13 |
| Prince Albert | C | Winnipeg | +36 | 50 | +64 |
| Prince Rupert | P | Winnipeg | +12 | 50 | +40 |
| Québec | E | Ottawa | -18 | 45 | -15 |
| Regina | C | Winnipeg | +30 | 50 | +58 |
| St. Catharines | E | Toronto | 0 | 45 | +17 |
| St. Hyacinthe | E | Ottawa | -11 | 45 | - 8 |
| Saint John, NB | A | Ottawa | +22 | 45 | +24 |
| St. John's NF | N | Vancouver | -11 | 50 | + 1 |
| Sarnia | E | Toronto | +12 | 45 | +30 |
| Saskatoon | C | Winnipeg | +38 | 50 | +66 |
| Sault Ste. Marie | E | Ottawa | +34 | 45 | +37 |
| Shawinigan | E | Ottawa | -12 | 45 | - 9 |
| Sherbrooke | E | Ottawa | -14 | 45 | -12 |
| Stratford | E | Toronto | + 6 | 45 | +24 |
| Sudbury | E | Ottawa | +21 | 45 | +24 |
| Sydney | A | Ottawa | - 2 | 45 | + 1 |
| The Pas | C | Winnipeg | +16 | 50 | +44 |
| Trois-Rivières | E | Ottawa | -12 | 45 | - 9 |
| Thunder Bay | E | Vancouver | +44 | 50 | +57 |
| Timmins | E | Vancouver | +13 | 50 | +25 |
| Toronto | E | Toronto | 0 | 45 | +18 |
| Trail | P | Vancouver | -22 | 50 | -10 |
| Truro | A | Ottawa | +10 | 45 | +13 |
| Vancouver | P | Vancouver | 0 | 50 | +12 |
| Victoria | P | Vancouver | +2 | 50 | +14 |
| Windsor | E | Toronto | +14 | 45 | +32 |
| Winnipeg | C | Winnipeg | 0 | 50 | +28 |

## AZIMUTHS OF THE POINTS OF RISING AND SETTING OF THE SUN FOR LATITUDES 43°N TO 52°N

In Degrees East of North for Rising and West of North for Setting

| | | | 43°N | 44°N | 45°N | 46°N | 47°N | 48°N | 49°N | 50°N | 51°N | 52°N |
|---|---|---|---|---|---|---|---|---|---|---|---|---|
| Jan. 2 | and | Dec. 11 | 122 | 123 | 124 | 124 | 125 | 126 | 127 | 127 | 128 | 129 |
| Jan. 10 | and | Dec. 3 | 121 | 121 | 122 | 123 | 123 | 124 | 125 | 126 | 127 | 127 |
| Jan. 16 | and | Nov. 27 | 119 | 120 | 120 | 121 | 122 | 122 | 123 | 124 | 125 | 126 |
| Jan. 21 | and | Nov. 22 | 118 | 118 | 119 | 120 | 120 | 121 | 121 | 122 | 123 | 124 |
| Jan. 25 | and | Nov. 17 | 116 | 117 | 117 | 118 | 119 | 119 | 120 | 120 | 121 | 122 |
| Jan. 29 | and | Nov. 14 | 115 | 115 | 116 | 116 | 117 | 118 | 118 | 119 | 119 | 120 |
| Feb. 2 | and | Nov. 10 | 114 | 114 | 114 | 115 | 115 | 116 | 116 | 117 | 118 | 118 |
| Feb. 5 | and | Nov. 6 | 112 | 113 | 113 | 113 | 114 | 114 | 115 | 115 | 116 | 116 |
| Feb. 9 | and | Nov. 3 | 111 | 111 | 111 | 112 | 112 | 113 | 113 | 114 | 114 | 115 |
| Feb. 12 | and | Oct. 31 | 109 | 110 | 110 | 110 | 111 | 111 | 112 | 112 | 113 | 113 |
| Feb. 15 | and | Oct. 28 | 108 | 108 | 109 | 109 | 109 | 110 | 110 | 110 | 111 | 111 |
| Feb. 18 | and | Oct. 25 | 107 | 107 | 107 | 107 | 108 | 108 | 108 | 109 | 109 | 110 |
| Feb. 20 | and | Oct. 22 | 105 | 105 | 106 | 106 | 106 | 106 | 107 | 107 | 108 | 108 |
| Feb. 23 | and | Oct. 19 | 104 | 104 | 104 | 104 | 105 | 105 | 105 | 106 | 106 | 106 |
| Feb. 26 | and | Oct. 17 | 102 | 103 | 103 | 103 | 103 | 104 | 104 | 104 | 104 | 105 |
| Mar. 1 | and | Oct. 14 | 101 | 101 | 101 | 102 | 102 | 102 | 102 | 102 | 103 | 103 |
| Mar. 3 | and | Oct. 11 | 100 | 100 | 100 | 100 | 100 | 100 | 101 | 101 | 101 | 101 |
| Mar. 6 | and | Oct. 9 | 98 | 98 | 98 | 99 | 99 | 99 | 99 | 99 | 100 | 100 |
| Mar. 8 | and | Oct. 6 | 97 | 97 | 97 | 97 | 97 | 97 | 98 | 98 | 98 | 98 |
| Mar. 11 | and | Oct. 4 | 95 | 96 | 96 | 96 | 96 | 96 | 96 | 96 | 96 | 96 |
| Mar. 13 | and | Oct. 1 | 94 | 94 | 94 | 94 | 94 | 94 | 95 | 95 | 95 | 95 |
| Mar. 16 | and | Sept. 28 | 93 | 93 | 93 | 93 | 93 | 93 | 93 | 93 | 93 | 93 |
| Mar. 18 | and | Sept. 26 | 91 | 91 | 91 | 91 | 91 | 92 | 92 | 92 | 92 | 92 |
| Mar. 21 | and | Sept. 23 | 90 | 90 | 90 | 90 | 90 | 90 | 90 | 90 | 90 | 90 |
| Mar. 23 | and | Sept. 21 | 89 | 89 | 89 | 89 | 89 | 88 | 88 | 88 | 88 | 88 |
| Mar. 26 | and | Sept. 18 | 87 | 87 | 87 | 87 | 87 | 87 | 87 | 87 | 87 | 87 |
| Mar. 28 | and | Sept. 16 | 86 | 86 | 86 | 86 | 86 | 86 | 85 | 85 | 85 | 85 |
| Mar. 31 | and | Sept. 13 | 85 | 84 | 84 | 84 | 84 | 84 | 84 | 84 | 84 | 84 |
| Apr. 3 | and | Sept. 10 | 83 | 83 | 83 | 83 | 83 | 83 | 82 | 82 | 82 | 82 |
| Apr. 5 | and | Sept. 8 | 82 | 82 | 82 | 81 | 81 | 81 | 81 | 81 | 80 | 80 |
| Apr. 8 | and | Sept. 5 | 80 | 80 | 80 | 80 | 80 | 80 | 79 | 79 | 79 | 79 |
| Apr. 11 | and | Sept. 2 | 79 | 79 | 79 | 78 | 78 | 78 | 78 | 78 | 77 | 77 |
| Apr. 13 | and | Aug. 30 | 78 | 77 | 77 | 77 | 77 | 76 | 76 | 76 | 76 | 75 |
| Apr. 16 | and | Aug. 28 | 76 | 76 | 76 | 76 | 75 | 75 | 75 | 74 | 74 | 74 |
| Apr. 19 | and | Aug. 25 | 75 | 75 | 74 | 74 | 74 | 73 | 73 | 73 | 72 | 72 |
| Apr. 22 | and | Aug. 22 | 73 | 73 | 73 | 73 | 72 | 72 | 72 | 71 | 71 | 70 |
| Apr. 25 | and | Aug. 19 | 72 | 72 | 71 | 71 | 71 | 70 | 70 | 70 | 69 | 69 |
| Apr. 28 | and | Aug. 16 | 71 | 70 | 70 | 70 | 69 | 69 | 68 | 68 | 67 | 67 |
| May 1 | and | Aug. 12 | 69 | 69 | 69 | 68 | 68 | 67 | 67 | 66 | 66 | 65 |
| May 5 | and | Aug. 9 | 68 | 67 | 67 | 67 | 66 | 66 | 65 | 65 | 64 | 63 |
| May 8 | and | Aug. 5 | 66 | 66 | 66 | 65 | 65 | 64 | 64 | 63 | 62 | 62 |
| May 12 | and | Aug. 2 | 65 | 65 | 64 | 64 | 63 | 62 | 62 | 61 | 61 | 60 |
| May 16 | and | July 28 | 64 | 63 | 63 | 62 | 61 | 61 | 60 | 60 | 59 | 58 |
| May 21 | and | June 24 | 62 | 62 | 61 | 60 | 60 | 59 | 59 | 58 | 57 | 56 |
| May 26 | and | June 19 | 61 | 60 | 60 | 59 | 58 | 58 | 57 | 56 | 55 | 54 |
| June 1 | and | July 12 | 59 | 59 | 58 | 57 | 57 | 56 | 55 | 54 | 53 | 53 |
| June 10 | and | July 3 | 58 | 57 | 56 | 56 | 55 | 54 | 53 | 53 | 52 | 51 |

## AZIMUTH OF THE SUN AT RISING AND SETTING

Only twice a year, namely about March 21 and September 23, does the sun rise and set more or less exactly in the east and west respectively. It is of interest and sometimes of value to know the position of Sunrise and Sunset at other times. The table above tabulates these in degrees east of north and west of north for Sunrise and Sunset respectively for a selection of latitudes and dates. For latitudes and dates other than those tabulated take simple proportions.

## REFERENCES

The tables and charts in the *Canadian Almanac* are intended for simple astronomical observations. To make more extensive observations the following are recommended: *The Observer's Handbook* (obtainable from the Royal Astronomical Society of Canada, 136 Dupont St., Toronto, ON M5R 1V2); *Astronomical Phenomena* (obtainable from The Superintendent of Documents, U.S. Government Printing Office, Washington, D.C.). See also "Suggestions for Further Reading".

## NOTES ON THE ASTRONOMICAL TABLES

The purpose of the following notes is to explain those tables which are not self-explanatory and to illustrate how they may be used for places other than those specified.

These tables give Standard Times of Sunrise and Sunset for the four Canadian cities listed. When Daylight Saving Time is in effect, of course, one hour must be added to the listed times. The calculations are for the upper limb (edge) of the sun and for the astronomical (sea) horizon. Accordingly the actual observation of Sunrise or Sunset will differ from the tabulated value if the observer is below or above the level of his visible horizon at the point of Sunrise or Sunset.

The listed times of Moonrise and Moonset have been calculated for places at the stated latitudes and for longitude 5 hours west.

To obtain the approximate times of Sunrise, Sunset, Moonrise and Moonset for other Canadian cities and towns proceed as indicated in the table on page 1-6. The errors for Sunrise and Sunset by this approximate method will seldom exceed 10 minutes in winter and summer or 4 minutes in spring and fall, and for Moonrise and Moonset they will seldom exceed 15 minutes.

The tables have been calculated using a computer program written by Li Sen, using algorithms given in *Astronomy with your Personal Computer* (second edition), by Peter Duffett-Smith (Cambridge University Press, 1990).

**JANUARY 1998**

| Moon's Phases E.S.T. | d | h | m |
|---|---|---|---|
| First Quarter | 5 d | 9 h | 18 m |
| Full Moon | 12 d | 12 h | 24 m |
| Last Quarter | 20 d | 14 h | 40 m |
| New Moon | 28 d | 1 h | 1 m |

| Day of Yr. | Day of Mo. | Day of Wk. | Ottawa E.S.T. Rises | Ottawa E.S.T. Sets | Toronto E.S.T. Rises | Toronto E.S.T. Sets | Winnipeg C.S.T. Rises | Winnipeg C.S.T. Sets | Vancouver P.S.T. Rises | Vancouver P.S.T. Sets | Moon Lat. 45° Rises | Moon Lat. 45° Sets | Moon Lat. 50° Rises | Moon Lat. 50° Sets | Day of Wk. | Day of Mo. |
|---|---|---|---|---|---|---|---|---|---|---|---|---|---|---|---|---|
| | | | h m | h m | h m | h m | h m | h m | h m | h m | h m | h m | h m | h m | | |
| 1 | 1 | Thu | 7 42 | 16 30 | 7 51 | 16 51 | 8 26 | 16 38 | 8 07 | 16 24 | 9 32 | 20 11 | 9 43 | 20 01 | Thu | 1 |
| 2 | 2 | Fri | 7 42 | 16 30 | 7 51 | 16 52 | 8 26 | 16 39 | 8 07 | 16 25 | 10 10 | 21 22 | 10 18 | 21 16 | Fri | 2 |
| 3 | 3 | Sat | 7 42 | 16 31 | 7 51 | 16 53 | 8 26 | 16 40 | 8 07 | 16 26 | 10 45 | 22 34 | 10 49 | 22 31 | Sat | 3 |
| 4 | 4 | Sun | 7 42 | 16 32 | 7 51 | 16 54 | 8 26 | 16 41 | 8 07 | 16 28 | 11 18 | 23 45 | 11 18 | 23 46 | Sun | 4 |
| 5 | 5 | Mon | 7 42 | 16 33 | 7 51 | 16 55 | 8 26 | 16 42 | 8 06 | 16 29 | 11 50 | -- -- | 11 47 | -- -- | Mon | 5 |
| 6 | 6 | Tue | 7 42 | 16 34 | 7 51 | 16 56 | 8 25 | 16 43 | 8 06 | 16 30 | 12 23 | 0 56 | 12 17 | 1 01 | Tue | 6 |
| 7 | 7 | Wed | 7 42 | 16 35 | 7 51 | 16 57 | 8 25 | 16 44 | 8 06 | 16 31 | 12 59 | 2 06 | 12 49 | 2 14 | Wed | 7 |
| 8 | 8 | Thu | 7 42 | 16 36 | 7 50 | 16 58 | 8 24 | 16 46 | 8 05 | 16 32 | 13 38 | 3 14 | 13 26 | 3 26 | Thu | 8 |
| 9 | 9 | Fri | 7 41 | 16 37 | 7 50 | 16 59 | 8 24 | 16 47 | 8 05 | 16 34 | 14 22 | 4 21 | 14 07 | 4 35 | Fri | 9 |
| 10 | 10 | Sat | 7 41 | 16 38 | 7 50 | 17 00 | 8 24 | 16 48 | 8 04 | 16 35 | 15 11 | 5 23 | 14 55 | 5 39 | Sat | 10 |
| 11 | 11 | Sun | 7 41 | 16 39 | 7 50 | 17 01 | 8 23 | 16 50 | 8 04 | 16 36 | 16 05 | 6 19 | 15 48 | 6 36 | Sun | 11 |
| 12 | 12 | Mon | 7 40 | 16 41 | 7 49 | 17 02 | 8 22 | 16 51 | 8 03 | 16 38 | 17 02 | 7 09 | 16 47 | 7 25 | Mon | 12 |
| 13 | 13 | Tue | 7 40 | 16 42 | 7 49 | 17 03 | 8 22 | 16 52 | 8 03 | 16 39 | 18 02 | 7 53 | 17 48 | 8 07 | Tue | 13 |
| 14 | 14 | Wed | 7 40 | 16 43 | 7 48 | 17 05 | 8 21 | 16 54 | 8 02 | 16 40 | 19 02 | 8 31 | 18 51 | 8 43 | Wed | 14 |
| 15 | 15 | Thu | 7 39 | 16 44 | 7 48 | 17 06 | 8 20 | 16 55 | 8 01 | 16 42 | 20 02 | 9 04 | 19 55 | 9 13 | Thu | 15 |
| 16 | 16 | Fri | 7 38 | 16 46 | 7 47 | 17 07 | 8 20 | 16 57 | 8 01 | 16 43 | 21 02 | 9 34 | 20 57 | 9 40 | Fri | 16 |
| 17 | 17 | Sat | 7 38 | 16 47 | 7 47 | 17 08 | 8 19 | 16 58 | 8 00 | 16 45 | 22 00 | 10 02 | 21 59 | 10 05 | Sat | 17 |
| 18 | 18 | Sun | 7 37 | 16 48 | 7 46 | 17 09 | 8 18 | 17 00 | 7 59 | 16 46 | 22 59 | 10 29 | 23 00 | 10 28 | Sun | 18 |
| 19 | 19 | Mon | 7 37 | 16 49 | 7 45 | 17 11 | 8 17 | 17 01 | 7 58 | 16 48 | 24 00 | 10 55 | 24 00 | 10 52 | Mon | 19 |
| 20 | 20 | Tue | 7 36 | 16 51 | 7 45 | 17 12 | 8 16 | 17 03 | 7 57 | 16 49 | -- -- | 11 22 | -- -- | 11 16 | Tue | 20 |
| 21 | 21 | Wed | 7 35 | 16 52 | 7 44 | 17 13 | 8 15 | 17 05 | 7 56 | 16 51 | 0 56 | 11 52 | 1 04 | 11 43 | Wed | 21 |
| 22 | 22 | Thu | 7 34 | 16 53 | 7 43 | 17 15 | 8 14 | 17 06 | 7 55 | 16 52 | 1 55 | 12 25 | 2 06 | 12 13 | Thu | 22 |
| 23 | 23 | Fri | 7 33 | 16 55 | 7 43 | 17 16 | 8 13 | 17 08 | 7 54 | 16 54 | 2 55 | 13 02 | 3 09 | 12 48 | Fri | 23 |
| 24 | 24 | Sat | 7 33 | 16 56 | 7 42 | 17 17 | 8 12 | 17 09 | 7 53 | 16 56 | 3 55 | 13 46 | 4 11 | 13 30 | Sat | 24 |
| 25 | 25 | Sun | 7 32 | 16 58 | 7 41 | 17 19 | 8 11 | 17 11 | 7 52 | 16 57 | 4 54 | 14 37 | 5 10 | 14 20 | Sun | 25 |
| 26 | 26 | Mon | 7 31 | 16 59 | 7 40 | 17 20 | 8 09 | 17 13 | 7 51 | 16 59 | 5 49 | 15 36 | 6 06 | 15 19 | Mon | 26 |
| 27 | 27 | Tue | 7 30 | 17 00 | 7 39 | 17 21 | 8 08 | 17 14 | 7 50 | 17 00 | 6 40 | 16 41 | 6 55 | 16 27 | Tue | 27 |
| 28 | 28 | Wed | 7 29 | 17 02 | 7 38 | 17 23 | 8 07 | 17 16 | 7 48 | 17 02 | 7 26 | 17 51 | 7 39 | 17 40 | Wed | 28 |
| 29 | 29 | Thu | 7 28 | 17 03 | 7 37 | 17 24 | 8 05 | 17 18 | 7 47 | 17 04 | 8 07 | 19 05 | 8 17 | 18 57 | Thu | 29 |
| 30 | 30 | Fri | 7 27 | 17 05 | 7 36 | 17 25 | 8 04 | 17 19 | 7 46 | 17 05 | 8 45 | 20 19 | 8 50 | 20 15 | Fri | 30 |
| 31 | 31 | Sat | 7 26 | 17 06 | 7 35 | 17 27 | 8 03 | 17 21 | 7 44 | 17 07 | 9 19 | 21 33 | 9 21 | 21 32 | Sat | 31 |

**FEBRUARY 1998**

| Moon's Phases E.S.T. | d | h | m |
|---|---|---|---|
| First Quarter | 3 d | 17 h | 53 m |
| Full Moon | 11 d | 5 h | 23 m |
| Last Quarter | 19 d | 10 h | 27 m |
| New Moon | 26 d | 12 h | 26 m |

| Day of Yr. | Day of Mo. | Day of Wk. | Ottawa E.S.T. Rises | Ottawa E.S.T. Sets | Toronto E.S.T. Rises | Toronto E.S.T. Sets | Winnipeg C.S.T. Rises | Winnipeg C.S.T. Sets | Vancouver P.S.T. Rises | Vancouver P.S.T. Sets | Moon Lat. 45° Rises | Moon Lat. 45° Sets | Moon Lat. 50° Rises | Moon Lat. 50° Sets | Day of Wk. | Day of Mo. |
|---|---|---|---|---|---|---|---|---|---|---|---|---|---|---|---|---|
| | | | h m | h m | h m | h m | h m | h m | h m | h m | h m | h m | h m | h m | | |
| 32 | 1 | Sun | 7 25 | 17 08 | 7 34 | 17 28 | 8 01 | 17 23 | 7 43 | 17 09 | 9 53 | 22 45 | 9 51 | 22 49 | Sun | 1 |
| 33 | 2 | Mon | 7 23 | 17 09 | 7 33 | 17 29 | 8 00 | 17 25 | 7 42 | 17 10 | 10 27 | 24 00 | 10 21 | -- -- | Mon | 2 |
| 34 | 3 | Tue | 7 22 | 17 11 | 7 32 | 17 31 | 7 58 | 17 26 | 7 40 | 17 12 | 11 02 | -- -- | 10 53 | 0 04 | Tue | 3 |
| 35 | 4 | Wed | 7 21 | 17 12 | 7 31 | 17 32 | 7 57 | 17 28 | 7 39 | 17 14 | 11 40 | 1 06 | 11 28 | 1 17 | Wed | 4 |
| 36 | 5 | Thu | 7 20 | 17 13 | 7 29 | 17 34 | 7 55 | 17 30 | 7 37 | 17 15 | 12 21 | 2 13 | 12 07 | 2 26 | Thu | 5 |
| 37 | 6 | Fri | 7 18 | 17 15 | 7 28 | 17 35 | 7 54 | 17 31 | 7 36 | 17 17 | 13 08 | 3 16 | 12 52 | 3 31 | Fri | 6 |
| 38 | 7 | Sat | 7 17 | 17 16 | 7 27 | 17 36 | 7 52 | 17 33 | 7 34 | 17 19 | 13 59 | 4 13 | 13 42 | 4 29 | Sat | 7 |
| 39 | 8 | Sun | 7 16 | 17 18 | 7 26 | 17 38 | 7 51 | 17 35 | 7 32 | 17 20 | 14 54 | 5 04 | 14 38 | 5 20 | Sun | 8 |
| 40 | 9 | Mon | 7 14 | 17 19 | 7 24 | 17 39 | 7 49 | 17 37 | 7 31 | 17 22 | 15 51 | 5 50 | 15 37 | 6 04 | Mon | 9 |
| 41 | 10 | Tue | 7 13 | 17 21 | 7 23 | 17 40 | 7 47 | 17 38 | 7 29 | 17 24 | 16 51 | 6 29 | 16 39 | 6 42 | Tue | 10 |
| 42 | 11 | Wed | 7 12 | 17 22 | 7 22 | 17 42 | 7 46 | 17 40 | 7 28 | 17 25 | 17 51 | 7 04 | 17 42 | 7 14 | Wed | 11 |
| 43 | 12 | Thu | 7 10 | 17 24 | 7 20 | 17 43 | 7 44 | 17 42 | 7 26 | 17 27 | 18 51 | 7 36 | 18 45 | 7 43 | Thu | 12 |
| 44 | 13 | Fri | 7 09 | 17 25 | 7 19 | 17 44 | 7 42 | 17 43 | 7 24 | 17 29 | 19 50 | 8 04 | 19 47 | 8 08 | Fri | 13 |
| 45 | 14 | Sat | 7 07 | 17 27 | 7 17 | 17 46 | 7 40 | 17 45 | 7 22 | 17 30 | 20 48 | 8 31 | 20 48 | 8 32 | Sat | 14 |
| 46 | 15 | Sun | 7 06 | 17 28 | 7 16 | 17 47 | 7 38 | 17 47 | 7 21 | 17 32 | 21 46 | 8 58 | 21 50 | 8 56 | Sun | 15 |
| 47 | 16 | Mon | 7 04 | 17 29 | 7 15 | 17 49 | 7 37 | 17 49 | 7 19 | 17 34 | 22 45 | 9 24 | 22 51 | 9 20 | Mon | 16 |
| 48 | 17 | Tue | 7 03 | 17 31 | 7 13 | 17 50 | 7 35 | 17 50 | 7 17 | 17 35 | 23 43 | 9 53 | 23 52 | 9 45 | Tue | 17 |
| 49 | 18 | Wed | 7 01 | 17 32 | 7 12 | 17 51 | 7 33 | 17 52 | 7 15 | 17 37 | -- -- | 10 23 | -- -- | 10 13 | Wed | 18 |
| 50 | 19 | Thu | 6 59 | 17 34 | 7 10 | 17 53 | 7 31 | 17 54 | 7 13 | 17 39 | 0 42 | 10 58 | 0 54 | 10 45 | Thu | 19 |
| 51 | 20 | Fri | 6 58 | 17 35 | 7 08 | 17 54 | 7 29 | 17 55 | 7 12 | 17 40 | 1 40 | 11 38 | 1 55 | 11 23 | Fri | 20 |
| 52 | 21 | Sat | 6 56 | 17 37 | 7 07 | 17 55 | 7 27 | 17 57 | 7 10 | 17 42 | 2 38 | 12 24 | 2 54 | 12 08 | Sat | 21 |
| 53 | 22 | Sun | 6 55 | 17 38 | 7 05 | 17 57 | 7 25 | 17 59 | 7 08 | 17 44 | 3 34 | 13 17 | 3 50 | 13 01 | Sun | 22 |
| 54 | 23 | Mon | 6 53 | 17 39 | 7 04 | 17 58 | 7 23 | 18 00 | 7 06 | 17 45 | 4 26 | 14 18 | 4 42 | 14 03 | Mon | 23 |
| 55 | 24 | Tue | 6 51 | 17 41 | 7 02 | 17 59 | 7 21 | 18 02 | 7 04 | 17 47 | 5 14 | 15 26 | 5 28 | 15 13 | Tue | 24 |
| 56 | 25 | Wed | 6 50 | 17 42 | 7 01 | 18 00 | 7 19 | 18 04 | 7 02 | 17 49 | 5 58 | 16 38 | 6 09 | 16 28 | Wed | 25 |
| 57 | 26 | Thu | 6 48 | 17 44 | 6 59 | 18 02 | 7 17 | 18 05 | 7 00 | 17 50 | 6 38 | 17 54 | 6 46 | 17 47 | Thu | 26 |
| 58 | 27 | Fri | 6 46 | 17 45 | 6 57 | 18 03 | 7 15 | 18 07 | 6 58 | 17 52 | 7 15 | 19 10 | 7 19 | 19 08 | Fri | 27 |
| 59 | 28 | Sat | 6 44 | 17 46 | 6 56 | 18 04 | 7 13 | 18 09 | 6 56 | 17 53 | 7 50 | 20 26 | 7 50 | 20 28 | Sat | 28 |

## MARCH 1998

| | | | | Moon's Phases E.S.T. |
|---|---|---|---|---|
| First Quarter | 5 d | 3 h | 41 m | |
| Full Moon | 12 d | 23 h | 34 m | |
| First Quarter | 21 d | 2 h | 38 m | |
| New Moon | 27 d | 22 h | 14 m | |

| Day of Yr. | Day of Mo. | Day of Wk. | SUNRISE AND SUNSET Ottawa E.S.T. Rises | Ottawa E.S.T. Sets | Toronto E.S.T. Rises | Toronto E.S.T. Sets | Winnipeg C.S.T. Rises | Winnipeg C.S.T. Sets | Vancouver P.S.T. Rises | Vancouver P.S.T. Sets | MOONRISE AND MOONSET Local Mean Time Lat. 45 ° Rises | Lat. 45 ° Sets | Lat. 50 ° Rises | Lat. 50 ° Sets | Day of Wk. | Day of Mo. |
|---|---|---|---|---|---|---|---|---|---|---|---|---|---|---|---|---|
| | | | *h m* | *h m* | *h m* | *h m* | *h m* | *h m* | *h m* | *h m* | *h m* | *h m* | *h m* | *h m* | | |
| 60 | 1 | Sun | 6 43 | 17 48 | 6 54 | 18 06 | 7 11 | 18 10 | 6 54 | 17 55 | 8 25 | 21 41 | 8 21 | 21 47 | Sun | 1 |
| 61 | 2 | Mon | 6 41 | 17 49 | 6 52 | 18 07 | 7 09 | 18 12 | 6 52 | 17 57 | 9 01 | 22 54 | 8 54 | 23 03 | Mon | 2 |
| 62 | 3 | Tue | 6 39 | 17 51 | 6 51 | 18 08 | 7 07 | 18 14 | 6 50 | 17 58 | 9 39 | -- -- | 9 28 | -- -- | Tue | 3 |
| 63 | 4 | Wed | 6 37 | 17 52 | 6 49 | 18 10 | 7 05 | 18 15 | 6 48 | 18 00 | 10 20 | 0 04 | 10 07 | 0 16 | Wed | 4 |
| 64 | 5 | Thu | 6 36 | 17 53 | 6 47 | 18 11 | 7 03 | 18 17 | 6 46 | 18 01 | 11 06 | 1 09 | 10 50 | 1 24 | Thu | 5 |
| 65 | 6 | Fri | 6 34 | 17 55 | 6 45 | 18 12 | 7 01 | 18 19 | 6 44 | 18 03 | 11 55 | 2 09 | 11 39 | 2 25 | Fri | 6 |
| 66 | 7 | Sat | 6 32 | 17 56 | 6 44 | 18 13 | 6 59 | 18 20 | 6 42 | 18 05 | 12 49 | 3 02 | 12 33 | 3 18 | Sat | 7 |
| 67 | 8 | Sun | 6 30 | 17 57 | 6 42 | 18 15 | 6 57 | 18 22 | 6 40 | 18 06 | 13 46 | 3 49 | 13 31 | 4 04 | Sun | 8 |
| 68 | 9 | Mon | 6 28 | 17 59 | 6 40 | 18 16 | 6 55 | 18 24 | 6 38 | 18 08 | 14 44 | 4 30 | 14 31 | 4 43 | Mon | 9 |
| 69 | 10 | Tue | 6 26 | 18 00 | 6 38 | 18 17 | 6 53 | 18 25 | 6 36 | 18 09 | 15 43 | 5 06 | 15 33 | 5 16 | Tue | 10 |
| 70 | 11 | Wed | 6 25 | 18 01 | 6 37 | 18 18 | 6 50 | 18 27 | 6 34 | 18 11 | 16 42 | 5 38 | 16 35 | 5 46 | Wed | 11 |
| 71 | 12 | Thu | 6 23 | 18 03 | 6 35 | 18 20 | 6 48 | 18 28 | 6 32 | 18 12 | 17 41 | 6 07 | 17 37 | 6 12 | Thu | 12 |
| 72 | 13 | Fri | 6 21 | 18 04 | 6 33 | 18 21 | 6 46 | 18 30 | 6 30 | 18 14 | 18 40 | 6 34 | 18 39 | 6 36 | Fri | 13 |
| 73 | 14 | Sat | 6 19 | 18 05 | 6 31 | 18 22 | 6 44 | 18 32 | 6 27 | 18 16 | 19 38 | 7 01 | 19 41 | 7 00 | Sat | 14 |
| 74 | 15 | Sun | 6 17 | 18 07 | 6 30 | 18 23 | 6 42 | 18 33 | 6 25 | 18 17 | 20 37 | 7 27 | 20 42 | 7 24 | Sun | 15 |
| 75 | 16 | Mon | 6 15 | 18 08 | 6 28 | 18 24 | 6 40 | 18 35 | 6 23 | 18 19 | 21 35 | 7 55 | 21 43 | 7 48 | Mon | 16 |
| 76 | 17 | Tue | 6 13 | 18 09 | 6 26 | 18 26 | 6 38 | 18 36 | 6 21 | 18 20 | 22 33 | 8 25 | 22 44 | 8 15 | Tue | 17 |
| 77 | 18 | Wed | 6 11 | 18 11 | 6 24 | 18 27 | 6 35 | 18 38 | 6 19 | 18 22 | 23 31 | 8 57 | 23 45 | 8 45 | Wed | 18 |
| 78 | 19 | Thu | 6 10 | 18 12 | 6 22 | 18 28 | 6 33 | 18 39 | 6 17 | 18 23 | -- -- | 9 34 | -- -- | 9 20 | Thu | 19 |
| 79 | 20 | Fri | 6 08 | 18 13 | 6 21 | 18 29 | 6 31 | 18 41 | 6 15 | 18 25 | 0 28 | 10 17 | 0 44 | 10 01 | Fri | 20 |
| 80 | 21 | Sat | 6 06 | 18 15 | 6 19 | 18 31 | 6 29 | 18 43 | 6 13 | 18 26 | 1 23 | 11 06 | 1 40 | 10 49 | Sat | 21 |
| 81 | 22 | Sun | 6 04 | 18 16 | 6 17 | 18 32 | 6 27 | 18 44 | 6 10 | 18 28 | 2 15 | 12 01 | 2 32 | 11 45 | Sun | 22 |
| 82 | 23 | Mon | 6 02 | 18 17 | 6 15 | 18 33 | 6 25 | 18 46 | 6 08 | 18 29 | 3 04 | 13 04 | 3 19 | 12 49 | Mon | 23 |
| 83 | 24 | Tue | 6 00 | 18 19 | 6 13 | 18 34 | 6 22 | 18 47 | 6 06 | 18 31 | 3 48 | 14 12 | 4 01 | 14 00 | Tue | 24 |
| 84 | 25 | Wed | 5 58 | 18 20 | 6 12 | 18 35 | 6 20 | 18 49 | 6 04 | 18 32 | 4 29 | 15 25 | 4 39 | 15 16 | Wed | 25 |
| 85 | 26 | Thu | 5 56 | 18 21 | 6 10 | 18 37 | 6 18 | 18 51 | 6 02 | 18 34 | 5 07 | 16 40 | 5 13 | 16 36 | Thu | 26 |
| 86 | 27 | Fri | 5 54 | 18 23 | 6 08 | 18 38 | 6 16 | 18 52 | 6 00 | 18 36 | 5 43 | 17 57 | 5 45 | 17 57 | Fri | 27 |
| 87 | 28 | Sat | 5 52 | 18 24 | 6 06 | 18 39 | 6 14 | 18 54 | 5 58 | 18 37 | 6 18 | 19 15 | 6 17 | 19 18 | Sat | 28 |
| 88 | 29 | Sun | 5 51 | 18 25 | 6 04 | 18 40 | 6 12 | 18 55 | 5 56 | 18 39 | 6 54 | 20 31 | 6 49 | 20 39 | Sun | 29 |
| 89 | 30 | Mon | 5 49 | 18 26 | 6 03 | 18 41 | 6 09 | 18 57 | 5 53 | 18 40 | 7 33 | 21 45 | 7 23 | 21 57 | Mon | 30 |
| 90 | 31 | Tue | 5 47 | 18 28 | 6 01 | 18 43 | 6 07 | 18 58 | 5 51 | 18 42 | 8 14 | 22 55 | 8 02 | 23 10 | Tues | 31 |

## APRIL 1998

| | | | | Moon's Phases E.S.T. |
|---|---|---|---|---|
| First Quarter | 3 d | 15 h | 18 m | |
| Full Moon | 11 d | 17 h | 23 m | |
| Last Quarter | 19 d | 14 h | 53 m | |
| New Moon | 26 d | 6 h | 41 m | |

| Day of Yr. | Day of Mo. | Day of Wk. | SUNRISE AND SUNSET Ottawa E.S.T. Rises | Ottawa E.S.T. Sets | Toronto E.S.T. Rises | Toronto E.S.T. Sets | Winnipeg C.S.T. Rises | Winnipeg C.S.T. Sets | Vancouver P.S.T. Rises | Vancouver P.S.T. Sets | MOONRISE AND MOONSET Local Mean Time Lat. 45 ° Rises | Lat. 45 ° Sets | Lat. 50 ° Rises | Lat. 50 ° Sets | Day of Wk. | Day of Mo. |
|---|---|---|---|---|---|---|---|---|---|---|---|---|---|---|---|---|
| | | | *h m* | *h m* | *h m* | *h m* | *h m* | *h m* | *h m* | *h m* | *h m* | *h m* | *h m* | *h m* | | |
| 91 | 1 | Wed | 5 45 | 18 29 | 5 59 | 18 44 | 6 05 | 19 00 | 5 49 | 18 43 | 8 59 | 24 00 | 8 45 | -- -- | Wed | 1 |
| 92 | 2 | Thu | 5 43 | 18 30 | 5 57 | 18 45 | 6 03 | 19 01 | 5 47 | 18 45 | 9 49 | -- -- | 9 33 | 0 16 | Thu | 2 |
| 93 | 3 | Fri | 5 41 | 18 32 | 5 55 | 18 46 | 6 01 | 19 03 | 5 45 | 18 46 | 10 43 | 0 57 | 10 27 | 1 14 | Fri | 3 |
| 94 | 4 | Sat | 5 39 | 18 33 | 5 54 | 18 47 | 5 59 | 19 05 | 5 43 | 18 48 | 11 39 | 1 47 | 11 24 | 2 03 | Sat | 4 |
| 95 | 5 | Sun | 5 37 | 18 34 | 5 52 | 18 49 | 5 57 | 19 06 | 5 41 | 18 49 | 12 38 | 2 30 | 12 24 | 2 44 | Sun | 5 |
| 96 | 6 | Mon | 5 36 | 18 35 | 5 50 | 18 50 | 5 54 | 19 08 | 5 39 | 18 51 | 13 37 | 3 08 | 13 26 | 3 20 | Mon | 6 |
| 97 | 7 | Tue | 5 34 | 18 37 | 5 48 | 18 51 | 5 52 | 19 09 | 5 37 | 18 52 | 14 36 | 3 41 | 14 28 | 3 50 | Tue | 7 |
| 98 | 8 | Wed | 5 32 | 18 38 | 5 47 | 18 52 | 5 50 | 19 11 | 5 35 | 18 54 | 15 35 | 4 10 | 15 30 | 4 17 | Wed | 8 |
| 99 | 9 | Thu | 5 30 | 18 39 | 5 45 | 18 53 | 5 48 | 19 12 | 5 33 | 18 55 | 16 33 | 4 38 | 16 31 | 4 41 | Thu | 9 |
| 100 | 10 | Fri | 5 28 | 18 41 | 5 43 | 18 55 | 5 46 | 19 14 | 5 31 | 18 57 | 17 32 | 5 04 | 17 33 | 5 05 | Fri | 10 |
| 101 | 11 | Sat | 5 26 | 18 42 | 5 41 | 18 56 | 5 44 | 19 16 | 5 28 | 18 58 | 18 30 | 5 31 | 18 34 | 5 28 | Sat | 11 |
| 102 | 12 | Sun | 5 24 | 18 43 | 5 40 | 18 57 | 5 42 | 19 17 | 5 26 | 19 00 | 19 29 | 5 58 | 19 36 | 5 52 | Sun | 12 |
| 103 | 13 | Mon | 5 23 | 18 44 | 5 38 | 18 58 | 5 40 | 19 19 | 5 24 | 19 01 | 20 27 | 6 27 | 20 38 | 6 18 | Mon | 13 |
| 104 | 14 | Tue | 5 21 | 18 46 | 5 36 | 18 59 | 5 38 | 19 20 | 5 22 | 19 03 | 21 25 | 6 58 | 21 39 | 6 47 | Tue | 14 |
| 105 | 15 | Wed | 5 19 | 18 47 | 5 35 | 19 01 | 5 36 | 19 22 | 5 20 | 19 04 | 22 23 | 7 34 | 22 38 | 7 20 | Wed | 15 |
| 106 | 16 | Thu | 5 17 | 18 48 | 5 33 | 19 02 | 5 34 | 19 23 | 5 18 | 19 06 | 23 18 | 8 14 | 23 35 | 7 58 | Thu | 16 |
| 107 | 17 | Fri | 5 16 | 18 50 | 5 31 | 19 03 | 5 32 | 19 25 | 5 16 | 19 07 | -- -- | 9 00 | -- -- | 8 43 | Fri | 17 |
| 108 | 18 | Sat | 5 14 | 18 51 | 5 30 | 19 04 | 5 30 | 19 26 | 5 14 | 19 09 | 0 11 | 9 52 | 0 27 | 9 36 | Sat | 18 |
| 109 | 19 | Sun | 5 12 | 18 52 | 5 28 | 19 05 | 5 28 | 19 28 | 5 13 | 19 10 | 0 59 | 10 50 | 1 15 | 10 35 | Sun | 19 |
| 110 | 20 | Mon | 5 10 | 18 53 | 5 26 | 19 06 | 5 26 | 19 30 | 5 11 | 19 12 | 1 44 | 11 54 | 1 58 | 11 41 | Mon | 20 |
| 111 | 21 | Tue | 5 09 | 18 55 | 5 25 | 19 08 | 5 24 | 19 31 | 5 09 | 19 13 | 2 24 | 13 03 | 2 35 | 12 53 | Tue | 21 |
| 112 | 22 | Wed | 5 07 | 18 56 | 5 23 | 19 09 | 5 22 | 19 33 | 5 07 | 19 15 | 3 02 | 14 15 | 3 10 | 14 08 | Wed | 22 |
| 113 | 23 | Thu | 5 05 | 18 57 | 5 22 | 19 10 | 5 20 | 19 34 | 5 05 | 19 16 | 3 37 | 15 29 | 3 41 | 15 27 | Thu | 23 |
| 114 | 24 | Fri | 5 04 | 18 59 | 5 20 | 19 11 | 5 18 | 19 36 | 5 03 | 19 18 | 4 12 | 16 45 | 4 12 | 16 47 | Fri | 24 |
| 115 | 25 | Sat | 5 02 | 19 00 | 5 19 | 19 12 | 5 16 | 19 37 | 5 01 | 19 19 | 4 47 | 18 02 | 4 43 | 18 08 | Sat | 25 |
| 116 | 26 | Sun | 5 00 | 19 01 | 5 17 | 19 14 | 5 14 | 19 39 | 4 59 | 19 21 | 5 24 | 19 19 | 5 16 | 19 28 | Sun | 26 |
| 117 | 27 | Mon | 4 59 | 19 02 | 5 15 | 19 15 | 5 12 | 19 40 | 4 58 | 19 22 | 6 04 | 20 33 | 5 53 | 20 46 | Mon | 27 |
| 118 | 28 | Tue | 4 57 | 19 04 | 5 14 | 19 16 | 5 10 | 19 42 | 4 56 | 19 24 | 6 48 | 21 43 | 6 34 | 21 58 | Tue | 28 |
| 119 | 29 | Wed | 4 56 | 19 05 | 5 13 | 19 17 | 5 09 | 19 43 | 4 54 | 19 25 | 7 37 | 22 46 | 7 21 | 23 02 | Wed | 29 |
| 120 | 30 | Thu | 4 54 | 19 06 | 5 11 | 19 18 | 5 07 | 19 45 | 4 52 | 19 27 | 8 31 | 23 41 | 8 14 | -- -- | Thu | 30 |

| MAY 1998 | | | | | Moon's Phases E.S.T. |
|---|---|---|---|---|---|
| | First Quarter................ | 3 d | 5 h | 4 m | |
| | Full Moon................. | 11 d | 9 h | 29 m | |
| | Last Quarter............. | 18 d | 23 h | 35 m | |
| | New Moon............... | 25 d | 14 h | 32 m | |

| Day of Yr. | Day of Mo. | Day of Wk. | SUNRISE AND SUNSET Ottawa E.S.T. Rises | Sets | Toronto E.S.T. Rises | Sets | Winnipeg C.S.T. Rises | Sets | Vancouver P.S.T. Rises | Sets | MOONRISE AND MOONSET Local Mean Time Lat. 45 ° Rises | Sets | Lat. 50 ° Rises | Sets | Day of Wk. | Day of Mo. |
|---|---|---|---|---|---|---|---|---|---|---|---|---|---|---|---|---|
| | | | *h m* | *h m* | *h m* | *h m* | *h m* | *h m* | *h m* | *h m* | *h m* | *h m* | *h m* | *h m* | | |
| 121 | 1 | Fri | 4 18 | 19 43 | 5 10 | 19 20 | 5 05 | 19 47 | 4 50 | 19 28 | 9 28 | -- -- | 9 12 | 24 00 | Fri | 1 |
| 122 | 2 | Sat | 4 51 | 19 09 | 5 08 | 19 21 | 5 03 | 19 48 | 4 49 | 19 30 | 10 28 | 0 28 | 10 13 | -- -- | Sat | 2 |
| 123 | 3 | Sun | 4 49 | 19 10 | 5 07 | 19 22 | 5 01 | 19 50 | 4 47 | 19 31 | 11 28 | 1 08 | 11 16 | 1 21 | Sun | 3 |
| 124 | 4 | Mon | 4 48 | 19 11 | 5 05 | 19 23 | 5 00 | 19 51 | 4 45 | 19 33 | 12 28 | 1 43 | 12 19 | 1 53 | Mon | 4 |
| 125 | 5 | Tue | 4 47 | 19 13 | 5 04 | 19 24 | 4 58 | 19 53 | 4 44 | 19 34 | 13 27 | 2 14 | 13 21 | 2 21 | Tue | 5 |
| 126 | 6 | Wed | 4 45 | 19 14 | 5 03 | 19 25 | 4 56 | 19 54 | 4 42 | 19 36 | 14 26 | 2 42 | 14 23 | 2 47 | Wed | 6 |
| 127 | 7 | Thu | 4 44 | 19 15 | 5 02 | 19 27 | 4 55 | 19 56 | 4 41 | 19 37 | 15 24 | 3 09 | 15 25 | 3 10 | Thu | 7 |
| 128 | 8 | Fri | 4 42 | 19 16 | 5 00 | 19 28 | 4 53 | 19 57 | 4 39 | 19 39 | 16 23 | 3 35 | 16 26 | 3 33 | Fri | 8 |
| 129 | 9 | Sat | 4 41 | 19 18 | 4 59 | 19 29 | 4 52 | 19 59 | 4 37 | 19 40 | 17 21 | 4 01 | 17 28 | 3 57 | Sat | 9 |
| 130 | 10 | Sun | 4 40 | 19 19 | 4 58 | 19 30 | 4 50 | 20 00 | 4 36 | 19 42 | 18 20 | 4 29 | 18 30 | 4 22 | Sun | 10 |
| 131 | 11 | Mon | 4 38 | 19 20 | 4 57 | 19 31 | 4 49 | 20 01 | 4 34 | 19 43 | 19 19 | 5 00 | 19 32 | 4 49 | Mon | 11 |
| 132 | 12 | Tue | 4 37 | 19 21 | 4 55 | 19 32 | 4 47 | 20 03 | 4 33 | 19 44 | 20 18 | 5 34 | 20 33 | 5 21 | Tue | 12 |
| 133 | 13 | Wed | 4 36 | 19 22 | 4 54 | 19 33 | 4 46 | 20 04 | 4 32 | 19 46 | 21 15 | 6 13 | 21 31 | 5 57 | Wed | 13 |
| 134 | 14 | Thu | 4 35 | 19 24 | 4 53 | 19 34 | 4 44 | 20 06 | 4 30 | 19 47 | 22 09 | 6 57 | 22 26 | 6 40 | Thu | 14 |
| 135 | 15 | Fri | 4 33 | 19 25 | 4 52 | 19 36 | 4 43 | 20 07 | 4 29 | 19 48 | 22 59 | 7 47 | 23 15 | 7 30 | Fri | 15 |
| 136 | 16 | Sat | 4 32 | 19 26 | 4 51 | 19 37 | 4 41 | 20 08 | 4 28 | 19 50 | 23 44 | 8 43 | 24 00 | 8 27 | Sat | 16 |
| 137 | 17 | Sun | 4 31 | 19 27 | 4 50 | 19 38 | 4 40 | 20 10 | 4 26 | 19 51 | -- -- | 9 45 | -- -- | 9 31 | Sun | 17 |
| 138 | 18 | Mon | 4 30 | 19 28 | 4 49 | 19 39 | 4 39 | 20 11 | 4 25 | 19 52 | 0 25 | 10 50 | 0 37 | 10 39 | Mon | 18 |
| 139 | 19 | Tue | 4 29 | 19 29 | 4 48 | 19 40 | 4 37 | 20 13 | 4 24 | 19 54 | 1 02 | 11 59 | 1 11 | 11 51 | Tue | 19 |
| 140 | 20 | Wed | 4 28 | 19 30 | 4 47 | 19 41 | 4 36 | 20 14 | 4 23 | 19 55 | 1 37 | 13 10 | 1 43 | 13 06 | Wed | 20 |
| 141 | 21 | Thu | 4 27 | 19 32 | 4 46 | 19 42 | 4 35 | 20 15 | 4 21 | 19 56 | 2 10 | 14 23 | 2 12 | 14 23 | Thu | 21 |
| 142 | 22 | Fri | 4 26 | 19 33 | 4 45 | 19 43 | 4 34 | 20 16 | 4 20 | 19 58 | 2 43 | 15 37 | 2 42 | 15 41 | Fri | 22 |
| 143 | 23 | Sat | 4 25 | 19 34 | 4 44 | 19 44 | 4 33 | 20 18 | 4 15 | 19 59 | 3 18 | 16 52 | 3 12 | 17 00 | Sat | 23 |
| 144 | 24 | Sun | 4 24 | 19 35 | 4 44 | 19 45 | 4 32 | 20 19 | 4 14 | 20 00 | 3 55 | 18 07 | 3 46 | 18 19 | Sun | 24 |
| 145 | 25 | Mon | 4 23 | 19 36 | 4 43 | 19 46 | 4 31 | 20 20 | 4 13 | 20 01 | 4 36 | 19 20 | 4 24 | 19 34 | Mon | 25 |
| 146 | 26 | Tue | 4 22 | 19 37 | 4 42 | 19 47 | 4 30 | 20 21 | 4 12 | 20 02 | 5 23 | 20 27 | 5 08 | 20 44 | Tue | 26 |
| 147 | 27 | Wed | 4 21 | 19 38 | 4 41 | 19 48 | 4 29 | 20 23 | 4 11 | 20 03 | 6 15 | 21 28 | 5 58 | 21 45 | Wed | 27 |
| 148 | 28 | Thu | 4 21 | 19 39 | 4 41 | 19 49 | 4 28 | 20 24 | 4 10 | 20 05 | 7 12 | 22 21 | 6 55 | 22 36 | Thu | 28 |
| 149 | 29 | Fri | 4 20 | 19 40 | 4 40 | 19 49 | 4 27 | 20 25 | 4 10 | 20 06 | 8 12 | 23 05 | 7 57 | 23 19 | Fri | 29 |
| 150 | 30 | Sat | 4 19 | 19 41 | 4 40 | 19 50 | 4 26 | 20 26 | 4 09 | 20 07 | 9 14 | 23 43 | 9 01 | 23 55 | Sat | 30 |
| 151 | 31 | Sun | 4 19 | 19 42 | 4 39 | 19 51 | 4 25 | 20 27 | 4 08 | 20 08 | 10 16 | -- -- | 10 05 | -- -- | Sun | 31 |

| JUNE 1998 | | | | | Moon's Phases E.S.T. |
|---|---|---|---|---|---|
| | First Quarter............. | 1 d | 20 h | 45 m | |
| | Full Moon................ | 9 d | 23 h | 18 m | |
| | Last Quarter.............. | 17 d | 5 h | 38 m | |
| | New Moon................ | 23 d | 22 h | 50 m | |

| Day of Yr. | Day of Mo. | Day of Wk. | SUNRISE AND SUNSET Ottawa E.S.T. Rises | Sets | Toronto E.S.T. Rises | Sets | Winnipeg C.S.T. Rises | Sets | Vancouver P.S.T. Rises | Sets | MOONRISE AND MOONSET Local Mean Time Lat. 45 ° Rises | Sets | Lat. 50 ° Rises | Sets | Day of Wk. | Day of Mo. |
|---|---|---|---|---|---|---|---|---|---|---|---|---|---|---|---|---|
| | | | *h m* | *h m* | *h m* | *h m* | *h m* | *h m* | *h m* | *h m* | *h m* | *h m* | *h m* | *h m* | | |
| 152 | 1 | Mon | 4 18 | 19 43 | 4 38 | 19 52 | 4 25 | 20 28 | 4 07 | 20 09 | 11 16 | 0 16 | 11 09 | 0 25 | Mon | 1 |
| 153 | 2 | Tue | 4 17 | 19 43 | 4 38 | 19 53 | 4 24 | 20 29 | 4 07 | 20 10 | 12 16 | 0 46 | 12 12 | 0 51 | Tue | 2 |
| 154 | 3 | Wed | 4 17 | 19 44 | 4 37 | 19 53 | 4 23 | 20 30 | 4 06 | 20 11 | 13 15 | 1 13 | 13 14 | 1 15 | Wed | 3 |
| 155 | 4 | Thu | 4 16 | 19 45 | 4 37 | 19 54 | 4 23 | 20 31 | 4 05 | 20 11 | 14 14 | 1 39 | 14 16 | 1 38 | Thu | 4 |
| 156 | 5 | Fri | 4 16 | 19 46 | 4 37 | 19 55 | 4 22 | 20 32 | 4 05 | 20 12 | 15 12 | 2 05 | 15 17 | 2 01 | Fri | 5 |
| 157 | 6 | Sat | 4 15 | 19 47 | 4 36 | 19 56 | 4 22 | 20 33 | 4 04 | 20 13 | 16 11 | 2 32 | 16 19 | 2 26 | Sat | 6 |
| 158 | 7 | Sun | 4 15 | 19 47 | 4 36 | 19 56 | 4 21 | 20 33 | 4 04 | 20 14 | 17 10 | 3 01 | 17 22 | 2 52 | Sun | 7 |
| 159 | 8 | Mon | 4 15 | 19 48 | 4 36 | 19 57 | 4 21 | 20 34 | 4 04 | 20 15 | 18 10 | 3 34 | 18 24 | 3 22 | Mon | 8 |
| 160 | 9 | Tue | 4 14 | 19 49 | 4 35 | 19 58 | 4 20 | 20 35 | 4 03 | 20 15 | 19 08 | 4 11 | 19 24 | 3 56 | Tue | 9 |
| 161 | 10 | Wed | 4 14 | 19 49 | 4 35 | 19 58 | 4 20 | 20 36 | 4 03 | 20 16 | 20 04 | 4 53 | 20 21 | 4 37 | Wed | 10 |
| 162 | 11 | Thu | 4 14 | 19 50 | 4 35 | 19 59 | 4 20 | 20 36 | 4 03 | 20 17 | 20 56 | 5 42 | 21 13 | 5 25 | Thu | 11 |
| 163 | 12 | Fri | 4 14 | 19 51 | 4 35 | 19 59 | 4 19 | 20 37 | 4 02 | 20 17 | 21 44 | 6 37 | 22 00 | 6 20 | Fri | 12 |
| 164 | 13 | Sat | 4 14 | 19 51 | 4 35 | 20 00 | 4 19 | 20 37 | 4 02 | 20 18 | 22 27 | 7 38 | 22 40 | 7 23 | Sat | 13 |
| 165 | 14 | Sun | 4 13 | 19 52 | 4 35 | 20 00 | 4 19 | 20 38 | 4 02 | 20 18 | 23 05 | 8 42 | 23 16 | 8 30 | Sun | 14 |
| 166 | 15 | Mon | 4 13 | 19 52 | 4 35 | 20 01 | 4 19 | 20 38 | 4 02 | 20 19 | 23 40 | 9 50 | 23 47 | 9 41 | Mon | 15 |
| 167 | 16 | Tue | 4 13 | 19 52 | 4 35 | 20 01 | 4 19 | 20 39 | 4 02 | 20 19 | -- -- | 11 00 | -- -- | 10 54 | Tue | 16 |
| 168 | 17 | Wed | 4 13 | 19 53 | 4 35 | 20 01 | 4 19 | 20 39 | 4 02 | 20 20 | 0 13 | 12 10 | 0 17 | 12 09 | Wed | 17 |
| 169 | 18 | Thu | 4 13 | 19 53 | 4 35 | 20 02 | 4 19 | 20 40 | 4 02 | 20 20 | 0 45 | 13 22 | 0 45 | 13 24 | Thu | 18 |
| 170 | 19 | Fri | 4 13 | 19 54 | 4 35 | 20 02 | 4 19 | 20 40 | 4 02 | 20 20 | 1 18 | 14 35 | 1 14 | 14 41 | Fri | 19 |
| 171 | 20 | Sat | 4 14 | 19 54 | 4 35 | 20 02 | 4 19 | 20 40 | 4 02 | 20 21 | 1 52 | 15 47 | 1 45 | 15 57 | Sat | 20 |
| 172 | 21 | Sun | 4 14 | 19 54 | 4 35 | 20 02 | 4 19 | 20 40 | 4 03 | 20 21 | 2 30 | 16 59 | 2 19 | 17 12 | Sun | 21 |
| 173 | 22 | Mon | 4 14 | 19 54 | 4 36 | 20 03 | 4 16 | 20 41 | 4 03 | 20 21 | 3 13 | 18 08 | 2 59 | 18 24 | Mon | 22 |
| 174 | 23 | Tue | 4 14 | 19 55 | 4 36 | 20 03 | 4 16 | 20 41 | 4 03 | 20 21 | 4 01 | 19 12 | 3 45 | 19 29 | Tue | 23 |
| 175 | 24 | Wed | 4 14 | 19 55 | 4 36 | 20 03 | 4 16 | 20 41 | 4 03 | 20 21 | 4 56 | 20 09 | 4 39 | 20 26 | Wed | 24 |
| 176 | 25 | Thu | 4 15 | 19 55 | 4 37 | 20 03 | 4 17 | 20 41 | 4 04 | 20 21 | 5 55 | 20 58 | 5 38 | 21 13 | Thu | 25 |
| 177 | 26 | Fri | 4 15 | 19 55 | 4 37 | 20 03 | 4 17 | 20 41 | 4 04 | 20 21 | 6 57 | 21 40 | 6 42 | 21 53 | Fri | 26 |
| 178 | 27 | Sat | 4 15 | 19 55 | 4 37 | 20 03 | 4 18 | 20 41 | 4 05 | 20 21 | 8 00 | 22 16 | 7 48 | 22 26 | Sat | 27 |
| 179 | 28 | Sun | 4 16 | 19 55 | 4 38 | 20 03 | 4 18 | 20 41 | 4 05 | 20 21 | 9 02 | 22 47 | 8 53 | 22 54 | Sun | 28 |
| 180 | 29 | Mon | 4 16 | 19 55 | 4 38 | 20 03 | 4 19 | 20 41 | 4 06 | 20 21 | 10 03 | 23 15 | 9 57 | 23 19 | Mon | 29 |
| 181 | 30 | Tue | 4 17 | 19 55 | 4 39 | 20 03 | 4 19 | 20 40 | 4 06 | 20 21 | 11 03 | 23 42 | 11 01 | 23 43 | Tue | 30 |

## JULY 1998

| Moon's Phases E.S.T. | d | h | m |
|---|---|---|---|
| First Quarter | 1 d | 13 h | 43 m |
| Full Moon | 9 d | 11 h | 1 m |
| Last Quarter | 16 d | 10 h | 13 m |
| New Moon | 23 d | 8 h | 44 m |
| First Quarter | 31 d | 7 h | 5 m |

| Day of Yr. | Day of Mo. | Day of Wk. | SUNRISE AND SUNSET Ottawa E.S.T. Rises | Sets | Toronto E.S.T. Rises | Sets | Winnipeg C.S.T. Rises | Sets | Vancouver P.S.T. Rises | Sets | MOONRISE AND MOONSET Local Mean Time Lat. 45 ° Rises | Sets | Lat. 50 ° Rises | Sets | Day of Wk. | Day of Mo. |
|---|---|---|---|---|---|---|---|---|---|---|---|---|---|---|---|---|
| | | | h m | h m | h m | h m | h m | h m | h m | h m | h m | h m | h m | h m | | |
| 182 | 1 | Wed | 4 17 | 19 55 | 4 39 | 20 03 | 4 20 | 20 40 | 4 07 | 20 20 | 12 02 | -- -- | 12 03 | -- -- | Wed | 1 |
| 183 | 2 | Thu | 4 18 | 19 54 | 4 40 | 20 02 | 4 20 | 20 40 | 4 07 | 20 20 | 13 01 | 0 08 | 13 05 | 0 06 | Thu | 2 |
| 184 | 3 | Fri | 4 18 | 19 54 | 4 40 | 20 02 | 4 21 | 20 39 | 4 08 | 20 20 | 14 00 | 0 35 | 14 07 | 0 29 | Fri | 3 |
| 185 | 4 | Sat | 4 19 | 19 54 | 4 41 | 20 02 | 4 22 | 20 39 | 4 09 | 20 19 | 14 59 | 1 03 | 15 09 | 0 55 | Sat | 4 |
| 186 | 5 | Sun | 4 20 | 19 54 | 4 42 | 20 02 | 4 23 | 20 38 | 4 10 | 20 19 | 15 58 | 1 33 | 16 11 | 1 22 | Sun | 5 |
| 187 | 6 | Mon | 4 20 | 19 53 | 4 42 | 20 01 | 4 23 | 20 38 | 4 10 | 20 19 | 16 57 | 2 08 | 17 12 | 1 55 | Mon | 6 |
| 188 | 7 | Tue | 4 21 | 19 53 | 4 43 | 20 01 | 4 24 | 20 37 | 4 11 | 20 18 | 17 55 | 2 48 | 18 11 | 2 33 | Tue | 7 |
| 189 | 8 | Wed | 4 22 | 19 53 | 4 40 | 20 00 | 4 25 | 20 37 | 4 12 | 20 17 | 18 49 | 3 30 | 19 06 | 3 14 | Wed | 8 |
| 190 | 9 | Thu | 4 18 | 19 52 | 4 40 | 20 00 | 4 26 | 20 36 | 4 13 | 20 17 | 19 40 | 4 24 | 19 56 | 4 07 | Thu | 9 |
| 191 | 10 | Fri | 4 19 | 19 52 | 4 41 | 20 00 | 4 27 | 20 36 | 4 14 | 20 16 | 20 26 | 5 27 | 20 40 | 5 11 | Fri | 10 |
| 192 | 11 | Sat | 4 20 | 19 51 | 4 42 | 19 59 | 4 28 | 20 35 | 4 15 | 20 15 | 21 06 | 6 32 | 21 18 | 6 18 | Sat | 11 |
| 193 | 12 | Sun | 4 21 | 19 50 | 4 43 | 19 58 | 4 29 | 20 34 | 4 16 | 20 15 | 21 43 | 7 40 | 21 52 | 7 30 | Sun | 12 |
| 194 | 13 | Mon | 4 22 | 19 50 | 4 43 | 19 58 | 4 30 | 20 33 | 4 17 | 20 14 | 22 17 | 8 50 | 22 22 | 8 43 | Mon | 13 |
| 195 | 14 | Tue | 4 23 | 19 49 | 4 44 | 19 57 | 4 31 | 20 32 | 4 18 | 20 13 | 22 49 | 10 01 | 22 50 | 9 58 | Tue | 14 |
| 196 | 15 | Wed | 4 23 | 19 48 | 4 49 | 19 57 | 4 32 | 20 31 | 4 19 | 20 12 | 23 21 | 11 13 | 23 19 | 11 14 | Wed | 15 |
| 197 | 16 | Thu | 4 24 | 19 48 | 4 50 | 19 56 | 4 33 | 20 30 | 4 20 | 20 11 | 23 55 | 12 24 | 23 48 | 12 29 | Thu | 16 |
| 198 | 17 | Fri | 4 29 | 19 47 | 4 51 | 19 55 | 4 34 | 20 29 | 4 21 | 20 10 | -- -- | 13 36 | -- -- | 13 44 | Fri | 17 |
| 199 | 18 | Sat | 4 30 | 19 46 | 4 52 | 19 54 | 4 36 | 20 28 | 4 22 | 20 09 | 0 26 | 14 46 | 0 16 | 14 58 | Sat | 18 |
| 200 | 19 | Sun | 4 31 | 19 45 | 4 53 | 19 54 | 4 41 | 20 27 | 4 27 | 20 08 | 1 06 | 15 55 | 0 53 | 16 09 | Sun | 19 |
| 201 | 20 | Mon | 4 32 | 19 45 | 4 54 | 19 53 | 4 42 | 20 26 | 4 29 | 20 07 | 1 50 | 16 59 | 1 35 | 17 16 | Mon | 20 |
| 202 | 21 | Tue | 4 33 | 19 44 | 4 55 | 19 52 | 4 43 | 20 25 | 4 30 | 20 06 | 2 41 | 17 58 | 2 24 | 18 15 | Tue | 21 |
| 203 | 22 | Wed | 4 34 | 19 43 | 4 56 | 19 51 | 4 44 | 20 24 | 4 31 | 20 05 | 3 37 | 18 50 | 3 20 | 19 06 | Wed | 22 |
| 204 | 23 | Thu | 4 35 | 19 42 | 4 57 | 19 50 | 4 46 | 20 23 | 4 32 | 20 04 | 4 41 | 19 35 | 4 26 | 19 49 | Thu | 23 |
| 205 | 24 | Fri | 4 36 | 19 41 | 4 58 | 19 49 | 4 47 | 20 21 | 4 33 | 20 03 | 5 44 | 20 13 | 5 30 | 20 25 | Fri | 24 |
| 206 | 25 | Sat | 4 37 | 19 40 | 4 59 | 19 48 | 4 48 | 20 20 | 4 35 | 20 01 | 6 47 | 20 47 | 6 36 | 20 55 | Sat | 25 |
| 207 | 26 | Sun | 4 38 | 19 39 | 5 00 | 19 47 | 4 50 | 20 19 | 4 36 | 20 00 | 7 49 | 21 17 | 7 42 | 21 22 | Sun | 26 |
| 208 | 27 | Mon | 4 40 | 19 38 | 5 01 | 19 46 | 4 51 | 20 17 | 4 37 | 19 59 | 8 50 | 21 44 | 8 46 | 21 46 | Mon | 27 |
| 209 | 28 | Tue | 4 41 | 19 36 | 5 02 | 19 45 | 4 52 | 20 16 | 4 39 | 19 57 | 9 50 | 22 11 | 9 49 | 22 10 | Tue | 28 |
| 210 | 29 | Wed | 4 42 | 19 35 | 5 03 | 19 44 | 4 54 | 20 15 | 4 40 | 19 56 | 10 49 | 22 37 | 10 51 | 22 33 | Wed | 29 |
| 211 | 30 | Thu | 4 43 | 19 34 | 5 04 | 19 43 | 4 55 | 20 13 | 4 41 | 19 54 | 11 47 | 23 04 | 11 53 | 22 57 | Thu | 30 |
| 212 | 31 | Fri | 4 44 | 19 33 | 5 05 | 19 41 | 4 56 | 20 12 | 4 43 | 19 53 | 12 46 | 23 33 | 12 55 | 23 24 | Fri | 31 |

## AUGUST 1998

| Moon's Phases E.S.T. | d | h | m |
|---|---|---|---|
| Full Moon | 7 d | 21 h | 10 m |
| Last Quarter | 14 d | 14 h | 48 m |
| New Moon | 21 d | 21 h | 3 m |
| First Quarter | 30 d | 0 h | 6 m |

| Day of Yr. | Day of Mo. | Day of Wk. | SUNRISE AND SUNSET Ottawa E.S.T. Rises | Sets | Toronto E.S.T. Rises | Sets | Winnipeg C.S.T. Rises | Sets | Vancouver P.S.T. Rises | Sets | MOONRISE AND MOONSET Local Mean Time Lat. 45 ° Rises | Sets | Lat. 50 ° Rises | Sets | Day of Wk. | Day of Mo. |
|---|---|---|---|---|---|---|---|---|---|---|---|---|---|---|---|---|
| | | | h m | h m | h m | h m | h m | h m | h m | h m | h m | h m | h m | h m | | |
| 213 | 1 | Sat | 4 45 | 19 32 | 5 06 | 19 40 | 4 58 | 20 10 | 4 44 | 19 52 | 13 45 | 24 00 | 13 56 | 23 53 | Sat | 1 |
| 214 | 2 | Sun | 4 46 | 19 30 | 5 07 | 19 39 | 4 59 | 20 09 | 4 45 | 19 50 | 14 43 | -- -- | 14 57 | -- -- | Sun | 2 |
| 215 | 3 | Mon | 4 47 | 19 29 | 5 08 | 19 38 | 5 01 | 20 07 | 4 47 | 19 48 | 15 41 | 0 39 | 15 57 | 0 24 | Mon | 3 |
| 216 | 4 | Tue | 4 49 | 19 28 | 5 09 | 19 37 | 5 02 | 20 05 | 4 48 | 19 47 | 16 37 | 1 22 | 16 54 | 1 05 | Tue | 4 |
| 217 | 5 | Wed | 4 50 | 19 26 | 5 10 | 19 35 | 5 03 | 20 04 | 4 49 | 19 45 | 17 30 | 2 11 | 17 47 | 1 54 | Wed | 5 |
| 218 | 6 | Thu | 4 51 | 19 25 | 5 11 | 19 34 | 5 05 | 20 02 | 4 51 | 19 44 | 18 18 | 3 12 | 18 34 | 2 52 | Thu | 6 |
| 219 | 7 | Fri | 4 52 | 19 24 | 5 12 | 19 33 | 5 06 | 20 00 | 4 52 | 19 42 | 19 02 | 4 16 | 19 15 | 4 01 | Fri | 7 |
| 220 | 8 | Sat | 4 53 | 19 22 | 5 14 | 19 31 | 5 08 | 19 59 | 4 54 | 19 40 | 19 42 | 5 24 | 19 51 | 5 12 | Sat | 8 |
| 221 | 9 | Sun | 4 55 | 19 21 | 5 15 | 19 30 | 5 09 | 19 57 | 4 55 | 19 39 | 20 18 | 6 35 | 20 24 | 6 27 | Sun | 9 |
| 222 | 10 | Mon | 4 56 | 19 19 | 5 16 | 19 28 | 5 11 | 19 55 | 4 56 | 19 37 | 20 51 | 7 48 | 20 54 | 7 43 | Mon | 10 |
| 223 | 11 | Tue | 4 57 | 19 18 | 5 17 | 19 27 | 5 12 | 19 53 | 4 58 | 19 35 | 21 24 | 9 01 | 21 23 | 9 01 | Tue | 11 |
| 224 | 12 | Wed | 4 58 | 19 16 | 5 18 | 19 25 | 5 14 | 19 52 | 4 59 | 19 33 | 21 57 | 10 14 | 21 52 | 10 18 | Wed | 12 |
| 225 | 13 | Thu | 4 59 | 19 15 | 5 19 | 19 24 | 5 15 | 19 50 | 5 01 | 19 32 | 22 32 | 11 27 | 22 24 | 11 34 | Thu | 13 |
| 226 | 14 | Fri | 5 01 | 19 13 | 5 20 | 19 23 | 5 17 | 19 48 | 5 02 | 19 30 | 23 11 | 12 38 | 22 59 | 12 48 | Fri | 14 |
| 227 | 15 | Sat | 5 02 | 19 11 | 5 21 | 19 21 | 5 18 | 19 46 | 5 04 | 19 28 | 23 53 | 13 46 | 23 39 | 14 00 | Sat | 15 |
| 228 | 16 | Sun | 5 03 | 19 10 | 5 23 | 19 19 | 5 19 | 19 44 | 5 05 | 19 26 | -- -- | 14 52 | -- -- | 15 07 | Sun | 16 |
| 229 | 17 | Mon | 5 04 | 19 08 | 5 24 | 19 18 | 5 21 | 19 42 | 5 06 | 19 24 | 0 37 | 15 51 | 0 20 | 16 08 | Mon | 17 |
| 230 | 18 | Tue | 5 05 | 19 07 | 5 25 | 19 16 | 5 22 | 19 40 | 5 08 | 19 22 | 1 30 | 16 44 | 1 13 | 17 01 | Tue | 18 |
| 231 | 19 | Wed | 5 07 | 19 05 | 5 26 | 19 15 | 5 24 | 19 39 | 5 09 | 19 21 | 2 31 | 17 31 | 2 15 | 17 46 | Wed | 19 |
| 232 | 20 | Thu | 5 08 | 19 03 | 5 27 | 19 13 | 5 25 | 19 37 | 5 11 | 19 19 | 3 32 | 18 11 | 3 18 | 18 24 | Thu | 20 |
| 233 | 21 | Fri | 5 09 | 19 02 | 5 28 | 19 12 | 5 27 | 19 35 | 5 12 | 19 17 | 4 34 | 18 46 | 4 23 | 18 56 | Fri | 21 |
| 234 | 22 | Sat | 5 10 | 19 00 | 5 29 | 19 10 | 5 28 | 19 33 | 5 14 | 19 15 | 5 36 | 19 17 | 5 28 | 19 24 | Sat | 22 |
| 235 | 23 | Sun | 5 11 | 18 58 | 5 30 | 19 08 | 5 30 | 19 31 | 5 15 | 19 13 | 6 38 | 19 46 | 6 32 | 19 49 | Sun | 23 |
| 236 | 24 | Mon | 5 13 | 18 56 | 5 32 | 19 07 | 5 31 | 19 29 | 5 17 | 19 11 | 7 38 | 20 13 | 7 36 | 20 13 | Mon | 24 |
| 237 | 25 | Tue | 5 14 | 18 55 | 5 33 | 19 05 | 5 33 | 19 27 | 5 18 | 19 09 | 8 38 | 20 39 | 8 39 | 20 36 | Tue | 25 |
| 238 | 26 | Wed | 5 15 | 18 53 | 5 34 | 19 03 | 5 34 | 19 25 | 5 19 | 19 07 | 9 37 | 21 06 | 9 41 | 21 00 | Wed | 26 |
| 239 | 27 | Thu | 5 16 | 18 51 | 5 35 | 19 02 | 5 36 | 19 22 | 5 21 | 19 05 | 10 35 | 21 34 | 10 42 | 21 25 | Thu | 27 |
| 240 | 28 | Fri | 5 18 | 18 49 | 5 36 | 19 00 | 5 37 | 19 20 | 5 22 | 19 03 | 11 33 | 22 05 | 11 44 | 21 53 | Fri | 28 |
| 241 | 29 | Sat | 5 19 | 18 48 | 5 37 | 18 58 | 5 39 | 19 18 | 5 24 | 19 01 | 12 31 | 22 39 | 12 44 | 22 25 | Sat | 29 |
| 242 | 30 | Sun | 5 20 | 18 46 | 5 38 | 18 56 | 5 40 | 19 16 | 5 25 | 18 59 | 13 28 | 23 19 | 13 44 | 23 03 | Sun | 30 |
| 243 | 31 | Mon | 5 21 | 18 44 | 5 39 | 18 55 | 5 42 | 19 14 | 5 27 | 18 57 | 14 24 | 24 00 | 14 41 | 23 47 | Mon | 31 |

**SEPTEMBER 1998**

| | | | | Moon's Phases E.S.T. |
|---|---|---|---|---|
| Full Moon | 6 d | 6 h | 21 m | |
| Last Quarter | 12 d | 20 h | 58 m | |
| New Moon | 20 d | 12 h | 1 m | |
| First Quarter | 28 d | 16 h | 11 m | |

| Day of Yr. | Day of Mo. | Day of Wk. | SUNRISE AND SUNSET: Ottawa E.S.T. Rises | Ottawa Sets | Toronto E.S.T. Rises | Toronto Sets | Winnipeg C.S.T. Rises | Winnipeg Sets | Vancouver P.S.T. Rises | Vancouver Sets | MOONRISE AND MOONSET Local Mean Time: Lat. 45 ° Rises | Lat. 45 ° Sets | Lat. 50 ° Rises | Lat. 50 ° Sets | Day of Wk. | Day of Mo. |
|---|---|---|---|---|---|---|---|---|---|---|---|---|---|---|---|---|
| | | | h m | h m | h m | h m | h m | h m | h m | h m | h m | h m | h m | h m | | |
| 244 | 1 | Tue | 5 22 | 18 42 | 5 41 | 18 53 | 5 43 | 19 12 | 5 28 | 18 55 | 15 18 | 24 00 | 15 35 | -- -- | Tue | 1 |
| 245 | 2 | Wed | 5 24 | 18 40 | 5 42 | 18 51 | 5 45 | 19 10 | 5 30 | 18 53 | 16 08 | 0 53 | 16 24 | 0 36 | Wed | 2 |
| 246 | 3 | Thu | 5 25 | 18 38 | 5 43 | 18 49 | 5 46 | 19 08 | 5 31 | 18 50 | 16 53 | 1 56 | 17 07 | 1 41 | Thu | 3 |
| 247 | 4 | Fri | 5 26 | 18 36 | 5 44 | 18 48 | 5 48 | 19 06 | 5 32 | 18 48 | 17 35 | 3 02 | 17 46 | 2 49 | Fri | 4 |
| 248 | 5 | Sat | 5 27 | 18 35 | 5 45 | 18 46 | 5 49 | 19 03 | 5 34 | 18 46 | 18 13 | 4 12 | 18 21 | 4 02 | Sat | 5 |
| 249 | 6 | Sun | 5 28 | 18 33 | 5 46 | 18 44 | 5 51 | 19 01 | 5 35 | 18 44 | 18 48 | 5 26 | 18 52 | 5 19 | Sun | 6 |
| 250 | 7 | Mon | 5 30 | 18 31 | 5 47 | 18 42 | 5 52 | 18 59 | 5 37 | 18 42 | 19 22 | 6 41 | 19 23 | 6 39 | Mon | 7 |
| 251 | 8 | Tue | 5 31 | 18 29 | 5 48 | 18 40 | 5 54 | 18 57 | 5 38 | 18 40 | 19 57 | 7 57 | 19 53 | 7 58 | Tue | 8 |
| 252 | 9 | Wed | 5 32 | 18 27 | 5 50 | 18 39 | 5 55 | 18 55 | 5 40 | 18 38 | 20 32 | 9 12 | 20 25 | 9 18 | Wed | 9 |
| 253 | 10 | Thu | 5 33 | 18 25 | 5 51 | 18 37 | 5 57 | 18 53 | 5 41 | 18 36 | 21 10 | 10 26 | 20 59 | 10 36 | Thu | 10 |
| 254 | 11 | Fri | 5 35 | 18 23 | 5 52 | 18 35 | 5 58 | 18 50 | 5 42 | 18 33 | 21 52 | 11 37 | 21 38 | 11 50 | Fri | 11 |
| 255 | 12 | Sat | 5 36 | 18 21 | 5 53 | 18 33 | 6 00 | 18 48 | 5 44 | 18 31 | 22 38 | 12 45 | 22 22 | 13 00 | Sat | 12 |
| 256 | 13 | Sun | 5 37 | 18 19 | 5 54 | 18 31 | 6 01 | 18 46 | 5 45 | 18 29 | 23 30 | 13 47 | 23 13 | 14 03 | Sun | 13 |
| 257 | 14 | Mon | 5 38 | 18 18 | 5 55 | 18 29 | 6 02 | 18 44 | 5 47 | 18 27 | -- -- | 14 42 | -- -- | 14 58 | Mon | 14 |
| 258 | 15 | Tue | 5 39 | 18 16 | 5 56 | 18 28 | 6 04 | 18 42 | 5 48 | 18 25 | 0 26 | 15 30 | 0 05 | 15 45 | Tue | 15 |
| 259 | 16 | Wed | 5 41 | 18 14 | 5 57 | 18 26 | 6 05 | 18 40 | 5 50 | 18 23 | 1 25 | 16 11 | 1 10 | 16 25 | Wed | 16 |
| 260 | 17 | Thu | 5 42 | 18 12 | 5 58 | 18 24 | 6 07 | 18 37 | 5 51 | 18 21 | 2 26 | 16 47 | 2 13 | 16 58 | Thu | 17 |
| 261 | 18 | Fri | 5 43 | 18 10 | 6 00 | 18 22 | 6 08 | 18 35 | 5 53 | 18 18 | 3 27 | 17 19 | 3 18 | 17 27 | Fri | 18 |
| 262 | 19 | Sat | 5 44 | 18 08 | 6 01 | 18 20 | 6 10 | 18 33 | 5 54 | 18 16 | 4 29 | 17 48 | 4 22 | 17 53 | Sat | 19 |
| 263 | 20 | Sun | 5 45 | 18 06 | 6 02 | 18 18 | 6 11 | 18 31 | 5 55 | 18 14 | 5 29 | 18 15 | 5 26 | 18 17 | Sun | 20 |
| 264 | 21 | Mon | 5 47 | 18 04 | 6 03 | 18 17 | 6 13 | 18 29 | 5 57 | 18 12 | 6 29 | 18 42 | 6 29 | 18 40 | Mon | 21 |
| 265 | 22 | Tue | 5 48 | 18 02 | 6 04 | 18 15 | 6 14 | 18 26 | 5 58 | 18 10 | 7 28 | 19 08 | 7 31 | 19 03 | Tue | 22 |
| 266 | 23 | Wed | 5 49 | 18 00 | 6 05 | 18 13 | 6 16 | 18 24 | 6 00 | 18 08 | 8 26 | 19 35 | 8 33 | 19 28 | Wed | 23 |
| 267 | 24 | Thu | 5 50 | 17 58 | 6 06 | 18 11 | 6 17 | 18 22 | 6 01 | 18 06 | 9 25 | 20 05 | 9 34 | 19 55 | Thu | 24 |
| 268 | 25 | Fri | 5 52 | 17 56 | 6 08 | 18 09 | 6 19 | 18 20 | 6 03 | 18 03 | 10 22 | 20 38 | 10 35 | 20 25 | Fri | 25 |
| 269 | 26 | Sat | 5 53 | 17 54 | 6 09 | 18 07 | 6 20 | 18 18 | 6 04 | 18 01 | 11 19 | 21 15 | 11 34 | 20 59 | Sat | 26 |
| 270 | 27 | Sun | 5 54 | 17 52 | 6 10 | 18 06 | 6 22 | 18 15 | 6 06 | 17 59 | 12 15 | 21 57 | 12 31 | 21 40 | Sun | 27 |
| 271 | 28 | Mon | 5 55 | 17 51 | 6 11 | 18 04 | 6 23 | 18 13 | 6 07 | 17 57 | 13 08 | 22 45 | 13 25 | 22 28 | Mon | 28 |
| 272 | 29 | Tue | 5 57 | 17 49 | 6 12 | 18 02 | 6 25 | 18 11 | 6 09 | 17 55 | 13 58 | 23 40 | 14 15 | 23 24 | Tue | 29 |
| 273 | 30 | Wed | 5 58 | 17 47 | 6 13 | 18 00 | 6 26 | 18 09 | 6 10 | 17 53 | 14 45 | -- -- | 15 00 | -- -- | Wed | 30 |

**OCTOBER 1998**

| | | | | Moon's Phases E.S.T. |
|---|---|---|---|---|
| Full Moon | 5 d | 15 h | 12 m | |
| Last Quarter | 12 d | 6 h | 11 m | |
| New Moon | 20 d | 5 h | 9 m | |
| First Quarter | 28 d | 6 h | 46 m | |

| Day of Yr. | Day of Mo. | Day of Wk. | SUNRISE AND SUNSET: Ottawa E.S.T. Rises | Ottawa Sets | Toronto E.S.T. Rises | Toronto Sets | Winnipeg C.S.T. Rises | Winnipeg Sets | Vancouver P.S.T. Rises | Vancouver Sets | MOONRISE AND MOONSET Local Mean Time: Lat. 45 ° Rises | Lat. 45 ° Sets | Lat. 50 ° Rises | Lat. 50 ° Sets | Day of Wk. | Day of Mo. |
|---|---|---|---|---|---|---|---|---|---|---|---|---|---|---|---|---|
| | | | h m | h m | h m | h m | h m | h m | h m | h m | h m | h m | h m | h m | | |
| 274 | 1 | Thu | 5 59 | 17 45 | 6 15 | 17 58 | 6 28 | 18 07 | 6 12 | 17 51 | 15 27 | 0 41 | 15 40 | 0 27 | Thu | 1 |
| 275 | 2 | Fri | 6 00 | 17 43 | 6 16 | 17 57 | 6 30 | 18 05 | 6 13 | 17 48 | 16 06 | 1 48 | 16 15 | 1 36 | Fri | 2 |
| 276 | 3 | Sat | 6 02 | 17 41 | 6 17 | 17 55 | 6 31 | 18 02 | 6 15 | 17 46 | 16 42 | 2 59 | 16 48 | 2 51 | Sat | 3 |
| 277 | 4 | Sun | 6 03 | 17 39 | 6 18 | 17 53 | 6 33 | 18 00 | 6 16 | 17 44 | 17 17 | 4 13 | 17 19 | 4 09 | Sun | 4 |
| 278 | 5 | Mon | 6 04 | 17 37 | 6 19 | 17 51 | 6 34 | 17 58 | 6 18 | 17 42 | 17 51 | 5 30 | 17 49 | 5 29 | Mon | 5 |
| 279 | 6 | Tue | 6 05 | 17 35 | 6 20 | 17 49 | 6 36 | 17 56 | 6 19 | 17 40 | 18 26 | 6 47 | 18 21 | 6 51 | Tue | 6 |
| 280 | 7 | Wed | 6 07 | 17 34 | 6 22 | 17 48 | 6 37 | 17 54 | 6 21 | 17 38 | 19 04 | 8 04 | 18 55 | 8 12 | Wed | 7 |
| 281 | 8 | Thu | 6 08 | 17 32 | 6 23 | 17 46 | 6 39 | 17 52 | 6 22 | 17 36 | 19 46 | 9 20 | 19 33 | 9 32 | Thu | 8 |
| 282 | 9 | Fri | 6 09 | 17 30 | 6 24 | 17 44 | 6 40 | 17 50 | 6 24 | 17 34 | 20 32 | 10 32 | 20 17 | 10 47 | Fri | 9 |
| 283 | 10 | Sat | 6 10 | 17 28 | 6 25 | 17 42 | 6 42 | 17 48 | 6 25 | 17 32 | 21 23 | 11 39 | 21 07 | 11 55 | Sat | 10 |
| 284 | 11 | Sun | 6 12 | 17 26 | 6 26 | 17 41 | 6 43 | 17 45 | 6 27 | 17 30 | 22 19 | 12 38 | 22 02 | 12 55 | Sun | 11 |
| 285 | 12 | Mon | 6 13 | 17 24 | 6 28 | 17 39 | 6 45 | 17 43 | 6 28 | 17 28 | 23 19 | 13 29 | 23 03 | 13 45 | Mon | 12 |
| 286 | 13 | Tue | 6 14 | 17 23 | 6 29 | 17 37 | 6 47 | 17 41 | 6 30 | 17 26 | -- -- | 14 12 | -- -- | 14 27 | Tue | 13 |
| 287 | 14 | Wed | 6 16 | 17 21 | 6 30 | 17 36 | 6 48 | 17 39 | 6 31 | 17 24 | 0 19 | 14 50 | 0 06 | 15 02 | Wed | 14 |
| 288 | 15 | Thu | 6 17 | 17 19 | 6 31 | 17 34 | 6 50 | 17 37 | 6 33 | 17 22 | 1 21 | 15 23 | 1 10 | 15 32 | Thu | 15 |
| 289 | 16 | Fri | 6 18 | 17 17 | 6 32 | 17 32 | 6 51 | 17 35 | 6 34 | 17 20 | 2 22 | 15 52 | 2 14 | 15 58 | Fri | 16 |
| 290 | 17 | Sat | 6 20 | 17 15 | 6 34 | 17 31 | 6 53 | 17 33 | 6 36 | 17 18 | 3 22 | 16 19 | 3 18 | 16 22 | Sat | 17 |
| 291 | 18 | Sun | 6 21 | 17 14 | 6 35 | 17 29 | 6 55 | 17 31 | 6 37 | 17 16 | 4 22 | 16 45 | 4 20 | 16 45 | Sun | 18 |
| 292 | 19 | Mon | 6 22 | 17 12 | 6 36 | 17 27 | 6 56 | 17 29 | 6 39 | 17 14 | 5 21 | 17 11 | 5 23 | 17 08 | Mon | 19 |
| 293 | 20 | Tue | 6 24 | 17 10 | 6 37 | 17 26 | 6 58 | 17 27 | 6 41 | 17 12 | 6 19 | 17 38 | 6 25 | 17 32 | Tue | 20 |
| 294 | 21 | Wed | 6 25 | 17 09 | 6 39 | 17 24 | 6 59 | 17 25 | 6 42 | 17 10 | 7 18 | 18 07 | 7 26 | 17 57 | Wed | 21 |
| 295 | 22 | Thu | 6 26 | 17 07 | 6 40 | 17 23 | 7 01 | 17 23 | 6 44 | 17 08 | 8 16 | 18 38 | 8 28 | 18 26 | Thu | 22 |
| 296 | 23 | Fri | 6 28 | 17 05 | 6 41 | 17 21 | 7 03 | 17 22 | 6 45 | 17 06 | 9 14 | 19 13 | 9 28 | 18 59 | Fri | 23 |
| 297 | 24 | Sat | 6 29 | 17 04 | 6 43 | 17 20 | 7 04 | 17 20 | 6 47 | 17 05 | 10 10 | 19 53 | 10 26 | 19 37 | Sat | 24 |
| 298 | 25 | Sun | 6 30 | 17 02 | 6 44 | 17 18 | 7 06 | 17 18 | 6 48 | 17 03 | 11 03 | 20 39 | 11 21 | 20 21 | Sun | 25 |
| 299 | 26 | Mon | 6 32 | 17 00 | 6 45 | 17 17 | 7 08 | 17 16 | 6 50 | 17 01 | 11 54 | 21 30 | 12 11 | 21 13 | Mon | 26 |
| 300 | 27 | Tue | 6 33 | 16 59 | 6 46 | 17 15 | 7 09 | 17 14 | 6 52 | 16 59 | 12 40 | 22 27 | 12 57 | 22 12 | Tue | 27 |
| 301 | 28 | Wed | 6 35 | 16 57 | 6 48 | 17 14 | 7 11 | 17 12 | 6 53 | 16 57 | 13 23 | 23 30 | 13 37 | 23 16 | Wed | 28 |
| 302 | 29 | Thu | 6 36 | 16 56 | 6 49 | 17 12 | 7 13 | 17 11 | 6 55 | 16 56 | 14 02 | -- -- | 14 13 | -- -- | Thu | 29 |
| 303 | 30 | Fri | 6 37 | 16 54 | 6 50 | 17 11 | 7 14 | 17 09 | 6 56 | 16 54 | 14 37 | 0 37 | 14 45 | 0 27 | Fri | 30 |
| 304 | 31 | Sat | 6 39 | 16 53 | 6 52 | 17 09 | 7 16 | 17 07 | 6 58 | 16 52 | 15 11 | 1 47 | 15 16 | 1 41 | Sat | 31 |

## NOVEMBER 1998

| Moon's Phases E.S.T. | d | h | m |
|---|---|---|---|
| Full Moon | 4 d | 0 h | 18 m |
| Last Quarter | 10 d | 19 h | 28 m |
| New Moon | 18 d | 23 h | 27 m |
| First Quarter | 26 d | 19 h | 23 m |

| Day of Yr. | Day of Mo. | Day of Wk. | Ottawa E.S.T. Rises | Ottawa Sets | Toronto E.S.T. Rises | Toronto Sets | Winnipeg C.S.T. Rises | Winnipeg Sets | Vancouver P.S.T. Rises | Vancouver Sets | Moonrise and Moonset (Local Mean Time) Lat. 45° Rises | Lat. 45° Sets | Lat. 50° Rises | Lat. 50° Sets | Day of Wk. | Day of Mo. |
|---|---|---|---|---|---|---|---|---|---|---|---|---|---|---|---|---|
| | | | h m | h m | h m | h m | h m | h m | h m | h m | h m | h m | h m | h m | | |
| 305 | 1 | Sun | 6 40 | 16 51 | 6 53 | 17 08 | 7 17 | 17 05 | 7 00 | 16 51 | 15 45 | 3 01 | 15 45 | 2 58 | Sun | 1 |
| 306 | 2 | Mon | 6 41 | 16 50 | 6 54 | 17 07 | 7 19 | 17 04 | 7 01 | 16 49 | 16 19 | 4 16 | 16 15 | 4 18 | Mon | 2 |
| 307 | 3 | Tue | 6 43 | 16 48 | 6 55 | 17 05 | 7 21 | 17 02 | 7 03 | 16 47 | 16 55 | 5 34 | 16 47 | 5 40 | Tue | 3 |
| 308 | 4 | Wed | 6 44 | 16 47 | 6 57 | 17 04 | 7 22 | 17 00 | 7 05 | 16 46 | 17 35 | 6 52 | 17 24 | 7 02 | Wed | 4 |
| 309 | 5 | Thu | 6 46 | 16 46 | 6 58 | 17 03 | 7 24 | 16 59 | 7 06 | 16 44 | 18 20 | 8 08 | 18 05 | 8 22 | Thu | 5 |
| 310 | 6 | Fri | 6 47 | 16 44 | 6 59 | 17 02 | 7 26 | 16 57 | 7 08 | 16 43 | 19 10 | 9 21 | 18 54 | 9 37 | Fri | 6 |
| 311 | 7 | Sat | 6 48 | 16 43 | 7 01 | 17 00 | 7 27 | 16 56 | 7 09 | 16 41 | 20 06 | 10 26 | 19 49 | 10 43 | Sat | 7 |
| 312 | 8 | Sun | 6 50 | 16 42 | 7 02 | 16 59 | 7 29 | 16 54 | 7 11 | 16 40 | 21 07 | 11 23 | 20 50 | 11 40 | Sun | 8 |
| 313 | 9 | Mon | 6 51 | 16 40 | 7 03 | 16 58 | 7 31 | 16 53 | 7 13 | 16 38 | 22 09 | 12 11 | 21 55 | 12 26 | Mon | 9 |
| 314 | 10 | Tue | 6 53 | 16 39 | 7 05 | 16 57 | 7 32 | 16 51 | 7 14 | 16 37 | 23 12 | 12 51 | 23 00 | 13 04 | Tue | 10 |
| 315 | 11 | Wed | 6 54 | 16 38 | 7 06 | 16 56 | 7 34 | 16 50 | 7 16 | 16 35 | -- -- | 13 26 | -- -- | 13 36 | Wed | 11 |
| 316 | 12 | Thu | 6 55 | 16 37 | 7 07 | 16 55 | 7 36 | 16 48 | 7 17 | 16 34 | 0 14 | 13 57 | 0 05 | 14 03 | Thu | 12 |
| 317 | 13 | Fri | 6 57 | 16 36 | 7 09 | 16 54 | 7 37 | 16 47 | 7 19 | 16 33 | 1 15 | 14 24 | 1 09 | 14 28 | Fri | 13 |
| 318 | 14 | Sat | 6 58 | 16 35 | 7 10 | 16 53 | 7 39 | 16 46 | 7 21 | 16 32 | 2 15 | 14 50 | 2 12 | 14 51 | Sat | 14 |
| 319 | 15 | Sun | 7 00 | 16 33 | 7 11 | 16 52 | 7 40 | 16 44 | 7 22 | 16 30 | 3 14 | 15 16 | 3 15 | 15 13 | Sun | 15 |
| 320 | 16 | Mon | 7 01 | 16 32 | 7 12 | 16 51 | 7 42 | 16 43 | 7 24 | 16 29 | 4 13 | 15 42 | 4 17 | 15 36 | Mon | 16 |
| 321 | 17 | Tue | 7 02 | 16 31 | 7 14 | 16 50 | 7 44 | 16 42 | 7 25 | 16 28 | 5 11 | 16 10 | 5 19 | 16 01 | Tue | 17 |
| 322 | 18 | Wed | 7 04 | 16 30 | 7 15 | 16 49 | 7 45 | 16 41 | 7 27 | 16 27 | 6 10 | 16 40 | 6 20 | 16 28 | Wed | 18 |
| 323 | 19 | Thu | 7 05 | 16 30 | 7 16 | 16 48 | 7 47 | 16 40 | 7 28 | 16 26 | 7 08 | 17 14 | 7 21 | 17 00 | Thu | 19 |
| 324 | 20 | Fri | 7 06 | 16 29 | 7 18 | 16 48 | 7 48 | 16 39 | 7 30 | 16 25 | 8 05 | 17 52 | 8 21 | 17 36 | Fri | 20 |
| 325 | 21 | Sat | 7 08 | 16 28 | 7 19 | 16 47 | 7 50 | 16 38 | 7 31 | 16 24 | 9 00 | 18 36 | 9 17 | 18 18 | Sat | 21 |
| 326 | 22 | Sun | 7 09 | 16 27 | 7 20 | 16 46 | 7 51 | 16 37 | 7 33 | 16 23 | 9 52 | 19 25 | 10 10 | 19 08 | Sun | 22 |
| 327 | 23 | Mon | 7 10 | 16 26 | 7 21 | 16 45 | 7 53 | 16 36 | 7 34 | 16 22 | 10 40 | 20 20 | 10 57 | 20 03 | Mon | 23 |
| 328 | 24 | Tue | 7 12 | 16 25 | 7 23 | 16 45 | 7 55 | 16 35 | 7 36 | 16 21 | 11 23 | 21 20 | 11 38 | 21 05 | Tue | 24 |
| 329 | 25 | Wed | 7 13 | 16 25 | 7 24 | 16 44 | 7 56 | 16 34 | 7 37 | 16 20 | 12 02 | 22 24 | 12 15 | 22 12 | Wed | 25 |
| 330 | 26 | Thu | 7 14 | 16 24 | 7 25 | 16 44 | 7 57 | 16 33 | 7 39 | 16 19 | 12 38 | 23 31 | 12 47 | 23 23 | Thu | 26 |
| 331 | 27 | Fri | 7 16 | 16 23 | 7 26 | 16 43 | 7 59 | 16 32 | 7 40 | 16 19 | 13 11 | -- -- | 13 17 | -- -- | Fri | 27 |
| 332 | 28 | Sat | 7 17 | 16 23 | 7 27 | 16 43 | 8 00 | 16 32 | 7 41 | 16 18 | 13 43 | 0 40 | 13 45 | 0 36 | Sat | 28 |
| 333 | 29 | Sun | 7 18 | 16 22 | 7 28 | 16 42 | 8 02 | 16 31 | 7 43 | 16 17 | 14 15 | 1 52 | 14 13 | 1 52 | Sun | 29 |
| 334 | 30 | Mon | 7 19 | 16 22 | 7 30 | 16 42 | 8 03 | 16 30 | 7 44 | 16 17 | 14 48 | 3 06 | 14 43 | 3 10 | Mon | 30 |

## DECEMBER 1998

| Moon's Phases E.S.T. | d | h | m |
|---|---|---|---|
| Full Moon | 3 d | 10 h | 19 m |
| Last Quarter | 10 d | 12 h | 54 m |
| New Moon | 18 d | 17 h | 42 m |
| First Quarter | 26 d | 5 h | 46 m |

| Day of Yr. | Day of Mo. | Day of Wk. | Ottawa E.S.T. Rises | Ottawa Sets | Toronto E.S.T. Rises | Toronto Sets | Winnipeg C.S.T. Rises | Winnipeg Sets | Vancouver P.S.T. Rises | Vancouver Sets | Moonrise and Moonset (Local Mean Time) Lat. 45° Rises | Lat. 45° Sets | Lat. 50° Rises | Lat. 50° Sets | Day of Wk. | Day of Mo. |
|---|---|---|---|---|---|---|---|---|---|---|---|---|---|---|---|---|
| | | | h m | h m | h m | h m | h m | h m | h m | h m | h m | h m | h m | h m | | |
| 335 | 1 | Tue | 7 20 | 16 21 | 7 31 | 16 41 | 8 04 | 16 30 | 7 45 | 16 16 | 15 25 | 4 22 | 15 16 | 4 30 | Tue | 1 |
| 336 | 2 | Wed | 7 22 | 16 21 | 7 32 | 16 41 | 8 06 | 16 29 | 7 47 | 16 16 | 16 06 | 5 39 | 15 53 | 5 50 | Wed | 2 |
| 337 | 3 | Thu | 7 23 | 16 21 | 7 33 | 16 41 | 8 07 | 16 29 | 7 48 | 16 15 | 16 53 | 6 54 | 16 38 | 7 09 | Thu | 3 |
| 338 | 4 | Fri | 7 24 | 16 20 | 7 34 | 16 41 | 8 08 | 16 28 | 7 49 | 16 15 | 17 48 | 8 04 | 17 30 | 8 21 | Fri | 4 |
| 339 | 5 | Sat | 7 25 | 16 20 | 7 35 | 16 40 | 8 09 | 16 28 | 7 50 | 16 14 | 18 47 | 9 08 | 18 30 | 9 25 | Sat | 5 |
| 340 | 6 | Sun | 7 26 | 16 20 | 7 36 | 16 40 | 8 11 | 16 28 | 7 52 | 16 14 | 19 51 | 10 02 | 19 35 | 10 18 | Sun | 6 |
| 341 | 7 | Mon | 7 27 | 16 19 | 7 37 | 16 40 | 8 12 | 16 27 | 7 53 | 16 14 | 20 56 | 10 48 | 20 43 | 11 02 | Mon | 7 |
| 342 | 8 | Tue | 7 28 | 16 19 | 7 38 | 16 40 | 8 13 | 16 27 | 7 54 | 16 14 | 22 01 | 11 26 | 21 50 | 11 38 | Tue | 8 |
| 343 | 9 | Wed | 7 29 | 16 19 | 7 39 | 16 40 | 8 14 | 16 27 | 7 55 | 16 14 | 23 04 | 11 59 | 22 57 | 12 07 | Wed | 9 |
| 344 | 10 | Thu | 7 30 | 16 19 | 7 40 | 16 40 | 8 15 | 16 27 | 7 56 | 16 13 | -- -- | 12 28 | 24 00 | 12 33 | Thu | 10 |
| 345 | 11 | Fri | 7 31 | 16 19 | 7 41 | 16 40 | 8 16 | 16 27 | 7 57 | 16 13 | 0 05 | 12 55 | -- -- | 12 57 | Fri | 11 |
| 346 | 12 | Sat | 7 32 | 16 19 | 7 41 | 16 40 | 8 17 | 16 27 | 7 58 | 16 13 | 1 05 | 13 21 | 1 05 | 13 19 | Sat | 12 |
| 347 | 13 | Sun | 7 33 | 16 19 | 7 42 | 16 40 | 8 18 | 16 27 | 7 59 | 16 14 | 2 04 | 13 46 | 2 07 | 13 42 | Sun | 13 |
| 348 | 14 | Mon | 7 34 | 16 19 | 7 43 | 16 40 | 8 19 | 16 27 | 7 59 | 16 14 | 3 03 | 14 13 | 3 09 | 14 06 | Mon | 14 |
| 349 | 15 | Tue | 7 34 | 16 20 | 7 44 | 16 41 | 8 20 | 16 27 | 8 00 | 16 14 | 4 01 | 14 42 | 4 11 | 14 32 | Tue | 15 |
| 350 | 16 | Wed | 7 35 | 16 20 | 7 44 | 16 41 | 8 20 | 16 27 | 8 01 | 16 14 | 5 00 | 15 14 | 5 12 | 15 01 | Wed | 16 |
| 351 | 17 | Thu | 7 36 | 16 20 | 7 45 | 16 41 | 8 21 | 16 27 | 8 02 | 16 14 | 5 58 | 15 51 | 6 13 | 15 35 | Thu | 17 |
| 352 | 18 | Fri | 7 37 | 16 20 | 7 46 | 16 42 | 8 22 | 16 28 | 8 02 | 16 15 | 6 55 | 16 33 | 7 11 | 16 16 | Fri | 18 |
| 353 | 19 | Sat | 7 37 | 16 21 | 7 46 | 16 42 | 8 22 | 16 28 | 8 03 | 16 15 | 7 49 | 17 20 | 8 06 | 17 03 | Sat | 19 |
| 354 | 20 | Sun | 7 38 | 16 21 | 7 47 | 16 42 | 8 23 | 16 29 | 8 04 | 16 15 | 8 39 | 18 14 | 8 56 | 17 57 | Sun | 20 |
| 355 | 21 | Mon | 7 38 | 16 21 | 7 48 | 16 43 | 8 24 | 16 29 | 8 04 | 16 16 | 9 24 | 19 13 | 9 40 | 18 58 | Mon | 21 |
| 356 | 22 | Tue | 7 39 | 16 22 | 7 48 | 16 43 | 8 24 | 16 30 | 8 05 | 16 16 | 10 05 | 20 16 | 10 19 | 20 03 | Tue | 22 |
| 357 | 23 | Wed | 7 40 | 16 22 | 7 49 | 16 44 | 8 24 | 16 30 | 8 05 | 16 17 | 10 41 | 21 22 | 10 52 | 21 12 | Wed | 23 |
| 358 | 24 | Thu | 7 40 | 16 23 | 7 49 | 16 45 | 8 25 | 16 31 | 8 06 | 16 18 | 11 15 | 22 30 | 11 22 | 22 24 | Thu | 24 |
| 359 | 25 | Fri | 7 40 | 16 24 | 7 49 | 16 45 | 8 25 | 16 31 | 8 06 | 16 18 | 11 46 | 23 39 | 11 50 | 23 37 | Fri | 25 |
| 360 | 26 | Sat | 7 41 | 16 24 | 7 50 | 16 46 | 8 26 | 16 32 | 8 06 | 16 19 | 12 17 | -- -- | 12 17 | -- -- | Sat | 26 |
| 361 | 27 | Sun | 7 41 | 16 25 | 7 50 | 16 47 | 8 26 | 16 33 | 8 06 | 16 20 | 12 48 | 0 50 | 12 44 | 0 52 | Sun | 27 |
| 362 | 28 | Mon | 7 41 | 16 26 | 7 50 | 16 47 | 8 26 | 16 34 | 8 07 | 16 20 | 13 21 | 2 02 | 13 14 | 2 08 | Mon | 28 |
| 363 | 29 | Tue | 7 42 | 16 26 | 7 50 | 16 48 | 8 26 | 16 35 | 8 07 | 16 21 | 13 59 | 3 15 | 13 48 | 3 25 | Tue | 29 |
| 364 | 30 | Wed | 7 42 | 16 27 | 7 51 | 16 49 | 8 26 | 16 35 | 8 07 | 16 22 | 14 41 | 4 29 | 14 27 | 4 42 | Wed | 30 |
| 365 | 31 | Thu | 7 42 | 16 28 | 7 51 | 16 50 | 8 26 | 16 36 | 8 07 | 16 23 | 15 30 | 5 41 | 15 14 | 5 57 | Thu | 31 |

## PRINCIPAL (MEAN) ELEMENTS OF THE SOLAR SYSTEM

| Object | Equatorial Diameter (miles) | Equatorial Diameter (km) | Mass (earth=1) | Axial Rotation (days) | Magnitude at brightest | Mean Dist. from Sun (mill. miles) | Mean Dist. from Sun (mill. km) | Per. of Revol. | Eccentricity | Inclination (deg.) |
|---|---|---|---|---|---|---|---|---|---|---|
| Sun | 865,000 | 1,392,000 | 332,946 | 24.7** | -26.8 | | | | | |
| Moon | 2,159 | 3,475 | 0.0123 | 27.3217 | -12.6 | | | | | |
| Mercury | 3,032 | 4,879 | 0.0553 | 58.646 | -1.9 | 36.0 | 57.9 | 88.0d | .206 | 7.0 |
| Venus | 7,521 | 12,104 | 0.8150 | 243.019*** | -4.7 | 67.2 | 108.2 | 224.7 | .007 | 3.4 |
| Earth | 7,926 | 12,756 | 1.0000 | 0.9973 | | 93.0 | 149.6 | 365.3 | .017 | (0.0) |
| Mars | 4,222 | 6,794 | 0.1074 | 1.0260 | -2.8 | 141.6 | 227.9 | 687.0 | .093 | 1.8 |
| Jupiter | 88,846* | 142,984* | 317.833 | 0.410** | -2.5 | 483.7 | 778 | 11.86y | .048 | 1.3 |
| Saturn | 74,898* | 120,536* | 95.159 | 0.44401 | -0.4 | 888 | 1,429 | 29.42 | .056 | 2.5 |
| Uranus | 31,763* | 51,118* | 14.500 | 0.71833*** | +5.7 | 1,786 | 2,875 | 83.75 | .046 | 0.8 |
| Neptune | 30,775* | 49,528* | 17.204 | 0.67125 | +7.6 | 2,799 | 4,504 | 163.7 | .009 | 1.8 |
| Pluto | 1,430 | 2,302 | 0.0025 | 6.3872*** | +14.0 | 3,676 | 5,916 | 248.0 | .249 | 17.1 |

*at pressure 1 bar (101.325 kPa) ** at equator *** retrograde

## PLANETARY CONFIGURATIONS, 1998

UNIVERSAL (GREENWICH) TIME

| | *d* | *h* | |
|---|---|---|---|
| January | 4 | 21 | Earth at perihelion (distance 147,099,440 km) |
| | 6 | 15 | Mercury at greatest elongation W. (23°) |
| | 9 | 17 | Venus 4° N. of Neptune |
| | 16 | 11 | Venus in inferior conjunction |
| | 19 | 23 | Neptune in conjunction with Sun |
| | 21 | 01 | Mars 0.2° S. of Jupiter |
| | 26 | 17 | Mercury 8° S. of Venus |
| | 28 | 20 | Uranus in conjunction with Sun |
| February | 2 | 11 | Mercury 2° S. of Neptune |
| | 5 | 18 | Venus stationary |
| | 8 | 05 | Mercury 1.4° S. of Uranus |
| | 20 | 02 | Venus at greatest brilliancy (-4.6) |
| | 22 | 08 | Mercury in superior conjunction |
| | 23 | 09 | Jupiter in conjunction with Sun |
| | 26 | 17 | Eclipse of Sun (page 1-22) |
| March | 7 | 10 | Venus 4° N. of Neptune |
| | 11 | 15 | Mercury 1.2° N. of Mars |
| | 12 | 16 | Pluto stationary |
| | 13 | 05 | Penumbral eclipse of Moon (page 1-22) |
| | 19 | 07 | Venus 3° N. of Uranus |
| | 20 | 04 | Mercury at greatest elongation E. (19°) |
| | 20 | 20 | Equinox. Northern spring begins |
| | 27 | 15 | Mercury stationary |
| | 27 | 19 | Venus at greatest elongation W. (47°) |
| | 30 | 05 | Mercury 4° N. of Mars |
| April | 6 | 17 | Mercury in inferior conjunction |
| | 13 | 12 | Saturn in conjunction with Sun |
| | 19 | 02 | Mercury stationary |
| | 23 | 02 | Venus 0.3° N. of Jupiter |
| May | 4 | 11 | Neptune stationary |
| | 4 | 17 | Mercury at greatest elongation W. (27°) |
| | 12 | 16 | Mercury 0.8° S. of Saturn |
| | 12 | 20 | Mars in conjunction with Sun |
| | 17 | 20 | Uranus stationary |
| | 28 | 05 | Pluto at opposition |
| | 29 | 02 | Venus 0.3° N. of Saturn |
| June | 10 | 07 | Mercury in superior conjunction |
| | 21 | 14 | Solstice. Northern summer begins |
| | 27 | 11 | Mercury 5° S. of Pollux |
| July | 3 | 05 | Venus 4° N. of Aldebaran |
| July | 4 | 00 | Earth at aphelion (distance 152,095,706 km) |
| | 17 | 03 | Mercury at greatest elongation E. (27°) |
| | 18 | 18 | Jupiter stationary |
| | 23 | 20 | Neptune at opposition |
| | 30 | 05 | Mercury stationary |
| August | 3 | 07 | Uranus at opposition |
| | 5 | 03 | Venus 0.8° S. of Mars |
| | 8 | 02 | Penumbral eclipse of Moon (page 1-22) |
| | 8 | 18 | Venus 7° S. of Pollux |
| | 11 | 21 | Mars 6° S. of Pollux |
| | 14 | 00 | Mercury in inferior conjunction |
| | 16 | 16 | Saturn stationary |
| | 18 | 19 | Pluto stationary |
| | 22 | 02 | Eclipse of Sun (page 1-22) |
| | 23 | 05 | Mercury stationary |
| | 25 | 23 | Mercury 3° S. of Venus |
| | 31 | 09 | Mercury at greatest elongation W. (18°) |
| September | 6 | 10 | Venus 0.8° N. of Regulus |
| | 6 | 11 | Penumbral eclipse of Moon (page 1-22) |
| | 7 | 19 | Mercury 0.8° N. of Regulus |
| | 11 | 00 | Mercury 0.4° N. of Venus |
| | 16 | 03 | Jupiter at opposition |
| | 23 | 06 | Equinox. Northern autumn begins |
| | 25 | 20 | Mercury in superior conjunction |
| October | 06 | 16 | Mars 0.9° N. of Regulus |
| | 11 | 11 | Neptune stationary |
| | 19 | 01 | Uranus stationary |
| | 23 | 19 | Saturn at opposition |
| | 30 | 0 | Venus in superior conjunction |
| November | 9 | 09 | Mercury 1.9° N. of Antares |
| | 11 | 09 | Mercury at greatest elongation E. (23°) |
| | 14 | 01 | Jupiter stationary |
| | 21 | 14 | Mercury stationary |
| | 30 | 08 | Pluto in conjunction with Sun |
| December | 1 | 15 | Mercury in inferior conjunction |
| | 11 | 06 | Mercury stationary |
| | 20 | 04 | Mercury at greatest elongation W. (22°) |
| | 22 | 02 | Solstice. Northern winter begins |
| | 22 | 06 | Mercury 7° N. of Antares |
| | 30 | 16 | Saturn stationary |

This table includes configurations involving the sun, planets, and bright zodiacal stars. The meaning of the terms is as follows:

**Aphelion:** the point at which a planet is furthest from the sun.

**Conjunction:** in the same direction as another object--the sun, unless otherwise stated. Mercury and Venus can be at inferior conjunction (closer than the sun) or superior conjunction (beyond the sun).

**Elongation:** the angle between the planet and the sun.

**Opposition:** opposite another object (the sun, unless otherwise stated).

**Perihelion:** the point at which a planet is closest to the sun.

**Stationary:** motionless relative to the background stars. Because of the orbital motions of the planet and the earth, the planet normally moves eastward or westward relative to the background stars. At the moment when its motion changes from eastward to westward, or vice versa, the planet is said to be stationary.

## SYMBOLS AND ABBREVIATIONS

SUN, MOON AND PLANETS

| | |
|---|---|
| ☉ The Sun | ♃ Jupiter |
| ☾ The Moon | ♄ Saturn |
| ☿ Mercury | ♅ Uranus |
| ♀ Venus | ♆ Neptune |
| ⊕ The Earth | ♇ Pluto |
| ♂ Mars | |

SIGNS OF THE ZODIAC

| | | | |
|---|---|---|---|
| 1. ♈ Aries | 7. ♎ Libra | N. North | ′ Minutes of Arc |
| 2. ♉ Taurus | 8. ♏ Scorpius | S. South | ″ Seconds of Arc |
| 3. ♊ Gemini | 9. ♐ Sagittarius | E. East | h Hours |
| 4. ♋ Cancer | 10. ♑ Capricornus | W. West | m Minutes of Time |
| 5. ♌ Leo | 11. ♒ Aquarius | ° Degrees | s Seconds of Time |
| 6. ♍ Virgo | 12. ♓ Pisces | | |

## METEORS, METEORITES, AND METEOR SHOWERS

A *meteor* or "shooting star" appears momentarily in the sky when a particle from beyond the earth enters the earth's atmosphere at a high velocity. Most visible meteors are caused by particles smaller than a grape or marble, and these small particles are completely vaporized in the atmosphere at a height of about 80 km. A spectacular meteor, known as a *fire-ball*, is caused by a larger body which may fall to the earth's surface in one or more pieces. Particles seen thus to fall, or subsequently found by analysis to be of this nature, are called *meteorites*.

Meteorites may be divided into two main classes--the irons, which are almost pure nickel-iron, and the stones. Any freshly-fallen meteorite is characterized by a dark, smooth crust caused by the fusion of the outer part.

Meteors may be observed on any clear, moonless night at an average rate of about five an hour. At times *meteor showers* occur, when meteors are seen with much greater frequency and appear to radiate from a particular part of the sky which is called the *radiant*. This is an effect of perspective, the radiant being the vanishing point of the parallel tracks of the meteors. Meteor showers usually repeat themselves annually, and in some cases have been associated with the orbits of comets. When the earth passes through or near the orbit of a comet it can intercept the small particles (meteoroids) which cause meteors. The principal meteor showers for the northern hemisphere are listed below.

The study of meteors and meteorites adds to our knowledge of the nature and origin of the solar system and also to our knowledge of the earth's outer atmosphere.

### COMETS IN 1998

Comets Hyakutake and Hale-Bopp were outstanding performers in 1996 and 1997, respectively. At present (August 1997), astronomers are not expecting any bright comets to appear in 1998. It is possible, though, that a bright comet could be discovered between now and the beginning of the year, just as Comet Hyakutake was discovered early in 1996 - only a few weeks before it became clearly visible to the unaided eye.

### THE LEONID METEOR SHOWER IN 1998 & 1999

Meteor showers occur at the same time each year because the earth, in its orbit, intersects the orbit of a comet, and encounters a stream of particles which were once part of the comet. If the density of particles is high, the meteor shower is intense. Some astronomers predict that this will occur with the Leonid meteor shower in November 1998 and 1999. Thousands of meteors may be seen each hour, especially from a clear, dark location.

## MAPS OF THE NIGHT SKY

The maps on the next six pages cover the northern sky. Stars are shown down to a magnitude of 4.5 or 5, i.e. those which are readily apparent to the unaided eye on a reasonably dark night.

The maps are drawn for 45°N latitude, but are useful for latitudes several degrees north or south of this. They show the hemisphere of sky visible to an observer at various times of the year. Because the aspect of the night sky changes continuously with both longitude and time, while time zones change discontinuously with both longitude and time of year, it is not possible to state simply when, in general, a particular observer will find that his or her sky fits exactly one of the six maps. The month indicated below each map is the time of year when the map will match the "late evening" sky. On any particular night, successive maps will represent the sky as it appears every four hours later. For example, at 2 or 3 am on a March night, the May map should be used. Just after dinner on a January night, the November map will be appropriate. The centre of each map is the zenith, the point directly overhead; the circumference is the horizon. To identify the stars, hold the map in front of you so that the part of the horizon which you are facing (west, for instance) is downward. (The four letters around the periphery of each map indicate compass directions.)

On the maps, stars forming the usual constellation patterns are linked by straight lines, constellation names being given in upper case letters. The names in lower case are those of first magnitude stars, except Algol and Mira which are famous variable stars, and Polaris which is near the north celestial pole. Small clusters of dots indicate the positions of bright star clusters, nebulae, or galaxies. Although a few of these are just visible to the naked eye, and most can be located in binoculars, a telesope is needed for good views of these objects. The pair of wavy, dotted lines indicates roughly the borders of the Milky Way. Small asterisks locate the directions of the galactic centre (GC), the north galactic pole (NGP), and the south galactic pole (SGP). Two dashed lines appear on each of the six maps. The one with the more dashes is the celestial equator. Tick marks along this indicate hours of right ascension, the odd hours being labelled. The line with fewer dashes is the ecliptic, the apparent annual path of the Sun across the heavens. Letters along this line indicate the approximate position of the Sun at the beginning of each month. Also located along the ecliptic are the vernal equinox (VE), summer solstice (SS), autumnal equinox (AE), and winter solstice (WS). Moon and the other eight planets are found near the ecliptic, but since their motions are not related in a simple way to our year, it is not feasible to show them on a general set of maps.

The text above, and the six star charts on the following pages, were prepared by Professor Roy L. Bishop, Editor of the annual *Observer's Handbook of the Royal Astronomical Society of Canada* (RASC). They are copyright RASC 1996. They are used here with the kind permission of Professor Bishop and the RASC.

**PRINCIPAL ANNUAL METEOR SHOWERS FOR THE NORTHERN HEMISPHERE (UNIVERSAL TIME)**

| Shower | Location of Radiant | Date of Maximum Frequency | Hourly Number | Duration (in days) |
|---|---|---|---|---|
| Quadrantids | Bootes | Jan. 3 | 40 | 1 |
| Lyrids | Lyra | Apr. 22 | 15 | 2 |
| Eta Aquarids | Aquarius | May 5 | 20 | 3 |
| Delta Aquarids | Aquarius | July 28 | 20 | -- |
| Perseids | Perseus | Aug. 13 | 50 | 5 |
| Orionids | Orion | Oct. 22 | 25 | 2 |
| Taurids | Taurus | Nov. 3 | 15 | -- |
| Leonids | Leo | Nov. 17 | 15 | -- |
| Geminids | Gemini | Dec. 14 | 50 | 3 |
| Ursids | Ursa Minor | Dec. 23 | 15 | 2 |
| Quadranids | Bootes | Jan. 3/99 | 40 | 1 |

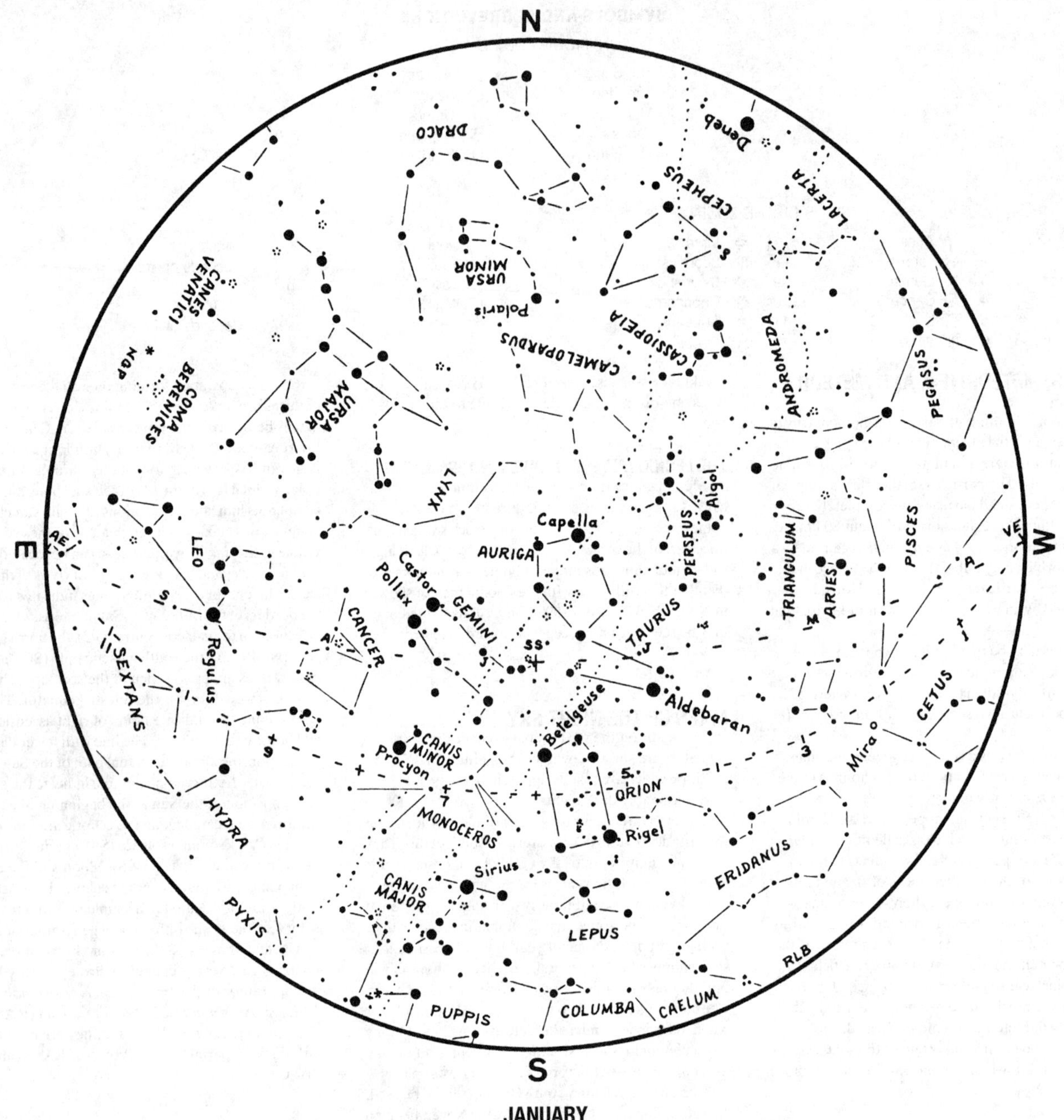


**JANUARY**

## THE NAKED-EYE PLANETS FOR 1998

The planets do *not* appear on the bimonthly star maps. They move slowly, relative to the background stars, near the *ecliptic*, which *is* shown on the maps. Mercury is never more than about 25° from the sun. Venus is very bright and is never more than about 45° from the sun. Mars is reddish. Jupiter is bright. Mercury, Mars and Saturn are comparable in brightness with the brightest stars.

### January

MERCURY may be visible early in the month, very low in the southeast, just before sunrise.

VENUS is best visible early in the month, when it is a brilliant object, very low in the southwest, just after sunset.

MARS moves from Capricorn into Aquarius during the month. It is visible low in the south-west, just after sunset, and sets a few hours later. On the 20th, it is in conjunction with Jupiter, only 0.2° apart.

JUPITER moves from Capricorn into Aquarius during the month. It is visible low in the south-west at sunset, and sets a few hours later. It is in conjunction with Mars on the 21st, only 0.2° apart.

SATURN, in Pisces, is east of south at sunset, and sets after midnight.

### February

MERCURY may be seen with great difficulty, at the beginning of the month, very low in the southeast, just before sunrise. It is in conjunction with the sun on the 22nd.

VENUS is at greatest brilliancy on the 20th, but it is visible only with difficulty, very low in the southeast, just before sunrise.

MARS moves from Aquarius into Pisces during the month. It is visible with difficulty, very low in the south-west, just after sunset.

JUPITER is not visible this month; it is in conjunction with the sun on the 23rd.

SATURN, in Pisces, is west of south at sunset, and sets before midnight.

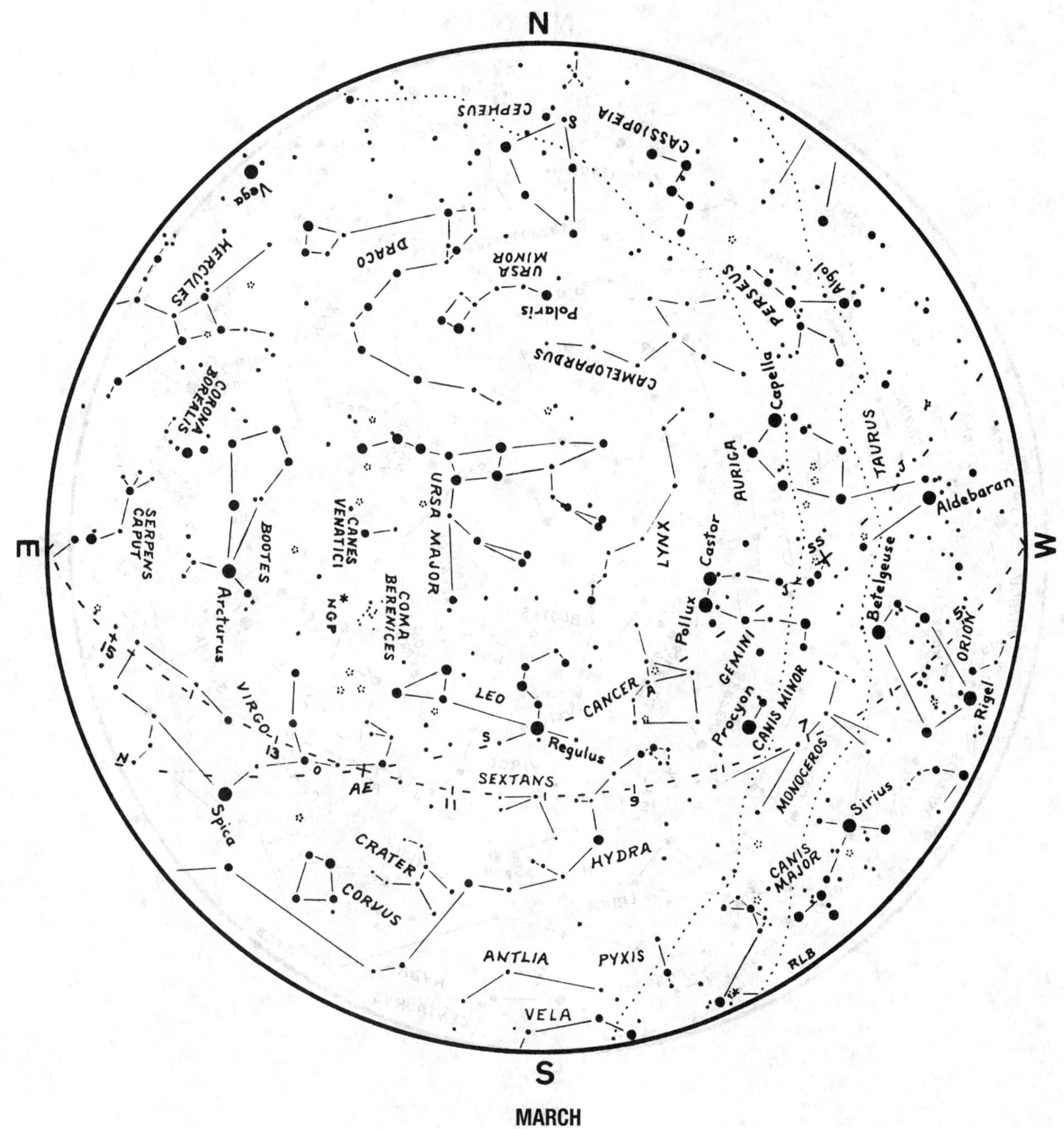


**MARCH**

## THE NAKED-EYE PLANETS FOR 1998

The planets do *not* appear on the bimonthly star maps. They move slowly, relative to the background stars, near the *ecliptic,* which *is* shown on the maps. Mercury is never more than about 25° from the sun. Venus is very bright and is never more than about 45° from the sun. Mars is reddish. Jupiter is bright. Mercury, Mars and Saturn are comparable in brightness with the brightest stars.

### March

MERCURY is visible, starting about the second week of the month, low in the south-west, just after sunset. It is at greatest elongation east on the 20th, and in conjunction with Mars on the 11th and 30th.

VENUS is at greatest elongation west on the 27th; it is visible in the south-east before sunrise, but is rather low because of the shallow angle between the ecliptic and the horizon.

MARS may be visible with difficulty, early in the month, very low in the south-west, just after sunset. It is in conjunction with Mercury on the 11th and the 30th.

JUPITER is in Aquarius. It may be visible, late in the month, very low in the south-east, just before sunrise. On the 26th, there is an occultation of Jupiter by the moon, visible from parts of North America.

SATURN, in Pisces, may be visible with difficulty, early in the month, very low in the west, just after sunset.

### April

MERCURY is not visible this month; it is in conjunction with the sun on the 6th.

VENUS is visible, low in the south-east, just before sunrise. It is in conjunction with Jupiter on the 23rd, when the two planets appear only 0.3° apart in the sky.

MARS is not visible this month.

JUPITER, in Aquarius, rises about 2 h before the sun, and is visible, very low in the south-east, just before sunrise. It is in conjunction with Venus on the 23rd, when the two planets appear only 0.3° apart.

SATURN is not visible this month; it is in conjunction with the sun on the 13th.

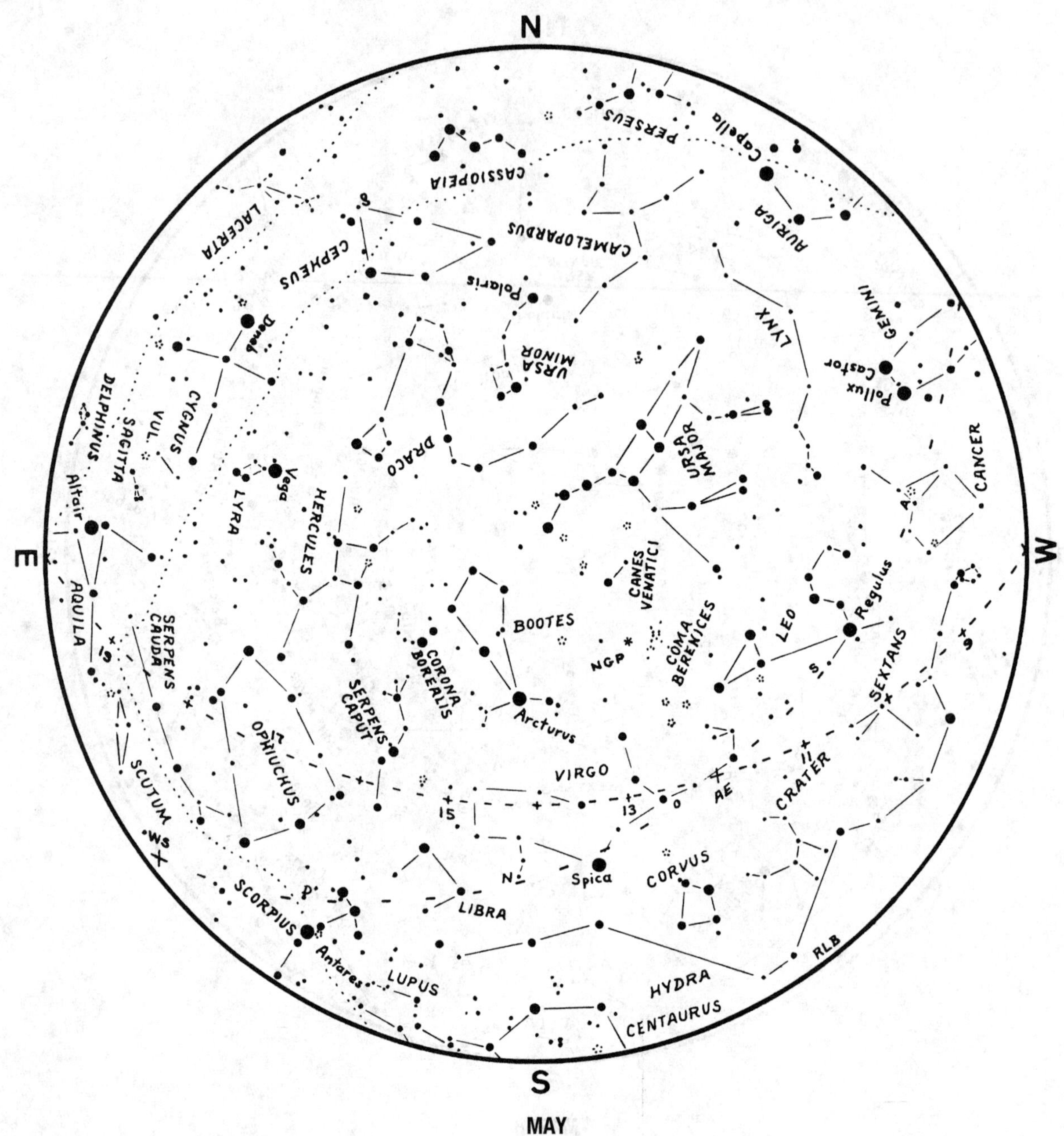


MAY

## THE NAKED-EYE PLANETS FOR 1998

The planets do *not* appear on the bimonthly star maps. They move slowly, relative to the background stars, near the *ecliptic*, which *is* shown on the maps. Mercury is never more than about 25° from the sun. Venus is very bright and is never more than about 45° from the sun. Mars is reddish. Jupiter is bright. Mercury, Mars and Saturn are comparable in brightness with the brightest stars.

### May

MERCURY is at greatest elongation west on the 4th, but this is not a favourable elongation; the planet is visible only with great difficulty, very low in the east, just before sunrise.

VENUS is visible, low in the east, just before sunrise. It is in conjunction with Saturn on the 29th, when the two planets appear only 0.3° apart in the sky.

MARS is not visible this month; it is in conjunction wih the sun on the 12th.

JUPITER, in Aquarius, rises about 3 h before the sun, and is visible, low in the south-east, just before sunrise.

SATURN, in Pisces, may be visible late in the month, very low in the east, just before sunrise. It is in conjunction with Venus on the 29th, when the two planets appear only 0.3° apart in the sky.

### June

MERCURY may be visible at the end of the month, very low in the west, just after sunset.

VENUS is a brilliant object, visible low in the east before sunrise.

MARS is not visible this month.

JUPITER moves from Aquarius into Pisces during the month. It rises about midnight, and is low in the south by sunrise.

SATURN, in Pisces, rises about 3 h before the sun, and is low in the south-east at sunrise.

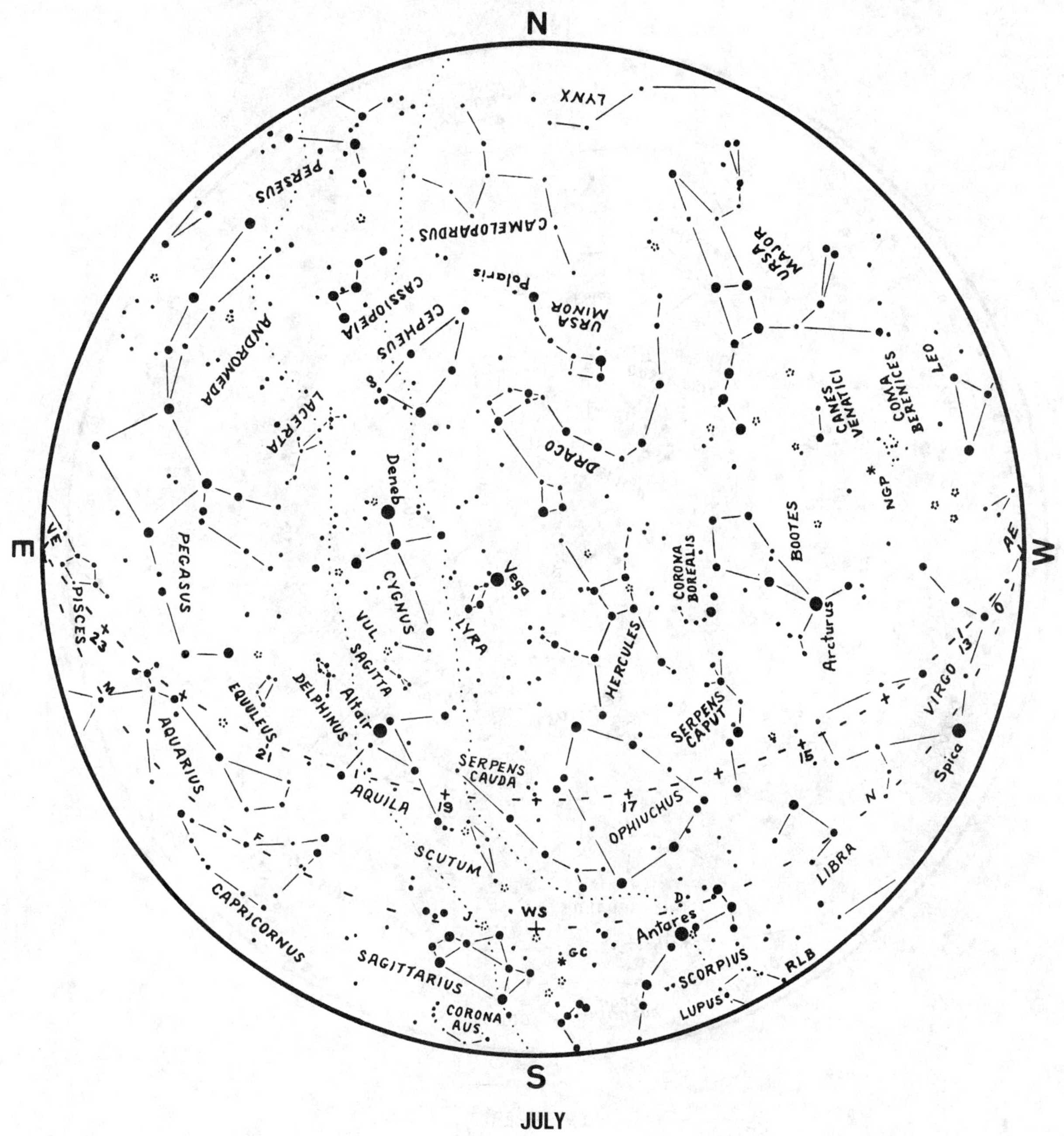


**JULY**

## THE NAKED-EYE PLANETS FOR 1998

The planets do *not* appear on the bimonthly star maps. They move slowly, relative to the background stars, near the *ecliptic*, which *is* shown on the maps. Mercury is never more than about 25° from the sun. Venus is very bright and is never more than about 45° from the sun. Mars is reddish. Jupiter is bright. Mercury, Mars and Saturn are comparable in brightness with the brightest stars.

### July

MERCURY is visible, very low in the west, just after sunset. It is at greatest elongation east on the 17th.

VENUS is a brilliant object, visible low in the east before sunrise.

MARS, in Gemini, may be visible late in the month, very low in the east, just before sunrise.

JUPITER, in Pisces, rises about midnight, and is west of south by sunrise.

SATURN moves from Pisces into Cetus during the month. It rises about 5 h before the sun, and is high in the south-east by sunrise.

### August

MERCURY may be visible with difficulty, at the beginning of the month, very low in the west, just after sunset. By the 14th, it is in conjunction with the sun. By the end of the month, it is again visible, low in the east, just before sunrise. It is at greatest elongation west on the 31st.

VENUS is a bright object, low in the east, just before sunrise. On the 5th, it is in conjunction with Mars (only 0.8° separated), and on the 25th, it is in conjunction with Mercury.

MARS moves from Gemini into Cancer during the month, passing 6° south of Pollux on the 11th. It is in conjunction with Venus on the 5th, (only 0.8° separated).

JUPITER moves from Pisces back into Aquarius during the month. It rises in mid-evening, and is low in the south-west by sunrise.

SATURN, in Cetus, rises about midnight, and is west of south by sunrise.

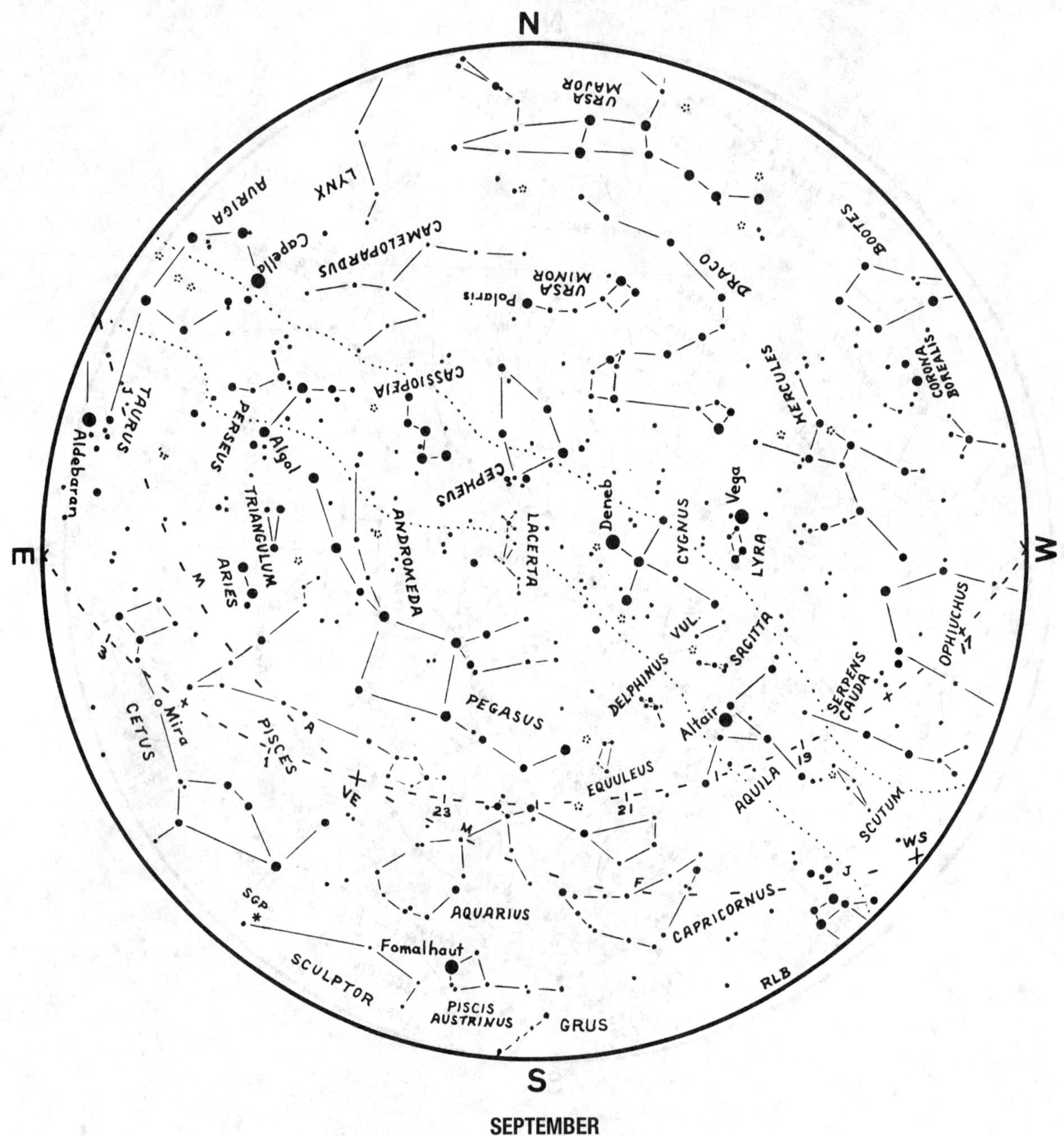


**SEPTEMBER**

## THE NAKED-EYE PLANETS FOR 1998

The planets do *not* appear on the bimonthly star maps. They move slowly, relative to the background stars, near the *ecliptic*, which *is* shown on the maps. Mercury is never more than about 25° from the sun. Venus is very bright and is never more than about 45° from the sun. Mars is reddish. Jupiter is bright. Mercury, Mars and Saturn are comparable in brightness with the brightest stars.

### September

MERCURY is visible in the first half of the month, very low in the east, just before sunrise. It passes 0.8° north of Regulus on the 7th, and is in conjunction with Venus (only 0.4° separated) on the 11th.

VENUS is a bright object, visible very low in the east, just before sunrise; by month's end, it will be difficult to see. On the 6th, it passes only 0.8° north of Regulus, and on the 11th, it is in conjunction with Mercury (only 0.4° separated).

MARS moves from Cancer into Leo during the month. It rises after midnight, and is well up in the south-east by sunrise.

JUPITER, in Aquarius, rises about sunset, and sets about sunrise. It is at opposition to the sun on the 16th.

SATURN moves from Cetus back into Pisces during the month. It rises in the evening, and is low in the south-west by sunrise.

### October

MERCURY is not easily visible this month.

VENUS is not easily visible this month. It is in conjunction with the sun on the 30th.

MARS is in Leo, passing only 0.9° north of Regulus on the 6th. It rises about 5 h before the sun, and is high in the south-east by sunrise.

JUPITER, in Aquarius, is low in the south-east at sunset, and sets after midnight.

SATURN, in Pisces, rises about sunset, and sets about sunrise. It is in opposition to the sun on the 23rd.

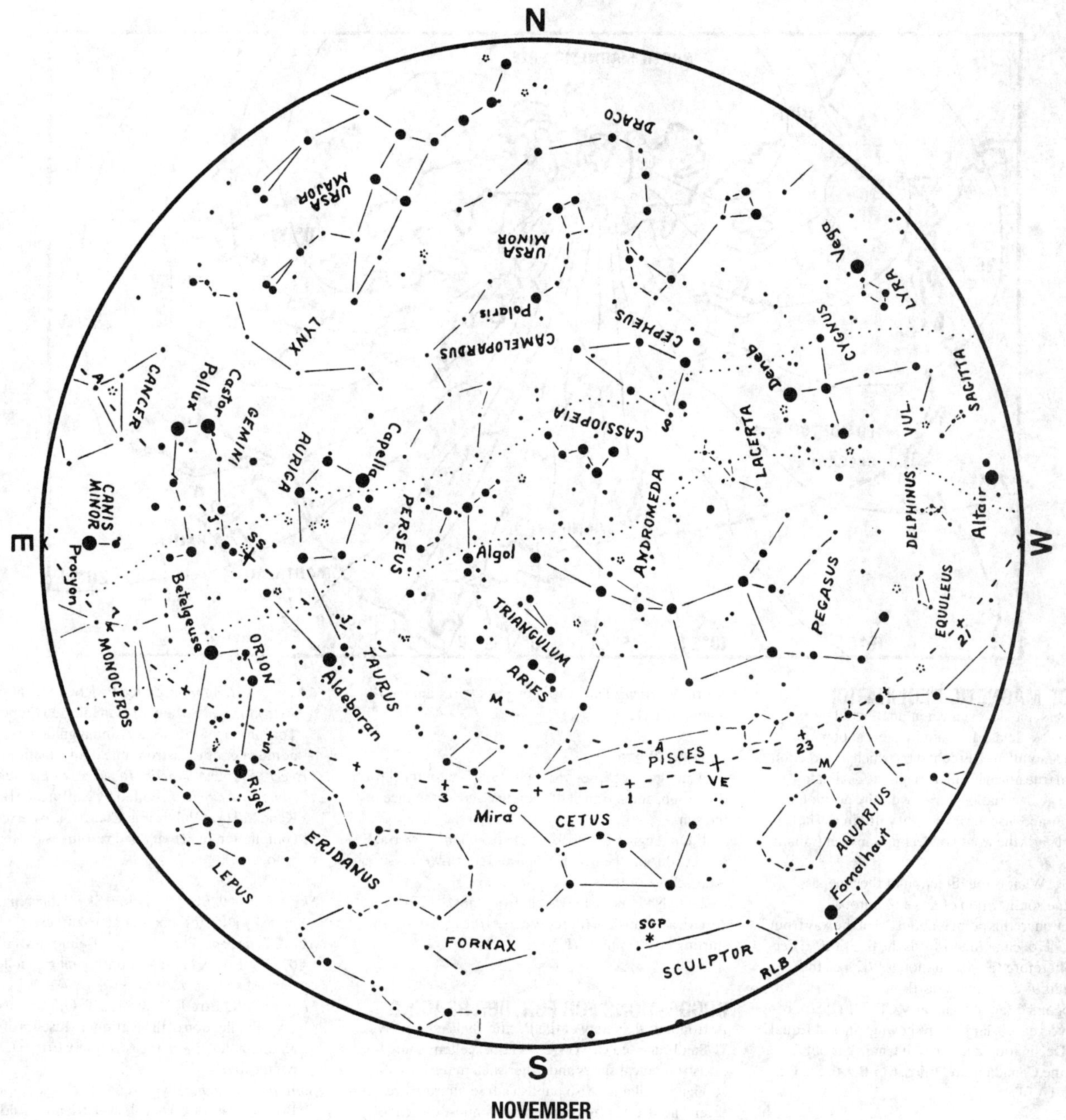


**NOVEMBER**

## THE NAKED-EYE PLANETS FOR 1998

The planets do *not* appear on the bimonthly star maps. They move slowly, relative to the background stars, near the *ecliptic*, which *is* shown on the maps. Mercury is never more than about 25° from the sun. Venus is very bright and is never more than about 45° from the sun. Mars is reddish. Jupiter is bright. Mercury, Mars and Saturn are comparable in brightness with the brightest stars.

### November

MERCURY is at greatest elongation east on the 11th, but this is not a favourable elongation, and the planet is visible only with great difficulty, very low in the south-west, just after sunset.

VENUS is not visible this month.

MARS moves from Leo into Virgo during the month. It rises about 6 h before the sun, and is in the south at sunrise. On the 13th, there is an occultation of Mars by the moon, visible from west and central North America.

JUPITER, in Aquarius, is east of south at sunset, and sets after midnight.

SATURN, in Pisces, is low in the south-east at sunset, and sets after midnight.

### December

MERCURY is visible late in the month, very low in the south-east, just before sunrise. It is at greatest elongation west on the 20th.

VENUS is visible low in the south-west, just after sunset.

MARS, in Virgo, rises about midnight, and is west of south by sunrise.

JUPITER, in Aquarius, is low in the south at sunset, and sets about midnight.

SATURN, in Pisces, is well up in the south-east at sunset, and sets after midnight.

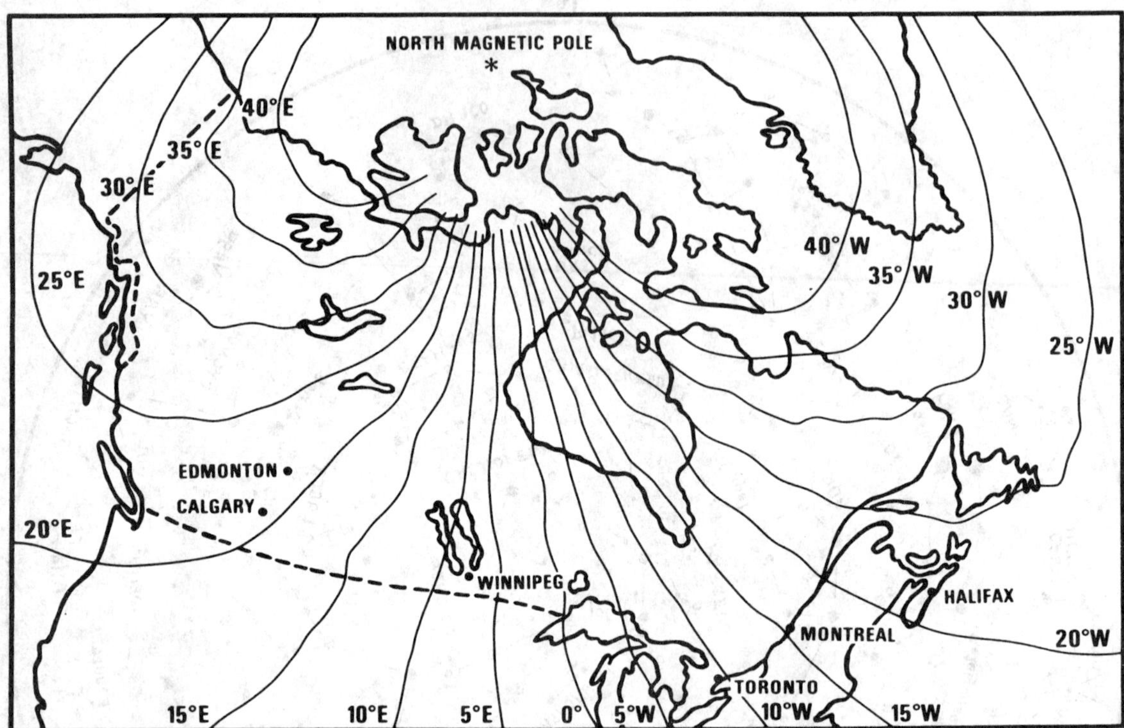


## CHART OF MAGNETIC DECLINATION

A compass needle, even when unaffected by extraneous magnetic fields, does not in general point due north. The amount and direction by which its direction differs from true north is called magnetic declination or variation. The declination varies with the position of the observer and also varies slowly with time. The above chart gives the values of declination over Canada as of 1980.

Example: What is the direction of the compass needle at the southern tip of Lake Manitoba?

From the chart this point is about 3/4 of the way from the line of 5°E declination towards the line of 10°E declination. Therefore the declination is 9°E, i.e., the needle points 9° east of true north.

The Isogonic Map of Canada MCR 701 (1980), revised every 5 years, a large map showing lines of Equal Magnetic Declination and Annual Change is obtainable from the Canada Map Office, 615 Booth St., Ottawa ON K1A 0E9.

## ECLIPSES DURING 1998

In 1998, there will be five eclipses - two of the sun, and three of the moon.

1. A **total eclipse of the sun** on February 26. The path of totality crosses Panama, the extreme northern part of South America east of Panama, and some of the islands of the Caribbean. A partial eclipse will be visible in south-eastern Canada.

2. A **penumbral eclipse of the moon** (not a very spectacular phenomenon), on March 12-13, visible from North America except the north-west corner. The eclipse begins at 9:14 pm, March 12, EST.

3. Another **penumbral eclipse of the moon** on August 7-8, visible from eastern North America. The eclipse begins at 9:32 pm, August 7, EDT.

4. An **annular eclipse of the sun** on August 21-22. The path of annularity passes north of Australia. Neither the annular nor the partial phases are visible from North America.

5. Another **penumbral eclipse of the moon** on September 6, the beginning visible from North America except the extreme east, and the end visible in western North America. The eclipse begins at 5:14 am, September 6, EDT.

### Looking Ahead:

Among the eclipses visible in 1999 is a total eclipse of the sun, and a transit of Mercury across the face of the sun.

1. On August 11, 1999, visible from a narrow track passing through central Europe and south-west Asia, a total eclipse of the sun.

2. On November 15, visible from most of North America, a transit of Mercury across the face of the sun, starting at 4:15 pm, EST.

## SUGGESTIONS FOR FURTHER READING

Astronomical Society of the Pacific, 390 Ashton Ave., San Francisco CA USA 94112. Excellent source of astronomical slides and other such material; catalogue available. Also publish a free quarterly teachers' newsletter (to obtain, mail request on school letterhead).

*Astronomy*, PO Box 1612, Waukesha WI USA 53187. Popular non-technical monthly magazine for general astronomy readers.

*The Backyard Astronomer's Guide*, by Terence Dickinson & Alan Dyer. Camden House Publishing, 1991. The best guide to equipment & techniques.

*The Beginner's Observing Guide*, by Leo Enright. Royal Astronomical Society of Canada, 136 Dupont St., Toronto ON M5R 1V2. A simple but serious introduction to the night sky. (3rd edtion: 1996-2000)

*The Cold Light of Dawn*, by Richard Jarrell. University of Toronto Press, 1988. An authoritative and comprehensive history of Canadian astronomy.

*Exploring the Night Sky*, by Terence Dickinson. Camden House Publishing, 1987. An award-winning guide, especially for young people.

*Looking Up*, by Peter Broughton. Dundurn Press, 1993. A history of the Royal Astronomical Society of Canada, illustrated.

*Nightwatch*, by Terence Dickinson. Camden House Publishing, 1989. Excellent introduction to the night sky.

*Observer's Handbook*, edited by Roy L. Bishop. Royal Astronomical Society of Canada, 136 Dupont St., Toronto ON M5R 1V2. Annual guide to sky phenomena & other astronomical information.

*Project SPICA: A Teacher Resource to Enhance Astronomy Education*, edited by N. Butcher Ball et al. Kendall/Hunt Publishing Co., 1994. An excellent compilation of activity and resources for teaching grades 3
to 12.

*Sky Atlas 2000.0*, by Wil Tirion. Sky Publishing. A popular sky atlas for amateur astronomers.

*Sky & Telescope*, PO Box 9111, Belmont MA USA 02178-9111. A popular monthly magazine for amateur astronomers.

*SkyNews.* PO Box 9724, Station T, Ottawa ON K1G 5A3. Publication of the National Museum of Science & Technology; general astronomy from a Canadian perspective.

*Summer Stargazing*, by Terence Dickinson. Firefly Books, 1996. A practical, user-friendly guide.

*The Universe at your Fingertips*, edited by Andrew Fraknoi et al. Astronomical Society of the Pacific, 390 Ashton Avenue, San Francisco CA USA 94112. Another excellent collection of teaching activities & resources.

## CANADIAN ASTRONOMY WEB SITES

Almost all of the astronomical institutions mentioned on page 1-1, and many of the branches of the Royal Astronomical Society of Canada, have sites on the World Wide Web. They can be accessed from the following key sites:

Canadian Astronomical Society:
http://www.astro.queensu.ca/~casca

Department of Astronomy, University of Toronto: http://www.astro.utoronto.ca/home.html

Herzberg Institute of Astrophysics:
http://www.hia.nrc.ca

Royal Astronomical Society of Canada:
http://www.rasc.ca

## NATIONAL ANTHEM: O CANADA

From "Chapter 5, Statues of Canada 1980; proclaimed July 1, 1980." Composed by Calixa Lavallée; French lyrics written by Judge Adolphe-Basile Routhier; English lyrics written by Robert Stanley Weir (with some changes incorporated in 1967).

O Canada! Our home and native land!
True patriot love in all thy sons command.
With glowing hearts we see thee rise, The True North strong and free!
From far and wide, O Canada, We stand on guard for thee.
God keep our land glorious and free!
O Canada, we stand on guard for thee.
O Canada, we stand on guard for thee.

O Canada! Terre de nos aïeux!
Ton front est ceint de fleurons glorieux!
Car ton bras sait porter l'épée, Il sait porter la croix!
Ton histoire est une épopée Des plus brillants exploits.
Et ta valeur, de foi trempée,
Protégera nos foyers et nos droits,
Protégera nos foyers et nos droits.

## FATHERS OF CONFEDERATION

Three conferences helped to pave the way for Confederation — those held at Charlottetown (September, 1864), Québec City (October, 1864) and London (December, 1866). As all the delegates who were at the Charlottetown conferences were also in attendance at Québec, the following list includes the names of all those who attended one or more of the three conferences.

*Hewitt Bernard was John A. Macdonald's private secretary. He served as secretary of both the Québec and London conferences.

### DELEGATES TO THE CONFEDERATION CONFERENCES, 1864-1866

| LEGEND: | Charlottetown, 1 September, 1864 | C |
|---|---|---|
| | Québec, 10 October, 1864 | Q |
| | London, 4 December, 1866 | L |

#### CANADA

| | |
|---|---|
| John A. Macdonald | C Q L |
| George E. Cartier | C Q L |
| Alexander T. Galt | C Q L |
| William McDougall | C Q L |
| Hector L. Langevin | C Q L |
| George Brown | C Q |
| Thomas D'Arcy McGee | C Q |
| Alexander Campbell | C Q |
| Sir Etienne P. Taché | Q |
| Oliver Mowat | Q |
| J.C. Chapais | Q |
| James Cockburn | Q |
| W.P. Howland | L |
| *Hewitt Bernard | |

#### NOVA SCOTIA

| | |
|---|---|
| Charles Tupper | C Q L |
| William A. Henry | C Q L |
| Jonathan McCully | C Q L |
| Adams G. Archibald | C Q L |
| Robert B. Dickey | Q |
| J.W. Ritchie | L |

#### NEW BRUNSWICK

| | |
|---|---|
| Samuel L. Tilley | C Q L |
| J.M. Johnson | C Q L |
| William H. Steeves | C Q |
| E.B. Chandler | C Q |
| John Hamilton Gray | C Q |
| Peter Mitchell | Q L |
| Charles Fisher | Q L |
| R.D. Wilmot | L |

#### PRINCE EDWARD ISLAND

| | |
|---|---|
| John Hamilton Gray | C Q |
| Edward Palmer | C Q |
| William H. Pope | C Q |
| A.A. Macdonald | C Q |
| George Coles | C Q |
| T.H. Haviland | Q |
| Edward Whelan | Q |

#### NEWFOUNDLAND

| | |
|---|---|
| F.B.T. Carter | Q |
| Ambrose Shea | Q |

## PARTICIPANTS TO THE FIRST MINISTERS' CONSTITUTIONAL CONFERENCE ON PATRIATION OF THE CONSTITUTION

**(held in Ottawa from September 2 to 5, 1981)**

The Right Honourable Pierre Elliott Trudeau, P.C., Q.C., M.P., Prime Minister of Canada;
The Honourable William G. Davis, Q.C., Premier of Ontario;
The Honourable René Lévesque, Premier of Québec;
The Honourable John M. Buchanan, Q.C., Premier of Nova Scotia;
The Honourable Richard B. Hatfield, Premier of New Brunswick;
The Honourable Sterling R. Lyon, Q.C., Premier of Manitoba;
The Honourable W.R. Bennett, Premier of British Columbia;
The Honourable J. Angus MacLean, P.C., D.F.C., C.D., Premier of Prince Edward Island;
The Honourable Allan Blakeney, Q.C., Premier of Saskatchewan;
The Honourable Peter Lougheed, Q.C., Premier of Alberta;
The Honourable Brian Peckford, Premier of Newfoundland.

## TABLE OF PRECEDENCE FOR CANADA

**(As revised on June 8, 1993)**

1. The Governor General of Canada or the Administrator of the Government of Canada. (Notes 1, 2 and 2.1).
2. The Prime Minister of Canada. (Note 3).
3. The Chief Justice of Canada. (Note 4).
4. The Speaker of the Senate.
5. The Speaker of the House of Commons.
6. Ambassadors, High Commissioners, Ministers Plenipotentiary. (Note 5).
7. Members of the Cabinet with relative precedence governed by the date of their appointment to the Queen's Privy Council for Canada.
8. The Leader of the Opposition. (Subject to Note 3).
9. The Lieutenant Governor of Ontario;
The Lieutenant Governor of Québec;
The Lieutenant Governor of Nova Scotia;
The Lieutenant Governor of New Brunswick;
The Lieutenant Governor of Manitoba;
The Lieutenant Governor of British Columbia;
The Lieutenant Governor of Prince Edward Island;
The Lieutenant Governor of Saskatchewan;
The Lieutenant Governor of Alberta;
The Lieutenant Governor of Newfoundland (Note 6).
10. Members of the Queen's Privy Council for Canada, not of the Cabinet, in accordance with the date of their appointment to the Privy Council.
11. Premiers of the Provinces of Canada in the same order as Lieutenant Governors. (Note 6).
12. The Commissioner of the Northwest Territories; The Commissioner of the Yukon Territory
13. Government Leader of the Northwest Territories; The Government Leader of the Yukon Territory
14. Representatives of Faith Communities. (Note 7).
15. Puisne Judges of the Supreme Court of Canada.
16. The Chief Justice and the Associate Chief Justices of the Federal Court of Canada.
17. (a) Chief Justices of the highest court of each province and territory;
(b) Chief Justices and Associate Chief Justices of the other superior courts of the provinces and territories; with precedence within sub-categories (a) and (b) governed by the date of appointment as chief justice.
18. (a) Judges of the Federal Court of Canada.
(b) Puisne Judges of the superior courts of the provinces and territories.
(c) The Chief Judge of the Tax Court of Canada;
(d) The Associate Chief Judge of the Tax Court of Canada;
(e) Judges of the Tax Court of Canada; with precedence within each sub-category governed by date of appointment.
19. Senators of Canada.
20. Members of the House of Commons.
21. Consuls General of countries without diplomatic representation.
22. The Chief of the Defence Staff and the Commissioner of the Royal Canadian Mounted Police. (Note 8).
23. Speakers of Legislative Assemblies, within their Provinces and Territory.
24. Members of the Executive Councils, within their Provinces and Territory.
25. Judges of Provincial and Territorial Courts, within their Province and Territory.
26. Members of Legislative Assemblies, within their Provinces and Territory.

**NOTES**

1. The presence of The Sovereign in Canada does not impair or supersede the authority of the Governor General to perform the functions delegated to him under the Letters Patent. The Governor General, under all circumstances, should be accorded precedence immediately after The Sovereign.
2. Precedence to be given immediately after the Chief Justice of Canada to former Governors General, with relative precedence among them governed by the date of their leaving office.

2.1 Precedence to be given immediately after the former Governors General to surviving spouses of deceased former Governors General (applicable only where the spouse was married to the Governor General during the latter's term of office), with relative precedence among them governed by the dates on which the deceased former Governor General left office.

3. Precedence to be given immediately after the surviving spouses of deceased former Governors General referred to in Note 2.1 to former Prime Ministers, with relative precedence governed by the date of their first assumption of office.
4. Precedence to be given immediately after former Prime Ministers to former Chief Justices of Canada, with relative precedence among them governed by the dates of their appointment as Chief Justice of Canada.

5. Precedence among Ambassadors and High Commissioners, who rank equally, to be determined by the date of the presentation of their credentials. Precedence to be given to Chargés d'Affaires immediately after Ministers Plenipotentiary.
6. This provision does not apply to such ceremonies and occasions as are of a provincial nature.
7. The religious dignitaries will be senior Canadian representatives of faith communities having a significant presence in a relevant jurisdiction. The relevant precedence of the representatives of faith communities is to be governed by the date of their assumption in their present office, their representatives being given the same relative precedence.
8. This precedence to be given to the Chief of the Defence Staff and the Commissioner of the R.C.M.P. on occasions when he has official functions to perform, otherwise the Chief of the Defence Staff and the Commissioner of the R.C.M.P. to have equal precedence with Deputy Ministers with their relative position to be determined according to the respective dates of their appointments to office. The relative precedence of the Chief of the Defence Staff and R.C.M.P. Commissioner, Deputy Ministers and other high officials of the public service to be determined from time to time by the Secretary of State of Canada in consultation with the Prime Minister.

## TABLE OF TITLES TO BE USED IN CANADA

**(As revised June 18, 1993)**

1. The Governor General of Canada to be styled "Right Honourable" for life and to be styled "His Excellency" and his wife "Her Excellency", or "Her Excellency" and her husband "His Excellency", as the case may be, while in office.
2. The Lieutenant Governor of a Province to be styled "Honourable" for life and to be styled "His Honour" and his wife "Her Honour", or "Her Honour" and her husband "His Honour", as the case may be, while in office.
3. The Prime Minister of Canada to be styled "Right Honourable" for life.
4. The Chief Justice of Canada to be styled "Right Honourable" for life.
5. Privy Councillors of Canada to be styled "Honourable" for life.
6. Senators of Canada to be styled "Honourable" for life.
7. The Speaker of the House of Commons to be styled "Honourable" while in office.
8. The Commissioner of a Territory to be styled "Honourable" while in office.
9. Puisne Judges of the Supreme Court of Canada and Judges of the Federal Courts and the Tax Court of Canada as well as the Judges of the undermentioned Courts in the Provinces and Territories:
   *Ontario* — Court of Appeal and the Ontario Court of Justice (General Division)
   *Québec* — The Court of Appeal and the Superior Court of Québec
   *Nova Scotia* — The Court of Appeal and the Supreme Court of Nova Scotia
   *New Brunswick* — The Court of Appeal and the Court of Queen's Bench of New Brunswick
   *Manitoba* — The Court of Appeal and the Court of Queen's Bench for Manitoba
   *British Columbia* — The Court of Appeal and the Supreme Court of British Columbia
   *Prince Edward Island* — The Supreme Court of Prince Edward Island
   *Saskatchewan* — The Court of Appeal and the Court of Queen's Bench for Saskatchewan
   *Alberta* — The Court of Appeal and the Court of Queen's Bench of Alberta
   *Newfoundland* — The Supreme Court of Newfoundland
   *Northwest Territories* — The Supreme Court of Northwest Territories
   *Yukon Territory* — The Supreme Court of Yukon to be styled "Honourable" while in office.
   (b) The Judges of the County and District Courts to be styled "Honourable" while in office.
10. Presidents and Speakers of the Legislative Assemblies of the Provinces and Territories to be styled "Honourable" while in office.
11. Members of the Executive Councils of the Provinces and Territories to be styled "Honourable" while in office.
12. Judges of Provincial and Territorial Courts (appointed by the Provincial and Territorial Governments) to be styled "Honourable" while in office.
13. The following are eligible to be granted permission by the Governor General, in the name of Her Majesty The Queen, to retain the title of "Honourable" after they have ceased to hold office:
    (a) Speakers of the House of Commons;
    (b) Commissioners of Territories;
    (c) Judges designated in item 9.
14. The title "Right Honourable" is granted for life to the following eminent Canadians:
    The Right Honourable Martial Asselin
    The Right Honourable Ellen L. Fairclough
    The Right Honourable Francis Alvin George Hamilton
    The Right Honourable Donald F. Mazankowski, P.C., M.P.
    The Right Honourable Jean-Luc Pepin
    The Right Honourable John Whitney Pickersgill

The Right Honourable Robert Lorne Stanfield

## CANADIAN HONOURS SYSTEM

For some years after Confederation, awards were made of a few hereditary honours and some knighthoods and companionships in orders of chivalry, and this policy continued until the end of the first World War.

From 1919 until 1933 no titular honours were granted. There was a brief revival of the defunct honours policy during the Conservative administration of R.B. Bennett, and several distinctions were awarded from 1934 to 1935, but the prohibition was reinstated with the return of the Liberals to office in 1935. Consequently, at the outset of the second World War, Canadians in the armed services were not entitled to receive awards in the order of chivalry for which other Commonwealth personnel were eligible. A parliamentary committee appointed in 1943 recommended that the ban on non-titular honours be lifted, clearing the way for members of the military and civilians to receive recognition for wartime services.

The hundredth anniversary of Confederation, July 1st, 1967, was the occasion on which the Order of Canada was created as the first component of a distinctly Canadian honours system. More information concerning Order, Decorations and Medals (as well as various Governor General's awards) may be obtained by writing to: Public Information Directorate, Government House, 1 Sussex Dr., Ottawa ON K1A 0A1.

### HERALDRY

Coats-of-arms, flags, badges and other heraldic devices are marks of honour and symbols of identity, authority and, in some cases, sovereignty. Each is granted by the Crown under an exercise of the Sovereign's prerogative to create heraldic honours.

Until June 4, 1988, Canadian corporations and individuals wishing to bear lawful arms petitioned the Sovereign's traditional heraldic officers in Londn and Edinburgh. On that date, by Royal Letters Patent, the Queen transferred the exercise of her heraldic prerogative, as Queen of Canada, to the Governor General who now heads a new office, the Canadian Heraldic Authority. With the act, heraldry, which has a long history in Canada, has been fully patriated.

These vice-regal responsibilities are administered by Canadian officers of arms appointed by commission under the Governor General's privy seal: the Herald Chancellor (the Secretary to the Governor General), the Deputy Herald Chancellor (the Deputy Secretary, Chancellery) and the Chief Herald of Canada (Director, Heraldry). He is assisted by three officers of arms: Saint-Laurent, Athabaska, and Fraser heralds, and one officer of arms extraordinary, Dauphin Herald.

New heraldic emblems are granted, and existing ones registered, by the Chief Herald upon receipt of an enabling Warrant from the Herald Chancellor or the Deputy Herald Chancellor acting on behalf of the Governor General. Grants and registrations are made by Letters Patent, documents that set out the Governor General's heraldic responsibilities, describe the emblem granted, and feature a representation of the Governor General's personal arms. To ensure a lasting record, the newly granted and registered emblems are entered in Canada's national armorial, the Public Register of Arms, Flags and Badges of Canada. Since the Authority was created, hundreds of petitions have been received from every part of the country, most for new grants of arms.

## CANADIAN HONOURS LIST

### ORDER OF CANADA

As mentioned above, the Order of Canada was created July 1, 1967. Her Majesty The Queen is Sovereign of the Order of Canada and the Governor General is, by virtue of that office, Chancellor and Principal Companion. She is assisted in the administration of the Order by an Advisory Council which comprises:

a) the Chief Justice of Canada (Chairman)
b) the Clerk of the Privy Council
c) the Deputy Minister, Canadian Heritage
d) the Chair of the Canada Council
e) the President of the Royal Society of Canada
f) the Chair of the Board of the Association of Universities and Colleges of Canada
g) not more than two other members, when considered appropriate by the Governor General, can be appointed for three-year terms.

The Secretary to the Governor General is, by his/her office, Secretary General of the Order.

The Order of Canada is designed to honour Canadian citizens for outstanding achievement and service to the country or to humanity at large and also for distinguished service in particular localities and fields of activity. The Order comprises three levels of membership: Companion, Officer, and Member. Up to 15 Companions may be appointed annually, but the total number of living Companions may not exceed 165. Up to 50 Officers and 100 Members may be appointed annually with no over-all limit.

The Order includes no titles of honour and confers no special privileges, hereditary or otherwise. Awards are made solely on the basis of merit. Members of the Order are entitled to place after their names the letters "C.C." for Companions, "O.C." for Officers, and "C.M." for Members.

Any person or organization may make nominations for appointment to the Order by writing to the Chancellery, Rideau Hall, Ottawa. The Advisory Council submits to the Governor General lists of those nominees who, in the opinion of the Council, are of greatest merit. Appointments to the Order are made by the Sovereign of the Order on the recommendation of the Governor

General as Chancellor of the Order, under an instrument sealed with the Seal of the Order.

Non-Canadians whom the Government desires to honour may be accorded honourary membership in the Order.

**Companions of the Order of Canada/Compagnons de l'Ordre du Canada (C.C.)**

*** indicates a promotion within the Order**

**(Appointed November 14, 1996)**

Albert W. Johnson, C.C. (Public Service), Ottawa, ON*
Roger D. Landry, C.C., O.Q. (Mass Media), Montréal, QC*
Mary Frances Pratt, C.C. (Visual Arts), St. John's, NF

**(Appointed April 17, 1997)**

Harold Scott MacDonald Coxeter, C.C. (Science), Toronto, ON
The Honourable Goldwin Arthur Martin, C.C. (Law), Willowdale, ON*
The Honourable Gordon F. Osbaldeston, P.C., C.C. (Public Service), London, ON*
Robert Bruce Salter, C.C. (Health Care), Schomberg, ON*
Thomas H.B. Symons, C.C. (Education), Peterborough, ON*

**Officers of the Order of Canada/Officiers de l'Ordre du Canada (O.C.)**

**(Appointed November 14, 1996)**

The Right Honourable Martial Asselin, P.C., O.C. (Public Service), Sillery, QC
Jean M. Be@langer, O.C. (Engineering/Environment), Ottawa, ON
John Bragg, O.C. (Industry/Commerce/Business), Collingwood, NS
Peter Frederick Bronfman, O.C. (Deceased) (Philanthropy), Toronto, ON
Tirone E. David, O.C., O.Ont. (Health Care), Toronto, ON
Jacques de Champlain, O.C. (Health Care), Outremont, QC
James Downey, O.C. (Education), Waterloo, ON
Jack Lawrence Granatstein, O.C. (History), Toronto, ON
Arthur Edward Cleeve Horne, O.C., O.Ont. (Visual Arts), Toronto, ON
James Kenneth Irving, O.C. (Industry/Commerce/Business), Saint John, NB
The Honourable Serge Joyal, P.C., O.C. (Arts/Patron), Montréal, QC
Malak Karsh, O.C. (Photography), Ottawa, ON
k.d. lang, O.C. (Music), Alberta & USA
Claude Léveillée, O.C. (Music), St-Benoît, QC
Kenneth William McNaught, O.C. (Education), Toronto, ON
Gérard Poirier, O.C. (Performing Arts), Montréal, QC
Frank Shuster, O.C. (Performing Arts), Toronto, ON
Charles Richard Stelck, O.C. (Science), Edmonton, AB
The Honourable William Alexander Stevenson, O.C. (Law), Edmonton, AB

**(Appointed April 17, 1997)**

Bruce Alexander Aikenhead, O.C. (Science), Salmon Arm, BC
John Kim Bell, O.C. (Arts/Music), Toronto, ON*
Avie Bennett, O.C., O.Ont. (Philanthropy), Toronto, ON*
William R.C. Blundell, O.C. (Voluntarism), Toronto, ON
James P. Bruce, O.C. (Public Service), Ottawa, ON
Kenneth G. Davey, O.C. (Science), Thornhill, ON
Richard Francis Haskayne, O.C. (Industry/Commerce/Business), Calgary, AB
Robert Wilson Jackson, O.C. (Health Care), Ontario & USA
René J.A. Lévesque, O.C. (Science), Outremont, QC
John David Francis MacNaughton, O.C. (Engineering), Mississauga, ON
Sandy Auld Mactaggart, O.C. (Industry/Commerce/Business), Edmonton, AB
Ali H. Rajput, O.C., S.O.M. (Health Care), Saskatoon, SK
George J. Rosengarten, O.C. (Philanthropy), Montréal, QC
Buffy Sainte-Marie, O.C. (Music), Saskatchewan & USA
Ernest Lionel Samuel, O.C. (Philanthropy), Oakville, ON
Harold Oaser Seigel, O.C. (Industry/Commerce/Business), North York, ON
Samuel Solomon, O.C. (Science), Westmount, QC
Éric St-Pierre, O.C. (Social Service), St-Césaire, QC
James Hutchings Taylor, O.C. (Public Service), Ottawa, ON
Lynton Ronald Wilson, O.C. (Industry/Commerce/Business), Montréal, QC

**Members of the Order of Canada/Membres de l'Ordre du Canada (C.M.)**

**(Appointed November 14, 1996)**

The Honourable Alan Rockwell Abraham, C.M., C.D. (Public Service), Halifax, NS
Anne-Marie Alonzo, C.M. (Literary Arts), Laval, QC
Sarah Anala, C.M. (Voluntarism), Saint John, NB
Simon Baker, C.M. (Voluntarism), North Vancouver, BC
Mona Blair Bandeen, C.M. (Industry/Commerce/Business), Toronto, ON
B. Norman Barwin, C.M. (Health Care), Nepean, ON
H. Thomas Beck, C.M., O.Ont. (Voluntarism), Toronto, ON
Jenny Belzberg, C.M. (Arts/Patron), Calgary, AB
Edward Isaac Bickert, C.M. (Music), Toronto, ON
The Honourable Rémi Bujold, P.C., C.M. (Public Service), Sillery, QC
Rita Marjorie Cox, C.M. (Heritage), Toronto, ON
Anthony R.C. Dobell, C.M. (Health Care), Montréal, QC
Francis Patrick Doyle, C.M. (Voluntarism), Ste. Anne, MB
Jacques Duchesneau, C.M. (Protective Services), Montréal, QC
Arthur P. Earle, C.M. (Industry/Commerce/Business), Beaconsfield, QC
John N. Economides, C.M. (Voluntarism), Montréal, QC
André Gagnon, C.M. (Law), Québec, QC
Clara Gallant, C.M. (Voluntarism), Summerside, PE
Ronald A. Gould, C.M. (Public Service), Ottawa, ON
Frank H. Gunston, C.M. (Health Care), Brandon, MB
Joan Fletcher Harrison, C.M. (Health Care), Toronto, ON
Gerald G. Hatch, C.M. (Engineering), Islington, ON
Simma Holt, C.M. (Mass Media), Coquitlam, BC
Catherine Hooper, C.M. (Voluntarism), Châteauguay, QC
Gilles Houde, C.M. (Social Service), Magog, QC
Mary John, C.M. (Voluntarism), Vanderhoof, BC
A. Richard Johnston, C.M. (Music), Calgary, AB
Rev. Arthur Lacerte, C.M. (Education), St. Boniface, MB
David M. Lank, C.M. (Heritage), Westmount, QC
Charles E. Linkletter, C.M. (Industry/Commerce/Business), Summerside, PE
Jean Loiselle, C.M. (Social Service), Montréal, QC
Edith Jacobson Low-Beer, C.M. (Philanthropy), Montréal, QC
Richard Gordon Margolese, C.M. (Health Care), Westmount, QC
Wendy Burdon McDonald, C.M. (Industry/Commerce/Business), North Vancouver, BC
Scott McIntyre, C.M. (Mass Media), North Vancouver, BC
Donald McKinnon, C.M. (Industry/Commerce/Business), Timmins, ON
Harold S. Millican, C.M. (Voluntarism), Calgary, AB
Lawrence A. Mysak, C.M. (Science), Montréal, QC
Sarah Weintraub Paltiel, C.M. (Education), Montréal, QC
Marilyn Ruth Peers, C.M. (Social Service), Halifax, NS
Jean-Henri Picard, C.M. (Industry/Commerce/Business), Montréal, QC
Grace Davis Pine, C.M. (Voluntarism), Saskatoon, SK
Charles-Albert Poissant, C.M. (Industry/Commerce/Business), Montréal, QC
Benjamin Windsor Powell, C.M. (Industry/Commerce/Business), Charlottetown, NF
Bernard E. Riedel, C.M. (Health Care), Vancouver, BC
Raymond C. Setlakwe, C.M. (Voluntarism), Thetford Mines, QC
Helene Shingles, C.M. (Health Care), Sarnia, ON
Bernard Snell, C.M. (Health Care), Edmonton, AB
Charles Alexander Thompson, C.M. (Health Care), London, ON
Albert Samuel Waxman, C.M. O.Ont. (Performing Arts), Toronto, ON
Irving Zucker, C.M. (Philanthropy), Hamilton, ON

**(Appointed April 17, 1997)**

Lois Etherington Betteridge, C.M. (Visual Arts), Guelph, ON
Gurcharan Singh Bhatia, C.M. (Voluntarism), Edmonton, AB
Leonard Austin Braithwaite, C.M. (Public Service), Etobicoke, ON
Rachel Browne, C.M. (Dance), Winnipeg, MB
Douglas Campbell, C.M. (Theatre), Toronto, ON
James Campbell, C.M. (Music), Ontario & USA
Warren Chippindale, C.M. (Philanthropy), Mont-Tremblant, QC
Jean Côté, C.M. (Voluntarism), Beauport, QC
Richard J. Currie, C.M. (Industry/Commerce/Business), Toronto, ON
William Lindemere Day, C.M. (Education), Surrey, BC
Naranjan S. Dhalla, C.M. (Health Care), Winnipeg, MB
John W. Dobson, C.M. (Industry/Commerce/Business), Montréal, QC
Ralph Colin Ellis, C.M. (Mass Media), North York, ON
Gathie Falk, C.M. (Visual Arts), Vancouver, BC
Morris Flewwelling, C.M. (Voluntarism), Red Deer, AB
John K. Friesen, C.M., D.F.C. (Education), Vancouver, BC
Andrée Dalcourt Gauvin, C.M. (Health Care), Outremont, QC
James Alan Longmore Gilbert, C.M. (Health Care), Edmonton, AB
Peter Harris, C.M. (Science), Lethbridge, AB
J.A. Euclide Herie, C.M. (Social Service), Don Mills, ON
Barbara Campbell Smith Ivey, C.M. (Voluntarism), Toronto, ON
William Klinck, C.M. (Voluntarism), Coaticook, QC
Jack Lambourne Locke, C.M. (Science), Ottawa, ON
Janet Louise Lunn, C.M., O.Ont. (Writing), Hillier, ON
Abbyann Day Lynch, C.M., O.Ont. (Health Care), Toronto, ON
David S. Mulder, C.M. (Health Care), Westmount, QC
Louis Lawrence Odette, C.M. (Philanthropy), Toronto, ON
Earl Herbert Orser, C.M. (Industry/Commerce/Business), London, ON
Alice V. Payne, C.M. (Science), Calgary, AB
Ian Job Reid, C.M. (Voluntarism), St. John's, NF
Sigmund Reiser, C.M. (Voluntarism), Willowdale, ON
Dorothy Reitman, C.M. (Voluntarism), Montréal, QC
John Edgar Sandison, C.M., C.D. (Voluntarism), Regina, SK

Barbara Scott, C.M. (Politics), Calgary, AB
Wladimir Smirnoff, C.M. (Science), Ste-Foy, QC
Ann Margaret Spicer, C.M. (Social Service), Victoria, BC
Boris Spremo, C.M. (Photography), Toronto, ON
Raymond G. Squires, C.M. (Voluntarism), St. Anthony, NF
George Terry, C.M. (Voluntarism), Moose Jaw, SK
Vance Toner, C.M. (Education/Athletics), Riverview, NB
Huguette Tourangeau, C.M. (Music), Montréal, QC
Rosario Tremblay, C.M. (Industry/Commerce/Business), Levis, QC
Milton K. Wong, C.M. (Voluntarism), Vancouver, BC
Robert James Wright, C.M. (Law), Willowdale, ON
Joseph Zatzman, C.M. (Industry/Commerce/Business), Halifax, NS

## ORDER OF MILITARY MERIT

The Order of Military Merit was created on July 1, 1972 to recognize meritorious service and devotion to duty by members of the Canadian Forces. The Order has three grades of membership: Commander (C.M.M.), Officer (O.M.M.) and Member (M.M.M.). The annual number of appointments is limited to one-tenth of one percent of the number of persons in the Canadian Forces in the preceding year.

### Commanders of the Order of Military Merit/ Commandeurs de l'Ordre du mérite militaire (C.M.M.)

*** indicates a promotion within the Order**

**(Announced December 17, 1996)**

M.Gen. R.A. Dallaire, C.M.M., M.S.C., C.D., Ottawa, ON*
Rear Admiral J.A. King, C.M.M., C.D., Ottawa, ON
L.Gen. D.N. Kinsman, C.M.M., C.D., Ottawa, ON
M.Gen. W.C. Leach, C.M.M., C.D., Ottawa, ON*
M.Gen. G.E.C. MacDonald, C.M.M., M.V.O., C.D., Ottawa, ON

### Officers of the the Order of Military Merit/Officiers de l'Ordre du mérite militaire (O.M.M.)

**(Announced, December 17, 1996)**

Maj. J.M. Andruszka, O.M.M., C.D., Ottawa, ON
Capt. (N) C.J. Brooks, O.M.M., C.D., Downsview, ON
L.Col. L.J. Colwell, O.M.M., C.D., Jemseg, NB
B.Gen. J.-M. Comtois, O.M.M., C.D., Montréal, QC
Col. J.R.G. Côté, O.M.M., C.D., Rimouski, QC
L.Col. J.F. Cruse, O.M.M., C.D., Kemptville, ON
Maj. C.R. Cue, O.M.M., C.D., Victoria, BC
L.Col. J.P. Culligan, O.M.M., C.D., Brantford, ON
Col. D.D. Dalziel, O.M.M., C.D., Ottawa, ON
L.Col. J.A.A. Diening, O.M.M., C.D., Toronto, ON
Col. M.J. Dumais, O.M.M., C.D., Trenton, ON
L.Col., D.E. Fraser, O.M.M., C.D., Sydney Mines, NS
Cdr. F.B. Frewer, O.M.M., C.D., Ottawa, ON
Col. E.H. Gosden, O.M.M., C.D., Montréal, QC
L.Col. E.W. Graham, O.M.M., C.D., Victoria, BC
Cdr. G.W. Gray, O.M.M., C.D., Palmerston, ON
Col. L.M. Lashkevich, O.M.M., C.D., Toronto, ON
L.Col. J.A.L. Lehoux, O.M.M., C.D., St-Basile le Grand, QC
Cdr. W.E. MacDonald, O.M.M., C.D., Victoria, BC
Capt. (N) I.D. Mack, O.M.M., C.D., Ottawa, ON
L.Col. Y.A. Martin, O.M.M., C.D., Laval, QC
L.Col. R.G. Parsons, O.M.M., C.D., Glace Bay, NS
Col. J.P.D. Robinson, O.M.M., C.D., Ottawa, ON
Maj. J.H.J. Russell, O.M.M., C.D., Calgary, AB
Cdr. H.R. Smith, O.M.M., C.D., Ottawa, ON
Col. P.S. Tanton, O.M.M., C.D., London, UK
L.Col. J.R.A. Têtu, O.M.M., C.D., Charlesbourg, QC
L.Cdr. J.M. Thibault, O.M.M., C.D., Champlain, QC
L.Col. J.R.A. Tremblay, O.M.M., C.D., Montréal, QC
Capt. (N) P.C.B. Young, O.M.M., C.D., Halifax, NS

### Members of the Order of Military Merit/Membres de l'Ordre du mérite militaire (M.M.M.)

**(Announced December 17, 1996)**

Chief Warrant Officer H.E. Austen, M.M.M., C.D., Cookstown, ON
Chief Warrant Officer L.D. Black, M.M.M., C.D., Trenton, ON
Master Warrant Officer J.R.R.R. Boivin, M.M.M., C.D., Québec, QC
Chief Warrant Officer J.R. Bouchard, M.M.M., C.D., Madawaska, NB
Chief Petty Officer 2nd Class E.M.A. Carberry, M.M.M., C.D., Corner Brook, NF
Master Warrant Officer D.B. Chipman, M.M.M., C.D., Gloucester, ON
Chief Warrant Officer F.W. Churchill, M.M.M., C.D., Lance Cove, NF
Capt. J.M.J. Coiteux M.M.M., C.D., Montréal, QC
Chief Warrant Officer R.V. Cooke, M.M.M., C.D., Edmonton, AB
Chief Petty Officer 2nd Class R.K. Cooper, M.M.M., C.D., Scarborough, ON
Master Warrant Officer J.M. Dempsey, M.M.M., C.D., Bathurst, NB
Chief Warrant Officer A.L. Dewar, M.M.M., C.D., Thornhill, ON
Chief Warrant Officer D.R. Dupuis, M.M.M., C.D., Saint John NB
Chief Petty Officer 2nd Class C.E. Dykman, M.M.M., C.D., Hamilton, ON
Master Warrant Officer J.E. Forest, M.M.M., C.D., Saint John, NB
Chief Warrant Officer R.H. Francis, M.M.M., C.D., Borden, ON
Chief Petty Officer 1st Class D.P. Garrett, M.M.M., C.D., New Glasgow, NS
Master Warrant Officer J.J.P. Gaudreau, M.M.M., C.D., Halifax, NS
Chief Warrant Officer J.H. Gelina, M.M.M., C.D., Windsor, ON
Master Warrant Officer D.L. Gingras, M.M.M., C.D., Pembroke, ON
Master Warrant Officer R.S. Goch, M.M.M., C.D., St. Catharines, ON
Chief Petty Officer 2nd Class M.P. Gourley, M.M.M., C.D., Halifax, NS
Master Warrant Officer L.M. Grant, M.M.M., C.D., Fredericton, NB
Chief Warrant Officer D.L. Hale, M.M.M., C.D., Stellarton, NS
Warrant Officer M.K. Hartling, M.M.M., C.D., Petawawa, ON
Warrant Officer B.R. Henwood, M.M.M., C.D., Shilo, MB
Warrant Officer C.E. Ives, M.M.M., C.D., Liverpool, NS
Chief Petty Officer 1st Class K.R. Johnston, M.M.M., C.D., Vancouver, BC
Chief Warrant Officer M.R. Kelly, M.M.M., C.D., Montréal, QC
Chief Warrant Officer G.A. Leach, M.M.M., C.D., Sydney, NS
Chief Warrant Officer J.J.Y. Leclerc, M.M.M., C.D., St-Germain, QC
Master Warrant Officer V.B. Lévesque, M.M.M., C.D., Murdochville, QC
Master Warrant Officer J.L.J. Lindsay, M.M.M., C.D., Jonquière, QC
Chief Petty Officer 1st Class R.M.J. Lupien, M.M.M., C.D., Victoria, BC
Sergeant K.D. MacWilliams, M.M.M., C.D., Borden, PE
Capt. R.A. Mader, M.M.M., C.D., Halifax, NS
Chief Petty Officer 1st Class T.A. Malmloff, M.M.M., C.D., Kirkland Lake, ON
Master Warrant Officer M. McBride, M.M.M., C.D., New Westminster, BC
Chief Petty Officer 1st Class W.R. Naylor, M.M.M., C.D., Roberts Creek, BC
Master Warrant Officer D.T. O'Connor, M.M.M., C.D., Tecumseh, ON
Capt. W.B. Papineau, M.M.M., C.D., Kingston, ON
Master Warrant Officer D. Paquette, M.M.M., C.D., Borden, ON
Master Warrant Officer R.W. Pellerin, M.M.M., C.D., Madawa, ON
Master Warrant Officer R.F. Perrone, M.M.M., C.D., Exeter, ON
Chief Petty Officer 2nd Class D.J. Puls, M.M.M., C.D., Victoria, BC
Chief Warrant Officer J.M. Reid, M.M.M., C.D., St. John's, NF
Chief Warrant Officer T.D. Restoule, M.M.M., C.D., Embrun, ON
Chief Warrant Officer F.J. Ritchie, M.M.M., C.D., Calgary, AB
Master Warrant Officer H.E.H. Soper, M.M.M., C.D., Carbonear, NF
Sgt. E.A.C. Stoneham, M.M.M., C.D., Fredericton, NB
Master Warrant Officer R.W. Ryan, M.M.M., C.D., Sydney, NS
Chief Warrant Officer R.C. Switzer, M.M.M., C.D., Fenelon Falls, ON
Master Warrant Officer C. Tkacz, M.M.M., C.D., Calgary, AB
Master Warrant Officer R.M. Torrie, M.M.M., C.D., Dauphin, MB
Master Warrant Officer J.R.M. Tremblay, M.M.M., C.D., Chicoutimi, QC
Master Corporal P.W. Vallée, M.M.M., Kirkland, QC
Warrant Officer J.E.V.N. Viau, M.M.M., C.D., Baylon, ON
Chief Warrant Officer R.K. Walker, M.M.M., C.D., Alderpoint, NS
Sgt. F.P. Walsh, M.M.M., C.D., Labrador City, NF
Warrant Officer R.J.M.Y. Whelan, M.M.M., C.D., Pembrooke, ON
Chief Warrant Officer J.A.Y. Williamson, M.M.M., C.D., Montréal, QC

## CANADIAN BRAVERY DECORATIONS/DÉCORATIONS CANADIENNES POUR ACTES DE BRAVOURE

The Decorations for Bravery, consisting of the Cross of Valour, the Star of Courage, and the Medal of Bravery, were instituted and created on May 10, 1972. They may be awarded to Canadian citizens or to non-Canadians who have performed an act of bravery in Canada, or outside Canada if the act was in Canada's interest. The Decorations for Bravery may be awarded posthumously.

The Cross of Valour is awarded for acts of the most conspicuous courage in circumstances of extreme peril. The Star of Courage is awarded for acts of conspicuous courage in circumstances of great peril. The Medal of Bravery is awarded for acts of bravery in hazardous circumstances.

### Star of Courage/Étoile du courage (S.C.)

**(Date of Announcement, March 21, 1996)**

Roger Boivin, S.C., Sudbury, ON

**(Date of Announcement, Nov. 18, 1996)**

Frank Stanley De Dobbelaer, S.C., Courtland, ON
Maj. Keith David Sawatzky, S.C., C.D., M.D., North York, ON

**(Announced February 7, 1997)**

Glen Mifsud, S.C., Mississauga, ON

**(Announced April 7, 1997)**

Constable Alexander Stephen Graham, S.C., C.D., Moonstone, ON

**(Announced May 8, 1997)**

Boyd Gavin, S.C., Hampden, NF

**Medal of Bravery/Médaille de la bravoure (M.B.)**
**(Announced September 23, 1996)**
Richard Harvie, M.B., Gold River, BC
Christian Houle, M.B., Drummondville, QC
Kerry-Jo Savana Klingbeil, M.B., Surrey, BC
Brenton Christopher Marchuk, M.B., Kamloops, BC
Patricia Carman Newell, M.B., Plympton Twp., ON
Jeffrey Richard Somerville, M.B., Plympton Twp., ON
Dwight Stanley Sadek, M.B., Slocan Park, BC
Philip Tassi, M.B., Hamilton, ON
Roy Kevin Yowney, M.B., Colinton, AB

**(Announced November 18, 1996)**
Susan Altimas, M.B., Montréal, QC
Blaine Blair Claybourne, M.B., Calgary, AB
Luke Alphonse Decloet, M.B., Langton, ON
William Mahar, M.B. (Posthumous), Faro, YT
Darren Meery, M.B., Scotchtown, NS
Eric Meunier, M.B., St-Mathias, QC
Kevin Schmalz, M.B., Calgary, AB
Doug Van De Kerckhove, M.B., Fleming, SK
Jean-Claude Landry, Rimouski, QC

**(Announced November 25, 1996)**
Cpl. Stacy Vance Merriam, M.B., Edmonton, AB

**(Announced February 7, 1997)**
Constable Marc Bergeron, M.B., Jonquière, QC
Steven Burtt, M.B., Campbellford, ON
Susan Leona Campbell, M.B., Richmond, BC
Douglas Chevrier, M.B., Kipawa, QC
Michael Bryan Hawley, M.B., Perth, ON
Constable Dany Levesque, M.B., Jonquière, QC
Chad Ronald Pettit, M.B. (Posthumous), London, ON

**(Announced April 7, 1997)**
Richard Thomas Boase, M.B., Hopedale, NF
James Steven Brown, M.B., Nairn Centre, ON
Patrick Émond, M.B. (Posthumous), Ste-Pétronille, QC
Kerrick (Kerry) Flatt, M.B., Burlington, ON
Michael Franz Ponty, M.B., Sorrento, BC
Terrance Frederick Rye, M.B. (deceased), Kindersley, SK
Maurice Sheehan, M.B., New Westminster, BC
Christine Tanguay, M.B., Dunham, QC
Ian Richard Tinker, M.B., Vancouver, BC
Joseph Paul Todd, M.B., Peterborough, ON

**Announced May 8, 1997)**
Alain Bérubé, M.B., Nanaimo, BC
William Boncheff, M.B., Etobicoke, ON
Master Cpl. Marie Sylvie Boudreau, M.B., C.D., Barrie, ON
Jacques Champagne, M.B., Aylmer, QC
Jean-Louis Fortin, M.B., Charlesbourg, QC
Gaétan Lapointe, M.B., Ville des Laurentides, QC
Warrant Officer Frances Dianne MacTaggart, M.B., C.D., Borden, ON
Keegan William Alan McLevin, M.B., Red Deer, AB
Ashford Steven Penner, M.B., North Battleford, SK
Edgar Stephen Scheer, M.B., Osoyoos, BC
Rodney Michael Simpson, M.B., Nanaimo, BC
John Joseph Timpson, M.B., Stittsville, ON

**MERITORIOUS SERVICE DECORATIONS/DÉCORATIONS POUR SERVICE MÉRITOIRE**

Approved by Her Majesty the Queen on July 10, 1991, the Meritorious Service Decorations were created to honour Canadians & foreigners (military & civil) for commendable actions performed on or after June 11, 1984.
The Meritorious Service Cross (Military Division) is awarded for the performance of a military deed or a military activity in an outstandingly professional manner or of a rare high standard that brings considerable benefit or great honour to the Canadian Forces.
The Meritorious Service Cross (Civil Division) is awarded for the performance of a deed or activity in an outstandingly professional manner or of an uncommonly high standard that brings considerable benefit or great honour to Canada.
The Meritorious Service Medal (Military Division) is awarded for the performance of a military deed or a military activity in a highly professional manner or of a very high standard that brings benefit or honour to the Canadian Forces.
The Meritorious Service Medal (Civil Division) is awarded for the performance of a deed or activity in a highly professional manner or of a very high standard that brings benefit or honour to Canada.

**Meritorious Service Cross/M.S.C. (Civil)/La Croix du service méritoire (civile)**

**Meritorious Service Cross/M.S.C. (Military)/La Croix du service méritoire (militaire)**
**(Announced January 31, 1996)**
M.Gen. Roy Raymond Crabbe, O.M.M., M.S.C., C.D., Winnipeg, MB

**(Announced May 10, 1996)**
B.Gen. Alain J.R.A.P. Forand, S.C., M.S.C., C.D., Québec, QC

**(Announced August 23, 1996)**
Gen. Joseph W. Ashy, M.S.C., United States Air Force

**(Announced August 29, 1996)**
Maj. Daniel Robert Burden, M.S.C., Salmon Arm, BC

**(Announced April 10, 1997)**
Gen. Bernard Louis Antonin Janvier, M.S.C., France
Col. William Joseph Fulton, M.S.C., C.D., Ottawa, ON
M.Gen. Guy Claude Tousignant, O.M.M., M.S.C., C.D., Ottawa, ON

**Meritorious Service Medal/M.S.M. (Civil)/La Médaille du service méritoire (civile)**
**(Announced April 4, 1996)**
Lois Maureen Burdett, M.S.M., Stratford, ON
Sgt. Terrance A. Cameron, M.S.M., London, ON
Jeffrey De Fourestier, M.S.M., Vanier, ON
Priscilla De Villiers, M.S.M., Burlington, ON
Victor Hugo Fernandez Meyer, M.S.M., St. Albert, AB
Edwin Roger Forde, M.S.M., Montréal, QC
John Alan Gardam, O.M.M., M.S.M., C.D., Nepean, ON
John A. Griffith, M.S.M., Navan, ON
Mikhail Malakhov, M.S.M., Ryazan, Russia
Robert Misericordia, M.S.M., Sooke, BC
Constable Claude Majella Monfort, M.S.M., Marathon, ON
Edward Nurse, M.S.M., Montréal, QC
Derek Porter, M.S.M., Victoria, BC
Richard Weber, M.S.M., Cantley, QC

**(Announced October 21, 1996)**
Willem J.C. Tensen, M.S.M., The Netherlands

**(Announced January 28, 1997)**
Rourk E.C. Simon, M.S.M., Montréal, QC

**(Announced May 15, 1997)**
Barbara Clark Smith, M.S.M., Peterborough, ON
Sophia Glezos Demetelin, M.S.M., Montréal, QC
George Heller, M.S.M., Le Vesinet, France
Guillaume François Jonckheer, M.S.M., Curacao, Netherlands Antilles
Anup Singh Jubbal, M.S.M., Burnaby, BC
David Alexander Nairn, M.S.M., C.D., Hull, QC
Richard Paquin, M.S.M., St-Didace, QC
Victor P. Poleschuk, M.S.M., Kamloops, BC
Cpl. Barry Gray Shannon, M.S.M., London, ON
Robert J. Tracy, M.S.M., C.D., Ottawa, ON

**Meritorious Service Medal M.S.M. (Military)/La Médaille du service méritoire (militaire)**
**(Announced January 31, 1996)**
L.Col., Richard David Francis Froh, M.S.M., C.D., Toronto, ON

**(Announced March 12, 1996)**
M.Gen. Cesky Krumlov, Czech Republic

**(Announced August 29, 1996)**
L.Cdr. William K. Erhardt, M.S.M. (USN), Richboro, PA
L.Col. David Allison Fraser, M.S.M., C.D., Calgary, AB
Capt. Gordon F. Sharpe, M.S.M., Winnipeg, MB
Sgt. Frederick Vallis, M.S.M., C.D., Lourdes, NF

**(Announced November 25, 1996)**
Sgt. Paul McMillan, M.S.M., Orillia, ON

**(Announced April 10, 1997)**
Warrant Office Andrew Macfarlane Ainslie, M.S.M., C.D., Trenton, ON
Sgt. Joseph Robert Yves Gagnon, M.S.M., C.D., Bagotville, QC
Master Cpl. Daniel Christien Lamoureux, M.S.M., Belleville, ON
Col. Andrew Brooke Leslie, M.S.M., C.D., Edmonton, AB
Sgt. Joseph Léonide Serge Marcotte, M.S.M., C.D., Courcelette, QC
Lieutenant (N) Kent Arthur Page, M.S.M., C.D. (Ret'd), Mississauga, ON
Cdr. Gary Alfred Paulson, M.S.M., C.D., Victoria, BC
Master Warrant Officer Joseph Daniel Maurice Santerre, M.S.M., C.D., Sherbrooke, QC

**(Announced April 15, 1997)**
Master Cpl. Joseph Benoit Michaël Gaudreau, M.S.M., Granby, QC
Master Cpl. Mark Christopher Holoshka, M.S.M., C.D., Ottawa, ON
Master Cpl. Donald David Peters, M.S.M., C.D. (Ret'd), Ottawa, ON

## BRITISH AND COMMONWEALTH HONOURS

In earlier times Canadians could receive hereditary titles, knighthoods and other such honours under the British system of honours, and this is still the case with Canadians who pursue careers in the United Kingdom. Furthermore, the Canadian military system of decorations was based on the British system and many Canadians hold British honours as a result of service in Canadian, British or other Commonwealth forces. While Canada has developed its own honours system, honours are still from time to time granted by the Sovereign to Canadians for, among other things, service to the Commonwealth.

**VICTORIA CROSS (V.C.)**

L.Col. Charles Cecil Ingersoll Merritt, V.C.
Sgt. Ernest Alvia Smith, V.C.
The Victoria Cross was founded by Queen Victoria at the close of the Crimean War in 1856, but made retroactive to 1854. It is described as a Maltese cross, made of gun metal, with a Royal Crest in the centre and underneath it an escroll bearing the inscription "For Valour". It is awarded, irrespective of rank, to members of any branch of Her Majesty's services, either in the British Forces or those of any Commonwealth realm, dominion, colony or dependency, the Mercantile Marine, nurses or staffs of hospitals, or to civilians of either sex while serving in either regular or temporary

capacity during naval, military, or air force operations. It is awarded only "for most conspicuous bravery or some daring or pre-eminent act of valour or self-sacrifice or extreme devotion to duty in the presence of the enemy." For additional conduct of similar bravery, a Bar is added. The ribbon was formerly red for the Army and blue for the Navy, but it is now red (a dull crimson) for all services. Since June 17th, 1943, the financial responsibility for a stipend to Canadian recipients has been assumed by the Canadian Government. Ninety-six V.C.s have been awarded to Canadians or to foreigners serving in Canadian or Commonwealth forces.

### GEORGE CROSS (G.C.)

Arthur Richard Cecil Butson, G.C., O.M.M., C.St.J., C.D., M.A., M.D., F.R.C.S. (Eng.), F.R.C.S.C.C.
John McClymont, G.C.
In 1940, King George VI instituted the George Cross for civilians and members of the services alike, male or female, who performed "acts of the greatest heroism or of the most conspicuous courage in circumstances of extreme danger." This decoration—the second highest Commonwealth award for bravery — is a plain silver cross bearing in the centre a representation of Saint George slaying the dragon and the words: "For Gallantry". The ribbon is garter blue. Eleven Canadians, and a Bermudian serving in a Canadian unit, have won the G.C. Not all were members of the armed forces.

### ALBERT MEDAL (A.M.)

Ernest Alfred Wooding, A.M., R.C.N.V.R.
Queen Elizabeth II requested that all living Albert Medal recipients convert their Albert Medal to a George Cross. For some reason Mr. Wooding did not convert his Albert Medal.

### ROYAL HONOURS (COMMONWEALTH)

The Order of Baronets, the lowest Hereditary rank, was instituted in 1611; a Baronet is designated "Sir John Smith, Baronet." The abbreviation Bt. is used in Court Circulars and has been generally adopted in lieu of "Bart." Taking precedence to Baronets are members of The Most Honourable Privy Council, who are addressed "Right Honourable."

The Most Noble Order of the Garter, instituted 1349. — K.G.

The Most Ancient and Most Noble Order of the Thistle, instituted 1687. — K.T.

The Most Honourable Order of the Bath, instituted in 1399, and revived in 1725, is divided into three classes — Knights Grand Cross, G.C.B.; Knights Commanders, K.C.B.; and Companions, C.B.

The Order of Merit, O.M., carries no title.

The Most Distinguished Order of St. Michael and St. George, instituted in 1818, has three classes — Knights Grand Cross, G.C.M.G.; Knights Commanders, K.C.M.G.; Companions, C.M.G.

The Most Eminent Order of the Indian Empire instituted 1877, has three classes — Knights Grand Commanders, G.C.I.E.; Knights Commanders, K.C.I.E.; Companions, C.I.E. (This Order has not been conferred since 1947.)

The Royal Victorian Order, instituted in 1896, has five classes — Knights Grand Cross, G.C.V.O.; Knights Commanders, K.C.V.O.; Commanders, C.V.O.; Members 4th and 5th classes — M.V.O. Ribbon, blue with red and white edges.

The Most Excellent Order of the British Empire, instituted in 1917, has five classes — Knights (or Dames) Grand Cross, G.B.E.; Knights Commanders, K.B.E.; Dames Commanders, D.B.E.; Commanders, C.B.E.; Officers, O.B.E.; and Members, M.B.E. Ribbon (Military) rose pink, pearl grey edging, vertical pearl stripe in centre; (Civil) rose pink, pearl grey edging, and no central vertical stripe.

Knights Bachelors are gentlemen unconnected with any order who have received the honour of Knighthood, and are entitled to the prefix "Sir". They rank immediately after Knights Commanders of the British Empire.

The Companions of Honour, C.H., instituted in 1917 rank immediately after Knights (Dames) Grand Cross of the Order of the British Empire. Membership is limited and carries no title.

In all Orders of Knighthood the Knights Grand Cross and the Knights Commanders have the prefix "Sir" with the initials of their class following the name. Companions and Members bear no title, but have the letters C.B., C.M.G., L.V.O., M.V.O., as the case may be, attached to their names.

The Garter, the Thistle, The Order of Merit and the Royal Victorian Order are all in the personal bestowal of the Sovereign. Appointments to the other Orders are made by Her Majesty on recommendation of the Prime Ministers of Commonwealth countries who wish to secure such appointments. Premiers of individual Australian states may also make recommendations.

### MARQUESS

The Most Hon. the Marquess of Exeter, Michael Anthony Cecil, 8th Marquess
The Most Hon. the Marquess of Ely, Charles John Tottenham, 8th Marquess

### EARLS

The Right Hon. the Earl of Egmont, Frederick George Moore Perceval, 11th Earl and 15th Baronet
The Right Hon. the Earl Grey, Richard Fleming George Charles Grey, 6th Earl
The Right Hon. the Earl Winterton, Donald David Turnour, 8th Earl

### VISCOUNTS

The Right Hon. the Viscount Charlemont, John Day Caulfeild, 14th Viscount
The Right Hon. the Viscount Galway, L.Cdr. George Rupert Monckton, R.C.N. (Ret'd), 12th Viscount
The Right Hon. the Viscount Greenwood, Sir David Henry Hamar Greenwood, Bt., F.R.G.S., 2nd Viscount
The Right Hon. the Viscount Hardinge, Charles Henry Nicholas Hardinge, 6th Viscount

### OLD CANADIAN TITLE

The title of Baron de Longueuil existed prior to the Treaty of Paris (1763), and was duly recognized by Queen Victoria pursuant to that treaty.
Baron de Longueuil, Raymond Grant de Longueuil, 11th Baron

### BARONS

The Right Hon. the Lord Aylmer, Michael Anthony Aylmer, 13th Baron
The Right Hon. the Lord Beaverbrook, Maxwell William Henry Aitken, 3rd Baron and 3rd Baronet
The Right Hon. the Lord Chatfield, Ernle David Lewis Chatfield, 2nd Baron
The Right Hon. the Lord Martonmere, John Stephen Robinson, 2nd Baron
The Right Hon. the Lord Morris, Michael David Morris, 3rd Baron
The Right Hon. the Lord Rodney, George Brydges, 10th Baron and 10th Baronet
The Right Hon. the Lord Shaughnessy, William Graham Shaughnessy, 3rd Baron
The Right Hon. the Lord Strathcona and Mount Royal, Hon. Col. Donald Euan Palmer Howard, 4th Baron
The Right Hon. the Lord Thomson of Fleet, Kenneth Roy Thomson, 2nd Baron

### BARONETS

Sir Richard Aylmer (16th Bt.)
Sir Christopher Hilaro Barlow (7th Bt.)
Sir Harold Boulton (4th Bt.)
Sir Alexander Boyd (3rd Bt.)
Sir Theodore Brinckman (6th Bt.)
Maj. Sir Hervey Bruce (7th Bt.)
Sir Lauder Brunton (3rd Bt.)
Sir Herbert Burbidge (5th Bt.)
Sir Michael Butler (3rd Bt.)
Sir Robert Cave-Brown-Cave (16th Bt.)
Sir George Reginald Chaytor (8th Bt.)
Sir Arthur Chetwynd (8th Bt.)
Sir John Davis (3rd Bt.)
Sir David Dyke (10th Bt.)
Sir David Flavelle (3rd Bt.)
The Revd. Sir Christopher Gibson, Bt., C.P. (4th Bt.)
Sir George Philip Grant-Suttie (8th Bt.)
Sir Philip Grotrian (3rd Bt.)
Sir Charles Gunning C.D., (8th Bt.)
Sir Charles Knowles (7th Bt.)
Sir Peter Johnson (7th Bt.)
Sir Peter Lambert (10th Bt.)
Sir Richard Latham (3rd Bt.)
Sir Edwin MacGregor (7th Bt.)
Sir Roderick McQuhae MacKenzie (12th Bt.)
Sir Robert Morris (10th Bt.)
Sir Richard Musgrave (7th Bt.)
Sir Christopher Oakes (3rd Bt.)
Sir Christopher Philipson-Stow, D.F.C. (5th Bt.)
Sir James Piers (11 Bt.)
Sir Francis Price, Bt. (7th Bt.)
Sir Christopher Robinson (8th Bt.)
Sir John James Michael Laud Robinson (11th Bt.)
Sir Julian Rose (5th Bt.)
Sir Charles Rugge-Price (9th Bt.)
Sir John Samuel (5th Bt.)
Sir Robert Shaw (7th Bt.)
Sir John Simeon (7th Bt.)
Sir Thomas Staples (15th Bt.)
The Rev. Sir Michael Stonhouse (19th Bt.)
Sir Adrian Stott (4th Bt.)
Sir John Stracey (9th Bt.)
Sir Philip Stuart (9th Bt.)
Sir Richard Sullivan (9th Bt.)
Sir Robert Synge (8th Bt.)
Sir Rodney Touche (2nd Bt.)
Sir Charles Hibbert Tupper (5th Bt.)
Sir Christopher Wells, M.D. (3rd Bt.)
Sir Donald Williams (10th Bt.)

### Knight Grand Cross of the Most Honourable Order of the Bath (G.C.B.)

Air Chief Marshal Sir David Evans, G.C.B., C.B.E.

### Knight Grand Cross of the Most Distinguished Order of St. Michael and St. George (G.C.M.G.)

Sir John Shaw Rennie, G.C.M.G., O.B.E.

### Knight Grand Cross or Dame Grand Cross of the Most Excellent Order of the British Empire (G.B.E.)

Sir Peter Gadsden, G.B.E.
Sir Francis Aimé Vallat, G.B.E., K.C.M.G., Q.C.

### Member of the Order of the Companions of Honour (C.H.)

Pierre Elliott Trudeau, C.C., C.H., P.C.

### Knight Commander of the Most Honourable Order of the Bath (K.C.B.)

Air Marshal Sir Richard Nelson, K.C.B., O.B.E., M.D.

### Knight Commander of the Most Distinguished Order of St. Michael and St. George (K.C.M.G.)

Sir Edwin Leather, K.C.M.G, K.C.V.O.

### Knight Commander of the Royal Victorian Order (K.C.V.O.)

Sir Conrad Swan, K.C.V.O.

**Knight Commander of the Most Excellent Order of the British Empire (K.B.E.)**
Sir David Bate, K.B.E.
Hon. Sir Nigel Bowen, K.B.E.

**KNIGHTS BACHELOR**
Sir Graham Day
Sir Stanley Matthews, C.B.E.
Sir Neil Shaw

**Companion of the Most Honourable Order of the Bath (C.B.)**
Air Vice-Marshal George Brookes, C.B., O.B.E.
M.Gen. Bertram Meryl Hoffmeister, C.B., C.B.E., D.S.O.

**Companion of the Most Distinguished Order of St. Michael and St. George (C.M.G.)**
H.J. Carmichael, C.M.G.
Edmond Cloutier, C.M.G., B.A., L.Ph.
Eleanor Emery, C.M.G.
Donovan Bartley Finn, C.M.G., M.Sc., Ph.D., F.R.S.C., F.C.I.C.
George H. McIvor, C.M.G.
Hector Brown McKinnon, C.C., C.M.G.
Alexander Ross, C.M.G.
Reginald McCartney Samples, C.M.G., D.S.O., O.B.E.
Joseph Emile St. Laurent, C.M.G.
Ivor Otterbein Smith, C.M.G., O.B.E.

**Companion of the Most Eminent Order of the Indian Empire (C.I.E.)**
Maj. Frederick Wernham Gerrard, C.I.E.
Capt. John Ryland, C.I.E., R.C.N.
Maj. Frederick Augustus Berrill Sheppard, C.I.E., O.B.E.

**Commander of the Royal Victorian Order (C.V.O.)**
Leopold Henry Amyot, C.V.O.
Col. John Gilbert Bourne, C.V.O., C.D.
Henry E. Davis, C.V.O., C.M.
Michel Gauvin, C.V.O., D.S.O.
John Reginald Gorman, C.V.O., C.B.E., M.C.
The Hon. David C. Lam, C.V.O., C.M., K.St.J., O.B.C., B.A.(Econ.), M.B.A., L.L.D., D.Mil.Sc., D.H.L., D.H.
Veronica Jane Langton, C.V.O.
Hartland Molson MacDougall, C.V.O.
Capt. Donald Curtis McKinnon, C.V.O., C.D., R.C.N.
Cdr. G.J. Manson, C.V.O., C.D., R.C.N.
John Crosbie Perlin, C.V.O.
Peter Michael Pitfield, C.V.O., P.C., Q.C.
M.Gen. Roy A. Reid, C.V.O., C.M., M.C., C.D.
L.Cdr. Lawrence James Wallace, C.V.O., O.C., O.B.C., R.C.N.V.R.

**Commander of the Order of the British Empire (C.B.E.)**
William Eric Adams, C.B.E.
James Pomeroy Anderson, C.B.E.
Brig. Gerald Gardiner Anglin, C.B.E., M.C., E.D.
Brig. Walter A. Bean, C.B.E., E.D., C.D.
Brig. John Arthur Watson Bennett, C.B.E., C.D.
Brig. John Francis Bingham, C.B.E.
Brig. Dudley Kingdon Black, C.B.E., D.S.O.
M.Gen. Mortimer Patrick Bogert, C.B.E., D.S.O.
George Herbert Bowler, C.B.E.
Garrett Brownrigg, C.B.E.
John Burke, C.B.E.
Alfred Charpentier, C.B.E.
Howard Brown Chase, C.B.E.
John Horrell Collier-Wright, C.B.E.
L.Gen. Samuel Findlay Clark, C.B.E., C.D.
Brig. Frederick Graham Coleman, C.B.E.
Brig. J. A. de Lalanne, C.B.E., M.C., E.D.
V.Adm. Harry George De Wolf, C.B.E., D.S.O., D.S.C., R.C.N.
Air Marshal Clarence Rupert Dunlap, C.B.E., C.D., R.C.A.F.
Philip Sydney Fisher, O.C., C.B.E., D.S.O., D.S.C., D.C.L., LL.D.
Conrad Trelawny Fitz-Gerald, C.B.E., M.D.
Brig. Frank James Fleury, C.B.E.
Charles Gavsie, C.B.E., Q.C.
Gerald Godsoe, C.B.E., Q.C.
Alexander Grant, C.B.E.
Joseph Ernest Gregoire, C.B.E.
Frank Sydney Grisdale, C.B.E.
Raymond Gushue, O.C., C.B.E., Q.C.
M.Gen. Lewis John Harris, C.B.E.
Wallace Bruce Haughan, C.B.E.
Brig. Robert James Henderson, C.B.E.
Harold Ferguson Hodgson, C.B.E.
Capt. Francis Deschamps Howie, C.B.E., D.S.O., R.N.
Alexander George Irvine, C.B.E.
Eric Campbell Judd, C.B.E., M.V.O.
Lester Millman Keachie, C.B.E., Q.C.
Capt. Thomas Douglas Kelly, C.B.E., R.C.N.R.
M.Gen. George Kitching, C.B.E., D.S.O., M.C.
Allan Collingwood Travers Lewis, C.B.E., Q.C.
Col. Edward Raymond Lewis, C.B.E.
Wilfrid Bennett Lewis, C.B.E.
Gordon Clapp Lindsay, C.B.E.
Air Vice-Marshal Ralph Edward McBurney, C.B.E., C.D., R.C.A.F.
John Struthers McNeil, C.B.E.
E.J. Mackie, C.B.E.
Raymond Charles Manning, C.B.E.
John Emile Marks, C.B.E.
Walter Melvill Marshall, C.B.E.
James Matson, C.B.E.
Ronald Henry Moray Mavor, C.B.E.
Air Chief Marshal Frank Robert Miller, C.B.E., C.D., R.C.A.F.
Edwin Mirvish, O.C., C.B.E.
E.C. O'Brien, C.B.E.
Air Vice-Marshal Walter Alyn Orr, C.B.E., C.D., R.C.A.F.
Luke William Pearsall, C.B.E.
M.Gen. Matthew Howard Somers Penhale, C.B.E., C.D.
Cyril Horace Frederick Pierrepont, C.B.E., E.D.
Air Vice-Marshal John Lawrence Plant, C.B.E., A.F.C., R.C.A.F.
Louis Rasminsky, C.C., C.B.E.
M.Gen. Norman Elliott Rodger, C.B.E.
James Joseph Alexander Ross, C.B.E., C.D.
T.H. Savage, C.B.E.
Lynn Seymour, C.B.E.
Air Vice-Marshal Douglas McCully Smith, C.B.E., C.D.
Brig. Gerald Lucian Morgan Smith, C.B.E., C.D.
George Spence, C.B.E., LL.D.
William Leonard O'Brien Stallard, C.B.E.
Basil Otto Stevenson, C.B.E.
Air Cdre. Stanley Gibson Tackaberry, C.B.E.
Kenneth Wiffin Taylor, O.C., C.B.E.
George Gamlin Thomas, C.B.E.
Lyman Trumbull, C.B.E.
L.Gen. Geoffrey Walsh, C.B.E., D.S.O., C.D.
M.Gen. Arthur Egbert Wrinch, C.B.E., C.D.
Henry Wrong, C.B.E.

**IMPERIAL SERVICE ORDER (I.S.O.)**
George Clayton Anderson
Robert Albert Andison
Arthur Barnstead
Avila Bedard
Peter Cooligan
Henri Fortier
Frank Henry French
Arthur Leigh Jolliffe
Edward Jost
Louis MacMillan
Walter Clifton Ronson
David John Scott
Ivan Vallee

**ROYAL VICTORIAN CHAIN**
Bestows no precedence; currently not held by anyone.

# ORDER OF PRECEDENCE FOR ORDERS, DECORATIONS AND MEDALS

**(as revised November, 1994)**

**SEQUENCE 1**
1. The sequence for wearing the insignia of Canadian orders, decorations and medals is, and the post-nominal letters associated with such orders, decorations and medals, as approved by Orders in Council, are:

**Victoria Cross (V.C.)**

**Cross of Valour (C.V.)**

**NATIONAL ORDERS**
Companion of the Order of Canada (C.C.)
Commander of the Order of Military Merit (C.M.M.)
Commander of the Royal Victorian Order (C.V.O.)
Officer of the Order of Canada (O.C.)
Officer of the Order of Military Merit (O.M.M.)
Lieutenant of the Royal Victorian Order (L.V.O.)
Member of the Order of Canada (C.M.)
Member of the Order of Military Merit (M.M.M.)
Member of the Royal Victorian Order (M.V.O.)
The Most Venerable Order of the Hospital of St. John of Jerusalem (All Grades) (no post-nominal letters)

**PROVINCIAL ORDERS**
Ordre national du Québec (G.O.Q., O.Q., C.Q.)
The Saskatchewan Order of Merit (S.O.M.)
The Order of Ontario (O.Ont.)
The Order of British Columbia (O.B.C.)
Alberta Order of Excellence (A.O.E.)

**DECORATIONS**
Star of Military Valour (S.M.V.)
Star of Courage (S.C)
Meritorious Service Cross (M.S.C.)
Medal of Military Valour (M.M.V.)
Medal of Bravery (M.B.)
Meritorious Service Medal (M.S.M.)
Royal Victorian Medal (R.V.M.)

**WAR MEDALS**
1939-1945 Star
Atlantic Star
Air Crew Europe Star
Africa Star
Pacific Star
Burma Star
Italy Star
France and Germany Star
Defence Medal
Canadian Volunteer Service Medal (C.V.S.M.)/Newfoundland Volunteers War Service Medal (N.V.W.S.M.)
War Medal (1939-1945)
Korea Medal
Canadian Volunteer Service Medal for Korea (C.V.S.M.K.)
Gulf and Kuwait Medal

**SPECIAL SERVICE MEDAL (S.S.M.) WITH BARS FOR:**
Pakistan (1989-1990)
Alert
Humanitas
NATO/ORAN
Peace/Paix

**UNITED NATIONS MEDALS**
UN Service (Korea) (1950-1954)
UN Emergency Force (1956-1967)
UN Truce Supervision Organization in Palestine (1948-) (U.N.T.S.O.) and Observer Group in Lebanon (1958)
UN Military Observation Group in India and Pakistan (1949-1979) (U.N.M.O.G.I.P.)
UN Organization in Congo (1960-1964)
UN Temporary Executive Authority in West New Guinea (1962-1963) (U.N.T.E.A.)
UN Yemen Observation Mission (1963-1964) (U.N.Y.O.M.)
UN Force in Cyprus (1965-1993) (U.N.F.C.Y.P.)
UN India Pakistan Observation Mission (1965-1966) (U.N.M.O.G.I.P.)
UN Emergency Force Middle East (1973-1979)
UN Disengagement Observation Force Golan Heights (1974-) (U.N.D.O.F.)
UN Interim Force in Lebanon (1978) (U.N.F.I.L.)
UN Iran/Iraq Military Observation Group (1989) (U.N.I.M.O.G.)
UN Transition Assistance Group (Namibia) (1989-1990) (U.N.T.A.G.)
UN Observer Group in Central America (1989-1992) (U.N.U.C.A.)
UN Iraq/Kuwait Observer Mission (1991) (U.N.I.K.O.M.)
UN Angola Verification Mission II (1991-1993) (U.N.A.V.E.M.)
UN Mission for the Referendum in Western Sahara (1991) (M.I.N.U.R.S.O.)
UN Observer Mission in El Salvador (1991) (O.N.U.S.A.L.)
UN Protection Force (Yugoslavia) (1992-) (U.N.P.R.O.F.O.R.)
UN Advance Mission in Cambodia (1992) (U.N.A.M.I.C.)
UN Transitional Authority in Cambodia (1992-1993) (U.N.T.A.C.)
UN Operation in Somalia (1992-1994) (O.N.U.S.O.M.)
UN Operation in Mozambique (1992-) (U.N.U.M.O.Z.)
UN Assistance Mission in Rwanda (1993-) (U.N.I.M.I.R.)

**INTERNATIONAL COMMISSION MEDALS**
International Commission for Supervision and Control (Indo-China) (1954-73)
International Commission for Control and Supervision (Vietnam) (1973)
Multinational Force and Observers (Sinai 1987-)
European Community Monitor Mission (Yugoslavia) (1991-)

**COMMEMORATIVE MEDALS**
Canadian Centennial Medal (1967)
Queen Elizabeth II's Silver Jubilee Medal (1977)
125th Anniversary of the Confederation of Canada Medal (1992)

**LONG SERVICE AND GOOD CONDUCT MEDALS**
RCMP Long Service Medal
Canadian Forces Decoration (C.D.)

**EXEMPLARY SERVICE MEDALS**
Police Exemplary Service Medal
Corrections Exemplary Service Medal
Fire Services Exemplary Service Medal
Canadian Coast Guard Exemplary Service Medal
Emergency Medical Services Exemplary Service Medal (created August 3, 1994)

**OTHER MEDALS**
Queen's Medal for Champion Shot
Service Medal of the Most Venerable Order of the Hospital of St. John of Jerusalem

2. The Bar to the Special Service Medal is worn centred on the ribbon. If there is more than one Bar, they are spaced evenly on the ribbon with the most recent uppermost.
3. Commonwealth orders, decorations and medals, the award of which is approved by the Government of Canada, are worn after Canadian orders, decorations and medals listed in Section 1, the precedence in each category being set by the date of appointment or award.
4. Foreign orders, decorations and medals, the award of which is approved by the Government of Canada, are worn after those referred to in Sections 1 and 3, the precedence in each category being set by the date of appointment or award.
5. The Newfoundland Volunteer War Service Medal has the same precedence as the Canadian Volunteer Service Medal.
6. The insignia of orders, decorations and medals not listed in this directive, as well as foreign awards, the award of which has not been approved by the Government of Canada, will not be mounted or worn in conjunction with orders, decorations and medals listed in this directive.
The insignia of orders, decorations and medals shall not be worn by anyone other than the recipient of such order, decoration or medal.

**SEQUENCE 2**
NOTWITHSTANDING THE ABOVE, a person who, **prior to 1 June, 1972**, was a member of a British Order or the recipient of a British decoration or medal referred to in this section, should wear the insignia, decoration or medal, together with the insignia of any Canadian Order or any Canadian decoration or medal that the recipient is entitled to wear, in the following sequence:
Victoria Cross (V.C.)
George Cross (G.C.)
Cross of Valour (C.V.)
Order of Merit (O.M.)
Order of the Companions of Honour (C.H.)
Companion of the Order of Canada (C.C.)
Commander of the Order of Military Merit (C.M.M.)
Officer of the Order of Canada (O.C.)
Companion of the Order of the Bath (C.B.)
Companion of the Order of St. Michael and St. George (C.M.G.)
Commander of the Royal Victorian Order (C.V.O.)
The Most Venerable Order of the Hospital of St. John of Jerusalem (All Grades) (No post-nominals)
Commander of the Order of the British Empire (C.B.E.)
Distinguished Service Order (D.S.O.)
Officer of the Order of Military Merit (O.M.M.)
Lieutenant of the Royal Victorian Order (L.V.O.)
Officer of the Order of the British Empire (O.B.E.)
Imperial Service Order (I.S.O.)
Member of the Order of Canada (C.M.)
Member of the Order of Military Merit (M.M.M.)
Member of the Royal Victorian Order (M.V.O.)
Member of the Order of the British Empire (M.B.E.)
Member of the Royal Red Cross (R.R.C.)
Distinguished Service Cross (D.S.C.)
Military Cross (M.C.)
Distinguished Flying Cross (D.F.C.)
Air Force Cross (A.F.C.)
Star of Courage (S.C.)
Meritorious Service Cross (M.S.C.)
Medal of Bravery (M.B.)
Meritorious Service Medal (M.S.M.)
Associate of the Royal Red Cross (A.R.R.C.)
Distinguished Conduct Medal (D.C.M.)
Conspicuous Gallantry Medal (C.G.M.)
George Medal (G.M.)
Distinguished Service Medal (D.S.M.)
Military Medal (M.M.)
Distinguished Flying Medal (D.F.M.)
Air Force Medal (A.F.M.)
Queen's Gallantry Medal (Q.G.M.)
Royal Victorian Medal (R.V.M.)
British Empire Medal (B.E.M.)

**WAR MEDALS**
Africa General Service Medal (1902-1956)
India General Service Medal (1908-1935)
Naval General Service Medal (1915-1962)
India General Service Medal (1936-39)
General Service Medal - Army and Air Force (1918-1962)
1914 Star
1914-15 Star
British War Medal (1914-18)
Mercantile Marine War Medal (1914-18)
Victory Medal (1914-18)
Territorial Force War Medal (1914-19)
1939-45 Star
Atlantic Star
Air Crew Europe Star
Africa Star
Pacific Star
Burma Star
Italy Star
France and Germany Star
Defence Medal
Canadian Volunteer Service Medal
War Medal (1939-45)
Korea Medal
Canadian Volunteer Service Medal for Korea
Gulf and Kuwait Medal
NOTE: Newfoundland Volunteer War Service Medal has the same precedence as the Canadian Volunteer Service Medal.

**UNITED NATIONS MEDALS**
As in Sequence 1.

**INTERNATIONAL COMMISSION MEDALS**
As in Sequence 1.

**POLAR MEDALS**
In order of date awarded.

**COMMEMORATIVE MEDALS**
King George V's Silver Jubilee Medal (1935)
King George VI's Coronation Medal (1937)
Queen Elizabeth II's Coronation Medal (1953)
Canadian Centennial Medal (1967)
Queen Elizabeth II's Silver Jubilee Medal (1977)
125th Anniversary of the Confederation of Canada Medal (1992)

**LONG SERVICE AND GOOD CONDUCT MEDALS**
Army Long Service and Good Conduct Medal
Naval Long Service and Good Conduct Medal
Air Force Long Service and Good Conduct Medal
RCMP Long Service Medal
Volunteer Officer's Decoration (V.D.)
Volunteer Long Service Medal
Colonial Auxiliary Forces Officer's Decoration (V.D.)
Colonial Auxiliary Forces Long Service Medal
Efficiency Decoration (E.D.)
Efficiency Medal
Naval Volunteer Reserve Decoration (V.R.D.)
Naval Volunteer Reserve Long Service and Good Conduct Medal
Air Efficiency Award
The Queen's Medal for Champion Shot
Canadian Forces Decoration (C.D.)
Exemplary Service Medals as in Sequence 1.
Other Medals as in Sequence 1.

**COMMONWEALTH (less U.K.) ORDERS, DECORATIONS AND MEDALS,**
the award of which must be approved by the Government of Canada, are worn after those listed above in the sequence of Orders, Decorations and Medals,

the precedence in each category by date of appointment or award.

**ALL OTHER FOREIGN AWARDS APPROVED BY THE GOVERNMENT OF CANADA,**

the award of which is approved by the Government of Canada, are worn after those listed above in the sequence of Orders, Decorations and Medals, the precedence in each category by date of appointment or award.

The numerous Orders, Decorations and Medals not listed above and those Foreign Awards for which official approval has not be granted will not be mounted or worn in conjunction with the official awards.

The insignia of Orders, Decorations and Medals may not been worn by anyone other than the recipient.

## ABBREVIATIONS INDICATING HONOURS AND DECORATIONS

A.F.C. – Air Force Cross. Ribbon, wide diagonal stripes of white and red.

A.F.M. – Air Force Medal. Ribbon, narrow diagonal stripes of white and red.

A.M. – Albert Medal, gold (Sea). Ribbon, nine alternate narrow stripes of blue and white.

Albert Medal, gold (Land). Ribbon, nine alternate narrow stripes of red and white.

Albert Medal, bronze (Sea). Ribbon, blue ground with two wide stripes of white.

Albert Medal, bronze (Land). Ribbon, red ground with two wide stripes of white.

B.E.M. – British Empire Medal.

Bt. – Baronet

C.B. – Companion of the Most Honourable Order of the Bath.

C.B.E. – Commander of the Order of the British Empire.

C.C. – Companion of the Order of Canada.

C.D. – Canadian Forces Decoration.

C.G.M. – Conspicuous Gallantry Medal; Navy and Air Force. It carries a cash grant. The Navy Medal ribbon is white with dark blue edges; the Air Force ribbon is light blue with dark blue edges.

C.H. – Member of the Order of the Companions of Honour.

C.I.E. – Companion of the Most Eminent Order of the Indian Empire.

C.M. – Member of the Order of Canada.

C.M.G. – Companion of the Most Distinguished Order of St. Michael and St. George.

C.M.M. – Commander of the Order of Military Merit.

C.S.I. – Companion of the Most Exalted Order of the Star of India.

C.V. – Cross of Valour.

C.V.O. – Commander of the Royal Victorian Order.

D.C.M. – Distinguished Conduct Medal. Ribbon, red ground, dark blue stripe in centre.

D.F.C. – Distinguished Flying Cross. Ribbon, wide diagonal stripes of violet and white.

D.F.M. – Distinguished Flying Medal. Ribbon, narrow diagonal stripes of white and violet.

D.S.C. – Distinguished Service Cross. Ribbon, three broad bands, dark blue, white, dark blue.

D.S.M. – Distinguished Service Medal.

D.S.O. – Companion of the Distinguished Service Order. Instituted 1886. Ribbon, dark red with dark blue stripe at each end.

E.D. – Canadian Efficiency Decoration for Officers of Military Auxiliary Forces.

E.M. – Edward Medal. Posthumous award.

E.M. – Efficiency Medal.

G.B.E. – Knight Grand Cross or Dame Grand Cross of the Most Excellent Order of the British Empire.

G.C. – George Cross.

G.C.B. – Knight Grand Cross of the Most Honourable Order of the Bath.

G.C.I.E. – Knight Grand Commander of the Most Eminent Order of the Indian Empire.

G.C.M.G. – Knight Grand Cross of the Most Distinguished Order of St. Michael and St. George.

G.C.S.I. – Knight Grand Commander of the Most Exalted Order of the Star of India.

G.C.V.O. – Knight Grand Cross of the Royal Victorian Order.

G.M. – George Medal.

I.S.M. – Imperial Service Medal.

I.S.O. – Companion of the Imperial Service Order. Instituted 1902.

K.B.E. – Knight Commander of the Most Excellent Order of the British Empire.

K.C.B. – Knight Commander of the Most Honourable Order of the Bath.

K.C.I.E. – Knight Commander of the Most Eminent Order of the Indian Empire.

K.C.M.G. – Knight Commander of the Most Distinguished Order of St. Michael and St. George.

K.C.S.I. – Knight Commander of the Most Exalted Order of the Star of India.

K.C.V.O. – Knight Commander of the Royal Victorian Order.

K.G. – Knight of the Most Noble Order of the Garter.

K.P. – Knight of the Most Illustrious Order of St. Patrick.

Kt. – Knight Bachelor.

K.T. – Knight of the Most Ancient and Most Noble Order of the Thistle.

L.V.O. – Lieutenant of the Royal Victorian Order.

M.B. – Medal of Bravery.

M.B.E. – Member of the Order of the British Empire.

M.C. – Military Cross. Instituted 1915. Ribbon, white with broad band of blue in centre.

M. du C. – Canada Medal.

M.M. – Military Medal.

M.M.M. – Member of the Order of Military Merit.

M.V.O. – Member of the Royal Victorian Order.

M.S.C. – Meritorous Service Cross.

M.S.M. – Meritorious Service Medal.

O.B.E. – Officer of the Order of the British Empire.

O.C. – Officer of the Order of Canada.

O.M. – Member of the Order of Merit.

O.M.M. – Officer of the Order of Military Merit.

P.C. – Privy Counsellor.

R.R.C. – Royal Red Cross. Instituted 1883. Ribbon, dark blue with narrow band of dark red at each end.

R.V.M. – Royal Victorian Medal.

S.C. – Star of Courage.

U.E. – Unity of Empire. Descendants of United Empire Loyalists.

V.C. – Victoria Cross.

V.D. – Auxiliary Forces (Volunteer) Officers' Decoration.

V.R.D. – Naval Volunteer Reserve Decoration.

## FORMS OF ADDRESS

The "Salutation and Closing" portions below have been used with the permission of the copyright holder, Michael Measures, from the book "Styles of Address" by Howard Measures. The content of each such portion is listed in order of diminishing formality.

### GOVERNMENT

**THE GOVERNOR GENERAL OF CANADA:**

Address — His/Her Excellency The Governor General, Government House, Ottawa.

Address — His/Her Excellency the Rt. Hon. (name), P.C., C.C., Governor General of Canada, Government House, Ottawa

Salutation and Closing —
(Sir/Madam)
I have the honour to be, Sir/Madam,
Your Excellency's obedient servant,
or, (Dear Governor General)
Believe me, Your Excellency,
Yours sincerely,
or, (My dear Governor General)
With kind regards,
Yours very sincerely,

*Note:* If the Governor General has military and other titles, the title His/Her Excellency precedes the others. If the Governor General is a Prince or a Royal Duke, the title His Royal Highness and the salutation Your Royal Highness are used instead of His Excellency and Your Excellency. The wife/husband of the Governor General is accorded the title Her/His Excellency. The Governor General and spouse together — Their Excellencies.

**LIEUTENANT GOVERNOR OF A PROVINCE:**

Address — His/Her Honour, The Lieutenant Governor of (the Province of) ______, Government House, ______. or,

Address — His/Her Honour the Hon. (name), Lieutenant Governor of (the Province of) ______, Government House, ______.

Salutation and Closing —
(Sir/Madam)
I am, Your Honour,
Yours very truly,
or, (Dear Sir/Madam),
Yours sincerely,
or, (My dear Lieutenant Governor)
I am, my dear Lieutenant Governor
Yours sincerely,
or, (Dear Mr., Mrs., Miss, ...)
With kind regards,
Yours sincerely,

*Note:* A lieutenant governor of a province of Canada retains the title Honourable for life.

**THE PRIME MINISTER OF CANADA:**

Address — The Right Honourable John/Jean M. Blank, P.C., M.P., Prime Minister of Canada, Ottawa.

Salutation and Closing —
(Dear Sir/Madam)
Yours very truly,
or, (Dear Mr./Madam Prime Minister)
Yours sincerely,
or, (Dear Prime Minister)
With kind regards,
Yours sincerely,

*Note:* The Prime Minister of Canada is a member of the Queen's Privy Council for Canada and has the title "The Right Honourable" for life.

**THE PREMIER OF A PROVINCE OF CANADA:**

Address — The Honourable John/Jean M. Blank, M.L.A., Premier of (the Province of) ______,

Salutation and Closing —
(Dear Sir/Madam)
Yours very truly,
or, (My dear Premier)
Believe me, my dear Premier, Yours sincerely,
or, (Dear Mr., Mrs., Miss, ...)
With kindest regards,
Yours sincerely,

*Note:* The Premier of a Province of Canada has the title "The Honourable" during his or her term of office. The Premier is head of the government of the Province, i.e., the First Minister; he or she is generally the President of the Executive Council of the Province. In Québec the Premier is styled "Prime Minister" instead of "Premier."

**MEMBER OF THE FEDERAL CABINET, MEMBER OF THE PRIVY COUNCIL NOT OF THE CABINET, AND MEMBER OF THE EXECUTIVE COUNCIL OF A PROVINCE:**

Address — The Honourable John/Jean M. Blank, Minister of,

Salutation and Closing —
(Dear Sir) (Dear Madam)
Yours very truly,
or, (Dear Mr. ...) (Dear Mrs., Miss, ...)
With kind regards,
Yours sincerely,

*Note:* If also a member of the United Kingdom Privy Council, he or she is addressed "The Right Honourable" for life. The letters P.C. are placed after the names of members of the Privy Council of Canada but not of the United Kingdom unless he/she is a peer. One member of the Cabinet addressing another uses the salutation "My dear Colleague". Members of the Privy Council of Canada are appointed, and have the title "The Honourable", for life. Members of Executive Councils of the Provinces have the title of Honourable only during their terms of office.

**MEMBER OF THE SENATE:**

Address — The Honourable John M. Blank, *or* The Honourable Jean M. Blank, The Senate, Ottawa.

Salutation and Closing —
(Dear Sir/Madam)
Yours very truly,
or, (Dear Senator ...)
I am, dear Senator ...
Yours sincerely,
or, (My dear Senator)
Believe me,
Yours sincerely,

*Note:* A senator who is a member of the Canadian Privy Council is addressed "Senator the Honourable John/Jean M. Blank". A Senator who is a member of the United Kingdom Privy Council is addressed "Senator the Right Honourable John/Jean M. Blank".

**MEMBER OF THE HOUSE OF COMMONS:**

Address — Mr./Mrs. or Miss John/Jean M. Blank, M.P., House of Commons,Ottawa.

Salutation and Closing —
(Dear Sir) (Dear Madam)
Yours very truly,
or, (Dear Mr. ...) (Dear Mrs., Miss, ...)
Yours sincerely,

**DEPUTY MINISTER OF A DEPARTMENT:**

Address — Mr./Mrs. or Miss John/Jean M. Blank, Deputy Minister of ________ .

Salutation and Closing —
(Sir/Madam)
Yours truly,
or, (Dear Sir/Madam)
Yours sincerely,
or, (Dear Mr., Mrs., Miss, ...)
With kind regards,
Yours sincerely,

**MEMBER OF A PROVINCIAL LEGISLATURE:**

Address — Mr./Mrs. or Miss John/Jean M. Blank, M.L.A., Member of the Legislative Assembly, (Legislative Bldgs., Edmonton; Parliament Bldgs., Victoria; Legislative Bldg., Winnipeg; Legislative Bldg., Fredericton;Confederation Bldg., St. John's; Province House, Halifax; Parliament Bldgs.,Toronto; Province Bldg., Charlottetown; Hotel du gouvernement, Québec; Legislative Bldgs., Regina).

Salutation and Closing —
(Dear Sir/Madam)
Yours very truly,
or, (Dear Mr., Mrs., Miss, ...)
Believe me,
Yours sincerely,

*Note:* In the case of the Province of Québec use M.N.A.; Ontario use M.P.P.; Newfoundland and Nova Scotia use M.H.A. instead of M.L.A.

**MAYOR OF A CITY OR TOWN:**

If the name is used:

Address — His Worship Mayor John M. Blank, *or* Her Worship Mayor Joan M. Blank, City Hall.

If the name is not used:

His Worship the Mayor of. Her Worship the Mayor of.

Salutation and Closing —
(Dear Sir) (Dear Madam)
Yours very truly,
or, (Dear Mr. Mayor) (Dear Madam Mayor)
Believe me, dear Mr./Madam Mayor,
Yours sincerely,

## JUDGES

**CANADA:**

In Canada there are two broad classes of courts — superior courts and county (or district) courts. Judges of the superior courts are addressed "The Honourable Mr./Madam Justice ________ " and judges of the county or district courts are addressed "The Honourable ________ , Judge." The Supreme Court of Canada and the Federal Court of Canada are also superior courts. The Supreme Courts of the Yukon and the Northwest Territories are superior courts.

There are two classes of Chief Justices — The Chief Justice of Canada or of a province on the one hand, and the Chief Justice of a court on the other. The Chief Justice of the Supreme Court of Canada is styled the Chief Justice of Canada; similarly, there is a Chief Justice for each of the provinces. Other courts in the provinces, namely, the trial courts, usually have a Chief Justice also and he or she is known as the Chief Justice of that court.

**CHIEF JUSTICE:**

The Chief Justice of Canada:

Address — The Right Honourable The Chief Justice of Canada, Supreme Court of Canada, Ottawa.

Or — The Right Honourable ________ , P.C., Chief Justice of Canada, Ottawa.

Salutation and Closing —
(Sir/Madam)
I am, Sir/Madam,
Yours very truly,
or, (Dear Sir/Madam)
Yours faithfully,
or, (Dear Mr./Madam Chief Justice)
Yours sincerely,

Chief Justice of a Province or Territory:

Address — The Honourable ________ , Chief Justice of ________,

Salutation and Closing —
(Sir/Madam)
I am, Sir/Madam,
Yours very truly,
or, (Dear Sir/Madam)
I am, Sir/Madam,
Yours sincerely,
or, (Dear Mr./Madam Chief Justice)
Believe me, dear Mr./Madam Chief Justice,
Yours sincerely,

**JUDGES:**

Supreme Court of Canada, Federal Court of Canada, Courts of Appeal, Courts of the Queen's Bench, Superior Court of the Province of Québec, Supreme Courts of the Provinces and Territories:

Address — The Honourable Mr. Justice John M. Blank, *or* The Honourable Madam Justice Jean M. Blank.

Salutation and Closing —
(Sir) (Madam)
I am, Sir/Madam,
Yours very truly,
or, (Dear Mr./Madam Justice ...)
Believe me,
Dear Mr./Madam Justice ...
Yours sincerely,

**JUDGES:**

County and District Courts:

Address — The Honourable John/Jean M. Blank, Judge,

Salutation and Closing —
(Sir/Madam)
I am, Sir/Madam,
Yours very truly,
or, (Dear Judge Smith)
Believe me, dear Judge Smith,
Yours sincerely,

## RELIGION

### Anglican Church of Canada

**ARCHBISHOP:**

Address — The Most Reverend ________ , D.D., Archbishop of ________.

Salutation and Closing —
(Most Reverend Sir)
I have the honour to be,
Most Reverend Sir,
Your obedient servant,
or, (Dear Archbishop)
Yours sincerely,

**BISHOP:**

Address — The Right Reverend ________ , D.D., Bishop of ________.

Salutation and Closing —
(Right Reverend Sir)
I am, Right Reverend Sir,
Respectfully yours,
or, (Dear Bishop ...)
Believe me, dear Bishop ...
Yours sincerely,
or, (My dear Bishop)
Believe me, my dear Bishop,
Yours sincerely,

**ARCHDEACON:**

Address — The Venerable The Archdeacon of ________ , *or*, The Venerable Archdeacon ________ .

Salutation and Closing —
(Venerable Sir)
I am, Venerable Sir,
Yours sincerely,
or, (Dear Mr. Archdeacon)
I am, dear Mr. Archdeacon,
Yours sincerely,

**DEAN:**

Address — The Very Reverend John M. Blank, Dean of ________ .

Salutation and Closing —
(Very Reverend Sir)
I am, Very Reverend Sir,
Yours very truly,
or, (Dear Mr. Dean)
Believe me, dear Mr. Dean,
Yours sincerely,

**CANON:**

Address — The Reverend Canon John M. Blank,

Salutation and Closing —
(Reverend Sir)
Yours very truly,
or, (Dear Canon ...)

Believe me, dear Canon ...
Yours faithfully,

## Minister of Religion

Address — The Reverend John M. Blank,
Salutation and Closing —
(Sir)
I am, Reverend Sir, (or, Sir),
Yours very truly,
or, (Reverend Sir)
Yours sincerely,
or, (Dear Mr. ...)
Believe me, dear Mr. ...
Yours sincerely,

## Moderator (Canada)

Address — The Right Reverend ________, D.D., Moderator of the ________ Church,
Salutation and Closing —
(Right Reverend Sir)
I am, Right Reverend Sir,
Yours sincerely,
or, (Dear Dr. ...)
Believe me, dear Dr. ...
Yours sincerely,

## Roman Catholic

**CARDINAL:**

Address — His Eminence John Cardinal Blank, Archbishop of ________.
Salutation and Closing —
(Your Eminence)
I have the honour to be, Your Eminence,
Your obedient servant,
or, (Your Eminence)
I am, Your Eminence,
Yours sincerely,
or, (Dear Cardinal ...)
Believe me, dear Cardinal ...
Yours sincerely,

**ARCHBISHOP:**

Address — The Most Reverend John M. Blank, Archbishop of ________.
Salutation and Closing —
(Your Excellency)
I have the honour to be,
Your Excellency,
Respectfully yours,
*(ecclesiastical use).*
or, (Most Reverend Sir)
I am, Most Reverend Sir,
Yours very truly,
or, (Dear Archbishop)
Yours sincerely,

**BISHOP:**

Address — The Most Reverend John M. Blank, Bishop of ________ *(ecclesiastical use).*
or, The Right Reverend John M. Blank, Bishop of ________.
Salutation and Closing —
(Your Excellency)
I am, Your Excellency,
Respectfully yours,
*(ecclesiastical use).*
or, (Right Reverend Sir)
I am, Right Reverend Sir,
Yours sincerely,
or, (Dear Bishop ...)
Believe me, dear Bishop ...
Yours sincerely,
or, (Dear Bishop)
With kind regards, dear Bishop,
Sincerely yours,

**MONSIGNOR:**

Address — The Right Reverend John M. Blank.
Salutation and Closing —
(Right Reverend Monsignor)
I am, Right Reverend Monsignor,
Yours sincerely,
or, (My dear Monsignor ...)
Believe me, my dear Monsignor ...
Yours sincerely,

**CANON:**

Address — The Very Reverend John M. Blank.
Salutation and Closing —
(Very Reverend Canon)
Very truly yours,
or, (My dear Canon ...)
Sincerely yours,

**MOTHER SUPERIOR:**

Address — The Reverend Mother Superior, The Congregation of ________.
Salutation and Closing —
(Dear Madam)
I am, dear Madam,
Yours respectfully,
or, (Reverend Mother Superior)
I remain,
Reverend Mother Superior,
Yours sincerely,
or, (Dear Mother Superior)
Believe me, dear Mother Superior,
Yours sincerely,

**PRIEST**

Address — The Reverend John M. Blank.
Salutation and Closing —
(Reverend Sir)
Yours sincerely,
or, (Dear Father ...)
Believe me, dear Father ...
Yours sincerely,

## Jewish

**CHIEF RABBI:**

Address — The Very Reverend John M. Blank, Chief Rabbi.
Salutation and Closing —
(Dear Sir)
I remain, Sir,
Yours very truly,
or, (Dear Chief Rabbi)
I am, dear Chief Rabbi,
Sincerely yours,

**RABBI:**

Address — The Reverend Rabbi John M. Blank.
Salutation and Closing —
(Dear Sir)
I am, Sir,
Yours very truly,
or, (Dear Rabbi ...)
I am, my dear Rabbi ...
Yours sincerely,

## PROFESSIONAL

**ADVOCATE, NOTARY, PHYSICIAN, DENTIST, CHARTERED ACCOUNTANT, OPTOMETRIST, ETC.:**

Address — John/Jean M. Blank, Esq., Q.C., John/Jean M. Blank, Esq., Advocate; Dr. John/Jean M. Blank, or J.M. Blank, Esq., M.D. (*Never* use both Dr. and M.D.); Dr. John/Jean M. Blank, or J.M. Blank, Esq., D.D.S. (*Never* use both Dr. and D.D.S.); J.M. Blank, Esq., C.A.; Optometrist John/Jean M. Blank, or J.M. Blank, O.D., or Dr. John/Jean M. Blank.
Salutation and Closing —
(Dear Sir/Madam)
Yours very truly,

## DIPLOMATIC

**AMBASSADORS of foreign countries in Canada:**

Address — His/Her Excellency John/Jean M. Blank, Ambassador of ________, Ottawa.
Salutation and Closing —
(Excellency)
Accept, Excellency, the assurances of my highest consideration *(formal diplomatic usage).*
or, (Excellency)
Yours very truly,
or, (Dear Mr./Madam Ambassador)
I am, dear Mr./Madam Ambassador,
Yours sincerely,
or, (Dear Mr., Mrs., Miss, ...)
I am, dear Mr., Mrs., Miss, ...
Yours sincerely,

**HIGH COMMISSIONERS of British Commonwealth countries in Canada:**

Address — His/Her Excellency John/Jean M. Blank, High Commissioner for ________, Ottawa.
Salutation and Closing —
(Your Excellency)
Accept, Your Excellency, the assurances of my highest consideration *(formal diplomatic usage).*
or, (Dear Sir/Madam)
Yours sincerely,
or, (Dear High Commissioner)
Believe me, dear High Commissioner,
Yours sincerely,
or, (Dear Mr., Mrs., Miss, ...)
With kind regards,
Yours very sincerely,

**MINISTERS PLENIPOTENTIARY of foreign countries in Canada:**

Address — His/Her Excellency John/Jean M. Blank, Minister of ________, Ottawa.
Salutation and Closing —
(Excellency)
Accept, Excellency, the assurances of my highest consideration *(formal diplomatic usage).*
or, (Dear Mr./Madam Minister)
I remain, dear Mr./Madam Minister,
Yours sincerely,
or, (Dear Mr., Mrs., Miss, ...)
Believe me, dear Mr., Mrs., Miss, ...
Yours sincerely,

**CANADIAN AMBASSADORS abroad from a Canadian citizen:**

Address — Mr./Mrs. or Miss John/Jean M. Blank, Canadian Ambassador to ________, ________.
Salutation and Closing —
(Dear Sir/Madam)
Yours very truly,
or, (Dear Ambassador)
I am, dear Ambassador,
Yours sincerely,
or, (Dear Mr., Mrs., Miss, ...)
With kind regards,
Yours sincerely,

**CANADIAN AMBASSADORS abroad from a foreign citizen:**

Address — His/Her Excellency John/Jean M. Blank, Canadian Ambassador to ________, ________.
Salutation and Closing —
(Your Excellency)
Accept, Your Excellency, the (renewed) assurances of my highest consideration *(formal diplomatic usage).*
or, (Dear Mr./Madam Ambassador)
I am, dear Mr./Madam Ambassador,

Yours sincerely,
or, (Dear Mr., Mrs., Miss, ...)
I am, dear Mr., Mrs., Miss, ...
Yours sincerely,

**CANADIAN HIGH COMMISSIONERS abroad:**
Address — Mr./Mrs. or Miss John/Jean M. Blank, High Commissioner for Canada.
Salutation and Closing —
(Dear Sir/Madam)
Yours very truly,
or, (Dear High Commissioner)
Believe me, dear High Commissioner,
Yours sincerely,
or, (Dear Mr., Mrs., Miss, ...)
With kind regards,
Yours sincerely,

**CANADIAN MINISTERS PLENIPOTENTIARY abroad from a Canadian citizen:**
Address — Mr./Mrs. or Miss John/Jean M. Blank, Canadian Minister to ________, ________.
Salutation and Closing —
(Sir/Madam)
I am, Sir/Madam,
Yours very truly,
or, (Dear Sir/Madam)
Yours very truly,
or, (Dear Mr., Mrs., Miss, ...)
With kind regards,
Yours sincerely,

**CANADIAN MINISTERS PLENIPOTENTIARY abroad from a foreign citizen:**
Address — His/Her Excellency John/Jean M. Blank, Canadian Minister to ________, ________.
Salutation and Closing —
(Your Excellency)
Accept, Your Excellency, the (renewed) assurances of
my highest consideration *(formal diplomatic usage)*.
or, (Dear Mr./Madam Minister)
I remain, dear Mr./Madam Minister,
Yours sincerely,
or, (Dear Mr., Mrs., Miss, ...)
Believe me, dear Mr., Mrs., Miss, ...
Yours sincerely,

# ABBREVIATIONS

**Indicating Academic, Ecclesiastical and other Degrees, membership in Societies and Institutions, military ranks, etc., appearing in the Canadian Almanac and Directory. For other lists of abbreviations, see Index.**

A.A.C.C.A. Associate of Association of Certified Accountants & Corporate Accountants (British)
A.A.C.I. Accredited Appraiser Canadian Institute
A.A.E. Associate of Accountants' & Executives' Corp. of Canada
A.A.G.O. -- of the American Guild of Organists
A.A.S.A. -- of the Alberta Society of Artists
A.B. Bachelor of Arts, American (Artium Baccalaureus)
A.C. "Advanced Certification" Canadian Association of Medical Radiation Technologists
A.C.A. Associate of Institute of Chartered Accountants (Eng.)
A.C.C.O. -- of Canadian College of Organists
AccS.C.R.P. -- of Canadian Public Relations Society Inc.
A.C.D. Archaeologiae Christianae Doctor
A.C.G.I. Associate of the City & Guilds of London Institute
A.C.I.C. -- of Canadian Institute of Chemistry
A.C.Inst.M. -- of the Institute of Marketing
A.C.I.S. -- of Chartered Institute of Secretaries (British)
A.C.S.M. -- of Cambourne School of Mines
Adm. Admiral
A.F.R.A.S. (A.F.R.Ae.S.) Fellow of the Royal Aeronautical Society
Ag. de l'U (Paris) Honorary Professor of University of Paris (Agrégé de l'Université Paris)
Ag. de Phil. Professor of Philosophy (Agrégé en Philosophie Louvain)
A.G.S.M. Associate of the Guildhall School of Music (British)
A.I.C. -- of the Institute of Chemistry (British)
A.I.I.C. -- of the Insurance Institute of Canada
A.K.C. -- of King's College (London)
A.L.C.M. -- of London (Canada) Conservatory of Music
A.L.S. Commissioned Alberta Land Surveyor
A.M. Master of Arts (Artium Magister)
A.M.E.I.C. Associate Member of the Engineering Institute of Canada
A.M.I.C.E. -- Member of the Institution of Civil Engineers (British)
A.M.I.E.E. -- Member of the Institute of Electrical Engineers
A.M.I.Mech.E. -- Member of the Institution of Mechanical Engineers (British)
A.Mus. -- of Music
A.P.A. -- Member of the Institute of Accredited Public Accountants (British)
A.P.H.A. -- Member of the Public Health Association (British)
A.P.R. Accredited Member of the Canadian Public Relations Society
A.R.A. Associate of the Royal Academy (honorary)
A.R.C.D. -- of the Royal College of Dancing
A.R.C.M. -- of the Royal College of Music
A.R.C.O. -- of the Royal College of Organists (Canadian)
A.R.C.S. (A.R.C.Sc.) -- of the Royal College of Science
A.R.C.T. -- of the Royal Conservatory of Music of Toronto
A.R.C.V.S. -- of the Royal College of Veterinary Surgeons
A.R.D.I.O. -- of Registered Interior Designers of Ontario
A.R.D.S. -- of the Royal Drawing Society (London, Eng.)
A.R.I.B.A. -- of the Royal Institute of British Architects
A.R.I.C. -- of the Royal Institute of Chemistry
A.R.S.H. -- of the Royal Society of Health
A.R.S.M. -- of the Royal School of Mines
A.R.S.M. -- of the Royal School of Music
A.Sc.T. Applied Science Technologist
Assoc. Inst. M.M. Associate of the Institute of Mining and Metallurgy (British)
A.T.C.L. -- of Trinity College, London (Eng.)
A.T.C.M. -- of the Toronto Conservatory of Music
A.Th. -- in Theology
B.A. Bachelor of Arts
B.A.A. -- of Applied Arts
B.Acc. -- of Accountancy
B.Adm. (B.Admin.) -- of Administration
B.Adm.Pub. -- Baccalauréat spécialisé en administration publique
B.Ae.E. (B.Aero.E.) Bachelor of Aeronautical Engineering
B.A.I. -- of Engineering (U. of Dublin)
B.A.L.S. -- of Arts in Library Science
B.A.O. -- of Obstetrics
B.Arch. -- in Architecture
B.A.S. (B.A.Sc.) -- of Applied Science
B.A.S.M. -- of Arts, Master of Science
B.A.Theo. -- of Arts in Theology
B.B.A. -- of Business Administration
B.C.D. Bachelier en Chirurgie Dentale
B.C.E. Bachelor of Civil Engineering
B.Ch. (Ch.B.) -- in Surgery (British)
B.Ch.E. -- in Chemical Engineering (American)
B.C.L. -- of Civil Law (or Canon Law)
B.Com. (B. Comm.) -- of Commerce
B.Comp.Sc. -- of Computer Science
B.D. -- of Divinity
B.D.C. Bachelier en droit canonique
B.Des. Bachelor of Design
B.D.S. -- of Dental Surgery (British)
B.E. (B.Eng.) -- of Engineering
B.Ed. (B.E.A.D.) -- of Education
B.E.D.S. -- of Environmental Design Studies
B.E.E. -- of Electrical Engineering (American)
B. en Ph. Bachelier en Philosophie
B. en Sc. Com. -- en Science Commerciale
B.E.S. Bachelor of Environmental Sciences (or Studies)
B. ès A. Bachelier ès Arts
B. ès L. -- ès Lettres
B. ès Sc. -- ès Science
B. ès Sc. App. -- ès Science Appliquée
B.F. Bachelor of Forestry (American)
B.F.A. -- of Fine Arts
B.Gen. Brigadier-General
B.H.E. (B.H.Ec.) Bachelor of Home Economics
B.H.Sc. -- of Household Science
B.J. -- of Journalism
B.J.C. -- in Canon Law
B.L. -- in Literature (or of Laws)
B.L.A. -- of Landscape Architecture
B.Litt. -- of Literature (American & British)
B.L.S. -- of Library Science
B.M. -- of Medicine
B.Mus. -- of Music
B.M.V. Bachelier en Médecine Vetérinaire
B.N. Bachelor of Nursing
B.N.Sc. -- of Nursing Science
B. Paed. (Péd.) -- of Pedagogy
B.P.A. -- of Public Administration
B.P.E. -- of Physical Education
B.Ph. (B.Phil.) -- of Philosophy
B.P.H.E. -- of Physical & Health Education
B.Ps. Baccalauréat en Psychologie
Br. Brother
B.S. Bachelor of Science (or of Surgery) (American)
B.S.A. -- of Science in Agriculture (or in Accounting, or in Administration)
B.Sc. -- of Science
B.Sc.A. Bachelier ès science appliquées
B.Sc.B. -- en Bibliothéconomie
B.Sc.(CE) Bachelor of Science in Civil Engineering
B.Sc.Com. -- of Commercial Science
B.Sc.Dom. Baccalauréat en Sciences Domestiques
B.Sc.F. (B.S.F.) Bachelor of Science in Forestry
B.Sc.F.E. -- of Science in Forestry Engineering
B.Sc.H. Bachelier en Sciences Hospitalières
B.Sc.N. (or B.S.N. or B.Sc. (Nurs.)) Bachelor of Science in Nursing
B.Sc.(OT) (or B.Sc.(Occ.Ther.)) -- of Science in Occupational Therapy
B.Sc.Phm. (B.S.P.) -- of Science in Pharmacy
B.Sc.Soc. -- of Social Science

B.S.C.E. -- of Science in Civil Engineering
B.S.Ed. -- of Science in Education
B.S.E.E. -- of Science in Electrical Engineering
B.S.S. -- of Social Sciences
B.S.W. -- of Social Work (or Welfare)
B.Tech. -- of Technology
B.Th. -- of Theology
B.T.S. -- of Technological Science (Edinburgh)
B.V.Sc. -- of Veterinary Science
C.A. Chartered Accountant
C.A.A.P. Certified Advertising Agency Practitioner
C.A.E. -- Association Executive
C.A.E./c.a.é. Chartered Account Executive
C.A.P. Certificat d'Aptitude Pedagogique
Capt. (or Capt.(N)) Captain (or Captain (Naval))
C.B.E. Commander, Order of the British Empire
C.B.V. Chartered Business Valuator
C.C. Chartered Cartographer
C.C. Companion, Order of Canada
C.D. Canadian Forces Decoration
Cdr. Commander
C.E. Civil Engineer
C.E.A. Certified Environmental Auditor
Cer.E. Ceramic Engineer
C.E.S. Certificat d'Études Secondaires (La Sorbonne)
C.F.A. Chartered Financial Analyst
C.F.P. Chartered Financial Planner
C.G.A. Certified General Accountant
Chan. Chanoine (Canon)
C.H.E. Certified Health Executive
Chem. Ing. Ingénieur Chimiste Diplomé (Swiss Fed. Inst. Technology)
C.I.F. Canadian Institute of Forestry
C.I.M. Certificate in Management
C.I.M. Certified Industrial Manager
C.I.S.&P. Canadian Inst. of Surveying & Photogrammetry
C.L.A. Canadian Library Association
C.L.S. Canada Land Surveyor
C.L.U. Chartered Life Underwriter
C.M. Master in Medicine (British)
C.M. Member, Order of Canada
C.M.A. Certified Management Accountant (or Canadian Medical Association or Canadian Management Association)
C.M.C. Certified Management Consultant
Cmd.O. Commissioned Officer
Cmdre. Commodore
C.M.M. Certified Municipal Manager (Ontario)
C.M.M. Commander, Order of Military Merit
C.O.A. Certified Office Administrator
Col. Colonel
C.P.A. Certified Public Accountant
C.P.C. -- Personnel Consultant
C.P.M. Certificate in Personnel Management
C.P.P.M.A. -- in Public Personnel Management Association
C.P.P.O. Certified Public Purchasing Officer
C.P.P. -- Professional Purchaser
C.R. (c.r.) Conseiller de la Reine (Queen's Counsel)
C.R.A. Canadian Residential Appraiser
C.S.R. Chartered Stenographic Reporter
C.T.C. Certified Travel Counsellor
C.Tech. -- Technician
C.W.O. Chief Warrant Officer
D.A. Doctor of Arts (honorary)
D.A. -- of Archaeology (Laval)
D.Arch. -- of Architecture
D.A.Sc. -- in Applied Sciences
D.C. -- of Chiropractic

D.C.D. Docteur en Chirurgie Dentale
D.Ch. Doctor of Surgery (British)
D.Ch.E. -- of Chemical Engineering (American)
D.C.L. -- of Civil Law (or Canon Law)
D.D. -- of Divinity
D.D.C. Doctorat Droit Canonique
D. de l'Un. -- de l'Université
D.D.S. Doctor of Dental Surgery (British)
D.D.T. -- of Drugless Therapy
D.Ed. -- of Education
D.Eng. -- of Engineering
D. en Méd. Vet. Docteur en Médecine Vetérinaire
D. en Ph. -- en Philosophie
D. ès L. -- ès Lettres (Doctor of Letters)
D. ès Sc. App. Doctor of Applied Science
D.F. -- of Forestry (American)
D.F.A. -- of Fine Arts (often honorary)
D.F.Sc. -- of Financial Science (Laval)
D.I.C. Diploma of Membership of Imperial College of Science & Technology (British)
Dip. Bact. -- in Bacteriology
Dip. d'É. Diplome d'Études
Dip. de l'U. (P) Diploma of the U. of Paris
Dip. d'É. Sup. or Dip.E.S. Diplome d'Études Supérieures, Paris
Dip. Ing. Diploma in Engineering
D.Jour Doctor of Journalism
D. Lit. (D. Litt.) -- of Letters (or Literature)
D.L.O. Diploma in Laryngology & Otology
D.L.S. Dominion Land Surveyor (or Doctor of Library Science)
D.M. Doctorat Médecine
D.M.D. Doctor of Dental Medicine
D. Ms. -- in Missionology
D. Mus. Doctorat en Musique
D.M.R. (D. or T.) Diploma in Medical Radiology (Royal Coll. of Surgeons, London)
D.M.T. -- in Tropical Medicine
D.M.T. & H. (Eng.) -- in Tropical Medicine & Hygiene
D.N.S. D.N.Sc.) Doctor of Nursing Science
D.O. -- of Osteopathy
Doct. Arch. -- of Christian Archaeology (Pontifical Institute, Rome)
D. Paed. (Péd.) -- of Paedagogy
D.P.E. Diploma in Physical Education
D.Ph. (D.Phil. or Ph.D.) Doctor of Philosophy
D.P.Ec. -- of Political Economy
D.P.H. -- (or Diploma) in Public Health
D.Ps. (D.Psy.) -- of Psychologie
D.P.Sc. -- of Political Science
D. Psych. -- (or Diploma) in Psychiatry
D.P.T. -- of Physio-Therapy
Dr. Doctor
D.R. Doctor of Radiology
Dr.Com.Sc. -- of Commercial Science
Dr. de l'U. (P) -- of the U. of Paris
Dr. ès Lettres -- of Letters (History of Literature)
Dr. jur. -- of Law (Dr. Juris)
Dr. rer. pol. -- of Political Economy (Dr. Rerum Politicarum) (Docteur des Sciences Politiques)
D.S.A. (D.Sc.A.) Docteur ès science appliqués
D.Sc. Doctor of Science
D.Sc.Mil. -- of Military Science
D.S.L. -- of Sacred Letters
D.Sc.Com. -- of Commercial Science
D.Sc.Fin. -- of Financial Science
D.Sc.Nat. -- in Natural Science
D.Sc.Soc. -- of Social Science

D.Th. -- of Theology
D.V.M. (D.M.V.) -- of Veterinary Medicine
D.V.Sc. -- of Veterinary Science
Ed.D. -- of Education
Ed.M. Master of Education (Harvard)
E.E. Electrical Engineer
E.M. Mining Engineer
E.T.C.M. Graduate of Eastern Townships Conservatory of Music
F.A.A.O. Fellow of the American Academy of Optometry
F.A.A.O.Dip. Diplomatic Fellow of the American Academy of Optometry
F.A.C.D. Fellow of the American College of Dentists
F.A.C.O. -- of the American College of Organists
F.A.C.P. -- of the American College of Physicians
F.A.C.R. -- of the American College of Radiology
F.A.C.S. -- of the American College of Surgeons
F.A.E. -- of the Accountants' & Executives' Corp. of Canada
F.A.G.S. -- of the American Geographical Society
F.A.I.A. -- of the American Institute of Actuaries
-- of the American Institute of Architects
F.A.I.A. Association of International Accountants
F.A.O.U. Fellow of the American Ornithologists Union
F.A.P.H.A. -- of the American Public Health Association
F.A.P.S. -- of the American Physical Society
F.A.S. -- of the Actuarial Society
F.B.A. -- of the British Academy (honorary)
F.B.O.A. -- of British Association of Optometrists
F.C.A. -- of the Institute of Chartered Accountants (British)
F.C.B.A. -- of Canadian Bankers' Association
F.C.C.A. -- of the Association of Certified Accountants
F.C.C.O. -- of the Canadian College of Organists
F.C.C.T. -- of the Canadian College of Teachers
F.C.C.U.I. -- of the Canadian Credit Union Institute
F.C.G.I. -- of the City & Guilds of London Institute
F.C.I. -- of the Canadian Credit Institute
F.C.I.C. -- of the Chemical Institute of Canada
F.C.I.I. -- of the Chartered Insurance Institute (British)
F.C.I.S. -- of the Chartered Institute of Secretaries (British)
F.C.O.G. -- of the College of Obstetricians & Gynaecologists (British)
F.C.A.M.R.T. -- of Canadian Association of Medical Radiation Technologists
FCMA -- of the Society of Management Accountants of Canada
F.C.S.I. -- of the Canadian Securities Institute
F.C.T.C. -- of the Canadian Institute of Travel Counsellors
F.E. Forest Engineer
F.E.I.C. Fellow of the Engineering Institute of Canada
F.F.A. -- of the Faculty of Actuaries (Scotland)
F.F.R. -- of the Faculty of Radiologists (British)
F.G.S. -- of the Geological Society (British)
F.G.S.A. -- of the Geological Society of America
F.I.A. -- of the Institute of Actuaries (British)
F.I.C. -- of the Institute of Chemistry

| | |
|---|---|
| F.I.C.B. | -- of the Institute of Canadian Bankers |
| F.I.C.E. | -- of the Institution of Civil Engineers |
| F.I.E.E. | -- of the Institution of Electrical Engineers |
| F.I.I.C. | -- of the Insurance Institute of Canada |
| F.I.L. | -- of the Institute of Linguists (British) |
| F.L.A. | -- of the Library Association (England) |
| F.M.S.A. | -- of the Mineralogical Society of America |
| Fr. | Father |
| F.R.A.I. | Fellow of the Royal Anthropological Institute |
| F.R.A.I.C. | -- of the Royal Architectural Institute of Canada |
| F.R.A.M. | -- of the Royal Academy of Music |
| F.R.A.S. | -- of the Royal Astronomical Society |
| F.R.C.C.O. | -- of the Royal Canadian College of Organists |
| F.R.C.M. | -- of the Royal College of Music |
| F.R.C.O. | -- of the Royal College of Organists |
| F.R.C.O.G. | -- of the Royal College of Obstetricians & Gynaecologists |
| F.R.C.P. | -- of the Royal College of Physicians of London |
| F.R.C.P.(C) | -- of the College of Physicians of Canada |
| or (E) or (I) or (Glas) | -- of the College of Physicians of Edin burgh or of Ireland or of Glasgow |
| F.R.C.S. | -- of the Royal College of Surgeons of England |
| F.R.C.S.(C.) | -- of the Royal College of Surgeons of Canada |
| or (E) or (I) or (Glas) or (Glas) | -- of the Royal College of Sur geons of Edinburgh or of Ireland or of Glasgow |
| F.R.G.S. | -- of the Royal Geographical Society |
| F.R.Hist.S. | -- of the Royal Historical Society |
| F.R.Hort.S. | -- of the Royal Horticultural Society |
| F.R.I.B.A. | -- of the Royal Institute of British Architects |
| F.R.I.C. | -- of the Royal Institute of Chemistry |
| F.R.I.C.S. | -- of the Royal Institution of Chartered Surveyors |
| F.R.M.C.M. | -- of Royal Manchester College of Music |
| F.R.M.S. (F.R.Met.S.) | -- of the Royal Meteorological Society |
| F.R.S. | -- of the Royal Society (honorary) |
| F.R.S.A. | -- of the Royal Society of Arts |
| F.R.S.C. | -- of the Royal Society of Canada |
| F.R.S.E. | -- of the Royal Society of Edinburgh |
| F.R.S.H. | -- of the Royal Society of Health |
| F.R.S.L. | -- of the Royal Society of Literature |
| F.S.A. | -- of the Society of Actuaries (or of Antiquaries) (honorary) |
| F.S.S. | -- of the Royal Statistical Society |
| F.T.C.L. | -- of Trinity College of Music (London) |
| F.Z.S. | -- of the Zoological Society (British) |
| Gen. | General |
| G.J. | Graduate Jeweller |
| H.A.R.C.V.S. | Honorary Associate of Royal College of Veterinary Surgeons |
| Ing.E.T.P. | Diplome de l'École Spéciale des Travaux Publiques |
| J.C.B. | Bachelor of Canon Law |
| J.C.D. | Doctor of Canon Law (or of Civil Law) |
| J.C.L. | Licentiate in Canon Law (Juris Canonici Licentiatus) |
| J.D. | Doctor of Jurisprudence |
| J.D.S. | -- of Jurisdical Science |
| Jr. | Junior |
| J.U.L. | Licentiate of Law in Utroque (both Civil & Canon Law) |
| Jur.M. | Master of Jurisprudence |
| Jur. utr. Dr. | Juris utriusque doctor, Equiv. to LL.D. |
| L.A.B. | Licentiate of the Assoc. Bd. of Royal Schools of Music (London, Eng.) |
| L.Cdr. | Lieutenant-Commander |
| L.C.L. | Licentiate in Canon Law |
| L.C.M.I. | -- of the Cost & Management Institute |
| L.Col. | Lieutenant-Colonel |
| L.D.C. | Licencié ès Droit Canonique |
| L.D.S. | Licentiate in Dental Surgery (British) |
| L. ès L. | Licencié ès Lettres |
| L. ès Sc. | -- ès Sciences |
| L.Gen. | Lieutenant-General |
| L.G.S.M. | Licentiate of the Guildhall School of Music & Drama (London, Eng.) |
| Litt.D. | Doctor of Letters (or Literature) |
| Litt.L. | Licence ès Lettres |
| Litt.M. | Master of Letters (or Literature) |
| L.J.C. | Licentiatus Juris Canonici |
| L.L. | License in Civil Law |
| LL.B. | Bachelor of Laws (Legum Baccalaureus) |
| LL.D. | Doctor of Laws (usually honorary) |
| LL.L. | Licence en droit |
| LL.M. | Master of Law |
| L. Mus. | Licentiate in Music |
| L.M.U.S. | -- in Music of the Univ. of Saskatchewan |
| L. Mus. T.C.L. | -- in General Musicianship of Trinity College, London |
| L.Péd. | Licence en Pédagogie |
| L.Ph. | -- en Philosophie |
| L.Psych. | Licencié en Psychologie |
| L.R.A.M. | Licentiate of the Royal Academy of Music (London) |
| L.R.C.M. | -- of the Royal College of Music (London) |
| L.R.C.P. | -- of the Royal College of Physicians |
| L.R.C.S. | -- of the Royal College of Surgeons |
| L.R.C.T. | -- of the Royal Conservatory of Toronto |
| L.R.E. | -- in Religious Education |
| L.R.S.M. | -- of the Royal Schools of Music (London) |
| L.S. | Land Surveyor |
| L.S.A. | Licentiate in Agricultural Science |
| L.Sc.Com. | -- in Commercial Science |
| L.Sc.O. | Licence en optométrie |
| L.S.Sc. | Licentiate in Sacred Scriptures |
| L.Sc.Soc. | Licence in Social Science |
| L.S.T. | Licentiate in Sacred Theology |
| Lt. (or Lt.(N)) | Lieutenant (or Lieutenant (Naval)) |
| L.T.C.L. | -- of Trinity College of Music (London) |
| L.T.C.M. | -- of the Toronto Conservatory of Music |
| L.Th | Licentiate in Theology |
| M. | Monsieur |
| M.A. | Master of Arts |
| M.Acc. | -- of Accountancy |
| M.A.C.F. | Membre de l'Académie canadienne-française |
| M.Ae.E. | Master of Aeronautical Engineering |
| M.A.I.E.E. | Member of American Institute of Electrical Engineers |
| M.A.I.M.E. | -- of American Institute of Mining Engineers |
| Maj. | Major |
| M.A.L.S. | Master of Arts in Library Science |
| M.A.P. | Maîtrise en administration publique |
| M.Arch. | Master of Architecture |
| M.A.S. | -- of Archival Studies |
| M.A.Sc. (M.A.S.) | -- of Applied Science |
| M.A.S.C.E. | Member of the American Society of Civil Engineers |
| M.A.S.M.E. | -- of the American Society of Mechanical Engineers |
| M.Aust. I.M. | -- of the Australian Institute of Mining & Metallurgy |
| M.B. | Bachelor of Medicine (British) |
| M.B.A. | Master in Business Administration |
| M.C.E. | -- of Civil Engineering |
| M.Ch. (Ch.M.) | -- of Surgery (British) |
| M.Ch.E. | -- of Chemical Engineering (American) |
| M.C.I. | Member of the Credit Institute |
| M.C.I.C. | -- of the Chemical Institute of Canada |
| M.C.I.F. | -- of the Canadian Institute of Forestry |
| M.C.I.M. | -- of the Canadian Institute of Mining |
| M.C.I.M.M. | -- of the Canadian Institute of Mining & Metallurgy |
| M.C.Inst.M. | -- of the Canadian Institute of Marketing |
| M.C.L. | Master of Civil Law |
| M.Com. | -- of Commerce |
| M.Comp. | -- of Canon Law |
| M.Comp.Sc. | -- of Computer Science |
| M.D. | Doctor of Medicine |
| M.D.C. | Master of Canon Law |
| M.D.C.M. | Doctor of Medicine & Master of Surgery |
| M.Des. | Master of Design |
| M.Div. | -- of Divinity |
| M.D.S. | -- of Dental Surgery (British) |
| M.D.V. | Doctor of Veterinary Medicine |
| Me | Maître |
| M.E. | Master of Mechanical Engineering |
| M.Ed. (M.A.Ed.) | -- of Education |
| M.E.D.S. | -- of Environmental Design Studies |
| M.E.E. | -- of Electrical Engineering (American) |
| M.E.I.C. | Member of the Engineering Institute of Canada |
| M.Eng. | Master of Engineering |
| M.F. | -- of Forestry |
| M.F.A. | -- of Fine Arts |
| M.Gen. | Major-General |
| Mgr. | Monsignor (or Manager or Monseigneur) |
| M.H.A. | Master of Health (or Hospital) Administration |
| M.H.E. (M.H.Ec.) | -- of Home Economics |
| M.I.C.E. | Member of the Institution of Civil Engineers (British) |
| M.I.C.I.A. | -- of Industrial, Commercial & Institutional Accountants |
| M.I.E.E. | -- of the Institution of Electrical Engineers (British) |
| M.I.M.M. | -- of the Institute of Mining & Metallurgy (British) |
| M.I.N.A. | -- of the Institute of Naval Architects |
| M.I.R.E. | -- of the Institute of Radio Engineers |
| M.J. | Master of Journalism |
| M.Litt. | -- of Letters (or Literature) |
| M.L.I.S. | -- of Library & Information Science |
| M.L.S. | -- of Library Science (or Licentiate in Medieval Studies) |
| M.M. (M.Mus.) | -- of Music |
| M.M.M. | Member, Order of Military Merit |
| M.N. (M.Nurs.) | Master of Nursing |
| M.P. | -- of Planning |
| M.P. | Member of Parliament |
| M.P.E. | Master of Physical Education |
| M.Ph. (M.Phil.) | -- of Philosophy |
| M.P.M. | -- of Pest Management |
| M.P.P. | Member of Provincial Parliament |
| M.Ps. (M.Psy.) | Master of Psychology |
| M.R.A.I.C. | Member of the Royal Architectural Institute of Canada |
| M.R.C.O.G. | -- of the Royal College of Obstetricians & Gynaecologists |
| M.R.C.P. | -- of the Royal College of Physicians |
| M.R.C.P.(E) or (I) or (Glas) | -- of the Royal College of Physicians of Edinburgh (or Ireland or Glasgow) |
| M.R.C.S. | -- of the Royal College of Surgeons |
| M.R.C.S.(E) | -- of the Royal College of Surgeons of Edinburgh |
| M.R.C.V.S. | -- of the Royal College of Veterinary Surgeons |

| | |
|---|---|
| M.R.M. | Master of Resource Management |
| M.R.S.C. | Member of the Royal Society of Canada |
| M.R.S.H. | -- of the Royal Society of Health |
| M.R.S.T. | -- of the Royal Society of Teachers |
| M.S. | Master of Surgery (British) |
| M.S.A. | -- of Science in Agriculture |
| M.Sc. | -- of Science |
| M.Sc.A. | -- of Applied Science |
| M.S.C.E. | -- of Science in Civil Engineering |
| M.Sc.F. | -- of Science in Forestry |
| M.Sc.(Med.) | -- of Science in Medicine |
| M.Sc.N. (M.S.N.) | -- of Science in Nursing |
| M.Sc.Phm. | -- of Science in Pharmacy |
| M.Sc.Soc. | -- in Social Sciences |
| M.S.Ed. | -- of Science in Education |
| M.S.Litt. | -- of Sacred Letters |
| M.S.P.E. | McGill School of Physical Education |
| M.S.R.C. | Membre Société Royale du Canada |
| M.S.S. | Master of Social Science |
| M.S.W. | -- of Social Work |
| M.U.Dr. | Medecinae Universae Doctor (Prague) (Dentistry & Medicine) |
| M.U.P. | Master of Planning |
| M.U.R.P. | -- of Urban & Rural Planning |
| Mus. Bac. (Mus.B.) | Bachelor of Music |
| Mus. Doc. (Mus.D.) | Doctor of Music |
| Mus. G. Paed. | Musicae Graduatus Paedagogus (Graduate Teacher in Music) |
| Mus.M. | Master of Music |
| M.V. | Médécin Vétérinaire |
| M.V.Sc. | Master of Veterinary Science |
| N.D.A. | National Diploma in Agriculture (Royal Ag. Soc. of Engineering) |
| N.D.D. | National Diploma in Dairying (Scotland) |
| N.P. | Notary Public |
| O.A. | Officier d'Académie (France) |
| O.C. | Order of Canada |
| O.D. | Doctor of Optometry |
| O.I.P. | Officier de l'Instruction Publique |
| O.L.S. | Ontario Land Surveyor |
| O.M.M. | Officer, Order of Military Merit |
| O.S.A. | Ontario Society of Artists |
| P.C. | Privy Councillor |
| P.D. | Doctor of Parapsychology |
| P.E. | Professional Engineer |
| P.Eng. | Registered Professional Engineer |
| Ph.B. | Bachelor of Philosophy |
| Ph.C. | Philosopher of Chiropractic |
| Ph.D. | Doctor of Philosophy |
| Ph.T.D. | Physical Therapy Doctor |
| Ph.L. | Licentiate in Philosophy |
| P.L.S. | Professional Legal Secretary |
| P.Mgr. | -- Manager |
| P.P. | -- Purchaser |
| P.P.B. | -- Public Buyer |
| Prof. | Professor |
| P.T.I.C. | Patent & Trade Mark Institute of Canada |
| Q.A.A. | Qualified Administrative Assistant |
| Q.C. | Queen's Counsel |
| Q.L.S. | Québec Land Surveyor |
| R.A. | Royal Academy (honorary) |
| R.Adm. | Rear-Admiral |
| R.A.M. | Royal Academy of Music (Budapest) |
| R.A.S. | Royal Aeronautical Society |
| R.B.A. | Royal Society of British Artists |
| R.C.A. | Royal Canadian Academy of Arts |
| R.C.A.M. | Royal College & Academy of Music (Budapest) |
| R.C.M. | Royal Conservatory of Music (Leipzig) |
| R.E. | Royal Engineers |
| Rev. | Reverend |
| R.F.P. | Registered Financial Planner |
| R.M.S. | Royal Society of Miniature Painters |
| R.M.T. | Registered Music Teacher |
| R.N. | -- Nurse |
| R.O.I. | Royal Institute of Oil Painters |
| R.P. | Member of the Royal Society of Portrait Painters |
| R.P. | Révérend Père (Reverend Father) |
| R.P.A. | Registered Public Accountant |
| R.P.Bio. | -- Professional Biologist |
| R.P.Dt. | -- Professional Dietitian |
| R.P.F. | -- Professional Forester |
| R.R.L. | -- Record Librarian |
| R.S.H. | Royal Society of Health |
| R.S.W. | Registered Specification Writer |
| R.T. | -- Technician of the Cdn. Association of Medical Radiation Technologists |
| S.C. | Senior Counsel (Eire) equivalent of Q.C. |
| Sc.D. | Doctorat ès Sciences |
| Sc.L. | Licence ès Sciences |
| Sc. Soc. B. | Bachelier Science Sociale |
| Sc. Soc. D. | Doctor of Social Science |
| Sc. Soc. L. | License in Social Science |
| S.J. | Society of Jesus |
| S.L.S. | Saskatchewan Land Surveyor |
| S.Lt. | Sub-Lieutenant |
| S.M. | Master of Science |
| Sr. | Senior |
| Sr. | Sister |
| S.S.B. | Bachelier en Science Sacrée |
| S.S.C. | Sculptors' Society of Canada |
| S.S.L. | Licentiate in Sacred Scripture |
| S.T.B. (S.Th.B.) | Bachelor of Sacred Theology |
| S.T.D. (S.Th.D.) | Doctor of Sacred Theology |
| S.T.L. (S.Th.L.) | Sacrae Theologiae Licentiatus (Licentiate in Sacred Theology) |
| S.T.M. | Master of Sacred Theology |
| T.C.L. | Trinity College, London |
| T.M.M.G. | Teacher, Massage & Medical Gymnastics |
| Th.D. | Doctor of Theology |
| V.Adm. | Vice-Admiral |
| V.G. | Vicar-General |
| V.S. | Veterinary Surgeon |

## BUSINESS AND SHIPPING ABBREVIATIONS

**As shipping terms vary in different countries, insurance or shipping agents should be consulted.**

For other lists of abbreviations, academic, etc., see Index.

| | |
|---|---|
| a/c | Account |
| Ad val. | Ad valorem |
| avoir | Avoirdupois |
| bbl. | Barrel |
| B/L. | Bill of Lading |
| b.m. | Board Measure |
| B.O. | Buyer's Option |
| B/P. | Bills Payable |
| B/R. | Bills Receivable |
| B/S. | Bill of Sale |
| c. | Hundred |
| C or Cent. | Centigrade |
| cf. | Compare |
| C. and F. | Cost & Freight |
| Cie | Compagnie |
| c.i.f. | Cost insurance & freight |
| C.L. | Car Load (of freight) |
| Co. | Company |
| C.O.D. | Cash on Delivery |
| C. of F. | Cost of Freight |
| Cr. | Credit |
| C.W.O. | Cash with Order |
| Cwt. | Hundredweight |
| D/A. | Documents Attached, also Deposit Account |
| Dis. (Disct.) | Discount |
| Dl. (or Tl.) | Double (or triple) first class |
| D.O.A. | Deliver Documents on Acceptance of Draft |
| D.O.P. | Deliver Documents on Payment of Draft |
| Dr. | Debit |
| D.V. | God willing (Deo volente) |
| e.g. | For example (exempli gratia) |
| E.&.O.E. | Errors & omissions excepted |
| Est. Wt. | Estimated Weight |
| et seq. | And the following (et sequens) |
| Ex. Div. | Without Dividend |
| Ex-Warehouse | Purchaser pays carriage charges & assumes risks from seller's warehouse |
| F. | Fahrenheit |
| F.a.a. | Free of Average (marine insurance) |
| F.A.S. | Free Alongside (Seller assumes risks & delivers goods to alongside of steamer free of carriage charges) |
| F.O.B. | Free on Board (Purchaser pays carriage charges & assumes risks from point specified) |
| F.P.A. | Free of Particular Average (Insured can recover only for a total loss, subject to other conditions of the contract) |
| Franco. | Pre-paid free of expense to point specified |
| G.A. | General Average (All owners of cargo & vessel share in any loss arising from expense incurred to preserve ship & contents from greater loss) |
| gm. | Grammes |
| gr. | Grain; grains, or gross |
| ibid. | In the same place (ibidem) |
| i.e. | That is (id est) |
| Inc. | Incorporated |
| Int. | Interest |
| K.D. | Knocked down |
| lb. (libra) | Pound |
| L/C. | Letter of Credit |
| L.C.L. | Less than Car Load (of freight) |
| Limited; Ltd. | Limited Liability (Shareholders are "limited" in liability to the amount of their subscribed stock in certain companies) |
| L.P. | List Price |
| M. | Thousand (Mille) |
| MS., MSS. | Manuscript(s) |
| N.E.S. (N.O.P.) | Not Otherwise Provided For (Customs) |
| N.O.S. | Not Otherwise Specified |
| N.S.F. | Not Sufficient Funds (re cheques) |
| Nstd. | Nested |
| O.K. | Correct |
| op. cit. | In the work quoted (opere citato) |
| O.R. | At Owner's Risk |
| O.R.B. | At Owner's Risk of Breakage |
| oz. | Ounce |
| P.A. | Particular Average (As used in Marine Insurance, means damage to the goods caused by perils insured against & named in the contract. This form is often written with a Franchise Clause, & means there will be no claim unless the loss exceeds the percentage named) |
| P/A. | Power of Attorney |
| P & D. | Pick Up & Deliver |
| pp. | Pages |
| Pro forma | As a Matter of Form |
| P.S. | Postscript |
| q.v. | Which see (quod vide) |

| | |
|---|---|
| R.R. | Rural Route (Postal delivery) |
| S.B. | Shipping Bill |
| s.s. | Steamship |
| s/o | Ship's Option, weight or measurement |
| S.U. | Set Up (meaning article is complete) |
| T.B.L. | Through Bill of Lading |
| Tare | Weight of Container (Deducting tare from "gross weight" gives "net weight") |
| Ton | 2,000 (short ton) or 2,240 (long ton) lbs. avoirdupois. A cubic ton in marine freight = 40 cubic feet |
| Ton wt/M. | Ton, weight or measurement (ship's option) |
| vide | See |
| viz | Namely; to wit (videlicet) |

# CUSTOMS REGULATIONS FOR CANADIANS RETURNING FROM ABROAD

Canadians returning to Canada may bring any amount of goods into the country subject to duties and any provincial or territorial assessments, with the exception of restricted items. Duties represent duty, excise taxes and the Goods & Services Tax (GST). Provincial and territorial taxes are not included in duties unless a relationship has been established between the federal government and a province or territory whereby the federal government collects the provincial or territorial taxes, levies and fees on their behalf.

Goods included in personal exemptions must be for personal or household use, souvenirs or gifts. Goods brought in for commercial use, or on behalf of another person do not qualify and are subject to full duties.

On your return to Canada, you must declare all goods acquired (purchases, gifts, awards, prizes, and purchases made at Canadian or foreign duty-free shops and still in your possession) and repairs or modifications you made to your vehicle, vessel or aircraft while outside Canada.

## Personal Exemptions

To qualify for personal exemptions you must be:
-Canadian resident returning from a trip abroad;
-former resident of Canada returning to live in Canada; or
-temporary resident of Canada.

Children and infants qualify for personal exemptions as long as the goods are for the use of the child or infant. The parent or guardian makes the customs declaration for the child.

Personal exemptions are applicable after the following minimum absences:

1. After an absence of 24 hours or more: up to a value of $50 in total (with the exception of tobacco and alcoholic beverages) any number of times a year. If the value of the goods exceeds $50 you pay duty on the full value (exemption cannot be claimed). The goods must accompany you on your return to Canada. A written declaration may be necessary.

2. After an absence of 48 hours or more: up to $200 in total any number of times in a year. You may have to make a written declaration. The goods must accompany you on your return to Canada.

3. After an absence of seven days or more: up to $500 any number of times in a year. You may have to make a written declaration. Goods you claim under this exemption may follow you by mail or other means, with the exception of alcoholic beverages or tobacco. You require a Form E24, "Returning Persons Declaration", obtainable from a customs officer, to claim your goods when they arrive. Goods must be claimed within 40 days of their arrival in Canada; duty is then payable, along with a processing fee. You may pay the duty and then apply to Revenue Canada for a refund (if the personal exemption applies) or refuse delivery; following a review that determines if the goods are eligible for free importation, the goods will be released to you without an assessment.

Persons residing outside Canada for part of the year are considered to be residents of Canada and are entitled to the above personal exemptions.

Exemptions cannot be transferred to another person or combined with another person's personal exemption. You cannot combine a 24-hour ($50) or 48-hour ($200) or the seven-day ($500) exemption when claiming an exemption. Nor can you carry over an unused portion of an exemption for another period of absence.

## Tobacco & Alcohol

Tobacco & alcoholic beverages must accompany you in your hand or checked luggage and may be included in the 48-hour ($200) or the seven-day ($500) exemptions, but not in the 24-hour ($50) exemption. You must meet the age requirements set by the province or territory where you enter Canada. In addition the following conditions apply:

1. You may bring in up to 200 cigarettes, 50 cigars or cigarillos, 400 tobacco sticks and 400 grams of manufactured tobacco. Duty must be paid on anything above this allowance, plus any applicable provincial or territorial limits or assessments.

2. You may include up to 1.14 litres (40 ounces) of wine or liquor, or 24 335 ml (12-ounce) cans or bottles (8.5 litres) of beer or ale. Wine coolers are classified as wine; beer coolers are classified as beer. Beer or wine that contains 0.5% alcohol by volume or less is not classifed as an alcoholic beverage, so no quantity limits apply. You may bring in more than this allowance of alcohol anywhere in Canada (with the exception of the Northwest Territories) as long as the quantities are within the limits set by the province. In most cases you must carry the allowance with you. If bringing in more than the free allowance, you must pay customs and provincial/territorial assessments; check with the appropriate provincial/territorial liquor control agency prior to leaving Canada for more information.

## Gifts

While abroad, you may send gifts duty-free and tax-free to recipients in Canada. The gift must be valued at $60 or less and cannot be an alcoholic beverage, tobacco product or advertising material. Gifts in excess of $60 require duty payment by the recipient on the excess amount. Gifts that accompany you on your return to Canada must be included in your personal exemption, while gifts you send from abroad are not included. Some conditions apply; contact your nearest Revenue Canada customs office for details.

## Prizes & Awards

In most cases, you pay regular duty on prizes or awards received outside Canada. Contact Revenue Canada customs offices for more information.

## Paying Duties

Duties may be paid by cash or travellers' cheques. Personal cheques are also acceptable (for amounts of $2500 or less and with proper identification); VISA and MasterCard are accepted at most customs locations.

For information on duty rates for particular items, contact your nearest Revenue Canada customs office.

## Special Duty Rate

After any trip abroad of 48 hours or longer you are entitled to a special duty rate on goods worth up to $300 more than your personal exemption. The goods must accompany you. The special duty rate does not apply to tobacco or alcoholic beverages. The special duty rate for goods not eligible under NAFTA, when combined with the GST, works out to about 15%.

## NAFTA Special Duty Rate

Goods qualify for a lower duty rate under NAFTA if they are:
-for personal use; and
-marked as made in the U.S., Mexico or Canada; or
-not marked or labelled to indicate they were made anywhere other than in the U.S., Mexico or Canada.

If you do not qualify for a personal exemption or if you exceed your exemption limit, you will have to pay GST over and above applicable duty or taxes on the portion not eligible under your exemption.

United States: The special duty rate on eligible goods will be reduced annually until 1998, when only GST will apply. The special duty rate, when combined with the GST rounded to the nearest half percent is 7% (1998).

Mexico: The special duty rate for eligible goods, when combined with the GST, is 8% (1995 rate). The combined rate will decrease each year until 2003, when only the GST will apply.

For information on goods eligible for the special duty rate under NAFTA, contact your nearest Revenue Canada customs office.

## Regular Duty Rates

If you do not qualify for a personal exemption, or you exceed your exemption limit, you will pay GST over and above all duties, taxes and assessments that apply on the portion not eligible under your exemption. The rates vary according to the goods, their country of origin and the country from which you are importing them.

## GATT (General Agreement on Tariffs & Trade)

Since January 1, 1995, duty on a wide range of products originating in non-NAFTA countries has been eliminated or will be reduced to zero within the next ten years. NAFTA goods also qualify for the GATT rate, so if the rate on the goods you are importing is lower under GATT than under NAFTA, the lower rate will automatically by applied.

## Value for Duty/Foreign Sales Tax

Value for duty is the amount used to calculate duty and is generally the price you paid for the item. Foreign sales tax is included in the price and forms part of the value of the item.

## Declaration

When returning to Canada by commercial aircraft, a traveller declaration card is distributed for completion before arrival. The cards are also used at some locations for people arriving by train, vessel or bus. If arriving by a private vehicle (eg., automobile), you must make an oral declaration unless you are claiming the $500 exemption.

Customs officials are legally entitled to examine luggage; you are responsible for opening, unpacking and repacking the luggage. Retain receipts of purchases and repairs made to verify length of stay and value of goods or repairs. Failure to declare or a false declaration may result in the seizure of goods. Penalties range from 25 to 80% of the value of the seized goods. Vehicles used to transport unlawfully imported goods may also be seized, with a penalty imposed before the vehicle can be returned. Commodities such as alcohol and tobacco are seized and not returned.

## Restrictions

Firearms: Contact a Revenue Canada customs office.

Explosives, fireworks, ammunition: You require authorization and you may also need a permit. Contact Chief Inspector of Explosives Division, Natural Resources Canada, 580 Booth St., Ottawa ON K1A 0E4, 613/995-2388.

Motor Vehicles: Import restrictions apply to most used or second-hand cars, generally from countries other than the United States. Under NAFTA, restrictions do not apply to vehicles imported from the U.S.; special duty rates, as outlined above, apply. Duty rates on vehicles drop annually, until they become duty-free in 1998 (excise tax and GST continue to apply in the usual way). Under NAFTA, customs restrictions continue to apply to vehicles imported from Mexico until 2009, when you will be able to import vehicles ten years or older. The age restriction will drop every second year until the restriction is dropped altogether in 2019. Vehicles imported from Mexico become duty-free in 2003. Under Transport Canada restrictions, all imported vehicles less than fifteen years old must comply with Canadian federal safety and emission standards. The person importing the vehicle is responsible for ensuring it meets the standards. For information, contact: Road Safety & Motor Vehicle Regulation Directorate, Transport Canada, 344 Slater St., 13th Fl., Ottawa ON K1A 0N5, 613/998-2174, 1-800-333-0558 (outside Ottawa area). Your vehicle may be subject to provincial or territorial sales tax; contact your provincial or territorial department of motor vehicles for information. In addition, you may need to meet some requirements in the country from which the vehicle is being exported.

Import Controls: Certain goods are monitored for their effect on Canadian manufacturers. You may need a permit to import, even if you qualify for a personal exemption. For information, contact Export & Import Permits Bureau, Dept. of Foreign Affairs & International Trade, Ottawa ON K1A 0G2, 613/952-1362.

Meat, dairy products, fresh fruit & vegetables: Complex requirements & restrictions exist; some importation of meat & dairy products from the U.S. is allowed. Limits exist for small amounts or for foodstuffs you can import under your personal exemption; if above those limits, duty ranges from 150 to 350% and you may require an agricultural inspection certificate. Contact regional Revenue Canada customs offices.

Cultural property: Antiquities or cultural objects of significance in the country of origin cannot be imported into Canada. For information, contact Movable Cultural Property, Cultural Development & Heritage, Dept. of Canadian Heritage, #500, 300 Slater St., Ottawa, ON K1A 0C8, 613/990-4161, Fax: 613/954-8826.

Agricultural products: Restrictions exist on live animals & animal products, meat & poultry products, dairy products, egg & egg products, fresh fruit & vegetables, seeds & grains, animal feeds, plant & plant products, forestry products, soil & fertilizers, pest control products, biological products. Contact a district office of the Food Production & Inspection Branch, Agriculture & Agri-Food Canada.

Endangered species: Canada is a signatory to an international agreement restricting the sale, trade or movement of a large number of endangered animals, birds, reptiles, fish, insects and certain forms of plant life; the restrictions also apply to their parts or products made from their parts. For information, contact Convention Administrator, Canadian Wildlife Service, Environment Canada, Ottawa ON K1A 0H3, 819/997-1840.

### Appeals

Disagreements about the amount of duty paid should be directed to your nearest Revenue Canada customs office; if not satisfactorily resolved, a formal appeal may be undertaken. If goods have been seized and you disagree with the action taken, you must notify Revenue Canada in writing within 30 days of the seizure date of your intention to appeal.

### Precautions

Carry proper identification and identification for children travelling with you; customs officials look for missing children and may ask questions about the children travelling with you.

"Identification of Articles for Temporary Exportation": Revenue Canada customs offices offer a free identification program for valuables; a list of your valuables (excluding jewellery) and their serial numbers on a wallet-sized form will show customs officials that the items were previously purchased in Canada or that you lawfully imported them prior to your current time abroad. In the case of jewellery, carry an appraisal of the item(s) from a gemologist, jeweller or insurance agent, together with a signed and dated photograph and a written declaration that the items in the photograph are those described in the appraisal report. If previously imported, carry a copy of the customs receipt.

If you take any item outside Canada and modify it, it is considered to be a new item and its full value will need to be declared. Similarly, under Canadian law, any repairs or modifications to a vehicle that increase its value, improve its condition or modify it while abroad may require that you pay duty on its full value on your return to Canada. This does not apply to incidental repairs to keep the car in operational condition while abroad, although you may be required to pay duty on the repairs and parts. A special provision is available that waives duties payable in such cases. Contact Revenue Canada for information.

### Regional Customs Offices

| | |
|---|---|
| Atlantic | 902/426-2911 |
| Québec | 418/648-4445 |
| Montréal Region | 514/283-9900 |
| Northern Ontario | 613/993-0534 |
| (after 4:30 pm & weekends) | 613/998-3326 |
| Southern Ontario | 416/973-8022 |
| (weekends & holidays) | 416/676-3643 |
| Hamilton Region | 905/308-8715 |
| Windsor Region | 519/257-6400 |
| Prairies | 204/983-6004 |
| Calgary Region | 403/292-8750, 4660 |
| Pacific | 604/666-0545 |
| Website | http://www.revcan.ca |

## ELECTION REGULATIONS

According to the Canada Elections Act, and subject to certain exceptions, the general rule as to the franchise of electors at a federal election is that every person in Canada is qualified as an elector if such person

(a) is of the full age of 18 years;

(b) is a Canadian citizen.

Among persons disqualified are certain officials charged with administering the elections, individuals who have lost their right to vote for a specified period for the commission of an election-related offence.

Writs for an election (general or by-election) are issued before the date fixed for polling day.

Similar qualifications apply in the Provinces and Territories, although for provincial and territorial elections there is usually a residence requirement of either six or twelve months before the date of the issue of the writ of election. The age requirement is 18 years.

To contact election officers see Index, "Elections, Govt. Info. Sources".

## LIQUOR REGULATIONS

**For names of personnel of the various Liquor Control Boards see index "Liquor Board, Commission, or Control."**

### Alberta

Liquor (wine, beer, cider, spirits) for off-premises consumption is sold from private retail liquor stores, general merchandise liquor stores & hotels authorized for off-sales. Some restrictions may apply.

Legal drinking age is 18 years.

Liquor may be sold in licensed premises whose primary source of business is the sale of food or liquor. Liquor may also be sold in a licensed canteen, casino facility, club, racetrack stadium (except where prohibited by local by-law), at professional sports or entertainment events, recreational facility, theatre, post-secondary institution, senior citizens' institution, traveller's lounge, aircraft, bus, train or water excursion craft for consumption on the premises.

Licensees purchase liquor from authorized retail liquor stores & warehouse facilities under certain conditions. Licenses are normally issued for a maximum two-year period. Fees vary with the type of license.

Alberta Gaming & Liquor Commission, 50 Corriveau Ave., St. Albert AB T8N 3T5 – 403/447-8737; Fax: 403/447-8908.

### British Columbia

The Liquor Control & Licensing Branch administers the Liquor Control & Licensing Act & Regulations & is responsible for:

- Issuing, renewing & transferring licenses for the sale of liquor;
- Licensing breweries, distilleries, wineries & their agents;
- Inspecting licensed premises;
- Approving & monitoring advertising of beer, wine & liquor;
- Enforcing the Liquor Control & Licensing Act & Regulations.

The Branch issues 10 types of liquor licenses for the sale of liquor. Each type of license has different licensing requirements.

"A" licenses, mainly hotels, resorts & clubs;
"B" restaurants;
"C" cabarets;
"D" neighbourhood public houses;
"E" stadium & concert hall;
"F" marine public house;
"G" & "H" licensee retail stores or cold beer & wine stores;
"I" restoration public house;
"J" winery lounge license.

British Columbia Liquor Control & Licensing Branch, 1019 Wharf St., Victoria BC V8W 2Y9; 250/387-1254; Fax: 250/387-9184

### Manitoba

Persons over the age of 18 years & who are not otherwise prohibited may purchase & consume spirits, wine & beer in premises licensed by the Liquor Control Commission. Further, those persons may purchase from a Liquor Control Commission store, liquor vendor or specialty wine store for consumption in a residence.

Beer may also be purchased from beer vendor depots located in most hotels throughout the province.

Parents dining with their children may purchase alcoholic beverages for the latter, for consumption with meals, only in licensed restaurants, dining rooms, cocktail lounges or cabarets.

Beverage rooms & cocktail rooms must be vacated within 30 minutes after the hour at which sale of liquor must cease.

Manitoba Liquor Control Commission, 1555 Buffalo Place, PO Box 1023, Winnipeg MB R3C 2X1 – 204/284-2501; Fax: 204/475-7666

### New Brunswick

Intoxicating liquor is sold in sealed packages at Liquor Stores. Where a permit &/or a license has been obtained, liquor may be sold by the glass in dining rooms, restaurants, taverns, cabarets, lounges, beverage rooms, & clubs. Age of majority is 19.

New Brunswick Liquor Corp., PO Box 20787, Fredericton NB E3B 5B8 – 506/452-6826; Fax: 506/452-9890

### Newfoundland

The importation, manufacture, & sale of Alcoholic Beverages through Retail Liquor outlets is the responsibility of the Newfoundland Liquor Corp.

The Newfoundland Liquor Corporation is also responsible for the issuing of all licenses, including those to manufacture & to sell packaged beer, & enforcement of regulations including, but not limited, to the following:

All liquor sold upon licensed premises shall be consumed thereon.

All liquor served in licensed premises shall be dispensed from the original container in which the liquor is purchased from or under the authority of the Liquor Corp.

The drinking age in Newfoundland is 19 years.

Nfld. Liquor Corp., PO Box 8750, Stn A, St. John's NF A1B 3V1 – 709/724-1100; Fax: 709/754-0321; TLX: 016-4923.

### Northwest Territories

The Northwest Territories Act, Chapter 331 of the Revised Statutes of Canada, 1952, authorizes the Commissioner in Council of the Northwest Territories to make acts respecting intoxicants.

The Liquor Licensing Board, established under Part I of the Liquor Act, controls the conduct of licensees & operation of licensed premises; grants, renews & transfers licenses &, after a hearing, may cancel or suspend licenses. There are presently twelve types of licenses issued by the Board. Part I also provides for plebiscites to be held concerning new liquor license applications & also concerning restriction or prohibition in a community.

Part II of the Liquor Act establishes a Liquor Commission. The Minister responsible for this Part may designate his powers to the Liquor Commission to operate liquor stores & to purchase, sell & distribute liquor in the Northwest Territories. The Liquor Commission operates liquor warehouses in Iqaluit & Yellowknife. Through agency agreements, private contractors operate retail liquor stores on behalf of the Liquor Commission in Fort Simpson, Fort Smith, Hay River, Inuvik, Yellowknife, Norman Wells & liquor warehouses in Hay River & Inuvik.

Northwest Territories Liquor Commission, PO Box 1130, Hay River NT X0E 0R0

### Nova Scotia

All liquor is sold through Government Stores.

Generally local option vote applies.

Eating establishment liquor licenses, lounges, clubs & cabarets serve spirits, draught beer, bottled beer & wine.

The legal minimum drinking age is 19 years.

Nova Scotia Liquor License Bd., #401, 277 Pleasant St., Dartmouth NS B2Y 4B7 – 902/424-6160; Fax: 902/424-8987

Nova Scotia Liquor Commission, PO Box 8720, Stn A, Halifax NS B3K 5M4 – 902/450-6752; Fax: 902/453-1153

### Ontario

In accordance with the provisions of the Liquor Control Act of Ontario, the Liquor Control Board buys wine, spirits & beer from all over the world for distribution & sale to Ontario consumers & licensed establishments.

To provide this service, the LCBO operates five major regional storage & distribution centres which supply more than 600 retail liquor stores. Through this vast network, over 3,000 products are available to consumers either by direct purchase or special order. As an additional service, customers can obtain products from around the world, that are not available in Ontario, through an LCBO private stock order.

The LCBO also operates a number of special outlets, known as Vintages stores, which offer consumers a wide variety of premium wines, spirits & special releases. Vintages products are also available in special sections of many regular LCBO stores. In addition, consumers can order from the full list of Vintages items at any LCBO outlet.

In the interests of consumer protection, the LCBO also regularly tests all alcoholic beverages sold in Ontario. This "quality control" testing ensures that all products carried by LCBO stores, Ontario winery stores & Brewers Retail outlets comply with the standards required under the Federal Food & Drug Act & Regulations.

Pursuant to the Liquor License Act of Ontario, the Liquor License Board of Ontario is responsible for the licensing & inspecting of approved premises which sell liquor (spirits, wine or beer) to the general public for on-premises consumption. Liquor may be sold in licensed premises in municipalities where the municipal electors have decided in favour of such sale. In addition, Special Occasion Permits are issued for occasional use only & not for private profit. Special events include weddings, receptions, banquets, charitable fundraisers, & community festivals. The LLBO also licenses manufacturers to sell to the LCBO & approves all liquor advertising pursuant to the Advertising Guidelines.

The drinking age in Ontario is 19.

The Liquor License Bd. of Ont., 55 Lake Shore Blvd. East, Toronto ON M5E 1A4 – 416/326-0308

Liquor Control Bd. of Ont., 55 Lake Shore Blvd. East, Toronto ON M5E 1A4 – 416/864-2400; Fax: 416/864-2476; URL: http//www.lcbo.com

### Prince Edward Island

Spirits, wines & beer in sealed packages may be purchased at Commission Stores throughout the Province by any person over the age of 19 who is not otherwise disqualified.

Spirits by the glass, & beer & wine by the open bottle or glass, may be purchased in dining rooms, cocktail lounges, clubs & military canteens licensed by the Commission.

Prince Edward Island Liquor Control Commission, 3 Garfield St., PO Box 967, Charlottetown PE C1A 7M4 – 902/368-5710; Fax: 902/368-5735

### Québec

Spirits & wines are sold by Québec Liquor Corporation stores only.

Spirits, beer & wine may be sold to the public by restaurants, bars & clubs under permit for consumption on the premises. Taverns may sell beer & cider. Pubs may sell beer, draught wine & cider.

A licensed grocery store may sell beer & certain designated wines & the product must not be consumed on the premises.

Persons under the age of 18 years old cannot be admitted into bars, pubs & taverns & at no time may alcoholic beverages be sold to them in other establishments.

Régie des Alcools, des courses et des jeux, 1, rue Notre-Dame est, Montréal PQ H2Y 1B6 – 514/873-3577; 1281, boul Charest ouest, Québec PQ G1N 2C9 – 418/643-7667

### Saskatchewan

The Saskatchewan Liquor & Gaming Authority, a Treasury Board Crown corporation, regulates liquor & gaming activities in the province. It is responsible for the control, sale & distribution of liquor in the province, & also licenses & regulates bingos, raffles, casinos, & breakopen tickets. The Liquor & Gaming Authority also controls the Video Lottery Terminal network through the province.

The minimum drinking age is 19.

Saskatchewan Liquor & Gaming Authority, PO Box 5054, Regina SK S4P 3M3 – 306/787-4213; Fax: 306/787-8468

### Yukon Territory

The Yukon Act, Chapter Y-2 of the Revised Statutes of Canada, 1970, authorizes the Commissioner in Executive Council, Yukon Territory, to make acts respecting intoxicants.

By virtue of Chapter 105 cited as the Liquor Act, established the laws governing the importation, distributing, licensing & retailing of alcoholic beverages in Yukon.

The formation of the Yukon Liquor Corporation by means of amendments to the Liquor Act came into force on April 1st, 1977. The separation as a Corporate entity resulted in increased responsibility & full accountability in all areas except major government policy.

The five members of the Board of Directors are appointed by the Commissioner in executive council to hold office at pleasure.

The President & Chief Executive Officer of the Corporation, is charged with the general direction, supervision & control of the Corporation & the administration of the Act.

Yukon Liquor Corp., 9031 Quartz Road, Whitehorse YT Y1A 4P9 – 403/667-5245; Fax: 403/393-6306

## MARRIAGE REGULATIONS

### Divorce Act in Canada

Divorce grounds in Canada, under the Divorce Act, 1985:

Breakdown of marriage, established by:

Spouses intentionally living separate and apart at least one year with the idea that the marriage is over,

or

Since the marriage, either spouse has:

Committed adultery, or

Treated the other spouse with physical or mental cruelty rendering continued cohabitation intolerable.

### Alberta

Marriageable age:

--Without parental consent: 18 years

--With parental consent: 16 years

--A female, under the age of 16, may be married without parental consent & proof that she is the mother of a living child or proof that she is expecting a child.

Blood Test: not required

Waiting Period: None. Marriage Licence is valid immediately & is valid for 3 months (from date of issuance).

Licence fee: $40.00

Civic Marriage ceremony fee: $50.00

### British Columbia

Marriageable age:

--Without parental consent: 19 years

With parental consent: 16 to 18 years

--A court order of consent: under 16 years

Blood test: not required

Waiting period for licence: none

Marriage Licence: $75.00

Civil Marriage Ceremony: $80.25

### Manitoba

Marriageable age:

--Without parental consent: 18 years

--With parental consent: 16 years (Persons under 16 years of age can be married only with the consent of a judge of the Family Court.)

Blood test: not required

Waiting period for licence: none

Waiting period after issuance of licence: 24 hours (This may be waived by person performing ceremony.)
Licence fee: $60.00. Licence valid for 3 months.

### New Brunswick
Marriageable age:
--Without parental consent: 18 years
--With parental consent: under 18 years
--Under 16 years: a declaration of a Judge of the Court of Queen's Bench that the proposed marriage may take place is necessary.
Blood test: not required
Waiting period for licence: none
Licence fee: $100.00

### Newfoundland
Marriageable age:
--Greater than or equal to 19 years: without parental consent
--Greater than or equal to 18 years: without parental consent in certain circumstances
--Greater than or equal to 16 years and less than 19 years: with the applicable parental, guardian or Director of Child Welfare consent (Consent may be dispensed within exceptional cases.)
--Less than 16 years: where by reason of pregnancy a judge issues a licence
Blood test: not required
Licence fee: $50.00

### Northwest Territories
Marriageable age:
--Without parental consent: 19 years
--At least 18 years of age if
(a) parent whose consent is required is not a resident of the NWT & minor has been a resident of the NWT for 12 months
(b) minor has been living apart from his or her parents (or guardian) and has not received financial aid from the parents (or guardian) for not less than 6 months preceding the date of delivery of a prescribed statutory declaration to the member of the clergy who is to proclaim the banns or to the issuer of marriage licences;
(c) father & mother of minor are dead & minor has no guardian;
(d) parents (surviving parent) of minor are (is) patients (patient) in a mental institution & minor has no guardian.
--With parental consent: 15 years
Blood test: not required
Waiting period for licence: none
Licence fee: $25.00

### Nova Scotia
Marriageable age:
--Without parental consent: 19 years or over
--With parental consent, or if a widow, widower, or divorcee: 16 years
--With court order: under 16 years
Blood test: not required
Waiting period for licence: 5 days
Licence fee: $100.00

### Ontario
Marriageable age:
--Without parental consent: 18 years
--With parental consent: 16 years
Blood test: not required
Waiting period after issuance of licence: none
Licence fee: $75.00
Fee for solemnization of marriage by judge or justice of the peace: $75.00

### Prince Edward Island
Marriageable age:
--Without parental consent: 18 years
--With parental consent: under 18 years
Other requirements: birth certificates and Social Insurance Numbers; in the case of a widow or widower, death certificate; in the case of a divorced person, certified copy of the Decree Absolute or Certificate of Divorce
Waiting period for licence: none
Licence fee: $100.00

### Québec
Marriageable age:
--Minimum age: 16 years
(ref.: art. 373, Code Civil du Québec)
--Moreover, a minor (under 18 years of age) must have the authorization of his or her parent(s) or tutor to get married.
Blood test: not required
Waiting period for licence: none
Fee for civil marriage: $186.89 (taxes included)

### Saskatchewan
Marriageable age:
--Without parental consent: 18 years
--With parental consent: 16 to 18 years
--With parental and court consent: under 16 years
Blood test: not required
Licence fee: $50.00

### Yukon Territory
Marriageable age:
--Without parental consent: 19 years (In the case of an 18 year old person who has lived apart from his parents/guardians for at least 6 months and received no financial aid from them during that time, no consent is needed.)
Blood test: not required
Waiting period for licence: none
Waiting period after issuance of licence: 24 hours
Licence fee: $20.00

# POSTAL INFORMATION

Services & rates quoted are as of October 31, 1997. The following products & services are currently undergoing change & simplification. Verify with local Canada Post postal outlets for more details.

## COMMUNICATIONS & ADVERTISING SERVICES:

#### LETTERMAIL RATES FOR DELIVERY IN CANADA
Includes letters, postcards, greeting cards & business correspondence.

**Standard Lettermail:**
Up to 30 g. . . . . . . . . . . . . . . . . . . . . . . . . . . . . $0.45
Over 30 g to 50 g . . . . . . . . . . . . . . . . . . . . . . . . 0.71

**Non-Coded Lettermail; Business Mail Only:**
Up to 30 g. . . . . . . . . . . . . . . . . . . . . . . . . . . . . 0.58
Over 30 g to 50 g . . . . . . . . . . . . . . . . . . . . . . . . 0.82

**Other Lettermail Incl. Non-Standard & Oversize:**
Up to 100 g. . . . . . . . . . . . . . . . . . . . . . . . . . . . 0.90
Over 100 g to 200 g . . . . . . . . . . . . . . . . . . . . . . 1.45
Over 200 g to 500 g . . . . . . . . . . . . . . . . . . . . . . 2.05

Oversize Letter Rates apply to all letters with any dimension greater than 24.5 cm (length) x 15 cm (width) x .5 mm (thickness), but not greater than 38 cm (length) x 27 cm (width) x 2 cm (thickness). Maximum weight for Lettermail is 500g. Items with any dimension exceeding the maximum dimension for Oversize Lettermail or exceeding 500g must be paid at parcel rates. Incentive Rates are available under sales agreements for customers whose mailing meets standard volume, frequency & preparation conditions. For details, please contact a Canada Post Corp. representative.

Canada Post is committed to consistently deliver properly prepared lettermail as follows: within two business days for letters whose destination is within the same major urban centre; within three business days for letters whose destination is in a major urban centre in the same province; in no more that four business days, for letters whose destination is in another major urban centre in another province. Service performance evaluation conducted by an outside party reveal that the Corporation is consistently meeting its targets 96-97% of the time.

#### ACKNOWLEDGEMENT OF RECEIPT CARDS (CANADA)
a) At time of mailing . . . . . . . . . . . . . . . . . . . . . . $0.90
b) Subsequent to the mailing (Canada only). . . . $1.60

U.S.A. & international found below under "Rates to the United States" & "International Rates".

#### ADDRESS ACCURACY
Address Accuracy is offered as an option to Electronic Lettermail & Electronic Admail mailings. Alternatively, mailers can have their lists updated through National Change of Address (NCOA), found below. Canada Post checks your mailing list & makes sure it meets the Canadian Addressing Standard to ensure valid & correct addresses. Consistent & accurate addressing eliminates the need for extra handling by the mailer or re-delivery by Canada Post Corporation (CPC).

#### ADDRESSED ADMAIL
Addressed Admail must bear the correct postal code & meet size & weight requirements. Rates are based on volume & level of mail preparation. Letter Carrier Presort requires an LCP Sales Agreement. Using the National distribution Guide requires the use of a Statement of Mailing. All mailings (LC, NDG) must be accompanied by a complete Statement of Mailing.

#### BUSINESS REPLY MAIL (CANADA)
Business Reply Mail is an efficient, cost-effective way to receive accurate & timely hard copy responses from customers. The image put forth is a positive one - a company with the foresight to offer prepaid postage to its customers. You only pay for the pieces returned to you.

#### CONTRACT CERTIFIED MAIL (CANADA)
Contract Certified is an optional service for domestic Lettermail products available by Sales Agreements only. The recipient's signature is automatically returned to the sender as legal proof of delivery & a copy is retained at the office of delivery for 24 months. There is no computerized information retrieval for this option.

Contract Certified Mail consists of a prepaid envelope which has a computer track perforated edge for efficient bulk preparation by the mailer. An adhesive label is located in the upper left hand corner of the envelope which serves as the sender's return address label & is affixed to the Acknowledgement of Receipt (AR) card by the delivery employee.

Lettermail service standards (2 days local, 3 days regional & 4 days national) apply to Contract Certified items. Standards are measured from date of acceptance to the date of first delivery attempt. See Service Performance below for more details. Contract Certified items can be deposited at any postal outlet or in street letter boxes. Contract Certified is available on an order basis at any retail outlet or through the National Philatelic Centre in Antigonish by calling 1-800-565-4362.

Contract Certified envelopes are sold in packs of 100 up to 10 packs (1,000). For purchases over 10 packs, there are volume discounts available. The price for 1 to 5 packs is $396.00 per pack & $345.00 per pack for 6 to 10 packs.

#### DOCUPOST
DocuPost is a document storage, retrieval & distribution service. DocuPost is an ideal way to handle ongoing routine document requests. DocuPost com-

bines the technologies of fax, electronic & hard copy mail delivery, along with Canada Post's existing mail delivery structure. Any information (text, graphic or audio) can be stored & distributed by DocuPost. Maximum flexibility & ease of access is provided through a 1-800 toll free line. Customers can access your information anytime from any place & choose the way they receive it - either by fax, 24 hours a day, 7 days a week, by phone, mail or email. DocuPost is ideal for documents that are updated frequently, such as application forms, price lists or schedules, catalogues, registration kits. For more information on DocuPost, please call 1-800-714-9996.

#### ELECTRONIC ADMAIL

Electronic Admail is a computerized mail production & delivery service supported by a network of distributed print sites, which means faster delivery & responses to your messages. Electronic Admail is used by businesses mailing a minimum of 1,000 pieces of advertising material, solicitations, notices, bulletins & more. The Mail Piece provides the same message to a multitude of recipients with the name & address field personalized. Highlight Colour is a simple, cost-effective, attention-grabbing feature that can be added to your mailings. You can choose from red, green, blue, magenta & cyan. Colour adds variety & appeal to your mailings, which means they are more likely to be read & responded to. For more information on Electronic Admail, please call 1-800-363-4763.

#### ELECTRONIC LETTERMAIL

Electronic Lettermail is a computerized mail production & delivery service supported by a network of distributed print sites, which means faster delivery & responses to your messages. Electronic Lettermail is ideal for customized applications with variable data fields in the body of the message such as those required for invoices, monthly statements & billings, & time sensitive notices. Our Quick Response Program (QRP) is perfect for customers requiring an all inclusive service for general customer communication programs that require fast turnaround, such as promotional letters, product recalls & collection letters. Creation & production can be turned around within seven days. Highlight colour is a simple, cost-effective, attention-grabbing feature that adds variety & appeal to your mailings, which means they are more likely to be read. You can choose from red, green, blue, magenta & cyan. To find out more about Electronic Lettermail, please call 1-800-363-4763.

#### NATIONAL CHANGE OF ADDRESS PROGRAM (NCOA)

NCOA service is the most accurate, comprehensive & up-to-date mover information available in Canada. Of the 16-18% of Canadians who move each year, over 70% notify Canada Post through the use of a Change of Notification form. NCOA service provides for the electronic matching of name & address fields of mailing lists. NCOA data comprises name(s), old addresses & new addresses, & effective date of the change. When a match occurs, the new address from the NCOA database is provided. Whether you are a lettershop, service bureau or other large volume mailer, the NCOA service will improve your service offering to clients, reduce volume of undelivered mail, reduce postage costs & wasted materials. For more information on NCOA, please call 1-800-363-4763 or for a list of NCOA licensees call 1-800-714-9996 & request document #8000.

#### PUBLICATIONS MAIL

Publications Mail includes domestic & international newspapers & periodicals mailed to subscribers, non-subscribers & news dealers in Canada, the United States or abroad. There are two categories of Publications Mail rates: commercial & funded.

Commercial Publications Mail includes magazines & newspapers mailed in Canada which qualify for distribution rates that are lower than regular mail rates. Funded Publications Mail includes magazines & newspapers mailed in Canada that meet certain criteria to qualify them for federal postage subsidies. The Government of Canada has been subsidizing the cost of delivering eligible publications to Canadians since Confederation through a program called the Publications Assistance Program. For details, please contact a Canada Post Corp. representative.

#### REGISTERED MAIL (CANADA)

Add-on service to Lettermail items that do not require the extra security or indemnity of the Security Registered product. The mailer will be provided with a proof of mailing & a signature will be obtained from the addressee or his/her representative before the delivery is completed. The fee is $3.15 plus applicable Lettermail postage. Upon payment of the appropriate fee, the acknowledgement of receipt service is also available.

#### SECURITY REGISTERED MAIL

Security Registered involves a high security processing stream making the product ideal for mailing lettermail items or parcels with an insurable value. The product provides proof of mailing, signature upon delivery, & an option of having a copy of the recipient's signature returned to the mailer.

The fee for Security Registered within Canada is $5.60 plus the applicable Lettermail rate. The Xpresspost rates plus the Security Registered service fee determine the rate for parcels.

#### TRACE MAIL (CANADA)

Common to all of the Trace Mail options, is the ability of Canada Post to provide immediate response to customer inquiries for delivery status information on items to be delivered in Canada. Customers are able to obtain delivery status information through a 1-800 number.

#### UNADDRESSED ADMAIL

Unaddressed Admail is one of Canada Post's direct mail services. It gets your message to the homes & businesses in a defined area that offer you the greatest potential. Because it's delivered by Canada Post's letter carriers with the regular mail, your flyer, brochure, catalogue or sample arrives in a low-clutter environment & is more likely to be seen & read. For details about our Unaddressed Admail service & rates, please call our Business Access Hotline at 1-800-260-7678.

### DISTRIBUTION SERVICES:

#### PRIORITY COURIER ™

Priority Courier is a fully featured, domestic courier service providing next business day delivery between most major centres & an on-time delivery guarantee. A range of Advance Purchase Products is also available. Information regarding delivery status & additional product information is available from local Priority Courier centres or by calling the 1-800-661-3434 or via the Internet at http://www.mailpost.ca. International courier service is offered through the SkyPak product (see below).

Priority Courier: 1-800-661-3434

Locally:

Edmonton: .................... 403/944-3100
Fredericton .................... 506/443-3278
London: .................... 519/645-4355
Montréal: .................... 514/633-8483
Ottawa/Hull: .................... 613/526-3278
Toronto: .................... 416/673-3278
Vancouver: .................... 604/482-4000
Winnipeg: .................... 204/987-5400

#### XPRESSPOST®

XPRESSPOST is an affordable, simple to use delivery service for packages & documents which provides an on-time delivery guarantee & confirmation of delivery. Positioned right in the middle between Priority Courier & Regular Post in terms of price, service & features, XPRESSPOST offers next business day local; two business day regional/national delivery between major Canadian centres & a full range of Advance Purchase Products. Customers can verify delivery of their items or obtain product information by calling 1-800-565-5880, or by accessing the Internet.

#### REGULAR POST

Regular Post is the most economical, domestic, ground parcel service. There are two delivery service levels available. **Expedited** service is the our fastest ground service providing an on-time delivery guarantee (next business day local, 2-5 business day regional & 5-7 business day national between major centres) & a full range of Advance Purchase Parcel Labels. **Regular** service is for non time-sensitive shipments ( 3-12 business days) & offers the most economical rates.

### OTHER SERVICES:

#### PROOF OF DELIVERY (CANADA)

Add-on service to Regular & Expedited services that provides delivery confirmation via Canada Post's automated telephone inquiry system & the Internet. The fee is $1.00 per item & includes $100 indemnity coverage. Additional coverage may be purchased for $0.50 for each additional $100 up to a maximum of $2,500.

#### INSURANCE FEES

Insurance is a service where Canada Post provides compensation for the loss, rifling or damage of mailable items if the requirements of indemnity subjects are met.

**Lettermail:**

a) Within Canada:
Insurance up to $100 .................... $0.45
& $0.45 for each additional $100 coverage up to a maximum $1,000.

**Parcels:**

a) Regular Post (within Canada): see Proof of Delivery
b) Priority Courier & Xpresspost within Canada: $0.50 per $100. Coverage up to a maximum of $2,500 with the first $100 free.
c) To the USA (parcels only) $1.00 for each $100. Coverage up to a maximum of $1,000. The first $100 coverage is included in the airmail postage.
d) To international destinations (parcels only): $1.00 for each additional $100. Coverage up to a maximum of $1,000. The first $100 coverage is included in the airmail parcel postage.

#### C.O.D. FEE (CANADA)

C.O.D. is a service for Regular Post & Xpresspost only. An amount due to the sender, up to a maximum of $1,000, is collected from the addressee upon delivery of the item. Customers wishing to use C.O.D. on document-sized items must pay the appropriate Xpresspost rate plus the C.O.D. fee.

The fee is $5.00 (no basic indemnity) plus appropriate postage & indemnity can be purchased at $0.50 per $100 up to $1,000.

#### MONEY ORDER FEES

A Money Order is a funds transmission document which may be purchased for values not exceeding $999.99 in Cdn$ & U.S.$ & £100 at postal outlets. Money orders are to be drawn in Canadian currency for payment in CANADA & the following countries:

Anguilla, Antigua & Bermuda, Bahamas, Barbados, Belize, Cayman Islands, Dominica, Fiji, Grenada, Haiti, Jamaica, Nevis, St. Kitts, St. Lucia, St. Vincent & Grenadines, Trinidad & Tobago. The fee is as follows:

Up to $999.99 maximum .................... $2.25

Money orders are to be drawn in U.S. currency for payment in the UNITED STATES. The fee is as follows:

Up to $999.99 maximum .................. $3.50

In the UNITED KINGDOM & GUYANA. The fee is as follows:

From £100 maximum..................... $4.50

Money orders are to be drawn in Canadian currency for all other countries except Poland (U.S. currency) & requires the preparation of a Canadian Postal Money Order Advice form which must accompany the money to be sent to the Ottawa Money Order Exchange office using a pre-addressed envelope. The fee is as follows:

Up to $999.99 maximum .................. $5.00

#### REDIRECTION SERVICES

The redirection services offered by Canada Post Corporation ensure that mail addressed to your old address is redirected to your new address on a permanent or temporary basis. Canada Post also offers a service where your mail can be held at your delivery office from a specified period of time. In all cases, you must complete a Change of Address Notification (NCOA) form, which is available at all postal outlets.

The fees for this service are as follows.

When mail is redirected within Canada & the request is permanent:

Residential (for individuals & families): $30 for each 6 month period

Business/Non-residential: $130 for each 6 month period

When mail is redirected outside Canada:

Residential (for individuals & families): $60 for each 6 month period

Businss/Non-residential: $300 for each 6 month period

Change of Address Announcement cards, used by the public to notify their correspondents, are available at postal outlets. The announcement cards require lettermail postage.

There is no charge for submitting a Change of Address Notification on behalf of a deceased person's estate.

#### TEMPORARY REDIRECTION

Temporary redirection is a service available to Canada Post customers when they wish to have their mail redirected to a temporary address.

The fees for this service are as follows.

When mail is redirected within Canada on a temporary basis:

Residential (for individuals & families): $27 initial fee for 3 months; $9 for each additional month

Business/Non-residential: $65 each month (no minimum)

When mail is redirected outside Canada:

Residential (for individuals & families): $54 for each 6 month period; $18 for each additional month

Business/Non-residential: $150 each month (no minimum)

#### HOLD MAIL

When you purchase this service your local delivery unit will hold your mail for the requested period of time.

Residential (for individuals & families): $6 for first 2 weeks (minimum); $3 for each addditional week

Business/Non-Residential addresses: $27.50 first week (minimum); $5.50 each additional day

Canada Post also offers Redirection & Hold Mail services for schools. Canada Post will hold the school's mail at the local delivery unit for a school representative to pick it up or will redirect all the school's mail to a specific address. Mail will wither be redirected or held during all school breaks.

School Temporary Redirection: $120/year

School Hold Mail Service: $150/year

#### RETURNED MAIL MANAGEMENT

Return Mail Management reduces the frustration & expense caused by undeliverable mail. Canada Post creates your mail piece with a bar code, & as undeliverables are returned to a Canada Post centre, the barcode is scanned & generates an electronic report. You can use this electronic file to update your mailinglist.

#### MAIL MANAGEMENT SERVICES (MMS)

Mail Management Services are designed to assist business, government & institutions in areas which can be privatized or outsourced, yet have a significant impact on business activities, costs & service to customers. MMS will provide management services by providing customized solutions from mailroom activities, internal mail delivery, outgoing mail preparation & distribution. MMS expertise is in mail generation, fulfillment, distribution, & other related business processes. For details about Mail Management Services, call our customer service representative at 1-800-363-4763.

### RATES TO THE UNITED STATES (its Territories & Possessions):

#### LETTERMAIL

**Weight Steps:**

Up to & including 30 g ...................... $0.52
Over 30 g to 50 g ............................ 0.77
Oversize letter rates (max. 500g)
Up to & including 100 g ...................... 1.17
100 g to 200 g ............................... 2.23
Over 200 g to 500 g .......................... 3.80
Lettermail more than 27 cm (width) x 38 cm (length) x 2 cm (thickness) up to 105 cm longest side x 200 cm (longest side plus girth)
Up to an including 250 g...................... 3.60
Over 250 g to 500 kg ......................... 4.85

USA Incentive Lettermail offers Canadian mailers significant postage savings & improved service performance linked to volume, & quality of mail preparation. For various USA Incentive Lettermail rates, please inquire at a postal outlet.

#### SPECIAL DELIVERY

Special Delivery to the USA is $4.60 plus applicable postage & can be used for expedited delivery of letters, postcards, & small airmail packets.

#### SECURITY REGISTERED MAIL

Available for airmail lettermail items. Fees to the USA- $5.60 plus the applicable postage which includes a basis indemnity of $1,000. Additional indemnity is available for $1.00 up to $1,000.

#### ACKNOWLEDGEMENT OF RECEIPT CARDS

At time of mailing is only $0.90.

#### PRINTED PAPERS (US)

| Weight Steps | Surface Mail |
|---|---|
| Up to & including 30 g | 0.52 |
| Over 30 g to 100 g | 0.96 |
| Over 100 g to 200 g | 1.43 |
| Over 200 g to 300 g | 2.00 |
| Over 300 g to 400 g | 2.70 |
| Over 400 g to 500 g | 3.55 |
| Over 500 g to 1 kg | 6.20 |

"M" bags (direct bags) of printed papers - $6.20 for the first kilogram plus $2.50 for each additional kilogram or fraction up to 30 kg (surface only).

#### SMALL PACKETS (US)

| Weight Steps | Surface Mail | Air Mail |
|---|---|---|
| Up to & including 250 g | $ 2.30 | $3.60 |
| Over 250 g to 500 g | 3.55 | 4.85 |
| Over 500 g to 1 kg | 6.20 | 8.55 |

#### PARCEL SERVICE (US)

Parcel rate (surface) starts at $6.90 depending on destination for the first 1.5 kg. For details inquire at a postal outlet.

Parcel rate (air) starts $11.50 for the first half kilogram. For details inquire at a postal outlet.

Parcels are subject to customs inspection & must bear a properly completed customs document (43-074-013). Completion of the customs document in English is preferred.

### INTERNATIONAL RATES

All countries except the U.S.A., its Territories & Possessions, St. Pierre & Miquelon, Canadian Forces post offices & Fleet Mail Offices.

#### LETTERMAIL

| Weight Steps | Air Mail |
|---|---|
| Up to & including 20 g | $0.90 |
| Over 20 g to 50 g | 1.37 |
| Over 50 g to 100g | 2.25 |
| Over 100 g to 250 g | 5.05 |
| Over 250 g to 500 g | 9.90 |
| Over 500 g to 1 kg | 18.55 |
| Over 1 kg to 2 kg | 37.10 |

#### AEROGRAMMES & POSTCARDS

All countries .......................... $0.90 each

#### SECURITY REGISTERED MAIL

Available for airmail lettermail items. Fees for International distinations - $5.60 plus the applicable postage which includes a maximum indemnity of $60.00.

#### ACKNOWLEDGEMENT OF RECEIPT CARDS

At time of mailing is only $0.90.

#### PRINTED PAPERS (INTERNATIONAL)

The Printed Papers service includes printed paper, "M" bags (directed bags) for printed paper & books. Fees are for "M" bags of printed papers - surface only: $7.20 for the first kilogram & $3.85 for each additional kilogram or fraction up to 30 kg maximum.

| Weight Steps | Air Mail | Surface Mail |
|---|---|---|
| Up to & including 20 g | $ 0.73 | $0.52 |
| Over 20 g to 50 g | 1.16 | 0.80 |
| Over 50 g to 100 g | 2.20 | 1.44 |
| Over 100 g to 250 g | 4.10 | 2.60 |
| Over 250 g to 500 g | 8.05 | 4.10 |
| Over 500 g to 1 kg | 16.10 | 7.20 |
| Over 1 kg to 2 kg | 26.80 | 10.20 |

#### SMALL PACKETS INTERNATIONAL

| Weight Steps | Air Mail | Surface Mail |
|---|---|---|
| Up to & including 100 g | $ 2.20 | $1.44 |
| Over 100 g to 250 g | 4.10 | 2.60 |
| Over 250 g to 500 g | 8.05 | 4.10 |
| Over 500 g to 1 kg | 16.10 | 7.20 |
| Over 1 kg to 2 kg | 26.80 | 10.20 |

#### INTERNATIONAL REPLY COUPONS

International Reply Coupons may be purchased in Canada for $3.50 each & are exchangeable in any countries of the Universal Postal Union for the minimum postage payable for an unregistered letter upon presentation of a sufficient number of reply coupons. An International Reply Coupon is exchangeable at any Canadian post outlet for $0.90 in Canadian postage stamps.

#### SPECIAL DELIVERY

Special Delivery to available to most international destinations for $4.60 plus applicable postage & can be used for expedited delivery of letters, postcards, small airmail packets, & airmail printed papers.

## MAP OF CANADA

### PARCEL SERVICE (INTERNATIONAL)

International Air & Surface parcel rates depend on the weight & destination. For details, please inquire at a postal outlet.

The prohibitions, restrictions, conditions, requirements & rates vary from country to country. For details, please inquire at a postal outlet.

### SKYPAK INTERNATIONAL COURIER

SkyPak International Courier is a fully featured International Courier service owned by GD Express Worldwide & sold by Canada Post Corporation.

SkyPak provides delivery to all destinations in the United States & to over 200 countries worldwide; next day a.m. service from major cities in Canada to major cites in the United States; delivery to PO Box addresses in the United States, acceptable to a PO Box address worldwide with the receiver's telephone number, money-back guarantee for items to guaranteed destinations. Prepaid envelopes for documents only are available in 2 sizes: 350 grams & 1 kilogram for items destined for Europe, Pacific, U.S.A. & International.

Information regarding delivery status & additional product information is available by calling 1-800-661-3434 or on the Internet at http://www.skypak. com.

#### SkyPak Prepaid Products (Advance Purchase Products)

Discounts available beginning with quantities of five prepaid envelopes.

#### Prepaid Letters (Max. 350 gr):

| Quantity | Zone 1 U.S.A. | Zone 2 Europe | Zone 3 Pacific | Zone 4/5 Int'l. |
|---|---|---|---|---|
| 1 | $25.20 | $37.80 | $42.00 | $63.00 |
| 5 | 24.15 | 35.70 | 39.90 | 60.90 |
| 10 | 23.10 | 33.60 | 37.80 | 57.75 |
| 30 | 21.00 | 30.45 | 34.65 | 55.65 |
| 50 | 18.90 | 8.35 | 32.55 | 53.55 |
| 100 | 17.85 | 25.20 | 29.40 | 51.45 |
| 250 | 16.28 | 24.15 | 27.83 | 49.35 |
| 500 | 15.75 | 23.10 | 26.51 | 46.20 |

#### Prepaid Pack (Max. 1 kg):

| Quantity | Zone 1 U.S.A. | Zone 2 Europe | Zone 3 Pacific | Zone 4/5 Int'l. |
|---|---|---|---|---|
| 1 | $33.60 | $54.60 | $63.00 | $89.25 |
| 5 | 32.55 | 52.50 | 60.90 | 86.10 |
| 10 | 31.50 | 49.35 | 57.75 | 84.00 |
| 30 | 29.40 | 47.25 | 55.65 | 81.90 |
| 50 | 27.30 | 45.15 | 53.55 | 79.80 |
| 100 | 25.20 | 39.90 | 48.30 | 74.55 |
| 250 | 24.15 | 35.70 | 44.10 | 70.35 |
| 500 | 23.10 | 33.60 | 42.00 | 68.25 |

## GENERAL INFORMATION:

### POSTAGE NOT REQUIRED

No postage is required on mail addressed to the Governor General, or Secretary to the Governor General, the Speaker or the Clerk of the Senate or House of Commons, the parliamentary librarian or associate parliamentary librarian, members of the Senate & members of the House of Commons.

### LITERATURE FOR THE BLIND (CANADA)

The following items can be mailed free of postage when bearing the label or words "Literature for the Blind" on the top right hand corner of the address: Items impressed in Braille or similar raised type; plates for printing literature for the blind; tapes & records posted by the blind in Canada for delivery in Canada; recording tapes, records, special writing paper intended solely for use of the blind when mailed by or addressed to a recognized institution for the blind.

### RETURN TO SENDER PROGRAM

Unpaid or shortpaid mail is mail for which the postage or fees have not been paid or fully paid. Lettermail & Parcels, with or without special services (such as Insurance, Security Registered, Registered, XPRESSPOST (domestic mail only), COD) are returned to sender for the collection of adequate postage, instead of penalizing the addressee.

### PROHIBITED ARTICLES

It is forbidden to post for delivery or transmission by or through Canada Post any prohibited items. Prohibited items are defined as any item which is prohibited by law or which contains products or substances that could harm Canada Post employees, soil or damage equipment or other shipments. For a complete list of items please consult a Canada Post Customer Service representative or visit your local postal outlet.

#### POSTAL CODE DIRECTORY

Postal code directories are available in two formats. The National Directory is $25.95 & the Regional Directories (Eastern, Central, Western) are $11.95 each (plus applicable taxes). You may purchase the Directory by sending a cheque or money order, payable to Canada Post Corporation, to the National Philatelic Centre (address below) or by calling 1-800-565-4362. Postal code information is also available through the Corporation's web site on the Internet. Please see the electronic address below.

#### PROVINCIAL SYMBOLS

Standard two-letter postal abbreviations for the provinces & territories are as follows:

Alberta........................AB
British Columbia................BC
Manitoba......................MB
New Brunswick.................NB
Newfoundland & Labrador.......NF
Northwest Territories...........NT
Nova Scotia....................NS
Ontario........................ON
Prince Edward Island............PE
Québec........................QC
Saskatchewan..................SK
Yukon Territory................YT

#### STAMP & COLLECTOR SERVICES

Stamps & other related products, such as Official First Day Covers, Prestamped Envelopes, Annual Souvenir Collections & Commemorative Stamp Packs are available at most post offices, philatelic counters & by mail order through the National Philatelic Centre.

Publications such as Collections of Canada & Canada's Stamp Details provide descriptions, visuals & details of these quality philatelic products. Both of these publications can be obtained by writing or calling: National Philatelic Centre, Canada Post Corporation, 75 St. Ninian St., Antigonish NS B2G 2R8; from Canada & the USA call toll-free 1-800-565-4362, & from other countries call 902/863-6550.

#### CUSTOMER SERVICE

Further information on Canada Post's products & services can be obtained through your local postal outlets, postal directory, your local customer service representative, or by calling one of the following numbers:

Toll Free (English): ......1-800-267-1177
Toll Free (French):.......1-800-267-1155
Montréal:..............514/344-8822
Toronto:................416/979-8822
Hearing Impaired with
TTY-Teletyping: ......1-800-267-2797

Customers may also contact Canada Post via the Internet : http://www.mailposte.ca

Email: service@mailposte.ca

Canada Post Corporation, 2701 Riverside Dr., Ottawa ON K1A 0B1.

# STATISTICAL INFORMATION

## CANADIAN POPULATION & PERCENTAGE DISTRIBUTION BY PROVINCES AND TERRITORIES, 1961 TO 1996 (CENSUS)

| PROVINCE AND TERRITORY | 1961<br>% | 1971<br>% | 1981<br>% | 1991[1]<br>% | 1996[1]<br>% |
|---|---|---|---|---|---|
| Newfoundland | 457,853<br>2.51 | 522,104<br>2.42 | 567,681<br>2.33 | 568,474<br>2.08 | 551,792<br>1.91 |
| Prince Edward Island | 104,629<br>0.58 | 111,641<br>0.52 | 122,506<br>0.50 | 129,765<br>0.46 | 134,557<br>0.46 |
| Nova Scotia | 737,007<br>4.04 | 788,960<br>3.66 | 847,442<br>3.48 | 899,942<br>3.30 | 909,282<br>3.15 |
| New Brunswick | 597,936<br>3.28 | 634,557<br>2.94 | 696,403<br>2.86 | 723,900<br>2.65 | 738,133<br>2.55 |
| Québec | 5,259,211<br>28.84 | 6,027,764<br>27.95 | 6,438,403<br>26.44 | 6,895,963<br>25.26 | 7,138,795<br>24.74 |
| Ontario | 6,236,092<br>34.19 | 7,703,106<br>35.71 | 8,625,107<br>35.43 | 10,084,885<br>36.9 | 10,753,573<br>37.27 |
| Manitoba | 921,686<br>5.05 | 988,247<br>4.58 | 1,026,241<br>4.21 | 1,091,942<br>4.00 | 1,113,898<br>3.86 |
| Saskatchewan | 925,181<br>5.07 | 926,242<br>4.29 | 968,313<br>3.97 | 988,928<br>3.62 | 990,237<br>3.43 |
| Alberta | 1,331,944<br>7.30 | 1,627,874<br>7.55 | 2,237,724<br>9.19 | 2,545,553<br>9.33 | 2,696,826<br>9.34 |
| British Columbia | 1,629,082<br>8.93 | 2,184,621<br>10.13 | 2,744,467<br>11.27 | 3,282,061<br>12.02 | 3,724,500<br>12.91 |
| Yukon | 14,628<br>0.08 | 18,388<br>0.09 | 23,153<br>0.09 | 27,797<br>0.10 | 30,766<br>0.10 |
| Northwest Territories | 22,998<br>0.13 | 34,807<br>0.16 | 45,741<br>0.18 | 57,649<br>0.21 | 64,402<br>0.22 |
| TOTALS<br>100 | 18,238,247<br>100 | 21,568,311<br>100 | 24,343,181<br>100 | 27,296,859<br>100 | 28,846,761<br>100 |
| Rural | 5,537,857 | 5,157,525 | 5,907,254 | 6,389,724 | 6,385,551 |
| Urban | 12,700,390 | 16,410,785 | 18,435,927 | 20,907,135 | 22,461,210 |

1.Excluding census data for one or more incompletely enumerated Indian reserves or Indian settlements. In 1991 and 1996, the Census of Population included both permanent and non-permanent residents.

Source: 1996 Census of Population, A National Overview (Catalogue 93-357-XPB), Statistics Canada.

## POPULATION OF METROPOLITAN AREAS AS OF JUNE 4, 1996 CENSUS WITH THOSE OF THE 1991 CENSUS

| | 1991 | 1996 |
|---|---|---|
| Calgary, AB | 754,033 | 821,628 |
| Chicoutimi-Jonquière, PQ | 160,928 | 160,454 |
| Edmonton, AB | 839,924 | 862,597 |
| Halifax, NS | 320,521 | 332,518 |
| Hamilton, ON | 599,760 | 624,360 |
| Kitchener, ON | 356,421 | 382,940 |
| London, ON | 381,522 | 398,616 |
| Montréal,PQ | 3,127,242 | 3,326,510 |
| Oshawa, ON | 240,104 | 268,773 |
| Ottawa-Hull, ON, PQ | 920,857 | 1,010,498 |
| Ontario (part) | 693,900 | 763,426 |
| Québec (part) | 226,957 | 247,072 |
| Québec, PQ | 645,550 | 671,889 |
| Regina, SK | 191,692 | 193,652 |
| St. John, NB | 124,981 | 125,705 |
| Saskatoon, SK | 210,023 | 219,056 |
| Sherbrooke, PQ | 139,194 | 147,384 |
| St. Catharines-Niagara, ON | 364,552 | 372,406 |
| St. John's, NF | 171,859 | 174,051 |
| Sudbury, ON | 157,613 | 160,488 |
| Thunder Bay, ON | 124,427 | 125,562 |
| Toronto, ON | 3,893,046 | 4,263,757 |
| Trois-Rivières, PQ | 136,303 | 139,956 |
| Vancouver, BC | 1,602,502 | 1,831,665 |
| Victoria, BC [1] | 287,897 | 304,287 |
| Windsor, ON | 262,075 | 278,685 |
| Winnipeg, MB | 652,354 | 667,209 |

1.Excluding census data for one or more incompletely enumerated Indian reserves or Indian settlements.
Source: 1996 Census of Population, A National Overview, Population and Dwelling Counts (Catalogue 93-357-XPB) Statistics Canada

## VITAL STATISTICS COMPARED WITH MACROREGIONS & REGIONS 1990-95

| MACRO REGIONS AND REGIONS | BIRTH RATE 0/000 | DEATH RATE 0/000 |
|---|---|---|
| **World** | **25** | **9** |
| **Africa** | **42** | **14** |
| Eastern Africa | 46 | 16 |
| Middle Africa | 46 | 15 |
| Northern Africa | 31 | 9 |
| Southern Africa | 32 | 9 |
| Western Africa | 46 | 16 |
| **Northern America** | **16** | **9** |
| **Latin America** | **26** | **7** |
| Caribbean | 24 | 8 |
| Central America | 30 | 6 |
| South America | 25 | 7 |
| **Asia** | **25** | **8** |
| Eastern Asia | 18 | 7 |
| South Central Asia | 31 | 10 |
| South Eastern Asia | 27 | 8 |
| Western Asia | 32 | 7 |
| **Europe** | **12** | **11** |
| Eastern Europe | 12 | 12 |
| Northern Europe | 14 | 11 |
| Southern Europe | 11 | 10 |
| Western Europe | 12 | 11 |
| **Oceania** | **19** | **8** |
| Australia and New Zealand | 15 | 8 |
| Melanesia | 32 | 9 |
| Micronesia | 33 | 6 |
| Polynesia | 31 | 6 |

Source: Statistical Yearbook
(Forty-first issue) - United Nations

## BIRTH AND DEATH RATES, CANADA 1995

| PROVINCE | LIVE BIRTHS Number | LIVE BIRTHS Rate [2] | DEATHS Number | DEATHS Rate [2] | INFANT DEATHS [1] Number | INFANT DEATHS [1] Rate [3] |
|---|---|---|---|---|---|---|
| Newfoundland | 5,859 | 10.2 | 3,935 | 6.8 | 46 | 7.9 |
| Prince Edward Island | 1,754 | 12.9 | 1,153 | 8.5 | 8 | 4.6 |
| Nova Scotia | 10,726 | 11.4 | 7,687 | 8.2 | 52 | 4.8 |
| New Brunswick | 8,563 | 11.3 | 5,938 | 7.8 | 41 | 4.8 |
| Québec | 87,417 | 11.9 | 52,734 | 7.2 | 477 | 5.5 |
| Ontario | 146,263 | 13.2 | 78,479 | 7.1 | 870 | 5.9 |
| Manitoba | 16,113 | 14.2 | 9,658 | 8.5 | 123 | 7.6 |
| Saskatchewan | 13,499 | 13.3 | 8,495 | 8.4 | 123 | 9.1 |
| Alberta | 38,914 | 14.1 | 15,895 | 5.8 | 274 | 7.0 |
| British Columbia | 46,820 | 12.4 | 26,375 | 7.0 | 280 | 6.0 |
| Yukon | 470 | 15.5 | 157 | 5.2 | 6 | 12.8 |
| Northwest Territories | 1,613 | 24.5 | 227 | 3.4 | 21 | 13.0 |
| TOTALS | 378,011 | 12.8 | 210,733 | 7.1 | 2,321 | 6.1 |

1.Children under one year of age.
2.Rate per 1,000 population.
3.Rate per 1,000 live births.

Source: Statistics Canada, Catalogue 84-210-XPB, Births and Deaths

## DEATHS, CANADA, 1995

| | DEATHS BOTH SEXES | DEATHS FEMALES | DEATHS MALES | CRUDE RATES [1] BOTH SEXES | CRUDE RATES [1] FEMALES | CRUDE RATES [1] MALES |
|---|---|---|---|---|---|---|
| Canada | 210,733 | 99,337 | 111,396 | 7.1 | 6.6 | 7.6 |
| Newfoundland | 3,935 | 1,703 | 2,232 | 6.8 | 5.9 | 7.7 |
| Prince Edward Island | 1,153 | 522 | 631 | 8.5 | 7.6 | 9.4 |
| Nova Scotia | 7,687 | 3,638 | 4,049 | 8.2 | 7.7 | 8.8 |
| New Brunswick | 5,938 | 2,684 | 3,254 | 7.8 | 7.0 | 8.6 |
| Québec | 52,734 | 24,762 | 27,972 | 7.2 | 6.6 | 7.7 |
| Ontario | 78,479 | 37,900 | 40,579 | 7.1 | 6.8 | 7.4 |
| Manitoba | 9,658 | 4,646 | 5,012 | 8.5 | 8.1 | 8.9 |
| Saskatchewan | 8,495 | 3,854 | 4,641 | 8.4 | 7.5 | 9.2 |
| Alberta | 15,895 | 7,268 | 8,627 | 5.8 | 5.3 | 6.2 |
| British Columbia | 26,375 | 12,210 | 14,165 | 7.0 | 6.5 | 7.6 |
| Yukon | 157 | 58 | 99 | 5.2 | 3.9 | 6.4 |
| Northwest Territories | 227 | 92 | 135 | 3.4 | 2.9 | 3.9 |

1.Per 1,000 population.

Source: Statistics Canada, Catalogue 84-210-XPB, Births and Deaths

## LEADING CAUSES OF DEATH, 1995

| FEMALE CAUSE | RANK | NUMBER | PERCENT | RATE [1] |
|---|---|---|---|---|
| Diseases of the circulatory system | 1 | 39,023 | 39.3 | 261.2 |
| Ischaemic heart disease | | 19,729 | 19.9 | 132.1 |
| Stroke | | 8,951 | 9.0 | 59.9 |
| Cancer | 2 | 26,475 | 26.7 | 177.2 |
| Lung | | 5,307 | 5.3 | 35.5 |
| Breast | | 4,922 | 5.0 | 32.9 |
| Respiratory diseases | 3 | 8,677 | 8.7 | 58.1 |
| Pneumonia and influenza | | 3,916 | 3.9 | 26.2 |
| Other chronic airways obstruction | | 2,739 | 2.8 | 18.3 |
| Accidents and adverse effects | 4 | 4,331 | 4.4 | 29.0 |
| Accidents falls | | 1,369 | 1.4 | 9.2 |
| Motor vehicle accidents | | 1,018 | 1.0 | 6.8 |
| Diseases of the digestive system | 5 | 3,683 | 3.7 | 24.7 |
| Chronic liver disease and cirrhosis | | 732 | 0.7 | 4.9 |
| Noninfective enteritis and colitis | | 612 | 0.6 | 4.1 |
| Endocrine diseases, etc. | 6 | 3,622 | 3.6 | 24.2 |
| Diabetes mellitus | | 2,768 | 2.8 | 18.5 |
| Fluid, electrolyte and acid-base balance | | 311 | 0.3 | 2.1 |
| Diseases of the nervous system | 7 | 3,468 | 3.5 | 23.2 |
| Alzheimer's disease | | 1,759 | 1.8 | 11.8 |
| Parkinson's disease | | 521 | 0.5 | 3.5 |
| Mental disorders | 8 | 3,081 | 3.1 | 20.6 |
| Senile and presenile dementia | | 1,482 | 1.5 | 9.9 |
| Alcoholic psychoses, etc. | | 172 | 0.2 | 1.2 |
| All other causes | | 6,967 | 7.0 | 46.7 |
| **ALL CAUSES** | | 99,327 | 100.0 | 664.9 |

| MALES CAUSE | RANK | NUMBER | PERCENT | RATE [1] |
|---|---|---|---|---|
| Diseases of the circulatory system | 1 | 40,085 | 36.0 | 273.1 |
| Ischaemic heart disease | | 24,331 | 21.8 | 165.8 |
| Stroke | | 6,586 | 5.9 | 44.9 |
| Cancer | 2 | 31.329 | 28.1 | 213.5 |
| Lung | | 9,768 | 8.8 | 66.6 |
| Prostate | | 3,760 | 3.4 | 25.6 |
| Respiratory diseases | 3 | 10,209 | 9.2 | 69.6 |
| Other chronic airways obstruction | | 4,308 | 3.9 | 29.4 |
| Pneumonia and influenza | | 3,465 | 3.1 | 23.6 |
| Accidents and adverse effects | 4 | 9,220 | 8.3 | 62.8 |
| Suicide | | 3,152 | 2.8 | 21.5 |
| Motor vehicle accidents | | 2,239 | 2.0 | 15.3 |
| Diseases of the digestive system | 5 | 3,933 | 3.5 | 26.8 |
| Chronic liver disease and cirrhosis | | 1,503 | 1.3 | 10.2 |
| Noninfective enteritis and colitis | | 371 | 0.3 | 2.5 |
| Endocrine diseases, etc. | 6 | 3,420 | 3.1 | 23.3 |
| Diabetes mellitus | | 2,728 | 2.4 | 18.6 |
| Fluid, electrolyte and acid-base balance | | 178 | 0.2 | 1.2 |
| Diseases of the nervous system | 7 | 2,766 | 2.5 | 18.8 |
| Alzheimer's disease | | 894 | 0.8 | 6.1 |
| Parkinson's disease | | 617 | 0.6 | 4.2 |
| Infectious and parasitic diseases | 8 | 2,481 | 2.2 | 16.9 |
| HIV infection | | 1,637 | 1.5 | 11.2 |
| Septicaemia | | 401 | 0.4 | 2.7 |
| All other causes | | 7,936 | 7.1 | 54.1 |
| **ALL CAUSES** | | 111,379 | 100.0 | 758.9 |

1.Per 100,000 population.

Source: Statistics Canada, Catalogue 84-503-XPB, The Leading Causes of Death at Different Ages

| MARRIAGES, 1995 | | | | | | | | | | | | | |
|---|---|---|---|---|---|---|---|---|---|---|---|---|---|
| | CANADA | NFLD. | P.E.I. | N.S. | N.B. | QUÉ. | ONT. | MAN. | SASK. | ALTA. | B.C. | YUKON | N.W.T. |
| Marriages | 160,256 | 3,404 | 877 | 5,329 | 4,257 | 24,238 | 67,583 | 6,703 | 5,799 | 18,044 | 23,597 | 207 | 218 |
| Marriage Rate [1] | 5.4 | 5.9 | 6.5 | 5.7 | 5.6 | 3.3 | 6.1 | 5.9 | 5.7 | 6.6 | 6.3 | 6.8 | 3.3 |
| **Mean age at marriage:** | | | | | | | | | | | | | |
| Grooms | 32.8 | 30.9 | 32.2 | 32.8 | 32.1 | 33.5 | 32.7 | 31.8 | 31.5 | 32.2 | 34.0 | 33.8 | 33.0 |
| Brides | 30.4 | 28.6 | 29.7 | 30.5 | 29.5 | 30.9 | 30.4 | 29.4 | 29.0 | 29.7 | 31.3 | 31.9 | 29.8 |
| **Mean age at marriage of single persons:** | | | | | | | | | | | | | |
| Grooms | 29.0 | 28.4 | 28.7 | 28.9 | 28.2 | 29.6 | 29.1 | 28.4 | 28.0 | 28.6 | 29.5 | 29.3 | 30.5 |
| Brides | 27.1 | 26.4 | 26.7 | 27.0 | 26.1 | 27.7 | 27.2 | 26.2 | 25.7 | 26.3 | 27.4 | 27.7 | 28.1 |
| **Mean age at marriage of divorced persons:** | | | | | | | | | | | | | |
| Grooms | 42.5 | 41.5 | 41.8 | 42.6 | 42.5 | 44.2 | 42.0 | 41.4 | 41.3 | 41.6 | 43.3 | 42.3 | 44.7 |
| Brides | 38.9 | 38.1 | 39.2 | 39.5 | 39.1 | 40.7 | 38.5 | 38.8 | 38.0 | 38.0 | 39.4 | 38.5 | 38.3 |

1.Per 1,000 population.

Source: Statistics Canada Catalogue 84-212-XPB, Marriages

| MOTHER TONGUE, 1991 | |
|---|---|
| LANGUAGE | MOTHER TONGUE |
| English | 16,454,515 |
| French | 6,623,235 |
| Italian | 538,690 |
| German | 490,650 |
| Chinese | 516,875 |
| Spanish | 187,615 |
| Portuguese | 220,630 |
| Ukrainian | 201,315 |
| Polish | 200,395 |
| Dutch | 146,420 |
| Punjabi | 147,265 |
| Arabic | 119,255 |
| Greek | 132,980 |
| Tagalog | 115,980 |
| Vietnamese | 83,630 |
| Hindi | 40,575 |
| Hungarian | 83,915 |
| Cree | 82,070 |
| Russian | 38,030 |
| Gujari | 42,175 |

Source: Statistics Canada, Catalogue 96-304, 1991 Census Highlights

| RELIGION, 1991 | |
|---|---|
| | TOTAL POPULATION |
| All religions | 26,994,040 |
| Catholic | 12,335,255 |
| Protestant | 9,780,715 |
| United Church | 3,093,120 |
| Anglican | 2,188,110 |
| Presbyterian | 636,295 |
| Lutheran | 636,205 |
| Baptist | 663,360 |
| Pentecostal | 436,435 |
| Eastern Orthodox | 387,390 |
| Jewish | 318,070 |
| Eastern non-Christian | 747,455 |
| Islam | 253,260 |
| Buddist | 163,415 |
| Hindu | 157,010 |
| Sikh | 147,440 |
| Para-religious | 28,160 |
| No religious affiliation | 3,386,365 |

Source: Statistics Canada, Catalogue 96-304, 1991 Census Highlights

| SELECTED CRIMINAL CODE INCIDENTS, 1996 [1] | | |
|---|---|---|
| CRIMES | NUMBER | RATE[2] |
| Homicide | 633 | 2.1 |
| Sexual Assault (1,2,3) | 26,762 | 89 |
| Assault (1,2,3) | 215,653 | 720 |
| Robbery | 31,242 | 104 |
| **Violent Crime - (Total)** | **291,437** | **973** |
| Breaking & Entering | 396,085 | 1,322 |
| Motor Vehicle Theft | 178,580 | 596 |
| Other Theft | 849,529 | 2,835 |
| **Property Crime - (Total)** | **1,555,800** | **5,192** |
| Offensive Weapons | 16,132 | 54 |
| Mischief | 364,021 | 1,215 |
| **Other Criminal Code - (Total)** | **776,911** | **2,593** |
| **Criminal Code - (Total)** | **2,624,148** | **8,758** |

1.Excludes traffic crimes.
2.Rates are calculated on the basis of 100,000 population.

Source: Statistics Canada, Catalogue 85-002-XPE, Juristat

## LABOUR FORCE ESTIMATES, ANNUAL AVERAGES

| | POPULATION AGED 15 AND OVER | LABOUR FORCE TOTAL | EMPLOYMENT | UNEMPLOYMENT | PARTICIPATION RATE | UNEMPLOYMENT RATE | EMPLOYMENT/ POPULATION RATIO |
|---|---|---|---|---|---|---|---|
| | (000's) | | (000'S) | | (%) | (%) | (%) |
| 1949 | 9,268 | 5,055 | 4,913 | 141 | 54.5 | 2.8 | 53.0 |
| 1959 | 11,605 | 6,242 | 5,870 | 372 | 53.8 | 6.0 | 50.6 |
| 1969 | 14,162 | 8,194 | 7,832 | 362 | 57.9 | 4.4 | 55.3 |
| 1970 | 14,528 | 8,395 | 7,919 | 476 | 57.8 | 5.7 | 54.5 |
| 1971 | 14,872 | 8,639 | 8,104 | 535 | 58.1 | 6.2 | 54.5 |
| 1972 | 15,186 | 8,897 | 8,344 | 553 | 58.6 | 6.2 | 54.9 |
| 1973 | 15,526 | 9,276 | 8,761 | 515 | 59.7 | 5.5 | 56.4 |
| 1974 | 15,924 | 9,639 | 9,125 | 514 | 60.5 | 5.3 | 57.3 |
| 1975 | 16,323 | 9,974 | 9,284 | 690 | 61.1 | 6.9 | 56.9 |
| 1976 | 16,701 | 10,203 | 9,477 | 726 | 61.1 | 7.1 | 56.7 |
| 1977 | 17,051 | 10,500 | 9,651 | 849 | 61.6 | 8.1 | 56.6 |
| 1978 | 17,377 | 10,895 | 9,987 | 908 | 62.7 | 8.3 | 57.5 |
| 1979 | 17,702 | 11,231 | 10,395 | 836 | 63.4 | 7.4 | 58.7 |
| 1980 | 18,053 | 11,573 | 10,708 | 865 | 64.1 | 7.5 | 59.3 |
| 1981 | 18,368 | 11,899 | 11,001 | 898 | 64.8 | 7.5 | 59.9 |
| 1982 | 18,608 | 11,926 | 10,618 | 1,308 | 64.1 | 11.0 | 57.1 |
| 1983 | 18,805 | 12,109 | 10,675 | 1,434 | 64.4 | 11.8 | 56.8 |
| 1984 | 18,996 | 12,316 | 10,932 | 1,384 | 64.8 | 11.2 | 57.5 |
| 1985 | 19,190 | 12,532 | 11,221 | 1,311 | 65.3 | 10.5 | 58.5 |
| 1986 | 19,397 | 12,746 | 11,531 | 1,215 | 65.7 | 9.5 | 59.4 |
| 1987 | 19,642 | 13,011 | 11,861 | 1,150 | 66.2 | 8.8 | 60.4 |
| 1988 | 19,890 | 13,275 | 12,245 | 1,031 | 66.7 | 7.8 | 61.6 |
| 1989 | 20,968 | 14,151 | 12,086 | 1,065 | 67.5 | 7.5 | 62.4 |
| 1990 | 21,227 | 14,329 | 13,165 | 1,163 | 67 | 8.1 | 61.9 |
| 1991 | 21,612 | 14,407 | 12,916 | 1,491 | 66 | 10.4 | 59.8 |
| 1992 | 21,986 | 14,482 | 12,842 | 1,640 | 65 | 11.3 | 58.4 |
| 1993 | 22,371 | 14,663 | 13,014 | 1,648 | 65 | 11.2 | 58.2 |
| 1994 | 22,716 | 14,832 | 13,291 | 1,540 | 65 | 10.4 | 58.5 |
| 1995 | 23,027 | 14,927 | 13,506 | 1,422 | 64 | 9.5 | 58.6 |
| 1996 | 23,351 | 15,145 | 13,676 | 1,469 | 64 | 9.7 | 58.6 |

Source: Statistics Canada, Household Surveys Division, Catalogue 71-220-XPB, Labour Force Annual Averages

## EMPLOYMENT BY DETAILED OCCUPATION, CANADA, ANNUAL AVERAGES, 1991 TO 1996

| | 1991 | 1992 | 1993 | 1994 | 1995 | 1996 |
|---|---|---|---|---|---|---|
| | | | THOUSANDS | | | |
| All Occupations | 12,916 | 12,842 | 14,663 | 14,832 | 14,927 | 15,145 |
| Managerial and other professional | 4,081 | 4,095 | 4,438 | 4,507 | 4,623 | 4,653 |
| Managerial and administrative | 1,735 | 1,735 | 1,848 | 1,841 | 1,970 | 1,960 |
| Other professional | 2,347 | 2,359 | 2,590 | 2,665 | 2,652 | 2,692 |
| Natural sciences, engineering and mathematics | 517 | 483 | 542 | 556 | 567 | 567 |
| Social sciences | 275 | 288 | 311 | 328 | 309 | 319 |
| Religion | 30 | 29 | 34 | 37 | 33 | 34 |
| Teaching | 582 | 629 | 657 | 680 | 675 | 662 |
| Medicine and health | 699 | 692 | 749 | 750 | 747 | 762 |
| Artistic, literary and recreational | 243 | 239 | 295 | 313 | 319 | 345 |
| Clerical | 2,122 | 2,083 | 2,200 | 2,142 | 2,092 | 2,073 |
| Sales | 1,247 | 1,274 | 1,368 | 1,415 | 1,416 | 1,453 |
| Service | 1,721 | 1,749 | 1,986 | 1,997 | 2,004 | 2,064 |
| Primary occupations | 621 | 595 | 685 | 663 | 670 | 685 |
| Farming, horticulture & animal husbandry | 470 | 455 | 515 | 485 | 488 | 510 |
| Fishing and trapping | 44 | 37 | 46 | 43 | 36 | 38 |
| Forestry and logging | 50 | 52 | 68 | 74 | 82 | 72 |
| Mining and quarrying | 58 | 51 | 55 | 59 | 64 | 63 |
| Processing machining and fabricating etc. | 1,528 | 1,487 | 1,644 | 1,682 | 1,741 | 1,803 |
| Processing | 359 | 340 | 379 | 369 | 386 | 397 |
| Machining | 192 | 194 | 209 | 230 | 238 | 236 |
| Fabricating, assembling and repairing | 977 | 953 | 1,056 | 1,081 | 1,116 | 1,169 |
| Construction | 697 | 670 | 820 | 836 | 814 | 797 |
| Transport equipment operating | 474 | 466 | 506 | 541 | 559 | 557 |
| Material handling and other crafts | 425 | 423 | 483 | 514 | 520 | 541 |
| Material handling | 266 | 264 | 314 | 345 | 349 | 373 |
| Other crafts | 159 | 160 | 168 | 168 | 170 | 168 |
| Unclassified | | | 529 | 531 | 483 | 515 |

Source: Statistics Canada, Household Surveys Division, Catalogue 71F0004-XCB, Historical Labour Force CD-ROM

## LABOUR FORCE PARTICIPATION RATES OF WOMEN BY AGE AND EDUCATION, CANADA, 1991

| EDUCATION | TOTAL | AGE GROUPS 15-19 | 20-24 | 25-34 | 35-44 | 45-54 | 55-64 | 65 & OVER |
|---|---|---|---|---|---|---|---|---|
| Total | 59.9 | 47.5 | 81.1 | 78.5 | 79.6 | 71.9 | 39.2 | 5.7 |
| Less than Grade 9 | 24.3 | 24.5 | 44.6 | 48.5 | 56.0 | 49.5 | 25.2 | 3.5 |
| Grade 9-13 without certificate or diploma | 46.9 | 37.6 | 64.1 | 65.5 | 71.3 | 65.8 | 37.4 | 5.1 |
| Grade 9-13 with certificate or diploma | 64.3 | 57.1 | 80.5 | 75.9 | 79.1 | 73.6 | 42.0 | 6.7 |
| Trades certificate or diploma[1] | 72.0 | 71.8 | 86.7 | 81.1 | 82.8 | 79.4 | 50.9 | 8.2 |
| Some university or other non-university without certificate or diploma[2] | 71.5 | 78.0 | 83.3 | 78.9 | 80.6 | 76.9 | 47.2 | 7.9 |
| University or other non-university with Certificate or diploma[3] | 77.9 | 81.0 | 90.2 | 87.2 | 87.2 | 83.5 | 54.4 | 9.7 |
| University degree | 83.3 | 72.7 | 88.4 | 88.9 | 88.0 | 88.3 | 59.9 | 14.2 |

1.Includes persons with a trades certificate or diploma only and persons with other non-university education and a trades certificate or diploma.
2.Includes persons with some university education (with or without other non-university education) with a trades certificate or diploma.
3.Does not include persons with other non-university education and a trades certificate or diploma, or persons with some university education (with or without other non-university education) with a trades certificate or diploma.

Source: 1991 Census of Canada, unpublished data, Labour Household Survey Analysis Division

## MINIMUM HOURLY WAGE RATES FOR EXPERIENCED ADULT WORKERS, YOUNG WORKERS & STUDENTS

| JURISDICTION | EXPERIENCED ADULT WORKERS (INCLUDING DOMESTICS) | EFFECTIVE DATE | YOUNG WORKERS & STUDENTS [1] | EFFECTIVE DATE |
|---|---|---|---|---|
| Federal | Same as adult minimum wage rate in each provincial & territorial jurisdiction on July 17, 1996 | 18/12/96 | Employees under 17; same as the adult minimum wage rate in each provincial and territorial jurisdiction on July 1, 1996 | 18/12/96 |
| Alberta | $5.00 | 01/04/92 | Employees under 18 attending school: $4.50 | 01/04/92 |
| British Columbia | $7.00 | 01/10/95 | Same as adult rate | |
| Manitoba | $5.40 | 01/01/96 | Same as adult rate | |
| New Brunswick | $5.50 | 01/07/96 | Same as adult rate | |
| Newfoundland [2] | $5.25 | 01/04/97 | Same as adult rate | |
| Nova Scotia | $5.50 | 01/02/97 | Same as adult rate | |
| Ontario | $6.85 | 01/01/95 | Students under 18 emplyed for not more than 28 hours in a week or during a school holiday: $6.40 | 01/01/95 |
| Prince Edward Island | $5.40 | 01/09/97 | Same as adult rate | |
| Québec | $6.80 | 01/10/97 | Same as adult rate | |
| Saskatchewan | $5.60 | 01/12/96 | Same as adult rate | |
| Northwest Territories [2] | $6.50<br>$7.00 [3] | 01/04/91<br>01/04/91 | Employees under 16: $6.00<br>$6.50 [3] | 01/04/91<br>01/04/91 |
| Yukon Territory | $6.86 | 01/10/95 | Same as adult rate | |

1.Alberta, Ontario & the Northwest Territories have special rates for young workers or students.
2.Sixteen years of age & over.
3.For areas distant from the NWT highway system.
Source: Human Resources Development Canada, External Cooperation Division, September 1996

## AVERAGE EARNINGS OF MEN & WOMEN IN CANADA[1]

| | 1985 | 1986 | 1987 | 1988 | 1989 | 1990 | 1991 | 1992 | 1993 | 1994 | 1995 |
|---|---|---|---|---|---|---|---|---|---|---|---|
| Males[2] $ | 30,152 | 30,609 | 30,832 | 31,509 | 31,598 | 32,027 | 31,144 | 31,042 | 30,407 | 31,770 | 31,053 |
| Females[2] $ | 16,940 | 17,569 | 17,772 | 18,080 | 18,634 | 19,166 | 19,166 | 19,831 | 19,566 | 19,784 | 20,219 |
| **Earnings Ratio %** | | | | | | **59.8** | **61.5** | **63.9** | **64.3** | **62.3** | **65.1** |
| Males[3] $ | 39,115 | 39,361 | 39,820 | 40,302 | 40,113 | 41,183 | 40,870 | 41,270 | 40,441 | 41,611 | 40,610 |
| Females[3] $ | 25,403 | 25,905 | 26,257 | 26,323 | 26,409 | 27,885 | 28,458 | 29,669 | 29,207 | 29,047 | 29,700 |
| **Earnings Ratio %** | | | | | | **67.7** | **69.6** | **71.9** | **72.2** | **69.8** | **73.1** |

1.Constant (1995) dollars, for the years 1990-1995.
2.All earners.
3.Full year full time workers.
Source: Statistics Canada, Catalogue 13-217-XPB, Earnings of Men & Women

## AVERAGE FAMILY INCOME, 1991/1992/1994/1995

| | 1991 $ | 1992 $ | 1994 $ | 1995 $ |
|---|---|---|---|---|
| Canada | 51,856 | 52,504 | 52,858 | 54,161 |
| Newfoundland | 40,250 | 40,933 | 41,474 | 42,328 |
| Prince Edward Island | 43,171 | 44,519 | 45,369 | 45,450 |
| Nova Scotia | 44,113 | 45,541 | 45,436 | 44,826 |
| New Brunswick | 42,914 | 45,049 | 44,530 | 44,545 |
| Québec | 47,960 | 48,060 | 48,488 | 49,498 |
| Ontario | 56,727 | 57,071 | 57,482 | 59,356 |
| Manitoba | 46,214 | 49,545 | 48,809 | 51,467 |
| Saskatchewan | 45,685 | 47,720 | 46,507 | 50,065 |
| Alberta | 53,999 | 53,538 | 54,344 | 53,361 |
| British Columbia | 53,602 | 55,089 | 55,358 | 56,925 |

Source: Statistics Canada, Catalogue 13-208-XPB, Family Income

## AVERAGE HOUSEHOLD EXPENDITURE 1990/1992

| | 1990 $ | 1992 $ |
|---|---|---|
| Food | 5,977 | 5,686 |
| Shelter | 8,229 | 8,102 |
| Household operation | 1,907 | 1,974 |
| Household furnishings and equipment | 1,425 | 1,372 |
| Clothing | 2,596 | 2,222 |
| Transportation | 5,603 | 5,640 |
| Health Care | 848 | 867 |
| Personal Care | 887 | 844 |
| Recreation | 2,358 | 2,300 |
| Reading materials & other printed matter | 272 | 248 |
| Education | 424 | 430 |
| Tobacco products & alcoholic beverages | 1,276 | 1,410 |
| Gifts & contributions | 1,734 | 1,464 |
| Miscellaneous | 1,294 | 1,322 |

Source: Statistics Canada, Catalogue 62-555-XPB, Family Expenditure in Canada, Household Surveys Division

## NEW HOUSING PRICE INDEXES ANNUAL AVERAGES[1]

1986 = 100

| | CANADA | ATLANTIC PROVINCES | QUÉBEC | ONTARIO | PRAIRIE PROVINCES | BRITISH COLUMBIA |
|---|---|---|---|---|---|---|
| 1986 | 97.2 | 99.5 | 97.7 | 95.3 | 99.3 | 99.9 |
| 1987 | 113.6 | 102.8 | 110.9 | 121.5 | 103.1 | 103.0 |
| 1988 | 123.0 | 106.1 | 121.6 | 133.2 | 106.8 | 108.8 |
| 1989 | 134.7 | 109.8 | 126.7 | 150.1 | 108.7 | 121.3 |
| 1990 | 135.3 | 110.8 | 130.6 | 145.7 | 119.3 | 127.3 |
| 1991 | 125.2 | 113.2 | 131.0 | 128.5 | 117.7 | 118.2 |
| 1992 | 124.5 | 114.3 | 130.1 | 125.2 | 117.9 | 124.2 |
| 1993 | 125.5 | 116.0 | 130.9 | 123.5 | 123.1 | 128.8 |
| 1994 | 125.5 | 118.0 | 131.3 | 123.2 | 125.9 | 126.4 |
| 1995 | 124.2 | 119.9 | 132.9 | 123.4 | 126.4 | 117.5 |
| 1996 | 121.5 | 119.8 | 132.7 | 121.7 | 127.7 | 107.7 |

1.Twenty cities, house only.
Source: Statistics Canada, Prices, CANSIM- Time Series D698201, D698798, D698803, D698804, D698805, D698809

## USE OF SELECTED MEDIA, 1996 (PER THOUSAND HOUSEHOLDS)

| | TELEPHONE | CELLULAR PHONE | RADIO | TELEVISION | CABLE TELEVISION | VIDEO RECORDER | HOME COMPUTERS[1] | COMPUTER MODEMS[2] | INTERNET |
|---|---|---|---|---|---|---|---|---|---|
| CANADA | 11,268 | 1,611 | 11,258 | 11,305 | 1,260 | 9,534 | 3,603 | 1,772 | 844 |
| Newfoundland | 186 | 11 | 189 | 191 | 156 | 160 | 41 | 20 | 9 |
| Prince Edward Island | 48 | 4 | 49 | 49 | 33 | 41 | 11 | 5 | -- |
| Nova Scotia | 351 | 49 | 351 | 353 | 264 | 289 | 93 | 52 | 29 |
| New Brunswick | 280 | 31 | 280 | 284 | 197 | 240 | 61 | 29 | 13 |
| Québec | 2,959 | 213 | 2,967 | 2,977 | 1,997 | 2,349 | 719 | 290 | 123 |
| Ontario | 4,144 | 707 | 4,125 | 4,160 | 3,281 | 3,604 | 1,503 | 740 | 363 |
| Manitoba | 417 | 66 | 419 | 418 | 294 | 345 | 109 | 61 | 27 |
| Alberta | 1,027 | 216 | 1,026 | 1,025 | 738 | 307 | 108 | 46 | 18 |
| Saskatchewan | 377 | 71 | 377 | 377 | 230 | 911 | 393 | 217 | 104 |
| British Columbia | 1,479 | 241 | 1,474 | 1,472 | 1,260 | 1,287 | 565 | 312 | 156 |

1.Excludes systems which can only be used to play games or are used exclusively for business purposes.
2.Includes internal and external units.
Source: Household Facilities and Equipment (Catalogue 64-202-XPB), Statistics Canada

## CONSUMER PRICE INDEX

1986 - 1996; January 1996- July 1997

(1986 = 100)

| | Food | Shelter | Household Operations & Furnishings | Clothing & Footwear | Transportation | Health & Personal Care | Recreation, Reading & Education | Alcohol Beverages & Tobacco Products | All-items Index |
|---|---|---|---|---|---|---|---|---|---|
| 1986 | 100.0 | 100.0 | 100.0 | 100.0 | 100.0 | 100.0 | 100.0 | 100.0 | 100.0 |
| 1987 | 104.4 | 104.0 | 102.9 | 104.2 | 103.6 | 105.0 | 105.4 | 106.7 | 104.4 |
| 1988 | 107.2 | 108.6 | 106.8 | 109.6 | 105.6 | 109.6 | 111.3 | 114.6 | 108.6 |
| 1989 | 111.1 | 114.3 | 110.7 | 114.1 | 111.1 | 114.4 | 116.2 | 125.2 | 114.0 |
| 1990 | 115.7 | 119.5 | 112.9 | 117.3 | 117.3 | 120.0 | 121.3 | 136.1 | 119.5 |
| 1991 | 121.2 | 124.7 | 117.3 | 128.4 | 119.4 | 128.4 | 130.2 | 159.5 | 126.2 |
| 1992 | 120.8 | 126.4 | 117.9 | 129.5 | 121.8 | 131.3 | 131.9 | 169.0 | 128.1 |
| 1993 | 122.8 | 128.0 | 119.0 | 130.8 | 125.7 | 134.8 | 135.3 | 171.7 | 130.4 |
| 1994 | 123.3 | 128.5 | 119.3 | 131.8 | 131.3 | 136.1 | 139.3 | 143.6 | 130.7 |
| 1995 | 126.3 | 134.0 | 121.6 | 131.8 | 138.1 | 135.9 | 142.9 | 143.5 | 133.5 |
| 1996 | 128.0 | 134.2 | 124.1 | 131.3 | 143.5 | 136.6 | 146.3 | 146.3 | 135.6 |
| **1996** | | | | | | | | | |
| Jan. | 127.6 | 134.3 | 123.2 | 130.1 | 140.5 | 135.9 | 142.0 | 144.9 | 134.2 |
| Feb. | 126.8 | 134.3 | 123.5 | 132.0 | 140.4 | 136.0 | 142.9 | 145.3 | 134.4 |
| Mar. | 127.1 | 134.2 | 124.0 | 132.7 | 141.7 | 136.0 | 143.6 | 145.4 | 134.9 |
| Apr. | 128.3 | 134.1 | 123.9 | 132.0 | 143.1 | 136.7 | 144.0 | 145.5 | 135.3 |
| May | 127.8 | 134.2 | 124.0 | 131.5 | 144.9 | 136.7 | 145.7 | 146.3 | 135.7 |
| June | 128.6 | 134.0 | 124.5 | 129.4 | 143.8 | 136.5 | 145.8 | 146.5 | 135.6 |
| July | 128.3 | 134.1 | 124.5 | 129.5 | 142.4 | 136.6 | 149.2 | 146.3 | 135.6 |
| Aug. | 127.9 | 133.9 | 124.7 | 131.0 | 142.7 | 136.8 | 149.1 | 146.3 | 135.7 |
| Sept | 127.5 | 134.1 | 124.8 | 132.2 | 142.9 | 136.8 | 149.8 | 146.5 | 135.9 |
| Oct | 128.3 | 134.7 | 124.3 | 133.0 | 143.1 | 136.9 | 149.5 | 146.7 | 136.2 |
| Nov | 129.3 | 134.3 | 124.1 | 131.6 | 147.9 | 137.4 | 147.5 | 146.8 | 136.8 |
| Dec. | 128.9 | 134.5 | 124.2 | 130.0 | 148.3 | 137.3 | 146.7 | 148.9 | 136.8 |
| **1997** | | | | | | | | | |
| Jan. | 129.5 | 134.8 | 125.5 | 130.2 | 148.1 | 137.6 | 146.2 | 149.3 | 137.1 |
| Feb. | 129.8 | 134.7 | 125.5 | 131.6 | 147.9 | 138.1 | 147.2 | 149.9 | 137.3 |
| Mar. | 129.8 | 134.8 | 125.9 | 133.2 | 148.0 | 138.2 | 148.1 | 150.0 | 137.6 |
| Apr. | 129.4 | 134.7 | 125.9 | 134.6 | 147.5 | 139.3 | 148.3 | 150.0 | 137.6 |
| May | 129.9 | 134.4 | 125.7 | 133.5 | 147.5 | 139.2 | 149.7 | 151.0 | 137.7 |
| June | 130.4 | 134.5 | 125.5 | 132.7 | 148.0 | 139.6 | 151.4 | 151.3 | 138.0 |
| July | 131.0 | 134.5 | 125.4 | 131.4 | 147.2 | 139.3 | 152.3 | 150.6 | 138.0 |

Source: Statistics Canada, Catalogue 62-001-XPB, The Consumer Price Index

## PRINCIPAL TRADING PARTNERS IN 1996

| COUNTRIES | IMPORTS | EXPORTS |
|---|---|---|
| | Millions Canadian $, Custom Basis | |
| USA | 157,344 | 210,071 |
| Japan | 10,439 | 10,377 |
| United Kingdom | 5,908 | 3,808 |
| Germany | 4,820 | 3,149 |
| Korea, South | 2,727 | 2,676 |
| France | 3,399 | 1,671 |
| Italy | 2,718 | 1,307 |
| China, People's Republic | 4,925 | 2,706 |
| Taiwan | 2,863 | 1,362 |
| Mexico | 6,012 | 1,171 |
| Netherlands | 931 | 1,559 |
| Norway | 2,777 | 820 |
| Malaysia | 1,580 | 499 |
| Belgium | 816 | 1,473 |
| Hong Kong | 1,143 | 1,109 |
| Australia | 1,291 | 969 |
| Singapore | 1,190 | 529 |
| Brazil | 1,132 | 22 |
| Switzerland | 937 | 905 |
| **Total (includes all countries)** | **232,937** | **258,418** |

Source: Statistics Canada, International Trade Division

## IMPORTS AND EXPORTS - CANADA

**Value of merchandise imported and exported during the twelve months ended December 31st, 1996.**

| COMMONWEALTH AND PREFERENTIAL COUNTRIES | IMPORTS (millions of dollars) | EXPORTS (millions of dollars) |
|---|---|---|
| Australia | 1,291 | 1,017 |
| Bahamas | 23 | 21 |
| Bahrain | 1 | 15 |
| Bangladesh | 87 | 62 |
| Barbados | 15 | 37 |
| Belize | 7 | 2 |
| Bermuda | 2 | 34 |
| Cyprus | 3 | 15 |
| Fiji | 9 | 5 |
| Gibraltar | - | - |
| Ghana | 2 | 78 |
| Guyana | 204 | 11 |
| Hong Kong | 1,143 | 1,219 |
| India | 603 | 352 |
| Ireland | 590 | 240 |
| Jamaica | 239 | 94 |
| Kenya | 18 | 33 |
| Malawi | 2 | 6 |
| Malaysia | 1,580 | 536 |
| Malta | 58 | 4 |
| Mauritius | 18 | 3 |
| New Zealand | 322 | 227 |
| Nigeria | 311 | 42 |
| Pakistan | 165 | 85 |
| Papua, N.G. | - | 7 |
| Qatar | - | 17 |
| Sierra Leone | 14 | 1 |
| Singapore | 1,190 | 574 |
| South Africa | 439 | 233 |
| Sri Lanka | 71 | 52 |
| Tanzania, United Republic of | 1 | 18 |
| Trinidad and Tobago | 46 | 86 |
| Uganda | 12 | 12 |
| United Kingdom | 5,909 | 4,035 |
| Zambia | 5 | 6 |
| Zimbabwe | 13 | 12 |
| **FOREIGN COUNTRIES** | | |
| Albania Republic | - | 1 |
| Algeria | 738 | 418 |
| Angola | 165 | 7 |
| Argentina | 186 | 205 |
| Austria | 607 | 424 |
| Azerbaijin Republic | - | - |
| Belarus Republic | 5 | 3 |
| Belgium | 817 | 1,530 |
| Benin | - | 3 |
| Bolivia | 17 | 26 |
| Brazil | 1,133 | 1,428 |
| Bulgaria | 49 | 13 |
| Burkino Faso | - | 2 |
| Cameroon | 1 | 12 |
| Chile | 342 | 417 |
| China, People's Republic of | 4,925 | 2,971 |
| Colombia | 296 | 512 |
| Costa Rica | 146 | 50 |
| Côte d'Ivoire | 35 | 16 |
| Cuba | 401 | 289 |
| Czech Republic | 95 | 71 |
| Denmark | 354 | 122 |
| Dominican Republic | 91 | 78 |
| Ecuador | 128 | 72 |
| Egypt | 19 | 154 |
| El Salvador | 27 | 11 |
| Estonia Republic | 7 | 14 |
| Ethiopia | 6 | 22 |
| Finland | 417 | 206 |
| France | 3,399 | 1,750 |
| Gabon | - | 5 |
| Germany | 4,820 | 3,336 |
| Greece | 67 | 120 |
| Greenland | 2 | 8 |
| Guatemala | 103 | 67 |
| **FOREIGN COUNTRIES (continued)** | | |
| Guinea | 25 | 11 |
| Haiti | 2 | 31 |
| Honduras | 51 | 16 |
| Hungary | 47 | 48 |
| Iceland | 129 | 21 |
| Indonesia | 625 | 946 |
| Iran, Islamic Republic of | 237 | 561 |
| Iraq | - | - |
| Israel | 267 | 237 |
| Italy | 2,719 | 1,363 |
| Japan | 10,443 | 11,159 |
| Kazakhstan, Republic of | 4 | 13 |
| Korea, North | - | - |
| Korea, South | 2,727 | 2,812 |
| Kuwait | - | 77 |
| Kyrgyzstan, Republic of | - | 27 |
| Laos Peoples Democratic Republic | 1 | - |
| Latvia, Republic of | 6 | 9 |
| Lebanon | 5 | 68 |
| Liberia | - | 3 |
| Libyan Arab Jamahiriya | - | 137 |
| Lithuania, Republic of | 14 | 9 |
| Luxembourg | 36 | 19 |
| Madagascar | 5 | - |
| Mali | 2 | 11 |
| Mexico | 6,033 | 1,251 |
| Morocco | 82 | 200 |
| Mozambique | - | 17 |
| Myanmar | 14 | 1 |
| Nepal | 4 | 3 |
| Netherlands | 931 | 1,652 |
| Netherlands Antilles | 31 | 27 |
| Nicaragua | 9 | 16 |
| Niger | 14 | 12 |
| Norway | 2,777 | 847 |
| Oman (Muscat) | - | 11 |
| Panama | 23 | 48 |
| Paraguay | 2 | 6 |
| Peru | 126 | 179 |
| Philippines | 552 | 290 |
| Poland | 144 | 180 |
| Portugal | 176 | 100 |
| Romania | 50 | 102 |
| Russia Federation | 449 | 332 |
| Saudi Arabia | 650 | 636 |
| Senegal | 1 | 22 |
| Slovakia | 20 | 15 |
| Somalia | - | - |
| Spain | 687 | 523 |
| St. Pierre and Miquelon | 2 | 30 |
| Sudan | - | 8 |
| Surinam | 26 | 5 |
| Sweden | 1,201 | 281 |
| Switzerland | 937 | 940 |
| Syrian Arab Republic | 29 | 21 |
| Taiwan | 2,863 | 1,416 |
| Thailand | 1,043 | 572 |
| Togo | 44 | - |
| Tunisia | 3 | 41 |
| Turkey | 151 | 266 |
| Ukraine | 16 | 37 |
| United Arab Emirates | 14 | 172 |
| United States | 157,493 | 223,478 |
| Uruguay | 33 | 26 |
| Uzbekistan, Republic | 18 | 8 |
| Venezuela | 725 | 621 |
| Viet Nam | 97 | 49 |
| Yemen | 11 | 5 |
| Yugoslavia (Former) | 2 | 6 |
| Zaire | 20 | 12 |
| **Total (all countries)** | **233,113** | **275,921** |

Source: Statistics Canada, Catalogue 65-202-XPB, Imports, Merchandise Trade; Statistics Canada, Catalogue 65-203-XPB, Exports, Merchandise Trade

Note: Dash (-) in the above table indicates imports/exports less than $1 million.

# STATISTICS OF GROWTH AND PROGRESS IN CANADA

## GROWTH STATISTICS: AGRICULTURE/FISHERIES

| | POPULATION [1] | WHEAT PRODUCTION [2] | TOTAL CANADIAN CROPS [2, 3] | FARM CASH RECEIPTS FOR TOTAL PRODUCTS [2] | FARM CASH RECEIPTS FOR LIVESTOCK & LIVESTOCK PRODUCTS [2, 4] | DAIRY PRODUCTS INDUSTRY [5] VALUE OF SHIPMENTS | FISHERIES PRODUCTION [5, 6] |
|---|---|---|---|---|---|---|---|
| | | '000 BUSHELS | '000 ACRES | $000,000 | $000,000 | | |
| 1985 | 25,165 (ID) | 891,076 | 111,863 | 8,100 | 9,803 | 6,410,570 | 2,337,990 |
| 1986 | 25,309 (C) | 1,152,260 | 110,420 | 7,875 | 10,248 | 6,667,646 | 2,928,808 |
| 1987 | 25,617 (PD) | 953,340 | 110,484 | 7,342 | 10,619 | 6,883,944 | 3,164,390 |
| 1988 | 25,909 (PD) | 584,691 | 111,492 | 8,291 | 10,698 | 7,195,000 | 3,204,826 |
| 1989 | 26,240 (PD) | 911,071 | 112,063 | 8,764 | 10,843 | 7,349,000 | 2,857,530 |
| 1990 | 27,790 (IR) | 1,179,373 | 111,486 | 8,882 (R) | 11,195 (R) | 7,530,676 | 2,967,120 |
| 1991 | 28,120 (PD) | 1,173,802 | 110,702 | 8,732 (R) | 10,856 (R) | 7,576,415 | 2,935,130 |
| 1992 | 28,542 (PD) | 1,097,853 | 111,601 | 8,545 (R) | 11,335 (R) | 7,461,886 | 2,877,970 |
| 1993 | 28,946 (PR) | 1,000,594 | 112,715 (R) | 9,023 (R) | 12,280 (R) | 7,318,954 | 2,978,550 (R) |
| 1994 | 29,255 (PR) | 842,650 (R) | 110,319 (R) | 11,499 (R) | 12,495 (R) | 7,412,945 | 3,149,960 |
| 1995 | 29,615 (PR) | 919,227 (R) | 110,568 | 13,032 (R) | 12,670 | 7,795,466 (R) | -- -- -- |
| 1996 | 29,963 (PP) | 1,095,008 | 110,481 | 13,598 | 13,702 | 7,501,996 (P) | -- -- -- |

1.Statistics Canada, Catalogue 91-213-XPB, Annual Demographic Statistics
2.Statistics Canada, Agriculture Division
3.Includes grains, specialty crops, summerfallow, hay and improved pasture area.
4.Total livestock and livestock products (including poultry and animals on fur farms).
5.Statistics Canada, Industry Division
6.New series beginning in 1977 includes marketed values for sea fisheries only.

-- Not available
(ID) Final intercensal estimates
(C) Census Population
(PD) Final Postcensal estimates
(PR) Updated Postcensal estimates
(PP) Preliminary Postcensal estimates
(R) Revised
(P) Preliminary

## GROWTH STATISTICS: PRODUCTION OF SELECTED MINERALS/METALS

| | PIG IRON PRODUCTION | CRUDE PETROLEUM | COPPER TONS | NICKEL TONS | NATURAL GAS MILLION CU. FT. | IRON ORE | ZINC TONS | ASBESTOS TONS | CEMENT | VALUE OF TOTAL MINERAL PRODUCTION |
|---|---|---|---|---|---|---|---|---|---|---|
| | '000 metric tonnes | '000 BBL cubic metres | '000 kgs | '000 kgs | '000 cubic metres) | '000 tons metric tonnes | '000 kgs | metric tonnes | '000 tons metric tonnes | $000,000 |
| 1985 | 9,665 | 85,564 | 738,637 | 169,971 | 84,344 | 39,502 | 1,049,275 | 750 | 10,192 | 44,734 |
| 1986 | 9,249 | 85,468 | 698,527 | 163,639 | 71,896 | 36,167 | 988,173 | 662 | 10,611 | 32,447 |
| 1987 | 9,719 | 89,149 | 794,149 | 189,086 | 78,267 | 37,702 | 1,157,936 | 665 | 12,603 | 36,342 |
| 1988 | 9,498 | 93,806 | 758,478 | 198,744 | 90,911 | 39,934 | 1,370,000 | 710 | 12,350 | 36,955 |
| 1989 | 10,138 | 90,641 | 704,432 | 95,554 | 96,117 | 39,445 | 1,272,854 | 701 | 12,591 | 39,259 |
| 1990 | 7,346 | 90,279 | 771,443 | 195,004 | 98,771 | 35,670 | 1,179,300 | 686 | 11,745 | 40,778 |
| 1991 | 8,268 | 89,788 | 780,362 | 188,098 | 105,244 | 35,421 | 1,083,008 | 686 | 9,372 | 35,190 |
| 1992 | 8,621 | 93,256 | 761,694 | 177,555 | 116,664 | 31,582 | 1,195,736 | 587 | 8,598 | 35,404 |
| 1993 | 8,633 | 97,342 | 709,650 | 178,529 | 128,817 | 33,228 | 990,727 | 523 | 9,394 | 36,564 |
| 1994 | 8,106 | 110,452 | 590,784 | 141,974 | 138,856 | 36,416 | 976,309 | 531 | 10,584 | 41,150 |
| 1995(R) | 8,464 | 114,372 | 700,843 | 172,107 | 148,203 | 36,628 | 1,094,703 | 516 | 10,440 | 43,360 |
| 1996(P) | 8,638 | 116,832 | 655,891 | 184,548 | 152,985 | 36,030 | 1,187,829 | 521 | 11,050 | 49,171 |

Sources: Statistics Canada, Catalogue 41-001-XPB, Primary Iron and Steel; Statistics Canada, 26-202-XPB, Canada's Mineral Production
(P) Preliminary (R) Revised

## GROWTH STATISTICS: IMPORTS & EXPORTS

| | EXPORTS (INCLUDING RE-EXPORTS) | IMPORTS | IMPORTS OF RAW SUGAR, CANE [1] | IMPORTS OF CRUDE NATURAL RUBBER (EXCLUDING LATEX) [1] | IMPORTS OF RAW COTTON [1] | IMPORTS OF CRUDE PETROLEUM |
|---|---|---|---|---|---|---|
| | $000,000 | $000,000 | '000 kg | '000 kg | '000kg | '000 cubic metres |
| 1985 | 119,475 | 104,355 | 982 | 101,657 | 50,144 | 15,862,657 |
| 1986 | 120,669 | 112,511 | 1,090 | 91,302 | 58,332 | 20,166,763 |
| 1987 | 125,087 | 116,238 | 740 | 96,563 | 48,538 | 21,767,007 |
| 1988 | 138,498 | 131,171 | 732 | 81,206 | 40,666 | 23,475,727 |
| 1989 | 138,701 | 135,191 | 611 | 82,870 | 47,277 | 28,300,175 |
| 1990 | 148,979 | 136,245 | 911 | 75,116 | 39,197 | 31,846,753 |
| 1991 | 146,006 | 135,461 | 823 | 68,388 | 43,306 | 30,822,958 |
| 1992 | 162,823 | 148,017 | 891 | 81,500 | 44,876 | 29,383,477 |
| 1993 | 187,515 | 170,121 | 997 | 61,418 | 46,063 | 32,957,060 |
| 1994 | 226,475 | 202,737 | 995 | 101,814 | 44,961 | 36,237,601 |
| 1995 | 264,306 (R) | 225,628 (R) | 919 | 115,606 | 50,347 | 39,866,227 |
| 1996 | 275,921 | 232,937 | 1,227 | 113,374 | 58,922 | 43,237,525 |

1.From 1988, based on Harmonized System

Sources: Statistics Canada, Catalogue 65-202-XPB Exports Merchandise Trade; Statistics Canada, Catalogue 65-203-XPB Imports Merchandise Trade; Statistics Canada, Catalogue 65-007-XPB Imports By Commodity

## GROWTH STATISTICS: TRANSPORT/TRANSPORTATION

| | RAILWAY GROSS REVENUE [1] | RAILWAY OPERATING EXPENSES [1] | TONNE KILOMETRES REVENUE FREIGHT [1] | MOTOR VEHICLE REGISTRATION |
|---|---|---|---|---|
| | $000,000 | $000,000 | '000,000 | '000 |
| 1985 | 7,452 | 7,179 | 231,977 | 14,819 |
| 1986 | 7,377 | 7,243 | 236,331 | 15,336 |
| 1987 | 7,717 | 7,325 | 261,704 | 15,794 |
| 1988 | 7,778 | 7,291 | 263,635 | 16,336 |
| 1989 | 7,234 | 7,176 | 240,519 | 16,720 |
| 1990 | 6,875 | 6,737 | 239,807 | 16,981 |
| 1991 | 7,015 | 7,013 | 252,939 | 17,223 |
| 1992 | 6,748 | 7,013 | 243,662 | 17,412 |
| 1993 | 6,859 | 6,904 | 249,854 | 17,586 |
| 1994 | 7,370 (R) | 7,021(R) | 280,481(R) | 17,794 |
| 1995 | 7,062 | 7,415 | 271,032 | 17,047 |

1. 7 major railways representing about 95% of the industry in terms of operating revenues and other performance indicators.

Sources: Statistics Canada, Catalogue 52-003-XPB Railway Operating Statistics; Statistics Canada, Catalogue 53-219-XPB, Road Motor Vehicles

(R) Revised

## GROWTH STATISTICS: FINANCIAL

| | | CHARTERED BANKS [1] | | | | | LIFE INSURANCE | FEDERAL FINANCE [2] | | |
|---|---|---|---|---|---|---|---|---|---|---|
| | BANK OF CANADA NOTES IN CIRCULATION | ASSETS | LIABILITIES EXCLUDING CAPITAL RESERVES | DEMAND DEPOSITS | NOTICE DEPOSITS | TOTAL LOANS | NET AMOUNT LIFE INSURANCE IN FORCE DEC.31 [3] | TOTAL GROSS REVENUE [4] | TOTAL GROSS EXPENDITURE [4] | NET DEBT [5] |
| | $000,000 | $000,000 | $000,000 | $000,000 | $000,000 | $000,000 | $000,000 | $000,000 | $000,000 | $000,000 |
| 1985 | 16,672 | 443,761 | 423,555 | 19,267 | 164,149 | 308,767 | 693,310 | 78,055(R) | 115,039 | 202,104(R) |
| 1986 | 17,911 | 467,972 | 444,495 | 20,123 | 177,464 | 315,891 | 776,718 | 83,060 | 116,911 | 239,888 |
| 1987 | 19,447 | 486,384 | 463,038 | 22,532 | 192,910 | 332,846 | 833,013 | 90,145 | 120,826 | 270,873 |
| 1988 | 21,032 | 508,652 | 475,792 | 24,424 | 215,281 | 344,748 | 843,142 | 103,089 | 130,720 | 298,103 |
| 1989 | 22,093 | 550,939 | 522,339 | 24,526 | 248,031 | 382,785 | 923,359 | 109,506 | 136,334 | 326,484 |
| 1990 | 22,970 | 609,867 | 577,807 | 24,015 | 270,944 | 420,830 | 1,008,526 | 120,748 | 148,748 | 354,848 |
| 1991 | 24,481 | 635,912 | 599,518 | 35,082 | 146,211 | 437,916 | 1,078,607 | 127,112 | 158,971 | 386,785 |
| 1992 | 25,609 | 677,650 | 642,126 | 41,332 | 141,420 | 470,464 | 1,123,191 | 129,169 (A) | 167,140 (A) | 421,316 |
| 1993 | 27,237 | 753,992 | 716,795 | 46,016 | 142,085 | 507,394 | 1,123,619 | 132,209 (A) | 171,404 (A) | 461,685 |
| 1994 | 28,329 | 841,037(R) | 799,284 | 51,370 | 140,282 | 550,444 | 1,234,746 | 129,364 (RE) | 171,039 (RE) | 503,766 |
| 1995 | 28,778 | 912,069 | 869,187 | 57,533 | 135,563 | 586,711 | 1,317,184 | 136,982 | 174,216(RE) | 541,128 |
| 1996 | 29,109 | 1,104,873 | 1,059,063 | 63,362 | 145,589 | 675,005 | 1,357,310 | 145,453(E) | 177,703(RE) | 569,604 (R) |

1.As of December of each year
2.Based on the Financial Management System (FMS)
3.Compiled by the Office of the Superientendent of Financial Institutions Canada. Includes federally registered companies and societies. Does not include provincial companies and excludes annuities.
4.Fiscal Year ended March 31.
5.As at March 31.

Source: Bank of Canada

(R) Revised (E) Estimate

## GROWTH STATISTICS: INDUSTRIAL/TELEPHONE/POSTAL

| | INDUSTRY PRODUCT PRICE INDEX FOR MANUFACTURING | INDUSTRIAL AGGREGATE [1] | STRIKES AND LOCKOUTS EMPLOYEES AFFECTED | STRIKES AND LOCKOUTS DAYS NOT WORKED | TOTAL TELEPHONE ACCESS LINES | REVENUE FROM POSTAL OPERATIONS [2] |
|---|---|---|---|---|---|---|
| | 1986=100 | $ | '000 | '000 | '000 | $000 |
| 1985 | 99.2 | -- | -- | -- | 15,974 | 2,500,248 |
| 1986 | 100.0 | 425.16 | 484 | 7,152 | 12,948 | 2,757,674 |
| 1987 | 102.8 | 441.23 | 582 | 3,812 | 13,444 | 2,970,056 |
| 1988 | 107.2 | 460.67 | 207 | 4,899 | 13,976 | 3,138,552 |
| 1989 | 109.4 | 484.23 | 444 | 3,701 | 14,648 | 3,411,216 |
| 1990 | 109.7 | 506.24 | 271 | 5,079 | 15,296 | 3,579,843 |
| 1991 | 108.6 | 529.48 | 253 | 2,516 | 15,815 | 3,739,000 |
| 1992 | 109.1 | 547.98 | 149 | 2,109 | 16,247 | 3,921,000 |
| 1993 | 112.7 | 557.94 | 101 | 1,519 | 16,716 | 4,118,000 |
| 1994 | 119.2 (R) | 568.27 | 81 | 1,606 | 17,250 | 4,748,000 |
| 1995 | 128.8 | 573.75 | 149 (R) | 1,582 (R) | 17,763 | 4,953,000 |
| 1996 | 129.5 | 586.06 | 283 | 3,339 | -- | -- |

1.Average weekly Earnings (including overtime) for all employees (Canada)
2.Fiscal year ended March 31.

Sources: Statistics Canada, Catalogue 62-011-XPB Industry Price Indexes; Annual Estimates of Employment, Earnings and Hours, Statistics Canada, Labour Division; Human Resources Development Canada; Catalogue 56-203-XPB Telephone Statistics; Statistics Canada, Public Institutions Division

(R) Revised

# WEIGHTS & MEASURES

## THE INTERNATIONAL SYSTEM OF UNITS (SI) (BASE & SUPPLEMENTARY UNITS)

With the permission of the Canadian Standards Association, material is reproduced from CSA Standard CAN/CSA-Z234.1-89 (Canadian Metric Practice Guide), which is copyrighted by CSA, 178 Rexdale Blvd., Etobicoke, ON M9W 1R3. While use of this material has been authorized, CSA shall not be responsible for the manner in which the information is presented, nor for any interpretations thereof.

### BASE UNITS

The International System of Units includes two classes of units: seven base units, and derived units. The base units are seven precisely defined units used internationally for teaching and scientific research.

**SI BASE UNITS**

| Quantity | Name | Symbol |
|---|---|---|
| length | metre | m |
| mass | kilogram | kg |
| time | second | s |
| electric current | ampere | A |
| thermodynamic temperature | kelvin | K |
| amount of substance | mole | mol |
| luminous intensity | candela | cd |

**SI PREFIXES**

| Multiplying Factor | Prefix | Symbol |
|---|---|---|
| 1 000 000 000 000 000 000 = $10^{18}$ | exa | E |
| 1 000 000 000 000 000 = $10^{15}$ | peta | P |
| 1 000 000 000 000 = $10^{12}$ | tera | T |
| 1 000 000 000 = $10^{9}$ | giga | G |
| 1 000 000 = $10^{6}$ | mega | M |
| 1 000 = $10^{3}$ | kilo | k |
| 100 = $10^{2}$ | hecto | h |
| 10 = $10^{1}$ | deca | da |
| 0.1 = $10^{-1}$ | deci | d |
| 0.01 = $10^{-2}$ | centi | c |
| 0.001 = $10^{-3}$ | milli | m |
| 0.000 001 = $10^{-6}$ | micro | µ |
| 0.000 000 001 = $10^{-9}$ | nano | n |
| 0.000 000 000 001 = $10^{-12}$ | pico | p |
| 0.000 000 000 000 001 = $10^{-15}$ | femto | f |
| 0.000 000 000 000 000 001 = $10^{-18}$ | atto | a |

SI Prefixes and their symbols given in the above table are used to form names and symbols of decimal multiples or sub-multiples of SI units.

**SI DERIVED UNITS WITH SPECIAL NAMES**

| Name | Symbol | Typical Form[1] | In Base Units | Quantity |
|---|---|---|---|---|
| becquerel | Bq | $s^{-1}$ | $s^{-1}$ | activity of radionuclides |
| coulomb | C | s•A | s•A | quantity of electricity, electric charge |
| degree Celsius | °C | K | K | Celsius Temperature [2] |
| farad | F | C/V | $m^{-2}$•$kg^{-1}$•$s^{4}$•$A^{2}$ | electric capacitance |
| gray | Gy | J/kg | $m^{2}$•$s^{-2}$ | absorbed dose of ionizing radiation |
| henry | H | Wb/A | $m^{2}$•kg•$s^{-2}$•$A^{-2}$ | inductance |
| hertz | Hz | $s^{-1}$ | $s^{-1}$ | frequency [3] |
| joule | J | N•m | $m^{2}$•kg•$s^{-2}$ | energy, work, quantity of heat |
| lumen | lm | cd•sr | cd | luminous flux |
| lux | lx | lm/$m^{2}$ | $m^{-2}$•cd | illuminance |
| newton | N | m•kg/$s^{2}$ | m•kg•$s^{-2}$ | force |
| ohm | Ω | V/A | $m^{2}$•kg•$s^{-3}$•$A^{-2}$ | electric resistance |
| pascal | Pa | N/$m^{2}$ | $m^{-1}$•kg•$s^{-2}$ | pressure, stress |
| radian | rad | m/m | m•$m^{-1}$ = 1 | plane angle |
| siemens | S | A/V | $m^{-2}$•$kg^{-1}$•$s^{3}$•$A^{2}$ | electric conductance |
| sievert | Sv | J/kg | $m^{2}$•$s^{-2}$ | dose equivalent of ionizing radiation |
| steradian | sr | $m^{2}$/$m^{2}$ | $m^{2}$•$m^{-2}$ = 1 | solid angle |
| tesla | T | Wb/$m^{2}$ | kg•$s^{-2}$•$A^{-1}$ | magnetic flux density |
| volt | V | W/A | $m^{2}$•kg•$s^{-3}$•$A^{-1}$ | electric potential, potential difference, electromotive force |
| watt | W | J/s | $m^{2}$•kg•$s^{-3}$ | power, radiant flux |
| weber | Wb | V•s | $m^{2}$•kg•$s^{-2}$•$A^{-1}$ | magnetic flux |

1.The formulae for derived units are not necessarily unique. For example, the volt may be defined as one joule per coulomb.
2.The Celsius temperature scale (previously called Centigrade, but renamed to avoid confusion with "centigrade", associated with the centesimal system of angular measurement) is the commonly used scale, except for certain scientific and technological purposes where the thermodynamic temperature scale is preferred. Note the use of uppercase C for Celsius.
3.The SI unit of frequency, the hertz, is one cycle per second. The reciprocal of the frequency is the period. The hertz should not be used as a measure of discrete items per unit of time, e.g. 5 boxes per second on an assembly line would not be referred to as 5 hertz, but may be referred to in terms of the reciprocal second i.e. $5s^{-1}$.

## EXAMPLE OF SI DERIVED UNITS WITHOUT SPECIAL NAMES

| Name | Typical Form | In Base Units | Quantity |
|---|---|---|---|
| ampere per metre | A/m | $A \bullet m^{-1}$ | magnetic field strength |
| ampere per square metre | $A/m^2$ | $A \bullet m^{-2}$ | current density |
| candela per square metre | $cd/m^2$ | $cd \bullet m^{-2}$ | luminance |
| coulomb per cubic metre | $C/m^3$ | $m^{-3} \bullet s \bullet A$ | electric charge density |
| coulomb per kilogram | C/kg | $A \bullet s \bullet kg^{-1}$ | exposure |
| coulomb per square metre | $C/m^2$ | $m^{-2} \bullet s \bullet A$ | surface density of charge, flux density |
| cubic metre | $m^3$ | $m^3$ | volume |
| cubic metre per kilogram | $m^3/kg$ | $m^3 \bullet kg^{-1}$ | specific volume |
| farad per metre | F/m | $m^{-3} \bullet kg^{-1} \bullet s^4 \bullet A^2$ | permittivity |
| gray per second | Gy/s | $m^2 \bullet s^{-3}$ | absorbed dose rate |
| henry per metre | H/m | $m \bullet kg \bullet s^{-2} \bullet A^{-2}$ | permeability |
| joule per cubic metre | $J/m^3$ | $m^{-1} \bullet kg \bullet s^{-2}$ | energy density |
| joule per kelvin | J/K | $m^2 \bullet kg \bullet s^{-2} \bullet K^{-1}$ | heat capacity, entropy |
| joule per kilogram kelvin | J/(kg•K) | $m^2 \bullet s^{-2} \bullet K^{-1}$ | specific heat capacity, specific entropy |
| joule per kilogram | J/kg | $m^2 \bullet s^{-2}$ | specific energy |
| joule per mole | J/mol | $m^2 \bullet kg \bullet s^{-2} \bullet mol^{-1}$ | molar energy |
| joule per mole kelvin | J/(mol•K) | $m^2 \bullet kg \bullet s^{-2} \bullet K^{-1} \bullet mol^{-1}$ | molar entropy, molar heat capacity |
| kilogram per cubic metre | $kg/m^3$ | $kg \bullet m^{-3}$ | density, mass density |
| metre per second | m/s | $m \bullet s^{-1}$ | speed - linear |
| metre per second squared | $m/s^2$ | $m \bullet s^{-2}$ | acceleration - linear |
| mole per cubic metre | $mol/m^3$ | $mol \bullet m^{-3}$ | concentration (of amount of substance) |
| newton metre | N•m | $m^2 \bullet kg \bullet s^{-2}$ | moment of force |
| newton per metre | N/m | $kg \bullet s^{-2}$ | surface tension |
| pascal second | Pa•s | $m^{-1} \bullet kg \bullet s^{-1}$ | dynamic viscosity |
| radian per second | rad/s | $s^{-1}$ | speed- angular |
| radian per second squared | $rad/s^2$ | $s^{-2}$ | acceleration- angular |
| reciprocal metre | $m^{-1}$ | $m^{-1}$ | wave number* |
| square metre | $m^2$ | $m^2$ | area |
| square metre per second | $m^2/s$ | $m^2 \bullet s^{-1}$ | kinematic viscosity |
| volt per metre | V/m | $m \bullet kg \bullet s^{-3} \bullet A^{-1}$ | electric field strength |
| watt per metre kelvin | W/(m•K) | $m \bullet kg \bullet s^{-3} \bullet K^{-1}$ | thermal conductivity |
| watt per square metre | $W/m^2$ | $kg \bullet s^{-3}$ | heat flux density, irradiance |
| watt per square metre steradian | $W/(m^2 \bullet sr)$ | $kg \bullet s^{-3}$ | radiance |
| watt per steradian | W/sr | $m^2 \bullet kg \bullet s^{-3}$ | radiant intensity |

## UNITS PERMITTED FOR USE WITH THE SI

| Quantity | UNIT Name | Symbol | Definition [1] |
|---|---|---|---|
| time | minute | min | 1 min = **60** s [2] |
| | hour | h | 1 h = **3600** s [2] |
| | day | d | 1 d = **86 400** s [2] |
| | year | a | |
| plane angle | degree | ° | 1° = (π/**180**) rad [3] |
| | minute | ' | 1' = (π/**10 800**) rad [3] |
| | second | " | 1" = (π/**648 000**) rad [3] |
| | revolution | r | 1 r = **2π** rad [4] |
| area | hectare | ha | 1 ha = **1** $hm^2$ = **10 000** $m^2$ [5] |
| volume | litre | L | 1 L = **1** $dm^3$ [6] |
| mass | metric ton or tonne | t | 1 t = **1000** kg [7] = **1** Mg |
| linear density | tex | tex | 1 tex = **1 x $10^{-6}$** kg/m [8] |
| energy | electronovolt | eV | * [9] |
| mass of atom | unified atomic mass unit | u | * [10] |
| length | astronomical unit parsec | pc | * [11, 12] |

1. Conversion factors that are exact are shown in boldface.
2. These sysmbols are used only in the sense of duration of time & not for expressing the time of day.
3. No space is left between these symbols & the last digit of a number. The unit "degree", with its decimal subdivisions, is used when the unit "radian" is not suitable.
4. The designations revolution per minute (r/min) and revolution per second (r/s) are widely used in connection with rotating machinery.
5. Because of the need for a unit similar to the acre, the hectare will continue to be recognized as a unit for use in surveying & agriculture.
6. The international symbol for litre is L or l. In order to avoid possible confusion with the number one, the "L" is preferred in Canada.
7. Care must be taken in the interpretation of the word "tonne" when it occurs in French text of Canadian origin, where the meaning may be a "ton of 2000 pounds".
8. The tex is used only in the textile industry.
9. One electronvolt is the kinetic energy acquired by an electron in passing through a potential difference of 1V in vacuum.
10. The unified atomic mass unit is equal to the fraction 1/12 of the mass of an atom of the nuclide $^{12}C$.
11. The astronomical symbol does not have an international symbol; abbreviations are used (e.g. AU in English, UA in French). The astronomical unit of distance is the length of the radius of the unperturbed circular orbit of a body of negligible mass moving around the sun with a sidereal angular velocity of 0.017 202 098 950 radian per day of 86 400 ephemeris seconds.
12. 1 parsec (pc) is the distance at which 1 astronomical unit subtends an angle of 1 second of arc.

## CONVERSION OF UNITS TO THE INTERNATIONAL SYSTEM OF UNITS (SI)

### Area

| Unit | SI |
|---|---|
| 1 acre | =0.404 685 6 ha |
| 1 arpent (French measure)* | =0.341 889 4 ha |
| 1 circular mil | =506.7 x 10$^{-6}$ or µm$^2$ |
| 1 legal subdivision (40 acres) | =0.161 874 2 km$^2$ |
| 1 perch (French measure)* | =34.188 94 m$^2$ |
| 1 rood (1210 square yards) | =0.101 171 4 ha |
| 1 section (1 mile square, 640 acres) | =2.589 988 km$^2$ |
| 1 square foot | =929.030 4 cm$^2$ |
| 1 square foot (French measure)* | =1 055.214 cm$^2$ |
| 1 square inch | =645.16 mm$^2$ |
| 1 square mile | =2.589 988 km$^2$ |
| 1 square yard | =0.836 127 4 m$^2$ |
| 1 township (36 sections) | =93.239 57 km$^2$ |

* Measures formerly used to describe certain land in the Province of Québec

### Energy

| Unit | SI |
|---|---|
| 1 British thermal unit (Btu) (International Table) | = 1.055 056 kJ |
| 1 British thermal unit (Btu) (mean) | = 1.055 87 kJ |
| 1 British thermal unit (Btu) (thermochemical) | = 1.054 35 kJ |
| 1 British thermal unit (Btu) (39° F) | = 1.059 67 kJ |
| 1 British thermal unit (Btu) (59° F, 15° C) | = 1.054 80 kJ |
| 1 British thermal unit (Btu) (60.5° F) | = 1.054 615 kJ |
| 1 Calorie (dietetic) | = 4.185 5 kJ |
| 1 calorie (International Table) | = 4.186 8 J |
| 1 calorie (thermochemical) | = 4.184 J |
| 1 calorie (15° C) | = 4.185 5 J |
| 1 calorie (15° C) | = 4.185 8 J |
| 1 electronovolt | = 0.160 217 7 aJ |
| 1 erg | = 0.1 µJ |
| 1 foot poundal | = 42.140 11 mJ |
| 1 foot pound-force | = 1.355 818 J |
| 1 horsepower hour | = 2.684 520 MJ |
| 1 kilowatt hour | = 3.6 MJ |
| 1 therm | = 105.506 MJ |
| 1 ton (nuclear equivalent of TNT) | = 4.2 GJ |
| 1 watt hour | = 3.6 kJ |
| 1 watt second | = 1 J |

### Force

| Unit | SI |
|---|---|
| 1 dyne | =10 µN |
| 1 kilogram-force | = 9.806 65 N |
| 1 kilopond | = 9.806 65 N |
| 1 kip (thousand pounds force) | = 4.448 222 kN |
| 1 ounce-force | = 0.278 013 9 N |
| 1 poundal | = 0.138 255 0 N |
| 1 pound-force | = 4.448 222 N |

### Length

| Unit | SI |
|---|---|
| 1 angstrom | =0.1 nm |
| 1 arpent (French measure)* | =58.471 31 m |
| 1 astronomical unit | =149.597 870 Gm |
| 1 chain (66 feet) | =20.116 8 m |
| 1 ell (45 inches) | =1.143 m |
| 1 fathom | =1.828 8 m |
| 1 fermi | =1 fm |
| 1 foot | =0.304 8 m |
| 1 foot (French measure)* | =0.324 840 6 m |
| 1 foot (US survey, limited usage) | =0.304 800 6 m |
| 1 furlong | =0.201 168 km |
| 1 inch | =25.4 mm |
| 1 league (Intl. nautical) | =5.556 km |
| 1 league (UK nautical) | =5.559 552 km |
| 1 league (US) | =4.828 032 km |
| 1 light year | =9.460 528 Pm |
| 1 link (1/100 chain) | =0.201 168 m |
| 1 microinch | =25.4 nm |
| 1 micron | =1 µm |
| 1 mil (0.001 inch) | =25.4 µm |
| 1 mile | =1.609 344 km |
| 1 mile (Intl. nautical) | =1.852 km |
| 1 mile (UK nautical) | =1.853 184 km |
| 1 mile (US nautical) | =1.852 km |
| 1 parsec | =30.856 78 Pm |
| 1 perch | =5.029 2 m |
| 1 perch (French measure)* | =5.847 130 8 m |
| 1 pica (printers) | =4.217 518 mm |
| 1 point (printers) | =0.351 459 8 mm |
| 1 pole | =5.029 2 m |
| 1 rod | =5.029 2 m |
| 1 yard | =0.914 4 m |

### Mass

| Unit | SI |
|---|---|
| 1 carat | =200 mg |
| 1 cental (100 lb) | =45.359 237 kg |
| 1 coal tub (100 lb, Newfoundland) | =45.359 237 kg |
| 1 drachm (apothecary) | =3.887 935 g |
| 1 dram (apothecary, US) | =3.887 935 g |
| 1 dram (avoirdupois) | =1.771 845 g |
| 1 gamma | =1 µg |
| 1 grain | =64.798 91 mg |
| 1 hundredweight (100 lb) | =45.359 237 kg |
| 1 hundredweight (long 112 lb, UK) | =50.802 35 kg |
| 1 ounce (avoirdupois) | =28.349 523 g |
| 1 ounce (troy or apothecary) | =31.103 476 8 g |
| 1 metric carat | =200 mg |
| 1 pennyweight | =1.555 174 g |
| 1 pound (avoirdupois) | =0.453 592 37 kg |
| 1 pound (troy or apothecary) | =373.241 721 6 g |
| 1 quarter (28 lb, UK) | =12.700 58 kg |
| 1 scruple (apothecary, 20 grains) | =1.295 978 g |
| 1 slug | =14.593 90 kg |
| 1 stone (14 lb, UK) | =6.350 293 kg |
| 1 ton (2240 lb, UK) | =1.016 046 908 8 Mg |
| 1 ton (short, 2000 lb) | =0.907 184 74 Mg |
| 1 unified atomic mass | =1.660 540 x 10$^{-27}$ kg |

### Power

| Unit | SI |
|---|---|
| 1 Btu (IT) per hour | =0.293 071 1 W |
| 1 Btu (thermochemical) per hour | =0.292 875 1 W |
| 1 Btu (thermochemical) per minute | =17.572 50 W |
| 1 Btu (thermochemical) per second | =1.054 350 kW |
| 1 foot pound-force per hour | =0.376 616 1 mW |
| 1 foot pound-force per minute | =22.596 97 mW |
| 1 foot pound-force per second | =1.355 818 W |
| 1 horsepower (boiler) | =9.809 50 kW |
| 1 horsepower (electric) | =746 W |
| 1 horsepower (metric, cheval vapeur) | =735.498 75 W |
| 1 horsepower (water) | =746.043 W |
| 1 horsepower (550 ft•lbf/s) | =745.699 9 W |

### Pressure or Stress (Force per Area)

| Unit | SI |
|---|---|
| 1 atmosphere, standard | =101.325 kPa (=760 torr) |
| 1 atmosphere, technical | =98.066 5 kPa (=1 kgf/cm$^2$) |
| 1 bar | =100 kPa |
| 1 foot of water (39.2° F, 4° C) | =2.988 98 kPa |
| 1 inch of mercury (conventional 32° F) | =3.386 39 kPa |
| 1 inch of mercury (60° F) | =3.376 85 kPa |
| 1 inch of mercury (68° F, 20° C) | =3.374 11 kPa |
| 1 inch of water (conventional) | =249.088 9 Pa |
| 1 inch of water (39.2° F, 4° C) | =249.082 Pa |
| 1 inch of water (60° F) | =248.843 Pa |
| 1 inch of water (68° F, 20° C) | =248.641 Pa |
| 1 ksi (1000 lbf/in$^2$) | =6.894 757 MPa |
| 1 poundal /square foot | =1.488 164 Pa |
| 1 pound-force/square foot | =47.880 26 Pa |
| 1 pound-force/square inch (psi) | =6.894 757 kPa |
| 1 ton-force/square inch | =13.789 514 MPa |
| 1 ton-force (UK)/square inch | =15.444 3 MPa |
| 1 torr | =133.322 4 Pa |

### Temperature

| Unit | SI |
|---|---|
| Celsius temperature | = temperature in kelvins - 273.15 |
| Fahrenheit temperature | = 1.8 (Celsius temperature) + 32 |
| Fahrenheit temperature | = 1.8 (temperature in kelvins) - 459.67 |
| Rankine temperature | = 1.8 (temperature in kelvins) |

### Velocity (Speed)

| Unit | SI |
|---|---|
| 1 foot per hour | =84.666 67 µm/s<br>=304.8 mm/h |
| 1 foot per minute | =5.08 mm/s<br>=304.8 mm/min |
| 1 foot per second | =304.8 mm/s |
| 1 inch per minute | =25.4 mm/min |
| 1 inch per second | =25.4 mm/s |
| 1 knot (International) | =1.852 km/h<br>=0.514 444 4 m/s |
| 1 knot (UK) | =1.853 184 km/h |
| 1 mile per hour | =0.447 04 m/s<br>=1.609 344 km/h |
| 1 mile per minute | =26.822 4 m/s |

### Volume

| Unit | SI |
|---|---|
| 1 acre foot | =1233.482 m$^3$ |
| 1 barrel (oil, 42 US gallons) | =0.158 987 3 m$^3$ |
| 1 barrel (US dry, 7056 in$^3$) | =0.115 627 1 m$^3$ |
| 1 barrel (US dry, cranberries, 5826 in$^3$) | =95.471 03 dm$^3$ |
| 1 barrel (36 UK gallons) | =0.163 659 2 m$^3$ |
| 1 board foot[a] | =2.359 737 dm$^3$ |
| 1 bushel | =36.368 72 dm$^3$ |
| 1 bushel (US dry, 2150.42 in$^3$) | =35.239 07 dm$^3$ |
| 1 cord (128 ft$^3$, 4 ft x 4 ft x 8 ft, stacked wood) | =3.624 556 m$^3$ |
| 1 cubic foot | =28.316 85 dm$^3$ |
| 1 cubic inch | =16.387 064 cm$^3$ |
| 1 cubic yard | =0.764 554 9 m$^3$ |
| 1 cunit (100 ft$^3$, solid wood) | =2.831 685 m$^3$ |
| 1 cup | =250 cm$^3$ |
| 1 demiard | =0.284 130 6 dm$^3$ |
| 1 drop (1/100 teaspoon) | =0.05 cm$^3$ |
| 1 fluid dram | =3.551 633 cm$^3$ |
| 1 fluid dram (US measure) | =3.696 691 cm$^3$ |
| 1 fluid ounce | =28.413 062 cm$^3$ |
| 1 fluid ounce (US) | =29.573 53 cm$^3$ |
| 1 gallon | =4.546 09 dm$^3$ |
| 1 gallon (US) | =3.785 412 dm$^3$ |
| 1 gill | =0.142 065 dm$^3$ |
| 1 gill (US) | =0.118 294 dm$^3$ |
| 1 herring barrel | =145.474 9 dm$^3$ |
| 1 herring tub | =72.737 44 dm$^3$ |
| 1 hogshead | =245.488 9 dm$^3$ |
| 1 lambda | =1 mm$^3$ |
| 1 minim | =59.193 9 mm$^3$ |
| 1 minim (US) | =61.611 52 mm$^3$ |
| 1 peck | =9.092 180 dm$^3$ |
| 1 peck (US dry) | =8.809 768 dm$^3$ |
| 1 Petrograd standard (165 ft$^3$, sawn timber) | =4.672 280 m$^3$ |
| 1 pint | =0.568 261 2 dm$^3$ |
| 1 pint (US dry) | =0.550 610 5 dm$^3$ |

1 pint (US liquid) =0.473 176 5 $dm^3$
1 quart =1.136 522 $dm^3$
1 quart (US dry) =1.101 221 $dm^3$
1 quart (US liquid) =0.946 352 9 $dm^3$
1 salt cart =490.977 7 $dm^3$
1 salt tub =81.829 62 $dm^3$
1 sand barrel =81.829 62 $dm^3$
1 tablespoon =15 $cm^3$
1 teaspoon =5 $cm^3$
1 ton (register) =2.831 685 $m^3$

a. The board foot is nominally 1x12x12 = 144 $in^3$. However, the actual volume of wood is about 2/3 of the nominal quality.
b. This applies to stacked wood, comprising wood, bark, & arispace, to a total volume of 128 $ft^3$.
c. Also referred to as the "imperial gallon".

## MEASURES HAVING FORMER HOUSEHOLD USAGE

1 cup (Canadian, 8 fluid ounces) =227 $cm^3$
1 cup (US, 8 fluid ounces) =236 $cm^3$
1 cup (UK, 10 fluid ounces) =284 $cm^3$
1 tablespoon (Canadian, 1/2 fluid ounce) =14.21 $cm^3$
1 tablespoon (UK, 5/8 fluid ounce) =17.8 $cm^3$
1 tablespoon (US, 1/2 fluid ounce) =14.8 $cm^3$
1 teaspoon (1/6 fluid ounce) =4.74 $cm^3$
1 teaspoon (UK, 5/24 fluid ounce) =5.92 $cm^3$
1 teaspoon (US, 1/6 fluid ounce) =4.93 $cm^3$
*1 $cm^3$ =1 ml

# LAND & FRESHWATER AREAS OF CANADA

| Province or Territory | Land ($km^2$) | Freshwater ($km^2$) | Total Area ($km^2$) | Percentage of Total Area |
|---|---|---|---|---|
| Newfoundland | 371,690 | 34,030 | 405,720 | 4.1 |
| Island of Newfoundland* | 105,700 | 5,690 | 111,390 | 1.1 |
| Prince Edward Island | 5,660 | — | 5,660 | 0.1 |
| Nova Scotia | 52,840 | 2,650 | 55,490 | 0.6 |
| New Brunswick | 72,090 | 1,350 | 73,440 | 0.7 |
| Québec | 1,356,790 | 183,890 | 1,540,680 | 15.5 |
| Ontario | 891,190 | 177,390 | 1,068,580 | 10.7 |
| Manitoba | 548,360 | 101,590 | 649,950 | 6.5 |
| Saskatchewan | 570,700 | 81,630 | 652,330 | 6.5 |
| Alberta | 644,390 | 16,800 | 661,190 | 6.6 |
| British Columbia | 929,730 | 18,070 | 947,800 | 9.5 |
| Yukon Territory | 478,970 | 4,480 | 483,450 | 4.8 |
| Northwest Territories | 3,293,020 | 133,300 | 3,426,320 | 34.4 |
| Districts of Franklin * | 1,423,560 | 19,430 | 1,442,990 | 14.5 |
| Keewatin * | 575,470 | 25,120 | 600,590 | 6.0 |
| Mackenzie * | 1,293,990 | 88,750 | 1,382,740 | 13.9 |
| Canada | 9,215,430 | 755,180 | 9,970,610 | 100.0 |

*Indicates portion of total.

# CANADIAN HERITAGE — NAVIGATION CANALS

| Name | Location | Length of Channel | Locks No. | Minimum Dimensions Length | Width | Depth |
|---|---|---|---|---|---|---|
| | | km | | m | m | m |
| *Atlantic Area* | | | | | | |
| St. Peters | St. Peter's Bay to Bras d'Or Lakes, Cape Breton, NS | 0.80 | 1 | 91.44 | 14.45 | 4.88 |
| *Richelieu River* | | | | | | |
| St-Ours | St. Ours, PQ | 0.10 | 1 | 99.6 | 13.41 | 3.66 |
| Chambly | Chambly to St-Jean, PQ | 18.96 | 9 | 33.52 | 6.70 | 1.98 |
| *Ottawa & Rideau/Cataraqui Rivers* | | | | | | |
| Ste-Anne-de-Bellevue | Junction of St. Lawrence & Ottawa River | 0.19 | 1 | 54.86 | 12.9 | 2.74 |
| Carillon | Carillon Rapids, Ottawa River | 0.8 | 1 | 54.86 | 12.9 | 2.7** |
| Rideau | Ottawa to Kingston | 202.0 | 45 | 27.4 | 8.5 | 1.22** |
| | Lower Rideau Lake to Perth (Tay Br.) | 10.0 | 2 | 27.4 | 8.5 | 1.22** |
| *Lake Ontario to Georgian Bay* | | | | | | |
| Trent-Severn Waterway | Trenton to Rice Lake | 91.7 | 18 | 46.9 | 9.75 | 2.4 |
| | Rice Lake to Kirkfield | 180.8 | 15 | 31.4 | 9.75 | 1.8 |
| | Kirkfield to Gamebridge | 18.31 | 5 | 36.5 | 9.75 | 1.8 |
| | Gamebridge to Port Severn | 96.3 | 5 | 25.6 | 7.0 | 1.8 |
| | Sturgeon Lake to Lindsay (Scugog Br.) | 29.19 | 1 | 36.5 | 9.75 | 1.2 |
| | Lindsay to Port Perry (Scugog Br.) | 42.9 | | — | — | 1.2 |
| Murray | Lake Ontario to Bay of Quinte | 12.1 | — | — | — | 2.9 |

Vessels drawing > 1.5 m must contact the TSW Peterborough (705/742-9267)
Overhead clearance 6.7 m
* Marine railway lift 17.3 m
** Vessels drawing > 1.22 m or with larger dimensions than above, are advised to contact the Rideau Canal (Superintendent, 613/283-5170)

## FACTORS GOVERNING THE TRANSIT OF VESSELS THROUGH THE ST. LAWRENCE SEAWAY LOCKS, CANALS & CHANNELS BETWEEN MONTRÉAL & LAKE ERIE

Channel widths vary from a minimum of 61 m between bridge abutments & canals flanked by two embankments, to at least 137 m in open reaches.
Minimum vertical overhead clearance of structures & cables crossing the Seaway is 36 m above high water.

**MAXIMUM VESSEL DIMENSIONS**

| | |
|---|---|
| Length | 222.50 m overall |
| Beam | 23.15 m extreme breadth excluding permanent fenders |

The channels & canals in the deep waterway between Port of Montréal & Lake Erie are designed to a minimum controlling depth of 8.23 m.
In the Seaway canals the maximum permitted draught will be currently prescribed by the St. Lawrence Seaway Authority & the St. Lawrence Seaway Development Corporation. The present maximum permissible draught is 79.5 dm.

| Lock | Normal Lift in Metres | Useable Length in Metres | Widthin Metres | Useable Length Lower Ent. in Metres | Useable Length Upper Ent. in Metres |
|---|---|---|---|---|---|
| St-Lambert (Montréal Harbour) | 4.5 | 222.5 | 24.38 | 653 | 458 |
| Côte Ste-Catherine | 10.0 | 222.5 | 24.38 | 319 | 318 |
| Lower Beauharnois | 12.2 | 222.5 | 24.38 | 379 | 503 |
| Upper Beauharnois | 11.3 | 222.5 | 24.38 | 503 | 575 |
| Snell | 14.0 | 222.5 | 24.38 | 449 | 212 |
| Eisenhower | 11.8 | 222.5 | 24.38 | 210 | 330 |
| Iroquois | 0.2 | 222.5 | 24.38 | 236 | 671 |

Minimum depth on Lock Gate Sills is 9.14 m.

## WELLAND CANAL LOCKS

| Lock No. | Type | Useable Length in Metres | Width in Metres | Normal Lift in Metres | Mileage From Port Weller (Nautical Miles)* | Useable Length Lower Ent. in Metres | Useable Length Upper Ent. in Metres |
|---|---|---|---|---|---|---|---|
| 1 | Single | 222.5 | 24.38 | 14 | 1.7 | 840 | 448 |
| 2 | Single | 222.5 | 24.38 | 14 | 3.2 | 458 | 507 |
| 3 | Single | 222.5 | 24.38 | 14 | 5.5 | 445 | 459 |
| 4 | Double | 222.5 | 24.38 | 15 | 6.8 | 223 | — |
| 5 | Double | 222.5 | 24.38 | 15 | 6.8 | — | — |
| 6 | Double | 222.5 | 24.38 | 13 | 6.8 | — | — |
| 7 | Single | 222.5 | 24.38 | 14 | 7.5 | 306 | 601 |
| 8 | Single | 350.0 | 24.38 | 2 | 21.3 | 342 | 382.5 |

*Distances are shown in nautical miles in keeping with an international maritime agreement. One nautical mile equals 1.852 km.

# CLIMATE

## Temperature Data for Representative Stations in Canada

Temperature in Degrees Celsius

| Station (Airport) | Elevation (metres) | Mean Daily Annual | Jan. | Apr. | July | Oct. | Extreme Max.* | Min.* (m) | Average Frost Dates Last in Spring | First in Fall |
|---|---|---|---|---|---|---|---|---|---|---|
| Newfoundland: | | | | | | | | | | |
| St. John's | 140 | 4.8 | -3.9 | 1.2 | 15.5 | 6.9 | 30.6 | -23.3 | June 1 | Oct. 11 |
| Prince Edward Island: | | | | | | | | | | |
| Charlottetown Int. | 55 | 5.4 | -7.1 | 2.3 | 18.3 | 8.1 | 34.4 | -28.1 | May 16 | Oct. 15 |
| Nova Scotia: | | | | | | | | | | |
| Halifax Int. | 145 | 6.1 | -6.0 | 3.3 | 18.2 | 8.6 | 34.5 | -26.1 | May 12 | Oct. 15 |
| Sydney | 62 | 5.7 | -4.7 | 2.0 | 17.7 | 8.4 | 35.0 | -25.6 | May 23 | Oct. 14 |
| Yarmouth | 43 | 6.9 | -2.7 | 4.7 | 16.3 | 9.5 | 30.0 | -21.1 | May 2 | Oct. 21 |
| New Brunswick: | | | | | | | | | | |
| Chatham | 34 | 4.8 | -9.7 | 3.0 | 19.2 | 7.1 | 37.8 | -35.0 | May 19 | Sept. 23 |
| Fredericton | 20 | 5.4 | -9.2 | 4.1 | 19.3 | 7.5 | 37.2 | -37.2 | May 19 | Sept. 23 |
| St. John | 109 | 5.0 | -7.8 | 3.2 | 16.9 | 7.6 | 34.5 | -36.7 | May 16 | Oct. 3 |
| Quebec: | | | | | | | | | | |
| Arvida | 102 | 3.0 | -15.0 | 2.9 | 18.4 | 6.1 | 35.6 | -41.7 | May 21 | Sept. 20 |
| Montréal Int. (Dorval) | 36 | 6.2 | -10.2 | 5.7 | 20.9 | 8.7 | 37.8 | -37.8 | May 3 | Oct. 8 |
| Point au Pere | 8 | 3.1 | -11.1 | 1.7 | 16.1 | 5.6 | 32.2 | -36.1 | May 22 | Sept. 26 |
| Québec | 73 | 4.1 | -12.1 | 3.3 | 19.1 | 6.6 | 35.6 | -36.1 | May 13 | Sept. 28 |
| Schefferville | 522 | -4.8 | -22.8 | -7.2 | 12.6 | -1.4 | 31.7 | -50.6 | June 17 | Sept. 3 |
| Sherbrooke | 241 | 4.0 | -11.7 | 3.6 | 17.8 | 6.6 | 33.3 | -40.0 | June 2 | Sept. 10 |
| Ontario: | | | | | | | | | | |
| Kapuskasing | 226 | 0.5 | -18.6 | 0.5 | 16.8 | 4.4 | 36.7 | -44.4 | May 10 | Sept. 2 |
| London | 278 | 7.3 | -6.6 | 6.4 | 20.3 | 9.4 | 36.7 | -31.7 | May 10 | Oct. 5 |
| Ottawa Int. | 114 | 5.7 | -10.9 | 5.6 | 20.6 | 8.1 | 37.8 | -36.1 | May 7 | Oct. 2 |
| Thunder Bay | 199 | 2.3 | -15.4 | 2.5 | 17.6 | 5.7 | 37.2 | -41.1 | May 30 | Sept. 12 |
| Toronto Int. | 173 | 7.3 | -6.7 | 6.2 | 20.6 | 9.3 | 38.3 | -31.1 | May 8 | Oct. 5 |
| Manitoba: | | | | | | | | | | |
| Churchill | 29 | -7.2 | -27.5 | -10.1 | 11.8 | -1.5 | 33.9 | -45.4 | June 24 | Sept. 9 |
| The Pas | 271 | -0.6 | -22.7 | 0.0 | 17.7 | 3.6 | 36.7 | -49.4 | May 24 | Sept. 17 |
| Winnipeg Int. | 239 | 2.2 | -19.3 | 3.4 | 19.6 | 6.1 | 40.6 | -45.0 | May 23 | Sept. 22 |
| Saskatchewan: | | | | | | | | | | |
| Prince Albert | 428 | 0.1 | -21.5 | 1.9 | 17.4 | 3.7 | 37.8 | -50.0 | June 1 | Sept. 5 |
| Regina | 577 | 2.2 | -17.9 | 3.3 | 18.9 | 5.2 | 43.3 | -50.0 | May 24 | Sept. 11 |
| Alberta: | | | | | | | | | | |
| Beaverlodge CDA | 732 | 1.6 | -15.9 | 2.6 | 15.2 | 4.4 | 36.7 | -47.8 | May 24 | Sept. 7 |
| Calgary Int. | 1,084 | 3.4 | -11.8 | 3.3 | 16.4 | 5.5 | 36.1 | -45.0 | May 25 | Sept. 15 |
| Edmonton Int. | 707 | 1.6 | -16.5 | 3.2 | 15.8 | 4.7 | 35.0 | -48.3 | May 25 | Sept. 8 |
| British Columbia: | | | | | | | | | | |
| Kamloops | 346 | 8.3 | -6.1 | 9.1 | 20.8 | 8.4 | 41.7 | -37.2 | May 4 | Oct. 1 |
| Prince George | 676 | 3.3 | -12.1 | 4.3 | 15.1 | 4.8 | 34.3 | -50.0 | June 6 | Aug. 31 |
| Prince Rupert | 34 | 6.7 | -0.2 | 5.4 | 12.8 | 7.9 | 32.2 | -21.1 | May 11 | Oct. 15 |
| Vancouver Int. | 3 | 9.8 | 2.5 | 8.8 | 17.3 | 10.0 | 33.3 | -17.8 | Mar. 31 | Nov. 3 |
| Victoria Gonzales HTS | 69 | 10.0 | 4.1 | 9.1 | 15.4 | 10.8 | 35.0 | -15.6 | Apr. 8 | Oct. 29 |
| Yukon Territory: | | | | | | | | | | |
| Dawson | 324 | -5.1 | -30.7 | -1.6 | 15.6 | -4.0 | 35.0 | -58.3 | May 28 | Aug. 28 |
| Whitehorse | 703 | -1.2 | -20.7 | 0.3 | 14.1 | 0.6 | 34.4 | -52.2 | June 8 | Aug. 30 |
| Northwest Territories: | | | | | | | | | | |
| Frobisher Bay | 34 | -9.3 | -25.6 | -14.3 | 7.6 | -5.0 | 24.4 | -45.6 | June 28 | Aug. 27 |
| Inuvik | 68 | -9.8 | -29.6 | -14.3 | 13.6 | -8.1 | 31.7 | -56.7 | June 23 | Aug. 14 |
| Resolute | 67 | -16.6 | -32.1 | -23.1 | 4.1 | -15.1 | 18.3 | -52.2 | July 10 | July 20 |
| Yellowknife | 205 | -5.4 | -28.8 | -6.9 | 16.3 | -1.6 | 32.2 | -51.1 | May 27 | Sept. 16 |

* Temperature extremes are for the total period of record to 1980

## Precipitation Data for Representative Stations in Canada

Temperature in Degrees Celsius

| Station (Airport) | Average Total Precipitation (mm.) Jan. | Feb. | Mar. | Apr. | May | June | July | Aug. | Sept. | Oct. | Nov. | Dec. | Ann. | Aver. Ann. Snowfall (cm) |
|---|---|---|---|---|---|---|---|---|---|---|---|---|---|---|
| Newfoundland: | | | | | | | | | | | | | | |
| St. John's | 155.8 | 140.1 | 131.9 | 115.6 | 101.8 | 85.6 | 75.3 | 121.6 | 116.7 | 145.5 | 162.5 | 161.2 | 1513.6 | 359.4 |
| Prince Edward Island: | | | | | | | | | | | | | | |
| Charlottetown Int. | 116.8 | 97.4 | 95.3 | 81.8 | 83.6 | 79.9 | 84.3 | 88.1 | 86.3 | 106.4 | 120.5 | 129.0 | 1169.4 | 330.6 |
| Nova Scotia: | | | | | | | | | | | | | | |
| Halifax Int. | 152.8 | 135.5 | 128.4 | 114.8 | 106.4 | 89.4 | 94.2 | 111.3 | 93.7 | 133.5 | 152.5 | 180.1 | 1490.6 | 271.0 |
| Sydney | 149.0 | 123.6 | 131.4 | 102.0 | 95.2 | 82.1 | 81.4 | 101.3 | 87.2 | 122.7 | 160.4 | 163.6 | 1399.9 | 317.9 |
| Yarmouth | 141.0 | 114.2 | 98.5 | 96.3 | 92.4 | 81.3 | 77.8 | 97.3 | 89.4 | 116.5 | 134.7 | 142.2 | 1281.6 | 208.3 |
| New Brunswick: | | | | | | | | | | | | | | |
| Chatham | 98.8 | 86.8 | 97.1 | 84.5 | 81.9 | 82.0 | 91.0 | 83.5 | 85.2 | 95.6 | 102.4 | 107.9 | 1096.7 | 333.1 |
| Fredericton | 103.3 | 89.7 | 84.7 | 79.9 | 83.1 | 85.0 | 88.8 | 87.0 | 86.8 | 97.1 | 106.1 | 117.8 | 1109.3 | 290.4 |
| St. John | 148.8 | 115.7 | 114.1 | 107.7 | 107.7 | 94.2 | 103.4 | 102.0 | 111.8 | 127.7 | 145.7 | 166.0 | 144.4 | 292.7 |
| Quebec: | | | | | | | | | | | | | | |
| Arvida | 62.6 | 57.2 | 48.9 | 45.6 | 66.8 | 89.7 | 120.7 | 96.2 | 102.1 | 69.3 | 68.5 | 80.7 | 908.3 | 271.2 |
| Montréal Int. (Dorval) | 72.0 | 65.2 | 73.6 | 74.1 | 65.6 | 82.2 | 90.0 | 91.9 | 88.4 | 75.5 | 81.0 | 86.7 | 946.2 | 235.1 |
| Point au Pere | 75.6 | 62.7 | 66.3 | 52.4 | 71.4 | 60.5 | 78.7 | 78.4 | 81.5 | 75.9 | 67.9 | 79.3 | 850.6 | 292.9 |
| Québec | 89.8 | 78.1 | 82.0 | 72.8 | 86.9 | 109.9 | 116.6 | 117.1 | 119.4 | 90.7 | 97.1 | 113.6 | 1174.0 | 343.4 |
| Schefferville | 46.9 | 43.0 | 41.6 | 45.4 | 49.4 | 73.7 | 96.8 | 98.2 | 83.4 | 75.6 | 65.7 | 49.0 | 768.7 | 386.5 |
| Sherbrooke | 71.1 | 61.7 | 73.2 | 74.3 | 86.8 | 98.7 | 117.4 | 121.1 | 101.8 | 87.1 | 90.2 | 91.7 | 1075.1 | 322.6 |
| Ontario: | | | | | | | | | | | | | | |
| Kapuskasing | 53.6 | 43.0 | 55.4 | 53.2 | 74.3 | 84.7 | 96.3 | 92.5 | 94.4 | 77.4 | 80.1 | 53.3 | 858.2 | 319.9 |
| London | 75.2 | 60.5 | 75.1 | 81.2 | 66.9 | 73.6 | 72.4 | 80.3 | 78.6 | 73.4 | 84.7 | 87.5 | 909.4 | 208.8 |
| Ottawa Int. | 1.0 | 60.3 | 67.5 | 69.1 | 67.9 | 73.4 | 85.9 | 88.4 | 79.3 | 68.1 | 77.7 | 80.7 | 879.3 | 227.3 |
| Thunder Bay | 40.9 | 28.3 | 45.0 | 50.7 | 73.3 | 76.6 | 75.4 | 83.1 | 89.1 | 54.8 | 52.9 | 41.7 | 711.8 | 213.0 |
| Toronto Int. | 50.4 | 46.0 | 61.1 | 70.0 | 66.0 | 67.1 | 71.4 | 76.8 | 63.5 | 61.8 | 62.7 | 64.7 | 761.5 | 131.2 |
| Manitoba: | | | | | | | | | | | | | | |
| Churchill | 15.3 | 13.1 | 18.1 | 22.9 | 31.9 | 43.5 | 45.6 | 58.3 | 50.9 | 43.0 | 38.8 | 20.9 | 402.3 | 195.5 |
| The Pas | 18.0 | 15.4 | 23.6 | 27.4 | 37.3 | 63.0 | 70.2 | 57.5 | 57.3 | 33.2 | 28.8 | 22.0 | 453.7 | 170.0 |
| Winnipeg Int. | 21.3 | 17.5 | 22.7 | 38.5 | 65.7 | 80.1 | 75.9 | 75.2 | 53.3 | 30.9 | 25.2 | 19.2 | 525.5 | 125.5 |
| Saskatchewan: | | | | | | | | | | | | | | |
| Prince Albert | 16.6 | 14.9 | 19.2 | 22.0 | 39.4 | 69.1 | 65.3 | 52.1 | 39.4 | 21.6 | 17.0 | 21.8 | 398.4 | 121.7 |
| Regina | 16.6 | 16.1 | 17.8 | 23.7 | 46.4 | 79.6 | 53.3 | 44.8 | 36.7 | 18.8 | 13.5 | 16.7 | 384.0 | 115.7 |
| Alberta: | | | | | | | | | | | | | | |
| Beaverlodge CDA | 33.0 | 25.4 | 24.6 | 19.3 | 39.0 | 68.4 | 64.0 | 63.8 | 42.0 | 28.6 | 26.8 | 32.1 | 467.0 | 195.2 |
| Calgary Int. | 16.2 | 15.5 | 16.1 | 32.6 | 48.7 | 89.4 | 65.4 | 55.4 | 38.2 | 17.6 | 12.7 | 16.0 | 423.8 | 152.5 |
| Edmonton Int. | 24.4 | 17.6 | 16.0 | 20.2 | 42.2 | 76.7 | 91.6 | 78.2 | 45.7 | 15.4 | 16.7 | 21.9 | 466.6 | 137.9 |
| British Columbia: | | | | | | | | | | | | | | |
| Kamloops | 31.6 | 16.0 | 9.7 | 10.4 | 18.4 | 29.9 | 22.5 | 27.5 | 21.4 | 15.2 | 22.0 | 32.2 | 265.5 | 91.5 |
| Prince George | 57.4 | 39.2 | 36.8 | 27.4 | 47.3 | 66.9 | 59.7 | 68.2 | 58.7 | 59.2 | 50.5 | 57.0 | 628.3 | 241.7 |
| Prince Rupert | 27.5 | 222.1 | 200.8 | 190.0 | 139.5 | 129.5 | 103.0 | 158.4 | 233.4 | 366.5 | 268.4 | 284.1 | 2523.2 | 151.7 |
| Vancouver Int. | 153.8 | 114.7 | 101.0 | 59.6 | 51.6 | 45.2 | 32.0 | 41.1 | 67.1 | 114.0 | 150.1 | 182.4 | 1112.6 | 60.4 |
| Victoria Gonzales HTS | 110.7 | 73.6 | 46.9 | 30.4 | 19.3 | 20.1 | 13.4 | 21.0 | 33.5 | 63.4 | 95.7 | 119.2 | 647.2 | 32.0 |
| Yukon Territory: | | | | | | | | | | | | | | |
| Dawson | 16.5 | 15.7 | 10.1 | 9.7 | 21.1 | 38.8 | 47.2 | 44.0 | 28.2 | 28.7 | 21.5 | 24.6 | 306.1 | 137.1 |
| Whitehorse | 17.7 | 13.3 | 13.5 | 9.5 | 12.9 | 30.7 | 33.9 | 37.9 | 30.3 | 21.5 | 19.8 | 20.2 | 261.2 | 136.6 |
| Northwest Territories: | | | | | | | | | | | | | | |
| Frobisher Bay | 26.1 | 23.3 | 23.3 | 26.4 | 25.3 | 39.4 | 63.3 | 58.9 | 46.0 | 44.1 | 34.4 | 22.1 | 432.6 | 255.5 |
| Inuvik | 17.9 | 10.5 | 12.0 | 14.8 | 17.6 | 23.5 | 33.6 | 43.6 | 23.9 | 33.4 | 17.9 | 17.4 | 266.1 | 176.6 |
| Resolute | 3.3 | 3.0 | 3.0 | 5.9 | 8.1 | 12.1 | 22.5 | 31.1 | 18.0 | 13.8 | 5.7 | 4.9 | 131.4 | 83.8 |
| Yellowknife | 13.3 | 11.2 | 12.4 | 10.3 | 17.2 | 16.8 | 33.8 | 44.0 | 30.5 | 34.5 | 24.5 | 18.2 | 266.7 | 135.4 |

*1 in. = 25.4 mm. = 2.54 cm.

## KILOMETRES

## MILES

| | BANFF | BRANDON | CALGARY | CHARLOTTETOWN | CHICOUTIMI | CORNER BROOK | DAWSON CREEK | EDMONTON | FLIN FLON | FORT SMITH | FREDERICTON | GANDER | GASPÉ | HALIFAX | HAMILTON | JASPER | KENORA | LETHBRIDGE | LONDON | MONCTON | MONTRÉAL | NIAGARA FALLS | NORTH BAY | OTTAWA | PORT AUX BASQUES | PRINCE ALBERT |
|---|---|---|---|---|---|---|---|---|---|---|---|---|---|---|---|---|---|---|---|---|---|---|---|---|---|---|
| BANFF | • | 782 | 80 | 3147 | 2702 | 3484 | 633 | 266 | 846 | 1094 | 2924 | 3725 | 2997 | 3225 | 2256 | 178 | 1037 | 216 | 2327 | 3047 | 2406 | 2299 | 2059 | 2288 | 3356 | 567 |
| BRANDON | 1259 | • | 702 | 2392 | 1920 | 2714 | 1082 | 715 | 451 | 1543 | 2142 | 2943 | 2215 | 2447 | 1474 | 944 | 255 | 622 | 1545 | 2292 | 1624 | 1517 | 1277 | 1506 | 2574 | 454 |
| CALGARY | 129 | 1130 | • | 3055 | 2622 | 3404 | 553 | 186 | 766 | 1011 | 2832 | 3633 | 2917 | 3133 | 2176 | 258 | 957 | 136 | 2247 | 2955 | 2326 | 2219 | 1979 | 2208 | 3264 | 487 |
| CHARLOTTETOWN | 5065 | 3850 | 4917 | • | 552 | 368 | 3442 | 3075 | 2787 | 3903 | 223 | 597 | 516 | 144 | 1143 | 3304 | 2105 | 3014 | 1184 | 100 | 736 | 1147 | 1083 | 854 | 228 | 2814 |
| CHICOUTIMI | 4348 | 3090 | 4220 | 888 | • | 901 | 3002 | 2635 | 2347 | 3463 | 329 | 1130 | 402 | 544 | 673 | 2864 | 1665 | 2542 | 744 | 452 | 296 | 716 | 643 | 414 | 761 | 2374 |
| CORNER BROOK | 5607 | 4368 | 5478 | 592 | 1450 | • | 3791 | 3424 | 3136 | 4252 | 572 | 229 | 865 | 402 | 1462 | 3653 | 2454 | 3336 | 1534 | 449 | 1085 | 1500 | 1432 | 1203 | 140 | 3163 |
| DAWSON CREEK | 1019 | 1741 | 890 | 5539 | 4831 | 6101 | • | 367 | 1020 | 640 | 3224 | 4020 | 3297 | 3525 | 2556 | 467 | 1337 | 689 | 2627 | 3342 | 2706 | 2599 | 2359 | 2588 | 3651 | 741 |
| EDMONTON | 428 | 1151 | 299 | 4949 | 4241 | 5510 | 591 | • | 653 | 828 | 2857 | 3653 | 2930 | 3158 | 2189 | 299 | 970 | 322 | 2260 | 2975 | 2339 | 2232 | 1992 | 2221 | 3284 | 374 |
| FLIN FLON | 1362 | 668 | 1233 | 4485 | 3777 | 5047 | 1642 | 1051 | • | 1481 | 2569 | 3365 | 2642 | 2870 | 1901 | 882 | 682 | 862 | 1972 | 2687 | 2051 | 1944 | 1704 | 1933 | 2996 | 279 |
| FORT SMITH | 1761 | 2483 | 1627 | 6281 | 5573 | 6843 | 1030 | 1333 | 2383 | • | 3685 | 4480 | 3758 | 3986 | 3017 | 995 | 1798 | 1150 | 3083 | 3803 | 3167 | 3055 | 2820 | 3049 | 4112 | 1202 |
| FREDERICTON | 4706 | 3447 | 4558 | 359 | 529 | 921 | 5189 | 4598 | 4134 | 5930 | • | 801 | 435 | 215 | 895 | 3086 | 1887 | 2764 | 966 | 123 | 518 | 938 | 865 | 636 | 432 | 2596 |
| GANDER | 5995 | 4736 | 5847 | 961 | 1819 | 369 | 6470 | 5879 | 5415 | 7210 | 1289 | • | 1094 | 631 | 1691 | 3882 | 2683 | 3560 | 1762 | 678 | 1314 | 1734 | 1661 | 1432 | 369 | 3392 |
| GASPÉ | 4823 | 3565 | 4694 | 830 | 647 | 1392 | 5306 | 4715 | 4252 | 6048 | 700 | 1761 | • | 587 | 968 | 3159 | 1960 | 2837 | 1039 | 416 | 591 | 1011 | 938 | 709 | 725 | 2669 |
| HALIFAX | 5190 | 3938 | 5042 | 232 | 875 | 647 | 5673 | 5082 | 4619 | 6415 | 346 | 1015 | 945 | • | 1196 | 3387 | 2188 | 3065 | 1267 | 171 | 819 | 1239 | 1166 | 937 | 262 | 2897 |
| HAMILTON | 3631 | 2372 | 3502 | 1839 | 1083 | 2353 | 4114 | 3523 | 3059 | 4855 | 1440 | 2721 | 1558 | 1925 | • | 2418 | 1219 | 2096 | 84 | 1013 | 377 | 43 | 250 | 290 | 1322 | 1928 |
| JASPER | 286 | 1519 | 415 | 5317 | 4609 | 5879 | 752 | 369 | 1419 | 1601 | 4966 | 6247 | 5084 | 5451 | 3891 | • | 1199 | 394 | 2489 | 3204 | 2568 | 2461 | 2221 | 2450 | 3513 | 603 |
| KENORA | 1669 | 410 | 1510 | 3388 | 2680 | 3949 | 2152 | 1561 | 1098 | 2894 | 3037 | 4318 | 3154 | 3521 | 1962 | 1930 | • | 877 | 1290 | 2005 | 1369 | 1262 | 1022 | 1251 | 2314 | 709 |
| LETHBRIDGE | 384 | 1001 | 219 | 4851 | 4091 | 5369 | 1109 | 518 | 1387 | 1851 | 4448 | 5729 | 4566 | 4933 | 3373 | 634 | 1411 | • | 2167 | 2882 | 2246 | 2139 | 1899 | 2128 | 3191 | 623 |
| LONDON | 3745 | 2486 | 3616 | 1905 | 1197 | 2469 | 4228 | 3637 | 3174 | 4962 | 1555 | 2836 | 1672 | 2039 | 135 | 4006 | 2076 | 3487 | • | 1084 | 448 | 126 | 321 | 361 | 1393 | 2009 |
| MONCTON | 4904 | 3689 | 4756 | 161 | 727 | 723 | 5378 | 4788 | 4324 | 6120 | 198 | 1091 | 669 | 275 | 1630 | 5156 | 3227 | 4638 | 1745 | • | 636 | 1056 | 983 | 754 | 309 | 2714 |
| MONTRÉAL | 3872 | 2614 | 3743 | 1184 | 476 | 1746 | 4355 | 3764 | 3301 | 5097 | 834 | 2115 | 951 | 1318 | 607 | 4133 | 2203 | 3615 | 721 | 1024 | • | 420 | 347 | 118 | 945 | 2078 |
| NIAGARA FALLS | 3700 | 2441 | 3571 | 1846 | 1152 | 2414 | 4183 | 3592 | 3129 | 4917 | 1510 | 2791 | 1627 | 1994 | 69 | 3961 | 2031 | 3442 | 203 | 1699 | 676 | • | 293 | 333 | 1365 | 1971 |
| NORTH BAY | 3314 | 2055 | 3185 | 1743 | 1035 | 2305 | 3796 | 3206 | 2742 | 4538 | 1392 | 2673 | 1510 | 1876 | 402 | 3574 | 1645 | 3056 | 517 | 1582 | 558 | 472 | • | 229 | 1292 | 1731 |
| OTTAWA | 3682 | 2424 | 3553 | 1374 | 666 | 1936 | 4165 | 3574 | 3111 | 4907 | 1024 | 2305 | 1141 | 1508 | 467 | 3943 | 2013 | 3425 | 581 | 1213 | 190 | 536 | 369 | • | 1063 | 1960 |
| PORT AUX BASQUES | 5401 | 4142 | 5253 | 367 | 1225 | 225 | 5876 | 5285 | 4822 | 6618 | 695 | 594 | 1167 | 422 | 2128 | 5654 | 3724 | 5135 | 2242 | 497 | 1521 | 2197 | 2079 | 1711 | • | 3023 |
| PRINCE ALBERT | 912 | 731 | 784 | 4529 | 3821 | 5090 | 1193 | 602 | 449 | 1934 | 4178 | 5459 | 4295 | 4662 | 3103 | 970 | 1141 | 1003 | 3233 | 4368 | 3344 | 3172 | 2786 | 3154 | 4865 | • |
| PRINCE GEORGE | 632 | 1865 | 761 | 5663 | 4955 | 6225 | 406 | 715 | 1765 | 1436 | 5312 | 6593 | 5430 | 5797 | 4237 | 346 | 2276 | 980 | 4352 | 5502 | 4479 | 4307 | 3920 | 4289 | 6000 | 1316 |
| PRINCE RUPERT | 1373 | 2606 | 1502 | 6404 | 5695 | 6965 | 1146 | 1455 | 2506 | 2176 | 6053 | 7334 | 6170 | 6537 | 4978 | 1086 | 3016 | 1720 | 5092 | 6243 | 5219 | 5047 | 4661 | 5029 | 6740 | 2057 |
| QUÉBEC | 4142 | 2884 | 4014 | 945 | 206 | 1506 | 4625 | 4035 | 3571 | 5367 | 586 | 1875 | 703 | 912 | 877 | 4403 | 2474 | 3885 | 991 | 784 | 270 | 946 | 829 | 460 | 1281 | 3615 |
| REGINA | 893 | 365 | 764 | 4163 | 3455 | 4725 | 1376 | 785 | 752 | 2118 | 3813 | 5094 | 3930 | 4297 | 2737 | 1154 | 776 | 636 | 2852 | 4002 | 2979 | 2807 | 2420 | 2789 | 4500 | 365 |
| RIVIÈRE-DU-LOUP | 4324 | 3066 | 4196 | 740 | 148 | 1302 | 4807 | 4216 | 3753 | 5549 | 381 | 1670 | 499 | 727 | 1059 | 4585 | 2655 | 4067 | 1173 | 579 | 452 | 1128 | 1011 | 642 | 1077 | 3796 |
| ROUYN | 3154 | 1896 | 3026 | 1828 | 1120 | 2390 | 3637 | 3046 | 2583 | 4379 | 1477 | 2758 | 1595 | 1962 | 694 | 3415 | 1485 | 2897 | 808 | 1667 | 644 | 763 | 291 | 552 | 2165 | 2626 |
| SAINT JOHN | 4812 | 3553 | 4664 | 309 | 616 | 871 | 5295 | 4704 | 4241 | 6037 | 106 | 1239 | 806 | 240 | 1547 | 5073 | 3143 | 4554 | 1661 | 148 | 940 | 1616 | 1498 | 1130 | 645 | 4284 |
| ST. JOHN'S | 6328 | 5073 | 6183 | 1294 | 2184 | 702 | 6803 | 6212 | 5749 | 7551 | 1622 | 333 | 2094 | 1349 | 3055 | 6581 | 4651 | 4453 | 3169 | 1424 | 2448 | 3124 | 3006 | 2638 | 927 | 5792 |
| SASKATOON | 748 | 623 | 620 | 4421 | 3713 | 4983 | 1118 | 528 | 613 | 1860 | 4070 | 5351 | 4188 | 4554 | 2995 | 896 | 1033 | 663 | 3109 | 4260 | 3236 | 3064 | 2678 | 3046 | 4757 | 164 |
| SAULT STE. MARIE | 2887 | 1629 | 2758 | 2169 | 1461 | 2731 | 3370 | 2779 | 2360 | 4112 | 1819 | 3100 | 1936 | 2303 | 744 | 3148 | 1218 | 2617 | 858 | 2008 | 985 | 813 | 426 | 795 | 2506 | 2359 |
| SEPT-ÎLES | 4796 | 3537 | 4667 | 855 | 620 | 1466 | 5279 | 4688 | 4225 | 6021 | 774 | 1835 | 481 | 1011 | 1530 | 5057 | 3127 | 4538 | 1645 | 744 | 924 | 1582 | 1482 | 1114 | 1241 | 4268 |
| SHERBROOKE | 4028 | 2770 | 3899 | 1136 | 420 | 1698 | 4511 | 3920 | 3457 | 5253 | 777 | 2066 | 895 | 1123 | 763 | 4289 | 2359 | 3771 | 877 | 975 | 156 | 832 | 715 | 346 | 1473 | 3500 |
| SUMMERSIDE | 5039 | 3780 | 4910 | 63 | 863 | 655 | 5514 | 4923 | 4459 | 6256 | 333 | 1024 | 805 | 303 | 1765 | 5292 | 3362 | 4773 | 1876 | 135 | 1159 | 1835 | 1717 | 1349 | 430 | 4503 |
| SYDNEY | 5401 | 4142 | 5253 | 367 | 1225 | 225 | 5876 | 5285 | 4822 | 6618 | 695 | 594 | 1167 | 422 | 2128 | 5654 | 3724 | 5135 | 2242 | 497 | 1521 | 2197 | 2079 | 1711 | 0 | 4865 |
| THE PAS | 1481 | 575 | 1352 | 4424 | 3664 | 4942 | 1630 | 1040 | 151 | 2372 | 4022 | 5311 | 4139 | 4506 | 2947 | 1408 | 985 | 1236 | 3061 | 4263 | 3188 | 3016 | 2630 | 2998 | 4717 | 438 |
| THUNDER BAY | 2179 | 921 | 2050 | 2878 | 2169 | 3439 | 2662 | 2071 | 1608 | 3404 | 2527 | 3808 | 2644 | 3011 | 1452 | 2440 | 510 | 1922 | 1566 | 2717 | 1693 | 1521 | 1135 | 1503 | 3214 | 1651 |
| TORONTO | 3563 | 2305 | 3434 | 1724 | 1015 | 2285 | 4046 | 3455 | 2992 | 4788 | 1373 | 2654 | 1490 | 1857 | 68 | 3824 | 1894 | 3306 | 182 | 1563 | 539 | 137 | 335 | 399 | 2060 | 3051 |
| VANCOUVER | 929 | 2187 | 1057 | 5985 | 5277 | 6547 | 1202 | 1244 | 2290 | 2232 | 5634 | 6915 | 5752 | 6119 | 4559 | 875 | 2597 | 1143 | 4674 | 5824 | 4801 | 4628 | 4242 | 4611 | 6322 | 1841 |
| VICTORIA | 995 | 2253 | 1123 | 6051 | 5343 | 6613 | 1268 | 1310 | 2356 | 2298 | 5700 | 6981 | 5818 | 6185 | 4625 | 941 | 2663 | 1209 | 4740 | 5890 | 4867 | 4694 | 4308 | 4677 | 6387 | 1907 |
| WHITEHORSE | 2514 | 3236 | 2385 | 7034 | 6326 | 7596 | 1495 | 2086 | 3137 | 2525 | 6684 | 7965 | 6801 | 7168 | 5609 | 2247 | 3647 | 2604 | 5710 | 6874 | 5850 | 5678 | 5279 | 5660 | 7371 | 2688 |
| WIINDSOR | 3954 | 2699 | 3825 | 2097 | 1381 | 2659 | 4395 | 3804 | 3357 | 5137 | 1738 | 3027 | 1856 | 2223 | 319 | 4241 | 2260 | 3697 | 203 | 1936 | 904 | 388 | 700 | 764 | 2433 | 3351 |
| WINNIPEG | 1465 | 206 | 1336 | 3592 | 2884 | 4154 | 1947 | 1357 | 893 | 2689 | 3241 | 4522 | 3359 | 3726 | 2166 | 1725 | 204 | 1207 | 2280 | 3431 | 2408 | 2235 | 1849 | 2218 | 3928 | 937 |
| YARMOUTH | 4917 | 3658 | 4768 | 414 | 740 | 911 | 5380 | 4809 | 4345 | 6141 | 211 | 1279 | 911 | 349 | 1651 | 5177 | 3248 | 4670 | 1765 | 253 | 1044 | 1720 | 1603 | 1234 | 686 | 4389 |
| YELLOWKNIFE | 1939 | 2662 | 1811 | 6460 | 5752 | 7022 | 1209 | 1511 | 2562 | 713 | 6109 | 7390 | 6227 | 6593 | 5034 | 1780 | 3072 | 2029 | 5148 | 6299 | 5275 | 5103 | 4717 | 5086 | 6796 | 2113 |

| | PRINCE GEORGE | PRINCE RUPERT | QUÉBEC | REGINA | RIVIÈRE-DU-LOUP | ROUYN | SAINT JOHN | ST. JOHN'S | SASKATOON | SAULT STE. MARIE | SEPT-ÎLES | SHERBROOKE | SUMMERSIDE | SYDNEY | THE PAS | THUNDER BAY | TORONTO | VANCOUVER | VICTORIA | WHITEHORSE | WINDSOR | WINNIPEG | YARMOUTH | YELLOWKNIFE |
|---|---|---|---|---|---|---|---|---|---|---|---|---|---|---|---|---|---|---|---|---|---|---|---|---|
| BANFF | 393 | 853 | 2574 | 555 | 2687 | 1960 | 2990 | 3932 | 465 | 1794 | 2980 | 2503 | 3131 | 3356 | 920 | 1354 | 2214 | 577 | 618 | 1562 | 2457 | 910 | 3055 | 1205 |
| BRANDON | 1159 | 1619 | 1792 | 227 | 1905 | 1178 | 2208 | 3152 | 387 | 1012 | 2198 | 1721 | 2349 | 2574 | 357 | 572 | 1432 | 1359 | 1400 | 2011 | 1677 | 128 | 2273 | 1654 |
| CALGARY | 473 | 933 | 2494 | 475 | 2607 | 1880 | 2898 | 3842 | 385 | 1714 | 2900 | 2423 | 3051 | 3264 | 840 | 1274 | 2134 | 657 | 698 | 1482 | 2377 | 830 | 2963 | 1125 |
| CHARLOTTETOWN | 3519 | 3979 | 587 | 2587 | 460 | 1136 | 192 | 804 | 2747 | 1348 | 531 | 706 | 39 | 228 | 2749 | 1788 | 1071 | 3719 | 3760 | 4371 | 1303 | 2232 | 257 | 4014 |
| CHICOUTIMI | 3079 | 3539 | 128 | 2147 | 92 | 696 | 383 | 1357 | 2307 | 908 | 385 | 261 | 536 | 761 | 2277 | 1348 | 631 | 3279 | 3320 | 3931 | 858 | 1792 | 460 | 3574 |
| CORNER BROOK | 3868 | 4328 | 936 | 2936 | 809 | 1485 | 541 | 436 | 3096 | 1697 | 911 | 1055 | 407 | 140 | 3071 | 2137 | 1420 | 4068 | 4109 | 4720 | 1652 | 2581 | 566 | 4363 |
| DAWSON CREEK | 252 | 712 | 2874 | 855 | 2987 | 2260 | 3290 | 4227 | 695 | 2094 | 3280 | 2803 | 3426 | 3651 | 1013 | 1654 | 2514 | 747 | 788 | 929 | 2731 | 1210 | 3343 | 751 |
| EDMONTON | 444 | 904 | 2507 | 488 | 2620 | 1893 | 2923 | 3860 | 328 | 1727 | 2913 | 2436 | 3059 | 3284 | 646 | 1287 | 2147 | 773 | 814 | 1296 | 2364 | 843 | 2988 | 939 |
| FLIN FLON | 1097 | 1557 | 2219 | 467 | 2332 | 1605 | 2635 | 3572 | 381 | 1439 | 2625 | 2148 | 2771 | 2996 | 94 | 999 | 1859 | 1423 | 1464 | 1949 | 2086 | 555 | 2700 | 1592 |
| FORT SMITH | 892 | 1352 | 3335 | 1316 | 3448 | 2721 | 3751 | 4692 | 1156 | 2555 | 3741 | 3264 | 3887 | 4112 | 1474 | 2115 | 2975 | 1387 | 1428 | 1569 | 3192 | 1671 | 3816 | 443 |
| FREDERICTON | 3301 | 3761 | 364 | 2369 | 237 | 918 | 66 | 1008 | 2529 | 1130 | 481 | 483 | 207 | 432 | 2499 | 1570 | 853 | 3501 | 3542 | 4153 | 1080 | 2014 | 131 | 3796 |
| GANDER | 4097 | 4557 | 1165 | 3165 | 1038 | 1714 | 770 | 207 | 3325 | 1926 | 1140 | 1284 | 636 | 369 | 3300 | 2366 | 1649 | 4297 | 4338 | 4949 | 1881 | 2810 | 795 | 4592 |
| GASPÉ | 3374 | 3834 | 437 | 2442 | 310 | 991 | 501 | 1301 | 2602 | 1203 | 299 | 556 | 500 | 725 | 2572 | 1643 | 926 | 3574 | 3615 | 4226 | 1153 | 2087 | 566 | 3869 |
| HALIFAX | 3602 | 4062 | 567 | 2670 | 452 | 1219 | 149 | 838 | 2830 | 1431 | 628 | 698 | 188 | 262 | 2800 | 1871 | 1154 | 3802 | 3843 | 4454 | 1381 | 2315 | 217 | 4097 |
| HAMILTON | 2633 | 3093 | 545 | 1701 | 658 | 431 | 961 | 1898 | 1861 | 462 | 951 | 474 | 1097 | 1322 | 1831 | 902 | 42 | 2833 | 2874 | 3485 | 198 | 1346 | 1026 | 3128 |
| JASPER | 215 | 675 | 2736 | 717 | 2849 | 2122 | 3152 | 4089 | 557 | 1956 | 3142 | 2665 | 3288 | 3513 | 875 | 1516 | 2376 | 544 | 585 | 1396 | 2635 | 1072 | 3217 | 1106 |
| KENORA | 1414 | 1874 | 1537 | 482 | 1650 | 923 | 1953 | 2890 | 642 | 757 | 1943 | 1466 | 2089 | 2314 | 612 | 317 | 1177 | 1614 | 1655 | 2266 | 1404 | 127 | 2018 | 1909 |
| LETHBRIDGE | 609 | 1069 | 2414 | 395 | 2527 | 1800 | 2830 | 2767 | 412 | 1626 | 2820 | 2343 | 2966 | 3191 | 768 | 1194 | 2054 | 710 | 751 | 1618 | 2297 | 750 | 2902 | 1261 |
| LONDON | 2704 | 3164 | 616 | 1772 | 729 | 502 | 1032 | 1969 | 1932 | 533 | 1022 | 545 | 1166 | 1393 | 1902 | 973 | 113 | 2904 | 2945 | 3548 | 126 | 1417 | 1097 | 3199 |
| MONCTON | 3419 | 3879 | 487 | 2487 | 360 | 1036 | 92 | 885 | 2647 | 1248 | 462 | 606 | 84 | 309 | 2649 | 1688 | 971 | 3619 | 3660 | 4271 | 1203 | 2132 | 157 | 3914 |
| MONTRÉAL | 2783 | 3243 | 168 | 1851 | 281 | 400 | 584 | 1521 | 2011 | 612 | 574 | 97 | 720 | 945 | 1981 | 1052 | 335 | 2983 | 3024 | 3635 | 562 | 1496 | 649 | 3278 |
| NIAGARA FALLS | 2676 | 3136 | 588 | 1744 | 701 | 474 | 1004 | 1941 | 1904 | 505 | 983 | 517 | 1140 | 1365 | 1874 | 945 | 85 | 2876 | 2917 | 3528 | 241 | 1389 | 1069 | 3171 |
| NORTH BAY | 2436 | 2896 | 515 | 1504 | 628 | 181 | 931 | 1868 | 1664 | 265 | 921 | 444 | 1067 | 1292 | 1634 | 705 | 208 | 2636 | 2677 | 3280 | 435 | 1149 | 996 | 2931 |
| OTTAWA | 2665 | 3125 | 286 | 1733 | 399 | 343 | 702 | 1639 | 1893 | 494 | 692 | 215 | 838 | 1063 | 1863 | 934 | 248 | 2865 | 2906 | 3517 | 475 | 1378 | 767 | 3160 |
| PORT AUX BASQUES | 3728 | 4188 | 796 | 2796 | 669 | 1345 | 401 | 576 | 2956 | 1557 | 771 | 915 | 267 | 0 | 2931 | 1997 | 1280 | 3928 | 3969 | 4580 | 1512 | 2441 | 426 | 4223 |
| PRINCE ALBERT | 818 | 1278 | 2246 | 227 | 2359 | 1632 | 2662 | 3599 | 102 | 1466 | 2652 | 2175 | 2798 | 3023 | 272 | 1026 | 1896 | 1144 | 1185 | 1670 | 2082 | 582 | 2727 | 1313 |
| PRINCE GEORGE | • | 460 | 2951 | 932 | 3064 | 2337 | 3367 | 4304 | 772 | 2163 | 3357 | 2880 | 3503 | 3728 | 1090 | 1731 | 2591 | 495 | 536 | 1181 | 2850 | 1287 | 3432 | 1003 |
| PRINCE RUPERT | 740 | • | 3411 | 1392 | 3524 | 2797 | 3827 | 4764 | 1232 | 2623 | 3817 | 3340 | 3963 | 4188 | 1550 | 2191 | 3051 | 955 | 996 | 1641 | 3310 | 1747 | 3892 | 1463 |
| QUÉBEC | 4749 | 5489 | • | 2019 | 127 | 568 | 418 | 1372 | 2179 | 780 | 406 | 133 | 571 | 796 | 2149 | 1220 | 503 | 3151 | 3192 | 3803 | 730 | 1664 | 495 | 3446 |
| REGINA | 1500 | 2240 | 3249 | • | 2132 | 1405 | 2435 | 3372 | 160 | 1231 | 2425 | 1948 | 2571 | 2796 | 373 | 799 | 1659 | 1132 | 1173 | 1784 | 1902 | 355 | 2507 | 1427 |
| RIVIÈRE-DU-LOUP | 4931 | 5671 | 204 | 3431 | • | 681 | 303 | 1245 | 2292 | 893 | 231 | 246 | 444 | 669 | 2262 | 1333 | 616 | 3264 | 3305 | 3916 | 843 | 1777 | 368 | 3559 |
| ROUYN | 3761 | 4501 | 914 | 2261 | 1096 | • | 984 | 1921 | 1565 | 446 | 974 | 497 | 1120 | 1345 | 1535 | 606 | 389 | 2537 | 2578 | 3189 | 616 | 1050 | 1049 | 2832 |
| SAINT JOHN | 5419 | 6159 | 673 | 3919 | 488 | 1584 | • | 977 | 2595 | 1196 | 547 | 537 | 176 | 401 | 2565 | 1636 | 919 | 3567 | 3608 | 4219 | 1146 | 2080 | 65 | 3862 |
| ST. JOHN'S | 6927 | 7667 | 2208 | 5427 | 2004 | 3092 | 1572 | • | 3532 | 2133 | 1347 | 1491 | 843 | 576 | 3507 | 2573 | 1856 | 4504 | 4545 | 5156 | 2088 | 3017 | 1012 | 4799 |
| SASKATOON | 1242 | 1983 | 3507 | 257 | 3689 | 2519 | 4176 | 5684 | • | 1391 | 2585 | 2108 | 2731 | 2956 | 346 | 959 | 1819 | 1042 | 1083 | 1624 | 2036 | 515 | 2660 | 1267 |
| SAULT STE. MARIE | 3481 | 4221 | 1255 | 1981 | 1437 | 718 | 1925 | 3422 | 2239 | • | 1186 | 709 | 1332 | 1557 | 1369 | 440 | 420 | 2363 | 2404 | 3015 | 647 | 884 | 1261 | 2666 |
| SEPT-ÎLES | 5403 | 6143 | 653 | 3903 | 372 | 1568 | 880 | 2168 | 4160 | 1909 | • | 539 | 515 | 771 | 2555 | 1626 | 909 | 3557 | 3598 | 4209 | 1136 | 2070 | 612 | 3852 |
| SHERBROOKE | 4635 | 5375 | 214 | 3135 | 396 | 800 | 864 | 2400 | 3392 | 1141 | 867 | • | 690 | 915 | 2078 | 1149 | 432 | 3080 | 3121 | 3732 | 659 | 1593 | 614 | 3375 |
| SUMMERSIDE | 5638 | 6378 | 919 | 4138 | 715 | 1802 | 283 | 1357 | 4395 | 2144 | 829 | 1110 | • | 267 | 2706 | 1772 | 1053 | 3703 | 3744 | 4355 | 1287 | 2216 | 241 | 3998 |
| SYDNEY | 6000 | 6740 | 1281 | 4500 | 1077 | 2165 | 645 | 927 | 4757 | 2506 | 1241 | 1473 | 430 | • | 2931 | 1997 | 1280 | 3928 | 3969 | 4580 | 1512 | 2441 | 426 | 4223 |
| THE PAS | 1754 | 2494 | 3458 | 600 | 3640 | 2470 | 4128 | 5644 | 557 | 2203 | 4112 | 3344 | 4355 | 4717 | • | 929 | 1789 | 1388 | 1429 | 1942 | 2008 | 485 | 2630 | 1585 |
| THUNDER BAY | 2786 | 3526 | 1963 | 1286 | 2145 | 975 | 2633 | 4141 | 1543 | 708 | 2617 | 1849 | 2852 | 3214 | 1495 | • | 860 | 1931 | 1972 | 2583 | 1087 | 444 | 741 | 2226 |
| TORONTO | 4170 | 4910 | 810 | 2670 | 991 | 626 | 1479 | 2987 | 2927 | 676 | 1463 | 695 | 1695 | 2060 | 2879 | 1384 | • | 2791 | 2832 | 3435 | 227 | 1304 | 984 | 3086 |
| VANCOUVER | 797 | 1537 | 5071 | 1822 | 5253 | 4083 | 5741 | 7248 | 1677 | 3803 | 5724 | 4957 | 5959 | 6322 | 2234 | 3108 | 4492 | • | 41 | 1676 | 3034 | 1487 | 3632 | 1498 |
| VICTORIA | 863 | 1603 | 5137 | 1818 | 5319 | 4149 | 5807 | 7314 | 1743 | 3869 | 5790 | 5023 | 6025 | 6387 | 2300 | 3174 | 4558 | 66 | • | 1717 | 3053 | 1528 | 3673 | 1539 |
| WHITEHORSE | 1901 | 2641 | 6120 | 2871 | 6302 | 5132 | 6790 | 8298 | 2614 | 4852 | 6774 | 6006 | 7009 | 7371 | 3125 | 4157 | 5528 | 2697 | 2763 | • | 3660 | 2190 | 4284 | 1680 |
| WIINDSOR | 4587 | 5327 | 1175 | 3061 | 1357 | 991 | 1844 | 3360 | 3277 | 1041 | 1828 | 1061 | 2071 | 2433 | 3232 | 1749 | 365 | 4883 | 4913 | 5890 | • | 1547 | 1211 | 3303 |
| WINNIPEG | 2071 | 2812 | 2678 | 571 | 2860 | 1690 | 3347 | 4855 | 829 | 1423 | 3331 | 2564 | 3566 | 3928 | 781 | 715 | 2099 | 2393 | 2459 | 3524 | 2490 | • | 2145 | 1782 |
| YARMOUTH | 5523 | 6264 | 797 | 4035 | 592 | 1688 | 105 | 1629 | 4281 | 2029 | 985 | 988 | 388 | 686 | 4233 | 1193 | 1584 | 5845 | 5911 | 6894 | 1949 | 3452 | • | 3927 |
| YELLOWKNIFE | 1614 | 2354 | 5546 | 2297 | 5728 | 4558 | 6215 | 7723 | 2039 | 4291 | 6199 | 5432 | 6418 | 6796 | 2551 | 3582 | 4966 | 2411 | 2477 | 2704 | 5316 | 2868 | 6320 | • |

**Source: National Atlas Service, Natural Resources Canada**

## AIRLINE COMPANIES

Aer Lingus
538 Braodhollow Rd., Melville NY USA 11747
Toll Free: 1-800-223-6537

Aeroflot, Russian International Airlines
615, boul de Maisonneuve ouest, Montréal QC H3A 1L8
514/288-2125; Fax: 514/288-5973; Telex: 05-25821
General Manager, G. Matveyev

Aerolineas Argentinas
#802, 1235 Bay St., Toronto ON M5R 3K4
416/967-6043; Toll Free: 1-800-688-0008

Air Canada
Air Canada Centre, PO Box 14000, Stn St-Laurent, Montréal QC H4Y 1H4
514/422-5000; Fax: 514/422-5909
URL: http://www.aircanada.ca
President & CEO, R. Lamar Durrett

Air Charter Systems
780, boul Magenta, Farnham QC J2N 1B8
514/293-3656; Fax: 514/293-5169; Toll Free: 1-888-293-3317
President, Edward C.C. Peagram

Air Club International
#205, 11905, route Cargo A-3, Mirabel QC J7N 1H1
514/476-3555; Fax: 514/476-9818
Vice-President, Flight Operations, Jean Côté

Air France
#1510, 2000, rue Mansfield, Montréal QC H3A 3A3
514/847-1106; Fax: 514/285-8994; Telex: 05-25304
General Manager for Canada, Michel J. Guiral, 514/285-5010

Air India
#908, 390 Bay St., Toronto ON M5H 2Y2
416/865-1030; Fax: 416/865-0716

Air Liberté
1125, boul de Maisonneuve ouest, Montréal QC H3A 3B6
514/985-2586; Fax: 514/985-2588

Air Transat
11600, rue Cargo A-1, Mirabel QC J7N 1G9
514/476-1011; Fax: 514/476-0338
Email: slandry@airtransat.com
Vice-President, Operations, Capt. Pierre Ménard

Alitalia
2055, rue Peel, Montréal QC H3A 1V8
514/842-8241; Fax: 514/842-5651
General Manager for Canada, Vincenzo Ursino

American Airlines Inc.
Lester B. Pearson Airport, PO Box 6005, Stn Toronto AMF, Mississauga ON L5P 1B6
905/612-7266; Fax: 905/612-0144
URL: http://www.amrcorp.com
General Manager, Toronto, A.W. Pliszka

Austrian Airlines
17-20, White Stone Expressway, White Stone NY USA 11357
Toll Free: 1-800-843-0002

Avianca
(Aerovias Nacionales de Colombia)
#1102, 1 St. Clair Ave. West, Toronto ON M4V 1K6
416/969-8817; Fax: 416/969-9926

British Airways
#100, 4120 Yonge St., North York ON M2P 2B8
416/250-0250; Fax: 416/250-1921
Vice-President/General Manager, Malcolm Freeman

BWIA International Airways
#401, 40 Holly St., Toronto ON M4S 3C3
416/440-0112; Fax: 416/440-1899
Regional Manager, Sales & Service (Canada), Thomas Luck

Canada 3000 Airlines Limited
27 Fasken Dr., Toronto ON M9W 1K6
416/674-0257; Fax: 416/674-0256

Canadian Airlines International Ltd./Lignes Aériennes Canadien International ltée
#2800, 700 - 2 St. SW, Calgary AB T2P 2W2
403/294-2000; Fax: 403/294-2066
URL: http://www.cdnair.ca
Chairman, Harry R. Steeles

Canadian Regional Airlines
Calgary International Airport, Hangar 101, Code CP, 8050 - 22 St. NE, Calgary AB T2E 7H6
403/974-2300; Fax: 403/974-7760
URL: http://www.cdnair.ca
President, Mary B. Jordan

Condor Flugdienst
PO Box 66178, Chicago IL USA 60666
312/686-8440

Continental Airlines
2929 Allan Pkwy., PO Box 4607, Houston TX USA 77210-4607
Toll Free: 1-800-231-0856

Cubana
#405, 4, Place Ville-Marie, Montréal QC H3B 2E7
514/871-1222; Fax: 514/871-1227

Czech Airlines
#1510, 401 Bay St., Toronto ON M5H 2Y4
416/363-3174; Fax: 416/363-0239; Toll Free: 1-800-641-0641
Email: czechAir@aol.com; URL: http://www.baxter.net/csa
Regional Director, Antonin Jakubse
Montréal Office: #2210, 2020, rue Université, Montréal QC H3A 2A5
514/844-4200; Fax: 514/844-5742; Toll Free: 1-800-561-5171
Email: czech airlines montreal@msn.com

El Al Israel Airlines
555, boul René-Lévesque ouest, Montréal QC H2Z 1B1
514/875-8910; Fax: 514/393-9170

Finnair
#402, 20 York Mills Rd., North York ON M2P 2C2
416/222-0740; Fax: 416/222-5004; Telex: 065-23360
Manager, Canadian Division, Jyrki Eriksson

Iberia
1235 Bay St., 8th Fl., Toronto ON M5R 3K4
416/964-6645; Fax: 416/964-7684

Icelandair
#410, 5950 Symphony Woods Rd., Columbia MD USA 21044
410/715-1600; Fax: 410/715-3547; Toll Free: 1-800-223-5500
URL: http://www.centrum.is/icelandair
Director, The Americas, Gunnar Eklund

Japan Airlines
#2110, 130 Adelaide St. West, Toronto ON M5H 3P5
416/364-7229; Fax: 416/364-6107; Toll Free: 1-800-525-3663
District Passenger Sales Manager, Tatsuo Kameda

KLM Royal Dutch Airlines
#2501, 777 Bay St., Toronto ON M5G 2C8
416/204-5151; Fax: 416/204-5167; Toll Free: 1-800-387-5600
Director, Passenger Sales, Chris Rivers

Korean Air
55 University Ave., Toronto ON M5J 2H7
416/862-8381; Fax: 416/862-2105

Lufthansa German Airlines
26 Wellington St. East, Toronto ON M5E 1S2
416/360-3600; Fax: 416/360-3605

Northern Thunderbird Air Inc.
(NT Air)
4245 Hangar Rd., Prince George BC V2N 4M6
250/963-9611; Fax: 250/963-8422; Toll Free: 1-800-963-9611
President/Manager, Vernon Martin

Northwest Airlines
5101 Northwest Dr., St. Paul MN USA 55111-3034
612/726-2111; Toll Free: 1-800-225-2525
URL: http://www.nwa.com

Olympic Airways
#503, 80 Bloor St. West, Toronto ON M5S 2V1
416/964-7137; Fax: 416/920-3686

PIA Pakistan International Airlines
#437, 131 Bloor St. West, Toronto ON M5S 1R1
416/926-8747; Fax: 416/926-0507

Qantas Airways
#1705, 1111 West Georgia St., Vancouver BC V6E 4M3
604/684-1055; Fax: 604/684-8617; Toll Free: 1-800-227-4500
Manager, Canada, William Duplak

Royal Aviation Inc.
#503, 6700, Côte de Liesse, Montréal QC H4T 1E3
514/739-7000; Fax: 514/739-7993
Vice-President, Operations & Maintenance, Maurice Dahan

Royal Jordanian
45 St. Clair Ave. West, Toronto ON M4V 1K9
416/962-3955; Fax: 416/960-9162

Skyservice
5501 Electra Rd., PO Box 160, Toronto AMF ON L5P 1B1
905/677-3300; Fax: 905/678-5654
Email: keith_levia@skysrvs.com
Director, Flight Operations, Capt. Arnie MacLeish

Swissair
#502, 2 Bloor St. West, Toronto ON M4W 3E2
416/960-4290; Fax: 416/960-4295

Trans North Air
Airport Hangar C, Whitehorse Airport, 917 Alaska Hwy., Whitehorse YT Y1A 3E4
867/668-2177; Fax: 867/668-3420
President, R.F. Connelly

United Airlines
#310, 180 Bloor St. West, Toronto ON M5S 2V6
416/923-2740; Fax: 416/923-4853
District Sales Manager, Patrick K. Dunne

US Air
#100, 4120 Yonge St., Toronto ON M2P 2B8
Toll Free: 1-800-428-4322
Canadian Sales Manager, Carle Chadillon

Varig
(Viacao Aerea Rio-Grandense)
#1108, 77 Bloor St. West, Toronto ON M5S 1M2
416/926-9511; Toll Free: 1-800-468-2744

Viasa
(Venezolana Int'l de Aviacion)
#802, 1235 Bay St., Toronto ON M5R 3K2
Toll Free: 1-800-468-4272

## RAILWAY COMPANIES

Algoma Central Railway Inc.
PO Box 9500, Sault Ste Marie ON P6A 6Y1
705/541-2905; Fax: 705/541-2909
URL: http://www.mcs.net/~dsdawdy/Canpass/acr/soo_her.html
Executive Representative, W.J. McComb
Rail service, Sault Ste. Marie to Hearst, Ont.

Amtrak (National Railroad Passenger Corporation)
Wilmington Station, 3rd Fl., 100 South French St., Wilmington DE USA 19801
302/661-6601; Fax: 302/661-6610
Email: amtsord@erols.com
General Manager, Operations, Standards & Compliance, C.W. Autro

BC Rail Ltd.
PO Box 8770, Vancouver BC V6B 4X6
604/986-2012; Fax: 604/984-5265
URL: http://www.bcrail.com/bcr/index.htm
President/CEO, Paul J. McElligott
Full & intermodal service with CP & CN connections

1,388 miles of track operated; 107 locomotives; 10,361 freight cars

Burlington Northern (Manitoba) Ltd.
963 Lindsay St., Winnipeg MB R3N 1X6
204/453-4415; Fax: 204/477-0046
President, J.R. Galassi

Burlington Northern Railroad
400 Brunette Ave., New Westminster BC V3L 3E8
604/520-5200; Fax: 604/520-5206
Chair/CEO, Gerald Grinstein
25,000 miles (181 miles in Canada); 58,343 railcars; 2,505 power

Canada & Gulf Terminal Railway Company/Le Chemin de fer de Matane et du Golfe
206, rue Hébert, CP 578, Mont-Joli QC G5H 3L3
418/775-4373; Fax: 418/775-8661
General Director, Pierre Chalifour
30 miles; 1 locomotive

Canadian National Railway Company/La Compagnie des chemins de fer nationaux du Canada
PO Box 8100, Stn A, Montréal QC H3C 3N4
514/399-4937; Fax: 514/399-6910
URL: http://www.cn.ca
Chair, David G.A. McLean
27,278 route km of track (includes Grand Trunk Corp., CN's rail network in US); 1,892 diesel locomotives; 62,703 freight cars

Cape Breton & Central Nova Scotia Railway
PO Box 4444, Port Hawkesbury NS B0E 2V0
902/625-5715; Fax: 902/625-5722
General Manager, M.H. Westerfield

Cartier Railway Company/Chemin de Fer Cartier (QCM Railway)
Rte. 138, Port Cartier QC G5B 2H3
514/285-2064; Fax: 514/285-1978
President/CEO, Guy Dufresne
416 km; 32 locomotives; 1,365 cars

Central Western Railway
Webber Centre, #1420, 5555 Calgary Trail South, Edmonton AB T6H 5P9
403/448-5855; Fax: 403/439-5658
President/COO, T. Payne

Consolidated Rail Corporation (ConRail)
#14A, 2001 Market St., PO Box 41414, Philadelphia PA USA 19101-1414
215/209-5583; Fax: 215/209-5582
Chairman/President/CEO, James A. Hagen
66 route miles in Québec, from New York-Québec border to Montréal. Includes owned lines, leased lines & trackage rights. Total route miles US & Canada, 13,068

CP Rail System (Canadian Pacific Railway)
CP 6042, Succ A, Montréal QC H3C 3E4
514/395-6850; Fax: 514/395-7165
Senior Vice-President, J.A. Linn

CSX Transportation Inc.
12780 Levan Rd., Livonia MI USA 48150
313/464-4948; Fax: 313/464-4893
Chairman, R.J. Kirk
166 miles in Canada

Devco Railway (Cape Breton Development Corporation)
PO Box 2500, Sydney NS B1P 6K9
902/564-7613; Fax: 902/564-7608
General Manager, Transportation & Processing, Al McNeil
88 miles; 10 locomotives; 550 cars

Esquimalt & Nanaimo Railway
#800, 200 Granville St., Vancouver BC V6C 2R3
604/643-3250; Fax: 604/643-3274
Express Co.-Canadian Pacific
195 miles (equipment included with CP Rail)

Essex Terminal Railwy Co.
1601 Lincoln Rd., PO Box 24025, Windsor ON N8Y 4Y9
519/973-8222; Fax: 519/973-7234
President, B.G. McKeown
Freight only; 24 miles of main track (CN CP CSX NS connect); 5 locomotives; 5 cars

GO Transit
#600, 20 Bay St., Toronto ON M5J 2W3
416/869-3600, ext.504; Fax: 416/869-3525
URL: http://www.mcs.net/~dsdawdy/Canpass/go/go_top.html
Executive Director, Operations, J.A. Brown

Goderich-Exeter Railway Company Ltd.
1 Maitland Rd., Goderich ON N7A 2W9
519/524-4024; Fax: 519/524-4026
General Manager, A.E. Parker

Greater Winnipeg Water District Railway
598 Plinguet St., Winnipeg MB R2J 2W7
204/986-4118; Fax: 204/237-6207
Railway Supervisor, D.E. Carr
Express Co.-None
92 miles; 3 locomotives; 150 cars

New Brunswick Southern Railway Company Limited
11 Gifford Rd., PO Box 5666, Saint John NB E2L 5B6
506/635-2200; Fax: 506/635-2239
Manager, S. Smith

Norfolk Southern Corporation
185 Spring St. SW, Atlanta GA USA 30303
404/529-1824; Fax: 404/529-1948
General Manager, L.D. Hale Jr.
Operating Subsidiaries: Norfolk Southern Railway Co., North American Van Lines
Track miles 14,842 (245 miles in Canada); 2, 140 locomotives; 12,051 road haul equipment

Ontario Northland Transportation Commission
555 Oak St. East, North Bay ON P1B 8L3
705/472-4500; Fax: 705/476-5598
URL: http://www.mcs.net/~dsdawdy/Canpass/onr/onr.html
Chairman, M. Rukavina
(Owned by Province of Ontario)
700 miles; 26 locomotives; 700 cars

Québec North Shore & Labrador Railway Company/Chemin de fer QNS&L
CP 1000, Sept-Îles QC G4R 4L5
418/968-7495; Fax: 418/968-7498
URL: http://www.mcs.net/~dsdawdy/Canpass/qnsl/qnsl.html
General Manager, M. Duclos

Roberval & Saguenay Railway Company/Compagnie du Chemin de Fer Roberval-Saguenay
CP 1277, Jonquiere QC G7S 4K8
418/699-2433; Fax: 418/699-2069
Superintendent, Railway Services, G. Grenon
Express Co.-None (Canadian National Railway connects)
54 miles; 10 locomotives; 189 cars

Southern Railway of British Columbia Limited
2102 River Dr., New Westminster BC V3M 6S3
604/521-1966; Fax: 604/526-0914
President, R. Stoeckly
(freight only)
75 miles; 19 locomotives; 475 cars

Via Rail Canada Inc.
CP 8116, Succ A, Montréal QC H3C 3N3
514/871-6190; Fax: 514/871-6641
URL: http://www.mcs.net/~dsdawdy/Canpass/via/via.html
Chair, Marc Lefrançois
(passenger services only)

Wabush Mines
CP 878, Sept-Îles QC G4R 4L4
418/964-3000; Fax: 418/962-9876
General Manager, D. Lebel
Wabush Mines represents both the Arnaud Railway Company & the Wabush Lake Railway

White Pass & Yukon Route
PO Box 435, Skagway AK USA 98840
907/983-2214; Fax: 907/983-2658
Email: ngauge73@aol.com; URL: http://whitepassrailroad.com
President, Thomas H. King
Express Co.-None
110 miles; 13 locomotives; 45 cars

Wisconsin Central Ltd.
One O'Hare Center, 6250 North River Rd., Rosemont IL USA 60018
708/318-4601; Fax: 708/318-4628
Chair, President & CEO, Edward A. Burkhardt

# MEETING, CONFERENCE, EXHIBIT & EVENT PLANNERS

## ALBERTA

### CALGARY

The Calgary Woman's Show Ltd., #202, 8 Parkdale Cres. NW, Calgary AB T2N 3T8 – 403/270-7274; Fax: 403/270-3037; URL: http://www.intervisual.com/cwc – President, Judy Markle

Canadian National Sportsmen's Shows, #340, 1032 - 17 Ave. SW, Calgary AB T2T 0A5 – 403/245-9008; Fax: 403/245-5100 – Paul Husband

Creative Outlet Ltd., 408 Arlington Dr. SE, Calgary AB T2H 1S3 – 403/255-5511; Fax: 403/255-5512; Email: creative@cadvision.com – President, Jeff Eichler

Details - Convention & Event Management Inc., #320, 1000 Centre St. North, Calgary AB T2E 7W6 – 403/277-7377; Fax: 403/277-1399 – Contact, Jean Silzer, C.M.P.

First Nations Conferences Inc., PO Box 1240, Stn M, Calgary AB T2P 2L2 – 403/261-3022; Fax: 403/261-5676; Email: aboriginalcongress@discoveryweb.com; URL: http://www.aboriginalnet.com/congress – President, Edmund A. Oliverio

Industrial Trade & Consumer Shows Inc., #2450, 101 - 6th Ave SW, Calgary AB T2P 3P4 – 403/266-8700; Fax: 403/266-6814 – Contact, Steve Henrich

Panex Show Services, 120 - 9 Ave. SE, Calgary AB T2G 0P3 – 403/261-8551, 8552; Fax: 403/261-8554 – Western Canada Manager, Terry Symington

Southex Exhibitions Inc., #300, 999 - 8 St. SW, Calgary AB T2R 1N7 – 403/244-6111; Fax: 403/245-8666; Toll Free: 1-800-387-2446; Email: info@petroleumshow.com; URL: http://www.southex.com – Pat Atkinson

Trade Show Managers Inc., 5512, 4 St. NW, PO Box 64024, Calgary AB T2K 6J0 – 403/274-8858; Fax: 403/274-9388; Email: slmorrow@aca.ucalgary.ca – Contact, Sandra Morrow

### EDMONTON

Cameo Convention Consultants Ltd., 7418 - 182 St., Edmonton AB T5T 2G7 – 403/481-6268; Fax: 403/243-0666 – President, Mamie Bercov

The Cana Globe Group Inc., 15016 - 77 Ave., Edmonton AB T5R 3B3 – 403/487-8102; Fax: 403/487-2417; Email: meetings@canaglobe.com; URL: http://www.canaglobe.com – President, Christine McLaren

Conference Services, Dept. of Housing and Food Services, 44 Lister Hall, Edmonton AB T6G 2H6 – 403/492-4281; Fax: 403/492-7032; Toll Free: 1-800-615-4807; Email: conference.services@ualberta.ca; URL: http://www.hfs.ualberta.ca – Conference Services Coordinator, Michelle Hoyle

Dominion Trade Show Management Inc., 4614 - 97 St., Edmonton AB T6E 4M7 – 403/436-8000; Fax: 403/436-8009 – Marketing Representative, Cathy Chaney

Edmonton Convention Planners, 18828 - 80 Ave., Edmonton AB T5T 5B4 – 403/486-4589; Fax: 403/486-4589 – Principal & General Manager, Lois Zapf

The Event Coordinators, 10977 - 141 St., Edmonton AB T5M 1T5 – 403/453-6962; Fax: 403/455-9029 – President, John Hohol

Harold Smith Travel, #205, 10104 - 103 Ave., Edmonton AB T5J 0H8 – 403/429-3420; Fax: 403/424-7144; Toll Free: 1-800-661-6975 – Contact, Harold Smith

#### LETHBRIDGE

University of Lethbridge, Conference Services, 4401 University Dr., Lethbridge AB T1K 3M4 – 403/329-2244; Fax: 403/329-5166; Email: confserv@gw.uleth.ca; URL: http://home.uleth.ca – Conference Associate, Robin Gardner

#### SAINT ALBERT

The Great Alberta Hospitality Company Ltd., 22 Estate Cr., St. Albert AB T8N 5X2 – 403/460-7207; Fax: 403/460-4699 – General Manager, Jill Douglas

## BRITISH COLUMBIA

#### BURNABY

Canadian National Sportsmen's Shows (1989) Ltd., #501, 4190 Lougheed Hwy., Burnaby BC V5C 6A8 – 604/294-1313; Fax: 604/294-4740 – Show Manager, Jim Carslake

Southex Exhibitions, 4285 Canada Way, Burnaby BC V5G 1H2 – 604/433-5121; Fax: 604/434-6853; Toll Free: 1-800-633-8332; URL: http://www.southex.com – Vice-President, Western Region, Fred Barnes

#### COQUITLAM

Classic Consulting International Inc., #201, 931 Brunette Ave., Coquitlam BC V3K 6T5 – 604/527-1045; Fax: 604/527-1046 – Managing Director, Dawn Williams

#### KAMLOOPS

Classic Moment Creative Events, 1255 Delta Ave., Kamloops BC V2B 3Y4 – 250/376-7934; Fax: 250/376-7927 – Event Producer/Owner, Judy Basso

Showest Management Inc., PO Box 300, Kamloops BC V2C 5K6 – 250/851-2145; Fax: 250/851-0551 – President, Gerry K. Hartley

#### RICHMOND

Levy Show Service Ltd., 11160 Silversmith Place, Richmond BC V7A 5E4 – 604/277-1726; Fax: 604/277-1736 – General Manager, Henry Levy

#### VANCOUVER

Cantrav West Services Ltd., #300, 238 - 2nd Ave. East, Vancouver BC V5T 1B7 – 604/879-0950; Fax: 604/879-0949; Email: cantrav@cantrav.com; URL: http://www.cantrav.com – Contact, Janice Cann

Congress Canada, 827 West Pender St., Vancouver BC V6C 3G8 – 604/682-2199; Fax: 604/689-5284 – President, Pam Graham

Contacts Pacific Services Inc., #280, 1090 West Georgia St., Vancouver BC V6E 3V7 – 604/683-2174; Fax: 604/688-6972; Toll Free: 1-800-661-4646 – Contact, George Bartel

Events by Design Inc., #601, 325 Howe St., Vancouver BC V6C 1Z7 – 604/669-7175; Fax: 604/669-7083 – Director/Partner, Janna Shillington

The Famous Events Group, #504, 68 Water St., Vancouver BC V6B 1A4 – 604/689-3448, 649-6944; Fax: 604/689-5245 – President, Richard Lowy

International Conference Services, #604, 850 West Hastings St., Vancouver BC V6C 1E1 – 604/681-2153; Fax: 604/681-1049; Email: 74161.347@compuserve.com; URL: http://www.meet.ics.com – President, Franziska Kaltenegger

Music West Festival, #306, 21 Water St., Vancouver BC V6B 1A1 – 604/684-9338; Fax: 604/684-9337; Email: info@musicwest.com; URL: http://www.musicwest.com – President, Maureen Jack

Passport Planners, #308, 1345 Comox St., Vancouver BC V6E 4E4 – 604/687-3277; Fax: 604/687-2123 – President, George Brakey

Square Feet Northwest Event Management Inc., 1030 Mainland St., Vancouver BC V6B 2T4 – 604/683-4393; Fax: 604/688-0270; Email: mgmt@sqftevent.com – Blaine Woit

Venue West Conference Services Ltd., #645, 375 Water St., Vancouver BC V6B 5C6 – 604/681-5226; Fax: 604/681-2503; Email: congress@venuewest.com; URL: http://www.venuwest.com – B. Lou Cox

Westcoast Agenda, #708, 1755 Robson St., Vancouver BC V6G 3B7 – 604/688-8584; Fax: 604/669-9611 – Meeting Planner, Donna Reid

#### VICTORIA

Conference Management, Division of Continuing Studies, University of Victoria, PO Box 3030, Victoria BC V8W 3N6 – 250/721-8465; Fax: 250/721-8774; Email: morourke@uvic.ca; URL: http://www.uvcs.uvic.ca/conferce/ – Contact, Mary O'Rourke

Connections Victoria Ltd., PO Box 40046, Victoria BC V8W 3N3 – 250/382-0332; Fax: 250/382-2076; Email: connvic@octonet.com; URL: http://www.octonet.com/connvic/ – Managing Director, Ann Moxley

#### WEST VANCOUVER

Pacific Promotions Ltd., 138 Stevens Dr., West Vancouver BC V7S 1C4 – 604/925-3333, 2222; Fax: 604/925-4454 – President, David M. Frinton

#### WESTBANK

Home Business Exhibitions, 2956 Shannon Lake Rd., Westbank BC V4T 1T6 – 250/768-9561

#### WHISTLER

Destination Leisure Productions Ltd., PO Box 720, Whistler BC V0N 1B0 – 604/938-3350; Fax: 604/938-3485 – Managing Director, Laurin Kyle Boyle

#### WHITE ROCK

M. Van Keken & Associates Ltd., #303, 15047 Marine Dr., White Rock BC V4B 1C5 – 604/535-0944; Fax: 604/535-2744 – President/Executive Producer, Martin Van Keken

## MANITOBA

#### BRANDON

Brandon Economic Development Board, 1043 Rosser Ave., Brandon MB R7A 0L5 – 204/728-3287; Fax: 204/728-1092; Toll Free: 1-888-799-1111; Email: bedb@docker.com; URL: http://www.docker.com/~bedb/brandon.html – General Manager, Don Allan

#### WINNIPEG

Berkowitz Ltd., #242, 375 York Ave., Winnipeg MB R3C 3J3 – 204/957-7312; Fax: 204/943-0397 – Contact, Ivan Berkowitz

Frontline Associates, 676 Borebank St., Winnipeg MB R3N 1G2 – 204/254-2293; Fax: 204/257-5205; Email: frontlin@escape.ca; URL: http://www.escape.ca/~frontlin – Carmen Neufeld

Hank Hartloper Agency, #2, 1575 Seel Ave., Winnipeg MB R3T 1C8 – 204/925-1620; Fax: 204/925-1623 – Owner, Hank Hartloper

IN-KA Meeting Planners, #202, 16 Albert St., Winnipeg MB R3B 1G4 – 204/949-1653; Fax: 204/956-1700 – Contact, Gail Hall

## NEW BRUNSWICK

#### SAINT JOHN

Global Convention Services, PO Box 2329, Saint John NB E2L 3V6 – 506/658-0506; Fax: 506/658-0750 – General Manager, Ian Galbraith

Master Promotions Ltd., PO Box 565, Saint John NB E2L 3Z8 – 506/658-0018; Fax: 506/658-0750 – Show Manager, Sydney Jane Brittain

## NEWFOUNDLAND

#### CONCEPTION BAY

McCarthy's Party, Tour & Convention Services Topsail, General Delivery, Topsail, Conception Bay NF A0A 3Y0 – 709/781-2244; Fax: 709/781-2233; Email: mccarthys.party@nf.sympatico.ca – President, Regina McCarthy

#### GANDER

Atlantic Expositions Ltd, PO Box 402, Gander NF A1V 1W8 – 709/651-3315; Fax: 709/256-4051 – Manager, Keith Brown

#### SAINT JOHNS

The Fulcrum Group, #301, 140 Water St., St. John's NF A1C 6H6 – 709/753-1015; Fax: 709/753-1016

## NOVA SCOTIA

#### DARTMOUTH

Creative Convention Consultants, 11 Pettipas Dr., Unit M, Dartmouth NS B3B 4K1 – 902/468-9101; Fax: 902/468-8938 – President, David M. Alexander

Denex Group Inc., Burnside Industrial Park, 192 Joseph Zatzman Dr., Dartmouth NS B3B 1N4 – 902/468-4999; Fax: 902/468-2795; Email: denman@ns.sympatico.ca; URL: http://www.denexgroup.com – President, Jon Denman

Meetings Plus Ltd., 4 Applewood Lane, Dartmouth NS B2X 2Z6 – 902/462-1929; Fax: 902/462-4275; Email: amirault@netcom.ca – President, Leslie Amirault

#### HALIFAX

A.B. Thompson Associates Ltd., PO Box 9410, Stn A, Halifax NS B3K 5S3 – 902/425-2445; Fax: 902/425-2441; Toll Free: 1-800-200-PATH; Email: pathfndr@fox.nstn.ca – Contact, John Sutherland

DMS Enterprises Ltd., 5647 Morris St., Halifax NS B3J 1C4 – 902/425-5656 – Coordinator, Donna Susnick

Downeast Entertainment & Meeting Specialists, #116, 1585 Barrington St., Halifax NS B3J 1Z8 – 902/423-1974; Fax: 902/429-8002; Email: dwneast@fox.nstn.ca – Contact, Bill Norton

Lewis Conference Services International, Richmond Terminal, Pier 9, 3295 Barrington St., Halifax NS B3K 5X8 – 902/492-4988; Fax: 902/492-4781 – Contact, Trudy Lewis

On Site Meeting Planners Ltd., PO Box 2627, Stn M, Halifax NS B3J 3P7 – 902/461-0230; Fax: 902/465-2233 – President, Lynn Buckley

## ONTARIO

### AJAX

Metropolitan Promotions, PO Box 193, Ajax ON L1S 3C3 – 905/428-7610; Fax: 905/428-7046 – Show Manager, Tom Glaesser

### ASHBURN

Bar Hodgson Productions Inc., 8780 Baldwin St., RR#1, Ashburn ON L0B 1A0 – 905/655-5403; Fax: 905/655-3812; Email: supersho@idirect.com – President, Bar Hodgson

### BRAMPTON

Creative Meeting & Marketing Services, 74 Mara Cres., Brampton ON L6V 4B7 – 905/456-0438; Fax: 905/456-9429; Email: norrish@interlog.com – Ingrid Norrish

### BURLINGTON

Meeting Management Services Inc., 2267 Abbotsbury St., Burlington ON L7P 4H7 – 905/335-7993; Fax: 905/332-1587; Email: rdewar@ibm.net – Ronald F. Dewar

### CONCORD

Multimedia Trade Shows Inc., #7, 70 Villarboit Cres., Concord ON L4K 4C7 – 905/660-2491; Fax: 905/660-2492; Email: bcole@multimedia.ca; URL: http://www.newmedia.ca – President, Bruce Cole

### CUMBERLAND

Larabie Entertainment Productions, 2491 Ferry Rd., Cumberland ON K4C 1C6 – 613/833-3256; Fax: 613/834-7073 – Contact, Ted Larabie

### EXETER

AIS Communications Ltd., 145 Thames Rd. West, Exeter ON N0M 1S3 – 519/235-2400; Fax: 519/235-0798 – Contact, Peter Phillips

### GRIMSBY

Toronto Show Promotions, PO Box 217, Grimsby ON L3M 4G3 – 905/945-2775; Fax: 905/945-3199 – Doug Jarvis

### HAMILTON

About Town - Event & Meeting Planners, 494 Mary St., Hamilton ON L8L 4X4 – 905/529-6956; Fax: 905/529-1108 – Owner, Joan Balinson

Kelly-Alexander Inc., 875 Main St. West, Hamilton ON L8S 4R1 – 905/522-9422; Fax: 905/529-2242 – Show Manager, Paul McNair

Town Publishing Inc., Show Division, 875 Main St. West, Hamilton ON L8S 4R1 – 905/522-6117; Fax: 905/529-2242 – Show Manager, Lea Narciso

### HAVELOCK

Neveu Productions Inc., PO Box 659, Havelock ON K0L 1Z0 – 705/778-2275; Fax: 705/778-2275; Toll Free: 1-800-461-6568; Email: natlmcswapmeet@accel.net – Carolyn Neveu

### KINGSTON

Events & Management Plus Inc., 190 Railway St., PO Box 1570, Kingston ON K7L 5C8 – 613/531-9210; Fax: 613/531-0626; Email: events@adan.kingston.net – Owner, E. Hooper

### LONDON

London Show Productions, RR#5, London ON N6A 4B9 – 519/455-5888; Fax: 519/455-7780 – President, Arthur Bacon

### MARKHAM

Canadian Tel-A-Views Ltd., #12, 115 Apple Creek Blvd., Markham ON L3R 6C9 – 905/477-2677; Fax: 905/477-7872; Toll Free: 1-800-891-4859 – President, Fred Cox

Hugh Wilson & Associate Consultants Ltd., #204, 500 Alden Rd., Markham ON L3R 5H5 – 905/475-7531; Fax: 905/475-1916 – Contact, Emoke Nadai

Meridican Travel Inc., #1, 7225 Woodbine Ave., Markham ON L3R 1A3 – 905/477-7700; Fax: 905/477-7580 – President, Anthony Byron

### MISSISSAUGA

Automotive Video Productions, #17, 5004 Timberlea Blvd., Mississauga ON L4W 5C5 – 416/206-1304; Fax: 416/206-1170; Toll Free: 1-800-275-4287 – President, Ron Baker

Kerrwil Show & Conference Group, 395 Matheson Blvd. East, Mississauga ON L4Z 2H2 – 905/890-1846; Fax: 905/890-5769; Email: aschacht@kerrwil.com; URL: http://www.kerrwilshow.com – Manager, Anita Schachter

Lakeview Publications, #27, 1200 Aerowood Dr., Mississauga ON L4W 2S7 – 905/624-8100; Fax: 905/624-1760; Email: info@ept.ca; URL: http://www.ept.ca – President, Robert C. Luton

Meetings Professional International - Toronto, 6519B Mississauga Rd., Mississauga ON L5N 1A6 – 905/567-9591; Fax: 905/567-9961 – Executive Director, Leslie Wright

Ontario Trade Shows Ltd., #8, 1606 Sedlescomb Dr., Mississauga ON L4X 1M6 – 905/625-7070; Fax: 905/625-4856; Toll Free: 1-800-331-7408 – Alexander Donald

Opportunities Canada, #42, 2550 Goldenridge Rd., Mississauga ON L4X 2S3 – 905/277-5600; Fax: 905/277-3397 – Sales Manager, Cheryl Higgins

Travel Trust International Canada, #300, 2810 Matheson Blvd. East, Mississauga ON L4W 4X7 – 905/629-9975; Fax: 905/629-0361 – Manager, Corporate Planning Group, Doreen Ostrowski

Winexpo Productions Inc., #11, 5080 Timberlea Blvd., Mississauga ON L4W 4M2 – 905/629-7469; Fax: 905/629-3823; URL: http://www.toronto.com/winexpo – General Manager, Megan Parry

### MOUNT ALBERT

Marketer Shows Inc., 18540 Centre St., Mount Albert ON L0G 1M0 – 905/473-7009; Fax: 905/473-5217 – Terrence Kehoe

### NEPEAN

Intertrade Communications Inc., #203, 43 Roydon Place, Nepean ON K2E 1A3 – 613/224-3013; Fax: 613/224-4533; Toll Free: 1-888-662-6660; Email: trades@magi.com – Show Manager, Pauline Gaudet

### OAKVILLE

Jenkins Show Productions, 1076 Skyvalley Cr., Oakville ON L6M 3L2 – 905/827-4632; Fax: 905/827-8139; Toll Free: 1-800-465-1073 – President, Dave Jenkins

Premier Consumer Shows, City Parent Newsmagazine, 467 Speers Rd., Oakville ON L6K 3S4 – 905/815-0017; Fax: 905/815-0511; Toll Free: 1-800-387-7682 – Show Coordinator, Darren Melanson

Ten Star Productions Inc., 155 Castle Cr., Oakville ON L6J 5H4 – 905/845-2644; Fax: 905/333-1097 – Show Manager, Roberta Said

### OTTAWA

Conference Coll Inc., 1138 Sherman Dr., Ottawa ON K2C 2M4 – 613/224-1741(bus.); 225-4229(res.); Fax: 613/224-9685; Email: cci@sce.carleton.ca – President, Marg Coll

Connelly Business Exhibitions Inc., #214, 2487 Kaladar Ave., Ottawa ON K1V 8B9 – 613/731-9850; Fax: 613/731-2407 – Vice-President, Marketing, Dan Hamilton

DeLaurier Brown Associates, #20, 99 - 5th Ave., Ottawa ON K1S 5P5 – 613/823-6986; Fax: 613/823-6992 – President, Jean Brown

Golden Planners Inc., #401, 126 York St., Ottawa ON K1N 5T5 – 613/241-9333; Fax: 613/565-2173; Email: gpi@intranet.ca – President, Hélène Lamadeleine

Impact Management International, #250, 2415 Holly Lane, Ottawa ON K1V 7P2 – 613/523-0974 – Contact, Sheila McKirdy

Intertask Ltd., 275 Bay St., Ottawa ON K1R 5Z5 – 613/238-4075; Fax: 613/238-3805 – President, Paul Akehurst

The Organizing Solution Inc., 174 Hickory St., Ottawa ON K1Y 3T6 – 613/724-9900; Fax: 613/724-4851; Toll Free: 1-800-363-4988 – President, Patti Mordasewicz

Player Expositions International, 255 Clemow Ave., Ottawa ON K1S 2B5 – 613/567-6408; Fax: 613/567-2718 – Show Organizer, Halina Player

Richmor Enterprises, #201, 251 Laurier Ave. West, Ottawa ON K1P 5J6 – 613/563-0093; Fax: 613/236-4351; Email: richmor@cyberus.ca – Conference Manager, Bernadette Dawson

Southex Exhibitions Inc., #440, 47 Clarence St., Ottawa ON K1N 9K1 – 613/241-2888; Fax: 613/241-1827 – Group Show Manager, Ray Fahey

Taylor & Associates Convention Management, 676 Shefford Ct., Ottawa ON K1J 6X3 – 613/747-0262; Fax: 613/745-1846 – President, April Taylor

The Willow Group, 582 Somerset West, Ottawa ON K1R 5K2 – 613/237-2324; Fax: 613/237-9900; Email: moreinfo@thewillowgroup.com; URL: http://thewillowgroup.com/willow/ – Contact, Benoit Comeau

### PETERBOROUGH

Dawn Morris Productions Inc., #3, 1434 Chemong Rd., RR#1, Peterborough ON K9J 6X2 – 705/741-2536; Fax: 705/741-2539; Email: cifes@dawnmorris.on.ca; URL: http://www.dawnmorris.on.ca – Show Manager, Lesley Nicholson

### STOUFFVILLE

The Profile Group, #301, 37 Sandiford Dr., Stouffville ON L4A 7X5 – 905/640-7700; Fax: 905/640-7714

### SUDBURY

DAC Marketing Ltd., PO Box 2837, Stn A, Sudbury ON P3A 5J3 – 705/673-5588; Fax: 705/525-0626 – President, Darren A. Ceccarelli

### THORNHILL

Sheldon Kagan International Ltd., #14, 7420 Bathurst St., Thornhill ON L4J 6X4 – 905/764-0697; Fax: 905/764-0697; URL: http://www.sheldonkagan.com – President, Sheldon Kagan

### TORONTO

1071269 Ontario Inc., PO Box 1500-1288, Etobicoke ON M9C 4V5 – 416/620-6620; Fax: 416/621-6688 – Monique Trotter

Accent Toronto Inc./Insight Planners, One Sultan St., Toronto ON M5S 1L6 – 416/944-3631

Aldel Ltd., 1126B The Queensway, Etobicoke ON M8Z 1P7 – 416/259-3713; Fax: 416/259-8566; Email: jclare@aims.on.ca – Contact, Jim Clare

Backyard Living Productions, PO Box 1500-1288, Etobicoke ON M9C 4V5 – 416/620-6620; Fax: 416/621-6688 – Shirley Trotter

Barslow Communications & Marketing, 65 Helena Ave., Toronto ON M6G 2H3 – 416/653-4986; Fax: 416/653-2291; Email: barslow@to.org – President/CEO, Joyce Barslow

Base Services Canada Inc., #301, 250 Consumers Rd., North York ON M2J 4V6 – 416/494-1440; Fax: 416/495-8723; Email: base@onramp.ca – President, Brian Lechem

Business & Industry Services, 205 Humber College Blvd., Toronto ON M9W 5L7 – 416/675-6622; Fax: 416/675-0135; Email: swithenbank@admin.humberc.on.ca – Manager, Maggie Swithenbank

The Canadian Institute, 1329 Bay St., 3rd Fl., Toronto ON M5R 2C4 – 416/927-0718; Fax: 416/927-1061, 966-0175; Email: mktg@cicomm.com – Contact, Cynthia Mathieson

Canadian National Sportsmen's Shows (1989) Ltd., #202, 703 Evans Ave., Toronto ON M5C 5E9 – 416/695-0311; Fax: 416/695-0381 – President, Walter Oster

Canadian Shows & Special Events Inc., #1801, One Yonge St., Toronto ON M5E 1W7 – 416/363-1292; Fax: 416/369-0515 – Marketing & Sales Manager, Josie Graziosi

Communiqué Group Inc., 370 King St. West, Toronto ON M5V 2J9 – 416/593-1212; Fax: 416/593-7008 – President, Geoff Genovese

Congress Canada, #100, 49 Bathurst St., Toronto ON M5V 2P2 – 416/504-4500; Fax: 416/504-4505; Email: sales@congresscan.com – President, Pam Graham

Contemporary Craft Shows Ltd., 37 Langley Ave., Toronto ON M4K 3V9 – 416/465-2379; Fax: 416/465-2379 – Casey Sadaka

Convention Planners International Inc., #302, 234 Eglinton Ave. East, Toronto ON M4P 1K5 – 416/482-2992; Fax: 416/482-2714; Email: mail@cpitrul.com; URL: http://www.cpitrul.com – President, Aubrey Harmes

Creative Consulting, #2510, 44 St. Joseph St., Toronto ON M4Y 2W4 – 416/929-5135; Fax: 416/929-5135 – President, Christine Z. Adelhardt, C.M.P.

Creative Events Management, 55 Vansco Rd., Toronto ON M8Z 5Z8 – 416/259-1346; Fax: 416/259-2053 – President, Margi Taylor

Distinctive Meetings & Occasions, #408, 4576 Yonge St., North York ON M2N 6N4 – 416/441-9238; Fax: 416/441-9278 – President, Angela Tomsic

Farewell Tours, #420, 48 Yonge St., Toronto ON M5E 1G6 – 416/366-3901; Fax: 416/363-5561 – Contact, Nagel Andrews

Genigraphics Canada Inc., #400, 49 Spadina Ave., Toronto ON M5V 2J1 – 416/595-1335 – Contact, Michael Turney

Glavin & Associates, #301, 40 Holly St., Toronto ON M4S 3C3 – 416/482-3030; Fax: 416/482-3051; Email: glavin@magic.ca – Contact, Ingrid Rubin

Hospitality Tours, 180 Bloor St. West, Main Concourse, Toronto ON M5S 2V6 – 416/968-3481; Fax: 416/968-9053

Impact Event Management, 358 Danforth Ave., PO Box 65060, Toronto ON M4K 3Z2 – 416/461-5306; Fax: 416/461-8460; Email: dn@caribphoto.com; URL: http://www.caribphoto.com/psychic.htm – Donald Nausbaum

InAdvance, 59 Hogarth Ave., Toronto ON M4K 1K2 – 416/465-1430; Fax: 416/462-3750 –

Incentives International Inc., 160 Bloor St. East, Toronto ON M4W 1B9 – 416/928-5829; Fax: 416/928-7798 – President, J. Duff Shaw, C.M.P., C.I.T.E.

International Show Productions Inc., 36 Fallingbrook Dr., Scarborough ON M1N 1B6 – 416/691-2852; Fax: 416/691-2891; Toll Free: 1-800-265-3673 – Steve Nichols

International Tradeshow Services Inc., 20 Butterick Rd., Toronto ON M8W 3Z8 – 416/252-7791; Fax: 416/252-9848; Email: jimm@intltradeshows.com; URL: http://www.intltradeshows.com – President, James K. Mahon

Kerbel Communications Inc., 40 Holly St., 6th Fl., Toronto ON M4S 3C3 – 416/489-1414; Fax: 416/489-9940; Toll Free: 1-800-625-3625; Email: kerbel@inforamp.net – Event Manager, Shari Koladich

Klanside Inc., 401 Magnetic Dr., Unit 21, North York ON M3J 3H9 – 416/661-2056; Fax: 416/661-2904

The Mariposa Group Inc., 147 Liberty St., Toronto ON M6K 3G3 – 416/588-6699; Fax: 416/532-7736 – CEO, Greg Cochrane

MCC Planners Inc. (Meetings, Conventions, Conferences), #201N, 310 North Queen St., Toronto ON M9C 1K4 – 416/621-6622; Fax: 416/621-0363 – President, Marsha Jones

Meteor Show Productions Inc., 298 Sheppard Ave. East, North York ON M2N 3B1 – 416/229-2060; Fax: 416/223-2826; Toll Free: 1-800-896-7469; Email: weil@meteorshows.com; URL: http://www.meteorshows.com – President, Ralph Weil

MW Productions, #4, 88 Courcelette Rd., Scarborough ON M1N 2T2 – 416/691-6526; Fax: 416/691-6928; Toll Free: 1-800-267-4529; Email: ron.mackenzie@mwprod.com; URL: http://www.mwprod.com – Ron MacKenzie

Ontario Marketing Productions, 109 Scollard St., Toronto ON M5R 1G4 – 416/961-2999; Fax: 416/961-1157 – Contact, Linda Watt

Ontario Out of Doors Magazine, 777 Bay St., 6th Fl., Toronto ON M5W 1A7 – 416/596-5908; Fax: 416/596-2517; Email: 102677.1125@compuserve.com; URL: http://www.cyberplex.com/fishontario – Show Manager, Lynda Watson

Perdue Show Management, 378 Evans Ave., Etobicoke ON M8Z 1K6 – 416/503-8240; Fax: 416/503-8130 – President, Elizabeth Fairley

Peter Milne Consulting, 88 Patterson Ave., Scarborough ON M1L 3Y4 – 416/694-6059; Fax: 416/694-6059; Email: ptmilne@the-wire.com – President, Peter Milne

Plesman Expositions & Conferences Inc., 2005 Sheppard Ave. East, 4th Fl., North York ON M2J 5B1 – 416/497-9562; Fax: 416/497-9427; Toll Free: 1-800-387-5012; URL: http://www.netcon.plesman.com – Show Coordinator, Sean Wainwright

Promex Productions Inc., 118 Indian Rd., 2nd Fl., Toronto ON M6R 2V4 – 416/531-2121; Fax: 416/531-2194 – Show Manager, Angela Abromaitis

Promosalons, #503, 1200 Bay St., Toronto ON M5R 2A5 – 416/929-2562; Fax: 416/929-2564; Toll Free: 1-800-387-2566; Email: info@promosalons.com; URL: http://www.promosalons.com

Reed Exhibition Companies Inc., 3761 Victoria Park Ave., Scarborough ON M1W 3S2 – 416/491-7565; Fax: 416/491-5088

Ryerson Polytechnic University, 350 Victoria St., Toronto ON M5B 2K3 – 416/979-5184; Fax: 416/979-5148 – Program Director, Continuing Education, Diana E. Hennessy

Shield Associates Ltd., 25 Bradgate Rd., Don Mills ON M3B 1J6 – 416/444-5225; Fax: 416/444-8268; Email: sal@myna.com; URL: http://www.cmxshow.com – Show Coordinator, Patrick Shield

Show Fest Productions Inc., #5, 60 St. Clair Ave. West, Toronto ON M4V 1M7 – 416/925-4533; Fax: 416/925-7701; Email: gendel@compfest.com; URL: http://www.compfest.com – David Carter

Showcase Marketing Ltd., #410, 1110 Sheppard Ave. East, North York ON M2K 2W2 – 416/512-1305; Fax: 416/512-9998 – Paul Newdick

Sierra Corporate Productions Inc., #302, 102 Atlantic Ave., Toronto ON M6K 1X9 – 416/531-8757; Fax: 416/531-2602 – President, Bill Greenbaum

Sightlines Productions Ltd., #129, 6 Lansing Sq., North York ON M2J 1T5 – 416/499-5068; Fax: 416/492-4108 – President, Frank Bayley

Southex Exhibitions Inc., Head Office, #800, 1 Concorde Gate, North York ON M3C 3N6 – 416/385-1880; Fax: 416/385-1855; Toll Free: 1-888-823-7469; URL: http://www.southex.com – Research Manager, Sandy Zeidenberg

Taylor Enterprises Ltd., #310, 2175 Sheppard Ave. East, North York ON M2J 1W8 – 416/491-2897; Fax: 416/491-1670; Toll Free: 1-800-208-9398; Email: taylor@interlog.com; URL: http://www.interlog.com/~taylor/htehome.html – President, Joan Milne

Toronto International Bicycle Show, #1801, 1 Yonge St., Toronto ON M5E 1W7 – 416/363-1292; Fax: 416/369-0515 – Show Manager, Josie Graziosi

Two Plus One Group, #611, 220 Duncan Mill Rd., North York ON M3B 3J5 – 416/510-0114; Fax: 416/510-0165 – President, Alice Chee

#### UTOPIA

Marty Kay Productions Inc., RR#1, Utopia ON L0M 1T0 – 705/424-2668; Fax: 705/424-5202 – Contact, Marty Kay

## QUÉBEC

#### BROSSARD

Yves Barré & Associés, 6940, rue Barry, Brossard QC J4Z 1V1 – 514/443-3131; Fax: 514/443-8415 – Président, Yves Barré

#### HULL

Communications Show, CP 1241, Succ B, Hull QC J8X 3X7 – 418/877-8898; Fax: 418/877-9711 – Président, Roch Gamache

#### LONGUEUIL

Marcel Gaudreault, Consultant, 1431, Bourgeoys, Longueuil QC J4M 1Z5 – 514/647-5530; Fax: 514/647-1031 – Président, Marcel Gaudreault

#### MONTREAL

AFLD Consultants Inc., 3565, rue Edgar Leduc, Lachine QC H8T 3L5 – 514/639-6806; Fax: 514/639-6629; Email: afld@videotron.ca – Show Manager, Lucie Desharnais

Canadian National Sportsmen's Shows (1989) Ltd., #1630, 1155, rue Metcalfe, Montréal QC H3B 2V6 – 514/866-5409; Fax: 514/866-4092 – Show Manager, Diane Laporte

Clarkson-Conway Inc., CP 216, Succ Place Bonaventure, Montréal QC H5A 1A9 – 514/861-9694; Fax: 514/392-1577 – General Manager, Marilyn Meikle

Communications Savoir Faire, 4119, rue Sherbrooke ouest, Montréal QC H3Z 1B6 – 514/935-7776; Fax: 514/935-3825 – Président, Gina Roitman

Coplanor Congrès inc., #600, 511, Place d'Armes, Montréal QC H2Y 2W7 – 514/848-1133; Fax: 514/288-6469; Email: conf@coplanor.qc.ca – Executive Director, Carol Langevin

Events International Meeting Planners Inc., #700, 759, Carré Victoria, Montréal QC H2Y 2J7 – 514/286-0855; Fax: 514/286-6066; Email: info@eventsintl.com

Gerry Lou & Associates, #211, 1224, rue Stanley, Montréal QC H3B 2S7 – 514/878-2530; Fax: 514/878-2532 – Director, Client Services, Guylaine Pauld

GroupExpo, 101, rue Laurier ouest, Montréal QC H2T 2N6 – 514/272-0606; Fax: 514/272-6699

International Motivation & Incentive Consultants, 5427 Robert Burns St., Montréal QC H4W 2B5 – 514/482-3553; Fax: 514/482-9785; Telex: ITT 4951939 – President, Stephen P. Libman

JPdL Multi Management Inc., #609, 1410, rue Stanley, Montréal QC H3A 1P8 – 514/287-1070; Fax: 514/287-1248; Toll Free: 1-800-361-1070 – Président, Jean-Paul de Lavison

Maestro Innovations, #500, 1410, rue Stanley, Montréal QC H3A 1P8 – 514/287-1465; Fax: 514/843-5680 – Vice-President, Joan Macklin

Martin International, #2910, 500, Place des Armes, Montréal QC H2Y 2W2 – 514/288-3931; Fax: 514/288-0641 – General Manager, Lorraine Boisvenue

McGill University Conference Office, #490, Tour Ouest, 550, rue Sherbrooke ouest, Montréal QC H3A 1B9 – 514/398-3770; Fax: 514/398-4854; Email: MCO@ums1.ian.mcgill.ca; URL: http://www.mcgill.ca/mco – Contact, Joan Gross

Mobilvision Inc., 9200, boul Henri-Bourassa ouest, Montréal QC H4S 1L5 – 514/334-7277; Fax: 514/334-1180; Toll Free: 1-800-668-3976 – Président, Jacques Forest

Multicom International Montréal, Place Bonaventure, Door 4, PO Box 523, Montréal QC H5A 1C3 – 514/875-2789; Fax: 514/272-8879; Telex: 05-268769 – President, Sigrid Chatel

P.R. Charette Inc., 35, Promenade Westland, Montréal-Ouest QC H4X 1M3 – 514/489-8671; Fax: 514/487-3230 – Contact, Bob Charette

Promexpo Inc., 801, rue Sherbrooke est, 10e étage, Montréal QC H2L 1K7 – 514/527-9221; Fax: 514/527-8449 – General Manager, Vic Côté

Sensix Communications & Events Inc., #201, 8225 Mayrand Ave., Montréal QC H4P 2C7 – 514/739-2309; Fax: 514/342-1682; Email: sensix@aol.com – President, Michael Caplan

Sheldon Kagan International Ltd., 35, McConnell, Dorval QC H9S 5L9 – 514/631-2160; Fax: 514/631-4430; Email: sheldon@sheldonkagan.com; URL: http://www.sheldonkagan.com – President, Sheldon Kagan

Sorelcomm (1985) Inc., 1801, av McGill College, Montréal QC H3A 2N4 – 514/499-8920; Fax: 514/499-8921 – President, Denise L. Duhaime

#### QUEBEC

Forum Québec, 30, rue Grande Allée ouest, Québec QC G1R 2G6 – 418/524-8093; Fax: 418/529-1172 –

Omnitour, 105, Côte de la Montagne, Québec QC G1R 4P3 – 418/692-1223; Fax: 418/692-4537 – President, Jacques Morissette

Pro-Expo Inc., #115, 200, rue St-Jean-Baptiste, Québec QC G2E 5E8 – 418/871-6130; Fax: 418/871-3831 – President, Gaétan Marcoux

Les Promotions André Pageau Inc., 1627, boul St-Joseph, Québec QC G2K 1H1 – 418/623-3383; Fax: 418/623-5033; Email: info@promoapageau.qc.ca; URL: http://www.promoapageau.qc.ca – Président, André Pageau

#### SAINT LAMBERT

Destination à la Carte inc., #24, 680, av Victoria, Mezzanine, Saint-Lambert QC J4P 3S1 – 514/466-9342; Fax: 514/465-9949 – Président, Ken Ondrick

### SASKATCHEWAN

#### REGINA

Dawn Redmond & Associates Ltd., 2352 Smith St., Regina SK S4P 2P6 – 306/781-7300; Fax: 306/565-0881 – President, Dawn Redmond-Bradley

Dimension 11 Ltd., 2301 - 15th Ave., Regina SK S4P 1A3 – 306/586-2315; Fax: 306/721-6602; Toll Free: 1-800-303-2315; Email: dimension@net1fx.com – Contact, Sherry Knight

Merle Kennedy Consulting Inc., 3623 McCallum Ave., Regina SK S4S 0S6 – 306/586-0081 – Contact, Merle Kennedy

#### SASKATOON

Saskatoon Prairieland Exhibition Corporation, PO Box 6010, Saskatoon SK S7K 4E4 – 306/931-7149; Fax: 306/931-7886 – General Manager, Mark Regier

## EXHIBITIONS, SHOWS & EVENTS

The following list includes Consumer & Trade shows, Public Events, Conferences, Festivals arranged by category of interest. The addresses given are the office addresses of associations/sponsors. Focus is on events of an ongoing annual or biennial nature. The lists are not complete, but are fairly representative of shows held throughout Canada. Users are cautioned that dates or venues may alter.

#### ABORIGINAL *See* MULTICULTURAL

### ACCOUNTING

The Bottom Line, Reed Exhibition Companies Inc., 3761 Victoria Park Ave., Scarborough ON M1W 3S2 – 416/491-7565; Fax: 416/491-5088 – Sept.

National Conference, Society of Management Accountants of Canada, #850, 120 King St. West, PO Box 176, Hamilton ON L8N 3C3 – 905/525-4100; 416/847-0373 (Toronto line); Fax: 905/525-4533; Tollfree: 1-800-263-7622; URL: http://www.cma-canada.org – President & CEO, Robert W. Dye – July 14-17 1998 – Vancouver BC

### ADVERTISING

The Motivational Marketing Expo, Southex Exhibitions Inc., Head Office, #800, 1 Concorde Gate, North York ON M3C 3N6 – 416/385-1880; Fax: 416/385-1855; Tollfree: 1-888-823-7469; URL: http://www.southex.com – Show Manager, Ross Horton – Annual trade show, Sept. – Metro Toronto Convention Centre,

National Convention & Trade Show, Canadian Direct Marketing Association, #607, One Concorde Gate, North York ON M3C 3N6 – 416/391-2362; Fax: 416/441-4062; Email: nadiav@cdma.org; URL: http://www.cdma.org – Show Manager, Linda Kuschnir – Annual. Direct marketing & tele-marketing, April 21-23 1998 – Westin Harbour Castle, Toronto ON

#### AGRICULTURE *See* FARM BUSINESS/ AGRICULTURE

### AIR SHOWS/AVIATION

Abbotsford International Airshow, 30470 Approach Dr., Abbotsford BC V2T 6H5 – 604/852-8511; Fax: 604/852-6093; Tollfree: 1-888-852-8511; Email: airshow@uniserve.com; URL: http://www.harbour.com/commorgs/airshow – Managing Director, Bob McFarland – Large static display. Six hour flying show, August

Airshow, International Air Show Society of Whitehorse, PO Box 5108, Whitehorse YT Y1A 4S3 – 867/667-2148 – May – Whitehorse YT

Airshow Canada, PO Box 6, Abbotsford BC V2S 4N9 – 604/852-4600; Fax: 604/852-3704 – Held in conjunction with the Canadian Business Aircraft Association Exhibition – Annual trade show & symposium, August

Armed Forces Day, Harman Field, Stephenville NF A2N 2Y7 – 709/643-9123 – July

Canadian International Airshow, Press Bldg., Exhibition Place, 2nd Fl., Toronto ON M6K 3C3 – 416/393-6061, 6062; Fax: 416/393-6259 – Coordinator, Lisa Natale – Annually, three days of the Labour Day Weekend

CFB Comox Airshow, CFB Comox, Lazo BC V0R 2K0 – 250/339-8210; Fax: 250/339-8142 – Chief Officer, Major Drew Foulds – Biennial, July 1998

Festival of Flight, PO Box 280, Gander NF A1V 1W6 – 709/651-2656; Fax: 709/256-2124; Email: estaple@newcomm.net – Tourism Officer, Gail Hoyles – A celebration of Gander's aviation history, July/Aug.

Friendship Festival International Air Show, PO Box 1241, Fort Erie ON L2A 5Y2 – 905/871-6454; Fax: 905/871-1266; Tollfree: 1-888-333-1987; URL: http://www.friendshipfestival.com – Tracy Leblanc – Annual, July

Hamilton International Airshow, Hamilton International Airshow Foundation, #418, 150 King St. East, Hamilton ON L8N 1B2 – 905/528-4425; Fax: 905/528-8499 – Director of Operations, Sandra J. Kleus – June

Kamloops Air Show, PO Box 866, Kamloops BC V2C 5M8 – 250/828-1404 – Chair, Holly Schwieger, August

Lethbridge International Airshow, 1610 - 15 Ave. South, Lethbridge AB T1K 0W7 – 403/328-7605 – Annual – August

London International Airshow, 26 Duncan Cres., London ON N5V 4E8 – 519/659-3298; URL: http://www.airshow.org/lias.html – June

National Capital Airshow, #250, 108 Airport Service Rd., Gloucester ON K1V 9B4 – 613/526-1030; Fax: 613/526-1035 – July

Nova Scotia International Air Show, PO Box 218, Shearwater NS B0J 3A0 – 902/465-2725; Fax: 902/465-1221; URL: http://www3.ns.sympatico.ca/nsias – Chair, Fred MacGillivray – Canada's largest annual air show. Industrial displays, static aircraft, flying display, marching bands, Sept.

Saskatchewan Air Show, PO Box 5000, Moose Jaw SK S6H 7Z8 – 306/694-2600; Fax: 306/694-2602; Tollfree: 1-800-461-7469 – Capt. Andrew Mackenzie – July

Sourdough Days Airshow, Yukon Sourdough Rendezvous Society, PO Box 5108, Whitehorse YT Y1A 4S3 – 867/667-2148; Fax: 867/668-6755; Tollfree: 1-888-386-6766; Email: ysr@hypertech.yk.ca; URL: http://www.haylow.yk.net/rendez – Jack Kingscote – One of the last free airshows of its size in Canada, Feb. 20-22 1998 – Whitehorse YT

Victoria Airshow, #15, 9600 Canora Rd., Sidney BC V8L 4R1 – 250/656-3337; Fax: 250/655-3766 – August

### ANTIQUES

Annual Consumer Show, Ontario Steam & Antique Preservers Association, 5511 - 3rd Line, RR#1, Milton ON L9T 2X5 – 905/878-3205 – Secretary, Gordon Rayner – Parades, races, competitions, toy shows, August – Milton Fairgrounds, Milton ON

Antiques Bonaventure/Antiquités Bonaventure, Antiquités Obsession Ltée, 1886, rue Notre-Dame ouest, Montréal QC H3J 1M6 – 514/933-6375 – Robert Ness – Annual trade & consumer show, June – Montréal PQ

Blue Mountain's Antiques Show, Blue Mountain Promotions, #1323N, 6455 Macleod Trail, PO Box 30009, Calgary AB T2H 2V8 – 403/264-0792; Fax: 403/755-4081 – John Humphrey – Semi-annual (Apr. & Sept.), antiques & collectibles show – Roundup Centre, Stampede Grounds, Calgary AB

Capital Antique Show, Antiquités Obsession Ltée, 1886, rue Notre-Dame ouest, Montréal QC H3J 1M6 – 514/933-6375 – Robert Ness – Annual trade & consumer show, April 3-5 1998 – Ottawa Congress Centre, Ottawa ON

Carswell Collectables Antiques Show & Sale, Carswell Collectables, PO Box 1036, Red Deer AB T4N 6S5 – 403/324-2943; Fax: 403/347-7633 – Rae Carswell – April – Memorial Centre, Lacombe AB

The Christmas Holiday, Doll & Teddy Bear Show, Toronto Show Promotions, PO Box 217, Grimsby ON L3M 4G3 – 905/945-2775; Fax: 905/945-3199 – Doug Jarvis – Annual; antique, collectibles, artist dolls, teddy bears & collectible holiday decorations, Nov. – Toronto ON

Depression Glass Show & Sale, Hacking Antiques, 1026 Forestwood Dr., Mississauga ON L8H 7S7 – 905/277-1221 – Edith Hacking – Semi-annual consumer show – Toronto ON

The Montréal Winter Antique Show, Antiquités Obsession Ltée, 1886, rue Notre-Dame ouest, Montréal QC H3J 1M6 – 514/933-6375 – Robert Ness – Annual trade & consumer show, Dec. – Place Bonaventure, East Hall, Montréal PQ

Toronto Antique Show, c/o Exhibition Place, Toronto ON M6K 3C3 – 416/939-8437

Toronto Collectibles Extravaganza, Toronto Show Promotions, PO Box 217, Grimsby ON L3M 4G3 – 905/945-2775; Fax: 905/945-3199 – Doug Jarvis – Annual; nostalgia & antique show, Oct. – Toronto ON

Toronto International Toy Collectors Show, Toronto Show Promotions, PO Box 217, Grimsby ON L3M 4G3 – 905/945-2775; Fax: 905/945-3199 – Doug Jarvis – Annual; antique & collectible childhood memorabilia, Nov. – Toronto ON

The Toronto Toy Show, Toronto Show Promotions, PO Box 217, Grimsby ON L3M 4G3 – 905/945-2775; Fax: 905/945-3199 – Doug Jarvis – Annual consumer show; antique & collectible childhood memorabilia, April – Toronto ON

Yesteryear Heritage Fair, Nepean Sportsplex, 101 Centrepointe Dr., Nepean ON K2G 5K7 – 613/727-6641; Fax: 613/727-6613 – Projects Co-ordinator, Billie Swartzack – Feb. – Ottawa ON

**APPAREL *See* FASHION**

**ARCHITECTURE *See* CONSTRUCTION**

## ART/ARTS

***See Also* First Night; Crafts; Music; Events**

Arnold Mikelson Festival of Arts, 13743 - 16 Ave., White Rock BC V4A 1P7 – 604/536-6460 – Mary Mikelson – July – Three acres of beautiful gardens filled with over 100 of the artists' creations, paintings, pottery, woodsculpture, etc.

Artfocus Artist's Show, Artfocus Indoor Artists' Show, c/o Artfocus Magazine, PO Box 1063, Stn F, Toronto ON M4V 2T7 – 416/925-5564; Fax: 416/925-5564; Email: info@artfocus.com; URL: http://www.artfocus.com – President, Pat Fleisher – Semi-annual (spring & fall) consumer show. Paintings, photography, sculpture, prints, drawings, electronic art, etc. – Rotunda/Metro Hall, Toronto ON

Atlantic Theatre Festival, 356 Main St., Wolfville NS B0P 1X0 – 902/542-1515; Fax: 902/542-1526 – Produces & encourages creation of classic epic drama

Banff Arts Festival, The Banff Centre, PO Box 1020, Banff AB T0L 0C0 – 403/762-6300; Fax: 403/762-6483; URL: http://www.banffcentre.ab.ca – Vice-President/Director, Carol J. Phillips – Early June to late August

Blyth Festival, 107 Queen St. North, PO Box 10, Blyth ON N0M 1H0 – 519/523-4345; Fax: 519/523-9804 – Artistic Director, Janet Amos – Canadian plays festival, Summer – Blyth Memorial Hall

Charlottetown Festival, Confederation Centre of the Arts, 145 Richmond St., Charlottetown PE C1A 1J1 – 902/566-1267; Fax: 902/566-4648; Tollfree: 1-800-565-0278; URL: http://www.confederationcentre.com – Executive Director & CEO, Curtis Barlow – Annually, June - September. Musical & dramatic entertainment

du Maurier World Stage Theatre Festival, Harbourfront Centre, #100, 410 Queens Quay West, Toronto ON M5V 2Z3 – 416/973-4600; Fax: 416/973-6055; Email: publicity@harbourfront.on.ca; URL: http://www.harbourfront.on.ca – Artistic Director, Don Shipley

Festival Antigonish Summer Theatre, PO Box 5000, Antigonish NS B2G 2W5 – 902/867-2100; Fax: 902/867-5111 – Summer program of three main-stage, two children's & two late-night new works

Festival by the Sea, PO Box 6848, Stn A, Saint John NB E2L 4S3 – 506/632-0086; Fax: 506/632-0994 – General Manager, Gary D. Arthurs, C.A. – Annually, August. Performing arts. Ten days

The Fringe of Toronto Festival, Fringe of Toronto Festival, #303, 720 Bathurst St., Toronto ON M5S 2R4 – 416/534-5919; Fax: 416/534-6021 – Producer, Nancy Webster – Non-juried theatre festival features over 80 local, North American & international companies, July

Fringe Theatre Event, 10330 - 84 Ave., Edmonton AB T6E 2G9 – 403/448-9000; Fax: 403/431-1893; URL: http://www.alberta.com/fringe – General Manager, Shannon Paddon – August

Kingston Summer Festival, 218 Princess St., Kingston ON K7L 1B2 – 613/546-4465; Fax: 613/531-0591 – General Manager/Executive Producer, Nancy Helwig – Theatre, music & comedy festival

Manitoba Holiday Festival of the Arts, PO Box 147, Neepawa MB R0J 1H0 – 204/476-2927 – Doreen Sage – Classes, workshops for all ages. First two weeks of July

Nova Scotia Folk Art Festival, RR#3, East LaHave, Bridgewater NS B4V 2W2 – 902/766-4382; Fax: 902/766-4382 – Coordinator, Patricia Wyllie – Annual, August – Lunenburg NS

Shakespeare on the Saskatchewan Festival, PO Box 1646, Saskatoon SK S7K 3R8 – 306/653-2300; Fax: 306/653-2357; URL: http://www.zu.com/shakespeare – Artistic Director, Henry Woolf, July/August

Stephenville Festival, 129 Montana Dr., Stephenville NF A2N 2T4 – 709/643-4982; Fax: 709/643-9160 – Summer theatre festival

Winnipeg Fringe Festival, Manitoba Theatre Centre, 174 Market Ave., Winnipeg MB R3B 0P8 – 204/956-1340; Fax: 204/947-3741; URL: http://www.mtc.mb.ca – Bertram Schneider, July 17-26 1998

Women in View, 314 Powell St., Vancouver BC V6A 1G4 – 604/685-6684; Fax: 604/685-6649; URL: http://www.ffa.ucalgary.ca/vca/wmnvie.htm – Executive Director, Dawn Brennan – Multi-disciplinary festival, Jan. – Vancouver BC

## AUTOMOTIVE

Auto Show, VIEX Events Ltd., #2, 31 Bushby St., Victoria BC V8S 1B3 – 250/370-2983; Fax: 250/370-1733; URL: http://www.vicnet.net/~viex – Sales & Marketing Director, Patrick Doyle – June 3-7 1998 – Mayfair Shopping Centre, Victoria BC

Autorama, 16 Wakefield Cres., London ON N5X 1Z7 – 519/451-5368 – Show Producer, Don Cook – Annual consumer show. Custom built autos, hot rods, race cars, antiques, classics, commercial exhibitors, Feb. – Western Fairgrounds, London ON

Autorama, D&R Promotions, 2568 Carp Rd., Carp ON N6A 4G8 – 613/686-2200; Fax: 613/686-2202 – Doug McDougall – Annual consumer show, April – Ottawa ON

Big Rig National Truck Show, 490 Bethune St., Peterborough ON K92 3Z3 – 705/743-6671 – President, Kim Wallace – Annual consumer & trade show. Truck trailers, truck bodies, parts & accessories, engine power train components, service shop equipment, & supplies, truck & stock car race, June – Cayuga Speedway, Caledonia ON

Calgary International Auto & Truck Show, Calgary Motor Dealers Association, 3320 - 9 St. SE, Calgary AB T2G 3C3 – 403/287-3893; Fax: 403/243-0666 – Executive Manager, Jack Thompson – Annual consumer show: new vehicle displays, March – Calgary AB

Cam-Expo Québec, Pro-Expo Inc., #115, 200, rue St-Jean-Baptiste, Québec QC G2E 5E8 – 418/871-6130; Fax: 418/871-3831 – President, Gaétan Marcoux – Biennial trade & consumer show, Nov.

Canadian International Automotive Show, Automotive Industries Association of Canada, 1272 Wellington St., Ottawa ON K1Y 3A7 – 613/728-5821; Fax: 613/728-6021; Email: aia@aiacanada.com; URL: http://www.aftmkt.com – Vice-President, Yaroslaw Zajac – Biennial trade show, April 25-27 1998 – International Centre, Toronto ON

Canadian International Motorcycle Super Show, Bar Hodgson Productions Inc., 8780 Baldwin St., RR#1, Ashburn ON L0B 1A0 – 905/655-5403; Fax: 905/655-3812; Email: supersho@idirect.com – President, Bar Hodgson – Annual consumer show, Jan. – International Centre, Toronto ON

The Canadian Motorcycle & Powersports Business Show, Bar Hodgson Productions Inc., 8780 Baldwin St., RR#1, Ashburn ON L0B 1A0 – 905/655-5403; Fax: 905/655-3812; Email: supersho@idirect.com – President, Bar Hodgson – Annual trade show, Jan. – International Centre, Toronto ON

The Canadian Truck Show, AGM & Conference, Manitoba Trucking Association, 25 Bunting St., Winnipeg MB R2X 2P5 – 204/632-6600; Fax: 204/694-7134 – Show Contact, Bob Wilks – Biennial trade show. HD trucks, equipment, RMO supplies & related services, April – Winnipeg Convention Centre, Winnipeg MB

Car & Accessory Show, Greater Charlottetown Chamber of Commerce, 127 Kent St., PO Box 67, Charlottetown PE C1A 7K2 – 902/628-2000; Fax: 902/368-3570; Email: charcham@atcon.com – Ernest J. Dorion – Annual consumer show, May – Charlottetown PE

Classic Car Show, 2021 Wiggins Ave., Saskatoon SK S7J 1W2 – 306/343-0567; Fax: 306/343-5670 – Annie McDonald – 1955-1957 Chevrolets, Chev & GMC Trucks, Corvettes, Pontiacs. First long weekend in August

Cloverdale Fall RV Sale, Recreation Vehicle Dealers Association of British Columbia, #209, 20353 - 64 Ave., Langley BC V2Y 1N5 – 604/533-4200; Fax: 604/533-0795 – Contact, Lynn Thompson – Annually, Sept.

Edmonton International Auto & Truck Show, Edmonton Motor Dealers Association, 9249 - 48 St., Edmonton AB T6B 2R9 – 403/468-9552; Fax: 403/465-6201; Email: emda@compusmart.ab.ca – Show Manager, Elaine Babiy – Annual consumer show, March

Expo-Moto Montréal, Turbopress Inc., #600A, 5000, rue Buchan, Montréal QC H4P 1T2 – 514/738-9439; Fax: 514/738-4929 – Contact, Roger Saint-Laurent – Montréal QC

Expocam, Southex Exhibitions Inc., Head Office, #800, 1 Concorde Gate, North York ON M3C 3N6 – 416/385-1880; Fax: 416/385-1855; Tollfree: 1-888-823-7469; URL: http://www.southex.com – Show Manager, Chris Gowe – Biennial trade show. Trucks, trailers, bodies, heavy duty parts & services & accessories, engine & power train components, service shop equipment, Oct. 1999 – Montréal QC

Hamilton International Auto Show, Kelly-Alexander Inc., 875 Main St. West, Hamilton ON L8S 4R1 – 905/522-9422; Fax: 905/529-2242 – Show Manager, Paul McNair – Nov. – Copps Coliseum, Hamilton ON

Hamilton Travelcamping Show, Ontario Recreation Vehicle Dealers Association, PO Box 270, Brechin ON L0K 1B0 – 705/484-0295; Fax: 705/484-5740 – Executive Director, William A. Mallatratt – Annual consumer show. RVs, trailers, truck campers, campgrounds, etc., Feb.

Kelowna RV Show, c/o Recreation Dealers Association of BC, #201, 19623 - 56 Ave., Langley BC V3A 3X7 – 604/533-4200; Fax: 604/533-0795 – Marketing Manager, Lynn Thompson – Annual consumer show. RV dealers, RV lifestyle, parks & destinations, April

Kelowna RV Show, Recreation Vehicle Dealers Association of British Columbia, #209, 20353 - 64 Ave., Langley BC V2Y 1N5 – 604/533-4200; Fax: 604/533-0795 – Contact, Lynn Thompson – Annually, April – Kelowna BC

Molson Indy Vancouver at Pacific Place, 765 Pacific Blvd. South, Vancouver BC V6B 4Y9 – 604/684-4639; Fax: 604/684-1482 – Contact, Rena Shanaman – Annual Indy car race & show, August

Montréal International Auto Show, 2335, rue Guénette, St-Laurent QC H4R 2E9 – 514/331-6571; Fax: 514/331-2045; Email: info@ccam.qc.ca; URL: http://www.ccam.qc.ca – Directeur exécutif, Diane Bélair – Annual consumer show. New cars, light trucks, accessories, Jan. – Olympic Stadium, Montréal QC

The Motor Home & Trailer Show, Holger Enge Promotions, 204 Richmond St. West, Toronto ON M5H 2K1 – 416/777-1672; Fax: 416/777-1674 – Holger Enge – Annual consumer show; recreational vehicles, March – Mississauga ON

National Motorcycle Swap Meet & Bike Show, Neveu Productions Inc., PO Box 659, Havelock ON K0L 1Z0 – 705/778-2275; Fax: 705/778-2275; Tollfree: 1-800-461-6568; Email: natlmcswapmeet@accel.net – President, Robert Neveu – Annual consumer show. Retail motorcycle show & sale, March – West Annex, Ntl. Trade Centre, Exhibition Place, Toronto ON

Ottawa-Hull International Auto Show, Ottawa-Hull International Auto Show Inc., 234, boul Gingras, Fossambault-sur-le-Lac QC G0A 3N0 – 418/875-1883; Fax: 418/875-1715 – Richard Cantin – Annual consumer show, Feb. 4-8 1998 – Ottawa Congress Centre, Ottawa ON

Pacific International Auto & Light Truck Show, 3657 Wayburne Dr., Burnaby BC V5G 3L1 – 604/294-8330; Fax: 604/294-8359; Email: autoshow@bcada.org; URL: http:www.helix.net/bcauto/pias.html – Show Manager, Paul Cramp – Annual consumer show. New autos, related products & services, educational activities, aftermarket, Jan.

R.V. Exposition & Sale, Recreation Vehicle Dealers Association of Alberta, 11217 - 143 St., Edmonton AB T5M 3P8 – 403/455-8562; Fax: 403/453-3927; Tollfree: 1-888-858-7878; Email: rvda@planet.eon.net; URL: http://www.rvda-alberta.com – Executive Vice-President, John Milligan – Annual consumer show held in Calgary & Edmonton

R.V. Super Sale, Recreation Vehicle Dealers Association of Manitoba, 58 Leger Cres., Winnipeg MB R3X 1J4 – 204/256-6119; Fax: 204/256-6119 – Manager, Susan Andree – Annual consumer show, March – Winnipeg MB

Salon Auto-Sport, Compagnie d'expositions d'automobiles du Québec, CP 53025, Québec QC G1J 5K3 – 418/827-3420; Fax: 418/827-5331 – Jacques Picard – Annual sport car consumer show, April 1998 – Centre de foires de Québec, Québec QC

Salon de l'Auto de Québec/Québec City Auto Show, #325, 5600, boul des Galeries, Québec QC G2K 2H6 – 418/624-2290; Fax: 418/624-4929 – General Manager, Jean-Guy Bégin – Consumer show, March – PEPS of Laval University, Québec QC

Salon de la Moto de Montréal, Turbopress Inc., #600A, 5000, rue Buchan, Montréal QC H4P 1T2 – 514/738-9439; Fax: 514/738-4929 – Contact, Roger Saint-Laurent – Annual consumer show, Feb. – Montréal QC

Salon de la Moto de Québec, Turbopress Inc., #600A, 5000, rue Buchan, Montréal QC H4P 1T2 – 514/738-9439; Fax: 514/738-4929 – Contact, Roger Saint-Laurent – Annual consumer show, Feb. – Québec QC

Salon international des Véhicules récréatifs de Québec, Pro-Expo Inc., #115, 200, rue St-Jean-Baptiste, Québec QC G2E 5E8 – 418/871-6130; Fax: 418/871-3831 – President, Gaétan Marcoux – Annual show, March

Snowbird RV Show & Sale, Recreation Vehicle Dealers Association of British Columbia, #209, 20353 - 64 Ave., Langley BC V2Y 1N5 – 604/533-4200; Fax: 604/533-0795 – Contact, Lynn Thompson – Annually, Oct.

Speedorama, Speedorama Shows Inc., PO Box 442, Ajax ON L1S 3C5 – 905/427-2100; Fax: 905/427-2158 – Show Manager, Mike Shane – Annual trade & consumer show. Customs, hot rods, motorcycles, commercial exhibitors, feature cars, racing personalities, Feb.

Toronto Expo-Moto, Turbopress Inc., #600A, 5000, rue Buchan, Montréal QC H4P 1T2 – 514/738-9439; Fax: 514/738-4929 – Contact, Roger Saint-Laurent

Toronto International Spring Bike Show, Bar Hodgson Productions Inc., 8780 Baldwin St., RR#1, Ashburn ON L0B 1A0 – 905/655-5403; Fax: 905/655-3812; Email: supersho@idirect.com – President, Bar Hodgson, April – International Centre, Toronto ON

Toronto RV Show, Ontario Recreation Vehicle Dealers Association, PO Box 270, Brechin ON L0K 1B0 – 705/484-0295; Fax: 705/484-5740 – Executive Director, William A. Mallatratt – Annual consumer show, Jan. – Toronto ON

Truckcan, Southex Exhibitions Inc., Head Office, #800, 1 Concorde Gate, North York ON M3C 3N6 – 416/385-1880; Fax: 416/385-1855; Tollfree: 1-888-823-7469; URL: http://www.southex.com – Show Manager, Chris Seeney – Biennial trade show. Trucks, trailers, bodies, heavy duty parts & accessories, engine & power train components, service shop equipment, signs & decals, Oct. – International Centre, Mississauga ON

Truxpo '98, British Columbia Trucking Association, PO Box 381, Port Coquitlam BC V3C 4K6 – 604/942-3200; Fax: 604/942-3191; Tollfree: 1-800-565-2282 – Show Manager, Jerry Peters – Biennial trade show, Oct. 1-3 1998 – Abbotsford BC

Vancouver RV Show, Recreation Vehicle Dealers Association of British Columbia, #209, 20353 - 64 Ave., Langley BC V2Y 1N5 – 604/533-4200; Fax: 604/533-0795 – Contact, Lynn Thompson – Annual consumer show, March – Vancouver BC

Vancouver Summer Motorcycle Show, Canadian National Sportsmen's Shows (1989) Ltd., #501, 4190 Lougheed Hwy., Burnaby BC V5C 6A8 – 604/294-1313; Fax: 604/294-4740 – Show Contact, Paul McGeachie – Annual consumer show, July – Vancouver BC

World of Wheels, Master Promotions Ltd., PO Box 565, Saint John NB E2L 3Z8 – 506/658-0018; Fax: 506/658-0750 – Show Manager, Sydney Jane Brittain – Saint John NB

World of Wheels Show, Championship Auto Shows of Canada Inc., 6841 North Rochester Rd., Rochester NY 48306 – 810/650-5560; Fax: 810/650-5571 – Contact, Tom Williams – Annual consumer show. Sports & vintage cars. Held in Calgary, Edmonton, Winnipeg.

**BLUEGRASS *See* MUSIC**

## BOATING

Boat Show, VIEX Events Ltd., #2, 31 Bushby St., Victoria BC V8S 1B3 – 250/370-2983; Fax: 250/370-1733; URL: http://www.vicnet.net/~viex – Sales & Marketing Director, Patrick Doyle – Feb. 20-22 1998 – Cedar Hill Recreation Centre,

Calgary Boat & Sportsmen's Show, Canadian National Sportsmen's Shows, #340, 1032 - 17 Ave. SW, Calgary AB T2T 0A5 – 403/245-9008; Fax: 403/245-5100 – Paul Husband – Annual consumer show, Feb. – Roundup Centre, Stampede Park, Calgary AB

Classic Boat Festival, c/o Victoria Real Estate Board, 3035 Nanaimo St., Victoria BC V8T 4W2 – 250/385-7766; Fax: 250/385-8773 – Communications Manager, Michael Sampson – Annually, Labour Day weekend – Victoria BC

Edmonton Boat & Sportsmen's Show, Canadian National Sportsmen's Shows, #340, 1032 - 17 Ave. SW, Calgary AB T2T 0A5 – 403/245-9008; Fax: 403/245-5100 – Paul Husband – Annual consumer show, March – Northlands Agricom, Edmonton AB

Fraser Valley Boat & Sportsmen's Show, Square Feet Northwest Event Management Inc., 1030 Mainland St., Vancouver BC V6B 2T4 – 604/683-4393; Fax: 604/688-0270; Email: mgmt@sqftevent.com – Blaine Woit – Annual consumer show, March – Fraser Valley Trade & Exhibition Centre, Abbotsford BC

Halifax International Boat Show, Master Promotions Ltd., PO Box 565, Saint John NB E2L 3Z8 – 506/658-0018; Fax: 506/658-0750 – Show Manager, Sydney Jane Brittain – Annual consumer show, Feb. – Halifax NS

London International Boat Show, 743 Wellington Rd. South, London ON N6C 4R5 – 519/686-3121; Fax: 519/686-3658 – General Manager, Jeff Guy – Consumer show, March – London ON

Muskoka Boat Show, 20 Edgevalley Dr., Etobicoke ON M9A 4N7 – Show Manager, Henry Timothy – Annual trade & consumer show, July – Barrie Arena Complex, Barrie ON

New Brunswick International Boat Show, Master Promotions Ltd., PO Box 565, Saint John NB E2L 3Z8 – 506/658-0018; Fax: 506/658-0750 – Show Manager, Sydney Jane Brittain – Annual consumer show, March – Exhibition Harbour Station, Saint John NB

Ottawa Boat & Sportsmen's Show/Ottawa Cottage Show, Canadian National Sportsmen's Shows (1989) Ltd., #202, 703 Evans Ave., Toronto ON M5C 5E9 – 416/695-0311; Fax: 416/695-0381 – Show Manager, Sherri Verdec – Annual consumer show. Boating, hunting, fishing, travel, Feb. – Civic Centre, Lansdowne Park,

Toronto In-water Boat Show & Sale, #810, 310 Front St. East, Toronto ON M5V 3B5 – 416/591-6772; Fax: 416/591-3582, Sept. – Toronto ON

Vancouver International Boat Show, Canadian National Sportsmen's Shows (1989) Ltd., #501, 4190 Lougheed Hwy., Burnaby BC V5C 6A8 – 604/294-1313; Fax: 604/294-4740 – Show Manager, Jim Carslake – Annual consumer show. Sail & powerboats, sailboards, inflatables, canoes, marine electronics, charters, sailing schools, travels, Feb. – BC Place Stadium, Vancouver BC

## BOOKS

Annual Conference & Trade Show, Ontario Library Association, #303, 100 Lombard St., Toronto ON M5C 1M3 – 416/363-3388; Fax: 416/941-9581; Email: ola@interlog.com; URL: http://www.ola.amlibs.ca – Executive Director, Larry Moore – Nov.

CLA Conference, Canadian Library Association, #602, 200 Elgin St., Ottawa ON K2P 1L5 – 613/232-9625; Fax: 613/563-9895; Email: ai077@freenet.carleton.ca; URL: http://www.cla.amlibs.ca – Events Coordinator, Susanne Fletcher – June

Convention & Trade Show, Canadian Booksellers Association, 301 Donlands Ave., Toronto ON

M4J 3R8 – 416/467-7883; Fax: 416/467-7886; Email: enquiries@cbabook.org; URL: http://www.cbabook.org – Executive Director, John Finlay, CAE – Annual trade show, June

Montréal Book Fair/Salon du livre de Montréal, Salon du livre de Montréal, #202, 480, boul St-Laurent, Montréal QC H2Y 3Y7 – 514/845-2365; Fax: 514/845-7119 – Exhibits Manager, Noreen Bélanger – Annual consumer show, Nov. – Montréal QC

Salon du Livre de Québec, #203, 1026, rue St-Jean, Québec QC G1R 1R7 – 418/692-5420; Fax: 418/692-0794; Email: bookfair@accent.net; URL: http://www.accent.net/bookfair – General Manager, Denis Lebrun – Annual consumer show, Sept. – Québec QC

Vancouver International Writers Festival, 1243 Cartwright St., Vancouver BC V6H 4B7 – 604/681-6330; Fax: 604/681-8400; Email: viwf@axionet.com; URL: http://www.axionet.com/writerfest – Producer, Alma Lee – Five-day literary arts festival, Oct. – Vancouver BC

The Word on the Street, #107, 100 West Pender St., Vancouver BC V6B 1R8 – 604/684-8266; Fax: 604/684-5788; Email: vanbook@cafe.net; URL: http://sites.sympatico.ca/wots – Producer, Kelly Juhasz – Book & magazine fair, last Sunday in Sept. – Vancouver BC

## BRIDAL

Bridal Show, VIEX Events Ltd., #2, 31 Bushby St., Victoria BC V8S 1B3 – 250/370-2983; Fax: 250/370-1733; URL: http://www.vicnet.net/~viex – Sales & Marketing Director, Patrick Doyle – Feb. 18-22 1998 – Mayfair Shopping Centre, Victoria BC

Canada's Bridal Show, 460 Hanlan Dr., 2nd Fl., Woodbridge ON L4L 1A6 – 905/264-7000; Fax: 905/264-7300 – Lorie Sansone – Annual consumer show. Bridal fashion shows, gifts, florists, photography, entertainment, travel, Jan. & Oct. – Toronto ON

National Bridal Show, Klanside Inc., 401 Magnetic Dr., Unit 21, North York ON M3J 3H9 – 416/661-2056; Fax: 416/661-2904 – Kathy O'Hara – Annual consumer show. Fashion shows, seminars & wedding-related exhibitors, Feb. – Exhibition Place, Toronto ON

Le Salon de la Mariée, Sheldon Kagan International Ltd., 35, McConnell, Dorval QC H9S 5L9 – 514/631-2160; Fax: 514/631-4430; Email: sheldon@sheldonkagan.com; URL: http://www.sheldonkagan.com – President, Sheldon Kagan – Annual consumer show, Jan. – Palais des Congrès, Montréal QC

Le Salon National des Futurs Mariés, Salon International des Futures Mariés Inc., #2, 1179, boul Décarie, St-Laurent QC H4L 3M8 – 514/748-2015; Fax: 514/748-2427 – Mike S. Homsy – Annual consumer show, Jan. – Montréal QC

Sudbury Wedding Show, DAC Marketing Ltd., PO Box 2837, Stn A, Sudbury ON P3A 5J3 – 705/673-5588; Fax: 705/525-0626 – President, Darren A. Ceccarelli – Jan. – Sudbury ON

The Total Wedding Show, Ten Star Productions Inc., 155 Castle Cr., Oakville ON L6J 5H4 – 905/845-2644; Fax: 905/333-1097 – Show Manager, Roberta Said – Annual consumer show, Jan.

Tropical Wedding & Honeymoon Show, International Tradeshow Services Inc., 20 Butterick Rd., Toronto ON M8W 3Z8 – 416/252-7791; Fax: 416/252-9848; Email: jimm@intltradeshows.com; URL: http://www.intltradeshows.com – President, James K. Mahon – May 8-10 1998 – Trade & Convention Centre, Vancouver BC

Wedding Dreams, Bingemans Conference & Recreation Centre, 1380 Victoria St. North, Kitchener ON N2B 3E2 – 519/744-1555; Fax: 519/744-1985 – Contact, Doris Hauck – Annual consumer show. Fashion shows, wedding exhibits, Jan. 10-11 1998

Wedding Wishes, Thunder Bay Chamber of Commerce Trade Show, 857 North May St., Thunder Bay ON P7C 3S2 – 807/622-9882; Fax: 807/622-7752; Email: chamber@tb-chamber.on.ca; URL: http://www.tb-chamber.on.ca – Show Manager, Arleene Mapledoram – Annual consumer show, Nov. – Thunder Bay ON

## BUSINESS

Annual Conference & Trade Show, Canadian Society of Association Executives, #1100, 10 King St. East, Toronto ON M5C 1C3 – 416/363-3555; Fax: 416/363-3630; Email: csae@csae.com – Executive Vice-President, Wayne Amundson, CAE, Email: w.amundson@csae.com – July – Hamilton Convention Centre, Hamilton ON

Business Expo, Saskatoon Chamber of Commerce, 345 - 3 Ave. South, Saskatoon SK S7K 1M6 – 306/244-2151; Fax: 306/244-8366 – President, Betty Ann Latrace-Henderson, 306/242-7268 – Oct.

Business Expo, Town Publishing Inc., Show Division, 875 Main St. West, Hamilton ON L8S 4R1 – 905/522-6117; Fax: 905/529-2242 – Show Manager, Lea Narciso – Annual consumer & trade show – Convention Centre, Hamilton ON

Business Start-up Exhibition, Martin International, #2910, 500, Place des Armes, Montréal QC H2Y 2W2 – 514/288-3931; Fax: 514/288-0641 – General Manager, Lorraine Boisvenue – Consumer show, Jan.

Business World Exhibition, Martin International, #2910, 500, Place des Armes, Montréal QC H2Y 2W2 – 514/288-3931; Fax: 514/288-0641 – General Manager, Lorraine Boisvenue – Trade show. International showcase, technology shows, finance, advertising, small business, home office, Jan.

Canadian Business Hall of Fame, Junior Achievement of Canada, One Westside Dr., Toronto ON M9C 1B2 – 416/622-4602; Fax: 416/622-6861; Tollfree: 1-800-265-0699 – President/CEO, George Habib – Consumer trade show. Showcase of student-manufactured products, April

Canadian National Franchising Exposition, Opportunities Canada, #42, 2550 Goldenridge Rd., Mississauga ON L4X 2S3 – 905/277-5600; Fax: 905/277-3397 – Sales Manager, Cheryl Higgins – Consumer show. Franchising opportunities, Feb.

Careers Marketplace, Martin International, #2910, 500, Place des Armes, Montréal QC H2Y 2W2 – 514/288-3931; Fax: 514/288-0641 – General Manager, Lorraine Boisvenue – Annual consumer show. Technological & scientific job market; franchising; office equipment, Jan.

Cash & Treasury Management Conference, Treasury Management Association of Canada, #1010, 8 King St. East, Toronto ON M5C 1B5 – 416/367-8500; Fax: 416/367-3240; Email: info@tmac.ca; URL: http://www.tmac.ca – Manager of Administration, Patricia Wood, Email: pchiasson@tmac.ca – Annual trade show. Bank products, communication systems, financial software, pension management, brokers, dealers, stock exchanges, commercial paper & computers, October

Expo International, Blackpages Network Inc., #1201, 347 Bay St., Toronto ON M5H 2R7 – 416/364-1900; Fax: 416/366-5385; Email: info@blackpages.net; URL: http://www.blackpages.net – Tony Ukonga – Annual trade & consumer show; business networking show for ethnic communities, Oct. – Toronto ON

Financial Forum, #235, 180 Shirreff Ave., North Bay ON P1B 7K9 – 705/495-4215; Fax: 705/495-4414; URL: http://www.finforum.com – Contact, Steven Kizell – Annual consumer show, Feb.

Financial Solutions, Canadian Tel-A-Views Ltd., #12, 115 Apple Creek Blvd., Markham ON L3R 6C9 – 905/477-2677; Fax: 905/477-7872; Tollfree: 1-800-891-4859 – President, Fred Cox – Held in Calgary & Ottawa, January/February

Franchise & Business Opportunities Expo, Prestige Promotions, PO Box 135, Etobicoke ON M9C 4V2 – 905/238-3320; Fax: 905/277-3397 – Bob Sinclair – Held in Kitchener, London, Ottawa, Toronto, Moncton, Halifax, Winnipeg. Vancouver, Victoria. Annual consumer shows

Home-Based Business & Opportunities Shows, Home Business Exhibitions, 2956 Shannon Lake Rd., Westbank BC V4T 1T6 – 250/768-9561 – Annually in Edmonton, Calgary, Vancouver & Abbotsford

The London Business-To-Business Show, Jenkins Show Productions, 1076 Skyvalley Cr., Oakville ON L6M 3L2 – 905/827-4632; Fax: 905/827-8139; Tollfree: 1-800-465-1073 – President, Dave Jenkins – Feb. – London Convention Centre, London ON

Metro North Business Show & Conference, Canadian Tel-A-Views Ltd., #12, 115 Apple Creek Blvd., Markham ON L3R 6C9 – 905/477-2677; Fax: 905/477-7872; Tollfree: 1-800-891-4859 – President, Fred Cox – Annual consumer show. Products & services for business, plus franchising & dealership opportunities, September/October

Ottawa Business Show, Connelly Business Exhibitions Inc., #214, 2487 Kaladar Ave., Ottawa ON K1V 8B9 – 613/731-9850; Fax: 613/731-2407 – Vice-President, Marketing, Dan Hamilton – Annual trade show. Office equipment & systems, computers, communications, financial & investment services, advertising & marketing products; local, national & international, May – Ottawa ON

Salon international de la franchise et des réseaux d'affaires/International Franchising & Business Network Show, Promexpo Inc., 801, rue Sherbrooke est, 10e étage, Montréal QC H2L 1K7 – 514/527-9221; Fax: 514/527-8449 – Jacques Lasnier – Annual consumer show, Oct.

Saving & Investment Marketplace, Martin International, #2910, 500, Place des Armes, Montréal QC H2Y 2W2 – 514/288-3931; Fax: 514/288-0641 – General Manager, Lorraine Boisvenue – Annual trade & consumer show. RRSPs, mutual funds, real estate tax shelters, Jan.

Services & Suppliers Exposition, Human Resources Professionals Association of Ontario, #1902, 2 Bloor St. West, Toronto ON M4W 3E2 – 416/923-2324 (Office & Resource Line); Fax: 416/923-7264; Tollfree: 1-800-387-1311; Email: info@hrpao.org; URL: http://www.hrpao.org – Trade Show Manager, Marta Pawych – Annual trade show, Feb.

Thunder Bay Chamber of Commerce Trade Show, 857 North May St., Thunder Bay ON P7C 3S2 – 807/622-9882; Fax: 807/622-7752; Email: chamber@tb-chamber.on.ca; URL: http://www.tb-chamber.on.ca – Show Manager, Arleene Mapledoram – Annual trade & consumer show, May

Vancouver Island Business Trade Show, Greater Nanaimo Chamber of Commerce, 777 Poplar St., Nanaimo BC V9S 2H7 – 250/753-1191; Fax: 250/754-5186; Email: chamber@island.net; URL: http://www.island.net/~chamber/ – Executive Director, Jane Hutchins – Annual trade show, Sept.

Yukon Trade Show, PO Box 4044, Whitehorse YT Y1A 3S9 – 867/668-7979 – Contact, Al Dibbs – Annually, April – Mount McIntyre Recreation Centre & Takhini Arena

**CARS *See* AUTOMOTIVE**

## CHEMISTRY

Canadian Society of Clinical Chemists Annual Meeting, Events & Management Plus Inc., 190 Railway St., PO Box 1570, Kingston ON K7L 5C8 – 613/531-9210; Fax: 613/531-0626; Email: events@adan.kingston.net – Owner, E. Hooper – June

## CHILDREN

Canadian Juvenile Products Trade Show, Canadian Toy Association, PO Box 294, Kleinburg ON L0J 1C0 – 905/893-1689; Fax: 905/893-2392 – Executive Director, Sheila Edmondson – Jan.

City Parent Family Show, Premier Consumer Shows, City Parent Newsmagazine, 467 Speers Rd., Oakville ON L6K 3S4 – 905/815-0017; Fax: 905/815-0511; Tollfree: 1-800-387-7682 – Show Coordinator, Darren Melanson – Annual consumer show, July – Toronto ON

Edmonton International Children's Festival, c/o Citadel Theatre, 9828 - 101A Ave., Edmonton AB T5J 3C6 – 403/428-4811 – May

Milk International Children's Festival, Harbourfront Centre, #100, 410 Queens Quay West, Toronto ON M5V 2Z3 – 416/973-4600; Fax: 416/973-6055; Email: publicity@harbourfront.on.ca; URL: http://www.harbourfront.on.ca – Artistic Director, Don Shipley

Northern Alberta International Children's Festival, c/o 5 St. Anne St., St. Albert AB T8N 3Z9 – 403/459-1693; Fax: 403/458-5417; Email: gailb@st-albert.net; URL: http://www.discoveralberta.com/childfest – May/June – St. Alberta AB

Northern Saskatchewan International Children's Festival, PO Box 1642, Saskatoon SK S7K 3R8 – 306/664-3378; Fax: 306/664-2344 – Artistic Co-Director, Cass Cozens – Annually, June. Four day international festival of the performing arts for children

Regina International Children's Festival, 2201 Hamilton St., Regina SK S4P 2E7 – 306/352-7655; Fax: 306/525-6947 – Producer, Christa Donaldson – Annually, June. Four day festival & cultural activities for children

**CHRISTMAS CRAFTS *See* CRAFTS**

## CLEANING

Can-Clean, Canadian Sanitation Supply Association, #G10, 300 Mill Rd., Etobicoke ON M9C 4W7 – 416/620-9320; Fax: 416/620-7199; Email: cssa@the_wire.com; URL: http://www.cssa.com – Executive Director, Diane Gosling – Sanitation & maintenance chemicals; equipment & industrial cleaning supplies; for distributors & end-users, April – Exhibition Place, Toronto ON

CLATA Update '98: Canadian Launderers & Dry Cleaners Exposition, International Tradeshow Services Inc., 20 Butterick Rd., Toronto ON M8W 3Z8 – 416/252-7791; Fax: 416/252-9848; Email: jimm@intltradeshows.com; URL: http://www.intltradeshows.com – Glenn Watermann – Quadrennial trade show, April 1998 – Toronto Congress Centre, Toronto ON

## COMMUNICATIONS

Annual Conference, Canadian Association of Broadcasters, #306, 350 Sparks St., PO Box 627, Stn B, Ottawa ON K1P 5S2 – 613/233-4035; Fax: 613/233-6961; URL: http://www.cab-acr.ca – President & CEO, Michael McCabe – Annual trade show, Oct. 19-21 1997 – Metro Toronto Convention Centre, Toronto ON

Annual Convention & Cablexpo, Canadian Cable Television Association, #1010, 360 Albert St., Ottawa ON K1R 7X7 – 613/232-2631; Fax: 613/232-2137 – President, Richard Stursberg – Cable TV products & technologies, May 18-21 1998 – Montréal QC

CCBE Broadcast Equipment Trade Show, c/o Secretariat, CCBE, 1466 Kalligan Court, Mississauga ON L4X 1A8 – 905/566-9654; Fax: 905/270-5521 – George Roach – Annual trade show

International Communications Conference, Venue West Conference Services Ltd., #645, 375 Water St., Vancouver BC V6B 5C6 – 604/681-5226; Fax: 604/681-2503; Email: congress@venuewest.com; URL: http://www.venuwest.com – President, Betty Fata – May 29 - June 4 1999

MultiMedia, Multimedia Trade Shows Inc., #7, 70 Villarboit Cres., Concord ON L4K 4C7 – 905/660-2491; Fax: 905/660-2492; Email: bcole@multimedia.ca; URL: http://www.newmedia.ca – President, Bruce Cole – Annual trade show & conference featuring film & video production, electronic design & visual communications, May 12-15 1998 – Metro Toronto Convention Centre, Toronto ON

Multimedia in Education, Multimedia Trade Shows Inc., #7, 70 Villarboit Cres., Concord ON L4K 4C7 – 905/660-2491; Fax: 905/660-2492; Email: bcole@multimedia.ca; URL: http://www.newmedia.ca – Jai Cole – Annual trade show & conference for public education, post-secondary & training, May 12-15 1998 – Metro Toronto Convention Centre, Toronto ON

Production '97, c/o Production APIIS Inc., 1276, rue Amherst, Montréal QC H2L 3K8 – 514/842-5333; Fax: 514/842-6717 – Contact, Claudine Letourneau – Annual trade show, May

Salon des communications canadien/Canadian Communications Show, Communications Show, CP 1241, Succ B, Hull QC J8X 3X7 – 418/877-8898; Fax: 418/877-9711 – Président, Roch Gamache – Nov.

Showcase on Production, Multimedia Trade Shows Inc., #7, 70 Villarboit Cres., Concord ON L4K 4C7 – 905/660-2491; Fax: 905/660-2492; Email: bcole@multimedia.ca; URL: http://www.newmedia.ca – Jai Cole – Annual trade show & conference. Film, video, television, broadcast, audio visual, sound & multimedia production, May 12-15 1998

TeleCon - CBTA Exposition & Conference, International Tradeshow Services Inc., 20 Butterick Rd., Toronto ON M8W 3Z8 – 416/252-7791; Fax: 416/252-9848; Email: jimm@intltradeshows.com; URL: http://www.intltradeshows.com – Show Manager, Glen Waterman – Annual trade show, Sept. 1-3 1998 – Metro Toronto Convention Centre, Toronto ON

Televolution, MW Productions, #4, 88 Courcelette Rd., Scarborough ON M1N 2T2 – 416/691-6526; Fax: 416/691-6928; Tollfree: 1-800-267-4529; Email: ron.mackenzie@mwprod.com; URL: http://www.mwprod.com – Ron MacKenzie – Annual trade show, March – Metro Toronto Convention Centre, Toronto ON

Televolution East, MW Productions, #4, 88 Courcelette Rd., Scarborough ON M1N 2T2 – 416/691-6526; Fax: 416/691-6928; Tollfree: 1-800-267-4529; Email: ron.mackenzie@mwprod.com; URL: http://www.mwprod.com – Ron MacKenzie – Annual trade show. Telecommunications equipment, Oct. – Saint John NB

VICOM, Multimedia Trade Shows Inc., #7, 70 Villarboit Cres., Concord ON L4K 4C7 – 905/660-2491; Fax: 905/660-2492; Email: bcole@multimedia.ca; URL: http://www.newmedia.ca – President, Bruce Cole – May 12-15 1998

VoicePower, #808, 15 Gervais Dr., North York ON M3C 1Y8 – 416/449-7229; Fax: 416/449-8944 – Contact, Jacob Gordon – Annual conference & trade show of the voice/fax processing industry

## COMPUTERS

Atlantic Canada Business & Computer Show, Denex Group Inc., Burnside Industrial Park, 192 Joseph Zatzman Dr., Dartmouth NS B3B 1N4 – 902/468-4999; Fax: 902/468-2795; Email: denman@ns.sympatico.ca; URL: http://www.denexgroup.com – President, Jon Denman – Annual, Sept. – Halifax NS

Calgary Business Computer Show, Industrial Trade & Consumer Shows Inc., #2450, 101 - 6th Ave SW, Calgary AB T2P 3P4 – 403/266-8700; Fax: 403/266-6814 – Contact, Steve Henrich – Annual trade show & conference. Computer products & information, management technology, including hardware, software, open systems, multimedia, peripherals; home-based office & mobile office products, Oct. – Stampede Park, Calgary AB

Canadian Conference & Showcase on Object Technology, Plesman Expositions & Conferences Inc., 2005 Sheppard Ave. East, 4th Fl., North York ON M2J 5B1 – 416/497-9562; Fax: 416/497-9427; Tollfree: 1-800-387-5012; URL: http://www.netcon.plesman.com – Show Coordinator, Sean Wainwright – Annual trade & consumer show, Nov. – Toronto ON

Canadian Integrated Manufacturing & Design Show, Reed Exhibition Companies Inc., 3761 Victoria Park Ave., Scarborough ON M1W 3S2 – 416/491-7565; Fax: 416/491-5088

COMDEX/Canada, Softbank Comdex, 300 First Ave., Needham MA 02194-2722 – 617/449-6600, 416/283-3334; Fax: 617/449-6617; Email: http://www.comdex.com – Robert Berkowitz – Annual trade show & conference (July) in up-scale information systems for volume buyers of computer & communications products; also COMDEX/Pacific Rim in Vancouver (January) & COMDEX/Québec in Montréal (October)

Computer Fest, Show Fest Productions Inc., #5, 60 St. Clair Ave. West, Toronto ON M4V 1M7 – 416/925-4533; Fax: 416/925-7701; Email: gendel@compfest.com; URL: http://www.compfest.com – David Carter – Consumer show (Feb., Apr., Sept., Nov.). Computers & internet products, services, seminars, demonstrations & information for home, business & education – Toronto ON

Connected Computing, Softbank Comdex, 300 First Ave., Needham MA 02194-2722 – 617/449-6600, 416/283-3334; Fax: 617/449-6617; Email: http://www.comdex.com – Robert Berkowitz – Annual trade show, July – Toronto ON

Edmonton Computer & Business Show, Industrial Trade & Consumer Shows Inc., #2450, 101 - 6th Ave SW, Calgary AB T2P 3P4 – 403/266-8700; Fax: 403/266-6814 – Contact, Steve Henrich – Annual trade show: hardware, software, office equipment, networking, peripherals, integrated systems, Oct. – Edmonton Convention Centre, Edmonton AB

Electronic Design Showcase, Multimedia Trade Shows Inc., #7, 70 Villarboit Cres., Concord ON L4K 4C7 – 905/660-2491; Fax: 905/660-2492; Email: bcole@multimedia.ca; URL: http://www.newmedia.ca – Jai Cole – Annual trade show & conference. Design communications, including graphic design, publication & art direction, electronic design, prepress, typography, illustration, printing & service bureau services, May 12-15 1998

Executive Symposium & Showcase on Open Client/Server Computing, Plesman Expositions & Conferences Inc., 2005 Sheppard Ave. East, 4th Fl., North York ON M2J 5B1 – 416/497-9562; Fax: 416/497-9427; Tollfree: 1-800-387-5012; URL: http://www.netcon.plesman.com – Show Coordinator,

Sean Wainwright – Annual trade & consumer show, May

Focus on Video, Promex Productions Inc., 118 Indian Rd., 2nd Fl., Toronto ON M6R 2V4 – 416/531-2121; Fax: 416/531-2194 – Show Manager, Angela Abromaitis – Annual trade show. Video hardware, software, accessories & systems, Sept.

La Foire du Micro-Ordinateur, c/o Gestion Micro-Québec, 726, av Glazier, Vanier QC G1M 2Z2 – 418/527-6648; Fax: 418/527-2067 – Annual consumer show, Nov.

Game Fest, Show Fest Productions Inc., #5, 60 St. Clair Ave. West, Toronto ON M4V 1M7 – 416/925-4533; Fax: 416/925-7701; Email: gendel@compfest.com; URL: http://www.compfest.com – David Carter – Computer games for sales, in demonstration & in test-drive centres, Nov. – Arrow Hall, International Centre, Mississauga ON

International Symposium on Robotics & Exhibition, Golden Planners Inc., #401, 126 York St., Ottawa ON K1N 5T5 – 613/241-9333; Fax: 613/565-2173; Email: gpi@intranet.ca – Senior Associate, Phil Ecclestone – May 14-17 2000 – Montréal QC

Internet Forum, Show Fest Productions Inc., #5, 60 St. Clair Ave. West, Toronto ON M4V 1M7 – 416/925-4533; Fax: 416/925-7701; Email: gendel@compfest.com; URL: http://www.compfest.com – David Carter – Internet services, seminars, demonstrations & information, April – Arrow Hall, International Centre, Mississauga ON

Mac Expo, Show Fest Productions Inc., #5, 60 St. Clair Ave. West, Toronto ON M4V 1M7 – 416/925-4533; Fax: 416/925-7701; Email: gendel@compfest.com; URL: http://www.compfest.com – David Carter – Macintosh computers, software, services, seminars, demonstrations & information for home, business & education, Feb. – Automotive Bldg., Exhibition Place, Toronto ON

Micro Expo, Groupe Expocor Inc., #G-03, 360, rue Notre-Dame ouest, Montréal QC H2Y 1T9 – 514/844-0502; Fax: 514/849-9517; Email: admi@expocor.qc.ca; URL: http://www.expocor.qc.ca – Show Coordinator, Claude Thibault – Semi-annual consumer show (March & November)

National Factory Automation Show, Reed Exhibition Companies Inc., 3761 Victoria Park Ave., Scarborough ON M1W 3S2 – 416/491-7565; Fax: 416/491-5088 – Show Manager, Glen Chiasson – Annual trade show alternating between Toronto & Montréal, Sept.

Netcon, Plesman Expositions & Conferences Inc., 2005 Sheppard Ave. East, 4th Fl., North York ON M2J 5B1 – 416/497-9562; Fax: 416/497-9427; Tollfree: 1-800-387-5012; URL: http://www.netcon.plesman.com – Show Coordinator, Sean Wainwright – Annual trade show for computer networking & connectivity; also Montréal, Ottawa, Calgary, Vancouver, Sept. – Toronto ON

Ontario Computer Fairs, 185 Macdonell Ave., Toronto ON M6R 2A4 – 416/535-3761; Fax: 416/535-8091, April 1997 – Kitchener Memorial Auditorium Complex, Kitchener ON

VARDEX Exhibition & Conference, Reed Exhibition Companies Inc., 3761 Victoria Park Ave., Scarborough ON M1W 3S2 – 416/491-7565; Fax: 416/491-5088 – Show Manager, Janet Whidett – Annual trade show, May – Toronto ON

Virtual Reality World, Multimedia Trade Shows Inc., #7, 70 Villarboit Cres., Concord ON L4K 4C7 – 905/660-2491; Fax: 905/660-2492; Email: bcole@multimedia.ca; URL: http://www.newmedia.ca – President, Bruce Cole – May 12-15 1998

Windows World, Softbank Comdex, 300 First Ave., Needham MA 02194-2722 – 617/449-6600, 416/283-3334; Fax: 617/449-6617; Email: http://www.comdex.com – Robert Berkowitz – Annual trade show. Windows products, tools, platforms, July – Metro Toronto Convention Centre, Toronto ON

## CONSTRUCTION & BUILDING PRODUCTS

Atlantic Building Materials Show, Atlantic Building Supply Dealers Association, #203, 95 Foundry St., Moncton NB E1C 5H7 – 506/858-0700; Fax: 506/859-0064; Tollfree: 1-800-561-7114; Email: absda@fox.nstn.ca; URL: http://Fox.nstn.ca/~absda/ – President, John J. Ward – Annual trade show, March

Best Ottawa/Buildex, Intertrade Communications Inc., #203, 43 Roydon Place, Nepean ON K2E 1A3 – 613/224-3013; Fax: 613/224-4533; Tollfree: 1-888-662-6660; Email: trades@magi.com – Event Manager, Pauline Gaudet – Nov. – Ottawa Civic Centre, Ottawa ON

Buildex, RK Communications, #306, 1755 West Broadway, Vancouver BC V6J 4S5 – 604/739-2112; Fax: 604/739-2124 – Regional Manager, Mark Stephenson, Email: marks@mediaedge.ca – Annual trade show, March – Vancouver Trade & Convention Centre,

Canadian Construction Show, Southex Exhibitions, 4285 Canada Way, Burnaby BC V5G 1H2 – 604/433-5121; Fax: 604/434-6853; Tollfree: 1-800-633-8332; URL: http://www.southex.com – Vice-President, Western Region, Fred Barnes – Feb. 18-20 1998 – Toronto ON

Canadian Rental Mart, AIS Communications Ltd., 145 Thames Rd. West, Exeter ON N0M 1S3 – 519/235-2400; Fax: 519/235-0798 – Contact, Peter Phillips – Annual trade show. Construction equipment, power tools & party goods, March – International Centre, Toronto ON

CanGlass, AIS Communications Ltd., 145 Thames Rd. West, Exeter ON N0M 1S3 – 519/235-2400; Fax: 519/235-0798 – Contact, Peter Phillips – Annual trade show. Architecture, auto glass, June – Royal Constellation Hotel, Toronto ON

Expo-Rencontre Contech Inc., 257, rue Saint-Jean, Longueuil QC J4H 2X4 – 514/646-1833; Fax: 514/646-3918 – Show Manager, Lise Monette – Annual trade show, October in Montréal, & November in Québec City

Salon Constructo, 1500, boul Jules-Poitras, Saint-Laurent QC H4N 1X7 – 514/745-5720; Fax: 514/339-2267 – Show Manager, Mark Perlstein – Annual trade show, November

## COSMETICS

Esthetics 2000, #14, 1380 Matheson Blvd. East, Mississauga ON L4W 4P8 – 905/238-6875; Fax: 905/238-6876 – Annual trade show, May

## CRAFTS

Annual Christmas Fair, Prince Edward Island Crafts Council, 156 Richmond St., Charlottetown PE C1A 1H9 – 902/892-5152; Fax: 902/628-8740; URL: gopher://gopher.well.sf.ca.us/00/Art/PEI.Crafts.Council – Nov. – Confederation Centre, Charlottetown PE

Art Market, Art Market Productions, PO Box 385, Banff AB T0L 0C0 – 403/762-2345 – Marlene Loney – Annual consumer show; art & craft sale, Nov. – Calgary AB

Atlantic Craft Trade Show, Nova Scotia Development & Tourism, PO Box 519, Halifax NS B3J 2R7 – 902/424-8609; Fax: 902/424-5739; Email: econ.jgillis@gov.ns.ca – Trade Officer, Peter L. Giffin – Annual trade show. Juried craft & giftware products, Feb.

Bazaart, MacKenzie Art Gallery, 3475 Albert St., Regina SK S4S 6X6 – 306/522-4242; Fax: 306/569-8191 – Bonnie Schaffer – Juried outdoor art show & sale; complete range of crafts

Big M Craft & Bake Sale, Manitoba Stampede & Exhibition, PO Box 849, Morris MB R0G 1K0 – 204/746-2552; Fax: 204/746-2900 – Contact, Allen Recksiedler – Oct.

Cameo's Canadian Spring Craft Sale, Cameo Convention Consultants Ltd., 7418 - 182 St., Edmonton AB T5T 2G7 – 403/481-6268; Fax: 403/243-0666 – President, Mamie Bercov – Annual consumer show, April

Cameo's Christmas Craft Sale, Cameo Convention Consultants Ltd., 7418 - 182 St., Edmonton AB T5T 2G7 – 403/481-6268; Fax: 403/243-0666 – President, Mamie Bercov – Annual consumer show, Nov.

Christmas at the Forum - Festival of Crafts, Antiques, Art & Foods, DMS Enterprises Ltd., 5647 Morris St., Halifax NS B3J 1C4 – 902/425-5656 – Coordinator, Donna Susnick – Annual consumer show, Nov. – Halifax NS

Christmas Craft & Gift Show, Canadian Shows & Special Events Inc., #1801, One Yonge St., Toronto ON M5E 1W7 – 416/363-1292; Fax: 416/369-0515 – Marketing & Sales Manager, Josie Graziosi – Annual consumer show for all age groups, Nov. – Toronto Congress Centre, Toronto ON

Christmas Tradition, DAC Marketing Ltd., PO Box 2837, Stn A, Sudbury ON P3A 5J3 – 705/673-5588; Fax: 705/525-0626 – President, Darren A. Ceccarelli – Annual consumer shows. Various locations throughout Ontario

Country Decorating & Collectibles Show & Sale, Synergic Media Ltd., RR#4, Uxbridge ON L9P 1R4 – 905/649-2480; Fax: 905/649-1022 – Show Producer, Ian Russell – Consumer show held in March, June, September & November – Markham Fairgrounds, Markham ON

Craft & Trade Show, Town of Springdale, PO Box 52, Springdale NF A0J 1T0 – 709/673-4313; Fax: 709/673-4969 – Recreation Director, Greg Hillier – Annually, third weekend of September

Craft Christmas Gift Sale, Nepean Sportsplex, 101 Centrepointe Dr., Nepean ON K2G 5K7 – 613/727-6641; Fax: 613/727-6613 – Projects Co-ordinator, Billie Swartzack – Annual consumer show, Nov.

Craft Fairs, Newfoundland & Labrador Crafts Development Association, Devon House, 59 Duckworth St., St. John's NF A1C 1E6 – 709/753-2749; Fax: 709/753-2766; Email: anne_manuel@porthole.entnet.nf.ca – Executive Director, Anne Manuel – St. John's (July, October, November); Corner Brook (November)

Craft-Ex, DAC Marketing Ltd., PO Box 2837, Stn A, Sudbury ON P3A 5J3 – 705/673-5588; Fax: 705/525-0626 – President, Darren A. Ceccarelli – Annual consumer show in Timmins & Sudbury, April

Crafts, Fabrics & More, Canadian Craft & Hobby Association, #24, 1410 - 40 Ave. NE, Calgary AB T2E 6L1 – 403/291-0559; Fax: 403/291-0675; Tollfree: 1-888-991-0559; Email: ccha@cadvision.com; URL: http://www.cdncraft.org – Executive Director, Patrice Baron-Parent – May 23-25 1998 – Calgary AB

Craftworld, Cryderman Productions, 136 Thames St., Chatham ON N7L 2Y8 – 519/351-8344; Fax: 519/351-8345 – John Cryderman – Semi-annual shows in Chatham, Kitchener, London, Sarnia; annual shows in Stratford, Surrey

Elegance Christmas Craft Show, Contemporary Craft Shows Ltd., 37 Langley Ave., Toronto ON M4K 3V9 – 416/465-2379; Fax: 416/465-2379 – Casey Sadaka – Nov.

Metro Toronto Christmas Gift Show & Sale, Metro Toronto Christmas Show, Lawrence Plaza, PO Box 54045, Toronto ON M6A 3B7 – 416/789-1925 – Sam

Davis – Annual consumer show, Dec. – Skydome, Toronto ON

Na'Amat Shoppers' Fair & Auction at Toronto Congress Centre, c/o 272 Codsell Ave., North York ON M3H 3X2 – 416/636-5425; Fax: 416/636-5248 – Lorraine Levene – Annually, November – Toronto ON

One of a Kind Christmas Canadian Craft Show & Sale, The Canadian Craft Show Ltd., 21 Grenville St., Toronto ON M4Y 1A1 – 416/960-3680; Fax: 416/923-5624 – Show Coordinator, Patti Stewart – Annual consumer show, November/December – Toronto ON

One of a Kind Springtime Canadian Craft Show & Sale, The Canadian Craft Show Ltd., 21 Grenville St., Toronto ON M4Y 1A1 – 416/960-3680; Fax: 416/923-5624 – Show Coordinator, Patti Stewart – Annual consumer show, March/April – Automotive Building, Exhibition Place, Toronto ON

ORIGINALS - The Spring Craft Sale, Southex Exhibitions Inc., #440, 47 Clarence St., Ottawa ON K1N 9K1 – 613/241-2888; Fax: 613/241-1827 – Show Manager, Tom Gamble – Consumer show, April 1997 – Civic Centre, Lansdowne Park, Ottawa ON

Ottawa Christmas Craft Sale, Southex Exhibitions Inc., #440, 47 Clarence St., Ottawa ON K1N 9K1 – 613/241-2888; Fax: 613/241-1827 – Show Manager, Tom Gamble – Consumer show, Dec. – Civic Centre, Lansdowne Park, Ottawa ON

Pine Tree Potters Sale, 22 Church St., Aurora ON L4G 1G4 – 905/727-1278 – April & November

Plein Art Québec, Conseil des métiers d'art du Québec, 378, rue St-Paul ouest, Montréal QC H2Y 2A6 – 514/287-7555; Fax: 514/287-9923 – Directeur général, Yvan Gauthier – Annual consumer show, August – Québec QC

Salon des métiers d'arts, Conseil des métiers d'art du Québec, 378, rue St-Paul ouest, Montréal QC H2Y 2A6 – 514/287-7555; Fax: 514/287-9923 – Directeur général, Yvan Gauthier – Annual consumer show, Dec. – Montréal QC

Saskatchewan Handcraft Festival, 813 Broadway Ave., Saskatoon SK S7N 1B5 – 306/653-3616; Fax: 306/244-2711 – Marketing Coordinator, Chris Jones – Annual three-day festival, July – Battleford SK

Sew Creative, Craft & Quilting Show, Hank Hartloper Agency, #2, 1575 Seel Ave., Winnipeg MB R3T 1C8 – 204/925-1620; Fax: 204/925-1623 – Owner, Hank Hartloper – Oct. 16-17 1998 – Winnipeg MB

Signatures in Christmas Craft, Contemporary Craft Shows Ltd., 37 Langley Ave., Toronto ON M4K 3V9 – 416/465-2379; Fax: 416/465-2379 – Casey Sadaka – Annual consumer show, Dec.

Signatures Québec, Contemporary Craft Shows Ltd., 37 Langley Ave., Toronto ON M4K 3V9 – 416/465-2379; Fax: 416/465-2379 – Casey Sadaka – Annual consumer show, Nov. – Québec QC

Springtime at the Forum - Festival of Crafts, Antiques, Art & Foods, DMS Enterprises Ltd., 5647 Morris St., Halifax NS B3J 1C4 – 902/425-5656 – Coordinator, Donna Susnick – Annual consumer show, May – Halifax NS

Sundog Handcraft Fair, PO Box 7183, Saskatoon SK S7K 4J1 – 306/384-7364; Fax: 306/384-7364 – Coordinator, Diane Boyko Horbay – Juried three-day craft market plus continuous stage acts & gourmet food court. Annually, first weekend of December

Victoria Park Arts/Crafts Fair, 655 Main St., Moncton NB E1C 1E8 – 506/853-3516; Fax: 506/859-2629 – Contact, Linda O'Neill – Annually, August

Wintergreen, 813 Broadway Ave., Saskatoon SK S7N 1B5 – 306/653-3616; Fax: 306/244-2711 – Marketing Coordinator, Chris Jones – Annual. Three day Christmas craft market, Nov. – Regina SK

**DANCE *See* MUSIC**

**DECORATING *See* HOME SHOWS**

## DENTAL

Annual Spring Meeting, Ontario Dental Association, 4 New St., Toronto ON M5R 1P6 – 416/922-3900; Fax: 416/922-9005; URL: http://www.oda.on.ca/ – Coordinator, Diana Thorneycroft – Dental products, equipment & services, May

Canadian Association of Orthodontists, Taylor Enterprises Ltd., #310, 2175 Sheppard Ave. East, North York ON M2J 1W8 – 416/491-2897; Fax: 416/491-1670; Tollfree: 1-800-208-9398; Email: taylor@interlog.com; URL: http://www.interlog.com/~taylor/htehome.html – President – Joan Milne, Oct. 1998

Winter Clinic, Toronto Academy of Dentistry, #902, 170 Bloor St. West, Toronto ON M5S 1T9 – 416/967-5649; Fax: 416/967-5081 – Executive Administrator, Raisyl Wagman – Annual trade show, Nov. – Metro Toronto Convention Centre, Toronto ON

## ELECTRICAL/ELECTRONICS

Armed Forces Communications Electronics Association Show, Richmor Enterprises, #201, 251 Laurier Ave. West, Ottawa ON K1P 5J6 – 613/563-0093; Fax: 613/236-4351; Email: richmor@cyberus.ca – Conference Manager, Bernadette Dawson – April – Congress Centre, Ottawa ON

The Canadian Consumer Electronics Exposition, PO Box 1500-1288, Etobicoke ON M9C 4V5 – 416/620-6620; Fax: 416/621-6688 – Shirley Trotter – Annual trade & consumer show, Sept.

Canadian High Technology Show, Reed Exhibition Companies Inc., 3761 Victoria Park Ave., Scarborough ON M1W 3S2 – 416/491-7565; Fax: 416/491-5088 – Group Show Manager, Mike Sweetman – Annual (Toronto) & biennial (Ottawa) trade show. Electronic components, robotics, communications systems

Electrical Showcase '2000, Manitoba Electrical League, #14, 395 Berry St., Winnipeg MB R3J 1N6 – 204/885-3668; Fax: 204/885-3678 – Executive Director, Larry McLennan – Triennial trade show

Eptech, Lakeview Publications, #27, 1200 Aerowood Dr., Mississauga ON L4W 2S7 – 905/624-8100; Fax: 905/624-1760; Email: info@ept.ca; URL: http://www.ept.ca – President, Robert C. Luton – Trade show held in various locations. Electronic components, systems

ExpoLectria, Corporation des maîtres électriciens du Québec, #100, 5925, boul Décarie, Montréal QC H3W 3C9 – 514/738-2184; Fax: 514/738-2192; Tollfree: 1-800-361-9061 – Directeur général et secrétaire executif, Yvon Guilbault – Annual trade show, May

## ENVIRONMENT

Calgary Environmental Tradeshow & Conference, Southex Exhibitions Inc., #300, 999 - 8 St. SW, Calgary AB T2R 1N7 – 403/244-6111; Fax: 403/245-8666; Tollfree: 1-800-387-2446; Email: info@petroleumshow.com; URL: http://www.southex.com – Pat Atkinson – Annual trade show for environmental technology, products & services, Oct. – Convention Centre, Calgary AB

Canadian Environmental Technology Showcase, Reed Exhibition Companies Inc., 3761 Victoria Park Ave., Scarborough ON M1W 3S2 – 416/491-7565; Fax: 416/491-5088 – Annual trade show, May – Place Bonaventure, Montréal QC

CETECH - Canadian Environmental Technology Pavilion, Reed Exhibition Companies Inc., 3761 Victoria Park Ave., Scarborough ON M1W 3S2 – 416/491-7565; Fax: 416/491-5088 – Environmental products, technology & services; part of Canadian Manufacturing Week, Oct. – International Centre, Toronto ON

Globe '98 International Trade Fair & Conference on Business & the Environment, The Globe Foundation of Canada, #504, 999 Canada Place, Vancouver BC V6C 3E1 – 604/775-1994; Fax: 604/666-8123; Email: info@globe.apfnet.org; URL: http://www.globe.ca – President & CEO, Dr. John D. Wiebe – Sixth in a biennial series of trade fairs & conferences on developing the business of the environment; only major international event in North America for the environment industry, the corporate sector & the finance & investment community; offers exhibitors access to the Asia Pacific, North American & Latin American marketplaces, March 17-20 1998 – Vancouver Trade & Convention Centre, Vancouver BC

International Association on Water Quality, Venue West Conference Services Ltd., #645, 375 Water St., Vancouver BC V6B 5C6 – 604/681-5226; Fax: 604/681-2503; Email: congress@venuewest.com; URL: http://www.venuwest.com – President, Betty Fata – June 20-29 1998

International Environment & Economy Crossroads, 1431, Bourgeoys, Longueuil QC J4M 1Z4 – 514/647-5530; Fax: 514/647-1031 – Show Manager, Marcel Gaudreault – Annual trade & consumer show. Innovation showcase, four-day conference & gala, May

Plast-X '98, Environment & Plastics Industry Council, #500, 5925 Airport Rd., Mississauga ON L4V 1W1 – 905/678-7748; Fax: 905/678-0774 – President, Sandra Birkenmayer – Oct. 1998 – International Centre, Toronto ON

Toronto Environmental Tradeshow & Conference, Southex Exhibitions Inc., #300, 999 - 8 St. SW, Calgary AB T2R 1N7 – 403/244-6111; Fax: 403/245-8666; Tollfree: 1-800-387-2446; Email: info@petroleumshow.com; URL: http://www.southex.com – Pat Atkinson – Environmental technology, products & services relating to: air pollution control; consulting; water & wastewater treatment; laboratory analysis & testing; solid & hazardous waste; transportation handling & disposal; site remediation; health, safety & protection; treatment of contaminated underground water, May 1998 – International Centre, Toronto ON

**ETHNIC *See* MULTICULTURAL**

## EVENTS

***See Also* Specific categories for events such as Winter Carnivals, Music Festivals, Rodeos, Exhibitions, etc.**

Atlantic Canada Bicycle Rally, PO Box 1555, Stn M, Halifax NS B3J 2Y3 – 902/423-2453; URL: http://home.istar.ca/~cycling – Gary Conrod – Largest bicycle event in Atlantic Canada, August

Benson & Hedges Inc. Symphony of Fire, c/o 1500 Don Mills Rd., North York ON M3B 3L1 – Annual fireworks competitions at Montreal, Toronto & Vancouver

Billy Barker Days, PO Box 4441, Quesnel BC V2J 3J4 – 250/992-1234 – July 16-19 1998

Blossom Festival, PO Box 329, Creston BC V0B 1G0 – 250/428-4342 – May, long weekend

Brantford's Riverfest, 1 Sherwood Dr., Brantford ON N3T 1N3 – 519/751-9900; Tollfree: 1-800-265-6299; Email: riverfest@bfree.on.ca; URL: http://www.bfree.on.ca/comdir/festivals/riverfest – Celebration of the Grand River, May

Brockville Riverfest, Waterfront, c/o, PO Box 1341, Brockville ON K6V 5Y6 – 613/342-8975 – June

The Canadian Tulip Festival, PO Box 394, Stn A, Ottawa ON K1N 8V4 – 613/562-1480 – May

Canadian Turtle Derby, PO Box 1220, Boissevain MB R0K 0E0 – 204/534-6000; Fax: 204/534-6825 – Contact, Ivan Strain – Annually, July

Charleswood In-Motion Days, 625 Municipal Rd., Winnipeg MB R3R 1J2 – 204/837-7356 – Chairman, Ed McTaggart – Annually, June. Business displays, stage performances, carnival, youth soccer tournament

CHIN International Picnic, Exhibition Place, Toronto ON M6K 3C3 – 416/531-9991 – June/July

Chocolate Fest, PO Box 5002, St. Stephen NB E3L 2X5 – 506/465-5616; Fax: 506/465-5610; URL: http://www.pcsolutions.nb.ca/ganong – Chair, Derek O'Brien – Annually, August

Colonial Harvest Week Festival, Craigflower Farmhouse, c/o Heritage Properties Branch, 800 Johnston St., 5th Fl., Victoria BC V8V 1X4 – 250/387-4697 – October

Dakota Ojibway Tribal Days, Dakota Ojibway Tribal Council, c/o Tribal Administrator, 702 Douglas St., PO Box 1148, Brandon MB R7A 6A4 – Office Manager, A. Chalmers, Jan. 30 - Feb. 1 1998 – Keystone Centre, Brandon MB

Discovery Days, Discovery Days Festival, PO Box 308, Dawson City YT Y0B 1G0 – 867/993-7400; Fax: 867/993-7434 – Contact, Peter G. Menzies – August

Exploit's Valley Salmon Festival, Grand-Falls-Windsor NF – 709/489-2728 – Music, horse show, dance, salmon dinner; largest festival in Newfoundland, July

Feast of St. Louis, PO Box 160, Louisbourg NS B0A 1M0 – 902/733-2280; Fax: 902/733-2362; Email: louisbourg@info.pch.qc.ca – Manager, Heritage Presentation, Anne O'Neill – Eighteenth-century celebrations in honour of St. Louis, August – Louisbourg NS

Festival du Voyageur, 768, av Taché, Winnipeg MB R2H 2C4 – 204/237-7692; Fax: 204/233-7576; Email: voyageur@festivalvoyageur.mb.ca; URL: http://www.festivalvoyageur.mb.ca – Communications Officer, Francine Champagne – Annually, February. Ten day winter festival celebrating the voyageur & fur trade era

The Friendship Festival, Friendship Festival International Air Show, PO Box 1241, Fort Erie ON L2A 5Y2 – 905/871-6454; Fax: 905/871-1266; Tollfree: 1-888-333-1987; URL: http://www.friendshipfestival.com – Tracy Leblanc – June 20 - July 5 1998

Gold Panning Championships, PO Box 300, Taylor BC V0C 2K0 – 250/789-3004; Fax: 250/789-9076 – Fred Jarvis – Annually, August long weekend

Gold Rush Bathtub Race, Yukon Sourdough Rendezvous Society, PO Box 5108, Whitehorse YT Y1A 4S3 – 867/667-2148; Fax: 867/668-6755; Tollfree: 1-888-386-6766; Email: ysr@hypertech.yk.ca; URL: http://www.haylow.yk.net/rendez – Executive Director, Derek Charlton – Longest & hardest bathtub race. Two days, 486 miles, Yukon River

Halifax Highland Games, 7 Tay Ave., Dartmouth NS B2X 1K5 – Bob Findlay – July – Halifax NS

Heritage Canoe Festival, (Lift Lock), c/o Friends of the Trent Severn, PO Box 572, Peterborough ON K9J 6Z6 – 705/742-2251; Fax: 705/750-4816; Tollfree: 1-800-663-7628; URL: http://www.frsw.com – Mary Lyons – Annually, 2nd weekend in May

Humber Valley Strawberry Festival, PO Box 989, Deer Lake NF A0K 2E0 – 709/635-3861; Fax: 709/635-5103; Email: humberva@terra.nlnet.nf.ca – Co-ordinator, Bonnie Paul – July/Aug.

Icelandic Festival of Manitoba, 281 Wildwood Ave., Winnipeg MB R3T 0E5 – 204/284-2169

Just for Laughs Festival, 51, rue Sherbrooke ouest, Montréal QC H2X 1X2 – 514/845-3155; Fax: 514/845-4140; Email: info@hahaha.com; URL: http://www.hahaha.com – Contact, Robin Altman – July. 450 comics from 11 countries

Kitchener-Waterloo Oktoberfest, 17 Benton St., PO Box 1053, Kitchener ON N2G 4G1 – 519/570-4267; Fax: 519/742-3072; Email: info@oktoberfest.ca; URL: http://www.oktoberfest.ca – Executive Director, Larry Blundell – Annually, October. Bavarian festival: foods, entertainment, parades

Labrador Straits Bakeapple Folk Festival, PO Box 22, Forteau NF A0K 2P0 – 709/931-2908; Fax: 709/931-2306 – Annually, August

Leacock Heritage Festival, c/o 150 Front St. South, Orillia ON L3V 4S7 – 705/325-3261 – July/August

Louis Riel Day, 216 - 1st Ave. North, Saskatoon SK S7K 3W3 – 306/665-8600; Fax: 306/665-0450; Email: bacton@baton.com – Promotion Manager, Bruce Acton – July 5 1998

Manitoba Oktoberfest, 375 York Ave., 2nd Fl., Winnipeg MB R3C 3J3 – 204/956-1720 – Director of Sales & Marketing, Terry O'Reilly

Manitoba Sunflower Festival, PO Box 1630, Altona MB R0G 0B0 – 204/324-9005; Fax: 204/324-1550; URL: http://www.town.altona.mb.ca – Chair, Ron Epp – Annual, last weekend of July

Minto Coal Mining Festival, PO Box 7, Minto NB E0E 1J0 – 506/327-3383 – Contact, Rose Collette – June

Northern Manitoba Trappers' Festival, Inc., PO Box 475, The Pas MB R9A 1K6 – 204/623-2912 – Annually, February

Northwest Territorial Days, c/o, PO Box 668, North Battleford SK S9A 2Y9 – 306/445-2024 – July

Nova Scotia Gaelic Mod, PO Box 9, Baddeck NS B0E 1B0 – 902/295-3411 – Sam McPhee – Four-day festival, August – Gaelic College, St. Ann's NS

Nova Scotia International Tattoo, PO Box 3233 South, Halifax NS B3J 3H5 – 902/420-1114; Fax: 902/423-6621 – Assistant Producer, George Tibbetts – Annually, June/July

Okanagan Wine Festival, 185 Lakeshore Dr., Penticton BC V2A 1B7 – 250/493-4055 – Annually, end September or beginning October

Oktoberfest, 375 York Ave., Winnipeg MB R3C 3J3 – 204/956-1720; Fax: 204/943-0310; Tollfree: 1-800-565-7776; Email: info@wpgconvctr.mb.ca – Director of Entertainment, Terry O'Reilly – September

Penticton Peach Festival, c/o 184 West Lakeshore Dr., Penticton BC V2A 1B7 – 250/493-4055 – August

Peterborough Summer Festival of Lights, c/o City Hall, 500 George St. North, Peterborough ON K9H 3R9 – 705/876-4611; Fax: 705/876-8797 – Entertainment Chair, Royce Williamson – June to August every Wednesday & Saturday evenings at Del Crary Park

Pictou Lobster Carnival, PO Box 1480, Pictou NS B0K 1H0 – 902/485-5150 – Gerard McIsaac – Annual, July

Pile O Bones Sunday, c/o Regina Exhibition Association, PO Box 167, Regina SK S4P 2Z6 – 306/781-9200 – July

Québec International Summer Festival, 160, rue St-Paul, CP 25, Québec QC G1K 7A1 – 418/692-4540 – Contact, Gilles Laforce – Entertainment in the streets & parks of Old Québec

Royal St. John's Regatta, St. John's NF – 709/576-8511 – North America's oldest continuing sporting event, August – St. John's NF

Sam Steele Days, c/o, PO Box 115, Cranbrook BC V1C 4H6 – 250/426-4161; Fax: 250/426-3873 – Louie Musso – June 18-21 1998

Shediac Lobster Festival, PO Box 1923, Shediac NB E0A 3G0 – 506/532-1122; Fax: 506/532-1122; Email: lobsterf@nbnet.nb.ca – Emery Bourque – Annually, first week of July

Shelburne County Lobster Festival, PO Box 280, Shelburne NS B0T 1W0 – 902/875-3544; Fax: 902/875-1278; Email: munshel@atcon.com – Secretary, Marilyn Johnston – Annually, June; seaside celebration with delicious lobster

Shelburne Founder's Days, PO Box 699, Shelburne NS B0T 1W0 – 902/875-3873; Fax: 902/875-3932 – Chair, Jerry Locke – Annually, July

Shippagan Provincial Fisheries Festival, PO Box 1004, Shippagan NB E0B 2P0 – 506/336-8726 – Secretary, Claire Robichaud – Annually, July

Steinbach Pioneer Days, c/o Peter Goertzen, PO Box 1136, Steinbach MB R0A 2A0 – 204/326-9661

Storytelling Festival, c/o The Storytellers' School of Toronto, 412A College St., Toronto ON M5T 1T3 – Held annually at North York Library for two days, February

Summerfest: Edmonton Street Performers Festival, #901, 10136 - 100 St., Edmonton AB T5J 0P1 – 403/425-5162 – July

Threshermen's Show & Seniors' Festival, PO Box 98, Yorkton SK S3N 2V6 – 306/783-8361 – Chairman, Susan Mandzluk – Annually, August

Trinity Conception Fair, c/o Harbour Grace Stadium, Harbour Grace NF A0A 2M0 – 709/945-5140; Fax: 709/596-1919; Tollfree: 1-800-596-3233 – Chair, Gordon Pike – Annually, September

Welland Rose Festival, c/o Chamber of Commerce, 32 East Main St., Welland ON L3B 3W3 – 905/732-6603 – Annually, June. Rose show, lobsterfest, sporting events, moonlight canal cruises, juried art show, seniors' events, multi-cultural dancers, day-in-the-park, craft show, fishing derby, children's events, grand parade

Winnipeg Beach Boardwalk Summer Festival, Winnipeg Beach MB R0C 3G0 – 204/389-2698 – Norma Giller

Yukon Gold Panning Championships, Yukon Gold-Panning Championships, Klondike Visitors Association, PO Box 389, Dawson City YT Y0B 1G0 – 867/993-5575; Fax: 867/993-6415; Email: kva@dawson.net – On Canada Day, July – Dawson City YT

Yukon Sourdough Rendezvous, Yukon Sourdough Rendezvous Society, PO Box 5108, Whitehorse YT Y1A 4S3 – 867/667-2148; Fax: 867/668-6755; Tollfree: 1-888-386-6766; Email: ysr@hypertech.yk.ca; URL: http://www.haylow.yk.net/rendez – Executive Director, Derek Charlton – Annually. Celebrates the gold rush times. Mad trapper, flour packing, tug-a-truck contests, fiddle show, lyp sync & queen contests, Feb.

## EXHIBITIONS

***See Also* Farm Business/Agriculture, Rodeos**

Buffalo Days Exhibition, Regina Exhibition Park, PO Box 167, Regina SK S4P 2Z6 – 306/781-9200; Fax: 306/565-3443; Tollfree: 1-888-734-3975 – Marketing Manager, Tom Mullin – July 25 - Aug. 2 1998

Calgary Exhibition & Stampede, PO Box 1060, Stn M, Calgary AB T2P 2K8 – 403/261-0101; Fax: 403/265-7197; Tollfree: 1-800-661-1260 – General Manager, Steve Edwards – Annual city-wide festival; agricultural exhibits, July – Stampede Fairgrounds, Calgary AB

Canadian Lakehead Exhibition, 425 Northern Ave., Thunder Bay ON P7C 2V7 – 807/622-6473; Fax: 807/623-5540 – Administrative Clerk, Dulcie Prystanski – Annually, June

Canadian National Exhibition, Canadian National Exhibition Association, Exhibition Place, Toronto ON M6K 3C3 – 416/393-6000; Fax: 416/393-6259 – General Manager, Peter Moore – Annual public show, Aug. - Sept. – Exhibition Place, Toronto ON

Edmonton's Klondike Days Exposition, PO Box 1480, Edmonton AB T5J 2N5 – 403/471-7210; Fax: 403/471-8176 – Contact, Bob Gray – Annual consumer show, July – Northlands Exposition Grounds,

Expo Québec, La Commission de l'Exposition provinciale de Québec, 250, boul Wilfrid-Hamel, Québec QC G1L 5A7 – 418/691-7110; Fax: 418/691-7249 – General Manager, René Proulx – Annual exhibition. Industrial, agricultural, food, August – City Fairgrounds, Québec QC

Fredericton Exhibition, PO Box 235, Stn A, Fredericton NB E3B 4Y9 – 506/458-8819; Fax: 506/458-9294; Email: frex@nb.net.nb.ca – Contact, Brian Embleton – Annual, begins on Labour Day, Sept.

Home Town Fair, c/o Moose Jaw Exhibition Co. Ltd., PO Box 1467, Moose Jaw SK S6H 4R3 – 306/692-2723; Fax: 306/692-2762 – Chair, Stu Anderson – Annually, June

Interior Provincial Exhibition, PO Box 490, Armstrong BC V0E 1B0 – 250/546-9406; Fax: 250/546-6181 – Manager, Mike McCarty – Annual consumer agricultural fair & show, Sept.

Kamloops Exhibition, 479 Chilcotin St., Kamloops BC V2H 1G4 – 250/828-3590 – Annual agricultural fair & show, September

Lindsay Central Exhibition, 37 Adelaide St. North, Lindsay ON K9V 4K8 – 705/324-5551; Fax: 705/324-8111 – Secretary/Manager, Stephanie Sollitt – Annual consumer agricultural fair & show, Sept.

Markham Agricultural Fair, 10801 McCowan Rd., Markham ON L3P 3J3 – 905/642-3247; Fax: 905/640-8458 – Manager, David Morrison – Annual consumer show, September/October

Medicine Hat Exhibition & Stampede, PO Box 1298, Medicine Hat AB T1A 7N1 – 403/527-1234 – General Manager, Dann Sodero – Annual consumer show, August

New Atlantic National Exhibition, PO Box 284, Saint John NB E2L 3Y2 – 506/633-2020; Fax: 506/636-6958 – Contact, J. Charles Swanton – Annual, August

Niagara Regional Exhibition, 1100 Niagara St. North, Welland ON L3C 1M6 – 905/735-6413 – Annual consumer agricultural fair & show, September

Northwest Roundup & Exhibition, PO Box 116, Swan River MB R0L 1Z0 – 204/734-3718

Nova Scotia Provincial Exhibition, PO Box 192, Truro NS B2N 5C5 – 902/893-9222 – Paul R. Roy – Agricultural exhibition, August – Bible Hill NS

Pacific National Exhibition, PO Box 69020, Vancouver BC V5K 4W3 – 604/253-2311 – Public Relations Manager, Roger Young – Annual event; agricultural competitions, parade, Aug. - Sept. – Exhibition Park, Vancouver BC

Prince Albert Exhibition, Prince Albert Exhibition Association, PO Box 1538, Prince Albert SK S6V 5T1 – 306/764-1711; Fax: 306/764-5246; Email: paex@sk.sympatico.ca; URL: http://www.sasknet.com./~citynews/paex.htm – Manager, Doug MacKenzie – Annual, August – Prince Albert SK

Provincial Exhibition of Manitoba, #3, 1175 - 18th St., Brandon MB R7A 7C5 – 204/726-3590; Fax: 204/725-0202 – General Manager, Dave Wowchuk – Annual summer fair & pro rodeo, June – Keystone Centre, Brandon MB

Red River Exhibition, Red River Exhibition Association, 876 St. James St., Winnipeg MB R3G 3J7 – 204/772-9464; Fax: 204/775-9695 – Manitoba's largest fair & single-site entertainment event. Annually, 10 days, last two weeks in June

Regina Buffalo Days Exhibition, Regina Exhibition Association Ltd., PO Box 167, Regina SK S4P 2Z6 – 306/781-9200; Fax: 306/565-3443 – Secretary, Isabel Sheltgen – Annual consumer show, July – Exhibition Grounds, Regina SK

Saskatoon Exhibition, Saskatoon Prairieland Exhibition Corporation, PO Box 6010, Saskatoon SK S7K 4E4 – 306/931-7149; Fax: 306/931-7886 – General Manager, Mark Regier – Commercial exhibits & agricultural shows, July – Prairieland Exhibition Park, Saskatoon SK

## FARM BUSINESS/AGRICULTURE

***See Also* Exhibitions, Rodeos**

Ag-Expo, Lethbridge & District Exhibition, 3401 Parkside Dr. South, Lethbridge AB T1J 4R3 – 403/328-4491; Fax: 403/320-8139; Email: whoopup@agt.net; URL: http://www.telusplanet.net/public/whoopup – Agricultural Coordinator, Twyla Gurr – Annual agricultural exhibition which includes the North American seed fair, March

AgVenture, Medicine Hat & District Chamber of Commerce, 413 - 6th Ave. SE, Medicine Hat AB T1A 2S7 – 403/527-5214; Fax: 403/527-5182 – President, Leigh Smythe – March – Cypress Centre, Medicine Hat AB

Annual Convention & Trade Show, Canadian Association of Agri-Retailers, #107, 1090 Waverley St., Winnipeg MB R3T 0P4 – 204/989-9300; Fax: 204/989-9306; Email: caar@mb.sympatico.ca – Executive Director, Jacqueline Ryrie – Feb. – Regina Exhibition Park, Regina SK

Atlantic Winter Fair, 200 Prospect Rd., Goodwood NS B3T 1P2 – 902/876-8221; Fax: 902/876-8551 – Contact, David Coombes – Annual consumer exhibition, October

Canada Dairy Expo, Saskatoon Prairieland Exhibition Corporation, PO Box 6010, Saskatoon SK S7K 4E4 – 306/931-7149; Fax: 306/931-7886 – General Manager, Mark Regier – Largest national dairy cattle show & sale; comprehensive dairy industry exhibitions; trade show, April – Prairieland Exhibition Park, Saskatoon SK

Canadian International Farm Equipment Show, Dawn Morris Productions Inc., #3, 1434 Chemong Rd., RR#1, Peterborough ON K9J 6X2 – 705/741-2536; Fax: 705/741-2539; Email: cifes@dawnmorris.on.ca; URL: http://www.dawnmorris.on.ca – Show Manager, Lesley Nicholson – Annual trade show, Feb. – Toronto ON

Canadian Western Agribition, Canadian Western Agribition Association, Regina Exhibition Park, Canada Centre Bldg., 2nd Fl., PO Box 3535, Regina SK S4P 3J8 – 306/565-0565; Fax: 306/757-9963; URL: http://www.sasknet.com/corporate/Agribition/ – Wayne Gamble – Annual trade & consumer show, Nov. – Exhibition Park, Regina SK

Chinook Livestock Classic, Lethbridge & District Exhibition, 3401 Parkside Dr. South, Lethbridge AB T1J 4R3 – 403/328-4491; Fax: 403/320-8139; Email: whoopup@agt.net; URL: http://www.telusplanet.net/public/whoopup – Agricultural Coordinator, Twyla Gurr – Annual purebred beef cattle show, Oct. – Exhibition Grounds, Lethbridge AB

Estevan Farmer's Day, c/o Estevan Chamber of Commerce, 1102 - 4th St., Estevan SK S4A 0W7 – 306/634-2828; Fax: 306/634-6729 – Manager, Linda Mack – Annually, March

Fall Fair, Provincial Exhibition of Manitoba, #3, 1175 - 18th St., Brandon MB R7A 7C5 – 204/726-3590; Fax: 204/725-0202 – General Manager, Dave Wowchuk – Ag Ex, Winter Expressions, MRCA Rodeo finals, Nov. – Keystone Centre, Brandon MB

Fall Fair & Mexabition, Saskatoon Prairieland Exhibition Corporation, PO Box 6010, Saskatoon SK S7K 4E4 – 306/931-7149; Fax: 306/931-7886 – General Manager, Mark Regier – Annual livestock & agricultural trade show featuring nine purebred beef cattle shows, Nov. – Prairieland Exhibition Park, Saskatoon SK

Farmers' Field Day & Open House, c/o St. John's Research Station, Agriculture Canada, Brookfield Rd., PO Box 39088, St. John's NF A1E 5Y7 – 709/772-4619; Fax: 709/772-6064; Email: henderf@em.agr.ca; URL: http://res.agr.ca/stjohns – Coordinator, Frank Hender – Annually, 4th Saturday in August

Food & Livestock Show, PO Box 8700, St. John's NF A1B 4J6 – 709/729-6716; Fax: 709/729-6046 – Coordinator, Denise Murphy – Annually, September/October

International Plowing Match & Farm Machinery Show, Ontario Plowmen's Association, 367 Woodlawn Rd. West, Guelph ON N1H 7K9 – 519/767-1967; Fax: 519/661-7569; Tollfree: 1-800-661-7569 – General Manager, John Fennell – Annual, Sept. – Barrie ON

International Potato Technology Exposition, Master Promotions Ltd., PO Box 565, Saint John NB E2L 3Z8 – 506/658-0018; Fax: 506/658-0750 – Show Manager, Mark Cusack – Feb. – Civic Centre, Charlottetown PE

International Salon of Farm Machinery, Les Productions Jacqueline Vézina inc., #3000, 926, St-Maurice, Montréal QC H3C 1L7 – 514/861-8241; Fax: 514/861-8246 – Présidente, Jacqueline Vézina

Norfolk County Fair & Horse Show, Norfolk County Agricultural Society, 172 South Dr., Simcoe ON N3Y 1G6 – 519/426-7280 – Secretary-Manager, S.J. Culver – Annual consumer show, Oct. – Simcoe ON

Northlands Farmfair, PO Box 1480, Edmonton AB T5J 2N5 – 403/471-7210; Fax: 403/471-8169; Email: npevents@planet.eon.net – Annually, November

Nova Scotia 4-H Show, c/o NS Dept. of Agriculture & Marketing, PO Box 550, Truro NS B2N 5E3 – 902/893-6585, ext.310; Fax: 902/893-2757; Email: ecrousc@cs.nsac.ns.ca – Supervisor, Elizabeth Crouse – Annual consumer show, October

Ontario Dairy Expo, Western Fair Association, PO Box 4550, Stn D, London ON N5W 5K3 – 519/438-7203; Fax: 519/679-3124 – Annual trade show, August – London ON

Ottawa Winter Fair, 466 Pleasant Park Rd., Ottawa ON K1H 5N1 – 613/733-6218 – Contact, Margaret Harrison – October

Paris Fall Fair, PO Box 124, Paris ON N3L 3E7 – 519/442-2823; Fax: 519/442-5121; URL: http://www.niche.on.ca/parisfair/ – Manager, Harry Emmott – Annual Labour Day weekend consumer show

Perth County Farm Progress Show, Perth County Agricultural Week, 20 Glastonbury Dr., PO Box 901, Stratford ON N5A 6W3 – 519/271-5130; Fax: 519/271-5832 – Manager, Brian Gropp – Annual consumer show, February

Poultry Industry Conference & Exhibition, Western Fair Association, PO Box 4550, Stn D, London ON N5W 5K3 – 519/438-7203; Fax: 519/679-3124 – Annual trade show, April – Western Fairgrounds, London ON

Prairie Ventures, Saskatoon Prairieland Exhibition Corporation, PO Box 6010, Saskatoon SK S7K 4E4 – 306/931-7149; Fax: 306/931-7886 – General Manager, Mark Regier – Annual consumer show. Specialty: livestock, fruit, vegetable growers, Feb. – Prairieland Exhibition Park, Saskatoon SK

Provincial Livestock Show, c/o NB Dept. of Agriculture, PO Box 6000, Fredericton NB E3B 5H1 – 506/453-6610 – Contact, Deborah Graye – Annual, Sept.

Regional Potato Festival, PO Box 1166, Grand Falls NB E3Z 1C5 – 506/475-1816 – President, Denise Leclerc, June 28 - July 5 1998

Royal Agricultural Winter Fair, Royal Agricultural Winter Fair Association, Coliseum, Exhibition Place, Toronto ON M6K 3C3 – 416/393-6400; Fax: 416/393-6488; Email: rwfair@ican.net; URL: http://www.royalfair.org – CEO, David E. Garrick – Annual consumer show. World's largest indoor agricultural fair & equestrian event, Nov. – Exhibition Place, Toronto ON

Royal Manitoba Winter Fair, Provincial Exhibition of Manitoba, #3, 1175 - 18th St., Brandon MB R7A 7C5 – 204/726-3590; Fax: 204/725-0202 – General Manager, Dave Wowchuk – Annual consumer show; agricultural machinery, products & services; horse shows, March – Keystone Centre, Brandon MB

Salon de l'Agriculteur, 2285, St-Germain, CP 123, St-Hyacinthe QC J2S 8N7 – 514/771-1226; Fax: 514/771-1226 – Florent Fortier – Annual trade show. Agricultural products, Jan. – St-Hyacinthe QC

Salon de l'Agriculture de l'Alimentation et de la Consommation, Association des étudiants de l'Université Laval, #0110, Cité Universitaire, Pavillon Paul Comtois, Ste-Foy QC G1K 7P4 – 418/656-2131; Fax: 418/656-2610 – Michel Delisle – Annual consumer show, Feb. – Centre de foires de Québec, Québec QC

Summerside Agricultural Exhibition, PO Box 1295, Summerside PE C1N 4K2 – 902/436-7139, 8324 – Colleen Marsh, Sept.

Western Canada Farm Progress Show, PO Box 167, Regina SK S4P 2Z6 – 306/781-9200; Fax: 306/565-3443; Tollfree: 1-888-734-3975; Email: wcfps@sasknet.sk.ca; URL: http://www.wcfps.com – Show Administrator, Jack Shaw – Annual consumer & trade show, June – Regina Exhibition Park, Regina SK

Western Canadian Crop Production Show, Saskatoon Prairieland Exhibition Corporation, PO Box 6010, Saskatoon SK S7K 4E4 – 306/931-7149; Fax: 306/931-7886 – General Manager, Mark Regier – Annual consumer show, Jan. – Prairieland Exhibition Park, Saskatoon SK

Western Fair, Western Fair Association, PO Box 4550, Stn D, London ON N5W 5K3 – 519/438-7203; Fax: 519/679-3124 – Annual consumer show, Sept. – Queen's Park, London ON

Western Farm Fair Show, Western Fair Association, PO Box 4550, Stn D, London ON N5W 5K3 – 519/438-7203; Fax: 519/679-3124 – Annual consumer show, March – Western Fairgrounds, London ON

Western Nova Scotia Exhibition, PO Box 425, Yarmouth NS B5A 4B3 – 902/742-8222; Fax: 902/742-0458 – Frank Anderson – Six-day agricultural fair & talent competition, July or Aug. – Yarmouth NS

Whoop Up Bull Show & Sale, Lethbridge & District Exhibition, 3401 Parkside Dr. South, Lethbridge AB T1J 4R3 – 403/328-4491; Fax: 403/320-8139; Email: whoopup@agt.net; URL: http://www.telusplanet.net/public/whoopup – Agricultural Coordinator, Twyla Gurr – Show & sale of purebred bulls, March

## FASHION

Imprinted Sportswear Show, Miller Freeman Expositions, #500, 13760 Noel Rd., Dallas TX 75240 – 972/239-3060; Fax: 972/419-7855; Tollfree: 1-800-527-0207; Email: iss@mfi.com; URL: http://iss.shows.com – Kelly McKibben – Annual trade show, April – Toronto ON

Mode Accessories Show, Two Plus One Group, #611, 220 Duncan Mill Rd., North York ON M3B 3J5 – 416/510-0114; Fax: 416/510-0165 – President, Alice Chee – Semi-annual trade show (January & August) – International Plaza Hotel, Toronto ON

National Apparel Technology Show/Salon National de la Technologie du Vêtement, P.R. Charette Inc., 35, Promenade Westland, Montréal-Ouest QC H4X 1M3 – 514/489-8671; Fax: 514/487-3230 – Contact, Bob Charette – April – Palais de Congrès de Montréal, Montréal QC

Ontario Fashion Exhibitors Inc. Fashion Market, Ontario Fashion Exhibitors Inc., #219, 111 Peter St., Toronto ON M5V 2H1 – 416/596-2401; Fax: 416/596-1808 – Marketing Director, Lynn Radmore – Trade show held four times annually. Women's fashions & accessories; children's wear

**FESTIVALS *See* EVENTS**

## FILM & VIDEO FESTIVALS & SPECIAL EVENTS

Alberta Film & Television Awards, Alberta Motion Picture Industries Association, 606 Midland Walwyn Tower, Edmonton Centre, Edmonton AB T5J 2Z2 – 403/944-0707; Fax: 403/426-3057 – President, Andy Thomson, 403/482-2022 – Feb.

Atlantic Film & Video Producers Conference, PO Box 2726, Charlottetown PE C1A 8C3 – 902/892-3131; Fax: 902/566-1724 – June

Atlantic Film Festival/Festival du Film de l'Atlantique, Atlantic Film Festival, PO Box 36139, Halifax NS B3J 3S9 – 902/422-3456; Fax: 902/422-4006; Email: aff@screen.com; URL: http://www.screen.com/atlanticfilm.html – Executive Director, Gordon Whittaker – Films & videos. Competition, seminars & workshops, Sept. – Halifax NS

Banff Festival of Mountain Films, 107 Tunnel Mountain Dr., PO Box 1020, Stn 38, Banff AB T0L 0C0 – 403/762-6125; Fax: 403/762-6277; Email: cmc@banffcentre.ab.ca; URL: http://www.banffcentre.ab.ca/cmc/index.html – Festival Coordinator, Deb Smythe – Annual festival, Nov. – Banff Centre, Banff AB

Banff Television Festival, 1516 Railway Ave., Canmore AB T1W 1P6 – 403/678-9260; Fax: 403/678-9269; URL: http://www.banfftvfest.com – President & CEO, W. Paterson Ferns – Television films & programs. Competition, seminars & workshops, June – Banff AB

Canadian International Annual Film Festival, 25 Eugenia St., Barrie ON L4M 1P6 – 705/737-2729; Fax: 705/737-2729; Email: ciaff@iname.com – Director, Ben Andrews – Judging takes place in June (categories: Independent Filmmakers, Film Students, Amateurs); Festival in the fall

Le Carrousel international du film de Rimouski, CP 1462, Rimouski QC G5L 8M3 – 418/722-0103; Fax: 418/724-9504; Email: cifr@carrousel.qc.ca; URL: http://www.carrousel.qc.ca – Directrice générale, Sylvie Blanchette – Films for children. Competition, workshops, Sept. – Rimouski QC

Cinéfest - The Sudbury International Film Festival, #218, 40 Elm St., Sudbury ON P3C 1S8 – 705/688-1234; Fax: 705/688-1351; Email: cinefest@vianet.on.ca; URL: http://www.cinefest.com – Executive Director, Tammy Frick – Full-length feature festival with over 100 Canadian & international films, animations, shorts, Midnight Madness, documentary & children's film series, Sept. – Sudbury ON

Colloque de l'Association québécoise des études cinématographiques, 335, boul de Maisonneuve est, Montréal QC H2X 1K1 – 514/842-9763; Fax: 514/842-1816 – November

Festival de l'audiovisuel, CP 68, Succ Ahuntsic, Montréal QC H3L 3W5 – 514/334-4084 – May/June

Festival du cinéma international, Festival du cinéma international des Premières Oeuvres dans les villes de Ste-Thérèse, Ste-Adèle et St-Jérôme, 34, rue Blainville ouest, Ste-Thérèse QC J7E 1W9; Email: festival@odyssee.net; URL: http://www.odyssee.net/~festival – Coordinator, Judith Hamel – Francophone feature films. People's choice awards, seminars, Oct..

Festival du cinéma international en Abitibi-Témiscamingue, 215, av Mercier, Rouyn-Noranda QC J9X 5W8 – 819/762-6212; Fax: 819/762-6762; Email: fciat@sympatico.ca; URL: http://www.telebec.qc.ca/fciat/ – Executive Director, Jacques Matte – Features, medium-length & short films. Competition; regional jury award for short or medium-length film; people's choice award for feature & animation, Oct. – Rouyn-Noranda QC

Festival du film étudiant canadien/Canadian Student Film Festival, Festival du film étudiant canadien, 1432, rue de Bleury, Montréal QC H3A 2J1 – 514/848-7186; Fax: 514/848-3886 – Coordonnatrice, Danièle Cauchard – Films & videos by Canadian students. Film competition, August – Montréal QC

Festival international du film de Baie-Comeau, 70, av Michel-Hémon, Baie-Comeau QC G4Z 2A5 – 418/296-8379; Fax: 418/296-8399 – Coordinator, André Thalabot – Feature films, people's choice awards, Jan. – Baie-Comeau QC

Le Festival International du Film Scientifique du Québec - Téléscience, Cybermonde, 85, rue St-Paul ouest, Montréal QC H2Y 3V4 – 514/849-1612; Fax: 514/982-0064; Email: cite@artech.org; URL: http://cite.artech.org – Président, Hervé Fischer, Oct.

Festival international du nouveau cinéma et de la vidéo/Montréal International Festival of New Cinema & Video, Festival international du nouveau cinéma et de la vidéo, 3726, boul St-Laurent, Montréal QC H2X 2V8 – 514/843-4725, 4711; Fax: 514/843-4631 – Directeur, Claude Chamberlan – New trends in cinema & video. Competition, Québec Critics' awards for feature & short films. Jury award for video production, Oct. – Montréal QC

Film Studies Association of Canada Conference, Film Studies Association of Canada, Film & Communications, Brock University, St Catharines ON L2S 3A1 – 905/688-5550, ext.3214; Fax: 905/688-2789; Email: jeanette@spartan.ac.brocku.ca; URL: http://www.film.queensu.ca/FSAC/Home.html – President, Graham Petrie – May/June annually, held at a different university each year

Genie, Gemini, Gémeaux Awards, Academy of Canadian Cinema & Television, 158 Pearl St., Toronto ON M5H 1L3 – 416/591-2040; Fax: 416/591-2157; Tollfree: 1-800-644-5194; URL: http://www.academy.ca – CEO, Maria Topalovich – Annual awards show

Image & Nation gaie et lesbienne, festival international du cinéma et de vidéo de Montréal, CP 1595, Succ Place de P, Montréal QC H2W 2R6 – 514/526-7221 – Autumn

Images du futur, Cybermonde, 85, rue St-Paul ouest, Montréal QC H2Y 3V4 – 514/849-1612; Fax: 514/982-0064; Email: cite@artech.org; URL: http://cite.artech.org – Président, Hervé Fischer – May to October, annually; art, new technologies & communications

Images Festival of Independent Film & Video, #448, 401 Richmond St. West, Toronto ON M5V 3A8 – 416/971-8405; Fax: 416/971-7412; Email: images@interlog.com; URL: http://www.interlog.com/~images/ – Executive Director, Deirdre Logue – Annual. Independent films & videos. Workshops, April – Toronto ON

In-Sight: Festival of Women's Films, 9722 - 102 St., 2nd Fl., Edmonton AB T5K 0X4 – 403/448-0703; Fax: 403/495-6412 – Coordinator, Nancy Poole – Biennial. Women's films & videos. Seminars, Nov. 1998 – Edmonton AB

Indian Summer, World Festival of Aboriginal Motion Pictures, c/o, PO Box 1280, Pincher Creek AB T0K 1W0 – 403/627-4813; Fax: 403/627-4957 – September

International Film Festival of Québec City, #50, 35, rue Dalhousie, Québec QC G1K 8W6 – 418/694-9920;

Fax: 418/694-0632 – Coordinator, Marie Talbot – Feature films. Competition, people's choice awards, Sept. – Québec QC

L'Annuelle des Professionnels des Industries de L'Image et du Son/Image & Sound Industries Annual Conference & Forum, 1276, rue Amherst, Montréal QC H2L 3K8 – 514/842-5333; Fax: 514/842-6717, May

Les Journées africaines et créoles, Les Journées africaines et créole, 67, rue Ste-Catherine ouest, 5e étage, Montréal QC H2X 1Z7 – 514/284-3322; Fax: 514/845-0631; Email: vuesda@cam.org; URL: http://www.vuesdafrique.org – President, Gérard Le Chêne – Competition. Films by & about African & Creole peoples, April – Montréal QC

Les Rendez-vous du cinéma québécois, 4545, av Pierre-De Coubertin, CP 1000, Succ M, Montréal QC H1V 3R2 – 514/252-3021; Fax: 514/251-8038; Email: rendez-vous@coproductpons.com; URL: http://www.coproductpons.com/rendez-vous/ – Directeur, Michel Coulombe – Restrospective of recent Québec productions. Competition, Feb. – Montréal QC

Local Heroes, 10022 - 103 St., 3rd Fl., Edmonton AB T5J 0X2 – 403/421-4084; Fax: 403/425-8098; Tollfree: 1-800-480-4084; Email: filmhero@nsi-canada.ca; URL: http://www.nsi-canada.ca – Executive Director, Jan Miller – Feature, medium-length & short films. Workshops, March 8-14 1998 – Edmonton AB

Making Scenes Film & Video Festival, National Gallery of Canada; URL: http://fox.nstn.ca/~scenes/ – Annual lesbian & gay film & video festival, May – National Gallery of Canada, Ottawa ON

Montreal International Chinese Film Festival/Festival international du cinéma chinois de Montréal, #393, 1600, de Lorimier, Montréal QC H2K 3W5 – 514/527-3981; Fax: 514/521-7081 – Coordinator, Suzanne Girard – Film screenings: Vancouver, mid-May, Montréal, end of May, Toronto, early June, Ottawa/Hull, early June. Exhibition: Montréal, mid-May to early June

Ottawa International Animation Festival, Canadian Film Institute, 2 Daly Ave., Ottawa ON K1N 6E2 – 613/232-8769; Fax: 613/232-6315; Email: olaf@ottawa.com; URL: http://olaf.ottawa.com – Director, Chris Robinson – Biennial. Animation films & videos. Workshops & panels, Sept./Oct. – Ottawa ON

Saskatchewan Film & Video Showcase, 2431 - 8th Ave., Regina SK S4R 5J7 – 306/525-9899; Fax: 306/569-1818 – President, Jack Walton – Retrospective of recent Saskatchewan productions. Competition, forum & workshops, Nov. – Regina SK

St. John's Women's Film & Video Festival, PO Box 984, St. John's NF A1C 5C2 – 709/772-0359; Fax: 709/772-4808 – Festival Director, Alyson Dyer – Women's films & videos. Workshops & panels, Oct. – St. John's NF

Summer Institute of Film & Television/Rencontre Estivale ciné-vidéo, Summer Institute of Film & Television, Algonquin College, 2 Daly Ave., 2nd Fl., Ottawa ON K1P 6E3 – 613/727-4723, ext.6150; Fax: 613/733-6170 – Coordinator, Lawry Trevor-Deutsch – Features, medium-length & short films. Workshops, June – Ottawa ON

Toronto International Film Festival, #1600, 2 Carlton St., Toronto ON M5B 1J3 – 416/967-7371; Fax: 416/967-9477; Email: tiffg@torfilmfest.ca; URL: http://www.bell.ca/toronto/filmfest – Managing Director, Suzanne Weiss – Features & theatrical shorts. Competition. Awards for excellence in Canadian production. People's choice & film critics awards. Symposium, workshops, sales office, Sept. – Toronto ON

Vancouver International Film Festival, #410, 1008 Homer St., Vancouver BC V6B 2X1 – 604/685-0260; Fax: 604/688-8221; Email: viff@viff.org; URL: http://www.viff.org.viff – Executive Director, Alan Franey – Features, medium-length & short films. Competition; juried awards for best Canadian screenplay, best new western Canadian director & best East Asian film; people's choice award for most popular foreign film & for most popular Canadian film. Trade forum, Oct. – Vancouver BC

World Film Festival, Montréal World Film Festival, 1432, rue de Bleury, Montréal QC H3A 2J1 – 514/848-3883; Fax: 514/848-3886; Email: ffm@interlink.net; URL: http://www.ffm-montreal.org/ – President & Executive Director, Serge Losique – Features, medium-length & short films. Competition, symposium, markets, August – Montréal QC

Yorkton Short Film & Video Festival, 49 Smith St. East, Yorkton SK S3N 0H4 – 306/782-7077; Fax: 306/782-1550 – Finance Director, Rob Dewhirst – Canadian short films & videos. Competition, seminars & workshops, May – Yorkton SK

## FIRST NIGHT CELEBRATIONS

First Night Banff, c/o Banff Allied Arts Council, PO Box 1343, Banff AB T0L 0C0 – 403/762-8562; Fax: 403/762-4286 – General Manager, Special Events, Judy Anderson-Hansen

First Night Comox Valley, c/o Comox Valley Chamber of Commerce, 2040 Cliffe Ave., Courtenay BC V9N 2L3 – 250/338-1210; Fax: 250/334-1384 – Coordinator, Liz Wouters

First Night Edmonton, 7 Sir Winston Churchill Sq., 6th Fl., Edmonton AB T5J 2V4 – 403/448-9200; Fax: 403/426-7608; Email: firstni@planet.eon.net; URL: http://www.1stnight.ab.ca – Producer, Linda Brenneman-Snider – Dec. 27-31

First Night Kamloops, PO Box 1166, Kamloops BC V2C 6H3 – 250/374-4634; Fax: 250/374-4621 – Executive Director, Marg Marshall

First Night Maple Ridge, 11925 Haney Pl., Maple Ridge BC V2X 6G2 – 604/463-5244; Fax: 604/463-8336 – Marilyn Jollymore

First Night Ottawa-Carleton, c/o Sparks Street Mall Management Board, 151 Sparks St., 2nd Fl., Ottawa ON K1P 5E3 – 613/230-0984; Fax: 613/230-7671 – Executive Director, Ken Dale

First Night Qualicum Beach, PO Box 154, Qualicum Beach BC V9K 1S7 – 250/752-6841 – Margot Cyr

First Night Saint John, PO Box 6355, Stn A, Saint John NB E2L 4R8 – 506/632-0086; Fax: 506/632-0994 – General Manager, Gary Arthurs

First Night Toronto, #116-58, 65 Front St. West, Toronto ON M5J 1E6 – 416/362-3692; Fax: 416/362-4430 – Producer, Laurel Smith-Devlin

First Night Vancouver, c/o Pacific National Exhibition, PO Box 69020, Vancouver BC V5K 4W3 – 604/253-2311; Fax: 604/251-7726 – Division Manager, Hammy McClymont

First Night Victoria Celebration of the Arts Society, c/o #710, 1175 Douglas St., Victoria BC V8W 2E1 – 250/382-2160; Fax: 250/655-3655 – Producer, Debora Johns

First Night Whistler, 4010 Whistler Way, Whistler BC V0N 1B4 – 604/932-3928; Fax: 604/932-7231 – Contact, Maureen Douglas

Gabriola First Night Arts Society, PO Box 217, Gabriola BC V0R 1X0 – 250/247-9901; Fax: 250/247-9915 – President, Alan Howardson

## FISHING/AQUACULTURE

Adams River Sockeye Salmon Run, PO Box 101, Celesta BC V0E 1L0 – 250/955-6279 – October

Atlantic Aquaculture Fair, Master Promotions Ltd., PO Box 565, Saint John NB E2L 3Z8 – 506/658-0018; Fax: 506/658-0750 – Show Manager, Sydney Jane Brittain – Canada's largest aquaculture event, June

Eastern Canadian Fisheries Exposition, South West Nova Fisheries Exposition, PO Box 425, Yarmouth NS B5A 4B3 – 902/742-8222; Fax: 902/742-0458; Email: crosby@klis.com – Frank Anderson – Occupational & recreational technology & equipment, April 2-4 1999 – Yarmouth NS

Flin Flon Trout Festival, PO Box 751, Flin Flon MB R8A 1N6 – 204/687-5166, June – Flin Flon MB

Great Northern Pike Festival, PO Box 160, Nipawin SK S0E 1E0 – 306/356-8692 – June & mid-August – Lynn Lake MB

Nova Scotia Fisheries Exhibition & Fishermen's Reunion, PO Box 308, Lunenburg NS B0J 2C0 – 902/634-3025 – August

Salmon Festival, c/o, PO Box 234, Campbellton NB E3N 3G4 – 506/753-7767 – July

Seafood Festival, PO Box 1220, Shippagan NB E0B 2P0 – 506/336-4116 – June

Spring Fishing Show, Ontario Out of Doors Magazine, 777 Bay St., 6th Fl., Toronto ON M5W 1A7 – 416/596-5908; Fax: 416/596-2517; Email: 102677.1125@compuserve.com; URL: http://www.cyberplex.com/fishontario – Show Manager, Lynda Watson – Feb.

## FLOWERS/LANDSCAPING/GARDENING

CAN WEST Horticultural Show, British Columbia Nursery Trades Association, #101, 5830 - 176A St., Surrey BC V3S 4E3 – 604/574-7772; Fax: 604/574-7773; Email: bhardy@direct.ca – Show Director, Jane Stock – Sept.

Canada Blooms, Civic Garden Centre, 777 Lawrence Ave. East, North York ON M3C 1P2 – 416/447-5218; Fax: 416/447-2154 – President, Mary Mingie – Annually, March

Canadian Garden & Flower Show, Klanside Inc., 401 Magnetic Dr., Unit 21, North York ON M3J 3H9 – 416/661-2056; Fax: 416/661-2904 – Show Manager, Kathy O'Hara – Annual consumer show, March/April

Floriculture, c/o 54 Lochinvar Ave., Winnipeg MB R2J 1R4 – 204/253-4022 – B. Hildebrand – July/August

Flower & Vegetable Show, Newfoundland Horticultural Society, PO Box 84, Goulds NF A1S 1G3 – 709/737-8590; Fax: 709/772-6064 – President, Ron Taggart – August – St. John's NF

Gardenscape, Saskatoon Prairieland Exhibition Corporation, PO Box 6010, Saskatoon SK S7K 4E4 – 306/931-7149; Fax: 306/931-7886 – Maurice Neault – Annual consumer show. Care & creation of yards & gardens; displays, exhibits, information & demonstrations, March – Trade Centre, Prairieland Exhibition Park, Saskatoon SK

Hamilton & Burlington Rose Society Show, Royal Botanical Gardens, PO Box 399, Hamilton ON L8N 3H8 – 905/527-1158; Fax: 905/577-0375 – Director, Sharilyn J. Ingram – June

Hamilton Orchid Show, Royal Botanical Gardens, PO Box 399, Hamilton ON L8N 3H8 – 905/527-1158; Fax: 905/577-0375 – Director, Sharilyn J. Ingram, March

Ikenobo Ikebana Japanese Flower Show, Royal Botanical Gardens, PO Box 399, Hamilton ON L8N 3H8 – 905/527-1158; Fax: 905/577-0375 – Director, Sharilyn J. Ingram – Sept.

The Landscaping Show/Salon de l'aménagement extérieur, Promexpo Inc., 801, rue Sherbrooke est, 10e étage, Montréal QC H2L 1K7 – 514/527-9221; Fax: 514/527-8449 – General Manager, Vic Côté – Annual consumer show

Manitoba Horticulture Industry Days, 676 Borebank St., Winnipeg MB R3N 1G2 – 204/254-2293 – Coordinator, Carmen Neufeld – Annual trade show,

November. Floral & nursery stock, computers, seed, chemicals, equipment

Ontario Garden Show, Town Publishing Inc., Show Division, 875 Main St. West, Hamilton ON L8S 4R1 – 905/522-6117; Fax: 905/529-2242 – Show Manager, Lea Narciso – Annual consumer show, April – Royal Botanical Gardens, Hamilton ON

Provincial Rose Show, 6955 Ward Ave., Halifax NS B3L 2K3 – 902/453-6801 – Marjorie Fowler – Competitive show for rose growers in Nova Scotia, July – Spring Garden Place, Halifax NS

Saskatoon Horticultural Society Annual Show, 1420 Alexander Ave., Saskatoon SK S7K 3B9 – 306/652-8864 – Contact, Amanda Ryce – August

South Burnaby Garden Club, 15675 - 91 Ave., Surrey BC V4N 2X2 – 604/434-2100 – Secretary, D. Heys – September

Spring Flower Exhibition, Newfoundland Horticultural Society, PO Box 84, Goulds NF A1S 1G3 – 709/737-8590; Fax: 709/772-6064 – President, Ron Taggart – May – Oxen Pond, Memorial University, St. John's NF

World Orchid, Venue West Conference Services Ltd., #645, 375 Water St., Vancouver BC V6B 5C6 – 604/681-5226; Fax: 604/681-2503; Email: congress@venuewest.com; URL: http://www.venuwest.com – President, Betty Fata – April 22 - May 2 1999

## FOOD & BEVERAGE

***See Also* Hospitality Industry**

AGM, Canadian Institute of Food Science & Technology, #1105, 191 The West Mall, Etobicoke ON M9C 5K8 – 416/626-3140; Fax: 416/620-5392 – Ingredients, lab services & other services for food manufacturers, August

AGM & Hostex Show, Ontario Restaurant Association, #1201, 121 Richmond St. West, Toronto ON M5H 2K1 – 416/359-0533; Fax: 416/359-0531; Tollfree: 1-800-668-8906 – Contact, Jane Anderson – Oct. – International Centre, Mississauga ON

ARFEX - Alberta Restaurant & Foodservices Exposition, Alberta Restaurant & Foodservices Association, 10085 - 166 St., Edmonton AB T5P 4Y1 – 403/444-9494; Fax: 403/481-8727; Tollfree: 1-800-461-9762 – President, Elizabeth Kuhnel – Annual, April

Bakery Showcase, PH#3, 3300 Don Mills Rd., North York ON M2J 4X7 – 416/490-7910; Fax: 416/490-6931 – Sec.-Treas., Alex Telfer – Biennial trade show, Oct. – Toronto ON

Canadian Automatic Merchandising Show, Canadian Automatic Merchandising Association, #301, 885 Don Mills Rd., Toronto ON M3C 1V9 – 416/441-3737; Fax: 416/441-3782 – Executive Director, Caroline Manton – March 1998 – Toronto ON

Canadian Fine Food Show, Meteor Show Productions Inc., 298 Sheppard Ave. East, North York ON M2N 3B1 – 416/229-2060; Fax: 416/223-2826; Tollfree: 1-800-896-7469; Email: weil@meteorshows.com; URL: http://www.meteorshows.com – Director, Marketing & Sales, Richard B. Swayze – Annual trade show, May 3-5 1998 – International Centre, Toronto ON

Canadian Food Technology Show, 850 Boundary Rd., Cornwall ON K6H 5R5 – 613/936-2698; Fax: 613/936-2716 – Annual trade show, June

Canadian Natural Product Spring Show, Canadian Health Food Association, 370 Steelcase Rd. East, Markham ON L3R 1G2 – 905/479-6939; Fax: 905/479-1516 – Executive Director, Bill Reynolds – Organic & natural products; homeopathy, food supplements & herbs, April

FAB - Food & Beverage Shows, #105, 10544 - 114 St., Edmonton AB T5H 3J7 – 403/420-6336; Fax: 403/426-7862 – Contact, Rick Young – Annual consumer show. Food, wine & other spirits tasting, seminars, & entertainment, March

Flavour: Atlantic Canada's Food, Wine & Vacation Show, Denex Group Inc., Burnside Industrial Park, 192 Joseph Zatzman Dr., Dartmouth NS B3B 1N4 – 902/468-4999; Fax: 902/468-2795; Email: denman@ns.sympatico.ca; URL: http://www.denexgroup.com – President, Jon Denman – Annual consumer show, April

Food & Hospitality Show, Restaurant & Foodservices Association of British Columbia & the Yukon, #140, 475 West Georgia St., Vancouver BC V6B 4H9 – 604/669-2239; Fax: 604/669-6175; Tollfree: 1-800-663-4482; URL: http://www.yes.net/RFABCY/ – Show Coordinator, George Acs – Annual trade show, April

The Good Food Festival & Market, 117 Evelyn Ave., Toronto ON M6J 4G7 – 416/766-2880; Fax: 416/762-9942 – Manager, Lynda Chubak – Annual consumer festival, May – Automotive Bldg., Exhibition Place,

Gourmet Food & Wine Expo, Winexpo Productions Inc., #11, 5080 Timberlea Blvd., Mississauga ON L4W 4M2 – 905/629-7469; Fax: 905/629-3823; URL: http://www.toronto.com/winexpo – General Manager, Megan Parry – Consumer show, Nov. – Metro Toronto Convention Centre, Toronto ON

Grocery Showcase Canada '98, Canadian Federation of Independent Grocers, #902, 2235 Sheppard Ave. East, North York ON M2J 5B5 – 416/492-2311; Fax: 416/492-2347; Tollfree: 1-800-661-2344 – President, John F.T. Scott – Annual trade show, Oct.

Meteors Western Food & Beverage Show, Meteor Show Productions Inc., 298 Sheppard Ave. East, North York ON M2N 3B1 – 416/229-2060; Fax: 416/223-2826; Tollfree: 1-800-896-7469; Email: weil@meteorshows.com; URL: http://www.meteorshows.com – Director, Marketing & Sales, Richard B. Swayze – Sept. 16-17 1998 – PNE Coliseum, Vancouver BC

Okanagan Wine Festival, 185 Lakeshore Dr., Penticton BC V2A 1B7 – 250/490-8866; Fax: 250/492-6119 – Held annually at various Okanagan Valley locations

Ottawa Wine & Food Show, Player Expositions International, 255 Clemow Ave., Ottawa ON K1S 2B5 – 613/567-6408; Fax: 613/567-2718 – Show Organizer, Halina Player – Annual trade & consumer show, Oct./Nov.

Salon des vins, bières et spiritueux de Montréal, AFLD Consultants Inc., 3565, rue Edgar Leduc, Lachine QC H8T 3L5 – 514/639-6806; Fax: 514/639-6629; Email: afld@videotron.ca – Show Manager, Lucie Desharnais – Biennial trade show 1998

SIVS International Wine & Spirits Show / Salon International des Vins et Spiriteux, #1100, 300, Léo Pariseau, CP 159, Montréal QC H2W 2N9 – 514/289-9669; Fax: 514/289-8711; Tollfree: 1-800363-2806 – General Manager, Alain Bellefeuille – Biennial consumer show. Sale by the bottle or case of alcoholic beverages & private stocks, March

SSA International - Super Salon de l'alimentation, #1100, 300, rue Léo Pariseau, CP 159, Montréal QC H2W 2N9 – 514/289-9669; Fax: 514/289-8711; Tollfree: 1-800-363-2806 – Director, Sales & Operations, Hélène Bourgault – Annual trade show for the food retail industry including food & beverage products & store equipment, April

Toronto Wine & Cheese Show, Meteor Show Productions Inc., 298 Sheppard Ave. East, North York ON M2N 3B1 – 416/229-2060; Fax: 416/223-2826; Tollfree: 1-800-896-7469; Email: weil@meteorshows.com; URL: http://www.meteorshows.com – Director, Marketing & Sales, Richard B. Swayze – Annual consumer show, March 20-22 1998 – International Centre, Toronto ON

## FOREST INDUSTRY

Demo, Canadian Pulp & Paper Association, Sun Life Building, 1155, rue Metcalfe, 19e étage, Montréal QC H3B 4T6 – 514/866-6621; Fax: 514/866-3035; Email: cppacda@ibm.net; URL: http://www.open.doors.cppa.ca/ – Asst. Manager, Wayne Novak – Active demonstrations of all types of industrial woodlands equipment. Harvesting, silviculture, transportation & handling, Sept.

Exfor, Canadian Pulp & Paper Association, Sun Life Building, 1155, rue Metcalfe, 19e étage, Montréal QC H3B 4T6 – 514/866-6621; Fax: 514/866-3035; Email: cppacda@ibm.net; URL: http://www.open.doors.cppa.ca/ – Chair, K. Linn Macdonald – Largest annual exhibition & conference devoted to the manufacturing of pulp & paper products

Forest Expo, #106, 3851 - 18th Ave., Prince George BC V2N 1B1 – 250/563-8833; Fax: 250/563-8909; URL: http://www.forestexpo.bc.ca – Show Manager, Trudy Swaan – Biennial, May

Truck Loggers Association Convention & Trade Show, The Truck Loggers Association, #725, 815 Hastings St. West, Vancouver BC V6C 1B4 – 604/684-4291; Fax: 604/684-7134 – Office Manager, Dave Webster – Annual trade & consumer show, Jan. – Vancouver BC

## FUNERALS

Canadian Funeral Trade Show, PO Box 97507, Scarborough ON M1C 4Z1 – 416/281-5460; Fax: 416/282-9095 – Executive Director, Brenda Broughton – Annual trade show, May

**FURNITURE *See* HOME SHOWS**

**GARDENING *See* FLOWERS**

## GIFTS & JEWELLERY

Alberta Fall Gift Show, Southex Exhibitions, 4285 Canada Way, Burnaby BC V5G 1H2 – 604/433-5121; Fax: 604/434-6853; Tollfree: 1-800-633-8332; URL: http://www.southex.com – Group Show Manager, Peter Henderson – Annual trade show: giftware, stationery, kitchenware, luggage & leathergoods, pottery, china, glass & jewellery, August – Edmonton AB

Alberta Spring Gift Show, Southex Exhibitions, 4285 Canada Way, Burnaby BC V5G 1H2 – 604/433-5121; Fax: 604/434-6853; Tollfree: 1-800-633-8332; URL: http://www.southex.com – Group Show Manager, Peter Henderson – Annual trade show: giftware, stationery, kitchenware, luggage & leathergoods, pottery, china, glass & jewellery, Feb. – Edmonton AB

Expo-Achats Bijouterie/Jewellery Buy Mart, Corporation des bijoutiers du Québec, #0.1, 7585, rue Lacordaire, St-Léonard QC H1S 2A6 – 514/251-2410; Fax: 514/251-1702 – Directrice générale, Lise Petitpas, August – Palais des Congrès, Montréal QC

The Last Minute Christmas Show & Sale, PO Box 54045, Toronto ON M6A 3B7 – 416/789-1925 – Sam Davis – Annual consumer show, Dec. – International Centre, Mississauga ON

Montréal Fall Gift Show/Le Salon du Cadeau - Montréal - Automne, Southex Exhibitions Inc., Head Office, #800, 1 Concorde Gate, North York ON M3C 3N6 – 416/385-1880; Fax: 416/385-1855; Tollfree: 1-888-823-7469; URL: http://www.southex.com – Show Manager, Mary Cartan – Annual trade show. Giftware, stationery, kitchenware, luggage & leathergoods, pottery, china, glass, jewellery, August – Montréal QC

Montréal Spring Gift Show/Le Salon du Cadeau - Montréal - Printemps, Southex Exhibitions Inc., Head Office, #800, 1 Concorde Gate, North York ON M3C 3N6 – 416/385-1880; Fax: 416/385-1855; Tollfree: 1-888-823-7469; URL: http://www.southex.com – Show Manager, Margaret Johnston – Annual trade show. Giftware, stationery, kitchenware, luggage & leathergoods, pottery, china, glass, jewellery, March – Montréal QC

Ontario North Gift Show, North Bay Chamber of Commerce, PO Box 747, North Bay ON P1A 8J8 – 705/472-8480; Fax: 705/472-8027 – Contact, Lisa Lassman – Annual trade show, April

Toronto Spring Gift Show, Southex Exhibitions Inc., Head Office, #800, 1 Concorde Gate, North York ON M3C 3N6 – 416/385-1880; Fax: 416/385-1855; Tollfree: 1-888-823-7469; URL: http://www.southex.com – Show Manager, Mary Carton – Annual trade show. Giftware, stationery, kitchenware, luggage & leathergoods, pottery, china, glass, jewellery, Feb. – Toronto ON

Treasures, Heirloom Arts & Crafts Show, Synergic Media Ltd., RR#4, Uxbridge ON L9P 1R4 – 905/649-2480; Fax: 905/649-1022 – Show Producer, Ian Russell – Consumer show held in March & November – Markham Fairgrounds, Markham ON

Vancouver Fall Gift Show, Southex Exhibitions, 4285 Canada Way, Burnaby BC V5G 1H2 – 604/433-5121; Fax: 604/434-6853; Tollfree: 1-800-633-8332; URL: http://www.southex.com – Group Show Manager, Peter Henderson – Annual trade show. Giftware, housewares, luggage & leathergoods, jewellery, Sept. – Vancouver BC

Vancouver Island Gift Show, #2, 31 Bushby St., Victoria BC V8S 1B3 – 250/370-2983; Fax: 250/380-1733 – Annual trade show

Vancouver Spring Gift Show, Southex Exhibitions, 4285 Canada Way, Burnaby BC V5G 1H2 – 604/433-5121; Fax: 604/434-6853; Tollfree: 1-800-633-8332; URL: http://www.southex.com – Group Show Manager, Peter Henderson – Annual trade show. Giftwares, housewares, luggage & leathergoods, jewellery, March – Vancouver BC

Victoriana - A Celebration of Elegance, Perdue Show Management, 378 Evans Ave., Etobicoke ON M8Z 1K6 – 416/503-8240; Fax: 416/503-8130 – Show Manager, Sandra Durbach – Spring & winter shows – King Edward Hotel, Toronto ON

Wholesale Gift Show, VIEX Events Ltd., #2, 31 Bushby St., Victoria BC V8S 1B3 – 250/370-2983; Fax: 250/370-1733; URL: http://www.vicnet.net/~viex – Sales & Marketing Director, Patrick Doyle – Spring Show – Cedar Hill Recreation Centre,

## GOVERNMENT

Government Technology Exhibition & Conference, Connelly Business Exhibitions Inc., #214, 2487 Kaladar Ave., Ottawa ON K1V 8B9 – 613/731-9850; Fax: 613/731-2407 – Vice-President, Marketing, Dan Hamilton – Sept.

Québec Municipalities Show/Salon de la municipalité du Québec, Promexpo Inc., 801, rue Sherbrooke est, 10e étage, Montréal QC H2L 1K7 – 514/527-9221; Fax: 514/527-8449 – General Manager, Ginette Gauthier – Annual trade show. Consultant services, environment, recreation, culture, GIS, April

## GRAPHIC ARTS

Canadian Community Newspapers Association Convention, Canadian Community Newspapers Association, #206, 90 Eglinton Ave. East, Toronto ON M4P 2Y3 – 416/482-1090; Fax: 416/482-1908; Email: ccna@sentex.net; URL: http://www.sentex.net/~ccna – Executive Director, Michael Anderson – Annual trade show, July 22-25 1998 – Winnipeg MB

Graphics Canada, Southex Exhibitions Inc., Head Office, #800, 1 Concorde Gate, North York ON M3C 3N6 – 416/385-1880; Fax: 416/385-1855; Tollfree: 1-888-823-7469; URL: http://www.southex.com – Research Manager, Sandy Zeidenberg – Biennial trade show for graphic arts industry, Nov. 1999 – Toronto ON

Ontario Community Newspapers Association Convention, Ontario Community Newspapers Association, #103, 3050 Harvester Rd., Burlington ON L7N 3J1 – 905/639-8720; Fax: 905/639-6962; Email: info@ocna.org; URL: http://www.ocna.org – Executive Director, Don Lamont – Annual trade show, March – Toronto ON

Print Ontario '98, Ontario Trade Shows Ltd., #8, 1606 Sedlescomb Dr., Mississauga ON L4X 1M6 – 905/625-7070; Fax: 905/625-4856; Tollfree: 1-800-331-7408 – Show Manager, Alexander Donald – Biennial trade show, Nov. 21-23 1998 – Automotive Building, Exhibition Place, Toronto ON

## HAIRDRESSING

Educational Hair Dressing Show, Allied Beauty Association, #325, 3625 Dufferin St., Toronto ON M3K 1Z2 – 416/635-1282; Fax: 416/635-1205 – Executive Director, Marc Speir – Held in various locations, September/October

## HARDWARE

The Western Show, Canadian Hardware & Housewares Manufacturers' Association, #101, 1335 Morningside Ave., Scarborough ON M1B 5M4 – 416/282-0022; Fax: 416/282-0027 – Show Manager, Maureen Hizaka, Oct. – BC Place Stadium, Vancouver BC

## HEALTH

Annual Health Conference & Exhibition, Manitoba Health Organizations, #600, 360 Broadway, Winnipeg MB R3C 4G6 – 204/942-6591; Fax: 204/956-1373 – President, Ronald G. Birt – Nov.

International Psychogeriatric Association, Venue West Conference Services Ltd., #645, 375 Water St., Vancouver BC V6B 5C6 – 604/681-5226; Fax: 604/681-2503; Email: congress@venuewest.com; URL: http://www.venuwest.com – President, Betty Fata – Aug. 15-21 1999

International Society for Experimental Hematology, Venue West Conference Services Ltd., #645, 375 Water St., Vancouver BC V6B 5C6 – 604/681-5226; Fax: 604/681-2503; Email: congress@venuewest.com; URL: http://www.venuwest.com – President, Betty Fata – Aug. 1-7 1998

Schizophrenia 1988, Venue West Conference Services Ltd., #645, 375 Water St., Vancouver BC V6B 5C6 – 604/681-5226; Fax: 604/681-2503; Email: congress@venuewest.com; URL: http://www.venuwest.com – President, Betty Fata – July 26-30 1998

Whole Life Expo, 356 Dupont Ave., Toronto ON M5R 1V9 – 416/515-1330 – Julia Woodford – Annual consumer show. Herbal & natural products, Nov. – Metro Toronto Convention Centre, Toronto ON

World Association for Social Psychiatry, Venue West Conference Services Ltd., #645, 375 Water St., Vancouver BC V6B 5C6 – 604/681-5226; Fax: 604/681-2503; Email: congress@venuewest.com; URL: http://www.venuwest.com – President, Betty Fata – Aug. 17-21 1998

World Congress of Medical Technology, Venue West Conference Services Ltd., #645, 375 Water St., Vancouver BC V6B 5C6 – 604/681-5226; Fax: 604/681-2503; Email: congress@venuewest.com; URL: http://www.venuwest.com – President, Betty Fata – Aug. 20-25 2000

## HEATING, PLUMBING & AIR CONDITIONING

***See Also* Hardware**

CIPHEX '99, CIPHEX, c/o #330, 295 The West Mall, Etobicoke ON M9C 4Z4 – 416/695-0447; Fax: 416/695-0450; Email: ciph@ican.net; URL: http://www.ciph.com – Show Manager, Elizabeth McCullough – Oct. 1999 – Toronto ON

CIPHEX West 2000, CIPHEX, c/o #330, 295 The West Mall, Etobicoke ON M9C 4Z4 – 416/695-0447; Fax: 416/695-0450; Email: ciph@ican.net; URL: http://www.ciph.com – Show Manager, Elizabeth McCullough – April 2000

Climatex, Corporation des maîtres entrepreneurs en réfrigération du Québec, #301, 6525, boul Décarie, Montréal QC H3W 3E3 – 514/735-1131; Fax: 514/735-3509 – Sylvain Roy – Annual trade show, March – Montréal QC

CMX '2000, Shield Associates Ltd., 25 Bradgate Rd., Don Mills ON M3B 1J6 – 416/444-5225; Fax: 416/444-8268; Email: sal@myna.com; URL: http://www.cmxshow.com – Show Coordinator, Patrick Shield – Biennial trade show. Heating, ventilation, plumbing, air conditioning, ventilation & refrigeration, March 30 - April 1 2000

CMX '98, Shield Associates Ltd., 25 Bradgate Rd., Don Mills ON M3B 1J6 – 416/444 5225; Fax: 416/444-8268; Email: sal@myna.com; URL: http://www.cmxshow.com – Show Coordinator, Patrick Shield – Biennial trade show. Heating, ventilation, plumbing, air conditioning & refrigeration, March 26-28 1998

Mécanexpo-CIPHEX, CIPHEX, c/o #330, 295 The West Mall, Etobicoke ON M9C 4Z4 – 416/695-0447; Fax: 416/695-0450; Email: ciph@ican.net; URL: http://www.ciph.com – Show Manager, Elizabeth McCullough – Biennial trade show. Plumbing, heating, cooling & piping exhibits & conference, April 1999

## HOBBIES

***See Also* Crafts**

Annual Stamp Exhibition & Sale of Stamps, Coins & Sports Cards, Regina Philatelic Club, PO Box 1891, Regina SK S4P 3E1 – 306/586-8152, Feb. 25-26 – Regina SK

Montréal Hobby & Craft Show, CP 343, Succ Notre-Dame, Montréal QC H4A 3P5 – 514/484-9414; Fax: 514/485-6579 – Annual consumer show, Oct.

Toronto Model Railway Show, 25 Lippincott St. West, Etobicoke ON M9N 1B3 – 416/249-4563 – Show Coordinator, Jack Bell – Annual consumer show, March

**HOME ENTERTAINMENT *See* ELECTRICAL/ ELECTRONICS**

## HOME SHOWS

Atlantic National Home Show, Master Promotions Ltd., PO Box 565, Saint John NB E2L 3Z8 – 506/658-0018; Fax: 506/658-0750 – Show Manager, Brian McKiel – Annual consumer show, March – Saint John NB

BC Fall Home Show, Southex Exhibitions, 4285 Canada Way, Burnaby BC V5G 1H2 – 604/433-5121; Fax: 604/434-6853; Tollfree: 1-800-633-8332;

URL: http://www.southex.com – Show Manager, Rob Haynes – Annual consumer show, Oct.

BC Home & Garden Show, Southex Exhibitions, 4285 Canada Way, Burnaby BC V5G 1H2 – 604/433-5121; Fax: 604/434-6853; Tollfree: 1-800-633-8332; URL: http://www.southex.com – Show Manager, Rob Haynes – Annual trade & consumer show, Feb.

BC Interior Home & Garden Show, Showest Management Inc., PO Box 300, Kamloops BC V2C 5K6 – 250/851-2145; Fax: 250/851-0551 – Show Manager, Gerry Hartley – Annual consumer show, February/March

Bridge City Cosmopolitan Home Show, Bridge City Cosmopolitan Club, PO Box 351, Saskatoon SK S7K 3L3 – 306/653-1888 – Terry Akister, Feb. – Saskatchewan Place, Saskatoon SK

Burlington Lifestyle Home Show, Jenkins Show Productions, 1076 Skyvalley Cr., Oakville ON L6M 3L2 – 905/827-4632; Fax: 905/827-8139; Tollfree: 1-800-465-1073 – President, Dave Jenkins – Annual consumer show, April – Burlington ON

Calgary Renovation Show, Young Marketing Services Inc., #105, 10544 - 114 St., Edmonton AB T5H 3J7 – 403/423-4060; Fax: 403/426-7862 – Show Manager, Rick Young – Annual consumer show, Jan. – Stampede Park, Calgary AB

Canadian Pool & Spa Conference & Expo, National Spa & Pool Institute of Canada, #5, 7370 Bramalea Rd., Mississauga ON L5S 1N6 – 905/676-1591; Fax: 905/676-1598; Tollfree: 1-800-879-7066 – Show Manager, Nancy Lumb – Annual trade show, Dec. 2-3 1998 – Toronto ON

Canadian Pool, Spa & Patio Show, "Splish Splash", c/o The Profile Group, #301, 37 Sandiford Dr., Stouffville ON L4A 7X5 – 905/640-7700; Fax: 905/640-7714 – Show Manager, George Zarras – Annual consumer show. Pools, spas, patios, decks, fencing & related leisure products, Feb.

Colchester County Home Show, Master Promotions Ltd., PO Box 565, Saint John NB E2L 3Z8 – 506/658-0018; Fax: 506/658-0750 – Show Manager, Brian McKeil – April – Legion Stadium, Truro NS

Cottagefest, Jenkins Show Productions, 1076 Skyvalley Cr., Oakville ON L6M 3L2 – 905/827-4632; Fax: 905/827-8139; Tollfree: 1-800-465-1073 – President, Dave Jenkins – Annual consumer show. Cottage country businesses; cottage-related products & services, June

Design Forum, Perdue Show Management, 378 Evans Ave., Etobicoke ON M8Z 1K6 – 416/503-8240; Fax: 416/503-8130 – President, Elizabeth Fairley – Annual home furnishings trade show, August

Edmonton Home Show, Young Marketing Services Inc., #105, 10544 - 114 St., Edmonton AB T5H 3J7 – 403/423-4060; Fax: 403/426-7862 – Show Manager, Rick Young – Annual consumer show, Sept. – Edmonton AB

Edmonton Renovation Show, Young Marketing Services Inc., #105, 10544 - 114 St., Edmonton AB T5H 3J7 – 403/423-4060; Fax: 403/426-7862 – Show Manager, Rick Young – Annual consumer show, Jan. – Edmonton Northlands, Edmonton AB

Expo Habitat Québec, Association provinciale des constructeurs d'habitations Québec, 2825, boul Wilfrid-Hamel, Québec QC G1P 2H9 – 418/682-3353; Fax: 418/682-3851 – Mildred Charlton – Feb. – Patinodrome, Ste-Foy QC

Fredericton Spring Lifestyles, Master Promotions Ltd., PO Box 565, Saint John NB E2L 3Z8 – 506/658-0018; Fax: 506/658-0750 – Show Manager, Brian McKeil, March/April – Capital Exhibit Centre, Fredericton NB

Hamilton Home Show, Ontario Marketing Productions, 109 Scollard St., Toronto ON M5R 1G4 – 416/961-2999; Fax: 416/961-1157 – Contact, Linda Watt – Annual consumer show, March – Hamilton Convention Centre, Hamilton ON

Home & Garden Show, VIEX Events Ltd., #2, 31 Bushby St., Victoria BC V8S 1B3 – 250/370-2983; Fax: 250/370-1733; URL: http://www.vicnet.net/~viex – Sales & Marketing Director, Patrick Doyle – April 1-5 1998 – Mayfair Shopping Centre,

Home Show, Thunder Bay Chamber of Commerce Trade Show, 857 North May St., Thunder Bay ON P7C 3S2 – 807/622-9882; Fax: 807/622-7752; Email: chamber@tb-chamber.on.ca; URL: http://www.tb-chamber.on.ca – Show Manager, Arleene Mapledoram – Sept. – Thunder Bay ON

Home, Garden & Leisure Show, Medicine Hat & District Chamber of Commerce, 413 - 6th Ave. SE, Medicine Hat AB T1A 2S7 – 403/527-5214; Fax: 403/527-5182 – Anna Steckle – Consumer show, March – Cypress Centre, Stampede Park, Medicine Hat AB

Indoor Living Show, Southex Exhibitions Inc., Head Office, #800, 1 Concorde Gate, North York ON M3C 3N6 – 416/385-1880; Fax: 416/385-1855; Tollfree: 1-888-823-7469; URL: http://www.southex.com – Show Manager, Arnie Hingston – Annual consumer show, Oct.

Interiors Decor Showcase, Decor Showcase, c/o Paint & Decorating Retailer Association, #5, 7895 Tranmere Dr., Mississauga ON L5S 1V9 – 905/678-0331; Fax: 905/678-0335 – Contact, Rosemary Schooley – Annual trade show. Home decorating products, paint & coatings, sundries, wallcovering, window treatments, decorative fabrics & floor coverings, Feb.

International Home & Garden Show, Showcase Marketing Ltd., #410, 1110 Sheppard Ave. East, North York ON M2K 2W2 – 416/512-1305; Fax: 416/512-9998 – Paul Newdick – Annual consumer show, March

International Home Show, Showcase Marketing Ltd., #410, 1110 Sheppard Ave. East, North York ON M2K 2W2 – 416/512-1305; Fax: 416/512-9998 – Paul Newdick – Annual consumer show, Nov. – International Centre, Toronto ON

Kitchener-Waterloo HomExpo, Ontario Marketing Productions, 109 Scollard St., Toronto ON M5R 1G4 – 416/961-2999; Fax: 416/961-1157 – Contact, Linda Watt – Consumer show, Feb. – Kitchener Memorial Auditorium, Kitchener ON

Landscape Pool & Patio Show, c/o Bingemans Conference & Recreation Centre, 1380 Victoria St. North, Kitchener ON N2B 3E2 – 519/744-1555; Fax: 519/744-1985 – Marketing Manager, Brian Banks – Annual consumer show. Pools, spas, decks, landscaping, patio furniture. Manufacturers & services, Feb. 27 - March 1 1998

The London Convention Centre Fall Home Show, Jenkins Show Productions, 1076 Skyvalley Cr., Oakville ON L6M 3L2 – 905/827-4632; Fax: 905/827-8139; Tollfree: 1-800-465-1073 – President, Dave Jenkins – Oct. – London ON

London Home & Garden Show, London Show Productions, RR#5, London ON N6A 4B9 – 519/455-5888; Fax: 519/455-7780 – President, Arthur Bacon – Consumer show, April – London ON

The London Home Builders' Association Lifestyle Home Show, Jenkins Show Productions, 1076 Skyvalley Cr., Oakville ON L6M 3L2 – 905/827-4632; Fax: 905/827-8139; Tollfree: 1-800-465-1073 – President, Dave Jenkins, Feb. – London ON

Mall Home Shows, Jenkins Show Productions, 1076 Skyvalley Cr., Oakville ON L6M 3L2 – 905/827-4632; Fax: 905/827-8139; Tollfree: 1-800-465-1073 – President, Dave Jenkins – Shows at shopping centres throughout Ontario in March, October, November

Markham Home Show, Canadian Tel-A-Views Ltd., #12, 115 Apple Creek Blvd., Markham ON L3R 6C9 – 905/477-2677; Fax: 905/477-7872; Tollfree: 1-800-891-4859 – Lynn McVey – Oct.

Metro East Home Show, Metropolitan Promotions, PO Box 193, Ajax ON L1S 3C3 – 905/428-7610; Fax: 905/428-7046 – Show Manager, Tom Glaesser, Feb. – Metro East Trade Centre, Pickering ON

Metro Home Show, Southex Exhibitions Inc., Head Office, #800, 1 Concorde Gate, North York ON M3C 3N6 – 416/385-1880; Fax: 416/385-1855; Tollfree: 1-888-823-7469; URL: http://www.southex.com – Show Manager, Norm Shulz – Annual consumer show, Jan. – National Trade Centre, Exhibition Place, Toronto ON

The Metro West Fall Home Show, Jenkins Show Productions, 1076 Skyvalley Cr., Oakville ON L6M 3L2 – 905/827-4632; Fax: 905/827-8139; Tollfree: 1-800-465-1073 – President, Dave Jenkins – Oct. – Oakville ON

Miramichi Lifestyle, Master Promotions Ltd., PO Box 565, Saint John NB E2L 3Z8 – 506/658-0018; Fax: 506/658-0750 – Brian McKeil – April – Miramichi Civic Centre, Miramichi NB

Montréal Kitchen & Bath Expo, Interface Design, 5318, boul St-Laurent, Montréal QC H2T 1S1 – 514/273-4030; Fax: 514/273-3649 – Présidente, Ginette Gadoury – Montréal QC

Montréal National Home Show/Salon National de l'habitation de Montréal, Promexpo Inc., 801, rue Sherbrooke est, 10e étage, Montréal QC H2L 1K7 – 514/527-9221; Fax: 514/527-8449 – Michele Tessier – Annual consumer show, February/March – Montréal QC

National Home Show, Southex Exhibitions Inc., Head Office, #800, 1 Concorde Gate, North York ON M3C 3N6 – 416/385-1880; Fax: 416/385-1855; Tollfree: 1-888-823-7469; URL: http://www.southex.com – Show Manager, Maureen Eckford – Annual consumer show, April – Coliseum Bldg., Exhibition Place, Toronto ON

National Home Show/National Kitchen & Bath Showcase, Southex Exhibitions Inc., Head Office, #800, 1 Concorde Gate, North York ON M3C 3N6 – 416/385-1880; Fax: 416/385-1855; Tollfree: 1-888-823-7469; URL: http://www.southex.com – Show Manager, Ross Horton, April – National Trade Centre, Exhibition Place, Toronto ON

National Housewares Show, International Tradeshow Services Inc., 20 Butterick Rd., Toronto ON M8W 3Z8 – 416/252-7791; Fax: 416/252-9848; Email: jimm@intltradeshows.com; URL: http://www.intltradeshows.com – President, James K. Mahon, June 1-2 1998 – Congress Centre, Toronto ON

Niagara Lifestyle Home Show, Jenkins Show Productions, 1076 Skyvalley Cr., Oakville ON L6M 3L2 – 905/827-4632; Fax: 905/827-8139; Tollfree: 1-800-465-1073 – President, Dave Jenkins – Annual consumer show, April – Garden City/Rex Stimers Arena, St Catharines ON

Nova Scotia Ideal Home Shows, Denex Group Inc., Burnside Industrial Park, 192 Joseph Zatzman Dr., Dartmouth NS B3B 1N4 – 902/468-4999; Fax: 902/468-2795; Email: denman@ns.sympatico.ca; URL: http://www.denexgroup.com – Group Show Manager, Bev Campbell – Consumer shows held in April & September

Oakville Lifestyle Home Show, Jenkins Show Productions, 1076 Skyvalley Cr., Oakville ON L6M 3L2 – 905/827-4632; Fax: 905/827-8139; Tollfree: 1-800-465-1073 – President, Dave Jenkins – Annual consumer show, April – Glen Abbey Recreation Centre, Oakville ON

Ottawa Fall Home Show, Southex Exhibitions Inc., #440, 47 Clarence St., Ottawa ON K1N 9K1 – 613/241-2888; Fax: 613/241-1827 – Show Manager, Paul Le Guerrier – Annual consumer show, Sept. – Civic Centre, Lansdowne Park, Ottawa ON

Ottawa Spring Home Show, Southex Exhibitions Inc., #440, 47 Clarence St., Ottawa ON K1N 9K1 – 613/241-2888; Fax: 613/241-1827 – Show Manager, Paul

Le Guerrier – Annual consumer show, April 1997 – Civic Centre, Lansdowne Park, Ottawa ON

PEI Provincial Home Show, Master Promotions Ltd., PO Box 565, Saint John NB E2L 3Z8 – 506/658-0018; Fax: 506/658-0750 – Show Manager, Mark Cusack – March – Charlottetown PE

Pool, Spa & Patio Show, Backyard Living Productions, PO Box 1500-1288, Etobicoke ON M9C 4V5 – 416/620-6620; Fax: 416/621-6688 – Shirley Trotter, March – International Centre, Toronto ON

Québec National Home Show/Salon National de l'habitation de Québec, Promexpo Inc., 801, rue Sherbrooke est, 10e étage, Montréal QC H2L 1K7 – 514/527-9221; Fax: 514/527-8449 – General Manager, Audrey Robitaille – Annual consumer show, March – Québec QC

Red Deer Home Ideas, Home Ideas & Lifestyles, #10, 7895 - 49 Ave., Red Deer AB T4P 2B4 – 403/346-5321; Fax: 403/342-1301; Email: cahba@rttinc.com; URL: http://www.albertaweb.com/cahba – Contact, Patrick Kennedy – Annual, Feb./March

Renovations - The Kitchen, Bath & Window Show, Southex Exhibitions Inc., #440, 47 Clarence St., Ottawa ON K1N 9K1 – 613/241-2888; Fax: 613/241-1827 – Show Manager, Paul Le Guerrier – Annual trade & consumer show, Jan. – Civic Centre, Lansdowne Park, Ottawa ON

Saint John Home & Garden Show, Master Promotions Ltd., PO Box 565, Saint John NB E2L 3Z8 – 506/658-0018; Fax: 506/658-0750 – Show Manager, Sydney Jane Brittain – Saint John NB

Salon international du mueble de Toronto/Toronto International Home Furnishings Market, Association des fabricants de meubles du Québec inc., #101, 1111, rue St-Urbain, Montréal QC H2Z 1Y6 – 514/866-3631; Fax: 514/871-9900 – Director of Exhibitions, Rita Hanson – Annual trade & consumer show, Jan. – International Centre, Toronto ON

Sarnia CHOK Home & Recreation Show, Sarnia CHOK, 148 North Front St., Sarnia ON N7T 7K5 – 519/336-1070 – Show Manager, Penni Steele – Annual consumer show, May – Clearwater Arena, Sarnia ON

Showcase, Medicine Hat & District Chamber of Commerce, 413 - 6th Ave. SE, Medicine Hat AB T1A 2S7 – 403/527-5214; Fax: 403/527-5182 – Jeanette Frost – Annual consumer show, Nov.

Showmart - Home & Leisure Show, c/o CHWK, PO Box 386, Chilliwack BC V2P 6J7 – 604/795-5711; Fax: 604/795-6643; Email: showmart@fraservalley.com; URL: http://www.fraservalley.com/showmart – Sales, Steve Hemenway – Annual consumer show, Feb.

Western Canada Kitchen & Bath Expo, Hank Hartloper Agency, #2, 1575 Seel Ave., Winnipeg MB R3T 1C8 – 204/925-1620; Fax: 204/925-1623 – Owner, Hank Hartloper – Annual consumer show, Jan. – Winnipeg Convention Centre, Winnipeg MB

Western Canadian Pool & Spa Conference & Expo, National Spa & Pool Institute of Canada, #5, 7370 Bramalea Rd., Mississauga ON L5S 1N6 – 905/676-1591; Fax: 905/676-1598; Tollfree: 1-800-879-7066 – Executive Director, Nancy Lumb – Annual trade & consumer show, Jan. 28-29 1999 – Vancouver Trade Centre, Vancouver BC

Win Door, Shield Associates Ltd., 25 Bradgate Rd., Don Mills ON M3B 1J6 – 416/444-5225; Fax: 416/444-8268; Email: sal@myna.com; URL: http://www.cmxshow.com – Show Coordinator, Patrick Shield – Windows & doors show, new products & technologies, Nov. 18-20 1998

## HORSES

The Masters Show Jumping Show, Spruce Meadows, RR#9, Calgary AB T2J 5G5 – 403/974-4200; Fax: 403/974-4266 – Contact, Curtis Reid – Annual consumer show. Includes Equi-Fair, Breeds for the World, Festival of Nations, Sept.

Royal Red Arabian Horse Show, PO Box 167, Regina SK S4P 2Z6 – 306/781-4216; Fax: 306/565-3443 – Facility Contact, Lea Kennedy – Annual, August

Whoop Up Spring Quarter Horse Show, Lethbridge & District Exhibition, 3401 Parkside Dr. South, Lethbridge AB T1J 4R3 – 403/328-4491; Fax: 403/320-8139; Email: whoopup@agt.net; URL: http://www.telusplanet.net/public/whoopup – Agricultural Coordinator, Twyla Gurr – Annual trade & consumer show, April

## HORTICULTURE *See* FLOWERS

## HOSPITAL

Convention, Provincial Health Authorities of Alberta, 44 Capital Blvd., #200, 10044 - 108 St. NW, Edmonton AB T5J 3S7 – 403/426-8502; Fax: 403/424-4309 – Coordinator, Christine Y. Chepyha – Annual trade show, Nov.

Convention & Exhibition, Ontario Hospital Association, #2800, 200 Front St. West, Toronto ON M5V 3L1 – 416/205-1300; Fax: 416/205-1301; URL: http://www.oha.com – Maria Batt – Annual trade show, Nov.

## HOSPITALITY INDUSTRY (HOTEL, MOTEL, RESTAURANT)

***See Also* Food & Beverage**

Annual Convention & Exposition, British Columbia & Yukon Hotels Association, 948 Howe St., 2nd Fl., Vancouver BC V6Z 1N9 – 604/681-7164; Fax: 604/681-7649; Tollfree: 1-800-663-3153; URL: http://www.fleethouse.com/fhcanada/bc-acco.htm – Event Coordinator, Marilyn Pierlet – Annual trade show, Nov./Dec.

HostEx, Canadian Restaurant & Foodservices Association, 316 Bloor St. West, Toronto ON M5S 1W5 – 416/923-8416; Fax: 416/923-1450; Tollfree: 1-800-387-5649; Email: 102477.3104@compuserve.com – Chairman, Paul Hollands – Annual trade show, Oct.

Salon Rendez-vous, Association des fournisseurs d'hôtels et restaurants inc., 2435, rue Guénette, Saint Laurent QC H4R 2E9 – 514/334-5161; Fax: 514/334-1279; Tollfree: 1-800-567-2347; Email: afhr@sympatico.ca; URL: http://www.afhr.com – Trésorier, Sylvain Inkel – Annual trade show, Feb. – Montréal QC

Salon Reste-Hôte, Association des restaurateurs du Québec, 2485, rue Sherbrooke est, Montréal QC H2K 1E8 – 514/527-9801; Fax: 514/527-3066; Tollfree: 1-800-463-9801 – Exhibits Manager, F. Gadbois – Annual trade show. Equipment, services & food products for restaurants, hotels & institutions, March – Québec QC

## IMPORT/EXPORT

World Trade, Canadian International Trade Association, #611, 2 Carlton St., Toronto ON M5B 1J3 – 416/351-9728; Fax: 416/351-9911 – President, Sydney King – Annual trade show. Agents & distributors locator & recruiter show, Oct.

## INDUSTRIAL

Atlantic Industrial Exhibition, Reed Exhibition Companies Inc., 3761 Victoria Park Ave., Scarborough ON M1W 3S2 – 416/491-7565; Fax: 416/491-5088 – Show Manager, Tracy McKnight – Biennial trade show; Moncton (1998), Sept.

Canadian Hospital Engineers Society, Taylor Enterprises Ltd., #310, 2175 Sheppard Ave. East, North York ON M2J 1W8 – 416/491-2897; Fax: 416/491-1670; Tollfree: 1-800-208-9398; Email: taylor@interlog.com; URL: http://www.interlog.com/~taylor/htehome.html – President, Joan Milne – Oct. 1998 – Victoria BC

Halifax Industrial Exhibition, Reed Exhibition Companies Inc., 3761 Victoria Park Ave., Scarborough ON M1W 3S2 – 416/491-7565; Fax: 416/491-5088 – Annual trade show; machine tools, Sept.

Industrial Expo New Brunswick, Master Promotions Ltd., PO Box 565, Saint John NB E2L 3Z8 – 506/658-0018; Fax: 506/658-0750 – Show Manager, Mark Cusack – May – Saint John NB

Industrial Expo Nova Scotia, Master Promotions Ltd., PO Box 565, Saint John NB E2L 3Z8 – 506/658-0018; Fax: 506/658-0750 – Mark Cusack – Biennial show, May 1999

Montréal Fabricating & Machine Tool Show/Le Salon du Travail des Métaux et de la Machine Outil de Montréal, Reed Exhibition Companies Inc., 3761 Victoria Park Ave., Scarborough ON M1W 3S2 – 416/491-7565; Fax: 416/491-5088 – National Accounts Manager, Bob Mathieu – Biennial trade show, May 1998 – Montréal QC

Plant Maintenance & Engineering Show/Le Salon Industriel de la Maintenance et de l'Ingenierie, Reed Exhibition Companies Inc., 3761 Victoria Park Ave., Scarborough ON M1W 3S2 – 416/491-7565; Fax: 416/491-5088 – Show Manager, Bob Mathieu – Annual trade show, May – Montréal QC

Salon industriel de l'Estrie, Les Promotions André Pageau Inc., 1627, boul St-Joseph, Québec QC G2K 1H1 – 418/623-3383; Fax: 418/623-5033; Email: info@promoapageau.qc.ca; URL: http://www.promoapageau.qc.ca – Président, André Pageau – Biennial trade show, May 2000 – Sherbrooke QC

Salon industriel de Montréal/Montéregie, Les Promotions André Pageau Inc., 1627, boul St-Joseph, Québec QC G2K 1H1 – 418/623-3383; Fax: 418/623-5033; Email: info@promoapageau.qc.ca; URL: http://www.promoapageau.qc.ca – Président, André Pageau – Oct. 26-28 1999 – St-Hyacinthe QC

Salon Industriel de Québec, Les Promotions André Pageau Inc., 1627, boul St-Joseph, Québec QC G2K 1H1 – 418/623-3383; Fax: 418/623-5033; Email: info@promoapageau.qc.ca; URL: http://www.promoapageau.qc.ca – Président, André Pageau – Biennial trade show, Oct. 6-8 1998 – Québec QC

Salon Industriel du Saguenay/Lac-St-Jean, Les Promotions André Pageau Inc., 1627, boul St-Joseph, Québec QC G2K 1H1 – 418/623-3383; Fax: 418/623-5033; Email: info@promoapageau.qc.ca; URL: http://www.promoapageau.qc.ca – Président, André Pageau – Biennial, May 4-6 1999 – Chicoutimi QC

Southwestern Ontario Industrial Show, Reed Exhibition Companies Inc., 3761 Victoria Park Ave., Scarborough ON M1W 3S2 – 416/491-7565; Fax: 416/491-5088 – Trade show, May 26-28 1998 – Kitchener ON

Vancouver Industrial Exhibition, Reed Exhibition Companies Inc., 3761 Victoria Park Ave., Scarborough ON M1W 3S2 – 416/491-7565; Fax: 416/491-5088 – Show Manager, Sharon Freedman – Biennial trade show, June 2-4 1998 – Abbotsford BC

Weld Expo Canada, Reed Exhibition Companies Inc., 3761 Victoria Park Ave., Scarborough ON M1W 3S2 – 416/491-7565; Fax: 416/491-5088 – Show Manager, Terry Lynn Weiss – Trade show, Oct.

Windsor Mold Show, Reed Exhibition Companies Inc., 3761 Victoria Park Ave., Scarborough ON M1W 3S2 – 416/491-7565; Fax: 416/491-5088 – Show Manager, Charlene Jennings – Biennial trade show, Oct. 1998 – Ciocciaro Club, Windsor ON

## INSURANCE

Annual Convention, Insurance Brokers Association of Ontario, 90 Eglinton Ave. East, 2nd Fl., Toronto ON M4P 2Y3 – 416/488-7422; Fax: 416/488-7526 – Executive Director, Robert J. Carter – Annual trade show, Oct.

## INTERIOR DESIGN/DECORATING

***See Also* Home Shows**

Designers' Weekend, Venue West Conference Services Ltd., #645, 375 Water St., Vancouver BC V6B 5C6 – 604/681-5226; Fax: 604/681-2503; Email: congress@venuewest.com; URL: http://www.venuwest.com – President, Betty Fata – Annual trade show, Feb. – Vancouver BC

IIDEX - International Interior Design Exposition, Association of Registered Interior Designers of Ontario, 717 Church St., Toronto ON M4W 2M5 – 416/921-2127; Fax: 416/921-3660; Tollfree: 1-800-334-1180 – Contact, Cathy Clark – Nov.

International Decor Showcase, Canadian Decorating Products Association, #5, 7895 Tranmere Dr., Mississauga ON L5S 1V9 – 905/678-0331; Fax: 905/678-0335 – Show Manager, Mary Schooley – Feb. – Automotive Bldg., Exhibition Place, Toronto ON

SIDIM - Montréal International Interior Design Show, Interface Design, 5318, boul St-Laurent, Montréal QC H2T 1S1 – 514/273-4030; Fax: 514/273-3649 – Présidente, Ginette Gadoury – Trade & consumer show, May 29-31 1997 – Montréal QC

**JEWELLERY *See* GIFTS**

**LANDSCAPING *See* FLOWERS**

## LEGAL

Canadian Association of Law Libraries, Events & Management Plus Inc., 190 Railway St., PO Box 1570, Kingston ON K7L 5C8 – 613/531-9210; Fax: 613/531-0626; Email: events@adan.kingston.net – Owner, E. Hooper – May 31 - June 3 1998 – Hamilton ON

Canadian Bar Association, International Tradeshow Services Inc., 20 Butterick Rd., Toronto ON M8W 3Z8 – 416/252-7791; Fax: 416/252-9848; Email: jimm@intltradeshows.com; URL: http://www.intltradeshows.com – President, James K. Mahon – Aug. 24-26 1998 – St. John's NF

Technology for Lawyers/Technologie juridique, Canadian Society for the Advancement of Legal Technology, #200, 20 Toronto St., Toronto ON M5C 2B8 – 416/663-5290; Fax: 416/663-6502 – Conference Coordinator, Tricia W. Sands – Annual two-day event open to public. Application of technology to the practice of law, April

**LEISURE *See* SPORTS & RECREATION**

## LIGHTING

International Lighting Exposition, Kerrwil Show & Conference Group, 395 Matheson Blvd. East, Mississauga ON L4Z 2H2 – 905/890-1846; Fax: 905/890-5769; Email: aschacht@kerrwil.com; URL: http://www.kerrwilshow.com – Manager, Anita Schachter – Biennial trade show. Residential, commercial, industrial, landscape, emergency lighting, Oct. 1999 – Metro Toronto Convention Centre, Toronto ON

## LOGISTICS

Logistech - The International Materials Handling & Distribution Show, Southex Exhibitions Inc., Head Office, #800, 1 Concorde Gate, North York ON M3C 3N6 – 416/385-1880; Fax: 416/385-1855; Tollfree: 1-888-823-7469; URL: http://www.southex.com – Chris Seeney, Show Manager – Biennial trade show, Sept. 21-23 1998 – International Centre, Toronto ON

## MACHINERY & MANUFACTURING

***See Also* Industrial**

Canadian Machine Tool Show, Reed Exhibition Companies Inc., 3761 Victoria Park Ave., Scarborough ON M1W 3S2 – 416/491-7565; Fax: 416/491-5088 – Show Manager, Elaine Dale Harris – Biennial trade show, Sept. 1997 – Toronto ON

## MAGAZINES

Magazines, Ontario Trade Shows Ltd., #8, 1606 Sedlescomb Dr., Mississauga ON L4X 1M6 – 905/625-7070; Fax: 905/625-4856; Tollfree: 1-800-331-7408 – Alexander Donald – Annual conference & trade show for publishing professionals, June – The Old Mill, Toronto ON

## MARINE

***See Also* Fishing; Boating**

Canadian Shipbuilding & Offshore Exhibition, Shipbuilding Association of Canada, #1502, 222 Queen St., Ottawa ON K1P 5V9 – 613/232-7127; Fax: 613/238-5519 – Director, Administration & Finance, Joy MacPherson – Annual trade show, Feb. – Ottawa ON

Toronto International Marine Trade Show, The National Marine Manufacturers Association, #804, 370 King St. West, Toronto ON M5V 1J9 – 416/591-6772; Fax: 416/591-3582 – Show Manager, Carol Bell – Jan. – Toronto ON

**MARKETING *See* ADVERTISING**

**MATERIALS HANDLING *See* LOGISTICS**

## MEDICAL

Annual Congress, Canadian Society of Laboratory Technologists, PO Box 2830, Stn A, Hamilton ON L8N 3N8 – 905/528-8642; Fax: 905/528-4968; URL: http://www.cslt.com – Executive Director, E. Valerie Booth – Annual trade show, June

Annual Meeting, Canadian Paediatric Society, #100, 2204 Walkley Rd., Ottawa ON K1G 4G8 – 613/526-9397, ext.231; Fax: 613/526-3332; Email: info@cps.ca; URL: http://www.cps.ca – Stephanie Mutschler, Conference Coordinator, June 24-28 1998 – Hamilton Convention Centre, Hamilton ON

Canadian Cardiovascular Society Annual Scientific Meeting & Exhibition, Venue West Conference Services Ltd., #645, 375 Water St., Vancouver BC V6B 5C6 – 604/681-5226; Fax: 604/681-2503; Email: congress@venuewest.com; URL: http://www.venuwest.com – President, Betty Fata – Trade show, Oct. – Ottawa ON

COS Annual Meeting & Exhibition, Canadian Ophthalmological Society, #610, 1525 Carling Ave., Ottawa ON K1Z 8R9 – 613/729-6779; Fax: 613/729-7209; Tollfree: 1-800-267-5763; Email: cos@eyesite.ca; URL: http://eyesite.ca – Executive Director, Hubert Drouin, June 26-29 1998 – Calgary Convention Centre, Calgary AB

Mayfest, Canadian Hearing Society, 271 Spadina Rd., Toronto ON M5R 2V3 – 416/964-9595; TTY: 416/964-0023; Fax: 416/928-2506; Tollfree: 1-800-465-4327; Email: info@chs.ca; URL: http://www.chs.ca – President, Keith Golem – Latest innovations & access for deaf, deafened & hard of hearing people, May – Toronto ON

Medical & Surgical Exposition, The Royal College of Physicians & Surgeons of Canada, 774 Echo Dr., Ottawa ON K1S 5N8 – 613/730-8177; Fax: 613/730-8833; Tollfree: 1-800-668-3740; Email: communications@rcpsc.edu; URL: http://rcpsc.medical.org – Executive Director, Hugh M. Scott – Annual trade show, Sept. 24-27 1998 – Convention Centre, Toronto ON

## MILITARY

ARMX '99, 310 Dupont St., Toronto ON M5R 1V9 – 416/968-7252; Fax: 416/968-2377 – Contact, Wolfgang Schmidt – Biennial. Aerospace & defence equipment exhibition for the Canadian government. Seminars on training & simulation. International exhibitions, May

## MINING & MINERALS

Canadian Mining & Industrial Exposition, DAC Marketing Ltd., PO Box 2837, Stn A, Sudbury ON P3A 5J3 – 705/673-5588; Fax: 705/525-0626 – President, Darren A. Ceccarelli – April 28-29 1998 – Garson Arena, Sudbury ON

**MOTORCYCLES *See* AUTOMOTIVE**

## MULTICULTURAL

Acadian Festival, Caraquet NB E0B 1K0 – 506/727-6515 – August

Can-Irish Harmony: Canada's Irish Festival on the Miramichi, Irish Canadian Cultural Association of New Brunswick, 109 Roy Ave., Miramichi NB E1V 3N8 – 506/622-4007 – President, Farrell McCarthy – July – Miramichi NB

Canada's National Ukrainian Festival, 119 Main St. South, Dauphin MB R7N 1K4 – 204/638-5645; Fax: 204/638-5851 – Manager, Pat Maksymchuk – Annual. Three days of song, dance, music, costume, cuisine, culture, August

Carrousel of the Nations, c/o 370 Victoria Ave., Windsor ON N9A 4M6 – 519/255-1127; Fax: 519/255-1435 – Executive Director, Kathie Thomas – Annually. Thirty ethnocultural villages, June

Celebration Multicultural Festival, Multicultural Association of Nova Scotia, #901, 1809 Barrington St., Halifax NS B3J 3K8 – 902/423-6534; Fax: 902/422-0881; Email: multicul@fox.nstn.ca; URL: http://fox.nstn.ca/~multicul/ – Executive Director, Barbara Campbell – Annual festival, June 20-22 – Dartmouth NS

Festival Acadien de Clare, PO Box 282, Meteghan NS B0W 2J0 – 902/645-3168; Fax: 902/769-2408 – Annually. Five days. Musical, cultural, sports, July

Le Festival de l'Escaouette, a/s Les Trois Pignons, PO Box 430, Cheticamp NS B0E 1H0 – 902/224-2642 – Assistant Manager, Daniel Aucoin – Annually. Acadian folklore, traditions, culture, August

Foire Brayonne, c/o Box 338, Edmundston NB E3V 3K9 – 506/739-6608 – July/August. Brayon heritage festival

Folkfest, 233 Ave. C South, Saskatoon SK S7M 1N3 – 306/931-0100; Fax: 306/665-3421 – Coordinator, Deneen Gudjonson – Annual. Three days. Twenty or more ethnic pavilions, August

Folklorama - Canada's Cultural Celebration, #300, 180 King St., Winnipeg MB R3B 3G8 – 204/982-6210; Fax: 204/943-1956; Email: folkarts@mts.net; URL: http://www.folklorama.ca – Director, Claudette Leclerc – Annual. Fourteen days. More than forty ethnic pavilions, August

Loyalist Days, c/o Delta Hotel, #207, 39 King St., Saint John NB E2L 4W3 – 506/634-8123, July

Manitoba Highland Gathering, PO Box 59, Selkirk MB R1A 2B1 – 204/757-2365 – Annual, July

Metro International Caravan, 253 Adelaide St. West, Toronto ON M5H 1Y2 – 416/977-0466 – Leon Kossar – Annual, mid-June. Nine days. 40 international pavilions

MOSAIC - Regina's Annual Festival of Cultures, Regina Multicultural Council, 2144 Cornwall St., Regina SK S4P 2K7 – 306/757-5990; Fax: 306/780-9407 – Executive Director, Joanne Grant – Annual. First weekend in June. Twenty ethno-cultural pavilions

Opasquiak Indian Days, PO Box 297, The Pas MB R9A 1K8 – 204/623-5483 – Caroline Constant – Traditional native events, August

Ukrainian Pysanka Festival, c/o, PO Box 877, Vegreville AB T9C 1R9 – 403/632-2771 – Music, folk art, Pysanka writing, Easter egg painting, July

Vesna Festival, 205 Sturgeon Pl., Saskatoon SK S7K 4C5 – 306/931-8659 – Don Gabruch – Annual Spring celebration. Two days of entertainment, dancing, cultural demonstrations & displays. "The World's Largest Ukrainian Cabaret", May

## MUSIC

Atlantic Jazz Festival, PO Box 33043, Halifax NS B3L 4T6 – 902/422-8221 – Contact, Susan Hunter – July

Big Valley Jamboree, 200 Lakeshore Dr., Regina SK S4P 3V7 – 306/565-4500; Fax: 306/565-3274 – Louise Yates – July. Country music

Brandon Folk Music & Arts Festival, PO Box 2047, Brandon MB R7A 6S8 – 204/727-3928; Fax: 204/726-8139; URL: http://207.61.175.2/folk/ – Artistic Director, Donna Lowe – Annually, last weekend in July

Canadian Open Old Time Fiddler's Contest, Sports Complex, c/o, PO Box 27, Shelburne ON L0N 1S0 – 519/925-3551; Fax: 519/925-1105 – Manager, Bob Carruthers, Aug. 6-9 1998

Central Canada's Fiddlers' Festival, PO Box 10, Austin MB R0H 0C0 – 204/637-2354 – Contact, Terry Farley

Classical Music Festival, c/o, PO Box 181, Whistler BC V0N 1B0 – 604/932-3928 – August

Dawson City Music Festival, PO Box 456, Dawson City YT Y0B 1G0 – 867/993-5584; Fax: 867/993-5510; URL: http://www.dcmf.com – Annually, third weekend in July

Dockside Ceilidh, c/o 89 King St., North Sydney NS B2A 2T3 – 902/794-3772 – President, Northside Highland Dancers' Association, Kay Batherson – Daily, summer. Cultural music & entertainment at Marine Atlantic Ferry Terminal

Downtowners Optimist Band Festival, 1544 Albert St., Regina SK S40 2S4 – 306/757-7172; Fax: 306/757-0577 – Co-Chairman, Greg Way – Annually, March. Band & vocal jazz festival

Edmonton Folk Music Festival, PO Box 4130, Edmonton AB T6E 4T2 – 403/429-1899 – August. Blues, jazz, country, Celtic, bluegrass. arts & crafts

Elora Festival, c/o, PO Box 990, Elora ON N0B 1S0 – 519/846-0331 – July - Aug. Choral & contemporary Canadian music

Festival International de Jazz de Montréal, 822, rue Sherbrooke est, Montréal QC H2L 1K4 – 514/523-FEST; Fax: 514/525-5609; URL: http://www.montrealjazzfestival.worldlinx.com/ – Contact, Caroline Jamet – Annual. Over 1,500 musicians & 350 shows, July – Montréal QC

Festival Mondial de Folklore de Drummondville, 405, rue Saint-Jean, Drummondville QC J2B 5L7 – 819/472-1184; Fax: 819/474-6585 – Contact, Maurice Rhéaume – July. Ten days, over 20 countries, 300 shows

Folk on the Rocks, PO Box 326, Yellowknife NT X1A 2N3 – 867/920-7806 – Annual. Two days. Inuit, Dene, other northern & southern folk groups, July

Given'er on the Green, Town of Springdale, PO Box 52, Springdale NF A0J 1T0 – 709/673-4313; Fax: 709/673-4969 – Recreation Director, Greg Hillier – Annually, last weekend of June. Celebration of Newfoundland & Labrador musicians

International Festival of Baroque Music, International Baroque Music Festival, PO Box 644, Lameque NB E0B 1V0 – 506/344-5846; Fax: 506/344-3266; Tollfree: 1-800-320-2276 – Early music festival with five productions, last week of July (Northeastern New Brunswick, on Lameque Island)

International Jazz Festival, 435 West Hastings St., Vancouver BC V6B 1L4 – 604/682-0706; Fax: 604/682-0704; Tollfree: 1-888-438-5200; URL: http://www.jazzfest.bc.sympatico.ca – Executive Director, Robert Ken – June

Jazz City International Festival, 10516 - 77 Ave., Edmonton AB T6E 1N1 – 403/432-7166 – Annually June. Ten days

Kamloops Big Band Spectacular, c/o Kamloops Parks & Recreation Services, 7 Victoria St., Kamloops BC V2C 1A2 – 250/828-3552; Fax: 250/372-1573 – Contact, K. Sean-Smith – May

Kinsmen International Band & Choral Festival, Moose Jaw Kinsmen Club, PO Box 883, Moose Jaw SK S6H 4P5 – 306/693-5933 – Russ McKnight – 3,000 musicians, evening concerts, parade. Annual, May – Moose Jaw SK

Kiwanis Music Festival of Greater Toronto, 3315 Yonge St., 2nd Fl., Toronto ON M4N 2L9 – 416/487-5885; Fax: 416/487-5784 – General Manager, Eileen Keown, Feb. 7-21 1998 – Toronto ON

Maritime Old Time Fiddling Contest & Jamboree, PO Box 3037, Dartmouth East NS B2W 4Y3 – 902/434-5466; Fax: 902/435-7267; Email: whebby@fox.nstn.ca; URL: http://fox.nstn.ca/~whebby – James Delaney – July

Miramichi Folk Song Festival, PO Box 13, Miramichi NB E1V 3M2 – 506/773-4469 – August

Newfoundland & Labrador Folk Festival, c/o Tourism St. John's, PO Box 908, St. John's NF A1C 5P3 – 709/576-8508 – August. Traditional Newfoundland & Labrador music & dance

Northern Lights Festival Boréal, Northern Lights Festival, Bell Park Amphitheatre, c/o, PO Box 1236, Stn B, Sudbury ON P3E 4S7 – 705/674-5512; Fax: 705/671-1998; Email: nlfbnet@vianet.on.ca – Audrey Dumanski – July

Nova Scotia Bluegrass Oldtime Music Festival, PO Box 546, Elmsdale NS B0N 1M0 – 902/883-7189; Fax: 902/450-5073 – Jerry Murphy – Annually, July. Three days

Nova Scotia Kiwanis Music Festival, PO Box 1623, Halifax NS B3J 2Z1 – 902/423-6147 – Sharon Holland – Adjudicated music festival & closing concert, Feb. – Halifax NS

Old Time Fiddle & Step Dancing Championships, PO Box 1329, Deep River ON K0J 1P0 – 613/584-3377 – Chair, Jim Hickey – Labour Day weekend, annually, Aug.

Ottawa International Jazz Festival, Confederation Park, c/o, PO Box 3104, Stn D, Ottawa ON K1P 6H7 – 613/594-3580 – July

Polkafest, Manitoba Stampede & Exhibition, PO Box 849, Morris MB R0G 1K0 – 204/746-2552; Fax: 204/746-2900 – Contact, Allen Recksiedler, Sept.

Regina Folk Festival, PO Box 1203, Regina SK S4P 3B4 – 306/757-7684; Fax: 306/525-4009; Email: slimguy@sk.sympatico.ca; URL: http://bfsmedia.com/rbcs/rff – Contact, Greg Bodnarchuk – Annual three day folk-based music festival, Aug.

Saskatchewan Jazz Festival, PO Box 1593, Saskatoon SK S7K 3R3 – 306/652-1421; Fax: 306/934-5014; Tollfree: 1-800-638-1211; Email: sask.jazz@sk.sympatico.ca; URL: http://www.sasknet.com/jazz/ – Festival Manager, Sonia Morgan, June 19-28 1998 – Saskatoon SK

Scotia Festival of Music, #317, 1541 Barrington St., Halifax NS B3J 1Z5 – 902/429-9467; Fax: 902/425-6785; Email: scotia.festival@sympatico.ns.ca; URL: http://www3.sympatico.ns.ca/scotia.festival – Contact, Christopher Wilcox – Annually, May. Chamber music

Sound of Music Festival, #210, 460 Brant St., Burlington ON L7R 4B6 – 905/333-6364; Fax: 905/333-1245 – Chair/President, Brian Ellis – Third weekend in June

TerrifVic Dixieland Jazz Party, TerrifVic Jazz Party, #211, 633 Courtney St., Victoria BC V8W 1B9 – 250/953-2011; Fax: 250/381-3010; URL: http://www.islandnet.com/~bbs/jazz.html – Annually, April

Victoriaville International Festival of New Music, CP 460, Victoriaville QC G6P 6T3 – 819/752-7912; Fax: 819/758-4370 – Contact, Michel Levasseur – 25 concerts in 5 days, musicians from 12 different countries, May

Welcome to the Ceilidh, 2360 Armcrescent West, Halifax NS B3L 3E3 – 902/422-3143 – Contact, Anita MacDougall – Annually, June. Highland, national & choreographed Scottish dancers

Western Canada Olde Tyme Fiddling Championship, 841 - 8th Ave. NE, Swift Current SK S9H 2R6 – 306/773-8924 – Contact, Don MacRae – Annual, Sept.

Winnipeg Folk Festival, 264 Taché Ave., Winnipeg MB R2H 1Z9 – 204/231-0096; URL: http://www.magic.mb.ca/~wff/ – Annually, July

Winnipeg Jazz Festival, #501, 100 Arthur St., Winnipeg MB R3B 1H3 – 204/942-1654; URL: http://www.xpressnet.com/~cohenm/jazzwpg/ – Neal Kimelman – June

## OFFICE EQUIPMENT

COMDA Product Show, Canadian Office Machine Dealers Association, #204, 3464 Kingston Rd., Scarborough ON M1M 1R5 – 416/261-1607; Fax: 416/261-1679 – Executive Director, Don Vickery

The COPA Show, Canadian Office Products Association, #911, 1243 Islington Ave., Toronto ON M8X 1Y9 – 416/239-2737; Fax: 416/239-1553; URL: http://www.copa.ca – Manager, Conference Services, Gerald Petkau – Annual trade show. Office products, furniture, equipment, Apr. 20-21 – International Centre, Toronto ON

Home Office Expo, Show Fest Productions Inc., #5, 60 St. Clair Ave. West, Toronto ON M4V 1M7 – 416/925-4533; Fax: 416/925-7701; Email: gendel@compfest.com; URL: http://www.compfest.com – David Carter – Home office products, services, seminars, demonstrations & information, Sept. – Automotive Bldg., Exhibition Place, Toronto ON

**OKTOBERFESTS** *See* EVENTS

## PACKAGING

PAC-EX, Packaging Association of Canada, 2255 Sheppard Ave. East, #E330, North York ON M2J 4Y1 – 416/490-7860; Fax: 416/490-7844 – Show Manager, Steve Utting – Biennial trade show, Sept.

Packaging Forum d'Emballage, Packaging Association of Canada, 2255 Sheppard Ave. East, #E330, North York ON M2J 4Y1 – 416/490-7860; Fax: 416/490-7844 – Show Manager, Steve Utting – Biennial trade show, June 9-11 1998 – Palais des congrès, Montréal QC

**PARENTS *See* CHILDREN**

## PETROLEUM

Calgary Oil & Gas Show - Inter-Can, Southex Exhibitions Inc., #300, 999 - 8 St. SW, Calgary AB T2R 1N7 – 403/244-6111; Fax: 403/245-8666; Tollfree: 1-800-387-2446; Email: info@petroleumshow.com; URL: http://www.southex.com – Pat Atkinson – Biennial trade show. Petroleum & natural gas products, services & technology; exploration, production, transmission, processing, marketing, June 1999 – Roundup Centre, Stampede Park, Calgary AB

Fort McMurray Oil Sands Tradeshow, Southex Exhibitions Inc., #300, 999 - 8 St. SW, Calgary AB T2R 1N7 – 403/244-6111; Fax: 403/245-8666; Tollfree: 1-800-387-2446; Email: info@petroleumshow.com; URL: http://www.southex.com – Pat Atkinson – Biennial trade show; products, services & technology for the mining & processing of oil sands, Sept. 1998 – MacDonald Island Centre, Fort McMurray AB

Horizontal Well Technology Trade Show, Southex Exhibitions, 4285 Canada Way, Burnaby BC V5G 1H2 – 604/433-5121; Fax: 604/434-6853; Tollfree: 1-800-633-8332; URL: http://www.southex.com – Vice-President, Western Region, Fred Barnes, Nov. 9-11 1998 – Calgary AB

National Petroleum Show, Southex Exhibitions Inc., #300, 999 - 8 St. SW, Calgary AB T2R 1N7 – 403/244-6111; Fax: 403/245-8666; Tollfree: 1-800-387-2446; Email: info@petroleumshow.com; URL: http://www.southex.com – Pat Atkinson – Biennial, June 1998 – Stampede Park, Calgary AB

Offshore Newfoundland Oil & Gas Exhibition, Atlantic Expositions Ltd, PO Box 402, Gander NF A1V 1W8 – 709/651-3315; Fax: 709/256-4051 – Manager, Keith Brown – Annual trade show, June – St. John's NF

## PETS

All About Pets, William Peddie Show Productions Inc., 21 Lorraine Gardens, Etobicoke ON M9B 4Z5 – 416/231-9992; Fax: 416/233-9725 – Show Manager, Gregory Williams – Annual consumer show, April – Toronto ON

PIJAC Canada National Pet & Trade Show, PIJAC Canada, #308, 189, boul Hymus, Pointe-Claire QC H9R 1E9 – 514/630-7878; Fax: 514/630-7444; Tollfree: 1-800-667-7452; Email: pijac@odyssee.net; URL: http://www.pijaccanada.com – Show Committee Chair, Bob Stevens – Annual trade show, Sept. 19-20 1998 – Toronto ON

## PHARMACEUTICALS

***See Also* Medical**

International Conference, Canadian Pharmaceutical Association, 1785 Alta Vista Dr., 2nd Fl., Ottawa ON K1G 3Y6 – 613/523-7877; Fax: 613/523-0445; Tollfree: 1-800-917-9489; Email: cpha@cdnpharm.ca; URL: http://www.cdnpharm.ca – Executive Director, L.C. Fevang – Aug./Sept.

## PLASTICS & RUBBER

Expoplast, Canadian Plastics Industry Association, #500, 5925 Airport Rd., Mississauga ON L4V 1W1 – 905/678-7748; Fax: 905/678-0774; Email: national@cpia.ca; URL: http://www.plastics.ca – Show Manager, Jack McLean – Triennial trade show: plastics machinery, raw materials suppliers, mold makers, processors, fabricators, auxilliary equipment, Oct. 2000

Plast-ex, Canadian Plastics Industry Association, #500, 5925 Airport Rd., Mississauga ON L4V 1W1 – 905/678-7748; Fax: 905/678-0774; Email: national@cpia.ca; URL: http://www.plastics.ca – President, Pierre Dubois – Triennial trade show, May 1998

**PRINTING *See* GRAPHIC ARTS**

## PSYCHIC PHENOMENA

ESP Psychic Expo, Impact Event Management, 358 Danforth Ave., PO Box 65060, Toronto ON M4K 3Z2 – 416/461-5306; Fax: 416/461-8460; Email: dn@caribphoto.com; URL: http://www.caribphoto.com/psychic.htm – Donald Nausbaum – Annual consumer show. Psychics, astrologers, natural healing, crystals, books, tapes, computers, Oct.

Psychic, Mystics & Seers Fair, Impact Event Management, 358 Danforth Ave., PO Box 65060, Toronto ON M4K 3Z2 – 416/461-5306; Fax: 416/461-8460; Email: dn@caribphoto.com; URL: http://www.caribphoto.com/psychic.htm – Donald Nausbaum – Consumer show. Psychics, astrologers, tarot card readers, holistic health, computers, Feb. – National Trade Centre, West Annex, Toronto ON

## REAL ESTATE

National Annual Conference, The Canadian Real Estate Association, Minto Place, The Canada Bldg., #1600, 344 Slater St., Ottawa ON K1R 7Y3 – 613/237-7111; Fax: 613/234-2567; Email: info@crea.ca; URL: http://www.mls.ca – Coordinator, Gail McHardy – Annual trade show, Oct.

Real Estate Show, Martin International, #2910, 500, Place des Armes, Montréal QC H2Y 2W2 – 514/288-3931; Fax: 514/288-0641 – General Manager, Lorraine Boisvenue – Annual consumer show. Commercial real estate, professional services, financing & insuring, vacation homes, luxury homes, homes of the future. Québec City & Montréal, Jan.

**RECREATIONAL VEHICLES *See* AUTOMOTIVE**

## RENTALS

Canadian Rental Mart, AIS Communications Ltd., 145 Thames Rd. West, Exeter ON N0M 1S3 – 519/235-2400; Fax: 519/235-0798 – Contact, Peter Phillips – March 10-11 1998

## RODEOS

***See Also* Exhibitions, Farm Business/Agriculture**

Agribition Rodeo, Canadian Western Agribition Rodeo, c/o Public Relations Office, Canadian Western Agribition, PO Box 3535, Regina SK S4P 3J8 – 306/565-0565; Fax: 306/757-9963; URL: http://www.sasknet.com/agribition – Executive Vice-President, Wayne Gamble – Annually, November

CCA Finals Rodeo, c/o Canadian Cowboys Association, PO Box 1877, Lloydminster SK S9V 1N4 – 306/825-7116; Fax: 306/825-7762 – General Manager, Bob Phipps – Annually, Oct./Nov. Four days

Hometown Rodeo, c/o Moose Jaw Exhibition Co. Ltd., PO Box 1467, Moose Jaw SK S6H 4R3 – 306/692-2723 – Annually, April & September

Manitoba Stampede & Exhibition, PO Box 849, Morris MB R0G 1K0 – 204/746-2552; Fax: 204/746-2900 – Contact, Allen Recksiedler – Four days, July 16-19 1998

Maple Creek Cowtown Rodeo, PO Box 1091, Maple Creek SK S0N 1N0 – 306/662-3667 – Jim Montgomery – Annually, May

Silver Buckle Rodeo, Westerner Exposition Association, 4847A - 19 St., Red Deer AB T4R 2N7 – 403/343-7800; Fax: 403/341-4699 – General Manager, John Harms – Annual four-day event; western clothing, art & rodeo, April – Westerner Park, Red Deer AB

Williams Lake Stampede, c/o 1148 South Broadway, Williams Lake BC V2G 1A2 – 250/392-5025

**RVS *See* AUTOMOTIVE; SPORTS & RECREATION**

## SAFETY

Conference, Canada Safety Council, 1020 Thomas Spratt Place, Ottawa ON K1G 5L5 – 613/739-1535; Fax: 613/739-1566; Email: csc@safety-council.org; URL: http://www.safety-council.org – President, Émile-J. Thérien – Annual trade show. Safety-related products & services for workplace, traffic, home & leisure, April

Health & Safety Conference & Trade Show, Industrial Accident Prevention Association Ontario, Eaton Tower, 250 Yonge St., 28th Fl., Toronto ON M5B 2N4 – 416/506-8888; Fax: 416/506-8880; Tollfree: 1-800-669-4939; Email: feedback@iapa.on.ca; URL: http://www.iapa.on.ca – CEO, Maureen C. Shaw – April

## SCIENCE

Annual Meeting, Canadian Federation of Biological Societies, #104, 1750 Courtwood Cres., Ottawa ON K2C 2B5 – 613/225-8889; Fax: 613/225-9621; Email: cfbs@igs.net; URL: http://www.fermentas.com/cfbs/ – Executive Director, Dr. Paul Hough, Ph.D. – June

Mines & Minerals Symposia, c/o Ministry of Northern Development & Mines, #A3, 933 Ramsey Lake R, Sudbury ON P3E 6B5 – 705/670-5627; Fax: 705/670-5622 – Annual trade show & seminar in April (Northern Ontario) & December (Toronto)

## SENIOR CITIZENS

Great Canadian Maturity Show & Travel Show, Premier Consumer Shows, City Parent Newsmagazine, 467 Speers Rd., Oakville ON L6K 3S4 – 905/815-0017; Fax: 905/815-0511; Tollfree: 1-800-387-7682 – Show Coordinator, Darren Melanson – Semi-annual consumer show in April & October (Toronto); various annual shows in Ontario centres

Salon des Aînés et Salon Vacances Loisirs, Expositions André Guillemette, #302, 2900, rue Quatre-Bourgeois, Ste-Foy QC G1N 1Y4 – 418/657-7949; Fax: 418/650-6393 – André Guillemette – Annual consumer show; travel & other services for seniors, May

Yorton Threshermen's Show & Seniors' Festival, Yorkton Threshermen's Show & Seniors' Festival, Western Development Museum, PO Box 98, Yorkton SK S3N 2V6 – 306/783-8361 – Event Chairman, Susan Mandziuk – Annual, July – Western Development Museum, Yorkton SK

**SEWING *See* CRAFTS**

## SPORTS & RECREATION

***See Also* Boating; Automotive, for combined auto/ RV shows**

Alberta Camping & Cottage Show, Uniglobe International Exhibitions Ltd., #240, 4936 - 87 St., Edmonton AB T6E 5W3 – 403/469-2400; Fax: 403/ 469-1398 – President, Tom McCaffrey – Annual consumer show; products & services related to camping, cottage & tourist industry; held in Edmonton (Feb.) & Calgary (Mar.)

Atlantic Canada Snowmobile Show, Snowtime, #131, 393 University Ave., Charlottetown PE C1A 4N4 – 902/628-5290; Fax: 902/566-1651; Email: acss@ auracom.com – Art Gennis – Annual trade & consumer show, Oct.

Atlantic Outdoor Sports & RV Show, PO Box 2968, Dartmouth East NS B2W 4Y2 – 902/827-3572 – Manager, Darrelyn Sapp – Annual consumer show. Trailer & motor homes, 4x4s, tent trailers, boats, motors, hunting, fishing & camping, tourism & sporting goods, March

Campex, Ontario Private Campground Association, RR#5, Owen Sound ON N4K 5N7 – 519/371-3393; Fax: 519/371-5315; Email: opca@headwaters.com; URL: http://www.campgrounds.org – Managing Director, Marcel Gobeil – Trade show, Oct.

Canadian Outdoor Retailers Show, Toronto International Bicycle Show, #1801, 1 Yonge St., Toronto ON M5E 1W7 – 416/363-1292; Fax: 416/ 369-0515 – Show Manager, Josie Graziosi – Sept. 12-14 1998 – National Trade Centre, Exhibition Place, Toronto ON

Canadian Power Toboggan Championship, PO Box 22, Beausejour MB R0E 0C0 – 204/268-2049 – Annual, March

Canoe Expo, c/o The Profile Group, #301, 37 Sandiford Dr., Stouffville ON L4A 7X5 – 905/640-7700; Fax: 905/640-7714 – Show Producer, George Zarras – Annual consumer show. Canoes, kayaks, location camps & outfitters, April

CHALLENGE - Canada's Sports, Fitness & Music Show, 65 Helena Ave., Toronto ON M6G 2H3 – 416/652-1302; Fax: 416/653-2291 – Executive Producer, Joyce Barslow – Annual consumer show. Health & fitness, leisure, fashion, April

Country Living Show, Square Feet Northwest Event Management Inc., 1030 Mainland St., Vancouver BC V6B 2T4 – 604/683-4393; Fax: 604/688-0270; Email: mgmt@sqftevent.com – Blaine Woit – Annual consumer show, Jan. – Pacific Coliseum, Vancouver BC

Fall Hunting Show, Ontario Out of Doors Magazine, 777 Bay St., 6th Fl., Toronto ON M5W 1A7 – 416/ 596-5908; Fax: 416/596-2517; Email: 102677.1125@ compuserve.com; URL: http://www.cyberplex.com/ fishontario – Show Manager, Lynda Watson – Annual consumer show: hunting equipment, "World & Canadian Calling Contest"; shooting range; seminars, Sept.

Ironman Canada Triathlon Championship, 199 Ellis St., Penticton BC V2A 4L4 – 250/490-8787; Fax: 250/490-8788; Email: dburtch@vip.net; URL: http://www.ironman.ca – Race Director, Dr. David Burtch – Annual three-day trade expo staged as part of the events prior to the Ironman race, Aug.

K-W Outdoors Show, c/o Bingemans Conference & Recreation Centre, 1380 Victoria St. North, Kitchener ON N2B 3E2 – 519/744-1555; Fax: 519/ 744-1985 – Contact, Doris Hauck – Annual consumer show. Hunting & fishing equipment, charters, boats, campgrounds, Feb. 7-8 1998

London Sports Show, Western Fair Association, PO Box 4550, Stn D, London ON N5W 5K3 – 519/438-7203; Fax: 519/679-3124 – Annual consumer show, Feb. – Western Fairgrounds, London ON

MISE - Montréal International Sports Exhibition, Canadian Sporting Goods Association, #510, 455, rue Saint-Antoine ouest, Montréal QC H2Z 1J1 – 514/393-1132; Fax: 514/393-9513; Email: sportind@ csga.ca; URL: http://www.globalsports.com/csga – President & CEO, Yves Paquette – Annual trade show, Jan.

The Montréal Golf & Travel Show, International Show Productions Inc., 36 Fallingbrook Dr., Scarborough ON M1N 1B6 – 416/691-2852; Fax: 416/691-2891; Tollfree: 1-800-265-3673 – Steve Nichols – Annual consumer show, March

Motorhead Snowmobile, Watercraft & ATV Show, Marketer Shows Inc., 18540 Centre St., Mount Albert ON L0G 1M0 – 905/473-7009; Fax: 905/473-5217 – Terrence Kehoe – Annual consumer show, March – Toronto International Centre, Toronto ON

National Outfitter's Hunting & Fishing Show, Mobilvision Inc., 9200, boul Henri-Bourassa ouest, Montréal QC H4S 1L5 – 514/334-7277; Fax: 514/ 334-1180; Tollfree: 1-800-668-3976 – Président, Jacques Forest – Feb. 28 - March 1 1998 – Montréal Congress Centre,

NSIA Ski, Snowboard & Outdoor Trade Show, National Snow Industries Association, #810, 245, av Victoria, Montréal QC H3Z 2M6 – 514/939-7370; Fax: 514/939-7371; Tollfree: 1-800-263-6742; Email: nsia@netc.net – Executive Director, Anna DiMeglio – Annual trade show, Feb. 1998 – Montréal QC

"One Big Canadian Show"; Fall Market & BTAC Outdoor Show, Canadian Sporting Goods Association, #510, 455, rue Saint-Antoine ouest, Montréal QC H2Z 1J1 – 514/393-1132; Fax: 514/ 393-9513; Email: sportind@csga.ca; URL: http:// www.globalsports.com/csga – President & CEO, Yves Paquette – Annual trade show, Sept. – Toronto Congress Centre, Toronto ON

Ottawa Ski & Snowboard Show, Intertrade Communications Inc., #203, 43 Roydon Place, Nepean ON K2E 1A3 – 613/224-3013; Fax: 613/224-4533; Tollfree: 1-888-662-6660; Email: trades@ magi.com – Event Manager, Pauline Gaudet – Consumer show, Oct.

Red Deer Sportsman Show, Westerner Exposition Association, 4847A - 19 St., Red Deer AB T4R 2N7 – 403/343-7800; Fax: 403/341-4699 – General Manager, John Harms – Annual consumer show, March – Western Exposition Grounds, Red Deer AB

Salon Camping, Plein Air, Chasse et Pêche de Montréal/Montréal Sportsmen's Show, Canadian National Sportsmen's Shows (1989) Ltd., #1630, 1155, rue Metcalfe, Montréal QC H3B 2V6 – 514/ 866-5409; Fax: 514/866-4092 – Show Manager, Diane Laporte – Annual consumer show: camping, fishing, hunting, RVs, tourism, April – Place Bonaventure, Montréal QC

Salon Camping, Plein Air, Chasse et Pêche de Québec/ Québec City Sportsmen's Show, Canadian National Sportsmen's Shows (1989) Ltd., #1630, 1155, rue Metcalfe, Montréal QC H3B 2V6 – 514/866-5409; Fax: 514/866-4092 – Show Manager, Diane Laporte – Annual consumer show: camping, fishing, hunting, RVs, tourism, March – Parc de l'Exposition, Québec QC

Salon Sports Plein Air Outaouais/The Outaouais Sports Outdoors Exhibition, Salon Sports Plein Air Outaouais/The Outaouais Sports Outdoor Exhibition, CP 1151, Succ B, Hull QC J8X 3X7 – 819/457-2063; Fax: 819/457-1805 – Promoter, Richard Sarrasin – Annual consumer show. Outfitters & nautical section, Feb. – Robert Guertin Arena, Hull QC

Ski & Winter Holiday Show, Denex Group Inc., Burnside Industrial Park, 192 Joseph Zatzman Dr., Dartmouth NS B3B 1N4 – 902/468-4999; Fax: 902/ 468-2795; Email: denman@ns.sympatico.ca; URL: http://www.denexgroup.com – Show Manager, Bob Dunnington – Consumer show, Sept.

Sports, Recreation & Leisure Trade Show, c/o South East Alberta Travel & Convention Association, PO Box 605, Medicine Hat AB T1A 7G5 – 403/527-6422; Fax: 403/528-2683 – Annual consumer show, Feb.

The Summer Holiday Show/Salon Vacances et Loisir d'été, Promexpo Inc., 801, rue Sherbrooke est, 10e étage, Montréal QC H2L 1K7 – 514/527-9221; Fax: 514/527-8449 – General Manager, Maguy Rigaud – Annual consumer show held in Montréal & Québec, April

Supertrax International Snowmobilers Show, Marketer Shows Inc., 18540 Centre St., Mount Albert ON L0G 1M0 – 905/473-7009; Fax: 905/473-5217 – Terrence Kehoe – Annual consumer show, Oct. – Markham ON

The Toronto Golf & Travel Show, International Show Productions Inc., 36 Fallingbrook Dr., Scarborough ON M1N 1B6 – 416/691-2852; Fax: 416/691-2891; Tollfree: 1-800-265-3673 – Steve Nichols – Annual consumer show, February/March

Toronto International Bicycle Show, #1801, 1 Yonge St., Toronto ON M5E 1W7 – 416/363-1292; Fax: 416/369-0515 – Show Manager, Josie Graziosi – March – Automotive Bldg., Exhibition Place, Toronto ON

Toronto Ski & Snowboard Show, Canadian National Sportsmen's Shows (1989) Ltd., #202, 703 Evans Ave., Toronto ON M5C 5E9 – 416/695-0311; Fax: 416/695-0381 – Show Manager, Tim Kennedy – Annual consumer show, Oct. – National Trade Centre, Exhibition Place, Toronto ON

Toronto Sportsmen's Show, Canadian National Sportsmen's Shows (1989) Ltd., #202, 703 Evans Ave., Toronto ON M5C 5E9 – 416/695-0311; Fax: 416/695-0381 – Show Manager, Tim Kennedy – Annual consumer show, March – National Trade Centre, Exhibition Place, Toronto ON

Vancouver Fishing Show, Square Feet Northwest Event Management Inc., 1030 Mainland St., Vancouver BC V6B 2T4 – 604/683-4393; Fax: 604/ 688-0270; Email: mgmt@sqftevent.com – Bruce Guerin, Blaine Woit – Annual consumer show, Jan. – Pacific Coliseum, Vancouver BC

Vancouver Ski Show, Vancouver Ski Foundation, #306, 1367 West Broadway, Vancouver BC V6H 4A9 – 604/878-0754; Fax: 604/878-0754 – Producer, Valerie Lang – Annual consumer show, Oct. – BC Place Stadium, Vancouver BC

Vancouver Sportsmen's Show, Canadian National Sportsmen's Shows (1989) Ltd., #501, 4190 Lougheed Hwy., Burnaby BC V5C 6A8 – 604/294-1313; Fax: 604/294-4740 – Show Manager, Jim Carslake – Annual consumer show, February/ March – Pacific National Exhibition, Vancouver BC

**STAMPEDES *See* RODEOS**

**THEATRE *See* ARTS**

## TOYS & GAMES

BC Teddy Event, Trade Show Managers Inc., 5512, 4 St. NW, PO Box 64024, Calgary AB T2K 6J0 – 403/ 274-8858; Fax: 403/274-9388; Email: slmorrow@ aca.ucalgary.ca – Contact, Sandra Morrow – March – White Rock BC

The Bear Fair, Trade Show Managers Inc., 5512, 4 St. NW, PO Box 64024, Calgary AB T2K 6J0 – 403/274-8858; Fax: 403/274-9388; Email: slmorrow@aca.ucalgary.ca – Contact, Sandra Morrow – Oct. – Calgary AB

Canadian Toy & Decoration Fair, Canadian Toy Association, PO Box 294, Kleinburg ON L0J 1C0 – 905/893-1689; Fax: 905/893-2392 – Executive Director, Sheila Edmondson – Annual trade show, Jan.

May Madness, Trade Show Managers Inc., 5512, 4 St. NW, PO Box 64024, Calgary AB T2K 6J0 – 403/274-8858; Fax: 403/274-9388; Email: slmorrow@aca.ucalgary.ca – Contact, Sandra Morrow – May – Toronto ON

Salon international de la Video et di Divertissement familial, Yves Barré & Associés, 6940, rue Barry, Brossard QC J4Z 1V1 – 514/443-3131; Fax: 514/443-8415 – Président, Yves Barré – Nov. – Place Bonaventure, Montréal QC

The Toronto Christmas Train Show, Toronto Show Promotions, PO Box 217, Grimsby ON L3M 4G3 – 905/945-2775; Fax: 905/945-3199 – Doug Jarvis – Annual; operating train layouts, memorabilia, Nov. – Toronto ON

## TRANSPORTATION

***See Also* Automotive**

Annual Convention & Trade Show, Ontario School Bus Association, #100, 295 The West Mall, Etobicoke ON M9C 4Z4 – 416/695-9965; Fax: 416/695-9977 – Events Coordinator, Rebecca Jasas – Annual conference & trade show. Safety, fuel economy, buses & accessories, computers, July – Toronto ON

International Air Cargo Show, International Tradeshow Services Inc., 20 Butterick Rd., Toronto ON M8W 3Z8 – 416/252-7791; Fax: 416/252-9848; Email: jimm@intltradeshows.com; URL: http://www.intltradeshows.com – President, James K. Mahon – May 14-15 1998 – Congress Centre, Ottawa ON

Transfreight, c/o Groupe Bomart, #103, 7493 Trans Canada Hwy., St-Laurent QC H4T 1T3 – 514/337-9043; Fax: 514/337-1862 – Contact, Jean-Pierre Emmanuel – Annual multimodal transportation trade show & conference, Sept.

## TRAVEL & TOURISM

Canadian Meetings & Incentive Travel Symposium & Trade Show, 777 Bay St., 5th Fl., Toronto ON M5W 1A7 – 416/596-5165; Fax: 416/596-5810 – Richard Elliott – Annual trade show & conference, August

The London Travel Show, Motivations International Inc., 14 Rowan Ave., Toronto ON M4N 2X9 – 416/481-6384; Fax: 416/483-6791 – Coordinator, John Stephenson – Semi-annual consumer show (March & October) – London ON

Southwestern Ontario Golf & Vacation Show, Western Fair Association, PO Box 4550, Stn D, London ON N5W 5K3 – 519/438-7203; Fax: 519/679-3124 – Annual consumer show; equipment, destinations, demonstrations, Feb. – London ON

The Travel & Vacation Show, Player Expositions International, 255 Clemow Ave., Ottawa ON K1S 2B5 – 613/567-6408; Fax: 613/567-2718 – Show Organizer, Halina Player – Annual consumer show, April – Ottawa ON

Travel Technology Conference & Trade Show, Baxter Travel Group, 310 Dupont St., Toronto ON M5R 1V9 – 416/968-7252; Fax: 416/968-2377 – Special Projects Manager, Alan Crockford – Annual trade show, March

**TRUCKS *See* AUTOMOTIVE**

**TVS, STEREOS *See* ELECTRICAL/ELECTRONICS**

**VIDEO *See* COMMUNICATIONS**

## WINTER CARNIVALS

Banff/Lake Louise Winter Festival, PO Box 1298, Banff AB T0L 0C0 – 403/762-1200; Fax: 403/762-8461 – Feb.

Bon Soo Winter Carnival, PO Box 781, Sault Ste. Marie ON P6A 5N3 – 705/759-3000; Fax: 705/759-6950 – General Manager, Donna Gregg – Late January/early February. Ten days. More than 125 indoor & outdoor events & activities – Sault Ste. Marie ON

Carnaval de Québec, 290, rue Joly, Quebec QC G1L 1N8 – 418/626-3716; Fax: 418/626-7252; URL: http://www.carnival.qc.ca – General Manager, Denis Rhéaume – Eleven days, major winter event, Feb.

Carnaval-Souvenir de Chicoutimi, 67, Jacques-Cartier ouest, Chicoutimi QC G7J 1E9 – 418/543-4438; Fax: 418/543-4884 – Ten days, major winter event, Feb.

Charlottetown Winter Carnival, PO Box 3027, Charlottetown PE C1A 7N9 – 902/892-5708 – Feb.

Conception Bay South Winterfest, Conception Bay South NF – 709/834-2093 – Feb.

Corner Brook Winter Carnival, c/o, PO Box 886, Corner Brook NF A2H 6H6 – 709/632-5343; Fax: 709/632-5344 – President, Jeannette Christopher – Annually, 10 days, Feb. 20 - March 1 1998

Elliot Lake Winterfest, c/o, PO Box 1, Elliot Lake ON P5A 1Z5 – 705/461-7233 – Feb.

Fête des Neiges, Société du Parc des Îles, Île Notre-Dame, Montréal QC H3C 1A9 – 514/872-6093; Fax: 514/872-9969 – Mireille Caron – 16 day major winter event. Sports, cultural, ice sculptures, Feb.

Hamilton Winterfest, c/o 555 Bay St. North, Hamilton ON L8L 1H1 – 905/546-4646 – Feb.

Huntsville Winter Wonderfest, c/o, PO Box 1470, Huntsville ON P0A 1K0 – 705/789-8113 – Feb.

Jasper in January, c/o, PO Box 98, Jasper AB T0E 1E0 – 403/852-3858; Fax: 403/852-4932 – Jan.

Kapuskasing Winter Carnival, 88 Riverside Dr., Kapuskasing ON P5N 1B3 – 705/335-2341 – February & March

Kirkland Lake Winter Carnival, c/o PO Bag 1757, Kirkland Lake ON P2N 3P4 – 705/567-9361 – March

Labrador City Winter Carnival, PO Box 1237, Wabush NF A0R 1B0 – 709/944-3602; Fax: 709/282-5106

Mount Pearl Frosty Festival, Mount Pearl NF – 709/748-1008 – Feb.

Nova Scotia Smelt Tournament, 2228 Conquerall Rd., Bridgewater NS B4V 2W3 – 902/543-7090; Fax: 902/543-9122; Email: icefish@istar.ca; URL: http://www.isisnet.com/jmailman/fishing.html – Martin Bell – Largest ice fishing tournament, Eastern Canada, Feb.

Prince Albert Winter Festival, PO Box 1388, Prince Albert SK S6V 5S9 – 306/764-7595, Feb.

Red Deer Family Winter Fest, c/o Recreation Parks & Culture Dept., PO Box 5008, Red Deer AB T4N 3T4 – 403/342-6100; Fax: 403/342-6073; URL: http://www.city.red-deer.ab.ca – Feb.

Regina Waskimo Winter Festival, PO Box 7111, Regina SK S4P 3S7 – 306/522-3661; Fax: 306/565-2742 – Executive Director, J.B. Paterson – Annual, third weekend in February

Richmond Hill Winter Carnival, c/o, PO Box 155, Richmond Hill ON L4C 4Y2 – 905/737-6101 – Jan.

Riverview Winter Carnival, 30 Honour House Court, Riverview NB E1B 3Y9 – 506/387-2037; Fax: 506/387-7455 – Brian Frontain – Feb.

Salmon Arm Winterfest, c/o, PO Box 669, Salmon Arm BC V1E 4N8 – 250/832-6247 – Jan.

Saskatoon Winterfest, c/o Meewasin Valley Authority, 402 - 3rd Ave. South, Saskatoon SK S7K 3G5 – 306/665-6887

Sudbury Snowflake Festival, 100 Ramsey Lake Rd., Sudbury ON P3E 5S9 – 705/522-3701; Fax: 705/522-4954; Email: dugas@sciencenorth.on.ca – Coordinator, Audrey Dugas – Feb.

Vernon Winter Carnival, 3303 - 35th Ave., Vernon BC V1T 2T5 – 250/545-2236; Fax: 250/545-0006 – Feb.

Winterfest, Gander NF – 709/651-2930 – Feb.

Winterlude, 161 Laurier Ave. West, Ottawa ON K1P 6J6 – 613/239-5145; Fax: 613/239-5333 – Thérèse St-Onge, 613/239-5278 – Major winter festival, first three weekends of February. Skating on Rideau Canal - the world's longest skating rink, international ice & snow sculpture competitions, musical & figure skating shows, North America's largest winter playground for kids, various sporting & social events, fireworks, stage performances & buskers, Feb.

Winterlude, Grand Falls-Windsor NF – 709/489-2728 – Feb.

## WOMEN

Calgary Woman's Show, The Calgary Woman's Show Ltd., #202, 8 Parkdale Cres. NW, Calgary AB T2N 3T8 – 403/270-7274; Fax: 403/270-3037; URL: http://www.intervisual.com/cwc – President, Judy Markle – Annual consumer show: products & services, Oct. – Calgary AB

Spring Fever, The Calgary Woman's Show Ltd., #202, 8 Parkdale Cres. NW, Calgary AB T2N 3T8 – 403/270-7274; Fax: 403/270-3037; URL: http://www.intervisual.com/cwc – President, Judy Markle – Annual consumer show: products & services, April – Calgary AB

Toronto Women's Show, Toronto Women's Show Inc., PO Box 6465, Stn A, Toronto ON M5W 1X3 – 905/274-0888; Fax: 905/274-0434 – Show Manager, Brian MacLean – Annual consumer show, March – Queen Elizabeth Bldg., Exhibition Place, Toronto ON

Women in Focus, Classic Moment Creative Events, 1255 Delta Ave., Kamloops BC V2B 3Y4 – 250/376-7934; Fax: 250/376-7927 – Event Producer/Owner, Judy Basso – Annual spring trade show, work shops

Women's Showcase, PO Box 29217, London ON N6K 1M6 – 519/472-8565 – Contact, Diann Vail – Annual consumer show, winter. Fashion, health, business, home

World of Women, 3017 - 50 Ave., Red Deer AB T4N 5Y6 – 403/347-4491; Fax: 403/343-6188; URL: http://wow.reddeer.net – Contact, Sherall Kennedy, September

## WOOD/WOODWORKING

The Brantford Woodshow, PO Box 852, Brantford ON N3T 5R7 – 519/449-2444; Fax: 519/449-2445; Email: fulcher@worldchat.com – Manager, Paul Fulcher – Annual consumer show, Nov.

Salon Industriel du Bois Ouvre, Reed Exhibition Companies Inc., 3761 Victoria Park Ave., Scarborough ON M1W 3S2 – 416/491-7565; Fax: 416/491-5088 – Show Coordinator, Elaine Nichol – Biennial trade show, Sept. 1998 – Montréal QC

Woodtech Canada, Southex Exhibitions Inc., Head Office, #800, 1 Concorde Gate, North York ON M3C 3N6 – 416/385-1880; Fax: 416/385-1855; Tollfree: 1-888-823-7469; URL: http://www.southex.com – Research Manager, Sandy Zeidenberg – Biennial trade show, Sept. 23-25 1998

Woodworking Machinery & Supply Expo, Reed Exhibition Companies Inc., 3761 Victoria Park Ave., Scarborough ON M1W 3S2 – 416/491-7565; Fax: 416/491-5088 – Show Coordinator, Elaine Nicol – Biennial trade show; industrial woodworking & furniture manufacturing equipment, systems, supplies & finishing machinery, Oct. 1999

Woodworking Show, Cryderman Productions, 136 Thames St., Chatham ON N7L 2Y8 – 519/351-8344; Fax: 519/351-8345 – John Cryderman – Annual consumer show held in various locations (Edmonton, Ottawa, Surrey); woodworking products

# CANADIAN AWARDS

**(including Scholarships, Grants, Bursaries)**

Awards are listed under the following categories:



NOTE: Contact people for awards are listed at the end of the award description, where available.

## ADVERTISING & PUBLIC RELATIONS

### The Advertising & Design Club of Canada

#207, 109 Vanderhoof Ave., Toronto ON M4G 2H7
416/423-4113; Fax: 416/422-3762

**The Advertising & Design Club of Canada Awards**

Main categories of awards are: Print, Broadcast & Multimedia, Graphic, Editorial, & Interactive Design; winners receive gold, silver or merit awards

### Association of Canadian Advertisers Inc. / Association canadienne des annonceurs

South Tower, #307, 175 Bloor St. East, Toronto ON M4W 3R8
416/964-3805; Fax: 416/964-0771; Toll Free: 1-800-565-0109
Email: aca@sympatico.ca;
URL: http://www3.sympatico.ca/aca/

**ACA Gold Medal**

Established in 1941 to encourage high standards of personal achievement in advertising - for introducing new concepts or techniques, for significantly improving existing practices, or for enhancing the stature of advertising

### Canadian Direct Marketing Association / Association canadienne du marketing direct

#607, One Concorde Gate, North York ON M3C 3N6
416/391-2362; Fax: 416/441-4062
Email: nadiav@cdma.org; URL: http://www.cdma.org

**RSVP Awards**

24 categories of direct response awards; Director's Choice Award for the company judged by the CDMA Board of Directors to have made the most outstanding contribution to direct marketing industry; open to both CDMA members & non-members; direct response campaigns from all media are considered

### Institute of Canadian Advertising

#500, 2300 Yonge St., PO Box 2350, Toronto ON M4P 1E4
416/482-1396; Fax: 416/481-1856; Toll Free: 1-800-567-7422
Email: ica@goodmedia.com;
URL: http://www.goodmedia.com/ica/

**Cassie Awards**

Established 1993; jointly administered with the Association of Canadian Advertisers; Cassies - an acronym for Canadian Advertising Success Stories - are judged on their effectiveness in attaining the advertiser's objectives; 10 gold awards presented bi-annually

### Marketing Magazine

777 Bay St., 5th Fl., Toronto ON M5W 1A7
416/596-5858; Fax: 416/593-3170

**The Marketing Awards**

Annual advertising awards offering 20 Gold Awards in the following categories: television/cinema, radio, magazine, newspaper, transit, business press, direct mail, outdoor, point-of-purchase/interior store design, multimedia campaign, & public service. Silver Awards, Bronze Awards, & Certificates of Excellence are also awarded. Entries must have run in the previous year & must have been conceived & created by people working in English in the Canadian advertising business

### Outdoor Advertising Association of Canada / L'Association canadienne de l'affichage extérieur

#100, 21 St. Clair Ave. East, Toronto ON M4T 1L9
416/968-3435; Fax: 416/968-0154

**Billi Awards**

Established in 1978, the awards recognize creative excellence in English outdoor ad design, primarily in billboard & transit-shelter formats

### Le Publicité club de Montréal

#1220, 500, rue Sherbrooke ouest, Montréal QC H3A 3C6
514/842-5681
Email: pubclub@cam.org;
URL: http://www.pcm.montreal.qc.ca/

**Les Prix coq d'or**

Definitive French language advertising awards

## AGRICULTURE & FARMING

### Canadian Society of Animal Science / Société canadienne de zootechnie

#1112, 141 Laurier Ave. West, Ottawa ON K1P 5J3
613/232-9459; Fax: 613/594-5190
URL: http://tdg.res.uoguelph.ca/~aic/csas.html

**Animal Industries Award in Extension & Public Service**

Recognizes outstanding service to the animal industries of Canada in technology transfer, leadership & education in animal production

**Award for Excellence in Genetics & Physiology**

Recognizes excellence in teaching, research, or technology transfer in the areas of animal breeding or physiology

**Award for Excellence in Nutrition & Meat Sciences**

Recognizes excellence in teaching, research, or technology transfer in the area of animal nutrition of meat science

### Provincial Exhibition of Manitoba

#3, 1175 - 18th St., Brandon MB R7A 7C5
204/726-3590; Fax: 204/725-0202

**Royal Manitoba Winter Fair Awards**

Prizes given in various categories for best of show for agricultural products, animals & crops; several equestrian events offer prizes for best in competition

### Royal Agricultural Winter Fair Association / Foire agricole royale d'hiver

Coliseum, Exhibition Place, Toronto ON M6K 3C3
416/393-6400; Fax: 416/393-6488
Email: rwfair@ican.net;
URL: http://www.royalfair.org

**Agricultural Awards**

Grand Champion is the highest honour in the following categories: dairy, beef, sheep, goats, swine, market livestock, field crops, vegetables, honey & maple, poultry, jams/jellies/pickles, dairy products, square dancing, fiddling, fleece wool, rabbits, & eight youth activities

**Breeding Horse Awards**

17 sections award prizes in this category

**Performance Horse Awards**

35 divisions & classes offer prizes; Leading International Rider is the highest honour in the horse show


**ARCHITECTURE See CULTURE, VISUAL ARTS & ARCHITECTURE**

**ART See CULTURE, VISUAL ARTS & ARCHITECTURE**

**BRAVERY See CITIZENSHIP & BRAVERY**


## BROADCASTING & FILM

### Academy of Canadian Cinema & Television / Académie canadienne du cinéma et de la télévision

158 Pearl St., Toronto ON M5H 1L3
416/591-2040; Fax: 416/591-2157;
Toll Free: 1-800-644-5194
URL: http://www.academy.ca

**Prix Gémeaux**

For excellence & achievement in French-language television production; held annually & presented in 50 categories covering Programs, Performance & Crafts; nominations & voting by peer groups composed of academy members

**The Gemini Awards**

The nationally telecast awards for excellence & achievement in Canadian television production are awarded annually & presented to winners in more than 50 categories covering Best Program, Best Performance & Best Craft, as well as three special awards following nomination & voting by a peer group

**The Genie Awards**

The nationally telecast Genie Awards celebrate excellence in Canadian cinema. The annual awards cover 21 categories from Best Picture to Best Sound, as well as the Golden Reel award for the top Canadian box office gross. Special achievement awards are voted by members of the academy. The Claude Jutra Award for Direction of a First Feature Film was added in 1993

### Alberta Motion Picture Industries Association

606 Midland Walwyn Tower, Edmonton Centre, Edmonton AB T5J 2Z2
403/944-0707; Fax: 403/426-3057

**Alberta Film & Television Awards**

Annual awards established in 1973; "Rosies" presented to Albertans responsible for creating outstanding film & television works; presentation alternates between Calgary & Edmonton

**Billington Awards**

Lifetime achievement in the motion picture industry in Alberta

### The Alliance for Children & Television / Alliance pour l'enfant et la télévision

#1002, 60 St. Clair Ave. East, Toronto ON M4T 1N5
416/515-0466; Fax: 416/515-0467
Email: acttv@interlog.com

**Awards of Excellence**

For children's TV programs produced in Canada

### Banff Television Festival

1516 Railway Ave., Canmore AB T1W 1P6
403/678-9260; Fax: 403/678-9269
Email: banfftv@screen.com; URL: http://www.banfftvfest.com

**Banff Rockie Awards**

Annual television awards for: made-for-TV-movies; mini-series; continuing series; short dramas; comedies; social & political documentaries; popular science programs; arts documentaries; performance specials; animation; sports, & children's programs. Also a grand prize winner & two special jury awards. All entries must be made for television & either in English or French

**Canwest Global Outstanding Achievement Award**

Given annually to an individual, organization or production unit for exceptional achievement

### Canadian Association of Broadcasters / Association canadienne des radiodiffuseurs

#306, 350 Sparks St., PO Box 627, Stn B, Ottawa ON K1P 5S2
613/233-4035; Fax: 613/233-6961
URL: http://www.cab-acr.ca

**BBM Scholarship**

Established in 1986; $2,500 awarded annually to a student in a graduate study program, or final year of an Honours degree with the intention of entering a graduate program at a Canadian university or post-secondary institution, who has demonstrated achievement in & knowledge of statistical &/or quantitative research methodology

**Jim Allard Broadcast Journalism Scholarship**

Established 1983; $2,500 awarded annually to the student who best combines academic achievement with natural talent

**Raymond Crépault Scholarship**

Established in 1975 by Radiomutuel with the association; $5,000 awarded annual to French Canadian students with broadcasting experience who are enrolled in, or wish to begin or complete a program of studies in communcations at the university level

**Ruth Hancock Memorial Scholarships**

$1,500 award established jointly in 1975 by the association & the CTV Television Network; presented annually to three Canadian students enrolled in recognized communications courses

### Canadian Conference of the Arts / Conférence canadienne des arts

189 Laurier Ave. East, Ottawa ON K1N 6P1
613/238-3561; Fax: 613/238-4849; Toll Free: 1-800-463-3561
Email: cca@mail.culturenet.ca; URL: http://www.culturenet.ca

**Rogers Communications Inc. Media Award for Coverage of the Arts**

Established 1991; recognizes & appreciates the consistent &/or innovative creation & production of arts programming in the Canadian electronic media; nominations are made by CCA members & by media colleagues

### Canadian Film & Television Production Association / Association canadienne de production de film et télévision

#806, 175 Bloor St. East, Toronto ON M4W 3R8
416/927-8942; Fax: 416/922-4038

**Chetwynd Award for Entrepreneurial Excellence**

Sponsored by Atlantis Films & presented to an individual or partnership that has demonstrated private sector entrepreneurial achievement in the motion picture &/ or television industry

**Jack Chisholm Award for Lifetime Contribution**

Sponsored by Kodak Canada & presented to an individual who has demonstrated noteworthy contributions to the success & progress of the motion picture &/ or television industry

### Canadian Heritage

Jules Léger Bldg., 6th Fl., 25 Eddy St., Hull QC K1A 0H3
819/997-7603

**Jeanne Sauvé Award for Women in Communications**

Established in 1994; jointly administered by the Department of Canadian Heritage & Canadian Women in Radio & Television; the award takes the form of three-month internships with Canadian Heritage enabling the winners to gain first-hand knowledge & insight into federal communications policy & legislation – Alison Taylor, 819/990-4152

### Canadian International Annual Film/Video Festival

25 Eugenia St., Barrie ON L4M 1P6
705/737-2729; Fax: 705/737-2729
Email: ciaff@iname.com; URL: http://cn.camriv.bc.ca/~george/ciaff/canadian.html

**Canadian International Annual Film/Video Awards**

Awards in three categories: amateur film/video maker; independent film/video maker, & pre-professional students of film/video

### Canadian Society of Cinematographers

571 Jarvis St., Toronto ON M4Y 2J1
416/966-6710

**Canadian Society of Cinematography Awards**

Twelve awards given annually: Best Commercial Cinematography; Best Documentary Cinematography; Best Dramatic Short; Best Industrial Cinematography; Best TV Series Cinematography; Best Unique Cinematography; The Bill Hilson Award for Outstanding Achievement; The Fuji Award; The Kodak New Century Award; The Roy Tash Newsfilm Award; The Stan Clinton News Essay Award, & The Telefilm Canada Student Cinematography Award

### Festival international du court métrage de Montréal / Montréal International Short Film Festival

#326, 4205, rue St-Denis, Montréal QC H2J 2K9
514/990-9676; Fax: 514/285-2886

**International Animation Competition**

The following prizes are awarded for the best international animated short film (includes Canadian entries): Grand Prize of $1,000 to the director; TV 5 Kaleidoscope Prize, & Public Prize

**International Competition**

The following prizes are awarded for the best international short films (includes Canadian entries): Grand Prize, $2,000 for the director; Société Radio-Canada Prize; Best Screenplay; Youth Prize; Public Prize; C/FP Prize

**Long Night of the Short**

Prize given for the most bizarre film

**Québec University Competition & Québec College Competition**

Prizes given for the best short film produced by university students & the best produced by college students

### ITVA CANADA

PO Box 1156, Stn Adelaide, Toronto ON M5C 2K5
416/733-3757; Fax: 416/733-1741
Email: itvacda@inforamp.net

**EVA Awards**

Variety of awards presented annually covering: Internal Communications; Training; Recruiting; Medical/ Health Issues; Corporate Image; Sales & Marketing; Specialty Channels; Multimedia; The Peter Llewellin Award for Student Achievement; Writing; Directing; Performance; Graphics & Animation; Editing; Music; Excellence in Technical Imagery; Excellence in Production Achievement

### National Screen Institute - Canada / Institute national des arts de l'écran - Canada

10022 - 103 St., 3rd Fl., Edmonton AB T5J 0X2
403/421-4084; Fax: 403/425-8098; Toll Free: 1-800-480-4084
Email: filmhero@nsi-canada.ca; URL: http://www.nsi-canada.ca

**Drama Prize**

This national competition for emerging filmmakers has three components - competition, production/training, exhibition; the completed productions are premiered at the Local Heroes Film Festival
Six teams receive prizes of $6,000 each towards the production of a 10-minute dramatic film, augmented by up to $5,500 in equipment & services sponsorships; as well, an established filmmaker in their area acts as the production's mentor & assists in script development, fundraising & finding distribution opportunities

### Société Radio-Canada

CP 6000, Succ Centre-ville, Montréal QC H3C 3A8
514/597-4510; Fax: 514/597-4807
URL: http://www.radio-canada.com

**Grands Prix Société Radio-Canada des scénaristes, nouvellistes et poétes**

Ce concours, lancé en 1996, remplace le "Concours d'oeuvres dramatiques radiophoniques" et le "Concours de nouvelles". Il vise á favoriser l'émergence de nouveaux talents, à stimuler la création radiophonique et à récompenser la meilleure écriture de fiction dans les catégories dramatique, nouvelle et poésie. ler prix: 5 000$ dans les trois catégories; 2e prix: 3 000$ dans les trois catégories

### Toronto International Film Festival / Festival international du film de Toronto

2 Carlton St., 16th Fl., Toronto ON M5B 1J3
416/967-7371; Fax: 416/967-9477
Email: tiffg@torfilmfest.ca; URL: http://www.bell.ca/filmfest

**Air Canada People's Choice Award**

Sponsored by Air Canada & voted best film of the festival by festival audiences

**Metro Media Award & FIPRESCI Award**

Metro Media Award is voted by the press corps at the festival, & the FIPRESCI Award is voted by the international film critics attending the festival

**Toronto-City Award for Best Canadian Feature Film**

Jointly sponsored by the City of Toronto & Citytv; $25,000 awarded to the Best Canadian Feature Film

### TVOntario

2180 Yonge St., PO Box 200, Stn Q, Toronto ON M4T 2T1
416/484-2600; Fax: 416/484-2725
URL: http://www.tvo.org/

**Prix TVOntario Awards**

Established 1991 to showcase the best educational broadcasters in Canada, the United States & abroad; awarded every two years

## BUSINESS & TRADE

### Caldwell Partners

64 Prince Arthur Ave., Stn F, Toronto ON M5R 1B4
416/920-7702; Fax: 416/922-8646
URL: http://www.ceoaward-canada.org/ceo.htm

**Outstanding CEO of the Year Award**

The annual award takes into consideration the candidate's leadership, innovation, business achievements, corporate performance, social responsibility, sense of vision & global competitiveness

**Top 40 Under 40**

Established in 1996 & sponsored by CIBC, Canadian Airlines, CTV, The Financial Post & Caldwell Partners; recognizes 40 of Canada's new entrepeneurs, executives & professionals who have reached a level of success but haven't yet reached 40 years of age

### Canadian Association of Family Enterprise / Association canadienne des enterprises familiales

1163 Sylvester St., PO Box 136, Lefroy ON L0L 1W0
705/456-4900; Fax: 705/456-4962
Email: ucstaff@cafe-uc.on.ca;
URL: http://www.cafe-uc.on.ca/

**CAFE-Jaguar Award for Family Enterprise of the Year**

Established to recognize the importance of family enterprise; looks at: job creation, technological advancement, environment, innovation & entrepeneurial success; open to any family enterprise, private or publicly owned

### The Conference Board of Canada

255 Smyth Rd., Ottawa ON K1H 8M7
613/526-3280; Fax: 613/526-4857
Email: infoserv@conferenceboard.ca;
URL: http://www.conferenceboard.ca/nbec

**National Awards for Excellence in Business-Education Partnership**

Awarded to partnerships that have a demonstrated record of success in promoting the importance of science, technology &/or mathematics; linking education & the world of work, promoting teacher development, encouraging students to stay in school, expanding vocational &/or apprenticeship training – Mary Ann McLaughlin

### Entrepreneur of the Year Institute

Ernst & Young Tower, TD Centre, 222 Bay St., PO Box 251, Toronto ON M5K 1J7
416/943-3144; Fax: 416/943-3767; Toll Free: 1-888-946-3694
URL: http://www.eycan.com/special/special/htm

**Entrepreneur of the Year**

Founded in 1994 & co-sponsored by Ernst & Young, Canadian Business magazine, Bank of Montréal, Nesbitt Burns, McCarthy Tétrault, & Air Canada, the awards recognize successful business owners & also promote the beneficial impact the entrepreneurial spirit has on Canada's local & national economies; nominees must be owner-managers who are primarily responsible for the recent performance of their company; regional winners are honoured in fall banquets across the country & the national Entrepreneur of the Year award recipients are announced in November

### The Financial Post

333 King St. East, Toronto ON M5A 4N2
416/350-6200; Fax: 416/350-6201

**Financial Post Annual Reports Awards**

Presented annually in 12 industry categories for excellence in communicating with shareholders & the public

### Foreign Affairs & International Trade Canada

Canada Export Award Program, Team Canada Division (TBC), 125 Sussex Dr., Tower C, 5th Fl., Ottawa ON K1A 0G2
Fax: 613/996-8688; Toll Free: 1-800-267-8376
URL: http://www.dfait-maeci.gc.ca/english/trade/award-e/htm; http://www.dfait-maeci.gc.ca/english/trade/invitee.htm

**Canada Export Award**

Honours those firms from across Canada who have demonstrated superior performance in the export arena

Open to all firms or divisions of firms resident in Canada, that have been exporting goods or services for three or more years; this includes trading houses & banks, as well as transport, market research, packaging & promotion firms; selection is based on but not limited to the extent to which the firm has shown significant increases in its export sales, success in breaking into new markets, success in introducing export products into world markets; other achievements by firms in export markets that contribute to Canada's economic well-being or to the reputation of the organization as a world-class exporter will also be considered

Award is a plaque bearing the Canada Export Award logo & a brief citation of the firm's accomplishments; firms receiving an award are welcome to use the logo on their letterhead, advertisements & other promotional material for a period of up to three years after its presentation; national & local promotion will be given to firms receiving the award

### Information Highways Magazine

162 Joicey Blvd., Toronto ON M5M 2V2
416/488-7372; Fax: 416/488-7078
Email: info@tce.on.ca

**Canadian Online Product Awards**

Honours online products designed for Canadian organizations & consumers; open to companies & individuals who develop or market products to Canadians in the following categories: general business, finance, legal, engineering, scientific, medical, consumer, library, internet search & retrieval technology & internet-enabled decision support products. Entry fee of $160.50 for each entry required

### National Quality Institute / Institut national de la qualité

#307, 2275 Lakeshore West Blvd., Etobicoke ON M8V 3Y3
416/251-7600; Fax: 416/251-9131; Toll Free: 1-800-263-9648
Email: info@nqionline.com;
URL: http://www.nqi.com

**Canada Awards for Excellence**

Previously called the Canada Awards for Business Excellence & established by the Government of Canada in 1984, the awards have been expanded to recognize excellence in Education, Government & Health Care; those who apply for the Canada Awards for Excellence will receive a confidential assessment & written feedback report from the examiners on how far their organization has travelled on the road to excellence; three categories of awards - Entrepreneurship Award, Innovation Award & Quality Award

Winners receive export assistance to help them access world markets, exposure through national advertising, & lifetime use of the Canada Awards for Excellence logo on corporate literature & products

### National Transportation Week Inc.

2323 St. Laurent Blvd., Ottawa ON K1G 4J8
613/736-1350; Fax: 613/736-1395

**Award of Achievement**

Established 1987; awarded to those who have brought about positive & measurable developments of significant & lasting benefit to transportation in Canada

**Award of Excellence**

Established 1975; for an outstanding contribution to the betterment of the transportation industry

### University of Alberta

Faculty of Business, 25 University Campus NW, Calgary AB T6G 2E8
403/492-5693; Fax: 403/492-2997
URL: http://www.registrar.ualberta.ca/awards/awards.html

**Canadian Business Leader Award**

Annual award recognizes distinguished professional achievements & contributions to the community

### The Women's Entrepreneurship Program

The Joseph L. Rotman Centre for Management, Univ. of Toronto, 105 George St., Toronto ON M5S 3E6
416/978-5703; Fax: 416/978-5433
Email: mbaprog@fmgmt.mgmt.utoronto.ca;
URL: http://www.mgmt.utoronto.ca

**Canadian Woman Entrepreneur of the Year Awards**

Start-Up Award for a woman in business at least three years, but less than five, whose venture provides a product, service or marketing strategy that is innovative & supported by a solid plan for growth; Lifetime Achievement Award for a woman who has owned her business for at least 20 years; Quality Plus Award for demonstrated ability to develop & maintain excellence; Impact on Local Economy Award for a woman who has contributed significantly to the development of local economy through her business; International Competitiveness Award for a company that has increased sales by developing global markets, & Turnaround Award for a woman who has applied management skills to revitalize a declining or moribund business

**CINEMA See BROADCASTING & FILM**

## CITIZENSHIP & BRAVERY

### Bridgestone/Firestone Canada Inc.

#400, 5770 Hurontario St., Mississauga ON L5R 3G5
905/890-1990; Fax: 905/890-1991

**National Truck Hero Award**

Established 1956; endorsed by the Canada Safety Council, the Traffic Injury Research Foundation & the trucking industry; designed to promote highway safety by focusing public attention on acts of bravery performed by professional Canadian truck drivers in the course of their daily work

### The Canadian Council of Christians & Jews / Conseil canadien des chrétiens et des juifs

#820, 2 Carleton St. West, Toronto ON M5B 1J3
416/597-9693; Fax: 416/597-9775; Toll Free: 1-800-663-1848
Email: cccj@interlog.com;
URL: http://www.interlog.com/~cccj/

**Good Servant Medal**

Created to commemorate the retirement of Richard D. Jones, O.C., LL.D., after 30 years of continuous service to CCCJ, as founder & principal officer, 1947-1977; recognizes individuals who have rendered extraordinary service to their community beyond the call of duty without seeking public recognition

### The Canadian Council of the Blind / Le Conseil canadien des aveugles

#405, 396 Cooper St., Ottawa ON K2P 2H7
613/567-0311; Fax: 613/567-2728

**Book of Fame Citation**

The Book of Fame was donated to the Council in 1958 by the disbanded Comrades Club of Toronto; it contains the names & citations of outstanding blind Canadians selected yearly by the eight divisions & the National Board of Directors of the Council; each recipient of a citation is presented with a framed photograph of the appropriate page in the book

### Canadian Decorations for Bravery

Canadian Decorations Advisory Committee, Rideau Hall, One Sussex Drive, Ottawa ON K1A 0A1
613/993-8200; Fax: 613/990-7636

**Canadian Decorations for Bravery**

The Canadian Honours System provides three decorations for Bravery to express the nation's gratitude to those people who risk their lives to save or protect others, defying in the process the instinct for self-preservation. See the Canadian Honours List in this section for a list of recent recipients

### Canadian Native Arts Foundation / Fondation canadienne des arts autochtones
#508, 77 Mowat Ave., Toronto ON M6K 3E3
416/926-0775; Fax: 416/588-9198

**National Aboriginal Achievement Awards**

Established in 1993 & awarded to aboriginal achievers from the First Nations, Inuit & Metis communities; nominees are outstanding achievers working in any occupational area

### The Duke of Edinburgh's Award
#406, 207 Queens Quay West, PO Box 124, Toronto ON M5J 1A7
416/203-0674; Fax: 416/203-0676

**Young Canadians Challenge**

Established in Canada in 1963 with His Royal Highness Prince Philip as Patron, the award recognizes personal achievement in a voluntary program of activities by young people in the age range of 14-25

Open to all Canadian youth; young people participate independently or through youth groups, clubs, schools, etc.; program is operated throughout Canada, with divisional offices located in each of the ten provinces

Award is in the form of a pin & an inscribed certificate representing Gold, Silver, & Bronze levels; Gold awards are presented by His Excellency The Governor General of Canada, or a member of the Royal Family, at national awards ceremonies

### The National Citizens' Coalition
#907, 100 Adelaide St. West, Toronto ON M5H 1S3
416/869-3838; Fax: 416/869-1891

**The Colin M. Brown Freedom Medal**

Established 1987; a medal is awarded annually to an individual who best typifies the principles of political & economic freedom which the Coalition espouses

### National Transportation Week Inc.
2323 St. Laurent Blvd., Ottawa ON K1G 4J8
613/736-1350; Fax: 613/736-1395

**Award of Valor**

Established 1979; awarded for "an exemplary act of bravery in perilous circumstances"

### Ontario Ministry of Citizenship, Culture & Recreation
Ontario Honours & Awards ,77 Bloor St. West, 9th Fl., Toronto ON M7A 2R9
416/314-7526; Fax: 416/314-7743

**The Ontario Medal for Firefighters Bravery**

Established 1976 to recognize acts of superlative courage & bravery performed in the line of duty by members of Ontario's firefighting forces

**The Ontario Medal for Good Citizenship**

Established 1973 to recognize & pay tribute to citizens who, through their selflessness, humanity & kindness, make Ontario a better province in which to live

**The Ontario Medal for Police Bravery**

Established 1976 to recognize acts of superlative courage & bravery performed in the line of duty by members of Ontario's police forces

**The Order of Ontario**

Established 1986 to recognize those men & women who have rendered service of the greatest distinction & of singular excellence in all fields of endeavour benefiting society in Ontario & elsewhere

### The Royal Bank of Canada
1, Place Ville-Marie, 4e étage sud, Montréal QC H3C 3A9
514/874-8549; Fax: 514/874-3890

**Royal Bank Award**

Established 1967 to acknowledge the accomplishments of Canadian citizens, or persons living in Canada, whose unique work has benefited society at large

Candidate must be a Canadian citizen or a person domiciled in Canada; award may be shared & not necessarily conferred each year; institutions & corporations are not eligible; award consists of a gold medal, $125,000 to the winner & $125,000 to be donated to the winner's charity of choice

### St. John Ambulance / Ambulance Saint-Jean
312 Laurier Ave. East, Ottawa ON K1N 6P6
613/236-7461; Fax: 613/236-2425
Email: nhq@nhq.sja.ca; URL: http://www/sja.ca

**Life-saving Awards of the Order of St. John**

Awarded to individuals who apply first aid to a victim or endanger their own life in saving or attempting to save a life

### Toronto Life Fashion Magazine
59 Front St. East, 2nd Fl., Toronto ON M5E 1B3
416/364-3334; Fax: 416/594-3374
Email: fashion@istar.ca

**Women Who Make a Difference**

Awarded annually to Toronto area women who have had noteworthy success in their field & who have made a vital contribution to life in the city; awards are given in the following categories: Business Professional, Community Affairs, Entrepreneur, Communications, the Arts, Early Achiever – Publicity & Promotion Director, Cynthia Evans

### United Nations Association in Canada / Association canadienne pour les Nations-Unies
#900, 130 Slater St., Ottawa ON K1P 6E2
613/232-5751; Fax: 613/563-2455
Email: unac@magi.com; URL: http://www.unac.org

**Pearson Peace Medal**

Awarded to a Canadian who has contibuted significantly to humanitarian causes

### YTV Canada Inc.
64 Jefferson Ave., Unit 18, Toronto ON M6K 3H3
416/534-1191; Fax: 416/533-0346

**YTV Achievement Awards**

Recognize outstanding accomplishments & contributions made to society by young Canadians (19 years or younger) in: Acting, Band, Bravery, Dance, Entrepreneurship, Environmental, Innovation, Instrumental, Public Service, Specialty Performance, Sports, Terry Fox Award (for spirit & determination), Visual Arts, Vocal, & Writing

$3,000 & a statuette presented on the YTV awards show each spring

**COMMUNICATIONS See JOURNALISM**

**CRAFTS See CULTURE, VISUAL ARTS & ARCHITECTURE**

## CULTURE, VISUAL ARTS & ARCHITECTURE

### Arts Foundation of Greater Toronto
#365 Richmond St. West, PO Box 124, Toronto ON M5V 3A8
416/597-8223; Fax: 416/597-6956
Email: jhowell@interlog.com

**The Toronto Arts Awards**

Awarded annually to encourage & promote the creative arts in Toronto; award recipients must be Canadian citizens, landed immigrants or long-term residents of Canada & must show that they have had an ongoing association with Toronto & have contributed significantly to the arts & culture of the city

Eight awards of $2,500 to purchase or commission an original work by a less-established Toronto artist are presented covering the following disciplines: media arts, writing & publishing, performing arts, music, visual arts, architecture & design, & two for lifetime achievement

### The Canada Council for the Arts / Conseil des Arts du Canada
350 Albert St., PO Box 1047, Ottawa ON K1P 5V8
613/566-4414, ext.4116; Fax: 613/566-4416; Toll Free: 1-800-263-5588
URL: http://www.canadacouncil.ca

**Bell Canada Award in Video Art**

$10,000 awarded annually to a Canadian video artist who has made an exceptional contribution to the advancement of video art in Canada through his/her video tapes or video installations; candidates are nominated by three professional curators &/or critics who are specialists in Canadian video art; the winner is selected by the committee of professional video artists convened by the Council

**Canada Council Molson Prizes**

Funded from an endowment by the Molson Family Foundation, two prizes of $50,000 each awarded annually to distinguished Canadians, one in the arts, one in social sciences & humanities; acknowledges Canadian citizens whose contributions have enriched the cultural or intellectual heritage of Canada & to encourage Canadians honoured with this distinction to continue contributing to the cultural & intellectural heritage of Canada

**Duke & Duchess of York Prize in Photography**

Endowed by the Government of Canada in 1986 on the occasion of Prince Andrew's marriage; up to $17,000 awarded annually to cover living expenses, project costs & travel to a professional Canadian artist for personal creative work or advanced study in photography; winner is chosen from the recipients of the "Creation/ Production Grants to Professional Artists" in photography

**J.B.C. Watkins Award**

A bequest from the estate of the late John B.C. Watkins, provides special fellowships of $5,000 (awarded in addition to the regular grant) to Canadian artists in any field who are graduates of a Canadian university or postsecondary art institution or training school; preference is given to those who wish to carry out their postgraduate studies in Denmark, Norway, Sweden or Iceland, but applications are accepted for studies in any country other than Canada

**Joseph S. Stauffer Prizes**

Each year the Canada Council designates up to three Canadians who have been awarded an arts grant in the fields of music, visual arts & literature as winners; the prizes, worth an additional $4,000 each, honour the memory of the benefactor whose bequest to the Canada Council enables it to "encourage young Canadians of outstanding promise or potential"

**Petro-Canada Award in Media Arts**

Endowed by Petro-Canada in 1987 to celebrate the centenary of engineering in Canada; $10,000 awarded approximately every three years to a professional Canadian artist who has demonstrated outstanding & innovative use of new technology in the media arts

**Prix de Rome in Architecture**

Established 1987; designed to recognize the work of a Canadian citizen actively engaged in the field of contemporary architecture whose career is well under way & whose personal work shows exceptional talent.

Grant of $34,000 & use of a live-in studio in the Trastevere quarter of Rome for 12 months

**Ronald J. Thom Award for Early Design Achievement**

$10,000 awarded every two years to a Canadian in the early stages of his/her career who demonstrates both outstanding creative talent & exceptional potential in architectural design

Sensitivity to architecture's allied arts, crafts & professions in the context of the integrated building environment must be evident in all work

**Saidye Bronfman Awards**

Funded by the Samuel & Saidye Bronfman Family Foundation, $20,000 prise is awarded annually to an exceptional craftsperson; in addition to the cash award, works by the recipient are acquired by the Canadian Museum of Civilization.

Candidates must be nominated by the national or provincial crafts council, a previous recipient of the awards, a member association of the Canadian Craft Council or a single media guild

**Victor Martyn Lynch-Staunton Awards**

Each year the Canada Council designates three Canadian artists who have been awarded grants in music & visual arts as holders of Victor Martyn Lynch-Staunton Awards; this designation is made to honour the memory of the benefactor whose bequest to the Council enables it to increase the number of grants available to senior or established artists; the awards increase the grants by $4,000

## Canadian Conference of the Arts / Conférence canadienne des arts

189 Laurier Ave. East, Ottawa ON K1N 6P1
613/238-3561; Fax: 613/238-4849; Toll Free: 1-800-463-3561
Email: cca@mail.culturenet.ca;
URL: http://www.culturenet.ca

**Diplôme d'Honneur**

Established in 1954; presented annually to Canadians who have contributed outstanding service to the arts; recipients have included Vincent Massey, Wilfrid Pelletier, Maureen Forrester, Floyd Chalmers, Gabrielle Roy, Glenn Gould, Alfred Pellan, Bill Reid, Antonine Maillet

## Canadian Historical Association / Société historique du Canada

395 Wellington St., Ottawa ON K1A 0N3
613/233-7885; Fax: 613/567-3110
Email: jmineault@archives.ca

**Albert B. Corey Prize**

Established 1966 & jointly sponsored by the CHA & the American Historical Association; $1,000 awarded every two years to the best book dealing with the history of Canadian-American relations or the history of both countries

**The Wallace K. Ferguson Prize**

Established 1979; $1,000 awarded annually for a outstanding work in a field of history other than Canadian

## The City of Toronto

Corp. Servs., Human Resources, 100 Queen St. West, 1st Fl., Toronto ON M5H 2N2
416/392-7855; Fax: 416/392-0006

**City of Toronto Fashion Awards**

A series of awards including: Designer of the Year, Industry Achievement, Couturier, Most Promising Fashion Graduate & Most Promising New Designer – Laurie Belzak, 416/392-7571

**Urban Design Awards**

Awarded every two years for urban development in Toronto – Planning & Development Dept., 416/392-1526

## Conseil de la vie française en Amérique

56, rue Saint-Pierre, 1er étage, Québec QC G1K 4A1
418/692-1150; Fax: 418/692-4578

**L'Ordre de la fidélité française**

Établi en 1947; destiné à reconnaître les mérites exceptionnels d'un francophone ayant apporté une contribution significative au progrès des francophones et à la promotion des facteurs de vie et de la culture française en Amérique du Nord

**Prix littéraire Champlain**

1 500 $; vise à encourager en Amérique du Nord la production littéraire chez les francophones qui vivent à l'extérieur du Québec, d'une part, et à susciter chez les Québécois un intérêt pour les francophones qui sont en situation de minorité hors du Québec en Amérique du Nord

## Heritage Canada / La Fondation Héritage Canada

412 MacLaren St., PO Box 1358, Stn B, Ottawa ON K1P 5R4
613/237-1066; Fax: 613/237-5987
Email: hercanot@sympatico.ca

**Achievement Awards**

Established 1989, these awards recognize individuals or groups for achievements in the conservation of heritage in the natural or cultural environments; designed to be presented jointly by Heritage Canada & established provincial or territorial umbrella groups or associations that are members of Heritage Canada & that have juried awards programs & awards ceremonies; each group or association, called a partner, will be fully responsible for choosing its candidate within prescribed criteria & eligibility rules; in this way, Heritage Canada also recognizes these partners for their dedication & commitment to excellence in heritage preservation

**Gabrielle Léger Award**

Recognizes outstanding work in architectural conservation in Canada; this is an annual national award to an individual who has contributed outstanding community service in the cause of heritage conservation

**Lieutenant Governor's Award**

Established 1979 to recognize outstanding work in architectural conservation on a provincial level by an individual or group

It must be demonstrated that the applicant's continuous efforts in the field of heritage conservation have benefited the province where the foundation's annual meeting is being held; applicants must be sponsored by an organized heritage group &/or elected officials at any level of government

## Ontario Arts Council / Conseil des arts de l'Ontario

#600, 151 Bloor St. West, Toronto ON M5S 1T6
416/961-1660; Fax: 416/961-7796;
Toll Free: 1-800-387-0058
Email: oac@gov.on.ca

**Emerging Artists Award**

$7,500 award established by the K.M. Hunter Charitable Foundation; the winners are selected from a batch of applicants recommended by Ontario Arts Council juries; awards rotate each year through film, photography, video, dance, literature, theatre, music & visual arts

**Lieutenant-Governor's Awards**

Approximately $300,000 to be awarded annually for the visual & performing arts that recognize institutional achievements rather than celebrating particular productions or artists; established in 1995 & co-sponsored by the J.P. Bickell Foundation

**The Jean A. Chalmers Award for Crafts**

Annual award of $20,000 honours individual Canadian craftspersons whose work continues to influence creativity & to set significant standards for innovation & excellence

**The Jean A. Chalmers Award for Visual Arts**

Annual award of $20,000 recognizes individual Canadian artists who have created a substantial body of work which influences creativity

**The Venture Fund**

Assists in artistic projects that embody a sense of challenge, experimentation or risk

## PEI Council of the Arts

115 Richmond St., Charlottetown PE C1A 1H7
902/368-4410; Fax: 902/368-4418

**Senior Arts Award**

$5,000 awarded every two years to a PEI professional artist with an accumulated body of work who has contributed in general to art in PEI

## Québec Ministère de la culture et des communications

225, Grande Allée est, Bloc C, 3e étage, Québec QC G1R 5G5
418/643-2183; Fax: 418/643-4457
Email: dc@mcc.gouv.qc.ca;
URL: http://www.mcc.gouv.qc.ca

**Les Prix du Québec:**

**Prix Albert-Tessier**

$30,000, a silver medal & a scroll awarded for excellence in cinema

**Prix Gérard-Morisset**

$30,000, a silver medal & scroll awarded for excellence in heritage

**Prix Georges-Émile-Lapalme**

$30,000, et une médaille en argent; attribué annuellement pour la qualité et le rayonnement de la langue française parlée ou écrite au Québec

**Prix Paul-Émile-Borduas**

$30,000, a silver medal & a scroll awarded for excellence in architecture, design, visual arts, & crafts

## Royal Architectural Institute of Canada / Institut royal d'architecture du Canada

#330, 55 Murray St., Ottawa ON K1N 5M3
613/241-3600; Fax: 613/241-5750
Email: info@raic.org;
URL: http://www.aecinfo.com/raic/index.html

**Governor General's Medals for Architecture**

Defined by the Governor General for recognition of outstanding achievement in the field of Canadian architecture

**RAIC Allied Arts Medal**

Established 1953; silver medals awarded at intervals of not less than one year & not more than three years for outstanding achievement in the arts which are allied to architecture, such as mural paintings, sculpture, decoration, stained glass, industrial design

**RAIC Gold Medal**

Established 1930; gold medals awarded annually in recognition of a person of science or letters related to architecture & the arts, in addition to an architect, for great achievement & contribution to the architectural profession

## The Royal Society of Canada / La Société royale du Canada

#308, 225 Metcalfe St., Ottawa ON K2P 1P9
613/991-6990; Fax: 613/991-6996
Email: adminrsc@rsc.ca; URL: http://www.rsc.ca

**Centenary Medal**

Established 1982; awarded at irregular intervals in recognition of achievements in scholarship & research

**Sir John William Dawson Medal**

Established 1985; $2,000 & a silver medal awarded for important & sustained contributions by one individual in at least two different fields in the general areas of interest of the society or in a broad domain that transcends the usual disciplinary boundaries

**The J.B. Tyrrell Historical Medal**

Established 1927; awarded at least every two years for outstanding work in the history of Canada

## Social Sciences & Humanities Research Council of Canada

350 Albert St., 10th Fl., PO Box 1610, Ottawa ON K1P 6G4
613/992-0530; Fax: 613/992-1787
Email: z-info@sshrc; URL: http://www.sshrc.ca

**The Bora Laskin National Fellowship in Human Rights Research**

To support interdisciplinary or multidisciplinary research & the development of expertise in the field of human rights, with emphasis on Canadian human rights issues

$45,000 stipend pluas $10,000 for research & research-related travel expenses

**The Jules & Gabrielle Léger Fellowship**
Awarded to promote research & writing on the historical contribution of the Crown & its representatives, federal & provincial, to the political, constitutional, cultural, intellectual & social life of the country
Award is for $40,000, plus $10,000 for research & research-travel expenses

## La Société Saint-Jean-Baptiste de Montréal

82, rue Sherbrooke ouest, Montréal QC H2X 1X3
514/843-8851; Fax: 514/844-6369

**Prix Esdras-Minville**
Established 1978; $1,500 & a medal awarded annually to a French Canadian in recognition of outstanding achievement in Human Science (History, Sociology, Economics, Politics, etc.) in serving the higher interests of the French Canadian people

**Prix Philippe-Hébert**
Established 1971; $1,500 & a medal awarded annually to a French Canadian in recognition of outstanding achievement in the plastic arts in serving the higher interests of the French Canadian people

**Prix Victor-Morin**
Established 1962; $1,500 & a medal awarded annually to a French Canadian in recognition of outstanding achievement in theatre, television, or film, in serving the higher interests of the French Canadian people

## Toronto Arts Council

141 Bathurst St., Toronto ON M5V 2R2
416/392-6800; Fax: 416/392-6920
Email: tac@city.toronto.on.ca;
URL: www.city.toronto.on.ca/4edc/tac.htm

**Margo Bindhardt Award**
$10,000 prize awarded every second year to recognize individuals whose leadership & vision, through their creative work or activism, have had a significant impact on the arts & arts awareness in Toronto

**William Kilbourn Award**
Established in 1995 & to be awarded every second year from 1998 on

## Yorkdale Shopping Centre

#412, One Yorkdale Rd., Toronto ON M6A 3A1
416/789-3261

**Yorkdale Designer of the Year Award**
Annual award of $10,000; fashion designer must be Canadian & have presented at least six collections; second award of $2,500 for designing a special theme outfit for the annual fall show at Yorkdale – Fruitman Communications Group, 416/628-8366

**Yorkdale New Designer Discovery Award**
Annual award of $5,000 & use of a cart/kiosk in the mall for one month (value $2,500) for the best new fashion designer; must have a collection of at least 10 outfits & a minimum of three years experience in the fashion industry; second award of $2,500 for designing a special theme outfit for the annual spring fashion show at Yorkdale – Fruitman Communications Group, 416/638-8366

**DANCE See PERFORMING ARTS**

**DRAMA See PERFORMING ARTS**

# EDUCATIONAL

## Alberta Education

Devonian Building, West Tower, 11160 Jasper Ave., Edmonton AB T5K 0L2
403/422-9327; Fax: 403/422-4199

**Excellence in Teaching Awards**
Recognizes outstanding Alberta teachers; honours creative, innovative & effective teaching; focuses public attention on the teaching profession; involves Albertans in celebrating teaching excellence

## Alberta Heritage Scholarship Fund

9940 - 106 St., 6th Fl., Edmonton AB T5K 2V1
403/427-8640; Fax: 403/422-4516
32 scholarships & awards are available in various fields of study

## Association for Media & Technology in Education in Canada / Association des média et de la technologie en éducation au Canada

#1318, 3-1750 The Queensway, Etobicoke ON M9C 5H5
604/323-5627; Fax: 604/323-5577
Email: maepp@langara.bc.ca;
URL: http://www.camosun.bc.ca/~amtec/

**AMTEC Leadership Award & the SONY Award**
Two awards recognize outstanding individual achievement & leadership in the field of educational media & technology

## Association of Canadian Universities for Northern Studies / Association universitaire canadienne d'études nordiques

#405, 17 York St., Ottawa ON K1N 9J6
613/562-0515; Fax: 613/562-0533
Email: acuns@cyberus.ca; URL: http://www.geog.mcgill.ca/northern/acunhome.html

**Royal Canadian Geographical Society Studentship in Northern Geography**
Based on academic excellence; $10,000 awarded to a graduate student engaged in northern geographical research

**Studentships in Northern Studies**
Research culminating in a thesis or similar document involving direct northern experience; $10,000 for students enrolled in graduate & undergraduate degree programs or other courses of study recognized at a Canadian university with special relevance to Canada's northern territories & adjacent regions

## Association of Universities & Colleges of Canada / Association des Universités et Collèges du Canada

#600, 350 Albert St., Ottawa ON K1R 1B1
613/563-1236; Fax: 613/563-9745
Email: info@aucc.ca; URL: http://www.aucc.ca

**C.D. Howe Memorial Foundation Engineering Awards**
Two $6,000 scholarships (one male, one female) for students who have completed the first year of an engineering program

**C.D. Howe Scholarship Program**
Two $5,000 scholarships open to all disciplines but for students from Thunder Bay or the following school boards: Lakehead, Lakehead District R.C., Lake Superior, North of Superior District R.C., Geraldton, Geraldton District R.C., Nipigon-Red Rock, & Hornepayne

**Cable Telecommunications Research Fellowship Program**
Two $5,000 fellowships to assist in completing a graduate degree which includes a thesis on a topic in the engineering of broadband communications systems or computer science

**Department of National Defence Security and Defence Forum**
Four $12,000 (master's), $16,000 (doctorate) scholarships in studies relating to current & future Canadian natural security & defence issues. Six internships of up to 12 months worth $16,000 to help recent MA graduates obtain work experience in security & defence studies by working in this field in the non-governmental or private sectors

**Emergency Prepardness Canada Research Fellowship in Honour of Stuart Nesbitt White**
Provides support of up to $10,000 per annum for research in the area of disaster/emergency research & planning; preference is given to applicants who hold a Master's degree & who are planning research in the following fields: Urban & Regional Planning, Economics, Earth Sciences, Risk Analysis & Management, Systems Science, Social Sciences, Business Administration & Health Administration – Michelyne Léger, 613/563-1236, ext.266; email: mleger@aucc.ca

**Fessenden-Trott Awards**
Four $9,000 scholarships open to all disciplines; restricted to Ontario in 1997, to Western provinces in 1998, to Québec in 1999 & Atlantic provinces in 2000

**Frank Knox Memorial Fellowship Program**
Up to two $14,500 US awards, plus tuition fees & health insurance for Canadian citizens who have graduated from a AUCC member institution & wish to study at Harvard in the following disciplines: arts & sciences (including engineering), business administration, design, divinity studies, education, law, public administration, medicine, dental medicine & public health

**Frederick T. Metcalf Award Program (Canadian Cable Television Association)**
A $5,000 scholarship awarded annually to students pursing a master's degree in any discipline directly related to the development & delivery of cable in Canada

**National Access Awareness Week Student Awards Program**
Maximum of $3,500 awarded to undergraduate, graduate or college diploma program students with a disability; number of awards determined annually

**Queen Elizabeth Silver Jubilee Endowment Fund for Study in a Second Official Language Award Program**
Six $5,000 (plus travel costs) scholarships open to all disciplines, except translations, for students studying in their second language

## Association des professionnels en ressources humaines du Québec / Association of Human Resources Professionals of the Province of Québec

#820, 1253, av McGill Collège, Montréal QC H3B 2Y5
514/879-1636; Fax: 514/879-1722

**Inter-University Excellence Contest**
Established in 1987 to promote teaching of human resources management in Québec universities that prepare students for the job market; open to students at Québec universities; amounts of 2 000$, 1 500$ & 1 000$

## BC Ministry of Education, Skills & Training

Parliament Bldgs., Victoria BC V8V 1X4
250/387-4611

**Governor General's Academic Medal Award**
Established to encourage academic students; awards medals to students achieving the highest academic standing in the graduating class

**Lieutenant Governor's Silver Medal Award**
Each college & institute in BC is eligible to present one medal each year to a student who has excelled academically, & has contributed to the life of their college, institute, or community

**Premier's Excellence Award**
Award provides a $5,000 bursary to the top all-around graduating Grade 12 student in each of the 15 college regions in BC who will attend one of the province's post-secondary institutions

**United World College Scholarships**
The Government of BC funds 14 World College Scholarships annually; each scholarship is valued at $16,500; each year seven new scholarships are funded in addition to seven scholarships to students returning for their second year of study; students attending United World Colleges follow a two-year program leading to the International Baccalaureate, accepted by major international universities as equivalent to the final year of senior secondary school & first year university

## Black Business & Professional Association

#203, 675 King St. West, Toronto ON M5V 1M9
416/504-4097; Fax: 416/504-7343

**Harry Jerome Scholarships**
Five annual awards of $2,000 aimed at helping young people who may lack resources for further education

## The Canada Council for the Arts / Conseil des Arts du Canada

350 Albert St., PO Box 1047, Ottawa ON K1P 5V8
613/566-4414, ext.4116; Fax: 613/566-4416; Toll Free: 1-800-263-5588
URL: http://www.canadacouncil.ca

**Coburn Fellowships**

Two $20,000 fellowships are awarded annually to a Canadian student (at Vicoria University of the University of Toronto) & an Israeli student, studying in the fields of fine arts or humanities, to study on a reciprocal basis; the winners are chosen by Victoria University

**John G. Diefenbaker Award**

Funded by the Government of Canada, this annual award honours the memory of former Prime Minister John G. Diefenbaker; it enables a German scholar to spend up to 12 months in Canada to pursue research in any of the disciplines in the social sciences & humanities; candidates must be nominated by university departments or research institutes in Canada. Value of full award is $75,000; in addition, the Social Sciences & Humanities Research Council of Canada provides a travel allowance of up to $20,000

## Canada Post Corporation

#N0610, 2701 Riverside Dr., Ottawa ON K1A 0B1
613/734-7610; Fax: 613/734-8814
URL: http://www.mailposte.ca

**Flight for Freedom Literacy Awards**

The five annual award categories recognize the contributions of businesses, literacy organizations, educators, & individuals to the cause of literacy in Canada: the Governor General's Flight for Freedom Literacy Award to a literacy organization, the Government of Canada Literacy Innovation Award, Corporate Canada Literacy Award to a business/industry, Literacy Education Award (one English, one French) to an educator & Individual Achievement Literacy Award (one English, one French) for participation in a community literacy program

## Canadian Mathematical Society / Société mathématique du Canada

#109, 577 King Edward St., PO Box 415, Stn A, Ottawa ON K1N 6N5
613/562-5702; Fax: 613/565-1539
Email: office@cms.math.ca;
URL: http://camel.math.ca

**Canadian Mathematical Olympiad**

Annual mathematics competition established to provide an opportunity for students to perform well on the Canadian Open Mathematics Challenge & to complete on a national basis. Fifteen cash prizes

## Canadian Sociology & Anthropology Association / Société canadienne de sociologie et d'anthropologie

1455, boul de Maisonneuve ouest, Montréal QC H3G 1M8
514/848-8780; Fax: 514/848-4539
Email: csaa@vax2.concordia.ca

**John Porter Award**

Recognizes the best sociology book published in Canada in the past three years

**Special Contribution Awards**

Given to recognize the work of eminent sociologists & anthropologists

## Canadian Teachers' Federation / Fédération canadienne des enseignantes et enseignants

110 Argyle Ave., Ottawa ON K2P 1B4
613/232-1505; Fax: 613/232-1886
Email: info@ctf-fce.ca; URL: http://www.ctf-fce.ca

**Hilroy Fellowship Program**

Twenty-eight awards given each year to encourage & reward active classroom teachers who have developed new ideas for the improvement of teaching practices; awarded through annual competition
Twenty provincial & one territorial award in the amount of $2,500 each; six national awards for Great Merit in the amount of $5,000 each & one national award for Outstanding Merit in the amount of $10,000

## CIDA Awards Program

Canadian Bureau for International Education
#1100, 220 Laurier Ave. West, Ottawa ON K1P 5Z9
613/237-4820; Fax: 613/237-1073
Email: ctaha@cbie; GBeaudoin@cbie; URL: http://www.cbie.ca

**Awards for Canadians**

A program funded by CIDA & managed by the Canadian Bureau for International Education; CIDA wishes to increase the number of Canadian professionals capable of working in the international arena by providing funding up to $15,000 for short-term, overseas work experiences
Must possess a university degree, college diploma or professional designation, have substantial work experience, two years of which have involved using specific skills necessary to undertake the proposed project. For information on fields of specialization & eligible countries, contact CIDA Communications Branch, 200 Promenade du Portage, Hull PQ K1A 0G4; 819/997-5006; Fax: 819/953-6088. Other information & applications should be sent to the CBIE at the above address

## The City of Toronto

Corp. Servs., Human Resources, 100 Queen St. West, 1st Fl., Toronto ON M5H 2N2
416/392-7855; Fax: 416/392-0006

**City of Toronto Scholarships**

Awarded each year on Civic Honours Day (on the anniversary of the incorporation of Toronto in March)

## The Commonwealth of Learning

#600, 1285 West Broadway, Vancouver BC V6H 3X8
604/775-8200; Telex: 04507508 COMLEARN;
Fax: 604/775-8210
Email: info@col.org; URL: http://www.col.org

**COL/ICDE Awards of Excellence**

Recognizes individual & institutional achievement in distance education

## Foundation for Educational Exchange Between Canada & the United States of America

#2015, 350 Albert St., Ottawa ON K1R 1A4
613/237-5366; Fax: 613/237-2029
Email: info@fulbright.ca; URL: http://www.usis-canada.usia.gov/fulbrigh.htm

**Canada-US Fulbright Program**

To expand research, teaching & study opportunities for Canadian & American faculty & students engaged in the study of Canada, the United States & the relationship between the two countries; based on academic excellence & the merit of the applicant's proposed project, awards given annually for study in a number of different fields including conservation, ecology, environmental management, resource analysis & environmental policy. Applicants must relocate from the U.S. to Canada, or Canada to the U.S.
$15,000 US for graduate students; $25,000 US for faculty

## Institute of Environmental Studies

#1016, 33 Wilcocks St., Toronto ON M5S 3E8
416/978-7077; Fax: 416/978-3884
Email: ies.gradinfo@utoronto.ca; URL: http://www/utoronto.ca/env/es.htm

**Canadian Environmental Directory Publisher's Award**

First awarded in 1996; annual award to a student in environmental studies

## The Japan Foundation, Toronto

#213, 131 Bloor St. West, Toronto ON M5S 1R1
416/966-1600; Fax: 416/966-9773
Email: jftor@interlog.com
Offers a broad range of programs designed to further cultural exchange with Japan, with an emphasis on Japanese studies at the post-secondary level & Japanese langugage study, including:

**The Japan Foundation Fellowships**

Scholars, researchers, artists & other professionals are provided an opportunity to conduct research or pursue projects in Japan. Term of award is from two to 14 months, depending on category; annual application deadline is Dec. 1 for funding year beginning the following April 1

## Ontario Council on Graduate Studies

#203, 444 Yonge St., Toronto ON M5B 2H4
416/979-2165; Fax: 416/979-8635

**John Charles Polanyi Prizes**

In honour of the achievement of John Charles Polanyi, co-recipient of the 1986 Nobel Prize in Chemistry, the Government of Ontario has established a fund to provide annually up to five prizes to persons continuing to post-doctoral studies at an Ontario university

## Photographic Historical Society of Canada

1712 Avenue Rd., PO Box 5420, Stn Avenue/Fairlawn, Toronto ON M5M 4N5
416/691-1555; Fax: 416/693-0018
Email: phsc@onramp.ca;
URL: http://web.onramp.ca/phsc

**Kodak Canada Award**

$500 presented annually for the best student paper on original research into any aspect of Canadian photographic history; $250 second prize also presented

**Publication Grant**

Up to $1,000 awarded to aid the publication, in book or monograph form, of original research into Canada's photographic history

## The Royal Society of Canada / La Société royale du Canada

#308, 225 Metcalfe St., Ottawa ON K2P 1P9
613/991-6990; Fax: 613/991-6996
Email: adminrsc@rsc.ca; URL: http://www.rsc.ca

**Innis-Gérin Medal**

Established 1966; awarded every two years for a distinguished & sustained contribution to the literature of the social sciences including human geography & social psychology

**NATO Fellowship Programme**

To promote study & research leading to publication on the common interests, traditions & outlook of the countries of the North Atlantic Alliance; for social science researchers

**Pierre Chauveau Medal**

Established 1951; awarded every two years (since 1966) for a distinguished contribution to knowledge in the humanities other than Canadian literature & Canadian history

**Sir Arthur Sims Scholarships**

Established 1952; aims to encourage Canadian students to undertake postgraduate work in Great Britain; one to be awarded for outstanding merit & promise in any subject of the humanities or social sciences; one to be awarded for outstanding merit & promise in any subject of the natural sciences

## SaskPower

PO Box 220, Beauval SK S0M 0G0
306/288-2258; Fax: 306/288-4667;
Toll Free: 1-800-864-3022
Email: northern.enterprise.fund@sk.sympatico.ca

**Northern Enterprise Fund Scholarship Program**

To promote entrepreneurial spirit in Northern Saskatchewan by providing scholarships to students enrolled in courses related to business or based on occupational shortages in the north
Five $2,500 university scholarships & five $2,500 institute scholarships are awarded to full-time students who are permanent residents of the SaskPower Northern

Enterprise Fund Administration District; priority will be given to applicants showing intention of returning to, or remaining in the north

### Social Sciences & Humanities Research Council of Canada

350 Albert St., 10th Fl., PO Box 1610, Ottawa ON K1P 6G4
613/992-0530; Fax: 613/992-1787
Email: z-info@sshrc; URL: http://www.sshrc.ca

**The Thérèse F.-Casgrain Fellowship**

$40,000 stipend awarded every second year (1998, 2000, etc.) to support research on women & social change in Canada

### Yukon Government

PO Box 2703, Whitehorse YT Y1A 2C6
867/667-5127; Fax: 867/667-6339

**Innovations in Education Awards**

Awarded to individuals or groups that have demonstrated innovation, superior dedication or outstanding service to education in the Yukon; winners may receive a $2,000 education bursary & a specially commissioned artwork

**ENGINEERING See SCIENTIFIC, ENGINEERING, TECHNICAL**

## ENVIRONMENTAL

### Alberta Emerald Foundation for Environmental Excellence

#600, 12220 Stony Plain Rd., Edmonton AB T5J 3L2
403/413-9629; Fax: 403/482-9100; Toll Free: 1-800-219-8329

**Emerald Awards**

Awarded to Albertans who have made a significant contribution to the protection or enhancement of the environment

Nominations are open to individual, not-for-profit organizations, business & industry, communities & government, educational institutions & volunteer organizations excelling in environmental achievements

### Alberta Environmental Protection

Natural Resources Service
9915 - 108 St., 10th Fl., Edmonton AB T5K 2C9
403/427-6749; Fax: 403/422-6068

**Order of the Big Horn**

Fish & wildlife conservation awards presented to individuals, organizations & corporations for their outstanding contributions to fish & wildlife conservation in Alberta – Program Manager, Vonn Bricker

### Atlantic Salmon Federation / Fédération du saumon atlantique

PO Box 429, St. Andrews NB E0G 2X0
506/529-4581; Fax: 506/529-4438
Email: asf@nbnet.nb.ca; URL: http://www.flyfishing.com/asf/

**Olin Fellowship**

$1,000-$3,000 fellowships offered annually to individuals seeking to improve their knowledge or skills in fields dealing with current problems in biology, management, or conservation of Atlantic salmon & its habitat; the fellowship may be applied toward a wide range of endeavours such as graduate work, sabbatical research, management experience, etc.; tenable at any accredited university or research laboratory, or in an active management program

**Roll of Honour**

Presented annually to individuals who exhibit outstanding commitment to salmon conservation at the grassroots level

### BC Ministry of Environment, Lands & Parks

Public Affairs & Communications Branch
810 Blanshard St., 1st Fl., Victoria BC V8V 1X4
250/387-9422; Fax: 250/356-6464

**Minister's Environmental Awards**

Awarded for identifying, reducing, solving or avoiding an environmental problem; demonstrating consistently responsible environmental management practices; promoting active concern for the enhancement & protection of the environment; or improving public awareness & understanding of an environmental problem or solution

Categories include individual citizen, youth group, non-profit organization, community or municipality, business or industry, environmental education, communications or media; by nomination. Selection of award winners is made by the Minister

### Canadian Industrial Innovation Centre

156 Columbia St. West, Waterloo ON N2L 3L3
519/885-5870; Fax: 519/885-5729; Toll Free: 1-800-265-4559
Email: info@innovationcentre.ca;
URL: http://www.innovationcentre.ca

**Excellence in Invention**

The contest awards $1,000 each to the top two inventors whose innovations will improve or assist in environmentally friendly activities. Its goal is to raise public awareness of the issues involved & the efforts Canadian innovators are making to provide global solutions

Each invention must be submitted to the Inventor's Assistance Program, Critical Factor Assessment Process & receive a positive rating; judging occurs in April

### Canadian Land Reclamation Association / Association canadienne de réhabilitation des sites dégradés

PO Box 61047, RPO Kensington, Calgary AB T2N 4S6
403/289-9435; Fax: 403/289-9435

**The Noranda Award**

Presented annually by the association on behalf of Noranda Mines Inc. in recognition of superior research or field work in reclamation; not restricted to members

### Canadian Nature Federation / Fédération canadienne de la nature

#606, One Nicholas St., Ottawa ON K1N 7B7
613/562-3447; Fax: 613/562-3371; Toll Free: 1-800-267-4088
Email: cnf@web.net; URL: http://www.web.net/~cnf

**Douglas H. Pimlott Award**

Given in recognition of outstanding lifetime achievement in wildlife conservation

### Canadian Wildlife Federation / Fédération canadienne de la faune

2740 Queensview Dr., Ottawa ON K2B 1A2
613/721-2286; Fax: 613/721-2902;
Toll Free: 1-800-563-9453

**Canadian Conservation Achievement Awards Program:**

**Canadian Outdoorsman of the Year Award**

Presented annually to an outdoorsperson who has demonstrated an active commitment to conservation in Canada

**Roderick Haig-Brown Memorial Award**

Awarded annually to an individual who has made a significant contribution to furthering the sport of angling &/or conservation & wise use of Canada's recreational fisheries resources

**Roland Michener Conservation Award**

A trophy is given annually in recognition of an individual's outstanding achievement in the field of conservation in Canada

### Conservation Council of Ontario / Le Conseil de conservation de l'Ontario

#506, 489 College St., Toronto ON M6G 1A5
416/969-9637; Fax: 416/960-8053
Email: cco@web.apc.org

**The Lieutenant Governor's Conservation Award**

Recognizes outstanding accomplishments in the conservation & protection of Ontario's natural environment; three categories of awards: individuals, non-profit/non-governmental organizations, & corporate/institutional or business associations

### Energy Probe Research Foundation

225 Brunswick Ave., Toronto ON M5S 2M6
416/964-9223; Fax: 416/964-8239; Toll Free: 1-800-263-2784
Email: EnergyProbe@nextcity.com;
URL: http://www.nextcity.com/EnergyProbe/

**The Margaret Laurence Fund**

Grants & scholarships are made to foster an understanding of peace & the environment upon which the fate of the planet rests

Recipients of the grants & scholarships are limited to students, authors, researchers, & publishers, working with the foundation in collaborative projects approved by the directors

### Environment Canada

Inquiry Centre
351 St. Joseph Blvd., Hull QC K1A 0H3
819/997-2800; Fax: 819/953-2225; Toll Free: 1-800-668-6767
Email: enviroinfo@ec.gc.ca; URL: http://www.dec.gc.ca

**Action 21 Network**

Established to create public awareness for positive environmental actions being taken by Canadians & to celebrate our environmental heroes; the objective is to demonstrate how people are contributing to a healthier environment & thereby encourage others to take similar actions right across the coutnry. Stories of individuals & groups whose actions are having a positive environmental impact should be submitted Feb. 1, May 1 & Oct. 1 to become members of the Action 21 Network – Deborah Spurr, Communications & Consultants, Action 21, 10 Wellington St., 27th Fl., Les Terrasses de la Chaudière, Hull, QC K1A 0H3, 819/953-9450

### The Financial Post

333 King St. East, Toronto ON M5A 4N2
416/350-6200; Fax: 416/350-6201

**Environment Awards for Business:**

**Business Partnership Award**

Awarded for environmental partnerships between business & community organizations that contribute to the reduction or elimination of pollution; sponsored by Syncrude Canada Ltd.

**Ecotourism Award**

Awarded to Canadian organizations in the tourism industry that have incorporated sustainable development & environmental concerns into their operations

**Education Award**

Awarded for an educational awareness program aimed at students or consumers to raise their awareness of the environment & environmental issues

**Environmental Management Award**

Awarded for the integration of ecological considerations into organizational decision-making

**Environmental Technology Award**

Awarded for the development of new Canadian technology either contributing to the reduction or elimination of pollution at its source or providing for cost effective remediation of environmental contamination

**Product Stewartship Award**

Awarded for organizations that have applied a product life cycle approach to the development of products or services in order to minimize the environmental impact resulting from the manufacture, use & disposal of products

### George Cedric Metcalf Charitable Foundation
105 Pears Ave., Toronto ON M5R 1S9
416/926-0366
**George Cedric Metcalf Charitable Foundation**
Support for charitable organizations concerned with social services, arts/culture, education, environment, wildlife, & international development; Projects may be in Canada or in developing countries through Canadian-based organizations
Canadian registered charities only
Range: $500 to $45,000; median grant: $5,000 – Coordinator, Josie Romita

### International Development Research Centre / Centre de recherches pour le développement international
250 Albert St., 10th Fl., PO Box 8500, Ottawa ON K1G 3H9
613/236-6163; Fax: 613/563-0815
Email: cta@idrc.ca; URL: http://www.idrc.ca
**IDRC Doctoral Research Awards (IDRA)**
$20,000 per year provided for Ph.D. research in the areas of sustainable & equitable development in the following themes: food security; equity in natural resource use; biodiversity conservation; sustainable employment' strategies & policies for healthy societies; information & communications
**John G. Bene Fellowship in Social Forestry**
$7,000 awarded to M.Sc. or Ph.D. students interested in social sciences combined with forestry or agroforestry from an international development perspective; must spend at least part of thesis research overseas

### Manitoba Heritage Federation Inc.
21 - 2nd Ave. NW, 2nd Fl., Dauphin MB R7N 1H1
204/638-9154; Fax: 204/638-0683
Email: mhf@mb.sympatico.ca; URL: http://www.mts.net/~mhf
**D.L. Campbell Award**
Recognizes outstanding achievement of an individual to support, enhance & promote heritage for all Manitobans
**Heritage Preservation Award**
Recognizes a project or work concerned with preserving Manitoba's heritage
**Outstanding Contribution to Manitoba's Heritage**
Awarded to one recipient from any of seven heritage disciplines who has made an outstanding contribution to Manitoba's heritage

### Manitoba Sustainable Development Coordination Unit
#305, 155 Carlton St., Winnipeg MB R3C 3H8
204/945-1124; Fax: 204/945-0090
**The Award of Excellence Program for Sustainable Development**
Awarded to Manitobans (groups or individuals) for undertaking projects which exemplify the fundamental principles & guidelines of sustainable development

### Newfoundland & Labrador Department of Environment & Labour
Public Relations Office
Confederation Bldg., PO Box 8700, St. John's NF A1B 4J6
709/729-2575
Email: TRYAN@env.gov.nf.ca;
URL: http://www.gov.nf.ca
**Environmental Awards Program**
Sponsored & managed by the Department & administered by the Newfoundland & Labrador Women's Institutes, the awards, which began in 1990, recognize people from all walks of life who have contributed in a meaningful way to the preservation, protection, & restoration of the environment; awrads are given in six categories: individual, citizen's group or organization, education, youth, business, & municipal – Newfoundland & Labrador Women's Institutes, Executive Director, Sylvia Manning, 709/753-8780

### OH & S Canada Magazine & Southam Information & Technology Group
c/o Occupational Health, Safety & Environment Group, 1450 Don Mills Rd., North York ON M3B 2X7
416/442-2035; Fax: 416/442-2200
**Awards of Excellence**
To recognize & honour outstanding contributions & innovations by Canadian occupational health & safety individuals or corporations; awards include: Lifetime Achievement Award, Professional of the Year Award, Most Promising Professional Award, Most Significant Individual Contribution Award, Training Award, Outstanding Contribution - Labour - Award, Best Occupational, Health & Safety Program - Company Award, Most Innovative Product or Service Award (Special Supplier Award)
Each winner receives $1,000 & an OSH trophy

### Recycling Council of Ontario / Conseil du recyclage de l'Ontario
#504, 489 College St., Toronto ON M6G 1A5
416/960-1025; Fax: 416/960-8053; Toll Free: 1-800-263-2849
Email: rco@web.net; URL: http://www.web.net/rco
**Ontario Waste Minimization Awards**
A series of awards for outstanding achievement in recycling: includes 3Rs initiatives in commercial, industrial & institutional settings; Outstanding Municipal, Non-profit Organization, Recycling Program Operator; Outstanding School Program, & Media Contribution Award

### The Royal Society of Canada / La Société royale du Canada
#308, 225 Metcalfe St., Ottawa ON K2P 1P9
613/991-6990; Fax: 613/991-6996
Email: adminrsc@rsc.ca; URL: http://www.rsc.ca
**Miroslaw Romanowski Medal**
Established in 1993; $2,000 & a medal awarded every year in recognition of noteworthy scientific contributions in the environmental sciences

### Wildlife Habitat Canada / Habitat faunique Canada
#200, 7 Hinton Ave. North, Ottawa ON K1Y 4P1
613/722-2090; Fax: 613/722-3318
Email: jladd@whc.org
**Graduate Scholarship Program**
$10,000 a year for a maximum of two years for a Master's degree & a maximum of $12,000 per year for three years for a Ph.D. for student research in the area of conservation of wildlife habitat

**FILM See BROADCASTING & FILM**

**GOVERNMENTAL See LEGAL, GOVERNMENTAL, PUBLIC ADMINISTRATION**

## HEALTH & MEDICAL

### Canada Safety Council / Conseil canadien de la sécurité
1020 Thomas Spratt Place, Ottawa ON K1G 5L5
613/739-1535; Fax: 613/739-1566
Email: csc@safety-council.org;
URL: http://www.safety-council.org
**Dr. Stuart Wiberg Memorial Safety Award**
Presented annually to an individual who has made an outstanding contribution to the field of public safety, primarily in a voluntary capacity
**Gold/Silver Seal Certificates**
Established by the Canadian Industrial Safety Association to stimulate interest in the prevention of occupational accidents & diseases & to recognize meritorious achievement in resolving safety issues; the award certificates are available on a non-competitive basis for in-plant recognition of a company's own injury-free record
**Occupational Safety & Health Achievement Award**
Provides visible recognition to individuals for outstanding contributions to the prevention of death, injury & disease in the Canadian workplace

### Canadian Association of Medical Radiation Technologists / Association canadienne des technologues en radiation médicale
#601, 294 Albert St., Ottawa ON K1P 6E6
613/234-0012; Fax: 613/234-1097
**CAMRT Awards**
Administers awards for students & registered technologists including; Dr. M. Mallett Student Award, Dr. Petrie Memorial Award, George Reason Memorial Cup, E.I. Hood Award, CAMRT Student Achievement Award, Philips Rose Bowl, PACS Technology Award

### Canadian Nurses Association / Association des infirmières et infirmiers du Canada
50 Driveway, Ottawa ON K2P 1E2
613/237-2133; Fax: 613/237-3520
Email: commdiv@cna-nurses.ca
**CNA Media Awards**
Annual awards for media reports that foster public understanding of the values & objectives of the Canadian health system & an award for excellence in international health reporting; awards open to print, radio & television

### Canadian Nurses Foundation / Fondation des infirmières et infirmiers du Canada
50 Driveway, Ottawa ON K2P 1E2
613/237-2133; Fax: 613/237-3520
**Ross Award for Nursing Leadership**
Recognizes an outstanding leader in the field of Canadian nursing, for a major contribution to nursing research or education in any of its aspects

### Canadian Society of Hospital Pharmacists / Société canadienne des pharmaciens d'hôpitaux
#350, 1145 Hunt Club Rd., Ottawa ON K1V 0Y3
613/736-9733; Fax: 613/736-5660
Email: bleslie@worldlink.ca; URL: http://www.cshp.ca/~cshp
**CSHP Awards Program**
The association offers 19 awards some of which are co-sponsored by various pharmaceutical companies

### Canadian Society of Laboratory Technologists / Société canadienne des technologistes de laboratoire
PO Box 2830, Stn A, Hamilton ON L8N 3N8
905/528-8642; Fax: 905/528-4968
URL: http://www.cslt.com
**CSLT Student Scholarship Program**
The association awards 5 scholarships of $500 each to the best students who are enrolled in general medical laboratory technology, cytotechnology, or cytogenetics studies

### Canadian Veterinary Medical Association / Association canadienne des médecins vétérinaires
339 Booth St., Ottawa ON K1R 7K1
613/236-1162; Fax: 613/236-9681
URL: http://www.upei.ca/~cvma/
**The CVMA Humane Award**
Established 1987 to encourage care & well-being of animals; awarded to an individual (veterinarian or non-veterinarian) whose work is judged to have contributed significantly to the welfare of animals; $1,000 & a plaque awarded

**The Schering Veterinary Award**

Established 1985 to enhance progress in large animal medicine & surgery; award made to a veterinarian whose work in large animal practice, clinical research or basic sciences is judged to have contributed significantly to the advancement of large animal medicine, surgery & theriogenology, including herd health management; $1,000 & a plaque awarded

**The Small Animal Practitioner Award**

Established 1987 to encourage progress in the field of small animal medicine & surgery; awarded to a veterinarian whose work in small animal practice, clinical research or basic sciences is judged to have contributed significantly to the advancement of small animal practice, including the advancement of the public's knowledge of the responsibilities of pet ownership; $1,000 & a plaque awarded

## Catholic Health Association of Canada / Association catholique canadienne de la santé

1247 Kilborn Pl., Ottawa ON K1H 6K9
613/731-7148; Fax: 613/731-7797
Email: chac@web.net; URL: http://www.net-globe.com/chac/

**Performance Citation Award**

Established 1981; awarded annually to an individual who makes an outstanding contribution to health care in a Christian context, who exhibits exemplary leadership of a national effort at building the Christian community & unselfish dedication to others

## College of Family Physicians of Canada / Collège des médecins de famille du Canada

2630 Skymark Ave., Mississauga ON L4W 5A4
905/629-0900; Fax: 905/629-0893
Email: info@cfpc.ca; URL: http://www.cfpc.ca

**D.I. Rice Merit Award**

$5,000, plus travel expenses awarded annually to a renowned leader in family medicine to allow travel for a period of approximately one month in order to engage in educational activities

**D.M. Robb Research Award**

$2,500 awarded annually to a community-based family physician to conduct research in family medicine

**Family Physician of the Year Award**

Sponsored by Janseen Ortho; awarded to physicians who have been in family practice for a minimum of 15 years & members of the college for at least 10 years, & who have made outstanding contributions to family medicine, to their communities & to the college
$1,000 plus travel costs & accommodation for the recipient & spouse to attend the assembly at which the award is presented

## Easter Seals/March of Dimes National Council / Conseil National des Timbres de Pâques et de la Parade des dix sous

#511, 90 Eglinton Ave. East, Toronto ON M4P 2Y3
416/932-8382; Fax: 416/932-9844

**The Easter Seals Canada Award**

**The Keith S. Armstrong Award**

Established 1976; plaque awarded to recognize & pay tribute to an individual employed in a non-government rehabilitation organization who, over a period of years, has provided exceptional service in the interests of physically handicapped persons

**The March of Dimes/Ability Fund Canada Award**

**The Sun Life Group Benefits Award**

**The Walter Dinsdale Award**

Established 1982; plaque awarded to an individual or organization for outstanding achievement in the area of technical aids for the benefit of disabled persons

**The Whipper Watson Award**

Awarded to an individual or business that has made significant progress in integrating people with disabilities into the workplace

## Epilepsy Canada / Epilepsie Canada

#745, 1470, rue Peel, Montréal QC H3A 1T1
514/845-7855; Fax: 514/845-7866; Toll Free: 1-800-860-5499
Email: epilepsy@epilepsy.ca; URL: http://www.epilepsy.ca

**Epilepsy Canada/Parke-Davis Canada Research Fellowship**

To develop expertise in clinical or basic epilepsy research & to enhance the quality of care for epilepsy patients in Canada; $35,000 awarded annually to a Ph.D. or M.D. for clinical research at a Canadian institution; designed as a training program & not intended for those holding faculty appointments

## Medical Research Council of Canada

Holland Cross, Tower B, 5th Fl., 1600 Holland St., Ottawa ON K1A 0W9
613/954-1812; Fax: 613/954-1800
Email: dsaintjean@hpb.hwx.xa; URL: http://www.hwc.ca:8100/

**Michael Smith Award for Excellence**

A medal plus $50,000 research grant awarded annually to an outstanding Canadian researcher who has demonstrated innovation, creativity & dedication to health research

## Planned Parenthood Federation of Canada / Fédération pour le planning des naissances du Canada

#430, One Nicholas St., Ottawa ON K1N 7B7
613/241-4474; Fax: 613/241-7550
Email: ppfed@web.net

**Norman Barwin Scholarship**

Established 1987; $2,500 awarded to a full-time graduate student in the field of reproductive health

## The Royal College of Physicians & Surgeons of Canada / Le Collège royal des médecins et chirurgiens du Canada

774 Echo Dr., Ottawa ON K1S 5N8
613/730-8177; Fax: 613/730-8833; Toll Free: 1-800-668-3740
Email: communications@rcpsc.edu; URL: http://rcpsc.medical.org

**Detweiler Travelling Fellowships**

$1,750 per month up to $21,000 to enable five Fellows to visit medical centres in Canada or abroad to study or gain experience in the use of application of new knowledge or techniques in surgical practice

**International Travelling Fellowship**

$1,750 per month, up to $21,000 to enable Fellows outside of Canada to study in a medical centre in Canada; or to enable Fellows residing in Canada to practice & teach in a lesser developed country

**Medical Education Travelling Fellowship**

$1,750 per month up to $21,000 for the recipient to acquire knowledge & expertise in the field of medical education

**RCPSC-MRC-Sandoz Clinical Research Fellowship**

$45,000 per year for two years to enable young physicians to acquire skill in the research field, including clinical investigation for further application as a career clinical scientist; preference given to those who train in Canada & intend to remain in this country

**Royal College Fellowship in Studies in Medical Education**

$45,000 per year of study to a maximum of three years to help increase the number & quality of professionally trained medical educators in Canada by providing training in the science of medical education

**The Royal College of Physicians & Surgeons of Canada Medals**

Established 1946; $5,000 & a bronze medal awarded annually for original scientific work judged best in the Division of Medicine, & the Division of Surgery; the purpose of the awards is to provide national recognition to original work by young clinicians & investigators

**Walter C. MacKenzie, Johnson & Johnson Fellowship**

$1,750 per month up to $21,000 to allow Fellow to vist one or more centres to acquire surgical research or clinical surgical expertise

## The Royal Society of Canada / La Société royale du Canada

#308, 225 Metcalfe St., Ottawa ON K2P 1P9
613/991-6990; Fax: 613/991-6996
Email: adminrsc@rsc.ca; URL: http://www.rsc.ca

**Jason A. Hannah Medal**

Established 1976; $1,500 & a bronze medal awarded annually for an important publication in the history of medicine

**The McLaughlin Medal**

$1,500 & a medal awarded annually for important research of sustained excellence in any branch of medical science

**HERITAGE See CULTURE**

**HISTORY See CULTURE**

**HORTICULTURE See AGRICULTURE & FARMING**

# JOURNALISM

## Atlantic Journalism Awards

University of Kings College, Halifax NS B3H 2A1
902/422-1271, ext. 158
Email: skimber@is.doc.ca; URL: http://www.uking@ns.ca/aja.aja.html

**Journalism Awards**

A program of the University of King's College School of Journalism established in 1981 to recognize excellence & achievement in work by Atlantic Canadian journalists; covers work in English or French; 8 award categories featuring work published or broadcast in the news media of Atlantic Canada
Winners in individual categories will receive an awards certificate & $300

## Canadian Association of Journalists / L'Association canadienne des journalistes

St. Patrick's Building, Carleton University, 1125 Colonel By Dr., Ottawa ON K1S 5B6
613/526-8061; Fax: 613/521-3904
Email: cf408@freenet.carleton.ca; URL: http://www.eagle.ca/caj/

**The CAJ Awards**

$1,000 awards presented for the top investigative report published or broadcast in the following media: Newspaper (open category), Newspaper (circulation under 25,000), Magazine, Network, Regional TV, Network Radio, Regional Radio

## Canadian Business Press

#201, 40 Shields Crt., Unionville ON L3R 0M5
905/946-8889

**Kenneth Wilson Awards**

Recognize excellence in writing & graphic design in specialized business/professional publications; open to all business publications, regardless of CBP membership, that are published in English &/or French; all awards, except the Harvey Southam Editorial Career Award, require an entry fee

## Canadian Community Newspapers Association

#206, 90 Eglinton Ave. East, Toronto ON M4P 2Y3
416/482-1090; Fax: 416/482-1908
Email: ccna@sentex.net; URL: http://www.sentex.net/~ccna

**General Excellence Awards**

Awards are presented to newspapers for general excellence by circulation category, & include presentations to the Best All-Round Newspaper, Best Front Page, & Best Editorial Page

**Premier Awards**

Awards are presented in the following categories: Outstanding Columnist, Local Cartoon, Editorial Writing, Community Service, Agricultural Edition, House Ad, Reporter Initiative, News Story, Environmental Writing, National Newspaper Week coverage

**Special Competition Awards**

Awards are given in following areas: Best Spot News Photo, Best Feature Photo, Best Sports Photo, Best Christmas Edition, Best Sports Page, Best Special Section, Best Historical Story, Best Newspaper Promotion, Best Feature Story, Best Photo Essay, Most Creative Ad, Car Care Pages, Car Care Section, Best Feature Series

## Canadian Newspaper Association / Association canadienne des journaux

#200, 890 Yonge St., Toronto ON M4W 3P4
416/923-3567; Fax: 416/923-7206
Email: bcantley@cna-acj.ca; URL: http://www.cna-acj.ca/

**National Newspaper Awards/Concours canadien de journalisme**

Awards are presented annually in early spring in 15 categories: Spot News Reporting, Enterprise Reporting, Special Project, Layout & Design, Critical Writing, Sports Writing, Feature Writing, Cartooning, Columns, Business Reporting, International Reporting, Spot News Photography, Feature Photography, Sports Photography, Editorial Writing

Eligible are those employed by or freelance for daily newspapers or wire services in French or English; awards are governed by an independent board of governors consisting of newspaper & pubilc representatives

Winners receive $2,500 plus certificates; two runners-up in each category receive citations of merit & $250

## Canadian Scene News Services for the Ethnic Media

#301, 73 Simcoe St., Toronto ON M5J 1W9
416/593-0439; Fax: 416/593-0448

**Canadian Scene Awards**

Established 1991 to mark the 40th anniversary of the multilingual news service; one plaque is given to an individual for an article &/or a radio/television program best promoting intercultural understanding

## Canadian Science Writers' Association / Association canadienne des rédacteurs scientifiques

PO Box 75, Stn A, Toronto ON M5W 1A2
416/928-9624; Fax: 416/960-0528
Email: cswa@interlog.com; URL: http://www.interlog.com/~cswa

**Canadian Forest Service-Ontario Journalism Award**

Open to print journalists who have published an article concerning some aspect of forestry in Ontario during the previous calendar year

**Greg Clark Outdoor Writing Award**

Open to Canadian print entries for work appearing in an Ontario publication during the previous year & related to natural resources in Ontario

## Canadian Society of Magazine Editors

c/o Canadian Living, #100, 25 Sheppard Ave. West, North York ON M2N 6S7
416/596-5177

**The Editors Choice Awards**

Awards are presented in three categories: fewer than 50,000 circulation; 50,000-250,000 circulation; more than 250,000 circulation

## International Development Research Centre / Centre de recherches pour le développement international

250 Albert St., 10th Fl., PO Box 8500, Ottawa ON K1G 3H9
613/236-6163; Fax: 613/563-0815
Email: cta@idrc.ca; URL: http://www.idrc.ca

**Fellowship in Journalism with L'Agence Périscoop Multimédia**

$30,000 fellowship awarded

**Internship with Gemini News Service**

$30,000 provided for an internship with Gemini News Service

## National Magazine Awards Foundation / Fondation nationale des prix du magazine canadien

#207, 109 Vanderhoof Ave., Toronto ON M4G 2H7
416/422-1358; Fax: 416/422-3762

**National Magazine Awards**

Awards are presented annually in 26 categories including Personal Journalism, Arts & Entertainment, Humour, Business, Science, Health & Medicine, Sports & Recreation, Fiction, Poetry, Travel, Magazine Illustration, Photojournalism, Art Direction, Magazine Covers, & Photography; all above awards go to individual magazine writers, photographers, illustrators, or art directors; Magazine of the Year recognizes continual overall excellence, The President's Medal is awarded to an article from the text categories & offers a prize of $3,000; The Foundation Award for Outstanding Achievement was introduced in 1990 & recognizes an individual's innovation & creativity through career-long contributions to the magazine industry

Awards are gold or silver scrolls with $1,500 & $500 cash prizes respectively

## La Société Saint-Jean-Baptiste de Montréal

82, rue Sherbrooke ouest, Montréal QC H2X 1X3
514/843-8851; Fax: 514/844-6369

**Prix Olivar-Asselin**

Established 1955; $1,500 & a medal awarded annually to a French Canadian in recognition of outstanding achievement in journalism in serving the higher interests of the French Canadian people

## Toronto Press Club

PO Box 263, Stn Commerce Court South, Toronto ON M5L 1E8
416/363-0651; Fax: 416/363-9717

**Canadian News Hall of Fame**

Toronto Press Club is custodian of the Hall of Fame dedicated to those people who have contributed regularly to journalism as staffers

**National Newspaper Awards**

Established 1949; awarded annually to print men & women employed regularly on the staffs of Canadian daily newspapers

**Norman DePoe Memorial Scholastic Fund**

A bursary awards program to students in the media

## Western Canadian Magazine Awards Foundation

PO Box 2131, Stn Main P.O., Vancouver BC V6B 3P8
604/984-7525

**The Western Magazine Awards**

Twenty-six categories of awards for editorial excellence in Western Canadian magazine writing, photography, illustration & art direction

## Western Ontario Newspaper Awards

225 Fairway Rd., PO Box R1200, Kitchener ON N2G 4E5
519/894-2231, ext.602

**Ford Motor Company of Canada Limited Trophies**

Family Section Feature Writing Trophy; Ford Spot News Photography Trophy; Ford Feature Photography Trophy; Ford Trophy for Writing Excellence

**Southam Newspapers Trophies**

Southam Business Writing Trophy; Southam Spot News Trophy; Sandy Baird Humourous Writing Trophy; K.J. Strachan Editorial Writing Trophy, & Southam Sports Photography Trophy

**Special Awards & Trophies**

C.B. Schmidt Award; John E. Motz Memorial Trophy; Joan May Memorial Trophy; Richard Sutton Memorial Trophy; Winnifred M. Stokes Hill Memorial Trophy; Gene Florcyk Memorial Award; Edward J. Hayes Award; Windsor Star Trophy; Walter J. Blackburn Award; Sault Star Award; Larry N. Smith Award; Norma R. Bidwell Award; Robert J. Hanley Award; Press Institute of Canada Award; Jack Bowman Memorial Award; The Del Bell Trophy; Carl Morgan Award, & the Martha G. Blackburn Award

**LANGUAGES See CULTURE**

# LEGAL, GOVERNMENTAL, PUBLIC ADMINISTRATION

## Alberta Human Rights & Citizenship Commission

Standard Life, #1600, 10405 Jasper Ave., Edmonton AB T5J 4R7
403/427-7661

**Alberta Human Rights Award**

A citation & a specially commissioned glass trophy awarded to the individual who made a significant contribution to the promotion of human rights in Alberta

## Alberta Justice

Public Security Division
10365 - 97 St., 10th Fl., Edmonton AB T5J 3W7
403/427-3457; Fax: 403/427-5916

**Crime Prevention Awards**

Awards recognize the contributions of individuals, businesses, & special interest groups towards establishing & maintaining safer communities; awards are presented in three categories: individuals, businesses, & community programs/organizations; nominees must play a role in establishing, coordinating or maintaining a specific crime prevention practice in their community – Gloria Ohrt, Manager, Family Violence & Crime Prevention

## Crime Prevention Ontario

23 Cedar St. North, Timmins ON P4N 6H8
705/264-4276; Toll Free: 1-800-668-0261

**Crime Prevention Ontario Community Awards**

Established 1984; awards recognize outstanding contributions made by community organizations, volunteers, police services & individual police officers, in the prevention of crime in Ontario; participation is open to all residents of Ontario, to organizations operating in Ontario, & to Ontario police services

Certificates are presented at regional ceremonies held throughout the province from Ontario Crime Prevention Week in November to mid-March the following year

**Crime Prevention Ontario Provincial Awards**

Awarded to the best of the Crime Prevention Ontario Community Award winners; plaques presented by the Solicitor General at the Annual Crime Prevention Ontario Symposium in April each year

## Government Finance Officers Association of the US & Canada

#800, 180 North Michigan Ave., Chicago IL 60601
312/977-9700; Fax: 312/977-4806

**The Canadian Award for Financial Reporting**

Established in 1990; goal of the program is to encourage municipal governments throughout Canada to publish high-quality financial reports & to provide peer recognition & technical guidance for officials preparing these reports; awards are valid for one year & may be granted in successive years to qualified governments; submissions & judging are conducted in either English or French

**The Distinguished Budget Presentation Award**

Established 1984; recognizes excellence in governmental budgeting by state, provincial & local governments in the US & Canada; awards are valid for one year & may be granted successively to qualified organizations

### Institute of Public Administration of Canada / Institut d'administration publique du Canada

#401, 1075 Bay St., Toronto ON M5S 2B1
416/924-8787; Fax: 416/924-4992
Email: ntl@ipaciapc.ca; URL: http://www.ipaciapc.ca

**IPAC/IBM Award for Innovative Management**

Awarded in recognition of outstanding organizational achievement in the public sector

**Vanier Medal**

A gold medal is awarded annually as a mark of distinction & exceptional achievement to a person who has shown outstanding leadership in public administration in Canada

### Justice Canada

Programs Directorate, Justice Bldg., Ottawa ON K1A 0H8
613/957-4344

**Civil Law/Common Law Exchange Program**

To give civil & common law students from across Canada the opportunity to learn about & compare Canada's two legal systems; the program also promotes bilingualism within educational & cultural activities
Open to individuals enrolled in a three-year law program in a Canadian university; preference is given to students in their second & third year of law studies
A scholarship of $1,500 is awarded to participants who successfully complete both sessions of the program; all travel & living expenses associated with the program are paid & each student receives an incidental expense allowance

**Legal Studies for Aboriginal People Program**

A grants & scholarship program to encourage Metis & Non-Status Indians to enter the legal profession by providing financial assistance through a pre-law orientation course & a three-year scholarship program
Open to Aboriginal People (Metis & Non-Status Indians)

### Professional Institute of The Public Service of Canada / Institut professionnel de la fonction publique du Canada

53 Auriga Dr., Nepean ON K2E 8C3
613/228-6310; Fax: 613/228-9048; Toll Free: 1-800-267-0446

**Professional Institute Gold Medals**

Established 1937; two gold medals are presented biennially. Those eligible are scientific, professional, or technical workers or groups of workers employed by the federal, provincial, or municipal government services of Canada who have made a contribution of outstanding importance to national or world well-being in either pure or applied science or in some field outside pure or applied science

### Society of Composers, Authors & Music Publishers of Canada / Société canadienne des auteurs, compositeurs et éditeurs de musique

41 Valleybrook Dr., North York ON M3B 2S6
416/445-8700; Fax: 416/445-7108; Toll Free: 1-800-557-6226
Email: socan@socan.ca; URL: http://www.socan.ca

**Gordon F. Henderson/SOCAN Copyright Competition**

$2,000 presented annually to a law student or articling lawyer for an essay on the subject of copyright & music

## LITERARY ARTS, BOOKS & LIBRARIES

### Association des écrivains de langue française

14, rue Broussais, F75014 Paris
01/43-219599; Fax: 01/43-201222

**Prix France-Québec/Jean-Hamelin**

Fondé en 1965 par l'A.D.E.L.F. avec la Délégation générale du Québec à Paris, ce prix est attribué annuellement à un écrivain québécois d'expression française pour un ouvrage publié depuis le 1er janvier de l'année précédente et avant le 15 juin de l'année d'attribution (date limite de rigueur pour le dépot des candidatures, en dix exemplaires). Le montant du prix est de Frs.5.000.- offert par le Gouvernement du Québec; les frais de voyage et de séjour (pour venir à Paris recevoir le prix) sont pris en charge par le Gouvernement français

### Association pour l'avancement des sciences et des techniques de la documentation

#202, 3414, av du Parc, Montréal QC H2X 2H5
514/281-5012; Fax: 514/281-8219
Email: info@asted.org; URL: http://www.asted.org

**Prix Marie-Claire-Daveluy**

Established 1970; awarded annually to encourage young authors to write for young people & to promote the production of Canadian writing for young people
Open to any French-speaking person between the ages of 15 & 20; must be a resident of Canada; prize of $500 for 15-17 years, & $500 for 18-20 years

### B.C. BookWorld

3516 - 13th Ave., Vancouver BC V6R 2S3
604/736-4011; Fax: 604/736-4011
Email: bcbookworld@msn.com

**VanCity Book Prize**

$4,000 awarded to the best B.C. book pertaining to women's issues (fiction or non-fiction); sponsored by VanCity, Vancouver Public Library, B.C. Ministry of Women's Equality & B.C. BookWorld

### Book Publishers Association of Alberta

#123, 10523 - 100 Ave., Edmonton AB T5J 0A8
403/424-5060; Fax: 403/424-7943
Email: bpaa@planet.eon.net

**The Alberta Book Industry Awards**

To recognize outstanding achievements in Alberta publishing; five awards are given - Alberta Publisher of the Year, Alberta Book of the Year, Alberta Book Design Award, Alberta Book Promotion Award, Alberta Educational Book of the Year
Stone carvings by Brian Clark are presented & kept by the winner in the award year & exchanged for plaques the following year

### Books in Canada

30A Hazelton Ave., Toronto ON M5R 2E2
416/924-2777
Email: binc@istar.ca

**Chapters/Books in Canada First Novel Award**

Established 1976 by *Books in Canada* magazine; co-sponsored by Chapters to promote & encourage Canadian writing
Winner receives $5,000 & his/her books are made available in Chapters bookstores across Canada

### British Columbia Historical Federation

PO Box 5254, Stn B, Victoria BC V8R 6N4
250/825-4743
Email: welwood@selkirk.bc.ca

**Writing Awards**

Established 1983; Lieutenant-Governor's Medal for Historical Writing, three Certificates of Merit, & cash awards given annually to authors of best books on any facet of BC history

### The Canada Council for the Arts / Conseil des Arts du Canada

350 Albert St., PO Box 1047, Ottawa ON K1P 5V8
613/566-4414, ext.4116; Fax: 613/566-4416; Toll Free: 1-800-263-5588
URL: http://www.canadacouncil.ca

**Canada-Japan Book Award**

$10,000 awarded annually for a book in English or French about Japan by a Canadian author, or for a book by a Japanese author translated by a Canadian into English or French; the translated work or the work by the Canadian author must have been published during the year preceding the award. Publishers of eligible books may nominate books for this award

**The Governor General's Literary Awards**

$10,000 each awarded annually to the best English-language & best French-language work in each of the following categories: children's literature (text & illustration), drama, fiction, poetry, literary non-fiction, & translation
Books must be by Canadian authors, illustrators & translators, published in Canada or abroad during the previous year; in the case of translation, the original work must also be a Canadian-authored title; juries select the winning titles from the books submitted by the publishers; a formal application from the publisher is required

### Canadian Association of Children's Librarians

c/o Canadian Library Association, #602, 200 Elgin St., Ottawa ON K2P 1L5
613/232-9625; Fax: 613/563-9895
Email: ai077@freenet.carleton.ca

**Amelia Frances Howard-Gibbon Illustrators Medal**

Established 1971; a silver medal awarded annually for outstanding illustrations in a children's book published in Canada; the illustrator must be a Canadian or a Canadian resident

**Book of the Year for Children Medal**

A silver medal awarded annually for the outstanding children's book published during the calendar year; book must have been written by a Canadian or a resident of Canada

### Canadian Association of College & University Libraries

c/o Canadian Library Association, #602, 200 Elgin St., Ottawa ON K2P 1L5
613/232-9625; Fax: 613/563-9895
URL: http://www.cla.amlibs.ca

**Innovation Achievement Award**

To recognize academic libraries which, through innovation in ongoing programs/services or in a special event/project, have contributed to academic librarianship & library development; a framed acknowledgement & a $1,500 gift certificate is offered for the vendor of the institution's choice

**Outstanding Academic Librarian Award**

Awarded to a librarian who has made a notable contribution to the field of academic librarianship

### Canadian Association of Public Libraries

c/o Beth Houius, Hamilton Public Library, 55 York Blvd., PO Box 2700, Stn LCD 1, Hamilton ON L8N 4E4
905/546-3285; Fax: 905/546-3282
Email: bhouius@hpl.hamilton.on.ca; URL: http://www.cla.amlibs.ca

**Outstanding Public Library Service Award**

Awarded annually for outstanding service in the field of public librarianship

### Canadian Authors Association

27 Doxsee Ave. North, PO Box 419, Campbellford ON K0L 1L0
705/653-0323; Fax: 705/653-0593
Email: canauth@redden.on.ca; URL: http://www.CanAuthors.org/national.html

**Canadian Authors Association/Air Canada Award**

To encourage younger (30 years old or under) Canadian writers of promise; Air Canada offers the winner two return tickets anywhere within its system

Work may be published in any form; nominations are made by CAA branches & other writers organizations

**The Vicky Metcalf Awards**

Awarded annually for works of interest to Canadian youth; given to stimulate writing for children; presented annually at CAA conference

Cash prize of $10,000 (fiction, nonfiction, or picture book); $3,000 (short story for children published in magazine, periodical or anthology published in the calendar year); $1,000 (editor of a winning story if published in a Canadian book or periodical)

## Canadian Booksellers Association

301 Donlands Ave., Toronto ON M4J 3R8
416/467-7883; Fax: 416/467-7886
Email: enquiries@cbabook.org; URL: http://www.cbabook.org

**Barry Britnell Award**

Presented annually to the bookseller of the year

**Best Author of the Year**

Presented annually to an author who has produced a substantial body of work & has made a significant contribution to the Canadian book industry

**Publisher of the Year**

Recognizes overall achievement with special reference to elements of particular concern to the bookselling community

## The Canadian Children's Book Centre

35 Spadina Rd., Toronto ON M5R 2S9
416/975-0010; Fax: 416/975-1839
Email: ccbc@lglobal.com; URL: http://www.lglobal.com/~ccbc/

**The Geoffrey Bilson Award for Historical Fiction**

Rewards excellence in outstanding work of historical fiction for young people by a Canadian author, published in previous calendar year; judges are: a writer, bookseller, children's books specialist, historian, librarian; award is in the amount of $1,000

## Canadian Historical Association / Société historique du Canada

395 Wellington St., Ottawa ON K1A 0N3
613/233-7885; Fax: 613/567-3110
Email: jmineault@archives.ca

**François-Xavier Garneau Medal**

The Senior CHA Prize; $2,000 awarded every five years to a book which represents an outstanding Canadian contribution to history

**Sir John A. Macdonald Prize**

Established 1976; $1,000 awarded annually for the nonfiction work of Canadian history "judged to have made the most significant contribution to an understanding of the Canadian past"

## Canadian Library Association

#602, 200 Elgin St., Ottawa ON K2P 1L5
613/232-9625; Fax: 613/563-9895
Email: ai077@freenet.carleton.ca; URL: http://www.cla.amlibs.ca

**Dafoe Scholarship**

$1,750 awarded annually to a student entering an accredited Canadian library school

**H.W. Wilson Scholarship**

$2,000 presented annually to a student entering an accredited Canadian library school

**Howard V. Phalin - World Book Scholarship in Library Science**

$2,500 scholarship given annually to be used for a program of study or series of courses either leading to a further library degree or related library work in which the candidate is currently engaged

**Young Adult Canadian Book Award**

Presented to recognize the best English-language fiction for young adults by a Canadian author

## Canadian Library Trustees Association

c/o Canadian Library Association, #602, 200 Elgin St., Ottawa ON K2P 1L5
613/232-9625; Fax: 613/563-9895

**Achievement in Literacy Award**

Through this award, CLTA endorses the initiatives of the public library systems which have structured literacy programs as a component of library services to the community

## Canadian School Library Association

c/o Canadian Library Association, #602, 200 Elgin St., Ottawa ON K2P 1L5
613/232-9625; Fax: 613/563-9895

**Margaret B. Scott Award of Merit**

Awarded annually to recognize outstanding achievement in school librarianship in Canada

**National Book Service Teacher-Librarian of the Year Award**

To honour a school-based teacher-librarian who has made an outstanding contribution to school librarianship by planning & implementing an exemplary school library program based on a collaborative model; award is sponsored by National Book Service

## Canadian Science Writers' Association / Association canadienne des rédacteurs scientifiques

PO Box 75, Stn A, Toronto ON M5W 1A2
416/928-9624; Fax: 416/960-0528
Email: cswa@interlog.com; URL: http://www.interlog.com/~cswa

**Science in Society Journalism Awards**

Open to Canadian journalists in all media for work appearing in the previous calendar year; categories include newspapers, magazines, trade publications, radio, television, children's books & general books; awards total $12,000

## Carousel Magazine

UC Room 274, University of Guelph, Guelph ON N1G 2W1
519/824-4120, ext.6748; Fax: 519/673-9603
Email: daniel@uoguelph.ca

**Carousel Writing Contest**

First awarded in 1996, $400 prize for fiction & $400 prize for poetry

## Christie Brown & Co.

2150 Lakeshore Blvd. West, Toronto ON M8V 1A3
416/503-6000; Fax: 416/503-6010

**Mr. Christie's Book Award**

Prizes total $45,000 & are awarded to the best children's book (one English & one French) in three age categories: ages four to eight; nine to 11, & 12 & over; the author &/or illustrator must be Canadian, & the books must be written/illustrated for children

## The City of Toronto

Corp. Servs., Human Resources, 100 Queen St. West, 1st Fl., Toronto ON M5H 2N2
416/392-7855; Fax: 416/392-0006

**Book Awards**

In 1973, City Council established a Book Award Selection Committee to select an annual winner or winners of a literary prize; committee selects a short list of nominees whose books are about Toronto & published in the preceding year

## Coopers & Lybrand

145 King St. West, Toronto ON M5H 1V8
416/869-1130; Fax: 416/941-8345
URL: http://www.ca.coopers.com

**National Business Book Award**

Established 1985; annual prize of $10,000 awarded to author of book containing key material on business in Canada

## Corporation des bibliothécaires professionnels du Québec / Corporation of Professional Librarians of Québec

#320, 307, rue Ste-Catherine ouest, Montréal QC H2X 2A3
514/845-3327; Fax: 514/845-1618
Email: info@cbpq.qc.ca; URL: http://www.cbpq.qc.ca

**Merite annuel de la CBPQ - Bibliothécaire professionnel(le)**

Stimuler et reconnaître l'excellence parmi les membres; attirer l'attention des médias sur les récipiendaires de cette distinction honorifique et sur la nature des réalisations primées; orienter des perceptions; le prix comporte les volets suivants: distinction honorifique, remise d'une épinglette en or, publicité entourant l'événement

## Corporation du Grand Prix de la science-fiction et du fantastique québécois

3194, terrasse Sagard, Longueuil QC J4L 3J9
514/674-0869

**Grand Prix de la science-fiction et du fantastique québécois**

Institué en 1984, une bourse de 2 000 $ est remise au lauréat

## The Crime Writers of Canada

3007 Kingston Rd., PO Box 113, Scarborough ON M1M 1P1
416/782-3116; Fax: 416/789-4680
Email: ap113@torfree.net; URL: http://www.swifty.com/cwc/cwchome.htm

**The Arthur Ellis Awards**

Established 1984; awarded annually in the following categories: best crime novel (by a previously published novelist), best crime non-fiction, best first crime novel (by a previously unpublished novelist), best crime short story, best crime juvenile novel, & best play with a criminous theme

**The Derrick Murdoch Award**

Established 1984; presented to an individual or organization which has made a significant & lasting contribution to the craft of crime writing in Canada

## Le Fondation Émile-Nelligan

261, rue Bloomfiled, Outremont QC H2V 3R6
514/522-0652

**Prix Gilles-Corbeil**

Ce prix (100 000 $) décerné pour la première fois en 1990, est triennal; le candidat doit être l'auteur d'une oeuvre écrite en français et citoyen du Canada ou des États-Unis

## Fondation Les Forges

3231, rue Notre-Dame ouest, CP 232, Pointe-du-Lac QC G0X 1Z0
819/379-9813; Fax: 819/376-0774

**Grand Prix de poésie de la Fondation Les Forges**

Le Fesitval international de la poésie remet une bourse de 5 000 $ au lauréat lors de l'ouverture officielle du festival; le candidat doit: être de citoyenneté canadienne et avoir déjà publié trois ouvrages de poésie chez un éditeur reconnu

**Prix Piché de poésie - Le Sortilège**

Les bourse sont offertes par la Société des alcools du Québec; ler prix, 2 000 $, 2e prix, 500 $; le candidat doit être de citoyenneté canadienne et n'avoir jamais publié d'ouvrage de poésie chez un éditeur reconnu

## The Giller Prize

c/o Kelly Duffin, 21 Steepleview Cres., Richmond Hill ON L4C 9R1
905/508-5146; Fax: 905/508-4469

**The Giller Prize**

$25,000 award to the author of the best Canadian novel or collection of short stories published in English

## International Board on Books for Young People - Canadian Section / Union internationale pour les livres de jeunesse

c/o Canadian Children's Book Centre, 35 Spadina Rd., Toronto ON M5R 2S9
416/393-7653; Fax: 416/975-1839

**Claude Aubry Award**
$1,000 awarded biennially for distinguished contributions to Canadian children's literature by a librarian, teacher, author, illustrator, publisher, bookseller, or editor

**Elizabeth Mrazik-Cleaver Picture Book Award**
$1,000 awarded for distinguished Canadian picture book illustration; submissions to Children's Literature Service, National Library of Canada, 395 Wellington St., Ottawa, ON K1A 0N4

**Frances E. Russell Award**
Awarded to initiate & encourage research in children's literature in Canada; award is in the amount of $1,000

## The League of Canadian Poets

54 Wolseley St., 3rd Fl., Toronto ON M5T 1A5
416/504-1657; Fax: 416/703-0059
Email: league@ican.net; URL: http://www.swifty.com/lc/

**Canadian Chapbook Manuscript Competition**
$12 per entry, no limit on the number of manuscripts submitted; 15-24 pages of poems; first prize $1,000 plus a published chapbook, 50 copies, second prize $750, third prize $500

**Gerald Lampert Memorial Award**
Established 1979; $1,000 awarded annually for excellence in a first book of poetry, written by a Canadian citizen or landed immigrant, & published in the preceding year

**National Poetry Contest Prizes**
$6 per entry; there is no limit on the number of poems a person may submit; poems should be previously unpublished & under 75 lines in length
First Prize: $1,000; Second: $750; Third: $500; the three winners, plus 47 finalists, are also published in the contest anthology

**Pat Lowther Memorial Award**
$1,000 awarded annually for excellence in a book of poetry, written by a Canadian female citizen or landed immigrant, & published in the preceding year

## The Lionel Gelber Prize

c/o Prize Manager, Lionel Gelber Prize, 112 Braemore Gdns., Toronto ON M6G 2C8
416/652-1947; Fax: 416/656-3722
Email: oomfpub@pathcom.com

**The Lionel Gelber Prize**
This $50,000 prize is the largest of its kind in the world; a legacy of Lionel Gelber, internationalist writer who died in 1989 & who was much acclaimed for his service to Canada; the prize is "designed to stimulate authors of any nationality who write about international relations, & to encourage the audience for these books to grow"
Books published in English or French translation, must be copyrighted in the year in which the prize is awarded; books must be published or distributed in Canada; submissions by publishers only

## Literary Translators' Association of Canada / Association des traducteurs et traductrices littéraires du Canada

3492, av Laval, Montréal QC H2X 3C8
514/849-8540
Email: alterego@rocler.qc.ca

**Glassco Translation Prize**
$500 & one year's membership in the association awarded annually for a translator's first work in book-length literary translation into French or English, published in Canada during the previous calendar year

## Manitoba Writers' Guild

#206, 100 Arthur St., Winnipeg MB R3B 1H3
204/942-6134; Fax: 204/942-5754
Email: mbwriter@escape.ca; URL: http://www.mbwriter.mb.ca

**Heaven Chapbook Prize**
$250 awarded biennially for the best literary chapbook by a Manitoba writer

**John Hirsch Award for Most Promising Manitoba Writer**
$2,500 awarded annually to the most promising Manitoba writer working in poetry, fiction, creative non-fiction or drama

**Le Prix littéraire des caisses populaires**
Biennial award of $1,000 presented to the author whose published book or play is judged to be the best French language work by a Manitoba author

**Manitoba Book Design of the Year Awards**
For the best overall design in Manitoba book publishing in two categories: adult & childrens

**McNally Robinson Award for Manitoba Book of the Year**
$2,500 to the Manitoba author judged to have written the best book in the calendar year

**McNally Robinson Book for Young People Award**
$1,000 awarded annually to the writer whose young person's book is judged the best written by a Manitoba author

## McClelland & Stewart

#900, 481 University Ave., Toronto ON M5G 2E9
416/598-1114; Fax: 416/598-7764

**The Journey Prize**
"The Journey Prize Anthology" presents accomplished writings by outstanding new Canadian writers who have had prior publication in a Canadian literary journal; one of these is chosen as winner
$10,000 cash prize donated by James Michener; the journal that submitted the winning piece will be awarded $2,000 by M&S; submissions from authors not accepted

## The Municipal Chapter of Toronto IODE

#205, 40 St. Clair Ave. East, Toronto ON M4T 1M9
416/925-5078; Fax: 416/925-5127

**IODE Book Award**
Established in 1975; an inscribed scroll & not less than $1,000 awarded annually to the author or illustrator of the best children's book written or illustrated by a Canadian resident in Toronto or surrounding area & published by a Canadian publisher within the preceding 12 months

## The National Chapter of Canada IODE

#254, 40 Orchard View Blvd., Toronto ON M4R 1B9
416/487-4416; Fax: 416/487-4417

**National Chapter of Canada IODE Violet Downey Book Award**
$3,000 awarded annually for the best English-language book, containing at least 500 words of text in any category suitable for children aged 13 & under

## Nova Scotia Library Association

c/o Nova Scotia Provincial Library, 3770 Kempt Rd., Halifax NS B3K 4X8
902/424-2478; Fax: 902/424-0633
Email: mahm1@ponyx.nsh.library.ns.ca; URL: http://www.library.ns.ca/nsla

**Ann Connor Brimer Award**
$500 awarded to the author of fiction or non-fiction books published in Canada currently in print & intended for children up the the age of 15; writer must be residing in Atlantic Canada – Heather Mackenzie, Halifax City Regional Library, 5381 Spring Garden Rd., Halifax NS B3J 1E9

## Ontario Arts Council / Conseil des arts de l'Ontario

#600, 151 Bloor St. West, Toronto ON M5S 1T6
416/961-1660; Fax: 416/961-7796; Toll Free: 1-800-387-0058
Email: oac@gov.on.ca

**Floyd S. Chalmers Canadian Play Award**
Four $10,000 awards may be given annually for outstanding plays performed in Metropolitan Toronto

**Ruth Schwartz Children's Book Award**
Two awards presented annually; $3,000 for best picture book & $2,000 for best young adult/middle reader book; in conjunction with the Canadian Booksellers Association

**The Chalmers Canadian Children's Play Awards**
Established 1973; awarded annually to recognize outstanding new Canadian plays for young audiences performed in the Metropolitan Toronto area; $10,000 for an outstanding play & $5,000 each for two runners-up

## Ontario Library Association / Association des bibliothèques de l'Ontario

#303, 100 Lombard St., Toronto ON M5C 1M3
416/363-3388; Fax: 416/941-9581
Email: ola@interlog.com; URL: http://www.ola.amlibs.ca

**Silver Birch Awards**
Reading program for children in Ontario in grades 4, 5 & 6, established in 1994 (approximately 40,000 children take part); children register through their school or public library to read 20 Canadian books, half fiction & half non-fiction; those who have read five of the books can then vote for their favourite; winners receive a tactile image of a silver birch tree at a luncheon held each June in Toronto

## Ontario Ministry of Citizenship, Culture & Recreation

Ontario Publishing Centre, 77 Bloor St. West, 2nd Fl., Toronto ON M7A 2R9
416/314-7745

**Trillium Book Award/Prix Trillium**
Awarded annually to an Ontario author of a book of excellence; the winning book must have been published within the preceding 12 months; books in English or French in any genre are eligible; winner receives $12,000 & the publisher receives $2,500

## PEI Council of the Arts

115 Richmond St., Charlottetown PE C1A 1H7
902/368-4410; Fax: 902/368-4418

**Island Literary Awards**
Established in 1987 in recognition of Island writers in six categories: Short Story, Poetry, Children's Literature, Feature Article, Creative Writing for Children, Playwriting; an additional award is made "for distinguished contribution to the literary arts"; awards of $500, $200 & $100

## Periodical Marketers of Canada

South Tower, #1007, 175 Bloor St. East, Toronto ON M4W 3R8
416/968-7218; Fax: 416/968-6182

**Canadian Letters Awards**
Established 1996; recognises an individual who has made an outstanding contribution to writing, publishing, teaching or literary administration; award consists of a statuette & a $5,000 donation to the charitable literary organizatin or educational institution of the winner's choice

## Phoenix Community Works Foundation

316 Dupont St., Toronto ON M5R 1V9
416/964-7919; Fax: 416/964-6941

**The bp nichol Chap-book Award**
$1,000 awarded for the best poetry chap-book in English, published in Canada; entries must be from 10-48 pages in length

## Prism International

#E462, Dept. of Creative Writing, UBC, 1866 Main Mall, Vancouver BC V6T 1Z1
604/822-2514

Email: prism@unixg.ubc.ca; URL: http://www.arts.ubc.ca/crwr/prism/prism/html

**Prism Short Fiction Contest**

$3,000 in prizes for annual short fiction contest

### Québec Ministère de la culture et des communications

225, Grande Allée est, Bloc C, 3e étage, Québec QC G1R 5G5
418/643-2183; Fax: 418/643-4457
Email: dc@mcc.gouv.qc.ca; URL: http://www.mcc.gouv.qc.ca

**Les Prix du Québec:**

**Prix Athanase-David**

La plus haute distinction du gouvernement du Québec en littérature; le lauréat reçoit 30 000 $ et une médaille en argent; attribué annuellement pour l'ensemble de l'oeuvre littéraire d'un créateur québécois

### Québec Ministère des Relations internationales

Édifice Hector-Fabre, 525, boul René-Lévesque, Québec QC G1R 5R2

**Prix Québec-Paris**

Originellement appelé Prix France-Canada, ce prix a été fondé en 1958 par la Commission culturelle de l'Association France-Canada, á laquelle s'est associée, dès a création en 1961, la Délégation générale du Québec; le prix est attribué à un écrivain d'expression français, québécois ou canadien français, dont l'ouvrage a été publié au Canada ou en France au cours de l'année pour laquelle le prix et attribué
Le lauréat reçoit une bourse de 2 000 $ offerts par le gouvernement du Québec, plus une contribution de 4 000 FF offerte par la Ville de Paris; de plus, le gouvernement français prend en charge les frais de voyage et de séjour en France du lauréat – Direction générale France, 418/649-2330

**Prix Québec/Wallonie-Bruxelles du livre de la jeunesse**

Le prix a été créé en 1978 dans le but d'encourager le developpement de la littérature de jeunesse at de faire connaître aux deux communautés, québécoise et français de Belgique, leur production respective; le prix est de 105 000 FB ou 3 500 $, auxquels s'ajoute une aide financière à l'éditeur de 180 000 FB ou 6 000 $ – Direction générale de l'Europe, 418/649-2308

### Québec Society for the Promotion of English Language Literature / Société québécoise pour la promotion de la littérature de la langue anglaise

1200 Atwater Ave., Montréal QC H3Z 1X4
514/933-0878; Fax: 514/933-0878
Email: qspell@total.net

**QSPELL Prizes**

Established 1988; awards three annual prizes of $2,000 each to honour literary excellence: The A.M. Klein poetry prize, The Hugh MacLennan fiction prize & the Royal Bank of Canada non-fiction prize
Books can be submitted by publishers or authors; three copies, accompanied by entry form & $10 registration fee per title; authors must have lived in Québec three of the past five years

**QSPELL/FEWQ First Book Award**

$500 award established in 1996 to an author not previously published in book form

### Real Estate Institute of Canada / Institut canadien de l'immeuble

#208, 5407 Eglinton Ave. West, Toronto ON M9C 5K6
416/695-9000; Fax: 416/695-7230; Toll Free: 1-800-542-7342
Email: infocentral@reic.com; URL: http://www.reic.ca

**Morguard Literary Awards**

Co-sponsored by REIC & Morguard Investments Limited, this competition is open to any topic pertaining to the Canadian real estate industry; subject matter may include, but is not limited to, real estate law, architecture, legislation, property management, appraisal, & ethics; competition consists of two categories, including academic writers & practising industry lay writers
An award of $2,000 is presented to the winner in each category, & the winning submissions will be featured in a future edition of Pro-Act

### The Royal Society of Canada / La Société royale du Canada

#308, 225 Metcalfe St., Ottawa ON K2P 1P9
613/991-6990; Fax: 613/991-6996
Email: adminrsc@rsc.ca; URL: http://www.rsc.ca

**Lorne Pierce Medal**

Established 1926; awarded every two years for an achievement of special significance & conspicuous merit in imaginative or critical literature written in either English or French, & preferably dealing with a Canadian subject

### Salon du livre de Québec

#203, 1026, rue Saint-Jean, Québec QC G1R 1R7
418/692-5420; Fax: 418/692-0794

**Prix des libraires du Québec**

Ce prix fut créé en 1993; il souligne l'excellence d'un roman québécois par sa qualité d'écriture et son originalité; une bourse de 2 000 $ est offerte au lauréat par Le Journal de Québec

### Saskatchewan Book Awards

PO Box 1921, Regina SK S4P 3E1
306/569-1585; Fax: 306/569-4187

**Brenda MacDonald Riches First Book Award**

$1,000 to the author of the best first book by a Saskatchewan writer; sponsored by Agrium Inc.

**Children's Literature Award**

$1,000 awarded to the author of the best book of children's literature by a Saskatchewan author; sponsored by SaskEnergy

**City of Regina Book Award**

$1,000 to the author of the best book by a Regina writer; sponsored by the city of Regina

**Fiction Award**

$1,000 presented to the author of the best book of fiction (novel or short fiction) by a Saskatchewan author; sponsored by SaskPower

**Non-Fiction Award**

$1,000 award sponsored by Wascana Energy for the best book of non-fiction by a Saskatchewan author

**Poetry Award**

$1,000 awarded to the best book of poetry by a Saskatchewan author; sponsored by the Saskatchewan Arts Board

**Saskatchewan Award for Publishing**

A commemorative plaque for the publisher & a certificate for the author presented to the best book published in Saskatchewan; judged on overall quality of design, production, marketing, content & significance; sponsored by Saskatchewan Municipal Government

**Saskatchewan Book of the Year Award**

Sponsored by Regina News-Midwest News; $1,000 awarded to the author of a book in one of the following categories: children's books, drama, fiction, non-fiction or poetry

**Saskatchewan First Peoples Publishing Award**

Commemorative certificates for the writer & publisher of the best book with First Nations, Metis, or non-status Indian content written, or in the case of an anthology, edited by a person of First Nations, Metis, or non-status Indian descent; based on the quality of publisher's craft, editing, & literary or artistic value; sponsored by Casino Regina

**Saskatchewan Publishing in Education Award**

Commemorative certificates for the writer or editor & publisher of the best books produced as an educational resource, judged on the quality of the publisher's craft, editing & its value to educators at primary, secondary or post secondary levels; sponsored by the Reader's Digest Foundation of Canada

### Saskatchewan Library Association

PO Box 3388, Regina SK S4P 3H1
306/780-9413; Fax: 306/780-9447
Email: sla@pleis.lib.sk.ca; URL: http://www.lib.sk.ca/sla/

**The Frances Morrison Award**

Awarded for outstanding service to libraries

**The Mary Donaldson Award**

Awarded for excellence to a student studying at a library education institution in Saskatchewan

### Saskatchewan Writers Guild Inc.

PO Box 3986, Regina SK S4P 3R9
306/757-6310; Fax: 306/565-8554
Email: swg@sk.sympatico.ca; URL: http://www.sasknet.com/~skwriter

**City of Regina Writing Award**

$4,000 to a Regina writer to reward merit & enable a writer to work on a specific writing project; funded by the City of Regina Arts Commission & administered by the SWG

### La Société Saint-Jean-Baptiste de Montréal

82, rue Sherbrooke ouest, Montréal QC H2X 1X3
514/843-8851; Fax: 514/844-6369

**Prix Duvernay**

Le prix a été crée en 1944 afin de signaler les mérites d'un compatriote dont la compétence et le rayonnement dans le domaine intellectuel et littéraire servent les intérêts supéricurs de la nation québécoise; le prix est de 3 000 $, accompagne une médaille, et est attribué à tous les trois ans

### Stephen Leacock Associates

PO Box 854, Orillia ON L3V 6K8
705/325-6546

**Stephen Leacock Memorial Medal**

Established 1946 to encourage the writing & publishing of humorous works in Canada; given annually for the best Canadian book of humour published in the preceding year
Winner receives the medal & a cash award of $5,000 donated by Manulife Bank of Canada

**The Order of Mariposa**

Awarded occasionally to someone who has contributed significantly to humour in Canada

### Stephen Leacock Heritage Festival

PO Box 2305, Orillia ON L3V 6S3
705/325-3261

**Leacock Limerick Awards**

Annual cash award of $1,000 for best limerick with 2nd & 3rd place prizes; entries must include $5 registration fee; winners announced Aug 1.

### Union des écrivaines et écrivains québécois

La Maison des écrivains, 3492, av Laval, Montréal QC H2X 3C8
514/849-8540; Fax: 514/849-6239
Email: ecrivez@uneq.qc.ca; URL: http://www.uneq.qc.ca

**Prix Émile Nelligan**

Le prix est accordé à un poète nord-américain de langue français de 35 ans ou moins
5 000 $ et une médaille à l'effigie du poète sont remises par la Fondation Émile-Nelligan

### University of British Columbia

President's Office, 6328 Memorial Rd., Vancouver BC V6T 1Z2
604/822-8310; Fax: 604/822-3134

**Medal for Canadian Biography**

Established 1952; awarded annually for the best biography written either about or by a Canadian & published in the preceding year

### Ville de Montréal
Service de la culture
5650, d'Iberville, 5e étage, Montréal QC H2G 3E4
514/872-5579

**Grand Prix du livre de Montréal**
Le prix est offert par la Ville de Montréal à l'auteur ou aux co-auteurs d'un ouvrage de langue française ou anglaise, pour la facture exceptionnelle et l'apport original de cette publication; le prix consiste en une bourse de 10 000 $ pour un résident de la Communauté urbaine de Montréal

### West Coast Book Prize Society
#700, 1033 Davie St., Vancouver BC V6E 1M7
604/687-2405; Fax: 604/687-2405
URL: http://www.harbour.sfu.ca/bcbook

**BC Book Prizes:**
Established 1985; awards of $2,000 presented to winners in each of six categories; the the book may have been published anywhere in the world; $25 fee per entry:

**Dorothy Livesay Poetry Prize**
Awarded to the author of the best work of poetry; the writer must have lived in BC for three of the preceding five years

**The Bill Duthie Booksellers' Choice Prize**
Awarded for the best book in terms of public appeal, initiative, design, production & content; the book must have been published in BC

**The Ethel Wilson Fiction Prize**
Awarded to the author of the best work of fiction; the writer must have lived in BC for three of the preceding five years

**The Hubert Evans Non-Fiction Prize**
Awarded to the author of the best original non-fiction literary work (philosophy, belles lettres, biography, history, etc.); the writer must have lived in BC for three of the preceding five years

**The Roderick Haig-Brown Regional Prize**
Awarded to the author of the book that contributes most to the enjoyment & understanding of BC; the book may deal with any aspect of the province & should epitomize the BC experience

**The Sheila A. Egoff Children's Prize**
Awarded to the author of the best book for young people aged 16 & under; the author or illustrator must have lived in BC for three of the preceding five years

### Writers Guild of Alberta
Percy Page Centre, 11759 Groat Rd., 3rd Fl., Edmonton AB T5M 3K6
403/422-8174; Fax: 403/422-2663; Toll Free: 1-800-665-5354
Email: writers@compusmart.ab.ca; URL: http://www.rtt.ab.ca/rtt.writers

**Annual Awards Program**
Established 1982 to recognize excellence in writing by Alberta authors; published books may be entered in any of the following categories: Children's Literature (any genre), Drama, Novel, Non-Fiction, Poetry, Short Fiction, Best First Book; winners receive leather-bound copy of their book & $500 cash award

### The Writers' Development Trust / Société d'encouragement aux auteurs
The Writers' Centre, #201, 24 Ryerson Ave., Toronto ON M5T 2P3
416/504-8222; Fax: 416/504-9090
Email: writers.trust@sympatico.ca

**Rogers Communiations Writers' Trust Prize for Canadian Fiction**
Established in 1997, $10,000 awarded annually to the author of the novel or short-story collection published in the calendar year that the jury believes is the year's best fiction book

**The Bronwen Wallace Memorial Award**
$1,000 awarded annually to a Canadian writer under the age of 35 who is not yet published in book form; award alternates each year between poetry & short fiction

**The Gordon Montador Award**
Established 1993; $2,000 awarded annually for the year's best book on contemporary social issues

**The Marian Engel Award**
Established 1986; $10,000 awarded annually for outstanding prose writing by a Canadian woman

**Viacom Canada Writers' Trust Prize for Canadian Non-Fiction**
Established in 1997, $10,000 awarded annually to the author of non-fiction published in the calendar year that the judges believe shos the highest literary merit; four runner-up prizes of $1,000 each awarded to other shortlisted authors

### Writers' Federation of Nova Scotia
#901, 1809 Barrington St., Halifax NS B3J 3K8
902/423-8116; Fax: 902/422-0881
Email: writers1@fox.nstn.ca; URL: http://www.chebucto.ns.ca/Culture/WFNS/

**Evelyn Richardson Memorial Literary Trust Award**
$1,000 award was established in 1978 to recognize outstanding work in non-fiction by a Nova Scotian writer (native or resident)

**Thomas H. Raddall Atlantic Fiction Prize**
$4,000 award honours the best writing by an Atlantic Canadian writer

### The Writers' Union of Canada
24 Ryerson Ave., Toronto ON M5T 2P3
416/703-8982; Fax: 416/703-0826
Email: twuc@the-wire.com;
URL: http://www.swifty.com/twuc

**Short Prose Competition for Developing Writers**

**Writing for Children Competition**

**MEDICAL See HEALTH & MEDICAL**

**MULTICULTURAL See CITIZENSHIP & BRAVERY**

**MUSIC See PERFORMING ARTS**

## PERFORMING ARTS

### Alberta Heritage Scholarship Fund
9940 - 106 St., 6th Fl., Edmonton AB T5K 2V1
403/427-8640; Fax: 403/422-4516

**Alberta Foundation for the Arts Scholarships**
Five awards of $10,000 at graduate level for study in music, drama, dance & the visual arts & up to $50,000 is available to assist Alberta artists to further their training through non-academic short-term courses & internship or apprenticeship programs

### Alberta Recording Industries Association
#1205, 10109 - 106 Street, Edmonton AB T5J 3L7
403/428-3372; Fax: 403/426-0188; Toll Free: 1-800-465-3117

**ARIA Craft Awards**
Annual awards in the following categories: Recording Engineer of the Year, Record Producer of the Year, Recording Studio of the Year, Record Company of the Year, Publishing Company of the Year, Best Compilation Album of the Year, Best Album Design of the Year, Best Music Score of the Year, Best Music Video, Best Booking Agent, Manager of the Year, & Musician of the Year

**ARIA Performance Awards**
Annual awards for Alberta artists in the following categories: People's Choice Award, Female Recording Artist of the Year, Male Recording Artist of the Year, Group Recording of the Year, Most Promising Artist, Best Pop/Light Rock, Best Rock/Heavy Metal, Best Alternative, Best Country, Best Blues/R&B/Soul, Best Roots/Traditional/Ethnic, Best Rap/Dance/Rhythm, Best Jazz, Best Classical, Best Children's, Songwriter/Composer of the Year, Single of the Year, Album of the Year, Award of Distinction, & Award of Excellence

### The Banff Centre
PO Box 1020, Banff AB T0M 0E0
403/762-6193; Fax: 403/762-6444

**The Clifford E. Lee Choreography Award**
Established 1978; awarded annually in recognition of outstanding Canadian choreography & jointly sponsored by the Banff Centre & the Edmonton-based Clifford E. Lee Foundation
Winner receives a $5,000 cash prize & a commission to mount a new work for premiere at the Banff Festival of the Arts – George Ross

### The Canada Council for the Arts / Conseil des Arts du Canada
350 Albert St., PO Box 1047, Ottawa ON K1P 5V8
613/566-4414, ext.4116; Fax: 613/566-4416; Toll Free: 1-800-263-5588
URL: http://www.canadacouncil.ca

**Canada Council Instrument Bank**
The Council owns a Stradivarius violin & a Brott-Turner-Tecchler cello which are loaned to gifted Canadian musicians of exception solo career potential following a competition held every three years

**Glenn Gould Prize**
$50,000 international prize awarded every three years to an individual who has earned international recognition as the result of a highly exceptional contribution to music & its communication, through any of the communications technologies
Individuals from a broad range of fields, including musical creation or performance, film, video, television, radio & recordings, musical theatre, & writing are eligible; candidates may not put forward their own nomination; they must be nominated by three specialists in the particular field or a related one

**Healey Willan Prize**
$5,000 awarded every two years to the Canadian amateur choir that gives the best performance in terms of musicianship, technique & program in the CBC National Radio Competition for Amateur Choirs

**Jacqueline Lemieux Prize**
$3,000 awarded twice annually to the most talented Canadian candidate in the "Projects in Dance - Discovery Component" competition

**Jean-Marie Beaudet Award in Orchestra Conducting**
$1,000 awarded annually to a young Canadian orchestra conductor selected by the Music Advisory Committee of the Canada Council's Music Section from among staff conductors with Canadian orchestras

**John Hirsh Prize**
$6,000 awarded annually to a new & developing theatre director who has demonstrated great potential for future excellence & exciting artisitc vision; alternates each year between French & English theatre

**Jules Léger Prize for New Chamber Music**
Annual $7,500 prize designed to encourage Canadian composers to write for chamber music groups & to foster the performance of Canadian chamber music by these groups; the Canadian Music Centre administers the award, the Canada Council funds the award & selects the jury of musicians to study the submitted scores; the CBC broadcasts the winning work of its English- & French-language stereo networks; submissions to The Canadian Music Centre, 20 St. Joseph St., Toronto ON M4Y 1J9

**Peter Dwyer Scholarships**
Annual scholarships totalling $20,000 awarded to the most promising Canadian students at the National Ballet School & the National Theatre School; each school is awarded $10,000 & chooses the winner on behalf of the Canada Council

**Robert Fleming Prizes**
The annual $1,500 prize in memory of Robert Fleming is intended to encourage the careers of young creators of music; awarded to the most talented Canadian music

composer in the competition for the "Grants to Musicans" program in music composition

**Sir Ernest MacMillan Memorial Prize in Choral Conducting**

$2,000 provided by the Toronto Mendelssohn Choir Foundation & awarded annually to a Canadian candidate in the competition for grants in choral conducting

**Sylva Gelber Foundation Award**

Established 1981; approximately $15,000 awarded annually to the most talented Canadian artist under the age of 30 in the "Grants to Musicians" competition for performers in classical music

**Virginia Parker Award**

Approximately $25,000 awarded annually to a young Canadian classical musician, instrumentalist, or conductor who has received at least one Canada Council grant from a juried program; the prize is intended to assist a young performer in furthering his/her career & is awarded on the recommendation of the Music Advisory Committee of the Canada Council's Music Section

## Canadian Academy of Recording Arts & Sciences / Académie canadienne des arts et des sciences de l'enregistrement

124 Merton St., 3rd Fl., Toronto ON M4S 2Z2
416/485-3135; Fax: 416/485-4978
URL: http://www.juno-awards.ca

**Juno Awards**

Annual awards for: Album of the Year, Single of the Year, Bestselling Album (foreign/domestic), Bestselling Francophone Album, Female Vocalist of the Year, Male Vocalist of the Year, Group of the Year, Instrumental Artist(s) of the Year, Best New Solo Artist, Best New Group, Songwriter of the Year, Country Female Vocalist of the Year, Country Male Vocalist of the Year, Country Group or Duo of the Year, Best Children's Album, Best Roots & Traditional Album (one award Solo, one Group), Best Classical Album: Solo or Chamber Ensemble, Best Classical Album: Large Ensemble or Soloist(s) with Large Ensemble Accompaniment, Best Classical Album: Vocal or Choral Performance, Best Classical Composition, Best Contemporary Jazz Album, Best Mainstream Jazz Album, Best R&B/Soul Recording, Best Dance Recording, Best Rock Album, Best Rap Recording, Best Rap Recording, Best Reggae Recording, Best Blues/Gospel Album, Best Music of Aboriginal Canada Recording, Best Global Recording, Best Alternative Album

Also: Producer of the Year, Recording Engineer of the Year, Best Video, Best Album Design, Hall of Fame Award, Walt Grealis Special Achievement Award, & International Achievement Award (not awarded every year)

## Canadian Broadcasting Corporation

CBC Radio Music, PO Box 500, Stn A, Toronto ON M5W 1E6
416/205-3311
URL: http://www.radio.cbc.ca

**National Radio Competition for Amateur Choirs**

Established 1975; awarded biennially; prizes offered in following categories: Children's, Youth, Large, Adult Mixed Chamber, Adult Equal Voice, Traditional & Ethno-Cultural, & Contemporary Choral Music

Eight first prizes of $3,000 each; eight 2nd prizes of $2,000 each; $1,000 for best performance of a Canadian work

**National Radio Competition for Young Composers**

Established 1973; competition sponsored every two years by CBC & the Canada Council; entrants must be Canadian citizens or landed immigrants, 30 years of age or under, & must not be employees of the CBC

Up to 10 prizes are given: three 1st prizes of $5,000 each; three 2nd prizes of $4,000 each; three 3rd prizes; a $5,000 Grand Prize; a performance of the winning works is given on CBC English & French radio networks

## Canadian Country Music Association / Association de la musique country canadienne

#127, 3800 Steeles Ave. West, Woodbridge ON L4L 4G9
905/850-1144; Fax: 905/850-1330
Email: ccma@sprynet.com; URL: http://www.ccma.org

**Music Awards & Citations**

Awards in 10 categories are presented annually to outstanding performers; 29 citations honour individuals & organizations that have made a significant contribution to country music

## Canadian Theatre Critics Association / Association des critiques de théâtre du Canada

#700, 250 Dundas St. West, Toronto ON M5T 2Z5
416/367-8896; Fax: 416/367-5992

**The Nathan Cohen Award**

Named in honour of the distinguished theatre critic of the Toronto Star; award is presented annually to help recognize high critical standards & to give encouragement to those working professionally in the field of theatre criticism

Entry categories in the English language division are: reviews of up to 750 words; reviews, profiles & other theatrical features of 750 words to a maximum of 3,000 words; up to three items may be submitted in either or both categories; one winner will be chosen from each category; each of the two winners receives a cheque for $500 & a framed certificate

## Council for Business & the Arts in Canada / Conseil pour le monde des affaires et des arts du Canada

#705, 165 University Ave., Toronto ON M5H 3B8
416/869-3016; Fax: 416/869-0435

**Edmund C. Bovey Award**

To recognize individual members of the business community who contribute leadership, time, money & expertise to the arts

A sculpture to the winner & $20,000 distributed to the arts in a way specified by the winner

**Financial Post Awards for Business in the Arts**

Established in 1979 to encourage the corporate sector's involvement with the visual & performing arts in Canada & to recognize this involvement

## Dance Ontario Association / Association Ontario Danse

179 Richmond St. West, Toronto ON M5V 1V3
416/204-1083; Fax: 416/204-1085; Toll Free: 1-800-363-6087
Email: danceont@iComm.ca; URL: http://www.icomm.ca/danceon

**Dance Ontario Award**

Recognizes a lifetime commitment to dance

## Dreamspeakers Festival Society

#201, 15620 - 111 Ave., Edmonton AB T5M 4R7
403/451-5033; Fax: 403/452-9042

**Aboriginal Film Awards**

Established in 1996 to recognize outstanding achievement in the aboriginal filmmaking industry

## Governor General's Performing Arts Foundation

PO Box 1534, Stn B, Ottawa ON K1P 5W1
613/996-5051; Fax: 613/996-2828

**Governor General's Performing Arts Awards**

Established in 1992; honours six performing artists for their lifetime achievement & contribution to the cultural enrichment of Canada; each recipient is awarded $10,000 & a commemorative medal

**Ramon John Hnatyshyn Award for Voluntarism in the Performing Arts**

Recognizes outstanding service to the performing arts; the recipient is presented with a specially commissioned artwork by Canadian glass artist Daniel Crichton

**The National Arts Centre Award**

Recognizes work of an extraordinary nature & significance in the performing arts by an individual artist &/ or company in the past performance year; recipients receive a $10,000 cash award donated by the NAC Foundation & an original sculpture by Stephen Braithwaite

## The Jazz Report

14 London St., Toronto ON M6G 1M5
416/533-2813

**The Jazz Report Awards**

Established 1993; annual awards in 36 categories determined by readers & contributors to the quarterly

## The National Music Festival / Festival national de musique

1034 Chestnut Ave., Moose Jaw SK S6H 1A6
306/693-7087; Fax: 306/693-7087

**Competition Awards**

Ten separate provincial competitions are held throughout May & June & the winners of these compete for national honours each August in a different province each year; the Festival is organized by the Federation of Canadian Music Festivals, in cooperation with the hosting provincial association

Cash awards of $1,500, $800 & $400 are presented to first, second, & third place winners in each of six categories: Voice, Piano, Strings, Woodwinds, Brass, Chamber Groups; Grand Award of $2,000 is given to the best performer at the Grand Award Competition of the six winners

## Ontario Arts Council / Conseil des arts de l'Ontario

#600, 151 Bloor St. West, Toronto ON M5S 1T6
416/961-1660; Fax: 416/961-7796; Toll Free: 1-800-387-0058
Email: oac@gov.on.ca

**Heinz Unger Award for Conducting**

Established 1968 & awarded biennially to honour the memory of the York Concert Society music director; administered by the Music Office of the Ontario Arts Council in cooperation with the Association of Canadian Orchestras

**Jean A. Chalmers Award for Creativity in Dance**

Biennial award of $20,000; honours an individual who has made an outstanding contribution to nuturing creativity in dance in Canada

**Jean A. Chalmers Award for Distinction in Choreography**

Established 1994; biennial $20,000 award honours prominent choreographers who have created a substantial body of work

**Jean A. Chalmers Awards for Musical Composition**

Established in 1993; two annual awards of $10,000 presented together; the Composers Award honours a Canadian composer of an outstanding work in a particular genre; the Presenters Award is given to an Ontario-based producer or commissioner of a new Canadian work in a particular genre

**John Adaskin Memorial Fund**

Established in memorial of the Canadian Music Centre's first executive secretary; supports a project that encourages the promotion & development of Canadian music in the school system

**Leslie Bell Scholarship for Choral Conducting**

Established 1973; up to $2,000 awarded biennially in competition; the purpose of the award is to help young emerging choral conductors in Ontario further their studies in the choral music field either in Canada or abroad; competition organized by the Ontario Choral Federation

**The Chalmers Performing Arts Training Grants**

Assist qualified professional performing artists to undertake intensive study projects or professional upgrading with outstanding master teachers or at highly-regarded institutions

**The Jean A. Chalmers Choreographic Award**

$10,000 national award is presented every two years to honour choreographers of outstanding potential

**The Jean A. Chalmers National Music Award**

Annual $20,000 award recognizes individual performers or ensembles making an outstanding contribution to Canadian musical creativity

**The John Hirsch Director's Award**

Established in 1993; awarded every three years to promising theatre directors

**The Pauline McGibbon Award**

Annual award of $7,000; alternates between designers, directors & production craftspersons

**The Vida Peene Fund**

Provides assistance to projects which benefit the orchestra community as a whole

**Tim Sims Encouragement Fund**

Established in 1995; $1,000 to be awarded annually to a promising young comedic performer or troupe

### Québec Ministère de la culture et des communications

225, Grande Allée est, Bloc C, 3e étage, Québec QC G1R 5G5
418/643-2183; Fax: 418/643-4457
Email: dc@mcc.gouv.qc.ca;
URL: http://www.mcc.gouv.qc.ca

**Les Prix du Québec:**

**Prix Denise-Pelletier**

$30,000, a silver medal & scroll awarded for excellence in performing arts

### RPM Weekly

6 Brentcliffe Rd., Toronto ON M4G 3Y2
416/425-0257; Fax: 416/425-8629

**Big Country Awards**

Annual awards to honour achievement by Canadian country music singers & composers; winners are selected by subscribers to the music trade magazine

### La Société Saint-Jean-Baptiste de Montréal

82, rue Sherbrooke ouest, Montréal QC H2X 1X3
514/843-8851; Fax: 514/844-6369

**Prix Calixa-Lavallee**

Established 1959; $1,500 & a medal awarded annually to a French Canadian in recognition of outstanding achievement in music in serving the higher interests of the French Canadian people

### Society of Composers, Authors & Music Publishers of Canada / Société canadienne des auteurs, compositeurs et éditeurs de musique

41 Valleybrook Dr., North York ON M3B 2S6
416/445-8700; Fax: 416/445-7108; Toll Free: 1-800-557-6226
Email: socan@socan.ca; URL: http://www.socan.ca

**SOCAN Awards**

Established 1990 for the purpose of recognizing SOCAN creators & their contribution to Canadian music; presented at the annual Awards Dinner; only SOCAN member writers, composers & music publishers are eligible

**SOCAN Awards for Young Composers**

Total of $16,500 awarded to encourage & recognize the creative talents of upcoming Canadian composers; The Sir Ernest MacMillan Awards for compositions for no fewer than 13 performers; The Serge Garant Awards for compositions for a minimum of three performers; The Pierre Mercure Awards for solo or duet compositions; The Hugh Le Caine Awards for compositions realized on tape with electronic means; The Godfrey Ridout Awards for choral compositions of any variety

### Toronto Arts Council

141 Bathurst St., Toronto ON M5V 2R2
416/392-6800; Fax: 416/392-6920
Email: tac@city.toronto.on.ca;
URL: www.city.toronto.on.ca/4edc/tac.htm

**Muriel Sherrin Award**

Funded through an endowment made possible by the former board of directors of the Toronto International Festival, the $10,000 prize is presented to artists & creators for international initiatives in the fields of music & dance; awarded every second year & alternates between music & dance

### Toronto Theatre Alliance

#403, 720 Bathurst St., Toronto ON M5S 2R4
416/536-6468; Fax: 416/536-3463; Toll Free: 1-800-541-0499
Email: tta@idirect.com; URL: http://www.ffa.ucalgary,ca/tta/

**Dora Mavor Moore Awards**

Established 1979; celebrating excellence in Toronto theatre, 36 awards in large, medium & small theatre divisions, Theatre for Young Audiences & New Choreography

### PUBLIC ADMINISTRATION See LEGAL, GOVERNMENTAL, PUBLIC ADMINISTRATION

## PUBLIC AFFAIRS

### B'nai Brith Canada

15 Hove St., North York ON M3H 4Y8
416/633-6224; Fax: 416/630-2159
URL: http://www.bnaibrith.ca

**Award of Merit & Humanitarian Awards**

Established 1981; presented annually at gala events in major communities across Canada

Selection of honourees based on outstanding achievement in their chosen fields as well as personal commitment over the years to the overall betterment of Canadian society

### The Canadian Council of Christians & Jews / Conseil canadien des chrétiens et des juifs

#820, 2 Carleton St. West, Toronto ON M5B 1J3
416/597-9693; Fax: 416/597-9775; Toll Free: 1-800-663-1848
Email: cccj@interlog.com; URL: http://www.interlog.com/~cccj/

**Human Relations Award**

Made to outstanding Canadians who have made a significant contribution towards bringing people together regardless of race, religion, or social status, in an atmosphere of understanding & respect; the award is made annually & is approved by a National Nominating Committee from the Board of Directors of CCCJ

### Canadian Council of Professional Engineers / Conseil canadien des ingénieurs

#401, 116 Albert St., Ottawa ON K1P 5G3
613/232-2474; Fax: 613/230-5759
Email: info@ccpe.ca; URL: http://www.ccpe.ca

**The Meritorious Service Award for Community Service**

Recognizes outstanding service & dedication to Canadian society through voluntary participation in community organizations, government-sponsored activities, or humanitarian work

### The Canadian Council of the Blind / Le Conseil canadien des aveugles

#405, 396 Cooper St., Ottawa ON K2P 2H7
613/567-0311; Fax: 613/567-2728

**Award of Merit**

Established 1952; presented to a Canadian, blind or sighted, who has rendered outstanding work for the blind

A gold medal & clasp, a specially printed & bound citation & honorary life membership in the CCB

### The City of Toronto

Corp. Servs., Human Resources, 100 Queen St. West, 1st Fl., Toronto ON M5H 2N2
416/392-7855; Fax: 416/392-0006

**Access Award**

Established 1982; presented to a group or organization which has made a significant contribution toward improving the quality of life for the city's residents who have a disability; the award honours those who are sensitive to the access needs of persons with disabilities when planning structures or programs (this could include consideration of access requirements in the design of new or renovated buildings, a job creation campaign, a transportation system, recreational program, etc.)

**Civic Award of Merit**

Established 1956; awarded to individuals who have attained distinction & renown in various fields of endeavour; award is in the form of an acrylic obelisk with medallion

**Constance E. Hamilton Award**

This award commemorates the Privy Council of Great Britain granting women status as persons in 1929; award is named after the first woman member of City Council; recipients are persons who have made a significant contribution to securing equitable treatment for Toronto women

**William P. Hubbard Race Relations Award**

Named for Toronto's first visible minority Member of Council & Acting Mayor, this award honours persons who have made a voluntary contribution to racial harmony in Toronto; award was presented for the first time in 1990

### Government of Newfoundland & Labrador

The Premier's Office, PO Box 8700, St. John's NF A1B 4J6
709/729-3570; Fax: 709/729-5875

**The Premier's Award for Access & Awareness**

Designed to reflect the aims & objectives of National Access Awareness Week; it is intended to recognize those exceptional individuals, organizations, & businesses that have made outstanding contributions to access & awareness for visible & nonvisible minorities

### Ontario Ministry of Citizenship, Culture & Recreation - Seniors' Issues Group

76 College St., 6th Fl., Toronto ON M7A 1N3
416/327-2433; Fax: 416/327-2425;
Toll Free: 1-800-267-7329

**Ontario Senior Achievement Award**

Presented annually to Ontario residents who have made a significant contribution to their communities after reaching 65 years of age; nominations may be made by any individual or organization – Kate Clark

### Planned Parenthood Federation of Canada / Fédération pour le planning des naissances du Canada

#430, One Nicholas St., Ottawa ON K1N 7B7
613/241-4474; Fax: 613/241-7550
Email: ppfed@web.net

**Phyllis Harris Scholarship**

$2,500 towards full-time study at a Canadian university for students who have worked or volunteered in the general field of human sexuality who intend to work for a degree in the field of family planning or population issues

### Québec Ministère de l'industrie, du commerce, de la science et de la technologie

Direction de la diffusion de la science et de la technologie , 710, Place d'Youville, 3e étage, Québec QC G1R 4Y4
418/691-5698, poste 4119
URL: http://www.micst.gouv.qc.ca;
http://www.mcc.gouv.qc.ca

**Prix Léon-Gérin**
$30,000, a silver medal & a scroll awarded for excellence in human sciences – Secrétariat des Prix du Québec dans le domaine scientifique

### Status of Women Canada
#700, 360 Albert St., Ottawa ON K1A 1C3
613/995-7835; Fax: 613/943-2386
**Governor General's Award in Commemoration of Persons Case**
Established 1979 to celebrate the 50th anniversary of the "Persons Case" which resulted in women being declared "persons" & thus eligible for appointment to the Senate; annual awards recognize contributions by individuals toward promoting the equality of women in Canada

**PUBLIC RELATIONS See ADVERTISING & PUBLIC RELATIONS**

**RADIO See BROADCASTING & FILM**

**RECREATION See SPORTS & RECREATION**

## SCIENTIFIC, ENGINEERING, TECHNICAL

### Association of Universities & Colleges of Canada / Association des Universités et Collèges du Canada
#600, 350 Albert St., Ottawa ON K1R 1B1
613/563-1236; Fax: 613/563-9745
Email: info@aucc.ca; URL: http://www.aucc.ca
**Petro-Canada Graduate Research Award Program**
Up to four awards of $10,000 for students working towards a master's or doctoral degree in a subject related to the oil & gas industry

### The Canada Council for the Arts / Conseil des Arts du Canada
350 Albert St., PO Box 1047, Ottawa ON K1P 5V8
613/566-4414, ext.4116; Fax: 613/566-4416; Toll Free: 1-800-263-5588
URL: http://www.canadacouncil.ca
**Isaak Walton Killam Memorial Prizes**
Up to three prizes of $50,000 each are given annually to eminent Canadian scholars in recognition of a distinguished career in & contribution to the natural sciences, the health sciences, & engineering; candidates must be nominated by three experts in their particular field
**Killam Research Fellowships**
Fellowships to a maximum of $53,000 offered on a competitive basis to support researchers in any of the following broad fields: humanities, social sciences, natural sciences, health sciences, engineering & studies linking any of the disciplines within these broad fields – Email: Killam@canadacouncil.ca

### Canadian Aeronautics & Space Institute / Institut aéronautique et spatial du Canada
#818, 130 Slater St., Ottawa ON K1P 6E2
613/234-0191; Fax: 613/234-9039
Email: casi@casi.ca; URL: http://www.casi.ca
**C.D. Howe Award**
Established 1966; a silver plaque presented annually for achievement in the fields of planning, policy making & overall leadership in Canadian aeronautics & space activities
**McCurdy Award**
Established 1954; a silver medal & trophy presented annually for outstanding achievement in art, science & engineering relating to aeronautics & space
**Romeo Vachon Award**
Established 1969; bronze plaque awarded annually for outstanding contribution of a practical nature to the art, science, & engineering of aeronautics & space in Canada
**Trans-Canada (McKee) Trophy**
Canada's oldest aviation award established 1927; presented annually except when no qualified recipient is nominated for outstanding achievement in the field of air operations

### Canadian Council of Professional Engineers / Conseil canadien des ingénieurs
#401, 116 Albert St., Ottawa ON K1P 5G3
613/232-2474; Fax: 613/230-5759
Email: info@ccpe.ca; URL: http://www.ccpe.ca
**Canadian Engineers' Gold Medal Award**
Established 1972; a national award designed to bestow distinction on outstanding engineers in Canada & to recognize exceptional achievements in their chosen fields, irrespective of any affiliation with a given society, institute or association; the award is also designed to assist in the furtherance of public understanding of the role of the engineer in Canadian society
**ENCON Insurance Managers Inc.**
$5,000 to a professional engineer wishing to pursue studies in the area of engineering failure investigation, risk management &/or materials testing to help in the prevention of accidents which may result from materials failure
**Manulife Financial Scholarship**
Offers three scholarships of $10,000 each annually to provide financial assistance to engineers returning to university for further study or research in an engineering field; candidates must be accepted or registered in a faculty of engineering
**Meloche Monnex Scholarship**
Two scholarships of $7,500 each to provide financial assistance to engineers returning to university to further study or research in a field other than engineering; field of study chosen should favour the acquisition of knowledge pertinent to enhancing the performance of the candidate in the engineering profession
**The Young Engineer Achievement Award**
Designed to bestow distinction on young outstanding engineers in Canada & to recognize exceptional achievements in their chosen fields, irrespective of any affiliation with a given society, institute or association; the presentation of this award is also designed to promote public understanding of the role of the professional engineer in Canadian society

### Canadian Information Processing Society / Association Canadienne de L'Informatique
#2401, 1 Yonge St., Toronto ON M5E 1E5
416/861-2477; Fax: 416/368-9972
Email: info@cips.ca; URL: http://www.cips.ca
**Canadian Information Technology Innovation**
For organizations or individuals who have demonstrated innovation in information technology; both commercial & non-commercial innovations are eligible
**Canadian Software Systems**
For a software system, originating in Canada, that has had a significant effect, as evidenced by new concepts, market acceptance, increased competitiveness, or influence on later software developments; the award may be for a product or project, & given to an organization or group

### Canadian Institute of Forestry / Institut forestier du Canada
#606, 151 Slater St., Ottawa ON K1P 5H3
613/234-2242; Fax: 613/234-6181
Email: cif@cif-ifc.org; URL: http://www.cif-ifc.org/
**Canadian Forestry Achievement Award**
Established 1966 & presented annually in recognition of superior accomplishments in forestry research &/or in recognition of outstanding administrative leadership in management, education, research, & affairs of professional & scientific societies
**Canadian Forestry Scientific Achievement Award**
Established 1980; presented annually in recognition of superior accomplishments in scientific forestry
**International Forestry Achievement Award**
Established 1980; presented in recognition of outstanding achievement in international forestry

### Canadian Institute of Mining, Metallurgy & Petroleum / Institut canadien des mines, de la métallurgie et du pétrole
#1210, 3400, boul de Maisonneuve ouest, Montréal QC H3Z 3B8
514/939-2710; Fax: 514/939-2714
URL: http://www.cim.org
**CIM Awards**
The institute administers 26 awards recognizing achievement in mining, metallurgy & petroleum industries

### The Canadian Network for the Advancement of Research, Industry & Education
#470, 410 Laurier Ave. West, Ottawa ON K1P 6H5
613/660-3634; Fax: 613/660-3806
Email: info@canarie.ca; URL: http://www.canarie.ca
**Canada's National Iway Award**
Awards recognize accomplishments of individuals who have demonstrated leadership in the development of Canada's emerging information society in the following categories: Product Development for an individual who has demonstrated creativity & leadership in the design & implementation of a product which supports the development & application of the Information Highway in Canada; Education/Public Awareness for an individual who has initiated uses of Canada's Information Highway that improve the quality, effectiveness, access to &/or outcome of education & training programs in educational institutions; Government Services for an individual who has initiated uses of Canada's Information Highway that save time & taxpayer dollars in the conduct of government operations. Joint initiative with the Canadian Advanced Technology Association, sponsored by Royal Bank

### Canadian Society for Chemical Engineering / Société canadienne du génie chimique
#550, 130 Slater St., Ottawa ON K1P 6E2
613/232-6252; Fax: 613/232-5862
Email: cic_adm@fox.nstn.ca;
URL: http://www.chem-inst-can.org
**The Canadian Society for Chemical Engineering Awards**
Offers several awards & scholarships in chemical engineering or industrial chemistry

### Canadian Society for Chemistry / Société canadienne de chimie
#550, 130 Slater St., Ottawa ON K1P 6E2
613/232-6252; Fax: 613/232-5862
Email: cic_adm@fox.nstn.ca; URL: http://www.chem-inst-can.org
**The Canadian Society for Chemistry Awards**
Several awards & scholarships are offered in organic chemistry, inorganic, bio-organic, analytical, pure or applied, physical, medicinal, & electrochemistry

### The Chemical Institute of Canada / Institut de chimie du Canada
#550, 130 Slater St., Ottawa ON K1P 6E2
613/232-6252; Fax: 613/232-5862
Email: cic_adm@fox.nstn.ca;
URL: http://www.chem-inst-can.org
**Chemical Institute of Canada Awards**
The institute administers several awards & scholarships in chemistry, chemical engineering, & macromolecular science or engineering

### E.W.R. Steacie Memorial Fund / Fondation E.W.R. Steacie
c/o Steacie Institute for Molecular Sciences, NRC Canada, 100 Sussex Dr., Ottawa ON K1A 0R6
613/990-0968, 993-1212; Fax: 613/954-5242
URL: http://www.sims.nrc.ca/sims/prize.htm

**The Steacie Prize**

Canada's most prestigious award for young scientists & engineers; named to honour the memory of Edgar William Richard Steacie, a physical chemist & former President of the National Research Council of Canada; established 1963; awarded annually to a person up to 40 years of age for outstanding scientific work in a Canadian context; winner receives a certificate & $8,000 – P. Hackett, DocuFax 613/954-5242; email Peter.Hackett@nrc.ca; Huguette.Morin-Dumais@nrc.ca

## The Engineering Institute of Canada / Institut canadien des ingénieurs

1980 Ogilvie Rd., PO Box 27078, RPO Gloucester Ctr, Gloucester ON K1J 9L9

613/742-5185; Fax: 613/742-5189

Email: ici.eic@nrc.ca; URL: http://www.eic-ici.ca

**The Sir John Kennedy Medal**

Established in 1927 in commemoration of the great services rendered in the field of engineering by Sir John Kennedy, a past president of the EIC; medal is awarded every two years by the council in recognition of outstanding merit in the profession or of noteworthy contributions to the science of engineering or to the benefit of the institute

## Ernest C. Manning Awards Foundation

#3900, 421 - 7th Ave. SW, Calgary AB T2P 4K9

403/266-7571; Fax: 403/266-8154

URL: http://www.manningawards.ca

**The Manning Awards**

Given annually to Canadian innovators who have conceived & developed new concepts, procedures, processes or products of benefit to Canada; awards may be in any area of activity

One $100,000 Principal Award; one $25,000 Award of Distinction; two $5,000 Innovation prizes, & four $4,000 Young Canadian Innovation Awards

## Natural Sciences & Engineering Research Council of Canada / Conseil de recherches en sciences naturelles et en génie

350 Albert St., Ottawa ON K1A 1H5

613/996-6266; Fax: 613/992-5337

URL: http://www.nserc.ca

**Canada Gold Medal for Science & Engineering**

Awarded annually to an individual who has made outstanding & sustained contributions to Canadian research in natural sciences & engineering; the gold medal will be awarded for any activity of exceptional importance & impact that leads to the enhancement of the research enterprise in Canada - such activities may include contributions to knowledge, the application of existing knowledge, to the novel solution of practical problems, the promotion or management of research activity, the leadership in the transfer of knowledge

The accomplishments for which the award is given must have been carried out in Canada & achieved over a substantial period of time; persons from any sector (academic, business & industry, or government) are eligible; current members of council are not eligible; awardee's performance in relation to the cited achievement must demonstrate an unusually high degree of ability & the application of such qualities as expertise, creativity, imagination, leadership, perseverance & dedication

**The E.W.R. Steacie Memorial Fellowships**

Awarded to enhance the career development of outstanding & highly promising scientists & engineers who are staff members of Canadian universities; successful fellows are relieved of any teaching & administrative duties, enabling them to devote all their time & energy to research; up to four fellowships are awarded annually for a one or two-year period; fellowships are held at a Canadian university or affiliated research institution

Steacie fellows receive their normal university salary, which is paid by NSERC, & are eligible for NSERC grants

## Québec Ministère de l'industrie, du commerce, de la science et de la technologie

Direction de la diffusion de la science et de la technologie

710, Place d'Youville, 3e étage, Québec QC G1R 4Y4

418/691-5698, poste 4119

URL: http://www.micst.gouv.qc.ca; http://www.mcc.gouv.qc.ca

**Prix Armand-Frappier**

$30,000, a silver medal & a scroll presented to recognize the career of a scientist who, in addition to having achieved excellence in his own research, has made exceptional contributions to the development of Québec's research institutions, & has promoted research or increased the Québec public's interest in science & technology – Secrétariat des Prix du Québec dans le domaine scientifique

**Prix Marie-Victorin**

$30,000, a silver medal & a scroll awarded for excellence in pure & applied science – Secrétariat des Prix du Québec dans le domaine scientifique

**Prix Wilder-Penfield**

$30,000, a silver medal & a scroll awarded for excellence in the biomedical domain; recognized disciplines include medical science, natural science, & engineering – Secrétariat des Prix du Québec dans le domaine scientifique

## Royal Astronomical Society of Canada / Société royale d'astronomie du Canada

136 Dupont St., Toronto ON M5R 1V2

416/924-7973; Fax: 416/924-2911

URL: http://www.rasc.ca

**Chant Medal**

Established 1940 in appreciation of the great work of the late Prof. C.A. Chant in furthering the interests of astronomy in Canada; silver medal is awarded no more than once a year to an amateur astronomer resident in Canada on the basis of the value of the work which he/she has carried out in astronomy & closely allied fields of original investigation

**Ken Chilton Prize**

Established 1977; plaque awarded annually to an amateur astronomer resident in Canada, in recognition of a significant piece of work carried out or published during the year

## The Royal Canadian Geographical Society / La Société géographique royale du Canada

39 McArthur Ave., Vanier ON K1L 8L7

613/745-4629; Fax: 613/744-0947

Email: rgs@cangeo.ca

**The Gold Medal**

Established 1972; to recognize a particular achievement of one or more individuals in the field of geography, or a significant national or international event – Coordinator, Society Programs, Karen Hallquist

**The Massey Medal**

Established 1959; awarded annually for outstanding personal achievement in the exploration, development, or description of the geography of Canada

## The Royal Society of Canada / La Société royale du Canada

#308, 225 Metcalfe St., Ottawa ON K2P 1P9

613/991-6990; Fax: 613/991-6996

Email: adminrsc@rsc.ca; URL: http://www.rsc.ca

**Bancroft Award**

Established 1968; $1,500 & a presentation scroll awarded every two years for publication, instruction, & research in the earth sciences that have conspicuously contributed to public understanding & appreciation of the subject

**Eadie Medal**

Established 1975; $1,500 & a bronze medal awarded annually in recognition of major contributions to any field in engineering or applied science with an emphasis on communications

**John L. Synge Award**

Established 1986; $1,500 & a diploma awarded at irregular intervals for outstanding research in any of the branches of mathematics

**Rutherford Memorial Medals: Chemistry & Physics**

Established 1980; two medals & $1,500 each awarded annually for outstanding research, one in chemistry, one in physics

**The Flavelle Medal**

Established 1924; awarded every two years (since 1966) for an outstanding contribution to biological science during the preceding 10 years or for significant additions to a previous outstanding contribution to biological science

**The Henry Marshall Tory Medal**

Established 1941; awarded every two years (since 1947) for outstanding research in a branch of astronomy, chemistry, mathematics, physics, or an allied science

**The McNeil Medal**

$1,500 bursary & a medal awarded to encourage communication of science to students & the public

**Willet G. Miller Medal**

Established 1943; awarded every two years for outstanding research in any branch of the earth sciences

## Science Council of British Columbia

#800, 4710 Kingsway, Burnaby BC V5H 4M2

604/438-2752; Fax: 604/438-6564; Toll Free: 1-800-665-7222

Email: info@scbc.org; URL: http://www.scbc.org

**BC Science & Technology Awards**

Up to six gold medals awarded each year for outstanding achievements by BC scientists, engineers, industrial innovators & science communicators. The awards are: Industrial Innovation, Business/Education Partnership, Solutions Through Research, New Frontiers in Research, Cecil Green Award for Technology Entrepreneurship, Science Council Chairman's Award for Career Achievement, & Eve Savory Award for Science Communication

## Social Sciences & Humanities Research Council of Canada

350 Albert St., 10th Fl., PO Box 1610, Ottawa ON K1P 6G4

613/992-0530; Fax: 613/992-1787

Email: z-info@sshrc; URL: http://www.sshrc.ca

**Doctoral Fellowships**

Must have completed one year of doctoral study or a master's degree leading to a Ph.D. or equivalent; disciplines include: Geography, Health Studies, Applied Health Studies & Environmental Studies

Approx. $14,400 per year

**Postdoctoral Fellowships**

To suppport a core of the most promising new scholars in the social sciences & humanities & to assist them in establishing a research base at an important time in their research career; provides stipendiary support to non-tenured PhD graduates who are undertaking new research, publishing research findings, developing & expanding personal research networks, broadening teaching experience & preparing to become competitive in national research competitions

Approximately $28,000 per year (for a maximum of two years) plus a $5,000 accountable research allowance

## Society of Chemical Industry - Canadian Section

c/o Praxair Canada Inc., One City Centre Dr., Mississauga ON L5B 1M2

905/803-1703; Fax: 905/803-1696

**Canada Medal Award**

Established 1939; awarded every two years for outstanding services in the Canadian chemical industry; recipient delivers an address at a meeting of the society

**International Award**

Established 1976; award is presented in recognition of outstanding service in the chemical industry in the international sphere, preferably to Canadians or persons who have contributed measurably to the Canadian chemical scene

**Le Sueur Memorial Award**

Established 1955 to commemorate Ernest A. Le Sueur; award is presented in recognition of outstanding innovation in the Canadian chemical industry

## SPORTS & RECREATION

### Canadian Amateur Boxing Association / Association canadienne de boxe amateur

#711, 1600 James Naismith Dr., Gloucester ON K1B 5N4

613/748-5611; Fax: 613/748-5740

Email: caba@boxing.ca; URL: http://www.boxing.ca

**Outstanding Boxer of the Canada Cup Tournament**

### Canadian Association for Health, Physical Education, Recreation & Dance / Association canadienne pour la santé, l'éducation physique, le loisir et la danse

#809, 1600 James Naismith Dr., Gloucester ON K1B 5N4

613/748-5622; Fax: 613/748-5737

Email: CAHPERD@rtm.activeliving.ca; ACSEPLD@rtm.activeliving.ca; URL: http://www.activeliving.ca/activeliving/cahperd/indexfr.html

**R. Tait McKenzie Awards of Honour**

Instituted at the Montreal Convention in 1948, this is the most prestigious award presented by CAHPERD; named after the distinguished Canadian physician, sculptor & physical educator, Dr. Robert Tait McKenzie; candidate shall have performed distinguished, meritorious service as a recognized leader regionally & nationally in his/her field

### Canadian Association for the Advancement of Women & Sport & Physical Activity / Association canadienne pour l'avancement des femmes du sport et de l'activité physique

#308A, 1600 James Naismith Dr., Gloucester ON K1B 5N4

613/748-5793; Fax: 613/748-5775

URL: http://infoweb.magi.com/~wmnsport/index.html

**Breakthrough Awards**

Annual awards in recognition of women's achievements in sports

### Canadian Curling Association / Association canadienne de curling

#511, 1600 James Naismith Dr., Gloucester ON K1B 5N4

613/748-5628; Fax: 613/748-5713

Email: cca@curling.ca; URL: http://www.curling.ca

**Award of Achievement**

Commemorative plaque presented in recognition of individuals who have contributed significantly to any aspect of Canadian curling operations

**Ray Kingsmith Executive of the Year**

Awarded to an individual who parallels the level of involvement & commitment exemplified by Ray Kingsmith

### Canadian Sport Council / Conseil canadien du sport

#301A, 1600 James Naismith Dr., Gloucester ON K1B 5N4

613/748-5670; Fax: 613/748-5732

**Bruce Taylor Memorial Award**

A trophy is awarded to an individual deemed to have made an outstanding lifetime contribution to amateur sport in a builder capacity, at the provincial, national, or international level, or a combination of all three

**Canadian Airlines Athlete of the Month**

Each month winners are chosen by a selection committee of the federation & receive a commemorative plaque & an airline pass to any Canadian Airlines destination in the world

**Corporate Recognition Awards**

Presented annually to the top 10 corporations deemed to have made significant contributions to the development of sport in Canada

**Dick Ellis Trophy**

Trophy is awarded to Canada's most outstanding national amateur team of the year

**Elaine Tanner Award**

Established 1972; trophy is awarded to Canada's most outstanding junior (under 20 years old) amateur female athlete of the year

**Johnny F. Bassett Memorial Award**

Presented by the Government of Canada through the Dept. of Canadian Heritage; presented to a citizen of the Canadian sport community who has displayed a combination of sporting excellence & community work

**Norton H. Crowe Award**

Established 1932; a medal is awarded to Canada's most outstanding amateur male athlete of the year selected from nominations from sport governing bodies

**Tom Longboat Award**

Awarded occasionally by National Indian Brotherhood to male/female athlete of the year

**Velma Springstead Award**

Established 1934; a silver bowl awarded to Canada's most outstanding amateur female athlete of the year

**Viscount Alexander Trophy**

A trophy is awarded to Canada's most outstanding junior (under 20 years old) amateur male athlete of the year

### Ontario Ministry of Citizenship, Culture & Recreation

Recreation Programs Branch, 77 Bloor St. West, 8th Fl., Toronto ON M7A 2R9

416/314-7696; Fax: 416/314-7458

**Corps d'Elite Ontario Award**

Established 1986; designed to acknowledge those residents of Ontario whose voluntary efforts have had a significant impact on the development of recreation in Ontario

### La Société Saint-Jean-Baptiste de Montréal

82, rue Sherbrooke ouest, Montréal QC H2X 1X3

514/843-8851; Fax: 514/844-6369

**Prix Maurice-Richard**

Established 1979; $1,500 & a medal awarded annually to a French Canadian in recognition of outstanding achievement in sports & athletics in serving the higher interests of the French Canadian people

### Swimming/Natation Canada

#503, 1600 James Naismith Dr., Gloucester ON K1B 5N4

613/748-5673; Fax: 613/748-5715

Email: natloffice@swimming.ca; URL: http://www.swimming.ca

**Female/Male Swimmer of the Year**

Best international swimmer of the year; winner receives a plaque & gift

**Recognition of Disabled Athletes**

Best international swimmer with a disability of the year; winner receives a plaque & gift

**TECHNICAL See SCIENTIFIC, ENGINEERING, TECHNICAL**

**TELEVISION See BROADCASTING & FILM**

**THEATRE See PERFORMING ARTS**

**TRADE See BUSINESS & TRADE**

**VISUAL ARTS See CULTURE, VISUAL ARTS & ARCHITECTURE**

**VOLUNTEERISM See CITIZENSHIP & BRAVERY**

**WRITING See LITERARY ARTS, BOOKS & LIBRARIES**

# SECTION 2

## ORGANIZATIONS DIRECTORY



See ADDENDA at the back of this book for late changes & additional information.

# RELIGIOUS DENOMINATIONS

### Ahmadiyya Movement in Islam (Canada)/ Mouvement Ahmadiyya en Islam (Canada) (1966)
10610 Jane St., Maple, ON L6A 1S1
905/832-2669, Fax: 905/832-3220, Email: info@islam.ahmadiyya.org
President & Missionary-in-Charge, Naseem Mahdi
General Secretary, Malik Lal Khan
Secretary External Affairs, Hasanat Ahmad Syed
Publications: Ahmadiyya Gazette

### The Anglican Church of Canada/L'Église anglicane (ACC) (1893)
Anglican Church House, 600 Jarvis St., Toronto, ON M4Y 2J6
416/924-9192; Book Centre: 924-1332, Fax: 416/968-7983
Primate of the Anglican Church of Canada, The Most Rev. Michael Peers, B.A., L.Th., D.D.
Treasurer, Robert G. Armstrong, C.A.
Publications: Anglican Journal/Journal Anglican; Anglican Church Directory

### The Antiochan Orthodox Christian Archdiocese of North America (1905)
St. George's Orthodox Church, #555, 575, rue Jean Talon est, Montréal, QC H2R 1T8
514/276-8533, Fax: 514/276-6740
His Eminence Metropolitan, Philip Saliba
Archpriest, Antony Gabriel

### The Apostolic Church in Canada
27 Castlefield Ave., Toronto, ON M4R 1G3
416/489-0453
President, Rev. John Kristensen
National Secretary/Missionary Secretary, Rev. J. Karl Thomas

### Apostolic Church of Pentecost of Canada Inc./ Église apostolique de Pentecôte du Canada inc. (ACOP) (1921)
General Office, #200, 809 Manning Rd. NE, Calgary, AB T2E 7M9
403/273-5777, Fax: 403/273-8102, Email: acop@compuserve.com, URL: http://www.illuminart.com/acop/
Moderator, Rev. Gil Killam
Administrator, Rev. Wes Mills
Missions Director, Rev. Rick Parkyn
Publications: Harvestime; Focus
Affiliates: Evangelical Fellowship of Canada

### Armenian Evangelical Church
c/o Armenian Evangelical Union of North America, 42 Glenforest Rd., Toronto, ON M4N 1Z8
Contact, Rev. Y. Sarmazian

### Armenian Holy Apostolic Church - Canadian Diocese (AHAC) (1984)
615, av Stuart, Outremont, QC H2V 3H2
514/276-9479, Fax: 514/276-9960
Archbishop, His Eminence Hovnan W. Derderian
Publications: Noragenounk
Affiliates: Canadian Council of Churches

### Associated Gospel Churches of Canada/ Association des églises évangélique (AGC) (1925)
3228 South Service Rd., Burlington, ON L7N 3T9
905/634-8184, Fax: 905/634-6283, Email: agc@ftn.net, URL: http://www.agcofcanada.com/home/
President, Dr. Donald Hamilton
Moderator, Rev. Vern Trafford
Publications: Advance Magazine
Affiliates: World Relief; World Team; UFM International; Evangelical Fellowship of Canada
Eastern Office: 5500, rue Grenier, Saint-Hubert, QC J3Y 1N7, 514/678-6345
Western Office: 1613 Early Dr., Saskatoon, SK S7H 3K1, 306/477-2321

### Atlantic Canada Association of Free Will Baptists (1898)
RR#6, Woodstock, NB E0J 2B0
506/325-9381
Moderator, Licentiate Oral McAffee

### The Baha'i Faith in Canada (1844)
Baha'i National Centre, 7200 Leslie St., Thornhill, ON L3T 6L8
905/889-8168, Fax: 905/889-8184, Telex: 06 96413, Email: nsacan@interlog.com
General Secretary, Reginald Newkirk
Public Affairs, Gerald Filson, Ph.D
Publications: Baha'i Canada
Affiliates: Baha'i International Community

### Baptist General Conference of Canada (BGC) (1981)
4306 - 97 St., Edmonton, AB T6E 5R9
403/438-9127, Fax: 403/435-2478, Email: bgcc@datanet.ab.ca, URL: http://www.datanet.ab.ca/users/bgcc/
Executive Director, Abe Funk
Publications: BGC Canada News
Baptist General Conference in Alberta: District Executive Minister, Dr. Cal Netterfield, 5011 - 122A St., Edmonton, AB T6H 3S8, 403/438-9126, Fax: 403/438-5258
Baptist General Conference in Saskatchewan: District Executive Minister, Rev. Charles Lees, PO Box 419, Loon Lake, SK S0M 1L0, 306/837-4711, Fax: 306/837-2376
British Columbia Baptist Conference: District Executive Minister, Rev. Walter W. Wieser, 7600 Glover Rd., Langley, BC V3A 6H4, 604/888-2246, Fax: 604/888-0046
Central Canada Baptist Conference: District Executive Minister, Rev. Alf Bell, #19, 130 Ulster St., Winnipeg, MB R3T 3A2, 204/261-9113, Fax: 204/261-9176

### Brethren in Christ (1788)
2619 Niagara Pkwy., Fort Erie, ON L2A 2Z4
905/871-9991, Fax: 905/871-6330
Bishop, Dale Shaw
Secretary, Betty Albraht
Treasurer, Doug Winger
Publications: Evangelical Visitor

### British Methodist Episcopal Church Conference of Canada (1856)
460 Shaw St., Toronto, ON M6G 3L3
416/534-3831, Fax: 416/383-6856
General Superintendent, Rt. Rev. Dr. D.D. Rupwate
General Secretary, Rev. Maurice M. Hicks
Publications: BME Church Newsletter
Affiliates: Canadian Council of Churches

### Buddhist Churches of Canada
4860 Garry St., Richmond, BC V7A 2B2
604/272-3330, Fax: 604/272-6865

### Canadian Baptist Ministries/Ministères Baptist Canadiens (1912)
Canadian Baptist Place, 7185 Millcreek Dr., Mississauga, ON L5N 5R4
905/821-3533, Fax: 905/826-3441, Email: cbmadmin@inforamp.com, URL: http://www.cbmin.org
General Secretary, Rev. David K. Phillips
President, Carmen Moir
Communications, David Rogelstad
Publications: The Enterprise; Infomission, m.
Affiliates: Baptist World Alliance

#### BAPTIST CONVENTION OF ONTARIO & QUÉBEC (BCOQ) (1887)
#414, 195 The West Mall, Etobicoke, ON M9C 5K1
416/622-8600, Fax: 416/622-2308
Email: info@baptist.ca, URL: http://www.baptist.ca
Executive Minister, Rev. Dr. Ken Bellous
Publications: The Canadian Baptist; BCOQ Directory, a.

#### THE BAPTIST UNION OF WESTERN CANADA (BUWC) (1908)
#605, 999 - 8 St. SW, Calgary, AB T2R 1J5
403/228-9559, Fax: 403/228-9048, Toll Free: 1-800-820-2479
Email: buwcmain@ab.imag.net
Executive Minister, Rev. G. Fisher
Publications: Share; Baptist Union Yearbook
Affiliates: Baptist World Alliance

#### UNION D'ÉGLISES BAPTISTES FRANÇAISES AU CANADA/UNION OF FRENCH BAPTIST CHURCHES IN CANADA (UEBF) (1969)
2285, av Papineau, Montréal, QC H2K 4J5
514/526-6643, Téléc: 514/526-9269
Executive Officer, Dr. J. Boillat
Publications: Le Trait d'Union
Organisation(s) affiliée(s): Alliance Baptiste Mondiale

#### UNITED BAPTIST CONVENTION OF THE ATLANTIC PROVINCES/LA CONVENTION BAPTISTE DES PROVINCES DE L'ATLANTIQUE (UBCAP) (1906)
**Atlantic United Baptist Convention**
1655 Manawagonish Rd., Saint John, NB E2M 3Y2
506/635-1922, Fax: 506/635-0366
Email: ubcap@nbnet.nb.ca
Executive Minister/Editor of the Year Book, Dr. Harry G. Gardner
Director of Administration/Treasurer, Daryl W. Mackenzie
Publications: The Atlantic Baptist
Affiliates: Baptist World Alliance

### Canadian Conference of Mennonite Brethren Churches (1945)
#3, 169 Riverton Ave., Winnipeg, MB R2L 2E5
204/669-6575, Fax: 204/654-1865, Email: rpauls@cdnmbconf.ca, URL: http://www.cdnmbconf.ca/mb/mbdoc.htm
Executive Minister, Reuben Pauls
Publications: Manitoba Herald

### Canadian Convention of Southern Baptists (1987)
PO Box 300, Cochrane, AB T0L 0W0
403/932-5688, Fax: 403/932-4937, Toll Free: 1-888-442-2272, Email: 70420,2230@compuserve.com
Executive Director, Allen E. Schmidt
President, Clare Cremer
Publications: The Baptist Horizon
Affiliates: Southern Baptist Convention

### Canadian Council for Conservative Judaism (CCCJ) (1982)
#112, 1520 Steeles Ave., Concord, ON L4K 3B9
905/738-1717, Fax: 905/738-1331, Email: 71263.302@compuserve.com
President, David Greenberg
Executive Secretary, Rhonda Schild
Publications: CCCJ/Mercaz/Masorti Update
Affiliates: United Synagogue of Conservative Judaism; World Council of Synagogues

### Canadian Council for Reform Judaism
36 Atkinson Ave., Thornhill, ON L4J 8C9
905/709-2275, Fax: 905/709-1895
President, Charles Rothschild

### Canadian Council of Reform Rabbis
c/o Temple Binai Tikvav, 1607 - 90 Ave. SW, Calgary, AB T2V 4V7
613/224-1802
Contact, Rabbi Jordan Goldsom

### Canadian District of the Moravian Church in America, Northern Province
2304 - 38 St., Edmonton, AB T6L 4K9
403/467-6745, Fax: 403/467-0411
President, Ruth Humphreys

### Canadian Friends Service Committee (CFSC) (1931)
**Religious Society of Friends**
60 Lowther Ave., Toronto, ON M5R 1C7
416/920-5213
Coordinator, Peter Chapman
Clerk, Mona Callin
Publications: Quaker Concern
Canadian Yearly Meeting: 91A Fourth Ave., Ottawa, ON K1S 2L1, 613/235-8553, Fax: 613/235-8553

### Canadian Islamic Organization Inc. (1985)
2069 Kempton Park Dr., Mississauga, ON L5M 2Z4
905/820-4655, Fax: 905/820-0382
General Secretary, Fareed Ahmad Khan

### The Canadian Orthodox Church/L'Église Orthodoxe canadienne (COC) (1970)
37323 Hawkins Pickle Rd., Dewdney, BC V0M 1H0
604/826-9336, Fax: 604/820-9758
Archbishop, Lazar Puhalo
Publications: Canadian Orthodox Missionary; Synakis: Canadian Orthodox Journal of Theology, q.
Affiliates: The Nemanjic Institute for Serbo-Byzantine Studies; Centre for Canadian Orthodox Studies

### Canadian Unitarian Council/Conseil Unitarien du Canada (CUC) (1960)
**Unitarian Church**
#706, 188 Eglinton Ave. East, Toronto, ON M4P 2X7
416/489-4121, Fax: 416/489-9010, Email: cuc@web.net, URL: http://www.web.net/~cuc
Executive Director, Ellen K. Campbell
Administrator, Carol Dahlquist
Publications: The Canadian Unitarian
Affiliates: Unitarian Universalist Association; International Association for Religious Freedom; International Council of Unitarians & Universities

### Christian Brethren Church in the Province of Québec/l'Église des frères chrétiens dans la Province du Québec (CBCPQ) (1942)
**Plymouth Brethren**
358, rue Wellington sud, Sherbrooke, QC J1H 5E4
819/820-1693, Fax: 819/821-9287
Secretary, Norman Buchanan

### Christian Church (Disciples of Christ) in Canada/Église Chrétienne (Disciples du Christ) au Canada (DISCAN) (1922)
PO Box 64, Guelph, ON N1H 6J6
519/823-5190, Fax: 519/823-5766
Executive Regional Minister, Rev. Dr. Robert W. Steffer
Moderator, Rev. Mervin Bailey
Publications: The Canadian Disciple
Affiliates: The Christian Church (Disciples of Christ) in USA

### Christian Episcopal Church of Canada
St. Saviour's Parish, 4300 Corless Rd., Richmond, BC V7C 4S2
604/275-7422
Diocesan Bishop, The Rt. Rev. A. Donald Davies
Vicar General for the Diocese of Canada, The Rev. Robert D. Redmile, BA, B.Ed.

### The Christian & Missionary Alliance in Canada/Alliance chrétienne et missionaire au Canada (C&MA) (1972)
**The Alliance Church**
PO Box 7900, Stn B, North York, ON M2K 2R6
416/492-8775, Fax: 416/492-7708, Email: nationaloffice@cmacan.org
President, Dr. Arnold Cook
Vice-President, Canadian Ministries, Dr. C. Stuart Lightbody
Vice-President, Finance, M.H. Quigg
Vice-President, Personnel/Missions, Rev. Wally Albrecht
Vice-President, General Services, K.R. Paton
Publications: Briefing; Inside Story, s-a.; Alliance Life, bi-m.; Canadian Alliance News, 3 pa; Alliance Men in Action, s-a.; CMAC Official Directory, a.; Prayer Directory, a.; CMAC Yearbook; CMAC Statistical Report, a.; Prayer Line, m.; Praise & Prayer, m.
Affiliates: Alliance World Fellowship - International
Canadian Midwest District Office: District Superintendent, Rev. Bill Parsons, 2950 Arens Rd. East, Regina, SK S4V 1N8, 306/586-3549, Fax: 306/584-0399
Canadian Pacific District Office: District Superintendent, Rev. Brian Thom, #201, 11471 Blacksmith Pl., Richmond, BC V7A 4T7, 604/277-1983, Fax: 604/277-2003
Eastern & Central Canadian District Offices: Superintendent, Central Canadian District, Rev. David Lewis; Superintendent, Eastern Canadian District, Rev. Douglas Wiebe, 155 Panin Rd., Burlington, ON L7V 1A1, 905/639-9615, Fax: 905/634-7044
St. Lawrence District Office: District Superintendent, Rev. Yvan Fournier, #201, 964, rue Mainguy, Ste-Foy, QC G1V 3S4, 418/659-3313, Fax: 418/659-4306
Western Canadian District Office: District Superintendent, Rev. Arnold Downey, 907A - 9 Ave. SW, Calgary, AB T2P 1L3, 403/265-7900, Fax: 403/265-4599

### Christian Reformed Church in North America (CRCNA) (1857)
2850 Kalamazoo Ave. SE, Grand Rapids, MI 49560 USA
616/241-1691, Fax: 616/246-0834
General Secretary, Dr. David H. Engelhard
Executive Director of Ministries, Dr. Peter Borgdorff
Publications: The Banner
Affiliates: National Association of Evangelicals; North American Presbyterian & Reformed Council; Reformed Ecumenical Council
Canada: Contact, Terry Veldboom, 3475 Mainway, PO Box 5070, Burlington, ON L7R 3Y8, 905/336-2920, Fax: 905/336-8344

### Christian Science (1879)
The First Church of Christ, Scientist, 175 Huntington Ave., Boston, MA 02115 USA
617/450-3301, Fax: 617/450-3325
Manager, Committee on Publication, Victor Westberg
Manager, Communications Division, Norm Bleichman, Bus: 617/450-3309
Publications: The Christian Science Journal; The Christian Science Monitor, daily; The Herald of Christian Science, m.; The Christian Science Sentinel, w.

### The Church Army in Canada (1929)
Headquarters & College of Evangelism, 397 Brunswick Ave., Toronto, ON M5R 2Z2
416/924-9279, Fax: 416/924-2931
National Director, Bruce Smith
Warden, The Rev. Duke Vipperman
Publications: The Crusader
Affiliates: Anglican Church of Canada

### Church of God, Anderson (1920)
Eastern Canada, 38 James St., Dundas, ON L9H 2J6
905/627-5236, Email: jr_wiebe@ecunet.org
Chairperson, Jim Wiebe
Publications: The Messenger
Affiliates: Church of God, Anderson, Indiana
Western Canada Assembly: Chairperson, Jack Wagner; Church Service/Mission Coordinator, John D. Campbell, 4717 - 56th St., Camrose, AB T4V 2C4, 403/672-0722, Fax: 403/672-6888

### Church of God of Prophecy in Canada
RR#2, Brampton, ON L6V 1A1
905/843-2379
National Overseer, Canada East, Bishop Wade H. Phillips
National Overseer, Canada West, Bishop Vernon Van Deventer
Publications: Canadian Trumpeter (Canada West); Torch Light (Canada East)

### Church of Jesus Christ of Latter-Day Saints (Mormons) (1830)
1185 Eglinton Ave. East, PO Box 116, North York, ON M3C 3C6
416/424-2485, Fax: 416/424-3326
Commnications Officer, Bruce Smith
Communications Officer, Donna Smith

### Church of The Nazarene Canada (1902)
#7, 3800 - 19 St. NE, Calgary, AB T2E 6V2
403/250-5166, Fax: 403/250-5183
Administrator, Dr. Neil E. Hightower
Chairman, Dr. William Stewart
Vice-Chairman, Dr. Charles Muxworthy
Secretary, Rev. Clair MacMillan
Publications: Spotlight

### Conference of Mennonites in Canada (CMC) (1903)
600 Shaftesbury Blvd., Winnipeg, MB R3P 0M4
204/888-6781, Fax: 204/831-5675, Email: cmc@mbnet.mb.ca
General Secretary, Helmut Harder
Publications: Nexus

### Congregational Christian Churches in Canada (CCCC) (1821)
#202, 222 Fairview Dr., Brantford, ON N3T 2W9
519/751-0606, Fax: 519/751-0852, URL: http://www.cccc.ca
Executive Director, Rev. W. Riegert
President, Jim Potter, Email: jpotter@ican.net
Publications: Communications

### The Coptic Orthodox Church (Canada)
St. Mark's Coptic Orthodox Church, 41 Glendinning Ave., Scarborough, ON M1W 3E2
416/494-4449, Fax: 416/494-2631
Archpriest, Fr. M.A. Marcos
Publications: Coptologia

### L'Église Réformée du Québec
5377, Maréchal-Joffre, Charny, QC G6X 3C9
Courrier électronique: Farel@qbc.clic.net
Secrétaire, François Cordey
Publications: En Lui
Organisation(s) affiliée(s): Christian Reformed Church; Presbyterian Church of North America

### Estonian Evangelical Lutheran Church (EELK) (1950)
383 Jarvis St., Toronto, ON M5B 2C7
416/923-5172, Fax: 416/923-5688
Archbishop, Rev. Udo Petersoo
Publications: Eesti Kirik
Affiliates: Lutheran World Federation; World Council of Churches

### The Evangelical Alliance Mission of Canada Inc. (TEAM) (1969)
PO Box 56030, RPO Airways, Calgary, AB T2E 8K5

403/250-2140, Fax: 403/291-2857
Canadian Director, Rev. Norman Niemeyer
Publications: TEAM Horizons; Wherever, 3 pa; TEAM Prayer Directory, a.

### Evangelical Covenant Church of Canada
245 - 21st St. East, Prince Albert, SK S6V 1L9
306/922-3449, Fax: 306/922-5414
Superintendent, Rev. Jerome Johnson
Publications: The Covenant Messenger

### Evangelical Fellowship of Canada/Alliance évangélique du Canada (EFC) (1964)
PO Box 3745, Markham, ON L3S 0Y4
905/479-5885, Fax: 905/479-4742, Email: efc@efc-canada.com, URL: http://www.efc-canada.com
President, Gary R. Walsh
Corporate Affairs Director, Lorna A. Renkema
Publications: Faith Today; Canada Watch Bulletin, q.

### Evangelical Lutheran Church in Canada (ELCIC) (1986)
1512 St. James St., Winnipeg, MB R3H 0L2
204/786-6707, Fax: 204/783-7548, URL: http://info.wlu.ca/~wwwsem/elcic/ehome.html
Secretary, Rev. Leon C. Gilbertson
Bishop, Rev. Telmor G. Sartison
Publications: Canada Lutheran
Affiliates: The Lutheran World Federation; World Council of Churches
The Lutheran Council in Canada: President, Rev. Dr. Edwin Lehman; Vice-President, Bishop Telmor Sartison, 1512 St. James St., Winnipeg, MB R3H 0L2, 204/783-7548
British Columbia Synod: Bishop, Marlin B. Aadland, Ph.D., 80 - 10 Ave. East, New Westminster, BC V3L 4R5, 604/524-1318, Fax: 604/524-9255
Eastern Synod: Bishop, Rev. William D. Huras, #340, 50 Queen St. North, Kitchener, ON N2H 6P4, 519/743-1461, Fax: 519/743-4291
Manitoba/Northwestern Ontario Synod: Rev. Richard M. Smith, #201, 3657 Roblin Blvd., Winnipeg, MB R3R 0E2, 204/889-3760, Fax: 204/896-0272
Saskatchewan Synod: Bishop, Rev. Allan A. Grundahl, Bessborough Towers, #707, 601 Spadina Cres. East, Saskatoon, SK S7K 3G8, 306/244-2474, Fax: 306/664-8677
Synod of Alberta & the Territories: Bishop, Rev. P. Kristenson, 10014 - 81 Ave., Edmonton, AB T6E 1W8, 403/439-2636, Fax: 403/433-6623

### Evangelical Mennonite Conference (EMC) (1812)
PO Box 1268, Steinbach, MB R0A 2A0
204/326-6401, Fax: 204/326-1613, Email: emconf@mts.net
Executive Secretary, Don Thiessen
Publications: Messenger
Affiliates: Mennonite Central Committee

### Evangelical Mennonite Mission Conference (EMMC) (1959)
PO Box 52059, Stn Niakwa, Winnipeg, MB R2M 5P9
204/253-7929, Fax: 204/256-7384
Executive Secretary, Henry Dueck
Publications: The Recorder

### Fellowship of Evangelical Baptist Churches in Canada
679 Southgate Dr., Guelph, ON N1G 4S2
519/821-4830, Fax: 519/821-9829, Email: 103227.1367@compuserve.com
President, Rev. Terry Cuthbert
Publications: Evangelical Baptist

### Foursquare Gospel Church of Canada (1981)
#100, 8459 - 160th St., Surrey, BC V3S 3T9
604/543-8414, Fax: 604/543-8417, Email: fgcc@portal.ca
President/General Supervisor, Timothy J. Peterson
Publications: Foursquare World Advance

### Free Methodist Church in Canada/Église méthodiste libre au Canada (1880)
4315 Village Centre Ct., Mississauga, ON L4Z 1S2
905/848-2600, Fax: 905/848-2603, Email: fmccan@inforamp.net, URL: http://www.fmc-canada.org
President, Bishop Keith A. Elford
Secretary, David N. Ashton
Treasurer, Brian R. Cooke
Publications: The Free Methodist Herald
Affiliates: Evangelical Fellowship of Canada; Canadian Council of Christian Charities; World Methodist Council

### Fung Loy Kok Institute of Taoism
1376 Bathurst St., 2nd Fl., Toronto, ON M5R 3J1
416/656-7479

### General Church of the New Jerusalem in Canada
279 Burnhamthorpe Rd., Etobicoke, ON M9B 1Z6
519/748-5802, Fax: 519/748-6435
Rev. Michael D. Gladish

### Greek Orthodox Church (Canada)
Greek Orthodox Diocese of Toronto, 27 Teddington Park Ave., Toronto, ON M4N 2C4
416/322-5055, Fax: 416/485-5929
Bishop of Toronto (Canada), The Rt. Rev. Sotirios Athanassoulas
Publications: The Orthodox Way

### Independent Assemblies of God - Canada
1211 Lancaster St., London, ON N5V 2L4
519/451-1751
General Secretary, Rev. Harry O. Wuerch
Publications: The Canadian Mantle

### Inter-Varsity Christian Fellowship of Canada (IVCF) (1929)
#17, 40 Vogell Rd., Richmond Hill, ON L4B 3N6
905/884-6880, Fax: 905/884-6550, Toll Free: 1-800-668-9766, Email: national@ivcf.dar.com, URL: http://www.dar.com/ivcf/
General Director, James E. Berney
Chairperson, David Bogart
Publications: The Intercessor
Affiliates: International Fellowship of Evangelical Students; Evangelical Fellowship of Canada; Canadian Council of Christian Charities; Coalition for Religious Freedom in Education

### ISKCON Toronto - Hare Krishna Movement (1966)
**International Society for Krishna Consciousness**
243 Avenue Rd., Toronto, ON M5R 2J6
416/922-5415, Fax: 416/964-9509
Director, Kala Das
Publications: Back to Godhead

### Italian Pentecostal Church of Canada (1912)
6724, rue Fabre, Montréal, QC H2G 2Z6
514/593-1944, Fax: 514/593-1835
General Superintendent, Rev. Daniel Ippolito
General Secretary, John Della Foresta
Publications: Voce Evangelica

### Mennonite Central Committee Canada (MCCC) (1963)
134 Plaza Dr., Winnipeg, MB R3T 5K9
204/261-6381, Fax: 204/269-9875, URL: http://www.mennonitecc.ca/mcc
Executive Director, Marv Frey, Email: MF@mennonitecc.ca
Affiliates: Conference of Mennonites in Canada; Canadian Conference of Mennonite Brethren Churches; Canadian Conference of the Brethren in Christ Church; Evangelical Mennonite Brethren Conference; Evangelical Mennonite Mission Conference; Mennonite Conference of Eastern Canada; Northwest Mennonite Conference; Old Colony Mennonite Church; Sommerfelder Mennonite Church; Evangelical Mennonite Conference
MCC Alberta: Executive Director, Dick Neufeld, 76 Skyline Cres. NE, Calgary, AB T2K 5X7, 403/275-6935, Fax: 403/275-3711
MCC British Columbia: Executive Director, Ed Janzen, 31872 South Fraser Way, PO Box 2038, Clearbrook, BC V2T 3T8, 604/850-6639, Fax: 604/850-8734, Email: mccbc@web.apc.org
MCC Canada Ottawa Office: #803, 63 Sparks St., Ottawa, ON K1P 5A6, 613/238-7224, Fax: 613/238-7611, Email: mccott@web.apc.org
MCC Manitoba: Executive Director, Peter Peters, 134 Plaza Dr., Winnipeg, MB R3T 5K9, 204/261-6381, Fax: 204/269-9875
MCC Ontario: Executive Director, Dave Worth, 50 Kent Ave., Kitchener, ON N2G 3R1, 519/745-8458, Fax: 519/745-0064, Email: mccon@web.apc.org
MCC Saskatchewan: Executive Director, Werner Froese, 600 - 45 St. West, Saskatoon, SK S7L 5W9, 306/665-2555, Fax: 306/665-5564

### Mennonite Conference of Eastern Canada (MCEC) (1988)
4489 King St. East, RR#3, Kitchener, ON N2G 3W6
Moderator, Ron Sawatsky

### New Apostolic Church - Canada
65 Northfield Dr., PO Box 1615, Waterloo, ON N2J 4J2
519/884-2862, Fax: 519/884-3438
President, E. Wagner
Treasurer, T. Witt

### New Life League (1986)
PO Box 4083, Ponoka, AB T4J 1R5
403/783-6986, Fax: 403/783-6986
Director, Cliff Reimer
Treasurer, Don Hogman
Publications: Newsletter

### North American Baptist Conference - Canadian Headquarters
11525 - 23 Ave., Edmonton, AB T6J 4T3
403/438-8852, Fax: 403/434-9170, Email: rberg@enabel.ab.ca
Rev. Ron Berg
Publications: NAB Today
Affiliates: Edmonton Baptist Seminary; North American Baptist College

### Northwest Mennonite Conference
9505 - 79 St., Edmonton, AB T6C 2S1
403/468-1003, Fax: 403/465-7313
Moderator, Jim Miller
Publications: Northwest Mennonite Conference Newsletter

### The Old Holy Catholic Church in Canada (OHCC) (1939)
**Sancta Vetus Catholica Ecclesia Canadiensis**
PO Box 899, Hawkesbury, ON K6A 3E1
613/632-1210, Fax: 613/632-4812
Presiding Archbishop, Rainer Laufers
Chancellor, Rev. Fr. Ryan Perkins
Publications: OHCC Newsletter

### Old Order Amish Church
c/o Heritage Historical Library, RR#4, Aylmer West, ON N5H 2R3
Contact, David Luthy

### Orthodox Church in America - Archdiocese of Canada (OCA ADOC) (1902)
Office of the Bishop, PO Box 179, Spencerville, ON K0E 1X0
613/925-5226, Fax: 613/925-5221
HG Bishop Seraphim (Storheim)
Publications: Canadian Orthodox Messenger
Bishop's Office West: Dn. Andrew Piasta, Box 24, Site 5, RR#2, Winterburn, AB T0E 2N0, 403/987-4833, Fax: 403/987-4500
Chancery: Chancellor, Archpriest John Tkachuk, CP 1390, Succ Place Bonaventure, Montréal, QC H5A 1H3, 514/481-5093, Fax: 514/481-2256

### Orthodox Missionary Church of Canada (OMCC) (1968)
Sts. Cyril & Methodius Parish, #514, 186 King St., London, ON N6A 1C7
519/438-0734, URL: http://phobos.astro.uwo.ca/~arenburg/omcc.html
Missionary Vicar, The Very Rev. Andrei Bazilsky
Publications: Orthodoxy for Canada
Affiliates: Autocephalous Holy Orthodox Church of America

### Patriarchal Parishes of the Russian Orthodox Church in Canada (1897)
St. Barbara's Russian Orthodox Cathedral, 10105 - 96th St., Edmonton, AB T5H 2G3
403/422-0277
Administrator, Rt. Rev. Bishop Mark

### The Pentecostal Assemblies of Canada/Les Assemblées de la Pentecôte du Canada (PAoC) (1919)
6745 Century Ave., Mississauga, ON L5N 6P7
905/542-7400, Fax: 905/542-7313, Email: admin@paoc.org
General Superintendent, Rev. William D. Morrow
General Sec.-Treas., Rev. David Ball
Executive Director, Overseas Missions, Rev. E.S. Hunter
Executive Director, Canadian Ministries, Rev. K.B. Birch
Publications: The Pentecostal Testimony; Resource, m.
Affiliates: World Pentecost; Pentecostal/Charismatic Churches of North America

### Pentecostal Assemblies of Newfoundland (PAON) (1925)
PO Box 8248, St. John's, NF A1B 3T2
709/753-6314, Fax: 709/753-4945, Email: paon@paon.nf.ca
General Superintendent, Roy D. King
Publications: Good Tidings
Affiliates: Pentecostal Fellowship of North America

### Polish National Catholic Church of Canada
St. John's Cathedral, 186 Cowan Ave., Toronto, ON M6K 2N6
416/532-8249, Fax: 416/532-4653
Bishop Administrator, The Rt. Rev. Thaddeus Peplowski

### Presbyterian Church in Canada/Église Presbytérienne au Canada (PCC) (1875)
50 Wynford Dr., North York, ON M3C 1J7
416/441-1111, Fax: 416/441-2825, Email: pccweb@presbycan.ca, URL: http://www.presbycan.ca/index.html
Moderator, Tamiko Corbett, B.A.
Principal Clerk, The Rev. Dr. T. Gemmell, B.A., B.D., D.D.
Deputy Clerk, Barbara M. McLean
Deputy Clerk, The Rev. Dr. Tony Plomp, B.A., B.D., D.D.
General Secretary, Life & Mission Agency, The Rev. J.P. Morrison
General Secretary, Service Agency, Rev. K.A. Hincke
Chief Financial Officer, Donald A. Taylor
Principal, Knox College, Toronto, Dr. A. Van Seters
Principal, Presbyterian College, Montréal, Dr. W.J. Klempa
WMS President, The Rev. Rosemary Doran
AMS President, Marlene Sinnis
Executive Director, Women's Missionary Society, Charlotte Brown
Publications: The Presbyterian Record; Glad Tidings

### The Reformed Episcopal Church of Canada - Diocese of Eastern Canada
PO Box 2532, New Liskeard, ON P0J 1P0
705/647-4565, Fax: 705/647-5429, Email: fed@nt.net
President, Rt. Rev. Dr. Michael Fedechko
Publications: The Messenger

### The Reformed Episcopal Church of Canada - Diocese of Western Canada (1874)
626 Blanshard St., Victoria, BC V8W 3G6
250/383-8915, Fax: 250/727-3722, Email: recwcan@acts.bc.ca
Bishop, Rt. Rev. Charles W. Dorrington
Publications: The Grape Vine

### Regional Synod of Canada Inc. - Reformed Church in America (RSC) (1993)
Reformed Church Centre, RR#4, Cambridge, ON N1R 5S5
519/622-1777, Fax: 519/622-1993, Email: RSCMoerman@aol.com
Executive Secretary, Rev. James Moerman
Publications: The Pioneer
Affiliates: The Reformed Church in America - HQ: New York, NY, USA

### Reorganized Church of Jesus Christ of Latter Day Saints (Canada) (RLDS) (1830)
**Saints' Church**
390 Speedvale Ave. East, Guelph, ON N1E 1N5
519/822-4150, Fax: 519/822-4151
Bishop of Canada & Regional Bishop, Jim Poirier
Regional President, Larry Windland
Publications: Saint's Herald

### Roman Catholic Church in Canada
Apostolic Nunciature, 724 Manor Ave., Ottawa, ON K1M 0E3
613/746-4914, Fax: 613/746-4786
Apostolic Pro-Nuncio to Canada, Most Reverend Carlo Curis
Counsellor, Msgr. Vito Rallo, P.H.
Secretary of the Apostolic Nunciature, Rev. Henri-Marie Guindon, S.M.M.
Assemblée des évêques du Québec: Secrétaire général, Clément Vigneault, 1225, boul St-Joseph est, Montréal, QC H2J 1L7, 514/274-4323, Téléc: 514/274-4383
Atlantic Episcopal Assembly: Contact, Most Rev. J. Faber MacDonald, PO Box 771, Grand Falls-Windsor, NF A2A 2M4, 709/489-2778
Canadian Conference of Catholic Bishops: President, Most Rev. Francis J. Spence; General Secretary, Rev. Douglas Crosby, o.m.i.; M. Émilius Goulet, p.s.s., 90 Parent Ave., Ottawa, ON K1N 7B1, 613/241-9461, Fax: 613/241-8117, Toll Free: 1-800-769-1147, Email: cecc@cccb.ca, URL: http://www.cam.org/~cccb
Ontario Conference of Catholic Bishops: General Secretary, Tom Reilly, #800, 10 St. Mary St., Toronto, ON M4V 1P9, 416/923-1423, Fax: 416/923-1509
Ordinariat militaire du Canada: Evêque, André Vallée, p.m.é; Aumônier général, B.Gen. Jean Pelletier, Ordinaire militaire, 1247, Place Kilborn, Ottawa, ON K1H 6K9, 613/990-7824, Téléc: 613/991-1056
The Western Catholic Conference: President, Most Rev. Paul O'Byrne, 1916 - 2 St. SW, Calgary, AB T2S 1S3, 403/228-4501, Fax: 403/228-7704

### Romanian Orthodox Church in America (Canadian Parishes)
St. Demetrios Romanian Orthodox Church, 103 Furby St., Winnipeg, MB R3C 2A4
204/775-6472
Contact, Rev. Father Victor Malanca
Treasurer, Terry Holunga
Publications: Credinta - the Faith

### The Salvation Army in Canada (1882)
Territorial Headquarters, Canada & Bermuda, 2 Overlea Blvd., Toronto, ON M4H 1P4
416/425-2111, Fax: 416/422-6157, URL: http://www.sallynet.org
Territorial Commander, Commissioner Donald Kerr
Chief Secretary, Colonel John Busby
Field Secretary, Personnel, Lt.Col. John Carew
Program Secretary, Lt.Col. Ralph Stanley
Secretary, Business Administration, Lt.Col. Clyde Moore
Assistant Chief Secretary, Lt.Col. William Wilson
Secretary, Social Services, Major Ray Moulton
Editor-in-Chief & Literary Secretary, Major Edward Forster
Education Secretary, Major Cecil Cooper
Financial Secretary, Major Glen Shepherd
Government Relations Officer & Director of Overseas Projects, Lt.Col. Elva Jolley
President, C.B.C.C., Winnipeg, Major Lloyd Hetherington
Principal, C.F.O.T., Toronto, Major Douglas Moore
Principal, C.F.O.T., St. John's, Major David Hiscock
Property Secretary, Major Donald Copple
Trade Secretary, Major Ronald Goodyear
Secretary, Ministry to Women, Major Mary Moore
Secretary, League of Mercy, Lt.Col. Verna Carew
Secretary, Music, Brian Burditt
Secretary, Public Relations, Lt.-Col. Melvin Bond
Secretary, Youth, Major Gregory Simmonds
Publications: The War Cry; En Avant, w.; The Young Soldier, w.; Sally Ann, m.; The Edge, m.; Horizons, bi-m.

### Serbian Orthodox Church - Diocese of Canada (1983)
RR#3, Campbellville, ON L0P 1B0
905/878-0043, Fax: 905/878-1909
Serbian Orthodox Bishop of Canada, His Grace The Rt. Rev. Georgije Djokic
Publications: Istocnik

### Seventh-Day Adventist Church in Canada/Église Adventiste du Septième Jour au Canada
1148 King St. East, Oshawa, ON L1H 1H8
905/433-0011, Fax: 905/433-0982, Email: 74617.3630@compuserve.com
President, Orville Parchment
Secretary, Claude Sabot
Treasurer, Don Upson
Communications, Ralph Janes
Publications: Canadian Adventist Messenger

### The Society of Saint Peter the Apostle (1889)
3329 Danforth Ave., Scarborough, ON M1L 4T3
416/699-7077, Fax: 416/699-9019, Email: missions@eda.net, URL: http://www.eda.net/~missions/peter.htm
National Director, Sr. L. Spencer

### The Spiritual Science Fellowship of Canada (1977)
Spiritualist Yoga Fellowship
PO Box 1387, Stn H, Montréal, QC H3G 2N3
514/937-8539, Fax: 514/937-5380
President, Marilyn Zwaig Rossner, Ph.D.
Publications: SSF Events
Affiliates: International Council of Community Churches

### Student Christian Movement of Canada/ Mouvement d'étudiant(e)s chrétien(ne)s (SCM) (1921)
#C3, 310 Danforth Ave., Toronto, ON M4K 1N6
416/463-4312
General Secretary, Jean Ann Ledwell
Publications: All Things New

### Ukrainian Orthodox Church of Canada
9 St. Johns Ave., Winnipeg, MB R2W 1G8
204/586-3093, 582-8709, Fax: 204/582-5241
Primate, The Most Rev. Metropolitan Fedak Wasyly
Auxillary Bishop, Rt. Rev. Yurij Kalistchuk
Archbishop, Rt. Rev. John Stinka
Chairman of the Presidium, Very Rev. Fr. William Makarenko
Publications: The Herald

### Union of Spiritual Communities of Christ
Orthodox Doukhobors in Canada
PO Box 760, Grand Forks, BC V0H 1H0
250/442-8252, Fax: 250/442-3433
Chairperson, Andrew Evin
Administrator, S.W. Babakaiff
Publications: Iskra

### Union of the Vietnamese Buddhist Churches in Canada (1983)
4450, av Van Horne, Montréal, QC H3S 1S1
514/733-3841, Fax: 514/733-5860
Président, Ven Thich Thiên Nghi
Publications: Hoa Dao Magazine

### The United Brethren Church in Canada (1856)
501 Whitelaw Rd., Guelph, ON N1K 1E7
519/836-0180, Fax: 519/837-2219
President, Rev. Brian K. Magnus
Treasurer, Bryan Winger
Secretary, Joan Sider
Publications: U.B.
Affiliates: Evangelical Fellowship of Canada

### The United Church of Canada/Église unie du Canada (UCC) (1925)
3250 Bloor St. West, Etobicoke, ON M8X 2Y4
416/231-5931, Fax: 416/231-3103, Info Line: 416/231-7680
Moderator/General Council, Marion Best
General Secretary, Virginia Coleman
Communications Officer, Mary Frances
Publications: The United Church Observer; Mandate, bi-m.; The United Church of Canada Yearbook & Directory, a.
Conferences
Alberta & Northwest Conference: Executive Secretary, Rev. Dr. George H. Rodgers, 9911 - 48 Ave., Edmonton, AB T6E 5V6, 403/435-3995, Fax: 403/438-3317
All Native Circle Conference: Speaker, Rev. Grafton Antone, #18, 399 Berry St., Winnipeg, MB R2W 4X3, 204/831-0740, Fax: 204/837-9703
Bay of Quinte Conference: Executive Secretary, Rev. David M. Iverson, 218 Barrie St., Kingston, ON K7L 3K3, 613/549-2503, Fax: 613/549-1050
British Columbia Conference: Executive Secretary, Rev. Brian D. Thorpe, #200, 1955 West 4 Ave., Vancouver, BC V6J 1M7, 604/734-0434, Fax: 604/734-7024
Hamilton Conference: PO Box 100, Carlisle, ON L0R 1H0, 905/659-3343, Fax: 905/659-7766
London Conference: Executive Secretary, Rev. W. Peter Scott, 359 Windermere Rd., London, ON N6G 2K3, 519/672-1930, Fax: 519/439-2800
Manitoba & Northwestern Ontario Conference: Executive Secretary, H. Dianne Cooper, 120 Maryland St., Winnipeg, MB R3G 1L1, 204/786-8911, Fax: 204/774-0159
Manitou Conference: Executive Secretary, Rev. J. Stewart Bell, 1402 Regina St., North Bay, ON P1B 2L5, 705/474-3350, Fax: 705/497-3597
Maritime Conference: Executive Secretary, Rev. Robert H. Mills, PO Box 1560, Sackville, NB E0A 3C0, 506/536-1334, Fax: 506/536-2900
Montréal & Ottawa Conference: Executive Secretary, Rev. Tad Mitsui, 225 - 50 Ave., Lachine, QC H8T 2T7, 514/634-7015, Fax: 514/634-2489
Newfoundland & Labrador Conference: Executive Secretary, Rev. Boyd L. Hiscock, 320 Elizabeth Ave., St. John's, NF A1B 1T9, 709/754-0386, Fax: 709/754-8336
Saskatchewan Conference: Executive Secretary, Rev. Wilbert R. Wall, 418A McDonald St., Regina, SK S4N 6E1, 306/721-3311, Fax: 306/721-3171
Toronto Conference: Executive Secretary, Rev. Albion Wright, 65 Mayall Ave., North York, ON M3L 1E7, 416/241-2677, Fax: 416/241-2689

### Watch Tower Bible & Tract Society of Canada
Jehovah's Witnesses
PO Box 4100, Georgetown, ON L7G 4Y4
905/873-4100, Fax: 905/873-4554
Executive Director, Kenneth A. Little
Information Officer, Warren Shewfelt
Publications: The Watchtower; Awake, s-m.

### The Wesleyan Church of Canada (1897)
The Wesleyan Methodist Church of Canada
Central Canada District, #101, 3 Applewood Dr., Belleville, ON K8P 4E3
613/966-7527, Fax: 613/968-6190, Email: c.can.dist@intranet.ca
District Superintendent, Rev. Donald E. Hodgins
Publications: Clarion
Atlantic District: District Superintendent, Ray Barnwell Sr., PO Box 20, Sussex, NB E0E 1P0, 506/433-1007, Fax: 506/432-6668

## RELIGIOUS ORGANIZATIONS

### Africa Inland Mission International (Canada)/ Mission à l'intérieur de l'Afrique (Canada) (AIM) (1895)
AIM Canada
1641 Victoria Park Ave., Scarborough, ON M1R 1P8
416/751-6077, Fax: 416/751-3467, Email: aim-can@aimint.org
Director, Dr. John Brown
Personnel Director, Robert Cousins
Publications: Africa Inland Mission International

### Association of Christian Churches in Manitoba/ Association des les églises chrétiennes du Manitoba (ACCM) (1990)
484 Maryland St., Winnipeg, MB R3G 1M5
204/774-3143
Rev. Ted Chell

### Association des parents catholiques du Québec (APCQ) (1966)
#406, 7400, boul Saint-Laurent, Montréal, QC H2R 2Y1
514/276-8068; 8075, Téléc: 514/948-2595
Présidente, Jocelyne St.-Cyr
Publications: Famille - Québec
Organisation(s) affiliée(s): Organisation internationale de l'enseignement catholique (OIEC)

### Association of Regular Baptist Churches (1957)
130 Gerrard St. East, Toronto, ON M5A 3T4
416/925-3261, Fax: 416/925-8305
President, Rev. Stephen Kring
Secretary, Rev. W.P. Bauman
Publications: The Gospel Witness

### Atlantic Ecumenical Council of Churches (1951)
c/o Immaculate Conception Church, Saint-Louis, QC C0B 1Z0
902/882-2622
President, David Luker
Secretary, Rev. Arthur Pendergast
Publications: Friends of AEC

### The Bible Holiness Movement/Mouvement de sainteté biblique (1949)
PO Box 223, Stn A, Vancouver, BC V6C 2M3
250/498-3895
Bishop-General (International Leader), Evangelist Wesley H. Wakefield
Publications: Hallelujah
Affiliates: Religious Freedom of Council of Christian Minorities; Christians Concerned for Racial Equality

### The Bible League of Canada/Société canadienne pour la distribution de la Bible (1949)
PO Box 5037, Burlington, ON L7R 3Y8
905/319-9500, Fax: 905/319-0484, Toll Free: 1-800-363-9673, Email: bibleag@worldchat.com, URL: http://www.worldchat.com/public/bibleag/
Executive Director, J.G. Klomps
President, J. Walhout
Publications: The Bible League Report
Affiliates: The Bible League

### Buddhist Association of Canada (1974)
1330 Bloor St. West, Toronto, ON M6H 1P2
416/537-1342, Fax: 416/537-1342
Chairman, Dr. Clement Wong
Publications: Prazna; Newsletter

### Canada's National Bible Hour (1925)
PO Box 1210, St Catharines, ON L2R 7A7
905/684-1401
Founder, Ernest C. Manning
President, James O. Blackwood

### Canadian African Missions Foundation
251 Head St. North, Simcoe, ON N3Y 3X8
519/426-0511, Fax: 519/426-1149
Vice-President, Jeff Campbell
Affiliates: Association of Faith Churches & Ministries (Canada)

### Canadian Bible Society/Société biblique canadienne (1804)
10 Carnforth Rd., Toronto, ON M4A 2S4
416/757-4171, Fax: 416/757-3376, Toll Free: 1-800-465-2425, URL: http://www.canbible.ca
National Director, Rev. Gregory Bailey
Executive Director & Finance, Wallis Sherwin
Director, Ministry Funding, Barbara Walkden
Director, Secteur francophone, Serge Rhéaume, Bus: 514/524-7873
Publications: Canadian Bible Society Newsletter

### Canadian Centre for Ecumenism/Centre canadien d'oecuménisme (1963)
2065, rue Sherbrooke ouest, Montréal, QC H3H 1G6
514/937-9176, Fax: 514/937-2684, Email: 76261.716@compuserve.com
Director, Fr. Philippe Thibodeau

Chairman, Richard Bowie
Publications: Ecumenism/Oecumenisme
Affiliates: Canadian Conference of Catholic Bishops

### Canadian Centre for Law & Justice (1993)
1318 Wellington St., PO Box 36038, Ottawa, ON K1Y 4V3
Fax: 613/778-3443

### Canadian Chapter of the International Council of Community Churches/Section canadienne du conseil international des églises communautaires (CCICCC) (1989)
30 Briermoor Cres., Ottawa, ON K1T 3G7
613/738-2942, Fax: 613/738-7835, Email: saterio@istar.ca, URL: http://www.angelfire.com/biz/saterio/index.html
General Superintendent for Canada, Bishop S.A. Thériault, Ph.D., Th.D.
Sec.-Treas., The Rev. J. Venne, L.Th.
Publications: CCICC Info SCCIEC
Affiliates: World Council of Churches; National Council of Churches
English-speaking Sector: Rev. Leona Hartman, O.Tr., PO Box 1387, Stn A, Montréal, QC H3G 2N3, 514/937-8359
French-speaking Sector: Rev. Jacques Lefebvre, SPS, CP 403, Succ. A, Hull, QC J8Y 6M9, 613/238-2213

### The Canadian Churches' Forum for Global Ministries/Le forum des églises canadiennes pour les ministères globaux (1921)
11 Madison Ave., Toronto, ON M5R 2S2
416/924-9351, Fax: 416/924-5356, Email: ccforum@web.apc.org
Coordinator, Outreach & Communication, Robert Faris
Coordinator, Education & Training, Kevin Anderson
Coordinator, Finance & Administration, Mary Lou Smith
Publications: Focus
Affiliates: Canadian Council of Churches

### The Canadian Council of Christians & Jews/Conseil canadien des chrétiens et des juifs (CCCJ) (1947)
#601, 25 Adelaide St. East, Toronto, ON M5C 1A3
416/364-3101, Fax: 416/364-5705, Toll Free: 1-800-663-1848, Email: cccj@interlog.com, URL: http://www.interlog.com/~cccj/
National Executive Director, Elyse Graff
Publications: Newsletter
Affiliates: International Council of Christians & Jews

### The Canadian Council of Churches/Conseil canadien des églises (CCC) (1944)
#201, 40 St. Clair Ave. East, Toronto, ON M4T 1M9
416/921-4152, Fax: 416/921-7478, Email: ccchurch@web.net, URL: http://www.web.net/~ccchurch
President, Bishop Barry Curtis
General Secretary, Janet Somerville
Communications Officer, Iman Nashed
Publications: CCC-Echo-CCE
Affiliates: Members include - Anglican Church of Canada, Armenian Orthodox Church, Baptist Convention of Ontario & Quebec, Canadian Conference of Catholic Bishops, Christian Church (Disciples of Christ), Coptic Orthodox Church, Ethiopian Orthodox Church, Greek Orthodox Church, Evangelical Lutheran Church in Canada, Orthodox Church in America, Polish National Catholic Church of Canada, Presbyterian Church in Canada, Reformed Church in America (Ont.), Religious Society of Friends, Salvation Army, United Church, Ukrainian Orthodox Church

### Canadian Council of Muslim Women/Conseil canadien des femmes musulmanes (CCMW) (1982)
#513, 2400 Dundas St., Toronto, ON L5K 2R8
905/823-3804, Fax: 905/333-4131
Email: LALH68A@prodigy.com, URL: http://www.qucis.queensu.ca/home/fevens/ccmw.html
Founding President, Dr. Lila Fahlman
Publications: The Muslim Woman
Affiliates: World Council of Muslim Women

### Canadian Lutheran World Relief (CLWR) (1946)
1080 Kingsbury Ave., Winnipeg, MB R2P 1W5
204/694-5602, Fax: 204/694-5460, Toll Free: 1-800-661-2597, Email: clwr@mbnet.mb.ca
Executive Director, Ruth E. Jensen

### Canadian-Muslim Civil Liberties Association/Association canadienne-musulman des libertés civiles (CMCLA) (1995)
#200, 200 Consumers Rd., North York, ON M2J 4R4
416/496-9666, Fax: 416/496-9530, Email: cmcla@torfree.net
President, Faisal M. Kutty
Executive Director, Imran Yousuf
Vice-President, Fayaz Karin
Public Relations, Sajidah Kutty
Communications, Irfan Khan
Fundraising, Sagib Meer
Publications: CMCLA News; CMCLA Alert
Affiliates: Council on American Islamic Relations

### Canadian Religious Conference/Conférence religieuse canadienne (CRC) (1954)
219 Argyle Ave., Ottawa, ON K2P 2H4
613/236-0824, Fax: 613/236-0825, Email: crcn@web.net, URL: http://www.crc.ca/crcn/
Publications: CRC Bulletin

### Canadian Theological Society (CTS) (1955)
Wycliffe College, 5 Hoskin Ave., Toronto, ON M5S 1H7
403/596-2439, Fax: 403/979-1471
Secretary, Prof. Brian Walsh
Publications: CTS Newsletter/Communiqué de la STC

### Canadian Tract Society (1970)
26 Hale St., PO Box 2156, Brampton, ON L6T 3S4
905/457-4559, Fax: 905/457-4559
Publications: Order Form

### Catholic Biblical Association of Canada (CBAC) (1974)
3275 St. Clair Ave. East, Scarborough, ON M1L 1W2
416/285-9552, Fax: 416/285-9174
Executive Director, Jocelyn Monette
Publications: The Word Is Life
Affiliates: Catholic Biblical Federation

### Child Evangelism Fellowship of Canada/Association de l'évangelisation des enfants (CEF) (1937)
PO Box 165, Winnipeg, MB R3C 2G9
204/943-2774, Email: 103442.1544@compuserve.com
National Director, Don Collins
Chairman, Jim Pride
Publications: Evangelizing Today's Child
Affiliates: Child Evangelism Fellowship Inc.; CEF of Nations

### Christian Aid Mission (CAM) (1953)
201 Stanton St., Fort Erie, ON L2A 3N8
905/871-1773, Fax: 905/871-5165, Email: friends@christianaid.ca, URL: http://www.christianaid.ca
President, James S. Eagles
Publications: Christian Mission; Prayerline

### Christian Children's Fund of Canada (CCFC) (1960)
1027 McNicoll Ave., Scarborough, ON M1W 3X2
416/495-1174, Fax: 416/495-9395, Telex: 06-986703
National Director, Peter G. Harris
Director of Development, Mary Lynne Stewart
Publications: Canadaid
Affiliates: Canadian Direct Marketing Association; National Society of Fundraising Executives

### Christian Reformed World Relief Committee of Canada (CRWRC) (1962)
3475 Mainway, PO Box 5070, Burlington, ON L7R 3Y8
905/336-2920, Fax: 905/336-8344, Toll Free: 1-800-730-3490, Email: CRWRC@crcna.org, URL: http://www.kingsu.ab.ca/~jake/crwrc.htm
Director, Wayne Dejong
Coordinator of Communications, Keith Knight
Coordinator of Church Relations, Rick DeGraaf
Publications: In Touch
Affiliates: Christian Reformed World Relief Committee

### Council of Muslim Communities of Canada
#1010, 4 Forest Lawn Way, North York, ON M2N 5X8
416/512-2106, Fax: 416/512-2106
President, Hanny Hassan
Coordinator, Muin Muinuddin
Publications: Islam Canada

### Ecumenical Coalition for Economic Justice/Coalition oecuménique pour la justice économique (1973)
#402, 77 Charles St. West, Toronto, ON M5R 2S2
416/921-4615, Fax: 416/922-1419, Email: gattfly@web.net
Publications: Economic Justice Report
Affiliates: Canadian Council of Churches

### Federation of Islamic Associations
73 Patricia Ave., North York, ON M2M 1J1
416/222-2794, Fax: 416/674-8168
President, Ayube Ally

### Focus on The Family (Canada) Association (1982)
PO Box 9800, Vancouver, BC V6B 4G3
604/684-8333, Fax: 604/684-8653
President, Dr. Bruce Gordon
Publications: Focus on the Family; Teachers in Focus

### Gideons International in Canada (1911)
501 Imperial Rd. North, Guelph, ON N1H 6T9
519/823-1140, Fax: 519/767-1913
Executive Director, Graham Sawer
Publications: The Canadian Gideon

### Global Outreach Mission Inc. (1943)
PO Box 1210, St Catharines, ON L2R 7A7
905/684-1401
President, James O. Blackwood
Sec.-Treas., Douglas Waters
Comptroller, Alvin Voth
Affiliates: Interdenominational Foreign Mission Association

### Gospel Missionary Union of Canada (GMU) (1949)
2121 Henderson Hwy., Winnipeg, MB R2G 1P8
204/338-7831, Fax: 204/339-3321, Email: 76756.2126@compuserve.com
Canadian Director, Grant Morrison
Publications: The Gospel Message

### Habitat for Humanity Canada (HFHC) (1985)
40 Albert St., Waterloo, ON N2L 3S2
519/885-4565, Fax: 519/885-5225, Toll Free: 1-800-667-5137, Email: hfhc@sentex.net, URL: http://www.sentex.net/~hfhc/

President & CEO, Wilmer Martin
Publications: Habitat Spirit

### Holy Childhood Association (1843)
**Children Helping Children**
3329 Danforth Ave., Unit D, Scarborough, ON M1L 4T3
416/699-7077, Fax: 416/699-9019
Associate Director, Margaret T. Tipping

### Jesuit Fathers & Brothers (1540)
**Society of Jesus**
69 Marmaduke St., Toronto, ON M6R 1T3
416/763-4664, Fax: 416/763-4666
National Superior, Rev. David E. Nazar, S.J.
Assistant to the National Superior, Rev. Geoffrey B. Williams, S.J.
Publications: Compass

**CANADIAN JESUIT MISSIONS**
1190 Danforth Ave., Toronto, ON M4J 1M6
416/465-1824, Fax: 416/465-1825
CEO, Michael Murray, S.J.
Director, Dr. Jim Thompson
International Executive Officer, J.P. Horigan

**THE JESUIT CENTRE FOR SOCIAL FAITH & JUSTICE (1979)**
947 Queen St. East, Toronto, ON M4M 1J9
416/469-1123, Fax: 416/469-3579
Director, Kevin Arsenault
Coordinator, Bob Jeffcott
Publications: The Moment Refugee Update; Central America Update, bi-m.

### The Missionary Union of the Clergy & Religious (1916)
3329 Danforth Ave., Scarborough, ON M1L 4T3
416/699-7077, Fax: 416/699-9019, Email: missions@eda.net
National Director, Sr. L. Spencer

### Multifaith Action Society (1973)
385 Boundary Road, Vancouver, BC V5K 4S1
604/291-1865
Coordinator, Joan Craker
President, Rev. Dr. Phillip Hewett
Publications: Multifaith News; The Multifaith Calendar

### OMF International - Canada (1865)
**Overseas Missionary Fellowship**
5759 Coopers Ave., Mississauga, ON L4Z 1R9
905/568-9971, Fax: 905/568-9974, Email: gdykema@cproject.com
National Director, Rev. William Fietje
Director, Administration & Finance, Ron Adams
Publications: East Asians Millions
Affiliates: Evangelical Fellowship of Canada

### Operation Mobilization Canada (1966)
**Send the Light**
104 Culham St., Oakville, ON L6H 1G5
905/338-8106, Fax: 905/849-3501
Director, Steve Hawkins
Publications: Canadian Monthly

### Organisation catholique canadienne pour le développement et la paix/Canadian Catholic Organization for Development & Peace (OCCDP) (1967)
**Development & Peace**
5633, rue Sherbrooke est, Montréal, QC H1N 1A3
514/257-8711, Téléc: 514/257-8497, Ligne sans frais: 1-888-234-8533, Courrier électronique: info@devp.org, URL: http://www.devp.org
Directeur général, Fabien Leboeuf
Président, Raymond Boucher
Publications: Solidarités; Global Village Voice, q.
Organisation(s) affiliée(s): Asia Partnership for Human Development; Coopération internationale pour le développement et la solidarité

### Society for the Propagation of the Faith for Canada (1822)
English Sector, 3329 Danforth Ave., Unit D, Scarborough, ON M1L 4T3
416/699-7077, Fax: 416/699-9019, Email: missions@eda.net, URL: http://www.eda.net~missions
National Director, Sr. L. Spencer
Publications: Missions Today

**OEUVRE PONTIFICALE DE LA PROPAGATION DE LA FOI - SECTEUR FRANÇAIS DU CANADA**
2269, ch Saint-Louis, Sillery, QC G1T 1R5
418/687-9531, Téléc: 418/687-9057
Directeur national, Jean-Marc Daoust
Publications: Univers

### Taskforce on the Churches & Corporate Responsibility/Comité inter-Églises sur les responsabilités des corporations (TCCR) (1975)
129 St. Clair Ave. West, Toronto, ON M4V 1N5
416/923-1758, Fax: 416/927-7554, Email: tccr@web.net
Coordinator, Daniel M. Gennarelli
Publications: TCCR Mailing
Affiliates: Anglican Church of Canada; Canadian Conference of Catholic Bishops; Evangelical Lutheran Church in Canada; Presbyterian Church in Canada; Religious Society of Friends (Quakers); United Church of Canada; CUSO; YWCA

### Unitarian Service Committee of Canada/Comité du service unitaire du Canada (1945)
**USC Canada**
#705, 56 Sparks St., Ottawa, ON K1P 5B1
613/234-6827, Fax: 613/234-6842, Email: uscanada@web.net
CEO, John Martin
Director, Canadian Programs, Friederike Knabe
Director of Finance, Francine Longtin
Communications Manager, Susan Fisher
Publications: 56 Sparks
BC Provincial Office: Contact, David Love, #402, 207 West Hastings, Vancouver, BC V6B 1H7, 604/682-0486, Fax: 604/682-0340, Email: uscbc@axionet.com
Ontario Provincial Office: Contact, Tim D'Souza, 89 King St. North, Waterloo, ON N2J 2X3, 519/884-6276, Fax: 519/746-4096

### VISION TV Canada's Faith Network (1988)
80 Bond St., Toronto, ON M5B 1X2
416/368-3194, Fax: 416/368-9774, Email: visiontv@web.apc.org
President & CEO, Fil Fraser
Vice-President, Programming & Development, Peter Flemington
Vice-President, Production & Presentation, Rita Deverell
Director, Finance & Administration, Susan Bower
Publications: Great Viewers' Guide; Social Justice Calendar, bi-m.; Faith Matters Calendar, bi-m.

### World Congress of Faiths (1936)
2 Market St., Oxford 0X1 3EF UK
/(44 86) 520 2751, Fax: /(44 86) 520 2746
Chair, Rev. Marcus Braybrooke
Hon. Sec.-Treas., David Potter
Publications: World Faiths Encounter

# ORGANIZATIONS

**(Including Associations, Societies, Institutes, Research Organizations, Relief Agencies, Support Groups and Centres)**

**ABORIGINAL PEOPLES *see* NATIVE PEOPLES**

**ABORTION *see* REPRODUCTIVE ISSUES**

**ACCIDENT PREVENTION *see* SAFETY & ACCIDENT PREVENTION**

## ACCOUNTING

### Canadian Academic Accounting Association/Association canadienne des professeurs de comptabilité (CAAA) (1976)
Faculty of Management, University of Toronto, #850, 120 King St. West, PO Box 176, Hamilton, ON L8N 3C3
905/525-1884, Fax: 905/525-3046, Email: vfortunato@cma-canada.org
Administrative Officer, Vittoria Fortunato
President, Howard Teall
Publications: Canadian Accounting Education & Research News; Contemporary Accounting Research, q.
Affiliates: American Accounting Association

### Canadian Comprehensive Auditing Foundation/Fondation canadienne pour la vérification intégrée (CCAF) (1980)
#210, 55 Murray St., Ottawa, ON K1N 5M3
613/241-6900, Fax: 613/241-6900, Email: ccaf@istar.ca
President, J.P. Boisclair, FCA, CMC
Publications: CCAF Update

### Canadian Institute of Chartered Accountants/Institut canadien des comptables agréés (CICA)
**Chartered Accountants of Canada**
277 Wellington St. West, Toronto, ON M5V 3H2
416/977-3222, Fax: 416/977-8585, URL: http://www.cica.ca/
President, Michael Rayner, FCA
Chair, Donald H. Penny, FCA
Executive Vice-President, Nigel F. Byars, CA
Vice-President, Communications, Randall Pearce
Director, Communications, Loretta O'Connor
Publications: CA Magazine
Affiliates: International Accounting Standards Committee; International Federation of Accountants

**ATLANTIC SCHOOL OF CHARTERED ACCOUNTANCY**
PO Box 489, Halifax, NS B3J 2R7
902/425-7974, Fax: 902/423-9784
Executive Director, J.D. Trainor, C.A.

**CHARTERED ACCOUNTANTS INSTITUTE OF BERMUDA (1973)**
PO Box 1625, Hamilton HM GX Bermuda
809/292-7479, Fax: 809/295-3121
Executive Director, Sandra Mayor

**INSTITUTE OF CHARTERED ACCOUNTANTS OF ALBERTA**
Manulife Place, #580, 10180 - 101 St., Edmonton, AB T5J 4R2
403/424-7391, Fax: 403/425-8766
URL: http://www.icaa.ab.ca
Executive Director, S.J. Glover, FCA

**INSTITUTE OF CHARTERED ACCOUNTANTS OF BRITISH COLUMBIA (ICABC) (1905)**
1133 Melville St., Vancouver, BC V6E 4E5
604/681-3264, Fax: 604/681-1523, Toll Free: 1-800-663-2677

Email: exec.dir@sfu.ca, URL: http://www.ica.bc.ca
CEO, R.W. McCloy, FCA
President, Alison Morse
Communications Officer, Sarah Good
Publications: CommuniCAtion Magazine
Affiliates: All provincial CA institutes in Canada & Bermuda

**INSTITUTE OF CHARTERED ACCOUNTANTS OF MANITOBA (1886)**
#1200, 363 Broadway, Winnipeg, MB R3C 3N9
204/942-8248, Fax: 204/943-7119
Executive Vice-President, G.B.J. Hannaford, FCA
Publications: Folio

**INSTITUTE OF CHARTERED ACCOUNTANTS OF NEWFOUNDLAND (1949)**
**CA Newfoundland**
Box 103, 570 Newfoundland Dr., St. John's, NF A1A 5B1
709/753-7566, Fax: 709/753-3609
Executive Director, Nina Adey, FCA

**INSTITUTE OF CHARTERED ACCOUNTANTS OF THE NORTHWEST TERRITORIES**
PO Box 2433, Yellowknife, NT X1A 2P8
867/873-3680, Fax: 867/920-4135
Administrative Assistant, Dorothy Davis

**INSTITUTE OF CHARTERED ACCOUNTANTS OF NOVA SCOTIA**
#1104, 1791 Barrington St., Halifax, NS B3J 3L1
902/425-3291, Fax: 902/423-4505
Executive Director, Ross Towler, FCA

**INSTITUTE OF CHARTERED ACCOUNTANTS OF ONTARIO/INSTITUT DES COMPTABLES AGRÉÉS DE L'ONTARIO (ICAO) (1879)**
69 Bloor St. East, Toronto, ON M4W 1B3
416/962-1841, Fax: 416/962-8900, Toll Free: 1-800-387-0735
Email: exof@icao.on.ca, URL: http://www.icao.on.ca
Chief Executive Officer, David A. Wilson, MBA, FCA
Director of the Executive Office, Brendan Wycks, MBA
Publications: CheckMark

**INSTITUTE OF CHARTERED ACCOUNTANTS OF PRINCE EDWARD ISLAND (1921)**
PO Box 301, Charlottetown, PE C1A 7K7
902/894-4290, Fax: 902/894-4791
Executive Director, Edison Shea, FCA
Publications: Bottom Line

**INSTITUTE OF CHARTERED ACCOUNTANTS OF SASKATCHEWAN**
#900, 1867 Hamilton St., Regina, SK S4P 2C2
306/359-1010, Fax: 306/569-8288
Executive Director, Nola Dianne Joorisity
Publications: CHAFF

**NEW BRUNSWICK INSTITUTE OF CHARTERED ACCOUNTANTS/INSTITUT DES COMPTABLES AGRÉÉS DU NOUVEAU-BRUNSWICK (NBICA) (1916)**
93 Prince William St., 4th Fl., Saint John, NB E2L 2B2
506/634-1588, Fax: 506/634-1015
Executive Director, J. Blackier, CA
Publications: Interim Report

**ORDRE DES COMPTABLES AGRÉÉS DU QUÉBEC (OCAQ) (1880)**
680, rue Sherbrooke ouest, 7e étage, Montréal, QC H3A 2S3
514/288-3256, Téléc: 514/843-8375, Ligne sans frais: 1-800-363-4688
URL: http://www.uquebec.ca/comptables/agrees
Directeur général et secrétaire, Gérard Caron, FCA
Président, Jean-Pierre Dubeau
Directrice des communications, Francine Cléroux
Publications: Bilans; Répertoire de cours, semi-annuel

## Canadian Institute of Financial Accountants (1988)
2380 Holly Lane, 2nd Fl., Ottawa, ON K1V 7P2
613/521-0620, Fax: 613/521-1185
President, Andrew Yeung
Publications: Newsletter
Affiliates: Canadian Association of Certified Executive Accountants

## Canadian Insurance Accountants Association/Association canadienne des comptables d'assurance (CIAA) (1934)
2150 Portway Ave., Mississauga, ON L5H 3M7
905/274-2422, Fax: 905/274-4059
Executive Director, Paul D. Mann

## Certified General Accountants Association of Canada (1913)
**CGA - Canada**
#700, 1188 Georgia St. West, Vancouver, BC V6E 4A2
604/669-3555, Fax: 604/689-5845, URL: http://www.cga-canada.org
President & COO, Guy Legault, B.Sc., MBA, FCGA, CAE
Chairman & CEO, Ruby J. Howard, FCGA
Communications, Elaine Allan
Publications: CGA Magazine
Affiliates: International Federation of Accountants Council (IFAC); Confederation of Asian & Pacific Accountants (CAPA); International Accounting Standards Committee; Asia Pacific Accounting Association (APAA); China Accounting Research & Education (CARE); Fédération Internationale des Experts Comptables Francophones (FIDEF); Institute of Chartered Accountants of the Caribbean (ICAC); Interamerican Accounting Association (IAA); International Association of Accounting Education & Research (IAAER)

**CERTIFIED GENERAL ACCOUNTANTS ASSOCIATION OF ALBERTA**
**CGA - Alberta**
#1410, 555 - 4 Ave. SW, Calgary, AB T2P 3E7
403/299-1300, Fax: 403/299-1339, Toll Free: 1-800-661-1078
URL: http://www.cga-canada.org/alberta/
Director, Communications, Corinne Wilkinson, Bus: 403/299-1326
Publications: Insight

**CERTIFIED GENERAL ACCOUNTANTS ASSOCIATION OF ONTARIO (1913)**
**CGA Ontario**
240 Eglinton Ave. East, Toronto, ON M4P 1K8
416/322-6520, Fax: 416/322-5594, Toll Free: 1-800-668-1454
Email: webspinner@cga-ontario.org, URL: http://www.cga-ontario.org
Executive Director, Gordon W. Fuller, FCGA
President & CEO, 1997/98, John C. Wright, FCGA
Executive Vice-President, 1997/98, J. Thomas McCallum, CBV, FCGA
First Vice-President/Secretary, Jeannine Brooks, CGA
Second Vice-President/Treasurer, Laurie Ouellette, FCGA
Public Relations Officer, Elizabeth Lewis
Publications: Statements

**ATLANTIC REGION EDUCATION ASSOCIATION**
Commerce House, 236 St. George St., PO Box 5100, Moncton, NB E1C 8R2
506/857-2204, Fax: 506/852-4450

**CERTIFIED GENERAL ACCOUNTANTS ASSOCIATION OF BRITISH COLUMBIA**
**CGA - British Columbia**
1555 - 8th Ave. West, Vancouver, BC V6J 1T5
604/732-1211, Fax: 604/732-1252
URL: http://www.cga-bc.org/
Executive Director, R.W. Caulfield
Public Relations Coordinator, Maureen Sydor

**CERTIFIED GENERAL ACCOUNTANTS ASSOCIATION OF MANITOBA (1973)**
**CGA Manitoba**
4 Donald St. South, Winnipeg, MB R3L 2T7
204/477-1256, Fax: 204/453-7176, Toll Free: 1-800-282-8001
Executive Director, L.W. Hampson, FCGA
Publications: Newsletter

**CERTIFIED GENERAL ACCOUNTANTS ASSOCIATION OF NEW BRUNSWICK/ASSOCIATION DES COMPTABLES GÉNÉRAUX LICENCIÉS DU NOUVEAU-BRUNSWICK (1962)**
**CGA - New Brunswick**
236 St. George St., PO Box 1395, Moncton, NB E1C 8T6
506/857-0939, Fax: 506/855-0887
President, Murray Lambert, BA, CGA
Administrative Assistant, Trudy Dryden
Publications: CGA-NB Newsletter

**CERTIFIED GENERAL ACCOUNTANTS ASSOCIATION OF NEWFOUNDLAND**
**CGA - Newfoundland**
685 Water St. West, PO Box 5010, St. John's, NF A1C 5V3
709/579-1863, Fax: 709/579-0838
President, Judy Summers, CGA

**CERTIFIED GENERAL ACCOUNTANTS ASSOCIATION OF THE NORTHWEST TERRITORIES (1977)**
**CGA - Northwest Territories**
PO Box 128, Yellowknife, NT X1A 2N1
867/873-5620, Fax: 867/873-4469
Email: cganwt@cga-canada.org
Executive Director, Angie Dumbrille, B.Sc.
Publications: Northern Accounts

**CERTIFIED GENERAL ACCOUNTANTS ASSOCIATION OF NOVA SCOTIA**
**CGA - Nova Scotia**
#416, 5251 Duke St., Halifax, NS B3J 1P3
902/425-4923, Fax: 902/425-4983
President, G. Angus MacGillivray, BBA, CGA

**CERTIFIED GENERAL ACCOUNTANTS ASSOCIATION OF PRINCE EDWARD ISLAND**
**CGA - Prince Edward Island**
178 Fitzroy St., 2nd Fl., PO Box 812, Charlottetown, PE C1A 7L9
902/892-3787, Fax: 902/368-3627
President, David A. Wright, CGA

**CERTIFIED GENERAL ACCOUNTANTS ASSOCIATION OF SASKATCHEWAN (1978)**
**CGA - Saskatchewan**
#4, 2345 Ave. C North, Saskatoon, SK S7L 5Z5
306/955-4622, Fax: 306/373-9219, Toll Free: 1-800-667-5745
Email: cgasask@eagle.wbm.ca, URL: http://www.cga-canada.org/saskatchewan
Executive Director, Howard L. Janzen, FCGA
Publications: CGA Saskatchewan Newsletter

**CERTIFIED GENERAL ACCOUNTANTS ASSOCIATION OF YUKON**
**CGA - Yukon**
PO Box 5358, Whitehorse, YT Y1A 4Z2
867/668-4461, Toll Free: 1-800-565-1211
President, Elaine Carlyle, CGA
Publications: Newsletter

**CGA - CANADA RESEARCH FOUNDATION (CGARF) (1981)**
#700, 1188 West Georgia St., Vancouver, BC V6E 4A2
604/669-3555, Fax: 604/689-5845
President, Jean Précourt
Manager of Research, Stephen Spector
Publications: Research Review
Affiliates: American Accounting Association; Canadian Academic Accounting Association

**ORDRE DES COMPTABLES GÉNÉRAUX LICENCIÉS DU QUÉBEC (1908)**
**CGA - Québec**
#450, 445, boul St-Laurent, Montréal, QC H2Y 2Y7
514/861-1823, Téléc: 514/861-7661, Ligne sans frais: 1-800-463-0163
Courrier électronique: cga-quebec@sympatico.ca, URL: http://www.cga-quebec.org
Directeur général, Marcel Godbout Lavoie, CGA
Président, Michel Guindon, FCGA
Directrice des communications, France Goyette
Publications: Bulletin CGA

### Guild of Industrial, Commercial & Institutional Accountants/Guilde des comptables industriels, commerciaux et institutionnels (1961)
**Guild of ICIA**
PO Box 7, Stn C, Toronto, ON M6J 3M7
905/278-7846, Fax: 905/795-0621
President, Norbert Bajcar, FICIA
Registrar, Garfield Brown, FICIA
Publications: Guild of ICIA Journal

### The Institute of Internal Auditors/L'Institut des vérifacateurs internes (IIA) (1941)
249 Maitland Ave., Altamonte Springs, FL 32701-4201 USA
407/830-7600, Fax: 407/831-5171, Email: iia@theiia.org, URL: http://www.theiia.org
International President, William G. Bishop III, CIA
Publications: Internal Auditor; IIA Today, bi-m.; Pistas de Auditoria; IIA Educator

### Petroleum Accountants Society of Canada (1953)
#750, 700 - 4 Ave. SW, Calgary, AB T2P 3J4
403/262-4744, Fax: 403/266-1525, Email: petasocc@cadvision.com, URL: http://www.cadvision.com/pasc
President, Murray Montgomery
Secretary, Bill Bruggencate
Treasurer, John Topping
Publications: The Ledger

### Society of Management Accountants of Canada/Société des comptables en management du Canada (SMAC) (1920)
#850, 120 King St. West, PO Box 176, Hamilton, ON L8N 3C3
905/525-4100; 416/847-0373 (Toronto line), Fax: 905/525-4533, Toll Free: 1-800-263-7622, URL: http://www.cma-canada.org
President & CEO, Robert W. Dye
Chair, Derrick Struge, B.Comm., MBA, CA, CMA, FCMA
Publications: CMA, the Management Accounting Magazine
Affiliates: Confederation of Asian & Pacific Accountants; International Federation of Accountants

**CERTIFIED MANAGEMENT ACCOUNTANTS SOCIETY OF BRITISH COLUMBIA (CMA) (1945)**
#1575, 650 West Georgia St., PO Box 11548, Vancouver, BC V6B 4W7
604/687-5891, Fax: 604/687-6688, Toll Free: 1-800-663-9646
Email: feedback@cmabc.com, URL: http://www.cmabc.com
Colin Bennett
Publications: CMA Update

**ORDRE DES COMPTABLES EN MANAGEMENT ACCRÉDITÉS DU QUÉBEC (1941)**
715, square Victoria, 3e étage, Montréal, QC H2Y 2H7
514/849-1155, Téléc: 514/849-9674, Ligne sans frais: 1-800-263-5390
Président/Directeur général, François Renauld, CMA
Publications: Elite C.M.A.

**SOCIETY OF MANAGEMENT ACCOUNTANTS OF ALBERTA (1944)**
One Palliser Sq., #1800, 125 - 9 Ave. SE, Calgary, AB T2G 0P6
403/269-5341, Fax: 403/262-5477, Toll Free: 1-800-332-1106
Email: cma@istar.ca, URL: http://www.cmaab.com
Executive Director, Sterling Eddy, CMA, CMC, FCMA
Publications: Management Accounter

**SOCIETY OF MANAGEMENT ACCOUNTANTS OF THE ATLANTIC PROVINCES**
Purdy's Tower 2, Box 42, #1309, 1969 Upper Water St., Halifax, NS B3J 3R7
902/422-5836, Fax: 902/423-1605
Executive Director, G.D. Pollock, Ph.D.

**SOCIETY OF MANAGEMENT ACCOUNTANTS OF MANITOBA (1947)**
#808, 386 Broadway, Winnipeg, MB R3C 3R6
204/943-1538, 1539, Fax: 204/947-3308, Toll Free: 1-800-841-7148
Executive Director, Steve Vieweg

**SOCIETY OF MANAGEMENT ACCOUNTANTS OF NEWFOUNDLAND**
PO Box 28090, RPO Avalon Mall, St. John's, NF A1B 4J8
709/726-3652

**SOCIETY OF MANAGEMENT ACCOUNTANTS OF THE NORTHWEST TERRITORIES**
PO Box 512, Yellowknife, NT X1A 2N4
867/873-2875, Fax: 867/920-2503
Executive Director, Nieta World
Publications: CMA News

**SOCIETY OF MANAGEMENT ACCOUNTANTS OF ONTARIO (1941)**
#300, 70 University Ave., Toronto, ON M5J 2M4
416/977-7741, Fax: 416/977-6079, Toll Free: 1-800-387-2991
Email: info@cma-ontario.org, URL: http://www.cma-ontario.org
Executive Director, R.W. Dye, FCMA
President, Terry Pringle, CMA
Vice-President, Angela Holtham, CMA
2nd V-P & Treasurer, Marie Campagna, CMA
Secretary, Ivan Fraser, CMA
Publications: The Management Accountants Handbook; Directions

**SOCIETY OF MANAGEMENT ACCOUNTANTS OF SASKATCHEWAN (1929)**
#202, 1900 Albert St., Regina, SK S4P 4K8
306/359-6461, Fax: 306/347-8580
Executive Director, John Hartney, BA, B.Admin., CMA

**SOCIETY OF MANAGEMENT ACCOUNTANTS OF THE YUKON (SMAY) (1975)**
PO Box 4823, Whitehorse, YT Y1A 4N6
867/668-3388, Fax: 867/668-2402

**ACTUARIES *see* INSURANCE INDUSTRY**

## ADDICTION

### Addiction Research Foundation/Fondation de la recherche sur la toxicomanie (ARF) (1949)
33 Russell St., Toronto, ON M5S 2S1
416/595-6000, Fax: 416/595-5017, Info Line: 416/595-6111, Toll Free: 1-800-463-6273, Email: sanohelp@arf.org, URL: http://www.arf.org
President, Dr. Perry Kendall
Publications: The Journal
Affiliates: World Health Organization; United Nations; International Council of Alcohol & Addiction; International Labour Organization

### Addictions Foundation of Manitoba/Fondation manitobaine de lutte contre les dépendances (AFM) (1956)
1031 Portage Ave., Winnipeg, MB R3G 0R8
204/944-6200, Fax: 204/786-7768, URL: http://afm.mb.ca
Executive Director, Herb Thompson
Publications: Inside View

### Adult Children of Alcoholics (ACA)
20 Bloor St. East, PO Box 75061, Toronto, ON M4W 3T3
416/593-5147
Contact, Dianne Dogherty
Publications: Serenity

### Against Drunk Driving (ADD) (1983)
**The Neil Gray Memorial Fund**
PO Box 397, Stn A, Brampton, ON L6V 2L3
905/793-4233, Fax: 905/793-4233, Email: add@netcom.ca, URL: http://www.netmediapro.com/add/
Co-Chair, John Hymers
Co-Chair, Tom Tumilty
Office Manager, Kathleen Close
Publications: ADDvisor Newsletter; Grieving Process; Operation Lookout Network News
Affiliates: Ontario Community Council on Impaired Driving

### Al-Anon Family Groups
**National Public Information Canada/Information publique nationale du Canada**
1771 Avenue Rd., PO Box 54533, North York, ON M5M 4N5
416/366-4072, Toll Free: 1-800-443-4525

### Alcoholics Anonymous (AA) (1939)
#202, 234 Eglinton Ave. East, Toronto, ON M4P 1K5
416/487-5591, Fax: 416/487-5855
Office Manager, Carole Keenan

### Canadian Centre on Substance Abuse/Centre canadien de lutte contre l'alcoolisme et les toxicomanies (CCSA) (1988)
#300, 75 Albert St., Ottawa, ON K1P 5E7
613/235-4048, Fax: 613/235-8101, Toll Free: 1-800-559-4514, Email: jlecaval@ccsa.ca, URL: http://www.ccsa.ca
CEO, Jacques LeCavalier
Policy Associate, Dr. Eric Single
Communications Associate, Richard Garlick
Publications: Action News; Action nouvelles
Policy & Research Unit: Banting Institute, #207, 100 College St., Toronto, ON M5G 1L5, 416/978-1772, Fax: 416/971-1365

### Concerns, Canada (1934)
**Alcohol & Drug Concerns, Inc.**
#112H, 4500 Sheppard Ave. East, Scarborough, ON M1S 3R6
416/293-3400, Fax: 416/293-1142
President, Rev. Larry Gillians
Publications: Concerns

### Council on Drug Abuse (CODA)
#17, 698 Weston Rd., Toronto, ON M6N 3R3
416/763-1491, Fax: 416/767-6859
President, Frederick J. Burford
Secretary, Wendy Gidge
Treasurer, G. Ernest Jackson
Chairman, Frank C. Buckley
Publications: CODA

**The Council for a Drug-Free Workplace/Le Conseil pour une entreprise sans drogues (1989)**
44 King St. West, 12th Fl., Toronto, ON M5H 1H1
416/866-3699, Fax: 416/933-2388, Toll Free: 1-800-563-5000
Executive Director, Jacques Perras
Publications: Taking a Stand

**MADD Canada (1982)**
**Mothers Against Drunk Driving**
#36, 5160 Explorer Dr., Mississauga, ON L4W 4T7
905/624-5364, Fax: 905/624-8920
Chairman, Dave King
Administrator, L. Waywell
Publications: MADD Canada Report

**Narcotics Anonymous (1953)**
PO Box 5700, Toronto, ON M5W 1N8
416/691-9519
Chairperson, Public Information, Philip Horgan
Publications: Narcotics Anonymous

**Parents Against Drugs (PAD) (1983)**
7 Hawksdale Rd., North York, ON M3K 1W3
416/395-4970, Fax: 416/395-4972
Executive Director, Diane Buhler
Chairman, Michelle DiCarlo
Publications: PAD Parent Handbook
Affiliates: Council on Drug Abuse

**Physicians for a Smoke-Free Canada/Médecins pour un Canada sans fumée (1985)**
PO Box 4849, Stn E, Ottawa, ON K1S 5J1
613/233-4878, Fax: 613/748-0835
Executive Director, Catherine A. Rudick
Affiliates: International Organization of Consumers Unions

**ADMINISTRATION *see* MANAGEMENT & ADMINISTRATION**

## ADVERTISING & MARKETING

**Advertising Agency Association of Alberta**
#2401, 10104 - 103 Ave., Edmonton, AB T5J OH8
403/424-5944, Fax: 403/428-0970
President, Russell B. Hakes

**Advertising Agency Association of British Columbia (AAABC)**
#1723, 595 Burrard St., PO Box 49122, Vancouver, BC V7X 1J1
604/682-1291, Fax: 604/682-1291
President, Steve Vrlak

**Advertising Agency Print Production Association (AAPPA)**
1881 Yonge St, PO Box 48027, Toronto, ON M4S 3C4
President, Jane Sallows, Bus: 416/480-6678
Publications: PPA Update

**The Advertising & Design Club of Canada (1948)**
#207, 109 Vanderhoof Ave., Toronto, ON M4G 2H7
416/423-4113, Fax: 416/422-3762
President, Doug Robinson
Publications: Directions

**Agency Owners Roundtable (AOR) (1979)**
RR#1, Brandy Crest Rd., Port Carling, ON P0B 1J0
705/764-8791, Fax: 705/764-8735
Executive Director/Sec.-Treas., R.A. McCall
Publications: AOR News Bulletin

**American Marketing Association (AMA) (1937)**
#200, 250 South Wacker Dr., Chicago, IL 60606-5819 USA
312/648-0536, Fax: 312/993-7542
Contact, Anne Carey
Publications: Marketing Management; Marketing Research, q.; Marketing News, bi-weekly; Journal of Marketing, q.; Journal of Marketing Research, q.; Journal of Health Care Marketing, q.; Journal of Public Policy and Marketing, biennial; Services Marketing Today, bi-m.
British Columbia Chapter: Member Recruitment, Celina Benndorf, #122, 980 West First St., North Vancouver, BC V7P 3N4, 604/986-5050, Fax: 604/988-5226
Calgary Chapter: Contact, Edith Wenzel, #1000, 734 - 7th Ave. SW, Calgary, AB T2P 3P8, 403/269-3734, Fax: 403/237-8186
Montréal Chapter: President, Pierre Trudel, 4316, boul St-Laurent, Montréal, QC H2W 1Z3, 514/499-1391, Fax: 514/842-2422
Ottawa Chapter: President, Ken Lambert, PO Box 224, Stn B, Ottawa, ON K1P 1C4, 613/786-1166
Toronto Chapter: Association Manager, Renée Auer, 246 Sherbourne St., Toronto, ON M5A 2S1, 416/413-0170, Fax: 416/413-0485

**Association des agences de publicité du Québec/Association of Québec Advertising Agencies (AAPQ) (1988)**
#1220, 500, rue Sherbrooke ouest, Montréal, QC H3A 3C6
514/848-1732, Téléc: 514/848-1950, Courrier électronique: aapq@aapq.qc.ca, URL: http://www.aapq.qc.ca
Directeur général, Joseph Mullie

**Association of Canadian Advertisers Inc./Association canadienne des annonceurs (ACA) (1914)**
South Tower, #307, 175 Bloor St. East, Toronto, ON M4W 3R8
416/964-3805, Fax: 416/964-0771, Toll Free: 1-800-565-0109, Email: aca@sympatico.ca, URL: http://www3.sympatico.ca/aca/
President & CEO, Ronald S. Lund
Chair, Katherine Macmillan
Vice-President, Joan Curran

**ASSOCIATION CANADIENNE DES ANNONCEURS INC.**
1080, Côte du Beaver Hall, Montréal, QC H2Z 1S8
514/861-0422, Téléc: 514/861-7740
Vice-président principal, Maurice Brisebois

**Audit Bureau of Circulations (ABC) (1914)**
Canadian Member Service Office, #850, 151 Bloor St. West, Toronto, ON M5S 1S4
416/962-5840, Fax: 416/962-5844
Senior Vice-President, Canada, Robert White
Supervisor, Canadian Member Services, Marian C. Robertson

**Canadian Advertising Foundation/Fondation canadienne de la publicité (CAF) (1957)**
#402, 350 Bloor St. East, Toronto, ON M4W 1H5
416/961-6311, Fax: 416/961-7904
CEO/President, Linda Nagel, CAE
Chairman, Peter Elwood
Publications: Pulse
Advertising Standards Council - Atlantic Region: PO Box 3112, Halifax, NS B3J 3G6
Advertising Standards Council - BC Region: PO Box 3005, Vancouver, BC V6B 3X5, 604/681-2674
Advertising Standards Council - Saskatchewan: Chairman, Gus Sanheim, PO Box 1322, Regina, SK S4P 3B8
Alberta Advertising Standards Council - Calgary: 215 - 16 St. SE, PO Box 2400, Stn M, Calgary, AB T2P 0W8
Le Conseil des normes de la publicité: Directeur général, Niquette Delage, #130, 4823 rue Sherbrooke ouest, Montréal, QC H3Z 1G7, 514/931-8060, Téléc: 514/931-2797

**Canadian Advertising Research Foundation/Fondation canadienne de recherche en publicité (CARF) (1949)**
South Tower, #307, 175 Bloor St. East, Toronto, ON M4W 3R8
416/964-3832, Fax: 416/964-0771, Email: shirleyu@inforamp.net
Administrative Board Assistant, Shirley Uyesugi
Chairman, Geoff Parker
Publications: CARF Newsletter
Affiliates: Advertising Research Foundation, New York

**Canadian Association of Marketing Research Organizations/Association canadienne des organisations de recherche en marketing (CAMRO) (1975)**
#1105, 191 The West Mall, Etobicoke, ON M9C 5K8
416/620-7420, Fax: 416/620-5392, Email: bbandc@enterprise.ca
Executive Director, Dave Stark
Association Coordinator, Laurie Watson
Publications: CAMRO News

**Canadian Automatic Merchandising Association/L'Association Canadienne d'Auto-Distribution (CAMA) (1953)**
#301, 885 Don Mills Rd., Toronto, ON M3C 1V9
416/441-3737, Fax: 416/441-3782
Executive Director, Caroline Manton
Publications: CAMA Update

**Canadian Direct Marketing Association/Association canadienne du marketing direct (CDMA) (1967)**
#607, One Concorde Gate, North York, ON M3C 3N6
416/391-2362, Fax: 416/441-4062, Email: nadiav@cdma.org, URL: http://www.cdma.org
President/CEO, John R. Gustavson, Bus: 416/391-2362, ext.228
Director of Communications, Scott McClellan
Membership Sales & Marketing Manager, Gilles Latour
Publications: Communicator
Affiliates: European Direct Marketing Association; Direct Marketing Association - USA

**Canadian Institute of Marketing/Institut canadien du marketing (CIM) (1982)**
41 Capital Dr., Nepean, ON K2G 0E7
613/727-0954, Fax: 613/228-8398
National Chair, Roger Walsh
Director General, John Harte
National Vice-Chair, Jim Schauer
Publications: Communicate; CIM Information Letter
Affiliates: Affiliated with 13 other Institutes of Marketing around the world

**Canadian Media Directors' Council**
c/o SMW Advertising, 565 Bloor St. East, Toronto, ON M4V 1L5
416/925-7733
President, Sue Jaffe

**Canadian Outdoor Measurement Bureau (COMB)**
#302, 1300 Yonge St., Toronto, ON M4T 1X3
416/968-3823, Fax: 416/968-0154
Manager, Danielle Parent

**Canadian Print Marketers Association/Association canadienne des courtiers en imprimerie (CPMA) (1991)**
#4, 110 West Beaver Creek Rd., Richmond Hill, ON L4B 1J9
905/764-6116, Fax: 905/764-6904

Director, David F. Fleiner
Publications: Newsline

**Canadian Telemarketing Association**
36 Adelaide St. East., PO Box 1113, Toronto, ON M5C 2K5
416/581-1236, ext.29, Fax: 416/599-5058, Toll Free: 1-800-363-4822
Executive Director, Don MacLeod

**Chartered Institute of Marketing Management of Ontario (CIMMO) (1988)**
19 Bartley Dr., RR#3, Caledon East, ON L0N 1E0
905/880-2964, Fax: 905/880-1970, Email: goodall@netcom.ca
Chairman, Nigel Goodall

**Conseil des directeurs médias du Québec (CDMQ)**
143, rue des Intendants, Varennes, QC J3X 2C3
514/652-6834, Téléc: 514/652-6283
Secretaire, Michelle Valiquette

**Industrial Marketing & Research Association of Canada/Association canadienne de recherche et marketing industriel (IMRAC) (1977)**
#224, 6 Lansing Sq., North York, ON M2J 1T5
416/492-6628, Fax: 416/493-1226
President, Roger Briers
Publications: IMRAC Network; Canadian Guide to Industrial Marketing Information

**Institute of Canadian Advertising (ICA) (1905)**
#500, 2300 Yonge St., PO Box 2350, Toronto, ON M4P 1E4
416/482-1396, Fax: 416/481-1856, Toll Free: 1-800-567-7422, Email: ica@goodmedia.com, URL: http://www.goodmedia.com/ica/
President, Rupert T.R. Brendon
Director, Education Services, Janice Schenk

**MediaWatch/Évaluations - Media (1981)**
**National Watch on Images of Women in the Media**
#204, 517 Wellington St. West, Toronto, ON M5V 1G1
416/408-2065, Fax: 416/408-2069, Email: mediawatch@myna.com, URL: http://www.myna.com/~mediawat/
Executive Director, Linda Hawke
Publications: Action Bulletin

**National Advertising Benevolent Society/Société nationale de bienfaisance en publicité (NABS) (1983)**
South Tower, #307, 175 Bloor St. East, Toronto, ON M4W 3R8
416/962-0446, Fax: 416/944-3797, Toll Free: 1-800-661-6227, Email: nabs@nabs.org, URL: http://www.nabs.org
Executive Director, Patricia Crosbie
President, Esmé Carroll
Publications: NABS News
NABS Atlantic: Contact, Donna Alteen, 2584 Agricola St., Halifax, NS B3K 4C4, Fax: 902/422-1199, Toll Free: 1-800-661-6227
NABS West: General Manager, Michael Godin, #401, 68 Water St., Vancouver, BC V6B 1A4, 604/688-3087, Fax: 604/689-7167, Email: nabswest@nabswest.org, URL: http://www.nabswest.org

**National Association of Major Mail Users, Inc./Association nationale des grands usagers postaux inc. (NAMMU) (1983)**
CP 481, Succ Desjardins, Montréal, QC H5B 1B6
905/278-6737, Fax: 905/278-7357
President, Don McArthur
Publications: NAMMU Bulletin; ANGUP Bulletin

**Newspaper Marketing Bureau Inc.**
#201, 10 Bay St., Toronto, ON M5J 2R8
416/364-3744, Fax: 416/363-2568
President, John Finneran
Montréal Office: #1328, 2020, rue University, Montréal, QC H3A 2A5, 514/282-1542, Fax: 514/843-4354
Vancouver Office: Marketing Manager, Elena Dunn, #1005, 1166 Alberni St., Vancouver, BC V6E 3Z3, 604/669-8796, Fax: 604/683-1240

**Outdoor Advertising Association of Canada/L'Association canadienne de l'affichage extérieur (OAAC) (1903)**
#100, 21 St. Clair Ave. East, Toronto, ON M4T 1L9
416/968-3435, Fax: 416/968-0154
Executive Assistant, Brenda Carroll
Publications: Outdoor Views

**Print Measurement Bureau (PMB)**
#1502, 77 Bloor St. West, Toronto, ON M5S 1M2
416/961-3205, Fax: 416/961-5052
President, John Chaplin
Director of Operations, Joanne Van der Burgt

**Professional Marketing Research Society/Association professionnelle de recherche en marketing (PMRS) (1960)**
#110, 2175 Sheppard Ave. East, Toronto, ON M2J 1W8
416/493-4080, Fax: 416/491-1670
President, Mike Nestler
Adminstrator, Jennifer Rogers
Publications: Imprints; Canadian Journal of Marketing Research, a.

**Promotional Products Association of Canada Inc./Association de la publicité par l'objet du Canada (PPAC) (1956)**
#305, 4920, boul de Maisonneuve ouest, Montréal, QC H3Z 1N1
514/489-5359, Fax: 514/489-7760, Toll Free: 1-800-489-8741, Email: ppacapoc@vir.com, URL: http://www.promotionalproducts.com/ppac
Executive Director, Kurt Reckziegel
President, Michel Gratton
Publications Editor, Carol Phillips
Publications: Image News/Nouvelles Image

**Le Publicité club de Montréal (PCM)**
#1220, 500, rue Sherbrooke ouest, Montréal, QC H3A 3C6
514/842-5681, Courrier électronique: pubclub@cam.org, URL: http://www.pcm.montreal.qc.ca/
Président, Alain Richard
Secrétaire-trésorier, Georges E. Gaucher

**Radio Marketing Bureau (RMB) (1961)**
146 Yorkville Ave., Toronto, ON M5R 1C2
416/922-5757, Fax: 416/922-6542, Toll Free: 1-800-667-2346
President/CEO, Brian M. Jones
Affiliates: Radio Advisory Board of Canada
Ottawa Office: Senior Vice-President, T. Leadman, PO Box 3914, Stn C, Ottawa, ON K1Y 4M5, 613/729-7474, Fax: 613/725-2642

**Sign Association of Canada**
#500, 7030 Woodbine Ave., Markham, ON L3R 1A2
905/470-9787, Fax: 905/470-8993
General Manager, E.D. Gagnon

**Society of Ontario Advertising Agencies (SOAA) (1970)**
#205, 660 Eglinton Ave. West, Toronto, ON M5N 1C3
416/782-8908, Fax: 416/782-8908
Contact, Rita Otis
Publications: Meeting Notice

**Trans-Canada Advertising Agency Network (T-CAAN) (1963)**
3390 Bayview Ave., North York, ON M2M 3S3
416/221-8883, Fax: 416/221-8260
President, Phil Chant
Managing Director, W.S. Whitehead
Publications: T-CAAN 'Tattler'
Affiliates: Inter-Market Association of Advertising Agencies - USA

**AEROSPACE INDUSTRY *see* AVIATION & AEROSPACE**

## AGRICULTURE & FARMING

***see also* Animal Breeding; Poultry & Eggs**

**Agricultural Groups Concerned About Resources & the Environment**
**AGCare**
491 Eglinton Ave. West, 5th Fl., Toronto, ON M5N 3A2
416/485-7330, Fax: 416/485-9528, Email: agcare@agcare.org, URL: http://www.agcare.org
Chairman, Jeff Wilson
Vice-Chairman, Bill Allison, Jr.
2nd Vice-Chairman, James Fischer
Technical Advisor, Michael Mazur
Communications Advisor, Terry Boland
Public Information Coordinator, Mary Wiley, Bus: 519/837-1326
Secretary, Dave Armitage
Publications: AGCare Update
Affiliates: Ontario Soybean Growers' Marketing Board; Ontario Fruit & Vegetable Growers' Association; Ontario Corn Producers' Association; Ontario Wheat Producers' Marketing Board; Ontario Bean Producers' Marketing Board; Ontario Seed Growers' Association; Ontario Red Wheat Association; Ontario Soil & Crop Improvement Association; Ontario Federation of Agriculture; Flowers Canada (Ontario); Ontario Flue-Cured Tobacco Growers' Marketing Board

**Agricultural Institute of Canada/Institut agricole du Canada (AIC) (1920)**
#1112, 141 Laurier Ave. West, Ottawa, ON K1P 5J3
613/232-9459, Fax: 613/594-5190, Email: info@aic.ca, URL: http://www.aic.ca
Executive Director, Roy Carver
Communications Coordinator, Brenda Heald
Publications: National Report; Canadian Journal of Animal Science; Canadian Journal of Plant Science; Canadian Journal of Soil Science; Canadian Journal of Agricultural Economics
Affiliates: Canadian Economics & Farm Management Society; Canadian Consulting Agrologists' Association; Canadian Society of Agronomy; Canadian Society of Animal Science; Canadian Society of Extension; Canadian Society for Horticultural Science; Canadian Society of Soil Science; Canadian Society of Agrometeorology; British Columbia Institute of Agrologists; Alberta Institute of Agrologists; Saskatchewan Institute of Agrologists; Manitoba Institute of Agrologists; Ontario Institute of Agrologists; New Brunswick Institute of Agrologists; Nova Scotia Institute of Agrologists; PEI Institute of Agrologists; Newfoundland/Labrador Institute of Agrologists

**ALBERTA INSTITUTE OF AGROLOGISTS**
PO Box 5097, Airdrie, AB T4B 2B2
403/948-1231, Fax: 403/948-3141
Email: P.Ag.@aia.ab.ca, URL: http://www.aia.ab.ca
President, Roger Lore
Publications: Calgary News Brief

**BRITISH COLUMBIA INSTITUTE OF AGROLOGISTS**
#302, 34252 Marshall Rd., Abbotsford, BC V2S 5E4
604/855-9291, Fax: 604/853-3556
Email: info@bcia.com, URL: http://www.bcia.com
Registrar, Garth Bean

**MANITOBA INSTITUTE OF AGROLOGISTS (MIA) (1950)**
16 Lowell Pl., Winnipeg, MB R3T 4H8
204/275-3721, Fax: 204/261-6565
Email: murphy@mia.mb.ca, URL: http://www.mia.mb.ca
Executive Director, Lee Anne Murphy, P.Ag.
Publications: The Manitoba Agrologist

**NEW BRUNSWICK INSTITUTE OF AGROLOGISTS/L'INSTITUT DES AGRONOMES DU NOUVEAU-BRUNSWICK (NBIA)**
PO Box 3479, Stn B, Fredericton, NB E3B 5H2
506/453-2717
Email: estabrookse@em.agr.ca
Registrar, Evans N. Estabrooks
Publications: NBIA Newsletter

**NEWFOUNDLAND & LABRADOR INSTITUTE OF AGROLOGISTS**
PO Box 978, Mount Pearl, NF A1N 3C9
709/772-4170
President, Edward Woodrow
Sec.-Treas., Gary Bishop

**NOVA SCOTIA INSTITUTE OF AGROLOGISTS (NSIA) (1953)**
Nova Scotia Agricultural College, PO Box 550, Truro, NS B2N 5E3
902/893-6520, Fax: 902/893-6393
Email: NSIA_info@nsac.ns.ca, URL: http://www.nsac.ns.ca/nsdam/nsia/
Registrar, Dave Livingstone
Publications: NSIA Newsletter

**ONTARIO INSTITUTE OF AGROLOGISTS (OIA) (1960)**
1 Stone Rd. West, 1st Fl., Guelph, ON N1G 4Y2
519/826-4226, Fax: 519/826-4228
Email: oia@freespace.net, URL: http://www.freespace.net/~oia
Executive Director, Ruth Friendship-Keller, P.Ag.
President, George McLaughlin, CM, P.Ag.
Publications: OIA Newsletter
Affiliates: Ontario Farm Animal Council; Conservation Council of Ontario

**PRINCE EDWARD ISLAND INSTITUTE OF AGROLOGISTS (PEIIA)**
PO Box 2712, Charlottetown, PE C1A 8C3
902/629-1229, Fax: 902/629-1229
Email: kimpinskij@em.agr.ca
President, Les Haliday
Sec.-Treas., Maria MacDonald
Publications: Newsletter

**SASKATCHEWAN INSTITUTE OF AGROLOGISTS (SIA) (1946)**
#7, 3012 Louise St., Saskatoon, SK S7J 3L8
306/242-2606, Fax: 306/955-5561
Executive Director, Glen Hass, P.Ag.
Publications: Agrologist

### Alberta Association of Agricultural Societies (AAAS) (1947)
J.G. O'Donoghue Building, #201, 7000 - 113 St., Edmonton, AB T6H 5T6
403/427-2174, Fax: 403/422-7755
President, Ernie Romaniuk
Administrator, Wendy Pruden
Publications: AG Society News

### Alberta Canola Producers Commission (1989)
#170, 14315 - 118 Ave., Edmonton, AB T5L 4S6
403/452-6487, Fax: 403/451-6933
General Manager, H. Bruce Jeffery
Chairman, Reece Kindt
Publications: Alberta Canola Grower

### Alberta Conservation Tillage Society (ACTS) (1978)
PO Box 326, Carbon, AB T0M 0L0
403/572-3600, Fax: 403/572-3605, Toll Free: 1-800-251-6846, Email: acts@telusplanet.net, URL: http://www.actsagtec.com
President, Spencer Hilton
Vice-President, Walter MacKoway
Vice-President, Vern McNeely
Executive Manager, Russell Evans
Publications: Conservation Tillage News
Affiliates: Alberta Reduced Tillage Initiative

### Alberta Milk Producers' Society (1989)
14904 - 121A Ave., Edmonton, AB T5V 1A3
403/453-5942, Fax: 403/455-2196
General Manager, Bob Tchir

### Alberta Wheat Pool (AWP) (1923)
505 - 2 St. SW, PO Box 2700, Calgary, AB T2P 2P5
403/290-4910, Fax: 403/290-5550, URL: http://www.awp.com/
Director, Corporate Affairs, Dale Riddell
Affiliates: Prairie Pools Inc.; Prairie Sun Grains; Western Cooperative Fertilizers Ltd.; XCANGrain Pool Ltd.

### Association of British Columbia Grape Growers (ABCGG) (1960)
#5, 1864 Spall Rd., Kelowna, BC V1Y 4R1
250/762-4652, Fax: 250/862-8870, Email: bcgrapegrowers@awinc.com
Secretary, Connie Bielert

### Association des jeunes ruraux du Québec (AJRQ) (1974)
#304, 1140, rue Taillon, Québec, QC G1N 3T9
418/681-4847, Téléc: 418/654-0451, Courrier électronique: lynx@cmg.qc.ca
Directeur général, Maurice Le Pesant
Publications: Info-Rural
Organisation(s) affiliée(s): Conseil des 4-H du Canada

### Association professionnelle des meuniers du Québec/Québec Feed Manufacturer's Association (APMQ) (1963)
#115, 2323, boul Versant nord, Ste-Foy, QC G1N 4P4
418/688-9227, Téléc: 418/688-3575
Directeur général, André J. Pilon
Publications: Le Meunier

### Association des technologistes agro-alimentaires inc./Agricultural Technologists Association Inc. (ATA) (1964)
3230, rue Sicotte, CP 70, Saint Hyacinthe, QC J2S 7B3
514/774-8969, Téléc: 514/743-0612
Secrétaire exécutive, Mylène Mongeau

### Atlantic Dairy Council (ADC)
PO Box 9410, Stn A, Halifax, NS B3K 5S3
902/425-2445, Fax: 902/425-2441, Email: pathfndr@fox.nstn.ca
Executive Secretary, John K. Sutherland

### Atlantic Farmers Council (1937)
PO Box 750, Moncton, NB E1C 8N5
506/858-6555, Fax: 506/858-6379
Executive Secretary, John Eaton
President, John Shenkels

### BC Milk Producers Association
846 Broughton St., Victoria, BC V8W 1E4
250/383-7171, Fax: 250/383-5031
Secretary, Andy Dolberg

### Beef Information Centre
Head Office, #100, 2233 Argentia Rd., Toronto, ON L5N 2X7
905/821-4900, Fax: 905/821-4915
Executive Manager, Carolyn McDonell
National Public Relations Manager, Marg Thibeault

### British Columbia Certified Seed Potato Growers' Association (1920)
4119 - 40 St., Ladner, BC V4K 3N2
604/946-8338
Secretary, Noel Roddick

### British Columbia Fruit Growers' Association
1473 Water St., Kelowna, BC V1Y 1J6
250/762-5226, Fax: 250/861-9089
General Manager, Stephen Thomson

### Canada Grains Council
#330, 360 Main St., Winnipeg, MB R3C 3Z3
204/942-2254, Fax: 204/947-0992, Email: office@canadagrainscouncil.ca, URL: http://www.canadagrainscouncil.ca
Executive Director & CEO, A. Douglas Mutch, Email: dmutch@canadagrainscouncil.ca

### Canadian 4-H Council/Conseil des 4-H du Canada (1933)
#208, 1690 Woodward Dr., Ottawa, ON K2C 3R8
613/723-4444, Fax: 613/723-0745
Executive Director, Mike Nowosad
President, Keith Wilkinson
Publications: Forum; 4-H Council Directory, a.
Affiliates: Canadian 4-H Foundation; National 4-H Council (USA)
Member Councils
Alberta: Head, Home Economics & 4H Branch, R.T. (Ted) Youck, Alberta Agriculture, J.G. O'Donoghue Bldg., #200, 7000 - 113 St., Edmonton, AB T6H 5T6, 403/427-4462, Fax: 403/422-7755
British Columbia: Manager, Youth Development Farm, Gordon Bryant, P.Ag., #101, 3547 Skaha Lake Rd., Penticton, BC V2A 7K2, 250/492-1320, Fax: 250/492-1309, Email: gbryant@galaxy.gov.bc.ca
Manitoba: Chief, Youth Section/Marketing, Shaunda Rossington, Manitoba Agriculture, #916, 401 York Ave., Winnipeg, MB R3C 0P8, 204/945-4526, Fax: 204/945-6134
New Brunswick: Director, Communications & Education Branch, Serge Michaud, NB Department of Agriculture, PO Box 6000, Fredericton, NB E3B 5H1, 506/453-2666, Fax: 506/453-7978
Newfoundland: 4-H Youth Program Specialist, Robyn Moss, Dept. of Forest Resources & Agrifoods, Manitoba Dr., PO Box 569, Clarenville, NF A0E 1J0, 709/466-2558, Fax: 709/466-3644
Nova Scotia: 4-H & Rural Youth Supervisor, Elizabeth Crouse, P.Ag., Nova Scotia Dept. of Agriculture & Marketing, MacRae Library, 137 College Rd., Truro, NS B2N 5E3, 902/893-6587, Fax: 902/895-7693, Email: ecrouse@es.nsac.ns.ca
Ontario: 4-H Program Consultant, Cathy Wilson Pinkney, Ontario Ministry of Agriculture, Food & Rural Affairs, PO Box 1030, Guelph, ON N1H 6N1, 519/767-3150, Fax: 519/837-3049
PEI: 4-H Administrator, Heather Tweedy, PEI Dept. of Agriculture, Fisheries & Forestry, 420 University Ave., Charlottetown, PE C1A 7N8, 902/368-4833, Fax: 902/368-7204, Email: j.macquara@peinet.pe.ca
Saskatchewan: Executive Director, Janice Myers, Rural Service Centre, 3735 Thatcher Ave., Saskatoon, SK S7K 2H6, 306/933-7729, Fax: 306/933-7352

### Canadian Co-operative Association (CCA) (1987)
#400, 275 Bank St., Ottawa, ON K2P 2L6
613/238-6711, Fax: 613/567-0658, Email: support@coopcca.com, URL: http://www.coopcca.com
Executive Director, Nora Sobolov
Executive Assistant, Cathi Wilkins

### Canadian Consulting Agrologists Association/ L'Association canadienne des agronomes-conseils (CCAA) (1973)

11 Lynnhaven Cres., Nepean, ON K2E 5K3
613/224-4471, Fax: 613/224-0785, URL: http://www.igw.ca/ccaa
Manager, Henry F. Heald, P.Ag.
President, Ralph Ashmead, P.Ag., CAC
Publications: CCAA Directory; CCAA News, q.

### Canadian Federation of Agriculture/Fédération canadienne de l'agriculture (CFA) (1935)

#1101, 75 Albert St., Ottawa, ON K1P 5E7
613/236-3633, 9997, Fax: 613/236-5749, Email: cfafca@fox.nstn.ca, URL: http://www.cfa-fca.ca
Executive Director/Treasurer, Sally Rutherford
President, Jack Wilkinson
Communications Coordinator, Kevin Carmichael
Publications: Update
Affiliates: BC Federation of Agriculture; Unifarm (Alberta); Keystone Agricultural Producers (Manitoba); Ontario Federation of Agriculture; L'Union des producteurs agricoles (Québec); Coopérative fédérée de Québec; NB Federation of Agriculture; NS Federation of Agriculture; PEI Federation of Agriculture; Canadian Chicken Marketing Agency; Canadian Egg Producers Council; Canadian Egg Marketing Agency; Canadian Turkey Marketing Agency; Dairy Farmers of Canada; Canadian Horticultural Council; Prairie Pools Inc.; Canadian Broiler Hatching Egg Marketing Agency; Canadian Sugar Beet Producers Association; Newfoundland & Labrador Federation of Agriculture

#### BRITISH COLUMBIA FEDERATION OF AGRICULTURE (BCFA) (1935)

846 Broughton St., Victoria, BC V8W 1E4
250/383-7171, Fax: 250/383-5031
Email: mdean@bcfa.bc.ca, URL: http://www.bcfa.bc.ca/bcfa
Jake Jansen
Publications: Country Life

#### CANADIAN SUGAR BEET PRODUCERS' ASSOCIATION (CSBPA) (1943)

PO Box 190, Taber, AB T0K 2G0
403/223-1110, Fax: 403/223-1022
Ron Hanzel
Affiliates: World Association of Beet & Cane Growers

#### COOPÉRATIVE FÉDÉRÉE DU QUÉBEC (CFQ) (1922)

#200, 9001, boul de l'Acadie, Montréal, QC H4N 3H7
514/384-6450, Téléc: 514/384-8772
Courrier électronique: lebrune@coopfed.qc.ca, URL: http://www.coopfed.qc.ca
Directeur général, Jean-Pierre Deschênes
Publications: Le Coopérateur Agricole

#### DAIRY FARMERS OF CANADA/LES PRODUCTEURS LAITIERS DU CANADA (1934)

#1101, 75 Albert St., Ottawa, ON K1P 5E7
613/236-9997, Fax: 613/236-0905
Executive Director, Richard Doyle
President, Claude Rivard
Vice-President, Barron Blois
Administrative Assistant, Elizabeth Medwenitsch
Publications: DFC Newsletter; Facts & Figures at a Glance, a.

#### GROUPE LACTEL, SOCIÉTÉ EN COMMANDITE (1990)

1205, rue Ampére, Boucherville, QC J4B 7M6
514/449-6113, Téléc: 514/449-6297
URL: http://www.lactel.com
Directeur général, Jean-François Robert
Publications: LACTuel

#### KEYSTONE AGRICULTURAL PRODUCERS (KAP) (1985)

437 Assiniboine Ave., Winnipeg, MB R3C 0Y5
204/943-2509, Fax: 204/957-1742
General Manager, Craig Douglas
Publications: KAP News

#### NEW BRUNSWICK FEDERATION OF AGRICULTURE/FÉDÉRATION D'AGRICULTURE DU NOUVEAU-BRUNSWICK (NBFA) (1876)

#206, 1115 Regent St., Fredericton, NB E3B 3Z2
506/452-8101, Fax: 506/452-1085
Email: nbfa@nbnet.nb.ca, URL: http://personal.nbnet.nb.ca/nbfa/nbfa.htm
President, Maarten van Oord
Office Manager, Nicole Arseneau

#### NOVA SCOTIA FEDERATION OF AGRICULTURE (NSFA)

PO Box 784, Truro, NS B2N 5E8
902/893-2293, Fax: 902/893-7063
Executive Director, Dermott English

#### ONTARIO FEDERATION OF AGRICULTURE (OFA) (1936)

40 Eglinton Ave. West, 5th Fl., Toronto, ON M4P 3A2
416/485-3333, Fax: 416/485-9027
Email: info@ofa.on.ca, URL: http://www.ofa.on.ca
President, Tony Morris, Email: ofapres@flexnet.com
General Manager, Gerry Gartner, Email: gerry@ofa.on.ca
Publications: Farm & Country Journal; Members' Digest
Affiliates: AG Care

#### PRAIRIE POOLS INC.

#724, 90 Sparks St., Ottawa, ON K1P 5B4
613/594-4976, Fax: 613/232-7043
Contact, Gordon Pugh

#### PRINCE EDWARD ISLAND FEDERATION OF AGRICULTURE

Farm Centre, 420 University Ave., Charlottetown, PE C1A 7Z5
902/892-6913, Fax: 902/368-7204
Contact, Anne Boswall

### Canadian Feed Industry Association/Association canadienne des industries de l'alimentation animale (CFIA) (1929)

#625, 325 Dalhousie St., Ottawa, ON K1N 7G2
613/241-6421, Fax: 613/241-7970
General Manager, Christine Mercier
Chairman, Glenn Ravnsborg
Manager, Technical Services, Nancy Fischer
Publications: CFIA Newsletter
Affiliates: Canola Council of Canada; Canada Grains Council; Canadian Egg Marketing Agency; Canadian Chicken Marketing Agency; Canadian Turkey Marketing Agency

### Canadian Feed Information Centre (CFIC) (1986)

PO Box 1251, Swift Current, SK S9H 3X4
306/773-5401, Fax: 306/773-3955
Contact, Dr. J.E. Knipfel

### Canadian Honey Council/Conseil canadien du miel (1940)

PO Box 1566, Nipawin, SK S0E 1E0
306/862-3844, Fax: 306/862-5122, Toll Free: 1-800-663-2827
Sec.-Treas., Linda Gane
Publications: Hive Lights; Canadian Honey Council Information Letter; Canadian Honey Council Statistical Material
Affiliates: Apimondia

### Canadian Honey Packers' Association/ Association canadienne des emballeurs de miel (1984)

530, rang Nault, Victoriaville, QC G6P 7R5
819/758-3877, Fax: 819/758-9386, Email: mlabonte@ivic.qc.ca, URL: http://www.worldexport.com/labonte/
President, Jean Marc Labonté
Affiliates: Canadian Honey Council

### Canadian Mushroom Growers' Association/ Association des champignonnistes du Canada (CMGA) (1955)

26 Alderbrook Dr., Nepean, ON K2H 5W5
613/820-6302, Fax: 613/820-6009
President, John Kristalyn
Executive Vice-President, H.R. Taylor
Publications: Mushroom World; CMGA Roster, a.
Affiliates: International Society for Mushroom Science (ISMS)

### Canadian Organic Growers Inc. (COG) (1975)

PO Box 6408, Stn J, Ottawa, ON K2A 3Y6
613/256-1848, Fax: 613/256-4453, Email: braybrok@istar.ca
President, Mary Alice Johnson
Vice-President, Tomàs Nimmo, Bus: 705/444-0923
Membership Secretary, Kathy Lamarche
Publications: COGnition; Directory of Organic Agriculture; Organic Field Crop Handbook
Affiliates: International Federation of Organic Agriculture Movements; Organic Trade Association

### Canadian Pest Management Society/Société canadienne de lutte contre les organismes nuisibles (CPMS) (1954)

Agriculture Canada, PO Box 1000, Agassiz, BC V0M 1A0
604/796-2221, Fax: 604/796-0359, Email: brookes@bcrsag.agr.ca
Sec.-Treas., Victoria R. Brookes
Publications: Canadian Pest Management Society Newsletter
Affiliates: Agricultural Institute of Canada

### Canadian Plowing Organization (1955)

43 Ewen Dr., Uxbridge, ON L9P 1L5
905/852-6221, Fax: 905/852-6221
Secretary, Robert Timbers
President, Lars Skjaveland
Vice-President, James Sache
Affiliates: World Ploughing Organization

### Canadian Seed Growers' Association/ Association canadienne des producteurs de semences (1904)

PO Box 8455, Ottawa, ON K1G 3T1
613/236-0497, Fax: 613/563-7855
Executive Director, W.K. Robertson

### Canadian Seed Trade Association/Association canadienne du commerce des semences (CSTA) (1923)

#302, 39 Robertson Rd., Ottawa, ON K2H 8R2
613/829-9527, Fax: 613/829-3530, Email: csta@hookup.net, URL: http://www.hookup.net/~csta/
Executive Vice-President, W.C. Leask

### Canadian Society of Agricultural Engineering/ Société canadienne de génie rural (CSAE) (1958)

PO Box 381, RPO University, Saskatoon, SK S7N 4J8
306/966-5335, Fax: 306/966-5334, URL: http://www.engr.usask.ca/societies/csae/
Manager, D.I. Norum, Bus: 306/966-5319, Email: norum@sask.usask.ca
Publications: Canadian Agricultural Engineering
Affiliates: American Society of Agricultural Engineers

### Canadian Society of Agronomy

#907, 151 Slater St., Ottawa, ON K1P 5H4
613/232-9459, Fax: 613/594-5190
Secretary, B.G. Rossnagel

### Canadian Society of Extension/Société canadienne de la vulgarisation agricole (CSE)

14815 - 119 Ave., Edmonton, AB T5L 2N9

403/451-5959, Fax: 403/452-5385, URL: http://tdg.uoguelph.ca/cse
President, Rob McNabb
Secretary, John Melicher
Publications: Extension Information Bulletin

### Canadian Sphagnum Peat Moss Association (CSPMA) (1988)
4 Wycliff Pl., St Albert, AB T8N 3Y8
403/460-8280, Fax: 403/459-0939, Toll Free: 1-888-873-7328, URL: http://www.peatmoss.com
President, Gerry Hood, Email: ghood@peatmoss.com
Publications: Bale Mail; CSPMA Retailer Newsletter, s-a.

### Canola Council of Canada (1967)
#400, 167 Lombard Ave., Winnipeg, MB R3B 0T6
204/982-2100, Fax: 204/942-1841, Email: chabihb@canola-council.org, URL: http://www.canola-council.org
President, Dale Adolphe
Manager, Information Services, Dave Wilkins
Publications: Canola Digest

### Christian Farmers Federation of Ontario/Fédération des agriculteurs chrétiens de l'Ontario (CFFO) (1954)
115 Woolwich St., Guelph, ON N1H 3V1
519/837-1620, Fax: 519/824-1835, Email: cffomail@christianfarmers.org, URL: http://www.christianfarmers.org
Contact, Elbert van Donkersgoed
Affiliates: AG Care; Christian Farmers Federation of Alberta; Christian Environmental Council; Rural Development Advisory Committee

#### JUBILEE CENTRE FOR AGRICULTURAL RESEARCH (1983)
115 Woolwich St., Guelph, ON N1H 3V1
519/837-1620, Fax: 519/824-1835
Email: cffomail@christianfarmers.org, URL: http://www.christianfarmers.org
Research Director, Elbert van Donkersgoed
Chair, Tom Oegema
Publications: Earthkeeping Ontario

### Co-op Atlantic/Co-op Atlantique (1927)
PO Box 750, Moncton, NB E1C 8N5
506/858-6000, Fax: 506/858-6477, URL: http://www.co-op-atlantic.ca
CEO, Eric Claus
Publications: Co-op Express

### Conseil de l'industrie laitière du Québec inc./Québec Dairy Council Inc. (CILQ) (1963)
#310, 8585, boul St-Laurent, Montréal, QC H2P 2M9
514/381-5331, Téléc: 514/381-6677
Président exécutif, Claude Lambert
Président du conseil d'administration, Guy Domingue
Adjointe administrative, Yolaine Villeneuve
Publications: Mise à Jour

### Cooperative of Maple Syrup Producers of New Brunswick Inc./Cooperative des producteurs de sirop d'érable du Nouveau-Brunswick inc. (1988)
9 Industrielle St., PO Box 951, Saint-Quentin, NB E0K 1J0
506/235-3438, Fax: 506/235-3529
President, Denis Cote
Marketing Director, J.L. Paul Ouellet
Affiliates: International Maple Syrup Institute; Conseil acadien de la coopération; Canadian Federation of Chefs & Cooks

### Crop Protection Institute of Canada/Institut canadien pour la protection des cultures (CPIC) (1953)
#627, 21 Four Seasons Pl., Etobicoke, ON M9B 6J8
416/622-9771, Fax: 416/622-6764, Email: rosew@cropro.org, URL: http://www.cropro.org
President, J.S. King
Communication Manager, Wendy Rose
Publications: Newsletter

### Dairy Farmers of Ontario (DFO)
6780 Campobello Rd., Mississauga, ON L5N 2L8
905/821-8970, Fax: 905/821-3160, URL: http://www.milk.org
General Manager, Bob Bishop
Publications: Ontario Milk Producer

### Dairy Nutrition Council of Alberta (DNCA) (1988)
14904 - 121A Ave., Edmonton, AB T5V 1A3
403/453-5942, Fax: 403/455-2196, Toll Free: 1-800-252-7530, URL: http://www.dnca.ab.ca
Manager, C. Thorvaldson
Publications: Fast Facts
Affiliates: Dairy Farmers of Canada

### Dairyworld Foods (1992)
**Agrifoods International Cooperative Ltd.**
425 Winnipeg St., Regina, SK S4P 3A5
306/924-1300
Wendy Kelly
Publications: Dairyworld Digest; Agrifoods Milkline

### Earthkeeping: Food & Agriculture in Christian Perspective (1978)
#205, 10711 - 107 Ave., Edmonton, AB T5H 0W6
403/428-6981, Fax: 403/428-1581, Email: earthkeeping@enabel.ccinet.ab.ca
President, Herman Bulten
Administrative Assistant, Rita Anema
Coordinator, Research & Policy, Kathryn W. Olson
Publications: Earthkeeping Alberta
Affiliates: Alberta Environment Network

### Fédération des agricultrices du Québec
555, boul Roland-Therrien, Longueuil, QC J4H 3Y9
514/679-0530, Téléc: 514/679-2652
Secrétaire, Lise Dufort

### Fédération d'agriculture biologique du Québec
555, boul Roland-Therrien, Longueuil, QC J4H 3Y9
514/679-0530, Téléc: 514/679-5436
Secrétaire, Alyne Savary

### Fédération des producteurs de lait du Québec (FPLQ) (1983)
555, boul Roland-Therrien, Longueuil, QC J4H 3Y9
514/679-0530, Téléc: 514/679-5899, Courrier électronique: fplq@upa.qc.ca
Directrice générale, Guylaine Gosselin
Publications: Le Producteur de lait québécois
Organisation(s) affiliée(s): Union des producteurs agricoles

### Fédération des producteurs de porc du Québec (FPPQ) (1966)
555, boul Roland-Thérrien, Longueuil, QC J4H 3Y9
514/679-0530, Téléc: 514/679-0102, Ligne sans frais: 1-800-363-7672, Courrier électronique: fppq@netaxis.qc.ca
Secrétaire, Benoît Desilet
Publications: Porc Québec
Organisation(s) affiliée(s): Union des producteurs agricoles du Québec

### Flax Council of Canada (1985)
#465, 167 Lombard Ave., Winnipeg, MB R3B 0T6
204/982-2115, Fax: 204/942-1841, Email: flax@flaxcouncil.ca, URL: http://www.flaxcouncil.ca
President, Donald H. Frith
Chairman, Garvin Hanley
Publications: Flax Focus

### Flax Growers Western Canada
PO Box 832, Regina, SK S4P 3B1
306/781-7475, Fax: 306/525-4173
Contact, Donald R. Jaques

### International Flying Farmers - Canadian Branch
910 Crescent Ave., High River, AB T1V 1H2
403/652-7373
Secretary, Lenora Jones

### National Dairy Council of Canada/Conseil national de l'industrie lactière du Canada
221 Laurier Ave. East, Ottawa, ON K1N 6P1
613/238-4116, Fax: 613/238-6247, Telex: 053-3952
President & CEO, Kempton L. Matte

### National Farmers Union/Syndicat national des cultivateurs (NFU) (1969)
250C - 2 Ave. South, Saskatoon, SK S7K 2M1
306/652-9465, Fax: 306/664-6226, URL: http://www.wbm.ca/users/farmers
President, Nettie Wiebe, Bus: 306/493-2569
Vice-President, Chris Tait, Bus: 204/252-2773
Women's President, Karen Fyfe, Bus: 902/886-2993
Youth President, Karen Pedersen, Bus: 306/398-2795
Executive Secretary, Darrin Qualman, Bus: 306/652-9465, Email: farmers@eagle.wbm.ca
Publications: Union Farmer; Union Farmer Quarterly
Affiliates: Action Canada Network

### Northern Ontario Dairymen's Association (1948)
PO Box 445, Kirkland Lake, ON P2N 3J1
705/567-3377
President, Michael Holland
Sec.-Treas., Dean Archer

### Nova Scotia Beekeepers Association
RR#2, Berwick, NS B0P 1E0
902/538-7527
Manager, Joanne Moran

### Nova Scotia Fruit Growers' Association (NSFGA) (1863)
Kentville Agricultural Centre, 32 Main St., Kentville, NS B4N 1J5
902/678-1093, Fax: 902/679-1567
Secretary Manager, Janice Lutz
Affiliates: Nova Scotia Federation of Agriculture

### Nova Scotia Milk Producers Association
347 Willow St., PO Box 784, Truro, NS B2N 5E8
902/893-2293, Fax: 902/893-7063
Sec.-Treas., Donna Langille
Publications: Newsletter

### Ontario Beekeepers' Association (OBA) (1881)
RR#3, Bayfield, ON N0M 1G0
519/565-2622, Fax: 519/565-5452, Email: ontbee@tcc.on.ca, URL: http://www.tdg.ca/ontag/bee
President, Henry Hiemstra
Business Administrator, Patricia A. Westlake
Publications: The Sting

### Ontario Creamerymen's Association (1935)
26 Dominion St., Alliston, ON L9R 1L5
705/435-6751
President, Lloyd Kennedy
Publications: Newsletter

### Ontario Dairy Council (ODC) (1971)
6533D Mississauga Rd., Mississauga, ON L5N 1A6
905/542-3620, Fax: 905/542-3624, Email: ondrycnl@idirect.com
President, Tom Kane
Chairman, Nick Quickert
Publications: News & Views
Affiliates: National Dairy Council; International Dairy Federation

**Ontario Fruit & Vegetable Growers' Association/ L'Association des fruitculteurs et des maraîchers de l'Ontario (OFVGA) (1859)**
#103, 355 Elmira Rd. North, Guelph, ON N1K 1S5
519/763-6160, Fax: 519/763-6604, Email: gayle@in.on.ca, URL: http://www.tdg.ca/ontag/ofvga
Executive Secretary, Michael Mazur
Publications: The Grower

**Ontario Grain & Feed Association (1965)**
#106, 1400 Bishop St., Cambridge, ON N1R 6W8
519/622-3800, Fax: 519/622-3590
Executive Vice-President, D.O. Buttenham
Publications: Bulletin; Trade Directory, a.

**Ontario Maple Syrup Producers' Association (OMSPA) (1966)**
RR#6, Strathroy, ON N7G 3H7
519/232-4596, Fax: 519/232-9166, Email: kenneth.mcgregor@sympatico.ca, URL: http://www.tdg.ca/ontag/omspa/
Sec.-Treas., Kenneth McGregor
Publications: Maple Mainline

**Ontario Plowmen's Association (1913)**
367 Woodlawn Rd. West, Guelph, ON N1H 7K9
519/767-1967, Fax: 519/661-7569, Toll Free: 1-800-661-7569
General Manager, John Fennell

**Ordre des agronomes du Québec/Order of Agrologists of Québec (OAQ) (1974)**
#710, 1259, rue Berri, Montréal, QC H2L 4C7
514/844-3833, Téléc: 514/844-7462
Présidente, Josée DeGrandmont
Chargée de projets, Chantal Paul
Publications: Agro-Nouvelles

**PEI Dairy Producers Association (1976)**
PO Box 335, Charlottetown, PE C1A 7K7
902/892-5331, Fax: 902/566-2755
Chairman, Casey Van Diepen

**Preservation of Agricultural Lands Society (PALS) (1977)**
PO Box 1090, St Catharines, ON L2R 7A3
905/468-2841, Fax: 905/468-7614
Contact, Gracia Janes
President, John Bacher
Vice-President, Joan Ashcroft
Publications: Pals Newsletter
Affiliates: Ontario Environmental Network Land Use Caucus

**Prince Edward Island Soil & Crop Improvement Association (1971)**
PO Box 1600, Charlottetown, PE C1A 7N3
902/628-6997, Fax: 902/628-6998
President, Ronnie Gallant
Secretary, Marilyn Haslam

**Prince Edward Island Vegetable Growers Co-op Association**
81 Sherwood Rd., PO Box 1494, Charlottetown, PE C1A 7N1
902/892-5361, Fax: 902/566-2383
Manager, Don Read

**Québec Farmers' Association (QFA) (1957)**
PO Box 80, Ste-Anne-de-Bellevue, QC H9X 3L4
514/457-2010, Fax: 514/398-7972
Executive Director, Hugh Maynard
President, Douglas Mackinnon
Publications: Québec Farmers' Advocate

**Québec Young Farmers (1969)**
PO Box 80, Ste-Anne-de-Bellevue, QC H9X 3L4
514/457-2010, Fax: 514/398-7972
President, Amber Heatlie
Publications: News Spreader

**Saskatchewan Association of Agricultural Societies & Exhibitions (SAASE) (1987)**
PO Box 7602, Saskatoon, SK S7K 4R4
306/664-6654, Fax: 306/664-6654
Executive Director, Judy Reimer
Publications: Newsletter
Affiliates: Canadian Association of Fairs & Exhibitions

**Saskatchewan Canola Growers Association (1969)**
#210, 111 Research Dr., Saskatoon, SK S7N 3R2
306/668-2380, Fax: 306/975-1126
President, Ken Mannle
Executive Director, Holly Rask
Administrative Assistant, Shelley Braun
Publications: Canola Country

**Saskatchewan Dairy Foundation (SDF) (1981)**
445 Winnipeg St., PO Box 1294, Regina, SK S4P 3B8
306/949-6999, Fax: 306/949-2605
President, M. Pearson
Vice-President, C. Baerg
Publications: Milk & More

**Saskatchewan Game Farmers Association**
2341 Robin Pl., North Battleford, SK S9A 3T6
306/445-7412, Fax: 306/445-4007
Executive Director, Terri Harris
Affiliates: Saskatchewan Stock Growers Association

**SeCan Association/Association SeCan (1976)**
#200, 57 Auriga Dr., Nepean, ON K2E 8B2
613/225-6891, Fax: 613/225-6422, Email: secan@ott.hookup.net
General Manager, L.R. White
President, Grant Datway
Publications: SeCan News

**Society of Ontario Nut Growers (SONG) (1972)**
RR#2, 1540 Concession 6 Rd., Niagara on the Lake, ON L0S 1J0
905/682-4966
Secretary, G. Robert Hambleton
Publications: SONG News

**Sustainable Agriculture Association (SAA) (1985)**
PO Box 1181, Stn M, Calgary, AB T2P 2K9
Fax: 403/728-2395, Toll Free: 1-800-699-1477
President, Brad McNish
Publications: News & Notes from the Back 40

**Union des producteurs agricoles (UPA) (1924)**
555, boul Roland-Therrien, Longueuil, QC J4H 3Y9
514/679-0530; 4943, Téléc: 514/679-5436, URL: http://www.upa.qc.ca/
Directeur général, Claude Lafleur
Publications: La Terre de chéz-nous

**Vegetable Growers' Association of Manitoba (1953)**
808 Muriel St., Winnipeg, MB R2Y 0Y3
204/888-8989, Fax: 204/888-0944
Executive Secretary, Evelyn MacKenzie-Reid
Publications: Newsletter

**Vegetable & Potato Producers' Association of Nova Scotia**
Kentville Agricultural Centre, 32 Main St., Kentville, NS B4N 1J5
902/678-9335
Secretary Manager, Tammy Hall

**Western Barley Growers Association (WBGA) (1973)**
#232, 2116 - 27 Ave. NE, Calgary, AB T2E 7A6
403/291-3630, Fax: 403/291-9841
President, Buck Spencer
Vice-President, Greg Rockafellow
Alberta Vice-President, Doug Robertson
Saskatchewan Vice-President, Darwin Kells
Treasurer, Marvin Fowler
Publications: The Barley Grower

**Western Canadian Wheat Growers Association (WCWGA) (1970)**
1836 Victoria Ave. East, Regina, SK S4N 7K1
306/586-5866, Fax: 306/586-2707, Toll Free: 1-888-776-3276
Executive Director, Alanna Koch
President, Larry Maguire
Publications: The Wheatgrower; Pro-Farm, bi-m.

**Western Grains Research Foundation (WGRF) (1981)**
118 Veterinary Rd., Saskatoon, SK S7N 2R4
306/975-0060, Fax: 306/975-3766
Chairman, Cam Henry
Executive Director, L.I. Peterson, Email: lpeterson@mail.innovplace.saskatoon.sk.c
Affiliates: United Grain Growers; Western Canadian Wheat Growers Association; Western Barley Growers Association; Flax Growers Western Canada; Canadian Canola Growers Association; Wild Rose Agricultural Products; Keystone Agricultural Producers; Oat Producers of Alberta; Canadian Seed Growers Association; Alberta Wheat Pool; Saskatchewan Wheat Pool; Manitoba Pool Elevators; National Farmers Union; Alberta Winter Wheat Commission; BC Grain Producers Association

**Wild Rose Agricultural Producers (1996)**
14815 - 119 Ave., Edmonton, AB T5L 4W2
403/451-5912, Fax: 403/453-2669, Email: wrap@planet.eon.net
Executive Director, Rod Scarlett
Publications: Wild Rose News

## AIDS

**The AIDS Foundation of Canada Inc. (1986)**
#1000, 885 Dunsmuir, Vancouver, BC V6C 1N5
604/688-7294, Fax: 604/689-4888
President, Nathan S. Ganapathi

**Canadian AIDS Society/Société canadienne du sida (CAS) (1986)**
#400, 100 Sparks St., Ottawa, ON K1P 5B7
613/230-3580, Fax: 613/563-4998, Email: cdnaids@cyberus.ca, URL: http://www.cdnaids.ca
Executive Director, Russell Armstrong
Manager of Finance, Kelly James Masterson
Development Officer, Susan McIntosh
Communications Officer, Bob Daley
Publications: InfoCAS/InfoSCS
Affiliates: International Council of AIDS Service Organizations

**AIDS VANCOUVER (1983)**
**Vancouver AIDS Society**
c/o Pacific AIDS Resource Centre, 1107 Seymour St., Vancouver, BC V6B 5S8
604/681-2122, Fax: 604/893-2211, Info Line: 604/687-2437, TDD: 604/893-2215
URL: http://mindlink.net/aids_vancouver/
Executive Director, Rick Marchand

**BLACK COALITION FOR AIDS PREVENTION (1987)**
**BLACK CAP**
#940, 790 Bay St., Toronto, ON M5G 1N8
416/977-7725, Fax: 416/977-2325
Email: blackcap@web.net
Executive Director, Dionne A. Falconer
Publications: Black CAP Links

**CANADIAN HIV/AIDS LEGAL NETWORK/RÉSEAU JURIDIQUE CANADIEN SUR LE VIH/SIDA (1992)**
4007, rue de Mentana, Montréal, QC H2L 3R9
514/526-1796, Fax: 514/526-5543
Email: aidslaw@web.net, URL: http://www.odyssee.net/~jujube
Ralf Jurgens
Publications: HIV/AIDS Policy & Law Newsletter

**COALITION DES ORGANISMES COMMUNAUTAIRES QUÉBÉCOIS DE LUTTE CONTRE LE SIDA (COCQ-SIDA) (1990)**
#320, 4205, rue St-Denis, Montréal, QC H2J 2K9
514/844-2477, Téléc: 514/844-2498
Directrice générale, Lyse Pinault
Président, Jacques Gélinas
Publications: iti

### Canadian Foundation for AIDS Research/Fondation canadienne de recherche sur le SIDA (CANFAR) (1987)
#901, 165 University Ave., Toronto, ON M5H 3B8
416/361-6281, Fax: 416/361-5736, Toll Free: 1-800-563-2873
General Manager, Roger C. Bullock
Publications: The Catalyst

### AIR CONDITIONING *see* HEATING, AIR CONDITIONING, PLUMBING

### AIR SHOWS *see* EVENTS

## ANIMAL BREEDING
***see also* Fur Trade**

### The Animal Health Trust of Canada/La Fondation canadienne de la santé animale (1972)
#1801, One Yonge St., Toronto, ON M5E 1W7
416/368-7914, Fax: 416/369-0515, Toll Free: 1-800-565-5235
Executive Director, Marcia Darling
Publications: Insight
Affiliates: Canadian Veterinary Medical Association (founding body)

### Appaloosa Horse Club of Canada (ApHCC) (1954)
PO Box 940, Claresholm, AB T0L 0T0
403/625-3326, Fax: 403/625-2274, Email: appaloos@agt.net, URL: http://www.agt.net/public/appaloos/
Executive Secretary, Lorna Guitton
Publications: The Appaloosa

### Ayrshire Breeders Association of Canada (ABAC)
**Ayrshire Canada**
Glenaladale House, 21111 Lakeshore Rd., PO Box 188, Ste-Anne-de-Bellevue, QC H9X 3V9
514/398-7970, Fax: 514/398-7972, Email: info@ayrshire-canada.com, URL: http://www.ayrshire-canada.com
General Manager, Yvon Rioux
Publications: Canadian Ayrshire Review

### Canada Fox Breeder's Association
286 Fitzroy St., Summerside, PE C1N 1J2
902/436-9547, Fax: 902/436-1994
Sec.-Treas., Robynn Quinn
Affiliates: 9 provincial affiliates

### Canada Mink Breeders Association/Association des éleveurs de visons du Canada (CMBA) (1953)
65B Skyway Ave., Etobicoke, ON M9W 6C7
416/675-9400, Fax: 416/675-9401
Executive Secretary, Karlene Hart
Publications: Newsletter
Affiliates: Majestic Fur Association

### Canada Sheep Council
10 Campbell Cres., North York, ON M2P 1P2
416/489-4487
Executive Director, D.J. Sloan

### Canadian Angus Association/L'Association canadienne Angus (1906)
#214, 6715 - 8 St. NE, Calgary, AB T2E 7H7
403/571-3580, Fax: 403/571-3599, Toll Free: 1-888-571-3580, Email: cdnangus@cadvision.com
General Manager, Doug Fee
Publications: Aberdeen Angus World

### Canadian Arabian Horse Registry (1958)
801 Terrace Plaza, 4445 Calgary Trail South, Edmonton, AB T6H 5R7
403/436-4244, Fax: 403/438-2971
Registrar/Administrator, Phyllis Kinsella
Publications: Canadian Arabian News
Affiliates: World Arabian Horse Registry; Canadian Equestrian Federation

### Canadian Association of Animal Breeders/Association canadienne des éleveurs de bétail (CAAB) (1984)
PO Box 817, Woodstock, ON N4S 8A3
519/539-0662, Fax: 519/537-5391
Executive Director, R.J. McDonald

### Canadian Belgian Horse Association
RR#3, Schomberg, ON L0G 1T0
905/939-7497
Secretary, Barb Meyers

### Canadian Bison Association/Association canadienne du bison (CBA) (1984)
PO Box 1387, Morden, MB R0G 1J0
204/822-3219, Fax: 204/822-4328
President, Len Ross
Show/Sale Chairman, Don Scott
Executive Secretary, Gail Reichert
Publications: Smoke Signals
Affiliates: American Bison Association - USA; National Bison Association - USA; Peace River Bison Association

### Canadian Blonde d'Aquitaine Association (1972)
1608A Centre St. North, Calgary, AB T2E 2R9
403/276-5771, Fax: 403/276-7577
President, Lyle Hamann
Publications: Blonde Advantage

### Canadian Brown Swiss & Braunvieh Association (1914)
#9, 350 Speedvale Ave. West, Guelph, ON N1H 7M7
519/821-2811, Fax: 519/821-2723, Email: browncow@jerseycanada.com, URL: http://www.jerseycanada.com/browncow
Sec.-Manager, Bill Prins
Publications: The Bell/La Cloche

### Canadian Cattle Breeders' Association/Société des éleveurs de bovins canadiens (CCBA) (1895)
468, rue Dolbeau, Sherbrooke, QC J1G 2Z7
819/346-1258, Fax: 819/346-1258
Secretary, Jean-Guy Bernier
Publications: Entre-Nous

### Canadian Cattlemen's Association (1932)
#215, 6715 - 8 St. NE, Calgary, AB T2E 7H7
403/275-8558, Fax: 403/274-5686, URL: http://www.cattle.ca
Executive Vice-President, Dennis Laycraft
Animal Health & Meat Inspection Committee, Heidi Grogan
Environmental Coordinator, Peggy Strankman
Ottawa Office: Assistant General Manager, Jim Caldwell, #602, 150 Metcalf St., Ottawa, ON K2P 1P1, 613/233-9375, Fax: 613/233-2860

### Canadian Charolais Association (CCA) (1958)
2320 - 41 Ave. NE, Calgary, AB T2E 6W8
403/250-9242, Fax: 403/291-9324, Email: cca@charolais.com, URL: http://www.charolais.com
General Manager, Dale Kelly, P.Ag.
Publications: Charolais Banner

### Canadian Co-operative Wool Growers Ltd. (1918)
PO Box 130, Carleton Place, ON K7C 3P3
613/257-2714, Fax: 613/257-8896
General Manager, Eric Bjergso
Publications: Canadian Wool Grower

### Canadian Cutting Horse Association (CCHA) (1953)
540 McIntosh Rd. NE, Calgary, AB T2E 5Z3
403/276-6448, Fax: 403/276-6452
Dave Whittal
Publications: The Canadian Cutter

### Canadian Dexter Cattle Association (CDCA) (1986)
2417 Holly Lane, Ottawa, ON K1V 0M7
613/731-7110, Fax: 613/731-0704, URL: http://www.hookup.net/~jbush/
Secretary, Ron Black
Publications: CDCA Newsletter
Affiliates: Canadian Livestock Records Corporation

### Canadian Donkey & Mule Association (CDMA)
c/o Northfolk Minature Donkeys, RR#2, Site 1, Box 15, Rocky Mountain House, AB T0M 1T0
403/845-5308
Karen Anderson
Publications: CDMA News
Affiliates: American Donkey & Mule Society; British Donkey Breed Society; Breed Societies of Britain, Australia, Sweden, Holland, Germany, New Zealand

### Canadian Fjord Horse Association
PO Box 1, Site 203, RR#2, Tofield, AB T0B 4J0
403/922-6231
President, Keith Kemp

### Canadian Galloway Association (1882)
1 Hallstone Rd., Brampton, ON L6V 3N2
905/459-0650, Fax: 905/459-0650
Sec.-Treas., Brigitte Morris
Publications: Newsletter; Canadian Galloway Advance, a.

### Canadian Gelbvieh Association (1972)
#A123, 2116 - 27 Ave. NE, Calgary, AB T2E 7A6
403/250-8640, Fax: 403/291-5624
Secretary Manager, Wendy Belcher
Publications: Gelbvieh Guide

### Canadian Goat Society/La Société canadienne des éléveurs de chèvres (CGS) (1917)
2417 Holly Lane, Ottawa, ON K1V 0M7
613/731-9894
Secretary Manager, Sharon Hunt
Publications: Canadian Goat Society Quarterly q.

### Canadian Guernsey Association (1905)
368 Woolwich St., Guelph, ON N1H 3W6
519/836-2141, Fax: 519/824-9250

Secretary Manager, Vivianne Macdonald
Publications: Canadian Guernsey Journal
Affiliates: Canadian Dairy Breeds; Canadian Livestock Records Corporation; Joint Classification Board; Agriculture & Agri-Food Canada; Canadian Dairy Network

**Canadian Hays Converter Association (1976)**
#450, 1207 - 11 Ave. SW, Calgary, AB T3C 0M5
403/245-6923, Fax: 403/244-3128
Office Manager, Terri Worms
Publications: Newsletter
Affiliates: Beef Improvement Federation; Canadian Beef Breeds Council; Saskatchewan Livestock Centre

**Canadian Hereford Association (1890)**
5160 Skyline Way NE, Calgary, AB T2E 6V1
403/275-2662, Fax: 403/295-1333
General Manager, Duncan J. Porteous
Publications: Canadian Hereford Digest

**Canadian Highland Cattle Society/Société canadienne des éleveurs de bovins Highland (CHCS) (1964)**
Maple Lea Farm, 307 Spicer, Knowlton, QC J0E 1V0
514/243-5543, Fax: 514/243-1150
Secretary-Manager, Margaret Badger
Publications: The Kyloe Cry

**Canadian Icelandic Horse Federation (CIHF) (1979)**
5435 Rochdell Rd., Vernon, BC V1B 3E8
250/545-2336, Fax: 250/549-9116, Toll Free: 1-800-255-2336, Email: rhood@junction.net
Secretary, Christine Schwartz
Publications: CIHF Newsletter

**Canadian Landrace Swine Breeders Association/Club des porcs Landrace (1990)**
PO Box 34, Beebe, QC J0B 1E0
819/876-5103, Fax: 819/876-7986
Secretary, Allan Smith
Affiliates: Purebred Swine Breeders Association of Canada

**Canadian Limousin Association (1970)**
5663 Burleigh Cres. SE, Calgary, AB T2H 1Z7
403/253-7309, Fax: 403/253-1704
Executive Manager, Beverly J. Leavitt
Publications: Limousin Leader

**Canadian Livestock Records Corporation/Société canadienne d'enregistrement des animaux (CLRC) (1905)**
2417 Holly Lane, Ottawa, ON K1V 0M7
613/731-7110, Fax: 613/731-0704, Email: clrc@clrc.on.ca, URL: http://www.clrc.on.ca
General Manager, Bruce E. Hunt
Publications: CLRC Newsletter

**Canadian Maine-Anjou Association (CMAA) (1970)**
#110, 3016 - 19 St. NE, Calgary, AB T2E 6Y9
403/291-7077, Fax: 403/291-0274
General Manager, Rod McLeod
Publications: Maine-Anjou International

**Canadian Milking Shorthorn Society**
RR#1, 3071 Range Allan, Kinnear's Mills, QC G0N 1K0
418/424-3246, Fax: 418/424-3528
President, Dale Nugent
Secretary, Patricia Knott
Publications: The Improver

**Canadian Morgan Horse Association Inc./Association des chevaux Morgan canadien inc. (CMHA) (1968)**
PO Box 286, Port Perry, ON L9L 1A3
905/985-1691, Fax: 905/985-3385, Email: cmha@osha.igs.net, URL: http://www.osha.igs.net/~cmha/.index.htm
Office Administrator, Nancy Kavanagh
President, Ivan Mackenzie
Publications: The Canadian Morgan
Affiliates: American Morgan Horse Association

**Canadian Murray Grey Association (1970)**
PO Box 605, Red Deer, AB T4N 5G6
403/343-1355, Fax: 403/346-4910
President, Kevin E. Willis
1st Vice-President, Harley Herman
2nd Vice-President, Doug Holtby
Sec.-Treas., Doris Burrington
Publications: MG National

**Canadian Palomino Horse Association (1942)**
631 Hendershott Rd., RR#1, Hannon, ON L0R 1P0
905/692-4328
President, Cliff Wismer
Secretary, Lorraine Holdaway
Publications: Gold Horse News; Palomino Horse Breeders, q.

**Canadian Percheron Association**
PO Bag 200, Crossfield, AB T0M 0S0
403/946-5426
Sec.-Treas., Cathie James

**Canadian Pinto Horse Association**
RR#1, Andrew, AB T0B 0C0
403/895-7399
Secretary, Georgina Campbell
Publications: Canadian Pinto Review

**Canadian Pinzgauer Association (CPA) (1974)**
PO Box 248, Nanton, AB T0L 1R0
403/646-2193, Fax: 403/646-2193
Executive Secretary, Terry A. Place
Publications: CPA News
Affiliates: Alberta Pinzaguer Association

**Canadian Pork Council/Conseil canadien du porc (CPC) (1966)**
75 Albert St., Ottawa, ON K1P 5E7
613/236-9239, Fax: 613/236-6658, Email: cpc@fox.nstn.ca, URL: http://www.canpork.ca
Executive Secretary, Martin Rice

**Canadian Quarter Horse Association**
PO Box 1258, Stony Plain, AB T0E 2G0
403/963-3612, Fax: 403/963-8612
President, Peter Rice

**Canadian Red Poll Cattle Association (1906)**
RR#3, Ponoka, AB T4J 1R3
403/783-5951, Fax: 403/783-6722
President, Carl Blach
Secretary, Jackie Fleming
Publications: Canadian Red Poll Cattle Association Newsletter; Breeders List
Affiliates: Canadian Livestock Records Corporation

**Canadian Romagnola-Marchigiana Association**
**Romark**
PO Box 37, Priddis, AB T0L 1W0
403/931-2415, Fax: 403/931-2415
Secretary Manager, Janet Carscallen

**Canadian Sheep Breeders Association/La Société Canadienne des Éleveurs de Moutons**
c/o Francis Winger, RR#4, Mount Forest, ON N0G 2L0
519/323-0360, Fax: 519/323-0468
President, D.E. Acres, Bus: 613/623-5260

**Canadian Shorthorn Association**
Gummer Bldg., 5 Douglas St., Guelph, ON N1H 2S8
519/822-6841, Fax: 519/822-9753
Sec.-Treas., Patricia Coulson
Publications: Shorthorn News Magazine

**Canadian Simmental Association (1969)**
#13, 4101 - 19 St. NE, Calgary, AB T2E 7C4
403/250-7979, Fax: 403/250-5121
General Manager, Barry Bennett

**Canadian Standardbred Horse Society/Société canadienne du cheval Standardbred (CSHS) (1909)**
2150 Meadowvale Blvd., Mississauga, ON L5N 6R6
905/858-3060, Fax: 905/858-8047, Email: cantrot@io.org, URL: http://home.ican.net/~troton
General Manager, Ted Smith
Publications: Trot

**Canadian Swine Breeders' Association (1889)**
#215, 2435 Holly Lane, Ottawa, ON K1V 7P2
613/731-5531, Fax: 613/731-6655
Manager, Ron James
Publications: Canadian Swine

**Canadian Tarentaise Association (1974)**
PO Box 5097, Airdrie, AB T4B 2B2
403/948-3141, Fax: 403/481-2819
President, Paulette Martin
Sec.-Treas., Jan Petterson
Publications: Tarentaise Today
Affiliates: American Tarentaise Association; SOPEXA - Cambery, France

**Canadian Thoroughbred Horse Society/Société canadienne du cheval thoroughbred (CTHS) (1906)**
PO Box 172, Etobicoke, ON M9W 5L1
416/675-1370, Fax: 416/675-9525, Email: cths@idirect.com
National Executive Secretary, Fran Okihiro

**Canadian Trakehner Horse Society (CTHS) (1974)**
PO Box 1270, New Hamburg, ON N0B 2G0
519/662-3209, Fax: 519/662-3209, Email: cantrakhsiuh@golden.net
President, Desmond Leeper
Registrar/Secretary, Ingrid Von Hausen
Publications: CTHS Newsletter

**Canadian Welsh Black Cattle Society**
PO Box 147, Hanna, AB T0J 1P0
403/579-2409
Secretary, Marlene Wallace

**La Fédération des producteurs de bovins du Québec/Federation of Québec Beef Producers (FPBQ) (1974)**
555, boul Roland-Therrien, Longueuil, QC J4H 3Y9
514/679-0530, Téléc: 514/442-9348, Courrier électronique: fpbq@upa.qc.ca
Secrétaire-trésorier, Gaetan Bélanger
Publications: La Minute Bovine; Bovins du Québec, trimestriel
Organisation(s) affiliée(s): Union des producteurs agricoles

**GENCOR (1969)**
**Western Ontario Breeders Inc.**
RR#5, Guelph, ON N1H 6J2
Fax: 519/763-6582, Toll Free: 1-888-821-2150
General Manager, Paul Larmar
Contact, Wendy Robinson
Publications: WOBI News

### Holstein Association of Canada/Association Holstein du Canada (HAC) (1884)
**Holstein Canada**

171 Colborne St., PO Box 610, Brantford, ON N3T 5R4
519/756-8300, Fax: 519/756-5878, Email: general@holstein.ca, URL: http://www.holstein.ca/
Secretary Manager, Keith Flaman
Publications: Info Holstein; Who's Who; Better Breeding Directory

### Jersey Canada (1901)
#9, 350 Speedvale Ave. West, Guelph, ON N1H 7M7
519/821-1020, Fax: 519/821-2723, Email: info@jerseycanada.com, URL: http://www.jerseycanada.com
Executive Sec.-Treas., Russell G. Gammon
President, J.D. Livock, Bus: 905/257-1945
Publications: Canadian Jersey Breeder
Affiliates: World Jersey Cattle Bureau

### National Chinchilla Breeders of Canada (NCBC) (1946)
RR#10, Brampton, ON L6V 3N2
905/451-8736, Fax: 905/457-5326
Sec.-Treas., Betty Stone
Publications: Canada Chinchilla, The Bulletin
Affiliates: Agriculture Canada

### Nova Scotia Mink Breeders' Association (1938)
RR#2, Weymouth, NS B0W 3T0
902/837-5565
Secretary, Austin Mullen

### The Ontario Farm Animal Council (OFAC) (1988)
7195 Millcreek Dr., Mississauga, ON L5N 4H1
905/821-3880, Fax: 905/858-1589, Email: ofac@milk.org, URL: http://www.milk.org/ofac.htm
Executive Director, Leslie Ballentine
Chairman, Mike Cooper
Publications: FAC's

### Salers Association of Canada
#228, 2116 - 27 Ave. NE, Calgary, AB T2E 7A6
403/291-2620, Fax: 403/291-2176
Publications: Salers Magazine

### Saskatchewan Stock Growers Association (1913)
PO Box 4752, Regina, SK S4P 3Y4
306/757-8523, Fax: 306/569-8799
President, Wilfred Campbell
Manager, Pamela Mitchell
Publications: Saskatchewan Stockgrower
Affiliates: Saskatchewan Angus Association; Saskatchewan Cattle Breeders Association; Saskatchewan Game Farmers Association; Saskatchewan Hereford Association; Saskatchewan Limousin Association; Saskatchewan Maine-Anjou Association; Saskatchewan Shorthorn Association; Saskatchewan Simmental Association; Saskatchewan Swine Breeders Association

### Western Stock Growers' Association (WSGA) (1896)
Stockmen's Centre, #101, 2116 - 27 Ave. NE, Calgary, AB T2E 7A6
403/250-9121, Fax: 403/250-9122
President, Norm Ward
Manager, Pam Miller
Publications: Western Stock Growers Newsletter

### World Jersey Cattle Bureau (Canadian Office)
PO Box 90, Richmond Hill, ON L4C 4X9
905/832-2229, Fax: 905/832-2229
Member, F. Redelmeier
Affiliates: Jersey Cattle Association of Canada

## ANIMALS & ANIMAL SCIENCE

### Animal Alliance of Canada/Alliance Animale du Canada (AAC) (1990)
#101, 221 Broadview Ave., Toronto, ON M4M 2G3
416/462-9541, Fax: 416/462-9647, Email: aac@inforamp.net, URL: http://www.inforamp.net/~aac/
Contact, Jacqui Barnes
Publications: Take Action; Legislative Newsletter; Compassionate Shopping Guide

### Animal Defence League of Canada (ADLC) (1958)
PO Box 3880, Stn C, Ottawa, ON K1Y 4M5
613/233-6117
Office Manager, J. Bélair
Publications: News Bulletin

### ARK II
**Canadian Animal Rights Network**

PO Box 687, Stn Q, Toronto, ON M4T 2N5
416/223-4141, Fax: 416/730-8550, Info Line: 416/730-8552
President, Susan Hargreaves
Executive Consultant, Don Reobuck
Publications: The Ark II Activist

### Canadian Animal Health Institute/Institut canadien de la santé animale (CAHI) (1968)
27 Cork St. West, Guelph, ON N1H 2W9
519/763-7777, Fax: 519/763-7407, Email: jszk@cahi-icsa.ca
President, Jean Szkotnicki
Executive Assistant, Jean Wood
Publications: Inforum; CAHI Directory

### Canadian Association of Animal Health Technologists & Technicians/Association canadienne des techniciens et technologistes en santé animale (CAAHTT) (1989)
PO Box 91, Grandora, SK S0K 1V0
306/329-8660, Fax: 306/329-4700
Office Coordinator, Sandy Hass
Publications: Newsletter

### Canadian Association for Laboratory Animal Science (CALAS)
Biosciences Animal Service, University of Alberta, CW 401, Biological Science Bldg., Edmonton, AB T6G 2E9
403/492-5193, Fax: 403/492-7257
Executive Sec.-Treas., Donald G. McKay
Affiliates: International Council for Laboratory Animal Science

### Canadian Association of Zoological Parks & Aquariums (CAZPA) (1975)
c/o Calgary Zoo, PO Box 3036, Stn B, Calgary, AB T2M 4R8
President, David R. Banks, Bus: 403/232-9300
Publications: CAZPA Newsletter; CAZPA Roster, a.

### Canadian Council on Animal Care/Conseil canadien de protection des animaux (CCAC) (1968)
Constitution Square, Tower II, #315, 350 Albert St., Ottawa, ON K1R 1B1
613/238-4031, Fax: 613/238-2837, Email: lroach@bart.ccac.ca
Executive Director, Donald Boisvert, M.D., Ph.D.
Information Officer, Dr. Gillian Griffin
Publications: Resource/Ressource

### Canadian Federation of Humane Societies/Fédération des sociétés canadiennes d'assistance aux animaux (CFHS) (1957)
#102, 30 Concourse Gate, Nepean, ON K2E 7V7
613/224-8072, Fax: 613/723-0252, Email: cfhs@magi.com
Executive Director, Frances Rodenburg
President, Eleanor Dawson
Publications: Animal Welfare in Focus; Farm Animal Welfare in Focus; Caring for Animals; Whalekind; Humane Education
Affiliates: American Humane Association; World Society for the Protection of Animals; Canadian Nature Federation; Delta Society
Alberta Society for the Prevention of Cruelty to Animals: Executive Director, Neil McDonald; President, Joy Ripley, 10806 - 124 St., Edmonton, AB T5M 0H3, 403/447-3600; Animal Abuse Line: 403/451-2273, Fax: 403/447-4748
Brandon Humane Society: PO Box 922, Brandon, MB R7A 5Z9, 204/728-1333
British Columbia Society for the Prevention of Cruelty to Animals: Stephen Huddart, #322, 470 Granville St., Vancouver, BC V6C 1V5, 604/681-7271, Fax: 604/681-7022, Email: bches@mindlink.bc.ca
Calgary Humane Society: President, Greg Kelly, 1323 - 36 Ave. NE, Calgary, AB T2E 6T6, 403/250-7722, Fax: 403/291-9818
Carleton County Animal Shelter Inc.: Dan Dobbelsteyn, RR#5, Debec, NB E0J 1J0, 506/277-1104
Fort McMurray Society for the Prevention of Cruelty to Animals: President, Brenda Tolen, PO Box 5604, Fort McMurray, AB T9H 3G5, 403/743-8997
Gloucester County Society for the Prevention of Cruelty to Animals: RR#1, Site 37, PO Box 4, Bathurst, NB E2A 3Y5, 506/548-8537
Humane Society Yukon: President, Andrea Lemphers; Secretary, Sandra Richardson, PO Box 5564, Whitehorse, YT Y1A 4Z2, 867/633-4337
London Humane Society: 624 Clarke Rd., London, ON N5V 3K5, 519/451-0630
Montréal SPCA: Executive Director, Tom Knott, 5215, rue Jean Talon ouest, Montréal, QC H4P 1X4, 514/735-2711, Fax: 514/735-7448
New Brunswick Society for the Prevention of Cruelty to Animals: Executive Director, Raymond Ward; President, Ken Machin, PO Box 23100, Moncton, NB E1A 6S8, 506/857-8698, Fax: 506/383-8000
Newfoundland Society for the Prevention of Cruelty to Animals: President, David G.L. Buffett, LL.B.; Honorary Secretary, Hilda Smith, PO Box 1533, St. John's, NF A1C 5N8, 709/726-0301, Fax: 709/576-7333
Northwest Territories Society for the Prevention of Cruelty to Animals: Treasurer, Sabrina A. Port; President, Colin E.H. Port, PO Box 2278, Yellowknife, NT X1A 2P7, 867/920-4255, Fax: 867/920-4258
Nova Scotia Society for the Prevention of Cruelty: President, William Caudle, #422, 1600 Bedford Hwy., Bedford, NS B4A 1E8, 902/835-4798, Fax: 902/835-7885
Ontario Society for the Prevention of Cruelty to Animals: CEO, Victoria E.R. Earle; Chairman, Donald Cobb, 16640 Yonge St., Newmarket, ON L3Y 4V8, 905/898-7122, Fax: 905/853-8643
Parkland Society for the Prevention of Cruelty to Animals: President, Charlene Waines, PO Box 931, Red Deer, AB T4N 5H3, 403/342-7722, Fax: 403/341-3147
Prince Edward Island Humane Society: President, James Schurman, PO Box 20022, Sherwood, PE C1A 9E3, 902/892-1190, Fax: 902/892-1190, Toll Free: 1-800-892-1191
Regina Humane Society Inc.: President, Joan Ennis; General Manager, Cathy Lauritsen, PO Box 3143, Regina, SK S4P 3G7, 306/543-6363, Fax: 306/545-7661, Email: humane@max.infosys.com, URL: http://www.maxinfosys.com/~humane
Saskatchewan Society for the Prevention of Cruelty to Animals: President, Dr. Ernest Olfert; Secretary,

Arlene Eberhardt, PO Box 37, Saskatoon, SK S4P 3G7, 306/382-7722
Société protectrice des animaux de Québec: Présidente, Ginette Garon; Secrétaire, M. George Thompson, 1130, de Galilée, Québec, QC G1P 4B7, 418/527-9104, Téléc: 418/527-6685
Société québécoise pour la défense des animaux: Directeur général, Hélène Laferrière; Présidente, Johanne Fortin, #401, 1645, boul de Maisonneuve ouest, Montréal, QC H3H 2N3, 514/932-4260, Téléc: 514/939-0919
Toronto Humane Society: COO, Kathleen Hunter, 11 River St., Toronto, ON M5A 4C2, 416/392-2273, Fax: 416/392-9978

### Canadian Kennel Club/Club Canin Canadien (CKC) (1888)
#100, 89 Skyway Ave., Etobicoke, ON M9W 6R4
416/675-5511, Fax: 416/675-6506, URL: http://www.ncf.carleton.ca/freeport/community.associations/kennel-club/menu
CEO, Bryan Hocking
Publications: Dogs in Canada

### Canadian Police Canine Association/Association canadienne de chiens policiers
8004 - 4A St. NE, Calgary, AB T2K 5W8
403/274-7401
President, A.B. Amm

### Canadian Shire Horse Society
#1882, Concession 10, RR#2, Blackstock, ON L0B 1B0
905/263-8629
Secretary, Peggy Chapman

### Canadian Society of Animal Science/Société canadienne de zootechnie (CSAS) (1951)
#1112, 141 Laurier Ave. West, Ottawa, ON K1P 5J3
613/232-9459, Fax: 613/594-5190, URL: http://tdg.res.uoguelph.ca/~aic/csas.html
President, Valerie Stevens, Ph.D., P.Ag., Email: stevensv@em.agr.ca
Sec.-Treas., Dr. Roland Rotter
Publications: Canadian Journal of Animal Science; CSAS Newsletter, q.
Affiliates: World Association for Animal Production

### Canadian Society of Zoologists/Société canadienne de zoologie (CSZ) (1961)
Université du Québec à Rimouski, Dép. d'Océanographie, 300, allée des Ursulines, Québec, QC G5L 3A1
418/723-1986, ext.1704, Email: jocelyne_pellerin@uqar.uquebec.ca
Président, Dr. John Webster
President Elect, William Marshall
Secrétaire, Dr. Jocelyne Pellerin-Massicotte
Publications: Bulletin
Affiliates: Canadian Council on Animal Care

### Canadian Vegans for Animal Rights (C-VAR) (1986)
Hudson Bay Centre, 20 Bloor St. East, PO Box 75054, Toronto, ON M4W 3T3
416/924-1377
Director, Michael Schwab

### Canadian Veterinary Medical Association/Association canadienne des médecins vétérinaires (CVMA) (1948)
339 Booth St., Ottawa, ON K1R 7K1
613/236-1162, Fax: 613/236-9681, URL: http://www.upei.ca/~cvma/
Executive Director, Claude Paul Boivin
Publications: Canadian Veterinary Journal; Canadian Journal of Veterinary Research, q.

#### ALBERTA VETERINARY MEDICAL ASSOCIATION (AVMA) (1905)
#100, 8615 - 149 St., Edmonton, AB T5R 1B3
403/489-5007, Fax: 403/484-8311
President, Dr. Les Byers
Registrar, Dr. Malcolm Gray
Publications: AVMA Newsletter

#### BRITISH COLUMBIA VETERINARY MEDICAL ASSOCIATION (BCVMA) (1907)
#155, 1200 West 73 St., Vancouver, BC V6P 6G5
604/266-3441, Fax: 604/266-8447
Registrar, Dominic Leung
Director of Member Services, Ilona Rule
President, Dr. Ann Lawson
Publications: The Bulletin

#### MANITOBA VETERINARY MEDICINE ASSOCIATION
#203, 2989 Pembina Hwy., Winnipeg, MB R3T 2H5
204/269-0625, Fax: 204/269-1129
President, Dr. Ron Mentz
Registrar, Sandra McKinnon

#### NEW BRUNSWICK VETERINARY MEDICAL ASSOCIATION (1919)
PO Box 1065, Moncton, NB E1C 8P2
506/851-7654, Fax: 506/851-2524
President, Dr. Emery Leger
Executive Director, Dr. R. Pattie
Publications: NBVMA Newsletter

#### NEWFOUNDLAND & LABRADOR VETERINARY MEDICAL ASSOCIATION (NLVMA)
PO Box 818, Mount Pearl, NF A1N 3C8
709/576-2131, Fax: 709/576-6046
President, Beverly Dawe
Sec.-Treas., Alan Pater
Publications: NALVMA Newsletter

#### NOVA SCOTIA VETERINARY MEDICAL ASSOCIATION
15 Cobequid Rd., Lower Sackville, NS B4C 2M9
902/865-1876, Fax: 902/865-3759
President, Dr. Tom Hutchison
Secretary Registrar, Dr. Frank Richardson
Publications: NSVMA Newsletter

#### ONTARIO VETERINARY MEDICAL ASSOCIATION
245 Commercial St., Milton, ON L9T 2J3
905/875-0756, Fax: 905/875-0958
Executive Director, M.M. (Marty) Smart-Wilder, CAE

#### PRINCE EDWARD ISLAND VETERINARY MEDICAL ASSOCIATION (1920)
PO Box 100, Montague, PE C0A 1R0
902/838-2281, Fax: 902/838-5077
Sec.-Treas., Dr. David Lister

#### SASKATCHEWAN VETERINARY MEDICAL ASSOCIATION
#104, 112 Research Dr., Saskatoon, SK S7N 3R3
306/955-7862
President, Dr. Don Wilson
Registrar, K. Ron Presnell
Publications: SVMA Directory

### Canadians for Ethical Treatment of Food Animals (CETFA)
2225 West 41st Ave., PO Box 18024, Vancouver, BC V6M 4L3
604/261-3801, Fax: 604/261-3801
National Coordinator, Tina Harrison

### College of Veterinarians of Ontario (CVO) (1872)
2106 Gordon St., Guelph, ON N1L 1G6
519/824-5600, Fax: 519/824-6497
Registrar, Dr. John L. Henry
Publications: Update
Affiliates: American Veterinary Medical Association; American Animal Hospital Association

### Horse Council of BC (HCBC) (1980)
5746B - 176A St., Cloverdale, BC V3S 4C7
604/576-2722, Fax: 604/576-0401, Toll Free: 1-800-345-8055, Email: hcbc@uniserve.com
Executive Director, Laurel Wood
Publications: Horse Industry Directory

### Jardin zoologique du Québec (JZQ) (1931)
9141, av du Zoo, Charlesbourg, QC G1G 4G4
418/622-0313, Téléc: 418/644-9004
Directeur, Jean-Paul Bédard

### National Retriever Club of Canada
RR#2, 1348 Mills Rd., Sidney, BC V8L 3S1
250/656-5987
Sec.-Treas., Jane Schmidt

### Ordre des médecins vétérinaires du Québec (OMVQ) (1902)
#200, 795, av du Palais, Saint-Hyacinthe, QC J2S 5C6
514/774-1427, Téléc: 514/774-7635, Ligne sans frais: 1-800-267-1427
Directeur général/Secrétaire, Dr. Marcel Bouvier
Présidente, Dr. Christiane Gagnon
Publications: Vétérinarius; Le Médecine vétérinaire du Québec, trimestriel

### PIJAC Canada
**Pet Industry Joint Advisory Council of Canada**
#308, 189, boul Hymus, Pointe-Claire, QC H9R 1E9
514/630-7878, Fax: 514/630-7444, Toll Free: 1-800-667-7452, Email: pijac@odyssee.net, URL: http://www.pijaccanada.com
Executive Director, Louis McCann

### Société des parcs de sciences naturelles du Québec
8173, av du Zoo, Charlesbourg, QC G1G 4G4
418/622-0313, Téléc: 418/646-9239
Directeur, Jardin zoologique, Jean-Paul Bédard

### Western Federation of Individuals & Dog Organizations (1973)
**FIDO**
8160 Railway Ave., Richmond, BC V7C 3K2
604/681-1929, Fax: 604/277-4285
President, Frances Clark

### World Society for the Protection of Animals/Société mondiale pour la protection des animaux (WSPA) (1953)
#1310, 44 Victoria St., Toronto, ON M5C 1Y2
416/369-0044, Fax: 416/369-0147, Toll Free: 1-800-363-9772, Email: wspacanada@compuserve.com, URL: http://www.way.net/wspa/
Director, Canadian Operations, Silia Coiro-Smith
Publications: WSPA News

### ZOOCHECK Canada Inc.
#1729, 3266 Yonge St., Toronto, ON M4N 3P6
416/696-0241, Fax: 416/696-0370, Email: zoocheck@idirect.com
Rob Laidlaw
Holly Penfound
Barry MacKay
Julie Woodyer
Lesli Bisgould
Andrea Villiers
Publications: Newsletter
Affiliates: American Association of Zookeepers; Canadian Association of Zoological Parks & Aquariums; Canadian Federation of Humane Societies

### Zoological Society of Metropolitan Toronto (1969)
PO Box 370, Scarborough, ON M1E 4Y9
416/392-9114, Fax: 416/392-9115
President, Calvin White
Chair, Peter Evans

Publications: News Prints; Collections
Affiliates: Canadian Association of Zoos, Parks & Aquariums; American Association of Zoos, Parks & Aquariums; Canadian Centre for Philanthropy

**Zoological Society of Montréal/Société zoologique de Montréal (1964)**
2055 Peel, Montréal, QC H3A 1V4
514/845-8317
Contact, Marlene Harris
Contact, George E. Midgley
Publications: The Zoological Society Newsletter

## ANTIQUES

**Antiquarian Booksellers' Association of Canada/Association de la librairie ancienne du Canada (ABAC) (1966)**
145 Main St. West, Port Colborne, ON L3K 3V3
905/834-5323, Fax: 905/834-5323, Email: alphabet@iaw.com, URL: http://206.217.21.64/ca/index.html
President, Richard Shuh, Bus: 905/834-5323
Secretary, Cameron Treleaven, Bus: 403/282-5832
Publications: ABAC/ALAC National Newsletter

**Antique Automobile Club of America**
501 West Governor Rd., Hershey, PA 17033 USA
717/534-1910
Executive Director, William H. Smith
Publications: Antique Automobile
Lord Selkirk Region: Contact, S. Jerry McCreery, #709, 595 River Ave., Winnipeg, MB R3L 0E6
Maple Leaf Region: Contact, David J. Gurney, PO Box 809, Richmond Hill, ON K0A 2Z0
Ontario Region: Contact, Bob Kelly, RR#2, Peterborough, ON K9J 6X3
St. Lawrence Valley Region: Contact, Steven J. Latimer, RR#4, Brockville, ON K6V 5T4

**Antique & Classic Boat Society Inc. (Toronto) (1980)**
PO Box 305, Islington, ON M9A 4X3
416/299-3311
President, Andrew Dyment
Publications: Classic Boat

**Antique & Classic Car Club of Canada**
41 Summer Dr., Scarborough, ON M1K 3E4
416/261-5571
Contact, Bud Murray
Publications: The Reflector

**Canadian Antique Dealers Association (CADA)**
250 Eglinton Ave. East, PO Box 89544, Toronto, ON M4P 3E1
416/961-6211
President, Robert Dirstein

**Historic Vehicle Society of Ontario (HVSO) (1959)**
PO Box 221, Harrow, ON N0R 1G0
519/776-6909, Fax: 519/776-8321
Administrator, Georgia Klym Skeates
Publications: HVSO Newsletter

**Manitoba Antique Association (1967)**
PO Box 2881, Winnipeg, MB R3C 4B4
Secretary, Gathorne Burns, Bus: 204/885-2781
Publications: Newsletter

**Vintage Automobile Racing Association of Canada**
2467 Yonge St., Toronto, ON M4P 2H6
416/487-8166, 416/482-4017, Fax: 416/488-9013
President, Mike Rosen

**Vintage Locomotive Society Inc. (1968)**
PO Box 33021, RPO Polo Park, Winnipeg, MB R3G 3N4
204/832-5259
Sec.-Treas., K. Gordon Younger
Publications: The Journal Box

**ARBITRATION *see* LABOUR RELATIONS**

## ARCHAEOLOGY

**Archaeological Society of British Columbia (ASBC) (1966)**
PO Box 520, Stn A, Vancouver, BC V6C 2N3
604/822-2567, Fax: 604/822-6161
President, Joyce Johnson
Publications: The Midden
Affiliates: Society of American Archaeology

**Canadian Archaeological Association/Association d'archéologie canadienne (1968)**
Space 162 - Box 127, 3170 Tillicum Rd., Victoria, BC V9A 7H7
250/478-1147, Fax: 250/388-7373
Executive Secretary, Bjorn O. Simonsen
Publications: Canadian Journal of Archaeology/Journal canadien d'archéologie; Canadian Archaeological Association Newsletter, s-a.
Affiliates: Society of American Archaeology

**ARCHAEOLOGICAL SOCIETY OF ALBERTA (ASA) (1975)**
1202 Lansdowne Ave. SW, Calgary, AB T2S 1A6
403/243-4340
Executive Sec.-Treas., Jeanne Cody
Publications: Alberta Archaeological Review

**ASSOCIATION DES ARCHÉOLOGUES DU QUÉBEC (AAQ) (1979)**
CP 322, Succ Haute-Ville, Québec, QC G1R 4P8
514/523-1960, Téléc: 514/776-8300
Courrier électronique: jean-pierre.chrestien@civilisations.ca
Président, Christian Bélanger

**NOVA SCOTIA ARCHAEOLOGY SOCIETY**
PO Box 36090, Halifax, NS B3J 3S9
902/823-1879
President, Dr. David Keenleyside
Treasurer, Lynne Schwarz

**SASKATCHEWAN ARCHAEOLOGICAL SOCIETY (SAS) (1963)**
#5, 816 - 1 Ave. North, Saskatoon, SK S7K 1Y3
306/664-4124, Fax: 306/665-1928
Email: ad583@sfn.saskatoon.sk.ca
Executive Director, Tim Jones
Business Administrator, Linda Drever
Publications: Saskatchewan Archaeological Society Newsletter; Saskatchewan Archaeology, a.

**Manitoba Archaeological Society Inc. (MAS) (1961)**
PO Box 1171, Winnipeg, MB R3C 2Y4
204/942-7243, Fax: 204/942-3749
President, Leslie Burns
First Vice-President, Kevin Brownlee
Publications: Manitoba Archaeological Journal

**Newfoundland & Labrador Association of Amateur Archaeologists**
108 New Cove Rd., St. John's, NF A1A 2C2
709/753-0665
President, Bruce Ryan

**The Ontario Archaeological Society Inc. (1950)**
126 Willowdale Ave., North York, ON M2N 4Y2
416/730-0797, Fax: 416/730-0797, Email: oas@io.org
Executive Director, Ellen Blaubergs
President, Henry van Lieshout
Publications: Arch Notes; Ontario Archaeology, a.

**Ontario Society of Industrial Archaeology (OSIA) (1982)**
88 Upper Canada Dr., North York, ON M2P 1S4
416/207-5872, Fax: 416/207-5911
President, Ian Livsey
Publications: OSIA Bulletin
Affiliates: The International Committee for the Conservation of the Industrial Heritage

**Save Ontario Shipwrecks (SOS) (1981)**
#310, 2175 Sheppard Ave. East, North York, ON M2J 1W8
416/491-2373, Fax: 416/491-1670, URL: http://yoda.sscl.uwo.ca/assoc/sos/
President, Barry Lyons
Publications: S.O.S. News
Affiliates: Underwater Council

**Underwater Archaeological Society of British Columbia (1975)**
c/o Vancouver Maritime Museum, 1905 Ogden Ave., Vancouver, BC V6J 1A3
604/980-0354, Fax: 604/980-0358
Executive Director, David Stone
President, Robyn Woodward
Publications: The FogHorn

## ARCHITECTURE

**Alberta Association of Architects (AAA) (1906)**
Duggan House, 10515 Saskatchewan Dr., Edmonton, AB T6E 4S1
403/432-0224, Fax: 403/439-1431, Email: info@aaa.ab.ca, URL: http://www.aaa.ab.ca
Executive Director, Penny A. Cairns
President, Richard Lindseth, MRAIC
Publications: Columns: the Newsletter of the Alberta, Saskatchewan & Manitoba Associations of Architects

**Architects Association of New Brunswick/Association des architectes du Nouveau-Brunswick (AANB) (1933)**
73 Duke St., Saint John, NB E2L 1N4
506/658-6116
Executive Director, N. Lynn Cornfield
Publications: Searching for Context

**Architects Association of Prince Edward Island (AAPEI)**
PO Box 1766, Charlottetown, PE C1A 7N4
902/892-8908, Fax: 902/368-7403
President, Larry Jones

**The Architectural Conservancy of Ontario (ACO) (1933)**
#204, 10 Adelaide St. East, Toronto, ON M5C 1J3
416/367-8075, Fax: 416/367-8630
President, Alice King Sculthorpe
Consulting Heritage Manager, Paul Dilse
Publications: Acorn
Affiliates: Ontario Heritage Alliance

**Architectural Institute of British Columbia (AIBC) (1914)**
#103, 131 Water St., Vancouver, BC V6B 4M3
604/683-8588, Fax: 604/683-8568, Toll Free: 1-800-667-0753, Email: aibc@aibc.bc.ca, URL: http://www.aibc.bc.ca
Executive Director, Cheryl Williams
President, Bryce Rositch
Publications: AIBC Newsletter

**Association of Architectural Technologists of Ontario (AATO) (1969)**
#407, 150 Consumers Rd., North York, ON M2J 1P9
416/493-6758, Fax: 416/493-9245 (voice req.), Toll Free: 1-800-563-2286, URL: http://www.aato.on.ca
Administrative Secretary, Rita Staniforth
Publications: AATO News Reports

**Design Exchange (DX) (1987)**
**The Group for the Creation of a Design Centre in Toronto**
Toronto Dominion Centre, 234 Bay St., PO Box 18, Toronto, ON M5K 1B2
416/363-6121, Fax: 416/368-0684, URL: http://www.hyperm.com/dxsite
President, Howard Cohen

**Manitoba Association of Architects (MAA)**
137 Bannatyne Ave., 2nd Fl., Winnipeg, MB R3B 0R3
204/925-4620, Fax: 204/925-4624, URL: http://cad9.cadlab.umanitoba.ca/MAA.html
Executive Director, Judy Pestrak
Publications: Columns: the Newsletter of the Alberta, Saskatchewan & Manitoba Associations of Architects

**Newfoundland Association of Architects**
PO Box 5204, St. John's, NF A1C 5V5
709/726-8550, Fax: 709/726-1549
President, Paul Blackwood
Administrative Assistant, Lynda Hayward

**Northwest Territories Architectural Society**
PO Box 1394, Yellowknife, NT X1A 2P1
867/920-2609, Fax: 867/920-4261
Contact, Darrell Vikse

**Nova Scotia Association of Architects (NSAA) (1932)**
1361 Barrington St., Halifax, NS B3J 1Y9
902/423-7607, Fax: 902/425-7024
Executive Director, Diane Scott-Stewart
President, Tom Connell, MRAIC

**Ontario Association of Architects (OAA) (1889)**
111 Moatfield Dr., North York, ON M3B 3L6
416/449-6898, Fax: 416/449-5756, Toll Free: 1-800-565-2724, Email: oaamail@orgx.com, URL: http://www.oaa.on.ca
Executive Director, Brian Watkinson
President, James J. Nowski
Director of Communications, Phyllis Clasby
Publications: Directory of Architects; Perspectives

**Ordre des architectes du Québec (OAQ) (1890)**
1825, boul René-Lévesque ouest, Montréal, QC H3H 1R4
514/937-6168, Téléc: 514/933-0242, Ligne sans frais: 1-800-599-6168, Courrier électronique: oaq@videotron.ca, URL: http://www.oaq.com
Directrice générale, Claude LeTarte
Publications: Esquisses

**Royal Architectural Institute of Canada/Institut royal d'architecture du Canada (RAIC) (1907)**
#330, 55 Murray St., Ottawa, ON K1N 5M3
613/241-3600, Fax: 613/241-5750, Email: info@raic.org, URL: http://www.aecinfo.com/raic/index.html
Executive Director, Timothy Kehoe
President, Barry J. Hobin
Director of Services, Alexandra Fitzgerald
Publications: RAIC Update; En Bref; Canadian Architectural Directory; RAIC Directory of Scholarships & Awards for Architecture; Advanced Buildings, bi-m.

**Saskatchewan Association of Architects (SAA) (1911)**
#200, 642 Broadway Ave., Saskatoon, SK S7N 1A9
306/242-0733, Fax: 306/664-2598, URL: http://cad9.cadlab.umanitoba.ca/SAA.html
Executive Director, Margaret Topping
Publications: Columns: the Newsletter of the Alberta, Saskatchewan & Manitoba Associations of Architects

**Society for the Study of Architecture in Canada/ Société pour l'étude de l'architecture au Canada (SSAC) (1974)**
PO Box 2302, Stn D, Ottawa, ON K1P 5W5
President, Dorothy Field
Vice-President, Rhodri Windsor-Liscombe
Publications: Society for the Study of Architecture in Canada Bulletin/Bulletin de la Société pour l'étude de l'architecture au Canada
Affiliates: Society of Architectural Historians

**ARCHIVES *see* LIBRARIES & ARCHIVES**

**ARMED FORCES *see* MILITARY & VETERANS**

**ARMS CONTROL *see* INTERNATIONAL COOPERATION/INTERNATIONAL RELATIONS**

**ART FESTIVALS *see* EVENTS**

## ARTS

***see also* Visual Art, Crafts, Folk Arts**

**Alberta Foundation for the Arts (1991)**
Standard Life Centre, 10405 Jasper Ave., Edmonton, AB T5E 2R7
403/427-9968, Fax: 403/422-1162, Email: cpadfield@mcd.gov.ab.ca
Executive Director, Clive Padfield
Publications: Bulletin

**Arts Foundation of Greater Toronto (1986)**
#365 Richmond St. West, PO Box 124, Toronto, ON M5V 3A8
416/597-8223, Fax: 416/597-6956, Email: jhowell@interlog.com
Executive Director, Julia Howell
President, Richard Ouzounian

**Assembly of BC Arts Councils**
#201, 3737 Oak St., Vancouver, BC V6H 2M4
604/738-0749, Fax: 604/738-5161
Executive Director, Deborah Meyers

**Association of National Non-Profit Artists' Centres/Regroupement des artistes des centres alternatifs (ANNPAC) (1976)**
183 Bathurst St., Main Fl., Toronto, ON M5T 2R7
416/869-1275, 3854, Fax: 416/360-0781
President, Roger Lee
Publications: Parallélogramme
Affiliates: National Association of Artists' Organizations; Canadian Artists Representation; Canadian Conference of the Arts

**Canadian Artists' Representation/Le Front des artistes canadiens (CARFAC) (1968)**
21, rue Forest, Aylmer, QC J9H 4E3
819/682-4183
National Director, Greg Graham
National Representative, Glen MacKinnon
Communications Officer, Flora Kallies
Publications: CARNET
Affiliates: International Association of Art; Canadian Conference of the Arts

**Canadian Arts Presenting Association/ l'Association canadienne des organismes artistiques (CAPACOA) (1985)**
#200, 17 York St., Ottawa, ON K1N 9J6
613/562-3515, Fax: 613/562-4005, Email: capacoa@magi.com, URL: http://www.culturenet.ca/capacoa/
Executive Director, Peter Feldman
Publications: CAPACOA Newsletter; CAPACOA Presenting Profile, biennial

**Canadian Association of Artists Managers/ Association canadienne de direction d'artistes (CAAM)**
c/o Renée Simmons Artists Management, 117 Ava Rd., Toronto, ON M6C 1W2
416/782-7712, Fax: 416/256-7657

**Canadian Celtic Arts Association**
University of Toronto, St. Michael's College, 81 St. Mary St., Toronto, ON M5S 1J4
416/926-7145, Fax: 416/926-7276
Membership Secretary, Jean Talman
Publications: CCAA Newsletter; Garm Lu, s-a.

**Canadian Conference of the Arts/Conférence canadienne des arts (CCA) (1945)**
189 Laurier Ave. East, Ottawa, ON K1N 6P1
613/238-3561, Fax: 613/238-4849, Toll Free: 1-800-463-3561, Email: cca@mail.culturenet.ca, URL: http://www.culturenet.ca
National Director, Keith Kelly
President, Mireille Gagné
Publications: Directory of the Arts/l'Annuaire des arts; Blizzart, q.

**Canadian Institute of the Arts for Young Audiences/Institut canadien des arts pour jeunes publics**
#302, 601 Cambie St., Vancouver, BC V6B 2P1
604/687-7697, Fax: 604/669-3613, Email: kidsfest@youngarts.ca, URL: http://www.wimsey.com/Youngarts/
Executive Director, Marjorie MacLean

**Conseil des arts et des lettres du Québec**
#1500, 500, Place d'Armes, Montréal, QC H2Y 2W2
514/864-3350, Téléc: 514/864-4160, Ligne sans frais: 1-800-608-3350

**Council for Business & the Arts in Canada/ Conseil pour le monde des affaires et des arts du Canada (CBAC) (1974)**
#705, 165 University Ave., Toronto, ON M5H 3B8
416/869-3016, Fax: 416/869-0435
President & CEO, Sarah Iley
Publications: CBAC News; CBAC Survey of Performing Arts Organizations, a.; CBAC Survey of Public Museums & Arts Galleries; CBAC Survey of Corporate Donations

**Federation of Canadian Artists (FCA) (1989)**
1241 Cartwright St., Vancouver, BC V6H 4B7
604/681-8534, Fax: 604/681-2740
President, Joyce Kamikura
Gallery Manager, Katie Reid
Publications: FCA News

**Governor General's Performing Arts Foundation (1992)**
PO Box 1534, Stn B, Ottawa, ON K1P 5W1
613/996-5051, Fax: 613/996-2828
Co-Chair, Peter Herrndorf
Co-Chair, Monique Mercure

**Manitoba Arts Council/Conseil des Arts du Manitoba (MAC) (1969)**
#525, 93 Lombard Ave., Winnipeg, MB R3B 3B1

204/945-2237, Fax: 204/945-5925, Email: manart1@mts.net, URL: http://www.infobahn.mb.ca/mac
Executive Director, Victor Jerrett Enns
Publications: ArtVentures Newsletter

### New Brunswick Arts Council Inc. (NBAC) (1979)
Brunswick Sq., 3rd Level, 39 King St., Saint John, NB E2L 4W3
506/635-8019, Fax: 506/635-8603
Coordinator, Sandra Donnelly
President, Jill Smith
Publications: Newsletter

### Newfoundland & Labrador Arts Council (NLAC) (1980)
PO Box 98, Stn C, St. John's, NF A1C 5H5
709/726-2212, Fax: 709/726-0619, Email: rfollett@nfld.com
Chairman, Arthur Griffin

### Northwest Territories Arts Council (1985)
c/o NWT Education, Culture & Employment, PO Box 1320, Stn Main, Yellowknife, NT X1A 2L9
867/920-3103, Fax: 867/873-0205
Arts & Culture Officer, Evelyn Dhont

### Ontario Arts Council/Conseil des arts de l'Ontario (OAC)
#600, 151 Bloor St. West, Toronto, ON M5S 1T6
416/961-1660, Fax: 416/961-7796, Toll Free: 1-800-387-0058, Email: oac@gov.on.ca
Executive Director, Gwenlyn Setterfield

### Organization of Saskatchewan Arts Councils (OSAC) (1968)
1102 - 8 Ave., Regina, SK S4R 1C9
306/586-1250, Fax: 306/586-1550
Executive Director, Dennis Garreck
Communications Coordinator, Michelle Lavallee
Publications: OSAC News

### PAPA: The Association for Communication Specialists in Arts & Entertainment (PAPA) (1976)
c/o Ontario Arts Council, #600, 151 Bloor St. West, Toronto, ON M5S 1T6
416/698-0607, Fax: 416/698-0607, Email: papa@sympatico.ca
Chairman, Teri MacFarlane
Publications: PAPA Press

### PEI Council of the Arts (1974)
115 Richmond St., Charlottetown, PE C1A 1H7
902/368-4410, Fax: 902/368-4418
Executive Director, Judy MacDonald
Publications: PEI Council of Arts
Affiliates: West Prince Arts Council; East Kings Arts Council; Conseil des arts evangeline; Southern Kings Arts Council; South Shore Arts Council; Malpak Arts Council

### Saskatchewan Arts Alliance Corp. (SAA) (1984)
PO Box 3765, Regina, SK S4P 3N8
306/652-6122, Fax: 306/652-6628
President, Terry Schwalm
Treasurer, Karen Haggman
Administrator, Mark Rudoff

### Vancouver Cultural Alliance (VCA) (1986)
#100, 938 Howe St., Vancouver, BC V6Z 1N9
604/681-3535, Fax: 604/681-7848, Email: arts_yvr@cyberstore.net, URL: http://www.culturenet.ca/vca
Executive Director, Lori Baxter
Communications Manager, Manuela Bizzotto
Publications: VCA News

### Yukon Arts Council (YAC) (1971)
PO Box 5120, Whitehorse, YT Y1A 4S3
867/668-6284, Info Line: 403/667-2787
Resource Administrator, Lilyan Grubach
Publications: Yukon Arts Council Newsletter

**AUDITING *see* ACCOUNTING**

## AUTOMOTIVE
*see also* **Transportation & Shipping**

### Association des propriétaires d'autobus du Québec/Québec Bus Owners Association (APAQ) (1927)
#107, 225, boul Charest est, Québec, QC G1K 3G9
418/522-7131, Téléc: 418/522-6455, Courrier électronique: apaq@apaq.qc.ca, URL: http://www.apaq.qc.ca
Vice-président exécutif/Directeur général, Jacques Guay
Publications: Le Billet du bus; La Revue du bus, 10 fois par an

### Automobile Dealers Association of Newfoundland
81 Smallwood Dr., Mount Pearl, NF A1N 1B2
709/364-9474, Fax: 709/364-9474
Business Manager, Fred J. Marshall

### Automobile Journalists Association of Canada/Association des journalistes automobile du Canada (AJAC)
77 Wembley Dr., Toronto, ON M4L 3C9
416/463-2658, Fax: 416/463-0866
Administrator, Bert Coates
President, Alex Law
Publications: Express; Directory, s-a.

### Automobile Protection Association/Association pour la protection automobile (APA)
292, boul St. Joseph ouest, Montréal, QC H2V 2N7
514/272-5555, Fax: 514/273-0797
Président - directeur général, George Iny
Coordinateur administrative, Dany Duchemin
Publications: Roulez sans vous faire rouler Lemon Aid

### Automotive Industries Association of Canada/Association des industries de l'automobile (AIA Canada) (1964)
1272 Wellington St., Ottawa, ON K1Y 3A7
613/728-5821, Fax: 613/728-6021, Email: aia@aiacanada.com, URL: http://www.aftmkt.com
President, Dean Wilson
Vice-President, Yaroslaw Zajac
Vice-President, Administration, Beverlie Cook
Manager, Communications Services, Denise Faguy
Manager, Marketing, Marc Brazeau
Publications: Aftermarket Update; Aftermarket Watch

### Automotive Parts Manufacturers' Association/Association des fabricants de pièces d'automobile (APMA) (1952)
#516, 195 The West Mall, Etobicoke, ON M9C 5K1
416/620-4220, Fax: 416/620-9730, Email: apma@interware.net, URL: http://www.capma.com
President, Gerald B. Fedchun
Director, Environment, Peter Corbyn, P.Eng.
Publications: Industry Outlook; APMA News

### Automotive Retailers Association of British Columbia (1951)
#1, 8980 Fraserwood Ct., Burnaby, BC V5J 5H7
604/432-7987, Fax: 604/432-1756
Executive Director, D. Robert Clarke
Publications: Automotive Retailer

### Automotive Trades Association (Manitoba) Inc. (ATA) (1937)
#105, 1200 Pembina Hwy., Winnipeg, MB R3T 2A6
204/475-3235, Fax: 204/453-5743
President, Herb Wittenberg
Business Manager, J. Henry Brodersen
Publications: Newsletter
Affiliates: Society of Collision Repair Specialists

### Canadian All-Terrain Vehicle Distributors Council/Conseil canadien des distributeurs de véhicules tout terrain (CATV) (1984)
#235, 7181 Woodbine Ave., Markham, ON L3R 1A3
905/470-9406, Fax: 905/470-9407
Executive Director, Robert Ramsay

### Canadian Association of Japanese Automobile Dealers (CAJAD) (1982)
#101, One Eva Rd., Etobicoke, ON M9C 4Z5
416/620-9717, Fax: 416/620-0392, Toll Free: 1-800-263-4340
Executive Director, Brian B. Caldwell
Director, Public Affairs, Michael Edmonds
Publications: Connections/Connexions

### Canadian Automobile Association/Association canadienne des automobilistes (CAA) (1913)
#200, 1145 Hunt Club Rd., Ottawa, ON K1V 0Y3
613/247-0117, Fax: 613/247-0118, URL: http://www.caa.ca
President & CEO, Brian A. Hunt
Chairman, Raymond A. Cadieux, C.A.
Publications: Autopinion; The Motorist's Advocate
Affiliates: Alliance internationale de tourisme; Fédération internationale de l'automobile; Federacion interamericana de touring y automovil-clubes; Commonwealth Motoring Conference; American Automobile Association

#### ALBERTA MOTOR ASSOCIATION
10310 G.A. MacDonald Ave., Edmonton, AB T6J 6R7
403/430-5555, Fax: 403/430-5676, Toll Free: 1-800-642-3810
Contact, David Barr

#### BRITISH COLUMBIA AUTOMOBILE ASSOCIATION (BCAA) (1906)
4567 Canada Way, Burnaby, BC V5G 4T1
604/268-5000, Fax: 604/268-5560, Toll Free: 1-800-663-1956
URL: http://www.bcaa.bc.ca
President & CEO, William G. Bullis
Director, Public Affairs, Ellen Chesney, Bus: 604/268-5340
Publications: Westworld

#### CAA MANITOBA MOTOR LEAGUE
870 Empress St., Winnipeg, MB R3C 2Z3
204/987-6161, Fax: 204/775-9989
Contact, Donna Wankling

#### CANADIAN AUTOMOBILE ASSOCIATION MARITIMES
**CAA Maritimes**
737 Rothesay Ave., Saint John, NB E2H 2H6
506/634-1400, Fax: 506/653-9500, Toll Free: 1-800-561-8807
President, Steve McCall

#### CANADIAN AUTOMOBILE ASSOCIATION QUÉBEC (1904)
**CAA Québec**
444, rue Bouvier, Québec, QC G2J 1E3
418/624-2424, Téléc: 418/624-3297, Ligne sans frais: 1-800-463-7232
Courrier électronique: info@caa.quebec.qc.ca, URL: http://www.caa-quebec.qc.ca
Président-directeur général, Paul A. Pelletier
Publications: Touring; Accès Québec, trimestriel
Organisation(s) affiliée(s): Alliance internationale du Tourisme; Fédération internationale de l'automobile

**CANADIAN AUTOMOBILE ASSOCIATION SASKATCHEWAN**
**CAA Saskatchewan**
200 Albert St. North, Regina, SK S4R 5E2
306/791-4321, Fax: 306/791-4321
Contact, Gerald Butler

**CANADIAN AUTOMOBILE ASSOCIATION CENTRAL ONTARIO (1903)**
**CAA Central Ontario**
60 Commerce Valley Dr. East, Thornhill, ON L3T 7P9
905/771-3000, Fax: 905/771-3101
President, Stephen A. Wilgar
Publications: LeisureWays

**CANADIAN AUTOMOBILE ASSOCIATION ELGIN NORFOLK**
**CAA Elgin Norfolk**
1091 Talbot St., St Thomas, ON N5P 1G4
519/631-6490, Fax: 519/631-6578, Toll Free: 1-800-265-4343
Contact, Ms. Pat Jackson

**CANADIAN AUTOMOBILE ASSOCIATION MID-WESTERN ONTARIO (1915)**
**CAA Mid-Western Ontario**
PO Box 9030, Stn C, Kitchener, ON N2G 4W8
519/894-2582, Fax: 519/893-5512, Toll Free: 1-800-265-8975
President, Grady Liddle
Publications: Leisure World

**CANADIAN AUTOMOBILE ASSOCIATION NIAGARA**
**CAA Niagara**
3271 Schmon Pkwy., Thorold, ON L2V 4Y6
905/984-8585, Fax: 905/688-0289, Toll Free: 1-800-263-7272
Contact, Robert J. Spence

**CANADIAN AUTOMOBILE ASSOCIATION NORTHEASTERN ONTARIO (1964)**
**CAA Northeastern Ontario**
The Oaks Mall, 2140 Regent St., Sudbury, ON P3E 5S8
705/522-0000, Fax: 705/522-5202, Toll Free: 1-800-461-7111
President & CEO, R.J. Smith

**CANADIAN AUTOMOBILE ASSOCIATION OTTAWA**
**CAA Ottawa**
2525 Carling Ave., Ottawa, ON K2B 7Z2
613/820-1890, Fax: 613/820-4646
President, Brian A. Hunt

**CANADIAN AUTOMOBILE ASSOCIATION PETERBOROUGH**
**CAA Peterborough**
680 The Queensway, PO Box 1957, Peterborough, ON K9J 7X7
705/743-4343, Fax: 705/743-9740

**CANADIAN AUTOMOBILE ASSOCIATION THUNDER BAY**
**CAA Thunder Bay**
585 Memorial Ave., Thunder Bay, ON P7B 3Z1
807/345-1261, Fax: 807/345-8944
Contact, Greg Fayrik

**CANADIAN AUTOMOBILE ASSOCIATION WINDSOR**
**CAA Windsor**
1215 Ouellette Ave., Windsor, ON N8X 1J3
519/255-1212, Fax: 519/255-7379, Toll Free: 1-800-265-5681
Contact, Keith Robinson

### Canadian Automobile Dealers Association (CADA) (1941)
85 Renfrew Dr., Markham, ON L3R 0N9
905/940-4959, Fax: 905/940-6870, Toll Free: 1-800-463-5289
President, Richard C. Gauthier
Chairman, E.A. Knight
Publications: Newsline

### Canadian Automobile Sport Clubs - Ontario Region Inc. (CASC-OR) (1964)
703 Petrolia Rd., North York, ON M3J 2N6
416/667-9500, Fax: 416/667-9555, Email: casc.or@sympatico.ca, URL: http://www3.sympatico.ca/casc.or/
Business Manager, R.M. Varey
President, Peter Jackson
Publications: Region News

### Canadian Automotive Repair & Service Council (1991)
**CARS Council**
#230, 440 Laurier Ave. West, Ottawa, ON K1R 7X6
613/782-2402, Fax: 613/782-2362
President, Daniel Bell
Chairman, Norman Clark
Secretary, Kenneth R. Graydon
Treasurer, William Burkimsher
Publications: CARS Insider; L'Autoscope CARS, trimestriel
Affiliates: CARS Institute

### Canadian Automotive Repair & Service Institute/Institut du service d'entretien et de reparation automobiles du Canada (1991)
**CARS Institute**
#230, 440 Laurier Ave. West, Ottawa, ON K1R 7X6
613/782-2402, Fax: 613/782-2362, Toll Free: 1-800-661-2277
Executive Director, Keith Lancastle
Affiliates: CARS Council

### Canadian Tire Dealers Association
#1707, 2200 Yonge St., Toronto, ON M4S 2C6
416/486-8032, Fax: 416/484-6902
Executive Director, Terry Connoy

### Canadian Towing Society/Société canadienne de remorquage (1985)
PO Box 128, Bancroft, ON K0L 1C0
613/332-1666, Fax: 613/332-0623
Administrator, Brent Anderson

### Corporation des concessionnaires d'automobiles du Québec inc. (CCAQ) (1945)
#750, 140, Grande-Allée est, Québec, QC G1R 5M8
418/523-2991, Téléc: 418/523-3725
Président-directeur général, Jacques Béchard
Secrétaire, Suzanne Gauthier
Relationiste, Jean Cadoret
Publications: Bref; Contact, trimestriel
Organisation(s) affiliée(s): Eastern Townships Automobile Dealers Association; Eastern Québec Automobile Dealers Association; Laurentian Automobile Dealers Association; Mauricie Automobile Dealers Association; Montréal Automobile Dealers Association; North-Western Québec Automobile Dealers Association; Outaouais Automobile Dealers Association; Québec Automobile Dealers Association; Richelieu Automobile Dealers Association; Saguenay-Lac-St-Jean Automobile Dealers Association

### Japan Automobile Manufacturers Association of Canada (JAMA Canada) (1984)
#460, 151 Bloor St. West, Toronto, ON M5S 1S4
416/968-0150, Fax: 416/968-7095, Email: jamacan@interlog.com
Executive Director, David Worts

### Manitoba Motor Dealers Association (1944)
#203, 2281 Portage Ave., Winnipeg, MB R3J 0M1
204/889-4924, Fax: 204/885-6552
Executive Director, Shirley Canty

### Motor Dealers' Association of Alberta (1950)
9249 - 48 St., Edmonton, AB T6B 2R9
403/468-9552, Fax: 403/465-6201, URL: http://www.compusmart.ab.ca/mdaalta
President, Bill Watkin
Publications: Driveline
Affiliates: Automotive Service Repair Association (ASRA)

### Motor Dealers' Association of BC (1943)
**MDA of BC**
3657 Wayburne Dr., Burnaby, BC V5G 3L1
604/294-8330, Fax: 604/298-8726
Executive Vice-President, Marion Keys
Publications: Signals
Affiliates: Automobile Dealers' Association of Greater Vancouver (same address & contact)

### Motor Vehicle Manufacturers' Association/Association des fabricants de véhicules à moteur (MVMA) (1926)
#1602, 25 Adelaide St. East, Toronto, ON M5C 1Y7
416/364-9333, Fax: 416/367-3221
President, Mark A. Nantais
Chairman, G. Yves Landry

### National Auto League
248 Pall Mall St., PO Box 5845, London, ON N6A 4T4
519/434-3221, Fax: 519/434-5220
President, Glen Bessey
Affiliates: National Truck League
Regional Offices

### National Automotive Equipment Association (NAEA) (1989)
#11-12, 1520 Trinity Dr., Mississauga, ON L5T 1N9
905/564-7373, Fax: 905/564-7408
President, David Clarke
Secretary, Robert McVey

### New Brunswick Automobile Dealers' Association
202 Pleasant St., PO Box 294, Newcastle, NB E1V 3M4
506/622-1422, Fax: 506/622-4498
Manager, George E. Irlam

### Nova Scotia Automobile Dealers' Association (NSADA)
PO Box 9410, Stn A, Halifax, NS B3K 5S3
902/425-2445, Fax: 902/425-2441, Email: pathfndr@fox.nstn.ca
Executive Vice-President, John K. Sutherland
Publications: Pathfinder Dealer Update

### Ontario Automobile Dealer Association
85 Renfrew Dr., 2nd Fl., Markham, ON L3R 0N9
905/940-6232, Fax: 905/940-6235
Director General, Bill Davis
Publications: Automobile Journal

### Organization of Registered Automobile Dealers in Ontario (ORADIO)
97 Guildwood Pkwy., PO Box 11021, Scarborough, ON M1E 5G5
416/283-1937
Managing Director, Clint McCormack

### PEI Automobile Dealers Association
PO Box 22004, Parkdale, PE C1A 7J0
902/368-7116, Fax: 902/368-7116
Secretary, Norma Proud

### Recreation Vehicle Dealers Association of Canada/Association des commerçants de véhicules recréatifs du Canada (RVDA) (1981)
#209, 20353 - 64 Ave., Langley, BC V2Y 1N5
604/533-4010, Fax: 604/533-0795, Email: ernie_hamm@vancouver.net, URL: http://www.rvda.ca

Executive Vice-President, Ernie Hamm
Executive Assistant, Eléonore Hamm
Affiliates: Recreation Vehicle Dealers of America
Atlantic Recreation Vehicle Dealers Association: Representative, Derek Dobson, PO Box 635, Saint John, NB E2L 4A5, 506/849-3363, Fax: 506/847-4377

**ONTARIO RECREATION VEHICLE DEALERS ASSOCIATION (ORVDA) (1979)**
PO Box 270, Brechin, ON L0K 1B0
705/484-0295, Fax: 705/484-5740
Executive Director, William A. Mallatratt
Publications: ORVDA News

**RECREATION VEHICLE DEALERS ASSOCIATION OF ALBERTA (1978)**
**RVDA of Alberta**
11217 - 143 St., Edmonton, AB T5M 3P8
403/455-8562, Fax: 403/453-3927, Toll Free: 1-888-858-7878
Email: rvda@planet.eon.net, URL: http://www.rvda-alberta.com
Executive Vice-President, John Milligan
Publications: RV Viewpoints

**RECREATION VEHICLE DEALERS ASSOCIATION OF BRITISH COLUMBIA (1974)**
**RVDA of British Columbia**
#209, 20353 - 64 Ave., Langley, BC V2Y 1N5
604/533-4200, Fax: 604/533-0795
Executive Director, Janet Marwick
Publications: Newsletter

**RECREATION VEHICLE DEALERS ASSOCIATION OF MANITOBA**
58 Leger Cres., Winnipeg, MB R3X 1J4
204/256-6119, Fax: 204/256-6119
Manager, Susan Andree

**RECREATION VEHICLE DEALERS ASSOCIATION OF NOVA SCOTIA**
**RVDA of Nova Scotia**
PO Box 621, New Glasgow, NS B2H 5E7
902/752-3164, Fax: 902/755-3029
President, Kim Stone

**RECREATION VEHICLE DEALERS ASSOCIATION OF QUÉBEC**
**RVDA of Québec**
#110, 560, Henri Bourassa ouest, Montréal, QC H3L 1P4
514/338-1471, Téléc: 514/335-6250
Directeur général, Michel Gagné

**RECREATION VEHICLE DEALERS ASSOCIATION OF SASKATCHEWAN**
PO Box 1983, Regina, SK S4P 3E1
306/525-5666, Fax: 306/757-3670
President, Bill Ortman

### Saskatchewan Automobile Dealers Association (SADA)
#330, 3303 Hillsdale St., Regina, SK S4S 6W9
306/721-2208, Fax: 306/721-2200
Executive Vice-President, Ben R. Holden, BSP

### Société de l'assurance automobile du Québec (1978)
333, boul Jean-Lesage, CP 19 600, Québec, QC G1K 8J6
418/528-4290, Téléc: 418/644-0339
Jean-Yves Gagnon

### Used Car Dealers Association of Ontario (UCDA) (1984)
#205, 4174 Dundas St. West, Toronto, ON M8X 1X3
416/231-2600, Fax: 416/232-0775, Toll Free: 1-800-268-2598, Email: bobucda@ucda.org, URL: http://www.ucda.org
Executive Director, Robert G. Beattie
Publications: Members' Briefs

### Vehicle Information Centre of Canada/Centre d'information sur les véhicules du Canada (VICC) (1989)
#220, 175 Commerce Valley Dr. West, Markham, ON L3T 7P6
905/764-5560, Fax: 905/764-6846
President, Henning M. Norup, AIIC
Vice-President, Roch Lacroix
Publications: How Cars Measure Up; Choosing Your Car; Auto Insurance Rate Group Tables; Car Theft

## AVIATION & AEROSPACE
*see also* **Aerospace Industry**

### Aerospace Industries Association of Canada/Association des industries aérospatiales du Canada (AIAC) (1962)
#1200, 60 Queen St., Ottawa, ON K1P 5Y7
613/232-4297, Fax: 613/232-1142, Email: aiac@fox.nstn.ca, URL: http://www.aiac.ca
President, Peter R. Smith
Publications: Aerospace News

### Air Transport Association of Canada/Association du transport aérien du Canada (ATAC) (1934)
#1100, 255 Albert St., Ottawa, ON K1P 6A9
613/233-7727, Fax: 613/230-8648, Email: atac@pop.infoshare, URL: http://www.atac.ca
President/CEO, John W. Crichton
Publications: ATAC Newsletter
Affiliates: Alberta Aviation Council; BC Aviation Council; Canadian Business Aircraft Association; Helicopter Association International; National Air Transporation Association; Northern Air Transport Association; Saskatchewan Aviation Council; Federation of Canadian Municipalities

### Aircraft Engineers Association (Atlantic) Inc. (AEA) (1980)
837 Charlotte St., Fredericton, NB E3B 1M7
506/452-1809, Fax: 506/452-8251
President, Ben L. McCarty
Secretary, Dario Mazzorana
Publications: Newsletter

### Airport Management Conference of Ontario
PO Box 179, Perkinsfield, ON L0L 2J0
705/526-8086, Fax: 705/526-1769
President, Don Timlin
Secretary Manager, John O'Hara

### Alberta Aviation Council (AAC) (1962)
67 Airport Rd., Edmonton, AB T5G 0W6
403/414-6191, Fax: 403/479-6296, Toll Free: 1-888-289-4222, Email: aac@planet.eon.net
Association Manager, Monika Burckhardt
Publications: Flight Times
Affiliates: Civil Air Rescue Emergency Services

### British Columbia Aviation Council
#303, 5360 Airport Rd. South, Richmond, BC V7B 1B4
604/278-9330, Fax: 604/278-8210
Chairman, Jack Cameron

### Canadian Aeronautics & Space Institute/Institut aéronautique et spatial du Canada (CASI) (1954)
#818, 130 Slater St., Ottawa, ON K1P 6E2
613/234-0191, Fax: 613/234-9039, Email: casi@casi.ca, URL: http://www.casi.ca
Executive Director, Ian M. Ross
Publications: The Canadian Aeronautics & Space Journal; CASI Log, q.
Affiliates: International Congress of Aeronautical Sciences; International Astronautical Federation

### Canadian Airports Council/Conseil des aéroports du Canada (CAC) (1991)
#2100, 1100, boul René-Lévesque ouest, Montréal, QC H3B 4X8
514/394-7200, Fax: 514/394-7356
Contact, J.G. Auger, FCIT

### Canadian Aviation Historical Society (CAHS) (1963)
PO Box 224, Stn A, North York, ON M2N 5S8
416/488-2247, Fax: 416/488-2247
President, Jack Gow
Treasurer, Terry Judge
Secretary, Ed Rice
Publications: Outbound; CAHS Journal, q.

### Canadian Aviation Maintenance Council/Conseil canadien de l'entretien des aéronefs (CAMC) (1992)
#290, 955 Green Valley Cres., Ottawa, ON K2C 3V4
613/727-8272, Fax: 613/727-7018, Toll Free: 1-800-448-9715, Email: camc@secretariat.ca
Executive Director, William Weston
Publications: Update

### Canadian Federation of AME Associations
**Aircraft Maintenance Engineers Association**
55 Archer Cres., Elmvale, ON L0L 1P0
705/322-9637, Fax: 705/322-8337
Chairperson, D. Snedden

### Canadian Owners & Pilots Association (COPA) (1954)
#1001, 75 Albert St., Ottawa, ON K1P 5E7
613/236-4901, Fax: 613/236-8646, Email: copa@copanational.org, URL: http://www.copanational.org
Executive Vice-President, Kevin Psutka, Email: kpsutka@copanational.org
Publications: Canadian Flight News; Canadian Ultralight News, m.; Canadian Homebuilt Aircraft News, m.; Canadian Plane Trade, m.; Canadian Warplane Heritage News/Flightlines, bi-m.; Canadian Flight Annual

### Canadian Seaplane Pilots Association
RR#6, Orillia, ON L3V 6H6
705/325-6153, Fax: 705/325-6377, Email: cspa@copanational.org
President, R. Vodarek

### The De Havilland Moth Club of Canada (1981)
305 Old Homestead Rd., Keswick, ON L4P 1E6
905/476-4225
Founder/Director, R. de H. "Ted" Leonard
Publications: DH Moth Newsletter

### Institute for Aerospace Studies (UTIAS) (1949)
University of Toronto, 4925 Dufferin St., North York, ON M3H 5T6
416/667-7701, Fax: 416/667-7799, Email: info@utias.utoronto.ca, URL: http://www.utias.utoronto.ca/
Director, Dr. A.A. Haasz
Publications: Annual Progress Report

### International Air Transport Association (IATA) (1945)
2000, rue Peel, Montréal, QC H3A 2R4
514/844-6311, Fax: 514/844-5286
Director General, Pierre Jeanniot
General Counsel/Corporate Secretary, Lorne Clark
Manager, Public Relations, Wanda Potrykus
Affiliates: International Civil Aviation Organization

**International Airline Passengers Association of Canada/Association canadienne des passagers de lignes aériennes internationales**
12 Inglewood Cres., Kirkland, QC H9J 2M6
Contact, Terry A. Evans
Contact, Martin Castonguay

**International Civil Aviation Organization/Organisation de l'aviation civile internationale (ICAO) (1947)**
999, rue Université, Montréal, QC H3C 5H7
514/954-8219, Fax: 514/954-6077, Telex: 05-24513, Email: icaohg@icao.org, URL: http://www.cam.org/~icao/
President, Dr. Assad Kotaite
Secretary General, Dr. Philippe Rochat
Publications: ICAO Journal

**International Industry Working Group (IIWG) (1970)**
International Air Transport Association, 2000, rue Peel, Montréal, QC H3A 2R4
514/844-6311, Fax: 514/844-6727, URL: http://www.iata.org
Secretary, M. O'Brien
Chairman, Boeing Commercial Airplane Group, Seattle WA, USA, Edward L. Gervais

**The Ninety-Nines Inc./International Women Pilots**
7100 Terminal Drive, PO Box 965, Oklahoma City, OK 73159 USA
405/685-7969
President, Joyce Wells
Publications: The Ninety-Nines
East Canada Section: Governor, Joy Parker Blackwood, 221 Whitehall Dr., Markham, ON L3R 9T1, 905/841-7930, Fax: 905/475-7212
West Canada Section: Governor, Sonja Wilford, 725 Franklin Rd., Kamloops, BC V2B 6G5, 250/579-8584, Fax: 250/372-0330

**Northern Air Transport Association (NATA) (1977)**
PO Box 2457, Yellowknife, NT X1A 2P8
867/920-2985, Fax: 867/873-8077
Executive Director, Stu Grant
President, Al Kapty

**Recreational Aircraft Association Canada (RAAC) (1983)**
152 Harwood Ave. South, Ajax, ON L1S 2H6
905/683-3517, Fax: 905/428-2415, Toll Free: 1-800-387-1028
President, Barry Miller
Publications: Recreational Flyer

**SEDS - Canada (1980)**
**Students for the Exploration & Development of Space**
York University, Student Centre Building, Rm. 333, 4700 Keele St., North York, ON M3J 1P3
Email: seds@seds.ca, URL: http://www.seds.ca
Chair, H. Peter White, Bus: 416/650-9890, Email: white@eol.ists.ca
Secretary, Christine Marton, Bus: 416/699-0591, Email: cmarton.@epas.utoronto.ca
Publications: Ylem

**Ultralight Pilots Association of Canada/Association canadienne des pilots d'avions ultra-legers (UPAC)**
Hunters Gate Plaza, #6, 14845 Yonge St., Aurora, ON L4G 6H8
905/833-3467, Fax: 905/833-1336
Vice-President, Membership & Administration, Peter Henshall

**BANKING *see* FINANCE**

**BARS *see* RESTAURANTS, BARS, FOOD SERVICES**

**BETTER BUSINESS BUREAUX *see* BUSINESS**

**BEVERAGE INDUSTRY *see* FOOD & BEVERAGE INDUSTRY**

**BIRTH *see* CHILDBIRTH**

**BOOK TRADE *see* PUBLISHING**

**BOOKKEEPING *see* ACCOUNTING**

**BREEDERS *see* ANIMAL BREEDING**

## BROADCASTING

***see also* Film & Video; Telecommunications**

**The Alliance for Children & Television/Alliance pour l'enfant et la télévision (ACT) (1974)**
#205, 344 Dupont St., Toronto, ON M5R 1V9
416/515-0466, Fax: 416/515-0467, Email: acttv@interlog.com
Executive Director, Kealy Wilkinson
Operations Manager, Judith Pyke
Chairman, Alan Mirabelli
Publications: Alliance Info
Montréal Office: #102, 3774, rue Saint-Denis, Montréal, QC H2W 2M1, 514/844-6513, Téléc: 514/284-0168

**Association for the Study of Canadian Radio & Television/Association pour les études sur la radio-télévision canadienne (ASCRT) (1978)**
c/o Centre for Broadcasting Studies, Concordia University, 1455, boul de Maisonneuve ouest, Montréal, QC H3G 1M8
514/848-2385, Fax: 514/848-4501
President, Prof. Howard Fink
Publications: ASCRT/AERTC Bulletin; Frequency/Fréquence

**Audio Engineering Society**
Box 292, #200, 131 Bloor St. West, Toronto, ON M5S 1R8
416/863-0898, Fax: 416/863-1047
Chair, D. Tremblay
Treasurer, R. Lynch
Communications, A. Reynolds

**BBM Bureau of Measurement/Sondages BBM (1944)**
#305, 1500 Don Mills Rd., North York, ON M3B 3L7
416/445-9800, Fax: 416/445-8644, Telex: 06-986-198, URL: http://www.bbm.ca/
President, Owen Charlebois
Publications: In Sync

**Broadcast Educators Association of Canada/Association canadienne des éducateurs en radiodiffusion (BEAC) (1977)**
741 Colborne St., Brantford, ON N3S 3R9
519/753-1058, Fax: 519/753-1682, Email: bradfoj@operatns.mohawkc.on.ca
Executive Director, John Bradford
President, Jane Bonisteel
Vice-President, Donna Leon-Millen
Publications: Communiqué
Affiliates: Canadian Association of Broadcasters

**Broadcast Executives Society (BES) (1961)**
#700, 890 Yonge St., Toronto, ON M4W 3P4
416/961-3201
Administrator, Deanna Toshack

**Broadcast Research Council of Canada (BRC)**
Box 409, #100, 2 Bloor St. West, Toronto, ON M4W 3E2
Fax: 416/929-2529
President, Daphne Hubble, Bus: 416/596-2489

**Canadian Association of Broadcast Consultants**
500 Van Buren St., PO Box 550, Kemptville, ON K0G 1J0
613/258-5928, Fax: 613/258-7418
President, Pierre Labarre
Sec.-Treas., M.A. Tilston

**Canadian Association of Broadcasters/Association canadienne des radiodiffuseurs (CAB) (1926)**
#306, 350 Sparks St., PO Box 627, Stn B, Ottawa, ON K1P 5S2
613/233-4035, Fax: 613/233-6961, URL: http://www.cab-acr.ca
President & CEO, Michael McCabe
Executive Vice-President, Michel Tremblay
Senior Vice-President, Peter Miller
Vice-President, Radio, Elisabeth Ostiguy
Vice-President, Television, Rob Scarth
Communications Coordinator, Michael Buzzell
Publications: Radio Plus; TV Plus, m.; Info Plus, m.

**ALBERTA BROADCASTERS ASSOCIATION**
c/o CFRN-TV, PO Box 5030, Stn E, Edmonton, AB T5P 4C2
403/483-3311, Fax: 403/484-4426
President, Fred Filthaut

**ASSOCIATION CANADIENNE DE LA RADIO ET TÉLÉVISION DE LANGUE FRANÇAISE (ACRTF)**
CP 127, Saint-Lambert, QC J4P 3N4
514/923-5455, Téléc: 514/923-5525
Président, Michel Arpin

**ATLANTIC ASSOCIATION OF BROADCASTERS (AAB)**
c/o CFSX Radio, 30 Oregon Dr., Stephenville, NF A2N 2X9
709/643-2191, Fax: 709/643-5025
President, G. Murphy

**BRITISH COLUMBIA ASSOCIATION OF BROADCASTERS (BCAB) (1946)**
c/o Okanagan Radio Ltd., 2419 Hwy. 97 North, Kelowna, BC V1X 4J2
250/868-4713, Fax: 250/860-8856
Email: petrie@osgltd.com, URL: http://www.bcab.org
President, E. Petrie

**BROADCASTERS ASSOCIATION OF MANITOBA**
c/o CKY TV, Polo Park, Winnipeg, MB R3G 0L7
204/788-3300, Fax: 204/788-3399
President, Vaughan Tozer

**CENTRAL CANADA BROADCASTERS' ASSOCIATION (CCBA) (1950)**
c/o CJOH-TV, 1500 Merivale Rd., Ottawa, ON K2E 6Z5
613/224-1313, Fax: 613/224-7998
President, A. MacKay

**ONTARIO ASSOCIATION OF BROADCASTERS**
57 Cherrywood Dr., Nepean, ON K2H 6H1
613/829-0284
Executive Director, Gerry Acton

**SASKATCHEWAN ASSOCIATION OF BROADCASTERS**
c/o CJYM, 208 Hwy. 4, PO Box 490, Rosetown, SK S0L 2V0
306/882-2686, Fax: 306/882-3037
Sec.-Treas., Wax Williams

#### WESTERN ASSOCIATION OF BROADCASTERS (WAB) (1934)
c/o Alberta Hospitality, 22 Estate Cres., St Albert, AB T8N 5X2
403/460-7207, Fax: 403/460-4699
President, Doug Shillington
Sec.-Treas., J. Douglas, Bus: 403/460-7207

### Canadian Association of Captioning Consumers/Association canadienne pour le sous-titrage (CACC) (1993)
#203, 627 Lyons Lane, Oakville, ON L6J 5Z7
905/338-1246, Fax: 905/338-7483
President, Ellen Rusi
Publications: Captioning Today

#### REGROUPEMENT QUÉBÉCOIS POUR LE SOUS-TITRAGE INC. (RQST) (1992)
#376, 65, rue de Castelnau ouest, Montréal, QC H2R 2W3
514/278-8722, Téléc: 514/278-8704, Ligne sans frais: 1-800-742-0529
URL: http://www.surdite.org/
Directeur général, Richard McNicoll
Publications: Bulletin RQST

### Canadian Association of Ethnic (Radio) Broadcasters/Association canadienne des radiodiffuseurs éthniques (CAEB) (1981)
622 College St., Toronto, ON M6G 1B6
416/531-9991, Fax: 416/531-5274, URL: http://www.chinradio.com
Executive Director, Johnny Lombardi

### Canadian Cable Television Association/Association canadienne de télévision par cable (CCTA) (1957)
#1010, 360 Albert St., Ottawa, ON K1R 7X7
613/232-2631, Fax: 613/232-2137
President, Richard Stursberg
Sr. Vice-President, Public Affairs, Elizabeth Roscoe
Publications: Cable Communiqué

### Canadian Satellite Users Association
#1105, 191 The West Mall, Etobicoke, ON M9C 5K8
416/620-4332, Fax: 416/620-5392, Email: bbande@enterprise.ca, URL: http://www.bbande.com
Executive Director, Don Braden
Chair, John Riley

### Conseil international des radios-télévisions d'expression française (CIRTEF)
a/s Société Radio-Canada, 1400, boul René-Lévesque est, Montréal, QC H2L 2M2
514/597-4700, Téléc: 514/597-4599
Président, Paul Saint-Pierre

### Fédération professionnelle des réalisateurs de télévision et de cinéma
#1231, rue Panet, CP 870, Succ. C, Montréal, QC H2L 4L6
514/525-8599, Téléc: 514/526-4124
Président, Jean Gagne

### Friends of Canadian Broadcasting (FCB) (1984)
#200/238, 131 Bloor St. West, Toronto, ON M5R 1B2
416/968-7496, Fax: 416/968-7406, Email: friends@hookup.net, URL: http://friendscb.org
Spokesperson, Ian Morrison

### ITVA CANADA (1989)
PO Box 1156, Stn Adelaide, Toronto, ON M5C 2K5
416/733-3757, Fax: 416/733-1741, Email: itvacda@inforamp.net
General Manager, Tosca Gazer
National President, Mark Arlett
Publications: Videosync

### National Campus/Community Radio Association/Association nationale des radio étudiantes & communautaires (NCRA) (1986)
c/o CFRU-FM, #273, University Centre, Guelph, ON N1G 2W1
President, Alka Sharma, Bus: 519/824-4120
Vice-President, Internal, Susan Kennard, Bus: 403/271-6477
Publications: Voices; NCRA Directory, a.; National Music Chart, a.; NCRN, q.
Affiliates: World Association of Community Broadcasters (AMAC)

### Radio Advisory Board of Canada/Conseil consultatif canadien de la radio (RABC) (1944)
#201, 880 Lady Ellen Pl., Ottawa, ON K1Z 5L9
613/728-8692, Fax: 613/728-3278
General Manager, P.G. Bowie
President, P.J. Saunders

### Radio Amateurs of Canada/Radio amateurs du Canada (RAC) (1993)
#6, 614 Norris Ct., Kingston, ON K7P 2R9
613/634-4184, Fax: 613/634-7118, URL: http://www.rac.ca/
General Manager, Deborah F. Norman
President, J. Farrell Hopwood
Publications: The Canadian Amateur

### Radio Television News Directors' Association (Canada)/Association canadienne des directeurs de l'information en radio-télévision (RTNDA) (1961)
#310, 2175 Sheppard Ave. East, North York, ON M2J 1W8
416/756-2213, Fax: 416/491-1670, Email: taylor@interlog.com, URL: http://www.vvv.com/~rtnda/
President, Hudson Mack
Administrator, Diane Gaunt
Publications: Newsletter
Affiliates: Radio-Television News Directors Association International

### Society of Television Lighting Directors Canada/Société des directeurs d'éclairage de télévision (STLDC) (1978)
46 Ladysbridge Dr., Scarborough, ON M1G 3H7
416/439-2875, Fax: 416/424-4682, URL: http://web.idirect.com/~stld
Chair, Bruce Whitehead, Bus: 416/424-4284, Fax: 416/424-4682
Treasurer, Alf Hunter
Publications: Television Lighting; STLDC Newsletter
Affiliates: Society of Television Lighting Directors - United Kingdom

### Telecaster Committee of Canada Inc./Le Comité des télédiffuseurs du Canada inc. (1972)
#604, 890 Yonge St., Toronto, ON M4W 3P4
416/928-6046, Fax: 416/924-7644
President, P.A. Beatty

### Television Bureau of Canada, Inc./Bureau de la télévision du Canada, inc. (1961)
**TVB of Canada Inc.**
#700, 890 Yonge St., Toronto, ON M4W 3P4
416/923-8813, Fax: 416/923-8739, URL: http://www.tvb.ca
President & CEO, Jim Patterson
Director, Marketing, Jim Quance
Director, Research, Suzanne Marshall
Publications: TV Basics
Affiliates: Television Bureau of Advertising - New York, USA
Montréal Branch Office: Vice-President, J.R. Genin, #980, 550, rue Sherbrooke ouest, Montréal, QC H3A 1B9, 514/284-0425, Fax: 514/284-0698

### Western Association of Broadcast Engineers
CFCN Radio-Broadcast House, PO Box 7060, Stn E, Calgary, AB T3C 3L9
403/240-5769, Fax: 403/240-5883
President, J. Bruins

### Women in Film & Television - Toronto (1984)
**WIFT-T**
#902, 20 Eglinton St. West, PO Box 2009, Toronto, ON M4R 1K8
416/322-3430, Fax: 416/322-3703, Email: wift-admin@goodmedia.com, URL: http://www.goodmedia.com/wift/
Executive Director, Joan Jenkinson
Publications: Changing Focus

## BUILDING & CONSTRUCTION
*see also* **Equipment & Machinery; Housing**

### Aggregate Producers' Association of Ontario (APAO) (1956)
#2, 365 Brunel Rd., Mississauga, ON L4Z 1Z5
905/507-0711, Fax: 905/507-0717
Executive Director, Robert Cook
Manager, Environment & Resources, Moreen Miller
Executive Assistant, Sonja Hamilton

### Architectural Metal Association
#200, 670 Bloor St. West, Toronto, ON M6G 1L2
416/533-7800, Fax: 416/533-4795
Executive Director, Don Mockford

### Architectural Woodwork Manufacturers Association of Canada (AWMAC) (1967)
925 - 5 St. West, High River, AB T1V 1A7
250/652-3666, Fax: 250/652-7384
President, Casey Beyers Bergen
Secretary/Manager, Frank Van Donzel

### Association béton Québec (ABQ)
#107, 85, rue St-Charles ouest, Longueuil, QC J4H 1C5
514/463-3569, Téléc: 514/463-1704
Directeur général, J. Gaétan Trudeau
Publications: L'Ere du béton

### Béton Canada/Concrete Canada (1990)
Dépt. de génie civil, Université de Sherbrooke, Sherbrooke, QC J1K 2R1
819/821-8061, Téléc: 819/821-6949, Courrier électronique: concrete@andrew.sca.usherb.ca, URL: http://www.usherb.ca/beton/
Network Manager, Yves Delagrave

### Building Maintenance Contractors Association
#1219, 1644 Bayview Ave., Toronto, ON M4G 4E9
416/421-1598, Fax: 416/421-1598
Executive Director, Carla Kelman

### Canadian Cement Council/Conseil canadien du ciment (1992)
Box 74, #1600, 350 Albert St., Ottawa, ON K1R 1A4
613/238-3348, Fax: 613/238-6594
Executive Director, Kenneth G. Whiting

### Canadian Concrete Masonry Producers Association/Association canadienne des manufacturiers de maçonnerie en béton (CCMPA) (1949)
#101, 1013 Wilson Ave., Downsview, ON M3K 1G1
416/630-9944, Fax: 416/630-1916
Executive Director, M.A. Patamia
Publications: Update
Affiliates: National Concrete Masonry Association (U.S.)

## Canadian Concrete Pipe Association/Association canadienne des fabricants de tuyaux de béton (CCPA) (1992)

#508, 6299 Airport Rd., Mississauga, ON L4V 1N6
905/677-1010, Fax: 905/677-1007, Toll Free: 1-800-435-0116
Chair, Edwin Kling
Vice-Chair, Bill Dunn
Manager, Grant Lee
Sec.-Treas., Ed McMenamin
Publications: Concrete Pipe Journal
Affiliates: Ontario Concrete Pipe Association; Tubecon; American Concrete Pipe Association

## Canadian Construction Association/Association canadienne de la construction (CCA) (1918)

85 Albert St., 10th Fl., Ottawa, ON K1P 6A4
613/236-9455, Fax: 613/236-9526, Email: cca@cca-acc.com, URL: http://www.cca-acc.com
President/CEO, Michael Atkinson
Chairman, Brian Scroggs
Publications: National Review

#### ALBERTA CONSTRUCTION ASSOCIATION (ACA) (1958)

10949 - 120 St., Edmonton, AB T5H 3R2
403/455-1122, Fax: 403/451-2152
Operations Manager, Shelley Andrea
Executive Director, Merv Ellis
Publications: Alberta Construction
Affiliates: Alberta Construction Safety Association; Alberta Construction Tendering System

#### ALBERTA ROADBUILDERS & HEAVY CONSTRUCTION ASSOCIATION (1954)

#201, 9333 - 45 Ave., Edmonton, AB T6E 5Z7
403/436-9860, Fax: 403/436-4910
President, Barrie McPhalen
Publications: Roadrunner; Directory, a.
Affiliates: Western Canada Roadbuilders Association; Alberta Construction Safety Association; Roads & Transportation Association Canada

#### ASSOCIATION DES CONSTRUCTEURS DE ROUTES ET GRANDS TRAVAUX DU QUÉBEC/QUÉBEC ROAD BUILDERS & HEAVY CONSTRUCTION ASSOCIATION (ACRGTQ) (1944)

435, av Grande-Allée est, Québec, QC G1R 2J5
418/529-2949, Téléc: 418/529-5139, Ligne sans frais: 1-800-463-4672
Directrice générale par intérim, Maître Gisèle Bourque
Publications: Dossiers

#### ASSOCIATION DE LA CONSTRUCTION DU QUÉBEC/CONSTRUCTION ASSOCIATION OF QUÉBEC (ACQ) (1989)

#205, 7400, boul les Galeries d'Anjou, Anjou, QC H1M 3M2
514/354-0609, Téléc: 514/354-8292, Ligne sans frais: 1-888-868-3424
Président, Réjean Tardif
Secrétaire général, Michel Paré
Publications: Construire

#### ASSOCIATION DES ENTREPRENEURS EN CONSTRUCTION DU QUÉBEC/ASSOCIATION OF BUILDING CONTRACTORS OF QUÉBEC (AECQ) (1976)

#101, 7905, boul Louis-H-Lafontaine, Anjou, QC H1K 4E4
514/353-5151, Téléc: 514/353-6689, Ligne sans frais: 1-800-361-4304
Directeur général, Pierre Dion

#### BRITISH COLUMBIA CONSTRUCTION ASSOCIATION (BCCA) (1969)

#400, 3795 Carey Rd., Victoria, BC V8Z 6T8
250/475-1077, Fax: 250/475-1078
Email: bcca@bccassn.com, URL: http://www.bccassn.com
President, David Robertson
Executive Assistant, Kim Haakonson
Publications: Membership Directory & Buyer's Guide; The Bulletin, m.

#### BRITISH COLUMBIA ROAD BUILDERS & HEAVY CONSTRUCTION ASSOCIATION (1965)

#165, 10711 Cambie Rd., Richmond, BC V6X 3G5
604/276-0202, Fax: 604/276-2647
President, S. Anthony Toth
Publications: Bulletin
Affiliates: Western Canada Roadbuilders Association

#### CONSTRUCTION ASSOCIATION OF NEW BRUNSWICK INC. (CANB)

190 Brunswick St., Fredericton, NB E3B 1G6
506/459-5770, Fax: 506/457-1913
Email: canb@nbnet.nb.ca
Executive Secretary, Margaret A. Wilby

#### CONSTRUCTION ASSOCIATION OF NOVA SCOTIA

PO Box 47040, Halifax, NS B3K 5Y2
902/429-6760, Fax: 902/429-3965
President, Carol MacCulloch

#### CONSTRUCTION ASSOCIATION OF PEI

Holland College Royalty Centre, 40 Enman Cres., PO Box 728, Charlottetown, PE C1A 7L3
902/368-3303, Fax: 902/894-9757
General Manager, Francis Reid
Affiliates: Canadian Electrical Contractors Association

#### MANITOBA HEAVY CONSTRUCTION ASSOCIATION INC.

1236 Ellice, Winnipeg, MB R3G 0E7
204/947-1379, Fax: 204/943-2279
Executive Director, Chirs Lorenc

#### NEWFOUNDLAND & LABRADOR CONSTRUCTION ASSOCIATION

78 O'Leary Ave., PO Box 8008, St. John's, NF A1B 3M7
709/753-8920, Fax: 709/754-3968
Email: nlca@nfld.com, URL: http://www.netfx.iom.net/nlca/
President, Lawrence J. Rossiter

#### NEWFOUNDLAND & LABRADOR ROAD BUILDERS ASSOCIATION (1968)

26 Rostellan Pl., St. John's, NF A1B 2T9
709/722-2446
Manager, Rudy Wasmeier
President, Dave Burnell
Vice-President, Len Knox

#### NORTHERN BRITISH COLUMBIA CONSTRUCTION ASSOCIATION (NBCCA) (1979)

3851 - 18 Ave., Prince George, BC V2N 1B1
250/563-1744, Fax: 250/563-1107
President, Rosalind Thorn
Publications: The Northern Report

#### NORTHWEST TERRITORIES CONSTRUCTION ASSOCIATION (1976)

#201, 4817 - 49 St., Yellowknife, NT X1A 3S7
867/873-3949, Fax: 867/873-8366
Executive Director, Richard Bushey
Office Manager, Rosemarie Laine
Publications: Weekly Bulletin; Construction North of 60, a.

#### NOVA SCOTIA ROAD BUILDERS ASSOCIATION (1948)

109 Chain Lake Dr., Halifax, NS B3S 1B3
902/450-1433, Fax: 902/450-1424
Managing Director, Steven Williams

#### ONTARIO GENERAL CONTRACTORS ASSOCIATION (OGCA) (1939)

#703, 6299 Airport Rd., Mississauga, ON L4V 1N3
905/671-3969, Fax: 905/671-8212
President, Don J. Cameron
Publications: OGCA News
Affiliates: Council of Ontario Construction Associations

#### ONTARIO ROAD BUILDERS' ASSOCIATION

#1, 365 Brunel Rd., Mississauga, ON L4Z 1Z5
905/507-1107, Fax: 905/890-8122
Executive Director, Rob Bradford

#### PEI ROADBUILDERS & HEAVY CONSTRUCTION ASSOCIATION (1962)

Holland College Royalty Centre, 40 Enman Cres., PO Box 1901, Charlottetown, PE C1A 7N5
902/894-9514, Fax: 902/894-9512
Email: pei.roadbuilders@pei.sympatico.ca, URL: http://www3.sympatico.ca/pei.roadbuilders/
Manager, Roger Perry

#### ROAD BUILDERS ASSOCIATION OF NEW BRUNSWICK (1958)

606 Queen St., PO Box 1061, Fredericton, NB E3B 5C2
506/454-5079, Fax: 506/452-7646
Secretary Manager, J.A. Hughson
President, Malcolm MacAfee

#### ROADBUILDERS & HEAVY CONSTRUCTION ASSOCIATION OF SASKATCHEWAN (1956)

3026 Kings Rd., Regina, SK S4S 2H6
306/586-1805, Fax: 306/585-3750
Email: vjakub@ucomnet.unibase.com
Executive Administrator, Val Jakubowski
Publications:
Affiliates: Western Canada Roadbuilders & Heavy Construction Association

#### SASKATCHEWAN CONSTRUCTION SAFETY ASSOCIATION INC. (1995)

1939 Elphinstone St., Regina, SK S4T 3N3
306/525-0171, Fax: 306/347-8595, Toll Free: 1-800-817-2079
Publications: Advocate

#### SOUTHERN INTERIOR CONSTRUCTION ASSOCIATION (SICA) (1969)

710 Laval Cres., Kamloops, BC V2C 5P3
250/372-3364, Fax: 250/828-6634
Email: sica@netshop.net
President, Debra Hicks
Publications: SICA Bulletin

#### TORONTO CONSTRUCTION ASSOCIATION

1 Sparks Ave., North York, ON M2H 2W1
416/499-4101, Fax: 416/499-5890
Executive Vice-President, Temple W. Harris
Director, Labour Relations, Brian M. Foote
Affiliates: International Council for Building Research Studies and Documentation

#### WESTERN CANADA ROADBUILDERS ASSOCIATION (1975)

1236 Ellice Ave., Winnipeg, MB R3G 0E7
403/947-1379, Fax: 403/943-2279
Executive Director, Chris Lorenc
President, Colleen Munro
Affiliates: Roads & Transportation Association of Canada

#### WINNIPEG CONSTRUCTION ASSOCIATION

**Manitoba Construction Association**

290 Burnell St., PO Box 737, Winnipeg, MB R3G 2L4
204/775-8664, Fax: 204/783-6446
Email: info@wpgca.com, URL: http://www.wpgca.com/
Executive Vice-President, Gervin L. Greasley
President, David Bockstael

## Canadian Masonry Contractors' Association (CMCA) (1972)

360 Superior Blvd., Mississauga, ON L5T 2N7
905/564-6622, Fax: 905/564-5744
Executive Administrator, Carol S. Elford
Publications: On the Level; Annual Masonry Magazine
Affiliates: Ontario Masonry Contractors' Association; Metro Mason Contractors Association; Canada Masonry Centre

## Canadian Paint & Coatings Association/ L'Association canadienne de l'industrie de la peinture et du revêtement (CPCA) (1913)
#103, 9900, boul Cavendish, Saint Laurent, QC H4M 2V2
514/745-2611, Fax: 514/745-2031
President, Dick Murry
Publications: Associ-Action

## Canadian Portland Cement Association/ Association canadienne du ciment Portland (CPCA)
#206, 60 Queen St., Ottawa, ON K1P 5Y7
613/236-9471, Fax: 613/563-4498, Email: 75201.3423@ compuserve.com, URL: http:// www.buildingweb.com/cpca/index.html
Director, National Operations, Norman F. Macleod

## Canadian Prestressed Concrete Institute/Institut canadien du béton précontraint (CPCI) (1961)
#100, 196 Bronson Ave., Ottawa, ON K1R 6H4
613/232-2619, Fax: 613/232-5139, Email: cpci@ fox.nstn.ca, URL: http://www.buildingweb.com/ cpci/
President, J.R. Fowler
Executive Secretary, Donna White
Publications: Update

## Canadian Ready Mix Concrete Association
365 Brunel Rd., Mississauga, ON L4Z 1Z5
905/507-1122, Fax: 905/890-8122
Sec.-Treas., John D. Hull

#### ALBERTA READY-MIXED CONCRETE ASSOCIATION (1961)
#201, 9333 - 45 Ave., Edmonton, AB T6E 5Z7
403/436-5645, Fax: 403/436-4910
Email: armca@connect.ab.ca, URL: http:// www.constructworld.com/armca/
Executive Administrator, Ed Kalis
Publications: The Mixer

#### ATLANTIC PROVINCES READY-MIXED CONCRETE ASSOCIATION/ ASSOCIATION DES FABRICANTS DE BÉTON PRÉPARÉ DES PROVINCES ATLANTIQUES (APRMCA) (1966)
PO Box 99, Lakeside, NS B3T 1M6
902/454-0139, Fax: 902/454-0164
Marketing Director, John M. Connely
Publications: Ready Mix News
Affiliates: Canadian Portland Cement Association

#### MANITOBA READY-MIXED CONCRETE ASSOCIATION INC.
14 Mitchelson Way, Winnipeg, MB R2G 4E1
204/667-8539
President, Gary Kurz
Secretary, Angie Both

#### READY MIXED CONCRETE ASSOCIATION OF ONTARIO (RMCAO) (1959)
365 Brunel Rd., Mississauga, ON L4Z 1Z5
905/507-1122, Fax: 905/890-8122
Executive Director, John D. Hull
Publications: Flash; Directory of Members & Reference Manual, s-a.

#### SASKATCHEWAN READY-MIXED CONCRETE ASSOCIATION INC.
1024 Winnipeg St., Regina, SK S4R 8P8
306/757-2788, Fax: 306/757-5410
Executive Director, Garth Sanders

## Canadian Renovators' Council
c/o A.B. Cameron, #850, 10201 Southport Rd. SW, Calgary, AB T2W 4X9
403/531-2700, Fax: 403/531-2707
Secretary, Alexander B. Cameron

## Canadian Retail Building Supply Council/Conseil canadian des détaillants de matériaux de construction (CRBSC)
#1004, 213 Notre Dame Ave., Winnipeg, MB R3B 1N3
204/957-1077, Fax: 204/947-5195, Toll Free: 1-800-661-0253
President, Judy Huston

#### ASSOCIATION DES DÉTAILLANTS DE MATÉRIAUX DE CONSTRUCTION DU QUÉBEC/QUÉBEC BUILDING MATERIALS DEALERS ASSOCIATION (ADMACQ) (1940)
474, Place Trans-Canada, Longueuil, QC J4G 1N8
514/646-5842, Téléc: 514/646-6171
Vice-président exécutif, Gabriel Pollender
Président, Renelle Anctil
Secrétaire-administrative, Lisette Leduc
Publications: Quart de Rond; Répertoire annuel
Organisation(s) affiliée(s): Conseil québécois du commerce de détail

#### ATLANTIC BUILDING SUPPLY DEALERS ASSOCIATION (ABSDA) (1954)
#203, 95 Foundry St., Moncton, NB E1C 5H7
506/858-0700, Fax: 506/859-0064, Toll Free: 1-800-561-7114
Email: absda@fox.nstn.ca, URL: http://Fox.nstn.ca/ ~absda/
President, John J. Ward
Chairman of the Board, Joe Corcoran
Publications: Atlantic Building Supply News

#### BUILDING SUPPLY DEALERS ASSOCIATION OF BRITISH COLUMBIA (1938)
#2, 19299 - 94 Ave., Surrey, BC V4N 4E6
604/513-2205, Fax: 604/513-2206
Executive Director, George R. Tracy
Publications: BSDA News Magazine; Annual Directory

#### LUMBER & BUILDING MATERIALS ASSOCIATION OF ONTARIO (LBMAO) (1917)
4500 Sheppard Ave. East, Unit F, Scarborough, ON M1S 3R6
416/298-1731, Fax: 416/298-4865, Toll Free: 1-800-465-5270
Executive Director, Stephen J. Johns
Publications: Directory of Ontario Lumber & Building; LBMAO Reporter
Affiliates: Retail Council of Canada

#### WESTERN RETAIL LUMBERMEN'S ASSOCIATION INC. (WRLA) (1890)
#1004, 213 Notre Dame Ave., Winnipeg, MB R3B 1N3
204/957-1077, Fax: 204/947-5195, Toll Free: 1-800-661-0253
Email: wrla@wrla.org
Executive Director, Judy Huston
President, Chuck Fischer
Publications: Yardstick; WRLA Directory, a.

## Canadian Roofing Contractors' Association/ Association canadienne des entrepreneurs en couverture (CRCA) (1960)
#1300, 155 Queen St., Ottawa, ON K1P 6L1
613/232-6724, Fax: 613/232-2893
Executive Director, John E. Hill
Publications: Roofing Canada
Affiliates: Construction Specifications Canada

#### ALBERTA ROOFING CONTRACTORS ASSOCIATION LTD. (ARCA) (1961)
2725 - 12 St. NE, Calgary, AB T2E 7J2
403/250-7055, Fax: 403/250-1702, Toll Free: 1-800-382-8515
Executive Manager, Dennis Looten
Affiliates: National Roofing Contractors Association USA

#### ASSOCIATION DES MAÎTRES COUVREURS DU QUÉBEC/QUÉBEC MASTER ROOFERS ASSOCIATION (AMCQ) (1967)
#3001, boul Tessier, Laval, QC H7S 2M1
514/973-2322, Téléc: 514/973-2321
Directrice administrative, Micheline Bonnaud
Publications: Nouvelles AMCQ; Membres, annuel

#### NEW BRUNSWICK ROOFING CONTRACTORS ASSOCIATION, INC.
PO Box 7242, Saint John, NB E2L 4S6
506/652-7003, Fax: 506/634-8765
Manager, Sean Darrah

#### ONTARIO INDUSTRIAL ROOFING CONTRACTORS' ASSOCIATION (OIRCA) (1964)
#207, 5233 Dundas St. West, Islington, ON M9B 1A6
416/239-9655, Fax: 416/239-6693
Executive Director, Don B. Marks
Publications: Ontario Roofing News

#### ROOFING CONTRACTORS ASSOCIATION OF BRITISH COLUMBIA (RCABC) (1958)
RCABC Roofing Institute
9734 - 201st St., Langley, BC V1M 3E8
604/882-9734, Fax: 604/882-1744
Email: roofing@rcabc.org, URL: http://www.rcabc.org
Executive Vice-President, George Fraser, CAE
Publications: RCABC on Top
Affiliates: International Federation of Roofing Contractors

#### ROOFING CONTRACTORS ASSOCIATION OF MANITOBA INC. (RCAM) (1966)
290 Burnell St., Winnipeg, MB R3G 2A7
204/783-6365, Fax: 204/783-6446
Secretary Manager, R.M. Stefanick

#### ROOFING CONTRACTORS' ASSOCIATION OF NOVA SCOTIA
112 Blue Water Rd., Bedford, NS B4B 1G7
902/835-0113, Fax: 902/835-4888
Secretary, Marg Woodworth

#### SASKATCHEWAN ROOFING CONTRACTORS ASSOCIATION
1935 Elphinstone St., Regina, SK S4T 3N3
306/721-8020, Fax: 306/565-2840
Manager, Marlene McLarty

## Canadian Welding Bureau (1947)
7250 West Credit Ave., Mississauga, ON L5N 5N1
905/542-1312, Fax: 905/542-1318, Email: info@ cwbgroup.com, URL: http://www.cwbgroup.com
President/CEO, D.E.H. Reynolds
Publications: CWB Net

## Clay Brick Association of Canada/Association canadienne de brique d'argile cuite (CBAC) (1973)
#105, 5409 Eglinton Ave., Etobicoke, ON M9C 5K6
416/695-8388, Fax: 416/695-8399
National Accounts Executive, Peter Quigley
Office Manager, Michelle Hoby

## Conseil provincial du Québec des métiers de la construction (CPQMC)
#228, 4881, rue Jarry est, Montréal, QC H1R 1Y1
514/323-9770, Téléc: 514/323-5042
Directeur général, Maurice Pouliot

## Construction Specifications Canada/Devis de construction Canada (CSC) (1954)
#200, 100 Lombard St., Toronto, ON M5C 1M3
416/777-2198, Fax: 416/777-2197, Email: 74722.520@ compuserve.com, URL: http://www.csc-dcc.ca
Executive Director, Nick Franjic, CAE
President, Gerry Wilson, RSW
Publications: Construction Canada; The Specifier, m.
Affiliates: Construction Specification Foundation; Construction Specifications Canada/Alberta Section Training Trust Fund; Construction Specifications Institute; Canadian Standards Association; Mechanical Contractors Association of Canada; Ontario Bid Depository Council; Alberta Building Envelope Council; Alberta Roofing Contractor's Association; Canadian Institute of

Plumbing & Heating; Association of Professional Engineers of Canada; Royal Architectural Institute of Canada; Canadian Contruction Association; Toronto Constuction Association; Society of the Plastics Industry of Canada; Thermal Insulation Association of Canada

**Council of Ontario Construction Associations (COCA) (1974)**
#602, 920 Yonge St., Toronto, ON M4W 3C7
416/968-7200, Fax: 416/968-0362
Executive Vice-President, David Frame
President, David Surplis

**Master Insulators' Association of Ontario Inc.**
The Airway Centre, #525, 5915 Airport Rd., Mississauga, ON L4V 1T1
905/673-0004
Manager, Peter Woloszanskyj
Affiliates: Chapter of Thermal Insulation Association of Canada

**Master Painters & Decorators Association of British Columbia (1911)**
4090 Graveley St., Burnaby, BC V5C 3T6
604/298-7578, Fax: 604/298-5183
President, Alan Kelly
Manager, Barry G. Law

**Mechanical Contractors Association of Canada/ Association des entrepreneurs en mécanique du Canada**
#408, 116 Albert St., Ottawa, ON K1P 5G3
613/232-0492, Fax: 613/235-2793
President, Richard McKeagan
Affiliates: Council of Construction Trade Associations

**MECHANICAL CONTRACTORS ASSOCIATION OF ALBERTA**
#204, 2725 - 12 St. NE, Calgary, AB T2E 7J2
403/250-7237, Fax: 403/291-0551
Contact, H. Tiedemann

**MECHANICAL CONTRACTORS ASSOCIATION OF BRITISH COLUMBIA (MCA-BC) (1902)**
3210 Lake City Way, Burnaby, BC V5A 3A4
604/420-9714, Fax: 604/420-0127
Executive Vice-President, Dana M. Taylor
President, Keith Hodgson
Manager, Membership Services, Aryeh Meir
Publications: Report to Members; Mechanical Contractor, q.

**MECHANICAL CONTRACTORS ASSOCIATION OF MANITOBA (MCAM) (1970)**
860 Bradford St., Winnipeg, MB R3H 0N5
204/774-2404, Fax: 204/772-0233
Executive Director, Don Shannon
Publications: MCAM Newsletter

**MECHANICAL CONTRACTORS ASSOCIATION OF NEW BRUNSWICK/ ASSOCIATION DES ENTREPRENEURS EN MÉCHANIQUE DU N.-B. (1976)**
105 Prospect St., Fredericton, NB E3B 2T7
506/452-0150, Fax: 506/450-8106
Email: bdixon@nbnet.nb.ca
President, Bill Dixon
Publications: Mechanical News & Views
Affiliates: Canadian Construction Association

**MECHANICAL CONTRACTORS ASSOCIATION OF NEWFOUNDLAND & LABRADOR**
PO Box 22, Pouch Cove, NF A0A 3L0
709/335-2875
Contact, Mary O'Keefe

**MECHANICAL CONTRACTORS ASSOCIATION OF NOVA SCOTIA**
c/o Constuction Association of Nova Scotia, PO Box 47040, Halifax, NS B3K 5Y2
902/429-6760, Fax: 902/429-3965
Manager, Donna Lewis

**MECHANICAL CONTRACTORS ASSOCIATION OF ONTARIO**
#105, 7 Director Ct., Woodbridge, ON L4L 4S5
905/856-0342, Fax: 905/856-0385
Executive Vice-President, Steve Coleman

**MECHANICAL CONTRACTORS ASSOCIATION OF PRINCE EDWARD ISLAND**
c/o Construction Association of PEI, PO Box 728, Charlottetown, PE C1A 7L3
902/368-3303, Fax: 902/894-9757
Manager, Francis Reid

**MECHANICAL CONTRACTORS ASSOCIATION OF SASKATCHEWAN INC.**
#32, 1736 Quebec Ave., Saskatoon, SK S7K 1V9
306/664-2154, Fax: 306/653-7233
Executive Director, Judy Nagus

**National Building Envelope Council**
18 Crispin Private, Ottawa, ON K1K 2T8
613/747-0251
Executive Director, Rick Quirouette

**National Elevator & Escalator Association (NEEA) (1977)**
#708, 6299 Airport Rd., Mississauga, ON L4V 1N3
905/678-9940, Fax: 905/677-7634
Executive Director, Andrew Reistetter

**Ontario Carpentry Contractors Association**
#305, One Greensboro Dr., Etobicoke, ON M9W 1C8
416/248-6213
Executive Director, Mauro Angeloni

**Ontario Concrete Block Association (OCBA) (1962)**
#101, 1013 Wilson Ave., Downsview, ON M3K 1G1
416/630-9944, Fax: 416/630-1916
Executive Director, M.A. Patamia
Publications: Block Focus; Design Focus, s-a.

**Ontario Concrete & Drain Contractors Association (1981)**
#6, 400 Creditstone Rd., Concord, ON L4K 3Z3
905/660-7676, Fax: 905/660-7611
Managing Director, P. Celsi

**Ontario Concrete Pipe Association (OCPA) (1957)**
#508, 6299 Airport Rd., Mississauga, ON L4V 1N6
905/677-1010, Fax: 905/677-1007, Toll Free: 1-800-435-0116, Email: ccpa@ican.ca, URL: http://www.ccpa.com
Marketing Director, A. Grant Lee
Chair, Sue Tanenbaum
Sec.-Treas., Ed McMenamin
Affiliates: Municipal Engineers Association; Canadian Concrete Pipe Association; Tubecon; American Concrete Pipe Association; Canadian Portland Cement Association; Water Environment Association of Ontario; Canadian Public Works Association; Ontario Sewer & Watermain Construction Association

**Ontario Erectors Association**
#210, 277 Lakeshore Rd. East, Oakville, ON L6J 1H9
905/849-7219, Fax: 905/849-6798
President, William Jemison

**Ontario Painting Contractors Association (OPCA) (1976)**
#305, 211 Consumers Rd., North York, ON M2J 4G8
416/498-1897, Fax: 416/498-6757, Toll Free: 1-800-461-3630
Executive Director, Maureen Marquardt, CAE
Publications: Brush Strokes
Affiliates: Federation of Painting & Decorating Contractors of Toronto

**Ontario Sewer & Watermain Construction Association (OSWCA) (1970)**
#300, 5045 Orbitor Dr., Unit 12, Mississauga, ON L4W 4Y4
905/629-7766, Fax: 905/629-0587
Executive Director, Sam Morra
Assistant Executive Director, J. Flannigan
Publications: The Undergrounder

**Pipe Line Contractors Association of Canada (PLCAC) (1954)**
#720, 5915 Airport Rd., Mississauga, ON L4V 1T1
905/673-0544, Fax: 905/673-0546
Executive Director, Barry L. Brown
Publications: Pipeline

**Sealant & Waterproofing Association (SWA) (1989)**
70 Leek Cres., Richmond Hill, ON L4B 1H1
416/499-4000, Fax: 416/499-8752
Secretary, Mary Thorburn

**Structural Board Association/Association du panneaux structural (SBA) (1976)**
#412, 45 Sheppard Ave. East, North York, ON M2N 5W9
416/730-9090, Fax: 416/730-9013, URL: http://www.sba-osb.com/
President, John D. Lowood, P.Eng

**Terrazzo Tile & Marble Association of Canada**
#5, 30 Capstan Gate, Concord, ON L4K 3E8
905/660-9640, Fax: 905/660-5706
Executive Director, Bob Sanelli

## BUSINESS

***see also* Consumers; Management & Administration; Retail Trade; Trade**

**Business Council of British Columbia (1966)**
#810, 1050 Pender St. West, Vancouver, BC V6E 3S7
604/684-3384, Fax: 604/684-7957
President/CEO, Jerry L. Lampert
Vice-President, Finance & Administration, Barbara Seymour-Gray
Chairman, Jim Shepard
Publications: Industrial Relations Bulletin; Government Directory, a.; Policy Perspectives; President's Report; BC Economic Update, q.; Collective Bargaining Review & Outlook, a.

**Business Council on National Issues/Conseil canadien des chefs d'entreprise (BCNI) (1976)**
Royal Bank Centre, #806, 90 Sparks St., Ottawa, ON K1P 5B4
613/238-3727, Fax: 613/236-8679
President/Chief Executive, Thomas d'Aquino
Vice-President, Finance & Administration, Patricia A. Longino

**Calmeadow (1983)**
#600, 365 Bay St., Toronto, ON M5H 2V1
416/362-9670, Fax: 416/362-0769, Email: calmead@inforamp.net
President, Martin P. Connell
Vice-President, Linda Haynes
COO, Paul Royds

**Canadian Association for Corporate Growth (CACG) (1973)**
c/o ABN AMRO Bank Canada, 15th Fl., Aetna Tower, T-D Centre, PO Box 114, Stn Toronto Dominion, Toronto, ON M5K 1G8

416/365-2932, Fax: 416/367-1485
President, Mark Borkowski
Administrator, Barbara Corder

### Canadian Association of Family Enterprise/ Association canadienne des enterprises familiales (CAFE) (1983)
1163 Sylvester St., PO Box 136, Lefroy, ON L0L 1W0
705/456-4900, Fax: 705/456-4962, Email: ucstaff@cafe-uc.on.ca, URL: http://www.cafe-uc.on.ca/
Publications: The Family Enterpriser

### The Canadian Centre for Business in the Community/Le Centre Canadien des Relations Entre L'Enterprise et la Collectivité (IDPAR)
255 Smyth Rd., Ottawa, ON K1H 8M7
613/526-3280, Fax: 613/526-4857
Director, George M. Khoury
Publications: Campaigns Outlook; Corporate Community Investment in Canada; The IDPAR Newsletter, 3 pa

### Canadian Council of Better Business Bureaus/ Conseil canadien des bureaux d'éthique commerciale (CCBBB) (1972)
#368, 7330 Fisher St. SE, Calgary, AB T2H 2H8
403/531-8686, Fax: 403/531-8697
President, Wayne Lovely
Chairman, Raymond Whalen

#### BETTER BUSINESS BUREAU OF CENTRAL & NORTHERN ALBERTA (1957)
Capitol Place, #514, 9707 - 110 St., Edmonton, AB T5K 2L9
403/482-2341, Fax: 403/482-1150
President, P. Ross Bradford

#### BETTER BUSINESS BUREAU OF MAINLAND BC (1939)
#404, 788 Beatty St., Vancouver, BC V6B 2M1
604/682-2711, Fax: 604/681-1544
Email: bbbmail@bbbmbc.com, URL: http://www.bbbmbc.com
Executive Vice-President, Carol E. Tulk
Publications: Newsletter; Business Advisor, a.; Buyers' Guide

#### BETTER BUSINESS BUREAU OF MID-WESTERN ONTARIO
354 Charles St., Kitchener, ON N2G 4L5
519/579-3080, Fax: 519/570-0072
President, Patricia J. Tallman

#### BETTER BUSINESS BUREAU OF NEWFOUNDLAND
360 Topsail Rd., PO Box 516, St. John's, NF A1E 2B6
709/364-2222, Fax: 709/364-2255
Manager, Betty Mulrooney

#### BETTER BUSINESS BUREAU OF NOVA SCOTIA (1949)
#601, 1888 Brunswick St., Halifax, NS B3J 3J8
902/422-6581, Fax: 902/429-6457
Email: bbbns@bbbns.com, URL: http://www.bbbns.com/bbbns
Executive Director, Louis A. Gannon Jr.

#### BETTER BUSINESS BUREAU OF OTTAWA & HULL (1937)
#603, 130 Albert St., Ottawa, ON K1P 5G4
613/237-4856, 233-3562, Fax: 613/237-4878
Executive Director, Leslie King
Publications: Newsletter

#### BETTER BUSINESS BUREAU OF SASKATCHEWAN
#302, 2080 Broad St., Regina, SK S4P 1Y3
306/352-7601, Fax: 306/565-6236
Executive Director, Eileen McLeod

#### BETTER BUSINESS BUREAU OF SOUTH CENTRAL ONTARIO (1973)
100 King St. East, Hamilton, ON L8N 1A8
905/526-1112, Fax: 905/526-1225

#### BETTER BUSINESS BUREAU OF SOUTHERN ALBERTA (1955)
#350, 7330 Fisher St. SE, Calgary, AB T2H 2H8
403/531-8784
President, Norman Haines
General Manager, V.A. Briggs
Publications: Examiner

#### BETTER BUSINESS BUREAU OF VANCOUVER ISLAND (1962)
#201, 1005 Langley St., Victoria, BC V8W 1V7
250/386-6348, Fax: 250/386-2367
Contact, Susan Brice, Bus: 250/386-1416, Fax: 250/386-2367
Publications: The Better Business Bureau of Vancouver Island Membership Directory/ Consumer Guide

#### BETTER BUSINESS BUREAU OF WESTERN ONTARIO (1983)
#616, 200 Queens Ave., London, ON N6A 1J3
519/673-3222, Fax: 519/673-5966
President, Janet B. Delaney
Publications: Membership Directory & Information Guide

#### BETTER BUSINESS BUREAU OF WINDSOR & SOUTHERN ONTARIO
500 Riverside Dr. West, Windsor, ON N9A 5K6
519/258-7222, Fax: 519/258-1198
Email: wbbb@wincom.net, URL: http://www.wincom.net/wbbb/
President, Joseph L. Amort

#### BETTER BUSINESS BUREAU OF WINNIPEG & MANITOBA (1930)
#301, 365 Hargrave St., Winnipeg, MB R3B 2K3
204/989-9010, Fax: 204/989-9016
Manager, T.S. Durham
Publications: Dateline Winnipeg

#### BUREAU D'ÉTHIQUE COMMERCIALE DE MONTRÉAL INC./BETTER BUSINESS BUREAU OF MONTRÉAL INC. (1928)
#460, 2055, rue Peel, Montréal, QC H3A 1V4
514/286-1236, Téléc: 514/286-2658
Présidente, Johanne Bouchard
Publications: Annuaire de la Confiance

#### BUREAU D'ÉTHIQUE COMMERCIALE DE QUÉBEC INC./BETTER BUSINESS BUREAU OF QUÉBEC INC. (1947)
485, rue Richelieu, Québec, QC G1R 1K2
418/523-2555, Téléc: 418/523-2444
Vice-président executif, Jules Martineau

### Canadian Council for International Business/ Conseil canadien pour le commerce international (CCIB) (1990)
**Canadian Secretariat ICC/BIAC**
#1160, 55 Metcalfe St., Ottawa, ON K1P 6L2
613/230-5462, Fax: 613/230-7087
President/CEO, Timothy I. Page
Publications: CCIB Newsletter
Affiliates: International Chamber of Commerce; Business & Industry Advisory Committee to the OECD

### Canadian Council for Public-Private Partnerships/Le conseil canadien des sociétés publiques-privées (C2P3) (1993)
#4700, Toronto Dominion Bank Tower, PO Box 48, Stn Toronto Dominion, Toronto, ON M5K 1E6
416/601-8333, Fax: 416/868-0673, Email: partners@pppcouncil.ca, URL: http://www.inforamp.net/~partners
Executive Administrator, Anne Dudman
President, Glenna Carr
Chair, The Hon. Donald S. Macdonald
Vice-President, Blair Cowper-Smith
Publications: Public-Private Review
Affiliates: Federation of Canadian Municipalities; Canadian Water & Wastewater Association

### Canadian Federation of Independent Business/ Fédération canadienne de l'entreprise indépendante (CFIB) (1972)
#401, 4141 Yonge St., North York, ON M2P 2A6
416/222-8022, Fax: 416/222-4337, Email: cfib@cfib.ca, URL: http://www.cfib.ca
Chairman & CEO, John Bulloch
President, Catherine Swift
Senior Vice-President, Communications, Dave Hill
Bureau du Québec: Press Attaché, Delphine Mantha, #900, 500, boul René-Lévesque ouest, Montréal, QC H2Z 1W7, 514/861-3234, Téléc: 514/861-1711

### Canadian Franchise Association/Association canadienne de la franchise (CFA) (1989)
#201, 5045 Orbitor Dr., Bldg. 12, Mississauga, ON L4W 4Y4
905/625-2896, Fax: 905/625-9076, Toll Free: 1-800-665-4232, Email: info@cfa.ca, URL: http://www.cfa.ca
President, Richard Cunningham

### Canadian Institute of Chartered Business Valuators (CICBV) (1971)
277 Wellington St. West, Toronto, ON M5V 3H2
416/204-3396, Fax: 416/977-8585
Executive Director, Denis R.T. White
Administrator, Kitty Jones
President, D. Jeffrey Harder, CBV
Vice-President, Peter A. Miller
Sec.-Treas., Donald M. Spence
Publications: The Business Valuator; Journal of Business Valuation, a.; Valuation Law Review; Business Valuator Digest

### Canadian International Institute of Applied Negotiation/L'Institut international canadien de la négociation pratique (CIIAN) (1992)
#1422, 50 O'Connor St., Ottawa, ON K1P 6L2
613/237-9050, Fax: 613/230-1651, Email: conciian@intranet.on.ca
CEO, Benjamin Hoffman

### Canadian Labour Market & Productivity Centre/ Centre canadien du marché du travail et de la productivité (CLMPC) (1984)
55 Metcalfe St., 15th Fl., Ottawa, ON K1P 6L5
613/234-0505, Fax: 613/234-2482, Email: clmpc@magi.com, URL: http://www.clmpc.ca
CEO, Shirley Seward
Publications: Working Together

### Canadian Organization of Small Business Inc. (COSBI) (1979)
**The Voice of Business**
PO Box 11246, Stn Main, Edmonton, AB T5H 3J5
403/423-2672, Fax: 403/423-2751
Managing Director, Donald Richard Eastcott
Chairman, Roy E. Shannon, C.A.
Publications: The Voice of Business
Eastern Office: Manager, Leonard Domino, Skymark Place, 3555 Don Mills Rd., Unit 6-105, North York, ON M2H 3N3, 416/539-7324, Fax: 416/537-7324

### Canadian Professional Sales Association/ Association canadienne des professionnels de la vente (CPSA) (1874)
#310, 145 Wellington St. West, Toronto, ON M5J 1H8
416/408-2685, Fax: 416/408-2684, Toll Free: 1-800-267-2772, Email: membership@cpsa.com, URL: http://www.cpsa.com
President, Terry J. Ruffell
Director, Sharon Armstrong
Publications: Contact; Travel Services, a.; Professional Development Services; Business Travel Survey; Guide to Car Costs & Policies; Canadian Sales Management Manual

**Canadian Quality Council**
1229 Meadow Brook Dr., Airdrie, AB T4A 1W7
403/948-3959, Fax: 403/948-3959
President, Kenneth Kivenko
Managing Director, Dirk Bannister
Event Manager, Sarah Kennedy
Publications: Canada Quality Journal

**Canadian Society of Customs Brokers/Société canadienne des courtiers en douane (CSCB) (1991)**
111 York St., Ottawa, ON K1N 5T4
613/562-3543, Fax: 613/562-3548, Email: cscb@cscb.ca, URL: http://www.cscb.ca
President, Carol West
Senior Policy Officer, M. Janice McBride
Publications: CSCB Bulletin
Affiliates: International Federation of Customs Brokers Associations

**Canadian Turnaround Management Association/Association canadienne de redressement d'entreprises (CTMA) (1983)**
1980, rue Sherbrooke ouest, 10e étage, Montréal, QC H3H 1E5
514/937-6392, Fax: 514/933-9710
National Chairman, Harry H. Feldman, FCA
Vice-President, Bob Coffey
Secretary, Alan Mass
Treasurer, Stuart Mitchell
Publications: Journal of Corporate Renewal
Affiliates: Turnaround Management Association of America (TMA)

**Canadian Youth Business Foundation/La Fondation canadienne des jeunes entrepreneurs (CYBF) (1996)**
#221, 40 Dundas St. West, PO Box 44, Toronto, ON M5G 2C2
416/408-2923, Fax: 416/408-3234, Toll Free: 1-800-464-2923, Email: info@cybf.ca, URL: http://www.cybf.ca
Executive Director, Anne Cira
Publications: Youth Business

**Conseil du patronat du Québec (CPQ) (1969)**
#606, 2075, rue Université, Montréal, QC H3A 2L1
514/288-5161, Téléc: 514/288-5165
Président, Ghislain Dufour
Publications: Bulletin d'information

**Foundation for the Advancement of Canadian Entrepreneurship (FACE)**
49 Wellington St. East, Toronto, ON M5E 1C9
416/363-9182

**Hong Kong-Canada Business Association/L'Association commerciale Hong Kong-Canada (HKCBA) (1984)**
9 Temperance St., 2nd Fl., Toronto, ON M5H 1Y6
416/368-8277, Fax: 416/368-4321, Email: davidhui@netcom.ca, URL: http://www.hkcba.com
National Executive Director, David Hui
National Chair, David I. Matheson, QC, Bus: 416/865-3430, Fax: 416/863-1515
Publications: Hong Kong Monitor

**International Association of Business Communicators/Toronto (1942)**
**IABC/Toronto**
#1807, 365 Bloor St. East, Toronto, ON M4W 3L4
416/968-0264, Fax: 416/968-6818, Email: info@iabctoronto.com, URL: http://www.iabctoronto.com
President, Karen Schwartz, ABC
Account Manager, Eden Spodek

**Meeting Professionals International (MPI) (1972)**
#5018, 1950 Stemmons Freeway, Dallas, TX 75207-3109 USA
214/712-7750, Fax: 214/746-7770, Telex: 535109 MPL
CEO, Edwin L. Griffin, Jr., CAE
Director of Marketing, Gary E. Boyler
Publications: The Meeting Manager; Membership Directory, a.; MPI Express
Toronto Chapter: Executive Director, Leslie Wright; President, Marsha Jones, CMP, 6519B Mississauga Rd., Mississauga, ON L5N 1A6, 905/567-9591, Fax: 905/567-9961

**Mouvement québécois de la qualité**
#L600, 455, rue Saint-Antoine ouest, Montréal, QC H2Z 1J1
514/874-9933, Téléc: 514/866-4600
Directrice administrative, Johanne Cholette
Publications: Forum Qualité; Qualité totale, trimestriel

**The National Citizens' Coalition (1967)**
#907, 100 Adelaide St. West, Toronto, ON M5H 1S3
416/869-3838, Fax: 416/869-1891
President, David E.T. Somerville
Chairman, Colin T. Brown

**National Quality Institute/Institut national de la qualité (NQI) (1992)**
#307, 2275 Lakeshore West Blvd., Etobicoke, ON M8V 3Y3
416/251-7600, Fax: 416/251-9131, Toll Free: 1-800-263-9648, Email: info@nqionline.com, URL: http://www.nqi.com
Executive Director, John Perry
COO, Ken Scott, CMA
Publications: NQI Newsletter

**Ontario Public Buyers Association, Inc. (OPBA) (1952)**
Ridley Square, #361, 111 Fourth Ave., St Catharines, ON L2S 3P5
905/682-3788, Fax: 905/682-3788, URL: http://vaxxine.com/opba
President, Kathryn Davey
Vice-President, Patricia Baird
Secretary, Lynda Allair
Treasurer, David Farrar
Publications: Caveat Emptor; Purchasing Manual
Affiliates: National Institute of Governmental Purchasing, Inc.; Institute of Purchasing & Supply of Great Britain; International Federation of Purchasing & Materials Management

**Pacific Corridor Enterprise Council (PACE) (1990)**
#1300, 720 Olive Way, Seattle, WA 98101-1812 USA
206/626-5474, Fax: 206/223-8984, Toll Free: 1-800-800-PACE
Chairman, Warren Wheeler
President, P. J. Fraser
Publications: Keeping PACE

**CARGO HANDLING *see* TRANSPORTATION & SHIPPING**

**CASH MANAGEMENT *see* FINANCE**

**CENTRAIDE *see* SOCIAL RESPONSE/SOCIAL SERVICES**

## CHEMICAL INDUSTRY

**Canadian Association of Chemical Distributors/Association canadienne des distributeurs de produits chimiques (CACD) (1986)**
#301, 627 Lyons Lane, Oakville, ON L6J 5Z7
905/844-9140, Fax: 905/844-5706, Email: cacd@cacd.ca
Executive Director, Aud Harlow

**Canadian Chemical Producers' Association/Association canadienne des fabricants de produits chimiques (CCPA) (1962)**
#805, 350 Sparks St., Ottawa, ON K1R 7S8
613/237-6215, Fax: 613/237-4061, Toll Free: 1-800-267-6666, Email: ciric@ccpa.ca, URL: http://www.ccpa.ca
President & CEO, Richard Paton
Vice-President, Business Development/Sec.-Treas., D.W. Goffin
Vice-President, Technical Affairs, G.E. Lloyd
Director of Public Affairs, E.E. Alexander
Vice-President, Responsible Care, B.R. Wastle
Executive Assistant, Charlaine Gendron
Publications: Reducing Emissions Report

**Canadian Explosives Distributors Association/Association des distributeurs d'explosifs du Canada**
**CEDEC**
35 Phylis St., Nepean, ON K2J 1W5
613/825-2989, Fax: 613/723-0013
Manager, René A. Morin
Manager, Doris Morin

**Canadian Fertilizer Institute/L'Institut Canadien des Engrais (CFI)**
#1540, 222 Queen St., Ottawa, ON K1P 5V9
613/230-2600, Fax: 613/230-5142
Managing Director, Roger L. Larson

**ASSOCIATION DES FABRICANTS D'ENGRAIS DU QUÉBEC/QUÉBEC FERTILIZER MANUFACTURERS ASSOCIATION (AFEQ) (1956)**
CP 218, Saint-Hyacinthe, QC J2S 7B4
514/779-5081, Téléc: 514/779-3967
Directeur administratif, Donald Côté

**THE ATLANTIC FERTILIZER INSTITUTE (AFI)**
21 Macmillan Cres., Charlottetown, PE C1A 8G3
902/894-9361
Sec.-Treas., Jack Cutcliffe

**CANADIAN ASSOCIATION OF AGRI-RETAILERS (CAAR) (1978)**
#107, 1090 Waverley St., Winnipeg, MB R3T 0P4
204/989-9300, Fax: 204/989-9306
Email: caar@mb.sympatico.ca
Executive Director, Jacqueline Ryrie
Publications: Input; Communicator, q.

**THE FERTILIZER INSTITUTE OF ONTARIO INC. (TFIO)**
#104, 1400 Bishop St., Cambridge, ON N1R 6W8
519/622-4011, Fax: 519/622-7566
Email: tfio@sympatico.ca
Executive Vice-President, Tom G. Sawyer

**Canadian Manufacturers of Chemical Specialties Association/Association canadienne des manufacturiers de spécialités chimiques (CMCS) (1958)**
#702, 56 Sparks St., Ottawa, ON K1P 5A9
613/232-6616, Fax: 613/233-6350, Email: assoc@cmcs.org, URL: http://www.cmcs.org
President, Dr. David Halton
Publications: Microgram; Formulator, a.

**The Chemical Institute of Canada/Institut de chimie du Canada (CIC) (1945)**
#550, 130 Slater St., Ottawa, ON K1P 6E2
613/232-6252, Fax: 613/232-5862, Email: cic_adm@fox.nstn.ca, URL: http://www.chem-inst-can.org
Executive Director, Anne E. Alper
Chair, B. Henry
Publications: Canadian Chemical News/L'Actualité chimique canadienne

**CANADIAN SOCIETY FOR CHEMICAL ENGINEERING/SOCIÉTÉ CANADIENNE DU GÉNIÉ CHIMIQUE (CSCE) (1966)**
#550, 130 Slater St., Ottawa, ON K1P 6E2
613/232-6252, Fax: 613/232-5862
Email: cic_adm@fox.nstn.ca, URL: http://www.chem-inst-can.org
President, Maya Veljkovic
Executive Secretary, Anne E. Alper
Publications: Canadian Journal of Chemical Engineering; Canadian Chemical News, 10 pa

**CANADIAN SOCIETY FOR CHEMICAL TECHNOLOGY/SOCIÉTÉ CANADIENNE DE TECHNOLOGIE CHIMIQUE (CSCT) (1971)**
#550, 130 Slater St., Ottawa, ON K1P 6E2
613/232-6252, Fax: 613/232-5862
Email: cic_adm@fox.nstn.ca, URL: http://www.chem-inst-can.org
Executive Secretary, Anne E. Alper
President, Eric Mead

**CANADIAN SOCIETY FOR CHEMISTRY/SOCIÉTÉ CANADIENNE DE CHIMIE (CSC) (1985)**
#550, 130 Slater St., Ottawa, ON K1P 6E2
613/232-6252, Fax: 613/232-5862
Email: cic_adm@fox.nstn.ca, URL: http://www.chem-inst-can.org
Executive Secretary, Anne E. Alper
President, L. Weiler

**Oil & Colour Chemists' Organization of Ontario (OCCO) (1975)**
125 Jeffcoat Dr., Etobicoke, ON M9W 3B9
416/247-6681, Fax: 416/247-7432
Secretary, John F. Ambury
Chair, David R. Hammett
Education Officer, M. Miller
Affiliates: Oil & Colour Chemists' Association (UK)

**Potash & Phosphate Institute of Canada/Institut potasse et phosphate de Canada (PPIC) (1971)**
704 CN Tower, Midtown Plaza, Saskatoon, SK S7K 1J5
306/652-3535, Fax: 306/664-8941, Email: ldoell@ppi-far.com
President, Dr. Mark D. Stauffer
Publications: Better Crops

**Society of Chemical Industry - Canadian Section (1881)**
c/o Praxair Canada Inc., One City Centre Dr., Mississauga, ON L5B 1M2
905/803-1703, Fax: 905/803-1696
Honorary Secretary, Don Kirkwood
Publications: Chemistry & Industry

**CHILD & FAMILY SERVICES *see* SOCIAL RESPONSE/SOCIAL SERVICES**

## CHILDBIRTH

**Alberta Association of Midwives (AAM)**
#1616, 20 A St. NW, Calgary, AB T2N 2L5
403/289-8334, Fax: 403/932-7777
Joy West/Eklund
Publications: AAM News
Affiliates: International Confederation of Midwives

**Association of Ontario Midwives/Association des sages-femmes de l'Ontario (AOM) (1985)**
#102, 562 Eglinton Ave. East, Toronto, ON M4P 1B9
416/481-2811, Fax: 416/481-7547, Email: midwives@interlog.com
President, Carol Cameron
Publications: AOM Journal

**Infant Feeding Action Coalition**
**INFACT Canada**
10 Trinity Sq., Toronto, ON M5G 1B1
416/595-9819, Fax: 416/598-0292, Email: infact@ftn.net
National Coordinator, Elisabeth Sterken
Publications: INFACT Canada Newsletter

**International Society for the Study of Hypertension in Pregnancy (Canada) Inc./Société internationale pour l'étude de l'hypertension en frossesse (Canada) inc. (ISSHP) (1986)**
Hôpital St-François D'Assise, Dept. OB-GYN, 10, rue de l'Espinay, Québec, QC G1L 3L5
418/525-4461, Fax: 418/525-4481, Email: jean-marie.moutquin@crsfa.ulaval.ca
President, Jean-Marie Moutquin
Publications: Hypertension in Pregnancy

**La Leche League Canada (LLLC) (1961)**
18C Industrial Dr., Chesterville, ON K0C 1H0
613/448-1842, Fax: 613/448-1845
Executive Director, Carol Luck
Publications: New Beginnings
Affiliates: La Leche League International

**Midwifery Task Force of British Columbia**
1108 Rose St., Vancouver, BC V5L 4K8
604/251-5976
Coordinator, Lisa Huggins

**Midwives Association of British Columbia (MABC) (1981)**
#55, 2147 Commercial Dr., Vancouver, BC V5N 5A3
604/436-6007, Fax: 604/255-1076, Info Line: 604/254-0744
Secretary, Sandy Anthony
Publications: MABC Newsletter
Affiliates: International Confederation of Midwives

**Parents of Multiple Births Association of Canada Inc./Association de parents de naissances multiples du Canada inc. (POMBA) (1978)**
240 Graff Ave., PO Box 22005, Stratford, ON N5A 7V6
519/272-2203, Fax: 519/272-1926, Email: office@pomba.org, URL: http://www.pomba.org
President, Lynda P. Haddon
Business Services Director, Anita Grant
Publications: Double Feature; POMBA Reporter, q.

**Serena Canada**
151 Holland Ave., Ottawa, ON K1Y 0Y2
613/728-6536
Executive Director, Marie-Paule Doyle
Affiliates: International Federation for Family Life Promotion

**Vaginal Birth After Caesarean Canada/Accouchement vaginal après césarienne du Canada (1990)**
**VBAC/AVAC Canada**
291 Glencairn Ave., Toronto, ON M5N 1T8
416/489-7710
Coordinator, Caroline Sufrin-Disler
Publications: VBAC/AVAC Canada Newsletter
Alberta: Contact, Bev Yadlowski, 8403 - 77 St., Edmonton, AB T6C 2L7, 403/465-2822
British Columbia: Contact, Laurie Brant, 4006 Nithsdale St., Burnaby, BC V5G 1P6, 604/433-5827

## CHILDREN & YOUTH
***see also* Social Response/Social Services**

**Alberta Associations for Bright Children (AABC) (1981)**
The Bright Site, #1280, 6240 - 113 St., Edmonton, AB T6H 3L2
403/422-0362, Fax: 403/413-1631, Email: aabc@freenet.edmonton.ab.ca, URL: http://www.freenet.edmonton.ab.ca/aabc/
President, Debra Chinchilla
Publications: News Notes

**Association for Bright Children (Ontario)/Société pour enfants doués et surdoués (Ontario) (ABC) (1975)**
#100, 2 Bloor St. West, PO Box 156, Toronto, ON M4W 2G7
416/925-6136, Info Line: 416/925-6136
President, Joanne Lee
Publications: ABC Newsmagazine

**Association for Bright Children of Manitoba (ABC) (1993)**
307 Country Club Blvd., Winnipeg, MB R3K 1X4
204/896-1649, Fax: 204/896-3989
President, Judith Neumann
Publications: Exceptional Times

**B'nai Brith Youth Organization Canada (BBYO)**
**BBYO Canada**
4600 Bathurst St., North York, ON M2R 3V3
416/631-5724, Fax: 416/631-5718
Director, Elizabeth Sokolsky

**Boys & Girls Clubs of Canada/Clubs garçons et filles du Canada (1947)**
#405, 7100 Woodbine Ave., Markham, ON L3R 5G2
905/477-7272, Fax: 905/477-2056, Email: info@bgccan.com, URL: http://www.bgccan.com
National President, William R. Turner
Director, Resource Development, Michael Meadows
Publications: Canada's Kids

**Canadian Association for Young Children/L'Association canadienne pour les jeunes enfants (CAYC) (1974)**
5417 Rannock Ave., Winnipeg, MB R3R 0N3
204/831-1658
President, Gayle Karen Robertson
Publications: Canadian Children

**Canadian Child Care Federation/Fédération canadienne des services de garde à l'enfance (CCCF) (1987)**
#306, 120 Holland Ave., Ottawa, ON K1Y 0X6
613/729-5289, Fax: 613/729-3159
Executive Director, Dianne Bascombe
President, Cathy McCormack
Publications: Interaction; Directory of Canadian Child Care Organizations, biennial

**The Canadian Council for Exceptional Children/Le Conseil canadien de l'enfance exceptionnelle**
#36, 101 Polytek Ct., Gloucester, ON K1J 9J2
613/747-9226, Fax: 613/745-9282
Director, Bill Gowling
Publications: Keeping-in-Touch

**Canadian Young Judaea**
#205, 788 Marlee Ave., Toronto, ON M6B 3K1
416/781-5156, Fax: 416/787-3100
National Executive Director, Risa Epstein-Gamliel
Publications: The Judaean

**Canadian Youth Foundation/La Fondation canadienne de la jeunesse (CYF) (1992)**
215 Cooper St., 3rd Fl., Ottawa, ON K2P 0G2
613/231-6474, Fax: 613/231-6497, Email: cyf@cyf.ca, URL: http://www.cyf.ca
Executive Director, Lucie Bohac Konrad
President, David McGown
Affiliates: Canadian Youth Business Foundation

**Child Find Canada Inc. (1983)**
#508, 710 Dorval Dr., Oakville, ON L6K 3V7

905/845-3463, Fax: 905/845-9621, Toll Free: 1-800-387-7962, Email: childcan@aol.com, URL: http://www.childfind.ca
President, Manuel Legacy
Publications: Missing

#### CHILD FIND ALBERTA (CFA) (1983)
#101, 424 - 10 St. NW, Calgary, AB T2N 1V9
403/270-3463, Fax: 403/270-8355, Toll Free: 1-800-561-1733
Email: childab@aol.com
Executive Director, Eric R. Sommerfeldt
Affiliates: Reseau Enfants Retour

#### CHILD FIND BRITISH COLUMBIA
#200, 1334 Saint Paul St., Kelowna, BC V1Y 2E1
604/763-2022, Fax: 604/860-0843
Executive Director, Maryann Fiske

#### CHILD FIND MANITOBA (1985)
#1110, 405 Broadway, Winnipeg, MB R3C 3L6
204/945-5735, Fax: 204/948-2461, Toll Free: 1-800-387-7962
Email: childmb@aol.com
Executive Director, Myrna Driedger
Administrative Assistant, Michele A. Pitre
Publications: Findings

#### CHILD FIND NEW BRUNSWICK
210 Brunswick St., Fredericton, NB E3B 1G9
506/459-7250, Fax: 506/459-8742
Email: childnb@aol.com
Executive Director, Keith Ross

#### CHILD FIND NEWFOUNDLAND/LABRADOR
Empire West Plaza, #3, 391-95 Empire Ave., St. John's, NF A1E 1W6
709/738-4400, Fax: 709/738-0550
President, Maura Beam

#### CHILD FIND ONTARIO (1983)
#210, 710 Dorval Dr., Oakville, ON L6K 3V7
905/842-5353, Fax: 905/842-5383, Toll Free: 1-800-387-7962
Email: childfind@spectranet.ca
Executive Director, Jackie Cutmore
President, Bev Kennedy

#### CHILD FIND PEI INC. (CFPEI) (1988)
PO Box 1092, Charlottetown, PE C1A 7M4
902/368-1678, Fax: 902/368-1389, Toll Free: 1-800-387-7962
Email: cfpei@isn.net
President, Mary Scott

#### CHILD FIND SASKATCHEWAN INC. (1984)
#41, 1002 Arlington Ave., Saskatoon, SK S7H 2X7
306/955-0070, Fax: 306/373-1311, Toll Free: 1-800-513-3463
Email: childfind@sk.sympatico.ca
President, Phyllis Hallatt

### The Children's Wish Foundation of Canada/ Fondation canadienne rêves d'enfants (1984)
#404, 95 Bayly St. West, Ajax, ON L1S 7K8
905/420-4055, Fax: 905/420-9671, Toll Free: 1-800-267-9474, Email: wishes.national@sympatico.ca, URL: http://www.childrenswish.ca
Executive Director, Laura Cole
National President, Dan Schonberg
Vice-President, Ciro Cucciniello
National Chairman, Lloyd Matthews
Director, PR & Communications, Wendy A. Murray
Publications: Chapters/Chapitres

### Gifted Children's Association of BC (GCA/ BC) (1983)
PO Box 56589, RPO Lougheed Mall, Burnaby, BC V3J 7W2
604/534-6343, Fax: 604/534-9143; URL: http://www.vcn.bc.ca/gca/
President, Rae Desaulniers
Publications: Bright Connections
Affiliates: Coalition for Students with Special Needs

### Giftedness Québec
École secondaire Lemoyne d'Iberville, 560, boul Lemoyne, Longueuil, QC J4H 1X3
514/463-2900, Téléc: 514/463-3954
Personne resource, Anna-Maria F. Dumont

### Girl Guides of Canada/Guides du Canada (1910)
50 Merton St., Toronto, ON M4S 1A3
416/487-5281, Fax: 416/487-5570, URL: http://www.girlguides.ca
Chief Commissioner, Marsha Ross
Executive Director, Christine A. Featherstone
President, Rosalyn Schmidt
Communications Manager, Barbara Crocker
Publications: Canadian Guider
Affiliates: National Youth Serving Agencies; National Voluntary Organizations; Coalition on Rights of the Child; National Council of Women of Canada; Canadian Centre for Philanthropy; Canadian Camping Association; Canadian Council for Adult Education

### Guides francophones du Canada (1962)
3827, rue St. Hubert, Montréal, QC H2L 4A4
514/524-3753, Téléc: 514/524-3755
Présidente, Gilberte Gougeon
Directrice générale, Rita L. Lévesque
Commissaire nationale, Odette Lepage
Publications: Revue

### Heritage of Children of Canada (1984)
73-1/2 Day Ave., Toronto, ON M6E 3W1
416/656-5408
Founder, Sylvia Lusher
Affiliates: Queens Park Legislature, all parties

### Junior Achievement of Canada/Jeunes entreprises du Canada (JACAN) (1967)
One Westside Dr., Toronto, ON M9C 1B2
416/622-4602, Fax: 416/622-6861, Toll Free: 1-800-265-0699
President/CEO, George Habib
Chairman, George E. Harvey
Publications: Revue

### Kids Help Foundation/La fondation Jeunesse (1981)
#410, 60 Bloor St. West, Toronto, ON M4W 1A1
416/920-5437, Fax: 416/920-0651, Toll Free: 1-800-268-3062
National Executive Director, Heather Sproule
President, Stephen Graham
Manager of Development, Sylvia Kadlick

### Manitoba Child Care Association (1974)
364 McGregor St., Winnipeg, MB R2W 4X3
204/586-8587, Fax: 204/589-5613
Executive Director, Dorothy Dudek
Publications: Child Care Focus

### National CGIT Association (CGIT) (1915)
**Canadian Girls in Training**
#414, 195 The West Mall, Etobicoke, ON M9C 5K1
416/622-3979, Fax: 416/622-8356
National Coordinator, Susan Rogers
Publications: Torch; Carrying the Torch, a.; Creating Great Ideas Together, 3 pa
Affiliates: Canadian Baptist Federation; Christian Church (Disciples of Christ) in Canada; The Presbyterian Church in Canada; The United Church of Canada

### Newfoundland & Labrador Association for Gifted Children (NLAGC)
PO Box 21364, St. John's, NF A1A 5G6
President, Susan Duffett
Publications: Newsletter

### Réseau enfants retour Canada/Missing Children's Network Canada (1985)
#406, 231, rue Saint-Jacques, Montréal, QC H2Y 1M6
514/843-4333, Téléc: 514/843-8211, Courrier électronique: missing_children@alliance9000.com, URL: http://www.alliance9000.com/E/MCNC/11.html
Directrice générale, Susan Armstrong
Organisation(s) affiliée(s): Plaidoyer victimes - Montréal; Défense des droits des enfants internationale

### SAFE KIDS Canada/Enfants en Sécurité (1993)
#1300, 180 Dundas St. West, Toronto, ON M5G 1Z8
416/813-6766, Fax: 416/813-4986
Executive Director, Dianne Merrick
Communications Coordinator, Christine Hudson
Publications: Snapshots

### Saskatchewan Council on Children & Youth
PO Box 570, Pilot Butte, SK S0G 3Z0
306/352-1694
Sec.-Treas., Eunice M. Halen

### Scouts Canada (1914)
**Boy Scouts of Canada**
1345 Baseline Rd., PO Box 5151, LCD Merivale, Ottawa, ON K2C 3G7
613/224-5131, Fax: 613/224-3571, Email: mailbox@scouts.ca, URL: http://www.scouts.ca
Chief Executive, John C. Pettifer
President, David Rattray
Executive Director, Operations, Bob Hallett
Director, Sponsor Relations, Bryon Milliere
Executive Director, Communication & Revenue Development, John Rietveld
Director, Communications, Andy McLaughlin
Executive Director, Program Services, Robert J. Stewart
Executive Director, Supply Services, Ben Kruser
Executive Director, International Relations/Special Events, Robert C. Butcher
National Commissioner, Herbert C. Pitts
Information Systems Management, W. Thomas Obright
Publications: Canadian Leader
Affiliates: World Scout Bureau

## CITIZENSHIP & IMMIGRATION

### Canadian Citizenship Federation/Fédération canadienne du civisme (1968)
#402, 396 Cooper St., Ottawa, ON K2P 2H7
613/235-1467, Fax: 613/235-3233
Executive Secretary, Read E. Brook
President, E.J. Desjardins
Treasurer, Pearl Dobson
Publications: Views & News/Nouvelles et idées
Edmonton Chapter: President, Rajendra S. Chopra, 11233 - 34A Ave., Edmonton, AB T6J 3M4
Saint John Chapter: Secretary, Eric L. Teed, O.C., Q.C., PO Box 6446, Stn A, Saint John, NB E2L 4R8, 506/672-6856
Calgary Canadian Citizenship Council: Gita Boyd, #204, 4202 - 17 Ave. SE, Calgary, AB T2A 0T2, 403/272-9455
Greater Victoria Citizenship Council: President, Gladys Swityk, 1113 Fairfield Rd., Victoria, BC V8V 3A8, 250/382-0553

Montréal Citizenship Council: Menelaos Pavlides, 11227, James Morrice, Montréal, QC H3M 2E6, 514/331-5318
Thompson Citizenship Council: Executive Director, Sukh D.H. Khokhar, 97 McGill Pl., Thompson, MB R8N 0H9, 204/677-3981, Fax: 204/778-5145
Vancouver Citizenship Council: President, Rudyard Spence, 7067 Ramsay Ave., Burnaby, BC V5E 3L3, 604/521-8793, Fax: 604/521-8793, Email: rspence@bcit.bc.ca

**Canadian Ukrainian Immigrant Aid Society (CUIAS) (1977)**
#96, 2150 Bloor St. West, Toronto, ON M6S 1M8
416/767-4595, Fax: 416/767-2658
Executive Director, Eugen Duvalko
Affiliates: Ukrainian Canadian Congress

**Chinese Information & Community Services of Greater Toronto (CICS) (1968)**
#310, 3852 Finch Ave. East, Toronto, ON M5T 1N6
416/292-7510, Fax: 416/292-9120, Info Line: 292-7244, Email: cics@ipoline.com, URL: http://www.ipoline.com/cics
Executive Director, Eliot Yip

**Citizenship BC Society (1991)**
268 - 59th Ave. West, Vancouver, BC V5X 1X2
604/321-5223, Fax: 604/321-5283
President, Susan French
Publications: Citizenship BC Newsletter

**Citizenship Council of Manitoba Inc./Conseil Manitobain de la citoyenneté inc. (1948)**
**International Centre of Winnipeg**
406 Edmonton St., Winnipeg, MB R3B 2M2
204/943-9158, Fax: 204/949-0734, Email: miicwpg@web.net
Executive Director, Tom R. Denton
President, R. Kaval Chohan
Publications: Daily
Affiliates: Canadian Council for Refugees

**Cross Cultural Communication Centre (CCCC) (1971)**
2909 Dundas St. West, Toronto, ON M6P 1Z1
416/760-7855, Fax: 416/767-4352
Chairperson, Angela Robertson
Publications: Cross Cultural Communication Centre Newsletter; Toronto Immigrant Services Directory, biennial

**Jewish Immigrant Aid Services of Canada/Services canadiens d'assistance aux immigrants juifs (JIAS) (1922)**
#325, 4600 Bathurst St., North York, ON M2R 3V3
416/630-6481, Fax: 416/630-1376
Director, Perry Romberg

**National Organization of Immigrant & Visible Minority Women of Canada/Organisation nationale des femmes immigrantes et des femmes appartenant à une minorité visible du Canada (NOIVMWC) (1986)**
#504, 251 Bank St., Ottawa, ON K2P 1X3
613/232-0689, Fax: 613/232-0988
Executive Director, Shelley Das
Publications: NOIVMWC News

**Ontario Council of Agencies Serving Immigrants (OCASI) (1977)**
110 Eglinton Ave. West, 2nd Fl., Toronto, ON M4R 1A3
416/322-4950, Fax: 416/322-8082, Email: ocasi1@web.apc.org
Executive Director, Sharmini Peries
President, Kay Blair
Publications: OCASI Newsletter

**Organization of Professional Immigration Consultants (OPIC) (1991)**
Scotia Plaza, #6200, 40 King St. West, Toronto, ON M5H 3Z7
416/495-7965, Fax: 416/495-6373, URL: http://opic.org
President, Charles W. Pley
Publications: Topic

**Ottawa-Carleton Immigrant Services Organization/Organisation des services aux immigrants d'Ottawa-Carleton (OCISO) (1976)**
959 Wellington St., Ottawa, ON K1Y 4W1
613/725-0202, Fax: 613/725-9054, URL: http://www.ncf.carleton.ca/freeport/social.services/cis/ociso/menu
Executive Director, Nancy Worsfold
Publications: Newcomers' Guide to Education in Ottawa-Carleton

**Portuguese Social Service Centre (PSSC) (1969)**
1115 College St., Toronto, ON M6H 1B5
416/533-5507, Fax: 416/533-7175
Executive Director, Vasco Cabral

**Somali Immigrant Aid Organization (1992)**
#21, 698 Weston Rd., Toronto, ON M6N 3R3
416/766-7326, Fax: 416/769-9217
Executive Director, Dr. Mohammed H. Ali

**CIVIL LIBERTIES *see* HUMAN RIGHTS & CIVIL LIBERTIES**

**COLLEGES *see* EDUCATION**

**COMMUNICATIONS *see* TELECOMMUNICATIONS**

**COMMUNITY LIVING ASSOCIATIONS *see* DISABLED PERSONS**

**COMMUNITY PLANNING *see* PLANNING & DEVELOPMENT**

**COMPUTERS *see* INFORMATION TECHNOLOGY**

**CONSERVATION *see* ENVIRONMENTAL**

**CONSTRUCTION *see* BUILDING & CONSTRUCTION**

## CONSUMERS
***see also* Standards & Testing**

**Association des consommateurs du Québec (ACQ)**
7383, rue de la Roche, Montréal, QC H2R 2T4
514/278-5514, Téléc: 514/278-5515
Président, Alain Paquet

**Canadian Society of Consumer Affairs Professionals**
64 Mortimer Ave., Toronto, ON M4K 2A1
416/422-4049
Administrator, Constance Puotinen

**Consumers' Association of Canada/Association des consommateurs du Canada (CAC) (1947)**
#307, 267 O'Connor St., PO Box 9300, Ottawa, ON K1G 3T9
613/238-2533, Fax: 613/563-2254
Executive Director, Marnie McCall
Affiliates: Consumers International, UK; Consumers Union, USA
CAC Alberta: President, Wendy Armstrong, #304, 10136 - 100 St., Edmonton, AB T5J 0P1, 403/426-3270, Fax: 403/425-9578
CAC British Columbia: President, Evelyn Fox, #306, 198 West Hastings St., Vancouver, BC V6B 1H2, 604/682-3535, Fax: 604/682-2920
CAC Manitoba: President, Jackey Wasney, #21, 222 Osborne St. South, Winnipeg, MB R3L 1Z3, 204/452-2572, Fax: 204/284-1876
CAC New Brunswick: President, Mary Wood, PO Box 704, Rothesay, NB E2E 5A8, 506/849-1807
CAC Newfoundland: President, Dr. Robert W. Sexty, 92 Old Topsail Rd., St. John's, NF A1E 2A8, 709/737-4514, Fax: 709/737-7680
CAC Northwest Territories: President, Ruth Spence, 5007 - 50 St., PO Box 995, Yellowknife, NT X1A 2N7, 867/920-8845, Fax: 867/873-4058
CAC Nova Scotia: President, Hanson Dowell, QC, 250 Main St., PO Box 910, Middleton, NS B0S 1P0, 902/825-3059
CAC Québec: Président, Jean Carouzet, #225, 4823, rue Sherbrooke ouest, Montréal, QC H3Z 1G7, 514/931-8556, Téléc: 514/938-1311
CAC Saskatchewan: President, Gales Barnes, 116 - 103 St. East, Saskatoon, SK S7N 1Y7, 306/242-4909, Fax: 306/373-5810
CAC Yukon: President, John Willson, c/o 11 Fiesta Lane, Etobicoke, ON M8Y 1V3, 416/255-1486, Fax: 416/255-0514

**Fédération nationale des associations de consommateurs du Québec (FNACQ) (1978)**
#103, 1215, rue de la Visitation, Montréal, QC H2L 3B5
514/521-6820, Téléc: 514/521-0736
Personne ressource, Francesca Dalio
Secrétaire, Linda Mainville
Organisation(s) affiliée(s): International Organization of Consumers Unions

**CONTRACEPTION *see* REPRODUCTIVE ISSUES**

**COOPERATIVE HOUSING *see* HOUSING**

**COPYRIGHT *see* PATENTS & COPYRIGHT**

**CORRECTIONAL SERVICES *see* LAW**

**COURTS *see* LAW**

**CRAFTS *see* VISUAL ART, CRAFTS, FOLK ARTS**

**CREDIT MANAGEMENT *see* FINANCE**

**CRISIS INTERVENTION *see* SOCIAL RESPONSE/SOCIAL SERVICES**

## CULTURE
***see also* Multiculturalism**

**Alliance for the Preservation of English in Canada (APEC) (1977)**
#5068, 3080 Yonge St., Toronto, ON M4N 3N1
416/482-2732, Fax: 416/482-2732
President, Ronald P. Leitch
Publications: APEC Newsletter

**Alliance Québec (1982)**
#930, 630, boul René-Lévesque ouest, Montréal, QC H3B 1S6
514/875-2771, Fax: 514/875-7507, Email: aqinfo@aq.qc.ca, URL: http://www.aq.qc.ca
Executive Director, David Birnbaum
President, Michael Hamelin
Director of Communications, Rob Bull
Publications: Québecer, q.

**Assemblée internationale des parlementaires de langue française (AIPLF) (1992)**
Région Amérique, 1025, rue St-Augustin, Bur. RC-13, Québec, QC G1A 1A3
418/643-7391, Téléc: 418/643-1865, URL: http://www.regionamerique.aiplf.org
Secrétaire administrative régionale, Marie-Hélène Bergeron
Publications: Bulletin Amérique

**Association of Canadian Clubs/Association des cercles canadiens (1909)**
237 Nepean St., Ottawa, ON K2P 0B7
613/236-8288, Fax: 613/236-8299
National Director, Barbara E. Crowder
President, The Hon. Lincoln Alexander

**Centre culturel franco-manitobain (CCFM)**
340, boul Provencher, Winnipeg, MB R2H 0G7
204/233-8972, Téléc: 204/233-3324, URL: http://francoculture.ca/ccfm
Responsable, Shane Barnabé

**Chateauguay Valley English-Speaking Peoples' Association (CVESPA) (1983)**
27 Prince St., PO Box 1597, Huntingdon, QC J0S 1H0
514/264-5386, Fax: 514/264-5387, Toll Free: 1-800-665-9841
President, Maurice J. King
Executive Director, Janet Hicks
Publications: CVESPA Newsletter

**Compagnie des cent-associés francophones (1980)**
182 Tanguay Ave., Sudbury, ON P3C 5G5
705/674-0281, Téléc: 705/674-0281
Président, Rhéal Perron

**Congrès mondial acadien (CMA)**
CP 4530, Dieppe, NB E1A 6G1
506/859-1994, Téléc: 506/857-2252
Directeur général, Wilfred Roussel

**Conseil des organismes francophones du Toronto Métropolitain (COFTM) (1977)**
**Centre Francophone**
20 Lower Spadina Ave., Toronto, ON M5V 2Z1
416/203-1220, Téléc: 416/203-1165
Directeur, Rosanna Bravar
Publications: Annuaire des ressources francophones du Grand Toronto
Organisation(s) affiliée(s): Assemblée des centres culturels de l'Ontario; Centraide

**Conseil de la vie française en Amérique (CVFA) (1937)**
56, rue Saint-Pierre, 1er étage, Québec, QC G1K 4A1
418/692-1150, Téléc: 418/692-4578
Directeur général, Yvan Forest
Président, Gérard Lévesque
Secrétaire général, Roland G. La Flèche
Publications: Répertoire de la vie française en Amérique; Le Franc-Contact, trimestriel

**The Council of Canadians/Le Conseil des Canadiens (COC) (1985)**
#904, 251 Laurier Ave. West, Ottawa, ON K1P 5J6
613/233-2773, Fax: 613/233-6776, Toll Free: 1-800-387-7177, Email: coc@web.net, URL: http://www.web.net/coc
Executive Director, Peter Bleyer
Chairperson, Maude Barlow
Publications: Canadian Perspectives; ActionLink, irreg.
BC Office: BC Organizer, Steven Staples, #711, 207 West Hastings St., Vancouver, BC V6X 3J9, 604/688-8846, Email: bccoc@web.net

**English-Speaking Union of Canada (ESU)**
#101, 485 Eglinton Ave. East, Toronto, ON M4P 1N2
416/481-8648, Fax: 416/485-5562
National President, Jean Horsey
Canadian National Secretary, Marion Owston
President, H.R.H. The Prince Philip Duke of Edinburgh, KG, KT
Publications: Canadian Concord

**Fédération des communautés francophones et acadienne du Canada (FCFAC)**
#1404, One Nicholas St., Ottawa, ON K1N 7B7
613/241-7600, Téléc: 613/241-6046, URL: http://www.franco.ca/fcfa
Directeur général, Yvon Samson
Président, Jacques Michaud
Québec: #416, 2, Place Québec, Québec, QC G1R 2B5, 418/523-8471, Téléc: 418/522-6449

**ASSOCIATION CANADIENNE-FRANÇAISE DE L'ALBERTA (ACFA) (1926)**
#303, 8527, rue Marie-Anne-Gaboury, Edmonton, AB T6C 3N1
403/466-1680, Téléc: 403/465-6773
Courrier électronique: acfaprov@datanet.ab.ca, URL: http://francalta.ab.ca
Directeur, Georges Arès
Président, John Moreau
Publications: Le Franco
Organisation(s) affiliée(s): Fédération culturelle canadienne-française

**ASSOCIATION CANADIENNE-FRANÇAISE DE L'ONTARIO (ACFO) (1910)**
#1711, 2, rue Carlton, Toronto, ON M5B 1J3
416/595-5585, Téléc: 416/595-0202
Courrier électronique: acfo@franco.ca, URL: http://www.franco.ca/acfo
Directrice générale, Lorraine Gandolfo
Présidente, Treva Cousineau

**ASSOCIATION CULTURELLE FRANCO-CANADIENNE DE LA SASKATCHEWAN (1912)**
2132 Broad St., Regina, SK S4P 1Y5
306/569-1912, Téléc: 306/781-7916
Courrier électronique: acfc@franco.ca, URL: http://www.dlcwest.com/~acfc/
Directeur général, Louis Émond

**ASSOCIATION FRANCO-YUKONNAISE (AFY) (1982)**
CP 5205, Whitehorse, YT Y4A 4Z1
867/668-2663, Téléc: 867/663-3511
Courrier électronique: francoyk@yknet.yk.ca, URL: http://francoculture.ca/afy
Directeur général, Pierre Bourbeau
Secrétaire, Martine Caron
Publications: L'Aurore boréale

**FÉDÉRATION ACADIENNE DE LA NOUVELLE-ECOSSE/ACADIAN FEDERATION OF NOVA SCOTIA (FANE) (1968)**
1106 South Park St., Halifax, NS B3H 2W7
902/421-1772, Téléc: 902/422-3942
Directeur de l'information, Karl Roach
Directrice générale, Vaughne Madden

**FÉDÉRATION DES FRANCOPHONES DE TERRE-NEUVE ET DU LABRADOR (FFTNL) (1973)**
265 Duckworth St., St. John's, NF A1C 1G9
709/722-0627, Téléc: 709/722-9904, Ligne sans frais: 1-800-563-9898
Courrier électronique: fftnl@franco.ca, URL: http://www.franco.ca/fftnl/index.htm
Directrice générale, Hélène Davis
Président, Jean-Guy Dionne
Publications: Le Caboteur

**FÉDÉRATION DE LA JEUNESSE CANADIENNE-FRANÇAISE INC. (FJCF) (1974)**
#440, 325 Dalhousie, Ottawa, ON K1N 7G2
613/562-4624, Téléc: 613/562-3995
Courrier électronique: fjcf@franco.ca, URL: http://www.franco.ca/fjcf
Directeur général, Gilles Vienneau
Présidente, Mona Fortier
Publications: Nouvelles en bref

**SOCIÉTÉ DES ACADIENS ET ACADIENNES DU NOUVEAU-BRUNSWICK (SAANB)**
CP 670, Petit-Rocher, NB E0B 2E0
506/783-4205, Téléc: 506/783-0629
Courrier électronique: saanbpro@nbnet.nb.ca, URL: http://www.rbmulti.nb.ca/saanb/saanb.htm
Directrice générale, Michèle Doiron
Présidente, Lise Ouellette

**SOCIÉTÉ FRANCO-MANITOBAINE (SFM) (1969)**
#212, 383 Provencher Blvd., Winnipeg, MB R2H 0G9
204/233-4915, Téléc: 204/233-1017, Ligne sans frais: 1-800-665-4443
Courrier électronique: sfm@franco-manitobain.org, URL: http://www.franco-manitobain.org
Directeur général, Daniel Boucher
Communications, Michel Loiselle
Publications: Annuaire des services en français au Manitoba

**Fédération culturelle canadienne-française (FCCF) (1977)**
Place de la francophonie, #405, 450, rue Rideau, Ottawa, ON K1N 5Z4
613/241-8770, Téléc: 613/241-6064, Ligne sans frais: 1-800-267-2005, Courrier électronique: fccf@franco.ca, URL: http://francoculture.ca/fccf/
Directeur général, Sylvio Boudreau
Publications: Qui vive

**L'Institut canadien de Québec (1848)**
350, rue Saint-Joseph est, Québec, QC G1K 3B2
418/529-0924, Téléc: 418/529-1588, Courrier électronique: courrier@icqbdq.qc.ca, URL: http://www.icqbdq.qc.ca
Directeur général, Jean Payeur

**The Royal Commonwealth Society of Canada/La Société royale du Commonwealth du Canada (RCS)**
PO Box 691, Stn Adelaide, Toronto, ON M5C 2J8
905/372-8323, Fax: 905/372-8323
Chairman, Sir Arthur Chetwynd, Bt
Publications: Commonwealth Notes

**Servas Canada (1960)**
229 Hillcrest Ave., North York, ON M2N 3P3
URL: http://servas.org
Coordinator, Michael Al Johnson
Publications: Bulletin, Servas International
Affiliates: Servas International

**Société de développement des entreprises culturelles (SODEC) (1984)**
#200, 1755, boul René-Lévesque est, Montréal, QC H2K 4P6
514/873-7768, Téléc: 514/873-4388
Directrice de la planification, Martine-Andrée Racine

**Société nationale de l'Acadie (SNA) (1881)**
415, rue Notre-Dame, Dieppe, NB E1A 2A8
506/853-0404, Téléc: 506/853-0400
Présidente, Liane Roy
Secrétaire général, René Légère

**La Société Saint-Jean-Baptiste de Montréal (SSJBM) (1834)**
82, rue Sherbrooke ouest, Montréal, QC H2X 1X3
514/843-8851, Téléc: 514/844-6369
Président général, François Lemieux
Publications: Bulletin

**Townshippers' Association/Association des townshippers (TA) (1979)**
#204, 1945, rue Belvedere sud, Ascot, QC J1H 5Y3
819/566-5717, Fax: 819/566-0271
President, David Morgan
Executive Director, Susan C. Mastine
Publications: Crossroads
Affiliates: Alliance Québec; Châteauguay Valley English Speaking People's Association; Coasters Association; Committee for Anglophone Social Action; Outaouais Alliance; Voice of English Québec

**Union culturelle des franco-ontariennes (UCFO) (1936)**
#212, 435 St-Laurent Blvd., Ottawa, ON K1K 2Z8
613/741-1334, Téléc: 613/741-8577
Directrice générale, Guylaine Leclerc
Présidente, Madeleine Paquette
Publications: Communiqué
Organisation(s) affiliée(s): Fédération nationale des femmes canadiennes françaises; Match International; Réseau national d'action education femmes; Regroupement des organismes du patrimoine franco-ontarien; Table féministe francophone de concertation provinciale de l'Ontario

**DATA PROCESSING *see* INFORMATION TECHNOLOGY**

**DEFENCE *see* MILITARY & VETERANS**

## DENTAL

**Association des denturologistes du Québec (ADQ) (1971)**
Complexe Raycom, #820, 5100, rue Sherbrooke est, Montréal, QC H1V 3R9
514/252-0270, Téléc: 514/252-0392, Ligne sans frais: 1-800-563-6273, Courrier électronique: denturo@mlink.net, URL: http://www.adq-qc.com
Directeur générale, Claude Chartier
Publications: Le Denturo

**Canadian Academy of Endodontics/L'Académie canadienne d'endodontie (1964)**
#1250, 10665 Jasper Ave., Edmonton, AB T5J 3S9
403/425-8930, Fax: 403/420-1744
Executive Director, Dr. Carl Hawrish
Publications: Newsletter of the C.A.E.
Affiliates: Canadian Dental Association

**Canadian Academy of Oral Pathology/Académie canadienne de pathologie buccale (CAOP)**
University of Western Ontario, Dept. of Oral Pathology, London, ON N6A 5C1
519/679-2111, Fax: 519/661-3370
President, Dr. T.D. Dailey

**Canadian Academy of Oral Radiology/Académie canadienne de radiologie buccale (CAOR)**
University of Toronto, Faculty of Dentistry, 124 Edward St., Toronto, ON M5G 1G6
416/979-4932, ext.4365, Fax: 416/979-4936
President, Dr. P.A. Sikorski
Sec.-Treas., Dr. G. Petrikowski

**Canadian Association for Dental Research/Association canadienne de recherches dentaires**
University of Alberta, Faculty of Dentistry, #3036, 46 University Campus NW, Edmonton, AB T6G 2N8
403/492-3631, Fax: 403/491-1624
Sec.-Treas., Dr. Carl Osadetz

**Canadian Association of Orthodontists/Association canadienne des orthodontists (CAO) (1949)**
#310, 2175 Sheppard Ave. East, North York, ON M2J 1W8
416/491-3186, Fax: 416/491-1670, Email: taylor@interlog.com
Administrator, Diane Gaunt
Publications: CAO Newsletter

**Canadian Association of Public Health Dentistry (CAPHD)**
c/o Alberta Dental Association, #101, 8230 - 105th St., Edmonton, AB T6E 5H9
403/432-1012, Fax: 403/432-4864
President, G. Thompson
Secretary, E.C.S. Swan
Publications: Journal of Community Dentistry
Affiliates: Canadian Dental Association

**Canadian Dental Assistants Association (CDAA) (1945)**
#105, 1785 Alta Vista Dr., Ottawa, ON K1G 3Y6
613/521-5495, Fax: 613/521-5572, Toll Free: 1-800-345-5137, Email: cdaa@cyberus.ca
Executive Director, Jill Ramsey
Publications: CDAA Journal

**Canadian Dental Association/L'Association dentaire canadienne (CDA) (1902)**
1815 Alta Vista Dr., Ottawa, ON K1G 3Y6
613/523-1770, Fax: 613/523-7736, URL: http://www.cda-adc.ca
Executive Director, Jardine Neilson
President, Toby Gushue
Manager, Information Systems, Shameer Kanji, Email: skanji@cda-adc.ca
Publications: Journal of Canadian Dental Association
Affiliates: Fédération dentaire internationale

**ALBERTA DENTAL ASSOCIATION**
#101, 8230 - 105 St., Edmonton, AB T6E 5H9
403/432-1012, Fax: 403/433-4864
Executive Director, Gordon Thompson
Registrar, Dr. B.E. Leroy

**ASSOCIATION DES CHIRURGIENS DENTISTES DU QUÉBEC**
#1425, 425, boul de Maisonneuve ouest, Montréal, QC H3A 3G5
514/282-1425, Téléc: 514/282-0255, Ligne sans frais: 1-800-361-3794
Président, Daniel Pelland

**COLLEGE OF DENTAL SURGEONS OF BRITISH COLUMBIA (CDSBC) (1908)**
#500, 1765 - 8th Ave. West, Vancouver, BC V6J 5C6
604/736-3621, Fax: 604/734-9448, Toll Free: 1-800-663-9169
Executive Director, Dr. G.R. Thordarson
Registrar, Dr. E. McNee
Publications: Bulletin

**COLLEGE OF DENTAL SURGEONS OF SASKATCHEWAN (1906)**
#202, 728 Spadina Cres. East, Saskatoon, SK S7K 4H7
306/244-5072, Fax: 306/244-2476
Registrar, Dr. G.H. Peacock

**DENTAL ASSOCIATION OF PRINCE EDWARD ISLAND**
184 Belvedere Ave., Charlottetown, PE C1A 2Z1
902/566-5199, Fax: 902/892-4470
Secretary, Dr. B.D. Barrett

**MANITOBA DENTAL ASSOCIATION (MDA) (1983)**
#103, 698 Corydon Ave., Winnipeg, MB R3M 0X9
204/453-0055, Fax: 204/453-0108
Registrar, Dr. M.A. Lasko
Publications: The Bulletin

**NEW BRUNSWICK DENTAL SOCIETY/SOCIÉTÉ DENTAIRE DU NOUVEAU-BRUNSWICK (1890)**
Carleton Place, #820, 520 King St., PO Box 488, Stn A, Fredericton, NB E3B 4Z9
506/452-8575, Fax: 506/452-1872
Executive Director, Barbara Wishart
Registrar, Dr. Philip Cyr

**NEWFOUNDLAND DENTAL ASSOCIATION**
139 Water St., 9th Fl., St. John's, NF A1C 1B2
709/579-2362, Fax: 709/579-1250
Executive Director, Dr. Gary MacDonald

**NOVA SCOTIA DENTAL ASSOCIATION (NSDA) (1891)**
#604, 5991 Spring Garden Rd., Halifax, NS B3H 1Y6
902/420-0088, Fax: 902/423-6537
Email: nsda@fox.nstn.ca
Executive Director, D.V. Pamenter
Publications: Dispatch; NS Dentist, bi-m.

**ONTARIO DENTAL ASSOCIATION (ODA)**
4 New St., Toronto, ON M5R 1P6
416/922-3900, Fax: 416/922-9005
URL: http://www.oda.on.ca/
Executive Director, John C. Gillies, CAE
President, Dr. Jack Cottrell

**Canadian Dental Hygienists' Association/Association canadienne des hygiènistes denteurs (CDHA) (1963)**
96 Centrepointe Dr., Nepean, ON K2G 6B1
613/224-5515, Fax: 613/224-7283
Executive Director, Carol Matheson Worobey
Publications: Probe; Explorer, bi-m.

**College of Dental Technologists of Ontario**
#321, 2100 Ellesmere Rd., Scarborough, ON M1H 3B7
416/438-5003, Fax: 416/438-5004
Registrar, E. Cheung
Chairman, Joseph B. Nagy, RDT
Publications: Advisor

**Commercial Dental Laboratory Conference (CDLC) (1969)**
PO Box 272, Kingston, ON K7L 4V8
613/531-8336, Fax: 613/548-8188, Toll Free: 1-800-461-2577
Treasurer, Rick King

**CUMBA (1944)**
562 Eglinton Ave. East, Toronto, ON M4P 1B9
416/487-5451, Fax: 416/487-3379
President/CEO, C.J. McCrodan

**Dentistry Canada Fund/Fonds dentaire canadien (DCF) (1994)**
427 Gilmour St., Ottawa, ON K2P 0R5
613/236-4763, Fax: 613/236-3935, Email: dcfsjw@magi.com
Executive Vice-President, Douglas Smith
Affiliates: Canadian Dental Association

**Denturist Association of Canada/Association des denturologistes du Canada (DAC) (1971)**
PO Box 46114, RPO Westdale, Winnipeg, MB R3R 3S3
204/897-1087, Fax: 204/895-9595, Toll Free: 1-800-773-0099, Email: dentcda@mb.sympatico.ca
President, Tony Sarrapuchiello
Chief Administrative Officer, Gerry Hansen
Publications: Journal of Canadian Denturism

**ALBERTA DENTURIST SOCIETY (1980)**
#1240, 10060 Jasper Ave., Edmonton, AB T5J 3R8
403/429-2330 (Edmonton & area), Fax: 403/429-2336, Toll Free: 1-800-260-2742
Administrator, Lorrie Rees
Affiliates: National Council of Denturist Governing Bodies; National Council of Denturist Educators

**DENTURIST ASSOCIATION OF MANITOBA (1970)**
PO Box 46105, RPO Westdale, Winnipeg, MB R3R 3S3
204/897-1087, Fax: 204/895-9595
Administrator, Gerry Hansen
President, David L. Hicks

**DENTURIST ASSOCIATION OF NEWFOUNDLAND & LABRADOR**
PO Box 10, Harbour Grace, NF A0A 3P0
709/596-7647, Fax: 709/596-1602
Email: carbone.austin@nf.sympatico.ca
Secretary, Austin J. Carbone

**DENTURIST ASSOCIATION OF ONTARIO (DAO)**
#200, 5925 Airport Rd., Mississauga, ON L4V 1W1
905/405-6258, Fax: 905/405-6259
Executive Director, Clifford Muzylowsky
Executive Secretary, Freida Steward
Publications: The Denturist

**DENTURIST SOCIETY OF BRITISH COLUMBIA**
#C312, 9801 King George Hwy., Surrey, BC V3T 5H5
604/582-6823, Fax: 604/582-6823
Sec.-Treas., Dorothy L. MacArthur

**DENTURIST SOCIETY OF NOVA SCOTIA**
209 High St., Bridgewater, NS B4V 1W2
902/543-5067, Fax: 902/543-6278
President, Ken Edwards

**DENTURIST SOCIETY OF PRINCE EDWARD ISLAND**
151 Hanover St., Summerside, PE C1N 1E5
902/436-3295
President, Boyd P. Bernard

**DENTURIST SOCIETY OF SASKATCHEWAN**
210 - 2 Ave. North, Saskatoon, SK S7K 2B5
306/244-1717
James Hoffart, DD

**NEW BRUNSWICK DENTURISTS SOCIETY/SOCIÉTÉ DES DENTUROLOGISTES DU NOUVEAU-BRUNSWICK (1973)**
PO Box 106, Hampton, NB E0G 1Z0
506/832-7678, Fax: 506/832-4860
Secretary, C. Scovil Brown, DD

**YUKON DENTURIST ASSOCIATION**
#1, 106 Main St., Whitehorse, YT Y1A 2A7
867/668-6818, Fax: 867/668-6811
President, Peter Allen, DD

### National Dental Examining Board of Canada
#203, 100 Bronson Ave., Ottawa, ON K1R 6G8
613/236-5912, Fax: 613/236-8386
Registrar & Executive Director, Dr. Jack D. Gerrow

### Newfoundland Dental Board
139 Water St., 6th Fl., St. John's, NF A1C 1B2
709/579-2391, Fax: 709/579-2392
Secretary Registrar, Dr. Charles P. Daly

### Ontario Dental Nurses & Assistants Association
869 Dundas St., London, ON N5W 2Z8
519/679-2566, Fax: 519/679-8494
CEO, Ian Tripp
Publications: The Journal
Affiliates: Canadian Dental Assistants Association (CDAA)

### Ordre des dentistes du Québec (ODQ) (1973)
625, boul René-Lévesque ouest, 15e étage, Montréal, QC H3B 1R2
514/875-8511, Téléc: 514/393-9248, Ligne sans frais: 1-800-361-4888, URL: http://www.odq.qc.ca/
Directeur général et secrétaire, Paul J. Thériault
Publications: Journal dentaire du Québec
Organisation(s) affiliée(s): Association dentaire canadienne

### Ordre des denturologistes du Québec (ODQ) (1973)
#106, 45, Place Charles Lemoyne, Longueuil, QC J4K 5G5
514/646-7922, Téléc: 514/646-2509, Ligne sans frais: 1-800-567-2251
Directrice générale et secrétaire, Monique Bouchard
Publications: Présence

### Provincial Dental Board of Nova Scotia
#602, 5991 Spring Garden Rd., Halifax, NS B3H 1Y6
902/420-0083, Fax: 902/492-0301
Registrar, Dr. D.M.J. Bonang

### Provincial Dental Council of Prince Edward Island
184 Belvedere Ave., Charlottetown, PE C1A 2Z1
902/566-5199
Registrar, Dr. Ray Wenn

### Royal College of Dental Surgeons of Ontario (1868)
**RCDS of Ontario**
6 Crescent Rd., 5th Fl., Toronto, ON M4W 1T1
416/961-6555, Fax: 416/961-5814, Toll Free: 1-800-565-4591
Registrar, Dr. Minna H. Stein
Publications: Dispatch

### Royal College of Dentists of Canada
#1706, 365 Bloor St. East, Toronto, ON M4W 3L4
416/929-2722, Fax: 416/929-5924
Executive Director, Kay Montgomery

**DEVELOPING COUNTRIES *see* INTERNATIONAL COOPERATION/INTERNATIONAL RELATIONS**

**DEVELOPMENT EDUCATION RELATIONS *see* INTERNATIONAL COOPERATION/INTERNATIONAL RELATIONS**

## DISABLED PERSONS

### AboutFace (1985)
99 Crowns Lane, 4th Fl., Toronto, ON M5R 3P4
416/944-3223, Fax: 416/944-2488, Toll Free: 1-800-665-3223, Email: abtface@interlog.com, URL: http://www.interlog.com/~abtface/
Executive Director, Anna Pileggi
Office Manager, Consuelo McQueen
Communications & Marketing Manager, Lorna Renooy
Community Outreach Coordinator, Linda Walters
Publications: AboutFace

### Advocacy Resource Centre for the Handicapped/Centre de la Défense des Droits des Handicapés (ARCH) (1980)
#255, 40 Orchard View Blvd., Toronto, ON M4R 1B9
416/482-8255, Fax: 416/482-2981, TDD: 416/482-1254, Email: arch@indie.ca, URL: http://www.indie.ca/arch
Executive Director, David Baker
President, Ron McInnes
Publications: ARCH-TYPE

### Alberta Association of Rehabilitation Centres (AARC) (1972)
Box 105, 2725 - 12 St. NE, Calgary, AB T2E 7J2
403/250-9495, Fax: 403/291-9864
Executive Director, Gail Roberson
President, Rita Thompson
Publications: Network

### Alberta Committee of Citizens with Disabilities (ACCD) (1973)
Princeton Place, #707, 10339 - 124 St., Edmonton, AB T5N 3W1
403/488-0988, Fax: 403/488-3757, TDD: 403/488-9090, Toll Free: 1-800-387-2514, Email: accd@oanet.com, URL: http://www.indie.ca/accd
Executive Director, Beverley D. Matthiessen
Publications: Action News
Affiliates: Council of Canadians with Disabilities

### Association for the Neurologically Disabled of Canada (AND)
59 Clement Rd., Etobicoke, ON M9R 1Y5
416/244-1992, Fax: 416/244-4099, Toll Free: 1-800-561-1497, Email: andc@idirect.com, URL: http://www.and.ca/
Executive Director, Kathleen Haswell
President, Robert S. Nelson
Publications: A.N.D. - NOW

### Association du Québec pour enfants avec problèmes auditifs (AQEPA) (1969)
#427, 3700, rue Berri, Montréal, QC H2L 4G9
514/842-8706, Téléc: 514/849-3002, URL: http://www.craph.org/craph/associat/aqepa.htm
Directrice générale, Pauline Lazure
Publications: Entendre

### Association québécoise de loisir pour personnes handicapées/Québec Leisure Association for Handicapped Persons (AQLPH) (1979)
4545, av Pierre de Coubertin, CP 1000, Succ. M, Montréal, QC H1V 3R2
514/252-3144, Téléc: 514/252-3164
Directrice générale, Madeleine Cruvelier
Publications: Habilités loisirs; Centre de doc., annuel
Organisation(s) affiliée(s): Regroupement loisir Québec; Confédération des organismes provinciaux de personnes handicapées du Québec

### Association for Vaccine Damaged Children (1986)
56 Brisco St., Brampton, ON L6V 1W8
905/454-2237
Contact, Nancy Howes

### BALANCE (1986)
#302, 4920 Dundas St. West, Etobicoke, ON M9A 1B7
416/236-1796, Fax: 416/236-4280, Email: khunt@ican.net
Executive Director, Susan Archibald
Chairperson, Nayla Farah

### Bob Rumball Centre for the Deaf (BRCD) (1979)
2395 Bayview Ave., North York, ON M2L 1A2
416/449-9651 (Voice & TDD), Fax: 416/449-8881, Toll Free: 1-800-841-9663
Interim Executive Director, Rev. Robert Rumball
Chairman, Alistair M. Fraser
Supervisor of Centre Programs, Shirley Cassel
Manager of Finance, James Pennock

### Canadian Association for Community Living/Association canadienne pour l'intégration communautaire (CACL) (1958)
Kinsmen Building, York University Campus, 4700 Keele St., North York, ON M3J 1P3
416/661-9611, Fax: 416/661-5701, Email: info@cacl.ca, URL: http://indie.ca/cacl/index.htm
President, Julie Stone
Executive Vice-President, Diane Richler
Publications: Newsbreak

**ALBERTA ASSOCIATION FOR COMMUNITY LIVING (AACL) (1954)**
11724 Kingsway Ave., Edmonton, AB T5G 0X5
403/451-3055, Fax: 403/453-5779, Toll Free: 1-800-252-7556

Email: aacl@ccinet.ab.ca, URL: http://www.ccinet.ab.ca/aacl/
Executive Director, Bruce Uditsky
President, Zuhy Sayeed
Publications: Bulletin; Connections, q.
Affiliates: Alberta Community Living Foundation

**ASSOCIATION FOR COMMUNITY LIVING - MANITOBA**
#1, 90 Market Ave., Winnipeg, MB R3B 0P3
204/947-1118, Fax: 204/949-1464
Executive Director, Dale Kendel
President, Moira Grahame

**ASSOCIATION DU QUÉBEC POUR L'INTÉGRATION SOCIALE/QUÉBEC ASSOCIATION FOR COMMUNITY LIVING (AQIS) (1951)**
3958, rue Dandurand, Montréal, QC H1X 1P7
514/725-7245, Téléc: 514/725-2976
Directrice générale, Diane Milliard
Présidente, Danielle Chrétien
Conseillère aux communications, Sylvie Carle
Publications: L'Ebruiteur

**BRITISH COLUMBIA ASSOCIATION FOR COMMUNITY LIVING (BCACL) (1955)**
#300, 30 - 6th Ave. East, Vancouver, BC V5T 4P4
604/875-1119, Fax: 604/875-6744
Email: info@bcacl.org, URL: http://www.vcn.bc.ca/bcacl
Executive Director, Judy Carter-Smith
President, Anita Dadson
Publications: BCACL Chapter Information List; Community Living News, q.

**NEW BRUNSWICK ASSOCIATION FOR COMMUNITY LIVING/ASSOCIATION DU NOUVEAU-BRUNSWICK POUR L'INTÉGRATION COMMUNAUTAIRE (1957)**
86 York St., 2nd Fl., Fredericton, NB E3B 3N5
506/458-8866, Fax: 506/452-9791
Executive Director, Lorraine Silliphant
President, Joanne Kraftcheck

**NEWFOUNDLAND ASSOCIATION FOR COMMUNITY LIVING (NACL) (1976)**
Prudential Bldg., 49 Elizabeth Ave., PO Box 5453, Stn C, St. John's, NF A1C 5W4
709/722-0790, Fax: 709/722-1325
Executive Director, Michele T. Neary
President, Florence Paul
Publications: Gateway

**NOVA SCOTIA ASSOCIATION FOR COMMUNITY LIVING**
10 Portland St., Dartmouth, NS B2Y 1G9
902/469-1174, Fax: 902/461-0196
Executive Director, Mary Rothman
President, Tim Boulton

**THE ONTARIO ASSOCIATION FOR COMMUNITY LIVING/ASSOCIATION POUR L'INTÉGRATION COMMUNAUTAIRE DE L'ONTARIO (OACL) (1953)**
#403, 240 Duncan Mill Rd., North York, ON M3B 1Z4
416/447-4348, Fax: 416/447-8974
URL: http://www.acl.on.ca
Executive Director, Keith Powell
President, Lee Holling
Publications: Directions; OACL Directory, bi-a.

**PRINCE EDWARD ISLAND ASSOCIATION FOR COMMUNITY LIVING (1986)**
1 Rochforn Ave., PO Box 280, Charlottetown, PE C1A 7K4
902/566-4844, Fax: 902/368-8057
Executive Director, Madonna Fradsham
President, Mary McPhee
Publications: Connections

**SASKATCHEWAN ASSOCIATION FOR COMMUNITY LIVING (SACL) (1955)**
3031 Louise St., Saskatoon, SK S7J 3L1
306/955-3344, Fax: 306/373-3070
URL: http://www.usask.ca/education/SACL/
Executive Director, Karen Rongve
President, Greg Plosz
Publications: Dialect

**YELLOWKNIFE ASSOCIATION FOR COMMUNITY LIVING**
4912 - 53 St., PO Box 981, Yellowknife, NT X1A 2N7
867/920-2644, Fax: 867/920-2348
Executive Director, Lanny Cooke
President, Don Clunie

**YUKON ASSOCIATION FOR COMMUNITY LIVING (1964)**
PO Box 4853, Whitehorse, YT Y1A 4N6
867/667-4606, Fax: 867/667-4606
President, Kathleen Curtis
Program Coordinator, Vicki Wilson
Publications: Visions

### Canadian Association of the Deaf/Association des sourds du Canada (CAD) (1940)
#205, 2435 Holly Lane, Ottawa, ON K1V 7P2
613/526-4785, Fax: 613/526-4718
Executive Director, James D. Roots
Publications: Deaf Canada/CAD Chat
Affiliates: World Federation of the Deaf; Council of Canadians with Disabilities

### Canadian Association of Independent Living Centres/Association canadienne des centres de vie autonome (CAILC) (1985)
#1004, 350 Sparks St., Ottawa, ON K1R 7S8
613/563-2581, Fax: 613/235-4497
National Director, Traci Walters
Publications: CAILC Communique

### Canadian Brain Injury Coalition/La coalition canadienne des traumatisés craniens (CBIC) (1989)
29 Pearce Ave., Winnipeg, MB R2V 2K3
204/334-0471, Fax: 204/339-1034, Email: cbic@pcs.mb.ca
Executive Director, Diane Bastiaansson
Publications: Newsletter

### The Canadian Council of the Blind/Le Conseil canadien des aveugles (CCB) (1945)
#405, 396 Cooper St., Ottawa, ON K2P 2H7
613/567-0311, Fax: 613/567-2728
Executive Director, M.L. Moran
Affiliates: World Blind Union

### Canadian Council on Rehabilitation & Work/Le Conseil canadien de la réadaptation et du travail (CCRW) (1976)
20 King St. West, 9th Fl., Toronto, ON M5H 1C4
416/974-3201; TTY/ATS: 416/974-2636, Fax: 416/974-5577, Email: info@ccrw.org, URL: http://www.ccrw.org
Executive Director, Joan Westland
Publications: Ability & Enterprise

### Canadian Cultural Society of The Deaf, Inc. (1973)
11337 - 61 Ave, House 144, Edmonton, AB T6H 1M3
403/436-2599, Fax: 403/430-9489
Contact, Carolyn Anne Fritz
Publications: CCSD Newsletter

### Canadian Deafened Persons Association (CDPA) (1987)
310 Elmgrove Rd., Ottawa, ON K1A 3L1
613/729-6274, Fax: 613/729-5265
Publications: CDPA Newsletter
Affiliates: Canadian Association of Captioning Consumers

### Canadian Deafness Research & Training Institute/Institut canadien de recherche et de formation sur la surdité (CDRTI) (1988)
2300, boul René-Lévesque ouest, Québec, QC H3H 2R5
514/937-2191, Fax: 514/937-2284
President, Dr. J.C. MacDougall

### Canadian Foundation for Physically Disabled Persons (1984)
731 Runnymede Rd., Toronto, ON M6N 3V7
416/760-7351, Fax: 416/760-9405
Administrator, Barbara Logan
Chairman, Vim Kochhar
Publications: WhyNot

### Canadian Guide Dogs for the Blind (CGDB) (1984)
4120 Rideau Valley Dr. North, PO Box 280, Manotick, ON K4M 1A3
613/692-7777, Fax: 613/692-0650
Vice-President, Jane Thornton

### Canadian Hard of Hearing Association/Association des malentendants canadiens (CHHA) (1982)
#205, 2435 Holly Lane, Ottawa, ON K1V 7P2
613/526-1584; TTY 613/526-2692, Fax: 613/526-4718, Toll Free: 1-800-263-8068, Email: chhanational@cyberus.ca
National Coordinator, Janice McNamara
President, Fred Clark
Publications: Listen/Écoute

### Canadian Hearing Society (CHS) (1940)
271 Spadina Rd., Toronto, ON M5R 2V3
416/964-9595; TTY: 416/964-0023, Fax: 416/928-2506, Toll Free: 1-800-465-4327, Email: info@chs.ca, URL: http://www.chs.ca
Executive Director, David Allen
President, Keith Golem
Executive Assistant, Angela Pearl
Assistant Executive Director, Iris Boshes
Director, Social Services Development, Gary Malkowski
Director, Hearing Health Care, Joanne Deluzio
Director, Finance & Support Services, Tom McNeil
Director, Human Resources, Edna Soostar
Director, Information & Public Relations, Susan Main
Publications: Vibes
Affiliates: Canadian Hearing Society Foundation

### The Canadian National Institute for the Blind/L'Institut national canadien pour les aveugles (CNIB) (1918)
1929 Bayview Ave., Toronto, ON M4G 3E8
416/480-7580, Fax: 416/480-7677, Email: irc@lib.cnib.ca, URL: http://www.cnib.ca
President/CEO, Euclid J. Herie
Chairman, National Council, F. Garrick Homer
Vice-President, Marketing, Communications, & Foundations, Gerrard Grace
Publications: CNIB National Annual Review
Affiliates: World Blind Union
Division du Québec: Interim Executive Director, Jim Sanders, 3622, rue Hochelaga, Montréal, QC H1W 1J1, 514/529-2040, Téléc: 514/529-4662, Ligne sans frais: 1-800-465-4622

### Canadian Speech Communicators Association (CSCA) (1967)
c/o Lethbridge Community College, 3000 South College Dr., Lethbridge, AB T1K 1L6
403/758-6608, Fax: 403/320-1461
Contact, Yvonne Hohm
Publications: Spectrum

**Christian Record Services Inc. (1899)**
**National Camps for the Blind**
#119, 1300 King St. East, Oshawa, ON L1H 8N9
905/436-6938, Fax: 905/436-7102
Executive Director, Patricia L. Page
Publications: Christian Record; Christian Record Talking Magazine, bi-m.; Young & Alive, q.; Lifeglow, q.

**Consumer Organization of Disabled People of Newfoundland & Labrador (COD) (1980)**
PO Box 422, Stn C, St. John's, NF A1C 5K4
709/722-7011, Fax: 709/722-4424
Executive Director, Mary Ennis
Publications: COD-E-BATE
Affiliates: Council of Canadians with Disabilities

**Council of Canadians with Disabilities/Conseil des Canadiens avec déficiences (CCD) (1976)**
#926, 294 Portage Ave., Winnipeg, MB R3C 0B9
204/947-0303, Fax: 204/942-4625, Telex: 23 7601197, Email: ccd@pcs.mb.ca, URL: http://www.pcs.mb.ca/~ccd/
National Coordinator, Laurie Beachell
Research Analyst, April D'Aufin
Publications: A Voice of Our Own
Affiliates: Consumer Organization of Disabled People of Newfoundland & Labrador; PEI Council of the Disabled; Nova Scotia League for Equal Opportunities; PUSH-Ontario; Manitoba League of the Physically Handicapped; Saskatchewan Voice of the Handicapped; Alberta Committee of Disabled Citizens; British Columbia Coalition of the Disabled; Association canadienne des sourds; DAWN Canada; National Network on Mental Health; Thalidomide Victims of Canada; National Education Association of Disabled Students; People First of Canada

**Deaf Youth Canada/Jeunesse sourde canadienne (1975)**
c/o Alberta School for the Deaf, 6240 - 113 St., Edmonton, AB T6H 3L2
403/422-0244, Fax: 403/422-2036
President, Joe McLaughlin
Affiliates: Canadian Association of the Deaf

**Easter Seals/March of Dimes National Council/ Conseil National des Timbres de Pâques et de la Parade des dix sous (1962)**
**Canadian Rehabilitation Council for the Disabled**
#511, 90 Eglinton Ave. East, Toronto, ON M4P 2Y3
416/932-8382, Fax: 416/932-9844, TDD: 416/250-7490
National Executive Director, Heather Stonehouse
Publications: Rehabilitation Digest; The Lily Tree
Affiliates: Canadian Life & Health Insurance Association; Insurance Bureau of Canada; National Voluntary Organizations Committee; National Voluntary Health Agencies Committee; Canadian Council on Health Services Accreditation; Canadian Standards Association; National Institute for Disability Management & Research

**ABILITIES FOUNDATION OF NOVA SCOTIA (1931)**
**Easter Seals**
3670 Kempt Rd., Halifax, NS B3K 4X8
902/429-3420, Fax: 902/454-6121
Email: abfound@ns.sympatico.ca
President & CEO, Thomas G. Merriam
Publications: Abilities Foundation

**ALBERTA REHABILITATION COUNCIL FOR THE DISABLED**
**Easter Seal Ability Council**
#400, 10909 Jasper Ave., Edmonton, AB T5J 3L9
403/429-0137, Fax: 403/429-1937, TDD: 403/429-2065
Email: easter@telusplanet.net
Executive Director, Jim Killick
Provincial Administrator, Karon Shaw

**CENTRE DE RÉADAPTATION CONSTANCE-LETHBRIDGE/ CONSTANCE LETHBRIDGE REHABILITATION CENTRE (CRCL) (1945)**
7005, boul de Maisonneuve ouest, Montréal, QC H4B 1T3
514/487-1891, Téléc: 514/487-5494
Directrice générale, Ghislaine Prata
Organisation(s) affiliée(s): Confédération québécoise des centres d'hébergement et de réadaptation
Easter Seal Research Institute: President, George Doty; Director, Anne Michie, #200, 250 Ferrand Dr., North York, ON M3C 3P2, 416/421-8377, Fax: 416/696-1035, Toll Free: 1-800-668-6252, Email: info@easterseals.org

**THE EASTER SEAL SOCIETY (ONTARIO)/SOCIÉTÉ DU TIMBRE DE PÂQUES DE L'ONTARIO (TESS) (1922)**
**Ontario Society for Crippled Children**
#200, 250 Ferrand Dr., North York, ON M3C 3P2
416/421-8377, Fax: 416/696-1035, Toll Free: 1-800-668-6252
URL: http://www.easterseals.org
Executive Director, Peter Ely
President, John Logan
Vice-President, Paul Truelove
Secretary, John Wheatley
Treasurer, Alison Morse
Publications: Update

**KINSMEN REHABILITATION FOUNDATION OF BRITISH COLUMBIA (KRF) (1952)**
#300, 999 West Broadway, Vancouver, BC V5Z 4R1
604/736-8841, Fax: 604/738-0015, TDD: 604/738-0603
Email: kathy@kinsmen.mlnet.com, URL: http://mindlink.net/kinsmen_rehab/
CEO, Andy Danyliu
Manager, Education & Information Services, Kathy Ellis
Publications: Know No Limits News

**NEWFOUNDLAND SOCIETY FOR THE PHYSICALLY DISABLED INC. (NSPD) (1950)**
#712, 100 Forest Rd., St. John's, NF A1A 1E5
709/754-1399, Fax: 709/754-1398
President, J.M. O'Keefe
Vice-President, Bruce Callahan
Honorable Treasurer, Christine Stratton
Honorable Secretary, June Perry

**ONTARIO MARCH OF DIMES/MARCHE DES DIX SOUS DE L'ONTARIO (OMOD) (1951)**
**Rehabilitation Foundation for the Disabled**
10 Overlea Blvd., Toronto, ON M4H 1A4
416/425-3463, Fax: 416/425-1920, Toll Free: 1-800-263-3463
Email: omod@inforamp.net, URL: http://www.omod.org
Executive Director, Andria Spindel
Publications: The Dime Planner; Dimensions; PoliOntario Newsletter; C.E. Bulletin
Affiliates: Stroke Recovery Association of Ontario; Positive Action for Conductive Education

**QUÉBEC EASTER SEAL SOCIETY/SOCIÉTÉ DES TIMBRES DE PÂQUES DU QUÉBEC (1949)**
#1220, 615, boul René-Lévesque ouest, Montréal, QC H3B 1P5
514/866-1969, Fax: 514/866-6124, Toll Free: 1-800-263-1969
Executive Director, Robert C. Bédard

**THE REHABILITATION CENTRE/LE CENTRE DE RÉADAPTATION (1981)**
**Royal Ottawa Health Care Group**
505 Smyth Rd., Ottawa, ON K1H 8M2
613/737-7350, Fax: 613/737-7056
Executive Director, George Langill
Associate Executive Director, Irene Giustini
Publications: Perspective
Affiliates: University of Ottawa

**SASKATCHEWAN ABILITIES COUNCIL (1950)**
2310 Louise Ave., Saskatoon, SK S7J 2C7
306/374-4448, Fax: 306/373-2665
Executive Director, Kirsti Clarke
Director of Central Services, Ian Wilkinson
Publications: SAC Bulletin; Handi Farmer, q.

**SOCIÉTÉ POUR LES ENFANTS HANDICAPÉS DU QUÉBEC/QUÉBEC SOCIETY FOR DISABLED CHILDREN (1930)**
2300, boul René-Lévesque ouest, Montréal, QC H3H 2R5
514/937-6171, Téléc: 514/937-0082
Directeur général, Diane Tétreault
Président, John Penhale
Directeur, Communication, Michel Gailloux
Contrôleur, Richard Rioux
Publications: Papillon
Organisation(s) affiliée(s): Centre canadien de philanthropie; Conseil québécois pour l'enfance et la jeunesse

**SOCIETY FOR MANITOBANS WITH DISABILITIES INC. (SMD) (1946)**
825 Sherbrook St., Winnipeg, MB R3A 1M5
204/786-5601, Fax: 204/783-2919, TDD: 204/784-3710, Toll Free: 1-800-282-8041
Communications Manager, Katherine Murdock
Executive Director, David L. Steen
President, David Hargrave
Publications: Annual Report; Communiqué, s-a.

**John Milton Society for the Blind in Canada/ Société John Milton pour les aveugles du Canada (JMS) (1970)**
#202, 40 St. Clair Ave. East, Toronto, ON M4T 1M9
416/960-3953
President, James MacMillan
Publications: JMS Newsletter; Intouch; Insound, q.; Insight, bi-m.

**Low Vision Association of Ontario**
#101, 263 Russell Hill Rd., Toronto, ON M4V 2T4
416/921-6609
Contact, Karen Skead
Managing Director, Bill Carroll
Publications: Eye Trumpets; Cornets Visuels

**Ontario Federation for Cerebral Palsy**
#104, 1630 Lawrence Ave. West, Toronto, ON M6A 1C8
416/244-9686, Fax: 416/244-6543, Email: ofcp@the.connection.com, URL: http://www.connection.com/ofcp/
Executive Director, Clarence Meyers

**Ontario Rehabilitation & Work Council**
700 Caledonia Rd., North York, ON M6B 4H9
416/789-7925, Fax: 416/789-3499
Manager, Dorothy Solate

**People First Society of Alberta**
11720 Kingsway Ave., Edmonton, AB T5G 0X5
403/453-3047, Fax: 403/453-5779
Publications: The Question Mark
Affiliates: National People First

**Prince Edward Island Council of the Disabled (1975)**
#302, 134 Kent St., PO Box 2128, Charlottetown, PE C1A 7N7
902/892-9149, Fax: 902/566-1919, Toll Free: 1-800-653-5999
Information & Development Coordinator, Teresa MacKinnon

**R.C.L. (Québec) for the Disabled/R.C.L. (Québec) pour les Handicapés (1956)**
#410, 1000, rue Saint-Antoine ouest, Montréal, QC H3C 3R7
514/866-3689, Fax: 514/866-6303

**The Roeher Institute/L'Institut Roeher (1970)**
Kinsmen Building, York University, 4700 Keele St., North York, ON M3J 1P3
416/661-9611, Fax: 416/661-5701, Toll Free: 1-800-856-2207, Email: info@roeher.ca, URL: http://indie.ca/roeher/
President, Marcia H. Rioux, Ph.D.
Publications: Entourage
Affiliates: International Association for Scientific Study of Intellectual Deficiency; Canadian Association for Community Living

**Silent Voice Canada Inc.**
699 Coxwell Ave., Toronto, ON M4C 3C1
416/463-1105, TDD: 416/463-3928
Executive Director, Beverly Pageau
Publications: Silent Echo

**Speech Foundation of Ontario (SFO) (1977)**
10 Buchan Ct., North York, ON M2J 1V2
416/491-7771, Fax: 416/491-7215, Email: sfotcc@pathcom.com
Program Director, Margit Pukonen
Chairman, Gerald Brown

**Speech & Hearing Association of Nova Scotia**
PO Box 775, Halifax Central CRO, Halifax, NS B3J 2V2
902/423-9331, Fax: 902/423-0981
President, Janice Whebby
Publications: Ripples
Affiliates: Canadian Association of Speech-Language Pathologists & Audiologists (CASLPA)

**Speech Language Hearing Association of Alberta (SHAA)**
#2210, 10060 Jasper Ave., Edmonton, AB T5J 3R8
403/944-1609, Fax: 403/426-6882
Contact, Christine Seskus
Publications: The SHAA Journal
Affiliates: Canadian Association of Speech-Language Pathologists & Audiologists

**Vision Institute of Canada (VIC) (1981)**
York Mills Centre, #110, 16 York Mills Rd., North York, ON M2P 2E5
416/224-2273, Fax: 416/224-9234
Chief of Clinical Services, Dr. Catherine Chiarelli
Executive Director, Dr. Mitchell Samek
Publications: Vision Institute

**Vocational & Rehabilitation Research Institute (VRRI) (1966)**
3304 - 33 St. NW, Calgary, AB T2L 2A6
403/284-1121, Fax: 403/289-6427, Email: vrri@cadvision.com, URL: http://www.vrri.org
Executive Director, Leslie Tamagi
Chairman, Dr. Bob Sainsbury
Publications: Journal of Practical Approaches to Developmental Handicap; Bridges, s-a.

**DISARMAMENT *see* INTERNATIONAL COOPERATION/INTERNATIONAL RELATIONS**

## DRILLING

**Canadian Association of Drilling Engineers (CADE) (1974)**
#800, 540 - 5 Ave. SW, Calgary, AB T2P 0M2
403/264-4311, Fax: 403/263-3796, URL: http://www.lexicom.ab.ca/~cade
President, Fred Yurkiw
Vice-President, Doug Long
Publications: CADEnews
Affiliates: Canadian Association of Oilwell Drilling Contractors

**Canadian Association of Oilwell Drilling Contractors (CAODC) (1949)**
#800, 540 - 5 Ave. SW, Calgary, AB T2P 0M2
403/264-4311, Fax: 403/263-3796, Email: info@caodc.ca, URL: http://www.caodc.ca/
Managing Director, Don Herring
Coordinator, Technical Services, Diana Dennis
Publications: CAODC Membership Directory; Cost Study, a.; CAODC Newsletter, m.

**Canadian Drilling Association (CDA) (1938)**
#306, 222 McIntyre St. West, North Bay, ON P1B 2Y8
705/476-6992, Fax: 705/476-9494
Secretary Manager, Richard Niels
Publications: Drill Press; Directory of Goods & Services for the Drilling Industry

**Canadian Ground Water Association/Association canadienne des eaux souterraines (CGWA) (1976)**
PO Box 60, Lousana, AB T0M 1K0
403/749-2331, Fax: 403/749-2958
President, Martin Hammond
1st Vice-President, Jamie McDonald
2nd Vice-President, Guy Rohne
Secretary-Manager, Maurice Lewis
Publications: CGWA Newsletter
Affiliates: Canadian Earth Energy Association

**ALBERTA WATER WELL DRILLING ASSOCIATION (AWWDA) (1958)**
PO Box 130, Lougheed, AB T0B 2V0
403/386-2335, Fax: 403/386-2344
Sec.-Treas., Carol Larson
Publications: AWWDA Newsletter

**ASSOCIATION DES EAUX SOUTERRAINES DU QUÉBEC**
5930, boul Louis-H. Lafontaine, Anjou, QC H1M 1S7
514/353-9960, Téléc: 514/353-4825
Directeur général, Gilles Doyon

**BRITISH COLUMBIA GROUND WATER ASSOCIATION**
1708 - 197A St., Langley, BC V2Z 1K2
604/530-8934
Secretary, Joan Perry

**MANITOBA WATER WELL ASSOCIATION**
PO Box 1648, Winnipeg, MB R3C 2Z6
204/231-3728
Secretary Manager, Judy Stevens

**NEW BRUNSWICK GROUND WATER ASSOCIATION**
30 Blair St., Fredericton, NB E3B 5X3
506/455-8913, Fax: 506/454-9834
Executive Director, T.R. Mockler

**NEWFOUNDLAND & LABRADOR WATER WELL CORPORATION**
PO Box 249, Clarkes Beach, NF A0A 1W0
709/786-3561, Fax: 709/786-7386
Contact, Martin B. Hammond

**NOVA SCOTIA GROUNDWATER ASSOCIATION**
#219, 114 Woodlawn Rd., Dartmouth, NS B2W 2S7
902/435-6636, Fax: 902/434-7827
Sec-Treas., Patti Josey

**ONTARIO GROUND WATER ASSOCIATION (OGWA) (1951)**
2995 Delia Cres., Brights Grove, ON N0N 1C0
519/869-8933, Fax: 519/869-8940
Sec.-Treas., Judy Lethbridge
Publications: The Source

**PRINCE EDWARD ISLAND GROUND WATER ASSOCIATION**
RR#2, PO Box 857, Cornwall, PE C0A 1H0
902/675-2360, Fax: 902/675-2360
Contact, E. Watson MacDonald

**SASKATCHEWAN GROUND WATER ASSOCIATION (SGWA)**
PO Box 9434, Saskatoon, SK S7K 7E9
306/244-7551, Fax: 306/343-0001
Executive Secretary, Kathleen Watson
Publications: The Groundwater Journal

## ECONOMICS

**Association des économistes québécois (ASDÉQ)**
#3200, 380, rue Saint-Antoine ouest, Montréal, QC H2Y 3X7
514/284-2427, Téléc: 514/287-9057
Directrice exécutive, Marie-Lise Cote

**Association des professionnels en développement économique du Québec/Economic Development Professionals Association of Québec (APDEQ) (1959)**
#1000, 625, av du Président Kennedy, Montréal, QC H3A 1K2
514/845-8275, Téléc: 514/845-4071, Ligne sans frais: 1-800-361-8470, Courrier électronique: apdeq@generation.net
Présidente, Carole Voyzelle
1er Vice-Président, Laurent Thauvette
2e Vice-Président, Daniel Dicaire
3e Vice-Président, Claude Robichaud
Secrétaire-trésorier, Howard R. Silverman
Publications: Apdéquat

**Atlantic Association of Applied Economists (AAAE)**
c/o Nova Scotia Economic Renewal Agency, #708, 1800 Argyle St., PO Box 519, Halifax, NS B3J 2R7
902/424-6172, Fax: 902/424-5739, Email: econ.fmorley@gov.ns.ca
President, Fred Morley

**Atlantic Provinces Economic Council/Conseil Économique des Provinces de l'Atlantique (APEC) (1954)**
#500, 5121 Sackville St., Halifax, NS B3J 1K1
902/422-6516, Fax: 902/429-6803, Email: apec@fox.nstn.ns.ca, URL: http://ttg.sba.dal.ca/apec/
Chair, Aldea Landry
President & CEO, Elizabeth Beale
Publications: Atlantic Report

**Canada West Foundation (CWF)**
#550, 630 - 3rd Ave. SW, Calgary, AB T2P 4L4
403/264-9535, Fax: 403/269-4776, Email: cwf@freenet.calgary.ab.ca, URL: http://www.cwf.ca
President, David K. Elton, Email: delton@freenet.calgary.ab.ca
Administrative Officer, Lori Zaremba, Email: zaremba@freenet.calgary.ab.ca

**Canadian Agricultural Economics & Farm Management Society/Société canadienne d'économie rurale et de gestion agricole**
#907, 151 Slater St., Ottawa, ON K1P 5H4
613/232-9459, Fax: 613/594-5190
Secretary, Jeff Corman
Publications: Revue canadienne d'économie rurale; Canadian Journal of Agricultural Economics, 5 pa
Affiliates: Agricultural Institute of Canada

**Canadian Association for Business Economics, Inc./Association canadienne de science économique des affaires, inc. (CABE)**
Ontario Teachers' Pension Plan Board, 5650 Yonge St., North York, ON M2M 4H5
416/730-5375, Fax: 416/730-3773, URL: http://www.cabe.ca
Vice-President, Research & Economics, Leo De Bever, Email: Leo_deBever@otppb.com
Affiliates: International Federation of Associations of Business Economists

**Canadian Economics Association/Association canadienne d'economique (1967)**
Dept. of Economics, University of Toronto, 150 Saint George St., Toronto, ON M5S 3G7
416/978-6295, Fax: 416/978-6713, Email: cea@qed.econ.queensu.ca, URL: http://pacific.commerce.ubc.ca/cea/
President, Robin Broadway
Sec.-Treas., Prof. Michael Denny
Publications: The Canadian Journal of Economics/La Revue canadienne d'économique; Canadian Public Policy/Analyse de politique; CEA Newsletter, s-a.

**C.D. Howe Institute/Institut C.D. Howe (1973)**
125 Adelaide St. East, Toronto, ON M5C 1L7
416/865-1904, Fax: 416/865-1866, Email: cdhowe@cdhowe.org, URL: http://www.cdhowe.org
Executive Vice-President, Angela Ferrante
President & CEO, Tom Kierans
Secretary, Joyce Vaz
Director of Publications, Barry A. Norris

**Centre de recherche et développement en économique (CRDE) (1970)**
Pavillon Lionel-Groulx, Université de Montréal, CP 6128, Succ Centre-Ville, Montréal, QC H3C 3J7
514/343-6557, Téléc: 514/343-5831, Courrier électronique: crde@ere.umontreal.ca, URL: http://tornade.ere.umontreal.ca/crde/
Directeur, Jean-Marie Dufour
Secrétaire administrative, Josée Vignola

**Community Economic Development Institute (1986)**
University College of Cape Breton, PO Box 5300, Sydney, NS B1P 6L2
902/564-1366, Fax: 902/564-1366
CEO, Dr. Gerth MacIntyre
Publications: Centre for Community Economic Development

**The Conference Board of Canada (1954)**
255 Smyth Rd., Ottawa, ON K1H 8M7
613/526-3280, Fax: 613/526-4857, Telex: 053-3343, Email: infoserv@conferenceboard.ca, URL: http://www.conferenceboard.ca/nbec
President, James R. Nininger
Senior Vice-President, Charles Barrett

**Economic Developers Association of Canada/Association canadienne de développement économique (EDAC) (1968)**
#7, 714 Lakeshore Rd. East, Mississauga, ON L5G 1J6
905/891-8771, Fax: 905/891-8411
Executive Director, Penny A. Gardiner
Publications: Communiqué; Economic Development Papers, a.

**Economic Developers Council of Ontario Inc. (EDCO) (1957)**
PO Box 127, Fergus, ON N1M 2W7
519/787-1255, Fax: 519/787-1330, Email: edco@sympatico.ca, URL: http://www.edco.on.ca
Executive Director, Gladys M. Schmidt
President, Greg Borduas, Ph.D.
Publications: EDCO Journal; EDCO News, m.; Ontario - Canada's Business Centre, a.

**The Fraser Institute (1974)**
626 Bute St., 2nd Fl., Vancouver, BC V6E 3M1
604/688-0221, Fax: 604/688-8539, Toll Free: 1-800-665-3558, Email: info@fraserinstitute.ca, URL: http://www.fraserinstitute.ca
Executive Director, Dr. Michael A. Walker
Director, Kristin McCahon
Director, David Hanley
Director, Brian April
Director, V. Waese
Publications: Fraser Forum; On Balance, 10 pa; Critical Issues Bulletins; Fraser Folio
Toronto Office: T-D Centre, #2550, 55 King St. West, Toronto, ON M5K 1E7, 416/363-6575, Fax: 416/601-7322

**Institute for Policy Analysis (IPA) (1967)**
University of Toronto, #707, 140 Saint George St., Toronto, ON M5S 1A1
416/978-4854, Fax: 416/978-5519
Contact, Prof. James E. Pesando

**The North-South Institute/L'Institut Nord-Sud (NSI) (1976)**
#200, 55 Murray St., Ottawa, ON K1N 5M3
613/241-3535, Fax: 613/241-7435, Telex: 053-3300, Email: nsi@nsi-ins.ca, URL: http://www.nsi-ins.ca
President, Dr. Roy Culpeper
Publications: Review

**EDITORS *see* WRITERS & EDITORS**

## EDUCATION

*see also* **Research & Scholarship**

**Agence francophone pour l'enseignement supérieur et la recherche (AUPELF-UREF) (1961)**
Direction générale-Rectorat, CP 400, Succ Côte des Neiges, Montréal, QC H3C 2S7
514/343-6630, Téléc: 514/343-2107, Télex: 055-60955, Courrier électronique: syfed@refer.qc.ca, URL: http://www.refer.qc.ca
Directeur général-Recteur, Michel Guillou
Documentaliste, Céline Brunel
Publications: Universités

**Alberta Catholic School Trustees Association**
#107, 17704 - 103 Ave., Edmonton, AB T5S 1J9
403/484-6209, Fax: 403/484-6248
Executive Director, J. Kevin McKinney
Affiliates: Canadian Catholic School Trustees Association

**Alliance canadienne des responsables et enseignants en français (Langue maternelle)/Canadian Association for the Teachers of French as a First Language (ACREF) (1989)**
Faculté d'éducation, Université d'Ottawa, 145, rue Jean-Jacques Lussier, CP 415, Succ. A, Ottawa, ON K1N 6N5
613/562-5800, ext.4144, Téléc: 613/562-5146
Président, Benoît Cazabon
Publications: Le Trait d'Union

**Association for Baha'i Studies/Association d'études Baha'ies (ABS) (1975)**
34 Copernicus St., Ottawa, ON K1N 7K4
613/233-1903, Fax: 613/233-3644, Email: as929@freenet.carleton.ca
Executive Secretary, Christine Zerbinis
Academic Director, Pierre-Yves Mocquais
Publications: Journal of Baha'i Studies; Baha'i Studies, irreg.; ABS Bulletin, s-a.; Campus Association, s-a.
Affiliates: International Fraternal Association for Baha'i Studies

**Association of British Columbia Teachers of English as an Additional Language (BC TEAL) (1967)**
#177, 4664 Lougheed Hwy., Burnaby, BC V5C 5T5
604/294-8325, Fax: 604/294-8355, Email: bcteal@unixg.ubc.ca
President, Christine Stechishin
Publications: TEAL Newsletter
Affiliates: Affiliation of Multicultural Societies & Service Agencies of B.C.

**Association of Business Teacher Educators of Canada**
Faculty of Education, University of Regina, Regina, SK S4S 0A2
306/585-4610, Fax: 306/585-4880
President, Prof. Nancy Hicks

**Association des cadres scolaires du Québec**
#170, 1195, rue de Lavigerie, Ste-Foy, QC G1V 4N3
418/654-0014, Téléc: 418/654-1719
Directeur général, Jacques Fortin
Publications: Réussir; En Bloc, tous les 2 mois

**Association of Canadian Bible Colleges (ACBC)**
PO Box 4311, Three Hills, AB T0M 2N0
403/443-5511, Fax: 403/443-5540
President, Dr. Larry McKinney
Vice-President, Rev. David Boyd
Sec.-Treas., Peter Doell
Publications: Association of Canadian Bible Colleges Directory

**Association of Canadian Community Colleges/Association des collèges communautaires du Canada (ACCC) (1972)**
#200, 1223 Michael St. North, Ottawa, ON K1J 7T2
613/746-2222, Fax: 613/746-6721, URL: http://www.accc.ca
President, Tom Norton
Vice-President, International Services, Jean-Robert Vaillancourt
Vice President, National Services, Terry Anne Boyles
Publications: ACCC Community; The National Advocate/Le Porte-Parole, bi-m.; ACCC International, q.; International Update, bi-m.

**Association of Canadian Medical Colleges/L'Association des facultés de médecine du Canada (ACMC) (1943)**
774 Echo Dr., Ottawa, ON K1S 5P2
613/730-0687, Fax: 613/730-1196, Email: dhawkins@acmc.ca, URL: http://www.acmc.ca
Executive Director, Dr. David Hawkins
President, Dr. Louis Larochelle
Director, Administration, Janet Watt-Lafleur
Publications: ACMC Forum; Admission Requirements to Canadian Faculties of Medicine & their Selection Policies, biennial; Canadian Medical Education Statistics, a.
Affiliates: Canadian Medical Association; Association of Universities & Colleges of Canada

**Association for Canadian Studies/Association d'études canadiennes (ACS) (1973)**
c/o UQAM, V-5130, CP 8888, Succ Centre-Ville, Montréal, QC H3C 3P8
514/987-7784, Fax: 514/987-8210, Email: acs-aec@uqam.ca, URL: http://www.er.uqam.ca/nobel/c1015/
Administrative Director, Vincent Masciotra
President, Gwynneth Evans

Treasurer, Elizabeth Beaton
Publications: ACS Bulletin AEC; Directory to Canadian Studies in Canada; Canadian Issues, a.

**Association canadienne d'éducation de langue française (ACELF) (1947)**
268, rue Marie-de-l'Incarnation, Québec, QC G1N 3G4
418/681-4661, Téléc: 418/681-3389, Courrier électronique: informat@acelf.ca, URL: http://www.acelf.ca
Président, Louis-Gabriel Bordeleau
Secrétaire général par intérim, Fernand Langlais
Publications: Éducation et francophonie; Au fil des jours, 5 fois par an
Organisation(s) affiliée(s): UNESCO

**Association canadienne française pour l'avancement des sciences (ACFAS) (1923)**
425, rue de la Gauchetière est, Montréal, QC H2L 2M7
514/849-0045, Téléc: 514/849-5558
Directeur général, Germain Godbout
Présidente, Jennifer Stoddart
Chargée de programmes, Patricia Legault
Publications: Interface

**Association canadienne des professeurs d'immersion/Canadian Association of Immersion Teachers (ACPI) (1977)**
#310, 176, rue Gloucester, Ottawa, ON K2P 0A6
613/567-2223, Téléc: 613/230-5940, Courrier électronique: acpi@magi.com, URL: http://www.sfu.ca/cprf/acpi/
Secrétaire, Nicole Sangemino
Présidente, Marie-Christine Halliday
Publications: Le Journal de l'Immersion

**Association of Colleges of Applied Arts & Technology of Ontario/Association des collèges d'arts appliquées et de technologie de l'Ontario (ACAATO)**
#1010, 655 Bay St., Toronto, ON M5G 2K4
416/596-0744, Fax: 416/596-2364, URL: gopher://info.senecac.on.ca:2000/
Executive Director, Joan S. Homer
Publications: Ontario College News

**Association des collèges privés du Québec (1968)**
1940, boul Henri-Bourassa est, Montréal, QC H2B 1S2
514/381-8891, Téléc: 514/381-4086
Secrétaire général, Jacques N. Tremblay
Président, Benoit Lauzière
Tech. administration, Francine Bisson
Publications: Annuaire administratif

**Association des directeurs généraux des commissions scolaires du Québec (ADIGECS)**
50, boul Taschereau, La Prairie, QC J5R 4V3
514/444-4484, Téléc: 514/659-7131
Président, Gilles Taillon

**Association of Early Childhood Educators, Ontario (AECEO) (1950)**
#211, 40 Orchard View Blvd., Toronto, ON M4R 1B9
416/487-3157, Fax: 416/487-3758, Toll Free: 1-800-463-3391
Executive Director, Robyn Gallimore
Publications: The ECE Link

**Association of Educational Research Officers of Ontario/Association ontarienne des agents de recherche en éducation (AERO) (1972)**
Board of Education, 5050 Yonge St., North York, ON M2N 5N8
416/395-8147, Fax: 416/395-8346
President, Sylvia Larter
President Elect, Sandra Sangster
Publications: AERO Newsletter
Affiliates: American Educational Research Association

**Association des enseignantes et des enseignants franco-ontariens/Franco-Ontarian Teachers' Association (AEFO) (1939)**
681 Belfast Rd., Ottawa, ON K1G 0Z4
613/244-2336, Téléc: 613/563-7718
Directeur général, Guy Matte
Publications: En bref; Réseau, 5 fois par an
Organisation affiliée: Ontario Teachers' Federation

**Association française des conseils scolaires de l'Ontario**
#211, 435 St. Laurent Blvd., Ottawa, ON K1K 2Z8
613/745-3195, Téléc: 613/745-4772
Directeur général, J. Ladouceur

**Association francophone internationale des directeurs d'établissements scolaires (AFIDES) (1983)**
500, boul Crémazie est, Montréal, QC H2P 1E7
514/383-7335, Téléc: 514/384-2139, Courrier électronique: afides@grics.qc.ca, URL: http://grics.qc.ca/afides
Secrétaire général, Richard Charron
Présidente du C.A., Khadidjatou Ka Sarr
Publications: La Revue des échanges

**Association des institutions d'enseignement secondaire (AIES) (1968)**
1940, boul Henri-Bourassa est, Montréal, QC H2B 1S2
514/381-8891, Téléc: 514/381-4086, Courrier électronique: info@cadre.qc.ca, URL: http://www.cadre.qc.ca
Directrice générale, Micheline Lavallée

**Association des institutions de niveaux préscolaire et élémentaire du Québec (AIPÉQ)**
1940, boul Henri-Bourassa est, Montréal, QC H2B 1S2
514/381-8891, Téléc: 514/381-4086, Ligne sans frais: 1-800-381-8891
Présidente, Renée Champagne
Contacte, Rose-Aimée Michaud

**Association for Media & Technology in Education in Canada/Association des média et de la technologie en éducation au Canada (AMTEC) (1970)**
#1318, 3-1750 The Queensway, Etobicoke, ON M9C 5H5
604/323-5627, Fax: 604/323-5577, Email: maepp@langara.bc.ca, URL: http://www.camosun.bc.ca/~amtec/
President, Dr. Katy Campbell, Email: katy.campbell@ualberta.ca
President-Elect, Dr. Genevieve Gallant, Email: ggallant@morgan.ucs.mun.ca
Sec.-Treas., Mary Anne Epp, Email: maepp@langara.bc.ca
Publications: Canadian Journal of Educational Communication; Media News, 3 pa
Affiliates: Canadian School Library Association; Canadian Association for Distance Education; Canadian Education Association; Pacific Instructional Media Association; Association for Educational Communications & Technology; Society for Instructional Technology/Edmonton

**Association of New Brunswick Professional Educators/Association des éducateurs professionnels du Nouveau-Brunswick**
91 Carlisle Rd., Fredericton, NB E3B 7X5
506/444-5331, Fax: 506/453-3325
President, Onil Dumont
Sec.-Treas., Mike Logue

**Association québécoise du personnel de direction des écoles (AQPDE) (1967)**
2965, boul Rive Sud, St-Romuald-d'Etchemin, QC G6W 6N6
418/838-1088, Téléc: 418/838-1091, Courrier électronique: aqpde@globetrotter.qc.ca, URL: http://grics.qc.ca/aqpde/
Présidente, Liliane Marcoux
Publications: Le Lien

**Association québécoise des professeures et professeurs de français (AQPF) (1967)**
#222, 2095, boul Charest ouest, Ste-Foy, QC G1N 4L8
418/683-0947, Téléc: 418/527-4765, Ligne sans frais: 1-800-267-0947
Présidente, Huguette Lachapelle
Publications: Québec français
Organisation(s) affiliée(s): Fédération internationale des professeurs de français

**Association of Universities & Colleges of Canada/Association des Universités et Collèges du Canada (AUCC) (1911)**
#600, 350 Albert St., Ottawa, ON K1R 1B1
613/563-1236, Fax: 613/563-9745, Email: info@aucc.ca, URL: http://www.aucc.ca
President & CEO, Robert Giroux
Senior Vice-President, Sally Brown
Corporate Secretary, Rosemary Cavan
Director, Government Relations & Public Affairs, Robert Best
Director, International & Canadian Programs Branch, François Beslisle
Director, Research & Policy Analysis, Robert Davidson
Director, International Policy & Liaison, Karen McBride
Director, Publications & Communications, Christine Tausig Ford
Publications: Canadian University Distance Education Directory; Directory of Canadian Universities, a.; University Affairs, 10 pa; Financial Statistics of Universities & Colleges, a.; Universities Telephone Directory, a.; Uniworld, a.; Trends: The Canadian University in Profile, a.; Research File, a.

**ASSOCIATION OF ATLANTIC UNIVERSITIES/ASSOCIATION DES UNIVERSITÉS DE L'ATLANTIQUE (AAU) (1964)**
#403, 5657 Spring Garden Rd., Halifax, NS B3J 3R4
902/425-4230, Fax: 902/425-4233
Executive Director, Anne Marie MacKinnon
Publications: Association of Atlantic Universities Calendar

**ASSOCIATION OF CANADIAN FACULTIES OF DENTISTRY/ASSOCIATION DES FACULTÉS DENTAIRES DU CANADA (ACFD)**
427 Gilmour St., Ottawa, ON K2P 0R5
613/236-4763, Fax: 613/236-3935
Email: dcf-acfd@sympatico.ca
Executive Sec.-Treas., Lorraine Emmerson
Publications: Forum

**ASSOCIATION OF CANADIAN UNIVERSITIES FOR NORTHERN STUDIES/ASSOCIATION UNIVERSITAIRE CANADIENNE D'ÉTUDES NORDIQUES (ACUNS) (1977)**
#405, 17 York St., Ottawa, ON K1N 9J6
613/562-0515, Fax: 613/562-0533
Email: acuns@cyberus.ca, URL: http://www.geog.mcgill.ca/northern/acunhome.html
President, Dr. Roger H. King
Vice-President, Dr. Jill Oakes
Sec.-Treas., Frank Duerden
Publications: Northline/Point nord

**ASSOCIATION OF CANADIAN UNIVERSITY PLANNING PROGRAMS (ACUPP)**
Dept. of City Planning, University of Manitoba, Winnipeg, MB R3T 2N2
204/474-8761, Fax: 204/275-7198

President, Dr. Christine McKee
Sec.-Treas., Peter Boothroyd
Affiliates: Canadian Institute of Planners

**ASSOCIATION OF DEANS OF PHARMACY OF CANADA (ADPC)**
Faculty of Pharmacy, University of Alberta, 3118 Dentistry/Pharmacy Bldg., Montréal, T6 T6G 2N8
403/492-0204, Fax: 403/492-1843
Email: rmoskalyk@pharmacy.ualberta.ca
President, Richard Moskalyk, Ph.D.

**ASSOCIATION OF DIRECTORS OF JOURNALISM PROGRAMS IN CANADIAN UNIVERSITIES/ASSOCIATION DES DIRECTEURS ET COORDONNATEURS DE PROGRAMMES DE JOURNALISME DES UNIVERSITÉS CANADIENNES (1982)**
Director's Office, School of Journalism & Communication, Carleton U., Ottawa, ON K1S 5B6
613/520-7404, Fax: 613/520-6690
Dean, Peter Johansen

**ASSOCIATION DES ÉCOLES D'OPTOMÉTRIE DU CANADA/ ASSOCIATION OF SCHOOLS OF OPTOMETRY OF CANADA (1972)**
École d'optométrie, Université de Montréal, CP 6128, Succ. A, Montréal, QC H3C 3J7
514/343-7537, Téléc: 514/343-2382
Président, Dr. Roland Giroux
Organisation(s) affiliée(s): Association of Schools & Colleges of Optometry

**ASSOCIATION OF REGISTRARS OF THE UNIVERSITIES & COLLEGES OF CANADA/ASSOCIATION DES REGISTRAIRES DES UNIVERSITÉS ET COLLÈGES DU CANADA (ARUCC) (1964)**
Bishop's University, Lennoxville, QC J1M 1Z7
819/822-9675, Fax: 819/822-9616
Email: amontgom@admin.ubishops.ca
President, Ann Montgomery
Publications: Contact; ARUCC Directory, a.

**ASSOCIATION OF UNIVERSITY FORESTRY SCHOOLS OF CANADA/ ASSOCIATION DES ÉCOLES FORESTIÈRES UNIVERSITAIRES DU CANADA (AUFSC)**
Faculté de foresterie et de géomatique, Université Laval, CP 2208, Succ Terminus, Ste-Foy, QC G1K 7P4
418/656-2116, Fax: 418/656-3177
Sec.-Treas., Prof. Claude Godbout

**CANADIAN ASSOCIATION OF COLLEGE & UNIVERSITY STUDENT SERVICES/ASSOCIATION DES SERVICES AUX ÉTUDIANTS DES UNIVERSITÉS ET COLLÈGES DU CANADA (CACUSS) (1977)**
Dept. of Residences, Maritime Hall, University of Guelph, #158, 50 Stone Rd. East, Guelph, ON N1G 2W1
519/824-4120, ext.3052, Fax: 519/767-1670
Assistant Director of Residences, Blair Capes
Publications: CACUSS Communiqué; Membership Directory, a.

**CANADIAN ASSOCIATION FOR GRADUATE STUDIES/ASSOCIATION CANADIENNE DES ÉTUDES AVANCÉES (CAGS) (1962)**
Hagen Hall, Room 205, University of Ottawa, 115 Seraphin Marion St., Ottawa, ON K1N 6N5
613/562-5291, Fax: 613/562-5292
Email: cags@uottawa.ca, URL: http://www.uottawa.ca/associations/cags-acea/
President, Dr. Joseph De Koninck
Publications: CAGS Statistical Report; CAGS Newsletter, s-a.

**CANADIAN ASSOCIATION OF SCHOOLS OF SOCIAL WORK/ ASSOCIATION DES ÉCOLES DE SERVICE SOCIAL (CASSW)**
#100-B, 30 Rosemount Ave., Ottawa, ON K1Y 1P4
613/722-2974, Fax: 613/722-5661
Executive Director, Ann D. Sharp, MSW
Publications: Canadian Social Work Review

**CANADIAN ASSOCIATION OF UNIVERSITY BUSINESS OFFICERS/ ASSOCIATION CANADIENNE DE PERSONNEL ADMINISTRATIF UNIVERSITAIRE (CAUBO) (1937)**
#320, 350 Albert St., Ottawa, ON K1R 1B1
613/563-1236, ext.268, Fax: 613/563-7739
Email: mcohen@aucc.ca
Executive Director, Maurice Cohen
President, Glenn Harris
Publications: University Manager; Financial Statistics

**CANADIAN ASSOCIATION OF UNIVERSITY RESEARCH ADMINISTRATORS/ASSOCIATION CANADIENNE D'ADMINISTRATEURS DE RECHERCHE UNIVERSITAIRE (CAURA) (1972)**
McMaster University, Gilmour Hall, #110B, 1280 Main St. West, Hamilton, ON L8S 4S8
905/529-7070, ext.24519, Fax: 905/540-8019
President, Kevin Keough
Vice-President, Noli Swatman
Sec.-Treas., Emmi Morwald
Publications: CAURA Bulletin

**CANADIAN ASSOCIATION OF UNIVERSITY SCHOOLS OF NURSING/ ASSOCIATION CANADIENNE DES ÉCOLES UNIVERSITAIRES DE NURSING (CAUSN) (1942)**
#325, 350 Albert St., Ottawa, ON K1R 1B1
613/563-1236, ext.280, Fax: 613/563-7739
Executive Director, Wendy McBride
Publications: CAUSN Newsletter/Bulletin d'information

**CANADIAN COUNCIL OF UNIVERSITY BIOLOGY CHAIRS/CONSEIL UNIVERSITAIRE DES DIRECTEURS DE BIOLOGIE DU CANADA (CCUBC)**
c/o Dept. of Botany, Axelrod Bldg., Univ. of Guelph, Guelph, ON N1G 2W1
519/824-4120, ext.6000, Fax: 519/767-1991
Email: lpeterso@uoguelph.ca
Sec.-Treas., John Vierula
Publications: CCUBC Newsletter

**CANADIAN INTERUNIVERSITY ATHLETIC UNION/UNION SPORTIVE INTERUNIVERSITAIRE CANADIENNE (CIAU)**
Place R. Tait McKenzie, 1600 James Naismith Dr., 3rd Fl., Gloucester, ON K1B 5N4
613/748-5619, Fax: 613/748-5764
Email: national@ciau.ca, URL: http://www.ciau.ca
President, Tom Allen
Publications: CIAU Directory
Affiliates: Fédération internationale du sport universitaire (CIAU is official Canadian representative); Atlantic Universities Athletic Association; Fédération québécoise du sport étudiant; Ontario Universities Athletic Association; The Great Plains Athletic Conference; Canada West Universities Athletic Association

**CONFEDERATION OF CANADIAN FACULTIES OF AGRICULTURE & VETERINARY MEDICINE/CONFÉDÉRATION DES FACULTÉS D'AGRICULTURE ET DE MÉDÉCINE VÉTÉRINAIRE DU CANADA (CCFAVM) (1990)**
Ontario Agricultural College, Univ. of Guelph, Dean's Office, 50 Stone Rd. East, Guelph, ON N1G 2W1
519/763-5350, Fax: 519/763-5350
Executive Director, Dr. C.M. Switzer

**COUNCIL OF CANADIAN LAW DEANS/CONSEIL DES DOYENS ET DES DOYENNES DES FACULTÉS DE DROIT DU CANADA (CCLD)**
Faculty of Law, University of Ottawa, 57 Louis Pasteur, PO Box 415, Stn A, Ottawa, ON K1N 6N5
613/562-5889, Fax: 613/562-5121
Executive Director, Mistrale Goudreau

**COUNCIL OF CANADIAN UNIVERSITY CHEMISTRY CHAIRMEN**
Dept. of Chemistry, University of Manitoba, Winnipeg, MB R3T 2N2
204/474-9321, Fax: 204/275-0905
Sec.-Treas., Prof. Harry Duckworth

**COUNCIL OF WESTERN CANADIAN UNIVERSITY PRESIDENTS (COWCUP)**
University of Regina, #100, 3737 Wascana Pkwy., Regina, SK S4S 0A2
306/585-4382, Fax: 306/585-5200
Chair, Donald O. Wells, B.Sc., M.Sc., Ph.D.

**DEANS & DIRECTORS OF HOME ECONOMICS & RELATED AREAS IN CANADIAN UNIVERSITIES (1942)**
Université de Montréal, Fac. of Medicine, Dept. of Nutrition, CP 6128, Succ Centre Ville, Montréal, QC H3C 3J7
514/343-6401, Fax: 514/343-7395
Suzanne Simard Mavrikakis

### Atlantic Provinces Education Foundation/ Fondation d'éducation des provinces Atlantiques (APEF)
PO Box 2044, Halifax, NS B3J 2Z1
902/424-5352, Fax: 902/424-8976, Email: premiers@fox.nstn.ns.ca
Information Officer, Kim Thomson

### Canadian Alliance of Student Associations/ Alliance canadienne des associations étudiantes (CASA)
PO Box 3408, Stn D, Ottawa, ON K1P 6H8
613/236-3457, Fax: 613/236-2386, URL: http://www.casa.ca
National Director, R. Hoops Harrison

### Canadian Asian Studies Association/Association canadienne des études asiatiques (CASA) (1968)
Centre d'Études de l'Asie de l'Est, Université de Montréal, PO Box 6128, Stn A, Montréal, QC H3C 3J7
514/343-6569, Fax: 514/343-7716, Email: denm@ere.umontreal.ca, URL: http://tornade.ere.umontreal.ca/~denm/casa.htm
Contact, Loy Denis
Publications: Contact
Affiliates: International Association of Sanskrit Studies

### Canadian Association for Adult Education
29 Prince Arthur Ave., Toronto, ON M5R 1B2
416/964-0559, Fax: 416/964-9226
Executive Director, Ian Morrison
President, Teresa MacNeil
Contact, Daniel Benedict

### Canadian Association for the Advancement of Netherlandic Studies/Association canadienne pour l'avancement des études néerlandaises (CAANS) (1971)
Dept. of Classics, Acadia University, Wolfville, NS B0P 1X0
902/585-1267, Fax: 902/585-1070, Email: bverstra@ace.acadian.ca
President, Beert Verstraete
Publications: Canadian Journal of Netherlandic Studies

### Canadian Association of African Studies/ Association canadienne des études africaines (CAAS) (1971)
855, rue Sherbrooke ouest, Montréal, QC H3A 2T7
514/398-4800, Fax: 514/398-1770
Contact, Prof. Frank Kanz
Publications: Canadian Journal of African Studies; Canadian Association of African Studies Newsletter

### Canadian Association for American Studies/ Association d'études américaines au Canada (CAAS) (1964)
Dept. of English, University of Guelph, MacKinnon Bldg., Guelph, ON N1G 2W1
519/824-4120, Fax: 519/766-0844
President, Christine Bold
Publications: Canadian Review of American Studies

Affiliates: American Studies Association; British Association of American Studies; European Studies of American Studies

### Canadian Association of Business Education Teachers/Association canadienne du personnel enseignant en commerce (1967)
c/o The Halton Board of Education, 2050 Guelph Line, PO Box 5005, Burlington, ON L7R 3Z2
905/335-3663, Fax: 905/335-9802
Executive Director, Lily Kretchman
President, Al Renner
Publications: The Canadian Journal of Business Education
Affiliates: National Business Educators Association; International Society of Business Educators

### Canadian Association for Co-operative Education/Association canadienne de l'enseignement coopératif (CAFCE) (1973)
#310, 55 Eglinton Ave. East, Toronto, ON M4P 1G8
416/483-3311, Fax: 416/483-3365, Email: co-oped@idirect.com, URL: http://www.sfu.ca/cafce
Richard Murphy
Carol Cox
Publications: CAFCE News; Co-op Education, a.; CAFCE Co-op Program Directory

### Canadian Association for Distance Education/Association canadienne de l'éducation à distance (CADE) (1984)
#205, One Stewart St., Ottawa, ON K1N 6H7
613/230-3630, Fax: 613/230-2746, Email: cade@csse.ca, URL: http://www.cade-aced.ca
President, May Maskow
Executive Secretary, Tim Howard
Publications: Journal of Distance Education; Communiqué, q.

### Canadian Association of Foundations of Education/Association canadienne des fondements de l'éducation (CAFE) (1971)
c/o Research Services, Ryerson University, 350 Victoria St., Toronto, ON M3B 2K3
416/979-5000, ext.7521, Fax: 416/979-5336, Email: mowen@acs.ryerson.ca
President, Dr. Michael Owen, Ph.D.
Publications: CAFE Newsletter
Affiliates: Canadian Philosophy of Education Society; Canadian History of Education Society

### Canadian Association of Geographers/Association canadienne des géographes (CAG) (1951)
Burnside Hall, McGill University, 805, rue Sherbrooke ouest, Montréal, QC H3A 2K6
514/398-4946, Fax: 514/398-7437, Email: cag@felix.geog.mcgill.ca
President, Bryan Massam
Sec.-Treas., Mark Rosenberg
Publications: The Canadian Geographer; CAG Newsletter, bi-m.
Affiliates: Represented on the Canadian Commission for UNESCO, the Social Science Federation of Canada, & the Canadian Committee of the International Geographical Union

### Canadian Association of Hispanists
Dept. of Modern Languages, University of Ottawa, PO Box 450, Stn A, Ottawa, ON K1N 6N5
613/564-2305, Fax: 613/564-9527
President, Nigel Dennis
Sec.-Treas., Marian G.R. Coope

### Canadian Association of Independent Schools (CAIS) (1979)
PO Box 1502, St Catharines, ON L2R 7J9
905/688-4866, Fax: 905/688-5778, Email: cais@ridley.on.ca
Executive Director, Janet M. Lewis

### Canadian Association for Pastoral Practice & Education/Association canadienne pour la pratique et l'éducation pastorales (CAPPE) (1965)
47 Queen's Park Cres., Toronto, ON M5C 2C3
416/977-3700, Fax: 416/978-7821, Email: krausj@ican.net, URL: http://www3.ns.sympatico.ca/cappe/home.htm
Executive Director, Rev. Jan K. Kraus
Publications: Newsletter/Nouvelles
Affiliates: American Association of Pastoral Counselling; Association for Clinical Pastoral Education

### Canadian Association of Principals (CAP) (1977)
#36B, 1010 Polytek Ct., Gloucester, ON K1J 9J2
613/745-8472, Fax: 613/745-6325, Email: caphk@istar.ca
Office Administrator, Marie Budarick
Publications: CAP INFO; CAP Journal, q.

### Canadian Association of School Social Workers & Attendance Counsellors (CASSWAC) (1982)
c/o London Board of Education, 1250 Dundas St. East, London, ON N6A 5L1
519/452-2125, Fax: 519/455-3545
President, Edward James
Treasurer, Gayle Stewart
Publications: CASSWAC News

### Canadian Association for Scottish Studies (CASS) (1971)
Dept. of History, University of Guelph, Guelph, ON N1G 2W1
519/824-4120, ext.3209, Fax: 519/766-1384, Email: scottish@arts.uoguelph.ca
General Editor, Scott McLean
Review Editor, Scott Moir
Publications: Scottish Tradition
Affiliates: Scottish Studies Foundation

### Canadian Association of Second Language Teachers/Association canadienne des professeurs de langue seconde (CASLT) (1970)
#310, 176 Gloucester St., Ottawa, ON K2P 0A6
613/234-6567, Fax: 613/230-5940, Email: caslt@mts.net, URL: http://www2.tvo.org/education/caslt
Office Manager, Brigitte Roy
President, Bev Anderson
Publications: Réflexions

### Canadian Association of Slavists/Association canadienne des slavistes (CAS) (1956)
Dept. of Modern Langs. & Comparative Studies, University of Alberta, Edmonton, AB T6G 2E6
403/492-2566, Fax: 403/492-2715
Sec.-Treas., Maxim Tarnawsky
President, Joan DeBardeleben
Publications: CAS Newsletter; Canadian Slavonic Papers, q.
Affiliates: International Conference of Slavic & East European Studies

### Canadian Association for Teacher Education/Association canadienne pour la formation des enseignants (CATE) (1978)
Faculté des sciences de l'éducation, Université Laval, Laval, QC G1K 7P4
418/656-2131, ext.5480, Fax: 418/656-7347, Email: tlaf@fse.ulaval.ca
President, Dr. Thérèse Laferriere
Vice-President, Dr. Alice Colins
Sec.-Treas., Dr. Joe Engemann
Affiliates: Canadian Association for Research in Early Childhood/Association canadienne pour la recherche préscolaire; Association of Business Teacher Educators of Canada/Association des professeurs en enseignement commercial au Canada

### Canadian Association of Teachers of Community Health/Association canadienne des professeurs de santé communautaire (CATCH) (1967)
Dept. of Epidemiology & Community Medicine, University of Ottawa, 451 Smyth Rd., Ottawa, ON K1H 8M5
613/787-6458, Fax: 613/787-6472
President., Dr. J. Segovia, M.D.
Sec.-Treas., Dr. W. Thurston, Ph.D.
Publications: CATCH Newsletter
Affiliates: Canadian Public Health Association

### Canadian Association of Teachers of Technical Writing
Dept. of English & Communications, Douglas College, PO Box 2503, New Westminster, BC V3L 5B2
604/527-5400
President, Diana Wagner

### Canadian Association for University Continuing Education/Association pour l'éducation permanente dans les universités du Canada (CAUCE) (1974)
#600, 350 Albert St., Ottawa, ON K1R 1B1
613/563-1236, Fax: 613/563-9745
Email: cauce@aucc.ca, URL: http://www.tile.net/tile/listserv/caucel.html
Executive Coordinator, Beverlee Stevenson
President, Jim Sharpe
Publications: Bulletin; Canadian Journal of University Continuing Education, s-a.; Yearbook of Exemplary Practice, a.; Canadian University Distance Education Directory, a.; The Handbook, a.

### Canadian Association of University Teachers/Association canadienne des professeures et professeurs d'université (CAUT) (1951)
2675 Queensview Dr., Ottawa, ON K2B 8K2
613/820-2270, Fax: 613/820-7244, Email: acppu@caut.ca, URL: http://www.caut.ca
Executive Director, Dr. Donald C. Savage
Associate Executive Director, Gordon Piché
Director, Member Services, Rosalind Riseborough
Publications: CAUT Bulletin

#### CONFEDERATION OF ALBERTA FACULTY ASSOCIATIONS (CAFA)
University of Alberta, 11043 - 90 Ave., Edmonton, AB T6G 2E1
403/492-5630, Fax: 403/492-6145
Email: cafa@gpu.srv.ualberta.ca, URL: http://www.ualberta.ca/~cafa/
President, Rick Szostak

#### CONFEDERATION OF UNIVERSITY FACULTY ASSOCIATIONS OF BRITISH COLUMBIA (CUFA/BC)
515 West Hastings St., Vancouver, BC V6B 5K3
604/291-5201, Fax: 604/291-5202
Executive Director, Robert Clift

#### FEDERATION OF NEW BRUNSWICK FACULTY ASSOCIATIONS/FÉDÉRATION DES ASSOCIATIONS DE PROFESSEURS D'UNIVERSITÉ DU NOUVEAU-BRUNSWICK (FNBFA) (1973)
#297, 65 Brunswick St., Fredericton, NB E3B 1G5
506/458-8977, Fax: 506/458-5620
Email: fnbfa@nbnet.nb.ca
Executive Director, Desmond A. Morley
Secretary, Patricia Lewington
Publications: Bulletin

**FÉDÉRATION QUÉBÉCOISE DES PROFESSEURES ET PROFESSEURS D'UNIVERSITÉ/QUÉBEC FEDERATION OF UNIVERSITY PROFESSORS (FQPPU)**
#405, 4446, boul St-Laurent, Montréal, QC H2W 1Z5
514/843-5953, Téléc: 514/843-6928
Président, Roch Denis

**MANITOBA ORGANIZATION OF FACULTY ASSOCIATIONS (MOFA)**
Collège Universitaire de St-Boniface, 200 Cathedral Ave., Winnipeg, MB R2H 0H7
204/235-4486, Fax: 204/237-3240
President, Luc Cote

**ONTARIO CONFEDERATION OF UNIVERSITY FACULTY ASSOCIATIONS/UNION DES ASSOCIATIONS DES PROFESSEURS DES UNIVERSITÉS DE L'ONTARIO (OCUFA) (1964)**
#400, 27 Carlton St., Toronto, ON M5B 1L2
416/979-2117, Fax: 416/593-5607
Email: ocufa@ocufa.on.ca
Executive Director, Marion Perrin
Secretary, Lisa Alexis
Publications: Forum

### Canadian Bureau for International Education/Bureau canadien de l'éducation internationale (CBIE) (1966)
#1100, 220 Laurier Ave. West, Ottawa, ON K1P 5Z9
613/237-4820, Fax: 613/237-1073, Telex: 053-3255, Email: jfox@cbie.ca, URL: http://www.cbie.ca
President, James W. Fox
Publications: Synthesis/Synthèse
Affiliates: UNESCO Canada; National Consortium of Scientific & Educational Societies

### Canadian Catholic School Trustees' Association/Association canadienne des commissaires d'écoles catholique (CCSTA) (1960)
80 Sheppard Ave. East, North York, ON M2N 6E8
416/229-5326, Fax: 416/229-5345
President, Dorothy Fortier
Executive Secretary, Dr. John J. Flynn
Publications: Catholic Schools in Toronto; Reading for Catholic Teachers; CCSTA Newsletter, 3 pa

### Canadian College of Teachers/Collège canadien des enseignants (1958)
2010A Sherwood Dr., PO Box 57157, Stn Eastgate, Sherwood Park, AB T8A 5L7
403/922-6668, Fax: 403/922-2885
Sec.-Treas., Ronald E. Johnston
Publications: CCT News

### Canadian Council for the Advancement of Education/Le Conseil canadien pour l'avancement de l'éducation (CCAE) (1993)
#301, 250 Consumers Rd., North York, ON M2J 4V6
416/494-1440, Fax: 416/495-8723, Email: base@onramp.ca, URL: http://www.stmarys.ca/partners/ccae/ccae.htm
President, St. Mary's University, Chuck Bridges
Publications: Ensemble

### Canadian Council for Multicultural & Intercultural Education/Conseil canadien pour l'éducation multiculturelle et interculturelle (CCMIE) (1983)
#200, 144 O'Connor St., Ottawa, ON K1P 5M9
613/233-4916, Fax: 613/233-4735, Email: national-office@ccmie.ca, URL: http://www.intranet.on.ca/~ccmie/
National Office & Resource Manager, Kamal Eddine Firdaous
President, Dr. Leticia Marques de Sa Messier
Publications: Multiculturalism/Multiculturalisme
Affiliates: International Association for Intercultural Education

### Canadian Council of Teachers of English Language Arts (CCTELA) (1967)
c/o Association Management Centre, PO Box 4143, Stn C, Calgary, AB T2R 5M9
204/474-8564, Fax: 204/275-5962
Executive Director, Marita Watson
Publications: English Quarterly; CCTE Newsletter, q.
Affiliates: International Federation of Teachers of English; NCTE

### Canadian Education Association/Association canadienne d'éducation (CEA) (1891)
#8-200, 252 Bloor St. West, Toronto, ON M5S 1V5
416/924-7721, Fax: 416/924-3188, Email: acea@hookup.net, URL: http://www.acea.ca
Executive Director, Penny Milton
Publications: Education Canada; Newsletter/le bulletin, 8 pa

### Canadian Ethnic Studies Association/Société canadienne d'études ethniques (CESA) (1977)
a/s Centre d'études ethniques, Université de Montréal, PO Box 6128, Stn Centre-Ville, Montréal, QC H3C 3J7
President, Dr. Natalia Aponiuk
Sec.-Treas., Denis Hlynka
Publications: Canadian Ethnic Studies; CESA Bulletin, s-a.

### Canadian Federation of Business School Deans/Fédération canadienne des doyens des écoles d'administration (1979)
#1005, 116 Albert St., Ottawa, ON K1P 5G3
613/564-3301, Fax: 613/564-7695
Director of Operations, Karen Fleming
Publications: Bulletin

### Canadian Federation of Students/Fédération canadienne des étudiantes et étudiants (CFS) (1981)
#500, 170 Metcalfe St., Ottawa, ON K2P 1P3
613/232-7394, Fax: 613/232-0276, URL: http://www.cfs-fcee.ca
National Chairperson, Brad Lavigne
Publications: Student Advocate; Student Association Directory, a.

### Canadian Federation of Students Services/Fédération canadienne des étudiantes et étudiants services (1982)
**CFS-Services**
243 College St., Toronto, ON M5T 2Y1
416/977-3703, Fax: 416/977-4796, Telex: 06-22436
Executive Director, David A. Jones
Publications: The Student Traveller; The Student Association Directory, a.

### Canadian Federation of University Women/Fédération canadienne des femmes diplômées des universités (CFUW) (1919)
Head Office, #600, 251 Bank St., Ottawa, ON K2P 1X3
613/234-8252, Fax: 613/234-8221
Executive Director, Kim Young
President, Betty Bayless
Publications: The Communicator/La Communicatrice
Affiliates: International Federation of University Women

### Canadian Foundation for Economic Education/Fondation d'éducation économique (CFEE) (1974)
#501, 2 St. Clair Ave. West, Toronto, ON M4V 1L5
416/968-2236, Fax: 416/968-0488
President, Gary Rabbior

### Canadian Home Economics Association/Association canadienne d'économie familiale (CHEA) (1939)
#307, 151 Slater St., Ottawa, ON K1P 5H3
613/238-8817, Fax: 613/238-8972, Email: cheagen@web.net
Executive Director, Ellen Boynton
President, Nancy Cook
International Development Program Manager, Nicole Pelletier
Development Education Officer, Pat Ulrich
Publications: ID Connections; Canadian Home Economics Journal, q.; Rapport; Membership Directory
Affiliates: Canadian Council on Social Development; World Food Day Association; International Federation for Home Economics; Canadian Council for International Cooperation; National Council of Women of Canada; Vanier Institute of the Family

### Canadian Home Economics Association Foundation/Fondation de l'association canadienne d'économie familiale (CHEAF) (1980)
303 Ashland Ave., Winnipeg, MB R3L 1L6
204/475-1508
Secretary, Dr. Margaret I. Morton
Chairperson, Dr. Elizabeth Feniak
Affiliates: Canadian Home Economics Association

### Canadian Home & School Federation/Fédération canadienne des associations foyer-école (CHSF) (1927)
#104, 858 Bank St., Ottawa, ON K1S 3W3
613/234 7292, Fax: 613/234 3913, Email: chspft@cyberus.ca, URL: http://cnet.unb.ca/cap/partners/chsptf/
Acting Executive Director, G.T. Durkin
Publications: Newsletter

**ALBERTA HOME & SCHOOL COUNCILS' ASSOCIATION**
#102, 12310 - 105 Ave., Edmonton, AB T5N 0Y4
403/454-9867, Fax: 403/455-0167, Toll Free: 1-800-661-3470
President, Elizabeth Dobrovolsky
Publications: Newsletter

**BRITISH COLUMBIA CONFEDERATION OF PARENT ADVISORY COUNCILS (BCCPAC)**
#1540, 1185 Georgia St. West, Vancouver, BC V6E 4E6
604/687-4433, Fax: 604/687-4488
Email: bccpac@direct.ca, URL: http://www.discoverlearning.com
President, Silvia Dyck
Executive Director, Hélène Cameron
Publications: BCCPAC Bulletin; BCCPAC Newsletter, 4-5 pa

**MANITOBA ASSOCIATION OF PARENT COUNCILS**
#309, 1181 Portage Ave., Winnipeg, MB R3G 0T3
204/786-4722, Fax: 204/774-8553

**NEW BRUNSWICK FEDERATION OF HOME & SCHOOL ASSOCIATIONS (NBFHSA) (1938)**
RR#1, PO Box 367, Scoudouc, NB E0A 1N0
506/532-6775
Provincial Secretary, Patricia Lee
President, Linda Bateman
Publications: News & Views

**NEWFOUNDLAND & LABRADOR HOME & SCHOOL FEDERATION (NLHSF) (1979)**
33 Pippy Pl., PO Box 23140, St. John's, NF A1B 4J9
709/739-4830, Fax: 709/739-4833
Email: nlhsf@calvin.stemnet.nf.ca, URL: http://www.stemnet.nf.ca/Organizations/NLHSF/
President, Marie Law
Executive Director, Eva Whitmore
Publications: The Cuffer

**NOVA SCOTIA FEDERATION OF HOME & SCHOOL ASSOCIATIONS**
PO Box 91, La Have, NS B0R 1C0
902/688-2463
Director, Anne White
President, Sandra Himmelman

**ONTARIO FEDERATION OF HOME & SCHOOL ASSOCIATIONS INC. (1916)**
#551, 1260 Bay St., Toronto, ON M5R 2B7
416/924-7491, Fax: 416/924-5354
Executive Secretary, Beth McGuire
President, Pat Johansen
Publications: OFHSA Bulletin

**PRINCE EDWARD ISLAND HOME & SCHOOL FEDERATION (1953)**
3 Queen St., PO Box 1012, Charlottetown, PE C1A 7M4
902/892-0664, Fax: 902/628-1844, Toll Free: 1-800-916-0664
Executive Director, Shirley Jay
President, Audrey Newcombe

**QUÉBEC FEDERATION OF HOME & SCHOOL ASSOCIATIONS/ FÉDÉRATION DES ASSOCIATIONS FOYER-ÉCOLE DU QUÉBEC (QFHSA) (1944)**
#562, 3285, boul Cavendish, Montréal, QC H4B 2L9
514/481-5619, Fax: 514/481-5619
Email: qfhsa@discovland.net
President, Patricia Waters
Executive Secretary, Donna Sauriol
Publications: Québec Home & Safety School News

**SASKATCHEWAN ASSOCIATION OF SCHOOL COUNCILS (SASC) (1938)**
221 Cumberland Ave. North, Saskatoon, SK S7N 1M3
306/955-5723, Fax: 306/955-5723
Executive Director, Joy Bastness
President, Deborah Agema
Publications: Newsletter

## Canadian Industrial Arts Association
#45333, Faculty of Education BS, University of New Brunswick, Fredericton, NB E3B 6E3
506/453-3508, Fax: 506/453-3569
President, Alfred T. Steeves

## Canadian School Boards Association/ Association canadienne des commissions/ conseils scolaires (CSBA) (1923)
#600, 130 Slater St., Ottawa, ON K1P 6E2
613/235-3724, Fax: 613/238-8434, Email: admin@CdnSBA.org, URL: http://www.cdnsba.org/
President, Donna Cansfield
Executive Director, Marie Pierce
First Vice-President, Eric Jonasson
Second Vice-President, Dr. Roy Wilson
Publications: CSBAction

**ALBERTA SCHOOL BOARDS ASSOCIATION (ASBA) (1907)**
12310 - 105 Ave., Edmonton, AB T5N 0Y4
403/482-7311, Fax: 403/482-5659
Executive Director, David Anderson
President, Dr. Roy Wilson
Publications: Spectrum

**ASSOCIATION QUÉBÉCOISE DES COMMISSIONS SCOLAIRES/ QUÉBEC SCHOOL BOARDS ASSOCIATION (1929)**
#520, 4999, rue Ste-Catherine ouest, Montréal, QC H3Z 1T3
514/482-7522, Fax: 514/482-9399
Email: cscott@login.net, URL: http://www.login.net/qsba
Executive Director, Jeff Polenz

**MANITOBA ASSOCIATION OF SCHOOL TRUSTEES**
191 Provencher Blvd., Winnipeg, MB R2H 0G4
204/233-1595, Fax: 204/231-1356
Executive Director, Dr. J.B. MacNeil

**NEW BRUNSWICK SCHOOL TRUSTEES' ASSOCIATION**
701 Churchill Row, Fredericton, NB E3B 1P7
506/450-4066, Fax: 506/450-8204
Executive Director, Marven Betts

**NEWFOUNDLAND & LABRADOR SCHOOL BOARDS' ASSOCIATION (NLSBA) (1969)**
#117, 19 Crosbie Pl., St. John's, NF A1B 3W9
709/722-7171, Fax: 709/722-8214
Executive Director, Myrle Vokey
Publications: Tidbits

**NOVA SCOTIA SCHOOL BOARDS ASSOCIATION (NSSBA) (1954)**
PO Box 605, Stn M, Halifax, NS B3J 2R7
902/420-9191, Fax: 902/429-7405
Email: sharon@nssba.ednet.ns.ca
Executive Director, Frank Barteaux
Communications Manager, Sharon MacPhee
Publications: NSSBA Matters

**SASKATCHEWAN SCHOOL TRUSTEES ASSOCIATION (SSTA) (1915)**
#400, 2222 - 13 Ave., Regina, SK S4P 3M7
306/569-0750, Fax: 306/352-9633
Executive Director, J.C. Melvin
Publications: School Trustee

## Canadian Society of Biblical Studies/Société canadienne des études bibliques (CSBS) (1933)
Dept. of Religious Studies, Memorial University, PO Box 4200, Stn C, St. John's, NF A1C 5S7
709/737-8166, Fax: 709/737-4569
Executive Secretary, Prof. David J. Hawkin
Publications: Studies in Religion/Sciences religieuses; Bulletin, a.
Affiliates: Canadian Corporation for the Study of Religion; Canadian Federation of Humanities

## Canadian Society for Education through Art/ Société canadienne d'éducation par l'art (CSEA) (1955)
675, Samuel de Champlain, Boucherville, QC J4B 6C4
514/655-2435, Fax: 514/655-4379, Email: louise.filion@enter-net.com
President, Judy Freedman
Secretary, Louise Filion
Publications: CSEA/SCEA Newsletter; Canadian Review of Art Education; Research Review, s-a.
Affiliates: British Columbia Art Teachers' Association; Fine Arts Council, Alberta Teachers' Association; Saskatchewan Society for Education through Art; Manitoba Association of Art Educators; Ontario Society for Education through Art; Provincial Association of Art Teachers; Association québécoise des éducateurs spécialisés en arts plastiques; New Brunswick Arts Education Council; Nova Scotia Art Teachers' Association; PEI Art Teachers' Association; Art Council of the Newfoundland Teachers' Association; Canadian Art Gallery Educators

## Canadian Society for the Study of Education/ Société canadienne pour l'étude de l'éducation (CSSE) (1972)
#205, One Stewart St., Ottawa, ON K1N 6H7
613/230-3532, Fax: 613/230-2746, Email: csse@csse.ca
Administrator, Tim Howard
President, Yvonne Hébert, Ph.D.
Publications: CSSE News/Nouvelles SCÉÉ; Canadian Journal of Education, q.; Yearbook

## Canadian Society for the Study of Higher Education/Société canadienne pour l'étude de l'enseignement supérieur (CSSHE) (1970)
#320, 350 Albert St., Ottawa, ON K1R 1B1
613/563-1236, Fax: 613/563-7739, Email: kclements@aucc.ca
President, Glen Jones
Executive Secretary, Kenneth Clements
Publications: Canadian Journal of Higher Education; CSSHE Bulletin, 5 pa; CSSHE Directory, a.; Professional File, 3 pa

## Canadian Teachers' Federation/Fédération canadienne des enseignantes et enseignants (CTF) (1920)
110 Argyle Ave., Ottawa, ON K2P 1B4
613/232-1505, Fax: 613/232-1886, Email: info@ctf-fce.ca, URL: http://www.ctf-fce.ca
President, Maureen Morris
Secretary-General, Jacques Schryburt

**ALBERTA TEACHERS' ASSOCIATION (ATA) (1918)**
Barnett House, 11010 - 142 St., Edmonton, AB T5N 2R1
403/453-2411, Fax: 403/455-6481
URL: http://www.teachers.ab.ca
Executive Secretary, Julius S. Buski
Publications: ATA News; The ATA Magazine, q.; ATA Directory & Information Guide, a.

**ASSOCIATION DES ENSEIGNANTES ET DES ENSEIGNANTS FRANCOPHONES DU NOUVEAU-BRUNSWICK (AEFNB) (1970)**
CP 712, Fredericton, NB E3B 5B4
506/452-8921, Téléc: 506/453-9795
Directeur général, Ronald LeBreton
Publications: Nouvelles

**BRITISH COLUMBIA TEACHERS' FEDERATION/FÉDÉRATION DES ENSEIGNANTS DE LA COLOMBIE-BRITANNIQUE (BCTF) (1916)**
#100, 550 - 6th Ave. West, Vancouver, BC V5Z 4P2
604/871-2283, Fax: 604/871-2294
URL: http://www.bctf.bc.ca
Executive Director, Elsie McMurphy
President, Alice McQuade
Publications: Teacher

**MANITOBA TEACHERS' SOCIETY (MTS) (1919)**
191 Harcourt St., Winnipeg, MB R3J 3H2
204/888-7961, Fax: 204/831-0877
Email: mbteach@mb.sympatico.ca, URL: http://www.mts.net/teachers/
General Secretary, Art Reimer
Publications: The Manitoba Teacher

**NEW BRUNSWICK TEACHERS' FEDERATION (1902)**
PO Box 1535, Fredericton, NB E3B 5R6
506/452-8921, Fax: 506/453-9795
Executive Director, Edouard Allain
Publications: NBTA News

**NEWFOUNDLAND & LABRADOR TEACHERS' ASSOCIATION/ ASSOCIATION DES ENSEIGNANTS DE TERRE-NEUVE (NLTA) (1890)**
3 Kenmount Rd., St. John's, NF A1B 1W1
709/726-3223, Fax: 709/726-4302, Toll Free: 1-800-563-3599
Email: nlta@calvin.stemnet.nf.ca, URL: http://www.stemnet.nf.ca/Organizations/NLTA/
Publications: NTA Bulletin

**NORTHWEST TERRITORIES TEACHERS' ASSOCIATION/ ASSOCIATION DES ENSEIGNANTS DES TERRITOIRES DU NORD-OUEST**
5018 - 48 St., PO Box 2340, Yellowknife, NT X1A 2P7
867/873-8501, Fax: 867/873-2366
Email: nwtta@nwtta.nt.ca, URL: http://www.nwtta.nt.ca
Executive Director, Blake W. Lyons
Publications: Communicate; Professional Development & Teacher Welfare Bulletins

**NOVA SCOTIA TEACHERS UNION/SYNDICAT DES ENSEIGNANTS DE LA NOUVELLE-ÉCOSSE (NSTU) (1895)**
3106 Dutch Village Rd., Armdale, NS B3L 4L7
902/477-5621, Fax: 902/477-3517, Toll Free: 1-800-565-6788

URL: http://fox.nstn.ca/~nstu/
Executive Director, James MacKay
Publications: The Teacher; Aviso, 3 pa

**ONTARIO TEACHERS' FEDERATION/FÉDÉRATION DES ENSEIGNANTES ET DES ENSEIGNANTS DE L'ONTARIO (OTF) (1944)**
#700, 1260 Bay St., Toronto, ON M5R 2B5
416/966-3424, Fax: 416/966-5450
President, Bill Martin
Sec.-Treas., Susan Langley
Publications: Interaction

**PRINCE EDWARD ISLAND TEACHERS' FEDERATION/FÉDÉRATION DES ENSEIGNANTS DE L'ÎLE-DU-PRINCE-EDOUARD (PEITF) (1880)**
PO Box 6000, Charlottetown, PE C1A 8B4
902/569-4157, Fax: 902/569-3682
President, Ralph Grant
Executive Assistant, Bob MacRae
Executive Assistant, Allan Murphy
General Secretary, James L. Blanchard
Publications: PEITF Newsletter

**PROVINCIAL ASSOCIATION OF PROTESTANT TEACHERS OF QUÉBEC/ASSOCIATION PROVINCIALE DES ENSEIGNANTS PROTESTANTS DU QUÉBEC (PAPT) (1864)**
#1, 17035 Brunswick Blvd., Kirkland, QC H9H 5G6
514/694-9777, Fax: 514/694-0189
Executive Director, Alan Lombard
Publications: Sentinel/Sentinelle

**SASKATCHEWAN TEACHERS' FEDERATION/FÉDÉRATION DES ENSEIGNANTS ET DES ENSEIGNANTES DE LA SASKATCHEWAN (STF)**
2317 Arlington Ave., Saskatoon, SK S7K 2H8
306/373-1660, Fax: 306/374-1122
Email: src@stf.sk.ca, URL: http://www.stf.sk.ca
President, Carol Moen
Publications: Saskatchewan Bulletin

**YUKON TEACHERS' ASSOCIATION/ASSOCIATION DES ENSEIGNANTS DU YUKON (YTA) (1955)**
2064 - 2 Ave., Whitehorse, YT Y1A 1A9
867/668-6777, Fax: 867/667-4324
President, Terry Price
Publications: YTA Note

### Canadian Test Centre Inc./Services d'évaluation pédagogique (CTC) (1990)
#7, 85 Citizen Court, Markham, ON L6G 1A8
905/513-6636, Fax: 905/513-6639, Toll Free: 1-800-668-1006, Email: echeng@ctest.com
Managing Director, Ernest W. Cheng
Director, S. Shiu, CPA, CGA

### Canadian University & College Conference Officers Association/Association des coordonnateurs de congrès des universités et des collèges du Canada (CUCCOA)
c/o Ryerson Polytechnic University, 160 Mutual St., Toronto, ON M5B 2M2
416/979-5284, Fax: 416/979-5212
Publications: CUCCOA Clips

### Canadian University & College Counselling Association/Association canadienne de counselling universitaire et collégial (CUCCA) (1963)
Centre for Student Development, McMaster University, 409 Hamilton Hall, Hamilton, ON L8S 4K1
905/525-9140, ext.24711, Fax: 905/529-8972, Email: nifakis@mcmaster.ca
President, Dr. Debbie Nifakis
Publications: Coast to Coast with CUCCA
Affiliates: Canadian Association of College & University Student Services (CACUSS)

### Canadian Vocational Association/Association canadienne de la formation professionnelle (CVA) (1960)
PO Box 3435, Stn D, Ottawa, ON K1P 6L4
613/722-7696, Fax: 613/722-7696, Email: cva_acfp@magi.com, URL: http://www.cva.ca
President, Anna Kae Todd
Office Manager, P. McMahon
Publications: Canadian Vocational Journal

### Centre d'animation de développement et de recherche en éducation (CADRÉ) (1968)
1940, boul Henri-Bourassa est, Montréal, QC H2B 1S2
514/381-8891, Téléc: 514/381-4086, Ligne sans frais: 1-888-381-8891, Courrier électronique: info@cadre.qc.ca, URL: http://www.cadre.qc.ca
Directrice générale, Micheline Lavallée

### Centre franco-ontarien de ressources pédagogiques (CFORP) (1974)
290 Dupuis St., Vanier, ON K1L 1A2
613/747-8000, Téléc: 613/747-2808
Directrice générale, Bernadette LaRochelle
Publications: Ressources

### Co-operative, Career & Work Education Association of Canada/Association canadienne pour l'alternance travail-études (CCWEAC) (1983)
**National Co-operative Education Centre**
2 King St. West, Hamilton, ON L8P 1A1
905/523-6682, Fax: 905/523-7753
President, Hilda Pollard
Publications: CCWEAC Newsletter

### Coalition for Education Reform
65 Parkway Ave., Markham, ON L3P 2G8
Affiliates: Organization for Quality Education; Quality Education Network; Educators' Association for Quality Education

### College Institute Educators' Association of BC (CIEA) (1980)
#301, 555 - 8 Ave. West, Vancouver, BC V5Z 1C6
604/873-8988, Fax: 604/873-8865, Email: admin@ciea.bc.ca
President, Ed Lavalle
Publications: Profile
Affiliates: BC Federation of Labour; Canadian Association of University Teachers

### The Commonwealth of Learning (COL) (1988)
#600, 1285 West Broadway, Vancouver, BC V6H 3X8
604/775-8200; Telex: 04507508 COMLEARN, Fax: 604/775-8210, Email: info@col.org, URL: http://www.col.org
Chairman, Dr. H. Ian Macdonald
President, Dato' Prof. Gajaraj Dhanarajan
Public Affairs Officer, Dave Wilson, CAE, Email: dwilson@col.org
Publications: Connections

### Comparative & International Education Society of Canada/Société canadienne d'éducation comparée et internationale (CIESC/SCECI) (1967)
Faculty of Education, Queen's University, Kingston, ON K7L 3N6
613/545-6000, ext.7410, Fax: 613/545-6584
President, Dr. Eva Krugley-Smolska
Secretary, Iain Munro
Publications: CIESC Newsletter; Canadian & International Education, s-a.

### Conférence des recteurs et des principaux des universités du Québec/Conference of Rectors & Principals of Quebec Universities (CREPUQ) (1963)
#1200, 300, Léo Pariseau, CP 952, Succ Place du Parc, Montréal, QC H2W 2N1
514/288-8524, Téléc: 514/288-0554, Courrier électronique: crepuq@crepuq.qc.ca, URL: http://www.crepuq.qc.ca
Directeur général, Jacques Bordeleau
Publications: Répertoire des regroupements de recherche des établissements universitaires du Québec; CREPUQ en Bref; Répertoire des bibliothèques universitaires québécoises

### Conseil des écoles françaises de la communauté urbaine de Toronto/Metro Toronto French-Language School Council (CEFCUT) (1988)
#207, One Concorde Gate, North York, ON M3C 3N6
416/391-1264, Téléc: 416/391-3892
Responsable/Communications, Alice Ducharme
Publications: En Somme

### Corporate-Higher Education Forum/Forum entreprises-universités (C-HEF) (1983)
#440, 1010 - 8 Ave. SW, Calgary, AB T2P 1J2
514/543-1171, Fax: 514/543-1175, Email: cheforum@aol.com, URL: http://www.work.org/C-HEF/
President, Norman E. Wagner
Publications: Rapport

### Council of Ontario Universities/Conseil des universités de l'Ontario (COU) (1962)
#203, 444 Yonge St., Toronto, ON M5B 2H4
416/979-2165, Fax: 416/979-8635, Email: postmaster@coupo.cou.on.ca, URL: http://www.cou.on.ca
President, Bonnie M. Patterson
Chairperson, Dr. J Robert S. Prichard
Executive Director, Public Affairs, Arnice Cadieux
Executive Director, Research, Analysis & Policy,
Executive Director, Office for Partnerships for Advanced Skills, Dr. Norm Shulman
Executive Director, Ontario Council on Graduate Studies, Dr. Nicole Bégin-Heick
Publications: COU Newsletter
Affiliates: Some 28 councils, committees & associations; contact head office for a complete list

### Council of Outdoor Educators of Ontario (COEO) (1969)
#403, 1185 Eglinton Ave. East, North York, ON M3C 3C6
416/426-7276
Publications: Pathways; Directory of Programs Personnel

### Council for Second Languages Programs in Canada/Conseil des programmes de langues secondes au Canada
#320, 350 Albert St., Ottawa, ON K1R 1B1
613/563-1236, Fax: 613/563-7739
President, Adrien Roy
Contact, Kenneth Clements

### Educational Media Producers & Distributors Association of Canada/Association des producteurs et distributeurs du media d'education (1967)
3 Wellesley Ave., Toronto, ON M4X 1V2
416/923-7252, Fax: 416/929-2051
Executive Director, Jarvis Stoddart
Chairperson, Jennifer Baird

### Fédération des associations de parents francophones de l'Ontario (FAPFO) (1954)
#302, 1173 Cyrville, Gloucester, ON K1J 7S6
613/741-8846, Téléc: 613/741-7322, Courrier électronique: 103256.3630@compuserve.com

Présidente, Francesca Piredda
Publications: APrioI

### Fédération des cégeps (1969)
500, boul Crémazie est, Montréal, QC H2P 1E7
514/381-8631, Téléc: 514/381-2263, Courrier électronique: dg@fedecegeps.qc.ca, URL: http://www.fedecegeps.qc.ca
Directeur général, Gaëtan Boucher
Publications: Annuaire des cégeps; Cégepropos, trimestriel

### Fédération des comités de parents de la Province de Québec inc.
389, boul Rochette, Beauport, QC G1C 1A4
418/667-2432, Téléc: 418/667-6713
Directeur général, Jean-Pierre Jobidon
Publications: Veux-tu savoir?

### Fédération des commissions scolaires du Québec (FCSQ) (1947)
1001, av Bégon, CP 490, Ste-Foy, QC G1V 4C7
418/651-3220, Téléc: 418/651-2574, URL: http://grics.qc.ca/fcsq/accueil.htm
Directeur général, Fernand Paradis
Présidente, Diane Drouin
Publications: Commissaires d'écoles

### Federation of Independent Schools in Canada/Fédération canadienne des écoles privées (FISC) (1980)
9125 - 50 St., Edmonton, AB T6B 2H3
403/469-9868, Fax: 403/469-9880, Email: gduthler@kingsu.ab.ca
Executive Director, Gary Duthler

#### ASSOCIATION OF INDEPENDENT SCHOOLS & COLLEGES IN ALBERTA (AISCA) (1965)
9125 - 50 St., Edmonton, AB T6B 2H3
403/469-9868, Fax: 403/469-9880
Email: gduthler@kingsu.ab.ca
Executive Director, Gary Duthler
Publications: AISCA Directory of Independent Schools in Alberta

#### CONFERENCE OF INDEPENDENT SCHOOLS (ONTARIO) (CIS)
PO Box 1502, St Catharines, ON L2R 7J9
905/688-4866, Fax: 905/688-5778
Email: cis@ridley.on.ca
Executive Director, Janet M. Lewis

#### FÉDÉRATION DES ASSOCIATIONS DE L'ENSEIGNEMENT PRIVÉS (FAEP) (1991)
1940, boul Henri-Bourassa est, Montréal, QC H2B 1S2
514/381-8891, Téléc: 514/381-4086
Directeur exécutif, Auguste Servant

#### FEDERATION OF INDEPENDENT SCHOOL ASSOCIATIONS OF BC (FISA) (1966)
150 Robson St., Vancouver, BC V6B 2A7
604/684-6023, Fax: 604/684-3163
Executive Director, Fred Herfst
President, A. Blesch
Vice-President, Dr. L. Hollaar
Secretary, G. Baldwin
Treasurer, P. Vanderpol
Publications: Independent Schools Directory; Newsletter

#### MANITOBA FEDERATION OF INDEPENDENT SCHOOLS INC. (MFIS) (1974)
23 Pinecrest Bay, Winnipeg, MB R2G 1W2
204/667-9971, Fax: 204/661-5357
Executive Administrator, John Doornbos
President, Bill Gortemaker
Publications: MFIS Newsletter

#### ONTARIO ALLIANCE OF CHRISTIAN SCHOOLS (OACS) (1952)
617 Hwy. 53 East, Ancaster, ON L9G 3K9
905/648-2100, Fax: 905/648-2110
Email: oacs@oacs.org, URL: http://www.oacs.org
Executive Director, Adrian Guldemond
Publications: The Communicator; The Digest
Affiliates: Christian Schools International

#### ONTARIO FEDERATION OF INDEPENDENT SCHOOLS (OFIS) (1974)
2199 Regency Terrace, Ottawa, ON K2C 1H2
613/596-4013, Fax: 613/596-4971
Acting Executive Director, Elaine Hopkins
Publications: OFIS News

#### SASKATCHEWAN ASSOCIATION OF HISTORICAL HIGH SCHOOLS (SAHHS)
c/o Lutheran College Bible Institute, PO Box 459, Outlook, SK S0L 2N0
306/867-8344, Fax: 306/867-9947
President, Daniel A. Haugen

#### SASKATCHEWAN ASSOCIATION OF INDEPENDENT CHURCH SCHOOLS
c/o Saskatoon Christian Centre, 102 Pinehouse Dr., Saskatoon, SK S7K 5H7
306/242-7141
President, Lou Brunelle

### Fédération nationale des enseignants et des enseignantes du Québec/National Federation of Québec Teachers (FNEEQ) (1969)
1601, av de Lorimier, Montréal, QC H2K 4M5
514/598-2241, Téléc: 514/598-2190, Courrier électronique: fneeq@accent.net
Président, Pierre Patry
Secrétaire général, Hélène Boileau
Publications: FNEEQ-Actualité

### Fédération des parents francophones de l'Alberta/Federation of Francophone Parents of Alberta (FPFA) (1986)
#205, 8925 - 82 Ave., Edmonton, AB T6C 0Z2
403/468-6934, Téléc: 403/469-4799, Courrier électronique: fpfa@connect.ab.ca
Directrice générale, Mariette Rainville
Publications: Le Chaînon

### Fédération provinciale des comités de parents du Manitoba (FPCP) (1976)
531 Marion St., Winnipeg, MB R2J 0J9
204/237-9666, Téléc: 204/231-1436, Courrier électronique: fpcp@solutions.mb.ca
Directrice générale, Hélène d'Auteuil
Publications: Entre parents

### Fédération québécoise des directeurs et directrices d'établissements d'enseignement (FQDE) (1961)
#100, 7855, boul Louis-H-Lafontaine, Anjou, QC H1K 4E4
514/353-7511, Ligne sans frais: 1-800-361-4258
Président, Guy Lessard

### Federation of Women Teachers' Associations of Ontario/Fédération des associations des enseignantes de l'Ontario (FWTAO) (1918)
1260 Bay St., Toronto, ON M5R 2B8
416/964-1232, Fax: 416/964-0512, URL: http://www.fwtao.on.ca
Executive Director, Joan Westcott
Publications: FWTAO Newsletter
Affiliates: Ontario Teachers' Federation

### Foundation for Educational Exchange Between Canada & the United States of America (1990)
**The Fulbright Program**
#2015, 350 Albert St., Ottawa, ON K1R 1A4
613/237-5366, Fax: 613/237-2029, Email: info@fulbright.ca, URL: http://www.usis-canada.usia.gov/fulbrigh.htm
Executive Director, Dr. Victor Konrad
Program Officer, Denise Yap
Publications: The Canada-US Fulbright Program

### Humanities & Social Sciences Federation of Canada/Fédération canadienne des sciences humaines et sociales (HSSFC) (1996)
#415, 151 Slater St., Ottawa, ON K1P 5H3
613/238-6112, Fax: 613/238-6114, Email: fedcan@hssfc.ca, URL: http://www.hssfc.ca
Executive Director, Marcel Lauzière
Publications: Bulletin

### Institut canadien d'éducation des adultes
#300, 5225, rue Berri, Montréal, QC H2J 2S4
514/948-2044, Téléc: 514/948-2040
Directrice général, Diane Laberge

### International Association for Better Basic Education (1975)
34 Broadway Ave., Ottawa, ON K1S 2V6
613/232-3014
Secretary, F.D. Richardson

### International Association of Master Penmen & Teachers of Handwriting (1950)
34 Broadway Ave., Ottawa, ON K1S 2V6
613/232-3014
Secretary, F.D. Richardson
Publications: Penmen's Newsletter
Affiliates: International Association for Better Basic Education

### International Council for Adult Education/Conseil international d'éducation des adultes (ICAE) (1973)
#500, 720 Bathurst St., Toronto, ON M5S 2R4
416/588-1211, Fax: 416/588-5725, Email: icae@web.net, URL: http://www.web.net/icae/
Executive Director, Raymond Desrochers
President, Lalita Ramdas
Publications: Convergence; ICAE News/Nouvelles du CIEA, q.

### International Federation of Institutes for Advanced Study/Fédération internationale des instituts des hautes études (IFIAS) (1972)
39 Spadina Rd., Toronto, ON M5R 2S9
416/926-7570, Fax: 416/926-9481, Email: ifiastor@vm.utcs.toronto.ca, URL: http://www.ifias.ca/
Director, Robert I.G. McLean
Associate Director/Secretary, Peter Main
Chairman, Sir Hermann Bondi
Publications: IFIAS News; Member Institute Directory, a.; Latin American Scientists on Global Change (HDGC Program), a.

### Learning Disabilities Association of Canada/Troubles d'apprentissage - Association canadienne (LDAC) (1971)
#200, 323 Chapel St., Ottawa, ON K1N 7Z2
613/238-5721, Fax: 613/235-5391, Email: ldactaac@fox.nstn.ca, URL: http://edu-ss10.educ.queensu.ca/~lda/
President, Linda Jeppesen
Publications: National
Affiliates: Canadian Coalition for Prevention of Developmental Disabilities

#### ASSOCIATION QUÉBÉCOISE POUR LES TROUBLES D'APPRENTISSAGE/LEARNING DISABILITIES ASSOCIATION OF QUÉBEC (AQETA) (1966)
#300, 284, rue Notre-Dame ouest, Montréal, QC H2Y 1T7
514/847-1324, Téléc: 514/281-5187
Directrice générale, Denise D. Marquez
Publications: Rendez-vous

**LEARNING DISABILITIES ASSOCIATION OF ALBERTA/TROUBLES D'APPRENTISSAGE - ASSOCIATION DE L'ALBERTA (LDAA) (1968)**
#145, 11343 - 61 Ave., Edmonton, AB T6H 1M3
403/448-0360, Fax: 403/438-0665, Info Line: 403/988-3349
Email: ldaa@compusmart.ab.ca
Provincial Coordinator, David Barnum
Publications: Agenda

**LEARNING DISABILITIES ASSOCIATION OF BRITISH COLUMBIA/ TROUBLES D'APPRENTISSAGE - ASSOCIATION DE LA COLOMBIE-BRITANNIQUE (LDABC) (1974)**
#203, 15463 - 104 St., Surrey, BC V3R 1N9
604/588-6322, Fax: 604/588-6344
Executive Director, Marny Ryan
Publications: The Advocate

**LEARNING DISABILITIES ASSOCIATION OF MANITOBA/TROUBLES D'APPRENTISSAGE - ASSOCIATION DE MANITOBA (1966)**
60 Maryland St., 2nd Fl., Winnipeg, MB R3G 1K7
204/774-1821, Fax: 204/788-4090
Executive Director, Jan Thiessen
Office Manager, Jan Kaludjer
Publications: Newslines

**LEARNING DISABILITIES ASSOCIATION OF NEW BRUNSWICK/ TROUBLES D'APPRENTISSAGE - ASSOCIATION DU NOUVEAU-BRUNSWICK (LDANB) (1980)**
88 Prospect St. West, Fredericton, NB E3B 2T8
506/459-7852, Fax: 506/458-1352
Email: mckayf@nald.ca, URL: http://www.nald.ca/ldanb.htm
President, Millie LeBlanc
Publications: Reflections

**LEARNING DISABILITIES ASSOCIATION OF NEWFOUNDLAND/ TROUBLES D'APPRENTISSAGE - ASSOCIATION DE TERRE-NEUVE (1981)**
PO Box 26036, St. John's, NF A1E 5T9
709/754-3665, Fax: 709/754-3665
President, Diane White
Vice-President, Roger Deveaux
Publications: Newsletter

**LEARNING DISABILITIES ASSOCIATION OF THE NORTHWEST TERRITORIES**
PO Box 242, Yellowknife, NT X1A 2N2
867/873-6378, Fax: 867/873-6378
Contact, Irene Birin

**LEARNING DISABILITIES ASSOCIATION OF NOVA SCOTIA/ TROUBLES D'APPRENTISSAGE - ASSOCIATION DE LA NOUVELLE ÉCOSSE (LDANS) (1988)**
55 Ochterloney St., Dartmouth, NS B2Y 1C3
902/464-9751, Fax: 902/464-9167
Executive Director, Lori Steeves
President, David Muldoon
Publications: News & Events

**LEARNING DISABILITIES ASSOCIATION OF ONTARIO/TROUBLES D'APPRENTISSAGE - ASSOCIATION DE L'ONTARIO (LDAO) (1964)**
Box 39, #1004, 365 Bloor St. East, Toronto, ON M4W 3L4
416/929-4311, Fax: 416/929-3905
Executive Director, Carol Yaworksi
Publications: Communiqué

**LEARNING DISABILITIES ASSOCIATION OF PRINCE EDWARD ISLAND**
PO Box 1081, Charlottetown, PE C1A 7M4
902/892-9664, Fax: 902/368-4548
Executive Director, Mike Howatt

**LEARNING DISABILITIES ASSOCIATION OF SASKATCHEWAN/ TROUBLES D'APPRENTISSAGE - ASSOCIATION DE LA SASKATCHEWAN**
Albert Community Centre, #26, 610 Clarence Ave. South, Saskatoon, SK S7H 2E2
306/652-4114, Fax: 306/652-3220
Executive Director, Laurie Garcea
Publications: The Provincial

**LEARNING DISABILITIES ASSOCIATION OF YUKON TERRITORY (LDAY) (1973)**
#205, 4133 - 4 Ave., PO Box 4853, Stn Main, Whitehorse, YT Y1A 4N6
867/668-5167, Fax: 867/668-6504
Executive Director, George Green
Publications: LDAY News; Learning Disabilities in the Classroom
Affiliates: Yukon Association for Community Living; Special Olympics; Yukon Literacy Council

**Learning Enrichment Foundation (LEF) (1979)**
116 Industry St., Toronto, ON M6M 4L8
416/769-0830, Fax: 416/769-9912
Executive Director, Eunice Grayson
Publications: LEF Rep; LEF Update

**Manitoba Association for Bilingual Education**
1574 Main St., Winnipeg, MB R2W 5J8
204/338-0395
Albert Christ
Betty Ann Watts

**Manitoba Association of School Business Officials Inc.**
19 Trowbridge Bay, St Vital, MB R2N 2V9
204/254-7570, Fax: 204/254-3606
Executive Director, Ede Fast

**Manitoba Association of School Superintendents (MASS)**
200 St. Mary's Rd., Winnipeg, MB R2H 1H9
204/231-1241, Fax: 204/231-1912, Email: sups@mbnet.mb.ca
Executive Director, Strini Reddy
Publications: MASS Communications
Affiliates: Canadian Association of School Administrators

**Manitoba Parents for German Education Inc. (MPGE) (1981)**
#15, 1110 Henderson Hwy., Winnipeg, MB R2G 1L1
204/338-7405
President, Leona Rew
Administrative Secretary, Anita Riedl
Publications: MPGE Newsletter
Affiliates: Manitoba Association for Bilingual Education

**Mensa Canada Society (1967)**
**The High IQ Society**
Box 11, #232, 329 March Rd., Kanata, ON K2K 2E1
613/599-5897, Email: bn628@freenet.toronto.on.ca, URL: http://www.rohcg.on.ca/mensa/mensa.html
Executive Director, Elizabeth Clarke
President, Bill Eggertson
Publications: mc2

**National Association of Career Colleges/ Association nationale des collèges carrières (NACC)**
PO Box 340, Brantford, ON N3T 5N3
519/753-8689, Fax: 519/753-4712
Chief Administration Officer, Anne Burns
President, Addie Jason
Publications: Careers; NACC National News, q.

**National Educational Association of Disabled Students/Association nationale des étudiants handicapés au niveau post-secondaire (NEADS) (1986)**
Carleton University, 4th Level Unicentre, 1125 Colonel By Dr., Ottawa, ON K1S 5B6
613/526-8008, Fax: 613/520-3704
Coordinator, Frank Smith
Publications: NEADS Newsletter
Affiliates: British Columbia Educational Association of Disabled Students; Nova Scotia Disability Action Committee; Association québécoise des étudiant(e)s handicapé(e)s au post-secondaire

**North American Jewish Students' Network**
#707, 40 Sheppard Ave. West, North York, ON M2N 6K9
416/512-0814, Fax: 416/512-9816, Email: jsnet@io.org
National Director, Howard Katz
National Chair, Talia Klein
Publications: Future Tense

**Ontario Association of Career Colleges (OACC) (1972)**
PO Box 340, Brantford, ON N3T 5N3
519/752-2124, Fax: 519/753-4712
Executive Director, Paul Kitchin
Administrative Assistant, Lorna Hillis

**Ontario Association for Curriculum Development (OACD) (1950)**
PO Box 931, London, ON N6A 5K1
519/438-8390, Fax: 519/679-6855
Executive Director, Jack D. Little
Publications: Curriculum Connections

**Ontario Association of Deans of Education (OADE)**
Faculty of Education, University of Western Ontario, London, ON N6G 1G7
519/661-2080, Fax: 519/661-3833
Contact, Dean Allen Pearson
Affiliates: Council of Ontario Universities

**Ontario Association of School Business Officials (OASBO) (1945)**
#5-110, 252 Bloor St. West, Toronto, ON M5S 1V5
416/923-3107, Fax: 416/923-3490
Executive Director, R.G. Jenkins
Administrative Assistant, S. Fernandes
Publications: The Advocate

**Ontario Cooperative Education Association (OCEA) (1976)**
939 Progress Ave., Scarborough, ON M1G 3T8
416/396-6329, Fax: 416/396-6739, Email: bmisener@interhop.net
President, Judi Misener
Publications: OCEA Exchange
Affiliates: Cooperative, Career, Work Education Association of Canada

**Ontario Council on Graduate Studies**
#203, 444 Yonge St., Toronto, ON M5B 2H4
416/979-2165, Fax: 416/979-8635

**Ontario Council for Leadership in Educational Administration**
#115, 252 Bloor St. West, Toronto, ON M5S 1V5
416/944-2652, Fax: 416/944-3822
Executive Director, Peter E. Angelini

**Ontario Council for University Lifelong Learning**
Dept. of Continuing Studies, University of Western Ontario, London, ON N6A 5B8
519/661-3631, Fax: 519/661-3799
President, Carole Farber
Affiliates: Council of Ontario Universities

**Ontario Educational Research Council/Conseil ontarien de recherches pédagogiques (OERC) (1959)**
35 Beechwood Ave., PO Box 74163, Toronto, ON K1M 2H9
613/744-4345, Fax: 613/744-7597, Email: direland@cyberus.ca

President, Jack MacFadden
Office Manager, David Ireland
Publications: Reporting Classroom Research; Math 4 Girls; Aspects of/de l'immersion; Faîtes qu'ils ne décrochent pas/Give Them a Reason To Stay; Coming of Age: Co-operative Education
Affiliates: Teachers Federation of Ontario

**Ontario English Catholic Teachers' Association/Association des enseignants catholiques de langue anglaise de l'Ontario (OECTA) (1944)**
#400, 65 St. Clair Ave. East, Toronto, ON M4T 2Y8
416/925-2493, Fax: 416/925-7764, Toll Free: 1-800-268-7230
General Secretary, James J. Carey
Publications: The Reporter; Agenda, m.
Affiliates: Ontario Teachers' Federation

**Ontario Federation of Catholic School Associations (OFCSA) (1940)**
#1216, 383 Richmond St., London, ON N6A 3C4
519/432-5573, Fax: 519/432-0126
President, Mary Ann Cuderman
Executive Director, Patrick Smith
Publications: FCPTAO Newsletter

**Ontario Principals' Association**
#12-115, 252 Bloor St. West, Toronto, ON M5S 1V5
905/274-3601
President, William N. Bone
Publications: Ontario Principal

**Ontario Public School Boards Association**
Phoenix House, 439 University Ave., 18th Fl., Toronto, ON M5G 1Y8
416/340-2540, Fax: 416/340-7571, Email: admin@opsba.org, URL: http://www.opsba.org/
Executive Director, Gail Anderson
President, Lynn Peterson
Executive Vice-President, Liz Sandals
Publications: Fast Reports; Education Today, 5 pa

**Ontario Public School Teachers' Federation/Fédération des enseignants des écoles publiques de l'Ontario (OPSTF) (1921)**
5160 Orbitor Dr., Mississauga, ON L4W 5H2
905/238-0200, Fax: 905/238-0201, Toll Free: 1-800-268-7221, URL: http://www.nt.net/~torino/opstf.htm
President, R. Ferland
Publications: OPSTF News; NewsToday, 10 pa
Affiliates: Ontario Teachers' Federation

**Ontario School Trustees' Council/Conseil ontarien des conseillers scolaires (OSTC) (1958)**
#1804, 20 Eglinton Ave. West, Toronto, ON M4R 1K8
Fax: 416/932-9458
Vice-President, Patrick Meany

**Ontario Secondary School Teachers' Federation/Fédération des enseignants des écoles secondaires de l'Ontario (OSSTF) (1919)**
60 Mobile Dr., Toronto, ON M4A 2P3
416/751-8300, Fax: 416/751-3394, URL: http://www.osstf.on.ca
President, Earl Manners
General Secretary, Malcolm Buchanan
Publications: Forum

**Ontario Separate School Trustees' Association**
#1804, 20 Eglinton Ave. West, Toronto, ON M4R 1K8
416/932-9460, Fax: 416/932-9459
Executive Director, P. Slack
Publications: The Catholic Trustee
Affiliates: Canadian Catholic School Trustees Association

**Parent Co-operative Preschools International (PCPI) (1962)**
3767 Northwood Dr., Niagara Falls, ON L2H 2Y5
905/374-6605
President, Marika Townsend
Publications: Co-operatively Speaking

**Provincial Association of Catholic Teachers/Association provinciale des enseignants catholiques (PACT) (1969)**
#330, 5800, boul Metropolitain est, Montréal, QC H1S 1A7
514/252-7946, Fax: 514/252-9003
President, Michael Palumbo
Publications: PACT

**Québec Association of Independent Schools/Association des écoles privées du Québec (QAIS) (1965)**
#206, 410, rue Gratton, Saint-Laurent, QC H4M 2E2
514/744-6711, Fax: 514/744-6523
Executive Director, Soryl Naymark
President, Elizabeth Scanlan

**Le Réseau d'enseignement francophone à distance du Canada (REFAD) (1988)**
CP 670, Succ. C, Montréal, QC H2L 4L5
514/523-3143, Téléc: 514/525-7763, Courrier électronique: refad@sympatico.ca, URL: http://www.franco.ca/refad/
Directrice générale, Nicole Lemire
Président, Pierre Pelletier
Publications: Connexion; Répertoire de l'enseignement à distance en français, annuel; Actes du Colloque de REFAD, annuel

**Saskatchewan Association for Multicultural Education (SAME) (1984)**
#201, 2205 Victoria Ave., Regina, SK S4P 0S4
306/780-9428, Fax: 306/525-4009, Email: same@sk.sympatico.ca
Executive Director, Estelle Anthony
President, Jim Greenlaw
Secretary, John Willms
Program Coordinator, Rhonda Rosenberg
Publications: S.A.M.E. Newsletter
Affiliates: Canadian Council for Multicultural & Intercultural Education

**SchoolNet National Advisory Board/Conseil consultatif national de Rescol (SNAB) (1993)**
235 Queen St. West, 8th Fl., Ottawa, ON K1A 0H5
613/993-5452, Fax: 613/941-1296, Toll Free: 1-800-461-5945, Email: schoolnet@ic.gc.ca, URL: http://www.schoolnet.ca/snab; http://www.rescol.ca/ccnr
Chair, Byron James
Secretary, Doug Hull
Director of Schoolnet, Elise Boisjoly
Publications: SchoolNet Newsletter

**Société pour la promotion de l'enseignement de l'anglais (langue seconde) au Québec/Society for the Promotion of the Teaching of English as a Second Language in Québec (SPEAQ) (1976)**
#530, 7400, boul Saint-Laurent, 5e étage, Montréal, QC H2R 2Y1
514/271-3700, Téléc: 514/948-1231, URL: http://cyberscol.qc.ca/partenaires/speaq/speaq.htm
President, Jacquelyne Lord, Courrier électronique: gelyne@mercure.net
Administrative Assistant, Louis Lagrois
Publications: SPEAQ Out
Organisation(s) affiliée(s): TESOL

**Society for Educational Visits & Exchanges in Canada/Société éducative de visites et d'échanges au Canada (SEVEC) (1981)**
#201, 57 Auriga Dr., Nepean, ON K2E 8B2
613/998-3760, Fax: 613/998-7094, Toll Free: 1-800-387-3832, Email: sevec@hookup.net
Executive Director, A.D.S. MacKay
Coordinator of Communications, Marc Bourgeois
Publications: infoSEVEC
Québec Regional Office: Coordonnatrice, Nathalie Bouchard, 51, rue des Jardins, Québec, QC G1R 4L6, 418/648-3588, Téléc: 418/648-4288

**Students' Union of Nova Scotia/Association étudiante de la Nouvelle-Écosse (SUNS) (1978)**
#1888, 501 Brunswick St., Halifax, NS B3J 3J8
902/423-6653, Fax: 902/423-7013, Email: suns@ns.sympatico.ca
President, Sheldon Shaw
Publications: Notes & News; SUNS Lobby Guide

**Superannuated Teachers of Ontario/Enseignants et enseignantes retraités de l'Ontario (STO) (1968)**
#200, 1260 Bay St., Toronto, ON M5R 2B1
416/962-9463, Fax: 416/962-1061, Toll Free: 1-800-361-9888

**TeleLearning Network of Centres of Excellence/Réseau de centres d'excellence en téléformation (TL-NCE) (1995)**
Room ASB 9701, Simon Fraser University, Burnaby, BC V5A 1S6
604/291-5396, Fax: 604/291-3439, Email: tlnce@telelearn.ca, URL: http://www.telelearn.ca
Executive Director, Joanne Curry, Email: joannec@sfu.ca
Dr. Linda Harasim
Dr. Tom Calvert
Publications: TL-NCE Update

**TESL Canada Federation (1978)**
**Teaching English as a Second Language Canada Federation**
PO Box 44105, Burnaby, BC V5B 4Y2
604/298-4210, Fax: 604/298-4210, Toll Free: 1-800-393-9199, Email: teslcan@unixg.ubc.ca, URL: http://www.tesl.ca/
Administrative Director, Carol May
President, William McMichael, Email: mcmichael@ritslab.ubc.ca
Vice-President, Silvia Begin, Email: gsabegin@oanet.com
Secretary, Linda Curtis, Email: 73322.2750@compuserve.com
Treasurer, Catherine Eddy, Email: ceddy@vsb.bc.ca
Publications: TESL Canada Journal/Revue TESL du Canada
Affiliates: Teachers of English to Speakers of Other Languages (TESOL); Société pour la promotion de l'enseignement de l'anglais (langue seconde) au Québec

**United World Colleges (UWC) (1974)**
Lester B. Pearson College of the Pacific, 650 Pearson College Dr., Victoria, BC V9C 4H7
250/391-2411, Fax: 250/391-2412, Email: admin@pearson-college.uwc.ca, URL: http://www.pearson-college.uwc.ca/pearson/
President, Dr. Peter D. Bovinton
Publications: Pearson Times

**EGGS *see* POULTRY & EGGS**

## ELECTRONICS & ELECTRICITY

**Aircraft Electronics Association of Canada (1960)**
**AEA Canada**
c/o Aeronautical Electronics, Toronto City Centre Airport, Hangar 6, Toronto, ON M5V 1A1
416/203-8845, Fax: 416/203-8846

Vice-President, E. Tom Sternig
Publications: Avionics News

### L'Alliance des manufacturiers et des exportateurs du Québec (1984)
#904, 1080, Côte du Beaver Hall, Montréal, QC H2Z 1S8
514/866-7774, Téléc: 514/866-3779, Ligne sans frais: 1-800-363-0226
Président, Gérald A. Ponton

### Canadian Electrical Contractors Association
#207, 23 Lesmill Rd., North York, ON M3B 3P6
416/391-3226, Fax: 416/391-3926
Executive Secretary, Eryl M. Roberts

#### CORPORATION DES MAÎTRES ÉLECTRICIENS DU QUÉBEC/ CORPORATION OF MASTER ELECTRICIANS OF QUÉBEC (CMEQ) (1950)
#100, 5925, boul Décarie, Montréal, QC H3W 3C9
514/738-2184, Téléc: 514/738-2192, Ligne sans frais: 1-800-361-9061
Directeur général et secrétaire executif, Yvon Guilbault
Publications: Electricité Québec

#### ELECTRICAL CONTRACTORS ASSOCIATION OF ALBERTA (ECA ALBERTA)
11302 - 119 St., Edmonton, AB T5G 2X4
403/451-2412, Fax: 403/455-9815
Area Manager, Sheri McLean

#### ELECTRICAL CONTRACTORS ASSOCIATION OF BC (ECA-BC) (1952)
#510, 5050 Kingsway, Burnaby, BC V5H 4C2
604/435-4186, Fax: 604/439-1194
Executive Director, Clifford L. Pilkey, CAE
Director of Communications, Rick Stewart
Line Trade Director, Paddy Hatca
Publications: Relay; Membership List, a.
Affiliates: National Electrical Contractors Association

#### ELECTRICAL CONTRACTORS ASSOCIATION OF NEW BRUNSWICK INC. (ECANB) (1964)
PO Box 322, Fredericton, NB E3B 4Y9
506/452-7627, Fax: 506/452-1786
Executive Director, David Ellis
Publications: ECANB Today
Affiliates: Construction Association of New Brunswick Inc.; Canadian Construction Association

#### ELECTRICAL CONTRACTORS ASSOCIATION OF ONTARIO (ECA ONTARIO)
#207, 23 Lesmill Rd., North York, ON M3B 3P6
416/391-3226, Fax: 416/391-3926
Executive Vice-President, Eryl M. Roberts
Executive Assistant, Jo-Anne Jackson-Thorne
Affiliates: Council of Ontario Construction Associations

#### ELECTRICAL CONTRACTORS ASSOCIATION OF SASKATCHEWAN
Construction House, 1939 Elphinstone St., Regina, SK S4T 3N3
306/525-0171, Fax: 306/347-8595
Executive Director, Manley McLachlan

### Canadian Electrical Manufacturers Representatives Association
#200, 670 Bloor St. West, Toronto, ON M6G 1L2
416/533-7800, Fax: 416/533-4795
Executive Director, Don Mockford

### Canadian Electricity Association/Association canadienne de l'électricité (CEA) (1891)
#1600, One Westmount Square, Montréal, QC H3Z 2P9
514/937-6181, Fax: 514/937-6498, Email: info@canelect.ca, URL: http://www.canelect.ca
President & CEO, Hans R. Konow
Secretary, I. Murray Phillips
Publications: Connections/Connexions

### Canadian Electronic & Appliance Service Association/Organisation canadienne de service d'appareils domestique (CEASA) (1977)
#115, 10 Wynford Heights Cres., North York, ON M3C 1K8
416/447-7469, Fax: 416/447-2511
Executive Director, S. Rubicini
Publications: Service Contacts

### Comité canadien des éléctrotechnologies/ Canadian Committee on Electrotechnologies (CCE) (1986)
1010, Ste-Catherine ouest, 9e étage, Montréal, QC H3C 4S7
514/392-8446, Téléc: 514/392-8416, Courrier électronique: cceinfo@cce.qc.ca, URL: http://www.cce.qc.ca
Directeur général, Raymond Mongeau

### Consumer Electronics Marketers of Canada (CEMC)
#210, 10 Carlson Ct., Etobicoke, ON M9W 6L2
416/674-7410, Fax: 416/674-7412
Vice-President, Alda M. Murphy

### Electrical Power Systems Construction Association (EPSCA)
c/o Ontario Hydro, #H2, 700 University Ave., Toronto, ON M5G 1X6
416/592-2547, Fax: 416/592-4229
Sec.-Treas., N.A. Donnelly

### Electro-Federation Canada Inc. (1995)
#210, 10 Carlson Ct., Etobicoke, ON M9W 6L2
416/674-7410, Fax: 416/674-7412
President & CEO, Jim McCarthy

### Electronic Industry Association of Alberta (1981)
9924 - 45 Ave., Edmonton, AB T6E 5J1
403/436-9750, Fax: 403/437-1240
Publications: Crosscurrents

### Electronics & Information Association of Manitoba (EIAM) (1983)
#476, 435 Ellice Ave., Winnipeg, MB R3B 1Y6
204/982-3426, Fax: 204/982-3420, Email: eiam@mbnet.mb.ca, URL: http://www.mbnet.mb.ca/~eiam/
President, Alan Pollard
1st Vice-President, Ray Huemsen
Publications: Networds; EIAM Membership Directory
Affiliates: Computer Technology Network;

### Institute of Electrical & Electronics Engineers Canada (1884)
IEEE Canada
86 Main St., PO Box 830, Dundas, ON L9H 2R1
905/628-9554, Fax: 905/628-9554
Email: member.services@ieee.ca, URL: http://www.ieee.ca
President, Linda Weaver
Publications: Canadian Review
Affiliates: The Engineering Institute of Canada

### Manitoba Electrical League (1957)
#14, 395 Berry St., Winnipeg, MB R3J 1N6
204/885-3668, Fax: 204/885-3678
Executive Director, Larry McLennan
Publications: Feedback

### Ontario Electrical League (1966)
#1000, 2 Lansing Sq., North York, ON M2J 4P8
416/495-0052, Fax: 416/495-1804, Email: bakerj@interlog.com
President, David Reid
Operations Manager, Jim Baker
Publications: Dialogue

## EMERGENCY RESPONSE
***see also* Safety & Accident Prevention**

### Canadian Avalanche Association (CAA) (1982)
Canadian Avalanche Centre
PO Box 2759, Revelstoke, BC V0E 2S0
250/837-2435, Fax: 250/837-4624, Email: canav@junction.net, URL: http://www.avalanche.ca/snow
President, Niko Weis
Manager, Alan Dennis
Publications: Avalanche News
Affiliates: Alpine Club of Canada; Canadian West Ski Areas; Association of Canadian Mountain Guides

### Canadian Lifeboat Institution Inc. (CLI) (1981)
One Passage Island, West Vancouver, BC V7W 1V7
604/290-2701
President, P. Matty
Publications: Newsletter
Affiliates: International Lifeboat Federation

### The Canadian Red Cross Society/La Société canadienne de la Croix-Rouge (1896)
1800 Alta Vista Dr., Ottawa, ON K1G 4J5
613/739-3000, Fax: 613/731-1411, Telex: 05-33784, Email: feedback@redcross.ca, URL: http://www.redcross.ca
Secretary General, Dr. Pierre Duplessis
President, Janet Davidson
Vice-President, Gene Durkin
Affiliates: International Committee of the Red Cross; International of Red Cross & Red Crescent Societies (Geneva)

### Civil Air Search & Rescue Association (CASARA) (1984)
1180 Graham St., Kelowna, BC V1Y 9P5
250/861-7328, Fax: 250/861-7585
National President, Charles Pachal

### Corporation des services d'ambulance du Québec
535, av des Oblats, Québec, QC G1N 1V5
418/522-3456, Téléc: 418/522-3337
Directeur général, Gilles Ricard

### Lifesaving Society/Société de sauvetage (1908)
287 McArthur Ave., Ottawa, ON K1L 6P3
613/746-5694, Fax: 613/746-9929, Email: experts@livesaving.ca, URL: http://www.lifesaving.ca
Executive Director, Rick Haga
Publications: The Communiqué
Affiliates: Royal Life Saving Society; International Life Saving Federation
Alberta & NWT Branch: 11759 Groat Rd., Edmonton, AB T5M 3K6, 403/453-8638, Fax: 403/447-4885, Email: experts@livesaving.org
BC & Yukon Branch: #112, 3989 Henning Dr., Burnaby, BC V5C 6N5, 604/299-5450, Fax: 604/299-5795, Email: lifesaving_society@bc.sympatico.ca
Manitoba Branch: Contact, Karine Levasseur, #504, 138 Portage Ave. East, Winnipeg, MB R3C 9Z9, 204/956-2124, Fax: 204/944-8546, Email: acquatics@lifesaving.ca
New Brunswick Branch: Maritime Opportunity Centre, 1216 Sand Cove Rd., Saint John, NB E2M 4Z8, 506/635-1552, Fax: 506/635-0988, Email: lifesavenb@netcity.ca
Newfoundland & Labrador Branch: PO Box 8065, Stn A, St. John's, NF A1B 3M9, 709/576-1953, Fax: 709/576-1953, Email: lifeguard@firstcity.net

Nova Scotia Branch: 5516 Spring Garden Rd., PO Box 3010, Halifax, NS B3J 3G6, 902/425-5450, Fax: 902/425-5606, Email: sportns@fox.nstn.ca
Ontario Branch: 322 Consumers Rd., North York, ON M2J 1P8, 416/490-8844, Fax: 416/490-8766, Email: experts@lifeguarding.com
PEI Branch: PO Box 2411, Sherwood, PE C1A 8G2, 902/368-7757, Fax: 902/368-7757, Email: pratt.lifesaving@pei.sympatico.ca
Québec Branch: 4545, av Pierre-de-Coubertin, CP 1000, Succ. M, Montréal, QC H1V 3R2, 514/252-3100, Téléc: 514/252-3232, Courrier électronique: alerte@sauvetage.ca
Saskatchewan Branch: #403, 2206 Dewdney Ave., Regina, SK S4R 1H3, 306/780-9255, Fax: 306/522-4820

### Occupational First Aid Attendants Association of British Columbia (1931)
#204, 3855 Henning Dr., Burnaby, BC V5C 6N3
604/294-0244, Fax: 604/294-0289, Toll Free: 1-800-667-4566, Email: ofaaa@lionsgate.com
President, Tanya Hollist
Publications: The Association News

### REACT Canada Inc. (1962)
**Radio Emergency Associated Communications Teams**
32 The Queensway North, Keswick, ON L4P 1E3
905/476-5556
Director, Ronald W. McCracken
Publications: The REACTivist; The REACTer, bi-m.; Team Topics; REACT Team Directory
Affiliates: REACT International Inc.; Salvation Army; Red Cross

### St. John Ambulance/Ambulance Saint-Jean (1883)
**The Priory of Canada of the Most Venerable Order of the Hospital of St. John of Jerusalem**
312 Laurier Ave. East, Ottawa, ON K1N 6P6
613/236-7461, Fax: 613/236-2425, Email: nhq@nhq.sja.ca, URL: http://www/sja.ca
Secretary/CEO, D.J. Phillips
Chancellor, David M. Johnston
Federal District Council (Ottawa Area): Executive Director, D.A.F. Spry, 30 The Driveway, Ottawa, ON K2P 1C9, 613/236-3626, Fax: 613/233-0672
Alberta Council: Executive Director, David Hook, 10975 - 124 St., Edmonton, AB T5M 0H9, 403/452-6565, Fax: 403/452-2835
BC Council: Executive Director, Lucille Johnstone, 6111 Cambie St., Vancouver, BC V5Z 3B2, 604/321-2652, Fax: 604/321-5316
Manitoba Council: St. John House, 535 Doreen St., Winnipeg, MB R3G 3H5, 204/784-7000, Fax: 204/786-2295
New Brunswick Council: Executive Director, John Yauss, PO Box 3599, Stn B, Fredericton, NB E3A 5J8, 506/458-9129, Fax: 506/452-8699
Newfoundland Council: Executive Director, John O'Brien, PO Box 5489, St. John's, NF A1C 5W4, 709/726-4200, Fax: 709/726-4117
Nova Scotia Council: St. John House, 88 Slayter St., Dartmouth, NS B3A 2A6, 902/463-5646, Fax: 902/469-9609
NWT Council: Executive Director, Nancy Heimbach, 5023 - 51 St., Yellowknife, NT X1A 1S5, 867/873-5658, Fax: 867/920-4458
Ontario Council: Executive Director, Robert V. Olsen, 46 Wellesley St. East, Toronto, ON M4Y 1G5, 416/923-8411, Fax: 416/923-8456
PEI Council: Executive Director, C.S. Crockett, PO Box 1235, Charlottetown, PE C1A 7M8, 902/569-1234, Fax: 902/368-3231
Québec Council: Directeur exécutif, Louise Boisvert, 1407, rue de la Montagne, Montréal, QC H3G 1Z3, 514/842-4801, Téléc: 514/842-4807
Saskatchewan Council: Executive Director, R.L. Rowlatt, 2625 - 3 Ave., Regina, SK S4T 0C8, 306/522-7226, Fax: 306/525-4177

## EMPLOYMENT & HUMAN RESOURCES
*see also* **Labour Relations**

### Action Group Against Harassment & Discrimination in the Workplace/Groupe d'action contre le harcèlement et discrimination au travail (AGAHD) (1991)
**Action Against Harassment**
49 Montpetit St., L'Orignal, ON K0B 1K0
613/632-9828, Fax: 613/632-9828
President, Bronwen Williams

### Association of Professional Placement Agencies & Consultants/Association de placement en personnel agences et conseillers (APPAC) (1962)
#L-109, 114 Richmond St. East, Toronto, ON M5C 1P1
416/362-0983, Fax: 416/360-5478
Executive Director, Jacqueline Carter
Publications: Dialogue
Affiliates: International Federation of Personnel Services Association

### Association of Professional Recruiters of Canada
2 Walton Ct., Ottawa, ON K1V 9T1
613/523-5957, Fax: 613/523-8505, Email: info@hrtoday.com, URL: http://www.hrtoday.com
Executive Director, Nathaly Pinchuk
President, Brian Pascal
Publications: HR Today Journal

### Association des professionnels en ressources humaines du Québec/Association of Human Resources Professionals of the Province of Québec (APRHQ) (1934)
#820, av 1253 McGill Collège, Montréal, QC H3B 2Y5
514/879-1636, Téléc: 514/879-1722
Directrice générale, Chantal Décarie
Publications: Info Ressources Humaines

### Association of Self Employment Developers of Ontario (ASEDO) (1994)
59 Welland Vale Rd., St Catharines, ON L2R 6V6
905/685-3418, Fax: 905/684-1282, Email: asedo@bigwave.ca
President, Sandie Heirwegh
Vice-President, Barbara Okanik
Sec.-Treas., David Jackson
Publications: Smart Starts

### Canadian Association of Career Educators & Employers/Association canadienne des spécialistes en emploi et des employeurs (CACEE) (1946)
#205, 1209 King St. West, Toronto, ON M6K 1G2
416/535-8126, Fax: 416/532-0934, Email: cacee@inforamp.net, URL: http://www.cacee.com/workweb
Executive Director, Graham B.F. Donald
Publications: Career Options

### Canadian Career Information Association/Association canadienne de documentation professionnelle (CCIA) (1975)
#205, 1209 King St. West, Toronto, ON M6K 1E2
416/588-0653, Fax: 416/532-0934, Email: claudia@cacee.com
Co-Chair, Jane Nares
Co-Chair, Gillian Boyce
Contact, Claudia Walker
Publications: Career INFOcus

### Corporation professionnelle des conseilliers et conseillières d'orientation du Québec (CPCCOQ) (1963)
#520, 1100, rue Beaumont, Montréal, QC H3P 3H5
514/737-4717, Téléc: 514/737-6431, Ligne sans frais: 1-800-363-2643
Secrétaire générale, Martine Lacharite
Présidente, Louise Landry
Publications: L'Orientation; Orientation Nouvelles, mensuel

### Employment & Staffing Services Association of Canada/Association des entreprises en placement et gestion de personnel (FTHS) (1968)
#1105, 191 The West Mall, Etobicoke, ON M9C 5K8
416/626-7130, Fax: 416/620-5392, Email: bbandc@enterprise.ca
Executive Director, Amanda Curtis, CAE
Publications: Legislative Watch

### Human Resources Professionals Association of Ontario (HRPAO) (1954)
#1902, 2 Bloor St. West, Toronto, ON M4W 3E2
416/923-2324 (Office & Resource Line), Fax: 416/923-7264, Toll Free: 1-800-387-1311, Email: info@hrpao.org, URL: http://www.hrpao.org
Executive Director, Anne CameronSmith
President, Timothy R. McConnell, CHRP
Communications Manager, Katherine Came
Publications: Human Resources Professional

### Institute of Equality & Employment/Institut d'égalité et d'emploi (1985)
#2500, 1250 boul René Lévesque ouest, Montréal, QC H3B 4Y1
514/846-1212, Fax: 514/846-3427
President, Roy L. Heenan

### International Association for Human Resource Information Systems/L'Association canadienne des professionnels en systèmes de ressources humaines (IHRIM) (1985)
c/o Base Service Canada Inc., #301, 250 Consumers Rd., North York, ON M2J 4V6
416/490-6566, Fax: 416/495-8723, Toll Free: 1-800-780-6566, Email: ihrim@onramp.ca
Director, Canada, Brian L.G. Lechem
Associate Director, Canada, Ruth Abrahamson
Publications: IHRIMLink
Affiliates: American Assn. of HR Systems Profls.

### The Professional Development Institute Inc./Institut supérieur de gestion (PDI) (1973)
**Proactive Management Group**
79 Fentiman Ave., Ottawa, ON K1S 0T7
613/730-7777, Fax: 613/235-1115
President, A.P. Martin
Publications: The Harvard Planner; Think Proactive/La Gestion proactive; Essence of a Proactive Life; Bringing Time to Life

## ENERGY
*see also* **Environmental**

### Association of Major Power Consumers in Ontario (AMPCO) (1975)
#500, 10 Lower Spadina Ave., Toronto, ON M5V 2Z2
416/260-0225, Fax: 416/260-0442
Executive Director, Arthur Dickinson
Chairman, Michael G. Ford, P.Eng.
Publications: The AMPCO Report

### Canadian Association of Energy Service Companies (CAESCO) (1987)
48 Reeve Dr., Markham, ON L3P 6B9
905/294-3366, Fax: 905/294-1560

President, Alan Levy
Executive Director, Marion Fraser
Information Contact, Michelle Dixon-Parent
Publications: CAESCO News; Directory, a.

### Canadian Coalition for Nuclear Responsibility/Regroupement pour la surveillance du nucléaire (1975)
PO Box 236, Stn Snowdon, Montréal, QC H3X 3T4
514/489-5118, Fax: 514/489-5118
President, Gordon Edwards
Sec.-Treas., Marc Chénier
Affiliates: Environment Liaison Centre - International; Friends of the Earth - Canada

### Canadian Energy Research Institute (CERI) (1975)
#150, 3512 - 33 St. NW, Calgary, AB T2L 2A6
403/282-1231, Fax: 403/284-4181, Email: cdneri@acs.ucalgary.ca, URL: http://www.ucalgary.ca/UofC/Others/CERI/index.htm
President, Dr. Gerry E. Angevine
Director, Conferences & Communications, R.J. Buchanan
Publications: CERI Insight

### Canadian Fluid Power Association/Association canadienne d'énergie fluide (CFPA) (1974)
c/o Trade Association Management Group, 208 Brimorton Dr., Scarborough, ON M1H 2C6
416/431-1330, Fax: 416/764-7463
Manager, John Martin
President, Al Trudelle
Publications: Fluid Power News

### Canadian Gas Research Institute/Institut canadien des recherches gazières (CGRI) (1974)
55 Scarsdale Rd., North York, ON M3B 2R3
416/447-6661, Fax: 416/447-6757, Email: cgri@hookup.net, URL: http://www.hookup.net/~cgri/
General Manager, Roger Barker
Publications: CGRI Monitor

### Canadian Institute of Energy (CIE) (1979)
#229, 640 - 5 Ave. SW, Calgary, AB T2P 0M6
403/262-6969, Fax: 403/269-2787
National President, Peter D. Faloon, Bus: 403/221-9011, Fax: 403/221-9010
Director, Eric Smith, Bus: 519/337-0511, Fax: 519/337-0519
Director, Julian Taylor, Bus: 604/691-5789, Fax: 604/691-5773
Treasurer, Sandy Constable, Bus: 604/688-1773, Fax: 604/669-4311
Publications: CIE National News
Affiliates: The Institute of Energy (UK); Canadian Institute of Fluidized Bed Technology; Canadian National Committee of the World Energy Congress

### Canadian Nuclear Association/Association nucléaire canadienne (CNA) (1960)
#475, 144 Front St. West, Toronto, ON M5J 2L7
416/977-6152, Fax: 416/979-8356, Toll Free: 1-800-387-4477, URL: http://www.cna.ca/weare.html
President, Jack Richman
Publications: Nuclear Canada/Canada nucléaire

### Canadian Nuclear Society/Société nucléaire canadienne (CNS)
#475, 144 Front St. West, Toronto, ON M5J 2L7
416/977-6152, Fax: 416/979-8356, Toll Free: 1-800-387-4477
President, Jerry Cuttler
Publications: Canadian Nuclear Society Bulletin

### Canadian Renewable Fuels Association/Association canadienne des carburants renouvelables (CRFA)
90 Woodlawn Rd. West, Guelph, ON N1H 1B2
519/767-0431, Fax: 519/837-1674, Email: crfa@greenfuels.org, URL: http://www.greenfuels.org
President, Jim Johnson
Vice-President, Doug MacKenzie
Public Affairs Advisor, Terry Boland
Publications: Green Fuels Today

### Canadian Solar Industries Association Inc./Association des industries solaires du Canada inc. (CanSIA) (1978)
#250, 2415 Holly Lane, Ottawa, ON K1V 7P2
613/736-9077, Fax: 613/736-8938, Email: cansia@magmacom.com, URL: http://www.newenergy.org/newenergy/cansia.html
Contact, Ortrud Seelemann
Publications: CanSIA Newsletter

### Canadian Wind Energy Association Inc./Association canadienne d'énergie écolienne (CanWEA) (1984)
#100, 3553 - 31 St. NW, Calgary, AB T2L 2K7
403/289-7713, Fax: 403/282-1238, Toll Free: 1-800-922-6932, Email: canwea@cadvision.com, URL: http://keynes.fb12.tu-berlin.de/luftraum/konst/canwea.html
Executive Coordinator, Cindy Bourns
Publications: Windsight
Affiliates: Solar Energy Society of Canada

### Energy Council of Canada (1924)
#400, 30 Colonnade Rd., Nepean, ON K2E 7J6
613/727-1881, 952-6469, Fax: 613/952-6470, Email: epc@energy.ca, URL: http://www.energy.ca
Executive Director, E. Philip Cockshutt
Publications: Proceedings: Canadian National Energy Forum

### Energy Pathways Inc. (EPI) (1979)
#500, 251 Laurier Ave. West, Ottawa, ON K1P 5J6
613/235-7976, Fax: 613/235-2190, Email: epi@epi.ca, URL: http://www.epi.ca/home.htm
President, Bill Armstrong
Vice-President, Consulting, Charles Hodgson
Publications: On-Site

### Energy Probe Research Foundation (EPRF) (1980)
225 Brunswick Ave., Toronto, ON M5S 2M6
416/964-9223, Fax: 416/964-8239, Toll Free: 1-800-263-2784, Email: EnergyProbe@nextcity.com, URL: http://www.nextcity.com/EnergyProbe/
Chairman, Walter Pitman
President, Patricia Adams
Sec.-Treas., Annetta Turner
Research Coordinator, Lawrence Solomon
Director, Nuclear Research & Senior Policy Analyst, Norman Rubin, Email: NormanRubin@nextcity.com
Utility Analyst, Tom Adams
Publications: EnergyFutures; Probe Alert; The Next City, q.

### Nuclear Awareness Project
PO Box 104, Uxbridge, ON L9P 1M6
905/852-0571, Fax: 905/852-0571, Email: nucaware@web.net
Contact, David Martin
Publications: Nuclear Awareness News; The Facts About Food Irradiation
Affiliates: Nuclear Information & Resource Service; Canadian Environment Network

### Planetary Association for Clean Energy, Inc./Société planétaire pour l'assainissement de l'énergie (PACE) (1975)
#1001, 100 Bronson Ave., Ottawa, ON K1R 6G8
613/236-6265, Fax: 613/235-5876
President, Andrew Michrowski
Publications: Newsletter

### Solar Energy Society of Canada Inc./Société d'énergie solaire du Canada inc. (SESCI) (1974)
#702, 116 Lisgar St., Ottawa, ON K1A 0K1
613/234-4151, Fax: 613/234-2988, Email: sesci@sympatico.ca, URL: http://www.newenergy.org/newenergy/sesci.html
Managing Director, Sheila McKirdy
Publications: SOL-A Voice of Conservation & Renewable Energy in Canada; Canadian Renewable Energy Guide
Affiliates: International Solar Energy Society

### Wood Energy Technology Transfer Inc. (WETT) (1993)
#1105, 191 The West Mall, Etobicoke, ON M9C 5K8
416/695-1676, Fax: 416/620-5392, Email: bbandc@onterprise.ca
Manager, Amanda Curtis, CAE
Publications: WETT Ink

## ENGINEERING & TECHNOLOGY

### American Society of Mechanical Engineers (ASME) (1880)
345 East 47 St., New York, NY 10017 USA
212/705-7722, Fax: 212/705-7674, Toll Free: 1-800-843-2763
Executive Director, David L. Belden
Publications: ASME News; Mechanical Engineering, m.; CIME (Computers in Mechanical Engineering), m.; Manufacturing Review, q.; Applied Mechanics Reviews

### Association of Consulting Engineers of Canada/Association des ingénieurs-conseils du Canada (ACEC) (1925)
#616, 130 Albert St., Ottawa, ON K1P 5G4
613/236-0569, Fax: 613/236-6193, Email: memserv@acec.ca, URL: http://www.acec.ca
Chairman & CEO, Philippe Lefebvre, eng.
President & COO, Pierre Franche
Communications Officer, J. Daniel Matko
Publications: Export Action; ACEC Directory of Canadian Consulting Engineers, a.; Canadian Consulting Engineer, bi-m.

#### ASSOCIATION OF CONSULTING ENGINEERS OF ALBERTA (CEA) (1978)
#1709 Toronto Dominion Tower, Edmonton, AB T5J 2Z1
403/420-6066, Fax: 403/420-6392, Telex: 037-2966
Executive Director, Allan C. Oliver
Executive Assistant, Elizabeth Hrushka
Publications: Newsletter
Affiliates: Alberta Construction Association; Alberta Chamber of Resources; Alberta Economic Development & Trade; Canadian Manufacturers' Association; International Federation of Consulting Engineers; Western Economic Diversification Canada; Alberta Association of Architects; Association of Professional Engineers, Geologists, & Geophysicists of Alberta; Alberta Society of Engineering Technologists; Alberta Research Council; Engineering Institute of Canada; Industry Canada

#### ASSOCIATION OF CONSULTING ENGINEERS OF MANITOBA INC. (ACEM) (1978)
4 Donald St. South, Winnipeg, MB R3L 2T7

204/475-7774, Fax: 204/475-7774
URL: http://www.tetres.ca/acem/index.html
Executive Director, Elaine P. Madison
President, K.G. Bolton, P.Eng.
Publications: ACEM Newsletter; ACEM Directory of Member Firms, biennial
Affiliates: Association of Professional Engineers of Manitoba; International Federation of Consulting Engineers; Manitoba Association of Architects

**ASSOCIATION OF CONSULTING ENGINEERS OF ONTARIO (CEO) (1975)**
#300, 86 Overlea Blvd., Toronto, ON M4H 1C6
416/425-8027, Fax: 416/425-8035
President, Donald Ingram
Publications: CEO Newsletter; Association of Consulting Engineers of Ontario Directory

**ASSOCIATION OF CONSULTING ENGINEERS OF SASKATCHEWAN (ACES) (1977)**
2123 Broad St., Regina, SK S4P 1Y6
306/359-3338, Fax: 306/522-5325
Executive Director, Ted Rey
Publications: ACES Newsletter

**ASSOCIATION OF CONSULTING ENGINEERS OF THE YUKON (CEY) (1983)**
c/o EBA Engineering Consultants Ltd., #6, 151 Industrial Rd., Whitehorse, YT Y1A 2V3
867/668-3068, Fax: 867/668-4349
Email: whitehorse@eba.ca
Executive Director, Richard Trimble

**ASSOCIATION DES INGÉNIEURS-CONSEILS DU QUÉBEC/ CONSULTING ENGINEERS OF QUÉBEC (AICQ) (1974)**
#1200, 2050, rue Mansfield, Montréal, QC H3A 1Y9
514/288-2032, Téléc: 514/288-2306
Vice-Présidente exécutive, Johanne Desrochers, BAA
Publications: Bulletin

**CONSULTING ENGINEERS OF BRITISH COLUMBIA (CEBC) (1976)**
#514, 409 Granville St., Vancouver, BC V6C 1T2
604/687-2811, Fax: 604/688-7110
Email: consulting_engineers@cebc.org
Executive Director, John Wilkins, B.Sc., DIC
Publications: Commentary; Directory of Member Firms; Industry Profile; Awards Magazine

**CONSULTING ENGINEERS OF NEW BRUNSWICK/LES INGENIEURS-CONSEILS DU NOUVEAU-BRUNSWICK (CENB) (1983)**
#105, 535 Beaverbrook Ct., Fredericton, NB E3B 1X6
506/458-8455, Fax: 506/452-2729
President, Andrew Steeves

**CONSULTING ENGINEERS OF NEWFOUNDLAND & LABRADOR**
140 University Ave., St. John's, NF A1B 1Z5
709/753-1014, Fax: 709/753-3466
Executive Director, Eric Mercer

**CONSULTING ENGINEERS OF NWT (CENT) (1990)**
c/o NAPEGG, #5, 4807 - 49 St., Yellowknife, NT X1A 3T5
867/920-4055, Fax: 867/873-4058
President, Gary Craig, P.Eng.

**NOVA SCOTIA CONSULTING ENGINEERS ASSOCIATION (1973)**
45 Hastings Dr., Dartmouth, NS B2Y 2C7
902/461-1325, Fax: 902/461-1321
Executive Director, P.S. Ferguson, P.Eng
Publications: Update; Newton, q.

### Association des ingénieurs municipaux du Québec/Association of Québec Municipal Engineers (AIMQ) (1963)
2020, rue Université, 18e étage, Montréal, QC H3A 2A5
514/649-7060, Téléc: 514/932-7149
Secrétaire, Alain Dulude
Publications: Contact Plus

### British Columbia Technology Industries Association (BCTIA) (1994)
#450, 1122 Mainland St., Vancouver, BC V6B 5L1
604/683-6159, Fax: 604/683-3879, Email: info@bctia.org, URL: http://www.bctia.org
General Manager, Kathleen Troupe
Publications: TIA Monitor
Affiliates: Information Technology Association of Canada

### Canadian Acoustical Association/Association canadienne d'acoustique
41 Watson Ave., Toronto, ON M6S 4C9
905/762-6093, Fax: 905/670-1698, Email: http://www.uwo.ca/hhcru/caa/
President, John Hemingway
Executive Secretary, John Bradley, Email: john.bradley@nrc.ca
Publications: Canadian Acoustics

### Canadian Advanced Technology Association/ Association canadienne de technologie de pointe (CATA) (1978)
388 Albert St., 2nd Fl., Ottawa, ON K1P 5H9
613/236-6550, Fax: 613/236-8189, Toll Free: 1-800-387-2282, Email: info@cata.ca, URL: http://www.cata.ca/
President, John Reid, Email: jonreid@ibm.net
Publications: CATAlist

### Canadian Air Cushion Technology Society (CACTS)
#818, 130 Slater St., Ottawa, ON K1P 6E2
613/234-0191, Fax: 613/234-9039, Email: casi@casi.ca, URL: http://www.casi.ca/
Executive Director, Ian M. Ross

### Canadian Association for Composite Structures & Materials/Association canadienne pour les structures et matériaux composites (CACSMA) (1988)
75, boul de Mortagne, Boucherville, QC J4B 6Y4
514/641-5139, Fax: 514/641-5117, Email: info@cacsma.ca, URL: http://www.cacsma.ca
Président, Nicolas Juillard
Publications: CACSMA Bulletin

### Canadian Council of Professional Engineers/ Conseil canadien des ingénieurs (CCPE) (1936)
#401, 116 Albert St., Ottawa, ON K1P 5G3
613/232-2474, Fax: 613/230-5759, Email: info@ccpe.ca, URL: http://www.ccpe.ca
President, Wendy Ryan-Bacon, P.Eng
Chairman, Pierre Desjarins, P.Eng.
Publications: Canadian Professional Engineer
Affiliates: World Federation of Engineering Organizations

**ASSOCIATION OF PROFESSIONAL ENGINEERS, GEOLOGISTS & GEOPHYSICISTS OF ALBERTA (APEGGA) (1920)**
Scotia Place, Tower One, 10060 Jasper Ave, 15th Fl., Edmonton, AB T5J 4A2
403/426-3990, Fax: 403/426-1877, Toll Free: 1-800-661-7020
Email: email@apegga.com, URL: http://www.apegga.com
Executive Director & Registrar, Robert Ross, P.Eng.
Deputy Registrar, Al Schuld, P.Eng.
Director, Special Projects, Stewart McIntosh, P.Eng.
Director, Registration & Compliance, Dave Todd, P.Eng.
Director, Communications, Trevor Maine, P.Eng.
Manager, Public Relations, Kimberly Nishikaze
Manager, Editorial Services, Nordahl Flakstad
Director, Professional Development, Len Shrimpton, P.Eng.
Director, Professional Practice, Ray Chopiuk, P.Eng.
Director, Administration, Melora Jones, CA
Publications: The PEGG

**ASSOCIATION OF PROFESSIONAL ENGINEERS, GEOLOGISTS & GEOPHYSICISTS OF THE NORTHWEST TERRITORIES (NAPEGG) (1979)**
#5, 4807 - 49 St., Yellowknife, NT X1A 3T5
867/920-4055, Fax: 867/873-4058
Email: napegg@tamarack.nt.ca, URL: http://www.napegg.nt.ca
Executive Director, Robert W. Spence, P.Eng.
Office Manager, Leigh Wells
Publications: NAPEGG Newsletter; NAPEGG Membership Directory, a.

**ASSOCIATION OF PROFESSIONAL ENGINEERS & GEOSCIENTISTS OF BRITISH COLUMBIA (APEGBC) (1920)**
#200, 4010 Regent St., Burnaby, BC V5C 6N2
604/430-8035, Fax: 604/430-8085, Email: comm@apeg.bc.ca, URL: http://www.apeg.bc.ca
Executive Director & Registrar, John Bremner, P.Eng.
Director, Registration, G.M. Pichler, P.Eng.
President, John Haythorne, P.Eng.
Publications: The BC Professional Engineer

**ASSOCIATION OF PROFESSIONAL ENGINEERS & GEOSCIENTISTS OF NEWFOUNDLAND (APEGN) (1952)**
PO Box 21207, St. John's, NF A1A 5B2
709/753-7714, Fax: 709/753-6131
Email: apegn@public.compusult.nf.ca, URL: http://www.apegn.nf.ca
Executive Director, Allen L. Steeves, P.Eng.
President, Darlene Whalen, P.Eng.
Publications: Dialogue for Engineers & Geoscientists

**ASSOCIATION OF PROFESSIONAL ENGINEERS & GEOSCIENTISTS OF SASKATCHEWAN (APEGS) (1930)**
#104, 2255 - 13 Ave., Regina, SK S4P 0V6
306/525-9547, Fax: 306/525-0851, Toll Free: 1-800-500-9547
Email: dkpaddock@apegs.sk.ca, URL: http://www.apegs.sk.ca
Executive Director/Registrar, Dennis Paddock, P.Eng.
Publications: The Professional Edge

**ASSOCIATION OF PROFESSIONAL ENGINEERS OF MANITOBA (APEM) (1920)**
850A Pembina Hwy., Winnipeg, MB R3M 2M7
204/474-2736, Fax: 204/474-5960
Executive Director, David A. Ennis, P.Eng.
Director of Admissions, S. Matile, P.Eng.

**ASSOCIATION OF PROFESSIONAL ENGINEERS OF NEW BRUNSWICK/ASSOCIATION DES INGÉNIEURS DU NOUVEAU-BRUNSWICK (APENB) (1920)**
#105, 535 Beaverbrook Ct., Fredericton, NB E3B 1X6
506/458-8083, Fax: 506/451-9629
Email: apenb@nbnet.nb.ca, URL: http://www.apenb.nb.ca
Executive Director, Eddie Kinley, P.Eng.
Publications: The Professional Engineer; Bulletin, q.

**ASSOCIATION OF PROFESSIONAL ENGINEERS OF NOVA SCOTIA (APENS) (1920)**
PO Box 129, RPO Central, Halifax, NS B3J 2M4
902/429-2250, Fax: 902/423-9769
Email: info@apens.ns.ca, URL: http://www.apens.ca
Executive Director, John Woods, P.Eng., Email: jwoods@apns.ns.ca
Director of Prof. Practice, Peter Mitchell, P.Eng.
Publications: The Engineer

**ASSOCIATION OF PROFESSIONAL ENGINEERS OF PRINCE EDWARD ISLAND (APEPEI) (1955)**
549 North River Rd., Charlottetown, PE C1E 1J6
902/566-1268, Fax: 902/566-5551
Email: apepei@peinet.pe.ca, URL: http://www.isn.net/virtual/apepei/
Executive Director/Registrar, Graeme A. Linkletter, P.Eng.

President, Kerry Taylor, P.Eng.
Publications: APEPEI Newsletter

**ASSOCIATION OF PROFESSIONAL ENGINEERS OF THE YUKON TERRITORY (APEY) (1955)**
PO Box 4125, Whitehorse, YT Y1A 3S9
867/667-6727, Fax: 867/667-6727
Sec.-Treas., Niels Jacobsen, P.Eng.
Publications: The Association Newsletter

**ORDRE DES INGÉNIEURS DU QUÉBEC (OIQ) (1920)**
2020, rue University, 18e étage, Montréal, QC H3A 2A5
514/845-6141, Téléc: 514/845-1833, Ligne sans frais: 1-800-461-6141
URL: http://www.oiq.qc.ca
Secrétaire/Directeur général, Hubert Stéphenne, ing.
Publications: Plan; Méga Plan, annuel
Organisation(s) affiliée(s): Conseil Interprofessionnel du Québec

**PROFESSIONAL ENGINEERS ONTARIO/ORDRE DES INGÉNIEURS DE L'ONTARIO (PEO) (1922)**
#1000, 25 Sheppard Ave. West, North York, ON M2N 6S9
416/224-1100, Fax: 416/224-8168
URL: http://www.peo.on.ca
Executive Director, Peter Large, P.Eng.
President, Christine Bell, P.Eng.
Manager, Public Relations, Virginia M. Brown
Publications: Engineering Dimensions; The Link, bi-m.

## Canadian Council of Technicians & Technologists/Conseil canadien des techniciens et technologues (CCTT)
285 McLeod St., 2nd Fl., Ottawa, ON K2R 1A1
613/238-8123, Fax: 613/238-8822, URL: http://www.cctt.ca/
Executive Director, C. Charles Brimley, C.E.T.

**ALBERTA SOCIETY OF ENGINEERING TECHNOLOGISTS (ASET) (1963)**
Canada Trust Tower, #2100, 10104 - 103 Ave. NW, Edmonton, AB T5J 0H8
403/425-0626, Fax: 403/424-5053, Toll Free: 1-800-272-5619
Email: asetadmin@worldgate.com, URL: http://aset.worldgate.com
Executive Director, Brian McCormack, CAE
Registrar, Don Byers
Director, Communications, Jay Fisher
Publications: Technology Alberta; Techline

**APPLIED SCIENCE TECHNOLOGISTS & TECHNICIANS OF BRITISH COLUMBIA (ASTTBC) (1958)**
10767 - 148 St., Surrey, BC V3R 0S4
604/585-2788, Fax: 604/585-2790, Toll Free: 1-800-410-2030
Email: techinfo@asttbc.org, URL: http://www.asttbc.org
Executive Director, John E. Leech, A.Sc.T., CAE
Publications: ASTT Newsletter; Applied Science Technologists & Technicians of BC Membership Directory, a.; News for BC MLAs & BC MPs, q.; News for BC Municipalities, q.; Careers in Technology; Career Manager

**ASSOCIATION OF ENGINEERING TECHNICIANS & TECHNOLOGISTS OF NEWFOUNDLAND (AETTN) (1968)**
PO Box 790, Mount Pearl, NF A1N 2Y2
709/747-2868, Fax: 709/747-2869
URL: http://www.cabot.nf.ca/aettn
Contact, Austin Sheppard
Publications: Technology Newfoundland & Labrador

**CERTIFIED TECHNICIANS & TECHNOLOGISTS ASSOCIATION OF MANITOBA (CTTAM) (1965)**
#602, 1661 Portage Ave., Winnipeg, MB R3J 3T7
204/783-0088, Fax: 204/783-6284
Email: cttam@mts.net, URL: http://www.cctt.ca/members/manitoba.htm
Executive Director, Kenneth G. Campbell, C.E.T.
Administrative Coordinator, Anne Sawatzky
Publications: Manitoba Technologist; TechLink, q.

**NEW BRUNSWICK SOCIETY OF CERTIFIED ENGINEERING TECHNICIANS & TECHNOLOGISTS/SOCIÉTÉ DES TECHNICIENS ET DES TECHNOLOGUES AGRÉÉS DU GÉNIE DU NOUVEAU-BRUNSWICK (NBSCETT) (1968)**
#115, 535 Beaverbrook Ct., Fredericton, NB E3B 1X6
506/454-6124, Fax: 506/452-7076
Executive Director, Edward F. Leslie, CAE
Registrar, Ken C. Brown, CET
Administrative Assistant, Marie Colwell
Publications: NBSCETT Technologist; NBSCETT News

**ONTARIO ASSOCIATION OF CERTIFIED ENGINEERING TECHNICIANS & TECHNOLOGISTS (OACETT) (1957)**
#404, 10 Four Seasons Pl., Etobicoke, ON M9B 6H7
416/621-9621, Fax: 416/621-8694
URL: http://www.onramp.ca/business/oacett/
Executive Director, Bruce G. Wells
President, Angelo J. Innocente
Registrar, J.D. Holmes
Publications: The Ontario Technologist

**ORDRE DES TECHNOLOGUES PROFESSIONNELS DU QUÉBEC (OTPQ) (1927)**
#720, 1265, rue Berri, Montréal, QC H2L 4X4
514/845-3247, Téléc: 514/845-3643, Ligne sans frais: 1-800-561-3459
Directeur général, Denis Daigneault
Publications: TP Express; Le Technologue, tous les 2 mois

**PRINCE EDWARD ISLAND SOCIETY OF CERTIFIED ENGINEERING TECHNOLOGISTS (PEISCET)**
PO Box 1436, Charlottetown, PE C1A 7N1
902/892-3085, Fax: 902/892-3085
President, Allan Lapp

**SASKATCHEWAN APPLIED SCIENCE TECHNOLOGISTS & TECHNICIANS (SASTT) (1965)**
363 Park St., Regina, SK S4N 5B2
306/721-6633, Fax: 306/721-0112
Email: sastt@sympatico.sk.ca
Executive Director/Registrar, Jaime Briltz, A.Sc.T.
President, John Walker, A.Sc.T.
Publications: SASTT Journal; Annual Salary Survey

**SOCIETY OF CERTIFIED ENGINEERING TECHNICIANS & TECHNOLOGISTS OF NOVA SCOTIA (SCETTNS)**
PO Box 159, Stn Main, Dartmouth, NS B2Y 3Y3
902/463-3236, Fax: 902/465-7567
President, Gabe Gallant
Publications: Technology Nova Scotia

## Canadian Institute of Marine Engineering
3530 Griffith St., Saint Laurent, QC H4T 1A7
514/735-1775, Fax: 514/735-0035
Executive Secretary, Gernot Seebacher
Publications: Marine Engineering Digest

## Canadian Remote Sensing Society/Société canadienne de télédétection (CRSS)
#818, 130 Slater St., Ottawa, ON K1P 6E2
613/234-0191, Fax: 613/234-9039
Executive Director, Ian M. Ross
Publications: Canadian Journal of Remote Sensing

## Canadian Society for Color in Art, Industry & Science/Société canadienne pour la couleur (CSC) (1972)
NRC Institute for National Measurement Standards, Bldg. M36, Rm. 1119, Montréal Rd., Ottawa, ON K1A 0R6
613/993-9347, Fax: 613/952-1394
Contact, Dr. A.R. Robertson

## Canadian Society for Professional Engineers (CSPE) (1979)
#303, 203 College St., Toronto, ON M5T 1P9
416/598-0520, Fax: 416/598-3679
President, Michael Robertson, P.Eng.
Communications Officer, E.K. Christian, P.Eng.
Publications: The CSPEaker

## Canadian Technical Asphalt Association/Association canadienne des techniques de l'asphalte (CTAA) (1955)
825 Fort St., 3rd Fl., Victoria, BC V8W 1H6
250/361-9187, Fax: 250/361-9187, Email: ctaavic@islandnet.com
Sec.-Treas., Robert Noble, P.Eng.
Publications: Newsletter; Journal, a.

## Consulting Engineers of Alberta (CEA)
#505, 22 Sir Winston Churchill Ave., St Albert, AB T8N 1B4
403/458-1852, Fax: 403/458-5225, Email: cea@caisnet.com, URL: http://www.caisnet.com/cea/
Executive Director, Shirley Mercier
President, Rick Prentice, P.Eng.
Publications: The Bullet; Showcase Directory, a.
Affiliates: Association of Professional Engineers, Geologists & Geophysicists of Alberta; Alberta Society of Engineering Technologists; Alberta Association of Architects

## Continental Automated Buildings Association/Association continentale pour l'automatisation des bâtiments (CABA) (1988)
1500 Montréal Rd., Ottawa, ON K1A 0R6
613/990-7407, Fax: 613/954-5984, Toll Free: 1-888-798-2222, Email: caba@caba.org, URL: http://www.caba.org
Executive Director, Ron Zimmer, CAE
President, Jack Fraser
Director, Communications, Marc Raidor
Publications: Home & Building Automation Quarterly; Information Series

## The Engineering Institute of Canada/Institut canadien des ingénieurs (EIC) (1887)
1980 Ogilvie Rd., PO Box 27078, RPO Gloucester Ctr, Gloucester, ON K1J 9L9
613/742-5185, Fax: 613/742-5189, Email: ici.eic@nrc.ca, URL: http://www.eic-ici.ca
Executive Director, Michael Bozozuk
President, John Seychuk
Publications: President's Letter

**CANADIAN GEOTECHNICAL SOCIETY/SOCIÉTÉ CANADIENNE DE GÉOTECHNIQUE (CGS) (1972)**
#501, 170 Attwell Dr., Etobicoke, ON M9W 6A3
514/674-0366, Fax: 514/674-9507
Email: cgs@inforamp.net, URL: http://www.inforamp.net/~cgs
Director General, A.G. Stermac
President, Jim Laing
Publications: Canadian Geotechnical Journal; Geotechnical News, q.
Affiliates: National Research Council, Institute for Research in Construction (IRC-NRC); Canadian Rock Mechanics Association; Tunnelling Association of Canada; Canadian Geoscience Council; International Society for Soil Mechanics & Foundation Engineering; International Society for Rock Mechanics; International Association of Engineering Geology; International Permafrost Association; International Geotextile Society; International Association of Hydrogeologists

**CANADIAN SOCIETY FOR CIVIL ENGINEERING/SOCIÉTÉ CANADIENNE DE GÉNIE CIVIL (CSCE) (1887)**
Tour Guy, #840, 2155, rue Guy, Montréal, QC H3H 2R9
514/933-2634, Fax: 514/933-3504
Email: csc@musica.mcgill.ca, URL: http://www.csce.ca
Director of Administration, Leslie C. West
Publications: Canadian Journal of Civil Engineering; Canadian Civil Engineer, bi-m.

**CANADIAN SOCIETY FOR ENGINEERING MANAGEMENT/SOCIÉTÉ CANADIENNE DE GESTION EN INGÉNIERE (CSEM) (1981)**
c/o Base Service Canada Inc., #301, 250 Consumers Rd., North York, ON M2J 4V6
416/494-1440, Fax: 416/495-8723
Email: base@onramp.ca
Sec.-Treas., J. Gordon Thomson
Chairman, John Dinsmore
Publications: Engineers Club

**CANADIAN SOCIETY FOR MECHANICAL ENGINEERING/SOCIÉTÉ CANADIENNE DE GÉNIE MÉCANIQUE (CSME) (1887)**
#405A, 130 Slater St, Ottawa, ON K1P 6E2
613/232-8811, Fax: 613/230-9607
Email: csocme@istar.ca, URL: http://home.istar.ca/~csocme/index.htm
Executive Director, T.C. Arnold
President, Dr. R. Seshadri
Publications: The Bulletin; Transactions, q.

### Industrial Research & Development Institute (IRDI) (1991)
649 Prospect Blvd., PO Box 518, Midland, ON L4R 4L3
705/526-2163, Fax: 705/526-2701, Email: admin@irdi.on.ca, URL: http://www.irdi.on.ca
President/CEO, C.M. Harper
Publications: IRDI Update

### Institute of Power Engineers (IPE) (1940)
3532 Commerce Ct., Burlington, ON L7N 3L7
905/333-3348, Fax: 905/333-9328
National President, R.C. Wennerstrom
1st National Vice-President, Alain Fournier
National Secretary, J.J. Kolibash
Publications: Canadian Power Engineer Magazine

### Intelligent Sensing for Innovative Structure/Systèmes intelligents pour structures innovatrices (ISIS) (1995)
227 Engineering Bldg., University of Manitoba, Winnipeg, MB R3T 5V6
204/474-8506, Fax: 204/474-7519, Email: central@isiscanada.com
Network Manager, Lloyd McGinnis
Publications: Innovator

### Municipal Engineers Association (1974)
#2, 530 Otto Rd., Mississauga, ON L5T 2L5
905/795-2555, Fax: 905/795-2660
President, Robert Davies
Publications: Municipal Engineers Association Newsletter

### NACE - International (1943)
**National Society of Corrosion Engineers**
1440 South Creek Dr., PO Box 218340, Houston, TX 77218-8340 USA
281/228-6200, Fax: 281/228-6300, URL: http://www.nace.org
President, Robert Puyear
Treasurer, Lee Bone
Publications: Materials Performance
Toronto Region: c/o Gaberial Ogundele, Ontario Hydro Technologies, 800 Kipling Ave. (KR 178), Toronto, ON M8Z 5S4, 416/207-6842

### National Optics Institute/Institut national d'Optique (NOI) (1985)
369, rue Franquet, Ste-Foy, QC G1P 4N8
418/657-7006, Fax: 418/657-7009, Email: info@ino.qc.ca, URL: http://www.ino.qc.ca
Jean-Guy Paquet
Robert J.L. Corriveau
Publications: NOI Bulletin
Affiliates: Optical Society of America

### Plant Engineering & Maintenance Association of Canada (PEMAC)
#18, 170 Wilkinson Rd., Brampton, ON L6T 4Z5
905/874-1154, Fax: 905/459-3690
Executive Director, Steve Galbauer
President, Brian Hurting
Publications: PEMACTION

### SHAD International (1981)
8 Young St. East, Waterloo, ON N2J 2L3
519/884-8844, Fax: 519/884-8191, Email: info@shad.ca, URL: http://www.shad.ca
President, Jack Pal
Vice-President, Ron Champion

### Society of Motion Picture & Television Engineers (SMPTE) (1916)
595 West Hartsdale Ave., White Plains, NY 10607-1824 USA
914/761-1100, Fax: 914/761-3115, Email: smpte@smpte.org, URL: http://www.smpte.org/
President, David L. George
Executive Vice-President, Charles Jablonski
Publications: SMPTE Journal

### Society of Tribologists & Lubrication Engineers/Société des tribologistes et ingénieurs en lubrification (1987)
840 Busse Hwy., Park Ridge, IL 60068-2376 USA
708/825-5536, Fax: 708/825-1456
Executive Director, Maxine E. Hensley
President, Curtis L. Gordon
Publications: Lubrication Engineering

## ENVIRONMENTAL
***see also* Naturalists**

### Air & Waste Management Association/Association pour la Prévention de la Contamination de l'Air et du Sol (A&WMA) (1907)
One Gateway Center, 3rd Fl., Pittsburgh, PA 15222 USA
412/232-3444, Fax: 412/232-3450, Email: info@awma.org, URL: http://www.awma.org
Executive Director, John Thorner
Deputy Director, Technical Programs, Steve Stasko
Canadian Office Director, Jane Meyboom
Chair, Atlantic Canada Section, Scott MacKnight, Bus: 902/463-0114, Fax: 902/466-5743
Chair, British Columbia & Yukon Section, Joffre Berry, Bus: 604/432-8401, Fax: 604/431-9258
Chair, Canadian Prairie & Northern Section, Lawrence Strachan, Bus: 204/945-7071, Fax: 204/945-5229
Chair, Ontario Section, Helle Tosine, Bus: 416/314-3920, Fax: 416/314-3225
Chair, Québec Section, Pierre Lupien, Bus: 514/499-4536, Fax: 514/499-4515
Chair, Vancouver Island Section, Michael Williams, Bus: 604/360-3092, Fax: 604/360-3079
Publications: The Journal of the Air & Waste Management Association; Directory & Resource Book; Environmental Manager
National Office: Director, Jane Meyboom, #1202, 155 Queen St., Ottawa, ON K1P 6L1, 613/233-2006, Fax: 613/233-8096

### Alberta Wilderness Association (AWA) (1969)
455 - 12 St. NW, PO Box 6398, Stn D, Calgary, AB T2P 2E1
403/492-2311, Fax: 403/492-2364
President, Glenda Hanna
1st Vice-President, Peter Sherrington
2nd Vice-President, Jennifer Klimek
Publications: Wild Lands Advocate; Eastern Slopes Wildlands: Our Living Heritage; Rivers on Borrowed Time; Action Alert - Wise Use Newsletter, q.
Affiliates: Environmental Resource Centre

### Association of Municipal Recycling Co-ordinators (AMRC) (1987)
25 Douglas St., Guelph, ON N1H 2S7
519/823-1990, Fax: 519/823-0084, Email: amrc@albedo.net
Executive Director, Linda Varangu
Co-Chair, Joe Davis
Co-Chair, Mark Collins
Publications: For R Information

### Association québécoise des techniques de l'eau (AQTE) (1962)
#220, 911, rue Jean-Talon est, Montréal, QC H2R 1V5
514/270-7110, Téléc: 514/270-7154, Courrier électronique: assqenv@login.net
Directeur général, Eric Bouchard
Présidente, Johnny Izzi
Publications: Sciences et techniques de l'eau; Répertoire de produits et services dans le domaine de l'eau, annuel; Effluent, 10 fois par an
Organisation(s) affiliée(s): Association romande pour la protection des eaux et de l'air (ARPEA)

### Association des récupérateurs du Québec, inc.
191, rue Saint-Joseph est, CP 2115, Succ. Québec, Québec, QC G1K 7M9
418/529-6001, Téléc: 418/686-0076

### British Columbia Water & Wastewater Association (BCWWA) (1964)
1777 Harbour Dr., Coquitlam, BC V3J 5W4
604/936-4982, Fax: 604/931-3880
President, Prad Khare
Executive Director, Catherine Gibson
Secretary, Chester Merchant
Publications: Watermark; BCWWA Membership Directory
Affiliates: American Water & Waste Association; Water Pollution Control Federation; Lower Mainland Water & Sewer Supervisors Association; American Society of Plumbing Engineers - BC Chapter

### Canadian Association for Environmental Analytical Laboratories/Association canadienne des laboratoires d'analyse environnementale (CAEAL) (1989)
#300, 265 Carling Ave., Ottawa, ON K1S 2E1
613/233-5300, Fax: 613/233-5501, Email: rwilson@caeal.ca, URL: http://www.caeal.ca
Executive Director, Rick Wilson
Publications: CAEAL/ACLAE Newsletter

### Canadian Association of Recycling Industries (CARI)
#502, 50 Gervais Dr., North York, ON M3C 1Z3
416/510-1244, Fax: 416/510-1248
Associate Manager, Donna Turner
Publications: CARI

### Canadian Association on Water Quality/ Association canadienne sur la qualité de l'eau (CAWQ) (1966)

**Canadian National Committee of the International Association on Water Quality**

Environmental Technology Centre, 3439 River Rd. South, Gloucester, ON K1A 0H3
613/990-9849, Fax: 613/990-9855
Executive Officer, Dr. H.R. Eisenhauer
President, Dr. J.D. Norman
Secretary, Dr. Y. Comeau
Publications: Water Quality Research Journal of Canada; R & D News in Environmental Science & Engineering, bi-m.

### Canadian Centre for Pollution Prevention/Centre canadien pour la prévention de la pollution (C2P2) (1992)

#112, 265 North Front St., Sarnia, ON N7T 7X1
519/337-3423, Fax: 519/337-3486, Toll Free: 1-800-667-9790, Email: c2p2@sarnia.com, URL: http://c2p2.sarnia.com
Executive Director, Stewart Forbes
Information Manager, Marianne Lines
Publications: At the Source

### Canadian Coalition for Ecology, Ethics & Religion (CCEER) (1991)

1021 Jackson St., Lot 75, Dauphin, MB R7N 2N5
204/638-4319, Fax: 204/638-5733, Email: frajotte@galaxy.mb.ca
Director, Dr. Freda Rajotte
Director, Peter Timmerman
Publications: Sacred Spaces
Affiliates: International Consultancy on Religion, Education & Culture; International Coordinating Committee on Religion & the Earth; North American Conference on Religion & Ecology; International Federation of Institutes for Advanced Study

### Canadian Conservation Institute/Institut canadien de conservation (CCI) (1972)

1030 Innes Rd., Ottawa, ON K1A 0M5
613/998-3721, Fax: 613/998-4721, Email: cci-icc_publications@pch.gc.ca
Director General, Bill Peters
Publications: CCI Newsletter/Bulletin de l'ICC

### Canadian Council for Human Resources in the Environment Industry/Le conseil canadien des ressources humaines de l'industrie de l'Environnement (CCHREI) (1993)

#700, 700 - 4th Ave. SW, Calgary, AB T2P 3J4
403/233-0748, Fax: 403/269-9544, Email: cchrei@netway.ab.ca, URL: http://www.chatsubo.com/cchrei
Executive Director & CEO, Grant Trump
Publications: Changing Times Newsletter; Compendium of Environmental Training Courses; Definition of Environmental Employment; Classification of Environmental Occupations; Skill Set Documentation
Affiliates: Canadian Environment Industry Association; Association of Universities & Colleges of Canada; Association of Canadian Community Colleges; Canadian Council of Professional Engineers; Association Québécois des Techniques de L'Eau; Chemical Institute of Canada; Industry Canada; Environment Canada; Human Resources Development Canada; Canadian Standards Association; Canadian Council of Technicians & Technologists

### Canadian Council of Ministers of the Environment

#360, 123 Main St., Winnipeg, MB R3C 1A3
204/948-2090, Fax: 204/948-2125, Email: lforand@ccme.ca, URL: http://www.ccme.ca/ccme
Director general, Liseanne Forand

### Canadian Earth Energy Association/Association canadienne de l'énergie du sol (CEEA) (1987)

#605, 130 Slater St., Ottawa, ON K1P 6E2
613/230-2332, Fax: 613/237-1480, Email: ceea@earthenergy.org, URL: http://www.earthenergy.org
Executive Director, Bill Eggertson
Publications: CEEA
Affiliates: International Ground Source Heat Pump Association; Geothermal Heat Pump Consortium

### Canadian Ecophilosophy Network (1983)

PO Box 5853, Stn B, Victoria, BC V8R 6S8
250/598-7004, Fax: 250/598-9901, Email: ecosophy@islandnet.com
Publications Editor, Alan R. Drengson
Publications: The Trumpeter: Journal of Ecosophy

### Canadian Environment Industry Association/ Association canadienne des industries de l'environnement (CEIA) (1988)

#208, 350 Sparks St., Ottawa, ON K1R 7S8
613/236-6662, Fax: 613/236-6850, Email: CEIAEA@capitalnet.com, URL: http://www.ceia.org
Executive Director, Ron Portelli
President, G. Steve Hart
Publications: CEIA Communiqué

#### L'ASSOCIATION DES ENTREPRENEURS DE SERVICES EN ENVIRONNEMENT DU QUÉBEC (AESEQ) (1959)

#220, 911, Jean Talon est, Montréal, QC H2R 1V5
514/270-7110, Téléc: 514/270-7154
Courrier électronique: assqenv@login.net
Directeur général, Eric Bouchard

#### CANADIAN ENVIRONMENT INDUSTRY ASSOCIATION - BRITISH COLUMBIA

**CEIA-BC**

World Trade Centre, #504, 999 Canada Pl., Vancouver, BC V6C 3E1
604/775-7266, Fax: 604/775-5168
Email: ceiabc@cyberstore.ca, URL: http://www.ceia-bc.com/
Administrator, Steve Greentree

#### CANADIAN ENVIRONMENT INDUSTRY ASSOCIATION - ONTARIO

**CEIA-Ontario**

63 Polson St., 2nd Fl., Toronto, ON M5A 1A4
416/778-6590, Fax: 416/778-5702
Email: ceiaon@web.apc.org
President, Gerry Rich

#### ENVIRONMENTAL SERVICES ASSOCIATION OF ALBERTA (ESAA) (1988)

#1710, 10303 Jasper Ave., Edmonton, AB T5J 3N6
403/429-6363, Fax: 403/429-4249, Toll Free: 1-800-661-9278
Email: info@esaa.org, URL: http://www.esaa.org
Managing Director, Tim Schultz, Email: schultz@esaa.org
Publications: The Insider; Directory & Buyer's Guide, a.

#### MANITOBA ENVIRONMENTAL INDUSTRIES ASSOCIATION INC. (MEIA)

895A Century St., Winnipeg, MB R3H 0M3
204/987-8505, Fax: 204/772-6705
Email: meia@canpay.com, URL: http://www.canpay.com/meia/
Executive Director, Monique Grabowski
President, Michael G. Van Wallenghem, BSA, B.Comm., Bus: 204/778-4969, Fax: 204/775-9381
Publications: MEIA Update

#### NEW BRUNSWICK ENVIRONMENT INDUSTRY ASSOCIATION

PO Box 637, Stn A, Fredericton, NB E3B 5B3
506/451-1991, Fax: 506/457-2100
Email: geobacnb@nbnet.nb.ca
President, Victor Nowicki

#### NEWFOUNDLAND ENVIRONMENTAL INDUSTRY ASSOCIATION (NEIA) (1992)

Parsons Bldg., 1st Fl., 90 O'Leary Ave., St. John's, NF A1B 2C7
709/722-3333, Fax: 709/722-3213
Email: hillyard.janice@cbsc.ic.gc.ca, URL: http://www.webpage.ca/neia/
Executive Director, Nancy Creighton
President, Padraic O'Flaherty, Bus: 709/726-5245, Email: padraic_oflaherty@stratos.ca

#### NOVA SCOTIA ENVIRONMENTAL INDUSTRY ASSOCIATION (NSEIA)

PO Box 563, Dartmouth, NS B2Y 3Y8
902/466-8421, Fax: 902/466-8421
Email: vision@ra.isisnet.com, URL: http://www.isisnet.com/nseia/
Contact, David W. Harrison

#### SASKATCHEWAN ENVIRONMENTAL MANAGERS' ASSOCIATION (SEMA)

PO Box 834, Regina, SK S4P 3B1
306/543-3831, Fax: 306/757-5410
Administrator, Robert Schultz

### Canadian Environmental Law Association/ Association canadienne du droit de l'environnement (CELA) (1970)

#401, 517 College St., Toronto, ON M6G 4A2
416/960-2284, Fax: 416/960-9392
Executive Director, Michelle Swenerchuk
Publications: Intervenor

### Canadian Environmental Network/Réseau canadien de l'environnement (CEN) (1977)

#1004, 251 Laurier Ave. West, Ottawa, ON K1R 5J6
613/228-9810, Email: cen@web.apc.org
Executive Director, Eva Shacherl
Information Coordinator, Lesley Cassidy
Publications: CEN Bulletin; The Green List
Affiliates: Environment Liaison Centre - International

#### ALBERTA ENVIRONMENTAL NETWORK (AEN) (1987)

10511 Saskatchewan Dr., Edmonton, AB T6E 4S1
403/433-9302, Fax: 403/433-9305
Office Manager, Sam Gunsch
Publications: Environment Network News

#### BC ENVIRONMENTAL NETWORK (BCEN) (1979)

1672 - 10th Ave. East, Vancouver, BC V5N 1X5
604/879-2279, Fax: 604/879-2272
Email: bcen@alternatives.com
Executive Director, Anne-Marie Sleeman
Administrative Coordinator, Sherry Reid
Publications: British Columbia Environmental Directory; The British Columbia Environmental Report, q.

#### MANITOBA ECO-NETWORK INC./RÉSEAU ÉCOLOGIQUE DU MANITOBA INC. (1988)

**Manitoba Environmental Network**

#2, 70 Albert St., Winnipeg, MB R3B 1E7
204/947-6511, Fax: 204/946-6514
Executive Director, Anne Lindsey
President, Steering Committee, Jack Dubois
Director, Communications, Toby Maloney
Publications: Eco-Journal; Springtide, a.; Due Process, a.; Our Common Future - A Public Forum on Environment & Development, a.; Green Guide to Winnipeg

#### NEW BRUNSWICK ENVIRONMENTAL NETWORK/RÉSEAU ENVIRONNEMENTAL DU NOUVEAU-BRUNSWICK (NBEN) (1990)

RR#4, Sussex, NB E0E 1P0
506/433-6101, Fax: 506/433-6101

Contact, Mary Ann Coleman
Publications: Network Update/Mise à jour

**NEWFOUNDLAND & LABRADOR ENVIRONMENTAL NETWORK (NLEN) (1989)**
PO Box 944, Corner Brook, NF A2H 6J2
709/634-2520, Fax: 709/634-2520
Email: nlen@web.net
Coordinator, Lori March
Publications: Environment Network News

**NORTHERN ENVIRONMENTAL NETWORK NORNET**
PO Box 3932, Whitehorse, YT Y1A 3S7
867/668-2482, Fax: 867/668-6637
Coordinator, J. Hicklin

**NOVA SCOTIA ENVIRONMENTAL NETWORK**
RR#5, New Glasgow, NS B2H 5C8
902/922-3314, Fax: 902/922-2283
Coordinator, Ishbel Munro
Publications: Atlantic Resource Directory

**ONTARIO ENVIRONMENTAL NETWORK (OEN) (1981)**
25 Douglas St., Guelph, ON N1H 2S7
519/837-2565, Fax: 519/837-8113
Email: oen@web.apc.org, URL: http://www.web.net/~oen
Coordinator, Cecilia Fernandez
Publications: Network News; Environmental Resource Book

**PRINCE EDWARD ISLAND ENVIRONMENTAL NETWORK (PEIEN) (1990)**
126 Richmond St., Charlottetown, PE C1A 1H9
902/566-4170, Fax: 902/566-4037
Co-Chair, Sharon Labchuk
Co-Chair, Gary Schneider
Office Coordinator, Susan Stephenson
Publications: The Networker

**RÉSEAU QUÉBÉCOIS DES GROUPES ÉCOLOGISTES (RQGE) (1983)**
#701, 460, rue Sainte-Catherine ouest, Montréal, QC H3B 1A7
514/392-0096, Téléc: 514/392-0952
Directrice générale, Gabrielle Pelletier
Publications: Bouquet Ecologique

**SASKATCHEWAN ECO-NETWORK (SEN) (1980)**
#203, 115 - 2 Ave. North, Saskatoon, SK S7K 2B1
306/652-1275, Fax: 306/665-2128
Email: sen@link.ca
Office Administrator, Bernadette Richards
Working Group Coordinator, Phillip Penna
Publications: Network News

### Canadian Environmental Technology Advancement Corporation - West (CETAC - WEST)
Alberta Regional Office, #420, 715 - 5 Ave. SW, Calgary, AB T2P 2X6
403/777-9595, Fax: 403/777-9599
President & CEO, Joe Lukacs

### The Canadian Institute for Environmental Investigations (CIEI) (1993)
#202, 70 Fulton Way, Richmond Hill, ON L4B 1J5
905/731-7788, Fax: 905/731-7870
Director of Education, D. James Hawkins
Executive Vice-President, Elaine Konstan, Bus: 905/731-7387
Affiliates: International Investigations Agency Inc.

### Canadian Institute for Environmental Law & Policy/Institut canadien du droit et de la politique de l'environnement (CIELAP) (1970)
#400, 517 College St., Toronto, ON M6G 4A2
416/923-3529, Fax: 416/923-5949, Email: cielap@web.net, URL: http://www.web.net/cielap
Executive Director, Anne Mitchell
Publications: Canadian Environmental Law Reports; Newsletter, q.
Affiliates: Canadian Environmental Network; Ontario Environmental Network, Great Lakes United

### Canadian Institute of Resources Law/Institut canadien du droit des ressources (CIRL) (1979)
PF-B 3330, University of Calgary, 2500 University Dr. NW, Calgary, AB T2N 1N4
403/220-3200, Fax: 403/282-6182, Email: cirl@acs.ucalgary.ca, URL: http://www.ucalgary.ca/~cirl/
Executive Director, J. Owen Saunders
Publications: Resources
Affiliates: Australian Mining & Petroleum Law Association; The Canadian Petroleum Law Foundation; Centre for Natural Resources Law - University of Melbourne - Australia; Centre for Petroleum & Mineral Law Studies, University of Dundee - Scotland; Dalhousie Ocean Studies Program - Halifax; Energy Law Center - Salt Lake City; International Bar Association (Section of Energy & Natural Resources Law); International Institute for Energy Law - Leiden; Japan Energy Law Research Institute - Tokyo; Rocky Mountain Mineral Law Foundation - Denver; Scandinavian Institute of Marine Law, University of Oslo - Norway; Westwater Research Center - Vancouver

### Canadian Land Reclamation Association/Association canadienne de réhabilitation des sites dégradés (CLRA)
PO Box 61047, RPO Kensington, Calgary, AB T2N 4S6
403/289-9435, Fax: 403/289-9435
Sec.-Treas., Linda Jones
Publications: CLRA-ASSMR Newsletter
Affiliates: American Society for Surface Mining & Reclamation

### The Canadian Network for Environmental Education & Communication/Réseau canadien d'éducation et de communication relatives à l'environnement (EECOM) (1993)
PO Box 948, Stn B, Ottawa, ON K1P 5P9
902/863-5984, Fax: 902/863-9481
Chairperson, Anne Camozzi
Publications: The EECOM Newsletter; The Canadian Environmental Educators Guide to the Internet
Affiliates: North American Association for Environmental Education

### Canadian Parks Partnership/Partenaires des parcs canadiens (CPP) (1986)
#360, 1414 - 8th St., Calgary, AB T2R 1J6
403/292-4212, Fax: 403/292-4214, Toll Free: 1-800-454-7275, Email: partners@cadvision.com, URL: http://www.parksday.ca
Executive Director, Jocelyne Daw
Publications: Partners

### Canadian Polystyrene Recycling Association/Association de recyclage du polystyréne du Canada (CPRA) (1989)
7595 Tranmere Dr., Mississauga, ON L5S 1L4
905/612-8290, Fax: 905/612-8024
President, Michael G. Scott
Publications: CPRA News

### Canadian Society of Environmental Biologists/La Société canadienne des biologistes de l'environnement (CSEB) (1943)
PO Box 962, Stn F, Toronto, ON M4Y 2N9
President, Sean Sharpe
Sec.-Treas., Gerry Leering, Bus: 705/743-5780, Fax: 705/743-9592, Email: gleering@trentu.ca
Publications: CSEB Newsletter

### Canadian Society for Peat & Peatlands/Société canadienne de la tourbe et des tourbières (CSPP) (1989)
RR#3, PO Box 4, Parrsboro, NS B0M 1S0
902/348-2304, Fax: 902/348-2304
President, Jean-Yves Daigle
Sec.-Treas., Ted E. Tibbetts
Publications: CSPP Newsletter
Affiliates: International Peat Society

### Canadian Steel Can Recycling - Sponsored by Dofasco (CSCR) (1983)
1330 Burlington St. East, PO Box 2460, Hamilton, ON L8N 3J5
905/548-4253, Fax: 905/545-3236
Manager, John Paulowich
Affiliates: Steel Recycling Institute - Pittsburgh, PA

### Canadian Water Quality Association/Association canadienne pour la qualité de l'eau (CWQA) (1960)
#330, 295 The West Mall, Etobicoke, ON M9C 4Z4
416/695-3068, Fax: 416/695-2945, Email: cwqa@ican.net
General Manager, Ralph P. Suppa, CAE
Publications: Communique

### Canadian Water Resources Association/Association canadienne des ressources hydriques (CWRA) (1948)
c/o Membership Office, PO Box 1329, Cambridge, ON N1R 7G6
519/622-4764, Email: cwranat@genie.geis.com, URL: http://www.cwra.org/cwra
President, F.A. Ross, Bus: 403/327-3302
Publications: Water News; Canadian Water Resources Journal, q.

### Canadian Water & Wastewater Association/Association canadienne des eaux potables et usées (CWWA) (1986)
#402, 45 Rideau St., Ottawa, ON K1N 5W8
613/241-5692, Fax: 613/241-5193, Email: admin@cwwa.ca, URL: http://www.cwwa.ca
Executive Director, T. Duncan Ellison
Publications: CWWA/ACEPU Bulletin
Affiliates: Water Environment Association of Ontario; Western Canada Water & Wastewater Association; Association québécoise des techniques de l'environnement; American Water Works Association - Atlantic & Ontario Sections

### Canadian Wildlife Federation/Fédération canadienne de la faune (CWF) (1961)
2740 Queensview Dr., Ottawa, ON K2B 1A2
613/721-2286, Fax: 613/721-2902, Toll Free: 1-800-563-9453
General Manager, Richard Leitch
Executive Vice-President, Colin Maxwell
Manager, Communications & Programs, Sandy Baumgartner
Publications: Your Big Backyard; Canadian Wildlife, a.; Biosphère; Wild

**ALBERTA FISH & GAME ASSOCIATION**
6924 - 104 St., Edmonton, AB T6H 2L7
403/437-2342, Fax: 403/438-6872
Executive Vice-President, Ron Houser
Publications: The Outdoor Edge

**BRITISH COLUMBIA WILDLIFE FEDERATION**
#303, 19292 - 60 Ave., Surrey, BC V3S 8E5
604/533-2293, Fax: 604/533-1592
President, Bob Morris
Publications: The Outdoorsman

**FÉDÉRATION QUÉBÉCOISE DE LA FAUNE/QUÉBEC WILDLIFE FEDERATION (1946)**
#109, 6780, 1re Avenue, Charlesbourg, QC G1H 2W8
418/626-6858, Téléc: 418/622-6168
Courrier électronique: fede@fqf.qc.ca, URL: http://www.fqf.qc.ca
Président, Claude Lamoureux
Publications: Info FQF

**MANITOBA WILDLIFE FEDERATION (1944)**
70 Stevenson Rd., Winnipeg, MB R3H 0W7
204/633-5967, Fax: 204/632-5200
President, Larry Thiessen
Publications: Outdoor Edge/Wildlife Crusader

**NEW BRUNSWICK WILDLIFE FEDERATION/FÉDÉRATION DE LA FAUNE DU NOUVEAU-BRUNSWICK (NBWF) (1924)**
PO Box 20211, Fredericton, NB E3B 7A2
506/457-7468, Fax: 506/451-0618
President, Dale Stickles

**NEWFOUNDLAND & LABRADOR WILDLIFE FEDERATION (1963)**
PO Box 13399, Stn A, St. John's, NF A1B 4B7
709/364-8415
Executive Director, Richard Bouzanne

**NORTHWEST TERRITORIES WILDLIFE FEDERATION (1985)**
5134 Forrest Dr. North, Yellowknife, NT X1A 2W4
867/873-3853
President, Lorne Schollar
Publications: Northwest Territories Wildlife Newsletter; Canadian Hunting & Fishing Annual

**NOVA SCOTIA WILDLIFE FEDERATION (1930)**
PO Box 654, Halifax, NS B3J 2T3
902/423-6793, Fax: 902/423-6793
Executive Director, Tony Rodgers

**PEI WILDLIFE FEDERATION**
PO Box 753, Charlottetown, PE C1A 7L3
902/687-3131, Fax: 902/687-2350
President, Steve Cheverie

**SASKATCHEWAN WILDLIFE FEDERATION (SWF) (1929)**
444 River St. West, PO Box 788, Moose Jaw, SK S6H 4P5
306/692-7772, Fax: 306/692-4370
Executive Director, Ed Begin
Publications: Outdoor Edge

**YUKON FISH & GAME ASSOCIATION (YFGA) (1945)**
PO Box 4095, Whitehorse, YT Y1A 3S9
867/667-4263, Fax: 867/667-4237
President, Russel Tait
Publications: Outdoor Edge

### Canadian Wildlife Foundation (1976)
2740 Queensview Dr., Ottawa, ON K2B 1A2
613/721-2286, Fax: 613/721-2902
Executive Secretary, Colin Maxwell
Affiliates: Canadian Wildlife Federation

### Canadians for a Clean Environment (CCE) (1981)
5017 Victoria Ave., Niagara Falls, ON L2E 4C9
905/356-1160, Email: cce@itcanada.com
Contact, Al Oleksuik
Publications: Clean Scene

### Citizens Network on Waste Management (CNWM) (1981)
17 Major St., Kitchener, ON N2H 4R1
519/744-7503, Fax: 519/744-1546
Coordinator, John Jackson

### Citizens' Clearinghouse on Waste Management (CCWM) (1989)
RR#2, Cameron, ON K0M 1G0
705/887-1553, Fax: 705/887-4401
Co-Director, Barbara Wallace
Co-Director, Milton Wallace

### The Clean Nova Scotia Foundation (CNSF) (1987)
1675 Bedford Row, PO Box 2528, Stn Central, Halifax, NS B3J 3N5
902/420-3474, Fax: 902/424-5334, Toll Free: 1-800-665-5377, Email: cnsf@loki.atcon.com, URL: http://www.ccn.cs.dal.ca/Environment/CNSF/cnsf.html
Executive Director, Meinhard Doelle
Project Officer, Scott McMillan
Project Officer, Heather Gordon
Development Officer, Hilary Rankin
Publications: Nova Scotia RENEWS
Affiliates: Pitch-In Canada; Centre for Marine Conservation - Washington DC, USA; Tree Canada Foundation

### The Composting Council of Canada/Le Conseil canadien du compostage (1991)
16 Northumberland St., Toronto, ON M6H 1P7
416/535-0240, Fax: 416/536-9892, Email: ccc@compost.org, URL: http://www.compost.org
Executive Director, Susan Antler
Publications: Communiqué; Decision-Makers Technology Guide
Affiliates: The Composting Council (USA)

### Conseil des bio-industries du Québec/Québec Bio-Industry Council (1991)
1555, boul Chomedy, Laval, QC H7V 3Z1
514/978-5973, Téléc: 514/978-5970
Directeur général, Renaud Levesque
Président, Dupuis Angers

### Conservation Council of New Brunswick/Conseil de la conservation du Nouveau-Brunswick (CCNB) (1969)
180 St. John St., Fredericton, NB E3B 4A9
506/458-8747, Fax: 506/458-1047, Email: ccnb@web.apc.org
Executive Director, Meredith Brewer
President, Janice Harvey
Honorary President, Dr. Reg E. Balch
Policy Director, David Coon
Publications: EcoAlert
Affiliates: Friends of the Earth Canada; linkage projects with Arbofilia in Costa Rica & MAN in Nicaragua

### Conservation Council of Ontario/Le Conseil de conservation de l'Ontario (CCO) (1952)
#506, 489 College St., Toronto, ON M6G 1A5
416/969-9637, Fax: 416/960-8053, Email: cco@web.apc.org
Executive Director, Chris Winter
President, Dr. Kenneth H. MacKay
Publications: Ontario Conservation News

### Conservation Ontario
Box 11, 120 Bayview Pkwy., Newmarket, ON L3R 4W3
905/895-0716, Fax: 905/895-0751
General Manager, James Anderson
Publications: Ruffwater News; Conservation Action Briefs, q.

### CSR: Corporations Supporting Recycling (CSR)
#601, 26 Wellington St. East, Toronto, ON M5E 1S2
416/594-3456, Fax: 416/594-3463, Toll Free: 1-888-277-2762, Email: info@csr.org, URL: http://www.csr.org
President/CEO, Damian Bassett
Vice-President, Municipal Development, Joseph P. Hruska
Manager, Information Systems, David Pederson
Publications: The Recycler; CSR Sheet; Recycling in Ontario
Affiliates: Ontario Newspaper Publishers; Grocery Products Manufacturers of Canada; Ontario Soft Drink Association; Canadian Council of Grocery Distributors; Society of Plastics Industry of Canada; Packaging Association of Canada

### Ducks Unlimited Canada/Canards Illimités Canada (DUC) (1937)
**DU Canada**
Oak Hammock Marsh Conservation Centre, 1 Mallard Bay at Hwy. 220, PO Box 1160, Oak Hammock Marsh, MB R0C 2Z0
204/467-3000, Fax: 204/467-9028, Toll Free: 1-800-665-3825, Email: webfoot@ducks.ca, URL: http://www.ducks.ca
Chairman of the Board, W.G. Turnbull
President, George C. Reifel
Executive Vice-President, Don A. Young
Manager, Conservation Programs, Rod Fowler
Chief Biologist, Brian Gray
Communications Manager, Bob Kindrachuk
Publications: Conservator; Conservationniste, 3 fois par an
Affiliates: Ducks Unlimited organizations in Australia, Europe, Mexico, New Zealand, the UK & the US; North American Waterfowl Management Plan

### Earth Day Canada/Jour de la terre Canada (EDC) (1991)
#250, 144 Front St. West, Toronto, ON M5J 2L7
416/599-1991, Fax: 416/599-3100, Toll Free: 1-900-561-3300
Executive Director, Robyn Jones-Martin
President, Jed Goldberg
Publications: Solutions

### Ecology Action Centre (EAC) (1971)
#31, 1568 Argyle St., Halifax, NS B3J 2B3
902/429-2202, Fax: 902/422-6410, Email: eac_hfx@istar.ca
Co-Director, Wendy MacGregor
Co-Director, Amanda Lavers
Publications: Between the Issues

### Elsa Wild Animal Appeal of Canada (1971)
2482 Yonge St., PO Box 45051, Toronto, ON M4P 3E3
416/489-8862, Fax: 416/489-4769
Contact, D.E. Henderson
Publications: Elsa Newsletter

### Enviro-Accès Inc. (1993)
**Centre pour l'avancement des technologies environnementales**
#310, 855, rue Pepin, Sherbrooke, QC J1L 2P8
819/823-2230, Téléc: 819/823-6632, Courrier électronique: enviro-a@enviroaccess.ca, URL: http://www.enviroaccess.ca/
Présidente - directrice générale, Manon Laporte
Directeur exécutif, Philippe Morel, Courrier électronique: pmorel@enviroaccess.ca
Publications: Biomasse-environnement; Répertoire de l'expertise de recherche en l'environnement; Répertoire des programmes d'aide; Fiches technologiques; Guide Fiscal

### Environment & Plastics Industry Council (EPIC) (1989)
#500, 5925 Airport Rd., Mississauga, ON L4V 1W1
905/678-7748, Fax: 905/678-0774
President, Sandra Birkenmayer
Vice-President, Dr. Fred Edgecombe
Director of Communications, Bob Hamp

### Environment Probe (1988)
225 Brunswick Ave., Toronto, ON M5S 2M6
416/964-9223, Fax: 416/964-8239, Email: ElizabethBrubaker@nextcity.com, URL: http://www.nextcity.com/EnvironmentProbe/
Executive Director, Elizabeth Brubaker

**The Environmental Coalition of PEI (1988)**
126 Richmond St., Charlottetown, PE C1A 1H9
902/566-4696, Fax: 902/566-4037, Email: peien@cycor.ca
Contact, Sharon Labchuk
Publications: ECO-News

**The Environmental Law Centre (Alberta) Society (ELC) (1981)**
#204, 10709 Jasper Ave., Edmonton, AB T5J 3N3
403/424-5099, Fax: 403/424-5133, Toll Free: 1-800-661-4238, Email: elc@web.net, URL: http://www.web.net/~elc
Executive Director, Donna Tingley
President, Judith Hanebury
Publications: Journal of Environmental Law & Practice; Environmental Law Centre News Brief, q.

**Environmental Youth Alliance (EYA) (1989)**
PO Box 34097, Stn D, Vancouver, BC V6J 3L1
604/873-0616, Email: dragon@wimsey.com
Contact, Doug Ragan
Publications: SCREAM

**Environnement jeunesse (1979)**
ENJEU
4545, av Pierre-de-Coubertin, CP 1000, Succ. M, Montréal, QC H1V 3R2
514/252-3016, Téléc: 514/254-5873
Directrice générale, Christiane Dinelle
Publications: L'ENJEU
Organisation(s) affiliée(s): Réseau québécois des groupes écologistes (RQGE); Association québécoise pour la promotion de l'éducation relative à l'environnement (AQPERE)

**The Evergreen Foundation/Fondation Evergreen (1991)**
#500, 355 Adelaide St. West, Toronto, ON M5V 1S2
416/596-1495, Fax: 416/596-1443, Email: 74744.2403@compuserve.com, URL: http://www.evergreen.ca/
Executive Director, Geoff Cape
Publications: Evergreen Foundation News; Evergreen World; Outdoor Classroom News, s-a.

**Fédération des associations pour la protection de l'environnement des lacs inc. (FAPEL) (1976)**
CP 51128, Succ. Centre, Montréal, QC H1N 3T8
514/256-6822, Téléc: 514/256-7005
Directrice générale, Lucie McNeil
Secrétaire, Lyne Vigneault

**Fondation de la faune du Québec (FFQ) (1985)**
#420, 1175, av Lavigerie, Ste-Foy, QC G1V 4P1
418/644-7926, Téléc: 418/643-7655
Président/directeur général, Bernard Beaudin
Publications: Nature

**Forest Alliance of British Columbia (FABC) (1991)**
1055 Dunsmuir St., PO Box 49312, Vancouver, BC V7X 1L3
604/685-7507, Fax: 604/685-5373, Toll Free: 1-800-567-8733, Email: fabc@mindlink.bc.ca, URL: http://www.forest.org
Executive Director, Tom Tevlin
Chairman, Jack Munro
Community Relations Manager, Donna Freeman
Publications: The Forest & the People; Choices - Issues & Options for BC Forests, q.

**Fort Whyte Centre for Environmental Education (1966)**
1961 McCreary Rd., PO Box 124, Winnipeg, MB R3Y 1G5
204/989-8355, Fax: 204/895-4700
President/CEO, Bill Elliott
Publications: Branta

**Friends of the Earth/Ami(e)s de la terre (FoE) (1978)**
#306, 47 Clarence St., Ottawa, ON K1N 9K1
613/241-0085, Fax: 613/241-7998, Email: foe@intranet.ca
CEO, Beatrice Olivastri
Publications: Earth Words
Affiliates: Canadian Environmental Network; Canadian Participatory Committee for UNCED

**The Gaia Group (1985)**
2108 Reynolds St., Regina, SK S4N 3N1
306/352-4804
President, Jim Elliott
Publications: Whisper in the Woods

**GreenLEAP (1991)**
The Independent Association of Legal, Engineering & Accounting Professionals for the Environment
#400, 70 Richmond St. East, Toronto, ON M5C 1N8
416/363-5577, Fax: 416/367-2653
Chief Administrative Officer, Glenna Ford
Publications: GreenLEAP; GreenNews, s-a.

**Greenpeace Canada (1971)**
#605, 250 Dundas St. West, Toronto, ON M5T 2Z5
416/597-8408, Fax: 416/597-8422, Toll Free: 1-800-320-7183, URL: http://www.greenpeacecanada.org/
Executive Director, Jeanne Moffat
Publications: Greenlink

**Harmony Foundation of Canada/Fondation Harmonie du Canada (1985)**
1183 Fort St., Victoria, BC V8V 3L1
250/380-3001, Fax: 250/380-0887, Email: harmony@islandnet.com, URL: http://www.harmonyfdn.bc.ca/~harmony
Executive Director, Michael Bloomfield
Publications: Workplace Guide: Practical Action for the Environment/Guide pour le milieu de travail vers la santé environnementale; Home & Family Guide: Practical Action for the Environment/Guide pour la famille et la maison: la protection de l'environnement au quotidien; Community Workshops for the Environment/Ateliers communautaires au sujet de l'environnement; Our Common Future: A Canadian Response to the Challenge of Sustainable Development; Earthworms, Nature's Recyclers; Greenworks: Building on Success; Environmental Considerations for Planning a Conference or Meeting; Strengthening Our Communities: A Guidebook for Community Youth Programs; Growing Up Green Action Wheel & Growing Up Green; Discovering Your Community: A Cooperative Process for Planning Sustanability
Affiliates: Centre for our Common Future; Canadian Environmental Network
Ottawa Office: #202A, 145 Spruce St., Ottawa, ON K1R 6P1, 613/230-5399, Fax: 613/238-6470

**Institut de recherche en biologie végétale (IRBV) (1990)**
4101, rue Sherbrooke est, Montréal, QC H1X 2B2
514/872-0272, Téléc: 514/872-9406, Courrier électronique: irbv@ere.umontreal.ca
Directeur général, Hargurdeep Saini

**Institute for Environmental Policy & Stewardship/Institut de politique et environmentales d'intendance (IEPS) (1989)**
Faculty of Environmental Sciences, Blackwood Hall, University of Guelph, Guelph, ON N1G 2W1
519/824-4120, ext.3798, 3072, Fax: 519/763-4686
Director, Isabel Hethcoate
Publications: The Green Web

**International Environmental Liability Management Association (IELMA)**
#2200, 181 University Ave., Toronto, ON M5H 3M7
416/601-6758, Fax: 416/863-1036, Email: actuarius@aol.com, URL: http://www.magic.ca/ielma/IELMA.html

**International Institute for Sustainable Development/Institut international du développement durable (IISD) (1990)**
161 Portage Ave. East, 6th Fl., Winnipeg, MB R3B 0Y4
204/958-7700, Fax: 204/958-7710, Email: info@iisd.ca, URL: http://iisd1.iisd.ca/
President/CEO, Arthur J. Hanson
Sec.-Treas., Ian R. Seymour, CA
Project Officer, Marlene Roy
Publications: Developing Ideas
Trade & Sustainable Development Program: Contact, David Runnalls, #1360, 250 Albert St., Ottawa, ON K1P 6M1, 613/238-2296, Fax: 613/238-8515

**International Society of Indoor Air Quality & Climate (ISIAQ) (1992)**
PO Box 22038, Sub 32, Ottawa, ON K1V 0W2
613/731-2559, Fax: 613/733-9394, Email: ae977@freenet.carleton.ca, URL: http://www.cyberus.ca/~dsw/
Secretary, Dr. Douglas Walkinshaw
President, Prof. Olli Seppänen
Publications: Indoor Air

**National Energy Conservation Association/Association nationale pour la conservation de l'énergie (NECA) (1983)**
#200, 281 McDermot Ave., Winnipeg, MB R3B 0S9
204/956-5888, Fax: 204/956-5819, Toll Free: 1-800-263-5974, Email: neca@neca.ca, URL: http://www.mbnet.mb.ca/~neca/
CEO/Sec.-Treas., Laverne Dalgleish
Manager, Trevor Anderson
Training Administrator, Kari Mackinnon
Chairman, Peter Etherington
Director, Len Wall
Publications: Visions

**The Nature Conservancy of Canada/Société canadienne pour la conservation de la nature (NCC) (1963)**
#400, 110 Eglinton Ave. West, Toronto, ON M4R 2G5
416/932-3202, Fax: 416/932-3208, Toll Free: 1-800-465-0029
Executive Director, John Eisenhauer
Publications: The Ark

**Newfoundland & Labrador Environmental Association**
#603, 140 Water St., St. John's, NF A1C 6H6
709/722-1740, Fax: 709/726-1813
President, Stan Tobin

**North American Recycled Rubber Association (NARRA) (1994)**
160 Baseline Rd., Bowmanville, ON L1C 1A2
905/623-8919, Fax: 905/623-1791, Email: narra@oix.com
Secretary & Director of Research, Philip E. Coulter, P.Eng.
Office Manager, Margaret Carter
Publications: NARRA News

**Nova Scotia Business Council on the Environment (NSBCE) (1992)**
12 Portland St., Dartmouth, NS B2Y 1G9
902/469-7110, Fax: 902/464-0365
Project Manager, David W. Harrison
Project Coordinator, Joanne Hurshman
Publications: Environmental Management

**Ocean Voice International, Inc./Echo de l'océan, inc. (OVI) (1987)**
PO Box 37026, Ottawa, ON K1V 0W0
613/264-8986, Fax: 613/521-4205, Email: mcall@superaje.com, URL: http://www.ovi.ca
President, Don E. McAllister
Vice-President, Jaime Baquero
Treasurer, Phyllis Kofmel
Secretary, Katjo Rodriguez
Publications: Sea Wind
Affiliates: Global Coral Reef Alliance

**Ontario Centre for Environmental Technology Advancement (OCETA) (1994)**
63 Polson St., 2nd Fl., Toronto, ON M5A 1A4
416/778-5624, Fax: 416/778-5624, Email: oceta@hookup.net, URL: http://www.oceta.on.ca
President & CEO, Ed Mallett
Chairman of the Board, Jane Pagel
Vice-President, Business Services, Brian Wanless, Bus: 416/778-5288
Vice-President, Technology & Research, Adele Buckley, Bus: 416/778-5281
Vice-President, Finance & Investment, Keith Lue, Bus: 416/778-5283
Publications: CEIA/OCETA Fax Newsletter
Affiliates: Ontario Environmental Training Consortium; Canadian Environmental Industry Association; Waste Technology International; Canadian Institute of Technology for the Environment

**Ontario Pollution Control Equipment Association (OPCEA) (1970)**
PO Box 137, Midhurst, ON L0L 1X0
705/725-0917, Fax: 705/725-1068
President, John Coomey
Publications: Product & Service Directory
Affiliates: Pollution Control Association of Ontario

**Ontario Toxic Waste Research Coalition (OTWRC) (1986)**
PO Box 35, Vineland Station, ON L0R 2E0
519/744-7503, Fax: 519/744-1546
CEO, John Jackson
Secretary, Ruth Burton, Bus: 905/563-8571
Affiliates: Concerned Citizens Group; Echo Site Study Committee; Niagara Citizens for Modern Waste Management; Niagara North Federation of Agriculture; Niagara Peninsula Fruit & Vegetable Growers; Niagara Residents for Safe Toxic Waste Disposal; Preservation of Agricultural Lands Society

**Ontario Waste Management Association/Société ontarienne de gestion des déchets (OWMA) (1977)**
#320, 4195 Dundas St. West, Etobicoke, ON M8X 1Y4
416/236-0172, Fax: 416/236-0174
Executive Director, Terry E. Taylor, CAE
General Manager, Nancy Crawford
Affiliates: National Solid Wastes Management Association

**Osgoode Hall Environmental Law Society (1991)**
Legal & Literary Society, Osgoode Hall Law School, York University, 4700 Keele St., North York, ON M3J 1P3
416/736-5027, Fax: 416/736-5736
Director, Colin Piercey
Director, Cheryl Sheruit
Director, Paul McCulloch
Director, Lara Edwards

**The Pembina Institute for Appropriate Development (PIAD) (1985)**
PO Box 7558, Drayton Valley, AB T7A 1S7
403/542-6272, Fax: 403/542-6464, Email: piad@ccinet.ab.ca, URL: http://www.piad.ab.ca
Executive Director, Thomas Marr-Laing
President, Wally Heinrichs
Publications: The Alberta Environmental Directory; Canadian Environmental Education Catalogue; enCompass, bi-m.

**Pitch-In Canada/Passons à l'action Canada (PIC) (1967)**
PO Box 45011, RPO Ocean Park, White Rock, BC V4A 9L1
604/290-0498, Fax: 604/535-4653, URL: http://www.pitch-in.ca/
President, Allard W. van Veen
Chairman, Bette Ballhorn
Publications: Pitch-In News
Affiliates: Clean World International - London, UK

**Pollution Probe Foundation (PPF) (1969)**
12 Madison Ave., Toronto, ON M5R 2S1
416/926-1907, Fax: 416/926-1601, Email: pprobe@web.net, URL: http://www.web.net/~pprobe/
Executive Director, Ken Ogilvie
Publications: ProbeAbilities
Affiliates: Clean Air Network

**Prairie Association for Water Management (PAWM) (1983)**
PO Box 1949, Hanna, AB T0J 1P0
403/854-2509
Coordinator, Candis Preston
President, Harry Gordon
Publications: PAWM

**Recycling Council of Alberta (RCA) (1987)**
PO Box 40552, RPO Highfield, Calgary, AB T2G 5G8
403/287-1477, Fax: 403/287-1942, Email: rca@cadvision.com; cseide@agt.net
Executive Director, Christina Seidel
Publications: The Connector

**Recycling Council of British Columbia (RCBC) (1974)**
#201, 225 Smithe St., Vancouver, BC V6B 4X7
604/683-6009, Fax: 604/683-7255, Toll Free: 1-800-667-4321, Email: rcbc@rcbc.bc.ca, URL: http://www.rcbc.bc.ca
Executive Director, Renie D'Aquila
Publications: Reiterate; Update, bi-m.

**Recycling Council of Ontario/Conseil du recyclage de l'Ontario (RCO) (1978)**
#504, 489 College St., Toronto, ON M6G 1A5
416/960-1025, Fax: 416/960-8053, Toll Free: 1-800-263-2849, Email: rco@web.net, URL: http://www.web.net/rco
Executive Director, John Hanson
Chair, John Lackie
Vice-Chair, Geoff Rathbone
Past Chair., Anne Mathewson
Publications: RCO Update

**Resource Conservation Manitoba Inc. (RCM) (1985)**
#2, 70 Albert St., Winnipeg, MB R3B 1E7
204/925-3777, Fax: 204/942-4207
Executive Director, Glen Koroluk
Publications: The R Report

**Resource Efficient Agricultural Production Canada (REAP-Canada) (1988)**
Sustainable Farming
Glenaladale House, Macdonald College, 21111 ch Lakeshore, PO Box 125, Ste-Anne-de-Bellevue, QC H9X 3V9
514/398-7743, Fax: 514/398-7972, Email: reap@interlink.net
President, Roger Samson
Publications: Sustainable Farming; Weed Management in Sustainable Agriculture; Priorities in Sustainable Agriculture Research
Affiliates: Canadian Organic Growers; Ecological Farmers Association of Ontario

**Saskatchewan Environmental Society (SES) (1970)**
#203, 115 - 2nd Ave. North, PO Box 1372, Saskatoon, SK S7K 3N9
306/665-1915, Fax: 306/665-2128, Email: saskenv@link.ca, URL: http://www.lights.com/ses/
Program Coordinator, Ann Coxworth
President, Bert Weichel
Sec.-Treas., Peter Krebs
Publications: SES Newsletter; SES Backgrounders, irreg.
Affiliates: Canadian Coalition for Nuclear Responsiblity; Canadian Environmental Network; Saskatchewan Eco-Network

**Saskatchewan Soil Conservation Association Inc. (SSCA) (1987)**
PO Box 1360, Indian Head, SK S0G 2K0
306/695-4235, Fax: 306/695-4236, Toll Free: 1-800-213-4287, Email: ssca@sk.sympatico.ca, URL: http://paridss.usask.ca/consgroups/ssca/sscahome.htm
President, Clint Steinley
Executive Manager, Doug McKell, P.Ag.
Office Manager, Clair Neill
Publications: Prairie Steward

**Saskatchewan Waste Reduction Council (SWRC) (1991)**
#203, 115 - 2nd Ave. North, Saskatoon, SK S7K 0G4
306/931-3242, Fax: 306/665-2128, Email: swrc@link.ca
Executive Director, Joanne Fedyk
Vice-Chair, Clayton Sampson
Chair, Bert Weichel
Publications: WasteWatch

**Sea Shepherd Conservation Society (SSCS) (1977)**
PO Box 48446, Vancouver, BC V7X 1A2
604/688-7325, Fax: 604/574-3161, Email: nvoth@estreet.com, URL: http://www.seashepherd.org
International Director, Lisa Distefano
Director, Paul Watson
Publications: The Sea Shepherd Log

**SEEDS Foundation (SEEDS) (1976)**
Society, Environment & Energy Development Studies Foundation
#440, 10169 - 104 St., Edmonton, AB T5J 1A5
403/424-0971, Fax: 403/424-2444, Toll Free: 1-800-661-8751, Email: stokerm@pschools.st-albert.ab.ca
Executive Director, Dan Stoker
Publications: PAGES

**Sierra Club of British Columbia (SCBC) (1969)**
1525 Amelia St., Victoria, BC V8W 2K1
250/386-5255, Fax: 250/386-4453, Email: scbcgis@cyberstore.ca
Contact, Vicky Husband
Publications: Sierra Report

**Sierra Club of Canada (1892)**
#620, One Nicholas St., Ottawa, ON K1N 7B7
613/241-4611, Fax: 613/233-2292
Executive Director, Elizabeth May
Affiliates: Canadian Coalition for Biodiversity

**Sierra Club of Eastern Canada (1972)**
#204, 517 College St., Toronto, ON M6G 4A2
416/960-9606, Fax: 416/960-9020, Email: sierraec@interlog.com
Contact, Kerry Wilkins
Publications: Sanctuary

Affiliates: Sierra Club of Western Canada; Sierra Club - USA

**Société québécoise d'assainissement des eaux (SQAE) (1980)**
1055, boul René-Lévesque est, 10e étage, Montréal, QC H2L 4S5
514/873-7411, Téléc: 514/873-7879, Courrier électronique: info@sqac.gouv.qc.ca, URL: http://www.sqac.gouv.qc.ca
Président-directeur général, Guy Leclerc
Vice-Président, Administration & finance, Jean Genest
Vice-président, Gestion des projets, François Rochette
Secrétaire général, Marc Pinsonnault

**Society Promoting Environmental Conservation (SPEC) (1968)**
2150 Maple St., Vancouver, BC V6J 3T3
604/736-7732, Fax: 604/736-7115
President, Paul Hundal
Publications: SPECtrum

**Soil Conservation Canada/Conservation des sols Canada (SCC) (1987)**
#907, 151 Slater St., Ottawa, ON K1P 5H4
Executive Director, Bryan James
President, Tom G. Sawyer
Publications: The Protector

**Solid Waste Association of North America (SWANA) (1961)**
PO Box 7219, Silver Spring, MD 20907 USA
301/585-2898, Fax: 301/589-7068, Email: swana@millkern.com, URL: http://www.swana.org
Executive Director/CEO, John H. Skinner, Ph.D.
COO, Lori Swain
CFO, Dawn M. Brown
Special Assistant to the Exec. Director, Intl. Board & Exec. Committee, Kathleen H. Lane
Canadian Representative/Manager, Solid Waste & Recycling, City of Lethbridge, Walter Brodowski, Bus: 403/320-3090, Fax: 403/329-4657
Publications: MSW Solutions

**United Nations Environment Programme/Programme des nations unies pour l'environnement (UNEP) (1972)**
Regional Office for North America, 2 United Nations Plaza, Rm. DC2-0803, New York, NY 10017 USA
212/963-8138, Fax: 212/963-7341, Telex: 422311 UN UI, Email: jfp@un.org, URL: http://www.unep.org
Director, Joanne Fox-Przeworski
Publications: Our Planet
Affiliates: Canadian Committee for UNEP

**Water Environment Association of Ontario (WEAO) (1971)**
63 Hollyberry Trail, North York, ON M2H 2N9
416/502-1440, Fax: 416/502-1786, Email: dfountai@pandr.com, URL: http://www.oww.org
President, Nels Conroy
Executive Administrator, Sandy M. Pickett, Bus: 416/502-1440
Publications: WEAO Newsletter
Affiliates: Water Environment Federation; Canadian Water & Wastewater Association

**Western Canada Water Environment Association (WCWEA) (1973)**
#203, 301 - 14 St. NW, Calgary, AB T2N 2A1
403/283-2003, Fax: 403/283-2007, Email: taylorj@wcwwa.ca, URL: http://www.wcwwa.ca
Manager, M.M. Janice Taylor
Chairman, Bill Brant

**Western Canada Water & Wastewater Association (WCWWA) (1948)**
#203, 301 - 14 St. NW, Calgary, AB T2N 2A1
403/283-2003, Fax: 403/283-2007, Email: taylorj@wcwwa.ca, URL: http://www.wcwwa.ca
Manager, M.M. Janice Taylor
President, Bill Brant
Publications: Water West; Who's Who, a.
Affiliates: Canadian Water & Wastewater Association

**Western Canada Wilderness Committee (WCWC) (1980)**
20 Water St., Vancouver, BC V6B 1A4
604/683-8220, Fax: 604/683-8229, Toll Free: 1-800-661-9453, Email: wc2wild@web.net, URL: http://www.web.net/wcwild/
Founder & Executive Director, Paul George
Executive Director, National Campaigns, Joe Foy
Executive Director, International Campaigns, Adriane Carr
Publications: Western Canada Wildnerness Committee Reports

**Wildlife Habitat Canada/Habitat faunique Canada (1984)**
#200, 7 Hinton Ave. North, Ottawa, ON K1Y 4P1
613/722-2090, Fax: 613/722-3318, Email: jladd@whc.org
Executive Director, David J. Neave
Chairperson, John C. Perlin

**Wildlife Preservation Trust Canada/Fiducie pour la faune au Canada (WPTC) (1985)**
Greey Bldg., #205, 56 The Esplanade, Toronto, ON M5E 1A7
416/368-3550, Fax: 416/368-0272, Email: wptc@inforamp.net
Executive Director, Elaine Williams
President, Graham F. Hallward
Treasurer, Eleanor Clitheroe
Publications: On the Edge
Affiliates: Jersey Wildlife Preservation Trust; Wildlife Preservation Trust International; International Union for Conservation & Nature

**World Wildlife Fund - Canada/Fonds mondial pour la nature (WWF) (1967)**
#504, 90 Eglinton Ave. East, Toronto, ON M4P 2Z7
416/489-8800, Fax: 416/489-3611, Toll Free: 1-800-267-2632, Email: panda@wwfcanada.org, URL: http://www.wwfcanada.org
President & CEO, Monte Hummel
Chairman, Dr. Donald A. Chant, O.C.
Communications Officer, Jeff Kenney, Email: jkenney@wwfcanada.org
Publications: Working for Wildlife; Schools for Wildlife
Affiliates: World Wide Fund for Nature (International)

**Yukon Conservation Society (YCS) (1968)**
302 Hawkins St., PO Box 4163, Whitehorse, YT Y1A 3T3
867/668-5678, Fax: 867/668-6637
Coordinator, Shelley Gerber
Director, Bob Van Dijken
Publications: Walk Softly
Affiliates: Canadian Environmental Network; Tatshenshini International; Canadian Nature Federation

## EQUIPMENT & MACHINERY

***see also* Building & Construction**

**Association des marchands de machines aratoires de la Province de Québec**
CP 590, Bedford, QC J0J 1A0
514/248-7946, Téléc: 514/248-3264
Directeur, René Maurice

**Association des professionnels à l'outillage municipal**
26, rue St-Raphael, Saint-Luc, QC J2W 1T1
514/348-6139, Téléc: 514/348-5889
Secrétaire, Robert Marjanek

**Canadian Association of Equipment Distributors**
#300, 1272 Wellington St., Ottawa, ON K1Y 3A7
613/722-4711, Fax: 613/722-0099
Executive Director, Nancy Leu

**Canadian Conveyor Manufacturers' Association**
#701, 116 Albert St., Ottawa, ON K1P 5G3
613/232-7213, Fax: 613/232-7381
President, Lloyd J. Beverly

**Canadian Crane Manufacturers' Association**
#701, 116 Albert St., Ottawa, ON K1P 5G3
613/232-7213, Fax: 613/232-7381
President, Lloyd J. Beverly

**Canadian Custom Engineered Machinery Manufacturers' Association**
#701, 116 Albert St., Ottawa, ON K1P 5G3
613/232-7213, Fax: 613/232-7381
President, Lloyd J. Beverly

**Canadian Environmental Equipment Manufacturers' Association**
#701, 116 Albert St., Ottawa, ON K1P 5G3
613/232-7213, Fax: 613/232-7381
President, Lloyd J. Beverly

**Canadian Farm & Industrial Equipment Institute**
#307, 720 Guelph Line, Burlington, ON L7R 4E2
905/632-8483, Fax: 905/632-7138
President, Brent M. Hamre

**Canadian Machine Tool Distributors' Association (CMTDA)**
208 Brimorton Dr., Toronto, ON M1H 2C6
416/431-1330, Fax: 416/431-5223
Sec.-Treas., John Martin

**Canadian Mining Equipment Manufacturers' Association**
#701, 116 Albert St., Ottawa, ON K1P 5G3
613/232-7213, Fax: 613/232-7381
President, Lloyd J. Beverly

**Canadian Outdoor Power Equipment Association**
208 Brimorton Dr., Toronto, ON M1H 2C6
416/431-1330, Fax: 416/431-5223
Manager, John Martin

**Canadian Packaging & Printing Machinery Manufacturers' Association**
#701, 116 Albert St., Ottawa, ON K1P 5G3
613/232-7213, Fax: 613/232-7381
President, Lloyd J. Beverly

**Canadian Petroleum Equipment Manufacturers' Association**
#701, 116 Albert St., Ottawa, ON K1P 5G3
613/232-7213, Fax: 613/232-7381
President, Lloyd J. Beverly

**Canadian Process Control Association (CPCA)**
4 St. Thomas St., Toronto, ON M5S 2B8
416/595-0103, Fax: 416/595-9880
Manager, Bruce G. Lawson

**Canadian Pulp & Paper Machinery Manufacturers' Association**
#701, 116 Albert St., Ottawa, ON K1P 5G3
613/232-7213, Fax: 613/232-7381
President, Lloyd J. Beverly

**Compressed Air & Gas Machinery Manufacturers' Association**
#701, 116 Albert St., Ottawa, ON K1P 5G3
613/232-7213, Fax: 613/232-7381
President, Arnold W.D. Garlick

**Machinery & Equipment Manufacturers' Association of Canada/Association des manufacturiers de machineries et d'équipements du Canada (MEMAC) (1955)**
#701, 116 Albert St., Ottawa, ON K1P 5G3
613/232-7213, Fax: 613/232-7381, URL: http://www.memac.org
President, Lloyd Beverly
Western Office: Vice-President, J. Stashuk, 1056 - 47th Ave. West, Vancouver, BC V6M 2L4, 604/266-3080

**Municipal Equipment & Operations Association (Ontario)**
City of Waterloo, PO Box 337, Waterloo, ON N2J 4A8
519/747-8619, Fax: 519/886-5788
President, Paul Udit

**Ontario Retail Farm Equipment Dealers' Association (ORFEDA) (1945)**
64 Temperance St., PO Box 430, Aurora, ON L4G 3L5
905/841-6888, Fax: 905/841-1214
Executive Vice-President, Glen E. Peart
Publications: ORFEDA Dealer Bulletin
Affiliates: North American Equipment Dealers Association

**Prairie Implement Manufacturers Association (PIMA) (1970)**
2152 Scarth St., Regina, SK S4P 2H6
306/522-2710, Fax: 306/781-7293, Toll Free: 1-888-999-7462, Email: pima@sk.sympatico.ca, URL: http://www.pima.ca
President, Larry Schneider
Manager, Member Services, Byron Irwin
Publications: PIMA Pulse

**ETHNIC GROUPS *see* MULTICULTURALISM**

## EVENTS

**Association des professionnels en exposition du Québec (APEQ) (1990)**
6940, rue Barry, Brossard, QC J4Z 1V1
514/443-1570, Téléc: 514/443-8415
Directeur général, Yves Barré
Présidente, Francine Bois
Publications: L'Exposé

**The BC Association of Festivals & Events (1976)**
**Festivals BC**
PO Box 538, Squamish, BC V0N 3G0
604/892-5977, Fax: 604/892-5978, Toll Free: 1-800-661-2295
Executive Director, Garth McCreedy
President, Bryan Pasch
Publications: Newsletter
Affiliates: Northwest Festivals Association; International Festival Association

**Canadian Association of Exposition Managers/Association canadienne des directeurs d'expositions (CAEM) (1983)**
Box 82, #239A, 6900 Airport Rd., Mississauga, ON L4V 1E8
905/678-9377, Fax: 905/678-9578
Executive Director, Carol Ann Burrell
Publications: Communiqué; Expresse; CAGM Buyers Guide and Directory

**Canadian Association of Fairs & Exhibitions/Association canadienne des foires et expositions (1926)**
PO Box 1172, Stn Main, Edmonton, AB T5J 2M4
403/474-1902, Fax: 403/471-4981, Email: cafe@planet.eon.net
Executive Director, Elwood F. Hart
President, Ruor Hoffman
Publications: Canadian Fair News; Directory of Canadian Fairs & Exhibitions Industry, a.
Affiliates: International Association of Fairs & Exhibitions; Provincial Associations of Agricultural Societies; Outdoor Amusement Business Association; Showmens League of Canada

**Carnaval de Québec/Québec Winter Carnival (1954)**
290, rue Joly, Québec, QC G1L 1N8
418/626-3716, Téléc: 418/626-7252
Directeur général, Denis Rhéaume
Directeur des commandités, Jean Pelletier
Directeur du marketing et des communications, Gabriel Béron

**Edmonton Klondike Days Association (1965)**
#1660, 10020 - 101A Ave., Edmonton, AB T5J 3G2
403/426-4055, Fax: 403/424-0418
General Manager, Don Gray
Affiliates: Northwest Festivals Association; International Festivals Association; Canadian Society of Association Executives; National Tour Association

**The Exhibit & Display Association of Canada (EDAC)**
#309, 2175 Sheppard Ave. East, North York, ON M2J 1W8
416/491-0308, Fax: 416/502-2115
Executive Director, Leona Crock
President, Sam Kohn

**Exhibition Association of Nova Scotia**
RR#2, Hubbards, NS B0J 1T0
902/857-3874
Administrator, D.C. Bishop

**Federation of Canadian Music Festivals/Fédération des festivals de musique du Canada (FCMF) (1949)**
1034 Chestnut Ave., Moose Jaw, SK S6H 1A6
306/693-7087, Fax: 306/693-7087, URL: http://www.planet.eon.net/~tuckey/NATIONAL.HTML
Executive Director, Sharon L. Penner
President, J. Alexander Clark
Publications: Piu Mosso; Digest Report, a.
Affiliates: Canadian Conference of the Arts

**ALBERTA MUSIC FESTIVAL ASSOCIATION (1963)**
4408 - 63 St., Camrose, AB T4V 2J4
403/672-5709
Executive Director, Sue Reesor
Publications: Alberta Music Festival Association Provincial Syllabus

**ASSOCIATED MANITOBA ARTS FESTIVALS, INC. (AMAF) (1977)**
#424, 100 Arthur St., Winnipeg, MB R3B 1H3
204/945-4578, Fax: 204/948-2073
Executive Director, Karen Oliver
Publications: Focus on Festivals

**BC ASSOCIATION OF PERFORMING ARTS FESTIVALS**
#288, 733 Johnson St., Victoria, BC V8W 3C7
604/920-7064, Fax: 604/920-7084
Executive Director, Helen Tuele

**FEDERATION OF MUSIC FESTIVALS OF NOVA SCOTIA**
49 MacDonald St., Antigonish, NS B2G 1M6
902/863-3179
Secretary, Mavis Murray

**NEW BRUNSWICK FEDERATION OF MUSIC FESTIVALS INC./LA FÉDÉRATION DES FESTIVALS DE MUSIQUE DU NOUVEAU-BRUNSWICK INC. (NBFMF) (1973)**
801 Mitchell St., Fredericton, NB E3B 6E8
506/452-1132, Fax: 506/444-5207
Executive Secretary, Gerald Goguen

**NEWFOUNDLAND FEDERATION OF MUSIC FESTIVALS (1969)**
101 LeMarchant Rd., St. John's, NF A1C 2H1
709/726-2831
Sec.-Treas., Dr. David K. Peters

**ONTARIO MUSIC FESTIVALS ASSOCIATION INC. (OMFA)**
3315 Yonge St., 2nd Fl., Toronto, ON M4N 2L9
416/487-5885, Fax: 416/487-5784
Executive Secretary, Mary Ann Griffin

**PEI MUSIC FESTIVAL ASSOCIATION**
RR#3, O'Leary, PE C0B 1V0
902/853-3435
Provincial Secretary, Susan Hardy

**QUÉBEC COMPETITIVE MUSIC FESTIVAL**
364, av Olivier, Westmount, QC H3Z 2C9
514/935-9074, Téléc: 514/935-4909
Secretary, Jan Simons

**SASKATCHEWAN MUSIC FESTIVAL ASSOCIATION INC. (1908)**
#201, 1819 Cornwall St., Regina, SK S4P 2K4
306/757-1722, Fax: 306/347-7789
URL: http://www.ffa.ucalgary.ca/scco/smea.html
Executive Director, Doris Lazecki

**Festivals Ontario (1986)**
PO Box 423, Orillia, ON L3V 6J8
705/325-0619, Fax: 705/325-7399
President, Jaye Robinson
Publications: Network/Réseau

**Greater Vancouver International Film Festival Society (VIFF) (1982)**
#410, 1008 Homer St., Vancouver, BC V6B 2X1
604/685-0260, Fax: 604/688-8221, Email: viff@viff.org, URL: http://viff.org/viff/
Festival Director, Alan Franey

**International Special Events Society - Toronto Chapter (1979)**
84 Seventh St., Toronto, ON M8V 3B4
416/252-9229, Fax: 416/252-7071, Toll Free: 1-800-688-4737, Email: ises@idirect.com, URL: http://www.ndgphoenix.com/ises.html
President, Georgina DeCarlo
President-Elect, Duane Brandow
Vice-President, Membership, Larry Cuthbertson
Vice-President, Education & Programming, Mike Heindl
Sec.-Treas., Leslee Bell
Association Manager, Shelley Macdonald
Publications: Toronto Chapter Newsletter

**Provincial Exhibition of Manitoba (1882)**
**Royal Manitoba Winter Fair**
#3, 1175 - 18th St., Brandon, MB R7A 7C5

204/726-3590, Fax: 204/725-0202, Info Line: 204/728-7769
General Manager, Dave Wowchuk

**Royal Agricultural Winter Fair Association/Foire agricole royale d'hiver (RAWF) (1922)**
Royal Winter Fair
Coliseum, Exhibition Place, Toronto, ON M6K 3C3
416/393-6400, Fax: 416/393-6488, Email: rwfair@ican.net, URL: http://www.royalfair.org
CEO, David E. Garrick
Marketing Manager, Sue Bundy
Publications: Around the Royal; Royal Horse Show Magazine, a.; Prize Lists, a.; RAWF Catalogue, a.

**Société des fêtes et festivals du Québec (SFFQ) (1976)**
4545, av Pierre-de-Coubertin, CP 1000, Succ. M, Montréal, QC H1V 3R2
514/252-3037, Téléc: 514/254-1617, Ligne sans frais: 1-800-361-7688
Directeur Général, Pierre-Paul Leduc
Publications: Festivals et Attractions; Le Bottin de l'industrie des festivals et attractions, annuel; Le Guide des festivals et attractions, annuel
Organisation(s) affiliée(s): International Festivals Association

**Toronto International Film Festival/Festival international du film de Toronto (1976)**
Cinematheque Ontario
2 Carlton St., 16th Fl., Toronto, ON M5B 1J3
416/967-7371, Fax: 416/967-9477, Info Line: 416/923-3456, Email: tiffg@torfilmfest.ca, URL: http://www.bell.ca/filmfest
Director, Piers Handling
Managing Director, Suzanne Weiss
Director, Communications, Michèle Maheux
Publications: Cinematheque Ontario Programme Guide; Programme Book, a.

**Western Association of Exposition Managers (WAEM)**
#523, 409 Granville St., Vancouver, BC V6C 1T2
604/669-3177, Fax: 604/604-669-5343
Executive Director, Tom Abbott

**Westerner Exposition Association (1891)**
4847A - 19 St., Red Deer, AB T4R 2N7
403/343-7800, Fax: 403/341-4699
General Manager, John Harms
Manager, Marketing & Sponsorship, Lisanne Ballantyne
Publications: The Westernews
Affiliates: International Association of Fairs & Exhibitions; International Association of Auditorium Management; Canadian Association of Fairs & Exhibitions

**EXECUTIVES *see* MANAGEMENT & ADMINISTRATION**

**EXHIBITIONS *see* EVENTS**

**EXPORT TRADE *see* TRADE**

**FAIRS *see* EVENTS**

**FARMING *see* AGRICULTURE & FARMING**

## FASHION & TEXTILES

**Allied Beauty Association (ABA) (1934)**
#325, 3625 Dufferin St., Toronto, ON M3K 1Z2
416/635-1282, Fax: 416/635-1205
Executive Director, Marc Speir

**Apparel Manufacturers Association of Ontario**
#605, 130 Slater St., Ottawa, ON K1P 6E2
613/565-3047, Fax: 613/231-2305, Toll Free: 1-800-661-1187
Executive Director, Stephen Beatty

**Association of Nova Scotia Hairdressers (ANSH) (1962)**
#9, 75 MacDonald Ave., Dartmouth, NS B3B 1S5
902/468-6477, Fax: 902/468-7147
Business Manager, Kimberly Carter
President, Larry MacDonald
Publications: Newsletter

**Barbers Association of British Columbia (1924)**
#411, 207 Hastings St. West, Vancouver, BC V6B 1H7
604/688-9731
Secretary, L.D. Carmichael

**Canadian Apparel Federation/Fédération canadienne du vêtement (CAF)**
#603, 130 Slater St., Ottawa, ON K1P 6E2
613/231-3220, Fax: 613/231-2305
Executive Director, Stephen Beatty
President, Jack Kivenko
Design Division: #112, 372 Richmond St. West, Toronto, ON M5V 1X6, 416/977-3620, Fax: 416/977-2637

**Canadian Association of Textile Colourists & Chemists/Association canadienne des coloristes et chimistes du textile**
269 MacDonald St., Woodstock, ON N4S 8C9
519/621-5722, Fax: 519/621-2420
Executive Director, Carl Webster
Publications: Canadian Textile Journal
Affiliates: Textile Federation of Canada

**Canadian Association of Wholesale Sales Representatives/Association canadienne des représentants de ventes en gros**
#336, 370 King St. West, PO Box 2, Toronto, ON M5V 1J9
416/593-6500, Fax: 416/593-5145
Executive Director, Karyn O'Neill
President, Julian Ernest
Administrator, S. Martineau
Publications: CAWS News

**ALBERTA FASHION MARKET**
#300L, 10403 - 172 St., Edmonton, AB T5S 1K9
403/484-7541
Administrator, Susan Brochu

**APPAREL SALESMEN'S MARKET**
3625, av Park, Montréal, QC H2X 3P8
514/849-9497, Fax: 514/849-9498
Marketing Manager, Susan Trudeau

**PRAIRIE APPAREL MARKET**
#77, 81 Garry St., Winnipeg, MB R3C 4J9
204/947-0561
Administrator, Pat Herzog

**WESTERN APPAREL MARKETS BC**
#28, 910 Mainland St., Vancouver, BC V6B 1A9
604/682-5719, Fax: 604/682-3892
Executive Director, Wayne Abrams

**WESTERN CANADA CHILDREN'S WEAR MARKETS (WCCWM) (1967)**
#407, 910 Mainland St., Vancouver, BC V6B 1A9
604/687-2778, Fax: 604/687-2779
President, John Knapton

**Canadian Laundry & Linen Institute (CLLI) (1981)**
PO Box 2277, Stn A, London, ON N6A 4E9
519/434-6261, Fax: 519/434-6261, Email: clli@odyssey.on.ca
Secretary, Ruth Baker
Education Director, Susan Wolnik

**Canadian Sewing & Needlecraft Association/Association canadienne des travaux d'aiguilles (CSNA) (1972)**
#204, 224 Merton St., Toronto, ON M4S 1A1
General Manager, Elizabeth Kelembet
Publications: CSNA Trade News

**Canadian Textiles Institute/Institut canadien des textiles (CTI) (1935)**
#1720, 66 Slater St., Ottawa, ON K1P 5H1
613/232-7195, Fax: 613/232-8722
President, Eric L. Barry

**Centre des technologies textiles/Textile Technology Centre (CTT) (1987)**
3000, rue Boullé, Saint-Hyacinthe, QC J2S 1H9
514/778-1870, Téléc: 514/778-3901
Président, Bernard Rose
Directeur général, Ray-Marc Dumoulin
Publications: InfoTex-Info Sageos
Organisation(s) affiliée(s): Fédération canadienne du textile; Association canadienne des coloristes et chimistes du textile; Société des textiles du Canada; Association des textiles des Cantons de l'Est; Institut canadien du tapis; Institut canadien des textiles; Institut québécois des revêtements de sol; Société des diplômes en textile
Textile Technology Centre: Stephen Laramee, #202, 53 Village Centre Pl., Mississauga, ON L4Z 1V9, 905/897-1474, Fax: 905/566-0177

**Children's Apparel Manufacturers Association/Association des Manufacturiers de Mode Enfantine (CAMA) (1951)**
#3110, 6900 Decarie Blvd., Montréal, QC H3X 2T8
514/731-7774, Fax: 514/731-7459
Executive Director, Murray W. Schwartz

**Footwear Council of Canada**
PO Box 644, Stn Don Mills, North York, ON M3C 2T6
Secretary, Sharon Maloney

**Garment Manufacturers Association of Western Canada**
#114, 85 Adelaide St., Winnipeg, MB R3A 0V9
204/943-2228
Executive Director, Allan Finkel

**Hairdressers' Association of British Columbia (HABC) (1929)**
899 West 8th Ave., Vancouver, BC V5Z 1E3
604/871-0222, Fax: 604/871-0299, Toll Free: 1-800-663-9283
Sec.-Treas., Theresia. Weigert
Publications: Snippets; Essentials, s-a.

**Institut des Manufacturiers du Vêtement du Québec/Apparel Manufacturers Institute of Québec (IMVQ) (1974)**
#801, 555, rue Chabanel ouest, Montréal, QC H2N 2H8
514/382-3846, Téléc: 514/383-1689
Directrice, Jane C. Binder
Publications: AMIQ Journal; AMIQ Apparel Directory; Internal AMIQ Newsletters, bi-m.; AMIQ Associate Directory

**Luggage, Leathergoods, Handbags & Accessories Association of Canada**
LLHA Association
#2112, 2330 Bridletowne Circle, Scarborough, ON M1W 3P6
416/491-5844, Fax: 416/496-9329
President, Sally MacGillivray
General Manager, Joyce Scobie

**Manitoba Fashion Institute**
#114, 85 Adelaide St., Winnipeg, MB R3A 0V9
204/942-7314, Fax: 204/943-2228
Executive Director, Allan Finkel

**Men's Clothing Manufacturers Association Inc./ Association des manufacturiers de vêtements pour hommes inc. (MCMA)**
#801, 555, rue Chabanel ouest, Montréal, QC H2N 2H8
514/382-3846, Fax: 514/383-1689
Executive Director, David Balinsky
Publications: On the Button
Affiliates: Associated Clothing Manufacturers of the Province of Quebec Inc./Les Manufacturiers associés du vêtement de la Province de Québec inc; Canadian Trimmers Manufacturing Association; Montreal Clothing Contractors Association Inc./ L'Association entrepreneurs en confection de Montréal inc; Quebec Council of Odd Pants Employers Inc./Conseil du patronat des fabricants de pantalons du Québec inc; Rainwear & Sportswear Manufacturers Association/ L'Association des fabricants de vêtements imperméables et vêtements sports

**New Brunswick Hairdressers Association**
440 Brunswick St., Fredericton, NB E3B 1H3
506/458-8087
Registrar, Gaye Cail

**Ontario Fashion Exhibitors Inc. (OFE) (1955)**
#219, 111 Peter St., Toronto, ON M5V 2H1
416/596-2401, Fax: 416/596-1808
Executive Director, Serge S. Micheli, CAE
President, Ronnie Kantor
Publications: OFE Buyers Guide
Affiliates: Canadian Association of Wholesale Sales Representatives

**Québec Fashion Apparel Manufacturers' Guild/ Guilde des manufacturiers de vêtement de mode du Québec (1938)**
#300, 9250, av du Parc, Montréal, QC H2N 1Z2
514/384-3800, Fax: 514/383-5411
Executive Director, S. Purcell
Office Manager, Francine Paquette

**Textile Federation of Canada/La Fédération canadienne du textile**
1 Pacifique, Ste-Anne-de-Bellevue, QC H9X 1C5
514/457-2347, Fax: 514/457-2147
Chairman, Ben Staving
Publications: Canadian Textile Journal

**Wool Bureau of Canada**
#820, 33 Yonge St., Toronto, ON M5E 1G4
416/361-1440, Fax: 416/361-3179, Toll Free: 1-800-986-9665, Email: woolmark@woolmark, URL: http://www.woolmark.com

**FESTIVALS *see* EVENTS**

## FILM & VIDEO

***see also* Broadcasting**

**Academy of Canadian Cinema & Television/ Académie canadienne du cinéma et de la télévision (ACCT) (1979)**
158 Pearl St., Toronto, ON M5H 1L3
416/591-2040, Fax: 416/591-2157, Toll Free: 1-800-644-5194, URL: http://www.academy.ca
CEO, Maria Topalovich
Chair, Rudy Buttignol
National Vice-Chair, David Cronenberg
Treasurer, John Vandervelde
Publications: Infocus; Who's Who in Canadian Film & TV

**Alberta Motion Picture Industries Association (AMPIA) (1973)**
606 Midland Walwyn Tower, Edmonton Centre, Edmonton, AB T5J 2Z2
403/944-0707, Fax: 403/426-3057
Executive Director, Deborah Braun
President, Andy Thomson, Bus: 403/482-2022
Executive Assistant, Catherine Morrison
Communications Officer, J. Margolis
Publications: AMPIA Directory; Moving Pictures, bi-m.

**Association des producteurs de films et de télévision du Québec (APFTQ)**
#201, 740, rue St-Maurice, Montréal, QC H3C 1L5
514/397-8600, Téléc: 514/392-0232
Présidente-directrice générale, Suzanne D'Amours
Organisation(s) affiliée(s): Canadian Association of Film Distributors & Exporters

**Association québécoise des réalisateurs et réalisatrices de cinéma et de télévision (AQRRCT) (1973)**
#122, 1600, rue de Lorimier, Montréal, QC H2K 3W5
514/521-1984, postes 436, 437; 514/527-2197, Téléc: 514/527-7699
Président, François Côté
Directrice, Martine Maltais
Publications: Action
Organisation(s) affiliée(s): Coalition des créateurs et titulaires de droits d'auteur; Association littéraire et artistique internationale

**Atlantic Filmmakers' Co-operative (AFCOOP) (1973)**
PO Box 2043, Stn M, Halifax, NS B3J 2Z1
902/423-8833, Fax: 902/425-7339
Lynda Rossborough
Publications: AFCOOP News
Affiliates: Independent Film & Video Alliance; Academy of Canadian Cinema & TV; Linda Joy Busby Media Arts Foundation; Atlantic Independent Media; Atlantic Film Festival

**Canadian Animation Producers Association (CAPA)**
c/o Nelvana Ltd., 32 Atlantic Ave., Toronto, ON M6K 1X9
416/588-5571, Fax: 416/588-5588
President, Michael Hirsh

**Canadian Association of Video Distributors (1985)**
4222 Manor St., Burnaby, BC V5G 1B2
604/433-3331, Fax: 604/433-4815
Executive Director, William McCartney

**Canadian Film Centre/Centre canadien du film (CFC) (1988)**
2489 Bayview Ave., North York, ON M2L 1A8
416/445-1446, Fax: 416/445-9481, URL: http://www.cdnfilmcentre.com
Executive Director, S. Wayne Clarkson
Chair, Barbara Barde
Founder & Chair Emeritus, Norman Jewison
Publications: at the centre

**Canadian Film Institute/Institut canadien du film (CFI) (1935)**
2 Daly Ave., Ottawa, ON K1N 6E2
613/232-8769, Fax: 613/232-6727, Info Line: 232-7662
President, Serge Losique
Director of Programming, Tom McSorley
Affiliates: Cinémathèque Canada

**Canadian Film & Television Production Association/Association canadienne de production de film et télévision (CFTPA) (1948)**
#806, 175 Bloor St. East, Toronto, ON M4W 3R8
416/927-8942, Fax: 416/922-4038
President, Elizabeth McDonald
Vice-President, Industrial Relations & Training, Mireille Watson
Publications: ACTION; CFTPA Directory of Members; The Guide, a.

**Canadian Filmmakers Distribution Centre (CFMDC) (1967)**
#220, 37 Hanna Ave., Toronto, ON M6K 1W8
416/588-0725, Fax: 416/588-7956, Email: cfmdc@gold.interlog.com
Alan McNairn
Publications: The Independent Eye; Film Catalogue, a.
Affiliates: Canadian Filmmakers Distribution West

**Canadian Motion Picture Distributors Association/Association canadienne des distributeurs de film (CMPDA) (1920)**
#1603, 22 St. Clair Ave. East, Toronto, ON M4T 2S3
416/961-1888, Fax: 416/968-1016
President, Hon. Douglas C. Frith, PC
Vice-President, Susan Peacock
Affiliates: Motion Picture Association of America, Inc.

**Canadian Picture Pioneers (CPP) (1940)**
#906, 21 Dundas Sq., Toronto, ON M5B 1B7
416/368-1139, Fax: 416/368-1130
President, Philip R. Carlton
Executive Assistant, Barry Chapman
Publications: CPP Newsletter

**La Cinémathèque québécoise (1963)**
**Musée au cinéma**
335, boul de Maisonneuve est, Montréal, QC H2X 1K1
514/842-9763, Téléc: 514/842-1816
Directeur à la conservation, Robert Daudelin
Directeur à la gestion, Charles-Mathieu Brunelle
Directeur des communications, Jean Hamel
Directeur des Services Techniques, François Auger
Publications: Revue de la Cinémathèque

**Directors Guild of Canada/La Guilde canadienne des réalisateurs (DGC) (1962)**
#401, 387 Bloor St. East, Toronto, ON M4W 1H7
416/972-0098, Fax: 416/972-6058
President, Allan King
National Executive Secretary, Pamela Brand
Publications: DGC National News
Affiliates: ACTRA; Directors' Guild of America

**Dreamspeakers Festival Society (1991)**
#201, 15620 - 111 Ave., Edmonton, AB T5M 4R7
403/451-5033, Fax: 403/452-9042
Executive Director, Sharon Shirt

**Independent Film & Video Alliance/Alliance de la vidéo et du cinéma indépendant (IFVA) (1980)**
#3000, 5505, boul St-Laurent, Montréal, QC H2T 1S6
514/277-0328, Fax: 514/277-0419, Toll Free: 1-800-567-0328, Email: ifva@cam.org, URL: http://www.ffa.ucalgary.ca/
National Coordinator, Peter Sandmark
President, Jean Claude Bustros
Publications: Alliance Bulletin/Le Bulletin de l'Alliance

**Motion Picture Theatre Associations of Canada/ Les associations des propriétaires des cinémas du Canada (MPTAC) (1967)**
1303 Yonge St., Toronto, ON M4T 2Y9
416/323-7214, Fax: 416/232-6633
Executive Director, Dina Lebo

**The Moving Pictures Travelling Canadian Film Festival Society (1993)**
#410, 1008 Homer St., Vancouver, BC V6B 2X1
604/685-8952, Fax: 604/688-8221
Festival Director, John Dippong
Publications: Newsletter

**National Screen Institute - Canada/Institute national des arts de l'écran - Canada (NSI) (1986)**
10022 - 103 St., 3rd Fl., Edmonton, AB T5J 0X2
403/421-4084, Fax: 403/425-8098, Toll Free: 1-800-480-4084, Email: filmhero@nsi-canada.ca, URL: http://www.nsi-canada.ca
Executive Director, Jan Miller
Office Manager, Debbie Yee
Publications: Screen Sheet
Affiliates: Canadian Conference of the Arts; Alberta Motion Pictures Industry Association

**Ontario Film Association, Inc. (OFA) (1949)**
**Association for the Advancement of Visual Media**
#1341, 3-1750 The Queensway, Etobicoke, ON M9C 5H5
416/761-6056
Executive Director, Margaret Nix, Fax: 905/820-7397
Publications: Visual Media/Medias visuels

**Saskatchewan Motion Picture Association (SMPIA) (1989)**
2431 - 8th Ave., Regina, SK S4R 5J7
306/525- 9899, Fax: 306/569-1818, Email: smpia@unibase.unibase.com, URL: http://midxpress.com/midxpress/smpia/main.htm
Executive Director, Elizabeth Verrall
Communications Officer, Colleen Mahoney
Publications: Storyboard; Saskatchewan Motion Picture Directory, s-a.

**FILM FESTIVALS *see* EVENTS**

## FINANCE

***see also* Taxation**

**Association des cadres financiers municipaux du Québec**
#690, 1265 rue Berri, Montréal, QC H2L 4X4
514/499-1130, Téléc: 514/499-1737, Télex: 051-3898
Diane Toupin

**Association of Canadian Financial Corporations/Association des compagnies financières canadiennes (ACFC) (1944)**
Sussex Centre, #401, 50 Burnhamthorpe Rd. West, Mississauga, ON L5B 3C2
905/949-4920, Fax: 905/896-9380
President, John Bohdan Gregorovich

**Association of Canadian Pension Management (ACPM) (1976)**
#1103, 60 Bloor St. West, Toronto, ON M4W 3B8
416/964-1260, Fax: 416/964-0567
Executive Director, Marcia Barrett
President, Andrea Vincent
Vice-President, Patricia Cox
Publications: ACPM Reporter; Supplement, q.; Penfacts: A Guide to Pensions in Canada, a.

**Association de planification fiscale et financière (APFF) (1976)**
#300, 445, boul Saint-Laurent, Montréal, QC H2Y 2Y7
514/866-2733, Téléc: 514/866-0113, Courrier électronique: apff@apff.org, URL: http://www.apff.org
Président et directeur général, Yvon L. Caron
Publications: Flash Fiscal; Livre du congrès, annuel; Revue de planification fiscale et successorale, trimestriel; Stratège, trimestriel

**The Canadian Association of Financial Planners (CAFP)**
#1710, 439 University Ave., Toronto, ON M5G 1Y8
416/593-6592, Fax: 416/593-8459, Toll Free: 1-800-346-2237, Email: planners@cafp.org, URL: http://www.cafp.org/
Executive Director, Farida Karim
National Chairman, Fred Smith, RFP
President, Gary R. Duncan, CA, RFP
Publications: The Canadian Financial Planner

**Canadian Association of Pension Supervisory Authorities/Association canadienne des organismes de contrôle des régimes de retraite (CAPSA)**
250 Yonge St., 29th Fl., Toronto, ON M5B 2N7
416/314-0660, Fax: 416/314-0650
Susan Ellis

**Canadian Association of Student Financial Aid Administrators**
Queens University, Student Awards Office, 110 Alfred St., Kingston, ON K7L 3N6
613/545-2216, Fax: 613/545-6409
Director, P. Bogstad

**Canadian Bankers Association/Association des banquiers canadiens (CBA) (1893)**
Commerce Court West, 30th Fl., PO Box 348, Stn Commerce Court, Toronto, ON M5L 1G2
416/362-6092, Fax: 416/362-7705, Toll Free: 1-800-263-0231, URL: http://www.cba.ca
President & CEO, Raymond J. Protti
Chairman, G.J. Feeney, Royal Bank of Canada
Vice-Chairman, L. Courville, National Bank of Canada
Vice-Chairman, H. Kluge, CIBC
Publications: Canadian Banker

**Canadian Corporate Shareholder Services Association/Association canadienne des services aux actionnaires (CCSSA) (1985)**
Royal Trust Tower, Toronto Dominion Centre, PO Box 110, Stn Toronto Dominion, Toronto, ON M5K 1G8
President, Francoise Bureau, Bus: 514/394-6081
Publications: Newsletter

**Canadian Council of Financial Analysts**
#1702, 390 Bay St., Toronto, ON M5H 2Y2
416/366-5755, Fax: 416/366-6716
Director, Deborah Kent

**Canadian Finance & Leasing Association/Association canadienne de financement et de location (CFLA) (1973)**
Box 7, #1210, 151 Yonge St., Toronto, ON M5C 2W7
416/860-1133, Fax: 416/860-1140, URL: http://www.inforamp.net/~mreid/cfla.html
President & COO, David Powell
Chairman, Tim Hammill
Publications: Voicebox
Affiliates: Equipment Lessors Association of America

**Canadian Insolvency Practitioners Association/Association canadienne des professionnels de l'insolvabilité (CIPA) (1979)**
277 Wellington St. West, Toronto, ON M5V 3H2
416/204-3242, Fax: 416/204-3410
Executive Director, Norman H. Kondo
President, Ralph W. Peterson, CA, CIP
Affiliates: The Canadian Institute of Chartered Accountants

**Canadian Institute of Financial Planning (CIFP)**
#503, 151 Yonge St., Toronto, ON M5C 2W7
416/865-1237, Fax: 416/861-9937
Executive Director, John W. Murray
Vice-President, Donald Johnston
Affiliates: Investment Funds Institute of Canada; Canadian Association of Financial Planners; Life Underwriters Association of Canada

**Canadian Payments Association/Association canadienne des paiements (CPA) (1980)**
#1212, 50 O'Connor St., Ottawa, ON K1P 6L2
613/238-4173, Fax: 613/233-3385
General Manager, Robert M. Hammond
Chairman, Serge Vachon
Publications: Forum; Review

**The Canadian Payroll Association/L'Association canadienne de la paie (CPA) (1978)**
#801, 1867 Yonge St., Toronto, ON M4S 1Y5
416/487-3380, Fax: 416/487-3384, Info Line: 416/487-3620, Toll Free: 1-800-387-4693, Email: infoline@payroll.ca, URL: http://www.payroll.ca
Chair & CEO, Renée Carr
Vice-President & COO, Bill Williams
Publications: Dialogue Magazine
Affiliates: American Payroll Association

**Canadian Pension & Benefits Institute/Institut canadien de la retraite et des avantages sociaux (1960)**
#305, 2035, rue Victoria, Saint-Lambert, QC J4S 1H1
514/465-4400, Fax: 514/465-1921
Executive Director, Louis-Joseph Regimbal
President, Robert Askew
Sec.-Treas., Pierre Laqueux
Publications: Forum

**The Canadian Securities Institute/Institut canadien des valeurs mobilières (CSI) (1970)**
#1550, 121 King St. West, PO Box 113, Toronto, ON M5H 3T9
416/364-9130, Fax: 416/359-0486
President, Dr. Roberta Wilton
Publications: CSI Impact
Affiliates: Investment Dealers Association of Canada; Montreal Exchange; Toronto, Alberta, & Vancouver Stock Exchanges

**Canadian Venture Capital Association/Association canadienne du capital de risque (CVCA)**
#706, 1881 Yonge St., Toronto, ON M4S 3C4
416/487-0519, Fax: 416/487-5899, Email: kryan@cvca.ca, URL: http://www.cvca.ca
President, Edward G. Anderson
Executive Director, Deborah Cummings
Administrator, Kathryn Ryan

**Confédération des caisses populaires et d'économie desjardins du Québec (CCPÉDQ)**
100, av des Commandeurs, Lévis, QC G6V 7N5
418/835-2253, Téléc: 418/833-4769, Télex: 051-3533, Ligne sans frais: 1-800-463-4810; URL: http://www.desjardins.com
Président et chef de la direction, Claude Béland
Président et chef des opérations, John Harbour
Directeur des affairs institutionnelles, André Chapleau

**Credit Association of Canada/Association des directeurs de crédit du Canada (CAC) (1944)**
St. Mary's Credit Union, 1515 - 20th St, Saskatoon, SK S7M 0Z5
306/382-1177, Fax: 306/382-7600
President, A. Musey
Publications: Credit Canada
Affiliates: International Credit Association

**Credit Institute of Canada/L'Institut canadien du crédit (CIC) (1928)**
#501, 5090 Explorer Dr., Mississauga, ON L4W 3T9
905/629-9805, Fax: 905/629-9809, Email: geninfo@creditedu.org, URL: http://www.creditedu.org
President & Dean, Carol A. Breining
General Manager, Brenda Cornell, Email: genmgr@creditedu.org
Publications: To Your Credit

**Credit Union Central of Canada/La Centrale des caisses de crédit du Canada (1953)**
300 The East Mall, 5th Fl., Toronto, ON M9B 6B7
416/232-1262, Fax: 416/232-9196, URL: http://www.cucentral.ca
President/CEO, William G. Knight
Director, Communications, Veronica Feldcamp
Publications: Briefs
Affiliates: World Council of Credit Unions

**Credit Union Institute of Canada (CUIC) (1972)**
#400, 275 Bank St., Ottawa, ON K2P 2L6
613/238-4940, Fax: 613/567-0658

**Fédération des associations coopérative d'économie familiale du Québec/Federation of Family Economics Cooperative Associations of Québec (FACEF) (1970)**
#305, 5225, rue Berri, Montréal, QC H2J 2S4
514/271-7004
Présidente, Louise Blain
Publications: Changements
Organisation(s) affiliée(s): International Organization of Consumers Unions

**Fédération des caisses d'économie Desjardins du Québec (1962)**
7755, boul Louis H. Lafontaine, Anjou, QC H1L 4R5
514/353-4960, Téléc: 514/353-0588
Directeur général, Gilles Lafleur
Publications: Journal d'entreprise

**Fédération des caisses populaires du Manitoba inc.**
#200, 605, rue Des Meurons, CP 68, Winnipeg, MB R2H 3B4
204/237-8988, Téléc: 204/233-6405
Directeur général, Fernand Vermette

**Fédération des caisses populaires de l'Ontario (FCPO) (1946)**
214, ch Montreal, Vanier, ON K1L 8L8
613/746-3276, Téléc: 613/746-3063
Directeur général, Pierre Lacasse
Administration et finance, Alain Boucher
Crédit et gestion réseau, Daniel Brault
Ressources humaines, Alain Kervran
Systèmes et marketing, Jean-Guy Laflèche
Publications: Info-Fédé
Organisation(s) affiliée(s): Mouvement Desjardins

**Financial Executives Institute Canada**
#1701, 141 Adelaide St. West, Toronto, ON M5H 3L5
416/366-3007, Fax: 416/366-3008
Director, Professional Affairs, Stan Udaskin
Publications: Newsletter

**Institute of Canadian Bankers/Institut des banquiers canadiens**
Tour Scotia, #1000, 1002, rue Sherbrooke ouest, 10e étage, Montréal, QC H3A 3M5
514/282-9480, Fax: 514/282-8881, URL: http://www.icb.org
Executive Director & CEO, Dr. Rosaire M. Couturier
Atlantic Regional Office: Queen's Court, #501, 5475 Spring Garden Rd., Halifax, NS B3J 1G2, 902/429-0440, Fax: 902/429-5478
Ontario Regional Office: Regional Director, Anne Wettlaufer, #1830, 199 Bay St., PO Box 348, Stn Commerce Court, Toronto, ON M5L 1G2, 416/362-6092, Fax: 416/362-7705
Québec Regional Office: #1000, 1002, rue Sherbrooke ouest, 10th Fl., Montréal, QC H3A 3M5, 514/282-9480, Téléc: 514/282-8881
Western Regional Office: #805, 550 - 6 Ave. SW, Calgary, AB T2P 0S2, 403/262-3422, Fax: 403/233-7698

**International Association of State Lotteries/Association internationale des loteries d'état (AILE) (1958)**
500, rue Sherbrooke ouest, Montréal, QC H3A 3G6
514/282-0273, Fax: 514/873-8999, Email: aile@cam.ort
General Secretary, Lynne Roiter
President, Enrique Augusto Gonella
Publications: AILE Directory; AILE Review, q.

**International Organization of Securities Commissions/Organisation internationale des commissions de valeurs (IOSCO) (1983)**
Stock Exchange Tower, 800 Square Victoria, 42th Fl., PO Box 171, Montréal, QC H4Z 1C8
514/875-8278, Fax: 514/875-2669, Telex: 05-26 8761
Secretary General, Eudald Canadell
Publications: Annual Report

**Investment Counsel Association of Ontario (ICAO) (1952)**
61 Shaw St., Toronto, ON M6J 2W3
416/504-1118, Fax: 416/504-1117
President, William E. Rogan
Vice-President, David Pennycook
Secretary, Robert R. McInnes
Treasurer, Robert Steinbach
Executive Director, Keith A. Douglas, CAE
Publications: Member Letter

**Investment Dealers Association of Canada/Association canadienne des courtiers en valeurs mobilières (IDA) (1916)**
#1600, 121 King St. West, Toronto, ON M5H 3T9
416/364-6133, Fax: 416/364-0753
President & CEO, Joseph J. Oliver
Chairman, W. David Wilson
Vice-President, Capital Markets, Ian Russell
Corporate Secretary & Vice-President, Operations, Eileen M. Andrews
Vice-President, Member Regulation, Gregory M. Clarke
Vice-President, Government & Member Relations, D.W. Grant
Publications: IDA Report; Provincial Economic Outlooks, a.; Capital Markets Update/Structural Trends in Canada Markets, s-a.; Economic Indicator Card, 3 pa; Statistical Bulletin, bi-m.; Fiscal Report Card; Bulletins
Affiliates: National Association of Securities Dealers; Securities Industry Association; Public Securities Association; Securities & Exchange Commission
Calgary Office: #2330, 355 - 4 Ave. SW, Calgary, AB T2P 0J1, 403/262-6393, Fax: 403/265-4603
Montréal Office: #2802, 1, Place Ville Marie, Montréal, QC H3B 4R4, 514/878-2854, Téléc: 514/878-3860
Vancouver Office: Bentall Four, #944, 1055 Dunsmuir St., PO Box 49151, Vancouver, BC V7X 1J1, 604/683-6222, Fax: 604/683-6050

**Investment Funds Institute of Canada/L'Institut des fonds d'investissement du Canada (IFIC) (1962)**
#503, 151 Yonge St., Toronto, ON M5C 2W7
416/363-2158, Fax: 416/861-9937, Email: ific@mutfunds.com, URL: http://www.mutfunds.com/ific
President & CEO, The Honourable Thomas A. Hockin
Chairman, Harold Hands
Publications: IFIC Update Newsletter

**Investor Learning Centre of Canada (ILC)**
121 King St. West, 15th Fl., Toronto, ON M5H 3T9
416/364-6666, Fax: 416/364-9315
Chair, Frederick Ketchen
Publications: Investment Facts
Affiliates: Canadian Securities Institute (CSI)

**Investors Association of Canada (IAC) (1986)**
#380, 26 Soho St., Toronto, ON M5T 1Z7
416/340-1722, Fax: 416/340-9202
Chairman, Chuck Chakrapani
Publications: Money Digest

**Municipal Finance Officers Association of Ontario**
121 John St., Toronto, ON M5V 2E2
416/979-1414, Fax: 416/979-1060
Executive Director, Heather Bell

**Ontario Association of Credit Counselling Services (OACCS) (1975)**
PO Box 278, Grimsby, ON L3M 4G5
905/945-5644, Fax: 905/945-4680, Toll Free: 1-800-263-0260
Executive Director, Patricia White
Board President, John Curran
Publications: Connections

**Ontario Mortgage Brokers Association (OMBA) (1960)**
#8, 951 Wilson Ave., Downsview, ON M3K 2A7
416/631-0320, Fax: 416/631-8165
Executive Director, Lorne H. Collis

**Ontario Society of Collection Agencies**
77 Samuel Cres., Georgetown, ON L7G 5J3
905/873-2920
Executive Director, Don Sinclair

**Pension Investment Association of Canada/Association Canadienne des Gestionnaires de Fonds de Retraite (PIAC) (1977)**
61 Shaw St., Toronto, ON M6J 2W3
416/504-1116, Fax: 416/504-1117
General Manager, Keith A. Douglas, CAE
Publications: Communique

**Social Investment Organization (SIO) (1989)**
#443, 366 Adelaide St. East, Toronto, ON M5A 3X9
416/360-6047, Fax: 416/360-6380, Email: sio@web.net
Executive Director, Robert Walker
Publications: The SIO Forum; The SIO Forum Back Issues; Social Investment Groups & Activities, a.

**Treasury Management Association of Canada/Association de gestion de trésorerie du Canada (TMAC) (1982)**
#1010, 8 King St. East, Toronto, ON M5C 1B5
416/367-8500, Fax: 416/367-3240, Email: info@tmac.ca, URL: http://www.tmac.ca
Executive Vice-President, John Bumister, Email: johnb@tmac.ca
President, Betty Hoffart, CMA
Manager of Administration, Patricia Wood, Email: pchiasson@tmac.ca
Director, Conferences & Education, Chris Pipe, Email: cpipe@tmac.ca
Director, Finance & Communications, Belinda Espley, Email: bespley@tmac.ca
Manager, Membership & Publications, Eileen Leung, Email: eleung@tmac.ca
Publications: The Canadian Treasurer
Affiliates: Canadian Institute of Chartered Accountants; Society of Management Accountants; Certified General Accountants; Canadian Payments Association; Association of Canadian

Pension Management; International Group of Treasury Associations

**The Trust Companies Association of Canada/ L'Association des compagnies de fiducie du Canada (1952)**
One Financial Place, #1002, 1 Adelaide St. East, PO Box 137, Toronto, ON M5C 2V9
416/866-8842, Fax: 416/866-2122
Corporate Secretary, Christine Kniehl

**Women in Capital Markets/Les femmes sur les marchés financiers (WCM) (1993)**
#300, 595 Bay St., Toronto, ON M5G 2C2
416/971-8805, Fax: 416/596-7894
President, Heather-Anne Irwin
Director & Secretary, C.L. Sugiyama
Publications: Women in Capital Markets

**FIRST AID & SAFETY *see* EMERGENCY RESPONSE**

## FISHERIES & FISHING INDUSTRY
***see also* Marine Trades**

**Alliance des pêcheurs professionnels du Québec**
#100, 56, rue St-Pierre, Québec, QC G1K 4A1
418/692-1148, Téléc: 418/692-1854
Directeur général, François Poulin

**Atlantic Salmon Federation/Fédération du saumon atlantique (ASF) (1948)**
PO Box 429, St. Andrews, NB E0G 2X0
506/529-4581, Fax: 506/529-4438, Email: asf@nbnet.nb.ca, URL: http://www.flyfishing.com/asf/
President, Bill Taylor
Director, Communications & Public Policy, Sue Scott
Publications: The Atlantic Salmon Journal
Affiliates: Federation of Fly Fishers; Theodore Gordon Flyfishers; Trout Unlimited; Canadian Wildlife Federation

**BC Salmon Farmers Association (BCSFA) (1984)**
#506, 1200 Pender St. West, Vancouver, BC V6E 2S9
604/682-3077, Fax: 604/669-6974, Toll Free: 1-800-661-7256
Executive Director, Greg D'Avignon
Publications: Newsletter

**BC Shellfish Growers Association (BCSGA) (1964)**
647A Bunting Place, Comox, BC V9M 3R1
250/339-7419, Fax: 250/339-7463
President, Dave Mitchell
Vice-President, Judith Reid
Office Manager, Dave Conley
Publications: BC Shellfish Growers Association

**BC Trout Farmers Association**
24831 - 80 Ave., Langley, BC V3A 4P9
604/888-0660
President, Juanita Bouwmeester
Affiliates: Canadian Aquaculture Producers' Council

**Canadian Aquaculture Industry Alliance/Alliance de l'industrie canadienne de l'aquiculture (CAIA) (1987)**
45 O'Connor St., 20th Fl., Ottawa, ON K1P 1A4
613/788-6851, Fax: 613/235-7012, Email: CAIAoffice@aol.com
Executive Director, Sharon Ford
President, William Thompson
Vice-President, Marli MacNeil
Sec.-Treas., Marc Kielley
Publications: Aquainfo
Affiliates: Aquaculture Association of Canada

**Canadian Association of Fish Exporters/ L'Association canadienne des exportateurs de poisson (CAFE) (1978)**
#212, 1770 Woodward Dr., Ottawa, ON K2C 0P8
613/228-9220, Fax: 613/228-9223, Email: csmith@seafood.ca, URL: http://www.seafood.ca
President, Jane Barnett, Ph.D., Email: jbarnett@seafood.ca
Operations Manager, Cynthia Smith
Publications: Newsfax; World Seafood Market Report, m.; Entrée Canada, 3 pa
Affiliates: BC Salmon Marketing Council; Canadian Aquaculture Industry Alliance

**Canadian Centre for Fisheries Innovation/Centre canadien d'innovations des pêches (CCFI) (1989)**
Ridge Rd., PO Box 4920, Stn C, St. John's, NF A1C 5R3
709/778-0517, Fax: 709/778-0516, Email: ccfi@gill.ifmt.nf.ca
Managing Director, Alastair O'Reilly
Chairman, Ian J. Reid
Affiliates: Memorial University of Newfoundland; Marine Institute

**Fisheries Council of British Columbia**
#1400, 1188 Georgia St. East, Vancouver, BC V6E 4A2
604/684-6454, Fax: 604/684-5109
President, Michael Hunter

**Fisheries Council of Canada/Conseil canadien des pêches (FCC) (1945)**
#806, 141 Laurier Ave. West, Ottawa, ON K1P 5J3
613/238-7751, Fax: 613/238-3542
President, Ronald W. Bulmer
Vice-President, P.J. McGuinness
Chairman, Cliff Doyle
Publications: Fish & Seafood Products & Services Directory
Affiliates: International Coalition of Fisheries Associations; North Atlantic Seafood Association

**CANADIAN ASSOCIATION OF PRAWN PRODUCERS/ASSOCIATION CANADIENNE DES PRODUCTEURS DE CREVETTE (CAPP) (1993)**
#310, 15 Dartmouth Rd., Bedford, NS B4A 3X6
902/832-7114, Fax: 902/832-7115
Executive Director, John Angel

**FISH & SEAFOOD ASSOCIATION OF ONTARIO**
c/o Clouston Foods Canada, 3800 Steeles Ave. West, Woodbridge, ON L4L 4G9
905/851-6771, Fax: 905/851-5703
President, Denis Galliera

**FISHERIES ASSOCIATION OF NEWFOUNDLAND & LABRADOR LTD. (1945)**
90 O'Leary Ave., PO Box 8900, Stn A, St. John's, NF A1B 3R9
709/726-7223, Fax: 709/754-3339
President, Alastair O'Rielly

**NEW BRUNSWICK FISH PACKERS' ASSOCIATION/L'ASSOCIATION DES EMPAQUETEURS DE POISSON DU NOUVEAU-BRUNSWICK (NBFPA) (1946)**
#104, 1133 St. George Blvd., Moncton, NB E1E 4E1
506/857-3056, Fax: 506/857-3059
Executive Director, Peter A. Dysart
Affiliates: Alliance of Manufacturers & Exporters Canada

**PRINCE EDWARD ISLAND SEAFOOD PROCESSORS ASSOCIATION**
c/o Atlantic Fish Specialties Ltd., 17 Walker Dr., Parkdale, PE C1A 8S5
902/894-7005, Fax: 902/566-3546
President, Jim Dunphy

**SEAFOOD PROCESSORS ASSOCIATION OF PRINCE EDWARD ISLAND**
c/o West Royalty Industrial Park, Charlottetown, PE C1E 1B0
902/629-1555, Fax: 902/368-1914
Administrator, Ron Mullins

**SEAFOOD PRODUCERS ASSOCIATION OF NOVA SCOTIA**
Queen Square, #1801, 45 Alderney Dr., PO Box 991, Dartmouth, NS B2Y 3Z6
902/463-7790, Fax: 902/469-8294
President, Roger C. Stirling

**New Brunswick Salmon Growers Association (1987)**
Lime Kiln Rd., RR#4, St. George, NB E0G 2Y0
506/755-3526, Fax: 506/755-6237
General Manager, William Thompson

**Nova Scotia Salmon Association (NSSA) (1965)**
6 Whidden St., Antigonish, NS B2Y 1S8
902/863-3986, Fax: 902/863-6055
Contact, K. Rice
Publications: Upstream

**Ontario Aquaculture Association**
PO Box 324, Elmira, ON N3B 2Z6
519/669-3400, Fax: 519/669 2864
Administrator, Laurie Taylor

**Prince Edward Island Fishermen's Association**
53 Queen St., PO Box 2224, Charlottetown, PE C1A 8B9
902/566-4050, Fax: 902/368-3748, Email: peifa@isn.net
Managing Director, Rory McLellan

**FOLK ARTS *see* VISUAL ART, CRAFTS, FOLK ARTS**

## FOOD & BEVERAGE INDUSTRY

**Association des brasseurs du Québec/Québec Brewers Association**
Tour Laurentienne, #475, 1981, av McGill College, Montréal, QC H3A 2W9
514/284-9199, Téléc: 514/284-0817
Directeur général, Yvon Millette

**Association of Canadian Biscuit Manufacturers/ Association canadienne des manufacturiers de biscuits (ACBM) (1965)**
885 Don Mills Rd., North York, ON M3C 1V9
416/510-8036
Executive Director, Carol A. Findlay
President, Gary MacLeod

**Association of Canadian Distillers/Association des distallateurs canadiens (ACD) (1947)**
#1100, 90 Sparks St., Ottawa, ON K1P 5T8
613/238-8444, Fax: 613/238-3411, Telex: 0533783, Email: 103115.1225@compuserve.com
President, Ronald Veilleux
Chairman, Manuel A. Diaz

**Association des manufacturiers de produits alimentaires du Québec/Québec Food Processors Association (AMPAQ) (1954)**
Édifice De Bleury, #102, 200, rue MacDonald, St-Jean-sur-Richelieu, QC J3B 8J6
514/349-1521, Téléc: 514/349-6923
Directeur général, André Latour, caé
Publications: Courrier

**Baking Association of Canada/Association canadienne de la boulangerie (BAC) (1947)**
#301, 885 Don Mills Rd., Toronto, ON M3C 1V9

416/510-8041, Fax: 416/510-8043
President, Paul Hetherington

### Breakfast Cereal Manufacturers of Canada (1983)
#301, 885 Don Mills Rd., North York, ON M3C 1V9
416/510-8036, Fax: 416/510-8043
Manager, Shelly Girvan
Affiliates: Grocery Products Manufacturers of Canada

### Brewers Association of Canada/Association des brasseurs du Canada (1943)
Heritage Place, #1200, 155 Queen St., Ottawa, ON K1P 6L1
613/232-9601, Fax: 613/232-2283, Email: office@brewers.ca, URL: http://www.brewers.ca
President & CEO, R.A. (Sandy) Morrison
Executive Assistant, Linda Andrusek
Publications: On Tap/En Fût

### Brewing & Malting Barley Research Institute/Institut de recherche - brassage et orge de maltage (BMBRI) (1948)
#206, 167 Lombard Ave., Winnipeg, MB R3B 0T6
204/942-1407, Fax: 204/947-5960
Managing Director, N.T. Kendall, Ph.D.
President, J.T. Steer
Publications: Barley Briefs

### Canadian Association of Specialty Foods/L'Association canadienne des aliments fins (CASF) (1985)
19 Burlingame Rd., Etobicoke, ON M8W 1Y7
416/255-7071, Fax: 416/253-6571
Executive Director, Loraine Longo
Publications: Communiqué

### Canadian Bottled Water Federation/Fédération canadienne des eaux embouteillées (CBWF) (1987)
#203-1, 70 East Beaver Creek Rd., Richmond Hill, ON L4B 3B2
905/886-6928, Fax: 905/886-9531, Email: ecgriswood@all.adl.com
Executive Director, Elisabeth Griswold-Woodworth
Publications: Water Power
Affiliates: Canadian Bottled Water Federation

### Canadian College & University Food Service Association (CCUFSA)
National Office, Drew Hall, University of Guelph, Guelph, ON N1G 2W1
519/824-4120, Fax: 519/837-9302, Email: dboeckne@uoguelph.ca
Executive Director, David Boeckner
Publications: CCUFSA Newsletter

### Canadian Council of Grocery Distributors/Conseil canadien de la distribution alimentaire (CCGD) (1987)
CP 1082, Succ Place-du-Parc, Montréal, QC H2W 2P4
514/982-0267, Fax: 514/849-3021
President/CEO, John F. Geci
Secretary, Francine Chevrier
Vice-President, Communications & Development, Monika Simon
Secretary, France Bessette
Publications: Precis; Bulletin; Communiqué
Affiliates: Retail Council of Canada

### Canadian Federation of Independent Grocers/Fédération canadienne des épiciers indépendants (CFIG) (1962)
#902, 2235 Sheppard Ave. East, North York, ON M2J 5B5
416/492-2311, Fax: 416/492-2347, Toll Free: 1-800-661-2344
President, John F.T. Scott
Executive Assistant, Leslie Johnston
Publications: The Independent Grocer; The Practical Grocer, q.

### Canadian Food Brokers Association/Association canadienne des courtiers en alimentation (CFBA) (1943)
#101, 58 Meadowbrook Ln., Unionville, ON L3R 2H9
905/477-4644, Fax: 905/477-9580, Email: kbray@idirect.com, URL: http://web.idirect.com/~cfba
President, Keith H. Bray
Publications: CFBA News; CFBA Directory

### Canadian Food Service Executives Association (CFSEA)
#3529, 1531 Bayview Ave., North York, ON M4G 4G8
416/421-5045, Fax: 416/421-5045
Business Manager, Carla Kelman

### Canadian Food Supervisors' Association
#2G, 57 Simcoe St. South, Oshawa, ON L1H 7N1
905/436-0145, Fax: 905/436-2969

### Canadian Health Food Association/Association canadienne des aliments de santé (CHFA) (1964)
370 Steelcase Rd. East, Markham, ON L3R 1G2
905/479-6939, Fax: 905/479-1516
Executive Director, Bill Reynolds

### Canadian Hospitality Foundation (1962)
#213, 300 Adelaide St. East, Toronto, ON M5A 1N1
416/363-3401, Fax: 416/363-3403
Executive Director, Rigzin Dolkar

### Canadian Industrial Sweetener Users (CISU) (1970)
#301, 885 Don Mills Rd., North York, ON M3C 1V9
416/510-8036, Fax: 416/510-8044, Info Line: 510-8044
Executive Director, David L. Armstrong
Affiliates: Grocery Products Manufacturers of Canada

### Canadian Meat Council/Conseil des viandes du Canada (CMC) (1919)
Dow's Lake Court, #410, 875 Carling Ave., Ottawa, ON K1S 5P1
613/729-3911, Fax: 613/729-4997
General Manager, Robert Weaver

### Canadian Meat Science Association
c/o Canadian Meat Council, #410, 875 Carling Ave., Ottawa, ON K1S 5P1
416/729-3911, Fax: 416/729-4997

### Canadian National Millers Association (CNMA)
#1127, 90 Sparks St., Ottawa, ON K1P 5B4
613/238-2293, Fax: 613/235-5866
President, Gordon Harrison

### Canadian Nut Council/Conseil canadien des noix (CNC) (1984)
#301, 885 Don Mills Rd., North York, ON M3C 1V9
416/510-8036, Fax: 416/510-8044
General Manager, Ileana Lima

### Canadian Produce Marketing Association/Association canadienne de la distribution de fruits et légumes (CPMA) (1924)
#310, 1101 Prince of Wales Dr., Ottawa, ON K2C 3W7
613/226-4187, Fax: 613/226-2984, Email: question@cpma.ca, URL: http://www.cpma.ca
Executive Vice-President, Dan Dempster
Publications: Communiqué
Affiliates: Canadian Horticultural Council

### Canadian Snack Food Association/Association canadienne des fabricants des grignotines (CSFA) (1956)
#301, 885 Don Mills Rd., Toronto, ON M3C 1V9
416/510-8036, Fax: 416/510-8044
Manager, Iliana Lima
Publications: CSFA Roster; Information Letter; Statistical Material
Affiliates: Canadian Horticultural Council

### Canadian Soft Drink Association/Association canadienne de l'industrie des boissons gazeuses (CSDA) (1942)
#330, 55 York St., Toronto, ON M5J 1R7
416/362-2424, Fax: 416/362-3229, Email: 102005.1662@compuserve.com, URL: http://www.softdrink.ca
President & CEO, Paulette Vinette, CAE
Publications: Perspectives; Packaging Stewardship Annual Report
Association des embouteilleurs des boissons gazeuses du Québec inc.: Vice-présidente régionale, Nycol Pageau-Goyette, #900, 500, rue Sherbrooke ouest, Montréal, QC H3A 3C6, 514/282-3804, Téléc: 514/844-7556, Courrier électronique: 102125.141@compuserve.com
Atlantic Region: Regional Vice-President, Calla Farn, #310, 1657 Barrington St., Halifax, NS B3J 2A1, 902/492-0910, Fax: 902/492-0090, Email: 102022.716@compuserve.com
Ontario Region: Regional Vice-President, Stuart Hartley, 32nd Floor, South Tower, Royal Bank Plaza, Box 32, Toronto, ON M5J 2J8, 416/369-3059, Fax: 416/865-0887, Email: 73772.1733@compuserve.com
Western Region: Regional Vice-President, John Nixon, #130, 10691 Shellbridge Way, Richmond, BC V6X 2W8, 604/244-2920, Fax: 604/244-2945, Email: 102363.3421@compuserve.com

### Canadian Spice Association/Association canadienne des épices (CSA) (1942)
885 Don Mills Rd., North York, ON M3C 1V9
416/510-8024, Fax: 416/510-8043

### Canadian Sugar Institute/Institut canadien du sucre (CSI) (1966)
Water Park Place, #620, 10 Bay St., Toronto, ON M5J 2R8
416/368-8091, Fax: 416/368-6426
President, Sandra Marsden
Publications: Sugar in Perspective/Parlons sucre

### Canadian Wine Institute/Institut du vin canadien (CWI) (1948)
#401, 50 Burnhamthorpe Rd. West, Mississauga, ON L5B 3C2
905/949-8463, Fax: 905/949-8465
President, Roger Randolph
Affiliates: Wine Council of Ontario; British Columbia Wine Institute

### Coffee Association of Canada/Association du café du Canada (CAC) (1991)
#301, 885 Don Mills Rd., North York, ON M3C 1V9
416/510-8032, Fax: 416/510-8044, Email: info@coffeeassoc.com
President, David Wilkes
Affiliates: Grocery Products Manufacturers of Canada

### Confectionery Manufacturers Association of Canada/Association canadienne des fabricants de confiseries (CMAC) (1919)
#301, 885 Don Mills Rd., North York, ON M3C 1V9
416/510-8034, Fax: 416/510-8044, Email: carolh@fcpmc.com
President, Carol L. Hochu
Chairman, Michael McKean
Publications: CMAC News Clips

**Conseil de la boulangerie du Québec/Québec Bakery Council (CBQ) (1938)**
Édifice de Bleury, #102, 200, rue MacDonald, St-Jean-sur-Richelieu, QC J3B 8J6
514/349-0107, Téléc: 514/349-6923
Directeur général, André Latour, caé
Publications: La Fournée
Organisation(s) affiliée(s): Conseil canadien de la boulangerie

**Consumers United to Stop Food Irradiation (CUSFI) (1986)**
RR#1, Ilderton, ON N0M 2A0
519/666-2072
President, Anne Marie Brown

**Flavour Manufacturers Association of Canada**
#301, 885 Don Mills Rd., North York, ON M3C 1V9
416/510-8036, Fax: 416/510-8043
Technical Chairman, Robert J. Gordon

**Food & Consumer Products Manufacturers of Canada/Fabricants de produits alimentaires et de consommation du Canada (FCPMC) (1959)**
#301, 885 Don Mills Rd., North York, ON M3C 1V9
416/510-8024, Fax: 416/510-8043, Email: info@fcpmc.com, URL: http://www.fcpmc.com
President/CEO, George Fleischmann
Publications: Outlook

**Food Industry Suppliers of Canada/Les Fournisseurs de l'industrie alimentaire du Canada (CDFISA) (1943)**
PO Box 152, Apple Hill, ON K0C 1B0
613/525-2775, Fax: 613/525-4328, Toll Free: 1-800-483-0016, Email: cdfisa@glen-net.ca
General Manager, Robin Flockton
Publications: The Window
Affiliates: International Association of Food Industry Suppliers

**Food Institute of Canada/Institut des aliments du Canada (FIC) (1989)**
#415, 1600 Scott St., Ottawa, ON K1Y 4N7
613/722-1000, Fax: 613/722-1404, Email: fic@foodnet.fic.ca, URL: http://foodnet.fic.ca/fic/fic.html
Executive Director, Christopher J. Kyte
Publications: Technical Communiqué; Executive Summary, m.; Frozen Food, bi-m.; Quarterly

**German Wine Society**
415 Yonge St., 10th Fl., Toronto, ON M5B 2E7
416/598-5528, Fax: 416/598-3584
Executive Director, Ron Fiorelli
Publications: German Wine in Canada

**Institute of Edible Oil Foods (IEOF) (1954)**
#301, 885 Don Mills Rd., North York, ON M3C 1V9
416/510-8036, Fax: 416/510-8044
Executive Director, Ileana Lima
Secretary, Paige Entwistle

**International Maple Syrup Institute/Institut international du sirop d'érable (1975)**
643, rue Grosvenor, Montréal, QC H3Y 2S9
514/842-9471, Fax: 514/842-3541
President, Lynn Reynolds
Director, Claude Tardif

**Master Brewers Association of The Americas (MBAA) (1887)**
#310, 2421 North Mayfair Rd., Wauwatosa, WI 53226 USA
414/774-8558, Fax: 414/774-8556, Email: channer@mbaa.com, URL: http://www.mbaa.com
Senior Administrator, Connie Hanner
Publications: Technical Quarterly

**Ontario Coffee & Vending Service Association (OCVSA)**
#301, 885 Don Mills Rd., North York, ON M3C 1V9
905/510-8036, ext.252, Fax: 905/510-8044
President, Sam Silvestro

**Ontario Flour Millers Association (1935)**
40 George St. North, Cambridge, ON N1S 2M8
519/621-4060, Fax: 519/740-3490, Toll Free: 1-800-665-3682
Secretary, R.L. Lovell
Affiliates: Canadian National Millers' Association

**Ontario Food Processors Association (OFPA) (1935)**
6533C Mississauga Rd., Mississauga, ON L5N 1A6
905/821-2321, Fax: 905/821-9702
Executive Vice-President, Jane Graham

**Ontario Tender Fruit Institute**
6533C Mississauga Rd., Mississauga, ON L5N 1A6
905/821-2321, Fax: 905/821-8702
Secretary, Jane Graham

**Organic Trade Association (OTA) (1985)**
PO Box 1078, Greenfield, MA 01302 USA
413/774-7511, Fax: 413/774-6432, Email: ota@igc.apc.org
Executive Director, Katherine Dimatteo
Publications: The Organic Report

**Pet Food Association of Canada/Association des fabricants d'aliments pour animaux familiers du Canada (PFAC) (1967)**
1435 Goldthorpe Ave., Mississauga, ON L5G 3R2
905/891-2921, Fax: 905/278-4778
Manager, J. David Mitchell
President, Shelley Martin

**Saskatchewan Brewers Association Limited**
380 Dewdney Ave. East, PO Box 3057, Regina, SK S4P 3G7
306/525-0376
Director of Brewery Operations, Larry Kitz

**Tea Association of Canada/Association du thé du Canada (TAC) (1991)**
#301, 885 Don Mills Rd., North York, ON M3C 1V9
416/510-8649, Fax: 416/510-8044
President, Danielle J. O'Rourke
Executive Assistant, Nancy O'Rourke

**Tea Council of Canada/Conseil canadien du thé (TCC)**
#301, 855 Don Mills Rd., North York, ON M3C 1V9
416/510-8647, Fax: 416/510-8044
President, Danielle J. O'Rourke
Executive Assistant, Nancy Ritchie

**Wine Council of Ontario (1974)**
#8205, 110 Hannover Dr., St Catharines, ON L2W 1A4
905/684-8070, Fax: 905/684-2993
Executive Director, Linda Franklin
Publications: Ontario Wine News

**FOOD SERVICES *see* RESTAURANTS, BARS, FOOD SERVICES**

## FORESTRY & FOREST PRODUCTS

**Alberta Forest Products Association (AFPA) (1960)**
#200, 11738 Kingsway Ave., Edmonton, AB T5G 0X5
403/452-2841, Fax: 403/455-0505
Executive Director, Garry Leithead
Affiliates: Alberta Forestry Association; Canadian Lumber Standards; Canadian Wood Council; Forintek Canada; National Lumber Grade Authority

**Association of British Columbia Professional Foresters (ABCPF) (1947)**
#1201, 1130 West Pender St., Vancouver, BC V6E 4A4
604/687-8027, Fax: 604/687-3264, Email: guest@rpf-bc.org
President, Henry J. Benskin, R.P.F.
Executive Director, E.V. Scoffield, R.P.F.
Registrar, Jerome Marburg, LL.B.
Publications: Forum

**Association des industries forestières du Québec ltée/Québec Forest Industries Association Ltd. (AIFQ) (1924)**
#102, 1200, av Germain-des-Prés, Ste-Foy, QC G1V 3M7
418/651-9352, Téléc: 418/651-4622, URL: http://www.aifq.qc.ca
Président/Directeur général, André Duchesne
Président du conseil d'administration, L. Olivier
Secrétaire, Julien Michaud
Publications: Le papetier

**Association des manufacturiers de bois de sciage du Québec/Québec Lumber Manufacturers Association (AMBSQ) (1953)**
#200, 5055, boul Hamel ouest, Québec, QC G2E 2G6
418/872-5610, Téléc: 418/872-3062, Courrier électronique: info@sciage-lumber.qc.ca, URL: http://www.sciage-lumber.qc.ca
Président/Directeur général, Gaston Déry
Directeur, Communications, Louis Boudreault
Publications: Pribec; Asso-Scié, trimestriel

**Association of Registered Professional Foresters of New Brunswick/Association des forestiers agréés du Nouveau-Brunswick (ARPFNB) (1937)**
c/o John Hugh Flemming Forestry Centre, RR#10, Fredericton, NB E3B 6H6
506/452-6933, Fax: 506/450-3128
President, Gilles Couturier, R.P.F.
Executive Director, T.E. Sifton, R.P.F.
Publications: Newsletter
Affiliates: Canadian Forestry Institute; Canadian Forestry Association; New Brunswick Forest Products Association

**Canadian Forest Industries Council/Conseil canadien des industries forestières**
#1200, 555 Burrard St., Vancouver, BC V7X 1S7
604/684-0211, Fax: 604/687-4930
President, Mike Apsey
Co-chairman, Jake Kerr

**Canadian Forestry Association/Association forestière canadienne (CFA) (1900)**
#203, 185 Somerset St. West, Ottawa, ON K2P 0J2
613/232-1815, Fax: 613/232-4210, Email: cfa@cyberus.ca
Executive Director, Glen Blouin
Publications: Forest Forum

**ALBERTA FORESTRY ASSOCIATION (1970)**
101 Alberta Block, 10526 Jasper Ave., Edmonton, AB T5J 1Z7
403/428-7582, Fax: 403/428-7557
Executive Director, Audrey Ruff
Publications: News & Views Newsletter

**BRITISH COLUMBIA FORESTRY ASSOCIATION (BCFA) (1925)**
**Forestry Education BC**
9800A - 140 St., Surrey, BC V3T 4M5
604/582-0100, Fax: 604/582-0101
President, Victor Godin

Vice-President, Finance, Don Gladwin
Manager, Dave Campbell
Publications: Landscapes

#### CANADIAN FORESTRY ASSOCIATION OF NEW BRUNSWICK/ ASSOCIATION FORESTIÈRE CANADIENNE DU NOUVEAU-BRUNSWICK (1939)
The Tree House, 124 St. John St., Fredericton, NB E3B 4A7
506/452-1339, Fax: 506/452-7950
Secretary Manager, David Folster
President, Robert Spurway
Publications: The Arbor Day Planter

#### MANITOBA FORESTRY ASSOCIATION INC. (1972)
900 Corydon Ave., Winnipeg, MB R3M 0Y4
204/453-3182, Fax: 204/477-5765
Executive Director, Dianne J. Beaven
President, James E. Potton
Publications: Adventuring in Conservation

#### NEWFOUNDLAND FOREST PROTECTION ASSOCIATION (1910)
c/o Corner Brook Pulp & Paper Ltd., PO Box 2001, Corner Brook, NF A2H 6J4
President, S.R. Weldon
Chairman, Education Committee, George VanDusen

#### NOVA SCOTIA FORESTRY ASSOCIATION (NSFA) (1959)
PO Box 1113, Truro, NS B2N 5G9
902/893-4653, Fax: 902/895-1197
Executive Director, Jeff Vroom

#### ONTARIO FORESTRY ASSOCIATION/ASSOCIATION FORESTIÈRE DE L'ONTARIO (OFA) (1949)
#502, 150 Consumers Rd., North York, ON M2J 1P9
416/493-4565, Fax: 416/493-4608
Email: oforest@interlog.com
Executive Director, Richard M. Monzon
Publications: OFA Newsletter

#### PEI FOREST IMPROVEMENT ASSOCIATION
Covehead Rd., RR#1, York, PE C0A 1P0
General Manager/Coordinator, Wanson Hemphill

#### SASKATCHEWAN FORESTRY ASSOCIATION (SFA) (1977)
PO Box 400, Prince Albert, SK S6V 5R7
306/763-2189, Fax: 306/764-7463
Manager, Marie Grono
President, Martha O'Sullivan
Publications: Tree Lines

### Canadian Hardwood Plywood Association/ Association canadienne du contreplaqué de bois dur (CHPA)
27 Goulburn Ave., Ottawa, ON K1N 8C7
613/233-6205, Fax: 613/233-1929, Email: chpa@sympatico.ca, URL: http://www.lumberweb.com/chpa/
Assistant Executive Vice-President, Richard Lipman
President, R. Staniforth
Publications: CHPA Membership & Product Directory/Répertoire des membres et produits de l'ACCBD

### Canadian Institute of Forestry/Institut forestier du Canada (CIF) (1908)
#606, 151 Slater St., Ottawa, ON K1P 5H3
613/234-2242, Fax: 613/234-6181, Email: cif@cif-ifc.org, URL: http://www.cif-ifc.org/
Executive Director, Ralph Roberts, RPF
President, Hap Oldham
Publications: The Forestry Chronicle

### Canadian Institute of Treated Wood/Institut canadien des bois traités (CITW) (1955)
#202, 2141 Thurston Dr., Ottawa, ON K1G 6C9
613/737-4337, Fax: 613/247-0540
Executive Director, Henry Walthert
Affiliates: Canadian Wood Council

### Canadian Lumber Standards Accreditation Board (CLSAB) (1960)
#103, 4400 Dominion St., Burnaby, BC V5G 4G3
604/451-7313, Fax: 604/451-7343
Executive Director, Nils Larsson

### Canadian Lumbermen's Association/Association canadienne de l'industrie du bois (CLA) (1908)
27 Goulburn Ave., Ottawa, ON K1N 8C7
613/233-6205, Fax: 613/233-1929, Email: cla@sympatico.ca, URL: http://www.lumberweb.com/cla/en/
Executive Director, R.H. Rivard
President, Léo Huard
Assistant Executive Director, Richard Lipman
Publications: Hardwood Bureau Membership & Product Directory/Répertoire des membres et services du bureau du bois dur de l'ACIB; Wood Products Manufacturing & Inspection Bureau Membership Product Directory

### Canadian Pallet Council/Conseil des palettes du Canada (1977)
208C Division St., Cobourg, ON K9A 3P7
905/372-1871, Fax: 905/373-0230, URL: http://www.cpcpallet.com
General Manager, Belinda Junkin
Publications: Newsletter

### Canadian Paper Trade Association (CPTA) (1922)
#200, 670 Bloor St. West, Toronto, ON M6G 1L2
416/533-7800, Fax: 416/533-4795
Executive Director, Don Mockford

### Canadian Particleboard Association/Association canadienne des fabricants de panneaux de particules (CPA)
4612, rue Sainte-Catherine ouest, Westmount, QC H3Z 1S3
514/989-1002, Fax: 514/989-9318
President, Kelly Shotbolt
Executive Vice-President, Michel G. Tremblay, CAE

### Canadian Pulp & Paper Association/Association canadienne des de pâtes et papier (CPPA) (1913)
Sun Life Building, 1155, rue Metcalfe, 19e étage, Montréal, QC H3B 4T6
514/866-6621, Fax: 514/866-3035, Email: cppacda@ibm.net, URL: http://www.open.doors.cppa.ca/
President & CEO, Lise Lachapelle
Chair, K. Linn Macdonald
Publications: CPPA Trade Directory; CPPA Monthly Statistical Report
Affiliates: Pulp & Paper Research Institute of Canada

### Canadian Well Logging Society (CWLS) (1957)
#1600, 734 - 7th Ave. SW, Calgary, AB T2P 3P8
403/269-9366, Fax: 403/269-2787, URL: http://www.canpic.ca/CWLS
President, Glenn W. Gray, Bus: 403/234-9144
Publications: CWLS Journal; Symposium Transactions, biennial; Insite, q.

### Canadian Wood Council/Conseil canadien du bois (CWC) (1959)
#350, 1730 St. Laurent Blvd., Ottawa, ON K1G 5L1
613/247-7077, Fax: 613/247-7856, URL: http://cwc.metrics.com/cwc.html
President, Kelly McCloskey
Chairman, David McElroy
Publications: Wood le Bois; Wood Leader, m.; CWC Directory, s-a.

### Canadian Wood Pallet & Container Association/ Association canadienne des manufacturiers de palettes et contenants (CWPCA) (1967)
PO Box 640, Pickering, ON L1V 3T3
905/831-3477, Fax: 905/831-3477
Executive General Manager, Gordon R. Hughes
Publications: CWPCA Newsletter/Bulletin; Pallet Enterprise, bi-m.; CWPCA Membership Guide, a.
Affiliates: National Wooden Pallet & Container Association; Western Pallet Association

### Canadian Wood Preservers Bureau/Bureau canadien de la préservation du bois (CWPB) (1988)
#202, 2141 Thurston Dr., Ottawa, ON K1G 6C9
613/737-4337, Fax: 613/247-0540
General Manager, Henry Walthert
President, Craig Wilson

### Cariboo Lumber Manufacturers' Association (CLMA) (1959)
#205, 197 North Second Ave., Williams Lake, BC V2G 1Z5
250/392-7778, Fax: 250/392-4692, Email: peterson@clma.cofi.org
President, J. Dave Peterson
Public Affairs, Heidi Frank
Forestry, Gord Rattray
Chief Quality Control Supervisor, Bob Onofrechuk
Aboriginal Affairs, Duncan Barnett
Publications: Member Mill Directory

### Christmas Tree Growers' Association of Ontario Inc. (1950)
RR#1, Lynden, ON L0R 1T0
519/647-3530, Fax: 519/647-3515, URL: http://www.christmastrees.on.ca
Manager, Hubert A. Will
Publications: OCT News

### Consulting Foresters of British Columbia
#600, 890 West Pender St., Vancouver, BC V6C 1J9
604/687-5500, Fax: 604/687-1327
Sec.-Treas., P.W. Appleby

### Council of Forest Industries (COFI)
#203, 197 Second Ave. North, Williams Lake, BC V2G 1Z5
250/392-7770, Fax: 250/392-5188
Vice President, Aboriginal Affairs, Marlie Beets

### La Fédération des producteurs de bois du Québec (FPBQ) (1970)
555, boul Roland-Therrien, Longueuil, QC J4H 3Y9
514/679-0530, Téléc: 514/679-5682
Directeur général, Victor Brunette, ing.f.
Publications: Forêt de Chez Nous
Organisation(s) affiliée(s): Union des producteurs agricoles

### Junior Forest Wardens Association of Canada
9920 - 108 St., 10th Fl., Edmonton, AB T5K 2M4
403/422-8474, Fax: 403/427-0292
Chief Warden, W.F. Myring

### Maritime Lumber Bureau/Bureau de bois de sciage des Maritimes (MLB) (1938)
PO Box 459, Amherst, NS B4H 4A1
902/667-3889, Fax: 902/667-0401, Toll Free: 1-800-667-9192, URL: http://www.mlb.ca
President & CEO, Diana L. Blenkhorn

### Mechanical Wood-Pulps Network/Réseau sur les pâtes de bois mécaniques (1990)
Wood-Pulps Network
570, boul Saint-Jean, Pointe-Claire, QC H9R 3J9
514/630-4100, Fax: 514/630-4107, Email: nce@paprican.ca
Network Manager, Dan Crosilla

### Millwork Manufacturers Association
#174, 4664 Lougheed Hwy., Burnaby, BC V5C 5R7
604/298-3555, Fax: 604/298-3558

Secretary-Manager, Edward V. Wheatley
Publications: Architectural Woodwork Digest

### National Aboriginal Forestry Association (NAFA) (1989)
Head Office, PO Box 200, Golden Lake, ON K0J 1X0
613/625-2245, Fax: 613/233-4329,
Email: nafa@web.net, URL: http://sae.ca/nafa/
Executive Director, Harry M. Bombay
Senior Advisor, Peggy Smith, RPF
Office Manager, Janet Pronovost
Branch Office: 875 Bank St., Ottawa, ON K1S 3W4, 613/233-5563, Fax: 613/233-4329

### New Brunswick Forest Products Association Inc.
Hugh John Flemming Forestry Centre, RR#10, Fredericton, NB E3B 6H6
506/452-6930, Fax: 506/450-3128
Executive Director, M.R. Cater

### Nova Scotia Forest Products Association
PO Box 696, Truro, NS B2N 5E5
902/895-1179, Fax: 902/893-1197
Executive Director, Steve Talbot

### Nova Scotia Forestry Exhibition Committee (NSFE) (1984)
PO Box 1149, Middleton, NS B0S 1P0
902/825-4344, Fax: 902/825-4634
Executive Manager, Dianne Hankinson LeGard
Publications: AVABT Action

### Ontario Forest Industries Association/l'Industrie forestière de l'Ontario (OFIA) (1943)
#1700, 130 Adelaide St. West, Toronto, ON M5H 3P5
416/368-6188, Fax: 416/368-5445, Email: 73573.2032@compuserve.com
President/CEO, R. Marie Rauter
Publications: Code of Forest Practices; Principes directeurs et code de pratiques forestières, annuel

### Ontario Lumber Manufacturers' Association/Association des manufacturiers de bois de sciage de l'Ontario (OLMA) (1966)
#1105, 55 University Ave., PO Box 8, Toronto, ON M5J 2H7
416/367-9717, Fax: 416/367-3415
President, David G. Milton, RPF
Manager, Eleanor Siegel
Chairman, Jules Fournier
Affiliates: Bureau de promotion des industries du bois; Canadian Forest Industry Council; Canadian Wood Council

### Ontario Professional Foresters Association (OPFA) (1957)
#102, 27 Beaver Creek Rd. West, Richmond Hill, ON L4B 1M8
905/764-2921, Fax: 905/764-2921
Executive Director, John W. Ebbs, R.P.F.
Publications: The Professional Forester

### Ontario Shade Tree Council (OSTC) (1964)
2842 Bloor St. West, Etobicoke, ON M8X 1B1
416/231-4181, Fax: 416/231-3863
President, Patricia Thomson
Treasurer, Mark Procunier
Publications: OSTC Yearbook; OSTC News, bi-m.

### Ordre des ingénieurs forestiers du Québec (OIFQ) (1921)
#380, 2750, rue Einstein, Québec, QC G1P 4R1
418/650-2411, Téléc: 418/650-2168
Président/Directeur général, Magella Morasse
Directeur des communications, Pierre Breton
Publications: L'Aubelle
Organisation(s) affiliée(s): Canadian Forestry Association/Fédération canadienne des associations d'ingénieurs forestiers

### Sustainable Forest Management Network of Centres of Excellence/Réseau de centres d'excellence sur la gestion durable des forêts (SFM) (1995)
208G Biological Sciences Bldg., University of Alberta, Edmonton, AB T6G 2E9
403/492-8161, Fax: 403/492-8160, Email: aboddy@gpu.srv.ualberta.ca
Dr. Ellie Prepas
Network Manager, Dr. Bruce MacLock

### Wholesale Lumber Dealers Association Inc. (WLDA) (1918)
#806, 5075 Yonge St., North York, ON M2N 6C6
416/222-7030, Fax: 416/222-7402, Toll Free: 1-800-363-2091
President, Ted Rowe

FRANCOPHONES IN CANADA *see* CULTURE

## FRATERNAL
*see also* Service Clubs

### Benevolent & Protective Order of Elks of Canada (1913)
**BPO Elks of Canada**
#100, 2629 - 29 Ave., Regina, SK S4G 2N9
306/359-9010, Fax: 306/565-2860, Toll Free: 1-888-843-3557
National Executive Director, William J. Blake, CAE
Publications: The Canadian Elk

### Canadian Association, Sovereign Military Order of Malta (1952)
**Knights of Malta**
1247 Kilborn Ave., Ottawa, ON K1H 6K9
613/731-8897, Fax: 613/731-1312
President, F. Vincent Regan, KM, Q.C.
Publications: Knights of Malta Newsletter

### Canadian Woman's Christian Temperance Union (1884)
Charles Promenade Building, #203, 730 Yonge St., Toronto, ON M4Y 2B7
416/921-4909
National Secretary, Wendy Harker

### Empire Club of Canada
Royal York Hotel, 100 Front St. West, Toronto, ON M5J 1E3
416/364-2878

### Grand Orange Lodge of Canada (1830)
**Loyal Orange Association**
94 Sheppard Ave. West, North York, ON M2N 1M5
416/223-1690, Fax: 416/223-1324, Toll Free: 1-800-565-6248, URL: http://www.orange.ca
Grand Secretary, Norman R. Ritchie
Publications: The Sentinel

**LADIES' ORANGE BENEVOLENT ASSOCIATION OF CANADA**
PO Box 435, Westville, NS B0N 1C0
902/396-4840
Grand Secretary, Dorothy Pushie

### The Independent Order of Foresters
Forester House, 789 Don Mills Rd., Don Mills, ON M3C 1T9
416/429-3000
Executive Secretary, J. Robert Heatley

### Knights of Columbus/Chevaliers de Colomb (1882)
PO Box 1670, New Haven, CT 06507 USA
203/772-2130, Fax: 203/865-2310, URL: http://www.kofc-supreme-council.org
Supreme Knight, Virgil C. Knight
Chief Agent, Kerry J. Soden, CA
Supreme Secretary, Charles P. Reisbeck, Jr.
Chief Agent & Assistant to Supreme Knight, Canadian Affairs, Edward J. Buckley
Publications: Columbia; Knightline

### Knights of Pythias - Domain of British Columbia (1880)
447 Penticton Ave., Penticton, BC V2A 2M5
250/492-6520, Fax: 250/492-6520
Grand Secretary, Marv Wilson
Publications: Pythian Record
Affiliates: Supreme Lodge Knights of Pythias

### The National Chapter of Canada IODE (IODE) (1900)
#254, 40 Orchard View Blvd., Toronto, ON M4R 1B9
416/487-4416, Fax: 416/487-4417
President, Sandra E. Connery
Publications: Echoes
Affiliates: IODE Bahamas; IODE Bermuda

### Order of The Eastern Star (Grand Chapter of Ontario)
18 Central Park Blvd. North, Oshawa, ON L1G 5Y2
905/728-8901
Grand Secretary, M. Ruth Wales

### Order of Sons of Italy in Canada (1919)
505, rue Jean Talon est, Montréal, QC H2R 1T6
514/271-2281, Fax: 514/271-2281
Secretary, F. Pantaleo
Publications: Newsletter

### Royal Arch Masons of Canada
361 King St. West, Hamilton, ON L8P 1B4
905/522-5775, Fax: 905/522-5099
Grand Scribe E., Ezra-Melvyn J. Duke

### Society of Kabalarians of Canada (1964)
**Kabalarian Philosophy**
5912 Oak St., Vancouver, BC V6M 2W2
604/263-9551, Fax: 604/263-5514, Email: admin@kabalarians.com, URL: http://www.kabalarians.com
President, Lorenda Bardell
Office Manager, Garett Hennigan
Publications: The Kabalarian Student

### Sons of Scotland Benevolent Association
#411, 90 Eglinton Ave. East, Toronto, ON M4P 2Y3
416/482-1250, Fax: 416/482-9576
Sec.-Treas., Effie MacFie

### Sovereign Order of St. John of Jerusalem, Knights of Malta, Grand Priory of Canada (OSJ) (1048)
**Knights Hospitallers of Cyprus, Rhodes, Malta & Russia**
Grand Chancery Canada, 52 Kingswood Dr., Bowmanville, ON L1E 1Z3
905/579-0326, Fax: 905/723-5392
Grand Chancellor, H.E. Marquis & Count Joseph Frendo Cumbo
Secretary General, Chev. Raymond Borg
Treasurer General, Chev. Alfred Bonello
Publications: OSJ News

### United Commercial Travelers of America (UCT)
#300, 901 Centre St. North, Calgary, AB T2E 2P6
403/277-0745, Fax: 403/277-6662, Toll Free: 1-800-267-2371
Chief Agent for Canada, Lindsay Maxwell

**FREIGHT FORWARDING *see* TRANSPORTATION & SHIPPING**

## FUNERAL SERVICES

**Alberta Funeral Service Association (AFSA) (1928)**
#130, 6715 - 8 St. NE, Calgary, AB T2E 7H7
403/274-1922, Fax: 403/274-8191, Toll Free: 1-800-803-8809
Executive Administrator, Gail Paget
Publications: AFSA
Affiliates: Funeral Service Association of Canada

**Cemetery & Crematorium Association of British Columbia (CCABC) (1970)**
15800 - 32 Ave., Surrey, BC V4P 2J9
604/531-2141, Fax: 604/536-8828
Sec.-Treas., Nunzio J. Defoe
Publications: Cemetery Dispatch

**Corporation des thanatologues du Québec (CTQ) (1958)**
945, rue Paradis, Roberval, QC G8H 2J9
418/275-4875, Téléc: 418/275-7496
Directeur général, Ghislain Harvey
Publications: Le Bulletin

**Funeral Advisory & Memorial Society (FAMS) (1956)**
**Toronto Memorial Society**
55 St. Phillips Rd., Etobicoke, ON M9P 2N8
416/241-6274
Executive Director, Sylvia Hill

**Funeral Service Association of BC**
1551 Pandora Ave., Victoria, BC V8R 6P9
250/388-7055, Fax: 250/388-6134
Contact, Janet Ricciuti
Affiliates: Funeral Service Association of Canada

**Funeral Service Association of Canada/ L'Association des services funéraires du Canada**
#201, 206 Harwood Ave. South, Ajax, ON L1S 2H6
905/619-0982, Fax: 905/619-0983
Executive Director, Susan MacKinnon

**Manitoba Funeral Service Association (1964)**
PO Box 243, Winnipeg, MB R3C 2G9
204/947-0927, Fax: 204/269-7148
Executive Secretary, Lorrie Waugh
Publications: Newsletter

**New Brunswick Funeral Directors & Embalmers Association**
343 Main St., PO Box 31, Hampton, NB E0G 1Z0
506/832-5541, Fax: 506/832-3082

**Newfoundland & Labrador Funeral Services Association**
PO Box 138, Winterton, NF A0B 3M0
709/583-2700
Secretary, Don Green
Affiliates: Funeral Service Association of Canada

**Nova Scotia Licensed Embalmers & Funeral Directors Association**
172 Main St., Kentville, NS B4N 1J8
902/678-1999, Fax: 902/679-2226
President, Wayne Eiffin
Affiliates: Funeral Service Association of Canada

**Ontario Association of Cemeteries**
PO Box 1156, Stn F, Toronto, ON M4Y 2T8
416/920-4823, Fax: 416/920-4135
President, André Arndt
Publications: The Journal

**Ontario Funeral Service Association Inc. (OFSA) (1922)**
#130, 320 North Queen St., Etobicoke, ON M9C 5K4
416/695-3434, Fax: 416/695-3583, Toll Free: 1-800-268-2727, Email: ofsa@interware.net, URL: http://www.ofsa.org
Executive Director, Sheelah H. Brodie
Publications: OFSA Newsletter
Affiliates: Funeral Service Association of Canada

**Prince Edward Island Funeral Directors & Embalmers Association**
RR#6, Kensington, PE C0B 1M0
902/836-3313, Fax: 902/886-4461
Treasurer, John MacIsaac
Affiliates: Funeral Service Association of Canada

**Saskatchewan Funeral Service Association**
#12, 2700 Montague St., Regina, SK S4S 0J9
306/584-1575, Fax: 306/584-9259
Contact, Gerri Monsees
Affiliates: Funeral Service Association of Canada

## FUR TRADE

***see also* Animal Breeding**

**Aboriginal Trappers Federation of Canada (ATFC) (1984)**
PO Box 1869, Cornwall, ON K6H 6N6
613/932-1258
Executive Director, Bob Stevenson

**Association for the Protection of Fur-Bearing Animals (1953)**
**The Fur Bearers**
2235 Commercial Dr., Vancouver, BC V5N 4B6
604/255-0411, Fax: 604/255-1491
Executive Director, Jennifer Deneen
Publications: The Furbearers

**Canadian Association for Humane Trapping (CAHT) (1954)**
#1202, 390 Bay St., Toronto, ON M5H 2Y2
416/363-2614, Fax: 416/363-8451
President, Robert Gardiner
Publications: CAHT Bulletin

**The Fur Council of Canada/Conseil canadien de la fourrure**
#1270, 1435, rue Saint-Alexandre, Montréal, QC H3A 2G4
514/844-1945, Fax: 514/844-8593
Executive Director, Del Haylock
Secretary, Angela Gurley

**Fur Institute of Canada/Institut de la fourrure du Canada (FIC) (1983)**
#804, 255 Albert St., Ottawa, ON K1P 6A9
613/231-7099, Fax: 613/231-7940
Executive Vice-Chairman, Douglas Pollock
Chairman, Bruce Williams
Affiliates: International Union for Nature & Natural Resources

**Fur Trade Association of Canada (Québec) Inc./ Association canadienne du commerce de la fourrure (Québec) inc.**
#1270, 1435, rue Saint-Alexandre, Montréal, QC H3A 2G4
514/844-1945, Fax: 514/844-8593
Executive Director, Del Haylock

**Furriers Guild of Canada**
#300, 461 King St. West, Toronto, ON M5V 1K4
416/593-0324, Fax: 416/593-1546
Executive Director, Linda Jagros-May

**Retail Fur Council of Canada/Conseil des détaillants en fourrures**
#1270, 1435, rue Saint-Alexandre, Montréal, QC H3A 2G4
514/844-1945, Fax: 514/844-8593
Contact, Del Haylock

## GALLERIES & MUSEUMS

***see also* Visual Art, Crafts, Folk Arts**

**Atlantic Provinces Art Gallery Association (APAGA) (1975)**
Acadia University Art Gallery, Wolfville, NS B0P 1X0
902/542-2201, ext.1166, Fax: 902/542-4727
President, Franziska Kruschen
Affiliates: Canadian Museums Association

**British Columbia Museums Association (BCMA) (1957)**
514 Government St., Victoria, BC V8V 4X4
250/387-3315, Fax: 250/387-1251, Email: bcma@MuseumsAssn.bc.ca, URL: http://www.MuseumsAssn.bc.ca/~bcma/
Executive Director, David Hemphill
Professional Development Coordinator, Lee Boyko
Dogwood Regional Network Coordinator, Cliff Quinn
Publications: Museum Round-Up; Directory of Museums, Galleries & Related Organizations in BC

**Canadian Art Museum Directors Organization/ Organisation des directeurs des musées d'art canadiens (CAMDO)**
c/o The Nickle Arts Museum, University of Calgary, 2500 University Dr. NW, Calgary, AB T2N 1N4
Email: nickle@acs.ucalgary.ca
President, Ann Davis
Affiliates: Canadian Conference of Arts

**Canadian Federation of Friends of Museums/ Fédération canadienne des amis de musées (CFFM)**
c/o Art Gallery of Ontario, 317 Dundas St. West, Toronto, ON M5T 1G4
416/979-6650, Fax: 416/979-6666
President, Dr. Sean B. Murphy
National Director, Carol Sprachman
Publications: Communiqué
Affiliates: World Federation of Friends of Museums - Brussels; Canadian Museums Association

**Canadian Museums Association/Association des musées canadiens (1947)**
280 Metcalfe St., Ottawa, ON K2P 1R7
613/567-0099, Fax: 613/233-5438, Email: info@museums.ca, URL: http://www.museums.ca
Executive Director, John G. McAvity
Business Manager, Robert Levesque
Publications: ND Reports; Muséogramme, m.; Muse, q.; Directory of Canadian Museums & Related Institutions, biennial

**ALBERTA MUSEUMS ASSOCIATION (AMA) (1971)**
Rossdale House, 9829 - 103 St., Edmonton, AB T5K 0X9
403/424-2626, Fax: 403/425-1679
Email: can-ama@immedia.ca
Executive Director, Adriana A. Davies
Publications: Alberta Museums Review; The Directory of Alberta Museums & Related Institutions, bi-a.

**ASSOCIATION OF MANITOBA MUSEUMS (AMM) (1972)**
#422, 167 Lombard Ave., Winnipeg, MB R3B 0T6
204/947-1782, Fax: 204/942-1555
Executive Director, Marilyn de von Flindt
President, Philippe Mailhot
Publications: AMM Newsletter; Dawson & Hind, irreg.

**ASSOCIATION MUSEUMS NEW BRUNSWICK/ASSOCIATION DES MUSÉES DU NOUVEAU-BRUNSWICK (AMNB) (1974)**
503 Queen St., PO Box 116, Stn A, Fredericton, NB E3B 4Y2
506/452-2908, Fax: 506/459-0481
Email: muse@nbnet.nb.ca, URL: http://www.amnb.nb.ca
President, Jeanne Mance Cormier
Publications: AMNB Bulletin; Directory of NB Museums & Related Institutions

**COMMUNITY MUSEUMS ASSOCIATION OF PRINCE EDWARD ISLAND (1983)**
PO Box 22002, Charlottetown, PE C1A 9S2
902/892-8837, Fax: 902/628-6331
Email: cmapei@isn.net
President, Barbara Boys MacCormac
Training Coordinator, Barry King
Publications: CMA PEI Newsletter

**ONTARIO MUSEUM ASSOCIATION/ASSOCIATION DES MUSÉES DE L'ONTARIO (OMA) (1972)**
George Brown House, 50 Baldwin St., Toronto, ON M5T 1L4
416/348-8672, Fax: 416/348-0438
Email: omachin@planeteer.com, URL: http://www.museumassn.on.ca
Executive Director, Marie G. Lalonde
Publications: Currently
Affiliates: Ontario Heritage Alliance

### ICOM Museums Canada/ICOM Musées Canada (1946)
**International Council of Museums**
#400, 280 Metcalfe St., Ottawa, ON K2P 1R7
613/567-0099, Fax: 613/233-5438
President, Johanne Landry
Publications: ICOM Canada Newsletter; UNESCO Museum Quarterly

### Museum Association of Newfoundland & Labrador (MANL)
One Springdale St., PO Box 5785, St. John's, NF A1C 5X3
709/722-9034, Fax: 709/722-9035, Email: can_manl@immedia.ca
Executive Director, Ute Okshevsky, MMST
President, Marilyn Dawe
Publications: MANL Newsletter
Affiliates: Heritage Canada

### Museums Association of Saskatchewan (MAS) (1967)
1808 Smith St., Regina, SK S4P 2N4
306/780-9279, Fax: 306/359-6758, Email: can-mas@immedia.ca
Executive Director, Gayl Hipperson
Communications Manager, Teresa Quilty
Publications: Bulletin

### Ontario Association of Art Galleries (OAAG) (1968)
#306, 489 King St. West, Toronto, ON M5V 1K4
416/598-0714, Fax: 416/598-4128, Email: oaag@interlog.com, URL: http://www.culturenet.ca/oaag/
Publications: Context

### Organization of Military Museums of Canada, Inc./L'Organisation des musées militaires du Canada inc. (OMMC Inc.) (1967)
72 Robertson Rd., PO Box 26106, Nepean, ON K2H 9R6
613/829-0280, Fax: 613/829-0280
Executive Director, Major R.K. Malott, MSc, BA, CD, FRPSC, Ret'd
President, L.Col. Donald Carrington, CD, Ret'd
Publications: The Bulletin
Affiliates: Friends of the Canadian War Museum; Directorate of Military History & Heritage; Military Collectors Club of Canada

### La Société des musées québécois (SMQ) (1958)
CP 8888, Succ Centre-Ville, Montréal, QC H3C 3P8
514/987-3264, Téléc: 514/987-3379, URL: http://www.uqam.ca/musees/
Directrice générale, Sylvie Gagnon
Publications: SMQ Bulletin; Musées, 3 fois par an

**GAMES *see* RECREATION, HOBBIES & GAMES**

**GARDENING *see* HORTICULTURE & GARDENING**

## GAS & OIL

### Canadian Association of Petroleum Producers/Association canadienne des producteurs pétroliers (CAPP) (1992)
#2100, 350 - 7 Ave. SW, Calgary, AB T2P 3N9
403/267-1100, Fax: 403/261-4622, Email: communication@capp.ca, URL: http://www.capp.ca
President, David J. Manning, Q.C.
Vice-President, Strategic Planning, Chris Peirce
Vice-President, Environment & Operations, Bill Harlan
Vice-President, Fiscal Policy & Corporate Services, Len Landry
Vice-President, Markets & Transportation, Richard Woodward
General Counsel, Nick Schultz
Publications: Crude Oil Report; Natural Gas Report, m.; ReCAPP, m.; Canada's Upstream Petroleum Industry, a.; CAPP Statistical Handbook, a.; Petrographs, a.; CAPP Perspective, 3 pa
Affiliates: Natural Gas Council

### Canadian Energy Pipeline Association (CEPA) (1993)
#1650, 801 - 6 Ave. SW, Calgary, AB T2P 3W2
403/221-8777, Fax: 403/221-8760, URL: http://www.cepa.com
President, Myron F. Kanik

### Canadian Gas Association/Association canadienne du gaz (CGA) (1907)
#1200, 243 Consumers Rd., North York, ON M2J 5E3
416/498-1994, Fax: 416/498-7465, Email: info@cga.ca, URL: http://www.cga.ca
President/CEO, Gerald Doucet
Publications: CGA Domestic Demand Forecast; Canadian Gas Facts, a.; Natural Gas Industry Data Tables, a.; Natural Gas Utility Directory, a.; Canadian Residential Heating Survey, a.; Gas Cogeneration Database, a.; Gas Cooling Database, a.; Canadian Gas Rates, a.; Areas Served by Natural Gas in Canada, biennial
Affiliates: International Gas Union; Canadian Gas Research Institute; Gas Technology Canada

### Canadian Gas Processors Association (CGPA) (1960)
900 - 6 Ave. SW, 5th Fl., Calgary, AB T2P 3K2
403/263-6881, Fax: 403/263-6886, Email: nstar@cadvision.com
President, Heather Douglas
Secretary, A. Apuzzo
Publications: News in Brief
Affiliates: Gas Processors Association (USA)

### Canadian Gas Processors Suppliers Association
#1600, 700 - 4 Ave. SW, Calgary, AB T2P 3J4
403/263-5388
President, Karsten Pedersen
Publications: The Downstream Review

### Canadian Petroleum Products Institute/Institut canadien des produits pétroliers (CPPI) (1989)
#1000, 275 Slater St., Ottawa, ON K1P 5H9
613/232-3709, Fax: 613/236-4280, Email: sharonwestbrook@cppi.ca
President, Alain Perez

### Canadian Society of Petroleum Geologists (CSPG) (1928)
#505, 206 - 7 Ave. SW, Calgary, AB T2P 0W7
403/264-5610, Fax: 403/264-5898, Email: cspg@cspg.org, URL: http://www.cspg.org
President, Gerry Reinson
Vice-President, Ric Sebastian
Publications: Bulletin of Canadian Petroluem Geology; The Reservoir, m.
Affiliates: Association of Professional Engineers, Geologists & Geophysicists of Alberta; Canadian Institute of Mining, Metallurgy & Petroleum; Geological Association of Canada; Petroleum Communications Foundation

### Compressed Gas Association - Canada (CGA-Canada)
44 Revcoe Dr., North York, ON M2M 2B8
905/278-2456
Executive Secretary, Lloyd R. Jacobson, Fax: 416/223-5747

### Industrial Gas Users Association/Association des consommateurs industriels de gaz (IGUA) (1973)
#900, 170 Laurier Ave. West, Ottawa, ON K1P 5V5
613/236-8021, Fax: 613/230-9531, Email: igua@hypernet.on.ca, URL: http://www.hypernet.on.ca/igua/
Executive Director, Peter Fournier
Office Manager, Margaret Blair

### Offshore Technologies Association of Nova Scotia (OTANS) (1982)
#813, 1800 Argyle St., Halifax, NS B3J 3N8
902/425-4774, Fax: 902/422-2332, Email: otans@istar.ca
Business Manager, Tina Battlock

### Ontario Natural Gas Association
#1104, 77 Bloor St. West, Toronto, ON M5S 1M2
416/961-2339, Fax: 416/961-1173, Email: onga@sympatico.ca
President, Paul E. Pinnington

### Petroleum Communication Foundation/Fondation des communications sur les ressources pétrolières (PCF) (1975)
#214, 311 - 6th Ave. SW, Calgary, AB T2P 3H2
403/264-6064, Fax: 403/237-6286, Email: pcomm@pcf.ab.ca, URL: http://www.pcf.ab.ca
Executive Director, Leonard F. Bradley
President, Jan Rowley
Information Coordinator, Tony Laramée
Publications: Connections

### Petroleum Recovery Institute (PRI) (1966)
#100, 3512 - 33 St. NW, Calgary, AB T2L 2A6

403/282-1211, Fax: 403/289-1988, Email: ayasse@pri.ab.ca, URL: http://www.pri.com
President & CEO, Dr. Conrad Ayasse
Publications: Partners

**Petroleum Services Association of Canada (PSAC) (1981)**
Aquitaine Tower, #1800, 540 - 5 Ave. SW, Calgary, AB T2P 0M2
403/264-4195, Fax: 403/263-7174, Email: info@psac.ca, URL: http://www.psac.ca
President, Roger Soucy
Publications: On Stream; Fastline, 9 pa

**Petroleum Society of CIM (1949)**
#320, 101 - 6 Ave. SW, Calgary, AB T2P 3P4
403/237-5112, Fax: 403/262-4792, Email: petsoc@canpic.ca, URL: http://www.canpic.ca/PETSOC/
Office Manager, Catherine Buchanan
Publications: JCPT

**Propane Gas Association of Canada Inc./Association canadienne du gaz propane inc. (PGAC) (1967)**
#1800, 300 - 5 Ave. SW, Calgary, AB T2P 3C4
403/543-6500, Fax: 403/543-6508, Email: info@propanegas.ca, URL: http://www.propanegas.ca
Chairman, Bob Bush
Managing Director, Bill Kurtze
Publications: C3 Sign Post

## GEMS & JEWELLERY

**Alberta Federation of Rock Clubs**
47 Garland Cres., Sherwood Park, AB T8A 2P7
403/467-0520
President, Dave Engberg
Affiliates: Gem & Mineral Federation of Canada

**Canadian Gemmological Association (1958)**
1767 Avenue Rd., Toronto, ON M5M 3Y8
416/785-0962, Fax: 416/785-9043
President, Duncan Parker
Publications: The Canadian Gemmologist; CGA Newsletter
Affiliates: Gemmological Association & Gem Testing Laboratory of Great Britain

**Canadian Institute of Gemmology/Institut canadien de gemmologie (CIG) (1983)**
**Pacific Institute of Gemmology**
PO Box 57010, Vancouver, BC V5K 5G6
604/530-8569, Fax: 604/530-8569, Toll Free: 1-800-294-2211, Email: wolf@kwantlen.bc.ca, URL: http://www.deepcove.com/cig/
Executive Director, Wolf Kuehn
Publications: Gemmology Canada
Affiliates: Allied Teaching Centre of the Gemmological Association; Gem Trading Lab of Great Britain

**Canadian Jewellers Association (CJA) (1922)**
Box 2021, #1108, 20 Eglinton Ave. West, Toronto, ON M4R 1K8
416/480-1424, Fax: 416/480-2342
General Manager, Karen Bassels
Publications: Jewellery World

**Corporation des bijoutiers du Québec/Québec Jewellers' Corporation (CBQ) (1952)**
#0.1, 7585, rue Lacordaire, St-Léonard, QC H1S 2A6
514/251-2410, Téléc: 514/251-1702
Directrice générale, Lise Petitpas
Publications: Bijouterie

**Gem & Mineral Federation of Canada/Fédération canadienne des gemmes et des minéraux (GMFC) (1977)**
#202, 237 Wellington Cres., Winnipeg, MB R3M 0A1
204/452-1035
President, Marjorie Reynolds
Membership Chair, Alice Clarke
Treasurer, Jack Wrightson
Historian, Margaret Lowe
Publications: GMFC Newsletter; GMFC Membership Directory

**Jewellers Vigilance Canada Inc. (JVC) (1987)**
20 Eglinton Ave. West, PO Box 2021, Toronto, ON M4R 1K8
416/480-1452, Fax: 416/480-2342, Toll Free: 1-800-636-9536, Email: jvc@maple.net
Executive Coordinator, Carla J. Adams
Publications: Action Update

**Jewellery Appraisers Association of Canada (1988)**
#13, 5501 - 204 St., PO Box 26003, Langley, BC V3A 5N0
604/530-6807, Fax: 604/530-8626
President, Geoffrey Dominy
Director, Anna Miller

**GENEALOGY *see* HISTORY, HERITAGE, GENEALOGY**

## GOVERNMENT & PUBLIC ADMINISTRATION
***see also* Politics**

**Alberta Association of Municipal Districts & Counties (1909)**
4504 - 101 St., Edmonton, AB T6E 5G9
403/436-9375, Fax: 403/437-5993
Executive Director, Larry Goodhope
President, Roelof Heinen

**Alberta Rural Municipal Administrators Association (1922)**
c/o County of Grande Prairie, 8611 - 108 St., Grande Prairie, AB T8V 4C5
403/532-9722, Fax: 403/532-4234
President, Ron Pfau

**Alberta Urban Municipalities Association (AUMA) (1905)**
8712 - 105 St., Edmonton, AB T6E 5V9
403/433-4431, Fax: 403/433-4454, Toll Free: 1-800-661-2862, Email: main@auma.ab.ca, URL: http://www.auma.ab.ca
Executive Director, John E. Maddison, CAE
Publications: Urban Perspective

**Association of Clerks-At-The-Table in Canada/Association des greffiers parlementaires du Canada (1969)**
Legislative Assembly, Legislative Assembly Bldg., PO Box 6000, Fredericton, NB E3B 5H1
403/453-2506, Fax: 403/453-7154, Email: loredana@gov.nb.ca
President, Loredana Catalli Sonier
Vice-President, Robert Vaive
Secretary, Deborah Deller

**Association des communicateurs municipaux du Québec (ACMQ) (1975)**
144, boul de l'Hôpital, Gatineau, QC J8T 7S7
819/243-2331, Téléc: 819/243-2338, Ligne sans frais: 1-800-668-8383
Président, Jean Boileau
Publications: Le Triangle
Organisation(s) affiliée(s): Sociétés des relationistes du Québec

**Association des directeurs généraux des municipalités du Québec (1973)**
51, rue Auteuil, Québec, QC G1R 4C2
418/694-1428, Téléc: 418/694-9462
Président, Denis Cassista
Secrétaire, Roger Noël
Publications: Bulletin éclair; Le Sablier, trimestriel

**Association internationale des maires francophones - Bureau à Québec (AIMF)**
51, rue d'Auteuil, Québec, QC G1R 4C2
418/694-1973, Téléc: 418/694-4649
Conseiller technique, Jean Lenoir

**Association of Municipal Administrators of New Brunswick/Association des administrateurs municipaux du Nouveau-Brunswick (1977)**
#402, 200 Prospect St. West, Fredericton, NB E3B 2T8
506/453-4229, Fax: 506/453-7954
Executive Director, Eva Turnbull
Publications: President's Newsletter

**Association of Municipal Administrators, Nova Scotia (AMANS) (1970)**
#1106, 1809 Barrington St., Halifax, NS B3J 3K8
902/423-2215, Fax: 902/425-5592
Administrative Director, Janice Wentzell
Publications: AMA Newsletter

**Association of Municipal Clerks & Treasurers of Ontario/Association des secrétaires et trésoriers municipaux de l'Ontario (AMCTO) (1937)**
#520, 2810 Matheson Blvd. East, Mississauga, ON L4W 4X7
905/602-4294, Fax: 905/602-4295
Executive Director, Kenneth S. Cousineau, CAE
President, Larry Simons, CMO
Publications: Municipal Monitor
Affiliates: Association of Municipalities of Ontario; International Institute of Municipal Clerks; Municipal Information Systems Association

**Association des municipalités du Nouveau-Brunswick (AMNB) (1989)**
702, rue Principale, CP 849, Petit-Rocher, NB E0B 2E0
506/542-2622, Téléc: 506/542-2618, Courrier électronique: amnb@nbnet.nb.ca
Directeur général, Léopold Chiasson
Président, Maire Réginald Poulin
Publications: L'Elue
Organisation(s) affiliée(s): Association internationale des maires et responsables des capitales et métropoles partiellement ou entièrement francophones (AIMF); Fédération canadienne des municipalités (FCM); Union des municipalités régionales de comté et des municipalités locales du Québec (UMRCQ)

**Association of Municipalities of Ontario (AMO) (1889)**
#1701, 393 University Ave., Toronto, ON M5G 1E6
416/971-9856, Fax: 416/971-6191, Email: amo@amo.municom.com, URL: http://www.amo.on.ca
Executive Director, Douglas Raven
President, Terry Mundell
Information Manager, Renata Kulpa
Director of Policy, Deborah Dubinofsky
Publications: Updates

**Association québécoise des directeurs et directrices du loisir municipal (AQDLM) (1966)**
55, du Carrefour Sportif, CP 820, Montréal, QC G0J 1B0
418/629-3355, Téléc: 418/629-4090
Président, Jean-Yves Fournier
Publications: Forum Loisir

**Association des urbanistes et des aménagistes municipaux du Québec**
295, boul Charest est, Québec, QC G1K 3G8
418/691-6855, Téléc: 418/691-3942
Présidente, Nathalie Prud'homme
Publications: URB-INFO

**Association of Yukon Communities (AYC) (1974)**
3128 3rd Ave., Whitehorse, YT Y1A 1E7
867/668-4388, Fax: 867/665-7574
Executive Director, Larry Bagnell
President, Barbara Harris
Affiliates: Federation of Canadian Municipalities

**Canadian Association of Municipal Administrators (CAMA)**
24 Clarence St., 2nd Fl., Ottawa, ON K1N 5P3
613/241-8444, Fax: 613/241-7440
Executive Director, Maria Hughes

**Canadian Council on Social Development/Conseil canadien de développement social (CCSD) (1920)**
441 MacLaren St., 4th Fl., Ottawa, ON K2P 2H3
613/236-8977, Fax: 613/236-2750, Email: council@achilles.net, URL: http://www.achilles.net/~council/
Executive Director, David Ross
President, Sharon Manson Singer
Communications Officer, Nancy Perkins
Publications: Vis-a-Vis; Perception, q.

**Cities of New Brunswick Association**
#404, 200 Prospect St., Fredericton, NB E3N 2T8
506/457-7297, Fax: 506/453-7954
Executive Director, Frederick Martin
President, Mayor Thomas Higgins

**City Clerks & Election Officers Association (1975)**
City of St. Albert, 5 St. Anne St., St Albert, AB T8N 3Z9
403/459-1633, Fax: 403/460-2394
Secretary, Adele Cordell
Publications: Minute Talk

**Corporation des officiers municipaux agréés du Québec/Corporation of Chartered Municipal Officers of Québec (COMAQ) (1968)**
#210, 1135, ch St-Louis, Sillery, QC G1S 1E7
418/527-1231, Téléc: 418/527-4462
Secrétaire général, Erick Parent
Publications: Le Carrefour; Répertoire des membres, annuel

**Corporation des secrétaires municipaux du Québec inc. (CSMQ) (1939)**
#500, 580, av Grande-Allée est, Québec, QC G1R 2K2
418/647-4518, Téléc: 418/647-4115
Directeur général, Marie-Andrée Levasseur
Publications: Le Scribe

**Federal Superannuates National Association/Association nationale des retraités fédéraux (FSNA) (1963)**
#401, 233 Gilmour St., Ottawa, ON K2P 0P2
613/234-9663, Fax: 613/234-2314, Email: info@fsna.com
National President, Claude A. Edwards
Executive Director, Jean-Guy Soulière
Publications: On Guard/En Garde
Affiliates: Coalition of Seniors for Social Equity; Seniors Health Action Group

**Federation of Canadian Municipalities/Fédération canadienne des municipalités (FCM) (1937)**
24 Clarence St., 2nd Fl., Ottawa, ON K1N 5P3
613/241-5221, Fax: 613/241-7440, Telex: 053-4451, Email: federation@fcm.ca, URL: http://www.fcm.ca
Executive Director, James W. Knight
President, Deputy Mayor Jae Eadie, City of Winnipeg
Administration & Finance, Sue Killam
Publications: Forum; Communiqué, irreg.

**Federation of Northern Ontario Municipalities (FONOM) (1960)**
81 St. Brendon St., Sudbury, ON P3E 1K4
705/669-0135, Fax: 705/669-0729
Executive Director, Phyllis Floyd

**Federation of Prince Edward Island Municipalities Inc. (FPEIM) (1957)**
1 Kirkdale Rd., Charlottetown, PE C1E 1R3
902/566-1493, Fax: 902/368-1239, Email: macbain@peinet.pe.ca
Executive Director, Lisa B. Doyle-MacBain
President, Doug Doncaster
Publications: FPEIM Municipal Directory; Information Update, m.
Affiliates: Association of Municipal Administrators, PEI; Maritime Municipal Training & Development Board

**Foreign Service Community Association/Association de la communauté du service extérieur (FSCA) (1976)**
c/o Dept. of External Affairs, 125 Sussex Dr., Ottawa, ON K1A 0G2
613/944-5729
Office Coordinator, Diane Villeneuve
Publications: Bulletin

**Government Finance Officers Association of the US & Canada**
#800, 180 North Michigan Ave., Chicago, IL 60601 USA
312/977-9700, Fax: 312/977-4806
Executive Director, Jeffrey L. Esser
President, Linda R. Savitsky

**Institute on Governance/Institut sur la gouvernance (IOG) (1990)**
122 Clarence St., Ottawa, ON K1N 5P6
613/562-0090, Fax: 613/562-0097, Email: info@igvn.ca, URL: http://www.igvn.ca
Managing Director, Tim Plumptre
Director, Kathleen Lauder
Director, Claire McQuillan
Director, Suzanne Taschereau

**Institute of Public Administration of Canada/Institut d'administration publique du Canada (IPAC) (1947)**
#401, 1075 Bay St., Toronto, ON M5S 2B1
416/924-8787, Fax: 416/924-4992, Email: ntl@ipaciapc.ca, URL: http://www.ipaciapc.ca
Executive Director, Joseph M. Galimberti
Publications: Canadian Public Administration/Administration publique du Canada; Public Sector Management, q.

**Local Government Administrators of Alberta**
4233 - 53 Ave., Red Deer, AB T4N 2E1
403/347-4782
Sec.-Treas., Lois Hyland

**Manitoba Association of Urban Municipalities (MAUM) (1950)**
#200, 611 Corydon Ave., Winnipeg, MB R3L 0P3
204/982-6286; Purchasing 1-800-563-6286, Fax: 204/478-1005
Executive Director, Rochelle Zimberg, CAE
Publications: Mirror on Urban Scene

**Manitoba Municipal Administrators Association Inc.**
PO Box 220, Rorketon, MB R0L 1R0
204/732-2333, Fax: 204/732-2557
Secretary, Elizabeth Tymchuk

**Municipal Officers' Association of British Columbia (1919)**
#200, 880 Douglas St., Victoria, BC V8W 2B7
250/383-7032, Fax: 250/384-3000
Executive Director, Lillian Whittier
President, Mike Phelan
Sec.-Treas., Patti Sawka
Publications: Chapter 290

**Newfoundland & Labrador Federation of Municipalities (NLFM) (1951)**
PO Box 5756, St. John's, NF A1C 5X3
709/753-6820, Fax: 709/738-0071
Chief Administrator, Patricia Hempstead
President, Sam Synard
Publications: Municipal News

**Northeastern Ontario Municipal Association**
220 Algonquin Blvd. East, Timmins, ON P4N 1B3
705/264-1331, Fax: 705/360-1392
Sec.-Treas., Amos Latta

**Northwest Territories Association of Municipalities**
Northwest Tower, #904, 5201 - 50 Ave., Yellowknife, NT X1A 3S9
867/873-8359, Fax: 867/873-5801
Executive Director, Yvette Gonzalez
President, Dennis Bevington

**Northwestern Ontario Municipal Association (1946)**
161 East Brock St., Thunder Bay, ON P7E 4H1
807/626-0155, Fax: 807/626-8163
Executive Director, Ken Taniwa
Affiliates: Association of Municipalities of Ontario

**Ontario Municipal Administrators' Association**
#101, 49 Emma St., Guelph, ON N1E 6X1
519/837-3369, Fax: 519/837-0729
Sec.-Treas., M.R. Sather

**Ontario Municipal Human Resources Association (1963)**
PO Box 400, Waterloo, ON N2J 4A9
519/886-0844, Fax: 519/886-1197, Email: omhra@golden.net
Administrative Officer, Terry Hallman

**Ontario Municipal Management Institute (OMMI) (1979)**
PO Box 58009, Oshawa, ON L1J 8L6
905/434-8885, Fax: 905/434-7381
Executive Director, Bill McKim
President, Mario Belvedere
Publications: You & Your Local Government; OMMI Quarterly Report; Network

**Organization of Small Urban Municipalities (Ontario)**
55 King St. West, Cobourg, ON K9A 2M2
905/372-4301, Fax: 905/372-1533
Executive Secretary, B.W. Baxter

**The Public Affairs Association of Canada/Association des affaires publiques du Canada (PAAC) (1988)**
#1105, 191 The West Mall, Etobicoke, ON M9C 5K8
416/620-5055, Fax: 416/626-5392
Association Manager, Brenda Looyenga
Publications: Public Affairs

**Rural & Improvement Districts Association of Alberta (RIDAA) (1976)**
Site 206, RR#2, PO Box 36, St Albert, AB T8N 1M9

403/973-6762, Fax: 403/973-6864
Executive Director, Shirley Mercier

### Rural Municipal Administrators' Association of Saskatchewan (RMAAS) (1955)

PO Box 146, Harris, SK S0L 1K0
306/656-2072, Fax: 306/656-2151
Executive Director, Jim Angus
President, Audrey Trombley
Publications: The Rural Administrator

### Saskatchewan Association of Rural Municipalities (SARM) (1905)

2075 Hamilton St., Regina, SK S4P 2E1
306/757-3577, Fax: 306/565-2141, Toll Free: 1-800-667-3604, Email: sarm.mg@sk.sympatico.ca
Executive Director, Ken Engel
Publications: The Rural Councillor

### Saskatchewan Urban Municipalities Association (SUMA) (1906)

#200, 1819 Cornwall St., Regina, SK S4P 2K4
306/525-3727, Fax: 306/565-3552
Executive Director, Keith Schneider
Publications: The Urban Voice

### Society of Local Government Managers of Alberta

4629 - 54 Ave., PO Box 308, Bruderheim, AB T0B 0S0
403/796-3836, Fax: 403/796-2081
Sec.-Treas., Linda M. Davies

### Union of BC Municipalities (1904)

#15, 10551 Shellbridge Way, Richmond, BC V6X 2W9
604/270-8226, Fax: 604/660-2271, Email: ubcm@civicnet.gov.bc.ca
Executive Director, Richard Taylor
President, Richard Trumper
Publications: UBCM News

### Union of Manitoba Municipalities (UMM) (1903)

PO Box 397, Portage La Prairie, MB R1N 3B7
204/857-8666, Fax: 204/239-5050
Executive Director, Jerome Mauws
Secretary, Connie Krawec
Publications: Keystone Municipal News

### Union des municipalités du Québec (UMQ) (1919)

#680, 680, rue Sherbrooke ouest, Montréal, QC H3A 2M7
514/282-7700, Téléc: 514/282-7711, Courrier électronique: umq@istar.ca
Directeur général, Raymond L'Italien
Président, Mario LaFramboise
Publications: Partenaires; Urba, 10 fois par an
Organisation(s) affiliée(s): Conseil du patronat du Québec; Fédération canadienne des municipalités;

### Union des municipalités régionales de comté et des municipalités locales du Québec (UMRCQ) (1944)

#560, 2954, boul Laurier, Ste-Foy, QC G1V 4T2
418/651-3343, Téléc: 418/651-1127, Courrier électronique: umrcq@umrcq.qc.ca, URL: http://www.umrcq.qc.ca
Directeur général, Michel Fernet
Publications: Quorum; L'Union, 5 fois par an

### Union of Municipalities of New Brunswick/Union des municipalités du Nouveau-Brunswick (UMNB) (1995)

115 Allan-a-dale Lane, Rothesay, NB E2E 1H2
506/849-5789, Fax: 506/849-5788, Email: ygibb@brunnet.net
Executive Director, Yvonne Gibb
President, Marcel Deschênes
Publications: Newsletter

### Union of Nova Scotia Municipalities (UNSM) (1905)

#1106, 1809 Barrington St., Halifax, NS B3J 3K8
902/423-8331, Fax: 902/425-5592, Email: unsm@istar.ca, URL: http://www.munisource.org/unsm
Executive Director, Kenneth Simpson
Administrative Assistant, Judy Webber
Publications: Municipal Open Line

### Urban Municipal Administrators' Association of Saskatchewan (UMAAS) (1974)

PO Box 730, Hudson Bay, SK S0E 0Y0
306/865-2261, Fax: 306/865-2800
Executive Director, Richard Dolezsar
President, John Wade
Publications: UMAAS Update

**GRAPHIC ARTS *see* PRINTING INDUSTRY & GRAPHIC ARTS**

**GROCERY TRADE *see* FOOD & BEVERAGE INDUSTRY**

## HEALTH & MEDICAL

***see also* AIDS; Dental; Disabled Persons; Hospitals; Mental Health; Nursing; Research & Scholarship;**

### Academy of Medicine, Toronto (1907)

704 Spadina Rd., PO Box 549, Stn P, Toronto, ON M5S 2T1
President, Dr. John H. Fowler, M.D., Bus: 416/465-2800
Publications: The Bulletin

### Acoustic Neuroma Association of Canada/Association pour les Neurinomes acoustiques du Canada (ANAC) (1984)

PO Box 369, Edmonton, AB T5J 2J6
403/428-3384, Toll Free: 1-800-561-2622, Email: anac@compusmart.ab.ca
President, Shirley Entis
Office Manager, Linda Gray
Publications: The Connection

### Acupuncture Foundation of Canada Institute/Institut de la Fondation d'Acupuncture du Canada (AFCI) (1995)

3003 Danforth Ave., PO Box 93688, RPO Shoppers World, Toronto, ON M4C 5R5
416/752-3988, Fax: 416/752-4398, Email: info@afcinstitute.com, URL: http://www.afcinstitute.com/afci.html
Executive Director, Cheryll A. Kwok
Executive President, Linda Rapson, MD
Publications: Acupuncture Canada
Affiliates: World Federation of Acupuncture Societies; Pan Pacific Medical Acupuncture Forum; NAFTA Acupuncture Commission

### African Medical & Research Foundation Canada (AMREF Canada) (1973)

59 Front St. East, Toronto, ON M5E 1B3
416/601-6981, Fax: 416/601-6984
Executive Director, Gillian Evans
Treasurer/Secretary, Bill Crawford
Chairman, Arthur S. Labatt
Publications: News Update
Affiliates: African Medical & Research Foundations Nairobi; Ontario Africa Working Group

### Alberta Association of Naturopathic Practitioners

921 - 17 Ave. SW, Calgary, AB T2T 0A4
403/244-4989, Fax: 403/228-6750
Executive Sec.-Treas., Dr. Karen Jansen

### Alberta Heritage Foundation for Medical Research

Manulife Place, #3125, 10180 - 101 St., Edmonton, AB T5J 3S4
403/423-5727, Fax: 403/429-3509
President, Matthew Spence
Contact, Public Relations, Lois Hammond

### Allergy Asthma Information Association/Association de l'information sur l'allergie et l'asthme (AAIA) (1964)

30 Eglinton Ave. West, Mississauga, ON L5R 3E7
905/712-2242, Fax: 905/712-2245
Executive Director, Susan Daglish
Operations Manager, Tom J. Christie
Publications: Newsletter
Affiliates: Canadian Society of Allergy & Clinical Immunology

### Allergy Foundation of Canada/Fondation du Canada des allergies (AFC) (1974)

PO Box 1904, Saskatoon, SK S7K 3S5
306/373-7591, Email: sswoynarski@sk.sympatico.ca
President, Sandy Woynarski
Publications: Allergy Alert

### Alliance of Physiotherapy Regulatory Boards/Alliance des corporations professionnelles de physiothérapeutes (1987)

230 Richmond St. West, 10th Fl., Toronto, ON M4V 1V6
416/591-3828, Fax: 416/591-3834
Executive Director, Susan G. Takahashi
Chair, Brenda Hudson
Publications: The Alliance Newsletter

### Alzheimer Society of Canada/Société Alzheimer du Canada (ASC) (1977)

#201, 1320 Yonge St., Toronto, ON M4T 1X2
416/925-3552, Fax: 416/925-1649, Toll Free: 1-800-616-8816, Email: info@alzheimer.ca, URL: http://www.alzheimer.ca
Executive Director, Stephen E. Rudin, M.Ed.
Director, Communications & Public Relations, Lisa Dower
Affiliates: HealthPartners

#### ALZHEIMER ASSOCIATION OF ALBERTA (1988)

#218A, 2323 - 32 Ave. NE, Calgary, AB T2E 6Z3
403/250-1303, Fax: 403/250-8241, Toll Free: 1-888-233-0332
Email: alzhab@agt.net, URL: http://www.telusplanet.net/public/alzhab/home.htm
Affiliates: Canadian Association on Gerontology; Alberta Association on Gerontology; Canadian Centre for Philanthropy

#### ALZHEIMER ASSOCIATION OF ONTARIO/ASSOCIATION ALZHEIMER D'ONTARIO (1983)

**Alzheimer Ontario**
#202, 1200 Bay St., Toronto, ON M5R 2A5
416/967-5900, Fax: 416/967-3826
Email: alzheimeront@sympatico.ca
Executive Director, John Ellis
President, John Carriere
Publications: Alzheimer Journal

#### ALZHEIMER ASSOCIATION OF SASKATCHEWAN INC. (1982)

#301, 2550 - 12th Ave., Regina, SK S4P 3X1
306/949-4141, Fax: 306/949-3069, Toll Free: 1-800-263-3367
Executive Director, Joan Kortje
Office Coordinator, Linda Orell
President, Barbara Wilson
Publications: Alzheimer Newsletter

#### ALZHEIMER MANITOBA (1982)

205 Edmonton St., Winnipeg, MB R3C 1R4

204/943-6622, Fax: 204/942-5408, Toll Free: 1-800-378-6699
Executive Director, Sylvia Rothney
Publications: Reflects

#### ALZHEIMER SOCIETY OF BC (1981)
#20, 601 West Cordova St., Vancouver, BC V6B 1G1
604/681-6530, Fax: 604/669-6907, Toll Free: 1-800-667-3742
Email: info@alzheimersociety.bc.ca
Executive Director, Ian Ross
Publications: Contact; In Touch, bi-m.

#### ALZHEIMER SOCIETY OF NEW BRUNSWICK/SOCIÉTÉ ALZHEIMER DU NOUVEAU BRUNSWICK (1987)
PO Box 1553, Stn A, Fredericton, NB E3A 5G2
506/459-4280, Fax: 506/452-0313, Toll Free: 1-800-664-8411
Executive Director, Gloria McIlveen
President, Exelda Gaston
Secretary, Joan McKell
Publications: The Beacon

#### ALZHEIMER SOCIETY OF NOVA SCOTIA (1983)
5954 Spring Garden Rd., Halifax, NS B3H 1Y7
902/422-7961, Fax: 902/422-7971
Email: alzheime@ra.isisnet.com
Executive Director, Kathryn Garden
Publications: Alzheimers Nova Scotia

#### ALZHEIMER SOCIETY OF PEI
166 Fitzroy St., Charlottetown, PE C1A 1S1
902/628-2257, Fax: 902/368-2715
Executive Director, Judy McCann-Beranger
Publications: Alzheimer PEI

#### FÉDÉRATION QUÉBÉCOISE DES SOCIÉTÉS ALZHEIMER (FQSA) (1985)
1474, rue Fleury est, Montréal, QC H2C 1S1
514/388-3148, Téléc: 514/381-3462, Ligne sans frais: 1-800-636-6473
Courrier électronique: alzqc@generation.net
Directrice générale, Dr. Lise Hébert

#### NEWFOUNDLAND ALZHEIMER ASSOCIATION INC. (1988)
Southcott Hall, #328-329, 100 Forest Rd., 3rd Fl., St. John's, NF A1A 1E5
709/576-0608, Fax: 709/576-0608
Email: sharing@avalon.nf.ca
President, Claude Hender
Executive Director, Shirley Barnes
Publications: Newsletter

### Amyotrophic Lateral Sclerosis Society of Canada/Société canadienne de la sclérose latérale amyotrophique (ALS) (1977)
**ALS Society of Canada**
#220, 6 Adelaide St. East, Toronto, ON M5C 1H6
416/362-0269, Fax: 416/362-0414, Toll Free: 1-800-267-4257, Email: alssoc@inforamp.net, URL: http://www.als.ca
President, W. Brian Smith
Director of Marketing & Communications, Geoff Dewar
Publications: ALS Outlook
Affiliates: Amyotrophic Lateral Sclerosis Association (USA)

### Aplastic Anemia Association of Canada (AAAC) (1987)
22 Aikenhead Rd., Etobicoke, ON M9R 2Z3
416/235-0468, Fax: 416/235-1756, Toll Free: 1-888-840-0039
Chairperson, Caroline Laughlin
Publications: Newsletter

### The Arthritis Society/Société d'arthrite (1948)
#901, 250 Bloor St. East, Toronto, ON M4W 3P2
416/967-1414, Fax: 416/967-7171, Toll Free: 1-800-321-1433, URL: http://www.arthritis.ca
Chairperson, Wm. Woloshyn
President/CEO, Denis Morrice, Sr.
Vice-President/Communications, Sharon McConnell
National Communications Manager, Joe Konecny, Email: jkonecny@arthritis.ca
Publications: Arthritis News; ArthroExpress, q.

### Association Canadienne de l'Ataxie de Friedreich/Canadian Association of Friedreich's Ataxia (ACAF) (1972)
**Fondation Claude St-Jean**
5620, rue C.A. Jobin, Montréal, QC H1P 1H8
514/321-8684, Téléc: 514/321-9257, Ligne sans frais: 1-800-222-3968
Président, Claude St-Jean
Publications: Eldorado
Bureau des Services sociaux: Personne ressource, Gina Tourigny, 3800, rue Radisson, Montréal, QC H1M 1X6, 514/899-1586, Téléc: 514/899-1586

### Association des chirurgiens généraux du Québec
#3000, 2, Complexe Desjardins, Montréal, QC H5B 1G8
514/350-5107, Téléc: 514/350-5157
Président, Michel Talbot
Secrétaire, Grégoire Bégin
Secrétariat, Marcelle Rousseau

### Association des conseils des médecins, dentistes et pharmaciens du Québec/Association of Councils of Physicians, Dentists & Pharmacists of Québec (1947)
308, boul St-Joseph est, Montréal, QC H2T 1J2
514/842-5059, Téléc: 514/842-5356, Courrier électronique: acmdp@sympatico.ca, URL: http://www.acmdp.qc.ca
Directrice générale, Françoise Cloutier
Ajointe administrative, Nicole Du Rand, Numéro au travail: 514/842-5050
Publications: Communiqué

### Association des dermatologistes du Québec/ Association of Dermatologists of Québec (ADQ) (1950)
#3000, 2, Complexe Desjardins, Montréal, QC H5B 1G8
514/350-5111, Téléc: 514/350-5161, Courrier électronique: dermato@fmsq.org
Président, Pierre Ricard, m.d.
Vice-président, Normand Doré, m.d.
Secrétaire, Jacques Tanguay, m.d.
Trésorier, Louis-Philippe Durocher, m.d.
Personne ressource, Francinc Labelle

### Association diabète Québec/Québec Diabetes Association (ADQ)
5635, rue Sherbrooke est, Montréal, QC H1N 1A2
514/259-3422, Téléc: 514/259-9286, Ligne sans frais: 1-800-361-3504
Président-Directeur General, Serge Langlois
Présidente, CPADQ, Jana Havrankova
Publications: Plein Soleil; Info-Diàbete; Info-ADQ
Organisation(s) affiliée(s): Canadian Diabetes Association

### Association of Local Public Health Agencies (ALPHA) (1986)
#1618, 415 Yonge St., Toronto, ON M5B 2E7
416/595-0006, Fax: 416/595-0030, Email: mail@alphaweb.org, URL: http://www.alphaweb.org
Executive Director, Gordon White
Coordinator, Association Services, Susan Lee

### Association des médecins de langue française du Canada (1902)
8355, boul Saint-Laurent, Montréal, QC H2P 2Z6
514/388-2228, Téléc: 514/388-5335, Ligne sans frais: 1-800-387-2228
Directeur général, André de Sève

### Association des médecins ophtalmologistes du Québec
#3000, 2, Complexe Desjardins, Montréal, QC H5B 1G8
514/350-5124
Président, Jean Deschênes
Secrétaire, Pierre Turcotte

### Association des médecins du travail du Québec/ Québec Occupational Medical Association
#505, 1100, av Beaumont, Mount Royal, QC H3P 3E5
514/344-1662, Téléc: 514/737-6431
Directrice administrative, Jocelyne Lessard
Président, Alain Gagnon

### Association des néphrologues du Québec
#3000, 2, Complexe Desjardins, Montréal, QC H5B 1G8
514/350-5134, Téléc: 514/350-5151
Président, Dr. Raymond Dandavino
Secrétaire, Robert Charbonneau
Secrétariat, Raymonde Dionne

### Association des neurochirurgiens du Québec
#3000, 2, Complexe Desjardins, Montréal, QC H5B 1G8
514/350-5120, Téléc: 514/350-5100
Président, Jacques Boucher
Secrétaire, Georges L'Espérance
Secrétariat, Raymonde Dionne

### Association des neurologues du Québec
#3000, 2, Complexe Desjardins, Montréal, QC H5B 1G8
514/350-5122, Téléc: 514/350-5100
Président, Yves Lapierre
Secrétaire, Michel Lebel

### Association des obstétriciens et gynécologues du Québec (AOGQ)
#3000, 2, Complexe Desjardins, Montréal, QC H5B 1G8
514/849-4969, Téléc: 514/849-5011
Directrice administrative, Francine Charlebois
Organisation(s) affiliée(s): Fédérations des médecins spécialistes du Québec

### Association d'orthopédie du Québec
#3000, 2, Complexe Desjardins, Montréal, QC H5B 1G8
514/844-0803 ou 350-5000, Téléc: 514/350-5100
Président, Gaétan Langlois
Secrétaire-trésorier, Charles Hilaire Rivard
Secrétariat, Louise Leclaire

### Association d'oto-rhino-laryngologie et de chirurgie cervico-faciale du Québec
#3000, 2, Complexe Desjardins, Montréal, QC H5B 1G8
514/350-5125
Président, Raynald Ferland
Secrétaire, Patrick Savard

### Association des pathologistes du Québec
#3000, 2, Complexe Desjardins, Montréal, QC H5B 1G8
514/350-5102, Téléc: 514/350-5100
Président, Rénald Morency
Secrétaire, Pierre Russo

### Association des pédiatres du Québec
#3000, 2, Complexe Desjardins, Montréal, QC H5B 1G8
514/350-5127, Téléc: 514/350-5100

Président, Claude Lemoine
Secrétaire, Pierre Gaudreault

### Association des pharmaciens des établissements de santé du Québec (APES) (1963)

#505, 50, boul Cremazie ouest, Montréal, QC H2P 2T2
514/381-7904, Téléc: 514/381-2781
Directrice générale, Manon Lambert
Publications: Pharmactuel

### Association des physiâtres du Québec

#3000, 2, Complexe Desjardins, Montréal, QC H5B 1G8
514/350-5119, Téléc: 514/350-5100
Président, Marcel Morand
Secrétaire-trésorier, Denis Raymond

### Association professionnelle des technologues diplômés en electrophysiologie médicale (APTDEPM) (1989)

1063A, av Larivière, Rouyn-Noranda, QC J9X 4K9
819/762-2376, Téléc: 819/762-2376
Président, Steve Girard
Secrétaire-trésorière, Isabelle Charbonneau
Administratrice, Marléne Galarneau
Directrice des comités, Annie Dubois
Publications: Le Potentiel

### Association québécoise de la fibrose kystique/ Québec Cystic Fibrosis Association (AQFK) (1981)

#2260, 800, boul René-Lévesque ouest, Montréal, QC H3B 1X9
514/877-6161, Téléc: 514/877-6116, Ligne sans frais: 1-800-363-7711
Directrice générale, Denise Ménard
Publications: Commentaires; À Propos, trimestriel; Santé vous bien, trimestriel; Info FK

### Association des radiologistes du Québec

#3000, 2, Complexe Desjardins, Montréal, QC H5B 1G8
514/350-5129, Téléc: 514/350-5100
Président, Guy Breton
Secrétaire, Jacques Lévesque

### Asthma Society of Canada/Société canadienne de l'asthme (ASC) (1974)

#425, 130 Bridgeland Ave., Toronto, ON M6A 1Z4
416/787-4050, Fax: 416/787-5807, Toll Free: 1-800-787-3880
Executive Director, Elizabeth Kovac
Publications: Attack on Asthma

### Autism Society Canada/Société canadienne d'autisme (ASC) (1976)

#202, 129 Yorkville Ave., Toronto, ON M5R 1C4
416/922-0302, Fax: 416/922-1032
Executive Director, David White
Publications: Rendezvous

#### AUTISM SOCIETY ALBERTA (ASA) (1972)

#101, 11720 Kingsway Ave., Edmonton, AB T5G 0X5
403/453-3971, Fax: 403/447-4948
Contact, Barbara Stewart

#### AUTISM SOCIETY OF BRITISH COLUMBIA (1974)

1584 Rand Ave., Vancouver, BC V6P 3G2
604/261-8888, Fax: 604/261-7898
Email: autismbc@mindlink.net
Executive Director, Rhonda Garside
Publications: Newsletter

#### AUTISM SOCIETY MANITOBA

825 Sherbrook St., 2nd Fl., Winnipeg, MB R3A 1M5
204/783-9563, Fax: 204/786-0860
President, Tony Schweitzer
Publications: Newsletter

#### AUTISM SOCIETY NEW BRUNSWICK

PO Box 635, Fredericton, NB E3B 5B4
506/363-3200, Fax: 506/363-4106
President, Karen Cunningham

#### AUTISM SOCIETY NEWFOUNDLAND & LABRADOR (ASNL) (1987)

PO Box 14078, Stn A, St. John's, NF A1B 4G8
709/722-2803
President, Joyce Churchill

#### AUTISM SOCIETY NOVA SCOTIA (ASNS) (1977)

PO Box 392, Sydney, NS B1P 6H2
902/539-8323
President, Phyllis Frost
Publications: Newsletter
Affiliates: Society for Treatment of Autism

#### AUTISM SOCIETY ONTARIO (1973)

#302, 300 Sheppard Ave. West, North York, ON M2N 1N5
416/512-9880, Fax: 416/512-8026
Executive Director, Jane Vinet
Publications: Newslink

#### AUTISM SOCIETY PEI

PO Box 75, York, PE C0A 1P0
902/368-2685
President, Carolyn Bateman

#### SASKATCHEWAN SOCIETY FOR THE AUTISTIC INC. (1976)

3510 - 25 Ave., Regina, SK S4S 1L8
306/586-4615, Fax: 306/586-4615
Email: DNesteg531@aol.com
President, Dennis Nestegard
Affiliates: Saskatoon Society for Autism; Regina District Society for the Autistic

#### SOCIÉTÉ QUÉBÉCOISE DE L'AUTISME/QUÉBEC SOCIETY FOR AUTISM (1976)

2300, boul René-Lévesque ouest, Montréal, QC H3H 2R5
514/931-2215, Téléc: 514/931-2397
Directrice générale, Manon Carle Dagenais
Publications: Express

### Autism Treatment Services of Canada

404 - 94 Ave. SE, Calgary, AB T2J 0E8
403/253-6961, Fax: 403/253-6974
Executive Director, Dr. Dave Mikkelson

### Breast Cancer Society of Canada/Société du cancer du sein du Canada

401 St. Clair St., Point Edward, ON N7V 1P2
519/336-6846
Contact, L.M. Greenaway

### British Columbia Cancer Foundation (BCCF) (1935)

601 West 10th Ave., Vancouver, BC V5Z 1L3
604/877-6040, Fax: 604/877-6161, Toll Free: 1-888-906-2873, URL: http://www.bccancer.bc.ca
President & CEO, Michael K. Petrie
Affiliates: British Columbia Cancer Research Centre; British Columbia Cancer Agency

### British Columbia Ear Bank (1973)

Burrard Bldg., St. Paul's Hospital, #B53, 1081 Burrard St., Vancouver, BC V6Z 1Y6
604/631-5636, Fax: 604/631-5705
Manager, Dr. Leo Yang
Director, Chee N. Thong

### British Columbia Health Association (BCHA) (1917)

#600, 1333 Broadway West, Vancouver, BC V6H 4C7
604/734-2423, Fax: 604/734-7202, Telex: 04-54300
Email: annis@bcha.bc.ca, URL: http://www.HINETBC.org/BCHA/BCHAhome.html
General Manager, David J. Annis
President/CEO, Mary Collins
Chair, Lorraine Grant
Publications: BCHA News; From the President, m.

### British Columbia Medical Services Foundation (1968)

Harbour Centre, #1200, 555 West Hastings St., PO Box 12132, Vancouver, BC V6B 4N6
604/688-2204, Fax: 604/688-4170, Email: info@vancouverfoundation.bc.ca
Program Associate, Marit Gilbert

### British Columbia Paraplegic Association (BCPA) (1957)

780 Marine Dr. SW, Vancouver, BC V6P 5Y7
604/324-3611, Fax: 604/324-3671
Executive Director, Norman Haw
Executive Assistant, M. Brownlee
Publications: Paragraphic
Affiliates: BC Injury Prevention Centre

### British Columbia Parkinson's Disease Association (BCPDA) (1969)

411 Dunsmuir St., 3rd Fl., Vancouver, BC V6B 1X4
604/662-3240, Fax: 604/662-3241, Toll Free: 1-800-668-3330
Executive Director, Lois Raphael
Publications: BCPDA Newletter

### British Columbia Transplant Society (BCTS) (1985)

East Tower, 555 West 12th Ave., 4th Fl., Vancouver, BC V5Z 3X7
604/877-2100, Fax: 604/877-2111, Toll Free: 1-800-663-6189
Director/CEO, Bill Barrable

### Canadian Academy of Facial Plastic & Reconstructive Surgery/Académie canadienne de chirurgie plastique et reconstructive faciale (CAFPRS) (1981)

#401, 600 University Ave., Toronto, ON M5G 1X5
905/569-6965, Toll Free: 1-800-545-8864
President, Dr. Joseph Wong
Executive Director, Marcy Binsky

### Canadian Anaesthetists' Society/Société canadienne des anesthésistes (CAS) (1943)

#208, One Eglinton Ave. East, Toronto, ON M4P 3A1
416/480-0602, Fax: 416/480-0320, Email: cas@multinet.org
Executive Director, Ann Andrews
President, Dr. Pierre Limoges
Meeting & Congress Coordinator, Annette Schilz
Publications: Canadian Journal of Anaesthesia; CAS Newsletter, triennial
Affiliates: World Federation of Societies of Anaesthesiologists; Royal College of Physicians & Surgeons of Canada; Canadian Medical Association; Canadian Standards Association; Society for Education in Anesthesia

### Canadian Association of Cardio-Pulmonary Technologists (CACPT) (1970)

PO Box 848, Stn A, Toronto, ON M5W 1G3
416/243-3600, ext.2201
President, John Fedirko
Treasurer, Lori Davis
Publications: C-P Update

### Canadian Association of Centres for the Management of Hereditary Metabolic Diseases

#### GARROD Association

c/o Winnipeg Children's Hospital, 840 Sherbrook St., FE229, Winnipeg, MB R3A 1S1

204/787-2494, Fax: 204/787-1419, Email: greenberg@cc.umanitoba.ca
Contact, Dr. Cheryl R. Greenberg

### Canadian Association of Child Neurology Corporation/Corporation de l'association canadienne de neurologie pédiatrique (1991)
Hospital for Sick Children, 555 University Ave., Toronto, ON M5G 1X8
416/813-6332, Fax: 416/813-6334
President, Dr. William J. Logan

### Canadian Association for Clinical Microbiology & Infectious Diseases/Association canadienne de microbiologie clinique et des maladies contagieuses (CACMID) (1980)
20045, Montée Sainte-Marie, Montréal, QC H9X 3R5
514/457-2070, Fax: 514/457-6346
Director, Head of Infectious Diseases, Dr. I. Salit
Sec.-Treas., Dr. Wayne C. Bradbury
Publications: CACMID Newsletter; Directory of Specialists in Microbiology & Infectious Disease, a.
Affiliates: Canadian Association of Medical Microbiologists; Canadian Infectious Diseases Society; Canadian Society of Microbiologists; Association des microbiologistes du Québec; Pan-American Group for Rapid Viral Diagnosis; Biological Implications of Pathogenicity Group; Canadian Society for International Health

### The Canadian Association of Emergency Physicians/L'Association canadienne des médecins d'urgence (CAEP)
#102, 1785 Alta Vista Dr., Ottawa, ON K1G 3Y6
613/523-3343, Fax: 613/521-4314, URL: http://unixg.ubc.ca:780/~grunfeld/caep.html
President, Dr. Garth Dickinson
Treasurer, Dr. Garnet Cummings
Secretary, Dr. John Talon
Publications: Communiqué; Journal of Emergency Medicine, bi-m.
Affiliates: Canadian Medical Association; Royal College of Physicians & Surgeons of Canada; International Federation of Emergency Medicine; American College of Emergency Physicians

### Canadian Association of Gastroenterology/Association canadienne de gastroentérologie
University of Calgary, Dept. of GI Research, #1709, 3330 Hospital Dr. NW, Calgary, AB T2N 4N1
403/220-4539, Fax: 403/283-3028
Executive Director, Dr. John L. Wallace
Affiliates: Canadian Medical Association; World Organization of Gastroenterology

### Canadian Association of General Surgeons/Association canadienne des chirurgiens généraux
Health Sciences Centre, 300 Prince Phillip Dr., St. John's, NF A1B 3V6
902/737-6558
President, Dr. Christopher Heughan
Secretary, Dr. Roger Keith
Affiliates: Canadian Medical Association

### Canadian Association of Internes & Residents/Association canadienne des internes et résidents
#500, 505 University Ave., Toronto, ON M5G 1X4
416/979-1182, Fax: 416/595-9778
Executive Director, Lois Ross

### Canadian Association of Medical Biochemists/Association des médecins biochimistes du Canada (CAMB) (1975)
Hôtel-Dieu de Québec, 11, Côte du Palais, Québec, QC G1R 2J6
418/691-5135, Fax: 418/691-5383
Sec.-Treas., Dr. Pierre Douville
Affiliates: Royal College of Physicians & Surgeons of Canada

### Canadian Association of Medical Microbiologists/Association canadienne des médecins microbiologistes (CAMM) (1961)
London Health Sciences Centre, 339 Windermere Rd., London, ON N6A 5A5
250/727-4494, Fax: 250/727-4480
President, Dr. David Colby, Bus: 519/663-3396
Affiliates: Canadian Medical Association; International Congress of Chemotherapy

### Canadian Association of Medical Oncologists/Association des oncologues médicaux du Canada
Cross Cancer Institute, 11560 University Ave., Edmonton, AB T6G 1Z2
403/492-8763, Fax: 403/432-7359
President, Dr. Anthony. Fields
Sec.-Treas., Dr. Glenwood Goss

### Canadian Association of Medical Radiation Technologists/Association canadienne des technologues en radiation médicale (CAMRT)
#601, 294 Albert St., Ottawa, ON K1P 6E6
613/234-0012, Fax: 613/234-1097
Executive Director, Dr. Richard Lauzon, Email: rlauzon@camrt.ca
President, Bill Brodie, Email: wbrodie@neuro_rad.lan.mcgill.ca
Director of Communications, Steven Brasier, Email: az972@freenet.carleton.ca
Registrar, Norma Saunders
Director of Education, Susan Ward
Publications: The Canadian Journal of Medical Radiation Technology; CAMRT News, 5 pa

### Canadian Association of Neuropathologists/Association canadienne de neuropathologistes (1960)
London Health Services Centre - Victoria Campus, 375 South St., London, ON N6A 4G5
519/667-6756, Fax: 519/667-6749, Email: davidr@lhsc.on.ca
President, Dr. S. Ludwin
Sec.-Treas., Dr. D.A. Ramsay
Affiliates: International Society of Neuropathology

### Canadian Association of Nuclear Medicine Inc./Association canadienne de médecine nucléaire
774 Echo Dr., Ottawa, ON K1S 5N8
613/730-6254, Fax: 613/730-1116, Email: canm@rcpsc.edu
President, Dr. Karen Gulchyn
Publications: Photon
Affiliates: Canadian Medical Association; Society of Nuclear Medicine - USA; Canadian Association of Radiation Protection

### Canadian Association of Occupational Therapists/Association canadienne des ergothérapeutes (CAOT) (1926)
Carleton Technology & Training Centre, #3400, 1125 Colonel By Dr., Ottawa, ON K1S 5R1
613/523-2268, Fax: 613/523-2552, Toll Free: 1-800-434-2268
President, Sandra Bressler
Executive Director, Anne Strickland
Publications: National; The Canadian Journal of Occupational Therapy, bi-m.

### Canadian Association of Optometrists/Association canadienne des optométristes (CAO) (1948)
234 Argyle Ave., Ottawa, ON K2P 1B9
613/235-7924, Fax: 613/235-2025, URL: http://fox.nstn.ca/~eyedocs/caoorg.html
CEO, Michael J. DiCola
Director of Administration, Chantale Wall
Publications: Canadian Journal of Optometry
Affiliates: American Optometric Association; International Federation of Asian & Pacific Associations of Optometrists; World Council of Optometry

#### ALBERTA ASSOCIATION OF OPTOMETRISTS
#902, 11830 Kingsway Ave., Edmonton, AB T5G 0X5
403/451-6824, Fax: 403/452-9918
Executive Director, R. Glenn Campbell
President, Dr. Dorrie Morrow

#### ASSOCIATION DES OPTOMÉTRISTES DU QUÉBEC (AOQ)
#740, 1265, rue Berri, Montréal, QC H2L 4X4
514/288-6272, Téléc: 514/288-7071
Président/Directeur général, Dr. Claude Neilson

#### BRITISH COLUMBIA ASSOCIATION OF OPTOMETRISTS (BCAO) (1921)
#125, 10451 Shellbridge Way, Richmond, BC V6X 2W8
604/270-9909
Email: bc-optom@mortimer.com, URL: http://www.optometrists.bc.ca
Executive Director, Thomas J. Little
President, Dr. Tim Allen
Publications: The Optometrist; Vision at Work, biennial

#### MANITOBA ASSOCIATION OF OPTOMETRISTS (MAO) (1909)
#878, 167 Lombard Ave., Winnipeg, MB R3B 0V3
204/943-9811, Fax: 204/943-1208
Executive Director, Carol Loyd
President, Dr. Jane Thrall

#### NEW BRUNSWICK ASSOCIATION OF OPTOMETRISTS/ASSOCIATION DES OPTOMÉTRISTES DU NOUVEAU-BRUNSWICK
20 Woodstock Rd., Fredericton, NB E3B 2H3
506/458-8759, Fax: 506/450-1271
Executive Director, Denise Roy
President, Dr. Lillian Linton

#### NEWFOUNDLAND ASSOCIATION OF OPTOMETRISTS
PO Box 2284, Stn C, St. John's, NF A1C 6E6
709/368-0380, Fax: 709/368-4139
Executive Director, Nap Dupuis
President, Dr. Ian Henderson
Publications: Update

#### NOVA SCOTIA ASSOCIATION OF OPTOMETRISTS
Comp 83, Caribou Wilds, RR#4, Lower Sackville, NS B4C 3B1
902/835-9318, Fax: 902/928-0933
President, Dr. Ray Wagg
Sec.-Treas., Dr. Carl Davis

#### ONTARIO ASSOCIATION OF OPTOMETRISTS (1909)
290 Lawrence Ave. West, Toronto, ON M5M 1B3
416/256-4411, Fax: 416/256-9881
Executive Director, Dennis E. Souder, CAE
President, Dr. Richard Kniaziew
Publications: Insight

#### PRINCE EDWARD ISLAND ASSOCIATION OF OPTOMETRISTS
111 Pownal St., PO Box 2847, Charlottetown, PE C1A 3W4
902/566-4418, Fax: 902/566-4694
President, Dr. Jane Toombs
Secretary, Dr. David McKenna

#### SASKATCHEWAN ASSOCIATION OF OPTOMETRISTS (SAO) (1909)
125 - 3 Ave. South, Saskatoon, SK S7K 1L6
306/652-2069, Fax: 306/652-2642
Email: saskop@sk.sympatico.ca
Executive Director, Donald D. Sauer
President, Dr. W. Bruce Robinson
Publications: SAO Newsletter

**Canadian Association of Oral & Maxillofacial Surgeons/Association canadienne de spécialistes en chirurgie buccale et maxillo-faciale (CAOMS) (1953)**
#304, 333 Wethersfield Dr., Vancouver, BC V5X 4M9
604/322-3025, Fax: 604/322-3025, Email: caoms@portal.ca
President, Dr. Douglas Vincelli
Executive Director, Dr. A.E. Swanson
Publications: The Voice
Affiliates: Canadian Dental Association

**Canadian Association of Paediatric Surgeons/Association de la chirurgie infantile canadienne**
Regina General Hospital, 1440 - 14th Ave., Regina, SK S4P 0W5
306/359-4542, Fax: 306/359-4723
President, Dr. Angus Juckes
Publications: Journal of Paediatric Surgery

**Canadian Association of Pathologists**
Toronto General Hospital, #EC4-316, 200 Elizabeth St., Toronto, ON M5G 2C4
416/340-3008, Fax: 416/340-4706
Sec.-Treas., Joan Sweet
Secrétaire-trésorier, Dr. Vincent Bernier
Publications: Newsletter

**Canadian Association of Physical Medicine & Rehabilitation/Association canadienne de médecine physique et de réadaptation (CAPMR)**
774 Echo Dr., Ottawa, ON K1S 5N8
613/730-6240, Fax: 613/730-1116, Email: capm&r@rcpsc.edu
President, Dr. Ron Bowie
Publications: CAPM&R News
Affiliates: Canadian Medical Association

**Canadian Association of Prosthetists & Orthotists/Association canadienne des prosthesistes et orthesistes (CAPO) (1955)**
#401, 225 Vaughan St., Winnipeg, MB R3C 1T7
204/949-4970, Fax: 204/947-3627
President, Allan O'Neill
Publications: CAPO Yearbook
Affiliates: Canadian Board for Certification of Prosthetists & Orthotists

**Canadian Association for Quality in Health Care/Association canadienne pour la qualité dans les services de santé (CAQHC) (1981)**
8 Astley Ave., Toronto, ON M4W 3B4
416/975-0204, Fax: 416/972-1366, Email: caqhc@highlander.cbnet.ns.ca, URL: http://highlander.cbnet.ns.ca/cbnet/healthca/caqhc/
President, Joanne Watson
Publications: QA Link; The Canadian Journal of Quality in Health Care

**Canadian Association of Radiologists/L'Association canadienne des radiologistes (CAR) (1937)**
#510, 5101, rue Buchan, Montréal, QC H4P 2R9
514/738-3111, Fax: 514/738-5199
Executive Director, Suzanne Charette
Publications: Canadian Association of Radiologists' Journal; Illuminator, bi-m.
Affiliates: Canadian Medical Association

**Canadian Association of Speech-Language Pathologists & Audiologists/Association canadienne des orthophonistes et audiologistes (CASLPA) (1965)**
#2006, 130 Albert St., Ottawa, ON K1P 5G4
613/567-9968, Fax: 613/567-2859, Toll Free: 1-800-259-8519, Email: caslpa@caslpa.ca, URL: http://www.caslpa.ca
Executive Director, Keith Christopher
President, Debbie Shugar
Manager, Publications & Communications, Karen McCarthy
Publications: Communiqué; Journal of Speech-Language Pathology & Audiology, q.
Affiliates: International Association of Logopedics & Phoniatrics

**Canadian Athletic Therapists Association/Association canadienne des thérapeutes du sport (CATA) (1965)**
Place R. Tait McKenzie, #507, 1600 James Naismith Dr., Gloucester, ON K1B 5N4
613/748-5876, Fax: 613/748-5850
President, Dale Butterwick
Program Coordinator, Laurel McDonald
Publications: CATA Newsletter; Journal of the Canadian Athletic Therapists' Association, a.

**Canadian Brain Tissue Bank**
Banting Institute, #127, 100 College St., Toronto, ON M5G 1L5
416/977-3398, Fax: 416/964-2165
Coordinator, Administration, R.D. Brown
Tissue Coordinator, M. Pataki
Medical Director, T.P. Morley

**Canadian Cancer Society/Société canadienne du cancer (1938)**
#200, 10 Alcorn Ave., Toronto, ON M4V 3B1
416/961-7223, Fax: 416/961-4189, Toll Free: 1-800-939-3333
CEO, Dorothy J. Lamont
Executive Director, Programs & Planning, Maaike Asselbergs
President, Dr. Ronald J. Potter
Director of Public Relations, Michael McFarland
Publications: National News; Progress Against Cancer, q.; Canadian Cancer Statistics, a.
Affiliates: International Union Against Cancer

**Canadian Cardiovascular Society/Societé canadienne de cardiologie (CCS) (1962)**
#401, 360, av Victoria, Westmount, QC H3Z 2N4
514/482-3407, Fax: 514/482-6574
Executive Director, Linda Theriault
Affiliates: International Society & Federation of Cardiology; Inter-American Society of Cardiology; Canadian Society of Clinical Perfusionists; Canadian Society of Cardiology Technologists; Canadian Association of Cardiopulmonary Technologists; Canadian Medical Association; Canadian Coalition for High Blood Pressure Prevention & Control

**Canadian Celiac Association/Association canadienne de la maladie coéliaque (CCA) (1976)**
**Celiac Canada**
6519B Mississauga Rd., Mississauga, ON L5N 1A6
905/567-7195, Fax: 905/567-0710, Toll Free: 1-800-363-7296
Executive Director, Judi Sennett
President, Gwen Shaver
Publications: Celiac News

**Canadian Chiropractic Association/Association chiropratique canadienne (CCA) (1943)**
1396 Eglinton Ave. West, Toronto, ON M6C 2E4
416/781-5656, Fax: 416/781-7344, Email: ccachiro@inforamp.net, URL: http://www.inforamp.net/~ccachiro
Executive Director, Edward Barisa
Publications: Journal of the Canadian Chiropractic Association; Chiropractic Business Magazine, bi-m.
Affiliates: Canadian Chiropractic Examining Board; Canadian Chiropractic Historical Association; Canadian Chiropractic Protective Association; Canadian Chiropractic Supply Division; Canadian Federation of Chiropractic Regulatory Boards; Canadian Memorial Chiropractic College; Chiropractic Foundation for Spinal Research; Council on Chiropractic Education (Canada); Module de chiropratique - L'UQTR

**ASSOCIATION DES CHIROPRATICIENS DU QUÉBEC**
7960, boul Metropolitain est, Anjou, QC H1K 1A1
514/355-0557, Téléc: 514/355-0070
Secrétaire exécutive, M. Marois
Président, Dr. C. Gelinas, Numéro au travail: 418/835-6064

**BRITISH COLUMBIA CHIROPRACTIC ASSOCIATION (BCCC) (1934)**
#102, 7031 Westminster Hwy., Richmond, BC V6X 1A3
604/270-1332, Fax: 604/278-0093
Executive Director, Dr. D. Nixdorf

**COLLEGE OF CHIROPRACTORS OF ALBERTA (1986)**
Manulife Place, #1870, 10180 - 101 St., Edmonton, AB T5J 3S4
403/420-0932, Fax: 403/425-6583
Executive Director, Debbie Manz
Publications: Portfolio; Bargain Finder, m.

**MANITOBA CHIROPRACTORS' ASSOCIATION (MCA) (1945)**
#2706, 83 Garry St., Winnipeg, MB R3C 4J9
204/942-3000, Fax: 204/942-3010
Email: mca@escape.ca
Registrar, Dr. E. Audrey Toth, DC
Publications: Newsletter

**NEW BRUNSWICK CHIROPRACTORS' ASSOCIATION (1958)**
PO Box 21046, Oromocto, NB E2V 2R9
506/450-0600
President, Dr. M.L. Blanchette, Bus: 506/548-9595
Secretary, Dr. C.J. Levere

**NEWFOUNDLAND & LABRADOR CHIROPRACTIC ASSOCIATION**
724 Water St., St. John's, NF A1E 1C2
709/726-4076
President, Dr. K. Beatty
President, Dr. L. Goyeche, Bus: 709/726-4076, Fax: 709/739-7762

**NOVA SCOTIA CHIROPRACTIC ASSOCIATION (1953)**
RR#1, Cleveland, NS B0E 1J0
902/625-0005, Fax: 902/625-1441
URL: http://www.medianet.ca/nsca/
President, Dr. M.I. Parker, Bus: 902/667-1236
Sec.-Treas., Dr. D. MacNeil
Publications: Spinal Column

**ONTARIO CHIROPRACTIC ASSOCIATION (OCA) (1929)**
#30, 5160 Explorer Dr., Mississauga, ON L4W 4T7
905/629-8211, Fax: 905/629-8214
Executive Director, Peter Waite, CAE

**PRINCE EDWARD ISLAND CHIROPRACTIC ASSOCIATION**
266 Read Dr., Summerside, PE C1N 5A9
902/436-7183
Sec.-Treas., Dr. Vincent Adams
President, Dr. R.J. Belyea, Bus: 902/892-6432

**Canadian Coalition for High Blood Pressure Prevention & Control/Coalition canadienne pour la prévention et le contrôle de l'hypertension artérielle (CCHBPPC) (1985)**
#200, 160 George St., Ottawa, ON K1N 9M2
613/241-4361, ext.317, Fax: 613/241-3278
President, Dr. Arun Chockalingam
Secretary, Sherron Elliot
Publications: Message
Affiliates: World Hypertension League

**Canadian College of Health Service Executives/ Collège canadien des directeurs de services de santé (CCHSE) (1970)**
#402, 350 Sparks St., Ottawa, ON K1R 7S8
613/235-7218, Fax: 613/235-5451, Email: cchse@hph.hwc.ca
Acting President, Don Schurman
Publications: Contact; Healthcare Management Forum, q.

**Canadian College of Medical Geneticists/Collège canadien de généticiens médicaux (CCMG) (1975)**
774 Echo Dr., Ottawa, ON K1S 5N8
613/730-6250, Fax: 613/730-1116, Email: ccmg@rcpsc.edu
Secretary, Dr. Alessandra Duncan
Publications: CCMG Newsletter
Affiliates: Royal College of Physicians & Surgeons of Canada

**Canadian Coordinating Office for Health Technology Assessment/Office canadien de coordination de l'évaluation des technolgies de la santé (CCOHTA) (1989)**
#110, 955 Green Valley Cres., Ottawa, ON K2C 3V4
613/226-2553, Fax: 613/226-5392, Email: pubs@ccohta.ca, URL: http://www.ccohta.ca
Publications: CCOHTA Update/Nouvelles de l'OCCETS

**Canadian Council for Tobacco Control/Conseil canadien pour le contrôle du tabac (CCTC) (1974)**
#1000, 170 Laurier Ave. West, Ottawa, ON K1P 5V5
613/567-3050, Fax: 613/567-2730, Email: jforsythe@ccsh.ca, URL: http://www.ccsh.ca
Executive Director, Janice Forsythe
President, Dexter Harvey

**Canadian Critical Care Society/Société canadienne de soins intensifs (CCCS)**
700 William Ave., Room GH 723, Winnipeg, MB R3E 0Z3
416/787-3112, Fax: 416/787-2823
Sec.-Treas., Dr. Hugh Devitt
Publications: CCCS Newsletter
Affiliates: Canadian Medical Association; World Federation of Societies of Intensive & Critical Care Medicine

**Canadian Cystic Fibrosis Foundation/Fondation canadienne de la fibrose kystique (CCFF) (1960)**
#601, 2221 Yonge St., Toronto, ON M4S 2B4
416/485-9149, Fax: 416/485-0960, Toll Free: 1-800-378-2233, Email: postmaster@ccff.ca, URL: http://www.ccff.ca/~cfwww/index.html
Executive Director, Cathleen Morrison
Assistant Executive Director, Rod Morrison
President, Denis Mouton
Vice-President, Peggy Gorman
Vice-President, Gord Thow
Publications: Candid Facts/A Propos
Affiliates: International Cystic Fibrosis (Mucoviscidosis) Association

**Canadian Deafblind & Rubella Association/ Association canadienne de la surdi-cécité et de la rubéole (CDBRA) (1976)**
c/o The W. Ross Macdonald School, 350 Brant Ave., Brantford, ON N3T 3J9
905/527-2110, Fax: 905/527-6384
President, Linda Mamer
Publications: Intervention

**Canadian Dermatology Association/Association canadienne de dermatologie**
#521, 774 Echo Dr., Ottawa, ON K1S 5N8
613/730-6262, Fax: 613/730-1116
Sec.-Treas., Paul Brisson
Publications: Canadian Dermatology Association Journal
Affiliates: Canadian Medical Association; American Academy of Dermatology

**Canadian Diabetes Association/Association canadienne du diabète (CDA) (1953)**
#800, 15 Toronto St., Toronto, ON M5C 2E3
416/363-3373, Fax: 416/363-3393, Toll Free: 1-800-226-8464, Email: info@cda-nat.org, URL: http://www.diabetes.ca/
Executive Director, Jim O'Brien
Publications: Canadian Diabetes; Canadian Journal of Diabetes Care; Diabetes Dialogue, q.
Affiliates: Association du diabète du Québec

**Canadian Dietetic Association/Association canadienne des diététistes (CDA) (1935)**
#601, 480 University Ave., Toronto, ON M5G 1V2
416/596-0857, Fax: 416/596-0603
CEO, Marsha Sharp
President, Kathy Morpurgo
Publications: Communiqué; Journal of the Canadian Dietetic Association, q.
Affiliates: 10 provincial dietetic associations

**BRITISH COLUMBIA DIETITIANS' & NUTRITIONISTS' ASSOCIATION (BCDNA) (1956)**
#402, 1755 West Broadway, Vancouver, BC V6J 4S5
604/736-3790, Fax: 604/736-5606
Executive Director, Janice Macdonald
Publications: BCDNA News

**MANITOBA ASSOCIATION OF REGISTERED DIETITIANS**
#700, 360 Broadway, Winnipeg, MB R3C 4G6
204/235-1792, Fax: 204/235-1792
Executive Director, Corinne Eisenbraun
Publications: MARD Matters

**NEW BRUNSWICK ASSOCIATION OF DIETITIANS/ASSOCIATION DES DIÉTÉTISTES DU NOUVEAU-BRUNSWICK (NBAD)**
PO Box 22024, RPO Lansdowne, Saint John, NB E2K 4T7
506/642-9058, Fax: 506/636-8900
Email: javw@nbnet.nb.ca

**NEWFOUNDLAND DIETETIC ASSOCIATION (NDA)**
PO Box 1756, Stn C, St. John's, NF A1C 5P5
709/778-4173, Fax: 709/778-4333
Email: hcc.scoma@hccsj.nf.ca
Chairperson, Marjorie Scott
Affiliates: HEAL (Health Action Lobby)

**NOVA SCOTIA DIETETIC ASSOCIATION (NSDA) (1953)**
PO Box 36104, RPO Spring Garden, Halifax, NS B3J 3S9
902/835-9706
President, Kimberlee A. Mitchell
Publications: NSDA Newsletter; Membership Directory, a.

**ORDRE PROFESSIONNEL DES DIÉTÉTISTES DU QUÉBEC (OPDQ) (1956)**
#703, 1425, boul René-Lévesque ouest, Montréal, QC H3G 1T7
514/393-3733, Téléc: 514/393-3582
Courrier électronique: opdq@opdq.org, URL: http://www.opdq.org
Directrice générale, Arlette Marcotte
Présidente, Micheline Seguin Bernier
Directrice des communications, Annie Langlois, Dt.P.
Publications: Diététique en action; Contact

**PRINCE EDWARD ISLAND DIETETIC ASSOCIATION**
PO Box 2575, Charlottetown, PE C1A 8C2
902/892-6004
Provincial Representative, Betty McNab
President, Margie Kays
Publications: Prince Edward Dietetic Association Newsletter

**SASKATCHEWAN DIETETIC ASSOCIATION (SDA) (1958)**
PO Box 3894, Regina, SK S4P 3R8
306/359-3040, Fax: 306/757-8161
Provincial President, Michael Chan
Administration, Teressa Isaac
Publications: SDA Newsletter 3-4 pa

**Canadian Down Syndrome Society/Société canadienne du Syndrome de Down (CDSS) (1987)**
#811 - 14 St. NW, Calgary, AB T2N 2A4
403/270-8500, Fax: 403/270-8291, Toll Free: 1-800-883-5608, Email: 702698@mail.ican.ca
Executive Director, Dianna Jossa
Publications: CDSS News

**Canadian Dyslexia Association/Association canadienne de la dyslexie (1991)**
25, rue St-Médard, Aylmer, QC J9H 1Z4
819/684-0542, Fax: 819/684-6157
Director, Louise Ward
Publications: Dyslexia Concerns Us

**Canadian Federation of Medical Students**
#500, 505 University Ave., Toronto, ON M5G 1X4
416/595-9778, Fax: 416/595-9778
President, Natasha Leighl
Vice-President, Education, Bridget Fernandez
Vice-President, Communications, Stephen Brown

**Canadian Foundation of Homeopathic Research & Development**
4624 - 99th St., Edmonton, AB T6E 5H5
403/438-4465
Executive Director, Anne MacFerlene

**Canadian Foundation for the Study of Infant Deaths/Fondation canadienne sur l'étude de la mortalité infantile (CFSID) (1973)**
**SIDS Foundation**
#308, 586 Eglinton Ave. East, Toronto, ON M4P 1P2
416/488-3260, Fax: 416/488-3864, Toll Free: 1-800-363-7437, Email: sidscanada@inforamp.net, URL: http://www.sidscanada.org/sids.html
Executive Director, Beverley De Bruyn
Publications: The Baby's Breath
Affiliates: SIDS International

**Canadian Health Coalition/Coalition canadienne de la santé (1979)**
2841 Riverside Dr., Ottawa, ON K1V 8X7
613/521-3400, Fax: 613/521-4655
Coordinator, Pam Fitzgerald
Publications: Medicare Monitor

**Canadian Health Economics Research Association/Association canadienne pour la recherche en économie de la santé (CHERA) (1982)**
Abramsky Hall, 3rd Fl., Queen's University, Kingston, ON K7L 3N6
613/545-6000, ext.4871, Fax: 613/545-6353, Email: chera@post.queensu.ca
Executive Coordinator, Bill Swan
President, Raisa Deber
Publications: CHERAction

**Canadian Hematology Society/Societe canadienne d'hematologie (1971)**
#206, 435 St. Laurent Blvd., Ottawa, ON K1H 8L6
613/737-8178, Fax: 613/737-8141, Email: cag@magi.com
Sec.-Treas., Gail Rock, Ph.D., M.D.
Publications: Canadian Hematology Newsletter

### Canadian Hemochromatosis Society/Société canadienne de l'hémochromatose (CHS) (1982)
#272, 7000 Minoru Blvd., Richmond, BC V6Y 3Z5
604/279-7135, Fax: 604/279-7138, Email: chcts@istar.ca
National Vice-President, Elizabeth Minish
National President, Charm Cottingham
Publications: Among Ourselves
Affiliates: Haemochromatosis Society of Great Britain; Haemochromatosis Society of Southern Africa; Haemochromatosis Research Foundation (Albany) New York; Association hémochromatose France; Haemochromatosis Society Australia

### Canadian Hemophilia Society/Société canadienne de l'hémophilie (CHS) (1953)
#1210, 625, av President Kennedy, Montréal, QC H3A 1K2
514/848-0503, Fax: 514/848-9661
Executive Director, Lindee David
Finance Manager, Pierre Latreille
Publications: Hemophilia Today
Affiliates: World Federation of Hemophilia

### Canadian Implant Association/L'Association canadienne des implantes intraoculaires (CIA) (1975)
5591, Côte des Neiges, Montréal, QC H3T 1Y8
514/735-1133, Fax: 514/731-0657
President, Dr. Marvin L. Kwitko
Affiliates: International Intraocular Implant Council

### Canadian Infectious Disease Society/Société canadienne de maladies infectieuses (CIDS) (1978)
774 Echo Dr., Ottawa, ON K1S 5N8
613/730-6251, Fax: 613/730-1116
President, Dr. Gary Garber
Secretary, Dr. Anne-Marie Bourgault
Publications: CIDS Newsletter

### Canadian Institute of Academic Medicine/Institut canadien de médecine académique (CIAM) (1990)
774 Echo Dr., Ottawa, ON K1S 5P2
613/730-0687, Fax: 613/730-1196
Contact, Dr. James C. Hogg

### Canadian Institute of Child Health/Institut canadien de la santé infantile (CICH) (1977)
#512, 885 Meadowlands Dr. East, Ottawa, ON K2C 3N2
613/224-4144, Fax: 613/224-4145, Email: cich@igs.net, URL: http://www.cich.ca
Executive Director, Denise Avard
Publications: Child Health
Affiliates: Canadian Coalition for the Prevention of Developmental Disabilities

### Canadian Institute of Health Care
1851 Eglinton Ave. West, Toronto, ON M6E 2J6
416/785-5572
Executive Director, M. Lapuente

### Canadian Institute of Hypnotism (CIH) (1953)
110, rue Greystone, Montréal, QC H9R 5T6
514/426-1010, Fax: 514/426-4680
Executive Director, Maurice Kershaw
Publications: Newsletter of CIH

### Canadian Institute of Public Health Inspectors/Institut canadien des inspecteurs en hygiène publique (CIPHI) (1934)
#201, 38 Auriga Dr., Nepean, ON K2E 8A5
613/224-7568, Fax: 613/224-6055
Executive Director, James D. Bradley
Publications: Environmental Health Review

### Canadian Liver Foundation/Fondation canadienne du foie (CLF) (1969)
#200, 365 Bloor St. East, Toronto, ON M4W 3L4
416/964-1953, Fax: 416/964-0024, Toll Free: 1-800-563-5483, Email: clf@liver.ca, URL: http://www.liver.ca
Executive Director, Donald R. Brown, QC
Publications: Liver Letter; Annual Research Report

### Canadian Lung Association/Association pulmonaire du Canada (CLA) (1900)
#508, 1900 City Park Dr., Gloucester, ON K1J 1A3
613/747-6776, Fax: 613/747-7430, Email: info@lung.ca, URL: http://www.lung.ca
President & CEO, Margo Craig Garrison
Affiliates: Canadian Nurses' Respiratory Society; Canadian Thoracic Society; Canadian Physiotherapy Cardio-Respiratory Society

#### ALBERTA LUNG ASSOCIATION
PO Box 4500, Edmonton, AB T6E 6K2
403/492-0354, Fax: 403/492-0362, Toll Free: 1-800-661-5864
Executive Director, Gary Lathan
Yellowknife Branch Office: PO Box 121, Yellowknife, NT X1A 2N1, 867/920-2929

#### ASSOCIATION PULMONAIRE DU QUÉBEC/QUÉBEC LUNG ASSOCIATION
#100, 4837, rue Boyer, Montréal, QC H2J 3E6
514/596-0805, Téléc: 514/596-1883
Directeur général, Claude Robitaille

#### BC LUNG ASSOCIATION (BCLA) (1903)
2675 Oak St., Vancouver, BC V6H 2K2
604/731-5864, Fax: 604/731-5810
Email: info@bc.lung.ca
Executive Director, Scott McDonald
President, Richard Gage
Publications: Your Health

#### CANADIAN THORACIC SOCIETY/SOCIÉTÉ CANADIENNE DE THORACOLOGIE (CTS) (1958)
c/o Canadian Lung Association, #508, 1900 City Park Dr., Gloucester, ON K1J 1A3
613/747-6776, Fax: 613/747-7430
URL: http://www.lung.ca/thorax/index.html
Sections Coordinator, Michelle Gaudreau
Publications: Airwaves
Affiliates: American Thoracic Society

#### THE LUNG ASSOCIATION OF NOVA SCOTIA
17 Alma Cres., Halifax, NS B3N 3E6
902/443-8141, Fax: 902/445-2573, Toll Free: 1-800-465-5864
Email: info@ns.lung.ca
Executive Director, Bill VanGorder

#### MANITOBA LUNG ASSOCIATION
629 McDermot Ave., 2nd Fl., Winnipeg, MB R3A 1P6
204/774-5501, Fax: 204/772-5083
Executive Director, Arlene Gibson

#### NEW BRUNSWICK LUNG ASSOCIATION/ASSOCIATION PULMONAIRE DU NOUVEAU-BRUNSWICK
Victoria Health Centre, #257, 65 Brunswick St., Fredericton, NB E3B 1G5
506/455-8961, Fax: 506/462-0939, Toll Free: 1-800-565-5864
Executive Director, Ken Maybee

#### NEWFOUNDLAND LUNG ASSOCIATION (NLA) (1944)
292 LeMarchant Rd., PO Box 5250, Stn C, St. John's, NF A1C 5W1
709/726-4664, Fax: 709/726-2550
Executive Director, Peggy Johnson

#### ONTARIO LUNG ASSOCIATION (OLA) (1945)
#201, 573 King St. East, Toronto, ON M5A 4L3
416/864-9911, Fax: 416/864-9916, Toll Free: 1-800-668-7682
Email: olalung@titan.tcn.net, URL: http://www.on.lung.ca
President & CEO, R. Ross Reid
Director, Marketing & Communications, Jill Palmer
Publications: LungLine; Ontario Respiratory Care Society Update, 3 pa; Ontario Thoracic Reviews
Affiliates: Ontario Thoracic Society; Ontario Respiratory Care Society

#### PRINCE EDWARD ISLAND LUNG ASSOCIATION (1936)
#2, 1 Rochford St., Charlottetown, PE C1A 9L2
902/892-5957, Fax: 902/368-7281
Email: info@pei.lung.ca, URL: http://www.lung.ca
Executive Director, Vicki Bryanton
Executive Assistant, Bernadette Flood
Affiliates: Canadian Thoracic Society; Canadian Nurses Respiratory Society; Canadian Physio-Cardio Respiratory Society

#### SASKATCHEWAN LUNG ASSOCIATION (SLA) (1911)
Saskatchewan Anti-Tuberculosis League
1231 - 8 St. East, Saskatoon, SK S7H 0S5
306/343-9511, Fax: 306/343-7007
Email: info@sk.lung.ca, URL: http://www.sk.lung.ca
Executive Director, Brian Graham, Ph.D.
Publications: Life & Breath

#### YUKON LUNG ASSOCIATION
PO Box 4754, Whitehorse, YT Y1A 4N6
867/668-6974
President, Marian Bakica

### Canadian Marfan Association/Association du syndrome de Marfan (1986)
4216 Pheasant Run, Mississauga, ON L5L 2B9
905/480-9449
Executive Director, Laura Libralesso
President, Anne Bakewell
Publications: NewsLinks

### Canadian Massage Therapist Alliance/Alliance canadienne de massothérapeutes (CMTA) (1991)
#1807, 365 Bloor St. East, Toronto, ON M4W 3L4
416/968-2149, Fax: 416/968-6818, Email: cmta@collinscan.com, URL: http://www.collinscan.com/~collins/clientspgs/cmtai.html
Chair, Monica Gillis
Publications: Hand in Hand

### Canadian Medical Association/Association médicale canadienne (CMA) (1867)
1867 Alta Vista Dr., Ottawa, ON K1G 3Y6
613/731-9331, Fax: 613/731-9013, Toll Free: 1-800-267-9703, URL: http://www.cma.ca
President, Dr. Victor Dirnfeld, M.D.
Secretary General, L.P. Landry
Publications: Canadian Medical Association Journal; Canadian Journal of Surgery; Humane Medicine; Canadian Journal of Respiratory Therapy; CMA News; Strategy
Affiliates: Association of Canadian Medical Colleges; Association of Canadian Pharmaceutical Physicians; Canadian Academy of Sport Medicine; Canadian Anaesthetists Society; Canadian Association of Emergency Physicians; Canadian Association of Gastroenterology; Canadian Association of General Surgeons; Canadian Association of Internes & Residents; Canadian Association of Medical Microbiologists; Canadian Association of Nuclear Medicine; Canadian Association of Pathologists; Canadian Association of Physical Medicine & Rehabilitation; Canadian Association of Radiologists; Canadian Cardiovascular Society; Canadian Critical Care Society; Canadian Dermatology Association; Canadian Life Insurance Medical Officers

Association; Canadian Medical Protective Association; College of Family Physicians of Canada; Royal College of Physicians & Surgeons of Canada; Society of Obstetricians & Gynaecologists of Canada

**ALBERTA MEDICAL ASSOCIATION**
#400, 12230 - 106 Ave. NW, Edmonton, AB T5N 3Z1
403/482-2626, Fax: 403/482-5445
Email: ama_mail@amda.ab.ca, URL: http://www.amda.ab.ca
Executive Director, Dr. Robert A. Burns
Assistant Executive Director, Ron Kustra

**ASSOCIATION MÉDICALE DU QUÉBEC/QUÉBEC MEDICAL ASSOCIATION (AMQ) (1929)**
#660, 1000, rue de La Gauchetière ouest, Montréal, QC H3B 4W5
514/866-0660, Téléc: 514/866-0670, Ligne sans frais: 1-800-363-3932
Directeur administratif, Gilles Bellefeuille
Agente de communication, Michelle Hébert
Publications: AMQ Express/QMA Express

**BRITISH COLUMBIA MEDICAL ASSOCIATION (BCMA) (1900)**
#115, 1665 Broadway West, Vancouver, BC V6J 5A4
604/736-5551, Fax: 604/736-4566
Email: nfinlays@bcma.bc.ca, URL: http://www.bcma.org
Executive Director, Dr. Norman D. Finlayson
President, Dr. Granger Avery
Communications Officer, David McPhee
Publications: The British Columbia Medical Journal; BCMA News, bi-m.

**MANITOBA MEDICAL ASSOCIATION/ASSOCIATION MÉDICALE DU MANITOBA (MMA)**
125 Sherbrook St., Winnipeg, MB R3C 2B5
204/786-7565, Fax: 204/775-9696
Executive Director, John A. Laplume
Communications Officer, Debbie Bride
Publications: Inter-Com

**MEDICAL SOCIETY OF NOVA SCOTIA (MSNS)**
City of Lakes Business Park, 5 Spectacle Lake Dr., Dartmouth, NS B3B 1X7
902/468-1866, Fax: 902/468-6578
Executive Director, Richard Dyke, MBA, CMA
President, Cynthia Forbes
Communications Officer, Camille Finlay
Publications: News

**MEDICAL SOCIETY OF PRINCE EDWARD ISLAND (MSPEI) (1855)**
559 North River Rd., Charlottetown, PE C1E 1J7
902/368-7303, Fax: 902/566-3934
Executive Director, Marilyn Lowther

**NEW BRUNSWICK MEDICAL SOCIETY/SOCIÉTÉ MÉDICALE DU NOUVEAU-BRUNSWICK (NBMS) (1867)**
176 York St., Fredericton, NB E3B 3N7
506/458-8860, Fax: 506/458-9853, Toll Free: 1-800-661-2001
Executive Director, David H. Balmain, CAE
Communications Officer, Janet Maston
Publications: NBMS Newsletter; President's Letter, bi-m.

**NEWFOUNDLAND & LABRADOR MEDICAL ASSOCIATION (NLMA) (1924)**
164 MacDonald Dr., St. John's, NF A1A 4B3
709/726-7424, Fax: 709/726-7525
Executive Director, Bruce Squires
Communications Officer, Lana Collins
Publications: Communiqué

**NORTHWEST TERRITORIES MEDICAL ASSOCIATION**
4920 - 47th St., 3rd Fl., PO Box 1709, Yellowknife, NT X1A 2P3
867/873-9253, Fax: 867/873-9254
CEO, Paula Lessard

**ONTARIO MEDICAL ASSOCIATION (OMA) (1880)**
#300, 525 University Ave., Toronto, ON M5G 2K7
416/599-2580, Fax: 416/599-9309
URL: http://www.oma.org
Chief Executive Officer, David Pattenden
Executive Director, Corporate Affairs & Administration, Tom Magyarody
President, John Gray
Publications: Ontario Medical Review

**SASKATCHEWAN MEDICAL ASSOCIATION (SMA) (1906)**
#200, 211 - 4th Ave. South, Saskatoon, SK S7K 1N1
306/244-2196, Fax: 306/653-1631, Toll Free: 1-800-667-3781
Email: SMA@sk.sympatico.ca
Executive Director, Dr. Brian Scharfstein
Communications Officer, Donna Hjertaas

**YUKON MEDICAL ASSOCIATION**
406 Lambert St., Whitehorse, YT Y1A 1Z7
867/667-4421, Fax: 867/668-3736
President, Dr. Roger Mitchell
Vice-President, Dr. Cindy Breitkreitz
Treasurer, Dr. Bruce Beaton
Affiliates: British Columbia Medical Association

### Canadian Medical Foundation
1867 Alta Vista Dr., Ottawa, ON K1G 3Y6
613/731-9331, Fax: 613/731-1779
Manager, Darlene Brown

### Canadian Medical Malpractice Prevention Association (CMMPA) (1987)
#90293, 2900 Warden Ave., Scarborough, ON M1W 3Y8
416/969-1587, Fax: 416/496-2825
President, Sharon Roberts
Vice-President, Suzanne Christie

### Canadian MedicAlert Foundation, Inc./Fondation canadienne MedicAlert, inc. (1961)
**MedicAlert**
#301, 250 Ferrand Dr., North York, ON M3C 3G8
416/696-0267, 0142, Fax: 416/696-0156, Toll Free: 1-800-668-1507
President, Shelagh Tippet-Fagyas
Chairman, Ivan C. Juul-Hansen
Affiliates: MedicAlert Foundation International

### Canadian Memorial Chiropractic College (CMCC) (1945)
1900 Bayview Ave., Toronto, ON M4G 3E6
416/482-2340, Fax: 416/482-9745, Email: communications@cmcc.ca, URL: http://www.cmcc.ca
Chair of the Board, Dr. David Gohn
President, Dr. J.A. Moss
Publications: Primary Contact

### Canadian Natural Health Association (1960)
#5, 439 Wellington St. West, Toronto, ON M5V 1E7
416/977-2642, Fax: 416/977-1536
Executive Director, Hélène Roussel
Publications: Living Naturally
Affiliates: American Natural Hygiene Society

### Canadian Naturopathic Association/Association canadienne de naturopathie (CNA) (1930)
PO Box 4520, Stn C, Calgary, AB T2T 5N3
403/244-4487, Fax: 403/244-2340, Info Line: 403/245-0633
Executive Director, Marjorie Zingle, CAE
National Coordinator, Heather MacFarlane
Publications: Journal of Naturopathic Medicine; Canadian Naturopathic Association Newsletter

### Canadian Network of Toxicology Centres/Réseau canadien des centres de toxicologie (CNTC) (1983)
Bovey Bldg., 2nd Fl., Gordon St., Guelph, ON N1G 2W1
519/837-3320, Fax: 519/837-3861, Email: dwarner@tox.uoguelph.ca, URL: http://www.uoguelph.ca/cntc
Executive Director, Dr. Len Ritter
Program Coordinator, Donna Warner
Controller, J.W. Cooper
Publications: CNTC News
Affiliates: Administrative office for the Canadian Network of Toxicology Centres

### Canadian Neurological Society/Société canadienne de neurologie (CNS)
#810, 906 - 12th Ave., Calgary, AB T2R 1K7
403/229-9544, Fax: 403/229-1661
President, Dr. N. Pillay
Executive Director, Lucile Edwards
Affiliates: Canadian Medical Association

### Canadian Occupational Therapy Foundation/La Fondation canadienne d'Ergothérapie (COTF) (1983)
#602, 55 Eglinton Ave. East, Toronto, ON M4P 1G8
416/487-5438
Executive Assistant, Charmaine Francis

### Canadian Ophthalmological Society/Société canadienne d'opthalmologie (COS) (1937)
#610, 1525 Carling Ave., Ottawa, ON K1Z 8R9
613/729-6779, Fax: 613/729-7209, Toll Free: 1-800-267-5763, Email: cos@eyesite.ca, URL: http://eyesite.ca
Executive Director, Hubert Drouin
Publications: Canadian Journal of Opthalmology; Perspectives, q.
Affiliates: Canadian Medical Association; Concilium Ophthalmological Universale

### Canadian Orthopaedic Foundation/Fondation orthopédique du Canada (COF) (1945)
#5100, One First Canadian Place, Toronto, ON M5X 1K2
800/461-3639, Fax: 800/244-8825
Executive Secretary, K. DeCruz
President, Michael A. Simurda
Secretary, Dr. Robert Hollinshead
Treasurer, Dr. Hubert Labelle
Publications: Bulletin
Affiliates: World Orthopaedic Concern; Canadian Medical Association

### Canadian Orthoptic Council
c/o University Hospital, Dept. of Ophthalmology, Saskatoon, SK S7N 0X0
306/966-8045
Contact, Dr. K. Romanchuk

### The Canadian Orthoptic Society (TCOS) (1967)
I.W.K. Children's Hospital, Orthoptic Clinic, 5850 University Ave., PO Box 3070, Halifax, NS B3J 3G9
902/428-8021, Fax: 902/428-3207
President, Brenda Hum-Boutilier

### Canadian Osteogenesis Imperfecta Society
128 Thornhill Cres., Chatham, ON N7L 4M3
Contact, Mary Lou Kearney
Publications: Connect

### Canadian Osteopathic Aid Society (COAS) (1960)
575 Waterloo St., London, ON N6B 2R2
519/439-5521
Executive Secretary, Marguerite Torney

### Canadian Osteopathic Association (1926)
575 Waterloo St., London, ON N6B 2R2

519/439-5521
Administrative Secretary, Marguerite Torney

### Canadian Paediatric Society/Société canadienne de pédiatrie (CPS) (1951)
#100, 2204 Walkley Rd., Ottawa, ON K1G 4G8
613/526-9397, ext.231, Fax: 613/526-3332, Email: info@cps.ca, URL: http://www.cps.ca
President, Dr. John Watts
Vice-President, Dr. Paul Munk
Publications: CPS News; Gazette SCP; Paediatrics & Child Health

### Canadian Pain Society/Société canadienne pour le traitement de la douleur (1982)
University of Vancouver, Dept. of Psychology, Vancouver, BC V6T 1Z4
604/822-3948, Fax: 604/822-6923
President, Kenneth Craig
Publications: Pain Research & Management
Affiliates: International Association for the Study of Pain

### Canadian Palliative Care Association/Association canadienne des soins palliatifs (CPCA) (1991)
5 Blackburn Ave., Ottawa, ON K1N 8A2
Toll Free: 1-800-668-2785
Executive Director, Linda Lysne
Publications: AVISO; Directory of Services

### Canadian Paraplegic Association/Association canadienne des paraplégiques (CPA) (1945)
#320, 1101 Prince of Wales Dr., Ottawa, ON K2C 3W7
613/723-1033, Fax: 613/723-1060, Email: eboyd@cyberplus.ca
Managing Director, Eric Boyd
President, Marie Trudeau
Publications: Caliper

### Canadian Paraplegic Association (Ontario)
**CPA Ontario**
520 Sutherland Dr., Toronto, ON M4G 3V9
416/422-5644, Fax: 416/422-5943, Email: on@canparaplegic.org
Executive Director, William Adair
Publications: Outspoken
Affiliates: National Rehabilitation Association; Canadian Association of Rehabilitation Professionals

### Canadian Pediatric Foundation/La fondation canadienne de pédiatrie (CPF) (1985)
#100, 2204 Walkley Rd., Ottawa, ON K1G 4G8
613/526-9397, ext.338, Fax: 613/526-3332, Toll Free: 1-800-580-0940, Email: cpf@cps.ca
President, Barrett A. Adams, Dr.

### Canadian Pelvic Inflammatory Disease Society/La Société canadienne AIP (1985)
**Canadian PID Society**
PO Box 33804, Stn D, Vancouver, BC V6J 4L6
604/684-5704, Info Line: 604/684-5704
Coordinator, Jill Weiss

### Canadian Peptic Ulcer Research Foundation
Manulife Centre, #3200, 10180 - 101 St., Edmonton, AB T5J 3W8
403/425-9510, Fax: 403/429-3044, Telex: 037-2073
Contact, Dr. Alan B. Thomson

### Canadian Physiotherapy Association/L'Association canadienne de physiothérapie (CPA) (1920)
#410, 2345 Yonge St., Toronto, ON M4P 2E5
416/932-1888, Fax: 416/932-9708, Toll Free: 1-800-387-8679, Email: information@physiotherapy.ca, URL: http://www.physiotherapy.ca
CEO, Dan Stapleton
Director, Administration & Membership Services, Elizabeth DiChiara
Director, Communications & Public Affairs, Katrina Schmitz
Director, Education, Practice & Research, Dianne Parker-Taillon
Director, Business Development, Melanie Gralvin
Publications: Physiotherapy Canada; Contact, bi-m.
Affiliates: World Confederation for Physical Therapy; Alliance of Physiotherapy Regulatory Boards of Canada; Canadian University Physiotherapy Academic Council; Health Action Lobby (HEAL); Physiotherapy Foundation of Canada; Accreditation Council for Canadian Physiotherapy Academic Programs

### Canadian Post-MD Education Registry/Système informatisé sur les stagiaires post-MD en formation clinique (CAPER) (1986)
774 Echo Dr., Ottawa, ON K1S 5P2
613/730-1204, Fax: 613/730-1196
Director, A.D. Thurber
Office Manager, K. Edmonds
Publications: The CAPER Annual Census of Post-M.D. Trainees
Affiliates: Association of Canadian Medical Colleges

### Canadian Psoriasis Foundation/Fondation canadienne du psoriasis (CPF) (1983)
#500A, 1306 Wellington St., Ottawa, ON K1Y 3B2
613/728-4000, Fax: 613/728-8913, Toll Free: 1-800-265-0926
National Coordinator, Patricia Normandeau
President, Susan Barylo
Executive Director, Don Rutherford
Publications: Canadian Psoriasis Foundation
Affiliates: US National Psoriasis Foundation; Psoriasis Association of Great Britain

### Canadian Public Health Association/Association canadienne de santé publique (CPHA) (1912)
#400, 1565 Carling Ave., Ottawa, ON K1Z 8R1
613/725-3769, Fax: 613/725-9826, Email: comm@cpha.ca, URL: http://www.cpha.ca
Executive Director, Gerald Dafoe
President, Dr. John Hastings
Assistant Executive Director, Management, Janet MacLachlan
Publications: Canadian Journal of Public Health; CPHA Health Digest, q.
Affiliates: Canadian Association of Teachers of Social & Preventive Medicine; The Canadian Society for International Health; Canadian Coalition for High Blood Pressure Prevention & Control; Society for the Study of Pathophysiology of Pregnancy

#### ALBERTA PUBLIC HEALTH ASSOCIATION (APHA) (1943)
11715 - 101 St., Peace River, AB T8S 1L8
403/624-7120, Fax: 403/624-7122
President, H. Campsall
Publications: The Promoter

#### ASSOCIATION POUR LA SANTÉ PUBLIQUE DU QUÉBEC/QUÉBEC PUBLIC HEALTH ASSOCIATION (ASPQ) (1943)
3958, rue Dandurand, Montréal, QC H1X 1P7
514/593-9939, Téléc: 514/593-4554
Directrice générale, Janine Dalaire
Président, Françoise Bouchard
Publications: Le périscoop; Bulletin de santé publique, trimestriel

#### BRITISH COLUMBIA PUBLIC HEALTH ASSOCIATION (BCPHA)
#101, 2182 - 12th St. West, Vancouver, BC V6K 2N4
604/731-4970, Fax: 604/731-5965
Executive Director, Kaela Jubas
President, Ann Geddes
Publications: The Public's Health

#### MANITOBA PUBLIC HEALTH ASSOCIATION (MPHA) (1940)
PO Box 22002, RPO Broadway, Winnipeg, MB R3C 4K6
204/477-6336
President, Brian Peel
Publications: MPHA Newsletter

#### NEWFOUNDLAND PUBLIC HEALTH ASSOCIATION
OXFAM Resource Centre, 382 Duckworth St., St. John's, NF A1C 1H8
709/753-2202, Fax: 709/753-4110
President, Linda Ross

#### ONTARIO PUBLIC HEALTH ASSOCIATION/ASSOCIATION POUR LA SANTÉ PUBLIQUE DE L'ONTARIO (OPHA) (1949)
#202, 468 Queen St. East, Toronto, ON M5A 1T7
416/367-3313, Fax: 416/367-2844, Toll Free: 1-800-267-6817
Executive Director, Peter R. Elson
President, Winston Miller
Publications: Health Beat; OPHA News
Affiliates: ANDSOOHA - Public Health Nursing Management; Association of Ontario Public Health Business Administrators; Association of Supervisory Public Health Inspectors; Canadian Institute of Public Health Inspectors (Ontario Branch); Ontario Society of Nutritionists in Public Health; RNAO (Community Health Nurses Interest Group); Ontario Society of Public Health Dentists; Ontario Association of Health Promotion Specialists in Public Health

#### PUBLIC HEALTH ASSOCIATION OF NOVA SCOTIA (PHANS)
PO Box 20129, RPO Spryfield, Halifax, NS B3R 2K9
902/477-6102, Fax: 902/479-1177
President, Marjorie Willison

#### SASKATCHEWAN PUBLIC HEALTH ASSOCIATION INC.
159 McKee Cres., Regina, SK S4S 5N7
President, Sandra Craig, Bus: 306/787-3180

### Canadian Rett Syndrome Association (CRSA)
#301, 555 Fairway Rd., Kitchener, ON N2C 1X4
416/494-1954, Fax: 519/893-1169
President, Eugene Bradley

### Canadian Rheumatology Association/Société canadienne de rhumatologie
2705, boul Laurier, Ste-Foy, QC G1V 4G2
418/654-2242, Fax: 418/654-2798, URL: http://www.arthritis.ca/cra/index.html
President, Dr. Simon Carette
Affiliates: Canadian Medical Association, Royal College of Physicians & Surgeons of Canada

### Canadian Sickle Cell Society/La société de l'anemie falciforme du Canada (1978)
#33, 6999, Côte des Neiges, Montréal, QC H3S 2B8
514/735-5109, Fax: 514/735-5100
Regional Director, Rosetta Cadogan

### Canadian Sleep Society/Société canadienne du sommeil (CSS) (1986)
#5055, 3080 Yonge St., Toronto, ON M4N 3N1
416/483-6260, Fax: 416/483-7081, URL: http://bisleep.medsch.ucla.edu/CSS/css.html
President, C.F.P. George, M.D., Email: cgeorge@julian.uwo.ca
Sec.-Treas., Sandra Halko, RPSGT, Email: sleeplab@vichosp.london.on.ca
Publications: Vigilance
Affiliates: Association of Professional Sleep Societies; World Federation of Sleep Research

### Canadian Society of Aerospace Medicine/Société médicale aéronautique du Canada (CSAM)
c/o Canadian Aeronautics & Space Institute, 818, 130 Slater St., Ottawa, ON K1P 6E2

613/234-0191, Fax: 613/234-9039, Email: casi@casi.ca, URL: http://www.casi.ca
Executive Director, Ian M. Ross
President, Dr. C. Thibeault
Publications: CASI Log
Affiliates: Canadian Medical Association; Aerospace Medical Association

**Canadian Society of Allergy & Clinical Immunology/Société canadienne d'allergie et d'immunologie clinique (CSACI) (1962)**
774 Echo Dr., Ottawa, ON K1S 5N8
613/730-6272, Fax: 613/730-1116, Email: csaci@rcpsc.edu
President, Dr. Zave Chad
Vice-President, Dr. A. Becker
Sec.-Treas., Dr. E. Leith
Publications: CJACI
Affiliates: Canadian Allergy, Asthma & Immunology Foundation

**Canadian Society of Cardiovascular & Thoracic Surgeons/Société des chirurgiens cardiovasculaires et thoraciques**
Ottawa Heart Institute, Civic Hospital, #211, 1053 Carling Ave., Ottawa, ON K1Y 4E9
613/761-4233, Fax: 613/761-5367
Secretary, Dr. Roy Masters
Publications: Newsletter

**Canadian Society for Clinical Investigation/Société canadienne de recherches cliniques (CSCI) (1951)**
774 Echo Dr., Ottawa, ON K1S 5N8
613/730-6240, Fax: 613/730-8194, Email: caroline.frewer@rcpsc.edu
Sec.-Treas., Dr. J.H. Matthews
President, Dr. Michel G. Bergeron
Executive Director, Caroline Frewer
Publications: Clinical & Investigative Medicine; CSCI News Bulletin, s-a.

**Canadian Society of Clinical Neurophysiologists/Société canadienne de neurophysiologistes cliniques (CSCN) (1958)**
PO Box 4220, Stn C, Calgary, AB T2T 5N1
403/229-9544, Fax: 403/229-1661, Email: brains@ccns.org, URL: http://www.ccns.org
Executive Director, Lucile Edwards
President, Dr. G.B. Young
Publications: Canadian Journal of Neurological Sciences
Affiliates: Canadian Medical Association; Canadian Association for Neuroscience; Canadian Association of Neuroscience Nurses; Canadian Stroke Society; Canadian League Against Epilepsy; Canadian Headache Society; Movement Disorders Group; Multiple Sclerosis Society of Canada; Amyotrophic Lateral Sclerosis Society of Canada; Canadian Peripheral Nerve Group

**Canadian Society of Cytology/Société canadienne de cytologie (CSC) (1961)**
Dept. of Pathology, McGill University, 3775 University St., Montréal, QC H3A 2B4
Fax: 514/398-2440
Sec.-Treas., Dr. M. Auger
Chairman, Dr. M.A. Duggan
Publications: CSC Bulletin
Affiliates: Canadian Association of Pathologists

**Canadian Society of Diagnostic Medical Sonographers (CSDMS) (1981)**
PO Box 1624, Yellowknife, NT X1A 2P2
867/743-2962, Fax: 867/743-2962, Toll Free: 1-800-273-6746, Email: csdms@nt.sympatico.ca
Executive Director, Sandra Mayer
Publications: Interface

**Canadian Society of Endocrinology & Metabolism/Société canadienne d'endocrinologie et métabolisme (CSEM) (1972)**
The Montreal Children's Hospital, 2300 Tupper St., #C1238, Montréal, QC H3H 1P3
514/934-4400, Fax: 514/934-4494
President, Dr. Otto Rorstad
Sec.-Treas., Dr. Cindy Goodyer
Publications: Newsletter; Membership Directory
Affiliates: Canadian Society of Clinical Investigation

**Canadian Society for the History of Medicine**
Memorial University of Newfoundland, Faculty of Medicine, St. John's, NF A1B 3V6
709/737-6592, Fax: 709/737-6400
Dr. John Crellin

**Canadian Society of Internal Medicine/Société canadienne de médecine interne (CSIM) (1984)**
774 Echo Dr., Ottawa, ON K1S 5N8
613/730-6244, Fax: 613/730-1116, Email: csim@rcpsc.edu
Head, M. Dallimore
Publications: CSIM Bulletin
Affiliates: Canadian Medical Association

**Canadian Society for International Health/Société canadienne de la santé internationale (CSIH) (1977)**
#902, 170 Laurier Ave. West, Ottawa, ON K1P 5V5
613/230-2654, Fax: 613/230-8401, Email: csih@fox.nstn.ca, URL: http://www.csih.org/csihmem.html
Executive Director, Charles A. Shields Jr., CAE
Publications: Synergy
Affiliates: Pan American Health Organization

**Canadian Society of Laboratory Technologists/Société canadienne des technologistes de laboratoire (CSLT) (1937)**
PO Box 2830, Stn A, Hamilton, ON L8N 3N8
905/528-8642, Fax: 905/528-4968, URL: http://www.cslt.com
Executive Director, E. Valerie Booth
Director of Communications, Kurt Davis, FCSLT, CAE
Publications: Canadian Journal of Medical Technology; Annual Roster
Affiliates: International Association of Medical Laboratory Technologists; Intersociety Council of Laboratory Medicine; Conjoint Council on Accreditation of Allied Programs in Health Care

**Canadian Society for Medical Mycology/Société canadienne de mycologie médicale (CSMM) (1987)**
Université de Montréal, Dept. of Microbiology & Immunology, PO Box 6128, Stn A, Montréal, QC H3C 3J7
514/343-7184, Fax: 514/343-5701, Email: louisr@globale.net
President, Dr. Louis de Repentigny
Publications: CSMM Newsletter
Affiliates: International Society for Human & Animal Mycology

**Canadian Society of Nephrology/Société canadienne de néphrologie (CSN) (1967)**
c/o Victoria General Hospital, Div. of Nephrology, #5076, 5820 University Ave., Halifax, NS B3H 1V8
902/473-4023, Fax: 902/473-2675
President, Dr. M.L. West, M.D.
Publications: ; Scientific Meeting Abstract, a.

**Canadian Society of Nutrition Management/Société canadienne de gestion de la nutrition**
#2M, 57 Simcoe St., PO Box 948, Oshawa, ON L1H 7N1
905/436-0145, Fax: 905/436-2969
Executive Director, Janet Milner

**Canadian Society of Orthopaedic Technologists/Société canadienne des technologistes en orthopédie (CSOT) (1972)**
#200, 4433 Sheppard Ave. East, Agincourt, ON M1S 1V3
416/292-0687, Fax: 416/292-1038, Email: cinacsot@idirect.com, URL: http://web.idirect.com/~csotcina/csot.html
Registrar/Office Manager, Pamela Smith
Publications: BodyCast; Newscast, q.

**Canadian Society of Otolaryngology - Head & Neck Surgery/Société canadienne d'otolaryngologie et de chirurgie cervico-faciale (CSO-HNS) (1947)**
55 MacGregor Ave., Toronto, ON M6S 2A1
519/439-1850, Fax: 519/672-4602
Administrator, Donna Humphrey
President, Dr. Murray Morrison
Publications: Journal of Otolaryngology
Affiliates: International Federation of Oto-Rhino-Laryngological Societies; Canadian Medical Association; Canadian Deaf & Hard of Hearing Forum

**Canadian Society of Plastic Surgeons/Société canadienne des chirurgiens plasticiens (CSPS) (1947)**
#917, 30, boul Saint-Joseph est, Montréal, QC H2T 1G9
514/843-5415, Fax: 514/843-5415, Toll Free: 1-800-665-5415, Email: csps_sccp@sympatico.ca, URL: http://www.plasticsurgery.ca
President, Dr. Gerald Moysa
Vice-President, Dr. D. Kimit Rai
Publications: CSPS News
Affiliates: Canadian Medical Association

**Canadian Society of Respiratory Therapists/La Société canadienne des thérapeutes respiratoires (CSRT) (1964)**
#102, 1785 Alta Vista Dr., Ottawa, ON K1G 3Y6
613/731-3164, Fax: 613/521-4314, Toll Free: 1-800-267-3422
Executive Director, Cheryl Homuth
Publications: RRT

**Canadian Society of Surgical Oncology/Société canadienne d'oncologie chirurgicale (CSSO)**
2075 Bayview Ave., #H326, North York, ON M4N 3M5
416/480-6950, Fax: 416/480-5253, Email: david.beatty@sunnybrook.on.ca
Secretary, Dr. D. Beatty
Affiliates: Canadian Oncology Society

**Canadian Society for Transfusion Medicine/Société canadienne de médecine transfusionnelle (CSTM) (1989)**
#306, 2311 McEown Ave., Saskatoon, SK S7J 2H3
306/374-7175
Director, Edna Blum
Publications: CSTM Bulletin

**Canadian Society for Vascular Surgery/Société canadienne de chirurgie vasculaire**
#100, 215 Bloor St. West, Toronto, ON M6S 1M8
416/763-3797, Fax: 416/763-3797
Secretary, Dr. Douglas Woostor

**Canadian Spinal Research Organization (CSRO) (1984)**
#1, 120 Newkirk Rd., Richmond Hill, ON L4C 9S7
905/508-4000, Fax: 905/508-4002, Toll Free: 1-800-361-4004, Email: csro@globalserve.net, URL: http://www.csro.com

President, Ray Wickson
Vice-President, Barry Munro
Publications: CSRO Quarterly

### Canadian Urological Association/Association canadienne d'urologie (1945)

Health Sciences Centre, Rm. GE446, 820 Sherbrook St., Winnipeg, MB R3A 1R9
204/787-3677, Fax: 204/787-3040, URL: http://www.cua.org
President, Dr. Philip Belitsky
Secretary, Denis H. Hosking
Publications: Newsletter
Affiliates: Canadian Medical Association

### Canadians for Health Research/Les Canadiens pour la recherche médicale (CHR) (1976)

PO Box 126, Westmount, QC H3Z 2T1
514/398-7478, Fax: 514/398-8361, Email: chrpat@total.net
President, Patricia Guyda
Administrative Assistant, Linda Bazinet
Publications: The Diary; Future Health/Perspectives Santé, q.

### Candlelighters Childhood Cancer Foundation Canada/Fondation des éclaireurs pour le cancer dans l'enfance Canada (CCCFC) (1987)

**Candlelighters Canada**

#401, 55 Eglinton Ave. East, Toronto, ON M4P 1G8
416/489-6440, Fax: 416/489-9812, Toll Free: 1-800-363-1062, Email: staff@candlelighters.ca, URL: http://www.candlelighters.ca
Executive Director, Eleanor G. Pask, RN, MScN, Ed.D.
President, Bill Buchanan, Email: buchanan@voyager.newcomm.net
Secretary, Richard A.B. Devenney
Treasurer, Winston Marcellin
Director, Fundraising, Karen Power
Director, Alberta, Valerie Figliuzzi, Bus: 403/460-8590
Director, BC, Ruth Morley, Bus: 604/372-3222
Director, Manitoba, Leslie Sneyd, Bus: 204/983-1067
Director, New Brunswick, Judy Allen, Bus: 506/847-9627
Director, Newfoundland, Pauline Hoseworthy, Bus: 709/726-1793
Director, Nova Scotia, Ainslie Machel-Campbell, Bus: 902/479-1549
Director, Ontario, Dr. Helen Pastoric, Email: pastoric@globalserve.net
Francophone Director, Camille de Varennes, Bus: 514/471-7498, Email: tulipe@accent.net
Director, Québec, Deborah McQuaig, Bus: 514/377-8800
Director, PEI, Janet MacQuarrie, Bus: 902/628-8195
Director, Saskatchewan, Chris Flogan, Bus: 306/764-1965
Publications: Contact; Resource Catalogue, a.

### Catholic Health Association of Canada/Association catholique canadienne de la santé (CHAC) (1939)

1247 Kilborn Pl., Ottawa, ON K1H 6K9
613/731-7148, Fax: 613/731-7797, Email: chac@web.net, URL: http://www.net-globe.com/chac/
President, Richard M. Haughian
Chairperson, Kateri Ghesquiere, SCJ
Publications: CHAC Info/Info ACCS; CHAC Review/Revue ACCS, q.

### Children's Oncology Care of Ontario Inc. (COCO) (1981)

**Ronald McDonald House**

26 Gerrard St. East, Toronto, ON M5B 1G3
416/977-0458, Fax: 416/977-8807
Executive Director, C. Kimpton
President, Betsy Wright
Publications: Ronald McDonald House Newsletter

### Children's Rehabilitation & Cerebral Palsy Association

The Neurological Centre, 2805 Kingsway, Vancouver, BC V5R 5H9
604/451-5511, Fax: 604/451-5651
Executive Director, Dot Ewen
Affiliates: International Cerebral Palsy Society

### Chinese Medicine & Acupuncture Association of Canada/L'Association de médecine chinoise et d'acupuncture du Canada (CMAAC)

154 Wellington St., London, ON N6B 2K8
519/642-1970, Fax: 519/642-2932
Director General, Hsi Ping Lin, Dr. Ac.

### Chronic Fatigue Syndrome/Myalgic Encephalomyelitis Group

**M.E. Association of Ontario**

PO Box 322, Stn K, Toronto, ON M4P 2G7
416/763-9025
Contact, Alan Stern

### College of Chiropractic Science

#235, 1333 Neilson Rd., Scarborough, ON M1B 4Y9
416/281-0640, Fax: 416/281-9519
President, Dr. Michael Willes
Affiliates: Canadian Chiropractic Association

### College of Dieticians of Ontario/L'Ordre des diététistes de l'Ontario (CDO)

700 Bay St., 14th Fl., Toronto, ON M5G 1Z6
416/327-8224, Fax: 416/327-0867
Registrar, Carol J. Shapiro
Publications: Resumé

### College of Family Physicians of Canada/Collège des médecins de famille du Canada (CFPC) (1954)

2630 Skymark Ave., Mississauga, ON L4W 5A4
905/629-0900, Fax: 905/629-0893, Email: info@cfpc.ca, URL: http://www.cfpc.ca
Executive Director, Dr. Calvin Gutkin
President, Dr. Nick Busing, MD, CCFP, FCFP
Publications: Canadian Family Physician
Alberta Chapter: President, Dr. Mary E. Hurlburt; Executive Secretary, Elaine R. Taschuk, #203, 12230 - 106 Ave., Edmonton, AB T5N 3Z1, 403/488-2395, Fax: 403/488-2396
British Columbia College of Family Physicians: Executive Director, Bev Kulyk; President, Dr. Kirstie L. Overhill, #350, 1665 West Broadway, Vancouver, BC V6J 1X1, 604/736-1877, Fax: 604/736-4675, Email: bccfp@bc.sympatico.ca
Manitoba Chapter: President, Dr. Kenneth L. Kliewer; Administrative Secretary, Susan Patek, PO Box 28076, RPO North Kildonan, Winnipeg, MB R2G 4E9, 204/668-3667, Fax: 204/668-3663
New Brunswick College of Family Physicians: President, Dr. Gregory C. Archibald; Executive Secretary, Louise Farr, 270 Keswick Ridge Rd., Mouth of Keswick, NB E0H 1N0, 506/363-2600, Fax: 506/363-2601, Email: nbcfp@nb.sympatico.ca
Newfoundland & Labrador Chapter: President, Dr. Chris Randell; Administrator, Debbie Rideout, c/o FPU Health Sciences Centre, Memorial University, 300 Prince Philip Dr., St. John's, NF A1B 3V6, 709/753-9041, Fax: 709/737-2040
Nova Scotia College of Family Physicians: President, Robert A. Oliver; Administrator, Beth MacPherson, RR#1, PO Box 925, Bedford, NS B0J 3J0, 902/823-1021, Fax: 902/823-1035, Email: nstn1829@fox.nstn.ca
Ontario College of Family Physicians: Executive Director, L. Cheryl Katz; President, Dr. Ralph Masi, #800, 357 Bay St., Toronto, ON M5H 2T7, 905/867-9646, Fax: 905/867-9990
Prince Edward Island Chapter: President, Dr. George Carruthers; Chapter Secretary, Elaine Caseley, RR#4, Kensington, PE C0B 1M0, 902/836-4638, Fax: 902/836-4638, Email: cfpc.pei@pei.sympatico.ca
Saskatchewan Chapter: President, Dr. Cheryl Zagozeski; Administrator, Mona Chappell, PO Box 7111, Saskatoon, SK S7K 4J1, 306/665-7714, Fax: 306/665-7714, Email: mchappel@eagle.wbm.ca
Section du Québec: Présidente, Dr. Francine Léger; Secrétaire administrative, Micheline Guilbault, #101, 310 av Victoria, Westmount, QC H3Z 2M9, 514/481-5962, Téléc: 514/481-6948

### College of Medical Laboratory Technologists of Ontario/Ordre des technologistes de laboratoire médical de l'Ontario (CMLTO) (1993)

#330, 10 Bay St., Toronto, ON M5J 2R8
416/861-9605, Fax: 416/861-0934, Toll Free: 1-800-323-9672, Email: swoodcock@cmlto.on.ca
Registrar, Sheila Woodcock
Publications: Focus

### Community & Hospital Infection Control Association Canada/Association pour la prévention des infections à l'hôpital et dans la communauté - Canada (1976)

**CHICA-Canada**

PO Box 46125, RPO Westdale, Winnipeg, MB R3R 3S3
250/897-5990, Fax: 250/895-9595, Email: chicacda@mb.sympatico.ca
President, Patricia Piaskowski
Publications: Canadian Journal of Infection Control
Affiliates: International Federation of Infection Control

### Consumer Health Organization of Canada (CHOC) (1975)

#205, 250 Sheppard Ave. East, North York, ON M2N 6M9
416/222-6517, Fax: 416/225-1243
President, Libby Gardon
Publications: Consumer Health Newsletter
Affiliates: National Health Federation in US

### Corporation professionnelle des acupuncteurs du Québec

6731, rue St-Denis, Montréal, QC H2S 2S3
514/464-0805
Président, Claude B. Prevost

### Corporation professionnelle des physiothérapeutes du Québec (CPPQ) (1973)

#530, 1100, av Beaumont, Montréal, QC H3P 3H5
514/737-2770, Téléc: 514/737-6431, Ligne sans frais: 1-800-361-2001
Présidente, France Hétu, pht, MBA
Publications: Physio-Québec

### Council on Chiropractic Education (Canada) (CCE(C))

103 Chisholm Rd., Regina, SK S4S 5N9
President, Dr. Alex Guy

### Crohn's & Colitis Foundation of Canada/Fondation canadienne des maladies inflammatoires de l'intestin (CCFC) (1974)

#301, 21 St. Clair Ave. East, Toronto, ON M4T 1L9
416/920-5035, Fax: 416/929-0364, Toll Free: 1-800-387-1479, Email: ccfc@cycor.ca, URL: http://www.ccfc.ca
National Executive Director, Michael J. Howorth
Director of Communications, Barbara Victor
Publications: The Journal

### DES Action Canada (1982)
#203, 5890 Monkland Ave., PO Box 233, Stn Snowdon, Montréal, QC H3X 3T4
514/482-3204, Fax: 514/482-1445, Toll Free: 1-800-482-1337, Email: desact@web.net, URL: http://www.web.net/~desact
Executive Director, Colette Godin
President, Shirley Simand
Publications: DES Action Newsletter
Affiliates: DES Action Australia; DES Action Britain; DES Action Italy; DES Action Germany; DES Action The Netherlands; DES Action USA; DES Action Ireland; Info DES France; DES Action Belgium

### Diabetes Research Foundation (1974)
89 Granton Dr., Richmond Hill, ON L4B 2N5
905/889-4171, Fax: 905/889-4209, Toll Free: 1-800-668-0274
Executive Director, Tim Feher
President/CEO, Terry A. Jackson
Publications: Countdown; Tielines
Affiliates: Juvenile Diabetes Foundation International; Diabetes Canada

### Dystonia Medical Research Foundation/Fondation de recherches médicales sur la dystonie (1976)
#116, 230 Heath St. West, Toronto, ON M5P 1N8
416/487-8326, Fax: 416/488-6974, Toll Free: 1-800-361-8061
Canadian Representative, Shirley Morris
Publications: Dystonia Dialogue

### Endometriosis Association, Inc./Association de l'endometriose inc. (1980)
International Headquarters, 8585 North 76th Place, Milwaukee, WI 53223 USA
414/355-2200, Fax: 414/355-6065, Toll Free: 1-800-426-2363, Email: endo@endometriosisassn.org, URL: http://www.endometriosisassn.org
Executive Director, Mary Lou Ballweg
Publications: Endometriosis Association Newsletter

### Epilepsy Canada/Epilepsie Canada (EC) (1966)
#745, 1470, rue Peel, Montréal, QC H3A 1T1
514/845-7855, Fax: 514/845-7866, Toll Free: 1-800-860-5499, Email: epilepsy@epilepsy.ca, URL: http://www.epilepsy.ca
National Executive Director, Denise Crépin
President, James LaMartina
National Director of Programs, Rebecca Rupp
Publications: Lumina

#### ASSOCIATION QUÉBÉCOISE DE L'ÉPILEPSIE (1960)
#111, 1015, Côte du Beaver Hall, Montréal, QC H2Z 1S1
514/875-5595, Téléc: 514/875-6734, Ligne sans frais: 1-888-875-5595
Courrier électronique: aqe@cam.org, URL: http://www.cam.org/~aqe/
Directrice générale, France Picard

### Epilepsy Ontario/Epilepsie Ontario (1956)
#308, 1 Promenade Circle, Thornhill, ON L4J 4P8
905/764-5099, Fax: 905/764-1231, Toll Free: 1-800-463-1119, Email: epilepsy@epilepsy.org, URL: http://www.epilepsy.org
Chief Executive Director, Dianne Findlay
Publications: Sharing
Affiliates: Epilepsy Association of Metropolitan Toronto

### Eye Bank of BC (EBBC) (1983)
Eye Care Centre, 2550 Willow St., Vancouver, BC V5Z 3N9
604/875-4567, Fax: 604/875-5316, Toll Free: 1-800-667-2060
Coordinator, Debbie Chow
Medical Director, Dr. J.S.F. Richards
Affiliates: Canadian National Institute for the Blind; Eye Bank Association of America; Canadian Ophthalmological Society

### Eye Bank of Canada - Ontario Division (1955)
**Ontario Eye Bank**
One Spadina Cres., Toronto, ON M5S 2J5
416/480-7465, 978-7355, Fax: 416/978-1522, Email: eye.bank@utoronto.ca
Administrator, Fides Coloma
Affiliates: Canadian National Institute for the Blind; University of Toronto

### Federation of Canadian Naturists (1985)
PO Box 186, Islington, ON M9A 4X2
416/267-2283, Email: naturist@torfree.net
President, David Basford, Fax: 905/627-9935
Publications: Going Natural
Affiliates: International Naturist Federation

### Fédération des médecins omnipraticiens du Québec/Québec Federation of General Practitioners (FMOQ) (1963)
#1000, 1440, rue Ste-Catherine ouest, Montréal, QC H3G 1R8
514/878-1911, Téléc: 514/878-4455, Ligne sans frais: 1-800-361-8499, Courrier électronique: directi@fmoq.org, URL: http://www.sante.qc.ca/synapses/fmoq.htm
Président, Dr. Renald Dutil
Publications: Le Médecin du Québec

### Fédération des médecins spécialistes du Québec (FMSQ) (1965)
#3000, 2, Complexe Desjardins, Montréal, QC H5B 1G8
514/350-5000, Téléc: 514/350-5100
Françoise Godbout

### Federation of Medical Licensing Authorities of Canada/Fédération des ordres des médecins du Canada (FMLAC) (1968)
PO Box 8234, Ottawa, ON K1G 3H7
613/738-0372, Fax: 613/738-8977, Email: fmlac@aol.com
President, Dr. K. Brown
Executive Secretary, Sylvia Smith
Publications: Communiqué

#### COLLÈGE DES MÉDECINS DU QUÉBEC/COLLEGE OF PHYSICIANS OF QUÉBEC (CMQ) (1847)
2170, boul René-Lévesque ouest, Montréal, QC H3H 2T8
514/933-4441, Téléc: 514/933-3112, Ligne sans frais: 1-800-633-3246
Courrier électronique: cdoccmq@interlink.net, URL: http://www.cmq.org
Président, Dr. Roch Bernier
Publications: Le Collège; Annuaire médical

#### COLLEGE OF PHYSICIANS & SURGEONS OF ALBERTA (CPSA) (1905)
#900, 10180 - 101 St., Edmonton, AB T5J 4P8
403/423-4764, Fax: 403/420-0651, Toll Free: 1-800-561-3899
Email: lwebb@cpsa.ab.ca, URL: http://www.cpsa.ab.ca
Registrar, L. Ohlhauser

#### COLLEGE OF PHYSICIANS & SURGEONS OF BRITISH COLUMBIA
1807 West 10th Ave., Vancouver, BC V6J 2A9
604/733-7758, Fax: 604/733-3503, Toll Free: 1-800-461-3008
Registrar, T.F. Handley

#### COLLEGE OF PHYSICIANS & SURGEONS OF MANITOBA (CPS MANITOBA) (1871)
494 St. James St., Winnipeg, MB R3G 3J4
204/774-4344, Fax: 204/774-0750
URL: http://www.umanitoba.ca/colleges/cps
Registrar, K. Brown
Publications: From the College

#### COLLEGE OF PHYSICIANS & SURGEONS OF NEW BRUNSWICK/COLLÈGE DES MÉDECINS ET CHIRURGIENS DU NOUVEAU-BRUNSWICK (1981)
#300, One Hampton Rd., Rothesay, NB E2E 5K8
506/849-5050, Fax: 506/849-5069, Toll Free: 1-800-667-4641
Email: cpsnb@netcity.ca, URL: http://www.cpsnb.org
Registrar, Ed Schollenberg, MD, LLB, FRCPC

#### COLLEGE OF PHYSICIANS & SURGEONS OF NOVA SCOTIA
5248 Morris St., Halifax, NS B3J 1B4
902/422-5823, Fax: 902/422-5035
Registrar, Dr. Cameron Little
Publications: Newsletter

#### COLLEGE OF PHYSICIANS & SURGEONS OF ONTARIO (1866)
80 College St., Toronto, ON M5G 2E2
416/967-2600
Registrar, Dr. Michael E. Dixon
Publications: Members' Dialogue

#### COLLEGE OF PHYSICIANS & SURGEONS OF PRINCE EDWARD ISLAND (1988)
199 Grafton St., Charlottetown, PE C1A 1L2
902/566-3861, Fax: 902/566-3861
President, Dr. Roy Montgomery
Office Secretary, Ruth Stavert
Registrar, H.E. Ross

#### COLLEGE OF PHYSICIANS & SURGEONS OF SASKATCHEWAN (CPSS) (1905)
211 - 4th Ave. South, Saskatoon, SK S7K 1N1
306/244-7355, Fax: 306/244-0090
Email: cpss@quadrant.net
Registrar, D.A. Kendel, M.D.
Deputy Registrar, Dr. L. Loewen
Director, Communications & Education, J. Wolan
Publications: The College Newsletter; Bulletin, q.

#### NEWFOUNDLAND MEDICAL BOARD (1893)
#6, 139 Water St., St. John's, NF A1C 1B2
709/726-8546, Fax: 709/726-4725
Registrar, R.W. Young
Publications: Newsletter

### Fédération québécoise des massothérapeutes (FQMM) (1979)
#204, 1265, Mont-Royal est, Montréal, QC H2J 1Y4
514/597-0505, Téléc: 514/597-0141, Ligne sans frais: 1-800-363-9609, URL: http://www.globale.com/data/fqm.htm
Directeur général, Daniel Bouffard
Publications: Le Massager

### Fondation de la banque d'yeux du Québec inc./Québec Eye Bank Foundation (1976)
5689, boul Rosemont, Montréal, QC H1T 2H1
514/252-3886, Téléc: 514/252-3821
Directrice administrative, Maryse Senécal
Publications: Les Amis de la banque d'yeux

### Fondation québécoise du cancer (1979)
2075, rue de Champlain, Montréal, QC H2L 2T1
514/527-2194, Téléc: 514/527-1943, Infoligne: 514/522-6237, Ligne sans frais: 1-800-361-4212
Directeur, Guy Germain

### Health Action Network Society (HANS) (1984)
#202, 5262 Rumble St., Burnaby, BC V5J 2B6
604/435-0512, Fax: 604/435-1561, Email: info@hans.org, URL: http://www.hans.org/

President, Lorna Hancock
Executive Administrator, Cathrine Gabriel
Publications: Health Action

### Health Care Public Relations Association of Canada/L'Association des relations publiques des organismes de la santé, Canada (HCPRA) (1973)
253 College St., PO Box 166, Toronto, ON M5T 1R5
416/699-6353, Fax: 416/699-6353
Executive Director, Judy Hodgson
Publications: Impressions
Affiliates: Canadian Healthcare Association

### Health Evidence Application & Linkage Network/Réseau de liaison et d'application de l'information sur la santé (HEALNet) (1995)
Dept. of Clinical Epidemiology & Biostatistics, McMaster University, 1200 Main St. West, Hamilton, ON L8N 3Z5
905/525-9140, ext.22162, Fax: 905/577-0017, Email: fraserp@fhs.mcmaster.ca, URL: http://hiru.mcmaster.ca/nce
Program Leader, Dr. George Browman, Email: browman@fhs.mcmaster.ca
Publications: Network Nexus

### Health Sciences Centre Foundation (1981)
MS7, 820 Sherbrook St., Winnipeg, MB R3A 1R9
204/787-2022, Fax: 204/787-4547, Info Line: 204/787-1900, Email: hscfound@mb.sympatico.ca
Executive Director, Janet Walker
Chairman, James A. Ferguson
Publications: Foundation Newsletter; Magazine, a.
Affiliates: Health Sciences Centre; Foundations for Health

### Heart & Stroke Foundation of Alberta (1957)
1825 Park Rd. SE, Calgary, AB T2G 3Y6
403/264-5549, Fax: 403/237-0803, Email: ramageb@hsfacal.org, URL: http://www.hsfacal.org/
Executive Director, John Paquet
Publications: Heart & Stroke Foundation of Alberta Lifelines

### Heart & Stroke Foundation of Canada/Fondation des maladies du coeur du Canada (HSFC) (1983)
#200, 160 George St., Ottawa, ON K1N 9M2
613/241-4361, Fax: 613/241-3278
National Executive Director, William G. Tholl
President, Gary M. Sutherland
Affiliates: International Society & Federation of Cardiology; Canadian Coalition for High Blood Pressure Prevention & Control

#### FONDATION DES MALADIES DU COEUR DU QUÉBEC/HEART & STROKE FOUNDATION OF QUÉBEC (FMCQ) (1955)
465, boul René-Lévesque ouest, 3e étage, Montréal, QC H2Z 1A8
514/871-1551, Téléc: 514/871-1464, Ligne sans frais: 1-800-361-7650
Directrice générale, Louise Bertrand
Président, Charles Bourgeois
Publications: Coeur à Coeur/Heart to Heart

### Hemophilia Ontario (1988)
#308, 60 St. Clair Ave. East, Toronto, ON M4T 1N5
416/972-0641, Fax: 416/972-0307
President, David Mitchell
Publications: Hemophilia Ontario
Affiliates: Ontario AIDS Network

### Huntington Society of Canada/Société Huntington du Canada (1973)
13 Water St. North, PO Box 1269, Cambridge, ON N1R 7G6
519/622-1002, Fax: 519/622-7370, Toll Free: 1-800-998-7398
Executive Director, Ralph M. Walker
President, Colin Patterson
Director of Communications, Isla Horvath
Publications: Horizon
Affiliates: Canadian Neurological Coalition; International Huntington Association

### Huntington Society of Québec/Société Huntington du Québec (1986)
4841, rue Rivard, Montréal, QC H2J 2N7
514/842-5740, Fax: 514/842-5740
Social Worker, France Leblanc
Publications: Horizon

### Interior Alzheimer Foundation (1981)
2020 Springfield Rd., Kelowna, BC V1Y 7V8
250/762-3312
President, Marjorie Chermishnuk
Publications: Sensor

### International Association for Medical Assistance to Travellers (IAMAT) (1960)
40 Regal Rd., Guelph, ON N1K 1B5
519/836-0102, Fax: 519/836-3412, Info Line: 416/652-0137, Email: iamat@sentex.net, URL: http://www.sentex.net/~iamat
President, M.A. Uffer-Marcolongo
Toronto Office: Contact, Nadia Sallese, #1, 1287 St. Clair Ave. West, Toronto, ON M6E 1B8, 416/652-0137

### Interstitial Cystitis Association of Canada/Association canadienne pour la cystite interstitielle (ICA) (1987)
PO Box 5814, Stn A, Toronto, ON M5W 1P2
416/920-8986, Fax: 416/968-9081
President, Helen Klukach
Vice-President & Treasurer, Sheila Holmes, Bus: 905/434-6858, Fax: 905/432-3847
Publications: National Report; Helpline, q.
Affiliates: Interstitial Cystitis Association - USA Head Office

### The Kidney Foundation of Canada/La Fondation canadienne du rein (KFOC) (1964)
#780, 5160, boul Décarie, Montréal, QC H3X 2H9
514/369-4806, Fax: 514/369-2472, Toll Free: 1-800-361-7494
National President, Owen Brown
National Executive Director, Gavin Turley
Publications: Let's Talk Research; Kidney Heart Watch

### Leprosy Mission Canada/La Mission évangélique contre la lèpre (Canada) (1892)
**TLM Canada**
#1410, 75 The Donway West, North York, ON M3C 2E9
416/441-3618, Fax: 416/441-0203, Email: tlm@tlmcanada.org, URL: http://www.tlmcanada.org
Executive Director, Peter Derrick
President, Dr. John Clement
Publications: The Leprosy Mission in Action
Affiliates: The Leprosy Mission International

### Lupus Canada (1989)
5512 - 4 St. NW, PO Box 64034, Calgary, AB T2K 6J1
403/274-5599, Fax: 403/274-5599, Toll Free: 1-800-661-1468, Email: lupuscan@cadvision.com
President, Mae Boa, Bus: 306/787-6066, Email: mboa@sasked.gov.sk.ca
National Office Coordinator, P.K. O'Brien
Publications: Lupus Canada Bulletin
Affiliates: Lupus Foundation of America

### Manitoba Cancer Treatment & Research Foundation
100 Olivia St., Winnipeg, MB R3E 0V9
204/787-2136, Fax: 204/783-6875, Email: donnac@mctrf.mb.ca
Donna Pacholok

### Manitoba Medical Service Foundation Inc.
100A Polo Park Centre, 1485 Portage Ave., Winnipeg, MB R3G 0W4
204/788-6801, Fax: 204/774-1761
Executive Director, John Wade

### Manitoba Paraplegia Foundation Inc. (1980)
825 Sherbrook St., Winnipeg, MB R3A 1M5
204/786-4753, Fax: 204/786-1140
President, Doug Finkbeiner, QC
Publications: Paratracks

### M.E. Association of Canada/Association E.M. du Canada (1988)
**Myalgic Encephalomyelitis/Chronic Fatigue Syndrome Association of Canada**
#400, 246 Queen St., Ottawa, ON K1P 5E4
613/563-1565, Fax: 613/567-0614, Info Line: 613/563-1565, Email: info@mecan.ca, URL: http://www.mecan.ca
Chairperson, Rod Blaker
Director, Membership & Support Group Services, Peter Bates
Publications: Messenger

### The Medical Council of Canada/Le Conseil médical du Canada (1912)
#100, 2283 St. Laurent Blvd., PO Box 8234, Stn T, Ottawa, ON K1G 3H7
613/521-6012, Fax: 613/521-9417, URL: http://www.mcc.ca
Executive Director/CEO, Dr. W. Dale Dauphinee
Publications: Echo

### Medical Devices Canada (MEDEC) (1973)
**MEDEC**
#510, 401 The West Mall, Etobicoke, ON M9C 5J5
416/620-1915, Fax: 416/620-1595
President, Dennis W. Bryant
Publications: Canadian Assistive Devices Directory; Medec Pulse, 10 pa; Medical Devices Industry Directory; Medec Membership Directory; Annual MEDCOMP Survey; Annual Survey of Industry Trends

### Medical Reform Group (1979)
PO Box 158, Stn D, Toronto, ON M6P 3J8
416/588-9167, Email: udiemer@sources.copy
Contact, Ulli Diemer
Publications: Medical Reform
Affiliates: International Organization of Consumers Unions

### The Michener Institute for Applied Health Sciences (1967)
222 St. Patrick St., Toronto, ON M5T 1V4
416/596-3101, ext.3123, Fax: 416/596-3123, Info Line: 416/596-3132, Email: cdandary@staff.michener.on.ca, URL: http://www.michener.on.ca
President & CEO, Renate Krakauer
Affiliates: 170 hospitals, labs, & clinics across Canada

### The Migraine Association of Canada (1974)
#1912, 365 Bloor St. East, Toronto, ON M4W 3L4
416/920-4916, Fax: 416/920-3677, Info Line: 416/920-4917, Toll Free: 1-800-663-3557, Email: cindy@migraine.ca, URL: http://www.migraine.ca
Executive Director, Anne Kerr
President, Bill Ross
Fund Development Manager, Cindy Stanleigh
Communications Manager, Shaaron McDonald
Publications: Headlines

**Multiple Organ Retrieval & Exchange Program of Ontario/Programme de récupération et d'échange de multiples organes de l'Ontario (MORE) (1988)**
#503, 984 Bay St., Toronto, ON M5S 2A5
416/921-1130, Fax: 416/921-7313, Toll Free: 1-800-263-2833
Executive Director, Gary Cooper
Acting Executive Secretary, Catherine Gilboord

**Multiple Sclerosis Society of Canada/Société canadienne de la sclérose en plaques (1948)**
**MS Society**
#1000, 250 Bloor St. East, Toronto, ON M4W 3P9
416/922-6065, Fax: 416/922-7538, Toll Free: 1-800-268-7582, Email: info@mssoc.ca, URL: http://www.mssoc.ca
President, Alistair M. Fraser
Chairman, Bruce R. Richmond, C.A.
Vice-President, Communications, Deanna Groetzinger
Publications: MS/SP Canada
Affiliates: Canadian Medical Association

**Muscular Dystrophy Association of Canada/Association canadienne de la dystrophie musculaire (MDAC) (1954)**
#900, 2345 Yonge St., Toronto, ON M4P 2E5
416/488-0030, Fax: 416/488-7523, Toll Free: 1-800-567-2873, URL: http://www.mdac.ca
National Executive Director, Chad Hanna
Executive Assistant, Rosanne Portelance
Publications: Connections/Connexions

**Myasthenia Gravis Association of British Columbia (1955)**
2805 Kingsway Ave., Vancouver, BC V5R 5H9
604/451-5511, Fax: 604/451-5651, Email: tnc@istar.ca, URL: http://home.istar.ca/ntnc
President, Brenda Kelsey
Publications: MGABC Bulletin

**National Cancer Institute of Canada/Institut national du cancer du Canada (NCIC)**
#200, 10 Alcorn Ave., Toronto, ON M4V 3B1
416/961-7223, Fax: 416/961-4189
CEO, Dorothy J. Lamont
Executive Director, Dr. D.J. Beatty
Publications: Journal of the National Cancer Institute

**National Clearinghouse on Tobacco & Health/Centre national de documentation sur le tabac et la santé (NCTH) (1988)**
#1000, 170 Laurier Ave. West, Ottawa, ON K1P 5V5
613/567-3050, Fax: 613/567-2730
Director, John Hamilton
Affiliates: Canadian Council on Smoking & Health

**National Eating Disorder Information Centre (NEDIC) (1985)**
College Wing 1-211, 200 Elizabeth St., Toronto, ON M5G 2C4
416/340-4156, Fax: 416/340-4736, Email: mbear@torhosp.toronto.on.ca
Programme Coordinator, Merryl Bear
Publications: Bulletin

**National Institute of Nutrition/Institut national de la nutrition (NIN) (1983)**
#302, 265 Carling Ave., Ottawa, ON K1S 2E1
613/235-3355, Fax: 613/235-7032, Email: nin@hpb.hwca.ca, URL: http://www.hwc.ca:8080/nin
President, Suzanne Hendricks
Chairman, Dr. George Ivany
Publications: Rapport; NIN Review/Le Point INN, q.
Affiliates: Agricultural Institute of Canada; Canadian Dental Association; Canadian Dental Hygienists' Association; Canadian Dietetic Association; Canadian Home Economics Association; Canadian Institute of Food Science & Technology; Canadian Medical Association; Canadian Nurses Association; Canadian Paediatric Society; Canadian Pharmaceutical Association; Canadian Public Health Association; Canadian Society for Nutritional Sciences; Canadian Society of Allergy & Clinical Immunology; College of Family Physicians of Canada; Organization for Nutrition Education; Sport Medicine Council of Canada

**North American Chronic Pain Association of Canada (NACPAC) (1986)**
#105, 150 Central Park Dr., Brampton, ON L6T 2T9
905/793-5230, Fax: 905/793-8781, Toll Free: 1-800-616-7246, Email: nacpac@sympatico.ca, URL: http://www3.sympatico.ca/nacpac/
President, Dr. Ric Edwards
Publications: ACPA Chronicle; The NacPac Track, q.
Affiliates: American Chronic Pain Association

**Occupational & Environmental Medical Association of Canada/Association canadienne de la médecine du travail et de l'environnement (OEMAC) (1983)**
54 Forward Ave., London, ON N6H 5C8
519/439-7970, Fax: 519/439-8840, Email: oemac@esc.net
OEMAC Secretariat, Lise Jamieson
President, Dr. Ciaran O'Shea
Publications: Liaison; Membership Directory, a.
Affiliates: Canadian Medical Association; Canadian Board of Occupational Medicine; Royal College of Physicians & Surgeons of Canada

**Ontario Association of Naturopathic Doctors (1950)**
Lambton Business Centre, #304, 4174 Dundas St. West, Etobicoke, ON M8X 1X3
416/233-2001, Fax: 416/233-2924
President, Pamela Milroy, ND
Office Coordinator, Heather Fleck
Publications: ONA Pulse

**Ontario Cancer Institute**
Princess Margaret Hospital, 610 University Ave., Toronto, ON M5G 2M9
416/946-4482, Fax: 416/946-2084
Chief Librarian, Carol Morrison

**Ontario Council on Community Health Accreditation (OCCHA) (1981)**
3370 South Service Rd., Burlington, ON L7N 3M6
416/639-6367, Fax: 416/639-6534, Email: occha@interlynx.net

**Ontario Podiatry Association**
#900, 2 Sheppard Ave. East, North York, ON M2N 5Y7
416/927-9111, Fax: 416/733-2491
Executive Secretary, Gloria Patterson

**Ordre des ergothérapeutes du Québec (OEQ) (1974)**
#710, 1259, rue Berri, Montréal, QC H2L 4C7
514/844-5778, Téléc: 514/844-0478, Ligne sans frais: 1-800-265-5778
Directeur général et secrétaire, Réjean Pedneault
Publications: Revue québécoise d'ergothérapie

**Ordre des orthophonistes et audiologistes du Québec (OOAQ) (1973)**
#730, 1265, rue Berri, Montréal, QC H2L 4X4
514/282-9123, Téléc: 514/282-9541
Présidente, Renée Boisclair-Papillon
Secrétaire, Jean-Philippe Legault
Trésorière, Carmen Phénix
Publications: Bulletin de l'OOAQ

**Ordre professionnel des technologistes médicaux du Québec (OPTMQ) (1973)**
#300, 1150, boul Saint-Joseph est, Montréal, QC H2J 1L5
514/527-9811, Téléc: 514/527-7314, Ligne sans frais: 1-800-567-7763
Directeur général, Alain Collette
Président, Richard Charette
Coordonnatrice des services professionnels, Marie France Gionet
Publications: Sommaire

**Organ Donors Canada/Donneurs d'organes du Canada (1974)**
5326 Ada Blvd., Edmonton, AB T5W 4N7
403/474-9363
Executive Director, Mae Cox

**Osteoporosis Society of Canada/La Société de l'ostéoporose du Canada (1982)**
33 Laird Dr., Toronto, ON M4G 3S9
416/696-2663, Fax: 416/696-2673, Toll Free: 1-800-463-6842
Executive Director, Joyce Gordon
Office Manager, Maxine Smith
Publications: Osteoblast

**Parkinson Foundation of Canada/La fondation canadienne du parkinson (1965)**
#710, 390 Bay St., Toronto, ON M5H 2Y2
416/366-0099, Fax: 416/366-9190, Toll Free: 1-800-565-3000
CEO, Trevor Williams
National Director, Finance, Carol Giannone
Publications: Network

**Post-Polio Awareness & Support Society of BC (PPASS) (1986)**
Depot#1, PO Box 6579, Victoria, BC V8P 5N7
250/477-8244, 6546, Fax: 250/477-8287
President, Alf Foxgord
Publications: PPASS News

**Post-Polio Network Manitoba Inc.**
825 Sherbrook St., 2nd F., Winnipeg, MB R3A 1M5
204/772-6979, Fax: 204/786-0860
Publications: Newsletter

**Psoriasis Society of Canada/Société psoriasis du Canada (1983)**
National Office, PO Box 25015, Halifax, NS B3M 4H4
902/443-8680, Fax: 902/457-1664, Toll Free: 1-800-656-4494
President, Judy Misner
Vice-President, John Merlini
Sec.-Treas., Diane Drake
Director, Robert Kotler
Publications: National Psoriasis Newsletter
Affiliates: Intl. Federation of Psoriasis Associations

**Respiratory Health Network of Centres of Excellence/Réseau de centres d'excellence en santé respiratoire (1990)**
**Inspiraplex**
Institut thoracique de Montréal, 3650, rue Saint-Urbain, Montréal, QC H2X 2P4
514/843-2096, Fax: 514/843-2098, Email: annev@meakins.lan.mcgill.ca, URL: http://www.meakins.mcgill.ca/Inspiraplex/index.html
Executive Director, Anne Vézina
Scientific Director, Dr. Peter Macklem
Associate Scientific Director, Dr. Quatayba Hamid
Publications: Inspiraplex

**The Royal College of Physicians & Surgeons of Canada/Le Collège royal des médecins et chirurgiens du Canada (RCPSC) (1929)**
774 Echo Dr., Ottawa, ON K1S 5N8

613/730-8177, Fax: 613/730-8833, Toll Free: 1-800-668-3740, Email: communications@rcpsc.edu, URL: http://rcpsc.medical.org
Executive Director, Hugh M. Scott
President, Dr. Luc Deschênes
Head, Communications Section, Pierrette Leonard
Publications: RCPSC Bulletin; Annals RCPSC, 8 pa
Affiliates: Canadian Medical Association; College of Family Physicians of Canada; Association of Canadian Medical Colleges

**RP Research Foundation - Fighting Blindness/ Fondation RP pour la recherche sur les yeux (1974)**
#910, 36 Toronto St., Toronto, ON M5C 2C5
416/360-4200, Fax: 416/360-0060, Toll Free: 1-800-461-3331
National Executive Director, Sharon Colle
President, Brian Larter
Publications: Vision
Affiliates: US RP Foundation

**Saint Elizabeth Health Care (1908)**
#320, 10 Gateway Blvd., North York, ON M3C 3A1
416/429-1234, Fax: 416/429-8244
President, Shirlee Sharkey
Communications Officer, Catherine Cameron
Publications: Elizabethan Times

**Sleep/Wake Disorders Canada/Affections du sommeil/eveil Canada (SWDC) (1975)**
#5055, 3080 Yonge St., Toronto, ON M4N 3N1
416/483-9654, Fax: 416/483-7081, Toll Free: 1-800-387-9253, Email: swds@globalserve.net
Ontario Coordinator, Wendy Stratton
Executive Director, Bev Devins
Publications: Good Night Good Day
Affiliates: Canadian Neurological Coalition

**Society of Obstetricians & Gynaecologists of Canada/Sociéte des obstétriciens et gynécologues du Canada (SOGC) (1944)**
774 Echo Dr., Ottawa, ON K1S 5N8
613/730-4192, Fax: 613/730-4314, Toll Free: 1-800-561-2416, Email: sogcwebmaster@medical.org, URL: http://www.medical.org/sogc_docs/SOGC.html
Executive Vice-President, Dr André Lalonde
Director, Finance, Brenda Dashney
Publications: SOGC News; SOGC Journal, m.

**Spina Bifida & Hydrocephalus Association of Canada/Association spina-bifida et d'hydrocephalie du Canada (SBHAC) (1981)**
#220, 388 Donald St., Winnipeg, MB R3B 2J4
204/957-1784, Fax: 204/957-1794, Toll Free: 1-800-565-9488, Email: spinab@mts.net, URL: http://www.sbhac.ca
Executive Director, Andrea Salmon
President, Colleen Talbot
Publications: Podium
Affiliates: International Federation for Hydrocephalus & Spina Bifida

**L'ASSOCIATION DE SPINA-BIFIDA ET D'HYDROCÉPHALIE DU QUÉBEC (ASBHQ) (1975)**
#425, 5757, rue Decelles, Montréal, QC H3S 2C3
514/340-9019, Téléc: 514/340-9109, Ligne sans frais: 1-800-567-1788
Directrice générale, Tina Marie Lalonde
Publications: Contact

**Stroke Recovery Association of Ontario (SRAO) (1975)**
#292, 10 Overlea Blvd., Toronto, ON M4H 1A4
416/425-4209, Fax: 416/425-1920
Provincial Coordinator, Cheryl L. Denomy
Publications: The Phoenix

**Thyroid Foundation of Canada/Fondation du Canada pour les maladies thyroidiennes (1980)**
1040 Gardiners Rd., Kingston, ON K7P 1R7
613/634-3426, Fax: 613/634-3483, Toll Free: 1-800-267-8822, Email: thyroid@limestone.kosone.com, URL: http://home.ican.net/~thyroid/Canada.html
Founder, Diana Meltzer Abramsky, C.M., B.A.
National Office Coordinator, Katherine Keen
Publications: Thyrobulletin

**Tourette Syndrome Foundation of Canada/La Foundation canadienne de la syndrome Tourette (TSFC) (1976)**
#203, 3675 Keele St., North York, ON M3J 1M6
416/636-2800, Fax: 416/636-1688, Toll Free: 1-800-361-3120, Email: tsfc.org@sympatico.ca
Executive Director, Rosie Wartecker
President, Judy Rogers
Publications: The Green Leaflet

**United Ostomy Association, Canada (1987)**
**UOA Canada**
5 Hamilton Ave., Hamilton, ON L8V 2S3
905/389-8822
President, Allan Porter
Publications: UOA Canada Talks
Affiliates: United Ostomy Association - USA

**HEART & STROKE ASSOCIATIONS *see* HEALTH & MEDICAL**

## HEATING, AIR CONDITIONING, PLUMBING

**American Society of Heating, Refrigerating & Air Conditioning Engineers - Toronto Chapter (ASHRAE)**
Bldg. 11, #300, 5045 Orbitor Dr., Mississauga, ON L4W 4Y4
905/602-4714, Fax: 905/602-1197
President, D. Taylor
Publications: Toronto Chapter Gazette

**American Society of Plumbing Engineers (ASPE) (1964)**
#210, 3617 Thousand Oaks Blvd., Westlake, CA 91362 USA
805/495-7120
British Columbia Chapter: President, Graham Aspinal, PO Box 2201, Stn Terminal, Vancouver, BC V6B 3W2, 604/688-8671
Montréal Chapter: Président, André Lavallée, c/o Cosertec, 5070, av des Sorbiers, Montréal, QC H1T 2H5, 514/382-1556
Québec City Chapter: President, Marcel Fortier, T.Sc.A., CIPE, 1937, rue Delisle, Bernières, QC G7A 2A3, 418/623-7013

**British Columbia Insulation Contractors Association (BCICA) (1958)**
#242, 4299 Canada Way, Burnaby, BC V5G 1H3
604/438-6616, Fax: 604/438-6525
Administrator, Debbie Hoover
Affiliates: Thermal Insulation Association of Canada

**Canadian Institute of Plumbing & Heating/ L'Institut canadien de plomberie et de chauffage (CIPH) (1933)**
#330, 295 The West Mall, Etobicoke, ON M9C 4Z4
416/695-0447, Fax: 416/695-0450, Email: ciph@ican.net, URL: http://www.ciph.com
President/General Manager, Edward R. Hardison
Program Manager, Ralph P. Suppa
Show Manager, Elizabeth McCullough
Publications: Pipeline; Canadian Institute of Plumbing & Heating Directory; Canadian Institute of Plumbing & Heating Statistics

**Canadian Refrigeration & Air Conditioning Contractors Association (CRACCA) (1972)**
Bldg. 11, #300, 5045 Orbitor Dr., Mississauga, ON L4W 4Y4
905/602-4700, Fax: 905/602-1197
Secretary, Warren J. Heeley

**Heating, Refrigerating & Air Conditioning Institute of Canada/Institut canadien du chauffage, de la climatisation et de la réfrigération (HRAI) (1969)**
Bldg. 11, #300, 5045 Orbitor Dr., Mississauga, ON L4W 4Y4
905/602-4700, Fax: 905/602-1197, Email: hrai@web.net, URL: http://www.hrai.ca
President, Warren J. Heeley
Manager, Member Services, Joanne Spurrell
Manager, Technical, Gord Arnott
Manager, Contractors, Martin Luymes
Manager, Manufacturers, Caroline Czajko
Manager, Wholesalers, Gerald Smith
Manager, Communications, Gerald J. Smith
Publications: HRAI News; HRAI Membership Directory; The HRAI Catalogue
Affiliates: North American Heating, Refrigeration & Air Conditioning Wholesalers, Heating, Refrigeration & Air Conditioning Contractors Section

**Independent Plumbing & Heating Contractors' Association (IPHCA) (1980)**
#305, 1 Greensboro Dr., North York, ON M9W 1C8
416/248-6213, Fax: 416/248-6214
Manager, Mauro Angeloni

**Ontario Plumbing Inspectors Association (OPIA) (1920)**
1677 Gregory Rd., RR#3, St Catharines, ON L2R 6P9
905/685-9402, Fax: 905/685-0640
Secretary, F. Penfold
Publications: OPIA Bulletin

**Ontario Refrigeration & Air Conditioning Contractors Association (ORAC)**
Office Mall II, #7A, 1400 Bayly St., Pickering, ON L1W 3R2
905/420-7272, Fax: 905/420-7288
President, Marv Lindgren
Secretary, Barry Eon
Affiliates: Heating, Refrigerating & Air Conditioning Institute of Canada

**Refrigeration Service Engineers Society (Canada) (RSES Canada) (1952)**
PO Box 1400, Stn A, North York, ON M2N 5T5
416/221-3538, Fax: 416/222-3927
President, Gary Struhar, CMS
First Vice-President, Wesley Maxfield, CM
Second Vice-President, Garry MacKenzie, CM
Secretary, Eglal Homsy
Treasurer, Stephen Manson
Executive Assistant, Norman B. Fraser
Publications: RSES Canada Bulletin

**Thermal Insulation Association of Canada/ Association canadienne de l'isolation thermique (TIAC) (1964)**
#210, 44 Byward Market Sq., Ottawa, ON K1N 7A2
613/562-1012, Fax: 613/562-1014
Executive Vice-President, Alison Bowick, MBA, CAE
Office Manager, Heather McIntosh
Publications: TIAC Times

**HERALDRY *see* HISTORY, HERITAGE, GENEALOGY**

**HERITAGE *see* HISTORY, HERITAGE, GENEALOGY**

## HISTORY, HERITAGE, GENEALOGY

*see also* Culture; Multiculturalism

### Alberta Family History Society (AFHS) (1980)
PO Box 30270, Stn B, Calgary, AB T2M 4P1
URL: http://www.freenet.calgary.ab.ca/science/afhs.html
Chair, Noreen Chambers
Queries Coordinator, Myrna Waldroff, Fax: 403/252-2957
Publications: Chinook
Affiliates: Federation of Family History Societies (England)

### Alberta Historical Resources Foundation (AHRF) (1976)
Old St. Stephen's College, 8820 - 112 St., Edmonton, AB T6G 2P8
403/431-2300, Fax: 403/432-1376
Director, Mark Rasmussen

### Alberta Pioneer Railway Association (1968)
PO Box 70014, Londonderry, AB T5C 3R6
403/472-6229
Contact, Herb Dickson
Publications: The Marker
Affiliates: Heritage Canada

### Association québécoise d'interprétation du patrimoine (AQIP) (1977)
82, Grande Allée ouest, CP 657, Succ. Haute-Ville, Québec, QC G1R 4S2
418/647-1927, Téléc: 418/647-6483
Présidente, Lise Drolet
Publications: Bulletin de Liaison

### Association québécoise pour le patrimoine industriel (AQPI) (1988)
2050, Amherst, Montréal, QC H2L 3L8
514/528-8444, Téléc: 514/528-8686
Présidente, Marie-Claude Robert
Publications: Bulletin
Organisation(s) affiliée(s): The International Committee for the Conservation of the Industrial Heritage

### British Columbia Genealogical Society (BCGS) (1971)
PO Box 88054, Lansdowne Mall, Richmond, BC V6X 3T6
604/502-9119, Fax: 604/263-4952, Email: bcgs@npsnet.com, URL: http://www.npsnet.com/bcgs
President, Keith Lachance
1st Vice-President, Susan Hyde
Corresponding Secretary, Marian Elder, Bus: 604/522-6453
Publications: The British Columbia Genealogist

### British Columbia Historical Federation (1922)
RR#1, S22, C1, Nelson, BC V1L 5P4
250/825-4743, Email: welwood@selkirk.bc.ca
President, Ron Welwood
Publications: BC Historical News

### British Columbia Railway Historical Association (BCRHA) (1961)
PO Box 8114, VCPO, Victoria, BC V8W 3R8
250/389-0584, Fax: 250/385-2760, Email: uah46@freenet.victoria.bc.ca
President, Paul J. Smith
Publications: Callboard

### Bus History Association, Inc. (BHA) (1963)
965 MacEwan, Windsor, ON N9B 2G1
519/977-0664
Chair, Paul Leger
Publications: Bus Industry; News

### Canada's National History Society/Société d'historie nationale du Canada (CNHS) (1993)
#478, 167 Lombard Ave., Winnipeg, MB R3C 0E7
204/988-9309, Fax: 204/988-9300, Email: beaver@cyberspc.mb.ca, URL: http://www.cyberspc.mb.ca/~otmw/cnhs/cnhs.html
Chairman & President, Joseph E. Martin
Vice-President, Laird Rankin
Publications: The Beaver

### Canadian Association of Professional Heritage Consultants/Association canadienne des consultants patrimoine (CAPHC) (1987)
PO Box 1023, Stn F, Toronto, ON M5A 2T7
President, Susan Maltby, B.A., M.A.C., Bus: 416/537-3446, Fax: 416/537-3446
Secretary, David Nasby
Treasurer, Bob Mitchell
Vice-President, Robert Shipley
Publications: The Heritage Consultants' Forum; Membership Directory, a.
Affiliates: ICOMOS International (International Council on Monuments & Sites); ICOMOS Canada - English-Speaking Committee

### Canadian Canal Society/Société des canaux du Canada (CCS) (1982)
PO Box 23016, RPO Midtown, St Catharines, ON L2R 7P6
905/688-5550, ext.3264, Fax: 905/988-5490
President, Robert Sparks
Secretary, Doris Bates
Treasurer, Carol Gaspari
Publications: Canals Canada/Canaux du Canada
Affiliates: Inland Waterways Association (UK)

### Canadian Catholic Historical Association - English Section/Société canadienne d'histoire de l'église catholique - Section anglaise (CCHA) (1933)
1155 Yonge St., Toronto, ON M4T 1W2
416/934-3400, ext.504, Fax: 416/934-3444, URL: http://www.umanitoba.ca/colleges/st_pauls/ccha/ccha.html
Secretary General, Rev. Edward Jackman
Publications: Canadian Catholic Historical Studies; Bulletin, s-a.

### Canadian Federation of Genealogical & Family History Societies Inc. (1984)
**CanFed**
227 Parkville Bay, Winnipeg, MB R2M 2J6
204/256-6176
Secretary, Cécile Alarie-Skene
Publications: CANFED Newsletter

### Canadian Friends Historical Association (CFHA) (1972)
60 Lowther Ave., Toronto, ON M5R 1C7
416/969-9675, URL: http://home.interhop.net/~aschrauwe/
Chairperson, Christopher Densmore
Publications: Canadian Quaker History Journal; Directory of Canadian Biography; Index of Quaker Records
Affiliates: Friends Historical Society

### Canadian Heritage Information Network/Réseau canadien d'information sur le patrimoine (CHIN) (1972)
15, rue Eddy, 4e étage, Hull, QC K1A 0M5
819/994-1200, Fax: 819/994-9555, Email: service@chin.gc.ca, URL: http://www.chin.gc.ca
Director General, Lynn Elliott-Sherwood
Director, Systems & Access, Gail Eagen
Publications: Network News

### Canadian Historical Association/Société historique du Canada (CHA) (1922)
395 Wellington St., Ottawa, ON K1A 0N3
613/233-7885, Fax: 613/567-3110, Email: jmineault@archives.ca
President, Judith Fingard
Administrative Assistant, Joanne Mineault
Publications: Register of Dissertations; CHA Bulletin, q.; Journal of the CHA, a.

### Canadian Institute for Historical Microreproductions/Institut canadien de microreproductions historiques (CIHM) (1978)
PO Box 2428, Stn D, Ottawa, ON K1P 5W5
613/235-2628, Fax: 613/235-9752, Email: cihmicmh@nlo.nlc.bnc.ca, URL: http://www.nlc-bnc.ca/cihm/
Executive Director, Pam Bjornson
Publications: Facsimile

### Canadian Oral History Association/Société canadienne d'histoire orale (COHA) (1974)
PO Box 2064, Stn D, Ottawa, ON K1P 5W3
613/996-6996, Fax: 613/995-6575
President, Janet Trimble
Vice-President, Joan Fairweather
Sec.-Treas., Carolyn Vachon
Publications: Canadian Oral History Association Journal; Canadian Oral History Association Newsletter

### Canadian Railroad Historical Association/Association canadienne d'histoire ferroviaire (CRHA) (1932)
120 rue St-Pierre, Saint-Constant, QC J5A 2G9
514/632-2410
President, Walter J. Bedbrook
Vice-President, Robert V.V. Nicholls
Treasurer, Robert Carlson
Publications: Canadian Rail

### Canadian Society of Church History/Société canadienne d'histoire de l'église (1960)
Dept. of History, University of Maine, Orono, ME 04469-5774 USA
207/581-1908, Fax: 207/581-1817
President, William Katerberg
Publications: Canadian Society of Church History Papers

### Canadian Society for Industrial Heritage/Société canadienne de l'héritage industriel (CSIH) (1991)
240 Sparks St., PO Box 55122, Ottawa, ON K1P 1A1
613/991-6705, Fax: 613/990-3636
Chairperson, Louise Trottier
Publications: Machines

### Canadian Society of Mayflower Descendants (1980)
2071 Wellington Ave., Burlington, ON L7R 1P4
Governor, Robert M. Cruikshank
Publications: Canadian Pilgrim
Affiliates: General Society of Mayflower Descendants - USA

### Canadian Society for the Study of Names/Société canadienne d'onomastique (CSSN) (1951)
c/o Geographical Names, 615 Booth St., Ottawa, ON K1A 0E9
613/992-3405, Fax: 613/943-8282, Email: hkerfoot@nrcan.gc.ca, URL: http://GeoNames.NRCan.gc.ca/english/CSSN.html
President, Helen Kerfoot
Publications: Onomastica Canadiana; The Name Gleaner, q.

### Canadian Steam Preservation & Industrial Archaeological Association
13541 - 62 Ave., Surrey, BC V3X 2J3

604/594-1970, Fax: 604/594-1820
Sec.-Treas., David Jackson
Publications: Industrial Age
Affiliates: The International Committee for the Conservation of the Industrial Heritage

**Canadian Warplane Heritage (CWH) (1971)**
**Canada's Flying Museum**
#300, 9300 Airport Rd., Mount Hope, ON L0R 1W0
905/679-4183, Fax: 905/679-4186, Email: museum@warplane.com, URL: http://www.warplane.com
President, Dennis Bradley
Publications: Flightlines

**Conseil des monuments et sites du Québec (CMSQ) (1975)**
82, Grande-Allée ouest, Québec, QC G1R 2G6
418/647-4347, Téléc: 418/647-6483, Ligne sans frais: 1-800-494-4347
Présidente, France Gagnon Pratte
Directrice, Marie Nolet
Publications: Continuité
Succursale de Montréal: 5695, rue Waverley, Montréal, QC H2T 2Y2, 514/270-8645, Téléc: 514/270-8355

**The Family History Association of Canada/Association canadienne de l'histoire des familles (1976)**
#404, 4620 West 10th Ave., Vancouver, BC V6R 2H2
250/222-2112
National Chairman, Gretha M. Warren

**Federation of Nova Scotian Heritage (FNSH) (1976)**
#901, 1809 Barrington St., Halifax, NS B3J 3K8
902/423-4677, Fax: 902/422-0881, Toll Free: 1-800-355-6873, Email: fnsh@fox.nstn.ca
Executive Director, Susan Charles
Publications: Federation News
Affiliates: Heritage Canada; Canadian Museums Association; Association for State & Local History

**Fédération québécoise des sociétés de généalogie (1984)**
CP 9454, Ste-Foy, QC G1V 4B8
418/653-3940, URL: http://www.gouv.qc.ca/francais/minorg/mccq/dpm/organis/fqsg/fqsg.htm
Présidente, Esther Taillon
Publications: Info-Généalogie

**Fédération des sociétés d'histoire du Québec (1965)**
4545, av Pierre-De-Coubertin, CP 1000, Succ. M, Montréal, QC H1V 3R2
514/252-3031, Téléc: 514/251-8038
Directeur général, Mario Boucher
Publications: Actualités Histoire Québec; Histoire Québec, semi-annuel

**Genealogical Association of Nova Scotia/Association généologique de la Nouvelle-Écosse (1982)**
PO Box 641, Halifax, NS B3J 2T3
Email: ab018@ccn.cs.dal.ca, URL: http://www.ccn.cs.dal.ca/Recreation/GANS/gans_homepage.html
President, Karen MacKay
Publications: Nova Scotia Genealogist

**Genealogical Institute of The Maritimes/Institut généalogique des Provinces Maritimes (GIM) (1983)**
PO Box 3142, Stn Halifax South, Halifax, NS B3J 3H5
902/424-6065
Registrar, Virginia Clark
President, Lois Yorke

**Heraldry Society of Canada/Société héraldique du Canada (1966)**
PO Box 8128, Stn T, Ottawa, ON K1G 3H9
613/737-4587, Fax: 613/737-4150, Email: hsc@hsc.ca, URL: http://www.hsc.ca/
President, Jean Matheson
Secretary, Howard Heck
International Correspondent, James Taylor
Publications: Heraldry in Canada
Affiliates: Commonwealth Heraldry Board

**Heritage Canada/La Fondation Héritage Canada (1973)**
**Heritage Canada Foundation**
412 MacLaren St., PO Box 1358, Stn B, Ottawa, ON K1P 5R4
613/237-1066, Fax: 613/237-5987, Email: hercanot@sympatico.ca
Executive Director, Brian Anthony
Director, Government & Public Relations, Douglas Franklin
Publications: The Heritage Directory; Heritage Canada, 5 pa; Press Review, m.
Affiliates: Canadian Heritage Network

**L'Héritage canadien du Québec/The Canadian Heritage of Québec (HCQ) (1960)**
1181, rue de la Montagne, Montréal, QC H3G 1Z2
514/393-1417, 481-5796, Fax: 514/393-9444
Executive Director, Arnold Sharp
Président, C. Robin Molson
Publications: Le Bulletin de l'Héritage canadien du Québec/The Canadian Heritage of Québec Newsletter

**Heritage Council of British Columbia (1988)**
c/o BC Museums Association, 514 Government St., Victoria, BC V8V 4X4
250/387-3315, Fax: 250/387-1251
Chair, Greg Evans
Affiliates: Archaeological Society of BC; Archives Association of BC; BC Museums Association; BC Historical Federation; Heritage Society of BC; Underwater Archaeological Society of BC

**Heritage Foundation of Newfoundland & Labrador (1984)**
PO Box 5171, St. John's, NF A1C 5V5
709/739-1892, Fax: 709/739-5413, Email: heritage@avalon.nf.ca, URL: http://www.avalon.nf.ca/heritage
Executive Secretary, George Chalker
Chairperson, Victoria Collins

**Historic Theatres' Trust/Société des salles historiques (1989)**
PO Box 387, Stn Victoria, Montréal, QC H3Z 2V8
514/933-8077, Fax: 514/933-8012
Sec.-Treas., Janet MacKinnon
President, Jim Leworthy
Vice-President, Claude Fortin
Publications: Bulletin

**Historical Society of Alberta (HSA) (1907)**
PO Box 4035, Stn C, Calgary, AB T2T 5M9
403/261-3662, Fax: 403/269-6029
President, Marcel M.C. Dirk
Publications: Alberta History; History Now; Edmonton & District Historical Society; Chinook Country Historical Society; Lethbridge Historical Society; Central Alberta Historical Society
Affiliates: Heritage Canada

**Huguenot Society of Canada/Société Huguenote du Canada (1966)**
#105, 4936 Yonge St., North York, ON M2N 6S3
Fax: 416/226-0043
President, Richard W. Pogson
Publications: Huguenot Trails
Affiliates: Ontario Historical Society

**International Council on Monuments & Sites Canada (ICOMOS Canada) (1975)**
PO Box 737, Stn B, Ottawa, ON K1P 5R4
613/749-0971, Fax: 613/749-0971, Email: icomosca@ottawa.icomos.org, URL: http://www.icomos.org/canada
President, François Leblanc
Président, Comité francophone, Michel Bonnette
President, English Committee, Alistair Kerr
Executive Assistant, Renée Leblanc
Publications: ICOMOS Canada
Affiliates: UNESCO; International Centre for the Study of the Preservation & Restoration of Cultural Property (ICCROM)

**J. Douglas Ferguson Historical Research Foundation (1971)**
654 Hiawatha Blvd., Ancaster, ON L9G 3A5
905/648-4041
Sec.-Treas., Dorte Brace
Chairperson, William H. McDonald

**Jewish Genealogical Society of Canada (JGSC) (1985)**
PO Box 446, Stn A, North York, ON M2N 2T1
416/638-3280, Email: henry_wellisch@tvo.org
President, Henry Wellisch
Publications: Shem Tov
Affiliates: Jewish Federation of Greater Toronto

**Literary & Historical Society of Québec (1824)**
44 St-Stanislas, Québec, QC G1R 4H3
418/694-9147
Librarian, Cynthia Dooley

**Manitoba Genealogical Society Inc. (1976)**
885 Notre Dame Ave., Winnipeg, MB R3E 0M4
204/944-1153, Fax: 204/783-0190
Library Chair, Louisa Shermerhorn
Publications: Generations

**Manitoba Heritage Federation Inc. (1985)**
21 - 2nd Ave. NW, 2nd Fl., Dauphin, MB R7N 1H1
204/638-9154, Fax: 204/638-0683, Email: mhf@mb.sympatico.ca, URL: http://www.mts.net/~mhf
President, Don Fyk
Vice-President, Joan Whiston
Treasurer, Jack Watts, CMA, FCMA
Secretary, Marci Crawford
Administrator, Sheila Goraluk
Publications: Heritage Now

**Manitoba Historical Society (MHS) (1879)**
#470, 167 Lombard Ave., Winnipeg, MB R3B 0T6
204/947-0559, Fax: 204/943-1093
President, Celine M. Kear
Publications: Manitoba History; Keywords, bi-m.; Manitoba Historical Atlas
Affiliates: Heritage Canada

**Monarchist League of Canada/Ligue Monarchiste du Canada (MLC) (1970)**
PO Box 1057, Oakville, ON L6J 5E9
905/482-4157, Fax: 905/972-9179, Toll Free: 1-800-465-6925, Email: john.aimers@sympatico.ca, URL: http://www.monarchist.ca
Chairman, John Aimers
Dominion Vice-Chairman & Editor, Arthur Bousfield
Dominion Vice-Chairman, Public Relations, Paul Benoit
Publications: Canadian Monarchist News; Monarchy Canada, q.
Affiliates: Canadian Royal Heritage Trust

**New Brunswick Genealogical Society (1979)**
PO Box 3235, Stn B, Fredericton, NB E3A 5G9
URL: http://degaulle.hil.unb.ca/genealogy/society.html
President, Joan Pearce
Publications: Generations

**New Brunswick Historical Society (1874)**
120 Union St., Saint John, NB E2L 1A3
506/652-3590
President, Dennis Knibb
Vice-President, Kathy Wilson
Secretary, Steven McNeil
Treasurer, George F. Teed
Publications: New Brunswick H.S. Newsletter

**Newfoundland Historical Society (1881)**
Colonial Building, Rm #15, St. John's, NF A1C 2C9
709/722-3191, Fax: 709/729-0578, URL: http://www.infonet.st-johns.nf.ca/nfldhist/
Office Manager, Mary Bridson
President, Dr. J.K. Hiller
Publications: Newfoundland Quarterly; Newfoundland Historical Society Newsletter
Affiliates: Heritage Canada

**Newfoundland & Labrador Genealogical Society Inc. (NLGS) (1984)**
Colonial Building, Military Rd., St. John's, NF A1C 2C9
709/754-9525, URL: http://infonet.st-johns.nf.ca/Community/Providers/NLGS/nlgs.html
President, Dianne Jackman
Publications: The Newfoundland Ancestor

**North-West Mounted Police Commemorative Association**
PO Box 876, Cochrane, AB T0L 0W0
403/932-4167
Contact, Cliff Christian

**Ontario Black History Society (OBHS) (1978)**
Ontario Heritage Centre, #202, 10 Adelaide St. East, Toronto, ON M5C 1J3
416/867-9420, Fax: 416/867-8691
President, Rosemary J. Sadlier
Publications: Ontario Black History News
Affiliates: Ontario Historical Society

**Ontario Electric Railway Historical Association (1953)**
**Halton County Radial Railway**
PO Box 578, Milton, ON L9T 5A2
519/856-9802
Contact, Garry Gladden
Publications: Radial Report
Affiliates: Association of Railway Museums; Ontario Museum Association; Canadian Museums Association

**Ontario Genealogical Society/Société de généalogie de l'Ontario (OGS) (1961)**
#102, 40 Orchard View Blvd., Toronto, ON M4R 1B9
416/489-0734, Fax: 416/489-9803, URL: htpp://www.interlog.com/~dreed/ogs_home.htm
President, Ann Ward
Publications: Newsleaf; Families, q.; Newsline
Affiliates: Ontario Heritage Alliance

**Ontario Heritage Foundation (OHF) (1967)**
10 Adelaide St. East, Toronto, ON M5C 1J3
416/325-5000, Fax: 416/314-4930
Chair, Joanna Bedard
Executive Director, Lesley Lewis
Director, Heritage Programs, Richard Moorhouse
Manager, Heritage Community Services, Brian Rogers
Manager, Marketing, John Ecker, Bus: 416/325-5013
Natural Heritage Consultant, James Duncan
Natural Heritage Consultant, Patti Priestman
Publications: Heritage Dimensions

**Ontario Historical Society/La Société historique de l'Ontario (OHS) (1888)**
34 Parkview Ave., North York, ON M2N 3Y2
416/226-9011, Fax: 416/226-2740
Executive Director, Dorothy Duncan
Communications Coordinator, Meribeth Clow
Publications: Ontario History; OHS Bulletin, bi-m.

**Pier 21 Society (1988)**
PO Box 611, Halifax, NS B3J 2R7
902/425-7770, Fax: 902/423-4045, Email: pier21@pier21.ns.ca, URL: http://pier21.ns.ca
President, Dr. Ruth M. Goldbloom
Manager, Information Services, Erez Segal

**Postal History Society of Canada (PHSC) (1972)**
216 Mailey Dr., Carleton Place, ON K7C 3X9
613/257-5453
President, D. Murray
Vice-President, Dr. Robert C. Smith
Secretary, R.F. Narbonne
Treasurer, Geoffrey R. Newman
Publications: PHSC Journal
Affiliates: American Philatelic Society; British North America Philatelic Society

**Prince Edward Island Genealogical Society Inc. (PEIGS)**
PO Box 9066, Charlottetown, PE C1A 8C4
President, Elizabeth Glen

**Prince Edward Island Museum & Heritage Foundation (PEIMHF) (1983)**
2 Kent St., Charlottetown, PE C1A 1M6
902/368-6600, Fax: 902/368-6608, Email: peimhf@cycor.ca, URL: http://www.peisland.com/peimuseum/welcome.htm
Executive Director, Chris Severance
Publications: The Island Magazine

**Québec Family History Society/Société de l'histoire des familles du Québec (QFHS) (1977)**
PO Box 1026, Pointe Claire, QC H9S 4H9
514/695-1502, URL: http://www.cam.org/~qfhs/index.html
President, G. Schroder
Publications: Connections
Affiliates: International Federation of Family History Societies

**Regroupement des organismes du patrimoine franco-ontarien (ROPFO) (1989)**
50 Maple Lane, Ottawa, ON K1M 1G8
613/744-7098
Présidente, Huguette Parent
Publications: Fleur de trille

**Richard III Society of Canada (1966)**
331 Rose Park Dr., Toronto, ON M4T 1R8
416/486-0031
Secretary, Noreen Armstrong
Publications: Newsletter

**The Royal Nova Scotia Historical Society (RNSHS) (1878)**
PO Box 2097, Dartmouth, NS B2W 3X8
902/424-6060, Fax: 902/424-0628, Email: omarc@istar.ca
President, David B. Flemming
Secretary, Rosemary Barbour
Publications: Collections of the RNSHS
Affiliates: Genealogical Association of Nova Scotia

**Saskatchewan Architectural Heritage Society (SAHS) (1987)**
Historic Strathdee Mall, #311, 2066 Dewdney Ave., Regina, SK S4R 1H3
306/359-0933, Fax: 306/359-3899
Executive Director, Michael Phelps
President, Kent Smith-Windsor
Publications: Facade; Saskatchewan Architectural Heritage Directory; Heritage Artisans Directory

**Saskatchewan Council of Cultural Organizations (SCCO) (1979)**
#210, 438 Victoria Ave. East, Regina, SK S4N 0N7
306/780-9284, Fax: 306/780-9252, Email: oshumski@unibase.unibase.com, URL: http://www.sasknet.com/~SCCO/
General Manager, Mary Mahon Jones
Communications Coordinator, Olivia Shumski, Email: olivia.shumski@sasknet.sk.ca
Publications: Cultural Report
Affiliates: Canadian Society of Association Executives

**Saskatchewan Cultural Exchange Society (SCES) (1979)**
2431 - 8 Ave., Regina, SK S4R 5J7
306/569-8966, Fax: 306/757-4422
Program Officer, Margaret Fry
President, Ross Taylor
Publications: The Exchange; Bulletin, m.

**Saskatchewan Genealogical Society (SGS) (1969)**
#201, 1870 Lorne St., PO Box 1894, Regina, SK S4P 3E1
306/780-9207, Fax: 306/781-6021, Email: margethomas.sgs@cabler.cableregina.com, URL: http://www.regina.ism.ca/orgs/sgs/index.htm
Executive Director, Marge Thomas
Publications: Bulletin
Affiliates: Saskatchewan Heritage Committee

**Société canadienne d'histoire de l'Église Catholique - Section française/Canadian Catholic Historical Association - French Section (SCHEC) (1933)**
175 Main St., Ottawa, ON K1S 1C3
613/237-0580, Téléc: 613/232-4064
Secrétaire trésorier, Romuald Boucher, O.M.I.
Publications: Études d'histoire religieuse; Bulletin de liaison, semi-annuel

**Société franco-ontarienne d'histoire et de généalogie (SFOHG) (1981)**
CP 1363, Succ. B, Sudbury, ON P3E 5K4
705/853-4849
Président, Richard Pelland
Publications: Le Chaînon

**Société généalogique canadienne-française (1943)**
CP 335, Succ. Place-d'Armes, Montréal, QC H2Y 3H1
514/729-8366, Téléc: 514/729-1180, URL: http://www.sgcf.com
Président, Normand Robert
Publications: Memoires de la Société généalogique canadienne-française

**La Société historique acadienne (1960)**
CP 632, Moncton, NB E1C 8M7
506/855-5918
Président, Léone Boudreau-Nelson
Secrétaire, E. Roy
Publications: Les Cahiers de la Société historique acadienne

**Société historique de Québec (1937)**
72, Côte de la Montagne, Québec, QC G1K 4E3
418/692-0556, Téléc: 418/692-0614

Président, Marc Beaudoin
Publications: Quebecensia

### United Empire Loyalists' Association of Canada (1914)
**UEL Association**
Dominion Office, The George Brown House, 50 Baldwin St., Toronto, ON M5T 1L4
416/591-1783, Fax: 416/591-1783
Executive Director, Dorothy Chisholm
Publications: The Loyalist Gazette

### West Coast Railway Association (WCRA) (1961)
PO Box 2790, Vancouver, BC V6B 3X2
604/524-1011, Fax: 604/522-1293, Toll Free: 1-800-722-1233, Email: don_evans@bc.sympatico.ca, URL: http://www.wcra.org
President, Bill Johnston, Bus: 604/524-1011
Publications: WCRA News

### Western Heritage Centre Society
105 River Ave., PO Box 1477, Cochrane, AB T0L 0W0
403/932-3514, Fax: 403/932-3515
General Manager, Norm Haines

### Yukon Historical & Museums Association (1977)
3126 - 3 Ave., PO Box 4357, Whitehorse, YT Y1A 3T5
867/667-4704
President, Brent Slobodin
Coordinator, Marjorie Copp
Publications: Yukon Historical & Museums Association Newsletter
Affiliates: Heritage Canada; BC Heritage Trust

### HOBBIES *see* RECREATION, HOBBIES & GAMES

### HOME & SCHOOL ASSOCIATIONS *see* EDUCATION

### HOME BUILDERS *see* HOUSING

## HOMOSEXUALITY

### Canadian Lesbian & Gay Archives (CLGA) (1973)
#201, 56 Temperance St., PO Box 639, Stn A, Toronto, ON M5W 1G2
416/777-2755, Email: queeries@clga.ca, URL: http://www.clga.ca/archives
President, Ray Brillinger
Publications: Lesbian & Gay Archivist
Affiliates: Association of Canadian Archivists; Ontario Association of Archives

### Coalition for Lesbian & Gay Rights in Ontario/Coalition pour les droits des lesbiennes et personnes gaies en Ontario (CLGRO) (1975)
PO Box 822, Stn A, Toronto, ON M5W 1G3
416/533-6824
Publications: CLGRO Newsletter
Affiliates: International Lesbian & Gay Association

### Council on Homosexuality & Religion/Conseil de l'homosexualité et la religion (CHR) (1976)
PO Box 1912, Winnipeg, MB R3C 3R2
204/474-0212, Fax: 204/478-1160, Info Line: 204/284-5208
President, Rev. A.E. Millward
Sec.-Treas., Chris Vogel

### Equality for Gays & Lesbians Everywhere/Égalité pour les gais et lesbiennes (EGALE) (1986)
#306, 177 Nepean St., Ottawa, ON K2P 0B4
613/230-1043, Fax: 613/230-9395, Email: egale@istar.ca
Executive Director, John Fisher
President, Carmen Paquette

### Integrity/Vancouver
PO Box 2797, Stn Main, Vancouver, BC V6B 3X2
604/432-1230
President, Lynette Ley
Affiliates: Integrity Inc. - USA

## HORTICULTURE & GARDENING

### Alberta Horticultural Association
1 Fenwick Cres., St Albert, AB T8N 1N5
403/460-1578
Sec.-Treas., Donna Dawson

### Les Amis du Jardin botanique de Montréal/Friends of the Montréal Botanical Garden (1975)
4101, rue Sherbrooke est, Montréal, QC H1X 2B2
514/872-1493, Téléc: 514/872-3765
Directrice générale, Karen Grislis
Président, Michel Labrecque
Secrétaire, Paule Lamontagne
Publications: Le Quatre-Temps

### Association des jardiniers maraîchers du Québec
#100, 905, rue du Marché Central, Montréal, QC H4N 1K2
514/387-8319, Téléc: 514/387-1406
Directeur général, Alain Gravel

### Canadian Gladiolus Society (CGS) (1921)
73 Bayview Cres., Cobourg, ON K9A 4C5
Email: mmcdonald@kraft.com
Sec.-Treas., Dr. M.S. McDonald
Publications: Fall Bulletin

### Canadian Horticultural Council/Conseil canadien de l'horticulture (CHC) (1922)
#310, 1101 Prince of Wales Dr., Ottawa, ON K2C 3W7
613/226-4187, Fax: 613/226-2984
Executive Vice-President, Dan Dempster
Assistant Executive Vice-President, Steven Whitney
Publications: Rapporteur
Affiliates: Canadian Federation of Agriculture

### Canadian Iris Society (CIS) (1946)
RR#9, 924 Bains Rd., Dunnville, ON N1A 2W8
416/774-8360
Secretary, Cathy Boyko
President, Jean Lederer
Publications: CIS Newsletter

### Canadian Nursery Trades Association (CNTA) (1968)
**Landscape Canada**
RR#4, Stn Main, 7856 Fifth Line South, Milton, ON L9T 2X8
905/875-1399, Fax: 905/875-1840, Toll Free: 1-888-446-3499, Email: cntalc@spectranet.ca
Executive Director, Chris D. Andrews
Publications: CNTA Newsbrief; CNTA Membership Directory, a.; Canadian Standards for Nursery Stock, biennial
Affiliates: Flowers Canada; Canadian Ornamental Plant Foundation; Associated Landscape Contractors of America; American Association of Nurserymen; International Garden Centres Association; North American Plant Protection Organization

#### BRITISH COLUMBIA NURSERY TRADES ASSOCIATION (BCNTA) (1964)
#101, 5830 - 176A St., Surrey, BC V3S 4E3
604/574-7772, Fax: 604/574-7773
Email: bhardy@direct.ca
Executive Director, Jane Stock
Program & Technology Coordinator, Bill Hardy
Publications: Dig This; Hortwest

#### LANDSCAPE ALBERTA NURSERY TRADES ASSOCIATION (LANTA) (1957)
10215 - 176 St., Edmonton, AB T5S 1M1
403/489-1991, Fax: 403/444-2152, Toll Free: 1-800-378-3198
Email: lanta@planet.eon.net
Executive Director, Nigel Bowles
Publications: Prairie Landscape; Clippings, m.

#### LANDSCAPE NEW BRUNSWICK
RR#1, Grand Dique, NB E0A 1S0
506/532-8787, Fax: 506/859-6919
Executive Secretary, Ellen Ruddick

#### LANDSCAPE NEWFOUNDLAND & LABRADOR (LNL)
PO Box 21328, St. John's, NF A1A 5G6
709/738-2374, Fax: 709/738-2374
Executive Secretary, Pamela Pippy

#### LANDSCAPE NOVA SCOTIA
Kentville Agricultural Centre, Blair House, Kentville, NS B4N 1J5
902/768-0533, Fax: 902/679-1074
Executive Secretary, Sonya MacKillop

#### LANDSCAPE ONTARIO HORTICULTURAL TRADES ASSOCIATION (LOHTA) (1973)
7856 Fifth Line South, RR#4, Milton, ON L9T 2X8
905/875-1805, Fax: 905/875-3942
Email: lo@mail.westonia.com, URL: http://www.hort-trades.com
Executive Director, Tony DiGiovanni
Publications: Landscape Trades; Horticulture Review

#### MANITOBA NURSERY & LANDSCAPE ASSOCIATION (MNLA) (1958)
**Landscape Manitoba**
808 Muriel St., Winnipeg, MB R2Y 0Y3
204/889-5981, Fax: 204/888-0944
Executive Secretary, Evelyn MacKenzie-Reid
Publications: Prairie East Horticultural News

#### SASKATCHEWAN NURSERY TRADES ASSOCIATION (SNTA)
8 Hamilton Pl., Saskatoon, SK S7L 3N3
306/384-9072, Fax: 306/384-9017
Executive Secretary, Kathy Evans

### Canadian Ornamental Plant Foundation/Fondation canadienne des plantes ornementales (COPF) (1964)
PO Box 21083, North Bay, ON P1B 7N8
705/495-2563, Fax: 705/495-1449
Managing Director, Peggy Walsh Craig
Publications: COPF News

### Canadian Rose Society (CRS) (1955)
10 Fairfax Cres., Scarborough, ON M1L 1Z8
416/757-8809, Fax: 416/757-4796
Secretary, Anne Graber
Publications: The Rosarian; The Canadian Rose Annual
Affiliates: World Federation of Rose Societies

### Canadian Society for Horticultural Science/Société canadienne de science horticole (CSHS) (1956)
c/o Agricultural Institute of Canada, #1112, 141 Laurier Ave. West, Ottawa, ON K1P 5J3
613/232-9459, Fax: 613/594-5190
Email: office@aic.ca, URL: http://www.aic.ca/members/cshs.html
Contact, David Wees, Email: Wees@agradm.lan.mcgill.ca
Publications: CSHS Newsletter; Canadian Journal of Plant Science, q.
Affiliates: International Society for Horticultural Science

### Canadian Wildflower Society
#228, 4981 Hwy. 7, Markham, ON L3R 1N1

Contact, James French
Publications: Wildflower

### City Farmer - Canada's Office of Urban Agriculture (1978)
#801, 318 Homer St., Vancouver, BC V6B 2V3
604/685-5832, Fax: 604/685-0431, Email: cityfarm@unixg.ubc.ca, URL: http://www.cityfarmer.org
Executive Director, Michael Levenston
Publications: Gardening with People with Disabilities; Urban Home Composting; Urban Agriculture Notes

### Fédération interdisciplinaire de l'horticulture ornementale du Québec (FIHOQ) (1976)
Pavillon Envirotron, Cité Universitaire, CP 2208, Succ. Terminus, Ste-Foy, QC G1K 7P4
418/659-3562, Téléc: 418/651-7439
Directrice administrative, Aline Munger
Publications: L'Actuel horticole
Organisation(s) affiliée(s): Association internationale des producteurs en horticulture; Conseil canadien de l'horticulture; Chambre de commerce du Québec; Conseil québécois de l'Horticulture

### Fédération des sociétés d'horticulture et d'écologie du Québec (FSHÉQ)
4545, av Pierre-de-Coubertin, CP 1000, Succ. M, Montréal, QC H1V 3R2
514/252-3010, Téléc: 514/251-8038
Président, René Paquet

### Flowers Canada Inc./Fleurs Canada inc. (FC) (1967)
7856 Fifth Line South, RR#4, Milton, ON L9T 2X8
519/875-0707, Fax: 519/875-3494, Email: flowers@spectranet.ca
Executive Director, Garry R. Watson
Publications: News Vine

### Ontario Horticultural Association (1951)
PO Box 842, Sutton, ON L0E 1R0
URL: http://www.interlog.com/~onthort
President, Jim Anderson

### Prince Edward Island Horticultural Association, Inc. (1984)
PO Box 2232, Charlottetown, PE C1A 8B9
902/566-2733, Fax: 902/566-2383
President, Ralph Yeo
Treasurer, Gerald Dykerman
Agrologist, Joanne Driscoll
Affiliates: PEI Vegetable Growers Cooperative; PEI Cole Crop Growers Co-op Ltd.; PEI Greenhouse Growers Association; PEI Federation of Agriculture; PEI Strawberry Growers Association; Canadian Horticulture Council

### Rhododendron Society of Canada (1971)
RR#2, St George Brant, ON N0E 1N0
519/448-1537
Contact, Dr. H.G. Hedges

### Royal Botanical Gardens/Les jardins botaniques royaux (RBG) (1932)
PO Box 399, Hamilton, ON L8N 3H8
905/527-1158, Fax: 905/577-0375
Director, Sharilyn J. Ingram
Publications: Pappus

### Saskatchewan Horticultural Association
PO Box 68, Parkside, SK S0J 2A0
306/747-3296
President, Helen Buchanan
Secretary, Alan Daku
Treasurer, Jean Procknow

### Seeds of Diversity Canada/Programme semencier du patrimoine (SODC) (1984)
PO Box 36, Stn Q, Toronto, ON M4T 2L7
905/623-0353
President, Garrett Pittenger
Publications: Seeds of Diversity; Seed Listing, a.; Resource List of Seeds Companies & Nurseries Selling Heirloom Varieties; How to Save Your Own Vegetable Seeds

### Southern Ontario Orchid Society
45 Stamford Sq. South, Scarborough, ON M1L 1X2
416/759-1439
Contact, Walter Norman

## HOSPITALS
*see also* Health & Medical; Nursing

### Association of Canadian Teaching Hospitals (ACTH) (1970)
#E408, 4500 Oak St., Vancouver, BC V6H 3N1
604/875-3468, Fax: 604/872-3290
Executive Director, James B. Flett
Affiliates: Association of Canadian Medical Colleges

### Association des centres hospitaliers et centres d'accueil privés du Québec (ACHAP) (1979)
#200, 204, rue Notre-Dame ouest, Montréal, QC H2Y 1T3
514/499-3630, Téléc: 514/873-7063
Directeur général, Jacques Renaud

### Association of Ontario Health Centres/Association des centres de santé de l'Ontario (AOHC) (1982)
#102, 5233 Dundas St. West, Etobicoke, ON M9B 1A6
416/236-2539, Fax: 416/236-0431, Email: mail@aohc.com, URL: http://www.aohc.org
Executive Director, Gary O'Connor
Publications: Healthlink; CHC News for CHC People, q.
Affiliates: Healthy Communities; Broader Health Sector Task Force

### British Columbia Association of Private Care (1978)
**BC Pricare**
#101, 1700 - 75th Ave. West, Vancouver, BC V6P 6G2
604/263-4223, Fax: 604/263-4229
Chief Executive Officer, Ed Helfrich
Coordinator, Board & Member Services, Pat Christie
Publications: BC Pricare News
Affiliates: Canadian College of Health Services Executives; Canadian & BC Gerontology Associations; Canadian Home Care Association; Canadian Association for Community Care; Quality Council of BC

### Canadian Administrative Housekeepers Association/L'Association Canadienne des Intendants Administratif (CAHA) (1972)
c/o Dryden District General Hospital, PO Box 3003, Dryden, ON P8N 2Z6
604/528-3868, Fax: 604/528-3871
President, Bonnie Suni, CAH
Director of Membership, Gordon Sisco, CAH
Sec.-Treas., Gillian Profitt, CAH
Publications: Magazine

### Canadian Association for Community Care/Association canadienne de soins et services communautaires (CACC) (1977)
**HomeSupport Canada**
#701, 45 Rideau St., Ottawa, ON K1N 5W8
613/241-7510, Fax: 613/241-5923, Email: cacc@trytel.com
Co-Executive Director, Dawn Walker
Co-Executive Director, Sharon Sholzberg-Gray
Publications: National Bulletin
Affiliates: Canadian Council on Health Services Accreditation; One Voice

#### ALBERTA LONG TERM CARE ASSOCIATION (ALTCA) (1980)
CN Tower, #910, 10004 - 104 Ave., Edmonton, AB T5J 0K1
403/421-1137, Fax: 403/426-0479
Executive Director, Claire Mills

#### ASSOCIATED HOMES FOR SPECIAL CARE, NOVA SCOTIA (1964)
#119, 2786 Agricola St., Halifax NS B3K 4E1
902/453-2977, Fax: 902/453-2967
Interim Executive Director, Julie Gibson

#### CONFÉDÉRATION QUÉBÉCOISE DES CENTRES D'HÉBERGEMENT ET DE RÉADAPTATION (CQCHR) (1974)
#1100, 1001, boul de Maisonneuve est, Montréal, QC H2L 4P9
514/597-1007, Téléc: 514/873-5411
Vice-président exécutif, Louis Champoux
Agente d'information, Nancy Leggett-Bachand
Publications: L'Accueil

#### NEW BRUNSWICK ASSOCIATION OF NURSING HOMES, INC./ASSOCIATION DES FOYERS DE SOINS DU NOUVEAU-BRUNSWICK, INC. (1972)
197 Main St., Fredericton, NB E3A 1E1
506/458-9466, Fax: 506/458-9206
Executive Director, Michel Desjardins
Publications: Intercom

#### NEWFOUNDLAND & LABRADOR ASSOCIATION OF HOMES FOR SPECIAL CARE
PO Box 95, Holyrood, NF A0A 2R0
709/229-7053
Sec.-Treas., Tom Power

#### NEWFOUNDLAND & LABRADOR HEALTH CARE ASSOCIATION (NLHCA) (1962)
Beclin Building, 1118 Topsail Rd., PO Box 8234, Stn A, St. John's, NF A1B 3N4
709/364-7701, Fax: 709/364-6460
Executive Director, John F. Peddle

#### NURSING HOME ASSOCIATION OF MANITOBA (NHAM) (1974)
#700, 360 Broadway, Winnipeg, MB R3C 4G8
204/956-1819, Fax: 204/943-5370
Executive Director, Isabel Rourke
President, R. Bazinet

#### ONTARIO ASSOCIATION OF NON-PROFIT HOMES & SERVICES FOR SENIORS (OANHSS) (1919)
#700, 7050 Weston Rd., Woodbridge, ON L4L 8G7
905/851-8821, Fax: 905/851-0744
Email: admin@oanhss.org
Executive Director, Michael Klejman
Publications: Action Update

### Canadian Association of Health-Care Auxiliaries/Association des auxiliaires bénévoles des établissements de santé du Canada (CAHA) (1951)
#100, 17 York St., Ottawa, ON K1N 9J6
613/241-8005, Fax: 613/241-5055
President, Carol Clemenhagen
Vice-President, Finance, Tim Julien
Publications: Volunteering for Health/Bénévole de la Santé
Affiliates: Canadian Hospital Association

#### ALBERTA HEALTH CARE AUXILIARIES ASSOCIATION (AHAA) (1948)
#334, 1480 Southview, Medicine Hat, AB T1B 3I3
403/527-6442, Fax: 403/529-5859
President, Mary Kundert
Publications: Around Alberta

**ASSOCIATION DES AUXILIAIRES BÉNÉVOLES DES ÉTABLISSEMENTS DE SANTÉ DU QUÉBEC/ASSOCIATION OF HOSPITAL AUXILIARIES OF THE PROVINCE OF QUÉBEC (ABESQ) (1952)**
#400, 505, boul de Maisonneuve ouest, Montréal, QC H3A 3C2
514/282-4264, Téléc: 514/282-4289
Présidente, Nicole Boisvert
Secrétaire, Andrée Quinn
Trésorière, Suzanne Gagnon
Publications: Servo

**BRITISH COLUMBIA ASSOCIATION OF HEALTH CARE AUXILIARIES (BCAHA)**
#600, 1333 West Broadway, Vancouver, BC V6H 4C7
604/734-2423, Fax: 604/734-7202
President, April Sear, Bus: 604/947-9190
Administrative Secretary, Irene Popil
Director, Communications, Elena Tighe, Bus: 604/758-0415
Publications: Auxiliary Action
Affiliates: BC Health Association; Canadian Association of Health Care Auxiliaries; Canadian Hospital Association

**HOSPITAL AUXILIARIES ASSOCIATION OF ONTARIO (HAAO) (1910)**
52 Karen Cres., Hamilton, ON L9L 5M6
905/574-0020, Fax: 905/574-1025
President, Dianne Jackson
Publications: The Volunteer

**MANITOBA HEALTH AUXILIARIES ASSOCIATION**
#8A, 2366 Portage Ave., Winnipeg, MB R3J 0N4
204/889-6150
President, Jessie Wright

**NEW BRUNSWICK ASSOCIATION OF HEALTHCARE AUXILIARIES**
770 Reid St., Fredericton, NB E3B 3V9
506/455-7359
Secretary/Archivist, R. John Booker
President, Helen MacTavish

**NEWFOUNDLAND/LABRADOR ASSOCIATION OF HEALTH CARE AUXILIARIES**
PO Box 29, Grand Bag East, Port Aux Basques, NF A0N 1K0
709/645-2480
President, Roslyn Tucker

**NOVA SCOTIA ASSOCIATION OF HEALTH AUXILIARIES**
PO Box 156, Hantsport, NS B0P 1P0
902/684-9448
President, Elizabeth Caldwell

**SASKATCHEWAN HEALTH CARE AUXILIARIES ASSOCIATION (1941)**
PO Box 85, Eyebrow, SK S0H 1L0
306/759-2132
Contact, Jean Gurney

### Canadian Association of Medical Clinics
The Raxlen Clinic, 500 Parliament St., Toronto, ON M4X 1P4
416/966-3641, Fax: 416/944-8662
Executive Director, Derek Evelyn

### Canadian Association of Paediatric Hospitals/Association canadienne des hôpitaux pédiatriques (1968)
#430, 1730 St. Laurent Blvd., Ottawa, ON K1G 5L1
613/738-7706, Fax: 613/738-7941
Executive Director, Diane C. Barei

### Canadian Association of Social Work Administrators in Health Facilities/Association canadienne des administrateurs de services sociaux en milieu de santé (CASWAHF) (1973)
Social Work Department, Kingston General Hospital, 76 Stuart St., Kingston, ON K7L 2V7
613/549-6666, ext.4443, Fax: 613/548-2354
President, Patrick F. Whalen-Browne
Publications: Connections

### Canadian Council on Health Services Accreditation/Conseil canadien d'agrément des services de santé (CCHSA) (1958)
#430, 1730 St. Laurent Blvd., Ottawa, ON K1G 5L1
613/738-3800, Fax: 613/738-3755, URL: http://www.cchsa.ca
Executive Director, Elma Heidemann
Affiliates: Association of Canadian Teaching Hospitals; Canadian Association for Community Care; Canadian College of Health Service Executives; Royal College of Physicians & Surgeons of Canada; The College of Family Physicians of Canada; Canadian Healthcare Association; Canadian Medical Association

### Canadian Healthcare Association/Association canadienne des soins de santé (1931)
17 York St., Ottawa, ON K1N 9J6
613/241-8005, Fax: 613/241-5055, URL: http://www.canadian-healthcare.org
President, Joyce Bailey
Chairman, John Baker
Affiliates: International Hospital Federation; American Hospital Association

**ASSOCIATION DES HÔPITAUX DU QUÉBEC/QUÉBEC HOSPITAL ASSOCIATION (AHQ)**
#400, 505, boul de Maisonneuve ouest, Montréal, QC H3A 3C2
514/842-4861, Téléc: 514/282-4271
Vice-président exécutif, Jacques A. Nadeau
Président, Serge Bélisle
Publications: Artére

**HEALTH ASSOCIATION OF PEI (HAPEI) (1961)**
10 Pownal St., PO Box 490, Charlottetown, PE C1A 7L1
902/368-3901, Fax: 902/368-3231
Executive Director, Carol Gabanna
Group Tendering Coordinator, Donna Butler

**MANITOBA HEALTH ORGANIZATIONS (MHO) (1921)**
#600, 360 Broadway, Winnipeg, MB R3C 4G6
204/942-6591, Fax: 204/956-1373
President, Ronald G. Birt
Chairman, Edwin H. Klassen
Communications Officer, Wendy Fox
Publications: Healthbeat

**NEW BRUNSWICK HEALTHCARE ASSOCIATION/ASSOCIATION DES SOINS DE SANTÉ DU NOUVEAU-BRUNSWICK (NBHA) (1962)**
861 Woodstock Rd., Fredericton, NB E3B 7R7
506/451-0750, Fax: 506/451-0760
Email: nbha@nbnet.nb.ca
Executive Director, Michel J. Poirier
Associate Executive Director, Dr. Karon Croll
Publications: Telescope

**NORTHWEST TERRITORIES HEALTH CARE ASSOCIATION (NWTHCA) (1965)**
#206, 4817 - 49 St., PO Box 1709, Yellowknife, NT X1A 2P3
867/873-9253, Fax: 867/873-9254
Executive Director, Persa Kovich
Publications: NWTHCA Newsletter

**NOVA SCOTIA ASSOCIATION OF HEALTH ORGANIZATIONS (NSAHO) (1960)**
Bedford Professional Centre, 2 Dartmouth Rd., Halifax, NS B4A 2K7
902/832-8500, Fax: 902/832-8505
Acting CEO, Robert Cook
Publications: Newsletter; Your Association this Week, w.; Clipboard, bi-weekly

**ONTARIO HOSPITAL ASSOCIATION (OHA) (1924)**
#2800, 200 Front St. West, Toronto, ON M5V 3L1
416/205-1300, Fax: 416/205-1301
URL: http://www.oha.com
President & CEO, David C. MacKinnon
Chair, Robert K. Muir
Corporate Secretary, M. Murray
Publications: Executive Report; Hospital Perspectives, q.

**PROVINCIAL HEALTH AUTHORITIES OF ALBERTA (1919)**
44 Capital Blvd., #200, 10044 - 108 St. NW, Edmonton, AB T5J 3S7
403/426-8502, Fax: 403/424-4309
Executive Director, Mike Higgins

**SASKATCHEWAN ASSOCIATION OF HEALTH ORGANIZATIONS (SAHO) (1993)**
1445 Park St., Regina, SK S4N 4C5
306/347-5500, Fax: 306/525-1960
President, Arliss Wright
Publications: SAHO News; Materials Manager

### Canadian Home Care Association/Association canadienne de soins et services à domicile (CHCA) (1990)
#401, 17 York St., Ottawa, ON K1R 7F8
613/569-1585, Fax: 613/569-1604
Executive Director, Lesley Larsen
President, Shirlee Sharkey
Publications: At Home/Chez Nous

### Hospital Engineers Association of Alberta
2007 - 14th St. SW, Calgary, AB T2V 1P9
403/541-3291
President, Allan Potter

### National Sanitarium Association
PO Box 100, Stn Commerce Court, Toronto, ON M5L 1B9
416/980-4457, Fax: 416/980-7012
Sec.-Treas., J.G. Barraclough

### Ontario Association of Directors of Volunteer Services in Healthcare (OADHVS) (1970)
#1437, 1011 Upper Middle Rd., Oakville, ON L6H 5Z9
416/926-4823, Fax: 416/926-4992, URL: http://www.interlog.com/~odvh/
President, Carol Dixon
Publications: Directions
Affiliates: Volunteer Ontario

### Ontario Association of Medical Laboratories (OAML) (1974)
#206, 4120 Yonge St., North York, ON M2P 2B8
416/250-8555, Fax: 416/250-8464
President, Paul J. Gould

### Ontario Nursing Home Association (ONHA) (1959)
#202, 345 Renfrew Dr., Markham, ON L3R 9S9
905/470-8995, Fax: 905/470-9595
Executive Director, Shelly Jamieson
President, David Cutler
Publications: Long Term Care

## HOUSING
*see also* **Real Estate**

### Association of Condominium Managers of Ontario (ACMO) (1977)
#1105, 191 The West Mall, Etobicoke, ON M9C 5K8
416/626-7895, Fax: 416/620-5392, Toll Free: 1-800-265-3263
Executive Director, Don Braden
Publications: The Condominium Manager

**Canadian Association of Home Inspectors (CAHI) (1992)**
PO Box 22010, RPO Capri Centre, Kelowna, BC V1Y 9N9
Fax: /1-800-610-5665, Toll Free: 1-800-610-5665, URL: http://www.bconnex.net/~jmlueck/cahi.html
Co-Chairman, Jeff Clarke
Affiliates: American Society of Home Inspectors; Canadian Council of Building Officials Associations; Interprovincial Building Codes Education Association

**Canadian Condominium Institute - National Chapter (CCI) (1982)**
#310, 2175 Sheppard Ave. East, North York, ON M2J 1W8
416/491-6216, Fax: 416/491-1670, Email: taylor@interlog.com
President, Rob Giesbrecht
Chairman, Mark Freedman
National Executive Director, Diane Gaunt
Publications: CCI Review

**Canadian Federation of Apartment Associations (CFAA) (1995)**
#203, 1847 West Broadway, Vancouver, BC V6J 1Y6
604/733-9440, Fax: 604/733-9420
President, Debbie Johnson

**Canadian Home Builders' Association/ Association canadienne des constructeurs d'habitations (CHBA) (1943)**
#200, 150 Laurier Ave. West, Ottawa, ON K1P 6M7
613/230-3060, Fax: 613/232-8214, Email: chba@chba.ca, URL: http://www.chba.ca
Chief Operating Officer, John K. Kenward
President, Gerhard Ruehr

**ASSOCIATION PROVINCIALE DES CONSTRUCTEURS D'HABITATIONS QUÉBEC/PROVINCIAL HOME BUILDERS ASSOCIATION OF QUÉBEC (APCHQ)**
2825, boul Wilfrid-Hamel, Québec, QC G1P 2H9
418/682-3353, Téléc: 418/682-3851
Directeur général, Jean-Pierre Sirard

**Canadian Housing & Renewal Association/ Association canadienne d'habitation et de rénovation urbaine (CHRA) (1968)**
#401, 251 Laurier Ave. West, Ottawa, ON K1P 5J6
613/594-3007, Fax: 613/594-9596
Executive Director, Sharon Chisholm
Office Manager, Elisa Ruiz
Publications: Canadian Housing/Habitation canadienne

**Canadian Manufactured Housing Association**
#200, 150 Laurier Ave. West, Ottawa, ON K1P 5J4
613/563-3520, Fax: 613/232-8600
Executive Vice-President, James R. Cooke

**Canadian Shareowners Association (1987)**
#1317, 2 Carlton St., Toronto, ON M5B 1J3
519/252-1555, Fax: 519/252-9570, Email: bart@shareowner.ca, URL: http://www.shareowner.ca
President, John Bart
Publications: Canadian Shareowner

**Co-operative Housing Federation of BC (CHF-BC) (1982)**
133 East 8th Ave., Vancouver, BC V5T 1R8
604/879-5111, Fax: 604/879-4611, Info Line: 604/879-5112, Email: mknaut@chf.bc.ca, URL: http://www.vcn.bc.ca/chfbc/
Executive Director, Mary Flynn
Publications: SCOOP

**Cooperative Housing Association of Newfoundland & Labrador**
PO Box 453, Mount Pearl, NF A1N 2C4
709/747-5615, Fax: 709/747-5606
Financial Services Officer, Dave Adams

**Cooperative Housing Federation of Canada/ Fédération de l'habitation coopérative du Canada (CHF) (1968)**
#311, 225 Metcalfe St., Ottawa, ON K2P 1P9
613/230-2201, Fax: 613/230-2231, Toll Free: 1-800-465-2752
Executive Director, Alexandra Wilson
Coordinator/Communications, Suzan Schmekel
Publications: Coopservations
Ontario Region: Managing Director, Dale Reagan, #207, 2 Berkeley St., Toronto, ON M5A 2W3, 416/366-1711, Fax: 416/366-3876

**Cooperative Housing Federation of Nova Scotia (CHFNS) (1981)**
#305, 3045 Robie St., Halifax, NS B3K 4P6
Publications: Co-op Housing News
Affiliates: Affordable Housing Association of Nova Scotia

**Federation of Metro Toronto Tenants' Associations (FMTA) (1974)**
#403, 344 Bloor St. West, Toronto, ON M5S 3A7
416/921-9494, Fax: 416/921-4177
Administrator, Charlene Baker
Chairperson, Kenn Hale
Vice-Chairperson, Henk Mulder
Policy Coordinator, Deborah Wandal
Publications: Tenants Bulletin
Affiliates: United Tenants of Ontario; Tenant Non-Profit Redevelopment Company; Metro Tenants Legal Service

**Federation of Ottawa-Carleton Tenants' Associations/Fédération des associations de locataires d'Ottawa-Carleton**
#1, 20 Rochester, Ottawa, ON K1R 7V3
613/594-5429, Fax: 613/594-5804, URL: http://www.ncf.carleton.ca/focta/
Executive Director, D. McIntyre

**Institute of Municipal Assessors of Ontario**
#303, 109 Railside Rd., North York, ON M3A 1B2
416/447-7213, Fax: 416/447-3452
Executive Director, W.J. Lettner
Publications: Assessors Review

**Manitoba Landlords Association**
738 Elgin Ave., Winnipeg, MB R3E 1B2
204/775-1726
Contact, L. Holubowich

**Manufactured Housing Association - Alberta & Saskatchewan (1976)**
#201, 4921 - 49 St., Red Deer, AB T4N 1V2
403/347-8925, Fax: 403/347-2505, Toll Free: 1-800-661-7444
Executive Director, Vi Tkachuk
Publications: Newsletter

**Multiple Dwelling Standards Association (MDSA) (1970)**
163 Beechwood Ave., North York, ON M2L 1J9
416/449-7700
President/General Manager, Jan Schwartz

**Nova Scotia Institute of Assessors (1967)**
PO Box 706, Sydney, NS B1P 6H7
902/563-2150
Secretary, Mora Smith

**Ontario Association of Property Standards Officers Inc.**
148 Braemar Rd., Kingston, ON K7M 4B8
613/544-7222, Fax: 613/546-0902
Secretary, P. Clark
Publications: The Property Standard

**Ontario Non-Profit Housing Association (ONPHA) (1988)**
#400, 489 College St., Toronto, ON M6G 1A5
416/927-9144, Fax: 416/927-8401
Executive Director, Robin Campbell
Publications: Connections

**Rental Housing Council of British Columbia**
#1011, 470 Granville St., Vancouver, BC V6C 1V5
604/681-0045, Fax: 604/681-4261
Executive Director, Edward N. Whitlock

**HUMAN RESOURCES *see* EMPLOYMENT & HUMAN RESOURCES**

## HUMAN RIGHTS & CIVIL LIBERTIES

**Amnesty International, Canadian Section (English Speaking)**
214 Montréal Rd., 4th Fl., Vanier, ON K1L 1A4
613/744-7667, Fax: 613/746-2411, Email: info@amnesty.ca
President, Donna Thiessen
Secretary General, Roger Clark
Communications, John Tackaberry
Documentalist, Lillibeth Ackbarali
Publications: The Activist
Affiliates: Formal relations with the United Nations Economic & Social Council (ECOSOC), UNESCO, the Council of Europe; the Organization of American States, the Organization of African Unity & the Inter-Parliamentary Union
Pacific Regional Office: #4, 3664 Hastings St. West, Vancouver, BC V5K 2A9, 604/294-5160, Fax: 604/294-5130
Toronto Regional Office: 400 Bloor St. West, 2nd Fl., Toronto, ON M5S 1X5, 416/929-9477, Fax: 416/929-0539

**Amnistie internationale, Section canadienne (Francophone) (1971)**
6250, boul Monk, Montréal, QC H4E 3H7
514/766-9766, Téléc: 514/766-2088, Courrier électronique: aimtl@cam.org, URL: http://www.amnistie.qc.ca
Directeur général, Michel Frenette
Responsable, Communications, Anne Sainte-Marie
Publications: Agir

**Canada Council on Human Rights & Race Relations (1988)**
**Human Rights & Race Relations Centre**
#1506, 141 Adelaide St. West, Toronto, ON M5H 3L5
416/440-1971, Fax: 416/481-7793, Toll Free: 1-888-667-5877
President, Hasanat Ahmad Syed
Secretary, Ismat Pasha
Publications: New Canada

**The Canadian Centre/International P.E.N. (PEN) (1926)**
**PEN Canada**
24 Ryerson Ave., Toronto, ON M5T 2P3
416/703-8448, Fax: 416/703-3870, Email: pencan@web.apc.org
President, Nino Ricci
Policy Director, Isabel Harry
Administrative Director, Margaret Purcell
Publications: Canadian PEN Newsletter

**Canadian Civil Liberties Association/Association canadienne des libertés civiles (CCLA) (1964)**
#403, 229 Yonge St., Toronto, ON M5B 1N9
416/363-0321, Fax: 416/861-1291
President, Sybil Shack
General Counsel, A. Alan Borovoy
Publications: CCLA Newsnotes

**ALBERTA CIVIL LIBERTIES RESEARCH CENTRE (ACLRC) (1982)**
c/o Faculty of Law, University of Calgary, 2500 University Dr. NW, Calgary, AB T2N 1N4
403/220-2505, Fax: 403/284-0945
Email: ac;rc@freenet.calgary.ab.ca, URL: http://www.FreeNet.Calgary.ab.ca/populati/communit/acl/aclrc.html
Executive Director, Linda McKay-Panos
Publications: Centrepiece

**MANITOBA ASSOCIATION FOR RIGHTS & LIBERTIES (1978)**
#502, 177 Lombard Ave., Winnipeg, MB R3B 0W5
204/947-0213, Fax: 204/946-0403
URL: http://www.winnipeg.freenet.mb.ca/marl/marl_hm.html
Executive Director, Valerie Price
President, Greg Tramley
Publications: MARL Newsletter

**SAINT JOHN CHARTER RIGHTS & CIVIL LIBERTIES ASSOCIATION (1971)**
PO Box 6446, Stn A, Saint John, NB E2L 4R8
506/632-0096, Fax: 506/634-7423
President, Fred D. Hodges, CM, LLD
Secretary, Eric L. Teed, OC, Q.C.

**The Canadian Free Speech League**
810 Courtney St., Victoria, BC V8W 1C4
250/385-1022, Fax: 250/479-3294
General Counsel, Douglas Christie
Publications: Friends of Freedom

**Canadian Human Rights Foundation/Fondation canadienne des droits humains**
#304, 1425, rue René-Levesque, Montréal, QC H3G 1T7
514/954-0382, Fax: 514/954-0659
Executive Director, Ruth Selwyn
President, Pearl Eliadis
Publications: Newsletter/Bulletin

**Canadian Tribute to Human Rights/Monument canadien pour les droits de la personne (1984)**
PO Box 510, Stn B, Ottawa, ON K1P 5P6
President, Stephen Naor
Sec.-Treas., George Wilkes

**Citizens for Public Justice (CPJ) (1963)**
#311, 229 College St., Toronto, ON M5T 1R4
416/979-2443, Fax: 416/979-2458, Email: cpj@web.net, URL: http://www.web.net/~cpj
Executive Director, Harry J. Kits
Chairman, Brian Walsh
Publications: The Catalyst

**Human Rights Institute of Canada/Institut canadien des droits humains (HRIC) (1974)**
#303, 246 Queen St., Ottawa, ON K1P 5E4
613/232-2920, Fax: 613/232-3735
President, Dr. Marguerite E. Ritchie
Publications: Research Studies & Submissions to Parliamentary Committees

**International Centre for Human Rights & Democratic Development/Centre international des droits de la personne et du développement démocratique (ICHRDD) (1988)**
#100, 63, rue de Bresoles, Montréal, QC H2Y 1V7
514/283-6073, Fax: 514/283-3792, Email: ichrdd@web.net, URL: http://www.ichrdd.ca
President, Warren Allmand
Publications: Libertas

**League for Human Rights of B'nai Brith Canada/Ligue des droits de la personne de B'nai Brith Canada (1965)**
15 Hove St., Downsview, ON M3H 4Y8
416/633-6227, Fax: 416/630-2159, Email: league@bnaibrith.ca, URL: http://www.bnaibrith.ca/league_f.htm
National Director, Dr. Karen Mock, Email: kmock@bnaibrith.ca
Publications: Review of Anti-Semitism in Canada; Research Reports on Hate Groups in Canada

**Macedonian Human Rights Movement of Canada/Mouvement canadien de défense des droits de la personne dans la communauté macédonienne (MHRMC) (1986)**
2376 Eglinton Ave. East, PO Box 44532, Toronto, ON M1K 5K3
416/202-8866, Fax: 416/412-3385, URL: http://www.mhrmc.on.ca
President, Dr. Andon Plukov
Secretary, Jamie Rapos
Treasurer, Bruce Nicov
Vice-President, Louie Opashinov
Publications: Human Rights Abuses Against Ethnic Macedonians

**Network on International Human Rights/Réseau des droits de la personne au plan international (NIHR) (1986)**
c/o CCIC, #300, One Nicholas St., Ottawa, ON K1N 7B7
613/241-7007, ext.361, Fax: 613/241-5302, Email: nihr@web.net
Coordinator, Myriam de Feyter

**Patients' Rights Association**
170 Merton St., Toronto, ON M4S 1A1
416/487-6287, Fax: 416/489-7533
Executive Director, Mary Margaret Steckle
Publications: The Patients' Advocate

**Vancouver Island Human Rights Coalition (VIHRC) (1982)**
#418, 620 View St., Victoria, BC V8W 1J6
250/382-3012
President, Ron MacIsaac
Director, Tom Loring
Publications: Newsletter

**Victoria Civil Liberties Association (VCLA) (1983)**
c/o Advanced Imaging Lab., Biology Dept., University of Victoria, PO Box 3020, Victoria, BC V8W 3N5
250/721-7134, Fax: 250/721-7120, Email: togo@uvic.ca
Contact, Tom Gore
Publications: VCLA News

**HUMANE SOCIETIES *see* ANIMALS & ANIMAL SCIENCE**

**ILLUSTRATION *see* VISUAL ART, CRAFTS, FOLK ARTS**

**IMMIGRATION *see* CITIZENSHIP & IMMIGRATION**

**IMPLEMENT MANUFACTURING *see* EQUIPMENT & MACHINERY**

**IMPORT TRADE *see* TRADE**

**INDUSTRIAL RELATIONS *see* LABOUR RELATIONS**

**INDUSTRY *see* MANUFACTURING & INDUSTRY**

**INFORMATION CENTRES *see* SOCIAL RESPONSE/SOCIAL SERVICES**

## INFORMATION TECHNOLOGY

**AFCOM - the Premier Association for Data Center, Network & Enterprize Systems Management (1980)**
742 East Chapman Ave., Orange, CA 92666 USA
714/997-7966, Fax: 714/997-9743
President, Leonard Eckhaus
Publications: Enterprise Management Issues; Communiqué

**ASM International (1947)**
**Association for Systems Management**
1433 West Bagley Rd., Berea, OH 44017 USA
216/243-6900, Fax: 216/234-2930, URL: http://www.asm-intl.org
Managing Director, Michael J. DeHaemer, Email: DeHaemer@po.asm-intl.org
President, Montréal Chapter, Lise Trudel, Bus: 514/481-4632
Contact, Ottawa Valley Chapter, Robert Elliott, Bus: 613/748-2816
Contact, London Chapter, Patricia White, Bus: 519/971-2908
Contact, Calgary Chapter, Eric Pattrie, Bus: 403/266-2266
Contact, Edmonton Chapter, Eddie Nealon, Bus: 403/420-8938
Contact, Vancouver Chapter, Sandra Cunningham, Bus: 604/986-6468
Publications: Journal of Systems Management

**Association of Professional Computer Consultants - Canada (1992)**
#310, 2175 Sheppard Ave. East, North York, ON M2J 1W8
416/491-2886, Fax: 416/491-1670
President, Frank McCrea
Administrator, Diane Gaunt
Publications: News & Information

**BC Advanced Systems Institute (ASI)**
#450, 1122 Mainland St., Vancouver, BC V6B 5L1
604/689-0551, Fax: 604/689-4198, Toll Free: 1-800-501-3388, Email: asi@asi.bc.ca, URL: http://www.asi.bc.ca/asi/
Executive Director, Brent Sauder, Email: bsauder@asi.bc.ca
Operations Manager, Carol M. Hassell, Email: hassell@asi.bc.ca
Industry Programs Manager, Vince Lum, Email: vincelum@asi.bc.ca

**Canada's Coalition for Public Information/Coalition canadienne de l'information publique (CPI) (1993)**
200 Adelaide St. West, 3rd Fl., Toronto, ON M5H 1W7
416/977-6018, Fax: 416/597-1617, Email: cpi@web.net, URL: http://www.canarie.ca/cpi
President, Maureen Cubberley
Chair, Liz Hoffman

**Canadian Alliance Against Software Theft/Alliance canadienne contre le vol de logiciels (CAAST) (1990)**
c/o Strategic Ampersand Inc., #1440, 250 Bloor St. East, Toronto, ON M4W 1E6
416/961-5595, Fax: 416/961-7955
Chief Counsel, Michael Eisen

**Canadian Association of Internet Providers (CAIP)**
#200, 5925 Airport Rd., Mississauga, ON L4V 1W1

905/405-6212, Fax: 905/405-6214, URL: http://www.caip.ca/
President, Ron Kawchuk, Email: kawchuk@io.org
Chair, Margo Langford

**Canadian Association of SAS Users/Association canadienne des utilisateurs SAS (CASU) (1991)**
BCE Place, #2220, 181 Bay St., PO Box 819, Toronto, ON M5J 2T3
416/363-4424, Fax: 416/363-5399
Contact, Jeff Read

**Canadian Children's Multimedia Foundation (CCMF) (1994)**
#404, 1080 Broughton St., Vancouver, BC V6G 2A8
604/662-3805
President, Sharon Lipovsky

**Canadian Community of Computer Educators (CCCE)**
15 Lone Oak Ave., Brampton, ON L6S 5V4
905/796-9311
President, Alania Baldwin
Consortium Training Director, Gord McDougall
Membership/Public Relations Director, Joyce Holland
Program Director, Annetta Wange

**Canadian Computer Dealer Association (CCDA) (1981)**
PO Box 21547, RPO Upper Canada Mall, Newmarket, ON L3Y 8J1
905/770-7648
General Manager, Bruce Hampson
Publications: Connections

**Canadian Human-Computer Communications Society**
#106, 430 King St. West, Toronto, ON M5V 1L5
416/593-4040, Fax: 416/593-5184
Chair, Dr. Wayne Davis

**Canadian Image Processing & Pattern Recognition Society/Association canadienne de traitement d'images et reconnaissance des formes (CIPPRS) (1984)**
Campus de l'Universite de Montreal, 2900, boul Édouard-Montpetit, Montréal, QC H3C 3A7
President, Prof. Réjean Plamondon, Bus: 514-340-4539, Fax: 514/340-4147, Email: ha03@music.mus.polymtl.ca
Affiliates: Canadian Information Processing Society

**Canadian Information & Image Management Society/Société canadienne de la gestion de l'information et des images (CIIMS) (1967)**
#207, 136 Randall St., Oakville, ON L6J 1P3
905/842-6067, Fax: 905/842-2646, Email: ciims@fox.nstn.ca, URL: http://www.ciims.ca
Executive Director, Donald Donahue
President, Kathryn Beaton
Secretary, Julie Donahue
Publications: Imaging Canada

**Canadian Information Processing Security SIG/Sécurité informatique canadienne**
**Security SIG**
#106, 430 King St. West., Toronto, ON M5V 1L5
416/593-4040, Fax: 416/593-5184
Chair, Peter Kingston

**Canadian Information Processing Society/Association Canadienne de L'Informatique (CIPS) (1958)**
#2401, 1 Yonge St., Toronto, ON M5E 1E5
416/861-2477, Fax: 416/368-9972, Email: info@cips.ca, URL: http://www.cips.ca
Executive Director, Mary Jean Kucerak
Publications: Canadian Computer Census

Affiliates: British Computer Society; Australian Computer Society; Association for Computing Machinery

**Canadian Society for Computational Studies of Intelligence/Société canadienne pour l'étude d'intelligence par ordinateur (CSCSI) (1973)**
c/o Dept. of Computer Science, University of Ottawa, Ottawa, ON K1N 6B5
613/564-5069, Fax: 613/564-9486, URL: http://cscsi.sfu.ca
President, Clare Cremer, I.S.P.
Secretary, Dr. F. Popowich, Email: popowich@cs.sfu.ca
Publications: Canadian AI Magazine

**CANARIE Inc. (1993)**
**Canadian Network for the Advancement of Research, Industry & Education**
#470, 410 Laurier Ave. West, Ottawa, ON K1P 6H5
613/660-3634, Fax: 613/660-3806, Email: info@canarie.ca, URL: http://www.canarie.ca
President & CEO, Andrew K. Bjerring, Email: Andrew.K.Bjerring@canarie.ca
Office Manager, Susy Carrière, Email: Susy.Carriere@canarie.ca
Communications Officer, Phil Sampson, Email: Phil.Sampson@canarie.ca

**Centre international pour le développement de l'inforoute en français (CIDIF)**
165, boul Hébert, Edmundston, NB E3V 2S8
506/737-5280, Téléc: 506/737-5281, Courrier électronique: info@cidif.org, URL: http://www.cidif.org/
Directeur général, Jocelyn Nadeau, Courrier électronique: jocelyn@cidif.org

**Chinese Canadian Information Processing Professionals (1981)**
**CIPro**
PO Box 361, North York, ON M3C 2S7
416/286-6584, Fax: 416/250-6873, Email: cipro@idirect.com
President, Auck Siu
Publications: CIPro News

**COACH, Canada's Health Informatics Association (COACH) (1975)**
**Canadian Organization for Advancement of Computers in Health**
#216, 10458 Mayfield Rd., Edmonton, AB T5P 4P4
403/489-4553, Fax: 403/489-3290, Email: coachorg@telusplanet.net, URL: http://www.telusplanet.net/public/coachorg/
Executive Director, Steven A. Huesing
Publications: Healthcare Computing & Communications Canada

**Communications Information Technology Ontario (CITO)**
D.L. Pratt Building, #286, 6 King's College Rd., Toronto, ON M5S 3H5
416/978-7203, Fax: 416/978-7207, Email: office@itrc.on.ca, URL: http://www.itrc.on.ca/
President, Peter Leach

**Electronic Commerce Canada**
582 Somerset St. West, Ottawa, ON K1R 5K2
613/237-2324, Fax: 613/237-9900, Email: office@ecc.ca, URL: http://www.ecc.ca
President, Norm Morrison
Vice-President, Jim Lowe
Sec.-Treas., Norman Henderson

**Electronic Commerce Council of Canada/Conseil canadien de l'échange électronique de données (EDI) (1985)**
**Electronic Data Interchange Council of Canada**
#203, 5401 Eglinton Ave. West, Etobicoke, ON M9C 5K6
416/621-7160, Fax: 416/620-9175, Email: edicc@idirect.com
President, Marshall A. Spence
Publications: EDIFact Trade Data Elements Directory; Interchange, bi-m.; Membership Directory
Atlantic Region Office: Executive Director, Dan DeMatteis, PO Box 962, Wolfville, NS B0P 1X0, 902/542-1113, Fax: 902/542-1714, Email: ddematte@fox.nstn.ns.ca
EDI Institute of Québec: President, André Vallerand; Director, Communications, Philip van Leeuwen; Senior Project Officer, Douglas Beeson, World Trade Centre, #3280, 380, rue Saint-Antoine ouest, Montréal, QC H2Y 3X7, 514/288-6346, Fax: 514/288-4199, Email: institute@ecworld.org
Western Regional Office: Executive Director, Jeff Connie, #450, 1122 Mainland St., Vancouver, BC V6B 5L1, 604/689-8220, Fax: 604/689-0141, Email: jconnie@cyberstore.ca

**Electronic Frontier Canada Inc.**
20 Richmond Ave., Kitchener, ON N2G 1Y7
Email: efc@efc.ca, URL: http://insight.mcmaster.ca/org/efc/efc.html

**Groupe interuniversitaire de recherche en informatique cognitive des organisations/Cognitive & Computer Science Interuniversity Research Group (GIRICO) (1986)**
#912, 276, rue St-Jacques, Montréal, QC H2Y 1N3
514/985-5459, Téléc: 514/985-2720
Président/Directeur général, Ghislain Lévesque
Publications: ICO Québec

**Information Resource Management Association of Canada (IRMAC) (1971)**
**Database Association of Ontario**
PO Box 5639, Stn A, Toronto, ON M5W 1N8
Email: irmac@io.org, URL: http://www.irmac.ca
President, Jim Sullivan, Bus: 905/837-3227, Email: jsullivan@clearnet.com
Secretary, Craig Lloyd, Bus: 416/228-5817
Treasurer, Ray Hensel, Bus: 416/365-3858
Publications: Primary Key

**Information Technology Association of Canada/Association canadienne de la technologie de l'information (ITAC) (1987)**
#402, 2800 Skymark Ave., Mississauga, ON L4W 5A6
905/602-8345, Fax: 905/602-8346, Email: info@itac.ca, URL: http://www.itac.ca/
President/CEO, Gaylen Duncan
Vice-President, Membership, Winston Kinch
Vice-President, Policy, Norine Heselton
Vice-President, Government Relations, Peter Broadmore
Publications: Fax Flash
Affiliates: Information Technology Industry Association of Nova Scotia (ITANS); Technologies Industry Association of British Columbia (TIA BC); ITAC Ontario; Québec Software Promotion Centre; New Brunswick Information Technology Alliance; Software Technology Centre Saskatchewan; Newfoundland & Labrador Alliance of Technical Industries (NATI); Alberta Information Technology Association (AITA); Information Technology Association of PEI (ITAP)

**Information Technology Industry Alliance of Nova Scotia (ITANS) (1989)**
#101, 1046 Barrington St., Halifax, NS B3J 2N7

902/423-5332, Fax: 902/423-9400, Email: uta.itans@purdyswharf.com, URL: http://www.seimac.com/~ITANS/
Chairman, David Bough
President, Geoff Allen
Office Manager, Uta Kielwein
Publications: Newsletter; Information Technology Industry Directory, biennial
Affiliates: Information Technology Association of Canada

**Instrument Society of America (ISA) (1945)**
67 Alexander Dr., PO Box 12277, Research Triangle Park, NC 27709 USA
919/549-8411, Fax: 919/549-8288, Telex: 802-540 ISA DUR, Email: info@isa.org, URL: http://www.isa.org
Executive Director, Glenn F. Harvey, Email: gharvey@isa.org
Contact, District 10, James S. Drennan, Bus: 403/255-7884, Fax: 253-6393
Contact, District 13, Ken K. Hamilton, Bus: 905/335-0989, Fax: 905/335-6512, Email: hamiltonk@bailey.ca
Publications: Intech; Industrial Computing, m.
Affiliates: American Association for the Advancement of Science; American Institute of Physics; International Measurement Confederation; National Institute for Certification in Engineering Technologies; National Inventors Hall of Fame; American National Standards Institute; American Society of Mechanical Engineers; Fluid Controls Institute; Institute of Electrical & Electronic Engineers;

**Interactive Multimedia Arts & Technologies Association/Association des arts et des technologies de l'interactivité et du multimedia (IMAT) (1995)**
#360, 144 Front St. West, Toronto, ON M5J 2L7
416/977-1801, Fax: 416/977-1802, Email: imat@goodmedia.com, URL: http://www.imat.ca/
Publications: Wave

**National Capital FreeNet/Libertel de la Capitale Nationale (NCF) (1993)**
c/o Carleton University, 1125 Colonel By Dr., Ottawa, ON K1S 5B6
613/520-9001, Fax: 613/520-3524, Email: office@freenet.carleton.ca; telnet: telnet.ncf.carleton.ca, URL: http://www.ncf.carleton.ca/
Executive Director, Lisa K. Donnelly, Email: lkd@freenet.carleton.ca
Chairman, David Sutherland
Publications: The Official FreeNet Survival Guide

**Net Active Canada**
#1105, 7400, rue Sherbrooke ouest, Montréal, QC H4B 1R8
514/481-9912, Email: jhs@well.com, URL: http://tdg.res.uoguelph.ca/~ipirg/
Coordinator, John Stevenson

**Newfoundland & Labrador Alliance of Technical Industries (NATI)**
Parsons Bldg., 1st Fl., 90 O'Leary Ave., St. John's, NF A1B 2C7
709/722-8324, Fax: 709/722-3213, Email: nati@nfld.com, URL: http://www.netfx.iom.net/nati/
Executive Director, Dr. Jack Botsford
Information Officer, Jennifer L. Bishop
Affiliates: Canadian Advanced Technology Association; Information Technology Association of Canada

**reBOOT Canada**
#111, 72 Fraser Ave., Toronto, ON M6K 3J7
416/534-6017, Fax: 416/534-6083, Email: info@reboot.on.ca, URL: http://www.reboot.on.ca
Director of Operations, Ron Piovesan

**Software Human Resource Council (Canada) Inc./Conseil des ressources humaines du logiciel (Canada) Inc. (SHRC)**
#608, 155 Queen St., Ottawa, ON K1P 6L1
613/237-8551, Fax: 613/230-3490
President & CEO, Paul Swinwood

## INSURANCE INDUSTRY

**Association of Canadian Insurers/Association des assureurs canadiens (ACI) (1990)**
181 University Ave., 13th Fl., Toronto, ON M5H 3M7
416/362-9729, Fax: 416/361-5952
President, Alain Thibault
Vice-President, Doug McIntyre

**Association des courtiers d'annuités**
1210, rue Sherbrooke ouest, 11e étage, Montréal, QC H3A 1H6
514/842-9526, Téléc: 514/847-0051
Président, Ted Fisher

**Association des intermédiaires en assurance de personnes du Québec/Life Intermediaries Association of Québec (AIAPQ) (1989)**
#500, 1, Westmount Sq., Montréal, QC H3Z 2P9
514/932-4277, Téléc: 514/932-6400, Courrier électronique: aiapq@cureka.qc.ca
Directrice générale, Lucie Granger
Publications: Prospective

**Association of Marine Underwriters of British Columbia (AMUBC)**
c/o Johnson & Higgins Ltd., #1700, 200 Granville St., Vancouver, BC V6C 2S2
604/681-6141, Fax: 604/681-9846
Secretary, Marilyn M. Randle

**Canadian Association of Blue Cross Plans**
c/o Alberta Blue Cross, 10009 - 108 St., Edmonton, AB T5J 3C5
403/498-8297, Fax: 403/498-8532
President, V. George Ward

**Canadian Association of Mutual Insurance Companies/Association canadienne des compagnies d'assurance mutuelles (CAMIC) (1980)**
#907, 325 Dalhousie St., PO Box 117, Stn B, Ottawa, ON K1P 6C3
613/789-6851, Fax: 613/789-6854, URL: http://www.camic.ca
President, Normand Lafrenière, BA; MPA, Email: nlafreniere@camic.ca
Publications: Reflexion; Taxletter, q.

**Canadian Board of Marine Underwriters (CBMU) (1917)**
#1105, 191 The West Mall, Etobicoke, ON M9C 5K8
416/626-7380, Fax: 416/620-5392, Email: cbmu@webcom.com, URL: http://www.webcom.com/cbmu/
Sec.-Treas., Brenda Looyenga
Publications: The Log

**Canadian Boiler & Machinery Underwriters' Association/Association canadienne des assureurs en bris des machines (1925)**
#1804, 33 Elmhurst Ave., North York, ON M2N 6G8
416/221-9755
Sec.-Treas., Margaret Wansbrough

**Canadian Council of Insurance Regulators**
Ontario Insurance, 5160 Yonge St., PO Box 85, Toronto, ON M2N 6L9
416/590-7272
Superintendent, Laurie Savage

**Canadian Foresters Life Insurance Society (1879)**
**Canadian Foresters**
PO Box 850, Brantford, ON N3T 5S3
905/525-9559
CEO, Donald G. Payne
President, William J. Taggart
Publications: Fraternal Newsletter; The Canadian Forester, a.

**Canadian Independent Adjusters' Association/Association canadienne des experts indépendants (CIAA) (1953)**
#1305, 55 Queen St. East, Toronto, ON M5C 1R6
416/362-7466, Fax: 416/362-8251
Executive Director, Ann M. Wolochatiuk
Publications: The Canadian Independent Adjuster
Affiliates: National Association of Independent Insurance Adjusters (USA); Chartered Institute of Loss Adjustors (UK)

**Canadian Industrial Risks Insurers (CIRI) (1973)**
#1906, 180 Dundas St. West, Toronto, ON M5G 1Z8
416/595-0155, Fax: 416/595-0948
Manager, Henry D. Ulozas
Publications: Inside IRI; Sentinel
Affiliates: International Risks Insurers

**Canadian Institute of Actuaries/Institut canadien des actuaires**
#820, 360 Albert St., Ottawa, ON K1R 7X7
613/236-8196, Fax: 613/233-4552, URL: http://www.actuaries.ca/CIA/CIA.html
Executive Director, Rick Neugebauer
President, Harry H. Panjer, Ph.D., FCIA, FSA
Affiliates: International Actuarial Association; American Academy of Actuaries; Society of Actuaries; Casualty Actuarial Society; Conference of Consulting Actuaries

**Canadian Life & Health Insurance Association Inc./Association canadienne des compagnies d'assurances de personnes inc. (CLHIA) (1894)**
#1700, One Queen St. East, Toronto, ON M5C 2X9
416/777-2221, Fax: 416/777-1895, Info Line: 416/777-2344, Toll Free: 1-800-268-8099, URL: http://www.inforamp.net/~clhia/
Chairman, President & CEO, The Mutual Life Assurance Co. of Canada, Robert M. Astley
President, Mark R. Daniels
Vice-President, Corporate & Member Services, Judy E. Barrie
Executive Vice-President, Policy Development, Gregory R. Traversy
Senior Advisor, Insurance Operations, Charles C. Black
Vice-President & General Counsel, J.P. Bernier
Senior Vice-President, Quebec Affairs, Yves Millette
Vice-President, Taxation & Research, James S. Witol
Assistant Vice-President, Finance & Administration, Angela M. Albini
Publications: Impact
Montréal Office: Senior Vice-President, Québec Affairs, Yves Millette, #630, 1001, boul de Maisonneuve ouest, Montréal, QC H3A 3C8, 514/845-9004, Téléc: 514/845-6182
Ottawa Office: Director, Federal Affairs, Andrew Casey, #400, 46 Elgin St., Ottawa, ON K1P 5K6, 613/230-0031, Fax: 613/230-0297

## Canadian Life Insurance Medical Officers Association/Association canadienne des directeurs médicaux en assurance-vie (CLIMOA)

142 Cassandra Blvd., North York, ON M3A 1S9
416/449-6791
Secretary, Dr. A.E. Wallace
Publications: Annual Proceedings
Affiliates: Canadian Medical Association

## Centre for Study of Insurance Operations (CSIO)

#402, 480 University Ave., Toronto, ON M5G 1V2
416/591-1773, Fax: 416/591-1482
Director of Communications, Terrie Dionne
President, Len W. Ashby, CMC
Publications: Connections

## Conseil des assurances de dommages (CAD) (1991)

#1919, 2020, rue University, Montréal, QC H3A 2A5
514/282-8765, Téléc: 514/282-7466, Ligne sans frais: 1-800-667-7089, Courrier électronique: info@conseilad.qc.ca, URL: http://www.conseilad.qc.ca
Directrice générale, Diane Paradis
Publications: Intermède; Intermède Plus

## Facility Association

#200, 20 Richmond St. East, Toronto, ON M5C 2R9
416/863-1750, Fax: 416/868-0894
President, Bernard Webber

## Groupement des assureurs automobiles (GAA) (1978)

#600, 500, rue Sherbrooke ouest, Montréal, QC H3A 3C6
514/288-1537, Téléc: 514/288-0753
Directeur général, Raymond Medza
Publications: Contact Info

## Insurance Brokers Association of Canada/ Association des courtiers d'assurances du Canada (IBAC) (1921)

#1902, 181 University Ave., Toronto, ON M5H 3M7
416/367-1831, Fax: 416/367-3687
Executive Director, Joanne Brown, AIIC

### ASSOCIATION DES COURTIERS D'ASSURANCES DE LA PROVINCE DE QUÉBEC/INSURANCE BROKERS ASSOCIATION OF QUÉBEC (ACAPQ)

500, rue Sherbrooke ouest, 7e étage, Montréal, QC H3A 3C6
514/842-2591, Téléc: 514/842-3138, Ligne sans frais: 1-800-361-7288
Directrice générale, Maya Raic
Président, Paul Andre

### INSURANCE BROKERS ASSOCIATION OF ALBERTA (1925)

#701, 10109 - 106 St., Edmonton, AB T5J 3L7
403/424-3320, Fax: 403/424-7418, Toll Free: 1-800-318-0197
Executive Director, Harold Baker
Publications: Alberta Broker

### INSURANCE BROKERS ASSOCIATION OF BRITISH COLUMBIA (1920)

#1300, 1095 West Pender St., Vancouver, BC V6E 2M6
604/683-8471, Fax: 604/683-7831
General Manager, Jack F. Hamilton
Publications: BC Broker

### INSURANCE BROKERS ASSOCIATION OF MANITOBA (IBAM) (1951)

#205, 530 Kenaston Blvd., Winnipeg, MB R3N 1Z4
204/488-1857, Fax: 204/489-0316, Toll Free: 1-800-204-5649
Executive Director, William T. O'Brien
Publications: The Manitoba Broker

### INSURANCE BROKERS ASSOCIATION OF NEW BRUNSWICK/ ASSOCIATION DES COURTIERS D'ASSURANCES DU NOUVEAU-BRUNSWICK

#409, 212 Queen St., Fredericton, NB E3B 5G2
506/450-2898, Fax: 506/450-1494
Email: ibanb@nbnet.nb.ca
Executive Director, Linda M. Dawe, FIIC, CAIB
Publications: News & Views

### INSURANCE BROKERS ASSOCIATION OF NEWFOUNDLAND

PO Box 275, Mount Pearl, NF A1N 2C3
709/726-4450, Fax: 709/754-4399
President, Elizabeth A. Cook, CCIB, FIIC

### INSURANCE BROKERS ASSOCIATION OF ONTARIO

90 Eglinton Ave. East, 2nd Fl., Toronto, ON M4P 2Y3
416/488-7422, Fax: 416/488-7526
Executive Director, Robert J. Carter

### INSURANCE BROKERS ASSOCIATION OF PRINCE EDWARD ISLAND

c/o Charlie Cook Insurance Agency Ltd., 125 Pownal St., Charlottetown, PE C1A 3W4
902/566-5666, Fax: 902/566-4662
Secretary, Jeff Cooke

### INSURANCE BROKERS ASSOCIATION OF SASKATCHEWAN (IBAS)

#310, 2631 - 28th Ave., Regina, SK S4S 6X3
306/525-5900, Fax: 306/569-3018
General Manager, Ernest J. Gaschler
Publications: IBAS Newsletter; Saskatchewan Insurance Directory, a.

### INSURANCE BROKERS' ASSOCIATION OF NOVA SCOTIA

14 Dufferin St., Bridgewater, NS B4V 2E8
902/543-5569, Fax: 902/543-8508
Executive Director, Heather A. Winters, AIIC, CAIB, CCIB, CRM

### REGROUPEMENT DES CABINETS DE COURTAGE D'ASSURANCE DU QUÉBEC/INSURANCE BROKERS' ASSOCIATION OF QUÉBEC - ASSEMBLY

#139, 955, rue D'Assigny, Longueuil, QC J4K 5C3
514/674-6258, Téléc: 514/674-3609
Directrice générale, Claudette Carrier

### TORONTO INSURANCE CONFERENCE (TIC) (1918)

c/o Base Service Canada Inc., #301, 250 Consumers Rd., North York, ON M2J 4V6
416/498-7722, Fax: 416/495-8723
Email: base@onramp.ca
Executive Secretary, Ruth Abrahamson

## Insurance Bureau of Canada/Bureau d'assurance du Canada (IBC) (1964)

#1800, 151 Yonge St., Toronto, ON M5C 2W7
416/362-2031, Fax: 416/361-5952, Toll Free: 1-800-387-2880, URL: http://www.ibc.ca
President, George D. Anderson
Vice-President, Policy Development, Paul Kovacs
Vice-President, Legel Counsel, Alex Kennedy
Vice-President, Public Affairs, Mary Lou O'Reilly
Publications: Facts of the General Insurance Industry in Canada; Perspective, q.; Between the Lines, q.
Affiliates: Canadian Coalition Against Insurance Fraud
Atlantic Canada Office: Regional Vice-President, Don Forgeron, Purdy's Wharf, Tower II, #1706, 1969 Upper Water St., PO Box 13, Halifax, NS B3J 3R7, 902/429-2730, Fax: 902/420-0157, Toll Free: 1-800-565-7189
British Columbia & Yukon Office: Regional Vice-President, Brian E. Stanhope, #550, 409 Granville St., Vancouver, BC V6C 1W9, 604/684-3635, Fax: 604/684-6235
Ottawa Office: Director, Government Relations, Mark Yakabuski, #1208, 155 Queen St., Ottawa, ON K1P 6L1, 613/236-5043, Fax: 613/236-5208
Prairies & Northwest Territories Office: Regional Vice-President, Alan D. Wood, #1105, 10080 Jasper Ave., Edmonton, AB T5J 1V9, 403/423-2212, Fax: 403/423-4796, Toll Free: 1-800-232-7275
Québec Office: Administrateur général, Raymond Medza, #900, 425, boul de Maisonneuve ouest, Montréal, QC H3A 3G5, 514/288-1563, Téléc: 514/288-0753, Ligne sans frais: 1-800-361-5131

## Insurance Council of British Columbia (1930)

Box 7, #300, 1040 West Georgia St., Vancouver, BC V6E 4H1
604/688-0321, Fax: 604/662-7767
General Manager, Jerry Matier

## Insurance Crime Prevention Bureau/Service anti-crime des assureurs (ICPB) (1923)

PO Box 919, Stn U, Toronto, ON M8Z 5P9
416/252-5215, Fax: 416/252-5226
President, J.C. Cloutier
Vice-President, Canada East, G.R. Garand
Publications: Communique

## Insurance Institute of Canada/Institut d'assurance du Canada (IIC) (1952)

18 King St. East, 6th Fl., Toronto, ON M5C 1C4
416/362-8586, Fax: 416/362-4239, Email: iican@ibm.net
CEO/President, J.C. Rhind
Publications: Perspectives; The Graduate, biennial; Exam Statistics, a.; Eduquorum, a.
Affiliates: Insurance Institute of America; Chartered Insurance Institute; Australian Insurance Institute; Insurance Institute of New Zealand; Insurance Institute of India; Insurance Institute of Malaysia

### L'INSTITUT D'ASSURANCE DE DOMMAGES DU QUÉBEC - BUREAU RÉGIONAL DE L'EST DU QUÉBEC

#305, 5400 boul des Galeries, Québec, QC G2K 2B5
418/623-3688, Fax: 418/623-6935
Christine Dufour
Carole Forcier

### L'INSTITUT D'ASSURANCE DE DOMMAGES DU QUÉBEC - BUREAU RÉGIONAL DE L'OUEST DU QUÉBEC (1927)

#2230, 1200, av McGill College, Montréal, QC H3B 4G7
514/393-8156, Téléc: 514/393-9222
Directrice générale, Diane Laflamme
Publications: Bulletin

### INSURANCE INSTITUTE OF BRITISH COLUMBIA (IIBC)

#410, 800 Pender St. West, Vancouver, BC V6C 2V6
604/681-5491, Fax: 604/681-5479
Manager, Malcolm C. Simpson
Publications: Newsletter

### INSURANCE INSTITUTE OF MANITOBA (IIM) (1923)

#533, 167 Lombard Ave., Winnipeg, MB R3B 0T6
204/956-1702, Fax: 204/956-0758
Manager, Marjorie J. Peabody
Publications: Insurance Omnibus

### INSURANCE INSTITUTE OF NEW BRUNSWICK (IINB) (1952)

Parrtown Place, 32 King St., 6th Fl., Saint John, NB E2L 1G3
506/658-0331, Fax: 506/658-0977
Manager, Janet Kyle

### INSURANCE INSTITUTE OF NEWFOUNDLAND INC. (IIN) (1956)

PO Box 576, Mount Pearl, NF A1N 2W4
709/754-4398, Fax: 709/754-4399
Manager, Bernadette Hughes

### INSURANCE INSTITUTE OF NORTHERN ALBERTA (IINA)

Oxford Tower, #602, 10235 - 101 St., Edmonton, AB T5J 3E8
403/424-1268, Fax: 403/420-1940
Education Co-ordinator, Christine J. Chaston
Education Co-ordinator, Donna McEwen
Publications: IINA Newsletter

**INSURANCE INSTITUTE OF NOVA SCOTIA (IINS) (1953)**
414 Duke Tower, Scotia Square, PO Box 1561, RPO Central, Halifax, NS B3J 2Y3
902/422-4112, Fax: 902/423-9307
Manager, Jennifer Simpson
Publications: Calendar of Events

**INSURANCE INSTITUTE OF ONTARIO (1899)**
18 King St. East, 6th Fl., Toronto, ON M5C 1C4
416/362-8586, Fax: 416/362-1126
General Manager, J.C. Rhind
Publications: In Ontario

**INSURANCE INSTITUTE OF PRINCE EDWARD ISLAND (IIPEI) (1960)**
75 King St., Charlottetown, PE C1A 1B4
902/892-1692, Fax: 902/368-2936
Manager, Violet L. MacDonald

**INSURANCE INSTITUTE OF SASKATCHEWAN (IIS)**
1424 Broad St., Regina, SK S4R 1Y9
306/525-9799, Fax: 306/569-3018
Manager, Donna Dunn
Publications: Newsletter

**INSURANCE INSTITUTE OF SOUTHERN ALBERTA (IISA) (1954)**
#801, 1015 - 4 St. SW, Calgary, AB T2R 1J4
403/266-3427, Fax: 403/269-3199
General Manager, Frances A. Lang
President, Jackie L. Tatebe
Publications: IISA Newsletter

### Insurers' Advisory Organization (1989) Inc. (IAO) (1883)
**IAO Commercial & Residental Risk Services**
#700, 18 King St. East, Toronto, ON M5C 1C4
416/368-1801, Fax: 416/368-0333, Info Line: 416/601-4532, Toll Free: 1-800-268-8080
President & CEO, Barry L. Wilson, BBA
Vice-President, Marketing, A. Lynne LeGallais
Atlantic Branch: Park Lane Terrace, #510, 5657 Spring Garden Rd., Halifax, NS B3J 3R4, 902/429-4333, Fax: 902/423-7376, Toll Free: 1-800-565-4333
British Columbia Branch Office: #1502, 1166 Alberni St., PO Box 73, Vancouver, BC V6E 3Z3, 604/681-3113, Fax: 604/688-6986, Toll Free: 1-800-665-5661
IAO School of Loss Control Technology: Coordinator, Training Solutions, Caroline Schweppe, #800, 18 King St. East, Toronto, ON M5C 1C4, 416/601-4550, Fax: 416/363-0330, Toll Free: 1-800-268-8080
Prairies & NWT Branch Office: Branch Manager, Gilles Proulx, #1750, 140 - 4 Ave. SW, Calgary, AB T2P 3N3, 403/262-7283, Fax: 403/262-8068
Québec Branch Office: Branch Manager, Sam Hasbani, #2600, 300, rue Léo Pariseau, CP 990, Succ. Place du Parc, Montréal, QC H2W 2N1, 514/285-1201, Téléc: 514/844-0777, Ligne sans frais: 1-800-363-9465
Winnipeg Customer Service Centre: #200, 428 Portage Ave., Winnipeg, MB R3C 0E2, 204/944-9756, Fax: 204/944-9550

### Life Insurance Institute of Canada/Institut d'assurance-vie du Canada (LIIC) (1936)
#1600, One Queen St. East, Toronto, ON M5C 2X9
416/359-2020, Fax: 416/359-9173
Executive Director, Debbie Cole-Gauer
Publications: LIIC News

### The Life Insurance Managers Association of Canada/Association des directeurs d'agence-vie du Canada (LIMAC) (1974)
#1700, One Queen St. East, Toronto, ON M5C 2X9
416/359-2000, Fax: 416/359-9173
Executive Vice-President, Gordon A. Dunn, Bus: 416/359-2005
Publications: LIMAC Newsletter

### Life Underwriters Association of Canada/L'Association des assureurs-vie du Canada (LUAC) (1906)
41 Lesmill Rd., North York, ON M3B 2T3
416/444-5251, Fax: 416/444-8031
President, David Thibaudeau
Executive Assistant, Shirley Fingler
Chair & CEO, John Dean
Publications: Forum

**CANADIAN INSTITUTE OF CHARTERED LIFE UNDERWRITERS & CHARTERED FINANCIAL CONSULTANTS**
41 Lesmill Rd., North York, ON M3B 2T3
416/444-5251, Fax: 416/444-8031
Chair, Leslie Macdonald Francis
Vice-President/Manager, Clifford Sadgrove

### Nuclear Insurance Association of Canada (NIAC)
#800, 18 King St. East, Toronto, ON M5C 1C4
416/601-1801, Fax: 416/368-0333
Manager, Elaine Collier, BA, FIIC
Assistant Manager, T. Soutar

### Ontario Insurance Adjusters Association
128 Queen St. South, PO Box 42254, Mississauga, ON L5M 4Z0
905/542-0576, Fax: 905/542-1301
Business Manager, Jackie Johnston-Schnurr
Publications: Without Prejudice

### Ontario Mutual Insurance Association
PO Box 3187, Cambridge, ON N3H 4S6
519/622-9220, Fax: 519/622-9227
President, Glen Johnson, CAE
Treasurer, Sarah Underwood

### Reinsurance Research Council/Conseil de recherche en réassurance (1973)
#1807, 365 Bloor St. East, Toronto, ON M4W 3L4
416/968-0183, Fax: 416/968-6818, Email: rrc@collinscan.com, URL: http://www.collinscan.com/~collins/clientspgs/rrc.html
Chair, David Wilmot
General Manager, Eden Spodek

### Risk & Insurance Management Society Inc. (RIMS) (1962)
1310 Ingledene Dr., Oakville, ON L6H 2G4
905/845-8226, Fax: 905/845-9578
Canadian Director, Risk Management, Legislative & Public Affairs, Lloyd Hackett
Publications: RIMSCAN; RIMSCOPE, q.; Risk Management, m.

### Saskatchewan Municipal Hail Association
2100 Cornwall St., Regina, SK S4P 2K7
306/569-1852
Secretary, Murray Otterson

### Society of Public Insurance Administrators of Ontario (SPIAO) (1977)
2141 Major Mackenzie Dr., Vaughan, ON L6A 1T1
905/832-2281, Fax: 905/832-8525
Public Relations Officer, Anita Moore

### Underwriters' Laboratories of Canada/Laboratoires des assureurs du Canada (ULC) (1920)
7 Crouse Rd., Scarborough, ON M1R 3A9
416/757-3611, Fax: 416/757-9540
President, Peter Higginson
Publications: ULC News
Montréal: #503, 650 - 32e av, Lachine, QC H8T 3K5, 514/639-5343, Téléc: 514/639-5313
Vancouver: #201, 3540 West 41st Ave., Vancouver, BC V6N 3E6, 604/264-1355, Fax: 604/264-1306

## INTERIOR DESIGN

### Associated Designers of Canada (ADC) (1965)
#7, 206 Bloor St. West, Toronto, ON M5S 1T8
416/960-5230, Fax: 416/960-2047, Email: homewood@interlog.com, URL: http://www.ffa.ucalgary.ca/adc/indexadc.htm
Executive Director, Chuck Homewood
Publications: ADC Newsletter; ADC Standards & Working Procedures

### Association of Canadian Industrial Designers/Association des designers industriels du Canada (ACID) (1948)
315, rue du St-Sacrement, 3e étage, Montréal, QC H2Y 1Y1
514/287-6531, Fax: 514/287-6532
President, Philippe Lalonde
Publications: ACID Leaf
Affiliates: International Council of Societies of Industrial Design - Helsinki, Finland

**ASSOCIATION OF CHARTERED INDUSTRIAL DESIGNERS OF ONTARIO (ACIDO) (1984)**
c/o Axis Group Inc., 65 Bellwoods Ave., Toronto, ON M6J 3N4
416/364-3388, Fax: 416/364-1530
President, Harry Mahler
Publications: ACIDO News

**ASSOCIATION DES DESIGNERS INDUSTRIELS DU QUÉBEC (ADIQ) (1984)**
#3, 360, Place Royale, Montréal, QC H2Y 2V1
514/287-6531, Téléc: 514/287-6532
Courrier électronique: adiq@sympatico.ca
Directrice générale, Florence Lebeau

**BRITISH COLUMBIA INDUSTRIAL DESIGNERS**
1050 Homer St., Vancouver, BC V6B 2W9
604/684-9890, Fax: 604/684-5447
President, Peter Busby

### Association of Registered Interior Designers of Ontario (ARIDO) (1984)
717 Church St., Toronto, ON M4W 2M5
416/921-2127, Fax: 416/921-3660, Toll Free: 1-800-334-1180
Contact, Cathy Clark
Publications: ARIDO Newsletter
Affiliates: Interior Designers Educators Council; National Council for Interior Design Education; American Society of Interior Designers; Foundation for Interior Design Education; International Federation of Interior Designers

### Interior Designers of Canada/Designers d'intérieur du Canada (IDC)
Ontario Design Centre, #414, 260 King St. East, Toronto, ON M5A 1K3
416/594-9310, Fax: 416/594-9313
Office Manager, Kymberley Krause
Affiliates: International Federation of Interior Architects/Interior Designers

**ASSOCIATION OF REGISTERED INTERIOR DESIGNERS OF NEW BRUNSWICK/ASSOCIATION DES DESIGNERS D'INTÉRIEUR IMMATRICULÉS DU NOUVEAU-BRUNSWICK (ARIDNB) (1985)**
PO Box 1541, Fredericton, NB E3B 5G2
506/459-3014, Fax: 506/853-4111
Sara Dunton
Publications: Perspective

**INTERIOR DESIGNERS OF ALBERTA (IDA)**
5512 - 4 St. NW, PO Box 64024, Calgary, AB T2K 6J0
403/274-9290, Fax: 403/274-9388
Association Manager, Sandra Morrow
Publications: Dimensions

**INTERIOR DESIGNERS INSTITUTE OF BRITISH COLUMBIA (IDI OF BC) (1950)**
#523, 409 Granville St., Vancouver, BC V5C 1T2
604/251-5343, Fax: 604/251-5347
Email: assn@portal.ca, URL: http://www.designsource.bc.ca
President, Ellen Collison
Association Manager, Sue Osterman
Publications: Dimensions
Affiliates: Design Resource Association

**INTERIOR DESIGNERS OF NOVA SCOTIA (IDNS)**
PO Box 2042, Stn M, Halifax, NS B3J 3B4
902/425-5397, Fax: 902/425-5606
President, Linda Rodie

**PROFESSIONAL INTERIOR DESIGNERS INSTITUTE OF MANITOBA**
137 Bannatyne Ave. East, 2nd Fl., Winnipeg, MB R3B 0R3
204/925-4625, Fax: 204/925-4624
Executive Secretary, Joyce Sandall

**SOCIÉTÉ DES DESIGNERS D'INTERIEURS DU QUÉBEC/INTERIOR DESIGNERS SOCIETY OF QUÉBEC (1935)**
#200, 354, rue Notre-Dame ouest, Montréal, QC H2Y 1T9
514/284-6263, Téléc: 514/284-6112, Ligne sans frais: 1-888-247-2790
Directrice exécutif, Sylvie Champeau
Publications: Image

## INTERNATIONAL COOPERATION /INTERNATIONAL RELATIONS

### AFS Interculture Canada (1978)
**Interculture Canada**
#505, 1231, rue Ste-Catherine ouest, Montréal, QC H3G 1P5
514/288-3282, Fax: 514/843-9119, Toll Free: 1-800-361-7248, URL: http://www.afs.org
National Director, Claude Roberge
National Chair, Paul Van Houtte
Publications: The Link/Le Lien
Affiliates: Scouts International

### Association canadienne des clubs UNESCO/ Canadian Association of UNESCO Clubs (1991)
#208, 420, rue St-Paul est, Montréal, QC H2Y 1H4
514/286-0087, Téléc: 514/281-5010
Secrétaire générale, France Alarie
Publications: Fréquence/Frequency

### Atlantic Council of Canada/Conseil atlantique du Canada (ACC) (1966)
Trinity College, 6 Hoskin Ave., Toronto, ON M5S 1H8
416/979-1875, Fax: 416/979-0825, Email: atlantic@idirect.com
President, Prof. Robert Spencer
Publications: The Atlantic Council Letter
Affiliates: NATO; Atlantic Treaty Association - Paris, France

### Bridgehead Inc. (1981)
20 James St., Ottawa, ON K2P 0T6
613/567-1455, Fax: 613/567-1468, Toll Free: 1-800-565-8563
Managing Director, Howard Esbin
Publications: Food for Thought

### Canada World Youth/Jeunesse Canada Monde (CWY) (1971)
2330, rue Notre-Dame Ouest, 3e étage., Montréal, QC H3J 1N4
514/931-3526, Fax: 514/939-2621, Telex: 055-60979, Email: jcmcwy@web.apc.org
Executive Director, Paul Shay
Communications Coordinator, Suzanne Hamel
Publications: Bulletin
Affiliates: World Assembly of Youth
Atlantic Regional Office: Regional Director, Matthew Pearce, #125, 1657 Barrington St., Halifax, NS B3J 2A1, 902/422-1782, Fax: 902/429-1274
British Columbia Regional Office: Regional Director, Gary Henkelmann, #201, 1894 West Broadway, Vancouver, BC V6J 1Y9, 604/732-5113, Fax: 604/732-9141
Ontario Regional Office: Regional Director, Anne Game, 386 Bloor St. West, 2nd Fl., Toronto, ON M5S 1X4, 416/922-0776, Fax: 416/922-3721
Prairies Regional Office: #205, 10816A - 82 Ave., Edmonton, AB T5H 2P2, 403/432-1877, Fax: 403/433-4489
Québec Regional Office: Directrice régionale, Joanne Bourgeois, 2330, rue Notre Dame ouest, 4e étage, Montréal, QC H3J 1N4, 514/931-3933, Téléc: 514/935-4580, Télex: 055-60979

### Canadian Association for the Study of International Development/L'Association canadienne d'études du développement international (CASID)
c/o The North-South Institute, #200, 55 Murray St., Ottawa, ON K1N 5M3
613/241-3535, Fax: 613/241-7435, Email: nsi@web.apc.org
President, Patricia Paton
Vice-President, Arpi Hamalian
Sec.-Treas., Rosalind Boyd, Bus: 514/398-3508, Fax: 514/398-8432
Publications: Canadian Journal of Development Studies

### Canadian Commission for UNESCO/Commission canadienne pour l'UNESCO (1957)
350 Albert St., PO Box 1047, Ottawa, ON K1P 5V8
613/566-4414, Fax: 613/566-4405, Toll Free: 1-800-263-5588
Acting Secretary-General, Louis Patenaude
President, Michel Agnaïeff
Vice-President, Marshall Wm. Conley
Publications: Bulletin

### Canadian Council for International Co-operation/ Conseil canadien pour la coopération internationale (CCIC) (1968)
#300, One Nicholas St., Ottawa, ON K1N 7B7
613/241-7007, Fax: 613/241-5302, Email: ccic@web.net, URL: http://www.web.net/ccic-ccci
President/CEO, Betty Plewes
Commuications Officer, Denise Fournier
Publications: Au Courant; Who's Who in International Development

### Canadian Foundation for the Americas/Fondation canadienne pour les Amériques (FOCAL) (1990)
#230, 55 Murray St., Ottawa, ON K1N 5M3
613/562-0005, Fax: 613/562-2525, Email: focal@focal.ca, URL: http://www.focal.ca
Executive Director, Dean J. Browne
Director of Communications, Judy Redpath
Publications: FOCAL Update/Le point FOCAL; The FOCAL Papers/Les cahiers de FOCAL, 5 pa

### Canadian Foundation for World Development (CFWD) (1977)
2441 Bayview Ave., North York, ON M2L 1A5
416/445-4740, Fax: 416/441-4025
President, Kenneth G. Davis
Secretary, R. Davis
Publications: Grassroots

### Canadian Friends of Burma/Les Amis canadiens de la Birmanie (CFOB) (1991)
#206, 145 Spruce St., Ottawa, ON K1R 6P1
613/237-8056, Fax: 613/563-0017, Email: cfob@web.net
Coordinator, Christine Harmston
Advisor, Executive Committee, Penny Sanger
Advisor, Executive Committee, Murray Thomson
Financial Officer, Khine Thinn
Publications: Burma Links
Affiliates: World University Service of Canada; Canadian Asia Pacific Working Group

### Canadian Friends of Soviet People (1918)
280 Queen St. West, Toronto, ON M5V 2A1
416/977-5819, Fax: 416/593-0781
President, Michael Lukas
Publications: Northstar Compass

### Canadian Hunger Foundation/Fondation canadienne contre la faim (CHF) (1961)
323 Chapel St., Ottawa, ON K1N 7Z2
613/237-0180, Fax: 613/237-5969, Email: chfott@web.apc.org
Executive Director, Bruce Moore
Deputy Director, Tom Taylor
Director, Finance & Administration, Marion Lacelle
Publications: Global Link

### Canadian Institute for Conflict Resolution/ Institute canadien pour la résolution des conflits (CICR) (1988)
St. Paul University, 223 Main St., Ottawa, ON K1S 1C4
613/235-5800, Fax: 613/782-3005
President, Robert P. Birt

### Canadian Institute of Cultural Affairs/Institut canadien des affaires culturelles (1976)
**ICA Canada**
579 Kingston Rd., Toronto, ON M4E 1R3
416/691-2316, Fax: 416/691-2491, Email: icacan@web.net, URL: http://www.web.net/~icacan/
Executive Director, T. Duncan Holmes
Publications: Edges: New Planetary Patterns
Affiliates: Part of a network of nationally autonomous ICAs in 29 countries; through ICA International in Brussels, ICA Canada has consultative status with the UN, UNICEF, the World Health Organization & the Food & Agricultural Organization

### Canadian Institute of International Affairs/ Institut canadien des affaires internationales (CIIA) (1928)
5 Devonshire Pl., Toronto, ON M5S 2C8
416/979-1851, Fax: 416/979-8575, Toll Free: 1-800-668-2442, Email: mailbox@ciia.org, URL: http://www.trinity.utoronto.ca/ciia/
President/CEO, Alan Sullivan
Chairman, Peter White
Publications: Behind the Headlines; International Journal, q.

### Canadian Peace Alliance/Alliance canadienne pour la paix (CPA) (1985)
#5, 555 Bloor St. West, Toronto, ON M5S 1Y6
416/588-5555, Fax: 416/588-5556, Email: cpa@web.net
Coordinator, Tryna Booth
Affiliates: Action Canada Network; International Peace Bureau

### Canadian Peace Congress
873 Jane St., PO Box 98516, Toronto, ON M6N 5A6
416/762-3874
President, Larri Prokop

### Canadian Physicians for Aid & Relief (CPAR) (1983)
#202, 111 Queen St. East, Toronto, ON M5C 1S2
416/369-0865, Fax: 416/369-0294, Toll Free: 1-800-263-2727, Email: cpar@web.net
Executive Director, Joy Woolfrey
President, Mark Doidge
Publications: CPAReport

Affiliates: Canadian Environmental Network; Canadian Centre for Philanthropy

### CARE Canada (1946)
6 Antares Dr., PO Box 9000, Ottawa, ON K1G 4X6
613/228-5600, Fax: 613/226-5777, Toll Free: 1-800-267-5232, Email: info@care.ca, URL: http://www.care.ca
Executive Director, A. John Watson
Chairman, Peter Crossgrove
Communications, Heather Rourke
Publications: CARE in Action
Affiliates: CARE International; Canadian Council for International Cooperation

### Carrefour de solidarité internationale inc. (1976)
**CSI - Sherbrooke**
555, rue Short, Sherbrooke, QC J1H 2E6
819/566-8595, Téléc: 819/566-8076, Courrier électronique: csi-sher@login.net
Coordonnateur général, François Faucher
Publications: CSI - Informe

### Centre canadien d'étude et de coopération internationale/Canadian Centre for International Studies & Cooperation (CECI) (1958)
180, rue Sainte-Catherine est, Montréal, QC H2X 1K9
514/875-9911, Téléc: 514/875-6469, Courrier électronique: ceci@web.apc.org
Directeur général, Yves Pétillon
Directrice des communications, Lise Londei
Publications: CECI Dit...
Bureau de Québec: 160, rue St-Joseph est, Québec, QC G1K 3A7, 418/523-6552, Téléc: 418/523-7525

### Child Haven International/Accueil international pour l'enfance (1985)
RR#1, Maxville, ON K0C 1T0
613/527-2829, Fax: 613/527-1118, Email: childha@glen-net.ca, URL: http://www.glen-net.ca/childha/
Director, Bonnie Cappuccino
Director, Fred Cappuccino
Publications: Child Haven International/Accueil international pour l'enfance
Affiliates: Child Haven International - USA, India, Nepal

### Children's International Summer Villages (Canada) Inc.
5 Dunvegan St., Ottawa, ON K1K 3E7
613/749-9680, Fax: 613/749-9680
National Secretary, Coreen Blackburn

### Citizens for Foreign Aid Reform Inc. (C-FAR)
PO Box 392, Etobicoke, ON M9W 5L3
905/897-7221, Fax: 905/897-3914
Director, Paul Fromm

### CNEC - Partners International
#48, 8500 Torbram Rd., Brampton, ON L6T 5C6
905/458-1202, Fax: 905/458-4339
President, Rev. Grover Crosby
Publications: Partners

### CODE (1959)
**Canadian Organization for Development through Education**
321 Chapel St., Ottawa, ON K1N 7Z2
613/232-3569, Fax: 613/232-7435, Toll Free: 1-800-661-2633, Email: codehq@codecan.com, URL: http://www.web.net/~code
President, Robert Dyck
Chair, Stan Hovdebo
Publications: NGOMA (Talking Drum)
Affiliates: International Book Bank; CODE Europe; CODE Inc.; CODE Foundation

### CoDevelopment Canada (CODEV) (1985)
#205, 2929 Commercial Dr., Vancouver, BC V5N 4C8
604/708-1495, Fax: 604/708-1497, Email: codev@web.apc.org
President, Bill Brassington

### Compassion Canada (1963)
PO Box 5591, London, ON N6A 5G8
519/668-0224, Fax: 519/685-1107, Toll Free: 1-800-563-5437, Email: bslauenwhite@capc.ci.org
President, Barry Slauenwhite
Publications: Compassion Today

### Conseil de la Coopération de l'Ontario (CCO) (1964)
450 Rideau St., Ottawa, ON K1N 5Z4
613/789-7777, Téléc: 613/789-3763, Courrier électronique: cco@cooperation-ont.org
Directrice générale, Ethel Côté
Président, Benoit Martin
Publications: Le Coopère-action
Organisation(s) affiliée(s): Association canadienne française de l'Ontario

### Conseil de la coopération du Québec (CCQ) (1939)
#304, 4950, boul de la Rive Sud, Lévis, QC G6V 4Z6
418/835-3710, Téléc: 418/835-6322
Président, Majella St-Pierre
Publications: Présence coopérative
Organisation(s) affiliée(s): Conseil canadien de la coopération; Alliance coopérative internationale

### CUSO (1961)
2255 Carling Ave., Ottawa, ON K2B 1A6
613/829-7445, Fax: 613/829-7996, Email: cusoppu@web.net
Executive Director, Melanie Macdonald
Chair, François Faucher
Publications: Forum; Solidarité; The Sustainable Times
Calgary Office: Regional Coordinator, Rebekah Seidel, 233 - 10th St. NW, Calgary, AB T2N 1V5, 403/283-2871, Fax: 403/283-2902, Email: cusoalbt@web.net
Halifax Office: Regional Coordinator, Linda Snyder, #508, 1657 Barrington St., Halifax, NS B3J 2A1, 902/423-6709, Fax: 902/423-9736, Email: cusoatl@web.net
Manitoba & Western Ontario Office: Regional Coordinator, George Harris, 60 Maryland St., Winnipeg, MB R3G 1K7, 204/774-8489, Fax: 204/786-3012, Email: cusoman@web.net
Québec Regional Office: Regional Coordinator, Francine Néméh, #380, 1600, av de Lorimier, Montréal, QC H2K 3W5, 514/528-8465, Fax: 514/528-1750, Email: cusoque@web.net
Saskatoon Office: Regional Coordinator, Don Kossick, 614B - 10th St. East, Saskatoon, SK S7H 0G9, 306/933-4141, Fax: 306/933-4346, Email: cusosask@web.net
Toronto Office: Regional Coordinator, Steve Seaborn, #200, 133 Richmond St. West, Toronto, ON M5H 2L3, 416/363-2191, Fax: 416/363-6041, Email: cusoont@web.net
Vancouver Office: Regional Coordinator, Brenda Kuecks, #914, 207 West Hastings St., Vancouver, BC V6B 1H6, 604/683-2099, Fax: 604/683-8536, Email: cusobc@web.net

### Four Arrows/Las Cuatro Flechas (1968)
PO Box 1332, Ottawa, ON K1P 5R4
613/234-5887, Fax: 613/234-5887
Coordinator, R. Rarihokwats

### Group of 78/Groupe des 78 (1980)
#206, 145 Spruce St., Ottawa, ON K1R 6P1
613/ 230-0860, Fax: 613/563-0017
Chairperson, Geoffrey Pearson

### HOPE International Development Agency (1985)
214 - 6 St., New Westminster, BC V3L 3A2
604/525-5481, Fax: 604/525-3471, Email: hope@web.apc.org
Executive Director, David S. McKenzie
Communications Director, John King
Chairman, Girve Fretz
Publications: HOPE Newsletter; Concern, q.

### Horizons of Friendship (HOF) (1973)
50 Covert St., PO Box 402, Stn Main, Cobourg, ON K9A 4L1
905/372-5483, Fax: 905/372-7095
Email: horizons@web.net
Executive Director, Rick Arnold
Publications: Horizons Newsletter
Affiliates: Americas Policy Group

### Inter Pares/Among Equals
58 Arthur St., Ottawa, ON K1R 7B9
613/563-4801, Fax: 613/594-4704
Director, Lise Latrémouille
Publications: Inter Pares Bulletin

### International Child Care (Canada) Inc. (ICC) (1973)
#103, 195 King St., PO Box 2125, Stn B, St Catharines, ON L2M 6P5
905/688-0632, Fax: 905/688-6069
Administrative Manager, Lorna Rogalski
Publications: Grace Notes

### International Development Education Resource Association (IDERA) (1974)
#200, 2678 Broadway Ave. West, Vancouver, BC V6K 2G3
604/732-1496; Film Line: 604/739-8815, Fax: 604/738-8400, Email: idera@web.net, URL: http://www.vcn.bc.ca/idera
Executive Director, Stuart Black
Film Programmer, Robyn Holland
Publications: IDERA Newsletter; Press Relief, a.
Affiliates: Independent Film & Video Alliance

### International Relief Agency Inc. (IRA) (1979)
95 Wood St., Toronto, ON M4Y 2Z3
416/922-7120, Fax: 416/928-0901, Email: ira@ica.net.ca
Director General, Adam A. Budzanowski
Office Manager, Eileen Brown
Chairman, Olivia Aquino
Publications: The Global Forum Magazine
Affiliates: Best of 7 Continents Inc.; International Hippocrates Foundation

### JCI - Global Strategists (CCGS) (1995)
**Global Strategists**
#704, 153 Nepean St., Ottawa, ON K2P 0B5
613/231-2428, Fax: 613/231-2428
President, Joanne Charnetski
Vice-President, Tariq Rauf
Publications: Policy Forum Notes

### Mahatma Gandhi Canadian Foundation for World Peace (1986)
PO Box 60002, RPO U of Alberta, Edmonton, AB T6G 2S4
403/492-5504
Vijay Bhardwaj

### Manitoba Council for International Cooperation/Conseil du Manitoba pour la coopération internationale (MCIC) (1974)
#202, 583 Ellice Ave., Winnipeg, MB R3B 1Z7
204/786-2106, Fax: 204/772-7179, Email: mcic@web.net, URL: http://www.escape.ca/~mcic
Publications: MCIC News; Getting Your Message Across: A Directory of Manitoba Media

### The Marquis Project, Inc. (1979)
#200, 107 - 7 St., Brandon, MB R7A 3S5
204/727-5675, Fax: 204/727-5683, Email: marquis@docker.com
Executive Director, Zack Gross
Publications: Newsletter
Affiliates: Canadian Council for International Cooperation; Manitoba Council for International Cooperation; Partnership Africa-Canada; Canadian Peace Alliance; Manitoba Eco-Network

### Mercy International Canada (1993)
#2400, 180 Dundas St. West, PO Box 44, Toronto, ON M5G 1Z8
416/971-9200, Fax: 416/971-5613, Toll Free: 1-800-465-0088
Executive Director, Janis Kazaks
Business Manager, Elizabeth Lin
Publications: Bringing Hope to Life
Mercy International Ottawa: Director, International Programs, Janis Kazaks, 629 Highland Ave., Ottawa, ON K2A 2K2, 613/728-7170, Fax: 613/728-0033

### Ontario Council for International Cooperation/Conseil de l'Ontario pour la coopération internationale (OCIC) (1988)
#612, 590 Jarvis St., Toronto, ON M4Y 2J4
416/972-6303, Fax: 416/972-6996, Email: ocic@web.net, URL: http://www.web.net/~ocic/
Executive Director, Tonia de Sousa-Shields
President, Linda Slavin
Publications: Bulletin

### Operation Eyesight Universal (OEU) (1963)
4 Parkdale Cres. NW, Calgary, AB T2N 3T8
403/283-6323, Fax: 403/270-1899, Toll Free: 1-800-585-8265, Email: oeuca@cadvision.com
Executive Director, John A. Huggett
Publications: Gift of Sight
Affiliates: Royal Commonwealth Society for the Blind; Kenya Society for the Blind; International Agency for the Prevention of Blindness
Central Canada Regional Office: Manager, Community Relations, Stephen Faul, #323, 2100 Ellesmere Rd., Scarborough, ON M1H 3B7, 416/438-3555, Fax: 416/438-6132

### Oxfam-Canada (1963)
#300, 294 Albert St., Ottawa, ON K1P 6E6
613/237-5236, Fax: 613/237-0524, Email: oxfam@web.net, URL: http://www.oxfam.ca
Executive Director, Chisanga Puta-Chekwe
Affiliates: Oxfam International

### Peace Brigades International (Canada) (PBI) (1981)
**Central American Projects Office/Peace Brigades International (Canada)**
#304, 192 Spadina Ave., Toronto, ON M5T 2C2
416/504-4429, Fax: 416/504-4430, Email: pbi@web.net, URL: http://www.ncf.carleton.ca/pbi
Coordinator, Louise Palmer
Publications: Project Bulletin

### Peacefund Canada/Fonds canadien pour la paix (PFC) (1986)
#206, 145 Spruce St., Ottawa, ON K1R 6P1
613/230-0860, Fax: 613/563-0017, Email: pfcan@web.net
Executive Secretary, Murray Thomson
Publications: Peacefund Canada
Affiliates: International Council for Adult Education; Canadian Association for Adult Education

### Physicians for Global Survival (Canada)/Association des médecins pour la survie mondiale (Canada) (PGS) (1980)
#208, 145 Spruce St., Ottawa, ON K1R 6P1
613/233-1982, Fax: 613/233-9028, Email: pgs@web.net, URL: http://www.web.net/~pgs/
Executive Director, Debbie Grisdale
President, Dr. Konia Trouton
Publications: Turning Point; Position Papers
Affiliates: International Physicians for the Prevention of Nuclear War (IPPNW)

### Project Peacemakers (1982)
745 Westminster Ave., Winnipeg, MB R3G 1A5
204/775-8178, Fax: 204/775-8178
Karen Schlichting-Enns
Publications: Peace Projections
Affiliates: Canadian Peace Alliance; Canadian Centre for Arms Control & Disarmament; Winnipeg Coordinating Committee for Disarmament; Project Ploughshares; Manitoba Environmental Network; Coalition of Organizations Against Apartheid; The IDEA Centre; Project Ploughshares

### Project Ploughshares (1976)
Institute of Peace & Conflict Studies, Conrad Grebel College, 84 Waterloo University Campus, Waterloo, ON N2L 3G6
519/888-6541, Fax: 519/885-0806, Email: plough@watservl.uwaterloo.ca, URL: http://watserv1.uwaterloo.ca/~plough/
Policy & Public Affairs Director, Ernie Regehr
Program Coordinator, Ken Epps
Director of Development & Administration, Nancy Regehr
Publications: Ploughshares Monitor; Peace Resource Catalogue; Armed Conflicts Report, a.
Affiliates: Canadian Council of Churches

### Saskatchewan Council for International Co-operation/Conseil de la Saskatchewan pour la co-opération internationale (SCIC) (1974)
2138 McIntyre St., Regina, SK S4P 2R7
306/757-4669, Fax: 306/757-3226, Email: scic@web.net
Publications: Earthbeat; Development Education Directory; Environment & Development Directory; One World, q.

### Save the Children - Canada/Aide à l'enfance - Canada (1946)
#6020, 3080 Yonge St., Toronto, ON M4N 3P4
416/488-0306, Fax: 416/483-4430, Toll Free: 1-800-668-5036, Email: sccan@web.apc.org
National Director, René De Grâce

### Save a Family Plan (SAFP) (1965)
1040 Waterloo St., PO Box 3622, London, ON N6A 4L4
519/672-1115, Fax: 519/672-6379
Executive Director, Fr. Sebastian Adayanthrath
President, Rev. Dr. Michael Ryan

### Science for Peace/Science et paix (SfP) (1981)
University of Toronto, University College, Toronto, ON M5S 3H8
416/978-3606, Fax: 416/978-3606, Email: sfp@physics.utoronto.ca, URL: http://www.math.yorku.ca/sfp/
President, L. Terrell Gardner
Vice-President, Eric Fawcett
Secretary, Phyllis Creighton
Treasurer, Maureen Kapral
Publications: SfP Bulletin
Affiliates: Canadian Peace Research & Education Association

### Ten Days for Global Justice/Dix jours pour le justice global (1973)
**Inter-Church Committee for World Development Education**
#401, 77 Charles St. West, Toronto, ON M5S 1K5
416/922-0591, Fax: 416/922-1419, Email: tendays@web.net, URL: http://www.web.net/~tendays/
National Coordinator, Dennis Howlett
Publications: Ten Days Update; Freedom From Debt, a.

### United Nations Association in Canada/Association canadienne pour les Nations-Unies (UNAC) (1946)
**UNA - Canada**
#900, 130 Slater St., Ottawa, ON K1P 6E2
613/232-5751, Fax: 613/563-2455, Email: unac@magi.com, URL: http://www.unac.org
Executive Director, Harry Qualman
Information Officer, Joan Broughton
Publications: Liaison
Affiliates: World Federation of United Nations Associations
Edmonton: President, Randy Palivoda, 85 Woodhaven Dr., Spruce Grove, AB T7X 1M9, 403/497-5326, Fax: 403/471-8811
Hamilton: President, Brian Reid, 25 Lynndale Dr., Dundas, ON L9H 3L4, 905/575-2143, Fax: 905/575-2441, Email: 661901@ican.net
Kootenay Region: President, J.J. Verigin, Jr., PO Box 760, Grand Forks, BC V0H 1H0, 250/442-8252, Fax: 250/442-3433
Montréal Office: Vice-Président, Paul Gagner, #1625, 2020, Université, Montréal, QC H3A 2A5, 514/362-8020, Fax: 514/362-8067
National Capital Region: President, Peter Stockdale, #900, 130 Slater St., Ottawa, ON K1P 6E2, 613/232-5751, ext.25, Fax: 613/563-2455
Québec Office: Présidente, Marie-Thérèse Wéra, 913, av Painchaud, Québec, QC G1S 4L7, 418/681-2991, Téléc: 418/681-9235, Courrier électronique: wera@pop.total.net
Quinte & District: President, Aruna Alexander, 186 Mill St., PO Box 806, Stirling, ON K0K 3E0, 613/395-2842
Saguenay/Lac-St-Jean: Président, Jules Dufour, a/s UQAC, 555, boul de l'Université, Chicoutimi, QC G7H 2B1, 418/545-5371, Téléc: 418/545-5012, Courrier électronique: jdufour@uqac.uquebec.ca
Saint John: President, Eric Teed, OC, CD, QC, PO Box 6446, Stn A, Saint John, NB E2L 4R8, 506/634-7320, Fax: 506/634-7423
St. John's: Branch Contact, Jerry Vink, 155 Water St., PO Box 683, St. John's, NF A1C 6J9, 709/754-0690, Fax: 709/778-0693, Email: nlhra@nf.sympatico.ca
Toronto Office: President, Anne D'Andrea, #116, 2 College St., Toronto, ON M6G 1K3, 416/929-0990, Fax: 416/929-8773
Vancouver Office: President, Gulzar Samji, #208, 1956 Broadway West, Vancouver, BC V6J 1Z2, 604/732-0448, Fax: 604/736-8963
Victoria Office: President, Mike Samo, #217, 620 View St., Victoria, BC V8W 1J6, 250/383-4635, Fax: 250/383-4635, Email: unavictoria@pine.com
Winnipeg Office: President, Elizabeth Willcock, 375 Jefferson Ave., Winnipeg, MB R2V 0N4, 204/586-0173, Fax: 204/582-6272, Email: msmith@magic.mb.ca

### World Federalists of Canada/Mouvement canadien pour une fédération mondiale (WFC) (1948)
#207, 145 Spruce St., Ottawa, ON K1R 6P1
613/232-0647, Fax: 613/562-0017
Executive Director, Fergus Watt
President, The Very Rev. Dr. Lois A. Wilson
Administrative Officer, D. Welch
Publications: Canadian World Federalist
Affiliates: World Federalist Movement

**World University Service of Canada/Entraide universitaire mondiale du Canada (WUSC) (1939)**
PO Box 3000, Stn C, Ottawa, ON K1Y 4M8
613/798-7477, Fax: 613/798-0990, Email: wusc@wusc.ca, URL: http://www.wusc.ca
Executive Director, Marc Dolgin
Deputy Executive Director, Ravi Gupta
Publications: Communiqué
Affiliates: Canadian Council for International Cooperation

**World Vision Canada/Vision Mondiale (WVC) (1950)**
6630 Turner Valley Rd., Mississauga, ON L5N 2S4
905/821-3030, Fax: 905/821-1354, Toll Free: 1-800-268-5863, Email: dave_toycen@worldvision.ca, URL: http://www.worldvision.ca
President, Dave Toycen
Publications: Childview; Traits D'Union, trimestriel; Context, q.; Voices, q.; Prospects, q.

**INTERNATIONAL TRADE *see* TRADE**

**INTERPRETERS *see* LANGUAGE, LINGUISTICS, LITERATURE**

**INVESTMENT *see* FINANCE**

**JEWELLRY *see* GEMS & JEWELLERY**

**JUDGES *see* LAW**

## LABOUR RELATIONS

***see also* Employment & Human Resources**

**Arbitration & Mediation Institute of Canada Inc./Institut d'arbitrage et de médiation du Canada inc. (AMIC) (1974)**
#2600, 160 Elgin St., Ottawa, ON K1P 1C3
613/786-8650, Fax: 613/563-9869
Executive Director, Robert M. Nelson
Publications: Canadian Arbitration & Mediation/Journal 'd Arbitrage et de Médiation Canadien

**ALBERTA ARBITRATION & MEDIATION SOCIETY (AAMS) (1982)**
University of Alberta, 110 Law Centre, Edmonton, AB TG6 2H5
403/433-4881, Fax: 403/433-9024, Toll Free: 1-800-232-7214
Executive Director, Peter Portlock
Publications: AAMS Newsletter; AAMS Directory, a.

**ARBITRATION & MEDIATION INSTITUTE OF MANITOBA INC.**
290 Burnell St., Winnipeg, MB R3G 2A7
204/783-0529, Fax: 204/783-6446
Chair, Barry Effler

**ARBITRATION & MEDIATION INSTITUTE OF ONTARIO INC.**
#602, 234 Eglinton Ave. East, Toronto, ON M4P 1K5
416/487-4447, Fax: 416/487-4429
Office Manager, Mena Peckan
President, David McCutcheon

**ARBITRATION & MEDIATION INSTITUTE OF SASKATCHEWAN INC. (AMIS) (1987)**
532 - 2nd Ave., Saskatoon, SK S7K 2C5
306/975-1245, Fax: 306/955-1239, Info Line: 306/975-1245
Email: r.graham@sk.sympatico.ca, URL: http://www.saskstar.sk.ca/amis/
President, Robert C. Graham, C.Arb.
Secretary, James N. Perry, C.Arb.
Publications: AMIS Newsletter

**ATLANTIC PROVINCES ARBITRATION & MEDIATION INSTITUTE**
PO Box 1C1, Site 8, RR#1, Boutiliers Point, NS B0J 1G0
902/826-7579, Fax: 902/826-7996
President, Deborah Baker

**BRITISH COLUMBIA ARBITRATION & MEDIATION INSTITUTE (1980)**
1628 - 7 Ave. West, Vancouver, BC V6J 1S5
604/736-6614, Fax: 604/736-6225
Administrator, Reva Lander

**INSTITUT D'ARBITRAGE ET DE MÉDIATION DU QUÉBEC**
#002, 4444, rue Ste-Catherine ouest, Montréal, QC H3Z 1R2
514/939-3849, Téléc: 514/939-0828
Directeur général, Pierre Lefort

**Association canadienne des relations industrielles/Canadian Industrial Relations Association (ACRI) (1963)**
Département des relations industrielles, Université Laval, Pavillon J.-A.-deSève, Québec, QC G1K 7P4
418/656-2468, Téléc: 418/656-3175
Secrétaire-trésorier, Anthony Giles
Organisation(s) affiliée(s): International Industrial Relations Association; Industrial Relations Research Association; La Fédération canadienne des sciences sociales

**Association of Workers' Compensation Boards of Canada/Association des commissions des accidents du travail du Canada (AWCBC) (1919)**
#1350, 10665 Jasper Ave., Edmonton, AB T5J 3S9
403/425-5462, Fax: 403/427-2385, Email: awcbc@compusmart.ab.ca
Executive Director, Brenda Croucher
Publications: Newsletter

**Canadian Association of Administrators of Labour Legislation/Association canadienne des administrateurs de la législation ouvrière**
c/o Federal-Provincial Relations Branch, Department of Labour, 165, rue Hôtel de Ville, Hull, QC K1A 0J2
819/997-1333, Fax: 819/997-0126
Secretary, Monique Poitras
Sec.-Treas., Louise Guertin

**Canadian Association of Labour Media/Association canadienne de la presse syndicale (CALM)**
c/o Canadian Labour Congress, 2841 Riverside Dr., Ottawa, ON K1V 8X7
613/521-3400, Fax: 613/521-4655, Email: calm@web.net, URL: http://www.calm.ca
President, Mike Freeman
Publications: Labour News & Graphics

**Canadian Committee on Labour History/Comité canadien sur l'histoire du travail (CCLH) (1971)**
History Dept., Memorial University of Newfoundland, PO Box 4200, Stn C, St. John's, NF A1C 5S7
709/737-2144, Fax: 709/737-4342, Email: joanb@plato.ucs.mun.ca, URL: http://www.mun.ca/cclh/
Editor, Dr. G.S. Kealey
Publications: Labour/Le Travail
Affiliates: International Association of Labour History Institutions; Canadian Historical Association; Canadian Association of Labour Media; Conference of Historical Journals; Council of Editors of Learned Journals

**Canadian Compensation Association/Association canadienne de rémuneration (1985)**
10435 Islington Ave., PO Box 294, Kleinburg, ON L0J 1C0
905/893-1689, Fax: 905/893-2392, Email: kleinbrg@netrover.com, URL: http://www.assn-office.com/cca
Executive Director, Wayne Glover, CAE
Affiliates: American Compensation Association

**Canadian Injured Workers Alliance/L'Alliance canadienne des victimes d'accidents et de maladies du travail (CIWA) (1990)**
PO Box 3678, Thunder Bay, ON P7E 6E3
807/345-3429, Fax: 807/345-7086, URL: http://indie.ca/ciwa/
Coordinator, Steve Mantis
Publications: Highlights

**Centre d'arbitrage commercial national et international du Québec/Québec National & International Commercial Arbitration Centre (CACNIQ) (1986)**
Édifice la Fabrique, #090, 295, boul Charest est, Québec, QC G1K 3G8
418/649-1374; Montréal: 519/393-3774, Téléc: 418/649-0845
Directeur général, Jean Gauthier
Président, Nabil Antaki

**Construction Labour Relations - An Alberta Association (CLRA) (1971)**
#207, 2725 - 12 St. NE, Calgary, AB T2E 7J2
403/250-7390, Fax: 403/250-5516, Toll Free: 1-800-308-9466, Email: neil@clra.org
President, R. Neil Tidsbury
Publications: Bulletin

**Construction Labour Relations Association of British Columbia (1969)**
97 - 6 St., PO Box 820, New Westminster, BC V3L 4Z8
604/524-4911, Fax: 604/524-3925
President, C.C. McVeigh
Office Manager, W. Mazur

**Construction Labour Relations Association of Manitoba (CLRAM)**
290 Burnell St., Winnipeg, MB R3G 2A7
204/775-0441, Fax: 204/783-7270, Email: CLRAM@mb.sympatico.ca
Executive Director, Peter Wightman

**Construction Management Bureau Ltd.**
#200, 5450 Cornwallis St., Halifax, NS B3K 1A9
902/429-6763, Fax: 902/422-5303
President, Hugh A.R. Simpson

**Inter-American Commercial Arbitration Commission (IACAC) (1934)**
OAS Administrative Building, Rm. 211, 19th & Constitution Ave. NW, Washington, DC 20006 USA
202/458-3249, Fax: 202/458-3293, Telex: 64128 ANSWERBAC
Director General, Guillermo Fernandez de Soto
President, Julio Gonzales Soria
Publications: IACAC Newsletter
Canadian National Section: Contact, Prof. Paul J. Davidson, Canadian Arbitration Centre & Amicable Composition Centre, Inc., Faculty of Law, Civil Law Section, University of Ottawa, PO Box 450, Stn A, Ottawa, ON K1N 6N5, 613/232-1476, Fax: 613/564-9800

**International Federation of Commercial Arbitration Institutions/Fédération internationale des institutions d'arbitrage commercial (IFCAI) (1985)**
140 West 51 St., 9th Fl., New York, NY 10023 USA
212/484-4110, Fax: 212/765-4874
President, Michael F. Hoellering
Sec.-Treas., B.W. Vigrass

Publications: International Federation of Commercial Arbitration Institutions Newsletter

**Newfoundland Construction Labour Relations Association (NCLRA)**
15 Hallett Cres., PO Box 28065, RPO Avalon Mall, St. John's, NF A1B 4J8
709/753-5770, Fax: 709/753-5771
Chairman, Craig Power
Publications: NCLRA Newsletter

**L'Ordre professionnel des conseillers en relations industrielles du Québec (OPCRIQ) (1971)**
#503, 1100, av Beaumont, Mount Royal, QC H3P 3E5
514/344-1609, Téléc: 514/344-1610, Courrier électronique: opcriq@opcriq.qc.ca, URL: http://www.opcriq.qc.ca
Directeur général, Florent Francoeur
Publications: Ecriteau

**Provincial Building & Construction Trades Council of Ontario (1959)**
**Provincial Building Trades Council**
#604, 15 Gervais Dr., North York, ON M3C 1Y8
416/449-4830, Fax: 416/449-5713
Business Manager/Sec.-Treas., Joseph Duffy
Publications: Naylor Communications
Affiliates: International Foundation of Employee Benefit Plans - Building Trades Department

**Pulp & Paper Employee Relations Forum**
#800, 505 Burrard St., Vancouver, BC V7X 1M4
604/683-8571, Fax: 604/683-4259
President, E.Y. Mitterndorfer

**Union of Injured Workers of Ontario, Inc.**
#1, 1474 St. Clair Ave. West, Toronto, ON M6E 1C6
416/657-1215, Fax: 416/657-8122
Executive Director, Philip Biggin
Publications: Injured Workers' Voice

**Western Employers Labour Relations Association**
#507, 4190 Lougheed Hwy., Burnaby, BC V5C 6A8
604/291-2871, Fax: 604/291-0538
Executive Vice-President, Jim Galbraith

## LANDSCAPE ARCHITECTURE

**Alberta Association of Landscape Architects (AALA) (1970)**
#2, 9804 - 47 Ave., Edmonton, AB T6E 5P3
403/435-9902, Fax: 403/435-7503
President, Brian Baker
Publications: AALA

**Association des architectes paysagistes du Québec (AAPQ)**
#811, 3575, boul St-Laurent, Montréal, QC H2X 2T7
514/990-7731
President, Vincent Guamis

**Atlantic Provinces Association of Landscape Architects (APALA)**
PO Box 3415, Stn South, Halifax, NS B3J 3J1
902/422-6514, Fax: 902/425-0402
President, Cary Vollick
Publications: APALA Newsletter

**British Columbia Society of Landscape Architects (BCSLA) (1964)**
#110, 355 Burrard St., Vancouver, BC V6C 2G8
604/682-5610, Fax: 604/681-3394
Email: bcsla@direct.ca
Secretary, Klaudia Brhlik
Publications: Sitelines

**Canadian Society of Landscape Architects/Association des architectes paysagistes du Canada (CSLA) (1934)**
Box 7, Site 5, RR#1, Okotoks, AB T0L 1T0
403/938-2476, Fax: 403/938-2476, Email: csla@agt.net, URL: http://www.clr.utoronto.ca/ORG/CSLA/
Executive Director, Larry Paterson
Secretary, Linda LeGeyt
Publications: CSLA Bulletin
Affiliates: International Federation of Landscape Architects; Landscape Alliance

**Manitoba Association of Landscape Architects (MALA) (1973)**
131 Callum Cres., Winnipeg, MB R2G 2C7
204/663-4863, Fax: 204/668-5662
Executive Secretary, Valerie Lindberg
Publications: MALA News

**Ontario Association of Landscape Architects (OALA) (1968)**
#101, 2842 Bloor St. West, Etobicoke, ON M8X 1B1
416/231-4181, Fax: 416/231-2679
Email: oala@interlog.com, URL: http://www.oala.on.ca
Executive Director, Arthur M. Timms, B.Sc., Ph.D., CAE
President, David Anselmi
Publications: OALA News
Affiliates: Conservation Council of Ontario

**Saskatchewan Association of Landscape Architects (SALA) (1979)**
#200, 642 Broadway Ave., Saskatoon, SK S7N 1A9
306/975-3238, Fax: 306/975-3034
President, Heather Edwards
Secretary, Michael Beresnak
Publications: SALA Digest
Affiliates: International Federation of Landscape Architects

## LANGUAGE, LINGUISTICS, LITERATURE

**ABC CANADA (1990)**
**ABC CANADA Literacy Foundation**
1450 Don Mills Rd., North York, ON M3B 2X7
416/442-2292, Fax: 416/442-2293, Toll Free: 1-800-303-1004, Email: abccanada@southam.ca, URL: http://www.abc-canada.org
Executive Director, Colleen Albiston
Chair, Peter Gilchrist
Contact, Sarah Canzano
Publications: Literacy at Work

**Association of Visual Language Interpreters of Canada, Inc./Association des interprêtes en langage visuel du Canada**
c/o Canadian Hearing Society, #502, 2197 Riverside Dr., Ottawa, ON K1H 7X3
613/521-0509, Fax: 613/521-0838
President, Susan Margaret
Affiliates: International Association of Logopedics & Phoniatrics

**The Brontë Society - Canada (1893)**
142 Glenforest Rd., Toronto, ON M4N 1Z9
416/488-0888
Canadian Representative, Judith Watkins-Kapsa

**Canadian Association for Commonwealth Literature & Language Studies/Association canadienne pour l'étude des langues et de la littérature du Commonwealth (CACLALS) (1973)**
Dept. of English, University of Calgary, 2500 University Dr. NW, Calgary, AB T2N 1N4
403/220-5470, Fax: 403/289-1123
President, Victor J. Ramraj
Sec.-Treas., Kelly Hewson
Publications: Chimo
Affiliates: Association for Commonwealth Literature & Language Studies (ACLALS)

**Canadian Comparative Literature Association/Association canadienne de littérature comparée (1969)**
Dept. of English, University of Victoria, Victoria, BC V8W 1W3
250/721-7240, Fax: 250/721-6498
President, Prof. Evelyn Cobley
Secretary, Hilary Clark
Treasurer, Richard Cavell
Publications: Canadian Review of Comparative Literature

**Canadian Give the Gift of Literacy Foundation (CGGLF) (1986)**
35 Spadina Rd., Toronto, ON M5R 2S9
416/975-9366, Fax: 416/975-1839
Chair, Anne Erickson
Coordinator, Sharon English
Publications: Literacy Letter

**Canadian Linguistic Association/Association canadienne de linguistique**
Dept. of Linguistics, Memorial University, St. John's, NF A1B 3X9
709/737-8134, Fax: 709/737-4000, URL: http://www.ucs.mun.ca/~cla-acl
Sec.-Treas., James Black
Publications: The Canadian Journal of Linguistics/La Revue canadienne de linguistique; Bulletin, a.
Affiliates: International Permanent Committee of Linguists

**Canadian Literary & Artistic Association/Association littéraire et artistique canadienne inc.**
**ALAI Canada**
c/o Ogivy Renault, #1000, 1981, av McGill College, Montréal, QC H3A 3C1
514/847-4512, Fax: 514/658-5993
President, Ghislain Roussel
Publications: ALAI Canada Newsletter

**Canadian Parents for French (CPF) (1977)**
#310, 176 Gloucester St., Ottawa, ON K2P 0A6
613/235-1481, Fax: 613/230-5940, Email: cpf@omnimage.ca, URL: http://www.cpf.ca
Executive Director, J. Elmer Hynes
National President, Kate Merry
Publications: CPF Immersion Registry; CPF National News, 3 pa
Affiliates: Fédération des communautés francophones et acadienne du Canada; Association canadienne des professeurs d'immersion; Canadian Association of Second Language Teachers

**Canadian Translators & Interpreters Council/Conseil des traducteurs et interprètes du Canada (1956)**
#1402, One Nicholas St., Ottawa, ON K1N 7B7
613/562-0379, Fax: 613/241-4098
President, Diane Blais-Ialenti
Executive Asssistant, Béatrice Dugué
Publications: Action CTIC

**ASSOCIATION DES TRADUCTEURS ET INTERPRÈTES DU MANITOBA/ASSOCIATION OF TRANSLATORS & INTERPRETERS OF MANITOBA**
200, av de la Cathédrale, CP 83, Winnipeg, MB R2H 0H7
204/233-1757

**ASSOCIATION OF TRANSLATORS & INTERPRETERS OF ALBERTA/ ASSOCIATION DES TRADUCTEURS ET INTERPRÈTES DE L'ALBERTA (ATIA) (1979)**
PO Box 2635, Stn M, Calgary, AB T2P 3C1
403/243-3477, Edmonton: 403/434-8384, Fax: 403/447-5834
URL: http://www.atia.ab.ca
President, Valerie Henitiuk
Publications: Transforum

**ASSOCIATION OF TRANSLATORS & INTERPRETERS OF ONTARIO/ ASSOCIATION DES TRADUCTEURS ET INTERPRÈTES DE L'ONTARIO (ATIO) (1921)**
#1202, One Nicholas St., Ottawa, ON K1N 7B7
613/241-2846, Fax: 613/241-4098, Toll Free: 1-800-234-5030
Administrative Director, Liette Poitras
President, Pascal Sabourin
Secretary, Michel Trahan
Treasurer, Creighton Douglas
Publications: informatio; Directory

**ASSOCIATION OF TRANSLATORS & INTERPRETERS OF SASKATCHEWAN/ASSOCIATION DES TRADUCTEURS ET INTERPRÈTES DE LA SASKATCHEWAN (ATIS) (1980)**
2341 Broad St., Regina, SK S4P 1Y9
306/522-2847
President, Catherine Laratte
Vice-President, Joan Boyer
Publications: Bulletin de l'ATIS Bulletin
Affiliates: Canadian Translators & Interpreters Council, Regional Center for North America (USA, Canada, Mexico); Fédération internationale des traducteurs

**CORPORATION DES TRADUCTEURS, TRADUCTRICES, TERMINOLOGUES ET INTERPRÈTES DU NOUVEAU-BRUNSWICK/ CORPORATION OF TRANSLATORS, TERMINOLOGISTS & INTERPRETERS OF NEW BRUNSWICK (CTINB) (1970)**
CP 427, Fredericton, NB E3B 4Z9
506/458-1519
Président, Gérard Snow
Publications: Bulletin de la CTINB/CTINB Bulletin; Répertoire/Directory, au deux ans
Organisation(s) affiliée(s): Fédération internationale des traducteurs

**INTERPRETERS/TRANSLATORS SOCIETY OF NORTHWEST TERRITORIES (1989)**
PO Box 995, Yellowknife, NT X1A 2N7
867/873-9715
President, Violet Hardisty

**ORDRE DES TRADUCTEURS ET INTERPRÈTES AGRÉÉS DU QUÉBEC (OTIAQ) (1992)**
#1108, 2021, rue Union, Montréal, QC H3A 2S9
514/845-4411, Téléc: 514/845-9903, Ligne sans frais: 1-800-265-4815
Courrier électronique: otiaq@odyssee.net, URL: http://www.otiaq.org
Directrice générale, Diane McKay
Président, Bruce Knowlden
Relations publiques, Georges Aubé
Publications: Antenne; Circuit, trimestriel; Répertoire annuel de tous les membres

**SOCIETY OF TRANSLATORS & INTERPRETERS OF BRITISH COLUMBIA/SOCIÉTÉ DES TRADUCTEURS ET INTERPRÈTES DE COLOMBIE-BRITANNIQUE (1981)**
#400, 905 Pender St. West, Vancouver, BC V6C 1L6
604/684-9371, Fax: 604/687-6130
President, Yolanda Hobrough
Publications: The Transletter; Directory, a.

**Centre international de recherche en aménagement linguistique/International Center for Research on Language Planning (CIRAL) (1967)**
Pav. Charles-de-Koninck, Cité Universitaire, Université Laval, CP 2208, Succ. Terminus, Ste-Foy, QC G1K 7P4
418/656-3232, Téléc: 418/656-7144, Courrier électronique: ciral@ciral.ulaval.ca, URL: http://www.ciral.ulaval.ca
Directrice, Denise Deshaies

**Dhe Internasional Union for Kanadan (IUK) (1987)**
92 Glenholm Ave., Toronto, ON M6H 3B1
Internasional Prezident, Jonathan Kates/Keets
Publications: Dhe Times uv Toronto; The Kanadan Nuuzletter, 3 pa

**Esperanto Association of Canada/Association canadienne d'esperanto (KEA) (1958)**
**Kanada Esperanto-Asocio**
PO Box 2159, Sidney, BC V8L 3S6
250/656-7012, Fax: 250/656-7012, Email: dutemple@islandnet.com, URL: http://www.engcorp.com/kea/indexa.html
President, Ciprian Jauca
Publications: Lumo; Esperanto Update, q.
Affiliates: Universal Esperanto Association - Rotterdam

**AKADEMIO DE ESPERANTO - SEKCIO FAKAJ TERMINAROJ/ ACADEMY OF ESPERANTO - SECTION DICTIONARIES FOR SPECIAL FIELDS (1978)**
54 Scriven Rd., RR#1, Bailieboro, ON K0L 1B0
705/939-6088
Director, R. Eichholz
Publications: Akademiaj Studoj
Affiliates: Akademio de Esperanto

**CANADIAN ESPERANTO YOUTH/JEUNESSE ESPERANTISTE CANADIENNE (JEK) (1976)**
**Junularo Esperantista Kanada**
PO Box 2159, Sidney, BC V8L 3S6
250/474-3137
Email: phopkins@sol.uvic.ca, URL: http://www.engcorp.com/kea/jek.html
Secretary, Bruce Arthur
Publications: Juna Alumeto
Affiliates: World Esperanto Youth Organization

**SOCIÉTÉ QUÉBÉCOISE D'ESPÉRANTO/ESPERANTO SOCIETY OF QUÉBEC (SQE) (1983)**
6358A, rue de Bordeaux, Montréal, QC H2G 2R8
514/272-0151, Téléc: 514/495-8442, Infoligne: 514/272-0151
Courrier électronique: normand.fleury@sympatico.ca, URL: http://www.cam.org/~mmaerten/esk.html
Président, Normand Fleury
Secrétaire-trésorier, Marco Maertens
Publications: La Riverego; Catalogue du service de librairie, annuel
Organisation(s) affiliée(s): Universala Esperanto-Asocio; Tutmonda Esperantista Junulara Organizo

**WORLD ESPERANTO ASSOCIATION (UEA) (1908)**
**Universala Esperanto Associo**
765 Braemar Ave., Sidney, BC V8L 5G5
250/656-1767
Email: uea@intern.nl.net
Canadian Representative, Olga du Temple

**Fédération canadienne pour l'alphabétisation en français (FCAF) (1991)**
#205, 235, ch Montréal, Vanier, ON K1L 6C7
613/749-5333, Téléc: 613/749-2252, Courrier électronique: alpha@fcaf.franco.ca, URL: http://www.franco.ca/alpha/
Directrice générale, Luce Lapierre
Publications: de A à Z

**International Reading Association (IRA) (1956)**
800 Barksdale Rd., PO Box 8139, Newark, DE 19714-8139 USA
302/731-1600, ext.220, Fax: 302/731-1057, Email: afarstrup@reading.org
Executive Director, Alan E. Farstrup
Public Information Coordinator, Janet Butler
Publications: Reading Today; The Reading Teacher; Journal of Adolescent & Adult Literacy; Reading Research Quarterly; Lecturay Vida

**Jane Austen Society of North America (JASNA) (1979)**
200 Kingsmount Blvd., Sudbury, ON P3E 1K9
705/670-1357
Canadian Membership Secretary, Nancy Thurston
President, E. Solender
Publications: Persuasions; JASNA News, s-a.

**Laubach Literacy Canada/Alphabétisation Laubach du Canada (1981)**
#225, 70 Crown St., Saint John, NB E2L 2X6
506/634-1980, Fax: 506/634-0944, Email: laubach@acces-cible.net, URL: http://www.nald.ca/llc.htm
President, Ms. D. Lark Gamey
Publications: Literacy Connections
Affiliates: Laubach Literacy International

**Literary Translators' Association of Canada/ Association des traducteurs et traductrices littéraires du Canada (LTCA) (1975)**
3492, av Laval, Montréal, QC H2X 3C8
514/849-8540, Email: alterego@rocler.qc.ca
Treasurer, Howard Scott
Publications: Transmission; Répertoire/ Directory, biennial

**Manitoba Association for the Promotion of Ancestral Languages (MAPAL) (1983)**
1574 Main St., Winnipeg, MB R2W 5J8
204/338-7951, Fax: 204/334-8277
Acting President, Laura Shabaga
Publications: Manitoba Heritage Review; Reaching Out

**Movement for Canadian Literacy/ Rassemblement canadien pour l'alphabétisation (MCL) (1977)**
458 MacLaren St., 2nd Fl., Ottawa, ON K1R 5K6
613/563-2464, Fax: 613/563-2504, Email: mcl@magi.com, URL: http://www.nald.ca/mcl/mcl2.htm
Executive Director, J. Craig McNaughton
President, Nayda Veeman
Publications: Literacy Bin

**Québec Society for the Promotion of English Language Literature/Société québécoise pour la promotion de la littérature de la langue anglaise (QSPELL) (1987)**
1200 Atwater Ave., Montréal, QC H3Z 1X4
514/933-0878, Fax: 514/933-0878, Email: qspell@total.net
President, Guy Rodgers
Secretary, Julie Keith

**Saskatchewan Elocution & Debate Association/ Association d'élocution et des débats de la Saskatchewan (SEDA) (1974)**
1860 Lorne St., Regina, SK S4P 2L7
306/780-9243, Fax: 306/781-6021
Executive Director, Tanya Sturgeon
Publications: Voice
Affiliates: Canadian Student Debating Federation

**Saskatchewan Organization for Heritage Languages Inc. (SOHL) (1985)**
2144 Cornwall St., Regina, SK S4P 2K7

306/780-9275, Fax: 306/780-9407, Toll Free: 1-800-780-9460, Email: schladmin@sasknet.sk.ca
Executive Director, Joan Kanigan-Fairen
Publications: SOHL Newsletter
Affiliates: Saskatchewan Council of Cultural Organizations

**Sweetgrass First Nations Language Council (1989)**
PO Box 22019, Brantford, ON N3S 7V1
519/759-2650, Fax: 519/759-8912, Email: angie@woodland-centre.on.ca
Speaker, Dorothy Lazore
Publications: Sweetgrass News

**World Literacy of Canada/Alphabétisation mondiale Canada (WLC) (1955)**
59 Front St. East, Toronto, ON M5E 1B3
416/863-6262, Fax: 416/601-6984
Executive Director, Mamta Mishra
Canadian Program Officer, Stephanie Garrow
Publications: Worldlit

## LAW

*see also* Prisoners & Ex-Offenders

**The Advocates' Society (1963)**
Campbell House, 160 Queen St. West, Toronto, ON M5H 3H3
416/597-0243, Fax: 416/597-1588
Executive Director, Alexandra Chyczij
Publications: The Advocates' Journal; The Advocates' Brief, 10 pa

**Alberta Civil Trial Lawyers' Association (ACTLA) (1986)**
#550, 10055 - 106 St., Edmonton, AB T5J 2Y2
403/429-1133, Fax: 403/429-1199, Toll Free: 1-800-665-7248, Email: admin@actla.com, URL: http://www.actla.com
Executive Director, Lyn Bromilow
President, Gary J. Bigg
Publications: The Barrister
Affiliates: Association of Trial Lawyers of America

**Alberta Federation of Police Associations (AFPA)**
9636 - 102 Ave., Edmonton, AB T5H 0G5
403/429-0557, Fax: 403/428-0374
President, Darryl da Costa
Affiliates: Canadian Police Association

**Alberta Government Civil Lawyers Association (AGCLA) (1976)**
Alberta Justice, Civil Law Division, Bowker Building, 9833 - 109 St., 5th Fl., Edmonton, AB T5K 2E8
403/498-3311, Fax: 403/425-0307, Info Line: 403/498-3300
President, Herb Schlotter

**Alberta Law Foundation (ALF) (1973)**
#300, 407 - 8 Ave. SW, Calgary, AB T2P 1E5
403/264-4701
Executive Director, Owen G. Snider, MBA
Affiliates: Association of Canadian Law Foundations

**Association of Canadian Courts Administrators (ACCA) (1975)**
Court Services, Dept. of Justice, 9833 - 109 St., Edmonton, AB T5K 2E8
403/427-9620, Fax: 403/422-9639
President, Rod Wacowich
Vice-President, Anne Roland
Secretary, Andre Garneau
Treasurer, Raynald Chartrand
Publications: Canadian Court Forum

**Association des directeurs de polices et pompiers du Québec**
1701, rue Parthenais, bur. C-1.12, Montréal, QC H2K 3S7
514/521-2311, Téléc: 514/521-3962
Directeur général, Laurin Audy

**Association des juristes d'expression française de l'Ontario (AJEFO) (1980)**
17 Copernicus St., Ottawa, ON K1N 6N5
613/562-5866, Téléc: 613/562-5245
Directeur général, Gérard Lévésque
Président, Michel Landry
Directeur adjoint, Christian Hyde
Publications: L'Expression

**Association des juristes d'expression française de la Saskatchewan/French Jurists Association of Saskatchewan (AJEFS) (1989)**
2132 Broad St., Regina, SK S4P 1Y5
306/565-2507, Téléc: 306/781-7916
Présidente, Suzanne B. Stradecki
Publications: Bulletin des juristes

**Association of Legal Court Interpreters & Translators/Association des interprètes et des traducteurs judiciares (1972)**
2114, boul Saint-Laurent, Montréal, QC H2X 2T2
514/845-3111, Fax: 514/845-3006
President, Henri Keleny
Translations Manager, Betty Farkas

**Atlantic Association of Chiefs of Police**
c/o Fredericton Police Department, 311 Queen St., Fredericton, NB E3B 1B1
506/452-9701, Fax: 506/450-2102
Sec.-Treas., R.M. Cronkhite
Publications: Atlantic News

**Barreau de Montréal/Bar of Montréal (1849)**
Palais de Justice, #980, 1, rue Notre Dame est, Montréal, QC H2Y 1B6
514/866-9392, Téléc: 514/866-1488
Directeur général, Maurice Boileau

**Barreau du Québec/Québec Bar Association (1849)**
Maison du Barreau, #600, 445, boul Saint-Laurent, Montréal, QC H2Y 3T8
514/954-3400, Téléc: 514/954-3407, Ligne sans frais: 1-800-361-8495, URL: http://www.barreau.qc.ca
Directeur général, Pierre Gauthier
Directeur général adjoint, Jacques Houle, Courrier électronique: jhoule@barreau.qc.ca
Communications, Léon Bédard, Courrier électronique: lbedard@barreau.qc.ca
Publications: Journal du Barreau; Revue de Barreau; Rapport Annuel
Organisation(s) affiliée(s): Fédération des professions juridiques du Canada

**Canadian Association of Chiefs of Police/Association canadienne des chefs de police (CACP) (1905)**
#1710, 130 Albert St., Ottawa, ON K1P 5G4
613/233-1106, Fax: 613/233-6960, Email: cacp@travel-net.com
Executive Director, Bryan McConnell
President, John D. Moodie
Administrative Assistant & Office Manager, Catherine Toner
Publications: Canadian Police Chief Newsletter; CACP Directory & Buyer's Guide, a.; Canadian Police Chief Magazine, a.

**Canadian Association on Competition Law/Association canadienne d'étude du droit de la concurrence**
55, rue Saint-Jacques, Montréal, QC H2Y 3X2
514/987-6242, Fax: 514/845-7874, Telex: 05-268656 ROBIC
President, Jacques A. Léger
Affiliates: International League of Unfair Competition - Paris, France

**Canadian Association of Crown Counsel**
55 Munsee St., Cayuga, ON N0A 1E0
905/772-5043, Fax: 905/772-3494
President, Jean-Pierre Major

**Canadian Association of Law Teachers/Association canadienne des professeurs de droit (CALT)**
c/o Canadian Bar Association, #902, 50 O'Connor St., Ottawa, ON K1P 6L2
President, Dr. Anne Stalker
Publications: CALT/ACPD Bulletin

**Canadian Association of Legal Assistants/Association canadienne des adjoints juridiques (CALA) (1980)**
PO Box 967, Stn B, Montréal, QC H3B 3K5
416/321-1000, ext.277, Email: cala@dyedurham.ca, URL: http://www.dyedurham.ca/cala/
President, Cathy Robinson
Publications: Liaison

**Canadian Association of Legal Support Staff (CALSS) (1978)**
PO Box 3186, Winnipeg, MB R3C 4E7
President, Sheila Down
Publications: Connection

**Canadian Association of Police Boards (CAPB) (1989)**
10 Peel Centre Dr., Brampton, ON L6T 4B9
905/458-1342, Fax: 905/458-7278
Executive Director, Frederick Biro, CAE
Publications: Police Board News; CAPB News, 10 pa

**Canadian Association of Provincial Court Judges/Association Canadienne des Juges des Cours Provinciales (CAPCJ) (1973)**
PO Box 5001, Moncton, NB E1C 8R3
506/856-2307, Fax: 506/856-3226
President, Judge Ann. Rounthwaite
Sec.-Treas., Judge Irwin Lampert
Publications: Provincial Judges Journal

**Canadian Bar Association/Association du barreau canadien (CBA) (1921)**
#902, 50 O'Connor St., Ottawa, ON K1P 6L2
613/237-2925, Fax: 613/237-0185, Toll Free: 1-800-267-8860, Email: info@cba.org, URL: http://cba.org/abc
Acting Executive Director, Steve Bresolin
President, P. André Gervais, Q.C.
Publications: National; Canadian Bar Review, q.; Ottawa Report, q.; Canadian Bar Association Directory, a.
Affiliates: Canadian Association of Law Teachers; Canadian Law Information Council; Commonwealth Bar Association; Inter-American Bar Association; International Bar Association; Union internationale des avocats

**Canadian Bar Foundation/Fondation du barreau canadien (1978)**
#902, 50 O'Connor St., Ottawa, ON K1P 6L2
613/237-2925, Fax: 613/237-0185
President, Gordon Proudfoot
Publications: Canadian Bar Review; National, m.

**Canadian Bar Insurance Association/Association d'assurance du barreau canadien (CBIA) (1966)**
#5070, 3080 Yonge St., Toronto, ON M4N 3R2
416/488-0702, Fax: 416/488-2254
Contact, Barry Reynolds

**Canadian Canon Law Society/Société canadienne de droit canonique (CCLS) (1966)**
223 Main St., Ottawa, ON K1S 1C4
613/236-1393, ext.2215, Fax: 613/236-5278
Sec.-Treas., Lucy Gorman-McCoy
Publications: Newsletter of the Canadian Canon Law Society/Bulletin de nouvelles de La Société canadienne de droit canonique

**The Canadian Corporate Counsel Association/ L'Association canadienne des conseillers juridiques d'entreprises**
#300, 20 Toronto St., Toronto, ON M5C 2B8
416/869-0522, Fax: 416/869-0946
Executive Director, Robert V.A. Jones, QC
President & CEO, Leo Chrzanowski
Treasurer, Michael P. Thompson

**Canadian Council on International Law/Conseil canadien de droit international (CCIL) (1972)**
#215, 236 Metcalfe St., Ottawa, ON K2P 1R3
613/235-0442, Fax: 613/230-5978
Executive Director, Madeleine Renaud
Publications: Newsletter; CCIL Conference Proceedings, a.
Affiliates: Société québécoise de droit international; American Society of International Law; Japanese Association of International Law

**Canadian Criminal Justice Association/ Association canadienne de justice pénale (CCJA) (1919)**
#304, 383 Parkdale Ave., Ottawa, ON K1Y 4R4
613/725-3715, Fax: 613/725-3720, Email: ccja@istar.ca
Executive Director, Gaston St-Jean
Publications: The Bulletin; Canadian Journal of Criminology, q.; Justice Report, 3 pa; Directory of Justice Services; Directory of Services to Victims of Crime
Affiliates: Alberta Criminal Justice Association; British Columbia Criminal Justice Association; Manitoba Criminal Justice Association; New Brunswick Chapter, Canadian Criminal Justice Association; Newfoundland & Labrador Criminology & Corrections Association; Nova Scotia Criminology & Corrections Association; Ontario Association of Corrections & Criminology; Saskatchewan Criminal Justice Association

**Canadian Institute for the Administration of Justice/Institut canadien d'administration de la justice (CIAJ) (1974)**
Faculté de droit, Université de Montréal, CP 6128, Stn Centre-Ville, Montréal, QC H3C 3J7
514/343-6157, Fax: 514/343-6296, Email: ciaj@umontreal.ca
Executive Director, Christine Robertson
Publications: CIAJ Newsletter

**Canadian Law & Society Association/Association canadienne de droit et société (CLSA) (1985)**
318 Osgoode, 4700 Keele St., Toronto, ON M3G 1P3
416/736-5037, Fax: 416/736-5615, Email: fzemans@yorku.ca, URL: http://www.juris.uqam.ca/rcds/INDEX_EN.HTM
President, Wes Pue
Sec.-Treas., Fred Zemans
Publications: Canadian Journal of Law & Society/ Revue canadienne de droit et société; ACDS/CLSA Bulletin

**Canadian Maritime Law Association/Association canadienne de droit maritime (1951)**
#2000, 360, rue Saint-Jacques, Montréal, QC H2Y 1P5
514/849-4161, Fax: 514/849-4167
Sec.-Treas., J.A. Cantello
Publications: Membres/Members

**Canadian Petroleum Law Foundation (1963)**
c/o Canadian Occidental Petroleum Ltd., #1500, 635 - 8 Ave. SW, Calgary, AB T2P 3Z1
403/234-6700, Fax: 403/234-6971
Secretary, John B. McWilliams
Publications: Petroleum Law Supplement of Alberta Law Review

**Canadian Police Association/L'Association canadienne des policiers (CPA) (1953)**
141 Catherine St., Ottawa, ON K2P 1C3
613/231-4168, Fax: 613/231-3254, Email: cpa@igs.net
Executive Officer, Scott Newark
Publications: Yearbook; CPANews, m.; Express, q.

**Canadian Society for the Advancement of Legal Technology/Association canadienne pour l'avancement de l'informatique juridique (CSALT)**
#200, 20 Toronto St., Toronto, ON M5C 2B8
416/663-5290, Fax: 416/663-6502
Administrator, Carolynn R. Parke, Bus: 416/420-2208, Fax: 416/420-3542
Publications: CSALT News; CSALT Review

**Chambre des notaires du Québec (1847)**
**Ordre des notaires du Québec**
Tour de la Bourse, #700, 800, Place Victoria, CP 162, Montréal, QC H4Z 1L8
514/879-2903, Téléc: 514/879-1923, Courrier électronique: gagnonri@cdnq.org, URL: http://www.cdnq.org
Directeur général, Richard Gagnon
Publications: Revue du notariat; Cours de perfectionnement du notariat, semi-annuel; Entracte, 18 fois par an
Organisation(s) affiliée(s): Fédération des professions juridiques

**Church Council on Justice & Corrections/Conseil des églises pour la justice et la criminologie (CCJC) (1974)**
507 Bank St., 2nd Fl., Ottawa, ON K2P 1Z5
613/563-1688, Fax: 613/237-6129, Email: ccjc@web.net
Communication Coordinator, Rick Prashaw
Publications: Update/À Jour

**Community Legal Education Association (Manitoba) Inc./Association d'éducation juridique communautaire (Manitoba) inc. (CLEA) (1985)**
#501, 294 Portage Ave., Winnipeg, MB R3C 0B9
204/943-2382; 943-2305 (legal info./lawyer ref.), Fax: 204/943-3600, Toll Free: 1-800-262-8800, Email: info@communitylegal.mb.ca, URL: http://www.acjnet.org/white/clea.html
Acting Executive Director, Barb Palace
President, Diane Dwarka
Publications: Manitoba Directory of Legal Services
Affiliates: Public Legal Education Association of Canada

**Community Legal Education Ontario (CLEO) (1975)**
#600, 119 Spadina Ave., Toronto, ON M5V 2L1
416/408-4420, Fax: 416/408-4424
Executive Director, Mary Marrone

**Community Legal Information Association of Prince Edward Island (1985)**
Sullivan Building, #158, 20 Fitzroy, PO Box 1207, Charlottetown, PE C1A 7M8
902/892-0853, Fax: 902/368-4096, Email: cliapei@web.net
Executive Director, Ann Sherman
Publications: Legal Information

**Continuing Legal Education Society of BC (1965)**
#300, 845 Cambie St., Vancouver, BC V6B 5T2
604/669-3544, Fax: 604/669-9260, Toll Free: 1-800-663-0437, Email: custserv@cle.bc.ca, URL: http://www.cle.bc.ca
Executive Director, Jack J. Huberman, Q.C.

**Court Interpreters Association of Ontario**
1396A Yonge St., Unit D, Toronto, ON M4T 1Y5
416/975-9564, Fax: 416/967-5281
President, Rajeshwar Singh

**Criminal Lawyers' Association of Ontario (1971)**
#800, 56 Temperance St., Toronto, ON M5H 3V5
416/214-9875, Fax: 416/214-9802, Email: crimlaw@ilap.com
Executive Director, Stephanie Mealing
Publications: Newsletter
Affiliates: Canadian Council of Criminal Defence Lawyers; National Association of Criminal Defense Lawyers - USA

**Federation of Law Reform Agencies of Canada**
c/o Manitoba Law Reform Commission, 405 Broadway, 12th Fl., Winnipeg, MB R3C 3L6
204/945-2900, Fax: 204/948-2184
President, Jeffrey A. Schnoor, Q.C., Email: jschnoor@jus.gov.mb.ca

**Federation of Law Societies of Canada/ Fédération des professions juridiques du Canada (1972)**
#480, 445, boul Saint-Laurent, Montréal, QC H2Y 2Y7
514/875-6350, Fax: 514/875-6115, Email: pafoley@flsc.ca, URL: http://www.flsc.ca/
Executive Director, Diane Bourque
President, Donald M. Little, Q.C.
Sec.-Treas., Patricia-Ann Foley

**Fondation du barreau du Québec**
#404, 445, boul Saint-Laurent, Montréal, QC H2Y 3T8
514/954-3461, Téléc: 514/954-3449
Président, Henri Grondin
Président du conseil d'administration, Guy Gilbert

**Foundation for Legal Research in Canada**
c/o Canadian Bar Association, #902, 50 O'Connor St., Ottawa, ON K1P 6L2
613/237-2925, Fax: 613/237-0185
Treasurer, Stephen Bresolin

**Institute of Law Clerks of Ontario (ILCO) (1968)**
#1150, 36 Toronto St., Toronto, ON M5C 2C5
416/214-6252; Employment Hotline: 416/214-6256
President, Giselle Piper
Secretary, Carolyn Keates
Publications: Law Clerks Review

**International Commission of Jurists (Canadian Section)/La Commission Internationale de Juristes (Section canadienne) (ICJ)**
#902, 50 O'Connor St., Ottawa, ON K1P 6L2
613/237-2925 (Wed. only), Fax: 613/237-0185
Présidente, The Honourable Madame le juge Michèle Rivet
Publications: Newsletter

**Law Foundation of British Columbia (1969)**
#1340, 605 Robson St., Vancouver, BC V6B 5J3

604/688-2337, Fax: 604/688-4586, Email: lfbc@bc.sympatico.ca
Executive Director, Jane MacFadgen

**Law Foundation of Newfoundland**
PO Box 5907, Stn C, St. John's, NF A1C 5X4
709/754-4424, Fax: 709/754-4320
Chairman, P.D. Lewis, Q.C.

**Law Foundation of Nova Scotia**
PO Box 325, Halifax, NS B3J 2N7
902/422-8335, Fax: 902/492-0424
Executive Director, Jane E. Holmes

**Law Foundation of Ontario/La fondation du droit de l'Ontario**
#2210, 20 Queen St. West, Toronto, ON M5H 3R3
416/598-1550, Fax: 416/598-1526
Controller & Secretary, Mary Shannon Brown
Chair, Roger D. Yachetti, Q.C.

**Law Foundation of Prince Edward Island (1972)**
49 Water St., Charlottetown, PE C1A 7K2
902/566-1666, Fax: 902/368-7557
Executive Director, Kathy Stuart
Chair, John Mitchell, LLB
Affiliates: Association of Canadian Bar Foundations

**Law Foundation of Saskatchewan**
#620, 2220 - 12 Ave., Regina, SK S4P 0M8
306/352-1121, Fax: 306/522-3499
Chairman, H. Harry Dahlem, Q.C.

**Law Society of Alberta (1907)**
#600, 919 - 11 Ave. SW, Calgary, AB T2R 1P3
403/229-4700, Fax: 403/228-1728, URL: http://www.law.ualberta.ca/lawsociety
Secretary, Peter L. Freeman, Q.C., Email: secretar@lawsocietyalberta.com
Publications: The Benchers' Advisory
Affiliates: Federation of Law Societies of Canada

**Law Society of British Columbia (1884)**
845 Cambie St., 8th Fl., Vancouver, BC V6B 4Z9
604/669-2533, Fax: 604/669-5232
Treasurer, Benjamin B. Trevino, Q.C.
Publications: Benchers' Bulletin
Affiliates: Federation of Law Societies of Canada

**Law Society of Manitoba (1877)**
219 Kennedy St., Winnipeg, MB R3C 1S8
204/942-5571, Fax: 204/956-0624, Email: mblaw@pangea.ca
CEO, Deborah J. McCawley, Q.C.
Publications: Communique
Affiliates: Federation of Law Societies of Canada

**Law Society of New Brunswick/Barreau du Nouveau-Brunswick (1847)**
Justice Bldg., #206, 1133 Regent St., Fredericton, NB E3B 3Z2
506/458-8540, Fax: 506/451-1421, Email: lawlibry@nbnet.nb.ca
President, Peter T. Zed
Vice-President, Gilles Godbout
Treasurer, Christopher Nagle
Executive Director, Michel Carrier
Affiliates: Federation of Law Societies of Canada

**Law Society of Newfoundland**
Atlantic Place, 5th Fl., 215 Water St., PO Box 1028, St. John's, NF A1C 5M3
709/722-4740, Fax: 709/722-8902, Email: pringrose@thezone.net
Executive Director, Peter G. Ringrose
Affiliates: Federation of Law Societies of Canada

**Law Society of the Northwest Territories/Le Barreau des Territoires du Nord-Ouest (1978)**
4918 - 50 St., PO Box 1298, Yellowknife, NT X1A 2N9
867/873-3828, Fax: 867/873-6344, Email: lawsocnt@ssimicro.com
Executive Director, Becky McCaffrey
Publications: Arctic Orbiter
Affiliates: Federation of Law Societies of Canada

**Law Society of Prince Edward Island (1876)**
49 Water St., PO Box 128, Charlottetown, PE C1A 7K2
902/566-1666, Fax: 902/368-7557, Email: lspei@isn.net
Sec.-Treas., Beverly Mills Stetson, LLB
Affiliates: Federation of Law Societies of Canada

**Law Society of Saskatchewan (LSS) (1907)**
#1100, 2500 Victoria Ave., Regina, SK S4P 3X2
306/569-8242, Fax: 306/352-2989
Secretary & Director of Administration, A. Kirsten Logan
General Counsel & Co-Director of Administration, Allan T. Snell
Publications: LSS Newsletter
Affiliates: Federation of Law Societies of Canada

**Law Society of Upper Canada/Barreau du Haut-Canada (LSUC) (1797)**
Osgoode Hall, 130 Queen St. West, Toronto, ON M5H 2N6
416/947-3300, Fax: 416/947-5967, Toll Free: 1-800-668-7380, URL: http://www.lsuc.on.ca/Welcome.html
CEO, John Saso
Publications: Benchers' Bulletin
Affiliates: Federation of Law Societies of Canada

**Law Society of Yukon (YLS) (1985)**
**Yukon Law Society**
#201, 302 Steele St., Whitehorse, YT Y1A 2C5
867/668-4231, Fax: 867/667-7556
Executive Secretary, Jan Graham
Publications: LSY Newsletter
Affiliates: Federation of Law Societies of Canada

**Legal Education Society of Alberta (LESA) (1975)**
Canada Trust Tower, #2610, 10104 - 103 Ave., Edmonton, AB T5J 0H8
403/420-1987, Fax: 403/425-0885, Toll Free: 1-800-282-3900, Email: lesa@lesa.org, URL: http://www.law.ualberta.ca/lesa/
Executive Director, Hugh A. Robertson, Q.C.

**Manitoba Association of Crown Attorneys/Association des avocats de la couronne du Manitoba (1974)**
405 Broadway Ave., Winnipeg, MB R3C 3L6
204/945-0242, Fax: 204/948-2041
President, Gord Hannon

**The Manitoba Law Foundation/La Fondation manitobaine du droit**
412 McDermot Ave., Winnipeg, MB R3A 0A9
204/947-3142, Fax: 204/942-3221
Executive Director, W.K. Greenaway, Ph.D., LL.B.

**Metropolitan Toronto Lawyers Association (1885)**
361 University Ave., Toronto, ON M5G 1T3
416/327-5700, Fax: 416/947-9148, Email: matthea@gov.on.ca
Executive Director, Anne Matthewman
Publications: Vox

**Municipal Law Enforcement Officers' Association (Ontario) Inc. (1979)**
PO Box 247, Wasaga Beach, ON L0L 2P0
705/429-2511
Executive Director, D.H. Kemp

President, B. Russell
Publications: The Summit

**National Judicial Institute/Institut national de la magistrature (NJI) (1988)**
#202, 100 Metcalfe St., Ottawa, ON K1P 5M1
613/237-1118, Fax: 613/237-6155
Executive Director, Judge Dolores Hansen
Coordinator, Research & Communications, Julie Dagenais Blackburn

**New Brunswick Law Foundation/Fondation pour l'avancement du droit au Nouveau-Brunswick (1975)**
#204, 1133 Regent St., Fredericton, NB E3B 3Z2
506/453-7776, Fax: 506/451-1421
Chairman, Harry H. Williamson

**New Brunswick Probation Officers Association Inc.**
Justice Bldg., Rm. 110, Queen St., Fredericton, NB E3B 5E2
506/453-2367
President, K. Douglas Pitts

**Northwest Territories Association of Provincial Court Judges**
Court House, PO Box 297, Iqaluit, NT X0A 0H0
867/979-5450, Fax: 867/979-6384
Judge Beverley Browne
Publications: Newsletter

**Northwest Territories Law Foundation**
PO Box 2594, Yellowknife, NT X1A 2P9
867/873-8275, Fax: 867/873-6383
Executive Manager, Wendy Carter

**Nova Scotia Barristers' Society (1857)**
1815 Upper Water St., Halifax, NS B3J 1S7
902/422-1491, Fax: 902/429-4869, Email: dpink@mail.nsbs.ca, URL: http://home.istar.ca/~nsbs/
Executive Director, Darrel I. Pink
Director, Administration, Victoria Rees
Publications: Society Record; Law News, bi-m.; Current Law, m.
Affiliates: Continuing Legal Education Society; Public Legal Education Society; Law Foundation; Canadian Bar Association

**Ontario Association of Chiefs of Police (OACP) (1952)**
PO Box 193, Sault Ste Marie, ON P6A 5L6
705/946-6389, Fax: 705/942-2093
Executive Director, William M. Malpass

**Ontario Association of Police Services Boards (OAPSB) (1962)**
#601, 920 Yonge St., Toronto, ON M4W 3C7
416/323-9343, Fax: 416/323-3955
Executive Director, Sandi L. Humphrey, CAE
Publications: PSB News

**Ontario Crown Attorneys Association (OCAA) (1946)**
#1420, 439 University Ave., Toronto, ON M5G 1Y8
416/599-4499, Fax: 416/599-4609
President, Paul Vesa

**Ontario Family Law Judges' Association/Association des juges de la cour de famille de l'Ontario**
80 Dundas St. East, PO Box 5600, Stn A, London, ON N6A 2P3
519/660-3045
Secretary, Judge Eleanor Schnall

### Ontario Judges Association/Association des juges provinciaux des tribunaux criminels de l'Ontario (1952)
c/o Ontario Court (Provincial Division), #1000, 200 Frederick St., Kitchener, ON N2H 6P1
519/741-3366, Fax: 519/741-3399
Judge Donald C. Downie
Affiliates: Canadian Association of Provincial Court Judges

### People's Law School
#150, 900 Howe St., Vancouver, BC V6Z 2M4
604/331-5400, Fax: 604/331-5401
Executive Director, Gordon Hardy

### Police Association of Ontario/Association des policiers de l'Ontario (PAO) (1944)
#1, 6730 Davand Dr., Mississauga, ON L5T 2K8
905/670-9770, Fax: 905/670-9755
Administrator, David Griffin
President, John Moor
Publications: News Bulletin

### Prince Edward Island Association of Chiefs of Police (PEIACP)
c/o Borden-Carleton Community Police, PO Box 69, Borden-Carleton, PE C0B 1X0
902/437-2228, Fax: 902/437-6049
Contact, Chief Jamie Fox

### Probation Officers Association of Ontario
PO Box 582, Cobourg, ON K9A 4C3
613/523-4985, Fax: 613/523-1096
President, Penny Arp

### Provincial Judges Association of Manitoba
Provincial Court, 408 York Ave., 5th Fl., Winnipeg, MB R3C 0P9
204/945-8005, Fax: 204/945-0552
Judge Ronald J. Meyers

### Provincial Prosecutors Association
c/o Court House, 155 Elm St. West, Sudbury, ON P3C 1T9
705/671-5900, Fax: 705/675-4146
President, Wayne Gervais

### The Public Interest Advocacy Centre/Centre pour la défense de l'intérêt public (PIAC) (1976)
#1204, One Nicholas St., Ottawa, ON K1N 7B7
613/562-4002, Fax: 613/562-0007, Email: piac@web.net, URL: http://www.web.net/piac/
Executive Director, Michael Janigan
Publications: Hotwire

### Public Legal Education Association of Saskatchewan, Inc. (PLEA Sask.) (1980)
#115, 701 Cynthia St., Saskatoon, SK S7L 6B7
306/653-1868, Fax: 306/653-1869, Email: pleasask@web.apc.org, URL: http://www.sfn.saskatoon.sk.ca/education/pleasask/index.html
Co-Director, Doug Surtees
Co-Director, Joel Janow
President, Lucille Lamb
Publications: PLEA

### Public Legal Education Society of Nova Scotia (PLENS) (1982)
#911, 6080 Young St., Halifax, NS B3K 5L2
902/454-2198, Fax: 902/455-3105, Info Line: 902/455-3135, Toll Free: 1-800-665-9779
Executive Director, Maria G. Franks
President, Carmen Moir
Publications: PLE News

### Public Legal Information Association of Newfoundland (PLIAN) (1984)
PO Box 1064, Stn C, St. John's, NF A1C 5M5
709/722-2643, Fax: 709/722-8902, Email: plian@nf.sympatico.ca
Executive Director, Heidi A. Wells, LL.B.

### Société de criminologie du Québec (SCQ)
#210, 2000, boul Saint-Joseph est, Montréal, QC H2H 1E4
514/529-4391, Téléc: 514/521-3753
Président, Juge Jacques Lamarche
Coordonnatrice, Sylvie Archambault
Publications: Ressources-et-vous

### The Society of Notaries Public of British Columbia (1926)
#621, 736 Granville St., Vancouver, BC V6Z 1G3
604/681-4516, Fax: 604/681-7258
Secretary, Stanley J. Nicol

### Yukon Law Foundation
PO Box 5330, Whitehorse, YT Y1A 4Z2
867/668-4231, Fax: 867/667-7556
Executive Secretary, Jan Graham

### Yukon Public Legal Education Association (YPLEA) (1984)
Yukon College, PO Box 2799, Whitehorse, YT Y1A 5K4
867/668-5297, Fax: 867/668-5541, Toll Free: 1-800-668-5297
Contact, Susan Dennehy

## LIBRARIES & ARCHIVES

### Administrators of Medium Public Libraries of Ontario (AMPLO)
c/o Brantford Public Library, 173 Colborne St., Brantford, ON N3T 2G8
519/756-2223, Fax: 519/756-4979, Email: wnewman@brantford.library.on.ca
Chair, Wendy Newman
Vice-Chair, Rod Hall, Email: rhall@hookup.net
Secretary, Lorane Sims, Email: linclib2@vaxxine.com
Treasurer, Gerda Molson

### Administrators of Small Public Libraries of Ontario (ASPLO) (1981)
St. Marys Public Library, 15 Church St. North, St Marys, ON N4X 1B4
519/284-3346, Fax: 519/284-2630, Email: smlib@execulink.com
Chairman, Barb Taylor
Publications: ASPLO Newsletter

### Alberta Association of College Librarians (AACL)
Grant MacEwan Community College, Learning Resources Centre, 10700 - 104 Ave., Edmonton, AB T5J 4S2
403/497-5894, Fax: 403/497-5895, Email: aaclserv@acd.mhc.ab.ca
Contact, Patricia Lloyd
Publications: AACL Newsletter

### Alberta Association of Library Technicians (AALT) (1974)
PO Box 700, Edmonton, AB T5J 2L4
403/422-8243, URL: http://www.FreeNet.Calgary.ab.ca/occupati/educatio/aalt/aalt2.html
President, Kim Varey
Publications: AALT Technician

### Alberta Government Libraries' Council (AGLC) (1975)
Cooperative Government Library Services Section, 902 Legislature Annex, 9718 - 107 St., Edmonton, AB T5K 1E4
403/427-3837, Fax: 403/427-1623, Email: kpowell@assembly.ab.ca
Coordinator, Karen Powell

### American Society for Information Science - Western Canada Chapter
**WesCan ASIS**
c/o University of Lethbridge Library, 4401 University Dr., Lethbridge, AB T1K 3M4
403/329-2008, Fax: 403/329-2022
Chair, Leona Jacobs

### Art Libraries Society of North America (ARLIS/NA)
#201, 4101 Lake Boone Trail, Raleigh, NC 27607 USA
919/787-5181, Fax: 919/787-4916, Toll Free: 1-800-892-7547, Email: arlisna@mercury.interpath.com, URL: http://caroline.eastlib.ufl.edu/arlis/
Executive Director, Penney De Pas, CAE

### Association des archivistes du Québec (AAQ) (1967)
CP 423, Sillery, QC G1T 2R8
418/652-2357, Téléc: 418/646-0868, Courrier électronique: aaq@microtec.ca, URL: http://www.archives.ca/aaq/
Directrice générale, Andrée Gingras
Publications: La Chronique; Archives, trimestriel

### Association des bibliothécaires professionel(le)s du Nouveau-Brunswick/Association of Professional Librarians of New Brunswick (ABPNB) (1992)
Oromocto Public Library, 54 Miramichi Rd., Oromocto, NB E2V 1S2
506/357-3329, Téléc: 506/357-2266
Présidente, Muriel Morton, Numéro au travail: 506/357-3329, Téléc: 506/357-2266
Vice-présidente, Sylvie Nadeau, Numéro au travail: 506/632-2807, Téléc: 506/632-2235
Trésorier, Jean-Claude Arcand
Secrétaire, Marilynn Rudi
Publications: Biblio-Net

### Association des bibliothécaires du Québec/Québec Library Association (ABQ) (1932)
525, Mount Pleasant, Westmount, QC H3Y 3H6
514/935-6357
Secrétaire exécutive, Marie Eberlin
Publications: Bulletin; Read: A Guide to Excellent Books for Children & Young Adults; Lire

### Association des bibliothèques de droit de Montréal/Montréal Association of Law Libraries (ABDM) (1987)
#900, 1000, rue de la Gauchetière, Montréal, QC H3B 4W5
514/954-3159, Téléc: 514/393-1919, Courrier électronique: charest@cam.org
Bibliothécaire, Ronald Charest
Publications: Info

### Association des bibliothèques publiques de l'Estrie (ABIPE) (1990)
5086, rue Frontenac, Lac Mégantic, QC G6B 1H3
819/583-0876, Téléc: 819/583-0878
Président, Yves Tanguay

### Association des bibliothèques de la région Mauricie-Bois-Francs (1985)
**Bibli-o-Coeur**
Bibliothèque de Shawinigan, 550, de l'Hôtel de Ville, CP 400, Shawinigan, QC G9N 6V3
819/536-7218, Téléc: 819/536-0808
Présidente, Charlotte Lecours-Picard

### Association of Canadian Archivists (ACA) (1975)
PO Box 2596, Stn D, Ottawa, ON K1P 5W6

613/443-0251, Fax: 613/443-0261, Email: ltardif@magmacom.com, URL: http://www.archives.ca/aca/
President, Terry Thompson
Sec.-Treas., Patrick Burden
Office Manager, Lyne St-Hilaire-Tardif
Publications: Archivaria; ACA Bulletin, bi-m.
Affiliates: Bureau of Canadian Archivists

**ARCHIVES ASSOCIATION OF ONTARIO/L'ASSOCIATION DES ARCHIVES DE L'ONTARIO (AAO) (1993)**
PO Box 46009, Stn College Park, Toronto, ON M5B 2L8
416/792-1173, Fax: 416/792-2530
President, Stephen Posner
Executive Assistant, Barbara Schon
Publications: Archives Grants Guide; Off the Record, bi-m.; Directory of Ontario Archives 1995
Affiliates: Ontario Heritage Foundation

**ASSOCIATION OF NEWFOUNDLAND & LABRADOR ARCHIVES (ANLA) (1982)**
Colonial Building, Military Rd., St. John's, NF A1C 2C9
709/726-2867, Fax: 709/729-0578
URL: http://www.infonet.st-johns.nf.ca/providers/anla/anlahome.html
President, Larry Dohey
Vice-President, Joan Ritcey
Secretary, Iris Power
Treasurer, Howard Brown
Publications: ANLA Bulletin; Directory of Archival Holdings in Newfoundland & Labrador

**SASKATCHEWAN ARCHIVISTS SOCIETY (SAS) (1988)**
#120, 3303 Hillsdale, Regina, SK S4S 6W9
306/787-0452, Fax: 306/787-0708
President, Trina Gillis
Vice-President, Linda Putz
Secretary, Anne Stoszek
Publications: Checklist

### Association of Canadian Map Libraries & Archives/Association des cartothèques et archives cartographiques du Canada (ACMLA) (1967)
Visual & Sound Archives Division, National Archives of Canada, 344 Wellington St., Ottawa, ON K1A 0N3
613/996-7620, Fax: 613/995-6575, URL: http://www.sscl.uwo.ca/assoc/acml/acmla.html
Membership Chairperson, Bruce Weedmark
President, Alberta Auringer Wood
Publications: ACMLA Bulletin; Directory of Canadian Map Collections; University Map Libraries in Canada: A Folio of Selected Plans; Guide for a Small Map Collection; Canadian Fire Insurance Plans in Ontario

### Association des directeurs de bibliothèques publiques du Québec
Bibliothèque Gabrielle-Roy, 350, rue Saint-Joseph est, Québec, QC G1K 3B2
418/529-0924, Téléc: 418/529-1588
Présidente, Jean Payer
Publications: DEFI

### Association of Parliamentary Librarians in Canada/Association des bibliothécaires parlementaires au Canada (ABPAC) (1975)
c/o Library of Parliament, 111 Wellington St., Ottawa, ON K1A 0A9
613/996-4934, Fax: 613/947-9235, Email: lemayf@parl.gc.ca
Contact, François Le May
Publications: APLIC Bulletin

### Association pour l'avancement des sciences et des techniques de la documentation (ASTED) (1973)
#202, 3414, av du Parc, Montréal, QC H2X 2H5
514/281-5012, Téléc: 514/281-8219, Courrier électronique: info@asted.org, URL: http://www.asted.org
Directeur général, Louis Cabral
Présidente, Joanne Cournoyer
Publications: Nouvelles ASTED; Documentation et bibliothèques, trimestriel
Organisation(s) affiliée(s): Fédération internationale des bibliothécaires (IFLA); Fédération internationale de documentation (FID); Fédération des associations de bibliothécaires, archivistes et documentalistes des états francophones (FABADEF)

### Association des responsables des bibliothèques/centres de documentation universitaires et recherche d'expression française au Canada (ABCDEF-Canada) (1991)
CP 400, Succ. Côte des Neiges, Montréal, QC H3S 2S7
URL: http://www.refer.qc.ca/ABCDEF/
Présidente, Monique Légère
Publications: Répertoire des Journaux et périodiques de langue française

### Atlantic Provinces Library Association (APLA) (1957)
School of Library & Information Studies, Dalhousie University, 6225 University Ave., Halifax, NS B3H 4H8
902/494-3656, Fax: 902/494-2319
President, Susan Libby
Publications: APLA Bulletin

### BC Courthouse Library Society
800 Smithe St., Vancouver, BC V6Z 2E1
604/660-2910, Fax: 604/660-9418, Toll Free: 1-800-665-2570, Email: bccls@bccls.bc.ca
Chief Librarian & Executive Officer, Maureen B. McCormick

### Bibliographical Society of Canada/Société bibliographique du Canada (BSC) (1946)
PO Box 575, Stn P, Toronto, ON M5S 2T1
416/946-3173, Email: dondertman@library.utoronto.ca, URL: http://www.library.utoronto.ca/~bsc
President, Anne Yandle
Secretary, Anne Dondertman
Publications: BSC Bulletin; Papers/Cahiers, s-a.

### Les Bibliothèques publics du Québec - Montérégie (1981)
Bibliothèque Municipale de Beloeil, 620, rue Richelieu, Beloeil, QC J3G 5E8
514/467-7872, Téléc: 514/467-3257
Présidente, Sylvie Provost
Vice-Présidente, Johanne Guevremont
Secrétaire, Alain Larouche

### Bibliothèques publiques du Bas-Saint-Laurent
CRSBP du Bas-St-Laurent, 465, rue St-Pierre, Rivière-du-Loup, QC G5R 4T6
418/867-1682
Présidente, Nicole Gagnon
Secrétaire-trésorier, Yves Savard

### Bibliothèques publiques de l'Île de Montréal/Public Libraries of the Island of Montréal (BPIM)
a/s Bibliothèque de Verdun, 5955, av Bannantyne, Montréal, QC H4H 1H6
514/765-7167
Président, Florian Dubois

### Les bibliothèques publiques des régions de Québec et Chaudière-Appalaches (1989)
250, 18ième rue, St-Georges, QC G5Y 4S9
418/226-2271, Téléc: 418/228-1321, Courrier électronique: sgbliol@quebectel.com, URL: http://www.bibliotheques.qc.ca/bsg/index.htm
Présidente, Julie Michaud

### British Columbia Library Association (BCLA) (1911)
#110, 6545 Bonsor Ave., Burnaby, BC V5H 1H3
604/430-9633, Fax: 604/430-8595, Email: bcla@unixg.ubc.ca, URL: http://www.interchg.ubc.ca/bcla
President, Frieda Wiebe
Publications: BCLA Reporter

### British Columbia Library Trustees Association (BCLTA) (1978)
#110, 6545 Bonsor Ave., Burnaby, BC V5H 1H3
604/430-9626, Fax: 604/430-8595, Email: bclta@mindlink.bc.ca
President, Daniel Greene
Publications: Open Door

### Bureau canadien des archivistes/Bureau of Canadian Archivists
CP 2485, Succ. D, Ottawa, ON K1P 5W6
613/996-7778, Téléc: 613/995-6226
Secrétaire générale, Sylvie Gervais

### Canadian Association of Children's Librarians (CACL)
c/o Canadian Library Association, #602, 200 Elgin St., Ottawa, ON K2P 1L5
613/232-9625, Fax: 613/563-9895, Email: ai077@freenet.carleton.ca
President, Joanne Griener

### Canadian Association of College & University Libraries (CACUL) (1963)
c/o Canadian Library Association, #602, 200 Elgin St., Ottawa, ON K2P 1L5
613/232-9625, Fax: 613/563-9895, URL: http://www.cla.amlibs.ca
President, Melody Burton, Bus: 613/545-6000, ext.4544, Email: burtonm@qucdn.queensu.ca

### The Canadian Association of Family Resource Programs/L'Association canadienne des programmes de ressources pour la famille (1975)
**FRP Canada**
#101, 30 Rosemount Ave., Ottawa, ON K1Y 1P4
613/728-3307, Fax: 613/729-5421
Executive Director, Alla Ivask
Publications: Play & Parenting Connections; FRP Canada Directory, a.

### Canadian Association for Information Science/Association canadienne des sciences de l'information (CAIS) (1974)
CAIS Secretariat, FIS, University of Toronto, 140 Saint George St., Toronto, ON M5S 1A1
416/978-8876, Fax: 416/971-1399
President, Albert Tabah
Ottawa Chapter President, Pat Johnston, Bus: 613/737-2207
West Chapter President, Jocelyn Godolphin, Bus: 604/228-2499
Publications: The Canadian Journal of Information & Library Science/Revue canadienne des sciences de l'information et de bibliotechéconomie

### Canadian Association of Law Libraries/Association canadienne des bibliothèques de droit (CALL) (1961)
190 Railway St., PO Box 1570, Kingston, ON K7L 5C8

613/531-9338, Fax: 613/531-0626, Email: call@adan.kingston.net, URL: http://www.kingston.net/iknet/call
Administrative Officer, Elizabeth Hooper
Publications: Canadian Law Libraries

## Canadian Association of Music Libraries, Archives & Documentation Centres Inc./ Association canadienne des bibliothèques, archives et centres de documentation musicaux inc. (CAML) (1973)

National Library of Canada, Music Division, 395 Wellington St., Ottawa, ON K1A 0N4
613/996-2300, Fax: 613/952-2895, Email: stm@psb.nlc-bnc.ca, URL: http://www.caml.yorku.ca/
President, Dr. S. Timothy Maloney
Publications: CAML Newsletter/Les Nouvelle de l'ACBM
Affiliates: International Association of Music Libraries, Archives & Documentation Centres

## Canadian Association of Public Libraries (CAPL) (1972)

c/o Beth Houius, Hamilton Public Library, 55 York Blvd., PO Box 2700, Stn LCD 1, Hamilton, ON L8N 4E4
905/546-3285, Fax: 905/546-3282, Email: bhouius@hpl.hamilton.on.ca, URL: http://www.cla.amlibs.ca
President, Virginia Van Vliet

## Canadian Association of Research Libraries/ Association des bibliothèques de recherche du Canada (CARL) (1976)

Morisset Hall, University of Ottawa, #602, 65 University St., Ottawa, ON K1N 9A5
613/562-5800, ext.3652, Fax: 613/562-5195
Email: carl@uottawa.ca, URL: http://www.uottawa.ca/library/carl
Interim Executive Director, Timothy Mark
President, Marnie Swanson
Publications: Annual Statistics

## Canadian Association of Special Libraries & Information Services (CASLIS) (1969)

#29, 3 Greystone Walk, Scarborough, ON M1K 5J4
403/261-1263
President, Mary-Lu Brennan
Publications: Special Issues

## Canadian Council of Archives/Conseil canadien des archives (CCA) (1985)

West Memorial Bldg., #1109, 344 Wellington St., Ottawa, ON K1A 0N3
613/995-2373, Fax: 613/947-6662
Email: mhoude@archives.ca, URL: http://www.CdnCouncilArchives.ca
Executive Director, Michel Houde
Chairperson, Diane Charland
Publications: Directory of Canadian Archives; Institutional Guidelines for Small Archives; CCA Newsletter, s-a.

#### ARCHIVES ASSOCIATION OF BRITISH COLUMBIA (AABC) (1990)

PO Box 78530, RPO University, Vancouver, BC V6T 1Z4
Email: aabc@harbour.com, URL: http://www.harbour.com/AABC/
President, Trevor Livelton, Bus: 250/361-0374
Publications: AABC Newsletter

#### ARCHIVES COUNCIL OF PRINCE EDWARD ISLAND (1987)

Public Archives, George Coles Bldg., PO Box 1000, Charlottetown, PE C1A 7M4
902/368-4351, Fax: 902/368-6327
President, Marilyn Bell

#### ARCHIVES SOCIETY OF ALBERTA (ASA) (1993)

PO Box 21080, RPO Dominion, Calgary, AB T2P 4H5
URL: http://www.lexicom.ab.ca/~glenbow/asa/home.htm
President, Bryan Corbett
Publications: ASA Newsletter

#### ASSOCIATION FOR MANITOBA ARCHIVES (1992)

PO Box 26005, RPO Westminster, Winnipeg, MB R3C 4K9
204/942-3491, Fax: 204/942-3492
Program Coordinator, Diane Haglund
Publications: Communique
Affiliates: Association of Canadian Archivists

#### COUNCIL OF ARCHIVES NEW BRUNSWICK/CONSEIL DES ARCHIVES DU NOUVEAU-BRUNSWICK (CANB) (1985)

c/o Provincial Archives of New Brunswick, PO Box 6000, Fredericton, NB E3B 5H1
506/453-2122, Fax: 506/453-3288
URL: http://moondog.usask.ca/cca/index.html
Contact, Fred Farrell
Publications: CANB Gazette

#### COUNCIL OF NOVA SCOTIA ARCHIVES (CNSA) (1983)

c/o Public Archives of Nova Scotia, 6016 University Ave., Halifax, NS B3H 1W4
902/424-7093, Fax: 902/424-0628
Email: cnsa@fox.nstn.ca, URL: http://Fox.nstn.ca/~cnsa/
President, Anita Price
Education & Outreach Archivist, Johanna Smith
Publications: Council of Nova Scotia Archives Newsletter
Affiliates: Federation of NS Heritage; Society of American Archivists; Association of Canadian Archivists

#### NORTHWEST TERRITORIES ARCHIVES COUNCIL (NWTAC) (1985)

c/o Northwest Territories Archives, Government of the Northwest Territories, PO Box 1320, Yellowknife, NT X1A 2L9
867/873-7698, Fax: 867/873-0205
President, Dr. Richard Valpy

#### RÉSEAU DES ARCHIVES DU QUÉBEC (RAQ) (1987)

CP 160, Succ. D, Montréal, QC H3K 3B9
514/596-6037, Téléc: 514/596-7780
URL: http://www.raq.qc.ca
Président, A. Boudreau
Secrétaire-trésorier, Agathe Dunan
Publications: Bulletin du RAQ

#### SASKATCHEWAN COUNCIL OF ARCHIVES (1987)

PO Box 22041, Regina, SK S4S 7G7
306/787-4066, Fax: 306/787-1975
URL: http://www.usask.ca/archives/sca.html
President, Trevor Powell

#### YUKON COUNCIL OF ARCHIVES (YCA) (1986)

PO Box 6053, Whitehorse, YT Y1A 5L7
867/667-5321, Fax: 867/393-6253
Email: Lesley.Buchan@gov.yk.ca, URL: http://moondog.usask.ca/cca/yuk1.html
President, Lesley Buchan
Publications: YCA Newsletter

## Canadian Council of Library Schools/Conseil canadien des écoles de bibliothéconomie (CCLS)

c/o Graduate School of Library & Information Studies, 3459 McTavish, Montréal, QC H3A 1Y1
514/398-4204, Téléc: 514/398-7193, Courrier électronique: inaw@musicb.mcgill.ca
Président, Prof. Gilles Deschatelets

## Canadian Health Libraries Association/ Association des bibliothèques de la santé du Canada (CHLA) (1976)

3332 Yonge St., PO Box 94038, Toronto, ON M4N 3R1
416/485-0377, Fax: 416/485-0377, Email: chla@inforamp.net
President, Lois Wyndham
Office of Secretariat, Dorothy Davey
Publications: Bibliotheca Medica Canadiana; Directory, a.
Affiliates: Ontario Hospital Libraries Association

#### ASSOCIATION DES BIBLIOTHÈQUES DE LA SANTÉ DE MONTRÉAL/ MONTRÉAL HEALTH LIBRARIES ASSOCIATION

2365, Côte de Liesse, Montréal, QC H4N 2M7
514/333-2057, Téléc: 514/335-4102
Présidente, Dona Gibson

#### CENTRAL ONTARIO HEALTH LIBRARIES ASSOCIATION

Library, Oshawa General Hospital, 24 Alma St., Oshawa, ON L1G 2B9
905/576-8711, ext.3334, Fax: 905/721-4759
Email: library@hospital.oshawa.on.ca
President, Susan Hendricks

#### GOLDEN HORSESHOE HEALTH LIBRARIES ASSOCIATION

Health Sciences Library, 1200 Main St. West, Hamilton, ON L8N 3Z5
905/525-9140, ext.22545, Fax: 905/528-3733
Email: bayley1@fhs.mcmaster.ca
President, Liz Bayley

#### HEALTH LIBRARIES ASSOCIATION OF BRITISH COLUMBIA (HLABC) (1980)

BC Cancer Agency, 600 - 10th Ave. West., Vancouver, BC V5Z 4E6
604/877-6000, ext.2692, Fax: 604/872-4596
Email: bccalib@wimsey.com
President, Beth Morrison
Publications: HLABC Forum

#### KINGSTON AREA HEALTH LIBRARIES ASSOCIATION (KAHLA)

Staff Library, Kingston Psychiatric Hospital, PO Box 603, Kingston, ON K7L 4X3
613/546-1101, ext.5745, Fax: 613/548-5588
Email: Envoy:ill.okph
President, Karen Gagnon

#### LONDON AREA HEALTH LIBRARIES ASSOCIATION (LAHLA)

Medical Library, London Psychiatric Hospital, PO Box 2532, Terminal A, London, ON N6A 4H1
519/455-5110, ext.2167, Fax: 519/455-9986
Email: mwhy@julian.uwo.ca
President, Mai Why

#### MANITOBA HEALTH LIBRARIES ASSOCIATION (MHLA) (1979)

Medical Library, Univ. of Manitoba, 770 Bannatyne Ave., Winnipeg, MB R3E 0W3
204/237-2808, Fax: 204/235-3339
Email: poluha@bldghsc.lan1.umanitoba.ca
President, David Colborne
Secretary, Mark Rabnett
Publications: MHLA News

#### MARITIMES HEALTH LIBRARIES ASSOCIATION/ASSOCIATION DES BIBLIOTHÈQUES DE LA SANTÉ DES MARITIMES (MHLA)

Dr. Everett Chalmers Hospital, 700 Priestman St., PO Box 9000, Fredericton, NB E3B 5N5
506/452-5432, Fax: 506/452-5571
Email: dlibrary@nbnet.nb.ca
President, Paul E. Clark
Publications: MHLA/ABSM Bulletin

#### NEWFOUNDLAND & LABRADOR HEALTH LIBRARIES ASSOCIATION (NLHLA) (1978)

School of Nursing Library, Salvation Army Grace General Hospital, 241 LeMarchant Rd., St. John's, NF A1E 1P9
709/778-6645, Fax: 709/722-0449
Email: doreilly@cabot.fac.nf.ca
President, Debbie O'Reilly

#### NORTHERN ALBERTA HEALTH LIBRARIES ASSOCIATION

6 Longview Cres., St Albert, AB T8N 2W2
403/459-4084
President, Georgia Makowski

**NORTHWESTERN ONTARIO HEALTH LIBRARIES ASSOCIATION**
Hargan Medical Library, Thunder Bay Regional Cancer Centre, 290 Munroe St., Thunder Bay, ON P7A 7T1
807/343-6732, Fax: 807/343-2630
Email: cwalsh@smtpgate.octrf.on.ca
President, Catherine Walsh

**OTTAWA VALLEY HEALTH LIBRARIES GROUP/ASSOCIATION DES BIBLIOTHÈQUES DE SANTÉ DE LA VALLÉE DE L'OUTAOUAIS**
Ottawa Civic Hospital, 1053 Carling Ave., Ottawa, ON K1Y 4E9
613/761-4000, ext.4459, Fax: 613/761-5292
Email: cna@hookup.net
President, Kyungja Shin

**SASKATCHEWAN HEALTH LIBRARIES ASSOCIATION (SHLA) (1988)**
PO Box 14, Richardson, SK S0G 4G0
306/586-8813, Fax: 306/766-4314
Email: rghlib@cableregina.com
President, Alice Lalonde
Secretary, Irene Frank

**SOUTHERN ALBERTA HEALTH LIBRARIES ASSOCIATION**
c/o Medical Library, University of Calgary, 3330 Hospital Dr. NW, Calgary, AB T2N 4N1
403/220-3752, Fax: 403/282-7992
President, Alix Hayden

**TORONTO HEALTH LIBRARIES ASSOCIATION (THLA) (1965)**
Science & Medicine Library, University of Toronto, 7 King's College Circle, Toronto, ON M5S 1A5
416/978-1331, Fax: 416/978-7666
Email: wright@library.utoronto.ca
President, Elaine Wright
Publications: THLA News
Affiliates: Ontario Hospital Libraries Association

**WELLINGTON/WATERLOO/DUFFERIN HEALTH LIBRARY NETWORK**
Groves Memorial Community Hospital, 235 Union St. East, Fergus, ON N1M 2W3
519/843-2010, ext.228, Fax: 519/843-7420
Co-chair, Elizabeth Andrushko

**WINDSOR AREA HEALTH LIBRARIES ASSOCIATION**
Medical Library, Hôtel Dieu Hospital, 1030 Ouellette Ave., Windsor, ON N9A 1E1
519/973-4411, ext.3178, Fax: 519/973-0642
Email: library@hdgh.org
President, Toni Janik

### Canadian Health Record Association/Association canadienne interprofessionnelle des dossiers de santé (CHRA) (1942)
**Canadian College of Health Record Administrators**
#501, 1090 Don Mills Rd., North York, ON M3C 3R6
416/447-4900, Fax: 416/447-4598, Email: chragen@ibm.net, URL: http://www.chra.ca
Executive Director, Deborah Del Duca
Publications: Canadian Health Record Association Position Statements
Affiliates: International Federation of Health Records Organizations

### Canadian Libraries in Occupational Safety & Health (1975)
c/o Alberta Labour Library, 10808 - 99 Ave, 3rd Fl., Edmonton, AB T5K 0G5
403/427-8533, Fax: 403/422-0084, Email: labour-library@gov.ab.ca
Librarian, Debbie Hunter
Publications: Health & Safety on the Job

### Canadian Library Association (CLA) (1946)
#602, 200 Elgin St., Ottawa, ON K2P 1L5
613/232-9625, Fax: 613/563-9895, Email: ai077@freenet.carleton.ca, URL: http://www.cla.amlibs.ca
Executive Director, Karen Adams
President, Paul Whitney, Bus: 604/436-5431
President-Elect, Syd Jones, Bus: 416/393-7214, Email: syd@mtrl.toronto.on.ca
Treasurer, Ruth Reedman, Bus: 204/983-3437, Email: ruth_reedman@cwb.ca
Publications: Feliciter; CLA Directory of Members
Affiliates: Canadian Association of Public Libraries; Canadian Association of College & University Libraries; Canadian Library Trustees Association; Canadian School Library Association; Canadian Association of Special Libraries & Information Services

### Canadian Library Trustees Association (CLTA)
c/o Canadian Library Association, #602, 200 Elgin St., Ottawa, ON K2P 1L5
613/232-9625, Fax: 613/563-9895
President, Gary Archibald, Bus: 902/742-4195, Email: nstn2360@fox.nstn.ns.ca

### Canadian School Library Association (CSLA)
c/o Canadian Library Association, #602, 200 Elgin St., Ottawa, ON K2P 1L5
613/232-9625, Fax: 613/563-9895
President, Mary Latham, Bus: 519/621-4171
Publications: School Libraries in Canada

### Chief Executives of Large Public Libraries of Ontario (CELPLO)
Etobicoke Public Libraries, PO Box 501, Toronto, ON M9C 5G1
416/394-5005, Fax: 416/394-5050
Chairperson, Jennifer Milne

### Church Library Association of Ontario (CLAO) (1969)
#2, 28 Saranac Blvd., Toronto, ON M6A 2G5
519/669-4789
President, Helen Sanderson
Publications: Library Lines
Affiliates: Church & Synagogue Library Association (USA)

### Comité des bibliothèques de la région du Nord de Montréal (COBREN) (1977)
a/s Bibliothèque municipale de Saint-Jérôme, 185, rue du Palais, St-Jérôme, QC J7Z 1X6
514/436-1511
Présidente, Renée Chalifoux-Massé

### Corporation des bibliothécaires professionnels du Québec/Corporation of Professional Librarians of Québec (CBPQ) (1969)
#320, 307, rue Ste-Catherine ouest, Montréal, QC H2X 2A3
514/845-3327, Téléc: 514/845-1618, Courrier électronique: info@cbpq.qc.ca, URL: http://www.cbpq.qc.ca
Directrice générale, Régine Horinstein
Président, Josée Saint-Marseille
Publications: Argus

### Council of Administrators of Large Urban Public Libraries (CALUPL) (1978)
281 Front St. East, Toronto, ON M5A 4L2
416/393-7550, Fax: 416/393-7544
Chair, Gabriele Lundeen

### Council of Federal Libraries/Conseil des bibliothèques du gouvernement fédéral (CFL) (1976)
National & International Programs, National Library of Canada, 395 Wellington St., Ottawa, ON K1A 0N4
613/995-3904, Fax: 613/947-2916, Email: claude.blanchard@nlc-bnc.ca, URL: http://www.nlc-bnc.ca/cfl-cbgf
Chairperson, Marianne Scott
Publications: Liaison

### Council of Head Librarians of New Brunswick/Conseil des directeurs de bibliothèques de Nouveau-Brunswick
Ward Chipman Library, University of New Brunswick, PO Box 5050, Saint John, NB E2L 4L5
506/648-5700, Fax: 506/648-5701
President, Susan Collins
Publications: Directory of New Brunswick Libraries

### Council of Prairie & Pacific University Libraries (COPPUL) (1991)
#2222, 246 Stewart Green St., Calgary, AB T3H 3C8
403/249-8626, Fax: 403/246-6976, Email: hafry@telusplanet.net, URL: http://library.usask.ca/coppul
Executive Director, Hazel Fry
Chair, Director of Libraries, University of Saskatchewan, Frank Winter

### County & Regional Municipality Librarians of Ontario (CARML)
c/o Frontenac County Library, Frontenac County Court House, Court St., Kingston, ON K7L 2N4
613/548-8657, Fax: 613/548-8193, Email: mwatkins@frontenac.county.library.on.ca
Chair, Marion Watkins
Affiliates: Southern Ontario Library Service

### Government Libraries Association of British Columbia (GLABC) (1976)
794 Fort St., PO Box 38044, Victoria, BC V8W 3N2
President, Rob Harvey
Vice-President, Janet Frost
Treasurer, Antje Helmuth
Publications: GLABC Newsletter; GLABC Directory

### Groupe biblio-santé de la région de Québec (1982)
L'Hotel-Dieu de Québec, 11, Côte du Palais, Québec, QC G1R 2J6
418/691-5073, Téléc: 418/691-5468
Présidente, Lisette Germain
Publications: Catalogue collectif des périodiques dans les bibliothèques de santé de la région de Québec

### Indexing & Abstracting Society of Canada/Société canadienne pour l'analyse des documents (IASC) (1977)
PO Box 744, Stn F, Toronto, ON M4Y 2N6
416/496-5025, Fax: 416/496-5068, URL: http://tornade.ere.umontreal.ca/~turner/iasc/home.html
President, Christine Jacobs, Email: cmjacobs@johnabbott.qc.ca
Vice-President, James Turner
Sec.-Treas., Noelina Bridge, Email: 74452.2615@compuserve.com
Central Canada Representative, Jin Tan
Publications: IASC/SCAD Bulletin; Register of Indexers/Répertoire des indexeurs
Affiliates: Society of Indexers; American Society of Indexers; Australian Society of Indexers

### Library Association of Alberta (LAA) (1939)
80 Baker Cres. NW, Calgary, AB T2L 1R4
403/284-5818, Fax: 403/282-6646, Email: shepparc@cadvision.com
President/Provincial Representative, Pilar Martinez
Executive Director, Christine Sheppard
Treasurer, Lisa-Jane Watson
Publications: Letter of the LAA

### Library Boards Association of Nova Scotia (LBANS) (1976)
c/o Pictou-Antigonish Regional Library, PO Box 276, New Glasgow, NS B2H 5E3

902/755-6031, Fax: 902/755-6775, Email: aripley@nsngp.library.ns.ca
Secretary, Ann Ripley

**Manitoba Association of Library Technicians (MALT) (1971)**
PO Box 1872, Winnipeg, MB R3C 3R1
President, Diana Pollock, Bus: 204/789-3466
Publications: MALT Newsletter

**Manitoba Government Libraries Council (MGLC)**
c/o Food Development Centre Library, 810 Phillips St., PO Box 1240, Portage La Prairie, MB R1N 3J9
204/239-3162, Fax: 204/239-3180, Toll Free: 1-800-870-1044, Email: lpetriuk@fdc.mb.ca, URL: http://www.gov.mb.ca/leg-lib/mglc.html
Chairperson, Linda Petriuk

**Manitoba Library Association (MLA) (1936)**
#208, 100 Arthur St., Winnipeg, MB R3B 1H3
204/943-4567, Fax: 204/942-1555, Email: cm@mts.net, URL: http://www.mbnet.mb.ca/cm
President, Karen Hunt
Publications: Newsline
Affiliates: Manitoba School Library Audio Visual Association; Manitoba Association of Library Technicians

**Manitoba Library Trustees Association**
PO Box 1168, Gimli, MB R0C 1B0
204/642-8860
President, Shirley Bergen

**Manitoba School Library Association (MSLA)**
c/o The Manitoba Teachers' Society, 191 Harcourt St., Winnipeg, MB R3J 3H2
204/888-7961, Fax: 204/831-0872
President, Barbara Kelly
President-Elect, Margaret Stimson
Publications: MSLA Journal
Affiliates: Manitoba Teachers' Society

**National Archival Appraisal Board/Conseil national d'évaluation des archives (NAAB) (1983)**
PO Box 69016, Stn Place de Ville, Ottawa, ON K1R 1A9
613/996-7604, Fax: 613/995-2267, Email: lpilon@archives.ca
Administrator, Louise Pilon

**New Brunswick Library Trustees' Association/Association des commissaires de bibliothèque du Nouveau-Brunswick, inc. (NBLTA) (1979)**
105 Scarlet Dr., Rothesay, NB E2E 1S3
506/847-7208
Chairman, Judy Heron
Publications: NBLTA Newsletter

**Northwest Territories Library Association (NWTLA) (1982)**
PO Box 2276, Yellowknife, NT X1A 2P7
867/920-6269, Fax: 867/873-0395, Email: bev_speight@gov.nt.ca
President, Bev Speight, Bus: 403/873-6444
Publications: Snowshoe; NWTLA Directory, biennial

**Nova Scotia Government Libraries Council (NSGLC)**
c/o Dept. of Natural Resources, PO Box 698, Halifax, NS B3J 2T9
Chairperson, Valerie Brisco, Bus: 902/424-8633

**Nova Scotia Library Association (NSLA) (1973)**
c/o Nova Scotia Provincial Library, 3770 Kempt Rd., Halifax, NS B3K 4X8
902/424-2478, Fax: 902/424-0633, Email: mahml@ponyx.nsh.library.ns.ca, URL: http://www.library.ns.ca/nsla
President, Heather MacKenzie
Publications: NSLA News

**Ontario Association of Library Technicians/Association des bibliotechniciens de l'Ontario (OALT) (1973)**
Abbey Market, 1500 Upper Middle Rd. West, PO Box 76010, Oakville, ON L6M 3H5
President, Penni Lee
Publications: Newsletter/Nouvelles

**Ontario College & University Library Association (OCULA) (1969)**
#303, 100 Lombard St., Toronto, ON M5C 1M3
416/363-3388, Fax: 416/941-9581, Email: jgilbert@interlog.com
Executive Director, Larry Moore
President, Martha Wolfe
Publications: Inside OCULA
Affiliates: Ontario Library Association

**Ontario Council of University Libraries (OCUL)**
University of Ottawa, 65 University, Ottawa, ON K1N 9A5
613/562-5883, Fax: 613/562-5195
Chief Librarian, Richard Greene

**Ontario Government Libraries Council (OGLC)**
Ferguson Block, 4th Fl., 77 Wellesley St. West, Toronto, ON M7A 1N3
416/327-2535, Fax: 416/327-2530
Chair, Maria Cece
Publications: Exchange

**Ontario Hospital Libraries Association (OHLA) (1985)**
#2800, 200 Front St. West, Toronto, ON M5V 3J1
613/737-8529, Fax: 613/737-8521
President, Jessie McGowan
Publications: OHLA Newsline
Affiliates: Canadian Hospital Libraries Association

**Ontario Library Association/Association des bibliothèques de l'Ontario (OLA) (1900)**
#303, 100 Lombard St., Toronto, ON M5C 1M3
416/363-3388, Fax: 416/941-9581, Email: ola@interlog.com, URL: http://www.ola.amlibs.ca
Executive Director, Larry Moore
President, Jane Horrocks
Publications: Inside OLA; Access, 3 pa
Affiliates: Divisions at same address: Ontario College & University Library Association; Ontario Library Trustees' Association; Ontario Public Library Association; Ontario School Library Association; Ontario Library & Information Technology Association

**Ontario Library & Information Technology Association (OLITA) (1992)**
#300, 100 Lombard St., Toronto, ON M5C 1M3
416/363-3388, Fax: 416/941-9581, Email: jgilbert@interlog.com
President, Bill Oldfield

**Ontario Library Trustees Association (OLTA)**
#300, 100 Lombard St., Toronto, ON M5C 1M3
416/363-3388, Fax: 416/941-9581
President, Maureen Rudaik
Publications: Inside OLTA
Affiliates: Ontario Library Association

**Ontario Public Library Association (OPLA)**
#303, 100 Lombard St., Toronto, ON M5C 1M3
416/363-3388, Fax: 416/941-9581, Email: jgilbert@interlog.com
President, Lynne Jordan
Vice-President, Ann Mckenzie
Publications: Inside OPLA

**Ontario School Library Association (OSLA) (1972)**
#303, 100 Lombard St., Toronto, ON M5C 1M3
416/363-3388, Fax: 416/941-9581, Email: jgilbert@interlog.com
President, Elizabeth Kerr
Publications: Inside OSLA

**Prince Edward Island Professional Librarians Association (1982)**
c/o Robertson Library Reference Dept., 550 University Ave., Charlottetown, PE C1A 4P3
902/368-4637
President, Brenda Brady
Vice-President, Johanne Jacob

**Rassemblement des bibliothèques publiques du Lac-Saint-Jean et Saguenay (RABLES) (1981)**
a/s Bibliothèque municipale d'Alma, 500, rue Collard, Alma, QC G8B 1N2
418/669-5140, Téléc: 418/669-5089, URL: http://www.crsbpslsj.biblio.qc.ca/regroupement.html
Président, Martin Bouchard
Publications: Rapport d'activités

**Regroupement des bibliothèques publiques de l'Abitibi-Témiscamingue (RBPAT) (1985)**
Bibliothèque municipale de Rouyn-Noranda, 201, av Dallaire, Rouyn-Noranda, QC J9X 4T5
819/762-0944, Téléc: 819/797-7136
Président, Luc Sigouin

**Regroupement des bibliothèques publiques de la Côte-Nord**
Bibliothèque centrale de prêt de la Côte-Nord, 59, rue Napoléon, Sept-Îles, QC G4R 5C5
418/962-1020
Président, Yvon Grondin

**Saskatchewan Association of Library Technicians (SALT)**
PO Box 9388, Saskatoon, SK S7K 7E9
306/477-2743, Fax: 306/975-7521
President, Louise Hajlasz
Membership Secretary, Elisabeth Eilingen
Publications: SALT Newsletter

**Saskatchewan Government Libraries Council**
c/o Saskatchewan Agriculture & Food Library, 3085 Albert St., #B5, Regina, SK S4S 0B1
306/787-5151, Fax: 306/787-0216
Contact, Helene Stewart

**Saskatchewan Library Association (SLA) (1942)**
PO Box 3388, Regina, SK S4P 3H1
306/780-9413, Fax: 306/780-9447, Email: sla@pleis.lib.sk.ca, URL: http://www.lib.sk.ca/sla/
Executive Director, Andrea Wagner
Publications: Forum

**Saskatchewan Library Trustees Association (SLTA) (1942)**
PO Box 67, Vanguard, SK S0N 2V0
306/582-2026, Fax: 306/582-4811
President, Dorothy Saunderson
Affiliates: Canadian Library Association

**Special Libraries Association**
1700 - 18 St. NW, Washington, DC 20009 USA
202/234-4700, Fax: 202/265-9317, Email: sla@sla.org, URL: http://www.sla.org/
Executive Director, David R. Bender, Ph.D.
Associate Executive Director, Lois Schoenbrun, CAE
President, Eastern Canada Chapter, Ruth L. Noble, Email: nobleL@vax2.concordia.ca
President, Toronto Chapter, Mary Hum, Email: mhumnnnn@reach.com
President, Western Canada Chapter, Rita M. Penco, Email: penco@ppc.ubc.ca

**Ukrainian Librarians Association of Canada**
St. Vladimir Institute Library, 620 Spadina Ave., Toronto, ON M5S 2H4
416/480-2440, Fax: 416/480-1247
President, Andrew Gregorovich

**Yukon Teacher-Librarians' Association (YTLA)**
2064 - 2nd Ave., Whitehorse, YT Y1A 1A9
867/668-6777, Fax: 867/667-4324
Affiliates: Association of Teacher Librarians in Canada; Canadian Special Library Association

**LIFESAVING *see* EMERGENCY RESPONSE**

**LINGUISTICS *see* LANGUAGE, LINGUISTICS, LITERATURE**

**LITERACY *see* LANGUAGE, LINGUISTICS, LITERATURE**

**LITERARY ARTS *see* WRITERS & EDITORS**

**LITERATURE *see* LANGUAGE, LINGUISTICS, LITERATURE**

**LIVESTOCK *see* ANIMAL BREEDING**

**LONG-TERM CARE *see* HOSPITALS**

**MACHINERY *see* EQUIPMENT & MACHINERY**

## MANAGEMENT & ADMINISTRATION

**Administrative Sciences Association of Canada/ Association des sciences administratives du Canada (ASAC) (1982)**
Dept. of Administrative Sciences, UQAM, PO Box 6192, Stn A, Montréal, QC H3C 4R2
514/987-3697, Fax: 514/987-3343
Secretary, Iréne Lepine
President, P. Andiappan
Publications: Canadian Journal of Administrative Sciences/Revue canadienne des sciences administratives; ASAC Bulletin, s-a.

**Association of Administrative Assistants/ Association des adjoints administratifs (AAA) (1951)**
PO Box 5107, Stn A, Toronto, ON M5W 1N4
416/760-6907
President, Linda Varsava, Q.A.A.
Publications: Communique

**Association des MBA du Québec (AMBAQ)**
#500, 407, boul Saint-Laurent, Montréal, QC H2Y 2Y5
514/874-3710, Téléc: 514/866-4020
Directeur général, Laurent Vezina
Publications: Ratio

**Association of Professional Executives of the Public Service of Canada/L'Association professionnelle des cadres de la fonction publique du Canada (APEX) (1984)**
LaSalle Academy Bldg., 65 Guigues St., PO Box 420, Stn A, Ottawa, ON K1N 8V4
613/995-6252, Fax: 613/943-8919
Executive Director, Pierre de Blois
Publications: Bulletin

**Association of Records Managers & Administrators**
**ARMA International**
#215, 4200 Somerset Dr., Prairie Village, KA 66208 USA
913/341-3808, Fax: 913/341-3742, Toll Free: 1-800-422-2762, Email: 76015.3151@compuserve.com, URL: http://www.arma.org/hq/
Executive Director, James P. Souders
Halifax Chapter: PO Box 2381, Stn M, Halifax, NS B3J 3E4, Email: corkettm@gov.ns.ca
Vancouver Chapter: #300, 3665 Kingsway, Vancouver, BC V5R 5W2, 604/435-2897, Fax: 604/435-8181

**Atlantic Canada Plus Association (1977)**
Metropolitan Place, #601, 6009 Quinpool Rd., PO Box 9410, Stn A, Halifax, NS B3K 5S3
902/492-3807, Fax: 902/425-2441
Executive Director, John K. Sutherland
Chairman, Don MacVey
Publications: ACP Membership Directory

**Canadian Association of School Administrators/ Association canadienne des administrateurs et des administratrices scolaires (CASA) (1975)**
#1133 - 160A St., White Rock, BC V4A 7G9
604/535-6330, Fax: 604/531-6454
Director, Programs & Services, Douglas S. McCall
Publications: The President Reports
Affiliates: Association of British Columbia Superintendents; Conference of Alberta School Superintendents; Saskatchewan League of Educational Administrators, Directors & Superintendents; Manitoba Association of School Superintendents; Ontario Catholic Supervisory Officers' Association; Québec Association of School Administrators; Association of Directors General of Protestant School Boards of Québec; New Brunswick School Superintendents Association; Association des directions générales scolaires du Nouveau-Brunswick; Association of Nova Scotia Educational Administrators; School Administrators of Prince Edward Island; Newfoundland & Labrador Association of Superintendents of Education

**Canadian Executive Service Organization/Service administratif canadien aux organismes (CESO) (1967)**
South Tower, #400, 175 Bloor St. East, Toronto, ON M4W 3R8
416/961-2376, Fax: 416/961-1096, Telex: 06-23583, Toll Free: 1-800-268-9052, Email: toronto@ceso-saco.com
CEO/President, Daniel W. Haggerty
Senior Vice-President, Andrew M. Salkeld
Sec.-Treas., Terry Brackenridge
Regional Manager, Québec, Jean-Louis Castonguay
Publications: Focus; Dreamcatcher - Aboriginal Services Newsletter
Alberta & Western Arctic Office: Regional Manager, George Ferrand; Secretary/Receptionist, Debra Racicot, Edmonton Centre, 1724 Royal Trust Tower, Edmonton, AB T5J 2Z2, 403/421-4740, Fax: 403/429-3186, Email: alberta@ceso-saco.com
Atlantic Region Office: Regional Manager, Paddy Moran, #305, 802 Prince St., Truro, NS B2N 1H1, 902/893-2477, Fax: 902/893-1159
Manitoba & Northwestern Ontario Office: Regional Manager, Gwen La Frenière; Administrative Assistant, Yvonne Dubois, #1000, 191 Lombard Ave., Winnipeg, MB R3B 0X1, 204/949-0177, Fax: 204/942-1647, Email: manitoba@ceso-saco.com
National Capital Region: Contact, Andrew M. Salkeld, 323 Chapel St., 2nd Fl., Ottawa, ON K1N 7Z2, 613/236-7763, Fax: 613/237-5969, Email: ottawa@ceso-saco.com
Ontario & Eastern Arctic Office/Operations Centre: Regional Manager, Laurie Blachford; Administrative Assistant, Sonya Mergler, #400, 175 Bloor St. East, Toronto, ON M4W 3R8, 416/961-2376, Fax: 416/961-1096, Email: toronto.centre@ceso-saco.com
Saskatchewan Office: Regional Manager, Murray McConnell; Administrative Assistant, Velma Krahenbil, #1050, 2002 Victoria Ave., Regina, SK S4P 0R7, 306/757-0651, Fax: 306/565-8741, Email: saskatchewan@ceso-saco.com

**Canadian Institute of Certified Administrative Managers (CICAM) (1979)**
#700, 2 Bloor St. West, Toronto, ON M4W 3R1
416/921-7962, Fax: 416/923-2071
Executive Director, Dr. Albert E. Ballantyne, DHL, M.Phil., FCAM
President, John E.G. Stone

**Canadian Institute of Management/Institut canadien de gestion (CIM) (1942)**
#110, 2175 Sheppard Ave. East, North York, ON M2J 1W8
416/493-0155, Fax: 416/491-1670, Toll Free: 1-800-387-5774
Executive Director, Joan L. Milne, P.Mgr., RMP
National President, Jim Peacock
Administrator, Carolyn Vigon
Publications: The Canadian Manager

**Canadian Institute for Organization Management (CIOM)**
#501, 350 Sparks St., Ottawa, ON K1R 7S8
613/238-4000, Fax: 613/238-7643, Email: ccr@chamber.ca, URL: http://www.chamber.ca
Director, Roger Stanion
Administrator, Linda Robert
Affiliates: Canadian Chamber of Commerce

**Canadian Management Centre of AMA (American Management Association) International**
150 York St., 5th Fl., Toronto, ON M5H 3S5
416/214-5678, Fax: 416/214-1453
Managing Director, William P. Sutton
Marketing Manager, Deborah Spencer
Affiliates: American Management Association International

**Canadian Public Personnel Management Association**
5 Tournament Dr., North York, ON M2P 1K1
416/362-2805
Director of Professional Development, Joseph Fernandes

**The Canadian Public Relations Society, Inc./La Société canadienne des relations publiques, inc. (CPRS) (1948)**
#720, 220 Laurier Ave. West, Ottawa, ON K1P 5Z9
613/232-1222, Fax: 613/232-0565, Email: cprs@cycor.ca, URL: http://www.cprs.ca/
Executive Director, Arbo A. Mattila, APR, CAE
Contact, A.M. St. Amour
Affiliates: International Public Relations Association; Public Relations Society of America

**Canadian Society of Association Executives/ Société canadienne des directeurs d'association (CSAE) (1951)**
#1100, 10 King St. East, Toronto, ON M5C 1C3
416/363-3555, Fax: 416/363-3630, Email: csae@csae.com
President, Judith Wiley, Email: j.wiley@csae.com
Chairperson, John O'Brien, CAE
Executive Vice-President, Wayne Amundson, CAE, Email: w.amundson@csae.com
Vice-President, Michel G. Tremblay, caé
Publications: CSAE News; Association, bi-m.; CSAE Membership Directory, a.; CSAE Salary Surveys, a.; The Association Agenda; Association Contact

Affiliates: European Society of Association Executives; American Society of Association Executives; Australian Society of Association Executives

### Canadian Society of Corporate Secretaries (CSCS) (1994)
#255, 55 St. Clair Ave. West, Toronto, ON M4V 2Y7
416/921-5449, Fax: 416/967-6320, Toll Free: 1-800-774-2850
Executive Director, Jacqueline Tilford
President, Katherine Calder
Publications: Professional Administrator

### Confédération nationale des cadres du Québec (CNCQ) (1992)
a/s Association des cadres des collèges du Québec, 6365, boul Hamel, L'Ancienne-Lorette, QC G2E 5W2
418/877-1500, Téléc: 418/877-4469
Président, Jean Perron
Organisation(s) affiliée(s): Conféderation internationale des cadres

### Couchiching Institute on Public Affairs (CIPA) (1931)
c/o Base Service Canada Inc., #301, 250 Consumers Rd., North York, ON M2J 4V6
416/494-1440, Fax: 416/495-8723, Email: base@onramp.ca, URL: http://www.couch.ca
Executive Director, Ruth Abrahamson
Publications: Couchiching News

### Fédération des secrétaires professionnelles du Québec (FSPQ)
#300, 1173, boul Charest ouest, Québec, QC G1N 2C9
418/527-5041, Téléc: 418/682-3430
Présidente, Louise M. Gosselin

### Foundation for Association Research & Education/La Fondation de recherche et d'enseignement pour l'avancement des associations (FARE) (1991)
c/o Canadian Society of Association Executives, #1100, 10 King St. East, Toronto, ON M5C 1C3
416/363-3555, Fax: 416/363-3630
Executive Director, Judith Wiley, Email: j.wiley@csae.com

### Institute of Certified Management Consultants of Canada/Institut des conseillers en management du Canada (ICMCC)
Heritage Bldg., BCE Place, PO Box 835, 181 Bay St., Toronto, ON M5J 2T3
416/869-3001, Fax: 416/860-1535, Email: icmcc@cmc-consult.org, URL: http://www.cmc-consult.org
Executive Director, Heather Osler, CAE
Publications: Common Body of Knowledge; Management Practices in Information Technology
Affiliates: International Council of Management Consulting Institutes

#### INSTITUTE OF CERTIFIED MANAGEMENT CONSULTANTS OF ALBERTA (ICMCA) (1977)
582 Manulife Place, 10180 - 101 St., Edmonton, AB T5J 3S4
403/424-2056, Fax: 403/425-8766, Toll Free: 1-800-565-0902
Executive Director, Linda Wood, CAE
Publications: Perspective; Member Directory

#### INSTITUTE OF CERTIFIED MANAGEMENT CONSULTANTS OF ATLANTIC CANADA (ICMCAC) (1982)
PO Box 1440, Sackville, NB E0A 3C0
Toll Free: 1-800-565-5314
Publications: Atlantic Update

#### INSTITUTE OF CERTIFIED MANAGEMENT CONSULTANTS OF BRITISH COLUMBIA (1973)
#1501, 650 Georgia St. West, PO Box 11606, Vancouver, BC V6B 4N9
604/681-1419, Fax: 604/687-6688
Executive Director, Jennie Ambrose
Publications: CMC Report

#### INSTITUTE OF CERTIFIED MANAGEMENT CONSULTANTS OF MANITOBA/INSTITUT MANITOBAIN DES CONSEILLERS EN ADMINISTRATION AGRÉÉS (ICMCM) (1977)
PO Box 23041, RPO McGillivray, Winnipeg, MB R3T 5S3
204/488-4507, Fax: 204/489-1749
Email: 102777.2033@compuserve.com
Executive Director, Barbara Campbell, CMC
Publications: Consulting Perspectives; Membership Directory, a.

#### INSTITUTE OF CERTIFIED MANAGEMENT CONSULTANTS OF ONTARIO (ICMCO) (1966)
Heritage Bldg., BCE Place, PO Box 835, 181 Bay St., Toronto, ON M5J 2T3
416/860-1515, Fax: 416/860-1535, Toll Free: 1-800-268-1148
Email: icmco@cmc-consult.org
Executive Director, Heather Osler, CAE
President, Richard M. Harris
Membership/Board Secretary, Marina Melrinho
Publications: Straight Forward

#### INSTITUTE OF CERTIFIED MANAGEMENT CONSULTANTS OF SASKATCHEWAN (ICMCS) (1990)
901 - 3rd Ave. North, 2nd Fl., Saskatoon, SK S7K 2K4
306/244-6061, Fax: 306/242-7844
President, Gilbert Ackerman

### Institute of Chartered Secretaries & Administrators in Canada/Institut des secrétaires et administrateurs agréés au Canada (ICSA) (1920)
#255, 55 St. Clair Ave. West, Toronto, ON M4V 2Y7
416/944-9727, Fax: 416/967-6320, Toll Free: 1-800-501-3440, Email: 103741.1135@compuserve.com
Executive Director, Lezlie Oler
Publications: Professional Administrator; Directory of Members, a.
Affiliates: International Institute of Chartered Secretaries & Administrators

### Institute of Corporate Directors/Institut des administrateurs des corporations (IOCD) (1980)
#255, 55 St. Clair Ave. West, Toronto, ON M4V 2Y7
416/944-8282, Fax: 416/967-6320
Executive Secretary, Leslie Oler
Publications: Director
Affiliates: Institute of Directors

### Institute of Professional Management
2 Walton Ct., Ottawa, ON K1V 9T1
613/523-5957, Fax: 613/523-8505
Executive Director, Peggy Winstan

### National Society of Fund Raising Executives
#700, 1101 King St., Alexandria, VA 22314-2967 USA
703/684-0410, Fax: 703/684-0540, Toll Free: 1-800-666-3863, URL: http://www.nsfre.org/
President, Patricia F. Lewis
Executive Assistant, Sandra J. Bond
Greater Toronto Chapter: President, Douglas McLaren, c/o CFRE, 15 Clarence Sq., Toronto, ON M5V 1H1, 416/596-6642

### Ontario Medical Secretaries' Association (OMSA) (1959)
#300, 525 University Ave., Toronto, ON M5G 2K7
416/599-2580, Fax: 416/599-9309, Toll Free: 1-800-268-7215
Administrator, Katharine Brown

### Ordre des administrateurs agréés du Québec (1973)
#640, 680, rue Sherbrooke ouest, Montréal, QC H3A 2M7
514/499-0880, Téléc: 514/499-0892, Ligne sans frais: 1-800-465-0880
Directeur général et vice-président exécutif, Richard Gagnon, Adm.A.
Directrice aux communications et au recrutement, Francine Labelle
Coordonnatrice, Lysane Martel
Publications: Dimensions
Organisation(s) affiliée(s): Institut des conseillers en management du Québec; Institut des planificateurs financiers du Canada

### The Presidents Association Canada
The Chief Executive Officers Division of the AMA International, 150 York St., 5th Fl., Toronto, ON M5H 3S5
416/214-5678, Fax: 416/214-1453
Executive Director, Dodie Teplinsky

### Professional Secretaries International - Canada District
Waterford Hospital, St. John's, NF A1E 4J8
Director, Dianne Clements, CPS
Publications: The Secretary
Eastern Canada Division: President, Patricia Mombourquette, CPS, 20 Joffre St., Dartmouth, NS B2Y 3C8
Ontario Division: President, Susan L. Martin, CPS, CAM, 233 Cheltonwood Cres., Waterloo, ON N2V 1X5
Western Canada Division: President, Cindy Caton, 435 Aldine St., Winnipeg, MB R3J 3B5

### Project Management Institute (PMI) (1969)
130 South State Rd., Upper Darby, PA 19082 USA
610/734-3330, Fax: 610/734-3266, URL: http://www.pmi.org
Executive Director, Deborah Bigelow
Manager, Membership & Marketing, Karen Alfons
Publications: PMI; PM Network, m.

### Purchasing Management Association of Canada/Association canadienne de gestion des achats (PMAC) (1919)
#1414, 2 Carlton St., Toronto, ON M5B 1J3
416/977-7111 (English), 514/255-8618 (Français), Fax: 416/977-8886, Email: info@pmac.ca, URL: http://www.pmac.ca
Executive Vice-President & COO, David S. Cameron
Director, Marketing & Communications, Alexandra Marshall
Publications: Progressive Purchasing
Affiliates: Canadian Purchasing Research Foundation

### Société des relationnistes du Québec inc.
#500, 407, boul St-Laurent, Montréal, QC H2Y 2Y5
514/874-3705, Téléc: 514/866-4020, Courrier électronique: srq@planetecom.net, URL: http://www.planetecom.net/srq/
Coordonnateur, Marc Goyette

### Strategic Leadership Forum, The International Society for Strategic Management/Toronto Chapter (1950)
26 Rose Park Dr., Toronto, ON M4T 1R1
416/481-7228, Fax: 416/489-3304, Email: mstreet@inforamp.net, URL: http://www.slf-canada.org
President, Karen Gorsline
Publications: Focus on Strategy; Strategy & Leadership, bi-m.

## MANUFACTURING & INDUSTRY

### Alliance of Manufacturers & Exporters Canada/ Alliance des manufacturiers et des exporteurs du Canada (1996)
75 International Blvd., 4th Fl., Toronto, ON M9W 6L9
416/798-8000, Fax: 416/798-8050, Email: national@the-alliance.com, URL: http://www.palantir.ca/the-alliance//
President, Stephen Van Houten
Senior Vice-President, Mark Drake
Controller, Dorothy Featherstone
Publications: In Focus; Export News, 15 pa
Ottawa Office: Vice-President, Special Services, Jacqueline J. Parent, #250, 99 Bank St., Ottawa, ON K1P 6B9, 613/238-8888, Fax: 613/563-9218, Email: ottawa@the-alliance.com
Alberta Division: #1531, 10060 Jasper Ave., Edmonton, AB T5J 3R8, 403/426-6622, Fax: 403/426-1509, Email: alberta@the-alliance.com
Alliance of Manufacturers & Exporters Newfoundland: Parsons Bldg., 90 O'Leary Ave., 1st Fl., St. John's, NF A1B 2C7, 709/772-3682, Fax: 709/772-3213, Email: nfld@the-alliance.com
Association des manufacturiers du Québec: #904, 1080, côte du Beaver Hall, Montréal, QC H2Z 1S8, 514/866-7774, Téléc: 514/866-3779, Courrier électronique: quebec@the-alliance.com
BC Manufacturers' Association: #1330, 1100 Melville St., Vancouver, BC V6E 4A6, 604/685-8131, Fax: 604/685-9623, Email: bc@the-alliance.com
Manitoba Division: Century Plaza, #100, One Wesley Ave., Winnipeg, MB R3C 4C6, 204/949-1454, Fax: 204/943-3476, Email: manitoba@the-alliance.com
New Brunswick Division: #104, 1133 St. George Blvd., Moncton, NB E1E 4E1, 506/857-3056, Fax: 506/857-3059, Email: nb@the-alliance.com
Nova Scotia Division: #1020, 1801 Hollis St., Halifax, NS B3J 3N4, 902/422-4477, Fax: 902/422-9563, Email: ns@the-alliance.com
Ontario Division: #400, 75 International Blvd., Toronto, ON M9W 6L9, 416/798-8000, Fax: 416/798-8050, Email: ontario@the-alliance.com
Ontario Division - Toronto Office: Hearst Block, #539A, 900 Bay St., Toronto, ON M7A 2E1, 416/325-6396, Fax: 416/325-6509
PEI Division: Administrator, Ronald Mullins, West Royalty Industrial Park, One First Ave., Charlottetown, PE C1E 1B0, 902/629-1555, Fax: 902/368-1914, Email: pei@the-alliance.com
Saskatchewan Division: 1024 Winnipeg St., Regina, SK S4R 8P8, 306/522-2773, Fax: 306/757-5410, Email: sask@the-alliance.com

### American Electroplaters & Surface Finishers Society/Association des galvanoplastes d'Amérique (AESF) (1909)
12644 Research Pkwy., Orlando, FL 32826 USA
407/281-6441, Fax: 407/281-6446, Telex: 5106016246
Executive Director, Ted Witt
Publications: Plating & Surface Finishing
Canadian Branches
Montréal Branch: President, Gerald Loh, CEF, #715, 717 av Lajoie, Dorval, QC H0P 1G7, 514/631-3730
Ottawa Branch: President, John Cody, c/o British American Bank Note Inc., PO Box 399, Stn A, Ottawa, ON K1N 8V4, 613/728-5854
Toronto Branch: Treasurer, Walter Nikaruk, 68 Burnamthorpe Cres., Islington, ON M9A 1G7, 416/237-1400
Western Ontario Branch: President, Paul Starr, 70 Book St., Wallaceburg, ON N8A 2T6, 519/627-1691

### American Foundrymen's Society (AFS) (1896)
505 State St., Des Plaines, IL 60016-8399 USA
708/824-0181, Fax: 708/824-7848, Toll Free: 1-800-537-4237
Executive Vice-President, Charles H. Jones
Publications: Modern Casting
Canadian Chapters
British Columbia Chapter: Chairman, Mike Johnston, Inproheat Industries Ltd., 680 Raymur Ave., Vancouver, BC V6A 2R1, 604/254-0461
Eastern Canada Chapter: Chairman, Yves Marchand, Sefford Foundry, 480 Robinson St., Granby, QC J2G 7N4, 514/777-1075
Manitoba Chapter: Chairman, Graham A. Corlett, PO Box 1090, Winkler, MB R6W 4B2, 204/325-4393
Ontario Chapter: Chairman, John E. Parr, c/o Dofasco, Inc., PO Box 2460, Hamilton, ON L8N 3J5, 905/544-3761

### Association of Independent Corrugated Converters (1975)
AICC Canada - Region Eleven
PO Box 10569, Winona, ON L8E 5R1
905/643-4550, Fax: 905/643-4550
Executive Director, Donald H. Lumb

### Association de manutention du Québec/Material Handling Association of Québec (AMQ) (1986)
62A, Labelle, Laval, QC H7N 2S3
514/662-3717, Téléc: 514/662-6096
Vice-président exécutif, Victor Vonka
Business Manager, Stephanie Vonka
Publications: Bulletin

### Association de la recherche industrielle du Québec (ADRIQ)
#100, 425, rue de la Gauchetière est, Montréal, QC H2L 2M7
514/847-7570, Téléc: 514/849-5558
Directeur général, Claude Demers

### Business & Institutional Furniture Manufacturers International
1150 Flint Rd., North York, ON M3J 2J5
416/661-3370, Fax: 416/661-4586
Acting Chairman, Monty Brown

### Canadian Appliance Manufacturers Association (CAMA)
#210, 10 Carlson Ct., Etobicoke, ON M9W 6L2
416/674-7410, Fax: 416/674-7412
Vice-President, Alda M. Murphy

### Canadian Association of Moldmakers (CAMM) (1991)
424 Tecumseh Rd. East, Windsor, ON N8X 2R6
519/255-7863, Fax: 519/255-9446, Toll Free: 1-800-567-2266
Executive Director, Jean H. Kroes
Executive Secretary, Patricia M. Papp
Treasurer, C. Butcher
Publications: The CAMM Newsletter

### Canadian Association for Production & Inventory Control/Association canadienne pour la gestion de la production et les stocks (CAPIC) (1962)
APICS Region VIII
#604, 3 Church St., Toronto, ON M5E 1M2
416/364-5007, Fax: 416/862-0315, Info Line: 364-5007, Toll Free: 1-800-567-8207
Administrator, Marilyn Ryder
Publications: APICS - The Performance Advantage; Production & Inventory Management, q.
Affiliates: American Production & Inventory Control Society

### Canadian Battery Association (CBA)
#1801, One Yonge St., Toronto, ON M5E 1W7
416/363-7845, Fax: 416/369-0515
Executive Director, Lois Marsh

### Canadian Boiler Society/Société canadienne de manufacturiers chaudières (CBS)
3266 Douglas St., Burlington, ON L7N 1G9
905/681-9886, Fax: 905/681-1533
Executive Director, J.R. Cassidy

### Canadian Brush, Broom & Mop Manufacturers Association/Association canadienne des fabricants de brosses, balais et vadrouilles (CBBMMA) (1944)
#200, 670 Bloor St. West, Toronto, ON M6G 1L2
416/533-7800, Fax: 416/533-4795
Executive Director, Don Mockford

### Canadian Carpet Institute
#605, 130 Slater St., Ottawa, ON K1P 6E2
613/232-7183, Fax: 613/232-3072
Executive Director, Michael B. Kronick

### Canadian Cosmetic, Toiletry & Fragrance Association/Association canadienne des cosmétiques, produit de toilette et parfums (CCTFA) (1928)
#510, 5090 Explorer Dr., Mississauga, ON L4W 4T9
905/629-0111, Fax: 905/629-0112
President, C.A. Low
Vice-President, Administration & Meetings, S. Wissler

### Canadian Council of Furniture Manufacturers/ Conseil canadien des fabricants de meubles (CCFM)
1873 Inkster Blvd., Winnipeg, MB R2R 2A6
204/694-5872, Fax: 204/694-1281
Acting President, Terry Clark

### Canadian Decorating Products Association/ Association canadienne de l'industrie de décoration (CDPA) (1949)
#5, 7895 Tranmere Dr., Mississauga, ON L5S 1V9
905/678-0331, Fax: 905/678-0335
Office Manager, Rosemary Schooley
Publications: Decorating Centre; Members Update, s-a.
Affiliates: National Decorating Products Association

### Canadian Die Casters Association/Association canadienne des mouleurs sous pressions
#307, 151 Slater St., Ottawa, ON K1P 5H3
613/232-8663, Fax: 613/230-9607
Executive Director, Donald P. Kennedy

### Canadian Fibreboard Manufacturers' Association/Association canadienne des manufacturiers d'isolant de fibre de bois (CFMA) (1958)
#200, 670 Bloor St. West, Toronto, ON M6G 1L2
416/533-7800, Fax: 416/533-4795
Executive Director, Don Mockford
President, Paul St. Louis

### Canadian Flexible Foam Manufacturers' Association (CFFMA) (1981)
#200, 6900 Airport Rd., PO Box 85, Mississauga, ON L4V 1E8
905/677-6594, Fax: 905/677-5212
Secretary, George D. Sinclair

### Canadian Gear Products Manufacturers' Association
#701, 116 Albert St., Ottawa, ON K1P 5G3
613/232-7213, Fax: 613/232-7381
President, Lloyd J. Beverly

**Canadian Hardware & Housewares Manufacturers' Association/Association canadienne des fabricants en quincaillerie et articles ménagers (CHHMA) (1966)**
#101, 1335 Morningside Ave., Scarborough, ON M1B 5M4
416/282-0022, Fax: 416/282-0027
President, Vaughn Crofford
Publications: CHHMA Newsletter

**Canadian Heat Exchange & Vessel Manufacturers Association (CHEVMA) (1976)**
#310, 2175 Sheppard Ave. East, North York, ON M2J 1W8
416/491-2886, Fax: 416/491-1670, Email: taylor@interlog.com
Administrator, Timothy A. Christie
Publications: CHEVMA Members Directory; Bulletin, q.

**Canadian Industrial Innovation Centre (CIIC/W) (1981)**
156 Columbia St. West, Waterloo, ON N2L 3L3
519/885-5870, Fax: 519/885-5729, Toll Free: 1-800-265-4559, Email: info@innovationcentre.ca, URL: http://www.innovationcentre.ca
Manager, Marketing Services Group, Gary Svoboda
Publications: Eureka; The Innovation Showcase

**Canadian Juvenile Products Association**
PO Box 294, Kleinburg, ON L0J 1C0
905/893-1689, Fax: 905/893-2392, Email: kleinbrg@netrover.com
Executive Director, Wayne Glover, CAE

**Canadian Kitchen Cabinet Association/Association canadienne de fabricants d'armoires de cuisine (CKCA)**
27 Goulburn Ave., Ottawa, ON K1N 8C7
613/233-6205, Fax: 613/233-1929, Email: ckca@sympatico.ca, URL: http://www.kitchenweb.com/ckca/en/
President, Bill Laurysen
Executive Vice-President, R.H. Rivard
Executive Secretary, Suzanne Cardinal

**Canadian Laboratory Suppliers Association/Association canadienne de fournisseurs de laboratoire**
94 Torrance Rd., Scarborough, ON M1J 2J4
416/431-4301, Fax: 416/431-5889
Administrator, Lorraine MacNevin

**Canadian Lamp & Fixture Manufacturers Association Inc. (CLFMA)**
30 Dovedale Crt., Scarborough, ON M1S 5A7
416/754-3377, Fax: 416/754-8077
Frank Delorey

**Canadian Plastics Industry Association/Association canadienne de l'industrie des plastiques (CPIA)**
#500, 5925 Airport Rd., Mississauga, ON L4V 1W1
905/678-7748, Fax: 905/678-0774, Email: national@cpia.ca, URL: http://www.plastics.ca
President, Pierre Dubois
Manager, Seminars, Paul Waller
Administrative Assistant, Liliane M.R. Veilleux
Communications, Karen Wolfe, Email: kwolfe@cpia.ca
Publications: Newsletter

**Canadian Pump Manufacturers' Association**
#701, 116 Albert St., Ottawa, ON K1P 5G3
613/232-7213, Fax: 613/232-7381
President, Lloyd J. Beverly

**Canadian Sanitation Supply Association/Association canadienne des fournisseurs de produits sanitaires (CSSA) (1957)**
#G10, 300 Mill Rd., Etobicoke, ON M9C 4W7
416/620-9320, Fax: 416/620-7199, Email: cssa@the_wire.com, URL: http://www.cssa.com
Executive Director, Diane Gosling
President, Mike Ambler
Publications: Update; Bulletin; CSSA Roster, a.

**Canadian Tobacco Manufacturers' Council/Conseil canadien des fabricants des produits de tabac (CTMC) (1963)**
#701, 99 Bank St., Ottawa, ON K1P 6B9
613/238-2799, Fax: 613/238-4463
President, Robert Parker
Director, Communications, Marie Josée Lapointe
Publications: Tobacco File

**Canadian Tooling & Machining Association (CTMA) (1963)**
#3, 140 McGovern Dr., Cambridge, ON N3H 4R7
519/653-7265, Fax: 519/653-6764, Email: info@ctma.com, URL: http://www.ctma.com
General Manager, Brian Naylor
Publications: CTMA View
Affiliates: Auto Parts; Canadian Foundry Association; Canadian Plastics Institute; GTMA England; PMPTB - Ohio, USA; SPI - Toronto; CAMM - Windsor

**Canadian Toy Association/L'Association canadienne du Jouet (1932)**
PO Box 294, Kleinburg, ON L0J 1C0
905/893-1689, Fax: 905/893-2392
Executive Director, Sheila Edmondson
Chairman, Sheldon Klein
Publications: The Insider; Canadian Toy & Decoration Fair

**Canadian Urethane Manufacturers Association (CUMA) (1974)**
32 Baleberry Cr., Weston, ON M9P 3L2
416/244-9859
Manager, Rodger G. Davis

**Canadian Valve Manufacturers' Association**
#701, 116 Albert St., Ottawa, ON K1P 5G3
613/232-7213, Fax: 613/232-7381
President, Arnold W.D. Garlick

**Canadian Window & Door Manufacturers Association/Association canadienne des manufacturiers de portes et de fenêtres (CWDMA) (1967)**
27 Goulburn Ave., Ottawa, ON K1N 8C7
613/233-9804, Fax: 613/233-1929, Email: cwdma@sympatico.ca, URL: http://www.windoorweb.com/cwdma
Executive Director, Richard Lipman
Executive Vice-President, R.H. Rivard
Publications: Membership & Product Directory

**Cellulose Insulation Manufacturers Association of Canada (CIMAC) (1978)**
PO Box 245, Stn Mont-Royal, Montréal, QC H3P 3C5
514/737-6482, Fax: 514/737-6929
Executive Director, Harry Hencher
President, Norman Carbonneau

**Door & Hardware Institute (1975)**
Canadian Headquarters, 208 Evans Ave., Toronto, ON M8Z 1J7
416/251-0702, Fax: 416/252-4064
Canadian Administrator, Les Groves
Publications: Doors & Hardware

**Hydrogen Industry Council/Conseil de l'industrie de l'hydrogène (HIC) (1982)**
#2610, 1800, av McGill College, Montréal, QC H3A 3J6
514/288-5139, Fax: 514/843-6079
Directeur général, Richard D. Champagne

**Insulating Glass Manufacturers Association of Canada/Association canadienne des manufacturiers de vitrage isolant (IGMAC) (1967)**
PO Box 25013, Brantford, ON N3T 6K5
519/449-2487, Fax: 519/449-2887
General Manager, Susan Macivor

**National Floor Covering Association**
#605, 130 Slater St., Ottawa, ON K1P 6E2
613/232-7845, Fax: 613/232-3072
Executive Director, Michael B. Kronick

**Office Products Manufacturers Association of Canada**
#240, 4600 Highway #7, Woodbridge, ON L4L 4Y7
905/850-3892, Fax: 905/850-3895
Executive Assistant, Jo Anne Falkenburger

**Organization of CANDU Industries/Association des industries CANDU (OCI) (1979)**
#1801, One Yonge St., Toronto, ON M5E 1W7
416/363-7845, Fax: 416/369-0515
General Manager, Jack R. Howett
Administrator, Lois Marsh
Publications: OCI Newsletter
Affiliates: Atomic Energy of Canada

**Portable Appliance Manufacturers Association of Canada (PAMA)**
#210, 10 Carlson Ct., Etobicoke, ON M9W 6L2
416/674-7410, Fax: 416/674-7412
Vice-President, Alda M. Murphy

**The Rubber Association of Canada/Association canadienne de l'industrie du caoutchouc (RAC) (1920)**
#308, 89 The Queensway West, Mississauga, ON L5B 2V2
905/270-8322, Fax: 905/270-2640, Email: rac@inforamp.net
President, Brian E. James
Chairman, Dan Patrick
Office Manager, Glenn Maidment
Publications: RAC News

**Soap & Detergent Association of Canada/Association des savonniers canadiens (SDAC) (1969)**
#301, 885 Don Mills Rd., North York, ON M3C 1V9
416/510-8036, Fax: 416/510-8044
Manager, Linda N. Reid
Affiliates: Grocery Products Manufacturers of Canada

**Tanners Association of Canada**
1969 Leslie St., North York, ON M3B 2M3
416/443-9794, Fax: 416/443-9795
President, Peter M. Stewart

**MAPPING *see* SURVEYING & MAPPING**

## MARINE TRADES

***see also* Fisheries & Fishing Industry; Transportation & Shipping**

**British Columbia Marine Trades Association**
#270, 1075 West Georgia St., Vancouver, BC V6E 3C9
604/683-5191, Fax: 604/688-3105, URL: http://bcmarine.com
President, Christopher Goulder
Publications: Marine BC

**British Columbia Maritime Employers Association**
#500, 349 Railway St., Vancouver, BC V6A 1A4
604/688-1155, Fax: 604/684-2397
CEO/President, R.V. Wilds
Director, Labour Relations, M.H. Cahan

**Canadian Centre for Marine Communications**
PO Box 8454, St. John's, NF A1B 3N9
709/579-4872, Fax: 709/579-0492, Email: wayneb@ccmpost.ifmt.f.ca
President & CEO, Wayne Buffey

**Canadian Marine Manufacturers Association**
Box 38, #804, 370 King St. West, Toronto, ON M5V 1J9
416/971-4240, Fax: 416/971-4275, Email: info@cmma.ca, URL: http://www.cmma.ca

**Canadian Navigation Society (CNS)**
#818, 130 Slater St., Ottawa, ON K1P 6E2
613/234-0191, Fax: 613/234-9039
Executive Director, Ian M. Ross

**Canadian Port & Harbour Association/Association des ports et havres du Canada (CPHA) (1959)**
8 Parmalea Cres., Toronto, ON M9R 2X7
416/245-1742, Fax: 416/245-1250, URL: http://www.newswire.ca/cpha/cpha1.htm
Executive Director, John Jursa
Publications: CPHA Newsletter; CPHA Monitor, s-a.
Affiliates: American Association of Port Authorities

**International Association of Great Lakes Ports (IAGLP) (1960)**
c/o Chamber of Maritime Commerce, #704A, 350 Sparks St., Ottawa, ON K1R 7S8
613/233-8779, Fax: 613/232-6211
Sec.-Treas., Genevieve Harrison

**Mid-Canada Marine Dealers Association**
23 Sage Cres., Winnipeg, MB R2Y 0X8
204/831-5438, Fax: 204/831-5438
President, Rene St. Onge
Executive Secretary, Brian Ans

**The National Marine Manufacturers Association (NMMA)**
#804, 370 King St. West, Toronto, ON M5V 1J9
416/591-6772, Fax: 416/591-3582
Show Manager, Carol Bell
Administrative Coordinator, Andrea Janko
Show Coordinator, D'Arcy McDonald
Affiliates: National Association of Boat Manufacturers; National Association of Marine Products & Services; Association of Marine Engine Manufacturers

**Shipbuilding Association of Canada/Association de la construction navale du Canada (1995)**
#1502, 222 Queen St., Ottawa, ON K1P 5V9
613/232-7127, Fax: 613/238-5519
President, Peter Cairns
Publications: Newsletter

**MARKETING *see* ADVERTISING & MARKETING**

**MASONIC ORDERS *see* FRATERNAL**

**MEDIATION *see* LABOUR RELATIONS**

**MEDICAL *see* HEALTH & MEDICAL**

## MENTAL HEALTH

**Agoraphobic Foundation of Canada Inc./Fondation canadienne pour les agoraphobes inc. (AFC) (1982)**
PO Box 132, Laval, QC H7W 4K2
514/628-5215
President, F. Rosen, Bus: 514/688-4726
Publications: AFC Newsletter

**Association des psychologues du Québec/Québec Psychological Association (APQ) (1989)**
#208, 1150 boul St-Joseph est, Montréal, QC H2J 1L5
514/528-7498, Téléc: 514/528-6020
Président, Daniel-Laurent Frégeau
Vice-Président, Richard Gauthier
Trésorier, Jean Grégoire
Publications: Bulletin

**Association des sexologues du Québec (ASQ) (1978)**
#300, 6915, rue St-Denis, Montréal, QC H2S 2S3
514/270-9289, Téléc: 514/270-9289
Directrice générale, Sylviane Larose
Présidente, Normande Couture
Publications: Sexologie Actuelle; Repertoire des sexologues, annuel; Les sexologues peuvent vous aider

**Canadian Art Therapy Association - Eastern Chapter (CATA) (1977)**
#601, 6-2400 Dundas St. West, Mississauga, ON L5K 2R8
905/858-9642, Fax: 905/542-7199
President, Lois Woolf
Publications: Journal of the Canadian Art Therapy Association

**Canadian Art Therapy Association - Western Chapter**
#350, 1425 Marine Dr., West Vancouver, BC V7T 1B9
604/926-9381, Fax: 604/926-5729
Contact, Lois Woolf

**Canadian Association of Psychoanalytic Child Therapists (CAPCT)**
42 Brookmount Rd., Toronto, ON M4L 3N2
416/690-5464, Fax: 416/690-2746
President, Janet Morrison, Bus: 416/925-2831

**Canadian Association for Suicide Prevention/L'Association canadienne pour la prévention du suicide (CASP) (1985)**
#201, 1615 - 10th Ave. SW, Calgary, AB T3C 0J7
403/245-3900, Email: siec@nucleus.com, URL: http://www3.sympatico.ca/masecard/index.html
Executive Director, G. Harrington
Publications: CASP/ACPS News

**Canadian Centre for Stress & Well-Being (1982)**
**Stress Management Centre**
#1801, One Yonge St., Toronto, ON M5E 1W7
416/363-6204, Fax: 416/367-1014
Director, Dr. Lucille C. Peszat, Ed.D.

**Canadian Group Psychotherapy Association (CGPA)**
11 Millstone Cres., Whitby, ON L1R 1T4
905/666-0555, Fax: 905/666-0000
Executive Secretary, Anne Eberle
President, Dr. Kent Mahoney
Publications: CGPA Chronicle

**Canadian Hypertension Society/Société canadienne d'hypertension artérielle (CHS) (1979)**
Dept. of Pharmacology, Chown Bldg., Univ. of Manitoba, #A329, 753 McDermot Ave., Winnipeg, MB R3E 0T6
204/789-3356, Fax: 204/783-6915
President, Dr. R.M.K.W. Lee, Bus: 905/521-2100, Fax: 905/523-1224
Sec.-Treas., Dr. Donald D. Smyth
Publications: Hypertension Canada
Affiliates: Canadian Society for Clinical Investigation; Royal College of Physicians & Surgeons of Canada

**Canadian Institute of Stress**
#500, 1235 Bay St., Toronto, ON M5R 3K4
416/961-8575, Fax: 416/237-1828
Contact, Dr. Richard Earle

**Canadian Mental Health Association/Association canadienne pour la santé mentale (CMHA) (1918)**
2160 Yonge St., Toronto, ON M4S 2Z3
416/484-7750, Fax: 416/484-4617
General Director, Edward J. Pennington
National President, Sharon Barnes
Director of Administration, Jeannine Hurd
Publications: Mental Health Matters

**Canadian Play Therapy Institute (CPTI) (1985)**
PO Box 2153, Kingston, ON K7L 5J9
613/384-2795, Fax: 613/634-0866, Email: cplayti@limestone.kosone.com, URL: http://www.playtherapy.org/
Executive Director, Viktoria Takacs, M.Ed.
Publications: Canadian Play Therapy Newsletter
Affiliates: Play Therapy International

**Canadian Psychiatric Association/Association des psychiatres du Canada (CPA) (1951)**
#200, 237 Argyle Dr., Ottawa, ON K2P 1B8
613/234-2815, ext.26, Fax: 613/234-9857, Toll Free: 1-800-267-1555, Email: cpa@medical.org, URL: http://medical.org
Chief Executive Officer, Alex Saunders
Manager, Communications, Sharon Petrie
Publications: Journal of Psychiatry & Neuroscience; Bulletin, bi-m.; The Canadian Journal of Psychiatry, 10 pa
Affiliates: Canadian Medical Association; World Psychiatric Association

**ALBERTA PSYCHIATRIC ASSOCIATION (APA)**
Holy Cross Hospital, Calgary, AB T5J 2J7
403/247-9507
President, Dr. Ron Aldons

**MANITOBA PSYCHIATRIC ASSOCIATION**
Room P2433, Dept. of Psychiatry, Health Sciences Centre, 771 Bannatyne Ave., Winnipeg, MB R3E 3N4
204/787-7056, Fax: 204/787-4879
President, Dr. Samia Barakat

**NEW BRUNSWICK PSYCHIATRIC ASSOCIATION**
PO Box 3220, Stn B, Saint John, NB E2M 4H7
506/672-7871, Fax: 506/635-1614
President, Dr. Roger. Guzman
Secretary, Jeanette Logan

**NEWFOUNDLAND PSYCHIATRIC ASSOCIATION**
Terrace Clinic, #8, 10 Rowan St., PO Box 15, St. John's, NF A1B 2X3
709/579-0138
Dr. John Angel
Nova Scotia Psychiatric Association: President, Dr. Simon Brooks, PO Box 280, Tatamagouche, NS B0K 1V0, 902/657-2009

**ONTARIO PSYCHIATRIC ASSOCIATION (OPA) (1920)**
Queen Street Mental Health Centre, 1001 Queen St. West, Toronto, ON M6J 1H4
416/535-8501, Fax: 416/583-4307
Executive Director, Allison Stuart
President, Clive Chamberlain
Publications: Dialogue

**PEI PSYCHIATRIC ASSOCIATION**
#10, 1 Rochford St., Charlottetown, PE C1A 3T1
902/628-6258, Fax: 902/628-2383
President, Dr. Ben Stears

**SASKATCHEWAN PSYCHIATRIC ASSOCIATION**
222 Ave. P South, Saskatoon, SK S7M 2W2
306/652-8777, Fax: 306/665-3304
President, Dr. Annu Thakur

**Canadian Psychiatric Research Foundation**
#307, 60 Bloor St. West, Toronto, ON M4W 3B8
416/975-9891
Executive Director, Ron Rea

**Canadian Psychoanalytic Society/Société canadienne de psychanalyse**
7000, ch Côte-des-Neiges, Montréal, QC H3S 2C1
514/738-6105, Fax: 514/738-6393, Email: psyanal@aei.ca
Administrative Director, Nadia Gargour

**Canadian Psychological Association/Société canadienne de psychologie (CPA) (1939)**
#205, 151 Slater St., Ottawa, ON K1P 5H3
613/237-2144, Fax: 613/237-1674, Email: cpa@cpa.ca, URL: http://www.cpa.ca
Executive Director, Dr. John C. Service
President, Dr. Janel Gauthier
Publications: Psynopsis; Canadian Psychology; Canadian Journal of Experimental Psychology; Canadian Journal of Behavioural Science
Affiliates: Canadian Register of Health Service Providers in Psychology; Social Science Federation of Canada; Correctional Services Canada; Council of Provincial Associations of Psychologists; International Union of Psychological Science; National Associations Active in Criminal Justice; Youth Science Foundation

**Canadian Schizophrenia Foundation (CSF) (1969)**
16 Florence Ave., North York, ON M2N 1E9
416/733-2117, Fax: 416/733-2352, Email: centre@orthomed.org, URL: http://www.orthomed.org
Executive Director, Steven Carter
Publications: Journal of Orthomolecular Medicine; Nutrition & Mental Health

**Child & Parent Resource Institute (CPRI) (1960)**
600 Sanitorium Rd., London, ON N6H 3W7
519/471-2540, Fax: 519/641-1922, URL: http://www.hometown.on.ca/cpri/
Administrator, E. Sorin

**Depressive & Manic Depressive Association of Ontario/L'Association ontarienne de la dépression et de la psychose maniaco-dépressive (DMDAO) (1989)**
#101, 214 Merton St., Toronto, ON M4S 1A6
416/481-5413, Fax: 416/481-5545
Executive Director, Sue Trevor, C.A.
President, Allan Strong
Publications: The Link

**Fédération des familles et amis de la personne atteinte de maladie mentale/Federation of Families & Friends of Persons with a Mental Illness (FFAPAMM) (1986)**
#203, 1990, rue Jean-Talon nord, Ste-Foy, QC G1N 4K8
418/687-0474, Téléc: 418/687-0123, Ligne sans frais: 1-800-323-0474
Directrice générale, Hélène Fradet
Publications: Le Porte Parole

**Manic Depressive Association of Metropolitan Toronto (MDAMT) (1984)**
#252, 40 Orchard View Blvd., Toronto, ON M4R 1B9
416/486-8046
Executive Director, Neasa Martin
President, Jack Norris
Publications: MDAMT Newsletter

**National Mental Health Fund (NMHF) (1986)**
#307, 60 Bloor St. West, Toronto, ON M4W 3B8
416/975-9891
Executive Director, Ron Rea
President, Timothy R. Price
Publications: NMHF Newsletter; Campaigner Update, q.
Affiliates: Canadian Mental Health Association; Canadian Psychiatric Research Foundation

**Ontario Association of Children's Mental Health Centres/Association ontarienne des centres de santé mentale pour enfants (OACMHC)**
#309, 40 St. Clair Ave. East, Toronto, ON M4T 1M9
416/921-2109, URL: http://www.oacmhc.org
Executive Director, Sheila Weinstock

**Ontario Psychological Association (OPA) (1946)**
#221, 730 Yonge St., Toronto, ON M4Y 2B7
416/961-5552, Fax: 416/961-5516, Email: ont@hookup.net
Executive Director, Dr. Ruth Berman
Administrative Officer, C. Mardoner
Publications: Psychology Ontario

**L'Ordre des psychologues du Québec (OPQ) (1962)**
#510, 1100, av Beaumont, Montréal, QC H3P 3H5
514/738-1881, Téléc: 514/737-6431, Infoligne: 514/738-1223, Ligne sans frais: 1-800-561-1223
Directeur général, René Corriveau
Publications: Psychologie-Québec
Organisation(s) affiliée(s): American Psychological Association

**Schizophrenia Society of Canada/Société canadienne de schizophrénie (SSC) (1979)**
#814, 75 The Donway West, North York, ON M3C 2E9
416/445-8204, Fax: 416/445-2270, Email: info@schizophrenia.ca, URL: http://www.schizophrenia.ca
Executive Director, Penelope Marrett
President, Ann Braden
Publications: The SSC Bulletin
Affiliates: Canadian Alliance for Research on Schizophrenia; World Schizophrenia Fellowship

**Society for the Treatment & Study of Stress/Société de traitement et d'étude sur le stress**
125, av Pagnuelo, Montréal, QC H2V 3C3
514/277-8696
President, J. Pierre Hogue

**Survivors of Suicide Support Program (1989)**
#301, 349A George St. North, Peterborough, ON K9H 3P9
705/748-6711, Fax: 705/748-2577
Executive Director, Mark Graham

**World Federation for Mental Health/Fédération mondiale pour la santé mentale (WFMH) (1948)**
1021 Prince St., Alexandria, VA 22314-2971 USA
703/838-7543, Fax: 703/519-7648
Secretary General, Dr. Eugene Brody
Deputy Secretary General, Richard Hunter
Publications: The WFMH Newsletter
North American Regional Council: PO Box 185, Lethbridge, AB T1J 3T5, 403/329-1008, Fax: 403/329-0264

**MENTALLY CHALLENGED PERSONS *see* DISABLED PERSONS**

**METAL INDUSTRIES *see* STEEL & METAL INDUSTRIES**

**METALLURGY *see* MINES & MINERAL RESOURCES**

**MIDWIFERY *see* CHILDBIRTH**

## MILITARY & VETERANS

**Air Cadet League of Canada/Ligue des cadets de l'air du Canada (1941)**
Constitution Bldg., 313 Rideau St., Ottawa, ON K1N 5Y4
613/991-4349, Fax: 613/991-4347, URL: http://www.isisnet.com/smacdouga/rcac.html
Executive Director, Richard Logan
President, W.C.F. Beattie
Publications: In-Formation

**Air Force Association of Canada/L'Association des forces aériennes du Canada (1948)**
PO Box 2460, Stn D, Ottawa, ON K1P 5W6
613/992-7482, Fax: 613/995-2196, Email: btracy@airforce.ca, URL: http://www.airforce.ca
Executive Director, Robert Tracy
Publications: Airforce
Affiliates: Air Force Association of United States; Royal Air Forces Association

**The Army Cadet League of Canada/Ligue des cadets de l'armée du Canada (1971)**
Constitution Bldg., 305 Rideau St., Ottawa, ON K1N 9E5
613/991-4348, Fax: 613/990-8701, Email: brianlockhart@igs.net, URL: http://ww2.isys.ca/army/index.html
Executive Director, C.J. Devaney
President, L.K. Deane
Publications: Journal
Affiliates: Army Cadet Force Association; Deutscher-Bundeswehr-Verband

**Army, Navy & Air Force Veterans in Canada/Les Anciens combattants de l'armée, de la marine et des forces aeriennes au Canada (ANAVETS) (1917)**
#2, 6 Beechwood Ave., Vanier, ON K1L 8B4
613/744-0222, Fax: 613/744-0208
Sec.-Treas., I.D. Inrig

**Canadian Battle of Normandy Foundation/Fondation canadienne de la Bataille de Normandie (CBNF) (1992)**
1650 Featherston Dr., Ottawa, ON K1H 6P2
613/731-7767, Fax: 613/731-6577
President, Cdr. W.A.B. Douglas, CD, Ph.D., RCN (Ret'd)
Honorary Patron, Col. the Hon. Brian Dickson, PC, CC, CD
General Manager, Lawrence E. Davies, CD
Publications: Normandy Newsletter

**Canadian Corps Association (1934)**
201 Niagara St., Toronto, ON M5V 1C9
416/504-6694
Dominion Secretary, Shirley Wood Heesaker

### The Canadian Corps of Commissionaires/Les Corps canadien des commissionnaires (1925)
**The Commissionaires**
#201, 100 Gloucester St., Ottawa, ON K2P 0A4
613/236-4936, Fax: 613/563-8508, Email: nhq@commissionaires.ca, URL: http://www.comnet.ca/~cccnhq/commish.htm
Chairman, Lt.Col. R.G. Smellie, CD, QC
Executive Secretary, Lt.Gen. J.A.R. Gutknecht, CMM, OStJ, CD

### Canadian Council of War Veterans' Associations
60 Morrow St., Peterborough, ON K9J 1X3
705/742-2901
President, John E. Denniston
Vice-President, Frank Caldwell
Treasurer, Bill Hughes

### Canadian Infantry Association/Association canadienne de l'infanterie (CIA) (1912)
PO Box 158, Anjou, QC H1K 4G6
514/355-2211, Fax: 514/355-2211
Sec.-Treas., LCol P. Caron, CD (Ret'd)

### Canadian Naval Association
14 Hayden St., Toronto, ON M4Y 1V8
416/924-2811
Executive Director, Jean Brodie

### Canadian Peacekeeping Veterans Association
PO Box 48197, Victoria, BC V8Z 7H6
604/383-7240, Fax: 604/383-7240, Email: duke@islandnet.com, URL: http://www.islandnet.com/~duke/cpva.htm
President, James P. MacMillan-Murphy, CD

### Commission canadienne d'histoire militaire/Canadian Commission of Military History (CCHM) (1973)
a/s Directeur - Historie et patrimoine, Quartier général de la Défense nationale, Ottawa, ON K1A 0K2
613/998-7063, Téléc: 613/990-8579
Secrétaire général, René Chartrand
Président, Dr. Serge Bernier
Trésorier, Jean Morin
Publications: Bibliographie d'historie militaire
Organisation(s) affiliée(s): Commission internationale d'histoire militaire

### Commonwealth War Graves Commission - Canadian Agency/Commission des sépultures de guerre du Commonwealth (CWGC) (1921)
#1707, 66 Slater St., Ottawa, ON K1A 0P4
613/992-3224, Fax: 613/995-0431
Secretary General, Daniel F. Wheeldon
Publications: Commonwealth War Graves Commission Annual Report
Affiliates: Commonwealth War Graves Commission

### Conference of Defence Associations (CDA) (1932)
#301, 359 Kent St., Ottawa, ON K2P 0R7
613/236-1252, Fax: 613/236-8191, Email: cda@istar.ca, URL: http://home.istar.ca/~cda
Executive Director, L.Col. V.A. Coroy, CD (Ret'd)
Executive Secretary, Cdr. J.D. Sine, CD (Ret'd)
Publications: CDAI Newsline; Vanguard, q.

### Defence Associations National Network/Réseau des associations de la défense nationale (DANN) (1989)
PO Box 17, Stn B, Ottawa, ON K1P 6C3
613/831-0294, Email: cjpierce@igs.net, URL: http://www.sfu.ca/~dann
Chairman, Vice-Admiral D.N. Mainguy, (Ret'd)
National Secretary, Clifford J. Pierce
Publications: National Network News
Affiliates: The Royal Canadian Legion; The Navy League of Canada; The Federation of Military & United Services Institutes of Canada; The Air Force Officers Advisory Group; The Business Council on National Issues; Aerospace Industries Association of Canada; Canadian Defence Preparedness Association; The Naval Officers Association of Canada; Canadian Maritime Industries Association; The Conference of Defence Associations

### Defence Research & Education Centre (DREC) (1985)
Site 4, Box 3B8, RR#1, Tantallon, NS B0J 3J0
902/823-2770, Fax: 902/823-3057
President, Commodore R.W. Crocks, Ret'd.
Executive Director, Mary Kitley
Publications: Next Steps in Canadian Foreign Policy; The Defence Debate in Canada; DREC Reports
Affiliates: Veterans Against Nuclear Arms

### Dominion Civil Service War Veterans Association (1947)
1403 Gerrard St. East, Toronto, ON M4L 1Z5
416/465-0477
President, Gordon F. Madden

### Federation of Military & United Services Institutes of Canada/Fédération des instituts militaires et des instituts des services unis du Canada (FMUSIC) (1973)
Fort Frontenac, Kingston, ON K7K 5L0
613/544-7307, Fax: 613/541-5944
Executive Vice-Chair, Col. W.B. MacLeod
Publications: FMUSIC Newsletter; Bulletin FIMIC

### Jewish War Veterans of Canada
#353, 1111 Finch Ave., Downsview, ON M3J 2E5
416/663-8387
Post Commander, Jack Cahan

### Korea Veterans Association of Canada Inc./Association canadienne des vétérans de la Corée (1974)
8 Moorside Dr., Ottawa, ON K2C 3P4
613/225-0443, Fax: 613/225-9935
President, H. St. Laurent
Secretary, Les Peate
Publications: National Report
Affiliates: International Federation of Korea War Veterans Associations

### Liaison Association of War Veterans/Association liaison des anciens combattants (1987)
CP 21, Succ Sainte-Anne-de-Bellevue, Montréal, QC H9X 3L4
514/457-3440, Fax: 514/457-2143
Secretary, Ivette Glimont

### Military Collectors Club of Canada (MCCC) (1963)
525 London St., PO Box 64009, Winnipeg, MB R2K 4K2
204/669-0871
Sec.-Treas., John Zabarylo
Publications: Journal of the MCC of C

### National Council of Veteran Associations
2827 Riverside Dr., Ottawa, ON K1V 0C4
613/731-3821, Fax: 613/731-3234
Chair, H. Clifford Chadderton
Director of Administration, Claire Roy

### The Naval Officers Association of Canada/L'Association des officiers de la marine du Canada (NOAC) (1946)
72 Robertson Rd., PO Box 26083, Nepean, ON K2H 9R6
613/832-3045, Fax: 613/832-3917, Email: duncan.mathieson@sympatico.ca, URL: http://www.naval.ca
Executive Director, R.N. Duncan Mathieson
President, E.R. Crickard, Bus: 709/753-0960
Director, Maritime Affairs, P.T. Haydon, Bus: 902/835-5994
Publications: Starshell; Niobe Papers, a.

### Navy League of Canada/Ligue navale du Canada (1895)
305 Rideau St., Ottawa, ON K1N 9E5
613/993-5415, Fax: 613/990-8701, Toll Free: 1-800-375-6289, Email: navylge@magi.com
Executive Director & National Secretary, Douglas J. Thomas, Bus: 613/998-0447
Publications: Info-clips
Affiliates: Conference of Defence Associates

### Princess Patricia's Canadian Light Infantry Association
Regimental Headquarters, 4520 Crowchild Trail SW, Calgary, AB T3E 1T8
403/974-2862, Fax: 403/974-2864, Email: ppcli@nucleus.com, URL: http://www.nucleus.com/ppcli
National President, Doug Bedford
Sec.-Treas., Capt. Steve Newman
Publications: Newsletter

### Royal Canadian Air Force Benevolent Fund/La Caisse de Bienfaisance de l'Aviation Royale du Canada (RCAF BF) (1944)
Berger Building, 100 Metcalfe St., Ottawa, ON K1A 0K2
613/992-6082
Secretary-Manager, J.G. Allen
Publications: Benevolent Fund News

### Royal Canadian Legion/Légion royale canadienne (RCL) (1925)
Dominion Secretary, Legion House, 359 Kent St., Ottawa, ON K2P 0R7
613/235-4391, Fax: 613/563-1670, Email: info@legion.ca, URL: http://www.legion.ca
Public Relations Manager, Robert J. Butt
Dominion President, Joe Kobolak
1st Vice-President, Chuck Murphy
Dominion Secretary, Duane Daly
Director of Administration, Jacques Coté
Publications: Legion
Affiliates: British Commonwealth Ex-Services League; National Council of Veterans Associations
Provincial Commands
Alberta & NWT Command: Secretary, Ron Rivard, PO Box 3067, Stn B, Calgary, AB T2M 4L6, 403/284-1161, Fax: 403/284-9899
Manitoba & Northwest Ontario Command: Secretary, Ronnie Lamontagne, 563 St. Mary's Rd., Winnipeg, MB R2M 3L6, 204/233-3405, Fax: 204/237-1775
New Brunswick Command: Secretary, Glen Stewart, PO Box 3426, Stn B, Saint John, NB E2M 4X9, 506/634-8850, Fax: 506/633-4836
Newfoundland & Labrador Command: Secretary, Sheila Lane, PO Box 5745, St. John's, NF A1E 5X3, 709/753-6666, Fax: 709/753-5514
Nova Scotia Command: Secretary, Frank Fudge, PO Box 9075, Stn A, Halifax, NS B3K 5M7, 902/429-6425, Fax: 902/429-7481
Ontario Command: Secretary, Marlene Lambros, 218 Richmond St. West, Toronto, ON M5V 1V8, 416/598-4466, Fax: 416/598-4256
Pacific Command: Secretary, Linda Sawyer, 3026 Arbutus St., Vancouver, BC V6J 4P7, 604/736-8166, Fax: 604/736-1635
PEI Command: Secretary, Betty MacLachlan, PO Box 20132, RPO Sherwood, Charlottetown, PE C1A 9E3, 902/892-2161, Fax: 902/368-8853

Québec Command: Secrétaire, Diane Lefrançois-Rogers, #410, 1000, rue Saint-Antoine ouest, Montréal, QC H3C 3R7, 514/866-7491, Téléc: 514/866-6303
Saskatchewan Command: Secretary, Brent G. Burns, 3079 - 5 Ave., Regina, SK S4T 0L6, 306/525-8739, Fax: 306/525-5023

### Royal Canadian Military Institute (RCMI) (1890)
426 University Ave., Toronto, ON M5G 1S9
416/597-0286, Fax: 416/597-6919
President, LCol. J.D. Gibson
Vice-President, Capt. Nicholas Stethem
Vice-President, LCol. E.B. Pinnington
General Manager, Norbert Luth
Publications: SITREP

### Royal Canadian Mounted Police Veterans' Association/Gendarmarie royale du Canada association des ancien (1924)
Dominion HQ Secretariat, 1200 Vanier Pkwy., Ottawa, ON K1A 0R2
613/993-6497, Fax: 613/993-4353
President, Keith Trail
Secretary, Frank Korycan
Treasurer, J.H. MacLaughlan
Chief Administrative Officer, K.E. Koch
Publications: Keeping in Touch

### Royal Canadian Naval Benevolent Fund (RCNBF) (1945)
PO Box 505, Stn B, Ottawa, ON K1P 5P6
613/996-5087, Fax: 613/236-8830
Sec.-Treas., L.F. Harrison
Eastern Committee: Secretary, René Cloutier, Canadian Forces Base Halifax, FMO Halifax, Halifax, NS B3K 2X0, 902/427-7825, Fax: 902/427-7824
Western Committee: Secretary, Don Ross, Canadian Forces Base Esquimalt, FMO Victoria, Victoria, BC V0S 1B0, 250/383-6264

### Veterans Against Nuclear Arms/Vétérans contre les armes nucléaires (VANA) (1982)
240 Holyrood Rd., North Vancouver, BC V7N 2R5
902/985-7147, Email: dmorgan@web.net
National President, David Morgan
Publications: VANA Update
Affiliates: Defence Research & Education Centre

## MINES & MINERAL RESOURCES

### The Asbestos Institute/Institut de l'amiante (1984)
#1750, 1002, rue Sherbrooke ouest, Montréal, QC H3A 3L6
514/844-3956, Fax: 514/844-1381, Email: ai@asbestos-institute.ca, URL: http://www.asbestos-institute.ca
Director General, Scott Houston
Publications: The Asbestos Institute

### Association of Exploration Geochemists (AEG) (1970)
72 Robertson Rd., PO Box 26099, Nepean, ON K2H 9R0
613/828-0199, Fax: 613/828-9288
President, William B. Coker
Business Manager, Betty Arseneault
Publications: Journal of Geochemical Exploration

### Association des mines d'amiante du Québec/Québec Asbestos Mining Association (AMAQ)
a/s Byers Casgrain, #3900, 1, Place Ville-Marie, Montréal, QC H3B 4M7
514/878-3711, Téléc: 514/866-2241
Directeur général, David McAuslad
Division protection de l'environnement: 4125, rue Garlock, Sherbrooke, QC J1L 1W9, 819/821-7633, Téléc: 819/821-7824

### Association of Mining Municipalities of Ontario
c/o Town of Kirkland Lake, PO Bag 1757, Kirkland Lake, ON P2N 3P4
705/567-9361, Fax: 705/567-3535
President, Joe Maurinac

### Association des prospecteurs du Québec/Québec Prospectors Association (APQ) (1975)
#203, 15 Gamble est, Rouyn-Noranda, QC J9X 3B6
819/762-1599, Téléc: 819/762-1522
Directrice générale, Chantal Patenaude
Publications: Bulletin

### Canadian Copper & Brass Development Association (1958)
#375, 10 Gateway Blvd., North York, ON M3C 3A1
416/421-0788, Fax: 416/421-8092
Executive Director, A. Arnold Knapp
President, G.N. White
Publications: Canadian Copper/Cuivre canadien
Affiliates: International Copper Association

### Canadian Institute of Mining, Metallurgy & Petroleum/Institut canadien des mines, de la métallurgie et du pétrole (CIM) (1898)
#1210, 3400, boul de Maisonneuve ouest, Montréal, QC H3Z 3B8
514/939-2710, Fax: 514/939-2714, URL: http://www.cim.org
Executive Director, Yvan Jacques
Publications: CIM Bulletin; Journal of Canadian Petroleum Technology, 10 pa; CIM Reporter, 3 pa; CIM Directory, a.; Canadian Metallurgical Quarterly

### Canadian Mineral Analysts/Analystes des minéraux canadiens (CMA) (1969)
PO Box 894, Lynn Lake, MB R0B 0W0
204/356-2902, Fax: 204/356-2902, URL: http://www.info-mine.com/assoc-inst/cma/
Managing Secretary, Sigrid Fast
Treasurer, Wes Johnson
Conference Chair, Marc Bisson
Publications: Alchemist's Digest

### Canadian Mining Contractors Association/Association des entrepreneurs miniers du Canada (1991)
1088 Staghorn Ct., Mississauga, ON L5C 3R2
905/279-0104, Fax: 905/279-1646, Email: bcampbell@istar.ca
President, Bruce Campbell

### The Coal Association of Canada/L'Association charbonnière canadienne (CAC) (1973)
#502, 205 - 9 Ave. SE, Calgary, AB T2G 0R3
403/262-1544, Fax: 403/265-7604, Toll Free: 1-800-910-2625, Email: showes@agt.net, URL: http://www.coal.ca
President, D.O. Downing
Publications: Canadian Coal

### International Council for Applied Mineralogy (ICAM) (1980)
c/o CANMET, 555 Booth St., Ottawa, ON K1A 0G1
613/992-1376, Fax: 613/996-9673
Canadian Representative, William Petruk
Chairman, S.A. de Waal
Publications: Proceedings Volume
Affiliates: National Mineralogical Association - USA, Australia, South Africa, Europe, Brazil, South America, Poland; International Mineralogical Association

### Mineralogical Association of Canada/Association minéralogique du Canada (MAC) (1957)
1460 Merivale Rd., PO Box 78087, RPO Merivale, Ottawa, ON K2E 1B1
613/226-4651, Fax: 613/226-4651
President, Dr. Roger Mitchell
Secretary, G.M. LeCheminant
Publications: MAC Newsletter; The Canadian Mineralogist, q.
Affiliates: International Mineralogical Association

### Mining Association of Canada/Association minière du Canada (MAC)
#1105, 350 Sparks St., Ottawa, ON K1R 7S8
613/233-9391, Fax: 613/233-8897, URL: http://www.mining.ca
President, Dr. C. George Miller

#### ASSOCIATION MINIÈRE DU QUÉBEC/QUÉBEC MINING ASSOCIATION (AMQ) (1936)
Place la Cité, #942, 2600, boul Laurier, Ste-Foy, QC G1V 4W2
418/657-2016, Téléc: 418/657-2154
Directeur général, Dan Tolgyesi
Secrétaire de direction, Lise Belisle
Publications: Filon de l'Association minière du Québec inc.

#### MINING ASSOCIATION OF BRITISH COLUMBIA (MABC)
840 West Hastings St., Vancouver, BC V6E 1C8
604/681-4321, Fax: 604/681-5305
Email: infodata@info-mine.com, URL: http://www.info-mine.com/assoc-inst/mabc/
President & CEO, Gary K. Livingstone

#### MINING ASSOCIATION OF MANITOBA INC. (1940)
#700, 305 Broadway Ave., Winnipeg, MB R3C 3J7
204/942-2789, Fax: 204/943-4371
Executive Vice-President, Ed Huebert

#### MINING ASSOCIATION OF NEWFOUNDLAND
c/o Iron Ore Company of Canada, PO Box 1000, Labrador City, NF A2V 2L8
709/944-8486, Fax: 709/944-8343
President, Reg Gagnon

#### MINING SOCIETY OF NOVA SCOTIA (1887)
88 Leeside Dr., Sydney, NS B1R 1S6
902/567-2147, Fax: 902/567-2147
Sec.-Treas., George Sigut
Affiliates: Canadian Institute of Mining, Metallurgy & Petroleum

#### NEW BRUNSWICK MINING ASSOCIATION/L'ASSOCIATION MINIÈRE DU NOUVEAU-BRUNSWICK
#104, 1133 St. George Blvd., Moncton, NB E1E 4E1
506/857-3056, Fax: 506/857-3059
Manager, Gerald R. Cluney

#### ONTARIO MINING ASSOCIATION (OMA)
#1501, 110 Yonge St., Toronto, ON M5C 1T4
416/364-9301, Fax: 416/364-5986
President, Patrick Reid
Publications: Mining in Ontario; Mining Matters, m.

#### SASKATCHEWAN MINING ASSOCIATION (1965)
1740 Avord Tower, 2002 Victoria Ave., Regina, SK S4P 0R7
306/757-9505, Fax: 306/569-1085
Executive Director, Robert M. Cunningham
President, Lorne Repka
Publications: Mining Issues; Mineral Scene, q.

### New Brunswick Prospectors & Developers Association
PO Box 1195, Bathurst, NB E2A 4H9
506/546-4779, Fax: 506/546-4088
President, Earnest Brooks, Bus: 506/548-2156

Secretary, Don Hoy, Bus: 506/548-2772, Fax: 506/546-2332
Affiliates: Prospectors & Developers Association of Canada

**Newfoundland & Labrador Explorationists (NALE) (1989)**
PO Box 23013, St. John's, NF A1B 4J9
709/747-4425, Fax: 709/747-4491
President, Peter Tallman
Affiliates: Canadian Mineral Industries Federation; Prospectors & Developers Association of Canada

**Prospectors & Developers Association of Canada/Association canadienne des prospecteurs & entrepreneurs (PDAC) (1932)**
34 King St. East, 9th Fl., Toronto, ON M5C 2X8
416/362-1969, Fax: 416/362-0101, Email: info@pdac.ca, URL: http://www.pdac.ca
Executive Director, Dr. Anthony Andrews
President, John B. Heslop
Publications: PDAC in Brief; Exploration & Development Highlights, a.; PDAC Communiqué, bi-m.
Affiliates: Mining Association of Canada

**MONUMENTS & SITES *see* HISTORY, HERITAGE, GENEALOGY**

**MOTOR LEAGUES *see* AUTOMOTIVE**

## MULTICULTURALISM

***see also* Culture**

**Affiliation of Multicultural Societies & Service Agencies of BC (AMSSA) (1977)**
385 South Boundary Rd., Vancouver, BC V5K 4S1
604/718-2777, Fax: 604/298-0747, Email: amssa@amssa.org, URL: http://www.amssa.org
Executive Director, Vera Radyo
President, Carmela Canino
Publications: Cultures West; Update Bulletin, q.

**Armenian National Committee of Canada (ANC)**
3401, rue Olivar-Asselin, Montréal, QC H4J 1L5
514/334-1299, Fax: 514/334-6853, Email: anc.canada@sympatico.ca
Executive Director, Asbed Avedissian
President, Dr. Girair Basmadjian
Publications: The Armenian Cause
Affiliates: Armenian National Federation

**Armenian National Federation (ANF)**
3401, rue Olivar-Asselin, Montréal, QC H4J 1L5
514/334-1299, Fax: 514/334-6853
President, Stepan Nadjarian
Affiliates: Armenian National Committee of Canada

**Association France-Canada Inc. (1948)**
11 Blythwood Gardens, Succ. A, Toronto, ON M4N 3L2
416/485-5044
Président, Pierre. Dionne
Publications: Bulletin de France-Canada
Organisation(s) affiliée(s): La Fédération canadienne France-Canada

**Association of Soviet Jewry in Canada (1980)**
#6, 5987 Bathurst St., North York, ON M2R 1Z3
416/229-6057, Fax: 416/229-2592
Coordinator, Ella Gurevich
President, Rudy Favelyukis
Affiliates: Jewish Foundation of Greater Toronto

**Association of United Ukrainian Canadians (AUUC) (1918)**
14615 - 124th Ave., Edmonton, AB T5L 3B2
416/455-8695, Fax: 416/453-2948, Info Line: 416/535-1063
National President, George Moskal
Publications: Ukrainian Canadian Herald

**Australia-New Zealand Association (ANZA) (1935)**
**The ANZA Club**
3 - 8th Ave. West, Vancouver, BC V5Y 1M8
604/876-7128, Fax: 604/872-0421
Manager, Paul Woodley
Publications: ANZA News

**B'nai Brith Canada (BBC)**
**Children of the Covenant**
15 Hove St., North York, ON M3H 4Y8
416/633-6224, Fax: 416/630-2159, URL: http://www.bnaibrith.ca
President, Lyle Smordin
Executive Vice-President, Frank Dimant
National Director, Field Services, Pearl Gladman
Publications: The Jewish Tribune; Annual Audit of Anti-Semitism, a.
Affiliates: B'nai Brith International
Midwestern Region: Regional Director, Sophie Tapper, 370 Hargrave St., Winnipeg, MB R3B 2K1, 204/942-2597, Fax: 204/956-2819
National Capital Region: Director, Government Relations, Ian J. Kagedan, 151 Chapel St., Ottawa, ON K1N 7Y2, 613/789-4922, Fax: 613/789-1325
Québec Region: Regional Director, Yechiel Glustein, #219, 6900, boul Decarie, Montréal, QC H3X 2T8, 514/733-5377, Fax: 514/342-9632
Western Region: 1607 - 90 Ave. SW, Calgary, AB T2V 4V7, 403/255-6554

**Baltic Federation in Canada**
4 Credit Union Dr., Toronto, ON M4A 2N8
416/755-2353, Fax: 416/755-1244
President, Viesturs Zarins

**ESTONIAN CENTRAL COUNCIL IN CANADA (1952)**
#308, 958 Broadview Ave., Toronto, ON M4K 2R6
416/465-2219, Fax: 416/461-0488
Secretary General, Peter P. Aruvald
President, Laas Leiviat
Publications: Estonian Central Council in Canada Newsletter

**LATVIAN NATIONAL FEDERATION IN CANADA**
4 Credit Union Dr., Toronto, ON M4A 2N8
416/755-2353, Fax: 416/755-1244
President, Ted Kronbertes

**THE LITHUANIAN CANADIAN COMMUNITY**
1011 College St., Toronto, ON M6H 1A8
416/533-3292, Fax: 416/533-2282
Executive Director, Darija Powell
President, Al Pacevious

**Bangladesh Awami League of Canada (1992)**
Parkview Towers, #1514, 2777 Kipling Ave., Etobicoke, ON M9V 4M2
416/742-3469, Fax: 416/742-9530, Email: fkhan@interlog.com, URL: http://www.interlog.com/~fkhan/; http://www.ica.net/pages/fkhan420
President, Farook H. Khan
Publications: Joy Bangla

**Belarusian Canadian Alliance (BCA) (1948)**
524 Clarens Ave., Toronto, ON M6H 3W7
416/530-1025, Fax: 416/267-0798
President, Mykolaj Ganko, Bus: 416/267-0798
Secretary, George Repetski, Bus: 905/564-3578
Publications: Info-BCA

**Belgo-Canadian Association (BCA) (1948)**
121 Chillery Ave., Scarborough, ON M1K 4T5
416/261-4603, 705/877-3072
President, Yvonne Kennedy
Publications: Newsletter

**Black Cultural Centre for Nova Scotia (1977)**
**Society for the Protection & Preservation of Black Culture in Nova Scotia**
1149 Main St., Dartmouth, NS B2Z 1A8
902/434-6223, URL: http://www.nstn.ca/bccns/bcc.html
President, Alma Johnston

**The Black Secretariat (1984)**
#202, 394A Euclid Ave., Toronto, ON M6G 2S9
416/924-1104, Fax: 416/924-3406
Chairperson, Enid Lee
Publications: Black Voices; The Black Directory, a.

**Canada-Israel Foundation for Academic Exchanges/Fondation Canada-Israel pour les échanges universitaires (CIFAE)**
255 Wychwood Park, London, ON N6A 3K7
519/661-3820
Academic Director, Alain Goldschlager, Email: agold@bosshog.arts.uwo.ca

**Canadian Arab Federation/Fédération Canado-Arabe (CAF) (1967)**
5298 Dundas St. West, Etobicoke, ON M9B 1B2
416/231-7524, Fax: 416/231-6850, Email: jehad@camnet.ca
Executive Director, Jehad Al-Tweiwi
President, Dr. John Asfour
Publications: Arab Canadian; CAF News, m.

**Canadian Centre for Jewish Community Studies/Centre canadien pour l'étude de la communauté juive (1980)**
**Jerusalem Centre for Public Affairs**
#414, 855, rue Sherbrooke ouest, Montréal, QC H3A 2T7
514/398-4806, Fax: 514/398-1770
President, Daniel J. Elazar
Director, Harold M. Waller

**The Canadian Doukhobor Society (CDS)**
RR#1, Site 2, CB4, Castlegar, BC V1N 3H7
250/365-5327, Fax: 250/365-5327
Sec.-Treas., Larry A.. Ewashen
Co-Chair, Alex A. Wishlow
Co-Chair, Ken P. Bonderoff
Publications: The Canadian Doukhobor Newsletter

**Canadian Ethnocultural Council/Conseil ethnoculturel du Canada (1980)**
#1100, 251 Laurier Ave. West, Ottawa, ON K1P 5J6
613/230-3867, Fax: 613/230-8051, Email: cec@web.net, URL: http://www.web.net/~cec/
Executive Director, Irene Kamchen
Publications: Ethno Canada

**Canadian Hispanic Congress**
#200, 1829 - 54 St. SE, Calgary, AB T2B 1N5
403/248-3457, Fax: 403/273-5100
Contact, Felix Mora

**Canadian Institute for Jewish Research/Institut canadien de recherche sur le Judaisme**
#550, 5250, boul Decarie, Montréal, QC H3X 2H9
514/486-5544, Fax: 514/488 3064
Director, Prof. Frederick Krantz
Publications: Israfax

**Canadian Jewish Congress/Congrès juif canadien (CJC) (1919)**
1590, av Docteur Penfield, Montréal, QC H3G 1C5

514/931-7531, Fax: 514/931-0548, Email: canadianjewishcongress@cjc.ca, URL: http://www.cjc.ca
National Executive Director, Jack Silverstone
President, Goldie Hershon
National Director of Communications, Michael J. Cohen
Publications: National Archives Newsletter; National Small Communities Newsletter; DAIS
Atlantic Jewish Community Council: Program Coordinator, John Goldberg, Lord Nelson Hotel, #305, 1515 South Park St., Halifax, NS B3J 2L2, 902/422-7491, Fax: 902/425-3722
Calgary Jewish Community Council: Executive Director, Joel Miller, 1607 - 90 Ave. SW, Calgary, AB T2V 4V7, 403/253-8600, Fax: 403/253-7915
Jewish Community Council of Ottawa: Executive Director, Stanley A. Urman, 151 Chapel St., Ottawa, ON K1N 7Y2, 613/789-7306, Fax: 613/789-4593
Jewish Federation of Edmonton: Chief Administrative Officer, Miriam Cooper, 7200 - 156 St., Edmonton, AB T5R 1X3, 403/487-0585, Fax: 403/481-1854
Ontario Region: Executive Director, Manuel Prutschi, 4600 Bathurst St., North York, ON M2R 3V2, 416/635-2883, ext.123, Fax: 416/635-1408
Pacific Region: Executive Director, Erwin Nest, 950 - 41st Ave. West, Vancouver, BC V5Z 2N7, 604/257-5101, Fax: 604/257-5131
Saskatchewan Region - Regina: Community Development Officer, Eileen Curtis, 4715 McTavish St., Regina, SK S4S 6H2, 306/569-8166, Fax: 306/352-3499
Saskatchewan Region - Saskatoon: Community Development Officer, Walter Gumprich, c/o Congregation Agudas Israel, 715 McKinnon Ave., Saskatoon, SK S7H 2G2, 306/343-7023, Fax: 306/374-7715
Winnipeg Jewish Community Council: Executive Director, Robert Freedman, #200, 370 Hargrave St., Winnipeg, MB R3B 2K1, 204/943-0406, Fax: 204/956-0609

**Canadian Latvian Business & Professional Association (CLBPA)**
123 Overland Dr., North York, ON M3C 2C7
416/444-5201, Fax: 416/444-5208
President, Alexander Budrevics
Publications: CLBPA Newsletter

**Canadian Polish Congress (CPC) (1944)**
Kongres Polonii Kanadyjskiej, 288 Roncesvalles Ave., Toronto, ON M6R 2M4
416/532-2876; 7197, Fax: 416/532-5730
Secretary General, Andrew Guzkowski
President, Marek Malicki
Executive Vice-President, Jan Kaszuba
Publications: Newsletter
Affiliates: Polonia of the Free World; Canadian Polish Research Institute; Adam Mickiewicz Foundation; Polish Combattants Association; Polish National Union

**Canadian Polish Society**
43 Facer St., St Catharines, ON L2M 5H4
905/937-1413
Financial Secretary, Teresa Spera

**Canadian Serbian National Committee (1965)**
One Secroft Cres., North York, ON M3N 1R5
416/663-3409; 769-7181, Fax: 416/604-8565
Contact, William Dyrovic
Publications: Fraternity Review

**Canadian Slavonic Association**
3431 av Mont-Royal est, Montréal, QC H1X 3H2
514/527-3720; 672-5262
National President, Gregoire Maksymiuk
Executive Director, Jean-Pierre Olinick

**Canadian Slovak League**
1736 Dundas St. West, Toronto, ON M6K 1V5
416/533-6924, Fax: 416/533-6924
Secretary, Helen Danko

**Canadian Tibetan Association of Ontario (1980)**
19 Collingwood St., Scarborough, ON M1S 1A4
416/298-0464, Fax: 416/240-2083
President, Rinchen Dakpa

**Canadian Zionist Federation/La fédération sioniste canadienne (CZF) (1967)**
#550, 5250, boul Decarie, Montréal, QC H3X 2H9
514/486-9526, Fax: 514/483-6392
National President, Kurt Rothschild
Affiliates: World Zionist Organization; Jewish Agency

**Caribbean Cultural Committee**
**Caribana**
#300, 474 Bathurst St., Toronto, ON M5J 2S6
416/925-5435, Fax: 416/925-1108
Contact, Rodney Davis

**Central Organization of Sudeten-German Clubs in Canada (1957)**
20 Banff Rd., Toronto, ON M4S 2V5
416/483-8240
President, Rolf Lorenz
Publications: Freund Schaft/Friendship

**Chinese Canadian Intercultural Association (1980)**
112 Huron St., Toronto, ON M5T 2B2
416/591-6347, Fax: 416/591-6347
Executive Director, Yiu-Kuen Chan
President, Mr. On-Po Sze

**Chinese Canadian National Council/Conseil national des canadiens chinois (CCNC) (1980)**
**Chinese Canadian National Council for Equality**
#605, 119 Spadina Ave., Toronto, ON M5V 2L1
416/977-9871, Fax: 416/977-1630, Email: ccncna@astral.magic.ca
Executive Director, Jonas Ma
Publications: Newsletter
Affiliates: Canadian Council for Refugees

**Clans & Scottish Societies of Canada (CASSOC) (1976)**
St. Andrews Church, 73 Simcoe St., Toronto, ON M5J 1W9
416/593-0518, Toll Free: 1-800-593-0518
Chairman, John H. MacDonald
Sec.-Treas., W. Neil Fraser
Publications: An Drochaid

**Congrès Hellenique du Québec**
a/s Centre Communautaire Grec, #211, 5777, rue Wilderton, Westmount, QC H3S 2V7
514/738-2421, Téléc: 514/340-3586
Directrice générale, Kalioki Hagiepepros

**Cypriot Federation of Canada**
1430 Ellice Ave., Winnipeg, MB R3G 0G4
204/774-4444, Fax: 204/774-2002
President, Costas Ataliotis

**Czech & Slovak Association of Canada (1939)**
740 Spadina Ave., Toronto, ON M5S 2J2
416/925-2241, Fax: 416/925-1940
Executive Director, Anna Otypka
President, Blanca Rohn
Publications: Vestnik

**Fédération des associations lao du Canada/ Federation of Lao Associations of Canada (FALC) (1987)**
833, rue Murdoch, Chicoutimi, QC G7H 3Z6
418/543-9960, Téléc: 418/545-5012, Courrier électronique: kmounivo@uqac.uquebec.ca
Président, Khamlay Mounivongs

**Federation of Cambodian Associations of Canada/Fédération des associations cambodgiennes du Canada**
PO Box 389, Stn Jean-Talon, Montréal, QC H1S 2G3
514/327-9129, Fax: 514/327-4940
Secretary General, Simon Yim

**Federation of Canada-China Friendship Associations**
2948 Scott St., Victoria, BC V8R 4J6
250/598-5962, Fax: 250/598-5962
President, Barbara Chen

**Federation of Canadian Turkish Associations (1985)**
660 Eglinton Ave. East, PO Box 50029, Toronto, ON M4G 4G1
416/480-0954, Fax: 416/480-0682
President, Demir Delen

**Federation of Chinese Canadian Professionals (Ontario)**
Market Village, Box 127, #A203, 4350 Steeles Ave. East, Markham, ON L3R 9V4
905/940-3227

**Federation of Chinese Canadian Professionals (Québec)/Fédération des professionnels chinois canadiens (Québec)**
1111, rue St-Urbain, #R16, Montréal, QC H2Z 1Y6
514/393-1071, Fax: 514/393-9709
President, Douglas Yip
Publications: Newsletter

**Federation of Danish Associations in Canada/ Fédération des associations danoises du Canada (1981)**
**The Danish Federation**
679 Eastvale Ct., Gloucester, ON K1J 6Z7
613/238-6464; 747-9764
President, Rolf Buschardt Christensen
Publications: Conference Book

**Federation of Italian Canadian Seniors Clubs**
Casa del Zotto, 3010 Dufferin St., Toronto, ON M6B 4J5
416/787-4340, Fax: 416/787-3745
Executive Director, Antonietta Gulli

**Federation of Russian Canadians (FRC) (1930)**
799 College St., Toronto, ON M6G 1C7
416/536-7330, Fax: 416/535-3265
Vice-President, Nita Miskevich
Secretary, Nicole Tichnovich
Treasurer, Emily Bradshaw
Publications: Vestnik
Affiliates: Association of Canadians of Russian Descent

**Federation of Scottish Clans in Nova Scotia**
6079 Compton Ave., Halifax, NS B3K 1E8
President, Fran Sutherland, Bus: 902/423-3095
Vice-President, Jean Watson, Bus: 902/864-8335

**Federation of Sikh Societies of Canada/ Fédération des sociétés Sikhs du Canada**
PO Box 91, Stn B, Ottawa, ON K1P 6C3
613/737-7296, Fax: 613/739-7153
President, Mohinder Singh Gosal

**Finnish Canadian Cultural Federation/Fédération culturelle finno-canadienne (1971)**
Kanadan Suomalainen Kultturiliitto, #1001, 470 Cambridge St. South, Ottawa, ON K1S 4H8

613/235-4216
President, Mauri A. Jalava
Affiliates: Finland Society, R.Y.; Finn Fest USA, Inc.

**Finnish Organization of Canada (1923)**
PO Box 65070, Toronto, ON M4K 3Z2
416/465-8981, Fax: 416/651-0236, Email: ejokinen@inforamp.net
President, Elsie Jokinen
Publications: KAIKU/ECHO

**Fondation de l'amitié libano-canadienne/Libano-Canadian Friendship Foundation (1988)**
82, rue de Paris, Dollard-des-Ormeaux, QC H9B 3E3
514/875-2033, Téléc: 514/685-5743
Président, Ayad Karkouti

**German-Canadian Congress/Congrès germano-canadien (GCC) (1985)**
DeutschKanadischer Kongress, 965 Richmond Rd., Ottawa, ON K2B 6R1
613/728-6850, Fax: 613/728-2875
Executive Director, Irene Kamchen
Publications: Kongressnachrichten; News...nouvelles...nachrichten, q.

**Goethe-Institut (Montréal)**
418, rue Sherbrooke est, Montréal, QC H2L 1J6
514/499-0159, Fax: 514/499-0905
Contact, Uwe Förster

**Goethe-Institut Toronto (1962)**
**German Cultural Centre**
163 King St. West, Toronto, ON M5H 4C6
416/593-5257, Fax: 416/593-5145, Email: goethetoront@cis.compuserve.com, URL: http://www.goethe.de/uk/tor
Director, Dr. Peter Hubrich
Administrator, Brigitte Furch

**Goethe-Institut/German Cultural Centre (Vancouver)**
944 - 8th Ave. West, Vancouver, BC V5Z 1E5
604/732-3966, Fax: 604/732-5062, URL: http://www.goethe.de/uk/van
Contact, Werner Wolf

**Hebrew Culture Organization of Canada (HCOC) (1949)**
#550, 5250, boul Décarie, Montréal, QC H3X 2H9
514/486-9526, Fax: 514/483-6392

**Holocaust Education & Memorial Centre of Toronto (HEMC) (1985)**
4600 Bathurst St., North York, ON M2R 3V2
416/631-5689, Fax: 416/635-0925, Email: pzilberman@feduja.org
Director, Pnina Zilberman
Publications: HEMC Newsletter

**Hungarian Canadian Federation**
840 St. Clair Ave. West, Toronto, ON M6C 1C1
416/654-4926

**Icelandic National League (INL)**
699 Carter Ave., Winnipeg, MB R3M 2C3
204/284-3402, Fax: 204/284-3870, URL: http://www.helix.net/~rasgeirs/
President, Laurence Johnson
Affiliates: INL USA; Icelandic International League

**Institut interculturel de Montréal/Intercultural Institute of Montréal (IIM) (1963)**
4917, rue St-Urbain, Montréal, QC H2T 2W1
514/288-7229, Téléc: 514/844-6800, Courrier électronique: andre_giguere@icmm.login.qc.ca
Présidente/Directrice générale, Kalpana Das
Président du C.A., Carlo Sterlin
Publications: Interculture; Babillard interculturel, mensuel

**Irish Canadian Cultural Association of New Brunswick (1983)**
109 Roy Ave., Miramichi, NB E1V 3N8
506/622-4007
President, Farrell McCarthy
Publications: The Shamrock Leaf

**Irish Freedom Association (IFA) (1981)**
PO Box 171, Stn F, Toronto, ON M4Y 2L5
416/778-7821
Secretary, Farha'd O'Neill
Chair, Rita Adams
Secretary, Michelle M'Sherry
Publications: The Harp
Affiliates: Québec Irlande (Montréal)

**Islamic Foundation of Toronto, Inc.**
441 Nugget Ave., Scarborough, ON M1S 5E1
416/321-0909, Fax: 416/321-1995

**Islamic Information Foundation (IIF) (1981)**
8 Laurel Lane, Halifax, NS B3M 2P6
902/445-2494, Fax: 902/445-2494
Chairperson, Jamal Badawi

**Italian Cultural Institute (1976)**
Istituto Italiano di Cultura, 496 Huron St., Toronto, ON M5R 2R3
416/921-3802, Fax: 416/962-2503, Email: iicto@italcultur.org, URL: http://www.iicto-ca.org
Director, Francesca Valente
Publications: News

**Jamaican Canadian Association (JCA)**
995 Arrow Rd., North York, ON M9M 2Z5
416/746-5772, Fax: 416/746-5772
Executive Director, Akwatu Khenti
Publications: In Focus
Affiliates: The Black Secretariat

**Japanese Canadian Citizens Association**
511 East Broadway, Vancouver, BC V5T 1X4
604/874-8187, Fax: 604/874-8164
President, Edward R. Ide

**Jewish Association for Development - Canada/Juifs associés pour le développement - Canada (JAD/Canada) (1987)**
151 Chapel St., Ottawa, ON K1N 7Y2
613/789-7306
President, Elaine Sigler
Vice-President, Dr. K. Hoffman
Sec.-Treas., Seymour Dubrow
Publications: JAD Report
Affiliates: American Jewish World Service

**The Jewish Federation of Greater Toronto (JFGT) (1917)**
4600 Bathurst St., North York, ON M2R 3V2
416/635-2883, Fax: 416/631-5715, URL: http://www.feduja.org/
Executive Director, Dr. Allan Reitzes
President, Sandra Brown

**Jewish National Fund of Canada**
#500, 1980, rue Sherbrooke ouest, Montréal, QC H3H 1E8
514/934-0313, Fax: 514/934-0382
Executive Vice-President, Avner Regev
Affiliates: World Zionist Organization

**Labor Zionist Alliance of Canada**
**Labor Zionist Movement of Canada**
#10, 7005, rue Kildare, Montréal, QC H4W 1C1
514/342-9710
Chairman, David Kofsky
Affiliates: World Labor Zionist Movement & Israel Labor Party
Central Region Office: Director, Hy Fogelman, 272 Codsell Ave., North York, ON M3H 3X2, 416/630-9444
Western Region Office: 1727 Main St., Winnipeg, MB R2V 1Z4

**Latin American Environment Group (LAENG) (1966)**
603 1/2 Parliament St., Toronto, ON M5S 2T2
416/966-4773, Fax: 416/921-0071, Email: laeng@web.net
Eduardo Geray
Roberta Rice
Adiro de Lopez
Publications: Eco-american Update
Affiliates: Canada-Latin America Resource Centre

**Lithuanian Canadian R.C. Cultural Society (1949)**
**Ziburiai - Lights of Homeland**
2185 Stavebank Rd., Mississauga, ON L5C 1T3
905/275-4672, Fax: 905/275-6755
President, Ramune Jonaitis
Editor, P. Gaida
Publications: Lights of Homeland

**Maltese Canadian Society of Toronto, Inc. (1922)**
3084 Dundas St. West, Toronto, ON M6P 1Z8
416/767-3645
Publications: Information Letter
Affiliates: Maltese-Canadian Federation Inc.

**Manitoba Intercultural Council Inc.**
#500, 283 Bannatyne Ave., Winnipeg, MB R3B 3B2
204/943-9196, Fax: 204/956-1137
President, Terry Prychitko
Administrative Secretary, Maria Bansee

**Manitoba Multicultural Resources Centre Inc. (MMRC) (1984)**
1910 Portage Ave., 2nd Fl., Winnipeg, MB R3J 0J2
204/831-6672, Fax: 204/986-3798, Email: mmrc@freenet.mb.ca
Chairperson, Betty Ann Watts
Vice-Chair, Beryle Jones
Treasurer, Alexa Saborowski
Secretary, Alissa Schacter
Publications: Ethnobank
Affiliates: Coalition for Human Equity

**Mizrachi-Hapoel Hamizrachi Organization of Canada**
296 Wilson Ave., North York, ON M3H 1S8
416/630-9266, Fax: 416/630-2305
National Executive Vice-President, Rabbi Menachem Gopin
Publications: Or Hamizrach
Montréal Regional Office: Director, Peter Berkovitch, #216, 5250, boul Decarie, Montréal, QC H3X 2H9, 514/483-3660, Fax: 514/483-6392

**Multicultural Association of Northwestern Ontario (MANWO) (1980)**
711 Victoria Ave. East, Thunder Bay, ON P7C 5X9
807/622-4666, Fax: 807/622-7271
Executive Director, Moffat S. Makuto
Resource Development Officer, Erika Rebernik
Publications: Regional Youth Council Newsletter; NWO Resource Directory, biennial

**Multicultural Association of Nova Scotia/Association multiculturelle de la Nouvelle-Écosse (MANS) (1975)**
#901, 1809 Barrington St., Halifax, NS B3J 3K8
902/423-6534, Fax: 902/422-0881, Email: multicul@fox.nstn.ca, URL: http://fox.nstn.ca/~multicul/

Executive Director, Barbara Campbell
President, Kulvinder Dhillon
Publications: Share News
Affiliates: Cultural Federations of Nova Scotia; Atlantic Multicultural Council

**Multicultural Council of Saskatchewan (MCoS) (1975)**
369 Park St., Regina, SK S4N 5B2
306/721-2767, Fax: 306/721-3342
General Manager, Wade F. Luzny
Publications: News Circular; Saskatchewan Multicultural Magazine, q.; Our Multicultural Wish, biennial
Affiliates: Saskatchewan Council of Cultural Organizations

**Multicultural History Society of Ontario (1976)**
43 Queen's Park Cres. East, Toronto, ON M5S 2C3
416/979-2973, Fax: 416/979-7947, Email: mhso.mail@utoronto.ca
Director & CEO, Prof. Paul R. Magocsi
Publications: Polyphony; Multicultural History Society of Ontario Newsletter

**Muslim Education & Welfare Foundation of Canada (MEWFC) (1987)**
Aljameeatul Islaameeyah Lit-Tarbeeya War-Riaayah (Canada), 2580 McGill St., Vancouver, BC V5K 1H1
604/255-9941, Fax: 604/255-9941
President, Shamim Ahmad Sambhali
Secretary, Syed E. Rehman
Treasurer, Basil Ahmad
Public Relations, Mohammed Akram Chaudhry
Properties, A.K. Ismail

**Muslim World League (1962)**
#1018, 191 The West Mall, Etobicoke, ON M9C 5K8
416/622-2184, Fax: 416/622-2618
Director, Dr. Arafat El-Ashi

**National Association of Canadians of Origin in India (NACOI) (1976)**
PO Box 2308, Stn D, Ottawa, ON K1P 5W5
613/235-7343, Fax: 613/567-0655
Executive Director, Harbans Singh
Publications: Forum

**National Association of Japanese Canadians (NAJC) (1947)**
404 Webb Pl., Winnipeg, MB R3B 3J4
204/943-2910, Fax: 204/947-3145, Email: najcwpg@istar.ca
President, Randy Enomoto
Administrative Assistant, Sean Brygidyr
Publications: Nikkei Voice
Affiliates: Canadian Ethnocultural Council; Canadian Council for Refugees; National Capital Alliance on Race Relations

**National Congress of Italian Canadians/Congrès national des italo-canadiens (NCIC) (1974)**
#7584, 9e av, Montréal, QC H2A 3C3
514/721-6182, Fax: 514/721-5097
Executive Director, Laura Del Bosco
President, Art Bossio
Publications: Il Congresso Nazionale

**National Council of Ghanaian-Canadians (NCGC)**
925 Albion Rd., Etobicoke, ON M9V 1A5
416/740-5554
President, Charles Agyei-Amoama

**National Council of Trinidad & Tobago Organizations in Canada (NCTTOC) (1983)**
#1, 66 Oakmeadow Blvd., Scarborough, ON M1E 4G5
416/283-9672, Fax: 416/283-9672
President, Emmanuel J. Dick
Publications: NCTTOC News

**National Federation of Pakistani Canadians Inc. (NFPC) (1982)**
#1100, 251 Laurier Ave. West, Ottawa, ON K1P 5J6
613/232-5346, Fax: 613/232-6607
Executive Director, Talat Ali
President, Ali Khan
Treasurer, Naki Chaudhary
Publications: NFPC Newsletter

**New Brunswick Multicultural Council/Conseil Multiculturel du Nouveau-Brunswick (NBMC) (1983)**
374 St. George St., Moncton, NB E1C 1X2
506/853-0013, Fax: 506/857-9430
Executive Director, Cynthia Black
Publications: NBMC Newsletter
Affiliates: Atlantic Multicultural Council; Canadian Federation of Multicultural Councils

**Ontario Korean Businessmen's Association (1973)**
One Mobile Dr., North York, ON M4A 1H5
416/285-1100, Fax: 416/285-1103
Administrator, Sam Chung
Publications: KBA News
Affiliates: Ontario Korean Businessmen's Association Cooperative

**Ontario Multicultural Association (OMAMO) (1983)**
#0116, 65 Front St. West, PO Box 137, Toronto, ON M5J 1E6
416/696-9071, Fax: 416/696-8706
President, Dr. Keith Lowe
Affiliates: Canadian Council for Multicultural & Intercultural Education

**ORT Canada (1944)**
**Organization for Educational Resources & Technological Training**
#208, 5165, rue Sherbrooke ouest, Montréal, QC H4A 1T6
514/481-2787, Fax: 514/481-4119
National President, Dr. Mel Schwartz
Publications: ORT Reporter
Affiliates: World ORT Union
Toronto: National Executive Director, Diane Uslaner; National Administrative Coordinator, Sandy Stern, #604, 3101 Bathurst St., Toronto, ON M6A 2A6, 416/787-0339, Fax: 416/787-9420

**Pan-Macedonian Association (1960)**
406 Danforth Ave., Toronto, ON M4K 1P3
416/297-9530
President, Dr. Basil Solkaridis
Secretary, Alec Kalasatis

**Polish Alliance of Canada**
1640 Bloor St. West, Toronto, ON M6P 4A8
416/531-4826

**Polonia Przyszlosci - Polonia for the Future (1996)**
**Polish Society in Canada**
215 Roncesvalles Ave., Toronto, ON M6R 2L6
416/531-3230, Fax: 416/531-3245, Email: severyn@idirect.com, URL: http://www.pol-net.com/polonia/
President, Zbigniew Belz
Vice-President, Dariusz Lempkowski, Fax: 416/245-5695
Vice-President, Jan Szarycz, Bus: 416/621-4779

**Progressive Pakistan Canadian Friendship Society (1992)**
4944 Joyce St., Vancouver, BC V5R 4G6
604/433-1859, Fax: 604/433-1859
President, M.Z. Khan
Affiliates: Vancouver Multicultural Society

**Romanian World Congress**
170 Garden Ave., Richmond Hill, ON L4C 6M2
905/889-8228, Fax: 905/881-8552
President, Tudor Bompa, Ph.D.
Publications: Stindardul Romanilor

**Russian Canadian Cultural Aid Society**
91 Kersdale Ave., Toronto, ON M6M 1E4
416/653-1361
President, Victor Popov

**Slavic Congress of Canada (1989)**
9 Helene St. South, Mississauga, ON L5G 3A8
905/278-3996, Fax: 905/278-3996
President, W. Strok

**Slovak Canadian National Council/Conseil national des slovaques canadiens**
#210, 50 MacIntosh Dr., Markham, ON L3R 9T3
905/513-1215, Fax: 905/513-1215
President, Margaret A. Dvorsky

**Slovak Heritage & Cultural Society of British Columbia (1990)**
3804 Yale St., Burnaby, BC V5C 1P6
604/291-8065, Fax: 604/291-1966, Email: vlinder@direct.ca
Chairperson, Vladimir Linder
Publications: Slovak Heritage Live

**Slovenian Christian Democratic Association of Canada (1965)**
251 Golfdale Rd., Toronto, ON M4N 2C2
416/488-3381, Fax: 416/486-2320
President, Peter Klopchic
Affiliates: International Union of Christian Democratic Parties; European Union of Christian Democratic Parties

**South Pacific Peoples Foundation of Canada (SPPF) (1975)**
1921 Fernwood Rd., Victoria, BC V8T 2Y6
250/381-4131, Fax: 250/388-5258, Email: sppf@sppf.org
Executive Director, Stuart Wulff
Publications: Tok Blong Pasifik
Affiliates: Nuclear Free & Independent Pacific Movement

**Toronto Jewish Historical Society (1948)**
402 Richview Ave., Toronto, ON M5P 3G6
416/486-7856
President, Dr. Gordon Kerbel

**Ukrainian Canadian Congress/Congrès des ukrainiens-canadiens (UCC) (1940)**
456 Main St., Winnipeg, MB R3B 1B6
204/942-4627, Fax: 204/947-3882, Email: ucc_hg@mbnet.mb.ca
Executive Director, Lydia Hawryshkiw
President, W. Oleh Romaniw, QC
Director of Public Relations, Ihor Shawarsky
Publications: The Bulletin; Congress Report, triennial
Affiliates: Ukrainian Catholic Brotherhood; Ukrainian Self-Reliance Association (Orthodox); Ukrainian National Federation; League of Ukrainian Canadians; Ukrainian Canadian Professional & Business Federation

**Ukrainian Canadian Research & Documentation Centre/Centre Canadien-Ukrainien de Recherches et de Documentation (1986)**
#200, 620 Spadina Ave., Toronto, ON M5S 2H4
416/966-1819, Fax: 416/966-1820
Executive Director, Andrew Gregorovich

President, Wasyl Janischewskyj
Publications: Visnyk Bulletin

### Ukrainian Canadian Research Foundation (1965)
4 Island View Blvd., Toronto, ON M8V 2P4
416/255-9090
President, S.T. Pawluk

### Ukrainian National Aid Association
140 Bathurst St., Toronto, ON M5V 2R3
416/703-0687, Fax: 416/703-0687
Contact, Walter Okipniuk

### Ukrainian National Association
Canadian Office, 18 Leland Ave., Toronto, ON M8Z 2X5
416/231-4685
Chief Agent, Yaroslava Zorych

### United Israel Appeal of Canada (1967)
UIA of Canada
#315, 4600 Bathurst St., North York, ON M2R 3V2
416/636-7655, Fax: 416/636-9897, Email: uiacan@cjf.noli.com
Executive Vice-President, Steven Ain

### Urban Alliance on Race Relations (UARR) (1975)
#202, 675 King St. West, Toronto, ON M5V 1M9
416/703-6607, Fax: 416/703-4415, Email: ashelton@uarr.org, URL: http://www.uarr.org
Executive Director, Antoni Shelton
Publications: Currents

### Vietnamese Canadian Federation/Fédération vietnamienne du Canada (1980)
249 Rochester St., Ottawa, ON K1R 7M9
613/230-8282, Fax: 613/230-8282, Email: vcf@comnet.ca
Executive Director, Diep Trinh
President, Vinh Q. Tang
Treasurer, Hoa Luong
Publications: Lien Hoi; Vietnamese Associations in Canada, a.; Bulletin, bi-m.
Affiliates: Canadian Ethnocultural Council

**MUSEUMS *see* GALLERIES & MUSEUMS**

**MUSIC FESTIVALS *see* EVENTS**

## NATIVE PEOPLES

### 2-Spirited People of the First Nations (TPFN) (1989)
#1419, 2 Carlton St., Toronto, ON M5B 1J3
416/944-9300, Fax: 416/944-8381
President, Board of Directors, Sue Lamure
Publications: The Sacred Fire

### Aboriginal Nurses Association of Canada/Association des infirmières et infirmiers autochtones du Canada (ANAC) (1974)
192 Bank St., Ottawa, ON K2P 1W8
613/236-3373, Fax: 613/236-3599
Executive Director, Serge Pesant
President, Lea Bill
Vice-President, Marsha Forrest
Sec.-Treas., Deborah Greyeyes
Publications: The Aboriginal Nurse
Affiliates: Health Canada; Canadian Nurses Association

### Aboriginal People's Business Association (APBA) (1985)
Centre for Native Small Business, #680, 1155 Georgia St. West, Vancouver, BC V6E 3H4
604/687-7166, Fax: 604/687-5519
Executive Director, David Anderson
Publications: The Native Entrepreneur

### Aboriginal Urban Alliance of Ontario (1990)
College Park, 444 Yonge St., PO Box 46035, Toronto, ON M5B 2L8
416/923-6453
Vice-President, Michael Cheena

### Assembly of First Nations/Assemblée des Premières Nations (AFN)
One Nicholas St., 10th Fl., Ottawa, ON K1N 7B7
613/241-6789, Fax: 613/241-5808, URL: http://www.afn.ca
Senior Manager, Special Projects, Gina Whiteduck, Email: ginaw@afn.ca
Media & Communications, Jean Larose, Email: jlarose@afn.ca
Biodiversity, Alexandra McGregor, Email: mcgregoa@afn.ca
Head Office: Territory of Akwesasne, Hamilton's Island, Summerstown, ON K0C 2E0, 613/241-6789, Fax: 613/241-5808

### Assembly of Manitoba Chiefs
260 St. Mary Ave., 2nd Fl., Winnipeg, MB R3C 0M6
204/956-0610, Fax: 204/956-2109
Grand Chief, Phil Fontaine
Affiliates: Assembly of First Nations

### Association of Iroquois & Allied Indians
Onyota'A:Ka, RR#2, Southwold, ON N0L 2G0
519/652-3251, Fax: 519/652-9287
Chief Doug Maracle

### Association for Native Development in the Performing & Visual Arts (ANDPVA) (1974)
39 Spadina Rd., 2nd Fl., Toronto, ON M5R 2S9
416/972-0871, Fax: 416/972-0892
Executive Director, Shelley Charles
Publications: Newsletter

### Canadian Aboriginal Science & Engineering Association (1993)
22 College St., 2nd Fl., Toronto, ON M5G 1K2
416/972-0212, Fax: 416/972-0217
Contact, M. Dewasha

### Canadian Alliance in Solidarity with the Native Peoples (CASNP) (1960)
39 Spadina Rd., PO Box 574, Stn P, Toronto, ON M5R 2S9
416/972-1573, Fax: 416/972-6232, Email: casnp@pathcom.com, URL: http://www.pathcom.com/~casnp/
National Coordinator, Jay Mason
Office Manager, Kay Murphy
Publications: The Phoenix

### Canadian Council for Aboriginal Business/Conseil canadien pour le commerce autochtone (CCAB) (1984)
204 Saint George St., 2nd Fl., Toronto, ON M5R 2N5
416/961-8663, Fax: 416/961-3995, Toll Free: 1-800-465-7078
Executive Director, Brenda Maracle-O'Toole
National Director, Internship, Jason Thibault
Publications: Contact
Affiliates: Foundation for the Advancement of Aboriginal Youth

### Canadian Native Arts Foundation/Fondation canadienne des arts autochtones (CNAF) (1985)
#508, 77 Mowat Ave., Toronto, ON M6K 3E3
416/588-3328, Fax: 416/588-9198
Founder/President, John Kim Bell

### Canadian Native Friendship Centre (CNFC) (1962)
11205 - 101 St. NW, Edmonton, AB T5G 2A4
403/479-1999, Fax: 403/479-0043
Executive Director, Donna Woodward
Publications: Edmonton Native News

### Chiefs of Ontario
22 College St., 2nd Fl., Toronto, ON M5G 1K2
416/972-0212, Fax: 416/972-0217
Ontario Regional Chief, Gordon B. Peters
Affiliates: Assembly of First Nations

### Congress of Aboriginal Peoples/Congrès des Peuples Autochtones
65 Bank St., 4th Fl., Ottawa, ON K1P 5N2
613/238-3511, Fax: 613/230-6273
President, Harry W. Daniels
Vice-President, Frank Palmater

#### ALLIANCE AUTOCHTONE DU QUÉBEC INC./NATIVE ALLIANCE OF QUÉBEC INC.
21, rue Brodeur, Hull, QC J8Y 2P6
819/770-7763, Téléc: 819/770-7764
Président & Grand Chief, Fern Chalifoux

#### THE COUNCIL OF YUKON FIRST NATIONS (CYI)
11 Nisutlin Dr., Whitehorse, YT Y1A 3S4
867/667-7631, Fax: 867/668-6577
Grand Chief, Shirley Adamson

#### FEDERATION OF NEWFOUNDLAND INDIANS
PO Box 956, Corner Brook, NF A2H 6J3
709/634-0996, Fax: 709/634-0997
President, Brendan Sheppard

#### INDIAN COUNCIL OF FIRST NATIONS OF MANITOBA, INC.
PO Box 2857, The Pas, MB R9A 1M6
204/623-7227, Fax: 204/623-4041
Grand Chief, Andrew Kirkness

#### LABRADOR METIS ASSOCIATION
PO Box 2164, Stn B, Happy Valley-Goose Bay, NF A0P 1E0
709/896-0592, Fax: 709/896-0594
President, Todd Russell

#### METIS NATION NORTHWEST TERRITORIES
PO Box 1375, Yellowknife, NT X1A 2P1
867/873-3505, Fax: 867/873-3395
President, Gary Bohnet
Vice-President, Michael Paulette

#### NATIVE COUNCIL OF CANADA (ALBERTA) (1984)
#45, 10350 - 124 St., PO Box 14, Edmonton, AB T5N 1R6
403/917-1203, Fax: 403/488-2741
President, Doris Ronnenberg
Publications: Aboriginal Women
Affiliates: Aboriginal Trappers Federation of Canada

#### NATIVE COUNCIL OF NOVA SCOTIA (NCNS) (1975)
324 Abenaki Rd., PO Box 1320, Truro, NS B2N 5N2
902/895-1524, 1525, Fax: 902/895-0024, Toll Free: 1-800-565-4372
Email: ncns@atcon.com
Administrator/Supervisor, Lee Paul
Financial Comptroller, Heather Joudrie
Director, RNH Housing, Mike Martin
Director, Education, Spencer Wilmot
APTEC Program Manager, Paul Marr
CHIP Co-ordinator, Donna Gillis
Prenatal Facilitator, April Hiltz
Wildlife Management, Tim Martin
Director, Youth Program, Bernadette Sylliboy
Housing Commission, Sidney Peters
Publications: NCNS Newsletter

#### NATIVE COUNCIL OF PRINCE EDWARD ISLAND
33 Allen St., Charlottetown, PE C1A 3B9

902/892-5314, Fax: 902/368-7464
President & Chief, Graham Tuplin
Vice-President, Josephine MacLean
Publications: Our People/Gigmanag

**NEW BRUNSWICK ABORIGINAL PEOPLES COUNCIL (NBAPC) (1972)**
320 St. Mary's St., Fredericton, NB E3A 2S4
506/458-8422, 8423, Fax: 506/451-6130
Email: nbapc@nbnet.ca
President, Sandra Splude
Vice-President, Betty-Ann Lavellee
Publications: Mal-I-Mic News

**ONTARIO METIS ABORIGINAL ASSOCIATION (OMAA) (1971)**
452 Albert St. East, 2nd Fl., Sault Ste Marie, ON P6A 2J8
705/946-5900, Fax: 705/946-1161, Toll Free: 1-800-461-5112
Email: rhaggart@omaa.org, URL: http://www.omaa.org
President, Michael McGuire
1st Vice-President, Henry Wetelainen
2nd Vice-President, Lorraine Gisborn
Publications: In Touch

**UNITED NATIVE NATIONS**
Regional Head Office, 736 Granville St., 8th Fl., Vancouver, BC V6Z 1G3
604/688-1821, Fax: 604/688-1823
President, Viola Thomas
Vice-President, Scott Clark

### Federation of Saskatchewan Indians
Executive Office, 109 Hodsman Rd., Regina, SK S4N 5W5
306/721-2822, Fax: 306/775-2994
Secretary/Receptionist, Sherry Andrews

### Grand Council of the Crees/Grand Conseil des Cris
2, rue Lakeshore, Nemaska, Némiscau, QC J0Y 3B0
819/673-2600, Fax: 819/673-2606
Grand Chief, Matthew Coon-Come

### Indian Association of Alberta
Head Office, Stoney Plain Reserve, PO Box 516, Winterburn, AB T0E 2N0
403/470-5751, Fax: 403/470-3077

### International Native Arts Festivals Association (INAF) (1989)
PO Box 502, Stn M, Calgary, AB T2P 2J1
403/233-0022, Fax: 403/233-7681
Executive Director, Maria Donato

### Inuit Art Foundation/Fondation d'Art Inuit (IAF) (1985)
2081 Merivale Rd., Nepean, ON K2G 1G9
613/224-8189, Fax: 613/224-2907, Email: iaf@inuitart.org, URL: http://www.inuitart.org
Executive Director, Marybelle Mitchell
President, Mattiusi Iyaituk
Publications: Inuit Art Quarterly

### Inuit Tapirisat of Canada (1971)
#510, 170 Laurier Ave. West, Ottawa, ON K1P 5V5
613/238-8181, Fax: 613/234-1991, Telex: 053-3517, Email: itc@magi.com
President, Mary Sillett

### Labrador Inuit Association
PO Box 70, Nain, NF A0P 1L0
709/922-2942, Fax: 709/922-2931
President, William Barber

### Makivik Corporation/Société Makivik (1978)
PO Box 179, Kuujjuaq, QC J0M 1C0
819/964-2925, Fax: 819/964-2613, URL: http://www.accent.net/adst/MakWeb/Index.html
President, Zebedee Nungak
Treasurer, Pita Aatami
Secretary, Sheila Watt-Cloot
Publications: Makivik News

### Manitoba Indian Cultural Education Centre (MICEC) (1995)
Branch Office, 119 Sutherland Ave., Winnipeg, MB R2W 3C9
204/942-0228, Fax: 204/947-6564, URL: http://www.schoolnet.ca/ext/aboriginal/micec/index.html
Executive Director, Dennis Daniels
Publications: MICEC Newsletter

### Manitoba Métis Federation/Fédération des Métis du Manitoba
Head Office, 408 McGregor St., Winnipeg, MB R2W 4X5
204/586-8474, Téléc: 204/947-1816
President, Billyjo DeLaRonde
Publications: Le Métis
Organisation(s) affiliée(s): Métis National Council

### Metis Nation of Alberta
13140 St. Albert Trail, Edmonton, AB T5L 4R8
403/455-2200, Fax: 403/452-8946
Acting President, Lyle Donald

### Métis Nation in BC
126 Braelyn Cres., Penticton, BC V2A 6V3
250/493-8090, Fax: 250/493-3082
Spokesperson, Rick Poitras
Affiliates: Métis National Council

### Métis Nation of Ontario
193 Holland Ave., Ottawa, ON K1Y 0Y3
613/798-1488, Fax: 613/722-4225
President, Tony Belcourt
Chairman, Ronald E. Swain
Affiliates: Métis National Council

### Métis Nation of Saskatchewan
219 Robin Cres., 2nd Fl., Saskatoon, SK S7L 6M8
306/343-8285, Fax: 306/343-0171
President, Jim Durocher
Affiliates: Métis National Council

### Métis National Council/Ralliement national des Métis (MNC) (1983)
#310, 50 O'Connor St., Ottawa, ON K1P 6L2
613/232-3216, Fax: 613/232-4262
CEO, Gerald Morin

### Métis National Council of Women (MNCW) (1992)
#600, 99 Bank St., Ottawa, ON K1P 6B9
613/566-7022, Fax: 613/233-9527
President, Shelia Genaille

### Metis Settlements General Council
**Alberta Federation of Metis Settlement Associations**
Mayfield Business Centre, 10525 - 170 St., Edmonton, AB T5P 4W2
403/427-1122, Fax: 403/489-9558
Executive Director, Thomas Droege

### National Association of Friendship Centres/Association nationale des centres d'amitié (NAFC) (1971)
#204, 396 Cooper St., Ottawa, ON K2P 2H7
613/563-4844, Fax: 613/594-3428
Executive Director, Terry Doxtator
Office Manager, Gary Peters

**ABORIGINAL FRIENDSHIP CENTRES OF SASKATCHEWAN**
1440 Scarth St., Regina, SK S4R 2E9
306/525-5469, Fax: 306/525-3005
President, Sharon Ironstar

**ALBERTA NATIVE FRIENDSHIP CENTRES ASSOCIATION (ANFCA)**
#1102, 10025 - 106 St., Edmonton, AB T5M 1R1
403/423-3138, Fax: 403/425-6227
Email: anfca@nativecentres.org, URL: http://www.nativecentres.org
Coordinator, Raymond Chambers
President, Berv Martin

**BRITISH COLUMBIA ASSOCIATION OF INDIAN FRIENDSHIP CENTRES**
#3, 2475 Mount Newton, Saanichton, BC V0S 1M0
250/652-0210, Fax: 250/652-3102
Coordinator, Florence Wylie
President, Marie Anderson

**FREDERICTON NATIVE FRIENDSHIP CENTRE (FNFC) (1986)**
266 Douglas Ave., Fredericton, NB E3A 2N7
506/459-5283, Fax: 506/459-1756
Executive Director, Phil Fraser
President, Duane Pluss
Publications: Mocassin Telegraph

**MANITOBA ASSOCIATION OF FRIENDSHIP CENTRES**
PO Box 716, Winnipeg, MB R3C 2K3
204/256-7443, Fax: 204/254-3834
Coordinator, Grace Buhr
President, David Chartrand

**MICMAC NATIVE FRIENDSHIP CENTRE (1973)**
2158 Gottingen St., Halifax, NS B3K 3B4
902/420-1576, Fax: 902/423-6130
Executive Director, Gordon King

**NORTHWEST TERRITORIES COUNCIL OF FRIENDSHIP CENTRES**
PO Box 470, Fort Simpson, NT X0E 0N0
867/695-2577, Fax: 867/695-2141
Secretary, Hilda Antoine

**ONTARIO FEDERATION OF INDIAN FRIENDSHIP CENTRES**
290 Shuter St., Toronto, ON M5A 1W7
416/956-7575, Fax: 416/956-7577
Executive Director, Sylvia Maracle
President, Vera Pawis-Tabobondung

**REGROUPEMENT DES CENTRES D'AMITIÉ AUTOCHTONES DU QUÉBEC (RCAAQ) (1976)**
225, rue Max-Gros-Louis, Village-des-Hurons, QC G0A 4V0
418/842-6354, Téléc: 418/842-9795
Directeur, Raymond Picard
Présidente, Edith Cloutier

### Native Alcoholism Council of Manitoba
160 Salter St., Winnipeg, MB R2W 4K1
204/586-8395, Fax: 204/589-3921
Executive Director, Bertha Fontaine
Supervisor/Outreach, Berry Fontaine
Supervisor/Rehab, Elizabeth Fontaine

### Native Business Institute of Canada (NBI)
#101, 2055 Carling Ave., Ottawa, ON K2A 1G6
613/761-9734, Fax: 613/725-9031
Executive Director, Frank Craddock
Program Manager, Dorothy McCue

### Native Counselling Services of Alberta (NCSA) (1970)
#208, 324 - 7 St. South, Lethbridge, AB T1J 2G2
403/423-2141, Fax: 403/380-2562, Email: ncsa@mail.compusmart.ab.ca, URL: http://www.compusmart.ab.ca/ncsa/home.html
Executive Director, Allen Benson

### Native Investment & Trade Association (NITA) (1989)
#410, 890 West Pender St., Vancouver, BC V6C 1J9

604/684-0880, Fax: 604/684-0881, Toll Free: 1-888-684-0881, Email: nita@express.ca, URL: http://www.native-invest-trade.com
President, Calvin Helin

### Native Women's Association of Canada (NWAC)
9 Melrose Ave., Ottawa, ON K1Y 1T8
613/722-3033, Fax: 613/722-7687

#### ABORIGINAL WOMEN'S COUNCIL OF SASKATCHEWAN (1972)
#101, 118 - 12th St. East, Prince Albert, SK S6V 1B6
306/763-6005, Fax: 306/922-6034
Provincial Coordinator, Julie Pitzel
Accountant, Gail Lamb

#### FEMMES AUTOCHTONES DU QUÉBEC INC./QUÉBEC NATIVE WOMEN'S ASSOCIATION INC.
#204, 1450, rue City Councillors, Montréal, QC H3A 2E5
514/844-9618, Téléc: 514/844-2108
Directrice générale, Beverly Sabourin

#### INDIGENOUS WOMEN'S COLLECTIVE OF MANITOBA
#120, 388 Donald St., Winnipeg, MB R3B 2J4
204/944-8709, Fax: 204/949-1336

#### LABRADOR NATIVE WOMEN'S ASSOCIATION
PO Box 516, Stn B, Happy Valley-Goose Bay, NF A0P 1E0
709/896-2125

#### NATIVE WOMEN'S ASSOCIATION OF THE NWT
PO Box 2321, Yellowknife, NT X1A 2P7
867/873-5509, Fax: 867/873-3152
Interim Executive Director, Bren Kolson

#### NEW BRUNSWICK NATIVE INDIAN WOMEN'S COUNCIL
Victoria Health Centre, 65 Brunswick St., Fredericton, NB E3B 1G5
506/458-1114, Fax: 506/451-9386

#### NOVA SCOTIA NATIVE WOMEN'S ASSOCIATION
PO Box 805, Truro, NS B2N 5E8
902/893-7402
President, Clara Gloade

#### ONTARIO NATIVE WOMEN'S ASSOCIATION (1972)
RR#4, Site 7, Comp. 144, Thunder Bay, ON P7C 4Z2
807/623-3442, Fax: 807/623-1104
Executive Director, Madeline Beardy
President, Shirley Salt

#### YUKON INDIAN WOMEN'S ASSOCIATION
11 Nisutlin Dr., Whitehorse, YT Y1A 3S4
867/667-6162, Fax: 867/668-7539
President, Linda MacDonald

### Ontario Native Council on Justice (ONCJ) (1977)
#1305, 2 Carleton St., Toronto, ON M5B 1J3
416/592-1393, Fax: 416/592-1394
Executive Director, Carol Montagnes
Publications: Council News

### The Pacific Metis Federation
225 Vancouver Ave., Nanaimo, BC V9S 4E9
250/753-6616, Fax: 250/753-8671

### Saskatchewan Indian Cultural Centre (1972)
120 - 33rd St. East, Saskatoon, SK S7K 0S2
306/244-1146, Fax: 306/665-6520, Email: sicc@sk.sympatico.ca, URL: http://www.lights.com/sicc/
Director, Jim Bruce

### Union of British Columbia Indian Chiefs (1969)
342 Water St., 5th Fl., Vancouver, BC V6B 1B6
604/602-9555, Fax: 604/684-5726, URL: http://www.indigenous.bc.ca
President/Chief, Saul Terry
Publications: Union of BC Indian Chiefs Newsletter

### Union of New Brunswick Indians
#105, 565 Priestman St., Fredericton, NB E3B 5X8
506/458-9444, Fax: 506/458-2850
Chief, Roger Augustine

### Union of Nova Scotia Indians
111 Membertou St., PO Box 961, Sydney, NS B1P 6J4
902/539-4107, Fax: 902/564-2137
Sec.-Treas., Carl Gould

### Union of Ontario Indians (UOI)
**Anishinabek**
Nipissing First Nation, PO Box 711, North Bay, ON P1B 8J8
705/497-9127, Fax: 705/497-9135
Grand Council Chief, Joe Hare
Deputy Grand Chief, Vernon Roote
Publications: Anishinabek News

### Woodland Cultural Centre (WCC) (1972)
184 Mohawk St., PO Box 1506, Brantford, ON N3T 5V6
519/759-2650, Fax: 519/759-8912, Email: woodland@worldchat.com, URL: http://www.ciphermedia.com/WOODLAND/MM.HTML
Executive Director, Joanna Bedard

## NATURALISTS
*see also* Environmental

### Avicultural Advancement Council of Canada (AACC) (1972)
PO Box 5126, Stn B, Victoria, BC V8R 6N4
250/477-9982, Fax: 250/477-9935, Email: aacc@islandnet.com, URL: http://www.islandnet.com/~aacc
Executive Director, Doreen E. Albion
President, Dunstan H. Browne, Email: browne@islandnet.com
Editor & Membership, Mark S. Curtis, Email: chemmark@islandnet.com
Publications: The Avicultural Journal
Affiliates: American Singer Canary Club of Canada; Association des amateurs d'oiseaux de la Maurice; Association des éléveurs d'oiseaux de Montréal; BC Avicultural Society; BC Exotic Bird Society; Budgerigar & Foreign Bird Society; Cage Bird Society of Hamilton; Calgary Canary Club; Canadian Dove Association; Canadian Gloster Club; Cowichan Valley & Upper Island Cage Bird Club; Durham Avicultural Society; Edmonton Avicultural Association; Essex-Kent Cage Bird Society; Feather Fanciers Club; Golden Triangle Parrot Club; Kamloops Aviculturalist Society; London & District Cage Bird Society; Manitoba Canary & Finch Club; Mid Island Exotic Bird Club; Montréal Cage Bird Society; Northern Alberta Cage Bird Society; Okanagan Bird Club; Ontario Cage Bird Society; Ottawa Cage Bird Society; Ottawa Parrot Club; Southern Alberta Cage Bird Society; Tri County Cage Bird Club; Vancouver Canary Club; Vancouver Island Cage Bird Society; Zebra Finch Society of Canada

### British Columbia Waterfowl Society (1961)
**Reifel Bird Sanctuary**
5191 Robertson Rd., RR#1, Delta, BC V4K 3N2
604/946-6980, Fax: 604/946-6980
Manager, John Ireland
President, Ken Hall
Publications: Marshnotes

### Canadian Nature Federation/Fédération canadienne de la nature (CNF) (1971)
#606, One Nicholas St., Ottawa, ON K1N 7B7
613/562-3447, Fax: 613/562-3371, Toll Free: 1-800-267-4088, Email: cnf@web.net, URL: http://www.web.net/~cnf
Executive Director, Julie Gelfand
President, Cliff Wallis
Vice-President, Suzanne Ryan
Secretary, Lance Laviolette
Publications: Nature Canada; Nature Alert, q.
Affiliates: International Union for the Conservation of Nature; Committee on the Status of Endangered Wildlife in Canada; International Council for Bird Preservation; Canadian Council on Ecological Areas

### Les Cercles des jeunes naturalistes (CJN) (1931)
a/s Jardin Botanique de Montréal, #263, 4101, rue Sherbrooke est, Montréal, QC H1X 2B2
514/252-3023, Téléc: 514/252-3023
Directeur général, Laure Bouchard
Publications: Les Feuillets du naturaliste

### Federation of Alberta Naturalists (FAN) (1970)
PO Box 1472, Edmonton, AB T5J 2N5
403/453-8629, Fax: 403/453-8553, Email: fan@connect.ab.ca, URL: http://www.connect.ab.ca/~fan
Executive Director, Glen Semenchuk
President, Jorden Johnston
Publications: Alberta Naturalist

### Federation of BC Naturalists (1970)
#321, 1367 Broadway West, Vancouver, BC V6H 4A7
604/737-3057, Fax: 604/738-7175, Email: fbcn@intergate.bc.ca, URL: http://www.nq.com/land4nature/
Office Manager, Leslie-Ann Drummond
Publications: BC Naturalist; Cordillera

### Federation of Nova Scotia Naturalists (FNSN) (1990)
c/o Nova Scotia Museum, 1747 Summer St., Halifax, NS B3H 3A6
902/467-3380, URL: http://ccn.cs.dal.ca/Environment/FNSN/hp-fnsn.html
President, Alice L. White
Publications: FNSN News

### Federation of Ontario Naturalists (FON) (1931)
355 Lesmill Rd., North York, ON M3B 2W8
416/444-8419, Fax: 416/444-9866, Toll Free: 1-800-440-2366, Email: fon@web.net, URL: http://www.web.net/fon
Executive Director, John Lounds
President, Jane Allen
Chief Administrative Officer, Jean Labrecque
Director, Conservation & Environment, John Riley
Manager, Conservation & Stewardship Programs, Judy Eising
Manager, Education & Interpretive Programs, Nancy Croome Makowski
Coordinator, Club & Region Support Services, Sandy Symmes
Publications: Seasons
Affiliates: Coalition on the Niagara Escarpment; Conservation Council of Ontario; Great Lakes United; International Union for Conservation of Nature & Natural Resources; International Committee for Bird Preservation

### Jack Miner Migratory Bird Foundation, Inc.
PO Box 39, Kingsville, ON N9Y 2E8
519/733-4034
Executive Director, Kirk W. Miner

### Manitoba Naturalists' Society (MNS) (1920)
#401, 63 Albert St., Winnipeg, MB R3B 1G4
204/943-9029, Fax: 204/943-9029
Executive Director, Herta Gudauskas

President, Ron Clay
Publications: MNS Bulletin

### Natural History Society of Newfoundland & Labrador (1963)
PO Box 1013, Stn C, St. John's, NF A1C 5M3
President, John McConnel, Bus: 506/459-8685
Publications: Osprey

### Natural History Society of Prince Edward Island (NHSPEI) (1969)
PO Box 2346, Charlottetown, PE C1A 1Y6
902/894-9297
President, Ray Cooke
Publications: Island Naturalist
Affiliates: Island Nature Trust; Canadian Nature Federation

### Nature Saskatchewan (1949)
**Saskatchewan Natural History Society**
#206, 1860 Lorne St., Regina, SK S4P 2L7
306/780-9273, Fax: 306/780-9263, Toll Free: 1-800-667-4668, Email: nature.sask@unibase.unibase.com, URL: http://www.unibase.com/~naturesk
Acting Administrative Manager, Shari Martinook
President, Bob Berthiaume
Publications: Blue Jay; Nature Views, q.; The Eskimo Curlew

### New Brunswick Federation of Naturalists/Fédération des naturalistes du Nouveau-Brunswick
277 Douglas Ave., Saint John, NB E2K 1E5
President, Jim Goltz, Bus: 506/489-8683
Publications: NB Naturalist/Le Naturaliste du NB

### Society of Canadian Ornithologists/Société des ornithologistes du Canada (SCO) (1983)
c/o Canadian Museum of Nature, PO Box 3443, Stn D, Ottawa, ON K1P 6P4
President, Henri Ouellet
Secretary, Dr. Nancy Ford, Bus: 604/828-5436
Membership Secretary, Nancy Flood
Publications: Picoides

### Union québécoise pour la conservation de la nature/Québec Union for Nature Conservation (UQCN) (1981)
690, Grande Allée est, 4e étage, Québec, QC G1R 2K5
418/648-2104, Téléc: 418/648-0991
Président, Harvey Mead
Publications: Franc-Vert

**NEWSPAPERS *see* PUBLISHING**

**NURSERY TRADE *see* HORTICULTURE & GARDENING**

## NURSING
***see also* Health & Medical; Hospitals**

### Academy of Canadian Executive Nurses (ACEN) (1982)
c/o Health Care Corporation 3, Le Marchant Rd., St. John's, NF A1C 5B8
709/758-1317
President, Louise Jones
Publications: Canadian Journal of Nursing Administration; Newsletter, a.

### British Columbia Nurses' Union/Syndicat des infirmières de la Colombie-Britannique (BCNU) (1981)
#100, 4259 Canada Way, Burnaby, BC V5G 1H1
604/433-2268, Fax: 604/433-7945, Toll Free: 1-800-663-9991
COO, Anne Harvey
President, Ivory Warner
Publications: BCNU Update

### Canadian Association of Burn Nurses/Association canadienne des infirmières et infirmiers en soins aux brûlés (CABN)
Ross Tilley Regional Burn Centre, The Wellesley Hospital, 160 Wellesley St. East, Toronto, ON M4Y 1J3
416/926-7021, Fax: 416/926-4858
President, Joy Kramarich
Publications: Newsletter
Affiliates: Canadian Nurses Association

### Canadian Association of Critical Care Nurses/Association canadienne des infirmières et infirmiers en soins de phase aiguë (CACCN) (1985)
PO Box 22006, London, ON N6C 5Y3
519/649-5284, Fax: 519/668-2499, Email: caccn@execulink.com, URL: http://www.execulink.com/~caccn
President, Colleen Shelton
Vice-President, Gwynne MacDonald
Secretary, Val Davies
Publications: Official Journal of CACCN

### Canadian Association for the History of Nursing (CAHN)
130 Caruthers Ave., Kingston, ON K7L 1M7
613/545-2668, ext.4757, Fax: 613/545-6770
President, Lynn Kirkwood
Affiliates: Canadian Nurses Association

### Canadian Association of Nephrology Nurses & Technologists/Association canadienne des infirmières/iers et technologues de néphrologie (CANNT) (1968)
PO Box 4091, Stn C, Calgary, AB T2T 5M9
403/244-4487, Fax: 403/244-2340
President, Anita Amos
Publications: CANNT Journal
Affiliates: Canadian Nurses Association

### Canadian Association of Neuroscience Nurses/Association canadienne des infirmières et infirmiers en soins neurologiques (CANN) (1969)
71 Inch Bay, Winnipeg, MB R2Y 0X2
204/787-3577, Fax: 204/831-0888
President, Kathy Doerksen
Publications: Axon
Affiliates: Canadian Congress of Neurological Sciences

### Canadian Association of Nurses in AIDS Care/Association canadienne des infirmières et infirmiers en sidologie (CANAC) (1991)
c/o Casey House Hospice, 9 Huntley St., Toronto, ON M4Y 2K8
416/962-7600, Fax: 416/962-5147
President, Antoinette Lambert
Publications: CANAC/ACIIS Newsletter
Affiliates: Canadian Nurses Association

### Canadian Association of Nurses in Independent Practice/Association canadienne des infirmiers/ères autorisés en service privé (CANIP)
RR#5, Lucknow, ON N0G 2H0
519/395-3515, Fax: 519/395-3515
President, Nancy Elliott-Greenwood
Vice-President, Mary Ratensperger
Treasurer, Jean Millar
Secretary, Kelly Doran
Publications: Visions

### Canadian Association of Nurses in Oncology/Association canadienne des infirmières en oncologie (CANO) (1983)
#219, 111 Peter St., Toronto, ON M5V 2H1
416/596-6565, Fax: 416/596-1808, Email: canoacio@interlog.com
Publications: Canadian Oncology Nursing Journal
Affiliates: Canadian Nurses Association; International Society of Cancer Nurses

### Canadian Association of Pediatric Nurses/Association canadienne des infirmières et infirmiers en pédiatrie (CAPN) (1988)
c/o Montréal Children's Hospital, 2300, rue Tupper, Montréal, QC H3H 1P3
514/934-4400, ext.2855, Fax: 514/934-4355
President, Franco Carnevale
Publications: Newsletter

### Canadian Clinical Nurse Specialist Interest Group (CCNSIG)
RR#2, Halifax County, NS B0J 1N0
902/827-4437, Fax: 902/496-2119, Email: martinm@fhs.mcmaster.ca
President, Deborah McLeod
Publications: The Canadian CNS
Affiliates: Canadian Nurses Association

### Canadian Council of Cardiovascular Nurses/Conseil canadien des infirmières(iers) en nursing cardiovasculaire (CCCN) (1973)
#200, 160 George St., Ottawa, ON K1N 9M2
613/241-4361, Fax: 613/241-3278
President, Lynne Maxwell
Publications: Canadian Journal of Cardiovascular Nursing
Affiliates: Heart & Stroke Foundation of Canada; Canadian Coalition for High Blood Pressure Prevention & Control

### Canadian Federation of Mental Health Nurses/Fédération canadienne des infirmières et infirmiers en santé mentale (CFMHN)
10820 - 58 Ave., Edmonton, AB T6H 1C2
403/492-5250, Fax: 403/492-2551, Email: waustin@ua.nursing.ualberta.ca
President, Wendy Austin, Bus: 403/492-5250
Publications: CFMHN Newsletter
Affiliates: Canadian Nurses Association

### Canadian Gerontological Nursing Association/Association canadienne des infirmières et infirmiers en gérontologie (CGNA) (1984)
3223 Kenmore Cr. SW, Calgary, AB T3E 6K4
403/240-6882, Fax: 403/240-6203
President, Jean Miller
Publications: The Canadian Gerontological Nurse
Affiliates: Canadian Nurses Association

### Canadian Holistic Nurses Association/Association canadienne des infirmières en approches holistiques de soins (CHNA) (1986)
#209, 6051 Gilbert Rd., Richmond, BC V7C 3V3
604/244-1096, Fax: 604/241-4580
President, Lois Ross
Publications: Insight
Affiliates: Canadian Nurses Association

### Canadian Intravenous Nurses Association/Association canadienne des infirmiers(ères) en soins intraveineux (CINA) (1975)
#200, 4433 Sheppard Ave. East, Agincourt, ON M1S 1V3
416/292-0687, Fax: 416/292-1038, Email: cinacsot@idirect.com, URL: http://web.idirect.com/~csotcina
President, Janet Jones
Publications: CINA Journal; Mainliner, q.

### Canadian Nurse Educators Association/Association des infirmières enseignantes (CNEA) (1990)
400 Waterloo St., Winnipeg, MB R3N 0F6
204/889-2986, Fax: 204/888-1805
President, Dorothy Froman
Publications: Canadian Nurse Educators Association Newsletter
Affiliates: Canadian Nurses Association

### Canadian Nurses Association/Association des infirmières et infirmiers du Canada (CNA) (1908)
50 Driveway, Ottawa, ON K2P 1E2
613/237-2133, Fax: 613/237-3520, Email: commdiv@cna-nurses.ca
Executive Director, Dr. Mary Ellen Jeans
President, Rachel Bard
Director of Communications, Maureen Farrington
Publications: The Canadian Nurse/L'infirmière canadienne

#### ALBERTA ASSOCIATION OF REGISTERED NURSES (AARN) (1916)
11620 - 168 St., Edmonton, AB T5M 4A6
403/451-0043, Fax: 403/452-3276, Toll Free: 1-800-252-9392
Executive Director, Elizabeth Turnbull
Information Officer, Micky Elabdi
Publications: AARN Newsletter

#### ASSOCIATION OF NURSES OF PRINCE EDWARD ISLAND (ANPEI) (1922)
17 Pownal St., Charlottetown, PE C1A 3V7
902/368-3767, Fax: 902/628-1430
Executive Director/Registrar, Becky Gosbee
Publications: ANPEI Update

#### ASSOCIATION OF REGISTERED NURSES OF NEWFOUNDLAND (ARNN) (1953)
55 Military Rd., PO Box 6116, Stn C, St. John's, NF A1C 5X8
709/753-6040, Fax: 709/753-4940
Email: arnn@nf.sympatico.ca
Executive Director, Elizabeth Adey
Publications: ARNN Access

#### MANITOBA ASSOCIATION OF REGISTERED NURSES (1913)
647 Broadway, Winnipeg, MB R3C 0X2
204/774-3477, Fax: 204/775-6052, Toll Free: 1-800-665-2027
Executive Director, Diana Davidson-Dick
Publications: Nurscene

#### NORTHWEST TERRITORIES REGISTERED NURSES ASSOCIATION (NWTRNA) (1974)
PO Box 2757, Yellowknife, NT X1A 2R1
867/873-2745, Fax: 867/873-2336
Email: nwtrna@internorth.com
Executive Director/Registrar, Karen Hilliard
Publications: Northwest Territories Registered Nurses Association Newsletter

#### NURSES ASSOCIATION OF NEW BRUNSWICK/ASSOCIATION DES INFIRMIÈRES ET INFIRMIERS DU NOUVEAU-BRUNSWICK (1916)
165 Regent St., Fredericton, NB E3B 3W5
506/458-8731, Fax: 506/459-2838
Email: nanb@nanb.nb.ca, URL: http://www.nanb.nb.ca
Executive Director, Lucille Auffrey
Publications: Info Nursing

#### REGISTERED NURSES ASSOCIATION OF BRITISH COLUMBIA (RNABC) (1912)
2855 Arbutus St., Vancouver, BC V6J 3Y8
604/736-7331, Fax: 604/738-2272, Toll Free: 1-800-565-6505
Email: info@rnabc.bc.ca, URL: http://www.rnabc.bc.ca
Executive Director, Pat Cutshall
President, Rob Calnan, RN
Publications: Nursing BC

#### REGISTERED NURSES ASSOCIATION OF NOVA SCOTIA (RNANS)
#104, 120 Eileen Stubbs Ave., Dartmouth, NS B3H 1Y1
902/468-9744, Fax: 902/468-9510
Executive Director, Carolyn Moore
Publications: Nurse to Nurse

#### REGISTERED NURSES ASSOCIATION OF ONTARIO/L'ASSOCIATION DES INFIRMIÈRES ET INFIRMIERS AUTORISES DE L'ONTARIO (RNAO) (1925)
#1600, 438 University Ave., Toronto, ON M5G 2K8
416/599-1925, Fax: 416/599-1926
Director, Finance & Administration, Nancy Campbell
Executive Director, Doris Grinspun
Publications: Registered Nurse Journal

#### SASKATCHEWAN REGISTERED NURSES ASSOCIATION (SRNA) (1917)
2066 Retallack St., Regina, SK S4T 7X5
306/757-4643, Fax: 306/525-0849, Toll Free: 1-800-667-9945
Executive Director, Marianne Hodgson
Publications: Concern

#### YUKON REGISTERED NURSES ASSOCIATION (YRNA) (1993)
#14, 1114 - 1 Ave., Whitehorse, YT Y1A 1A3
867/667-4062, Fax: 867/668-5123
Email: yrna@yukon.net
Executive Director, Patricia McGarr
President, Colleen Wirth
Publications: Nurses Notes

### Canadian Nurses Foundation/Fondation des infirmières et infirmiers du Canada (CNF) (1962)
50 Driveway, Ottawa, ON K2P 1E2
613/237-2133, Fax: 613/237-3520
Executive Director, Beverly A. Campbell
Publications: In Touch with the Foundation; Foundation Focus, a.

### Canadian Nurses Protective Society/Société de protection des infirmières et infirmiers du Canada (CNPS) (1988)
50 The Driveway, Ottawa, ON K2P 1E2
613/237-2133, Fax: 613/237-3520, Toll Free: 1-800-267-3390, Email: cnps@istar.ca
Managing Director, Patricia McLean
Publications: Infolaw/InfoDroit

### Canadian Nurses Respiratory Society/Société canadienne des infirmières en santé respiratoire (CNRS)
10 Cowan Ave., St. John's, NF A1E 3N5
709/737-4253, Fax: 709/737-6795
President, Pamela Baker
Publications: CNRS/SCISR Newsletter
Affiliates: Canadian Lung Association; Canadian Nurses Association; International Council of Nurses

### Canadian Obstetric, Gynecologic & Neonatal Nurses (COGNN)
315 Oakwood Ave., Winnipeg, MB R3L 1E8
204/774-6581, Fax: 204/774-7834
President, Vera Rosolwich
Affiliates: Canadian Nurses Association

### Canadian Occupational Health Nurses Association/Association canadienne des infirmières et infirmiers en santé du travail (COHNA) (1986)
c/o BC Telephone, #5, 3777 Kingsway, Burnaby, BC V5H 3Z7
604/432-4012, Fax: 604/432-9456, Email: sharon_blaney@bctel.com
President, Sharon Blaney
Affiliates: Canadian Nurses Association

### Canadian Orthopaedic Nurses Association/Association canadienne des infirmières et infirmiers en orthopédie (CONA) (1978)
Ottawa General Hospital, Nurse Clinical Rm. 4232, 501 Smythe Rd., Ottawa, ON K1H 8L6
613/737-8303, Fax: 613/737-8470
President, Hélène Rairville
Publications: CONA Newsletter
Affiliates: Canadian Nurses Association

### Canadian Practical Nurses Association (CPNA) (1975)
#200, 440 Laurier Ave. West, Ottawa, ON K1R 7X6
613/782-3104; Fax: 905/432-7604
National President, Shiela Arsenault
Secretary, Edna Sagrott
Publications: Across the Nation
Affiliates: The Health Action Lobby; Canadian Council on Health Facilities Accreditation

#### ASSOCIATION OF NEW BRUNSWICK REGISTERED NURSING ASSISTANTS/ASSOCIATION DES INFIRMIERS ET INFIRMIÈRES AUXILIAIRES IMMATRICULÉES DU NOUVEAU-BRUNSWICK (1965)
384 Smythe St., Fredericton, NB E3B 3E4
506/454-0747, Fax: 506/459-0503
President, Dianne Parent
Publications: The Blue Band

#### LICENSED NURSING ASSISTANTS ASSOCIATION OF PRINCE EDWARD ISLAND
PO Box 1254, Charlottetown, PE C1A 7M8
902/566-1512, Fax: 902/892-6315
Publications: Heart of Caring

#### LICENSED PRACTICAL NURSES ASSOCIATION OF BRITISH COLUMBIA (LPNA) (1965)
RR#1, S-17B, C-A5, Peachland, BC V0H 1X0
250/767-3384, Fax: 250/767-3384
President, Jan J. van Doorn
Publications: Dogwood News

#### MANITOBA ASSOCIATION OF LICENSED PRACTICAL NURSES (1945)
615 Kernaghan Ave., Winnipeg, MB R2C 2Z4
204/222-6743, Fax: 204/224-0166
Executive Director, Verna Holgate
Publications: Current Affairs
Affiliates: Manitoba Health Organization

#### NEWFOUNDLAND COUNCIL FOR NURSING ASSISTANTS
Lemarchant Road Medical Centre, 195 LeMarchant Rd., St. John's, NF A1C 2H5
709/579-3843, Fax: 709/579-8268
Executive Director, Anne Keough

#### NOVA SCOTIA CERTIFIED NURSING ASSISTANTS ASSOCIATION (1956)
Sunnyside Place, #212, 1600 Bedford Hwy., Bedford, NS B4A 3E4
902/835-9510, Fax: 902/835-9510, Toll Free: 1-800-565-9510
Executive Director, Albert MacIntyre
Publications: CNA News

#### ORDRE DES INFIRMIÈRES ET INFIRMIERS AUXILIAIRES DU QUÉBEC (OIIAQ) (1974)
531, rue Sherbrooke est, Montréal, QC H2L 1K2
514/282-9511, Téléc: 514/282-0631, Ligne sans frais: 1-800-283-9511
Directrice générale, Dominique Aubertin
Publications: Santé Québec; L'infirmière auxiliaire, 3 fois par an

#### PROFESSIONAL COUNCIL OF LICENSED PRACTICAL NURSES (1985)
10604 - 170 Ave., Edmonton, AB T5S 1P3
403/484-8886, Fax: 403/484-9069, Toll Free: 1-800-661-5877
President, Sally Hurley
Publications: News & Views

**REGISTERED PRACTICAL NURSES ASSOCIATION OF ONTARIO (1958)**
#200, Building 4, 5025 Orbitor Dr., Mississauga, ON L4W 4Y5
905/602-4664, Fax: 905/602-4666
Email: rpnao@istar.ca
Executive Director, Barbara A. Thornber
President, Linda LaHay
Publications: RPNAO Update; The Care Connection, q.

**SASKATCHEWAN ASSOCIATION OF LICENSED PRACTICAL NURSES (SALPN) (1957)**
2310 Smith St., Regina, SK S4P 2P6
306/525-1436, Fax: 306/347-7784
President, Pat Hood
Publications: Hand in Hand
Affiliates: Alzheimers Association

**College of Nurses of Ontario/Ordre des infirmières et infirmiers de l'Ontario (CNO) (1963)**
101 Davenport Rd., Toronto, ON M5R 3P1
416/928-0900, Fax: 416/928-6507, Toll Free: 1-800-387-5526
Executive Director, Margaret Risk
Publications: College Communiqué

**Community Health Nurses Association of Canada/Association canadienne des infirmières et infirmiers en santé communautaire (CHNAC) (1987)**
1329 Spadina Cres. East, Saskatoon, SK S7K 3J2
306/966-6237, Fax: 306/966-6703
President-Elect, Shirley Sterlinger
President, Barbara Mathur
Publications: CHMAC Newsletter
Affiliates: Canadian Nurses Association

**Fédération des infirmières et infirmiers auxiliaires du Québec/Québec Federation of Nurses' Aids (FIIAQ)**
5385 - 1e av, Charlesbourg, QC G1H 2V5
418/622-8077, Téléc: 418/622-8471, Ligne sans frais: 1-800-463-5664
Présidente, Johanne Morin
Publications: ECHO-FIIAQ

**Fédération des infirmières et infirmiers du Québec (FIIQ) (1987)**
2050, rue de Bleury, 4e étage, Montréal, QC H3A 2J5
514/987-1141, Téléc: 514/987-7273
Présidente, Jennie Skene
Secrétaire directrice, Danielle Y. Mailhot
Publications: FIIQ; Le Pouls, semi-annuel
Bureau régional: #300, 1260, boul Lebourgneuf, Québec, QC G2K 2G2, 418/626-2226

**Gerontological Nursing Association of Ontario (1974)**
PO Box 368, Stn K, Toronto, ON M4P 2G7
Publications: Perspectives
Affiliates: Registered Nurses Association of Ontario

**Manitoba Nurses' Union/Syndicat des infirmières du Manitoba (MNU) (1975)**
#502, 275 Broadway, Winnipeg, MB R3C 4M6
204/942-1320, Fax: 204/942-0958
Executive Director, Irene Giesbrecht
President, Vera Chernecki
Publications: Pulse

**National Emergency Nurses Affiliation/Affiliation des infirmières et infirmiers d'urgence (NENA)**
20 Jasper St., St. John's, NF A1A 4E2
709/737-7238, Fax: 709/737-6770
President, Louanne Kinsella
Affiliates: Canadian Nurses Association

**New Brunswick Nurses' Union/Syndicat des infirmières du Nouveau-Brunswick**
750 Brunswick St., Fredericton, NB E3B 1H9
506/453-0820, 0822, Fax: 506/453-0828
Executive Director, Thomas Mann
President, Linda Silas Martin
Publications: The Parasol

**Newfoundland & Labrador Nurses' Union/Syndicat des infirmières de Terre-Neuve et du Labrador**
59A Le Marchant Rd., PO Box 416, Stn C, St. John's, NF A1C 5J9
709/753-9961, Fax: 709/753-1210, Toll Free: 1-800-563-5100
President, Debbie Forward
Publications: In Touch

**Nova Scotia Nurses' Union/Syndicat des infirmières de la Nouvelle-Écosse (NSNU)**
65 Queen St., Dartmouth, NS B2Y 1G4
902/469-1474, Fax: 902/466-6935
Executive Director, Tom Patterson
Publications: NSNU Newsletter

**Ontario Nurses' Association/Association des infirmières et infirmiers de l'Ontario (ONA) (1973)**
#600, 85 Grenville St., Toronto, ON M5S 3A2
416/964-8833, Fax: 416/964-8864, Toll Free: 1-800-387-5580, Email: onamail@ona.org, URL: http://www.ona.org/
CEO, Lesley M. Bell
Director, External Relations, Noelle Andrews
Communications Officer, Melanie Pottins
Publications: ONA News

**Operating Room Nurses Association of Canada/Association des infirmières et infirmiers de sales d'opération du Canada (ORNAC) (1983)**
Queensway Carleton Hospital, 3045 Baseline Rd., Nepean, ON K2H 8P4
613/721-2000, ext.2901, Fax: 613/721-4774
President, Vija Hay
Publications: Canadian Operating Room Nurses Journal; Communiqué

**Ordre des infirmières et infirmiers du Québec (OIIQ) (1920)**
**Corporation professionnelle des infirmières et infirmiers du Québec**
4200, boul Dorchester ouest, Westmount, QC H3Z 1V4
514/935-2501, Téléc: 514/935-1799, Ligne sans frais: 1-800-363-6048, Courrier électronique: inf@oiiq.org, URL: http://www.oiiq.org
Présidente, Gyslaine Desrosiers
Directrice générale et secrétaire, Hélène Rajotte
Directrice, Communications, Guylaine Chabot
Publications: L'infirmière du Québec; Le journal de l'OIIQ, tous les 2 mois

**Practical Nurses Federation of Ontario (Ind.)**
Bldg. 4, #200, 5025 Orbitor Dr., Mississauga, ON L4W 4Y5
905/602-6705, Fax: 905/602-4666
President, Ruth Cartwright
Director of Labour Relations, Bill Sly
Publications: PNFO Newsletter

**Prince Edward Island Nurses' Union/Syndicat des infirmières de l'Île-du-Prince-Edouard (PEINU) (1987)**
25 Kensington Ct., Charlottetown, PE C1A 8K4
902/892-7152, Fax: 902/368-2974
Executive Director, Elizabeth MacFadyen
President, Beryl Chandler
Publications: Concerns

**Psychiatric Nurses Association of Canada (PNAC) (1951)**
509 Pandora Ave. West, Winnipeg, MB R2C 1M8
204/222-6984, Fax: 204/222-6984
President, Gary Thronberg
Executive Assistant, Beverley Hill

**REGISTERED PSYCHIATRIC NURSES ASSOCIATION OF ALBERTA**
#201, 9711 - 45 Ave., Edmonton, AB T6E 5V8
403/434-7666, Fax: 403/436-4165
Executive Director, Janice Trylinski
President, Judy Dahl

**REGISTERED PSYCHIATRIC NURSES ASSOCIATION OF BRITISH COLUMBIA (1974)**
#251, 3041 Anson Ave., Coquitlam, BC V3B 2H6
604/944-4941, Fax: 604/944-4945
Executive Director, Keith Best
President, Dorothy Jennings
Publications: Intercom

**REGISTERED PSYCHIATRIC NURSES ASSOCIATION OF MANITOBA (RPNAM) (1960)**
1854 Portage Ave., Winnipeg, MB R3J 0G9
204/888-4841, Fax: 204/888-8638
Email: aosted@psychiatricnurses.mb.ca, URL: http://www.psychiatricnurses.mb.ca/rpnam/index.html
Executive Director, Annette D. Osted
President, Cheryl Adams
Publications: R.P.N.A.M. Update; IBID, q.

**REGISTERED PSYCHIATRIC NURSES ASSOCIATION OF SASKATCHEWAN (RPNAS) (1948)**
#101, 2631 - 28th Ave., Regina, SK S4S 6X3
306/586-4617, Fax: 306/586-6000
Executive Director, Marion Rieger
President, Roger Bitschy
Publications: RP News

**St. Elizabeth Visiting Nurses Association (SEN) (1921)**
698 King St. West, Hamilton, ON L8P 1C7
905/522-6887, Fax: 905/522-5579, Toll Free: 1-800-463-6612, Email: sen@networx.on.ca
President & CEO, Rita M. Soluk

**Saskatchewan Union of Nurses/Syndicat des infirmières de la Saskatchewan (SUN) (1974)**
2330 - 2 Ave., Regina, SK S4R 1A6
306/525-1666, Fax: 306/522-4612, Email: sunregina@sk.sympatico.ca
President, Judy Junor
Publications: Sunspots; Spectrum, q.
Affiliates: Saskatchewan Federation of Labour; Canadian Labour Congress

**Staff Nurses Associations of Alberta/Association du personnel infirmier de l'Alberta (SNAP)**
#303, 10328 - 81 Ave., Edmonton, AB T6E 1X2
403/439-3788, Fax: 403/439-1036, Toll Free: 1-800-461-8612
President, Linda Sloan
Publications: SNAP

**Union of Psychiatric Nurses/Syndicat des infirmières psychiatriques (1966)**
#200, 508 Clarke Rd., Coquitlam, BC V3J 3X2
604/931-2471, Fax: 604/931-1070
President, Stew Johnson
Publications: Spotlite
Affiliates: B.C. Government Employees Union; B.C. Federation of Labour

**Union québécoise des infirmières et infirmiers/Québec Union of Nurses (UQII) (1988)**
9405, rue Sherbrooke est, Montréal, QC H1L 6P3
514/356-8888, Téléc: 514/356-9999
Présidente, Louise Chabot
Publications: L'Union

Organisation(s) affiliée(s): Centrale de l'enseignement du Québec (CEQ)

**United Nurses of Alberta/Infirmières unies de l'Alberta (UNA) (1977)**
Park Plaza, 10611 - 98 Ave., 9th Fl., Edmonton, AB T5K 2P7
403/425-1025, Fax: 403/426-2093
President, Heather Smith
Publications: UNA News Bulletin; UNA Stat, bi-weekly; UNA Frontline, bi-m.

**Victorian Order of Nurses for Canada/Infirmières de l'Ordre de Victoria du Canada (VON Canada) (1897)**
5 Blackburn Ave., Ottawa, ON K1N 8A2
613/233-5694, Fax: 613/230-4376, Toll Free: 1-888-866-2273, Email: rbv@von.ca, URL: http://www.von.ca
Chief Executive Officer, Donna Roe
Chair, Dr. Marion Allen
Publications: National Network; VON Canada Report, q.; Annual Report

**NUTRITION *see* HEALTH & MEDICAL**

**OIL *see* GAS & OIL**

## PACKAGING

**Canadian Corrugated Case Association/Association canadienne des fabricants de carton ondulé**
#402, 701 Evans Ave., Etobicoke, ON M9C 1A3
416/695-1062, Fax: 416/695-0693
Executive Director, Steve Purwitsky
Administrator, Donna W. Mehta

**Canadian Paper Box Manufacturers' Association Inc./Association canadienne des fabricants de boîtes en cartons (CPBMA) (1921)**
#400, 701 Evans Ave., Etobicoke, ON M9C 1A3
416/626-7056, Fax: 416/626-7054
Executive Director, Jim Thurston

**Canadian Seniors Packaging Advisory Council/Conseil consultatif canadien pour l'adaptation de l'emballage aux besoins des aînés (CASPAC) (1991)**
#407, 2255 Sheppard Ave. East, Toronto, ON M2J 4Y1
416/497-7511, Fax: 416/496-6160
Chairperson, Marina Kovrig
Project Manager, Karen Cuggy-Murphy

**Environmentally-Sound Packaging Coalition of Canada (1987)**
#404, 198 West Hastings St., Vancouver, BC V6B 1H2
604/689-3770, Fax: 604/689-3779
President, Ruth Lotzkar
Publications: ESP Newsletter

**Packaging Association of Canada/Association canadienne de l'emballage (PAC) (1949)**
2255 Sheppard Ave. East, #E330, North York, ON M2J 4Y1
416/490-7860, Fax: 416/490-7844
President/CEO, Alan M. Robinson
Chairman, J. Robert Lavery

**Paper & Paperboard Packaging Environmental Council/Conseil de l'environnement des emballages de papier et de carton (PPEC) (1990)**
#400, 701 Evans Ave., Etobicoke, ON M9C 1A3
416/626-0350, Fax: 416/626-7054
Executive Director, John Mullinder
Chairman, Cam Gentile
Publications: PPEC News
Affiliates: Recycling Council of Ontario; Recycling Council of BC; Recycling Council of Manitoba

## PATENTS & COPYRIGHT

**Canadian Copyright Institute (CCI) (1965)**
35 Spadina Rd., Toronto, ON M5R 2S9
416/975-1756, Fax: 416/975-1839
Chairman, Ron B. Thomson
Publications: CCI Newsletter
Affiliates: Canadian Conference of the Arts; Book & Periodical Council

**Canadian Copyright Licensing Agency (1988)**
**CANCOPY**
#900, 6 Adelaide St. East, Toronto, ON M5C 1H6
416/868-1620, Fax: 416/868-1621, Toll Free: 1-800-893-5777, URL: http://cancopy.com/
Executive Director, Andrew Martin, Email: amartin@cancopy.com
Associate Director, Lucy White, Email: lwhite@cancopy.com
Communications Manager, Alexandra Soiseth, Email: soiseth@cancopy.com
Publications: CANCOPY News; CANCOPY Update, m.
Affiliates: International Federation of Reproduction Rights Organization

**Canadian Musical Reproduction Rights Agency/Agence canadienne des droits de production musicaux limitée (CMRRA) (1976)**
#320, 56 Wellesley St. West, Toronto, ON M5S 2S3
416/926-1966, Fax: 416/926-7521, Email: inquiries@cmrra.ca, URL: http://www.cmrra.ca
President, David A. Basskin
Sec.-Treas., C.C. Devereux

**Canadian Society of Copyright Consumers/Societé canadienne des consommaters copyright (CSCC) (1927)**
2160 New St., Burlington, ON L7R 1H8
905/632-8404, Fax: 905/632-6520
Executive Vice-President, J. Lyman Potts, CM
President, John Riley
Publications: CSCC/SCCC Newsletter

**Copyright Collective of Canada/Société de perception de droit d'auteur du Canada (CCC) (1989)**
#1603, 22 St. Clair Ave. East, Toronto, ON M4T 2S4
416/961-1888, Fax: 416/968-1016
Vice-President, Susan Peacock

**Inventors Association of Canada**
PO Box 281, Swift Current, SK S9H 3V6
306/773-7762
General Manager, Phyllis Tengum

**Patent & Trademark Institute of Canada/Institut canadien des brevets et marques (PTIC) (1957)**
PO Box 1298, Stn B, Ottawa, ON K1P 5R3
613/234-0516
Executive Director, Jane Donaldson
Publications: Bulletin; Canadian Intellectual Property Review, s-a.; Centennial Index III - Index of Learned Papers on Intellectual Property Subjects
Affiliates: Industry Canada

**Society of Composers, Authors & Music Publishers of Canada/Société canadienne des auteurs, compositeurs et éditeurs de musique (SOCAN) (1990)**
41 Valleybrook Dr., North York, ON M3B 2S6
416/445-8700, Fax: 416/445-7108, Toll Free: 1-800-557-6226, Email: socan@socan.ca, URL: http://www.socan.ca
General Manager, Michael R. Rock
Publications: Words & Music; Paroles et musique

**PEACE *see* INTERNATIONAL COOPERATION/INTERNATIONAL RELATIONS**

**PENSION MANAGEMENT *see* FINANCE**

**PENSIONERS *see* SENIOR CITIZENS**

## PHARMACEUTICAL

**Association of Faculties of Pharmacy of Canada/Association des facultés de pharmacie du Canada (AFPC) (1969)**
425 Adelaide St., Saskatoon, SK S7J 0H9
306/653-3513, Fax: 306/665-1916
Executive Director, Kenneth A. Ready
Publications: AFPC Communications; Directory of Pharmaceutical Research in Canadian Faculties of Pharmacy, biennial
Affiliates: Canadian Pharmaceutical Association

**Association professionnelle des pharmaciens salariés du Québec (APPSQ)**
405, Place Damiens, CP 33016, Succ. Concorde, Laval, QC H7G 4X6
514/663-3731, Téléc: 514/667-9633
Président, René Dubois, p.d.g.
Publications: Activox

**Association québécoise des pharmaciens propriétaires/Québec Association of Pharmacy Owners (AQPP) (1970)**
4378, av Pierre-de-Coubertin, Montréal, QC H1V 1A6
514/254-0676, Téléc: 514/254-1288, Ligne sans frais: 1-800-361-7765
Directeur général, Normand Cadieux
Publications: Québec Pharmacie

**Atlantic Provinces Pharmacy Council**
1526 Dresden Rd., PO Box 3363, Halifax, NS B3J 3J1
902/422-8528, Fax: 902/422-2619
Registrar, Susan Wedlake

**British Columbia Pharmacy Association**
#150, 3751 Shell Rd., Richmond, BC V6X 2W2
604/279-2053, Fax: 604/279-2065
Executive Director, Frank M. Archer

**Canadian Association of Pharmacy Students & Interns/Association canadienne des étudiants et internes en pharmacie (CAPSI) (1968)**
50 Nanaimo Dr., Nepean, ON K2H 6Y3
613/820-3371, Email: ay043@freenet.carleton.ca
President, Sean Hopkins
Publications: CAPSIL
Affiliates: International Pharmacy Student Foundation; Canadian Pharmaceutical Association; Academy of Students; Canadian Society of Hospital Pharmacists

**The Canadian Council for Accreditation of Pharmacy Programs/Le Conseil canadien de l'agrément des programmes de pharmacie (CCAPP) (1993)**
Univ. of Sask. Campus, Thorvaldson Bldg., #123, 110 Science Place, Saskatoon, SK S7N 5C9
306/966-6388, Fax: 306/966-6377
Executive Director, Dr. Bruce R. Schnell
Publications: CCAPP Directory & Annual Report

### Canadian Drug Manufacturers Association/ L'Association canadienne des fabricants de produits pharmaceutiques (CDMA) (1984)
#409, 4120 Yonge St., Toronto, ON M2P 2B8
416/223-2333, Fax: 416/223-2425, Email: info@cdma-acfpp.org
President, Brenda Drinkwalter
Chairman, Jack Kay
Publications: Drug News & Views

### Canadian Foundation for Pharmacy/Fondation canadienne pour la pharmacie (CFP) (1945)
9 Hawthorn Cres., Brampton, ON L6S 1A9
905/454-4818, Fax: 905/454-4860
Executive Director, Dr. Stuart Ryan
Publications: Board Bulletin; Your Foundation News, s-a.
Affiliates: Canadian Pharmaceutical Association

### Canadian Pharmaceutical Association/ Association pharmaceutique canadienne (CPhA) (1907)
1785 Alta Vista Dr., 2nd Fl., Ottawa, ON K1G 3Y6
613/523-7877, Fax: 613/523-0445, Toll Free: 1-800-917-9489, Email: cpha@cdnpharm.ca, URL: http://www.cdnpharm.ca
Executive Director, L.C. Fevang
President, Tom Healy
Publications: Canadian Pharmaceutical Journal
Affiliates: Commonwealth Pharmaceutical Association; Fédération internationale pharmaceutique

#### ALBERTA PHARMACEUTICAL ASSOCIATION (APHA) (1911)
10130 - 112 St., 7th Fl., Edmonton, AB T5K 2K4
403/990-0321, Fax: 403/990-0328
Registrar, Greg Eberhart
Publications: APhA Newsletter

#### COLLEGE OF PHARMACISTS OF BRITISH COLUMBIA (1891)
#200, 1765 - 8th Ave. West, Vancouver, BC V6J 1V8
604/733-2440, Fax: 604/733-2493, Toll Free: 1-800-663-1940
Email: copbc@axionet.com
Registrar, Linda J. Lytle
Publications: The Bulletin

#### MANITOBA PHARMACEUTICAL ASSOCIATION
187 St. Mary's Rd., Winnipeg, MB R2H 1J2
204/233-1411, Fax: 204/237-3468
Registrar, S.G. Wilcox

#### NEW BRUNSWICK PHARMACEUTICAL SOCIETY
#204, 95 Foundry St., Moncton, NB E1C 5H7
506/857-8957, Fax: 506/857-8838
Email: nbphs@nbnet.nb.ca
Registrar, Bill Veniot

#### NEWFOUNDLAND PHARMACEUTICAL ASSOCIATION (NPHA) (1954)
Apothecary Hall, 488 Water St., St. John's, NF A1E 1B3
709/753-5877, Fax: 709/753-8615
Secretary Registrar, Donald F. Rowe
Publications: The Apothecary

#### ORDRE DES PHARMACIENS DU QUÉBEC (1974)
#301, 266, rue Notre Dame ouest, Montréal, QC H2Y 1T6
514/284-9588, Téléc: 514/284-3420, Ligne sans frais: 1-800-363-0324
Directeur général/Secrétaire, Alain Boisvert
Publications: L'Ordonnance

#### SASKATCHEWAN PHARMACEUTICAL ASSOCIATION (1911)
#700, 4010 Pasqua St., Regina, SK S4S 6X3
306/584-2292, Fax: 306/584-9695
Registrar, R.J. Joubert

### Canadian Society for Clinical Pharmacology/ Société canadienne de pharmacologie clinique (CSCP)
c/o Ms. C. Van Der Giessen, #947, 76 Grenville St., Toronto, ON M5S 1B2
416/323-7552, Fax: 416/323-7553, Email: c.vandergiessen@utoronto.ca
President, Dr. Jean Cusson
Sec.-Treas., Dr. Gideon Karen
Publications: The Canadian Journal of Clinical Pharmacology
Affiliates: Royal College of Physicians & Surgeons of Canada; Canadian Society for Clinical Investigation

### Canadian Society of Hospital Pharmacists/ Société canadienne des pharmaciens d'hôpitaux (CSHP) (1947)
#350, 1145 Hunt Club Rd., Ottawa, ON K1V 0Y3
613/736-9733, Fax: 613/736-5660, Email: bleslie@worldlink.ca, URL: http://www.cshp.ca/~cshp
Executive Director, William J. Leslie
Publications: Pharmascope; Canadian Journal of Hospital Pharmacy, bi-m.; The Employment Opportunities Bulletin, s-m.

### Canadian Wholesale Drug Association/ Association des grossistes en médicaments du Canada (CWDA) (1964)
#505, 5255 Yonge St., Toronto, ON M2N 6P4
416/222-3922, Fax: 416/222-8960, Email: theresaf@ican.net, URL: http://www.cwda.com
President & CEO, Theresa S. Firestone
Chairman, Ron Frisch
Publications: Fastforward; Industry Directory

### Conference of Pharmacy Registrars of Canada/ Association canadienne des secrétaires généraux de pharmacie
c/o Ordre des Pharmaciens du Québec, 266, rue Notre Dame ouest, Montréal, QC H2Y 1T6
514/284-9588, Fax: 514/284-3420
Chairman, S.G. Wilcox

### Council for the Accreditation of Pharmaceutical Manufacturers Representatives of Canada
3489, rue Ashby, Saint Laurent, QC H4R 2K3
514/333-8362, Fax: 514/333-1119
Executive Director, Gilles Lachance

### Manitoba Society of Pharmacists Inc. (MSP) (1973)
187 St. Mary's Rd., Winnipeg, MB R2H 1J2
204/233-6227, Fax: 204/237-3468
Executive Director, Doug Nanton
President, Ross Forsyth
Publications: Communication; MSP Newsletter, bi-m.

### National Association of Pharmacy Regulatory Authorities/Association nationale des organismes de réglementation de la pharmacie (NAPRA)
#1005, 116 Albert St., Ottawa, ON K1P 5G3
613/569-9658, Fax: 613/569-9659, Email: 102473.3160@compuserve.com, URL: http://www.napra.org
Executive Director, Barbara Wells

### New Brunswick Pharmacists' Association Inc./ Association des pharmaciens du Nouveau-Brunswick inc. (NBPA) (1981)
410, 212 Queen St., Fredericton, NB E3B 1A8
506/459-6008, Fax: 506/453-0736, Email: nbpa@nbnet.nb.ca
Executive Director, George L. Bastin
Publications: Activities Update

### Nonprescription Drug Manufacturers Association of Canada/Association canadienne des fabricants de médicaments sans ordonnance (NDMAC) (1896)
#406, 1111 Prince of Wales Dr., Ottawa, ON K2C 3T2
613/723-0777, Fax: 613/723-0779, Email: ndmac@ndmac.ca
President, David S. Skinner
Communications Officer, Mary Wyllie
Publications: Self-Medication Digest

### Nova Scotia Pharmaceutical Society (NSPS) (1876)
1526 Dresden Row, PO Box 3363, Halifax, NS B3J 3J1
902/422-8528, Fax: 902/422-2619, Email: nsps@atcon.com
Registrar, Susan Wedlake
Publications: The President's Bulletin

### Ontario College of Pharmacists
483 Huron St., Toronto, ON M5R 2R4
416/962-4861, Fax: 416/962-1619, Email: tlanglois@ocpharma.com, URL: http://www.ocpharma.com
Manager, Patient Relations Program, Christina M. Langlois
Publications: Pharmacy Connection

### Ontario Pharmacists' Association (OPA)
#301, 23 Lesmill Rd., North York, ON M3B 3P6
416/441-0788, Fax: 416/441-0791
CEO, Barbara Stuart
President, Wayne Marigold

### Ordre des chimistes du Québec (1926)
#1010, 300, rue Léo-Pariseau, CP 1089, Succ Place-du-Parc, Montréal, QC H2W 2P4
514/844-3644, Téléc: 514/844-9601
Directeur général, Gilles Leduc
Présidente, Éveline de Médicis
Publications: Chimiste

### Pharmaceutical Manufacturers Association of Canada/Association canadienne de l'industrie du médicament (PMAC) (1914)
#302, 1111 Prince of Wales Dr., Ottawa, ON K2C 3T2
613/727-1380, Fax: 613/727-1407, Email: info@pmac-acim.org, URL: http://www.pmac-acim.org
President, Judy Erola
Chairman, Ger van Amersfoort

### Pharmacy Association of Nova Scotia (PANS) (1979)
PO Box 3214, Stn South, Halifax, NS B3J 3H5
902/422-9583, Fax: 902/422-2619, Email: pans@ns.sympatico.ca
Executive Director, J. Patrick King
Publications: The Pharmacist

### The Pharmacy Examining Board of Canada/Le Bureau des examinateurs en pharmacie du Canada (1963)
#603, 123 Edward St., Toronto, ON M5G 1E2
416/979-2431, Fax: 416/599-9244
President, Garth McCutcheon
Director of Administration, Lori Horley
Registrar/Treasurer, Dr. John Pugsley

### Prince Edward Island Pharmacy Board (1983)
PO Box 89, Crapaud, PE C0A 1J0
902/658-2780, Fax: 902/658-2198
Registrar, Neila I. Auld
Publications: Newsletter

## PHOTOGRAPHY

### Canadian Association of Photographers & Illustrators in Communications/Association canadienne de photographes et illustrateurs de publicité (CAPIC) (1978)
#322, 100 Broadview Ave., Toronto, ON M4M 2E8
416/462-3700, Fax: 416/462-3678, Email: capic@astral.magic.ca, URL: http://www.capic.org
Executive Officer, Duncan Read
President, Struan Campbell-Smith
Executive Assistant, Sylvia Allen
Publications: CAPIC Newsletter

### Canadian Imaging Trade Association (1955)
145 Upper Canada Dr., North York, ON M2P 1S9
416/226-2750, Fax: 416/226-3347
General Manager, Dori Gospodaric
Publications: Image Line

### National Association for Photographic Art/Association nationale d'art photographique (NAPA) (1969)
31858 Hopedale Ave., Clearbrook, BC V2T 2G7
604/855-4848, Fax: 604/859-6288
President, Rosemarie Culver
Publications: Canadian Camera
Affiliates: Fédération internationale de l'art photographique

### Photo Marketing Association International - Canada (PMAI) (1924)
78 Lytton Blvd., Toronto, ON M4R 1L3
416/489-5614, Fax: 416/489-5780, Email: lmcgregor@msn.com, URL: http://www.pmai.org
Director/Canadian Activities, Lynn McGregor
Publications: Newsline Canada; Photo Marketing Magazine, m.; Industry Newsletter, bi-w.

### Photographers Gallery Society Inc. (PGS) (1971)
12 - 23 St. East, 2nd Fl., Saskatoon, SK S7K 0H5
306/244-8018, Fax: 306/665-6568
Director, Monte Greenshields
Publications: Newsletter

### Photographic Historical Society of Canada (PHSOC) (1974)
1712 Avenue Rd., PO Box 54620, Toronto, ON M5M 4N5
416/691-1555, Fax: 416/693-0018, Email: phsc@onramp.ca, URL: http://web.onramp.ca/phsc
President, Les Jones
Publications: Photographic Canadiana

### Professional Photographers of Canada/Photographes professionnelles du Canada (PPOC)
PO Box 337, Gatineau, QC J8P 6J3
819/643-5177, Fax: 819/643-7177, Email: ppoc@magi.com
Executive Director, Suzanne Despatie

#### ALBERTA PROFESSIONAL PHOTOGRAPHERS ASSOCIATION
16136 - 110B Ave, Edmonton, AB T5P 4E6
403/483-4275, Fax: 403/489-7724
Executive Secretary, Pat Eisenbarth

#### CORPORATION DES MAÎTRES PHOTOGRAPHES DU QUÉBEC INC./QUÉBEC CORPORATION OF MASTER PHOTOGRAPHERS INC. (CMPQ) (1950)
#202, 650, boul de Grande Prairie, St-Léonard, QC H1P 1A2
514/328-1071
URL: http://www.intertower.com/cmpq.html
Publications: Bulletin Image

#### MARITIME PROFESSIONAL PHOTOGRAPHERS ASSOCIATION (MPPA)
19 Hill St., Edmundston, NB E3V 1H7
506/735-8186, Fax: 506/849-9477
Email: bhart@nbnet.nb.ca
Michael Jessop
Publications: Developments

#### PROFESSIONAL PHOTOGRAPHERS ASSOCIATION OF MANITOBA INC.
PO Box 1575, Winnipeg, MB R3C 2Z4
204/482-4425
President, Thomas Podruchny
Publications: PPAM News

#### PROFESSIONAL PHOTOGRAPHERS OF ONTARIO INC. (PPO) (1884)
2833 Donnelly Dr., RR#4, Kemptville, ON K0G 1J0
613/258-5432, Fax: 613/258-5432, Toll Free: 1-800-368-6776
Executive Assistant, Eileen K. Gilbert
Publications: Exposure Ontario

#### SASKATCHEWAN PROFESSIONAL PHOTOGRAPHERS ASSOCIATION INC.
1475 Cornwall St., Regina, SK S4R 2H8
306/757-1470
Executive Secretary, Tanya Owen

### PHYSICALLY CHALLENGED PERSONS *see* DISABLED PERSONS

## PLANNING & DEVELOPMENT

### Canadian Association of Certified Planning Technicians (CACPT) (1979)
PO Box 3844, Stn C, Hamilton, ON L8H 7R6
905/578-4681, Fax: 905/578-4681, Email: cacpt@networx.on.ca, URL: http://www.networx.on.ca/~cacpt
Executive Director, Donna Madden
Publications: Tech Talk

### Canadian Institute for Development Management (CIDM) (1991)
#202, 1900 Merivale Rd., Nepean, ON K2G 4N4
613/723-8698, Fax: 613/723-7333
Contact, Keith A.J. Hay

### Canadian Institute of Planners/Institut canadien des urbanistes (CIP) (1919)
#801, 116 Albert St., Ottawa, ON K1P 5G3
613/237-7526, Fax: 613/237-7045, Toll Free: 1-800-207-2138, Email: general@cip-icu.ca, URL: http://www.cip-icu.ca
Executive Director, Rachel Corbett, MCIP
President Elect, Barbara Dembek, MCIP
President, Gerry Couture, MCIP
Publications: Plan Canada
Affiliates: Commonwealth Association of Planners

#### ALBERTA ASSOCIATION, CANADIAN INSTITUTE OF PLANNERS (AACIP) (1963)
PO Box 596, Edmonton, AB T5J 2K8
403/435-8716, Fax: 403/435-7503
Email: b.holtby@ccinet.ab.ca
Publications: Planning Digest

#### ATLANTIC PLANNING INSTITUTE/INSTITUT DES URBANISTES DE L'ATLANTIQUE
PO Box 2012, RPO Central, Halifax, NS B3J 2Z1
506/577-4391
Email: ncollins@fox.nstn.ca
Representative, Armand Robichaud, MCIP
Publications: Planners Pen

#### MANITOBA ASSOCIATION OF THE CANADIAN INSTITUTE OF PLANNERS
137 Bannatyne Ave., Winnipeg, MB R3B 0K3
204/943-3637
President, D.J. Kalcsics, MCIP
Treasurer, A.P. Regiec, MCIP

#### ONTARIO PROFESSIONAL PLANNERS INSTITUTE/INSTITUT DES PLANIFICATEURS PROFESSIONNELS DE L'ONTARIO (OPPI) (1986)
#201, 234 Eglinton Ave. East, Toronto, ON M4P 1K5
416/483-1873, Fax: 416/483-7830, Toll Free: 1-800-668-1448
Email: oppi@interlog.com, URL: http://www.interlog.com/~oppi
Executive Director, Susan Smith
President, V. Cranmer
Publications: Ontario Planning Journal

#### ORDRE DES URBANISTES DU QUÉBEC (OUQ) (1963)
85, rue St-Paul ouest, 4e étage, #B5, Montréal, QC H2Y 3V4
514/849-1177, Téléc: 514/849-7176
Directrice générale, Gisèle Floch Rousselle
Publications: En Bref

#### PLANNING INSTITUTE OF BRITISH COLUMBIA (PIBC)
#20, 10551 Shellbridge Way, Richmond, BC V6X 2W9
604/270-2061, Fax: 604/660-2271
URL: http://www.pibc.bc.ca
President, Rob Roycroft
Secretary, Gary Holisko
Publications: PIBC News

### Canadian Urban Institute/Institut urbain du Canada (CUI) (1991)
30 St. Patrick St., 6th Fl., Toronto, ON M5T 3A3
416/598-1606, Fax: 416/598-5145, URL: http://www.interlog.com/~cui
President, John Farrow

### Intergovernmental Committee on Urban & Regional Research/Comité intergouvernemental de recherches urbaines et régionales (ICURR) (1967)
#301, 150 Eglinton Ave. East, Toronto, ON M4P 1E8
416/973-5629, Fax: 416/973-1375, Email: mafar@icurr.org, URL: http://www.icurr.org/icurr/
Executive Director, André Lanteigne
Chairman, Ken MacLeod
Senior Information Officer, Victoria Gregor, Bus: 416/973-1339
Information Officer, John Slatcher, Bus: 416/973-9408
Information Officer, Michael Afar, Bus: 416/973-1331
Publications: Liaison

### Rural Dignity of Canada/Dignité rurale du Canada (1986)
PO Box 70, Barachois-de-Malbaie, QC G0C 1A0
418/645-3766, Fax: 418/645-3835
National Coordinator, Cynthia Patterson
Assistant to National Coordinator, Sandra LeMieux
Publications: Newsletter
Affiliates: Transport 2000 Canada

### Urban Development Institute of Canada/Institut de développement urbain du Canada (UDI)
717 Pender St. West, 3rd Fl., Vancouver, BC V6C 1G9
604/669-9585, Fax: 604/689-8691, URL: http://www.udi.bc.ca
Executive Director, Maureen Enser
National President, Jack Winberg
Shari Borger

### PLUMBING *see* HEATING, AIR CONDITIONING, PLUMBING

### POLICE *see* LAW

## POLITICS

*see also* **Government & Public Administration**

### Association Canado-Américaine (ACA) (1896)

898, rue Ste-Julie, Trois-Rivières, QC G9A 1Y2
819/376-2111, Téléc: 819/376-2662
Chief Agent, Henri Lemay
Président Général, Eugene A. Lemieux, Numéro au travail: 603/625-8577
Publications: Le Canado-Americain
Organisation(s) affiliée(s): Canadian Fraternal Association

### BC Social Credit Party

PO Box 26088, Richmond, BC V6Y 3V3
604/270-4040, Fax: 604/270-4726
President, Jane Sorko

### Bloc québécois (BQ) (1991)

#055, 1200, av Papineau, Montréal, QC H2K 4R5
514/526-3000, Téléc: 514/526-2868, Courrier électronique: infobloc@bloc.org, URL: http://blocquebecois.org
Chef, Gilles Duceppe
Directeur général, Yves Dufour

### Canadian Political Science Association/Association canadienne de science politique (CPSA) (1913)

#205, One Stewart St., Ottawa, ON K1N 6H7
613/564-4026, Fax: 613/230-2746, Email: cpsa@csse.ca, URL: http://www.sfu.ca/igs/CPSA.html
Publications: Canadian Journal of Political Science/Revue canadienne de science politique; Bulletin; Directory of Political Scientists in Canada

### Christian Heritage Party of Canada/Parti d'héritage du Canada (CHP) (1986)

800 Niagara St., PO Box 23033, RPO Seaway Mall, Welland, ON L3C 7E7
905/788-2238, Fax: 905/788-2943
National Leader, Ron Gray
Party President, Carol Speelmah
Party Secretary, Betty Schaap
Party Treasurer, Gerald Tot
Executive Director, Margaret Purcell
Publications: Ambassador
Affiliates: CHP New Zealand

### Comité Québécois pour le Canada/Québec Committee for Canada

#3040, 6900, boul Décarie, Montréal, QC H3X 2T8
514/344-2410, Fax: 514/344-2760

### The Confederation of Regions Party of New Brunswick (1989)

**CoR Party of New Brunswick**

PO Box 3322, Stn B, Fredericton, NB E3A 5H1
506/444-4040, Fax: 506/444-4053, Email: cor@nbnet.nb.ca
Interim Leader, Greg Hargrove
President, Tony Huntjens
Contact, R. Finley

### Le Conseil pour l'unité canadienne/The Council for Canadian Unity (CUC) (1964)

#2811, 1800, av McGill College, Montréal, QC H3A 3J6
514/849-5303, Téléc: 514/849-7402, Ligne sans frais: 1-800-363-0963, URL: http://www.ccu-cuc.ca/
Président et chef de la direction, Jocelyn L. Beaudoin, CM

### Family Coalition Party of Ontario/Parti de la coalition des familles de l'Ontario (FCP) (1987)

#19, 117 Ringwood Dr., Stouffville, ON L4A 8C1
416/640-6702, Fax: 416/640-8102
Party Leader, Don Pennell
Chief Financial Officer, Henri Cloudt
Publications: Impact

### Green Party of Canada/Parti vert du Canada (GPC) (1983)

**Canadian Greens/Canadiens Verts**

#5, 3147 Kingsway, Vancouver, BC V5R 5K2
604/436-1437, Fax: 604/436-1438
Leader, Wendy Priesnitz
Executive Secretary, Annie Humphries-Loutit
Treasurer, Eileen Stevens
Fundraising Coordinator, Eric Saumur
Publications Coordinator, Peggy Robinson
Membership Secretary, John Beverley

#### GREEN PARTY OF BRITISH COLUMBIA (1983)

#515, 620 View St., Vancouver, BC V8W 1J6
250/382-8378, Fax: 250/382-8378
Email: editor@greenparty.bc.ca, URL: http://www.greenparty.bc.ca
Chair, David G. Cursons
Provincial Party Leader, Stuart Parker
Secretary, Annie Humphries-Loutit
Provincial Treasurer, Eileen Stevens
Membership Chair, David Walters
Publications: BC Green Party News

#### THE ONTARIO GREENS

**Green Party of Ontario/Green Party of Canada - Ontario Wing**

PO Box 35101, Ottawa, ON K1Z 1A2
613/724-6061, Fax: 613/232-3081
Email: greenpty@freenet.toronto.on.ca
Information Officer, Sharon Tivers
Publications: Ontario Greenhouse; Ontario Green News

#### PARTI VERT DU CANADA (QUÉBEC)/GREEN PARTY OF CANADA (QUÉBEC) (1984)

**Les verts/The Greens**

CP 262, Succ. Jean-Talon, Montréal, QC H1S 2Z2
514/259-3580, Téléc: 514/843-3757
Coordonateur, Rolf Bramann
Secrétaire général, Jean Guérnon

#### PARTI VERT DU QUÉBEC/QUÉBEC GREEN PARTY (PVQ) (1985)

196, ch de la Côte St-Antoine, Montréal, QC H3Y 2J2
514/937-9399
Victor Martel
Bernard Cooper
Publications: Verus

### The Liberal Party of Canada/Le Parti Libéral du Canada (1867)

#400, 81 Metcalfe St., Ottawa, ON K1P 6M8
613/237-0740, Fax: 613/235-7208, Email: info@liberal.ca, URL: http://www.liberal.ca
Leader, Right Honourable Jean Chrétien
President, Senator Dan Hays
Vice-President, English, Mobina Jaffer
Vice-President, French, Pierre Isabelle
Sec.-Treas., Graham Pyle
National Director, Terry Mercer
Publications: The Liberal Times
Affiliates: Liberal International

#### ALBERTA LIBERAL PARTY

#100, 10045 - 111 St., Edmonton, AB T5K 2M5
403/482-3994, Fax: 403/488-7513
Executive Director, Rob Van Walleghem

#### THE LIBERAL PARTY OF CANADA (BRITISH COLUMBIA)/PARTI LIBÉRAL DU CANADA (COLOMBIE-BRITANNIQUE) (LPC(BC))

1447 Hornby St., Vancouver, BC V6Z 1W8
604/730-8933, Fax: 604/730-8919
Email: Admin@BC.Liberal.ca
President, Norman Morrison

#### LIBERAL PARTY OF CANADA (ONTARIO)/PARTI LIBÉRAL DU CANADA (ONTARIO) (LPC(O))

PO Box 1108, Stn F, Toronto, ON M4Y 2T8
416/921-2844, Fax: 416/921-3880, Toll Free: 1-800-361-3881
President, Stephen LeDrew
Executive Director, Henry Wright

#### THE LIBERAL PARTY OF CANADA IN ALBERTA (LPC(A))

Metropolitan Plaza, 520 - 10303 Jasper Ave. NW, Edmonton, AB T5J 3N6
403/424-1984, Fax: 403/424-1966
President, Randolph Langley
Office Manager, Delores Yuzda

#### THE LIBERAL PARTY IN MANITOBA/PARTI LIBÉRAL AU MANITOBA

#2, 140 Roslyn Rd., Winnipeg, MB R3L 0G8
204/453-7343, Fax: 204/284-1492
President, Zela Vermeulen
Executive Director, Donald T. Hillman

#### LIBERAL PARTY OF NEWFOUNDLAND & LABRADOR/PARTI LIBÉRAL DE TERRE-NEUVE ET DU LABRADOR

PO Box 998, Stn C, St. John's, NF A1C 5M3
709/754-1813, Fax: 709/754-0820
President, John O'Brien
Executive Director, Fred Rowe

#### LIBERAL PARTY OF PRINCE EDWARD ISLAND/PARTI LIBÉRAL DE L'ÎLE DU PRINCE ÉDOUARD

PO Box 2559, Charlottetown, PE C1A 8C4
902/368-3449, Fax: 902/368-3687
President, Joe Broderick
Executive Director, Linda MacInnis

#### NEW BRUNSWICK LIBERAL ASSOCIATION

715 Brunswick St., Fredericton, NB E3B 1H8
506/453-3950, Fax: 506/453-2476
President, Réginald Léger
Executive Director, Steven MacKinnon

#### NORTHWEST TERRITORIES LIBERAL ASSOCIATION/ASSOCIATION LIBÉRALE DES TERRITORIES DU NORD-OUEST

4514 School Draw Ave., Yellowknife, NT X1A 2K3
President, Ruth Spence

#### NOVA SCOTIA LIBERAL ASSOCIATION/ASSOCIATION LIBÉRALE DE LA NOUVELLE-ÉCOSSE

PO Box 723, Halifax, NS B3J 2T3
902/429-1993, Fax: 902/423-1624
President, Lloyd Campbell
Executive Director, Anna M. Redmond
Publications: Newsletter

#### PARTI LIBÉRAL DU CANADA (QUÉBEC)/LIBERAL PARTY OF CANADA (QUEBEC) (PLC(Q))

640, rue St-Paul ouest, Montréal, QC H3C 1L9
514/866-6391, Téléc: 514/866-8182, Ligne sans frais: 1-800-361-8839
Présidente, Françoise Patry
Directeur général, Michel Béliveau

#### PARTI LIBERAL DU QUÉBEC/QUÉBEC LIBERAL PARTY

4364, rue Saint-Denis, Montréal, QC H2J 2L1
514/288-4364, Téléc: 514/288-9455
Directeur général, Stéphane Bertrand

#### SASKATCHEWAN LIBERAL ASSOCIATION/ASSOCIATION LIBÉRALE DE LA SASKATCHEWAN

2054 Broad St., PO Box 4401, Regina, SK S4P 1Y3
306/522-8507, Fax: 306/569-9271
President, Anita Bergman

#### YUKON LIBERAL ASSOCIATION/ASSOCIATION LIBÉRALE DU YUKON

RR#1, Site 2, Comp 3, Whitehorse, YT Y1A 5V3
President, Larry Bagnell

### The Libertarian Party of Canada

#301, One St. John's Rd., Toronto, ON M6P 1T7

416/763-3688, Fax: 416/763-5306
President, Chris Blatchly
Contact, D. Kublas

**BRITISH COLUMBIA LIBERTARIAN PARTY (1986)**
922 Cloverley St., North Vancouver, BC V7L 1N3
604/980-7370, Fax: 604/980-6690
President, Bill Tomlinson
Affiliates: Foundation for Research on Economics & the Environment

**GREATER VANCOUVER LIBERTARIAN ASSOCIATION (1973)**
922 Cloverley St., North Vancouver, BC V7L 1N3
604/980-7370, Fax: 604/980-6690
Director, Bill Tomlinson
President, Kerry Pearson
Publications: West Coast Libertarian
Affiliates: Foundation for Research on Economics & the Environment - USA

**MANITOBA LIBERTARIAN ASSOCIATION**
PO Box 245, Winnipeg, MB R3C 3R3
204/474-1056
Contact, C. Smith

**New Democratic Party/Nouveau Parti Démocratique (NDP)**
Federal Headquarters, #900, 81 Metcalfe St., Ottawa, ON K1P 6K7
613/236-3613, Fax: 613/230-9950
Leader, Alexa McDonough
Director of Policy, Judy Randall
Federal President, Iain Angus
Treasurer, Armand Roy

**Parti communiste du Québec (1965)**
CP 29, Succ. C, Montréal, QC H2L 4J7
514/273-6577
André Cloutier
Panagiotis Vamvakaris
Publications: L'Alternative; Le Communiste
Organisation(s) affiliée(s): Solidarité populaire Québec; Ligue des droits et libertés

**Parti québécois (PQ) (1968)**
#150, 1200, av Papineau, Montréal, QC H2K 4R5
514/526-0020, Téléc: 514/526-0272, Ligne sans frais: 1-800-363-9531, Courrier électronique: pqnatio@cam.org
Directeur général, Yves Dufour
Président, Lucien Bouchard
1e Vice-président, Fabien Béchard
Directeur des communications, Michel Leveillé
Publications: La Lettre du Parti

**Progressive Conservative Party of Canada/Parti progressiste-conservateur du Canada**
#501, 275 Slater St., Ottawa, ON K1P 5H9
613/238-6111, Fax: 613/238-7429, Email: pcinfo@pcparty.ca, URL: http://www.pcparty.ca/
Leader, Honourable Jean Charest, PC, MP
National President, Pierre W. Fortier
National Director, Michael Allen
Secretary, Dr. Kellie Leitch
Treasurer, Rick Perkins
Progressive Conservative Youth Federation: National President, Tasha Kheiriddin, #501, 275 Slater St., Ottawa, ON K1P 5H9, 613/238-6111, Fax: 613/238-7429
Montréal Office: Contact, Sylvia English, Tour de la Bourse, #1225, 800, Place Victoria, CP 55, Montréal, QC H4Z 1A8, 506/875-5464, Téléc: 506/875-5981
Ontario Regional Office: Ontario Organizer, Suzanne Warren, 21 Howland Ave., Toronto, ON M4K 2Z4, 416/469-5525, Fax: 416/469-2671
BC Regional Office: Manager, Matt Burns, 1917 West 4th Ave., PO Box 360, Vancouver, BC V6J 1M7, 604/730-8451, Fax: 604/730-8471

**Reform Party of Canada/Parti reformiste du Canada (REF) (1987)**
#600, 833 - 4 Ave. SW, Calgary, AB T2P 0K5
403/269-1990, Fax: 403/269-4077, URL: http://www.reform.ca
Executive Director, Glenn McMurray
Leader, Preston Manning
Publications: Reformer

**Socialist Party of Canada/Parti Socialiste du Canada (SPC) (1931)**
PO Box 4280, Victoria, BC V8X 3X8
250/595-2144, Email: 72607.2404@compuserve.com, URL: http://www.tcel.com/~sp/
General Secretary, Steve Szalai
Publications: Socialist Standard; World Socialist Review, irreg.
Affiliates: World Socialist Movement

**POLLUTION *see* ENVIRONMENTAL**

## POULTRY & EGGS

**Alberta Egg Producers' Board**
#15, 1915 - 32 Ave. NE, Calgary, AB T2E 7C8
403/250-1197, Fax: 403/291-9216, Email: altaegg@cadvision.com
General Manager, Warren Chorney

**Atlantic Provinces Hatchery Federation**
Agriculture Centre, #B122, 32 Main St., Kentville, NS B4N 1J5
902/679-5333, Fax: 902/679-6062
Sec.-Treas., Herbert N. Jansen

**British Columbia Broiler Hatching Egg Producers' Association (1980)**
PO Box 667, Abbotsford, BC V2S 6R7
604/852-6233, Fax: 604/859-4431
President, Chris den Hertog
Affiliates: BC Broiler Hatching Egg Commission

**Canadian Broiler Hatching Egg Marketing Agency**
#705, 200 Elgin St., Ottawa, ON K2P 1L5
613/232-3023, Fax: 613/232-5241
Secretary, Paul Jelley

**Canadian Chicken Marketing Agency/Office canadien de commercialisation des poulets (CCMA) (1978)**
#300, 377 Dalhousie St., Ottawa, ON K1N 9N8
613/241-2800, Fax: 613/241-5999, Telex: 053-4518
General Manager, Cynthia Currie
Policy Manager, Albert Chambers
Communications Manager, Nicole Beauchamp
Publications: Chicken Forum

**Canadian Egg Marketing Agency/Office canadien de commercialisation des oeufs (CEMA) (1972)**
#1900, 320 Queen St., Ottawa, ON K1R 5A3
613/238-2514, Fax: 613/238-1967
Email: info@canadaegg.ca, URL: http://www.canadaegg.ca
Chief Executive, Neil Currie
Publications: Today's Egg Producer

**Canadian Egg Producers Council**
#1101, 75 Albert St., Ottawa, ON K1P 5E7
613/236-3633, Fax: 613/236-5749
Executive Secretary, Sally Rutherford

**Canadian Poultry & Egg Processors Council/Conseil canadien des transformateurs d'oeufs et de volailles (CPEPC) (1975)**
#600, 2 Gurdwara Rd., Ottawa, ON K2E 1A2
613/224-0001, Fax: 613/224-2023
Anne Brownrigg
Chairman, Pieter Vanderpol
Publications: Newsletter

**Canadian Turkey Marketing Agency/Office canadien de commercialisation du dindon (CTMA) (1974)**
#102, 969 Derry Rd. East., Mississauga, ON L5T 2J7
905/564-3100, Fax: 905/792-7535
Email: ctma@canturkey.ca, URL: http://www.canturkey.ca
Executive Director, Philip J. Boyd
Publications: Plume; Turkey Facts, a.

**Fédération des producteurs d'oeufs de consommation du Québec (1965)**
555, boul Roland-Therrien, Longueuil, QC J4H 3Y9
514/679-0530, Téléc: 514/679-0855
Président, Jacques Bouchard

**Fédération des producteurs de volailles du Québec/Federation of Quebec Poultry Producers**
555, boul Roland-Therrien, Longueuil, QC J4H 3Y9
514/679-0530, Fax: 514/679-5375
Président, Luc Lamy
Publications: PROVOQUE

**New Brunswick Poultry Council**
#103, 1115 Regent St., Fredericton, NB E3B 3Z2
506/452-8085, Fax: 506/451-2121

**Ontario Hatcheries Association**
#101, 49 Emma St., Guelph, ON N1E 6X1
519/763-6360, Fax: 519/837-0729

## PRINTING INDUSTRY & GRAPHIC ARTS

**Association des arts graphiques du Québec, inc. (AAGQ) (1983)**
#101, 65, rue de Castelnau ouest, Montréal, QC H2R 2W3
514/274-7446, Téléc: 514/274-7482, Ligne sans frais: 1-800-607-7446
Directrice générale, Hélène Lagadec
Président, Pierre Audet
Publications: Le Maître imprimeur
Organisation(s) affiliée(s): Association canadienne de l'imprimerie; Printing Industries of America

**Business Documents & Systems Association/Association des fabricants de systèmes et documents de gestion (BDSA) (1972)**
#906, 75 Albert St., Ottawa, ON K1P 5E7
613/236-7723, Fax: 613/236-7084, URL: http://www.bdsa.ca
Executive Director, Neil Fitzmaurice

**Canadian Printing Industries Association/Association canadienne de l'imprimerie (CPIA) (1958)**
#906, 75 Albert St., Ottawa, ON K1P 5E7
613/236-7208, Fax: 613/236-8169
President, Michael Makin
Publications: CPIA Membership Directory; National Communiqué, m.; National Impressions, m.
Affiliates: Graphic Arts Council of North America; Printing Industries of America
Printing & Graphics Industries Association of Alberta: President, Doug Sloane; Executive Sec.-Treas., Joan Kumlin, PO Box 21006, RPO Dominion, Calgary, AB T2P 4H5, 403/281-1421, Fax: 403/251-6702, Email: kumlinje@cadvision.com

**Canadian Printing Ink Manufacturers Association (CPIMA) (1936)**
1532 Greenridge Circle, Oakville, ON L6M 2J4

905/847-2838, Fax: 905/847-2838
Executive Director, John A. Nace
President, Ralph Marshall

**Council of Printing Industries of Canada**
#208, 510 Front St. West, Toronto, ON M5V 3H3
416/599-1931, Fax: 416/408-4704
General Manager, Jean-Marc Metthé

**Forms & Manuals Management Association**
PO Box 5338, Stn A, Toronto, ON M5W 1N6
416/285-2854, Fax: 416/285-2955
President, Carol MacDonald
Publications: Platform

**GraphComm Training Centre (1969)**
**Ontario Graphic Communications Training Centre**
#109, 80 Park Lawn Rd., Toronto, ON M8Y 3H8
416/251-5449
Mike Zajac
John Marc-Metthé

**Printing Equipment & Supply Dealers' Association of Canada (PESDA) (1975)**
#320, 304 East Mall, Etobicoke, ON M9B 6E2
416/236-3733, Fax: 416/236-2171
Contact, Jennifer Rogers

**Saskatchewan Graphic Arts Industries Association Inc. (SGAIA)**
c/o PrintWest, PO Box 2500, Saskatoon, SK S7K 2C4
306/665-3549, Fax: 306/653-1255
Contact, Don Breher

**Society of Graphic Designers of Canada/Société des graphistes du Canada (GDC)**
Arts Court, 2 Daly Ave., Ottawa, ON K1N 6E2
613/567-5400, Fax: 613/564-4428, Email: gdcnat@magi.com, URL: http://www.swifty.com/gdc/
President, Steven Rosenberg
Publications: Axis; Graphic Design Journal; The National
Affiliates: International Council of Graphic Design Associations

## PRISONERS & EX-OFFENDERS

*see also* Law

**British Columbia Borstal Association**
#202, 2425 Quebec St., Vancouver, BC V5T 4L6
604/879-3224
Executive Director, John A. Cooper

**Canadian Association of Elizabeth Fry Societies/Association canadienne des sociétés Elizabeth Fry (CAEFS) (1978)**
#701, 151 Slater St., Ottawa, ON K1P 5H3
613/238-2422, Fax: 613/232-7130, Email: kpate@web.net, URL: http://www.web.apc.org/~kpate
Executive Director, Kim Pate
President, Susan Hendricks
Affiliates: National Associations Active in Criminal Justice; National Action Committee on the Status of Women; National Association of Women & the Law; National Voluntary Organizations; Canadian Criminal Justice Association; Women's Legal & Education & Action Fund; National Council of Women of Canada; United Way National Agencies Committee

**The John Howard Society of Canada/Société John Howard du Canada**
771 1/2 Montreal St., Kingston, ON K7K 3J6
613/542-7547, Fax: 613/542-6824, Email: jhsc@web.net, URL: http://www.nald.ca/jhs.htm

Executive Director, Graham Stewart
President, Burt Galaway

**Operation Springboard (1974)**
**Springboard**
230 Richmond St. East, Toronto, ON M5A 1P4
416/367-4288, Fax: 416/367-4291
Executive Director, Diane Nicholls
Publications: Perspectives

**Prisoners' Rights Group (PRG) (1975)**
3570 Dease Lane, Vancouver, BC V5S 1M6
604/432-6132, Fax: 604/430-2019
Coordinator, Claire Culhane

**Quaker Committee on Jails & Justice (QCJJ) (1975)**
60 Lowther Ave., Toronto, ON M5R 1C7
416/920-5213
Program Associate, Marc Forget
Clerk, Marianne Ostopovich
Publications: QCJJ Newsletter
Affiliates: Alternatives to Violence Project - Canada

**St. Leonard's Society of Canada/Société Saint-Léonard du Canada (SLSC) (1967)**
#712, 151 Slater St., Ottawa, ON K1P 5H3
416/233-5170, Fax: 416/977-6698, Email: slsc@istar.ca
Executive Director, Elizabeth White
Publications: Coast to Coast

**Seventh Step Society of Canada**
10620 Waneta Cres. SE, Calgary, AB T2J 1J6
403/271-2278, Fax: 403/271-8907
Executive Director, Patrick Graham
Affiliates: Seventh Step Society International

**PRO-LIFE ORGANIZATIONS *see* REPRODUCTIVE ISSUES**

**PROFESSIONAL DEVELOPMENT *see* EMPLOYMENT & HUMAN RESOURCES**

**PROFIT SHARING *see* FINANCE**

**PSYCHIATRY *see* MENTAL HEALTH**

**PSYCHOLOGY *see* MENTAL HEALTH**

**PUBLIC ADMINISTRATION *see* GOVERNMENT & PUBLIC ADMINISTRATION**

**PUBLIC HEALTH *see* HEALTH & MEDICAL**

## PUBLIC UTILITIES

**Canadian Association of Members of Public Utility Tribunals (CAMPUT)**
#2601, 2300 Yonge St., PO Box 2319, Toronto, ON M4P 1E4
Chair, Gerry Forrest
Sec.-Treas., Carol Horwood
Affiliates: National Association of Regulatory Utility Commissioners

**Canadian Council of Electrical Leagues (1984)**
#1000, 2 Lansing Sq., North York, ON M2J 4P8
416/495-0052, Fax: 416/495-1804
Secretary, Richard McCarten

**Canadian Public Works Association (CPWA)**
3370 South Service Rd., Garden Level, Burlington, ON L7N 3M6
905/634-7736, Fax: 905/634-1304

**Electrical Utilities Safety Association of Ontario (EUSA) (1915)**
220 Traders Blvd. East, Mississauga, ON L4Z 1W7
905/890-1011, Fax: 905/890-9249
General Manager, C.J. Tallon
Publications: Safe-T-Line; Safety Topics, m.

**Municipal Electric Association (MEA) (1986)**
#500, 20 Eglinton Ave. West, PO Box 2004, Toronto, ON M4R 1K8
416/483-7739, Fax: 416/483-9039, Email: mea@med.on.ca
CEO, T. Jennings
Publications: Circuit Breaker

**Ontario Municipal Water Association (OMWA)**
#69, 225 Benjamin Rd., Waterloo, ON N2J 3Z4
519/888-6402, Fax: 519/725-5987
Executive Director, D.J. Black
Publications: OMWA Newsletter; Pipeline, q.
Affiliates: America Water Works Association

**Utility Contractors' Association of Ontario Inc. (UCA)**
#720, 5915 Airport Rd., Mississauga, ON L4V 1T1
905/673-0548, Fax: 905/673-0546
General Manager, Barry L. Brown

## PUBLISHING

***see also* Printing Industry & Graphic Arts; Writers & Editors**

**Alcuin Society (1965)**
PO Box 3216, Vancouver, BC V6B 3X8
604/872-2326, Fax: 604/872-4235
Secretary, Doreen E. Eddy, Bus: 604/888-9049
Publications: Amphora

**Alternative Newspapers Association**
NOW Communications, 150 Danforth Ave., Toronto, ON M4K 1N1
416/461-0871, Fax: 416/461-2886
Contact, Alice Klein

**Association of Book Publishers of British Columbia (ABPBC) (1974)**
#107, 100 West Pender St., Vancouver, BC V6B 1R8
604/684-0228, Fax: 604/684-5788, Email: admin@books.bc.ca, URL: http://www.books.bc.ca
Executive Director, Margaret Reynolds
President, Jean Wilson
Publications: ABPBC Directory
Affiliates: Association of Canadian Publishers

**Association of Canadian Publishers/Association des éditeurs canadiens (ACP) (1972)**
#301, 2 Gloucester St., Toronto, ON M4Y 1L5
416/413-4929, Fax: 416/413-4920, URL: http://www.publishers.ca
President, Jack Stoddart
Executive Director, Paul Davidson
Vice-President, Sibyl Frei
Treasurer, Mary Mahoney-Robson
Secretary, Robert Davies
Publications: Just the Fax; ACP Directory, a.
Affiliates: Association of Book Publishers of British Columbia; Book Publishers Association of Alberta; Saskatchewan Publishers Group; Association of Manitoba Book Publishers; Ontario Publishers Group; Association des editeurs anglophones du Québec; Atlantic Publishers Association

**ASSOCIATION DES ÉDITEURS ANGLOPHONES DU QUÉBEC/QUÉBEC ENGLISH LANGUAGE PUBLISHERS ASSOCIATION (1990)**
#3, 1200, av Atwater, Montréal, QC H3Z 1X4

514/932-5633, Téléc: 514/932-5456
Président, Robert Davies

#### ASSOCIATION OF MANITOBA BOOK PUBLISHERS
#404, 100 Arthur St., Winnipeg, MB R3B 1H3
204/947-3335, Fax: 204/942-1555
Executive Director, Maureen Devanik

#### ATLANTIC PUBLISHERS ASSOCIATION (APA)
Lord Nelson Arcade, #202, 5675 Spring Garden Rd., Halifax, NS B3J 1H1
902/420-0711, Fax: 902/423-4302
Executive Director, Paulette Soloman

#### BOOK PUBLISHERS ASSOCIATION OF ALBERTA (BPA) (1975)
#123, 10523 - 100 Ave., Edmonton, AB T5J 0A8
403/424-5060, Fax: 403/424-7943
Email: bpaa@planet.eon.net
Executive Director, Katherine Shute
Publications: Newsletter
Affiliates: Rocky Mountain Book Publishers Association

### Association of Canadian University Presses/Association des presses universitaires canadiennes (ACUP) (1965)
35 Spadina Rd., Toronto, ON M5R 2S9
416/978-5850, Fax: 416/978-4738, Email: bkper@interlog.com
Secretary, Kathryn Bennett
Publications: Directory of Members

### Association for the Export of Canadian Books/Association pour l'exportation du livre canadien (AECB) (1972)
#504, One Nicholas St., Ottawa, ON K1N 7B7
613/562-2324, Fax: 613/562-2329, Email: aecb@aecb.org, URL: http://aecb.org
Executive Director, Luc Jutras
President & Chairman, Andrew Shaw
Publications: Biblio Export; Books on Canada; Rights Canada/Droits du Canada, biennial
Affiliates: Association of Canadian Publishers; Canadian Book Publishers Council; Association of Canadian University Presses; Association nationale des éditeurs de livres

### Association des libraires du Québec (ALQ) (1969)
1306, rue Logan, Montréal, QC H2L 1X1
514/526-3349, Téléc: 514/526-3340, Courrier électronique: lucie.lachapelle@alq.qc.ca
Directrice générale, Lucie Lachapelle
Président, Guy Beaulieu
Vice-président, Robert Leroux
Trésorier, Jacques Boutin
Secrétaire, Lynne Magnan
Recherchiste et rédactrice, Francine Déry
Publications: Bulletin de nouvelles; Répertoire des éditeurs et de leurs distributeurs, trimestriel; Annuaire des membres, annuel

### Association nationale des éditeurs de livres (ANEL) (1991)
2514, boul Rosemont, Montréal, QC H1Y 1K4
514/273-8130, Téléc: 514/273-9657, Courrier électronique: anel@cam.org, URL: http://www.cam.org/~anel/index.htm
Directrice générale, Lise Oligny

### Association québécoise des presses universitaires (AQPU)
a/s Presses de l'Université Laval, CP 2208, Succ. Terminus, Québec, QC G1K 7R4
418/656-3001, Téléc: 418/656-3305
Denis Vaugeois

### Association québécoise des salons du livre (1978)
#202, 480, rue St-Laurent, Montréal, QC H2Y 3Y7
514/845-2365, Téléc: 514/845-7119, Courrier électronique: slm.info@videotron.ca
Président, Francine Bois
Secrétaire, Johanne Gaudreau

### Book & Periodical Council (BPC) (1975)
35 Spadina Rd., Toronto, ON M5R 2S9
416/975-9366, Fax: 416/975-1839, Email: bkper@interlog.com
Executive Director, Nancy Fleming
Chair, Genia Lorentowicz

### Book Promoters' Association of Canada (BPAC)
c/o Random House of Canada, #210, 33 Yonge St., Toronto, ON M5E 1G4
President, Sheila Kay, Bus: 416/777-9841
Publications: BPAC Newsletter

### Canadian Book Manufacturers' Association (CBMA)
#906, 75 Albert St., Ottawa, ON K1P 5E7
613/236-7208, Fax: 613/236-8169
Executive Director, Neil Fitzmaurice
Affiliates: Book Manufacturers' Institute Inc.

### Canadian Bookbinders & Book Artists Guild/Guilde canadienne des relieurs et des artisans du livre (CBBAG) (1983)
#309, 176 John St., Toronto, ON M5T 1X5
416/581-1071
President, Ann Douglas
Publications: The CBBAG Newsletter
Affiliates: Ontario Crafts Council

### Canadian Booksellers Association (CBA) (1952)
301 Donlands Ave., Toronto, ON M4J 3R8
416/467-7883, Fax: 416/467-7886, Email: enquiries@cbabook.org, URL: http://www.cbabook.org
Executive Director, John Finlay, CAE
President, Jane Conney
First Vice-President, Ron Johnson
Second Vice-President, Gailmarie Anderson
Treasurer, Wayne Oakley
Publications: The Canadian Bookseller

### The Canadian Children's Book Centre (CCBC) (1976)
35 Spadina Rd., Toronto, ON M5R 2S9
416/975-0010, Fax: 416/975-1839, Email: ccbc@lglobal.com, URL: http://www.lglobal.com/~ccbc/
Executive Director, Charlotte Teeple
Program Coordinator, Jeffrey Canton
Publications: Children's Book News

### Canadian Circulation Management Association/Association canadienne des chefs de tirage (CCMA) (1933)
298 Highfield St., Moncton, NB E1C 5R6
506/854-7091, Fax: 506/855-1334
Secretary, Dave Dorman
Publications: CCMA Newsletter
Affiliates: Newspaper Association of America

### Canadian Circulations Audit Board Inc./Office canadien de vérification de la diffusion (CCAB) (1937)
#304, 188 Eglinton Ave. East, Toronto, ON M4P 2X7
416/487-2418, Fax: 416/487-6405
General Manager/President, Patrick Sweeney
Publications: Circulate

### Canadian Community Newspapers Association (CCNA) (1919)
#206, 90 Eglinton Ave. East, Toronto, ON M4P 2Y3
416/482-1090, Fax: 416/482-1908, Email: ccna@sentex.net, URL: http://www.sentex.net/~ccna
Executive Director, Michael Anderson
Regional Services Director, Karen Hamilton

#### ALBERTA WEEKLY NEWSPAPERS ASSOCIATION (AWNA)
Terrace Plaza, #360, 4445 Calgary Trail South, Edmonton, AB T6H 5R7
403/434-8746, Fax: 403/438-8356
Email: info@awnet.net
Executive Director, Dennis Merrell, CAE

#### ATLANTIC COMMUNITY NEWSPAPERS ASSOCIATION (ACNA)
PO Box 2500, Lunenburg, NS B0J 2C0
902/634-9355, Fax: 902/634-9362
Email: acna@atcon.com
Executive Director, Shelah Allen

#### BRITISH COLUMBIA & YUKON COMMUNITY NEWSPAPERS ASSOCIATION (1916)
#230, 1380 Burrard St., Vancouver, BC V6Z 2B7
604/669-9222, Fax: 604/684-4713
Executive Director, Allen L. Treleaven
Publications: Communicator; Publishers' Update, bi-weekly

#### MANITOBA COMMUNITY NEWSPAPERS ASSOCIATION (MCNA) (1919)
#310, 275 Portage Ave., Winnipeg, MB R3B 2B3
204/947-1691, Fax: 204/947-1919
Email: mcna@mb.sympatico.ca, URL: http://mcna.com
Executive Director, Clint Szakacs
Publications: Reaching the Manitoba Market

#### ONTARIO COMMUNITY NEWSPAPERS ASSOCIATION (OCNA) (1950)
#103, 3050 Harvester Rd., Burlington, ON L7N 3J1
905/639-8720, Fax: 905/639-6962
Email: info@ocna.org, URL: http://www.ocna.org
Executive Director, Don Lamont
Publications: Newsclips

#### QUÉBEC COMMUNITY NEWSPAPER ASSOCIATION/ASSOCIATION DES JOURNAUX RÉGIONAUX DU QUÉBEC (QCNA) (1980)
Glenaladale House, MacDonald College, 21111, rue Lakeshore, Ste-Anne-de-Bellevue, QC H9X 3V9
514/398-7706, Fax: 514/398-7972
Email: qcna@ocna.org
Executive Director, Allan S. Davis, CAE
Publications: Intermedia; Québec Community Newspapers Databook, a.
Affiliates: Conseil du presse du Québec; Canadian Daily Newspapers Association

#### SASKATCHEWAN WEEKLY NEWSPAPERS ASSOCIATION (1913)
#4, 2155 Airport Dr., Saskatoon, SK S7G 6M5
306/382-9683, Fax: 306/382-9421
Sec.-Treas., Linda Bobowski
Publications: SWNA Publisher

### Canadian Magazine Publishers Association (CMPA) (1973)
#202, 130 Spadina Ave., Toronto, ON M5V 2L4
416/504-0274, Fax: 416/504-0437, Email: cmpainfo@cmpa.ca, URL: http://www.cmpa.ca/
President, Catherine Keachie
Director, Administration & New Media, Cindy Goldrick, Email: cindyg@cmpa.ca
Publications: CMPA Newsletter; Magazines for Everyone, a.
Affiliates: Book & Periodical Development Council; Canadian Copyright Institute; Periodical Writers' Association of Canada; Annual Magazines Conference; Cultural Resources Council

### Canadian Multilingual Press Federation
PO Bag 9033, Surrey, BC V3T 4X3

604/532-1733, Fax: 604/532-1734, Email: windmill@pro.net
President, A.A. Van Der Heide

### Canadian Music Publishers Association/Association canadienne des éditeurs de musique (CMPA) (1949)
#320, 56 Wellesley St. West, Toronto, ON M5S 2S3
416/926-1966, Fax: 416/926-7521
President, David A. Basskin
Secretary, Cyril Devereux
Publications: CMPA Newsletter
Affiliates: International Federation of Serious Music Publishers; International Federation of Popular Music Publishers; Canadian Conference of the Arts; Coalition of Canadian Copyright Owners & Creators; Music Copyright Action Group

### Canadian Newspaper Association/Association canadienne des journaux (CNA) (1996)
#200, 890 Yonge St., Toronto, ON M4W 3P4
416/923-3567, Fax: 416/923-7206, Email: bcantley@cna-acj.ca, URL: http://www.cna-acj.ca/
President & CEO, Richard Dicerni
Affiliates: Newspaper Association of America

### The Canadian Press/La Presse canadienne (1917)
36 King St. East, Toronto, ON M5C 2L9
416/364-0321; Broadcast News: 364-3172, Fax: 416/364-0207, Telex: 06-217715; 06-2, URL: http://www.xe.com/canpress/
Acting General Manager, Jim Poling
Office Manager, Lee White
Calgary Bureau: Steve Ewart, #507, 200 - 4th Ave. SW, Calgary, AB T2P 3N1, 403/233-7004, Fax: 403/262-7520
Edmonton Bureau: Chris Vaughan-Johnston, Cornerpoint Bldg., #305, 10179 - 105 St., Edmonton, AB T5J 3N1, 403/428-6107, Fax: 403/428-0663
Fredericton Bureau: Judy Monchuk, c/o Press Gallery, Box 6000, Queen St., Fredericton, NB E3B 5H1, 506/455-9493, Fax: 506/457-9708
Halifax Bureau: Trade Mart Bldg., #400, 2021 Brunswick St., Halifax, NS B3K 2Y5, 902/422-8496, Fax: 902/425-2675
London (England) Bureau: Helen Branswell, Associated Press House, 12 Norwich St., London EC4 1EJ UK, 011/44-171-353-6355, Fax: 011/44-171-583-4238
Montréal Bureau: Denis Tremblay, Place d'Armes, 245, rue St-Jacques ouest, CP 998, Montréal, QC H2Y 3J6, 514/849-3212, Téléc: 514/282-6915 (Editorial)
Ottawa Bureau: Bureau Chief, Gerry Arnold, 140 Wellington St., PO Box 595, Stn B, Ottawa, ON K1P 5P7, 613/238-4142, Fax: 613/238-4452
Regina Bureau: Sandra Cordon, #335, Press Gallery, Legislative Bldg., Regina, SK S4S 0B3, 306/585-1011, Fax: 306/585-1027
St. John's Bureau: Ian Bailey, Battery Hotel Media Centre, PO Box 5951, St. John's, NF A1C 5X4, 709/576-0687, Fax: 709/576-0049
Vancouver Bureau: Stephen Ward, #250, 840 Howe St., Vancouver, BC V6Z 2L2, 604/731-3191, Fax: 604/687-5040
Victoria Bureau: Michael Smyth, #350, Press Gallery, Legislative Building, Victoria, BC V8V 1X4, 250/384-4912, Fax: 250/356-8217
Washington Bureau: Christine Morris, #615, 1825 K St. NW, Washington, DC 20006-1253 USA, 202/828-9669, Fax: 202/778-0348
Winnipeg Bureau: Nelle Oosterom, #101, 386 Broadway, Winnipeg, MB R3C 3R6, 204/942-8188, Fax: 204/942-4788

### Canadian Publishers' Council (CPC) (1910)
#203, 250 Merton St., Toronto, ON M4S 1B1
416/322-7011, Fax: 416/322-6999, Email: pubadmin@pubcouncil.ca, URL: http://www.pubcouncil.ca
Executive Director, Jacqueline Hushion, Email: jhushion@pubcouncil.ca
President, Diane Wood
Publications: This Week...
Affiliates: International Publishers Association

### Canadian Telebook Agency (1981)
#301, 2 Gloucester St., Toronto, ON M4Y 1K5
416/929-7332, Fax: 416/929-3015, Email: admin@cta.geis.com
General Manager, Elizabeth Bryant

### Canadian University Press/Presse universitaire canadienne (CUP) (1938)
#404, 73 Richmond St., Toronto, ON M5H 1Z4
416/364-0258, Fax: 416/364-6512, Email: cup@interlog.com, URL: http://www.interlog.com/~cup/
President, Jen Horsey
Bureau Chief/Vice-President, Samer Muscati
National Conference Coordinator, Tracy Frauzel
Publications: CUP Newsex; Canadian Student Press Styleguide

### Commonwealth Press Union - Canadian Section
c/o Southam Newspapers, 1450 Don Mills Rd., North York, ON M3B 2X7
416/445-6641, Fax: 416/442-3386
Chairman, Bill Ardell

### Connexions Information Sharing Services (1975)
PO Box 158, Stn D, Toronto, ON M6P 3J8
416/537-3949, Email: connex@sources.com, URL: http://www.connexions.org
Coordinator, Ulli Diemer
Publications: Connexions Digest; Connexions Annual; Media Guide

### Conseil de presse du Québec/Québec Press Council (CPQ) (1973)
55 1/2, rue Saint-Louis, Québec, QC G1R 3Z2
418/692-3008, Téléc: 418/692-5148
Secrétaire général, Jean-Paul Sabourin
Publications: Rapport annuel

### Les Hebdos du Québec Inc. (1932)
**L'Association des Hebdos du Québec**
#1410, 625, boul René-Lévesque ouest, Montréal, QC H3B 2R2
514/861-2088, Téléc: 514/861-1966
Vice-présidente et directrice générale, Francine Bouchard
Publications: L'Éditeur Nouveau
Organisation(s) affiliée(s): Publicité Club de Montréal; Société des relationnistes du Québec

### International Association for Publishing Education
c/o Canadian Centre for Studies in Publishing, SFU at Harbour Centre, 515 Hastings St. West, Vancouver, BC V6B 5K3
604/291-5074
Anne Cowan

### International Board on Books for Young People - Canadian Section/Union internationale pour les livres de jeunesse (IBBY - Canada) (1980)
c/o Canadian Children's Book Centre, 35 Spadina Rd., Toronto, ON M5R 2S9
416/975-0010, Fax: 416/975-1839
President, Theo Hersh
Publications: IBBY - Canada Newsletter

### The Literary Press Group of Canada (LPG) (1976)
#301, 2 Gloucester St., Toronto, ON M4Y 1L5
416/413-1887, Fax: 416/413-9443, Toll Free: 1-888-717-7702
Email: claudrum@lpg.ca, URL: http://www.lpg.ca
General Manager, Craig Laudrum
Publications: Noteworthy
Affiliates: Association of Canadian Publishers

### Magazines Canada (1968)
**The Magazine Association of Canada**
777 Bay St., 7th Fl., Toronto, ON M5W 1A7
416/596-5382, Fax: 416/596-6043, Email: magscan@hookup.net
President, Maureen Werner
Chairman, Brian Segal

### Manitoba Press Council Inc. (1984)
#103, 2015 Portage Ave., Winnipeg, MB R3J 0K3
204/831-6359, Fax: 204/889-0021, Email: masw@magic.mb.ca
Executive Secretary, Diane Cullen

### Newsletter Publishers Association (1977)
#207, 1401 Wilson Blvd., Arlington, VA 22209 USA
703/527-2333, Fax: 703/841-0629, Toll Free: 1-800-356-9302
Acting Executive Director, Patricia M. Wysocki
Office Manager, Janine Lee
Publications: Hotline

### Ontario Press Council/Conseil de presse de l'Ontario (1972)
#206, 80 Gould St., Toronto, ON M5B 2M7
416/340-1981, Fax: 416/340-8724
Executive Secretary, Mel Sufrin
Chairman, Hon. Willard Z. Estey

### Periodical Marketers of Canada (PMC) (1942)
South Tower, #1007, 175 Bloor St. East, Toronto, ON M4W 3R8
416/968-7218, Fax: 416/968-6182
Executive Director, Ray Argyle
Asst. Executive Director, Janette Hatcher

### Saskatchewan Publishers Group (SPG) (1989)
1925 - 7th Ave., Regina, SK S4R 1C1
306/359-7466, Fax: 306/352-0991, Email: spg@dlcwest.com
Co-Executive Director, Brenda Niskala
Co-Executive Director, Rachael Von Fossenand
President, Bert Wolfe
Publications: SPG PaperCuts; Prairie Books Now
Affiliates: Association of Canadian Publishers

### Société de développement des périodiques culturels québécois (SODEP) (1978)
**Périodiques culturels québécois**
CP 786, Succ. Place d'Armes, Montréal, QC H2Y 3J2
514/523-7724, Téléc: 514/523-9401, Courrier électronique: sodep@sympatico.ca, URL: http://www3.sympatico.ca/sodep/
Directrice générale, Francine Bergeron
Président, Yves Beauregard
Publications: Le Québec en revues

### Toronto Press Club (TPC) (1944)
PO Box 263, Stn Commerce Court South, Toronto, ON M5L 1E8
416/363-0651, Fax: 416/363-9717
President, Ed Patrick, Bus: 416/964-8180
Publications: Quote

**PULP & PAPER *see* FORESTRY & FOREST PRODUCTS**

**RADIO BROADCASTING *see* BROADCASTING**

## REAL ESTATE

***see also* Housing**

### Alberta Real Estate Association (AREA) (1947)

828 - 12 Ave. SW, Calgary, AB T2R 0J3

403/264-5581, Fax: 403/266-1597, Toll Free: 1-800-661-0231

Executive Vice-President, Dan Russell

Brooks Real Estate Co-operative Ltd.: President, Karen Hazell, PO Box 997, Brooks, AB T1R 1B8, 403/362-0123, Fax: 403/362-8543

Calgary Real Estate Board Co-op Ltd.: Executive Vice-President, Ron Esch, FRI, 805 - 5 Ave. SW, Calgary, AB T2P 0N6, 403/263-0530, Fax: 403/262-4432

Edmonton Real Estate Board Co-operative Listing Bureau Ltd.: Executive Vice-President, Ronald Hutchinson, 14220 - 112 Ave., Edmonton, AB T5M 2T8, 403/451-6666, Fax: 403/452-1135

Fort McMurray Real Estate Board Co-operative Listing Bureau Ltd.: Executive Officer, Chris Moskolyk, 9912 Manning Ave., Fort McMurray, AB T9H 2B9, 403/791-1124, Fax: 403/743-4724

Grande Prairie Real Estate Board: Executive Officer, Norma Christie, #102, 9905 - 101 Ave., Grande Prairie, AB T8V 0X7, 403/532-4508, Fax: 403/539-3515

Lethbridge Real Estate Board: Executive Officer, Marilyn Baxter-Brown, 522 - 6 St. South, Lethbridge, AB T1J 2E2, 403/328-8838, Fax: 403/328-8906

Lloydminster Real Estate Board Association: Executive Officer, Karyn Ranger, #9, 5009 - 48th St., Lloydminster, AB T9V 0H7, 403/875-6939, Fax: 403/875-5560

Medicine Hat Real Estate Board Co-operative Ltd.: Executive Officer, Joan McKenna, 403 - 4 St. SE, Medicine Hat, AB T1A 0K5, 403/526-2879, Fax: 403/526-0307

Northeastern Alberta Real Estate Board Co-op Ltd.: Executive Officer, Mary Clarke, Lakecentre Plaza, PO Box 1678, Grand Centre, AB T0A 1T0, 403/594-5958, Fax: 403/594-3181

Red Deer & District Real Estate Board Co-op Ltd.: Executive Officer, Nick Medwid, 4922 - 45 St., Red Deer, AB T4N 1K6, 403/343-0881, Fax: 403/347-9080

West Central Real Estate Association: Executive Officer, Valerie Gregg, PO Box 2386, Hinton, AB T7V 1Y2, 403/865-7511, Fax: 403/865-7517

### Appraisal Institute of Canada/Institut canadien des évaluateurs (AIC) (1938)

1111 Portage Ave., Winnipeg, MB R3G 0S8

204/783-2224, Fax: 204/783-5575, Email: mail@escape.ca, URL: http://www.aicanada.org

Executive Vice-President, Terrence J. Gifford, CAE, Email: tgifford@aicanada.org

President, Doug Rundell, AACI

Executive Secretary, Darlene Brown

Publications: The Digest; The Canadian Appraiser, q.

#### ALBERTA ASSOCIATION OF THE APPRAISAL INSTITUTE OF CANADA (AA-AIC)

#740, 540 - 5 Ave. SW, Calgary, AB T2P 0M2

403/263-7722, Fax: 403/290-0899

Email: abaaic@agt.net, URL: http://www.cyberpage.com/appraisal/alberta/appraisal.html

President, Dallas Maynard

Executive Director, Suzanne E. Teal

Publications: Newsletter

#### BRITISH COLUMBIA ASSOCIATION OF THE APPRAISAL INSTITUTE OF CANADA

#590, 789 Pender St. West, Vancouver, BC V6C 1H2

604/685-4018, Fax: 604/685-7592

President, Keith Goodwin

Executive Director, Janice P. O'Brien

Publications: West Coast Appraiser

#### MANITOBA ASSOCIATION OF THE APPRAISAL INSTITUTE OF CANADA

23 Rosewood Pl., Winnipeg, MB R2H 1M5

204/986-6405, Fax: 204/944-8476

Secretary, Wendy Sigmar

President, Susan Gifford, AACI

#### NEW BRUNSWICK ASSOCIATION OF REAL ESTATE APPRAISERS/ ASSOCIATION DES ÉVALUATEURS IMMOBILIERS DU NOUVEAU-BRUNSWICK (NBAREA) (1995)

#204, 403 Regent St., Fredericton, NB E3B 3X6

506/450-2016, Fax: 506/450-3010

Email: nbarea@nbnet.nb.ca

Executive Director, Susan Keirstead

President, Daniel Doucet, AACI

Secretary, Christine Gorman

#### NEWFOUNDLAND ASSOCIATION OF THE APPRAISAL INSTITUTE OF CANADA

718 Water St., St. John's, NF A1E 1C1

709/753-7644, Fax: 709/753-7469

Executive Assistant, Gina Goodyear

President, Gordon A. Brewer

#### NOVA SCOTIA ASSOCIATION OF THE APPRAISAL INSTITUTE OF CANADA

PO Box 3093, Stn South, Halifax, NS B3J 3G6

902/422-5481, Fax: 902/429-7566

Administrative Secretary, Davida Mackay

President, Lorraine Porter, AACI, Bus: 902/453-7091

Vice-President, Keith Conrod, AACI, Bus: 902/426-8435

#### ONTARIO ASSOCIATION OF THE APPRAISAL INSTITUTE OF CANADA (OA-AIC)

#505, 295 The West Mall, Etobicoke, ON M9C 424

416/695-9333, Fax: 416/695-9321

President, Roly Mayr, AACI

Executive Director, Eileen Richmond

Publications: Quarterly

#### PRINCE EDWARD ISLAND ASSOCIATION OF THE APPRAISAL INSTITUTE OF CANADA

25 Westhill Dr., Charlottetown, PE C1E 1N9

902/368-6395, Fax: 902/368-6164

Secretary, D.B. Sinclair

#### SASKATCHEWAN ASSOCIATION OF THE APPRAISAL INSTITUTE OF CANADA

1935 Elphinstone St., Regina, SK S4T 3N3

306/352-4195, Fax: 306/565-2840

Executive Director, Marlene McLarty

President, Guy Carbonneau

### Association des propriétaires du Québec inc. (APQ)

#520, 50, place Crémazie ouest, Montréal, QC H2P 2T2

514/382-9670, Téléc: 514/382-9676

Directeur général, Jacques Couture

### British Columbia Real Estate Association (BCREA) (1967)

#309, 1155 Pender St. West, Vancouver, BC V6E 2P4

604/683-7702, Fax: 604/683-8601, Email: bcrea@helix.net, URL: http://www.bcrea.bc.ca

Executive Officer, Robin Hill

President, Stuart Kirkpatrick

Communications Director, Fred Morley

Education Director, June Piry

Publications: Bulletin; Legally Speaking, 18 pa; MLA Real Estate Industry News, q.; Regional Advisory Committee on Land Claims Newsletter

Affiliates: National Association of Realtors - USA

Cariboo Real Estate Association: Executive Officer, Dorothy D. Friesen, 2609 Queensway, Prince George, BC V2L 1N3, 250/563-1236, Fax: 250/563-3637

Chilliwack & District Real Estate Board: Executive Officer, Sharon J. Labiuk, #201, 9319 Nowell St., PO Box 339, Chilliwack, BC V2P 4V8, 604/792-0912, Fax: 604/792-6795

Fraser Valley Real Estate Board: Executive Officer, Kenneth E. MacKenzie, 15463 - 104 Ave., PO Box 99, Surrey, BC V3R 1N9, 604/588-6555, Fax: 604/588-0325

Kamloops & District Real Estate Association: Executive Officer, Patrick J. Lindsay; Financial Officer, Cathy Boer, #101, 418 St. Paul St., Kamloops, BC V2C 2J6, 250/372-9411, Fax: 250/828-1986, Email: kadrea@mail.netshop.net

Kootenay Real Estate Board: Office Manager, Irene Cook, #208, 402 Baker St., PO Box 590, Nelson, BC V1L 5R4, 250/352-5477, Fax: 250/352-7184

Northern Lights Real Estate Board: Executive Officer, Marie Chilton, 1101 - 103 Ave., Dawson Creek, BC V1G 2G8, 250/782-2412

Northwest Real Estate Board: Executive Officer, Myrna Rolfsen, #117, 4546 Park Ave., Terrace, BC V8G 1V4, 250/638-8491, Fax: 250/638-1837

Okanagan-Mainline Real Estate Board: Executive Officer, Roger I. Cottle, 1889 Spall Rd., Kelowna, BC V1Y 4R2, 250/860-6292, Fax: 250/860-7704, Email: admin@omreb.com

Powell River Sunshine Coast Real Estate Board: Executive Officer, Linda Shillito, 4699 Marine Ave., Powell River, BC V8A 2L2, 604/485-6944, Fax: 604/485-6974

Real Estate Board of Greater Vancouver: Executive Officer, Larry A. Buttress, 1101 West Broadway, Vancouver, BC V6H 1G2, 604/736-4551, Fax: 604/734-1778

South Okanagan Real Estate Board: Executive Officer, Margaret Van, #3, 212 Main St., Penticton, BC V2A 5B2, 250/492-0626, Fax: 250/493-0832

Vancouver Island Real Estate Board: Executive Officer, Donn Gardner, 6374 Metral Dr., PO Box 719, Nanaimo, BC V9R 5M2, 250/390-4212, Fax: 250/390-5014, Email: vireb@island.net

Victoria Real Estate Board: Executive Officer, Anthony C. Quarless, 3035 Nanaimo St., Victoria, BC V8T 4W2, 250/385-7766, Fax: 250/385-8773, Email: vreb@islandnet.com

### Building Inspectors Association of Nova Scotia

2343 Barrington St., Halifax, NS B3K 2X2

902/422-8316

President, Rick Fraser

Treasurer, Ed Thornhill

### Building Owners & Managers Association of the Greater Toronto Area

**BOMA Toronto**

#2012, 20 Queen St. W, Toronto, ON M5H 3R3

416/596-8065, Fax: 416/596-1085, URL: http://www.bomatoronto.org

Executive Director, Lynn Johnston

### Canadian Institute of Professional Home Inspectors Inc.

535 - 55th Ave. East, Vancouver, BC V5X 1N6

604/327-0262, Fax: 604/738-4080

President, Ed R.R. Witzke, B.A., B.Arch., MCHBA

Publications: The Complete Canadian Home Inspection Guide

### Canadian Institute of Public Real Estate Companies

#1210, 123 Edward St., Toronto, ON M5G 1E2

416/598-0694, Fax: 416/598-0779

Executive Director, Ronald A. Daniel

### The Canadian Real Estate Association/ Association canadienne de l'immeuble (CREA) (1943)

Minto Place, The Canada Bldg., #1600, 344 Slater St., Ottawa, ON K1R 7Y3
613/237-7111, Fax: 613/234-2567, Email: info@crea.ca, URL: http://www.mls.ca
CEO, Pierre J. Beauchamp, FRI (E)
President, Jean M. Crofts
Publications: Canadian Realtor News
Affiliates: National Association of Realtors; International Real Estate Federation

### Fédération des chambres immobilières du Québec

990, av Holland, Québec, QC G1S 3T1
418/682-6102, Téléc: 418/682-8107
Directeur général, Louis Renaud
Publications: Contact
Chambre d'immeubles de Québec: Directrice générale, Louise Clément, 990, av Holland, Québec, QC G1S 3T1, 418/688-3362, Téléc: 418/688-3577
Chambre immobilière de l'Abitibi-Témiscamingue Inc.: Directeur général, Gilles Langlais, #201, 80, Mgr-Tessier est, Rouyn-Noranda, QC J9X 3B9, 819/762-1777, Téléc: 819/762-4030
Chambre immobilière Centre du Québec Inc.: Secrétaire générale, Mariette Proulx, #101, 925 boul St-Joseph, Drummondville, QC J2C 2C4, 819/477-1033, Téléc: 819/474-7913
Chambre immobilière de l'Estrie inc.: Directrice générale, Anita Roy, #01, 21, rue Morris, Sherbrooke, QC J1J 2L8, 819/566-7616, Téléc: 819/566-7688
Chambre immobilière du Grand Montréal: Président, Serge Brousseau; Vice-président/Directeur général, Louis Cherrier, 600, ch du Golf, Île-des-Soeurs, QC H3E 1A8, 514/762-2440, Téléc: 514/762-1854
Chambre immobilière de la Haute Yamaska Inc.: Secrétaire exécutive, Carole Corbeil, #1, 32, rue Carrier, Granby, QC J2G 8C8, 514/378-6702, Téléc: 514/375-5268
Chambre immobilière de Lanaudière Inc.: Secrétaire exécutive, Élise Roch, 765, boul Manseau, Joliette, QC J6E 3E8, 514/759-8511, Téléc: 514/755-6557, Courrier électronique: superactif@pandore.qc.ca
Chambre immobilière des Laurentides: Directrice, Rose Girard, 555, boul Sainte-Adèle, CP 1615, Sainte-Adèle, QC J0R 1L0, 514/229-3511, Téléc: 514/229-3812
Chambre immobilière de la Mauricie Inc.: Secrétaire exécutif, Josée Charland, #102, 1640 - 6e rue, Trois-Rivières, QC G8Y 5B8, 819/379-9081, Téléc: 819/379-9262
Chambre immobilière de l'Outaouais: Directrice générale, Lise Guillemette, 197, boul St-Joseph, Hull, QC J8Y 3X2, 819/771-5221, Téléc: 819/771-8715
Chambre immobilière du Saguenay-Lac St-Jean Inc.: Directrice générale, Ginette Gaudreault, #106, 735, boul Barrette, Chicoutimi, QC G7J 4C4, 418/545-8187, Téléc: 418/545-6305
Chambre immobilière de St-Hyacinthe Inc.: Secrétaire, Monique Plaberge, CP 667, Saint-Hyacinthe, QC J2S 7P5, 514/771-0343

### International Institute of Public Appraisers Ltd. (1977)

404 Queen St., PO Box 3132, Stn B, Fredericton, NB E3A 5G9
506/458-9179, Fax: 506/453-0088
President, Beverly E. Doyle
Executive Secretary, Wanda L. Scott
Publications: International Estates

### Manitoba Building Officials Association

395 Main Street, 7th Fl., Winnipeg, MB R3B 3E1
204/986-2722, Fax: 204/942-2008
Sec.-Treas., Ron Jubinville

### Manitoba Real Estate Association (1949)

1240 Portage Ave., 2nd Fl., Winnipeg, MB R3G 0T6
204/772-0405, Fax: 204/775-3781, Toll Free: 1-800-267-6019, Email: bcollie@mrea.mb.ca, URL: http://www.manitobarealestate.com
Executive Director, Brian M. Collie
Publications: Real Estate Manitoba; MREAction, m.
Brandon Real Estate Board: Executive Officer, Bill Madder, 907 Princess Ave., Brandon, MB R7A 6E3, 204/727-4672, Fax: 204/727-8331
Portage La Prairie Real Estate Board: Executive Officer, Jo-Anne Knox, 19 Royal Rd. North, Portage La Prairie, MB R1N 1T9, 204/857-4111, Fax: 204/857-7207
Thompson Real Estate Board: Treasurer, Larry Reid, c/o GJ Sherry & Associates (1987) Ltd., 1B City Centre Mall, Thompson, MB R8N 0M2, 204/677-4538, Fax: 204/677-4530
Winnipeg Real Estate Board: Executive Director, Gary Simonsen, 1240 Portage Ave., Winnipeg, MB R3G 0T6, 204/786-8854, Fax: 204/783-9447, URL: http://www.mls.ca

### New Brunswick Building Officials Association

c/o City of Saint John, Bldg. Inspectors Office, PO Box 1971, Saint John, NB E2L 4L1
506/658-2911, Fax: 506/632-6199
Secretary, Rick Armstrong

### New Brunswick Real Estate Association/ Association des agents des immeubles du Nouveau-Brunswick (NBREA) (1958)

PO Box 774, Stn A, Fredericton, NB E3B 5B4
506/459-8055, Fax: 506/459-8057
Executive Officer, Karen Small
Greater Moncton Real Estate Board Inc.: Executive Officer, Faye Andersen, 107 Cameron St., Moncton, NB E1C 5Y7, 506/857-8200, Fax: 506/857-1760
Northern New Brunswick Real Estate Board Inc.: Executive Officer, Carmelle F. Mallet, #5, 360 Parkside Dr., PO Box 185, Bathurst, NB E2A 3Z2, 506/548-3045, Fax: 506/548-4002
Real Estate Board of the Fredericton Area Inc.: Executive Officer, Louise E. Mazerall, 544 Brunswick St., PO Box 1295, Fredericton, NB E3B 5C8, 506/458-8163, Fax: 506/459-8922
Saint John Real Estate Board Inc.: Executive Officer, Linda Rector, #P100, Place 400, 400 Main St., Saint John, NB E2K 4N5, 506/634-8772, Fax: 506/634-8775
Valley Real Estate Board Inc.: President, Nicole Lévesque, PO Box 1809, Grand Falls, NB E3Z 1E1, 506/473-4999, Fax: 506/473-6368, Email: nicole@nbnet.nb.ca, URL: http://www.valleyboard.ca

### Newfoundland Real Estate Association

251 Empire Ave., 2nd Fl., St. John's, NF A1C 3H9
709/739-8600, Fax: 709/726-4221
Executive Secretary, Dorothy V. Saunders
Central Newfoundland Real Estate Board: President, Owen Grimes, PO Box 733, Grand Falls-Windsor, NF A2A 2K2, 709/489-7000, Fax: 709/489-5601
Humber Valley Real Estate Board: President, Alan Robinson; Secretary, Melva Sims, PO Box 553, Corner Brook, NF A2H 6E6, 709/634-9400, Fax: 709/634-3251
St. John's Real Estate Board: Executive Officer, Dorothy V. Saunders, 77 Portugal Cove Rd., St. John's, NF A1B 2M4, 709/726-5110, Fax: 709/726-4221

### Nova Scotia Real Estate Association (NSREA) (1960)

7 Scarfe Ct., Dartmouth, NS B3B 1W4
902/468-2515, Fax: 902/468-2533
Executive Officer, Douglas Dixon
Publications: The Exchange
Annapolis Valley Real Estate Board: Executive Officer, Cathy Simpson, PO Box 117, Auburn, NS B0P 1A0, 902/847-9336, Fax: 902/847-9869
Cape Breton Real Estate Board: Executive Secretary, Carol Williston, 329 George St., Sydney, NS B1P 1J7, 902/562-8199, Fax: 902/564-2007
Halifax-Dartmouth Real Estate Board: Executive Officer, Al Demings, 7 Scarfe Ct., Dartmouth, NS B3B 1W4, 902/468-7681, Fax: 902/468-7684
Highland Real Estate Board: President, Valerie Chugg, c/o The Prudential Highland Properties, #104, 219 Main St., Antigonish, NS B2G 2C1, 902/863-1878, Fax: 902/863-1933
Northern Nova Scotia Real Estate Board: Executive Assistant, Carol Burgess, PO Box 1185, Truro, NS B2N 5H1, 902/895-5586, Fax: 902/893-4533
South Shore Real Estate Board: President, Mary MacDonald; Sec.-Treas., Jon Walker, PO Box 81, Bridgewater, NS B4V 2W6, 902/354-5775, Fax: 902/354-2735
Yarmouth Real Estate Board: President, Ray Nelson, c/o Vaughne Realty, #2000, 255 Main St., Yarmouth, NS B5A 1E2, 902/742-4545, Fax: 902/742-1067

### Ontario Building Officials Association Inc./ Association de l'Ontario des officers en bâtiment inc. (OBOA) (1956)

#46, 6770 Davand Dr., Mississauga, ON L5T 2G3
905/564-0364
Executive Director, Tracey Preston
President, Garry Davis
Publications: OBOA Journal

### Ontario Real Estate Association (OREA) (1922)

99 Duncan Mill Rd., North York, ON M3B 1Z2
416/445-9910, Fax: 416/445-2644
Executive Director, Don Richardson
President, Rose E. Leroux
Board & Member Services Coordinator, Lynn Buck
Conference & Meeting Coordinator, Dina Sibellino
Publications: News & Views
Bancroft District Real Estate Board: Executive Officer, Dana Yonemitsu, PO Box 1522, Bancroft, ON K0L 1C0, 613/332-3842, Fax: 613/332-3842
Barrie & District Real Estate Board Inc.: Executive Officer, Frances Clarke, 85 Ellis Dr., Barrie, ON L4M 6E7, 705/739-4650, Fax: 705/721-9101
Brampton Real Estate Board: Executive Director, Bruce S. Lupton, 119 West Dr., Brampton, ON L6T 2J6, 905/451-1515, Fax: 905/451-8034
Brantford Regional Real Estate Association Inc.: Executive Manager, Louise Sharland, 59 Roy Blvd., Brantford, ON N3R 7K1, 519/753-0308, Fax: 519/753-8638
Chatham-Kent Real Estate Board: Executive Officer, Dorothy Ritchie, 188 St. Clair St., PO Box 384, Chatham, ON N7M 5K5, 519/352-4351, Fax: 519/352-6938
Cobourg-Port Hope District Real Estate Board: Executive Officer, Donna Causton, Victoria Place, #23, 1011 William St., Cobourg, ON K9A 5J4, 905/372-8630, Fax: 905/372-1443
Cornwall & District Real Estate Board: Executive Officer, Johanna Murray, 25 Cumberland St., Cornwall, ON K6J 4G8, 613/932-6457, Fax: 613/932-1687
Durham Region Real Estate Board: Executive Officer, Barbara Cail Maclean, #14, 50 Richmond St. East, Oshawa, ON L1H 7L1, 905/723-8184, Fax: 905/723-7531, Email: drreb@mail.durham.net
Golden Triangle Real Estate Board: Executive Officer, Yvonne Klysen, 54 Third St., Collingwood, ON L9Y 1K3, 705/445-7295, Fax: 705/445-7253
Grey Bruce Real Estate Board: Executive Officer, Chris Ransome, 504 - 10th St., Hanover, ON

N4N 1R1, 519/364-3827, Fax: 519/364-6800, Email: gbreb@sos.on.ca
Guelph & District Real Estate Board: Executive Officer, Janet Ceolin, 400 Woolwich St., Guelph, ON N1H 3X1, 519/824-7270, Fax: 519/824-5510
Haliburton District Real Estate Board: Executive Officer, Susan Schell, PO Box 99, Haliburton, ON K0M 1S0, 705/457-9093, Fax: 705/457-9094
Huron Real Estate Board: Executive Officer, Patricia Spence, 60 East St., Goderich, ON N7A 1N3, 519/524-4191, Fax: 519/524-5093
Kingston & Area Real Estate Association: Executive Officer, Susan Swann, 720 Arlington Park Pl., Kingston, ON K7M 8H9, 613/384-0880, Fax: 613/384-0863
Kitchener-Waterloo Real Estate Board Inc.: Executive Officer, Valerie Feick, 540 Riverbend Dr., Kitchener, ON N2K 3S2, 519/576-1400, Fax: 519/741-5364
Lindsay & District Real Estate Board: Executive Officer, Muriel Trowsdale, 31 Kent St. East, Lindsay, ON K9V 2C3, 705/324-4515, Fax: 705/324-3916
London & St. Thomas Real Estate Board: Executive Director, Elizabeth Doré, 342 Commissioners Rd. West, London, ON N2J 1Y3, 519/641-1400, Fax: 519/641-1419
Metropolitan Hamilton Real Estate Board: Executive Officer, Karan Mechar, 505 York Blvd., Hamilton, ON L8R 3K4, 905/529-8101, Fax: 905/529-4349
Midland-Penetang District Real Estate Board Inc.: Executive Officer, Neil Grant, #2, 578 King St., PO Box 805, Midland, ON L4R 4P4, 705/526-8706, Fax: 705/526-0701
Mississauga Real Estate Board: Executive Director, Deborah Crook, #29, 3355 The Collegeway, Mississauga, ON L5L 5T3, 905/608-6732, Fax: 905/608-0045
Muskoka Real Estate Board: Executive Officer, Susan Glassford, 18 Chaffey St., Huntsville, ON P1H 1K7, 705/788-1504, Fax: 705/788-2040
Niagara Falls-Fort Erie Real Estate Association: Executive Officer, Joan Swartz; President, Elizabeth O'Brien, 4411 Portage Rd., PO Box 456, Niagara Falls, ON L2E 6V2, 905/356-7593
North Bay Real Estate Board: Executive Officer, Evelyn A. Reid, 926 Castle St., PO Box 774, North Bay, ON P1B 4A8, 705/472-6812, Fax: 705/472-0529
The Oakville, Milton & District Real Estate Board: General Manager, May Barrett, FRI, 125 Navy St., Oakville, ON L6J 2Z5, 905/844-6491, Fax: 905/844-6699
Orangeville & District Real Estate Board: Executive Officer, June Moir, 228 Broadway Ave., Orangeville, ON L9W 1K5, 519/941-4547, Fax: 519/941-8482
Orillia & District Real Estate Board: Executive Officer, Dorothy Young, 32 Matchedash St. North, PO Box 551, Orillia, ON L3V 6K2, 705/325-9958, Fax: 705/325-0605, Email: oriloreb@bconnex.net
Owen Sound & District Real Estate Board: Executive Officer, Joanne Green, 653 - 2nd Ave. East, Owen Sound, ON N4K 2G7, 519/371-1922, Fax: 519/376-8465
Parry Sound Real Estate Board: Executive Officer, Margaret Hammel, 33 James St., Parry Sound, ON P2A 1T6, 705/746-4020, Fax: 705/746-2955
Peterborough Real Estate Board Inc.: Executive Officer, Carolyn J. Mills, 273 Charlotte St., PO Box 1330, Peterborough, ON K9J 7H5, 705/745-5724, Fax: 705/745-9377
Quinte & District Real Estate Board: Executive Officer, Elaine O'Hara, PO Box 128, Cannifton, ON K0K 1K0, 613/969-7873, Fax: 613/962-1851
Real Estate Board of Cambridge: Executive Officer, Shirley Highfield, 75 Ainslie St. North, PO Box 693, Cambridge, ON N1R 5W6, 519/623-3660, Fax: 519/623-8253
Real Estate Board of Ottawa-Carleton: Executive Director, Carol Mallett, 1826 Woodward Dr., Ottawa, ON K2C 0P7, 613/225-2240, Fax: 613/225-6420, URL: http://www.ottawarealestate.org
Renfrew County Real Estate Board: Executive Officer, Ann Anderson, 377 Isabella St., Pembroke, ON K8A 5T4, 613/735-5840, Fax: 613/735-0405
Rideau-St. Lawrence Real Estate Board: Executive Officer, Wilda Brown, #12, 1275 Kensington Pkwy., Brockville, ON K6V 6C3, 613/342-3103
St. Catharines District Real Estate Board: Executive Officer, Nancy Dingman, 116 Niagara St., St Catharines, ON L2R 4L4, 905/684-9459, Fax: 905/687-7010, Email: scdreb@vaxxine.com
Sarnia-Lambton Real Estate Board: Executive Director, Tom Woods, 555 Exmouth St., Sarnia, ON N7T 5P6, 519/336-6871, Fax: 519/344-1928
Sault Ste. Marie Real Estate Board: Secretary Manager, Geri White, #1, 498 Queen St. East, Sault Ste Marie, ON P6A 1Z8, 705/949-4560, Fax: 705/949-5935
Simcoe & District Real Estate Board: Executive Officer, Yvonne Stewart, 44 Young St., Simcoe, ON N3Y 1Y5, 519/426-4454, Fax: 519/426-9330
Stratford & District Real Estate Board: Executive Officer, Gwen Kirkpatrick, 91 Brunswick St., Stratford, ON N5A 3L9, 519/271-6870, Fax: 519/271-3040
Sudbury Real Estate Board: Executive Officer, Myra Lahti, 190 Elm St., Sudbury, ON P3C 1V3, 705/673-3388, Fax: 705/673-3197
Thunder Bay Real Estate Board: Executive Officer, Irene Holowka, 1135 Barton St., Thunder Bay, ON P7B 5N3, 807/623-8422, Fax: 807/623-0375
Tillsonburg District Real Estate Board: Secretary Manager, Sharon Smith, 1 Library Lane, PO Box 35, Tillsonburg, ON N4G 4H3, 519/842-9361, Fax: 519/688-6850
Timmins Real Estate Board: Executive Officer, Margot Hamel, 7 Balsam St. South, Timmins, ON P4N 2C7, 705/268-5451, Fax: 705/264-6420
Toronto Real Estate Board: President, John England; Executive Vice-President, Brian Smith, 1400 Don Mills Rd., North York, ON M3B 3N1, 416/443-8100, 8142, Fax: 416/443-0028, 1495
Welland District Real Estate Board: Executive Officer, Tammy Smith; President, John Fletcher, 706 East Main St., Welland, ON L3B 3Y4, 905/735-3624, Fax: 905/735-8722
Windsor-Essex County Real Estate Board: Executive Director, Leona MacIntyre, CAE, 3005 Marentette Ave., Windsor, ON N8X 4G1, 519/966-6432, Fax: 519/966-4469
Woodstock-Ingersoll & District Real Estate Board: Executive Officer, Carol Smith-Gee, #6, 65 Springbank Ave., Woodstock, ON N4S 8V8, 519/539-3616, Fax: 519/539-1975
York Region Real Estate Board: Executive Director, Donna Metcalfe, 1111 Stellar Dr., Newmarket, ON L3Y 7B8, 905/895-7624, Fax: 905/895-9216

### Prince Edward Island Real Estate Association
75 St. Peter's Rd., Charlottetown, PE C1A 5N7
902/368-8451, Fax: 902/894-9487
Executive Officer, J. Earle Arsenault

### Real Estate Institute of Canada/Institut canadien de l'immeuble (REIC) (1955)
#208, 5407 Eglinton Ave. West, Toronto, ON M9C 5K6
416/695-9000, Fax: 416/695-7230, Toll Free: 1-800-542-7342, Email: infocentral@reic.com, URL: http://www.reic.ca
Executive Vice-President, E. Peter Jacobs, CAE
Manager, Marketing & Communications, Constance A. Wrigley, Email: constance_wrigley@reic.com
Publications: PRO ACT - The Official Publication of the Real Estate Institute of Canada

### Saskatchewan Building Officials Association
PO Box 1671, Prince Albert, SK S6V 5T2
306/975-3235, Fax: 306/975-7212
President, Terry Roulston
Sec.-Treas., LeRoy Evanson

### Saskatchewan Real Estate Association (SREA) (1949)
231 Robin Cres., Saskatoon, SK S7L 6M8
306/373-3350, Fax: 306/373-5377
Executive Vice-President, Kirk Bacon
Publications: Sequence
Association of Battlefords Realtors: Executive Officer, Nancy Wappel, #501, 1101 - 101 St., PO Box 611, North Battleford, SK S9A 2Y7, 306/445-6300, Fax: 306/445-9020
Association of Regina Realtors Inc.: Executive Officer, Gord Archibald, 1854 McIntyre St., Regina, SK S4P 2P9, 306/791-2700, Fax: 306/781-7940, Email: rrea@cableregina.com
Estevan Real Estate Board: Executive Officer, J. Fomwald, PO Box 445, Estevan, SK S4A 2A4, 306/634-7885, Fax: 306/634-8610
Melfort Real Estate Board: Executive Officer, Debby McAlister, 606 Bemister Ave. East, PO Box 3157, Melfort, SK S0E 1A0, 306/752-4994, Fax: 306/752-4994
Moose Jaw Real Estate Board: Executive Officer, Trudy Rees, 79 Hochelaga St. West, Moose Jaw, SK S6H 2E9, 306/693-9544, Fax: 306/692-4463
Prince Albert Real Estate Board: Executive Officer, Charlene Welch-Leachman, 218B South Industrial Dr., Prince Albert, SK S6V 7L8, 306/764-8755, Fax: 306/763-0555
Saskatoon Real Estate Board: Executive Officer, Bill Benoit, 1149 - 8th St. East., Saskatoon, SK S7H 0S3, 306/244-4453, Fax: 306/343-1420, Email: bbenoit@sreb.com, URL: http://www.saskstar.sk.ca/board/
Swift Current Real Estate Board: Executive Officer, Nancy Hunter, #211, 12 Cheadle St. West, Swift Current, SK S9H 0A9, 306/773-4326, Fax: 306/773-3917
Weyburn Real Estate Board: Executive Officer, Eric Douglas, 140 First St. NE, Weyburn, SK S4H 0T2, 306/842-0300, Fax: 306/842-5520
Yorkton Real Estate Association Inc.: Executive Officer, Nancy Kirschman, #040, 41 Broadway West, Yorkton, SK S3N 0L6, 306/783-3067, Fax: 306/786-3231

### Yellowknife Real Estate Board
#2, 5201 - 50 Ave., Yellowknife, NT X1A 3S9
867/920-4624, Fax: 867/873-6387
President, Dale Vance
Executive Officer/Sec.-Treas., Julia Mott

### Yukon Real Estate Association (1977)
PO Box 5292, Whitehorse, YT Y1A 4Z2
867/668-2070, Fax: 867/668-2070
Executive Officer, Nicholas Smart
President, Dan Lang

## RECREATION, HOBBIES & GAMES

### Alberta Snowmobile Association (ASA) (1972)
Percy Page Centre, 11759 Groat Rd., Edmonton, AB T5M 3K6
403/453-8668, Fax: 403/453-8553
Executive Director, Louise A. Sherren
Publications: The Alberta Snowmobiler
Affiliates: Canadian Council of Snowmobile Organizations; International Snowmobile Council

### Alberta Whitewater Canoe Association (1972)
Percy Page Centre, 11759 Groat Rd., Edmonton, AB T5M 3K6

403/453-8585
President, Rosemarie Chinchilla
Technical Director, Bruce Lord
Affiliates: Canadian Recreational Canoe Association

### Amusement Machine Operators of Canada/ Opérateurs d'appareils d'amusement du Canada
2684 Fenton Rd., Gloucester, ON K1T 3T7
613/822-6808, Fax: 613/822-2721
Coordinator, Gus Ragland

### Association des camps du Québec inc./Québec Camping Association (ACQ) (1961)
4545, av Pierre-de-Coubertin, CP 1000, Succ. M, Montréal, QC H1V 3R2
514/252-3113, Téléc: 514/252-1650, Ligne sans frais: 1-800-361-3586
Directeur général, Louis Jean
Président, Claude Jetté
Publications: L'Express; Répertoire des camps de vacances, annuel
Organisation(s) affiliée(s): Regroupement loisir Québec

### Association of Canadian Mountain Guides/ Association des guides de montagne canadiens (ACMG) (1963)
PO Box 1537, Banff, AB T0L 0C0
403/678-2885, Fax: 403/678-6464, Email: acmg@cariboo.bc.ca, URL: http://www.acmg.com
President, Hans Gmoser
Sec.-Treas., George Field
Technical Director, Colin Zacharias
Publications: ACMG Newsletter
Affiliates: Canada Avalanche Association; Alpine Club of Canada; World Wildlife Fund

### Association canadienne de la raquette inc./ Canadian Snowshoe Association Inc. (ACR) (1907)
9, rue Bériault, Hull, QC J8X 1A1
613/741-7874
Secretary, Audette LeBel
President, Maurice Pichette
Publications: Info-Raquette

### Association canadienne de saut de barils inc./ Canadian Barrel Jumping Association Inc. (1963)
1465, Place Louis-Frechette, Saint-Bruno, QC J3V 2T8
514/653-9460
Président, Gilles Leclerc

### Backpackers International Association (Canada)
**Backpackers Resorts Canada**
168 Maryland St., Winnipeg, MB R3G 1L3
204/772-1272, Fax: 204/772-4117, Email: BMacdonald@msn.com
President, Bill Macdonald
Affiliates: American Association of International Hostels

### BC Fishing Resorts & Outfitters Association
PO Box 3301, Kamloops, BC V2C 6B9
250/374-6836, Fax: 250/374-6640
Executive Director, J.R. McMaster

### BC Sailing
**BC Sailing Association**
#304, 1367 West Broadway, Vancouver, BC V6H 4A7
604/737-3126, Fax: 604/737-0677
Executive Director, Stephen Tupper
Publications: Yearbook; Commodore's Newsletter, q.

### BC Snowmobile Federation (BCSF) (1965)
PO Box 849, Valemount, BC V0E 2Z0
250/566-4627, Fax: 250/566-4622, Email: bcsfaw@vis.bc.ca, URL: http://www.bcsf.org/sledding
President, Debbie Paynton
Communications Officer, Arnold Wied
Publications: Sno-Scene
Affiliates: International Snowmobile Council; Canadian Council of Snowmobile Organizations

### The Bruce Trail Association (BTA) (1963)
PO Box 857, Hamilton, ON L8N 3N9
905/529-6821, Fax: 905/529-6823, Toll Free: 1-800-665-4453, Email: Bruce.Trail@freenet.Hamilton.on.ca, URL: http://www.brucetrail.org/
Executive Director, Jacqueline Winters
Publications: Bruce Trail News
Affiliates: Ontario Trails Council; National Trail Council; Coalition on the Niagara Escarpment; Federation of Ontario Naturalists

### Canadian Aerophilatelic Society/La société canadienne d'aerophilatélie (CAS) (1986)
16 Harwick Cres., Nepean, ON K2H 6R1
613/829-0280, Fax: 613/829-0280
President, Major R.K. Malott, MSc, BA, CD, FRPSC, Ret'd
Treasurer, Ivan W. MacKenzie
Secretary, Ronald Miyanishi
Publications: The Canadian Aerophilatelist
Affiliates: American Air Mail Society; Royal Philatelic Society of Canada; American Philatelic Society; British North America Society

### Canadian Association of Numismatic Dealers (CAND)
PO Box 10272, Stoney Creek, ON L8E 5R1
613/643-4988, Fax: 613/643-6329
Richard Simpson

### Canadian Association of Wooden Money Collectors (CAWMC)
592 Sheppard Ave. West, PO Box 77575, North York, ON M3H 6A7
416/633-8390
Membership Secretary, Don Robb
Publications: Timber Talk

### Canadian Baton Twirling Federation/Fédération baton canadienne
35 Traynor Bay, Winnipeg, MB R2M 4H7
204/257-2206, Fax: 204/253-6738
President, Gladys Peteleski
First Vice-President, Joyce Ormshaw

### Canadian Boating Federation
50, rue Jacques Cartier, Salaberry-de-Valleyfield, QC J6T 4R3
514/377-4122, Fax: 514/377-5282

### Canadian Body Building Federation/Fédération canadienne de culturisme amateur
1520 Brookmill Lane, Gloucester, ON R1B 5G4
613/746-2223
President, Syd Pukalo
General Secretary, Winston Roberts

### Canadian Bridge Federation
2719 East Jolly Place, Regina, SK S4V 0X8
306/761-1677, Fax: 306/761-1697, URL: http://www.cbf.ca/CBFHome.html
Executive Secretary, J. Anderson

### Canadian Camping Association/Association des camps du Canada (CCA) (1936)
#303, 1810 Avenue Rd., Toronto, ON M5M 3Z2
416/781-4717, Fax: 416/781-7875
President, Margaret Steel
Publications: Camps Canada

#### ALBERTA CAMPING ASSOCIATION (ACA) (1949)
Percy Page Centre, 11759 Groat Rd., Edmonton, AB T5M 3K6
403/453-8570, Fax: 403/453-8553
Email: abcamp@freenet.edmonton.ab.ca
President, Rob Pegg
Office Manager, Barb Lambert
Treasurer, Gordon Matchett
Publications: Camping News; Directory of Camps, a.; Camping Standards of the ACA

#### BRITISH COLUMBIA CAMPING ASSOCIATION
c/o Sasamat Outdoor Centre, 3302 Senkler Rd., Belcarra, BC V3H 4S3
604/875-6760, Fax: 604/875-6760
President, Carol Voorhoeve

#### CAMPING ASSOCIATION OF NOVA SCOTIA (CANS) (1941)
PO Box 3243, Stn South, Halifax, NS B3J 3H5
902/865-3523, Fax: 902/865-7703
URL: http://www.kidscamps.com/canadian-camping
President, Elayne Mott

#### MANITOBA CAMPING ASSOCIATION (1937)
194A Sherbrook St., Winnipeg, MB R3C 2B6
204/784-1134, Fax: 204/784-1133
President, Jason Bowers
Publications: Manitoba Camping Scene
Affiliates: Christian Camping International

#### NEWFOUNDLAND & LABRADOR CAMPING ASSOCIATION
c/o Circle Square Ranch, PO Box 1120, Manuels, NF A1W 1N6
709/781-5330, Fax: 709/781-5430
President, Cal Sparkes

#### ONTARIO CAMPING ASSOCIATION (OCA) (1933)
#302, 1810 Avenue Rd., Toronto, ON M5M 3Z2
416/781 0525, Fax: 416/781-7875
Email: oca@ontcamp.on.ca, URL: http://www.ontcamp.on.ca
President, Barb Gilbert
Office Administrator, Bev Jahnke
Publications: OCAsional News; The Camping Guide, a.

#### RECREATION & PARKS ASSOCIATION OF NEW BRUNSWICK INC. (RPANB) (1987)
#105, 440 Wilsey Rd., Fredericton, NB E3B 7G5
506/459-1929, Fax: 506/450-6066
Executive Director, Art Murphy
Administrative Assistant, Susan Hebert
Publications: RECorder

#### SASKATCHEWAN CAMPING ASSOCIATION (SCA) (1974)
c/o Saskatoon YMCA, 25 - 22 St. East, Saskatoon, SK S7K 0C7
306/652-7515, Fax: 306/652-2828
President, Felix Tillmanns
Publications: SCAN

### Canadian Canoe Association/Association canadienne de canotage (CCA) (1900)
Place R. Tait McKenzie, 1600 James Naismith Dr., Gloucester, ON K1B 5N4
613/748-5623, Fax: 613/748-5700, Telex: 053-3660 SPORTR, URL: http://www.openface.ca/paddle/
Director General, Anne Merklinger
Commodore, Sharon Mousseau
Publications: Paddles Up

#### ALBERTA FLATWATER CANOE ASSOCIATION
48 Redwood Meadow Dr., Redwood Meadows, AB T3Z 1A3
403/949-2873, Fax: 403/249-5277
President, Janet Davies

#### ASSOCIATION QUÉBÉCOISE DE CANOË-KAYAK DE VITESSE (AQCKV) (1979)
4545, av Pierre-de-Coubertin, CP 1000, Succ. M, Montréal, QC H1V 3R2
514/252-3086, Téléc: 514/252-3094

Président, Jean-Guy Lahaie
Publications: La Pagaie

#### MANITOBA PADDLING ASSOCIATION INC. (MPA) (1982)
200 Main St., Winnipeg, MB R3C 4M2
204/925-5681, Fax: 204/925-5703
Executive Director, Denis Van Laeken
Publications: MPA Newsletter

#### NEWFOUNDLAND & LABRADOR CANOE ASSOCIATION
PO Box 5961, Stn C, St. John's, NF A1C 5X4
Director, Phil Powers, Bus: 709/724-1134

#### SASKATCHEWAN CANOE ASSOCIATION
PO Box 6064, Saskatoon, SK S7K 4E5
306/653-5568
Contact, Margery McDougall, Bus: 306/653-5568

### Canadian Casting Federation (1978)
c/o Toronto Sportsmen's Association, 17 Mill St., North York, ON M2P 1B3
416/487-4477, Fax: 416/487-4478
Executive Director, Peter Edwards

### Canadian Correspondence Chess Association (CCCA)
1669 Front Rd. West, L'Orignal, ON K0B 1K0
613/632-3166, Email: ccca@hawknet.ca
General Secretary, Manny Migicovsky
Publications: Check

### Canadian Council of Snowmobile Organizations/ Conseil canadien des organismes de motoneige (CCSO) (1974)
#12, 106 Saunders Rd., Barrie, ON L4M 6E7
705/725-1121, Fax: 705/739-5005, Email: ccso@transdata.ca
President, Don Lumley
Executive Director, Marc Lacroix
Publications: Canadian Snowmobiler
Affiliates: International Snowmobile Manufacturers Association

### Canadian Fitness & Lifestyle Research Institute/ Institut canadien de la recherche sur la condition physique et le mode de vie (CFLRI) (1985)
#201, 185 Somerset St. West, Ottawa, ON K2P 0J2
613/233-5528, Fax: 613/233-5536, Email: cflri@hookup.net, URL: http://activeliving.ca/activeliving/cflri.html
President, Cora Lynn Craig
Chair, Lise Gauvin
Communications Officer, Angèle Beaulieu
Publications: The Research File; Progress in Prevention

### Canadian Flag Association/Association canadienne de vexillologie (CFA) (1985)
50 Heathfield Dr., Scarborough, ON M1M 3B1
416/267-9618, Fax: 416/267-9618
President, Kevin Harrington
Publications: Flagscan
Affiliates: North American Vexillological Association

### Canadian Go Kart Track Owners' Association
#1, 234 Clements Rd. West, Ajax, ON L1S 3K5
905/683-9700, Fax: 905/683-9828
Office Manager, Wendy Calhoun-Clark

### Canadian International Checkers Federation (1985)
6 Wellington St., Lindsay, ON K9V 3N1
705/324-3476
Vice-President, M. Jerry Van Halteren
Affiliates: Fédération mondiale du jeu de dames

### Canadian International DX Club (CIDX) (1962)
79, rue Kipps, Greenfield-Park, QC J4V 3B1
514/462-1459, Fax: 514/671-3775, Email: ve6jy@freenet.edmonton.ab.ca
President, Sheldon Harvey
Publications: Messenger

### Canadian Intramural Recreation Association/ Association canadienne de loisirs intramuros (CIRA) (1977)
Place R. Tait McKenzie, 1600 James Naismith Dr., Gloucester, ON K1B 5N4
613/748-5639, Fax: 613/748-5706, Telex: 053-3660, URL: http://www.cdnsport.ca/activeliving/cira.html
President, Lynn Dyck
President-Elect, Rob Stinson
Executive Vice-President, Rick Turnbull
Publications: CIRA Bulletin

### Canadian Long Distance Riding Association (CaLDRA) (1985)
RR#2, Flesherton, ON N0C 1E0
905/473-3688
President, Nancy Beacon

### Canadian Mariners Association (1979)
376 Orenda Dr., Brampton, ON L6T 1G1
905/790-0440, Fax: 905/790-0455
Contact, W.A. Milne
Publications: Newsletter

### Canadian Motorcycle Association/Association motocycliste canadienne (CMA) (1946)
PO Box 448, Stn LCD 1, Hamilton, ON L8L 8C4
905/522-5705, Fax: 905/522-5716
General Manager, Marilyn Bastedo
President, Joseph Godsall
Publications: The Link/Le Lien
Affiliates: Fédération internationale motocycliste

### Canadian Numismatic Association/Association canadienne de numismatique (CNA) (1950)
PO Box 226, Barrie, ON L4M 4T2
705/737-0845, Fax: 705/737-0845, Email: cna@barint.dn.ca, URL: http://home.ican.net/~nunetcan/
President, Yvon Marquis
Publications: Canadian Numismatic Journal

### Canadian Orienteering Federation/Fédération canadienne de course d'orientation (COF) (1967)
PO Box 62052, Stn Convent Glen, Orleans, ON K1C 7H8
613/830-1147, Fax: 613/830-0456
Executive Director, Colin Kirk, Email: ckirk@rtm.cdnsport.ca
President, Jack Forsyth
Publications: Orienteering Canada
Affiliates: International Orienteering Federation

### Canadian Outrigger Racing Association (CORA) (1992)
PO Box 216, Pemberton, BC V0N 2L0
604/894-5684, Fax: 604/894-6918
Contact, Hugh Fisher
Affiliates: Canadian Canoe Association

### Canadian Paper Money Society (CPMS) (1965)
PO Box 562, Pickering, ON L1V 2R7
905/509-1146, Email: cpms@idirect.com
Sec.-Treas., Dick Dunn
Publications: The Canadian Paper Money Journal

### Canadian Parks & Wilderness Society/Société pour la protection des parcs et des sites naturales du Canada (CPAWS) (1963)
#380, 401 Richmond St. West, Toronto, ON M5V 3A8
416/979-2720, Fax: 416/979-3155, Email: cpaws@web.net, URL: http://www.afternet.com/~tnr/cpaws/cpaws.html
President, Juri Peepre
Executive Director, Mary Granskou
Publications: The Wilderness Activist

### Canadian Parks/Recreation Association/ Association canadienne des loisirs/parcs (CP/RA) (1945)
#306, 1600 James Naismith Dr., Gloucester, ON K1B 5N4
613/748-5651, Fax: 613/748-5854, Telex: 053-3660, Email: cpra@activeliving.ca, URL: http://activeliving.ca/activeliving/cpra.html
Executive Director, Geraldine Hebert
President, Neil Semenchuk
Publications: Recreation Canada

#### ALBERTA RECREATION & PARKS ASSOCIATION
Percy Page Centre, 11759 Groat Rd. NW, Edmonton, AB T5M 3K6
403/453-8631, Fax: 403/453-8553
Executive Director, Paul Servos
President, Roger Smolnicky
Publications: Recreation Alberta

#### BRITISH COLUMBIA RECREATION & PARKS ASSOCIATION (BCRPA) (1954)
#30, 10551 Shellbridge Way, Richmond, BC V6X 2W9
604/273-8055, Fax: 604/273-8059
Executive Director, Gordon J. Stewart
Publications: Recreation BC Magazine

#### MANITOBA PARKS & RECREATION ASSOCIATION
2799 Roblin Blvd., Winnipeg, MB R3R 0B8
204/986-3700, Fax: 204/986-6637
Contact, Bob Jones

#### NEWFOUNDLAND & LABRADOR PARKS & RECREATION ASSOCIATION (NLPRA) (1971)
PO Box 8700, Stn A, St. John's, NF A1B 4J6
709/729-3892, Fax: 709/729-3814
Executive Director, Gary Milley
Program Officer, Joanne Bennett
Publications: Recreation Quarterly; NLPRA Membership Directory

#### NORTHWEST TERRITORIES RECREATION & PARKS ASSOCIATION (1989)
PO Box 841, Yellowknife, NT X1A 2N6
867/669-9129, Fax: 867/669-9129
Executive Director, Adrienne Forest
Publications: The Energizer
Affiliates: Sport North

#### PARKS & RECREATION ONTARIO/PARCS ET LOISIRS DE L'ONTARIO (PRO) (1984)
#406, 1185 Eglinton Ave. East, North York, ON M3C 3C6
416/426-7142, Fax: 416/426-7371
Email: pro@osrc.com
CEO, Larry Ketcheson
Publications: Pro Job Mart; PROfile

#### RECREATION ASSOCIATION OF NOVA SCOTIA (RANS) (1973)
PO Box 3010, Stn South, Halifax, NS B3J 3G6
902/425-1128, Fax: 902/425-5606
Executive Director, Jean Robinson-Dexter
Publications: Recreation Matters

#### SASKATCHEWAN PARKS & RECREATION ASSOCIATION (SPRA) (1962)
#210, 3303 Hillsdale St., Regina, SK S4S 6W9
306/780-9214, Fax: 306/780-9257
General Manager, Carol E. Brasok
Publications: Recreation Saskatchewan
Affiliates: Canadian Parks & Recreation Association

### Canadian Power & Sail Squadrons (Canadian Headquarters)/Escadrilles canadiennes de plaisance (CPS) (1938)
26 Golden Gate Ct., Scarborough, ON M1P 3A5
416/293-2438, Fax: 416/293-2445, Toll Free: 1-800-277-2628, Email: hgg@cps-ecp.ca, URL: http://www.cps-ecp.ca
President/Executive Director, Brian Burch
Chief Commander, Y.A. Ferland
Publications: The Port Hole

### Canadian Racing Pigeon Union (1929)
4500 Blakie Rd., London, ON N6L 1G5
519/652-5704, Fax: 519/652-6406
President, Bill Badgerow
Sec.-Treas., Dorothy Deveau
Affiliates: Fédération colombophile internationale

### Canadian Recreational Canoeing Association/Association canadienne de canotage récréatif (CRCA) (1971)
446 Main St. West, PO Box 398, Merrickville, ON K0G 1N0
613/269-2910, Fax: 613/269-2908, Email: staff@crca.ca, URL: http://www.crca.ca/
Executive Director, Joseph Agnew
Publications: KANAWA - Canada's Canoeing & Kayaking Magazine
Affiliates: American Rivers Conservation Council; Canadian Camping Association; Canadian Marathon Racing Canoe Association; Canadian Red Cross; National Council Boy Scouts of Canada; Canadian White Water Association; Royal Life Saving Society of Canada, Girl Guides of Canada; Canoe Canada; American Canoe Association; Canadian Heritage River System; Canadian Parks Service

#### ALBERTA RECREATIONAL CANOE ASSOCIATION
c/o Calgary Outdoor Area Council, 1111 Memorial Dr. NW, Calgary, AB T2N 3E4
403/270-2262, Fax: 403/270-3654
Director, Gordon Harris

#### CANOE NEW BRUNSWICK
PO Box 243, Moncton, NB E1C 8K9
506/859-3548, Fax: 506/859-3697
President, George W. Geldart

#### CANOE NOVA SCOTIA
5516 Spring Garden Rd., PO Box 3010, Stn South, Halifax, NS B3J 3G6
902/425-5450, Fax: 902/425-5606
Executive Director, Ike Whitehead

#### FÉDÉRATION QUÉBÉCOISE DU CANOT CAMPING INC. (1976)
4545, av Pierre-de-Coubertin, CP 1000, Succ. M, Montréal, QC H1V 3R2
514/252-3001, Téléc: 514/252-3091
Directeur général, Pierre Trudel
Président, Benoît Chartrand
Publications: Le Courant

#### MANITOBA RECREATIONAL CANOEING ASSOCIATION (MRCA)
PO Box 2663, Winnipeg, MB R3C 4B3
204/338-6722
URL: http://130.179.24.217/mrca/mrca.html
Publications: MRCA Bulletin
Affiliates: Manitoba Paddling Association

#### NORTHWEST TERRITORIES CANOEING ASSOCIATION
PO Box 2763, Yellowknife, NT X1A 2R1
867/873-2339, Fax: 867/920-7809, Toll Free: 1-800-661-0797
President, Hillary Pounsett
Treasurer, Gordon Stewart

#### ONTARIO RECREATIONAL CANOEING ASSOCIATION
**Canoe Ontario**
#104, 1185 Eglinton Ave. East, North York, ON M3C 3C6
416/426-7170, Fax: 416/426-7363
Executive Director, John Pugsley, Bus: 416/426-7172
Publications: Canews
Affiliates: Canoe Ontario

#### PEI RECREATIONAL CANOEING ASSOCIATION
RR#5, PO Box 5604, Charlottetown, PE C1A 7J8
902/368-6355, Fax: 902/368-6186
Chairman, Shawn Shea

#### RECREATIONAL CANOEING ASSOCIATION BC (RCA/BC)
1367 West Broadway, Vancouver, BC V6H 4A7
604/275-6651
Email: carey_robson@bc.sympatico.ca
President, Carey Robson, Bus: 604/437-1140

#### YUKON CANOE & KAYAK CLUB
PO Box 5546, Whitehorse, YT Y1A 5H4
Contact, Ingrid Wilcox, Bus: 403/668-6562, Fax: 403/633-5625

### Canadian Sport Parachuting Association/Association canadienne de parachutisme sportive (CSPA) (1956)
4185 Dunning Rd., RR#3, Navan, ON K4B 1J1
613/835-3731, Fax: 613/835-3731, Email: cspa@travel-net.com, URL: http://www.islandnet.com/~murrays/cspa.html
President, Aiden Walters
Office Manager, Cathy Johnson
Publications: CanPara

### Canadian Stamp Dealers' Association/Association canadienne des négociants en timbres-postes (CSDA) (1942)
PO Box 1123, Stn Adelaide, Toronto, ON M5C 2K5
416/979-3335, Fax: 416/979-1144, Email: csda@parrassoc.com
President, John Sheffield, Bus: 519/681-3420, Fax: 519/668-6872
Vice-President, Roy Houtby
Secretary, Rick Day
Treasurer, Emil Talacko
Publications: CSDA Directory; CSDA Newsletter, bi-m.

### Canadian Table Tennis Association/Association canadienne de tennis de table (CTTA) (1937)
**Table Tennis Canada**
Place R. Tait McKenzie, 1600 James Naismith Dr., Gloucester, ON K1B 5N4
613/748-5675, Fax: 613/746-5705, Email: ctta@ctta.ca
Director General, Mr. Adham Sharara
President, Bruce Burton
Publications: 20/20
Affiliates: Sports Council of Canada

### Canadian Toy Collectors' Society Inc. (CTCS) (1970)
#245, 91 Rylander Blvd., Unit 7, Toronto, ON M1B 5M5
416/633-7378
President, Ed Barclay
Publications: Canadian Toy Collector
Affiliates: Dufferin County Museum & Archives

### Canadian Trapshooting Association (1966)
17 Stirling Close, Red Deer, AB T4N 0A9
403/347-5284, Fax: 403/347-5284
President, Bob Brown

### Canadian Yachting Association/Association canadienne de yachting (CYA) (1931)
#504, 1600 James Naismith Dr., Gloucester, ON K1B 5N4
613/748-5687, Fax: 613/748-5688, Telex: 053-3660, URL: http://www.cdnsport.ca/~smorrow
Executive Director, Brian Lane
President, Chris Campbell
Publications: Canadian Sailing Review; Annual Directory
Affiliates: International Yacht Racing Union; International Sailing Schools Association

### Chess Federation of Canada/Fédération canadienne des échecs
2212 Gladwin Cr., #E1, Ottawa, ON K1B 5N1
613/733-2844, Fax: 613/733-2844, URL: http://www.globalx.net/cfc/
Executive Director, Hal Bond
President, Nathan Davinski
Publications: En Passant
Affiliates: Fédération internationale des échecs

### Classical & Medieval Numismatic Society (CMNS) (1991)
PO Box 956, Stn B, North York, ON M2K 2T6
416/490-8659, Fax: 416/490-6452, Email: billmcdo@idirect.com
Executive Sec.-Treas., W.H. McDonald
Publications: The Anvil; The Picus, a.

### Council of BC Yacht Clubs
1367 West Broadway, Vancouver, BC V6H 4E9
604/929-3235
President, Peter Lissett

### Dominion of Canada Rifle Association (1868)
PO Box 11160, Stn H, Nepean, ON K2H 7T9
613/829-8281, Fax: 613/990-0434
Executive Director, LCol (ret'd) T.J. Kaulbach
Executive Vice-President, S.E. Frost
Publications: The Canadian Marksman

### Elvis in Canada Fan Club (EIC) (1980)
PO Box 20236, RPO Upper James, Hamilton, ON L9C 7M8
President, Frances M. Roberts
Affiliates: National Association of Fan Clubs

### Fantasy Balloon Owners & Pilots Association (1989)
205 Bridge St., New Dundee, ON N0B 2E0
519/696-2414, Fax: 519/696-2414
Director, Karen Rosenthal

### Fédération des clubs de motoneigistes du Québec (FCMQ) (1974)
4545, av Pierre-de-Coubertin, CP 1000, Succ. M, Montréal, QC H1V 3R2
514/252-3076, Téléc: 514/254-2066, Courrier électronique: info@fcmq.qc.ca, URL: http://www.fcmq.qc.ca
Président, Richard Charbonneau
Agent d'Administration, Danielle Poirier
Publications: Motoneige Québec

### Federation of Mountain Clubs of British Columbia (1980)
#336, 1367 West Broadway, Vancouver, BC V6H 4A9
604/737-3053, Fax: 604/738-7175, Email: fmcbc@sport.bc.ca
Executive Director, Linda Coss

### Federation of Ontario Cottagers' Associations Inc. (FOCA) (1964)
#101, 215 Morrish Rd., Scarborough, ON M1C 1E9
416/284-2305, Fax: 416/284-7108
Executive Director, Wendy Moore

Environment Committee, Shannon McCorquodale
Publications: Lake Stewards Newsletter

**Fédération de pétanque du Québec**
4545, av Pierre-de-Coubertin, CP 1000, Succ. M, Montréal, QC H1V 3R2
514/252-3077, Téléc: 514/252-3169
Secrétaire administrative, Line M. Dalard

**Fédération québécoise de camping et de caravaning inc. (FQCC) (1967)**
4545, av Pierre-de-Coubertin, CP 1000, Succ. M, Montréal, QC H1V 3R2
514/252-3003, Téléc: 514/254-0694
Directeur général, Irman Bolduc
Directrice, Services aux membres et du développement régional, Francine Langevin
Publications: Camping Caravaning

**Fédération québécoise de canoë kayak d'eau vive**
4545, av Pierre-de-Coubertin, CP 1000, Succ. M, Montréal, QC H1V 3R2
514/252-3099, Téléc: 514/252-3232
Président, Jean Obry

**Fédération québécoise des échecs/Québec Chess Federation (FQE) (1967)**
CP 640, Succ. C, Montréal, QC H2L 4L5
514/252-3034, Téléc: 514/251-8038, Courrier électronique: fqechec@cam.org, URL: http://WWW.CAM.ORG/~fqechec
Directeur général, Robert Finta
Président, Luc Nolet
Publications: Échec+

**Fédération québécoise des jeux récréatifs (FQJR) (1975)**
4545, av Pierre-de-Coubertin, CP 1000, Succ. M, Montréal, QC H1V 3R2
514/252-3032, Téléc: 514/251-8038, Courrier électronique: jeuxrecr@fqjr.qc.ca, URL: http://www.fqjr.qc.ca/
Directeur général, André Leclerc
Publications: Récréation Québec

**Fédération québécoise de la marche (1982)**
4545, av Pierre-de-Coubertin, CP 1000, Succ. M, Montréal, QC H1V 3R2
514/252-3157, Téléc: 514/254-1363
Publications: Marche

**Fly Fishing Canada (FFC) (1987)**
#50, 7171 Torbram Rd., Mississauga, ON L4T 3W4
905/678-0422, Fax: 905/678-0424
Executive Director, Jack Simpson

**Guide Outfitters Association of British Columbia (GOABC) (1966)**
PO Box 94675, Richmond, BC V6Y 4A4
604/278-2688, Fax: 604/278-3440, Email: goabc@dowco.com
General Manager, Dale Drown
Publications: BC Hunter

**Hang Gliding & Paragliding Association of Canada/Association canadienne de vol libre (HPAC) (1977)**
21593 - 94A Ave., Langley, BC V1M 2A5
604/882-5090
Administrator, Barry Bateman
Publications: AIR

**Hike Ontario (1974)**
**Federation of Ontario Hiking Trail Associations**
#411, 1185 Eglinton Ave. East, North York, ON M3C 3C6
416/426-7362, Fax: 416/426-7362, Toll Free: 1-800-422-0552
President, Jeff Hemming
Publications: Outlook
Affiliates: Ontario Trails Council; National Trail Association of Canada

**Horseshoe Canada Association/Association canadienne de fer à cheval**
PO Box 548, Raymore, SK S0A 3J0
306/746-2041, Fax: 306/746-5811
President, Sharon Ellison
Treasurer, Jack E. Adams
Publications: Canadian Horseshoe Pitchers Year Book

**International Computer Chess Association (Canada) (ICCA) (1977)**
Dept. of Computing Science, University of Alberta, Edmonton, AB T6G 2H1
403/492-3971, Fax: 403/492-1071, Email: Tony.Marsland@ualberta.ca, URL: http://www.cs.unimaas.nl/
President, Prof. T.A. Marsland
Vice-President, David N.L. Levy
Sec.-Treas, D.F. Beal
Publications: Journal of the International Computer Chess Association

**International Laser Class Association (North American Region)**
#328, 8466 North Lockwood Ridge Rd., Sarasota, FL 34243 USA
813/359-1384, Fax: 813/359-1384, Telex: 05-839600 LASER
General Manager, Allan Broadribb

**Lawn Bowls Canada/Boulingrin Canada**
Place R. Tait McKenzie, #708, 1600 James Naismith Dr., Gloucester, ON K1B 5N4
613/748-5643, Fax: 613/748-5796, Telex: 053-3660 SPORT
Executive Director, Margot Clayton Jones
President, Jim Keeling

**Lionel Collectors Association of Canada (LCAC) (1978)**
PO Box 976, Oshawa, ON L1H 7N2
General Agent/COO, T.G.J. Gascoigne
Publications: LCAC Switch List

**Lottery Collectors Society (LCS) (1987)**
10760 Shellbridge Way, Richmond, BC V6X 3H1
Sec.-Treas., Richard Bertrand
Publications: Lotologist

**Maritime Boating Association**
Martins Brook, PO Box 448, Lunenburg, NS B0J 2C0
902/634-3173
Contact, Weldon W. Allen

**Model Aeronautics Association of Canada Inc. (MAAC) (1949)**
#9, 5100 South Service Rd., Burlington, ON L7L 6A5
905/632-9808, Fax: 905/632-3304, URL: http://www.maac.ca
Sec.-Treas., Linda Patrick
Publications: Model Aviation Canada
Affiliates: Aero Club of Canada; Fédération aeronautique internationale

**National Association of Watch & Clock Collectors (NAWCC) (1943)**
514 Poplar St., Columbia, PA 17512-2124 USA
717/684-8261, Fax: 717/684-0878, URL: http://www.nawcc.org
Executive Director, Thomas Bartels
Publications: Bulletin; Mart, bi-m.

**National Firearms Association (NFA) (1984)**
PO Box 1779, Edmonton, AB T5J 2P1
403/439-1394, Fax: 403/439-4091, Email: nfadat@agt.net, URL: http://www.nfa.ca
National President, David A. Tomlinson
Publications: Pointblank

**New Brunswick Camping Committee**
Park Office Centre, #105, 440 Wilsey Rd., Fredericton, NB E3B 7G5
506/459-1929, Fax: 506/450-6066
CCA Liaison, Dana Welner

**Ontario Federation of Anglers & Hunters (OFAH) (1928)**
PO Box 2800, Peterborough, ON K9J 8L5
705/748-6324, Fax: 705/748-9577, Email: ofah@oncomdis.on.ca
Executive Vice-President, Rick Morgan
Secretary, Nancy Cator
Publications: Call of the Loon; Hotline, m.; Hunter Education News, q.; Canadian Fishing & Hunting Trade News
Affiliates: Canadian Wildlife Federation

**Ontario Federation of Snowmobile Clubs (OFSC) (1966)**
PO Box 94, Barrie, ON L4M 4S9
705/739-7669, Fax: 705/739-5005, Email: ofsc@mail.transdata.ca, URL: http://www.transdata.ca/~ofsc/~ofsc.htm
President, Bert Grant
Manager, Ron Purchase
Publications: Main Trail

**Ontario Marina Operators Association (OMOA) (1967)**
#211, 4 Cataraqui St., Kingston, ON K7K 1Z7
613/547-6662, Fax: 613/547-6813, Email: hq@omoa.kosone.com
Executive Director, Michael S. Shaw
Publications: Marina News
Affiliates: Canadian Marine Trades Federation

**Ontario Municipal Recreation Association (OMRA)**
#404, 1185 Eglinton Ave. East, North York, ON M3C 3C6
416/426-7151, Fax: 416/426-7366
President, Rita McWhirter

**Ontario Numismatic Association (ONA) (1962)**
PO Box 40033, Stn Waterloo Square, Waterloo, ON N2J 4V1
519/745-3104
Membership Chairman, Bruce Raszmann
Publications: The Ontario Numismatic

**Ontario Parks Association (OPA) (1936)**
1185 Eglinton Ave. East, North York, ON M3C 3C7
416/426-7157, Fax: 416/426-7366, Email: opa@hookup.net, URL: http://www.hookup.net/~opa
Executive Director, Denyse A. Morrissey
Publications: Green Sward
Affiliates: Landscape Ontario; Ontario Association of Landscape Architects

**Ontario Recreation Facilities Association (ORFA) (1947)**
1185 Eglinton Ave. East, North York, ON M3C 3C7
416/426-7062, Fax: 416/426-7385, Toll Free: 1-800-661-6732, Email: orfa@pathcom.com, URL: http://www.pathcom.com/~orfa/
Executive Director, John Milton
Publications: Facility Forum

**Ontario Research Council on Leisure (ORCOL) (1975)**
School of Rural Planning & Development, University of Guelph, #158, 50 Stone Rd. E., Guelph, ON N1G 2W1
519/824-4120, Fax: 519/767-1690
Vice-President, Don Reid
Publications: Applied Leisure Research

**Ontario Sport Fishing Guides' Association (OSGA) (1980)**
40 Sherwood Rd. East, Ajax, ON L1T 2Y9
905/683-3214, Fax: 905/683-2872
President, Hugh Caulfield
Secretary, Doug Kettle
Publications: Charter Chatter

**Ontario Trails Council (1988)**
Trail Studies Unit, Environmental Sciences Bldg., Trent University, PO Box 4800, Peterborough, ON K9J 7B8
709/748-1419, Fax: 709/748-1205, URL: http://www.csp.trentu.ca/gomrm/otc.html
President, Paul Gleason
Vice-President, John Marsh
Publications: Greenways
Affiliates: Bruce Trail Association; Canadian Motorcycling Association; Guelph Trail Club; Hike Ontario; Kawartha Rail-Trail; Ontario Federation of Snowmobile Clubs; Ontario Cycling Association; Ontario Competitive Trail Riders Association; Ontario Working Dog Association; Parry Sound Rail Line Task Force; Rideau Trail Association; Northland Associates; Ontario Trail Riders Association; Rails to Trails Conservancy - USA; Credit Valley Conservation Authority; Georgian Cycle & Ski Trail Association; Grand Valley Trail Association; Southeastern Ontario Rails to Tracks

**Ontario Vintage Radio Association (OVRA) (1980)**
197 Humberside Ave., Toronto, ON M6P 1K7
416/769-9627
President, Ted Catton
Publications: OVRA Newsletter

**Outdoor Recreation Council of British Columbia (ORC) (1976)**
#334, 1367 Broadway West, Vancouver, BC V6H 4A7
604/737-3058, Fax: 604/737-3666, Email: outrec_council@sport.bc.ca, URL: http://mindlink.net/outrec_council/outrec.htm
Executive Director, Norma Wilson
Publications: The Outdoor Report

**Outward Bound Ontario (COBWS) (1976)**
**Canadian Outward Bound Wilderness School**
#302, 150 Laird Dr., Toronto, ON M4G 3V7
416/421-8111, Fax: 416/421-9062, Toll Free: 1-800-268-7329
Executive Director, Philip Blackford
Publications: Alumni News

**Outward Bound Western Canada (1969)**
#109, 1367 Broadway West, Vancouver, BC V6H 4A9
604/737-3093, Fax: 604/738-7175, Email: ob@uniserve.com, URL: http://www.infinity.ca/outwardbound/
Executive Director, Andrew Orr
Marketing Manager, Anne Marie Barrett

**Paddle Sport BC**
c/o Sport BC, 1367 Broadway West, Vancouver, BC V6H 4A9
604/275-6651, Fax: 604/275-6651
Treasurer, Brian Creer
Publications: Canews; Paddle Post

**Racetracks of Canada, Inc./Hippodromes du Canada inc. (ROC) (1965)**
2150 Meadowvale Blvd., Mississauga, ON L5N 6R6
905/821-7795, Fax: 905/858-3111
President, Bill Taylor
Executive Vice-President, Roly Roberts
Publications: Track Talk
Affiliates: Canadian Horse Racing Hall of Fame

**Recreation Facilities Association of British Columbia (RFABC) (1948)**
8550 Young Rd. South, Chilliwack, BC V2P 4P1
604/793-2904, Fax: 604/795-8443, Email: mulligan@gov.chilliwack.bc.ca
Sec.-Treas., Ryan Mulligan
President, Ray Boogaards
Publications: Facility to Facility

**Regroupement loisir Québec (1980)**
4545, av Pierre-de-Coubertin, CP 1000, Succ. M, Montréal, QC H1V 3R2
514/252-3126, Téléc: 514/253-7156
Directeur général, François Hamel
Organisation(s) affiliée(s): Association canadienne des loisirs/parcs

**Roller Sports Canada/Sports à roulettes du Canada**
c/o Roller Sports Manitoba, 200 Main St., Winnipeg, MB R3C 4M2
204/925-5699, Fax: 204/925-5703
Executive Director, Rick Bochinski
President, Norm Dawkin

**The Royal Philatelic Society of Canada/Société royale de philatélie du Canada (RPSC) (1887)**
PO Box 929, Stn Q, Toronto, ON M4T 2P1
416/979-7474, Fax: 416/979-1144, Email: rpsc@interlog.com, URL: http://www.interlog.com/~rpsc
President, William G. Robinson
Publications: The Canadian Philatelist

**The RPSC Philatelic Research Foundation/ Fondation de recherche philatélique de la SRPC (1986)**
PO Box 929, Stn Q, Toronto, ON M4T 2P1
613/738-2770, Fax: 613/738-7863, Email: vergec@sympatico.ca
President, Charles J.G. Verge
Secretary, Harry Sutherland, Q.C., R.D.P., F.R.P.S.C.
Publications: The Opusculum

**SALTS Sail & Life Training Society (1974)**
PO Box 5014, Stn B, Victoria, BC V8R 6N3
250/383-6811, Fax: 250/383-7781
Executive Director, Martyn Clark
Business Manager, Ron Howatson
Publications: Saltings

**Saskatchewan Association of Recreation Professionals (1969)**
**Saskatchewan Recreation Society**
2205 Victoria Ave., Regina, SK S4P 0S4
306/780-9267, Fax: 306/525-4009, Toll Free: 1-800-667-7780, Email: sask.rec.society@sk.sympatico.ca
Executive Director, Al Neufeld
Publications: Update
Affiliates: Saskatchewan Parks & Recreation Association

**Saskatchewan Snowmobile Association Inc. (SSA) (1971)**
PO Box 533, Regina Beach, SK S0G 4C0
306/729-3500, Fax: 306/729-3505
President, Chris Brewer
Manager, Jeannie Brewer
Publications: Saskatchewan Snowmobiler

**Sea Kayak Association of BC**
7955 - 161 St., Surrey, BC V3S 7H9
604/597-1122
President, Mercia Sixta

**Shooting Federation of Canada/Fédération de tir du Canada (1932)**
45 Shirley Blvd., Nepean, ON K2K 2W6
613/828-7338, Fax: 613/828-7333
President, David Hitchcock
Publications: Aim

**Sky Line Hikers of the Canadian Rockies (1933)**
PO Box 75055, Stn Cambrian, Calgary, AB T2K 6J8
403/240-4016
Sec.-Treas., Irene Garvin
Publications: Skyliner

**Snowmobilers Association of Nova Scotia (SANS) (1976)**
5516 Spring Garden Rd., PO Box 3010, Stn Parklane Centre, Halifax, NS B3J 3G6
902/425-5450, Fax: 902/425-5606
Executive Director, Robert Semple, CAE
Publications: Sno' Trails-SANS

**Soaring Association of Canada/Association canadienne de vol à voile (SAC) (1945)**
#101, 1090 Ambleside Dr., Ottawa, ON K2B 8G7
613/829-0536, Fax: 613/829-9497, Email: sac@comnet.ca, URL: http://www.sac.ca/
President, Pierre Pepin
Director, James F. McCullum
Publications: Free Flight
Affiliates: Aero Club of Canada

**Taoist Tai Chi Society of Canada (1970)**
1376 Bathurst St., Toronto, ON M5R 3J1
416/656-2110, Fax: 416/654-3937
President, Albert Chan
Founder, Moy Lin-shin

**Trail Riders of the Canadian Rockies (1923)**
PO Box 6742, Stn D, Calgary, AB T2P 2E6
403/264-8656, Fax: 403/264-8657, Email: trcr@canuck.com, URL: http://www.canuck.com/~trcr
President, Gordon Thomson
Executive Director, Barbara Rostron
Secretary, Penny Egeland
Publications: Ridin' High

**Tunnelling Association of Canada (TAC)**
Dept. of Civil Engineering, University of Toronto, Toronto, ON M5S 1A4
416/978-3115
President, Prof. A.M. Crawford
Publications: Canadian Tunnelling

**White Water Kayaking Association of British Columbia**
1367 West Broadway, Vancouver, BC V6H 4A9
604/275-6651
President, Simon Shutter
Publications: Paddle Post

**Wilderness Canoe Association (WCA)**
1881 Yonge St., PO Box 48022, Stn Davisville, Toronto, ON M4S 3C6
905/831-3554
Contact, Brian Buttigieg
Publications: Nastawgan

**Writing Instruments Collectors Club of Canada**
PO Box 1215, Stn Q, Toronto, ON M4T 2P4
416/260-8240
Chairman, Stephen Overbury

### YMCA Canada (1851)
The National Council of Young Men's Christian Associations of Canada
#200, 2160 Yonge St., Toronto, ON M4S 2A9
416/485-9447, Fax: 416/485-8228
CEO, Sol Kasimer
Chair, Edward G. Robinson
Director of Communications, Dianne LeBreton
Publications: Between the Lines; Entre les lignes, trimestriel
Affiliates: Canadian Centre for Philanthropy; Canadian Child Care Federation; Canadian Coalition for the Rights of Children; Canadian Council for International Cooperation; Canadian Council on Children & Youth; Canadian Learning Consortium; Canadian Recreational Canoeing Association; Canadian Society of Association Executives; Coalition on National Voluntary Organizations; Conference Board of Canada; Huronia Tourism Association; National Fitness Leadership Advisory Committee; National Life Guard Service; National Voluntary Health Agencies; National Youth Serving Agencies; Partnership Africa Canada; Resorts Ontario; Royal Life Saving Society

### YWCA of/du Canada (1893)
Young Women's Christian Association of Canada
590 Jarvis St., Toronto, ON M4Y 2J4
416/962-8881, Fax: 416/962-8084, Email: national@ywcacanada.ca
President, Mobina Jaffee
CEO, Elaine Teofilovici
Publications: Journal
Affiliates: Selective: Canadian Association for the Advancement of Women in Sports; Canadian Congress for Learning Opportunities for Women; Canadian Coalition for the Rights of the Child; Canadian Daycare Advocacy; Canadian Research Institute for the Advancement of Women; Federated Women's Institutes of Canada; National Action Committee on the Status of Women

**RECYCLING *see* ENVIRONMENTAL**

**RED CROSS *see* EMERGENCY RESPONSE**

**RENEWABLE FUELS *see* ENERGY**

## REPRODUCTIVE ISSUES

### Alliance for Life/Alliance pour la vie (1972)
#B1, 90 Garry St., Winnipeg, MB R3C 4H1
204/942-4772, Fax: 204/943-9283, Crisis-Line: 1-800-665-0570, Email: ikrueger@infobahn.mb.ca
Executive Director, Anna M. Desilets
Affiliates: Alliance Action Inc.

### Birthright/Accueil Grossesse (1968)
777 Coxwell Ave., Toronto, ON M4C 3C6
416/469-1111, Fax: 416/469-1772, Toll Free: 1-800-550-4900
Co-President, Stephenie Fox
Co-President, Mary Berney
Co-President, Louise R. Summerhill
Publications: Life Guardian

### Canadian Abortion Rights Action League/ Association canadienne pour le droit à l'avortement (CARAL) (1974)
#306, 344 Bloor St. West, Toronto, ON M5S 3A7
416/961-1507, Fax: 416/961-5771, Email: caral@interlog.com, URL: http://www.interlog.com/~caral
Executive Director, Jo Dufay
President, Pauline Raven
Publications: Pro-choice News

### Canadian Fertility & Andrology Society/Société canadienne de fertilité et d'andrologie (CFAS) (1954)
#409, 2065, rue Alexandre Desève, Montréal, QC H2L 2W5
514/524-9009, Fax: 514/524-2163
Executive Director, Susan Orr-Mongeau
Publications: Directory

### Childbirth By Choice Trust/Choisir de donner naissance (1982)
#306, 344 Bloor St. West, Toronto, ON M5S 3A7
416/961-1507, Fax: 416/961-5771, Email: cbctrust@idirect.com, URL: http://web.idirect.com/~cbctrust/
Administrator, Jane Koster

### Coalition for Reproductive Choice (1982)
PO Box 51, Stn L, Winnipeg, MB R3H 0Z4
204/946-5018
Director, Amanda Le Rougetel
Administrative Coordinator, Susan Riley
Publications: Manitoba Pro Choice News
Affiliates: Manitoba Federation of Labour; Women's Health Clinic; Canadian Abortion Rights Action League; National Council of Jewish Women; YWCA

### Fédération du Québec pour le planning des naissances (FQPN) (1972)
#302, 4428, boul St-Laurent, Montréal, QC H2W 1Z5
514/844-3721, Téléc: 514/844-8736
Coordonnatrice, Anne St-Cerny

### Infertility Awareness Association of Canada/ Association canadienne de sensibilisation à l'infertilité (IAAC) (1990)
#201, 396 Cooper St., Ottawa, ON K2P 2H7
613/730-1322, Fax: 613/730-1323, Toll Free: 1-800-263-2929, Email: ax626@freenet.carleton.ca
Executive Director, Trish Maynard
Publications: Infertility Awareness
Affiliates: Canadian Fertility & Andrology Society; Society of Obstetricians & Gynaecologists of Canada

### League for Life in Manitoba/Ligue pour la vie au Manitoba (1970)
579 Des Meurons St., Winnipeg, MB R2H 2P6
204/233-8047, 7283, Fax: 204/233-0523, Toll Free: 1-800-665-0570
Executive Director, Patricia Soenen
President, Laverne Hudson
Publications: League for Life News

### Natural Family Planning Association
#205, 3050 Yonge St., Toronto, ON M4N 2K4
416/481-5465
Executive Director, M. Isabel Graham
President, Merrilyn Currie
Publications: Newsletter

### Ontario Coalition for Abortion Clinics (OCAC)
PO Box 753, Stn P, Toronto, ON M5S 2Z1
416/969-8463
Coordinating Committee, Miriam Jones

### Planned Parenthood Federation of Canada/ Fédération pour le planning des naissances du Canada (PPFC) (1964)
#430, One Nicholas St., Ottawa, ON K1N 7B7
613/241-4474, Fax: 613/241-7550, Email: ppfed@web.net
Executive Director, Bonnie Johnson
Director, Resource Development, Sharon Bradford
Publications: PPFC Bulletin

#### PLANNED PARENTHOOD ALBERTA (PPA) (1973)
#304, 301 - 14 St. NW, Calgary, AB T2N 2A1
403/283-8591, Fax: 403/270-3209
Executive Director, Melanie Anderson
Publications: Newsletter
Affiliates: Calgary Birth Control Association; Planned Parenthood Association of Edmonton; Planned Parenthood Banff; Planned Parenthood Alberta - Medecine Hat

#### PLANNED PARENTHOOD ASSOCIATION OF BRITISH COLUMBIA (1963)
#201, 1001 West Broadway, Vancouver, BC V6K 2G8
604/731-4252, Fax: 604/731-4698, Toll Free: 1-800-739-7367
Email: p.pabc@express.ca
Executive Director, Marcena S. Croy
President, Dr. Sue Chalmers
Publications: Facts of Life

#### PLANNED PARENTHOOD MANITOBA (1966)
#206, 819 Sargent Ave., Winnipeg, MB R3E 0B9
204/982-7800, Fax: 204/982-7819
Executive Director, Miriam Baron
President, Roberta Ellis

#### PLANNED PARENTHOOD NEWFOUNDLAND/LABRADOR
203 Merrymeeting Rd., St. John's, NF A1C 2W6
709/579-1009, Fax: 709/726-2308
President, Alison Earle
Clinic Coordinator, Nancy Stokes

#### PLANNED PARENTHOOD NOVA SCOTIA
Quinpool Medical Centre, #100, 6156 Quinpool Rd., Halifax, NS B3L 1A3
902/492-0444, Fax: 902/492-7155
Executive Director, Cari Patterson

#### PLANNED PARENTHOOD ONTARIO (1975)
790 Bay St., 8th Fl., Toronto, ON M5S 2Z2
416/595-9989, Fax: 416/595-9984, Toll Free: 1-800-463-6739
Executive Director, Cheryll Corness
President, Joan Toogood
Publications: Choice Words

#### PLANNED PARENTHOOD SASKATCHEWAN
2006 York Ave., Saskatoon, SK S7J 1H6
306/343-9343
President, Linda Holmes

### Pro-Life Society of British Columbia
#204, 1755 Springfield Rd., Kelowna, BC V1Y 5V5
250/862-3731, Email: egerk@awinc.com
President, Ted Gerk

### Right to Life Association of Newfoundland
PO Box 5427, St. John's, NF A1C 5W2
709/579-1500, Fax: 709/579-3818
President, Philomena Rogers

### Right to Life Association of Toronto (1972)
#700, 120 Eglinton Ave. East, Toronto, ON M4P 1E2
416/483-7869, Fax: 416/483-7052, Email: right-to-life@sympatico.ca
President, June Scandiffio
Publications: Newsletter

### World Organization Ovulation Method Billings Inc.
WOOMB Canada Inc.
1506 Dansey Ave., Coquitlam, BC V3K 3J1
604/936-4472, Fax: 604/936-5690
President, Lou Specken
Vice-President, Sheila J. Howard
Affiliates: WOOMB International - Australia

## RESEARCH & SCHOLARSHIP

***see also* Education; Health & Medical; Scientific**

### APRO - The Canadian Technology Network (1984)
**Association of Provincial Research Organizations**
#1004, 280 Albert St., Ottawa, ON K1P 5G8
613/567-2993, Fax: 613/567-4562
Chairman, Brian Barge
President & CEO, Graham Taylor
Office Manager, Deborah Pelletier

### Canadian Association for HIV Research
c/o Jewish General Hospital, 3755, ch Côte-Ste-Catherine, Montréal, QC H3T 1E2
514/340-8260, Fax: 514/340-7537
President, Dr. Mark A. Wainberg
Publications: The Clarion

### Canadian Association for Research in Nondestructive Evaluation/Association canadienne de recherche en évaluation nondestructifs (CARNDE) (1987)
75, boul de Montagne, Boucherville, QC J4B 6Y4
514/641-5252, Fax: 514/641-5104
Contact, Dr. Jean Bussière
Publications: Canadian Association for Research
Affiliates: Canadian Society for Nondestructive Testing, Inc.

### Canadian Bacterial Diseases Network/Réseau canadian de recherche sur les bactérioses (CBDN) (1990)
282, Heritage Medical Research Bldg., University of Calgary, 3330 Hospital Dr. NW, Calgary, AB T2N 4N1
403/220-2562, Fax: 403/283-5241, URL: http://www.cbdn.ca
Managing Director, Karen Corraini, Email: karen@cbdn.ca
Scientific Director, Dr. D.E. Woods, Email: woods@acs.ucalgary.ca
Publications: Microbial Connections

### Canadian Carbonization Research Association (CCRA) (1965)
PO Box 85291, RPO Brant Plaza, Burlington, ON L7R 4K4
905/637-0666
Treasurer, G.A. Chapman
Chairman, Wayne Jonasson

### Canadian Centre for Policy Alternatives/Centre canadien de politique alternatives (CCPA) (1980)
#804, 251 Laurier Ave. West, Ottawa, ON K1P 5J6
613/563-1341, Fax: 613/233-1458, Email: ccpa@policyalternatives.ca, URL: http://www.policyalternatives.ca
Executive Director, Bruce Campbell
President, Duncan Cameron
Publications: CCPA Monitor
BC Office: Coordinator, Seth Klein, #815, 207 West Hastings St., Vancouver, BC V6B 1H7, 604/801-5121, Fax: 604/801-5122, Email: sethk@policyalternatives.ca

### Canadian Committee of Byzantinists
University of Waterloo, 200 University Ave. West, Waterloo, ON N2L 3G1
519/885-1211, ext.3565, Fax: 519/746-3097, Email: dsahas@uwaterloo.waterloo.ca
President, Daniel Sahas
Publications: Canadio-Byzantina
Affiliates: Association internationale des études byzantines

### Canadian Federation of the Theosophical Society in Canada (1919)
PO Box 123, Wellington, ON K0K 3L0
613/399-1359, Email: emswel@sympatico.ca
Regional Secretary, Elizabeth M. Smith
Publications: The Light Bearer

### Canadian Genetic Diseases Network/Réseau canadien sur les maladies génétiques (CGDN) (1990)
University of British Columbia, #349, 2125 East Mall, Vancouver, BC V6T 1Z4
604/822-7217, Fax: 604/822-7945, URL: http://data.ctn.nrc.ca/bc/content/type12/org319/parent.htm
Managing Director, Dr. David Shindler, Email: dshindler.cgdn@ubc.ca
Network Manager, Carol J. Smith, Email: csmith.cgdn@ubc.ca
Commercial Director, Margaret Moore

### Canadian Institute for Advanced Research/La fondation de l'institut canadien de recherches avancées
#701, 179 John St., Toronto, ON M5T 1X4
416/971-4252, Fax: 416/971-6169
President, Dr. J. Fraser Mustard
Vice-President, L. Douglas Todgham

### Canadian Institute for Mediterranean Studies/Institut canadien d'études méditerranéennes (1980)
c/o Italian Studies Dept., University of Toronto, 21 Sussex Ave., Ottawa, ON K1N 6S1
416/978-4399, Fax: 416/978-4399, Email: jandav.anido@sympatico.ca
President, Dr. Domenico Retropaulo
Publications: Bulletin; Scripta Mediterranea
Affiliates: Canadian Institute in Egypt; Canadian Archaeological Institute at Athens; Canadian Academic Centre in Italy

### Canadian Institute of Strategic Studies/Institut canadien d'études stratégiques (CISS) (1976)
Box 2321, #402, 2300 Yonge St., Toronto, ON M4P 1E4
416/322-8128, Fax: 416/322-8129, Toll Free: 1-800-831-5695, Email: info@ciss.ca, URL: http://www.ciss.ca
Executive Director, Alex Morrison
Director, Finance & Administration, Mark Larsen
Associate Executive Director, Jim Hanson
Director, Publications, Susan McNish
Publications: CISS Bulletin; McNaughton Papers; Strategic Datalinks, m.
The Lester B. Pearson Canadian International Peacekeeping Training Centre: President, Alex Morrison; Vice-President, Robert Hamilton, Cornwallis Park, PO Box 100, Clementsport, NS B0S 1E0, 902/638-8611, Fax: 902/638-8888, Email: presiden@ppc.cdnpeacekeeping.ns.ca, URL: http://www.cdnpeacekeeping.ns.ca

### Canadian Institute for the Study of the Soviet Union & East European Countries (1982)
72 Elise Terrace, North York, ON M2R 2X1
416/250-0269, Fax: 416/250-0269
President, Dr. Roman Fin

### Canadian Institute of Ukrainian Studies/Institut canadien d'études ukrainiennes (CIUS) (1976)
#352 Athabasca Hall, University of Alberta, 26 University Campus NW, Edmonton, AB T6G 2E8
403/492-2972, Fax: 403/492-4967, Telex: 037-2979, Email: cius@gpu.srv.ualberta.ca
Director, Dr. Zenon E. Kohut, Ph.D.
Publications: Journal of Ukrainian Studies; CIUS Newsletter, a.

### Canadian Mathematical Society/Société mathématique du Canada (CMS) (1945)
#109, 577 King Edward St., PO Box 415, Stn A, Ottawa, ON K1N 6N5
613/562-5702, Fax: 613/565-1539, Email: office@cms.math.ca, URL: http://camel.math.ca
President, Dr. Katherine Heinrich
Executive Director/Secretary, Graham P. Wright
Publications: Canadian Journal of Mathematics; Canadian Mathematical Bulletin, q.; Crux Mathematicorum with Mathematical Mayhem, 8 pa; CMS Notes, 9 pa

### Canadian Mining Industry Research Organization (CMIRO)
c/o Iron Ore Company of Canada, 100, rue Retty, Sept-Îles, QC G4R 3E1
418/968-7502, Fax: 418/968-7108
Chairman, Derek Rance

### Canadian Nautical Research Society/Société canadienne pour la recherche nautique (CNRS) (1982)
240 Sparks St., PO Box 55035, Ottawa, ON K1P 1A1
709/737-2602, Fax: 709/737-8427
President, G. Edward Reed
Secretary, Prof. Lewis Fischer, Email: lfisher@kean.ucs.mun.ca
Publications: Argonauta; The Northern Mariner/Le Marin du Nord, m.
Affiliates: International Commission for Maritime History

### Canadian Numismatic Research Society (CNRS) (1963)
PO Box 1351, Victoria, BC V8W 2W7
250/385-9703, Fax: 250/598-5539
Secretary, R. Greene
Publications: Transactions

### Canadian Operational Research Society/Société canadienne de recherche opérationelle (CORS)
PO Box 2225, Stn D, Ottawa, ON K1P 5W4
URL: http://www.ncf.carleton.ca/freeport/prof.assoc/cors/menu
Secretary, Dr. Sia Kahkeshan
Publications: INFOR - Information Systems & Operational Research

### Canadian Philosophical Association/Association canadienne de philosophie (1962)
Dept. of Philosophy, UQAM, 400, rue Ste-Catherine est, Montréal, QC H2X 3J8
514/987-3253, Fax: 514/987-8721, URL: http://www.uwindsor.ca/cpa
Présidente, Josiane Boulad Ayoub
Publications: Dialogue
Affiliates: Fédération internationale des sociétés de philosophie

### Canadian Quaternary Association
NBDNR Geological Surv., PO Box 6000, Fredericton, NB E3B 5H1
506/453-7947, Fax: 506/444-4176
Sec.-Treas., Toon Pronk
Publications: Newsletter/Bulletin; Géographie physique et quaternaire, 3 pa

### Canadian Research Institute for the Advancement of Women/Institut canadien de recherches sur les femmes (CRIAW) (1976)
#408, 151 Slater St., Ottawa, ON K1P 5H3
613/563-0681, Fax: 613/563-0682, Email: criaw@sympatico.ca, URL: http://www3.sympatico.ca/criaw
Executive Director, Linda Clippingdale

Publications: CRIAW Newsletter; The CRIAW Papers; Feminist Perspectives; Resources for Research & Action
Affiliates: National Action Committee on the Status of Women

### Canadian Society for Aesthetics/Société canadienne d'ésthetique (CSA) (1984)
Dept. of Theatre & Drama, University of Winnipeg, 515 Portage Ave., Winnipeg, MB R3B 2E9
204/786-9292, Fax: 204/453-5680
Co-President, Douglas Arrell
Co-President, Manon Regimbald

### Canadian Society for Eighteenth-Century Studies/Société canadienne d'étude du dix-huitième siècle (CSECS) (1969)
Dept. of English, Wilfred Laurier University, Waterloo, ON N2L 3C5
519/884-0710, ext.3581, Fax: 519/884-8854, Email: ety@mach1.wlu.ca,
URL: http://tornade.ere.umontreal.ca/~melancon/csecs.tdm.html
President, Peter Sabor
Sec.-Treas., Eleanor Ty
Publications: Bulletin; Lumen, a.
Affiliates: International Society for Eighteenth-Century Studies

### The Canadian Society for Mesopotamian Studies/La Société canadienne des études mésopotamiennes (CSMS) (1980)
4 Bancroft Ave., 4th Fl., Toronto, ON M5S 1A1
416/978-4531, Fax: 416/978-3305, URL: http://www.chass.utoronto.ca/nmc/rim/csms.html
Administrator, Linda Wilding
President, T. Cuyler Young, Jr.
Sec.-Treas., Ralph E. Warren
Publications: Bulletin of the CSMS
Affiliates: Canadian Mediterranean Institute; Royal Inscriptions of Mesopotamia Project

### Canadian Society of Patristic Studies/Association canadienne des études patristiques (CSPS) (1975)
Vancouver School of Theology, 6000 Long Dr., Vancouver, BC V6T 1L4
604/228-9031, Fax: 604/228-0189
President, Prof. Harry O. Maier
Secretary, Patrick T.R. Gray
Treasurer, Andrius Valecius
Publications: The Bulletin; Sciences Religieuses/Studies in Religion
Affiliates: Canadian Corporation for the Study of Religion

### Canadian Sociology & Anthropology Association/Société canadienne de sociologie et d'anthropologie (CSAA) (1966)
1455, boul de Maisonneuve ouest, Montréal, QC H3G 1M8
514/848-8780, Fax: 514/848-4539, Email: csaa@vax2.concordia.ca
Sec.-Treas., Suzanne Dubé
Publications: The Canadian Review of Sociology & Anthropology/La Revue canadienne de sociologie et d'anthropologie; Society/Société, 3 pa

### Canadian Technion Society (1945)
**Technion - Israel Institute of Technology**
#206, 970 Lawrence Ave. West, Toronto, ON M6A 3B6
416/789-4545, Fax: 416/789-0255, Toll Free: 1-800-935-8864
National Executive Director, Jerry Enchin
Executive Director, Cheryl Koperwas

### Cancer Research Society Inc./Société de recherche sur le cancer inc. (CRS) (1945)
#2332, 1, Place Ville Marie, Montréal, QC H3B 3M5
514/861-9227, Fax: 514/861-9220, Toll Free: 1-888-766-2262, Email: crs@cam.org, URL: http://www.cancer-research-society.ca
Executive Director, Ivy Steinberg
President/CEO, Dr. Guy Boileau
Vice-President, Jean-Jacques Gagnon
Treasurer, William Epstein, CA
Secretary, Gerald Snyder
Publications: CRS Update

### Centre for Research-Action on Race Relations/Centre de recherche-action sur les relations raciales (CRARR)
#801, 3465, Côte-des-Neiges, Montréal, QC H3H 1T7
514/939-3342, Fax: 514/939-9763
Executive Director, Fo Niemi
Publications: Newsletter
Affiliates: Canadian Ethnocultural Council

### Centre for Research on Latin America & The Caribbean (CERLAC) (1978)
240 York Lanes, York University, 4700 Keele St., North York, ON M3J 1P3
416/736-5237, Fax: 416/736-5737, Email: cerlac@yorku.ca
Director, Prof. Ricardo Grinsdun
Deputy Director, Prof. Patrick Taylor
Publications: CERLAC News
Affiliates: Canadian Association for Latin American & Caribbean Studies; Counterpoint: A Resource Centre for Global Analyses; Canada-Caribbean-Central America Policy Alternatives; Development Education Centre; International Council for Adult Education; Jesuit Centre for Social Faith & Justice; Latin American Working Group; OXFAM-Canada; Inter-Church Committee on Human Rights in Latin America; Centre for Caribbean Dialogue; Centre for Spanish Speaking People

### Classical Association of Canada/Société canadienne des études classiques (1946)
Dept. of Classics, University of Winnipeg, Winnipeg, MB R3B 2E9
204/786-9343, URL: http://137.122.12.15/Docs/Societies/ClassAc/Classic.Assoc.html
President, Andre Daviault
Secretary, Ivan Cohen
Treasurer, Craig Cooper
Publications: Phoenix; Classical Views, 3 pa
Affiliates: Canadian Federation for the Humanities

### Commission canadienne pour la théorie des machines et des mécanismes/Canadian Committee for the Theory of Machines & Mechanisms (CCToMM) (1993)
Université Laval, Génie Mécanique, Ste-Foy, QC G1K 7P4
418/656-3474, Téléc: 418/656-7415, Courrier électronique: cctomm@gmc.ulaval.ca
Secrétaire Général, Clément Gosselin
Président, Louis Cloutier
Publications: Bulletin de la CCToMM

### Forest Engineering Research Institute of Canada/Institut canadien de recherches en génie forestier (FERIC) (1974)
580, boul Saint-Jean, Pointe Claire, QC H9R 3J9
514/694-1140, Fax: 514/694-4351, Email: admin@mtl.feric.ca, URL: http://www.feric.ca
President/CEO, Dr. Gilbert G. Paillé
Sec.-Treas., Pierre Giguère
Affiliates: International Union of Forest Research Organizations; Canadian Pulp & Paper Association; Pulp & Paper Research Institute of Canada
Eastern Division: Manager, D.Y. Guimier, 580, boul Saint-Jean, Pointe Claire, QC H9R 3J9, 514/694-1140, Téléc: 514/694-4351
Western Division: Manager, Western Division, Alex W.J. Sinclair, 2601 East Mall, Vancouver, BC V6T 1Z4, 604/228-1555, Fax: 604/228-0999

### Great Lakes Institute for Environmental Research (GLIER) (1981)
University of Windsor, 304 Sunset Ave., Windsor, ON N9B 3P4
519/253-4232, Fax: 519/971-3616
Director, G.D. Haffner

### Humanist Association of Canada/Association humaniste du Canada (HAC) (1968)
PO Box 3736, Stn C, Ottawa, ON K1Y 4J8
613/739-9569, Fax: 613/738-1462, Email: hac@magi.com, URL: http://magi.com/~hac/hac.html
President, Colin Downie
Publications: Canadian Humanist News; Humanist in Canada, q.
Affiliates: International Humanist & Ethical Union (UK)

### Humanities Association of Canada/Association canadienne des humanités (1951)
Faculty of Philosophy, F.A. Savard Pavillion, Laval University, CP 2208, Succ Terminus, Québec, QC G1K 7P4
418/656-2244, Fax: 418/656-7267
President, Henri-Paul Cunningham
Sec.-Treas., Thomas Reisner

### Institut national de la recherche scientifique/National Scientific Research Institute (INRS)
#640, 2600, boul Laurier, CP 7500, Ste-Foy, QC G1V 4C7
418/654-2500, Téléc: 418/654-2525, URL: http://www.inrs-urb.uquebec.ca
Directeur général, Alain Soucy
Information et relations publiques, Diane Lespérance
Publications: INRS - Nouvelles

### Institute for Research on Public Policy/Institut de recherches politiques (1972)
#200, 1470, rue Peel, Montréal, QC H3A 1T1
514/985-2461, Fax: 514/985-2559
President/CEO, Monique Jérome-Forget
Executive Director, Marye Bos
Publications: Policy Options

### Institute for Robotics & Intelligent Systems/Institut de robotique et d'intelligence des systèmes (IRIS) (1990)
PRECARN Associates Inc., #300, 30 Colonnade Rd., Nepean, ON K2E 7J6
613/727-9507, ext.26, Fax: 613/727-5672, Email: johnston@precarn.ca, URL: http://www.precarn.ca
Network Manager, Paul Johnston
Publications: Intellinet
Affiliates: PRECARN Associates

### Institute of Speculative Philosophy (1988)
PO Box 913, Stn B, Ottawa, ON K1P 5P9
613/594-5881, Fax: 613/594-3952, Email: isp@raynon.com
President, Dr. Francis K. Peddle
Publications: Eleutheria

### Institute for Stuttering Treatment & Research (ISTAR) (1986)
8220 - 114 St., 3rd Fl., Edmonton, AB T6G 2P4
403/492-2619, Fax: 403/492-8457, Email: istar@gpu.srv.ualberta.ca
Executive Director, Deborah Kully
Chairman, Earl Howe

Office Manager, Shirley Vanaelst
Publications: Institute News; The Other Side of the Block; Stuttering: Current Status of Theory & Therapy; A Retrospective Look at Stuttering Therapy; Long-Term Results of an Intensive Therapy Program for Adult & Adolescent Stutterers
Affiliates: Alberta Stutterers Association; The University of Alberta; Speech & Hearing Association of Alberta; Canadian Association of Speech & Language Pathology & Audiology; American Speech & Hearing Association

**Institute of Urban Studies (IUS) (1969)**
University of Winnipeg, 346 Portage Ave., Winnipeg, MB R3C 0C3
204/982-1140, Fax: 204/943-4695, Email: ius@coned.uwinnipeg.ca
Director, Tom Carter
Administrative Officer, Mary Ann Beavis
Publications: Canadian Journal of Urban Research

**International Council for Canadian Studies (ICCS)/Conseil international d'études canadiennes (CIEC)**
#800, 325 Dalhousie St., Ottawa, ON K1N 7G2
613/789-7834, Fax: 613/789-7830, Email: contact@iccs-ciec.ca, URL: http://www.iccs-ciec.ca
Executive Director, Alain Guimont
President, Xavier Arbos
Director of Administration & Programs, Gaëtan Vallières
Academic & Public Relations Officer, Linda Jones
Publications Officer, Guy Leclair
Program Officer, Diane Cyr
Program Officer, Joanne Lortie

**International Council for Central & East European Studies (Canada)/Conseil international d'études centrales et est-européennes (Canada) (ICCEES) (1974)**
Dept. of Political Science, Glendon College, York University, 2275 Bayview Ave., Toronto, ON M4N 3M6
416/736-2100, ext.88327, Fax: 416/487-6728, Email: gl250114@venus.yorku.ca
Secretary, Prof. Stanislav J. Kirschbaum
President, Prof. Ferdinand J.M. Fledbrugge
Publications: International Newsletter

**International Geographical Union - Canadian Committee**
Dept. of Geography, University of Victoria, PO Box 3050, Victoria, BC V8W 3P5
506/721-7340
Secretary, Larry McCann

**International Society for Research in Palmistry Inc./Société internationale de recherches en chirologie inc.**
351, av Victoria, Westmount, QC H3Z 2N1
514/488-2292, Fax: 514/488-3822
Contact, Ghanshyam Singh

**Leukemia Research Fund of Canada (LRF) (1955)**
#220, 1110 Finch Ave. West, Toronto, ON M3J 2T2
416/661-9541, Fax: 416/661-7799, Toll Free: 1-800-268-2144
Executive Director, Mona Forrest
National Spokesperson, Bob Rae
Affiliates: Canadian Centre for Philanthropy

**Microelectronic Devices, Circuits & Systems for Ultra Large Scale Integration/Dispositifs, circuits et systèmes micro-électroniques intégres à ultra grande echelle (ULSI) (1990)**
**Micronet**
University of Toronto, 10 King's College Rd., Toronto, ON M5S 3G4
416/978-1638, Fax: 416/978-4516, URL: http://www.utoronto.ca/micronet
Program Leader, Dr. C.A.T. Salama
Network Manager, Maher Bitar, Email: maher@vrg.utoronto.ca
Publications: Micronet News; Micronet Quarterly

**The M.S.I. Foundation (1971)**
**Medical Services Incorporated**
#1220, 10405 Jasper Ave., Edmonton, AB T5J 3N4
403/421-7532, Fax: 403/425-4467
Chairperson, Dr. L.H. Le Riche
Associate Secretary, M. Yates
Publications: The M.S.I. Foundation Annual Report

**NeuroScience Network/Réseau NeuroSciences (1990)**
Room L7-132, 1650, av Cedar, Montréal, QC H3G 1A4
514/934-8290, Fax: 514/934-8216, Email: mc93@musica.mcgill.ca, URL: http://www.cns.ucalgary.ca/nce
Executive Director, Warren Bull

**Ontario Centres of Excellence**
2938 Dundas St. West, PO Box 70681, Toronto, ON M6P 4E7
416/767-3389, Email: oce@itrc.on.ca

**Ontario Public Interest Research Group/Groupe de recherche d'intérêt public de l'Ontario (OPIRG) (1976)**
#201, 455 Spadina Ave., Toronto, ON M5S 2G8
416/978-7770, Email: opirg@campuslife.utoronto.ca, URL: http://www.campuslife.utoronto.ca/groups/opirg/

**Protein Engineering Network of Centres of Excellence/Réseau de centres d'excellence en génie protéique (PENCE) (1990)**
University of Alberta, 750 Heritage Medical Research Centre, Edmonton, AB T6G 2S2
403/492-8851, Fax: 403/492-6995, URL: http://www.pence.ualberta.ca
Manager, Business Development & Marketing, James Chivers-Wilson, Email: james.chivers-wilson@ualberta.ca
Project Coordinator, Ann Liens, Email: ann.liens@ualberta.ca

**Pulp & Paper Research Institute of Canada/Institut canadien de recherches sur les pâtes et papiers (PAPRICAN) (1925)**
570, boul St-Jean, Pointe Claire, QC H9R 3J9
514/630-4100, Fax: 514/630-4105
President/CEO, Dr. Joseph D. Wright
Affiliates: Canadian Pulp & Paper Association

**The Royal Canadian Geographical Society/La Société géographique royale du Canada (RCGS) (1929)**
39 McArthur Ave., Vanier, ON K1L 8L7
613/745-4629, Fax: 613/744-0947, Email: rgs@cangeo.ca
Executive Director, Louise Maffett
President, Dr. Denis St-Onge
Publications: Canadian Geographic

**Royal Canadian Institute (RCI) (1849)**
196 Carleton St., Toronto, ON M5A 2K8
416/928-2096, URL: http://www.psych.utoronto.ca/people/vislab/RCI.html
President, Veronika Huta

**The Royal Society of Canada/La Société royale du Canada (RSC) (1882)**
**National Academy of Canada**
#308, 225 Metcalfe St., Ottawa, ON K2P 1P9
613/991-6990, Fax: 613/991-6996, Email: adminrsc@rsc.ca, URL: http://www.rsc.ca
President, Robert H. Haynes
Publications: Présentations; Transactions/Mémoires; Delta, q.; Proceedings/Délibérations, a.; Profile/Profil; ACTION: Newsletter of the Canadian National Committee, s-a.

**The Royal Society for the Encouragement of Arts, Manufactures & Commerce (RSA) (1754)**
8 John Adam St., London WC2N 6EZ UK
011/44-71-930-5115, Fax: 011/44-71-839-5805
Director, Peter Cowling
President, H.R.H. The Prince Philip, Duke of Edinburgh, KG, KT
Publications: RSA Journal
Atlantic Provinces Chapter: President, Prof. Ronald C. Gilkie, 1146 Studley Ave., Halifax, NS B3H 3R7

**Society of Applied Anthropology in Canada/Société d'anthropologie appliquée du Canada**
Département d'Anthropologie, Université de Montréal, CP 6128, Succ A, Montréal, QC H3C 3J7
President, Gilles Bibeau

**Society for the Study of Egyptian Antiquities (SSEA) (1969)**
PO Box 578, Stn P, Toronto, ON M5S 2T1
416/978-6838, Fax: 416/978-5294, Email: ssea@bigfoot.com, URL: http://www.geocities.com/TheTropics/1456/
President, Gayle Gibson
Secretary, Patricia Paice
Publications: SSEA Newsletter; SSEA Journal, a.
Affiliates: Canadian Institute in Egypt; Canadian Mediterranean Institute

**Traffic Injury Research Foundation of Canada/Fondation de recherches sur les blessures de la route au Canada (TIRF) (1963)**
#200, 171 Nepean St., Ottawa, ON K2P 0B4
613/238-5235, Fax: 613/238-5292, Email: tirf@sonetis.com
President & CEO, Dr. Herbert M. Simpson
Chairman, S.H. Van Houten

**RESOURCE MANAGEMENT *see* ENVIRONMENTAL**

## RESTAURANTS & FOOD SERVICES

**Association des fournisseurs d'hôtels et restaurants inc./Hotel & Restaurant Suppliers Association Inc. (AFHR) (1936)**
2435, rue Guénette, Saint Laurent, QC H4R 2E9
514/334-5161, Téléc: 514/334-1279, Ligne sans frais: 1-800-567-2347, Courrier électronique: afhr@sympatico.ca, URL: http://www.afhr.com
Directeur administratif, Jean Cyr
Président, Guy Lussier
Secrétaire, Jean-Pierre Verreault
Trésorier, Sylvain Inkel
Publications: Le Fournisseur

**Association des restaurateurs du Québec/Québec Restaurant Association (ARQ) (1938)**
2485, rue Sherbrooke est, Montréal, QC H2K 1E8
514/527-9801, Téléc: 514/527-3066, Ligne sans frais: 1-800-463-9801

Vice-président directeur général, Bernard Fortin
Publications: ARQ Info

### Canadian Culinary Institute (CCI)
#202, 738A Bank St., Ottawa, ON K1S 3V4
613/563-2433, Fax: 613/563-2317, Email: essence@ottawa.net
Chairman, Fred Malley, CCC
Affiliates: The educational arm of the Canadian Federation of Chefs & Cooks

### Canadian Federation of Chefs & Cooks/La Fédération canadienne des chefs et cuisiniers (CFCC) (1963)
#202, 738A Bank St., Ottawa, ON K1S 3V4
613/563-2433, Fax: 613/563-2317, Email: essence@ottawa.net, URL: http://www.cybersmith.net/cfcc/
President, Guy Ethier
Coordinator, National Office, Claire Forster
Publications: Essence; Chefs Directory, biennial
Affiliates: Canadian Culinary Institute; World Association of Cooks Societies

### Canadian Restaurant & Foodservices Association/Association canadienne des restaurateurs et des services alimentaires (CRFA) (1944)
316 Bloor St. West, Toronto, ON M5S 1W5
416/923-8416, Fax: 416/923-1450, Toll Free: 1-800-387-5649, Email: 102477.3104@compuserve.com
President, Douglas C. Needham
Senior Vice-President, David Harris
Vice-President, Government Affairs, Michael Ferrabee
Chairman, Paul Hollands
Publications: CRFA News; Membership Directory, a.; Foodservice Facts Magazine
Affiliates: Canadian Hospitality Foundation

#### ALBERTA RESTAURANT & FOODSERVICES ASSOCIATION (ARFA) (1977)
10085 - 166 St., Edmonton, AB T5P 4Y1
403/444-9494, Fax: 403/481-8727, Toll Free: 1-800-461-9762
President, Elizabeth Kuhnel
Publications: Provincial ARFA News; Alberta Restaurant News, q.; ARFA Membership Directory, a.

#### MANITOBA RESTAURANT & FOODSERVICES ASSOCIATION (MRFA)
#201, 698 Corydon Ave., Winnipeg, MB R3M 0X9
204/475-6660, Fax: 204/475-6661
Executive Director, Michael Moore

#### NEWFOUNDLAND RESTAURANT & FOODSERVICES ASSOCIATION
PO Box 402, Mount Pearl, NF A1N 2C4
709/753-2380
President, Brenda Power

#### NOVA SCOTIA RESTAURANT & FOODSERVICES ASSOCIATION
5411 Spring Garden Rd., Halifax, NS B3J 1G1
902/429-5343, Fax: 902/425-1025
Managing Director, Denise Burns

#### ONTARIO RESTAURANT ASSOCIATION (ORA) (1931)
#1201, 121 Richmond St. West, Toronto, ON M5H 2K1
416/359-0533, Fax: 416/359-0531, Toll Free: 1-800-668-8906
President, Paul Oliver
Publications: Buyers Guide Directory; Maincourse

#### PRINCE EDWARD ISLAND RESTAURANT & FOODSERVICES ASSOCIATION
PO Box 742, Charlottetown, PE C1A 7L3
902/963-2382, Fax: 902/963-2382
President, Dale Larkin

#### QUICK SERVICE RESTAURANT COUNCIL/CONSEIL DES RESTAURANTS À SERVICE RAPIDE (QSRC) (1991)
316 Bloor St. West, Toronto, ON M5S 1W5
416/923-8416, Fax: 416/923-1450, Toll Free: 1-800-387-5649

#### RESTAURANT & FOODSERVICES ASSOCIATION OF BRITISH COLUMBIA & THE YUKON (RFABCY) (1977)
#140, 475 West Georgia St., Vancouver, BC V6B 4H9
604/669-2239, Fax: 604/669-6175, Toll Free: 1-800-663-4482
URL: http://www.yes.net/RFABCY/
Executive Director, Earl Manning, CAE
Publications: Newsletter

#### SASKATCHEWAN RESTAURANT & FOODSERVICES ASSOCIATION (SRFA) (1979)
PO Box 1545, Saskatoon, SK S7K 3R5
306/665-1444, Fax: 306/665-1444
Executive Director, Michael van Grondelle
Publications: The Association Reporter

### Institute of Culinary Art & Technology
3 Kitsilano Cres., Richmond Hill, ON L4C 5A4
905/884-9380
Chancellor, Maurice Prior

### Société des chefs, cuisiniers et patissiers du Québec (SCCPQ) (1953)
3577, rue Ste-Catherine est, Montréal, QC H1W 2E6
514/528-1083, Téléc: 514/528-1037
Président, Denis Paquin, Numéro au travail: 514/463-3139
Secrétaire, Normand Corriveau
Agent Permanent, Mario Gringras
Publications: Le Pot-au-feu

## RETAIL TRADE

### Association des détaillants en alimentation du Québec/Québec Food Retailers' Association (ADA) (1955)
CP 455, Succ Place-du-Parc, Montréal, QC H2W 2N9
514/982-0104, Téléc: 514/849-3021, Ligne sans frais: 1-800-363-3923
Président/Directeur général, Michel Gadbois
Directrice, Affaires publiques et Communications, Diane Hétu
Publications: Bulletin Express; Info-Stats, 10 fois par an

### Association nationale des distributeurs de tabac et de confiserie/National Association of Tobacco & Confectionery Distributors (ANDTC) (1955)
#504, 3090, boul le Carrefour, Laval, QC H7T 2J7
514/682-6556, Téléc: 514/682-6732, Ligne sans frais: 1-888-686-2823, Courrier électronique: natcd@atmail.com
Vice-président exécutif, Luc A. Dumulong
Publications: Contact

### Canadian Association of Chain Drug Stores (CACDS) (1995)
#1210, 121 Bloor St. East, Toronto, ON M4W 3M5
416/922-1976, Fax: 416/922-6532
President & CEO, Sherry E. Porter

### Canadian Gift & Tableware Association/Association canadienne de cadeaux et d'accessoires de table (1976)
#301, 265 Yorkland Blvd., North York, ON M2J 1S5
416/497-5771, Fax: 416/497-8487, Toll Free: 1-800-750-1967, Email: info@gift.org, URL: http://www.cgta.org
President, Jack Shand
Publications: CGTA Retail News

### Canadian Office Machine Dealers Association/Association canadienne des distributeurs de machine de bureau (COMDA) (1942)
#204, 3464 Kingston Rd., Scarborough, ON M1M 1R5
416/261-1607, Fax: 416/261-1679
Executive Director, Don Vickery
Publications: COMDA Key
Affiliates: National Office Machine Dealers Association

### Canadian Office Products Association/Association canadienne des produits de bureau (COPA) (1933)
#911, 1243 Islington Ave., Toronto, ON M8X 1Y9
416/239-2737, Fax: 416/239-1553, URL: http://www.copa.ca
President, James Preece
Publications: COPA Conversation; Your Office, q.; Canadian Purchaser, q.
Affiliates: Retail Council of Canada; International Federation of Office Stationary Associations; International Stationary Press Association

### Canadian Retail Hardware Association/Association canadienne des détaillants en quincaillerie (CRHA) (1954)
6800 Campobello Rd., Mississauga, ON L5N 2L8
905/821-3470, Fax: 905/821-8946, Toll Free: 1-800-268-3965, Email: crha@crha.com
Executive Director, Thomas M. Ross
Director, Administration, Maura Bella
Director, Membership Services & Legislative Affairs, Linda Nolet
Publications: Reporter; Journaliste, 10 pa; Wage & Benefit Survey
Affiliates: National Retail Hardware Association - USA

### Canadian Sporting Goods Association/Association canadienne d'articles de sport (CSGA) (1945)
#510, 455, rue Saint-Antoine ouest, Montréal, QC H2Z 1J1
514/393-1132, Fax: 514/393-9513, Email: sportind@csga.ca, URL: http://www.globalsports.com/csga
President & CEO, Yves Paquette
Affiliates: World Federation of the Sporting Goods Industry

### Conseil québécois du commerce de détail/Retail Council of Québec (CQCD) (1978)
#710, 630, rue Sherbrooke ouest, Montréal, QC H3A 1E4
514/842-6681, Téléc: 514/842-7627, URL: http://www.cqcd.com
Directeur général, Gaston Lafleur

### Direct Sellers Association
#3, 100 West Beaver Creek Rd., Richmond Hill, ON L4B 1H4
905/886-8555, Fax: 905/885-8102
Contact, Ross Creber

### Fédération du détail et des services du Québec/Québec Federation of Retail & Service Organizations (1953)
CP 368, Sainte-Julienne, QC J0K 2T0
514/831-2748, Téléc: 514/831-2787
Directeur administratif, Gilles N. Rivet

### Gift Packaging & Greeting Card Association of Canada/Association canadienne du papier cadeau et de la carte de voeux (GPGCA)
1407 Military Trail, Scarborough, ON M1C 1A7
416/281-8147
Chairman, Don Bichard
Vice-Chairman, M. Dionne
Office Manager, Clancy Delbarre

**Independent Toy Store Association of Canada**
c/o Retail Council of Canada, #600, 210 Dundas St. West, Toronto, ON M5G 2E8
416/598-4684
Director, Marketing & Communications, Judy Johnson

**National Spa & Pool Institute of Canada (NSPI) (1958)**
#5, 7370 Bramalea Rd., Mississauga, ON L5S 1N6
905/676-1591, Fax: 905/676-1598, Toll Free: 1-800-879-7066
Executive Director, Nancy Lumb
Publications: NSPI of Canada Report; Membership Directory

**Retail Council of Canada/Le Conseil canadien du commerce de détail (RCC) (1963)**
#1210, 121 Bloor St. West, Toronto, ON M4W 3M5
416/922-6678, Fax: 416/922-8011, Toll Free: 1-888-373-8245, URL: http://www.retailcouncil.org
President/CEO, Diane J. Brisebois, CAE
Senior Vice-President, Peter Woolford
Publications: Canadian Retailer

**Retail Merchants Association of Canada (Alberta) Inc. (RMA) (1896)**
#205, 11125 - 107 Ave. NW, Edmonton, AB T5H 0X9
403/428-6781, Fax: 403/428-6785
Executive Director, Linda S. Gagnon
Publications: RMA News
Affiliates: Retail Council of Canada

**Retail Merchants Association of Canada, Inc. (RMA) (1910)**
1780 Birchmount Rd., Scarborough, ON M1P 2H8
416/291-7903, Fax: 416/291-5635
President, Sean McMahon
Publications: Retail Merchants News

**Retail Merchants' Association of BC (1911)**
1758 - 8th Ave. West, Vancouver, BC V6J 1V6
604/736-0368, Fax: 604/736-3154
President, Mark Startup, CAE
Publications: BC Retailer

**RETIREES *see* SENIOR CITIZENS**

## SAFETY & ACCIDENT PREVENTION

***see also* Emergency Response**

**Alberta Safety Council (1946)**
#201, 10526 Jasper Ave., Edmonton, AB T5J 1Z7
403/428-7555, Fax: 403/428-7557
Executive Director, Eya Zariwny
Program Director, Scott McLeod
Publications: Safety Counsellor
Affiliates: Canada Safety Council; National Safety Council

**Association of Canadian Fire Marshals & Fire Commissioners/L'Association canadienne des directeurs et commissaires des incendies (ACFM/FC) (1919)**
#508, 401 York Ave., Winnipeg, MB R3C 0P8
204/945-3322
Sec.-Treas., Robert Kearney
Publications: Fire Losses in Canada

**Association for Canadian Registered Safety Professionals/Association des professionnels en securité agréés du Canada (ACRSP) (1976)**
6519B Mississauga Rd., Mississauga, ON L5N 1A6
905/567-7198, Fax: 905/567-7191, Toll Free: 1-800-279-2777
Chair, Renzo Dalla Via
Executive Secretary, Peter Fletcher
Publications: Governor's Table

**Association des chefs de services d'incendie du Québec/Québec Fire Chief Association (ACSIQ) (1968)**
327, rue de Rouville, Beloeil, QC J3G 1X1
514/464-6413, Téléc: 514/467-6297, Courrier électronique: Information@acsiq.qc.ca, URL: http://www.acsiq.qc.ca
Secrétaire administrative, Nicole Aubin
Publications: L'Étincelle

**Association paritaire pour la santé et la sécurité du travail - Administration provinciale**
#10, 1220, boul Lebourgneuf, Québec, QC G2K 2G4
418/624-4801, Téléc: 418/624-4858
Directrice générale, Collette Trudel

**Association paritaire pour la santé et la sécurité du travail - Affaires municipales (APSAM) (1985)**
#710, 715, carré Victoria, Montréal, QC H2Y 2H7
514/849-8373, Téléc: 514/849-8873, Ligne sans frais: 1-800-465-1754, Courrier électronique: apsamnet@login.net
Directeur général, Alain Langlois
Publications: APSAM

**Association paritaire pour la santé et la sécurité du travail - Affaires sociales**
#950, 5100, rue Sherbrooke est, Montréal, QC H1V 3R9
514/253-6871, Téléc: 514/253-1443, Ligne sans frais: 1-800-361-4528
Directeur général, Gilles Le Beau

**Association paritaire pour la santé et la sécurité du travail - Construction (1985)**
ASP Construction
#301, 7905, boul Louis-H.-Lafontaine, Anjou, QC H1K 4E4
514/355-6190, Téléc: 514/355-7861, Ligne sans frais: 1-800-361-2061
Directeur général, Paul Héroux
Publications: Prévenir aussi

**Association paritaire pour la santé et la sécurité du travail - Habillement (1986)**
#1011, 9310, boul Saint-Laurent, Montréal, QC H2N 1N4
514/383-8317, Téléc: 514/383-7938, Courrier électronique: habillement@videotron.ca
Directeur général, Christian Millet

**Association paritaire pour la santé et la sécurité du travail - Imprimerie et activités connexes**
#300, 405, rue de la Concorde, Montréal, QC H3A 1J3
514/284-3318, Téléc: 514/284-9255
Directeur général, Claude Payette

**Association paritaire pour la santé et la sécurité du travail - Mines (APSM) (1986)**
#570, 979, av de Bourgogne, Ste-Foy, QC G1W 2L4
418/653-1933, Téléc: 418/653-7726
Directeur général, Pierre Lapointe
Publications: Vi.Ta.Mine

**Association paritaire pour la santé et la sécurité du travail - Produits en métal et électriques**
#201, 6705, rue Jean-Talon est, St-Léonard, QC H1S 1N2
514/253-5549, Téléc: 514/253-8193
Directeur général, Alain Langlois

**Association paritaire pour la santé et la sécurité du travail - Textiles primaires (1983)**
Préventex
#203, 2035, av Victoria, Saint-Lambert, QC J4S 1H1
514/671-6925, Téléc: 514/671-9267
Directeur général, Jean-Marc Champoux
Publications: Préventex

**Association québécoise des pompiers volontaires et permanents (1978)**
9401, Cote des Saintes, CP 206, Ste-Scholastique, QC J0N 1S0
514/478-8634, Téléc: 514/478-6962
Président, Claude Fortin
Publications: Info-Pompier

**Association de santé et sécurité des industries de la forêt du Québec inc./Québec Logging Health & Safety Association Inc. (ASSIFQ) (1969)**
#102, 1200, av Germain-des-Prés, Ste-Foy, QC G1V 3M7
418/657-2268, Téléc: 418/651-4622
Président - directeur général, J. Aurèle St-Pierre
Secrétaire, Suzanne Lavoie
Publications: Action Prévention
Organisation(s) affiliée(s): Association canadienne des producteurs de pâtes et papiers; Association des industries de la forêt du Québec ltée; Canadian Safety Council; Conseil du patronat du Québec; Canadian Society of Safety Engineering

**Association de santé et sécurité des pâtes et papiers du Québec inc./Québec Pulp & Paper Health & Safety Association Inc. (ASSPPQ) (1932)**
#102, 1200, av Germain-des-Prés, Ste-Foy, QC G1V 3M7
418/657-2267, Téléc: 418/651-4622
Président - directeur général, J. Aurèle St-Pierre
Publications: Action-Prévention
Organisation(s) affiliée(s): Association canadienne des producteurs de pâtes et papiers; Association des industries de la forêt du Québec ltée; Canadian Safety Council; Conseil du Patronat de Québec; Canadian Society of Safety Engineering

**Association sectorielle - Fabrication d'équipement de transport et machines/Sectorial Association - Transporation Equipment & Machinery Manufacturing (ASFETM) (1983)**
#202, 3565, rue Jarry est, Montréal, QC H1Z 4K6
514/729-6961, Téléc: 514/729-8628, Ligne sans frais: 1-888-527-3386
Directeur général, J. Adolphe Roy, c.r.
Responsable des communications, Suzanne Ready
Publications: Santé Securité +

**Association sectorielle transport entreposage (ASTE) (1983)**
#401, 6555, boul Métropolitain est, St-Léonard, QC H1P 3H3
514/955-0454, Téléc: 514/955-0449
Directeur général, Nicholas Lapierre

**British Columbia Safety Council (1945)**
#150, 6251 Graybar Rd., Burnaby, BC V6W 1H3
604/214-7433, Fax: 604/214-7434, Email: blowes@axionet.com, URL: http://www.safetycouncil.bc.ca
Executive Director, Bryan Lowes
President, Martin Pochurko
Publications: Safety First
Affiliates: Canada Safety Council; National Safety Council

**Canada Safety Council/Conseil canadien de la sécurité (CSC) (1968)**
1020 Thomas Spratt Place, Ottawa, ON K1G 5L5
613/739-1535, Fax: 613/739-1566, Email: csc@safety-council.org, URL: http://www.safety-council.org
President, Émile-J. Thérien
General Manager, Programs, Jack A. Smith
Publications: Living Safety; Safety Canada, q.

Affiliates: Canadian Standards Association; Environment Canada; Operation Lifesaver National Committee; Advisory Committee on International Driver Improvement - USA; Motorcycle & Moped Industry Council; Transport Canada; Canadian General Standards Board; National Research Council of Canada; Transportation Research Council of Canada; Transportation Research Board - USA; Canadian Association of Chiefs of Police; Institute of Transportation Engineers; Urban Transportation Engineers Council; Council of Uniform Traffic Control Devices for Canada; Selective Traffic Enforcement Committee; Canadian Automobile Association; Canadian Cycling Association; International Occupational Safety & Health Information Centre

**Canadian Alarm & Security Association/ Association canadienne de l'alarme et de la sécurité (CANASA) (1977)**
#201, 610 Alden Rd., Markham, ON L3R 9Z1
905/513-0622, Fax: 905/513-0624, Email: staff@canasa.org, URL: http://www.canasa.org
Executive Director, Norman Cheesman
Publications: Show Buyer's Guide & Directory; Security Pulse, q.

**Canadian Association of Fire Chiefs/Association canadienne des chefs de pompiers**
#1, 2425 Don Reid Dr., Ottawa, ON K1H 1A4
613/736-0576, Fax: 613/736-0684
Executive Director, Marcel Ethier

**Canadian Association of Poison Control Centres**
Children's Hospital, 840 Sherbrook St., Winnipeg, MB R3A 1S1
204/787-2591, Fax: 204/787-4807
Contact, Milton Tenenbein
Affiliates: World Federation of Associations of Clinical Toxicology & Poison Control Centres

**Canadian Automatic Sprinkler Association (CASA) (1961)**
#302, 335 Renfrew Dr., Markham, ON L3R 9S9
905/477-2270, Fax: 905/477-3611
President, John Galt
Administrator, Lisa Miles
Publications: CASA Notes

**Canadian Centre for Occupational Health & Safety/Centre canadien d'hygiène et de sécurité au travail (CCOHS) (1978)**
250 Main St. East, Hamilton, ON L8N 1H6
/Enquiries: 1-800-263-8466, Fax: /905/572-2206, Toll Free: 1-800-668-4284, Email: custserv@ccohs.ca, URL: http://www.ccohs.ca
President/CEO, S. Len Hong
Vice-President, P.K. Abeytunga
Manager, Inquiries Service, Roger Cockerline
Manager, Operations Support, Eleanor Irwin
Comptroller, Brian Hutchings
Manager, Health & Safety Products, Anne Gravereaux
Manager, Computer Systems, Ashok Setty
Publications: Operations; Materials; Working Environments; Work Related Diseases; Programs; Physical Agents; Statistics; Occupational Health & Safety Issues; Liaison, q.

**Canadian Fire Safety Association (CFSA) (1971)**
#310, 2175 Sheppard Ave. East, North York, ON M2J 1W8
416/492-9417, Fax: 416/491-1670, Email: taylor@interlog.com
President, Alan Speed
1st Vice-President, Brian Murphy
Administrator, Diane Gaunt
Publications: CFSA Newsletter

**Canadian Institute for Radiation Safety/Institut canadien de radioprotection (CAIRS) (1981)**
#607, 1120 Finch Ave. West, Toronto, ON M3J 3H7
416/650-9090, Fax: 416/650-9920, Toll Free: 1-800-263-5803, Email: info.cairs@cairs.ca
President/CEO, Dr. Fergal Nolan
Director, Science & Technology, Science & Technology, Dr. R. Moridi
National Laboratory & Centre for Public Education: Program Coordinator, Science & Technology, Brian Bjorndal, #102, 110 Research Dr., Saskatoon, SK S7N 3R3, 306/975-0566, Fax: 306/975-0494

**Canadian Society for Industrial Security Inc./La société canadienne de la sûreté industrielle inc. (CSIS Inc.) (1957)**
51 Lake Ave. West, Carleton Place, ON K7C 1L3
613/257-7203, Fax: 613/257-5383, Toll Free: 1-800-461-7748
National Sec.-Treas., L. Surrett
Publications: Forum

**Canadian Society of Safety Engineering, Inc./ Société canadienne de la santé et de la sécurité, inc. (CSSE) (1972)**
#602, 330 Bay St., Toronto, ON M5H 2S8
416/368-2230, Fax: 416/368-8429, URL: http://www.csse.org
Executive Manager, John H. Murphy
Publications: CSSE Contact
Affiliates: American Society of Safety Engineers

**Centre patronal de santé et sécurité du travail du Québec (CPSSTQ) (1982)**
#1000, 500, rue Sherbrooke ouest, Montréal, QC H3A 3C8
514/842-8401, Téléc: 514/842-9375, Courrier électronique: centrepatronalsst@sympatico.ca
Présidente-directrice générale, Denise Turenne, p.d.g.
Directeur des communications, Denis Michaud
Publications: Convergence

**Conseil des agences de securité et d'investigation du Québec inc. (CASIQ) (1966)**
#400, 5115, av de Gaspé, Montréal, QC H2T 3B7
514/273-8578, Téléc: 514/277-1922
Président, Louis J. Joron
Secrétaire-trésorier, Paul Guay, Numéro au travail: 514/935-2533, Téléc: 514/935-2996

**Council of Private Investigators**
#8, 130 Melford Dr., Scarborough, ON M1B 2X4
416/293-1479, Fax: 416/293-2390
President, Bud Davis
Publications: The Journal

**Farm Safety Association Inc.**
#22, 340 Woodlawn Rd. West, Guelph, ON N1H 1G8
519/823-5600, Fax: 519/823-8880
Public Relations Coordinator, Steve Zronik
Publications: Farmsafe

**Federal Association of Security Officials/ Association fédérale des représentants de la sécurité (FASO) (1992)**
PO Box 2384, Stn D, Ottawa, ON K1P 5W5
613/990-2615, Fax: 613/990-8297
Sec.-Treas., Sharon Savoie
Publications: News & Views

**Fire Prevention Canada Association**
**FIPRECAN**
#1, 2425 Don Reid Dr., Ottawa, ON K1H 1A4
613/736-8131, Fax: 613/736-0684
Sec.-Treas., Marcel Ethier

**Heavy Construction Association of Saskatchewan**
1939 Elphinstone St., Regina, SK S4T 3N3
306/757-2646, Fax: 306/757-2798
Safety Director, Steve Wallace
Publications: Badger

**Industrial Accident Prevention Association Ontario/Association pour la prévention des accidents industriels - Ontario (IAPA) (1917)**
Eaton Tower, 250 Yonge St., 28th Fl., Toronto, ON M5B 2N4
416/506-8888, Fax: 416/506-8880, Toll Free: 1-800-669-4939, Email: feedback@iapa.on.ca, URL: http://www.iapa.on.ca
CEO, Maureen C. Shaw
Publications: Accident Prevention; Update Releases; Impact, q.
Affiliates: Amalgamated Industry Groups - Ceramics & Stone Accident Prevention Association; Chemical Industries Accident Prevention Association; Food Products Accident Prevention Association; Grain, Feed & Fertilizer Accident Prevention Association; Leather, Rubber & Tanners Accident Prevention Association; Metal Trades Accident Prevention Association; Ontario Retail Accident Prevention Association; Printing Trades Accident Prevention Association; Textile & Allied Industries Accident Prevention Association; Woodworkers' Accident Prevention Association

**Industrial Accident Victims Group of Ontario (IAVGO) (1975)**
#203, 489 College St., Toronto, ON M6G 1A5
416/924-6477, Fax: 416/924-2472
Coordinator, Valerie Verah
Publications: Newsletter

**Institut de recherche en santé et en sécurité de travail - Québec/Québec Occupational Health & Safety Research Institute (IRSST) (1980)**
505, boul de Maisonneuve ouest, Montréal, QC H3A 3C2
514/288-1551, Téléc: 514/288-0998, Télex: 055 61348
Directeur général, Jean Yves Savoie
Directeur des opérations, Alain Lajoie
Directrice des communications, Françoise Cloutier
Publications: Prévention au travail
Organisation(s) affiliée(s): International Occupational Safety & Health Information Centre

**International Radiation Protection Association - Canadian Office/Association internationale de radioprotection - Bureau canadienne (IRPA)**
#820, 2155, rue Guy, Montréal, QC H3H 2R9
514/932-9552, Fax: 514/932-9419
President, Jean-Pierre Gauvin

**Ligue de sécurité du Québec/Québec Safety League (1923)**
2536, rue Lapierre, Lasalle, QC H8N 2W9
514/595-9110, Téléc: 514/595-3398
Président/Directeur général, Yvan R. Bastien
Publications: Signal

**Major Industrial Accidents Council of Canada/ Conseil canadien des accidents industriels majeurs (MIACC) (1987)**
#600, 265 Carling Ave., Ottawa, ON K1S 2E1
613/232-4435, Fax: 613/232-4915, Email: miacc@globalx.net, URL: http://hoshi.cic.sfu.ca/miacc/
Executive Director & CEO, Michael Salib, CAE
Chair, Allan G. Jones
Secretary, Paul A. Brazeau
Treasurer, David Egar
Director, Technical Programs, Roland Andersson
Publications: MIACC News; Life Cycle Management of Hazardous Substances

**Manitoba Safety Council (1920)**
#700, 213 Notre Dame Ave., Winnipeg, MB R3B 1N3
204/949-1085, Fax: 204/956-2897, Toll Free: 1-800-661-3321
Executive Director, Rita L. Borthwick
Publications: Spotlight Safety

**Mines Accident Prevention Association of Manitoba (MAPAM) (1962)**
#700, 305 Broadway, Winnipeg, MB R3C 3J7
204/942-2789, Fax: 204/943-4371
Executive Vice-President, Ed Huebert
Safety Director, B.D. Simoneau
Office Administrator, Sharon Schaubroeck

**New Brunswick Safety Council Inc./Conseil de sécurité du Nouveau-Brunswick inc. (NBSC) (1967)**
#204, 440 Wilsey Rd., Fredericton, NB E3B 7G5
506/458-8034, Fax: 506/444-0177
Business & Promotions Manager, Heather J. Wilson
President, Ron Carr
Affiliates: Canada Safety Council

**Newfoundland Safety Council**
354 Water St., PO Box 5123, St. John's, NF A1C 5V5
709/754-0210, Fax: 709/754-0010
President, Ray O'Neill
Affiliates: Canada Safety Council

**Nova Scotia Safety Council (1958)**
Bloomfield Centre, 2786 Agricola St., Halifax, NS B3K 4E1
902/454-9621, Fax: 902/454-6027
Executive Director, Thomas P. Haney
Publications: Safety Lines
Affiliates: Canada Safety Council

**Ontario Association of Fire Chiefs (OAFC) (1973)**
94 Nicholson Cres., Kingston, ON K7N 1X1
Fax: 613/634-2152, Toll Free: 1-800-774-6651
Sec.-Treas., Terry Landon
Publications: OAFC Newsletter

**Ontario Industrial Fire Protection Association (OIFPA) (1981)**
193 James St. South, Hamilton, ON L8P 3A8
905/527-0700, Fax: 905/527-6254
President, J. David Wallace
Publications: OIPFA Newsletter

**Ontario Natural Resources Safety Association/Association ontarienne de sécurité au travail - ressources naturelles (ONRSA) (1994)**
690 McKeown Ave., PO Box 2050, North Bay, ON P1B 9P1
705/474-7233, Fax: 705/472-5800, Toll Free: 1-800-850-5519, Email: onrsa@onlink.net
Executive Director, John J.G. Connors
Publications: Health & Safety Resource
Affiliates: Workplace Health & Safety Agency

**Ontario Safety League/Ligue de sécurité du Ontario (OSL) (1913)**
#100, 21 Four Seasons Pl., Etobicoke, ON M9B 6J8
416/620-1720, Fax: 416/620-5977, Email: info@osl.org, URL: http://www.osl.org
President & General Manager, Bert Killian
Publications: Safety Update; Fleet Safety & Health, m.; In the Drivers Seat, m.; Let's Talk Safety, m.; Catalogue of Safety Material; Film & Video Catalogue
Affiliates: Canada Safety Council; Provincial Safety Leagues/Councils

**Saskatchewan Professional Driver's Safety Council (SPDSC) (1947)**
1335 Wallace St., Regina, SK S4N 3Z5
306/569-9696, Fax: 306/781-7066, Toll Free: 1-800-563-7623
Affiliates: Canadian Trucking Association; Saskatchewan Trucking Association

**Saskatchewan Safety Council**
445 Hoffer Dr., Regina, SK S4N 6E2
306/757-3197, Fax: 306/569-1907
Executive Director, Harley P. Toupin

**Transportation Safety Association of Ontario/Association de sécurité dans les transports de l'Ontario (TSAO) (1942)**
#101, 555 Dixon Rd., Etobicoke, ON M9W 1H8
416/242-4771, Fax: 416/242-4714, Toll Free: 1-800-263-5016, Email: tsao@echo-on.net
Executive Director, William R. Boyle
Publications: Drivers' Newsletter; Bulletin, q.

**SAFETY & FIRST AID *see* EMERGENCY RESPONSE**

**SCHOLARLY *see* EDUCATION**

**SCHOOLS *see* EDUCATION**

## SCIENTIFIC

***see also* Education; Health & Medical; Research & Scholarship**

**Alberta Society of Professional Biologists (ASPB) (1973)**
#100, 4246 - 97 St., Edmonton, AB T6E 5Z9
403/434-5765, Fax: 403/435-7503, Email: aspb@ccinet.ab.ca, URL: http://www.ccinet.ab.ca/aspb/
Executive Director, Bonnie Holtby
Publications: ASPB Newsletter

**Arctic Institute of North America (AINA) (1945)**
University of Calgary, 2500 University Dr. NW, Calgary, AB T2N 1N4
403/220-7515, Fax: 403/282-4609, Email: mrobinso@ucdasvml.admin.ucalgary.ca, URL: http://www.ucalgary.ca/aina/
Executive Director, Michael P. Robinson
Publications: Arctic/InfoNorth

**Association de biodynamie du Québec inc./Bio-Dynamic Association of Québec Inc. (1979)**
416, rang 4 ouest, Baie-des-Sables, QC G0J 1C0
418/772-6574
Personne Ressource, Lise Beaulieu
Publications: Le Dynamot; Le Germe, trimestriel

**Association des biologistes du Québec (ABQ) (1973)**
#102, 1208, rue Beaubien est, Montréal, QC H2S 1T7
514/279-7115
Coordonnatrice, Nadège Marion
Président, Robert Hamelin
Publications: In Vivo

**Association des microbiologistes du Québec (AMQ)**
#102, 1208, rue Beaubien est, Montréal, QC H2S 1T7
514/279-7115, Téléc: 514/279-7115
URL: http://www.iaf.uquebec.ca/amq/
Président, Christian Beaulac, Courrier électronique: beaulacc@ere.umontreal.ca
Trésorier, Stéphane Bourget
Secrétaire, Michel Pronovost
Publications: Microcosmes

**Association of Professional Biologists of British Columbia (APB) (1980)**
#205, 733 Johnson St., Victoria, BC V8W 3C7
250/383-3306, Fax: 250/383-3306, Email: apbbc@tnet.net
Office Manager, Pat McLellan
Registrar, Linda Stordeur, R.P.Bio., Bus: 250/727-7612
President, Christopher J. Clement, R.P.Bio., A.Sc.T., R.P.F., Bus: 250/361-3979
Publications: BioLine; BioNews, bi-m.
Affiliates: BC Institute of Agrologists; Canadian Society of Professional Biologists; Professional Pest Management Association of BC; Association of BC Professional Foresters; Alberta Society of Professional Biologists; Association des biologistes du Québec; Association of Professional Engineers & Geoscientists; Applied Science Technologists & Technicians of BC

**Association for the Promotion & Advancement of Science Education (APASE) (1983)**
#200, 1111 Homer St., Vancouver, BC V6B 2Y1
604/687-8712, Fax: 604/687-8715, Email: info@apase.bc.ca, URL: http://www.apase.bc.ca
President, Barbara Moon
Executive Director, Connie Moffit
Publications: Diverse; Prism
Affiliates: Architectural Institute of BC; Association of Professional Engineers & Geoscientists; BC Teachers' Federation; Sierra Club Vancouver; CC West; SCWIST; BC Science Council

**Atlantic Provinces Council on the Sciences/Conseil des provinces atlantiques pour les sciences (APCS)**
Memorial University of Newfoundland, PO Box 4200, St. John's, NF A1B 3X7
709/737-8918, Fax: 709/737-4569
Executive Director, Joan Atkinson

**Canadian Association of Geoscience Companies (1990)**
#643, 7305 Woodbine Ave., Markham, ON L3R 3V7
905/513-1444, Fax: 905/475-8616
Managing Director, Frank Bottos

**Canadian Association of Palynologists/Association canadienne des palynologues (CAP) (1978)**
Dept. of Geology, Earth Sciences Centre, University of Toronto, 22 Russell St., Toronto, ON M5S 3B1
613/954-0355, Fax: 613/954-4724, URL: http://gpu.srv.ualberta.ca/~abeaudoi/cap/cap.html
President, Dr. Ian Campbell
President Elect, Dr. Rob Fensome
Sec.-Treas., Dr. Martin Head
CAP Councillor to IFPS, Dr. Julian Szeicz
Publications: CAP Newsletter
Affiliates: International Federation of Palynological Societies

**Canadian Association of Physicists/Association canadienne des physiciens et physiciennes (CAP) (1945)**
MacDonald Bldg., #112, 150 Louis Pasteur Ave., Ottawa, ON K1N 6NS
613/562-5614, Fax: 613/562-5615, Email: cap@physics.uottawa.ca, URL: http://www.cap.ca
President, Dr. Paul Vincett
Executive Director, Francine M. Ford
Publications: Physics in Canada; Directory of Employers of Physicists; Careers in Physics
Affiliates: Chemical Institute of Canada; Canadian Organization of Medical Physicists; American Physical Society

**Canadian Astronomical Society/Société canadienne d'astronomie (CASCA) (1971)**
Département de Physique, Université de Montréal, Montréal, QC H3C 3J7

514/343-2364, Fax: 514/343-2071, Email: casca@astro.umontreal.ca, URL: http://www.astro.queensu.ca/~casca/
Secretary, Serge Demers
Publications: Cassiopeia

### Canadian Botanical Association/Association botanique du Canada (CBA) (1965)
Dept. of Botany, University of Guelph, #158, 50 Stone Rd. East, Guelph, ON N1G 2W1
519/824-4120, ext.2745, Fax: 519/767-1991
Past President, Dr. U. Posluszny
Publications: The Bulletin of CBA/ABC

### Canadian College of Microbiologists
100 Richmond St. West, Toronto, ON M5H 3K6
416/777-0407

### Canadian College of Physicists in Medicine/Collège canadien des physiciens en médecine (CCPM) (1979)
11328 - 88 St., Edmonton, AB T5B 3P8
403/479-1110, Fax: 403/474-5894
Registrar, Alistair Baillie
Sec.-Treas., Karen Breitman
Publications: Canadian Medical Physics Newsletter
Affiliates: Canadian Organization of Medical Physicists

### Canadian Committee of Scientists & Scholars/Comité canadien des savants et scientifiques (CCSS) (1980)
Dept. of Physics, University of Toronto, 60 Saint George St., Toronto, ON M5S 1A7
416/978-5217, Fax: 416/978-7606, Email: fawcett@physics.utoronto.ca
Secretary, Eric Fawcett
President, John C. Polanyi
Vice-President, Ashok Vijh
Treasurer, Anton Kuerti

### Canadian Congress of Neurological Sciences/Congrès canadien des sciences neurologiques (CCNS)
906 - 12 Ave. SW, PO Box 4220, Stn C, Calgary, AB T2R 1K7
403/229-9544, Fax: 403/229-1661, Email: brains@ccns.org, URL: http://www.ccns.org
Executive Director, Lucile Edwards
Publications: Canadian Journal of Neurological Sciences

### Canadian Federation of Biological Societies/Fédération canadienne des sociétés de biologie (CFBS) (1957)
#104, 1750 Courtwood Cres., Ottawa, ON K2C 2B5
613/225-8889, Fax: 613/225-9621, Email: cfbs@igs.net, URL: http://www.fermentas.com/cfbs/
Executive Director, Dr. Paul Hough, Ph.D.
Publications: CFBS Newsletter

#### BIOPHYSICAL SOCIETY OF CANADA/LA SOCIÉTÉ DE BIOPHYSIQUE DU CANADA (BSC) (1985)
c/o Institute for Biodiagnostics, National Research Council, 435 Ellice Ave., Winnipeg, MB R3B 1Y6
204/984-5146, Fax: 204/984-6978
Email: deslauriers@ibd.nrc.ca, URL: http://www.ibd.nrc.ca/~bsc
Secretary, Dr. Roxanne Deslauriers, Bus: 204/984-5146
President, Peter B. Canham, Bus: 519/661-3053
Publications: Biophysical Society of Canada Newsletter

#### CANADIAN ASSOCIATION FOR ANATOMY, NEUROBIOLOGY & CELL BIOLOGY/ASSOCIATION CANADIENNE D'ANATOMIE, DE NEUROBIOLOGIE ET DE BIOLOGIE CELLULAIRE (CAANCB) (1956)
Dept. of Anatomy, University of Manitoba, 730 William Ave., Winnipeg, MB R3E 0W3
204/789-3796, Fax: 204/772-0622
Email: bruni@bldghsc.lanl.umanitoba.ca
President, Peter Haase
Publications: CAANCB/ACANBC Bulletin

#### CANADIAN PHYSIOLOGICAL SOCIETY/SOCIÉTÉ CANADIENNE DE PHYSIOLOGIE (CPS) (1935)
Dept. of Physiology, University of BC, 2146 Health Sciences Mall, Vancouver, BC V6T 1Z3
604/822-2083, Fax: 604/822-6048
Email: buchan@cs.ubc.ca
Secretary, A.M.J. Buchan
Publications: Physiology Canada
Affiliates: International Union of Physiological Sciences; Canadian Journal of Physiology & Pharmacology

#### THE CANADIAN SOCIETY OF BIOCHEMISTRY & MOLECULAR BIOLOGY/LA SOCIÉTÉ CANADIENNE DE BIOCHIMIE ET BIOLOGIE MOLÉECULAIRE (1958)
Dept. of Biochemistry, University of Western Ontario, London, ON N6A 5C1
519/661-3060, Fax: 519/661-3175
Secretary, Dr. Eugene Reno Tustanoff
Publications: Biochemistry & Cell Biology; The Bulletin of the Canadian Biochemical Society, s-a.

#### PHARMACOLOGICAL SOCIETY OF CANADA/SOCIÉTÉ DE PHARMACOLOGIE DU CANADA (PSC) (1957)
Dept. of Pharmacology & Toxicology, Queen's University, Kingston, ON K7L 3N6
613/545-6473, Fax: 613/545-6412
Email: bennett@post.queensu.ca, URL: http://www.pmcol.ualberta.ca/psc/
Secretary, Dr. Brian M. Bennett
Publications: Canadian Journal of Physiology & Pharmacology

### Canadian Geoscience Council/Conseil géoscientifique canadien (CGC) (1972)
Dept. of Earth Sciences, University of Waterloo, 200 University Ave. West, Waterloo, ON N2L 3G1
519/885-1211, ext.3029, Fax: 519/746-0183, Email: avmorgan@sciborg.uwaterloo.ca, URL: http://www.science.uwaterloo.ca/earth/cgc/cgc.html
Administrative Director, Alan V. Morgan
Financial Director, Ron McMillan

### Canadian Hydrographic Association/Association canadienne d'hydrographie (CHA)
162 Cleopatra Dr., Ottawa, ON K2G 5X2
613/224-9851, Fax: 613/224-9577, URL: http://www.cciw.ca/dfo/chs/cha/cha-home.html
President, Ken McMillan
Publications: Lighthouse
Affiliates: Canadian Institute of Surveying

### Canadian Institute of Biotechnology/Institut canadien de la biotechnologie (CIB) (1989)
#420, 130 Albert St., Ottawa, ON K1P 5G4
613/563-8849, Fax: 613/563-8850, Email: cib@biotech.ca, URL: http://www.biotech.ca
Executive Director, Rick Walter
Associate, Public Relations, Kathleen Vollrath
Coordinator, Special Projects, Tanya Taylor

### Canadian Institute of Food Science & Technology/Institut canadien de science et technologie alimentaires (1951)
#1105, 191 The West Mall, Etobicoke, ON M9C 5K8
416/626-3140, Fax: 416/620-5392
Publications: Food Research International

### Canadian Institute for Research in Atmospheric Chemistry/Institut canadien de la recherche en chimie atmosphérique (CIRAC) (1988)
#006, Steacie Building, York University, 4700 Keele St., North York, ON M3J 1P3
416/736-5586, Fax: 416/736-5690, Email: cirac@turing.sci.yorku.ca
Executive Director, Dr. David M. Halton
Publications: The Right Atmosphere

### Canadian Medical & Biological Engineering Society Inc./Société canadienne de génie biomédical inc. (CMBES) (1965)
National Research Council of Canada, Rm. 393, Bldg. M55, 1500 Montreal Rd., Ottawa, ON K1A 0R8
613/993-1686, Fax: 613/954-2216, Email: cmbes.society@nrc.ca, URL: http://www.bcit.bc.ca/~sohs/cmbes.htm
National Executive Secretary, Sally Chapman, Email: sally.chapman@nrc.ca
Publications: Newsletter
Affiliates: International Federation for Medical & Biological Engineering

### Canadian Meteorological & Oceanographic Society/Société canadienne de météorologie et d'océanographie (CMOS) (1967)
McDonald Bldg., #112, 150 Louis Pasteur Pvt., Ottawa, ON K1N 6N5
613/990-0300, Fax: 613/993-4658, Email: cmos@ottmed.meds.dfo.ca, URL: http://www.meds.dfo.ca/cmos/
Executive Director, Dr. Neil J. Campbell
President, Dr. Michel Beland
Publications: Atmosphere-Ocean; CMOS Bulletin SCMO, bi-m.

### Canadian Phytopathological Society/Société canadienne de phytopathologie (CPS) (1929)
MAPAQ Centre de Recherche, PO Box 455, Les Buissons, QC G0H 1H0
418/567-2235, Fax: 418/567-8791, URL: http://res.agr.ca/lond/pmrc/cps/cpshome.html
President, Dr. G. Lazarovitz
Secretary, Dr. B. Otrysko
Treasurer, Dr. R. Utkhede
Publications: CPS News; Canadian Journal of Plant Pathology, q.
Affiliates: International Society for Plant Pathology

### Canadian Science & Technology Historical Association/Association pour l'histoire de la science et de la technologie au Canada (CSTHA) (1980)
758 Holt Cres., Ottawa, ON K1G 2Y7
613/733-3188, Email: ae267@freenet.carleton.ca, URL: http://www.physics.uoguelph.ca/hist/CSTHA.html
President, Marianne Ainley
Sec.-Treas., Philip Enros
Publications: Scientia Canadensis; Dialogues, 3 pa

### Canadian Society of Exploration Geophysicists (CSEG) (1949)
#406, 206 - 7 Ave. SW, Calgary, AB T2P 0W7
403/262-0015, Fax: 403/262-7383, Email: cseg@cadvision.com, URL: http://www.geo.ucalgary.ca:80/cseg
Office Manager, Heather Payne
Publications: Recorder; Canadian Journal of Exploration Geophysics, bi-a.
Affiliates: Society of Exploration Geophysicists - USA; European Association of Geoscientists & Engineers - Netherlands

### Canadian Society of Forensic Science (CSFS) (1953)
#215, 2660 Southvale Cres., Ottawa, ON K1B 4W5

613/738-0001, Fax: 613/738-0001
Executive Secretary, Fredricka Monti
Publications: Canadian Society of Forensic Science - Journal

**Canadian Society for the History & Philosophy of Science/Société canadienne d'histoire et philosophie des sciences (1959)**
Department of History, Simon Fraser University, Burnaby, BC V5A 1S6
604/291-3521, Fax: 604/291-5837, Email: hgay@sfu.ca
Sec.-Treas., Prof. Hannah Gay
President, Maurice Gagnon, Bus: 819/821-7954, Fax: 819/821-7238
Publications: Communiqué
Affiliates: International Union for History & Philosophy of Science

**Canadian Society of Microbiologists/Société canadienne des microbiologistes (CSM) (1958)**
1200 Prince of Wales Dr., East, Ottawa, ON K2C 1M9
613/723-7233, Fax: 613/723-8792, Email: csm@istar.ca
President, D. Sprott
Secretariat, Lynn Anderson
Publications: CSM Newsletter
Affiliates: Youth Science Foundation; International Union of Microbiological Societies

**Canadian Society of Soil Science/Société canadienne de la science du sol (CSSS)**
PO Box 21018, RPO West End, Brandon, MB R7B 3W8
204/725-4336, Fax: 204/725-0624, URL: http://www.umanitoba.ca/CSSS
President, Al Fedkenheuer
Publications: Canadian Journal of Soil Science; Newsletter, q.
Affiliates: International Society of Soil Science

**Canadian Society for the Weizmann Institute of Science**
#218, 45 Sheppard Ave. East, North York, ON M2N 5W9
416/733-9220, Fax: 416/733-9430
Contact, Edie Bayer

**Canadian Space Society (1983)**
43 Moregate Cres., Bramalea, ON L6S 3K9
905/626-0505
Publications: Canadian Space Gazette

**Entomological Society of Canada/Société d'entomologie du Canada (ENTSOC) (1863)**
393 Winston Ave., Ottawa, ON K2A 1Y8
613/725-2619, Fax: 613/725-9349
President, Hugh Danks
Treasurer, Gary Gibson
Office Manager, A. Devine
Publications: ESC Bulletin; The Canadian Entomologist, bi-m.; Memoirs, irreg.

**Genetics Society of Canada/Société de génétique du Canada (GSC) (1956)**
#1112, 141 Laurier Ave. West, Ottawa, ON K1P 5J3
613/232-9459, Fax: 613/594-5190, Email: services@aic.ca
Coordinator, Joanne Lechuk
President, Ross Hodgetts
Publications: Bulletin of the GSC; Genome, q.
Affiliates: Canadian Federation of Biological Sciences; International Genetics Federation

**Geological Association of Canada/Association géologique du Canada (GAC) (1947)**
Dept. of Earth Sciences, Memorial University, 240 Prince Philip Dr., St. John's, NF A1B 3X5
709/737-8394, Fax: 709/737-2532, Email: gac@sparky2.esd.mun.ca, URL: http://www.esd.mun.ca/~gac/
President, Godfrey S. Nowlan, Email: nowlan@gsc.nrcan.gc.ca
Associate Sec.-Treas., Karen Johnston
Publications: Geoscience Canada; Geolog, q.
Affiliates: Canadian Society of Petroleum Geologists; Toronto Geological Discussion Group; Atlantic Geoscience Society; Canadian Quaternary Association; Canadian Geophysical Union

**Human Factors Association of Canada/Association canadienne d'ergonomie (HFAC) (1968)**
6519B Mississauga Rd., Mississauga, ON L5N 1A6
905/567-7193, Fax: 905/567-7191
Executive Manager, Peter Fletcher
President, Dr. Leslie Buck
Publications: Communiqué

**Industrial Biotechnology Association of Canada/Association canadienne de l'industrie de la biotechnologie (IBAC) (1987)**
#420, 130 Albert St., Ottawa, ON K1P 5G4
613/230-5585, Fax: 613/233-7541, Email: ibac@biotech.ca, URL: http://www.biotech.ca/members/ibac.htm
President, Joyce Groote
Chairman, Dr. Jack Wearing
Sec.-Treas., Dennis Lawson
Publications: Industry Directory; IBAC Focus; Position Papers

**Institute for Space & Terrestrial Science/Institut de science terrestre et spatiale (ISTS) (1988)**
4850 Keele St., 2nd Fl., North York, ON M3J 3K1
416/665-3311, Fax: 416/665-2032, Email: inquiries@ists.ca, URL: http://www.ists.ca
Executive Director, Dr. Ian Rowe
Communications Officer, Ian A. Thomson, Email: thomson@ists.ists.ca
Publications: Waves

**Institute of Textile Science/Institut des sciences textiles (ITS) (1956)**
1, rue Pacifique, Ste-Anne-de-Bellevue, QC H9X 1C5
514/457-2347
Secretary, Carmen Morosan

**International Association of Science & Technology for Development (IASTED) (1977)**
#80, 4500 - 16 Ave. NW, Calgary, AB T3B 0M6
403/288-1195, Fax: 403/247-6851, Toll Free: 1-800-995-2161, Email: iasted@cadvision.com, URL: http://www.iasted.com/
Conference Manager, Nadia Hamza
Publications: Control & Computers; Power & Energy Systems, 3 pa; International Journal of Modelling & Simulation, q.; Robotics & Automation, q.

**Microscopical Society of Canada (MSC) (1973)**
c/o Dept. of Pathology, McMaster University, 1200 Main St. West, Hamilton, ON L8N 3Z5
905/525-9140, ext.22496, Fax: 905/577-0198
Executive Secretary, Marie Colbert
Publications: Bulletin of the Microscopical Society of Canada

**Nova Scotian Institute of Science (NSIS) (1862)**
Science Services, University Library, Dalhousie University, 6225 University Ave., Halifax, NS B4H 4H8
902/494-2384, Fax: 902/494-2062, URL: http://www.ccn.cs.dal.ca/Science/NSIS/Home.html
President, Dr. Stan Heaps
Secretary, Dr. Sherry Niven
Publications: Proceedings of the Nova Scotia Institute of Science

**Oceans Institute of Canada/Institut canadien des océans (OIC) (1976)**
1226 LeMarchant St., Halifax, NS B3H 3P7
902/494-3879, Fax: 902/494-1334
Chairman, Management Committee, Board of Directors, Peter Duthil

**Ontario Herpetological Society (OHS)**
PO Box 244, Mississauga, ON L5G 4L8
416/285-6646, Fax: 416/285-9669
President, Grant Ankenman
Publications: The Ontario Herpetological Society News

**Ontario Kinesiology Association (OKA) (1982)**
6519B Mississauga Rd., Mississauga, ON L5N 1A6
905/567-7194, Fax: 905/567-7191, Email: oka@interlog.com, URL: http://www.interlog.com/~oka
Executive Manager, Leslie Wright
Publications: Kinnection

**Royal Astronomical Society of Canada/Société royale d'astronomie du Canada (RASC) (1903)**
136 Dupont St., Toronto, ON M5R 1V2
416/924-7973, Fax: 416/924-2911, URL: http://www.rasc.ca
National Secretary, R. Auclair
Executive Secretary, B. Bird
National Treasurer, R. Gupta
Publications: RASC Journal

**Science Alberta Foundation (1990)**
#2100, 700 - 6 Ave. SW, Calgary, AB T2P OT8
403/260-1996, Fax: 403/260-1165, Email: saf@freenet.calgary.ab.ca, URL: http://www.FreeNet.Calgary.ab.ca/science/sciencab.html
Executive Director, Anne Tingle
Publications: Between Friends

**Society of Toxicology of Canada/Société de toxicologie du Canada (STC) (1964)**
PO Box 517, Beaconsfield, QC H9W 5V1
514/428-2676, Fax: 514/428-2685
URL: http://meds-ss10.meds.queensu.ca/stcweb/
Executive Director, Gordon Krip
President, Dr. Gail D. Bellward
Treasurer, Dr. Michel Charbonneau
Secretary, Dr. Thomas E. Massey, Email: masseyt@post.queensu.ca
Publications: Canadian Journal of Physiology & Pharmacology; STC News/Nouvelles, 3 pa
Affiliates: Canadian Federation of Biological Societies; International Union of Toxicology

**Spectroscopy Society of Canada/Société de spectroscopie du Canada (SSC) (1957)**
PO Box 332, Stn A, Ottawa, ON K1N 8V3
613/597-1067
President, Dr. Ralph M. Paroli
Publications: Canadian Journal of Analytical Sciences & Spectroscopy; Canadian Spectroscopic News
Affiliates: Society for Applied Spectroscopy - USA; Colloquium Spectroscopicum Internationale; Chemical Institute of Canada; Canadian Society of Forensic Science

**Statistical Society of Canada/Société statistique du Canada (1977)**
582 Somerset St. West, Ottawa, ON K1R 5K2
613/234-0171, Fax: 613/237-9900, Email: ssc@thewillowgroup.com, URL: http://mast.queensu.ca/~ssc/en/welcome.html
Publications: Canadian Journal of Statistics; Liaison, q.; Directory of Statistics Programs in Canadian Universities, biennial

Affiliates: Committee of Presidents of Statistical Societies; International Statistical Institute

### Youth Science Foundation
#904, 151 Slater St., Ottawa, ON K1P 5H3
613/238-1671, Fax: 613/238-1677

**SEARCH & RESCUE *see* EMERGENCY RESPONSE**

**SECURITIES *see* FINANCE**

## SENIOR CITIZENS

### Advocacy Centre for the Elderly (ACE) (1984)
#701, 2 Carlton St., Toronto, ON M5B 1J3
416/598-2656, Fax: 416/598-7924
Executive Director, Judith A. Wahl
Publications: Newsletter

### Alberta Council on Aging (ACA)
#1740, 10130 - 103 St., Edmonton, AB T5J 3N9
403/423-7781, Fax: 403/425-9246, Email: acaging@compusmart.ab.ca
Executive Director, Christine Lawrence
Publications: ACA News

### Alberta Provincial Pensioners & Senior Citizens Organization
PO Box 266, Fort MacLeod, AB T0L 0Z0
President, Rulon Hirsche

### Alberta Senior Citizens Sport & Recreation Association (ASCSRA) (1980)
#203, 2616 - 18 St. NE, Calgary, AB T2E 7R1
403/297-2703, Fax: 403/297-2702
Executive Director, Ruth Becker
Publications: SeniorAction
Affiliates: Alberta Sport Council; Alberta Recreation, Parks & Wildlife Foundation

### L'Assemblée des Aînées at Aînés Francophones du Canada (1992)
#1404, 1 Nicholas, Ottawa, ON K1N 7B7
613/241-7600, Téléc: 613/241-6046
Président, André Lécuyer

### L'Association internationale francophone des aînés (AIFA) (1981)
150, boul René-Lévesque est, 7e étage, Québec, QC G1R 4Y1
418/646-9117, Téléc: 418/646-1305
Secrétaire général, Guy Desrosiers
Publications: Maturité
Section Montréal: Présidente, Ruth T. Mendes, 1474, rue Fleury est, Montréal, QC H2C 1S1, 514/383-6019, Téléc: 514/383-3462

### Canadian Association on Gerontology/Association canadienne de gérontologie (CAG) (1971)
#500, 1306 Wellington St., Ottawa, ON K1Y 3B2
613/728-9347, Fax: 613/728-8913, Email: cagacg@magi.com, URL: http://www.cagacg.ca
Executive Director, Linda O'Rourke, M.S.W., Bus: 613/728-8913
President, Colette Tracyk
Publications: Canadian Journal on Aging

### Canadian Association of Retired Persons/Association canadienne des individus retraités (CARP) (1976)
#1304, 27 Queen St. East, Toronto, ON M5C 2M6
416/363-8748, Fax: 416/363-8747, URL: http://www.fifty-plus.net/
Executive Director, Murray Morgenthau
President, Lillian Morgenthau
Publications: CARP News

### The Canadian Grey Panthers Advocacy Network
#20, 5225 Orbitor Dr., Mississauga, ON L4W 4Y8
905/624-1616, Fax: 905/624-0015, Toll Free: 1-800-561-4739, Email: panthers@io.org, URL: http://www.panthers.net
Executive Director & Founder, Joe Moniz
Communications Director, Isobel Warren
President, Frank Oliver

### Canadian Institute of Senior Centres
Northwood Multipurpose Centre, 2515 Northwood Terrace, Halifax, NS B3K 3S5
902/258-3264, Fax: 902/454-3352

### Canadian Pensioners Concerned Inc./Corporation canadienne des retraités concernés
#24, 830 McLean St., Halifax, NS B3H 2T8
902/455-7684
National President, M. Doreen E. Fraser

### Elderhostel Canada/Séjours culturels des aînés du Canada (1980)
4 Cataraqui St., Kingston, ON K7K 1Z7
613/530-2222, Fax: 613/530-2096, Email: ecmail@elderhostel.org, URL: http://www.elderhostel.org
Executive Director, Dr. Robert H. Williston
Director, Atlantic Region, Joyce Kennedy, Bus: 902/457-6327, Fax: 902/445-3960
Director, BC Region, Loretta Krauter, Bus: 604/494-4469
Director, Ontario Region, Sabrina Jakubzig, Bus: 613/530-2095
Director, Prairies Region, Diane Osberg, Bus: 403/949-2165
Director, Québec Region, Judy Swedburg, Bus: 514/848-3313
Directeur des programmes français, Daniel Lavoie, Bus: 819/376-5124, Fax: 819/376-5166
Publications: Elderhostel Canada Catalogue

### Fédération de l'âge d'or du Québec/Québec Federation of Senior Citizens (FADOQ) (1970)
4545, av Pierre-de-Couberin, CP 1000, Succ. M, Montréal, QC H1V 3R2
514/252-3017, 3145, Téléc: 514/252-3154
Directrice générale, Nicole T. Moir
Publications: Virage
Organisation(s) affiliée(s): Association québécoise de gérontologie; Conseil canadien de développement social; Réseau canadien des aînés (One Voice); l'Assemblée des aîné(e)s francophones du Canada

### Help the Aged (Canada)/Aide aux aînés (Canada) (HTA) (1975)
99 - 5 Ave., Ottawa, ON K1S 5K4
613/232-0727, Fax: 613/232-7625, Toll Free: 1-800-263-5463
Executive Director, Pierre Barbeau
Publications: Agecare/Secours aux Aînés
Affiliates: HelpAge International

### Manitoba Society of Seniors (MSOS) (1979)
#1700, 330 Portage Ave., Winnipeg, MB R3C 0C4
204/942-3147, Fax: 204/943-1290, Toll Free: 1-800-561-6767
Acting Executive Director, Tina Alto
Editor, Irv Kroeker
Publications: MSOS Journal

### National Pensioners & Senior Citizens Federation (NPSCF) (1945)
3033 Lake Shore Blvd. West, Toronto, ON M8V 1K5
416/251-7042, Fax: 416/252-5770
President, Don Holloway
Secretary, Edith M. Johnston
Publications: The National News
Affiliates: International Senior Citizens Association

### New Brunswick Senior Citizens Federation Inc./Fédération des citoyens ainés du Nouveau-Brunswick inc. (NBSCF) (1968)
#100E, 236 St. George St., Moncton, NB E1C 1W1
506/857-8242, Fax: 506/857-0315
Executive Director, Steven J. Boyce
Publications: Horizons

### Older Adult Centres' Association of Ontario/Association des centres pour aînés de l'Ontario (OACAO) (1972)
#604, 1185 Eglinton Ave. East, North York, ON M3C 3C6
416/426-7038, Fax: 416/426-7388, Email: oacao@planeteer.com
President, William Krever
Treasurer, Marilyn Latham
Secretary, Nancy Biddoe
Fundraising, Karen Bentham
Publications: OACAO MEMO; The Centre Member

### One Voice - The Canadian Seniors Network/La Voix - Le Réseau canadien des aîné(e)s (1987)
#1005, 350 Sparks St., Ottawa, ON K1R 7S8
613/238-7624, Fax: 613/235-4497, Email: onevoice.lavoix@sympatico.ca
National Secretary, Ivan Hale
Publications: One Voice/La Voix

### Ontario Coalition of Senior Citizens' Organizations (OCSCO) (1985)
25 Cecil St., 3rd Fl., Toronto, ON M5T 1N1
416/979-7057, Fax: 416/979-5826
Executive Director, Morris Jesion
Publications: OCSCO Newsletter

### Prince Edward Island Senior Citizens Federation Inc. (PEISCF) (1972)
420 Queen St., PO Box 152, Charlottetown, PE C1A 7K4
902/628-8388, Fax: 902/892-1843, Email: obryanto@peinet.pe.ca
President, Libby Smith
Coordinator, Olive Bryanton
Publications: Voice for Island Seniors

### Society for the Retired & Semi-Retired
15 Sir Winston Churchill Sq., Edmonton, AB T5J 2E5
403/423-5510, Fax: 403/426-5175
Executive Director, Walter Coombs
Publications: News for Seniors

### United Senior Citizens of Ontario Inc. (USCO) (1961)
3033 Lakeshore Blvd. West, Toronto, ON M8V 1K5
416/252-2021, Fax: 416/252-5770, Toll Free: 1-888-320-2222
President, Leonard Harrison
Publications: The Voice USCO

## SERVICE CLUBS
*see also* **Fraternal**

### Association des Grands Frères/Grandes Soeurs du Québec/Big Brothers/Big Sisters of Québec (1981)
2300, boul René-Lévesque ouest, Montréal, QC H3H 2R5
514/935-4252, Téléc: 514/935-6518, Ligne sans frais: 1-800-661-4252
Directrice générale, Lise Bouchard

**Big Brothers of British Columbia & Affiliated Big Sisters (1953)**
#800, 15355 - 24th Ave., Unit 371, Surrey, BC V4A 2H9
604/878-1037, Fax: 604/536-5717
President, Mike Hamel

**Big Brothers of Canada/Les Grands Frères du Canada (BBSC) (1964)**
**Big Brothers & Sisters of Canada**
5230 South Service Rd., Burlington, ON L7L 5K2
905/639-0461, Fax: 905/639-0124, Toll Free: 1-800-263-9133, Email: bbsc@bbsc.ca, URL: http://www.bbsc.ca
National Executive Director, Michael McKnight
President, Rich Bassett
Director of Marketing, Bruce MacDonald
Publications: Rapport
Atlantic Regional Office: Resource Coordinator, Betty Hitchcock, 29 Bedell Ave., Saint John, NB E2K 2C1, 506/648-9794, Fax: 506/633-7781
BC/Alberta Regional Office: Executive Director, George Alliston, Unit 371, #800, 15355 - 24 Ave., Surrey, BC V4A 2H9, 604/878-1037, Fax: 604/536-5717
Québec Regional Office: Directrice générale, Lise Bouchard, 2300, boul René-Lévesque ouest, Montréal, QC H3H 2R5, 514/935-4252, Téléc: 514/935-6518, Ligne sans frais: 1-800-661-4252

**Big Sisters Association of Ontario (BSAO) (1981)**
2750 Dufferin St., Toronto, ON M6B 3R4
416/789-7859, Fax: 416/789-7850
Executive Director, Madeline Bergin

**British Columbia Lions Society for Children with Disabilities (1952)**
#300, 177 - 7th Ave. West, Vancouver, BC V5Y 1K5
604/873-1865, Fax: 604/873-0166
Executive Director, William J. Townsend
Associate Executive Director, A.W. Connell
Assistant Executive Director, Linda Wells
Comptroller, William Simpson
Publications: Main Event
Affiliates: BC Lions Foundation; Custom Service Transit Society

**Canadian Progress Club/Club progrès du Canada (1922)**
2395 Bayview Ave., North York, ON M2L 1A2
416/446-1830, Fax: 416/446-6857
Executive Director, Lee Irwin
National President, Carlos Pardo
National Sec.-Treas., Mary Kutarna
Publications: Progression

**Federation of Junior Leagues of Canada/Fédération des jeunes ligues du Canada**
154 Oxford St., Winnipeg, MB R3M 3J5
204/489-2559

**Kinsmen & Kinette Clubs of Canada/Les clubs Kin du Canada (1920)**
1920 Hal Rogers Dr., PO Box KIN, Cambridge, ON N3H 5C6
519/653-1920, Fax: 519/650-1091, Toll Free: 1-800-742-5546, Email: kinhq@kinclubs.ca, URL: http://nucleus.com/~gedwards/kinsmen.html
Executive Director, Robert W. Elliott
Publications: Contact; Kin Magazine, q.

**Kiwanis International/Western Canada District**
125 Sheep River Bay, Okotoks, AB T0L 1T4
403/938-5985, Fax: 403/938-2703
Sec.-Treas., Walter P. Voth

**Last Post Fund/Fonds du souvenir (LPF) (1909)**
#916, 685, rue Cathcart, Montréal, QC H3B 1M7
514/866-2727, Fax: 514/866-2147, Toll Free: 1-800-465-7113
Executive Director, Lt. Col. P. Ranger
Alberta Branch: Sec.-Treas., J.W. Ritchie, Canada Place, #940, 9700 Jasper Ave., Edmonton, AB T5J 2J6, 403/495-3766, Fax: 403/495-6960, Toll Free: 1-888-495-3766
British Columbia Branch: Capt. Ronald D. Rowdon, #520, 510 Hastings St. West, Vancouver, BC V6B 1L8, 604/685-8833, Fax: 604/685-4521, Toll Free: 1-800-268-0248
Filiale du Québec: Sec.-Treas., René Pothier, #921, 685, rue Cathcart, Montréal, QC H3B 1M7, 514/866-2888, Téléc: 514/866-1471, Ligne sans frais: 1-800-866-5229
Manitoba Branch: Robert W. Rollings, 51 St. Anne's Rd., Winnipeg, MB R2M 1Y4, 204/233-3073, Fax: 204/237-1169
New Brunswick & Prince Edward Island Branch: Ida DeGrâce, 400 Main St., PO Box 2054, Saint John, NB E2L 3T5, 506/658-9707, Fax: 506/658-9623, Toll Free: 1-800-561-0505
Newfoundland Branch: Sec.-Treas., Hugh R. Peden, Prudential Bldg., 49 Elizabeth Ave., St. John's, NF A1A 1W9, 709/579-4288, Fax: 709/579-0966
Nova Scotia Branch: Lois Townsend, #1003, 6080 Young St., Halifax, NS B3K 5L2, 902/455-5283, Fax: 902/455-4058, Toll Free: 1-800-565-4777
Ontario Branch: Sec.-Treas., Richard Noble, #624, 55 St. Clair Ave. East, Toronto, ON M4T 1M2, 416/923-1608, Fax: 416/923-3695, Toll Free: 1-800-563-2508
Saskatchewan Branch: Major Gerry Barr, 506 Federal Bldg., 101 - 22 St. East, Saskatoon, SK S7K 0E6, 306/975-6045, Fax: 306/975-4306, Toll Free: 1-800-667-3668
United Kingdom Representative: MacDonald House, 1 Grosvenor Sq., London W1X 0AB UK, /011-441-71-258-6339, Fax: /011-441-71-258-6645

**Lions Clubs International - District A**
#9, 155 Beaver Creek Rd., Richmond Hill, ON L4B 2N1
416/771-6400, Fax: 416/771-6692
Secretary, Roger L. Lacroix

**Rotary Clubs in Canada (1905)**
1 Rotary Center, Evanston, IL 60201 USA
312/866-3000, Fax: 312/328-8554, Telex: 724-465
General Secretary, Herbert Pigman
Promotional Services Dept., Hank Ottery
Publications: The Rotarian

**Soroptimist Foundation of Canada (1963)**
#22, 185 Woodridge Dr. SW, Calgary, AB T2W 3X7
403/249-9191, Fax: 403/249-9199
Sec.-Treas., Marguerite Duguid
Affiliates: Soroptimist International of the Americas

**Variety - The Children's Charity (Ontario) (1945)**
#300, 37 King St. East, Toronto, ON M5C 1E9
416/367-2828, Fax: 416/367-0028
Director, Finance & Administration, Mary Anne Beatty
Chief Barker, Bruce Raymond
Publications: Tent Topics
Affiliates: Variety Village; Variety Ability Systems Inc.

**Variety Club of British Columbia, Tent 47 (1965)**
**Variety Club**
1250 Homer St., Vancouver, BC V6B 2Y5
604/669-2313, 7770, Fax: 604/683-1025, Toll Free: 1-800-381-2040, URL: http://www.variety.bc.ca
Chief Barker/President, J.J. Richards
Executive Director, Dan Morin
Publications: Voice of Variety

**Variety Club of Manitoba, Tent 58 Inc. (1979)**
611 Wellington Cres., Winnipeg, MB R3M 0A7
204/982-1058, Fax: 204/475-3198
Publications: Variety Views

**Variety Club of Southern Alberta, Tent 61 (1982)**
#202, 110 -11 Ave. SE, Calgary, AB T2G 0X5
403/261-0061, Fax: 403/264-9041
Chief Officer, Audreu Cunneyworth
Publications: Variety Voice

**SHIPPING *see* TRANSPORTATION & SHIPPING**

**SOCIAL CLUBS *see* FRATERNAL**

## SOCIAL RESPONSE/SOCIAL SERVICES

**Alberta Association for Marriage & Family Therapy (AAMFT) (1978)**
PO Box 52053, Edmonton, AB T6G 2T5
403/448-9497
Affiliates: American Association for Marriage & Family Therapy

**Alberta Association of Services for Children & Families (AASCF) (1967)**
#54, 9912 - 106 St., Edmonton, AB T5K 1C5
403/424-4498, Fax: 403/425-4828
Executive Director, Leslie McCallum
Publications: Post-It

**Alberta Association of Social Workers/Association des travailleurs sociaux de l'Alberta (AASW)**
#52, 9912 - 106 St., Edmonton, AB T5K 1C5
403/421-1167, Fax: 403/421-1168
Executive Director, Rod Adachi
Publications: The Advocate

**Association of Community Information Centres in Ontario (ACICO) (1980)**
#205, 5233 Dundas St. West, Etobicoke, ON M9B 1A6
416/237-0405, Fax: 416/237-1395, URL: http://www.web.apc.org/acico/
Executive Director, Serge Lavoie
President, Rosanna Thoms
Publications: A CICO Online; Profiles, a.
Toronto: Executive Director, Allyson Hewitt; President, Mahil Senathirajah, 425 Adelaide St. West, 2nd Fl., Toronto, ON M5V 3C1, 416/392-0505, Fax: 416/392-4404, Email: cicmt@web.net, URL: http://www.web.net/~cicmt/

**Association of Human Services in Alberta (AHSA) (1980)**
#205, 10426 - 81 Ave., Edmonton, AB T6E 1X5
403/431-0626, Fax: 403/431-0626, Email: ahsa@agt.net
Executive Director, Walter Walchuk
President, Gerrit Groeneweg
Publications: Human Services

**Association québécoise des personnes de petite taille (AQPPT) (1976)**
#205, 2177, rue Masson, Montréal, QC H2H 1B1
514/521-9671, Téléc: 514/521-3369
Directrice générale, Louiselle St-Pierre
Publications: Des nouvelles de notre association; Grandis ensemble, annuel

**Association québécoise plaidoyer-victimes (PV) (1984)**
**Plaidoyer-Victimes**
#201, 4305, rue Iberville, Montréal, QC H2H 2L5
514/526-9037, Téléc: 514/526-9951
Coordonnatrice, Josée Coiteux
Publications: Info PV

**Association des services de réhabilitation sociale du Québec inc./Association of Social Rehabilitation Agencies of Québec Inc. (ASRSQ) (1962)**
2000, boul St-Joseph est, 2e étage, Montréal, QC H2H 1E4
514/521-3733, Téléc: 514/521-3753
Directrice générale, Johanne Vallée
Publications: Porte Ouverte

**L'Autre Parole (1976)**
CP 393, Succ. C, Montréal, QC H2L 4K3
Responsable, Relations publiques, Yvette Laprise
Publications: L'Autre Parole

**BC Council for Families (BCCF) (1977)**
#204, 2590 Granville St., Vancouver, BC V6H 3H1
604/660-0675, Fax: 604/732-4813, Toll Free: 1-800-663-5638, Email: bccf@istar.ca, URL: http://www.bccf.bc.ca
President, Gwenn Cutler
Executive Director, Dr. Carol Matusicky
Publications: Family Connections

**BC Parents in Crisis Society (BCPIC) (1974)**
#620, 1155 West Pender St., Vancouver, BC V6E 2P4
604/669-1616, Fax: 604/669-1636, Toll Free: 1-800-665-6880
Executive Director, Julie Norton
Publications: Newsletter
Victoria Office: Sandra McConnell, 941 Kings Rd., Victoria, BC V8T 1W7, 250/384-8042, Fax: 250/388-4391

**Bereaved Families of Ontario (BFO) (1978)**
#204, 214 Merton St., Toronto, ON M4S 1A6
Toll Free: 1-800-236-6364, Email: bfo@inforamp.net, URL: http://www.inforamp.net/~bfo
Executive Director, Margaret McGovern

**Birthparent & Relative Group Society (BRGS) (1983)**
PO Box 20089, RPO Beverly, Edmonton, AB T2W 5E6
403/473-1912
President, Louise McLean
Publications: BRGS Newsletter

**Block Parent Program of Canada Inc./Programme parents-secours du Canada inc. (BPPCI) (1968)**
12206 - 86 Ave., Surrey, BC V3W 3H7
604/594-6788, Fax: 604/594-6788, Toll Free: 1-800-663-1134
President, Rose Marie Danylo Brien
Secretary, Joyce Algar
Finance Manager, Judy Vizbar
Vice-President, Linda Patterson
Publicity & Promotion Manager, Joan Barnhill
Publications: National Voice of Block Parents

**British Columbia Association of Social Workers/Association des travailleurs sociaux de la Colombie-Britannique (BCASW) (1956)**
#402, 1755 West Broadway, Vancouver, BC V6J 4S5
604/730-9111, Fax: 604/730-9112, Toll Free: 1-800-665-4747, Email: bcasw@amssa.bc.ca
Office Manager, Lisa Wong
Publications: Perspectives; The Social Worker, q.
Affiliates: End Legislated Poverty; End the Arms Race Coalition; BC Human Rights Coalition

**British Columbia Block Parent Program**
12070 - 96 Ave., Surrey, BC V3W 1W2
604/581-0678, Fax: 604/581-8633
Provincial Coordinator, Tani Berbenuik

**British Columbia Federation of Foster Parent Associations (BCFFPA) (1967)**
#206, 3680 East Hastings St., Vancouver, BC V5K 2A9
604/660-7696, Fax: 604/775-1183, Toll Free: 1-800-663-9999
Executive Director, Joan Wenstob
President, Doug Anderson
Publications: BCFFPA Newsletter

**Campaign 2000 (1991)**
22 Wellesley St. East, Toronto, ON M4Y 1G3
416/922-3126, Fax: 416/922-9235
Coordinator, Rosemarie Popham
Publications: Campaign 2000 Countdown
Affiliates: Canadian Academy of Child Psychiatry; Canadian Association of Social Workers; Canadian Association of Food Banks; Canadian Association of Toy Libraries & Parent Resource Centres; Canadian Council for Reform Judaism; Canadian Council on Social Development; Canadian Housing & Renewal Association; Canadian Institute of Child Health; Canadian Mental Health Association; Canadian Teachers' Federation; Catholic Health Association of Canada; Child Care Advocacy Association of Canada; Child Poverty Action Group; Child Welfare League of Canada; Family Service Canada; National Anti-Poverty Organization; National Organization of Immigrant & Visible Minority Women; Save the Children, Canada; YWCA of/du Canada

**Canadian Association Against Sexual Harassment in Higher Education/Association canadienne contre le harcèlement sexuel en milieu d'enseignement supérieur (CAASHHE) (1985)**
University of Victoria, School of Social Work, PO Box 1700, Victoria, BC V8W 2Y2
250/721-8044, Fax: 250/721-7067
President, Prof. Barbara Whittington

**Canadian Association of Food Banks/Association canadienne des banques alimentaires (CAFB) (1987)**
530 Lakeshore Blvd. West, Toronto, ON M5V 1A5
416/203-9241, Fax: 416/203-9244
Executive Director, Julia Bass
National Coordinator, Barry Davidson
Chairperson, Dianne Swinemar
Publications: Provisions
Affiliates: Campaign 2000

**Canadian Association of Neighbourhood Services (CANS) (1978)**
#203, 3102 Main St., Vancouver, BC V5T 3G7
604/875-9111, Fax: 604/875-1256
Executive Director, Doug Sabourin
Publications: Viewpoint
Affiliates: Association of Neighbourhood Houses of Greater Vancouver; Toronto Association of Neighbourhood Services; International Federation of Settlements

**Canadian Association of Sexual Assault Centres/Association canadienne des centres contre le viol (CASAC) (1977)**
77 - 20th Ave. East, Vancouver, BC V5V 1L7
604/872-8212, Fax: 604/876-8450
Contact, Lee Lakeman

**Canadian Association of Social Workers/Association canadienne des travailleurs sociaux (CASW) (1926)**
#402, 383 Parkdale Ave., Ottawa, ON K1Y 4R4
613/729-6668, Fax: 613/729-9608, Email: casw@casw-acts.ca, URL: http://www.intranet.ca/~casw-acts/
Executive Director, Eugenia Repeteur Moreno
Publications: The Social Worker/Le Travailleur social
Affiliates: International Federation of Social Workers

**Canadian Career Development Foundation/Fondation canadienne pour l'avancement de la carriere (CCDF) (1979)**
#202, 411 Roosevelt Ave., Ottawa, ON K2A 3X9
613/729-6164, Fax: 613/729-3515, Email: ccdffcac@magi.com, URL: http://infoweb.magi.com/~ccdffcac
Executive Director, M. Lynne Bezanson
Senior Consultant, K. Sareena Hopkins
Publications: The Career Counsellor/Regard sur l'orientation professionnelle
Affiliates: International Association for Educational & Vocational Guidance

**Canadian Centre for Philanthropy/Centre canadien de philanthropie (CCP) (1980)**
**IMAGINE**
1329 Bay St., 2nd Fl., Toronto, ON M5R 2C4
416/515-0764, Fax: 416/515-0773, Toll Free: 1-800-263-1178, Email: ccp@ccp.ca, URL: http://www.web.net/imagine/
President/CEO, Patrick Johnston
IMAGINE Program Director, Chris Pinney
Publications: The Canadian Directory to Foundations & Grants; Front & Centre

**Canadian Centre for Victims of Torture (CCVT) (1983)**
194 Jarvis St., Toronto, ON M5B 2B7
416/363-1066, Fax: 416/363-2122, Email: ccvt@icomm.ca
Executive Director, Mulugeta Abai
Publications: CCVT Newsletter

**Canadian Council for Refugees/Conseil canadien pour les réfugiés (CCR) (1978)**
#302, 6839, rue Drolet, Montréal, QC H2S 2T1
514/277-7223, Fax: 514/277-1447, Email: ccr@web.net, URL: http://www.web.net/~ccr/
President, Sharry Aiken
Publications: Contact

**Canadian Counselling & Guidance Association/Société canadienne d'orientation et de consultation (CCGA) (1965)**
#600, 220 Laurier Ave. West, Ottawa, ON K1P 5Z9
613/230-4236, Fax: 613/230-5884
President, Chris Cooper
Publications: Canadian Journal of Counselling
Affiliates: International Round Table for the Advancement of Counselling

**Canadian Crossroads International/Carrefour canadien international (CCI) (1958)**
31 Madison Ave., Toronto, ON M5R 2S2
416/967-0801, Fax: 416/967-9078, Email: cci@web.net
Executive Director, Jean-Guy Bigeau
Publications: Echo; Baobab, q.; Virage, bi-m.
Affiliates: Canadian Centre for Philanthropy
Atlantic Office: Wayne McGill, #525, 1657 Barrington St., Halifax, NS B3J 2A1, 902/422-2933, Fax: 902/423-0579
Bureau du centre: Frédéric Gordeau, 715, rue Richelieu, Québec, QC G1R 1K8, 418/525-9943, Téléc: 418/525-5283
Group Program Office: 912, rue Sherbrooke est, Montréal, QC H2L 1L2, 514/528-5363, Téléc: 514/528-5367
Western Office: Helen Rusich, #101, 10920 - 88 Ave., Edmonton, AB T6G 0Z1, 403/433-8015, Fax: 403/439-9677
Western Office: 1830 Cultra Ave., Saanichton, BC V0S 1M0, 250/544-1366

**Canadian Feed the Children (CFTC) (1986)**
174 Bartley Dr., Toronto, ON M4A 1E1
416/757-1220, Fax: 416/757-3318, Toll Free: 1-800-387-1221
Executive Director, Kevin J. O'Brien

**Canadian Fellowship for Romanian Orphans**
112 Peevers Cres., Newmarket, ON L3Y 7T2
905/898-2564
President, Mary-Lee Conte

**Canadian Foundation on Compulsive Gambling (Ontario) (CFCG(O)) (1983)**
#605, 505 Consumers Rd., North York, ON M2J 4V8
416/499-9800, Fax: 416/499-8260, Toll Free: 1-888-391-1111, Email: cfcg@netcom.ca, URL: http://www.netcom.ca/~cfcg/banner.html
Executive Director, Tibor I. Barsony
Executive Assistant, K. Raic

**Canadian Social Work Foundation/Fondation canadienne du service social**
1620 Scott St., PO Box 64177, Ottawa, ON K1Y 4V2
613/729-6668, Fax: 613/729-9608, Email: casw@casw-acts.ca
President, John Mould

**Canadian Society for the Prevention of Cruelty to Children (CSPCC)**
356 First St., PO Box 700, Midland, ON L4R 4P4
705/526-5647, Fax: 705/526-0214
President, E.T. Barker, M.D.
Publications: Empathic Parenting
Affiliates: The Robertson Centre, England; The Infant-Parent Institute, USA; Attachment Parenting International

**Canadians Addressing Sexual Exploitation/ Canadiens opposés à l'exploitation sexuelle (CASE) (1974)**
85 Ellesmere Rd., PO Box 62569, RPO Parkway, Scarborough, ON M1R 5G8
416/412-6065, Fax: 416/412-1321
President, Dolina Smith
Publications: CASE Newsletter

**Canadians Concerned About Violence in Entertainment (C-CAVE) (1983)**
167 Glen Rd., Toronto, ON M4W 2W8
416/961-0853, Fax: 416/929-2720, Email: rdyson@oise.utoronto.ca
Chairperson, Dr. Rose Anne Dyson, Ed.D.
Publications: C-CAVE News
Affiliates: Coalition for Responsible Television (CRTV)

**Catholic Charities of The Archdiocese of Toronto (1913)**
#400, 1155 Yonge St., Toronto, ON M4T 1W2
416/934-3401, Fax: 416/934-3402
Executive Director, Michael J. Fullan
Publications: Catholic Charities
Affiliates: Catholic Family Services of Toronto & 26 member agencies

**Child Abuse Research & Education Productions Association of British Columbia**
**CARE Productions**
12666 - 72nd St., Surrey, BC V3W 2M8
604/599-3040, Fax: 604/599-3050

**Child Care Advocacy Association of Canada/ Association canadienne pour la promotion des services de garde à l'enfance (CCAAC) (1982)**
323 Chapel St., Ottawa, ON K1N 7Z2
613/594-3196, Fax: 613/594-9375
Publications: Vision; Bulletin
Affiliates: Canadian Labour Congress; Public Service Alliance; Canadian Union of Public Employees

**Child Welfare League of Canada/La Ligue pour la protection de l'enfance du Canada (CWLC) (1994)**
#312, 180 Argyle Ave., Ottawa, ON K2P 1B7
613/235-4412, Fax: 613/788-5075, Email: cwlc@magi.com, URL: http://infoweb.magi.com/~cwlc/
Executive Director, Sandra Scarth
Publications: In Brief; Canada's Children, q.
Affiliates: Child Welfare League of America

**Coalition of National Voluntary Organizations/ Regroupement des organisations nationales bénévoles (NVO) (1973)**
**National Voluntary Organizations**
#420, 395 Cooper St., Ottawa, ON K2P 2H7
613/238-1591, Fax: 613/238-5257, Email: nvo@web.net
Executive Director, Al Hatton
Chair, Lynne Toupin
Publications: NVOn the Move

**Confédération des organismes familiaux du Québec inc. (COFAQ) (1972)**
4098, rue St-Hubert, Montréal, QC H2L 4A8
514/521-4777, Téléc: 514/521-6272, Courrier électronique: cofaq3ci@odyssee.net, URL: http://www.odyssee.net/~cofaq3ci/cofaq
Secrétaire général, Denis Perreault
Publications: Info-COFAQ

**COSTI (1981)**
1710 Dufferin St., Toronto, ON M6E 3P2
416/658-1600, Fax: 416/658-8537, Email: hq@costi.org
Executive Director, Mario J. Calla
Publications: The Newsletter
Affiliates: United Way

**Dying with Dignity/Mourir dans la dignité (DWD) (1980)**
#706, 188 Eglinton Ave. East, Toronto, ON M4P 2X7
416/486-3998, Fax: 416/489-9010, Toll Free: 1-800-495-6156, Email: dwdca@web.net, URL: http://www.web.net/dwd
Executive Director, Marilynne Seguin
President, Dan Atkinson
Publications: Dying with Dignity Newsletter
Affiliates: World Federation of Right to Die Societies

**Eastman Crisis Centre (1985)**
**Agape House**
PO Box 3130, Steinbach, MB R0A 2A0
204/326-6062, Fax: 204/326-2359, Crisis-Line: 1-800-326-3431
Executive Director, Debby Anderson
Publications: Agape House Newsletter
Affiliates: Manitoba Association of Women's Shelters

**Edmonton Social Planning Council (ESPC) (1940)**
#41, 9912 - 106 St., Edmonton, AB T5K 1C5
403/423-2031, Fax: 403/425-6244, Email: edmspc@compusmart.ab.ca, URL: http://www.compusmart.ab.ca/espc
Executive Director, Brian Bechtel
Publications: First Reading; Alberta Facts, q.

**Education Wife Assault (EWA) (1978)**
427 Bloor St. West, Toronto, ON M5S 1X7
416/968-3422, Fax: 416/968-2026, Email: ewa@web.net
Contact Person, Marsha Sfeir
Publications: EWA
Affiliates: The Black Secretariat; The National Action Committee on the Status of Women; MATCH International; Ontario Association of Interval & Transition Houses

**End Physical Punishment of Children - Canada**
**EPOCH - Canada**
c/o The Canadian Society for the Prevention of Cruelty to Children, PO Box 700, Midland, ON L4R 4P4
National Co-ordinator, James Lindfield, Bus: 604/255-5443

**Equal Justice for All (EJA) (1984)**
230 Ave R South, Saskatoon, SK S7M 2Z1
306/653-6260, Fax: 306/655-5895
Co-Chair, Mildred Kerr
Co-Chair, Earle Mireau
Co-Chair, Dorothy Daowst
Publications: News for Youse

**Family & Community Support Services Association of Alberta (FCSSAA) (1981)**
City Hall, PO Box 5008, Red Deer, AB T4N 3T4
403/342-8101, Fax: 403/347-4636
Secretary, Colleen Jensen
Publications: FCSS Community Connections

**Family Mediation Canada/Médiation familiale du Canada (FMC) (1985)**
123 Woolwich St., 2nd Fl., Guelph, ON N1H 3V1
519/836-7750, Fax: 519/836-7204, Email: fmcpyoung@web.net
Executive Director, Paul Young
Publications: Resolve

**Family Service Association of Metropolitan Toronto (FSA) (1914)**
355 Church St., Toronto, ON M5B 1Z8
416/595-9230, Fax: 416/595-0242
Executive Director, Paul Zarnke
Publications: On Record; Impact
Affiliates: Family Service Canada

**Family Service Canada/Services à la famille - Canada (1982)**
#600, 220 Laurier Ave. West, Ottawa, ON K1P 5Z9
613/230-9960, Fax: 613/230-5884, URL: http://www.familyforum.com/fsc/index.htm
CEO/President, Trevor C. Williams
Executive Assistant, Joanne Rivet

**Fédération des associations de familles monoparentales du Québec/Federation of Single-Parent Family Associations of Québec (FAFMRQ) (1974)**
8059, boul St-Michel, Montréal, QC H1Z 3C9
514/729-6666, Téléc: 514/729-6746
Directrice générale, Sylvie Lévesque
Publications: Bulletin de liaison

**Fédération des centres d'action bénévole du Québec (FCABQ) (1972)**
1246, rue Bishop, Montréal, QC H3G 2E3
514/866-6312, Téléc: 514/866-6315
Directrice générale, Daniele Feredj
Publications: Info éclair
Organisation(s) affiliée(s): International Association for Volunteer Effort

**Foster Parents Plan/Plan de Parrainage (1968)**
**PLAN International**
#1001, 95 St. Clair Ave. West, Toronto, ON M4V 3B5
416/920-1654, Fax: 416/920-9942, Toll Free: 1-800-387-1418, Email: n-cno@plan.geis.com
National Director, Carol A. Wilding
Director, Marketing, Lianne Bridges
Manager, Public Relations, Shauna McMahon
Publications: Plan News

**Frontiers Foundation/Fondation frontière (1968)**
**Operation Beaver**
#203, 2615 Danforth Ave., Toronto, ON M4C 1L6

416/690-3930, Fax: 416/698-9846, Toll Free: 1-800-668-4130
Executive Director, Charles R. Catto
President, Herb Nabigon
Publications: Program Report
Affiliates: Native Council of Canada

**Goodwill Rehabilitation Services of Alberta**
PO Box 1680, Edmonton, AB T5J 2N9
403/462-1666, Fax: 403/463-7396, Email: goodwill@ccinet.ab.ca
President, Kenneth W. Delooze
Affiliates: Alberta Easter Seal Ability Council; Canadian Council on Rehabilitation & Work; United Way of The Alberta Capital Region

**Goodwill Toronto (1935)**
234 Adelaide St. East, Toronto, ON M5A 1M9
416/362-4711, Fax: 416/362-0720
President, Jim Dreiling
Chairman, David Stevenson
Manager, Public Relations & Advertising, Jill Kehoe
Publications: Goodwill Works

**GRAND Society (1983)**
**Grandparents Requesting Access & Dignity**
219 Browning Ave., Toronto, ON M4K 3J5
416/469-5471
President, Joan Brooks
Publications: Newsletter

**International Social Service Canada/Service Social International Canada (ISS Canada) (1979)**
#714, 151 Slater St., Ottawa, ON K1P 5H3
613/236-6161, Fax: 613/233-7306, Email: issc@magmacom.com
Director of Services, Agnes Casselman
Publications: Global Outreach
Affiliates: International Social Service - Geneva, Switzerland

**Kids First Parent Association of Canada (1987)**
PO Box 5256, Airdrie, AB T4B 2B3
403/289-1440
President, Cathy Perri
National Secretary, Catherine Buchanan
Treasurer, Debbie Kusturin
Publications: Kids First Newsletter

**Kids Help Phone/Jeunesse j'écoute (KHP) (1989)**
439 University Ave., Toronto, ON M5G 1Y8
416/586-0100, Fax: 416/586-1880, Toll Free: 1-800-668-6868, Email: webmaster@kidshelp.sympatico.ca, URL: http://kidshelp.sympatico.ca
National Executive Director, Heather Sproule
Publications: Phone Link

**Lawyers for Social Responsibility/Avocats en faveur d'une conscience sociale (LSR) (1984)**
5120 Carney Rd. NW, Calgary, AB T2L 1T2
403/282-8260, Fax: 403/289-4272, Email: bdelong@web.apc.org
President, Beverley Delong
Publications: Newsletter
Affiliates: International Association of Laws Against Nuclear Arms; Mines Action Canada; Canadian Network for the Abolition of Nuclear Weapons

**Manitoba Anti-Poverty Organization Inc. (MAPO) (1982)**
#102, 365 McGee St., Winnipeg, MB R3G 3M5
204/786-3323
Organizational Coordinator, Diane Sovie
President, Gail Allard
Publications: The MAPO Memo
Affiliates: National Anti-Poverty Organization

**Manitoba Association of Social Workers/Association des travailleurs sociaux du Manitoba (MASW) (1961)**
#103, 2015 Portage Ave., Winnipeg, MB R3J 0K3
204/888-9477, Fax: 204/889-0021, Email: masw@magic.mb.ca
Administrative Coordinator, Diane Cullen
President, Brenda Douglas
Publications: The Manitoba Social Worker
Affiliates: Manitoba Institute of Registered Social Workers

**Manitoba Institute of Registered Social Workers (MIRSW) (1963)**
#103, 2015 Portage Ave., Winnipeg, MB R3J 0K3
204/888-9477, Fax: 204/889-0021, Email: masw@magic.mb.ca
Administrative Coordinator, Diane Cullen

**Missing Children Society of Canada (MCSC) (1986)**
#219, 3501 - 23rd St. NE, Calgary, AB T2E 6V8
403/291-0705, Fax: 403/291-9728, Toll Free: 1-800-661-6160, URL: http://www.childcybersearch.org/mcsc/
Chairman, Rhonda M. Morgan
Publications: The Missing Link
Affiliates: RCMP Missing Children's Registry, Ottawa
Eastern Canada Office: Case Director, Barb Snider, #814, 99 Bronte Rd., Oakville, ON L6K 3B7, 905/469-8826, Fax: 905/469-8828, Toll Free: 1-800-661-6160

**National Anti-Poverty Organization/Organisation nationale anti-pauvreté (NAPO) (1971)**
#440, 325 Dalhousie St., Ottawa, ON K1N 7G2
613/789-0096, Fax: 613/789-0141, Email: napo@web.apc.org, URL: http://www.napo-onap.ca
Executive Director, Lynne Toupin
Assistant Director, Michael Farrell
Publications: NAPO News

**New Brunswick Association of Food Banks (1989)**
PO Box 206, Newcastle, NB E1V 3M3
506/466-6292, Fax: 506/466-1119
Contact, Gwa Cockburn

**New Brunswick Association of Social Workers/Association des travailleurs sociaux du Nouveau-Brunswick (1965)**
PO Box 1533, Stn A, Fredericton, NB E3B 5G2
506/459-5595, Fax: 506/457-1421, Email: atsnbasw@nbnet.nb.ca

**Newfoundland & Labrador Association of Social Workers/Association des travailleurs sociaux de Terre-Neuve et Labrador (NLASW) (1970)**
PO Box 5244, St. John's, NF A1C 5W1
709/753-0200, Fax: 709/753-0120, Email: NLASW@newcomm.net
Executive Director/Registrar, Bruce Cooper
President, Beverley Clarke
Publications: NLASW Newsletter
Affiliates: Canadian Association of Social Workers

**Non-Smokers' Rights Association/Association pour les droits des non-fumeurs (NSRA) (1975)**
#221, 720 Spadina Ave., Toronto, ON M5S 2T9
416/928-2900, Fax: 416/928-1860, Email: nsra@io.org
Executive Director, Garfield Mahood
General Manager, Dr. C.F. Folz
Legal Counsel, David Sweanor
Publications: Indorair
Affiliates: Canadian Society of Association Executives; Canadian Centre of Philanthropy

**Nova Scotia Association of Social Workers/Association des travailleurs sociaux de la Nouvelle-Écosse (NSASW) (1963)**
#106, 1891 Brunswick St., Halifax, NS B3J 2G8
902/429-7799, Fax: 902/429-7650
Executive Director, Harold Beals
Publications: Connections

**One Parent Families Association of Canada (1973)**
#203, 6979 Yonge St., North York, ON M2M 3X9
416/226-0062, Fax: 416/226-3089
President, Christopher Wren

**Ontario Association of Children's Aid Societies/Association ontarienne des sociétés de l'aide à l'enfance (OACAS) (1912)**
75 Front St. East, 2nd Fl., Toronto, ON M5E 1V9
416/366-8115, Fax: 416/366-8317, Email: info@oacas.org, URL: http://www.oacas.org
Executive Director, Mary McConville
Executive Assistant, Andrea Mills
Publications: OACAS Journal; Municipal Directory for CAS Referrals, a.; Child Welfare Contacts in Canada, a.

**Ontario Association of Distress Centres (OADC) (1971)**
**Distress Centres Ontario**
#418, 99 Atlantic Ave., Toronto, ON M6K 3J8
416/537-7373, Fax: 416/537-6739, Email: dco@istar.ca
Executive Director, Ron Mighton
Publications: Focus on Listening
Affiliates: Canadian Association of Distress Centres

**Ontario Association of Interval & Transition Houses (OAITH) (1977)**
#1404, 2 Carleton St., Toronto, ON M5B 1J3
416/977-6619, Fax: 416/977-1227, Email: oaith@web.net
Lobby Coordinator, Eileen Morrow

**Ontario Association for Marriage & Family Therapy (OAMFT) (1974)**
660 Eglinton Ave. West, PO Box 50055, Toronto, ON M4G 4G1
416/364-2627, Fax: 416/829-9539, Toll Free: 1-800-267-2638, Email: jnyholt@netrover.com, URL: http://www.inforamp.net/~mbehar/index.htm
President, Vincent Poon
Publications: The Bond

**Ontario Association of Volunteer Bureaux/Centres/L'Association des centres d'action bénévole de l'Ontario (1979)**
**Volunteer Ontario**
#203, 2 Dunbloor Rd., Etobicoke, ON M9A 2E4
416/236-0588, Fax: 416/236-0590
Executive Director, Lorraine Street
Publications: Volunteer Ontario Newsletter; Volunteer Ontario Bulletin, m.

**Ontario Block Parent Program Inc. (OBPPI) (1977)**
83 Sherwood Forest Dr., Markham, ON L3P 1P9
905/294-7173, Fax: 905/294-7173, Toll Free: 1-800-563-2771
Chairman, Marianne MacBride
Publications: Newsletter

**Ontario Coalition for Better Child Care (OCBCC) (1981)**
**Better Child Care Ontario, Inc.**
500A Bloor St. West, 2nd Fl., Toronto, ON M5S 1Y3
416/538-0628, Fax: 416/538-6737, Email: ocbcc@pop.web.net, URL: http://worldchat.com/public/tab/ocbcc/ocbcc.htm
Executive Director, Kerry McCuaig

Publications: Network News
Affiliates: Canadian Child Care Advocacy Association

### Ontario Coalition of Rape Crisis Centres/Coalition des centres anti-viol de l'Ontario (OCRCC) (1980)
8 Essa Rd., Barrie, ON L4N 3K3
705/737-0464, Fax: 705/739-7268
Executive Director, Anne Marie Aikins

### Ontario Community Support Association/Association ontarienne de soutien communautaire (OCSA) (1992)
#104, 970 Lawrence Ave. West, Toronto, ON M6A 3B6
416/256-3010, Fax: 416/256-3021, Toll Free: 1-800-267-6272, Email: ocsainfo@ocsa.on.ca, URL: http://www.ocsa.on.ca
President, Elizabeth Fulford
Publications: OCSA News

### Ontario Municipal Social Services Association/Association des services sociaux des municipalités de l'Ontario (OMSSA) (1950)
#100, 5720 Timberlea Blvd., Mississauga, ON L4W 4W2
905/629-3115, Fax: 905/629-1633
Chief Administrative Officer, Pauline Carter
Publications: OMSSA Connection
Affiliates: Association of Municipal Employment Services; Association of Municipalities of Ontario

### Ontario Social Development Council
#402, 130 Spadina Ave., Toronto, ON M5V 2L4
416/703-5351, Fax: 416/703-0552
Executive Director, Malcolm Shookner

### Ordre professionnelle des travailleurs sociaux du Québec (OPTSQ) (1960)
#335, 5757, av Decelles, Montréal, QC H3S 2C3
514/731-3925, Téléc: 514/731-6785
Directeur général, René Pagé, T.S.
Publications: Intervention
Organisation(s) affiliée(s): Conseil interprofessionnel du Québec

### Parent Finders of Canada (1974)
**Canadian Adoption Reunion Register**
3998 Bayridge Ave., Vancouver, BC V7V 3J5
604/980-6005, Fax: 604/926-2037, Email: reunion@portal.ca, URL: http://www2.portal.ca/~reunion
National Director, Joan E. Vanstone
Affiliates: American Adoption Congress; International Soundex Reunion Register

### Pen-Parents of Canada (1993)
PO Box 52548, RPO Coquitlam Centre, Coquitlam, BC V3B 7J4
604/469-1272
Director, Patty Lou Bryant
Publications: The Pen-Parents of Canada Newsletter

### People, Words & Change/Monde des mots (PWC) (1979)
211 Bronson Ave., Ottawa, ON K1R 6H5
613/234-2494, Fax: 613/234-4223
Senior Counsellor, Kae Bee
Publications: The Reader; This Is It, a.

### PLAN International Canada
#305, 675 West Hastings St., Vancouver, BC V6B 1N2
604/682-3717, Fax: 604/681-6406
Catherine Sloot

### PRIDE Canada Inc. (1984)
**Parent Resources Institute for Drug Education**
College of Pharmacy, University of Saskatchewan, Saskatoon, SK S7N 0W0
306/975-3755, 931-9690, Fax: 306/975-0503, Toll Free: 1-800-667-3747
Executive Director, Eloise Opheim
Program Director/Parent Development Coordinator, Shelly Porter
Youth Coordinator, Michelle Basket
Office Administrator/Resource Coordinator, Marie Boechler
Volunteer Coordinator, Mary Snatinsky
Conference Coordinator, Diane Romanuck
Publications: Survival Tactics for Drug-Free Youth
Affiliates: PRIDE International

### Prince Edward Island Block Parent Program
PO Box 531, Alberton, PE C0B 1B0
902/853-4324
Chairperson, Pierre Legresley

### Reena Foundation (1975)
#200, 75 Dufflaw Rd., Toronto, ON M6A 2W4
416/787-0131, Fax: 416/787-8052, Email: skeshen@reena.org
Executive Director, Sandy Keshen
Publications: Kolreena

### Regroupement québécois des CALACS
**Centres d'aide et de lutte contre les agressions à caractère sexuel**
CP 267, Succ. De Lorimier, Montréal, QC H2H 2N6
514/529-5252, Téléc: 514/529-5255
Coordonnatrice, Diane Lemieux

### The Right to Die Society of Canada (RTDSC) (1991)
PO Box 39018, Victoria, BC V8V 4X8
250/380-1112, Fax: 250/386-3800, Email: rights@islandnet.com, URL: http://www.islandnet.com/~deathnet
Executive Director, John Hofsess
Head, Toronto Chapter, Ruth von Fuchs, Bus: 416/535-1323
Publications: Last Rights
Affiliates: World Federation of Right to Die Societies

### Ronald McDonald Children's Charities of Canada/Oeuvres de bienfaisance pour enfants Ronald McDonald du Canada (1982)
McDonald's Restaurants of Canada, McDonald's Place, Toronto, ON M3C 3L4
416/443-1000, Fax: 416/446-3415, Toll Free: 1-800-387-8808
Director, Heather Clark

### Royal Canadian Humane Association (1894)
PO Box 3948, Stn C, Hamilton, ON L8H 7P2
905/662-2800, Fax: 905/522-7266
President, Al Siaroff
Sec.-Treas., Jean Best

### Samaritan's Purse - Canada (1973)
**Operation Christmas Child**
PO Box 20100, RPO Calgary Place, Calgary, AB T2P 4J2
403/250-6565, Fax: 403/250-6567, Toll Free: 1-800-663-6500, Email: canada@samaritan.org, URL: http://www.samaritan.org
Executive Director, Sean P. Campbell
President, Franklin Graham
Communications Director, Mike Schroeder
Publications: Samaritan's Purse

### Saskatchewan Block Parent Advisory Committee Inc.
135 Brown Cres., Saskatoon, SK S7J 2R9
306/373-2559
President, Daphne Bahnmann

### Secours aux lépreux (Canada) inc./Leprosy Relief (Canada) Inc. (SLC) (1961)
#125, 1275, rue Hodge, Montréal, QC H4N 3H4
514/744-3199, Téléc: 514/744-9095
Président, P.E. Legault
Publications: Le secours aux lèpreux/Leprosy Relief

### Sex Information & Education Council of Canada/Conseil du Canada d'information et éducation sexuelles (SIECCAN) (1964)
850 Coxwell Ave., East York, ON M4C 5R1
416/466-5304, Fax: 416/778-0785, Email: sieccan@web.net
Chairperson, Michael Barrett
Publications: SIECCAN Newsletter; Canadian Journal of Human Sexuality, q.

### Sharelife (1976)
1155 Yonge St., Toronto, ON M4T 1W2
416/934-3411, Fax: 416/934-3412, Toll Free: 1-800-263-2595
Executive Director, Terry Thompson
Communications Director, Marilyn Burns
Publications: LifeLines; ShareLife at Work
Affiliates: Canadian Centre for Philanthropy

### Social Planning Council of Metropolitan Toronto
#1001, 2 Carleton St., Toronto, ON M5B 1J3
416/351-0095, Fax: 416/351-0107
Executive Director, Peter Clutterbuck

### Social Planning Council of Ottawa-Carleton/Conseil de planification sociale d'Ottawa-Carleton (1928)
#317, 256 King Edward Ave., Ottawa, ON K1N 7M1
613/789-3658, Fax: 613/789-6680, Email: spc@cyberus.ca, URL: http://www.cyberus.ca/~spc
Executive Director, Terry Gilhen
President, Eileen Dooley
Affiliates: District Health Council; Ontario Social Development Council

### Social Planning Council of Winnipeg
412 McDermot Ave., Winnipeg, MB R3A 0A9
204/943-2561, Fax: 204/942-3221
Executive Director, Wayne Helgason

### Social Planning & Research Council of BC (SPARC) (1966)
#106, 2182 - 12th Ave. West, Vancouver, BC V6K 2N4
604/736-8118, Fax: 604/736-8697, Email: sparc@amssa.bc.ca
Executive Director, Eva Cheung Robinson
President, Barbara Grantham
Publications: SPARC News: Community Affairs in British Columbia

### Société de St-Vincent de Paul
2010, Mathias Tellier, Québec, QC G1J 1G6
418/661-8600, Téléc: 418/661-9548
Présidente, Ellen Schryburt

### Society of Transition Houses - BC & Yukon
#1112, 409 Granville St., Vancouver, BC V6C 1T2
604/669-6943, Fax: 604/689-6962
Coordinator, Greta Smith

### SOS Children's Village BC (SOS-BC) (1986)
14851 - 66A Ave., Surrey, BC V3S 2A3
604/599-0887, Fax: 604/599-0854
Office Manager, Alana Hicik
Publications: SOS Newsletter
Affiliates: SOS - Kinderdorf International - Vienna, Austria

### SOS Children's Villages Canada/Villages d'enfants SOS Canada (1969)
**SOS - Canada**
#1203, 130 Albert St., Ottawa, ON K1P 5G4
613/232-3309, Fax: 613/232-6764, Toll Free: 1-800-505-5111, Email: sos@web.net, URL: http://www.web.net/~sos

National Director, Carol Faulkner
Publications: Newsletter
Affiliates: SOS-Kinderdorf International

### Streetkids' Foundation (1987)

First Global Place, #201, 7 Concorde Pk., North York, ON M3C 3N4
416/391-1801
President, J.H. Vowles
Affiliates: Childhope Foundation Canada; Street Kids International

### Suicide Information & Education Centre (SIEC) (1982)

#201, 1615 - 10 Ave. SW, Calgary, AB T3C 0J7
403/245-3900, Fax: 403/245-0299, Email: siec@nucleus.com, URL: http://www.siec.ca
Director, Gerry Harrington
Publications: Current Awareness Bulletin; SIEC Clipping Service, m.; SIEC Alert, bi-m.; SIEC on CD-ROM, a.
Affiliates: Canadian Mental Health Associaton - Alberta Division

### Thalidomide Victims Association of Canada (TVAC)

#607, 1105 Jalna Blvd., London, ON N6E 2S9
519/681-0357, Fax: 519/685-1518
CEO, R. Warren
Founder, H. Clifford Chadderton

### Thompson Crisis Centre (1977)

PO Box 1226, Thompson, MB R8N 1P1
204/677-9668; Crisis: 204/778-7273, Fax: 204/677-9042, Toll Free: 1-800-446-0613
Executive Director, Michelle Lacroix
Publications: Newsletter

### The TRIAD Society for Truth in Adoption of Canada (1986)

TRIAD

PO Box 5922, Stn B, Victoria, BC V8R 6S8
250/598-9887, Fax: 250/388-9423
President, Wayne Schultz, Bus: 403/229-0268
Vice-President, Audrey Scammell, Bus: 250/598-9887
Sec.-Treas., Brian K. Ritchie, Bus: 250/385-7884
Publications: TRIAD Tribune; Chapter Newsletter, q.
Affiliates: Canadian Adoption Reunion Registry; International Soundex Reunion Registry (assists with international searches)

### UNICEF Canada/Comité UNICEF Canada (1955)

Canadian UNICEF Committee

443 Mt. Pleasant Rd., Toronto, ON M4S 2L8
416/482-4444, Fax: 416/482-8035, Toll Free: 1-800-567-4483, Email: secretary@unicef.ca
Executive Director, Harry S. Black
Publications: Project's Communique

### United Way of Canada/Centraide Canada

#404, 56 Sparks St., Ottawa, ON K1P 5A9
613/236-7041, Fax: 613/236-3087, Toll Free: 1-800-267-8221, Email: office@uwc-cc.ca, URL: http://www.uwc-cc.ca
President, David Armour
Chair, Marc Jolicoeur
Publications: Flash-Info
Affiliates: United Way International
Affiliated United Way/Centraide Offices

Battlefords United Way Inc.: Administrator, Fran Sawula; President, Sheila Turuk; Treasurer, Edna Logan, PO Box 904, North Battleford, SK S9A 2Z3, 306/445-1717

Brandon & District United Way: Executive Director, Debbie Arsenault; Campaign Director, Donna August, 638 Princess Ave., Brandon, MB R7A 0P3, 204/727-5923, Fax: 204/727-8939

Brant United Way: Executive Director, Dawn Grainger; Campaign Manager, Karina Poplar; Finance/Systems Coordinator, Rassam Flsaad, 82 Charlotte St., Brantford, ON N3T 2X1, 519/752-7848, Fax: 519/752-7913

Campbell River & District United Way: Executive Director, Carol Marshall; Board Chair, Brenda Matthews, 1253 Ironwood Rd., PO Box 135, Campbell River, BC V9W 5A7, 250/287-3213

Castlegar District United Way: Administrator, Nona Paulson; President, Ann Pollock, 1995 - 6 Ave., Castlegar, BC V1N 4B7, 250/365-7331, Fax: 250/365-5778

Centraide Abitibi-Témiscamingue-Ungava: Directrice générale, Pierrette Theberge; Président, Claude Girard, 1755, ch Sullivan, CP 607, Val-d'Or, QC J9P 4P6, 819/825-7139, Téléc: 819/825-7155

Centraide Bas St-Laurent: Directrice générale, Denise Banville, 103, rue de l'Evêché ouest, CP 636, Rimouski, QC G5L 7C7, 418/723-1258, 1250, Téléc: 418/722-6128

Centraide Coeur du Québec: Directeur général, Pierre Métivier, #200, 154, rue Dunkin, Drummondville, QC J2B 5V1, 819/477-0505, Téléc: 819/477-6719

Centraide Côte-Nord/Secteur est: Directeur, Denis Auray, 410A, rue Évangéline, Sept-Îles, QC G4R 2N5, 418/962-2011, Téléc: 418/968-2923

Centraide Côte-Nord/Secteur ouest: Responsable administratrice, Muriel Phaneuf, #301, 858, rue de Puyjalon, Baie-Comeau, QC G5C 1N1, 418/589-5567, Téléc: 418/295-2567

Centraide Estrie: Directeur général, Claude Forgues, 1150, rue Belvédère sud, Sherbrooke, QC J1H 4C7, 819/569-9281, Téléc: 819/569-5195

Centraide Gaspésie Îles-de-la-Madeleine: Directeur général, Jean Martel; Présidente, Christiane Brinck, Pavillon de la Montagne, 230, route du Parc, CP 596, Ste-Anne-des-Monts, QC G0E 2G0, 418/763-2171, Téléc: 418/763-5631

Centraide Gatineau-Labelle-Hautes-Laurentides: Directeur général, Jean-Claude LeBel, 671, rue de la Madone, CP 154, Mont-Laurier, QC J9L 3G9, 819/623-4090, Téléc: 819/623-7646

Centraide du Grand Montréal: Présidente et Directrice générale, Michèle Thibodeau-DeGuire; Directeur, Allocation et analyse sociale, Jean-Guy Bissonnette; Directeur, Services administratifs, Jean Camerlain; Directeur de la campagne, Pierre-Marie Cotte; Secrétaire exécutive de la corporation, Solange Vincent; Directrice, Communications, Lucie Rémillard; Président du conseil d'administration, Jean-François de Grandpré, 493, rue Sherbrooke ouest, Montréal, QC H3A 1B6, 514/288-1261, Téléc: 514/844-9900

Centraide Lanaudière: Directrice générale, Simone Éthier, 54, Place Bourget nord, Joliette, QC J6E 5E4, 514/752-1999, Téléc: 514/752-2603

Centraide Laurentides: Directeur général, André Aubert; Président, Réjean Kingsbury; Directrice de la campagne, Suzanne Piché; Agente de communications, Violette Gingras, 281, rue Brière, CP 335, St-Jérôme, QC J7Z 5T9, 514/436-1584, Téléc: 514/436-3025

Centraide Mauricie: Présidente, Denise Tremblay; Trésorier, Denis Gervais; Secrétaire, Lisette Dionne; Directeur général, Faby N. Dresdell; Agente de communication, Carole Ebacher; Secrétaire, Sylvie Denis; Coordonnateur de la campagne de financement, Jean Yves Perron, 880, Place Boland, Trois-Rivières, QC G8Z 4H2, 819/374-6207, Téléc: 819/374-6857

Centraide Outaouais: Directeur général, Marie-France Gosselin; Directrice de la campagne, Sylvie Moisan; Directrice, Allocations et relations avec les organismes, Nathalie LeBlanc; Responsable du programme des déléguées et délégués sociaux, Michel Renaud, 74, boul Montclair, Hull, QC J8Y 2E7, 819/771-7751, Téléc: 819/771-0301

Centraide Portage-Taché: Directeur général, Fernand Heppel, Collège de Ste-Anne, #100, 4e av, CP 520, La Pocatière, QC G0R 1Z0, 418/856-3012

Centraide Québec: Directeur général, Pierre Métivier; Directrice de la campagne, Sylvie Simard; Directrice des communications, Andrée Lafleur, #101, 3100, av Bourg-Royal, Beauport, QC G1C 5S7, 418/660-2100, Téléc: 418/660-2111

Centraide Richelieu-Yamaska: Directeur général, Rheaume Fortin, 320, rue de la Concorde nord, Saint-Hyacinthe, QC J2S 4N7, 514/773-6679, Téléc: 514/773-4734

Centraide Saguenay-Lac St-Jean: Directeur général, Martin St-Pierre, 2876, Place Davis, Jonquière, QC G7S 2C5, 418/548-4686, Téléc: 418/548-9715

Centraide sud-ouest du Québec: Directeur général, Yves Fortin, 98, rue Champlain, CP 427, Salaberry-de-Valleyfield, QC J6S 4V7, 514/371-2061, Téléc: 514/377-2309

Central Okanagan United Way: Executive Director, Len Lifahus; President, Terry Rolfo, 480 Leon Ave., Kelowna, BC V1Y 6J3, 250/860-2356, Fax: 250/868-3206

Comox District United Way: Executive Director, Marie Gordon; President, Pamela Jolin, PO Box 3097, Courtenay, BC V9N 5N3, 250/338-1151, Fax: 250/338-0609

Cowichan United Way: Executive Director, J. Bodard; Secretary, Barbara Ziraldo, PO Box 11, Duncan, BC V9L 3X1, 250/748-1312, Fax: 250/748-1312, Email: unitedway@cowichan.com

Deep River District United Way: President, John G. Melvin; Secretary, Ruth Harrison; Treasurer, George Featherstone; Campaign Chair, Al Bancroft, PO Box 188, Deep River, ON K0J 1P0

Elgin-St.Thomas United Way Services: CEO, Terry Carroll; President, Elaine McGregor-Morris, 120 Centre St., St Thomas, ON N5R 2Z9, 519/631-3171, Fax: 519/631-9253, Toll Free: 1-800-233-9422

Elrose & District United Appeal: President, Jack Elliot; Secretary, Elizabeth Knorr, PO Box 591, Elrose, SK S0L 0Z0, 306/378-2927

Eston United Way: President, Sharon McNichol, PO Box 561, Eston, SK S0L 1A0, 306/962-4363

Grande Prairie & District United Way: President, Patricia G. Reid, 9902 - 101 St., Grande Prairie, AB T8V 2P5, 403/532-1105, Fax: 403/532-3532

Guelph & Wellington United Way Social Planning Council: Executive Director, Morris Twist; Campaign Director, Allison Haskin-Brown, 161 Waterloo Ave., Guelph, ON N1H 3H9, 519/821-0571, Fax: 519/821-7847, URL: http://www.unitedway.well-guelph.org/

Huron United Way: Office Administrator, Carol Randle, RR#5, Clinton, ON N0M 1L0, 519/482-7643

Kimberley & District United Way: President, Desiree McKay; Sec.-Treas., Bonnie Kreutz, 280 Spokane St., Kimberley, BC V1A 2E4, 250/427-2566

Kindersley & District United Appeal: President, Stan Humeny, Bus: 306/463-4131; Sec.-Treas., Sandy Grocholski, PO Box 489, Kindersley, SK S0L 1S0, 306/875-3743

Kirkland & District United Way: President, Bertha Boisvert; Secretary, Judy MacLeod, PO Box 313, Kirkland Lake, ON P2N 3H7, 705/567-6926

Lakeland United Way: President, Earla Burqe, #104, 311 - 10 St., Cold Lake, AB T0A 0V2, 403/639-2699, Fax: 403/594-2750

Metro United Way (Halifax-Dartmouth): President, Joanne Linzey; Director, Finance, Administration & Human Resources, Evelyn M. Barkhouse; Director, Development & Marketing, John Gullick; Director, Agency & Community Services, Peter Mortimer, Cogswell Tower, #506, 2000 Barrington St., Halifax, NS B3J 3K1, 902/422-1501, Fax: 902/423-6837, Email: united@fox.nstn.ca

Neepawa & District United Way: Chairman, Susan Hall, PO Box 1545, Neepawa, MB R0J 1H0, 204/476-2371

Nelson & District United Way: President, Joan Reichardt; Secretary, Leslie Bow, PO Box 89, Nelson, BC V1L 1P5, 250/352-7207

North Okanagan United Way: Executive Director, Janis Christofferson, #103, 3307 - 32 Ave., PO Box 533, Vernon, BC V1T 6M4, 250/549-1346, Fax: 250/549-1357

Northumberland United Way: Executive Director, Lynda Kay, 17 King St. East, PO Box 476, Cobourg, ON K9A 4L1, 905/372-6955, Fax: 905/372-4417, Toll Free: 1-800-833-0002

Porcupine United Way: Executive Director, Joanne Krakana; President, Joseph Ferrari, 98 Pine St. South, PO Box 984, Timmins, ON P4N 7H6, 705/268-9696, Fax: 705/268-9700

Portage Plains United Way: Executive Director, Kevin Lyons; President, Anna-Marie Brown, 165B Saskatchewan Ave. East, Portage La Prairie, MB R1N 0L7, 204/857-4440, Fax: 204/239-1740, Email: uwplap@cpnet.net

Powell River & District United Way: President, Terry Kruger, Bus: 604/485-3070, PO Box 370, Powell River, BC V8A 5C2

Prince George United Way: Executive Director, David Coflin; President, Don Hope, 1306 - 7 Ave., Prince George, BC V2L 3P1, 250/561-1040, Fax: 250/562-8102, Email: pgunited@netbistro.com, URL: http://www.pgonline.com/unitedway

Rossland United Way: President, Don Thompson, Bus: 604/362-5533, PO Box 154, Rossland, BC V0G 1Y0

Swift Current United Way: President, Archie Green; Executive Secretary, Marlene Arndt, Bus: 306/773-4828, c/o Swift Current Chamber of Commerce, Route 35, Mobile Delivery, Swift Current, SK S9H 3X6, Fax: 306/773-5686

The Pas & District United Way Inc.: President, Fletcher Stewart, Bus: 204/623-3311, PO Box 2998, The Pas, MB R9A 1R7

United Way of Ajax-Pickering: Executive Director, Peter Beattey; Executive Assistant, Susan Frudd, #407, 95 Bayly St. West, Ajax, ON L1S 7K8, 905/686-0606, Fax: 905/686-0609

United Way of the Alberta Capital Region: President, Anne Smith; Chair, Hal Neldner; Vice-President, Agency & Community Services, Don Taylor; Vice-President, Resource Development, George Smith; Labour Coordinator, Gordon Steele; Controller, Joe Lavorato, 10020 - 108 St., Edmonton, AB T5J 1K6, 403/990-1000, Fax: 403/990-1919

United Way of Barrie/South Simcoe: Executive Director, John McCullough, 165 Ferndale Dr., PO Box 73, Barrie, ON L4M 4S9, 705/726-2301, Fax: 705/726-4897, Email: uwbss@bconnex.net, URL: http://www.bconnex.net/~uwbss

United Way of Burlington, Hamilton-Wentworth: CEO, Jody Orr, 177 Rebecca St., Hamilton, ON L8R 1B9, 905/527-4543, Fax: 905/527-5152

United Way of Calgary & Area: Chairman, Alan Tamaki; President, Dr. Ed Johnston; Community Services Director, Patricia Bond; Director, Finance, Lorne Hutchison, 120 - 13 Ave. SE, Calgary, AB T2G 1B3, 403/231-6265, Fax: 403/266-1271

United Way of Cambridge & North Dumfries: Executive Director, Frank Adamson; President, John Beveridge; Campaign Director, Mary Park; VLD Coordinator, Diana Drackley; Labour Representative, Dennis Hillier, 24 Queens Sq., Cambridge, ON N1S 1H6, 519/621-1030, Fax: 519/621-6220

United Way of Cape Breton: Executive Director, Ken Willingston; President, David Reynolds, Cabot House, 500 Kings Rd., 2nd Fl., PO Box 1929, Sydney, NS B1P 6W4, 902/562-5226, Fax: 902/562-5721

United Way of Central Alberta: Executive Director, C. Scott Cameron, 4322 - 52 Ave., PO Box 97, Red Deer, AB T4N 5E7, 403/343-3900, Fax: 403/346-0280

United Way of Colchester County: Executive Assistant, Shelly Andrews, 30 Esplanade, PO Box 32, Truro, NS B2N 5B6, 902/895-9313, Fax: 902/895-5003

United Way of Cornwall & District: Administrator, Keith E. Jodoin; President, Ernie Jackson; Executive Secretary, Elaine Myers, 331 Water St. East, PO Box 441, Cornwall, ON K6H 5T2, 613/932-2051, Fax: 613/932-7534

United Way of Cranbrook: Executive Secretary, Sharen Malone; President, Joe Oviatt, PO Box 657, Cranbrook, BC V1C 4J2, 250/426-8833

United Way of Cumberland County: Executive Director, Marilyn Mitchell; President, James Black, 43 Prince Arthur St., PO Box 535, Amherst, NS B4H 4A1, 902/667-2203, Fax: 902/667-3819

United Way of Estevan: President, Debbie Gress; Sec.-Treas., Debra Salaway, 621 Henry St., PO Box 611, Estevan, SK S4A 2A5, 306/634-9484 (after 5:00 pm), Fax: 306/634-8922

United Way of Fort McMurray: Executive Director, Ruby Olson, PO Box 4011, Fort McMurray, AB T9H 3L3, 403/791-0077, Fax: 403/791-0088

United Way of the Fraser Valley: Executive Director, Ken Becotte, 2445B West Railway St., Abbotsford, BC V2S 2E3, 604/852-1234 (Abbotsford); 792-2979(Chilliwack), Fax: 604/852-1234

United Way of Greater Fort Erie: Executive Director, Colleen Hardie; President, Peter Collee, 427 Garrison Rd., Fort Erie, ON L2A 6E6, 905/871-5454, Fax: 905/871-2064

United Way of Greater Saint John Inc.: Executive Director, Ann-Marie Tingley; Labour Liaison Representative, Ron Oldfield, 69 King St., Saint John, NB E2L 1G5, 506/658-1212, Fax: 506/633-7724

United Way of Greater Toronto: President, Dr. Anne Golden; Chair, Bahadur Madhani, 26 Wellington St. East, 11th Fl., Toronto, ON M5E 1W9, 416/777-2001, Fax: 416/777-0962, Email: uweditor@uwgt.org, URL: http://www.uwgt.org

United Way of Greater Victoria: CEO, Maureen Duncan; Chair, Dick Cavaye; Labour Director, André Pel; Associate Director, Marketing & Communications, Jo-Anne Johnson; Associate Director, Agency & Community Service, Chris Poirier-Skelton; Director, Finance & Administration, Todd Abercrombie; Campaign Director, Craig Marlow, 1144 Fort St., Victoria, BC V8V 3K8, 250/385-6708, Fax: 250/385-6712

United Way of Haldimand-Norfolk: Executive Director, Vincent Taylor; President, Ron Roberts, PO Box 472, Simcoe, ON N3Y 4L5, 519/426-5660, Fax: 519/426-0017

United Way of Halton Hills: Executive Director, Kathleen Hayward; President, Jim Lindsay, 115 Main St. South., PO Box 286, Halton Hills, ON L7G 4Y5, 905/877-3066, Fax: 905/877-3067

United Way of Kamloops & Region: Executive Director, Ingrid Caines, #14, 219 Victoria St., Kamloops, BC V2C 2A1, 250/372-9933, Fax: 250/372-5926

United Way of Kent County: Executive Director, Karen S. Kirkwood-Whyte; President, Rick Bradley; Secretary, Helen McNaughton, 177 King St. East, PO Box 606, Chatham, ON N7M 5K8, 519/354-0430, Fax: 519/354-9511

United Way of Kingston & District: Executive Director, Jack Butt; President, Dene Latta; Finance Manager, Louise Adam; Administrative Assistant, Maria Smedes, 417 Bagot St., Kingston, ON K7K 3C1, 613/542-2674, Fax: 613/542-1379

United Way of Kitchener-Waterloo & Area: Executive Director, John Thompson; Director, Community Services & Administration, Janet Lawrence; Director, Development, Anne MacKay, #1100, 20 Erb St. West, Waterloo, ON N2L 1T2, 519/888-6100, Fax: 519/888-7737

United Way of Lanark County: Executive Director, Elizabeth Clarke, PO Box 3, Carleton Place, ON K7C 3P3, 613/624-5658, Fax: 613/624-5579

United Way of Leeds & Grenville: Executive Director, Judith Baril, #103, 187 King St. West, PO Box 576, Brockville, ON K6V 5V7, 613/342-8889, Fax: 613/342-8850

United Way of Lethbridge & District: Executive Director, Audrey Porter, Bill Kergan Centre, #230, 207 - 13 St. North, Lethbridge, AB T1H 2R6, 403/327-1700, Fax: 403/320-2046

United Way of London & Middlesex: Chair, Peter Polischuk; Executive Director, Peter Lea, 409 King St., London, ON N6B 1S5, 519/438-1721, Fax: 519/438-9938

United Way of the Lower Mainland: Executive Director, Gary McCarthy; President, Marguerite Ford; Campaign Director, Kim Fenlon; Director, Agency & Community Services, Gil Martin; Labour Staff Representative, Ken Isomura; Labour Participation Director, Mervyn Van Steinburg; Finance Director, Kim Lockhart; VLD Coordinator, Cheryl Milton; Communications Director, Rhoda MacKillop, 4543 Canada Way, Burnaby, BC V5G 4T4, 604/294-8929, Fax: 604/293-0220

United Way of Medicine Hat, Redcliff & District: Executive Director, Clarence Heringer; President, Julie Friesen, 457 - 3 St. SE, PO Box 783, Medicine Hat, AB T1A 7G7, 403/526-5544, Fax: 403/526-5244

United Way of Milton: Executive Director, Anne Eadie, PO Box 212, Milton, ON L9T 4N9, 905/875-2550, Fax: 905/875-2402

United Way of Moose Jaw: Chair, David Jukes, PO Box 1510, Moose Jaw, SK S6H 7A8, 306/693-0414

United Way of Morden & District Inc.: President, Lorne Stelmach, #2, 801 Stephen St., Morden, MB R6M 1G2, 204/822-4421, Fax: 204/822-4079

United Way of Nanaimo & District: Executive Director, Ron Walker, PO Box 1088, Nanaimo, BC V9R 5Z2, 250/753-8929, Fax: 250/753-7227

United Way of Niagara Falls: Executive Director, Janie Palmer; Campaign Manager, Carole Porter, 5017 Victoria Ave., Niagara Falls, ON L2E 4C9, 905/354-9342, Fax: 905/354-2717

United Way of Oakville: Executive Director, Julia Dumanian; President, Fran Richardson, #200, 466 Speers Rd., Oakville, ON L6K 3W9, 905/845-5571, Fax: 905/845-0166, Email: uwo_postoffice@msn.com

United Way of Oshawa-Whitby-Newcastle: Executive Director, Cindy J. Murray; President, Marianne Zakarow; Campaign Director, Robert Howard, 419 King St. West, Oshawa, ON L1J 2K5, 905/436-7377, Fax: 905/436-6414

United Way of Oxford: Executive Director, Marilyn Mann, 943 Dundas St., PO Box 354, Woodstock, ON N4S 7X6, 519/539-3851, Fax: 519/539-3209

United Way of Peel Region: CEO, Roy Spooner; Division Manager, Cathy Davis, #800, 151 City Centre Dr., Mississauga, ON L5B 1M7, 905/896-7335, Fax: 905/896-7338

United Way of Peterborough & District: Executive Director, Casey L. Ready, 277 Stewart St., Peterborough, ON K9J 3M8, 705/742-8839, Fax: 705/742-9186

United Way of Pictou County: Executive Director, Rae Foshay-Langille, PO Box 75, New Glasgow, NS B2H 5E1, 902/755-1754

United Way of Prince Albert: Administrator, Ivy Rue; President, Lawrence Joseph, #102, 1100 - 1 Ave East, PO Box 818, Prince Albert, SK S6V 5S4, 306/763-3686

United Way of Prince Edward Island: Executive Director, Anthony Sosnkowski, 129 Queen St., PO Box 247, Charlottetown, PE C1A 7K4, 902/894-8202

United Way of Quinte: Executive Director, Lillian Duffy; President, Teresa Holliday, 240 William St., Belleville, ON K8N 3K3, 613/962-9531, Fax: 613/962-4165

United Way of Regina: CEO, Wayne Hellquist; President, Paul Fudge; Director, Agency & Community Services, Karen Rowan; Director, Operations, Allen Lefebvre, 2022 Halifax St., Regina, SK S4P 1T7, 306/757-5671, Fax: 306/522-7199

United Way of St. Catharines & District: Executive Director, Larry Gemmel; Campaign Director, Carolyn Bones; Director, Labour Community Services, Mariea McNelis; Director, Finance & Administration, Bhavana Varma; Clerical, Janet Rouse, 55 St. Paul St., PO Box 816, St Catharines, ON L2R 6Y3, 905/688-5050, Fax: 905/688-2997

United Way of Sarnia-Lambton: Executive Director, Dave Brown; Campaign Coordinator, Pamela Bodkin; Planning/Allocations & Government Relations, Heather Sherlock, 507 Louisa St., PO Box 548, Sarnia, ON N7T 7J4, 519/336-5452, Fax: 519/383-6032, Info Line: 519/336-2422, Email: uwofs-l@ebtech.net, URL: http://www.sarnia.com/groups/unitedway/

United Way of Saskatoon: Executive Director, Arla Gustafson; President, Shelley Brown; Campaign Director, Bernie Sutton, 345A - 3 Ave. South, Saskatoon, SK S7K 1M6, 306/975-7700, Fax: 306/244-0583

United Way of Sault Ste. Marie: Executive Director, Carmen J. Borghese, 8 Albert St. East, Sault Ste Marie, ON P6A 2H6, 705/256-7476, Fax: 705/759-5899

United Way of Slave Lake Society: President, Tyler Bray, Bus: 403/849-3999, PO Box 1985, Slave Lake, AB T0G 2A0

United Way of South Georgian Bay: President, Peter Webb, 127 Hurontario St., Collingwood, ON L9Y 2L9, 705/444-1141, Fax: 705/444-1141

United Way of South Niagara: Executive Director, Gary W. Clement, CAE, Seaway Mall, 800 Niagara St., Welland, ON L3C 5Z4, 905/735-0490, Fax: 905/735-5432

United Way of Stratford-Perth: Executive Director, Judith Spicer; President, Bill Thorn, 38 Albert St., PO Box 21100, Stratford, ON N5A 7V4, 519/271-7730, Fax: 519/273-9350

United Way of Thompson Inc.: President, Manisha Pandya; Coordinator, Jeannette M. Clarke, PO Box 202, Thompson, MB R8N 1N1, 204/778-5564, Fax: 204/778-5564

United Way of Thunder Bay: Executive Director, Joanne Kembel; Campaign Director, Debbie Escott, #102, 130 South Brodie St., PO Box 876, Thunder Bay, ON P7C 4X7, 807/623-6420, Fax: 807/623-6180

United Way of Trail: President, Ron Joseph; Executive Secretary, Joyce Demore-Powell, 1145 Cedar Ave., Trail, BC V1R 4B8, 250/364-0999, Fax: 250/364-1564

United Way of Victoria County: Executive Director, Mike Puffer; President, John Bennett; Office Manager, Barbara Rose, #209, 189 Kent St. West, Lindsay, ON K9V 5G6, 705/878-5081, Fax: 705/878-0475, Email: lindsay.ont@resonet.com

United Way of Windsor-Essex County: Executive Director, Hilary Payne, 1695 University Ave. West, Unit A, Windsor, ON N9B 1C3, 519/258-3033, Fax: 519/258-2346

United Way of Winnipeg: Executive Director, Susan Lewis; President, Bill Bowles; Director, Communications, Marg Wedlake; Comptroller, Bev Passey, 5 Donald St, 3rd Fl., Winnipeg, MB R3L 2T4, 204/477-5360, Fax: 204/453-6198

United Way of York Region: Executive Director, Wyn Chivers, #201, 3950 - 14th Ave., Markham, ON L3R 0A9, 905/474-9974, 416/324-3331, Fax: 905/474-0051

United Way/Centraide (Central NB) Inc.: CEO, Clair F. Smith; President, Graham Fraser, Park Office Centre, #201, 440 Wilsey Rd., Fredericton, NB E3B 6E9, 506/459-7773, Fax: 506/451-1104

United Way/Centraide of the Moncton Region: Executive Director, Kim Halliday; Campaign Coordinator, Julie Arsenault, PO Box 768, Moncton, NB E1C 8M9, 506/858-8600, Fax: 506/858-0584

United Way/Centraide Ottawa-Carleton: Executive Director, Claude Léost; President, Marie-Josée Posen, 106 Colonnade Rd., Nepean, ON K2E 7P4, 613/228-6700, Fax: 613/228-6730, Email: parker@unitedwayoc.on.ca, URL: http://www.unitedwayoc.on.ca

United Way/Centraide Sudbury & District: Executive Director, Michele Liebrock; President, Ron Chrysler, #3, 764 Notre Dame, Sudbury, ON P3A 2T4, 705/560-3330, Fax: 705/560-3337

United Way/Centraide of the Upper Ottawa Valley: President, John Hempstead; Administrative Secretary, Catherine Dick, 214 Church St., PO Box 727, Pembroke, ON K8A 6X9, 613/735-0436, Fax: 613/735-0436

Weyburn & District United Way: President, Dennis Pilon, Bus: 306/848-3240; Sec.-Treas, Hannah Bell, Bus: 306/842-7529, PO Box 608, Weyburn, SK S4H 2K7

Winkler & District United Way: President, Shirley Banman; Treasurer, Mary Froese, PO Box 1528, Winkler, MB R6W 4B4, 204/325-6448

Yorkton & District United Way Inc.: President, Tom Seeley; Secretary, Carol Bobowski, Bus: 306/783-6566, PO Box 44, Yorkton, SK S3N 2V6, 306/783-9409, Fax: 306/786-7116

### Vanier Institute of The Family/Institut Vanier de la famille (VIF) (1965)

94 Centrepointe Dr., Nepean, ON K2G 6B1

613/228-8500, Fax: 613/228-8007, Email: 104767.561@compuserve.com, URL: http://www.cfc-efc.ca/vif/

President, Jerome Berthelette

Executive Director, Administration, Alan Mirabelli

Publications: Transition

### Volunteer Grandparents Society of British Columbia (VGPS) (1974)

1734 Broadway West, Vancouver, BC V6J 1Y1

604/736-8271, Fax: 604/736-8279

Executive Director, Hinda Simkin

Publications: Getting Started

### The War Amputations of Canada

2827 Riverside Dr., Ottawa, ON K1V 0C4

613/731-3821, Fax: 613/731-3234, Toll Free: 1-800-465-2677, URL: http://www.waramps.ca

CEO, H. Clifford Chadderton

National President, B. Alan Russell

Director of Administration, Claire Roy

Publications: The Fragment; Champ; Les Vainqueurs

### Yukon Block Parent Association (1989)

PO Box 5553, Whitehorse, YT Y1A 5H4

867/668-5840

Sec.-Treas., Jennifer Maura

Contact, Jan Hooper

**SOFT DRINK INDUSTRY *see* FOOD & BEVERAGE INDUSTRY**

**SPCAS *see* ANIMALS & ANIMAL SCIENCE**

## SPORTS

### Active Living Alliance for Canadians with a Disability/Alliance de vie active pour les canadiens/canadiennes ayant un handicap (ALACD)

#707A, 1600 James Naismith Dr., Gloucester, ON K1B 5N4

613/748-5747, Fax: 613/748-5782, Email: disability.alliance@rtm.activeliving.ca, URL: http://www.activeliving.ca/alliance/alliance.html

Director, Jane Arkell

Chair, Eric Boyd

Publications: Access

Affiliates: Canadian Amputee Sports Association; Canadian Association for Disabled Skiing; Canadian Association for Health, Physical Education, Recreation & Dance; Canadian Blind Sports Association; Canadian Cerebral Palsy Sports Association; Canadian Deaf Sports Association; Canadian Intramural Recreation Association; Canadian National Institute for the Blind; Canadian Paralympic Committee; Canadian Paraplegic Association; Canadian Parks/Recreation Association; Canadian Red Cross Society; Canadian Special Olympics; Learning Disabilities Association of Canada; National Network for Mental Health

### Alberta Broomball Association

Percy Page Centre, 11759 Groat Rd., Edmonton, AB T5M 3K6

403/453-8527

President, Greg Mastervick

Technical Director, George Paleniuk

### Alberta Schools' Athletic Association (ASAA) (1956)

Percy Page Centre, 11759 Groat Rd., Edmonton, AB T5M 3K6

403/453-8670, Fax: 403/415-1883, Email: asaa@compusmart.ab.ca, URL: http://www.afternet.com/ASAA/

Executive Director, John F. Paton

Administrative Assistant, Judye Sware

Special Projects Coordinator, Steven Patrick

Publications: ASAA Newsletter

Affiliates: National Federation of State High School Associations

### Alpine Club of Canada/Club national canadien d'alpinisme (ACC) (1906)

PO Box 8040, Canmore, AB T1W 2T8

403/678-3200, Fax: 403/678-3224, Email: acc@mail.culturenet.ca, URL: http://www.culturenet.ca/acc/

Provincial Coordinator, Leslie DeMarsh

Publications: The Gazette; Canadian Alpine Journal, a.

Affiliates: International Union of Alpinist Associations

### American & Canadian Underwater Certification Inc. (1968)

**ACUC International**

1264 Osprey Dr., Ancaster, ON L9G 3L2

905/648-5500, Fax: 905/648-5440, Email: acuc@acuc.ca, URL: http://www.acuc.es/

President, R.W. Cronkwright

Vice-President, Marg Cronkwright

Office Manager, Nancy Hilton

Publications: Contact

Affiliates: World Diving Federation; Undersea Hyperbaric Medical Society

### Aquatic Federation of Canada/Fédération canadienne des sports aquatiques (1964)
c/o Synchro Canada, #310, 1600 James Naismith Dr., Gloucester, ON K1B 5N4
613/748-5674, Fax: 613/748-5724
President, Rob Campbell
Affiliates: Synchro Canada; Canadian Amateur Diving Association Inc.; Water Polo Canada; Swimming Canada

### Arctic Winter Games International Committee (AWGIC) (1968)
c/o Community Development Division, Municipal & Community Affairs, #400, 5201 - 50th Ave., Yellowknife, NT X1A 3S9
867/873-7245, Fax: 867/920-6467, Email: ilegaree@maca.gov.nt.ca
President, Gerry Thick, Email: gthick@hypertech.yknet.yk.ca
Secretary, Wendell Shiffler
Treasurer, Peter Milner
Technical Director, Ian D. Legaree

### Association of Ontario Sport & Recreation Administrators (1979)
1185 Eglinton Ave. East, Toronto, ON M3C 3C6
416/426-7000, Fax: 416/426-7381
President, Sterling Ivany
Publications: The Sports & Recreation Insider
Affiliates: Ontario Sports & Recreation Centre

### Athletics Canada/Athlétisme Canada
#805, 1600 James Naismith Dr., Gloucester, ON K1B 5N4
613/748-5678, Fax: 613/748-5645, Telex: 053-3660 SPORTR, URL: http://canoe2.canoe.ca/athcan/
President/CEO, Rolf Lund
Président du conseil, Brian Langley
Publications: Athletics Canada; Track & Field Journal, q.
Affiliates: International Amateur Athletic Federation

### Badminton Canada
#603A, 1600 James Naismith Dr., Gloucester, ON K1B 5N4
613/748-5605, Fax: 613/748-5695, URL: http://www.badminton.ca/
CEO, Roy Roberts
President, Wayne Macdonnell
Affiliates: International Badminton Federation

#### ALBERTA BADMINTON ASSOCIATION
Percy Page Centre, 11759 Groat Rd., Edmonton, AB T5M 3K6
403/453-8536, Fax: 403/453-8553
President/Technical Director, Jeff Bell
Provincial Coach/Program Coordinator, Sonny Lee

#### BADMINTON BC (1925)
#328, 1367 West Broadway, Vancouver, BC V6H 4A7
604/737-3030, Fax: 604/737-3130, Toll Free: 1-800-483-2473
Executive Director, Denise Coutts
Office Manager, Judy Cowan
Publications: Courtlines

#### BADMINTON NEW BRUNSWICK
PO Box 149, RR#1, Scoudouc, NB E0A 1N0
President, Bob Lee
Provincial Secretary, Rheal Chiasson

#### BADMINTON NEWFOUNDLAND & LABRADOR INC.
PO Box 21248, St. John's, NF A1A 5B2
709/576-7606, Fax: 709/579-3355
President, Wayne Somers

#### FÉDÉRATION QUÉBÉCOISE DE BADMINTON INC. (1929)
Badminton Québec
#100, 5648, rue Hochelaga, Montréal, QC H1N 3L7
514/252-3066, Téléc: 514/252-3175
Directeur général, Gaetan Jean
Publications: Entrefilet/Badmintonien

### Baseball Canada/Fédération canadienne de baseball amateur (CFAB) (1962)
Canadian Federation of Amateur Baseball
#712, 1600 James Naismith Dr., Gloucester, ON K1B 5N4
613/748-5606, Fax: 613/748-5767, Info Line: 613/748-5754, URL: http://www.cdnsport.ca/baseball
President, Richard Bélec
Publications: Executive Director's Report; Directory, a.; RBI Newsletter
Affiliates: Canadian Olympic Association

#### BASEBALL ALBERTA
Percy Page Centre, 11759 Groat Rd., Edmonton, AB T5M 3K6
403/453-8601, Fax: 403/453-8603
President, Doug Jones
Publications: Hits, Runs & Errors

#### BASEBALL BC
#200, 1367 West Broadway, Vancouver, BC V6H 4A9
604/737-3031, 3037, Fax: 604/737-6043
Executive Director, Rob Arnold

#### BASEBALL NEW BRUNSWICK
14 Lloyd St., Hanwell, NB E3C 1M4
506/450-1891, Fax: 506/444-9889
Contact, Donna Whalen

#### BASEBALL NOVA SCOTIA
PO Box 3010, Stn South, Halifax, NS B3J 3G6
902/425-5450, ext.355
Contact, Grant McDonald

#### BASEBALL QUÉBEC
4545, av Pierre-de-Coubertin, CP 1000, Succ. M, Montréal, QC H1V 3R2
514/252-3075, Téléc: 514/252-3134
Directeur général, Sylvain Lalonde

#### MANITOBA BASEBALL ASSOCIATION
200 Main St., Winnipeg, MB R3C 4M2
204/985-4121, Fax: 204/640-6311
Contact, Guy Constant

#### NEWFOUNDLAND AMATEUR BASEBALL ASSOCIATION (1947)
PO Box 8700, St. John's, NF A1B 4J6
709/576-4935, Fax: 709/576-7493
Email: sad1024@infonet.st_johns.nf.ca
Executive Director, Ken Dawe, Bus: 709/576-4932
Publications: Baseball Scoop

#### ONTARIO BASEBALL ASSOCIATION (OBA) (1918)
Baseball Ontario
#16, 1425 Bishop St., Cambridge, ON N1R 6J9
519/740-3900, Fax: 519/740-6311
Administrator, Sam Besse
Publications: Baseball Bits
Affiliates: Little League Ontario

#### PEI AMATEUR BASEBALL ASSOCIATION (1967)
PO Box 92, Morell, PE C0A 1S0
902/961-2420, Fax: 902/961-3040
President & Secretary, George Morrison
Vice-President, Walter MacEwen

#### SASKATCHEWAN BASEBALL ASSOCIATION (SBA) (1953)
1870 Lorne St., Regina, SK S4P 2L7
306/780-9200, Fax: 306/352-3669
Email: skbaseball.regina@sk.sympatico.ca, URL: http://www.dlcwest.com/~skbaseball/
Executive Assistant, Sharon Bergerman
Publications: Reading the Pitch

### Basketball Canada (1972)
1600 James Naismith Dr., Gloucester, ON K1B 5N4
613/748-5607, Fax: 613/748-5741, Email: basketball.canada@cdnsport.ca, URL: http://www.cdnsport.ca/basketball/
Executive Director, Rick Traer
President, Tony Wakeham
Coordinator, Marketing/Communications, Brenda MacFee
Affiliates: 10 provincial + 2 territorial associations; Canadian Interuniversity Athletic Union; Canadian Colleges Athletic Association; Canadian School Sports Federation; Toronto Raptors; Vancouver Grizzlies; Canadian Wheelchair Basketball Association; Canadian Association of Basketball Officials; National Association of Basketball Coaches of Canada; Women's Basketball Coaches Association

#### BASKETBALL ALBERTA (1975)
Percy Page Centre, 11759 Groat Rd., Edmonton, AB T5M 3K6
403/453-8649, Fax: 403/453-8553
Email: bballab@basketballalberta.ab.ca, URL: http://www.basketballalberta.ab.ca
Executive Director, Douglas Baker
Publications: Zone Press

#### BASKETBALL BC
#410, 1367 West Broadway, Vancouver, BC V6H 4A7
604/737-3032, Fax: 604/738-7173, Telex: 04-51588
Executive Director, Michael Hind
Publications: The Baseline

#### BASKETBALL MANITOBA
200 Main St., Winnipeg, MB R3C 4M2
204/985-4119, Fax: 204/985-4028
Executive Director, Gail Kenoall

#### BASKETBALL NEW BRUNSWICK/BASKETBALL NOUVEAU-BRUNSWICK (BNB) (1973)
53D Clark Rd., Fairvale, NB E2E 2K9
506/849-4667, Fax: 506/849-4668
Email: bnb@nbnet.nb.ca, URL: http://www.nbi.ca/bnb
Executive Director, Cindy Floyd
President, Chuck Beyea
Publications: Pivot
Affiliates: New Brunswick Association of Approved Basketball Officials; New Brunswick Interscholastic Athletic Association

#### BASKETBALL NOVA SCOTIA
PO Box 3010, Stn Parklane Centre, Halifax, NS B3J 3G6
902/425-5450, Fax: 902/425-5606
Executive Director, Patti Dow
Publications: Full Court Press

#### BASKETBALL PEI
112 Heron Ave., Summerside, PE C1N 5R9
902/436-1943
President, Doug Dexter
Sec.-Treas., Dana Barron

#### BASKETBALL SASKATCHEWAN INC. (BSI) (1976)
2205 Victoria Ave., Regina, SK S4P 0S4
306/780-9290, Fax: 306/525-4009
Email: bballsask@cableregina.com
Executive Director, Bryan Nicurity
Publications: Tip-Off
Affiliates: Saskatchewan Sport

#### FÉDÉRATION DE BASKET-BALL DU QUÉBEC/QUÉBEC BASKETBALL FEDERATION (FBBQ) (1970)
Basketball Québec
4545, av Pierre-de-Coubertin, CP 1000, Succ. M, Montréal, QC H1V 3R2
514/252-3057, Téléc: 514/252-3357

Directeur des programmes, Louis McNulty
Publications: Info-Basket

**NEWFOUNDLAND & LABRADOR BASKETBALL ASSOCIATION (1988)**
PO Box 21029, St. John's, NF A1A 5B2
709/576-2047, Fax: 709/576-8787
Email: bmurphy@sympatico.nf.ca
President, Glenn Normore
Treasurer, Kathy Bolger
Secretary, Jamie Jennings
Technical Director, Bill Murphy
Publications: Key Points

**ONTARIO BASKETBALL ASSOCIATION (1977)**
#704, 1185 Eglinton Ave. East, North York, ON M3E 3C6
416/426-7200, Fax: 416/426-7360
Email: bballont@oscr.com
Executive Director, Leslie Dal Cin
Publications: Time Out; Vertical Reality, s-a.

### Biathlon Canada (1985)
#509, 1600 James Naismith Dr., Gloucester, ON K1B 5N4
613/748-5608, Fax: 613/748-5762, Telex: 053-3660
Executive Director, Terrence Sheahan
President, Ray Kokkonen
Publications: Biathlon Broadcast
Affiliates: International Biathlon Union; Canadian Olympic Association

### Bobsleigh Canada
#308, 1600 James Naismith Dr., Gloucester, ON K1B 5N4
613/748-5610, Fax: 613/748-5773, Telex: 053-3660 SPORTR, URL: http://www.cdnsport.ca/bobcan
Executive Director, Benoit Morin
President, Robert Storey
Affiliates: Fédération internationale de bobsleigh et de tobogganing

### Bowling Federation of Canada/Fédération des quilles du Canada
#3, 1475 Star Top Rd., Gloucester, ON K1B 3W5
613/744-5090, Fax: 613/744-2217
Executive Director, Kevin Jepson
President, John Hoffman
Program Coordinator, Sheila Carr

### Bowling Proprietors' Association of Canada
#10A, 250 Shields Ct., Markham, ON L3R 9W7
905/479-1560, Fax: 905/479-8613
Executive Director, Inge Malcolmson

### Canada Games Council/Conseil des jeux du Canada (1969)
#409, 1600 James Naismith Dr., Gloucester, ON K1B 5N4
905/746-5799, Fax: 905/748-5759
President/CEO, Lane MacAdam
Chairman, Jack Pelech

### Canadian 5 Pin Bowlers' Association/Association canadienne des cinq quilles (C5PBA) (1978)
#3, 1475 Star Top Rd., Gloucester, ON K1B 3W5
613/744-5090, Fax: 613/744-2217
Executive Director, Kevin Jepson
President, John Hoffman
Publications: Semi Annual & Annual Meetings; The Canadian Bowler, 3 pa
Affiliates: International Bowling Association

### Canadian Academy of Sport Medicine/Académie canadienne de médecine sportive (CASM) (1970)
1600 James Naismith Dr., Gloucester, ON K1B 5N4
613/748-5851, Fax: 613/748-5850
President, Dr. Nicholas Montadi
Programme Coordinator, Jacqueline Burke
Publications: Clinical Journal of Sport Medicine; Nouvelles/News, q.
Affiliates: Canadian Medical Association

### Canadian Adult Recreational Hockey Association (CARHA) (1975)
1600 James Naismith Dr., Gloucester, ON K1B 5N4
613/748-5646, Fax: 613/748-5714, Email: hockey@carha.ca, URL: http://www.carha.ca
Executive Director, Mike Peski
Publications: The Hockey Beat

### Canadian Amateur Boxing Association/Association canadienne de boxe amateur (1969)
#711, 1600 James Naismith Dr., Gloucester, ON K1B 5N4
613/748-5611, Fax: 613/748-5740, Email: caba@boxing.ca, URL: http://www.boxing.ca
Executive Director, Stuart Charbula
President, Jimmy MacInnis
Technical Director, Matt Mizerski
Secretary/National Registrar, Shelley Helmer
Publications: CABA News Bulletin
Affiliates: International Amateur Boxing Association

### Canadian Amateur Diving Association Inc./Association canadienne du plongeon amateur inc. (CADA) (1968)
#705, 1600 James Naismith Dr., Gloucester, ON K1B 5N4
613/748-5631, Fax: 613/748-5766, Telex: SPORTREC OTT 05, URL: http://www.diving.ca/diving/cada.html
Executive Director, Don Adams, CAE, Email: dadams@rtm.cdnsport.ca
President, Gordon Peterson
Publications: Bulletin
Affiliates: Aquatic Federation of Canada; Sport Federation of Canada

### Canadian Amateur Netball Association/Association canadienne de netball amateur
4948, rue Grey, Pierrefonds, QC H8Z 2T4
416/248-5884
President, Helen Norman
Affiliates: International Federation of Netball Associations

### Canadian Amateur Speed Skating Association/Association canadienne de patinage de vitesse amateur (CASSA) (1960)
**Speed Skating Canada**
#312, 1600 James Naismith Dr., Gloucester, ON K1B 5N4
613/748-5669, Fax: 613/748-5600, Email: ssc@speedskating-canada.ca, URL: http://www.speedskating-canada.ca
Executive Director, Jean R. Dupré
President, John Cavar
Affiliates: International Skating Union

### Canadian Amateur Wrestling Association/Association canadienne de lutte amateur (CAWA) (1970)
Place R. Tait McKenzie, #505, 1600 James Naismith Dr., Gloucester, ON K1B 5N4
613/748-5686, Fax: 613/748-5722, Telex: 053 3660, URL: http://www.cdnsport.ca/wrestling/
Executive Director, Greg Mathieu
President, Hank Lyth
Publications: Canadian Wrestler
Affiliates: International Amateur Wrestling Association

### Canadian Amputee Sports Association/Association canadienne des sports pour amputés (CASA) (1977)
428 Lake Bonavista Dr. SE, Calgary, AB T2J 0M1
403/278-8772, Fax: 403/271-1920
President, Robert Wade
Publications: Ampscan
Affiliates: Canadian Paralympic Committee; International Sports Organization for the Disabled

### Canadian Association for Disabled Skiing/Association canadienne des sports pour skieurs handicapés (CADS) (1976)
2860 Rotary Dr., PO Box 307, Kimberley, BC V1A 1E9
250/427-7712, Fax: 250/427-7715
Executive Director, Jerry Johnston
President, Henry Wohler
Publications: CADS Newsletter
Affiliates: International Paralympic Committee; Canadian Paralympic Committee; Canadian Ski Association

**CANADIAN ASSOCIATION FOR DISABLED SKIING - NEWFOUNDLAND DIVISION**
6 Albany Pl., St. John's, NF A1E 1Y2
709/753-3625
Contact, Marg Tibbo

**CANADIAN ASSOCIATION FOR DISABLED SKIING NEW BRUNSWICK**
**CADS New Brunswick**
#2, 69 Abbott Ct., Fredericton, NB E3B 5V8
506/458-3480, Fax: 506/458-6779
Contact, Lionel Proulx

**CANADIAN ASSOCIATION FOR DISABLED SKIING NOVA SCOTIA**
**CADS Nova Scotia**
RR#2, Mahone Bay, NS B0J 2E0
902/624-8051, Fax: 902/624-8051

**DISABLED SKIERS ALBERTA**
Percy Page Centre, 11759 Groat Rd., Edmonton, AB T5M 3K6
403/453-8691, Fax: 403/453-8553
President, Greg McAndrews
Executive Coordinator, Allyson Holgate
Publications: Newsletter

**DISABLED SKIERS ASSOCIATION OF BC (DSABC) (1973)**
#324, 1367 West Broadway, Vancouver, BC V6H 4A9
604/737-3042, Fax: 604/738-7175
Executive Director, Diane Urquhart
President, Martin Grundy
Publications: Snowdrift

**DISABLED SKIING ASSOCIATION OF MANITOBA (DSAM) (1974)**
130 Cree Cres., Winnipeg, MB R3J 3W1
204/889-9202, Fax: 204/831-6650

**ONTARIO ASSOCIATION FOR SKIERS WITH DISABILITIES**
RR#2, PO Box 97, Wakefield, QC J0X 3G0
819/459-2714, Fax: 819/459-2697

**SASKATCHEWAN SKI ASSOCIATION - DISABLED DIVISION**
17 Clark Cres., Saskatoon, SK S7H 3L8
306/374-7745

**SKI QUÉBEC**
165, Place Lilac, Pincourt, QC J7V 5B6
514/453-6351, Téléc: 514/453-6353
Contact, Henry Wohler

### Canadian Association for Health, Physical Education, Recreation & Dance/Association canadienne pour la santé, l'éducation physique, le loisir et la danse (CAHPERD) (1933)
#809, 1600 James Naismith Dr., Gloucester, ON K1B 5N4

613/748-5622, Fax: 613/748-5737, Email: CAHPERD@rtm.activeliving.ca; ACSEPLD@rtm.activeliving.ca, URL: http://www.activeliving.ca/activeliving/cahperd/indexfr.html
Executive Director, Sue Cousineau
President, Dr. Rick Bell
President-Elect, Dr. Colin Higgs
Vice-President, BC Representative, Ian Craigon
NB Representative, Garth Wade
Alberta Representative, Linda Thompson
Saskatchewan Representative, Ken Loehndorf
Manitoba Representative, Ernie Wilson
Québec Representative, Dr. Gaston Marcotte
NS Representative, Heather Morse
PEI Representative, Garth Turtle
Newfoundland Representative, Greg Wood
Ontario Representative, Herwig Baldauf
Publications: CAHPERD Journal; AVANTE, 3 pa; In Touch

**Canadian Association of Nordic Ski Instructors (CANSI) (1976)**
#409, 1185 Eglinton Ave. East, North York, ON M3C 3C6
416/426-7262, Fax: 416/426-7346
President, Kelly-Anne Rover
Publications: Snow News

**Canadian Association for Sport Heritage/Association canadienne pour l'heritage sportif (CASH) (1979)**
Canada's Sport Hall of Fame, Exhibition Place, Toronto, ON M6K 3C3
416/260-6789, Fax: 416/260-9347
President, Cheryl Rielly
Publications: Communique

**Canadian Ball Hockey Association/Association canadienne de hockey-balle**
Box 223, 21 - 10405 Jasper Ave., Edmonton, AB T5J 3S2
403/413-3474, Fax: 403/481-4619
President, Steve Posavec

**Canadian Blind Sports Association Inc./Association canadienne des sports pour aveugles inc. (1976)**
#606A, 1600 James Naismith Dr., Gloucester, ON K1B 5N4
613/748-5609, Fax: 613/748-5899
Executive Director, Ross Bales
President, Gerry York
Publications: Beyond Sight; Plein la Vue, q.
Affiliates: International Blind Sports Association; Canadian Paralympic Committee

**ALBERTA SPORTS & RECREATION ASSOCIATION FOR THE BLIND (ASRAB) (1975)**
PO Box 85056, RPO Albert Park, Calgary, AB T2A 7R7
403/262-5332, Fax: 403/265-7221
Executive Director, Shelley Allen
President, Darlene Murphy
Publications: ASRAB in Action

**ASSOCIATION SPORTIVE DES AVEUGLES DU QUÉBEC INC. (1986)**
4545, av Pierre-de-Coubertin, CP 1000, Succ. M, Montréal, QC H1V 3R2
514/252-3178, Téléc: 514/254-1303
Directrice, Jean Touchette

**BC BLIND SPORTS & RECREATION ASSOCIATION (BCBSRA) (1978)**
#317, 1367 Broadway West, Vancouver, BC V6H 4A7
604/325-1638, 8638, Fax: 604/325-1638
Email: bcbs@express.ca
Executive Director, Jane Blaine
Program Coordinator, Michael York
Publications: BCBSRA Newsletter
Affiliates: International Blind Sports Association

**MANITOBA BLIND SPORT ASSOCIATION**
200 Main St., Winnipeg, MB R3C 4M2
204/925-5694, Fax: 204/925-5703
Executive Director, Michelle Barclay
President, Wayne Peters
Publications: MBSA in Motion

**NEW BRUNSWICK RECREATION & SPORT ASSOCIATION FOR THE VISUALLY IMPAIRED INC./ASSOCIATION DES LOISIRS ET DU SPORT POUR LES PERSONNES HANDICAPÉES DE LA VUE DU NOUVEAU-BRUNSWICK (NBRSAVI) (1976)**
80 Riverside Dr., Fredericton, NB E3A 3Y1
506/472-5941
President, Bill Turney
Publications: Bulletin
Affiliates: Active Living Alliance; Sport New Brunswick

**NOVA SCOTIA BLIND SPORTS ASSOCIATION**
c/o CNIB, 6136 Almon St., Halifax, NS B3K 1T8
902/453-1480
President, Alfredo Abdo

**ONTARIO BLIND SPORT ASSOCIATION (1976)**
1185 Eglinton Ave. East, North York, ON M3C 3C6
416/426-7187, Fax: 416/426-7361
President, Shirley Shelby

**SASKATCHEWAN BLIND SPORTS ASSOCIATION INC.**
#210, 438 Victoria Ave. East, Regina, SK S4N 0N7
306/780-9425, Fax: 306/347-7500
Executive Director, Brian Fedler
President, Gerry Nelson

**Canadian Centre for Ethics in Sport/Centre canadien pour l'éthique dans le sport (CCES) (1991)**
#702, 1600 James Naismith Dr., Gloucester, ON K1B 5N4
613/748-5755, Fax: 613/748-5746, Email: info@cces.ca, URL: http://www.cces.ca
Chairperson, Dr. Andrew Pipe
CEO, Victor Lachance
Affiliates: Spirit of Sport Foundation

**Canadian Cerebral Palsy Sports Association/Association canadienne des sports de paralysie cérébrale (CCPSA) (1985)**
#607A, 1600 James Naismith Dr., Gloucester, ON K1B 5N4
613/748-5725, Fax: 613/748-5899
Administrative Assistant, Laura Belton
Affiliates: Canadian Paralympic Committee; Cerebral Palsy International Sport & Recreation Association

**Canadian Colleges Athletic Association/Association canadienne du sport collégial (1979)**
1600 James Naismith Dr., Gloucester, ON K1B 5N4
613/748-5626, Fax: 613/748-5757
Executive Director, Sandra Murray-MacDonell
President, Allan Ferchuk
Affiliates: Nova Scotia Colleges Athletic Association; Fédération québécoise du sport étudiant; Ontario Colleges Athletic Association; Prairie Athletic Conference; Alberta Colleges Athletic Conference; British Columbia Colleges Athletic Association

**Canadian Council of Provincial/Territorial Sport Federations**
PO Box 3010 South, Halifax, NS B3J 2G6
902/425-5450, Fax: 902/425-5606
Chairperson, Jim Newman
Sec.-Treas., David J. MacLean

**Canadian Cricket Association/Association canadienne de cricket (1892)**
46 Port St. East, Mississauga, ON L5G 1C1
905/278-5000, Fax: 905/278-5005
President, Dr. Geoff Edwards
Publications: The Canadian Cricketer
Affiliates: International Cricket Council; Kanga Ball Canada

**Canadian Curling Association/Association canadienne de curling**
#803, 1600 James Naismith Dr., Gloucester, ON K1B 5N4
613/748-5628, Fax: 613/748-5713, Email: cca@curling.ca, URL: http://www.curling.ca
General Manager, Dave W. Parkes
Affiliates: International Curling Federation

**Canadian Cycling Association/Association cycliste canadienne**
#212A, 1600 James Naismith Dr., Gloucester, ON K1B 5N4
613/748-5629, Fax: 613/748-5692, Telex: 053-3660
President, Richard Camirand
Director General, Andre Robitaille

**Canadian Deaf Sports Association/Association des sports des sourds du Canada (CDSA) (1965)**
#218, 1367 West Broadway, Vancouver, BC V6H 4A9
604/737-3041, Fax: 604/738-7175
President, Ron Fee
Treasurer, Derek Sweeting
Program/Technical Director, D.A. Shirton
Publications: Competitor
Affiliates: International Committee of Sports for the Deaf

**ALBERTA DEAF SPORTS ASSOCIATION (ADSA) (1974)**
**Federation of Silent Sports of Alberta**
#143, 11331 - 61 Ave., Edmonton, AB T6H 1M3
403/438-8079, Fax: 403/438-9114
Email: adsa@compusmart.ab.ca
President, Loreen Juhasz
Publications: Alberta Deaf Sports Association

**ASSOCIATION SPORTIVE DES SOURDS DU QUÉBEC INC. (ASSQ)**
4545, av Pierre-de-Coubertin, CP 1000, Succ. M, Montréal, QC H1V 3R2
418/252-3069
Présidente, Ghyslaine Fiset

**BC DEAF SPORTS FEDERATION (BCDSF) (1975)**
Deaf Sports Office, #218, 1367 Broadway West, Vancouver, BC V6H 4A7
604/737-3041, Fax: 604/737-6043, TDD: 604/783-7122
President, Bradford Bentley
Office Administrator, Derek Sweeting
Publications: Newsletter

**DEAF SPORTS NOVA SCOTIA**
PO Box 20030, Halifax, NS B3R 2K9
President, Garfield Fisher

**MANITOBA DEAF SPORTS ASSOCIATION**
#301, 285 Pembina Hwy., Winnipeg, MB R3L 2E1
204/453-1840
President, Lawrence Prokopchuk

**NEW BRUNSWICK DEAF SPORTS ASSOCIATION (1986)**
31 Arland Dr., Riverview, NB E3B 3V3
506/386-8091
President, Albert Buss
Affiliates: Moncton Deaf Sports Association; Saint John Deaf Sports Club; Fredericton Deaf Sports Association

**NEWFOUNDLAND DEAF SPORTS ASSOCIATION (NDSA) (1987)**
PO Box 21313, St. John's, NF A1A 5G6
709/576-4592, Fax: 709/576-7501

President, Judy Shea
Affiliates: Sport Newfoundland & Labrador

**SASKATCHEWAN DEAF SPORTS ASSOCIATION**
1816 Lorne St., Regina, SK S4P 3N8
306/787-3432, Fax: 306/781-6021
Contact, Dale Birley

## Canadian Equestrian Federation/Fédération équestre canadienne (CEF) (1977)
#501, 1600 James Naismith Dr., Gloucester, ON K1B 5N4
613/748-5632, Fax: 613/747-2920
Executive Director, Basil Collett
President, Don Martz
Publications: The Bulletin
Affiliates: Fédération équestre internationale

## Canadian Fencing Federation/Fédération canadienne d'escrime (CFF) (1971)
#305, 1600 James Naismith Dr., Gloucester, ON K1B 5N4
613/748-5633, Fax: 613/748-5742, Telex: 053-3660, Email: cff@fencing.ca, URL: http://www.fencing.ca
Executive Director, Jan Meyer
President, Marie-France Dufour
Publications: Fencing Forum/L'Écho de l'escrime
Affiliates: Fédération internationale d'escrime

## Canadian Figure Skating Association/ Association canadienne de patinage artistique (CFSA)
#403, 1600 James Naismith Dr., Gloucester, ON K1B 5N4
613/748-5635, Fax: 613/748-5718, Telex: 053-3660, Email: cfsa@cfsa.ca, URL: http://www.cfsa.ca/
Director General, David M. Dore
President, Jean MacLellan

## Canadian Football League/Ligue canadienne de football (CFL) (1958)
110 Eglinton Ave. West, 5th Fl., Toronto, ON M4R 1A3
416/322-9650, Fax: 416/322-9651, URL: http://www.cfl.ca/
Commissioner, Larry W. Smith
Sec.-Treas., Gregory B. Fulton
Events Manager, Sandra Taylor
Communications Manager, Jim Neish
Publications: CFL Facts, Figures & Records; CFL Rules & Regulations Handbook, a.; Weekly Statistics Package

## Canadian Freestyle Ski Association
**Canadian Ski Association - Freestyle**
1600 James Naismith Dr., Gloucester, ON K1B 5N4
613/748-5663, Fax: 613/748-5710, URL: http://infoweb.magi.com/freestyl/
Executive Director, Tom McIllfaterick
President, Chris Robinson

## Canadian Golf Foundation/Fondation du Golf du Canada (CGF) (1979)
1333 Dorval Dr., Oakville, ON L6J 4Z3
905/849-9700, Fax: 905/845-7040, Toll Free: 1-800-263-0009, Email: cgf@inforamp.net
Executive Director, Linnea Turnquist

## Canadian Golf Industry Association/Association canadienne de l'industrie du golf
54 Haileybury Dr., Scarborough, ON M1K 4X5
416/267-3802, Fax: 416/267-4959
Secretary, Carl Banks

## Canadian Golf Superintendents Association/ Association canadienne des surintendants de golf (CGSA) (1966)
#509, 5580 Explorer Dr., Mississauga, ON L4W 4Y1
905/602-8873, Fax: 905/602-1958, Toll Free: 1-800-387-1056
Executive Director, R. Vince Gillis, CAE
Publications: GreenMaster

## Canadian Handball Association/Fédération de balle au mur du Canada (CHA)
3 Milburn Pl., Sherwood Park, AB T8A 0T8
403/467-6829
Contact, Pat Brennan

## Canadian Hearing Impaired Hockey Association
1650 Lewes Way, Cooksville, ON L4W 3L2
705/624-7494
Executive Director, Roy Hysen

## Canadian Highland Games Council/Conseil canadien des jeux de Highland
87 Woodlawn Ave., Brantford, ON N3Y 1A6
519/753-5027
President, Eric Davidson

## Canadian Hockey (1969)
2424 University Dr. NW, Calgary, AB T2N 3Y9
403/777-3636, Fax: 403/777-3635
Director, Finance & Administration, Earl T. Young

## Canadian Hockey Association/Association canadienne de Hockey (CHA) (1914)
#607, 1600 James Naismith Dr., Gloucester, ON K1B 5N4
613/748-5613, Fax: 613/748-5709, URL: http://www.canadianhockey.ca
Chairman, Bob MacKinnon
President, Murray Costello
Publications: Canadian Hockey Magazine
Affiliates: International Ice Hockey Federation

**ALBERTA AMATEUR HOCKEY ASSOCIATION/ASSOCIATION DE HOCKEY AMATEUR DE L'ALBERTA**
#1, 7875 - 48 Ave., Red Deer, AB T4P 2K1
403/342-6777, Fax: 403/346-4277
Executive Director, Howard Wurban
President, Marv Bird

**BRITISH COLUMBIA AMATEUR HOCKEY ASSOCIATION/ ASSOCIATION DE HOCKEY AMATEUR DE LA COLOMBIE-BRITANNIQUE (1919)**
6671 Oldfield Rd., Saanichton, BC V8M 2A1
250/652-2978, Fax: 250/652-4536
Executive Director, Donald Freer
President, Florence Remple

**FÉDÉRATION QUÉBÉCOISE DE HOCKEY SUR GLACE/QUÉBEC ICE HOCKEY FEDERATION (FQHG) (1976)**
**Hockey Québec**
4545, av Pierre-de-Coubertin, CP 1000, Succ. M, Montréal, QC H1V 3R2
514/252-3079, Téléc: 514/252-3158
Président, René Marcil
Directeur Général, Guy Blondeau

**MANITOBA AMATEUR HOCKEY ASSOCIATION/ASSOCIATION DE HOCKEY AMATEUR DU MANITOBA**
200 Main St., Winnipeg, MB R3C 4M2
204/985-4240, Fax: 204/985-4246
President, Jeff Hnatiuk

**NEW BRUNSWICK AMATEUR HOCKEY ASSOCIATION/ ASSOCIATION DE HOCKEY DU NOUVEAU-BRUNSWICK (NBAHA) (1968)**
#4, 165 Regent St., PO Box 456, Fredericton, NB E3B 4Z9
506/453-0089, Fax: 506/452-8088
President, Doug Steeves
Executive Director, Derryl Smith
Publications: Newsletter

**NEWFOUNDLAND AMATEUR HOCKEY ASSOCIATION/ASSOCIATION DE HOCKEY AMATEUR DE TERRE-NEUVE (1935)**
15A High St., PO Box 176, Grand Falls-Windsor, NF A2A 2J4
709/489-5512, Fax: 709/489-2273
Executive Director, Barbara Power
Publications: Minor Hockey Directory; Minor Hockey News, a.

**NOVA SCOTIA HOCKEY ASSOCIATION/ASSOCIATION DE HOCKEY DE LA NOUVELLE-ÉCOSSE**
#910, 6080 Young St., Halifax, NS B3K 2A2
902/454-9400, Fax: 902/454-3883
Executive Director, Patricia MacDougall

**ONTARIO HOCKEY ASSOCIATION/ASSOCIATION DE HOCKEY DE L'ONTARIO (1890)**
#6, 1425 Bishop St., Cambridge, ON N1R 6J9
519/622-2402, Fax: 519/622-3550
President, Brent Ladds
Affiliates: International Ice Hockey Federation

**PEI HOCKEY ASSOCIATION/ASSOCIATION DE HOCKEY DE L'ÎLE-DU-PRINCE-EDOUARD**
20 Falconwood Rd., Sherwood, PE C1A 6B5
902/566-5171, Fax: 902/894-8412
Secretary/Manager, Gordie Lund

**SASKATCHEWAN AMATEUR HOCKEY ASSOCIATION/ASSOCIATION DE HOCKEY AMATEUR DE LA SASKATCHEWAN (SAHA) (1912)**
1844 Victoria Ave. East, Regina, SK S4N 7K3
306/789-5101, Fax: 306/759-6112
Executive Director, Kelly McClintock
Publications: Newsletter

## Canadian In-Line & Roller Skating Association/ Association canadienne de patins à roulettes et à roues alignées (CIRSA) (1994)
#117, 679 Queens Quay West, Toronto, ON M5V 3A9
416/260-5959, Fax: 416/260-0798, Toll Free: 1-800-958-0000, Email: cirsa@ican.net, URL: http://www.io.org/~cirsa/cirsa.html
Acting Managing Director, Sandy Nimmo
Publications: Freewheel'n
Affiliates: Canadian Amateur Speed Skating Association; Canadian Hockey Association

## Canadian Kendo Federation/Fédération canadienne de kendo
205 Riviera Dr., Markham, ON L3R 5J8
416/445-1481, Fax: 416/445-0519
President, Roy T. Asa
Secretary, Kiyoski Hao

## Canadian Lacrosse Association/Association canadienne de crosse (CLA) (1867)
#508, 1600 James Naismith Dr., Gloucester, ON K1B 5N4
613/748-5641, Fax: 613/748-5698, Telex: 053-3660, URL: http://www.lacrosse.ca/
Executive Director, Wes Clark
Chairman, William Hutton
Publications: Canadian Lacrosse News
Affiliates: International Lacrosse Federation; International Federation of Women's Lacrosse Associations; Fédération internationale d'Inter-crosse; Canadian Lacrosse Foundation; Sport Canada; Coaching Association of Canada; Canadian Sport & Fitness Administration Centre

## Canadian Ladies' Golf Association/Association canadienne des golfeuses (CLGA) (1913)
Golf House, Glen Abbey, 1333 Dorval Dr., Oakville, ON L6J 4Z3
905/849-2542, Fax: 905/849-0188, Toll Free: 1-800-455-2542
National Executive Director, Peggy Brown
President, Mary Drummie
Publications: CLGA Yearbook

Affiliates: World Amateur Golf Council; United States Golf Association; Royal & Ancient Golf Association; Ladies' Golf Union

**Canadian Luge Association/Association canadienne de luge (1990)**
#308, 1600 James Naismith Dr., Gloucester, ON K1B 5N4
613/748-5610, Fax: 613/748-5773, Telex: 053-3660
Executive Director, Terrence J. Sheahan
President, Don Vierboom
Technical Director, Wally Rauf
Publications: Luge News
Affiliates: Canadian Olympic Association; Fédération internationale de luge de course

**Canadian MasterAthlete Federation (CMAF) (1988)**
#8, 100 West Beaver Creek Rd., Richmond Hill, ON L4B 1H4
905/707-8464, Fax: 905/707-8464, Toll Free: 1-800-363-9709, Email: sports@passport.ca
President, Liz Roach
Vice-President, Jim Walker
Sec.-Treas., Iain Douglas

**Canadian Masters Cross-Country Ski Association/Association canadienne des maîtres en ski de fond (CMCSA) (1980)**
PO Box 702, Stephenville, NF A2N 3B5
National Director, Jack White
Publications: CMCSA Newsletter
Affiliates: World Masters Cross-Country Ski Association; Cross-Country Canada

**Canadian Masters Track & Field Association**
1185 Eglinton Ave. East, North York, ON M3C 3C6
416/426-7310, Fax: 416/426-7326

**Canadian Olympic Association/Association olympique canadienne (COA) (1907)**
#900, 21 St. Clair Ave. East, Toronto, ON M4T 1L9
416/962-0262, Fax: 416/967-4902
CEO/Secretary General, Carol Anne Letheren
Executive Director, Marketing, Paul Shugart
Montréal: Director, Corporate Affairs, Kathleen Giguère, 2380, av Pierre Dupuy, Montréal, QC H3C 3R4, 514/861-3371, Fax: 514/861-2896
Ottawa: Executive Director, Sports, Paul Dupré, #309, 1600 James Naismith Dr., Gloucester, ON K1B 5N4, 613/748-5647, Fax: 613/747-9483

**Canadian Paralympic Committee/Comité paralympique du Canada (CPC) (1982)**
#707A, 1600 James Naismith Dr., Gloucester, ON K1B 5N4
613/748-5630, Fax: 613/748-5731, Telex: 053-3660
Managing Director, Linda Hancock
President, Helen Manning
Publications: Resource Index for the Physically Disabled
Affiliates: International Paralympic Committee

**Canadian Polo Association (1985)**
**Polo Canada**
c/o Armadale Co. Ltd. Toronto Buttonville Airport, Markham, ON L3P 3J9
905/477-8000, Fax: 905/477-6897
Contact, Michael C. Sifton
Publications: The Corinthian Horse Sport

**Canadian Pony Club (1934)**
RR#2, Pitcaple Farm, Cambridge, ON N3C 2V4
519/822-1859, Fax: 519/822-0770
Secretary, Virginia Buchanan-Smith
Publications: The Pony Express

**Canadian Professional Boxing Federation**
RR#2, Site 16A, PO Box 187, Halifax, NS B3L 4J2
902/424-4560
Sec.-Treas., Ken Weston

**Canadian Professional Golfers' Association/Association canadienne des golfeurs professionels (CPGA) (1911)**
13450 Dublin Line, RR#1, Acton, ON L7J 2W7
519/853-5449, Fax: 519/853-5449
Executive Director, David J. Colling
Publications: CPGA Bulletin

**Canadian Professional Rodeo Association (1945)**
#223, 2116 - 27 Ave. NE, Calgary, AB T2E 7A6
403/250-7440, Fax: 403/250-6926, Email: prorodeo@iul-ccs.com, URL: http://www.rodeocanada.com
General Manager, Bob Falkenberg

**Canadian Racing Drivers Association**
#116, 295 The Westway, Etobicoke, ON M9C 4Z4
Vice-President, Paul Anderson

**Canadian Racquetball Association/Association canadienne de racquetball (CRA) (1972)**
**Racquetball Canada**
#303, 1600 James Naismith Dr., Gloucester, ON K1B 5N4
613/748-5653, Fax: 613/748-5644
Executive Director, Tom MacWilliam
President, David Bell
1st Vice-President, David Arsenault
Publications: First Service; Premier Service, q.
Affiliates: Canadian Sport Council; Canadian Olympic Association; Coaching Association of Canada

**Canadian Rhythmic Sportive Gymnastic Federation/Fédération canadienne de gymnastique rythmique sportive (CRSGF) (1970)**
Place R. Tait McKenzie, 1600 James Naismith Dr., Ottawa, ON K1B 5N4
613/748-5654, Fax: 613/748-5761, Telex: SPORTREC OTT 05
President, John Biggs
Publications: Techtalk

**Canadian School Sports Federation/Fédération canadienne du sport scolaire**
#218, 11 Victoria St., Barrie, ON L4N 6T3
705/739-7888, Fax: 705/739-7176
President, Colin Hood

**Canadian Ski Association/Association canadienne de ski**
PO Box 33, Priddis, AB T0L 1W0
403/520-4208, Fax: 403/931-4219
Executive Director, Neil MacDonald
President, Jim Gardner

**Canadian Ski Council/Conseil canadien du ski (CSC) (1977)**
#36, 7035 Fir Tree Dr., Mississauga, ON L5S 1V6
905/677-0020, Fax: 905/677-2055, Email: canski@interlog.com, URL: http://www.skicanada.org
President, Colin S. Chedore
Publications: Ski Focus
Affiliates: Canadian Association for Disabled Skiing; Canadian Association of Nordic Ski Instructors; Canadian Ski Area Operators' Association; Canadian Ski Association; Canadian Ski Instructors' Alliance; Canadian Ski Coaches Federation; Canadian Ski Patrol System; Canadian Association of Snowboard Instructors; National Ski Industries Association

**Canadian Ski Instructors' Alliance (CSIA) (1938)**
#310, 774, boul Décarie, Montréal, QC H4L 3L5
514/748-2648, Fax: 514/748-2476
Executive Director, André Derome
Publications: Ski-Pro
Affiliates: International Ski Instructors Association

**Canadian Ski Marathon/Marathon canadien de ski (CSM) (1967)**
CP 400, Gatineau, QC J8P 6T9
819/669-7383, Fax: 819/722-0666
President, Christopher Busby
Publications: Entry Brochure; Essential Information Bulletin; Results Brochure

**Canadian Ski Media Association/Association canadienne des journalistes de ski**
7 Macleod St., Ottawa, ON K2P 0Z4
613/230-4126
Guy Thibaudeau, Bus: 514/226-7258

**Canadian Ski Patrol System/Organisation de la patrouille canadienne de ski (CSPS) (1941)**
4531 Southclark Pl., PO Box 921, Ottawa, ON K1G 3N3
613/822-2245, Fax: 613/822-1088, Email: cspshq@ican.net
Executive Director, John Leu
National President, Ron Gathercole
Manager, Renée Scanlon
Publications: Sweep

**Canadian Soccer Association/Association canadienne de soccer (1912)**
c/o Place Soccer Canada, 237 Metcalfe St., Ottawa, ON K2P 1R2
613/237-7678, Fax: 613/237-1516
COO, Kevan Pipe
President, Terry Quinn

**ALBERTA SOCCER ASSOCIATION**
Commonwealth Stadium, 1100 Stadium Rd., Edmonton, AB T5H 4E2
403/474-2200, Fax: 403/474-6300, Telex: 037-41708
Executive Director, Gary Sampley
Publications: Soccer Express

**BRITISH COLUMBIA SOCCER ASSOCIATION**
1126 Douglas Rd., Burnaby, BC V5C 4Z6
604/299-6401, Fax: 604/299-9610
Contact, Alex Kemp

**FÉDÉRATION QUÉBÉCOISE DE SOCCER FOOTBALL (FQSF) (1911)**
**Soccer Québec**
4545, av Pierre-de-Coubertin, CP 1000, Succ. M, Montréal, QC H1V 3R2
514/252-3068, Téléc: 514/252-3162
Secrétaire général, Jean Gandubert
Publications: Québec Soccer

**MANITOBA SOCCER ASSOCIATION**
200 Main St., Winnipeg, MB R3C 4M2
204/985-4139, Fax: 204/985-4028
Executive Director, David Kerr

**NEWFOUNDLAND SOCCER ASSOCIATION**
PO Box 21029, St. John's, NF A1A 5B2
709/576-0601, Fax: 709/576-0588
Executive Director, Andrew Cameron
Publications: Kickoff

**ONTARIO SOCCER ASSOCIATION**
#606, 1185 Eglinton Ave. East, North York, ON M3C 3C6
416/426-7300, Fax: 416/426-7313, Telex: 06-986157
Executive Director, Brian Avey

**PEI SOCCER ASSOCIATION (PEISA)**
Confederation Court Mall, Lower Level, PO Box 1863, Charlottetown, PE C1A 7N5
902/368-6251, Fax: 902/368-6251
President, John Diamond

Secretary/Registrar, Daphne Andrews
Treasurer, Wendy Ripley
Office Manager, Anne Matheson

**SASKATCHEWAN SOCCER ASSOCIATION INC.**
1870 Lorne St., Regina, SK S4P 2L7
306/780-9225, Fax: 306/781-6021

**SOCCER NEW BRUNSWICK**
79 Hazen Ave., Renforth, NB E2H 1N9
506/849-4183, Fax: 506/849-4895
President, Alex Savoie

**SOCCER NOVA SCOTIA**
5516 Spring Garden Rd., 4th Fl., Halifax, NS B3J 3G6
902/425-5606
President, Peter Rogers
Publications: Spotlight on Soccer

## Canadian Society for Exercise Physiology/ Société canadienne de physiologie de l'exercice (CSEP) (1967)
#202, 185 Somerset St. West, Ottawa, ON K2P 0J2
613/234-3755, Fax: 613/234-3565
Executive Director, William Hearst
President, Hélène Perrault, Ph.D.
Publications: Canadian Journal of Applied Physiology
Affiliates: Canadian Fitness & Lifestyle Research Institute; Canadian Physiotherapy Association - Cardio-Respiratory Division; Canadian Association of Cardiac Rehabilitation; American College of Sports Medicine

## Canadian Society for Psychomotor Learning & Sport Psychology/Société canadienne du apprentissage psycho-motrice et psychologie du sport (SCAPPS) (1970)
Faculty of Kinesiology, University of Calgary, Calgary, AB T2N 1N4
403/220-3428, Fax: 403/289-9117, Email: tegabrie@acs.ucalgary.ca, URL: http://www.scapps.org
Sec.-Treas., Dr. T. Gabriele
President, Dr. J. Deakin
Publications: Newsletter
Affiliates: International Society of Sport Psychology

## Canadian Special Olympics Inc./Jeux olympiques spéciaux du Canada inc. (1969)
#209, 40 St. Clair Ave. West, Toronto, ON M4V 1M2
416/927-9050, Fax: 416/927-8475, Email: solympic@inforamp.net, URL: http://www.incontext.ca/cso/index.html
President, Jim Jordan
Executive Vice-President, Frank Selke
Chairman of the Board, Brian Etherington
Publications: National Office Bulletin
Affiliates: Special Olympics International

**ALBERTA SPECIAL OLYMPICS INC. (1980)**
Percy Page Centre, 11759 Groat Rd., Edmonton, AB T5M 3K6
403/453-8520, Fax: 403/453-8553
Executive Director, Dave Keating
President, Hans Tiedemann

**BRITISH COLUMBIA SPECIAL OLYMPICS (BCSO) (1980)**
#226, 1367 West Broadway, Vancouver, BC V6H 4A7
604/737-3078, Fax: 604/737-6043
Executive Director, Dan Howe
Publications: Newsletter

**MANITOBA SPECIAL OLYMPICS (1980)**
200 Main St., 4th Fl., Winnipeg, MB R3C 4M2
204/925-5628, Fax: 204/925-5635
Executive Director, Maureen Dowds
Publications: On Your Mark

**NEW BRUNSWICK SPECIAL OLYMPICS**
#207, 390 King St., Fredericton, NB E3B 1E3
506/459-3999
Program Director, Jennifer Bent

**NEWFOUNDLAND & LABRADOR SPECIAL OLYMPICS (1986)**
#201, 102 - 104 LeMarchant Rd., St. John's, NF A1C 2H2
709/738-1923, Fax: 709/238-0119
Executive Director, Michael J. Walsh

**NOVA SCOTIA SPECIAL OLYMPICS**
5516 Spring Garden Rd., PO Box 3010, Stn Parklane Cntr, Halifax, NS B3J 3G6
902/425-5450, Fax: 902/425-5606
Executive Director, Geraldine Dowling

**ONTARIO SPECIAL OLYMPICS (OSO) (1980)**
#503, 1185 Eglinton Ave. East, North York, ON M3C 3C6
416/426-7277, Fax: 416/426-7341, Toll Free: 1-888-333-5515
Executive Director, Glenn MacDonell
President, Mary Matthews
Publications: Torch

**PEI SPECIAL OLYMPICS (1987)**
PO Box 841, Charlottetown, PE C1A 7L9
902/368-4543, Fax: 902/368-4542
Executive Director, Angela Marchbank
President, Elmer Williams
Secretary, Florence Birch

**SASKATCHEWAN SPECIAL OLYMPICS SOCIETY**
353 Broad St., Regina, SK S4R 1X2
306/780-9247, Fax: 306/780-9441
Executive Director, Pat Stellek

**YUKON SPECIAL OLYMPICS (1981)**
PO Box 4007, Whitehorse, YT Y1A 3S9
867/668-6511, Fax: 867/667-4237
Executive Director, Renée Hartling
Publications: Rendezvous; Special Olympic News, 3 pa
Affiliates: Special Olympics International

## Canadian Sport Council/Conseil canadien du sport (1951)
#301A, 1600 James Naismith Dr., Gloucester, ON K1B 5N4
613/748-5670, Fax: 613/748-5732, Telex: 053-3660
Managing Partner, Deborah Evans
Managing Partner, Sandy Johnson
Publications: Sports Directory/Répertoire des sports; Coast to Coast, 4-6 pa

**SASK SPORT INC.**
1870 Lorne St., Regina, SK S4P 2L7
306/780-9302, Fax: 306/781-6021
Assistant General Manager, Paul Barnby
President, Dorothy Josephson
Program Manager, John Lee

**SPORT BC (1966)**
#509, 1367 Broadway West, Vancouver, BC V6H 4A9
604/737-3005, Fax: 604/737-3097, Info Line: 604/737-3000
Email: brenda_kent@sport.bc.ca, URL: http://www.sport.bc.ca/SportBC/
Executive Director, Sandra Stevenson, Email: sandra_stevenson@sport.bc.ca
Chair, Jim Carter

**SPORT MANITOBA (1996)**
200 Main St., Winnipeg, MB R3C 4M2
204/925-5605, Fax: 204/925-5916
Email: info@sport.mb.ca, URL: http://www.sport.mb.ca
President & CEO, Jeff Hnatiuk
Publications: Sport Report

**SPORT NEW BRUNSWICK/SPORT NOUVEAU-BRUNSWICK (SNB) (1968)**
#103, 565 Priestman St., Fredericton, NB E3B 5X8
506/451-1320, Fax: 506/451-1325
President, Harold Nicholson
Contact, Kathleen MacFarlane
Publications: Initiatives

**SPORT NEWFOUNDLAND & LABRADOR (1972)**
PO Box 8700, Stn A, St. John's, NF A1B 4J6
709/576-4932, Fax: 709/576-7493
President, Bill Halfyard
Administrative Officer, Lynn Hindy

**SPORT NORTH FEDERATION**
PO Box 336, Yellowknife, NT X1A 2N3
867/873-3032, Fax: 867/920-4047
Executive Director, David Hurley
President, Jean Hinton

**SPORT NOVA SCOTIA (1974)**
PO Box 3010, Stn South, Halifax, NS B3J 3G6
902/425-5450, Fax: 902/425-5606
Email: sportns@fox.nstn.ca, URL: http://fox.nstn.ca/~sportns/
Executive Director, Scott Logan
President, Bill Greenlaw
Publications: Amateur Sport Update

**SPORT ONTARIO (1969)**
1185 Eglinton Ave. East, North York, ON M3C 3C6
416/426-7310
Chairperson, Dr. Susan Vial
Publications: For the Love of Sport

**SPORT PEI INC. (1973)**
PO Box 302, Charlottetown, PE C1A 7K7
902/368-4110, Fax: 902/368-4548
Executive Director, David MacNeill
President, Mike Conroy
Public Relations Coordinator, Cy Yard
Sports Marketing & Development Officer, Kim Griffin
Publications: The Communicator; Island Sport Scene, q.; The Island Sport Directory, a.

**SPORT YUKON**
4061 - 4th Ave., Whitehorse, YT Y1A 1H1
867/668-4236, Fax: 867/667-4237
Executive Director, Vern Haggard
President, George Arcand

**SPORTS QUÉBEC**
**Société de sports du Québec**
4545, av Pierre-du-Coubertin, CP 1000, Succ. M, Montréal, QC H1V 3R2
514/252-3114, Téléc: 514/254-9621
Directeur général, Luc Gélineau

## Canadian Sport & Fitness Administration Centre/ Centre canadien d'administration du sport et de la condition physique (CSFAC) (1970)
#203, 1600 James Naismith Dr., Gloucester, ON K1B 5N4
613/747-2900, Fax: 613/748-5706, URL: http://www.cdnsport.ca/
President, Wilf Wedmann
Chief Operating Officer, Sue Killam
Vice-President, Business Affairs, John Restivo

## Canadian Sporting Arms & Ammunition Association (CSAAA) (1973)
PO Box 235, Cobourg, ON K9A 4K5
905/373-1623, Fax: 905/373-1706, Email: showgun@eagle.ca, URL: http://www.eagle.ca/showgun
Executive Director, René J.J. Roberge
Publications: Shooting Sports Today; Canadian Hunting & Shooting Sport Trade Magazine, a.

### Canadian Swimming Coaches Association (1991)
1950 Cedar Cres., Vancouver, BC V6J 2R6
Paul McKinnon

### Canadian Tennis Association/Association canadienne de tennis (1890)
**Tennis Canada**
3111 Steeles Ave. West, Downsview, ON M3J 3H2
416/665-9777, Fax: 416/665-9017, Email: commnctn@tenniscanada.com, URL: http://www.tenniscanada.com
Chair, Jacqueline Boutet
President & CEO, Robert H. Moffatt

#### ALBERTA TENNIS ASSOCIATION (1973)
**Tennis Alberta**
Percy Page Centre, 11759 Groat Rd., Edmonton, AB T5M 3K6
403/453-8611, Fax: 403/453-8553
Email: tennisab@oanet.com
Executive Director, Catherine Over
Publications: Volley
Affiliates: Alberta Games Council

#### FÉDÉRATION QUÉBÉCOISE DE TENNIS/QUÉBEC TENNIS FEDERATION (1899)
285, Faillon ouest, Montréal, QC H2R 2W1
514/270-6060, Téléc: 514/270-2700
Directeur général, Jean François Manibal
Président, Réjean Genois
Publications: Tennis-Mag

#### NATIONAL CAPITAL TENNIS ASSOCIATION
1 Donald St., Ottawa, ON K1K 4E6
613/742-7559
Office Manager, Beverley Verney
Publications: NCTA News

#### NEWFOUNDLAND & LABRADOR TENNIS ASSOCIATION
Provincial Recreation Centre, PO Box 8700, St. John's, NF A1B 4J6
709/576-0902, Fax: 709/576-7493
Executive Director, Rick Kirby

#### NOVA SCOTIA TENNIS ASSOCIATION
5516 Spring Garden Rd., Halifax, NS B3J 1G6
902/425-5450, Fax: 902/423-0574
Executive Director, Kevin Reidy

#### ONTARIO TENNIS ASSOCIATION (OTA) (1918)
#412, 1185 Eglinton Ave. East, North York, ON M3C 3C6
416/426-7135, Fax: 416/426-7353, Toll Free: 1-800-387-5066
Executive Director, Peter Budreo
President, Pam Olley
Publications: Ontario Tennis; Ontario Tennis Yearbook & Tournament Schedule, s-a.
Affiliates: International Tennis Federation

#### PEI TENNIS ASSOCIATION
5 Wyndwood Cres., Charlottetown, PE C1A 8S2
902/566-5051, Fax: 902/628-1514
Executive Director, Linda Durling

#### SASKATCHEWAN TENNIS ASSOCIATION
**Tennis Saskatchewan**
2205 Victoria Ave., Regina, SK S4P 0S4
306/780-9410, Fax: 306/525-4009
Executive Director, Rory Park
Publications: Court Talk
Affiliates: Sasksport

#### TENNIS BC (1978)
#204, 1367 Broadway West, Vancouver, BC V6H 4A7
604/737-3086, Fax: 604/737-6043
Email: tbc@tennis.bc.ca, URL: http://www.tennis.bc.ca
Executive Director, Tom Fawsitt
Publications: Match Point

#### TENNIS MANITOBA (1881)
**Manitoba Tennis Association**
#303, 200 Main St., Winnipeg, MB R3C 4M2
204/925-5660, Fax: 204/925-5663
Email: tennismb@escape.ca, URL: http://www.escape.ca/~tennismb
CEO, Mark Farand
Publications: Toba Tennis News

#### TENNIS NEW BRUNSWICK
PO Box 549, Moncton, NB E1C 8L9
506/853-7578, Fax: 506/857-8240
Program Director, Phyllis Cairns

### Canadian Tenpin Federation Inc./Fédération canadienne des dix quilles Inc.
530 Home St., Winnipeg, MB R3G 1X7
204/783-7453, Fax: 204/786-4856
President, Paul Foster
Sec.-Treas., Adrianne Bride
Affiliates: Fédération internationale des quilleurs

### Canadian Therapeutic Riding Association/Association canadienne d'équitation thérapeutique (1981)
**CanTRA**
PO Box 24009, Guelph, ON N1E 6V8
519/767-0700, Fax: 519/767-0435
President, Carol Morrison
Publications: CANTRA Caller

### Canadian Trotting Association
2150 Meadowvale Blvd., Mississauga, ON L5N 6R6
905/858-3060, Fax: 905/858-3111
Executive Director, Tom Gorman
Publications: Trot

### Canadian Weightlifting Federation/Fédération haltérophile canadienne
755, Croissant Savard, Longueuil, QC J4X 1X9
514/466-4476, Fax: 514/931-6868
President, Philippe Saint-Cyr
General Manager, Dan Steinwald
Affiliates: International Weightlifting Federation

### Canadian Wheelchair Basketball Association/Association Canadienne de Basketball en Fauteuil Roulant (CWBA) (1994)
#715, 1600 James Naismith Dr., Gloucester, ON K1B 5N4
613/748-5888, Fax: 613/748-5889, URL: http://www.cwba.ca/
Executive Director, Reg McClellan
President, Maureen Orchard
Publications: Communiqué; Give & Go/Passe et Va, bi-weekly

### Canadian Wheelchair Sports Association/Association canadienne des sports en fauteuil roulant (CWSA) (1967)
#212A, 1600 James Naismith Dr., Gloucester, ON K1B 5N4
613/748-5685, Fax: 613/748-5722, Email: cwsa@bpg.ca, URL: http://indie.ca/cwsa/
Director General, Clare Gillespie
President, Laurel Crosby
Affiliates: International Stoke Mandeville Wheelchair Sports Federation

### Coaching Association of Canada/Association canadienne des entraîneurs (CAC) (1971)
#604, 1600 James Naismith Dr., Gloucester, ON K1B 5N4
613/748-5624, Fax: 613/748-5707, Email: coach@coach.ca, URL: http://www.coach.ca/
President, Dr. Geoff R. Gowan
Vice-President, Technical, John Bales
Chairman, Ken Bellemare
Communications Director, Carole Slight
Affiliates: Professional Arm: Canadian Professional Coaches Association

### The Commonwealth Games Association of Canada Inc./Association canadienne des jeux du Commonwealth inc. (CGAC) (1977)
#105, 1600 James Naismith Dr., Gloucester, ON K1B 5N4
613/748-5625, Fax: 613/748-5781
President, Judy Kent
Affiliates: Commonwealth Games Federation - London, England

### Cross Country Canada/Ski de fond Canada
#407, 1600 James Naismith Dr., Gloucester, ON K1B 5N4
613/748-5662, Fax: 613/748-5703
Executive Director, Neil MacDonald
President, Guy Laviolette
Affiliates: Canadian Ski Association

### Dr. James Naismith Basketball Foundation/La Fondation du Basket-Ball Dr James Naismith
1 James Naismith Way, PO Box 1991, Almonte, ON K0A 1A0
613/256-0492, Fax: 613/256-0492
Honourary President, Jack Donahue

### Equestrian Association for the Disabled (TEAD) (1978)
6095 Dickenson Rd., RR#2, Hannon, ON L0R 1P0
905/679-8323, Fax: 905/679-1705
Program Director/Instructor, Hilary Webb
Publications: Rocking Horse Review
Affiliates: Ontario Therapeutic Riding Association

### Federation of Canadian Archers Inc./Fédération canadienne des archers inc. (FCA) (1927)
#211, 1600 James Naismith Dr., Gloucester, ON K1B 5N4
613/748-5604, Fax: 613/748-5785, Telex: 053-3660, Toll Free: 1-800-511-9999, Email: brian.macpherson@cdnsport.ca
Executive Director, Brian MacPherson
President, Al Wills
Technical Director, Pascal Colmaire
Affiliates: Federation internationale de tir à l'arc; Canadian Olympic Association

### Fédération d'Haltérophilie du Québec/Québec Weightlifting Federation (FHQ) (1969)
4545, av Pierre-de-Coubertin, CP 1000, Succ. M, Montréal, QC H1V 3R2
514/252-3046, Téléc: 514/254-4545
Directeur technique, Augustin Brassard
Publications: Coup d'oeil sur l'halterophilie

### Fédération de patinage artistique du Québec (FPAQ)
4545, av Pierre-de-Coubertin, CP 1000, Succ. M, Montréal, QC H1V 3R2
514/252-3073, Téléc: 514/252-3170
Directrice executive, Anita Choquet

### Fédération du plongeon amateur du Québec (FPAQ) (1971)
4545, av Pierre-de-Coubertin, CP 1000, Succ. M, Montréal, QC H1V 3R2
514/252-3096, Téléc: 514/252-3094, Courrier électronique: plongeon@mlink.ca, URL: http://www.cigp.com/atlanta/federati/plongeon/
Directeur exécutif, Donald Normand
Publications: La Vrille

**Fédération québécoise du sport étudiant (FQSE) (1988)**
4545, av Pierre-De Coubertin, CP 1000, Succ. M, Montréal, QC H1V 3R2
514/252-3300, Téléc: 514/254-3292
Directeur général, Jean Hamel
Président, Michel Carrières

**Fédération de rugby du Québec**
4545, av Pierre-de-Coubertin, CP 1000, Succ. M, Montréal, QC H1V 3R2
514/341-6780, Téléc: 514/341-7699
Secrétaire, Simon Davies

**Field Hockey Canada/Hockey sur gazon Canada**
#206, 1600 James Naismith Dr., Gloucester, ON K1B 5N4
613/748-5634, Fax: 613/748-5790, Email: fieldhockey@bpg.ca, URL: http://www.cyberus.ca/~fieldhockey/
President, Janet Ellis
Senior Manager, Suzzanne Nicholson
Affiliates: Fédération internationale de hockey

**Football Canada (CAFA) (1882)**
**Canadian Amateur Football Association**
Lansdowne Park Civic Centre, 1015 Bank St., Ottawa, ON K1S 3W7
613/564-2675, Fax: 613/564-6309
Executive Director, Jack Jordan
President, Joe Pistilli

**Gymnastics Canada Gymnastique**
#510, 1600 James Naismith Dr., Gloucester, ON K1B 5N4
613/748-5637, Fax: 613/748-5691, URL: http://www.capitalnet.com/~chiug/cangym.html
President & CEO, Bill Houldsworth
Publications: Gymnastics Canada
Affiliates: Fédération internationale de gymnastique

**Horse Trials Canada/Concours Complet Canada**
RR#1, Dwight, ON P0A 1H0
705/635-1569
Secretary, Nancy Tapley
Publications: The Eventer

**Jockey Club of Canada**
PO Box 156, Etobicoke, ON M9W 5L2
416/675-7756, Fax: 416/675-6378
Executive Director, Gary Loschke

**Judo Canada (1956)**
**Canadian Kodokan Black Belt Association**
#401, 1600 James Naismith Dr., Ottawa, ON K1B 5N4
613/748-5640, Fax: 613/748-5697, Telex: 053-3660, Email: judo@cdnsport.ca, URL: http://www.ccn.cs.dal.ca/SportFit/JNS/judocan.html
Executive Director, Gary Gardiner
President, Luc Larocque
Publications: Yudansha Journal
Affiliates: International Judo Federation

**Manitoba High Schools Athletic Association (1962)**
200 Main St., Winnipeg, MB R3C 4M2
204/925-5640, Fax: 204/925-5624
Dr. Ron Buzahora
Publications: Pacer
Affiliates: National Federation of State Associations

**National Karate Association of Canada/Association nationale de karaté (1974)**
#230, 2616 - 18 St. NE, Calgary, AB T2E 7R1
250/297-2720, Fax: 250/297-2702
President, Peter Brown

**National Snow Industries Association/Association nationale des industries de la neige (NSIA) (1962)**
#810, 245, av Victoria, Montréal, QC H3Z 2M6
514/939-7370, Fax: 514/939-7371, Toll Free: 1-800-263-6742, Email: nsia@netc.net
Executive Director, Anna DiMeglio
Director, Show Services, Carol Hopper

**National Youth Bowling Council**
#10A, 250 Shields Ct., Markham, ON L3R 9W7
905/479-1560, Fax: 905/479-8610
National Administrator, Inge Malcolmson

**Newfoundland & Labrador Curling Association**
PO Box 21238, St. John's, NF A1A 5B2
709/722-1156, Fax: 709/722-1156
Secretary, Eugene Trickett

**Newfoundland & Labrador High School Athletic Federation (NFHSAF) (1969)**
Torbay Airport, Bldg. 25, St. John's, NF A1B 4J6
709/729-2795, Fax: 709/576-7493, Email: krichard@calvin.stemnet.nf.ca
Executive Director, Karen Richard
Publications: High School Sports Group

**Nordic Combined Ski Canada**
#407, 1600 James Naismith Dr., Gloucester, ON K1B 5N4
613/748-5664, Fax: 613/748-5765
Executive & Marketing Director, Jean R. Dupré
Chairman, Bruce Keith

**Nova Scotia School Athletic Federation**
5516 Spring Garden Rd., PO Box 3010, Stn South, Halifax, NS B3J 3G6
902/425-5450, Fax: 902/425-5606
Executive Director, Ron O'Flaherty

**Ontario Federation of School Athletic Associations (OFSAA) (1948)**
11 Victoria St., Barrie, ON L4N 6T3
705/739-7888, Fax: 705/739-7176
Executive Director, Colin Hood
Publications: OFSAA Bulletin
Affiliates: International School Sport Federation; Canadian School Sport Federation; Ontario Physical & Health Education Association; Ontario Coalition of Women in Educational Athletics; National Federation of State High School Associations

**The Ontario Jockey Club**
PO Box 156, Etobicoke, ON M9W 5L2
416/675-6110, Fax: 416/213-2126

**Ontario Ladies' Golf Association (OLGA) (1926)**
#304, 1185 Eglinton Ave. East, North York, ON M3C 3C6
416/426-7090, Fax: 416/426-7379
Executive Director, Honey Crossley

**Ontario Minor Hockey Association (1935)**
#43, 40 Vogell Rd., Richmond Hill, ON L4B 3N6
905/780-6642, Fax: 905/780-0344, URL: http://www.omhahockey.com
President, Mike Hammond
Executive Director, Michael McCauley

**Ontario Sports & Recreation Centre Inc./Centre ontarien des sports et des loisirs inc.**
1185 Eglinton Ave. East, North York, ON M3C 3C6
416/426-7000, Fax: 416/426-7381
General Manager, Guy Bradbury

**PEI Men's Golf Association (PEIGA) (1971)**
PO Box 51, Charlottetown, PE C1A 7K2
902/894-8462, Fax: 902/628-1759
Executive Director, Fred Coady, Bus: 902/368-1177
Publications: PEI Golf Record

**PEI Recreation & Sports Association for the Physically Challenged (PEIRSAPC)**
PO Box 841, Charlottetown, PE C1A 7L9
902/368-4540, Fax: 902/368-4542
Recreation & Sport Consultant, Frank MacIntyre, Bus: 902/368-4540

**PEI School Athletic Association**
c/o Dept. of Education, PO Box 2000, Charlottetown, PE C1A 7N8
President, Walter MacEwen
Sec.-Treas., Clem Gallant
Executive Secretary, Lyall Huggan, Bus: 902/368-4672

**Régie de la sécurité dans les sports du Québec (RSSQ) (1980)**
#302, 100, rue Laviolette, Trois-Rivières, QC G9A 5S9
819/371-6033, Téléc: 819/371-6992
URL: http://www.rssq.gouv.qc.ca
Président, Roger Landry
Publications: Le Sécuritaire

**Ringette Canada/Ringuette Canada (1975)**
#806, 1600 James Naismith Dr., Gloucester, ON K1B 5N4
613/748-5655, Fax: 613/748-5860, Telex: 053-3660 SPORTR, URL: http://www.ringette.ca/
Executive Director, Carolyne Hudson
President, Grant Crawford
Publications: Ringette Review

**Rowing Canada Aviron (RCA)**
**Canadian Amateur Rowing Association**
#716, 1600 James Naismith Dr., Gloucester, ON K1B 5N4
613/748-5656, Fax: 613/748-5712
Executive Director, Alan Roof
President, Joe Grey
Publications: Rowing Canada Aviron
Affiliates: Fédération Internationale des Sociétés d'Aviron

**Royal Canadian Golf Association/Association royale de golf du Canada (RCGA) (1895)**
Golf House, 1333 Dorval Dr., Oakville, ON L6J 4Z3
905/849-9700, Fax: 905/845-7040, Email: golfhous@rcga.org, URL: http://www.rcga.org
Executive Director, Stephen D. Ross
Publications: Golf Canada
Affiliates: World Amateur Golf Council

**ALBERTA GOLF ASSOCIATION (AGA) (1912)**
#104, 4116 - 64 Ave. SE, Calgary, AB T2B 2C3
403/236-4616, Fax: 403/236-2915
Email: altagolf@agt.net
Executive Director, Brent Ellenton
Publications: The AGA Director; The Alberta Golfer, a.

**ASSOCIATION DE GOLF DU QUÉBEC/QUÉBEC GOLF ASSOCIATION (AGQ) (1920)**
CP 399, Pierrefonds, QC H9H 4L1
514/620-6565, Téléc: 514/620-3413
Courrier électronique: golf.quebec@sympatico.ca, URL: http://www.memocard.com/QGA/
Directeur général, Phil Gribbin

**BRITISH COLUMBIA GOLF ASSOCIATION (BCGA) (1922)**
Sperling Plaza 2, #150, 6450 Roberts St., Burnaby, BC V5G 4E1
604/294-1818, Fax: 604/294-1819, Toll Free: 1-888-833-2242
Email: golfbc@bcga.org, URL: http://www.bcga.org
Executive Director, Kris Jonasson

Administrative Manager, Betty Clark
Affiliates: Canadian Golf Foundation; Professional Golf Association of BC; Canadian Ladies Golf Association of BC; Golf Course Superintendents Association of BC; International Association of Golf Administrators; National Golf Foundation; Pacific Coast Golf Association; Pacific Northwest Golf Association

**MANITOBA GOLF ASSOCIATION INC.**
#211, 200 Main St., Winnipeg, MB R3C 4M2
204/925-5730
Executive Director, Don Craig

**NEW BRUNSWICK GOLF ASSOCIATION/ASSOCIATION DE GOLF DU NOUVEAU BRUNSWICK (1934)**
#103, 565 Priestman St., Fredericton, NB E3B 5X8
506/451-1324, Fax: 506/451-1325
Email: nbgolf@nbnet.nb.ca
Executive Director, Steven Young

**NEWFOUNDLAND/LABRADOR GOLF ASSOCIATION**
PO Box 5361, St. John's, NF A1C 5W2
709/754-1090
Contact, Charles Cook

**NOVA SCOTIA GOLF ASSOCIATION (NSGA) (1931)**
14 Limardo Dr., Dartmouth, NS B3A 3X4
902/465-7306, Fax: 902/465-7306
Executive Director, Warren MacDonald

**ONTARIO GOLF ASSOCIATION (OGA) (1923)**
RR#3, Newmarket, ON L3Y 4W1
905/853-8511, Fax: 905/853-0803
Email: golf@netrover.com, URL: http://www.oga.org
Executive Director, Anne Edgar Dodds-Hebron
Publications: Ontario Golf News

**PRINCE EDWARD ISLAND GOLF ASSOCIATION**
PO Box 2245, Charlottetown, PE C1A 8B9
902/894-8462
Executive Director, Fred Coady

**SASKATCHEWAN GOLF ASSOCIATION (1914)**
510 Cynthia St., Saskatoon, SK S7L 7K7
306/975-0834, Fax: 306/242-8007
Executive Director, Bill Taylor
Publications: SGA Newsletter

## Ski Jumping Canada/Saut en ski Canada
#407, 1600 James Naismith Dr., Gloucester, ON K1B 5N4
613/748-5665, Fax: 613/748-5765, URL: http://www.cdnsport.ca/jump
Chairman, Rob McCormack
Executive & Marketing Director, Jean R. Dupré

## Softball Canada (1967)
**Canadian Amateur Softball Association**
#802, 1600 James Naismith Dr., Gloucester, ON K1B 5N4
613/748-5668, Fax: 613/748-5760, Email: softball@rtm.cdnsport.ca, URL: http://www.cdnsport.ca/softball/
CEO, Rick Johnson
President, Dale McMann

## Sport for Disabled - Ontario (SDO)
1185 Eglinton Ave. East, North York, ON M3C 3C6
416/426-7187, Fax: 416/426-7361, Toll Free: 1-800-265-1539, Email: sdoont@osrc.com
Acting Executive Director, Faye Blackwood
Affiliates: Ontario Amputee Sports Association; Ontario Blind Sports Association; Ontario Cerebral Palsy Sports Association; Ontario Wheelchair Sports Association

## Sport Medicine & Science Council of Canada/ Conseil canadien de la médecine sportive (SMCC) (1978)
1600 James Naismith Dr., Gloucester, ON K1B 5N4
613/748-5671, Fax: 613/748-5729
Executive Director, Rick Nickelchok
President, Mike Plyley
Publications: Sport Med Connection; Sport Med Info, q.; SMSCC Directory, a.
Affiliates: Fédération internationale de médecine sportive

## Sports Physiotherapy Division of the Canadian Physiotherapy Association/Groupe de physiothérapie sportive d'Association canadienne de physiothérapie (SPD)
#507, 1600 James Naismith Dr., Gloucester, ON K1B 5N4
613/748-5794, Fax: 613/748-5850
Program Coordinator, Gary Leslie

## Squash Canada (1914)
#603, 1600 James Naismith Dr., Gloucester, ON K1B 5N4
613/748-5672, Fax: 613/748-5861, Email: squash.canada@bpg.ca
General Manager, Richard Bennett
President, Jim McAuliffe
Technical Manager, Linda MacPhail
Publications: Canadian Squash

## Swimming/Natation Canada (1909)
#503, 1600 James Naismith Dr., Gloucester, ON K1B 5N4
613/748-5673, Fax. 613/748-5715, Email: natloffice@swimming.ca, URL: http://www.swimming.ca
CEO, Harold Cliff
Corporate Communications Director, Penny Joyce
Affiliates: Aquatic Federation of Canada

## Synchro Canada/Association canadienne de nage synchronisée amateur
**Canadian Amateur Synchronized Swimming Association**
1600 James Naismith Dr., Gloucester, ON K1B 5N4
613/748-5674, 746-0060, Fax: 613/748-5724
Executive Director, Jost am Rhyn
President, Joan Roberts

## Vélo-Québec
1251, rue Rachel est, Montréal, QC H2J 2J9
514/521-8356, Téléc: 514/521-5711, Ligne sans frais: 1-800-567-8356, Courrier électronique: jean-francois_pronovost@velo.qc.ca, URL: http://www.velo.qc.ca
Directeur général, Jean-François Pronovost
Publications: Le Bulletin de la Route Verte; Info Velo Québec, trimestriel

## Volleyball Canada (1973)
**Canadian Volleyball Association**
#811, 1600 James Naismith Dr., Gloucester, ON K1B 5N4
613/748-5681, Fax: 613/748-5727, Toll Free: 1-800-461-0124, Email: volleyball.canada@cdnsport.ca
Director General, Sylvie Bigras
President, Alan Ahac
Affiliates: International Volleyball Association; Canadian Olympic Association; Coaching Association of Canada

**ALBERTA VOLLEYBALL ASSOCIATION (AVA) (1957)**
Percy Page Centre, 11759 Groat Rd., Edmonton, AB T5M 3K6
403/453-8530, Fax: 403/453-8532
President, Bruce Kirkland
Executive Director, Terry Archer
Publications: Volleyball Today; Volley Notes, q.
Affiliates: Federation of Outdoor Volleyball Associations

**BRITISH COLUMBIA VOLLEYBALL ASSOCIATION (1965)**
#405, 1367 Broadway West, Vancouver, BC V6H 4A9
604/737-3087, Fax: 604/738-7175
Email: bcvolleyball@sport.bc.ca
Executive Director, Tom Caverly

**FÉDÉRATION DE VOLLEY-BALL DU QUÉBEC (FVBQ) (1968)**
**Volleyball Québec**
4545, av Pierre-de-Coubertin, CP 1000, Succ. M, Montréal, QC H1V 3R2
514/252-3065, Téléc: 514/252-3176
Directrice générale, Elaine Lauzon
Président, Raymond Côté
Publications: Smash
Organisation(s) affiliée(s): Sports Québec; Regroupement loisirs Québec

**MANITOBA VOLLEYBALL ASSOCIATION**
200 Main St., Winnipeg, MB R3C 4M2
204/925-5783, Fax: 204/925-5786
Executive Director, Greg Guenther
President, Kolleen Picklyk

**NEWFOUNDLAND & LABRADOR VOLLEYBALL ASSOCIATION**
PO Box 21248, St. John's, NF A1A 5B2
709/576-0817, Fax: 709/576-7493
Program Coordinator, Craig Neil
President, Todd Martin

**NORTHWEST TERRITORIES VOLLEYBALL ASSOCIATION**
c/o Sport North, PO Box 336, Yellowknife, NT X1A 2N3
867/873-3032, Fax: 867/920-4047, Toll Free: 1-800-661-0797
President, Rob Meckling

**ONTARIO VOLLEYBALL ASSOCIATION (OVA) (1929)**
#507, 1185 Eglinton Ave. East, North York, ON M3C 3C6
416/426-7316, Fax: 416/426-7109, Toll Free: 1-800-563-5938
Email: ovavol@osrc.com
Executive Director, Diane Wood
Publications: INFO; True North, bi-m.

**PRINCE EDWARD ISLAND VOLLEYBALL ASSOCIATION**
150 Gardiner St., Summerside, PE C1N 5J2
902/436-3933, Fax: 902/436-0133
President, Freddy Martin
Publications: Tip Off the Block
Affiliates: Sport PEI

**SASKATCHEWAN VOLLEYBALL ASSOCIATION**
1870 Lorne St., Regina, SK S4P 2L7
306/780-9250, Fax: 306/780-9288
Executive Director, Tim Bjornson
Publications: The Scoop

**VOLLEYBALL NEW BRUNSWICK**
PO Box 638, Stn A, Fredericton, NB E3B 5A6
506/458-1386, Fax: 506/452-0986
Director, Judy Hogan

**VOLLEYBALL NOVA SCOTIA**
5516 Spring Garden Rd., Halifax, NS B3J 1G6
902/425-5450, Fax: 902/425-5606
Director, June Lumsden

**VOLLEYBALL YUKON**
4061 - 4th Ave., Whitehorse, YT Y1A 1H1
867/633-4599, Fax: 867/667-4237
Sport Coordinator, Darlene Ries

## Water Polo Canada
#708, 1600 James Naismith Dr., Gloucester, ON K1B 5N4

613/748-5682, Fax: 613/748-5777, Email: susanfh@rtm.cdnsport.ca, URL: http://www.waterpolo.ca
Executive Director, Michel Langelier
President, Victor Tetreault
Publications: Inside 4 Metres
Affiliates: Aquatic Federation of Canada

### Water Ski Canada/Ski nautique Canada
#606B, 1600 James Naismith Dr., Gloucester, ON K1B 5N4
613/748-5683, Fax: 613/748-5867, Telex: 53-3660, URL: http://www.utoronto.ca/ski/water/ca/index.html
Executive Director, Hugh Mitchener
President, Peter Person
Publications: Ski Nautique News

### World University Games/Jeux mondiaux universitaires
c/o Canadian Intervuniversity Athletic Union, #302, 1600 James Naismith Dr., Gloucester, ON K1B 5N4
613/748-5619, Fax: 613/748-5764
Director, Promotions & Communications, Jennifer Brenning

## STANDARDS & TESTING
*see also* Consumers

### Cable Television Standards Foundation/Fondation des normes de télévision par câble (1988)
**Standards Foundation**
#1910, 350 Albert St., Ottawa, ON K1R 1A4
613/230-5442, Fax: 613/230-5679, Toll Free: 1-800-426-4170, URL: http://ctsc.ca
President & CEO, Gérald Lavallée
Affiliates: Canadian Cable Television Association

### Canadian Educational Standards Institute (CESI) (1986)
3 Elm Ave., Toronto, ON M4W 1M8
416/488-2244, Fax: 416/488-1773
Director, Solette N. Gelberg
Publications: CESI Newsletter

### Canadian Evaluation Society/Société canadienne l'évaluation (CES) (1981)
582 Somerset St. West, Ottawa, ON K1R 5K2
613/230-1007, Fax: 613/237-9900, Email: ces@cdnevalsociety.ca, URL: http://www.unites.uqam.ca/ces/ces-sce.html
Executive Secretary, Kathy Jones
President, Linda E. Lee
Publications: CES Newsletter; Canadian Journal of Program Evaluation, s-a.
Affiliates: American Evaluation Society; Australasian Evaluation Society

### Canadian General Standards Board/Office des normes générales du Canada (CGSB) (1934)
#1402, 222 Queen St., Ottawa, ON K1A 1G6
613/941-8709, 8703 (Sales Centre), Fax: 613/941-8706, Toll Free: 1-800-665-2472
Director General, B. Geiger
Chief of Sales Centre, Debra Imre
Publications: Calibre
Affiliates: Canadian Society for Nondestructive Testing, Inc.

### Canadian Society for Nondestructive Testing, Inc./Société canadienne pour essais nondestructifs, inc. (CSNDT) (1964)
#7, 966 Pantera Dr., Mississauga, ON L4W 2S1
905/238-4846, Fax: 905/238-0689, Email: csndt@canlinks.com, URL: http://www.csndt.org
President, Douglas Marshall
Administrator, Angie Giglio
Publications: CSNDT Journal

### Canadian Standards Association/Association canadienne de normalisation (CSA) (1919)
178 Rexdale Blvd., Etobicoke, ON M9W 1R3
416/747-4007, Fax: 416/747-2475, Telex: 06-989344, Toll Free: 1-800-463-6727, URL: http://www.csa.ca/
President/CEO, John E. Kean
Chairman, Robert T.E. Gillespie, P.Eng.
Vice-President, Standards Development, Pat Keindel
Vice-President, Certification & Testing, Pat Paladino
Vice-Chairman, David C. Colville
Vice-President, Marketing, Grant Carter
Vice-President, Finance, Peter Henderson
Vice-President, Corporate Secretary, Thane Crozier
Publications: Information Update
Central Region: 178 Rexdale Blvd., Etobicoke, ON M9W 1R3, 416/747-4044, Fax: 416/747-2475
Eastern Region: Manager, Terry Drew, 865, rue Ellingham, Pointe Claire, QC H9R 5E8, 514/694-8110, Fax: 514/694-5001
Western Region: Operations Manager, James M. Brown, Bus: 403/490-2007, 1707 - 94 St., Edmonton, AB T6N 1E6, 403/450-2111, Fax: 403/461-5322
Pacific Region: Director, Serge F. Bousquet, 13799 Commerce Pkwy., Richmond, BC V6V 2N9, 604/273-4581, Fax: 604/273-5815

### Canadian Toy Testing Council/Conseil canadien d'évaluation des jouets (CTTC) (1952)
22 Hamilton St. North, 2nd Fl., Ottawa, ON K1Y 1B6
613/729-7101, Fax: 613/729-7185
Executive Director, Leigh A. Poirier
Chairperson, Maxine Whelan
Communications/Program Manager, Marie C. Levine
Publications: Toy Report

### Société québécoise d'évaluation de programmes/Québec Society of Program Evaluation (SQEP) (1988)
199, boul Val Cartier, Loretteville, QC G2A 2M8
418/847-9850, Téléc: 418/847-9850
Président, Jean-René Bibeau
Publications: Bulletin de la SQEP

## STEEL & METAL INDUSTRIES

### Association de l'industrie de l'aluminium du Québec (AIAQ)
#1509, 1010, rue Sherbrooke ouest, Montréal, QC H3A 2R7
514/288-4842, Téléc: 514/288-0944
Directeur général, Christian L. Van Houtte

### Canadian Foundry Association/Association des fonderies canadiennes (CFA) (1975)
#405A, 130 Slater St., Ottawa, ON K1P 6E2
613/232-2645, Fax: 613/230-9607
Director, Operations, Judith Arbour, CAE
Publications: Report to Members

### Canadian Institute of Steel Construction/Institut canadien de la construction en acier (CISC) (1942)
#300, 201 Consumers Rd., North York, ON M2J 4G8
416/491-4552, Fax: 416/491-6461, Email: cisc_mike_gilmor@compuserve.com, URL: http://www.cisc-icca.ca
President, Hugh A. Krentz
Affiliates: Canadian Steel Construction Council; Steel Structures Education Foundation

### Canadian Sheet Steel Building Institute/Institut canadien de la tôle d'acier pour le bâtiment (CSSBI) (1961)
#2A, 652 Bishop St. North, Cambridge, ON N3H 4V6
519/650-1285, Fax: 519/650-8081
General Manager, Steven R. Fox

### Canadian Steel Construction Council/Conseil canadien de la construction en acier (CSCC) (1960)
#300, 201 Consumers Rd., North York, ON M2J 4G8
416/491-9898, Fax: 416/491-6461, Email: 76331.1001@compuserve.com
Chairman, H.A. Krentz
Affiliates: Canadian Institute of Steel Construction; Steel Structures Education Foundation

### Canadian Steel Producers Association/L'Association canadienne des producteurs d'acier (CSPA) (1986)
#1425, 50 O'Connor St., Ottawa, ON K1P 6L2
613/238-6049, Fax: 613/238-1832, Email: cspacpa@magmacom.com, URL: http://www.canadiansteel.ca
President, Jean Van Loon
Chairman, John Mayberry
Publications: Steel

### Canadian Steel Service Centre Institute/Institut canadien des centres de service des produits métallurgiques (CSSCI) (1957)
#104, 370 York Blvd., Hamilton, ON L8R 3L1
905/524-1100, Fax: 905/524-5600
President, David R. Roland
Vice-President, Robert J. Miller

### Canadian Steel Trade & Employment Congress
#501, 234 Eglinton Ave. East, Toronto, ON M4P 1K7
416/480-1797, Fax: 416/480-2986
Executive Director, George Nakitsas
Publications: Steel Trade Between the USA & Canada; Newsletter, 3 pa

### Corrugated Steel Pipe Institute/Institut pour tuyaux de tôle ondulée
#2A, 652 Bishop St. North, Cambridge, ON N3H 4V6
519/650-8080, Fax: 519/650-8081
Manager, Steven Fox
Publications: Railways Renew with Corrugated Steel; Timber Resource Roads Save with 'Soil-Steel' Engineering; CSP Void Forms Fill Bridge Overpass Design Requirements; Fully Perforated CSP Key To Disposal of Storm-Water Runoff; Perforated CSP for 'Recharge to Ground' of Storm Water Runoff; Quality Control Guidelines for CSP & SPCSP Products

### Nickel Development Institute (NiDI) (1984)
#510, 214 King St. West, Toronto, ON M5H 3S6
416/591-7999, Fax: 416/591-7987, Telex: 06-218565
President, Michael O. Pearce
Publications: Nickel; Communiqué

### Ontario Sheet Metal & Air Handling Group (1967)
#310, 1110 Sheppard Ave. East, North York, ON M2K 2W2
416/226-5533, Fax: 416/226-9277
Executive Director, William H. Gardner
Publications: Crossflow
Affiliates: Sheet Metal & Air Conditioning Contractors' National Association

### Reinforcing Steel Institute of Canada/Institut d'acier d'armature du Canada (RSIC) (1976)
70 Leek Cres., Richmond Hill, ON L4B 1H1
416/499-4000, ext.28, Fax: 416/499-8752
Publications: Reinforcing Steel Manual of Standard Practice

**INSTITUT D'ACIER D'ARMATURE DU QUÉBEC**
4970, place de la Savane, Montréal, QC H4P 1Z6
514/345-1655, Téléc: 514/739-2409
Contact, André Morin

**WESTERN REINFORCING CONTRACTORS ASSOCIATION**
3636 - 4 Ave. East, Vancouver, BC V5N 1M3
604/294-3766

### Sheet Metal & Air Conditioning Contractors' National Association (SMACNA) (1943)
4201 Lafayette Center Dr., Chantilly, VA 22021-1209 USA
703/803-2989, Fax: 703/803-3732
Executive Vice-President, John W. Sroka
Publications: SMACNews; Technical Manuals & Standards

## SURVEYING & MAPPING

### Association of Ontario Land Economists (1963)
#650, 144 Front St. West, Toronto, ON M5J 1G2
416/340-7818, Fax: 416/979-9159
Office Manager, Mary Sargent
Publications: The Land Economist

### Association québécoise de cartographie (1981)
CP 8684, Ste-Foy, QC G1V 4N6
418/776-2624
Président, Alain Laliberté
Secrétaire trésorier, Michel Dufault
Publications: Revue de carto Québec

### Canadian Cartographic Association/Association canadienne de cartographie (CCA) (1975)
Geography Dept., University of Calgary, 2500 University Dr. NW, Calgary, AB T2N 1N4
403/278-5069, Fax: 403/282-6561, Email: mkrieger@acs.ucalgary.ca
President, Dr. Janet Mersey
Publications: Cartouche; Cartographica, q.
Affiliates: International Cartographic Association

### Canadian Council of Land Surveyors/Conseil canadien des arpenteurs-géomètres (CCLS)
PO Box 5378, Stn Merivale, Ottawa, ON K2C 3J1
613/228-8519, Fax: 613/224-9577
Office Manager, Diane Sims
Sec.-Treas., Gerry Hawryluk
Publications: Focus; Bulletin, q.

**ALBERTA LAND SURVEYORS' ASSOCIATION (ALSA) (1910)**
#2501, 10004 - 104 Ave., Edmonton, AB T5J 0K1
403/428-8805, Fax: 403/429-3374, Toll Free: 1-800-665-2572
Executive Director, Brian Munday
Publications: ALS News

**ASSOCIATION OF MANITOBA LAND SURVEYORS (1881)**
#202, 83 Garry St., Winnipeg, MB R3C 4J9
204/943-6972, Fax: 204/957-7602
Sec.-Treas., Selwyn L. Sanderson
Administrative Assistant, Carol Lee
Publications: Association of Manitoba Land Surveyors Newsletter; The Quarter Post
Affiliates: Canadian Institute of Surveying & Mapping; Western Canadian Board of Examiners for Land Surveyors

**ASSOCIATION OF NEW BRUNSWICK LAND SURVEYORS/ ASSOCIATION DES ARPENTEURS-GÉOMÈTRES DU NOUVEAU-BRUNSWICK (ANBLS) (1954)**
#120, 535 Beaverbrook Ct., Fredericton, NB E3B 1X6
506/458-8266, Fax: 506/458-8267
Email: abbls@m1.net
Sec.-Treas., Douglas E. Morgan
President, Paul E. Ingraham
Publications: Annual Report

**ASSOCIATION OF NEWFOUNDLAND LAND SURVEYORS (1953)**
78 O'Leary Ave., St. John's, NF A1B 2C7
709/722-2031, Fax: 709/722-4104
Email: nfsurvey@thezone.net
Sec.-Treas., Dominic J. Howard
Publications: The Newfoundland Surveyor

**ASSOCIATION OF NOVA SCOTIA LAND SURVEYORS (1951)**
#301, 159 Portland St., Dartmouth, NS B2Y 1H9
902/469-7962, Fax: 902/469-7963
Executive Director, Robert Daniels
Publications: Nova Scotia Surveyor

**ASSOCIATION OF ONTARIO LAND SURVEYORS**
1043 McNicoll Ave., Scarborough, ON M1W 3W6
416/491-9020, Fax: 416/491-2576
Executive Director, Carl J. Rooth

**ASSOCIATION OF PRINCE EDWARD ISLAND LAND SURVEYORS**
PO Box 818, Charlottetown, PE C1A 7L9
902/894-5531, Fax: 902/566-4134
Sec.-Treas., Derek French

**CORPORATION OF LAND SURVEYORS OF THE PROVINCE OF BRITISH COLUMBIA (BCLS) (1905)**
**BC Land Surveyors**
#306, 895 Fort St., Victoria, BC V8W 1H7
250/382-4323, Fax: 250/382-5092
Email: corpbcls@islandnet.com, URL: http://www.islandnet.com/~bclsweb/
Sec.-Treas./Registrar, Gordon McKay Thomson, BCLS
President, Jon M. Magwood
Publications: The Link; Circular Letters, m.
Affiliates: Canadian Institute of Geomatics

**ORDRE DES ARPENTEURS-GÉOMETRES DU QUÉBEC/QUÉBEC LAND SURVEYORS ASSOCIATION (OAGQ) (1882)**
#350, 2954, boul Laurier, Ste-Foy, QC G1V 4T2
418/656-0730, Téléc: 418/656-6352
Président, Jean-Luc Léger
Publications: Arpenteur-Géometre; La Source
Organisation(s) affiliée(s): Fédération des arpenteurs-géometres du Québec

**SASKATCHEWAN LAND SURVEYORS' ASSOCIATION (SLSA) (1910)**
2402 - 2nd Ave., 2nd Fl., Regina, SK S4R 1A6
306/352-8999, Fax: 306/352-8366
Email: slsa@sk.sympatico.ca, URL: http://www.gov.sk.ca/spmc/sgd/sls/slsahome.htm
Executive Director, A. Carl Shiels
Publications: SLSA Newsletter

### Canadian Geophysical Union/Union géophysique canadienne (CGU) (1973)
Biological & Geological Sciences Bldg., Univ. of Western Ontario, London, ON N6A 5B7
519/661-3190, Fax: 519/661-3198, Email: cgu@seis.gp.uwo.ca, URL: http://www.cg.nrcan.gc.ca/cgu/cgu.html
Secretary, David Eaton
President, Larry Mayer
Treasurer, Ron Kurtz
Publications: Elements

### Canadian Institute of Geomatics/Association canadienne des sciences géomatiques (CIG) (1882)
#120, 162 Cleopatra Dr., Ottawa, ON K2G 5X2
613/224-9851, Fax: 613/224-9577, Email: cig-acsg@inasec.ca
Executive Director, Susan Pugh
President, Dave McKellar
Publications: Geomatica
Affiliates: International Federation of Surveyors; International Society for Photogrammetry & Remote Sensing; International Cartographic Association; Commonwealth Association of Canada Lands Surveyors; Canadian Council of Land Surveyors; Canadian Hydrographic Association

### Canadian Institute of Quantity Surveyors
PO Box 124, Stn R, Toronto, ON M4G 3Z3
416/471-0882, Fax: 416/471-7545, Email: information@ciqs.org, URL: http://www.ciqs.org
Executive Director, Lois Metcalfe, Email: exec_dir@ciqs.org
President, E. Stregger, Email: president@ciqs.org
Affiliates: Commonwealth Association of Surveying & Land Economy

### Geomatics Industry Association of Canada/ Association canadienne des entreprises de géomatique (GIAC) (1961)
#1204, 170 Laurier Ave. West, Ottawa, ON K1P 5V5
613/232-8770, Fax: 613/232-4908, Email: giac@globalx.net
President, Ed Kennedy
Chairman, Clark Beattie
Publications: Canadian GIS Source Book

**SUSTAINABLE DEVELOPMENT *see* ENVIRONMENTAL**

## TAXATION
***see also* Finanace**

### Association of Municipal Tax Collectors of Ontario
PO Box 69, Stn A, Toronto, ON M5W 1A2
905/725-0019, URL: http://www.intranet.ca/amtco/
President, Arthur Welsh
Publications: Tax Collectors Journal

### Canadian Federation of Tax Consultants
#502, 161 Eglinton Ave. East, Toronto, ON M4P 1J5
416/488-5404
Jack Poolc

### Canadian Institute of Taxation
Boughton, Peterson, Yang, Anderson, #2500, 1055 Dunsmuir St., PO Box 49290, Vancouver, BC V7X 1S8
604/687-6789, Fax: 604/683-5317

### Canadian Petroleum Tax Society
PO Box 2562, Stn M, Calgary, AB T2P 3K8
Fax: 403/261-6355
Secretary, John Nichol
Publications: Canadian Petroleum Tax Journal

### Canadian Property Tax Association, Inc. (1967)
#225, 6 Lansing Sq., North York, ON M2J 1T5
416/493-3276, Fax: 416/493-3905, Email: cpta@pathcom.com, URL: http://www.cpta.org
National Office Coordinator, Carole Munn
Publications: Communication Update

### Canadian Tax Foundation/Association canadienne d'études fiscales (CTF) (1945)
#1800, One Queen St. East, Toronto, ON M5C 2Y2
416/863-9784, Fax: 416/863-9585, URL: http://www.ctf.ca
Director, Robin J. MacKnight
Secretary, Patricia Hillmer
Treasurer, Brian Horychka
Publications: Canadian Tax Journal; Tax Papers; The National Finances; Canadian Tax Highlights, m.; Tax Memos
Affiliates: Canadian Bar Association; Canadian Institute of Chartered Accountants

Québec: Directrice régionale, Louise Beaugrand-Champagne, #2935, 1250, boul René-Lévesque ouest, Montréal, QC H3B 4W8, 514/939-6323, Téléc: 514/939-7353

**Canadian Taxpayers Federation - Ontario**
Manulife Centre, 55 Bloor St. West, PO Box 19518, Toronto, ON M4W 3T9
705/277-9429, Fax: 705/277-9430, Toll Free: 1-800-265-0442, Email: taxpayer@oncomdis.on.ca
Executive Director, Paul Pagnuelo
Affiliates: Canadian Taxpayers Federation

**Canadian Taxpayers Federation - Saskatchewan (CTF) (1989)**
#105, 438 Victoria Ave. East, Regina, SK S4N 0N7
306/352-7199, Fax: 306/352-7203, Toll Free: 1-800-667-7933, Email: adolter@sk.sympatico.ca
Executive Director, Moira Wright
Research Associate, Mark Lee
Publications: The Taxpayer
Affiliates: Alberta Taxpayers Association; British Columbia Taxpayers Association; Manitoba Taxpayers Association; Ontario Taxpayers Federation; Saskatchewan Taxpayers Association

**Taxpayers Coalition - Niagara (TCN) (1990)**
70 St. Paul St. West, PO Box 86, St Catharines, ON L2R 6R4
905/688-3713, Fax: 905/688-6454
Contact, Frank Sheehan

**TEACHING *see* EDUCATION**

**TECHNOLOGY *see* ENGINEERING & TECHNOLOGY**

## TELECOMMUNICATIONS
***see also* Broadcasting**

**Air Force Telecom Association (AFTA) (1985)**
PO Box 2058, Kingston, ON K7L 5J8
613/549-3582, Fax: 613/549-4557
Chairman, Capt. H.F. Huggins
Sec.-Treas., Sgt. R.A. Koopman
Publications: Newsletter

**Association des câblodistributeurs du Québec inc. (ACQ) (1974)**
#002, 1755, boul René-Lévesque est, Montréal, QC H2K 4P6
514/525-1083, Téléc: 514/525-1186
Directrice générale, Lysline Parenteau
Publications: Tête de ligne

**Association of Competitive Telecommunications Suppliers (ACTS)**
#1105, 191 The West Mall, Etobicoke, ON M9C 5K8
416/620-5393, Fax: 416/620-5392
President, Don Braden

**Canadian Association of Message Exchanges, Inc./Association canadienne d'échange de messages, inc. (CAM-X) (1964)**
37 Park Rd. South, PO Box 373, Grimsby, ON L3M 4H8
905/309-0224, Fax: 905/309-0225
Manager, Barbara Clausen
Publications: Cam-X Communiqué

**Canadian Business Telecommunications Alliance/L'Alliance canadienne des télécommunications de l'entreprise (CBTA) (1962)**
Canada Trust Tower, Box 705, #3650, 161 Bay St., Toronto, ON M5J 2S1
416/865-9993, Fax: 416/865-0859, Toll Free: 1-800-668-2282, Email: cbta@inforamp.net, URL: http://www.telecon.ca
Executive Director, Patrick M. Daly
Chairman/CEO, Majid Shahidi
President, Douglas Robson
General Manager & Controller, Alan E. Gaffen, B.Sc., CGA
Publications: Contact; Direct Line, m.; Making the Connections; Canadian Telecom Alert

**Canadian Independent Telephone Association/Association canadienne du téléphone indépendant (CITA) (1938)**
c/o CEM, 55 Vansco Rd., Toronto, ON M8Z 5Z8
416/259-7308, Fax: 416/259-2053
General Manager, Margi Taylor
Publications: CITA Communicator

**Canadian Institute for Telecommunications Research/Institut canadien de recherches en télécommunications (CITR) (1990)**
Department of Electrical Engineering, McGill University, #633, 3480 University St., Montréal, QC H3A 2A7
514/398-7475, Fax: 514/398-3127, URL: http://www.citr.ee.mcgill.ca
President, Dr. Maier Blostein
Network Manager, Lynn-Marie Holland, Email: lynn@citr.ee.mcgill.ca

**Canadian Telecommunications Consultants Association (CTCA) (1985)**
#604, 3 Church St., Toronto, ON M5E 1M2
416/860-1774, Fax: 416/862-0315, Toll Free: 1-800-463-2569, Email: office@ctca.ca, URL: http://www.ctca.ca
President, Betty Hodkinson, Bus: 416/594-2015

**Canadian Wireless Telecommunications Association/Association canadienne des télécommunications sans fil (CWTA) (1970)**
#2004, 275 Slater St., Ottawa, ON K1P 5H9
613/233-4888, Fax: 613/233-2032, URL: http://www.cwta.ca
President/CEO, Roger Poirier
Chairman, Frank Maw
Publications: Wireless Telecom

**Frequency Co-ordination System Association/Association pour la coordination des fréquences (FCSA) (1983)**
#700, One Nicholas St., Ottawa, ON K1N 7B7
613/241-3080, Fax: 613/241-9632, Email: lburns.fcsa@sympatico.ca
General Manager/Sec.-Treas., J. Burns
President, D.W. Varey
Vice-President, G. Nedoborski
Publications: Microwave Radio Catalog

**International Interactive Communications Society - Toronto Chapter (IICS) (1986)**
c/o Tayson Information Technology Inc., 275 Comstock, Scarborough, ON M1L 2H2
416/288-0550, Fax: 416/285-4395, Email: iics@tayson.com, URL: http://www.tayson.com/iics/
President, Peter Richardson
Publications: www.iics.org

**Ontario Cable Telecommunications Association**
#1304, 2025 Sheppard Ave. East, North York, ON M2J 1V6
416/498-1515, Fax: 416/498-1559
Executive Director, Roy O'Brien
Publications: CableOntario

**Telecommunications Research Institute of Ontario (TRIO) (1988)**
36 Steacie Dr., Kanata, ON K2K 2A9
613/592-9211, Fax: 613/592-8163, Email: telecom@trio.ca, URL: http://www.trio.ca/
President, Peter Leach
Director of Operations, Marc Diguer
Publications: TRIO Network

**TELEVISION *see* BROADCASTING**

**TENANTS & LANDLORDS *see* HOUSING**

**TESTING *see* STANDARDS & TESTING**

**TEXTILES *see* FASHION & TEXTILES**

**THIRD WORLD *see* INTERNATIONAL COOPERATION/INTERNATIONAL RELATIONS**

## TOURISM & TRAVEL

**Accommodation Motel Ontario Association (AMOA) (1949)**
**Motels Ontario**
347 Pido Rd., RR#6, Peterborough, ON K9J 6X7
705/745-4982, Fax: 705/745-4983, Toll Free: 1-800-461-1972, Email: motels@oncomdis.on.ca, URL: http://www.motelsontario.on.ca
President, Bruce M. Gravel
Publications: Newsline; Accommodator, q.; Buyers Guide/Member Directory, a.
Affiliates: Accommodation Canada; Canadian Federation of Independent Business; Canadian Tourism Research Institute; Tourism Federation of Ontario

**Alberta League for Environmentally Responsible Tourism (ALERT) (1979)**
PO Box 1288, Rocky Mountain House, AB T0M 1T0
403/845-4667, Fax: 403/845-5377
Contact, Martha Kostuch

**Algoma Kinniwabi Travel Association (1974)**
#1, 553 Queen St. East, Sault Ste Marie, ON P6A 2M3
705/254-4293, Fax: 705/254-4892, Toll Free: 1-800-263-2541
President, Ian McMillan
Publications: Algoma Outdoors

**Almaguin-Nipissing Travel Association (1974)**
**Ontario's Near North**
PO Box 351, North Bay, ON P1B 8H5
705/474-6634, Fax: 705/474-9271, Toll Free: 1-800-387-0516
Executive Director, Ted Day
Publications: Near North Newsletter

**Associated Canadian Travellers**
116 - 16th Ave. NE., Calgary, AB T2E 1J5
403/277-0745, Fax: 403/277-6662
General Manager, Yvette Stewart

**Association of Canadian Travel Agents (ACTA) (1977)**
#201, 1729 Bank St., Ottawa, ON K1V 7Z5
613/521-0474, Fax: 613/521-0805, Email: acta.ntl@sympatico.ca, URL: http://www.acta.net
Executive Director, Terry Ohman
President, Hugh Campbell
Affiliates: Universal Federation of Travel Agency Associations

**ASSOCIATION OF CANADIAN TRAVEL AGENTS - ALBERTA (ACTA - ALBERTA) (1977)**
625 - 25 Ave. NE, Calgary, AB T2E 1Y6

403/277-9445
Email: waym@cia.com
Contact, Jona Way
Publications: ACTA Advisor

**ASSOCIATION OF CANADIAN TRAVEL AGENTS - ATLANTIC (ACTA - ATLANTIC) (1976)**
**Atlantic Travel Industry Conference**
#423, 1800 Argyle St., PO Box 3131, Stn Halifax South, Halifax, NS B3J 3N8
902/422-7311, Fax: 902/492-5657
Email: andread@fox.nstn.ca
Contact, Andrea Davidson
Publications: News & Views

**ASSOCIATION OF CANADIAN TRAVEL AGENTS - BRITISH COLUMBIA (ACTA - BC)**
#905, 850 West Hastings St., Vancouver, BC V6C 1E1
604/688-0516, Fax: 604/688-6056
Executive Director, Glen Steeves
Publications: ACTA BC Communicates

**ASSOCIATION OF CANADIAN TRAVEL AGENTS - MANITOBA (1978)**
#17, 399 Berry St., Winnipeg, MB R3J 1N6
204/831-0831, Fax: 204/885-3764
Contact, Veronica Lopez
Publications: Travel Talk

**ASSOCIATION OF CANADIAN TRAVEL AGENTS - ONTARIO (OTIC) (1974)**
#4020, 3080 Yonge St., Toronto, ON M4N 3N1
416/488-2282, Fax: 416/488-2686, Toll Free: 1-888-257-2282
Executive Director, Marion Graber

**ASSOCIATION OF CANADIAN TRAVEL AGENTS - QUÉBEC/ ASSOCIATION DES AGENTS DE VOYAGES DU QUÉBEC (ACTA-QUÉBEC)**
#6600, 515, rue Ste-Catherine ouest, CP 8000, Succ. Centre Ville, Montréal, QC H3C 3L4
514/987-8733, Téléc: 514/987-3571
Contact, Louise Hodder

**ASSOCIATION OF CANADIAN TRAVEL AGENTS - SASKATCHEWAN**
122 Wood Cres., PO Box 1149, Assiniboia, SK S0H 0B0
306/642-5500, Fax: 306/642-4700
Contact, Judy Silzer
Publications: Saskatchewan

## Association of National Tourist Organization Representatives - Canada
c/o Netherlands Board of Tourism, #710, 25 Adelaide St. East, Toronto, ON M5C 1Y2
416/363-1577, ext.7, Fax: 416/363-1470
President, Jan Zandboer

## Association des terrains de camping du Québec (1962)
**Camping Québec**
#700, 2001, rue de la Metropole, Longueuil, QC J4G 1S9
514/651-7396, Téléc: 514/651-7397, Ligne sans frais: 1-800-363-0457, Courrier électronique: camping@ interlink.net
Vice-président executif, Maryse Catellier

## Associations touristiques régionales associées du Québec/Québec Regional Tourist Associations Inc. (ATRAQ) (1981)
#300, 3333, boul du Souvenir, Laval, QC H7V 1X1
514/686-8358, Téléc: 514/686-9630
Directrice générale, Louise Nadeau
Association touristique de l'Abitibi-Témiscamingue: Directeur général, Louis Laliberte, #103, 170, av Principale, Rouyn-Noranda, QC J9X 4P7, 819/762-8181, Téléc: 819/762-5212, Ligne sans frais: 1-800-808-0706
Association touristique du Bas-Saint-Laurent: 189, rue Hôtel-de-Ville, Rivière-du-Loup, QC G5R 5C4, 418/867-3015, Téléc: 418/867-3245, Ligne sans frais: 1-800-563-5268, Courrier électronique: atrbsl@icrdl.net, URL: http:// www.tourismebas-st-laurent.com
Association Touristique des Cantons-de-l'Est: Directeur général, Alain Larouche; Président, Jacques Robidas, 20, rue Don-Bosco sud, Sherbrooke, QC J1L 1W4, 819/820-2020, Téléc: 819/ 566-4445, Ligne sans frais: 1-800-355-5755, Courrier électronique: ate@multi-medias.ca, URL: http:// www.tourisme-estrie.qc.ca
Association touristique de Charlevoix: 630, boul de Comporté, CP 275, La Malbaie, QC G5A 1T8, 418/ 665-4454, Téléc: 418/665-3811, Ligne sans frais: 1-800-667-2276
Association touristique de Chaudière-Appalaches: 800, autoroute Jean-Lesage, Bernières, QC G7A 1C9, 418/831-4411, Téléc: 418/831-8442, Courrier électronique: atr.ch.app@mercure.net, URL: http://www.chaudapp.qc.ca
Association touristique du Coeur-du-Québec: 1180, rue Royale, 2e étage, Trois-Rivières, QC G9A 4J1, 819/375-1222, Téléc: 819/375-0301, Ligne sans frais: 1-800-567-7603
Association touristique de la Gaspésie: Denis-Paul Bouffard, 357, route de la Mer, Ste-Flavie, QC G0J 2L0, 418/775-2223, Téléc: 418/775-2234, Ligne sans frais: 1-800-463-0323, Courrier électronique: info@tourisme-gaspesie.qc.ca, URL: http://www.tourisme-gaspesie.qc.ca
Association touristique des Îles-de-la-Madeleine: 128, rue Principale, CP 1028, Cap-aux-Meules, QC G0B 1B0, 418/986-2245, Téléc: 418/986-2327, URL: http://www.ilesdelamadeleine.com/ tourisme.htm
Association touristique de Lanaudière: 3643, rue Queen, CP 1210, Rawdon, QC J0K 1S0, 514/834-2535, Téléc: 514/834-8100, Ligne sans frais: 1-800-363-2788, Courrier électronique: info@tourisme-lanaudiere.qc.ca, URL: http://tourisme-lanaudiere.qc.ca
Association touristique des Laurentides: 14142, rue de Lachapelle, RR#1, St-Jérôme, QC J7Z 5T4, 514/ 436-8532, Téléc: 514/436-5309
Association touristique de Manicouagan: 847, rve de Puyjalon, CP 2366, Baie-Comeau, QC G5C 2T1, 418/589-5319, Téléc: 418/589-9546
Association touristique de Mauricie-Bois-Francs: 1180, rue Royale, 2e étage, Trois-Rivières, QC G9A 4J1, 819/375-1222, Téléc: 819/375-0301
Association touristique de l'Outaouais: Directeur général, Gilles Picard, 103, rue Laurier, Hull, QC J8X 3V8, 819/778-2222, Téléc: 819/778-7758, Ligne sans frais: 1-800-265-7822, Courrier électronique: ato@achilles.net, URL: http:// www.achilles.net/~ato/
Association Touristique Régionale de Duplessis: 865, boul Laure, Sept-Îles, QC G4R 1Y6, 418/962-0808, Téléc: 418/962-6518, Courrier électronique: atrd@ bbsi.net, URL: http://www.bbsi.net/atrd/
Association touristique régionale de la Montérégie: Directeur général, Denis Brisebois, #989, rue Pierre-Dupuy, Longueuil, QC J4K 1A1, 514/674-5555, Téléc: 514/463-2876
Association touristique du Saguenay-Lac-Saint-Jean: #210, 198, rue Racine est, Chicoutimi, QC G7H 1R9, 418/543-9778, Téléc: 418/543-1805, Courrier électronique: atrsaglac@d4m.com, URL: http:// www.atrsaglac.d4m.com
Office des congrès et du tourisme du Grand Montréal: Vice-President, Sales & Promotions, Claude Zalloni, #600, 1555, rue Peel, Montréal, QC H3A 3L8, 514/844-5400, Téléc: 514/844-5757, Courrier électronique: info@octgm.cum.qc.ca, URL: http://www.cum.qc.ca/octgm/Welcome.html
Office du tourisme et des congrès de la communauté urbaine de Québec: Directeur, Pierre Fabrie; Director, Sales & Marketing, Claire Verreault; Director, Advertising & Communication, Daniel Gagnon; Director, Tourism & Membership, Jean J. Frenette, Communauté urbaine de Québec, 399, rue St-Joseph est, Québec, QC G1K 8E2, 418/522-3511, Téléc: 418/529-3121, Courrier électronique: pierre.labrie@cuq.qc.ca, URL: http:// www.quebec-region.cuq.qc.ca
Office du tourisme de Laval: 2900, boul Saint-Martin ouest, Laval, QC H7T 2J2, 514/682-5522, Téléc: 514/ 682-7304, Ligne sans frais: 1-800-463-3765, Courrier électronique: info@tourismelaval.qc.ca, URL: http://www.tourismelaval.qc.ca

## BC Motels, Campgrounds, Resorts Association (1944)
#209, 3003 St. John's St., Port Moody, BC V3H 2C4
604/945-7676, Fax: 604/945-7606, Email: bcmcra@ camping.bc.ca
Executive Director, Joss Pendy
Publications: The Dogwood Express; Super Camping BC

## Burlington Visitor & Convention Bureau
1340 Lakeshore Rd., Burlington, ON L7S 1Y2
905/634-5594, Fax: 905/634-7220
General Manager, Elaine Scrivener

## Cambridge Visitor & Convention Bureau (1981)
531 King St. East, Cambridge, ON N3H 3N4
519/653-1424, Fax: 519/653-1734, Toll Free: 1-800-749-7560, Email: cchamber@golden.net
Coordinator, Debbie Yantzi
Affiliates: Ontario Motor Coach Association; Festival Country Travel Association

## Canadian Association of Retail Travel Agents (CARTA)
765 Barton St. East, Hamilton, ON L8L 3A9
905/547-1324, Fax: 905/522-1752
President, Caesar Tam

## Canadian Business Travel Association/ Association canadienne des chargés de voyages (CBTA) (1983)
Deloitte & Touche, #2000, 1055 Dunsmuir St., PO Box 49279, Vancouver, BC V7X 1P4
604/669-4466, Fax: 604/684-0458
President, Pat Haygarth
CBTA Vancouver: Contact, Pat Haygarth, Bus: 604/ 669-4466
CBTA Calgary: Contact, Peggy Orchard, Bus: 403/233-6000
CBTA Winnipeg: Contact, Helen Mitchell, Bus: 204/ 942-5466
CBTA Toronto: Contact, Michele Butt, Bus: 416/920-8100
CBTA Ottawa: Contact, Lisa O'Driscoll, Bus: 613/232-2000
CBTA Montreal: Contact, Bryan Williams, Bus: 514/ 428-3260
Publications: Connector
Affiliates: National Business Travel Association, USA; International Business Travel Association

## Canadian Business Travel Association - Montréal/Association canadienne des chargés de voyages - Montréal (CBTA) (1968)
29, Hazelwood, Dollard-des-Ormeaux, QC H9A 2N7
514/990-2228, Fax: 514/637-1880
President, Andi La Rivière
Vice-President, Feride Bekbay
Secretary, Jeannine Duchesne
Treasurer, A. Leblanc
Publications: The Connector

### Canadian Hotel Marketing & Sales Executives, BC Chapter (CHMSE) (1985)
#100, 951 - 16th St., West Vancouver, BC V7V 3S4
604/926-2056, Fax: 604/926-4115
Executive Director, Mary Hiscox
Publications: BC Chapter Newsletter

### Canadian Hotel Marketing & Sales Executives, Ontario Chapter (CHMSE) (1982)
84 Seventh St., Toronto, ON M8V 3B4
416/252-9800, Fax: 416/252-7071
Executive Director, Shelley Macdonald
President, Scott T. Duff
Vice-President, Kelly Breen
Vice-President, Cathy Wallbank
Association Manager, Shelley Macdonald
Publications: Hospitality Update

### Canadian Institute of Travel Counsellors of Ontario (1967)
**CITC - Ontario**
#209, 55 Eglinton Ave. East, Toronto, ON M4P 1G8
416/484-4450, Fax: 416/484-4140, Toll Free: 1-800-589-5776, Email: info@citcontario.com, URL: http://www.citcontario.com
Executive Director, Steve Gillick
President, Shane Joseph, CTM
Publications: Professional Travel Counselling; The Inside Track

### Canadian National Aboriginal Tourism Association/Association canadienne nationale des autochtones pour le tourisme (CNATA)
875 Bank St., Ottawa, ON K1S 3W4
613/567-7566, Fax: 613/233-4329, URL: http://www.v1i.ca/clients/abc/cnata/cnata3.htm
President, Barry Parker
Chairperson, Anna Nibby-Woods
Head Office: Wahpeton Dakota Nation, PO Box 128, Prince Albert, SK S9V 5R4

### Canadian Recreational Vehicle Association (CRVA) (1975)
#200, 670 Bloor St. West, Toronto, ON M6G 1L2
416/533-7800, Fax: 416/533-4795
Executive Vice-President, Don Mockford

### Canadian Resort Development Association (CRDA) (1980)
48 Hayden St., Toronto, ON M4Y 1V8
416/960-4930, Fax: 416/923-8348
Director/President, Gloria A. Collinson
Publications: CRDA Newsletter
Affiliates: American Resort & Residential Development Association - Washington DC

### Canadian Tourism Research Institute
255 Smyth Rd., Ottawa, ON K1H 8M7
613/526-4306, Fax: 613/526-4857, Telex: 053-3333
Director, Harry French

### Cochrane Timiskaming Travel Association (1974)
**James Bay Frontier Travel Association**
76 McIntyre Rd., PO Box 920, Schumacher, ON P0N 1G0
705/360-1989, Fax: 705/268-5526, Toll Free: 1-800-461-3766
Manager, Guy Lamarche
Executive Secretary, Lynda Fortier
Publications: James Bay Frontier; Newsletter, q.

### Convention & Visitors Bureau of Windsor (1980)
City Centre, #103, 333 Riverside Dr. West, Windsor, ON N9A 5K4
519/255-6530, Fax: 519/255-6192, Toll Free: 1-800-265-3633, Email: ehamel@city.windsor.on.ca, URL: http://www.city.windsor.on.ca/cvb
General Manager, Elizabeth Hamel
Publications: Membership Matters; Visitor Guide, a.

### Cornwall & Seaway Valley Tourism (1993)
231 Augustus St., Cornwall, ON K6J 3W2
613/938-4748, Fax: 613/938-4751, Toll Free: 1-800-937-4748, Email: dmurray@cnwl.igs.net, URL: http://www.visit.cornwall.on.ca
Executive Manager, Dawn Murray
Publications: Calendar of Events

### Council of Tourism Associations of British Columbia (COTA) (1991)
PO Box 28005, RPO Harbour Centre, Vancouver, BC V6B 5L8
604/685-5956, Fax: 604/730-4801, Email: cota@travel.bc.ca
President, Pat Corbett
Publications: COTA Newsfax
Cariboo Tourism Association: Managing Director, G.R. Drew, 190 Yorsten St., PO Box 4900, Williams Lake, BC V2G 2V8, 250/392-2226, Fax: 250/392-2838, Toll Free: 1-800-663-5885, Email: cariboo@netshop.ca
High Country Tourism Association: General Manager, Lee Morris, #2, 1490 Pearson Pl., Kamloops, BC V1S 1J9, 250/372-7770, Fax: 250/828-4656
Kootenay Country Tourist Association: Executive Director, Geoff Sturgeon, 610 Railway St., Nelson, BC V1L 1H4, 250/352-6033, Fax: 250/352-1656, Toll Free: 1-800-661-6603, Email: kcta@worldtel.com, URL: http://travel.bc.ca/region/kootenay/index.html
North by Northwest Tourism Association of BC: General Manager, Marilyn Quilley, 3736 - 16th Ave., PO Box 1030, Smithers, BC V0J 2N0, 250/847-5227, Fax: 250/847-7585
Okanagan Similkameen Tourism Association: Executive Director, Deanna Rainey; President, Allen Tozer, 1332 Water St., Kelowna, BC V1Y 9P4, 250/860-5999, Fax: 250/861-7493, Email: osta@awinc.com, URL: http://www.travel.bc.ca/region/ok
Peace River Alaska Highway Tourism Association: Manager, Ella Fraser, 10631 - 100th St., PO Box 6850, Stn Main, Fort St. John, BC V1J 4J3, 250/785-2544, Fax: 250/785-4424, Toll Free: 1-888-785-2544, Email: prahta@awinc.com
Tourism Association of Vancouver Island: Managing Director, David Mailloux, #302, 45 Bastion Sq., Victoria, BC V8W 1J1, 250/382-3551, Fax: 250/382-3523, Email: tavi@islands.bc.ca
Tourism Rockies: Managing Director, Chris Dadson; President, Mike Smith, 905 Warren Ave., PO Box 10, Kimberley, BC V1A 2Y5, 250/427-4838, Fax: 250/427-3344, Email: bcrockies@cyberlink.bc.ca
Tourism Vancouver/Greater Vancouver Convention & Visitors Bureau: President & CEO, Rick Antonson, #210, 200 Burrard St., Vancouver, BC V6C 3L6, 604/682-2222, Fax: 604/682-1717, URL: http://www.tourism-vancouver.org
Tourism Victoria/Greater Victoria Visitors & Convention Bureau: CEO, Lorne Whyte, #710, 1175 Douglas St., Victoria, BC V8W 2E1, 250/382-2160, Fax: 250/361-9733, Info Line: 250/953-2033, Toll Free: 1-800-663-3883, Email: info@travel.victoria.bc.ca, URL: http://travel.victoria.bc.ca/
Vancouver Coast & Mountains Tourism Region: Executive Director, Kevan Ridgway, #204, 1755 Broadway West, Vancouver, BC V6J 4S5, 604/739-9011, Fax: 604/739-0153, Toll Free: 1-800-667-3306, Email: vcm.tourism@mindlink.bc.ca, URL: http://travel.bc.ca

### The Georgian Triangle Tourist Association & Convention Bureau (1978)
601 First St., Collingwood, ON L9Y 4L2
705/445-7722, Fax: 705/444-6082
Executive Director, Sheila Metras
President, D.J. McNichol
Publications: Georgian Triangle Newsletter; Georgian Triangle Visitor Guide, a.

### Greater Hamilton Tourism & Convention Services
One James St. South, 3rd Fl., Hamilton, ON L8P 4R5
905/546-4222, Fax: 905/546-4107, Toll Free: 1-800-263-8590
Manager, Joseph Fardell

### Hostelling International - Canada (HI-C) (1933)
**Canadian Hostelling Association**
#400, 205 Catherine St., Ottawa, ON K2P 1C3
613/237-7884, Fax: 613/237-7868, Telex: 053-3660, URL: http://www.HostellingIntl.ca/
Executive Director, Richard McCarron
President, François Vidal
Affiliates: International Youth Hostel Federation

### Hotel Association of Canada Inc./Association des hôtels du Canada (HAC) (1913)
#1016, 130 Albert St., Ottawa, ON K1P 5G4
613/237-7149, Fax: 613/238-3878, Email: hac@hotels.ca
President, Anthony P. Pollard, Bus: 613/237-7149, Fax: 613/238-3878
Chairman, Julian Koziak
Sec.-Treas., John D. Read, Bus: 204/942-0671, Fax: 204/942-6719
Publications: HAC Newsletter
Affiliates: American Hotel & Motel Association; International Hotel & Restaurant Association

#### ALBERTA HOTEL ASSOCIATION (1920)
#401, 5241 Calgary Trail South, Edmonton, AB T6H 5G8
403/436-6112, Fax: 403/436-5404
Email: aha@albertahotels.ab.ca, URL: http://www.albertahotels.ab.ca
Executive Vice-President, James P. Hansen

#### L'ASSOCIATION DES HÔTELIERS DU QUÉBEC/QUÉBEC HOTEL KEEPERS' ASSOCIATION (AHDQ) (1949)
#0.04, 425, rue Sherbrooke est, Montréal, QC H2L 1J9
514/282-5135, Téléc: 514/849-1157
URL: http://www.destinationquebec.com
Directeur général, Jean Lauzon
Publications: L'Hôtelier

#### BRITISH COLUMBIA & YUKON HOTELS ASSOCIATION
948 Howe St., 2nd Fl., Vancouver, BC V6Z 1N9
604/681-7164, Fax: 604/681-7649, Toll Free: 1-800-663-3153
URL: http://www.fleethouse.com/fhcanada/bc-acco.htm
Executive Vice-President, James C. Chase, C.M.A., DMATP
Publications: Inn Touch; Inn Focus, q.

#### HOTEL ASSOCIATION OF NOVA SCOTIA
PO Box 473, Stn M, Halifax, NS B3J 2P8
902/443-3635, Fax: 902/457-3304
Administrator, Jose Cabrita

#### HOTEL/MOTEL ASSOCIATION OF PRINCE EDWARD ISLAND
455 University Ave., Charlottetown, PE C1A 4NA
902/566-3137, Fax: 902/368-3806
President, Kevin Murphy

#### HOTELS ASSOCIATION OF SASKATCHEWAN
1054 Winnipeg St., Regina, SK S4R 8P8
306/522-1664, Fax: 306/525-1944
Executive Director, Bill Nelson

#### MANITOBA HOTEL ASSOCIATION (MHA) (1927)
#1505, 155 Carlton St., Winnipeg, MB R3C 3H8
204/942-0671
Executive Vice-President, John D. Read

Publications: Newsletter
Affiliates: Manitoba Chamber of Commerce; Tourism Association of Manitoba

#### NORTHWEST TERRITORIES HOTELS' ASSOCIATION
Yellowknife Inn, PO Box 490, Yellowknife, NT X1A 2N4
867/873-2601, Fax: 867/873-2602
Acting President, Jack Walker

#### ONTARIO HOTEL & MOTEL ASSOCIATION (OH&MA) (1924)
#220, 2560 Matheson Blvd. East, Mississauga, ON L4W 4Y9
905/602-9650, Fax: 905/602-9654, Toll Free: 1-800-387-0010
Email: info@ohma.com, URL: http://www.ohma.com
President, Rod Seiling
Publications: InnTouch; OH & MA Directory
Affiliates: American Hotel & Motel Association

### Huronia Tourism Association (HTA) (1969)
Simcoe County Bldg., Midhurst, ON L0L 1X0
705/726-9300, Fax: 705/726-3991
President, Julian H. Huffer, Bus: 705/726-8502
Chair, Michael J. Stewart
Vice-Chair, Josephine Martensson
Publications: In Brief; Huronia Vacation Planner, a.; Huronia Guide Map

### Institut de tourisme et d'hôtellerie du Québec (ITHQ) (1968)
401, rue de Rigaud, Montréal, QC H2L 4P3
514/282-5108, Téléc: 514/282-5163, Ligne sans frais: 1-800-361-5111
Directrice générale, Christine Martel
Agente d'information, Service des communications, Jacqueline Limoges

### Kitchener-Waterloo Area Visitor & Convention Bureau (KWAVCB) (1992)
2848 King St. East, Kitchener, ON N2A 1A5
519/748-0800, Fax: 519/748-6411, Toll Free: 1-800-265-6959
General Manager, Jane Falconer
Publications: Tourism Matters

### Metropolitan Toronto Convention & Visitors Association/Association du tourisme et des congrès du Toronto métropolitain (MTCVA) (1926)
**Tourism Toronto**
Queen's Quay Terminal at Harbourfront, #590, 207 Queen's Quay West, PO Box 126, Toronto, ON M5J 1A7
416/203-2600, Fax: 416/203-6753, Info Line: 416/203-2500, Toll Free: 1-800/363-1990, Email: mtcvacom@pathcom.com, URL: http://www.tourism-toronto.com
President, Kirk Shearer
Publications: Business Briefs; Membership Directory, a.
Affiliates: International Association of Convention & Visitor Bureaux; Metropolitan Toronto Board of Trade; American Society of Association Executives

### Motel Association of Alberta (MAA) (1948)
#202, 10335 - 178 St., Edmonton, AB T5S 1R5
403/944-1199, Fax: 403/455-6675
Executive Director, Roger E. Pollok
President, Mary Chamaschuk
Publications: Checking-In
Affiliates: Motels Ontario; BC Motels, Campgrounds & Resorts Association

### Muskoka Tourism (MTMA) (1984)
RR#2, Kilworthy, ON P0E 1G0
705/689-0660, Fax: 705/689-7118, Toll Free: 1-800-267-9700
General Manager, Dave Thomas

### Niagara Falls, Canada Visitor & Convention Bureau
5433 Victoria Ave., Niagara Falls, ON L2G 3L1
905/356-6061, Fax: 905/356-5567, Toll Free: 1-800-563-2557, Email: nfcvcb@tourismniagara.com, URL: http://www.tourismniagara.com/nfcvcb/
General Manager, Noel Buckley

### North of Superior Tourism Association (NOSTA) (1974)
**North of Superior Travel Association Inc.**
1119 East Victoria Ave., Thunder Bay, ON P7C 1B7
807/626-9420, Fax: 807/626-9421, Toll Free: 1-800-265-3951, Email: nosta@microage-tb.com, URL: http://www.nosta.on.ca
Managing Director, Bruce C. Hole
Publications: Summer Travel Guide; Winter Travel Guide

### North West Commercial Travellers' Association of Canada (NWCTA) (1882)
28 Main St. South, Winnipeg, MB R3L 2R1
204/284-8900, Fax: 204/284-8909, Toll Free: 1-800-665-6928
General Manager, Terry D. Carruthers
Publications: The Travellers; Hotel/Motel Directory, a.
Affiliates: Maritime Commercial Travellers Association; Canadian Professional Sales Association; The Order of United Commercial Travellers of America

### Northern Frontier Visitors Association
#4, 4807 - 49th St., Yellowknife, NT X1A 3T5
867/873-4262, Fax: 867/873-3654, Email: nfva@internorth.com
Manager, Melissa Daoust
President, Jonathan Cross
Publications: Northern Bound

### Northern Ontario Tourist Outfitters Association (NOTO) (1951)
#408, 269 Main St. West, North Bay, ON P1B 2T8
705/472-5552, Fax: 705/472-0621, Email: noto@onlink.net, URL: http://www.virtualnorth.com/noto/
Executive Director, Jim Grayston
Publications: The Outfitter

### Nunavut Tourism (1995)
PO Box 1450, Iqaluit, NT X0A 0H0
867/979-6551, Fax: 867/979-1261, Toll Free: 1-800-491-7910, Email: nunatour@nunanet.com, URL: http://www.nunatour.nt.ca
President, Paul Landry
Vice-President, John Hickes
Publications: Tourism Bulletin; Arctic Travellers, biennial

### Ontario East Tourism Association (OETA) (1974)
RR#1, Lansdowne, ON K0E 1L0
613/659-4300, Fax: 613/659-4306, Toll Free: 1-800-567-3278
Executive Director, Rose Wakim
President, Ronald Huck
Publications: Ontario East Discovery Map

### Ontario Hostelry Institute (OHI)
#213, 300 Adelaide St. East, Toronto, ON M5A 1N1
416/363-3401, Fax: 416/363-3403
Executive Director, Rigzin Dolkar

### Ontario Private Campground Association (OPCA) (1969)
RR#5, Owen Sound, ON N4K 5N7
519/371-3393, Fax: 519/371-5315, Email: opca@headwaters.com, URL: http://www.campgrounds.org
Managing Director, Marcel Gobeil
Publications: Update; Camping in Ontario, a.

### Ontario Ski Resorts Association (OSRA)
#22, 850 Tapscott Rd., Scarborough, ON M1X 1N4
416/321-2252, Fax: 416/321-2336
President, Donald K. McIlveen

### Ontario's Sunset Country Travel Association (1974)
PO Box 647, Kenora, ON P9N 3X6
807/468-5853, Fax: 807/468-5484, Info Line: 1-800-665-7567, Email: info@ontariossunsetcountry.ca, URL: http://www.ontariossunsetcountry.ca
Executive Director, Neil McInnis

### Ottawa Tourism & Convention Authority/L'Administration du tourisme et des congrès d'Ottawa (OTCA) (1972)
#1800, 130 Albert St., Ottawa, ON K1P 5G4
613/237-5150, Fax: 613/237-7339, Info Line: 613/237-5158, Toll Free: 1-800-363-4465, URL: http://www.tourottawa.org
President, Leslie Miller
Chair, Pat Kelly
Publications: Visitor Guide; Destination Planners' Guide, a.; Dining Guide; Member Directory

### Pacific Asia Travel Association (PATA) (1951)
Telesis Tower, #1000, 1 Montgomery St., San Francisco, CA 94104 USA
415/986-4646, Fax: 415/986-3458
President & CEO, Lakshman Ratnapala
Publications: PATA Travel News; Membership Directory

### Peterborough Kawartha Tourism & Convention Bureau (PKTCB) (1982)
175 George St. North, Peterborough, ON K9J 3G6
705/742-2201, Fax: 705/742-2494, Toll Free: 1-800-461-6424
General Manager, Glenda Hunter
Chairperson, Anne Marshall

### Rainbow Country Travel Association
Cedar Point Mall, 1984 Regent St. South, Sudbury, ON P3E 5S1
705/522-0104, Fax: 705/522-3132, Toll Free: 1-800-465-6655
Executive Director, Erin Downey

### Resorts Ontario (1942)
**Association of Tourist Resorts of Ontario**
29 Albert St. North, Orillia, ON L3V 5J9
705/325-9115, Fax: 705/325-7999, Toll Free: 1-800-363-7227, Email: escapes@resorts-ontario.com, URL: http://www.resorts-ontario.com
Managing Director, Grace Cerniuk, CAE
Publications: Resort News

### Sarnia/Lambton Visitor & Convention Bureau (VCB)
224 North Vidal St., Sarnia, ON N7T 5Y3
519/336-3232, Fax: 519/336-3278, Toll Free: 1-800-265-0316
Manager, Pat Laframboise
Publications: Convention & Facilities Guide; Travel Guide

### Sault Ste. Marie Hospitality & Travel (1982)
99 Foster Dr., 3rd Fl., Sault Ste Marie, ON P6A 5X6

705/759-5432, Fax: 705/759-2185, Toll Free: 1-800-461-6020
President, David Saunders
Managing Director, Suzanne J. Curran
Publications: Tourism Yearbook

**Sudbury Convention & Visitors Services**
PO Box 5000, Stn A, Sudbury, ON P3A 5P3
705/674-3141, Fax: 705/671-8145
Manager, Paul Brokenshire

**Tourism Brantford (1990)**
3 Sherwood Dr., Brantford, ON N3T 1N3
519/751-9900, Fax: 519/759-5975, Toll Free: 1-800-265-6299
Manager, Tourism & Marketing, Valerie Wilson
Publications: What's On in Brantford & Brant County; Brantford & Brant County Visitor Guide, a.
Affiliates: Festival Country; Ontario Motor Coach Association

**Tourism Industry Association of Canada/ Association de l'industrie touristique du Canada (TIAC) (1931)**
#1016, 130 Albert St., Ottawa, ON K1P 5G4
613/238-3883, Fax: 613/238-3878, Email: tiac@achilles.net
President, Debra Sara Ward
Chairman, John Gow
Publications: Update
Affiliates: Heritage Canada

**Tourism Industry Association of New Brunswick Inc./Association de l'industrie touristique du Nouveau-Brunswick inc. (TIANB) (1978)**
Prospect Place, #206, 191 Prospect St., Fredericton, NB E3B 2T7
506/458-5646, Fax: 506/459-3634
President, Patrick Valardo
General Manager, Graham McOuat
Publications: The Open Door
Fredericton Visitor & Convention Bureau: Manager, Nancy Lockerbie, PO Box 130, Fredericton, NB E3B 4Y7, Fax: 506/452-9509, Toll Free: 1-888-888-4768, Email: tourism@city.fredericton.nb.ca, URL: http://www.city.fredericton.nb.ca
Saint John Visitor & Convention Bureau: #360, 560 Main St., Saint John, NB E2K 1J5, 506/658-2990, Fax: 506/658-2879

**Tourism Industry Association of Newfoundland & Labrador (1983)**
**Hospitality Newfoundland & Labrador**
107 LeMarchant Rd., St. John's, NF A1C 2H1
709/722-2000, Fax: 709/722-8104, Toll Free: 1-800-563-0700
Executive Director, Cathy Duke
Publications: Tourism Times

**Tourism Industry Association of Nova Scotia (TIANS) (1977)**
The World Trade & Convention Centre, #402, 1800 Argyle St., Halifax, NS B3J 3N8
902/423-4480, Fax: 902/422-0184, Toll Free: 1-800-948-4267
Managing Director, J.B. Cabrita
Affiliates: Innkeepers Guild of Nova Scotia; Adventure Tourism Association of Nova Scotia
Cape Breton Tourist Association: Executive Director, Don Blackwood, 10 Keltic Dr., Sydney, NS B1S 1P5, 902/539-9876, Fax: 902/539-8430
Central Nova Tourist Association: Executive Director, Sally Anderson; Office Manager, Suzanne Waeelock, PO Box 1761, Truro, NS B2N 5Z5, 902/893-8782, Fax: 902/897-6641
Evangeline Trail Tourism Association: Executive Director, Beth Caldwell; Administrative Assistant, Krista Menzies, 5518 Prospect Rd., New Minas, NS B4N 3K8, 902/681-1645, Fax: 902/681-2747, Email: etta@fox.nstn.ca, URL: http://www.valleyweb.com/evangelinetrail/
Pictou County Tourist Association: Executive Director, Kimberly Dickson, 980 East River Rd., New Glasgow, NS B2H 3S8, 902/755-5180, Fax: 902/755-2848, URL: http://www.animax.com/pcta
Tourism Halifax: Director, Lewis M. Rogers, PO Box 1749, Halifax, NS B3J 3A5, 902/421-6448, Fax: 902/421-2842, Telex: 019-22641

**Tourism Industry Association of the NWT**
#2, 4807 - 49th St., Yellowknife, NT X1A 3T5
867/873-2122, Fax: 867/873-3654
Executive Director, Jackie Coulter
President, Yvonne Quick
Arctic Coast Tourism Association: PO Box 91, Cambridge Bay, NT X0C 0C0, 867/983-2224, Fax: 867/983-2302
Big River Tourism Association: PO Box 185, Hay River, NT X0E 0R0, 867/874-2422, Fax: 867/874-2027
Nahanni-Ram Tourism Association: PO Box 177, Fort Simpson, NT X0E 0N0, 867/695-3182, Fax: 867/695-2511

**Tourism Industry Association of PEI (TIAPEI)**
64 Great George St., PO Box 2050, Charlottetown, PE C1A 7N7
902/566-5008, Fax: 902/368-3605, Email: tiapei@peinet.pe.ca, URL: http://www.gov.pe.ca/conv/tiapei.html
General Manager, Don Cudmore
Publications: Tourism Tides

**Tourism Industry Association of Saskatchewan**
**TISASK**
2154 Airport Dr., Saskatoon, SK S7L 6M6
306/343-3610, Fax: 306/664-1971
Executive Director, Stephen McLellan
Hugh Vassos
Tourism Regina/Regina Convention & Visitors Bureau: Executive Director, Steve Mclellan; Marketing Manager, Gayle E. Zimmerman, Hwy. 1 East, PO Box 3355, Regina, SK S4P 3H1, 306/789-8166, Fax: 306/789-3171, Toll Free: 1-800-661-5099
Tourism Saskatoon: Executive Director, Susan Lamb; Director of Marketing, Jan Desrosiers, #6, 305 Idylwyld Dr. North, Saskatoon, SK S7L 0Z1, 306/242-1206, Fax: 306/242-1955, Toll Free: 1-800-567-2444, Email: toursaskatoon@sk.sympatico.ca, URL: http://www.city.saskatoon.sk.ca/tourism

**Tourism Industry Association of the Yukon (1972)**
**TIA Yukon**
1109 - 1st Ave., Whitehorse, YT Y1A 2A9
867/668-3331, Fax: 867/667-7379, Email: tiayukon@yknet.yk.ca
Executive Director, Lowry Toombs
Publications: TIA Yukon Newsletter
Klondike Visitors Association: Executive Director, Denny Kobayashi, PO Box 389, Dawson, YT Y0B 1G0, 867/993-5575, Fax: 867/993-6415, Email: kva@dawson.net, URL: http://www.dawsoncity.com

**Tourism Industry of Manitoba Inc. (TIM) (1969)**
c/o Viscount Gort Hotel, #104, 1670 Portage Ave., Winnipeg, MB R3C 0C9
204/774-8406, Fax: 204/774-8420, Email: tourism@solutions.mb.ca
President, Lilian Tankard
Publications: Tourism Journal of Manitoba

**Tourism London (1997)**
300 Dufferin Ave., London, ON N6B 1Z2
519/661-5000, Fax: 519/661-6160, Toll Free: 1-800-265-2602
General Manager, Michael Harris

**Tourism Stratford (1990)**
88 Wellington St., PO Box 818, Stratford, ON N5A 6W1
519/271-5140, Fax: 519/273-1818, Toll Free: 1-800-561-7926
Tourism Manager, Barbara Quarry
Publications: Festive Stratford Visitors' Guide
Affiliates: National Tour Association

**Tourism Thunder Bay (1970)**
**Visitors & Convention Bureau of Thunder Bay**
500 Donald St. East, Thunder Bay, ON P7E 5V3
807/625-2149, Fax: 807/623-3768, Info Line: 807/346-4636, Toll Free: 1-800-667-8386
Manager, Patricia Forrest, Bus: 807/625-2565
Publications: Thunder Bay - Superior By Nature

**Tourism Winnipeg (1988)**
#320, 25 Forks Market Rd., Winnipeg, MB R3C 4S8
204/943-1970, Fax: 204/942-4043, Toll Free: 1-800-665-0204, Email: WpgInfo@Tourism.Winnipeg.MB.ca, URL: http://www.tourism.winnipeg.mb.ca
Executive Director, P. McMillan
Publications: Meeting & Convention Resource Guide; Visitors Guide, a.; Passport to Winnipeg, s-a.

**Tourisme Jeunesse (1989)**
4545, av Pierre-de-Coubertin, Montréal, QC H1V 3R2
514/252-3117, Téléc: 514/252-3119, Ligne sans frais: 1-800-461-8585, Courrier électronique: info@tourismej.qc.ca, URL: http://www.tourismej.qc.ca
Directeur général, Joël Marier
Présidente, Claude Moreau
Publications: Tourisme Jeunesse; Les Auberges au Québec, annuel
Organisation(s) affiliée(s): Fédération internationale des auberges de jeunesse; Regroupment loisir Québec; Bureau canadian de l'éducation internationale

**Travel Alberta (1995)**
#500, 999 - 8 St. SW, Calgary, AB T2R 1J5
403/297-2957, Fax: 403/297-5068, URL: http://www.atp.ab.ca/
President & CEO, Tom McCabe
Executive Assistant, Joanna Suehwold
Calgary Convention & Visitors Bureau: Manager, Diana Bergdahl; President & CEO, Henry Kutarna, 237 - 8 Ave. SE, Calgary, AB T2G 0K8, 403/263-8510, Fax: 403/262-3809, Toll Free: 1-800-661-1678, URL: http://www.visitor.calgary.ab.ca/
Greater Edmonton Visitor & Convention Association: General Manager, Cindy Béland, 9797 Jasper Ave., Edmonton, AB T5J 1N9, 403/429-9915, Fax: 403/425-0725
Red Deer Visitor & Convention Bureau: Manager, Wendy Martindale; Chairperson, Merv Phillips, PO Box 5008, Red Deer, AB T4N 3T4, 403/346-0180, Fax: 403/346-5081, Toll Free: 1-800-215-8946

**Travellers' Aid Society of Metropolitan Toronto**
Room B23, Union Station, Toronto, ON M5J 1E6
416/366-7788, Fax: 416/366-0829
Executive Director, Helen Heffernan
Publications: Newsletter

**WorldHomes Holiday Exchange (WHE) (1986)**
**HomeLink International Canada**
1707 Platt Cres., North Vancouver, BC V7J 1X9
604/987-3262, Fax: 604/987-3262, Email: jgraber@direct.ca, URL: http://www.homelink.org
Director, Jack Graber
Publications: Holiday Exchange Book

## TRADE

*see also* Retail Trade

### Action Canada Network/Réseau canadien d'action (ACN) (1987)

#804, 251 Laurier Ave. West, Ottawa, ON K1P 5J6
613/233-1764, Fax: 613/233-1458, Email: actcan@web.apc.org
Administrative Coordinator, Mandy Rocks
National Co-Chair, Jean Claude Parrot
Communications Coordinator, Marcella Munro
Publications: Action Dossier; Action Bulletin

### Asia Pacific Foundation of Canada/Fondation Asie Pacifique du Canada (APFC) (1984)

#666, 999 Canada Pl., Vancouver, BC V6C 3E1
604/684-5986, Fax: 604/681-1370, URL: http://www.apfc.ca
President/CEO, Dr. William Saywell
Executive Vice-President, Dr. John D. Wiebe
Information Resources Coordinator, Rachel Charron
Publications: Dialogue

### Canada Beef Export Federation

#235, 6715 - 8 St. NE, Calgary, AB T2E 7H7
403/274-0005, Fax: 403/274-7275, Email: canada@cbef.com, URL: http://www.cbef.com
Executive Director, Ted Haney

### Canadian Association of Regulated Importers/Association canadienne des importateurs réglementés (CARI) (1986)

#203, 2525 St. Laurent Blvd., Ottawa, ON K1H 8P5
613/738-1729, Fax: 613/733-9501
General Manager, Robert De Valk
Publications: Importers Edge

### Canadian Courier Association

555 Dixon Rd., Etobicoke, ON M9W 1H8
905/242-2570, Fax: 905/242-9874
Executive Director, Douglas Moffatt
President, Kal Tobias

### Canadian Importers Association Inc./Association des importateurs canadiens inc. (1932)

#700, 210 Dundas St. West, Toronto, ON M5G 2E8
416/595-5333, Fax: 416/595-8226, Email: info@importers.ca, URL: http://www.importers.ca
Associate Executive Director, Adrian Bradford
President, Robert Armstrong
Publications: Importweek; Import Canada
Affiliates: National Trade Committees - Association of International Automobile Manufacturers of Canada; Canadian Meat Importers Committee; Canadian Association of Footwear Importers, Inc., Customs & Legislation Committee; Electronics Import Committee; International Cheese Council of Canada

#### ASSOCIATION OF INTERNATIONAL AUTOMOBILE MANUFACTURERS OF CANADA/ASSOCIATION DES FABRICANTS INTERNATIONAUX D'AUTOMOBILES DU CANADA (AIAMC) (1973)

#700, 210 Dundas St. West, Toronto, ON M5G 2E8
416/595-5333, Fax: 416/595-8226
President, Robert Armstrong
Associate Executive Director, Adrian Bradford, CAE
Publications: International Automobile Manufacturers Update

#### CANADIAN ASSOCIATION OF FOOTWEAR IMPORTERS INC. (CAFI)

#700, 210 Dundas St. West, Toronto, ON M5G 2E8
416/595-5333, Fax: 416/595-8226
Chair, Claude Church
Corporate Secretary, Catherine McPherson

#### CANADIAN MEAT IMPORTERS COMMITTEE (CMIC) (1969)

#700, 210 Dundas St. West, Toronto, ON M5G 2E8
416/595-5333, Fax: 416/595-8226
Email: info@importers.ca, URL: http://www.importers.ca
Executive Director, Fée Kiessling
Chairman, William Fenton

#### CUSTOMS & LEGISLATION COMMITTEE

#700, 210 Dundas St. West, Toronto, ON M5G 2E8
416/595-5333, Fax: 416/595-8226
Chair, Bud Hollings
Corporate Secretary, Catherine McPherson

#### ELECTRONICS IMPORT COMMITTEE (EIC)

#700, 210 Dundas St. West, Toronto, ON M5G 2E8
416/595-5333, Fax: 416/595-8226
Chair, Trent Cosgrove
Corporate Secretary, Catherine McPherson
Publications: Importweek

#### INTERNATIONAL CHEESE COUNCIL OF CANADA/CONSEIL CANADIEN DES FROMAGES INTERNATIONAUX (ICCC) (1975)

#700, 210 Dundas St. West, Toronto, ON M5G 2E8
416/595-5333, Fax: 416/595-8226
Chair, Peter Couture
Vice-Chair, Doug Smith
Treasurer, Walter Pelley
Secretary, Donald R. McArthur

### Canadian International Trade Association (CITA) (1988)

#611, 2 Carlton St., Toronto, ON M5B 1J3
416/351-9728, Fax: 416/351-9911
President, Sydney King
Vice-President, Lee Meister
Publications: World Trade Showguide

### Citizens Concerned About Free Trade (CCAFT)

PO Box 8052, Saskatoon, SK S7K 4R7
306/244-5757, Fax: 306/244-3790
National Chairman, David Orchard
National Organizer/Editor, Marjaleena Repo
Publications: True North: The Voice of Canadian Independence

### Club export agro-alimentaire du Québec/Québec Agri-Food Export Club (1990)

Édifice de Bleury, #102, 200, rue MacDonald, St-Jean-sur-Richelieu, QC J3B 8J6
514/349-1521, Téléc: 514/349-6923, Ligne sans frais: 1-800-563-9767
Secrétaire général, André Latour, caé
Publications: Exportise

### Federation of Export Clubs Canada (1980)

**Export Club**

#1402, 67 Yonge St., Toronto, ON M5E 1J8
416/364-4112, Fax: 416/364-4074
Chairman, H.J. Janthur

### France Technology Press Agency/Bureau de Presse France Technologies (1984)

**FRANTECH**

#2004, 20 Queen St. West, Toronto, ON M5H 3R3
416/977-2587, Fax: 416/977-9671, Email: 76001.2110@compuserve.com
Executive Director, Alexandra Sutton
Affiliates: French Trade Commission

### Hong Kong Trade Development Council

Office Tower, Convention Plaza, 1 Harbour Rd., 38th Fl., Wanchai Hong Kong
852/2584 4333, Fax: 852/2824 0249
Toronto Office: Director, Andrew Yui; Trade Enquiry Officer, Lily Kam, #1100, 347 Bay St., Toronto, ON M5H 2R7, 416/366-3594, Fax: 416/366-1569, Telex: 06218056 HKTDC
Vancouver Office: 1500 West Georgia St., 11th Fl., Vancouver, BC V6G 2Z6, 604/685-0883, Fax: 604/681-0093

### Institute for Canadian Studies (ICS) (1992)

298 Garry St., Winnipeg, MB R3C 1H3
204/925-8781, Fax: 204/943-2261, Email: lisashaw@instcanstudies.mb.ca
Director, W.H. Loewen
Researcher, Lisa Shaw

### The Parliamentary Centre/Le Centre parlementaire (1968)

250 Albert St., 4th Fl., Ottawa, ON K1P 6M1
613/237-0143, Fax: 613/235-8237
Director, Peter C. Dobell

### World Trade Centre Montréal/Centre de commerce mondial de Montréal (1984)

#2100, 380, rue St-Antoine ouest, Montréal, QC H2Y 3X4
514/849-1999, Téléc: 514/847-8343, Courrier électronique: wicmtl@wtc-mtl.com, URL: http://www.wtc-mtl.com
Directeur général, Benoit Labonté
Publications: Commerce mondial/World Trade

**TRANSLATION *see* LANGUAGE, LINGUISTICS, LITERATURE**

## TRANSPORTATION & SHIPPING

*see also* Marine Trades

### American Bureau of Shipping - Canadian Division (ABS-Can)

1577 Thompson St., Mississauga, ON L5C 1B4
905/897-9110, Fax: 905/897-9110
Canadian Representative, G.H. Mason

### Association québécoise du transport et des routes inc. (AQTR) (1965)

#100, 1595, rue Saint-Hubert, Montréal, QC H2L 3Z2
514/523-6444, Téléc: 514/523-2666, Infoligne: 514/523-0413
Directrice générale, Catherine Hirou
Président, Claude Beaupré
Publications: Information; Revue routes et transports, trimestriel

### Atlantic Provinces Transportation Commission

#330, 1133 St. George Blvd., Moncton, NB E1E 4E1
506/857-2820, Fax: 506/857-2835, Email: aptc@aptc.nb.ca, URL: http://www.aptc.nb.ca
Executive Director, Peter Juillemot
Staff Secretary, Cathy Peters

### Canadian Bus Association/Association canadienne de l'autobus (CBA) (1935)

#600, 99 Bank St., Ottawa, ON K1P 6B9
613/238-1800, Fax: 613/233-9656, Email: dlong@istar.ca
Executive Director, David Long
Association Manager, S.M. Beaudin
Publications: Canadian Bus News

### Canadian Business Aircraft Association Inc. (CBAA) (1962)

#1421, 50 O'Connor St., Ottawa, ON K1P 6L2
613/236-5611, Fax: 613/236-2361, Email: cbaa@istar.ca
CEO/President, J.D. Lyon
Chairman, Doug Thierman
Publications: CBAA Newsbrief; CBAA Bulletin; Membership Directory, a.
Affiliates: National Business Aircraft Association; International Business Aircraft Council; European Business Aircraft Association

### Canadian Council of Motor Transport Administrators/Conseil canadien des administrateurs en transport motorisé (CCMTA) (1940)
2323 St. Laurent Blvd., Ottawa, ON K1G 4K6
613/736-1003, Fax: 613/736-1395, Email: ccmta-secretariat@ccmta.ca, URL: http://www.ccmta.ca/
Executive Director, Louise Pelletier, CAE
Publications: CCMTA News

### Canadian Industrial Transportation League
#602, 1090 Don Mills Rd., North York, ON M3C 3R6
416/447-7766, Fax: 416/447-7312
President, Maria Rehner

### Canadian Institute of Traffic & Transportation/Institute canadien du trafic et du transport (CITT) (1958)
10 King St. East, 4th Fl., Toronto, ON M5E 1G4
416/363-5696, Fax: 416/363-5698, Email: citt@citt.ca, URL: http://www.citt.ca
President & COO, P.E. Cullen

### Canadian International Freight Forwarders Association, Inc./Association des transitaires internationaux canadiens, inc. (CIFFA) (1948)
PO Box 929, Streetsville, ON L5M 2C5
905/567-4633, Fax: 905/542-2716, Email: admin@ciffa.com, URL: http://www.ciffa.com/ciffa/
President, William M. Gottlieb
Secretary Manager, Marilyn Massoud
Publications: CIFFA Newsletter; Membership Directory, a.
Affiliates: International Federation of Freight Forwarders Associations

### Canadian Professional Logistics Institute/Institut Canadien des Professionnels de la Logistique (1990)
**The Logistics Institute**
10 King St. East, 4th Fl., Toronto, ON M5C 1C3
416/363-3005, Fax: 416/363-5598, URL: http://www.loginstitute.ca
President, Victor S. Deyglio
Publications: Canadian Logistics Journal
Affiliates: Canadian Institute of Traffic & Transportation; Canadian International Freight Forwarders Association

### Canadian Shipowners Association/Association des armateurs canadiens (CSA) (1903)
#705, 350 Sparks St., Ottawa, ON K1R 7S8
613/232-3539, Fax: 613/232-6211, Email: csa@shipowners.ca, URL: http://www.shipowners.ca
President, T. Norman Hall
Manager, Marine Operations, Capt. Réjean Lanteigne
Sec.-Treas., Silvie Dagenais
Publications: Seaports

### Canadian Shippers' Council
48 Balsam Dr., Baie-d'Urfé, QC H9X 3K5
514/457-7268, Fax: 514/457-7269
Secretary, Walter Mueller

### Canadian Transportation Research Forum/Le Groupe de recherches sur les transports au Canada (CTRF) (1967)
#209, 15 Innovation Blvd., Saskatoon, SK S7N 2X8
306/668-2828, Fax: 306/668-7603, Email: gail.sparks@venax.ca, URL: http://www.venax.ca/ctrf/
President, Barry Prentice
Secretary, Gail Sparks
Publications: Forumation

### Canadian Trucking Association/L'Association canadienne du camionnage (CTA) (1937)
#1025, 130 Slater St., Ottawa, ON K1P 6E2
613/236-9426, Fax: 613/563-2701, Email: cta@magi.com, URL: http://www.cta.ca
Publications: CTA Bulletin

#### ALBERTA TRUCKING ASSOCIATION
#100, 907 - 34 Ave. SE, PO Box 5520, Stn A, Calgary, AB T2H 1X9
403/243-3767, Fax: 403/243-4610, Toll Free: 1-800-352-8225
URL: http://www.albertatrucking.com
General Manager, Collin Heath
Publications: Truxfax Bulletin

#### ASSOCIATION DU CAMIONNAGE DU QUÉBEC INC./QUÉBEC TRUCKING ASSOCIATION INC. (ACQ) (1951)
#200, 6450, rue Notre Dame ouest, Montréal, QC H4C 1C4
514/932-0377, Téléc: 514/932-1358, Ligne sans frais: 1-800-361-5813
Président, Serge Leclerc
Vice-président exécutif, Claude Pigeon
Publications: ACQ-Plus
Organisation(s) affiliée(s): Union Internationale des Transports Routiers - Genève; American Trucking Association - Washington, DC

#### ATLANTIC PROVINCES TRUCKING ASSOCIATION (APTA) (1950)
Executive Building, #14, One Trites Rd., Riverview, NB E1B 2V5
506/387-4413, Fax: 506/387-7424
Executive Director, Ralph Boyd
Publications: APTA Newsletter; Atlantic Trucking, q.

#### BRITISH COLUMBIA TRUCKING ASSOCIATION (BCTA) (1913)
PO Box 381, Port Coquitlam, BC V3C 4K6
604/942-3200, Fax: 604/942-3191, Toll Free: 1-800-565-2282
President, Paul Landry
Chair, John Bourbonniere
Manager, Administration & Member Services, Karen Westerby
Publications: News & Views; BC Motor Transport Directory, a.; BCTA Membership Roster, a.

#### MANITOBA TRUCKING ASSOCIATION
25 Bunting St., Winnipeg, MB R2X 2P5
204/632-6600, Fax: 204/694-7134
General Manager, Bob Dolyniuk
Publications: Manitoba Highway News & Manitoba Ship-by-Truck Directory

#### NORTHWEST TERRITORIES MOTOR TRANSPORT ASSOCIATION (NWTMTA) (1971)
PO Box 574, Yellowknife, NT X1A 2N4
867/873-2831, Fax: 867/255-2724
President, Charlie Fair
Director, Public Affairs, Keith Mundy
Publications: NWTMTA Newsletter

#### ONTARIO TRUCKING ASSOCIATION (1926)
555 Dixon Rd., Etobicoke, ON M9W 1H8
416/249-7401, Fax: 416/245-6152
Email: info@ontruck.org, URL: http://www.ontruck.org
President, David H. Bradley
Manager, Safety & Operations, Barrie Montague
Manager, Membership & Accounting, Barbara P. Cole
Communications Manager, Rebecka Torn
Manager, Government Affairs, Michael Burke
Manager, Special Projects, Betsy Sharples
Publications: Update; Ship By Truck, s-m.

#### SASKATCHEWAN TRUCKING ASSOCIATION (STA) (1937)
1335 Wallace St., Regina, SK S4N 3Z5
306/569-9696, Fax: 306/781-7066, Toll Free: 1-800-563-7623
General Manager, Warren Smith

### Canadian Urban Transit Association/Association canadienne du transport urbain (CUTA) (1904)
#901, 55 York St., Toronto, ON M5J 1R7
416/365-9800, Fax: 416/365-1295
Executive Vice-President, Al Cormier, CAE
Affiliates: Ontario Urban Transit Association

### Chartered Institute of Transport in North America/Institut agrée des transports Amérique du Nord (CIT) (1919)
**CIT in North America**
#600, 99 Bank St., Ottawa, ON K1P 6B9
613/566-7033, Fax: 613/233-9656, Email: cit@comnet.ca, URL: http://www.cit.ca
Executive Director, Sheilagh Beaudin
Publications: CIT Newsletter; North American Transport, a.

### The Company of Master Mariners of Canada (1967)
401 East Waterfront Rd., Vancouver, BC V6A 4G9
604/253-6576, Fax: 604/253-0874, Email: national@axionet.com
National Master, Capt. D.J. Wilson
National Deputy Master, Capt. A. Knight
National Assistant Master, Capt. A.S. Monaghan
National Secretary, Capt. D.J. Bremner
National Treasurer, Capt. A. Whitelaw
Publications: From the Bridge
Affiliates: Master Mariner organizations in the UK, USA, South Africa, Australia & NZ

### Electric Vehicle Association of Canada/Association canadienne du véhicule électrique (1978)
#11, 21 Concourse Gate, Nepean, ON K2E 7S4
613/723-3127, Fax: 613/723-8275, Email: evac@evac.ca, URL: http://ww.evac.ca
Executive Director, Tom Lewinson
Publications: Electric Propulsion
Affiliates: Association européenne des véhicules électriques routiers; World Electric Vehicle Association; Electric Vehicle Association of Americas

### Freight Carriers Association of Canada (FCA) (1939)
660 Garrison Rd., Fort Erie, ON L2A 5M9
905/994-0560, Fax: 905/994-0117
Executive Vice-President, Micheline S. Tansey
Publications: News
Affiliates: Niagara Frontier Tariff Bureau

### Industrial Truck Association of Canada (1967)
c/o Trade Association Management Group, 208 Brimorton Dr., Scarborough, ON M1H 2C6
416/431-1330, Fax: 416/431-5223
Manager, John Martin

### Motorcycle & Moped Industry Council/Le Conseil de l'industrie de la motocyclette et du cyclomoteur (MMIC) (1971)
#235, 7181 Woodbine Ave., Markham, ON L3R 1A3
905/470-6123, Fax: 905/470-9407, Email: mtrcycl@ibm.net
Executive Director, Robert Ramsay
Publications: MMIC Bulletin

### Ontario Good Roads Association (OGRA) (1894)
#2, 530 Otto Rd., Mississauga, ON L5T 2L5
905/795-2555, Fax: 905/795-2660
Executive Director, Sheila Richardson
Office Manager, Cathy Houston
Publications: Municipal Routes

### Ontario Movers Association (OMA)
555 Dixon Rd., Etobicoke, ON M9W 1H8

416/249-7401, Fax: 416/245-6152
Publications: OMA Newsletter

**Ontario Traffic Council (OTC)**
#121, 20 Carlton St., Toronto, ON M5B 2H5
416/598-4138, Fax: 416/598-0449
Administrative Assistant, Judy Woodley

**Ontario Urban Transit Association**
#901, 55 York St., Toronto, ON M5J 1R7
416/365-9800, Fax: 416/365-1295
Executive Director, Dave Roberts

**Private Motor Truck Council of Canada/ Association canadienne du camionnage d'entreprise (PMTC) (1977)**
#11, 1155 North Service Rd. West, Oakville, ON L6M 3E3
905/827-0587, Fax: 905/827-8212, Email: trucks@pmtc.ca, URL: http://www.pmtc.ca
President, Bruce J. Richards
Chairman, G. Dennis
Vice-Chairman, P. Roy
Publications: News Briefs; The Counsellor, q.
Affiliates: National Private Truck Council

**The Railway Association of Canada/ L'Association des chemins de fer du Canada (RAC) (1917)**
#1105, 800, boul René-Lévesque ouest, Montréal, QC H3B 1X9
514/879-8555, Fax: 514/879-1522, Email: rac@railcan.ca, URL: http://www.railcan.ca
President, R.H. Ballantyne
Vice-President, M.D. Lacombe
Publications: Railway Trends
Affiliates: Association of American Railroads

**The Shipping Federation of Canada/La Fédération maritime du Canada (1903)**
#326, 300, rue St-Sacrement, Montréal, QC H2Y 1X4
514/849-2325, Fax: 514/849-6992, Telex: 055-61042
President, Francis C. Nicol
Publications: Maritime Perspective

**Transport 2000 Canada (1977)**
#102, 111 Metcalfe St., PO Box 858, Stn B, Ottawa, ON K1P 5P9
613/594-3290, Fax: 613/594-3271, Info Line: 613/594-3291
National Office Manager, Dirk Partridge
President, David W. Glastonbury
Vice-President, Harry Gow
Secretary, Anton Turrittin
Membership Secretary, John deWit
Publications: Transport Action
Affiliates: Transport 2000 International
Transport 2000 Alberta: President, John Bakker; Treasurer, Frank J. Testin, PO Box 4385, Edmonton, AB T6E 4T5, 403/458-2225
Transport 2000 Atlantic: President, John Pearce; Treasurer, William T. McIntyre, 40 Lorne Ave., Dartmouth, NS B2Y 3E7, 902/469-3474, Fax: 902/466-8832
Transport 2000 British Columbia: President, Ian Fisher, #213, 1728 Alberni St., Vancouver, BC V6G 1B2, 604/687-6219
Transport 2000 Ontario: President, Elizabeth Hill; Secretary, David G. Scott, 28 Vradenberg Dr., Scarborough, ON M1T 1M6, 416/497-6090
Transport 2000 Québec: Président, Luc Côté, 2520, rue Lionel-Groulx, 2e étage, Montréal, QC H3J 1J8, 514/932-8008, Téléc: 514/932-2024
Transport 2000 Saskatchewan: President, Jim Richards, PO Box 2134, Melfort, SK S0E 1A0, 306/752-2603

**Transportation Association of Canada/ Association des transports du Canada (TAC) (1970)**
2323 St. Laurent Blvd., Ottawa, ON K1G 4K6
613/736-1350, Fax: 613/736-1395, Email: secretariat@tac-atc.ca
Executive Director, Louise Pelletier, CAE
Publications: TAC News/Nouvelles de L'ATC; Transportation Forum, irreg.

**Western Canada Motor Coach Association (WCMCA) (1961)**
PO Box 4520, Stn C, Calgary, AB T2T 5N3
403/244-4487, Fax: 403/244-2340, Email: amc@incentre.net
Executive Director, Simone Hambly
President, Damian Opel
Publications: Headlights

**Western Transportation Advisory Council (WESTAC) (1973)**
#1140, 800 Pender St. West, Vancouver, BC V6C 2V6
604/687-8691, Fax: 604/687-8751
President, B. Maureen Melville
Vice-President/Corporate Secretary, Paul Ovimet
Transportation Analyst, Amanda Levey

**TRAVEL *see* TOURISM & TRAVEL**

**TREASURY MANAGEMENT *see* FINANCE**

**TRUCKING *see* TRANSPORTATION & SHIPPING**

**UNDERWATER ARCHAEOLOGY *see* ARCHAEOLOGY**

**UNDERWRITERS *see* INSURANCE INDUSTRY**

**UNITED WAY *see* SOCIAL RESPONSE/SOCIAL SERVICES**

**UNIVERSITIES *see* EDUCATION**

**URBAN DEVELOPMENT *see* PLANNING & DEVELOPMENT**

**USER GROUPS *see* INFORMATION TECHNOLOGY**

**VACATION INDUSTRY *see* TOURISM & TRAVEL**

**VENTURE CAPITAL *see* FINANCE**

**VETERANS *see* MILITARY & VETERANS**

**VETERINARY MEDICINE *see* ANIMALS & ANIMAL SCIENCE**

**VIDEO *see* FILM & VIDEO**

## VISUAL ART, CRAFTS, FOLK ARTS

***see also* The Arts; Galleries & Museums**

**Alberta Craft Council (ACC) (1979)**
10106 - 124 St., Edmonton, AB T5N 1P6
403/488-6611, Fax: 403/488-8855, Toll Free: 1-800-362-7238, Email: acc@compusmart.ab.ca
Chairman, Arne Handley
Publications: Alberta Craft Magazine

**Artists in Stained Glass (AISG)**
c/o Ontario Crafts Council, 35 McCaul St., Toronto, ON M5T 1V7
416/977-3551, Fax: 416/977-3552
Co-Chair, Sue Obata
Co-Chair, Robert Brown
Publications: A Flat Glass Journal

**Association des collections d'entreprises/ Corporate Art Collectors Association (1990)**
Secrétariat: Banque nationale du Canada, 600, rue de la Gauchetière ouest, 8e étage, Montréal, QC H3B 4L2
514/394-8533, Téléc: 514/394-6258
Président, Maurice Forget
Secrétaire, Francine Paul

**The Canadian Art Foundation (1991)**
70 The Esplanade, 2nd Fl., Toronto, ON M5E 1R2
416/368-8854, Fax: 416/368-6135
Contact, Richard Rhodes
Publications: Canadian Art

**Canadian Association of Film Distributors & Exporters/Association canadienne des distributeurs et exportateurs de films (CAFDE)**
62 Humewood Dr., Toronto, ON M6C 2W4
416/658-2929, Fax: 416/658-3176
President & CEO, Dan Johnson
Co-Chair, Victor Loewy
Co-Chair, Stephen Greenberg
Vice-Chair, Québec, Andre Link
Vice-Chair, Ontario, Bryan Gliserman
Sec.-Treas., Andy Myers
Affiliates: Association des producteurs de films et de television du Québec

**Canadian Association of Professional Conservators/Association canadienne des restaurateurs professionnels (1971)**
#400, 280 Metcalfe St., Ottawa, ON K2P 1R7
613/998-4971, Fax: 613/993-3412
Chairman, Gerald Fitzgerald
Secretary, Robert Arnold
Publications: Directory; CAPC News, s-a.

**Canadian Ceramic Society (CCS) (1901)**
#310, 2175 Sheppard Ave. East, North York, ON M2J 1W8
416/491-2886, Fax: 416/491-1670, Email: taylor@interlog.com
President, Al Matthews
Vice-President, Brian Sellars
Administrator, Diane Gaunt
Publications: Canadian Ceramics Quarterly; The Journal of the Canadian Ceramic Society

**Canadian Craft & Hobby Association (CCHA) (1978)**
#24, 1410 - 40 Ave. NE, Calgary, AB T2E 6L1
403/291-0559, Fax: 403/291-0675, Toll Free: 1-888-991-0559, Email: ccha@cadvision.com, URL: http://www.cdncraft.org
Executive Director, Patrice Baron-Parent
Publications: Canadian Craft Trade; Craft & Needlework Age; Canadian Florist, Greenhouse & Nursery, Craftrends

**Canadian Crafts Council/Conseil canadien des métiers d'art (CCC) (1974)**
345 Lakeshore Rd. West, Oakville, ON L6K 1G3
905/845-5357, Fax: 905/845-8210, Email: kingfish@spectranet.ca
President, Jan Waldorf
Publications: CCC Bulletin

**Canadian Folk Arts Council/Conseil canadien des arts populaires**
263 Adelaide St. West, 5th Fl., Toronto, ON M5H 1Y2
416/977-7456
Director General, Leon Kossar

**Canadian Guild of Crafts Québec/Guild canadienne des métiers d'art Québec (1906)**
2025, rue Peel, Montréal, QC H3A 1T6
514/849-6091, Fax: 514/849-7351
Managing Director, Nairy Kalemkerian

**Canadian Quilters Association/Association canadienne de la courtepointe (CQA) (1981)**
PO Box 22010, RPO Herongate, Ottawa, ON K1V 0C2
URL: http://www.nt.net/~giselef/cqaacc1.htm
President, Jackie Philpott, Bus: 709/686-5007, Email: jphilptt@atcon.com
Treasurer, Carol Galloway, Bus: 204/269-9566, Email: cgallow@mts.net
Publicity, Nancy Cameron Armstrong, Bus: 604/538-7551, Email: narmstr@ibm.net
Publications: CQA/ACC Newsletter

**Canadian Society of Decorative Arts/Cercle canadien des arts décoratifs (CSDA) (1981)**
PO Box 4, Stn B, Toronto, ON M5T 2T2
Email: mbradley@chin.gc.ca
President, Merridy Bradley, Bus: 613/992-3333
Publications: Bulletin

**Canadian Society of Painters in Water Color/ Société canadienne de peintres en aquarelle (CSPWC) (1926)**
#102, 258 Wallace Ave., Toronto, ON M6P 3M9
416/533-5100
Administrator, Shirley Barrie
Publications: Watercolour Newsletter

**Conseil des arts textiles du Québec (CATQ) (1980)**
811A, rue Ontario est, Montréal, QC H2L 1P1
514/524-6645, Téléc: 514/525-2621
Présidente, Micheline Couture
Coordonnatrice, Jocelyne Gaudreau
Publications: Textile

**Conseil des métiers d'art du Québec/Québec Crafts Council (1985)**
378, rue St-Paul ouest, Montréal, QC H2Y 2A6
514/287-7555, Téléc: 514/287-9923
Directeur général, Yvan Gauthier
Présidente, Louise Lemieux Bérubé

**Crafts Association of British Columbia**
Granville Island, 1386 Cartwright St., Vancouver, BC V6H 3R8
604/687-6511
Ann Wray
Publications: Craft Contacts

**Crafts Guild of Manitoba Inc. (1928)**
183 Kennedy St., Winnipeg, MB R3C 1S6
204/943-1190, Fax: 204/989-2254
Manager, S. Sulkers
Publications: Newsletter

**Embroiderers' Association of Canada, Inc. (EAC) (1973)**
1311 Salisbury Rd., RR#1, Moncton, NB E1C 8J5
506/852-8816, Fax: 506/478-2879, Email: shorsman@nb.sympatico.ca, URL: http://www.eac.ca/embroidery/
President, Sheila Horseman
Past President, Barbara Gilbert
Secretary, Leslie Burrows
Vice-President, Joan Mills
Publications: Embroidery Canada

**Folklore Canada International (FCI) (1986)**
PO Box 9, Stn DeLorimier, Montréal, QC H2H 2N6
514/524-8552, Fax: 514/524-0269
Director General, Guy Landry
Publications: Folklore Canada Express; Directory of Living Heritage Festivals & Events in Canada

**Fondation d'art nationale du Canada**
#2500, 1155, boul René-Lévesque ouest, Montréal, QC H3B 2K4
514/876-1632, Téléc: 514/875-8967
Directeur général, Pierre Lorrain

**Fusion: The Ontario Clay & Glass Association**
The Gardener's Cottage, 225 Confederation Dr., Scarborough, ON M19 1B2
416/438-8946, Fax: 416/438-0192
Contact, Elizabeth Dingman
Publications: Fusion Magazine

**International Association of Art Critics (Canada) Inc./Association internationale des critiques d'art (Canada) inc.**
#706, 15 McMurrich St., Toronto, ON M5R 3M6
416/925-5564, Fax: 416/925-2972
President, Normand Biron
Treasurer, Pat Fleisher

**Manitoba Crafts Council (1978)**
**Council of Manitoba Artisans Inc.**
#003, 100 Arthur St., Winnipeg, MB R3B 1H3
204/942-1816, Fax: 204/989-2254
President, Ron Mark
Administrator, Mary Krieger
Publications: The Bulletin

**The Metal Arts Guild (MAG) (1946)**
#303, 80 Spadina Ave., Toronto, ON M5S 2J3
416/504-8453
President, Louise Jarvis
Administrator, Camille Anderson
Publications: MAGazine

**Newfoundland & Labrador Crafts Development Association (NLCDA) (1972)**
Devon House, 59 Duckworth St., St. John's, NF A1C 1E6
709/753-2749, Fax: 709/753-2766, Email: anne_manuel@porthole.entnet.nf.ca
Executive Director, Anne Manuel
Chairperson, Ray Will
Publications: NLCDA Newsletter
Affiliates: Canadian Crafts Council

**Nova Scotia Designer Crafts Council (NSDCC) (1973)**
#901, 1809 Barrington St., Halifax, NS B3J 3K8
902/423-3837, Fax: 902/422-0881, Email: nsdcc@mail.kayhay.com
Executive Director, Susan Hanrahan
Publications: Nova Scotia Craft News; NSDCC News Flash, q.

**Ontario Crafts Council (1976)**
Chalmer's Building, 35 McCaul St., Toronto, ON M5T 1V7
416/977-3551, Fax: 416/977-3552, URL: http://www.craft.on.ca/occ
Executive Director, Sarah Lupmanis
Publications: Ontario Craft

**Ontario Folk Arts Multicultural Council (1966)**
Ontario Heritage Centre, #101G, 10 Adelaide St. East, Toronto, ON M5C 1J3
416/367-8027, Fax: 416/367-8027
Executive Director, Bryn Lloyd
Publications: News & Views

**Ontario Society for Education Through Art**
345 Balliol St., Toronto, ON M4S 1E1
416/487-0705
President, Susan Brown

**Ontario Woodcarvers Association (OWCA)**
14 Rintella Ct., Scarborough, ON M1P 3V5
Contact, Donald Swenor
Publications: Ontario Woodcarver

**Prince Edward Island Crafts Council (PEICC) (1965)**
156 Richmond St., Charlottetown, PE C1A 1H9
902/892-5152, Fax: 902/628-8740, URL: gopher://gopher.well.sf.ca.us/00/Art/PEI.Crafts.Council
Publications: Craft News

**Professional Art Dealers Association of Canada Inc./Association professionnelle des galeries d'art du Canada inc. (PADAC) (1966)**
#307, 80 Spadina Ave., Toronto, ON M5V 2J3
416/703-0061, Fax: 416/703-0063
Executive Administrator, Louise Durham
Publications: Membership Directory

**Royal Canadian Academy of Arts/Académie royale des arts du Canada (1880)**
Office of the Secretary, 163 Queen St. East, PO Box 2, Toronto, ON M5A 1S1
416/363-9612, Fax: 416/363-9612
President, Ernest Annau, RCA
Sec.-Treas., Vello Hubel, RCA
Publications: RCA Newsletter
Affiliates: National Gallery of Canada (founded by RCA in 1880); Royal Academy, England

**Saskatchewan Crafts Council (SCC) (1975)**
813 Broadway Ave., Saskatoon, SK S7N 1B5
306/653-3616, Fax: 306/244-2711, URL: http://www.ffa.ucalgary.ca/scco/scc.html; http://www.sasknet.sk.ca/SCCO/SCC.html
Publications: The Bulletin; The Craft Factor, 3 pa
Affiliates: Canadian Craft Council

**Sculptor's Society of Canada/Société sculpteurs du Canada (SSC) (1928)**
Exchange Tower, First Canadian Place, 130 King St. West, PO Box 40, Stn 1st Canadian Place, Toronto, ON M5X 1B5
416/214-0389, Email: sculpcan@lglobal.com, URL: http://www.lglobal.com/sculpcan/Welcome.html
President, Desmond Scott
Publications: SSC Newsletter; Sculpture for the City Catalogue

**SIAS International Art Society (1986)**
PO Box 3039, Sherwood Park, AB T8A 2A6
403/922-5463, Fax: 403/922-5463
Managing Director/President, Klaus Bous
Associate Director, Horatio Venancio

**Society of Canadian Artists/Société des artistes canadiens (SCA) (1957)**
1435 Woodbine Ave., Toronto, ON M4C 4G8
President, George Sanders
Treasurer, Marg Nurse
Corresponding Secretary, Joy Orzy
Publications: Newsletter

**Visual Arts Nova Scotia (VANS) (1976)**
#901, 1809 Barrington St., Halifax, NS B3J 3K8
902/423-4694, Fax: 902/422-0881, Email: vans@fox.nstn.ca, URL: http://www.cfn.cs.dal.ca/Culture/VANS/index.html
Executive Director, Andrew Terris
Publications: Visual Arts News

**Visual Arts Ontario (VAO) (1974)**
439 Wellington St. West, 3rd Fl., Toronto, ON M5V 1E7
416/591-8883, Fax: 416/591-2432, Email: vao@castlecom.net

Executive Director, Hennie L. Wolff
Publications: Agenda; Hidden Agenda, m.

**Western Canada Art Association (WCAA) (1970)**
Kelowna Art Gallery, 470 Queensway, Kelowna, BC V1Y 6S7
250/762-2226
Sec.-Treas., Gerald Jessop
Publications: Wagon

**WATER & WASTEWATER *see* ENVIRONMENTAL**

**WATER RESOURCES *see* ENVIRONMENTAL**

**WILDLIFE *see* ENVIRONMENTAL**

## WOMEN

**Association of Canadian Women Composers/Association des femmes compositrices canadiennes (ACWC) (1980)**
20 St. Joseph St., Toronto, ON M4Y 1J9
416/239-5195
Chairperson, Jana Skarecky
Publications: ACWC Newsletter; Directory of Canadian Women Composers

**Association féminine d'éducation et d'action sociale/Feminine Association for Education & Social Action (AFEAS) (1966)**
5999, rue de Marseille, Montréal, QC H1N 1K6
514/251-1636, Téléc: 514/251-9023
Secrétaire générale, Lise Girard
Publications: Femmes d'ici
Organisation(s) affiliée(s): Union mondiale des organisations féminines catholiques (UMOFC)

**Association des femmes d'affaires du Québec (AFAQ)**
3702, rue St-Denis, Montréal, QC H2X 3L7
514/845-4281, Téléc: 514/845-3365
Présidente, Henriette Lanctot

**Breast Cancer Action/Sensibilisation au cancer du sein**
PO Box 39041, RPO Billings Bridge Plaza, Ottawa, ON K1H 1A1
613/736-5921, Fax: 613/736-8422, Email: bcanet@magi.com, URL: http://infoweb.magi.com/~bcanet/

**Canadian Association for the Advancement of Women & Sport & Physical Activity/Association canadienne pour l'avancement des femmes du sport et de l'activité physique (CAAWS) (1981)**
#308A, 1600 James Naismith Dr., Gloucester, ON K1B 5N4
613/748-5793, Fax: 613/748-5775, URL: http://infoweb.magi.com/~wmnsport/index.html
Executive Director, Marg McGregor
Publications: Action Bulletin
Affiliates: National Action Committee on the Status of Women

**Canadian Association of Women Executives & Entrepreneurs/Association canadienne des femmes cadres et entrepreneurs (CAWEE) (1976)**
#300, 595 Bay St., Toronto, ON M5G 2C2
416/482-2933, Fax: 416/596-7894
President, Dianna Rhodes
Manager, Linda Hatfield
Publications: Newsletter

**Canadian Congress for Learning Opportunities for Women/Congrès canadien pour la promotion des études chez la femme (CCLOW) (1979)**
47 Main St., Toronto, ON M4E 2V6
416/699-1909, Fax: 416/699-2145, Email: cclow@web.net, URL: http://www.nald.ca/cclow.htm
Executive Director, Aisla Thomson
President, Pamela Dos Ramos
Publications: Women's Education des femmes

**Canadian Federation of Business & Professional Women's Clubs/Fédération canadienne des clubs de femmes de carrières commerciales et professionnelles (CFBPWC) (1930)**
**BPW Canada**
#308, 56 Sparks St., Ottawa, ON K1P 5A9
613/234-7619, Fax: 613/234-7619, Email: selkirk@bpwcanada.com, URL: http://www.bpwcanada.com
General Secretary, Shirley Côté
President, Marge Donovan
Publications: The Business & Professional Woman

**Canadian Women in Communications/Association canadienne des femmes en communication (CWC) (1991)**
#804, 372 Bay St., Toronto, ON M5H 2W9
416/363-1880, Fax: 416/363-1882, Toll Free: 1-800-361-2978, Email: cwc.afc@sympatico.ca, URL: http://www.citytv.com/cwc/
Executive Director, Stephanie MacKendrick
Publications: CWC Newsletter

**Canadian Women's Foundation/Fondation des femmes canadiennes**
#504, 133 Richmond St. West, Toronto, ON M5H 2L3
416/365-1444, Fax: 416/365-1745, Email: info@cdnwomen.org, URL: http://www.cdnwomen.org
Executive Director, Beverley Wybrow
Publications: Initiatives

**Catholic Women's League of Canada**
#1, 160 Murray Park Rd., Winnipeg, MB R3J 3X5
204/885-4856, Fax: 204/831-9507
Executive Director, Carrie Ehman

**Congress of Black Women of Canada**
590 Jarvis St., Toronto, ON M4Y 2J4
416/961-2427, Fax: 416/961-8842
President, Cloe Calendar
Affiliates: The Black Secretariat

**Federated Women's Institutes of Canada/Fédération des instituts féminins du Canada (FWIC) (1919)**
#606, 251 Bank St., Ottawa, ON K2P 1X3
613/234-1090, Fax: 613/234-1090
Executive Director, Arlene Strugnell
President, Mildred Keith
Publications: Federated News
Affiliates: Associated Country Women of the World

**ALBERTA WOMEN'S INSTITUTES (AWI) (1909)**
10403 - 172 St., Edmonton, AB T5S 1K9
403/488-5282, Fax: 403/488-5282
Executive Secretary, Janet Halberg

**BRITISH COLUMBIA WOMEN'S INSTITUTES (BCWI) (1909)**
20510 Fraser Hwy., Langley, BC V3A 4G2
604/533-6564, Fax: 604/533-6564
Sec.-Treas., Jan Marshall
President, Patsy Nagel
Publications: Network News
Affiliates: BC Federation of Agriculture

**FEDERATED WOMEN'S INSTITUTES OF ONTARIO (FWIO) (1897)**
7382 Wellington Rd. 30, RR#5, Guelph, ON N1H 6J2
519/836-3078, Fax: 519/836-9456
President, Arthena Hecker
Public Relations Officer, Mary Janes
Publications: Home & Country

**MANITOBA WOMEN'S INSTITUTES (MWI) (1910)**
Norquay Bldg., #908, 401 York Ave., Winnipeg, MB R3C 0P8
204/945-8976, Fax: 204/945-6134
Executive Administrator, Shirley Bell
Publications: Institute News
Affiliates: Associated Country Women of the World; Provincial Council of Women

**NEW BRUNSWICK WOMEN'S INSTITUTE (NBWI) (1911)**
Victoria Health Centre, #251, 65 Brunswick St., Fredericton, NB E3B 1G5
506/454-0798, Fax: 506/458-2606
Administrative Officer, Stella Quartermain
Publications: For Home & Country
Affiliates: Associated Country Women of the World

**NEWFOUNDLAND & LABRADOR WOMEN'S INSTITUTES (NLWI) (1935)**
Arts & Culture Centre, PO Box 1854, Stn C, St. John's, NF A1C 5P9
709/753-8780, Fax: 709/753-8780
Executive Administrator, Sylvia O. Manning
Publications: The Newfoundland & Labrador Women's Institutes Newsletter
Affiliates: Associated County Women of the World

**PRINCE EDWARD ISLAND WOMEN'S INSTITUTE**
Department of Agriculture, PO Box 2000, Charlottetown, PE C1A 7N8
902/368-4860, Fax: 902/368-5651
Liaison, Karen Lee Craig

**QUÉBEC WOMEN'S INSTITUTES (QWI) (1911)**
Macdonald Campus, McGill University, 21111 ch Lakeshore, PO Box 58, Montréal, QC H9X 3V9
514/398-7705, Fax: 514/398-7955
Kathryn Pryce
Publications: Québec Women's Institutes Newsletter
Affiliates: Associated Country Women of the World

**SASKATCHEWAN WOMEN'S INSTITUTES**
#137, Kirk Hall, University of Saskatchewan, 117 Science Pl., Saskatoon, SK S7N 0W0
306/966-5566, Fax: 306/966-8717
Administrative Coordinator, Beth Ratzlaff
Publications: The Second Penny
Affiliates: Saskatchewan Council of Women; Saskatchewan Safety Council; Saskatchewan Federation of Agriculture; Saskatchewan Farm Vacation Association; Saskatchewan Action Committee, Status of Women; Saskatchewan Agricultural Hall of Fame; Saskatchewan Committee on Rural Area Development

**WOMEN'S INSTITUTES OF NOVA SCOTIA (WINS) (1913)**
NSAC, PO Box 550, Truro, NS B2N 5E3
902/893-6520, Fax: 902/893-6393
Theresa Osborne
Publications: Home & Country; Nova Scotia Farm Women, q.
Affiliates: Associated Country Women of the World

**Fédération des femmes du Québec (FFQ) (1966)**
#100, 5225, rue Berri, Montréal, QC H2J 2S4
514/948-3262, Téléc: 514/948-3264
Directrice générale, Céline Signori

**Federation of Medical Women of Canada/Fédération des femmes médecins du Canada (FMWC) (1924)**
#107, 1815 Alta Vista Dr., Ottawa, ON K1G 3Y6
613/731-1026, Fax: 613/731-8748
Executive Coordinator, Kay Moffatt
Publications: FMWC Newsletter
Affiliates: Canadian Medical Association; Medical Women's International Association

**Fédération nationale des femmes canadiennes-françaises (FNFCF) (1914)**
#302, 450 Rideau St., Ottawa, ON K1N 5Z4
613/241-3500, Téléc: 613/241-6679
Directrice générale, Diane Vachon
Présidente, Ghislaine Foulem
Ressource de l'information, Nicole Pigeon
Publications: Concert action
Organisation(s) affiliée(s): Fédération des communautés francophones et acadienne du Canada; Comité canadien d'action sur le statut de la femme

**Hadassah-WIZO Organization of Canada (1917)**
#900, 1310, av Greene, Montréal, QC H3Z 2B8
514/937-9431, Fax: 514/933-6483
Executive Vice-President, Lily Frank
National President, Judy Mandleman
Publications: Orah
Affiliates: Canadian Jewish Congress; Canadian Zionist Federation; National Council of Women of Canada; United Nations Association; Women's International Zionist Organization

**Immigrant & Visible Minority Women Against Abuse (IVMWAA) (1989)**
PO Box 67041, Ottawa, ON K2A 0E0
613/729-3145, Fax: 613/729-9308
Executive Director, Lucya Spencer

**Jewish Women International of Canada (JWIC)**
#210, 638A Sheppard Ave. West, Downsview, ON M3H 2S1
416/630-9313, Fax: 416/630-9319
Executive Director, Penny Krowitz, CAE
Publications: Canadian Scene
Affiliates: Jewish Women International

**MATCH International Centre/Centre international Match (1977)**
#1102, 200 Elgin St., Ottawa, ON K2P 1L5
613/238-1312, Fax: 613/238-6867, Email: matchint@web.apc.org
Executive Director, Madonna Larbi
Accounting Officer, Sandy Wood
Publications: Match News

**Na'amat Canada Inc. (1924)**
#6, 7005, rue Kildare, Montréal, QC H4W 1C1
514/488-0792, Fax: 514/487-6727, Email: naamat@total.net
National Executive Director, Vivian Reisler
Publications: Na'amat Canada
Affiliates: Canadian Jewish Congress; National Action Committee on the Status of Women

**National Action Committee on the Status of Women/Comité canadien d'action sur le statut de la femme (NAC) (1971)**
#203, 234 Eglinton Ave. East, Toronto, ON M4P 1K5
416/932-1718, Fax: 416/932-0646, Toll Free: 1-800-665-5124, Email: nac@web.net
President, Sunera Thobani
Executive Coordinator, Beverly Bain
Treasurer, Maureen Leyland
Secretary, Laura Sky
Publications: Action Now

**National Association of Women in Construction (NAWIC) (1955)**
327 South Adams St., Fort Worth, TX 76104 USA
817/877-5551, Fax: 817/877-0324, Toll Free: 1-800-552-3506, Email: nawic@onramp.net, URL: http://www.nawic.org
Executive Vice-President, Dede Hughes
Publications: The NAWIC Image

**National Association of Women & the Law/Association nationale de la femme et du droit (NAWL) (1974)**
#604, 1 Nicholas St., Ottawa, ON K1N 7B7
613/241-7570, Fax: 613/241-4657, Email: nawl@ftn.net
Executive Director, Carolyn Karpoff
Coordinator, National Steering Committee, Darlene Jamieson
Publications: Jurisfemme

**National Council of Jewish Women of Canada**
#118, 1588 Main St., Winnipeg, MB R2V 1Y3
204/339-9700, Fax: 204/334-3779

**The National Council of Women of Canada/Le conseil national des femmes du Canada (NCWC) (1893)**
#33, 270 MacLaren St., Ottawa, ON K2P 0M3
613/232-5025, Fax: 613/232-8419, Email: ncwc@intranet.ca
President, Win Whitfield
Publications: NCWC News

**The Older Women's Network Co-op (OWN) (1988)**
115 The Esplanade, Toronto, ON M5E 1Y7
416/214-1518, Fax: 416/214-1541, Email: ownmetro@mail.rose.com
Executive Director, Moira Bacon
Chair, Helen Riley
Publications: Contact

**Réseau d'action et d'information pour les femmes (RAIF) (1973)**
CP 36088, CSP Place Ste-Foy, Ste-Foy, QC G1V 1C0
418/658-1973
Coordonnatrice, Marcelle Dolment
Publications: RAIF

**Réseau national d'action-éducation des femmes (1983)**
#208, 435 boul St-Laurent, Ottawa, ON K1K 2Z8
613/741-9978, Téléc: 613/741-3805
Présidente nationale, Monique Hébert
Directrice générale, Monique Roy

**Society for Canadian Women in Science & Technology/Société des canadiennes dans la science et la technologie (SCWIST) (1981)**
#417, 535 Hornby St., Vancouver, BC V6C 2E8
604/895-5814, Fax: 604/684-9171, Email: scwist@sfu.ca, URL: http://www.harbour.sfu.ca/scwist/
President, Hiromi Matsui
Publications: SCWIST News
Affiliates: BC Ministry of Advanced Education, Training & Technology; Industry, Science & Technology Canada; BC Ministry of Education; Canada Employment & Immigration Council; Secretary of State Canada, Women's Program; University of BC, Faculty of Science; Simon Fraser University; BC Institute of Technology; Capilano College; Vancouver School Board; Knowledge Network; Vancouver Foundation; Immigrant Women in Science Program; Douglas College

**Voice of Women/La Voix des femmes (VOW) (1960)**
**Canadian Voice of Women for Peace**
#215, 736 Bathurst St., Toronto, ON M5S 2R4
416/537-9343, Fax: 416/531-6214
Chair, Joy Warner
Publications: Voices
Affiliates: NGO status at the United Nations

**Western Businesswomen's Association (WBA)**
#302, 1107 Homer St., Vancouver, BC V6B 2Y1
604/688-0951, Fax: 604/681-4545
Administrator, Teena Keizer
Publications: WBA Newsletter

**Womanpower Inc. (1974)**
#604, 171 Queens Ave., London, ON N6A 5J7
519/438-1782, Fax: 519/438-7904
Coordinator, Darlene Labadie
Chair, Board of Directors, Eleanor Carvana

**Women Entrepreneurs of Canada/Les Femmes chefs d'entreprises du Canada (WEC) (1992)**
#604, 3 Church St., Toronto, ON M5E 1M2
416/361-7036, Fax: 416/862-0315
President, Nancy Adamo
Vice-President, Administration, Carol Denman
Publications: WECan

**The Women & Environments Education & Development Foundation (1987)**
**The WEED Foundation**
736 Bathurst St., Toronto, ON M5S 2R4
416/516-2600, Fax: 416/531-6214, Email: weed@web.apc.org, URL: http://www.web.net/~weed/
Office Manager, Jennifer Jackson
Publications: Women & Environments; WE International, q.
Affiliates: National Action Committee on the Status of Women

**Women in Music (WIM) (1991)**
**Society for Women in Music**
#1212, 207 West Hastings St., Vancouver, BC V6B 1H7
604/684-9461, Fax: 604/684-1543, Email: marian rose@mindlink.bc.ca
President, Gayle Webster
Publications: Brava

**Women in Science & Engineering Corporation/Corporation des femmes en sciences et en génie (WISE) (1977)**
6519B Mississauga Rd., Mississauga, ON L5N 1A6
905/567-7190, Fax: 905/567-7191
National President, Elza Seregelyi, Bus: 613/763-5994, Fax: 709/729-5878
Publications: WISE/CFSG National Newsletter

**Women of Unifarm (1970)**
14815 - 119 Ave., Edmonton, AB T5L 4W2
403/451-5912, Fax: 403/453-2669

**Women's Art Association of Canada (WAA) (1887)**
**Lyceum Club & Women's Art Association of Canada**
23 Prince Arthur Ave., Toronto, ON M5R 1B2
416/922-2060
President, A.L. Cumine
Publications: Bulletin
Affiliates: Lyceum Club (International)

**Women's Art Resource Centre (WARC) (1984)**
#389, 401 Richmond St. West, Toronto, ON M5V 3A8
416/977-0097, Fax: 416/977-7425, Email: warc@interlog.com
Director, Z. Packer
Director, Irene Abrahams
Publications: Matriart: A Canadian Visual Art Journal

**Women's Counselling & Referral & Education Centre (WCREC) (1975)**
525 Bloor St. West, Toronto, ON M5S 1Y4
416/534-7501, TTY: 416/534-5078, Fax: 416/534-1704
Publications: WCREC Newsletter

**Women's Enterprise Bureau (1990)**
30 Harvey Rd., St. John's, NF A1C 2G1
709/754-5555, Fax: 709/754-0079
Executive Director, Susan J. Adams, CAE
Chairperson, Ann Bell
Publications: Women Business Owners Directory
Affiliates: Provincial Advisory Council on the Status of Women

**Women's Inter-Church Council of Canada/ Conseil oécumenique des chrétiennes du Canada (WICC) (1918)**
#402, 815 Danforth Ave., Toronto, ON M4J 1L2
416/462-2528, Fax: 416/462-3915
Executive Director, Karen Hincke
President, Ann Austin-Cardwell
Publications: The Wick
Affiliates: International Committee for World Day of Prayer; International Committee for the Fellowship of the Least Coin

**Women's International League for Peace & Freedom (WILPF) (1915)**
PO Box 4781, Stn E, Ottawa, ON K1S 5H9
Fax: 613/567-2384
President, Marcelene Holyk
Publications: WILPF News

**Women's Legal Education & Action Fund/Fonds d'action et d'éducation juridiques pour les femmes (LEAF) (1985)**
#403, 489 College St., Toronto, ON M6G 1A5
416/963-9654, Fax: 416/963-8455
Chair, Joyce Burpee
Publications: LEAF Lines

**Women's Network PEI (1984)**
PO Box 233, Charlottetown, PE C1A 7K4
902/368-5040, Fax: 902/368-5039, Email: wnpei@isn.net
Project Coordinator, Deborah Conners
Publications: Newsletter

**Women's Research Centre (1973)**
#101, 2245 Broadway West, Vancouver, BC V6K 2E4
604/734-0485, Fax: 604/734-0484
Research Associate, Jan Barnsley

## WRITERS & EDITORS

*see also* Publishing

**Association canadienne des rédacteurs agricoles de langue française (ACRA) (1956)**
1001, boul de Maisonneuve ouest, 10e étage, Montréal, QC H3A 3E1
514/843-2112, Téléc: 514/845-6261
Secrétaire-trésorière, Sylvie Bouchard, agr.
Publications: ARADITION

**Association de la presse francophone (APF) (1976)**
#702, 325, rue Dalhousie, Ottawa, ON K1N 7G2
613/241-1017, Téléc: 613/241-6193, Courrier électronique: pressapf@globalx.net
Président, Roger Duplantie
Directeur, Yves Chartrand
Vice-Président, Jean Mongenais
Vice-Président, François Pageau
Trésorier, François Bélair
Secrétaire, Jacinthe LaFrance

**Canadian Association of Journalists/ L'Association canadienne des journalistes (CAJ) (1978)**
St. Patrick's Building, Carleton University, 1125 Colonel By Dr., Ottawa, ON K1S 5B6
613/526-8061, Fax: 613/521-3904, Email: cf408@freenet.carleton.ca, URL: http://www.eagle.ca/caj/
Executive Director, Rob Henderson
Publications: Media

**Canadian Authors Association (CAA) (1921)**
27 Doxsee Ave. North, PO Box 419, Campbellford, ON K0L 1L0
705/653-0323, Fax: 705/653-0593, Email: canauth@redden.on.ca, URL: http://www.CanAuthors.org/national.html
Administrator, Alec McEachern
National President, Murphy Shewchuk
National Vice-President, Gail Corbett
Sec.-Treas., Roger Tulk
Membership Chair, Deborah Ranchuk
Awards Chairman, Gillian Foss
Publications: Canadian Author; The Canadian Writer's Guide; National Newsline, q.
Affiliates: La Société des écrivains canadiens

**Canadian Farm Writers' Federation (1955)**
c/o Office of Research, University of Guelph, Guelph, ON N1G 2W1
519/824-4120, ext.8278, Fax: 519/821-5236, URL: http://www.uoguelph.ca/Research/cfwf
President, Owen Roberts, Email: owen@ornet.or.uoguelph.ca
Publications: Farm Journalist
Affiliates: British Columbia Farm Writers' Association; Alberta Farm Writers' Association; Saskatchewan Farm Writers' Association; Manitoba Farm Writers' & Broadcasters' Association; Eastern Canada Farm Writers' Association

**Canadian Journalism Foundation/La Fondation pour le journalisme canadien (CJF) (1990)**
TD Bank Tower, 5402, 66 Wellington St. West, PO Box 166, Toronto, ON M5K 1H6
416/366-8573, Fax: 416/367-2339
Chair, Knowlton Nash
Executive Director, William Wilton
Sec.-Treas., Donald J. Crawford

**Canadian Science Writers' Association/ Association canadienne des rédacteurs scientifiques (CSWA) (1971)**
PO Box 75, Stn A, Toronto, ON M5W 1A2
416/928-9624, Fax: 416/960-0528, Email: cswa@interlog.com, URL: http://www.interlog.com/~cswa
Administrative Director, Andy F. Visser-deVries
Publications: Science Link; CSWA Directory, a.

**Canadian Society of Children's Authors, Illustrators & Performers/La société canadienne des auteurs, illustrateurs et artistes pour enfants (CANSCAIP) (1977)**
35 Spadina Rd., Toronto, ON M5R 2S9
416/515-1559, Fax: 416/515-7022, Email: canscaip@interlog.com, URL: http://www.interlog.com/~canscaip
President, Sharon Jennings
Publications: CANSCAIP News

**Canadian Society of Magazine Editors (CSME) (1990)**
c/o Canadian Living, #100, 25 Sheppard Ave. West, North York, ON M2N 6S7
416/596-5177
President, Brian Banks, Bus: 416/596-5177
Membership Director, Christine Langlois, Bus: 416/733-7600

**The Crime Writers of Canada (CWC) (1981)**
3007 Kingston Rd., PO Box 113, Scarborough, ON M1M 1P1
416/782-3116, Fax: 416/789-4680, Email: ap113@torfree.net, URL: http://www.swifty.com/cwc/cwchome.htm
President, Peter Robinson
Sec.-Treas., Rick Blechta
Publications: Fingerprints; In Cold Blood

**Editors' Association of Canada/Association canadienne des rédacteurs-réviseurs (EAC) (1979)**
35 Spadina Rd., Toronto, ON M5R 2S9
416/975-1379, Fax: 416/975-1839, Email: editors@web.net, URL: http://www.web.net/eac-acr
President, Rosemary Tanner
Secretary, Jane Broderick
Treasurer, Vivian Elias
Publications: Active Voice/Voix active; Members' Handbook, a.; Directory of Members, a.
Affiliates: Book & Periodical Council; Canadian Conference of the Arts

**Federation of British Columbia Writers (FBCW) (1976)**
#600, 890 West Pender St., PO Box 2206, Stn Main, Vancouver, BC V6B 3W2
604/683-2057, Fax: 604/683-8269, Email: fedbcwrt@pinc.com, URL: http://www.swifty.com/bcwa/index.html
Executive Director, Corey Van't Haaff
President, D.C. Reid
Publications: Wordworks

**Fédération internationale des écrivains de langue française (FIDELF)**
3492, rue Laval, Montréal, QC H2X 3C8
514/849-8540, Téléc: 514/849-6239
Secrétaire général, Ronald Fornerod

**The League of Canadian Poets (LCP) (1966)**
54 Wolseley St., 3rd Fl., Toronto, ON M5T 1A5
416/504-1657, Fax: 416/703-0059, Email: league@ican.net, URL: http://www.swifty.com/lc/
Executive Director, Edita Petrauskaite
Program Manager, Sandra Drzewiecki
Publications: LCP Newsletter; Museletter, s-a.; Members Directory
Affiliates: Book & Periodical Council

**Loisir littéraire du Québec (LLQ) (1961)**
**Fédération québécoise du loisir littéraire**
4545, av Pierre-de-Coubertin, CP 1000, Succ. M, Montréal, QC H1V 3R2
514/252-3033, Téléc: 514/251-8038
Directrice générale, Ghislaine Lacasse
Président du conseil, François Rajotte
Publications: Le Courlis

**Manitoba Writers' Guild (MWG) (1981)**
#206, 100 Arthur St., Winnipeg, MB R3B 1H3
204/942-6134, Fax: 204/942-5754, Email: mbwriter@escape.ca, URL: http://www.mbwriter.mb.ca
Executive Director, Robyn Maharaj
Publications: Wordwrap

**Periodical Writers Association of Canada (PWAC) (1976)**
#203, 54 Wolseley St., Toronto, ON M5T 1A5
416/504-1645, Fax: 416/703-0059, Email: pwac@cycor.ca
Executive Director, Ruth Biderman
President, Danny Kucharsky
Publications: PWAContact; Directory of Members

**Saskatchewan Writers Guild Inc. (SWG) (1969)**
PO Box 3986, Regina, SK S4P 3R9
306/757-6310, Fax: 306/565-8554, Email: swg@sk.sympatico.ca, URL: http://www.sasknet.com/~skwriter
Executive Director, Mary Drover
President, Judy McCrosky
Publications: FreeLance; Grain, q.; Readings & Workshops Guide, a.; WindScript

**Société des écrivains canadiens (SEC) (1936)**
a/s Fondation Macdonald-Stewart, 1195, rue Sherbrooke ouest, Montréal, QC H3A 1H9
514/733-0754, Téléc: 514/342-3866
Secrétaire général, Jacques Constantin
Président général, Jacques G. Ruelland
Publications: Parléecrit; L'Écritoire, trimestriel

**Société professionelle des auteurs et des compositeurs du Québec (SPACQ) (1981)**
#420, 759, Square Victoria, Montréal, QC H2Y 2J7
514/845-3739, Téléc: 514/845-1903
Directrice générale, Francine Bertrand-Venne
Organisation(s) affiliée(s): Coalition des créateurs et titulaires de droits d'auteurs; Groupe action musique pour le droit d'auteur (GAMDA)

**Society of American Travel Writers - Canadian Chapter (SATW) (1964)**
5 Runnymede Rd., Toronto, ON M6S 2Y1
416/766-6522
Chairman, Joanna Ebbutt
Publications: Maple Leaf Rag

**Union des écrivaines et écrivains québécois (UNEQ) (1977)**
La Maison des écrivains, 3492, av Laval, Montréal, QC H2X 3C8
514/849-8540, Téléc: 514/849-6239, Courrier électronique: ecrivez@uneq.qc.ca, URL: http://www.uneq.qc.ca
Directeur général, Pierre Lavoie
Président, Louis Gauthier
Directrice des communications, Nicole Blouin
Publications: Bulletin UNEQ

**Writers Association for Romance & Mainstream (WARM) (1983)**
#7, 436 Terrasse Talbot, Longueuil, QC J4L 1T5
514/468-5410
President, Jeanette Paul
Treasurer, Kenneth Gee
Publications: Warm Times

**Writers Guild of Alberta (WGA) (1980)**
Percy Page Centre, 11759 Groat Rd., 3rd Fl., Edmonton, AB T5M 3K6
403/422-8174, Fax: 403/422-2663, Toll Free: 1-800-665-5354, Email: writers@compusmart.ab.ca, URL: http://www.rtt.ab.ca/rtt.writers
Executive Director, Miki Andrejevic
President, Fred Stenson
Publications: Directory of AB Writers; WestWord, bi-m.
Affiliates: Manitoba Writers' Guild; Federation of BC Writers; Saskatchewan Writers' Guild; Writers' Union of Canada; Newfoundland & Labrador Guilds; Periodical Writers' Association of Canada; League of Canadian Poets

**Writers Guild of Canada (WGC) (1991)**
35 McCaul St., Toronto, ON M5T 1V7
416/979-7907, Fax: 416/979-9273, Toll Free: 1-800-567-9974
President, Pete White
Manager, Member & Information Services, Sarah Dearing
Publications: WGC News

**Writers' Alliance of Newfoundland & Labrador (WANL) (1987)**
#102, 155 Water St., PO Box 2681, St. John's, NF A1C 5M5
709/739-5215, Fax: 709/739-5215, Email: wanl@public.nfld.com, URL: http://www.infonet.st-johns.nf.ca/providers/writers/writers.html
Executive Director, Patricia Warren
Publications: Word

**The Writers' Development Trust/Société d'encouragement aux auteurs**
The Writers' Centre, #201, 24 Ryerson Ave., Toronto, ON M5T 2P3
416/504-8222, Fax: 416/504-9090, Email: writers.trust@sympatico.ca
Executive Director, Nancy Kroeker
Publications: Literary Life

**Writers' Federation of New Brunswick (WFNB) (1983)**
PO Box 37, Stn A, Fredericton, NB E3B 4Y2
506/459-7228, Fax: 506/459-7228, URL: http://www.sjfn.nb.ca/community_hall/W/Writers_Federation_NB/index.htm
President, Heather Browne Prince
Treasurer, Kathy D. Leveille
Secretary, Jeanne Whitehead
Publications: New Brunswick ink

**Writers' Federation of Nova Scotia (WFNS) (1975)**
#901, 1809 Barrington St., Halifax, NS B3J 3K8
902/423-8116, Fax: 902/422-0881, Email: writers1@fox.nstn.ca, URL: http://www.chebucto.ns.ca/Culture/WFNS/
Executive Director, Jane Buss
Executive Assistant, Joanne Merriam
Publications: EastWord
Affiliates: Cultural Federation of Nova Scotia; Writers' Development Trust; Coalition of Copyright Owners; Canadian Copyright Institute; Metro Council on Continuing Education; Canadian Children's Book Centre

**The Writers' Union of Canada (TWUC) (1972)**
24 Ryerson Ave., Toronto, ON M5T 2P3
416/703-8982, Fax: 416/703-0826, Email: twuc@the-wire.com, URL: http://www.swifty.com/twuc
Executive Director, Penny Dickens
Chair, Paul Quarrington
Publications: Who's Who in the Writers' Union of Canada: A Directory of Members; The Writers' Union of Canada Newsletter, 9 pa
Affiliates: Canadian Copyright Institute; Canadian Conference of the Arts; Canadian Reprography Collective; Writers Development Trust; Give the Gift of Literacy

**YOUTH *see* CHILDREN & YOUTH**

# LABOUR UNIONS

**Aircraft Operations Group Association (Ind.)/Association du groupe des opérations d'aéronefs (ind.) (AOGA)**
#330, 130 Slater St., Ottawa, ON K1P 6E2
613/230-5476, 5758, Fax: 613/230-2668
Chairman, Wayne C. Foy
Vice-Chairman, G. Dewar
Sec.-Treas., R. Walker
Publications: AOGA Bulletin

**Alberta Dairy Employees & Driver Salesmen (Ind.)/Employés laitiers et des chauffeur-vendeurs de l'Alberta (ind.)**
10515 Princess Elizabeth Ave., Edmonton, AB T5G 0Y5
403/474-3255, Fax: 403/479-5722
President, Robert Paquin
Publications: Bread & Butter Gazette

**Alliance of Canadian Cinema, Television & Radio Artists (CLC)/Alliance des artistes canadiens du cinéma, de la télévision et de la radio (ACTRA) (1963)**
2239 Yonge St., Toronto, ON M4S 2B5
416/489-1311, Fax: 416/489-1435
National President, Alexander (Sandy) Crawley
National Vice-President, Mitch O'Connor
National Treasurer, Brian Gromoff
President, Performers Guild, Dan MacDonald
Chair, Media Guild (Broadcast Journalists), Mitch O'Connor
Chair, Media Guild (ACTRA Writers Guild), Mark O'Neill
National Executive Director, Performers Guild, Stephen Waddell
National Executive Director, Media Guild, Christine Jacobs
Director, Communications & Research, Catherine Allman
Director, Management Information Services, Bernie Metzner
Executive Director, Writers Guild of Canada, Margaret Collier
President, Writers Guild, Jack Gray
Publications: Actrascope; Face to Face with Talent, biennial; Writers Directory, biennial
British Columbia Office: Branch Representative, Louise Chwin, #301, 1622 West 7 Ave., Vancouver, BC V6J 1S5, 604/734-1414, Fax: 604/734-1417
Calgary Office: Branch Representative, Joan Frank, Mount Royal Place, #260, 1414 - 8 St. SW, Calgary, AB T2R 1J6, 403/228-3123, Fax: 403/228-3299
Edmonton Office: Branch Representative, Sharon Killey, #201, 10816A - 82 Ave., Edmonton, AB T6E 2B3, 403/433-4090, Fax: 403/433-4099
Maritimes Office: Branch Representative, Ed J. Frenette, 5510 Spring Garden Rd., Halifax, NS B3J 1G5, 902/420-1404, Fax: 902/422-0589
Montréal Office: Branch Representative, Arden Ryshpan, #530, 1450, rue City Councillors, Montréal, QC H3A 2E6, 514/844-3318, 3319, Fax: 514/844-2068
Newfoundland Office: Branch Representative, Marlene Cahill, 210 Water St., PO Box 575, St. John's, NF A1C 5K8, 709/722-0430, Fax: 709/722-2113
Ottawa Office: Branch Representative, Betty Hackett, #808, 130 Slater St., Ottawa, ON K1P 6E2, 613/230-0327, 0328, Fax: 613/230-2473
Saskatchewan Office: Branch Representative, Bill Siggins, #212, 1808 Smith St., Regina, SK S4P 2N4, 306/757-0885, Fax: 306/359-0044
Toronto Office: 2239 Yonge St., Toronto, ON M4S 2B5, 416/489-1311, Fax: 416/489-1435
Winnipeg Office: Branch Representative, Susan Robinson, Phoenix Building, #110, 388 Donald St., Winnipeg, MB R3B 2J4, 204/943-1307, 2365, Fax: 204/947-5664

**Alliance professionnelle des infirmières et infirmiers auxiliaires du Québec (ind.)**
3868, boul Sainte-Rose, Fabreville, QC H7P 1C9
514/963-5400, Téléc: 514/963-5231
Directrice générale, Monique Leroux
Vice-président, Luc Séguin
Secrétaire, Heather L'Heureux
Publications: L'Envoi

**Aluminum, Brick & Glass Workers International Union (AFL-CIO/CLC)/Syndicat international des ouvriers de l'aluminum, de la brique et du verre (FAT-COI/CTC) (ABGWIU)**
3362 Hollenberg Dr., Bridgeton, MO 63044 USA
314/739-6142, Fax: 314/739-1216
President, Ernest J. LaBaff
Sec.-Treas., Harvey Martin
Canadian Office: Canadian Director, Rodney Bezo, #2, 406 North Service Rd. East, Oakville, ON K6G 5R2, 905/842-9710, Fax: 905/842-9713

**Amalgamated Clothing & Textile Workers Unions (AFL-CIO/CLC)/Travailleurs amalgamés du vêtement et du textile (FAT-COI/CTC) (1914)**
15 Union Sq., New York, NY 10003 USA
212/242-0700, Fax: 212/255-8169
General President, Jack Sheinkman
General Sec.-Treas., Arthur Loevy
Publications: ABG Light
Canadian Office: Canadian Director, John Alleruzzo, #700, 15 Gervais Dr., North York, ON M3C 1Y8, 416/441-1806, Fax: 416/441-9680

**Amalgamated Transit Union (AFL-CIO/CLC)/Syndicat uni du transport (FAT-COI/CTC)**
5025 Wisconsin Ave. NW, Washington, DC 20016 USA
202/537-1645, Fax: 202/244-7824
President, James LaSala
Sec.-Treas., Oliver Green
Canadian Office: Canadian Director, Ken Foster, #603, 15 Gervais Dr., Don Mills, ON M3C 1Y8, 416/445-6204, Fax: 416/445-6208

**American Federation of Grain Millers (AFL-CIO/CLC)/Fédération américaine des meuniers (FAT-COI/CTC) (AFGM) (1936)**
4949 Olson Memorial Hwy., Minneapolis, MN 55422 USA
612/545-0211, Fax: 612/545-5489
General President, Larry R. Jackson
General Sec.-Treas., Larry Barber
Publications: Grain Miller News
Canadian Office: Trustee, D. Maldeis, 287 Second St., Midland, ON L4R 3R2, 705/526 8342

**American Federation of Labor & Congress of Industrial Organizations (AFL-CIO)/Fédération Américaine du travail et congrès des organisations industrielles (FAT-COI) (AFL-CIO)**
AFL-CIO Building, 815 - Sixteenth St. NW, Washington, DC 20006 USA
202/637-5000, Fax: 202/637-5058, URL: http://www.aflcio.org
President, John J. Sweeney
Sec.-Treas., Richard Trumka
Executive Vice-President, Linda Chavez-Thomson
Canadian Office - Building & Construction Trades Dept.: Executive Secretary, Guy Dumoulin, #910, 350 Sparks St., Ottawa, ON K1R 7S8, 613/236-0653, Fax: 613/230-5138

**American Federation of Musicians of the United States & Canada (AFL-CIO/CLC)/Fédération des musiciens des États-Unis et du Canada (FAT-COI/CTC) (AFM) (1896)**
Paramount Building, #600, 1501 Broadway, New York, NY 10036 USA
212/869-1330, Fax: 212/764-6134
President, Steve Young
Secretary, Stephen R. Sprague
Publications: International Musician
Canadian Office: Canadian Vice-President, David J. Jandrisch, #1010, 75 The Donway West, North York, ON M3C 2E9, 416/391-5161, Fax: 416/391-5165, Toll Free: 1-800-463-6333

**American Federation of Television & Radio Artists (AFL/CIO)**
260 Madison Ave., New York, NY 10016 USA
National Executive Director, Bruce York
President, Reed Farrell
Canadian Office: Shop Steward, Lyn Martin; Shop Steward, Lorna McCormick, 1640 Ouellette Ave., Windsor, ON N8X 1K9, 519/258-8888, Fax: 519/966-1090

**American Guild of Variety Artists (AFL-CIO)/Guilde américaine des artistes de variétés (FAT-COI) (AGVA) (1939)**
184 Fifth Ave., New York, NY 10010 USA
212/675-1003, Fax: 212/633-0097
President, Rod McKuen
Sec.-Treas., Frances Gaar

**Association of Allied Health Professionals: Newfoundland & Labrador (Ind.)/Association des professionnels unis de la santé: Terre-Neuve et Labrador (ind.) (AAHP) (1975)**
538 Water St., St. John's, NF A1E 1B7
709/722-3353, Fax: 709/722-3353
President, Nena Sandoval
Secretary, Noel Browne
Publications: News & Views

**Association of Allied Health Professionals, Ontario (Ind.)/Association des professionnels unis de la santé, Ontario (ind.) (AAHP-O) (1975)**
#305, 234 Eglinton Ave. East, Toronto, ON M4P 1K5
416/484-9685, Fax: 416/484-9959
Executive Director, Catherine E. Bowman
Publications: AAHPO - Update

**Association of Canadian Film Craftspeople (Ind.)/Association des artisans du film canadien (ind.) (ACFC)**
#105, 65 Heward Ave., Toronto, ON M4M 2T5
416/462-0211, Fax: 416/462-3248
President, John Subotich
Business Agent, Ray Stringer
Publications: Newsletter
BC Office: Contact, Brenda Collins, #140C, 555 Brooksbank Ave., North Vancouver, BC V7J 3S5, 604/983-5450, Fax: 604/983-5451
Manitoba Office: Office Manager, Darrell Varga, #302, 63 Albert St., Winnipeg, MB R3B 1G4, 204/943-1866, Fax: 204/943-1860

**Association canadienne des métiers de la truelle, section locale 100 (CTC)/Trowel Trades Canadian Association, Local 100 (CLC)**
9083, boul Saint-Michel, Montréal, QC H1Z 3G6
514/326-3691, Téléc: 514/326-5562
Président, Luc Chalifoux
Secrétaire, Christian Thomassin
Publications: L'Éclaireur

**Association des employés en service social de la Province du Québec (ind.)/Association of Social Service Employees of the Province of Québec (1972)**
#850, 1001, rue Sherbrooke est, Westmount, QC H2L 1L3
514/521-2514, Téléc: 514/521-0086
Président, Daniel Citrome
Publications: Action notes
Organisation(s) affiliée(s): Centrale des Profesionnel en Santé

**Association des manoeuvres interprovinciaux (CTC)/Interprovincial Labourers Association (CLC) (AMI)**
#910, 545, boul Crémazie est, Montréal, QC H2M 2V1
514/374-8780, Téléc: 514/381-4614
Directeur général, Ludger Synnett
Publications: Journal AMI

**Association nationale des ferblantiers et couvreurs, section locale 2020 (CTC)/National Association of Tinsmiths & Tilers, Local 2020 (CLC) (ANFC) (1982)**
#203, 3730, boul Crémazie est, Montréal, QC H2A 1B4
514/374-1515, Téléc: 514/374-2282
Directeur provincial, Pierre Lavoie
Publications: L'Informateur 2020
Organisation(s) affiliée(s): Fédération des travailleurs et travailleuses du Québec - Construction

**Association nationale des mécaniciens industriels, section local 1981 (CTC)/National Association of Industrial Mechanics, Local 1981 (CLC)**
#307, 3750, boul Crémazie est, Montréal, QC H2A 1B6
514/374-4527, Téléc: 514/374-2140, Ligne sans frais: 1-800-361-6585
Président, Gilles Pichette
Publications: L'Indicateur

**Association nationale des peintres et métiers connexes, section locale 99 (CTC)/National Association of Painters & Allied Trades, Local 99 (CLC)**
#1401, 3637, boul Crémazie est, Montréal, QC H1Z 2J9
514/593-5413
Directeur, Marc Lirette

**Association nationale des travailleurs en réfrigération, climatisation et protection-incendie, section locale 3 (CTC)/National Association of Refrigeration, Air-Conditioning & Fire Protection Workers, Local 3 (CLC)**
#340, 5800, boul Métroplitain est, Montréal, QC H1S 1A7
514/253-7475, Téléc: 514/253-7028
Directeur général, Jules Bergeron

**Association nationale des travailleurs en tuyauterie et calorifugeurs, section locale 618 (CTC)/National Association of Plumbers, Pipe Fitters & Insulators, Local 618 (CLC)**
#206, 3730, boul Crémazie est, Montréal, QC H2A 1B4
514/723-0618, Téléc: 514/721-6204
Directeur général, Claude Allard
Publications: Le 618

**Association des perfusionnistes du Québec/Association of Perfusionnistes of Quebec**
31, rue Leroy, Repentigny, QC J6A 1P7
514/934-4400, Téléc: 514/934-4368
Président, David Edgell

**Association des policiers provinciaux du Québec (ind.)/Québec Provincial Police Association (Ind.) (APPQ) (1966)**
1981, Léonard-de-Vinci, Sainte-Julie, QC J3E 1Y9
514/922-5414, Téléc: 514/922-5417
Président, Tony Cannavino
Vice-président, Discipline et déontologie, Michel Meunier
Vice-président, Griefs et formation, Réjean Corriveau
Vice-président, Ressources humaines et matérielles, Gaston Pomerleau
Secrétaire général, Daniel Langlois
Trésorier, Jean-Guy Dagenais
Publications: Au Devoir

**Association of Postal Officials of Canada (Ind.)/Association des officiers des postes du Canada (ind.) (APOC) (1966)**
#201, 28 Concourse Gate, Nepean, ON K2E 7T7
613/727-1310, Fax: 613/727-5354, Email: apoci@istar.ca
National President, Ronald Goodwin
Sec.-Treas., Michel Taddeo
Publications: APOC Bulletin

**Association of Professional Student Services Personnel (Ind.)/Association du personnel professionnel des services aux étudiants (ind.) (APSSP) (1975)**
#168, 615 Mount Pleasant Rd., Toronto, ON M4S 3C5
416/367-5267, Fax: 416/367-5267

President, Richard Waugh
Publications: APSSP Newsletter; APSSP Directory, a.

**Association professionnelle des gardes du corps du gouvernement du Québec (ind.)/Professional Association of Body Guards of the Government of Quebec (Ind.)**
#15, 5350, boul Henri-Bourassa, Charlesbourg, QC G1H 6Y8
418/628-7856, Téléc: 418/628-3122
Président, Réal Lizotte

**Association professionnelle des ingénieurs du gouvernement du Québec (ind.)/Association of Professional Engineers of the Government of Québec (Ind.) (APIGQ) (1986)**
#201, 455, rue Marais, Vanier, QC G1M 3A2
418/683-3633, Téléc: 418/683-6878
Président, Gaétan Lefebvre, ing.
Publications: L'Info

**Association professionnelle des inhalothérapeutes du Québec (ind.)/Professional Association of Inhalation Therapists of Québec (Ind.)**
#201, 3925, rue Rachel est, Montréal, QC H1X 3G8
514/251-8050, Téléc: 514/259-8084
Président, Michel Talbot
Publications: L'Informapiq

**Association professionnelle des technologistes médicaux du Québec (ind.)/Québec Professional Association of Medical Technologists (Ind.) (1955)**
1595, rue St-Hubert, 3e étage, Montréal, QC H2L 3Z2
514/524-3734, Téléc: 514/524-7863, Ligne sans frais: 1-800-361-4306
Présidente, Francine Genest
Publications: L'Express; Point d'interrogation, au deux ans; Rapport Annuel

**Association of Public Service Financial Administrators (Ind.)/Association des gestionnaires financiers de la Fonction publique (ind.) (APSFA) (1989)**
#302, 666 Kirkwood Ave., Ottawa, ON K1Z 5X9
613/728-0695, Fax: 613/761-9568
President, Merdon Hosking
Publications: FI Newsletter

**Association for Residential Treatment Concepts (CNFIU)/Association pour concept de traitement résidentiel (FCNSI)**
256 King St. North, PO Box 38012, Waterloo, ON N2J 4T9
519/740-1338, Fax: 519/622-7241
President, Mary Withers

**Association des techniciennes et techniciens en diététique du Québec (ind.)/Québec Association of Dietary Technicians (Ind.) (ATDQ) (1975)**
#850, 1001, rue Sherbrooke est, Montréal, QC H2L 1L3
514/522-1153, Téléc: 514/521-0086
Présidente, Luce Leblanc
Vice-présidente, Christiane Bénard
Organisation(s) affiliée(s): Centrale des professionnelles et professionels de la santé (CPS)

**Atlantic Communication & Technical Workers' Union (Ind.)/Syndicat des travailleurs de l'Atlantique (ind.) (AC & TWU) (1984)**
6148 Quinpool Rd., Halifax, NS B3L 1A2
902/425-2440, Fax: 902/422-4647, Toll Free: 1-800-565-2289
Business Manager, Carl E. Simpson
Publications: Info Update

**Atlantic Oil Workers (CCU)/Travailleurs du pétrole de l'Atlantique (CSC)**
PO Box 3138, Dartmouth, NS B2W 4Y3
902/365-6340
President, Michael Williams

**Bakery, Confectionery & Tobacco Workers International Union (AFL-CIO/CLC)/Syndicat international des travailleurs et travailleuses de la boulangerie, de la confiserie et du tabac (FAT-COI/CTC)**
10401 Connecticut Ave., Kensington, MD 20895-3961 USA
301/933-8600
President, Frank Hurt
Sec.-Treas., Gene McDonald
Canadian Office: International Vice-President, Alphonse De Césaré; Executive Vice-President & Director or Organization, David B. Durkee, 3329, rue Ontario est, Montréal, QC H1W 1P8, 514/527-9371, Fax: 514/527-8105

**Bricklayers, Masons Independent Union of Canada (CLC)/Syndicat indépendant des briqueteurs et des maçons du Canada (CTC)**
#105, 1263 Wilson Ave., North York, ON M3M 3G2
416/247-9841, Fax: 416/247-7346
President, Giuseppe Bellotto
Secretary, John Meiorin

**British Columbia Federation of Police Officers (Ind.)/Fédération des agents de police de la Colombie-Britannique (ind.)**
#603, 190 Alexander St., Vancouver, BC V6A 1B5
250/383-6182
President, Daryl Tottenhan

**British Columbia Ferry & Marine Workers' Union (CLC)/Syndicat des travailleurs marins et de bacs de la Colombie-Britannique (CTC) (BCFMWU) (1977)**
**Ferry Workers' Union**
#301, 710 Redbrick St., Victoria, BC V8T 5J3
250/382-2119, Fax: 250/385-9042, Email: bcfmwu@islandnet.com
President, Ken Michael
Executive Assistant, P. Crawford
Affiliates: BC Federation of Labour; National Union of Public & General Employees (NUPGE)

**Brotherhood of Maintenance of Way Employees (AFL-CIO/CLC)/Fraternité des préposés à l'entretien des voies (FAT-COI/CTC)**
#200, 26555 Evergreen Rd., Southfield, MI 48076-4225 USA
313/948-1010, Fax: 313/948-7150
International President, Mac A. Fleming
Sec.-Treas., William E. LaRue
Canadian Office: Vice-President, Gary D. Housch; Vice-President, Ken Deptuck; Director of Communications, Martine Bouchard, #1, 2775 Lancaster Rd., Ottawa, ON K1B 4V8, 613/731-7356, Fax: 613/733-3158

**Canadian Actors' Equity Association (CLC)/Association canadienne des artistes de la scène (CTC) (CAEA) (1976)**
**Actors' Equity**
44 Victoria St., 12th Fl., Toronto, ON M5C 3C4
416/867-9165, Fax: 416/867-9246, Email: mail@caea.com
Executive Director, Susan Wallace
President, Terry Tweed
Communications & Special Projects Coordinator, David Caron
Publications: The News

Western Office: Business Representative, Colleen A. Fee, 505 Hudson House, 321 Water St., Vancouver, BC V6B 1B8, 604/682-6173, Fax: 604/682-6174

**Canadian Air Line Dispatchers Association (CLC)/Association canadienne des régulateurs de vols (CTC)**
35 Devonshire Dr., Brampton, ON L6T 3G5
905/791-4680
President, D. Michael McLeod

**Canadian Air Line Pilots Association (Ind.)/Association canadienne des pilotes de ligne aérienne (ind.) (CALPA) (1937)**
1300 Steeles Ave. East, Brampton, ON L6T 1A2
905/453-8210, Fax: 905/453-8757
President, Capt. D. Johnny
First Vice-President, Capt. J.R. Saunders
Vice-President, Finance, Capt. K. Freeman
Publications: Pilot; CALPA Newsletter, m.
Affiliates: International Federation of Air Line Pilots' Associations

**Canadian Air Traffic Control Association (Ind.)/Association canadienne du contrôle du trafic aérien (ind.) (CATCA) (1959)**
Camelot Business Park, 162 Cleopatra Dr., Nepean, ON K2G 5X2
613/225-3553, Fax: 613/225-8448, Email: catca@catca.ca, URL: http://www.catca.ca
Managing Director, Joanne St-Gelais, CAE
President, Dave Lewis
Publications: CATCA News
Affiliates: International Federation of Air Traffic Control Associations

**Canadian Association of Firefighters (Ind.)/Association canadienne des pompiers (ind.) (CAFF) (1979)**
11J Rayborn Cres., St Albert, AB T8N 5C3
403/458-2503, Fax: 403/458-2503, Toll Free: 1-800-661-4924
President, Maurice Sandford
Sec.-Treas., Tom Burton
Publications: The Canadian

**Canadian Association of Professional Radio Operators (Ind.)/Association canadienne des professionnels de l'exploitation radio (ind.) (CAPRO)**
#402, 120 Holland Ave., Ottawa, ON K1Y 0X6
613/761-7711, Fax: 613/761-7712
National President, Gary Wilson
Publications: ROCOM

**Canadian Association of Simulator Technologists (Ind.) (1990)**
c/o Canadian Airlines International, 6001 Grant McConachie Way, Richmond, BC V7B 1K3
604/270-5090, Fax: 604/276-3620
Chairman, Bruce Fingarson

**Canadian Farmworkers Union (CLC)/Syndicat canadien des travailleurs agricoles (CTC) (CFU) (1980)**
#1, 10667 - 135 A St., Surrey, BC V3T 4E3
604/583-9334, Fax: 604/583-9334
President, Jawala Singh Grewal
Publications: The Farmworker

**Canadian Federation of Labour/Fédération canadienne du travail (CFL) (1982)**
**CF of L**
#300, 107 Sparks St., Ottawa, ON K1P 5B5
613/234-4141, Fax: 613/234-5188
President, James A. McCambly
Sec.-Treas., Terry D. Boudreau
Publications: Federation Update

Affiliates: American Federation of Labor & Congress of Industrial Organizations
Provincial Councils of Labour with Presidents
Alberta & Northwest Territories (District of MacKenzie) Council of Labour: President, John Lester, 5649 Burbank Rd. SE, Calgary, AB T2H 1Z5, 403/252-1166
British Columbia & Yukon Territory: President, Harry Cossey, #290, 2885 Boys Rd., Duncan, BC V9L 4Y9, 250/748-8491
Conseil du Québec: Président, Mario Di Pesa, #201, 9203, boul St-Laurent, Montréal, QC H2N 1N2, 514/385-0131
Manitoba Council: President, Ron McLean, #26B, 1313 Border St., Winnipeg, MB R3H 0X4, 204/697-3277, Fax: 204/697-3278
New Brunswick Council: President, Larry Calhoun, 138 Neill St., Fredericton, NB E3A 2Z6, 506/450-8888
Newfoundland & Labrador Council: President, Mike Power, 25 Nelder Dr., Mount Pearl, NF A1N 4M2, 709/747-4239
Nova Scotia Council: President, Charles Weir Jr., PO Box 419, Lower Sackville, NS B4C 2T2, 902/865-8811, Fax: 902/865-7317
Ontario Council: President, Reg Conrad, 30 Greendowns Dr., Scarborough, ON M1M 2G7, 416/266-3825, Fax: 416/266-0377
Prince Edward Island Council: President, Ted Crockett, 25 Kensington Ct., Charlottetown, PE C1A 8K4, 902/566-3255
Saskatchewan Council: President, Brian Woznesensky, 1402 Rose St., Regina, SK S4N 6C4, 306/569-8787

## Canadian Football League Players' Association (Ind.)/Association des joueurs de la ligue de football canadienne (ind.) (CFLPA)

#700, 10104 - 103 Ave., Edmonton, AB T5J 0H8
403/426-4535
President, Dan Ferrone
Publications: CFLPA Newsletter

## Canadian Health Care Guild (Ind.)/Guilde canadienne des soins de la santé (ind.)

#200, 17410 - 107 Ave., Edmonton, AB T5S 1E9
403/483-8126, Fax: 403/484-3341, Toll Free: 1-800-252-7984
President, Robert Metheral
Vice-President, Myrna Wright
Publications: Pulse

## Canadian Iron, Steel & Industrial Workers' Union (Ind.)/Syndicat canadien des travailleurs du fer, des métallurgistes et des travailleurs industriels (ind.)

17 East Broadway, Vancouver, BC V5T 1V4
604/879-8137, Fax: 604/873-9112
President, Frank Nolan
Publications: The Canadian Unionist

## Canadian Labour Congress/Congrès du travail du Canada (CLC) (1956)

2841 Riverside Dr., Ottawa, ON K1V 8X7
613/521-3400, Fax: 613/521-4655, Telex: 053-4750
President, Robert White
Sec.-Treas., Richard Martin
Executive Vice-President, Jean-Claude Parrot
Executive Vice-President, Nancy Riche
Financial Advisor/Controller, Pierre Ouimet
National Director, Environment, Dave Bennett
Canadian Health Coalition, Michael McBane
National Representative, Health & Safety, Amber Hockin
National Director, International Affairs, Stephen Benedict
National Director, Organization & Education Services, Martin J. Hanratty
National Director, Technical Services, Bob Baldwin
Director, Political Action, Patrick Kerwin
National Director, Women & Human Rights, Penni Richmond
Regions
Atlantic Regional Office: Regional Director, Linda Gallant, 2282 Mountain Rd., Moncton, NB E1G 1B4, 506/858-9350
Ontario Regional Office: Regional Director, Michael MacIssac, #305, 15 Gervais Dr., North York, ON M3C 1Y8, 416/441-3710, Fax: 416/441-4073
Pacific Regional Office: Regional Director, Rick Byrne, 1888 Angus St., Regina, SK S4T 1Z4, 604/525-6137
Prairie Regional Office: Regional Director, David Rice, 7621 Kingsway, Burnaby, BC V3N 3C7, 604/524-0391
Provincial Federations of Labour

#### ALBERTA FEDERATION OF LABOUR/FÉDÉRATION DU TRAVAIL DE L'ALBERTA (AFL) (1912)

#350, 10451 - 170 St., Edmonton, AB T5P 4T2
403/483-3021, Fax: 403/484-5928
URL: http://www.afl.org
President, Audrey M. Cormack
Publications: Labour News

#### BRITISH COLUMBIA FEDERATION OF LABOUR/FÉDÉRATION DU TRAVAIL DE LA COLOMBIE-BRITANNIQUE (BCFL) (1956)

4279 Canada Way, Burnaby, BC V5G 4P1
604/430-1421, Fax: 604/430-5917
Email: bcfed@bc.sympatico.ca, URL: http://www.bcfed.com
President, Ken Georgetti
Director of Communications, Bill Tieleman
Sec.-Treas., Angela Schira
Publications: The Bulletin
Affiliates: Canadian Centre for Policy Alternatives; Canadian Association of Labour Media

#### FÉDÉRATION DES TRAVAILLEURS ET TRAVAILLEUSES DU QUÉBEC/QUÉBEC FEDERATION OF LABOUR (FTQ) (1957)

545, boul Crémazie est, 17e étage, Montréal, QC H2M 2V1
514/383-8000, Téléc: 514/383-8001
Courrier électronique: ftq@montrealnet.ca
Président, Clément Godbout
Secrétaire général, Henri Massé
Directeur des communications, Louis Fournier
Publications: Le Monde ouvrier

#### MANITOBA FEDERATION OF LABOUR/FÉDÉRATION DU TRAVAIL DU MANITOBA (1956)

#101, 275 Broadway, Winnipeg, MB R3C 4M6
204/947-1400, Fax: 204/943-4276
President, Rob Hilliard
Publications: News & Views

#### NEW BRUNSWICK FEDERATION OF LABOUR/FÉDÉRATION DU TRAVAIL DU NOUVEAU-BRUNSWICK (NBFL) (1914)

96 Norwood Ave., Moncton, NB E1C 6L9
506/857-2125, Fax: 506/383-1597
President, John McEwen
Publications: Newsletter

#### NEWFOUNDLAND & LABRADOR FEDERATION OF LABOUR/FÉDÉRATION DU TRAVAIL DE TERRE-NEUVE ET DU LABRADOR (NLFL) (1936)

PO Box 8597, Stn A, St. John's, NF A1B 3P2
709/754-1660, Fax: 709/754-1220
President, Elaine Price
Sec.-Treas., Wayne Butler

#### NORTHWEST TERRITORIES FEDERATION OF LABOUR/FÉDÉRATION DU TRAVAIL DES TERRITOIRES DU NORD-OUEST (NWTFL) (1980)

PO Box 2787, Yellowknife, NT X1A 2R1
867/873-3695
President, James Evoy
Sec.-Treas., Sharon Burns

#### NOVA SCOTIA FEDERATION OF LABOUR/FÉDÉRATION DU TRAVAIL DE LA NOUVELLE-ECOSSE

#218, 3700 Kempt Rd., Halifax, NS B3K 4X8
902/892-7331
President, Rick Clarke
Executive Secretary, Alex MacDonald

#### ONTARIO FEDERATION OF LABOUR/FÉDÉRATION DU TRAVAIL DE L'ONTARIO (OFL) (1957)

#202, 15 Gervais Dr., North York, ON M3C 1Y8
416/441-2731, Fax: 416/441-0722
URL: http://www.ofl-fto.on.ca
President, Gordon F. Wilson
Executive Vice-President, Ken Signoretti
Sec.-Treas., Ethel Lavalley
Publications: Focus; The Advocate, q.; Women's Bulletin, q.

#### PRINCE EDWARD ISLAND FEDERATION OF LABOUR/FÉDÉRATION DU TRAVAIL DU L'ÎLE-DU-PRINCE-EDOUARD

184 Belvedere Ave., Charlottetown, PE C1A 2Z1
902/368-3068, Fax: 902/368-3192
President, Sandy MacKay
Treasurer, Heath Ellis

#### SASKATCHEWAN FEDERATION OF LABOUR/FÉDÉRATION DU TRAVAIL DE LA SASKATCHEWAN

#103, 2709 - 12 Ave., Regina, SK S4T 1J3
306/525-0197, Fax: 306/525-8960
President, Barbara Byers
Treasurer, Larry Hubich
Publications: Labour Report

#### YUKON FEDERATION OF LABOUR/FÉDÉRATION DU TRAVAIL DU YUKON (1980)

106 Strickland St., Whitehorse, YT Y1A 2J5
867/667-6676, Fax: 867/633-5558
President, Michael Miller

## Canadian Marine Officers' Union (AFL-CIO/CLC)/Syndicat canadien des officiers de la marine marchande (FAT-COI/CTC)

9670, rue Notre-Dame est, Montréal, QC H1L 3P8
514/354-8321, Fax: 514/354-8368
President/Sec.-Treas., Richard Vézina
Vice-President, Non-Maritime, Jean Brisebois
Vice-President, Robert Ford
Affiliates: Seafarers International Union of North America/Syndicat international des marins de l'Amérique du Nord

## Canadian Media Guild/La Guilde canadienne des médias (CMG) (1950)

#300, 144 Front St. West, Toronto, ON M5J 2L7
416/591-5333, Fax: 416/591-7278
President, Ray Aboud
Administrative Officer, Kathy Viner
Publications: SCAN

## Canadian Merchant Service Guild (CLC)/Guilde de la marine marchande du Canada (CTC)

1150 Morrison Dr., Ottawa, ON K2H 8S9
613/829-9531, Fax: 613/596-6079
National President, Maury R. Sjoquist
National Sec.-Treas., Larry Dempsey
Publications: CMSG News
Eastern Branch: Sec.-Treas., Earle Simpson, 3235, av Granby, Montréal, QC H1N 2Z8, 514/254-4571, Fax: 514/254-2141
Western Branch: Sec.-Treas., Leo M. Gray, 230 West Broadway, Vancouver, BC V5Y 1P7, 604/872-7811, Fax: 604/872-5323

#### CANADIAN ASSOCIATION OF MASTERS & CHIEF ENGINEERS (CLC)/ASSOCIATION DES CAPITAINES ET CHEFS INGÉNIEURS DU CANADA (CTC)

22 Cabot St., St Anthony, NF A0K 4S0
President, Capt. Herb Murrin

**CANADIAN MARINE PILOTS' ASSOCIATION (CLC)/ASSOCIATION DES PILOTES DE LA MARINE CANADIENNE (CTC)**
1311, av Allard, Ste-Foy, QC G1W 3G3
President, Capt. Michel Pouliot

### Canadian National Federation of Independent Unions/Fédération canadienne nationale des syndicats indépendants (CNFIU) (1980)
136 East Main St., Welland, ON L3B 3W6
905/735-0531, Fax: 905/788-9700
President, Vince Vocal
Sec.-Treas., Bryan Harris

### Canadian National Railways Police Association (Ind.)/Association des policiers des chemins de fer nationaux du Canada (ind.)
6479 Miller's Grove, Mississauga, ON L5N 3E5
905/824-0856, Fax: 905/824-4584
National President, Frank Morgan

### Canadian Overseas Telecommunications Union (CCU)/Syndicat canadien des télécommunications transmarines (CSC)
#200, 440, boul René-Lévesque ouest, Montréal, QC H2Z 1V7
514/866-9015, Fax: 514/868-8364
President, Carlos Saldanha
Vice-President, Daniel McDuff
Treasurer, Daniel Séguin

### Canadian Pacific Police Association (Ind.)/Association des policiers du Canadien Pacifique (ind.) (CPPA) (1972)
1237, Vallée, Chambly, QC J3L 5K4
514/678-4906, Fax: 514/658-6212
National President, François Dubuc

### Canadian Postmasters & Assistants Association/Association canadienne des maîtres de poste et adjoints (CPAA) (1902)
281 Queen Mary St., Ottawa, ON K1K 1X1
613/745-2095, Fax: 613/745-5559
National President, Leroy H. Kuan
Senior National Vice-President, Rowena J. Anderson
National Vice-President, Leslie Schous
National Sec.-Treas., Gerard J. Bourque
Publications: The Canadian Postmaster/Le Maître de poste canadien; CPAA/ACMPA Bulletin, m.
Affiliates: Canadian Labour Congress

### Canadian Red Cross Blood Transfusion Service Employees Association (Ind.)/Association des employés des services de transfusion sanguine de la Croix-Rouge (ind.)
850 Commissioners Rd. East, London, ON N6C 2V5
519/681-6781
President, Bea Dykeman

### Canadian Staff Union (Ind.)/Syndicat canadien du personnel (ind.)
2100, av Papineau, Montréal, QC H2K 4J4
514/527-9681
President, André Lamoureux

### Canadian Telephone Employees' Association (Ind.)/Association canadienne des employés de téléphone (ind.)
#360, Place du Canada, Montréal, QC H3B 2N2
514/861-9963
President, Judith King
Publications: Teleforum/Téléforum

### Canadian Transport Workers Union (Ind.)/Syndicat canadien des travailleurs du transport (ind.) (CTWU)
266 Livingstone Ave. North, Listowel, ON N4W 1P9
519/886-1603
President, Bill Johnston
Vice-President, Don Spence
General Secretary, Bev Strachan
Publications: News Letter

### Canadian Union of Operating Engineers & General Workers (Ind.)/Syndicat canadien des techniciens de chaufferies et des manoeuvres (ind.)
#106, 2087 Dundas St. East, Mississauga, ON L4X 2V7
905/238-8823
President, Bob Souliere
Vice-President, Douglas Draycott
Sec.-Treas., Allen Nesbitt

### Canadian Union of Postal Workers (CLC)/Syndicat des travailleurs et travailleuses des postes (CUPW)
377 Bank St., Ottawa, ON K2P 1Y3
613/236-7238, Fax: 613/563-7861
National President, Darrell Tingley
National Sec.-Treas., George Kuehnbaum
Publications: CUPW/SPC

### Canadian Union of Professional & Technical Employees (Ind.)/Syndicat canadien des employés professionnels et techniques (ind.) (CUPTE)
#1610, 85 Albert St., Ottawa, ON K1P 6A4
613/230-4747, Fax: 613/230-6399
President, Line Niquet
Publications: TR Newsletter; CUPTE News, q.

### Canadian Union of Public Employees (CLC)/Syndicat canadien de la fonction publique (CTC) (CUPE) (1963)
21 Florence St., Ottawa, ON K2P 0W6
613/237-1590, Fax: 613/237-5508, URL: http://www.cupe.ca
National President, Judy Darcy
National Sec.-Treas., Geraldine McGuire
Publications: Organize
Affiliates: Canadian Labour Congress
Airline Division Office: President, Denise Hill, #600, 180 Attwell Dr., Etobicoke, ON M9W 6A9, 416/798-3399, Fax: 416/798-3411
Canadian Broadcast Employees Union: President, Glenn Gray, #413, 1840 Victoria Park Ave., Scarborough, ON M1R 1S9
Regions
Alberta Division: Recording Secretary, Richard Scarfe, #210, 534 - 17 Ave. SW, Calgary, AB T2S 0B1
BC Division: Sec.-Treas., Colleen Jordan, #500, 4940 Canada Way, Burnaby, BC V5G 4T3, 604/291-1940, Fax: 604/291-1194
Division du Québec: Secrétaire archiviste, Henri Massé, 545, boul Crémazie, 12e étage, Montréal, QC H2M 2V1
Manitoba Division: Recording Secretary, Bernice Bryan, 743 McPhillips St., Winnipeg, MB R2X 2J1
New Brunswick Division: Sec.-Treas., Claire Doiron, #222, 96 Norwood Ave., Moncton, NB E1C 6L9
Newfoundland & Labrador Division: Recording Secretary, Dawn Lahey, 205 New Pennywell Rd., St. John's, NF A1B 1C5
Nova Scotia Division: Sec.-Treas., Betty Warrell, 12 Smith Ave., Dartmouth, NS B2V 1M4
Ontario Division: President, Sid Ryan; Sec.-Treas., Terry O'Connor, 156 Shorting Rd., Scarborough, ON M1S 3S6
Prince Edward Island Division: Recording Secretary, Rosalie Wade, 106 York Point Rd., RR#4, Cornwall, PE C0A 1H0
Saskatchewan Divison: Recording Secretary, Judy Henley, 26 Matheson Cres., Yorkton, SK S3N 3M3

### Canadian Union of Restaurant & Related Employees (Ind.)/Syndicat canadien des employé(e)s restaurantation et des employé(e)s relié(e)s (ind.)
94 Kenhar Dr., Weston, ON M9L 1N2
416/665-3842
President, James Whyte

### Canadian Union of Transportation Employees (CCU)/Syndicat canadien des employés du transport (CSC)
1615B - 6 Ave., Prince George, BC V2L 3N5
250/562-4272, Fax: 250/562-4279
President, Ron Stavast

### Cariboo Woodworkers Association (Ind.)/Association des travailleurs du bois de Cariboo (ind.)
PO Box 1798, 100 Mile House, BC V0K 2E0
250/395-5332
Secretary, Paul Klassen

### Centrale de l'enseignement du Québec/Québec Teaching Congress (CEQ) (1946)
9405, rue Sherbrooke est, Montréal, QC H1L 6P3
514/356-8888, Téléc: 514/356-9999, Courrier électronique: communications.montreal@ccq.qc.ca, URL: http://ceq.qc.ca
Présidente, Lorraine Pagé
Directrice générale, Claire Lalande
Publications: Nouvelles CEQ

**ALLIANCE DES PROFESSEURES ET PROFESSEURS DE MONTRÉAL (APPM) (1919)**
8225, boul Saint-Laurent, Montréal, QC H2P 2M1
514/383-4880, Téléc: 514/384-5756
Directeur général, Fernand Gauvreau
Publications: L'Alliance

**FÉDÉRATION DES ENSEIGNANTES ET ENSEIGNANTS DE CÉGEPS**
9405, rue Sherbrooke est, Montréal, QC H1L 6P3
514/354-9112 ou 356-8888, Téléc: 514/354-8535
Président, Réal Trottier
Publications: L'Enjeu

**FÉDÉRATION DES ENSEIGNANTES ET ENSEIGNANTS DE COMMISSIONS SCOLAIRES (CEQ) (FECS) (1988)**
#300, 1170, boul Lebourgneuf, Québec, QC G2K 2G1
418/627-8888, Téléc: 418/627-9999
Courrier électronique: fecs@ceq.qc.ca
Directrice générale, Diane Fortin
Publications: Bulletin FECS

**FÉDÉRATION DU PERSONNEL DES ÉTABLISSEMENTS DE LOISIR/FEDERATION OF RECREATION CENTRES' STAFF (FPEL)**
9405, rue Sherbrooke est, Montréal, QC H1L 6P3
514/356-8888, Téléc: 514/356-9999
Président, Martin Plourde

**FÉDÉRATION DU PERSONNEL DES ÉTABLISSEMENTS PRIVÉS D'ENSEIGNEMENT/FEDERATION OF PRIVATE TEACHING INSTITUTIONS STAFF (FPEPE) (1986)**
9405, rue Sherbrooke est, Montréal, QC H1L 6P3
514/356-8888, Téléc: 514/356-1866
Présidente, Francine Lamoureux
Publications: Le Bulletin

**FÉDÉRATION DU PERSONNEL PROFESSIONNEL DES COLLÈGES (CEQ) (1975)**
9405, rue Sherbrooke est, Montréal, QC H1L 6P3
514/356-8888, Téléc: 514/356-3377
Courrier électronique: fppc@ceq.qc.ca
Président, Jacques Legault
Publications: La Chronique

**FÉDÉRATION DU PERSONNEL PROFESSIONNEL DES UNIVERSITÉS (CEQ) (FPPU) (1993)**
9405, rue Sherbrooke est, Montréal, QC H1L 6P3

514/356-8888, Téléc: 514/356-9999
Présidente, Carole Demers

**FÉDÉRATION DU PERSONNEL DE LA SANTÉ ET DES SERVICES SOCIAUX/FEDERATION OF HEALTH & SOCIAL SERVICES STAFF (FPSSS)**
9405, rue Sherbrooke est, Montréal, QC H1L 6P3
514/356-8888, Téléc: 514/356-2845
Président, André Rodrigue
Publications: La Gazette Officielle

**FÉDÉRATION DU PERSONNEL DE SOUTIEN/FEDERATION OF SUPPORT STAFF**
9405, rue Sherbrooke est, 4e étage, Montréal, QC H1L 6P3
514/356-8888, Téléc: 514/493-3697
Présidente, Christiane Bigras
Publications: Le Relais

**FÉDÉRATION DES PROFESSIONNELLES ET PROFESSIONNELS DE L'ÉDUCATION DU QUÉBEC/QUÉBEC FEDERATION OF PROFESSIONAL EMPLOYEES IN EDUCATION (FPPE) (1985)**
9405, rue Sherbrooke est, Montréal, QC H1L 6P3
514/356-0505, Téléc: 514/356-1324
Président, Pierre Tellier
1er Vice-président, Yves Lanctôt
Vice-président aux affaires administratives, François Ferland
3e Vice-présidente, Francine Paquin
4e Vice-président, Richard Gardner
Publications: Le Passerelle

**SYNDICAT DES EMPLOYÉS EN RADIO-TÉLÉDIFFUSION DE RADIO-QUÉBEC/RADIO-QUÉBEC TELEVISION BROADCAST EMPLOYEES' UNION**
2480, rue Sainte-Catherine est, Montréal, QC H2K 4N7
514/525-2922, Téléc: 514/525-6375
Président, Jacques Poulin

**SYNDICAT PROFESSIONNEL DES INFIRMIÈRES ET INFIRMIERS DE TROIS-RIVIÈRES**
#204, 1300, rue Sainte-Marguerite, Trois-Rivières, QC G8Z 1V7
819/379-4121, Téléc: 819/379-0322
Présidente, Nicole Boudreau

**SYNDICAT DES PROFESSIONNELS ET DES TECHNICIENS DE LA SANTÉ DU QUÉBEC/QUÉBEC UNION OF HEALTH PROFESSIONALS & TECHNICIANS (SPTSQ)**
#850, 1001, rue Sherbrooke est, Montréal, QC H2L 1L3
514/526-1214, Téléc: 514/521-0086
Présidente, Carolle Dubé

## Centrale des professionnelles et professionnels de la santé (CPS) (1988)
#850, 1001, rue Sherbrooke est, Montréal, QC H2L 1L3
514/521-4469, Téléc: 514/521-0086
Directrice générale, Huguette Côté
Président, Jacques Paradis
Publications: Proposyndical

## Centrale des syndicats démocratiques/Congress of Democratic Unions (CSD) (1972)
5100, rue Sherbrooke est, 8e étage, Montréal, QC H1V 3R9
514/899-1070, Téléc: 514/899-1216
Président, Claude Gingras
Vice-président, Claude Faucher
Trésorier, Serge Tremblay
Secrétaire, Robert Légaré
Publications: La Base
Organisation(s) affiliée(s): Fédération démocratique de la métallurgie, des mines et des produits chimiques; Fédération des syndicats du textile et du vêtement (CSD) inc.

## Christian Labour Association of Canada (Ind.)/Association chrétienne du travail du Canada (ind.) (CLAC) (1952)
5920 Atlantic Dr., Mississauga, ON L4W 1N6
905/670-7383, Fax: 905/670-8416
Executive Director, Ed Grootenboer
President, Stan Baker
Director of Research & Education, Harry Antonides
Publicity Director, Ray Pennings
Publications: The Guide

## Communications, Energy & Paperworkers Union of Canada (CLC)/Syndicat canadien des communications, de l'énergie et du papier (CTC) (CEP) (1992)
350 Sparks St., 19th Fl., Ottawa, ON K1R 1A4
613/230-5200, Fax: 613/230-5801, Email: info@cep.ca, URL: http://www.cep.ca/cep/
President, Fred W. Pomeroy
Executive Vice-President, John McInnes
Executive Vice-President, Reg Basken
Publications: CEP Journal/Journal SCEP
Affiliates: Canadian Labour Congress; Ontario Federation of Labour
Section locale 145: Président, Gilles Leblanc, #201, 4555, boul Metropolitain est, St-Léonard, QC H1R 1Z4, 514/593-5323

## Communications Workers of America (AFL-CIO/CLC)/Travailleurs en communication d'Amérique (FAT-COI/CTC)
501 Third St. NW, Washington, DC 20001-2797 USA
202/434-1100, Fax: 202/434-1279
President, Morton Bahr
President, Printing, Publishing & Media Workers Sector, William J. Boarman
Canadian Office: Representative, David Esposti, #B, 288 Dalhousie St., Ottawa, ON K1N 7E6, 613/234-9159, Fax: 613/241-4120

## Compensation Employees' Union (Ind.)/Syndicat des employés d'indemnisation (ind.)
#241, 7080 River Rd., Richmond, BC V6X 1X5
604/278-4050, Fax: 604/278-5002
President, Bill Hawkins
Publications: Newsletter; Newspaper, q.; Newsletter/Womens' Issues, q.

## Confederation of Canadian Unions/Confédération des syndicats canadiens (CCU) (1969)
PO Box 1159, Gold River, BC V0P 1G0
250/283-7111, Fax: 250/283-2451, Email: ccu@goldrvr.island.net
President, Garry Gifford
Sec.-Treas., Karen Cooling
Publications: CCU Bulletin

## Confédération des syndicats nationaux/Confederation of National Trade Unions (CSN) (1921)
1601, av de Lorimier, Montréal, QC H2K 4M5
514/598-2121, Téléc: 514/598-2089, URL: http://www.accent.net/csn/
Secrétaire général, Pierre Paquette
Président, Gérald Larose
Trésorier, Léopold Beaulieu
Publications: Nouvelles CSN

## Congress of Union Retirees Canada (CLC)/Association des syndicalistes retraités du Canada (CURC) (1993)
2841 Riverside Dr., Ottawa, ON K1V 8X7
613/521-3400, Fax: 613/521-0423
President, Edith M. Johnston
1st Vice-President, Larry Wagg
Publications: Union Retiree
Affiliates: Canadian Labour Congress

## Conseil des syndicats hospitaliers de Montréal inc. (Ind.)/Montréal Council of Hospital Syndicates Inc. (Ind.) (CSHM)
#1610, 2050, rue Mansfield, Montréal, QC H3A 1Y9
514/844-9569, Téléc: 514/844-9560
Présidente, Mary Ann Korabel
Secrétaire administrative, Guylaine Guay

## Custodial & Maintenance Association (CNFIU)/Association du personnel de conciergerie et d'entretien (FCNSI) (CAMA) (1968)
c/o Rockway Public School, 70 Vanier Dr., Kitchener, ON N2C 1J5
519/745-5266
President, David Weiler
Publications: CAMA News

## Distillery, Wine & Allied Workers' International Union (AFL-CIO/CLC)/Union internationale des employés de distilleries, vins et industries connexes (FAT-COI/CTC) (DWAW)
66 Grand Ave., PO Box 567, Englewood, NJ 07631 USA
President, George J. Orlando
Publications: DWAW Journal; News Letter/Lettre d'information, q.
Canadian Office: Vice-President/Canadian Director, Raymond Bisson, 11, rue Monette, Delson, QC J0L 1G0, 514/632-4700

## Engineers & Scientists Association (Marconi) (Ind.)/Association des ingénieurs et des scientifiques (Marconi) (ind.)
600, boul Frederick Phillips, St-Laurent, QC H4M 2S9
514/748-3150, Fax: 514/748-3136
President, Henri Noory

## ESSA/AESS (1915)
#700, 220 Laurier Ave. West, Ottawa, ON K1P 5Z9
613/236-9181, Fax: 613/236-6017, Toll Free: 1-800-265-9181
Executive Director, Marvin Gandall
President, W.E. Krause
Publications: ESSA Bulletin/Bulletin AESS
Affiliates: International Labour Organization

## Federal Government Dockyard Chargehands Association (Ind.)/Association des chefs d'équipe des chantiers maritimes du gouvernement (ind.) (FGDCA) (1988)
C.F.B. Halifax, F.M.O., Halifax, NS B3K 2X0
902/429-9426, Fax: 902/421-1095
President, Darryl Roode
Vice-President, Tom Hillier
Treasurer, Bill Johnson
Secretary, Willie Courtney

## Fédération des affaires sociales inc. (CSN)/Social Affairs Federation Inc. (CNTU)
1601, av de Lorimier, Montréal, QC H2K 4M5
514/598-2210, Téléc: 514/598-2223
Président, Sylvio Robinson
Secrétaire générale, Cécile Côté
Trésorière, Lucille Poirier
Publications: Fas aux défis

## Fédération autonome du collégial (ind.)/Autonomous Federation of Collegial Staff (Ind.) (FAC) (1988)
1067, rue St-Denis, Montréal, QC H2X 3J3
514/848-9977, Téléc: 514/848-0166
Président, Michel Duffy
Publications: FACsimilé; FACtuel, 3 fois par an

## Fédération du commerce inc. (CSN)/Commerce Federation Inc. (CNTU)
#122, 1601, av de Lorimier, Montréal, QC H2K 4M5
514/598-2353, Téléc: 514/598-2304

Présidente, Lise Poulin
Publications: Info-Commerce

**Fédération CSN - Construction (CSN)/CNTU Federation - Construction (CNTU)**
1594, av de Lorimier, Montréal, QC H2K 3W5
514/598-2044, Téléc: 514/598-2040
Président, Olivier Lemieux
Publications: Batisseur

**Fédération démocratique de la métallurgie, des mines et des produits chimiques (CSD)/Metal Trades, Mines & Chemical Products Democratic Federation (CSD)**
801, 4e rue, Québec, QC G1J 2T7
418/529-2956, Téléc: 418/529-0483
Président, Jean Roy

**Fédération des employées et employés de services publics inc. (CSN)/Federation of Public Service Employees Inc. (CNTU) (FEESP)**
1601, av de Lorimier, Montréal, QC H2K 4M5
514/598-2231, Téléc: 514/598-2398
Présidente, Ginette Guérin
Publications: Nouvelles CSN
Organisation(s) affiliée(s): Confederation des syndicats nationaux

**Federation of Engineering & Scientific Associations/Fédération d'associations d'ingénieurs et de scientifiques (FESA)**
#206, 3199 Bathurst St., Toronto, ON M6A 2B2
416/784-1284, Fax: 416/784-1366
President, Leo J. Kok
Administrative Officer, Gordon Flowers
Publications: Information Digest
Affiliates: Association of Northern Telecom Engineers & Scientists; Canadian Standards Association Professional Engineers Association; Northern Electric London Professional Association; Salaried Employees Alliance, Computing Devices Company; Society of Ontario Hydro Professional & Administrative Employees; Society of Professional Engineers & Associates - CANDU Operations, Atomic Energy of Canada Limited; SPAR Engineers & Scientists Association; SPAR Professional & Allied Technical Employees Association
Montréal Office: Personne ressource, Suzanne Béliveau, #500, 7575, rte. Transcanadienne, Saint Laurent, QC H4T 1V6, 514/331-1403

**Fédération indépendante des syndicats affiliés (ind.)/Independent Federation of Affiliated Unions (Ind.) (FISA) (1947)**
1250 - 3e av, Québec, QC G1L 2X7
418/529-4571, 4572, Téléc: 418/529-4695, Ligne sans frais: 1-800-407-3472
Président, Paul Talbot
Publications: Info-FISA

**Fédération des intervenantes en garderie (CEQ)**
9405, rue Sherbrooke est, Montréal, QC H1L 6P3
514/356-8888, Téléc: 514/356-0202
Présidente, Denise Dextraze

**Fédération des médecins résidents du Québec inc. (ind.)/Québec Federation of Residents (Ind.) (FMRQ) (1970)**
445, rue Sherbrooke ouest, Montréal, QC H3A 1B6
514/282-0256, Téléc: 514/282-0471, Ligne sans frais: 1-800-465-0215
Président, Denis Soulières
Secrétaire, Dr. Pierre Lacaille-Bélanger
Publications: Le Bulletin

**Fédération de la métallurgie (CSN)/Federation of Metal Trades (CNTU) (1944)**
#204, 2100, boul de Maisonneuve est, Montréal, QC H2K 4S1
514/529-4937, Téléc: 514/529-4935
Président, Alain Lampron
Publications: Fer de Lance

**Fédération nationale des communications (CSN)/National Federation of Communication Workers (CNTU) (FNC) (1972)**
1601, av de Lorimier, Montréal, QC H2K 4M5
514/598-2132, Téléc: 514/598-2431, Courrier électronique: FNC@odyssee.net
Présidente, Chantale Larouche
Publications: La Dépêché

**Fédération des policiers du Québec (ind.)/Québec Federation of Policemen (Ind.)**
7955, boul. Louis-H. Lafontaine, Anjou, QC H1K 4E4
514/356-3321, Téléc: 514/356-1158
Président, Jean-Guy Roch
Directeur exécutif, Guy Marcil

**Fédération des professionnels et des professionnelles salarié(e)s et des cadres du Québec (CSN)/Quebec Federation of Managers & Professional Salaried Workers (CNTU) (FPPSCQ)**
1601, av de Lorimier, Montréal, QC H2K 4M5
514/598-2143, Téléc: 514/598-2491, Courrier électronique: fppcsn@accent.net
Président, Michel Kane, Courrier électronique: mkane@accent.net

**Fédération des syndicats du secteur de l'aluminium inc. (ind.)/Federation of Aluminum Unions Inc. (Ind.) (FSSA) (1972)**
1924, boul Mellon, Jonquière, QC G7S 3H3
418/548-7075, Téléc: 418/548-7992
Président, Raymond Labonté
Secrétaire exécutif, Romain Tremblay
Publications: Contact

**Fédération des syndicats du textile et du vêtement (C.S.D.) inc. (CSD) (1993)**
#800, 5100, rue Sherbrooke est, Montréal, QC H1V 3R9
514/899-5990, Téléc: 514/899-5901
Directeur professionnel, Yvon Jacques

**Fédération des travailleurs forestiers du Québec (ind.)/Québec Woodworkers Federation (Ind.) (FTFQ) (1965)**
422, rue Racine est, Chicoutimi, QC G7H 1T3
418/549-7353, Téléc: 418/543-4873
Président, Serge Théberge

**Fédération des travailleuses et travailleurs du papier et de la forêt (CSN)/Federation of Paper & Forest Workers (CNTU) (FTPF) (1937)**
155, boul Charest est, Québec, QC G1K 3G6
418/647-5775, Téléc: 418/647-5884
Président, Claude Plamondon
Coordonnateur, Claude Rioux
Publications: Le Travailleur
Organisation(s) affiliée(s): Fédération internationale des syndicats des travailleurs à la chimie, de l'énergie, des mines et des industries diverses (ICEM)

**Fraternité des constables du contrôle routier de la Sûreté du Québec (ind.)/Brotherhood of Constables of Highway Traffic Controllers of the Québec Provincial Police (Ind.)**
4165, rue Chauveau, Sherbrooke, QC J1L 1R9
819/567-9784
Président, Guy Lalumière
Publications: Le Fraternel

**Fraternité des constables spéciaux d'Hydro-Québec (ind.)/Brotherhood of Special Constables of Hydro-Québec (Ind.)**
2713, rue Lupien, Saint-Hubert, QC J3Y 6C4
514/462-1653
Président, Richard Seyer

**Fraternité inter-provinciale des poseurs d'acier d'armature/Interprovincial Brotherhood of Structural Steel Workers**
#307A, 3750, boul Crémazie est, Montréal, QC H2A 1B6
514/374-4620, Téléc: 514/374-2140
Directeur, Robert Paul

**Fraternité interprovinciale des ouvriers en électricité (CTC)/Interprovincial Brotherhood of Electrical Workers (CLC) (FIPOÉ)**
#1600, 545, boul Crémazie est, Montréal, QC H2M 2V1
514/385-3476, Téléc: 514/385-9298
President, André Farley
Publications: Journal FIPOE

**Fraternité nationale des charpentiers-menuisiers, forestiers et travailleurs d'usine (CTC)/National Brotherhood of Carpenters, Joiners, Foresters & Industrial Workers (CLC) (1981)**
#101, 2, boul Desaulniers, Saint-Lambert, QC J4P 1L2
514/374-0952, Téléc: 514/374-8800, Ligne sans frais: 1-800-465-9791
Président, Gaston Boudreau
Secrétaire, Diane Lanthier
Publications: La Fraternité
Organisation(s) affiliée(s): Congrès du travail du Canada; Fédération des travailleurs et travailleuses de Quebec

**Fraternité nationale des monteurs d'acier de structure, serruriers de bâtiments et chaudronniers, section locale 737 (CTC)/National Brotherhood of Structural Steel Erectors, Building Locksmiths & Boilermakers, Local 737 (CLC)**
#301, 3730, boul Crémazie est, Montréal, QC H2A 1B4
514/374-2326, Téléc: 514/374-2140
Président, Gérald Ducharme

**General Workers Union of Canada - Local 1 (Ind.)/Syndicat des travailleurs généraux du Canada - section locale 1 (ind.)**
#202, 460 Nanaimo St., Vancouver, BC V5L 4W3
604/253-6066, Fax: 604/253-5103
President, Rocco Salituro

**Glass, Molders, Pottery, Plastic & Allied Workers International Union (AFL-CIO/CLC)/Union internationale des travailleurs du verre, mouleurs, poterie, plastique et autres (FAT-COI/CTC)**
**GMP International Union**
608 East Baltimore Pike, PO Box 607, Media, PA 19063-0607 USA
610/565-5051, Fax: 610/565-0983
International President, Frank W. Carter
Sec.-Treas., James Rankin
Director, Research & Education, Joseph Galvin, Jr.
Canadian Office: Director of Canada, Rod Briggs, #103, 61 International Blvd., Etobicoke, ON M9W 6K4, 416/674-4690, Fax: 416/674-1690

**Grain Services Union (CLC)/Syndicat des services du grain (CTC) (GSU)**
2334 McIntyre St., Regina, SK S4P 2S2
306/522-6686, Fax: 306/565-3430
President, Garnet Lee
Secretary-Manager, Hugh J. Wagner
Publications: GSU News

**Graphic Communications International Union (AFL-CIO/CLC)/Syndicat international des communications graphiques (FAT-COI/CTC) (GCIU)**
1900 L St. NW, Washington, DC 20036 USA
212/462-1400, Fax: 212/331-9516
International President, James J. Norton
Canadian Office: Canadian Vice-President, James Cowan, #600, 1110 Finch Ave. West, North York, ON M3J 2T2, 416/661-9761

**Health Care Employees Union of Alberta (Ind.)/Syndicat des employés des soins de la santé de l'Alberta (ind.)**
10540 - 106 St., Edmonton, AB T5H 2X6
403/433-5800, Fax: 403/424-1230
President, Benjamin P. Horvath
Executive Sec.-Treas., Ken Archer

**Health Sciences Association of Alberta (Ind.)/Association des sciences de la santé de l'Alberta (ind.)**
10340 - 124 St., Edmonton, AB T5N 1R2
403/488-0168, Fax: 403/488-0534
President, Patricia Ennis
Publications: The Bulletin

**Health Sciences Association of Saskatchewan (Ind.)/Association des sciences de la santé de la Saskatchewan (ind.) (HSAS) (1972)**
#2, 3002 Louise St., Saskatoon, SK S7J 3L8
306/955-3399, Fax: 306/955-3396, Toll Free: 1-888-565-3399
Executive Director, Tim Slattery
President, Ted Makeechak
Publications: Dispatches

**Hospital Employees Union (CLC)/Syndicat des employés d'hôpitaux (CTC) (1944)**
2006 - 10 Ave. West, Vancouver, BC V6J 4P5
604/734-3431, Fax: 604/734-3163
Provincial President, Julie Eckert
Publications: The Hospital Guardian

**Hotel Employees & Restaurant Employees' International Union (AFL-CIO/CLC)/Union internationale des employés d'hôtels et de restaurants (FAT-COI/CTC)**
1219 - 28 St. NW, Washington, DC 20007 USA
202/393-4373, Fax: 202/333-0468
General President, Edward T. Hanley
General Sec.-Treas., Herman Leavitt
Canadian Regional Office: International Representative, Paul Clifford, 20 Austin Cres., Toronto, ON M5R 3E3

**Independent Canadian Extrusion Workers Union (CNFIU)**
PO Box 752, Midland, ON L4R 4P4
705/526-6783
Director, Steve Miller
President, Steve Bonnett

**Independent Canadian Transit Union (CCU)/Syndicat canadien indépendant du transport (CSC)**
#206, 5050 Kingsway, Burnaby, BC V5H 4H2
604/433-1892, Fax: 604/435-0160
National President, Hunter Wallace
Eastern Vice-President, Dan Carriere
Western Vice-President, Joe Elworthy
National Sec.-Treas., Neal Barreca
Publications: Progress

**Independent Paperworkers of Canada (Ind.) (IPC) (1992)**
#D412, 1450 Glen Abbey Gate, Oakville, ON L6M 2V7
905/825-2593, Fax: 905/825-2593

General Administrator, Gary Buccella
Publications: The Independent

**Independent Union of Precision Diecasters (CNFIU)/Syndicat indépendant de Precision Diecasters (FCNSI)**
PO Box 1295, Peterborough, ON K9J 5T2
705/745-6428
President, Jon Lunt

**International Alliance of Theatrical Stage Employees & Moving Picture Machine Operators of the United States & Canada (AFL-CIO/CLC)/Alliance internationale des employés de la scène et des projectionnistes des États-Unis et du Canada (FAT-COI/CTC) (IATSE)**
#601, 1515 Broadway, New York, NY 10036 USA
212/730-1770, Fax: 212/921-7699
President, Alfred W. Ditolla
Canadian Office: Canadian Vice-President, Alan L. Cowley, Bus: 416/281-5054, Fax: 416/441-4073; International Representative, East Coast, Robert Thomson, Bus: 902/883-8346; International Representative, West Coast, Gus Bottas, Bus: 403/456-7156, 6 Havilland Dr., West Hill, ON M1C 2T6, 416/441-3710, Fax: 416/441-4073

**International Allied Printing Trades Association/Association internationale des métiers alliés de l'imprimerie (1911)**
501 - 3 St. NW, Washington, DC 20001-2797 USA
202/434-1238, Fax: 202/434-1245
President, William J. Boarman
Sec.-Treas., Gerald H. Deneau

**International Association of Bridge, Structural & Ornamental Iron Workers (AFL-CIO)/Association internationale des travailleurs de ponts, de fer structural et ornemental (FAT-COI)**
#400, 1750 New York Ave. NW, Washington, DC 20006 USA
202/383-4800
President, Jacob West
General Secretary, Leroy Worley
Publications: The Ironworker
Canadian Office: General Vice-President, James Phair, 1350 L'Heritage Dr., Sarnia, ON N7S 6H8, 519/542-1413, Fax: 519/542-3790

**International Association of Fire Fighters (AFL-CIO/CLC)/Association internationale des pompiers (FAT-COI/CTC)**
1750 New York Ave. NW, Washington, DC 20006 USA
202/737-8484
General President, Alfred K. Whitehead
Canadian Office: Canadian Director, Doug Coupar, #403, 350 Sparks St., Ottawa, ON K1R 7S8, 613/567-8988, Fax: 613/567-8986

**International Association of Heat & Frost Insulators & Asbestos Workers (AFL-CIO/CLC)/Association internationale des isolateurs en amiante (FAT-COI/FCT)**
#301, 1776 Massachusetts Ave. NW, Washington, DC 20036-1989 USA
202/785-2388, Fax: 202/429-0568
General President, William G. Bernard
Publications: The Asbestos Worker
Canadian Office: Canadian Vice-President, André Chartrand, 3585, av Diane, Terrebonne, QC J6Y 1A2, 514/433-2926, Fax: 514/353-8653

**International Association of Machinists & Aerospace Workers (AFL-CIO/CLC)/Association internationale des machinistes et des travailleurs de l'aérospatiale (FAT-COI/CTC)**
Machinists Bldg., 9000 Machinists Place, Upper Marlboro, MD 20772 USA
301/967-4500, Fax: 301/967-4588
President, George J. Kourpias
Canadian Office: General Vice-President, Valérie E. Bourgeois, #300, 100 Metcalfe St., Ottawa, ON K1P 5M1, 613/236-9761, Fax: 613/563-7830

**International Brotherhood of Boilermakers, Iron Ship Builders, Blacksmiths, Forgers & Helpers (AFL-CIO)/Fraternité internationale des chaudronniers, constructeurs de navires en fer, forgerons, forgeurs et aides (FAT-COI) (IBB) (1880)**
**Boilermakers**
New Brotherhood Bldg., #570, 753 State Ave., Kansas City, KS 66101 USA
913/371-2640, Fax: 913/281-8101
Email: pamd@boilermakers.org
URL: http://www.boilermakers.com
International President, Charles W. Jones
International Sec.-Treas., Jerry Z. Willburn
Publications: The Boilermaker Reporter
Eastern Canadian Office: International Vice-President, Eastern Canada, Alexander C. MacDonald#139, 1216 Sandcove Rd., PO Box 3279, Stn B, Saint John, NB E2M 4X8 ,506/634-8203, Fax: 506/634-0307
Western Canada Office: International Vice-President, Western Canada, Richard C. Albright, #206, 17205 - 106 A Ave., Edmonton, AB T5S 1M7, 403/483-0823, Fax: 403/489-3043

**International Brotherhood of Electrical Workers (AFL-CIO/CFL)/Fraternité internationale des ouvriers en électricité (FAT-COI/FCT) (IBEW) (1891)**
1125 - 15th St. NW, Washington, DC 20005 USA
202/833-7000, Fax: 202/467-6316
International President, John J. Barry
International Secretary, Jack F. Moore
International Representative, Lawrence Liles, Bus: 202/728-6107
Publications: IBEW Journal
Canadian Office: International Vice-President, Ken J. Woods, #401, 45 Sheppard Ave. East, North York, ON M2N 5Y1, 416/226-5155, Fax: 416/226-1492

**International Brotherhood of Firemen & Oilers (AFL-CIO/CLC)/Fraternité internationale des chauffeurs et huileurs (FAT-COI/CTC) (IBF&O) (1898)**
1100 Circle, 75 Pkwy., #350, Atlanta, GA 30339 USA
404/933-9104, Fax: 404/933-0361
President, Jimmy L. Walker
Canadian Office: Canadian International Vice-President, Domenic Mancini, #6, 648 Finch Ave. East, North York, ON M2K 2E6, 416/221-5200, Fax: 416/221-5207

**International Brotherhood of Locomotive Engineers/Fraternité internationale des ingénieurs de locomotives (BLE) (1863)**
Standard Building, Mezzanine, 1370 Ontario St., Cleveland, OH 44113-1702 USA
216/241-2630, Fax: 216/861-0932
International President, Ronald P. McLaughlin
Public Relations Director, Stephen W. FitzGerald
Publications: Locomotive Engineers Journal; Locomotive Engineers Magazine, q.
Canadian Office: Vice-President/Director, Gilles Hallé, #1401, 150 Metcalfe St., Ottawa, ON K2P 1P1, 613/235-1828, Fax: 613/235-1069

**International Brotherhood of Painters & Allied Trades (AFL-CIO/CFL)/Fraternité internationale des peintres et métiers connexes (FAT-COI/FCT)**
1750 New York Ave. NW, Washington, DC 20006 USA
202/637-0700, Fax: 202/637-0771
President, A.L. (Mike) Monroe

Canadian Office: General Vice-President, 8th District, Armando Colafranceschi, 12 Morgan Ave., Thornhill, ON L3T 1R1, 905/882-6490, Fax: 905/882-9604

**International Brotherhood of Teamsters (AFL-CIO/CLC)/Fraternité internationale des teamsters (FAT-COI/CTC)**
25 Louisiana Ave. NW, Washington, DC 20001 USA
202/624-6800
General President, Ron Carey

**International Federation of Professional & Technical Engineers (AFL-CIO/CLC)/Fédération internationale des ingénieurs et techniciens (FAT-COI/CTC)**
#701, 8701 Georgia Ave., Silver Springs, MD 20910 USA
301/565-9016
President, James E. Sommerhauser
Canadian Office: Canadian International Representative Vice-President, Desmond Cupid, 24 Port Royal Trail, Scarborough, ON M1V 2G5

**International Longshoremen's Association (AFL-CIO/CLC)/Association internationale des débardeurs (FAT-COI/CTC) (ILA)**
#1530, 17 Battery Pl., New York, NY 10004 USA
212/425-1200, Fax: 212/809-6826
President, John Bowers
Publications: ILA News
Canadian Division: Canadian Vice-President, David W. Quinn, 1 Seaview Ave., Halifax, NS B3P 2A6, 902/479-1732

**International Longshoremen's & Warehousemen's Union (CLC)/Syndicat international des débardeurs et magasiniers (CTC)**
1188 Franklin St., San Francisco, CA 94109 USA
President, David Arian
Canadian Office: President, Gordie Westrand, #020, 1880 Triumph St., Vancouver, BC V5L 1K3, 604/254-8141, Fax: 604/254-8183

**International Plate Printers, Die Stampers, & Engravers Union of North America (AFL-CIO/CLC)/Syndicat international des graveurs et matriceurs de l'Amérique du Nord (FAT-COI/CTC)**
906 Dennis Ave., Silver Springs, MD 20901 USA
International President, Daniel Bradley
Canadian Contact: Secretary, Glen Bull, #26A, 778 St. Andre Dr., Orleans, ON K1C 4R6, 613/824-8568

**International Union of Allied Novelty & Production Workers (AFL-CIO/CLC)/Syndicat international des employés de la production de la nouveauté et autres travailleurs assimilés (FAT-COI/CTC)**
25 Rosalyn Rd., Mineola, NY 11501 USA
212/889-1212
President, Julius Isaacson
Canadian Office: Canadian Representative, Frank Johnston, 34 Madison Ave., Toronto, ON M5R 3N6, 416/960-5523, Fax: 416/960-1093

**International Union of Bricklayers & Allied Craftsmen (AFL-CIO/CFL)/Union internationale des briqueteurs et métiers connexes (FAT-COI/FCT)**
Bowen Bldg., 815 - 15 St. NW, Washington, DC 20005 USA
202/783-3788, Fax: 202/393-0219
President, John T. Joyce
Canadian Office: Director, Canadian Operation, Brian Strickland, 3 Forwell Rd., Kitchener, ON N2B 1W3, 519/576-4610, Fax: 519/576-7382

**International Union of Electronic, Electrical, Salaried, Machine & Furniture Workers (AFL-CIO)/Syndicat international des travailleurs de l'électricité, salariés, de machines et de meubles (FAT-COI)**
1126 - 16 St. NW, Washington, DC 20036 USA
202/296-1200
President, William H. Bywater
Canadian Office: President, Earl Staples, 55 Columbia St. East, Waterloo, ON N2J 4N7, 519/746-8140, Fax: 519/746-5414

**International Union of Elevator Constructors (AFL-CIO/CFL)/Union internationale des constructeurs d'ascenseurs (FAT-COI/FCT) (IUEC) (1901)**
#310, 5565 Sterrett Pl., Columbia, MD 21044 USA
410/997-9000, Fax: 410/997-0243
General President, John N. Russell
General Sec.-Treas., Richard W. Scariot
Canadian Office: Canadian Vice-President & Director, J. Warner Baxter, 108 Teal Ave., Stoney Creek, ON L8E 3B4, 416/849-6288, Fax: 416/849-7342

**International Union of Operating Engineers (AFL-CIO/CFL)/Union internationale des opérateurs de machines lourdes (FAT-COI/FCT)**
1125 - 17 St. NW, Washington, DC 20036 USA
202/429-9100
President, Frank Hanley
Publications: The International Operating Engineer
Canadian Office: Canadian Regional Director, J.V. Biddle, #401, 4211 Kingsway, Burnaby, BC V5H 1Z6, 403/438-1616, Fax: 403/439-2459

**International Union, United Automobile, Aerospace & Agricultural Implement Workers of America, Local 251 (CLC)/Syndicat international des travailleurs unis de l'automobile, de l'aérospatiale et de l'outillage agricole d'Amérique (CTC)**
8000 East Jefferson Ave., Detroit, MI 48214 USA
313/926-5000
President, Owen Bieber
Canadian Office: President, Jim Lee, PO Box 22024, Wallaceburg, ON N8A 5G4, 519/627-1629, Fax: 519/627-2055

**International Union, United Plant Guard Workers of America (Ind.)/Syndicat international des gardiens d'usine d'Amérique (ind.) (UPGWA)**
25510 Kelly Rd., Roseville, MI 48066 USA
313/772-7250, Fax: 313/772-9644
President, Eugene P. McConville
Publications: The Security Link
Region 12 - Canada: Director/Region 12, Watson E. Cook, #204, 5468 Dundas St. West, Toronto, ON M9B 6E3, 416/236-7523, Fax: 416/234-1564

**IWA - Canada (CLC) (1985)**
#500, 1285 West Pender St., Vancouver, BC V6E 4B2
604/683-1117, Fax: 604/688-6416
President, G.A. Stoney
Publications: IWA Canada Lumber Worker
Affiliates: British Columbia Federation of Labour

**Laborers' International Union of North America (AFL-CIO/CLC)/Union internationale des journaliers d'Amérique (FAT-COI/CTC) (LIUNA) (1903)**
905 - 16 St. NW, Washington, DC 20006 USA
202/737-8320, Fax: 202/737-2754
President, Arthur A. Coia
General Sec.-Treas., R.P. Vinall
Publications: The Laborer
Affiliates: American Federation of Labour & Congress of Industrial Organizations; Canadian Labour Congress

Canadian Office: Canadian Director & Vice-President, Enrico H. Mancinelli; Sub-Regional Manager, Eastern Canada, Nello Scipioni; Sub-Regional Manager, Central Canada, Joseph S. Mancinelli; Sub-Regional Manager, Western Canada, Victor Morden, #44 Hughson St. South, Hamilton, ON L8N 2A7, 905/522-7177, Fax: 905/522-9310

**Major League Baseball Players' Association (Ind.)/Association des joueurs de la Ligue majeure de baseball (ind.)**
12 East 49th St., New York, NY 10002 USA
212/826-0808, Fax: 212/752-3649
Executive Director, Donald M. Fehr

**Management & Professional Employees Society (Ind.)/Société des employés professionnels et administratifs (ind.) (MAPES)**
#523, 409 Granville St., Vancouver, BC V6C 1T2
604/669-3177, Fax: 604/669-5343
Executive Director, Thomas Abbott, CAE
Publications: MAPES Newsletter

**Manitoba Association of Health Care Professionals (CFL)/Association des professionnels de la santé du Manitoba (FCT) (MAHCP)**
#216, 819 Sargent Ave., Winnipeg, MB R3E 0B9
204/772-0425, Fax: 204/775-6829
President, C. Mark
Executive Director, Ron Wally
Publications: MAHCP Newsletter

**Marine Workers' Federation (CLC)/Fédération des travailleurs de construction navale (CTC) (1945)**
#200, 3700 Kempt Rd., Halifax, NS B3K 4X8
902/455-7279, Fax: 902/455-4716
President, Gary Marr

**Maritime Fishermen's Union (CLC)/Union des pêcheurs des Maritimes (CTC)**
1200 Main St., PO Box 1418, Shediac, NB E0A 3G0
506/532-2485, Fax: 506/532-2487, Email: muupm@nbnet.nb.ca
President, Guy Cormier
Sec.-Treas., Léo-Paul Guimond

**Metal Polishers, Buffers, Platers & Allied Workers International Union (AFL-CIO/CLC)/Syndicat international des polisseurs de métal, plaqueurs et travailleurs assimilés (FAT-COI/CTC)**
5578 Montgomery Rd., Cincinnati, OH 45212 USA
President/Sec.-Treas., Glenn Holt
Canadian Representation: Recording & Financial Sec.-Treas., Maud Doyle; President, Local 19, Bernice Baker, 39 Beachall St., Scarborough, ON M1S 3B3, 416/759-2211, Fax: 416/752-2854

**Miramichi Trades & Labour Union (Ind.)/Syndicat des métiers et du travail de la Miramichi (ind.)**
PO Box 684, Newcastle, NB E1V 3M5
506/622-1792
President, Greg Sullivan

**National Automobile, Aerospace, Transportation & General Workers Union of Canada (CLC)/Syndicat national de l'automobile, de l'aérospatiale, du transport et des autres travailleurs et travailleuses du Canada (CTC) (CAW-Canada) (1985)**
**Canadian Auto Workers Union**
205 Placer Ct., North York, ON M2H 3H9
416/497-4110, Fax: 416/495-6559, Email: caw@caw.ca, URL: http://www.caw.ca/caw/
National President, Basil "Buzz" Hargrove
National Sec.-Treas., Jim O'Neil

Quebec Director, Luc Desnoyers
Publications: Contact

### National Federation of Nurses' Unions/Fédération nationale des syndicats d'infirmières et d'infirmiers (1981)

377 Bank St., Ottawa, ON K2P 1Y3
613/233-1018, Fax: 613/233-3892
President, Kathleen Connors
Sec.-Treas., D. Bragg
Publications: Front Lines

### National Hockey League Players' Association (Ind.)/Association des joueurs de la ligue nationale de hockey (ind.) (NHLPA) (1967)

#2300, One Dundas St. West, Toronto, ON M5G 1Z3
416/408-4040, Fax: 416/408-3685, URL: http://www.nhlpa.com
Executive Director, Robert W. Goodenow
President, Mike Gartner
Publications: Goals

### National Union of Public & General Employees/ Syndicat national des employés généraux et du secteur public (NUPGE) (1976)

#204, 2841 Riverside Dr., Ottawa, ON K1V 8N4
613/526-1663, Fax: 613/526-0477, URL: http://www.nupge.ca
National President, James Clancy
National Sec.-Treas., Larry Brown
Publications: National News; Economic Indicators, s-m.; Bagdad Café, q.
Affiliates: Public Services International; Canadian Labour Congress
Member Unions

#### ALBERTA UNION OF PROVINCIAL EMPLOYEES/SYNDICAT DE LA FONCTION PUBLIQUE DE L'ALBERTA

10451 - 170 St., Edmonton, AB T5P 4S7
403/930-3300, Fax: 403/930-3392
President, Carol Anne Dean
Contact, Public Relations, Don McMann
Publications: Impact

#### BREWERY, GENERAL & PROFESSIONAL WORKERS UNION

238 Jane St., Toronto, ON M6S 3Z1
416/762-7477, Fax: 416/762-0182
President, Cam Nelson
Business Agent, George Redmond
Publications: Local 304 News

#### BRITISH COLUMBIA GOVERNMENT & SERVICE EMPLOYEES' UNION/SYNDICAT DES FONCTIONNAIRES PROVINCIAUX ET DE SERVICE DE LA COLOMBIE-BRITANNIQUE

4911 Canada Way, Burnaby, BC V5G 3W3
604/291-9611, Fax: 604/291-6030
President, John Shields
Sec.-Treas., Diane Wood
Affiliates: BC Federation of Labour; Canadian Labour Congress

#### CANADIAN UNION OF BREWERY & GENERAL WORKERS, LOCAL 325/SYNDICAT CANADIEN DES TRAVAILLEURS DE BRASSERIES ET TRAVAILLEURS EN GÉNÉRAL, SECTION LOCALE 325

One Carlingview Dr., Etobicoke, ON M9W 5E5
416/675-2648, Fax: 416/675-6694
President, Greg Greco

#### HEALTH SCIENCES ASSOCIATION OF BRITISH COLUMBIA/ ASSOCIATION DES SCIENCES DE LA SANTÉ DE LA COLOMBIE-BRITANNIQUE (HSA) (1971)

#600, 4710 Kingsway, Burnaby, BC V5H 4M6
604/439-0994, Fax: 604/439-0976, Toll Free: 1-800-663-2017
President, Cindy Stewart
Publications: The Report
Affiliates: BC Federation of Labour; Canadian Labour Congress

#### MANITOBA GOVERNMENT EMPLOYEES' UNION/ASSOCIATION DE LA FONCTION PUBLIQUE DU MANITOBA (MGEU)

#601, 275 Broadway, Winnipeg, MB R3C 4M6
204/982-6432, Fax: 204/942-2146, Toll Free: 1-800-262-8891
President, Peter Olfert
Publications: Contact

#### NEW BRUNSWICK GOVERNMENT EMPLOYEES UNION/SYNDICAT DES EMPLOYÉS DU GOUVERNEMENT DU NOUVEAU-BRUNSWICK (NBGEU)

500 Beaverbrook Ct., Ground Fl., Fredericton, NB E3B 5X4
506/453-9929, Fax: 506/458-9358
President, Alfred Watson
Director, Jerry Dunnett
Publications: NBGEU Bulletin

#### NEWFOUNDLAND ASSOCIATION OF PUBLIC EMPLOYEES/ ASSOCIATION DE LA FONCTION PUBLIQUE DE TERRE-NEUVE (NAPE)

PO Box 8100, St. John's, NF A1B 3M9
709/754-0700, Fax: 709/754-0726, Toll Free: 1-800-563-4442
President, Dave Curtis
Sec.-Treas., Allan Carter
Public Relations/Communications/Research, Trudi Brake
Publications: The Communicator
Affiliates: Newfoundland Federation of Labour

#### NOVA SCOTIA GOVERNMENT EMPLOYEES UNION/SYNDICAT DE LA FONCTION PUBLIQUE DE LA NOUVELLE-ÉCOSSE (NSGEU)

100 Eileen Stubbs Ave., Dartmouth, NS B3B 1Y6
902/424-4063, Fax: 902/455-2749
President, Dave Peters
Publications: NSGEU Newsletter

#### ONTARIO LIQUOR BOARD EMPLOYEES' UNION/SYNDICAT DES EMPLOYÉS DE LA RÉGIE DES ALCOOLS DE L'ONTARIO

5757 Coopers Ave., Mississauga, ON L4Z 1R9
905/712-2912, Fax: 905/712-2916
President, John Coones
Executive Officer, Sharon McTamaney
Publications: Echo

#### ONTARIO PUBLIC SERVICE EMPLOYEES UNION/SYNDICAT DES EMPLOYÉES ET EMPLOYÉS DE LA FONCTION PUBLIQUE DE L'ONTARIO (OPSEU) (1911)

100 Lesmill Rd., North York, ON M3B 3P8
416/443-8888, Fax: 416/443-9670, Toll Free: 1-800-268-7376
URL: http://www.inforamp.net/~opseu/
President, Leah Casselman
Publications: OPSEU News Update; Voices, q.
Affiliates: Canadian Labour Council; Ontario Federation of Labour

#### PRINCE EDWARD ISLAND UNION OF PUBLIC SECTOR EMPLOYEES/ SYNDICAT DE LA FONCTION PUBLIQUE DE L'ÎLE-DU-PRINCE-EDOUARD

PO Box 1116, Charlottetown, PE C1A 7M8
902/892-5335, Fax: 902/892-0978
President, Mike Butler
Publications: Accent; The Advocate, q.

#### SASKATCHEWAN GOVERNMENT EMPLOYEES' UNION/SYNDICAT DE LA FONCTION PUBLIQUE DE LA SASKATCHEWAN (SGEU)

1440 Broadway Ave., Regina, SK S4P 1E2
306/522-8571, Fax: 306/352-1969
CEO, Pat Gallagher
President, Barry Nowoselsky
Publications: Common Ground

### Native Brotherhood of British Columbia (Ind.)/ Fraternité des Indiens de la Colombie-Britannique (ind.)

#200, 1755 East Hastings St., Vancouver, BC V5L 1T1
604/255-3137, Fax: 604/251-7107, Telex: 04-51439
President, Cecil Hill
Publications: Native Voice

### New Brunswick Public Employees Association (Ind.)/Association des employés de la Fonction publique du Nouveau-Brunswick (ind.)

238 King St., PO Box 95, Fredericton, NB E3B 4Y2
506/458-8440, Fax: 506/450-8481
President, Ian MacMichael
Publications: Newsline/Bulletin

### New Brunswick School Business Employees' Association (Ind.)/Association des employés de l'administration des écoles du Nouveau-Brunswick (ind.)

PO Box 190, Chipman, NB E0E 1C0
506/339-7000, Fax: 506/339-7001
President, Wesley Miller

### New Brunswick School Supervisor's Organization (Ind.)/Association des conseillers en pédagogie du Nouveau-Brunswick (ind.) (NPSSO)

c/o School District 15, 1077 St. George Blvd., PO Box 1058, Moncton, NB E2A 4H8
506/547-2777, Fax: 506/547-2783
President, Kathy Baldwin
Publications: NBSSO Newsletter/ACPNB Bulletin de nouvelles

### The Newspaper Guild (AFL-CIO/CLC)/La Guilde des journalistes (FAT-COI/CTC) (TNG) (1933)

8611 Second Ave., Silver Spring, MD 20907 USA
301/585-2990, Fax: 301/585-0668
President, Charles Dale
Publications: The Guild Reporter
Affiliates: International Federation of Journalists
Canadian Region: Canadian Director, Mike Bocking, #103, 30 Concourse Gate, Nepean, ON K2E 7V7, 613/727-0990, Fax: 613/723-9236

### Nova Scotia Union of Public Employees (Ind.)/ Syndicat des employés du secteur public de la Nouvelle-Écosse (ind.)

6309 Chebucto Rd., Halifax, NS B3L 1K9
902/429-7655, Fax: 902/422-6055
Business Agent, R.A. Stockton
President, Cathie Osborne

### Office & Professional Employees International Union (AFL-CIO/CLC)/Union internationale des employés professionnels et de bureau (FAT-COI/CTC)

#606, 815 - 16 St. NW, Washington, DC 20006 USA
President, John Kelly
Canadian Office: Canadian Director & International Vice-President, Michel Lajeunesse, #630, 1265, rue Berri, Montréal, QC H2L 4C6, 514/288-6511, Fax: 514/288-6540

### Ontario Hospital Association/Blue Cross Employees Association (CNFIU)/Association des employés de la Croix-Bleue/Association des hôpitaux de l'Ontario (FCNSI)

150 Ferrand Dr., North York, ON M3C 1H6
416/429-2661, Fax: 416/429-2773
President, Marie Samuel-Andrew

### Ontario Professional Fire Fighters Association (Ind.)/Association des pompiers professionnels de l'Ontario (ind.) (OPFFA) (1970)

#7, 871 Equestrian Ct., Oakville, ON L6L 6L7
905/847-1060, Fax: 905/847-9725
Executive Sec.-Treas., Wayne De Mille
Affiliates: Canadian Association of Fire Fighters

**Ontario Provincial Police Association (Ind.)/ Association de la sûreté provinciale de l'Ontario (ind.) (OPPA) (1954)**
119 Ferris Lane, Barrie, ON L4M 2Y1
705/728-6161, Fax: 705/721-4867, Toll Free: 1-800-461-4282
Administrator, Jim Drennan
Publications: OPPA Newsletter

**Operative Plasterers' & Cement Masons' International Association of the US & Canada (AFL-CIO/CFL)/Association internationale des plâtiers et des finisseurs en ciment des États-Unis et du Canada (FAT-COI/FCT)**
#300, 14405 Laurel Pl., Laurel, MD 20707 USA
301/470-4200, Fax: 301/470-2502
General President, John J. Dougherty

**Operative Plasterers' & Cement Masons' International Association of the US & Canada (AFL-CIO/CFL) - Canadian Office**
1413 Hayes St., Orleans, ON K1E 3M8
613/824-5973, Fax: 613/837-7156
Vice-President, Canadian Consultant, Director of Jurisdiction, Michael J. Gannon
Publications: The Plasterer & Cement Mason

**Police Association of Nova Scotia (Ind.)/ Association des policiers de la Nouvelle-Écosse (ind.) (PANS)**
PO Box 1557, RPO Central, Halifax, NS B3J 2Y3
902/468-7555, Fax: 902/468-2202
Executive Director, Joe Ross
Publications: Police Review Magazine

**Police Brotherhood of the Royal Newfoundland Constabulary Association (Ind.)/Fraternité des policiers de la gendarmerie royale de Terre-Neuve (ind.)**
PO Box 7444, Stn C, St. John's, NF A1E 3Y4
709/739-5946, Fax: 709/739-6276
President, J. Gullage

**Professional Association of Foreign Service Officers (Ind.)/L'Association professionnelle des agents du service extérieur (ind.) (PAFSO)**
#412, 47 Clarence St., Ottawa, ON K1N 9K1
613/241-1391, Fax: 613/241-5911, Email: info@pafso.com, URL: http://www.pafso.com
Executive Director, Peter Cenne
Director of Administration, Debra Hulley
President, Gilbert Laurin
Publications: Bout de papier

**Professional Association of Internes & Residents of Alberta (Ind.)/Association professionnelle des internes et résidents de l'Alberta (ind.) (PAIRA) (1975)**
#460, 8409 - 112 St., Edmonton, AB T6G 1K6
403/432-1749, Fax: 403/432-1778, Email: paira@planet.eon.net
Executive Director, Connie Becker
Publications: PAIRAphrase

**Professional Association of Internes & Residents of Newfoundland (Ind.)/Association professionnelle des internes et résidents de Terre-Neuve (ind.) (PAIRN)**
c/o Faculty of Medicine, Student Affairs, Memorial University, 300 Prince Philip Dr., St. John's, NF A1B 3V6
709/737-7118, Fax: 709/737-6968
President, Michael Green, M.D.

**Professional Association of Internes & Residents of Ontario (Ind.)/Association professionnelle des internes et résidents de l'Ontario (ind.)**
505 University Ave., Toronto, ON M5G 1X4
416/979-1182
President, Steven Tishler

**Professional Association of Internes & Residents of Saskatchewan (Ind.)/Association professionnelle des internes et résidents de la Saskatchewan (ind.) (PAIRS) (1976)**
Royal University Hospital, Box 23, 103 Hospital Dr., Saskatoon, SK S7N 0W8
306/655-2134, Email: pairs@link.ca
President, Dr. Steve Kraus
Publications: Pairscript

**Professional Association of Residents & Internes of British Columbia (Ind.)/Association professionnelle des résidents et internes de la Colombie-Britannique (ind.)**
#900, 601 West Broadway,Vancouver, BC V5Z 4C2
604/876-7636, Fax: 604/876-7690
President, Dr. Eric Webber
Publications: PARI Scope

**Professional Association of Residents & Internes of Manitoba (Ind.)/Association professionnelle des résidents et internes du Manitoba (ind.) (PARIM) (1976)**
**PARI Manitoba**
#AD107, 720 McDermot Ave., Winnipeg, MB R3E 0T3
204/787-3673, Fax: 204/787-2692
President, Dr. Andrew Hall
Vice-President, Dr. Sowmil Mehta
Publications: PARIM News

**Professional Association of Residents & Interns of the Maritime Provinces (Ind.)/Association professionnelle des résidents et internes des provinces maritimes (ind.)**
Room 564, Bethune Building, Victoria General Hospital, 1278 Tower Rd., Halifax, NS B3H 2Y9
902/428-4091
President, E. Mackay

**Professional Employees Association (Ind.)/ Association des employés professionnels (ind.) (1974)**
#201, 1001 Wharf St., Victoria, BC V8W 1T6
250/385-8791, Fax: 250/385-6629
Executive Director, Alan MacLeod
Publications: The Professional
Vancouver Office: Senior Staff Officer, Doug Hensby, #390, 6450 Roberts St., Burnaby, BC V5G 4E1, 604/299-6677, Fax: 604/299-2717

**Professional Institute of The Public Service of Canada/Institut professionnel de la fonction publique du Canada (PIPSC) (1920)**
53 Auriga Dr., Nepean, ON K2E 8C3
613/228-6310, Fax: 613/228-9048, Toll Free: 1-800-267-0446
President, Steve Hindle
Executive Secretary, Lorraine Neville
Publications: Communications; Dialogue with Parliament/Dialogue parlementaire, a.
Regional Offices
Atlantic Regional Office - Fredericton: Regional Representative, Yvette G. Michaud, #211, 1133 Regent St., Fredericton, NB E3B 3Z2, 506/459-3471, Fax: 506/450-3271, Toll Free: 1-800-561-0027
Atlantic Regional Office - Halifax: Regional Representative, Wayne Rogers, #1081, 5161 George St., Halifax, NS B3J 1M7, 902/420-1519, Fax: 902/422-8516, Toll Free: 1-800-565-0727
BC-Yukon-Inuvik Regional Office: Regional Representative, Dave Riffel; Labour Relations Officer, Evan Heidinger, #1385, 200 Granville St., Vancouver, BC V6C 1S4, 604/688-8238, Fax: 604/688-8290, Toll Free: 1-800-663-0485
Edmonton Regional Office: Regional Representative, Joe Ahren; Labour Relations Officer, Ed Gilles, #955, 10020 - 101A Ave., Edmonton, AB T5J 3G2, 403/428-1347, Fax: 403/426-5962, Toll Free: 1-800-661-3939
Ontario Regional Office: Regional Representative, Dan Rafferty; Labour Relations Officer, Marija Dolenc, #253, 40 Orchard View Blvd., Toronto, ON M4R 1B9, 416/487-1114, Fax: 416/487-7268, Toll Free: 1-800-668-3943
Québec Regional Office: Représentant régional, Pierrette Gosselin; Agente des relations du travail, Suzelle Brosseau, #1920, 1200, av McGill College, Montréal, QC H3B 4G7, 514/878-1159, Téléc: 514/878-4650, Ligne sans frais: 1-800-363-0622
Winnipeg Regional Office: Regional Representative, George Smith; Office Administrator, D'Arcy Brown, #570, 125 Garry St., Winnipeg, MB R3C 3P2, 204/942-1304, Fax: 204/942-4348, Toll Free: 1-800-665-0094

**Provincial Federation of Ontario Firefighters (PFOFF)**
#310, 2630 Skymark Ave., Mississauga, ON L4W 5A3
905/602-9501, Fax: 905/602-9504
President, Bruce Carpenter
Vice-President, Jim Simmons
Sec.-Treas., Larry Staples
Affiliates: International Association of Fire Fighters; Ontario Federation of Labour; Canadian Labour Congress

**Public Service Alliance of Canada (CLC)/Alliance de la fonction publique du Canada (CTC) (PSAC) (1966)**
233 Gilmour St., Ottawa, ON K2P 0P1
613/560-4200, Fax: 613/567-0385, Email: aec@psac.com, URL: http://www.psac.com/
National President, Daryl T. Bean
National Executive Vice-President, Nycole Turmel
Regional Executive Vice-President, Ontario, Susan Giampietri
Regional Executive Vice-President, NCR, John Baglow
Vice-présidente exécutive régionale, Québec, Joane Hurens
Regional Executive Vice-President, Atlantic, Paul Ducey
Regional Executive Vice-President, Marian Meagher
Regional Executive Vice-President, Prairies, Albert Beal
Regional Executive Vice-President, North, Jean-François Des Lauriers
Publications: Alliance; PSAC Union Update/AFPC Parlons Syndicat, w.
Affiliates: Canadian Labour Congress; Public Services International
Components of PSAC
Agriculture Union: National President, Larry Leng, #1000, 233 Gilmour St., Ottawa, ON K2P 0P2, 613/560-4306
National Component/Elément national: National President, Doug Chalk, #301, 233 Gilmour St., Ottawa, ON K2P 0P2, 613/560-4364
Canada Employment & Immigration Union/Syndicat de l'emploi et de l'immigration du Canada: National President, Cres Pascucci, #1004, 233 Gilmour St., Ottawa, ON K2P 0P2, 613/236-9634, Fax: 613/236-7871
Customs Excise Union/Douanes Accise: National President, Mansel Legacy, 1741 Woodward Dr., Ottawa, ON K2C 0P9, 613/723-8008
Environment Component/Elément de l'environnement: National President, Joe Pacholik, 2181 Thurston Dr., Ottawa, ON K1G 4Z2, 613/736-5533
National Health & Welfare Union/Syndicat de la Santé nationale et du Bien-être social: National President,

Al MacIntyre, #1202, 233 Gilmour St., Ottawa, ON K2P 0P2, 613/237-2732

SECO Component/Elément SECO: National President, John Carter, #1001, 233 Gilmour St., Ottawa, ON K2P 0P2, 613/560-4334

Supply & Services Union/Syndicat des approvisionnements et services: National President, Valerie Denesiuk; Administrative Officer, Laura J. Griffin, #400, 233 Gilmour St., Ottawa, ON K2P 0P2, 613/560-4282, Fax: 613/569-2669

Union of Canadian Transport Employees/Union canadienne des employés des transports: National President, Robert Desfonds, #302, 275 Bank St., Ottawa, ON K2P 2L6, 613/238-4003

Union of Energy, Mines & Resources Employees/ Syndicat des employés de l'Energie, Mines et Ressources: National President, Bernice Miller, #803, 233 Gilmour St., Ottawa, ON K2P 0P1, 613/ 560-4378

Union of National Defence Employees/Union des employés de la Défense nationale: National President, Paul Millette, 330 McLeod St., Ottawa, ON K2P 2C5, 613/594-4505

Union of Northern Workers/Syndicat des travailleurs du Nord: President, Darm Crook, #200, 5112 - 52 St., Yellowknife, NT X1A 1T6, 867/873-5668, Fax: 867/ 920-4448

Union of Postal Communications Employees/Syndicat des employés des postes et des communications: National President, Stephen White, #701, 233 Gilmour St., Ottawa, ON K2P 0P2, 613/560-4342

Union of Public Works Employees/Syndicat des employés des travaux publics: National President, John Gordon, #705, 233 Gilmour St., Ottawa, ON K2P 0P2, 613/560-4393

Union of Solicitor General Employees/Syndicat des employés du Solliciteur général: National President, Lynn Ray, #603, 233 Gilmour St., Ottawa, ON K2P 0P2, 613/232-4821

Union of Taxation Employees/Syndicat des employé(e)s de l'impôt: National President, David Flinn, #602, 233 Gilmour St., Ottawa, ON K2P 0P2, 613/235-6704

Union of Veterans' Affairs Employees/Syndicat des employé(e)s des Affaires des anciens combattants: National President, Sandra L. Messer, #703, 233 Gilmour St., Ottawa, ON K2P 0P2, 613/560-5460

Yukon Employees Union/Syndicat des employés du Yukon: National President, David Hobbis, 208 Strickland St., Whitehorse, YT Y1A 2J8, 867/667-2332, Fax: 867/667-6521

### Pulp, Paper & Woodworkers of Canada (CCU) (PPWC) (1963)

#201, 1184 - 6 Ave. West, Vancouver, BC V6H 1A4
604/731-1909, Fax: 604/731-6448
President, Stan J. Shewaga
Publications: The Leaflet
Affiliates: Confederation of Canadian Unions

### Research Council Employees' Association (Ind.)/ Association des employés du conseil de recherches (ind.) (RCEA) (1967)

PO Box 8256, Ottawa, ON K1G 3H7
613/746-9341, Fax: 613/745-7868, Email: rcea@ftn.net, URL: http://ftn.net/~rcea/
President, Wayne J. Findlay
Publications: RCEA Newsletter/AECR Bulletin

### Retail, Wholesale & Department Store Union (AFL-CIO/CLC)/Union des employés de gros, de détail et de magasins à rayons (FAT-COI/ CTC) (RWDSU) (1937)

30 East 29 St., New York, NY 10016 USA
212/684-5300, Fax: 212/779-2809
President, Lenore Miller
Sec.-Treas., Stuart Appelbaum
Publications: RWDSU Record

### Retail Wholesale Union (CLC)/Syndicat des employés de gros et de détail (CTC)

4371 Fraser St., Vancouver, BC V5V 4G4
604/879-2996, Fax: 604/879-2456
President, Ron McCann
Publications: The Target

### Saskatchewan Joint Board, Retail, Wholesale & Department Store Union (CLC)/Conseil mixte du Syndicat des employés de gros, de détail et de magasins à rayons de la Saskatchewan (CTC)

1233 Winnipeg St., Regina, SK S4R 1K1
306/569-9311, Fax: 306/569-9521
President, Dennis Hicks

### Seafarers' International Union of Canada (AFL-CIO/CLC)/Syndicat international des marins canadiens (FAT-COI/CTC)

1333, rue Saint-Jacques, Montréal, QC H3C 4K2
514/931-7859, Fax: 514/931-3667
President, Roman Gralewicz
Publications: Canadian Sailor/Le Marin canadien
Affiliates: Seafarers' International Union of North America (AFL-CIO); International Transport Workers' Federation

### Service Employees International Union (AFL-CIO/ CLC)/Union internationale des employés des services (FAT-COI/CTC)

1313 L St. NW, Washington, DC 20005 USA
International President, John J. Sweeney
Canadian Office: Vice-President in Canada, S.E. (Ted) Roscoe; Vice-President in Canada, Louis Duvall, 1 Credit Union Dr., Toronto, ON M4A 2S6, 416/752-4073, Fax: 416/752-1966

### Sheet Metal Workers' International Association (AFL-CIO/CFL)/Association internationale des travailleurs du métal en feuilles (FAT-COI/FCT)

1750 New York Ave. NW, Washington, DC 20006-5386 USA
202/662-0842, Fax: 202/662-0894
General President, Arthur R. Moore
Canadian Office: Director of Canadian Affairs, Robert Belleville, #204, 2742 Saint Joseph Blvd., Orleans, ON K1C 1G4, 613/834-1816, Fax: 613/834-0501

#### CANADIAN COUNCIL OF SHEET METAL WORKERS

#4, 724 Bath Rd., Kingston, ON K7M 4Y2
613/384-2269, Fax: 613/384-7682
President, Leo Lavalle

### Shipyard General Workers' Federation of British Columbia (CLC)/Fédération des ouvriers des chantiers navals de la Colombie-Britannique (CTC)

#130, 111 Victoria Dr., Vancouver, BC V5L 4C4
604/254-8204, Fax: 604/254-7447
President, George MacPherson
General Secretary, Joe Hrgovic
Publications: Ship & Shop
Affiliates: Machinists, Fitters & Helpers Industrial Union #3, Marine Workers & Boilerworkers' Industrial Union #1, Shipwrights, Joiners & Caulkers' Industrial Union #9

### Société des auteurs, recherchistes, documentalistes et compositeurs (Ind.)/Society of Writers, Researchers & Composers (Ind.) (SARDEC) (1949)

1229, rue Panet, Montréal, QC H2L 2Y6
514/526-9196, Téléc: 514/526-4124
Directeur général, Yves Légaré
Présidente, Louise Pelletier
Publications: Info-SARDEC

### Society of Ontario Hydro Professional & Administrative Employees (Ind.)/Société des employés professionnels et administratifs de l'Hydro-Ontario (ind.) (1944)

#630, 525 University Ave., Toronto, ON M5G 2L3
416/979-2709, Fax: 416/979-5794, URL: http:// www.society.on.ca
Senior Staff Officer, Darlene M. Booth
President, John Wilson
Publications: Monitor; Directions, m.
Affiliates: Canadian Court of Utility Professionals & Associated Societies (CCUPAS)

### Syndicat des agents de conservation de la faune du Québec (ind.)/Québec Wildlife Conservation Employees' Union (Ind.) (SACFQ) (1982)

6953, boul St-Michel, Montréal, QC H2A 2Z3
514/722-0492, Téléc: 514/722-4569
Président, Paul Legault
Publications: Faune-éthique

### Syndicat des agents de maîtrise de Québec-Téléphone (ind.)/Québec-Telephone Professional Employees Union (Ind.) (SAQT) (1980)

216, rue de la Cathédrale, CP 126, Rimouski, QC G5L 7B7
418/722-6144
Présidente, Madeleine B. Hudon
Secrétaire, Lynda Fortin
Publications: Bulletin d'information

### Syndicat des agents de la paix en services correctionnels du Québec (ind.)/Union of Prison Guards of Québec (Ind.) (1982)

4906, boul Gouin est, Montréal, QC H1G 1A4
514/328-7774, Téléc: 514/328-0889, Ligne sans frais: 1-800-361-3559
Président national, Réjean Lagarde
Secrétaire général, Gilles Bergeron
Secrétaire administrative, Huguette Desbiens-Lafontaine
Publications: L'Horizon

### Syndicat canadien des employés de bureau (FCT)/Canadian Office Employees Union (CFL) (1977)

#203, 5584, ch Côte de Liesse, Mount Royal, QC H4P 1A9
905/737-6717
Président, Roméo Ethier
Publications: Bulletin

### Syndicat des constables spéciaux du gouvernement du Québec (ind.)/Union of Special Constables for the Government of Québec (Ind.)

#201, 650, rue Graham Bell, Ste-Foy, QC G1N 4H5
418/527-2512, Téléc: 418/527-2513, Ligne sans frais: 1-800-665-7880
Président, Gilles Tremblay
Publications: Assemblée nationale du Québec

### Syndicat construction Côte-Nord (ind.)/North Shore Construction Union Inc. (Ind.) (SCCN) (1975)

1045, av Boulle, CP 760, Saint-Hyacinthe, QC J2S 7P5
514/773-8833, Téléc: 514/773-2232
Président, Marcel Gendron

### Syndicat des employé(e)s de magasins et de bureau de la Société des alcools du Québec (ind.)/Québec Liquor Board Store & Office Employees Union (Ind.)

1065, rue St-Denis, Montréal, QC H2X 3J3
514/849-7754, Téléc: 514/849-7914
Président, Ronald Asselin
Publications: Le Pionnier

**Syndicat des employés de production du Québec et de l'Acadie (ind.) (SEPQA)**
1250, rue de la Visitation, Montréal, QC H2L 3B4
514/527-9869, Téléc: 514/527-6941
Président, Lillian Campbell

**Syndicat de la fonction publique du Québec inc. (ind.)/Québec Government Employees' Union (Ind.) (SFPQ) (1962)**
5100, boul des Gradins, Québec, QC G2J 1N4
418/623-2424, Téléc: 418/623-6109, Courrier électronique: presidence@sfpq.qc.ca
Président, Serge Roy

**Syndicat général du cinéma et de la télévision - Section Office national du film (ind.) (SGCT) (1968)**
#5-6A, 2360, ch Lucerne, Mont-Royal, QC H3R 2J8
514/344-9399, Téléc: 514/344-9509
Présidente, C.O. Hoedeman

**Syndicat du personnel technique et professionel de la Société des alcools du Québec (ind.)/ Québec Liquor Board's Union of Technical & Professional Employees (Ind.)**
905, rue de Lorimier, Montréal, QC H2K 3V9
514/873-5878
Président, Jacques Paquette
Publications: Bulletin-Communiqué

**Syndicat des physiothérapeutes et des thérapeutes en réadaptation physique du Québec (SPTRPQ) (1971)**
#850, 1001, rue Sherbrooke est, Montréal, QC H2L 1L3
514/526-3719, Téléc: 514/521-0086
Présidente, Marie Hélène Boudreau
Publications: L'Influx

**Syndicat des pompiers du Québec (CTC)/Québec Union of Firefighters (CLC) (SPQ) (1989)**
#430, 110, boul Crémazie ouest, Montréal, QC H2P 1B9
514/383-4698, Téléc: 514/383-6782
Président, Gilles Raymond
Publications: Pompier 90

**Syndicat des professeurs de l'État du Québec (ind.)/Union of Professors for the Government of Québec (Ind.) (SPEQ) (1965)**
#513, 801, rue Sherbrooke est, Montréal, QC H2L 1K7
514/525-7979, Téléc: 514/525-4655
Président, Luc Perron
Publications: L'Autre Dimension

**Syndicat professionnel des diététistes du Québec (ind.)/Québec Professional Union of Dieticians (Ind.) (SPDQ)**
#2, 6321, rue Marquette, Montréal, QC H2G 2Y3
514/274-5353, Téléc: 514/274-6114
Présidente, Claudette Péloquin
Publications: Informel

**Syndicat professionnel des ingénieurs d'Hydro-Québec (ind.)/Hydro-Québec Professional Engineers Union (Ind.) (SPIHQ) (1964)**
#200, 600, rue Sherbrooke est, Montréal, QC H2L 1K1
514/845-4239, Téléc: 514/845-0082, Ligne sans frais: 1-800-567-1260, Courrier électronique: spihq@mtl.net
Président, Louis Champagne
Adjointe administrative, Michèle Côté
Publications: Echo

**Syndicat professionnel des médecins du gouvernement du Québec (ind.)/Professional Union of Government of Québec Physicians (Ind.)**
3691, boul Neilson, Ste-Foy, QC G1W 1T3
418/656-1910; 682-5150
Président, Dr. Roland Leblanc

**Syndicat des professionnelles et professionnels du gouvernement du Québec (ind.)/Union of Professional Employees of the Québec Government (Ind.) (SPGA) (1966)**
7, rue Vallière, Québec, QC G1K 6S9
418/692-0022, Téléc: 418/692-1338, Ligne sans frais: 1-800-463-5079
Président, Robert Caron
Publications: Info-express

**Syndicat des technicien(ne)s et artisan(e)s du réseau français de Radio-Canada (ind.)/CBC French Network Technicians' Union (Ind.) (STARF)**
1250, rue de la Visitation, Montréal, QC H2L 3B4
514/524-1100, Téléc: 514/524-6023, Ligne sans frais: 1-888-838-1100
Président national, Alain Boissonneault

**Syndicat des technologues en radiologie du Québec (ind.)/Québec Professional Union of Medical Radiological Technicians (STRQ) (1965)**
#850, 1001, rue Sherbrooke est, Montréal, QC H2L 1L3
514/521-3999, Téléc: 514/521-0086
Président, Jacques Paradis

**Syndicat des travailleurs de la construction du Québec (CSD)**
**CSD - Construction**
801, 4e rue, Québec, QC G1J 2T7
418/522-3918, Téléc: 418/529-6323, Ligne sans frais: 1-800-463-4091
Président, Michel Fournier
Publications: Revue
Organisation(s) affiliée(s): Centrale des syndicats démocratiques

**Syndicat des travailleurs et travailleuses de produits manufacturés et de services (ind.)/ Manufactured Goods & Services Employees Union (Ind.) (STTPM)**
#210, 1010, rue Sherbrooke ouest, Montréal, QC H3A 2R7
514/843-8041, Téléc: 514/844-9330
Président, Pierre Collin

**Syndicat des travailleurs et travailleuses unis du Québec (ind.)/United Workers Union of Québec (Ind.)**
875, rue Coudret, Beauport, QC G1C 6A2
418/624-4012
Président, Paul Ringuette

**Teaching Support Staff Union (1978)**
Simon Fraser University, AQ 5129/30, Burnaby, BC V5A 1S6
604/291-4735, Fax: 604/291-5369, Email: tssu@sfu.ca
President, Colleen MacQuarrie
Publications: TSSU Newsletter

**Teamsters Canada (CLC) (CCT) (1976)**
#804, 2540, boul Daniel Johnson, Laval, QC H7T 2S3
514/682-5521, Téléc: 514/681-2244
Directeur, Louis Lacroix
Directeur, Affaires gouvernmentales et relations publiques, François Laporte
Organisation(s) affiliée(s): International Brotherhood of Teamsters
Central Region: 1194 Matheson Blvd., Mississauga, ON L4W 1Y2, 905/629-4144
Eastern Region: 19 Alma Cres., Halifax, NS B3N 2C4, 902/445-5301
Western Region: 899 West 8 Ave., Vancouver, BC V5Z 1E3, 604/875-9321

**Telecommunications Employees Association of Manitoba (Ind.)/Association des employés en télécommunications du Manitoba (ind.) (TEAM)**
#216, 666 St. James St., Winnipeg, MB R3G 3J6
204/784-2370
President, Arlene Verbrugghe
Business Manager, Bill Hales

**Telecommunications Workers' Union (CLC)/ Syndicat des travailleurs en télécommunications (CTC) (TWU) (1980)**
5261 Lane St., Burnaby, BC V5H 4A6
604/437-8601, Fax: 604/435-7760, Info Line: 604/435-2224
President, Rod Hiebert
Sec.-Treas., Carol Nagy
Director of Communications, Myron Johnson
Publications: Transmitter
Affiliates: BC Federation of Labour; Post, Telegraph & Telecommunications International

**Textile Processors, Service Trades, Health Care, Professional & Technical Employees International Union (Ind.)/Syndicat international des employés professionnels et techniques des soins de la santé, des métiers, des services, textiles (ind.)**
#905, 360 North Michigan Ave., Chicago, IL 60601 USA
General President, Frank A. Scalish
Canadian Office: International Vice-President, Thomas W. Corrigan, 34 Madison Ave., Toronto, ON M5R 3N6, 416/960-3359, Fax: 416/960-1093

**Transportation Communications International Union (AFL-CIO/CLC)/Syndicat international du transports communication (FAT-COI/CTC) (1899)**
3 Research Pl., Rockville, MD 20850 USA
301/948-4910, Fax: 301/330-7661
International President, Robert A. Scardelletti
Canadian Office: National President, Jack Boyce, #2285D, 11 St. Laurent Blvd., Ottawa, ON K1G 4Z7, 613/731-6315, Fax: 613/731-0233

**Union des artistes (FIA)/Artists' Union (UDA) (1937)**
3433, rue Stanley, Montréal, QC H3A 1S2
514/288-6682, Téléc: 514/288-7150
Directeur général, Jean-Robert Choquet
Publications: Union express

**Union des carreleurs et métiers connexes, section locale 1 (CTC)/Union of Tile Workers & Allied Trades, Local 1 (CLC)**
#1401, 3637, boul Crémazie est, Montréal, QC H1Z 2J9
514/727-2950, Téléc: 514/727-8331
Gérant d'affaires, Claude Labbé
Président, Mario Basilico

**Union nationale des poseurs de systèmes intérieurs, de revêtements souples et travailleurs d'usine, section locale 2366 (CTC)/National Union of Interior Systems, Resilient Floor Layers, & Plant Workers, Local 2366 (CLC)**
#202, 3730, boul Crémazie est, Montréal, QC H2A 1B4
514/723-2366, Téléc: 514/723-4130
Directeur, Leo Annett

**Union of Needletrades, Industrial & Textile Employees/Syndicat du vêtement, textile et autres industries (UNITE) (1995)**
1710 Broadway, New York, NY 10019 USA
212/265-7000, Fax: 212/265-3415
International President, Jay Mazur
Canadian Manager/Vice-President, International, Gérald Roy

Canadian Office: Canadian Director (ACTWU), John Alleruzzo, 15 Gervais Dr., North York, ON M3C 1Y8, 416/441-1806, Téléc: 416/441-9680

### Union des opérateurs de machinerie lourde, section locale 791 (CTC)

8350, boul St-Michel, Montréal, QC H1Z 4G3
514/374-0300, Téléc: 514/374-9725
Président, Michel Paquet

### Union of Rail Canada Traffic Controllers (CCU)/ Syndicat des contrôleurs de circulation ferroviaire du Canada (CSC) (RCTC)

**Brotherhood of Locomotive Engineers**

1002 Pembina Hwy., Winnipeg, MB R3T 1Z5
204/477-0260, Fax: 204/477-0998, Toll Free: 1-800-581-7282
General Chairman, Alan F. Owens
Publications: RCTC Newsletter

### United Association of Journeymen & Apprentices of the Plumbing & Pipe Fitting Industry of the U.S. & Canada (AFL-CIO/CFL)/Association unie des compagnons & apprentis de l'industrie de la plomberie & de la tuyauterie des Etats-Unis & du Canada (FAT/COI/FCT)

901 Massachusetts Ave. NW, PO Box 37800, Washington, DC 20013 USA
202/628-5823, Fax: 202/628-5024
President, Marvin J. Boede
General Sec.-Treas., Marion A. Lee
Canadian Office: Vice-President & Canadian Director, George Meservier, #316, 1959 - 152 St., Surrey, BC V4A 9E3, 604/531-0516, Fax: 604/531-0547

### United Brotherhood of Carpenters & Joiners of America (AFL-CIO/CLC)/Fraternité unie des charpentiers et menuisiers d'Amérique (FAT-COI/CTC)

101 Constitution Ave. NW, Washington, DC 20001 USA
202/546-6206, Fax: 202/543-5724
General President, Sigurd Lucassen
Canadian Office: Research Director, Derrick Manson, #807, 5799 Yonge St., North York, ON M2M 3V3, 416/225-8885, Fax: 416/225-5390

### United Fishermen & Allied Workers' Union (CLC)/ Syndicat des pêcheurs et travailleurs assimilés (CTC) (1945)

#160, 111 Victoria Dr., Vancouver, BC V5L 4C4
604/255-1336, Fax: 604/255-3162
President, John Radosevic
Publications: The Fisherman

### United Food & Commercial Workers' International Union (AFL-CIO/CLC)/Union internationale des travailleurs et travailleuses unis de l'alimentation et du commerce (FAT-COI/CTC)

1775 K St. NW, Washington, DC 20006 USA
202/223-3111, Fax: 202/466-1562
International President, Douglas H. Dority
Canadian Region: Canadian Director, Tom Kukovica, #300, 61 International Blvd., Etobicoke, ON M9W 6K4, 416/675-1104, Fax: 416/675-6919

### United Garment Workers of America (AFL-CIO/CLC)/Travailleurs unis du vêtement d'Amérique (FAT-COI/CTC)

4207 Lebanon Rd., Hermitage, TN 37076 USA
615/889-9221, Fax: 615/885-3102
President, David Johnson
Canadian Office: Representative, Eastern Canada, Nancy Depinto, Bus: 416/368-9841; Representative, Western Canada, Frank Dicesare, #103, 111 West Broadway, Vancouver, BC V5J 1P4, 604/875-0070, Fax: 604/875-0070

### United Mine Workers of America (CLC)/Mineurs unis d'Amérique (CTC)

900 - 15 St. NW, Washington, DC 20005 USA
202/842-7200
President, Richard Trumka
Canadian Office: Executive Board Member, District No. 18 (AB, SK & BC), Robin Campbell; Executive Board Member, District No. 26 (NS & NB), Don MacRae, 4718 - 1 St. SW, Calgary, AB T2G 0A2, 403/287-2155, Fax: 403/243-8006

### United Paperworkers International Union (AFL-CIO/CLC)/Syndicat international des travailleurs unis du papier (FAT-COI/CTC)

3340 Perimeter Hill Dr., PO Box 1475, Nashville, TN 37211 USA
615/834-8590, Fax: 615/834-7741
President, Wayne Glenn
Canadian Office: International Representative, Gary Talarico, Bus: 807/468-1898, 227 Otto St., Thunder Bay, ON P7A 2T4, 807/344-0844, Fax: 807/345-0375

### United Rubber, Cork, Linoleum & Plastic Workers of America (AFL-CIO/CLC)/Union des ouvriers unis du caoutchouc, liège, linoléum et plastique d'Amérique (FAT-COI/CTC)

570 White Pond Dr., Akron, OH 44320-1156 USA
216/869-0320, Fax: 216/869-5627
President, Kenneth L. Coss
Canadian Office: Canadian Director, Reginald Duguay, #202, 61 International Blvd., Rexdale, ON M9W 6K4, 416/674-2011, Fax: 416/674-6736

### United Steelworkers of America (AFL-CIO/CLC)/ Métallurgistes unis d'Amérique (FAT-COI/CTC)

5 Gateway Center, Pittsburgh, PA 15222 USA
URL: http://www.uswa.org
President, George Becker
Canadian Office: Director, District 6, Harry Hynd, #201, 885 Meadowlands Dr. East, Ottawa, ON K2C 3N2, 613/727-9397, Fax: 613/727-1825
Retail Wholesale Canada-Canadian Service Sector Division: Canadian Director/Vice-President, Thomas E. Collins, Bldg. 11, #200, 5045 Orbitor Dr., Mississauga, ON L4W 4Y4, 905/624-8800, Fax: 905/624-2314

### United Textile Workers of America (AFL-CIO/CLC)/Ouvriers unis des textiles d'Amérique (FAT-COI/CTC)

#5-6, 763 Walnut Knoll Ln., Cordova, TN 38018 USA
International President, Ron Myslowka
Canadian Office: President & Regional Director, Stanley Condie, #6, 4377, rue Notre Dame ouest, Montréal, QC H4C 1R9, 514/935-5213, Fax: 514/936-5214

### United Transportation Union - Canada (AFL-CIO/CLC)/Travailleurs unis des transports - Canada (FAT-CIO/CTC) (UTU)

#750, 1595 Telesat Ct., Gloucester, ON K1B 5R3
613/747-7979, Fax: 613/747-2815
National President, Larry H. Olson
Publications: UTU News Canada National President, Larry H. Olson, #750, 1595 Telesat Ct., Gloucester, ON K1B 5R3, 613/747-7979, Fax: 613/747-2815

## CANADIAN FOUNDATIONS

A World of Dreams Foundation Canada, #708, 465, rue St-Jean, Montréal QC H2Y 2R6 – 514/843-7254; Fax: 514/843-3822; Toll Free: 1-800-567-7254 – Executive Director/President, Deborah Sims

Abe & Sophie Bronfman Foundation, 4333, av Westmount, Montréal QC H3Y 1W2 – Chairperson, Mildred Lande, CM

Abe Stern Family Foundation, #1001, 9310, boul St-Laurent, Montréal QC H2N 1N4 – President, Abraham Stern

Abraham & Malka Green Charitable Foundation, c/o Greenwin Developments, #1600, 20 Eglinton Ave. West, Toronto ON M4R 2H1 – President, Abraham J. Green

A.D. Penner Family Foundation, PO Box 909, Steinbach MB R0A 2A0 – President, A.D. Penner

Aga Khan Foundation Canada, Constitution Square, #1820, 350 Albert St., Ottawa ON K1R 1A4 – 613/237-2532; Fax: 613/567-2532 – CEO, Nazeer Aziz Ladhani

The Albert & Nancy Friedberg Foundation, 347 Bay St., 2nd Fl., Toronto ON M5H 2R7 – President, Albert D. Friedberg

Albert & Temmy Latner Family Foundation, 69 Old Forest Hill Rd., Toronto ON M5P 2R3 – President, Albert J. Latner

Alberta Orange Foundation for Children, RR#3, Red Deer AB T4N 5E3 – 403/340-0077 – Secretary, L. Tiihonen

Alexandra Marine & General Hospital Foundation, 120 Napier St., Goderich ON N7A 1W5 – 519/524-8323; Fax: 519/524-5579 – Administrator, Ken Engelstad

The Allan & Susan Seidenfeld Charitable Foundation, 227 Bridgeland Ave., Toronto ON M6A 1Y7 – Director, Dr. Allan Seidenfeld

Allard Foundation Ltd., #210, 5324 Calgary Trail, Edmonton AB T6H 4J8 – Vice-President, Shirley C. Allard

Allen & Milli Gould Family Foundation, 310 Main St. West, Hamilton ON L8P 1J8 – 905/527-1531; Fax: 905/527-3624; Toll Free: 1-888-527-1531; Email: mgould1@compuserve.com – President, Allen H. Gould

Allstate Foundation of Canada, 10 Allstate Pkwy., Markham ON L3R 5P8 – 905/477-6900; Fax: 905/475-4488 – Executive Vice-President, Eric Pickering

Alva Foundation, 199 Albertus Ave., Toronto ON M4R 1J6 – ; Fax: 416/481-3014 – President, John P. Fisher

The Alvin & Mona Libin Foundation, Bow Valley Square III, #3200, 255 - 5 Ave. SW, Calgary AB T2P 3G6 – President, Mona Libin

D'Ancona Charitable Trust, 122 Barse St., Toronto ON M5M 4L4 – Trustee, David D'Ancona

Anglican Foundation of Canada, Anglican Church House, 600 Jarvis St., Toronto ON M4Y 2J6 – 416/924-9192; Fax: 416/968-7983 – Secretary, Rev. Canon A.G. Baker

Animal Welfare Foundation of Canada, 2126 Highview Dr., Burlington ON L7R 3Y4 – Sec.-Treas., M.J. Unsworth

Anna & Edward C. Churchill Foundation, c/o National Trust Co., 168 Wellington St., Kingston ON K7L 3E4 – 613/544-3033; Fax: 613/544-6060 – Sec.-Treas., Brenda Pearce

Anvil Foundation Inc., 273 Germain St., Saint John NB E2L 2G8 – Contact, Judith Meinert

The Arcangelo Rea Family Foundation, #5, 320 Ferndale Ave., London ON N6C 5P7 – Director, Juliann Good

Arthur & Margaret Weisz Family Foundation, c/o Weisz & Associaties, #200, 242 Main St. East, Hamilton ON L8N 1H5 – President, Thomas J. Weisz

Atkinson Charitable Foundation, One Yonge St., 5th Fl., Toronto ON M5E 1E5 – 416/368-5152; Fax: 416/865-3619; Email: cpascal@thestar.ca – President, Catherine Atkinson-Murray

Audrey S. Hellyer Charitable Foundation, #50, 1262 Don Mills Rd., North York ON M3B 2W7 – 416/445-1121 – Treasurer, Geoffrey Hobsbawn

Austrian Society Trust Fund, 2255, rue Dudemaine, Montréal QC H3M 1R4 – 514/335-5906 – Chairperson, Elfi Valenta

AWB Charitable Foundation, #4700, TD Bank Tower, Toronto ON M5K 1E6 – 416/601-7500; Fax: 416/868-1793 – Secretary, A.W. Baillie

Azrieli Foundation, 1155, rue Sherbrooke ouest, Montréal QC H3A 2N3

Banting Research Foundation, c/o Faculty of Medicine, McMurrich Building, University of Toronto, Toronto ON M5S 1A8 – 416/978-4952 – Chair, Dorothy M. Hellebust

Beaverbrook Canadian Foundation, #1506, 1260 Marlborough Ct., Oakville ON L6H 3H5 – 905/337-0215; Fax: 905/337-0215 – Sec.-Treas., Alfred Lang Madley

Bechtel Foundation of Canada, #200, 12 Concorde Pl., North York ON M3C 3T1 – 416/441-4900; Fax: 416/441-4941 – Secretary, Manuel T. Estima

Benjamin Family Foundation, 2401 Steeles Ave. West, Downsview ON M3J 2P1 – President, Michael C. Benjamin

Bennett Family Foundation, #902, 481 University Ave., Toronto ON M5G 2E9 – Director, Avram J. Bennett

Berman Family Foundation, #1207, 211 Queen's Quay West, Toronto ON M5J 2M6 – President, Joseph Berman

Bessin Family Foundation, 68 Hillmount Ave., Toronto ON M6B 1X4 – Vice-President, Berl Bessin

The B.I. Ghert Family Foundation, 5 Junewood Cres., North York ON M2L 2C3 – President, Bernard I. Ghert

Bill & Judith Rubinstein Charitable Foundation, #503, 3625 Dufferin St., North York ON M5K 1N4 – President, Bill Rubinstein

Birks Family Foundation, #534, 606, rue Cathcart, Montréal QC H3B 1K9 – 514/397-2567; Fax: 514/397-1121 – Chairman & Executive Director, G. Drummond Birks

Black Family Foundation, 10 Toronto St., Toronto ON M5C 2B7 – 416/363-8721 – Sec.-Treas., Cecelia Black

The Block Charitable Foundation, #800, 1030 West Georgia St., Vancouver BC V6E 3B9 – President, Henry J. Block

The Body Shop Charitable Foundation, 33 Kern Rd., North York ON M3B 1S9 – 416/441-4189, ext.296; Fax: 416/441-0712 – President, Margot Franssen

Boland Foundation, 161 Glenrose Ave., Toronto ON M4T 1K7 – Lawrence Hynes

Brandon Area Foundation, PO Box 216, Brandon MB R7A 58Y – Sec.-Treas., Zella Mills

Branscombe Family Foundation, 6746 Morrison St., PO Box 576, Niagara Falls ON L2E 6V2 – Vice-President, Frank A. Branscombe

Brawn Foundation, #500, 505 - 3rd St. SW, Calgary AB T2P 3E6 – 403/261-9010; Fax: 403/262-6977 – Managing Director, Kelley A. Buckley

The Brooke Foundation, #3106, 99 Harbour Sq., Toronto ON M5J 2H2 – Trustee, Barrie D. Rose

Bumper Foundation, #1501, 300 - 5 Ave. SW, Calgary AB T2P 3C4 – 403/266-9700; Fax: 403/265-8155

Burns Memorial Fund, Rocky Mountain Plaza, #1109, 615 MacLeod Trail SE, Calgary AB T2G 4T8 – 403/234-9396; Fax: 403/233-0513 – Executive Director, Pamela Burke

The Burton Charitable Foundation, 26 Swanhurst Blvd., Mississauga ON L5N 1B7 – 905/826-3952 – Sec.-Treas., Myrna R. Wagner

Butters Foundation, 109 William St., Cowansville QC J2K 1K9 – 514/263-4123 – Vice-Chairman, William D. Duke

Calgary Foundation, #1850, 540 - 5 Ave. SW, Calgary AB T2P 0M2 – 403/264-1662; Fax: 403/265-0152 – Executive Director, Sam W. Aylesworth

Canada Europe Foundation, #600, 99 Bank St., Ottawa ON K1P 6B9 – 613/748-3511; Fax: 613/749-1556 – CEO, Donald G. Mitchell

Canada Iceland Foundation, 54 Siddall Cres., Winnipeg MB R2K 3W6 – Treasurer, D. Olafson

Canada-Israel Cultural Foundation, #503, 2221 Yonge St., Toronto ON M4S 2B4 – 416/932-2260; Fax: 416/482-8281 – Secretary, Grace Brooker

Canadian Aldeburgh Foundation, 34 Glenallan Rd., Toronto ON M4N 1G8 – 416/481-1964 – President, M.B. Sutton

Canadian Foundation for Masorti Judaism, #112, 1520 Steeles Ave. West, Concord ON L3K 3B9 – 905/738-1717; Fax: 905/738-1331 – President, Ron Hoffman

Canadian Friends of the American Israel Medical Foundation, #656, 600 University Ave., Toronto ON M5G 1X5 – 416/596-4473 – Contact, Noe Zamel, MD, Email: noe@io.org

Canadian Pacific Charitable Foundation, One Palliser Square, #2300, 125 - 9th Ave. SE, Calgary AB T2G OP6

Canadian Progress Charitable Foundation, 2395 Bayview Ave., North York ON M2L 1A2 – 905/852-5300; Fax: 905/852-5301 – Chairman, Al Gordon

Canadian-Scandinavian Foundation, Geography Dept., McGill University, 805, rue Sherbrooke ouest, Montréal QC H3A 2K6 – 514/398-4304; Fax: 514/398-7437 – Contact, Dr. Jan Lundgren

Canadian Scholarship Trust Foundation, #200, 240 Duncan Mills Rd., North York ON M3B 3P1 – 416/445-7377; Fax: 416/445-1708; Toll Free: 1-800-387-4622; URL: http://www.ntgi.net/ntg/cst/ – Chair, David Baird

Canadian Television Series Development Foundation, 777 Bay St., 7th Fl., Toronto ON M5W 1A7 – 416/596-5878; Fax: 416/596-2650; Email: ipf@inforamp.net – Executive Director, Andra Sheffer

The Capitol Foundation, 12 Mill St. South, Port Hope ON L1A 2S5 – 905/885-1071; Fax: 905/885-9714; Email: capitol@eagle.ca; URL: http://www.eagle.ca/~capitol/

Carol & Morton Rapp Foundation, c/o Harold L. Wilson, #330, 100 Cowdray Ct., Scarborough ON M1S 5C8 – President, Morton Rapp

Carolyn Sifton Foundation, #1700, One Lombard Pl., Winnipeg MB R3B 0X2 – 204/942-7884; Fax: 204/943-8060 – President, Graeme D. Sifton

Carthy Foundation, #200, 707 - 7 Ave. SW, Calgary AB T2P 3H6 – President, Paul S. Christensen

Catherine & Maxwell Meighen Foundation, #1702, 110 Yonge St., Toronto ON M5C 1T4 – 416/366-2931 – President, Col. Maxwell C.G. Meighen

Catholic Education Foundation of Ontario, 80 Sheppard Ave. East, Toronto ON M2N 6E8 – 416/229-5326; Fax: 416/229-5345 – Executive Secretary, Dr. John J. Flynn

Central Okanagan Foundation, PO Box 1233, Stn A, Kelowna BC V1Y 7V8 – 250/861-6160; Fax: 250/861-6156 – Executive Director, Janice Henry

C.G. Jung Foundation of the Ontario Association of Jungian Analysts, 223 St. Clair Ave. West, 3rd Fl., Toronto ON M4V 1R3 – 416/961-9767 – Douglas Cann

Chalmers Fund, c/o Ontario Arts Council, 151 Bloor St. West, 6th Fl., Toronto ON M5S 1T6 – 416/961-1660; 969-7450; Fax: 416/961-7796; Toll Free: 1-800-387-0058 – Grant Coordinator, Linda Brown

Charles H. Ivey Foundation, #105, 201 Consumers Rd., North York ON M2J 4G8 – 416/498-1555 – Sec.-Treas., Mary D. Megson

The Charles Johnson Charitable Fund, #428, 1, carré Westmount, Montréal QC H3Z 2P9 – Chairman, Charles Johnson

The Charles Wilson Charitable Foundation, PO Box 1410, Saint John NB E2L 4J9 – Vice-President, Keith M. Wilson

Chastell Foundation, 1170, rue Peel, 8e étage, Montréal QC H3B 4P2 – Executive Director, Thomas X. Axeworthy

The Chawkers Foundation, 41 Union St., Ottawa ON K1M 1R5 – 613/741-1440 – President, Charles S. Alexander

Cheshire Homes Foundation Canada Inc., #215, 40 Orchard View Blvd., Toronto ON M4R 1B9 – 416/487-0443; Fax: 416/487-0624 – Chairman, John Brown

Chris Spencer Foundation, PO Box 48284, Stn Bentall Centre, Vancouver BC V7X 1A1 – 604/608-2560 – Chairman, Chris McGregor

CHUM Charitable Foundation, 1331 Yonge St., Toronto ON M4T 1Y1 – 416/925-6666; Fax: 416/926-4095; Telex: 06-22063 – Contact, Taylor Baiden

The CIBC Wood Gundy Children's Miracle Foundation, PO Box 500, Stn BCE Place, Toronto ON M5J 2S8 – Executive Assistant, C. Ferron

Citadel Charity Foundation, 12, rue des Grisons, Québec QC G1R 4M7 – Sec.-Treas., J. Michael McCormack

Clifford & Mabel Beckett Foundation, 10977 - 74 Ave., Edmonton AB T6G 0E5 – President, James M. Murland

Cole Foundation, #3050, 600, boul de Maisonneuve ouest, Montréal QC H3A 3J2 – President, John N. Cole

Columbus Charity Foundation, #12, 31255 Upper Maclure Rd., Abbotsford BC V2T 5N4 – Secretary, Lawrence A. King

Community Foundation for Greater Toronto, 1 Dundas St. West, 15th Fl., PO Box 78, Toronto ON M5G 1Z3 – President & CEO, Marjorie J. Sharpe

Community Foundation of Ottawa-Carleton, #301, 75 Albert St., Ottawa ON K1P 5E7 – 613/236-1616; Fax: 613/236-1621 – Chair, David Simmonds

Conn Smythe Foundation, c/o Fraser & Beatty, PO Box 100, Stn 1st Canadian Place, Toronto ON M5X 1B2 – President, Dr. Hugh Arthur Smythe

Cornerstone 52 Foundation, Royal Bank Plaza, North Tower, #1525, 200 Bay St., PO Box 75, Toronto ON M5J 2J2 – 416/214-0520; Fax: 416/214-0523; Email: cornerstone52@ediwise.com; URL: http://www.cornerstone52.org/

Counselling Foundation of Canada, #410, 1 Toronto St., Toronto ON M5C 2W3

C.P. Loewen Family Foundation, PO Box 2260, Steinbach MB R0A 2A0 – Sec.-Treas., C.N. Loewen

Crake Foundation Inc., 791 Brunswick St., Fredericton NB E3B 1H8 – Sec.-Treas., Bishop George Lemmon

The CRB Foundation, 1170, rue Peel, 8e étage, Montréal QC H3B 4P2 – 514/878-5263; Fax: 514/878-5299; URL: http://www2.excite.sfu.ca/default.html – Administrative Director, Ann Dadson

DAAT Charitable Foundation, 37 Main St. South, Georgetown ON L7G 3G2 – Secretary, Martin Vaughan

DAC Foundation for People with Special Needs, c/o National Trust Company, One Adelaide St. East, Toronto ON M5C 2W8 – 416/361-4096; Fax: 416/361-3717 – Senior Foundations Officer, David R. Windeyer

Dakamagaro Charitable Foundation, 9 Ava Rd., Toronto ON M5P 1X8 – Sec.-Treas., Gary Goldberg

Danbe Foundation Inc., c/o Minto Construction Ltd., PO Box 5152, Stn F, Ottawa ON K2C 3H8 – Sec.-Treas., Daniel Greenberg

Daryl K. Seaman Foundation, #1850, 540 - 5th Ave. SW, Calgary AB T2P 0M2 – 403/264-1662; Fax: 403/265-0152 – Daryl K. Seaman

The David Bloomfield Family Foundation, 80 Boundary Rd., Cornwall ON K6H 5V3

David & Dorothy Lam Foundation, #400, 576 Seymour St., Vancouver BC V6B 3K1 – President, David Lam

The Davies Charitable Foundation, Landmark Centre, 165 Ontario St., Kingston ON K7L 2Y6 – 613/546-

4000; Fax: 613/546-9130 – Executive Director, Eileen Bruce

DeFehr Foundation Inc., 55 Vulcan Ave., Winnipeg MB R2G 1B9 – President, A.A. DeFehr

D.E.K.E. Charitable Foundation, 47 Auckland Lane, RR#4, King City ON L0G 1K0 – Contact, Philip J. Wolfenden

Deloitte, Touche Foundation Canada, 800 Sun Life Tower, Box 40, 150 King St. West, Toronto ON M5H 1J9 – 416/351-3988; Fax: 416/599-2399 – Director, R.G. Harris

Devonian Foundation, #770, 999 - 8 St. SW, Calgary AB T2R 1J5 – Sec.-Treas., A.T. Bosovich

Diamond Foundation, 105 North Commercial Dr., Vancouver BC V5L 4V7 – President, G. Diamond

The Dominion Group Foundation, 165 University Ave., Toronto ON M5H 3B9 – President, George Cooke

Donald F. Hunter Charitable Foundation, Aldermines Corp., #2603, 130 Adelaide St. West, Toronto ON M3H 3P5

Donner Canadian Foundation, #402, 212 King St. West, Toronto ON M5H 1K5 – 416/593-5125 – President, Devon Gaffney Cross

Dr. Baxter Temple Carmichael Foundation, c/o Valin, Innes, #405, 96 Larch St., Sudbury ON P3E 1C1 – 705/673-3655; Fax: 705/673-8758

The Dr. David Friesen Family Corporation, #711, 213 Notre Dame Ave., Winnipeg MB R3B 1N3 – President, Dr. David Friesen

Dr. Helen Creighton Memorial Foundation, 6350 Cobourg Rd., Halifax NS B3H 2A1 – 902/422-1271, ext. 174; Fax: 902/423-3357 – President, Dr. Alan Wilson

E. & G. Odette Charitable Foundation, #410, 4120 Yonge St., North York ON M2P 2C8 – Director, Edmond G. Odette

E.A. Baker Foundation for the Prevention of Blindness, 1929 Bayview Ave., Toronto ON M4G 3E8 – 416/480-7587; Fax: 416/480-7000 – Administrative Secretary, Glacia d'Cambre

Eaton Foundation, 250 Yonge St., 8th Fl., Toronto ON M5B 1C8 – 416/343-3423; Fax: 416/343-3526 – Chairman, Patrick J. Wilson

Ed Mirvish Family Charitable Foundation, 581 Bloor St. West, Toronto ON M6G 1K3 – President, Eleanor Gene Misener

The Edith & Bernard Ennis Foundation, 177 Parkway Dr., Welland ON L3C 4C5 – President., Bernard Ennis

Edith H. Turner Foundation, #400, 21 King St. West, PO Box 990, Hamilton ON L8N 3R1 – 905/528-8411; Fax: 905/528-9008 – President, J. Benjamin Simpson

Edmonton Community Foundation, #601, 10117 Jasper Ave., Edmonton AB T5J 1W8 – President, Jean Forest

Educational & Charitable Fund of The Prince Edward Island Medical Society, 557 North River Rd., Charlottetown PE C1E 1J7 – 902/368-7303; Fax: 902/566-3934 – Executive Director, Marilyn Lowther

The Edward Bronfman Family Foundation, BCE Place, Box 778, 181 Bay St., PO Box 778, Toronto ON M5J 2T3 – Director, Dayle Rakowsky

Edward J. Freeland Foundation, 4741 Queen St., Niagara Falls ON L2E 2M2 – President, Edward James Freeland

Edwards Charitable Foundation, 9 Anewen Dr., Toronto ON M4A 1R9 – President, John Bruce McLellan

The EJLB Foundation, #1050, 1350, rue Sherbrooke ouest, Montréal QC H3G 1J1 – 514/843-5112; Fax: 514/843-4080 – Executive Director, Robert Alain

Eldee Foundation, #1720, 1080, Côte du Beaver Hall, Montréal QC H2Z 1S8 – 514/871-9261; Fax: 514/397-0816 – President, Neri J. Bloomfield

Elizabeth Greenshields Foundation, #1, 1814, rue Sherbrooke ouest, Montréal QC H3H 1E4 – 514/937-9225 – Secretary, Micheline Leduc

Emes Charitable Foundation, 32 Stormont Ave., Toronto ON M5N 2B9 – President, Leslie Z. Gerendasi

Emil Skarin Fund, c/o The Senate, 150 Athabasca Hall, University of Alberta, Edmonton AB T6G 2E8 – 403/492-2268; Fax: 403/492-2448; Email: senate.office@ualberta.ca – Executive Officer, Sandra Kereliuk

E.P. Taylor Equine Research Fund, c/o Ontario Jockey Club, PO Box 156, Etobicoke ON M9W 5L2 – 416/675-6110; Fax: 416/674-1958 – Sec.-Treas., Robert J. Careless

Eugene & Eva Kohn Family Foundation, 102 Caribou Rd., Toronto ON M5N 2A9 – Secretary-Treasurer, Eva Kohn

Evelyn Steinberg Alexander Family Foundation, #250, 5601, rue Paré, Montréal QC H4P 1P7 – Co-Chairperson, James Alexander

E.W. Bickle Foundation, Scotia Plaza, PO Box 105, Toronto ON M5H 3Y2 – 416/367-9003; Fax: 416/367-9004 – President, W.P. Wilder

The Farha Foundation, 7080, av du Parc, Montréal QC H3N 1X6 – 514/270-4900; Fax: 514/270-5363 – Executive Director, Francine Corbeil

Fast Foundation, #600, 4150, rue Ste-Catherine ouest, Montréal QC H3Z 2Y5 – President, Simone Fast

Federation of Chinese Canadian Professionals (Ontario) Education Foundation, 150 Heath St. West, PO Box 6402, Stn A, Toronto ON M4V 2Y4 – 416/635-2550 – President, Dr. John Chiu

F.K. Morrow Foundation, #402, 357 Bay St., Toronto ON M5H 2T7 – 416/364-4124 – President, Sr. M. Walters

Fleming Foundation, 223 Ontario St., Beamsville ON L0R 1B0 – President, Arthur DeWitt Fleming

Fondation Alfred Dallaire, 1120, rue Jean-Talon est, Montréal QC H2R 1V9 – 514/270-3111; Fax: 514/270-2493; Toll Free: 1-800-263-3811 – Présidente, Jocelyne Legare

Fondation Caldwell, 5151, côte Ste-Catherine, Montréal QC H3W 1M6 – Trésorier, Howard Gilmour

Fondation Cardinal-Villeneuve, 2975, ch Saint-Louis, Ste-Foy QC G1W 1P9 – 418/653-8766; Fax: 418/653-9263 – Directrice générale, Louise Berube

Fondation Caritas-Sherbrooke inc., 636, rue Québec, Sherbrooke QC J1H 3M2 – 819/566-6345; Fax: 819/566-6347 – Directeur, Abbé Desève Cormier

Fondation Caroline Durand, #2300, 630, boul René-Lévesque ouest, Montréal QC H3B 4T8 – Responsable, Pierre Venne

Fondation Charles Cusson, a/s Montreal Trust Company, CP 1900, Succ B, Montréal QC H3B 3L6 – 514/982-7000; Fax: 514/982-7069 – Secrétaire, Marcel Brochu

Fondation Charles LeMoyne, 3120, boul Taschereau, Greenfield-Park QC J4V 2H1 – 514/466-5487; Fax: 514/672-1716 – Directeur général, Denis Jacob

Fondation Charles O. Monat, 630, boul René-Lévesque ouest, Montréal QC H3B 4H7 – 514/876-7779 – Trésorier, Paul G. Côté

Fondation Desjardins, Complexe Desjardins Tour Sud, 40e étage, CP 7, Montréal QC H5B 1B2 – 514/281-7171; Fax: 514/281-2391; Toll Free: 1-800-443-8611 – Directeur administratif, P. de Montigny

Fondation Edward Assh, 842, rue St-Joseph est, CP 2036, Québec QC G1K 7N4 – 418/522-6458; Fax: 418/522-5414 – President, Maurice Assh

Fondation Felix Goyer, 1940, boul Henri-Bourassa est, Montréal QC H2B 1J1 – President, Jean-Claude Leclerc

Fondation Fournier-Ethier, a/s Trust Général du Canada, 1100, rue Université, Montréal QC H3B 2G7 – Trustee, Pierre Favreau

Fondation Guadeloupe, 9, rue Cayer, Hull QC J8Y 1K2 – 819/776-3877; Fax: 819/776-6358 – Responsable, Jacques Beaucage

Fondation Guy Vanier, 1981, av McGill College, Montréal QC H3A 2Y2 – Trustee, Therese Nguyen

Fondation J. Armand Bombardier, 1000, rue J.A. Bombardier, CP 370, Valcourt QC J0E 2L0 – 514/532-2258; Fax: 514/532-5499 – Directrice générale, France Bissonnette

La Fondation J. Raymond Pepin, #783, 3, de Longpré, Ste-Foy QC G1V 2S2 – Président, J.R. Pepin

Fondation J.A. De Seve, #2402, 505, rue Sherbrooke ouest, Montréal QC H2L 4N3 – Secrétaire, Thérèse de Grandpré

Fondation Jacques Francoeur, #1350, 1130, rue Sherbrooke ouest, Montréal QC H3A 2M8 – Coordonnateur des projets, Josée Francoeur

La Fondation Jean Beliveau, 2313, rue Ste-Catherine ouest, Montréal QC H3H 1N2 – Président, Jean Beliveau

Fondation Jean-Louis Lévesque, #2340, 2000, av McGill College, Montréal QC H3A 3H3 – President, Suzanne Lévesque

La Fondation Julius Richardson Inc., 5425, av Bessborough, Montréal QC H4V 2S7 – 514/483-1380; Fax: 514/483-4596 – Executive Director, Jean Michaud

Fondation Lionel-Groulx, 261, av Bloomfield, Outremont QC H2V 3R6 – 514/271-4759; Fax: 514/271-6369 – Directeur général, Jean-Marc Leger

Fondation Marcel Leger, 60, rue Saint-Jacques, 9e étage, Montréal QC H2Y 1L5 – 514/982-2464; Fax: 514/987-1960 – Jean-Marc Léger

La Fondation Marcelle et Jean Coutu, #101, 1374, Mont-Royal est, Montréal QC H2V 4P3 – Présidente, Marie-Josée Coutu

Fondation Ménopause Ostéoporose, #326, 2055, Northcliffe, Montréal QC H4A 3K6 – 514/482-7422; Fax: 514/482-7939; Toll Free: 1-800-977-1778 – Présidente, Lucille Rouleau-Ross

Fondation Monseigneur Victor Tremblay inc., 930, rue Jacques Cartier est, CP 456, Chicoutimi QC G7H 5C8 – 418/549-2805 – Secrétaire, Roland Bélanger

La Fondation Peladeau inc., 612, rue St-Jacques ouest, 13e étage, Montréal QC H3C 1C8 – Président, Pierre Peladeau

Fondation Père-Eusèbe-Ménard, 65, rue de Castelnau ouest, Montréal QC H2R 2W3 – 514/274-7645; Fax: 514/274-7647; Toll Free: 1-800-665-7645; Email: fondatio@odyssee.net; URL: http://www.odyssee.net/~fondatio/ – Directeur général, André Franche

Fondation des pompiers du Québec pour les grands brûlés, #204, 2600, boul Saint-Joseph est, Montréal QC H1Y 2A4 – 514/523-5325; Fax: 514/527-8119 – Sylvie Tremblay

Fondation québécoise des maladies mentales, #300, 801, rue Sherbrooke est, Montréal QC H2L 1K7 – 514/529-5354; Fax: 514/529-9877 – Directrice générale, Suzanne Dubois

Fondation Richelieu International, #200, 1173, ch Cyrville, Ottawa ON K1J 7S6 – 613/742-6911; Fax: 613/742-6916 – Directeur général, G. Mathias Pagé

Fondation des sourds du Québec, 3348, boul Mgr-Gauthier, Québec QC G1E 2W2 – 418/660-6800; Fax: 418/666-0123 – Président, Gaston Forgues

Fondation Tex-Scope inc., 3000, rue Boulle, Saint-Hyacinthe QC J2S 1H9 – 514/773-6800; Fax: 514/773-9971 – Secrétaire, Pierre Comtois

Fondation Yvon Boulanger, 2325, rue Deschamps, Repentigny QC J6A 2X9 – Trustee, Gaston Boulanger

Foster Hewitt Foundation, c/o Dixon Management Services, 34 Weatherstone Ct., PO Box 1090, Niagara on the Lake ON L0S 1J0 – Vice-President, Frederick E. Dixon

Francofonds inc., #242, 340, boul Provencher, Winnipeg MB R2H 0G9 – 204/237-5852; Fax: 204/233-3324 – Directrice générale, Maria Chaput

Frank Gerstein Charitable Foundation, c/o National Trust Co., National Trust Tower, One Financial Pl., One Adelaide St. East, Toronto ON M5C 2W8 – 416/361-4096 – Senior Foundations Officer, David R. Windeyer

The Frankel Family Foundation, 9 Dorchester Dr., North York ON M3H 3J2 – President, Aaron Frankel

Fraser Elliott Foundation, #5300, Commerce Court West, Toronto ON M5L 1B9 – President, Roy Fraser Elliott

Fredericton Foundation Inc., PO Box 130, Fredericton NB E3B 4Y7 – 506/455-8329 – Executive Director, Jack J. Kimm

Friends of the Environment Foundation, PO Box 5703, London ON N6A 4S4 – ; Toll Free: 1-800-361-5333; URL: http://www.fef.ca/ – Vice-President, Corporate Affairs, Dianne Smith-Sanderson

The Gairdner Foundation, #220, 255 Yorkland Blvd., North York ON M2J 1S3 – 416/493-3101; Fax: 416/493-8158 – Executive Director, Sally-Anne Hrica

Gamma-Rho Foundation Ltd., #630, 1980, rue Sherbrooke ouest, Montréal QC H3H 1G1 – President, James D. Raymond

Gelmont Foundation, #1901, 1, Place Ville-Marie, Montréal QC H3B 2C3 – President, Nahum Gelber

Genesis Research Foundation, 92 College St., Toronto ON M5G 1L4 – 416/978-2667; Fax: 416/978-8350 – Executive Director, Kathy Green

Geoffrey H. Wood Foundation, #750, 304 The East Mall, Etobicoke ON M9B 6E2 – 416/234-0240; Fax: 416/234-5140 – President & Executive Director, Samuel Tughan

George Cedric Metcalf Charitable Foundation, 105 Pears Ave., Toronto ON M5R 1S9 – 416/926-0366 – President, George Metcalf

George Hogg Family Foundation, 1205, rue Lucien l'Allier, Montréal QC H3G 2C4 – Secretary, Thomas S. Gillespie

George Lunan Foundation, c/o National Trust Company, National Trust Tower, One Financial Place, One Adelaide St. East, Toronto ON M5C 2W8 – 416/361-4095; Fax: 416/361-3717 – Senior Foundation Officer, David R. Windeyer

Georgina Foundation, 39 Maple Ave., Toronto ON M4W 2T8 – 416/921-7496 – Vice-President, Margaret Opekar

Gestetner Bros. Memorial Fund, 9101, Montée Louis H. Lafontaine, Anjou QC H1J 1Z1 – President, Alfred Gestetner

Good Foundation Inc., RR#1, Breslau ON N0B 1M0 – 519/648-2823 – Secretary, James M. Good

The Great Lakes Marine Heritage Foundation, 55 Ontario St., Kingston ON K7L 2Y2 – 613/542-2261; Fax: 613/542-0043; URL: http://www.marmus.ca – Contact, Maurice D. Smith

Greey-Lennox Charitable Foundation, c/o National Trust Company, National Trust Tower, One Financial Place, One Adelaide St. East, Toronto ON M5C 2W8 – 416/361-4096; Fax: 416/361-3717 – Treasurer, David R. Windeyer

Griffith Laboratories Foundation, 757 Pharmacy Ave., Scarborough ON M1L 3J8 – 416/288-3050; Fax: 416/288-3481

Grocery Industry Foundation...Together, #500, 1240 Bay St., Toronto ON M5R 2A7 – 416/975-8488; Fax: 416/922-8469 – Executive Director, John P. McNeil

Grotto Cerebral Palsy Foundation Inc., 324 Scarborough Rd., Toronto ON M4E 3M8 – 416/699-6297 – Executive Secretary, Charles M. Sinclair

Gustav Levinschi Foundation, #110, 1820, av Docteur Penfield, Montréal QC H3H 1B4 – Sec.-Treas., Anita David

Halifax Children's Foundation, PO Box 788, Halifax NS B3J 2V2 – 902/455-3846 – Chairperson, Ron MacDonald

Halton Region Conservation Foundation, 2596 Britannica Rd. West, RR#2, Milton ON L9T 2X6 – 905/336-1158; Fax: 905/336-7014

The Hamber Foundation, 1055 Dunsmuir St., PO Box 49390, Stn Bentall Centre, Vancouver BC V7X 1P3 – Chairman, G.W. MacLaren

Hamilton Community Foundation, Standard Life Centre, #205, 120 King St. West, Hamilton ON L8P 4V2 – 905/523-5600; Fax: 905/523-0741 – Executive Director, Judith McCulloch

Hans Klinkenberg Memorial Scholarship Fund, c/o The Canadian Institute of Geomatics, PO Box 5378, Stn F, Ottawa ON K2C 3J1 – 613/224-9851; Fax: 613/224-9577; Email: cig_acsg@inasec.ca – Executive Director, Susan Pugh

Harold Crabtree Foundation, Varette Building, #2005, 130 Albert St., Ottawa ON K1P 5G4 – 613/563-4589 – President, Sandra Crabtree

The Harold Greenberg Fund, BCE Place, Box 787, #100, 181 Bay St., Toronto ON M5J 2T3 – 416/956-5431; Fax: 416/956-2087 – Chairperson, Wendy MacKeigan

The Harry Bronfman Family Foundation, #1525, 1245, rue Sherbrooke ouest, Montréal QC H3G 1H4 – Contact, Charles R. Bronfman, PC, CC

Harry E. Foster Foundation, #209, 40 St. Clair Ave. West, Toronto ON M4V 1M2 – 416/927-9077; Fax: 416/927-8475 – Executive Assistant, Carol Davis-Kerr

The Harry & Max Korolnek Family Foundation, c/o Consolidated Bottle Co., PO Box 369, Stn D, Toronto ON M6P 3J9 – 416/656-7777; Fax: 416/656-6394 – President, Harry Korolnek

Harry A. Newman Memorial Foundation, 1268 Royal York Rd., Etobicoke ON M9A 4C5 – 416/231-3401 – Chairman, William DeLaurentis

Harry P. Ward Foundation, c/o Royal Trust Co., 55 Metcalfe St., Ottawa ON K1P 6L5 – Assistant Secretary, David W. Schiller

The Harweg Foundation, 23 Bedford Rd., Toronto ON M5R 2J9 – 416/925-3557 – Secretary, Jerome S. Cooper

Helen McCrea Peacock Foundation, PO Box 132, Midhurst ON L0L 1X0 – Sec.-Treas., Martha Tovee

Help Fill a Dream Foundation of Canada, 902 Hillside Ave., Victoria BC V8T 1Z8 – 250/382-3135; Fax: 250/382-2711 – President, Barry George

The Henry & Berenice Kaufmann Foundation, #210, 4670, rue Ste-Catherine ouest, Montréal QC H3Z 1S5 – Executive Vice-President, Marion Greenwood

The Henry N.R. Jackman Foundation, 165 University Ave., 10th Fl., Toronto ON M5H 3B8 – President, Henry N.R. Jackman

The Henry White Kinnear Foundation, #4700, Toronto Dominion Bank Tower, Toronto ON M5K 1E6 – 416/601-7500; Fax: 416/868-1793 – President, A.R.A. Scace, Q.C.

Herbert Marshall McLuhan Foundation, 122 St. Ninian St., Antigonish NS B2G 1Y9 – 902/863-2360; URL: http://www.mcluhan.ca/mcluhan/foundation.html – Director, George Sanderson

The Herschel Victor Foundation, 1250, rue Saint-Alexandre, Montréal QC H3B 3H6 – 514/866-4891 – President, Herschel Victor

H.G. Bertram Foundation, c.o Royal Trust Corp. of Canada, PO Box 7500, Stn A, Toronto ON M5W 1P9 – Trust Officer, Henri F. Ashley

Hofstedter Family Charitable Foundation, #503, 3625 Dufferin St., North York ON M3K 1N4 – President, S. Hofstedter

Hope Charitable Foundation, c/o National Trust Company, National Trust Tower, One Financial Pl., One Adelaide St. East, Toronto ON M5C 2W8 – 416/361-4096; Fax: 416/361-3717 – Senior Foundations Officer, David R. Windeyer

Hospital for Sick Children Foundation, 555 University Ave., Toronto ON M5G 1X8 – 416/813-6166; Fax: 416/813-5024 – Director, Communications, Natalie Jascott

Hospitals of Regina Foundation, PO Box 1697, Regina SK S4P 3Z6 – 306/766-7500; Fax: 306/766-7504; Toll Free: 1-888-766-7500 – Executive Director, John Dawes, CAE

HUME Foundation, #1, 125 Traders Blvd. East, Mississauga ON L4Z 2E5 – 905/568-8111 – Secretary, Barbara M. Humeniuk

Hylcan Foundation, #103, 4920, boul de Maisonneuve ouest, Montréal QC H3Z 1N1 – Secretary, Joan F. Sutherland

I.C.C. Foundation, #504, 170 Laurier Ave. W., Ottawa ON K1P 5V5 – 613/563-2642; Fax: 613/565-3089 – Executive Director, Corinne Gray

Ignat Kaneff Charitable Foundation, 1290 Central Pkwy. West, Mississauga ON L5C 4R3 – President, Dimitrina Kaneff

Imperial Oil Charitable Foundation, 111 St Clair Ave. West, Toronto ON M5W 1K3 – ; Fax: 416/968-4272; Toll Free: 1-800-668-3776 – Treasurer, Susan Young

Inter-Church action for Development, Relief & Justice, #404, 77 Charles St. West, Toronto ON M5S 1K5 – 416/944-8182; Fax: 416/922-1419; Email: icact@web.net – Executive Director, Dale Hildebrand

Ionic Lodge Foundation for Human Welfare, #245, 5180, rue Queen Mary, Montréal QC H3W 3E7 – 514/481-7761 – Chairperson, Stanley Litwin

Ireland Fund of Canada, 51 Front St. East, 2nd Fl., Toronto ON M5E 1B3 – 416/367-8311; Fax: 416/367-5931 – Executive Director, Paul Farrelly

Israel Cancer Research Fund, #1111, 20 Eglinton Ave. West, Toronto ON M4R 1K8 – 416/487-5246; Fax: 416/489-8932 – Executive Director, Suzanne Kaye

Israel Koschitzky Family Charitable Foundation, c/o Laven & Pittman, Western Canada Pl., #2200, 700 - 8 Ave. SW, Calgary AB T2P 3V4 – Secretary, David L. Laven

Jack Cooper Family Foundation, #206, 1 Eglinton Ave. East, Toronto ON M4P 3A1 – Director, Jack Cooper

Jackman Foundation, #1300, 44 Victoria St., Toronto ON M5C 1Y2 – 416/366-8567; Fax: 416/367-2339 – Secretary, Donald J. Crawford

Jacob & Dorothy Hendeles Foundation, c/o Robins, Appleny & Taub, #2500, 130 Adelaide St. West, PO Box 102, Toronto ON M5E 2M2 – President, Dorothy H. Hendeles

James Wallace McCutcheon Foundation, Toronto Dominion Centre, Box 35, Toronto ON M5K 1A1 – President & Chairman, J.W. McCutcheon

The Japan Foundation, Toronto, #213, 131 Bloor St. West, Toronto ON M5S 1R1 – 416/966-1600; Fax: 416/966-9773; Email: jftor@interlog.com – Director, Masamichi Sugihara

Jarislowsky Foundation, #2609, 1110, rue Sherbrooke ouest, Montréal QC H3A 1G8 – President, S.A. Jarislowsky

Jean Cameron Palliative Care Foundation, #777, 1130, rue Sherbrooke ouest, Montréal QC H3A 2M8 – 514/842-1714; Fax: 514/842-1718 – Vice-President, Gordon L. McGilton

Jewish Community Foundation of Greater Montréal, 5151, ch Côte-Sainte-Catherine, Montréal QC H3W 1M6 – 514/735-3541; Fax: 514/735-8972 – Executive Director, Robert Kleinman

Jewish Foundation of Manitoba, #204, 370 Hargrave St., Winnipeg MB R3B 2K1 – 204/958-4499; Fax: 204/958-4497 – Executive Director, David Cohen

The Jim Pattison Foundation, #1600, 1055 West Hastings St., Vancouver BC V6E 2H2 – Treasurer, M. Chant

The Joan & Clifford Hatch Foundation, 7130 Riverside Dr. East, Windsor ON N85 1C3 – President, H. Clifford Hatch

The Joe Brain Foundation, PO Box 24061, RPO Kenaston, Winnipeg MB R3N 2B1 – 204/897-3513; Fax: 204/897-3513 – President, Walter Dubowec, FCA

John Deere Foundation of Canada, PO Box 1000, Grimsby ON L3M 4H5 – President, G.J. Clark

The John Dobson Foundation, #1409, 1010, rue Sherbrooke ouest, Montréal QC H3A 2R7 – President, John W. Dobson

John H. McDonald Journalism Foundation, #206, 24 Ryerson Ave., Toronto ON M5T 2P3 – 416/504-4672; Fax: 416/504-3680

John Hardie Mitchell Family Foundation, 777 Dunsmuir St., PO Box 10426, Vancouver BC V7Y 1K3 – Secretary, Duncan Bell-Irving

John Labatt Foundation, 150 Simcoe St. North, London ON N6A 4M3 – Administrator, Carol Bober

John McKellar Charitable Foundation, #1600, 2 First Canadian Place, PO Box 480, Toronto ON M5X 1J5 – President, John D. McKellar

The John A. Sanderson & Family Trust, c/o Canada Trust., 70 Market St., Brantford ON N3T 2Z7 – Paul Read, QC

The Johnson Family Foundation, 95 Elizabeth Ave., PO Box 12049, St. John's NF A1B 1R7 – President, Paul J. Johnson

Joseph C. Edwards Foundation, Place Montréal Trust, 1900, av McGill College, Montréal QC H3A 3K9 – 514/982-7196; Fax: 514/982-7069 – Executive Vice-President, Dan J. Sullivan

Joseph Kerzner Charitable Foundation, #701, 1500 Don Mills Rd., North York ON M3B 3K4 – Director, Joseph Kerzner

The Joseph Louis Rotman Charitable Foundation, #1701, 22 St. Clair Ave. East, Toronto ON M4T 2J3 – President, Isaac Silverstein

The Joseph Segal Family Foundation, #520, 701 West Georgia St., Vancouver BC V7Y 1A1 – President, Joseph Segal

Joseph Tanenbaum Charitable Foundation, 1051 Tapscott Rd., Scarborough ON M1X 1A1 – President, Kurt Rothschild

The Joseph & Wolfe Lebovic Foundation, PO Box 1240, Stouffville ON L4A 8A2 – President, Joseph Lebovic

J.P. Bickell Foundation, c/o National Trust Company, National Trust Tower, One Financial Place, One Adelaide St. East, Toronto ON M5C 2W8 – 416/361-4096; Fax: 416/361-3717 – Secretary, David R. Windeyer

J.W. McConnell Family Foundation, #1800, 1002, rue Sherbrooke ouest, Montréal QC H3A 3L6 – 514/288-2133; Fax: 514/288-1479 – President & CEO, Tim Brodhead

J.W. Smith Foundation, 5657 Harold St., Vancouver BC V5R 5V6 – Vice-President, J.A. Gowans

Kahanoff Foundation, #4206, 400 - 3 Ave. SW, Calgary AB T2P 4H2 – 403/237-7896; Fax: 403/261-9614 – President, James B. Hume

Kaiser Youth Foundation, 1500 Georgia St. West, 19th Fl., Vancouver BC V6G 2Z8 – 604/681-9211; Fax: 604/685-9046; Email: kyf@wimsey.com; URL: http://www.tether.com/KYF – Executive Director, Diane Champion-Smith

Kamloops Foundation, PO Box 15, Kamloops BC V2C 5K3 – Sec.-Treas., Michael Black

Kathleen M. Richardson Foundation, Richardson Bldg., 1 Lombard Pl., 30th Fl., Winnipeg MB R3B 0Y1 – Secretary, Sheila A. Berthon

Kids Help Foundation, #410, 60 Bloor St. West, Toronto ON M4W 1A1 – 416/920-5437; Fax: 416/920-0651; Toll Free: 1-800-268-3062 – National Executive Director, Heather Sproule

The Kitchener & Waterloo Community Foundation, Marsland Centre, 20 Erb St. West, 11th Fl., Waterloo ON N2L 1T2 – 519/725-1806; Fax: 519/888-7737 – Executive Director, Jane Humphries

The Klemke Foundation, #1703, 9923 - 103 St., Edmonton AB T5K 2J3 – John Klemke

K.M. Hunter Charitable Foundation, #266, 171 Rink St. A, Peterborough ON K9J 2J6 – President, William T. Hunter

KPMG Charitable Foundation, Scotia Plaza, 20 King St. West, PO Box 122, Toronto ON M5H 3Z2 – 416/777-8500; Fax: 416/777-3969 – Sec.-Treas., Wayne Brownlee

Kroeker Foundation, Inc., PO Box 1450, Winkler MB R0G 2X0 – 204/325-4333 – Chairman, Walter E. Kroeker

Laidlaw Foundation, #2000, 365 Bloor St. East, Toronto ON M4W 3L4 – 416/964-3614; Fax: 416/975-1428; Email: laidlaw@web.net – Executive Director, Nathan Gilbert

Laura & B. Aaron Foundation, PO Box 984, Montréal QC H4L 4W3 – President, Arnold Aaron

Law for the Future Fund, c/o Canadian Bar Association, #902, 50 O'Connor St., Ottawa ON K1P 6L2 – Director, George Boros, LLM

The Lawson Foundation, #100, 248 Pall Mall St., London ON N6A 5P6 – Executive Director, Joan A. Francolini

Leon & Evelyn Kahn Family Charitable Foundation, #800, 1030 West Georgia St., Vancouver BC V6E 3B9 – Director, Leon Kahn

Leon & Thea Koerner Foundation, PO Box 39209, RPO Point Grey, Vancouver BC V6R 4P1 – 604/224-2611; Fax: 604/224-1059 – Executive Secretary, Alice Macaulay

Leonard Ellen Family Foundation, #1430, 5 Place Ville Marie, Montréal QC H3B 2G2 – 514/861-9666 – President, Leonard Ellen

Lethbridge Community Foundation, #200, 220 - 3rd Ave. South, Lethbridge AB T1J 0G9 – 403/328-5297; Fax: 403/328-9534 – Executive Director, Neil H. Manning

Lewis C. Smith Foundation, c/o Bessner, Gallay, Schapira, Kreisman, #812, 5250, rue Ferrier, Montréal QC H4P 1L4 – 514/341-5551; Fax: 514/341-2947 – Vice-President, Lawrence Bessner, F.C.A.

Lifeforce Foundation, PO Box 3117, Vancouver BC V6B 3X6 – 604/669-4673 – Consultant, Peter Hamilton

Lillian & Leroy Page Foundation, c/o National Trust Co., PO Box 2290, Hamilton ON L8N 3B5 – 905/526-1200 – Secretary, David G. Hartfield

Lithuanian Canadian Foundation, c/o Lithuanian Community Hall, 1573 Bloor St. West, Toronto ON M6P 1A6 – 416/532-3311 – President, J. Storvkus

Lloyd & Gladys Fogler Foundation, c/o Fogler, Rubinoff, #1400, 150 York St., Toronto ON M5H 3S5 – Director, Lloyd S.D. Fogler

Lloydminster Foundation, 5503 - 50 St., Lloydminster AB T9V 0Y4 – Sec.-Treas., Jean White

Lockwood Foundation, c/o National Trust Company, National Trust Tower, One Financial Pl., One Adelaide St. East, Toronto ON M5C 2W8 – 416/361-4096; Fax: 416/361-3717 – President, H.S. Lockwood

London Community Foundation, #100, 248 Pall Mall St., London ON N6A 5P6 – Executive Director, Terry Campbell

Lorne & Evelyn Johnson Foundation, 2400 - 13 Ave., Regina SK S4P 0V9 – 306/586-0944 – Executive Director, Douglas A. Lee, C.M.

Lovelight International Foundation, Inc., 4334, rue Fullum, Montréal QC H2H 2J5 – 514/931-9237; Telex: 524371

MacDonald Stewart Foundation, 1195, rue Sherbrooke ouest, Montréal QC H3A 1H9 – Executive Director, James P. Carroll

MAGFRAT Foundation (Magnus Fratres), c/o Big Brothers of Sarnia-Lambton, 193 George St., Sarnia ON N7T 4N6 – 519/336-0460 – President, Adrian Verstraaten

Malloch Foundation, c/o Lazier Hickey Langs O'Neal, 25 Main St. West, 17th Fl., Hamilton ON L8P 1H1 – 905/525-3652; Fax: 905/525-6278 – Sec.-Treas., Colin G. Lazier

The Manuel & Eva Kimel Foundation, 76 Miranda Ave., Toronto ON M6E 5A1 – Director, Manuel Kimel

Maple Leaf Foundation, 1055 Talbot St., St Thomas ON N5P 1G5 – Sec.-Treas., W.D. Husband

Maranatha Foundation, #201, 41 Valleybrook Dr., North York ON M3B 2S6 – Chairman, Donald Miller

Marion Ferguson Foundation, PO Box 752, Stn Adelaide, Toronto ON M5C 2K1

The Marjorie & Gerald Bronfman Foundation, #1525, 1245, rue Sherbrooke ouest, Montréal QC H3G 1H4 – President, Marjorie Bronfman

The Martin Foundation, c/o National Trust Co., 120 King St. West, PO Box 2290, Hamilton ON L8N 3B5 – 905/526-1200 – Sec.-Treas., David G. Hartfield

Masonic Foundation of Manitoba Inc., 420 Corydon, Winnipeg MB R3L 0N8 – 204/453-7410; Fax: 204/284-3527 – Sec.-Treas., Robert T. Crossley

Masonic Foundation of Ontario, 361 King St. West, Hamilton ON L8P 1B4 – Administrator, C. Moore

Masonic Foundation of Québec, 2295, rue Saint-Marc, Montréal QC H3H 2G9 – Treasurer, D. Drury

Matinée Ltd. Fashion Foundation, 3820, rue Saint-Antoine ouest, Montréal QC H4C 1B5

Maurice Joseph & Louis Weisfeld Charitable Foundation, 11 Chiltern Hill Rd., Toronto ON M6C 3B4 – Trustee, Louis Weisfeld

The Maurice Pollack Foundation, #801, 1 Westmount Sq., Montréal QC H3Z 2P9 – President, Florence P. Pedvis

Maurice & Tillie Wolfe Family Foundation, 302 The East Mall, Etobicoke ON M9B 6B8 – President, Rose Wolfe

Max Bell Foundation, #3516, Aetna Tower, Toronto-Dominion Centre, 79 Wellington St. West, PO Box 105, Stn Toronto Dominion, Toronto ON M5K 1G8 – 416/601-4770; Fax: 416/601-1630 – President, Donald S. Rickerd

The Max Clarkson Foundation, 23 Dunloe Rd., Toronto ON M4V 2W4 – President, Max B.E. Clarkson

Maxwell Cummings Family Foundation, 4115, rue Sherbrooke ouest, 6e étage, Montréal QC H3Z 1K1 – President, Robert M. Cummings

Maytree Foundation, #804, 170 Bloor St. West, Toronto ON M5S 1T9 – 416/944-2627; Fax: 416/944-8915 – President, Judy Broadbent

McGeachy Charitable Foundation, RR#3, Chatham ON N7M 5J3 – President, Neil Wallace McGeachy

McLean Foundation, #1008, 2 St. Clair Ave. West, Toronto ON M4V 1L5 – 804/964-6802; Fax: 804/964-2804 – Secretary, Elaine M. Kalm

McPherson Playhouse Foundation, 3 Centennial Square, Victoria BC V8W 1P5

Mennonite Foundation of Canada, #4, 117 Victor Lewis Dr., Winnipeg MB R3P 1J6 – 204/488-1985; Fax: 204/488-1986; Email: mfcwpg@mts.net – National Manager, Edgar Rempel

Milan Ilich Foundation, #201, 5631 No. 3 Rd., Richmond BC V6X 2C7 – Director, Milan Ilich

Mimi & Sam Pollock Foundation, #404, 625 Avenue Rd., Toronto ON M4V 2K7 – President, Samuel P.S. Pollock

Minerva Foundation, Edmonton House, #340, 10205 - 100 Ave., PO Box 3160, Edmonton AB T5J 2G7 – President, Douglas O. Goss

Minto Foundation, PO Box 5152, Stn F, Ottawa ON K2C 3H8 – President, Daniel Greenberg

The Miriam & Harold Green Family Foundation, #1600, 20 Eglinton Ave. West, Toronto ON M4R 2H1 – President, Harold Green

Mohawk College Foundation, PO Box 2034, Hamilton ON L8N 3T2 – 905/575-2066; Fax: 905/575-2443 – Executive Director, Richard Court

Molly Towell Perinatal Research Foundation, 1750 West 36th Ave., Vancouver BC V6M 1K2 – 604/261-4818 – Contact, J. Bryans

Molson Companies Donations Fund, Scotia Plaza, #3600, 40 King St. West, Toronto ON M5H 3Z5 – 416/860-6462 – Secretary & National Coordinator & Supt., Judy McClelland

The Molson Foundation, 1555, rue Notre Dame est, Montréal QC H2L 2R5 – 514/521-1786; Fax: 514/598-6866 – Secretary, Stephen T. Molson

Mon Sheong Foundation, 36 D'Arcy St., Toronto ON M5T 1J7 – 416/977-3762; Fax: 416/977-3231 – Executive Director, K.W. Cheng

Morley & Rita Cohen Foundation, c/o Ritaley Investments Inc., #1705, 1155, boul René-Lévesque ouest, Montréal QC H3B 4S5 – President, Morley M. Cohen

The Morrison Foundation, #1008, 341 Bloor St. West, Toronto ON M5S 1W8 – Treasurer, Tom Falls

Mr. and Mrs. P.A. Woodward's Foundation, c/o Medical Advisor, #710, 1155 Pender St. West, Vancouver BC V6E 2P4 – 604/682-8116; Fax: 604/682-8153 – Contact & Medical Advisor, Dr. Craig R. Arnold

Murphy Foundation Inc., #919, 167 Lombard Ave., Winnipeg MB R3B 0V3 – 204/942-5281 – Secretary, E.C. Fenton

Muttart Foundation, #530, 9919 - 105 St., Edmonton AB T5K 1B1 – 403/425-9616; Fax: 403/425-0282 – Executive Director, Robert S. Wyatt

Nancy's Very Own Foundation, 10 Cluny Dr., Toronto ON M4W 2P7 – 416/924-9799; Fax: 416/924-2933; Email: webmom@web.net; URL: http://www.coolwomen.org – President, Nancy Ruth

The Nat Christie Foundation, #1850, 540 - 5 Ave. SW, Calgary AB T2P 0M2 – 403/264-1662; Fax: 403/265-0152 – President, C. Peter Valentine

Nathan & Lily Silver Family Foundation, #510, 1 Yorkdale Rd., North York ON M6A 3A1 – President, Shoel Silver

Nathan Steinberg Family Foundation, 94 Forest Heights Blvd., North York ON M2L 2K8 – Secretary, H. Arnold Steinberg

National Magazine Awards Foundation, #207, 109 Vanderhoof Ave., Toronto ON M4G 2H7 – 416/422-1358; Fax: 416/422-3762 – Contact, Pat Kendall

N.E. Peters Foundation, #3000, 1 Place Ville Marie, Montréal QC H3B 4T9 – Sec.-Treas., Robert M. Rennie

Nelson Arthur Hyland Foundation, #601, 45 St. Clair Ave. West, Toronto ON M4V 1K9 – 416/920-6010 – President, Gerald F. Hayden, Q.C.

Nelson Lumber Foundation, PO Box 620, Lloydminster AB S9V 0Y8 – President, Raymond J. Nelson

Newman Foundation of Toronto, 89 St. George St., Toronto ON M5S 2E8 – 416/979-2468; Fax: 416/596-6920 – Administrative Coordinator, Pat Hayward

Nickle Family Foundation, Highstreet House, #401, 933 - 17 Ave. SW, Calgary AB T2T 5R6 – 403/244-4237; Fax: 403/244-3269; Email: peeverd@cadvision.com – President, Diana Nickle

Noranda Foundation, BCE Place, Box 755, #4100, 181 Bay St., Toronto ON M5J 2T3 – 416/982-7431; Fax: 416/982-7446 – Sec.-Treas., Janet Greaves

Norman & Margaret Jewison Charitable Foundation, 18 Gloucester Lane, 4th Fl., Toronto ON M4Y 1L5 – 416/923-2787; Fax: 416/923-8580 – Director, Ralph Brown, QC

Norwood Community Scholarship Foundation, #201, 65 Swindon Way, Winnipeg MB R3P 0T8 – 204/837-1830 – Secretary, B.V. Angus

Old Strathcona Foundation, #401, 10324 White Ave., Edmonton AB T6E 1Z8 – 403/433-5866; Fax: 403/431-1938 – Executive Director, Liz Iggulden

Ole Evinrude Foundation Canada Inc., 910 Monaghan Rd., Peterborough ON K9J 7B6 – 705/876-2699 – Sec.-Treas., C.F. Eagleson

Ontario Mental Health Foundation, #1708, 365 Bloor St. East, Toronto ON M4W 3L4 – 416/920-7721; Fax: 416/920-0026 – Executive Director, Dr. Howard Cappell

Ontario Trucking Association Education Foundation Inc., 555 Dixon Rd., Etobicoke ON M9W 1H8 – 416/249-7401; Fax: 416/245-6152 – Executive Director, Ana Ideias

The Oscar Ascher Schmidt Charitable Foundation, 3638 Bathurst St., Toronto ON M6A 2E5 – President, S. Schmidt

Oswald, Smith Foundation Society, #441, 1755 Robson St., Vancouver BC V6G 3B7 – President, K.O. Smith

Otnim Foundation Inc., PO Box 5152, Stn F, Ottawa ON K2C 3H8 – Vice-President, Robert Greenberg

Our Lady of The Prairies Foundation, 620 Spadina Cres. East, Saskatoon SK S7K 3G5 – 306/652-6767 – Chair, Joseph B. Leier

The P. Schwartz Family Foundation, #701, 2 St. Clair Ave. East, Toronto ON M4T 2T5 – President, Phineas Schwartz

Pfeiffer Family Charitable Trust, #400, 1085, rue Saint-Alexandre, Montréal QC H2Z 1P4 – 514/393-8122; Fax: 514/393-8120 – President, Dr. Julius Pfeiffer

Phillip Smith Foundation, c/o Montreal Trust, 15 King St. West, Toronto ON M5H 1B4 – 416/860-5555 – Sec.-Treas., Bruce Smith

Phoenix Community Works Foundation, 316 Dupont St., Toronto ON M5R 1V9 – 416/964-7919; Fax: 416/964-6941 – Executive Director, Larry Rooney

Physicians Services Inc. Foundation, #1006, 5160 Yonge St., North York ON M2N 6L9 – 416/226-6277; Fax: 416/226-6080 – Executive Director, Sandra Bennett

The Posluns Family Foundation, 637 Lakeshore Blvd. West, Toronto ON M5V 1A8 – President, Wilfred Posluns

Québec & Ontario Paper Company Foundation, 80 King St., 7th Fl., St Catharines ON L2R 7G2 – 905/688-5030 – Celine G. Arsenault

Quetico Foundation, #610, 48 Yonge St., Toronto ON M5E 1G6 – 416/941-9388; Fax: 416/941-9236 – Contact, Dave Taylor

QUNO Foundation, 80 King St., 7th Fl., St Catharines ON L2R 7G1 – Celine G. Arsenault

R. Howard Webster Foundation, #2912, 1155, boul René-Lévesque ouest, Montréal QC H3B 2L5 – Treasurer, Howard W. Davidson

R. Samuel McLaughlin Foundation, c/o National Trust Company, National Trust Tower, One Financial Pl., One Adelaide St. East, Toronto ON M5C 2W8 – 416/361-4096; Fax: 416/361-3717 – Secretary, David R. Windeyer

Rappaport Family Charitable Foundation, c/o Mintz & Partners, #100, 1446 Don Mills Rd., North York ON M3B 3N6 – Director, Abraham Rappaport

RBC Dominion Securities Foundation, PO Box 21, Stn Commerce Court, Toronto ON M5L 1A7 – Chairman, Derek Brown

Reader's Digest Foundation of Canada, 215, av Redfern, Montréal QC H3Z 2V9 – 514/934-0751; Fax: 514/932-3637 – President, Joe Beauduin

Recreation, Parks & Wildlife Foundation, Harley Court Bldg., 10045 - 111 St., 7th Fl., Edmonton AB T5K 1K4 – 403/482-6467; Fax: 403/488-9755 – Executive Director, Chuck Moser

The Red Deer Community Foundation, #503, 4808 Ross St., Red Deer AB T4N 1X5 – 403/341-6911; Fax: 403/341-4177 – Chairperson, Paul Meyette

Reichmann Charitable Trust, 2 First Canadian Place, 28th Fl., Toronto ON M5X 1B5 – Administrator, Lionel Weber

The Reimer Express Foundation Inc., 1400 Inkster Blvd., Winnipeg MB R2X 1R1 – Vice-President, Delbert J. Reimer

Rhodes Scholarship Trust, c/o McCarthy Tetrault, TD Centre, #4700, TD Bank Tower, Toronto ON M5K 1E6 – 416/601-7502; Fax: 416/868-1793 – Secretary, A.R.A. Scace, Q.C.

Richard & Edith Strauss Canada Foundation, #400, 1303, av Greene, Montréal QC H3Z 2A7 – President, Richard Strauss

Richard Ivey Foundation, 630 Richmond St., London ON N6A 3G6 – 519/673-1280; Fax: 519/672-4790; Email: 102704.353@compuserve.com – Executive Director, Marvi Ricker

Richard & Jean Ivey Fund, #508, 380 Wellington St., London ON N6A 5B5 – 519/679-0870 – Sec.-Treas., Keith L. Sumner

Richardson Century Fund, Richardson Bldg., 1 Lombard Pl., 30th Fl., Winnipeg MB R3B 0Y1 – Secretary, Sheila A. Berthon

Rita Steinberg Goldfarb Foundation, c/o Spiegel Sohmer, #1203, 5, Place Ville Marie, Montréal QC H3B 2G2 – President, Eileen Pelletier

Robert Campeau Family Foundation, 64 The Bridle Path, North York ON M3B 2B1 – Vice-President, Roland Villemarie

Rockwell International Canadian Trust, c/o Royal Trust Corp., PO Box 7500, Stn A, Toronto ON M5W 1P9 – 416/981-6243 – E. Leslie Frederick

Rona & Irving Levitt Family Foundation, c/o Forden Investments Inc., #1055, Place du Canada, Montréal QC H3B 2N2 – President, Irving Levitt

Rotary Club of Toronto Charitable Foundation, c/o Royal York Hotel, 100 Front St. West, Toronto ON M5J 1E4 – 416/363-8321 – Secretary, Eunice J. Doucette

Roy C. Hill Charitable Foundation, 147 McClure Dr., RR#4, King City ON L0G 1K0 – 905/833-0189 – Executive Director, Alan Coulter

Royal Bank of Canada Charitable Foundation, Royal Bank Plaza, South Tower, 9th Fl., Toronto ON M5J 2J5 – 416/974-3113; Fax: 416/974-0624 – Executive Director, Jacqueline Tuffin

Royal LePage Charitable Foundation, #400, 39 Wynford Dr., Toronto ON M5E 1S9 – President, George J. Cormack

The S. Schulich Foundation, 24 Junewood Cres., North York ON M2L 2C3 – President, Seymour Schulich

St. Andrew's Charitable Foundation, 51 Rosedale Rd., Toronto ON M4W 2P5 – Treasurer, C.B. Paterson

The Saint John Foundation, c/o Touche Ross & Co., PO Box 6549, Stn A, Saint John NB E2L 4R9 – Treasurer, John F. McCrossin

Sam Yakubowicz Family Foundation, 14 Banton Rd., North York ON M3H 3H1 – President, Sam Yakubowicz

Samuel & Bessie Orfus Family Foundation, 108 Vesta Dr., Toronto ON M5P 2Z9 – President, Howard Orfus

The Samuel H. Cohen Family Foundation, 5 Clarence Sq., Toronto ON M5V 1H1 – President, Samuel H. Cohen

Samuel Lunenfeld Charitable Foundation, #1609, 8 King St. East, Toronto ON M5C 1B5 – 416/363-9191 – Executive Director, Mitchell Kunin

Samuel & Saidye Bronfman Family Foundation, 1170, rue Peel, Montréal QC H3B 4P2 – 514/878-5270; Fax: 514/878-5293 – Executive Director, John Hobday

Samuel W. Stedman Foundation, 70 Market St., PO Box 751, Brantford ON N3T 2Z7 – Sec.-Treas., Vyrtle H. Sisson

Sandford Fleming Foundation, Room 4300, Carl Pollock Hall, University of Waterloo, Waterloo ON

N2L 3G1 – 519/888-4008; Fax: 519/746-1457 – Executive Director, Jeff Weller

The Sandra & Leo Kolber Foundation, 1170, rue Peel, 8e étage, Montréal QC H3B 4P2 – President, Sandra Kolber

Saskatchewan K of C Charitable Foundation, PO Box 73, Cupar SK S0G 0Y0 – 306/723-4484 – Executive Director, Lloyd Macknak

The Saskatoon Foundation, #101, 308 - 4 Ave. North, Saskatoon SK S7K 2L7 – 306/665-1766 – Executive Director, Moira R. Birney

Saul A. Silverman Family Foundation, 76 St. Clair Ave. West, 4th Fl., Toronto ON M4V 1N2 – President, Peter A. Silverman, QC

Savoy Foundation Inc., CP 69, St-Jean-sur-Richelieu QC J3B 6Z3 – 514/358-9779 – Directrice, Caroline Savoy

Scottish Rite Charitable Foundation of Canada, 152 George St., Hamilton ON L8P 1E5 – 905/522-0033 – Assistant Secretary, John I. Carrick

Scottish Studies Foundation Inc., 2482 Yonge St., PO Box 45069, Toronto ON M4P 3E3 – 416/359-8012 – Chairman, Alan McKenzie, FSA Scot

Seamont Foundation, #2600, 600, rue de la Gauchetière ouest, Montréal QC H3B 4M3 – President, Constance V. Pathy

Senator Norman M. Paterson Foundation, 1918 Yonge St., PO Box 664, Thunder Bay ON P7C 4W6 – 807/577-8421; Fax: 807/475-3493 – President & Sec.-Treas., Donald C. Paterson

Shaw Family Foundation, 4190 Marblethorne Ct., Mississauga ON L4W 2H9 – Secretary, Dianne Rowett

Shawbridge Foundation for Youth, #520, 5250, rue Ferrier, Montréal QC H4P 1L4 – 514/731-3419; Fax: 514/731-4999 – Executive Director, Peter L. Clement

Shiff Family Charitable Foundation, #412, 1867 Yonge St., Toronto ON M4S 1Y5 – Executive Director, Howard Driman

The Sikh Foundation, #4900, 40 King St. West, Toronto ON M5H 4A2 – 416/777-6697; Fax: 416/484-9656 – Contact, Kawal Kohli

Sir Ernest MacMillan Memorial Foundation, c/o McCarthy Tétrault, Toronto Dominion Centre, PO Box 48, Stn Toronto Dominion, Toronto ON M5K 1E6 – 416/601-7588; Fax: 416/868-1891 – President, John B. Lawson

Sir James Dunn Foundation, PO Box 6549, Stn A, Saint John NB E2L 3W8 – Vice-President, H.H. Stikeman

Sir Joseph Flavelle Foundation, c/o National Trust Company, National Trust Tower, One Financial Pl., One Adelaide St. East, Toronto ON M5C 2W8 – 416/361-4096; Fax: 416/361-3717 – Sec.-Treas., David R. Windeyer

Sky Works Charitable Foundation, 566 Palmerston Ave., Toronto ON M6G 2P7 – 416/536-6581; Fax: 416/536-7728 – Managing Director, Laura Sky

S.M. Blair Family Foundation, c/o National Trust Company, National Trust Tower, 21 King St. East, Toronto ON M5C 1B3 – 416/361-4096; Fax: 416/361-3717 – Assistant Sec.-Treas., David R. Windeyer

SMARTRISK Foundation, #301, 658 Danforth Ave., Toronto ON M4J 5B9 – 416/463-9878; Fax: 416/463-0137; Email: choose@smartrisk.ca – Executive Director, Dr. Robert Conn

The Sobey Foundation, 115 King St., Stellarton NS B0K 1S0 – President, D.F. Sobey

The Sonor Foundation, Toronto ON – 416/369-1499 – President, Michael R. Gardiner

Sons of Norway Foundation in Canada, 1020 Glenayre Dr., Port Moody BC V3H 1J6 – 604/937-7247 – Sec.-Treas., Ron Stubbings

South Saskatchewan Community Foundation, PO Box 277, Assiniboia SK S0H 0B0 – 306/642-4515 – Executive Director, Dianne Kessler

Steve Atanas Stavro Foundation, #202, 1900 Eglinton Ave. East, Scarborough ON M1L 2L9 – 416/751-4600; Fax: 416/751-3095 – President, Steve Stavro

Strathcona Trust, c/o Director General Reserves & Cadets, Dept. of National Trust, 101 Colonel By Dr., Ottawa ON K1A 0K2 – 613/992-3390 – Secretary, L.Col. W.J. Molnar

Stupp/Cohen Families Foundation, #1, 30 St. Clair Ave. West, Toronto ON M4V 3A1 – President, Jack Stupp

SUS Foundation of Canada, 620 Spadina Ave., Toronto ON M5S 2H4 – 416/923-3318; Fax: 416/923-8266 – President, William Kereliuk

Sydney & Florence Cooper Foundation, c/o TRL Investments Ltd., #1000, 920 Yonge St., Toronto ON M4W 3C7 – President, Sydney C. Cooper

T. Donald Miller Foundation, #801, 45 St. Clair Ave. West, Toronto ON M4V 1K9 – 416/920-6010; Fax: 416/920-6089 – President, Gerald F. Hayden, Q.C.

Tabachnick Foundation, c/o Rosenswig, Carere, McRae, #1134, 20 Dundas St. West, PO Box 134, Toronto ON M5G 2C2 – 416/977-6600; Fax: 416/927-5874 – Contact, Michael Rosenswig

TEAL Charitable Foundation, #177, 4664 Lougheed Hwy., Burnaby BC V5C 5T5 – 604/294-8325; Fax: 604/294-8355

tecNICA Foundation of Canada, 2060 Queen St. East, PO Box 51528, Toronto ON M4E 3V7 – 416/691-1529; Fax: 416/964-9226 – Chairperson, Juan Miranda

The Tecolote Foundation, Office of the President, 166 Pearl St., Toronto ON M5H 1L3 – Secretary, J. Ian Whitcomb

The Terry Fox Foundation, #605, 60 St Clair Ave. East, Toronto ON M4T 1N5 – 416/962-7866; Fax: 416/962-5677 – Breeda McClew

Thomas Beck Family Foundation, #502, 4100 Yonge St., North York ON M2P 2B5 – President, H. Thomas Beck

Thomas Sill Foundation Inc., #600, 175 Hargrave St., Winnipeg MB R3C 3R8 – Executive Director, C. Hugh Arklie

Tippet Foundation, #300, 95 Barber Greene Rd., North York ON M3C 3E9 – Sec.-Treas., John A.R. McCleery, CA

Tom & Annie Kohn Charitable Foundation, 103 Laurelcrest Ave., North York ON M3H 2B2 – President, Thomas Kohn

Toronto Hospital Foundation, Thomas J. Bell Wing, Rm.#614, 585 University Ave., Toronto ON M5G 2C4

The T.R. Meighen Foundation, #2, 260 Water St., PO Box 79, St. Andrews NB E0G 2X0 – 506/529-4882; Fax: 506/529-9181; Email: trmfound@nbnet.nb.ca – Manager, Ardeth Holmes

TREE Foundation for Youth Development, #520, 5250, rue Ferrier, Montréal QC H4P 1L4 – Executive Director, Peter L. Clement

Trillium Foundation, 21 Bedford Rd., 3rd Fl., Toronto ON M5R 2J9 – 416/961-0194; Fax: 416/961-9599 – Executive Director, Julie White

Two/Ten Charity Trust of Canada Inc., PO Box 4219, Stn Westmount, Montréal QC H3Z 3B6 – 514/671-3604; Fax: 514/671-3604 – Sec.-Treas., Diane Cappella

Ukranian Canadian Foundation of Taras Shevchenko, 456 Main St., Winnipeg MB R3B 1B6 – 204/942-4627; Fax: 204/947-3882 – Executive Director, Lydia Hawryshkiw

United Ukrainian Charitable Trust, 2445 Bloor St. West, Toronto ON M6S 1P7 – 416/763-4982; Fax: 416/766-5812 – President, Wasyl Bybyk

Vancouver Foundation, #1200, 555 West Hastings St., PO Box 12132, Vancouver BC V6B 4N6 – 604/688-2204; Fax: 604/688-4170 – President/CEO, Richard Mulcaster

Vancouver Ski Foundation, #306, 1367 West Broadway, Vancouver BC V6H 4A9 – 604/878-0754; Fax: 604/878-0754

Verda & Weldon Bateman Foundation, 4123 Whitemud Rd., Edmonton AB T6H 5R5 – President, Mary A. Radostits

The Vicbir Family Foundation, #609, 55 Water St. East, Brockville ON K6V 1A3 – President, Robert W.M. Birks

The Victoria Foundation, #118, 645 Fort St., Victoria BC V8W 1G2 – Executive Director, Sheila Henley

VideoFACT, A Foundation to Assist Canadian Talent, #508, 151 John St., Toronto ON M5V 2T2 – 416/596-8696; Fax: 416/596-6861 – Program Director, Beverley McKee

The Viliam Frankel Family Charitable Foundation, #510, 333, rue Chabanel ouest, Montréal QC H2N 2E7 – President, Viliam Frankel

Virginia Parker Moore Foundation, Canada Trust, 45 O'Connor St., 6th Fl., Ottawa ON K1P 1A4 – President, Martha C. Price

The Vivian & David Campbell Foundation, #706, 95 Wellington St. West, Toronto ON M5J 2N7 – Contact, Henry Campbell

The W. Garfield Weston Foundation, c/o George Weston Ltd., #2001, 22 St. Clair Ave. East, Toronto ON M4T 2S3 – 416/922-2500; Fax: 416/922-4394 – Executive Director, Garfield R. Mitchell

W. Maurice Young Foundation, PO Box 10053, Vancouver BC V7Y 1B6 – Chairman & President, W. Maurice Young

Walker Lynch Foundation, 72 Railside Rd., North York ON M3A 1A3 – 416/449-5464; Fax: 416/449-9165 – Director, Karl E.G. McIntyre

Walter C. Sumner Foundation, c/o Montreal Trust Co., 1690 Hollis St., Halifax NS B3J 3C5 – Vice President, Susan G. Byrne

Walter & Duncan Gordon Charitable Foundation, #307, 11 Church St., Toronto ON M5E 1W1 – 416/601-4776; Fax: 416/601-1689; Email: gordonfn@gordonfn.org – Executive Director, Christine Lee

The Walter J. Blackburn Federation, 369 York St., PO Box 2280, London ON N6A 4G1 – Administrator, Linda A. Callaghan

The Werner Family Foundation, 1191 Bathurst St., Toronto ON M5R 3H4 – President, Ernest Webster

West Vancouver Foundation, PO Box 91447, West Vancouver BC V7V 3P1 – 604/925-8153; Fax: 604/925-8153 – Chairman, J. Cowan McKinney

Wild Rose Foundation, Edmonton Centre, #2007, Toronto Dominion Tower, Edmonton AB T5J 2Z1 – 403/422-9305; Fax: 403/427-4155 – Executive Director, Stan C. Fisher

Windsor Foundation, c/o Montreal Trust Company of Canada, 1690 Hollis St., Halifax NS B3J 3C5 – Sec.-Treas., Paul Dyer

Winnipeg Foundation, #301, 161 Portage Ave. East, Winnipeg MB R3B 0Y4 – 204/944-9474 – Executive Director, Dan H. Kraayeveld, CA

Winspear Foundation, PO Box 1740, Stn Main, Edmonton AB T5J 2P1 – 403/425-0121; Fax: 403/425-0121 – Honorary Secretary, Judge Peter M. Caffaro

W.P. Scott Charitable Foundation, PO Box 26, Stn Toronto Dominion, Toronto ON M5K 1A1 – Sec.-Treas., Pamela J. Roumeliotis

Yukon Foundation, #200, 2131 Second Ave., Whitehorse YT Y1A 1C3 – Chair, R. Hougen

Zeller Family Foundation, c/o National Trust Company, #600, 2000, av McGill College, Montréal QC H3A 3H4 – Sec.-Treas., Gail Belanger, 514/985-5657

The Zoltan Freeman Family Foundation, 369 Ferrie St. East, Hamilton ON L8N 3G9 – President, Zoltan Freeman

Zukerman Charitable Foundation, 33 Prince Arthur Ave., 2nd Fl., Toronto ON M5R 1B2 – Trustee, Helen Zukerman

# SECTION 3

## GOVERNMENT DIRECTORY



**See ADDENDA at the back of this book for late changes & additional information.**

## GOVERNMENT QUICK REFERENCE

**Editor's Note:** Following are government agencies listed alphabetically under topics of frequent need or interest. Under each topic, federal agencies are listed first followed by provincial agencies. Applied titles are used. Only head office addresses are given. Refer to the in-depth government listings in this book for regional offices of the federal government.

If no government branch or division is given, address inquiries to Information/Communication Services.

**See GOVERNMENT, alphabetically following, for the main source of information in each province and for the federal government departments.**

Suggestions, corrections or additions to this table are welcome. Contact: The Editor, Section 3, Copp Clark Professional, 200 Adelaide St. West, 3rd Fl., Toronto ON M5H 1W7.

### ABORIGINAL AFFAIRS

Fisheries & Oceans Canada, Aboriginal Affairs, 200 Kent St., Ottawa ON K1A 0E6, 613/991-0181; Fax: 613/993-7651

Health Canada, First Nations & Inuit Health Program, Brooke Claxton Bldg., Tunney's Pasture, 120 Parkdale Ave., Ottawa ON K1A 0K9, 613/952-7177; Fax: 613/941-5366

Indian & Northern Affairs Canada, Claims & Indian Government Sector, Tour Nord, Les Terrasses de la Chaudière, 10 Wellington St., Hull QC K1A 0H4, 819/997-0380; Fax: 819/953-3017

Lands & Trusts Services Sector, Tour Nord, Les Terrasses de la Chaudière, 10 Wellington St., Hull QC K1A 0H4, 819/997-0380; Fax: 819/953-3017

Industry Canada, Aboriginal Business Canada, 235 Queen St., Ottawa ON K1A 0H5, 613/941-0222; Fax: 613/954-6436

National Aboriginal Management Board, Portage IV, #4F00, 140, Promenade du Portage, Hull QC K1A 0J9, 819/994-2274

**Alta:** Alberta Federal & Intergovernmental Affairs, Aboriginal Affairs, Commerce Place, 10155 - 102 St., Edmonton AB T5J 4G8, 403/422-0964; Fax: 403/427-0939

Alberta Justice, Aboriginal Justice Initiatives, J.E. Brownlee Bldg., 10365 - 97 St., Edmonton AB T5J 3W7, 403/422-2779; Fax: 403/427-4670

**B.C.:** Ministry of Aboriginal Affairs, PO Box 9100, Stn Prov. Gov't, Victoria BC V8W 9B1, 250/356-8281; Fax: 250/387-1785

Ministry of Children & Families, Aboriginal Services, 1022 Government St., 3rd Fl., Victoria BC V8V 1X4, 250/387-7091; Fax: 250/387-7914

Ministry of Education, Skills & Training, Aboriginal Education Branch (K-12), PO Box 9150, Stn Prov Govt, Victoria BC V8W 9H1, 250/387-1544; Fax: 250/387-1470

**Man.:** Manitoba Northern Affairs, Native Affairs Secretariat, 59 Elizabeth Dr., PO Box 37, Thompson MB R8N 1X4, 204/677-6607; Fax: 204/677-6753

**N.B.:** Department of Intergovernmental & Aboriginal Affairs, Aboriginal Affairs, PO Box 6000, Fredericton NB E3B 5H1, 506/453-2671; Fax: 506/453-2995

**NWT:** Ministry of Aboriginal Affairs, Precambrian Bldg., 7th Fl., PO Box 1320, Yellowknife NT X1A 2L9, 867/873-7143; Fax: 867/873-0233

**N.S.:** Nova Scotia Priorities & Planning Secretariat, Aboriginal Affairs, 1700 Granville St., 5th Fl., PO Box 1617, Halifax NS B3J 2Y3, 902/424-8910; Fax: 902/424-7638

**Ont.:** Ministry of Citizenship, Culture & Recreation, Native Community Branch, 77 Bloor St. West, 6th Fl., Toronto ON M7A 2R9, 416/314-7265; Fax: 416/314-7313

Ministry of Community & Social Services, Aboriginal Healing & Wellness, Hepburn Block, 80 Grosvenor St., 6th Fl., Toronto ON M7A 1E9, 416/326-6907; Fax: 416/326-7934

Ontario Native Affairs Secretariat, #1009, 595 Bay St., Toronto ON M5G 2C2, 416/326-4740; Fax: 416/326-4017

**Qué.:** Ministère de l'Environnement et de la Faune, Affaires institutionelles et des communications, Édifice Marie-Guyart, 675, boul René-Lévesque est, Québec QC G1R 5V7, 418/521-3823; Toll Free: 1-800-561-1616; Fax: 418/646-4762

Ministère des Affaires Municipales, Bureau de coordination des Affaires autochones, Édifice Cook-Chauveau, 20, rue Pierre-Olivier-Chauveau, Québec QC G1R 4J3, 418/691-2031; Fax: 418/643-8611

Secrétariat aux affaires autochtones, Edifice H, 875, Grande-Allée est, 2e étage, Québec QC G1R 4Y8, 419/644-3166; Fax: 419/646-4918

**Sask.:** Saskatchewan Indian & Metis Affairs Secretariat, 2151 Scarth St., 4th Fl., Regina SK S4P 3V7, 306/787-6250; Fax: 306/787-6336

**Yuk.:** Executive Council, Aboriginal Language Services, PO Box 2703, Whitehorse YT Y1A 2C6, 867/667-3737; Fax: 867/393-6229

Land Claims, Self Government & Devolution, PO Box 2703, Whitehorse YT Y1A 2C6, 867/667-5908; Fax: 867/393-6214

### ADOPTION *See* CHILD WELFARE

### AGRICULTURE

***See Also* Land Resources**

Agriculture & Agri-Food Canada, Sir John Carling Bldg., 930 Carling Ave., Ottawa ON K1A 0C5, 613/759-1000; Fax: 613/759-6726

Prairie Farm Rehabilitation Administration, CIBC Tower, #603, 1800 Hamilton St., Regina SK S4P 4L2, 306/780-6545; Fax: 306/780-5018

Canadian Grain Commission, #600, 303 Main St., Winnipeg MB R3C 3G8, 204/983-2734; Fax: 204/983-2751

Canadian Wheat Board, 423 Main St., PO Box 816, Winnipeg MB R3C 2P5, 204/983-0239, 3416; Fax: 204/983-3841

National Farm Products Council, Martel Bldg., 270 Albert, 13th Fl., PO Box 3430, Stn D, Ottawa ON K1P 6L4, 613/995-6752; Fax: 613/995-2097

**Alta:** Agriculture Financial Service Corporation, 4910 - 52 St., PO Box 5000, Camrose AB T4V 4E8, 403/679-1311; Fax: 403/679-1308 (Lending)

Alberta Agriculture, Food & Rural Development, 7000 - 113 St., Edmonton AB T6H 5T6, 403/427-2727; Fax: 403/427-2861

Alberta Agricultural Research Institute, J.G. O'Donoghue Bldg., #300, 7000 - 113 St., Edmonton AB T6H 5T6, 403/422-1072; Fax: 403/422-6317

**B.C.:** Ministry of Agriculture, Fisheries & Food, 808 Douglas St., Victoria BC V8W 2Z7, 250/387-5121; Fax: 250/387-5130

Risk Management Branch, 808 Douglas St., Victoria BC V8W 2Z7, 250/356-1615; Fax: 250/387-5130

Ministry of Health, Regional Programs, 1515 Blanshard St., 7th Fl., Victoria BC V8W 3C8, 250/952-3456

Provincial Agricultural Land Commission, #133, 4940 Canada Way, Burnaby BC V5G 4K6, 604/660-7000; Fax: 604/660-7033

**Man.:** Manitoba Agricultural Credit Corporation, #100, 1525 - 1 St., Brandon MB R7A 7A1, 204/726-6850; Fax: 204/726-6849

Manitoba Crop Insurance Corporation, #400, 50 - 24 St. NW, Portage la Prairie MB R1N 3V9, 204/239-3246; Fax: 204/239-3401

Manitoba Agriculture, Norquay Bldg., #809, 401 York Ave., Winnipeg MB R3C 0P8, 204/945-3433 (Administration); Fax: 204/945-5024

**N.B.:** Agricultural Development Board, c/o Department of Agriculture & Rural Development, PO Box 6000, Fredericton NB E3B 5H1, 506/453-2185; Fax: 506/453-7406

Department of Agriculture & Rural Development, PO Box 6000, Fredericton NB E3B 5H1, 506/453-2666; Fax: 506/453-7978

**Nfld.:** Department of Forest Resources & Agrifoods, Agrifoods Branch, Provincial Agriculture Bldg., Brookfield Rd., PO Box 8700, St. John's NF A1B 4J6, 709/729-4716

**N.S.:** Department of Agriculture & Marketing, Joseph Howe Bldg., #700, 1690 Hollis St., PO Box 190, Halifax NS B3J 2M4, 902/424-6734; Fax: 902/424-3948

Nova Scotia Farm Loan Board, PO Box 550, Truro NS B2N 5E3, 902/893-6506; Fax: 902/895-7693

**Ont.:** Agricultural Research Institute of Ontario, 1 Stone Rd. West, Guelph ON N1G 4Y2, 519/826-4166; Fax: 519/826-4211

Ministry of Agriculture, Food & Rural Affairs, Communications Branch, 1 Stone Rd. West, Guelph ON N1G 4Y2, 519/826-4240; Toll Free: 1-888-466-2372; Fax: 519/826-3262

Ontario Agricultural Licensing & Registration Review Board, Guelph Agriculture Centre, PO Box 1030, Guelph ON N1H 1G3, 519/767-3547

Ontario Agricultural Rehabilitation & Development Directorate, 1 Stone Rd. West, 2nd Fl., Guelph ON N1G 4Y2

**PEI:** Agricultural Development Corporation, PO Box 2000, Charlottetown PE C1A 7N8, 902/368-4830; Fax: 902/368-5743

Department of Agriculture & Forestry, Jones Bldg., 11 Kent St., PO Box 2000, Charlottetown PE C1A 7N8, 902/368-4880; Fax: 902/368-4857

**Qué.:** Ministère de l'Agriculture, des Pêcheries et de l'Alimentation, 200, ch Sainte-Foy, Québec QC G1R 4X6, 418/643-2673; Fax: 418/646-0829

Société québécoise d'initiatives agro-alimentaires, #284, 1275, ch Ste-Foy, Québec QC G1S 4S5, 418/643-2238; Fax: 418/643-2553

**Sask.:** Saskatchewan Agriculture & Food, Walter Scott Bldg., 3085 Albert St., Regina SK S4S 0B1, 306/787-5140; Fax: 306/787-0216

**Yuk.:** Yukon Renewable Resources, Agriculture Branch, PO Box 2703, Whitehorse YT Y1A 2C6, 867/667-5237; Fax: 867/393-6222

## AIDS

***See Also* Health Services; Sexually Transmitted Disease Control**

Health Canada, HIV/Aids Policy Coordination & Program Division, Brooke Claxton Bldg., Tunney's Pasture, 120 Parkdale Ave., Ottawa ON K1A 0K9, 613/952-5258; Fax: 613/941-5366

Laboratory Centre for Disease Control, Brooke Claxton Bldg., Tunney's Pasture, 120 Parkdale Ave., Ottawa ON K1A 0K9, 613/957-0315; Fax: 613/941-5366

**Alta:** Alberta Health, Disease Control & Prevention, PO Box 1360, Edmonton AB T5J 2N3, 403/427-5263; Fax: 403/422-6663

**Nfld.:** Department of Health, Disease Control & Epidemiology, West Block, Confederation Bldg., PO Box 8700, St. John's NF A1B 4J6, 709/729-3430; Fax: 709/729-5824

**NWT:** Department of Health & Social Services, Community Programs & Services, Centre Square Tower, 8th Fl., PO Box 1320, Yellowknife NT X1A 2L9, 867/920-6173; Fax: 867/873-0266

**N.S.:** Nova Scotia Advisory Commission on AIDS, Dennis Bldg., 1740 Granville St., 6th Fl., Halifax NS B3J 1X5, 902/424-5730; Fax: 902/424-4727

**Ont.:** Ministry of Health, Community Health Division, Hepburn Block, 8th Fl., Queen's Park, #1400, 80 Grosvenor St., Toronto ON M7A 1S2, 416/327-7225; Toll Free: 1-800-668-2437 (AIDS Bureau); Fax: 416/327-7230

**PEI:** Department of Health & Social Services, Jones Bldg., 11 Kent St., 2nd Fl., PO Box 2000, Charlottetown PE C1A 7N8, 902/368-4985; Fax: 902/368-4969

**Sask.:** Saskatchewan Health, Strategic Services Division, 3475 Albert St., Regina SK S4S 6X6, 306/787-8332; Fax: 306/787-8310

## AIR RESOURCES

***See Also* Environment**

Environment Canada, Air Pollution Prevention Directorate, Place Vincent-Massey, 351, boul St-Joseph, Hull QC K1A 0H3, 819/997-1298; Fax: 819/953-9547

Atmospheric Environment Service, 4905 Dufferin St., Downsview ON M3H 5T4, 416/739-4521; Fax: 819/953-2225

International Joint Commission, 100 Metcalfe St., Ottawa ON K1P 5M1, 613/995-2984; Fax: 613/993-5583

**Alta:** Alberta Environmental Protection, 9915 - 108 St., Edmonton AB T5K 2G8, 403/427-2739, 944-0313 (Information Centre)

Environmental Regulatory Service, 9915 - 108 St., Edmonton AB T5K 2G8, 403/427-2739, 944-0313 (Information Centre)

**B.C.:** Ministry of Environment, Lands & Parks, Air Resources Branch, 777 Broughton St., Victoria BC V8V 1X4, 250/387-9987; Fax: 250/356-9836

**Man.:** Manitoba Environment, #160, 123 Main St., Winnipeg MB R3C 1A5, 204/945-7100

Environmental Management Division, #160, 123 Main St., Winnipeg MB R3C 1A5, 204/945-7107; Fax: 204/945-5229

**N.B.:** Department of the Environment, Environmental Quality, 364 Argyle St., PO Box 6000, Fredericton NB E3B 5H1, 506/457-4844; Fax: 506/453-2265

**Nfld.:** Department of Environment & Labour, Environment Branch, Confederation Bldg., PO Box 8700, St. John's NF A1B 4J6; Fax: 709/729-1930

**NWT:** Department of Resources, Wildlife & Economic Development, Environmental Protection, PO Box 1320, Yellowknife NT X1A 2L9, 867/873-7654; Fax: 867/873-0221

**N.S.:** Department of the Environment, Air Quality Branch, 5151 Terminal Rd., 5th Fl., PO Box 2107, Halifax NS B3J 3B7, 902/424-2550; Fax: 902/424-0503

**Ont.:** Ministry of Environment & Energy, Conservation & Prevention Division, 135 St. Clair Ave. West, Toronto ON M4V 1P5, 416/323-4320; Fax: 416/323-4481

Environmental Monitoring & Reporting Branch, 135 St. Clair Ave. West, Toronto ON M4V 1P5, 416/235-6160; Fax: 416/235-6235

**PEI:** Department of Fisheries & Environment, Air Quality & Hazardous Materials Section, Jones Bldg., 11 Kent St., 4th Fl., PO Box 2000, Charlottetown PE CIA 7N8, 902/368-5037; Fax: 902/368-5830

**Qué.:** Ministère de l'Environnement et de la Faune, Milieu atmosphérique, Édifice Marie-Guyart, 675, boul René-Lévesque est, Québec QC G1R 5V7, 418/643-4588; Fax: 418/643-9591

**Sask.:** Saskatchewan Environment & Resource Management, Environmental Protection Branch, 3211 Albert St., Regina SK S4S 5W6, 306/787-6178; Fax: 306/787-0197

**Yuk.:** Yukon Renewable Resources, Environment Protection & Assessment Branch, PO Box 2703, Whitehorse YT Y1A 2C6, 867/667-5237; Fax: 867/393-6213

## AIRPORTS & AVIATION

***See Also* Transportation**

Canadian Transportation Agency, Les Terrasses de la Chaudière, 15 Eddy St., Hull QC K1A 0N9, 819/997-0344 (Communications); Fax: 819/953-8353

Air & Accessible Transportation Branch, Les Terrasses de la Chaudière, 15 Eddy St., Hull QC K1A 0N9, 819/953-5074; Fax: 819/953-8353

Civil Aviation Tribunal, 333 Laurier Ave. West, 12th Fl., Ottawa ON K1A 0N5, 613/998-1275; Fax: 613/990-9153

Industry Canada, Aerospace & Defence, C.D. Howe Bldg., 235 Queen St., Ottawa ON K1A 0H5, 613/954-3343; Fax: 613/941-2379

Institute for Aerospace Research, 1500 Montreal Rd., Ottawa ON K1A 0R6, 613/993-0141; Fax: 613/952-7214

National Defence (Canada), Air Command, MGen. George R. Pearkes Bldg., 101 Colonel By Dr., Ottawa ON K1A 0K2, 613/992-4581

Transport Canada, Safety & Security Group, Transport Canada Building, 330 Sparks St., Ottawa ON K1A 0N5, 613/990-2309; Fax: 613/954-4731

**Man.:** Manitoba Highways & Transportation, Northern Airports & Marine, 215 Garry St., 14th Fl., Winnipeg MB R3C 3Z1, 204/945-3421; Fax: 204/945-5539

**NWT:** Department of Transportation, Arctic Airports, Lahm Ridge Bldg., PO Box 1320, Yellowknife NT X1A 2L9, 867/920-3460; Fax: 867/873-0363

**Yuk.:** Yukon Community & Transportation Services, Aviation & Marine Branch, PO Box 2129, Haines Junction YT Y0B 1L0, 867/634-2035; Fax: 867/634-2131

**ALCOHOL & ALCOHOLISM *See* DRUGS & ALCOHOL; LIQUOR CONTROL**

## APPRENTICESHIP PROGRAMS

**Alta:** Alberta Advanced Education & Career Development, Apprenticeship & Industry Training Division, Commerce Place, 10155 - 102 St., 7th Fl., Edmonton AB T5J 4L5, 403/422-4488; Fax: 403/422-7376

**B.C.:** Ministry of Labour, Apprenticeship Initatives Division, 825 Fort St., 2nd Fl., PO Box 9570, Stn Prov. Gov't, Victoria BC V8W 9K1, 250/356-1487; Fax: 250/356-1653

**Man.:** Manitoba Education & Training, Apprenticeship, 185 Carlton St., 4th Fl., Winnipeg MB R3C 3J1, 204/945-3339; Fax: 204/948-2346

**N.B.:** Apprenticeship & Occupational Certification Board, PO Box 6000, Fredericton NB E3B 5H1, 506/453-2260; Fax: 506/453-3806

Department of Advanced Education & Labour, Collège Communautaire du NB, Edmundston, Chestnut Complex, 470 York St., PO Box 6000, Fredericton NB E3B 5H1, 506/735-2500; Fax: 506/735-1108

**NWT:** Department of Education, Culture & Employment, Career Development, PO Box 1320, Yellowknife NT X1A 2L9, 867/873-7146; Fax: 867/873-0155

Northwest Territories Apprenticeship & Trade Certification Board, PO Box 1192, Yellowknife NT X1A 2N8, 867/873-7357

**N.S.:** Department of Education & Culture, Apprenticeship Training Division, 2021 Brunswick St., PO Box 578, Halifax NS B3J 2S9, 902/424-8903; Fax: 902/424-0717

Nova Scotia Provincial Apprenticeship Board, PO Box 578, Halifax NS B3J 2S9, 902/424-0872; Fax: 902/424-0717

**Ont.:** Ministry of Education & Training, Apprenticeship Reform Project, Mowat Block, 900 Bay St., Toronto ON M7A 1L2, 416/314-5166; Fax: 416/325-2934

**Qué.:** Conseil consultatif du travail & de la main d'oeuvre, #2026, 800, Tour de la Place Victoria, CP 87, Montréal QC H4Z 1B7, 514/873-2880; Fax: 514/873-1129

Société québécoise de développement de la main-d'oeuvre, 425, rue St-Amable, Québec QC G1R 2C5, 418/643-1892; Fax: 418/643-1714

**Sask.:** Saskatchewan Post-Secondary Education & Skills Training, Training Programs Branch, 2220 College Ave., Regina SK S4P 3V7, 306/787-2093

**Yuk.:** Yukon Education, Training Programs, PO Box 2703, Whitehorse YT Y1A 2C6, 867/667-5140; Fax: 867/667-8555

## ARBITRATION *See* LABOUR

## ARCHIVES *See* HISTORY & ARCHIVES

## ARCTIC & NORTHERN AFFAIRS

Canadian Polar Commission, Constitution Square, #1710, 360 Albert St., Ottawa ON K1R 7X7, 613/943-8605; Fax: 613/943-8607

Indian & Northern Affairs Canada, Tour Nord, Les Terrasses de la Chaudière, 10 Wellington St., Hull QC K1A 0H4, 819/997-0380; Fax: 819/953-3017

Northern Affairs Sector, Tour Nord, Les Terrasses de la Chaudière, 10 Wellington St., Hull QC K1A 0H4, 819/997-0380; Fax: 819/953-3017

Office of the Nunavut Environmental Scientist, PO Box 1500, Yellowknife NT X1A 2R3, 867/920-8200; Fax: 867/920-7809

**Alta:** Northern Alberta Development Council, #206, Provincial Bldg., 9621 - 96 Ave., PO Bag 900-14, Peace River AB T8S 1T4, 403/624-6274; Fax: 403/624-6184

**Man.:** Manitoba Northern Affairs, 59 Elizabeth Dr., PO Box 37, Thompson MB R8N 1X4, 204/677-6607; Fax: 204/677-6753

**NWT:** Northwest Territories Development Corporation, Tower 7, PO Box 1437, Yellowknife NT X1A 2P1, 867/920-7700; Fax: 867/920-7701

**Ont.:** Ministry of Northern Development & Mines, Northern Development Division, #200, 70 Foster Dr., Sault Ste. Marie ON P6A 6V8, 705/945-5900; Fax: 705/945-5931

**Sask.:** Saskatchewan Northern Affairs, PO Box 5000, La Ronge SK S0J 1L0, 306/425-4200; Fax: 306/425-4349

**Yuk.:** Yukon Economic Development, 211 Main St., PO Box 2703, Whitehorse YT Y1A 2C6, 867/667-5466; Fax: 867/668-8601

## ARTS & CULTURE

Canada Council for the Arts, 350 Albert St., PO Box 1047, Ottawa ON K1P 5V8, 613/566-4365; Toll Free: 1-800-263-5588; Fax: 613/566-4390

Canadian Artists & Producers Professional Relations Tribunal, C.D. Howe Bldg., 240 Sparks St., 8th Fl. West, Ottawa ON K1A 1A1, 613/996-4052; Toll Free: 1-800-263-ARTS (2787); Fax: 613/947-4125

Canadian Broadcasting Corporation, 250 Lanark Ave., PO Box 3220, Stn C, Ottawa ON K1Y 1E4, 613/724-1200; TDD: 613/724-5173

Canadian Heritage, Jules Léger Bldg., 25 Eddy St., Hull QC K1A 1K5, 819/997-0055; TDD: 819/997-8776; Fax: 819/953-5382

National Archives of Canada, 395 Wellington St., Ottawa ON K1A 0N3, 613/995-5138; Fax: 613/995-6274

National Arts Centre, 53 Elgin St., PO Box 1534, Stn B, Ottawa ON K1P 5W1, 613/996-5051, 947-7000; Fax: 613/996-9578

National Film Board of Canada, 3155, rue Côte de Liesse, St-Laurent QC H4N 2N4, 514/283-9000; Fax: 514/283-8971

Natural Resources Canada, Mapping & Services Branch, 615 Booth St., Ottawa ON K1A 0E9, 613/995-4945; Fax: 613/995-8737

Telefilm Canada, Tour de la Banque Nationale, 600, De La Gauchetière ouest, 14e étage, Montréal QC H3B 4L8, 514/283-6363; Fax: 514/283-8212

**Alta:** Alberta Community Development, Arts & Libraries Branch, Standard Life Centre, 10405 Jasper Ave., 7th Fl., Edmonton AB T5J 4R7, 403/427-6315; Fax: 403/422-9132

Cultural Facilities & Historical Resources Division, Old St. Stephen's College, 8820 - 112 St., Edmonton AB T6G 2P8, 403/431-2300; Fax: 403/427-5598

**B.C.:** British Columbia Arts Council, 800 Johnson St., 5th Fl., Victoria BC V8V 1X4, 250/356-1718

British Columbia Festival of the Arts Society, 3577 Douglas St., Victoria BC V8Z 3L6, 250/383-4214

Ministry of Small Business, Tourism & Culture, Culture Division, 1405 Douglas St., Victoria BC V8W 3C1

**Man.:** Manitoba Arts Council, #525, 93 Lombard Ave., Winnipeg MB R3B 3B1, 204/945-2239; Fax: 204/945-5925

Manitoba Culture, Heritage & Citizenship, Culture, Heritage & Recreation Programs Division, 213 Notre Dame., Winnipeg MB R3B 1N3, 204/945-3729

**N.B.:** Department of Municipalities, Culture & Housing, Arts Branch, Marysville Place, 20 McGloin St., PO Box 6000, Fredericton NB E3B 5H1, 506/453-2555; Fax: 506/453-2416

**Nfld.:** Department of Tourism, Culture & Recreation, Confederation Bldg., PO Box 8700, St. John's NF A1B 4J6, 709/729-0928; Fax: 709/729-0662

Cultural Affairs Branch, Confederation Bldg., PO Box 8700, St. John's NF A1B 4J6, 709/729-0928; Fax: 709/729-0662

**NWT:** Department of Education, Culture & Employment, Culture & Heritage, PO Box 1320, Yellowknife NT X1A 2L9, 867/873-7551; Fax: 867/873-0155

Northwest Territories Arts Council, PO Box 1320, Stn Main, Yellowknife NT X1A 2L9

**N.S.:** Department of Education & Culture, Acadian & French Language Services Branch, 2021 Brunswick St., PO Box 578, Halifax NS B3J 2S9, 902/424-5168; Fax: 902/424-0511

Heritage & Culture Branch (Nova Scotia Museum), 2021 Brunswick St., PO Box 578, Halifax NS B3J 2S9, 902/424-5168; Fax: 902/424-0511

**Ont.:** Ministry of Citizenship, Culture & Recreation, Heritage, Arts & Cultural Industries Policy Branch, 77 Bloor St. West, 6th Fl., Toronto ON M7A 2R9, 416/314-7115; Fax: 416/314-7313

Ontario Arts Council, 151 Bloor St. West, 5th Fl., Toronto ON M5S 1T6, 416/961-1660; Fax: 416/969-7447

Royal Ontario Museum, 100 Queen's Park Cres., Toronto ON M5S 2C6, 416/586-5549; Fax: 416/586-5863

TV Ontario, 2180 Yonge St., 5th Fl., Toronto ON M4S 2C1, 416/484-2600; Fax: 416/484-4234

**PEI:** Department of Education, Culture, Heritage & Recreation, Sullivan Bldg., 16 Fitzroy St., PO Box 2000, Charlottetown PE C1A 7N8, 902/368-4789; Fax: 902/368-4663

**Qué.:** Conseil des arts et des lettres du Québec, #320, 79, boul René-Lévesque est, Québec QC G1R 5N5, 418/643-1707; Fax: 418/643-4558

Conseil des communautés culturelles & de l'immigration, #418, Tour de la Place-Victoria, CP 158, Montréal QC H4Z 1C3, 514/873-8501; Fax: 514/873-3469

Ministère de la Culture et des Communications, 225, Grand-Allée est, Québec QC G1R 5G5, 418/643-2183; Fax: 418/643-4457

**Sask.:** Saskatchewan Arts Board, T.C. Douglas Bldg., 3475 Albert St., 3rd Fl., Regina SK S4S 6X6, 306/787-4056; Toll Free: 1-800-667-7526 (Saskatchewan); Fax: 306/787-4199

**Yuk.:** Yukon Tourism, Arts Branch, PO Box 2703, Whitehorse YT Y1A 2C6, 867/667-8592; Fax: 867/667-8844

## ASTRONOMY *See* SPACE & ASTRONOMY

## ATOMIC ENERGY *See* NUCLEAR ENERGY

## ATTORNEYS-GENERAL *See* JUSTICE DEPARTMENTS

## AUDITS & AUDITORS-GENERAL

Auditor General of Canada, 240 Sparks St., Ottawa ON K1A 0G6, 613/995-3708; Fax: 613/957-4023

Public Works & Government Services Canada, Consulting & Audit Canada, Tower B, Place de Ville, 112 Kent St., Ottawa ON K1A 0S5, 613/996-0188

**Alta:** Alberta Office of the Auditor General, 9925 - 109 St., 8th Fl., Edmonton AB T5K 2J8, 403/427-4221; Fax: 403/422-9555

**B.C.:** Office of the Auditor General, 8 Bastion Sq., Victoria BC V8V 1X4, 250/387-6803; Fax: 250/387-1230

**Man.:** Office of the Provincial Auditor, 405 Broadway, 12th Fl., Winnipeg MB R3C 3L6, 204/945-3790; Fax: 204/945-2169

**N.B.:** Office of the Auditor General, PO Box 758, Fredericton NB E3B 5B4, 506/453-2243; Fax: 506/453-3067

**Nfld.:** Department of Finance, Confederation Bldg., PO Box 8700, St. John's NF A1B 4J6, 709/729-2700; Fax: 709/729-5970

**NWT:** Executive Council, Audit Bureau, PO Box 1320, Yellowknife NT X1A 2L9, 403/873-7106; Fax: 403/873-0209

Financial Management Board Secretariat, PO Box 1320, Yellowknife NT X1A 2L9

**N.S.:** Department of Finance, Internal Audit, PO Box 187, Halifax NS B3J 2N3, 902/424-2407; Fax: 902/424-0635

Office of the Auditor General, #302, 1888 Brunswick St., Halifax NS B3J 3J8, 902/424-5907; Fax: 902/424-4350

**Ont.:** Management Board of Cabinet, Audit Branch, Ferguson Block, 77 Wellesley St. West, 12th Fl., Toronto ON M7A 1N3, 416/314-3448; Fax: 416/314-3467

Office of the Provincial Auditor, #1530, 20 Dundas St. West, PO Box 105, Toronto ON M5G 2C2, 416/327-2381; Fax: 416/327-9862

**PEI:** Department of the Provincial Treasury, Office of the Comptroller, PO Box 2000, Charlottetown PE C1A 7N8, 902/368-4000; Fax: 902/368-5544

Office of the Auditor General, PO Box 2000, Charlottetown PE C1A 7N8, 902/368-4520; Fax: 902/368-4598

**Qué.:** Vérificateur général du Québec, #6.00, 900, Place d'Youville, Québec QC G1R 3P7, 418/691-5900; Fax: 418/646-1307

**Sask.:** Provincial Auditor Saskatchewan, #1500, 1920 Broad St., Regina SK S4P 3V7, 306/787-6398; Fax: 306/787-6383

**Yuk.:** Executive Council, Bureau of Management Improvement, PO Box 2703, Whitehorse YT Y1A 2C6, 867/667-5316; Fax: 867/667-8424

## AUTOMOBILE INSURANCE

***See Also* Insurance (Life, Fire, Property)**

**Alta:** Automobile Insurance Board, #407, Terrace Bldg., 9515 - 107 St., Edmonton AB T5K 2C3, 403/427-5428; Fax: 403/422-2175

**B.C.:** Insurance Corporation of BC (Autoplan), 151 West Esplanade, North Vancouver BC V7M 3H9, 604/661-2800; Fax: 604/661-2244

**Man.:** Manitoba Public Insurance, 234 Donald St., 9th Fl., PO Box 6300, Winnipeg MB R3C 4A4, 204/985-7000; Fax: 204/943-9851

**N.B.:** Board of Commissioners of Public Utilities, 110 Charlotte St., PO Box 5001, Saint John NB E2L 4Y9, 506/658-2504; Fax: 506/633-0163

**Nfld.:** Department of Government Services & Lands, Insurance & Pensions, PO Box 8700, St. John's NF A1B 4J6, 709/729-2594; Fax: 709/729-3205

**Ont.:** Ontario Insurance Commission, 5160 Yonge St., PO Box 85, Toronto ON M2N 6L9, 416/250-7250; Toll Free: 1-800-668-0128; Fax: 416/590-7070

**PEI:** Department of Community Affairs & Attorney General, Insurance & Real Estate Division, Shaw Building, 95 Rochford St., 4th Fl., PO Box 2000, Charlottetown PE C1A 7N8, 902/368-4564; Fax: 902/368-5283; 5355

**Qué.:** Société de l'assurance automobile du Québec, 333, boul Jean-Lesage, CP 19600, Québec QC G1K 8J6, 418/528-3100; Fax: 418/644-0339

**Sask.:** Saskatchewan Government Insurance, 2260 - 11 Ave., Regina SK S4P 0J9, 306/751-1200; Fax: 306/787-7477

## BANKING & FINANCIAL INSTITUTIONS

Auditor General of Canada, 240 Sparks St., Ottawa ON K1A 0G6, 613/995-3708; Fax: 613/957-4023

Bank of Canada, 234 Wellington St., Ottawa ON K1A 0G9, 613/782-8111; Fax: 613/782-8655

Business Development Bank of Canada, #400, 5, Place Ville Marie, Montréal QC H3B 5E7, 514/283-5904; Toll Free: 1-888-463-6232; Fax: 514/283-0617

Canada Deposit Insurance Corporation, 50 O'Connor St., 17th Fl., PO Box 2340, Stn D, Ottawa ON K1P 5W5, 613/996-2081; Toll Free: 1-800-461-2342; Fax: 613/996-6095

Office of the Superintendent of Financial Institutions, Kent Square, 255 Albert St., Ottawa ON K1A 0H2, 613/990-7788; Toll Free: 1-800-385-8647; Fax: 613/952-8219

Deposit Taking Institutions, Kent Square, 255 Albert St., Ottawa ON K1A 0H2, 613/990-7788; Toll Free: 1-800-385-8647; Fax: 613/952-8219

Revenue Canada, 875 Heron Rd., Ottawa ON K1A 0L8, 613/952-0384

Financial Industries Division, 123 Slater St., Ottawa ON K1A 0L8, 613/957-9767

Treasury Board of Canada, 140 O'Connor St., Ottawa ON K1A 0R5, 613/957-2400; Fax: 613/952-3658

**Alta:** Alberta Treasury, Banking & Cash Management, Terrace Bldg., 9515 - 107 St., Edmonton AB T5K 2C3, 403/427-3035; Fax: 403/422-2463

Financial Institutions, Terrace Bldg., 9515 - 107 St., Edmonton AB T5K 2C3, 403/427-3035; Fax: 403/422-2463

**B.C.:** Financial Institutions Commission, #1900, 1050 West Pender St., Vancouver BC V6E 3S7, 604/660-2947; Fax: 604/660-3170

International Finance Centre - Vancouver Society, World Trade Centre, #658, 999 Canada Place, Vancouver BC V6C 3E1, 604/683-6626; Fax: 604/683-6646

Ministry of Finance & Corporate Relations, 617 Government St., Victoria BC V8V 1X4, 250/387-9278

Banking & Cash Management, 620 Superior St., Victoria BC V8V 1X4, 250/387-9295; Fax: 250/387-3024

Credit Unions & Trust Companies, #1900, 1050 West Pender St., Vancouver BC V6E 3S7, 604/660-2947; Fax: 604/660-3170

**Man.:** Credit Union Deposit Guarantee Corporation, #100, 233 Portage Ave., Winnipeg MB R3B 2A7, 204/942-8480; Fax: 204/947-1723

Manitoba Agricultural Credit Corporation, #100, 1525 - 1 St., Brandon MB R7A 7A1, 204/726-6850; Fax: 204/726-6849

Manitoba Finance, Money Management & Banking, #109, Legislative Bldg., Winnipeg MB R3C 0V8, 204/945-3754; Fax: 204/945-8316

**N.B.:** Department of Justice, Corporate Affairs, #412, Centennial Bldg., PO Box 6000, Fredericton NB E3B 5H1, 506/453-3860; Fax: 506/453-2613

Credit Unions, Cooperatives & Trust Companies, #412, Centennial Bldg., PO Box 6000, Fredericton NB E3B 5H1, 506/457-4852; Fax: 506/453-7474

**Nfld.:** Credit Union Deposit Guarantee Corporation, PO Box 8700, St. John's NF A1B 4J6, 709/753-6498

Department of Finance & Treasury Board, Confederation Bldg., PO Box 8700, St. John's NF A1B 4J6, 709/729-2858

**NWT:** Department of Finance, PO Box 1320, Yellowknife NT X1A 2L9

Banking & Investment, PO Box 1320, Yellowknife NT X1A 2L9, 867/873-7496; Fax: 867/873-0325

Northwest Territories Business Credit Corporation, Northern United Place, 5004 - 54 St., PO Box 1320, Yellowknife NT X1A 2L9, 867/920-6454; Fax: 867/873-0308

Northwest Territories Development Corporation, Tower 7, PO Box 1437, Yellowknife NT X1A 2P1, 867/920-7700; Fax: 867/920-7701

**N.S.:** Department of Business & Consumer Services, Financial Institutions Division/Superintendent of Insurance, South Maritime Centre, #8, 1505 Barrington St., Halifax NS B3J 2X1, 902/424-6331; Fax: 902/424-5327

Department of Finance, PO Box 187, Halifax NS B3J 2N3, 902/424-5554; Fax: 902/424-0635

**Ont.:** Deposit Insurance Corporation of Ontario, #700, 4711 Yonge St., Toronto ON M2N 6K8

Financial Services Commission of Ontario, c/o Ministry of Finance, Frost Bldg. South, 7 Queen's Park Cres., Toronto ON M7A 1Y7

Ministry of Finance, Deposit Institutions Division, Frost Bldg. South, 7 Queen's Park Cres., Toronto ON M7A 1Y7, 416/325-0333 (Communications); Fax: 416/325-0339

Fiscal & Financial Policy Division, Frost Bldg. South, 7 Queen's Park Cres., Toronto ON M7A 1Y7, 416/325-0333 (Communications); Fax: 416/325-0339

Province of Ontario Savings Office, #1400, 1 Dundas St. West, Toronto ON M7A 1Y7, 416/325-8101; Fax: 416/325-8005

Revenue & Financial Institutions, Frost Bldg. South, 7 Queen's Park Cres., Toronto ON M7A 1Y7, 416/325-3300; Fax: 416/325-3295

Ontario Financing Authority, #1400, 1 Dundas St. West, Toronto ON M7A 1Y7

Ontario Mortgage Corporation, 62 Wellesley St. West, Toronto ON M5S 2X3, 416/314-3650

**PEI:** Department of Community Affairs & Attorney General, Securities & Consumer, Corporate & Insurance Services, Shaw Building, 95 Rochford St., 4th Fl., PO Box 2000, Charlottetown PE C1A 7N8, 902/368-4552; Fax: 902/368-5283; 5355

Department of the Provincial Treasury, PO Box 2000, Charlottetown PE C1A 7N8, 902/368-4000; Fax: 902/368-5544

**Qué.:** Caisse de dépôt et placement du Québec, 1981, av McGill College, Montréal QC H3A 3C7, 514/842-3261; Fax: 514/842-4833

Commission des valeurs mobilières du Québec, Tour de la Bourse, 800, Place Victoria, 17e étage, Montréal QC H4Z 1G3, 514/873-5326; Fax: 514/873-0711

L'Inspecteur général des Institutions financières, 800, place D'Youville, Québec QC G1R 4Y5, 418/694-5018 (Communications); Fax: 418/643-3336

Ministère des Finances, Politiques économiques, 12, rue St-Louis, Québec QC G1R 5L3, 418/691-2225; Fax: 418/646-6163

Politiques-Institutions Financières, 12, rue St-Louis, Québec QC G1R 5L3, 418/691-2233; Fax: 418/646-5643, 1631

**Sask.:** Saskatchewan Development Fund Corporation, #300, 2400 College Ave., Regina SK S4P 1C8, 306/787-1645; Fax: 306/787-8125

Saskatchewan Securities Commission, Toronto Dominion Bank Bldg., 1920 Broad St., 8th Fl., Regina SK S4P 3V7, 306/787-5645; Fax: 306/787-5899

Saskatchewan Finance, 2350 Albert St., Regina SK S4P 4A6, 306/787-6768; Fax: 306/787-6544

Saskatchewan Justice, Insurance, 1874 Scarth St., Regina SK S4P 3V7, 306/787-7881; Fax: 306/787-9779

**Yuk.:** Yukon Finance, PO Box 2703, Whitehorse YT Y1A 2C6, 867/667-5343; Fax: 867/393-6217

Yukon Justice, Corporate Affairs & Registrar of Securities, PO Box 2703, Whitehorse YT Y1A 2C6, 867/667-5225; Fax: 867/393-6272

## BANKRUPTCY

Industry Canada, Office of the Superintendent of Bankruptcy, Journal Tower South, 365 Laurier St. West, 8th Fl., Ottawa ON K1A 0C8, 613/941-1000; Fax: 613/941-2862

## BIBLIOGRAPHIC SERVICES

Library of Parliament, 111 Wellington St., Ottawa ON K1A 0A9, 613/995-1166; Fax: 613/992-1269

National Archives of Canada, 395 Wellington St., Ottawa ON K1A 0N3, 613/995-5138; Fax: 613/995-6274

National Research Council Canada, Canadian Institute for Scientific & Technical Information, Bldg. M-58, 1200 Montreal Rd., Ottawa ON K1A 0R6, 613/993-9101; Fax: 613/952-7928

**Alta:** Alberta Community Development, Arts & Libraries Branch, Standard Life Centre, 10405 Jasper Ave., 7th Fl., Edmonton AB T5J 4R7, 403/427-6315; Fax: 403/422-9132

Provincial Archives, 12845 - 102 Ave., Edmonton AB T5N 0H6, 403/427-1750; Fax: 403/427-4646

Alberta Justice, Provincial Court Library, Law Courts Bldg., 5th Fl., North, 1A Sir Winston Churchill Square, 2nd Fl. South, Edmonton AB T5J 0R2, 403/427-5579, 5580; Fax: 403/427-0481

**B.C.:** Ministry of Municipal Affairs & Housing, Library Services, Municipal Affairs, PO Box 9490, Victoria BC V8W 9N7, 250/356-1795; Fax: 250/387-4048

**Man.:** Manitoba Culture, Heritage & Citizenship, Public Library Services, #200, 1595 - 1 St., Brandon MB R7A 7A1, 204/726-6864; Fax: 204/726-6868

**N.B.:** Department of Municipalities, Culture & Housing, Marysville Place, 20 McGloin St., PO Box 6000, Fredericton NB E3B 5H1, 506/453-2354; Fax: 506/457-4991

**Nfld.:** Department of Tourism, Culture & Recreation, Provincial Archives, Confederation Bldg., PO Box 8700, St. John's NF A1B 4J6, 709/729-3065; Fax: 709/729-0578

**NWT:** Department of Education, Culture & Employment, NWT Public Library Services, PO Box 1100, Hay River NT X0E 0R0, 867/874-6531; Fax: 867/873-0155

**N.S.:** Department of Education & Culture, Provincial Library, 2021 Brunswick St., PO Box 578, Halifax NS B3J 2S9, 902/424-2457; Fax: 902/424-0633

**Ont.:** Ministry of Citizenship, Culture & Recreation, Libraries & Community Information Branch, 77 Bloor St. West, 6th Fl., Toronto ON M7A 2R9, 416/314-7265; Fax: 416/314-7313

Northern Ontario Library Service, 334 Regent St., Sudbury ON P3C 4E2, 705/675-6467; Fax: 705/675-6108

Southern Ontario Library Service, #50, 55 West Beaver Creek, Richmond Hill ON L4B 1K5, 905/771-1522; Fax: 905/771-1526

**PEI:** Department of Education, Provincial Libraries & Archives, Sullivan Bldg., 16 Fitzroy St., PO Box 2000, Charlottetown PE C1A 7N8, 902/368-4227; Fax: 902/368-6327

**Qué.:** Ministère de la Culture et des Communications, Archives nationales, Pavillon Louis-Jacques Casault, 1210 av du Séminaire, Ste-Foy QC G1N 4V1, 418/643-2183; Fax: 418/643-4457

**Sask.:** Saskatchewan Archives Board, University of Regina, 3737 Wascana Pkwy., Regina SK S4S 0A2, 306/787-4068; Fax: 306/787-1975

**Yuk.:** Yukon Education, Libraries & Archives, PO Box 2703, Whitehorse YT Y1A 2C6, 867/667-5309; Fax: 867/393-6254

## BILINGUALISM

Canadian Heritage, Official Languages, Jules Léger Bldg., 25 Eddy St., Hull QC K1A 1K5, 819/994-0943; Fax: 819/953-9353

Office of the Commissioner of Official Languages, 110 O'Connor St., Ottawa ON K1A 0T8, 613/996-6368; Fax: 613/993-5082

Treasury Board of Canada, Official Languages & Employment Equity Branch, 140 O'Connor St., Ottawa ON K1A 0R5, 613/952-2852; Fax: 613/941-4262

**Alta:** Alberta Education, Language Services, Devonian Bldg., 11160 Jasper Ave., Edmonton AB T5K 0L2, 403/427-2940; Fax: 403/422-1947

**B.C.:** Ministry of Education, Skills & Training, Policy, Planning & Special Programs Division, PO Box 9150, Stn Prov Govt, Victoria BC V8W 9H1, 250/356-2500; Fax: 250/356-5945

**Man.:** Le Centre Culturel franco-manitobain, 340, boul Provencher, St. Boniface MB R2H 0G7, 204/233-8972; Fax: 204/233-3324

Manitoba Culture, Heritage & Citizenship, Translation Services, 213 Notre Dame Ave., 2nd Fl., Winnipeg MB R3B 1N3, 204/945-3095; Fax: 204/945-5879

Manitoba Education & Training, Bureau de l'Education Française, #509. 1181 Portage Ave., Winnipeg MB R3C 0T3, 204/945-4325; Fax: 204/945-1291

**N.B.:** Department of Education, Educational Services Division (Anglophone), PO Box 6000, Fredericton NB E3B 5H1, 506/453-3678; Fax: 506/453-3325

Secteur des services Francophones d'éducation, PO Box 6000, Fredericton NB E3B 5H1, 506/453-3678; Fax: 506/453-3325

**NWT:** Executive Council, Office of Official Languages, PO Box 1320, Yellowknife NT X1A 2L9

Legislative Assembly, Office of the Languages Commissioner, PO Box 1320, Yellowknife NT X1A 2L9, 867/873-7034; Fax: 867/920-4735

**N.S.:** Department of Education & Culture, Acadian & French Language Services Branch, 2021 Brunswick St., PO Box 578, Halifax NS B3J 2S9, 902/424-5168; Fax: 902/424-0511

**Ont.:** Languages of Instruction Commission of Ontario, 56 Wellesley St. West, 11th Fl., Toronto ON M7A 2B7, 416/314-3500; Fax: 416/314-3502

Ministry of Education & Training, French-Language Education Policy & Programs, Mowat Block, 900 Bay St., Toronto ON M7A 1L2, 416/325-2127; Fax: 416/325-2934

Ministry of Municipal Affairs & Housing, Office of Francophone Municipal Relations, 777 Bay St., 17th Fl., Toronto ON M5G 2E5, 416/585-7556; Fax: 416/585-6227

Office of Francophone Affairs, Mowat Block, 900 Bay St., 4th Fl., Toronto ON M7A 1C2, 416/325-4949; Toll Free: 1-800-268-7507; Fax: 416/325-4980

**PEI:** Department of Community Affairs & Attorney General, Francophone Affairs Secretariat, PO Box 2000, Charlottetown PE C1A 7N8, 902/368-4509; Fax: 902/368-5283; 5355

Department of Education, French Programs & Services, Sullivan Bldg., 16 Fitzroy St., PO Box 2000, Charlottetown PE C1A 7N8, 902/368-4671; Fax: 902/368-4622

**Qué.:** Ministère de l'Éducation, Communauté anglophone, 600, rue Fullum, Montréal QC H2K 4L1, 514/873-4630; Fax: 514/873-1082

Secrétariat aux affaires intergouvernementales canadiennes, Bureaux coopération et francophonie, Edifice H, 3e étage, 875, Grande Allée est, Québec QC G1R 4Y8, 418/643-4011; Fax: 418/643-8730

**Sask.:** Saskatchewan Education, Official Minority Language Office Branch, 2220 College Ave., Regina SK S4P 3V7, 306/787-6089; Fax: 306/787-1300

Saskatchewan Intergovernmental Affairs, Office of French Language Coordination, 1919 Saskatchewan Dr., Regina SK S4P 3V7, 306/787-2028; Fax: 306/787-6352

**Yuk.:** Executive Council, Bureau of French Language Services, PO Box 2703, Whitehorse YT Y1A 2C6, 867/667-3775; Fax: 867/393-6226

## BIOTECHNOLOGY

Biotechnology Research Centre, 6100, av Royalmount, Montréal QC H4P 2R2, 514/496-6100; Fax: 514/496-6388

Industry Canada, Bio-Industries, C.D. Howe Bldg., 235 Queen St., Ottawa ON K1A 0H5, 613/954-3071; Fax: 613/952-4209

Institute for Biological Sciences, 1500 Montreal Rd., Ottawa ON K1A 0R6, 613/993-7506; Fax: 613/957-7867

Plant Biotechnology Institute, 110 Gymnasium Rd., Saskatoon SK S7N 0W9, 306/975-5248; Fax: 306/975-4839

**Alta:** Alberta Research Council, Biotechnology, 250 Karl Clark Rd., PO Box 8330, Edmonton AB T6H 5X2, 403/450-5319; Fax: 403/461-2651

**B.C.:** Science Council of British Columbia, #800, 4710 Kingsway, Burnaby BC V5H 4M2, 604/438-2752; Toll Free: 1-800-665-7222; Fax: 604/438-6564

**N.B.:** New Brunswick Research & Productivity Council, Chemical & Biotechnical Services, 921 College Hill Rd., Fredericton NB E3B 6Z9, 506/452-1369; Fax: 506/452-1395

**NWT:** Aurora Research Institute, c/o Aurora College, PO Box 1450, Inuvik NT X0E 0T0

Nunavut Research Institute, Aeroplex Bldg., PO Box 1720, Iqualuit NT X0A 0H0, 867/979-4115; Fax: 867/979-4681

**N.S.:** Nova Scotia Innovation Corporation, Woodside Industrial Park, 101 Research Dr., PO Box 790, Dartmouth NS B2Y 3Z7, 902/424-8670; Toll Free: 1-800-565-7051; Fax: 902/424-8679

**Ont.:** Ministry of Agriculture, Food & Rural Affairs, Education, Research & Laboratories Division, Communications Branch, 1 Stone Rd. West, Guelph ON N1G 4Y2, 519/826-3388; Fax: 519/826-4211

**PEI:** Department of Agriculture & Forestry, Research, Resources & Laboratories, PO Box 306, Kensington PE C0B 1M0, 902/368-5646; Fax: 902/368-5661

**Qué.:** Centre québécois de valorisation des biomasses et des biotechnologies, #620, 2875, boul Laurier, Ste-Foy QC G1V 2M2, 418/657-3853; Fax: 418/657-7934

**Sask.:** Saskatchewan Research Council, 15 Innovation Blvd., Saskatoon SK S7N 2X8, 306/933-5400; Fax: 306/933-7446

**BIRDS *See* WILDLIFE RESOURCES**

**BIRTH CERTIFICATES *See* VITAL STATISTICS**

**BOATS *See* LEISURE CRAFT & VEHICLE REGULATIONS**

## BROADCASTING

Canadian Broadcasting Corporation, 250 Lanark Ave., PO Box 3220, Stn C, Ottawa ON K1Y 1E4, 613/724-1200; TDD: 613/724-5173

Canadian Heritage, Broadcasting, Jules Léger Bldg., 25 Eddy St., Hull QC K1A 1K5, 819/997-7449; Fax: 819/947-9730

Canadian Radio-Television & Telecommunications Commission, 1, Promenade du Portage, Terrasses de la Chaudière, Hull QC J8X 4B1, 819/997-0313 (Public Affairs); Fax: 819/994-0218

House of Commons, Canada, Broadcasting Service, House of Commons, 111 Wellington St., PO Box 1103, Ottawa ON K1A 0A9, 613/995-3490

Industry Canada, Radio Communications & Broadcast Research, 3701 Carling Ave., PO Box 11490, Stn H, Ottawa ON K2H 8S2, 613/998-2332; Fax: 613/990-7986

**Ont.:** TV Ontario, 2180 Yonge St., 5th Fl., Toronto ON M4S 2C1, 416/484-2600; Fax: 416/484-4234

**Qué.:** Ministère de la Culture et des Communications, Inforoutes et multimédia, 225, Grand-Allée est, Québec QC G1R 5G5, 418/643-8096; Fax: 418/528-0874

Recherche, 225, Grand-Allée est, Québec QC G1R 5G5, 418/643-8824; Fax: 418/643-6214

Régie des télécommunications du Québec, #5.00, 900 place d'Youville, Québec QC G1R 3P7, 418/643-5560; Fax: 418/643-2960

Société de télédiffusion du Québec, 1000, rue Fullum, Montréal QC H2K 3L7, 514/521-2424; Toll Free: 1-800-361-4301; Fax: 514/873-7739

**Sask.:** Legislative Assembly, Broadcast Services, c/o Clerk's Office, #239, Legislative Bldg., 2405 Legislative Dr., Regina SK S4S 0B3, 306/787-2181; Fax: 306/787-0408

Saskatchewan Communications Network, North Block, 2440 Broad St., Regina SK S4P 3V7, 306/787-0490; Fax: 306/787-0496

**BUSINESS ASSISTANCE *See* INDUSTRY**

## BUSINESS DEVELOPMENT

***See Also* Industry; Science, Technology Development**

Agriculture & Agri-Food Canada, Market & Industry Services Branch, Sir John Carling Bldg., 930 Carling Ave., Ottawa ON K1A 0C5, 613/759-7561; Fax: 613/759-7497

Atlantic Canada Opportunities Agency, 644 Main St., 3rd Fl., PO Box 6051, Moncton NB E1C 9J8, 506/851-2271; Toll Free: 1-800-561-7862, TDD: 506/851-3540; Fax: 506/851-7403

Business Development Bank of Canada, #400, 5, Place Ville Marie, Montréal QC H3B 5E7, 514/283-5904; Toll Free: 1-888-463-6232; Fax: 514/283-0617

Canadian Commercial Corporation, Metropolitan Centre, #1100, 50 O'Connor St., Ottawa ON K1A 0S6, 613/996-0034; Fax: 613/995-2121

Export Development Corporation, 151 O'Connor St., Ottawa ON K1A 1K3, 613/598-2500; Fax: 613/237-2690

Federal Office of Regional Development (Québec), Tour de la Bourse, #3800, 800, Place Victoria, CP 247, Montréal QC H4Z 1E8, 514/283-6412; Toll Free: 1-800-322-4636; Fax: 514/283-3302

Industry Canada, C.D. Howe Bldg., 235 Queen St., Ottawa ON K1A 0H5, 613/941-0222; Fax: 613/954-6436

Aboriginal Business Canada, 235 Queen St., Ottawa ON K1A 0H5, 613/941-0222; Fax: 613/954-6436

National Secretariat, Canadian Business Service Centres, 235 Queen St., Ottawa ON K1A 0H5, 613/954-3576; Fax: 613/954-5463

National Research Council Canada, Industrial Research Assistance Program, Bldg. M-58, 1200 Montreal Rd., Ottawa ON K1A 0R6, 613/993-0695; Fax: 613/952-7928

Public Works & Government Services Canada, Supply Operations Service Branch, Place du Portage, Phase III, 11, rue Laurier, Hull QC K1A 0S5, 819/956-3115

Statistics Canada, Business & Trade Statistics, R.H. Coats Bldg., Tunney's Pasture, 120 Parkdale Ave., Ottawa ON K1A 0T6, 613/951-8116; Fax: 613/951-0581

Treasury Board of Canada, Office of Infrastructure, West Tower, 300 Laurier Ave. West, 3rd Fl., Ottawa ON K1A 0R5, 613/952-3171; Fax: 613/952-7979

Western Economic Diversification Canada, Canada Place, #1500, 9700 Jasper Ave., Edmonton AB T5J 4H7, 403/495-4164; Toll Free: 1-888-338-9378; Fax: 403/495-6223

**Alta:** Alberta Economic Development Authority, Commerce Place, 10155 - 102 St., 6th Fl., Edmonton AB T5J 4L6, 403/427-2251; Fax: 403/427-5922

Alberta Opportunity Company, 5110 - 49 Ave., PO Box 4040, Ponoka AB T4J 1R5, 403/783-7011; Toll Free: 1-800-661-3811; Fax: 403/783-7032

Alberta Economic Development & Tourism, Commerce Place, 10155 - 102 St., Edmonton AB T5J 4L6, 403/427-2280

Tourism, Trade & Investment, Commerce Place, 10155 - 102 St., Edmonton AB T5J 4L6, 403/427-2280; Fax: 403/427-1700

Northern Alberta Development Council, #206, Provincial Bldg., 9621 - 96 Ave., PO Bag 900-14, Peace River AB T8S 1T4, 403/624-6274; Fax: 403/624-6184

Sustainable Development Coordinating Council, South Petroleum Plaza, 9915 - 108 St., 10th Floor, Edmonton AB T5K 2G8, 403/427-6236; Fax: 403/422-6305

**B.C.:** Information, Science & Technology Agency, 563 Superior St., 3rd Fl., PO Box 9441, Victoria BC V8V 1X4, 250/387-0811; Fax: 250/356-9287

Ministry of Employment & Investment, British Columbia Trade & Investment Office, #730, 999 Canada Place, Vancouver BC V6C 3E1, 250/356-8702; Fax: 604/660-4048

Ministry of Small Business, Tourism & Culture, Business Equity Branch, 1405 Douglas St., Victoria BC V8W 3C1, 250/387-0225, 844-1823 (Vancouver); Fax: 250/387-1080

Premiers' Advisory Council on Science & Technology, #501, 168 Chadwick Ct., North Vancouver BC V7M 3L4, 604/987-8477; Fax: 604/987-5617

**Man.:** Economic Development Board Secretariat, #648, 155 Carlton St., Winnipeg MB R3C 3H8, 204/945-8221; Fax: 204/945-8229

Manitoba Development Corporation, #555, 155 Carlton St., Winnipeg MB R3C 3H8, 204/945-7626; Fax: 204/957-1793

Manitoba Industry, Trade & Tourism, 155 Carlton St., 6th Fl., Winnipeg MB R3C 3H8, 204/945-2066; Fax: 204/945-1354

Tourism & Business Development, 155 Carlton St., 6th Fl., Winnipeg MB R3C 3H8, 204/945-7731; Fax: 204/945-2804

**N.B.:** Canada/New Brunswick Business Service Centre, 570 Queen St., Fredericton NB E3B 6Z6, 506/444-6158; Toll Free: 1-800-668-1010

Department of Economic Development & Tourism, Centennial Bldg., 670 King St., 5th Fl., PO Box 6000, Fredericton NB E3B 5H1, 506/453-2850 (Communications & Promotion); Fax: 506/444-4586

Small Business Directorate, Centennial Bldg., 670 King St., 5th Fl., PO Box 6000, Fredericton NB E3B 5H1, 506/453-3890; Fax: 506/444-4182

New Brunswick Industrial Development Board, PO Box 6000, Fredericton NB E3B 5H1, 506/453-2474; Fax: 506/453-7904

Regional Development Corporation, 836 Churchill Row, PO Box 428, Fredericton NB E3B 5R4, 506/453-2277; Fax: 506/453-7988

**Nfld.:** Department of Industry, Trade & Technology, Business Development, Confederation Annex, 4th Fl., PO Box 8700, St. John's NF A1B 4J6, 709/729-5600; Fax: 709/729-5936

**NWT:** Northwest Territories Business Credit Corporation, Northern United Place, 5004 - 54 St., PO Box 1320, Yellowknife NT X1A 2L9, 867/920-6454; Fax: 867/873-0308

Northwest Territories Development Corporation, Tower 7, PO Box 1437, Yellowknife NT X1A 2P1, 867/920-7700; Fax: 867/920-7701

**N.S.:** Department of Business & Consumer Services, South Maritime Centre, #8, 1505 Barrington St., Halifax NS B3J 2X1, 902/424-7777; Fax: 902/424-7434

Nova Scotia Business Development Corporation, World Trade & Convention Centre, 1800 Argyle St., 6th Fl., Halifax NS B3J 2R7, 902/424-6488; Fax: 902/424-6823

Nova Scotia Innovation Corporation, Woodside Industrial Park, 101 Research Dr., PO Box 790, Dartmouth NS B2Y 3Z7, 902/424-8670; Toll Free: 1-800-565-7051; Fax: 902/424-8679

Nova Scotia Economic Renewal Agency, 1800 Argyle St., PO Box 519, Halifax NS B3J 2R7, 902/424-8920; Fax: 902/424-0582

**Ont.:** Innovation Ontario Corporation, 56 Wellesley St. West, 7th Fl., Toronto ON M7A 2E7, 416/326-1164; Fax: 416/326-1109

Ministry of Agriculture, Food & Rural Affairs, Farm Business Management & Western Region, Communications Branch, 1 Stone Rd. West, Guelph ON N1G 4Y2, 416/767-3151; Fax: 416/837-3049

Ministry of Consumer & Commercial Relations, Business Division, 250 Yonge St., Toronto ON M5B 2N5, 416/326-8575; Fax: 416/325-6192

Ministry of Economic Development, Trade & Tourism, Hearst Block, 900 Bay St., Toronto ON M7A 2E1, 416/325-6666; Fax: 416/325-6688

Business Development & Tourism Division, Hearst Block, 900 Bay St., Toronto ON M7A 2E1, 416/325-6666; Fax: 416/325-6688

Ontario Development Corporation, 56 Wellesley St. West, 6th Fl., Toronto ON M7A 2E7, 416/326-1070; Fax: 416/326-1073

**PEI:** Department of Economic Development & Tourism, Shaw Bldg., 95 Rochford St., 5th Fl., PO Box 2000, Charlottetown PE C1A 7N8, 902/368-4476; Fax: 902/368-4242

Business Support Programs, Holman Bldg., 25 University Ave., 3rd & 4th Fls., PO Box 910, Charlottetown PE C1A 7L9, 902/368-6300; Fax: 902/368-6301

Development Division, Shaw Bldg., 95 Rochford St., 5th Fl., PO Box 2000, Charlottetown PE C1A 7N8, 902/368-4476; Fax: 902/368-4242

Enterprise PEI, Holman Bldg., 25 University Ave., 3rd & 4th Fls., PO Box 910, Charlottetown PE C1A 7L9, 902/368-6300; Toll Free: 1-800-563-3734; Fax: 902/368-6301

**Qué.:** Ministère de l'Industrie, du commerce, de la Science et de la technologie, 710, Place d'Youville, 9e étage, Québec QC G1R 4Y4, 418/691-5950 (Renseignements); Fax: 418/644-0118

**Sask.:** Saskatchewan Development Fund Corporation, #300, 2400 College Ave., Regina SK S4P 1C8, 306/787-1645; Fax: 306/787-8125

Saskatchewan Opportunities Corporation, Grenfell Tower, 1945 Hamilton St., 6th Fl., Regina SK S4P 3V7, 306/787-8595; Fax: 306/787-8515

Saskatchewan Economic & Co-operative Development, 1919 Saskatchewan Dr., Regina SK S4P 3V7, 306/787-2232

**Yuk.:** Business Development Advisory Board, PO Box 2703, Whitehorse YT Y1A 2C6, 867/667-5470

Yukon Economic Development, 211 Main St., PO Box 2703, Whitehorse YT Y1A 2C6, 867/667-5466; Fax: 867/668-8601

Economic Development, 211 Main St., PO Box 2703, Whitehorse YT Y1A 2C6, 867/667-3013; Fax: 867/668-8601

## BUSINESS REGULATIONS

Industry Canada, C.D. Howe Bldg., 235 Queen St., Ottawa ON K1A 0H5, 613/941-0222; Fax: 613/954-6436

Revenue Canada, 875 Heron Rd., Ottawa ON K1A 0L8, 613/952-0384

Sherbrooke, 50, Place de la Cité, CP 1300, Sherbrooke QC J1H 5L8, 819/564-5888

**Alta:** Alberta Economic Development & Tourism, Business Finance, Commerce Place, 10155 - 102 St., Edmonton AB T5J 4L6, 403/427-3300; Fax: 403/422-9319

Alberta Municipal Affairs, Registries Division, John E. Brownlee Bldg., 10365 - 97 St., Edmonton AB T5J 3W7, 403/422-2362 (Edmonton), 403/297-8980 (Calgary); Toll Free: 1-800-465-5009 (in Alberta); Fax: 403/422-9105

**B.C.:** Ministry of Finance & Corporate Relations, Registries & Ministry Support Services, 617 Government St., Victoria BC V8V 1X4, 250/387-9278

**Man.:** Manitoba Consumer & Corporate Affairs, Companies Office, #317, 450 Broadway, Winnipeg MB R3C 0V8, 204/945-4206; Fax: 204/945-1459

**N.B.:** Department of Justice, Consumer Affairs, #412, Centennial Bldg., PO Box 6000, Fredericton NB E3B 5H1, 506/453-2682; Fax: 506/444-4494

Corporate Affairs, #412, Centennial Bldg., PO Box 6000, Fredericton NB E3B 5H1, 506/453-3860; Fax: 506/453-2613

**Nfld.:** Department of Government Services & Lands, Commercial & Corporate Affairs, PO Box 8700, St. John's NF A1B 4J6

Commercial Registrations, PO Box 8700, St. John's NF A1B 4J6, 709/729-3316; Fax: 709/729-0232

**NWT:** Northwest Territories Business Credit Corporation, Northern United Place, 5004 - 54 St., PO Box 1320, Yellowknife NT X1A 2L9, 867/920-6454; Fax: 867/873-0308

Northwest Territories Development Corporation, Tower 7, PO Box 1437, Yellowknife NT X1A 2P1, 867/920-7700; Fax: 867/920-7701

**N.S.:** Department of Business & Consumer Services, South Maritime Centre, #8, 1505 Barrington St., Halifax NS B3J 2X1, 902/424-7777; Fax: 902/424-7434

**Ont.:** Ministry of Consumer & Commercial Relations, Companies Branch, 393 University Ave., 2nd Fl.,

Toronto ON M7A 2H6, 416/596-3725; Fax: 416/596-0438

Registration Division, 393 University Ave., 4th Fl., Toronto ON M7A 2H6, 416/596-3600; Fax: 416/596-3802

**PEI:** Department of Community Affairs & Attorney General, Shaw Building, 95 Rochford St., 4th Fl., PO Box 2000, Charlottetown PE C1A 7N8, 902/368-4551; Fax: 902/368-5283

Consumer, Corporate & Insurance Division, Shaw Building, 95 Rochford St., 4th Fl., PO Box 2000, Charlottetown PE C1A 7N8, 902/368-4550; Fax: 902/368-5283; 5355

Securities & Consumer, Corporate & Insurance Services, Shaw Building, 95 Rochford St., 4th Fl., PO Box 2000, Charlottetown PE C1A 7N8, 902/368-4552; Fax: 902/368-5283; 5355

**Qué.:** L'Inspecteur général des Institutions financières, 800, place D'Youville, Québec QC G1R 4Y5, 418/694-5018 (Communications); Fax: 418/643-3336

Ministère de l'Industrie, du commerce, de la Science et de la technologie, 710, Place d'Youville, 9e étage, Québec QC G1R 4Y4, 418/691-5950 (Renseignements); Fax: 418/644-0118

**Sask.:** Saskatchewan Economic & Co-operative Development, Programs & Corporate Services Division, 1919 Saskatchewan Dr., Regina SK S4P 3V7, 306/787-2232

Saskatchewan Justice, Consumer Protection Branch, 1874 Scarth St., Regina SK S4P 3V7, 306/787-2952; Fax: 306/787-5550

Corporations Branch, 1874 Scarth St., Regina SK S4P 3V7, 306/787-2970; Fax: 306/787-8999

**Yuk.:** Yukon Economic Development, Strategic Management/Industry Trade & Investment, 211 Main St., PO Box 2703, Whitehorse YT Y1A 2C6, 867/667-5466; Fax: 867/668-8601

Yukon Justice, Consumer Services, PO Box 2703, Whitehorse YT Y1A 2C6, 867/667-5257; Fax: 867/393-6272

## CABINETS & EXECUTIVE COUNCILS

***See Also* Government (General Information); Parliament**

The Canadian Ministry, c/o Public Information Office, Library of Parliament, House of Commons, 111 Wellington St., Ottawa ON K1A 0A9, 613/992-4793; Fax: 613/992-1273

**Alta:** Executive Council, Legislature Bldg., 10800 - 97 Ave., Edmonton AB T5K 2B6, 403/427-2251; Fax: 403/427-1349

**B.C.:** , #156, Parliament Bldgs., 1150 McKenzie Ave., Victoria BC V8V 1X4

**Man.:** , Legislative Bldg., 450 Broadway, Winnipeg MB R3C 0V8

**N.B.:** , Centennial Bldg., PO Box 6000, Fredericton NB E3B 5H1

**Nfld.:** , Confederation Bldg., PO Box 8700, St. John's NF A1B 4J6, 709/729-5645

**NWT:** , PO Box 1320, Yellowknife NT X1A 2L9

**N.S.:** , One Government Place, PO Box 2125, Halifax NS B3J 3B7, 902/424-5970; Fax: 902/424-0667

**Ont.:** , Whitney Block, Queen's Park, 99 Wellesley St. West, 6th Fl., Toronto ON M7A 1A1, 416/325-7641

**PEI:** , Shaw Bldg., PO Box 2000, Charlottetown PE C1A 7N8

**Qué.:** Conseil exécutif, Hôtel du Parlement, Québec QC G1A 1A4

**Sask.:** Executive Council, Legislative Bldg., 2405 Legislative Dr., Regina SK S4S 0B3

**Yuk.:** , PO Box 2703, Whitehorse YT Y1A 2C6, 867/667-5812; Fax: 867/667-8424

**CANADA PENSION PLAN *See* PENSIONS**

## CAREER PLANNING

**Alta:** Alberta Advanced Education & Career Development, Learning Support & Accountability Division, Commerce Place, 10155 - 102 St., 11th Fl., Edmonton AB T5J 4L5, 403/422-4488; Fax: 403/422-5126

**B.C.:** Ministry of Education, Skills & Training, Career Programs Branch, PO Box 9150, Stn Prov Govt, Victoria BC V8W 9H1, 250/387-7044; Fax: 250/387-1418

Skills Development Division, PO Box 9150, Stn Prov Govt, Victoria BC V8W 9H1, 250/356-2500; Fax: 250/356-5945

**Man.:** Manitoba Education & Training, Workforce 2000 & Youth Programs, 185 Carlton St., 4th Fl., Winnipeg MB R3C 3J1, 204/945-6195; Fax: 204/945-1792

**N.B.:** Department of Advanced Education & Labour, Learning in the Workplace Initiative, Chestnut Complex, 470 York St., PO Box 6000, Fredericton NB E3B 5H1, 506/444-4331; Fax: 506/453-3300

Student Services, Chestnut Complex, 470 York St., PO Box 6000, Fredericton NB E3B 5H1, 506/453-3358; Fax: 506/444-4333

**Nfld.:** Department of Education, Advanced Studies Branch, Confederation Bldg., PO Box 8700, St. John's NF A1B 4J6, 709/729-5097; Fax: 709/729-5896

**NWT:** Department of Education, Culture & Employment, Career Development, PO Box 1320, Yellowknife NT X1A 2L9, 867/873-7146; Fax: 867/873-0155

**N.S.:** Department of Education & Culture, Student Services Division, 2021 Brunswick St., PO Box 578, Halifax NS B3J 2S9, 902/424-7454; Fax: 902/424-0749

**Ont.:** Ministry of Education & Training, Training Division, Mowat Block, 900 Bay St., Toronto ON M7A 1L2, 416/325-2929; Fax: 416/325-2934

**Sask.:** Saskatchewan Post-Secondary Education & Skills Training, 2220 College Ave., Regina SK S4P 3V7, 306/787-2010

**Yuk.:** Yukon Education, Training Programs, PO Box 2703, Whitehorse YT Y1A 2C6, 867/667-5140; Fax: 867/667-8555

## CENSORSHIP (MEDIA)

Canadian Heritage, Arts Policy, Jules Léger Bldg., 25 Eddy St., Hull QC K1A 1K5, 819/994-9529; Fax: 819/994-6249

**Alta:** Alberta Community Development, Film Classification Board, Standard Life Centre, 10405 Jasper Ave., 7th Fl., Edmonton AB T5J 4R7, 403/427-2006; Fax: 403/427-1496

**B.C.:** Motion Picture Appeal Board, #310, 435 Columbia St., New Westminster BC V3L 5N8, 604/660-8789; Fax: 604/660-8809

**Man.:** Film Classification Board (& Film Classification Appeal Board), #216, 301 Weston St., Winnipeg MB R3E 3H4, 204/945-8962; Fax: 204/945-0890

**N.B.:** New Brunswick Film Classification Board, c/o Dept. of Municipalities, Culture & Housing, 20 McGloin St., PO Box 6000, Fredericton NB E3B 5H1, 506/454-5475

**Ont.:** Ministry of Consumer & Commercial Relations, Entertainment Standards, 1075 Millwood Rd., Toronto ON M4G 1X6, 416/314-3626; Fax: 416/314-3632

Ontario Film Review Board, 1075 Millwood Rd., Toronto ON M4G 1X6, 416/314-3626

**Qué.:** Régie du Cinéma, 455, rue Ste-Hélène, Montréal QC H2Y 2L3, 514/873-2491; Fax: 514/873-8874

**Sask.:** Saskatchewan Film Classification Appeal Commission, 1871 Smith St., Regina SK S4P 3V7, 306/787-5884; Fax: 306/787-9779

Saskatchewan Film Classification Board, 1871 Smith St., Regina SK S4P 3V7, 306/787-5884; Fax: 306/787-9779

**CHEMICAL RELEASES *See* EMERGENCY RESPONSE**

## CHEMICALS

Environment Canada, Toxics Pollution Prevention Directorate, Place Vincent-Massey, 351, boul St-Joseph, Hull QC K1A 0H3, 819/953-1114; Fax: 819/953-5371

Industrial Materials Institute, 75, boul de Montagne, Boucherville QC J4B 6Y4, 514/641-5050; Fax: 514/641-5101

Industry Canada, Bio-Industries, C.D. Howe Bldg., 235 Queen St., Ottawa ON K1A 0H5, 613/954-3071; Fax: 613/952-4209

Institute for Chemical Process & Environmental Technology, 1500 Montreal Rd., Ottawa ON K1A 0R6, 613/993-4041; Fax: 613/957-8231

**Alta:** Alberta Environmental Protection, Environmental Regulatory Service, 9915 - 108 St., Edmonton AB T5K 2G8, 403/427-2739, 944-0313 (Information Centre)

**B.C.:** Ministry of Environment, Lands & Parks, Industrial Waste & Hazardous Contaminants Branch, 777 Broughton St., Victoria BC V8V 1X4, 250/387-9992; Fax: 250/387-9935

**Man.:** Manitoba Industry, Trade & Tourism, Industry Development, 155 Carlton St., 6th Fl., Winnipeg MB R3C 3H8, 204/945-7206; Fax: 204/945-3977

**N.B.:** New Brunswick Pesticides Advisory Council, c/o Department of the Environment, PO Box 6000, Fredericton NB E3B 5H1, 506/457-4848; Fax: 506/453-2893

New Brunswick Research & Productivity Council, Chemical & Biotechnical Services, 921 College Hill Rd., Fredericton NB E3B 6Z9, 506/452-1369; Fax: 506/452-1395

**Nfld.:** Department of Environment & Labour, Environment Branch, Confederation Bldg., PO Box 8700, St. John's NF A1B 4J6; Fax: 709/729-1930

**NWT:** Department of Resources, Wildlife & Economic Development, Environmental Protection, PO Box 1320, Yellowknife NT X1A 2L9, 867/873-7654; Fax: 867/873-0221

**N.S.:** Department of the Environment, Industrial Pollution Control Branch, 5151 Terminal Rd., 5th Fl., PO Box 2107, Halifax NS B3J 3B7, 902/424-2284; Fax: 902/424-0503

Pesticide Management Branch, 5151 Terminal Rd., 5th Fl., PO Box 2107, Halifax NS B3J 3B7, 902/424-2541; Fax: 902/424-0503

**Ont.:** Ministry of Environment & Energy, Environmental Sciences & Standards Division, 135 St. Clair Ave. West, Toronto ON M4V 1P5, 416/323-4512; Fax: 416/323-4396

**PEI:** Department of Agriculture & Forestry, Research, Resources & Laboratories, PO Box 306, Kensington PE C0B 1M0, 902/368-5646; Fax: 902/368-5661

Department of Fisheries & Environment, Environmental Protection Division, Jones Bldg., 11 Kent St., 4th Fl., PO Box 2000, Charlottetown PE CIA 7N8, 902/368-5024; Fax: 902/368-5830

**Qué.:** Ministère de l'Environnement et de la Faune, Édifice Marie-Guyart, 675, boul René-Lévesque est, Québec QC G1R 5V7, 418/643-3127; Toll Free: 1-800-561-1616; Fax: 418/646-5974

**Yuk.:** Yukon Renewable Resources, Environment Protection & Assessment Branch, PO Box 2703, Whitehorse YT Y1A 2C6, 867/667-5237; Fax: 867/393-6213

## CHILD WELFARE

***See Also* Day Care Services**

Justice Canada, Family, Children & Youth Section, Justice Bldg., 239 Wellington St., Ottawa ON K1A 0H8, 613/941-2339; Fax: 613/954-0811

**Alta:** Alberta Family & Social Services, Children's Services, Seventh St. Plaza, 10030 - 107 St., Edmonton AB T5J 3E4, 403/427-2734; Fax: 403/422-9044

Children's Services Division, Seventh St. Plaza, 10030 - 107 St., Edmonton AB T5J 3E4, 403/427-2734; Fax: 403/422-9044

Office of the Commissioner of Services for Children & Families, c/o Alberta Family & Social Services, Seventh St. Plaza, 10030 - 107 St., Edmonton AB T5J 3E4, 403/422-5011; Fax: 403/422-5036

**B.C.:** Ministry of Children & Families, Child, Family & Community Service, 1022 Government St., 3rd Fl., Victoria BC V8V 1X4, 250/356-3004; Fax: 250/356-3007 (Communications)

Children with Special Needs, 1022 Government St., 3rd Fl., Victoria BC V8V 1X4, 250/387-1275; Fax: 250/356-6534

**Man.:** Manitoba Family Services, #219, 114 Garry St., Winnipeg MB R3C 4V6, 204/945-2324 (Policy & Planning); Fax: 204/945-2156

Children's Special Services, #219, 114 Garry St., Winnipeg MB R3C 4V6, 204/945-3251; Fax: 204/945-2669

**N.B.:** Department of Health & Community Services, Family & Community Social Services Division, PO Box 5100, Fredericton NB E3B 5G8, 506/453-2536; Fax: 506/444-4697

Youth Council of New Brunswick, 736 King St., PO Box 6000, Fredericton NB E3B 5H1, 506/453-3271; Fax: 506/444-4413

**Nfld.:** Department of Human Resources & Employment, Child Welfare & Community Corrections, Confederation Bldg., PO Box 8700, St. John's NF A1B 4J6, 709/729-2668; Fax: 709/729-6996

**NWT:** Department of Health & Social Services, Family Support & Child Protection, Centre Square Tower, 8th Fl., PO Box 1320, Yellowknife NT X1A 2L9, 867/920-6255; Fax: 867/873-0444

**N.S.:** Department of Community Services, Family & Children's Services, Johnston Bldg., 5182 Prince St., 5th Fl., PO Box 696, Halifax NS B3J 2T7, 902/424-4326; Fax: 902/424-0708

**Ont.:** Ministry of Community & Social Services, Adoption Operational Services, 2 Bloor St. West, 24th Fl., Toronto ON M7A 1E9, 416/327-4930; Fax: 416/325-5172, 5171

Child Care Branch, Hepburn Block, 4th Fl., Toronto ON M7A 1E9, 416/327-4864; Fax: 416/327-0570

Ministry of the Attorney General, Office of the Official Guardian, 393 University Ave., 14th Fl., Toronto ON M5G 1W9, 416/314-8011; Fax: 416/314-8000

**Qué.:** Ministère de la Justice, Direction du droit de la jeunesse, 1200, rte de l'Église, Ste-Foy QC G1V 4M1, 418/643-5140 (Communications); Fax: 418/646-4449

Ministère de la Santé et des services sociaux, 1075, ch Ste-Foy, Québec QC G1S 2M1

Secrétariat à la famille, #3.300, 875, Grande-Allée est, Québec QC G1R 4Y8, 418/643-6414; Fax: 418/528-2009

**Sask.:** Saskatchewan Social Services, Child Day Care Division, 1920 Broad St., Regina SK S4P 3V6, 306/787-3855; Fax: 306/787-3441

Family & Youth Services Division, 1920 Broad St., Regina SK S4P 3V6, 306/787-7010; Fax: 306/787-0925

Protection & Children's Services, 2240 Albert St., Regina SK S4P 3V7, 306/787-2928; Fax: 306/694-3842

Saskatoon Child Centre, c/o Saskatchewan Justice, 1874 Scarth St., Regina SK S4P 3V7, 306/975-8250

**Yuk.:** Yukon Health & Social Services, Family/Children's Services, PO Box 2703, Whitehorse YT Y1A 2C6, 867/667-8117; Fax: 867/668-4613

Yukon Justice, Official Guardian's Office, PO Box 2703, Whitehorse YT Y1A 2C6, 867/667-5366; Fax: 867/393-6272

Victim Services/Family Violence Prevention Unit, PO Box 2703, Whitehorse YT Y1A 2C6, 867/667-3023; Fax: 867/393-6240

## CITIZENSHIP

Citizenship & Immigration Canada, Jean Edmonds Towers, 365 Laurier Ave. West, Ottawa ON K1A 1L1, 613/954-9019; Fax: 613/954-2221

Citizenship Services, Jean Edmonds Towers, 365 Laurier Ave. West, Ottawa ON K1A 1L1, 613/941-8405; Fax: 613/941-0061

Immigration & Refugee Board, 240 Bank St., Ottawa ON K1A 0K1, 613/995-6486; Fax: 613/996-0543

**Alta:** Alberta Community Development, Community & Citizenship Services Division, Standard Life Centre, 10405 Jasper Ave., 7th Fl., Edmonton AB T5J 4R7, 403/427-6530; Fax: 403/427-1496

Alberta Human Rights & Citizenship Commission, 10405 Jasper Ave., 16th Fl., Edmonton AB T5J 4R7, 403/427-7661; Fax: 403/422-3563

**B.C.:** Ministry of the Attorney General, Multiculturalism & Immigration Branch, #309, 703 Broughton St., Victoria BC V8W 1E2, 250/387-7970; Fax: 250/356-5316

**Man.:** Manitoba Culture, Heritage & Citizenship, Citizenship Division, 213 Notre Dame., Winnipeg MB R3B 1N3, 204/945-3729

**Ont.:** Ministry of Citizenship, Culture & Recreation, Communications Branch (Citizenship), 77 Bloor St. West, 6th Fl., Toronto ON M7A 2R9, 416/325-7725; Fax: 416/314-4965

Ontario Advisory Council on Multiculturalism & Citizenship, 35 McCaul St., 3rd Fl., Toronto ON M5T 1V7, 416/314-6650 (Voice & TDD); Fax: 416/314-6658

**Qué.:** Ministère des Relations avec les citoyens et de l'Immigration, 360, rue McGill, 4e étage, Montréal QC H2Y 2E9, 514/873-9940; Fax: 514/864-2899

## CLIMATE & WEATHER

Environment Canada, Atmospheric Environment Service, 4905 Dufferin St., Downsview ON M3H 5T4, 416/739-4521; Fax: 819/953-2225

Canadian Meteorological Centre (Montréal), 4905 Dufferin St., Downsview ON M3H 5T4, 514/421-4601; Fax: 514/421-4600

Climate & Atmospheric Research Directorate, 4905 Dufferin St., Downsview ON M3H 5T4, 416/739-4995; Fax: 416/739-4265

## COAL

***See Also* Energy**

Natural Resources Canada, Coal, Ferrous & Industrial Minerals Division, 580 Booth St., Ottawa ON K1A 0E4, 613/992-2018; Fax: 613/996-9094

Earth Sciences Sector, 580 Booth St., Ottawa ON K1A 0E4, 613/995-0947; Fax: 613/996-9094

Minerals & Metals Sector, 580 Booth St., Ottawa ON K1A 0E4, 613/995-0947; Fax: 613/996-9094

**Nfld.:** Department of Mines & Energy, Energy Branch, PO Box 8700, St. John's NF A1B 4J6, 709/729-2301

**N.S.:** Department of Natural Resources, Minerals & Energy Branch, Founder's Square, 1701 Hollis St., PO Box 698, Halifax NS B3J 2T9, 902/424-5346; Fax: 902/424-7735

**Qué.:** Ministère des Ressources Naturelles, Énergie, #B-302, 5700 - 4 av ouest, 3e étage, Charlesbourg QC G1H 6R1, 418/627-8600 (Renseignements); Fax: 418/643-0701

**Yuk.:** Yukon Economic Development, Mines & Resource Development, 211 Main St., PO Box 2703, Whitehorse YT Y1A 2C6, 867/667-5466; Fax: 867/668-8601

**COMMUNICATIONS *See* TELECOMMUNICATIONS**

**COMMUNITY HEALTH *See* HEALTH SERVICES; PUBLIC SAFETY**

## COMMUNITY SERVICES

Canadian Heritage, Citizenship & Canadian Identity Sector, Jules Léger Bldg., 25 Eddy St., Hull QC K1A 1K5, 819/997-0055; Fax: 819/953-5382

**Alta:** Alberta Municipal Financing Corporation, Terrace Bldg., #403, 9515 - 107 St., Edmonton AB T5K 2C3, 403/427-9711; Fax: 403/422-2175

Alberta Community Development, Standard Life Centre, 10405 Jasper Ave., 7th Fl., Edmonton AB T5J 4R7, 403/427-6530; Fax: 403/427-1496

Northern Alberta Development Council, #206, Provincial Bldg., 9621 - 96 Ave., PO Bag 900-14, Peace River AB T8S 1T4, 403/624-6274; Fax: 403/624-6184

**B.C.:** Ministry of Children & Families, Child, Family & Community Service, 1022 Government St., 3rd Fl., Victoria BC V8V 1X4, 250/356-3004; Fax: 250/356-3007 (Communications)

Community Support Services, 1022 Government St., 3rd Fl., Victoria BC V8V 1X4, 250/356-3004; Fax: 250/356-3007 (Communications)

**Man.:** Manitoba Family Services, Community Living Division, #219, 114 Garry St., Winnipeg MB R3C 4V6, 204/945-2324 (Policy & Planning); Fax: 204/945-2156

**N.B.:** Department of Health & Community Services, Family & Community Social Services Division, PO Box 5100, Fredericton NB E3B 5G8, 506/453-2536; Fax: 506/444-4697

Department of Municipalities, Culture & Housing, Municipal Government Services, Marysville Place, 20 McGloin St., PO Box 6000, Fredericton NB E3B 5H1, 506/453-2434; Fax: 506/457-4991

**Nfld.:** Department of Health, Community Health, West Block, Confederation Bldg., PO Box 8700, St. John's NF A1B 4J6, 709/729-5021; Fax: 709/729-5824

Department of Human Resources & Employment, Confederation Bldg., PO Box 8700, St. John's NF A1B 4J6, 709/729-2478; Fax: 709/729-6996

**NWT:** Department of Health & Social Services, Community Programs & Services, Centre Square Tower, 8th Fl., PO Box 1320, Yellowknife NT X1A 2L9, 867/920-6173; Fax: 867/873-0266

Department of Municipal & Community Affairs, #600, 5201 - 50 Ave., PO Box 1310, Yellowknife NT X1A 2L9, 867/873-7118; Fax: 867/873-0309

**N.S.:** Department of Community Services, Johnston Bldg., 5182 Prince St., 5th Fl., PO Box 696, Halifax NS B3J 2T7, 902/424-4326; Fax: 902/424-0502

**Ont.:** Ministry of Community & Social Services, Hepburn Block, 80 Grosvenor St., 6th Fl., Toronto ON M7A 1E9, 416/325-5666; Fax: 416/325-5172, 5171

Ministry of Health, Population Health & Community Services System Group, Hepburn Block, 8th Fl., Queen's Park, #1400, 80 Grosvenor St., Toronto ON M7A 1S2, Toll Free: 1-800-668-2437 (AIDS Bureau); Fax: 416/327-4389

**Sask.:** Saskatchewan Municipal Government, Municipal Services Division, 1855 Victoria Ave., Regina SK S4P 3V7, 306/787-8282; Fax: 306/787-4181

Sport, Recreation & Lotteries, 1855 Victoria Ave., Regina SK S4P 3V7, 306/787-5737; Fax: 306/787-8560

Saskatchewan Social Services, 1920 Broad St., Regina SK S4P 3V6, 306/787-3494; Fax: 306/787-1032

**Yuk.:** Yukon Community & Transportation Services, Community Services Branch, PO Box 2703, Whitehorse YT Y1A 2C6, 867/667-5299; Fax: 867/393-6404

## COMPENSATION *See* CRIMES COMPENSATION

## CONFLICT OF INTEREST

Industry Canada, Office of the Ethics Counsellor, 66 Slater St., 22nd Fl., Ottawa ON K1A 0C9, 613/995-0721; Fax: 613/995-7308

**Alta:** Alberta Office of the Ethics Commissioner, #410, 9925 - 109 St., Edmonton AB T5K 2J8, 403/422-2273; Fax: 403/422-2261

**B.C.:** Office of the Conflict of Interest Commissioner, #101, 431 Menzies St., Victoria BC V8V 1X4, 250/356-9283; Fax: 250/356-6580

**Ont.:** Office of the Integrity Commissioner, #1301, 101 Bloor St. West, Toronto ON M5S 2Z7, 416/314-8983; Fax: 416/314-8987

**Sask.:** Saskatchewan Justice, 1874 Scarth St., Regina SK S4P 3V7, 306/787-7872 (Communications); Fax: 306/787-3874

## CONSERVATION

### *See Also* Heritage Resources; Natural Resources

Auditor General of Canada, Environment & Sustainable Development, 240 Sparks St., Ottawa ON K1A 0G6, 613/995-3708; Fax: 613/957-4023

Canadian Heritage, Heritage, Jules Léger Bldg., 25 Eddy St., Hull QC K1A 1K5, 819/997-7782; Fax: 819/997-8392

Environment Canada, Environmental Conservation Service, Place Vincent-Massey, 351, boul St-Joseph, Hull QC K1A 0H3, 819/997-2800; Fax: 819/953-2225

Fisheries & Oceans Canada, Conservation & Protection, 200 Kent St., Ottawa ON K1A 0E6, 613/990-6012

Fisheries Resource Conservation Council, PO Box 2001, Stn D, Ottawa ON K1A 5W3

North American Wetlands Conservation Council (Canada), #200, 1750 Courtwood Cres., Ottawa ON K2C 2B5, 613/228-2601; Fax: 613/228-0206

**Alta:** Alberta Community Development, Cultural Facilities & Historical Resources Division, Old St. Stephen's College, 8820 - 112 St., Edmonton AB T6G 2P8, 403/431-2300; Fax: 403/427-5598

Alberta Environmental Protection, Land & Forest Service, 9915 - 108 St., Edmonton AB T5K 2G8, 403/427-2739, 944-0313 (Information Centre)

Natural Resources Service, 9915 - 108 St., Edmonton AB T5K 2G8, 403/427-2739, 944-0313 (Information Centre)

Natural Resources Conservation Board, Pacific Plaza, 10909 Jasper Ave., Edmonton AB T5J 2L9, 403/422-1977

Sustainable Development Coordinating Council, South Petroleum Plaza, 9915 - 108 St., 10th Floor, Edmonton AB T5K 2G8, 403/427-6236; Fax: 403/422-6305

**B.C.:** Ministry of Environment, Lands & Parks, 810 Blanshard St., Victoria BC V8V 1X5, 250/387-9419; Fax: 250/356-6464

Ministry of Forests, PO Box 9517, Stn Prov Govt, Victoria BC V8W 9C2, 250/387-5255; Fax: 250/387-8485

**Man.:** Ecological Reserves Advisory Committee, PO Box 355, Stn St. Vital, Winnipeg MB R2M 5C8, 204/942-6617

Endangered Species Advisory Committee, 200 Saulteaux Cr., PO Box 80, Winnipeg MB R3J 3W3, 204/945-6829

Manitoba Natural Resources, Resources Division, 200 Saulteaux Cres., PO Box 20, Winnipeg MB R3J 3W3, 204/945-4071; Fax: 204/945-3586

Manitoba Rural Development, Manitoba Conservation Districts Commission, Legislative Bldg., #309, 450 Broadway Ave., Winnipeg MB R3C 0V8, 204/945-7496; Fax: 204/945-5059

**N.B.:** Department of Natural Resources & Energy, Regional Support Services, PO Box 6000, Fredericton NB E3B 5H1, 506/453-2488; Fax: 506/453-2412

**Nfld.:** Department of Fisheries & Aquaculture, Licensing & Administration, Fisheries Bldg., 30 Strawberry Marsh Rd., PO Box 8700, St. John's NF A1B 4J6, 709/729-3723; Fax: 709/729-0360

**NWT:** Department of Resources, Wildlife & Economic Development, Environmental Protection, PO Box 1320, Yellowknife NT X1A 2L9, 867/873-7654; Fax: 867/873-0221

**N.S.:** Department of Natural Resources, Renewable Resources Branch, Founder's Square, 1701 Hollis St., PO Box 698, Halifax NS B3J 2T9, 902/424-5935; Fax: 902/424-7735

**Ont.:** Conservation Review Board, 77 Bloor St. West, 2nd Fl., Toronto ON M7A 2R9, 416/314-7125; Fax: 416/314-7175

Ministry of Environment & Energy, Conservation & Prevention Division, 135 St. Clair Ave. West, Toronto ON M4V 1P5, 416/323-4320; Fax: 416/323-4481

Ministry of Natural Resources, Water Management & Conservation Authorities, Whitney Block, #6540, 99 Wellesley St. West, Toronto ON M7A 1W3, 416/314-1977; Fax: 416/314-1995

**PEI:** Department of Fisheries & Environment, Conservation, Jones Bldg., 11 Kent St., 4th Fl., PO Box 2000, Charlottetown PE CIA 7N8, 902/368-4808; Fax: 902/368-5830

**Sask.:** Saskatchewan Conservation Data Centre, #326, 3211 Albert St., Regina SK S4S 5W6, 306/787-5021; Fax: 306/787-1349

Saskatchewan Wetland Conservation Corporation, #202, 2050 Cornwall St., Regina SK S4P 2K5, 306/787-0726; Fax: 306/787-0780

**Yuk.:** Yukon Renewable Resources, Environment Protection & Assessment Branch, PO Box 2703, Whitehorse YT Y1A 2C6, 867/667-5237; Fax: 867/393-6213

## CONSTITUTION

### *See Also* Federal-Provincial Affairs

Justice Canada, Communications & Executive Services Branch, Justice Bldg., 239 Wellington St., Ottawa ON K1A 0H8, 613/957-4222; Fax: 613/954-0811

National Archives of Canada, 395 Wellington St., Ottawa ON K1A 0N3, 613/995-5138; Fax: 613/995-6274

**Alta:** Alberta Federal & Intergovernmental Affairs, Federalism Constitution Team, Commerce Place, 10155 - 102 St., Edmonton AB T5J 4G8, 403/422-2300; Fax: 403/427-0939

**Ont.:** Ministry of Intergovernmental Affairs, 900 Bay St., 6th Fl., Toronto ON M7A 1C2, 416/325-4760 (Communications); Fax: 416/325-4759

**Sask.:** Saskatchewan Intergovernmental Affairs, Constitutional Relations, 1919 Saskatchewan Dr., Regina SK S4P 3V7, 306/787-8006; Fax: 306/787-1987

Saskatchewan Justice, Constitutional Law Branch, 1874 Scarth St., Regina SK S4P 3V7, 306/787-8385; Fax: 306/787-9111

## CONSTRUCTION

Canada Mortgage & Housing Corporation, 700 Montreal Rd., Ottawa ON K1A 0P7, 613/748-2000; Toll Free: 1-800-668-2642; Fax: 613/748-2098

Defence Construction Canada, Place de Ville, Tower B, 112 Kent St., 17th Fl., Ottawa ON K1A 0K3, 613/998-9548; Fax: 613/998-1061

Industry Canada, Service Industries & Capital Projects, C.D. Howe Bldg., 235 Queen St., Ottawa ON K1A 0H5, 613/954-2990; Fax: 613/952-9054

Institute for Research in Construction, 1500 Montreal Rd., Ottawa ON K1A 0R6, 613/993-3772; Fax: 613/941-0822

Treasury Board of Canada, Office of Infrastructure, West Tower, 300 Laurier Ave. West, 3rd Fl., Ottawa ON K1A 0R5, 613/952-3171; Fax: 613/952-7979

**Alta:** Alberta Transportation & Utilities, Contracts & Compliance, Twin Atria, 4999 - 98 Ave., Edmonton AB T6B 2X3, 403/427-2731; Fax: 403/422-2822

**B.C.:** Ministry of Municipal Affairs & Housing, Safety & Standards Department, Municipal Affairs, PO Box 9490, Victoria BC V8W 9N7, 250/387-4089; Fax: 250/356-1070

Ministry of Transportation & Highways, Planning & Major Projects Department, 940 Blanshard St., Victoria BC V8W 3E6, 250/387-3198; Fax: 250/387-6431

**Man.:** Manitoba Highways & Transportation, Construction & Maintenance Division, 215 Garry St., 16th Fl., Winnipeg MB R3C 3Z1, 204/945-3888; Fax: 204/945-3841

Manitoba Rural Development, Infrastructure Services (Manitoba Water Services Board), 2022 Currie Blvd., PO Box 22080, Brandon MB R7A 6Y9, 204/726-6073; Fax: 204/726-6290

**N.B.:** Department of Transportation, Construction, King Tower, Kings Pl., 2nd Fl., PO Box 6000, Fredericton NB E3B 5H1, 506/453-2673

New Brunswick, Buildings Group, PO Box 6000, Fredericton NB E3B 5H1, 506/453-3742; Fax: 506/444-4400

**Nfld.:** Department of Works, Services & Transportation, Confederation Bldg., PO Box 8700, St. John's NF A1B 4J6, 709/729-3676; Fax: 709/729-4285

Highway Design & Construction, Confederation Bldg., PO Box 8700, St. John's NF A1B 4J6, 709/729-3796; Fax: 709/729-4285

**NWT:** Department of Public Works & Services, Project Management Division, Bldg. YK, 7th Fl., PO Box 1320, Yellowknife NT X1A 2L9, 867/873-7829; Fax: 867/873-0264

Department of Transportation, Lahm Ridge Bldg., PO Box 1320, Yellowknife NT X1A 2L9, 867/920-3460; Fax: 867/873-0363

**N.S.:** Construction Industry Panel, PO Box 697, Halifax NS B3J 2T8, 902/424-6730; Fax: 902/424-3239

**Ont.:** Ministry of Municipal Affairs & Housing, Municipal Operations Divsion, 777 Bay St., 17th Fl., Toronto ON M5G 2E5, 416/585-7041 (Communications Branch); Fax: 416/585-6227

Ministry of Transportation, Quality & Standards Division, 301 St. Paul St., St. Catharines ON L2R 1W6

**PEI:** Department of Community Affairs & Attorney General, Inspection Services, PO Box 2000, Charlottetown PE C1A 7N8, 902/368-4884; Fax: 902/368-5544

Department of Transportation & Public Works, Buildings Division, Jones Bldg., PO Box 2000, Charlottetown PE C1A 7N8, 902/368-5100; Fax: 902/368-5395

**Qué.:** Ministère des Transports, Planification et technologie, 700, boul René-Lévesque est, 28e étage, Québec QC G1R 5H1, 418/528-0808; Fax: 418/643-9836

Régie du bâtiment du Québec, 545, boul Crémazie est, Montréal QC H2M 2V2, 514/873-0976; Toll Free: 1-800-361-0761; Fax: 514/873-7667

**Sask.:** Saskatchewan Municipal Government, Building Standards Branch, 1855 Victoria Ave., Regina SK S4P 3V7, 306/787-4517; Fax: 306/787-9273

**Yuk.:** Yukon Community & Transportation Services, Engineering & Development, PO Box 2703, Whitehorse YT Y1A 2C6, 867/667-5707; Fax: 867/393-6216

Transportation Engineering, PO Box 2703, Whitehorse YT Y1A 2C6, 867/633-7928; Fax: 867/393-6447

Yukon Housing Corporation, Program Administration, 410A Jarvis St., PO Box 2703, Whitehorse YT Y1A 2C6, 867/667-3549; Fax: 867/667-3664

## CONSUMER PROTECTION

### *See Also* Public Safety

Health Canada, Health Protection Branch, Brooke Claxton Bldg., Tunney's Pasture, 120 Parkdale Ave., Ottawa ON K1A 0K9, 613/957-2991; Fax: 613/941-5366

Industry Canada, Office of Consumer Affairs, C.D. Howe Bldg., 235 Queen St., Ottawa ON K1A 0H5, 613/941-0222; Fax: 613/954-6436

**B.C.:** Ministry of the Attorney General, Consumer Service Division, 1019 Wharf St., Victoria BC V8V 1X4, 250/356-9596 (Policy & Education); Fax: 604/356-1092

**Man.:** Manitoba Consumer & Corporate Affairs, Consumers' Bureau, #302, 258 Portage Ave., Winnipeg MB R3C 0B6, 204/945-3800; Fax: 204/945-0728

**N.B.:** Department of Justice, Consumer Affairs, #412, Centennial Bldg., PO Box 6000, Fredericton NB E3B 5H1, 506/453-2682; Fax: 506/444-4494

**Nfld.:** Department of Government Services & Lands, Commercial & Corporate Affairs, PO Box 8700, St. John's NF A1B 4J6

**Ont.:** Ministry of Consumer & Commercial Relations, Consumer Affairs Branch, 250 Yonge St., Toronto ON M5B 2N5, 416/326-8600; Fax: 416/326-8665

**PEI:** Department of Community Affairs & Attorney General, Consumer Services, Shaw Building, 95 Rochford St., 4th Fl., PO Box 2000, Charlottetown PE C1A 7N8, 902/368-4580; Fax: 902/368-5355

**Sask.:** Saskatchewan Justice, Consumer Protection Branch, 1874 Scarth St., Regina SK S4P 3V7, 306/787-2952; Fax: 306/787-5550

**Yuk.:** Yukon Justice, Consumer Services, PO Box 2703, Whitehorse YT Y1A 2C6, 867/667-5257; Fax: 867/393-6272

**CONVENTION FACILITIES *See* TOURISM & TOURIST INFORMATION**

**COPYRIGHT *See* PATENTS & COPYRIGHT**

## CORONERS

**Alta:** Alberta Justice, 7007 - 116 St. NW, Edmonton AB T6H 5R8, 403/427-4987; Fax: 403/422-1265

**B.C.:** British Columbia Coroner's Service, 4595 Canada Way, 2nd Fl., Burnaby BC V5G 4L9, 604/660-7739; Fax: 604/660-7776

**Man.:** Manitoba Justice, Office of the Chief Medical Examiner, #210, 1 Wesley Ave., Winnipeg MB R3C 4A5, 204/945-0571

**N.B.:** Department of the Solicitor General, Barker House, 4th Fl., PO Box 6000, Fredericton NB E3B 5H1, 506/453-3604; Fax: 506/453-3870

**Nfld.:** Department of Justice & Attorney General, Forensic Pathology, Health Sciences Complex, 300 Prince Philip Dr., St. John's NF A1B 3V6, 709/737-6402; Fax: 709/729-2129

**NWT:** Department of Justice, Coroner's Office, PO Box 1320, Yellowknife NT X1A 2L9, 867/873-7460

**N.S.:** Office of the Chief Medical Examiner, 5788 University Ave., Halifax NS B3H 1V8, 902/428-4052; Fax: 902/424-0607

**Ont.:** Ministry of the Solicitor General & Correctional Services, Office of the Chief Coroner, 26 Grenville St., 2nd Fl., Toronto ON M7A 2G9, 416/314-4000; Fax: 416/314-4030

**PEI:** Department of Community Affairs & Attorney General, Office of the Chief Coroner, PO Box 2000, Charlottetown PE C1A 7N8, 902/566-4100; Fax: 902/368-5283; 5355

**Qué.:** Bureau du coroner, 1200, route de l'Église, 5e étage, Ste Foy QC G1V 4Z7, 418/643-1845; Fax: 418/643-6174

**Sask.:** Saskatchewan Justice, Coroner's Branch, 1874 Scarth St., Regina SK S4P 3V7, 306/787-5541; Fax: 306/787-9111

**Yuk.:** Yukon Justice, Coroner's Service, PO Box 2703, Whitehorse YT Y1A 2C6, 867/667-5317; Fax: 867/393-6272

## CORRECTIONAL SERVICES

Correctional Service Canada, 340 Laurier Ave. West, Ottawa ON K1A 0P9, 613/995-5364 (Communications); Fax: 613/947-0091

Office of the Correctional Investigator, #402, 275 Slater St., Ottawa ON K1P 5H9, 613/990-2695; Toll Free: 1-800-267-5982; Fax: 613/990-9091

Solicitor General Canada, Sir Wilfrid Laurier Bldg., 340 Laurier Ave. West, Ottawa ON K1A 0P8, 613/991-3283; Fax: 613/993-7062

**Alta:** Alberta Justice, Correctional Services Division, 9833 - 109th St., Edmonton AB T5K 2E8, 403/427-2745; Fax: 403/427-5905

**B.C.:** Ministry of the Attorney General, Corrections Branch, PO Box 9282, Stn Prov. Gov't, Victoria BC V8W 9J7, 250/387-5059; Fax: 250/387-5698

**Man.:** Manitoba Justice, Adult Correctional Services, 405 Broadway, 8th Fl., Winnipeg MB R3C 3L6, 204/945-7307

**N.B.:** Department of the Solicitor General, Correctional Services, Barker House, 4th Fl., PO Box 6000, Fredericton NB E3B 5H1, 506/453-7414; Fax: 506/453-3870

**Nfld.:** Department of Justice & Attorney General, Adult Corrections Division, Confederation Bldg., PO Box 8700, St. John's NF A1B 4J6, 709/729-3880; Fax: 709/729-0416

**NWT:** Department of Justice, Corrections, PO Box 1320, Yellowknife NT X1A 2L9, 867/920-8922

**N.S.:** Correctional Services Division, PO Box 968, Stn M, Halifax NS, 902/424-6290; Fax: 902/424-0692

**Ont.:** Ministry of the Solicitor General & Correctional Services, Correctional Services Division, 101 Bloor St. West, 7th Fl., Toronto ON M5S 2Z7, 705/497-9500

**PEI:** Department of Community Affairs & Attorney General, PO Box 2000, Charlottetown PE C1A 7N8, 902/368-5250; Fax: 902/368-5283; 5355

**Qué.:** Ministère de la Sécurité publique, Services Correctionnels, Tour des Laurentides, 2525, boul Laurier, 5e étage, Ste-Foy QC G1V 2L2, 418/643-3500; Fax: 418/643-0275

**Sask.:** Saskatchewan Justice, Corrections Division, 1874 Scarth St., Regina SK S4P 3V7, 306/787-7872 (Communications); Fax: 306/787-8084

**Yuk.:** Yukon Justice, Community & Correctional Services Branch, PO Box 2703, Whitehorse YT Y1A 2C6, 867/667-8292 (Communications); Fax: 867/393-6272

**COURTS & JUDGES *See* JUSTICE DEPARTMENTS**

**CREDIT COUNSELLING *See* FINANCE**

## CRIMES COMPENSATION

Justice Canada, Communications & Executive Services Branch, Justice Bldg., 239 Wellington St., Ottawa ON K1A 0H8, 613/957-4222; Fax: 613/954-0811

**Alta:** Crimes Compensation Board, J.E. Brownlee Bldg., 10365 - 97 St., 10th Fl., Edmonton AB T5J 3W7, 403/427-7217; Fax: 403/422-4213

**B.C.:** Ministry of the Attorney General, Victim Services, PO Box 9282, Stn Prov. Gov't, Victoria BC V8W 9J7, 250/387-6848; Fax: 604/356-1092

**Man.:** Criminal Injuries Compensation Board, 763 Portage Ave., Winnipeg MB R3G 3N2, 204/775-7821; Fax: 204/784-1452

**N.B.:** Department of the Solicitor General, Victim & Community Services, Barker House, 4th Fl., PO Box 6000, Fredericton NB E3B 5H1, 506/453-2846; Fax: 506/453-3870

**Nfld.:** Department of Justice & Attorney General, Victim Services, Confederation Bldg., PO Box 8700, St. John's NF A1B 4J6, 709/729-0885; Fax: 709/729-2129

**NWT:** Department of Justice, Victims Services, PO Box 1320, Yellowknife NT X1A 2L9, 867/920-6911

Victims Assistance Committee, c/o Community Justice Division, PO Box 1320, Yellowknife NT X1A 2L9, 867/920-6911; Fax: 867/873-0299

**Ont.:** Criminal Injuries Compensation Board, 439 University Ave., 4th Fl., Toronto ON M5G 1Y8, 416/326-2900; Fax: 416/326-2883

**Qué.:** Ministère de la Justice, Bureau d'aide aux victimes d'actes criminels, 1200, rte de l'Église, Ste-Foy QC G1V 4M1, 418/643-5140 (Communications); Fax: 418/646-4449

**Sask.:** Saskatchewan Justice, Victims Services, 1874 Scarth St., Regina SK S4P 3V7, 306/787-0418; Fax: 306/787-9111

**Yuk.:** Yukon Justice, Consumer & Commercial Services Branch, PO Box 2703, Whitehorse YT Y1A 2C6, 867/667-8292 (Communications); Fax: 867/393-6272

**CROP MANAGEMENT *See* AGRICULTURE**

**CROWN LAND *See* LAND RESOURCES**

**CULTURE *See* ARTS & CULTURE**

## CURRENCY

Bank of Canada, 234 Wellington St., Ottawa ON K1A 0G9, 613/782-8111; Fax: 613/782-8655

Royal Canadian Mint, 320 Sussex Dr., Ottawa ON K1A 0G8, 613/993-3500

## CUSTOMS

Revenue Canada, Commercial Services Directorate, 875 Heron Rd., Ottawa ON K1A 0L8, 613/954-7190

Customs Border Services, 875 Heron Rd., Ottawa ON K1A 0L8, 613/952-0384

Travellers Directorate, 875 Heron Rd., Ottawa ON K1A 0L8, 613/954-6368

## DAIRYING

Agriculture & Agri-Food Canada, Dairy Section, 2200 Walkley Rd., 1st Fl., Ottawa ON K1A 0C5, 613/957-7078 ext.3010; Fax: 613/957-1527

Canadian Dairy Commission, Carling Executive Park, 1525 Carling Ave., Ottawa ON K1A 0Z2, 613/998-9490; Fax: 613/998-4492

Canadian Food Inspection Agency, Animal & Plant Health Directorate, 59 Camelot Dr., Nepean ON K1A 0Y9, 613/952-8000; Fax: 613/952-0677

Dairy, Fruit & Vegetable Division, 59 Camelot Dr., Nepean ON K1A 0Y9, 613/225-2342; Fax: 613/990-0607

**Alta:** Alberta Dairy Control Board, 5201 - 50 Ave., Wetaskiwin AB T9A 0S7, 403/361-1231; Fax: 403/361-1236

**B.C.:** British Columbia Milk Marketing Board, #105, 4664 Lougheed Hwy., Burnaby BC V5C 5T5, 604/294-6454; Fax: 604/294-4566

**Man.:** Manitoba Milk Producers' Marketing Board, 36 Scurfield Blvd., Winnipeg MB R3T 3N5, 204/488-6455; Fax: 204/488-4772

**N.B.:** New Brunswick Milk Marketing Board, Rochville Rd., PO Box 490, Sussex NB E0E 1P0, 506/432-9120; Fax: 506/432-9130

**Nfld.:** Newfoundland Milk Marketing Board, 655 Topsail Rd., St. John's NF A1E 2E3, 709/364-6634; Fax: 709/364-8364

**N.S.:** Nova Scotia Dairy Commission, PO Box 782, Truro NS B2N 5E8, 902/893-6379; Fax: 902/897-9768

**Ont.:** Ministry of Agriculture, Food & Rural Affairs, Dairy, Fruit & Vegetable Industry Inspection Branch, Communications Branch, 1 Stone Rd. West, Guelph ON N1G 4Y2, 519/837-5045; Fax: 519/767-0336

Ontario Milk Marketing Board, 6780 Campobello Rd., Mississauga ON L5N 2L8, 905/821-8970; Fax: 905/821-3160

**PEI:** Department of Agriculture & Forestry, Dairy Lab, 16 Walker Dr., Charolottetown PE C1A 8S6, 902/368-4480; Fax: 902/368-4486

**Qué.:** L'Union des Producteurs Agricoles, 555, boul Roland-Therrien, Longueuil QC J4H 3Y9, 514/679-0530; Fax: 514/679-5436

**Sask.:** Milk Control Board, #1210, 2500 Victoria Ave., Regina SK S4P 3X2, 306/787-5319; Fax: 306/787-1988

## DANGEROUS GOODS & HAZARDOUS MATERIAL

***See Also* Occupational Safety; Waste Management**

Environment Canada, Toxics Pollution Prevention Directorate, Place Vincent-Massey, 351, boul St-Joseph, Hull QC K1A 0H3, 819/953-1114; Fax: 819/953-5371

Health Canada, Environmental Health Directorate, Brooke Claxton Bldg., Tunney's Pasture, 120 Parkdale Ave., Ottawa ON K1A 0K9, 613/954-0291; Fax: 613/941-5366

National Defence (Canada), Air Command, MGen. George R. Pearkes Bldg., 101 Colonel By Dr., Ottawa ON K1A 0K2, 613/992-4581

Transport Canada, Transport Dangerous Goods, Transport Canada Building, 330 Sparks St., Ottawa ON K1A 0N5, 613/990-1147; Fax: 613/993-5925

**Alta:** Alberta Transportation & Utilities, Dangerous Goods Control, Twin Atria, 4999 - 98 Ave., Edmonton AB T6B 2X3, 403/422-9600; Fax: 403/415-0782

**B.C.:** Ministry of Environment, Lands & Parks, Industrial Waste & Hazardous Contaminants Branch, 777 Broughton St., Victoria BC V8V 1X4, 250/387-9992; Fax: 250/387-9935

**Man.:** Manitoba Environment, Transportation & Handling of Dangerous Goods, #160, 123 Main St., Winnipeg MB R3C 1A5, 204/945-7039; Fax: 204/945-5229

**N.B.:** Department of the Environment, Technical Approvals, 364 Argyle St., PO Box 6000, Fredericton NB E3B 5H1, 506/453-7945; Fax: 506/453-2893

New Brunswick Pesticides Advisory Council, c/o Department of the Environment, PO Box 6000, Fredericton NB E3B 5H1, 506/457-4848; Fax: 506/453-2893

**Nfld.:** Department of Environment & Labour, Environment Branch, Confederation Bldg., PO Box 8700, St. John's NF A1B 4J6; Fax: 709/729-1930

Department of Government Services & Lands, Motor Vehicles, 149 Smallwood Dr., PO Box 8710, Mount Pearl NF A1B 4J5, 709/729-2521; Fax: 709/729-6955

**Ont.:** Ministry of Transportation, Compliance Branch, 301 St. Paul St., St. Catharines ON L2R 1W6, 905/704-2507

**PEI:** Department of Fisheries & Environment, Air Quality & Hazardous Materials Section, Jones Bldg., 11 Kent St., 4th Fl., PO Box 2000, Charlottetown PE CIA 7N8, 902/368-5037; Fax: 902/368-5830

**Qué.:** Ministère de l'Environnement et de la Faune, Direction générale des opérations, Édifice Marie-Guyart, 675, boul René-Lévesque est, Québec QC G1R 5V7, 418/643-3127; Fax: 418/643-4747

Politiques du secteur industriel, Édifice Marie-Guyart, 675, boul René-Lévesque est, Québec QC G1R 5V7, 418/528-2363; Fax: 418/644-8562

**Sask.:** Saskatchewan Environment & Resource Management, Environmental Protection Branch, 3211 Albert St., Regina SK S4S 5W6, 306/787-6178; Fax: 306/787-0197

## DAY CARE SERVICES

***See Also* Child Welfare**

**Alta:** Alberta Family & Social Services, Day Care Programs, Seventh St. Plaza, 10030 - 107 St., Edmonton AB T5J 3E4, 403/427-4477; Fax: 403/422-9044

**B.C.:** Ministry of Children & Families, Day Care Subsidies/Community Projects, 1022 Government St., 3rd Fl., Victoria BC V8V 1X4, 250/387-1275; Fax: 250/356-6534

**Man.:** Economic Innovation & Technology Council, #648, 155 Carlton St., Winnipeg MB R3C 3H8, 204/945-5940; Fax: 204/945-8229

Manitoba Family Services, Child Day Care, #219, 114 Garry St., Winnipeg MB R3C 4V6, 204/945-2668; Fax: 204/948-2143

**N.B.:** Department of Health & Community Services, Family & Community Social Services Division, PO Box 5100, Fredericton NB E3B 5G8, 506/453-2536; Fax: 506/444-4697

**Nfld.:** Day Care & Homemaker Services Licensing Board, Confederation Bldg., PO Box 8700, St. John's NF A1B 4J6

Department of Human Resources & Employment, Program Development, Confederation Bldg., PO Box 8700, St. John's NF A1B 4J6, 709/729-2478; Fax: 709/729-6996

**NWT:** Department of Health & Social Services, Family Support & Child Protection, Centre Square Tower, 8th Fl., PO Box 1320, Yellowknife NT X1A 2L9, 867/920-6255; Fax: 867/873-0444

**Ont.:** Ministry of Community & Social Services, Child Care Branch, Hepburn Block, 4th Fl., Toronto ON M7A 1E9, 416/327-4864; Fax: 416/327-0570

Children, Family & Community Services Division, Hepburn Block, 80 Grosvenor St., 6th Fl., Toronto ON M7A 1E9, 416/325-5666; Fax: 416/325-5172, 5171

**PEI:** Department of Health & Social Services, Jones Bldg., 11 Kent St., 2nd Fl., PO Box 2000, Charlottetown PE C1A 7N8, 902/368-4900; Fax: 902/368-4969

**Sask.:** Saskatchewan Social Services, Child Day Care Division, 1920 Broad St., Regina SK S4P 3V6, 306/787-3855; Fax: 306/787-3441

Child Day Care Subsidy Unit, 1920 Broad St., Regina SK S4P 3V6, 306/787-3885; Fax: 306/787-1032

**Yuk.:** Yukon Health & Social Services, Family/Children's Services, PO Box 2703, Whitehorse YT Y1A 2C6, 867/667-8117; Fax: 867/668-4613

## DEATH CERTIFICATES *See* VITAL STATISTICS

## DEFENCE

***See Also* Emergency Response; Public Safety**

Foreign Affairs & International Trade Canada, Political & International Security Affairs Branch, Lester B. Pearson Bldg., 125 Sussex Dr., Ottawa ON K1A 0G2, 613/944-4000; Fax: 613/952-3904

National Defence (Canada), MGen. George R. Pearkes Bldg., 101 Colonel By Dr., Ottawa ON K1A 0K2, 613/992-4581

Emergency Preparedness Canada, Jackson Bldg., 122 Bank St., 2nd Fl., Ottawa ON K1A 0W6, 613/991-7077; Fax: 613/998-9589

## DELINQUENCY *See* YOUNG OFFENDERS

## DIPLOMATIC REPRESENTATIVES

***See Also* International Affairs**

Foreign Affairs & International Trade Canada, Diplomatic Corps Services, Lester B. Pearson Bldg., 125 Sussex Dr., Ottawa ON K1A 0G2, 613/995-5185; Fax: 613/943-1075

## DISABLED PERSONS SERVICES

**Alta:** Alberta Family & Social Services, Services to Persons with Disabilities, Seventh St. Plaza, 10030 - 107 St., Edmonton AB T5J 3E4, 403/422-0305; Fax: 403/422-9044

Premier's Council on the Status of Persons with Disabilities, #250, 11044 - 82 Ave., Edmonton AB T6G 0T2, 403/422-1095; Fax: 403/422-9691

**B.C.:** Ministry of Education, Skills & Training, Office for Disability Issues, PO Box 9150, Stn Prov Govt, Victoria BC V8W 9H1, 250/387-3813; Fax: 250/387-3114

**Man.:** Manitoba Family Services, Administration & Finance, #219, 114 Garry St., Winnipeg MB R3C 4V6, 204/945-5600; Fax: 204/948-2153

Vulnerable Persons' Commission Office, #219, 114 Garry St., Winnipeg MB R3C 4V6, 204/945-5039; Fax: 204/948-2603

**N.B.:** Premier's Council on the Status of Disabled Persons, #648, 440 King St., Fredericton NB E3B 5H8, 506/444-3000; Fax: 506/444-3001

**Nfld.:** Department of Human Resources & Employment, Family & Rehabilitative Services, Confederation Bldg., PO Box 8700, St. John's NF A1B 4J6, 709/729-2436; Fax: 709/729-6996

**NWT:** Department of Health & Social Services, Centre Square Tower, 8th Fl., PO Box 1320, Yellowknife NT X1A 2L9, 867/920-6173; Fax: 867/873-0266

**N.S.:** Department of Community Services, Mentally & Physically Challenged Children, Johnston Bldg., 5182 Prince St., 5th Fl., PO Box 696, Halifax NS B3J 2T7, 902/424-5863; Fax: 902/424-0708

Nova Scotia Disabled Persons Commission, #203, 2695 Dutch Village Rd., Halifax NS B3L 4T9, 902/424-8280; Toll Free: 1-800-565-8280 (within Nova Scotia); Fax: 902/424-0592

**Ont.:** Ministry of Citizenship, Culture & Recreation, Disability Issues Group, 700 Bay St., 3rd Fl., Toronto ON M5G 1Z6, 416/326-0201; Disability Issues Inquiry/Voice & TDD: 1-800-387-4456; 416/326-0111; Fax: 416/327-4080

Ontario Advisory Council on Disability Issues, 35 McCaul St., 3rd Fl., Toronto ON M5T 1V7, 416/314-6650 (Voice & TDD); Fax: 416/314-6658

**Qué.:** Bureau des personnes handicapées du Québec, 309, rue Brock, CP 820, Drummondville QC J2B 6X1, 819/477-7100; Fax: 819/477-8493

**Sask.:** Saskatchewan Health, 3475 Albert St., Regina SK S4S 6X6, 306/787-8332; Fax: 306/787-8310

**Yuk.:** Yukon Health & Social Services, PO Box 2703, Whitehorse YT Y1A 2C6, 867/667-3673 (Communications); Fax: 867/667-3096

## DISCRIMINATION & EMPLOYMENT EQUITY

Canadian Human Rights Commission, Place de Ville, Tower A, #1300, 320 Queen St., Ottawa ON K1A 1E1, 613/995-1151; TDD: 613/996-5211; Fax: 613/996-9661

**Alta:** Labour Relations Board/Public Service Employee Relations Board, #503, 10808 - 99 Ave., Edmonton AB T5K 0G5, 403/427-8547; Toll Free: 1-800-463-2572; Fax: 403/422-0970

**B.C.:** British Columbia Council of Human Rights, 844 Courtney St., 2nd. Fl., Victoria BC V8V 1X4, 250/387-3710; Fax: 250/387-3643

Ministry of the Attorney General, Employment Equity & Women's Programs, PO Box 9282, Stn Prov. Gov't, Victoria BC V8W 9J7, 250/387-3247; Fax: 250/356-5368

**Man.:** Human Rights Commission, #301, 259 Portage Ave., Winnipeg MB R3B 2A9, 204/945-3007; TDD: 945-3442; Fax: 204/945-1292

**N.B.:** New Brunswick Human Rights Commission, 751 Brunswick St., PO Box 6000, Fredericton NB E3B 5H1, 506/453-2301; Fax: 506/453-2653

**Nfld.:** Newfoundland & Labrador Human Rights Commission, PO Box 8700, St. John's NF A1B 4J6, 709/729-2709; Fax: 709/729-0790

**N.S.:** Pay Equity Commission, PO Box 697, Halifax NS B3J 1T8, 902/424-8595; Fax: 902/424-3239

**Ont.:** Ontario Human Rights Commission, 400 University Ave., 12th Fl., Toronto ON M7A 2R9, 416/314-4500; Fax: 416/314-4533

**PEI:** Prince Edward Island Human Rights Commission, 3 Queen St., PO Box 2000, Charlottetown PE C1A 7N8, 902/368-4180; Fax: 902/368-4236

**Sask.:** Saskatchewan Human Rights Commission, 122 - 3 Ave. North, 8th Fl., Saskatoon SK S7K 2H6, 306/933-5952; Fax: 306/933-7863

Saskatchewan Public Service Commission, Employee Relations, 2103 - 11 Ave., Regina SK S4P 3V7, 306/787-7606; Fax: 306/787-7533

**Yuk.:** Yukon Human Rights Commission, 205 Rogers St., Whitehorse YT Y1A 1X1, 867/667-6226

Yukon Public Service Commission, Staffing Relations Branch, PO Box 2703, Whitehorse YT Y1A 2C6, 867/667-5201; Fax: 867/667-6705

## DIVORCE

Justice Canada, Justice Bldg., 239 Wellington St., Ottawa ON K1A 0H8, 613/957-4222; Fax: 613/954-0811

**Alta:** Alberta Justice, Civil & Family Legal Services, 9833 - 109th St., Edmonton AB T5K 2E8, 403/422-9175; Fax: 403/425-0307

**B.C.:** Ministry of the Attorney General, PO Box 9282, Stn Prov. Gov't, Victoria BC V8W 9J7, 250/356-9596 (Policy & Education); Fax: 250/356-9037

**Man.:** Manitoba Justice, 405 Broadway, 5th Fl., Winnipeg MB R3C 3L6, 204/945-2852

**N.B.:** Department of Justice, #412, Centennial Bldg., PO Box 6000, Fredericton NB E3B 5H1, 506/453-2719 (Administration); Fax: 506/453-8718

**Nfld.:** Department of Justice & Attorney General, Confederation Bldg., PO Box 8700, St. John's NF A1B 4J6, 709/729-5942; Fax: 709/729-2129

**NWT:** Department of Justice, PO Box 1320, Yellowknife NT X1A 2L9, 867/920-6197

**N.S.:** Civil Litigation, 5151 Terminal Rd., PO Box 7, Halifax NS B3J 2L6, 902/424-4024; Fax: 902/424-0252

**Ont.:** Ministry of the Attorney General, Civil Law Division, 720 Bay St., 11th Fl., Toronto ON M5G 2K1, 416/326-2607; Fax: 416/326-4014

**PEI:** Department of Community Affairs & Attorney General, PO Box 2000, Charlottetown PE C1A 7N8, 902/368-4594; Fax: 902/368-4563

**Qué.:** Ministère de la Justice, 1200, rte de l'Église, Ste-Foy QC G1V 4M1, 418/643-5140 (Communications); Fax: 418/646-4449

**Sask.:** Saskatchewan Justice, Civil Law Division, 1874 Scarth St., Regina SK S4P 3V7, 306/787-7872 (Communications); Fax: 306/787-3874

**Yuk.:** Yukon Justice, PO Box 2703, Whitehorse YT Y1A 2C6, 867/667-8292 (Communications); Fax: 867/393-6272

## DRINKING DRIVING COUNTERMEASURES

Justice Canada, Policy Sector, Justice Bldg., 239 Wellington St., Ottawa ON K1A 0H8, 613/957-4222; Fax: 613/954-0811

**Alta:** Alberta Justice, Public Security Division, 10365 - 97 St., Edmonton AB T5J 3W7, 403/427-2745; Fax: 403/427-1194

**Nfld.:** Department of Health, Drug Dependency Services, West Block, Confederation Bldg., PO Box 8700, St. John's NF A1B 4J6, 709/729-0623; Fax: 709/729-5824

**N.S.:** Alcohol & Driving Countermeasures Office, 1690 Hollis St., PO Box 217, Stn M, Halifax NS B3J 2M4, 902/424-4673; Fax: 902/424-0700

**Ont.:** Ministry of the Attorney General, Drinking/Driving Countermeasures, 720 Bay St., 3rd Fl., Toronto ON M5G 2K1, 416/326-4408; Fax: 416/326-4007

**PEI:** Department of Transportation & Public Works, Safety, 17 Haviland St., 1st Fl., Charlottetown PE C1A 3S7, 902/368-5100; Fax: 902/368-5395

**Qué.:** Société de l'assurance automobile du Québec, 333, boul Jean-Lesage, CP 19600, Québec QC G1K 8J6, 418/528-3100; Fax: 418/644-0339

**Sask.:** Saskatchewan Justice, Public Law & Policy Division, 1874 Scarth St., Regina SK S4P 3V7, 306/787-7872 (Communications); Fax: 306/787-9111

## DRIVERS' LICENCES

**Alta:** Alberta Municipal Affairs, Registries Division, John E. Brownlee Bldg., 10365 - 97 St., Edmonton AB T5J 3W7, 403/422-2362 (Edmonton), 403/297-8980 (Calgary); Toll Free: 1-800-465-5009 (in Alberta); Fax: 403/422-9105

**B.C.:** Ministry of Transportation & Highways, Motor Vehicle Branch, 2631 Douglas St., Victoria BC V8T 5A3, 250/387-3140; Fax: 250/387-1169

**Man.:** Manitoba Highways & Transportation, Driver & Vehicle Licensing Division, 1075 Portage Ave., Winnipeg MB R3G 0S1, 204/945-3888; Fax: 204/948-2018

**N.B.:** Department of Transportation, Motor Vehicles & Policy, King Tower, Kings Pl., 2nd Fl., PO Box 6000, Fredericton NB E3B 5H1, 506/453-2552

**Nfld.:** Department of Government Services & Lands, Motor Registration Division, 149 Smallwood Dr., PO Box 8710, Mount Pearl NF A1B 4J5

**NWT:** Department of Transportation, Registration & Licensing, Lahm Ridge Bldg., PO Box 1320, Yellowknife NT X1A 2L9, 867/873-7418; Fax: 867/873-0363

**N.S.:** Department of Business & Consumer Services, Registry of Motor Vehicles, PO Box 1652, Halifax NS B3J 2Z3, 902/424-5851; Toll Free: 1-800-898-7668; Fax: 902/424-0544

**Ont.:** Licence Suspension Appeal Board, 700 Bay St., 24th Fl., PO Box 329, Toronto ON M5G 1Z6, 416/325-0209

Ministry of Transportation, Licensing & Control Branch, 301 St. Paul St., St. Catharines ON L2R 1W6, 416/235-4793

**PEI:** Department of Transportation & Public Works, Motor Vehicles, 17 Haviland St., 1st Fl., Charlottetown PE C1A 3S7, 902/368-5200; Fax: 902/368-5236

**Qué.:** Société de l'assurance automobile du Québec, 333, boul Jean-Lesage, CP 19600, Québec QC G1K 8J6, 418/528-3100; Fax: 418/644-0339

**Sask.:** Saskatchewan Government Insurance, Driver Licensing, 2260 - 11 Ave., Regina SK S4P 0J9, 306/751-1200; Fax: 306/787-7477

**Yuk.:** Yukon Driver Control Board, PO Box 2703, Whitehorse YT Y1A 2C6, 867/667-3638

Yukon Community & Transportation Services, Motor Vehicles, PO Box 2703, Whitehorse YT Y1A 2C6, 867/667-5315; Fax: 867/393-6404

## DRUGS & ALCOHOL

***See Also*** **Liquor Control**

Canadian Centre on Substance Abuse, #300, 75 Albert St., Ottawa ON K1P 5E7, 613/235-4048; Fax: 613/235-8101

Health Canada, Therapeutics Product Directorate, Brooke Claxton Bldg., Tunney's Pasture, 120 Parkdale Ave., Ottawa ON K1A 0K9, 613/957-0369; Fax: 613/941-5366

Justice Canada, Strategic Prosecution Policy, Justice Bldg., 239 Wellington St., Ottawa ON K1A 0H8, 613/952-7553; Fax: 613/954-0811

Patented Medicine Prices Review Board, Standard Life Centre, #1400, 333 Laurier Ave. West, PO Box L40, Ottawa ON K1P 1C1, 613/952-7360; Fax: 613/952-7626

**Alta:** AADAC Recovery Centre, 10302 - 107 St., Edmonton AB T5J 1K2, 403/427-4291; Fax: 403/422-2881

Alberta Alcohol & Drug Abuse Commission, Pacific Plaza Bldg., 10909 Jasper Ave., 6th Fl., Edmonton AB T5J 3M9, 403/427-2837; Fax: 403/423-1419

**B.C.:** Ministry of Health, 1515 Blanshard St., 7th Fl., Victoria BC V8W 3C8, 250/952-3456; Toll Free: AIDS Hotline 1-800-661-3886~

Ministry of the Attorney General, Liquor Control & Licensing Branch, 1019 Wharf St., Victoria BC V8V 1X4, 250/387-1254; Fax: 250/387-9184

Liquor Distribution Branch, 2625 Rupert St., Vancouver BC V5M 3T5, 604/252-3021; Fax: 604/252-3026

**Man.:** Drug Standards/Therapeutics Committee, #128, 599 Empress St., PO Box 925, Winnipeg MB R3C 2T6, 204/786-7233; Fax: 204/783-2171

Manitoba Health, Program Development, 599 Empress St., PO Box 925, Winnipeg MB R3C 2T6, 204/786-7312

**N.B.:** Department of Health & Community Services, PO Box 5100, Fredericton NB E3B 5G8, 506/453-3092; Fax: 506/444-4697

Prescription Drug Program, PO Box 5100, Fredericton NB E3B 5G8, 506/453-2415; Fax: 506/444-4697

**Nfld.:** Department of Health, Drug Dependency Services, West Block, Confederation Bldg., PO Box 8700, St. John's NF A1B 4J6, 709/729-0623; Fax: 709/729-5824

**NWT:** Department of Health & Social Services, Community Programs & Services, Centre Square Tower, 8th Fl., PO Box 1320, Yellowknife NT X1A 2L9, 867/920-6173; Fax: 867/873-0266

**N.S.:** Department of Health, Community Health Services, Joseph Howe Bldg., 1690 Hollis St., PO Box 488, Halifax NS B3J 2R8, 902/424-3749; Fax: 902/424-0550; 424-5769

**Ont.:** Ministry of Health, Community Health Division, Hepburn Block, 8th Fl., Queen's Park, #1400, 80 Grosvenor St., Toronto ON M7A 1S2, 416/327-7225; Toll Free: 1-800-668-2437 (AIDS Bureau); Fax: 416/327-7230

**Qué.:** Ministère de la Santé et des services sociaux, 1075, ch Ste-Foy, Québec QC G1S 2M1

**Sask.:** Saskatchewan Health, Prescription Drug Services Branch, 3475 Albert St., Regina SK S4S 6X6, 306/787-3301; Fax: 306/787-8679

Saskatchewan Liquor & Gaming Authority, 2500 Victoria Ave., PO Box 5054, Regina SK S4P 3M3, 306/787-4213; Fax: 306/787-8468

## ECONOMIC DEVELOPMENT *See* BUSINESS DEVELOPMENT

## EDUCATION

**Alta:** Alberta Advanced Education & Career Development, Commerce Place, 10155 - 102 St., 7th Fl., Edmonton AB T5J 4L5, 403/422-4488; Fax: 403/422-5126

Alberta Education, Devonian Bldg., 11160 Jasper Ave., Edmonton AB T5K 0L2, 403/427-7219; Fax: 403/427-0591

**B.C.:** British Columbia School Districts Capital Financing Authority, c/o Provincial Treasury, 620 Superior St., Victoria BC V8V 1X4, 250/387-7132; Fax: 250/387-3024

Ministry of Education, Skills & Training, PO Box 9150, Stn Prov Govt, Victoria BC V8W 9H1, 250/356-2500; Fax: 250/356-5945

**Man.:** Manitoba Education & Training, #168, Legislative Bldg., 401 York Ave., Winnipeg MB R3C 0P8, 204/945-4325; Fax: 204/945-1291

**N.B.:** Department of Advanced Education & Labour, Chestnut Complex, 470 York St., PO Box 6000, Fredericton NB E3B 5H1; Fax: 506/453-3806

Department of Education, PO Box 6000, Fredericton NB E3B 5H1, 506/453-3678; Fax: 506/453-3325

**Nfld.:** , Confederation Bldg., PO Box 8700, St. John's NF A1B 4J6, 709/729-5097; Fax: 709/729-5896

**NWT:** Department of Education, Culture & Employment, Educational Development Branch, PO Box 1320, Yellowknife NT X1A 2L9, 867/920-8061; Fax: 867/873-0155

**N.S.:** Department of Education & Culture, 2021 Brunswick St., PO Box 578, Halifax NS B3J 2S9, 902/424-5168; Fax: 902/424-0511

Nova Scotia Council on Higher Education, 2021 Brunswick St., PO Box 2086, Stn M, Halifax NS B3J 3B7, 902/424-6992; Fax: 902/424-0651

**Ont.:** Ministry of Education & Training, Organization Development & Services Division, Mowat Block, 900 Bay St., Toronto ON M7A 1L2, 416/325-2772; Fax: 416/325-2778

**PEI:** Department of Education, Sullivan Bldg., 16 Fitzroy St., PO Box 2000, Charlottetown PE C1A 7N8, 902/368-4600; Fax: 902/368-4663

**Qué.:** Ministère de l'Éducation, 1035, rue De La Chevrotière, 11e étage, Québec QC G1R 5A5, 418/643-7095; Fax: 418/646-6561; 528-2080

**Sask.:** Saskatchewan Education, 2220 College Ave., Regina SK S4P 3V7, 306/787-2010; Fax: 306/787-1300

**Yuk.:** Yukon Education, PO Box 2703, Whitehorse YT Y1A 2C6, 867/667-5141; Fax: 867/393-6254

## ELECTIONS

Elections Canada, The Jackson Bldg., 257 Slater St., Ottawa ON K1A 0M6, 613/993-2975; Toll Free: 1-800-463-6868, TDD: 1-800-361-8935; Fax: 613/954-8584

National Archives of Canada, 395 Wellington St., Ottawa ON K1A 0N3, 613/995-5138; Fax: 613/995-6274

**Alta:** Alberta Office of the Chief Electoral Officer, #100, 11510 Kingsway Ave., Edmonton AB T5G 2Y5, 403/427-7191; Fax: 403/422-2900

**B.C.:** Elections British Columbia, 1075 Pendergast St., Victoria BC V8V 1X4, 250/387-5305; Fax: 250/387-3578

**Man.:** Elections Manitoba, 200 Vaughan St., Main Fl., Winnipeg MB R3C 1T5, 204/945-3225; Fax: 204/945-6011

**N.B.:** Office of the Chief Electoral Officer, PO Box 6000, Fredericton NB E3B 5H1, 506/453-2218; Toll Free: 1-800-308-2922; Fax: 506/457-4926

**Nfld.:** , 39 Hallett Cr., St. John's NF A1B 4C4, 709/729-0712; Fax: 709/729-0679

**NWT:** Legislative Assembly, Elections NWT/Plebiscite Office, PO Box 1320, Yellowknife NT X1A 2L9, 867/920-6999; Fax: 867/920-4735

**N.S.:** Nova Scotia Elections Office, Joseph Howe Bldg., 9th Fl., PO Box 2246, Halifax NS B3J 3C8, 902/424-8584; Fax: 902/424-6622

**Ont.:** Elections Ontario, 51 Rolark Dr., Scarborough ON M1R 3B1, 416/321-3000; Toll Free: 1-800-668-2727; Fax: 416/321-6853

**PEI:** Elections Prince Edward Island, 180 Richmond St., 2nd Fl., PO Box 2000, Charlottetown PE C1A 7N8, 902/368-5895; Fax: 902/368-6500

**Qué.:** Élections du Québec, 3460, rue de La Pérade, Ste-Foy QC G1X 3Y5, 418/643-5380; Fax: 418/643-7291

Secrétariat à la réforme électorale et parlementaire, 875, Grande Allée est, Québec QC G1R 4Y8, 418/643-2483; Fax: 418/643-5612

**Sask.:** Office of the Chief Electoral Officer, 1702 Park St., Regina SK S4N 6B2, 306/787-4000; Fax: 306/787-4052

**Yuk.:** Legislative Assembly, c/o Clerk's Office, PO Box 2703, Whitehorse YT Y1A 2C6, 867/667-5498; Fax: 867/393-6280

## EMERGENCY RESPONSE

Environment Canada, Terrasses de la Chaudière, 10 Wellington St., Hull QC K1A 0H3, 819/997-2800; Toll Free: 1-800-668-6767; Fax: 819/953-2225

Fisheries & Oceans Canada, Rescue & Environmental Response, Canada Bldg., 344 Slater St., Ottawa ON K1A 0N7, 613/990-3110; Fax: 613/990-2780

National Defence (Canada), Emergency Preparedness Canada, Jackson Bldg., 122 Bank St., 2nd Fl., Ottawa ON K1A 0W6, 613/991-7077; Fax: 613/998-9589

National Search & Rescue Secretariat, Standard Life Bldg., 275 Slater St., 4th Fl., Ottawa ON K1A 0K2, 613/992-0054; Toll Free: 1-800-727-9414; Fax: 613/996-3746

Solicitor General Canada, National Security, Sir Wilfrid Laurier Bldg., 340 Laurier Ave. West, Ottawa ON K1A 0P8, 613/993-4136; Fax: 613/990-2632

Transport Canada, Security & Emergency Planning, Transport Canada Building, 330 Sparks St., Ottawa ON K1A 0N5, 613/990-3651; Fax: 613/996-6381

Transportation Safety Board of Canada, 200 Promenade du Portage, 4e étage, Hull QC K1A 1K8, 819/994-3741; Fax: 819/997-2239

**Alta:** Alberta Transportation & Utilities, Disaster Services, Twin Atria, 4999 - 98 Ave., Edmonton AB T6B 2X3, 403/422-9000; Fax: 403/415-0782

**B.C.:** British Columbia Provincial Emergency Program, 455 Boleskine Rd., Victoria BC V8Z 1E7, 250/387-5956; Fax: 250/952-4888

Ministry of Environment, Lands & Parks, Enforcement & Environmental Emergencies Branch, 810 Blanshard St., Victoria BC V8V 1X5, 250/387-9401; Fax: 250/387-1041

**Man.:** Manitoba Disaster Appeals Board, 405 Broadway Ave., 15th Fl., Winnipeg MB R3C 3L6, 204/945-3050; Fax: 204/945-4620

Manitoba Emergency Management Organization, #1510, 405 Broadway, Winnipeg MB R3C 3L6, 204/945-4772; Fax: 204/945-4620

Manitoba Environment, Environmental Operations Division, #160, 123 Main St., Winnipeg MB R3C 1A5, 204/945-7008; Fax: 204/945-5229

**Nfld.:** Department of Municipal & Provincial Affairs, Emergency Measures Division, West Block, Confederation Bldg., PO Box 8700, St. John's NF A1B 4J6, 709/729-3703; 24-hour Emergencies: 709/722-7107; Fax: 709/729-3857

**NWT:** Department of Municipal & Community Affairs, Emergency Services Division, #600, 5201 - 50 Ave., PO Box 1310, Yellowknife NT X1A 2L9, 867/873-7554; Fax: 867/873-8193

**N.S.:** Nova Scotia Emergency Measures Organization, PO Box 2107, Halifax NS B3J 3B7, 902/424-5620; Fax: 902/424-5376

**Ont.:** Ministry of Environment & Energy, Spills Action Centre, 5775 Yonge St., 10th Fl., Toronto ON M2M 4S1, 416/325-3000; Fax: 416/325-3011

Ministry of the Solicitor General & Correctional Services, Emergency Measures Ontario, 25 Grosvenor St., 19th Fl., Toronto ON M7A 1Y6, 416/314-3723; Fax: 416/314-3758

**PEI:** Prince Edward Island Emergency Measures Organization, East Prince Regional Service Centre, PO Box 2063, Summerside PE C1N 5L2, 902/888-8050; Fax: 902/888-8054

**Sask.:** Saskatchewan Environment & Resource Management, 3211 Albert St., Regina SK S4S 5W6, 306/787-2700; Toll Free: 1-800-667-2757; Fax: 306/787-3941

Saskatchewan Municipal Government, Emergency Planning, 1855 Victoria Ave., Regina SK S4P 3V7, 306/787-9567; Fax: 306/787-1694

## EMPLOYMENT

Human Resources Development Canada, Place du Portage, Phase IV, 140, Promenade du Portage, Hull QC K1A 0J9, 819/997-6481; Fax: 819/997-2407

Communications, Place du Portage, Phase IV, 140, Promenade du Portage, Hull QC K1A 0J9, 819/994-6013 (Communications)

National Defence (Canada), Canadian Forces Recruiting, Education & Training System, MGen. George R. Pearkes Bldg., 101 Colonel By Dr., Ottawa ON K1A 0K2, 613/992-4581

**Alta:** Alberta Advanced Education & Career Development, Learner Assistance Division, Commerce Place, 10155 - 102 St., 7th Fl., Edmonton AB T5J 4L5, 403/422-4488; Fax: 403/422-5126

Alberta Family & Social Services, Income & Employment Programs, Seventh St. Plaza, 10030 - 107 St., Edmonton AB T5J 3E4, 403/427-2635; Fax: 403/422-9044

Alberta Labour, Work Standards, 10808 - 99 Ave., Edmonton AB T5K 0G5, 403/427-8541; Fax: 403/422-3562

**B.C.:** Environmental Appeal Board, #125, 911 Yates St., Victoria BC V8V 1X5, 250/387-3464; Fax: 250/356-9923

Ministry of Education, Skills & Training, PO Box 9150, Stn Prov Govt, Victoria BC V8W 9H1, 250/356-2500; Fax: 250/356-5945

Ministry of Employment & Investment, 712 Yates St., Victoria BC V8W 9N1, 250/356-8702

Economic Development Division, 712 Yates St., Victoria BC V8W 9N1, 250/356-8702

Ministry of Labour, 825 Fort St., 2nd Fl., PO Box 9570, Stn Prov. Gov't, Victoria BC V8W 9K1, 250/356-1487; Fax: 250/356-1653

**Man.:** Manitoba Education & Training, Workforce 2000 & Youth Programs, 185 Carlton St., 4th Fl., Winnipeg MB R3C 3J1, 204/945-6195; Fax: 204/945-1792

**N.B.:** Department of Advanced Education & Labour, Labour & Employment Division, Chestnut Complex, 470 York St., PO Box 6000, Fredericton NB E3B 5H1; Fax: 506/453-3806

Department of Human Resources Development, 520 King St., 5th Fl., PO Box 6000, Fredericton NB E3B 5H1, 506/453-2001; Fax: 506/453-7478

New Brunswick Labour & Employment Board, 191 Prospect St., PO Box 908, Fredericton NB E3B 1B0, 506/453-2881; Fax: 506/453-3892

**Nfld.:** Department of Mines & Energy, PO Box 8700, St. John's NF A1B 4J6, 709/729-2301

**NWT:** Department of Education, Culture & Employment, Career Development, PO Box 1320, Yellowknife NT X1A 2L9, 867/873-7146; Fax: 867/873-0155

Culture & Careers Branch, PO Box 1320, Yellowknife NT X1A 2L9, 867/873-7252; Fax: 867/873-0155

**N.S.:** Department of Community Services, Income & Employment Support, Johnston Bldg., 5182 Prince St., 5th Fl., PO Box 696, Halifax NS B3J 2T7, 902/424-4326; Fax: 902/424-0721

Department of Human Resources, One Government Place, 1700 Granville St., PO Box 943, Halifax NS B3J 2V9, 902/424-7660; TDD: 424-3966; Fax: 902/424-0611

**Ont.:** Ministry of Community & Social Services, Social Assistance & Employment Opportunities Division, Hepburn Block, 80 Grosvenor St., 6th Fl., Toronto ON M7A 1E9, 416/325-5666; Fax: 416/325-5172, 5171

Ministry of Labour, Employment Practices Branch, 400 University Ave., 14th Fl., Toronto ON M7A 1T7, 416/326-7000; Fax: 416/326-7061

**PEI:** Department of Community Affairs & Attorney General, Labour & Industrial Relations Division, PO Box 2000, Charlottetown PE C1A 7N8, 902/368-5250; Fax: 902/368-5283; 5355

**Qué.:** Ministère du Travail, 200, ch Ste-Foy, 6e étage, Québec QC G1R 5S1, 418/643-4817; Fax: 418/644-6969

**Sask.:** Saskatchewan Post-Secondary Education & Skills Training, 2220 College Ave., Regina SK S4P 3V7, 306/787-2010

**Yuk.:** Employment Standards Board, PO Box 2703, Whitehorse YT Y1A 2C6

**EMPLOYMENT EQUITY *See* DISCRIMINATION & EMPLOYMENT EQUITY**

## ENERGY

***See Also* Natural Resources**

Atomic Energy of Canada Limited, 2251 Speakman Dr., Mississauga ON L5K 1B2, 905/823-9040; Fax: 905/823-8006

Energy Supplies Allocation Board, 580 Booth St., 17th Fl., Ottawa ON K1A 0E4, 613/995-5594; Fax: 613/992-8738

Indian Oil & Gas Canada, #100, 9911 Chula Blvd., Tsuu T'ina (Sarcee) AB T2W 6H6, 403/292-5625; Fax: 403/292-5618

National Energy Board, 311 - 6 Ave. SW, Calgary AB T2P 3H2, 403/292-4800; Fax: 403/292-5503

Natural Resources Canada, Canada Centre for Mineral & Energy Technology, 580 Booth St., Ottawa ON K1A 0E4, 613/995-0947; Fax: 613/996-9094

Energy Sector, 580 Booth St., Ottawa ON K1A 0E4, 613/996-7432; Fax: 613/992-1405

**Alta:** Alberta Energy, Petroleum Plaza, North Tower, 9945 - 108 St., Edmonton AB T5K 2G6, 403/427-7425; Fax: 403/427-3198

Alberta Research Council, Energy Technologies, 250 Karl Clark Rd., PO Box 8330, Edmonton AB T6H 5X2, 403/987-8119; Fax: 403/461-2651

**B.C.:** Ministry of Employment & Investment, Energy & Minerals Division, 1810 Blanshard St., 5th Fl., PO Box 9324, Victoria BC V8W 9N3, 250/356-8702

**Man.:** Manitoba Energy & Mines, #360, 1395 Ellice Ave., Winnipeg MB R3G 3P2, 204/945-4154; Fax: 204/945-0586, 1406

Petroleum & Energy Branch, #360, 1395 Ellice Ave., Winnipeg MB R3G 3P2, 204/945-6577; Toll Free: 1-800-282-8069 (Energy); Fax: 204/945-0586

**N.B.:** Department of Natural Resources & Energy, Mineral Resources & Energy, PO Box 6000, Fredericton NB E3B 5H1, 506/453-3826; Fax: 506/444-4367

**Nfld.:** Canada-Newfoundland Offshore Petroleum Board, TD Place, #500, 140 Water St., St. John's NF A1C 6H6, 709/778-1400; Fax: 709/778-1473

Department of Mines & Energy, Energy Branch, PO Box 8700, St. John's NF A1B 4J6, 709/729-2301

**N.S.:** Canada-Nova Scotia Offshore Petroleum Board, TD Centre, 1791 Barrington St., 6th Fl., Halifax NS B3J 3K9, 902/422-5588; Fax: 902/422-1799

Department of Natural Resources, Minerals & Energy Branch, Founder's Square, 1701 Hollis St., PO Box 698, Halifax NS B3J 2T9, 902/424-5346; Fax: 902/424-7735

Petroleum Development Agency, Founder's Square, 1701 Hollis St., PO Box 698, Halifax NS B3J 2T9, 902/424-5935; Fax: 902/424-7735

**Ont.:** Ministry of Environment & Energy, 135 St. Clair Ave. West, Toronto ON M4V 1P5, 416/325-4000 (Public Information Centre); Toll Free: 1-800-565-4923; Fax: 416/323-4564

Energy Conservation & Liaison, 135 St. Clair Ave. West, Toronto ON M4V 1P5, 416/323-5626; Fax: 416/323-5636

Ontario Energy Board, 2300 Yonge St., 26th Fl., Toronto ON M4P 1E4, 416/481-1967; Fax: 416/440-7656

Ontario Energy Corporation, South Tower, #905, 175 Bloor St. East, Toronto ON M4W 3R8, 416/926-4200; Fax: 416/926-9641

Ontario Hydro, 700 University Ave., Toronto ON M5G 1X6, 416/592-5111; Toll Free: 1-800-263-9000

**Qué.:** Ministère des Ressources Naturelles, Énergie, #B-302, 5700 - 4 av ouest, 3e étage, Charlesbourg QC G1H 6R1, 418/627-8600 (Renseignements); Fax: 418/643-0701

**Sask.:** Saskatchewan Energy & Mines, 1914 Hamilton St., Regina SK S4P 4V4, 306/787-2526; Fax: 306/787-7338

**Yuk.:** Yukon Economic Development, Mines & Resource Development, 211 Main St., PO Box 2703, Whitehorse YT Y1A 2C6, 867/667-5466; Fax: 867/668-8601

## ENVIRONMENT

Auditor General of Canada, Environment & Sustainable Development, 240 Sparks St., Ottawa ON K1A 0G6, 613/995-3708; Fax: 613/957-4023

Environment Canada, Terrasses de la Chaudière, 10 Wellington St., Hull QC K1A 0H3, 819/997-2800; Toll Free: 1-800-668-6767; Fax: 819/953-2225

Foreign Affairs & International Trade Canada, Environment & Sustainable Development, Lester B. Pearson Bldg., 125 Sussex Dr., Ottawa ON K1A 0G2, 613/944-0886; Fax: 613/944-0892

Indian & Northern Affairs Canada, Natural Resources & Environment Branch, Tour Nord, Les Terrasses de la Chaudière, 10 Wellington St., Hull QC K1A 0H4, 819/997-9381; Fax: 819/953-8766

Industry Canada, Environmental Affairs, C.D. Howe Bldg., 235 Queen St., Ottawa ON K1A 0H5, 613/954-3080; Fax: 613/952-9564

National Round Table on the Environment & Economy, Canada Bldg., #200, 344 Slater St., Ottawa ON K1R 7Y3, 613/992-7189; Fax: 613/992-7385

Natural Resources Canada, 580 Booth St., Ottawa ON K1A 0E4, 613/995-0947; Fax: 613/996-9094

**Alta:** Alberta Environmental Protection, 9915 - 108 St., Edmonton AB T5K 2G8, 403/427-2739, 944-0313 (Information Centre)

**B.C.:** Ministry of Environment, Lands & Parks, 810 Blanshard St., Victoria BC V8V 1X5, 250/387-9419; Fax: 250/356-6464

**Man.:** Manitoba Environment, #160, 123 Main St., Winnipeg MB R3C 1A5, 204/945-7100

**N.B.:** Department of the Environment, 364 Argyle St., PO Box 6000, Fredericton NB E3B 5H1, 506/453-3700; Fax: 506/453-3843

Corporate Services, 364 Argyle St., PO Box 6000, Fredericton NB E3B 5H1, 506/453-3703; Fax: 506/453-3843

**Nfld.:** Department of Environment & Labour, Confederation Bldg., PO Box 8700, St. John's NF A1B 4J6; Fax: 709/729-1930

**NWT:** Department of Resources, Wildlife & Economic Development, PO Box 1320, Yellowknife NT X1A 2L9

**N.S.:** Department of the Environment, 5151 Terminal Rd., 5th Fl., PO Box 2107, Halifax NS B3J 3B7, 902/424-5300; Fax: 902/424-0503

**Ont.:** Environmental Commissioner of Ontario, #605, 1075 Bay St., Toronto ON M5S 2B1, 416/325-3377; Toll Free: 1-800-701-6454; Fax: 416/325-3370

Ministry of Environment & Energy, 135 St. Clair Ave. West, Toronto ON M4V 1P5, 416/325-4000 (Public Information Centre); Toll Free: 1-800-565-4923; Fax: 416/323-4564

**PEI:** Department of Fisheries & Environment, Jones Bldg., 11 Kent St., 4th Fl., PO Box 2000, Charlottetown PE CIA 7N8, 902/368-5000; Fax: 902/368-5830

**Qué.:** Ministère de l'Environnement et de la Faune, Édifice Marie-Guyart, 675, boul René-Lévesque est, Québec QC G1R 5V7, 418/643-3127; Toll Free: 1-800-561-1616; Fax: 418/646-5974

**Sask.:** Saskatchewan Environment & Resource Management, 3211 Albert St., Regina SK S4S 5W6, 306/787-2700; Toll Free: 1-800-667-2757; Fax: 306/787-3941

**Yuk.:** Yukon Council on the Economy & the Environment, A-8E, PO Box 2703, Whitehorse YT Y1A 2C6, 867/667-5939; Fax: 867/668-4936

Yukon Renewable Resources, Environment Protection & Assessment Branch, PO Box 2703, Whitehorse YT Y1A 2C6, 867/667-5237; Fax: 867/393-6213

**EXPORTS *See* TRADE**

## EXPROPRIATION

Canada Lands Company, #1500, 200 King St. West, Toronto ON M5H 3T4, 416/974-9700; Fax: 416/974-9661

Justice Canada, Justice Bldg., 239 Wellington St., Ottawa ON K1A 0H8, 613/957-4222; Fax: 613/954-0811

National Defence (Canada), MGen. George R. Pearkes Bldg., 101 Colonel By Dr., Ottawa ON K1A 0K2, 613/992-4581

Public Works & Government Services Canada, Real Property Services Branch, Place du Portage, Phase III, 11, rue Laurier, Hull QC K1A 0S5, 819/956-3115

**Alta:** Alberta Public Works, Supply & Services, Land Acquisition Branch, 6950 - 113 St., 3rd Fl., Edmonton AB T6H 5V7, 403/422-1384; Fax: 403/422-5419

Land Compensation Board, Phipps-McKinnon Bldg., 10020 - 101A Ave., 18th Fl., Edmonton AB T5J 3G2, 403/427-2444; Fax: 403/427-5798

**B.C.:** Expropriation Compensation Board, 514 Government St., Victoria BC V8V 2L7, 250/387-4321; Fax: 250/387-0711

**Man.:** Manitoba Government Services, Land Management Agency, 25 Tupper St. North, Portage la Prairie MB R1N 3K1, 204/945-4800 (Administration)

**N.B.:** Expropriations Advisory Office, 295 boul St-Pierre ouest, CP 297, Caraquet NB E0B 1K0, 506/727-3481; Fax: 506/727-2783

**Nfld.:** Department of Government Services & Lands, Lands Branch, PO Box 8700, St. John's NF A1B 4J6

**N.S.:** Expropriations Compensation Board, 1601 Lower Water St., PO Box 1692, Stn M, Halifax NS B3J 3S3, 902/424-4448; Fax: 902/424-3919

**Ont.:** Ontario Municipal Board, 655 Bay St., 15th Fl., Toronto ON M5G 1E5, 416/326-6255; Fax: 416/326-5370

**PEI:** Department of Transportation & Public Works, Properties & Surveys Section, Jones Bldg., PO Box 2000, Charlottetown PE C1A 7N8, 902/368-5131; Fax: 902/368-5395

**Qué.:** Ministère de la Justice, 1200, rte de l'Église, Ste-Foy QC G1V 4M1, 418/643-5140 (Communications); Fax: 418/646-4449

Ministère des Transports, 700, boul René-Lévesque est, 28e étage, Québec QC G1R 5H1, 418/643-6740

Société immobilière du Québec, 475, rue St-Amable, Québec QC G1R 4X9, 418/646-1766 poste 3470; Fax: 418/643-7932

**Sask.:** Public & Private Rights Board, 2151 Scarth St., Regina SK S4P 3V7, 306/787-4071; Fax: 306/787-0088

Saskatchewan Property Management Corporation, 1840 Lorne St., Regina SK S4P 3V7, 306/787-6911; Fax: 306/787-1061

## EXTERNAL AFFAIRS *See* INTERNATIONAL AFFAIRS

## FAMILY BENEFITS

### *See Also* Income Security; Social Services

Human Resources Development Canada, Income Security Programs, Place Vanier, 120 Parkdale Ave., Ottawa ON K1A 0L1, 819/994-6013 (Communications)

Veterans Affairs Canada, Benefits, Daniel J. MacDonald Bldg., 161 Grafton St., PO Box 7700, Charlottetown PE C1A 8M9, 613/566-8808; Fax: 613/566-8073

**Alta:** Alberta Family & Social Services, Seventh St. Plaza, 10030 - 107 St., Edmonton AB T5J 3E4, 403/427-2734; Fax: 403/422-9044

Office of the Commissioner of Services for Children & Families, c/o Alberta Family & Social Services, Seventh St. Plaza, 10030 - 107 St., Edmonton AB T5J 3E4, 403/422-5011; Fax: 403/422-5036

**Man.:** Manitoba Family Services, #219, 114 Garry St., Winnipeg MB R3C 4V6, 204/945-2324 (Policy & Planning); Fax: 204/945-2156

**N.B.:** Department of Health & Community Services, Family & Community Social Services Division, PO Box 5100, Fredericton NB E3B 5G8, 506/453-2536; Fax: 506/444-4697

**Nfld.:** Department of Human Resources & Employment, Family & Rehabilitative Services, Confederation Bldg., PO Box 8700, St. John's NF A1B 4J6, 709/729-2436; Fax: 709/729-6996

**NWT:** Department of Health & Social Services, Family Support & Child Protection, Centre Square Tower, 8th Fl., PO Box 1320, Yellowknife NT X1A 2L9, 867/920-6255; Fax: 867/873-0444

**N.S.:** Department of Community Services, Family & Children's Services, Johnston Bldg., 5182 Prince St., 5th Fl., PO Box 696, Halifax NS B3J 2T7, 902/424-4326; Fax: 902/424-0708

**PEI:** Department of Health & Social Services, Jones Bldg., 11 Kent St., 2nd Fl., PO Box 2000, Charlottetown PE C1A 7N8, 902/368-4900; Fax: 902/368-4969

**Qué.:** Ministère de l'Emploi et de la Solidarité, 425, rue St-Amable, 2e étage, Québec QC G1R 4Z1, 418/643-9818; Toll Free: 1-800-361-4743; Fax: 418/646-5426

**Sask.:** Saskatchewan Social Services, Income Security Programs Division, 1920 Broad St., Regina SK S4P 3V6, 306/787-7469; Fax: 306/787-1032

**Yuk.:** Yukon Health & Social Services, Social Services Branch, PO Box 2703, Whitehorse YT Y1A 2C6, 867/667-3673 (Communications); Fax: 867/667-3096

## FEDERAL-PROVINCIAL AFFAIRS

Canadian Intergovernmental Conference Secretariat, 110 O'Connor St., PO Box 488, Stn A, Ottawa ON K1N 8V5, 613/995-2341; Fax: 613/996-6091

Citizenship & Immigration Canada, Corporate Governance, Jean Edmonds Towers, 365 Laurier Ave. West, Ottawa ON K1A 1L1, 613/957-4166; Fax: 613/957-5955

Federal Office of Regional Development (Québec), Tour de la Bourse, #3800, 800, Place Victoria, CP 247, Montréal QC H4Z 1E8, 514/283-6412; Toll Free: 1-800-322-4636; Fax: 514/283-3302

Finance Canada, Federal Provincial Relations & Social Policy Branch, Esplanade Laurier, 140 O'Connor St., Ottawa ON K1A 0G5, 613/992-1573; Fax: 613/996-8404

Human Resources Development Canada, Federal/Provincial, Place du Portage, Phase IV, 140, Promenade du Portage, Hull QC K1A 0J9, 819/994-4538; Fax: 819/953-4701

Industry Canada, Internal Trade, Consultations & Federal-Provincial Relations, C.D. Howe Bldg., 235 Queen St., Ottawa ON K1A 0H5, 613/954-9633; Fax: 613/954-8042

Office of Intergovernmental Affairs, c/o Privy Council Office, Langevin Block, 80 Wellington St., Ottawa ON K1A 0A3

Privy Council Office, Intergovernmental Affairs, Langevin Block, 80 Wellington St., Ottawa ON K1A 0A3, 613/947-5695; Fax: 613/995-0101

Treasury Board of Canada, Office of Infrastructure, West Tower, 300 Laurier Ave. West, 3rd Fl., Ottawa ON K1A 0R5, 613/952-3171; Fax: 613/952-7979

**Alta:** Alberta Federal & Intergovernmental Affairs, Commerce Place, 10155 - 102 St., 12th Fl., Edmonton AB T5J 4GB, 403/427-2611; Fax: 403/423-6654

**B.C.:** Ministry of Employment & Investment, International Branch, 712 Yates St., Victoria BC V8W 9N1, 250/952-0708; Fax: 250/952-0716

Ministry of Finance & Corporate Relations, Federal-Provincial Relations & Research, 617 Government St., Victoria BC V8V 1X4, 250/387-9018

**Man.:** Manitoba Finance, Federal-Provincial Relations & Research Division, #203, 333 Broadway Ave., Winnipeg MB R3C 0S9, 204/945-3754; Fax: 204/945-8316

**N.B.:** Department of Intergovernmental & Aboriginal Affairs, PO Box 6000, Fredericton NB E3B 5H1, 506/453-2384; Fax: 506/453-2995

Federal-Provincial Affairs, PO Box 6000, Fredericton NB E3B 5H1, 506/457-7275; Fax: 506/453-2995

**Nfld.:** Department of Municipal & Provincial Affairs, Canada/Newfoundland Infrastructure Program, West Block, Confederation Bldg., PO Box 8700, St. John's NF A1B 4J6, 709/729-5411

Executive Council, Intergovernmental Affairs Secretariat, Confederation Bldg., PO Box 8700, St. John's NF A1B 4J6, 709/729-5645; Fax: 709/729-5038

**NWT:** Ministry of Aboriginal Affairs, Precambrian Bldg., 7th Fl., PO Box 1320, Yellowknife NT X1A 2L9, 867/873-7143; Fax: 867/873-0233

**N.S.:** Executive Council, Intergovernmental Affairs, One Government Place, PO Box 2125, Halifax NS B3J 3B7, 902/424-4899; Fax: 902/424-0728

**Ont.:** Ministry of Finance, Intergovernmental Finance Policy Branch, Frost Bldg. South, 7 Queen's Park Cres., Toronto ON M7A 1Y7, 416/327-0140; Fax: 416/327-0160

Ministry of Intergovernmental Affairs, Constitutional Affairs, 900 Bay St., 6th Fl., Toronto ON M7A 1C2, 416/325-4804; Fax: 416/325-4759

**PEI:** Department of Health & Social Services, Administration & Federal-Provincial Relations, Jones Bldg., 11 Kent St., 2nd Fl., PO Box 2000, Charlottetown PE C1A 7N8, 902/368-4900; Fax: 902/368-4969

**Qué.:** Secrétariat aux affaires intergouvernementales canadiennes, Edifice H, 3e étage, 875, Grande Allée est, Québec QC G1R 4Y8, 418/643-4011; Fax: 418/643-8730

**Sask.:** Saskatchewan Finance, Taxation & Intergovernmental Affairs Branch, 2350 Albert St., Regina SK S4P 4A6, 306/787-6731; Fax: 306/787-6544

Saskatchewan Intergovernmental Affairs, 1919 Saskatchewan Dr., Regina SK S4P 3V7, 306/787-1643; Fax: 306/787-1987

**Yuk.:** Executive Council, Federal Relations Office, #707, 350 Sparks St., Ottawa ON K1R 7S8, 613/234-3206; Fax: 613/563-9602

## FILM CLASSIFICATION *See* CENSORSHIP (MEDIA)

## FILM PRODUCTION & COLLECTIONS

Canadian Broadcasting Corporation, 250 Lanark Ave., PO Box 3220, Stn C, Ottawa ON K1Y 1E4, 613/724-1200; TDD: 613/724-5173

National Film Board of Canada, 3155, rue Côte de Liesse, St-Laurent QC H4N 2N4, 514/283-9000; Fax: 514/283-8971

Telefilm Canada, Tour de la Banque Nationale, 600, De La Gauchetière ouest, 14e étage, Montréal QC H3B 4L8, 514/283-6363; Fax: 514/283-8212

**Alta:** Alberta Motion Picture Development Corporation, #690, 10020 - 101A Ave., Edmonton AB T5J 3G2, 403/424-8855; Fax: 403/424-7669

**B.C.:** Ministry of Small Business, Tourism & Culture, BC Film Commission, 1405 Douglas St., Victoria BC V8W 3C1, 604/660-2732; Fax: 604/660-4790

**Man.:** Manitoba Culture, Heritage & Citizenship, Arts Branch, 213 Notre Dame., Winnipeg MB R3B 1N3, 204/945-4579; Fax: 204/945-1684

**N.B.:** Department of Education, Instructional Resources, PO Box 6000, Fredericton NB E3B 5H1, 505/453-2319; Fax: 506/453-3325

**N.S.:** Department of Education & Culture, Learning Resources & Technology, 2021 Brunswick St., PO Box 578, Halifax NS B3J 2S9, 902/424-2462; Fax: 902/424-0633

Nova Scotia Film Development Corporation, 1724 Granville St., Halifax NS B3J 1X5, 902/424-7177, 7185

**PEI:** Department of Education, Provincial Libraries & Archives, Sullivan Bldg., 16 Fitzroy St., PO Box 2000, Charlottetown PE C1A 7N8, 902/368-4227; Fax: 902/368-6327

**Qué.:** Ministère de la Culture et des Communications, Archives nationales, Pavillon Louis-Jacques Casault, 1210 av du Séminaire, Ste-Foy QC G1N 4V1, 418/643-2183; Fax: 418/643-4457

**Sask.:** Saskatchewan Government Media Services, #3, Legislative Bldg., Regina SK S4S 0B3, 306/787-6281

**Yuk.:** Yukon Education, Libraries & Archives, PO Box 2703, Whitehorse YT Y1A 2C6, 867/667-5309; Fax: 867/393-6254

Yukon Tourism, Heritage Branch, PO Box 2703, Whitehorse YT Y1A 2C6, 867/667-5363; Fax: 867/667-8844

## FINANCE

### *See Also* Banking & Financial Institutions

Auditor General of Canada, 240 Sparks St., Ottawa ON K1A 0G6, 613/995-3708; Fax: 613/957-4023

Bank of Canada, 234 Wellington St., Ottawa ON K1A 0G9, 613/782-8111; Fax: 613/782-8655

Business Development Bank of Canada, #400, 5, Place Ville Marie, Montréal QC H3B 5E7, 514/283-5904; Toll Free: 1-888-463-6232; Fax: 514/283-0617

Canada Deposit Insurance Corporation, 50 O'Connor St., 17th Fl., PO Box 2340, Stn D, Ottawa ON K1P 5W5, 613/996-2081; Toll Free: 1-800-461-2342; Fax: 613/996-6095

Elections Canada, Election Financing, The Jackson Bldg., 257 Slater St., Ottawa ON K1A 0M6, 613/993-2975; Toll Free: 1-800-463-6868, TDD: 1-800-361-8935; Fax: 613/954-8584

Finance Canada, Esplanade Laurier, 140 O'Connor St., Ottawa ON K1A 0G5, 613/992-1573; TDD: 613/996-0035; Fax: 613/996-8404

Federal Provincial Relations & Social Policy Branch, Esplanade Laurier, 140 O'Connor St., Ottawa ON K1A 0G5, 613/992-1573; Fax: 613/996-8404

Financial Sector Policy Branch, Esplanade Laurier, 140 O'Connor St., Ottawa ON K1A 0G5, 613/992-1573; Fax: 613/996-8404

Office of the Superintendent of Financial Institutions, Kent Square, 255 Albert St., Ottawa ON K1A 0H2, 613/990-7788; Toll Free: 1-800-385-8647; Fax: 613/952-8219

Revenue Canada, Financial Industries Division, 123 Slater St., Ottawa ON K1A 0L8, 613/957-9767

Treasury Board of Canada, 140 O'Connor St., Ottawa ON K1A 0R5, 613/957-2400; Fax: 613/952-3658

**Alta:** Alberta Economic Development & Tourism, Business Finance, Commerce Place, 10155 - 102 St., Edmonton AB T5J 4L6, 403/427-3300; Fax: 403/422-9319

Alberta Treasury, Terrace Bldg., 9515 - 107 St., Edmonton AB T5K 2C3, 403/427-3035; Fax: 403/422-2463

Economics & Public Finance, Terrace Bldg., 9515 - 107 St., Edmonton AB T5K 2C3, 403/427-7546; Fax: 403/422-2164

Financial Institutions, Terrace Bldg., 9515 - 107 St., Edmonton AB T5K 2C3, 403/427-3035; Fax: 403/422-2463

**B.C.:** Financial Institutions Commission, #1900, 1050 West Pender St., Vancouver BC V6E 3S7, 604/660-2947; Fax: 604/660-3170

International Finance Centre - Vancouver Society, World Trade Centre, #658, 999 Canada Place, Vancouver BC V6C 3E1, 604/683-6626; Fax: 604/683-6646

Ministry of Finance & Corporate Relations, 617 Government St., Victoria BC V8V 1X4, 250/387-9278

**Man.:** Manitoba Finance, #109, Legislative Bldg., Winnipeg MB R3C 0V8, 204/945-3754; Fax: 204/945-8316

Treasury Board, #300, 333 Broadway, Winnipeg MB R3C 0S9, 204/945-1100; Fax: 204/945-4878

Manitoba Industry, Trade & Tourism, Financial Services, 155 Carlton St., 6th Fl., Winnipeg MB R3C 3H8, 204/945-2770; Fax: 204/945-1193

**N.B.:** Department of Finance, PO Box 6000, Fredericton NB E3B 5H1, 506/453-2286; Fax: 506/457-4989

**Nfld.:** Department of Finance & Treasury Board, Confederation Bldg., PO Box 8700, St. John's NF A1B 4J6, 709/729-2858

**NWT:** Department of Finance, PO Box 1320, Yellowknife NT X1A 2L9

**N.S.:** , PO Box 187, Halifax NS B3J 2N3, 902/424-5554; Fax: 902/424-0635

**Ont.:** Ministry of Finance, Frost Bldg. South, 7 Queen's Park Cres., Toronto ON M7A 1Y7, 416/325-0333 (Communications); Fax: 416/325-0339

Office of the Provincial Auditor, Finance, Public Accounts & General Government Portfolio, #1530, 20 Dundas St. West, PO Box 105, Toronto ON M5G 2C2, 416/327-2381; Fax: 416/327-9862

Ontario Financing Authority, #1400, 1 Dundas St. West, Toronto ON M7A 1Y7

**PEI:** Department of the Provincial Treasury, PO Box 2000, Charlottetown PE C1A 7N8, 902/368-4000; Fax: 902/368-5544

**Qué.:** Ministère des Finances, 12, rue St-Louis, Québec QC G1R 5L3, 418/691-2233; Fax: 418/646-5643, 1631

**Sask.:** Saskatchewan Finance, 2350 Albert St., Regina SK S4P 4A6, 306/787-6768; Fax: 306/787-6544

**Yuk.:** Yukon Finance, PO Box 2703, Whitehorse YT Y1A 2C6, 867/667-5343; Fax: 867/393-6217

## FINANCIAL INSTITUTIONS *See* BANKING & FINANCIAL INSTITUTIONS

## FIRE PREVENTION

Institute for Research in Construction, 1500 Montreal Rd., Ottawa ON K1A 0R6, 613/993-3772; Fax: 613/941-0822

Natural Resources Canada, 580 Booth St., Ottawa ON K1A 0E4, 613/995-0947; Fax: 613/996-9094

**Alta:** Alberta Labour, Office of the Provincial Fire Commissioner, 10808 - 99 Ave., Edmonton AB T5K 0G5, 403/427-8392; Fax: 403/422-3562

**B.C.:** Ministry of Municipal Affairs & Housing, Office of the Fire Commissioner, Municipal Affairs, PO Box 9490, Victoria BC V8W 9N7, 250/356-9000; Fax: 250/356-9019

**Man.:** Manitoba Labour, #156, Legislative Bldg., 450 Broadway, Winnipeg MB R3C 0V8, 204/945-3328; Fax: 204/948-2089

**N.B.:** Department of Municipalities, Culture & Housing, Office of the Fire Marshall, PO Box 6000, Fredericton NB E3B 5H1, 506/453-2004; Fax: 506/457-4899

Department of Natural Resources & Energy, Regional Operations, PO Box 6000, Fredericton NB E3B 5H1, 506/453-2207; Fax: 506/453-2930

**Nfld.:** Department of Works, Services & Transportation, Safety & Security, Confederation Bldg., PO Box 8700, St. John's NF A1B 4J6, 709/729-3443; Fax: 709/729-4285

Office of the Fire Commissioner, Bldg. 9001, Pleasantville, PO Box 8700, St. John's NF A1B 4J6, 709/726-1050; Fax: 709/729-2524

**NWT:** Department of Municipal & Community Affairs, #600, 5201 - 50 Ave., PO Box 1310, Yellowknife NT X1A 2L9, 867/873-7469; Fax: 867/873-8193

**N.S.:** Department of Labour, Fire Marshall's Office, 5151 Terminal Rd., PO Box 697, Halifax NS B3J 2T8, 902/424-4553; Fax: 902/424-3239

**Ont.:** Ministry of Natural Resources, Aviation, Flood & Fire Management, #400, 70 Foster Dr., Sault Ste. Marie ON P6A 6V5, 705/945-5937; Fax: 807/475-1503

Ministry of the Solicitor General & Correctional Services, Office of the Fire Marshal, 5775 Yonge St., North York ON M2M 4J1, 416/325-3100; Fax: 416/325-3119

Ontario Fire College, PO Box 850, Gravenhurst ON P0C 1G0, 705/687-2294; Fax: 705/687-7911

**PEI:** Department of Agriculture & Forestry, Forestry Division, J. Frank Gaudet Tree Nursery, Upton Rd., West Royalty, PO Box 2000, Charlottetown PE C1A 7N8, 902/368-4700; Fax: 902/368-4713

Department of Community Affairs & Attorney General, Office of the Fire Marshal, PO Box 2000, Charlottetown PE C1A 7N8, 902/368-4869; Fax: 902/368-5526

**Qué.:** Commissariat aux incendies, 455, rue Dupont, Québec QC G1K 6N2, 418/529-5706; Fax: 418/529-9922

Ministère de la Sécurité publique, Direction des affaires policières et de la sécurité incendie, 2525, boul Laurier, 6e étage, Ste-Foy QC G1V 2L2, 418/644-9774; Fax: 418/646-3564

**Sask.:** Saskatchewan Environment & Resource Management, Forest Fire Management, 3211 Albert St., Regina SK S4S 5W6, 306/953-2206; Fax: 306/953-2502

Saskatchewan Municipal Government, Municipal Boundary & Planning & Fire Prevention Appeals Committees, 2151 Scarth St., 4th Fl., Regina SK S4P 3V7, 306/787-6244; Fax: 306/787-1610

Office of the Fire Commissioner, 1855 Victoria Ave., Regina SK S4P 3V7, 306/787-4516; Fax: 306/787-9273

**Yuk.:** Yukon Community & Transportation Services, Office of the Fire Marshal, PO Box 2703, Whitehorse YT Y1A 2C6, 867/667-5217; Fax: 867/393-6404

## FIREARMS

Justice Canada, Canadian Firearms Centre, Justice Bldg., 239 Wellington St., Ottawa ON K1A 0H8, 613/952-3800; Fax: 613/954-0811

**Alta:** Alberta Justice, Provincial Firearms, 10365 - 97 St., Edmonton AB T5J 3W7, 403/427-0437; Fax: 403/427-1100

**B.C.:** Ministry of the Attorney General, PO Box 9282, Stn Prov. Gov't, Victoria BC V8W 9J7, 250/356-9596 (Policy & Education); Fax: 250/356-9037

**N.B.:** Department of the Solicitor General, Provincial Firearms Office, Barker House, 4th Fl., PO Box 6000, Fredericton NB E3B 5H1, 506/453-3775; Fax: 506/453-3870

**NWT:** Department of Justice, Firearms Office, PO Box 1320, Yellowknife NT X1A 2L9, 867/920-8714

**N.S.:** Licensing & Gun Control, 5151 Terminal Rd., PO Box 7, Halifax NS B3J 2L6, 902/424-6689; Fax: 902/424-0700

**Sask.:** Saskatchewan Justice, Provincial Firearms Office, 1874 Scarth St., Regina SK S4P 3V7, 306/787-9713; Fax: 306/787-9111

## FISHERIES

Fisheries & Oceans Canada, 200 Kent St., Ottawa ON K1A 0E6, 613/993-0999; TDD: 1-800-668-5228

Fisheries Resource Conservation Council, PO Box 2001, Stn D, Ottawa ON K1A 5W3

Foreign Affairs & International Trade Canada, Fisheries Conservation, Lester B. Pearson Bldg., 125 Sussex Dr., Ottawa ON K1A 0G2, 613/995-6907; Fax: 613/995-2188

Freshwater Fish Marketing Corporation, 1199 Plessis Rd., Winnipeg MB R2C 3L4, 204/983-6600; Fax: 204/983-6497

Gulf Fisheries Centre, PO Box 5030, Moncton NB E1C 9B6, 506/851-6227; Fax: 506/851-7732

Halifax Fisheries Research Laboratory, 1707 Lower Water St., PO Box 550, Halifax NS B3J 2S7, 902/426-7444; Fax: 902/426-2698

Northern Cod Research Program, PO Box 5667, St. John's NF A1C 5X1, 709/772-2051; Fax: 709/772-6100

Northwest Atlantic Fisheries Centre, PO Box 5667, St. John's NF A1C 5X1, 709/772-2020; Fax: 709/772-2156

**B.C.:** Ministry of Environment, Lands & Parks, Fisheries Branch, 780 Blanshard St., 2nd Fl., Victoria BC V8V 1X4, 250/387-9711; Fax: 250/387-9750

**Man.:** Manitoba Industry, Trade & Tourism, Master Angler Program, 155 Carlton St., 6th Fl., Winnipeg

MB R3C 3H8, 204/945-4254; Toll Free: 1-800-665-0040; Fax: 204/945-2302

Manitoba Natural Resources, Fisheries Branch, 200 Saulteaux Cres., PO Box 20, Winnipeg MB R3J 3W3, 204/945-7814; Fax: 204/945-2308

**N.B.:** Department of Natural Resources & Energy, Fish & Wildlife, PO Box 6000, Fredericton NB E3B 5H1, 506/453-2440; Fax: 506/453-6699

**Nfld.:** Department of Fisheries & Aquaculture, Fisheries Bldg., 30 Strawberry Marsh Rd., PO Box 8700, St. John's NF A1B 4J6, 709/729-3723; Fax: 709/729-6082

**NWT:** Department of Resources, Wildlife & Economic Development, Wildlife & Fisheries, PO Box 1320, Yellowknife NT X1A 2L9, 867/920-8716; Fax: 867/873-0221

**N.S.:** Department of Fisheries, Bank of Montreal Bldg., 5151 George St., 7th Fl., PO Box 2223, Halifax NS B3J 3C4, 902/424-4560; Fax: 902/424-4671

**Ont.:** Ministry of Natural Resources, Fish & Wildlife Branch, Whitney Block, #6540, 99 Wellesley St. West, Toronto ON M7A 1W3, 416/314-6132; Fax: 416/314-1994

**PEI:** Department of Agriculture & Forestry, Fisheries & Aquaculture Division, Jones Bldg., 11 Kent St., PO Box 2000, Charlottetown PE C1A 7N8, 902/368-5251; Fax: 902/368-5542

Department of Fisheries & Environment, Fish & Wildlife Division, Jones Bldg., 11 Kent St., 4th Fl., PO Box 2000, Charlottetown PE CIA 7N8, 902/368-4683; Fax: 902/368-5830

**Sask.:** Saskatchewan Environment & Resource Management, Fisheries Branch, 3211 Albert St., Regina SK S4S 5W6, 306/787-2884; Fax: 306/787-0737

**Yuk.:** Yukon Renewable Resources, Fisheries, PO Box 2703, Whitehorse YT Y1A 2C6, 867/667-5117; Fax: 867/393-6213

**FITNESS *See* RECREATION**

**FOOD *See* AGRICULTURE; NUTRITION**

**FOREIGN AFFAIRS *See* INTERNATIONAL AFFAIRS**

## FOREST RESOURCES

Industry Canada, Forest Industries & Building Products, C.D. Howe Bldg., 235 Queen St., Ottawa ON K1A 0H5, 613/957-0845; Fax: 613/952-8988

Natural Resources Canada, Canadian Forest Service, 580 Booth St., Ottawa ON K1A 0E4, 613/947-7399; Fax: 613/996-9094

**Alta:** Alberta Economic Development & Tourism, Forestry Industry Development, Commerce Place, 10155 - 102 St., Edmonton AB T5J 4L6, 403/422-7011; Fax: 403/427-5299

Alberta Environmental Protection, Forest Management Division, 9915 - 108 St., Edmonton AB T5K 2G8, 403/427-4566

**B.C.:** Forest Renewal BC, 727 Fisgard St., Victoria BC V8V 1X4, 250/387-2500

Ministry of Environment, Lands & Parks, Forest Practices Code, 965 Broughton St., 6th Fl., Victoria BC V8V 1X4, 250/387-6989; Fax: 250/953-5170

Ministry of Forests, PO Box 9517, Stn Prov Govt, Victoria BC V8W 9C2, 250/387-5255; Fax: 250/387-8485

**Man.:** Manitoba Natural Resources, Forestry Branch, 200 Saulteaux Crescent, PO Box 70, Winnipeg MB R3J 3W3, 204/945-7998; Fax: 204/948-2671

**N.B.:** Department of Natural Resources & Energy, Forest Management, PO Box 6000, Fredericton NB E3B 5H1, 506/453-2432; Fax: 506/453-6689

Forest Protection Limited, Comp 5, Site 24, RR#1, Fredericton NB E3B 4X2, 506/446-6930; Fax: 506/446-6934

New Brunswick Forest Products Commission, PO Box 6000, Fredericton NB E3B 5H1, 506/453-2196; Fax: 506/457-4966

**Nfld.:** Department of Forest Resources & Agrifoods, Forestry & Wildlife Branch, Confederation Complex, PO Box 8700, St. John's NF A1B 4J6, 709/729-4716

**NWT:** Department of Resources, Wildlife & Economic Development, Forest Management, PO Box 1320, Yellowknife NT X1A 2L9, 867/872-7700; Fax: 867/872-2077

**N.S.:** Department of Natural Resources, Forestry, Founder's Square, 1701 Hollis St., PO Box 698, Halifax NS B3J 2T9, 902/893-5749; Fax: 902/893-6102

**Ont.:** Algonquin Forestry Authority - Huntsville, 222 Main St. West, PO Box 1198, Huntsville ON P0A 1K0, 705/789-9647; Fax: 705/789-3353

Algonquin Forestry Authority - Pembroke, #84, 6 Isabella St., Pembroke ON K8A 5S5, 613/735-0173; Fax: 613/735-4192

Centre for Northern Forest Ecosystem Research, Lakehead University, 955 Oliver Rd., Thunder Bay ON P7B 5E1, 807/343-4016; Fax: 807/343-4001

Ministry of Natural Resources, Forest Management Branch, Whitney Block, #6540, 99 Wellesley St. West, Toronto ON M7A 1W3, 705/945-6660; Fax: 416/314-1994

**PEI:** Department of Agriculture & Forestry, Forestry Division, J. Frank Gaudet Tree Nursery, Upton Rd., West Royalty, PO Box 2000, Charlottetown PE C1A 7N8, 902/368-4700; Fax: 902/368-4713

**Qué.:** Ministère des Ressources Naturelles, Forêts, 880, ch Ste-Foy, Québec QC G1S 4X4, 418/627-8600 (Renseignements); Fax: 418/644-7160

Société de récupération, d'exploitation et de développement forestier, 1195, ave de Lavigerie, Ste-Foy QC G1V 4N3, 418/659-4530; Fax: 418/643-4037

**Yuk.:** Yukon Renewable Resources, PO Box 2703, Whitehorse YT Y1A 2C6, 867/667-5237; Toll Free: 1-800-661-0408 (Yukon)

**FUEL *See* NUCLEAR ENERGY; OIL & NATURAL GAS RESOURCES**

**GARBAGE *See* WASTE MANAGEMENT**

**GAS *See* OIL & NATURAL GAS RESOURCES**

## GEOLOGICAL SERVICES

Natural Resources Canada, Canada Centre for Mineral & Energy Technology, 580 Booth St., Ottawa ON K1A 0E4, 613/995-0947; Fax: 613/996-9094

Geological Survey of Canada, 601 Booth St., Ottawa ON K1A 0E8, 613/996-3919; Fax: 613/996-9990

Geomatics Canada, 580 Booth St., Ottawa ON K1A 0E4, 613/995-4321; Fax: 613/996-9094

**Alta:** Alberta Energy, Mineral Access, Geology & Mapping, Petroleum Plaza, North Tower, 9945 - 108 St., Edmonton AB T5K 2G6, 403/422-9466; Fax: 403/427-3198

**B.C.:** Ministry of Employment & Investment, Energy & Minerals Division, 1810 Blanshard St., 5th Fl., PO Box 9324, Victoria BC V8W 9N3, 250/356-8702

**Man.:** Manitoba Energy & Mines, Geological Services Branch, #360, 1395 Ellice Ave., Winnipeg MB R3G 3P2, 204/945-6567; Fax: 204/945-0586, 1406

**N.B.:** Department of Natural Resources & Energy, Geological Surveys Branch, PO Box 6000, Fredericton NB E3B 5H1, 506/453-2206; Fax: 506/453-3671

**Nfld.:** Department of Mines & Energy, Geological Survey, PO Box 8700, St. John's NF A1B 4J6, 709/729-2301; Fax: 709/729-3493

**NWT:** Department of Resources, Wildlife & Economic Development, Northwest Territories Remote Sensing Centre, PO Box 1320, Yellowknife NT X1A 2L9, 867/920-3329; Fax: 867/873-0221

**N.S.:** Department of Natural Resources, Surveys Division, Founder's Square, 1701 Hollis St., PO Box 698, Halifax NS B3J 2T9, 902/424-3145; Fax: 902/424-7735

**Ont.:** Ministry of Northern Development & Mines, Ontario Geological Survey, Resident Geologists Section, Willet Green Miller Centre, 933 Ramsey Lake Rd., 6th Fl., Sudbury ON P3E 6B5, 705/670-5955; Fax: 705/670-5953

Ontario Geological Survey, Sedimentary Geoscience Section, Willet Green Miller Centre, 933 Ramsey Lake Rd., 6th Fl., Sudbury ON P3E 6B5, 705/670-5902; Fax: 705/670-5904

**PEI:** Department of the Provincial Treasury, Geomatics Information Centre, PO Box 2000, Charlottetown PE C1A 7N8, 902/368-5165; Fax: 902/368-4399

**Qué.:** Ministère des Ressources Naturelles, Géologie, #B-302, 5700 - 4 av ouest, 3e étage, Charlesbourg QC G1H 6R1, 418/627-6274 poste 5021; Fax: 418/643-2816

**Sask.:** SaskGeomatics, 2151 Scarth St., Regina SK S4P 3V7, 306/787-2800

Saskatchewan Energy & Mines, Exploration & Geological Services Division, 1914 Hamilton St., Regina SK S4P 4V4, 306/787-2526; Fax: 306/787-7338

Geology & Petroleum Lands Branch, 1914 Hamilton St., Regina SK S4P 4V4, 306/787-2606; Fax: 306/787-2478

**Yuk.:** Yukon Economic Development, Geological Surveys, 211 Main St., PO Box 2703, Whitehorse YT Y1A 2C6, 867/667-8516; Fax: 867/668-8601

## GOVERNMENT (GENERAL INFORMATION)

Agriculture & Agri-Food Canada, Communications Branch, Sir John Carling Bldg., 930 Carling Ave., Ottawa ON K1A 0C5, 613/759-7976; Fax: 613/759-7969

Auditor General of Canada, 240 Sparks St., Ottawa ON K1A 0G6, 613/995-3708; Fax: 613/957-4023

Canadian Heritage, Communications Branch, Jules Léger Bldg., 25 Eddy St., Hull QC K1A 1K5, 819/997-0055; Fax: 819/953-5382

Citizenship & Immigration Canada, Jean Edmonds Towers, 365 Laurier Ave. West, Ottawa ON K1A 1L1, 613/954-9019; Fax: 613/954-2221

Correctional Service Canada, 340 Laurier Ave. West, Ottawa ON K1A 0P9, 613/995-5364 (Communications); Fax: 613/947-0091

Environment Canada, Terrasses de la Chaudière, 10 Wellington St., Hull QC K1A 0H3, 819/997-2800; Toll Free: 1-800-668-6767; Fax: 819/953-2225

Finance Canada, Consultations & Communications Branch, Esplanade Laurier, 140 O'Connor St., Ottawa ON K1A 0G5, 613/992-1573; Fax: 613/996-8404

Fisheries & Oceans Canada, 200 Kent St., Ottawa ON K1A 0E6, 613/993-0999; TDD: 1-800-668-5228

Foreign Affairs & International Trade Canada, Lester B. Pearson Bldg., 125 Sussex Dr., Ottawa ON K1A 0G2, 613/944-4000; Fax: 613/952-3904

Health Canada, Brooke Claxton Bldg., Tunney's Pasture, 120 Parkdale Ave., Ottawa ON K1A 0K9, 613/957-2991; Fax: 613/941-5366

House of Commons, Canada, House of Commons, 111 Wellington St., PO Box 1103, Ottawa ON K1A 0A9

Human Resources Development Canada, Place du Portage, Phase IV, 140, Promenade du Portage, Hull QC K1A 0J9, 819/994-6013 (Communications)

Indian & Northern Affairs Canada, Tour Nord, Les Terrasses de la Chaudière, 10 Wellington St., Hull QC K1A 0H4, 819/997-0380; Fax: 819/953-3017

Industry Canada, C.D. Howe Bldg., 235 Queen St., Ottawa ON K1A 0H5, 613/941-0222; Fax: 613/954-6436

Justice Canada, Communications & Executive Services Branch, Justice Bldg., 239 Wellington St., Ottawa ON K1A 0H8, 613/957-4222; Fax: 613/954-0811

National Defence (Canada), MGen. George R. Pearkes Bldg., 101 Colonel By Dr., Ottawa ON K1A 0K2, 613/992-4581

Natural Resources Canada, Communications Branch, 580 Booth St., Ottawa ON K1A 0E4, 613/992-0267; Fax: 613/996-9094

Office of the Prime Minister (Lib.), #309-S, Centre Block, House of Commons, 111 Wellington St., Ottawa ON K1A 0A2, 613/992-4211; Fax: 613/941-6900

Public Works & Government Services Canada, Communications, Place du Portage, Phase III, 11, rue Laurier, Hull QC K1A 0S5, 819/956-2304; TDD: 819/994-5389; Fax: 819/956-9062

Revenue Canada, Customs Border Services, 875 Heron Rd., Ottawa ON K1A 0L8, 613/952-0384

Solicitor General Canada, Communications Group, Sir Wilfrid Laurier Bldg., 340 Laurier Ave. West, Ottawa ON K1A 0P8, 613/991-2799; Fax: 613/993-7062

Statistics Canada, R.H. Coats Bldg., Tunney's Pasture, 120 Parkdale Ave., Ottawa ON K1A 0T6, 613/951-8116; Toll Free: 1-800-263-1136, TDD: 1-800-363-7629; Fax: 613/951-0581

Transport Canada, Transport Canada Building, 330 Sparks St., Ottawa ON K1A 0N5, 613/990-2309; Fax: 613/954-4731

Treasury Board of Canada, 140 O'Connor St., Ottawa ON K1A 0R5, 613/957-2400; Fax: 613/952-3658

Veterans Affairs Canada, Daniel J. MacDonald Bldg., 161 Grafton St., PO Box 7700, Charlottetown PE C1A 8M9, 902/566-8195; Fax: 902/566-8508

**Alta:** Alberta Public Affairs Bureau, Park Plaza, 10611 - 98 Ave., 6th Fl., Edmonton AB T5K 2P7, 403/427-2754; Fax: 403/422-4168

**B.C.:** British Columbia Government Communications Office, 612 Government St., Victoria BC V8V 1X4, 250/387-1337; Fax: 250/387-3534

Ministry of Finance & Corporate Relations, Enquiry BC, 525 Superior St., 1st Fl., Victoria BC V8V 1X4, 250/387-9273; Fax: 250/953-4302

**Man.:** Manitoba Information Services, Citizens' Inquiry Service, #511, 401 York Ave., Winnipeg MB R3C 0P8, 204/945-3744; Toll Free: 1-800-282-8060, TDD: 204/945-4796; Fax: 204/945-4261

**N.B.:** Communications New Brunswick, 225 King St., PO Box 6000, Fredericton NB E3B 5H1, 506/453-2240; Fax: 506/453-5329

**Nfld.:** Department of Government Services & Lands, PO Box 8700, St. John's NF A1B 4J6

**NWT:** Legislative Assembly, Public Information, c/o Clerk's Office, PO Box 1320, Yellowknife NT X1A 2L9, 867/669-2230; Toll Free: 1-800-661-0784; Fax: 867/920-4735

**N.S.:** Department of Business & Consumer Services, Access Nova Scotia, South Maritime Centre, #8, 1505 Barrington St., Halifax NS B3J 2X1, 902/424-7009; Toll Free: 1-800-225-8227; Fax: 902/424-2633

Communications Services/Public Inquiries Office, One Government Place, 1700 Granville St., Ground Fl., PO Box 608, Halifax NS B3J 2R7, 902/424-5200; Toll Free: 1-800-670-4357; Fax: 902/425-3026

**Ont.:** Management Board of Cabinet, Citizens' Inquiry Bureau, Ferguson Block, 77 Wellesley St. West, 12th Fl., Toronto ON M7A 1N3, 416/326-1234 (Ontario collect); TDD: 416/325-3408; Fax: 416/327-3517

Communications Services Branch, Ferguson Block, 77 Wellesley St. West, 12th Fl., Toronto ON M7A 1N3, 416/327-2789; Fax: 416/327-2817

**PEI:** Department of the Provincial Treasury, Island Information Service, 11 Kent St., PO Box 2000, Charlottetown PE C1A 7N8, 902/368-4000; Fax: 902/368-5544

**Qué.:** Ministère des Relations avec les citoyens et de l'Immigration, Communication-Québec, 1500-C, boul Charest Ouest, 1er étage, Ste-Foy QC G1N 2E5, 418/643-1430; Fax: 418/643-5190

**Sask.:** Saskatchewan Government Media Services, #3, Legislative Bldg., Regina SK S4S 0B3, 306/787-6281

**Yuk.:** Executive Council, Policy & Communications, PO Box 2703, Whitehorse YT Y1A 2C6, 867/667-5854, 5393, 5939; Fax: 867/393-6202

Yukon Government Services, Information Services, PO Box 2703, Whitehorse YT Y1A 2C6, 867/667-5436; Fax: 867/667-5304

## GOVERNMENT PURCHASING

Public Works & Government Services Canada, Open Bidding Service/MERX & Government Buiness Opportunities, OBS, c/o Information Systems Management Corporation, PO Box 22011, Ottawa ON K1V 0W2, 613/737-3374; Toll Free: 1-800-361-4637; Fax: 613/737-3643

Supply Operations Service Branch, Place du Portage, Phase III, 11, rue Laurier, Hull QC K1A 0S5, 819/956-3115

**Alta:** Alberta Public Works, Supply & Services, Purchasing Branch, 6950 - 113 St., 3rd Fl., Edmonton AB T6H 5V7, 403/427-3222 ext.223; Fax: 403/427-0812

**B.C.:** Ministry of Finance & Corporate Relations, British Columbia Purchasing Commission, #102, 1962 Canso Rd., PO Box 2190, Sidney BC V8L 3S8, 250/655-2400; Fax: 250/356-5851

**Man.:** Manitoba Government Services, Supply & Services Division, 270 Osborne St. North, Winnipeg MB R3C 1V7, 204/945-4800 (Administration)

**N.B.:** Department of Supply & Services, PO Box 6000, Fredericton NB E3B 5H1, 506/453-3742; Fax: 506/444-4400

**Nfld.:** Department of Works, Services & Transportation, Government Purchasing Agency, Confederation Bldg., PO Box 8700, St. John's NF A1B 4J6, 709/729-3343; Fax: 709/729-4285

**NWT:** Department of Public Works & Services, Bldg. YK, 7th Fl., PO Box 1320, Yellowknife NT X1A 2L9, 867/873-7114; Fax: 867/873-0264

**N.S.:** Department of Finance, Government Purchasing Agency/Public Tenders Office, Central Services Bldg., 6176 Young St., Suite 120, Halifax NS B3K 2A6, 902/424-5520; Fax: 902/463-5732

**Ont.:** Management Board of Cabinet, Supply & Service Division, Ferguson Block, 77 Wellesley St. West, 12th Fl., Toronto ON M7A 1N3, 416/327-3515; Fax: 416/327-3517

**PEI:** Department of the Provincial Treasury, Procurement Services, PO Box 2000, Charlottetown PE C1A 7N8, 902/368-4040; Fax: 902/368-5171

**Qué.:** Conseil du trésor, Approvisionnements, Édifice Cyrille-Duquet, 1500-H, rue Jean-Talon nord, Ste-Foy QC G1N 4T5, 418/643-5926; Fax: 418/643-7824

**Sask.:** Saskatchewan Property Management Corporation, 1840 Lorne St., Regina SK S4P 3V7, 306/787-6911; Fax: 306/787-1061

**Yuk.:** Yukon Government Services, Supply Services, PO Box 2703, Whitehorse YT Y1A 2C6, 867/667-5436; Fax: 867/393-6299

## GRANTS & SUBSIDIES

***See Also* Student Aid**

Atlantic Canada Opportunities Agency, 644 Main St., 3rd Fl., PO Box 6051, Moncton NB E1C 9J8, 506/851-2271; Toll Free: 1-800-561-7862, TDD: 506/851-3540; Fax: 506/851-7403

Business Development Bank of Canada, #400, 5, Place Ville Marie, Montréal QC H3B 5E7, 514/283-5904; Toll Free: 1-888-463-6232; Fax: 514/283-0617

Canada Council for the Arts, 350 Albert St., PO Box 1047, Ottawa ON K1P 5V8, 613/566-4365; Toll Free: 1-800-263-5588; Fax: 613/566-4390

Canada Mortgage & Housing Corporation, 700 Montreal Rd., Ottawa ON K1A 0P7, 613/748-2000; Toll Free: 1-800-668-2642; Fax: 613/748-2098

Farm Credit Corporation Canada, 1800 Hamilton St., PO Box 4320, Regina SK S4P 4L3, 306/780-8100; Toll Free: 1-800-387-3232; Fax: 306/780-5703

Federal Office of Regional Development (Québec), Tour de la Bourse, #3800, 800, Place Victoria, CP 247, Montréal QC H4Z 1E8, 514/283-6412; Toll Free: 1-800-322-4636; Fax: 514/283-3302

Human Resources Development Canada, Human Resources Investment, Place du Portage, Phase IV, 140, Promenade du Portage, Hull QC K1A 0J9, 819/994-6013 (Communications)

Indian & Northern Affairs Canada, Indian Program & Funding Allocation Directorate, Tour Nord, Les Terrasses de la Chaudière, 10 Wellington St., Hull QC K1A 0H4, 819/953-9540; Fax: 819/953-3017

Industry Canada, Industry Sector, C.D. Howe Bldg., 235 Queen St., Ottawa ON K1A 0H5, 613/941-0222; Fax: 613/954-6436

International Development Research Centre, PO Box 8500, Ottawa ON K1G 3H9, 613/236-6163; Fax: 613/238-7230

Medical Research Council of Canada, Tower B, Holland Cross, 1600 Scott St., 5th Fl., Ottawa ON K1A 0W9, 613/941-2672; Fax: 613/954-1800

National Film Board of Canada, 3155, rue Côte de Liesse, St-Laurent QC H4N 2N4, 514/283-9000; Fax: 514/283-8971

Natural Sciences & Engineering Research Council of Canada, Constitution Square, 350 Albert St., Ottawa ON K1A 1H5, 613/996-7235; Fax: 613/992-5337

Task Force on Incomes & Adjustment in the Atlantic Fishery, 200 Kent St., Ottawa ON K1A 0E6, 613/941-6502

Western Economic Diversification Canada, Canada Place, #1500, 9700 Jasper Ave., Edmonton AB T5J 4H7, 403/495-4164; Toll Free: 1-888-338-WEST (9378); Fax: 403/495-6223

**Alta:** Alberta Municipal Affairs, Grants, Subsidies & Recoveries, Commerce Place, 10155 - 102 St., Edmonton AB T5J 4L4, 403/427-6897; Fax: 403/427-4315

Local Government Services Division, Commerce Place, 10155 - 102 St., Edmonton AB T5J 4L4, 403/427-2732; Fax: 403/422-9105

**B.C.:** Ministry of Small Business, Tourism & Culture, Community & Regional Development Division, 1405 Douglas St., Victoria BC V8W 3C1, 250/356-7363; Fax: 250/387-5633

**Man.:** Manitoba Agricultural Credit Corporation, #100, 1525 - 1 St., Brandon MB R7A 7A1, 204/726-6850; Fax: 204/726-6849

Manitoba Culture, Heritage & Citizenship, Grants Administration, 213 Notre Dame., Winnipeg MB R3B 1N3, 204/945-4580; Fax: 204/945-5760

Multicultural Grants Advisory Council, 213 Notre Dame Ave., 4th Fl., Winnipeg MB R3B 1N3, 204/945-4458; Fax: 204/945-1675

**N.B.:** Department of Justice, Financial Services, #412, Centennial Bldg., PO Box 6000, Fredericton NB E3B 5H1, 506/453-2719 (Administration); Fax: 506/453-8718

New Brunswick Research & Productivity Council, IRAP, 921 College Hill Rd., Fredericton NB E3B 6Z9, 506/452-1385; Fax: 506/452-1395

**Nfld.:** Department of Municipal & Provincial Affairs, Canada/Newfoundland Infrastructure Program, West Block, Confederation Bldg., PO Box 8700, St. John's NF A1B 4J6, 709/729-5411

Department of Tourism, Culture & Recreation, Tourism & Crafts Branch, Confederation Bldg., PO Box 8700, St. John's NF A1B 4J6, 709/729-0928; Fax: 709/729-0662

Newfoundland Municipal Financing Corporation, Confederation Bldg., PO Box 8700, St. John's NF A1B 4J6, 709/729-6686; Fax: 709/729-2070

**NWT:** Department of Resources, Wildlife & Economic Development, Trade & Investment, PO Box 1320, Yellowknife NT X1A 2L9, 867/873-7361; Fax: 867/920-2756

**N.S.:** Department of Education & Culture, Grants & Audit Division, 2021 Brunswick St., PO Box 578, Halifax NS B3J 2S9, 902/424-3956; Fax: 902/424-0511

Department of Finance, PO Box 187, Halifax NS B3J 2N3, 902/424-5554; Fax: 902/424-0635

**Ont.:** Ministry of Citizenship, Culture & Recreation, Culture Division, 77 Bloor St. West, 6th Fl., Toronto ON M7A 2R9, 416/314-7265; Fax: 416/314-7313

Recreation Division, 77 Bloor St. West, 6th Fl., Toronto ON M7A 2R9, 416/327-2422

Ministry of Economic Development, Trade & Tourism, Business Development & Tourism Division, Hearst Block, 900 Bay St., Toronto ON M7A 2E1, 416/325-6666; Fax: 416/325-6688

Northern Ontario Heritage Fund Corporation, Roberta Bondar Place, #150, 70 Foster Dr., Sault Ste. Marie ON P6A 6V8, 705/945-6700; Fax: 705/945-6701

**PEI:** Department of the Provincial Treasury, PO Box 2000, Charlottetown PE C1A 7N8, 902/368-4000; Fax: 902/368-5544

**Qué.:** Société de développement industriel du Québec, Place Sillery, 1126, ch St-Louis, 5e étage, Québec QC G1S 1E5, 418/643-5172

**Sask.:** Saskatchewan Arts Board, T.C. Douglas Bldg., 3475 Albert St., 3rd Fl., Regina SK S4S 6X6, 306/787-4056; Toll Free: 1-800-667-7526 (Saskatchewan); Fax: 306/787-4199

Saskatchewan Economic & Co-operative Development, 1919 Saskatchewan Dr., Regina SK S4P 3V7, 306/787-2232

**Yuk.:** Yukon Community & Transportation Services, Sport & Recreation Branch, PO Box 2703, Whitehorse YT Y1A 2C6, 867/667-5608; Fax: 867/393-6416

Yukon Economic Development, Industry Trade & Investment, 211 Main St., PO Box 2703, Whitehorse YT Y1A 2C6, 867/667-5466; Fax: 867/668-8601

Yukon Tourism, Arts Branch, PO Box 2703, Whitehorse YT Y1A 2C6, 867/667-8592; Fax: 867/667-8844

### GUARANTEED INCOME *See* INCOME SECURITY

### HANDICAPPED SERVICES *See* DISABLED PERSONS SERVICES

## HEALTH CARE INSURANCE

Citizenship & Immigration Canada, Immigration Health Service, Jean Edmonds Towers, 365 Laurier Ave. West, Ottawa ON K1A 1L1, 613/954-4470; Fax: 613/941-2179

Health Canada, Health Promotions & Programs Branch, Brooke Claxton Bldg., Tunney's Pasture, 120 Parkdale Ave., Ottawa ON K1A 0K9, 613/957-2991; Fax: 613/941-5366

**Alta:** Alberta Health, Health Policy, PO Box 1360, Edmonton AB T5J 2N3, 403/427-7164 (Communications)

**B.C.:** Ministry of Health, Medical Services Plan Operations, 1515 Blanshard St., 7th Fl., Victoria BC V8W 3C8, 250/952-3187; Fax: 250/952-3131

Pharmacare, 1515 Blanshard St., 7th Fl., Victoria BC V8W 3C8, 250/952-1706; Fax: 250/952-2235

**Man.:** Manitoba Health, 599 Empress St., PO Box 925, Winnipeg MB R3C 2T6, 204/786-7191 (Finance & Administration Branch)

Health Services Insurance Fund, 447 Portage Ave., 12th Fl., Winnipeg MB R3B 3H5, 204/786-7191 (Finance & Administration Branch)

**N.B.:** Department of Health & Community Services, Medicare/Prescription Drug Program, PO Box 5100, Fredericton NB E3B 5G8, 506/453-2415; Fax: 506/444-4697

**Nfld.:** Department of Health, West Block, Confederation Bldg., PO Box 8700, St. John's NF A1B 4J6, 709/729-3127; Fax: 709/729-5824

Newfoundland Medical Care Commission, Elizabeth Towers, 100 Elizabeth Ave., St. John's NF A1C 5J3, 709/722-6980; Fax: 709/722-0718

**NWT:** Department of Health & Social Services, Health Services Administration, Centre Square Tower, 8th Fl., PO Box 1320, Yellowknife NT X1A 2L9, 867/873-7714; Fax: 867/873-0280

**N.S.:** Department of Health, Insured Programs Management & Clinical Rationalization Branch, Joseph Howe Bldg., 1690 Hollis St., PO Box 488, Halifax NS B3J 2R8, 902/424-4310; Fax: 902/424-0559

**Ont.:** Ministry of Health, Health Insurance & Related Programs, Hepburn Block, 8th Fl., Queen's Park, #1400, 80 Grosvenor St., Toronto ON M7A 1S2, 416/327-4327 (Health Information Centre); Fax: 416/327-4389

**Qué.:** Régie de l'Assurance-maladie du Québec, 1125, ch St-Louis, Québec QC G1K 7T3, 418/682-5111

**Sask.:** Saskatchewan Health, Insured Services Division, 3475 Albert St., Regina SK S4S 6X6, 306/787-8332; Fax: 306/787-8310

**Yuk.:** Yukon Health & Social Services, Health Care Insurance Services, PO Box 2703, Whitehorse YT Y1A 2C6, 867/667-5202; Fax: 867/668-3786

## HEALTH SERVICES

### *See Also* Health Care Insurance; Occupational Safety

Citizenship & Immigration Canada, Immigration Health Service, Jean Edmonds Towers, 365 Laurier Ave. West, Ottawa ON K1A 1L1, 613/954-4470; Fax: 613/941-2179

Correctional Service Canada, Health Care, 340 Laurier Ave. West, Ottawa ON K1A 0P9, 613/992-5713; Fax: 613/947-0091

Health Canada, Brooke Claxton Bldg., Tunney's Pasture, 120 Parkdale Ave., Ottawa ON K1A 0K9, 613/957-2991; Fax: 613/941-5366

Industry Canada, Health Industries, C.D. Howe Bldg., 235 Queen St., Ottawa ON K1A 0H5, 613/954-5258; Fax: 613/952-4209

Veterans Affairs Canada, Daniel J. MacDonald Bldg., 161 Grafton St., PO Box 7700, Charlottetown PE C1A 8M9, 902/566-8195; Fax: 902/566-8508

**Alta:** Alberta Health, PO Box 1360, Edmonton AB T5J 2N3, 403/427-7164 (Communications)

**B.C.:** Ministry of Health, 1515 Blanshard St., 7th Fl., Victoria BC V8W 3C8, 250/952-3456; Toll Free: AIDS Hotline 1-800-661-3886~

**Man.:** Manitoba Health, 599 Empress St., PO Box 925, Winnipeg MB R3C 2T6, 204/786-7191 (Finance & Administration Branch)

**N.B.:** Department of Health & Community Services, Communications, PO Box 5100, Fredericton NB E3B 5G8, 506/453-2536; Fax: 506/444-4697

**Nfld.:** Department of Health, West Block, Confederation Bldg., PO Box 8700, St. John's NF A1B 4J6, 709/729-5021; Fax: 709/729-5824

**NWT:** Department of Health & Social Services, Health Services Development, Centre Square Tower, 8th Fl., PO Box 1320, Yellowknife NT X1A 2L9, 867/920-6173; Fax: 867/873-0266

**N.S.:** Department of Health, Joseph Howe Bldg., 1690 Hollis St., PO Box 488, Halifax NS B3J 2R8, 902/424-4310; Toll Free: 1-800-387-6665; Fax: 902/424-0559

Emergency Health Services Branch, Joseph Howe Bldg., 1690 Hollis St., PO Box 488, Halifax NS B3J 2R8, 902/424-3928; Fax: 902/424-0647

**Ont.:** Ministry of Health, Communications & Information Branch, Hepburn Block, 8th Fl., Queen's Park, #1400, 80 Grosvenor St., Toronto ON M7A 1S2, 416/327-4352; Toll Free: 1-800-268-1153; Fax: 416/327-8791

**PEI:** Department of Health & Social Services, Jones Bldg., 11 Kent St., 2nd Fl., PO Box 2000, Charlottetown PE C1A 7N8, 902/368-4900; Fax: 902/368-4969

**Qué.:** Ministère de la Santé et des services sociaux, 1075, ch Ste-Foy, Québec QC G1S 2M1

**Sask.:** Saskatchewan Health, 3475 Albert St., Regina SK S4S 6X6, 306/787-8332; Fax: 306/787-8310

**Yuk.:** Yukon Health & Social Services, Health Services Branch, PO Box 2703, Whitehorse YT Y1A 2C6, 867/667-3673 (Communications); Fax: 867/667-3096

## HERITAGE RESOURCES

### *See Also* Land Resources; Parks

Canadian Heritage, Jules Léger Bldg., 25 Eddy St., Hull QC K1A 1K5, 819/997-0055; TDD: 819/997-8776; Fax: 819/953-5382

Canadian Heritage Information Network, Jules Léger Bldg., 25 Eddy St., Hull QC K1A 1K5, 819/994-1200; URL://www.chin.gc.ca/; Fax: 819/994-9555

National Archives of Canada, 395 Wellington St., Ottawa ON K1A 0N3, 613/995-5138; Fax: 613/995-6274

National Battlefields Commission, 390, av de Bernières, Québec QC G1R 2L7, 418/648-3506; Fax: 418/648-3638

**Alta:** Alberta Community Development, Cultural Facilities & Historical Resources Division, Old St. Stephen's College, 8820 - 112 St., Edmonton AB T6G 2P8, 403/431-2300; Fax: 403/427-5598

**B.C.:** Ministry of Small Business, Tourism & Culture, Heritage Branch, 1405 Douglas St., Victoria BC V8W 3C1, 250/356-1434; Fax: 250/356-7796

**Man.:** Heritage Grants Advisory Council, 213 Notre Dame Ave., 3rd Fl., Winnipeg MB R3B 1N3, 204/945-4580; Fax: 204/945-5760

Manitoba Heritage Council, 213 Notre Dame Ave., Main Fl., Winnipeg MB R3B 1N3, 204/945-4389; Fax: 204/948-2384

Manitoba Culture, Heritage & Citizenship, Culture, Heritage & Recreation Programs Division, 213 Notre Dame., Winnipeg MB R3B 1N3, 204/945-3729

**N.B.:** Department of Municipalities, Culture & Housing, Heritage Branch, Marysville Place, 20 McGloin St., PO Box 6000, Fredericton NB E3B 5H1, 506/453-2324; Fax: 506/453-2416

**Nfld.:** Department of Tourism, Culture & Recreation, Cultural Affairs Branch, Confederation Bldg., PO Box 8700, St. John's NF A1B 4J6, 709/729-0928; Fax: 709/729-0662

**NWT:** Department of Education, Culture & Employment, Culture & Heritage, PO Box 1320, Yellowknife NT X1A 2L9, 867/873-7551; Fax: 867/873-0155

**N.S.:** Department of Education & Culture, Heritage & Culture Branch (Nova Scotia Museum), 2021 Brunswick St., PO Box 578, Halifax NS B3J 2S9, 902/424-5168; Fax: 902/424-0511

**Ont.:** Ministry of Citizenship, Culture & Recreation, Heritage, Arts & Cultural Industries Policy Branch, 77 Bloor St. West, 6th Fl., Toronto ON M7A 2R9, 416/314-7115; Fax: 416/314-7313

Ontario Heritage Foundation, 10 Adelaide St. East, Toronto ON M5C 1J3, 416/325-5000; Fax: 416/325-5071

**PEI:** Department of Education, Culture, Heritage & Recreation, Sullivan Bldg., 16 Fitzroy St., PO Box 2000, Charlottetown PE C1A 7N8, 902/368-4789; Fax: 902/368-4663

**Qué.:** Commission des biens culturels du Québec, 12, rue Ste-Anne, 2e étage, Québec QC G1R 3X2, 418/643-8378; Fax: 418/643-8591

Ministère de la Culture et des Communications, Archives nationales, Pavillon Louis-Jacques Casault, 1210 av du Séminaire, Ste-Foy QC G1N 4V1, 418/643-2183; Fax: 418/643-4457

Centre de conservation du Québec, 1825, rue Semple, Québec QC G1N 4B7, 418/643-7001; Fax: 418/646-5419

**Sask.:** Saskatchewan Municipal Government, Culture & Recreation Division, 1855 Victoria Ave., Regina SK S4P 3V7, 306/787-8282; Fax: 306/787-4181

Heritage Branch, 1855 Victoria Ave., Regina SK S4P 3V7, 306/787-2809; Fax: 306/787-0069

**Yuk.:** Yukon Tourism, Heritage Branch, PO Box 2703, Whitehorse YT Y1A 2C6, 867/667-5363; Fax: 867/667-8844

## HISTORY & ARCHIVES

Canada Council for the Arts, 350 Albert St., PO Box 1047, Ottawa ON K1P 5V8, 613/566-4365; Toll Free: 1-800-263-5588; Fax: 613/566-4390

Library of Parliament, 111 Wellington St., Ottawa ON K1A 0A9, 613/995-1166; Fax: 613/992-1269

National Archives of Canada, 395 Wellington St., Ottawa ON K1A 0N3, 613/995-5138; Fax: 613/995-6274

**Alta:** Alberta Community Development, Historic Sites Service, Old St. Stephen's College, 8820 - 112 St., Edmonton AB T6G 2P8, 403/431-2310; Fax: 403/427-5598

Provincial Archives, 12845 - 102 Ave., Edmonton AB T5N 0H6, 403/427-1750; Fax: 403/427-4646

**B.C.:** Ministry of Finance & Corporate Relations, BC Archives & Records Services, 655 Belleville St., Victoria BC V8V 1X4, 250/387-5885; Fax: 250/387-2072

**Man.:** Manitoba Culture, Heritage & Citizenship, Historic Resources, 213 Notre Dame., Winnipeg MB R3B 1N3, 204/945-4389; Fax: 204/948-2384

Provincial Archives, 200 Vaughan St., Winnipeg MB R3C 1T5, 204/945-4233; Fax: 204/948-2008

**Nfld.:** Department of Tourism, Culture & Recreation, Cultural Affairs Branch, Confederation Bldg., PO Box 8700, St. John's NF A1B 4J6, 709/729-0928; Fax: 709/729-0662

Historic Resources, Confederation Bldg., PO Box 8700, St. John's NF A1B 4J6, 709/729-2460; Fax: 709/729-0870

**NWT:** Department of Education, Culture & Employment, PO Box 1320, Yellowknife NT X1A 2L9, 867/873-7657; Fax: 867/873-0155

Culture & Heritage, PO Box 1320, Yellowknife NT X1A 2L9, 867/873-7551; Fax: 867/873-0155

**N.S.:** Department of Education & Culture, Nova Scotia Museum of Natural History, 2021 Brunswick St., PO Box 578, Halifax NS B3J 2S9, 902/424-7353; Fax: 902/424-0560

Provincial Library, 2021 Brunswick St., PO Box 578, Halifax NS B3J 2S9, 902/424-2457; Fax: 902/424-0633

**Ont.:** Archives of Ontario, 77 Grenville St., Toronto ON M5S 1B3, 416/327-1600; Toll Free: 1-800-668-9933; Fax: 416/327-1999

**PEI:** Department of Education, Culture, Heritage & Recreation, Sullivan Bldg., 16 Fitzroy St., PO Box 2000, Charlottetown PE C1A 7N8, 902/368-4789; Fax: 902/368-4663

Provincial Libraries & Archives, Sullivan Bldg., 16 Fitzroy St., PO Box 2000, Charlottetown PE C1A 7N8, 902/368-4227; Fax: 902/368-6327

**Qué.:** Ministère de la Culture et des Communications, Archives nationales, Pavillon Louis-Jacques Casault, 1210 av du Séminaire, Ste-Foy QC G1N 4V1, 418/643-2183; Fax: 418/643-4457

**Sask.:** Saskatchewan Archives Board, University of Regina, 3737 Wascana Pkwy., Regina SK S4S 0A2, 306/787-4068; Fax: 306/787-1975

Saskatchewan Municipal Government, Heritage Branch, 1855 Victoria Ave., Regina SK S4P 3V7, 306/787-2809; Fax: 306/787-0069

**Yuk.:** Yukon Education, Libraries & Archives, PO Box 2703, Whitehorse YT Y1A 2C6, 867/667-5309; Fax: 867/393-6254

Yukon Tourism, Historic Sites, PO Box 2703, Whitehorse YT Y1A 2C6, 867/667-5295; Fax: 867/667-8844

## HOSPITALS

### *See Also* Health Care Insurance

Health Canada, Medical Services Branch, Brooke Claxton Bldg., Tunney's Pasture, 120 Parkdale Ave., Ottawa ON K1A 0K9, 613/957-2991; Fax: 613/941-5366

**Alta:** Alberta Health, Health Strategies & Research, PO Box 1360, Edmonton AB T5J 2N3, 403/427-7164 (Communications)

**B.C.:** Ministry of Health, Medical Services Commission, 1515 Blanshard St., 7th Fl., Victoria BC V8W 3C8, 250/952-3465; Fax: 250/952-3131

Strategic Services, 1515 Blanshard St., 7th Fl., Victoria BC V8W 3C8, 250/952-3456

**Man.:** Manitoba Health, Health Services Insurance Fund, 447 Portage Ave., 12th Fl., Winnipeg MB R3B 3H5, 204/786-7191 (Finance & Administration Branch)

Winnipeg Operations - Hospital Services, 599 Empress St., PO Box 925, Winnipeg MB R3C 2T6, 204/786-7138

**N.B.:** Department of Health & Community Services, Hospital Services, PO Box 5100, Fredericton NB E3B 5G8, 506/453-2283; Fax: 506/444-4697

**Nfld.:** Department of Health, Institutions, West Block, Confederation Bldg., PO Box 8700, St. John's NF A1B 4J6, 709/729-5021; Fax: 709/729-5824

Newfoundland Medical Care Commission, Elizabeth Towers, 100 Elizabeth Ave., St. John's NF A1C 5J3, 709/722-6980; Fax: 709/722-0718

**NWT:** Department of Health & Social Services, Health Services Development, Centre Square Tower, 8th Fl., PO Box 1320, Yellowknife NT X1A 2L9, 867/920-6173; Fax: 867/873-0266

**N.S.:** Department of Health, Operations & Regional Support Branch, Joseph Howe Bldg., 1690 Hollis St., PO Box 488, Halifax NS B3J 2R8, 902/424-4310; Fax: 902/424-0550; 424-5769

**Ont.:** Ministry of Health, Institutional Health & Community Services, Hepburn Block, 8th Fl., Queen's Park, #1400, 80 Grosvenor St., Toronto ON M7A 1S2, 416/327-4327 (Health Information Centre); Fax: 416/327-4389

**Qué.:** Ministère de la Santé et des services sociaux, 1075, ch Ste-Foy, Québec QC G1S 2M1

### HOUSE OF COMMONS *See* PARLIAMENT

## HOUSING

Canada Mortgage & Housing Corporation, 700 Montreal Rd., Ottawa ON K1A 0P7, 613/748-2000; Toll Free: 1-800-668-2642; Fax: 613/748-2098

**Alta:** Alberta Social Housing Corporation, 10155 - 102 St., 14th Fl., Edmonton AB T5J 4L4, 403/422-9222; Fax: 403/427-0961

**B.C.:** British Columbia Housing Management Commission/BC Housing, #1701, 4330 Kingsway, Burnaby BC V5H 4G7, 604/433-1711; Fax: 604/439-4722

Ministry of Municipal Affairs & Housing, Municipal Affairs, PO Box 9490, Victoria BC V8W 9N7, 250/387-4089; Fax: 250/356-1070

**Man.:** Manitoba Housing Authority, #303, 280 Broadway Ave., Winnipeg MB R3C 0R8, 204/945-3935; Fax: 204/945-0546

Manitoba Housing, #201, 280 Broadway Ave., Winnipeg MB R3C 0R8, 204/945-4692

**N.B.:** Department of Municipalities, Culture & Housing, Marysville Place, 20 McGloin St., PO Box 6000, Fredericton NB E3B 5H1, 506/453-2690; Fax: 506/457-4991

Community Services Division, Marysville Place, 20 McGloin St., PO Box 6000, Fredericton NB E3B 5H1, 506/453-2690; Fax: 506/453-2416

**Nfld.:** Newfoundland & Labrador Housing Corporation, 2 Canada Dr., PO Box 220, St. John's NF A1C 5J2, 709/724-3000; Fax: 709/724-3250

**NWT:** Northwest Territories Housing Corporation, Scotia Centre, PO Box 2100, Yellowknife NT X1A 2P6

**N.S.:** Department of Housing & Municipal Affairs, PO Box 216, Halifax NS B3J 2M4, 902/424-4141; Fax: 902/424-0531

**Ont.:** Ministry of Municipal Affairs & Housing, Housing Operations Division, 777 Bay St., 17th Fl., Toronto ON M5G 2E5, 416/585-7041 (Communications Branch); Fax: 416/585-6227

Ontario New Home Warranty Program, North East Tower, 6th Fl., 5160 Yonge St., Toronto ON M2N 6L9, 416/229-9200; Fax: 416/229-3800

**Qué.:** Société d'habitation du Québec, Bloc 2, 1054, Conroy, 4e étage, Québec QC G1R 5E7, 418/643-7676; Fax: 418/643-2166

**Sask.:** Saskatchewan Municipal Government, Housing Division, 1855 Victoria Ave., Regina SK S4P 3V7, Toll Free: 1-800-667-7567 (Saskatchewan); Fax: 306/787-4181

**Yuk.:** Yukon Housing Corporation, 410A Jarvis St., PO Box 2703, Whitehorse YT Y1A 2C6, 867/667-5759; Fax: 867/667-3664

## HUMAN RIGHTS

### *See Also* Boards of Review

Canadian Human Rights Commission, Place de Ville, Tower A, #1300, 320 Queen St., Ottawa ON K1A 1E1, 613/995-1151; TDD: 613/996-5211; Fax: 613/996-9661

Citizenship & Immigration Canada, Refugees, Jean Edmonds Towers, 365 Laurier Ave. West, Ottawa ON K1A 1L1, 613/957-5873; Fax: 613/957-5869

**Alta:** Alberta Community Development, Human Rights Secretariat, Standard Life Centre, 10405 Jasper Ave., 7th Fl., Edmonton AB T5J 4R7, 403/427-3116; Fax: 403/422-3563

Alberta Human Rights & Citizenship Commission, 10405 Jasper Ave., 16th Fl., Edmonton AB T5J 4R7, 403/427-7661; Fax: 403/422-3563

**B.C.:** British Columbia Council of Human Rights, 844 Courtney St., 2nd. Fl., Victoria BC V8V 1X4, 250/387-3710; Fax: 250/387-3643

**Man.:** Human Rights Commission, #301, 259 Portage Ave., Winnipeg MB R3B 2A9, 204/945-3007; TDD: 945-3442; Fax: 204/945-1292

**N.B.:** New Brunswick Human Rights Commission, 751 Brunswick St., PO Box 6000, Fredericton NB E3B 5H1, 506/453-2301; Fax: 506/453-2653

**Nfld.:** Newfoundland & Labrador Human Rights Commission, PO Box 8700, St. John's NF A1B 4J6, 709/729-2709; Fax: 709/729-0790

**N.S.:** Nova Scotia Human Rights Commission, Lord Nelson Arcade, 5675 Spring Garden Rd., 7th Fl., PO Box 2221, Halifax NS B3J 3C4, 902/424-4111; Fax: 902/424-0596

**Ont.:** Ontario Human Rights Commission, 400 University Ave., 12th Fl., Toronto ON M7A 2R9, 416/314-4500; Fax: 416/314-4533

**PEI:** Prince Edward Island Human Rights Commission, 3 Queen St., PO Box 2000, Charlottetown PE C1A 7N8, 902/368-4180; Fax: 902/368-4236

**Sask.:** Saskatchewan Human Rights Commission, 122 - 3 Ave. North, 8th Fl., Saskatoon SK S7K 2H6, 306/933-5952; Fax: 306/933-7863

**Yuk.:** Yukon Human Rights Commission, 205 Rogers St., Whitehorse YT Y1A 1X1, 867/667-6226

Yukon Human Rights Panel of Adjudicators, #202, 208 Main St., Whitehorse YT Y1A 2B2, 867/667-7667

## IMMIGRATION

***See Also* Citizenship**

Citizenship & Immigration Canada, Jean Edmonds Towers, 365 Laurier Ave. West, Ottawa ON K1A 1L1, 613/954-9019; Fax: 613/954-2221

Case Processing Centre - Vegreville, #6212, 55 Ave., Vegreville AB T9C 1W5, 403/632-8000; Fax: 403/632-8100

Refugees, Jean Edmonds Towers, 365 Laurier Ave. West, Ottawa ON K1A 1L1, 613/957-5873; Fax: 613/957-5869

Foreign Affairs & International Trade Canada, Passport Office, Place du Centre, 200, Promenade du Portage, 6e étage, Hull QC K1A 0G3, 819/994-3500; Toll Free: 1-800-567-6868, TDD: 613/994-3560; Fax: 819/953-5856

Immigration & Refugee Board, 240 Bank St., Ottawa ON K1A 0K1, 613/995-6486; Fax: 613/996-0543

**Alta:** Alberta Human Rights & Citizenship Commission, 10405 Jasper Ave., 16th Fl., Edmonton AB T5J 4R7, 403/427-7661; Fax: 403/422-3563

**B.C.:** Ministry of the Attorney General, Multiculturalism & Immigration Branch, #309, 703 Broughton St., Victoria BC V8W 1E2, 250/387-7970; Fax: 250/356-5316

**Man.:** Manitoba Culture, Heritage & Citizenship, Immigration/Settlement Policy & Planning Branch, 213 Notre Dame., Winnipeg MB R3B 1N3, 204/945-3729

**N.B.:** Department of Advanced Education & Labour, Multiculturalism & Immigration, Chestnut Complex, 470 York St., PO Box 6000, Fredericton NB E3B 5H1, 506/444-4331; Fax: 506/453-3300

## IMPORTS

***See Also* Trade**

Canadian International Trade Tribunal, Standard Life Centre, 333 Laurier Ave. West, Ottawa ON K1A 0G7, 613/990-2452; Fax: 613/990-2439

Foreign Affairs & International Trade Canada, Lester B. Pearson Bldg., 125 Sussex Dr., Ottawa ON K1A 0G2, 613/944-4000; Fax: 613/952-3904

Trade & Economic Policy Branch, Lester B. Pearson Bldg., 125 Sussex Dr., Ottawa ON K1A 0G2, 613/995-7972; Fax: 613/944-1471

North American Free Trade Agreement (NAFTA) Secretariat, Canadian Section, #705, 90 Sparks St., Ottawa ON K1P 5B4, 613/992-9388; Fax: 613/992-9392

**Alta:** Alberta Federal & Intergovernmental Affairs, Trade Policy Team, Commerce Place, 10155 - 102 St., 12th Fl., Edmonton AB T5J 4G8, 403/427-2611; Fax: 403/427-0699

**Man.:** Manitoba Industry, Trade & Tourism, Manitoba Trade/Manitoba Trading Corporation, 155 Carlton St., 4th Fl., Winnipeg MB R3C 3H8, 204/945-2466; Fax: 204/957-1793

## INCOME SECURITY

***See Also* Social Services**

Human Resources Development Canada, Income Security Programs, Place Vanier, 120 Parkdale Ave., Ottawa ON K1A 0L1, 819/994-6013 (Communications)

Veterans Affairs Canada, Veterans Services, Daniel J. MacDonald Bldg., 161 Grafton St., PO Box 7700, Charlottetown PE C1A 8M9, 902/566-8195; Fax: 902/566-8508

**Alta:** Alberta Family & Social Services, Income & Employment Programs, Seventh St. Plaza, 10030 - 107 St., Edmonton AB T5J 3E4, 403/427-2635; Fax: 403/422-9044

**B.C.:** Ministry of Human Resources, Income Support, Parliament Bldgs., Victoria BC V8V 1X4

**Man.:** Manitoba Family Services, Employment & Income Assistance Division, #219, 114 Garry St., Winnipeg MB R3C 4V6, 204/945-2324 (Policy & Planning); Fax: 204/945-2156

**N.B.:** Department of Human Resources Development, 520 King St., 5th Fl., PO Box 6000, Fredericton NB E3B 5H1, 506/453-2379; Fax: 506/453-7478

Social Welfare Appeals Board, PO Box 12999, Fredericton NB E3B 6C2, 506/525-4007

**Nfld.:** Department of Human Resources & Employment, Income Support, Confederation Bldg., PO Box 8700, St. John's NF A1B 4J6, 709/729-3243; Fax: 709/729-6996

**NWT:** Department of Education, Culture & Employment, Income Security Branch, PO Box 1320, Yellowknife NT X1A 2L9, 867/920-6160; Fax: 867/920-0443

**N.S.:** Department of Community Services, Income & Employment Support, Johnston Bldg., 5182 Prince St., 5th Fl., PO Box 696, Halifax NS B3J 2T7, 902/424-4326; Fax: 902/424-0721

**Ont.:** Ministry of Community & Social Services, Social Assistance & Employment Opportunities Division, Hepburn Block, 80 Grosvenor St., 6th Fl., Toronto ON M7A 1E9, 416/325-5666; Fax: 416/325-5172, 5171

**PEI:** Department of Health & Social Services, Jones Bldg., 11 Kent St., 2nd Fl., PO Box 2000, Charlottetown PE C1A 7N8, 902/368-4900; Fax: 902/368-4969

**Qué.:** Ministère de l'Emploi et de la Solidarité, 425, rue St-Amable, 2e étage, Québec QC G1R 4Z1, 418/643-9818; Toll Free: 1-800-361-4743; Fax: 418/646-5426

**Sask.:** Saskatchewan Social Services, Income Security, 2151 Scarth St., 1st Fl., Regina SK S4P 3V7, 306/787-3536; Fax: 306/694-3842

Income Security Programs Division, 1920 Broad St., Regina SK S4P 3V6, 306/787-7469; Fax: 306/787-1032

Saskatchewan Income Plan (SIP), 1920 Broad St., Regina SK S4P 3V6, 306/787-3389; Fax: 306/787-1032

**Yuk.:** Yukon Health & Social Services, PO Box 2703, Whitehorse YT Y1A 2C6, 867/667-3673 (Communications); Fax: 867/667-3096

**INCOME TAX *See* TAXATION**

## INCORPORATION OF COMPANIES & ASSOCIATIONS

Industry Canada, C.D. Howe Bldg., 235 Queen St., Ottawa ON K1A 0H5, 613/941-0222; Fax: 613/954-6436

Office of the Corporate Secretary, C.D. Howe Bldg., 235 Queen St., Ottawa ON K1A 0H5, 613/941-0222; Fax: 613/954-6436

**B.C.:** Ministry of Finance & Corporate Relations, Registries & Ministry Support Services, 617 Government St., Victoria BC V8V 1X4, 250/387-9278

**Man.:** Manitoba Consumer & Corporate Affairs, Companies Office, #317, 450 Broadway, Winnipeg MB R3C 0V8, 204/945-4206; Fax: 204/945-1459

**N.B.:** Department of Justice, Corporate Affairs, #412, Centennial Bldg., PO Box 6000, Fredericton NB E3B 5H1, 506/453-3860; Fax: 506/453-2613

**Nfld.:** Department of Government Services & Lands, Insurance & Pensions, PO Box 8700, St. John's NF A1B 4J6, 709/729-2594; Fax: 709/729-3205

**NWT:** Department of Justice, PO Box 1320, Yellowknife NT X1A 2L9, 867/920-6197

**N.S.:** Department of Business & Consumer Services, Registry of Joint Stock Companies, PO Box 1529, Halifax NS B3J 2Y4, 902/424-7742; Fax: 902/424-4633

**Ont.:** Ministry of Consumer & Commercial Relations, Companies Branch, 393 University Ave., 2nd Fl., Toronto ON M7A 2H6, 416/596-3725; Fax: 416/596-0438

**PEI:** Department of Community Affairs & Attorney General, Securities & Consumer, Corporate & Insurance Services, Shaw Building, 95 Rochford St., 4th Fl., PO Box 2000, Charlottetown PE C1A 7N8, 902/368-4552; Fax: 902/368-5283; 5355

**Qué.:** L'Inspecteur général des Institutions financières, 800, place D'Youville, Québec QC G1R 4Y5, 418/694-5018 (Communications); Fax: 418/643-3336

**Sask.:** Saskatchewan Justice, Registry Services Division, 1874 Scarth St., Regina SK S4P 3V7, 306/787-7872 (Communications); Fax: 306/787-3874

**Yuk.:** Yukon Justice, Corporate Affairs & Registrar of Securities, PO Box 2703, Whitehorse YT Y1A 2C6, 867/667-5225; Fax: 867/393-6272

**INDIANS *See* ABORIGINAL AFFAIRS**

## INDUSTRIAL DESIGN & INTELLECTUAL PROPERTY

Industry Canada, Canadian Intellectual Property Office, Place du Portage, Tour I, 50, rue Victoria, Hull QC K1A 0C9, 613/941-0222; Fax: 613/954-6436

Institute for Advanced Manufacturing Technology, 1500 Montréal Rd., Ottawa ON K1A 0R6, 613/993-5802; Fax: 613/952-6081

Institute for Information Technology, 1500 Montreal Rd., Ottawa ON K1A 0R6, 613/993-2491; Fax: 613/952-0074

**B.C.:** Ministry of Finance & Corporate Relations, Corporate & Personal Property, 617 Government St., Victoria BC V8V 1X4, 250/356-8658; Corporate Registry Hotline: 604/387-7848; Fax: 604/356-0206

**N.B.:** New Brunswick Research & Productivity Council, Product Innovation, 921 College Hill Rd., Fredericton NB E3B 6Z9, 506/452-0590; Fax: 506/452-1395

**INDUSTRIAL RELATIONS *See* LABOUR**

**INDUSTRIAL SAFETY *See* OCCUPATIONAL SAFETY**

## INDUSTRY

***See Also* Business Development**

Agriculture & Agri-Food Canada, Agricultural Industry Services Directorate, 2200 Walkley Rd., 1st Fl., Ottawa ON K1A 0C5, 613/759-7561; Fax: 613/957-1527

Business Development Bank of Canada, #400, 5, Place Ville Marie, Montréal QC H3B 5E7, 514/283-5904; Toll Free: 1-888-463-6232; Fax: 514/283-0617

Industry Canada, C.D. Howe Bldg., 235 Queen St., Ottawa ON K1A 0H5, 613/941-0222; Fax: 613/954-6436

National Research Council Canada, Industrial Research Assistance Program, Bldg. M-58, 1200 Montreal Rd., Ottawa ON K1A 0R6, 613/993-0695; Fax: 613/952-7928

Standards Council of Canada, #1200, 45 O'Connor St., Ottawa ON K1P 6N7, 613/238-3222; Fax: 613/995-4564

Statistics Canada, Large Enterprise Statistics, R.H. Coats Bldg., Tunney's Pasture, 120 Parkdale Ave., Ottawa ON K1A 0T6, 613/951-4055; Fax: 613/951-0581

**Alta:** Alberta Economic Development Authority, Commerce Place, 10155 - 102 St., 6th Fl., Edmonton AB T5J 4L6, 403/427-2251; Fax: 403/427-5922

Alberta Economic Development & Tourism, Commerce Place, 10155 - 102 St., Edmonton AB T5J 4L6, 403/427-2280

Industry Development, Commerce Place, 10155 - 102 St., Edmonton AB T5J 4L6, 403/427-2280

**B.C.:** Ministry of Employment & Investment, 712 Yates St., Victoria BC V8W 9N1, 250/356-8702

British Columbia Trade & Investment Office, #730, 999 Canada Place, Vancouver BC V6C 3E1, 250/356-8702; Fax: 604/660-4048

**Man.:** Economic Development Board Secretariat, #648, 155 Carlton St., Winnipeg MB R3C 3H8, 204/945-8221; Fax: 204/945-8229

Manitoba Industry, Trade & Tourism, Industry Development, 155 Carlton St., 6th Fl., Winnipeg MB R3C 3H8, 204/945-7206; Fax: 204/945-3977

**N.B.:** Department of Economic Development & Tourism, Corporate Services, Centennial Bldg., 670 King St., 5th Fl., PO Box 6000, Fredericton NB E3B 5H1, 506/453-2482; Fax: 506/453-5428

Small Business Directorate, Centennial Bldg., 670 King St., 5th Fl., PO Box 6000, Fredericton NB E3B 5H1, 506/453-3890; Fax: 506/444-4182

New Brunswick Industrial Development Board, PO Box 6000, Fredericton NB E3B 5H1, 506/453-2474; Fax: 506/453-7904

**Nfld.:** Department of Industry, Trade & Technology, Confederation Annex, 4th Fl., PO Box 8700, St. John's NF A1B 4J6, 709/729-5600; Toll Free: 1-800-563-2299; Fax: 709/729-5936

**NWT:** Department of Resources, Wildlife & Economic Development, PO Box 1320, Yellowknife NT X1A 2L9

Northwest Territories Development Corporation, Tower 7, PO Box 1437, Yellowknife NT X1A 2P1, 867/920-7700; Fax: 867/920-7701

**N.S.:** Nova Scotia Innovation Corporation, Woodside Industrial Park, 101 Research Dr., PO Box 790, Dartmouth NS B2Y 3Z7, 902/424-8670; Toll Free: 1-800-565-7051; Fax: 902/424-8679

Nova Scotia Economic Renewal Agency, 1800 Argyle St., PO Box 519, Halifax NS B3J 2R7, 902/424-8920; Fax: 902/424-0582

**Ont.:** Innovation Ontario Corporation, 56 Wellesley St. West, 7th Fl., Toronto ON M7A 2E7, 416/326-1164; Fax: 416/326-1109

Ministry of Economic Development, Trade & Tourism, Hearst Block, 900 Bay St., Toronto ON M7A 2E1, 416/325-6666; Fax: 416/325-6688

Ministry of Environment & Energy, Green Industry Office, 135 St. Clair Ave. West, Toronto ON M4V 1P5, 416/323-4578; Fax: 416/323-4436

**PEI:** Department of Economic Development & Tourism, Shaw Bldg., 95 Rochford St., 5th Fl., PO Box 2000, Charlottetown PE C1A 7N8, 902/368-4476; Fax: 902/368-4242

Enterprise PEI, Holman Bldg., 25 University Ave., 3rd & 4th Fls., PO Box 910, Charlottetown PE C1A 7L9, 902/368-6300; Toll Free: 1-800-563-3734; Fax: 902/368-6301

**Qué.:** Ministère de l'Industrie, du commerce, de la Science et de la technologie, 710, Place d'Youville, 9e étage, Québec QC G1R 4Y4, 418/691-5950 (Renseignements); Fax: 418/644-0118

Société de développement industriel du Québec, Place Sillery, 1126, ch St-Louis, 5e étage, Québec QC G1S 1E5, 418/643-5172

**Sask.:** Saskatchewan Crown Investments Corporation, #400, 2400 College Ave., Regina SK S4P 1C8, 306/787-6851; Fax: 306/787-8125

Saskatchewan Economic & Co-operative Development, 1919 Saskatchewan Dr., Regina SK S4P 3V7, 306/787-2232

Sector Development, 1919 Saskatchewan Dr., Regina SK S4P 3V7, 306/787-2246

**Yuk.:** Yukon Economic Development, 211 Main St., PO Box 2703, Whitehorse YT Y1A 2C6, 867/667-5466; Fax: 867/668-8601

Industry Trade & Investment, 211 Main St., PO Box 2703, Whitehorse YT Y1A 2C6, 867/667-5466; Fax: 867/668-8601

## INSURANCE (LIFE, FIRE, PROPERTY)

***See Also* Automobile Insurance; Health Care Insurance**

Canada Deposit Insurance Corporation, 50 O'Connor St., 17th Fl., PO Box 2340, Stn D, Ottawa ON K1P 5W5, 613/996-2081; Toll Free: 1-800-461-2342; Fax: 613/996-6095

Canada Mortgage & Housing Corporation, Insurance, 700 Montreal Rd., Ottawa ON K1A 0P7, 613/748-2779; Toll Free: 1-800-668-2642; Fax: 613/748-2098

Human Resources Development Canada, Insurance, Place du Portage, Phase IV, 140, Promenade du Portage, Hull QC K1A 0J9, 819/997-8662

Office of the Superintendent of Financial Institutions, Kent Square, 255 Albert St., Ottawa ON K1A 0H2, 613/990-7788; Toll Free: 1-800-385-8647; Fax: 613/952-8219

Insurance, Kent Square, 255 Albert St., Ottawa ON K1A 0H2, 613/990-7788; Toll Free: 1-800-385-8647; Fax: 613/952-8219

**Alta:** Alberta Treasury, Insurance, Terrace Bldg., 9515 - 107 St., Edmonton AB T5K 2C3, 403/427-1592; Fax: 403/422-2463

**B.C.:** Credit Union Deposit Insurance Corporation of British Columbia, #1900, 1050 West Pender St., Vancouver BC V6E 4K8, 604/660-2947; Fax: 604/660-3170

Insurance Council of British Columbia, #300, 1040 West Georgia St., PO Box 7, Vancouver BC V6E 4H1, 604/688-0321; Fax: 604/662-7767

Ministry of Finance & Corporate Relations, Insurance & IFBs, #1900, 1050 West Pender St., Vancouver BC V6E 3S7, 604/660-4825; Fax: 604/660-3170

**Man.:** Manitoba Public Insurance, 234 Donald St., 9th Fl., PO Box 6300, Winnipeg MB R3C 4A4, 204/985-7000; Fax: 204/943-9851

Manitoba Consumer & Corporate Affairs, Insurance, #1142, 405 Broadway, Winnipeg MB R3C 3L6, 204/945-2542; Fax: 204/948-2268

**N.B.:** Department of Justice, Insurance, #412, Centennial Bldg., PO Box 6000, Fredericton NB E3B 5H1, 506/453-2512; Fax: 506/453-2613

**Nfld.:** Department of Government Services & Lands, Insurance & Pensions, PO Box 8700, St. John's NF A1B 4J6, 709/729-2594; Fax: 709/729-3205

**NWT:** Department of Finance, Insurance Registry, PO Box 1320, Yellowknife NT X1A 2L9, 867/920-8056; Fax: 867/873-0325

**N.S.:** Department of Business & Consumer Services, Financial Institutions Division/Superintendent of Insurance, South Maritime Centre, #8, 1505 Barrington St., Halifax NS B3J 2X1, 902/424-6331; Fax: 902/424-5327

**Ont.:** Deposit Insurance Corporation of Ontario, #700, 4711 Yonge St., Toronto ON M2N 6K8

Ministry of Finance, Office of the Insurance Ombudsman, 5160 Yonge St., PO Box 85, Toronto ON M2N 6L9, 416/590-7063; Toll Free: 1-800-668-0128; Fax: 416/590-7070

Ontario Insurance Commission, 5160 Yonge St., PO Box 85, Toronto ON M2N 6L9, 416/250-7250; Toll Free: 1-800-668-0128; Fax: 416/590-7070

**PEI:** Department of Community Affairs & Attorney General, Insurance & Real Estate Division, Shaw Building, 95 Rochford St., 4th Fl., PO Box 2000, Charlottetown PE C1A 7N8, 902/368-4564; Fax: 902/368-5283; 5355

**Qué.:** Commission administrative des régimes de retraite et d'assurances (Québec), 2875, boul Laurier, 2e étage, Ste-Foy QC G1V 4J8, 418/644-8661; Fax: 418/646-8721

L'Inspecteur général des Institutions financières, 800, place D'Youville, Québec QC G1R 4Y5, 418/694-5011; Fax: 418/528-0835

Régie de l'assurance-dépôts du Québec, 800, place D'Youville, Québec QC G1R 4Y5, 418/694-5014; Fax: 418/643-3336

**Sask.:** Saskatchewan Crop Insurance Corporation, 484 Prince William Dr., PO Box 3000, Melville SK S0A 2P0; Fax: 306/728-7260

Saskatchewan Government Insurance, 2260 - 11 Ave., Regina SK S4P 0J9, 306/751-1200; Fax: 306/787-7477

Saskatchewan Justice, Insurance, 1874 Scarth St., Regina SK S4P 3V7, 306/787-7881; Fax: 306/787-9779

**Yuk.:** Yukon Justice, Consumer Services, PO Box 2703, Whitehorse YT Y1A 2C6, 867/667-5257; Fax: 867/393-6272

**INTERGOVERNMENTAL AFFAIRS *See* FEDERAL-PROVINCIAL AFFAIRS; INTERNATIONAL AFFAIRS**

## INTERNATIONAL AFFAIRS

***See Also* Diplomatic Representatives; Trade**

Canadian International Development Agency, Communications, Place du Centre, 200, Promenade du Portage, Hull QC K1A 0G4, 819/953-6535; TDD: 819/953-5023; Fax: 819/953-6088

Canadian International Trade Tribunal, Standard Life Centre, 333 Laurier Ave. West, Ottawa ON K1A 0G7, 613/990-2452; Fax: 613/990-2439

Environment Canada, Policy, Program & International Affairs, 4905 Dufferin St., Downsview ON M3H 5T4, 416/739-4344; Ottawa: 819/997-0142; Fax: 819/994-8854; Fax: 819/953-2225

Finance Canada, International Trade & Finance Branch, Esplanade Laurier, 140 O'Connor St., Ottawa ON K1A 0G5, 613/992-1573; Fax: 613/996-8404

Foreign Affairs & International Trade Canada, Lester B. Pearson Bldg., 125 Sussex Dr., Ottawa ON K1A 0G2, 613/944-4000; Fax: 613/952-3904

Diplomatic Corps Services, Lester B. Pearson Bldg., 125 Sussex Dr., Ottawa ON K1A 0G2, 613/995-5185; Fax: 613/943-1075

Political & International Security Affairs Branch, Lester B. Pearson Bldg., 125 Sussex Dr., Ottawa ON K1A 0G2, 613/944-4000; Fax: 613/952-3904

Industry Canada, International Business, C.D. Howe Bldg., 235 Queen St., Ottawa ON K1A 0H5, 613/954-3508; Fax: 613/957-4454

International Development Research Centre, PO Box 8500, Ottawa ON K1G 3H9, 613/236-6163; Fax: 613/238-7230

National Defence (Canada), MGen. George R. Pearkes Bldg., 101 Colonel By Dr., Ottawa ON K1A 0K2, 613/992-4581

Revenue Canada, Customs Border Services, 875 Heron Rd., Ottawa ON K1A 0L8, 613/952-0384

**B.C.:** International Finance Centre - Vancouver Society, World Trade Centre, #658, 999 Canada Place, Vancouver BC V6C 3E1, 604/683-6626; Fax: 604/683-6646

**Qué.:** Ministère des Relations Internationales, Édifice Hector-Fabre, 525, boul Réne-Levesque est, Québec QC G1R 5R9, 418/649-2300; Fax: 418/649-2656

## INTERNATIONAL AID

Canadian International Development Agency, Place du Centre, 200, Promenade du Portage, Hull QC K1A 0G4, 819/997-5456; TDD: 819/953-5023; Fax: 819/953-6088

International Development Research Centre, PO Box 8500, Ottawa ON K1G 3H9, 613/236-6163; Fax: 613/238-7230

**INUIT *See* ABORIGINAL AFFAIRS**

## INVESTMENT

***See Also* Business Development; Industry**

Business Development Bank of Canada, #400, 5, Place Ville Marie, Montréal QC H3B 5E7, 514/283-5904; Toll Free: 1-888-463-6232; Fax: 514/283-0617

Canada Investment & Savings, #1502, 110 Yonge St., Toronto ON M5C 1T4, 416/952-1252; Toll Free: 1-800-575-5151

Federal Office of Regional Development (Québec), Tour de la Bourse, #3800, 800, Place Victoria, CP 247, Montréal QC H4Z 1E8, 514/283-6412; Toll Free: 1-800-322-4636; Fax: 514/283-3302

Foreign Affairs & International Trade Canada, International Business & Communications Branch, Lester B. Pearson Bldg., 125 Sussex Dr., Ottawa ON K1A 0G2, 613/995-6877; Fax: 613/943-8819

Investment Development, Lester B. Pearson Bldg., 125 Sussex Dr., Ottawa ON K1A 0G2, 613/995-8400; Fax: 613/943-8819

Investment Trade Policy Division, Lester B. Pearson Bldg., 125 Sussex Dr., Ottawa ON K1A 0G2, 613/995-0990; Fax: 613/944-0679

Industry Canada, C.D. Howe Bldg., 235 Queen St., Ottawa ON K1A 0H5, 613/941-0222; Fax: 613/954-6436

**Alta:** Alberta Treasury, Investment Management, Terrace Bldg., 9515 - 107 St., Edmonton AB T5K 2C3, 403/427-3035; Fax: 403/422-2463

**B.C.:** Ministry of Employment & Investment, 712 Yates St., Victoria BC V8W 9N1, 250/356-8702

British Columbia Trade & Investment Office, #730, 999 Canada Place, Vancouver BC V6C 3E1, 250/356-8702; Fax: 604/660-4048

Investment Facilitation Branch, #730, 999 Canada Place, Vancouver BC V6C 3E1, 250/952-0648; Fax: 604/660-4048

**N.B.:** Department of Economic Development & Tourism, Centennial Bldg., 670 King St., 5th Fl., PO Box 6000, Fredericton NB E3B 5H1, 506/453-2850 (Communications & Promotion); Fax: 506/444-4586

Trade & Investment, Centennial Bldg., 670 King St., 5th Fl., PO Box 6000, Fredericton NB E3B 5H1, 506/453-2876; Fax: 506/453-3783

New Brunswick Investment Management Corporation, PO Box 6000, Fredericton NB E3B 5H1, 506/444-5800

**Nfld.:** Department of Industry, Trade & Technology, Marketing, Confederation Annex, 4th Fl., PO Box 8700, St. John's NF A1B 4J6, 709/729-5600; Fax: 709/729-5936

**NWT:** Department of Finance, Banking & Investment, PO Box 1320, Yellowknife NT X1A 2L9, 867/873-7496; Fax: 867/873-0325

Northwest Territories Development Corporation, Tower 7, PO Box 1437, Yellowknife NT X1A 2P1, 867/920-7700; Fax: 867/920-7701

**N.S.:** Department of Finance, Investments, Pensions & Treasury Services Branch, PO Box 187, Halifax NS B3J 2N3, 902/424-5554; Fax: 902/424-0635

Nova Scotia Innovation Corporation, Woodside Industrial Park, 101 Research Dr., PO Box 790, Dartmouth NS B2Y 3Z7, 902/424-8670; Toll Free: 1-800-565-7051; Fax: 902/424-8679

Nova Scotia Economic Renewal Agency, Investment & Trade, 1800 Argyle St., PO Box 519, Halifax NS B3J 2R7, 902/424-8920; Fax: 902/424-0582

**Ont.:** Innovation Ontario Corporation, 56 Wellesley St. West, 7th Fl., Toronto ON M7A 2E7, 416/326-1164; Fax: 416/326-1109

Ministry of Economic Development, Trade & Tourism, Investment, Hearst Block, 900 Bay St., Toronto ON M7A 2E1, 416/325-6758; Fax: 416/325-6688

**PEI:** Department of Economic Development & Tourism, Aerospace & Food, Holman Bldg., 25 University Ave., 3rd & 4th Fls., PO Box 910, Charlottetown PE C1A 7L9, 902/368-5957; Fax: 902/368-6301

Enterprise PEI, Holman Bldg., 25 University Ave., 3rd & 4th Fls., PO Box 910, Charlottetown PE C1A 7L9, 902/368-6300; Toll Free: 1-800-563-3734; Fax: 902/368-6301

**Qué.:** Groupe Société générale de financement - Québec, #1700, 600, rue de la Gauchetière ouest, Montréal QC H3B 4L8, 514/876-9290; Fax: 514/395-8055

**Sask.:** Saskatchewan Economic & Co-operative Development, Diversification Division, 1919 Saskatchewan Dr., Regina SK S4P 3V7, 306/787-2232

Investment Programs, 1919 Saskatchewan Dr., Regina SK S4P 3V7, 306/787-3524

Saskatchewan Finance, Investment & Liability Management Branch, 2350 Albert St., Regina SK S4P 4A6, 306/787-9474; Fax: 306/787-6544

**Yuk.:** Yukon Economic Development, 211 Main St., PO Box 2703, Whitehorse YT Y1A 2C6, 867/667-5466; Fax: 867/668-8601

Industry Trade & Investment, 211 Main St., PO Box 2703, Whitehorse YT Y1A 2C6, 867/667-5466; Fax: 867/668-8601

Yukon Finance, Investments & Debt Services, PO Box 2703, Whitehorse YT Y1A 2C6, 867/667-5346; Fax: 867/393-6217

## JUSTICE DEPARTMENTS

Canadian Judicial Council, #450, 112 Kent St., Ottawa ON K1A 0W8, 613/998-5182; Fax: 613/998-8889

Justice Canada, Justice Bldg., 239 Wellington St., Ottawa ON K1A 0H8, 613/957-4222; Fax: 613/954-0811

Solicitor General Canada, Sir Wilfrid Laurier Bldg., 340 Laurier Ave. West, Ottawa ON K1A 0P8, 613/991-3283; Fax: 613/993-7062

**Alta:** Alberta Justice, 9833 - 109th St., Edmonton AB T5K 2E8, 403/427-2745; Fax: 403/427-6821

**B.C.:** Ministry of the Attorney General, PO Box 9282, Stn Prov. Gov't, Victoria BC V8W 9J7, 250/356-9596 (Policy & Education); Fax: 250/356-9037

**Man.:** Manitoba Justice, 405 Broadway, 5th Fl., Winnipeg MB R3C 3L6, 204/945-2852

**N.B.:** Department of Justice, #412, Centennial Bldg., PO Box 6000, Fredericton NB E3B 5H1, 506/453-2719 (Administration); Fax: 506/453-8718

**Nfld.:** Department of Justice & Attorney General, Confederation Bldg., PO Box 8700, St. John's NF A1B 4J6, 709/729-5942; Fax: 709/729-2129

**NWT:** Department of Justice, PO Box 1320, Yellowknife NT X1A 2L9, 867/920-6197

**N.S.:** , 5151 Terminal Rd., PO Box 7, Halifax NS B3J 2L6, 902/424-7125; Fax: 902/424-0510

**Ont.:** Ministry of the Attorney General, 720 Bay St., 11th Fl., Toronto ON M5G 2K1, 416/326-2220; Fax: 416/326-4088

**PEI:** Department of Community Affairs & Attorney General, PO Box 2000, Charlottetown PE C1A 7N8, 902/368-5250; Fax: 902/368-5283; 5355

**Qué.:** Ministère de la Justice, 1200, rte de l'Église, Ste-Foy QC G1V 4M1, 418/643-5140 (Communications); Fax: 418/646-4449

**Sask.:** Saskatchewan Justice, 1874 Scarth St., Regina SK S4P 3V7, 306/787-7872 (Communications); Fax: 306/787-3874

**Yuk.:** Yukon Justice, PO Box 2703, Whitehorse YT Y1A 2C6, 867/667-8292 (Communications); Fax: 867/393-6272

**JUVENILES *See* YOUNG OFFENDERS; YOUTH SERVICES**

## LABOUR

Canada Labour Relations Board, 240 Sparks St., 4th Fl., Ottawa ON K1A 0X8, 613/996-9466; Fax: 613/947-5407

Human Resources Development Canada, Communications, Place du Portage, Phase IV, 140, Promenade du Portage, Hull QC K1A 0J9, 819/994-6013 (Communications)

Statistics Canada, National Accounts & Analytical Studies, R.H. Coats Bldg., Tunney's Pasture, 120 Parkdale Ave., Ottawa ON K1A 0T6, 613/951-8116; Fax: 613/951-0581

**Alta:** Alberta Labour, 10808 - 99 Ave., Edmonton AB T5K 0G5, 403/427-2723

Labour Relations Board/Public Service Employee Relations Board, #503, 10808 - 99 Ave., Edmonton AB T5K 0G5, 403/427-8547; Toll Free: 1-800-463-2572; Fax: 403/422-0970

**B.C.:** Labour Relations Board, 1125 Howe St., Vancouver BC V6Z 2K8, 604/660-1300; Fax: 604/660-1892

Ministry of Finance & Corporate Relations, Labour & Social Statistics, 617 Government St., Victoria BC V8V 1X4, 250/387-0374; Fax: 250/387-0380

Ministry of Labour, 825 Fort St., 2nd Fl., PO Box 9570, Stn Prov. Gov't, Victoria BC V8W 9K1, 250/356-1487; Fax: 250/356-1653

**Man.:** Manitoba Labour Board, A.A. Heaps Bldg., #402, 254-258 Portage Ave., Winnipeg MB R3C 0B6, 204/945-5873; Fax: 204/945-1296

Manitoba Labour, #156, Legislative Bldg., 450 Broadway, Winnipeg MB R3C 0V8, 204/945-4039 (Deputy Minister)

**N.B.:** Department of Advanced Education & Labour, Chestnut Complex, 470 York St., PO Box 6000, Fredericton NB E3B 5H1; Fax: 506/453-3806

New Brunswick Labour & Employment Board, 191 Prospect St., PO Box 908, Fredericton NB E3B 1B0, 506/453-2881; Fax: 506/453-3892

**Nfld.:** Department of Environment & Labour, Labour Relations Branch, Confederation Bldg., PO Box 8700, St. John's NF A1B 4J6; Fax: 709/729-1930

Department of Mines & Energy, PO Box 8700, St. John's NF A1B 4J6, 709/729-2301

Labour Relations Board, Beothuck Bldg., 20 Crosbie Rd., 3rd Fl., PO Box 8700, St. John's NF A1B 4J6, 709/729-2707; Fax: 709/729-5736

Labour Standards Board, Confederation Bldg., West Block, PO Box 8700, St. John's NF A1B 4J6, 709/729-2742; Fax: 709/729-6639

**NWT:** Department of Education, Culture & Employment, PO Box 1320, Yellowknife NT X1A 2L9, 867/920-6222 (Policy & Planning)

**N.S.:** Department of Labour, 5151 Terminal Rd., PO Box 697, Halifax NS B3J 2T8, 902/424-4125; Fax: 902/424-3239

Labour Relations Board, PO Box 697, Halifax NS B3J 2T8, 902/424-6730; Fax: 902/424-3239

Labour Standards Tribunal, PO Box 697, Halifax NS B3J 2T8, 902/424-6730; Fax: 902/424-3239

**Ont.:** Ministry of Labour, Communications & Marketing Branch, 400 University Ave., 14th Fl., Toronto ON M7A 1T7, 416/326-7400; Toll Free: 1-800-267-9517; Fax: 416/326-7406

Ontario Labour Relations Board, 400 University Ave., 4th Fl., Toronto ON M7A 1T7, 416/326-7500; Fax: 416/326-7531

**PEI:** Department of Community Affairs & Attorney General, Labour & Industrial Relations Division, PO Box 2000, Charlottetown PE C1A 7N8, 902/368-5250; Fax: 902/368-5283; 5355

Labour Relations Board, PO Box 2000, Charlottetown PE C1A 7N8, 902/368-5550; Fax: 902/368-5526

**Qué.:** Commission des normes du travail, 400, boul Jean-Lesage, Québec QC G1K 8W1, Toll Free: 1-800-265-1414; Fax: 514/864-4711

Conseil consultatif du travail & de la main d'oeuvre, #2026, 800, Tour de la Place Victoria, CP 87, Montréal QC H4Z 1B7, 514/873-2880; Fax: 514/873-1129

Ministère du Travail, 200, ch Ste-Foy, 6e étage, Québec QC G1R 5S1, 418/643-4817; Fax: 418/644-6969

Société québécoise de développement de la main-d'oeuvre, 425, rue St-Amable, Québec QC G1R 2C5, 418/643-1892; Fax: 418/643-1714

**Sask.:** Labour Relations Board, 1914 Hamilton St., Regina SK S4P 4V4, 306/787-2406; Fax: 306/787-2664

Office of the Worker's Advocate, 1870 Albert St., Regina SK S4P 3V7, 306/787-2456

Saskatchewan Labour, 1870 Albert St., Regina SK S4P 3V7, 306/787-4496; TDD: 306/787-2429; Fax: 306/787-2208

**Yuk.:** Yukon Justice, Labour Services, PO Box 2703, Whitehorse YT Y1A 2C6, 867/667-5944; Fax: 867/393-6272

## LAND RESOURCES

***See Also* Agriculture; Forest Resources; Parks**

Canada Lands Company, #1500, 200 King St. West, Toronto ON M5H 3T4, 416/974-9700; Fax: 416/974-9661

Canadian Heritage, Parks Canada Sector, Jules Léger Bldg., 25 Eddy St., Hull QC K1A 1K5, 819/997-0055; Fax: 819/953-5382

Indian & Northern Affairs Canada, Lands & Trusts Services Sector, Tour Nord, Les Terrasses de la Chaudière, 10 Wellington St., Hull QC K1A 0H4, 819/997-0380; Fax: 819/953-3017

Natural Resources Canada, 580 Booth St., Ottawa ON K1A 0E4, 613/995-0947; Fax: 613/996-9094

Nunavut Planning Commission, #1902, 130 Albert St., Ottawa ON K1P 5G4, 613/238-1155; Fax: 613/238-5724

**Alta:** Alberta Environmental Protection, Land & Forest Service, 9915 - 108 St., Edmonton AB T5K 2G8, 403/427-2739, 944-0313 (Information Centre)

**B.C.:** Ministry of Environment, Lands & Parks, Crown Land Registry Services Branch, 3400 Davidson Ave., Victoria BC V8V 1X4, 250/387-4461; Fax: 250/387-1830

**Man.:** Farm Lands Ownership Board, #915 Norquay Bldg., 401 York Ave., Winnipeg MB R3C 0P8, 204/945-3149; Fax: 204/945-6134

Manitoba Land Value Appraisal Commission, 800 Portage Ave., Winnipeg MB R3G 0N4; Fax: 204/948-2235

Manitoba Natural Resources, Land Information Centre, 1007 Century St., Winnipeg MB R3H 0W4, 204/945-4071; Fax: 204/945-3586

**N.B.:** Department of Municipalities, Culture & Housing, Land Use Planning Branch, Marysville Place, 20 McGloin St., PO Box 6000, Fredericton NB E3B 5H1, 506/453-2171; Fax: 506/457-4991

Department of Natural Resources & Energy, Crown Lands, PO Box 6000, Fredericton NB E3B 5H1, 506/453-2437; Fax: 506/457-4802

Department of the Environment, Environmental Planning, 364 Argyle St., PO Box 6000, Fredericton NB E3B 5H1, 506/457-4846; Fax: 506/457-7823

New Brunswick Geographic Information Corporation, 985 College Hill Rd., PO Box 6000, Fredericton NB E3B 5H1, 506/457-3581; Fax: 506/453-3898

**Nfld.:** Department of Government Services & Lands, Lands Branch, PO Box 8700, St. John's NF A1B 4J6

**NWT:** Department of Resources, Wildlife & Economic Development, Resources & Economic Development, PO Box 1320, Yellowknife NT X1A 2L9, 867/873-7115; Fax: 867/920-2756

**N.S.:** Department of Natural Resources, Land Administration, Founder's Square, 1701 Hollis St., PO Box 698, Halifax NS B3J 2T9, 902/424-4267; Fax: 902/424-3173

**Ont.:** Mining & Lands Commissioner, 700 Bay St., 24th Fl., Box 330, Toronto ON M5G 1Z6, 416/314-2320; Fax: 416/314-2327

Ministry of Natural Resources, Land Use Planning Branch, Whitney Block, #6540, 99 Wellesley St. West, Toronto ON M7A 1W3, 705/789-9611; Fax: 416/314-1994

Lands & Natural Heritage Branch, Whitney Block, #6540, 99 Wellesley St. West, Toronto ON M7A 1W3, 705/755-1212; Fax: 416/314-1994

Ontario Land Corporation, Ferguson Block, 77 Wellesley St. West, 13th Fl., Toronto ON M7A 1N3, 416/327-3937

**PEI:** Department of Fisheries & Environment, Habitat & Natural Areas Section, Jones Bldg., 11 Kent St., 4th Fl., PO Box 2000, Charlottetown PE CIA 7N8, 902/368-4807; Fax: 902/368-5830

**Qué.:** Commission de protection du territoire agricole, 200, ch Ste-Foy, 2e étage, Québec QC G1R 4X6, 418/643-3314; Fax: 418/643-2261

Ministère des Ressources Naturelles, Terres, #B-302, 5700 - 4 av ouest, 3e étage, Charlesbourg QC G1H 6R1, 418/627-8600 (Renseignements); Fax: 418/644-7160

**Sask.:** Saskatchewan Land Allocations Appeal Board, #302, 3085 Albert St., Regina SK S4S 0B1, 306/787-5955; Fax: 306/787-5134

Saskatchewan Agriculture & Food, Lands Branch, Walter Scott Bldg., 3085 Albert St., Regina SK S4S 0B1, 306/787-5180; Fax: 306/787-0216

Saskatchewan Environment & Resource Management, Sustainable Land Management, 3211 Albert St., Regina SK S4S 5W6, 306/787-7024; Fax: 306/787-1349

Saskatchewan Property Management Corporation, 1840 Lorne St., Regina SK S4P 3V7, 306/787-6911; Fax: 306/787-1061

**Yuk.:** Executive Council, Land Claims, Self Government & Devolution, PO Box 2703, Whitehorse YT Y1A 2C6, 867/667-5908; Fax: 867/393-6214

Yukon Community & Transportation Services, Lands & Property Assessment Branch, PO Box 2703, Whitehorse YT Y1A 2C6, 867/667-5218; Fax: 867/667-6258

## LAND TITLES

***See Also* Real Estate**

British Columbia Treaty Commission, #203, 1155 West Pender St., Vancouver BC V6E 2P4, 604/775-2075; Toll Free: 1-800-665-8330

Canada Lands Company, #1500, 200 King St. West, Toronto ON M5H 3T4, 416/974-9700; Fax: 416/974-9661

**Alta:** Alberta Municipal Affairs, John E. Brownlee Bldg., 10365 - 97 St., Edmonton AB T5J 3W7, 403/427-4095; Toll Free: 1-800-465-5009 (in Alberta); Fax: 403/422-0818

**B.C.:** Ministry of the Attorney General, Land Title Branch, 910 Government St., 1st Fl., Victoria BC V8V 1X4, 250/387-1903; Fax: 250/387-1763

**Man.:** Manitoba Consumer & Corporate Affairs, Land Titles & Personal Property, 405 Broadway, 10th Fl., Winnipeg MB R3C 3L6, 204/945-1718

Property Rights Division, 405 Broadway, 10th Fl., Winnipeg MB R3C 3L6, 204/945-1718

**N.B.:** New Brunswick Geographic Information Corporation, Legal, & Chief Registrar of Deeds, 985 College Hill Rd., PO Box 6000, Fredericton NB E3B 5H1, 506/457-7374; Fax: 506/453-3898

**Nfld.:** Department of Government Services & Lands, Lands Branch, PO Box 8700, St. John's NF A1B 4J6

**NWT:** Department of Justice, Legal Registries/Land Titles, PO Box 1320, Yellowknife NT X1A 2L9, 867/873-7490

**Ont.:** Assessment Review Board, 121 Bloor St. East, 3rd Fl., Toronto ON M4W 3H5, 416/314-6900; Toll Free: 1-800-263-3237; Fax: 416/314-6906

Ministry of Consumer & Commercial Relations, Real Property Registration, 393 University Ave., 4th Fl., Toronto ON M7A 2H6, 416/596-3643; Fax: 416/596-3802

**PEI:** Department of the Provincial Treasury, Deeds, PO Box 2000, Charlottetown PE C1A 7N8, 902/368-4591; Fax: 902/368-4399

**Yuk.:** Yukon Justice, Land Titles, PO Box 2703, Whitehorse YT Y1A 2C6, 867/667-5612; Fax: 867/393-6272

## LANDLORD & TENANT REGULATIONS

Justice Canada, Regulations Section, Justice Bldg., 239 Wellington St., Ottawa ON K1A 0H8, 613/957-0065; Fax: 613/954-0811

**Alta:** Alberta Justice, 9833 - 109th St., Edmonton AB T5K 2E8, 403/427-2745; Fax: 403/427-6821

**B.C.:** Ministry of Municipal Affairs & Housing, Shelter Aid for Elderly Renters, 1175 Douglas St., 4th Fl., Victoria BC V8W 2E1, 250/387-3461; Fax: 250/387-4264

Ministry of the Attorney General, Residential Tenancy Branch, 1019 Wharf St., Victoria BC V8V 1X4, 250/356-3413; Fax: 250/387-0271

**Man.:** Manitoba Consumer & Corporate Affairs, Residential Tenancies Branch, #317, 450 Broadway, Winnipeg MB R3C 0V8, 204/945-4069; Fax: 204/945-6273

**N.B.:** Department of Justice, Consumer Affairs, #412, Centennial Bldg., PO Box 6000, Fredericton NB E3B 5H1, 506/453-2682; Fax: 506/444-4494

**Nfld.:** Department of Government Services & Lands, Residential Tenancies, PO Box 8700, St. John's NF A1B 4J6, 709/729-2608; Fax: 709/729-6998

**Ont.:** Ministry of Municipal Affairs & Housing, Rent Registry, 415 Yonge St., 19th Fl., Toronto ON M5B 2E7, 416/326-0923; Fax: 416/326-0930

Rent Review Hearings Board, 77 Bloor St. West, 10th Fl., Toronto ON M5S 1M2, 416/314-0051; Fax: 416/314-0061

**PEI:** Department of Community Affairs & Attorney General, Consumer Services, Shaw Building, 95 Rochford St., 4th Fl., PO Box 2000, Charlottetown PE C1A 7N8, 902/368-4580; Fax: 902/368-5355

**Qué.:** Régie du logement, #11.65, 1, rue Notre-Dame est, Montréal QC H2Y 1B6, 514/873-6575; Fax: 514/873-6805

**Sask.:** Provincial Mediation Board/Office of the Rentalsman, 2103 - 11 Ave., 5th Fl., Regina SK S4P 3V7, 306/787-2699; Fax: 306/787-5574

**Yuk.:** Yukon Justice, Consumer Services, PO Box 2703, Whitehorse YT Y1A 2C6, 867/667-5257; Fax: 867/393-6272

## LANGUAGES (OFFICIAL) *See* BILINGUALISM

## LEGAL AID SERVICES

**Alta:** Alberta Legal Aid Society, Revlon Bldg., #300, 10320 - 102 Ave., Edmonton AB T5J 4A1, 403/427-7575; Fax: 403/427-5909

**B.C.:** Legal Services Society, #1500, 1140 West Pender St., PO Box 3, Vancouver BC V6E 4G1, 604/601-6000; Fax: 604/682-7967

**Man.:** Legal Aid Manitoba, #402, 294 Portage Ave., Winnipeg MB R3C 0B9, 204/985-8505; Fax: 204/944-8582

**N.B.:** Department of Justice, Legal Aid New Brunswick, #412, Centennial Bldg., PO Box 6000, Fredericton NB E3B 5H1, 506/451-1424; Fax: 506/451-1429

**Nfld.:** Newfoundland Legal Aid Commission, Centre Bldg., 21 Church Hill St., St. John's NF A1C 3Z8, 709/753-7860; Fax: 709/753-6226

**NWT:** Legal Services Board of the Northwest Territories, PO Box 1320, Yellowknife NT X1A 2L9, 867/873-7450; Fax: 867/873-5320

**N.S.:** Nova Scotia Legal Aid Commission, #401, 5475 Spring Garden Rd., Halifax NS B3J 3T2, 902/420-6584; Fax: 902/420-3471

**Ont.:** Ministry of the Attorney General, Legislative Counsel, Whitney Block, #3600, 99 Wellesley St. West, Toronto ON M7A 1A2, 416/326-2841; Fax: 416/326-2806

**PEI:** Department of Community Affairs & Attorney General, Legal Aid, PO Box 2000, Charlottetown PE C1A 7N8, 902/368-6042; Fax: 902/368-5283; 5355

**Qué.:** Fonds d'Aide aux Recours Collectifs, #1201, 360, rue St-Jacques ouest, Montréal QC H2Y 1P5, 514/864-2750; Fax: 514/864-2998

Ministère de la Justice, 1200, rte de l'Église, Ste-Foy QC G1V 4M1, 418/643-5140 (Communications); Fax: 418/646-4449

**Sask.:** Saskatchewan Legal Aid Commission, #820, 410 - 22 St. East, Saskatoon SK S7K 2H6, 306/933-5300; Fax: 306/933-6764

**Yuk.:** Yukon Legal Services Society/Legal Aid, 207 Strickland St., Whitehorse YT Y1A 2J7, 867/667-5210

Yukon Justice, Legal Aid, PO Box 2703, Whitehorse YT Y1A 2C6, 867/667-5210; Fax: 867/393-6272

**LEGISLATURES *See* PARLIAMENT**

## LEISURE CRAFT & VEHICLE REGULATIONS

Canadian Heritage, Parks Canada Sector, Jules Léger Bldg., 25 Eddy St., Hull QC K1A 1K5, 819/997-0055; Fax: 819/953-5382

Fisheries & Oceans Canada, Canadian Coast Guard, Canada Bldg., 344 Slater St., Ottawa ON K1A 0N7, 613/998-1574; Fax: 613/990-2780

Small Craft Harbours, 200 Kent St., Ottawa ON K1A 0E6, 613/993-3012; Fax: 613/952-6788

Transport Canada, Communications, Transport Canada Building, 330 Sparks St., Ottawa ON K1A 0N5, 613/990-6138; Fax: 613/995-0351

**Alta:** Alberta Municipal Affairs, Registries Division, John E. Brownlee Bldg., 10365 - 97 St., Edmonton AB T5J 3W7, 403/422-2362 (Edmonton), 403/297-8980 (Calgary); Toll Free: 1-800-465-5009 (in Alberta); Fax: 403/422-9105

**B.C.:** Ministry of Transportation & Highways, Motor Vehicle Branch, 2631 Douglas St., Victoria BC V8T 5A3, 250/387-3140; Fax: 250/387-1169

**Man.:** Manitoba Highways & Transportation, Driver & Vehicle Licensing Division, 1075 Portage Ave., Winnipeg MB R3G 0S1, 204/945-3888; Fax: 204/948-2018

**N.B.:** Department of Transportation, Motor Vehicles & Policy, King Tower, Kings Pl., 2nd Fl., PO Box 6000, Fredericton NB E3B 5H1, 506/453-2552

**Nfld.:** Department of Government Services & Lands, Motor Registration Division, 149 Smallwood Dr., PO Box 8710, Mount Pearl NF A1B 4J5

**NWT:** Department of Transportation, Motor Vehicles, Lahm Ridge Bldg., PO Box 1320, Yellowknife NT X1A 2L9, 867/920-8915; Fax: 867/873-0363

**N.S.:** Department of Business & Consumer Services, Registry of Motor Vehicles, PO Box 1652, Halifax NS B3J 2Z3, 902/424-5851; Toll Free: 1-800-898-7668; Fax: 902/424-0544

**Ont.:** Ministry of Transportation, Licensing & Control Branch, 301 St. Paul St., St. Catharines ON L2R 1W6, 416/235-4793

**PEI:** Department of Transportation & Public Works, Motor Vehicles, 17 Haviland St., 1st Fl., Charlottetown PE C1A 3S7, 902/368-5200; Fax: 902/368-5236

**Qué.:** Ministère des Transports, 700, boul René-Lévesque est, 28e étage, Québec QC G1R 5H1, 418/643-6740

**Sask.:** Saskatchewan Government Insurance, Vehicle Standards & Inspection, 2260 - 11 Ave., Regina SK S4P 0J9, 306/751-1200; Fax: 306/787-7477

**Yuk.:** Yukon Community & Transportation Services, Motor Vehicles, PO Box 2703, Whitehorse YT Y1A 2C6, 867/667-5315; Fax: 867/393-6404

**LIBRARIES *See* BIBLIOGRAPHIC SERVICES**

## LIQUOR CONTROL *See Also* Drugs & Alcohol

Canadian Centre on Substance Abuse, #300, 75 Albert St., Ottawa ON K1P 5E7, 613/235-4048; Fax: 613/235-8101

**Alta:** Alberta Gaming & Liquor Commission, 50 Corriveau Ave., St. Albert AB T8N 3T5, 403/447-8600; Fax: 403/447-8916

**B.C.:** Liquor Appeal Board, #1304, 865 Hornby St., Vancouver BC V6Z 2H4, 604/660-2987; Fax: 604/660-3372

Ministry of the Attorney General, Liquor Control & Licensing Branch, 1019 Wharf St., Victoria BC V8V 1X4, 250/387-1254; Fax: 250/387-9184

Liquor Distribution Branch, 2625 Rupert St., Vancouver BC V5M 3T5, 604/252-3021; Fax: 604/252-3026

**Man.:** Manitoba Liquor Control Commission, 1555 Buffalo Place, PO Box 1023, Winnipeg MB R3C 2X1, 204/284-2501

**N.B.:** New Brunswick Liquor Corporation, PO Box 20787, Fredericton NB E3B 5B8, 506/452-6826; Fax: 506/452-9890

Liquor Licensing Branch, PO Box 3000, Fredericton NB E3B 5G5, 506/453-3732; Fax: 506/457-7335

**Nfld.:** Newfoundland Liquor Corporation, Kenmount Rd., PO Box 8750, Stn A, St. John's NF A1B 3V1, 709/754-1100; Fax: 709/754-0321

**N.S.:** Nova Scotia Liquor Commission, 93 Chainlake Dr., PO Box 8720, Stn A, Halifax NS B3K 5M4, 902/450-6752; Fax: 902/453-1153

Nova Scotia Liquor Licence Board, PO Box 545, Dartmouth NS B2Y 3Y8, 902/424-3660; Fax: 902/424-8987

**Ont.:** Liquor Control Board of Ontario, 55 Lake Shore Blvd. East, Toronto ON M7A 2H6, 416/864-2570; Fax: 416/864-2476

Liquor Licence Board of Ontario, 55 Lake Shore Blvd. East, Toronto ON M5E 1A4; Fax: 416/326-0308

**PEI:** Prince Edward Island Liquor Control Commission, PO Box 967, Charlottetown PE C1A 7M4, 902/368-5710; Fax: 902/368-5735

**Qué.:** Société des alcools du Québec, 905, rue de Lorimier, Montréal QC H2K 3V9, 514/873-2020; Fax: 514/873-6788

**Sask.:** Saskatchewan Liquor & Gaming Authority, 2500 Victoria Ave., PO Box 5054, Regina SK S4P 3M3, 306/787-4213; Fax: 306/787-8468

**Yuk.:** Yukon Liquor Corporation, PO Box 2703, Whitehorse YT Y1A 2C6, 867/667-5245; Fax: 867/668-7806

## LOTTERIES & GAMING

**Alta:** Alberta Gaming & Liquor Commission, 50 Corriveau Ave., St. Albert AB T8N 3T5, 403/447-8600; Fax: 403/447-8916

**B.C.:** British Columbia Lottery Corporation, 74 West Seymour St., Kamloops BC V2C 1E2, 604/270-0649; Fax: 604/828-5637

**N.B.:** Atlantic Lottery Corporation, 770 St. George Blvd., PO Box 5500, Moncton NB E1C 8W6, 506/867-5800; Fax: 506/388-4246

**Ont.:** Gaming Control Commission, 1099 Bay St., 2nd Fl., Toronto ON M5S 2B3, 416/326-8880; Fax: 416/326-8711

Ontario Lottery Corporation, #800, 70 Foster Dr., Sault Ste. Marie ON P6A 6V2, 705/946-6400; Fax: 705/946-6846

Ontario Racing Commission, #1400, 180 Dundas St. West, Toronto ON M5G 1Z8, 416/327-0520; Fax: 416/325-3478

**Qué.:** Société des loteries du Québec, #2000, 500, rue Sherbrooke ouest, Montréal QC H3A 3G6, 514/282-8000; Fax: 514/873-8999

**Sask.:** Saskatchewan Liquor & Gaming Authority, 2500 Victoria Ave., PO Box 5054, Regina SK S4P 3M3, 306/787-4213; Fax: 306/787-8468

**Yuk.:** Yukon Lottery Appeal Board, c/o Consumer Services, PO Box 2703, Whitehorse YT Y1A 2C6, 867/667-5257

Yukon Lottery Commission, PO Box 2703, Whitehorse YT Y1A 2C6, 867/633-7890

**MANUFACTURING *See* INDUSTRY**

## MAPS, CHARTS & AERIAL PHOTOGRAPHS

Fisheries & Oceans Canada, Canadian Hydrographic Service, 200 Kent St., Ottawa ON K1A 0E6, 613/995-4413; Chart Distribution: 613/998-4931; Fax: 613/996-9053

Natural Resources Canada, Canada Centre for Remote Sensing, 588 Booth St., Ottawa ON K1A 0Y7, 613/947-1216; Fax: 613/947-3125

Centre for Topographic Information, #010, 2144, rue King ouest, Sherbrooke QC J1J 2E8, 819/564-5600; Fax: 819/564-5698

Legal Surveys Division, 615 Booth St., Ottawa ON K1A 0E9, 613/995-4356; Fax: 613/996-9990

**Alta:** Alberta Energy, Mineral Access, Geology & Mapping, Petroleum Plaza, North Tower, 9945 - 108 St., Edmonton AB T5K 2G6, 403/422-9466; Fax: 403/427-3198

Alberta Environmental Protection, Resource Data Division, 9915 - 108 St., Edmonton AB T5K 2G8, 403/427-5719; Fax: 403/422-0712

**B.C.:** Ministry of Environment, Lands & Parks, Geographic Data BC, 3400 Davidson Ave., Victoria BC V8V 1X4, 250/387-6316; Fax: 250/356-7831

**Man.:** Manitoba Energy & Mines, Maps, Reports & Publications, #360, 1395 Ellice Ave., Winnipeg MB R3G 3P2, 204/748-1557; Toll Free: 1-800-282-8069 (Energy); Fax: 204/945-0586

**N.B.:** Department of Natural Resources & Energy, Geological Surveys Branch, PO Box 6000, Fredericton NB E3B 5H1, 506/453-2206; Fax: 506/453-3671

**Nfld.:** Department of Mines & Energy, Geological Survey, PO Box 8700, St. John's NF A1B 4J6, 709/729-2301; Fax: 709/729-3493

**N.S.:** Department of Housing & Municipal Affairs, Nova Scotia Geomatics Centre, 16 Station St., Amherst NS B4H 3E3, 902/667-7231; Toll Free: 1-800-798-0706; Fax: 902/667-6008

Department of Natural Resources, Surveys Division, Founder's Square, 1701 Hollis St., PO Box 698, Halifax NS B3J 2T9, 902/424-3145; Fax: 902/424-7735

**Ont.:** Office of the Surveyor General, 90 Sheppard Ave. East, 4th Fl., North York ON M2N 3A1, 416/314-1286; Fax: 416/223-6215

**PEI:** Department of Transportation & Public Works, Properties & Surveys Section, Jones Bldg., PO Box 2000, Charlottetown PE C1A 7N8, 902/368-5131; Fax: 902/368-5395

Department of the Provincial Treasury, Geomatics Information Centre, PO Box 2000, Charlottetown PE C1A 7N8, 902/368-5165; Fax: 902/368-4399

**Qué.:** Ministère des Ressources Naturelles, Cadastre, #B-302, 5700 - 4 av ouest, 3e étage, Charlesbourg QC G1H 6R1, 418/644-6224; Fax: 418/644-7160

**Sask.:** SaskGeomatics, 2151 Scarth St., Regina SK S4P 3V7, 306/787-2800

Saskatchewan Energy & Mines, Northern Survey Branch, 1914 Hamilton St., Regina SK S4P 4V4, 306/787-2568; Fax: 306/787-2488

**Yuk.:** Yukon Renewable Resources, Geographic Information Section, PO Box 2703, Whitehorse YT Y1A 2C6, 867/667-8137; Fax: 867/667-3641

Geographic Information Section, PO Box 2703, Whitehorse YT Y1A 2C6, 867/667-8137; Fax: 867/667-3641

## MARINE NAVIGATION

Atlantic Pilotage Authority Canada, Purdy's Wharf, Tower 1, #1402, 1959 Upper Water St., Halifax NS B3J 3N2, 902/426-2550; Fax: 902/426-4004

Fisheries & Oceans Canada, Canadian Hydrographic Service, 200 Kent St., Ottawa ON K1A 0E6, 613/995-4413; Chart Distribution: 613/998-4931; Fax: 613/996-9053

Great Lakes Pilotage Authority Ltd., PO Box 95, Cornwall ON K6H 5R9, 613/933-2995; Fax: 613/932-3793

Pacific Pilotage Authority Canada, #300, 1199 West Hastings St., Vancouver BC V6E 4G9, 604/666-6771; Fax: 604/666-6093

St. Lawrence Seaway Authority, Place de Ville, Tower "B", 112 Kent St., 5th Fl., Ottawa ON K1P 5P2, 613/598-4626; Fax: 613/598-4620

### MARRIAGE LICENCES *See* VITAL STATISTICS

### MENTAL HEALTH *See* HEALTH SERVICES

## METALS

### *See Also* Minerals & Mining

Industry Canada, Metals & Minerals Processing, C.D. Howe Bldg., 235 Queen St., Ottawa ON K1A 0H5, 613/954-3176; Fax: 613/954-3079

Natural Resources Canada, Minerals & Metals Sector, 580 Booth St., Ottawa ON K1A 0E4, 613/995-0947; Fax: 613/996-9094

**Sask.:** Saskatchewan Energy & Mines, Metallic Minerals Branch, 1914 Hamilton St., Regina SK S4P 4V4, 306/787-2501; Fax: 306/787-2333

**Yuk.:** Yukon Economic Development, Mines & Resource Development, 211 Main St., PO Box 2703, Whitehorse YT Y1A 2C6, 867/667-5466; Fax: 867/668-8601

### METEOROLOGY *See* CLIMATE & WEATHER

## MINERALS & MINING

Industry Canada, Metals & Minerals Processing, C.D. Howe Bldg., 235 Queen St., Ottawa ON K1A 0H5, 613/954-3176; Fax: 613/954-3079

Natural Resources Canada, Canada Centre for Mineral & Energy Technology, 580 Booth St., Ottawa ON K1A 0E4, 613/995-0947; Fax: 613/996-9094

Earth Sciences Sector, 580 Booth St., Ottawa ON K1A 0E4, 613/995-0947; Fax: 613/996-9094

Geological Survey of Canada, 601 Booth St., Ottawa ON K1A 0E8, 613/996-3919; Fax: 613/996-9990

**Alta:** Alberta Energy, Mineral Operations Division, Petroleum Plaza, North Tower, 9945 - 108 St., Edmonton AB T5K 2G6, 403/427-7425; Fax: 403/427-3198

**B.C.:** British Columbia Advisory Council on Mining, 1810 Blanshard St., Victoria BC V8V 1X4, 250/952-0152

Ministry of Employment & Investment, Energy & Minerals Division, 1810 Blanshard St., 5th Fl., PO Box 9324, Victoria BC V8W 9N3, 250/356-8702

**Man.:** Manitoba Mining Board, #360, 1395 Ellice Ave., Winnipeg MB R3G 3P2, 204/943-6740

Manitoba Energy & Mines, #360, 1395 Ellice Ave., Winnipeg MB R3G 3P2, 204/945-4154; Fax: 204/945-0586, 1406

**N.B.:** Department of Natural Resources & Energy, Mineral Resources & Energy, PO Box 6000, Fredericton NB E3B 5H1, 506/453-3826; Fax: 506/444-4367

**Nfld.:** Department of Mines & Energy, Mines Branch, PO Box 8700, St. John's NF A1B 4J6, 709/729-2301; Fax: 709/729-6782

**NWT:** Department of Resources, Wildlife & Economic Development, Minerals, Oil & Gas, PO Box 1320, Yellowknife NT X1A 2L9, 867/920-3214; Fax: 867/873-0254

**N.S.:** Department of Natural Resources, Minerals & Energy Branch, Founder's Square, 1701 Hollis St., PO Box 698, Halifax NS B3J 2T9, 902/424-5346; Fax: 902/424-7735

**Ont.:** Mining & Lands Commissioner, 700 Bay St., 24th Fl., Box 330, Toronto ON M5G 1Z6, 416/314-2320; Fax: 416/314-2327

Ministry of Northern Development & Mines, Mines & Minerals Division, Willet Green Miller Centre, 933 Ramsey Lake Rd., 6th Fl., Sudbury ON P3E 6B5, 416/327-0633; Fax: 416/327-0634

**Qué.:** Ministère des Ressources Naturelles, Mines, #B-302, 5700 - 4 av ouest, 3e étage, Charlesbourg QC G1H 6R1, 418/627-8600 (Renseignements); Fax: 418/644-7160

Société québécoise d'exploration minière, Place Belle Cour, #2500, 2600, boul Laurier, Ste-Foy QC G1V 4M6, 418/658-5400; Fax: 418/658-5459

**Sask.:** Saskatchewan Energy & Mines, 1914 Hamilton St., Regina SK S4P 4V4, 306/787-2526; Fax: 306/787-7338

**Yuk.:** Yukon Economic Development, Mineral Resources Development, 211 Main St., PO Box 2703, Whitehorse YT Y1A 2C6, 867/667-8085; Fax: 867/668-8601

## MINIMUM WAGES

### *See Also* Labour

Human Resources Development Canada, Labour, Place du Portage, Phase IV, 140, Promenade du Portage, Hull QC K1A 0J9, 819/994-6013 (Communications)

**Alta:** Alberta Labour, Work Standards, 10808 - 99 Ave., Edmonton AB T5K 0G5, 403/427-8541; Fax: 403/422-3562

**B.C.:** Ministry of Labour, Employment Standards Headquarters, 825 Fort St., 2nd Fl., Victoria BC V8W 9K1, 250/387-3300; URL: http://labour.gov.bc.ca/esb; Fax: 250/356-1886

**Man.:** Manitoba Labour, Employment Standards Division, #156, Legislative Bldg., 450 Broadway, Winnipeg MB R3C 0V8, 204/945-4039 (Deputy Minister)

**N.B.:** Department of Advanced Education & Labour, Employment Standards Branch, Chestnut Complex, 470 York St., PO Box 6000, Fredericton NB E3B 5H1, 506/453-3902; Fax: 506/453-3806

**Nfld.:** Labour Standards Board, Confederation Bldg., West Block, PO Box 8700, St. John's NF A1B 4J6, 709/729-2742; Fax: 709/729-6639

**N.S.:** Department of Labour, Labour Standards, 5151 Terminal Rd., PO Box 697, Halifax NS B3J 2T8, 902/424-4311; Fax: 902/424-0648

**Ont.:** Ministry of Labour, Policy & Communications Division, 400 University Ave., 14th Fl., Toronto ON M7A 1T7, 416/326-7558; Fax: 416/326-7599

**PEI:** Department of Community Affairs & Attorney General, Employment Standards, PO Box 2000, Charlottetown PE C1A 7N8, 902/368-5550; Fax: 902/368-5283; 5355

**Qué.:** Commission des normes du travail, 400, boul Jean-Lesage, Québec QC G1K 8W1, Toll Free: 1-800-265-1414; Fax: 514/864-4711

**Sask.:** Minimum Wage Board, 1870 Albert St., Regina SK S4P 3V7, 306/787-2474; Fax: 306/787-4780

**Yuk.:** Employment Standards Board, PO Box 2703, Whitehorse YT Y1A 2C6

### MOTION PICTURES *See* FILM PRODUCTION & COLLECTIONS

### MOTOR VEHICLES *See* DRIVERS' LICENCES

## MULTICULTURALISM

Canadian Heritage, Citizens' Participation & Multiculturalism, Jules Léger Bldg., 25 Eddy St., Hull QC K1A 1K5, 819/994-2994; Fax: 819/953-8720

Citizenship & Canadian Identity Sector, Jules Léger Bldg., 25 Eddy St., Hull QC K1A 1K5, 819/997-0055; Fax: 819/953-5382

**Alta:** Alberta Community Development, Citizenship Services Branch, Standard Life Centre, 10405 Jasper Ave., 7th Fl., Edmonton AB T5J 4R7, 403/427-2927; Fax: 403/422-6438

Alberta Human Rights & Citizenship Commission, 10405 Jasper Ave., 16th Fl., Edmonton AB T5J 4R7, 403/427-7661; Fax: 403/422-3563

**B.C.:** Ministry of the Attorney General, Multiculturalism BC, #309, 703 Broughton St., Victoria BC V8W 1E2, 250/660-2395; Fax: 250/660-1150

**Man.:** Multicultural Grants Advisory Council, 213 Notre Dame Ave., 4th Fl., Winnipeg MB R3B 1N3, 204/945-4458; Fax: 204/945-1675

Multiculturalism Secretariat, 213 Notre Dame Ave., 5th Fl., Winnipeg MB R3B 1N3, 204/945-6300; Fax: 204/948-2256

**N.B.:** Department of Advanced Education & Labour, Multiculturalism & Immigration, Chestnut Complex, 470 York St., PO Box 6000, Fredericton NB E3B 5H1, 506/444-4331; Fax: 506/453-3300

Ministerial Advisory Committee on Multiculturalism, PO Box 6000, Fredericton NB E3B 5H1, 506/444-4331; Fax: 506/453-3300

**Nfld.:** Department of Tourism, Culture & Recreation, Cultural Affairs, Confederation Bldg., PO Box 8700, St. John's NF A1B 4J6, 709/729-3650; Fax: 709/729-5952

**NWT:** Department of Education, Culture & Employment, Culture & Heritage, PO Box 1320, Yellowknife NT X1A 2L9, 867/873-7551; Fax: 867/873-0155

**Ont.:** Ministry of Citizenship, Culture & Recreation, Culture Division, 77 Bloor St. West, 6th Fl., Toronto ON M7A 2R9, 416/314-7265; Fax: 416/314-7313

Ontario Advisory Council on Multiculturalism & Citizenship, 35 McCaul St., 3rd Fl., Toronto ON M5T 1V7, 416/314-6650 (Voice & TDD); Fax: 416/314-6658

**Qué.:** Ministère des Relations avec les citoyens et de l'Immigration, Secteur immigration et communautés culturelles, 360, rue McGill, 4e étage, Montréal QC H2Y 2E9, 514/499-2199; Fax: 514/873-1810

## MUNICIPAL AFFAIRS

Treasury Board of Canada, Office of Infrastructure, West Tower, 300 Laurier Ave. West, 3rd Fl., Ottawa ON K1A 0R5, 613/952-3171; Fax: 613/952-7979

**Alta:** Alberta Municipal Affairs, Commerce Place, 10155 - 102 St., Edmonton AB T5J 4L4, 403/427-2732; Fax: 403/422-9105

**B.C.:** Ministry of Employment & Investment, Community Development Unit, 1810 Blanshard St., 8th Fl., Victoria BC V8W 9N3, 604/775-1695; Fax: 604/775-1184

Ministry of Municipal Affairs & Housing, Municipal Affairs, PO Box 9490, Victoria BC V8W 9N7, 250/387-4089; Fax: 250/356-1070

**Man.:** Manitoba Municipal Board, #408, 800 Portage Ave., Winnipeg MB R3G 0N4, 204/945-1789; Fax: 204/948-2235

Manitoba Northern Affairs, Local Government Development Division, 59 Elizabeth Dr., PO Box 37, Thompson MB R8N 1X4, 204/677-6607; Fax: 204/677-6753

Manitoba Rural Development, Community Economic Development Branch, #301, 450 Broadway, Winnipeg MB R3C 0V8, 204/945-2192; Fax: 204/945-5059

Local Government Services Division, #609, 800 Portage Ave., Winnipeg MB R3G ON4; Fax: 204/945-1383

**N.B.:** Department of Municipalities, Culture & Housing, Marysville Place, 20 McGloin St., PO Box 6000, Fredericton NB E3B 5H1, 506/453-2690; Fax: 506/457-4991

**Nfld.:** Department of Municipal & Provincial Affairs, West Block, Confederation Bldg., PO Box 8700, St. John's NF A1B 4J6, 709/729-3053

Newfoundland Municipal Financing Corporation, Confederation Bldg., PO Box 8700, St. John's NF A1B 4J6, 709/729-6686; Fax: 709/729-2070

**NWT:** Department of Municipal & Community Affairs, #600, 5201 - 50 Ave., PO Box 1310, Yellowknife NT X1A 2L9, 867/873-7118; Fax: 867/873-0309

**N.S.:** Department of Housing & Municipal Affairs, PO Box 216, Halifax NS B3J 2M4, 902/424-4141; Fax: 902/424-0531

Nova Scotia Municipal Finance Corporation, 1601 Lower Water St., PO Box 850, Stn M, Halifax NS B3J 2V2, 902/424-4590; Fax: 902/424-0525

**Ont.:** Ministry of Municipal Affairs & Housing, Communications Branch, 777 Bay St., 17th Fl., Toronto ON M5G 2E5, 416/585-6900; Fax: 416/585-6227

Municipal Finance Branch, 777 Bay St., 17th Fl., Toronto ON M5G 2E5, 416/585-6951; Fax: 416/585-6227

Ontario Municipal Board, 655 Bay St., 15th Fl., Toronto ON M5G 1E5, 416/326-6255; Fax: 416/326-5370

**PEI:** Department of Community Affairs & Attorney General, PO Box 2000, Charlottetown PE C1A 7N8, 902/368-5250; Fax: 902/368-5283; 5355

**Qué.:** Ministère des Affaires Municipales, Édifice Cook-Chauveau, 20, rue Pierre-Olivier-Chauveau, Québec QC G1R 4J3, 418/691-2015; Fax: 418/643-7385

**Sask.:** Saskatchewan Municipal Board, 2151 Scarth St., 4th Fl., Regina SK S4P 3V7, 306/787-6221; Fax: 306/787-1610

Saskatchewan Municipal Government, Municipal Services Division, 1855 Victoria Ave., Regina SK S4P 3V7, 306/787-8282; Fax: 306/787-4181

**Yuk.:** Yukon Community & Transportation Services, Municipal & Community Affairs Division, PO Box 2703, Whitehorse YT Y1A 2C6, 867/667-5144; Fax: 867/393-6404

## MUSEUMS

Canadian Heritage, Cultural Development & Heritage Sector, Jules Léger Bldg., 25 Eddy St., Hull QC K1A 1K5, 819/997-0055; Fax: 819/953-5382

**Alta:** Alberta Community Development, Cultural Facilities & Historical Resources Division, Old St. Stephen's College, 8820 - 112 St., Edmonton AB T6G 2P8, 403/431-2300; Fax: 403/427-5598

**B.C.:** Ministry of Small Business, Tourism & Culture, Culture Division, 1405 Douglas St., Victoria BC V8W 3C1

**Man.:** Manitoba Culture, Heritage & Citizenship, Culture, Heritage & Recreation Programs Division, 213 Notre Dame., Winnipeg MB R3B 1N3, 204/945-3729

**N.B.:** Department of Municipalities, Culture & Housing, Cultural Affairs Division, Marysville Place, 20 McGloin St., PO Box 6000, Fredericton NB E3B 5H1, 506/453-2690; Fax: 506/453-2416

**Nfld.:** Department of Tourism, Culture & Recreation, Cultural Affairs Branch, Confederation Bldg., PO Box 8700, St. John's NF A1B 4J6, 709/729-0928; Fax: 709/729-0662

Historic Resources, Confederation Bldg., PO Box 8700, St. John's NF A1B 4J6, 709/729-2460; Fax: 709/729-0870

**NWT:** Department of Education, Culture & Employment, Culture & Heritage, PO Box 1320, Yellowknife NT X1A 2L9, 867/873-7551; Fax: 867/873-0155

**N.S.:** Department of Education & Culture, Heritage & Culture Branch (Nova Scotia Museum), 2021 Brunswick St., PO Box 578, Halifax NS B3J 2S9, 902/424-5168; Fax: 902/424-0511

**Ont.:** Ministry of Citizenship, Culture & Recreation, Culture Division, 77 Bloor St. West, 6th Fl., Toronto ON M7A 2R9, 416/314-7265; Fax: 416/314-7313

Royal Ontario Museum, 100 Queen's Park Cres., Toronto ON M5S 2C6, 416/586-5549; Fax: 416/586-5863

**PEI:** Department of Education, Sullivan Bldg., 16 Fitzroy St., PO Box 2000, Charlottetown PE C1A 7N8, 902/368-4600; Fax: 902/368-4663

**Sask.:** Saskatchewan Municipal Government, Heritage Branch, 1855 Victoria Ave., Regina SK S4P 3V7, 306/787-2809; Fax: 306/787-0069

Royal Saskatchewan Museum, College Ave. & Albert St., Regina SK S4P 3V7, 306/787-2813; Fax: 306/787-2820

**Yuk.:** Yukon Tourism, Heritage Branch, PO Box 2703, Whitehorse YT Y1A 2C6, 867/667-5363; Fax: 867/667-8844

**NATIVE AFFAIRS *See* ABORIGINAL AFFAIRS**

**NATURAL GAS *See* OIL & NATURAL GAS RESOURCES**

## NATURAL RESOURCES

Canadian Heritage, Parks Canada Sector, Jules Léger Bldg., 25 Eddy St., Hull QC K1A 1K5, 819/997-0055; Fax: 819/953-5382

Environment Canada, Terrasses de la Chaudière, 10 Wellington St., Hull QC K1A 0H3, 819/997-2800; Toll Free: 1-800-668-6767; Fax: 819/953-2225

Fisheries & Oceans Canada, 200 Kent St., Ottawa ON K1A 0E6, 613/993-0999; TDD: 1-800-668-5228

Natural Resources Canada, Communications Branch, 580 Booth St., Ottawa ON K1A 0E4, 613/992-0267; Fax: 613/996-9094

**Alta:** Alberta Energy, Petroleum Plaza, North Tower, 9945 - 108 St., Edmonton AB T5K 2G6, 403/427-7425; Fax: 403/427-3198

Alberta Environmental Protection, Natural Resources Service, 9915 - 108 St., Edmonton AB T5K 2G8, 403/427-2739, 944-0313 (Information Centre)

**B.C.:** Ministry of Employment & Investment, Energy & Minerals Division, 1810 Blanshard St., 5th Fl., PO Box 9324, Victoria BC V8W 9N3, 250/356-8702

Ministry of Environment, Lands & Parks, 810 Blanshard St., Victoria BC V8V 1X5, 250/387-9419; Fax: 250/356-6464

Crown Land Registry Services Branch, 3400 Davidson Ave., Victoria BC V8V 1X4, 250/387-4461; Fax: 250/387-1830

**Man.:** Manitoba Natural Resources, Management Services Division, 1577 Dublin Ave., Winnipeg MB R3E 3J5, 204/945-4071; Fax: 204/945-3586

**N.B.:** Department of Natural Resources & Energy, PO Box 6000, Fredericton NB E3B 5H1, 506/453-3826; Fax: 506/444-4367

**Nfld.:** Department of Forest Resources & Agrifoods, PO Box 8700, St. John's NF A1B 4J6, 709/729-4716

Department of Government Services & Lands, Lands Branch, PO Box 8700, St. John's NF A1B 4J6

Department of Mines & Energy, PO Box 8700, St. John's NF A1B 4J6, 709/729-2301

**NWT:** Department of Resources, Wildlife & Economic Development, PO Box 1320, Yellowknife NT X1A 2L9

Northwest Territories Water Board, PO Box 1500, Yellowknife NT X1A 2R3, 867/669-2772; Fax: 867/669-2719

**N.S.:** Department of Natural Resources, Founder's Square, 1701 Hollis St., PO Box 698, Halifax NS B3J 2T9, 902/424-5935; Fax: 902/424-7735

**Ont.:** Ministry of Natural Resources, Communications Services Branch, Whitney Block, 99 Wellesley St. West, Toronto ON M7A 1W3, 416/314-2119; Fax: 416/314-2051

**PEI:** Department of Fisheries & Environment, Jones Bldg., 11 Kent St., 4th Fl., PO Box 2000, Charlottetown PE CIA 7N8, 902/368-5000; Fax: 902/368-5830

**Qué.:** Ministère des Ressources Naturelles, #B-302, 5700 - 4 av ouest, 3e étage, Charlesbourg QC G1H 6R1, 418/627-8600 (Renseignements); Toll Free: 1-800-463-4558; Fax: 418/644-7160

**Sask.:** Saskatchewan Environment & Resource Management, 3211 Albert St., Regina SK S4S 5W6, 306/787-2700; Toll Free: 1-800-667-2757; Fax: 306/787-3941

Saskatchewan Northern Affairs, Resource Development Division, 1919 Saskatchewan Dr., Regina SK S4P 3V7, 306/787-2908; Fax: 306/425-4349

Saskatchewan Water Corporation (Sask Water), Water Resources Management, Victoria Place, 111 Fairford St. East, Moose Jaw SK S6H 7X9, 306/694-3950; Fax: 306/694-3944

**Yuk.:** Yukon Renewable Resources, PO Box 2703, Whitehorse YT Y1A 2C6, 867/667-5237; Toll Free: 1-800-661-0408 (Yukon)

## NUCLEAR ENERGY

Atomic Energy Control Board, 280 Slater St., PO Box 1046, Stn B, Ottawa ON K1P 5S9, 613/995-5894; Toll Free: 1-800-668-5284; Fax: 613/995-5086

Atomic Energy of Canada Limited, 2251 Speakman Dr., Mississauga ON L5K 1B2, 905/823-9040; Fax: 905/823-8006

Natural Resources Canada, Uranium & Nuclear Energy Branch, 580 Booth St., Ottawa ON K1A 0E4, 613/996-7432; Fax: 613/992-1405

**Ont.:** Ontario Hydro, 700 University Ave., Toronto ON M5G 1X6, 416/592-5111; Toll Free: 1-800-263-9000

**Qué.:** Hydro-Québec, 75, boul René-Lévesque ouest, Montréal QC H2Z 1A4, 514/289-2211; Fax: 514/843-3163

## NUTRITION

Agriculture & Agri-Food Canada, Food Bureau, Sir John Carling Bldg., 930 Carling Ave., Ottawa ON K1A 0C5, 613/759-7557; Fax: 613/759-7496

Health Canada, Health Promotions & Programs Branch, Brooke Claxton Bldg., Tunney's Pasture, 120 Parkdale Ave., Ottawa ON K1A 0K9, 613/957-2991; Fax: 613/941-5366

**Alta:** Alberta Health, Health Policy, PO Box 1360, Edmonton AB T5J 2N3, 403/427-7164 (Communications)

**B.C.:** Ministry of Health, Health Protection & Safety, 1515 Blanshard St., 7th Fl., Victoria BC V8W 3C8, 250/952-1731; Fax: 250/952-1486

**Man.:** Manitoba Health, Community & Mental Health Services Division, 599 Empress St., PO Box 925, Winnipeg MB R3C 2T6, 204/786-7191 (Finance & Administration Branch)

**N.B.:** Department of Health & Community Services, Public Health & Medical Services Division, PO Box 5100, Fredericton NB E3B 5G8, 506/453-2536; Fax: 506/444-4697

**Nfld.:** Department of Health, Health Promotion, West Block, Confederation Bldg., PO Box 8700, St. John's NF A1B 4J6, 709/729-3940; Fax: 709/729-5824

**NWT:** Department of Health & Social Services, Health Services Development, Centre Square Tower, 8th Fl., PO Box 1320, Yellowknife NT X1A 2L9, 867/920-6173; Fax: 867/873-0266

**N.S.:** Department of Health, Strategic Planning & Policy Development Branch, Joseph Howe Bldg., 1690 Hollis St., PO Box 488, Halifax NS B3J 2R8, 902/424-4310; Fax: 902/424-0730

**Ont.:** Ministry of Health, Community Health Branch, Hepburn Block, 8th Fl., Queen's Park, #1400, 80 Grosvenor St., Toronto ON M7A 1S2, 416/327-7535; Toll Free: 1-800-668-2437 (AIDS Bureau); Fax: 416/327-4389

**PEI:** Department of Health & Social Services, Jones Bldg., 11 Kent St., 2nd Fl., PO Box 2000, Charlottetown PE C1A 7N8, 902/368-4900; Fax: 902/368-4969

**Qué.:** Ministère de la Santé et des services sociaux, 1075, ch Ste-Foy, Québec QC G1S 2M1

**Sask.:** Saskatchewan Health, Wellness & Health Promotion Branch, 3475 Albert St., Regina SK S4S 6X6, 306/787-3083; Fax: 306/787-8310

**Yuk.:** Yukon Health & Social Services, Health Services Branch, PO Box 2703, Whitehorse YT Y1A 2C6, 867/667-3673 (Communications); Fax: 867/667-3096

## OCCUPATIONAL SAFETY

***See Also* Dangerous Goods & Hazardous Materials**

Canadian Centre for Occupational Health & Safety, 250 Main St. East, Hamilton ON L8N 1H6, 905/572-2981; Toll Free: 1-800-263-8466; Fax: 905/572-2206

Health Canada, Occupational & Environmental Health Services, Brooke Claxton Bldg., Tunney's Pasture, 120 Parkdale Ave., Ottawa ON K1A 0K9, 613/957-7699; Fax: 613/941-5366

**Alta:** Alberta Labour, Occupational Health & Safety, 10011 - 109 St., 5th Fl., Edmonton AB T5J 3S8, 403/427-6724; Fax: 403/427-5698

Occupational Health & Safety Council, 10808 - 99 Ave., Edmonton AB T5K 0G5, 403/427-8305; Fax: 403/422-9205

**B.C.:** Employment Standards Tribunal, #800, 360 West Georgia St., Vancouver BC V6B 6B2, 604/775-3512; Fax: 604/775-3372

Workers' Compensation Board of British Columbia, 6951 Westminster Hwy., Richmond BC V7C 1C6, 604/273-2266; Toll Free: 1-800-661-2112; Fax: 604/276-3151

**Man.:** Advisory Council on Workplace Safety & Health, #200, 401 York Ave., Winnipeg MB R3C 0P8, 204/945-3446; Fax: 204/945-4556

Manitoba Highways & Transportation, Occupational Health & Safety, 215 Garry St., 17th Fl., Winnipeg MB R3C 3Z1, 204/945-5819; Fax: 204/945-5115

Manitoba Labour, Workplace Safety & Health Division, #200, 401 York Ave., Winnipeg MB R3C 0P8, 204/945-3446; Fax: 204/945-4556

**N.B.:** Workplace Health, Safety & Compensation Commission of New Brunswick, 1 Portland St., PO Box 160, Saint John NB E2L 3X9, 506/632-2200; Toll Free: 1-800-222-9775; Fax: 506/632-2226

**Ont.:** Ministry of Labour, Occupational Health & Safety Branch, 400 University Ave., 14th Fl., Toronto ON M7A 1T7, 416/326-1359; Fax: 416/326-7761

Workplace Health & Safety Agency, #900, 121 Bloor St. East, Toronto ON M4W 3M5, 416/975-9728; Fax: 416/975-9775

**PEI:** Department of the Provincial Treasury, Occupational Health & Safety, PO Box 2000, Charlottetown PE C1A 7N8, 902/368-4200; Fax: 902/368-6622

**Qué.:** Commission de la santé et de la sécurité du travail du Québec, 1199, rue de Bleury, CP 6056, Succ Centre-Ville, Montréal QC H3C 4E1, 514/873-7183; Fax: 514/873-7007

**Sask.:** Office of the Worker's Advocate, 1870 Albert St., Regina SK S4P 3V7, 306/787-2456

Saskatchewan Labour, Occupational Health & Safety Division, 1870 Albert St., Regina SK S4P 3V7, Toll Free: 1-800-567-7233 (Saskatchewan); Fax: 306/787-2208

**Yuk.:** Yukon Workers' Compensation Health & Safety Board, Occupational Health & Safety, 401 Strickland St., Whitehorse YT Y1A 5N8, 867/667-8616; Toll Free: 1-800-661-0443; Fax: 867/393-6279

## OCCUPATIONAL TRAINING

Canadian Centre for Management Development, PO Box 420, Stn A, Ottawa ON K1N 8V4, 613/997-4163; Fax: 613/953-6240

Human Resources Development Canada, Communications, Place du Portage, Phase IV, 140, Promenade du Portage, Hull QC K1A 0J9, 819/994-6013 (Communications)

Public Service Commission of Canada, Training Programs Branch, 300 Laurier Ave. West, Ottawa ON K1A 0M7, 613/992-9562; Fax: 613/954-7561

**Alta:** Alberta Apprenticeship & Industry Training Board, 10155 - 102 St., 10th Fl., Edmonton AB T5J 4L5, 403/427-8765

Alberta Advanced Education & Career Development, Apprenticeship & Industry Training Division, Commerce Place, 10155 - 102 St., 7th Fl., Edmonton AB T5J 4L5, 403/422-4488; Fax: 403/422-7376

**B.C.:** Ministry of Education, Skills & Training, Skills Development Division, PO Box 9150, Stn Prov Govt, Victoria BC V8W 9H1, 250/356-2500; Fax: 250/356-5945

**Man.:** Manitoba Education & Training, Training & Advanced Education, 185 Carlton St., 4th Fl., Winnipeg MB R3C 3J1, 204/945-4325; Fax: 204/945-1291

**N.B.:** Department of Advanced Education & Labour, Chestnut Complex, 470 York St., PO Box 6000, Fredericton NB E3B 5H1; Fax: 506/453-3806

**NWT:** Department of Education, Culture & Employment, Career Development, PO Box 1320, Yellowknife NT X1A 2L9, 867/873-7146; Fax: 867/873-0155

**N.S.:** Department of Labour, Occupational Health, 5151 Terminal Rd., PO Box 697, Halifax NS B3J 2T8, 902/424-8055; Toll Free: 1-800-952-2687; Fax: 902/424-3239

**Ont.:** Ministry of Education & Training, Training Division, Mowat Block, 900 Bay St., Toronto ON M7A 1L2, 416/325-2929; Fax: 416/325-2934

**Qué.:** Société québécoise de développement de la main-d'oeuvre, 425, rue St-Amable, Québec QC G1R 2C5, 418/643-1892; Fax: 418/643-1714

**Sask.:** Saskatchewan Post-Secondary Education & Skills Training, Training Programs Branch, 2220 College Ave., Regina SK S4P 3V7, 306/787-2093

**Yuk.:** Yukon Education, Training Programs, PO Box 2703, Whitehorse YT Y1A 2C6, 867/667-5140; Fax: 867/667-8555

## OCEANOGRAPHY

Bayfield Institute for Marine Science & Surveys, 867 Lakeshore Rd., PO Box 5050, Burlington ON L7R 4A6, 905/336-4871; Fax: 905/336-6637

Bedford Institute of Oceanography, PO Box 1006, Dartmouth NS B2Y 4A2, 902/426-2373; Fax: 902/426-7827

Fisheries & Oceans Canada, Canadian Hydrographic Service, 200 Kent St., Ottawa ON K1A 0E6, 613/995-4413; Chart Distribution: 613/998-4931; Fax: 613/996-9053

Institute for Marine Biosciences, 1411 Oxford St., Halifax NS B3H 3Z1, 902/426-8332; Fax: 902/426-9413

Institute for Marine Dynamics, Memorial University, Kerwin Pl. & Arctic Ave., PO Box 12093, Stn A, St. John's NF A1B 3T5, 709/772-4939; Fax: 709/772-3101

Institute of Ocean Sciences, 9860 West Saanich Rd., PO Box 6000, Sidney BC V8L 4B2, 250/363-6517; Fax: 250/353-6807

Maurice Lamontagne Institute, 850, Rte de le Mer, CP 1000, Mont-Joli QC G5H 3Z4, 418/775-6553; Fax: 418/775-0542

## OIL & NATURAL GAS RESOURCES

***See Also* Energy; Natural Resources**

Indian Oil & Gas Canada, #100, 9911 Chula Blvd., Tsuu T'ina (Sarcee) AB T2W 6H6, 403/292-5625; Fax: 403/292-5618

National Energy Board, 311 - 6 Ave. SW, Calgary AB T2P 3H2, 403/292-4800; Fax: 403/292-5503

Natural Resources Canada, Canada Centre for Mineral & Energy Technology, 580 Booth St., Ottawa ON K1A 0E4, 613/995-0947; Fax: 613/996-9094

Energy Resources Branch, 580 Booth St., Ottawa ON K1A 0E4, 613/996-7432; Fax: 613/992-1405

**Alta:** Alberta Energy, Petroleum Plaza, North Tower, 9945 - 108 St., Edmonton AB T5K 2G6, 403/427-7425; Fax: 403/427-3198

**B.C.:** Ministry of Employment & Investment, Energy & Minerals Division, 1810 Blanshard St., 5th Fl., PO Box 9324, Victoria BC V8W 9N3, 250/356-8702

**Man.:** Manitoba Energy & Mines, Petroleum & Energy Branch, #360, 1395 Ellice Ave., Winnipeg MB R3G 3P2, 204/945-6577; Toll Free: 1-800-282-8069 (Energy); Fax: 204/945-0586

**N.B.:** Department of Natural Resources & Energy, Mineral Resources & Energy, PO Box 6000, Fredericton NB E3B 5H1, 506/453-3826; Fax: 506/444-4367

**Nfld.:** Canada-Newfoundland Offshore Petroleum Board, TD Place, #500, 140 Water St., St. John's NF A1C 6H6, 709/778-1400; Fax: 709/778-1473

Department of Mines & Energy, Energy Branch, PO Box 8700, St. John's NF A1B 4J6, 709/729-2301

Petroleum Resource Development, PO Box 8700, St. John's NF A1B 4J6, 709/729-2323

**NWT:** Department of Resources, Wildlife & Economic Development, Minerals, Oil & Gas, PO Box 1320, Yellowknife NT X1A 2L9, 867/920-3214; Fax: 867/873-0254

**N.S.:** Canada-Nova Scotia Offshore Petroleum Board, TD Centre, 1791 Barrington St., 6th Fl., Halifax NS B3J 3K9, 902/422-5588; Fax: 902/422-1799

Department of Natural Resources, Petroleum Development Agency, Founder's Square, 1701 Hollis St., PO Box 698, Halifax NS B3J 2T9, 902/424-5935; Fax: 902/424-7735

**Qué.:** Ministère des Ressources Naturelles, Gaz et pétrole, #B-302, 5700 - 4 av ouest, 3e étage, Charlesbourg QC G1H 6R1, 418/627-6390 poste 8251; Fax: 418/643-0701

Société québécoise d'initiatives pétrolières, #180, 1175, ave de Lavigerie, Ste-Foy QC G1V 4P1, 418/651-9543; Fax: 418/651-2292

**Sask.:** Saskatchewan Energy & Mines, Petroleum & Natural Gas Division, 1914 Hamilton St., Regina SK S4P 4V4, 306/787-2526; Fax: 306/787-2478

**Yuk.:** Yukon Economic Development, Mines & Resource Development, 211 Main St., PO Box 2703, Whitehorse YT Y1A 2C6, 867/667-5466; Fax: 867/668-8601

## OMBUDSMEN

Information Commissioner of Canada, Tower B, Place de Ville, 112 Kent St., 3rd Fl., Ottawa ON K1A 1H3, 613/995-2410; Toll Free: 1-800-267-0441; Fax: 613/995-1501

Office of the Commissioner of Official Languages, 110 O'Connor St., Ottawa ON K1A 0T8, 613/996-6368; Fax: 613/993-5082

Office of the Correctional Investigator, #402, 275 Slater St., Ottawa ON K1P 5H9, 613/990-2695; Toll Free: 1-800-267-5982; Fax: 613/990-9091

Privacy Commissioner of Canada, Tower B, Place de Ville, 112 Kent St., Ottawa ON K1A 1H3, 613/995-2410; Toll Free: 1-800-267-0441, TDD: 613/992-9190; Fax: 613/947-6850

**Alta:** Alberta Office of the Ombudsman, Phipps-McKinnon Bldg., #1630, 10020 - 101A Ave., Edmonton AB T5J 3G2, 403/427-2756; Fax: 403/427-2759

**B.C.:** Office of the Ombudsman, 931 Fort St., Victoria BC V8V 3K3, 250/387-5855; Toll Free: 1-800-567-3247; Fax: 250/387-0198

**Man.:** Manitoba Office of the Ombudsman, #750, 500 Portage Ave., Winnipeg MB R3C 3X1, 204/786-6483; Toll Free: 1-800-665-0531; Fax: 204/942-7803

**N.B.:** Office of the Ombudsman, 767 Brunswick St., PO Box 6000, Fredericton NB E3B 5H1, 506/453-2789; Fax: 506/453-5599

**N.S.:** , Lord Nelson Arcade, #300, 5675 Spring Garden Rd., PO Box 2152, Halifax NS B3J 3B7, 902/424-6780; Toll Free: 1-800-670-1111 (In Nova Scotia only); Fax: 902/424-6675

**Ont.:** Office of the Integrity Commissioner, #1301, 101 Bloor St. West, Toronto ON M5S 2Z7, 416/314-8983; Fax: 416/314-8987

Office of the Ombudsman, 125 Queen's Park, Toronto ON M5S 2C7, 416/586-3300; Toll Free: 1-800-263-1830 (English), TDD: 416/586-3510; Fax: 416/586-3485

**Qué.:** Protecteur du Citoyen, 2875, boul Laurier, 4e étage, Ste-Foy QC G1V 2M2, 418/643-2688; Fax: 418/643-8759

**Sask.:** Saskatchewan Ombudsman, #150, 2401 Saskatchewan Dr., Regina SK S4P 3V7, 306/787-6211; Fax: 306/787-9090

## PARKS

### *See Also* Land Resources

Canadian Heritage, Parks Canada Sector, Jules Léger Bldg., 25 Eddy St., Hull QC K1A 1K5, 819/997-0055; Fax: 819/953-5382

Citizenship & Immigration Canada, Canada Immigration Centres & Citizenship Offices, Jean Edmonds Towers, 365 Laurier Ave. West, Ottawa ON K1A 1L1, 613/954-9019; Fax: 613/954-2221

National Battlefields Commission, 390, av de Bernières, Québec QC G1R 2L7, 418/648-3506; Fax: 418/648-3638

Roosevelt Campobello International Park Commission, Campobello Island, Campobello Is. NB E0G 3H0, 506/752-2922; Fax: 506/752-6000

**Alta:** Alberta Sport, Recreation, Parks & Wildlife Foundation, Percy Page Centre, 11759 Groat Rd., Edmonton AB T5M 3K9, 403/427-1976; Fax: 403/488-9755

**B.C.:** Ministry of Environment, Lands & Parks, Parks Division (BC Parks), 800 Johnson St., 2nd Fl., Victoria BC V8V 1X4, 250/387 5002; Fax: 250/387-5757

**Man.:** Ecological Reserves Advisory Committee, PO Box 355, Stn St. Vital, Winnipeg MB R2M 5C8, 204/942-6617

Manitoba Natural Resources, Parks & Natural Areas Branch, 200 Saulteaux Cr., PO Box 50, Winnipeg MB R3J 3W3, 204/945-4362; Fax: 204/945-0012

**N.B.:** Department of Natural Resources & Energy, Parks & Natural Areas, PO Box 6000, Fredericton NB E3B 5H1, 506/453-2730; Fax: 506/453-6630

**Nfld.:** Department of Tourism, Culture & Recreation, Parks & Recreation Branch, Confederation Bldg., PO Box 8700, St. John's NF A1B 4J6, 709/729-0928; Fax: 709/729-0662

**NWT:** Department of Resources, Wildlife & Economic Development, Parks & Tourism, PO Box 1320, Yellowknife NT X1A 2L9, 867/873-7903; Fax: 867/873-0163

**N.S.:** Department of Natural Resources, Parks & Recreation (Belmont), Founder's Square, 1701 Hollis St., PO Box 698, Halifax NS B3J 2T9, 902/662-3030; Fax: 902/662-2160

**Ont.:** Ministry of Natural Resources, Ontario Parks, Whitney Block, #6540, 99 Wellesley St. West, Toronto ON M7A 1W3, 705/740-1224; Fax: 416/314-1994

Provincial Parks Council, 2450 McDougall St., Windsor ON N8X 3N6, 519/255-6731; Fax: 519/255-7990

**PEI:** Department of Economic Development & Tourism, Tourism PEI, Annex 1, West Royalty Industrial Park, 1 Watts Ave., Charlottetown PE C1E 1B0, 902/368-5540; Toll Free: 1-800-465-4734; Fax: 902/368-4438

**Qué.:** Ministère de l'Environnement et de la Faune, Direction générale du patrimoine faunique et naturel, Édifice Marie-Guyart, 675, boul René-Lévesque est, Québec QC G1R 5V7, 418/643-3127; Fax: 418/643-3619

Parcs québécois, Édifice Marie-Guyart, 675, boul René-Lévesque est, Québec QC G1R 5V7, 418/644-9393; Fax: 418/644-8932

**Sask.:** Saskatchewan Environment & Resource Management, Parks & Facilities, 3211 Albert St., Regina SK S4S 5W6, 306/787-2846; Fax: 306/787-7000

**Yuk.:** Yukon Renewable Resources, Parks & Outdoor Recreation Branch, PO Box 2703, Whitehorse YT Y1A 2C6, 867/667-5237; Fax: 867/668-7823

## PARLIAMENT

### *See Also* Government (General Information); Protocol (State)

House of Commons, Canada, House of Commons, 111 Wellington St., PO Box 1103, Ottawa ON K1A 0A9, 613/992-2986

Library of Parliament, 111 Wellington St., Ottawa ON K1A 0A9, 613/995-1166; Fax: 613/992-1269

Office of the Prime Minister (Lib.), #309-S, Centre Block, House of Commons, 111 Wellington St., Ottawa ON K1A 0A2, 613/992-4211; Fax: 613/941-6900

Privy Council Office, Langevin Block, 80 Wellington St., Ottawa ON K1A 0A3, 613/957-5153; Fax: 613/995-0101

Senate of Canada, Senate Bldg., 111 Wellington St., Ottawa ON K1A 0A4, 613/992-2493; Toll Free: 1-800-267-7362; Fax: 613/995-4998

**Alta:** Legislative Assembly, c/o Clerk's Office, #801, Legislature Annex, 9718 - 107 St., Edmonton AB T5K 1E4, 403/427-2478; Fax: 403/427-5688

**B.C.:** , c/o Clerk's Office, #221 Parliament Bldgs., Victoria BC V8V 1X4, 250/387-3785; Fax: 250/387-0942

**Man.:** , c/o Clerk's Office, Legislative Bldg., #237, 450 Broadway Ave., Winnipeg MB R3C 0V8, 204/945-3636; Fax: 204/948-2507

**N.B.:** , c/o Clerk's Office, Legislative Bldg., PO Box 6000, Fredericton NB E3B 5H1, 506/453-2506; Fax: 506/453-7154

**Nfld.:** House of Assembly, c/o Clerk's Office, Confederation Bldg., PO Box 8700, St.John's NF A1B 4J6, 709/729-3405; Fax: 709/729-4820

**NWT:** Legislative Assembly, c/o Clerk's Office, PO Box 1320, Yellowknife NT X1A 2L9, 867/669-2299, 669-2200; Toll Free: 1-800-661-0784; Fax: 867/920-4735

**N.S.:** Legislative House of Assembly, c/o Clerk's Office, Province House, 2nd Fl., PO Box 1617, Halifax NS B3J 2Y3, 902/424-5978; Fax: 902/424-0574

**Ont.:** Legislative Assembly, c/o Clerk's Office, #104, Legislative Bldg., Queen's Park, Toronto ON M7A 1A2, 416/325-7340; Fax: 416/325-7344

**PEI:** , c/o Clerk's Office, Province House, PO Box 2000, Charlottetown PE C1A 7N8, 902/368-5970; Fax: 902/368-5175

**Qué.:** Assemblée nationale, c/o Secrétariat général, Édifice Honoré-Mercier, #3.57, 1025, rue St-Augustin, Québec QC G1A 1A3, 418/643-2724; Fax: 418/643-5062

**Sask.:** Legislative Assembly, c/o Clerk's Office, #239, Legislative Bldg., 2405 Legislative Dr., Regina SK S4S 0B3, 306/787-2279; Fax: 306/787-0408

**Yuk.:** , c/o Clerk's Office, PO Box 2703, Whitehorse YT Y1A 2C6, 867/667-5498; Fax: 867/393-6280

## PAROLE BOARDS

### *See Also* Correctional Services

National Parole Board, 340 Laurier Ave. West, Ottawa ON K1A 0R1, 613/954-7474; Fax: 613/995-4380

Solicitor General Canada, Sir Wilfrid Laurier Bldg., 340 Laurier Ave. West, Ottawa ON K1A 0P8, 613/991-3283; Fax: 613/993-7062

**Alta:** Alberta Justice, Community Corrections & Release Programs Branch, 10365 - 97 St., Edmonton AB T5J 3W7, 403/422-5757; Fax: 403/422-3098

Criminal Justice Division, 9833 - 109th St., Edmonton AB T5K 2E8, 403/427-2745; Fax: 403/422-9639

**B.C.:** British Columbia Board of Parole, #301, 10090 - 152 St., Surrey BC V3R 8X8, 604/660-8846; Fax: 604/660-8877

**Man.:** Manitoba Justice, Corrections Division, 405 Broadway, 8th Fl., Winnipeg MB R3C 3L6, 204/945-2852

**N.B.:** Department of the Solicitor General, Barker House, 4th Fl., PO Box 6000, Fredericton NB E3B 5H1, 506/453-7414; Fax: 506/453-3870

**Nfld.:** Department of Justice & Attorney General, Adult Corrections Division, Confederation Bldg., PO Box 8700, St. John's NF A1B 4J6, 709/729-3880; Fax: 709/729-0416

**NWT:** Department of Justice, Solicitor General Branch, PO Box 1320, Yellowknife NT X1A 2L9, 867/873-7005

**N.S.:** Probate, 5151 Terminal Rd., PO Box 7, Halifax NS B3J 2L6, 902/424-7421; Fax: 902/424-0595

**Ont.:** Ontario Board of Parole, #201, 2195 Yonge St., Toronto ON M4S 2B1, 416/325-4480; Fax: 416/325-4485

**Qué.:** Commission québécoise des libérations conditionnelles, #200, 2055, rue Peel, Montréal QC H3A 1V4, 514/873-2230; Fax: 514/873-7580

**Sask.:** Saskatchewan Justice, Corrections Division, 1874 Scarth St., Regina SK S4P 3V7, 306/787-7872 (Communications); Fax: 306/787-8084

**Yuk.:** Yukon Justice, Adult Probation Unit, PO Box 2703, Whitehorse YT Y1A 2C6, 867/667-3586; Fax: 867/667-3446

## PASSPORT INFORMATION

### *See Also* Citizenship; Immigration

Foreign Affairs & International Trade Canada, Passport Office, Place du Centre, 200, Promenade du Portage, 6e étage, Hull QC K1A 0G3, 819/994-3500; Toll Free: 1-800-567-6868, TDD: 613/994-3560; Fax: 819/953-5856

## PATENTS & COPYRIGHT

Industry Canada, Canadian Intellectual Property Office, Place du Portage, Tour I, 50, rue Victoria, Hull QC K1A 0C9, 613/941-0222; Fax: 613/954-6436

Copyright & Industrial Design, Place du Portage, Tour I, 50, rue Victoria, Hull QC K1A 0C9, 819/997-1657; Fax: 819/953-6977

Patents, Place du Portage, Tour I, 50, rue Victoria, Hull QC K1A 0C9, 819/953-5864; Fax: 819/994-1989

Trade-Marks, Place du Portage, Tour I, 50, rue Victoria, Hull QC K1A 0C9, 819/997-2423; Fax: 819/997-1421

## PAY EQUITY

Human Resources Development Canada, Place du Portage, Phase IV, 140, Promenade du Portage, Hull QC K1A 0J9, 819/994-6013 (Communications)

Treasury Board of Canada, Official Languages & Employment Equity Branch, 140 O'Connor St., Ottawa ON K1A 0R5, 613/952-2852; Fax: 613/941-4262

**Alta:** Alberta Labour, Work Standards, 10808 - 99 Ave., Edmonton AB T5K 0G5, 403/427-8541; Fax: 403/422-3562

**B.C.:** Ministry of the Attorney General, Employment Equity & Women's Programs, PO Box 9282, Stn Prov. Gov't, Victoria BC V8W 9J7, 250/387-3247; Fax: 250/356-5368

**Man.:** Manitoba Labour, Employment Standards Division, #156, Legislative Bldg., 450 Broadway, Winnipeg MB R3C 0V8, 204/945-4039 (Deputy Minister)

**N.S.:** Pay Equity Commission, PO Box 697, Halifax NS B3J 1T8, 902/424-8595; Fax: 902/424-3239

**Ont.:** , 150 Eglinton Ave. East, 5th Fl., Toronto ON M4P 1E8, 416/481-4464; Fax: 416/314-8741

**PEI:** Labour Relations Board, PO Box 2000, Charlottetown PE C1A 7N8, 902/368-5550; Fax: 902/368-5526

**Sask.:** Saskatchewan Public Service Commission, Employee Relations, 2103 - 11 Ave., Regina SK S4P 3V7, 306/787-7606; Fax: 306/787-7533

## PENSIONS

Bureau of Pension Advocates, J. MacDonald Bldg., 2nd Fl., PO Box 7700, Charlottetown PE C1A 8M9, 902/566-8640; Fax: 902/566-7804

Finance Canada, Esplanade Laurier, 140 O'Connor St., Ottawa ON K1A 0G5, 613/992-1573; TDD: 613/996-0035; Fax: 613/996-8404

Human Resources Development Canada, Income Security Programs, Place Vanier, 120 Parkdale Ave., Ottawa ON K1A 0L1, 819/994-6013 (Communications)

Office of the Superintendent of Financial Institutions, Kent Square, 255 Albert St., Ottawa ON K1A 0H2, 613/990-7788; Toll Free: 1-800-385-8647; Fax: 613/952-8219

Revenue Canada, CPP/UI Division, 875 Heron Rd., Ottawa ON K1A 0L8, 613/957-2237

Registered Plans Division, 123 Slater St., Ottawa ON K1A 0L8, 613/954-0933

Veterans Review & Appeal Board, Daniel J. MacDonald Bldg., PO Box 7700, Charlottetown PE C1A 8M9, 902/566-8636; Fax: 902/566-7371

**Alta:** Alberta Pensions Administration, Park Plaza, 3rd Fl., 10611 - 98 Ave., Edmonton AB T5K 2P7, 403/427-2782; Fax: 403/427-1621

Alberta Labour, Pensions, 10808 - 99 Ave., Edmonton AB T5K 0G5, 403/427-8322; Fax: 403/422-4283

Alberta Treasury, Pensions Policy, Terrace Bldg., 9515 - 107 St., Edmonton AB T5K 2C3, 403/427-8730; Fax: 403/426-4564

**B.C.:** Ministry of Human Resources, Income Support, Parliament Bldgs., Victoria BC V8V 1X4

Ministry of Labour, Pension Benefits Standards, #210, 4946 Canada Way, Burnaby BC V5G 4J6, 604/775-1349; URL: http://labour.gov.bc.ca/psb; Fax: 604/660-6517

**Man.:** Manitoba Labour, Pension Commission, #156, Legislative Bldg., 450 Broadway, Winnipeg MB R3C 0V8, 204/945-2742; Fax: 204/945-2375

**N.B.:** Department of Advanced Education & Labour, Pensions Branch, Chestnut Complex, 470 York St., PO Box 6000, Fredericton NB E3B 5H1, 506/453-2055; Fax: 506/453-3806

**Nfld.:** Department of Finance & Treasury Board, Administration, Confederation Bldg., PO Box 8700, St. John's NF A1B 4J6, 709/729-5993

Debt Management & Pensions, Confederation Bldg., PO Box 8700, St. John's NF A1B 4J6, 709/729-2949; Fax: 709/729-2070

Department of Government Services & Lands, Insurance & Pensions, PO Box 8700, St. John's NF A1B 4J6, 709/729-2594; Fax: 709/729-3205

**N.S.:** Department of Finance, Investments, Pensions & Treasury Services Branch, PO Box 187, Halifax NS B3J 2N3, 902/424-5554; Fax: 902/424-0635

Pension Registration, PO Box 187, Halifax NS B3J 2N3, 902/424-8915; Fax: 902/424-0635

Pensions, PO Box 187, Halifax NS B3J 2N3, 902/424-5911; Fax: 902/424-0635

**Ont.:** Ontario Pension Board, #1200, 1 Adelaide St. East, Toronto ON M5C 2X6, 416/364-8558; Toll Free: 1-800-668-6203; Fax: 416/364-7578

Pension Commission of Ontario, 250 Younge St., 29th Fl., Toronto ON M5B 2N7, 416/314-0660; Fax: 416/314-0620

**PEI:** Department of Community Affairs & Attorney General, PO Box 2000, Charlottetown PE C1A 7N8, 902/368-5250; Fax: 902/368-5283; 5355

Department of Education, Teacher Certification & Pensions, Sullivan Bldg., 16 Fitzroy St., PO Box 2000, Charlottetown PE C1A 7N8, 902/368-4651; Fax: 902/368-4663

**Qué.:** Ministère de l'Emploi et de la Solidarité, 425, rue St-Amable, 2e étage, Québec QC G1R 4Z1, 418/643-9818; Toll Free: 1-800-361-4743; Fax: 418/646-5426

Ministère du Revenu, Perception automatique des pensions alimentaires, 3800, rue De Marly, Ste-Foy QC G1X 4A5, 418/643-7040; Fax: 418/646-8270

Régie des rentes, 2600, boul Laurier, Ste-Foy QC G1V 4T3, 418/643-8302; Fax: 418/643-9586

**Sask.:** Saskatchewan Finance, Public Employees Benefits Agency, 2350 Albert St., Regina SK S4P 4A6, 306/787-6757; Fax: 306/787-0244

Saskatchewan Pension Plan, 2350 Albert St., Regina SK S4P 4A6, 306/463-5412; Fax: 306/463-3500

Saskatchewan Justice, Pensions, 1874 Scarth St., Regina SK S4P 3V7, 306/787-2458; Fax: 306/787-9779

## PIPELINES

National Energy Board, 311 - 6 Ave. SW, Calgary AB T2P 3H2, 403/292-4800; Fax: 403/292-5503

Northern Pipeline Agency Canada, Lester B. Pearson Bldg., 125 Sussex Dr., Ottawa ON K1A 0G2, 613/993-7466; Fax: 613/998-8787

Transportation Safety Board of Canada, 200 Promenade du Portage, 4e étage, Hull QC K1A 1K8, 819/994-3741; Fax: 819/997-2239

**Alta:** Alberta Energy, Petroleum Plaza, North Tower, 9945 - 108 St., Edmonton AB T5K 2G6, 403/427-7425; Fax: 403/427-3198

**Man.:** Manitoba Energy & Mines, Pipelines & Surface Rights, #360, 1395 Ellice Ave., Winnipeg MB R3G 3P2, 204/945-6574; Toll Free: 1-800-282-8069 (Energy); Fax: 204/945-0586

**Qué.:** Régie du gaz naturel, Tour de la Bourse, #255, 800, Place Victoria, CP 001, Montréal QC H4Z 1A2, 514/873-2452; Fax: 514/873-2070

## POLICING SERVICES

Justice Canada, Legal Operations Sector, Justice Bldg., 239 Wellington St., Ottawa ON K1A 0H8, 613/957-4222; Fax: 613/954-0811

Royal Canadian Mounted Police, 1200 Vanier Pkwy., Ottawa ON K1A OR2, 613/993-1085; Fax: 613/993-5894

Solicitor General Canada, Policing & Law Enforcement, Sir Wilfrid Laurier Bldg., 340 Laurier Ave. West, Ottawa ON K1A 0P8, 613/990-2703; Fax: 613/993-5252

**Alta:** Alberta Justice, Public Security Division, 10365 - 97 St., Edmonton AB T5J 3W7, 403/427-2745; Fax: 403/427-1194

**B.C.:** British Columbia Police Commission, #405, 815 Hornby St., Vancouver BC V6Z 2E6, 604/660-2385; Fax: 604/660-1223

Ministry of the Attorney General, Police Services, PO Box 9282, Stn Prov. Gov't, Victoria BC V8W 9J7, 250/356-5483; Fax: 250/356-7747

**Man.:** Law Enforcement Review Agency, 405 Broadway, 14th Fl., Winnipeg MB R3C 3L6, 204/945-8667; Fax: 204/945-6692

Manitoba Justice, 405 Broadway, 5th Fl., Winnipeg MB R3C 3L6, 204/945-2852

**N.B.:** Department of the Solicitor General, Barker House, 4th Fl., PO Box 6000, Fredericton NB E3B 5H1, 506/453-3603; Fax: 506/457-4957

New Brunswick Police Commission, #103, 191 Prospect St. West, Fredericton NB E3B 2T7, 506/453-2069; Fax: 506/457-3542

**Nfld.:** Department of Justice & Attorney General, Royal Newfoundland Constabulary, Confederation Bldg., PO Box 8700, St. John's NF A1B 4J6, 709/729-8151; Inquiries: 709/729-8000; Fax: 709/729-2129

Royal Newfoundland Constabulary Public Complaints Commission, PO Box 21128, St. John's NF A1A 5B2, 709/729-0950

**NWT:** Department of Justice, Sheriff's Office, PO Box 1320, Yellowknife NT X1A 2L9, 867/920-6301

**N.S.:** Policing Services Division, 5151 Terminal Rd., PO Box 7, Halifax NS B3J 2L6, 902/424-2504; Fax: 902/424-0700

Nova Scotia Police Commission, #300, 1601 Lower Water St., Halifax NS B3J 2Y3, 902/424-3246; Fax: 902/424-3919

**Ont.:** Ministry of the Solicitor General & Correctional Services, Ontario Provincial Police, 50 Andrew St. South, 3rd Fl., Orillia ON L3V 7T5, 705/497-9500

Policing Services Division, 25 Grosvenor St., 9th Fl., Toronto ON M7A 2H3, 705/497-9500

**PEI:** Department of Community Affairs & Attorney General, PO Box 2000, Charlottetown PE C1A 7N8, 902/368-5250; Fax: 902/368-5283; 5355

**Qué.:** Ministère de la Sécurité publique, Tour des Laurentides, 2525, boul Laurier, 5e étage, Ste-Foy QC G1V 2L2, 418/643-3500; Fax: 418/643-0275

Sûreté du Québec, 1701, rue Parthenais, Montréal QC H2L 4K7, 514/598-4488; Fax: 514/598-4957

**Sask.:** Saskatchewan Police Commission, 1874 Scarth St., 7th Fl., Regina SK S4P 3V7, 306/787-6534

Saskatchewan Police Complaints Investigator, 2151 Scarth St., 3rd Fl., Regina SK S4P 3V7, 306/787-6519; Fax: 306/787-6528

Saskatchewan Justice, Law Enforcement Services, 1874 Scarth St., Regina SK S4P 3V7, 306/787-0400; Fax: 306/787-8084

Saskatchewan Municipal Government, Protection Services Branch, 1855 Victoria Ave., Regina SK S4P 3V7, 306/787-4509; Fax: 306/787-9273

**Yuk.:** Yukon Community & Transportation Services, Public Safety Branch, PO Box 2703, Whitehorse YT Y1A 2C6, 867/667-5824; Fax: 867/393-6249

## POLLUTION *See* AIR RESOURCES; WATER RESOURCES

## POPULATION

### *See Also* Statistics

National Archives of Canada, 395 Wellington St., Ottawa ON K1A 0N3, 613/995-5138; Fax: 613/995-6274

Statistics Canada, R.H. Coats Bldg., Tunney's Pasture, 120 Parkdale Ave., Ottawa ON K1A 0T6, 613/951-8116; Toll Free: 1-800-263-1136, TDD: 1-800-363-7629; Fax: 613/951-0581

**Alta:** Alberta Municipal Affairs, Registries Division, John E. Brownlee Bldg., 10365 - 97 St., Edmonton AB T5J 3W7, 403/422-2362 (Edmonton), 403/297-8980 (Calgary); Toll Free: 1-800-465-5009 (in Alberta); Fax: 403/422-9105

**B.C.:** Ministry of Finance & Corporate Relations, Population Statistics, 617 Government St., Victoria BC V8V 1X4, 250/387-0337; Fax: 250/387-0380

**Man.:** Manitoba Industry, Trade & Tourism, Manitoba Bureau of Statistics, #333, 260 St. Mary Ave., Winnipeg MB R3C 0M6, 204/945-2999; Fax: 204/945-0695

**N.B.:** Department of Finance, New Brunswick Statistics Agency, PO Box 6000, Fredericton NB E3B 5H1, 506/453-2381; Fax: 506/453-7970

**Nfld.:** Department of Government Services & Lands, 5 Mews Pl., PO Box 8700, St. John's NF A1B 4J6; Fax: 709/729-2071

**NWT:** Department of Finance, PO Box 1320, Yellowknife NT X1A 2L9, 867/873-7147; Fax: 867/873-0275

## POSTAL SERVICE

Canada Post Corporation, 2701 Riverside Dr., Ottawa ON K1A 0B1, 613/734-8440; Toll Free: 1-800-267-1177; Fax: 613/734-6084

## PREMIERS & LEADERS

### *See Also* Cabinets & Executive Councils; Government (General Information)

Office of the Prime Minister (Lib.), #309-S, Centre Block, House of Commons, 111 Wellington St., Ottawa ON K1A 0A2, 613/992-4211; Fax: 613/941-6900

**Alta:** Office of the Premier, Legislature Bldg., #307, 10800 - 97 Ave., Edmonton AB T5K 2B6, 403/427-2251; Fax: 403/427-1349

**B.C.:** , #156, West Annex, Legislative Bldgs., 1150 McKenzie Ave., Victoria BC V8V 1X4, 250/387-1715; Fax: 250/387-0087

**Man.:** , Legislative Bldg., #204, 450 Broadway, Winnipeg MB R3C 0V8, 204/945-3714; Fax: 204/949-1484

**N.B.:** , Centennial Bldg., 670 King St., PO Box 6000, Fredericton NB E3B 5H1, 506/453-2144; Fax: 506/453-7407

**Nfld.:** , Confederation Bldg., 8th Fl., PO Box 8700, St. John's NF A1B 4J6; Fax: 709/729-5875

**NWT:** , Legislative Assembly Bldg., PO Box 1320, Yellowknife NT X1A 2L9, 867/669-2311; 2322; Fax: 867/873-0385

**N.S.:** , One Government Place, 1700 Granville St., PO Box 726, Halifax NS B3J 1X5, 902/424-6600; Fax: 902/424-7648

**Ont.:** , Legislative Bldg., #281, 1 Queen's Park Cres. South, Toronto ON M7A 1A1, 416/325-1941; TDD: 416/325-7702; Fax: 416/325-7578

**PEI:** , Shaw Bldg., 95 Rochford St., 5th Fl. South, PO Box 2000, Charlottetown PE C1A 7N8, 902/368-4400; Fax: 902/368-4416

**Qué.:** Cabinet du premier ministre, Édifice J, 885, Grande-Allée est, 3e étage, Québec QC G1A 1A2, 418/643-5321; Fax: 418/643-3924

**Sask.:** Office of the Premier, 2405 Legislative Dr., Regina SK S4S 0B3, 306/787-9433; Fax: 306/787-0885

**Yuk.:** Office of the Government Leader, PO Box 2703, Whitehorse YT Y1A 2C6, 867/667-5885; Fax: 867/667-8424

## PRISONS *See* CORRECTIONAL SERVICES

## PROPERTY *See* REAL ESTATE

## PROTOCOL (STATE)

### *See Also* Parliament

Canadian Heritage, Citizenship & Canadian Identity Sector, Jules Léger Bldg., 25 Eddy St., Hull QC K1A 1K5, 819/997-0055; Fax: 819/953-5382

Foreign Affairs & International Trade Canada, Office of Protocol, Lester B. Pearson Bldg., 125 Sussex Dr., Ottawa ON K1A 0G2, 613/996-8683; Fax: 613/943-1075

Governor General & Commander-in-Chief of Canada, Rideau Hall, 1 Sussex Dr., Ottawa ON K1A 0A1, 613/993-8200; Fax: 613/990-7636

House of Commons, Canada, Parliamentary Exchanges & Protocol, House of Commons, 111 Wellington St., PO Box 1103, Ottawa ON K1A 0A9, 613/996-1102

**Alta:** Alberta Federal & Intergovernmental Affairs, Protocol Office, Commerce Place, 10155 - 102 St., 12th Fl., Edmonton AB T5J 4GB, 403/427-2611; Fax: 403/422-0786

**B.C.:** Ministry of Finance & Corporate Relations, Protocol & Events Branch, 617 Government St., Victoria BC V8V 1X4, 250/387-4304; Fax: 250/356-2814

**N.B.:** Department of Intergovernmental & Aboriginal Affairs, Office of Protocol, PO Box 6000, Fredericton NB E3B 5H1, 506/453-2671; Fax: 506/453-2995

**N.S.:** Executive Council, One Government Place, PO Box 2125, Halifax NS B3J 3B7, 902/424-4463; Fax: 902/424-4309

**Ont.:** Ministry of Economic Development, Trade & Tourism, International Relations, Hearst Block, 900 Bay St., Toronto ON M7A 2E1, 416/325-8545; Fax: 416/325-8550

**Qué.:** Ministère des Relations Internationales, Édifice Hector-Fabre, 525, boul Réne-Levesque est, Québec QC G1R 5R9, 418/649-2346; Fax: 418/649-2657

**Sask.:** Saskatchewan Intergovernmental Affairs, Protocol Office, 1919 Saskatchewan Dr., Regina SK S4P 3V7, 306/787-3109; Fax: 306/787-1269

## PUBLIC HEALTH *See* HEALTH SERVICES

## PUBLIC SAFETY

### *See Also* Occupational Safety

Atomic Energy Control Board, Reactor Regulation Directorate, 280 Slater St., PO Box 1046, Stn B, Ottawa ON K1P 5S9, 613/995-5894; Toll Free: 1-800-668-5284; Fax: 613/995-5086

Canadian Centre for Occupational Health & Safety, 250 Main St. East, Hamilton ON L8N 1H6, 905/572-2981; Toll Free: 1-800-263-8466; Fax: 905/572-2206

Canadian Transportation Agency, Les Terrasses de la Chaudière, 15 Eddy St., Hull QC K1A 0N9, 819/997-0344 (Communications); Fax: 819/953-8353

Fisheries & Oceans Canada, Canadian Coast Guard, Canada Bldg., 344 Slater St., Ottawa ON K1A 0N7, 613/998-1574; Fax: 613/990-2780

Foreign Affairs & International Trade Canada, International Security Bureau, Arms Control & CSCE Affairs, Lester B. Pearson Bldg., 125 Sussex Dr., Ottawa ON K1A 0G2, 613/992-3402; Fax: 613/952-3904

Health Canada, Health Protection Branch, Brooke Claxton Bldg., Tunney's Pasture, 120 Parkdale Ave., Ottawa ON K1A 0K9, 613/957-2991; Fax: 613/941-5366

Industry Canada, Office of Consumer Affairs, C.D. Howe Bldg., 235 Queen St., Ottawa ON K1A 0H5, 613/941-0222; Fax: 613/954-6436

National Defence (Canada), MGen. George R. Pearkes Bldg., 101 Colonel By Dr., Ottawa ON K1A 0K2, 613/992-4581

Royal Canadian Mounted Police, 1200 Vanier Pkwy., Ottawa ON K1A OR2, 613/993-1085; Fax: 613/993-5894

Solicitor General Canada, Canadian Security Intelligence Service, PO Box 9732, Ottawa ON K1G 4G4, 613/993-9620; Fax: 613/993-7062

National Security, Sir Wilfrid Laurier Bldg., 340 Laurier Ave. West, Ottawa ON K1A 0P8, 613/993-4136; Fax: 613/990-2632

Transport Canada, Safety & Security Group, Transport Canada Building, 330 Sparks St., Ottawa ON K1A 0N5, 613/990-2309; Fax: 613/954-4731

**Alta:** Alberta Health, Health Strategies & Research, PO Box 1360, Edmonton AB T5J 2N3, 403/427-7164 (Communications)

Alberta Justice, Public Security Division, 10365 - 97 St., Edmonton AB T5J 3W7, 403/427-2745; Fax: 403/427-1194

Alberta Transportation & Utilities, Disaster Services, Twin Atria, 4999 - 98 Ave., Edmonton AB T6B 2X3, 403/422-9000; Fax: 403/415-0782

**B.C.:** Ministry of the Attorney General, Public Safety & Regulatory Branch, PO Box 9282, Stn Prov. Gov't, Victoria BC V8W 9J7, 250/356-9596 (Policy & Education); Fax: 250/356-9037

**Man.:** Manitoba Health, Community & Mental Health Services Division, 599 Empress St., PO Box 925, Winnipeg MB R3C 2T6, 204/786-7191 (Finance & Administration Branch)

**N.B.:** Department of Municipalities, Culture & Housing, Community Services Division, Marysville Place, 20 McGloin St., PO Box 6000, Fredericton NB E3B 5H1, 506/453-2690; Fax: 506/453-2416

**Nfld.:** Department of Justice & Attorney General, Public Protection & Support Services, Confederation Bldg., PO Box 8700, St. John's NF A1B 4J6, 709/729-5942; Fax: 709/729-2129

**NWT:** Department of Justice, PO Box 1320, Yellowknife NT X1A 2L9, 867/920-6197

Department of Municipal & Community Affairs, Emergency Services Division, #600, 5201 - 50 Ave., PO Box 1310, Yellowknife NT X1A 2L9, 867/873-7554; Fax: 867/873-8193

**N.S.:** Department of Labour, Public Safety, 5151 Terminal Rd., PO Box 697, Halifax NS B3J 2T8, 902/424-4125; Fax: 902/424-3239

**Ont.:** Ministry of the Solicitor General & Correctional Services, Public Safety Division, 200 - 1 Ave. West,

North Bay ON P1B 9M3, 416/314-3382; Fax: 416/314-3388

**Qué.:** Ministère de la Sécurité publique, Tour des Laurentides, 2525, boul Laurier, 5e étage, Ste-Foy QC G1V 2L2, 418/643-3500; Fax: 418/643-0275

**Yuk.:** Yukon Community & Transportation Services, Public Safety Branch, PO Box 2703, Whitehorse YT Y1A 2C6, 867/667-5824; Fax: 867/393-6249

## PUBLIC TRUSTEE

**Alta:** Alberta Justice, Office of the Public Trustee, #400S, 10365 - 97 St., Edmonton AB T5J 3Z8, 403/427-2744; Fax: 403/422-9136

**B.C.:** Office of the Public Trustee, #600, 808 West Hastings St., Vancouver BC V6C 3L3, 604/660-4444; Fax: 604/660-4456

**Man.:** Manitoba Justice, Office of the Public Trustee, 405 Broadway, 7th Fl., Winnipeg MB R3C 3L6, 204/945-2703

**NWT:** Department of Justice, Public Trustee's Office, PO Box 1320, Yellowknife NT X1A 2L9, 867/873-7464

**Ont.:** Ministry of the Attorney General, Office of the Public Trustee, 720 Bay St., 11th Fl., Toronto ON M5G 2K1, 416/314-2690; General Inquiry: 416/314-2800; Fax: 416/314-2716

**Qué.:** Curateur public du Québec, #500, 600, boul René-Lévesque ouest, Montréal QC H3B 4W9, 514/873-4074; Fax: 514/873-4972

**Sask.:** Saskatchewan Justice, Public Trustees' Office, 1874 Scarth St., Regina SK S4P 3V7, 306/787-5427; Fax: 306/787-3874

**Yuk.:** Yukon Justice, Official Guardian's Office, PO Box 2703, Whitehorse YT Y1A 2C6, 867/667-5366; Fax: 867/393-6272

## PUBLIC UTILITIES

**Alta:** Alberta Energy & Utilities Board, 640 - 5 Ave. SW, Calgary AB T2P 3G4, 403/297-8311; Fax: 403/297-8398

Alberta Transportation & Utilities, Twin Atria, 4999 - 98 Ave., Edmonton AB T6B 2X3, 403/427-2731

**B.C.:** British Columbia Hydro & Power Authority, 6911 Southpoint Dr., Burnaby BC V3N 4X8, 604/528-1600; Fax: 604/623-3901

**Man.:** Public Utilities Board, 280 Smith St., 2nd Fl., Winnipeg MB R3C 1K2, 204/945-2638; Fax: 204/945-2643

**N.B.:** Board of Commissioners of Public Utilities, 110 Charlotte St., PO Box 5001, Saint John NB E2L 4Y9, 506/658-2504; Fax: 506/633-0163

**Nfld.:** Newfoundland & Labrador Hydro, PO Box 12400, St. John's NF A1B 4K7, 709/737-1400; Fax: 709/737-1231

Newfoundland & Labrador Public Utilities Commission, PO Box 21040, St. John's NF A1A 5B2, 709/726-0955; Fax: 709/726-9604

**NWT:** Northwest Territories Power Corporation, 4 Capital Drive, Hay River NT X0E 1G2, 867/874-5200; Fax: 867/874-5251

Northwest Territories Water Board, PO Box 1500, Yellowknife NT X1A 2R3, 867/669-2772; Fax: 867/669-2719

**N.S.:** Department of the Environment, Utilities Division, 5151 Terminal Rd., 5th Fl., PO Box 2107, Halifax NS B3J 3B7, 902/424-5300; Fax: 902/424-0503

Nova Scotia Utility & Review Board, #300, 1601 Lower Water St., PO Box 1692, Stn M, Halifax NS B3J 3S3, 902/424-4448; Fax: 902/424-3919

**Ont.:** Ontario Energy Board, 2300 Yonge St., 26th Fl., Toronto ON M4P 1E4, 416/481-1967; Fax: 416/440-7656

Ontario Hydro, 700 University Ave., Toronto ON M5G 1X6, 416/592-5111; Toll Free: 1-800-263-9000

**PEI:** Island Regulatory & Appeals Commission, #501, 134 Kent St., PO Box 577, Charlottetown PE C1A 7L1, 902/892-3501; Toll Free: 1-800-501-6268; Fax: 902/566-4076

**Qué.:** Hydro-Québec, 75, boul René-Lévesque ouest, Montréal QC H2Z 1A4, 514/289-2211; Fax: 514/843-3163

**Sask.:** SaskEnergy Incorporated, #1100, 1945 Hamilton St., Regina SK S4P 2C7, 306/777-9426; Fax: 306/777-9889

Saskatchewan Water Corporation (Sask Water), Victoria Place, 111 Fairford St. East, Moose Jaw SK S6H 7X9, 306/694-3900; Fax: 306/694-3944

**Yuk.:** Yukon Utilities Board, PO Box 6070, Whitehorse YT Y1A 5L7, 867/667-5058

Yukon Energy Corporation, PO Box 5920, Whitehorse YT Y1A 5L7, 867/667-5028; Fax: 867/393-6327

## PUBLIC WORKS & SERVICES

Canada Lands Company, #1500, 200 King St. West, Toronto ON M5H 3T4, 416/974-9700; Fax: 416/974-9661

Defence Construction Canada, Place de Ville, Tower B, 112 Kent St., 17th Fl., Ottawa ON K1A 0K3, 613/998-9548; Fax: 613/998-1061

Public Works & Government Services Canada, Place du Portage, Phase III, 11, rue Laurier, Hull QC K1A 0S5, 819/956-3115; TDD: 819/994-5389

**Alta:** Alberta Public Works, Supply & Services, 6950 - 113 St., 3rd Fl., Edmonton AB T6H 5V7, 403/427-7988; Fax: 403/427-0812

**B.C.:** Ministry of Transportation & Highways, Planning & Major Projects Department, 940 Blanshard St., Victoria BC V8W 3E6, 250/387-3198; Fax: 250/387-6431

**Man.:** Manitoba Government Services, Administration & Finance Division, 1700 Portage Ave., Main Fl., Winnipeg MB R3J 0E1, 204/945-4800 (Administration); Fax: 204/948-2016

**N.B.:** New Brunswick, Services Group, PO Box 6000, Fredericton NB E3B 5H1, 506/453-3742; Fax: 506/444-4400

**Nfld.:** Department of Works, Services & Transportation, Confederation Bldg., PO Box 8700, St. John's NF A1B 4J6, 709/729-3676; Fax: 709/729-4285

Works Branch, Confederation Bldg., PO Box 8700, St. John's NF A1B 4J6, 709/729-3676; Fax: 709/729-4285

**NWT:** Department of Public Works & Services, Bldg. YK, 7th Fl., PO Box 1320, Yellowknife NT X1A 2L9, 867/873-7114; Fax: 867/873-0264

**N.S.:** Department of Transportation & Public Works, 1969 Upper Water St., PO Box 186, Halifax NS B3J 2N2, 902/424-5837

**Ont.:** Management Board of Cabinet, Communications, Ferguson Block, 77 Wellesley St. West, 12th Fl., Toronto ON M7A 1N3, 416/326-9091; Fax: 416/327-3790

**PEI:** Department of Transportation & Public Works, Jones Bldg., PO Box 2000, Charlottetown PE C1A 7N8, 902/368-5100; Fax: 902/368-5395

**Qué.:** Ministère des Affaires Municipales, Développement des politiques et des programmes, Édifice Cook-Chauveau, 20, rue Pierre-Olivier-Chauveau, Québec QC G1R 4J3, 418/691-2040; Fax: 418/644-9863

Société immobilière du Québec, 475, rue St-Amable, Québec QC G1R 4X9, 418/646-1766 poste 3470; Fax: 418/643-7932

**Sask.:** Saskatchewan Municipal Government, Saskatchewan Infrastructure Program, 1855 Victoria Ave., Regina SK S4P 3V7, 306/787-8887; Fax: 306/787-3641

Saskatchewan Property Management Corporation, 1840 Lorne St., Regina SK S4P 3V7, 306/787-6911; Fax: 306/787-1061

**Yuk.:** Yukon Community & Transportation Services, Engineering & Development, PO Box 2703, Whitehorse YT Y1A 2C6, 867/667-5707; Fax: 867/393-6216

Yukon Government Services, Building Development, PO Box 2703, Whitehorse YT Y1A 2C6, 867/667-3064; Fax: 867/393-6218

## PUBLICATIONS

Canadian Heritage, Publishing Policy & Programs, Jules Léger Bldg., 25 Eddy St., Hull QC K1A 1K5, 819/997-4099; Fax: 819/997-4164

Public Works & Government Services Canada, Canada Communication Group Inc. (Queen's Printer for Canada), Place du Portage, Phase III, 11, rue Laurier, Hull QC K1A 0S5, Toll Free: 1-800-956-9111

Communications, Place du Portage, Phase III, 11, rue Laurier, Hull QC K1A 0S5, 819/956-2304; TDD: 819/994-5389; Fax: 819/956-9062

**Alta:** Alberta Public Affairs Bureau, Publication Services, 11510 Kingsway Ave., 2nd Fl., Edmonton AB T5G 2Y5, 403/422-2787; Fax: 403/452-0668

**B.C.:** Ministry of Finance & Corporate Relations, Queen's Printer & Product Sales & Services, #102, 1962 Canso Rd., PO Box 2190, Sidney BC V8L 3S8, 250/356-5849; Fax: 250/356-5851

Queen's Printer Financial & Administrative Services, #102, 1962 Canso Rd., PO Box 2190, Sidney BC V8L 3S8, 250/387-4180; Fax: 250/387-0388

**Man.:** Manitoba Culture, Heritage & Citizenship, Provincial Services Division, 200 Vaughan St., Winnipeg MB R3C 1T5, 204/945-3729; Fax: 204/948-2008

Statutory Publications, 155 Carlton St., 10th Fl., Winnipeg MB R3C 3H8, 204/945-3101; Fax: 204/945-7172

**N.B.:** Department of Justice, Office of the Queen's Printer, PO Box 6000, Fredericton NB E3B 5H1, 506/453-2520; Fax: 506/457-7899

**Nfld.:** Department of Works, Services & Transportation, Printing Services & Queen's Printer, Confederation Bldg., PO Box 8700, St. John's NF A1B 4J6, 709/729-3210; Fax: 709/729-4285

**Ont.:** Management Board of Cabinet, Publishing Inc., Ferguson Block, 77 Wellesley St. West, 12th Fl., Toronto ON M7A 1N3, 416/325-1353; Fax: 416/325-1367

Queen's Printer (Publications Ontario), Ferguson Block, 77 Wellesley St. West, 12th Fl., Toronto ON M7A 1N3, 416/326-5316; Fax: 416/327-3517

**PEI:** Department of the Provincial Treasury, PO Box 2000, Charlottetown PE C1A 7N8, 902/368-5190, 5084; Fax: 902/368-5168

**Qué.:** Ministère de la Culture et des Communications, Communications, 225, Grand-Allée est, Québec QC G1R 5G5, 418/643-6300; Fax: 418/643-4457

**Sask.:** Saskatchewan Justice, Queen's Printer, 1874 Scarth St., Regina SK S4P 3V7, 306/787-9345; Fax: 306/787-9111

**Yuk.:** Yukon Government Services, Queen's Printer, PO Box 2703, Whitehorse YT Y1A 2C6, 867/667-3585; Fax: 867/668-3585

**RADIO & TELEVISION *See* BROADCASTING**

## RAIL TRANSPORTATION

***See Also* Transportation**

Canadian National Railway Company, 935 la Gauchetière ouest, Montréal QC H3B 2M9, 514/399-5430; Fax: 514/399-5586, 5479

Transport Canada, Railway Legislation, Transport Canada Building, 330 Sparks St., Ottawa ON K1A 0N5, 613/993-7392; Fax: 613/990-7767

Transportation Safety Board of Canada, 200 Promenade du Portage, 4e étage, Hull QC K1A 1K8, 819/994-3741; Fax: 819/997-2239

Via Rail Canada Inc., 2, Place Ville-Marie, CP 8116, Succ A, Montréal QC H3C 3N3, 514/871-6000; Fax: 514/861-6463

**B.C.:** BC Rail Ltd., PO Box 8770, Vancouver BC V6B 4X6, 604/984-5001; Fax: 604/984-5201

**Ont.:** GO Transit, 1120 Finch Ave. West, Toronto ON M3J 3J8, 416/869-3600; Fax: 416/869-1755

Ministry of Transportation, Freight Transportation Policy, 301 St. Paul St., St. Catharines ON L2R 1W6, 416/235-4039

Ontario Northland, 555 Oak St. East, North Bay ON P1B 8L3, 705/472-4500; Fax: 705/476-5598

**Qué.:** Ministère des Transports, 700, boul René-Lévesque est, 28e étage, Québec QC G1R 5H1, 418/643-6740

**Sask.:** Saskatchewan Highways & Transportation, Grain & Rail Logistics, 1855 Victoria Ave., Regina SK S4P 3V5, 306/787-5311; Fax: 306/787-9777

## REAL ESTATE

### *See Also* Land Titles

Canada Mortgage & Housing Corporation, 700 Montreal Rd., Ottawa ON K1A 0P7, 613/748-2000; Toll Free: 1-800-668-2642; Fax: 613/748-2098

Justice Canada, Civil Litigation & Real Property Law (Québec) Section, Justice Bldg., 239 Wellington St., Ottawa ON K1A 0H8, 613/957-4657; Fax: 613/954-0811

**Alta:** Alberta Municipal Affairs, Registries Division, John E. Brownlee Bldg., 10365 - 97 St., Edmonton AB T5J 3W7, 403/422-2362 (Edmonton), 403/297-8980 (Calgary); Toll Free: 1-800-465-5009 (in Alberta); Fax: 403/422-9105

**B.C.:** Ministry of Environment, Lands & Parks, Crown Land Registry Services Branch, 3400 Davidson Ave., Victoria BC V8V 1X4, 250/387-4461; Fax: 250/387-1830

Real Estate Services Branch, 3400 Davidson Ave., Victoria BC V8V 1X4, 250/387-1934; Fax: 250/387-1830

Real Estate Council of British Columbia, #900, 750 West Pender St., Vancouver BC V6C 2T8, 604/683-9664; Fax: 604/683-9017

**Man.:** Manitoba Consumer & Corporate Affairs, Property Rights Division, 405 Broadway, 10th Fl., Winnipeg MB R3C 3L6, 204/945-1718

**N.B.:** Department of Justice, Consumer Affairs, #412, Centennial Bldg., PO Box 6000, Fredericton NB E3B 5H1, 506/453-2682; Fax: 506/444-4494

New Brunswick Real Estate Council, PO Box 785, Fredericton NB E3B 5B4, 506/455-9733; Fax: 506/450-8719

**Nfld.:** Department of Government Services & Lands, Residential Tenancies, PO Box 8700, St. John's NF A1B 4J6, 709/729-2608; Fax: 709/729-6998

**NWT:** Department of Justice, PO Box 1320, Yellowknife NT X1A 2L9, 867/920-6197

Legal Registries/Land Titles, PO Box 1320, Yellowknife NT X1A 2L9, 867/873-7490

**Ont.:** Management Board of Cabinet, Real Estate Services Division, 777 Bay St., 16th Fl., Toronto ON M5G 2E5, 416/585-6777; Fax: 416/585-7577

Ministry of Consumer & Commercial Relations, Real Estate & Business Brokers, 250 Yonge St., Toronto ON M5B 2N5, 416/326-8679; Fax: 416/326-8859

Ministry of Finance, Property Assessment Division, Frost Bldg. South, 7 Queen's Park Cres., Toronto ON M7A 1Y7, 416/325-0333 (Communications); Fax: 416/325-0339

**PEI:** Department of Community Affairs & Attorney General, Insurance & Real Estate Division, Shaw Building, 95 Rochford St., 4th Fl., PO Box 2000, Charlottetown PE C1A 7N8, 902/368-4564; Fax: 902/368-5283; 5355

**Qué.:** Ministère des Ressources Naturelles, Terres, #B-302, 5700 - 4 av ouest, 3e étage, Charlesbourg QC G1H 6R1, 418/627-8600 (Renseignements); Fax: 418/644-7160

**Sask.:** Saskatchewan Justice, Consumer Protection Branch, 1874 Scarth St., Regina SK S4P 3V7, 306/787-2952; Fax: 306/787-5550

**Yuk.:** Yukon Government Services, Property Management, PO Box 2703, Whitehorse YT Y1A 2C6, 867/667-5436; Fax: 867/393-6218

Yukon Justice, Land Titles, PO Box 2703, Whitehorse YT Y1A 2C6, 867/667-5612; Fax: 867/393-6272

## RECREATION

### *See Also* Tourism & Tourist Information

Canadian Heritage, Parks Canada Sector, Jules Léger Bldg., 25 Eddy St., Hull QC K1A 1K5, 819/997-0055; Fax: 819/953-5382

Sport Canada, Jules Léger Bldg., 25 Eddy St., Hull QC K1A 1K5, 819/956-8151; Fax: 819/956-8006

**Alta:** Alberta Sport, Recreation, Parks & Wildlife Foundation, Percy Page Centre, 11759 Groat Rd., Edmonton AB T5M 3K9, 403/427-1976; Fax: 403/488-9755

Alberta Community Development, Community & Citizenship Services Division, Standard Life Centre, 10405 Jasper Ave., 7th Fl., Edmonton AB T5J 4R7, 403/427-6530; Fax: 403/427-1496

**B.C.:** Ministry of Small Business, Tourism & Culture, Recreation & Sport Branch, 1405 Douglas St., Victoria BC V8W 3C1, 250/356-1160; Fax: 250/387-4253

**Man.:** Manitoba Culture, Heritage & Citizenship, Recreation & Wellness Promotion, 213 Notre Dame., Winnipeg MB R3B 1N3, 204/945-0487; Fax: 204/945-1684

**N.B.:** Department of Municipalities, Culture & Housing, Libraries Division, Marysville Place, 20 McGloin St., PO Box 6000, Fredericton NB E3B 5H1, 506/453-2690; Fax: 506/457-4991

**NWT:** Department of Municipal & Community Affairs, Community Development, #600, 5201 - 50 Ave., PO Box 1310, Yellowknife NT X1A 2L9, 867/873-7245; Fax: 867/920-6467

**N.S.:** Department of Natural Resources, Parks & Recreation (Belmont), Founder's Square, 1701 Hollis St., PO Box 698, Halifax NS B3J 2T9, 902/662-3030; Fax: 902/662-2160

**Ont.:** Industry Canada, East Tower, 235 Queen St. E., 4th Fl., Ottawa ON K1A 0H6, 613/954-3830; Fax: 613/952-9014

Ministry of Citizenship, Culture & Recreation, Recreation Division, 77 Bloor St. West, 6th Fl., Toronto ON M7A 2R9, 416/327-2422

Ministry of Consumer & Commercial Relations, Office of the Athletic Commissioner, 1075 Millwood Rd., Toronto ON M4G 1X6, 416/314-3630; Fax: 416/314-3623

**PEI:** Department of Economic Development & Tourism, Tourism PEI, Annex 1, West Royalty Industrial Park, 1 Watts Ave., Charlottetown PE C1E 1B0, 902/368-5540; Toll Free: 1-800-465-4734; Fax: 902/368-4438

Department of Education, Culture, Heritage & Recreation, Sullivan Bldg., 16 Fitzroy St., PO Box 2000, Charlottetown PE C1A 7N8, 902/368-4789; Fax: 902/368-4663

**Qué.:** Ministère des Affaires Municipales, Loisir et sports, Édifice Cook-Chauveau, 20, rue Pierre-Olivier-Chauveau, Québec QC G1R 4J3, 418/691-2096; Fax: 418/644-4517

Tourisme Québec, #412, 900, boul René-Lévesque est, Québec QC G1R 2B5, 418/643-5959; Toll Free: 1-800-363-7777 (Tourism Information); Fax: 418/646-8723

**Sask.:** Saskatchewan Municipal Government, Sport, Recreation & Lotteries, 1855 Victoria Ave., Regina SK S4P 3V7, 306/787-5737; Fax: 306/787-8560

**Yuk.:** Yukon Community & Transportation Services, Sport & Recreation Branch, PO Box 2703, Whitehorse YT Y1A 2C6, 867/667-5608; Fax: 867/393-6416

## RENT CONTROL *See* LANDLORD & TENANT REGULATIONS

## SALES TAX

Revenue Canada, GST Rulings & Interpretations, Tower C, Vanier Towers, 25 McArthur Rd., Ottawa ON K1A 0L5, 613/952-9198

**Alta:** Alberta Treasury, Tax & Revenue Administration, Terrace Bldg., 9515 - 107 St., Edmonton AB T5K 2C3, 403/427-3035; Fax: 403/422-2463

**B.C.:** Ministry of Finance & Corporate Relations, Revenue Division, 617 Government St., Victoria BC V8V 1X4, 250/387-9278

**Man.:** Manitoba Finance, Taxation Division, 401 York Ave., 4th Fl., Winnipeg MB R3C 0P8, 204/945-3754; Fax: 204/945-8316

**N.B.:** Department of Finance, Revenue Division, PO Box 6000, Fredericton NB E3B 5H1, 506/453-2286; Fax: 506/457-7335

**Nfld.:** Department of Finance & Treasury Board, Taxation, Confederation Bldg., PO Box 8700, St. John's NF A1B 4J6, 709/729-2966; Fax: 709/729-2856

**NWT:** Department of Finance, PO Box 1320, Yellowknife NT X1A 2L9

**N.S.:** Department of Business & Consumer Services, Provincial Tax Commission, PO Box 755, Halifax NS B3J 2V4, 902/424-4411; Toll Free: 1-800-565-2336; Fax: 902/424-0523

**Ont.:** Ministry of Finance, Retail Sales Tax Branch, Frost Bldg. South, 7 Queen's Park Cres., Toronto ON M7A 1Y7, 905/433-6156; Fax: 416/325-0339

**PEI:** Department of the Provincial Treasury, Tax Administration, PO Box 2000, Charlottetown PE C1A 7N8, 902/368-4146; Fax: 902/368-6164

**Qué.:** Ministère du Revenu, 3800, rue De Marly, Ste-Foy QC G1X 4A5

**Sask.:** Saskatchewan Finance, Revenue Division, 2350 Albert St., Regina SK S4P 4A6, 306/787-6768; Fax: 306/787-6544

Taxation & Intergovernmental Affairs Branch, 2350 Albert St., Regina SK S4P 4A6, 306/787-6731; Fax: 306/787-6544

## SCIENCE, TECHNOLOGY DEVELOPMENT

### *See Also* Business Development

Agriculture & Agri-Food Canada, Central Experimental Farm, Sir John Carling Bldg., 930 Carling Ave., Ottawa ON K1A 0C5, 613/759-7865; Fax: 613/759-1970

Bayfield Institute for Marine Science & Surveys, 867 Lakeshore Rd., PO Box 5050, Burlington ON L7R 4A6, 905/336-4871; Fax: 905/336-6637

Canadian Space Agency, 6767, rte de l'Aéroport, Saint-Hubert QC J3Y 8Y9, 514/926-4351; Fax: 514/926-4352

Foreign Affairs & International Trade Canada, Science & Technology Unit, Lester B. Pearson Bldg., 125 Sussex Dr., Ottawa ON K1A 0G2, 613/996-4819; Fax: 613/943-8819

Industry Canada, Advisory Council on Science & Technology Secretariat, C.D. Howe Bldg., 235 Queen St., Ottawa ON K1A 0H5, 613/993-6858; Fax: 613/954-6436

Spectrum, Information Technologies & Telecommunications, Journal Tower North, 300 Slater St., 20th Fl., Ottawa ON K1A 0C8, 613/941-0222; Fax: 613/954-6436

Institute of Ocean Sciences, 9860 West Saanich Rd., PO Box 6000, Sidney BC V8L 4B2, 250/363-6517; Fax: 250/353-6807

Medical Research Council of Canada, Tower B, Holland Cross, 1600 Scott St., 5th Fl., Ottawa ON K1A 0W9, 613/941-2672; Fax: 613/954-1800

National Research Council Canada, Bldg. M-58, 1200 Montreal Rd., Ottawa ON K1A 0R6, 613/993-9101; Fax: 613/952-7928

Natural Sciences & Engineering Research Council of Canada, Constitution Square, 350 Albert St., Ottawa ON K1A 1H5, 613/996-7235; Fax: 613/992-5337

Office of the Nunavut Environmental Scientist, PO Box 1500, Yellowknife NT X1A 2R3, 867/920-8200; Fax: 867/920-7809

**Alta:** Alberta Research Council, 250 Karl Clark Rd., PO Box 8330, Edmonton AB T6H 5X2, 403/450-5111; Fax: 403/461-2651

**B.C.:** Premiers' Advisory Council on Science & Technology, #501, 168 Chadwick Ct., North Vancouver BC V7M 3L4, 604/987-8477; Fax: 604/987-5617

Science Council of British Columbia, #800, 4710 Kingsway, Burnaby BC V5H 4M2, 604/438-2752; Toll Free: 1-800-665-7222; Fax: 604/438-6564

**Man.:** Economic Innovation & Technology Council, #648, 155 Carlton St., Winnipeg MB R3C 3H8, 204/945-5940; Fax: 204/945-8229

**N.B.:** Department of Economic Development & Tourism, Information Highway Secretariat, Centennial Bldg., 670 King St., 5th Fl., PO Box 6000, Fredericton NB E3B 5H1, 506/453-2850 (Communications & Promotion); Fax: 506/444-4586

New Brunswick Research & Productivity Council, 921 College Hill Rd., Fredericton NB E3B 6Z9, 506/452-8994; Fax: 506/452-1395

**Nfld.:** Department of Industry, Trade & Technology, Strategic Technologies, Confederation Annex, 4th Fl., PO Box 8700, St. John's NF A1B 4J6, 709/729-5652; Fax: 709/729-5936

Operation ONLINE, PO Box 8700, St. John's NF A1B 4J6, 709/729-0050

**NWT:** Aurora Research Institute, c/o Aurora College, PO Box 1450, Inuvik NT X0E 0T0

Nunavut Research Institute, Aeroplex Bldg., PO Box 1720, Iqualuit NT X0A 0H0, 867/979-4115; Fax: 867/979-4681

**N.S.:** Nova Scotia Technology & Science Secretariat, Maritime Centre, 1505 Barrington St., 14th Fl., PO Box 2311, Halifax NS B3T 3C8, 902/424-0377; Fax: 902/424-0129

**Ont.:** Ontario Science Centre, 770 Don Mills Rd., Toronto ON M3C 1T3, 416/696-2000; Fax: 416/696-3135

Science North, 100 Ramsey Lake Rd., Sudbury ON P3E 5S9, 705/522-3701; Fax: 705/522-4954

**Qué.:** Ministère de l'Industrie, du commerce, de la Science et de la technologie, Industrie et développement technologique, 710, Place d'Youville, 9e étage, Québec QC G1R 4Y4, 418/691-5950 (Renseignements); Fax: 418/644-0118

**Sask.:** Saskatchewan Research Council, 15 Innovation Blvd., Saskatoon SK S7N 2X8, 306/933-5400; Fax: 306/933-7446

## SECURITIES ADMINISTRATION

***See Also* Finance**

Bank of Canada, Financial Markets, 234 Wellington St., Ottawa ON K1A 0G9, 613/782-8111; Fax: 613/782-8655

Securities, Bank of Canada, 250 University Ave., Toronto ON M5H 3E5, 613/782-8111; Fax: 613/782-8655

Finance Canada, Security Services Division, Esplanade Laurier, 140 O'Connor St., Ottawa ON K1A 0G5, 613/995-5660; Fax: 613/996-8404

**Alta:** Alberta Securities Commission, 10025 Jasper Ave., 19th Fl., Edmonton AB T5J 3Z5, 403/427-5201; Fax: 403/422-0777

Alberta Treasury, Securities Administration, Terrace Bldg., 9515 - 107 St., Edmonton AB T5K 2C3, 403/427-3041 ext.271; Fax: 403/422-2463

**B.C.:** British Columbia Securities Commission, #1100, 865 Hornby St., Vancouver BC V6Z 2H4, 604/660-4800; Toll Free: 1-800-373-6393 (outside Vancouver area); Fax: 604/660-2688

**Man.:** Manitoba Securities Commission, #1128, 405 Broadway, Winnipeg MB R3C 3L6, 204/945-2548; Fax: 204/945-0330

**N.B.:** Department of Justice, Securities Administration, #412, Centennial Bldg., PO Box 6000, Fredericton NB E3B 5H1, 506/658-3060; Fax: 506/658-3059

Office of the Administrator of Securities, #606, 133 Prince William St., PO Box 5001, Saint John NB E2L 4Y9, 506/658-3060; Fax: 506/658-3059

**Nfld.:** Department of Government Services & Lands, Commercial & Corporate Affairs, PO Box 8700, St. John's NF A1B 4J6

**N.S.:** Department of Business & Consumer Services, Registry of Joint Stock Companies, PO Box 1529, Halifax NS B3J 2Y4, 902/424-7742; Fax: 902/424-4633

Nova Scotia Securities Commission, PO Box 458, Halifax NS B3J 2P8, 902/424-7768; Fax: 902/424-4625

**Ont.:** Ontario Securities Commission, #1800, 20 Queen St. West, Toronto ON M5H 3S8, 416/597-0681; Fax: 416/593-8240

**PEI:** Department of Community Affairs & Attorney General, Securities & Consumer, Corporate & Insurance Services, Shaw Building, 95 Rochford St., 4th Fl., PO Box 2000, Charlottetown PE C1A 7N8, 902/368-4552; Fax: 902/368-5283; 5355

**Qué.:** Commission des valeurs mobilières du Québec, Tour de la Bourse, 800, Place Victoria, 17e étage, Montréal QC H4Z 1G3, 514/873-5326; Fax: 514/873-0711

**Sask.:** Saskatchewan Securities Commission, Toronto Dominion Bank Bldg., 1920 Broad St., 8th Fl., Regina SK S4P 3V7, 306/787-5645; Fax: 306/787-5899

**Yuk.:** Yukon Justice, Corporate Affairs & Registrar of Securities, PO Box 2703, Whitehorse YT Y1A 2C6, 867/667-5225; Fax: 867/393-6272

## SENIOR CITIZENS SERVICES

Human Resources Development Canada, Income Security Programs, Place Vanier, 120 Parkdale Ave., Ottawa ON K1A 0L1, 819/994-6013 (Communications)

National Advisory Council on Aging, Postal Locator 4203A, 473 Albert St., 3rd Fl., Ottawa ON K1A 0K9, 613/957-1968; Fax: 613/957-7627

**Alta:** Seniors' Advisory Council for Alberta, 10025 Jasper Ave., Main Fl., Edmonton AB T5J 2N3, 403/422-2321; Fax: 403/422-3207

**B.C.:** Ministry of Children & Families, Adult Residential Care, 1022 Government St., 3rd Fl., Victoria BC V8V 1X4, 250/387-1275; Fax: 250/356-6534

Ministry of Health, Office for Seniors, 1515 Blanshard St., 7th Fl., Victoria BC V8W 3C8, 250/952-1238; Fax: 250/952-1159

**Man.:** Manitoba Seniors Directorate, #822, 155 Carlton St., Winnipeg MB R3C 3H8, 204/945-2127; Fax: 204/948-2514

**Nfld.:** Department of Health, Personal Care Home Program, West Block, Confederation Bldg., PO Box 8700, St. John's NF A1B 4J6, 709/772-3553; Fax: 709/729-5824

**NWT:** Department of Health & Social Services, Family Support & Child Protection, Centre Square Tower, 8th Fl., PO Box 1320, Yellowknife NT X1A 2L9, 867/920-6255; Fax: 867/873-0444

**N.S.:** Senior Citizens Secretariat, 1740 Granville St., 4th Fl., PO Box 2065, Halifax NS B3J 2Z1, 902/424-6322; Fax: 902/424-0561

**Ont.:** Ministry of Citizenship, Culture & Recreation, Seniors' Issues Group, 76 College St., 6th Fl., Toronto ON M7A 1N3, 416/327-2441; Fax: 416/327-2425

Ministry of Health, In-Home Services Branch, Hepburn Block, 8th Fl., Queen's Park, #1400, 80 Grosvenor St., Toronto ON M7A 1S2, 416/326-9750; Toll Free: 1-800-668-2437 (AIDS Bureau); Fax: 416/327-4389

Ontario Advisory Council on Senior Citizens, 35 McCaul St., 3rd Fl., Toronto ON M5T 1V7, 416/314-6650 (Voice & TDD); Fax: 416/314-6658

**PEI:** Department of Health & Social Services, Jones Bldg., 11 Kent St., 2nd Fl., PO Box 2000, Charlottetown PE C1A 7N8, 902/368-4900; Fax: 902/368-4969

**Qué.:** Conseil des aînes, 1005, ch Ste-Foy, Québec QC G1S 4N4, 418/643-6720; Fax: 418/646-9895

Ministère de la Santé et des services sociaux, 1075, ch Ste-Foy, Québec QC G1S 2M1

**Sask.:** Saskatchewan Social Services, Community Living Division, Central Office, #216, 110 Ominica St. West, Moose Jaw SK S6H 6V2, 306/694-3800; Fax: 306/694-3842

Income Security Programs Division, 1920 Broad St., Regina SK S4P 3V6, 306/787-7469; Fax: 306/787-1032

**Yuk.:** Yukon Health & Social Services, PO Box 2703, Whitehorse YT Y1A 2C6, 867/667-3673 (Communications); Fax: 867/667-3096

## SEXUALLY TRANSMITTED DISEASE CONTROL

***See Also* AIDS**

Health Canada, Laboratory Centre for Disease Control, Brooke Claxton Bldg., Tunney's Pasture, 120 Parkdale Ave., Ottawa ON K1A 0K9, 613/957-0315; Fax: 613/941-5366

**Alta:** Alberta Health, Disease Control & Prevention, PO Box 1360, Edmonton AB T5J 2N3, 403/427-5263; Fax: 403/422-6663

**B.C.:** Ministry of Health, Community Health Programs, 1515 Blanshard St., 7th Fl., Victoria BC V8W 3C8, 250/952-1544; Fax: 250/952-1426

**Man.:** Manitoba Health, Public Health, #301, 800 Portage Ave., Winnipeg MB R3G 0N4, 204/945-6720; Fax: 204/948-2190

**N.B.:** Department of Health & Community Services, PO Box 5100, Fredericton NB E3B 5G8, 506/453-3092; Fax: 506/444-4697

**Nfld.:** Department of Health, Disease Control & Epidemiology, West Block, Confederation Bldg., PO Box 8700, St. John's NF A1B 4J6, 709/729-3430; Fax: 709/729-5824

**NWT:** Department of Health & Social Services, Health Services Development, Centre Square Tower, 8th Fl., PO Box 1320, Yellowknife NT X1A 2L9, 867/920-6173; Fax: 867/873-0266

**N.S.:** Department of Health, Strategic Planning & Policy Development Branch, Joseph Howe Bldg., 1690 Hollis St., PO Box 488, Halifax NS B3J 2R8, 902/424-4310; Fax: 902/424-0730

**Ont.:** Ministry of Health, Health Information Centre, Hepburn Block, 8th Fl., Queen's Park, #1400, 80 Grosvenor St., Toronto ON M7A 1S2, 416/314-8337; Toll Free: 1-800-268-1153; Fax: 416/314-8721

**PEI:** Department of Health & Social Services, Jones Bldg., 11 Kent St., 2nd Fl., PO Box 2000, Charlottetown PE C1A 7N8, 902/368-4996; Fax: 902/368-4969

**Qué.:** Ministère de la Santé et des services sociaux, Santé publique, 1075, ch Ste-Foy, Québec QC G1S 2M1, 418/646-3487; Fax: 418/528-2651

**Sask.:** Saskatchewan Health, 3475 Albert St., Regina SK S4S 6X6, 306/787-1580; Fax: 306/787-8310

, 3475 Albert St., Regina SK S4S 6X6, 306/787-8332; Fax: 306/787-8310

Wellness & Health Promotion Branch, 3475 Albert St., Regina SK S4S 6X6, 306/787-3083; Fax: 306/787-8310

**Yuk.:** Yukon Health & Social Services, Health Services Branch, PO Box 2703, Whitehorse YT Y1A 2C6, 867/667-3673 (Communications); Fax: 867/667-3096

**SMALL BUSINESS DEVELOPMENT *See* BUSINESS DEVELOPMENT; INDUSTRY**

## SOCIAL SERVICES

***See Also* Community Services**

Citizenship & Immigration Canada, Social Policy, Jean Edmonds Towers, 365 Laurier Ave. West, Ottawa ON K1A 1L1, 613/957-5915; Fax: 613/957-5955

Human Resources Development Canada, Human Resources Investment, Place du Portage, Phase IV, 140, Promenade du Portage, Hull QC K1A 0J9, 819/994-6013 (Communications)

Veterans Affairs Canada, Veterans Services, Daniel J. MacDonald Bldg., 161 Grafton St., PO Box 7700, Charlottetown PE C1A 8M9, 902/566-8195; Fax: 902/566-8508

**Alta:** Alberta Family & Social Services, Seventh St. Plaza, 10030 - 107 St., Edmonton AB T5J 3E4, 403/427-2734; Fax: 403/422-9044

**Man.:** Manitoba Family Services, Finance & Administration, #219, 114 Garry St., Winnipeg MB R3C 4V6, 204/945-3080; Fax: 204/945-2760

**N.B.:** Department of Health & Community Services, Family & Community Social Services Division, PO Box 5100, Fredericton NB E3B 5G8, 506/453-2536; Fax: 506/444-4697

Department of Human Resources Development, 520 King St., 5th Fl., PO Box 6000, Fredericton NB E3B 5H1, 506/453-2001; Fax: 506/453-7478

**Nfld.:** Department of Human Resources & Employment, Confederation Bldg., PO Box 8700, St. John's NF A1B 4J6, 709/729-2478; Fax: 709/729-6996

Social Services Appeal Board, Confederation Bldg., PO Box 8700, St. John's NF A1B 4J6

**NWT:** Department of Health & Social Services, Community Programs & Services, Centre Square Tower, 8th Fl., PO Box 1320, Yellowknife NT X1A 2L9, 867/920-6173; Fax: 867/873-0266

**N.S.:** Department of Community Services, Family & Children's Services, Johnston Bldg., 5182 Prince St., 5th Fl., PO Box 696, Halifax NS B3J 2T7, 902/424-4326; Fax: 902/424-0708

**Ont.:** Ministry of Community & Social Services, Program Management Division, Hepburn Block, 80 Grosvenor St., 6th Fl., Toronto ON M7A 1E9, 416/325-5666; Fax: 416/325-5172, 5171

Social Assistance Review Board, 1075 Bay St., 7th Fl., Toronto ON M5S 2B1, 416/326-5104; Toll Free: 1-800-387-5655; Fax: 416/326-5135

**PEI:** Department of Health & Social Services, Jones Bldg., 11 Kent St., 2nd Fl., PO Box 2000, Charlottetown PE C1A 7N8, 902/368-4900; Fax: 902/368-4969

**Qué.:** Ministère de la Santé et des services sociaux, 1075, ch Ste-Foy, Québec QC G1S 2M1

**Sask.:** Saskatchewan Social Services, 1920 Broad St., Regina SK S4P 3V6, 306/787-3494; Fax: 306/787-1032

**Yuk.:** Yukon Health & Social Services, Social Services Branch, PO Box 2703, Whitehorse YT Y1A 2C6, 867/667-3673 (Communications); Fax: 867/667-3096

## SOLICITORS GENERAL

Solicitor General Canada, Sir Wilfrid Laurier Bldg., 340 Laurier Ave. West, Ottawa ON K1A 0P8, 613/991-3283; Fax: 613/993-7062

**Man.:** Manitoba Justice, 405 Broadway, 5th Fl., Winnipeg MB R3C 3L6, 204/945-2852

**N.B.:** Department of the Solicitor General, Barker House, 4th Fl., PO Box 6000, Fredericton NB E3B 5H1, 506/453-7414; Fax: 506/453-3870

**NWT:** Department of Justice, Solicitor General Branch, PO Box 1320, Yellowknife NT X1A 2L9, 867/873-7005

**Ont.:** Ministry of the Solicitor General & Correctional Services, Communications Branch, 200 - 1 Ave. West, North Bay ON P1B 9M3, 416/326-5010

**Qué.:** Ministère de la Sécurité publique, Tour des Laurentides, 2525, boul Laurier, 5e étage, Ste-Foy QC G1V 2L2, 418/643-3500; Fax: 418/643-0275

## SPACE & ASTRONOMY

Canadian Space Agency, 6767, rte de l'Aéroport, Saint-Hubert QC J3Y 8Y9, 514/926-4351; Fax: 514/926-4352

Environment Canada, Canadian Meteorological Centre (Montréal), 4905 Dufferin St., Downsview ON M3H 5T4, 514/421-4601; Fax: 514/421-4600

Herzberg Institute of Astrophysics, 5071 West Saanish Rd., Victoria BC V8X 4M6, 613/363-0040; Fax: 613/363-8483

Industry Canada, Aerospace & Defence, C.D. Howe Bldg., 235 Queen St., Ottawa ON K1A 0H5, 613/954-3343; Fax: 613/941-2379

Institute for Aerospace Research, 1500 Montreal Rd., Ottawa ON K1A 0R6, 613/993-0141; Fax: 613/952-7214

Natural Resources Canada, Canada Centre for Remote Sensing, 588 Booth St., Ottawa ON K1A 0Y7, 613/947-1216; Fax: 613/947-3125

**SPORTS *See* RECREATION**

## STANDARDS

Canadian Transportation Agency, Les Terrasses de la Chaudière, 15 Eddy St., Hull QC K1A 0N9, 819/997-0344 (Communications); Fax: 819/953-8353

Environment Canada, Environmental Protection Service, Place Vincent-Massey, 351, boul St-Joseph, Hull QC K1A 0H3, 819/997-2800; Fax: 819/953-2225

Institute for National Measurement Standards, 1500 Montreal Rd., Ottawa ON K1A 0R6, 613/990-9326; Fax: 613/952-5113

National Research Council Canada, 1500 Montreal Rd., Ottawa ON K1A 0R6, 613/990-9326; Fax: 613/952-5113

Public Works & Government Services Canada, Canadian General Standards Board, 222 Queen St., Ottawa ON K1A 1G6, 613/941-8709

Standards Council of Canada, #1200, 45 O'Connor St., Ottawa ON K1P 6N7, 613/238-3222; Fax: 613/995-4564

Transport Canada, Safety & Security Group, Transport Canada Building, 330 Sparks St., Ottawa ON K1A 0N5, 613/990-2309; Fax: 613/954-4731

Transportation Safety Board of Canada, 200 Promenade du Portage, 4e étage, Hull QC K1A 1K8, 819/994-3741; Fax: 819/997-2239

**Ont.:** Ministry of Consumer & Commercial Relations, Entertainment Standards, 1075 Millwood Rd., Toronto ON M4G 1X6, 416/314-3626; Fax: 416/314-3632

Technical Standards Division, West Tower, 3300 Bloor St. West, 4th Fl., Toronto ON M8X 2X4, 416/326-8555; Fax: 416/325-2000

## STATISTICS

***See Also* Vital Statistics**

Human Resources Development Canada, Workplace Information, Place du Portage, Phase IV, 140, Promenade du Portage, Hull QC K1A 0J9, 819/994-4204; Fax: 819/953-9582

Statistics Canada, R.H. Coats Bldg., Tunney's Pasture, 120 Parkdale Ave., Ottawa ON K1A 0T6, 613/951-8116; Toll Free: 1-800-263-1136, TDD: 1-800-363-7629; Fax: 613/951-0581

Statistics Canada Regional Reference Centres, R.H. Coats Bldg., Tunney's Pasture, 120 Parkdale Ave., Ottawa ON K1A 0T6, Toll Free: 1-800-263-1136, TDD: 1-800-363-7629; Fax: 613/951-0581

**Alta:** Alberta Municipal Affairs, Registries Division, John E. Brownlee Bldg., 10365 - 97 St., Edmonton AB T5J 3W7, 403/422-2362 (Edmonton), 403/297-8980 (Calgary); Toll Free: 1-800-465-5009 (in Alberta); Fax: 403/422-9105

**Man.:** Manitoba Industry, Trade & Tourism, Manitoba Bureau of Statistics, #333, 260 St. Mary Ave., Winnipeg MB R3C 0M6, 204/945-2999; Fax: 204/945-0695

**N.B.:** Department of Finance, New Brunswick Statistics Agency, PO Box 6000, Fredericton NB E3B 5H1, 506/453-2381; Fax: 506/453-7970

**NWT:** , PO Box 1320, Yellowknife NT X1A 2L9, 867/873-7147; Fax: 867/873-0275

**N.S.:** Statistics Division, PO Box 187, Halifax NS B3J 2N3, 902/424-5691; Fax: 902/424-0714

**Ont.:** Ministry of Consumer & Commercial Relations, Registrar General Branch, 189 Red River Rd., PO Box 4600, Thunder Bay ON P7B 6L8, 807/343-7414; Toll Free: 1-800-461-2156; Fax: 807/343-7411

**Qué.:** Bureau de la statistique du Québec, 200, ch Ste-Foy, 5e étage, Québec QC G1R 5T4, 418/691-2401; Toll Free: 1-800-463-4090; Fax: 418/643-4129

**Sask.:** Saskatchewan Finance, Bureau of Statistics, 2350 Albert St., Regina SK S4P 4A6, 306/787-6328; Fax: 306/787-6544

**Yuk.:** Executive Council, Bureau of Statistics, PO Box 2703, Whitehorse YT Y1A 2C6, 867/667-5640; Fax: 867/393-6203

## STUDENT AID

Indian & Northern Affairs Canada, Indian Program & Funding Allocation Directorate, Tour Nord, Les Terrasses de la Chaudière, 10 Wellington St., Hull QC K1A 0H4, 819/953-9540; Fax: 819/953-3017

**Alta:** Students Finance Board, Baker Centre, 10025 - 106 St., 10th Fl., Edmonton AB T5J 1G7, 403/427-2740; Fax: 403/422-4516

**B.C.:** Ministry of Education, Skills & Training, Policy, Planning & Special Programs Division, PO Box 9150, Stn Prov Govt, Victoria BC V8W 9H1, 250/356-2500; Fax: 250/356-5945

**Man.:** Manitoba Education & Training, Student Financial Assistance Program, Box 6, 693 Taylor Ave., Winnipeg MB R3M 3T9, 204/945-8729; Fax: 204/477-5596

**N.B.:** Department of Advanced Education & Labour, Student Services, Chestnut Complex, 470 York St., PO Box 6000, Fredericton NB E3B 5H1, 506/453-3358; Fax: 506/444-4333

**Nfld.:** Department of Education, Student Aid Division, Confederation Bldg., PO Box 8700, St. John's NF A1B 4J6, 709/729-5849; Fax: 709/729-5896

**NWT:** Department of Education, Culture & Employment, Early Childhood & School Services, PO Box 1320, Yellowknife NT X1A 2L9, 867/920-3491; Fax: 867/873-0155

**N.S.:** Department of Education & Culture, Student Assistance Office, 2021 Brunswick St., PO Box 578, Halifax NS B3J 2S9, 902/424-8433; Fax: 902/424-0540

**Ont.:** Ministry of Education & Training, Postsecondary Education Division, Mowat Block, 900 Bay St., Toronto ON M7A 1L2, 416/325-2929; Fax: 416/325-2934

**Qué.:** Ministère de l'Éducation, Statistiques et études quantitatives, 1035, rue De La Chevrotière, 11e étage, Québec QC G1R 5A5, 418/644-0383; Fax: 418/646-6561; 528-2080

**Yuk.:** Yukon Education, PO Box 2703, Whitehorse YT Y1A 2C6, 867/667-5929; Fax: 867/667-8555

## TAXATION

### *See Also* Sales Tax

Finance Canada, Tax Policy Branch, Esplanade Laurier, 140 O'Connor St., Ottawa ON K1A 0G5, 613/992-1573; Fax: 613/996-8404

Indian Taxation Advisory Board, 90 Elgin St., 2nd Fl., Ottawa ON K1A 0H4, 613/954-9769; Fax: 613/954-2073

Revenue Canada, 875 Heron Rd., Ottawa ON K1A 0L8, 613/952-0384

GST Rulings & Interpretations, Tower C, Vanier Towers, 25 McArthur Rd., Ottawa ON K1A 0L5, 613/952-9198

**Alta:** Alberta Treasury, Tax & Revenue Administration, Terrace Bldg., 9515 - 107 St., Edmonton AB T5K 2C3, 403/427-3035; Fax: 403/422-2463

Tax Policy, Terrace Bldg., 9515 - 107 St., Edmonton AB T5K 2C3, 403/427-8893; Fax: 403/426-4564

**B.C.:** Ministry of Finance & Corporate Relations, Revenue Division, 617 Government St., Victoria BC V8V 1X4, 250/387-9278

**Man.:** Manitoba Finance, Taxation Division, 401 York Ave., 4th Fl., Winnipeg MB R3C 0P8, 204/945-3754; Fax: 204/945-8316

**N.B.:** Department of Finance, Revenue Division, PO Box 6000, Fredericton NB E3B 5H1, 506/453-2286; Fax: 506/457-7335

Taxation & Fiscal Policy, PO Box 6000, Fredericton NB E3B 5H1, 506/453-2286; Fax: 506/453-2281

**Nfld.:** Department of Finance & Treasury Board, Fiscal & Tax Policy, Confederation Bldg., PO Box 8700, St. John's NF A1B 4J6, 709/729-2944; Fax: 709/729-2070

Taxation, Confederation Bldg., PO Box 8700, St. John's NF A1B 4J6, 709/729-2966; Fax: 709/729-2856

**NWT:** Department of Finance, Taxation, PO Box 1320, Yellowknife NT X1A 2L9, 867/920-3470; Fax: 867/873-0325

**N.S.:** Department of Business & Consumer Services, Provincial Tax Commission, PO Box 755, Halifax NS B3J 2V4, 902/424-4411; Toll Free: 1-800-565-2336; Fax: 902/424-0523

**Ont.:** Ministry of Finance, Office of the Budget & Taxation, Frost Bldg. South, 7 Queen's Park Cres., Toronto ON M7A 1Y7, 416/325-0333 (Communications); Fax: 416/325-0339

Tax Division, Frost Bldg. South, 7 Queen's Park Cres., Toronto ON M7A 1Y7, 416/325-0333 (Communications); Fax: 416/325-0339

**PEI:** Department of the Provincial Treasury, Tax Administration, PO Box 2000, Charlottetown PE C1A 7N8, 902/368-4146; Fax: 902/368-6164

Taxation & Property Records, PO Box 2000, Charlottetown PE C1A 7N8, 902/368-4000; Fax: 902/368-5544

**Qué.:** Ministère du Revenu, 3800, rue De Marly, Ste-Foy QC G1X 4A5

Direction générale des Contribuables, 3800, rue De Marly, Ste-Foy QC G1X 4A5

**Sask.:** Saskatchewan Finance, Revenue Division, 2350 Albert St., Regina SK S4P 4A6, 306/787-6768; Fax: 306/787-6544

Taxation & Intergovernmental Affairs Branch, 2350 Albert St., Regina SK S4P 4A6, 306/787-6731; Fax: 306/787-6544

**Yuk.:** Yukon Finance, Revenue Services, PO Box 2703, Whitehorse YT Y1A 2C6, 867/667-3074; Fax: 867/393-6217

## TELECOMMUNICATIONS

### *See Also* Broadcasting

Canadian Broadcasting Corporation, 250 Lanark Ave., PO Box 3220, Stn C, Ottawa ON K1Y 1E4, 613/724-1200; TDD: 613/724-5173

Canadian Radio-Television & Telecommunications Commission, 1, Promenade du Portage, Terrasses de la Chaudière, Hull QC J8X 4B1, 819/997-0313 (Public Affairs); Fax: 819/994-0218

Industry Canada, Communications Research Centre & Centre for Information Technologies Innovation, 3701 Carling Ave., PO Box 11490, Stn H, Ottawa ON K2H 8S2, 613/991-3313; Fax: 613/954-6436

Spectrum, Information Technologies & Telecommunications, Journal Tower North, 300 Slater St., 20th Fl., Ottawa ON K1A 0C8, 613/941-0222; Fax: 613/954-6436

Telecommunications Policy, Journal Tower North, 300 Slater St., 20th Fl., Ottawa ON K1A 0C8, 613/998-4241; Fax: 613/998-1256

**Alta:** Alberta Public Works, Supply & Services, Telecommunications, 6950 - 113 St., 3rd Fl., Edmonton AB T6H 5V7, 403/422-1140; Fax: 403/427-0238

**B.C.:** Information, Science & Technology Agency, 563 Superior St., 3rd Fl., PO Box 9441, Victoria BC V8V 1X4, 250/387-0811; Fax: 250/356-9287

**Man.:** Manitoba Government Services, Telecommunications, 270 Osborne St. North, Winnipeg MB R3C 1V7, 204/945-4800 (Administration)

Manitoba Industry, Trade & Tourism, Research & Economic Services, 155 Carlton St., 6th Fl., Winnipeg MB R3C 3H8, 204/945-8836; Fax: 204/945-1354

Manitoba Telecom Services, 489 Empress St., Winnipeg MB R3C 3V6, 204/941-4111; Fax: 204/772-6391

**Nfld.:** Department of Industry, Trade & Technology, Advanced Technology, Confederation Annex, 4th Fl., PO Box 8700, St. John's NF A1B 4J6, 709/729-5600; Fax: 709/729-5936

**Ont.:** Ministry of Economic Development, Trade & Tourism, Capital Goods & Technology Sectors Branch, Hearst Block, 900 Bay St., Toronto ON M7A 2E1, 416/326-9621; Fax: 416/325-6688

**Qué.:** Ministère de la Culture et des Communications, 225, Grand-Allée est, Québec QC G1R 5G5, 418/643-2183; Fax: 418/643-4457

Régie des télécommunications du Québec, #5.00, 900 place d'Youville, Québec QC G1R 3P7, 418/643-5560; Fax: 418/643-2960

**Sask.:** Saskatchewan Telecommunications (SaskTel), 2121 Saskatchewan Dr., Regina SK S4P 3Y2, 306/777-3737; Fax: 306/565-8717

### TELEPHONES *See* TELECOMMUNICATIONS

### TELEVISION *See* BROADCASTING

## TOURISM & TOURIST INFORMATION

Canadian Heritage, Parks Canada Sector, Jules Léger Bldg., 25 Eddy St., Hull QC K1A 1K5, 819/997-0055; Fax: 819/953-5382

Foreign Affairs & International Trade Canada, US General Relations Division, Lester B. Pearson Bldg., 125 Sussex Dr., Ottawa ON K1A 0G2, 613/944-7990; Fax: 613/944-8314

**Alta:** Alberta Economic Development & Tourism, Tourism, Trade & Investment, Commerce Place, 10155 - 102 St., Edmonton AB T5J 4L6, 403/427-2280; Fax: 403/427-1700

**B.C.:** Ministry of Small Business, Tourism & Culture, Tourism Division, 1405 Douglas St., Victoria BC V8W 3C1

**Man.:** Manitoba Industry, Trade & Tourism, Tourism, 155 Carlton St., 6th Fl., Winnipeg MB R3C 3H8, 204/945-3796; Toll Free: 1-800-665-0040; Fax: 204/945-2302

**N.B.:** Department of Economic Development & Tourism, Tourism & Parks, Centennial Bldg., 670 King St., 5th Fl., PO Box 6000, Fredericton NB E3B 5H1, 506/453-4283; URL: http://www.gov.nb.ca/tourism/index.htm; Fax: 506/444-4586

**Nfld.:** Department of Tourism, Culture & Recreation, Confederation Bldg., PO Box 8700, St. John's NF A1B 4J6, 709/729-0928; Fax: 709/729-0662

Tourism & Crafts Branch, Confederation Bldg., PO Box 8700, St. John's NF A1B 4J6, 709/729-0928; Fax: 709/729-0662

**NWT:** Department of Resources, Wildlife & Economic Development, Parks & Tourism, PO Box 1320, Yellowknife NT X1A 2L9, 867/873-7903; Fax: 867/873-0163

**N.S.:** Nova Scotia Economic Renewal Agency, Tourism Nova Scotia, 1800 Argyle St., PO Box 519, Halifax NS B3J 2R7, 902/424-8920; Fax: 902/424-0582

Travel Trade, 1800 Argyle St., PO Box 519, Halifax NS B3J 2R7, 902/424-4182; Fax: 902/424-0582

**Ont.:** Alberta Tourism Partnership, c/o Alberta Economic Development & Tourism, 10155 - 102 St., Edmonton ON T5J 4L6, 403/531-4671

Canadian Tourism Commission, East Tower, 235 Queen St. E., 4th Fl., Ottawa ON K1A 0H6, 613/954-3943; Fax: 613/954-3945

Ministry of Economic Development, Trade & Tourism, Business Development & Tourism Division, Hearst Block, 900 Bay St., Toronto ON M7A 2E1, 416/325-6666; Fax: 416/325-6688

**PEI:** Department of Economic Development & Tourism, Tourism PEI, Annex 1, West Royalty Industrial Park, 1 Watts Ave., Charlottetown PE C1E 1B0, 902/368-5540; Toll Free: 1-800-465-4734; Fax: 902/368-4438

**Qué.:** Tourisme Québec, #412, 900, boul René-Lévesque est, Québec QC G1R 2B5, 418/643-5959; Toll Free: 1-800-363-7777 (Tourism Information); Fax: 418/646-8723

**Sask.:** Saskatchewan Tourism Authority, #500, 1900 Albert St., Regina SK S4P 4L9, 306/787-9600; Toll Free: 1-800-667-7191; Fax: 306/787-0715

**Yuk.:** Yukon Tourism, PO Box 2703, Whitehorse YT Y1A 2C6, 867/667-5430; Fax: 867/667-8844

## TRADE

### *See Also* Business Development; Imports

Agriculture & Agri-Food Canada, Market & Industry Services Branch, Sir John Carling Bldg., 930 Carling Ave., Ottawa ON K1A 0C5, 613/759-7561; Fax: 613/759-7497

Business Development Bank of Canada, #400, 5, Place Ville Marie, Montréal QC H3B 5E7, 514/283-5904; Toll Free: 1-888-463-6232; Fax: 514/283-0617

Canadian International Grains Institute, #1000, 303 Main St., Winnipeg MB R3C 3G7, 204/983-5344; Fax: 204/983-2642

Canadian International Trade Tribunal, Standard Life Centre, 333 Laurier Ave. West, Ottawa ON K1A 0G7, 613/990-2452; Fax: 613/990-2439

Canadian Wheat Board, 423 Main St., PO Box 816, Winnipeg MB R3C 2P5, 204/983-0239, 3416; Fax: 204/983-3841

Export Development Corporation, 151 O'Connor St., Ottawa ON K1A 1K3, 613/598-2500; Fax: 613/237-2690

Finance Canada, International Trade & Finance Branch, Esplanade Laurier, 140 O'Connor St., Ottawa ON K1A 0G5, 613/992-1573; Fax: 613/996-8404

Foreign Affairs & International Trade Canada, International Business & Communications Branch, Lester B. Pearson Bldg., 125 Sussex Dr., Ottawa ON K1A 0G2, 613/995-6877; Fax: 613/943-8819

International Marketing Section, Lester B. Pearson Bldg., 125 Sussex Dr., Ottawa ON K1A 0G2, 613/995-0780; Fax: 613/992-2432, 992-6135

WIN Exports, Lester B. Pearson Bldg., 125 Sussex Dr., Ottawa ON K1A 0G2, 613/996-5701; Fax: 613/943-8819

Industry Canada, International Business, C.D. Howe Bldg., 235 Queen St., Ottawa ON K1A 0H5, 613/954-3508; Fax: 613/957-4454

North American Free Trade Agreement (NAFTA) Secretariat, Canadian Section, #705, 90 Sparks St., Ottawa ON K1P 5B4, 613/992-9388; Fax: 613/992-9392

Revenue Canada, Customs Border Services, 875 Heron Rd., Ottawa ON K1A 0L8, 613/952-0384

Trade Administration Branch, 875 Heron Rd., Ottawa ON K1A 0L8, 613/952-0384

Statistics Canada, Business & Trade Statistics, R.H. Coats Bldg., Tunney's Pasture, 120 Parkdale Ave., Ottawa ON K1A 0T6, 613/951-8116; Fax: 613/951-0581

Statistics Canada Regional Reference Centres, R.H. Coats Bldg., Tunney's Pasture, 120 Parkdale Ave., Ottawa ON K1A 0T6, Toll Free: 1-800-263-1136, TDD: 1-800-363-7629; Fax: 613/951-0581

**Alta:** Alberta Economic Development & Tourism, Tourism, Trade & Investment, Commerce Place, 10155 - 102 St., Edmonton AB T5J 4L6, 403/427-2280; Fax: 403/427-1700

Alberta Federal & Intergovernmental Affairs, Trade Policy Team, Commerce Place, 10155 - 102 St., 12th Fl., Edmonton AB T5J 4G8, 403/427-2611; Fax: 403/427-0699

**B.C.:** Ministry of Employment & Investment, British Columbia Trade & Investment Office, #730, 999 Canada Place, Vancouver BC V6C 3E1, 250/356-8702; Fax: 604/660-4048

Office of the Premier, British Columbia Trade Development Corporation (BC Trade), #730, 999 Canada Place, Vancouver BC V6C 3E1, 604/844-1900; Fax: 604/660-2457

**Man.:** Manitoba Development Corporation, #555, 155 Carlton St., Winnipeg MB R3C 3H8, 204/945-7626; Fax: 204/957-1793

Manitoba Industry, Trade & Tourism, 155 Carlton St., 6th Fl., Winnipeg MB R3C 3H8, 204/945-2066; Fax: 204/945-1354

Manitoba Trade/Manitoba Trading Corporation, 155 Carlton St., 4th Fl., Winnipeg MB R3C 3H8, 204/945-2466; Fax: 204/957-1793

**N.B.:** Department of Economic Development & Tourism, Centennial Bldg., 670 King St., 5th Fl., PO Box 6000, Fredericton NB E3B 5H1, 506/453-2850 (Communications & Promotion); Fax: 506/444-4586

**Nfld.:** Department of Industry, Trade & Technology, Confederation Annex, 4th Fl., PO Box 8700, St. John's NF A1B 4J6, 709/729-5600; Toll Free: 1-800-563-2299; Fax: 709/729-5936

**N.S.:** Nova Scotia Economic Renewal Agency, Investment & Trade, 1800 Argyle St., PO Box 519, Halifax NS B3J 2R7, 902/424-8920; Fax: 902/424-0582

**Ont.:** Ministry of Economic Development, Trade & Tourism, Marketing & Trade Division, Hearst Block, 900 Bay St., Toronto ON M7A 2E1, 416/325-6666; Fax: 416/325-6688

Trade Policy Branch, Hearst Block, 900 Bay St., Toronto ON M7A 2E1, 416/325-6930; Fax: 416/325-6949

**PEI:** Department of Agriculture & Forestry, Trade Relations, Jones Bldg., 11 Kent St., PO Box 2000, Charlottetown PE C1A 7N8, 902/368-5087; Fax: 902/368-4857

**Qué.:** Ministère de l'Industrie, du commerce, de la Science et de la technologie, Commerce extérieur et investissements étrangers, 710, Place d'Youville, 9e étage, Québec QC G1R 4Y4, 418/691-5950 (Renseignements); Fax: 418/644-0118

Ministère des Relations Internationales, Directions bilatérales; Institutions francophones et multilatérales, Édifice Hector-Fabre, 525, boul Réne-Levesque est, Québec QC G1R 5R9, 418/649-2300; Fax: 418/649-2656

**Sask.:** Saskatchewan Trade & Export Partnership, 1919 Saskatchewan Dr., Regina SK S4P 3V7, 306/787-9210; Fax: 306/787-6666

Saskatchewan Economic & Co-operative Development, Market Development, 1919 Saskatchewan Dr., Regina SK S4P 3V7, 306/787-0927

**Yuk.:** Yukon Economic Development, Industry Trade & Investment, 211 Main St., PO Box 2703, Whitehorse YT Y1A 2C6, 867/667-5466; Fax: 867/668-8601

## TRADE-MARKS *See* PATENTS & COPYRIGHT

## TRANSPORTATION

Centre for Surface Transportation Technology, U-89,, 1500 Montreal Rd., Ottawa ON K1A 0R6, 613/998-9639; Fax: 613/957-0831

Natural Resources Canada, Transportation Energy Use Division, 580 Booth St., Ottawa ON K1A 0E4, 613/996-7432; Fax: 613/992-1405

Transport Canada, Transport Canada Building, 330 Sparks St., Ottawa ON K1A 0N5, 613/990-2309; Fax: 613/954-4731

Transportation Safety Board of Canada, 200 Promenade du Portage, 4e étage, Hull QC K1A 1K8, 819/994-3741; Fax: 819/997-2239

**Alta:** Alberta Public Works, Supply & Services, Transportation Utility Corridor Management, 6950 - 113 St., 3rd Fl., Edmonton AB T6H 5V7, 403/422-1135; Fax: 403/422-2661

Alberta Transportation & Utilities, Twin Atria, 4999 - 98 Ave., Edmonton AB T6B 2X3, 403/427-2731

Traffic Safety Board, Twin Atria Bldg., 4999 - 98 Ave., 1st Fl., Edmonton AB T6B 2X3, 403/427-7178; Fax: 403/427-1740

**B.C.:** British Columbia Transportation Financing Authority, 2250 Granville Square, Vancouver BC V6C 1S4, 604/775-1174; Fax: 604/775-2792

Ministry of Transportation & Highways, 940 Blanshard St., Victoria BC V8W 3E6, 250/387-3198; Fax: 250/387-6431

**Man.:** Manitoba Highways & Transportation, 215 Garry St., Winnipeg MB R3C 3Z1, 204/945-3888; Fax: 204/945-7610

**N.B.:** Department of Transportation, King Tower, Kings Pl., 2nd Fl., PO Box 6000, Fredericton NB E3B 5H1, 506/453-3626

New Brunswick Transportation Agency, Kings Place, PO Box 6000, Fredericton NB E3B 5H1, 506/453-2802; Fax: 506/453-2900

**Nfld.:** Department of Works, Services & Transportation, Corporate Services, Confederation Bldg., PO Box 8700, St. John's NF A1B 4J6, 709/729-3676; Fax: 709/729-4285

**NWT:** Department of Transportation, Lahm Ridge Bldg., PO Box 1320, Yellowknife NT X1A 2L9, 867/920-3460; Fax: 867/873-0363

**Ont.:** Ministry of Transportation, 301 St. Paul St., St. Catharines ON L2R 1W6, Toll Free: 1-800-268-4686

Ontario Highway Transport Board, 151 Bloor St. West, 10th Fl., Toronto ON M5S 2T5, 416/326-6739; Fax: 416/326-6728

**PEI:** Department of Transportation & Public Works, Buildings Division, Jones Bldg., PO Box 2000, Charlottetown PE C1A 7N8, 902/368-5100; Fax: 902/368-5395

Highway Operations Division, Jones Bldg., PO Box 2000, Charlottetown PE C1A 7N8, 902/368-5100; Fax: 902/368-5395

**Qué.:** Conseil de la Recherche et du développement en transport, #1000, 545, boul Crémazie est, 9e étage, Montréal QC H2M 2V1, 514/523-3232; Fax: 514/523-2666

Ministère des Affaires Municipales, Développement des politiques et des programmes, Édifice Cook-Chauveau, 20, rue Pierre-Olivier-Chauveau, Québec QC G1R 4J3, 418/691-2040; Fax: 418/644-9863

Ministère des Transports, Planification et technologie, 700, boul René-Lévesque est, 28e étage, Québec QC G1R 5H1, 418/528-0808; Fax: 418/643-9836

**Sask.:** Saskatchewan Highways & Transportation, Logistics, Planning & Compliance Division, 1855 Victoria Ave., Regina SK S4P 3V5, 306/787-4804; Fax: 306/787-9777

Saskatchewan Municipal Government, Saskatchewan Infrastructure Program, 1855 Victoria Ave., Regina SK S4P 3V7, 306/787-8887; Fax: 306/787-3641

**Yuk.:** Yukon Community & Transportation Services, Transportation Engineering, PO Box 2703, Whitehorse YT Y1A 2C6, 867/633-7928; Fax: 867/393-6447

## TRAPPING & FUR INDUSTRY

Environment Canada, Canadian Wildlife Service, Place Vincent-Massey, 351, boul St-Joseph, Hull QC K1A 0H3, 819/997-1301; Fax: 819/953-7177

**B.C.:** Ministry of Environment, Lands & Parks, Wildlife Branch, 780 Blanshard St., Victoria BC V8V 1X4, 250/387-9731; Fax: 250/357-6750

**N.B.:** Department of Natural Resources & Energy, Fish & Wildlife, PO Box 6000, Fredericton NB E3B 5H1, 506/453-2440; Fax: 506/453-6699

**N.S.:** Department of Natural Resources, Enforcement & Hunter Safety, Founder's Square, 1701 Hollis St., PO Box 698, Halifax NS B3J 2T9, 902/424-5254; Fax: 902/424-7735

**PEI:** Department of Fisheries & Environment, Waterfowl & Furbearers Section, Jones Bldg., 11 Kent St., 4th Fl., PO Box 2000, Charlottetown PE CIA 7N8, 902/368-4666; Fax: 902/368-5830

**Sask.:** Saskatchewan Environment & Resource Management, Fish & Wildlife Branch, 3211 Albert St., Regina SK S4S 5W6, 306/787-2309; Email: dennis.sherratt.erm@govmail.gov.sk.ca; Fax: 306/787-9544

**Yuk.:** Yukon Renewable Resources, Wildlife Management, PO Box 2703, Whitehorse YT Y1A 2C6, 867/667-5177; Fax: 867/393-6213

## TREASURY SERVICES

### *See Also* Finance

**Alta:** Alberta Municipal Affairs, Commerce Place, 10155 - 102 St., Edmonton AB T5J 4L4, 403/427-2732; Fax: 403/422-9105

Alberta Treasury, Terrace Bldg., 9515 - 107 St., Edmonton AB T5K 2C3, 403/427-3035; Fax: 403/422-2463

**B.C.:** Ministry of Finance & Corporate Relations, Provincial Treasury, 620 Superior St., Victoria BC V8V 1X4, 250/387-9278

**Man.:** Manitoba Finance, Treasury Division, #109, Legislative Bldg., Winnipeg MB R3C 0V8, 204/945-3754; Fax: 204/945-8316

**N.B.:** Department of Finance, Treasury & Debt Management, PO Box 6000, Fredericton NB E3B 5H1, 506/453-2286; Fax: 506/453-2053

**Nfld.:** Department of Finance & Treasury Board, Confederation Bldg., PO Box 8700, St. John's NF A1B 4J6, 709/729-2858

Executive Council, Treasury Board Secretariat, Confederation Bldg., PO Box 8700, St. John's NF A1B 4J6, 709/729-2156

**NWT:** Department of Finance, Treasury, PO Box 1320, Yellowknife NT X1A 2L9; Fax: 867/873-0325

**N.S.:** Investments, Pensions & Treasury Services Branch, PO Box 187, Halifax NS B3J 2N3, 902/424-5554; Fax: 902/424-0635

**Ont.:** Ministry of Finance, Office of the Treasury, Frost Bldg. South, 7 Queen's Park Cres., Toronto ON M7A 1Y7, 416/325-0333 (Communications); Fax: 416/325-0339

**PEI:** Department of the Provincial Treasury, PO Box 2000, Charlottetown PE C1A 7N8, 902/368-4000; Fax: 902/368-5544

**Qué.:** Conseil du trésor, Edifice H, 4e étage, 875, Grande Allée est, Québec QC G1R 5R8, 418/643-5926; Fax: 418/643-7824

**Sask.:** Saskatchewan Finance, Treasury Board Branch, 2350 Albert St., Regina SK S4P 4A6, 306/787-6780; Fax: 306/787-3482

## UNEMPLOYMENT INSURANCE

Human Resources Development Canada, Insurance, Place du Portage, Phase IV, 140, Promenade du Portage, Hull QC K1A 0J9, 819/997-8662

**B.C.:** Ministry of Human Resources, Income Support, Parliament Bldgs., Victoria BC V8V 1X4

**Man.:** Manitoba Family Services, Employment & Income Assistance Division, #219, 114 Garry St., Winnipeg MB R3C 4V6, 204/945-2324 (Policy & Planning); Fax: 204/945-2156

**N.B.:** Department of Human Resources Development, Income Security Division, 520 King St., 5th Fl., PO Box 6000, Fredericton NB E3B 5H1, 506/453-2001; Fax: 506/453-7478

**Nfld.:** Department of Human Resources & Employment, Income Support, Confederation Bldg., PO Box 8700, St. John's NF A1B 4J6, 709/729-3243; Fax: 709/729-6996

**NWT:** Department of Education, Culture & Employment, Income Security Branch, PO Box 1320, Yellowknife NT X1A 2L9, 867/920-6160; Fax: 867/920-0443

**N.S.:** Department of Community Services, Income & Employment Support, Johnston Bldg., 5182 Prince St., 5th Fl., PO Box 696, Halifax NS B3J 2T7, 902/424-4326; Fax: 902/424-0721

## URBAN RENEWAL & DESIGN

### *See Also* Municipal Affairs

Canada Mortgage & Housing Corporation, 700 Montreal Rd., Ottawa ON K1A 0P7, 613/748-2000; Toll Free: 1-800-668-2642; Fax: 613/748-2098

Treasury Board of Canada, Office of Infrastructure, West Tower, 300 Laurier Ave. West, 3rd Fl., Ottawa ON K1A 0R5, 613/952-3171; Fax: 613/952-7979

**Alta:** Alberta Municipal Affairs, Local Government Services Division, Commerce Place, 10155 - 102 St., Edmonton AB T5J 4L4, 403/427-2732; Fax: 403/422-9105

**B.C.:** Ministry of Municipal Affairs & Housing, Local Government Services, Municipal Affairs, PO Box 9490, Victoria BC V8W 9N7, 250/387-4089; Fax: 250/356-1070

Ministry of Transportation & Highways, Planning & Major Projects Department, 940 Blanshard St., Victoria BC V8W 3E6, 250/387-3198; Fax: 250/387-6431

**Man.:** Manitoba Urban Affairs, #203, 280 Broadway Ave., Winnipeg MB R3C 0R8; Fax: 204/945-1249

**N.B.:** Department of Municipalities, Culture & Housing, Downtown Development Branch, Marysville Place, 20 McGloin St., PO Box 6000, Fredericton NB E3B 5H1, 506/457-4947; Fax: 506/458-9369

**Nfld.:** Department of Municipal & Provincial Affairs, Urban & Rural Planning, West Block, Confederation Bldg., PO Box 8700, St. John's NF A1B 4J6, 709/729-3090

Newfoundland & Labrador Housing Corporation, 2 Canada Dr., PO Box 220, St. John's NF A1C 5J2, 709/724-3000; Fax: 709/724-3250

**Ont.:** Ministry of Municipal Affairs & Housing, Municipal Operations Divsion, 777 Bay St., 17th Fl., Toronto ON M5G 2E5, 416/585-7041 (Communications Branch); Fax: 416/585-6227

Office for the Greater Toronto Area, Waterpark Pl., #300, 10 Bay St., Toronto ON M5J 2R8, 416/314-6400; Fax: 416/314-6440

Urban Economic Development, 777 Bay St., 17th Fl., Toronto ON M5G 2E5, 416/585-7474; Fax: 416/585-6227

**PEI:** Department of Economic Development & Tourism, Community Development Section, Shaw Bldg., 95 Rochford St., 4th Fl., Charlottetown PE C1A 7N8, 902/368-4476; Fax: 902/368-4242

**Qué.:** Ministère de la Métropole, Édifice H, #2.600, 875, Grande Allée Est, Québec QC G1R 4Y8, 418/646-3018; Fax: 418/643-6377

Société d'habitation du Québec, Bloc 2, 1054, Conroy, 4e étage, Québec QC G1R 5E7, 418/643-7676; Fax: 418/643-2166

**Sask.:** Saskatchewan Municipal Government, Municipal Development, 1855 Victoria Ave., Regina SK S4P 3V7, 306/787-2710; Fax: 306/787-4181

**Yuk.:** Yukon Economic Development, Economic Development, 211 Main St., PO Box 2703, Whitehorse YT Y1A 2C6, 867/667-3013; Fax: 867/668-8601

## VETERANS AFFAIRS

Veterans Affairs Canada, Daniel J. MacDonald Bldg., 161 Grafton St., PO Box 7700, Charlottetown PE C1A 8M9, 902/566-8195; Fax: 902/566-8508

**Ont.:** Soldiers Aid Commission, 2 Bloor St. West, 24th Fl., Toronto ON M7A 1E9, 416/327-4674

### VICTIM ASSISTANCE *See* CRIMES COMPENSATION; JUSTICE DEPARTMENTS

## VIOLENCE

### *See Also* Policing Services

Correctional Service Canada, Sex Offender Programming, 340 Laurier Ave. West, Ottawa ON K1A 0P9, 613/545-8248; Fax: 613/947-0091

**Alta:** Alberta Family & Social Services, Family Violence Prevention, Seventh St. Plaza, 10030 - 107 St., Edmonton AB T5J 3E4, 403/422-5916; Fax: 403/422-9044

Alberta Justice, Serious & Violent Crime Initiatives, Bowker Bldg., 9833 - 109 St., Edmonton AB T5K 2E8, 403/427-9030; Fax: 403/422-1330

**Man.:** Manitoba Family Services, Family Dispute Services, #219, 114 Garry St., Winnipeg MB R3C 4V6, 204/945-7259; Fax: 204/945-2156

**N.B.:** Department of Health & Community Services, Access/Assessment, Protection & Post Adoption Services, PO Box 5100, Fredericton NB E3B 5G8, 506/453-2040; Fax: 506/444-4697

**Ont.:** Ministry of Citizenship, Culture & Recreation, Ontario Anti-Racism Secretariat, 77 Bloor St. West, 6th Fl., Toronto ON M7A 2R9, 416/327-2422

Ministry of Community & Social Services, Children, Family & Community Services Division, Hepburn Block, 80 Grosvenor St., 6th Fl., Toronto ON M7A 1E9, 416/325-5666; Fax: 416/325-5172, 5171

**PEI:** Department of Community Affairs & Attorney General, Legal & Judicial Services Division, PO Box 2000, Charlottetown PE C1A 7N8, 902/368-5250; Fax: 902/368-5283; 5355

**Qué.:** Ministère de la Justice, Bureau d'aide aux victimes d'actes criminels, 1200, rte de l'Église, Ste-Foy QC G1V 4M1, 418/643-5140 (Communications); Fax: 418/646-4449

Ministère de la Sécurité publique, Direction Générale de la Sécurité et de la prévention, 2525, boul Laurier, 6e étage, Ste-Foy QC G1V 2L2, 418/646-8523; Fax: 418/646-5427

**Sask.:** Saskatchewan Justice, Victims Services, 1874 Scarth St., Regina SK S4P 3V7, 306/787-0418; Fax: 306/787-9111

Saskatchewan Social Services, Family & Youth Services Division, 1920 Broad St., Regina SK S4P 3V6, 306/787-7010; Fax: 306/787-0925

Protection & Children's Services, 2240 Albert St., Regina SK S4P 3V7, 306/787-2928; Fax: 306/694-3842

**Yuk.:** Yukon Justice, Victim Services/Family Violence Prevention Unit, PO Box 2703, Whitehorse YT Y1A 2C6, 867/667-3023; Fax: 867/393-6240

## VITAL STATISTICS

Statistics Canada, R.H. Coats Bldg., Tunney's Pasture, 120 Parkdale Ave., Ottawa ON K1A 0T6, 613/951-8116; Toll Free: 1-800-263-1136, TDD: 1-800-363-7629; Fax: 613/951-0581

Census & Demographic Statistics, R.H. Coats Bldg., Tunney's Pasture, 120 Parkdale Ave., Ottawa ON K1A 0T6, 613/951-6537; Fax: 613/951-0581

**Alta:** Alberta Municipal Affairs, Registries Division, John E. Brownlee Bldg., 10365 - 97 St., Edmonton AB T5J 3W7, 403/422-2362 (Edmonton), 403/297-8980 (Calgary); Toll Free: 1-800-465-5009 (in Alberta); Fax: 403/422-9105

**B.C.:** Ministry of Health, Vital Statistics, 818 Fort St., Victoria BC V8W 1H8, 250/952-2681; Fax: 250/952-2576

**Man.:** Manitoba Consumer & Corporate Affairs, 254 Portage Ave., Winnipeg MB R3C 0B8, 204/945-3701; Toll Free: Fax Certificate Requests: 204/948-3128; Fax: 204/945-0777

**N.B.:** Department of Health & Community Services, Vital Statistics, PO Box 5100, Fredericton NB E3B 5G8, 506/453-2536; Fax: 506/453-3245

**Nfld.:** Department of Government Services & Lands, 5 Mews Pl., PO Box 8700, St. John's NF A1B 4J6; Fax: 709/729-2071

**NWT:** Department of Finance, Bureau of Statistics, PO Box 1320, Yellowknife NT X1A 2L9; Fax: 867/873-0275

**N.S.:** Department of Business & Consumer Services, Vital Statistics, Halifax NS B3J 2M9, 902/424-8907; Fax: 902/424-0678

**Ont.:** Ministry of Consumer & Commercial Relations, Registrar General Branch, 189 Red River Rd., PO Box 4600, Thunder Bay ON P7B 6L8, 807/343-7414; Toll Free: 1-800-461-2156; Fax: 807/343-7411

**PEI:** Department of Health & Social Services, Jones Bldg., 11 Kent St., 2nd Fl., PO Box 2000, Charlottetown PE C1A 7N8, 902/368-4900; Fax: 902/368-4969

**Sask.:** Saskatchewan Health, Vital Statistics & Health Insurance Registration Branch, 1919 Rose St., Regina SK S4P 3V7, 306/787-1167; Fax: 306/787-8310

**Yuk.:** Yukon Health & Social Services, Vital Statistics, PO Box 2703, Whitehorse YT Y1A 2C6, 867/667-5207; Fax: 867/667-3096

### WAGES *See* LABOUR

## WASTE MANAGEMENT

***See Also* Dangerous Goods & Hazardous Materials**

Natural Resources Canada, Radioactive Waste Division, 580 Booth St., Ottawa ON K1A 0E4, 613/996-2395; Fax: 613/992-1405

**Alta:** Alberta Racing Commission, Sloane Square, #507, 5920 - 1A St. SW, Calgary AB T2H 0G3, 403/297-6551; Fax: 403/255-4078

**B.C.:** Ministry of Environment, Lands & Parks, Industrial Waste & Hazardous Contaminants Branch, 777 Broughton St., Victoria BC V8V 1X4, 250/387-9992; Fax: 250/387-9935

Municipal Waste Reduction Branch, 777 Broughton St., Victoria BC V8V 1X4, 250/387-9974; Fax: 250/356-9974

**Man.:** Manitoba Rural Development, Municipal Services, #609, 800 Portage Ave., Winnipeg MB R3G 0N4, 204/945-2570; Fax: 204/945-1994

**N.B.:** Department of the Environment, Municipal Services, 364 Argyle St., PO Box 6000, Fredericton NB E3B 5H1, 506/444-4599; Fax: 506/457-7805

**Nfld.:** Department of Environment & Labour, Pollution Prevention, Confederation Bldg., PO Box 8700, St. John's NF A1B 4J6, 709/729-2556; Fax: 709/729-1930

**NWT:** Department of Municipal & Community Affairs, #600, 5201 - 50 Ave., PO Box 1310, Yellowknife NT X1A 2L9, 867/873-7118; Fax: 867/873-0309

**N.S.:** Department of Housing & Municipal Affairs, Municipal Services Division, PO Box 216, Halifax NS B3J 2M4, 902/424-7415; Fax: 902/424-0531

Nova Scotia Resource Recovery Fund Board, PO Box 2107, Halifax NS B3J 3B7, 902/424-2577; Fax: 902/424-0503

**Ont.:** Ministry of Environment & Energy, Waste Reduction Branch, 40 St. Clair Ave. West, 7th Fl., Toronto ON M4V 1M2, 416/325-4440; Fax: 416/323-4481

**PEI:** Department of Fisheries & Environment, Solid Waste Section, Jones Bldg., 11 Kent St., 4th Fl., PO Box 2000, Charlottetown PE CIA 7N8, 902/368-5029; Fax: 902/368-5830

**Qué.:** Société québécoise de récupération et de recyclage, #500, 7171 rue Jean-Talon est, Anjou QC H1M 3N2, 514/352-5002; Fax: 514/873-6542

**Sask.:** Saskatchewan Environment & Resource Management, Environmental Protection Branch, 3211 Albert St., Regina SK S4S 5W6, 306/787-6178; Fax: 306/787-0197

Saskatchewan Municipal Government, Municipal Services Division, 1855 Victoria Ave., Regina SK S4P 3V7, 306/787-8282; Fax: 306/787-4181

**Yuk.:** Yukon Community & Transportation Services, Community Services Branch, PO Box 2703, Whitehorse YT Y1A 2C6, 867/667-5299; Fax: 867/393-6404

## WATER RESOURCES

***See Also* Environment; Oceanography**

Environment Canada, Environmental Protection Service, Place Vincent-Massey, 351, boul St-Joseph, Hull QC K1A 0H3, 819/997-2800; Fax: 819/953-2225

Federal Water Policy Office, Place Vincent-Massey, 351, boul St-Joseph, Hull QC K1A 0H3, 819/953-1513; Fax: 819/944-0237

Freshwater Institute, 501 University Cr., Winnipeg MB R3T 2N6, 204/983-5000; Fax: 204/983-6285

International Joint Commission, 100 Metcalfe St., Ottawa ON K1P 5M1, 613/995-2984; Fax: 613/993-5583

National Water Research Institute, 867 Lakeshore Rd., PO Box 5050, Burlington ON L7R 4A6, 905/336-4625; Fax: 905/336-4989

Nunavut Water Board, Gjoa Haven NT X0E 1J0

**Alta:** Alberta Agriculture, Food & Rural Development, Irrigation & Resource Management Division, 7000 - 113 St., Edmonton AB T6H 5T6, 403/422-4596; Fax: 403/422-0474

**B.C.:** Ministry of Environment, Lands & Parks, Water Resources Branch, 3400 Davidson Ave., Victoria BC V8V 1X4, 250/387-6945; Fax: 250/356-8298

**Man.:** Manitoba Water Services Board, 2022 Currie Blvd., PO Box 1059, Brandon MB R7A 6A3, 204/726-6076; Fax: 204/726-6290

Manitoba Natural Resources, Water Resources Branch, 1577 Dublin Ave., Winnipeg MB R3E 3J5, 204/945-7488; Fax: 204/945-7419

**NWT:** Northwest Territories Water Board, PO Box 1500, Yellowknife NT X1A 2R3, 867/669-2772; Fax: 867/669-2719

**N.S.:** Department of the Environment, Water Resources Branch, 5151 Terminal Rd., 5th Fl., PO Box 2107, Halifax NS B3J 3B7, 902/424-2554; Fax: 902/424-0503

**Ont.:** Ministry of Natural Resources, Water Management & Conservation Authorities, Whitney Block, #6540, 99 Wellesley St. West, Toronto ON M7A 1W3, 416/314-1977; Fax: 416/314-1995

Ontario Clean Water Agency, #700, 20 Bay St., Toronto ON M5J 2N8, 416/314-5600; Fax: 416/314-8300

**PEI:** Department of Fisheries & Environment, Water Resources Division, Jones Bldg., 11 Kent St., 4th Fl., PO Box 2000, Charlottetown PE CIA 7N8, 902/368-5028; Fax: 902/368-5830

**Qué.:** Société québécoise d'assainissement des eaux, 1055, boul René-Lévesque est, 10e étage, Montréal QC H2L 4S5, 514/873-7411; Fax: 514/873-7879

**Sask.:** Saskatchewan Environment & Resource Management, 3211 Albert St., Regina SK S4S 5W6, 306/787-2700; Toll Free: 1-800-667-2757; Fax: 306/787-3941

Saskatchewan Water Corporation (Sask Water), Victoria Place, 111 Fairford St. East, Moose Jaw SK S6H 7X9, 306/694-3900; Fax: 306/694-3944

**Yuk.:** Yukon Renewable Resources, PO Box 2703, Whitehorse YT Y1A 2C6, 867/667-5237; Toll Free: 1-800-661-0408 (Yukon)

## WEATHER

Environment Canada, Atmospheric Environment Service, 4905 Dufferin St., Downsview ON M3H 5T4, 416/739-4521; Fax: 819/953-2225

**WEED CONTROL *See* AGRICULTURE**

## WEIGHTS & MEASURES

Industry Canada, Measurement Canada, 3701 Carling Ave., PO Box 11490, Stn H, Ottawa ON K2H 8S2, 613/952-0655; Fax: 613/957-1265

Standards Council of Canada, #1200, 45 O'Connor St., Ottawa ON K1P 6N7, 613/238-3222; Fax: 613/995-4564

**WELFARE *See* INCOME SECURITY; SOCIAL SERVICES**

## WILDLIFE RESOURCES

Committee on the Status of Endangered Wildlife in Canada, Ottawa ON K1A 0H3, 819/997-4991; Fax: 819/953-6283

Environment Canada, Canadian Wildlife Service, Place Vincent-Massey, 351, boul St-Joseph, Hull QC K1A 0H3, 819/997-1301; Fax: 819/953-7177

National Wildlife Research Centre, 100, boul Gamelin, Hull QC K1A 0H3, 819/997-1092; Fax: 819/953-6612

North American Waterfowl Management Plan, c/o Canadian Wildlife Service, Place Vincent-Massey, 351, boul St-Joseph, 3e étage, Hull QC K1A 0H3, 819/997-2392; Fax: 819/994-4445

**Alta:** Alberta Sport, Recreation, Parks & Wildlife Foundation, Percy Page Centre, 11759 Groat Rd., Edmonton AB T5M 3K9, 403/427-1976; Fax: 403/488-9755

Alberta Environmental Protection, Fish & Wildlife, 9915 - 108 St., Edmonton AB T5K 2G8, 403/427-2739, 944-0313 (Information Centre)

**Man.:** Endangered Species Advisory Committee, 200 Saulteaux Cr., PO Box 80, Winnipeg MB R3J 3W3, 204/945-6829

Manitoba Natural Resources, Wildlife Branch, 200 Saulteaux Cr., PO Box 24, Winnipeg MB R3J 3W3, 204/945-7761; Fax: 204/945-3077

Saskeram Wildlife Management Area Advisory Committee, PO Box 2550, The Pas MB R9A 1M4, 204/627-8266

**N.B.:** Department of Natural Resources & Energy, Fish & Wildlife, PO Box 6000, Fredericton NB E3B 5H1, 506/453-2440; Fax: 506/453-6699

**Nfld.:** Department of Forest Resources & Agrifoods, Forestry & Wildlife Branch, Confederation Complex, PO Box 8700, St. John's NF A1B 4J6, 709/729-4716

**NWT:** Department of Resources, Wildlife & Economic Development, Wildlife & Fisheries, PO Box 1320, Yellowknife NT X1A 2L9, 867/920-8716; Fax: 867/873-0221

**N.S.:** Department of Natural Resources, Wildlife Division, PO Box 516, Kentville NS B4N 3X3, 902/678-6091; Fax: 902/679-6176

**Ont.:** Ministry of Natural Resources, Fish & Wildlife Branch, Whitney Block, #6540, 99 Wellesley St. West, Toronto ON M7A 1W3, 416/314-6132; Fax: 416/314-1994

**PEI:** Department of Fisheries & Environment, Fish & Wildlife Division, Jones Bldg., 11 Kent St., 4th Fl., PO Box 2000, Charlottetown PE CIA 7N8, 902/368-4683; Fax: 902/368-5830

**Qué.:** Ministère de l'Environnement et de la Faune, Direction générale du patrimoine faunique et naturel, Édifice Marie-Guyart, 675, boul René-Lévesque est, Québec QC G1R 5V7, 418/643-3127; Fax: 418/643-3619

**Sask.:** Saskatchewan Environment & Resource Management, Fish & Wildlife Branch, 3211 Albert St., Regina SK S4S 5W6, 306/787-2309; Email: dennis.sherratt.erm@govmail.gov.sk.ca; Fax: 306/787-9544

**Yuk.:** Yukon Renewable Resources, Wildlife Management, PO Box 2703, Whitehorse YT Y1A 2C6, 867/667-5177; Fax: 867/393-6213

## WOMEN'S ISSUES

***See Also* Pay Equity**

Canadian Heritage, Multiculturalism & Status of Women, Jules Léger Bldg., 25 Eddy St., Hull QC K1A 1K5, 819/997-9900; TDD: 819/997-8776; Fax: 819/953-8055

Health Canada, Women's Health Bureau, Brooke Claxton Bldg., Tunney's Pasture, 120 Parkdale Ave., Ottawa ON K1A 0K9, 613/957-1940; Fax: 613/941-5366

Status of Women Canada, #700, 360 Albert St., Ottawa ON K1A 1C3, 613/995-7835; Fax: 613/957-3359

**B.C.:** Ministry of Health, Women's Health Bureau, 1515 Blanshard St., 7th Fl., Victoria BC V8W 3C8, 250/952-1231; Fax: 250/952-1282

Ministry of Women's Equality, 756 Fort St., Victoria BC V8V 1X4, 250/387-3600; Fax: 250/356-1396

Ministry of the Attorney General, Employment Equity & Women's Programs, PO Box 9282, Stn Prov. Gov't, Victoria BC V8W 9J7, 250/387-3247; Fax: 250/356-5368

**Man.:** Executive Council, Culture, Heritage & Citizenship, Legislative Bldg., 450 Broadway, Winnipeg MB R3C 0V8, 204/945-3729; Fax: 204/945-5223

**Nfld.:** Provincial Advisory Council on the Status of Women, 131 Le Marchant Rd., St. John's NF A1C 2H3, 709/753-7270; Fax: 709/753-2606

**NWT:** Executive Council, Status of Women, PO Box 1320, Yellowknife NT X1A 2L9, 867/920-3106; Fax: 867/873-0122

Status of Women of the Northwest Territories, PO Box 1320, Yellowknife NT X1A 2L9, 867/920-6177

**N.S.:** Nova Scotia Advisory Council on the Status of Women, PO Box 745, Halifax NS B3J 2T3, 902/424-8662; Fax: 902/424-0573

**Ont.:** Ontario Womens Directorate, 900 Bay St., 6th Fl., Toronto ON M7A 1L2, 416/314-0300; Fax: 416/314-0247

**PEI:** Advisory Council on the Status of Women, PO Box 2000, Charlottetown PE C1A 7N8, 902/368-4510; Fax: 902/368-4516

**Qué.:** Secrétariat à la Condition féminine, #2.700, 875, Grande-Allée est, Québec QC G1R 5W5, 418/643-9052; Fax: 418/643-4991

Conseil du Statut de la Femme, #300, 8, rue Cook, Québec QC G1R 5J7, 418/643-4326; Fax: 418/643-8926

**Sask.:** Saskatchewan Women's Secretariat, 1855 Victoria Ave., 7th Fl., Regina SK S4P 3V5, 306/787-2329; Fax: 306/787-2058

**Yuk.:** Yukon Women's Directorate, PO Box 2703, Whitehorse YT Y1A 2C6, 867/667-3030; Fax: 867/393-6270

## WORKERS' COMPENSATION

Human Resources Development Canada, Place du Portage, Phase IV, 140, Promenade du Portage, Hull QC K1A 0J9, 819/994-6013 (Communications)

Merchant Seamen Compensation Board, Portage II, Place du Portage, 165 Hotel-de-Ville St., Ottawa ON K1A 0J2, 819/997-2555; Fax: 819/997-1664

**Alta:** Alberta Workers' Compensation Board, 9912 - 107 St., PO Box 2415, Edmonton AB T5J 2S5, 403/498-4000; Fax: 403/422-0972

**B.C.:** Workers' Compensation Board of British Columbia, 6951 Westminster Hwy., Richmond BC V7C 1C6, 604/273-2266; Toll Free: 1-800-661-2112; Fax: 604/276-3151

**Man.:** Manitoba Workers' Compensation Board, 333 Maryland St., Winnipeg MB R3G 1M2, 204/786-5471; Toll Free: 1-800-362-3340 (Manitoba); Fax: 204/786-3704

**N.B.:** Workplace Health, Safety & Compensation Commission of New Brunswick, 1 Portland St., PO Box 160, Saint John NB E2L 3X9, 506/632-2200; Toll Free: 1-800-222-9775; Fax: 506/632-2226

**Nfld.:** Newfoundland & Labrador Workers' Compensation Commission, #146, 148 Forest Rd., PO Box 9000, St. John's NF A1A 3B8, 709/778-1000; Fax: 709/738-1714

**NWT:** Northwest Territories Workers' Compensation Board, PO Box 8888, Yellowknife NT X1A 2R3, 867/920-3888; Fax: 867/873-4596

**N.S.:** Workers' Compensation Board of Nova Scotia, 5668 South St., PO Box 1150, Halifax NS B3J 2Y2, 902/424-8440; Fax: 902/424-0509

**Ont.:** Workers' Compensation Board, 2 Bloor St. East, 20th Fl., Toronto ON M4W 3C3, 416/927-4135; Fax: 416/927-5141

**PEI:** Prince Edward Island Workers' Compensation Board, PO Box 757, Charlottetown PE C1A 7L7, 902/368-5680; Fax: 902/368-5696

**Qué.:** Commission de la santé et de la sécurité du travail du Québec, 1199, rue de Bleury, CP 6056, Succ Centre-Ville, Montréal QC H3C 4E1, 514/873-7183; Fax: 514/873-7007

**Sask.:** Saskatchewan Workers' Compensation Board, #200, 1881 Scarth St., Regina SK S4P 4L1, 306/787-4370; Fax: 306/787-0213

**Yuk.:** Yukon Workers' Compensation Health & Safety Board, 401 Strickland St., Whitehorse YT Y1A 5N8, 867/667-5645; Toll Free: 1-800-661-0443; Fax: 867/393-6279

## YOUNG OFFENDERS

Justice Canada, Family, Children & Youth Section, Justice Bldg., 239 Wellington St., Ottawa ON K1A 0H8, 613/941-2339; Fax: 613/954-0811

**Alta:** Alberta Justice, Young Offender Branch, 10365 - 97 St., Edmonton AB T5J 3W7, 403/422-5019; Fax: 403/422-0732

**B.C.:** Ministry of the Attorney General, Family Justice Reform, PO Box 9282, Stn Prov. Gov't, Victoria BC V8W 9J7, 250/387-1111; Fax: 604/356-1092

**Man.:** Manitoba Justice, Community & Youth Correctional Services, 405 Broadway, 8th Fl., Winnipeg MB R3C 3L6, 204/945-7891; Fax: 204/948-2166

**N.B.:** Department of the Solicitor General, Institutional & Young Offender Services, Barker House, 4th Fl., PO Box 6000, Fredericton NB E3B 5H1, 506/453-2846; Fax: 506/453-2307

**Nfld.:** Department of Human Resources & Employment, Enquiries Division, Confederation Bldg., PO Box 8700, St. John's NF A1B 4J6, 709/729-2478; Fax: 709/729-6996

**NWT:** Department of Justice, Young Offenders, PO Box 1320, Yellowknife NT X1A 2L9, 867/920-8823

**Ont.:** Ministry of the Solicitor General & Correctional Services, Operational Support & Coordination Branch, 101 Bloor St. West, 7th Fl., Toronto ON M5S 2Z7, 705/494-3339

**Qué.:** Chambre de la jeunesse, 410, rue Bellechasse est, Montréal QC H2S 1X3, 514/495-5817; Fax: 514/873-8938

Ministère de la Justice, Direction du droit de la jeunesse, 1200, rte de l'Église, Ste-Foy QC G1V 4M1, 418/643-5140 (Communications); Fax: 418/646-4449

**Sask.:** Saskatchewan Social Services, Young Offenders, Central Office, #216, 110 Ominica St. West, Moose Jaw SK S6H 6V2, 306/787-9165; Fax: 306/694-3842

**Yuk.:** Yukon Health & Social Services, Social Services Branch, PO Box 2703, Whitehorse YT Y1A 2C6, 867/667-3673 (Communications); Fax: 867/667-3096

## YOUTH SERVICES

Human Resources Development Canada, Children & Youth, Place du Portage, Phase IV, 140, Promenade du Portage, Hull QC K1A 0J9, 613/953-8385; Fax: 613/953-0944

Justice Canada, Family, Children & Youth Section, Justice Bldg., 239 Wellington St., Ottawa ON K1A 0H8, 613/941-2339; Fax: 613/954-0811

**Alta:** Alberta Family & Social Services, Child Welfare, Seventh St. Plaza, 10030 - 107 St., Edmonton AB T5J 3E4, 403/422-5187; Fax: 403/422-9044

**B.C.:** Ministry of Children & Families, Child, Family & Community Service, 1022 Government St., 3rd Fl., Victoria BC V8V 1X4, 250/356-3004; Fax: 250/356-3007 (Communications)

Children with Special Needs, 1022 Government St., 3rd Fl., Victoria BC V8V 1X4, 250/387-1275; Fax: 250/356-6534

**Man.:** Manitoba Education & Training, Workforce 2000 & Youth Programs, 185 Carlton St., 4th Fl., Winnipeg MB R3C 3J1, 204/945-6195; Fax: 204/945-1792

Manitoba Family Services, Child & Family Services Division, #219, 114 Garry St., Winnipeg MB R3C 4V6, 204/945-2324 (Policy & Planning); Fax: 204/945-2156

**N.B.:** Youth Council of New Brunswick, 736 King St., PO Box 6000, Fredericton NB E3B 5H1, 506/453-3271; Fax: 506/444-4413

**Nfld.:** Department of Education, Youth Services Division, Confederation Bldg., PO Box 8700, St. John's NF A1B 4J6, 709/729-3503; Fax: 709/729-3669

**NWT:** Department of Education, Culture & Employment, Early Childhood & School Services, PO Box 1320, Yellowknife NT X1A 2L9, 867/920-3491; Fax: 867/873-0155

**N.S.:** Nova Scotia Youth Secretariat, One Government Place, 1700 Granville St., 5th Fl., PO Box 1617, Halifax NS B3J 2Y3, 902/424-3780; Fax: 902/424-7638

**Ont.:** Ministry of Environment & Energy, Environmental Youth Corps, 135 St. Clair Ave. West, Toronto ON M4V 1P5, 416/314-9387; General Inquiry: 416/314-5906; Fax: 416/323-4645

**PEI:** Department of Health & Social Services, Jones Bldg., 11 Kent St., 2nd Fl., PO Box 2000, Charlottetown PE C1A 7N8, 902/368-4900; Fax: 902/368-4969

**Qué.:** Ministère de la Santé et des services sociaux, 1075, ch Ste-Foy, Québec QC G1S 2M1

**Sask.:** Saskatchewan Social Services, Family & Youth Services Division, 1920 Broad St., Regina SK S4P 3V6, 306/787-7010; Fax: 306/787-0925

**Yuk.:** Yukon Health & Social Services, Social Services Branch, PO Box 2703, Whitehorse YT Y1A 2C6, 867/667-3673 (Communications); Fax: 867/667-3096

## ZONING

**Alta:** Alberta Municipal Affairs, Local Government Services Division, Commerce Place, 10155 - 102 St., Edmonton AB T5J 4L4, 403/427-2732; Fax: 403/422-9105

**B.C.:** British Columbia Assessment, 1537 Hillside Ave., Victoria BC V8T 4Y2, 250/595-6211; Fax: 250/595-6222

**Man.:** Manitoba Municipal Board, #408, 800 Portage Ave., Winnipeg MB R3G 0N4, 204/945-1789; Fax: 204/948-2235

Manitoba Natural Resources, Land Information Centre, 1007 Century St., Winnipeg MB R3H 0W4, 204/945-4071; Fax: 204/945-3586

Manitoba Rural Development, Assessment Branch, #609, 800 Portage Ave., Winnipeg MB R3G ON4, 204/945-2605; Fax: 204/945-1994

**N.B.:** Department of Municipalities, Culture & Housing, Land Use Planning Branch, Marysville Place, 20 McGloin St., PO Box 6000, Fredericton NB E3B 5H1, 506/453-2171; Fax: 506/457-4991

**Nfld.:** Department of Municipal & Provincial Affairs, Urban & Rural Planning, West Block, Confederation Bldg., PO Box 8700, St. John's NF A1B 4J6, 709/729-3090

**Ont.:** Ministry of Municipal Affairs & Housing, Plans Administration Branch (Central & Southwest), 777 Bay St., 17th Fl., Toronto ON M5G 2E5, 416/585-6025; Fax: 416/585-6227

**PEI:** Department of Community Affairs & Attorney General, Inspection Services, PO Box 2000, Charlottetown PE C1A 7N8, 902/368-4884; Fax: 902/368-5544

**Qué.:** Commission municipale du Québec, 20, rue Pierre-Olivier-Chauveau, 5e étage, Québec QC G1R 4J3, 418/691-2014; Fax: 418/644-4676

**Yuk.:** Yukon Community & Transportation Services, Municipal & Community Affairs Division, PO Box 2703, Whitehorse YT Y1A 2C6, 867/667-5144; Fax: 867/393-6404

# GOVERNMENT OF CANADA

**Seat of Government:** House of Commons, 111 Wellington St., PO Box 1103, Ottawa ON K1A 0A6
URL: http://canada.gc.ca
InfoCan URL: http://www.infocan.gc.ca/
All political authority in Canada is divided between the federal and provincial governments according to the provisions of the Constitution Act, 1867. Local municipalities are a concern of the provinces, and derive their authority from Acts of provincial legislation.
The Parliament of Canada consists of the Queen (represented in Canada by the Governor General), an Upper House called the Senate, and an elected House of Commons.

## GOVERNOR GENERAL & COMMANDER-IN-CHIEF OF CANADA/Gouverneur général et Commandant en chef du Canada

Rideau Hall, 1 Sussex Dr., Ottawa ON K1A 0A1
613/993-8200; Fax: 613/990-7636; URL: http://www.gg.ca
Canada is a constitutional monarchy; under the terms of its Constitution, Her Majesty Queen Elizabeth II is the Head of State. The Queen is represented in Canada by the Governor General who is also Commander-in-Chief of the Canadian Forces, Chancellor & Principal Companion of the Order of Canada, Chancellor & Commander of the Order of Military Merit, & Head of the Canadian Heraldic Authority.
The office of the Governor General encompasses a number of responsibilities, both constitutional & traditional in nature. These fall into six categories: the Crown in Canada, Canadian Sovereignty, Recognition of Excellence, National Identity, National Unity & Moral Leadership.
Canada's twenty-fifth Governor General, His Excellency the Right Honourable Roméo LeBlanc, was sworn in on February 8, 1995.
**Governor General**, His Excellency the Right Honourable Roméo LeBlanc, P.C., C.C., C.M.M., C.D.
**Secretary to the Governor General**, Judith A. LaRocque, C.V.O.
Personal Secretary, Kay Higgins
Executive Asst., Kevin Fram

### CHANCELLERY

Deputy Secretary, Lt.Gen. James C. Gervais, C.M.M., C.D.(Retired)
Director, Heraldry, Robert Watt
Director, Honours, Mary de Bellefeuille-Percy

### POLICY, PROGRAM & PROTOCOL

Deputy Secretary, Anthony P. Smyth, L.V.O.
Acting Director, Policy & Planning, Gabrielle Lappa
Acting Director, Public Information, Kate McGregor

## PRIVY COUNCIL OFFICE (PCO)/Bureau du Conseil privé (BCP)

Langevin Block, 80 Wellington St., Ottawa ON K1A 0A3
613/957-5153; Fax: 613/995-0101; URL: http://canada.gc.ca/depts/agencies/pcoind_e.html
The PCO is a public service department that provides advice to the Prime Minister with regard to the organization of the government and its relationships with Parliament, the Crown and other institutions; the delineation of responsibilities among Ministers; senior appointments; and matters for which the Prime Minister has a particular concern, such as national security. It supports the Prime Minister's power to organize Cabinet and the Cabinet decision-making process; and secretariat support to the Cabinet, its committees and their chairs. It also advises the Prime Minister regarding government priorities; the strategic handling of governmental issues; and government policies.
The Office has a special responsibility to ensure the continuity of government, which includes facilitating changes of government and briefing newly appointed Ministers. A member of the Privy Council is awarded the title "Honourable" for life. The Governor General, the Prime Minister and the Chief Justice of Canada are accorded the title "The Rt. Honourable" for life. The Canadian Transportation Accident & Safety Investigation Board and the Public Service Staff Relations Board report to Parliament through the President of the Privy Council.
Note: A list of Privy Council members may be obtained from: Orders-in-Council Division, #418, Blackburn Bldg., 85 Sparks St., Ottawa ON K1A 0A3, 613/957-5434; Fax: 613/957-5026

### ACTS ADMINISTERED

Canadian Transportation Accident Investigation & Safety Board Act
Oaths of Allegiance Act
Parliamentary Employment & Staff Relations Act
Public Service Staff Relations Act
Representation Act
**President of the Privy Council**, Hon. Stéphane Dion, 613/943-1838, Fax: 613/992-3700
Parliamentary Secretary, Office of the President, Paul De Villiers, House of Commons, Ottawa ON K1A 0A6, 613/992-6582
Executive Asst., Office of the President, Françoise Ducros, House of Commons, Ottawa ON K1A 0A6, 613/943-1838
**Clerk of the Privy Council & Secretary to the Cabinet**, Jocelyne Bourgon, 613/957-5400, Fax: 613/957-5729
Executive Asst., Marc O'Sullivan, 613/967-5403
Executive Asst., Guylaine Roy, 613/957-5270
Associate Secretary to the Cabinet & Deputy Clerk, Ronald Bilodeau, 613/957-5466, Fax: 613/957-5089
Senior Advisor, Privy Council Office & Coordinator, Security & Intelligence, John Tait, 613/957-5015
Deputy Clerk of the Privy Council & Counsel, Nicole Jauvin, 613/957-5696
Deputy Minister, Intergovernmental Affairs, George Anderson, 613/947-5695
Deputy Secretary to the Cabinet, Intergovernmental Operations, Michel Dorais, 613/957-7571
Deputy Secretary to the Cabinet, Intergovernmental Policy & Communications, Michael Horgan, 613/947-7569
Deputy Secretary to the Cabinet, Operations, Morris Rosenberg, 613/957-5418
Deputy Secretary to the Cabinet, Plans & Consultation, Wayne Wouters, 613/957-5390
Asst. Clerk of the Privy Council, Orders in Council, Michel Garneau, 613/957-5430
Asst. Deputy Minister, Corporate Services, Elisabeth Nadeau, 613/957-5151
Executive Director, Intelligence Assessment, Anthony Campbell, 613/957-5683
Asst. Secretary, Communications & Consultations, Ruth Cardinal, 613/957-5426
Asst. Secretary, Economic & Regional Development Policy, Jack Stagg, 613/957-5368
Asst. Secretary, Foreign & Defence Policy, Jim Bartleman, 613/957-5476
Asst. Secretary, Legislation & House Planning, Suzanne Poirier, 613/957-5792
Asst. Secretary, Liaison Secretariat for Macroeconomic Policy, Patrice Muller, 613/957-5473
Asst. Secretary, Machinery of Government, Vacant, 613/957-5491
Asst. Secretary, Management Priorities & Senior Personnel, David Holdsworth, 613/957-5293
Asst. Secretary, Priorities & Planning, Samy Watson, 613/957-5462
Asst. Secretary, Security & Intelligence, M. Purdy, 613/957-5275
Acting Asst. Secretary, Social Development, Roberta Santi, 613/957-5446

**Privy Council Members Organized by Date Sworn In:**

Privy Council Member, Hon. Walter Edward Harris, Jan. 18, 1950
Privy Council Member, Rt. Hon. John Whitney Pickersgill, June 12, 1953
Privy Council Member, Hon. Paul Theodore Hellyer, Apr. 26, 1957
Privy Council Member, Hon. Edmund Davie Fulton, June 21, 1957
Privy Council Member, Hon. Douglas Scott Harkness, June 21, 1957
Privy Council Member, Rt. Hon. Ellen Louks Fairclough, June 21, 1957
Privy Council Member, Hon. John Angus MacLean, June 21, 1957
Privy Council Member, Hon. Michael Starr, June 21, 1957
Privy Council Member, Rt. Hon. Frances Alvin George Hamilton, Aug. 22, 1957
Privy Council Member, H.R.H. Prince Philip, The Duke of Edinburgh, Oct. 14, 1957
Privy Council Member, Hon. Joseph-Pierre-Albert Sévigny, Aug. 20, 1959
Privy Council Member, Hon. Jacques Flynn, Dec. 28, 1961
Privy Council Member, Hon. Paul Martineau, Aug. 9, 1962
Privy Council Member, Hon. Marcel-Joseph-Aimé Lambert, Feb. 12, 1963
Privy Council Member, Hon. J.H. Théogène Ricard, Mar. 18, 1963
Privy Council Member, Hon. Frank Charles McGee, Mar. 18, 1963
Privy Council Member, Rt. Hon. Martial Asselin, Mar. 18, 1963
Privy Council Member, Hon. Mitchell William Sharp, Apr. 22, 1963
Privy Council Member, Hon. Allan Joseph MacEachen, Apr. 22, 1963
Privy Council Member, Hon. Hédard Robichaud, Apr. 22, 1963
Privy Council Member, Hon. Roger Joseph Teillet, Apr. 22, 1963
Privy Council Member, Hon. Yvon Dupuis, Feb. 3, 1964
Privy Council Member, Hon. Edgar John Benson, June 29, 1964
Privy Council Member, Hon. Léo Alphonse Joseph Cadieux, Feb. 15, 1965
Privy Council Member, Hon. Lawrence T. Pennell, July 7, 1965
Privy Council Member, Hon. Alan Aylesworth Macnaughton, Oct. 25, 1965
Privy Council Member, Hon. Joseph Julien Jean-Pierre Côté, Dec. 18, 1965
Privy Council Member, Rt. Hon. John Napier Turner, Dec. 18, 1965
Privy Council Member, Rt. Hon. Pierre Elliott Trudeau, Apr. 4, 1967
Privy Council Member, Rt. Hon. Jean Chrétien, Apr. 4, 1967
Privy Council Member, Hon. Louis Joseph Robichaud, July 5, 1967
Privy Council Member, Hon. Dufferin Roblin, July 5, 1967
Privy Council Member, Hon. Alexander Bradshaw Campbell, July 5, 1967
Privy Council Member, Rt. Hon. Robert L. Stanfield, July 7, 1967
Privy Council Member, Hon. Bryce Stuart Mackasey, Feb. 9, 1968

Privy Council Member, Hon. Donald Stovel Macdonald, Apr. 20, 1968
Privy Council Member, Hon. Gérard Pelletier, Apr. 20, 1968
Privy Council Member, Hon. Horace Andrew Olson, July 6, 1968
Privy Council Member, Hon. Jean-Eudes Dubé, July 6, 1968
Privy Council Member, Hon. Stanley Ronald Basford, July 6, 1968
Privy Council Member, Hon. Eric William Kierans, July 6, 1968
Privy Council Member, Hon. James Armstrong Richardson, July 6, 1968
Privy Council Member, Hon. Otto Emil Lang, July 6, 1968
Privy Council Member, Hon. Herb Gray, Oct. 20, 1969
Privy Council Member, Hon. Robert Douglas George Stanbury, Oct. 20, 1969
Privy Council Member, Hon. Jean-Pierre Goyer, Dec. 22, 1970
Privy Council Member, Hon. Alastair William Gillespie, Aug. 12, 1971
Privy Council Member, Hon. Martin Patrick O'Connell, Aug. 12, 1971
Privy Council Member, Hon. Patrick Morgan Mahoney, Jan. 28, 1972
Privy Council Member, Hon. Stanley Haidasz, Nov. 27, 1972
Privy Council Member, Hon. W. Warren Allmand, Nov. 27, 1972
Privy Council Member, Hon. James Hugh Faulkner, Nov. 27, 1972
Privy Council Member, Hon. André Ouellet, P.C., Q.C., Nov. 27, 1972
Privy Council Member, Hon. Marc Lalonde, Nov. 27, 1972
Privy Council Member, Hon. Lucien Lamoureux, June 10, 1974
Privy Council Member, Hon. Raymond Joseph Perrault, Aug. 8, 1974
Privy Council Member, Hon. Barnett Jerome Danson, Aug. 8, 1974
Privy Council Member, Hon. J. Judd Buchanan, Aug. 8, 1974
Privy Council Member, Hon. Roméo LeBlanc, Aug. 8, 1974
Privy Council Member, Hon. Muriel McQueen Ferguson, Nov. 7, 1974
Privy Council Member, Hon. Pierre Juneau, Aug. 29, 1975
Privy Council Member, Hon. Marcel Lessard, Sept. 26, 1975
Privy Council Member, Hon. Jack Sidney George Cullen, Sept. 26, 1975
Privy Council Member, Hon. Leonard Stephen Marchand, Sept. 15, 1976
Privy Council Member, Hon. John Roberts, Sept. 15, 1976
Privy Council Member, Hon. Monique Bégin, Sept. 15, 1976
Privy Council Member, Hon. Jean-Jacques Blais, Sept. 15, 1976
Privy Council Member, Hon. Francis Fox, Sept. 15, 1976
Privy Council Member, Hon. Anthony Chisholm Abbott, Sept. 15, 1976
Privy Council Member, Hon. Iona Campagnolo, Sept. 15, 1976
Privy Council Member, Hon. Joseph-Philippe Guay, Nov. 3, 1976
Privy Council Member, Hon. John Henry Horner, Apr. 21, 1977
Privy Council Member, Hon. Norman A. Cafik, Sept. 16, 1977
Privy Council Member, Hon. J. Gilles Lamontagne, Jan. 19, 1978
Privy Council Member, Hon. John M. Reid, Nov. 24, 1978
Privy Council Member, Hon. Pierre De Bané, Nov. 24, 1978
Privy Council Member, Rt. Hon. Charles Joseph Clark, June 4, 1979
Privy Council Member, Hon. Flora Isabel MacDonald, June 4, 1979
Privy Council Member, Hon. James Aloysius McGrath, June 4, 1979
Privy Council Member, Hon. Erik H. Nielsen, June 4, 1979
Privy Council Member, Hon. Allan Frederick Lawrence, June 4, 1979
Privy Council Member, Hon. John Carnell Crosbie, June 4, 1979
Privy Council Member, Hon. David Samuel Horne MacDonald, June 4, 1979
Privy Council Member, Hon. Lincoln MacCauley Alexander, June 4, 1979
Privy Council Member, Hon. Roch La Salle, June 4, 1979
Privy Council Member, Rt. Hon. Donald Frank Mazankowski, June 4, 1979
Privy Council Member, Hon. Elmer MacIntosh MacKay, June 4, 1979
Privy Council Member, Hon. Arthur Jacob Epp, June 4, 1979
Privy Council Member, Hon. John Allen Fraser, June 4, 1979
Privy Council Member, Hon. William H. Jarvis, June 4, 1979
Privy Council Member, Hon. Sinclair McKnight Stevens, June 4, 1979
Privy Council Member, Hon. John Wise, June 4, 1979
Privy Council Member, Hon. Ronald George Atkey, June 4, 1979
Privy Council Member, Rt. Hon. Ramon John Hnatyshyn, June 4, 1979
Privy Council Member, Hon. David Crombie, June 4, 1979
Privy Council Member, Hon. Robert René de Cotret, June 4, 1979
Privy Council Member, Hon. William Heward Grafftey, June 4, 1979
Privy Council Member, Hon. Perrin Beatty, June 4, 1979
Privy Council Member, Hon. J. Robert Howie, June 4, 1979
Privy Council Member, Hon. Arthur Ronald Huntington, June 4, 1979
Privy Council Member, Hon. Michael Holocombe Wilson, June 4, 1979
Privy Council Member, Hon. Renaude Lapointe, Nov. 30, 1979
Privy Council Member, Hon. Gerald Regan, Mar. 3, 1980
Privy Council Member, Hon. Mark R. MacGuigan, Mar. 3, 1980
Privy Council Member, Hon. Robert Phillip Kaplan, Mar. 3, 1980
Privy Council Member, Hon. James Sydney Fleming, Mar. 3, 1980
Privy Council Member, Hon. William H. Rompkey, Mar. 3, 1980
Privy Council Member, Hon. Pierre Bussières, Mar. 3, 1980
Privy Council Member, Hon. Charles Lapointe, Mar. 3, 1980
Privy Council Member, Hon. Edward C. Lumley, Mar. 3, 1980
Privy Council Member, Hon. Yvon Pinard, Mar. 3, 1980
Privy Council Member, Hon. Donald James Johnston, Mar. 3, 1980
Privy Council Member, Hon. Lloyd Axworthy, Mar. 3, 1980
Privy Council Member, Hon. Paul James Cosgrove, Mar. 3, 1980
Privy Council Member, Hon. Judith A. Erola, Mar. 3, 1980
Privy Council Member, Hon. James A. Jerome, Feb. 16, 1981
Privy Council Member, Hon. Jacob Austin, Sept. 22, 1981
Privy Council Member, Hon. Charles L. Caccia, Sept. 22, 1981
Privy Council Member, Hon. Serge Joyal, Sept. 22, 1981
Privy Council Member, Hon. W. Bennett Campbell, Sept. 22, 1981
Privy Council Member, Hon. Robert Gordon Robertson, Mar. 2, 1982
Privy Council Member, Hon. John Edward Broadbent, Apr. 17, 1982
Privy Council Member, Hon. William Grenville Davis, Apr. 17, 1982
Privy Council Member, Hon. Allan Emrys Blakeney, Apr. 17, 1982
Privy Council Member, Hon. E. Peter Lougheed, Apr. 17, 1982
Privy Council Member, Hon. William Richards Bennett, Apr. 17, 1982
Privy Council Member, Hon. John MacLennan Buchanan, Apr. 17, 1982
Privy Council Member, Hon. Alfred Brian Peckford, Apr. 17, 1982
Privy Council Member, Hon. James Matthew Lee, Apr. 17, 1982
Privy Council Member, Hon. Howard Russell Pawley, Apr. 17, 1982
Privy Council Member, Hon. Sterling Rufus Lyon, Apr. 17, 1982
Privy Council Member, Hon. David Michael Collenette, Aug 12, 1983
Privy Council Member, Hon. Céline Hervieux-Payette, Aug. 12, 1983
Privy Council Member, Hon. Roger Simmons, Aug. 12, 1983
Privy Council Member, Hon. David Paul Smith, Aug. 12, 1983
Privy Council Member, Hon. Roy MacLaren, Aug. 17, 1983
Privy Council Member, Rt. Hon. Robert George Brian Dickson, Apr. 19, 1984
Privy Council Member, Hon. Robert B. Bryce, Apr. 19, 1984
Privy Council Member, Hon. Peter Michael Pitfield, Apr. 19, 1984
Privy Council Member, Rt. Hon. Martin Brian Mulroney, May 7, 1984
Privy Council Member, Rt. Hon. Edward Richard Schreyer, June 3, 1984
Privy Council Member, Hon. Herb Breau, June 30, 1984
Privy Council Member, Hon. Joseph Roger Rémi Bujold, June 30, 1984
Privy Council Member, Hon. Jean-C. Lapierre, June 30, 1984
Privy Council Member, Hon. Ralph Ferguson, June 30, 1984
Privy Council Member, Hon. Douglas Cockburn Firth, June 30, 1984
Privy Council Member, Hon. Robert Carman Coates, Sept. 17, 1984
Privy Council Member, Hon. Jack Burnett Murta, Sept. 17, 1984
Privy Council Member, Hon. Harvie Andre, Sept. 17, 1984
Privy Council Member, Hon. Otto John Jelinek, Sept. 17, 1984
Privy Council Member, Hon. Charles James Mayer, Sept. 17, 1984
Privy Council Member, Hon. Thomas Edward Siddon, Sept. 17, 1984
Privy Council Member, Hon. William Hunter McKnight, Sept. 17, 1984

Privy Council Member, Hon. Walter Franklin McLean, Sept. 17, 1984
Privy Council Member, Hon. Thomas Michael McMillan, Sept. 17, 1984
Privy Council Member, Hon. Patricia Carney, Sept. 17, 1984
Privy Council Member, Hon. André Bissonnette, Sept. 17, 1984
Privy Council Member, Hon. Suzanne Blais-Grenier, Sept. 17, 1984
Privy Council Member, Hon. Benoît Bouchard, Sept. 17, 1984
Privy Council Member, Hon. Andrée Champagne, Sept. 17, 1984
Privy Council Member, Hon. Michel Côté, Sept. 17, 1984
Privy Council Member, Hon. James Francis Kelleher, Sept 17, 1984
Privy Council Member, Hon. Robert E.J. Layton, Sept. 17, 1984
Privy Council Member, Hon. Marcel Masse, Sept. 17, 1984
Privy Council Member, Hon. Barbara Jean McDougall, Sept. 17, 1984
Privy Council Member, Hon. Gerald Stairs Merrithew, Sept. 17, 1984
Privy Council Member, Hon. Monique Vézina, Sept. 17, 1984
Privy Council Member, Hon. Maurice Riel, Nov. 30, 1984
Privy Council Member, Hon. Cyril Lloyd Francis, Nov. 30, 1984
Privy Council Member, Hon. Saul Mark Cherniack, Nov. 30, 1984
Privy Council Member, Hon. Paule Gauthier, P.C., Q.C., Nov. 30, 1984
Privy Council Member, Hon. Lloyd Roseville Crouse, June 10, 1985
Privy Council Member, Hon. Stewart Donald McInnes, Aug. 20, 1985
Privy Council Member, Hon. Frank Oberle, Nov. 20, 1985
Privy Council Member, Hon. Gordon Francis Joseph Osbaldeston, Feb. 13, 1986
Privy Council Member, Hon. Lowell Murray, June 30, 1986
Privy Council Member, Hon. Paul Wyatt Dick, June 30, 1986
Privy Council Member, Hon. Pierre H. Cadieux, June 30, 1986
Privy Council Member, Hon. Jean Charest, June 30, 1986
Privy Council Member, Hon. Thomas Hockin, June 30, 1986
Privy Council Member, Hon. Monique Landry, June 30, 1986
Privy Council Member, Hon. Bernard Valcourt, June 30, 1986
Privy Council Member, Hon. Gerry Weiner, June 30, 1986
Privy Council Member, Hon. John William Bosley, June 30, 1987
Privy Council Member, Hon. Douglas Grinslade Lewis, Aug. 27, 1987
Privy Council Member, Hon. Pierre Blais, Aug. 27, 1986
Privy Council Member, Hon. Lucien Bouchard, Mar. 31, 1988
Privy Council Member, Hon. Gerry St. Germain, Mar. 31, 1988
Privy Council Member, Hon. John H. McDermid, Sept. 15, 1988
Privy Council Member, Hon. Shirley Martin, Sept. 15, 1988
Privy Council Member, Hon. Mary Collins, Jan. 30, 1989
Privy Council Member, Hon. Alan Redway, Jan. 30, 1989
Privy Council Member, Hon. William Charles Winegard, Jan. 30, 1989
Privy Council Member, Rt. Hon. A. Kim Campbell, Jan. 30, 1989
Privy Council Member, Hon. Jean Corbeil, Jan. 30, 1989
Privy Council Member, Hon. Gilles Loiselle, Jan. 30, 1989
Privy Council Member, Hon. John White Hughes Bassett, Nov. 30, 1989
Privy Council Member, Hon. Marcel Danis, Feb. 23, 1990
Privy Council Member, Rt. Hon. Joseph Antonio Charles Lamer, July 3, 1990
Privy Council Member, Hon. Audrey McLaughlin, Jan. 10, 1991
Privy Council Member, Hon. Pauline Browes, Apr. 21, 1991
Privy Council Member, Hon. Edmond Jacques Courtois, Dec. 5, 1991
Privy Council Member, Hon. J.J. Michel Robert, Dec. 5, 1991
Privy Council Member, Hon. Marcel Prud'homme, July 1, 1992
Privy Council Member, Hon. William C. Scott, July 1, 1992
Privy Council Member, Lorne Edmund Nystrom, July 1, 1992
Privy Council Member, Hon. Gerhard Herzberg, July 1, 1992
Privy Council Member, Hon. Arthur Tremblay, July 1, 1992
Privy Council Member, Hon. David Alexander Colville, July 1, 1992
Privy Council Member, Hon. Paul Desmarais, July 1, 1992
Privy Council Member, Hon. John Charles Polanyi, July 1, 1992
Privy Council Member, Hon. Maurice F. Strong, July 1, 1992
Privy Council Member, Hon. Antonine Maillet, July 1, 1992
Privy Council Member, Hon. Rita Joe, July 1, 1992
Privy Council Member, Hon. James Bourque, July 1, 1992
Privy Council Member, Hon. Richard Cashin, July 1, 1992
Privy Council Member, Hon. Paul M. Tellier, July 1, 1992
Privy Council Member, Hon. Patricia Helen Rogers, July 1, 1992
Privy Council Member, Hon. David Robert Peterson, July 1, 1992
Privy Council Member, Hon. Conrad M. Black, July 1, 1992
Privy Council Member, Hon. Charles Rosner Bronfman, Oct. 21, 1992
Privy Council Member, Hon. Maurice Richard, Oct. 30, 1992
Privy Council Member, Hon. William Ormond Mitchell, Nov. 5, 1992
Privy Council Member, Hon. Edwin A. Goodman, Nov. 30, 1992
Privy Council Member, Hon. George W. Vari, Dec. 23, 1992
Privy Council Member, Hon. Pierre H. Vincent, Jan. 4, 1993
Privy Council Member, Hon. Rosemary Brown, Apr. 20, 1993
Privy Council Member, Hon. James Stewart Edwards, June 25, 1993
Privy Council Member, Hon. Robert Douglas Nicholson, June 25, 1993
Privy Council Member, Hon. Barbara Jane Sparrow, June 25, 1993
Privy Council Member, Hon. Peter L. McCreath, June 25, 1993
Privy Council Member, Hon. Ian Angus Ross Reid, June 25, 1993
Privy Council Member, Hon. Larry Schneider, June 25, 1993
Privy Council Member, Hon. Garth Turner, June 25, 1993
Privy Council Member, Hon. David Anderson, Nov. 4, 1993
Privy Council Member, Hon. Ralph Goodale, Nov. 4, 1993
Privy Council Member, Hon. David Charle Dingwall, Nov. 4, 1993
Privy Council Member, Hon. Ron Irwin, Nov. 4, 1993
Privy Council Member, Hon. Brian Tobin, Nov. 4, 1993
Privy Council Member, Hon. Joyce Fairbairn, Nov. 4, 1993
Privy Council Member, Hon. Sheila Maureen Copps, Nov. 4, 1993
Privy Council Member, Hon. Sergio Marchi, Nov. 4, 1993
Privy Council Member, Hon. John Manley, Nov. 4, 1993
Privy Council Member, Hon. Diane Marleau, Nov. 4, 1993
Privy Council Member, Hon. Paul Martin, Nov. 4, 1993
Privy Council Member, Hon. Douglas Young, Nov. 4, 1993
Privy Council Member, Michel Dupuy, Nov. 4, 1993
Privy Council Member, Hon. Art Eggleton, Nov. 4, 1993
Privy Council Member, Hon. Marcel Massé, Nov. 4, 1993
Privy Council Member, Hon. Anne McLellen, Nov. 4, 1993
Privy Council Member, Hon. Allan Rock, Q.C., Nov. 4, 1993
Privy Council Member, Hon. Sheila Finestone, Nov. 4, 1993
Privy Council Member, Hon. Fernand Robichaud, Nov. 4, 1993
Privy Council Member, Hon. Ethel Blondin-Andrew, Nov. 4, 1993
Privy Council Member, Hon. Lawrence MacAulay, Nov. 4, 1993
Privy Council Member, Hon. Christine Stewart, Nov. 4, 1993
Privy Council Member, Hon. Raymond Chan, Nov. 4, 1993
Privy Council Member, Hon. Jon Gerrard, Nov. 4, 1993
Privy Council Member, Hon. Doug Peters, Nov. 4, 1993
Privy Council Member, Hon. Alfonso Gagliano, Sept. 15, 1994
Privy Council Member, Hon. Lucienne Robillard, Feb. 22, 1995
Privy Council Member, Hon. Fred J. Mifflin, Jan. 25, 1996
Privy Council Member, Hon. Jane Stewart, Jan. 25, 1996
Privy Council Member, Hon. Stéphane Dion, Jan. 25, 1996
Privy Council Member, Hon. Pierre S. Pettigrew, Jan. 25, 1996
Privy Council Member, Hon. Martin Cauchon, Jan. 25, 1996
Privy Council Member, Hon. Hedy Fry, Jan. 25, 1996
Privy Council Member, Hon. Don Boudria, Oct. 4, 1996
Privy Council Member, Hon. Guy Charbonneau, Oct. 17, 1996
Privy Council Member, Hon. Alasdair B. Graham, June 11, 1997
Privy Council Member, Hon. Lyle Vanclief, June 11, 1997
Privy Council Member, Hon. Harbance Singh Dhaliwal, June 11, 1997
Privy Council Member, Hon. Andy Scott, June 11, 1997
Privy Council Member, Hon. David Kilgour, June 11, 1997

Privy Council Member, Hon. Jim Peterson, June 11, 1997
Privy Council Member, Hon. Ronald J. Duhamel, June 11, 1997
Privy Council Member, Hon. Andy Mitchell, June 11, 1997
Privy Council Member, Hon. Gilbert Normand, June 18, 1997

#### Associated Agencies, Boards & Commissions

•Office of Intergovernmental Affairs
Listed alphabetically in detail, this section.

## SENATE OF CANADA/Sénat du Canada

Senate Bldg., 111 Wellington St., Ottawa ON K1A 0A4
613/992-1149; Fax: 613/995-4998; URL: http://www.parl.gc.ca/36/senmemb/senate/bio-e/bio-e.htm
Toll Free: 1-800-267-7362

*Senators* are appointed by the Governor General on the recommendation of the Prime Minister of Canada. Senators appointed prior to 2nd June 1965 hold their positions for life, but those appointed after that date hold their positions only until they attain the age of seventy-five years.

To be eligible for appointment, a senatorial candidate must be a Canadian citizen, or a British subject, and be at least thirty years of age. He must own real property worth a net of $4,000 in the province he represents and he must be worth at least $4,000 over and above all debts. He must be a resident of the province for which he was appointed or if he is appointed for Québec, he must either own his real property qualification or else be a resident in the electoral division for which he is appointed.

The *Speaker* of the Senate is appointed by the Governor General also on the recommendation of the Prime Minister.

The *Senate* can initiate any bills except those providing for expenditure of public money or imposing taxes. Although it can amend or reject any bill, it has seldom had to do either. No bill may become law unless it is passed by the Senate.

The main thrust of the Senate's work is carried out in committees, where bills are interpreted & reviewed clause by clause, & evidence is heard from groups & individuals who may be affected by the particular bill under review.

In recent decades, the Senate has begun examining major public concerns within Canada (including inflation, land use, international relations, unemployment, government efficiency). The Senate reports produced from such studies have proved to be valuable & less expensive than royal commissions or task forces, & have often led to changes in government policy or legislation. The Speaker of the Senate is appointed by the Governor General upon the recommendation of the Prime Minister. It is tradition to alternate between English-speaking & French-speaking selections as Speaker of the Senate.

#### Organization of the Senate

The Senate as originally constituted at Confederation consisted of 72 members. Through the addition of new provinces and the general growth of Canada it now has 104 regular members.

By provinces, representation is as follows:
Alta. 5; B.C. 6; Man. 6; N.B. 10; N.S. 10; N.W.T. 1; Nfld. 6; Ont. 24; P.E.I. 4; Qué. 24; Sask. 6; Yukon 1; Total 104.

By party affiliation, representation is as follows (September 22, 1997):
Lib. 52; PC 47; Ind. 3; Vacant 1; Total 103

**Speaker of the Senate**, Hon. Gildas L. Molgat, 613/992-4416
Government Leader, Hon. B. Alasdair Graham, 613/992-3770
Opposition Leader, Hon. John Lynch-Staunton, 613/943-1481
Government Whip, Hon. Jacques Hébert, 613/992-3756
Opposition Whip, Hon. Noel Kinsella, 613/943-0753

#### Officers of the Senate

**Clerk & Parliament Clerk**, Paul Bélisle, 613/992-2493
Clerk's Assistant, Richard G. Greene, 613/996-0397
Law Clerk & Parliamentary Counsel, Mark Audcent, 613/992-2416
Gentleman Usher of the Black Rod, Vacant, 613/992-8483
Director, Committees, Gary O'Brien, 613/990-0088
Director, Finance, Siroun Aghajanian, 613/992-7951
Director, Human Resources, Suzanne Beaudoin, 613/996-1096
Senior Asst. Editor, Debates, Jeanie Morrison, 613/996-0854
Communications Officer, Communications, Colette O'Brien, 613/992-1149

#### Senators with appointment year, political affiliation & phone no.

Senator, Hon. Willie Adams, 1977, Lib., 613/992-2753
Senator, Hon. Raynell Andreychuk, 1993, PC, 613/947-2239
Senator, Hon. David W. Angus, 1993, PC, 613/947-3193
Senator, Hon. Norman K. Atkins, 1986, PC, 613/992-7172
Senator, Hon. Jack Austin, 1975, Lib., 613/992-1437
Senator, Hon. Lise Bacon, 1994, Lib., 613/995-6194
Senator, Hon. James Balfour, 1979, PC, 613/995-2864
Senator, Hon. Marisa Ferrati Barth, 1997, Lib.
Senator, Hon. Gérald Beaudoin, 1988, PC, 613/995-6128
Senator, Hon. Eric Arthur Berntson, 1990, PC, 613/743-1424
Senator, Hon. Roch Bolduc, 1988, PC, 613/995-6185
Senator, Hon. M. Lorne Bonnell, 1971, Lib., 613/996-0370
Senator, Hon. Peter Bosa, 1977, Lib., 613/995-7235
Senator, Hon. John Bryden, 1994, Lib., 613/947-7305
Senator, Hon. John Buchanan, 1990, PC, 613/943-1409
Senator, Hon. Sr. Mary Alice (Peggy) Butts, 1997, Lib., 613/943-0695
Senator, Hon. Catherine Callbeck, 1997, Lib., 613/943-0686
Senator, Hon. Patricia Carney, 1990, PC, 613/943-1433
Senator, Hon. Sharon Carstairs, 1994, Lib., 613/947-7123
Senator, Hon. Ethel Cochrane, 1986, PC, 613/992-1577
Senator, Hon. Michel Cogger, 1986, PC, 613/992-2974
Senator, Hon. Erminie J. Cohen, 1993, PC, 613/947-3187
Senator, Hon. Gérald Joseph Comeau, 1990, PC, 613/934-1448
Senator, Hon. Anne C. Cools, 1984, Lib., 613/992-2808
Senator, Hon. Eymard Corbin, 1984, Lib., 613/996-8485
Senator, Hon. Pierre De Bané, 1984, Lib., 613/992-8289
Senator, Hon. Mabel Margaret DeWare, 1990, PC, 613/943-0759
Senator, Hon. Consiglio Di Nino, 1990, PC, 613/943-1454
Senator, Hon. C. William Doody, 1979, PC, 613/995-1144
Senator, Hon. Richard J. Doyle, 1985, PC, 613/995-7287
Senator, Hon. John Trevor Eyton, 1990, PC, 613/943-1460
Senator, Hon. Joyce Fairbairn, 1984, Lib., 613/996-4382
Senator, Hon. Jean B. Forest, 1996, Lib., 613/992-0648
Senator, Hon. J. Michael Forrestall, 1990, PC, 613/943-1442
Senator, Hon. Jean-Robert Gauthier, 1994, Lib., 613/947-7536
Senator, Hon. Ronald D. Ghitter, 1993, PC, 613/947-2220
Senator, Hon. Philippe D. Gigantès, 1984, Lib., 613/992-2852
Senator, Hon. Jerahmiel S. Grafstein, 1984, Lib., 613/992-2642
Senator, Hon. B. Alasdair Graham, 1972, Lib., 613/992-3770
Senator, Hon. Normand Grimard, 1990, PC, 613/943-1419
Senator, Hon. Leonard J. Gustafson, 1993, PC, 613/947-2233
Senator, Hon. Stanley Haidasz, 1978, Lib., 613/992-2713
Senator, Hon. Daniel Hays, 1984, Lib., 613/996-3485
Senator, Hon. Jacques Hébert, 1983, Lib., 613/992-3756
Senator, Hon. Céline Hervieux-Payette, 1995, Lib., 613/947-8008
Senator, Hon. Duncan J. Jessiman, 1993, PC, 613/947-2230
Senator, Hon. Janis Johnson, 1990, PC, 613/943-1430
Senator, Hon. James Kelleher, 1990, PC, 613/943-0762
Senator, Hon. William M. Kelly, 1982, PC, 613/992-0081
Senator, Hon. Colin Kenny, 1984, Lib., 613/996-2877
Senator, Hon. Wilbert Joseph Keon, 1990, PC, 613/943-1415
Senator, Hon. Noel Kinsella, 1990, PC, 613/943-0753
Senator, Hon. Michael Kirby, 1984, Lib., 613/992-2976
Senator, Hon. Leo Kolber, 1983, Lib., 613/992-2690
Senator, Hon. Thérèse Lavoie-Roux, 1990, PC, 613/943-1427
Senator, Hon. Edward M. Lawson, 1970, Ind., 613/996-5453
Senator, Hon. Marjory LeBreton, 1993, PC, 613/943-0756
Senator, Hon. P. Derek Lewis, 1978, Lib., 613/995-0765
Senator, Hon. Rose-Marie Losier-Cool, 1995, Lib., 613/947-8011
Senator, Hon. Paul Lucier, 1975, Lib., 613/992-2568
Senator, Hon. John Lynch-Staunton, 1990, PC, 613/943-1481
Senator, Hon. Finlay MacDonald, 1984, PC, 613/995-2150
Senator, Hon. Shirley Maheu, 1996, Lib., 613/947-2212
Senator, Hon. Len Marchand, 1984, Lib., 613/996-7282
Senator, Hon. Michael Arthur Meighen, 1990, PC, 613/943-1421
Senator, Hon. Leonce Mercier, 1996, Lib., 613/996-5620
Senator, Hon. Lorne Milne, 1995, Lib., 613/947-7695
Senator, Hon. Gildas L. Molgat, 1970, Lib., 613/992-4416
Senator, Hon. Wilfrid P. Moore, 1996, Lib., 613/947-1921
Senator, Hon. Lowell Murray, 1979, PC, 613/995-2407
Senator, Hon. Pierre-Claude Nolin, 1993, PC, 613/943-1451
Senator, Hon. Donald Oliver, 1990, PC, 613/943-1445
Senator, Hon. Gerald R. Ottenheimer, 1987, PC, 613/996-9389
Senator, Hon. Landon Pearson, 1994, Lib., 613/947-7134
Senator, Hon. Lucie Pépin, Lib.
Senator, Hon. Raymond J. Perrault, 1973, Lib., 613/992-2682
Senator, Hon. William J. Petten, 1968, Lib., 613/992-4294
Senator, Hon. Orville H. Phillips, 1963, PC, 613/992-5432
Senator, Hon. P.M. Pitfield, 1982, Ind., 613/992-2784
Senator, Hon. Marie-P. Poulin, 1995, Lib., 613/947-8005
Senator, Hon. Marcel Prud'homme, 1993, Ind., 613/947-2227
Senator, Hon. Maurice Riel, 1973, Lib., 613/996-9164
Senator, Hon. Jean-Claude Rivest, 1993, PC, 613/947-2236
Senator, Hon. Fernand Roberge, 1993, PC, 613/947-3250
Senator, Hon. Brenda M. Robertson, 1984, PC, 613/998-5585

Senator, Hon. Fernand Robichaud, 1997, Lib., 613/943-0675
Senator, Hon. Louis J. Robichaud, 1973, Lib., 613/996-4134
Senator, Hon. William Romkey, 1995, Lib., 613/947-9584
Senator, Hon. Eileen Rossiter, 1986, PC, 613/992-1650
Senator, Hon. Gerry St. Germain, 1993, PC, 613/947-2242
Senator, Hon. Marisa B. Sarretti, 1976, PC, 613/943-0679
Senator, Hon. Jean-Maurice Simard, 1985, PC, 613/995-0925
Senator, Hon. Herbert O. Sparrow, 1968, Lib., 613/996-5994
Senator, Hon. Mira Spivak, 1986, PC, 613/995-1488
Senator, Hon. Richard J. Stanbury, 1968, Lib., 613/992-6981
Senator, Hon. John B. Stewart, 1984, Lib., 613/992-2751
Senator, Hon. Peter Stollery, 1981, Lib., 613/992-3012
Senator, Hon. Terrance R. Stratton, 1993, PC, 613/947-2224
Senator, Hon. Nicholas W. Taylor, 1996, Lib., 613/947-1605
Senator, Hon. Andrew Thompson, 1967, Lib., 613/992-1306
Senator, Hon. David Tkachuk, 1993, PC, 613/947-3196
Senator, Hon. Charlie Watt, 1984, Lib., 613/992-2981
Senator, Hon. Dalia Wood, 1979, Lib., 613/992-3161

## HOUSE OF COMMONS, CANADA/Chambre des communes

House of Commons, 111 Wellington St., PO Box 1103, Ottawa ON K1A 0A9
URL: http://www.parl.gc.ca; gopher.parl.gc.ca/
Public Information Office:, 111 Wellington St., Ottawa ON K1A 0A6
613/992-4793, Fax: 613/992-1273
TDD: 613/995-2266

The House of Commons is the major law-making unit in Canada. The 301 members of the House represent each constituency, or riding, across Canada. Members are elected in general elections, held at least once every five years. During general elections one candidate per riding is elected, based on the largest number of votes, even if his or her vote is less than half the total. When a member resigns or dies between general elections, a by-election is held.

The party that wins the largest number of seats in the general election usually forms the government. The party with the second largest number of votes becomes the *Official Opposition*. If the government prior to a general election, comes out of the election without a clear majority, it has the right to meet the new House of Commons & determine whether it can develop enough support from the minor parties to give it a majority.

A *minority government* is created when one particular party holds no clear majority of seats in the House. In this case, the government is usually led by the party with the most seats in Parliament, providing it can sustain the support from other minor parties that enable it to pass legislation.

Any bills within federal jurisdiction must be passed by a majority of House members to become law. Members usually vote on proposed legislation according to party affiliation. They may vote against their party & may also leave their elected party to sit as an independent within the House.

The *Speaker* of the House of Commons is elected after each general election through a secret ballot process within the Commons Chamber. The person elected as Speaker must be a member of the House of Commons & is expected to be an impartial, nonpartisan & firm controller of all questions & procedures within it's confines. If the Speaker elected is an English-speaking member, it is customary that a French-speaking member be chosen as the Deputy Speaker.

**Speaker of the House**, Hon. Gilbert Parent, 613/992-5042
Deputy Speaker & Deputy Chairman, Committees of the Whole House, Ian McClelland
Deputy Speaker, Peter Milliken
Asst. Deputy Chair, Committees of the Whole House, Yolande Thibeault
Government Whip, Bob Kilger
Bloc Québécois Party Whip, Madeleine Dalphond-Guiral
Reform Party Whip, Chuck Strahl
NDP Party Whip, John Solomon
PC Party Whip, Vacant

#### House of Commons Staff

**Clerk of the House**, Robert Marleau, 613/992-2986
Deputy Clerk, Mary Anne Griffith, 613/996-0485
General Legal Counsel, Legal Services, Diane Davidson, 613/992-1511
Comptroller, John McCrae, 613/992-0100
Director General, Human Resources, Jacques Sabourin, 613/992-9721
Director, Information Systems, Louis Bard, 613/992-7363
Director General, Information Technologies, R.J. Desramaux, 613/992-1459
Director, Parliamentary Publications, A. Dambraskas, 613/992-2419
Director, Personnel Operations, Rose Bussière, 613/996-7883
Director, Program Evaluation & Review, L. McRae, 613/995-0224
Chief, Broadcasting Service, Philippe Parent, 613/995-3490

#### Parliamentary Precinct Services

Sergeant-at-Arms, Maj.-Gen. M.G. Cloutier, 613/995-7521
Director, Building Services, K.R. Macquarrie, 613/995-1990
Director, Security Services, Denis Gagnon, 613/995-7020

#### Procedural Services

Clerk Asst., Camille Montpetit, 613/995-5990
Principal Clerk, House Proceedings & Parliamentary Exchanges, William Corbett, 613/996-3611
Acting Deputy Principal Clerk, Parliamentary Exchanges & Protocol, Carol Chafe, 613/996-1102
Director, Committees & Parliamentary Associations & General Legislative Counsel, R.R. Walsh, 613/992-3150

### COMMITTEES OF THE HOUSE OF COMMONS

Following is a list of Standing Committees as set out in the Standing Orders. Each committee has between seven and 15 members except the Standing Committee on Procedure & House Affairs (formerly the Standing Committee on House Management) which consists of 14 members. The committee also acts as the Striking Committee.

There are also three Standing Joint Committees: Scrutiny of Regulations, Library of Parliament and Official Languages.

Committee members change frequently. Contact the Public Information Office listed above for an up-to-date list.

#### Standing Committees of the House

Aboriginal Affairs & Northern Development
Agriculture & Agri-Food
Canadian Heritage
Citizenship & Immigration
Environment & Sustainable Development
Finance
Fisheries & Oceans
Foreign Affairs & International Trade
Government Operations
Health
Human Resources Development
Human Rights & the Status of Persons with Disabilities
Industry
Justice & Legal Affairs
National Defence & Veterans Affairs
Natural Resources
Procedure & House Affairs
Public Accounts
Transport

## OFFICE OF THE PRIME MINISTER (LIB.)/ Cabinet du Premier ministre

#309-S, Centre Block, House of Commons, 111 Wellington St., Ottawa ON K1A 0A2
613/992-4211; Fax: 613/941-6900; Email: pm@pm.gc.ca; URL: http://pm.gc.ca/

The Prime Minister is the Head of Government in Canada & usually the leader of the party in power in the House of Commons. The Prime Minister recommends to the monarchy, the appointment of the Governor General & is responsible for selecting a team of ministers, who are then appointed by the Governor General to the Queen's Privy Council. In addition, he or she also controls the appointment of cabinet ministers, senators, judges & parliamentary secretaries. It is customary that the Prime Minister is also appointed to the Imperial Privy Council & is thus titled "The Right Honourable". The Prime Minister has the right to dissolve parliament & can therefore control the timing of general elections.

**Prime Minister/Premier ministre**, Rt. Hon. Jean Chrétien
Chief of Staff, Jean Pelletier, 613/957-5517
Senior Policy Advisor, Eddie Goldenberg, 613/957-5788
Executive Asst., Bruce Hartley, 613/957-5549
Legislative Asst., Graeme Clark, 613/957-5080
Director, Appointments, Vacant
Director, Communications, Peter Donolo, 613/957-5555
Director, Operations, Jean Carle, 613/957-5520
Director, Policy & Research, Chaviva Hosek, 613/957-5566
Press Secretary, Patrick Parisot, 613/957-5555
Manager, Correspondence, Mark Stokes, 613/957-5561
Manager, Finance, Personnel & Administration, Ray Monnot, 613/957-5564
Chief House Leader, Hon. Herb Gray, 613/995-7548
Chief Party Whip, Bob Kilger
Senior Deputy Whip, Marlene Catterall

### OFFICE OF THE DEPUTY PRIME MINISTER

Langevin Block, 80 Wellington St., Ottawa ON K1A 0A3
613/997-1441
Deputy Prime Minister, Hon. Herb Gray, 613/995-7548, Fax: 613/952-2240

## OFFICE OF THE LEADER, OPPOSITION, REFORM PARTY (REF.)

#409-S, Centre Block, House of Commons, 111 Wellington St., Ottawa ON K1A 0A6
613/996-6740; Fax: 613/947-0310; Email: info@reform.ca; URL: http://www.reform.ca
Toll Free: 1-888-REFORM-1
National Office Email: national-office@reform.ca
Reform Question Period Hotline Email: hotline@reform.ca
Membership Email: membership@reform.ca
Calgary Office: #600, 833 - 4 Ave. SW, Calgary AB T2P 0K5
403/269-1990, Fax: 403/269-4077

**Leader of the Reform Party**, Preston Manning, Email: pmanning@reform.ca

Chair, Caucus, Deborah Grey, Email: grey@reform.ca

House Leader, Randy White, Email: whiter@reform.ca

Deputy House Leader, Ken Epp, Email: epp@reform.ca

Coordinator, Question Period, Jim Hart, Email: hart@reform.ca

Chief Party Whip, Chuck Strahl, Email: strahl@reform.ca

Deputy Opposition Whip, Jay Hill, Email: hillj@reform.ca

Chair, Public Accounts Committee, John Williams, Email: williams@reform.ca

Chair, Scrutiny of Regulations Committee & Democratic Reform Critic, Ted White, Email: whitet@reform.ca

Special Projects, John Cummins, Email: cummins@reform.ca

## OFFICE OF THE LEADER, BLOC QUÉBÉCOIS (BQ)

#502-S, Centre Block, House of Commons, 111 Wellington St., Ottawa ON K1A 0A6

613/996-6779; Fax: 613/954-2121; URL: http://blocquebecois.org/

Montréal Office: #1475, 425, de Maisonneuve ouest, Montréal QC H3A 3G5

514/499-3000, Fax: 514/499-3638

Toll Free: 1-800-267-2562

**Leader of the Bloc Québécois**, Gilles Duceppe

Chief Party Whip, Stéphane Bergeron

Deputy Leader, Vacant, 613/995-7398

Director, Cabinet & Chief of Staff, Gilbert Charland, 613/996-6740

Senior Policy Advisor, Pierre-Paul Roy, 613/996-6740

## OFFICE OF THE LEADER, NEW DEMOCRATIC PARTY (NDP)

#900, 81 Metcalfe St., Ottawa ON K1P 6K7

613/236-3613; Fax: 613/230-9950; Email: ndpadmin@fed.ndp.ca; URL: http://www.fed.ndp.ca/fndp

**Leader of the New Democratic Party**, Alexa McDonough, Email: ndpadmin@fed.ndp.ca

New Democratic Party House Leader, William (Bill) Blaikie, #214, West Block, House of Commons, Ottawa ON K1A 0A6, 613/995-6339, Fax: 613/995-6688, Email: blaikb@parl.gc.ca

New Democratic Party Whip, John Solomon, 724 Confederation Bldg., House of Commons, Ottawa ON K1A 0A6, 613/992-4573, Fax: 613/996-6885, Email: solomj@parl.gc.ca

Principal Secretary, Dan O'Connor

## OFFICE OF THE LEADER, PROGRESSIVE CONSERVATIVE PARTY (PC)

#436-N, Centre Block, House of Commons, 111 Wellington St., Ottawa ON K1A 0A6

613/943-1106; Fax: 613/995-0364; URL: http://www.ncf.carleton.ca/freeport/government/fedelect/nat/pc/menu

**Leader, Progressive Conservative Party**, Hon. Jean Charest

National Director, Michael Allen

National President, Pierre Fortier

Chief of Staff, Janice Charette

Press Secretary, Rita Mezzanotte

Legislative Asst., Jessie Chauhan

Scheduling Asst., Danielle Labossière

Constituency Asst., Suzanne Poulin

Special Asst., Francine Carrier

Caucus Liaison, Chad Schella

## THE CANADIAN MINISTRY/The Cabinet

c/o Public Information Office, Library of Parliament, House of Commons, 111 Wellington St., Ottawa ON K1A 0A9

613/992-4793; Fax: 613/992-1273; URL: http://canada.gc.ca/howgoc/cab/cabind_e.html

The Canadian Ministry, or Cabinet, is the most significant of all federal government committees or councils. Cabinet members are selected & led by the Prime Minister, they must also be or become members of the Queen's Privy Council. Cabinet ministers determine specific policies & are responsible for them in the House of Commons. The Cabinet is responsible for initiating all public bills in the House of Commons, & in some instances can create regulations that have the strength of law, termed decisions of the Governor-in-Council.

Cabinet meetings are usually closed to the public, allowing members to discuss their opinions on particular policy in secret. Once decided, members usually support all policy uniformly. If a minister is unable to support the Ministry, he or she is obligated to resign.

Prime Minister, Rt. Hon. Jean Chrétien, #309-S, Centre Block, House of Commons, Ottawa ON K1A 0A6, 613/992-4211, Fax: 613/941-6900, Email: pm@pm.gc.ca

Minister, Fisheries & Oceans, Hon. David Anderson, #133, East Block, House of Commons, Ottawa ON K1A 0A6, 613/996-2358, Fax: 613/957-8844, Dept.: 613/992-3474; Fax: 613/990-7292

Minister, Foreign Affairs, Hon. Lloyd Axworthy, #418-N, Centre Block, House of Commons, Ottawa ON K1A 0A6, 613/995-0153, Fax: 613/953-2867, Dept: 613/995-1851; Fax: 613/996-3443

Secretary of State, Children & Youth, Hon. Ethel Blondin-Andrew, #249, West Block, House of Commons, Ottawa ON K1A 0A6, 613/992-4587, Fax: 613/992-7411, Dept.: 819/953-8385; Fax: 613/953-0944

Government House Leader, Hon. Don Boudria, #380, Confederation Bldg., House of Commons, Ottawa ON K1A 0A6, 613/996-2907, Fax: 613/996-9123

Secretary of State, Federal Office of Regional Development - Québec, Hon. Martin Cauchon, #264, West Block, House of Commons, Ottawa ON K1A 0A6, 613/995-7691, Fax: 613/995-0114, Dept.: 514/496-1282; Fax: 514/496-5096

Secretary of State, Asia-Pacific, Hon. Raymond Chan, #307, Confederation Bldg., House of Commons, Ottawa ON K1A 0A6, 613/996-1995, Fax: 613/995-9926, Dept: 613/995-1851; Fax: 613/996-3443

Minister, Transport, Hon. David Collenette, #104, East Block, House of Commons, Ottawa ON K1A 0A6, 613/995-4988, Fax: 613/995-1686, Dept.: 613/991-0700; Fax: 613/995-0327

Minister, Canadian Heritage, Hon. Sheila Copps, #511-S, Centre Block, House of Commons, Ottawa ON K1A 0A6, 613/995-2773, Fax: 613/992-2727, Dept.: 819/997-7788; Fax: 819/994-5987

Minister, National Revenue, Hon. Harbance Singh Dhaliwal, #121, East Block, 613/995-7052, Fax: 613/995-2962

President, Privy Council & Minister, Intergovernmental Affairs, Hon. Stéphane Dion, #276, Confederation Bldg., House of Commons, Ottawa ON K1A 0A6, 613/996-5789, Fax: 613/996-6562, Dept.: 613/943-1838

Secretary of State, Science, Research & Development & Western Economic Diversification, Hon. Ronald J. Duhamel, #325, East Block, House of Commons, Ottawa ON K1A 0A6, 613/995-0579, Fax: 613/996-7571, Dept.: 613/995-9001; 613/990-4056

Minister, National Defence, Hon. Art Eggleton, #365, West Block, House of Commons, Ottawa ON K1A 0A6, 613/941-6339, Fax: 613/941-2421, Dept.: 613/996-3100; Fax: 613/995-8189

Government Leader in the Senate, Hon. Joyce Fairbairn

Secretary of State, Multiculturalism & Status of Women, Hon. Hedy Fry, #583, Confederation Bldg., House of Commons, Ottawa ON K1A 0A6, 613/992-3213, Fax: 613/995-0056, Dept.: 819/997-9900; Fax: 819/953-8055

Minister, Public Works & Government Services, Hon. Alfonso Gagliano, #435-S, Centre Block, House of Commons, Ottawa ON K1A 0A6, 613/995-9414, Fax: 613/996-9768, Dept.: 819/997-5421; Fax: 819/953-1908

Minister, Natural Resources & Minister Responsible, Canadian Wheat Board, Hon. Ralph Goodale, #175, East Block, House of Commons, Ottawa ON K1A 0A6, Fax: 613/992-5098, Dept.: 613/996-2007; Fax: 613/996-4516

Deputy Prime Minister, Hon. Herb Gray, #231-S, Centre Block, House of Commons, Ottawa ON K1A 0A6, 613/995-7548, Fax: 613/952-2240

Secretary of State, Latin America & Africa, Hon. David Kilgour, #165, East Block, House of Commons, Ottawa ON K1A 0A6, 613/995-8695, Fax: 613/995-6465, Dept.: 613/992-6560; Fax: 613/996-3443

Minister, Labour, Hon. Lawrence MacAulay, #556, Confederation Bldg., House of Commons, Ottawa ON K1A 0A6, 613/995-9325, Fax: 613/995-2754, Dept.: 819953-5646; Fax: 994-5168

Minister, Industry, Hon. John Manley, #607, Confederation Bldg., House of Commons, Ottawa ON K1A 0A6, 613/992-3269, Fax: 613/995-1534, Dept.: 613/995-9001; Fax: 613/992-0302

Minister, International Trade, Hon. Sergio Marchi, #105-S, Centre Block, House of Commons, Ottawa ON K1A 0A6, Fax: 613/947-4452, Dept.: 613/992-7332; Fax: 613/996-8924

Minister, International Cooperation & Minister Responsible, Francophonie, Hon. Diane Marleau, #256, Confederation Bldg., House of Commons, Ottawa ON K1A 0A6, 613/996-8963, Fax: 613/995-2569, Dept.: 819/953-6238; Fax: 819/953-2903

Minister, Finance, Hon. Paul Martin, #515-S, Centre Block, House of Commons, Ottawa ON K1A 0A6, 613/992-4284, Fax: 613/992-4291, Email: pmartin@fin.gc.ca, Dept.: 613/996-7861; Fax: 613/995-5176

President, Treasury Board & Minster Responsible, Infrastructure, Hon. Marcel Massé, #314, West Block, House of Commons, Ottawa ON K1A 0A6, 613/952-5555, Fax: 613/992-6474, Dept.: 613/957-2666; Fax: 613/990-2806

Minister, Justice & Attorney General of Canada, Hon. Anne McLellan, #707, Confederation Bldg., House of Commons, Ottawa ON K1A 0A6, 613/992-4524, Fax: 613/943-0044, Dept.: 613/992-4621; Fax: 613/990-7255

Minister, Veterans Affairs & Secretary of State, Atlantic Canada Opportunities Agency, Hon. Fred J. Mifflin, #207, Confederation Bldg., House of Commons, Ottawa ON K1A 0A6, 613/992-4133, Fax: 613/992-7277, Dept.: 613/996-4649; Fax: 613/954-1054

Secretary of State, Parks, Hon. Andy Mitchell, #323, Confederation Bldg., House of Commons, Ottawa ON K1A 0A6, 613/996-3434, Fax: 613/991-2147

Secretary of State, Agriculture & Agri-food & Fisheries & Oceans, Hon. Gilbert Normand, #359, Confederation Bldg., House of Commons, Ottawa ON K1A 0A6

Secretary of State, International Financial Institutions, Hon. Jim Peterson, #426-N, Centre Block, House of Commons, Ottawa ON K1A 0A6, 613/992-4964, Fax: 613/992-1158, Dept.: 613/996-3170; 613/995-2355

Minister, Human Resources Development, Hon. Pierre S. Pettigrew, #507, Confederation Bldg., House of Commons, Ottawa ON K1A 0A6, 613/

995-8872, Fax: 613/953-2903, Dept.: 819/994-2482; Fax: 819/994-0448

Minister, Citizenship & Immigration, Hon. Lucienne Robillard, #107, Confederation Bldg., House of Commons, Ottawa ON K1A 0A6, 613/996-7267, Fax: 613/995-8632, Dept.: 613/954-1064; Fax: 613/957-2688

Minister, Health, Hon. Allan Rock, Q.C., #441-S, Centre Block, House of Commons, Ottawa ON K1A 0A6, 613/947-5000, Fax: 613/947-4276, Dept.: 613/957-0200; Fax: 613/952-1154

Solicitor General of Canada, Hon. Andy Scott, #230, Confederation Bldg., House of Commons, Ottawa ON K1A 0A6, 613/992-1067, Fax: 613/996-9955, Dept.: 613/991-2924; Fax: 613/996-2771

Minister, Environment, Hon. Christine Stewart, #484, Confederation Bldg., House of Commons, Ottawa ON K1A 0A6, 613/992-8585, Fax: 613/995-7536, Dept.: 819/997-1441; Fax: 819/953-3457

Minister, Indian Affairs & Northern Development, Hon. Jane Stewart, #549-D, Centre Block, House of Commons, Ottawa ON K1A 0A6, 613/992-3118, Fax: 613/992-6382, Dept.: 819/997-0002; Fax: 819/953-4941

Minister, Agriculture & Agri-Food, Hon. Lyle Vanclief, #356, Confederation Bldg., House of Commons, Ottawa ON K1A 0A6, 613/992-5321, Fax: 613/996-8652, Dept.: 613/759-1059; Fax: 613/759-1081

## THIRTY-SIXTH PARLIAMENT - CANADA

House of Commons, 111 Wellington St., Ottawa ON K1A 0A9

613/992-4793; URL: http://www.parl.gc.ca/english/index.html

Members of the House of Commons are elected by the people. The legal limit of duration for each House is five years, sitting at least once a year. The Speaker is elected by the House.

By virtue of the Constitution Act, after each decennial census the representation in the House of Commons is readjusted. Pursuant to the Electoral Boundaries Readjustment Act, and rule laid down therein, a representation order is prepared which redraws the constituency boundaries in each province.

Last General Election, June 2nd, 1997.

Legal duration, 5 years from the day of the return of the writs.

#### Political Party Leaders

Liberal, Rt. Hon. Jean Chrétien, P.C., Q.C.
Bloc Québécois, Gilles Duceppe
Reform Party, Preston Manning
New Democratic Party, Hon. Alexa McDonough
Progressive Conservative Party, Hon. Jean Charest, P.C.

#### Party Standings

By provinces, representation in the House of Commons is as follows:

Alta. 26; B.C. 34; Man. 14; N.B. 10; Nfld. 7; N.W.T. 2; N.S. 11; Ont. 103; P.E.I. 4; Qué. 75; Sask. 14; Yukon 1; Total 301

By party affiliation, representation is as follows (July 23, 1997):

Liberal (Lib.) 155; Reform (Ref.) 60; Bloc Québécois (BQ) 44; New Democratic Party (NDP) 21; Progressive Conservative Party (PC) 20; Independent (Ind.) 1; Total 301

#### Salaries & Allowances

The sessional allowance of each Member of Parliament is $64,400 plus a tax-free expense allowance of $21,300. Members representing the larger, more remote ridings (those electoral districts listed in Schedule III of the Canada Elections Act) receive a tax-free expense allowance of $26,200 per annum, while those from the Northwest Territories are entitled to $28,200. These allowances & entitlements have been in effect since January 1, 1991.

In addition to the salary & expense allowance, Members occupying certain positions in the House of Commons received the following supplementary annual allowances:

Prime Minister: $69,920*
Speaker of the House; & Leader of the Official Opposition: $49,100
Cabinet Ministers: $46,645*
Leaders of Other Opposition Parties: $29,500
Deputy Speaker of the House: $25,700
House Leader of the Official Opposition: $23,800
Government Whip; Official Opposition Whip: $13,200
Deputy Chair, House Committees; Asst. Deputy Chair, House Committees; Parliamentary Secretaries: $10,500
House Leaders of Other Parties: $10,100
Party Whips; Deputy Government Whip; Deputy Official Opposition Whip: $7,500

**Note:** *According to the 1992 budget, the Prime Minister & Cabinet Ministers took a five percent cut in ministerial pay effective April 1, 1992 as per Chapter 12 (1993) The Budget Implementation (fiscal measures) Act, 1992.

#### Members by Constituency

See also alphabetical list following. **Correspondence** to Members of the House of Commons should be addressed individually and may be sent postage free to the House of Commons, Ottawa, ON K1A 0A6. Listed here are constituency, name of member, party affiliatation, Ottawa phone/Fax number.

### Alberta

Athabasca, David Chatters, Ref., 613/996-1783, Fax: 613/995-1415
Calgary Centre, Eric Lowther, Ref., 613/995-1127, Fax: 613/995-7111
Calgary East, Deepak Obhrai, Ref., 613/947-4566, Fax: 613/947-4569
Calgary Northeast, Art Hanger, Ref., 613/947-4487, Fax: 613/947-4490
Calgary Southeast, Jason Kenney, Ref., 613/992-2235, Fax: 613/992-1920
Calgary Southwest, Preston Manning, Ref., 613/996-6740, Fax: 613/947-0310
Calgary West, Rob Anders, Ref., 613/992-3066, Fax: 613/992-3256
Calgary-Nose Hill, Diane Ablonczy, Ref., 613/996-2756, Fax: 613/995-2755
Crowfoot, Jack Ramsay, Ref., 613/947-4608, Fax: 613/947-4611
Edmonton East, Peter Goldring, Ref., 613/992-3821, Fax: 613/992-6898
Edmonton North, Deborah Grey, Ref., 613/996-9778, Fax: 613/996-0785
Edmonton Southeast, Hon. David Kilgour, Lib., 613/995-8695, Fax: 613/995-6465
Edmonton Southwest, Ian McClelland, Ref., 613/992-3594, Fax: 613/992-3616
Edmonton West, Hon. Anne McLellan, Lib., 613/992-4524, Fax: 613/943-0044
Edmonton-Strathcona, Rahim Jaffer, Ref., 613/995-7325, Fax: 613/995-5342
Elk Island, Ken Epp, Ref., 613/995-3611, Fax: 613/995-3612
Lakeland, Leon E. Benoit, Ref., 613/992-4171, Fax: 613/996-9011
Lethbridge, Rick Casson, Ref., 613/996-0633, Fax: 613/995-5752
Macleod, Dr. Grant Hill, Ref., 613/995-8471, Fax: 613/996-9770
Medicine Hat, Monte Solberg, Ref., 613/992-4516, Fax: 613/992-6181
Peace River, Charlie Penson, Ref., 613/992-5685, Fax: 613/947-4782
Red Deer, Bob Mills, Ref., 613/995-0590, Fax: 613/995-6831
St. Albert, John Williams, Ref., 613/996-4722, Fax: 613/995-8880
Wetaskiwin, Dale Johnston, Ref., 613/995-8886, Fax: 613/996-9860
Wild Rose, Myron Thompson, Ref., 613/996-5152, Fax: 613/947-4601
Yellowhead, Cliff Breitkreuz, Ref., 613/992-1653, Fax: 613/992-3459

### British Columbia

Burnaby-Douglas, Svend J. Robinson, NDP, 613/996-5597, Fax: 613/992-5501
Cariboo-Chilcotin, Philip Mayfield, Ref., 613/996-2205, Fax: 613/995-7139
Delta-South Richmond, John Cummins, Ref., 613/992-2957, Fax: 613/992-3589
Dewdney-Alouette, Grant McNally, Ref., 613/947-4613, Fax: 613/947-4615
Esquimalt-Juan de Fuca, Dr. Keith Martin, Ref., 613/996-2625, Fax: 613/996-9779
Fraser Valley, Chuck Strahl, Ref., 613/992-2940, Fax: 613/995-5621
Kamloops, Nelson A. Riis, NDP, 613/995-6931, Fax: 613/995-9897
Kelowna, Werner Schmidt, Ref., 613/992-7006, Fax: 613/992-7636
Kootenay-Columbia, Jim Abbott, Ref., 613/995-7246, Fax: 613/996-9923
Langley-Abbotsford, Randy White, Ref., 613/995-0183, Fax: 613/996-9795
Nanaimo-Alberni, Bill Gilmour, Ref., 613/992-5243, Fax: 613/996-9112
Nanaimo-Cowichan, Reed Elley, Ref., 613/943-2180, Fax: 613/993-5577
New Westminster-Coquitlam-Burnaby, Paul Forseth, Ref., 613/947-4455, Fax: 613/947-4458
North Vancouver, Ted White, Ref., 613/995-1225, Fax: 613/992-7319
Okanagan-Coquihalla, Jim Hart, Ref., 613/995-2581, Fax: 613/992-7200
Okanagan-Shuswap, Darrel Stinson, Ref., 613/995-9095, Fax: 613/992-3195
Port Moody-Coquitlam, Sharon Hayes, Ref., 613/947-4482, Fax: 613/947-4485
Prince George-Bulkley Valley, Richard M. Harris, Ref., 613/995-6704, Fax: 613/996-9850
Prince George-Peace River, Jay Hill, Ref., 613/947-4524, Fax: 613/947-4527
Richmond, Hon. Raymond Chan, Lib., 613/996-1995, Fax: 613/995-9926
Saanich-Gulf Islands, Gary Lunn, Ref., 613/996-1119, Fax: 613/996-0850
Skeena, Mike Scott, Ref., 613/993-6654, Fax: 613/993-9007
Surrey Central, Gurmant Grewal, Ref., 613/996-0666, Fax: 613/992-1965
Surrey North, Chuck Cadman, Ref., 613/992-2922, Fax: 613/992-0252
Surrey-White Rock-Langley, Val Meredith, Ref., 613/947-4497, Fax: 613/947-4500
Vancouver Centre, Hon. Hedy Fry, Lib., 613/992-3213, Fax: 613/995-0056
Vancouver East, Elizabeth Davies, NDP, 613/992-6030, Fax: 613/995-7412
Vancouver Island North, John Duncan, Ref., 613/992-2503, Fax: 613/996-3306
Vancouver Kingsway, M. Sophia Leung, Lib., 613/992-3302, Fax: 613/992-4466
Vancouver Quadra, Ted McWhinney, Lib., 613/992-2430, Fax: 613/995-0770
Vancouver South-Burnaby, Hon. Harbance Singh Dhaliwal, Lib., 613/995-7052, Fax: 613/995-2962
Victoria, Hon. David Anderson, Lib., 613/996-2358, Fax: 613/952-1458
West Kootenay-Okanagan, Jim Gouk, Ref., 613/996-8036, Fax: 613/943-0922

West Vancouver-Sunshine Coast, John Reynolds, Ref., 613/947-4617, Fax: 613/947-4620

## Manitoba

Brandon-Souris, Rick Borotsik, PC, 613/995-9372, Fax: 613/995-9109

Charleswood-Assiniboine, John Harvard, Lib., 613/995-5609, Fax: 613/992-3199

Churchill, Bev Desjarlais, NDP, 613/992-3018, Fax: 613/996-5817

Dauphin-Swan River, Inky Mark, Ref., 613/992-3176, Fax: 613/992-0930

Portage-Lisgar, Jake Hoeppner, Ref., 613/995-9511, Fax: 613/947-0313

Provencher, David Iftody, Lib., 613/992-3128, Fax: 613/995-1049

Saint-Boniface, Hon. Ronald J. Duhamel, Lib., 613/995-0579, Fax: 613/996-7571

Selkirk-Interlake, Howard Hilstrom, Ref., 613/992-2032, Fax: 613/992-6224

Winnipeg Centre, Pat Martin, NDP, 613/992-5308, Fax: 613/992-2890

Winnipeg North Centre, Judy Wasylycia-Leis, NDP, 613/996-6417, Fax: 613/996-9713

Winnipeg North-St. Paul, Dr. Rey Pagtakhan, Lib., 613/992-7148, Fax: 613/996-9125

Winnipeg South, Reg Alcock, Lib., 613/995-7517, Fax: 613/943-1466, Email: winnipeg_south@mbnet.mb.ca, URL: http://www.mbnet.mb.ca:80/wpgsth

Winnipeg South Centre, Hon. Lloyd Axworthy, Lib., 613/995-0153, Fax: 613/953-2867

Winnipeg Transcona, William (Bill) Blaikie, NDP, 613/995-6339, Fax: 613/995-6688

## New Brunswick

Acadie-Bathurst, Yvon Godin, NDP, 613/992-2165, Fax: 613/992-4558

Beauséjour-Petitcodiac, Angela Vautour, NDP, 613/992-1020, Fax: 613/992-3053

Charlotte, Greg Thompson, PC, 613/995-5550, Fax: 613/995-5226

Fredericton, Hon. Andy Scott, Lib., 613/992-1067, Fax: 613/996-9955

Fundy-Royal, John Herron, PC, 613/996-2332, Fax: 613/995-4286

Madawaska-Restigouche, Jean Dubé, PC, 613/995-0581, Fax: 613/996-9736

Miramichi, Charles Hubbard, Lib., 613/992-5335, Fax: 613/996-8418

Moncton, Claudette Bradshaw, Lib., 613/996-8072, Fax: 613/992-3459

Saint John, Elsie Wayne, PC, 613/947-4571, Fax: 613/947-4574

Tobique-Mactaquac, Gilles Bernier, PC, 613/947-4431, Fax: 613/947-4434

## Newfoundland

Bonavista-Trinity-Conception, Hon. Fred J. Mifflin, Lib., 613/992-4133, Fax: 613/992-7277

Burin-St. George's, Bill Matthews, PC, 613/992-8655, Fax: 613/992-5324

Gander-Grand Falls, George S. Baker, Lib., 613/996-1541, Fax: 613/992-5397

Humber-St. Barbe-Baie Verte, Gerry Byrne, Lib., 613/996-5509, Fax: 613/996-9632

Labrador, Lawrence O'Brien, Lib., 613/996-4630, Fax: 613/996-7132

St. John's East, Norman Doyle, PC, 613/996-7269, Fax: 613/992-2178

St. John's West, Charlie Power, PC, 613/992-0927, Fax: 613/995-7858

## Northwest Territories

Nunavut, Nancy Karetak-Lindell, Lib., 613/992-2848, Fax: 613/996-9764

Western Arctic, Hon. Ethel Blondin-Andrew, Lib., 613/992-4587, Fax: 613/992-7411

## Nova Scotia

Bras d'Or, Michelle Dockrill, NDP, 613/992-6756, Fax: 613/992-4053

Cumberland-Colchester, Bill Casey, PC, 613/992-3366, Fax: 613/992-7220

Dartmouth, Wendy Lill, NDP, 613/995-9378, Fax: 613/995-9379

Halifax, Alexa McDonough, NDP, 613/995-7224, Fax: 613/992-8569

Halifax West, Gordon Earle, NDP, 613/996-3085, Fax: 613/996-6988

Kings-Hants, Scott Brison, PC, 613/995-8231, Fax: 613/996-9349

Pictou-Antigonish-Guysborough, Peter Mackay, PC, 613/992-5041, Fax: 613/992-0877

Sackville-Eastern Shore, Peter Stoffer, NDP

South Shore, Gerald Keddy, PC

Sydney-Victoria, Peter Mancini, NDP, 613/995-6459, Fax: 613/995-2963

West Nova, Mark Muise, PC, 613/995-5711, Fax: 613/996-9857

## Ontario

Algoma-Manitoulin, Brent St. Denis, Lib., 613/996-5376, Fax: 613/995-6661

Barrie-Simcoe-Bradford, Aileen Carroll, Lib., 613/992-3394, Fax: 613/996-7923

Beaches-East York, Maria Minna, Lib., 613/992-2115, Fax: 613/992-8083

Bramalea-Gore-Malton, Gurbax Singh Malhi, Lib., 613/992-9105, Fax: 613/947-0443

Brampton Centre, Sarkis Assadourian, Lib., 613/995-4843, Fax: 613/995-7003

Brampton West-Mississauga, Colleen Beaumier, Lib., 613/996-2878, Fax: 613/995-6796

Brant, Hon. Jane Stewart, Lib., 613/992-3118, Fax: 613/992-6382

Broadview-Greenwood, Dennis J. Mills, Lib., 613/992-7771, Fax: 613/996-9884

Bruce-Grey, Ovid Jackson, Lib., 613/996-5191, Fax: 613/952-0979

Burlington, Paddy Torsney, Lib., 613/995-0881, Fax: 613/995-1091

Cambridge, Janko Peric, Lib., 613/996-1307, Fax: 613/996-8340

Carleton-Gloucester, Eugène Bellemare, Lib., 613/995-6296, Fax: 613/995-6298

Davenport, Hon. Charles Caccia, Lib., 613/992-2576, Fax: 613/995-8202

Don Valley East, Hon. David Collenette, Lib., 613/995-4988, Fax: 613/995-1686

Don Valley West, John Godfrey, Lib., 613/992-2855, Fax: 613/995-1635

Dufferin-Peel-Wellington-Grey, Murray Calder, Lib., 613/995-7813, Fax: 613/992-9789

Durham, Alex Shepherd, Lib., 613/996-4984, Fax: 613/996-4986

Eglinton-Lawrence, Joseph Volpe, Lib., 613/992-6361, Fax: 613/992-9791

Elgin-Middlesex-London, Gar Knutson, Lib., 613/990-7769, Fax: 613/996-0194

Erie-Lincoln, John Maloney, Lib., 613/995-0988, Fax: 613/995-5245

Essex, Susan Whelan, Lib., 613/992-1812, Fax: 613/995-0033

Etobicoke Centre, Hon. Allan Rock, Q.C., Lib., 613/947-5000, Fax: 613/947-4276

Etobicoke North, Roy Cullen, Lib., 613/995-4702, Fax: 613/995-8359

Etobicoke-Lakeshore, Jean Augustine, Lib., 613/995-9364, Fax: 613/992-5880

Glengarry-Prescott-Russell, Hon. Don Boudria, Lib., 613/996-2907, Fax: 613/996-9123

Guelph-Wellington, Brenda Chamberlain, Lib., 613/996-4758, Fax: 613/996-9922

Haldimand-Norfolk-Brant, Bob Speller, Lib., 613/996-4974, Fax: 613/996-9749

Halton, Julian Reed, Lib., 613/996-7046, Fax: 613/992-0851

Hamilton East, Hon. Sheila Copps, Lib., 613/995-2772, Fax: 613/992-2727

Hamilton Mountain, Beth Phinney, Lib., 613/995-9389, Fax: 613/992-7802

Hamilton West, Stan Keyes, Lib., 613/995-1757, Fax: 613/992-8356

Hastings-Frontenac-Lennox and Addington, Larry McCormick, Lib., 613/992-3640, Fax: 613/992-3642

Huron-Bruce, Paul Steckle, Lib., 613/992-8234, Fax: 613/995-6350

Kenora-Rainy River, Robert D. Nault, Lib., 613/996-1161, Fax: 613/996-1759

Kent-Essex, Jerry Pickard, Lib., 613/992-2612, Fax: 613/992-1852

Kingston and the Islands, Peter Milliken, Lib., 613/996-1955, Fax: 613/996-1958

Kitchener Centre, Karen Redman, Lib., 613/995-8913, Fax: 613/996-7329

Kitchener-Waterloo, Andrew Telegdi, Lib., 613/996-5928, Fax: 613/992-6251

Lambton-Kent-Middlesex, Rose-Marie Ur, Lib., 613/947-4581, Fax: 613/947-4584

Lanark-Carleton, Ian Murray, Lib., 613/947-2277, Fax: 613/947-2278

Leeds-Grenville, Jim Jordan, Lib., 613/992-8756, Fax: 613/996-9171

London North Centre, Joe Fontana, Lib., 613/992-0805, Fax: 613/992-9613

London West, Sue Barnes, Lib., 613/996-6674, Fax: 613/996-6772

London-Fanshawe, Pat O'Brien, Lib., 613/995-2901, Fax: 613/943-8717

Markham, Jim Jones, PC, 613/996-3374, Fax: 613/992-3921

Mississauga Centre, Carolyn Parrish, Lib., 613/995-7321, Fax: 613/992-6708

Mississauga East, Albina Guarnieri, Lib., 613/996-0420, Fax: 613/996-0279

Mississauga South, Paul Szabo, Lib., 613/992-4848, Fax: 613/996-3267

Mississauga West, Steve Mahoney, Lib., 613/995-7784, Fax: 613/996-9817

Nepean-Carleton, David Pratt, Lib., 613/992-2772, Fax: 613/992-1209

Niagara Centre, Hon. Gilbert Parent, Lib., 613/995-9579, Fax: 613/995-0244

Niagara Falls, Gary Pilliteri, Lib., 613/995-1547, Fax: 613/992-7910

Nickle Belt, Ray Bonin, Lib., 613/995-9107, Fax: 613/995-9109

Nipissing, Bob Wood, Lib., 613/995-6255, Fax: 613/996-7993

Northumberland, Hon. Christine Stewart, Lib., 613/992-8585, Fax: 613/995-7536

Oak Ridges, Bryon Wilfert, Lib., 613/992-3802, Fax: 613/996-1954

Oakville, Bonnie Brown, Lib., 613/995-4014, Fax: 613/992-0520

Oshawa, Ivan Grose, Lib., 613/996-4756, Fax: 613/992-1357

Ottawa Centre, Mac Harb, Lib., 613/996-5322, Fax: 613/996-5323

Ottawa South, Hon. John Manley, Lib., 613/992-3269, Fax: 613/995-1534

Ottawa West-Nepean, Marlene Catterall, Lib., 613/996-0984, Fax: 613/996-9880

Ottawa-Vanier, Mauril Bélanger, Lib., 613/992-4766, Fax: 613/992-6448

Oxford, John Finlay, Lib., 613/995-4432, Fax: 613/995-4433

Parkdale-High Park, Sarmite Bulte, Lib., 613/992-2936, Fax: 613/995-1629

Parry Sound-Muskoka, Hon. Andy Mitchell, Lib., 613/996-3434, Fax: 613/991-2147

Perth-Middlesex, John Richardson, Lib., 613/992-6124, Fax: 613/998-7902

Peterborough, Peter Adams, Lib., 613/995-6411, Fax: 613/996-9800
Pickering-Ajax-Uxbridge, Dan McTeague, Lib., 613/995-8082, Fax: 613/993-6587
Prince Edward-Hastings, Hon. Lyle Vanclief, Lib., 613/992-5321, Fax: 613/996-8652
Renfrew-Nipissing-Pembroke, Hec Cloutier, Lib., 613/992-7712, Fax: 613/995-9755
Sarnia-Lambton, Roger Gallaway, Lib., 613/957-2649, Fax: 613/957-2655
Sault Ste. Marie, Carmen Provenzano, Lib., 613/992-9723, Fax: 613/992-1954
Scarborough Centre, John Cannis, Lib., 613/992-6823, Fax: 613/943-1045
Scarborough East, John McKay, Lib., 613/992-1447, Fax: 613/992-8569
Scarborough Southwest, Tom Wappel, Lib., 613/995-0284, Fax: 613/996-6309
Scarborough-Agincourt, Jim Karygiannis, Lib., 613/992-4501, Fax: 613/995-1612
Scarborough-Rouge River, Derek Lee, Lib., 613/996-9681, Fax: 613/996-6643
Simcoe North, Paul DeVillers, Lib., 613/992-6582, Fax: 613/996-3128
Simcoe-Grey, Paul Bonwick, Lib., 613/992-4224, Fax: 613/992-2164
St. Catharines, Walt Lastewka, Lib., 613/992-3352, Fax: 613/947-4402
St. Paul's, Carolyn Bennett, Lib., 613/995-9666, Fax: 613/947-4622
Stoney Creek, Tony Valeri, Lib., 613/992-6535, Fax: 613/992-7764
Stormont-Dundas, Bob Kilger, Lib., 613/992-2521, Fax: 613/996-2119
Sudbury, Hon. Diane Marleau, Lib., 613/996-8963, Fax: 613/995-2569
Thornhill, Elinor Caplan, Lib., 613/992-0253, Fax: 613/992-0887
Thunder Bay-Atikokan, Stan Dromisky, Lib., 613/992-3061, Fax: 613/995-3315
Thunder Bay-Nipigon, Joe Comuzzi, Lib., 613/996-4792, Fax: 613/996-9785
Timiskaming-Cochrane, Benoît Serré, Lib., 613/992-2792, Fax: 613/992-2794
Timmins-James Bay, Réginald Bélair, Lib., 613/992-2919, Fax: 613/995-0747
Toronto Central-Rosedale, Bill Graham, Lib., 613/992-5234, Fax: 613/996-9607
Trinity-Spadina, Tony Ianno, Lib., 613/992-2352, Fax: 613/992-6301
Vaughan-King-Aurora, Maurizio Bevilacqua, Lib., 613/996-4971, Fax: 613/996-4973
Victoria-Haliburton, John O'Reilly, Lib., 613/992-2474, Fax: 613/996-9656
Waterloo-Wellington, Lynn Myers, Lib., 613/992-4633, Fax: 613/992-9932
Wentworth-Burlington, Hon. John Bryden, Lib., 613/995-8042, Fax: 613/996-1289
Whitby-Ajax, Judi Longfield, Lib., 613/992-6344, Fax: 613/992-8350
Willowdale, Hon. Jim Peterson, Lib., 613/992-4964, Fax: 613/992-1158
Windsor West, Hon. Herb Gray, Lib., 613/995-7548, Fax: 613/952-2240
Windsor-St. Clair, Shaughnessy Cohen, Lib., 613/947-3445, Fax: 613/947-3448
York Centre, Hon. Art Eggleton, Lib., 613/941-6339, Fax: 613/941-2421
York North, Karen Kraft Sloan, Lib., 613/996-7752, Fax: 613/992-8351
York South-Weston, John Nunziata, Ind., 613/995-0777, Fax: 613/992-2949
York West, Hon. Sergio Marchi, Lib., 819/992-7332, Fax: 819/947-4452

## Prince Edward Island

Cardigan, Hon. Lawrence MacAulay, Lib., 613/995-9325, Fax: 613/995-2754
Egmont, Joe McGuire, Lib., 613/992-9223, Fax: 613/992-1974
Hillsborough, George Proud, Lib., 613/996-4714, Fax: 613/995-7685
Malpeque, Wayne Easter, Lib., 613/992-2406, Fax: 613/995-7408

## Québec

Abitibi, Guy St-Julien, Lib., 613/996-3076, Fax: 613/996-0828
Ahuntsic, Eleni Bakopanos, Lib., 613/992-0983, Fax: 613/992-1932
Anjou-Rivière-des-Prairies, Yvon Charbonneau, Lib., 613/995-0580, Fax: 613/992-1710
Argenteuil-Papineau, Maurice Dumas, BQ, 613/992-0902, Fax: 613/992-2935
Beauce, Claude Drouin, Lib., 613/992-8053, Fax: 613/995-0687
Beauharnois-Salaberry, Daniel Turp, BQ, 613/992-5036, Fax: 613/995-7821
Beauport-Montmorency-Orléans, Michel Guimond, BQ, 613/995-9732, Fax: 613/996-2656
Bellechasse-Etchemins-Montmagny-L'Islet, Hon. Gilbert Normand, Lib., 613/992-2289, Fax: 613/992-6864
Berthier-Montcalm, Michel Bellehumeur, BQ, 613/992-0164, Fax: 613/992-5341
Bonaventure-Gaspé-Iles-de-la-Madeleine-Pabok, Yvan Bernier, BQ, 613/992-6188, Fax: 613/992-6194
Bourassa, Denis Coderre, Lib., 613/995-6108, Fax: 613/995-9755
Brome-Missisquoi, Denis Paradis, Lib., 613/947-8185, Fax: 613/947-8188
Brossard-La Prairie, Jacques Saada, Lib., 613/995-9287, Fax: 613/992-7273
Châteauguay, Maurice Godin, BQ, 613/996-7265, Fax: 613/996-9287
Chambly, Ghislain Lebel, BQ, 613/992-6035, Fax: 613/995-6223
Champlain, Réjean Lefebvre, BQ, 613/995-4895, Fax: 613/996-6883
Charlesbourg, Richard Marceau, BQ, 613/995-8857, Fax: 613/995-1625
Charlevoix, Gérard Asselin, BQ, 613/992-2363, Fax: 613/996-7954
Chicoutimi, André Harvey, PC, 613/995-8554, Fax: 613/992-0431
Compton-Stanstead, David Price, PC, 613/995-2024, Fax: 613/992-1696
Drummond, Pauline Picard, BQ, 613/947-4550, Fax: 613/947-4551
Frontenac-Mégantic, Jean-Guy Chrétien, BQ, 613/995-1377, Fax: 613/943-1562
Gatineau, Mark Assad, Lib., 613/992-4351, Fax: 613/992-1037
Hochelaga-Maisonneuve, Réal Ménard, BQ, 613/947-4576, Fax: 613/947-4579
Hull-Aylmer, Hon. Marcel Massé, Lib., 613/952-5555, Fax: 613/992-6474
Joliette, René Laurin, BQ, 613/996-6910, Fax: 613/995-2818
Jonquière, Jocelyne Girard-Bujold, BQ, 613/992-2617, Fax: 613/992-6069
Kamouraska-Rivière-du-Loup-Témiscouata-Les Basques, Paul Crête, BQ, 613/995-0265, Fax: 613/943-1229
Lac-Saint-Jean, Stéphan Tremblay, BQ, 613/947-2745, Fax: 613/947-2748
Lac-Saint-Louis, Clifford Lincoln, Lib., 613/995-8281, Fax: 613/995-0528
LaSalle-Émard, Hon. Paul Martin, Lib., 613/992-4284, Fax: 613/992-4291
Laurentides, Monique Guay, BQ, 613/992-3257, Fax: 613/992-2156
Laurier-Sainte-Marie, Gilles Duceppe, BQ, 613/992-6779, Fax: 613/943-1243
Laval Centre, Madeleine Dalphond-Guiral, BQ, 613/996-0864, Fax: 613/996-1195
Laval Ouest, Raymonde Folco, Lib., 613/992-2659, Fax: 613/992-9469
Laval-Est, Maud Debien, BQ, 613/992-0611, Fax: 613/992-8556
Lévis, Antoine Dubé, BQ, 613/992-7434, Fax: 613/995-6856
Longueuil, Caroline St-Hilaire, BQ, 613/992-8514, Fax: 613/992-2744
Lotbinière, Odina Desrochers, BQ, 613/992-2639, Fax: 613/992-1018
Louis-Hébert, Hélène Alarie, BQ, 613/995-4995, Fax: 613/996-8292
Manicouagan, Ghislain Fournier, BQ, 613/992-5681, Fax: 613/992-7276
Matapédia-Matane, René Canuel, BQ, 613/995-1013, Fax: 613/995-5184
Mercier, Francine Lalonde, BQ, 613/995-6327, Fax: 613/996-5173
Mont-Royal, Hon. Sheila Finestone, Lib., 613/995-0121, Fax: 613/990-5838
Notre-Dame-de-Grâce-Lachine, Marlene Jennings, Lib., 613/995-2251, Fax: 613/996-1481
Outremont, Hon. Martin Cauchon, Lib., 613/995-7691, Fax: 613/995-0114
Papineau-Saint-Denis, Hon. Pierre S. Pettigrew, Lib., 613/995-8872, Fax: 613/953-2903
Pierrefonds-Dollard, Bernard Patry, Lib., 613/992-2689, Fax: 613/996-8478
Pontiac-Gatineau-Labelle, Robert Bertrand, Lib., 613/992-5516, Fax: 613/992-6802
Portneuf, Pierre de Savoye, BQ, 613/992-2798, Fax: 613/995-1637
Québec, Christiane Gagnon, BQ, 613/992-8865, Fax: 613/995-2805
Québec-Est, Jean-Paul Marchand, BQ, 613/996-4151, Fax: 613/954-2269
Repentigny, Benoît Sauvageau, BQ, 613/992-5257, Fax: 613/996-4338
Richelieu, Louis Plamondon, BQ, 613/995-9241, Fax: 613/995-6784
Richmond-Arthabaska, André Bachand, PC, 613/992-4473, Fax: 613/995-2026
Rimouski-Mitis, Suzanne Tremblay, BQ, 613/992-5302, Fax: 613/996-8298
Roberval, Michel Gauthier, BQ, 613/992-2244, Fax: 613/993-5017
Rosemont, Bernard Bigras, BQ, 613/992-0423, Fax: 613/992-0878
Saint-Bruno-Saint-Hubert, Pierrette Venne, BQ, 613/996-2416, Fax: 613/995-6973
Saint-Eustache-Sainte-Thérèse, Gilles-A. Perron, BQ, 613/992-0336, Fax: 613/992-1160
Saint-Hyacinthe-Bagot, Yvan Loubier, BQ, 613/996-4585, Fax: 613/992-1815
Saint-Jean, Claude Bachand, BQ, 613/992-5296, Fax: 613/992-9849
Saint-Lambert, Yolande Thibeault, Lib., 613/998-5961, Fax: 613/954-0707
Saint-Laurent-Cartierville, Hon. Stéphane Dion, Lib., 613/996-5789, Fax: 613/996-6562
Saint-Léonard-Saint-Michel, Hon. Alfonso Gagliano, Lib., 613/995-9414, Fax: 613/996-9768
Shefford, Diane St-Jacques, PC, 613/992-5279, Fax: 613/992-7871
Sherbrooke, Hon. Jean Charest, PC, 613/943-1106, Fax: 613/995-0364
St. Maurice, Rt. Hon. Jean Chrétien, Lib., 613/992-4211, Fax: 613/941-6900
Témiscamingue, Pierre Brien, BQ, 613/996-3250, Fax: 613/992-3672
Terrebonne-Blainville, Paul Mercier, BQ, 613/947-4788, Fax: 613/947-4879
Trois-Rivières, Yves Rocheleau, BQ, 613/992-2349, Fax: 613/995-9498
Vaudreuil-Soulanges, Nunzio Discepola, Lib., 613/957-3744, Fax: 613/952-0874
Verchères, Stéphane Bergeron, BQ, 613/996-2998, Fax: 613/995-1062

Verdun-Saint-Henri, Raymond Lavigne, Lib., 613/995-6403, Fax: 613/995-6404

Westmount-Ville-Marie, Hon. Lucienne Robillard, Lib., 613/996-7267, Fax: 613/995-8632

## Saskatchewan

Battlefords-Lloydminster, Gerry Ritz, Ref., 613/995-7080, Fax: 613/996-8472

Blackstrap, Allan Kerpan, Ref., 613/995-5653, Fax: 613/995-0126

Churchill River, Rick Laliberte, NDP, 613/995-8321, Fax: 613/995-7697

Cypress Hills-Grasslands, Lee Morrison, Ref., 613/992-0657, Fax: 613/992-5508

Palliser, Dick Proctor, NDP, 613/992-9115, Fax: 613/992-0131

Prince Albert, Derrek Konrad, Ref., 613/995-3295, Fax: 613/995-6819

Qu'Appelle, Lorne Edmund Nystrom, NDP, 613/992-4593, Fax: 613/996-3120

Regina-Lumsden-Lake Centre, John Solomon, NDP, 613/992-4573, Fax: 613/996-6885

Saskatoon-Humboldt (49,294) Georgette Sheridan, Lib., 613/992-8052

Saskatoon-Humboldt, Jim Pankiw, Ref., 613/992-8052, Fax: 613/996-9899

Saskatoon-Rosetown-Biggar, Chris Axworthy, NDP, 613/995-1551, Fax: 613/996-8472

Souris-Moose Mountain, Roy Bailey, Ref., 613/992-7685, Fax: 613/995-8908

Wanuskewin, Maurice Vellacott, Ref., 613/992-1899, Fax: 613/992-3085

Wascana, Hon. Ralph Goodale, Lib., 613/996-3843, Fax: 613/992-5098

Yorkton-Melville, Garry Breitkruz, Ref., 613/992-4394, Fax: 613/992-8676

## Yukon

Yukon, Louise Hardy, NDP, 613/995-9368, Fax: 613/995-0945

#### MEMBERS (ALPHABETICAL)

See also Constituency List, preceding. **Correspondence** to Members of the House of Commons should be addressed individually and may be sent postage free to the House of Commons, Ottawa, ON K1A 0A6.

Listed here are: Name of member, constituency, party affiliation, province, Ottawa office phone number.

Jim Abbott, Kootenay-Columbia, Ref., BC, 613/995-7246, Fax: 613/996-9923

Diane Ablonczy, Calgary-Nose Hill, Ref., Alta., 613/996-2756, Fax: 613/995-2755

Peter Adams, Peterborough, Lib., Ont., 613/995-6411, Fax: 613/996-9800

Hélène Alarie, Louis-Hébert, BQ, Qué., 613/995-4995, Fax: 613/996-8292

Reg Alcock, Winnipeg South, Lib., Man., 613/995-7517, Fax: 613/943-1466, Email: winnipeg_south@mbnet.mb.ca, URL: http://www.mbnet.mb.ca:80/wpgsth

Rob Anders, Calgary West, Ref., Alta., 613/992-3066, Fax: 613/992-3256

Hon. David Anderson, Victoria, Lib., BC, 613/996-2358, Fax: 613/952-1458

Mark Assad, Gatineau, Lib., Qué., 613/992-4351, Fax: 613/992-1037

Sarkis Assadourian, Brampton Centre, Lib., Ont., 613/995-4843, Fax: 613/995-7003

Gérard Asselin, Charlevoix, BQ, Qué., 613/992-2363, Fax: 613/996-7954

Jean Augustine, Etobicoke-Lakeshore, Lib., Ont., 613/995-9364, Fax: 613/992-5880

Chris Axworthy, Saskatoon-Rosetown-Biggar, NDP, Sask., 613/995-1551, Fax: 613/996-8472

Hon. Lloyd Axworthy, Winnipeg South Centre, Lib., Man., 613/995-0153, Fax: 613/953-2867

André Bachand, Richmond-Arthabaska, PC, Qué., 613/992-4473, Fax: 613/995-2026

Claude Bachand, Saint-Jean, BQ, Qué., 613/992-5296, Fax: 613/992-9849

Roy Bailey, Souris-Moose Mountain, Ref., Sask., 613/992-7685, Fax: 613/995-8908

George S. Baker, Gander-Grand Falls, Lib., Nfld., 613/996-1541, Fax: 613/992-5397

Eleni Bakopanos, Ahuntsic, Lib., Qué., 613/992-0983, Fax: 613/992-1932

Sue Barnes, London West, Lib., Ont., 613/996-6674, Fax: 613/996-6772

Colleen Beaumier, Brampton West-Mississauga, Lib., Ont., 613/996-2878, Fax: 613/995-6796

Réginald Bélair, Timmins-James Bay, Lib., Ont., 613/992-2919, Fax: 613/995-0747

Mauril Bélanger, Ottawa-Vanier, Lib., Ont., 613/992-4766, Fax: 613/992-6448

Michel Bellehumeur, Berthier-Montcalm, BQ, Qué., 613/992-0164, Fax: 613/992-5341

Eugène Bellemare, Carleton-Gloucester, Lib., Ont., 613/995-6296, Fax: 613/995-6298

Carolyn Bennett, St. Paul's, Lib., Ont., 613/995-9666, Fax: 613/947-4622

Leon E. Benoit, Lakeland, Ref., Alta., 613/992-4171, Fax: 613/996-9011

Stéphane Bergeron, Verchères, BQ, Qué., 613/996-2998, Fax: 613/995-1062

Gilles Bernier, Tobique-Mactaquac, PC, NB, 613/947-4431, Fax: 613/947-4434

Yvan Bernier, Bonaventure-Gaspé-Iles-de-la-Madeleine-Pabok, BQ, Qué., 613/992-6188, Fax: 613/992-6194

Robert Bertrand, Pontiac-Gatineau-Labelle, Lib., Qué., 613/992-5516, Fax: 613/992-6802

Maurizio Bevilacqua, Vaughan-King-Aurora, Lib., Ont., 613/996-4971, Fax: 613/996-4973

Bernard Bigras, Rosemont, BQ, Qué., 613/992-0423, Fax: 613/992-0878

William (Bill) Blaikie, Winnipeg Transcona, NDP, Man., 613/995-6339, Fax: 613/995-6688

Hon. Ethel Blondin-Andrew, Western Arctic, Lib., NWT, 613/992-4587, Fax: 613/992-7411

Ray Bonin, Nickle Belt, Lib., Ont., 613/995-9107, Fax: 613/995-9109

Paul Bonwick, Simcoe-Grey, Lib., Ont., 613/992-4224, Fax: 613/992-2164

Rick Borotsik, Brandon-Souris, PC, Man., 613/995-9372, Fax: 613/995-9109

Hon. Don Boudria, Glengarry-Prescott-Russell, Lib., Ont., 613/996-2907, Fax: 613/996-9123

Claudette Bradshaw, Moncton, Lib., NB, 613/996-8072, Fax: 613/992-3459

Cliff Breitkreuz, Yellowhead, Ref., Alta., 613/992-1653, Fax: 613/992-3459

Garry Breitkruz, Yorkton-Melville, Ref., Sask., 613/992-4394, Fax: 613/992-8676

Pierre Brien, Témiscamingue, BQ, Qué., 613/996-3250, Fax: 613/992-3672

Scott Brison, Kings-Hants, PC, NS, 613/995-8231, Fax: 613/996-9349

Bonnie Brown, Oakville, Lib., Ont., 613/995-4014, Fax: 613/992-0520

Hon. John Bryden, Wentworth-Burlington, Lib., Ont., 613/995-8042, Fax: 613/996-1289

Sarmite Bulte, Parkdale-High Park, Lib., Ont., 613/992-2936, Fax: 613/995-1629

Gerry Byrne, Humber-St. Barbe-Baie Verte, Lib., Nfld., 613/996-5509, Fax: 613/996-9632

Hon. Charles Caccia, Davenport, Lib., Ont., 613/992-2576, Fax: 613/995-8202

Chuck Cadman, Surrey North, Ref., BC, 613/992-2922, Fax: 613/992-0252

Murray Calder, Dufferin-Peel-Wellington-Grey, Lib., Ont., 613/995-7813, Fax: 613/992-9789

John Cannis, Scarborough Centre, Lib., Ont., 613/992-6823, Fax: 613/943-1045

René Canuel, Matapédia-Matane, BQ, Qué., 613/995-1013, Fax: 613/995-5184

Elinor Caplan, Thornhill, Lib., Ont., 613/992-0253, Fax: 613/992-0887

Aileen Carroll, Barrie-Simcoe-Bradford, Lib., Ont., 613/992-3394, Fax: 613/996-7923

Bill Casey, Cumberland-Colchester, PC, NS, 613/992-3366, Fax: 613/992-7220

Rick Casson, Lethbridge, Ref., Alta., 613/996-0633, Fax: 613/995-5752

Marlene Catterall, Ottawa West-Nepean, Lib., Ont., 613/996-0984, Fax: 613/996-9880

Hon. Martin Cauchon, Outremont, Lib., Qué., 613/995-7691, Fax: 613/995-0114

Brenda Chamberlain, Guelph-Wellington, Lib., Ont., 613/996-4758, Fax: 613/996-9922

Hon. Raymond Chan, Richmond, Lib., BC, 613/996-1995, Fax: 613/995-9926

Yvon Charbonneau, Anjou-Rivière-des-Prairies, Lib., Qué., 613/995-0580, Fax: 613/992-1710

Hon. Jean Charest, Sherbrooke, PC, Qué., 613/943-1106, Fax: 613/995-0364

David Chatters, Athabasca, Ref., Alta., 613/996-1783, Fax: 613/995-1415

Rt. Hon. Jean Chrétien, St. Maurice, Lib., Qué., 613/992-4211, Fax: 613/941-6900

Jean-Guy Chrétien, Frontenac-Mégantic, BQ, Qué., 613/995-1377, Fax: 613/943-1562

Hec Cloutier, Renfrew-Nipissing-Pembroke, Lib., Ont., 613/992-7712, Fax: 613/995-9755

Denis Coderre, Bourassa, Lib., Qué., 613/995-6108, Fax: 613/995-9755

Shaughnessy Cohen, Windsor-St. Clair, Lib., Ont., 613/947-3445, Fax: 613/947-3448

Hon. David Collenette, Don Valley East, Lib., Ont., 613/995-4988, Fax: 613/995-1686

Joe Comuzzi, Thunder Bay-Nipigon, Lib., Ont., 613/996-4792, Fax: 613/996-9785

Hon. Sheila Copps, Hamilton East, Lib., Ont., 613/995-2772, Fax: 613/992-2727

Paul Crête, Kamouraska-Rivière-du-Loup-Témiscouata-Les Basques, BQ, Qué., 613/995-0265, Fax: 613/943-1229

Roy Cullen, Etobicoke North, Lib., Ont., 613/995-4702, Fax: 613/995-8359

John Cummins, Delta-South Richmond, Ref., BC, 613/992-2957, Fax: 613/992-3589

Madeleine Dalphond-Guiral, Laval Centre, BQ, Qué., 613/996-0864, Fax: 613/996-1195

Elizabeth Davies, Vancouver East, NDP, BC, 613/992-6030, Fax: 613/995-7412

Pierre de Savoye, Portneuf, BQ, Qué., 613/992-2798, Fax: 613/995-1637

Maud Debien, Laval-Est, BQ, Qué., 613/992-0611, Fax: 613/992-8556

Bev Desjarlais, Churchill, NDP, Man., 613/992-3018, Fax: 613/996-5817

Odina Desrochers, Lotbinière, BQ, Qué., 613/992-2639, Fax: 613/992-1018

Paul DeVillers, Simcoe North, Lib., Ont., 613/992-6582, Fax: 613/996-3128

Hon. Harbance Singh Dhaliwal, Vancouver South-Burnaby, Lib., BC, 613/995-7052, Fax: 613/995-2962

Hon. Stéphane Dion, Saint-Laurent-Cartierville, Lib., Qué., 613/996-5789, Fax: 613/996-6562

Nunzio Discepola, Vaudreuil-Soulanges, Lib., Qué., 613/957-3744, Fax: 613/952-0874

Michelle Dockrill, Bras d'Or, NDP, NS, 613/992-6756, Fax: 613/992-4053

Norman Doyle, St. John's East, PC, Nfld., 613/996-7269, Fax: 613/992-2178

Stan Dromisky, Thunder Bay-Atikokan, Lib., Ont., 613/992-3061, Fax: 613/995-3315

Claude Drouin, Beauce, Lib., Qué., 613/992-8053, Fax: 613/995-0687

Antoine Dubé, Lévis, BQ, Qué., 613/992-7434, Fax: 613/995-6856

Jean Dubé, Madawaska-Restigouche, PC, NB, 613/995-0581, Fax: 613/996-9736

Gilles Duceppe, Laurier-Sainte-Marie, BQ, Qué., 613/992-6779, Fax: 613/943-1243
Hon. Ronald J. Duhamel, Saint-Boniface, Lib., Man., 613/995-0579, Fax: 613/996-7571
Maurice Dumas, Argenteuil-Papineau, BQ, Qué., 613/992-0902, Fax: 613/992-2935
John Duncan, Vancouver Island North, Ref., BC, 613/992-2503, Fax: 613/996-3306
Gordon Earle, Halifax West, NDP, NS, 613/996-3085, Fax: 613/996-6988
Wayne Easter, Malpeque, Lib., PEI, 613/992-2406, Fax: 613/995-7408
Hon. Art Eggleton, York Centre, Lib., Ont., 613/941-6339, Fax: 613/941-2421
Reed Elley, Nanaimo-Cowichan, Ref., BC, 613/943-2180, Fax: 613/993-5577
Ken Epp, Elk Island, Ref., Alta., 613/995-3611, Fax: 613/995-3612
Hon. Sheila Finestone, Mont-Royal, Lib., Qué., 613/995-0121, Fax: 613/990-5838
John Finlay, Oxford, Lib., Ont., 613/995-4432, Fax: 613/995-4433
Raymonde Folco, Laval Ouest, Lib., Qué., 613/992-2659, Fax: 613/992-9469
Joe Fontana, London North Centre, Lib., Ont., 613/992-0805, Fax: 613/992-9613
Paul Forseth, New Westminster-Coquitlam-Burnaby, Ref., BC, 613/947-4455, Fax: 613/947-4458
Ghislain Fournier, Manicouagan, BQ, Qué., 613/992-5681, Fax: 613/992-7276
Hon. Hedy Fry, Vancouver Centre, Lib., BC, 613/992-3213, Fax: 613/995-0056
Hon. Alfonso Gagliano, Saint-Léonard-Saint-Michel, Lib., Qué., 613/995-9414, Fax: 613/996-9768
Christiane Gagnon, Québec, BQ, Qué., 613/992-8865, Fax: 613/995-2805
Roger Gallaway, Sarnia-Lambton, Lib., Ont., 613/957-2649, Fax: 613/957-2655
Michel Gauthier, Roberval, BQ, Qué., 613/992-2244, Fax: 613/993-5017
Bill Gilmour, Nanaimo-Alberni, Ref., BC, 613/992-5243, Fax: 613/996-9112
Jocelyne Girard-Bujold, Jonquière, BQ, Qué., 613/992-2617, Fax: 613/992-6069
John Godfrey, Don Valley West, Lib., Ont., 613/992-2855, Fax: 613/995-1635
Maurice Godin, Châteauguay, BQ, Qué., 613/996-7265, Fax: 613/996-9287
Yvon Godin, Acadie-Bathurst, NDP, NB, 613/992-2165, Fax: 613/992-4558
Peter Goldring, Edmonton East, Ref., Alta., 613/992-3821, Fax: 613/992-6898
Hon. Ralph Goodale, Wascana, Lib., Sask., 613/996-3843, Fax: 613/992-5098
Jim Gouk, West Kootenay-Okanagan, Ref., BC, 613/996-8036, Fax: 613/943-0922
Bill Graham, Toronto Central-Rosedale, Lib., Ont., 613/992-5234, Fax: 613/996-9607
Hon. Herb Gray, Windsor West, Lib., Ont., 613/995-7548, Fax: 613/952-2240
Gurmant Grewal, Surrey Central, Ref., BC, 613/996-0666, Fax: 613/992-1965
Deborah Grey, Edmonton North, Ref., Alta., 613/996-9778, Fax: 613/996-0785
Ivan Grose, Oshawa, Lib., Ont., 613/996-4756, Fax: 613/992-1357
Albina Guarnieri, Mississauga East, Lib., Ont., 613/996-0420, Fax: 613/996-0279
Monique Guay, Laurentides, BQ, Qué., 613/992-3257, Fax: 613/992-2156
Michel Guimond, Beauport-Montmorency-Orléans, BQ, Qué., 613/995-9732, Fax: 613/996-2656
Art Hanger, Calgary Northeast, Ref., Alta., 613/947-4487, Fax: 613/947-4490
Mac Harb, Ottawa Centre, Lib., Ont., 613/996-5322, Fax: 613/996-5323
Louise Hardy, Yukon, NDP, YT, 613/995-9368, Fax: 613/995-0945
Richard M. Harris, Prince George-Bulkley Valley, Ref., BC, 613/995-6704, Fax: 613/996-9850
Jim Hart, Okanagan-Coquihalla, Ref., BC, 613/995-2581, Fax: 613/992-7200
John Harvard, Charleswood-Assiniboine, Lib., Man., 613/995-5609, Fax: 613/992-3199
André Harvey, Chicoutimi, PC, Qué., 613/995-8554, Fax: 613/992-0431
Sharon Hayes, Port Moody-Coquitlam, Ref., BC, 613/947-4482, Fax: 613/947-4485
John Herron, Fundy-Royal, PC, NB, 613/996-2332, Fax: 613/995-4286
Dr. Grant Hill, Macleod, Ref., Alta., 613/995-8471, Fax: 613/996-9770
Jay Hill, Prince George-Peace River, Ref., BC, 613/947-4524, Fax: 613/947-4527
Howard Hilstrom, Selkirk-Interlake, Ref., Man., 613/992-2032, Fax: 613/992-6224
Jake Hoeppner, Portage-Lisgar, Ref., Man., 613/995-9511, Fax: 613/947-0313
Charles Hubbard, Miramichi, Lib., NB, 613/992-5335, Fax: 613/996-8418
Tony Ianno, Trinity-Spadina, Lib., Ont., 613/992-2352, Fax: 613/992-6301
David Iftody, Provencher, Lib., Man., 613/992-3128, Fax: 613/995-1049
Ovid Jackson, Bruce-Grey, Lib., Ont., 613/996-5191, Fax: 613/952-0979
Rahim Jaffer, Edmonton-Strathcona, Ref., Alta., 613/995-7325, Fax: 613/995-5342
Marlene Jennings, Notre-Dame-de-Grâce-Lachine, Lib., Qué., 613/995-2251, Fax: 613/996-1481
Dale Johnston, Wetaskiwin, Ref., Alta., 613/995-8886, Fax: 613/996-9860
Jim Jones, Markham, PC, Ont., 613/996-3374, Fax: 613/992-3921
Jim Jordan, Leeds-Grenville, Lib., Ont., 613/992-8756, Fax: 613/996-9171
Nancy Karetak-Lindell, Nunavut, Lib., NWT, 613/992-2848, Fax: 613/996-9764
Jim Karygiannis, Scarborough-Agincourt, Lib., Ont., 613/992-4501, Fax: 613/995-1612
Gerald Keddy, South Shore, PC, NS
Jason Kenney, Calgary Southeast, Ref., Alta., 613/992-2235, Fax: 613/992-1920
Allan Kerpan, Blackstrap, Ref., Sask., 613/995-5653, Fax: 613/995-0126
Stan Keyes, Hamilton West, Lib., Ont., 613/995-1757, Fax: 613/992-8356
Bob Kilger, Stormont-Dundas, Lib., Ont., 613/992-2521, Fax: 613/996-2119
Hon. David Kilgour, Edmonton Southeast, Lib., Alta., 613/995-8695, Fax: 613/995-6465
Gar Knutson, Elgin-Middlesex-London, Lib., Ont., 613/990-7769, Fax: 613/996-0194
Derrek Konrad, Prince Albert, Ref., Sask., 613/995-3295, Fax: 613/995-6819
Karen Kraft Sloan, York North, Lib., Ont., 613/996-7752, Fax: 613/992-8351
Rick Laliberte, Churchill River, NDP, Sask., 613/995-8321, Fax: 613/995-7697
Francine Lalonde, Mercier, BQ, Qué., 613/995-6327, Fax: 613/996-5173
Walt Lastewka, St. Catharines, Lib., Ont., 613/992-3352, Fax: 613/947-4402
René Laurin, Joliette, BQ, Qué., 613/996-6910, Fax: 613/995-2818
Raymond Lavigne, Verdun-Saint-Henri, Lib., Qué., 613/995-6403, Fax: 613/995-6404
Ghislain Lebel, Chambly, BQ, Qué., 613/992-6035, Fax: 613/995-6223
Derek Lee, Scarborough-Rouge River, Lib., Ont., 613/996-9681, Fax: 613/996-6643
Réjean Lefebvre, Champlain, BQ, Qué., 613/995-4895, Fax: 613/996-6883
M. Sophia Leung, Vancouver Kingsway, Lib., BC, 613/992-3302, Fax: 613/992-4466
Wendy Lill, Dartmouth, NDP, NS, 613/995-9378, Fax: 613/995-9379
Clifford Lincoln, Lac-Saint-Louis, Lib., Qué., 613/995-8281, Fax: 613/995-0528
Judi Longfield, Whitby-Ajax, Lib., Ont., 613/992-6344, Fax: 613/992-8350
Yvan Loubier, Saint-Hyacinthe-Bagot, BQ, Qué., 613/996-4585, Fax: 613/992-1815
Eric Lowther, Calgary Centre, Ref., Alta., 613/995-1127, Fax: 613/995-7111
Gary Lunn, Saanich-Gulf Islands, Ref., BC, 613/996-1119, Fax: 613/996-0850
Hon. Lawrence MacAulay, Cardigan, Lib., PEI, 613/995-9325, Fax: 613/995-2754
Peter Mackay, Pictou-Antigonish-Guysborough, PC, NS, 613/992-5041, Fax: 613/992-0877
Steve Mahoney, Mississauga West, Lib., Ont., 613/995-7784, Fax: 613/996-9817
Gurbax Singh Malhi, Bramalea-Gore-Malton, Lib., Ont., 613/992-9105, Fax: 613/947-0443
John Maloney, Erie-Lincoln, Lib., Ont., 613/995-0988, Fax: 613/995-5245
Peter Mancini, Sydney-Victoria, NDP, NS, 613/995-6459, Fax: 613/995-2963
Hon. John Manley, Ottawa South, Lib., Ont., 613/992-3269, Fax: 613/995-1534
Preston Manning, Calgary Southwest, Ref., Alta., 613/996-6740, Fax: 613/947-0310
Richard Marceau, Charlesbourg, BQ, Qué., 613/995-8857, Fax: 613/995-1625
Jean-Paul Marchand, Québec-Est, BQ, Qué., 613/996-4151, Fax: 613/954-2269
Hon. Sergio Marchi, York West, Lib., Ont., 819/992-7332, Fax: 819/947-4452
Inky Mark, Dauphin-Swan River, Ref., Man., 613/992-3176, Fax: 613/992-0930
Hon. Diane Marleau, Sudbury, Lib., Ont., 613/996-8963, Fax: 613/995-2569
Dr. Keith Martin, Esquimalt-Juan de Fuca, Ref., BC, 613/996-2625, Fax: 613/996-9779
Pat Martin, Winnipeg Centre, NDP, Man., 613/992-5308, Fax: 613/992-2890
Hon. Paul Martin, LaSalle-Émard, Lib., Qué., 613/992-4284, Fax: 613/992-4291
Hon. Marcel Massé, Hull-Aylmer, Lib., Qué., 613/952-5555, Fax: 613/992-6474
Bill Matthews, Burin-St. George's, PC, Nfld., 613/992-8655, Fax: 613/992-5324
Philip Mayfield, Cariboo-Chilcotin, Ref., BC, 613/996-2205, Fax: 613/995-7139
Ian McClelland, Edmonton Southwest, Ref., Alta., 613/992-3594, Fax: 613/992-3616
Larry McCormick, Hastings-Frontenac-Lennox and Addington, Lib., Ont., 613/992-3640, Fax: 613/992-3642
Alexa McDonough, Halifax, NDP, NS, 613/995-7224, Fax: 613/992-8569
Joe McGuire, Egmont, Lib., PEI, 613/992-9223, Fax: 613/992-1974
John McKay, Scarborough East, Lib., Ont., 613/992-1447, Fax: 613/992-8569
Hon. Anne McLellan, Edmonton West, Lib., Alta., 613/992-4524, Fax: 613/943-0044
Grant McNally, Dewdney-Alouette, Ref., BC, 613/947-4613, Fax: 613/947-4615
Dan McTeague, Pickering-Ajax-Uxbridge, Lib., Ont., 613/995-8082, Fax: 613/993-6587
Ted McWhinney, Vancouver Quadra, Lib., BC, 613/992-2430, Fax: 613/995-0770
Réal Ménard, Hochelaga-Maisonneuve, BQ, Qué., 613/947-4576, Fax: 613/947-4579
Paul Mercier, Terrebonne-Blainville, BQ, Qué., 613/947-4788, Fax: 613/947-4879
Val Meredith, Surrey-White Rock-Langley, Ref., BC, 613/947-4497, Fax: 613/947-4500
Hon. Fred J. Mifflin, Bonavista-Trinity-Conception, Lib., Nfld., 613/992-4133, Fax: 613/992-7277

Peter Milliken, Kingston and the Islands, Lib., Ont., 613/996-1955, Fax: 613/996-1958
Bob Mills, Red Deer, Ref., Alta., 613/995-0590, Fax: 613/995-6831
Dennis J. Mills, Broadview-Greenwood, Lib., Ont., 613/992-7771, Fax: 613/996-9884
Maria Minna, Beaches-East York, Lib., Ont., 613/992-2115, Fax: 613/992-8083
Hon. Andy Mitchell, Parry Sound-Muskoka, Lib., Ont., 613/996-3434, Fax: 613/991-2147
Lee Morrison, Cypress Hills-Grasslands, Ref., Sask., 613/992-0657, Fax: 613/992-5508
Mark Muise, West Nova, PC, NS, 613/995-5711, Fax: 613/996-9857
Ian Murray, Lanark-Carleton, Lib., Ont., 613/947-2277, Fax: 613/947-2278
Lynn Myers, Waterloo-Wellington, Lib., Ont., 613/992-4633, Fax: 613/992-9932
Robert D. Nault, Kenora-Rainy River, Lib., Ont., 613/996-1161, Fax: 613/996-1759
Hon. Gilbert Normand, Bellechasse-Etchemins-Montmagny-L'Islet, Lib., Qué., 613/992-2289, Fax: 613/992-6864
John Nunziata, York South-Weston, Ind., Ont., 613/995-0777, Fax: 613/992-2949
Lorne Edmund Nystrom, Qu'Appelle, NDP, Sask., 613/992-4593, Fax: 613/996-3120
Deepak Obhrai, Calgary East, Ref., Alta., 613/947-4566, Fax: 613/947-4569
Lawrence O'Brien, Labrador, Lib., Nfld., 613/996-4630, Fax: 613/996-7132
Pat O'Brien, London-Fanshawe, Lib., Ont., 613/995-2901, Fax: 613/943-8717
John O'Reilly, Victoria-Haliburton, Lib., Ont., 613/992-2474, Fax: 613/996-9656
Dr. Rey Pagtakhan, Winnipeg North-St. Paul, Lib., Man., 613/992-7148, Fax: 613/996-9125
Jim Pankiw, Saskatoon-Humboldt, Ref., Sask., 613/992-8052, Fax: 613/996-9899
Denis Paradis, Brome-Missisquoi, Lib., Qué., 613/947-8185, Fax: 613/947-8188
Hon. Gilbert Parent, Niagara Centre, Lib., Ont., 613/995-9579, Fax: 613/995-0244
Carolyn Parrish, Mississauga Centre, Lib., Ont., 613/995-7321, Fax: 613/992-6708
Bernard Patry, Pierrefonds-Dollard, Lib., Qué., 613/992-2689, Fax: 613/996-8478
Charlie Penson, Peace River, Ref., Alta., 613/992-5685, Fax: 613/947-4782
Janko Peric, Cambridge, Lib., Ont., 613/996-1307, Fax: 613/996-8340
Gilles-A. Perron, Saint-Eustache-Sainte-Thérèse, BQ, Qué., 613/992-0336, Fax: 613/992-1160
Hon. Jim Peterson, Willowdale, Lib., Ont., 613/992-4964, Fax: 613/992-1158
Hon. Pierre S. Pettigrew, Papineau-Saint-Denis, Lib., Qué., 613/995-8872, Fax: 613/953-2903
Beth Phinney, Hamilton Mountain, Lib., Ont., 613/995-9389, Fax: 613/992-7802
Pauline Picard, Drummond, BQ, Qué., 613/947-4550, Fax: 613/947-4551
Jerry Pickard, Kent-Essex, Lib., Ont., 613/992-2612, Fax: 613/992-1852
Gary Pilliteri, Niagara Falls, Lib., Ont., 613/995-1547, Fax: 613/992-7910
Louis Plamondon, Richelieu, BQ, Qué., 613/995-9241, Fax: 613/995-6784
Charlie Power, St. John's West, PC, Nfld., 613/992-0927, Fax: 613/995-7858
David Pratt, Nepean-Carleton, Lib., Ont., 613/992-2772, Fax: 613/992-1209
David Price, Compton-Stanstead, PC, Qué., 613/995-2024, Fax: 613/992-1696
Dick Proctor, Palliser, NDP, Sask., 613/992-9115, Fax: 613/992-0131
George Proud, Hillsborough, Lib., PEI, 613/996-4714, Fax: 613/995-7685
Carmen Provenzano, Sault Ste. Marie, Lib., Ont., 613/992-9723, Fax: 613/992-1954
Jack Ramsay, Crowfoot, Ref., Alta., 613/947-4608, Fax: 613/947-4611
Karen Redman, Kitchener Centre, Lib., Ont., 613/995-8913, Fax: 613/996-7329
Julian Reed, Halton, Lib., Ont., 613/996-7046, Fax: 613/992-0851
John Reynolds, West Vancouver-Sunshine Coast, Ref., BC, 613/947-4617, Fax: 613/947-4620
John Richardson, Perth-Middlesex, Lib., Ont., 613/992-6124, Fax: 613/998-7902
Nelson A. Riis, Kamloops, NDP, BC, 613/995-6931, Fax: 613/995-9897
Gerry Ritz, Battlefords-Lloydminster, Ref., Sask., 613/995-7080, Fax: 613/996-8472
Hon. Lucienne Robillard, Westmount-Ville-Marie, Lib., Qué., 613/996-7267, Fax: 613/995-8632
Svend J. Robinson, Burnaby-Douglas, NDP, BC, 613/996-5597, Fax: 613/992-5501
Yves Rocheleau, Trois-Rivières, BQ, Qué., 613/992-2349, Fax: 613/995-9498
Hon. Allan Rock, Q.C., Etobicoke Centre, Lib., Ont., 613/947-5000, Fax: 613/947-4276
Jacques Saada, Brossard-La Prairie, Lib., Qué., 613/995-9287, Fax: 613/992-7273
Benoît Sauvageau, Repentigny, BQ, Qué., 613/992-5257, Fax: 613/996-4338
Werner Schmidt, Kelowna, Ref., BC, 613/992-7006, Fax: 613/992-7636
Hon. Andy Scott, Fredericton, Lib., NB, 613/992-1067, Fax: 613/996-9955
Mike Scott, Skeena, Ref., BC, 613/993-6654, Fax: 613/993-9007
Benoît Serré, Timiskaming-Cochrane, Lib., Ont., 613/992-2792, Fax: 613/992-2794
Alex Shepherd, Durham, Lib., Ont., 613/996-4984, Fax: 613/996-4986
Georgette Sheridan, Saskatoon-Humboldt, Lib., Sask., 613/992-8052
Monte Solberg, Medicine Hat, Ref., Alta., 613/992-4516, Fax: 613/992-6181
John Solomon, Regina-Lumsden-Lake Centre, NDP, Sask., 613/992-4573, Fax: 613/996-6885
Bob Speller, Haldimand-Norfolk-Brant, Lib., Ont., 613/996-4974, Fax: 613/996-9749
Brent St. Denis, Algoma-Manitoulin, Lib., Ont., 613/996-5376, Fax: 613/995-6661
Caroline St-Hilaire, Longueuil, BQ, Qué., 613/992-8514, Fax: 613/992-2744
Diane St-Jacques, Shefford, PC, Qué., 613/992-5279, Fax: 613/992-7871
Guy St-Julien, Abitibi, Lib., Qué., 613/996-3076, Fax: 613/996-0828
Paul Steckle, Huron-Bruce, Lib., Ont., 613/992-8234, Fax: 613/995-6350
Hon. Christine Stewart, Northumberland, Lib., Ont., 613/992-8585, Fax: 613/995-7536
Hon. Jane Stewart, Brant, Lib., Ont., 613/992-3118, Fax: 613/992-6382
Darrel Stinson, Okanagan-Shuswap, Ref., BC, 613/995-9095, Fax: 613/992-3195
Peter Stoffer, Sackville-Eastern Shore, NDP, NS
Chuck Strahl, Fraser Valley, Ref., BC, 613/992-2940, Fax: 613/995-5621
Paul Szabo, Mississauga South, Lib., Ont., 613/992-4848, Fax: 613/996-3267
Andrew Telegdi, Kitchener-Waterloo, Lib., Ont., 613/996-5928, Fax: 613/992-6251
Yolande Thibeault, Saint-Lambert, Lib., Qué., 613/998-5961, Fax: 613/954-0707
Greg Thompson, Charlotte, PC, NB, 613/995-5550, Fax: 613/995-5226
Myron Thompson, Wild Rose, Ref., Alta., 613/996-5152, Fax: 613/947-4601
Paddy Torsney, Burlington, Lib., Ont., 613/995-0881, Fax: 613/995-1091
Stéphan Tremblay, Lac-Saint-Jean, BQ, Qué., 613/947-2745, Fax: 613/947-2748
Suzanne Tremblay, Rimouski-Mitis, BQ, Qué., 613/992-5302, Fax: 613/996-8298
Daniel Turp, Beauharnois-Salaberry, BQ, Qué., 613/992-5036, Fax: 613/995-7821
Rose-Marie Ur, Lambton-Kent-Middlesex, Lib., Ont., 613/947-4581, Fax: 613/947-4584
Tony Valeri, Stoney Creek, Lib., Ont., 613/992-6535, Fax: 613/992-7764
Hon. Lyle Vanclief, Prince Edward-Hastings, Lib., Ont., 613/992-5321, Fax: 613/996-8652
Angela Vautour, Beauséjour-Petitcodiac, NDP, NB, 613/992-1020, Fax: 613/992-3053
Maurice Vellacott, Wanuskewin, Ref., Sask., 613/992-1899, Fax: 613/992-3085
Pierrette Venne, Saint-Bruno-Saint-Hubert, BQ, Qué., 613/996-2416, Fax: 613/995-6973
Joseph Volpe, Eglinton-Lawrence, Lib., Ont., 613/992-6361, Fax: 613/992-9791
Tom Wappel, Scarborough Southwest, Lib., Ont., 613/995-0284, Fax: 613/996-6309
Judy Wasylycia-Leis, Winnipeg North Centre, NDP, Man., 613/996-6417, Fax: 613/996-9713
Elsie Wayne, Saint John, PC, NB, 613/947-4571, Fax: 613/947-4574
Susan Whelan, Essex, Lib., Ont., 613/992-1812, Fax: 613/995-0033
Randy White, Langley-Abbotsford, Ref., BC, 613/995-0183, Fax: 613/996-9795
Ted White, North Vancouver, Ref., BC, 613/995-1225, Fax: 613/992-7319
Bryon Wilfert, Oak Ridges, Lib., Ont., 613/992-3802, Fax: 613/996-1954
John Williams, St. Albert, Ref., Alta., 613/996-4722, Fax: 613/995-8880
Bob Wood, Nipissing, Lib., Ont., 613/995-6255, Fax: 613/996-7993

## FEDERAL GOVERNMENT DEPARTMENTS & AGENCIES

**Editor's Note:** The entries listed below are entered alphabetically, using "applied titles" as registered by the Federal Identity Program. Cross references are used to help you to locate the entry quickly. The two departments that incorporate "Department of" as part of their applied titles (Department of Finance Canada; Department of Justice Canada) are nevertheless listed alphabetically under Finance and Justice.

## AGRICULTURE & AGRI-FOOD CANADA/ Agriculture et Agro-alimentaire Canada

Sir John Carling Bldg., 930 Carling Ave., Ottawa ON K1A 0C5
613/759-1000; Fax: 613/759-6726; URL: http://aceis.agr.ca

The Department develops & implements national policies & programs to support the agriculture & agri-food sector in a manner that assures a dependable supply of safe, nutritious food at reasonable prices to consumers, with equitable returns to producers & processors. In addition, the Department participates in the development & implementation of federal policies & programs in the areas of socio-economic development, emergency response & international relations.

The Department meets its responsibilities through the Agri-Food Program, which is implemented in cooperation with the provincial governments, national & international agricultural organizations, universities, etc. The Department consults actively with its client groups including producers, processors, distributors, vendors & consumers of agricultural & agri-food products. Other federal departments with which elements of the Agri-Food Program work include

Environment Canada, Health Canada, the Department of Foreign Affairs & International Trade, Natural Resources Canada & Revenue Canada.
The Agri-Food program inludes the following activities:
• Agricultural Research & Development
• Policy & Farm Economic Programs
• Market & Industry Services
• Rural Prairie Rehabilitation, Sustainability & Development
• Corporate Management & Services
• Canadian Grain Commission

#### ACTS ADMINISTERED

Advance Payments for Crops Act
Agricultural Products Board Act
Agricultural Products Co-operative Marketing Act
Agricultural Products Marketing Act
Animal Pedigree Act
Canada Agricultural Products Act
Canada Grain Act
Canadian Dairy Commission Act
Canadian Food Inspection Agency Act
Canagrex Dissolution Act
Department of Agriculture & Agri-Food Act
Experimental Farm Stations Act
Farm Credit Corporation Act
Farm Debt Review Act
Farm Improvement & Marketing Cooperatives Loans Act
Farm Improvement Loans Act
Farm Income Protection Act
Farm Products Agencies Act
Financial Administration Act
Fish Inspection Act
Grain Futures Act
Hay & Straw Inspection Act
Livestock Feed Assistance Act
Prairie Farm Rehabilitation Act
Prairie Grain Advance Payments Act
Prairie Grain Provisional Payments Act

#### Acts Administered in Part by Agriculture & Agri-Food Canada

Consumer Packaging & Labelling Act (Canadian Food Inspection Agency)
Criminal Code (Justice & Attorney General)
Department of Foreign Affairs & International Trade Act (Foreign Affairs & International Trade)
Food & Drugs Act (Canadian Food Inspection Agency)
**Minister**, Hon. Lyle Vanclief, 613/759-1059, Fax: 613/759-1081
Secretary of State, Hon. Gilbert Normand, 613/947-4592, Fax: 613/947-4595
Deputy Minister, Frank Claydon, 613/759-1101, Fax: 613/759-1040

#### Communications Branch

613/759-7976; Fax: 613/759-7969
Acting Director General, G. Shaw
Director, Policy & Planning, Susan Leah, 613/759-7933
Acting Director, Strategic Planning & Operations Division, Eric Mikkelborg, 613/759-7903

### CORPORATE SERVICES BRANCH

613/759-6811; Fax: 613/759-6728
Asst. Deputy Minister & Director General, Finance & Resource Management Services, Andrew Graham
Director General, Finance & Resource Management Services, D. Kam, 613/759-6751
Director, Information Management Services, Victor Desroches, 613/759-7083, Fax: 613/759-6643

#### Human Resources Branch

613/759-1196; Fax: 613/759-1390
Director General, Jane Roszell
Director, Human Resources Management & Development Division, A. Ettinger, 613/759-1174
Director, Management Services Division, W. Newby, 613/759-1121
Director, Official Languages Division, C.R. Desrochers, 613/759-6453

### MARKET & INDUSTRY SERVICES BRANCH (MISB)

613/759-7561; Fax: 613/759-7497
Asst. Deputy Minister, Diane Vincent
Director General, International Markets Bureau, Lawrence T. Dickenson, Sir John Carling Bldg., 930 Carling Ave., 10th Fl., Ottawa ON K1A 0C5, 613/759-7684, Fax: 613/759-7499
Director General, International Trade Policy Directorate, Mike Gifford, Sir John Carling Bldg., 930 Carling Ave., 10th Fl., Ottawa ON K1A 0C5, 613/759-7675, Fax: 613/759-7503
Director General, Planning & Regional Operations Directorate, Phil Jensen, 613/759-7564
Director, Management Services Division, B. Cameron, 613/759-7613

#### Agricultural Industry Services Directorate

2200 Walkley Rd., 1st Fl., Ottawa ON K1A 0C5
Fax: 613/957-1527
Director General, Gilles Lavoie, 613/957-7078 ext. 3008
Director, Animal Industry Division, B. Howard, 613/957-7078 ext.3044, Fax: 613/957-1527
Director, Horticulture & Special Crops Division, M. Pearson, 613/957-7078 ext. 3063
Asst. Director, Dairy Section, P. Doyle, 613/957-7078 ext.3010
Asst. Director, Poultry Section, D. McGonnegal, 613/957-7078 ext. 3032
Asst. Director, Red Meat Section, John Ross, 613/957-7078 ext. 3007

#### Food Bureau

613/759-7557; Fax: 613/759-7496
Director General, André Charland
Director, Industry Analysis Division, G.M. McGregor, 613/759-7558
Director, Industry Services, R. Cooper, 613/759-7538

#### Market & Industry Regional Offices

Alberta: Canada Place, #810, 9700 Jasper Ave., Edmonton AB T5J 4G5 – 403/495-5525; Fax: 403/495-3324, Regional Director, Ken McCready
Atlantic (Overall): 440 University Ave., PO Box 2949, Charlottetown PE C1A 8C5 – 902/566-7300; Fax: 902/566-7316, Regional Director, Dave Faulkner
Atlantic (New Brunswick): #213, 633 Queen St., Fredericton NB E3B 1C3 – 506/452-3754; Fax: 506/452-3509, Asst. Director, Renald Cormier
Atlantic (Newfoundland): 354 Water St., 2nd Fl., PO Box 1878, St. John's NF A1C 5P9 – 709/772-4063; Fax: 709/772-4803, Asst. Director, Al McIssac
Atlantic (Nova Scotia): #200, 35 Commercial St., PO Box 698, Truro NS B2N 5E5 – 902/893-0068; Fax: 902/893-6777, Asst. Director, Janet Steele
Atlantic (Prince Edward Island): 500 Queen St., PO Box 2949, Charlottetown PE C1A 8C5 – 902/566-7311; Fax: 902/566-7316, Asst. Director, Rollin Andrew
British Columbia: #204, 620 Royal Ave., PO Box 2522, New Westminster BC V3L 5A8 – 604/666-6344; Fax: 604/666-7235, Regional Director, John Berry
Manitoba: #402, 303 Main St., Winnipeg MB R3C 3G7 – 204/983-3032; Fax: 204/983-4583, Regional Director, Bill Breckman
Ontario: 174 Stone Rd. West, Guelph ON N1G 4S9 – 519/837-9400; Fax: 519/837-9782, Regional Director, Conrad Paquette
Québec: Gare Maritime Champlain, #350-4, 901, Cap Diamant, Québec QC G1K 4K1 – 418/648-4775; Fax: 418/648-7342, Acting Regional Director, Jean Lamoureux
Montréal: 514/283-8888, ext. 502, Fax: 514/283-3143
Saskatchewan: #801, 1500 Hamilton St., PO Box 8035, Regina SK S4P 4C7 – 306/780-5545; Fax: 306/780-7360, Regional Director, Susie Miller

### POLICY BRANCH

613/759-7349; Fax: 613/759-7229
Asst. Deputy Minister, David Oulton
Director General, Strategic & Corporate Relations, G. O'Sullivan
Executive Director, Co-operatives Secretariat, Lynden Hillier, 613/759-7195, Fax: 613/759-7489

#### Adaptation & Grain Policy Directorate

#500, 303 Main St., Winnipeg MB R3C 3G7
204/983-8370; Fax: 204/983-5300
Sir John Carling Bldg., 930 Carling Ave., Ottawa ON K1A 0C5
613/759-7315, Fax: 613/759-6612
Director General, H. Migie
Acting Director, Environment Bureau, Michael Presley, Sir John Carling Bldg., 930 Carling Ave., Ottawa ON K1A 0C5, 613/759-7308, Fax: 613/759-7238
Director, Market Analysis Division, M. Liu, 204/983-8468
Director, Policy Development Division, Bruce Kirk, 204/984-7791

#### Economic & Policy Analysis Directorate

Executive Director, Ken Ash, 613/759-7423, Fax: 613/759-7236
Director, Economic & Industry Analysis Division, Jack Gellner, 613/759-7421, Fax: 613/759-7034

#### Farm Income Policy & Programs Directorate

613/759-7269; Fax: 613/759-7235
Director General, Dr. T.G. Richardson
Director, Insurance Division, M. Ellis, 613/759-2614, Fax: 613/759-7078
Director, Policy Development Division, R. Eyvindson, 613/759-7289, Fax: 613/759-7139

#### Industry Performance & Analysis Directorate

613/759-7369; Fax: 613/759-7237
Director General, Dr. D. Hedley
Director, Industry Information Program, B. Huff, 613/759-7465
Director, Marketing Policy Division, R. Tudor-Price, 613/759-7354

#### Net Income Stabilization Administration

PO Box 6100, Winnipeg MB R3C 3A4
204/983-0761; Fax: 204/983-7557
Toll Free: 1-800-665-NISA
A federal-provincial-farmer initiative designed to provide long-term income stabilization to farmers.
Executive Director, R. Charron

#### Rural Secretariat & Strategic Directorate

Executive Director, L. Johnson, 613/759-7113, Fax: 613/759-7105

### RESEARCH BRANCH

Sir John Carling Bldg., 930 Carling Ave., Ottawa ON K1A 0C5
613/759-7794; Fax: 613/759-7772
Asst. Deputy Minister, Dr. J.B. Morrissey

#### Research, Planning & Coordination Directorate

613/759-7792; Fax: 613/759-7769
Director General, Bruce Mitchell
Director, Financial & Administrative Services, D. Schmid, 613/759-1977

#### Central Experimental Farm

613/759-7865; Fax: 613/759-1970
Acting Director, Centre for Land & Biological Resources Research, M. Feldman, 613/759-1847

Acting Director, Plant Research Centre, Dr. H. Voldeng, 613/759-1652

#### Eastern Region Directorate

Research Stations at: St. John's Nfld., Charlottetown PEI, Fredericton NB, Kentville NS, Lennoxville Qué., Ste-Foy Qué., St-Hyacinthe Qué., St-Jean-sur-Richelieu Qué., London Ont., Harrow Ont, Ottawa Ont.

Director General, Dr. Yvon Martel, 613/759-7636, Fax: 613/759-7771

Director, Centre for Food & Animal Research, Dr. A. Lachance, 613/759-1435

#### Western Region Directorate

Research Stations at: Summerland BC, Lethbridge Alta., Lacombe Alta., Swift Current Sask., Saskatoon Sask., Brandon Man., Winnipeg Man.

Director General, Dr. R.G. Dorrell, 613/759-7865, Fax: 613/759-7770

### REVIEW BRANCH

613/759-6470; Fax: 613/759-6499

Director General, Elaine Lawson

Acting Director, Planning & Coordination, Frank Brunetta, 613/759-6471

### PRAIRIE FARM REHABILITATION ADMINISTRATION (PFRA)

CIBC Tower, #603, 1800 Hamilton St., Regina SK S4P 4L2

306/780-6545; Fax: 306/780-5018; URL: http://www.agr.ca/pfra

Shelterbelt Centre, Indian Head SK S0G 2K0

306/695-2284, Fax: 306/695-2568

Director General, Dr. Bernie Sonntag, 306/780-5081

Director, Ottawa Affairs, Jamshed Merchant, Sir John Carling Bldg., #4103, 930 Carling Ave., Ottawa ON K1A 0C5, 613/759-7225, Fax: 613/759-6623

#### PFRA Regional Offices

Northern Alberta: Royal Lepage Bldg., #1200, 10130 - 103 St., Edmonton AB T5J 3N9 – 403/495-4526; Fax: 403/495-4504, Regional Director, Fred Kraft

Southern Alberta: Harry Hays Bldg., #832, 220 - 4 Ave. SE, PO Box 2906, Calgary AB T2G 4X3 – 403/292-5641; Fax: 403/292-5659, Regional Director, Andrew Cullen

Manitoba Region: The Cargill Bldg., #238, 240 Graham Ave., Winnipeg MB R3C 0J7 – 204/983-3116; Fax: 204/983-2178, Regional Director, Erminio Caligiuri

Northern Saskatchewan: Peterson Bldg., University of Saskatchewan, North Rd., PO Box 908, Saskatoon SK S7K 3M4 – 306/975-4663; Fax: 306/975-4594, Regional Director, Brian Abrahamson

Southern Saskatchewan: 1800 Hamilton St., Regina SK S4P 4L2 – 306/780-5142; Fax: 306/780-5018, Regional Director, Gerry Wetterstrand

### ASSOCIATED AGENCIES, BOARDS & COMMISSIONS

Listed alphabetically in detail, this section.

Canadian Dairy Commission
Canadian Grain Commission
Canadian Wheat Board
Farm Credit Corporation
National Farm Products Council

## ATLANTIC CANADA OPPORTUNITIES AGENCY (ACOA)/Agence de promotion économique du Canada atlantique (APECA)

644 Main St., 3rd Fl., PO Box 6051, Moncton NB E1C 9J8

506/851-2271; Fax: 506/851-7403; URL: http://www.acoa.ca/

Toll Free: 1-800-561-7862, TDD: 506/851-3540

A federal government development agency providing support to entrepreneurs in the Atlantic Region. The goal of the ACOA is to improve the economy of Atlantic Canadian communities, through the successful development of businesses and job opportunities. The organization helps people set up new, and to expand existing businesses; market Atlantic Canada, nationally and internationally; works together with other federal departments, the provincial governments and private sector within the four Atlantic provinces to ensure maximum benefit for the region.

**Minister Responsible**, Hon. John Manley, 613/995-9001, Fax: 613/992-0302

**Secretary of State**, Hon. Fred J. Mifflin, 613/996-4649, Fax: 613/954-1054

President, J. David Nicholson, 506/851-6128

Vice-President, Programs, Peter Estey, 506/851-3550

Director, Trade, Innovation & Technology, Deborah Lyons, 506/851-6240

#### Regional Offices

Cape Breton: ACOA Cape Breton, 15 Dorchester St., 4th Fl., PO Box 2001, Sydney NS B1P 6K7 – 902/564-3614; Fax: 902/564-3825

New Brunswick: 570 Queen St., PO Box 578, Fredericton NB E3B 5A6 – 506/452-3184; Fax: 506/452-3285, Toll Free: 1-800-561-4030

Newfoundland: Atlantic Place, #801, 215 Water St., PO Box 1060, Stn C, St. John's NF A1C 5M5 – 709/772-2751; Fax: 709/772-2712, Toll Free: 1-800-563-5766

Nova Scotia: #600, 1801 Hollis St., PO Box 2284, Stn M, Halifax NS B3J 3C8 – 902/426-6743; Fax: 902/426-2054, Toll Free: 1-800-565-1228

Ottawa: PO Box 1667, Stn B, Ottawa ON K1P 5R5 – 613/954-2422; Fax: 613/954-0429

Prince Edward Island: 75 Fitzroy St., PO Box 40, Charlottetown PE C1A 7K2 – 902/566-7492; Fax: 902/566-7098

## ATLANTIC PILOTAGE AUTHORITY CANADA/ Administration de pilotage de l'Atlantique Canada

Purdy's Wharf, Tower 1, #1402, 1959 Upper Water St., Halifax NS B3J 3N2

902/426-2550; Fax: 902/426-4004; URL: http://canada.gc.ca/depts/agencies/apaind_e.html

The Authority operates a pilotage service within the Atlantic Region which includes all the compulsory pilotage waters of the four Atlantic provinces. Responsible for establishing, operating, maintaining and administering an efficient and economical pilotage service within the coastal waters of the Atlantic region. The authority prescribes tariffs of pilotage charges that are fair, reasonable and consistent with providing revenues allowing the Authority to operate on a self-sustaining financial basis. Reports to government through the Minister of Trasport.

**Chair**, R. Anthony McGuinness

## ATOMIC ENERGY OF CANADA LIMITED (AECL)/Énergie atomique du Canada Ltée (EACL)

2251 Speakman Dr., Mississauga ON L5K 1B2

905/823-9040; Fax: 905/823-8006; Email: webmaster@crl.aecl.ca; URL: http://www.aecl.ca

AECL develops, markets & manages the construction of CANDU power reactors & MAPLE research reactors.

**President & CEO**, J.R. Morden

## ATOMIC ENERGY CONTROL BOARD (AECB)/Commission de contrôle de l'énergie atomique (CCEA)

280 Slater St., PO Box 1046, Stn B, Ottawa ON K1P 5S9

613/995-5894; Fax: 613/995-5086; Email: info@atomcon.gc.ca; URL: http://www.gc.ca/aecb/

Toll Free: 1-800-668-5284

AECB derives authority from the Atomic Energy Control Act & is responsible for regulatory control of the health, safety, security & environmental aspects of the development, application & use of nuclear energy in Canada.

**President & CEO**, Dr. Agnes J. Bishop

Chair, Advisory Committee on Nuclear Safety, A Pearson

Director General, Administration Directorate, G.C. Jack

Director General, Analysis & Assessment Directorate, J.G. Waddington

Director General, Fuel Cycle & Materials Regulation Directorate, R.M. Duncan

Director General, Reactor Regulation Directorate, J.D. Harvie

Director General, Secretariat, J.P. Marchildon

Chief, Office of Public Information, H.J.M. Spence

Senior Counsel, A. Nowack

## AUDITOR GENERAL OF CANADA/ Vérificateur Général du Canada

240 Sparks St., Ottawa ON K1A 0G6

613/995-3708; Fax: 613/957-4023; Email: AG-Reports@oag-bvg.gc.ca; URL: http://www.oag-bvg.gc.ca/

Commissioner of the Environment & Sustainable Development URL: http://www.oag-bvg.gc.ca/oag-bvg/coe/html/env_e/menu_e.html; Email: green-report@oag-bvg.gc.ca

The Office of the Auditor General of Canada is responsible for examining the Public Accounts of Canada, including those relating to the Consolidated Revenue Fund, public property & various Crown Corporations, & also for conducting audits & studies involving the management of financial, physical & human resources of the federal government. The Auditor General must report annually to the House of Commons &, in addition, may report up to three times a year. He may also make a special report to the House on any matter that he feels should not be deferred. Following amendments to the Auditor General Act made in December 1995, the Auditor General is also required to report to the House of Commons annually on all significant matters related to the environment & sustainable development.

**Auditor General**, L. Denis Desautels, FCA, 613/992-2512

Deputy Auditor General, Audit Operations Branch, Raymond M. Dubois, 613/993-6309

Deputy Auditor General, Professional & Administrative Services Branch, Ronald Warme, 613/993-5456

Commissioner, Environment & Sustainable Development, Brian Emmett

Director, Public Affairs, John Zegers

#### Regional Offices

Edmonton: Manulife Place, #2460, 10180 - 101 St., Edmonton AB T5J 3S4 – 403/495-2028; Fax: 403/495-2031, Principal, Roger Simpton

Halifax: 1660 Hollis St., 4th Fl., Halifax NS B3J 1V7 – 902/426-7721; Fax: 902/426-8591, Principal, John O'Brien

Montréal: #1005, 685 rue Cathcart, Montréal QC H3B 1M7 – 514/283-6086; Fax: 514/283-1715, Principal, Francine Bissonette

Vancouver: #250, 757 West Hastings St., Vancouver BC V6C 1A1 – 604/666-3596; Fax: 604/666-6162, Principal, Alan Beaton
Winnipeg: #630, 240 Graham Ave., Winnipeg MB R3C 0J7 – 204/983-2426; Fax: 204/983-0003, Principal, John McCullough

## BANK OF CANADA/Banque du Canada

234 Wellington St., Ottawa ON K1A 0G9
613/782-8111; Fax: 613/782-8655; URL: http://www.bank-banque-canada.ca/english/intro-e.htm

The Bank is responsible for regulating "credit & currency in the best interests of the economic life of the nation". The Bank acts as fiscal agent for the Government of Canada in respect of the management of the public debt of Canada & the Exchange Fund Account. The sole right to issue paper money for circulation in Canada is vested in the Bank of Canada. Reports to government through the Minister of Finance.

**Governor**, Gordon Thiessen
Senior Deputy Governor, B. Bonin
Deputy Governor, C. Freedman
Deputy Governor, W. Paul Jenkins
Deputy Governor, S. Kennedy
Deputy Governor, T. Noël
Corporate Secretary, L. Theodore Requard
Chief, Banking Operations Department, B. Schwab
Chief, Financial Markets, B. Montador
Chief, Infrastructure Services, D.W. MacDonald
Chief, International Department, J.D. Murray
Chief, Management Services, J. Cosier
Chief, Market Operations & Analysis, Pat E. Demerse
Chief, Public Debt Department, R.L. Flett
Chief, Research Department, D.J. Longworth
Chief, Securities, S. Poirier, Bank of Canada, 250 University Ave., Toronto ON M5H 3E5

## BUSINESS DEVELOPMENT BANK OF CANADA (BDBC)/Banque de développement du Canada (BDC)

#400, 5, Place Ville Marie, Montréal QC H3B 5E7
514/283-5904; Fax: 514/283-0617; URL: http://www.bdc.ca/
Ligne sans frais: 1-888-463-6232

Financial Institution wholly owned by the Government of Canada. BDC plays a leadership role in delivering financial & managment services to Canadian small business, with a particular focus on the emerging & export sectors of the economy. BDC's range of development capital complements products available from other institutions. Financing instruments include micro-business loans, term loans, Working Capital for Growth loans, Working Capital for Exporters loans, Patient Capital loans, Venture Loans, Seed Capital & venture capital. BDC's management services include a wide range of business counselling, management support & mentoring services for new & expanding businesses, exporters, women, young entrepreneurs, & aboriginals. Services include include a training & counselling products for exporters called NEXPRO, as well as ISO certification assistance. BDC's services are made available across Canada through a broad network fo more than 80 branches.

**President/CEO**, François Beaudoin
Chair, Patrick J. Lavelle
Executive Vice-President/COO, John J. Ryan
Senior Vice-President, Corporate Affairs, Donald E. Layne
Senior Vice-President, Emerging Markets, David L. Mowat
Senior Vice-President, Operations, Luc Provencher
Vice-President & Treasurer, Clement Albert
Vice-President, Credit, Jacques Lemoine
Vice-President, Finance & CFO, Alan B. Marquis
Vice-President, Human Resources & Administration, Pauline Rochefort
Vice-President, Management Services, Norma Passaretti
Vice-President, Systems & Technology, Irène Nault
Director, Communications, Peter Stewart

#### BDC Regional Offices

Barrie: 151 Ferris Lane, PO Box 876, Barrie ON L4M 4Y6 – 705/739-0444
Bathurst: Harbourview Place, #205, 275 Main St., Bathurst NB E2A 1A9 – 506/548-7360
Brandon: 940 Princess Ave., PO Box 6, Brandon MB R7A 0P6 – 204/726-7570
Bridgewater: Eastside Plaza, 450 LaHave St., PO Box 540, Bridgewater NS B4V 2X6 – 902/527-5501
Calgary: Bow Valley Square 1, 202 - 6 Ave. SW, Calgary AB T2P 2R9 – 403/292-5000
Calgary North: 1935 - 32 Ave. NE, Calgary AB T2E 7C3 – 403/292-5333; Fax: 403/292-6651
Campbell River: Georgia Quay, #202, 909 Island Hwy., Campbell River BC V9W 2C2 – 250/286-5800; Fax: 250/286-5830
Charlottetown: 51 University Ave., 2nd Fl., PO Box 488, Charlottetown PE C1A 7L1 – 902/566-7454
Chicoutimi: #204A, 345, rue des Saguenéens, Chicoutimi QC G7H 6K9 – 418/698-5599
Corner Brook: Herald Towers, 4 Herald Ave., 1st Fl., Corner Brook NF A2H 4B4 – 709/637-4515
Cranbrook: 205 Cranbrook St. North, Cranbrook BC V1C 3R1 – 250/417-2200; Fax: 250/417-2213
Drummondville: 1010, boul René-Lévesque, Drummondville QC J2C 5W4 – 819/478-4951
Edmundston: Carrefour Assomption, #405, 121, rue de L'Eglise, Edmundston NB E3V 3L2 – 506/739-8311
Edmonton: First Edmonton Place, #200, 10665 Jasper Ave., Edmonton AB T5J 3S9 – 403/495-2277
Fort St. John: #7, 10230 - 100 St., Fort St. John BC V1J 3Y9 – 250/787-0622
Fredericton: The Barker House, #204, 570 Queen St., Fredericton NB E3B 5B4 – 506/452-3030
Granby: 619, rue Principale, Granby QC J2G 2Y1 – 514/372-5202
Grand Falls - Windsor: 42 High St., PO Box 744, Grand Falls-Windsor NF A2A 2M4 – 709/489-2181
Grande Prairie: Windsor Court, #102, 9835 - 101 Ave., Grande Prairie SK T8V 5V4 – 403/532-8875
Halifax: 1400 Cogswell Tower, Scotia Sq., PO Box 1656, Halifax NS B3J 2Z7 – 902/426-7860; Fax: 902/426-6783
Hamilton: #101, 25 Main St. West, Hamilton ON L8P 1H1 – 905/572-2954
Hull: #104, 259 boul St-Joseph, Hull QC J8Y 6T1 – 819/997-4434
Kamloops: #100, 63 West Victoria, Kamloops BC V2C 6L3 – 250/851-4900
Kelowna: 313 Bernard Ave., Kelowna BC V1Y 6N6 – 250/470-4812; Fax: 250/470-4832
Kenora: 227 Second St. South, Kenora ON P9N 1G1 – 807/467-3535; Fax: 807/467-3533
Kingston: Plaza 16, 16 Bath Rd., Kingston ON K7L 4V8 – 613/545-8636
Kitchener-Waterloo: Commerce House Bldg., 50 Queen St. North, 4th Fl., Kitchener ON N2H 6P4 – 519/571-6676
Langley: #101, 20316 - 56 Ave., Langley BC V3A 3Y7 – 250/532-5150; Fax: 250/532-5166
Laval: #700, 3090, boul Le Carrefour, Laval QC H7T 2J7 – 514/973-6868
Lethbridge: 520 - 5 Ave. South, Lethbridge AB T1J 0T8 – 403/382-3000
London: 380 Wellington St., London ON N6A 5B5 – 519/675-3101
Longueuil: #100, 550, ch Chambly, Longueuil QC J4H 3L8 – 514/928-4120
Mississauga: 3660 Hurontario St., 8th Fl., Mississauga ON L5B 3C4 – 905/566-6417
Moncton: Commercial Centre, 10 Commercial St., 4th Fl., PO Box 20019, Moncton NB E1C 9M1 – 506/851-6120
Montréal: BDC Bldg., #12525, 5, Place Ville Marie, Montréal QC H3B 2G2 – 514/496-7966; Fax: 514/496-7974
Montreal (De Maisonneuve): 6068, rue Sherbrooke est, Montreal QC H1N 1C1 – 514/283-5858
Nanaimo: #100, 235 Bastion St., Nanaimo BC V9R 3A3 – 250/754-0250; Fax: 250/754-0256
New Westminster: First Capital Place, #201, 960 Quayside Dr., New Westminster BC V3M 6G2 – 604/775-5400; Fax: 604/666-7750
North Bay: 222 McIntyre St. West, North Bay ON P1B 2Y8 – 705/495-5700; Fax: 705/495-5707
North Vancouver: #6, 221 West Esplande, North Vancouver BC V7M 3J3 – 604/666-7703; Fax: 604/666-1957
Oshawa: 17 King St. East, Oshawa ON L1H 1A8 – 905/725-3366
Ottawa: 280 Albert St., 3rd Fl., Ottawa ON K1P 5G8 – 613/995-0234
Peterborough: Peterborough Square Tower, 340 George St. North, 4th Fl., Peterborough ON K9J 7H6 – 705/750-4800
Prince Albert: 1100 - 1 Ave. East, PO Box 520, Prince Albert SK – 306/953-8580
Prince George: #100, 177 Victoria St., Prince George BC V2L 5R8 – 604/561-5323; Fax: 604/561-5512
Québec: 871, ch Saint-Louis, Québec QC G1S 1C1 – 418/648-3972
Red Deer: #107, 4815 - 50 Ave., Red Deer AB T4N 4A5 – 403/340-4203
Regina: Bank of Canada Bldg., #320, 2220 - 12 Ave., Regina SK S4P 0M8 – 306/780-6478
Rimouski: 391, boul Jessop, Rimouski QC G5L 1M9 – 418/722-3300
Rouyn-Noranda: #301, 139, boul Québec, Rouyn-Noranda QC J9X 6M8 – 819/764-6701
St Catharines: #100, 39 Queen St., St Catharines ON L2R 5G6 – 905/988-2874
St-Jerôme: #102, 55, rue Castonguay, St-Jerôme QC J7Y 2H9 – 514/432-7111; Fax: 514/432-8366
Saint John: 75 Prince William St., 2nd Fl., Saint John NB E2L 2B2 – 506/636-4751
St. John's: Atlantic Place, 215 Water St., 3rd Fl., St. John's NF A1C 5K4 – 709/722-5505
Saint-Laurent: #160, 3100, Cote Vertu, Saint-Laurent QC H4R 2J8 – 514/496-7500
Saint-Leonard: 6347, rue Jean-Talon est, Saint-Leonard QC H1S 3E7 – 514/251-2818
Saskatoon: Canada Bldg., 105 - 21st St. East, Saskatoon SK S7K 0B3 – 306/975-4822
Sault Ste. Marie: 153 Great Northern Rd., Sault Ste. Marie ON P6B 4Y9 – 705/941-3030; Fax: 705/941-3040
Scarborough: Metro East Corporate Centre, #112, 305 Milner Ave., Scarborough ON M1B 3V4 – 416/954-0709
Sept-Îles: #305, 106, rue Napoleon, Sept-Îles QC G4R 3L7 – 418/968-1420
Sherbrooke: 2532, rue King ouest, Sherbrooke QC J1J 2E8 – 819/564-5700
Stratford: 516 Huron St., Stratford ON N5A 5T7 – 519/271-5650
Sudbury: #10, 233 Brady Square, Sudbury ON P3B 4H5 – 705/670-6482
Surrey: London Stn, #160, 10362 King George Hwy., Surrey BC V3T 2W5 – 604/586-2400
Sydney: 225 Charlotte St., Sydney NS B1P 1C4 – 902/564-7700
Terrace: 3233 Emerson St., Terrace BC V8G 5L2 – 250/615-5300; Fax: 250/615-5320
Thunder Bay: #102, 1136 Alloy Dr., Thunder Bay ON P7B 6M9 – 807/346-1780; Fax: 807/346-1790
Timmins: Pine Plaza, #105, 119 Pine St. South, PO Box 1240, Timmins ON P4N 2K3 – 705/267-6416

Toronto: #100, 150 King St. West, Toronto ON M5H 1J9 – 416/973-0341; Fax: 416/954-5009
Toronto North: #600, 3901 Hwy.#7 West, Vaughan ON L4L 8L5 – 905/264-2100
Trois-Rivières: 1660, rue Royale, Trois-Rivières QC G9A 4K3 – 819/371-5215
Truro: 622 Prince St., PO Box 1378, Truro NS B2N 5N2 – 902/895-6377
Vancouver: #700, 601 West Hastings St., Vancouver BC V6B 5G9 – 604/666-7850; Fax: 604/666-7859
Victoria: 990 Fort St., Victoria BC V8V 3K2 – 604/363-0161; Fax: 604/363-8029
Whitehorse: 2090A - 2 Ave., Whitehorse YT Y1A 1B6 – 867/633-7510
Williams Lake: 94 North First Ave., Williams Lake BC V2G 1Y6 – 250/398-8233
Windsor: #604, 500 Ouellette Ave., Windsor ON N9A 1B3 – 519/257-6808
Winnipeg: #1100, 155 Carlton St., Winnipeg MB R3C 3H8 – 204/983-7900; Fax: 204/983-0870
Yellowknife: 4912 - 49 St., Yellowknife NT X1A 1P3 – 867/873-3565

## CANADA COUNCIL FOR THE ARTS/Conseil des Arts du Canada

350 Albert St., PO Box 1047, Ottawa ON K1P 5V8
613/566-4365; Fax: 613/566-4390; URL: http://www.canadacouncil.ca
Toll Free: 1-800-263-5588
An independent agency created by the Parliament of Canada in 1957 to foster & promote the arts. The Council provides a wide range of grants & services to professional Canadian artists & arts organizations in dance, media arts, music, theatre, writing, publishing & the visual arts. In addition to its primary role in the arts, the Council maintains the secretariat for the Canadian Commission for UNESCO & administers the Killam Program of Prizes & Fellowships to scholars of exceptional ability engaged in significant research projects. Reports to government through the Minister of Canadian Heritage.
**Chair**, Donna M. Scott
Vice-Chair, François Colbert

## CANADA DEPOSIT INSURANCE CORPORATION (CDIC)/Société d'assurance-dépôts du Canada (SADC)

50 O'Connor St., 17th Fl., PO Box 2340, Stn D, Ottawa ON K1P 5W5
613/996-2081; Fax: 613/996-6095; Email: info@cdic.ca; info@sadc.ca; URL: http://www.cdic.ca
Toll Free: 1-800-461-2342
CDIC was established in 1967 & membership is limited to banks, trust companies, & loan companies. Members may be either federally or provincially incorporated. Funding is provided by its members through premiums paid on insured deposits. Reports to government through the Minister of Finance.
CDIC responsibilities include:
• the provision of insurance against the loss of all or part of deposits;
• the promotion of sound business & financial practices for member institutions;
• to contribute to the stability of the Canadian financial system.
**Chair**, G.L. Reuber
President & CEO, J.P. Sabourin
Senior Vice-President, W. Acton
Senior Vice-President, G. Saint-Pierre
Vice-President, Corporate Services, B.C. Scheepers
Vice-President, Finance, J.R. Lanthier
Corporate Secretary & General Counsel, L.T. Lederman
Director, Communications & Public Affairs, M.A. Pearcy

## CANADA INVESTMENT & SAVINGS (CIS)/Placements Epargne Canada (PEC)

#1502, 110 Yonge St., Toronto ON M5C 1T4
416/952-1252; Email: cis@cis-pec.gc.ca; URL: http://www.cis-pec.gc.ca/
Toll Free: 1-800-575-5151
Provides Canadians with better access to existing Government of Canada securities, such as Canada Savings Bonds, Treasury Bills & Marketable Bonds. CIS also develops new investment products to help Canadians meet savings and investment needs.
**President & Chief Operating Officer**, Jacqueline Orange, 416/952-1250
President, Sales & Distribution, Hoda Masri, 416/952-1254
Vice-President, Marketing Services, Paul Bailey, 416/952-1256
Vice-President, Product Management, Clifford Prupas, 416/952-1258
Vice-présidente, Services intégrés, Chantale Cousineau Mahoney, 234 Wellington St., Ottawa ON K1A 0G9, 613/992-7214
Special Advisor, David Murchison, 234 Wellington St., Ottawa ON K1A 0G9, 613/996-3166
Administrative Officer, Anne L. Taillefer, 234 Wellington St., Ottawa ON K1A 0G9, 613/992-6790

## CANADA LABOUR RELATIONS BOARD (CLRB)/Conseil canadien des Relations du Travail (CCRT)

240 Sparks St., 4th Fl., Ottawa ON K1A 0X8
613/996-9466; Fax: 613/947-5407
The Board is an independent, administrative, quasi-judicial tribunal which administers Part I & certain provisions of Part II of the Canada Labour Code. Its responsibilities include the granting or revoking of collective bargaining rights, the mediation & adjudication of unfair labour practice complaints, the determination of unlawful strikes & lockouts, the disposition of appeals of a safety officer's decision, & other matters.
**Chair**, Ted Weatherill
Vice-Chair, L. Doyon
Vice-Chair, J.L. Guilbeault
Vice-Chair, Suzanne Handman
Vice-Chair, R.I. Hornung
Vice-Chair, P. Morneault

## CANADA LANDS COMPANY/Société Immobilière du Canada

#1500, 200 King St. West, Toronto ON M5H 3T4
416/974-9700; Fax: 416/974-9661; Email: clc@clc.ca; URL: http://www.clc.ca
The CLC is a Crown Corporation responsible for the management &/or disposal of certain surplus federal lands on behalf of the Government of Canada. The agency reports to government through the Minister of Public Works & Government Services.
**President & CEO**, Erhard Buchholz
Chair, Jon Grant
Secretary, Brian Way

### OLD PORT OF MONTRÉAL CORPORATION INC.

333, rue de la Commune ouest, Montréal QC H2Y 2E2
514/283-5256; Fax: 514/283-8423
President, Bernard Lamarre

## CANADA MORTGAGE & HOUSING CORPORATION (CMHC)/Société canadienne d'hypothèques et de logement (SCHL)

700 Montreal Rd., Ottawa ON K1A 0P7
613/748-2000; Fax: 613/748-2098; URL: http://www.cmhc-schl.gc.ca
Toll Free: 1-800-668-2642
Corporate Communications: 613/748-2521
Canadian Housing Information Centre: 613/748-2367
CMHC insures loans so that first time homebuyers can purchase a home with a five or ten percent downpayment.
Over 656,000 social housing units are supported on behalf of the federal government. All types of housing-related research & designed projects are conducted &/or funded by CMHC to improve the quality of housing & residential environments. Through its offices, CMHC provides service & advice to the public, mortgage lenders, real estate agents and the housing construction industry. Reports to government through Public Works & Government Services.

### ACTS ADMINISTERED

National Housing Act
**Minister Responsible**, Hon. Alfonso Gagliano, 613/997-5421, Fax: 613/953-1908
Chair, Peter Smith, 613/748-2786
President, Marc Rochon, 613/748-2900
Vice-President, Corporate Services, K.A. Kinsley, 613/748-2186
Vice-President, Insurance, W.G. Mulrihill, 613/748-2779
Vice-President, National & International Support, C. Poirier-Defoy, 613/748-2221
Vice-President, Strategy, D.A. Stewart, 613/748-2553

### CMHC Regional Offices

Atlantic: PO Box 9315, Stn A, Halifax NS B3K 5W9 – 902/426-3530; Fax: 902/426-9991, General Manager, J. Dalrymple
British Columbia & Yukon: #450, 999 Canada Pl., Vancouver BC V6C 3E1 – 604/666-2516; Fax: 604/666-3020, General Manager, J.T. Lynch
Ontario: 100 Sheppard Ave. East, North York ON M2M 6N5 – 416/221-2642; Fax: 416/218-3310, General Manager, P. Friedmann
Prairie & NWT: PO Box 2560, Calgary AB T2P 2N9 – 403/292-6200; Fax: 403/292-6238, General Manager, B. Zaccardi
Québec: Place du Canada, 1010, rue De La Gauchetière ouest, 11th Fl., Montréal QC H3B 2N2 – 514/283-4464; Fax: 514/283-7595, General Manager, J.F. Martin

## CANADA PLACE CORPORATION/Corporation Place du Canada

#1001, 999 Canada Pl., Vancouver BC V6C 3C1
604/666-7200; Fax: 604/666-0695
The Corporation is in charge of property management at Canada Place in Vancouver, which includes a cruise ship facility, a trade & convention centre, a hotel, an IMAX theatre, restaurants & a food fair/retail area.
**Chair**, Farouk Verjee
Vice-President & General Manager, William J. Watson

## CANADA PORTS CORPORATION (CPC)/Société canadienne des ports (SCP)

99 Metcalfe St., Ottawa ON K1A 0N6
613/957-6787; Fax: 613/996-9629; URL: http://canada.gc.ca/depts/agencies/cpoind_e.html
A federal system of ports administered pursuant to the Canada Ports Corporation Act, which was proclaimed in 1983. Seven of these ports are autonomous local port corporations located in Halifax, Montréal, Prince Rupert, Québec City, Saint John, St. John's & Vancouver. The other ports are directly administered by the Canada Ports Corporation & are located in Belledune, Churchill, Port Colborne, Port Saguenay/Baie des Ha!Ha!, Prescott, Sept-Îles & Trois-Rivières. In providing a public service, the ports are administered according to common commercial principles.
**Acting Chair**, Carole Taylor, 613/957-6794
President & CEO, Neil McNeil, 613/957-6700

**Local Port Corporations**

Halifax: PO Box 366, Halifax NS B3J 2P6 – 902/426-3643, David Bellefontaine

Montréal: Port of Montréal Bldg., 1 Cité du Havre, Montréal QC H3C 3R5 – 514/283-7042; Fax: 514/283-0829, Dominic Taddeo

Prince Rupert: 110 Third Ave. West, Prince Rupert BC V8J 1K8 – 250/627-7545; Fax: 250/627-7101, Don Krusel

Québec: CP 2268, Québec QC G1K 7P7 – 418/648-3558; Fax: 418/648-4160, Ross Gaudreault

Saint John: 133 Prince William St., PO Box 6429, Stn A, Saint John NB E2L 4R8 – 506/636-4869; Fax: 506/636-4443; Email: port@sjport.com; URL: http://www.sjport.com, Capt. Alwyn Soppitt

St. John's: PO Box 6178, St. John's NF A1C 5X8 – 709/772-4664; Fax: 709/772-4689, David Fox

Vancouver: #1900, 200 Granville St., Vancouver BC V6C 2P9 – 604/666-8978; Fax: 604/666-8916, N.C. Stark

**Divisional Ports**

Belledune: Port of Belledune, Belledune NB E0B 1G0 – 506/522-2859; Fax: 506/522-0803, Guy Desgagnes

Churchill: PO Box 217, Churchill MB R0B 0E0 – 204/675-8823; Fax: 204/675-2550, Ray Robusky, 613/957-6762 (Ottawa)

Port Colborne: PO Box 129, Port Colborne ON L3K 5V8 – 905/834-3644, Ray Robusky, 613/957-6762 (Ottawa)

Port Saguenay: CP 760, Chicoutimi QC G7H 5E1 – 418/543-0263; Fax: 418/543-4633, Ghyslaine Collard

Prescott: PO Box 520, Prescott ON K0E 1T0 – 613/925-4228; Fax: 613/925-5022, Ray Robusky, 613/957-6762 (Ottawa)

Sept-Îles: #202, 421, av Arnaud, Sept-Îles QC G4R 3B3 – 418/968-1231; Fax: 418/962-4445, Jean-Maurice Gaudreau

Trois-Rivières: CP 999, Trois-Rivières QC G9A 5K2 – 418/378-3939; Fax: 418/378-2487, Capt. Serge Tremblay

## CANADA POST CORPORATION/Société canadienne des postes

2701 Riverside Dr., Ottawa ON K1A 0B1

613/734-8440; Fax: 613/734-6084; URL: http://www.mailposte.ca

Toll Free: 1-800-267-1177

Ligne sans frais: 1-800-267-1155

Toll Free TDD: 1-800-267-2797

Federal government agency responsible for Canada's postal system. Reports to government through Public Works & Government Services. For postal rates, codes, abbreviations & other general information; *see* Postal Information in the main/global Index.

**Chair**, Hon. André Ouellet, P.C., Q.C.

President & CEO, Georges C. Clermont, Q.C.

National Vice-President, Sales, Stewart Bacon

Senior Vice-President & Chief Financial Officer, Ian A. Bourne

Senior Vice-President, Electronic Products & Services, Philippe Lemay

Senior Vice-President, Operations, Léo Blanchette

Senior Vice-President, Marketing & Product Management, C. Anne Joynt

Vice-President & Chief Information Officer, Gilles Farley

Vice-President, Administration, Hank J. Klassen

Vice-President, Electronic Services & Federal Government Accounts, Peter Melanson

Vice-President, Human Resources, André Villeneuve

Vice-President, Mail Operations, Tom Charlton

Vice-President, Central Area, Peter McInenly, Q.C.

Vice-President, Eastern Area, Jacques Brunelle

Vice-President, Western Area, John Drajawicz

Corporate Secretary & Secretary of the Board, Robert Y. Labelle

Corporate Treasurer, C. Derek Millar

**Canada Post Communications Offices**

Atlantic Division: PO Box 1689, Halifax NS B3J 2B1 – 902/494-4076; Fax: 902/494-4328

Huron Division: 955 Highbury Ave., London ON N5Y 1A3 – 519/646-5288; Fax: 519/646-5382

Pacific Division: 1010 Howe St., PO Box 2110, Vancouver BC V6B 4Z3 – 604/662-1388; Fax: 604/662-1710

Prairie Division: #1300, 10020 - 101A Ave., Edmonton AB T5J 4J4 – 403/944-3137; Fax: 403/944-3140

Winnipeg Office: #3M, 266 Graham Ave., Winnipeg MB R3C 0K0 – 204/987-5356, Fax: 204/987-5110

Québec Division: #100, 475, boul de l'Atrium, Charlesbourg QC G1H 7K2 – 418/624-6424; Fax: 418/624-6422

Montréal Office: #346, 1000, rue De La Gauchetière ouest, Montréal QC H3B 5B7 – 514/345-4569, Fax: 514/345-4307

York Division: #700, 1 Dundas St. West, Toronto ON M5G 2L5 – 416/204-4191; Fax: 416/204-4444

## CANADIAN ARTISTS & PRODUCERS PROFESSIONAL RELATIONS TRIBUNAL/ Tribunal canadien des relations professionnelles artistes-producteurs

C.D. Howe Bldg., 240 Sparks St., 8th Fl. West, Ottawa ON K1A 1A1

613/996-4052; Fax: 613/947-4125;

Email: tribunal.artists@ic.gc.ca; URL: http://homer.ic.gc.ca/capprt

Toll Free: 1-800-263-ARTS (2787)

The tribunal provides a framework for professional relations between self-employed artists & producers in the federal jurisdiction who use their services.

**ACTS ADMINISTERED**

Status of the Artist Act, S.C. 1992, c.33

**Acting Chair & CEO**, André Fortier

Secretary General, Elizabeth MacPherson

## CANADIAN BROADCASTING CORPORATION (CBC)/Société Radio-Canada (SRC)

250 Lanark Ave., PO Box 3220, Stn C, Ottawa ON K1Y 1E4

613/724-1200; URL: http://www.cbc.ca/

TDD: 613/724-5173

The Canadian Broadcasting Corporation (CBC) is a publicly owned corporation providing a national broadcasting service in Canada in two languages (English & French). The CBC was established by an Act of Parliament in 1936. The CBC reports to Parliament each year on its operations through the Minister of Canadian Heritage. The agency is governed by the 1991 Broadcasting Act & is subject to regulations of the Canadian Radio-television & Telecommunications Commission (CRTC).

**President & CEO**, Hon. Perrin Beatty

Senior Advisor to the President & CEO, Michael McEwen

Chair, Board of Directors, Guylaine Saucier

Executive Vice-President, James McCoubrey

Senior Vice-President, Media, Vacant

Senior Vice-President, Resources, Louise Tremblay

Vice-President, General Counsel & Corporate Secretary, Gerald Flaherty, Q.C.

Vice-President, Human Resources, George C.B. Smith

Vice-President, Internal Audit, Robert Hertzog

Senior Director, Corporate Communications & Public Affairs, Laurie Jones

**CBC OMBUDSMAN**

Ombudsman, English Services, David Bazay, PO Box 500, Stn A, Toronto ON M5W 1E6

Ombudsman, French Services, Mario Cardinal, 1400, boul René-Lévesque est, CP 6000, Montréal QC H3C 3A8

**ENGLISH NETWORKS**

PO Box 500, Stn A, Toronto ON M5W 1E6

416/205-3311

TDD: 416/205-6688

Vice-President, English Radio, Harold Redekopp

Vice-President, English Television Networks, Jim Byrd

Executive Director, Media Operations, Michael Harris

Executive Director, Network Programming, Slawko Klymkiw

Executive Director, News, Current Affairs & Newsworld, Television, Bob Culbert

Head, CBC Newsworld, Vince Carlin

Senior Director, Broadcast Communications, Diane Kenyon

Director, Media & Public Relations, Rob Mitchell

**FRENCH NETWORKS**

1400, boul René-Lévesque est, CP 6000, Montréal QC H3C 3A8

514/597-5970

TDD: 514/597-6013

Vice-President, French Radio, Marcel Pépin

Vice-President, French Television, Michèle Fortin

Director General, Communications, Raymond Guay

Director, Public Relations, Micheline Savoie

Executive Director, RDI, Renaud Gilbert

General Manager, TV5 (Consortium Québec-Canada), Guy Gougeon

**CBC ENGINEERING**

7925, rue Côte St-Luc, Montréal QC H4W 1R5

514/485-5401

Acting Senior Director, Corporate Engineering Services, George Jackson

**RADIO CANADA INTERNATIONAL**

1055, boul René-Lévesque est, CP 6000, Montréal QC H3C 3A8

514/597-7555

Acting Executive Director, Robert O'Reilly

Director, Operations, Jean-Claude Asselin

**CBC Regional Offices**

•Alberta (English & French): PO Box 555, Edmonton AB T5J 2P4 – 403/468-7500

Regional Director & Director Television (English Services), Judy Fantham

Director, Radio, French Services, Denis Collette

Coordinator, Program Marketing, Doug Ianson

Communications Manager, Radio & Television, Pierre Nöel

•Atlantic (French): 250 Archibald St., PO Box 950, Moncton NB E1C 8N8 – 506/853-6666

Director, Radio, Jules Chiasson

Director, Television, Louise Imbeault

Manager, Communications, Johanne Huard

•British Columbia (English & French): PO Box 4600, Vancouver BC V6B 4A2 – 604/662-6000

Regional Director & Director, Television (English Services), Donna Logan

Director, Radio (English Services), Susan Englebert

Director, Radio, French Services, Robert Groulx

Acting Manager, Communications, Dianne Warnick

•Manitoba (English & French): 491 Portage Ave., PO Box 160, Winnipeg MB R3C 2H1 – 204/788-3222 (English) – 204/788-3141 (French)

Acting Regional Director, English Services, Jane Chalmers

Director, French Radio Services, René Fontaine

Coordinator, Program Marketing, Laurie Wood

Manager, Communications, Huguette Le Gall

•Maritimes (English): 5600 Sackville St., PO Box 3000, Halifax NS B3J 3E9 – 902/420-8311
Acting Regional Director & Director, Television, Fred Mattocks
Regional Director, Radio, Susan Mitton
Senior Communications Manager, Eastern Canada, Jessie Clarey
•Newfoundland (English): Ayre's Centre, Pippy Place, PO Box 12010, Stn A, St. John's NF A1B 3T8 – 709/576-5000
Regional Director, Ron Crocker
Coordinator, Program Marketing, Heather Elliott
•Ontario (English): Broadcast Centre, 250 Front St. West, PO Box 500, Stn A, Toronto ON M5W 1E6 – 416/205-3700
Acting Regional Director & Director, Televsion (Windsor), Bruce Taylor
Director, Radio (Ottawa), Miriam Fry
Director, Radio (Toronto), Val Boser
•Ontario (French): 250 Lanark Ave., PO Box 3220, Stn C, Ottawa ON K1Y 1E4 – 613/724-1200
Director, Radio, Denis Pellerin
Director, Television, Christine Marais
Regional Manager, Communications, Maryse Lairot
•Québec (English): 1400, boul René-Lévesque est, CP 6000, Montréal QC H3C 3A8 – 514/ 597-5970
Regional Director & Director, Television, Nicole Bélanger
Director, Radio, Patricia Pleszczynska
Account Manager, Communications, Jackie Moore
•Québec City & Eastern Québec (French): 2475, boul Laurier, CP 10400, Ste-Foy QC G1V 2X2 – 418/654-1341, Director, Televsion, André Poirier, Manager, Communications, Ginette D'Aigle
•Saskatchewan (English & French): 2440 Broad St., Regina SK S4P 4A1 – 306/347-9540
Regional Director & Director, Television (English Services - Edmonton), Judy Fantham
Director, Radio, Evan Purchase
Director, Radio, French Services, Richard Marcotte
Director, Television for the Four Western Stations, French Services, Lionel Bonneville
Coordinator, Program Marketing, Chris Niemczyk
Manager, Communications, Françoise Sigur-Cloutier
•CBC North: 5129 - 49 St., PO Box 160, Yellowknife NT X1A 1P8 – 867/669-3500
Regional Director, Marie Wilson
Acting Senior Manager, Communications, Craig Yeo

## CANADIAN BUSINESS SERVICE CENTRE (CBSC)/Centres de services aux entreprises du Canada (CSEC)
235 Queen St., Ottawa ON K1A OH5
Fax: 613/954-4881; Email: cbsc@ic.gc.ca; URL: http://www.cbsc.org/

#### Regional Offices
The Business Link: Canada-Alberta Business Service Centre, #100, 10237 - 104 St., Edmonton AB T5J 1B1 – 403/422-7722; Fax: 403/422-0055; Email: buslink@cbsc.ic.gc.ca, Toll Free: 1-800-272-9675 – Info-Fax: 403/427-7971; Toll Free Info-Fax: 1-800-563-9926
Canada/British Columbia Business Service Centre: 601 West Cordova St., Vancouver BC V6B 1G1 – 604/775-5525; Fax: 604/775-5520, Toll Free: 1-800-667-2272 – Info-Fax: 604/775-5515
Canada Business Service Centre-Manitoba: 330 Portage Ave., 8th Fl., PO Box 2609, Winnipeg MB R3C 4B3 – 204/984-2272; Fax: 204/983-3852; Email: manitoba@cbsc.ic.gc.ca, Toll Free: 1-800-665-2019 – Info-Fax: 204/984-5527; Toll Free Info-Fax: 1-800-665-9386
Canada/New Brunswick Business Service Centre (CNBBSC): 570 Queen St., Fredericton NB E3B 6Z6 – 506/444-6140; Fax: 506/444-6172, Toll Free: 1-800-668-1010 – Info-Fax: 506/444-6169
Canada Businees Service Centre-Newfoundland: 90 O'Leary Ave., PO Box 8687, St. John's NF A1B 3T1 – 709/772-6022; Fax: 709/772-6090, Toll Free: 1-800-668-1010 – Info-Fax: 709/772-6030
Canada/NWT Business Service Centre: PO Box 1320, Yellowknife NT X1A 2L9 – 867/873-7958; Fax: 867/873-0574; Email: yel@cbsc.ic.gc.ca, Toll Free: 1-800-661-0599 – Info-Fax: 403/873-0575
Canada/Nova Scotia Business Service Centre (CNSBSC): 1575 Brunswick St., Halifax NS B3J 2G1 – 902/426-8604; Fax: 902/426-6530; Email: halifax@cbsc.ic.gc.ca, Toll Free: 1-800-668-1010 – Info-Fax: 902/426-3201; Toll Free Info-Fax: 1-800-401-3201
Canada/Ontario Business Call Centre (COBCC): 230 Richmond St. West, Toronto ON M5V 3E5 – 416/954-4636; Fax: 416/954-8597; Email: cobcc@cbsc.ic.gc.ca, Toll Free: 1-800-567-2345 – Info-Fax: 416/954-8555; Toll Free Info-Fax: 1-800/240-4192
Canada/Prince Edward Island Business Service Centre (CPEIBSC): 75 Fitzroy St., PO Box 40, Charlottetown PE C1A 7K2 – 902/368-0771; Fax: 902/566-7377, Toll Free: 1-800-668-1010 – Info-Fax: 902/368-0776; Toll Free Info-Fax: 1-800-401-3201
Info entrepreneurs: #12500, 5, Place Ville Marie, Montreal QC H3B 4Y2 – 514/496-4636; Fax: 514/496-5934, Ligne sans frais: 1-800-322-4636 – Info-Fax: 514-496-4010; Toll Free Info-Fax: 1-800-322-4010
Canada/Saskatchewan Business Service Centre (CSBSC): 122 - 3 Ave. North, Saskatoon SK S7K 2H6 – 306/956-2323; Fax: 306/956-2328, Toll Free: 1-800-667-4374 – Info-Fax: 306/956-2310; Toll Free Info-Fax: 1-800-667-9433
Canada/Yukon Business Service Centre: #201, 208 Main St., Whitehorse YT Y1A 2A9 – 867/633-6257, Toll Free: 1-800-661-0543

## CANADIAN CENTRE FOR MANAGEMENT DEVELOPMENT (CCMD)/Centre canadien de gestion (CCG)
PO Box 420, Stn A, Ottawa ON K1N 8V4
613/997-4163; Fax: 613/953-6240; Email: CCMD@on.infoshare.ca
Business Enquiries: 613/992-9045
Training and development programs for senior managers in the federal government. The institution is dedicated to providing public service executives with leading edge learning solutions through executive education and development.
**Principal**, Dr. Janet R. Smith, 613/992-8165, Fax: 613/943-1038
Director General, Business Centre/Communications & Marketing, D. Burke, 613/992-8059
Executive Director, Management Services, L. Durocher, 613/992-8171
Chief Operating Officer, E.P. Hossack, 613/947-4860
Vice-Principal, Executive Development Programs, B. Marson, 819/997-8735
Vice-Principal, Research, R. Heintzman, 613/995-5839
Head, Negotiation, Consultation & Conflict Management, Joseph Stanford, 613/943-2334

## CANADIAN CENTRE FOR OCCUPATIONAL HEALTH & SAFETY (CCOHS)/Centre canadien d'hygiène et de sécurité au travail (CCHST)
250 Main St. East, Hamilton ON L8N 1H6
905/572-2981; Fax: 905/572-2206; Email: custserv@ccohs.ca; URL: http://www.ccohs.ca
Toll Free: 1-800-263-8466
Inquiries: 905/572-4400; Fax: 905/572-4500
Provides occupational health & safety information in the form of publications, responses to inquiries & a computerized information service which is available both on-line & on CD-ROM. It is governed by a tripartite council representing employers, labour & governments. The Centre reports to Parliament through the Minister of Labour.
**Minister Responsible**, Hon. Lawrence MacAulay
President & CEO, Len Hong, 905/572-4432
Chair of the Council, Nicole Senécal
Vice-President, Dr. P.K. Abeytunga, 905/572-4537
Comptroller, Brian Hutchings, 905/572-4401
Manager, Computer Systems & Services, Ashok Setty, 905/572-4498
Manager, Health & Safety Products & Services, Anne Gravereaux, 905/572-4487
Manager, Inquiries Service, Dr. Roger Cockerline, 905/572-4523
Manager, Operations Support, Eleanor Irwin, 905/572-4408

## CANADIAN CENTRE ON SUBSTANCE ABUSE/Centre canadien de lutte contre l'alcoolisme et les toxicomanies
#300, 75 Albert St., Ottawa ON K1P 5E7
613/235-4048; Fax: 613/235-8101; URL: http://www.ccsa.ca
Established in 1988 under Canada's Drug Strategy, to determine methods of treating & preventing substance abuse. Works to minimize the harm associated with the use of alcohol, tobacco and other drugs.
**Chair**, William G. Deeks
CEO, Jacques LeCavalier
Director, Communications, Richard Garlick

## CANADIAN COMMERCIAL CORPORATION (CCC)/Corporation commerciale canadienne
Metropolitan Centre, #1100, 50 O'Connor St., Ottawa ON K1A 0S6
613/996-0034; Fax: 613/995-2121; Email: info@ccc.ca; URL: http://www.ccc.ca
Federal Crown Corporation which reports to Parliament through the Minister for International Trade. By serving as prime contractor, the Corporation facilitates exports of a wide range of goods & services from Canadian sources to foreign governments & international agencies.
In response to requests from foreign customers for individual products or services, CCC identifies Canadian firms capable of meeting the customer's requirements, executes prime as well as back-to-back contracts, & follows through with contract management, inspection, acceptance, & payment.
**Minister Responsible**, Hon. Sergio Marchi, 613/992-7332
Minister for International Trade & President of CCC, Robert G. Wright, 613/994-5000, Fax: 613/944-8493
Executive Vice-President & Chief Operating Officer, Douglas Patriquin, 613/996-0042
Director, Business Development, Stephen Bigsby, 613/995-9116
Head, Communications & Awareness, M.V. Asfar, 613/995-0560

## CANADIAN DAIRY COMMISSION (CDC)/Commission canadienne du lait (CCL)
Carling Executive Park, 1525 Carling Ave., Ottawa ON K1A 0Z2
613/998-9490; Fax: 613/998-4492; URL: http://www.cdc.ca
The CDC serves as an important dairy advisory body for the Minister of Agriculture & Agri-Food, given its key role in the national dairy industry. The Commission's mandate is to work with the Canadian dairy sector to develop policies, work towards consensus & administer programs that ensure the orderly production & marketing of milk in Canada with

a view to provide efficient producers & processors with the opportunity of obtaining a fair return for their labour & investments &, for consumers, an adequate supply of dairy products at reasonable prices.
**Chair**, Gilles Prégent
Vice-Chair, Louis Balcaen
Commissioner, Alvin Johnstone

## CANADIAN FOOD INSPECTION AGENCY (CFIA)/Agence canadienne d'inspection des aliments (ACIA)

59 Camelot Dr., Nepean ON K1A 0Y9
613/225-2342; Fax: 613/228-6634; URL: http://www.cfia-acia.agr.ca
Toll Free: 1-800-442-2342
Created in April 1997 this agency consolidates the delivery of federally-mandated food inspection & quarantine services previously provided by Agriculture & Agri-Food Canada, Health Canada, & Fisheries & Oceans Canada. All inspection services related to food safety, economic fraud, trade-related requirements, & animal & plant health programs are now provided by CFIA.
Also responsible for setting & enforcing standards to safeguard human, animal & plant health, to facilitate national & international trade & to support the protection of the environment through sustainable agricultural practices.

### ACTS ADMINISTERED

Consumer Packaging & Labelling Act (with Agriculture & Agri-Food Canada)
Feeds Act
Fertilizers Act
Financial Administration Act
Food & Drugs Act (with Agriculture & Agri-Food Canada)
Health of Animals Act
Meat Inspection Act
Plant Breeders' Rights Act
Plant Protection Act
Seeds Act
**Minister Responsible**, Hon. Ralph Goodale, 613/759-1059, Fax: 613/759-1081
President, Dr. Arthur Olson
Executive Vice-President, Ron Doering
Acting Vice-President, Human Resources, Rod Ballantyne
Acting Vice-President, Operations, Lynden Hillier
Acting Vice-President, Programs, Dr. André Gravel
Acting Vice-President, Public & Regulatory Affairs, Bob Ray
Acting Director General, Federal-Provincial Relations & Corporate Planning, Peter Brackenridge

### ANIMAL & PLANT HEALTH DIRECTORATE

613/952-8000; Fax: 613/952-0677
Director General, Dr. Norm G. Willis, 613/952-8000 ext.4192
Director, Animal Diseases Research Institute, Dr. P. Ide, 3851 Fallowfield Rd., Nepean ON K2H 8P9, 613/998-9320, Fax: 613/941-0891
Director, Animal Health Division, B. Stemshorn, 613/952-8000 ext.4601
Director, Central Issues & Strategies, Dr. R. Stevens, 613/952-8000 ext.4189
Director, Central Plant Health Laboratory, E. Singh, 613/998-9320 ext.5931, Fax: 613/996-2497
Director, Diagnostic Resource Centre, Dr. W. Sterritt, 613/998-9320 ext.4967, Fax: 613/991-6988
Director, Management Services, D. Buckland, 613/952-8000 ext.3854
Director, Plant Protection Division, Dr. Jean Hollebone, 613/952-8000 ext.4316

### FOOD INSPECTION DIRECTORATE

Director General, Dr. A. MacKenzie, 613/952-8000 ext.4188, Fax: 613/998-5967
Director, Dairy, Fruit & Vegetable Division, Peter Brackenridge, Fax: 613/990-0607
Acting Director, Food Division, Gerry Riasbeck, Fax: 613/993-8511
Director, Laboratory Services Division, Dr. W.P. Cochrane, 613/759-1207, Fax: 613/759-1277
Director, Meat & Poultry Products Division, Dr. M. Baker, Fax: 613/998-0958

## CANADIAN GRAIN COMMISSION/ Commission canadienne des grains

#600, 303 Main St., Winnipeg MB R3C 3G8
204/983-2734; Fax: 204/983-2751; URL: http://www.cgc.ca
General Inquiry: 1-800-665-9058; Client Feedback: 1-800-853-6705
Regulates grain handling in Canada & establishes & maintains quality standards for Canadian grains. Responsibilities include official inspection & grading of grain, weighing of grain at terminal & transfer elevators, licensing of grain elevators & dealers, conducting & publishing statistical & economic studies, & conducting basic & applied research on Canadian grain. Reports to government through the Minister of Agriculture & Agri-food.

### ACTS ADMINISTERED

Canada Grain Act
Grain Futures Act
**Chief Commissioner**, B. Senft
Asst. Chief Commissioner, D. Stow
Asst. Chief Commissioner, A. Shatzke
Executive Director, D.N. Kennedy
Director, Corporate Services Division, M. Kapitany
Director, Grain Research Laboratory, K.H. Tipples, Ph.D.
Director, Industry Services Division, Elizabeth Larmond

## CANADIAN HERITAGE/Patrimoine canadien

Jules Léger Bldg., 25 Eddy St., Hull QC K1A 1K5
819/997-0055; Fax: 819/953-5382; URL: http://www.pch.gc.ca/
TDD: 819/997-8776
Ensures the protection of Canada's natural heritage & historic sites, promotion of artistic development & Canadian heritage, & encourages full participation of all Canadians in our country's development.
Develops & administers policies & programs to promote Canadian values & identity. These policies & programs comprise the development of official languages minority communities & the recognition & use of English & French throughout Canadian society. Ensures the promotion of better understanding & respect among Canadians of all backgrounds & works to eliminate barriers to full integration of all Canadians (including the administration of the Canadian Multiculturalism Act).
Provides programming, largely managed by off-reserve Aboriginal people, to help them define & participate in solving social, cultural, political & economic issues affecting their lives. Coordinates Canada's international commitments on human rights & works to advance civic education & to provide young people greater opportunities to learn about Canada & to participate in their communities.
Promotes volunteerism, Canadian symbols & the organization of events of national significance.
Promotes amateur sport across the country, by providing policy leadership & financial cooperation to national sport organzations & athletes, as well as significant technical & financial support to major amateur sporting events, such as the Canada Games.

### ACTS ADMINISTERED

An Act to Incorporate the Jules & Paul-Émile Léger Foundation
Broadcasting Act
Canada Council Act
Canadian Film Development Corporation Act
Canadian Heritage Languages Institute Act
Canadian Multiculturalism Act
Canadian Race Relations Foundation Act
Canadian Radio-television & Telecommunications Commission Act
Corrupt Practices Inquiries Act
Cultural Property Export & Import Act
Department of Communications Act
Department of Multiculturalism & Citizenship Act
Department of State Act
Department of Transport Act
Disfranchising Act
Dominion Controverted Elections Act
Dominion Water Power Act
Federal Real Property Act
Fitness & Amateur Sport Act
Heritage Railway Stations Protection Act
Historic Sites & Monuments Act
Holidays Act
Laurier House Act
Lieutenant Governors Superannuation Act
Mingan Archipelago National Park Act
Museums Act
National Anthem Act
National Archives of Canada Act
National Arts Centre Act
National Battlefields at Québec Act
National Film Act
National Flag of Canada Manufacturing Standards Act
National Library Act
National Parks Act
National Symbol of Canada Act
Official Languages Act
Persons of Japanese Ancestry Ex Gratia Payments Order
Public Service Employment Act
Salaries Act
Status of the Artist Act
Trade-marks Act
**Minister**, Hon. Sheila Copps, 613/997-7788, Fax: 613/994-5987
**Secretary of State, Multiculturalism & Status of Women**, Hon. Hedy Fry, 819/997-9900, Fax: 819/953-8055
**Secretary of State, Parks Canada**, Hon. Andy Mitchell, 819/953-4077, Fax: 819/953-7343
Deputy Minister, Suzanne Hurtubise, 819/994-1132, Fax: 819/997-0913
Director General, Human Resources, Jacques Pelletier, 819/997-1873, Fax: 819/997-5893
General Counsel, Legal Services, Beverly Wilton, 819/997-2729, Fax: 819/997-2801

### CORPORATE SERVICES

Asst. Deputy Minister, Peter Homulos, 819/994-3046, Fax: 819/953-4796
Director General, Administrative Services, Daniel Giasson, 819/997-3717
Director General, Financial Management, Alain Latourelle, 819/997-1923, Fax: 819/953-2156
Director General, Information Management Branch, Peter Hall, 819/994-4689, Fax: 819/994-3681
Director, Central Correspondence & Documentation, Lisa Hartley, 819/994-3542, Fax: 819/997-4191

### CITIZENSHIP & CANADIAN IDENTITY SECTOR

Develops & administers policies, programs & services related to Canadian Identity such as official languages, amateur sports, muliticulturalism, Canadian symbols promotion & protocol, heritage cultures & languages, voluntary action, race relations & cross-cultural understanding, native citizens, human rights, Canadian studies & youth.

Asst. Deputy Minister, Norman Moyer, 819/994-2164, Fax: 819/953-7067

Director General, Citizens' Participation & Multiculturalism, Susan Scotti, 819/994-2994, Fax: 819/953-8720

Director General, Official Languages, Hilaire Lemoine, 819/994-0943, Fax: 819/953-9353

Acting Director General, Policy Coordination & Strategic Planning, Brian Gilhuly, 819/994-7996, Fax: 819/997-0743

Director General, Sport Canada, Dan Smith, 819/956-8151, Fax: 819/956-8006

#### Regional Offices

Atlantic: 1045, Main St., PO Box 106, Moncton NB E1G 1H1 – 506/851-7069; Fax: 506/851-7079, Regional Executive Director, Jean-Bernard Lafontaine

Ontario: North York City Centre, #500, 5160 Yonge St., Toronto ON M2N 6L9 – 416/954-0396; Fax: 416/954-2909, Regional Executive Director, Gilbert H. Scott

Prairies & Northwest Territories: 457 Main St., 9th Fl., Winnipeg MB R3B 3E8 – 204/983-2630; Fax: 204/984-6996, Regional Executive Director, Bill Balan

Québec: Complexe Guy-Favreau, Tour ouest, 200, boul René-Lévesque ouest, 6e étage, Montréal QC H2Z 1X4 – 514/283-5797; Fax: 514/283-7727, Regional Executive Director, Élisabeth Châtillon

Western: #300, 300 West Georgia St., Vancouver BC V6B 6C6 – 604/666-0146; Fax: 604/666-3508, Regional Executive Director, Orest Kruhlak

### CULTURAL DEVELOPMENT & HERITAGE SECTOR

Asst. Deputy Minister, Victor Rabinovitch, 819/994-1255, Fax: 819/994-5032

Director General, Arts Policy, Hubert Lussier, 819/994-9529, Fax: 819/994-6249

Director General, Broadcasting, Susan Baldwin, 819/997-7449, Fax: 819/947-9730

Director General, Canadian Conservation Institute, Bill Peters, 1030 Innes Rd., Ottawa ON K1A 0C8, 613/998-3721, Fax: 613/998-4721

Director General, Canadian Heritage Information Network, Lyn Elliott-Sherwood, 819/994-1200, Fax: 819/994-9555, URL://www.chin.gc.ca/

Director General, Heritage, Charles Gruchy, 819/997-7782, Fax: 819/997-8392

Acting Director General, Policy Coordination & Strategic Planning, David Walden, 819/997-7750, Fax: 819/997-7757

Chair, Canadian Cultural Property Export Review Board, Ian Christie Clark, 613/990-4161, Fax: 613/954-8826

#### Cultural Industries

Acting Director General, Susan Katz, 819/997-4455, Fax: 819/997-4464

Acting Director, Copyright Policy & Economic Planning, René Bouchard, 819/997-5683, Fax: 819/997-5685

Acting Director, Film, Video & Sound Recording Policy & Programs, J.-F. Bernier, 819/997-5918, Fax: 819/997-5709

Director, Publishing Policy & Programs, Allan Clarke, 819/997-4099, Fax: 819/997-4164

Manager, Book Publishing Industry Development Program (BPIDP), E. Rosenberg, 819/997-4696, Fax: 819/997-4169

### PARKS CANADA SECTOR

URL: http://parkscanada.pch.gc.ca/

Asst. Deputy Minister, Thomas E. Lee, 819/997-9525, Fax: 819/953-9745

Director General, National Historic Sites, Dr. Christina Cameron, 819/994-1808

Acting Director General, National Parks, Michael Porter, 819/994-2657

Director General, Strategies & Plans, Patrick Borbey, 819/953-4013

#### Canal Offices

Carillon: 210, rue du Barrage, Carillon QC J0V 1C0 – 514/537-3534; Fax: 514/537-3733

Chambly: 1899, boul. Périgny, Chambly QC J3L 4C3 – 514/658-0681; Fax: 514/658-2428

Lachine: Complex Guy-Favreau, Tour ouest, 200, boul. René-Lévesque ouest, Montréal QC H2Z 1X4 – 514/283-6054; Fax: 514/496-1263

Rideau: 34A Beckwith St. South, Smith Falls ON K7A 2A8 – 613/283-5170; Fax: 613/283-0677

St. Peters: PO Box 8, St. Peters NS B0E 3B0 – 902/535-2118 (seasonal), 902/733-2280 (year-round); Fax: 902/733-2362

Saint-Ours: 2930, ch des Patriotes, CP 7, Saint-Ours-sur-le-Richelieu QC J0G 1P0 – 514/785-2212

Sainte-Anne-de-Bellevue: 170, rue Ste-Anne, Sainte-Anne-de-Bellevue QC H9X 1N1 – 514/457-5546; Fax: 514/457-0378

Sault: One Canal Dr., Sault Ste. Marie ON P6A 1P0 – 705/942-6262; Fax: 705/942-2101

Trent-Severn Waterway: Ashburnham Dr., PO Box 567, Peterborough ON K9J 6Z6 – 705/750-4919; Fax: 705/742-9644

#### Parks Canada Regional Information Centres

Eastern Canada: Historic Properties Bldg., 1869 Upper Water St., Halifax NS B3J 1S9 – 902/426-3436; Fax: 902/426-6881, Director-General, J.J. O'Brien

Western Canada: #552, 220 - 4 Ave. SE, Calgary AB T2G 4X4 – 403/292-4401; Fax: 403/292-4242, Acting Director General, Western Canada, G. Fortin

#### Atlantic National Parks/National Historic Sites

Acadian Odyssey National Historic Site: #106, 1045 Main St., Moncton NB E1C 1H1 – 506/876-2443; Fax: 506/876-4802

Alexander Graham Bell Historic Site: PO Box 159, Baddeck NS B0E 1B0 – 902/295-2069; Fax: 902/295-3496

L'Anse au Meadows National Historic Site: PO Box 70, St-Lunaire-Griquet NF A0K 2X0 – 709/623-2608; Fax: 709/623-2028

Ardgowan National Historic Site: 2 Palmers Lane, Charlottetown PE C1A 5V6 – 902/566-7050; Fax: 902/566-7226

Bank Fishery National Heritage Exhibit: PO Box 9080, Stn A, Halifax NS B3K 5M7 – 902/634-4794; Fax: 902/634-8990

Beaubears Island National Historic Site: Kent County NB E0A 2A0 – 506/876-2443; Fax: 506/876-4802

Cape Breton Highlands National Park: Ingonish Beach NS B0C 1L0 – 902/285-2691; Fax: 902/285-2866

Cape Spear National Historic Site: PO Box 1268, St. John's NF A1C 5M9 – 709/772-5367; Fax: 709/772-6302

Carleton Martello Tower National Historic Site: PO Box 850, Moncton NB E1C 8N6 – 506/887-6000; Fax: 506/887-6008

Castle Hill National Historic Site: PO Box 10, Jerseyside, Placentia Bay NF A0B 2G0 – 709/227-2401; Fax: 709/227-2452

Fort Amherst National Historic Site: 2 Palmers Lane, Charlottetown PE C1A 5VL – 902/566-7050; Fax: 902/566-7226

Fort Anne National Historic Site: PO Box 9, Annapolis Royal NS B0S 1A0 – 902/532-2397; Fax: 902/532-2232

Fort Beausejour National Historic Site: #106, 1045 Main St., Moncton NB E1C 1H1 – 506/876-2443; Fax: 506/876-4802

Fort Edward National Historic Site: PO Box 150, Grand Pré NS B0P 1M0 – 902/542-3631; Fax: 902/542-1619

Fort McNab National Historic Site: PO Box 9080, Stn A, Halifax NS B3K 5M7 – 902/426-5080; Fax: 902/426-4228

Fortress of Louisbourg National Historic Site: PO Box 160, Louisbourg NS B0A 1M0 – 902/733-2280; Fax: 902/733-2362

Fundy National Park: PO Box 40, Alma NB E0A 1B0 – 506/887-6000; Fax: 506/887-6008

Georges Island National Historic Site: PO Box 9080, Stn A, Halifax NS B3K 5M7 – 902/426-5080; Fax: 902/426-4228

Grand Pré National Historic Site: Grand Pré NS B0P 1M0 – 902/542-3631; Fax: 902/542-1619

Grassy Island National Historic Site: PO Box 159, Baddeck NS B0E 1E0 – 902/295-2069; Fax: 902/295-3496

Green Gables House National Historic Site: 2 Palmer's Lane, Charlottetown PE C1A 5V6 – 902/672-6350; Fax: 902/672-6370

Gros Morne National Park: PO Box 130, Rocky Harbour NF A0K 4N0 – 709/458-2417; Fax: 709/458-2059

Halifax Citadel National Historic Site: PO Box 9080, Stn A, Halifax NS B3K 5M7 – 902/426-5080; Fax: 902/426-4228

Hawthorne Cottage National Historic Site: PO Box 5542, St. John's NF A1C 5X4 – 709/753-9262; Fax: 709/772-2940

Kejimkujik National Park: PO Box 236, Maitland Bridge NS B0T 1N0 – 902/682-2772; Fax: 902/682-3367

Kouchibouguac National Park: Kouchibouguac NB E0A 2A0 – 506/876-2443; Fax: 506/876-4802

Marconi National Historic Site: PO Box 159, Baddeck NS B0E 1B0 – 902/295-2069; Fax: 902/295-3496

New England Planters National Heritage Exhibit: PO Box 150, Grand Pré NS B0P 1M0 – 902/542-3631; Fax: 902/542-1619

Port aux Choix National Historic Site: PO Box 70, St-Lunaire-Griquet NF A0K 2X0 – 709/623-2607; Fax: 709/623-2028

Port-la-Joye National Historic Site: 2 Palmer's Lane, Charlottetown PE C1A 5V6 – 902/672-6350; Fax: 902/672-6370

Port Royal National Historic Site: PO Box 9, Annapolis Royal NS B0S 1A0 – 902/532-2397; Fax: 902/532-2232

Prince Edward Island National Park: 2 Palmer's Lane, Charlottetown PE C1A 5V6 – 902/566-7050; Fax: 902/566-7226

Prince of Wales Martello Tower National Historic Site: PO Box 9080, Stn A, Halifax NS B3K 5M7 – 902/426-5080; Fax: 902/426-4228

Province House National Historic Site: 2 Palmers Lane, Charlottetown PE C1A 5V6 – 902/566-7626; Fax: 902/566-7226

Red Bay National Historic Site: General Delivery, Red Bay NF A0X 4X0 – 709/920-2197; Fax: 709/920-9192

Ryan Premises National Historic Site: PO Box 1451, Bonavista NF A0C 1B0 – 709/468-1600; Fax: 709/468-1604

St. Andrews Blockhouse National Historic Site: #106, 1045 Main St., Moncton NB E1C 1H1 – 506/887-6000; Fax: 506/887-6008

St. Peter's Canal: PO Box 8, St. Peter's NS B0E 3B0 – 902/733-2280; Fax: 902/733-2362

Signal Hill National Historic Site: PO Box 1268, St. John's NF A1C 5M9 – 709/772-5367; Fax: 709/772-6302

Terra Nova National Park: Glovertown NF A0G 2L0 – 709/533-2801; Fax: 709/533-2706

York Redoubt National Historic Site: PO Box 9080, Stn A, Halifax NS B3K 5M7 – 902/426-5080; Fax: 902/426-5080

**Ontario National Parks/National Historic Sites**

Bellvue House National Historic Site: 35 Centre St., Kingston ON K7L 4E5 – 613/545-8666; Fax: 613/545-8721

Bethune Memorial House National Historic Site: 235 John St., Gravenhurst ON P0C 1G0 – 705/687-5443; Fax: 705/687-4935

Bruce Peninsula National Park: PO Box 189, Tobermory ON N0H 2R0 – 519/596-2233; Fax: 519/596-2298

Fathom Five National Marine Park: Tobermory ON – 519/596-2233; Fax: 519/596-2298

Fort George National Historic Site: 26 Queen St., PO Box 787, Niagara-on-the-Lake ON L0S 1J0 – 905/468-4257; Fax: 905/468-4638

Fort Malden National Historic Site: 100 Laird Ave., PO Box 38, Amherstburg ON N9V 2Z2 – 519/736-5416; Fax: 519/736-6603

Fort St. Joseph National Historic Site: PO Box 220, Richard's Landing ON P0R 1J0 – 705/246-2664; Fax: 705/246-1796

Fort Wellington National Historic Site: 370 Vankoughnet St., PO Box 479, Prescott ON K0E 1T0 – 613/925-2896; Fax: 613/925-1536

Georgian Bay Islands National Park: PO Box 28, Honey Harbour ON P0E 1E0 – 705/756-2415; Fax: 705/756-3886

Kingston Martello Towers: 35 Centre St., Kingston ON K7L 4E5 – 613/545-8666

Niagara National Historic Site: 26 Queen St., PO Box 787, Niagara-on-the-Lake ON L0S 1J0 – 905/468-4257; Fax: 905/468-4638

Point Pelee National Park: RR#1, Leamington ON N8H 3V4 – 519/322-2365; Fax: 519/322-1277

Pukaskwa National Park: Hwy 627, Hattie Cove, PO Box 39, Heron Bay ON P0T 1R0 – 807/229-0801; Fax: 807/229-2097

Queenston Heights & Brock's Monument: c/o Fort George National Historic Site, 26 Queen St., PO Box 787, Niagara-on-the-Lake ON L0S 1J0 – 905/468-4257; Fax: 905/468-4638

St. Lawrence Islands National Park: 2 County Rd. 5, RR#3, Mallorytown Landing ON K0E 1R0 – 613/923-5261; Fax: 613/923-2229

Woodside National Historic Site: 528 Wellington St. North, Kitchener ON N2H 5L5 – 519/571-5684; Fax: 519/571-5286

**Prairies & Northwest Territories National Parks/National Historic Sites**

Aulavik National Park: General Delivery, Sachs Harbour NT X0E 0T0 – 867/690-3904; Fax: 867/690-4808

Auyuittuq National Park: PO Box 353, Pangnirtung NT X0A 0R0 – 867/473-8828; Fax: 867/473-5612

Batoche National Historic Site: PO Box 999, Rosthern SK S0K 3R0 – 306/423-6227; Fax: 306/423-5400

Ellesmere Island National Park: PO Box 343, Pangnirtung NT X0A 0R0 – 867/473-8828; Fax: 867/473-8612

Fort Battleford National Historic Site: PO Box 70, Battleford SK S0M 0E0 – 306/937-2621; Fax: 306/937-3370

Fort Prince of Wales National Historic Site: PO Box 127, Churchill MB R0B 0E0 – 204/675-8863; Fax: 204/675-2026

Fort Walsh National Historic Site: PO Box 278, Maple Creek SK S0N 1N0 – 306/662-3590; Fax: 306/662-2711

Grasslands National Park: PO Box 150, Val Marie SK S0J 2P0 – 306/298-2257; Fax: 306/298-2042

Ivvavik National Park: PO Box 1840, Inuvik NT X0E 0T0 – 867/979-3248; Fax: 867/979-4491

Lower Fort Garry National Historic Site: PO Box 37, Group 343, RR#3, Selkirk MB R1A 2A8 – 204/785-6050; Fax: 204/482-5887

Motherwell Homestead National Historic Site: PO Box 247, Abernethy SK S0A 0A0 – 306/333-2116; Fax: 306/333-2210

Nahanni National Park Reserve: PO Box 348, Fort Simpson NT X0E 0N0 – 867/695-2713; Fax: 867/695-2446

Prince Albert National Park: PO Box 100, Waskesiu SK S0J 2Y0 – 306/663-4522; Fax: 306/663-5424

Riding Mountain National Park: Wasagaming MB R0J 2H0 – 204/848-7215; Fax: 204/848-2596

Riel House National Historic Site: 330 River Rd., PO Box 37, Winnipeg MB R3M 4A5 – 204/257-1783

St. Andrews Rectory National Historic Site: RR#3, Grp. 343, PO Box 37, Selkirk MB R1A 2A8 – 204/785-6050; Fax: 204/482-5887

The Forks National Historic Site: 45 Forks Market Rd., Winnipeg MB R3C 4T6 – 204/983-5988; Fax: 204/983-2221

Tutkut Nogait National Park: PO Box 1840, Inuvik NT X0E 0T1 – 867/979-3248; Fax: 867/979-4491

Wapusk National Park: PO Box 127, Churchill MB R0B 0E0 – 204/675-8863; Fax: 204/675-2026

Wood Buffalo National Park: PO Box 750, Fort Smith NT X0E 0P0 – 867/872-2349; Fax: 867/872-3910

York Factory National Historic Site: PO Box 127, Churchill MB R0B 0E0 – 204/675-8863; Fax: 204/675-2026

**Québec National Parks/National Historic Sites**

Artillery Park National Historic Site: 2, rue d'Auteuil, CP 2474, Succ Terminus postal, Québec QC G1K 7R3 – 418/648-4205; Fax: 418/648-4825

Carillon Barracks National Historic Site: 50, rue Principale, PO Box 5, Lachute QC J8H 3X2 – 514/537-3861

Cartier-Brébeuf National Historic Site: 175, rue de l'Espinay, CP 2474, Succ Terminus postal, Québec QC G1K 7R3 – 418/648-4038; Fax: 418/648-4367

Battle of the Châteauguay National Historic Site: 2371, rivière Châteauguay nord, PO Box 250, Howick QC J0S 1G0 – 514/829-2003; Fax: 514/829-3325

Battle of the Restigouche National Historic Site: Rte 132, CP 359, Pointe-à-la-Croix QC G0C 1L0 – 418/788-5676; Fax: 418/778-5895

Coteau-du-Lac National Historic Site: 308-A, ch du Fleuve, CP 550, Coteau-du-Lac QC J0P 1B0 – 514/763-5631; Fax: 514/763-1654

Forges du Saint-Maurice: 10000, boul des Forges, Trois-Rivières QC G9C 1B1 – 819/378-5116; Fax: 819/378-0887

Forillon National Park: 122, boul. Gaspé, CP 1220, Gaspé QC G0C 1R0 – 418/368-5505; Fax: 418/368-6837

Fort Chambly National Historic Site: 2, rue Richelieu, Chambly QC J3L 2B9 – 514/658-1585; Fax: 514/658-7216

Fort Lennox National Historic Site: 1 - 61e av, CP 90, St-Paul-de-l'Île-aux-Noix QC J0J 1G0 – 514/291-5700; Fax: 514/291-4389

Fort No. 1 at Pointe de Lévy National Historic Site: #1, 41, ch du Gouvernement, CP 2474, Succ Terminus postal, Québec QC G1K 7R3 – 418/835-5182; Fax: 418/835-5443

Fort Témiscamingue National Historic Site: 834, ch du Vieux-Fort, CP 636, Ville Marie QC J0Z 3W0 – 819/629-3222; Fax: 819/629-2977

Fortifications of Québec National Historic Site: 100, rue St-Louis, PO Box 2474, Stn Terminus postal, Québec QC G1K 7R3 – 418/648-7016; Fax: 418/648-4825

The Fur Trade at Lachine National Historic Site: 1255, boul Saint-Joseph, Lachine QC H8S 2M2 – 514/637-7433

Grande-Grave National Historic Site: 122, boul Gaspé, PO Box 1220, Gaspé QC G0C 1R0 – 418/368-5505

Grosse-Île & the Irish Memorial National Historic Site: CP 2474, Terminus postal, Québec QC G1K 7R3 – 418/563-4009; Fax: 418/563-1678

Jacques Cartier Monument National Historic Site: 122, boul. Gaspé, PO Box 1220, Gaspé QC G0C 1R0 – 418/368-5505

Louis-Joseph Papineau National Historic Site: 440, Bonsecours, Montréal QC H2Y 3C4

Louis S. St-Laurent National Historic Site: 6, rue Principale sud, Compton QC J0B 1L0 – 819/835-5448; Fax: 819/835-9101

Maillou House National Historic Site: 17, rue St-Louis, PO Box 430, Québec QC G1R 4R5 – 418/692-3853

Manoir Papineau National Historic Site: 500, rue Notre-Dame, CP 444, Montebello QC J0V 1L0 – 819/423-6965; Fax: 819/423-6455

La Mauricie National Park: Place Cascades, 794, 5e rue, CP 758, Shawinigan QC G9N 6V9 – 819/536-2638; Fax: 819/536-3661

Mingan Archipelago National Park Reserve: 1303, rue de la Digue, CP 1180, Havre-St-Pierre QC C0G 1P0 – 418/538-3331; Fax: 418/538-3595

Old Port of Québec Interpretation Centre: 100, rue Saint-André, CP 2474, Succ Terminus postal, Québec QC G1K 7R3 – 418/648-3300; Fax: 418/648-3678

Pointe-au-Père Lighthouse National Historic Site: 1034, rue du Phare, Pointe-au-Père QC G5M 1L8 – 418/724-6214; Fax: 418/724-6214

Québec Historic Canals: 1899, boul Périgny, Chambly QC J3L 4C3 – 514/658-0681; Fax: 514/658-2428

Saguenay St. Lawrence Marine Park: 182, rte de l'Église, CP 220, Tadoussac QC G0T 2A0 – 418/235-4703; Fax: 418/235-4686

Sir George-Étienne Cartier National Historic Site: 458, rue Notre-Dame est, Montréal QC H2Y 1C8 – 514/283-2282; Fax: 514/283-5560

Sir Wilfred Laurier National Historic Site: #205, 12e av, CP 70, Ville des Laurentides QC J0R 1C0 – 514/439-3702; Fax: 514/439-5721

**Western National Parks/National Historic Sites**

Banff National Park: PO Box 900, Banff AB T0L 0C0 – 403/762-1500; Fax: 403/762-3380

Bar J National Historic Site: PO Box 168, Longview AB T0L 1H0 – 403/395-2110; Fax: 403/395-2331

Chilkoot Trail National Historic Site: #205, 300 Main St., Whitehorse YT Y1A 2B5 – 867/667-3910; Fax: 867/393-6701

Elk Island National Park: RR#1, Site 4, Fort Saskatchewan AB T8L 2N7 – 403/992-5790; Fax: 403/992-3686

Fisgard Lighthouse National Historic Site: 603 Fort Rodd Hill Rd., Victoria BC V9C 2W8 – Fax: 604/478-8415

Fort Langley National Historic Site: 23433 Mavis St., PO Box 129, Fort Langley BC V1M 2R5 – 604/888-4424; Fax: 604/888-2577

Fort Rodd Hill National Historic Site: 603 Fort Rodd Hill Rd., Victoria BC V9C 2W8 – 250/478-5849; Fax: 250/478-8415

Fort St. James National Historic Site: PO Box 1148, Fort St. James BC V0J 1P0 – 250/996-7191; Fax: 250/996-8566

Glacier National Park: PO Box 350, Revelstoke BC V0E 2S0 – 250/837-7500; Fax: 250/837-7536

Gulf of Georgia Cannery National Historic Site: 12138 - 4 Ave., Richmond BC V7E 3J1 – 604/664-9327; Fax: 604/664-9008

Gwaii Haanas National Park Reserve: PO Box 37, Queen Charlotte BC V0T 1S0 – 250/559-8818; Fax: 250/559-8366
Jasper National Park: PO Box 10, Jasper AB T0E 1E0 – 403/852-6161; Fax: 403/852-5601
Kitwanga National Historic Site: PO Box 1148, Fort St. James BC V0J 1P0 – 250/996-7191; Fax: 250/996-8566
Klondike National Historic Sites: PO Box 390, Dawson City YT Y0B 1G0 – 867/993-7200; Fax: 867/993-7299
Kluane National Park Reserve: Haines Junction YT Y0B 1L0 – 867/634-7250; Fax: 867/634-7265
Kootenay National Park: PO Box 220, Radium Hot Springs BC V0A 1M0 – 250/347-9615; Fax: 250/347-9980
Mount Revelstoke National Park: PO Box 350, Revelstoke BC V0E 2S0 – 250/837-7500; Fax: 250/837-7536
Pacific Rim National Park: PO Box 280, Ucluelet BC V0R 3A0 – 250/726-7721; Fax: 250/726-4720
Rocky Mountain House National Historic Site: PO Box 2130, Rocky Mountain House AB T0M 1T0 – 403/845-3948; Fax: 403/845-5320
S.S. Klondide National Historic Site: #205, 300 Main St., Whitehorse YT Y1A 2B5 – 867/667-3910; Fax: 867/393-6701
Vuntut National Park: #205, 300 Main St., Whitehorse YT Y1A 2B5 – 867/667-3910; Fax: 867/393-6701
Waterton Lakes National Park: Waterton Park AB T0K 2M0 – 403/859-2224; Fax: 403/859-2650
Yoho National Park: PO Box 99, Field BC V0A 1G0 – 250/343-6324; Fax: 250/343-6330

#### STRATEGIC MANAGEMENT

Asst. Deputy Minister, Michael Wernick, 819/997-3772, Fax: 819/997-7117
Director General, Banque Internationale d'Information sur les états Francophones, Suzanne Richer, 819/997-3857, Fax: 819/953-8439
Director General, Corporate & Intergovernmental Affairs, Denny Gélinas, 819/994-1046, Fax: 819/953-2792
Director General, Corporate Review, Anne Scotton, 819/994-1018, Fax: 819/994-7080
Director General, International Exposition, Erika Bruce, 819/994-2061, Fax: 819/997-7624
Director General, Strategic Planning & Policy Coordination, Sean Berrigan, 819/994-5644, Fax: 819/997-5102

##### Communications Branch

Director General, Jean Chartier, 819/997-0231, Fax: 819/953-5382
Director, Citizenship & Canadian Identity Sector, Renée Saint-Arnaud-Watt, 819/994-5594, Fax: 819/994-7687
Director, Cultural Development & Heritage Sector, Wayne Scott, 613/990-4839, Fax: 613/957-2203
Director, Parks Canada Sector, Nicole Racette, 613/953-6782, Fax: 613/953-5523
Director, Strategic Communications Services, Denis Vezina, 819/953-6783, Fax: 819/953-5382
Director, Writing & Media Relations, Gilles Déry, 819/994-5606, Fax: 819/953-5382

##### Associated Agencies, Boards & Commissions

Listed alphabetically in detail, this section.
Canada Council/Conseil des Arts du Canada
Canadian Broadcasting Corporation/Société Radio-Canada (CBC)
Canadian Museum of Civilization/Musée canadien des civilisations (Listed in Section1; *see* Index.)
Canadian Museum of Nature/Musée canadien de la nature (Listed in Section 1; *see* Index.)
Canadian Radio-television & Telecommunications Commission/Conseil de la radiodiffusion et des télécommunications (CRTC)
National Archives of Canada/Archives nationales du Canada
National Arts Centre/Centre national des Arts (NAC)
National Battlefields Commission/Commission des champs de bataille nationaux
National Capital Commission/Commission de la Capitale nationale
National Film Board of Canada/Office national du film
National Gallery of Canada/Musée des Beaux-Arts du Canada (Listed in Section 1; *see* Index.)
National Library of Canada/Bibliothèque nationale du Canada (Listed in Section 1; *see* Index.)
National Museum of Science & Technology/Musée national des sciences et de la technologie (Listed in Section 1; *see* Index.)
Public Service Commission of Canada/Commission de la fonction publique du Canada
Telefilm Canada/Téléfilm Canada

### CANADIAN HUMAN RIGHTS COMMISSION/ Commission canadienne des droits de la personne

Place de Ville, Tower A, #1300, 320 Queen St., Ottawa ON K1A 1E1
613/995-1151; Fax: 613/996-9661; Email: info@chrc.ca; URL: http://www.chrc.ca/chrc.html
TDD: 613/996-5211
The Commission administers the Canadian Human Rights Act which applies to federal government departments & agencies, & businesses under federal jurisdiction. The Commission accepts complaints of discrimination based on race, national or ethnic origin, colour, religion, age, sex, marital & family status, pardoned offence, disability & sexual orientation. Collect calls accepted throughout Canada.
**Chief Commissioner**, Michelle Falardeau-Ramsay
Secretary General, John Hucker
Director, Corporate Services, Pierre Cousineau, 613/943-9031

##### Regional Offices

Alberta & Northwest Territories: Highfield Place, #308, 10010 - 106 St., Edmonton AB T5J 3L2 – 403/495-4040; Fax: 403/495-4044, TDD: 403/495-4108
Atlantic: 5657 Spring Garden Rd., 2nd Fl., PO Box 3545, Halifax NS B3J 3J2 – 902/426-8380; Fax: 902/426-2685, Toll Free: 1-800-565-1752, TDD: 902/426-9345
Ontario: #1002, 175 Bloor St. East, Toronto ON M4W 3R8 – 416/973-5527; Fax: 416/973-6184, TDD: 416/973-8912
Prairies: #242, 240 Graham St., Winnipeg MB R3C 0J8 – 204/983-2189; Fax: 204/983-6132, TDD: 204/983-2882
Québec: #470, 1253, av McGill College, Montréal QC H3B 2Y5 – 514/283-5218; Fax: 514/283-5084, TDD: 514/283-1869
Western: 800 Burrard St., 13th Fl., Vancouver BC V6Z 1X9 – 604/666-2251; Fax: 604/666-2386, TDD: 604/666-3071

### CANADIAN INTERGOVERNMENTAL CONFERENCE SECRETARIAT (CICS)/ Secrétariat des conférences intergouvernementales canadiennes

110 O'Connor St., PO Box 488, Stn A, Ottawa ON K1N 8V5
613/995-2341; Fax: 613/996-6091
CICS is a conference support body which provides the administrative services required for the planning & the conduct of federal-provincial & interprovincial conferences at the First Ministers, ministers & deputy ministers level. The agency is at the disposal of individual federal & provincial government departments which may be called upon to organize & chair such meetings.
**Secretary**, Stuart MacKinnon

### CANADIAN INTERNATIONAL DEVELOPMENT AGENCY (CIDA)/Agence canadienne de développement international (ACDI)

Place du Centre, 200, Promenade du Portage, Hull QC K1A 0G4
819/997-5456; Fax: 819/953-6088; URL: http://www.acdi.cida.gc.ca
TDD: 819/953-5023
Public Inquiries: 819/997-5006
Supports the efforts of the peoples of developing countries to achieve sustainable economic & social development by cooperating with them in development activities & by providing humanitarian assistance. The Official Development Assistance Program contributes to Canada's political & economic interests abroad in promoting social justice, international stability & long-term economic relationships. Reports to government through the Department of Foreign Affairs & International Trade.
**President**, Huguette Labelle, 819/997-7951, Fax: 819/953-3352
Vice-President, Africa & Middle East Branch, Carolyn McAskie, 819/997-1643
Vice-President, Americas Branch, Pierre Racicot, 819/997-3291
Acting Vice-President, Asia Branch, Jean-Marc Métivier, 819/997-1666
Acting Vice-President, Canadian Partnership Branch, Pierre David, 819/997-6057
Acting Vice-President, Corporate Management Branch, Claudia Roberts, 819/953-6596
Vice-President, Eastern & Central Europe Branch, Charles Bassett, 819/994-4787
Vice-President, Multilateral Programs Branch, Nicole Senécal, 819/997-7537
Vice-President, Personnel & Administration Branch, Nicole Charette, 819/997-6383
Vice-President, Policy Branch, John Robinson, 819/997-6133
Director General, Communications, Theresa M. Keleher, 819/953-6535

### CANADIAN INTERNATIONAL GRAINS INSTITUTE (CIGI)/Institut international du Canada pour le grain

#1000, 303 Main St., Winnipeg MB R3C 3G7
204/983-5344; Fax: 204/983-2642; URL: http://www.cigi.mb.ca
Established in 1972, the Institute is an instructional facility offering courses in grain handling, marketing & technology. A non-profit organization, it works in affiliation with the Canadian Wheat Board, the Canadian Grain Commission, & various departments of the federal government. It also works in cooperation with all segments of Canada's grain industry.
**Executive Director**, A.W. Tremere
Director, Feed Technology, D.R. Hickling
Director, Food Technology, A.R. Tweed
Director, Marketing, P.S. Westdal
Manager, Communications & Public Relations, V.S. Sloan
Manager, Finance & Administration, J.L. Peake
Executive Secretary, Mona Brisson

## CANADIAN INTERNATIONAL TRADE TRIBUNAL/Tribunal canadien du commerce extérieur

Standard Life Centre, 333 Laurier Ave. West, Ottawa ON K1A 0G7
613/990-2452; Fax: 613/990-2439; URL: http://canada.gc.ca/depts/agencies/cttind_e.html
The Tribunal is an independent, quasi-judicial body, which carries out both judicial & advisory functions relating to trade remedies. On December 31, 1988, it took over all of the inquiry & appeal functions of the Tariff Board, the Canadian Import Tribunal, & the Textile & Clothing Board, all of which no longer exist. With the proclamation of the North American Free Trade Agreement Implementation Act set on January 1, 1994, the Tribunal has been designated as the bid challenge authority for Canada. In this capacity, the Tribunal succeeds the Procurement Review Board of Canada. Reports to government through the Minister of Finance.

#### ACTS ADMINISTERED

Canadian International Trade Tribunal Act
Customs Act
Excise Tax Act
Special Import Measures Act
**Chair**, A.T. Eyton
Vice-Chairman, Patricia Close
Vice-Chairman, R.A. Guay
Vice-Chairman, A.B. Trudeau
Secretary, Michel P. Granger
Executive Director, Research, R.W. Erdmann
General Counsel, Gerry Stobo
Director, Procurement Division, Jean Archambault

## CANADIAN JUDICIAL COUNCIL/Conseil canadien de la magistrature

#450, 112 Kent St., Ottawa ON K1A 0W8
613/998-5182; Fax: 613/998-8889
The members of the Council include the Chief Justice of Canada (who acts as Chair), the Chief Justices & Associate Chief Justices of each Superior Court or Branch or Division thereof, the senior judges of the Supreme Court of the Yukon Territory & the Supreme Court of the Northwest Territories succeeding each other on the Council every two years, the Chief Judge and Associate Chief Judge of the Tax Court of Canada, & the Chief Justice of the Court Martial Court of Canada.
**Executive Director**, Jeannie Thomas

## CANADIAN MUSEUM OF CIVILIZATION/Musée Canadien des Civilisations

Listed in Section 6; *see* Index.

## CANADIAN MUSEUM OF NATURE/Musée Canadien de la Nature

Listed in Section 6; *see* Index.

## CANADIAN NATIONAL RAILWAY COMPANY (CNR)/Compagnie des chemins de fer nationaux du Canada

935 la Gauchetière ouest, Montréal QC H3B 2M9
514/399-5430; Fax: 514/399-5586, 5479
Emergency Numbers: Western Canada: 1-800-665-0581; Eastern Canada: 1-800-465-9239
The Company, incorporated in 1919 as a federal Crown corporation, is administered by a Board of Directors appointed by the Cabinet. It reports to Parliament through the Minister of Transport. CN's mandate is to operate a rail-based transportation system, offering rail and intermodal freight services across Canada. Other business units operate a freight railway network in the US, run the CN Tower in Toronto, develop the real estate and natural resource potentials of railway lands, provide technical consulting services, & invest the corporation's pension funds.
**Chair**, David McLean
President & CEO, Paul M. Tellier
Executive Vice-President & Chief Financial Officer, Y.H. Masse
Senior Vice-President, Marketing, Gerald Davies
Senior Vice-President, Western Canada, Rick Boyd
Vice-President, Investor Relations, Robert E. Noorigian, 514/399-0051
Treasurer & Principal Tax Counsel, Sean Finn
Operations (Edmonton), Parker Hogan, #10004, 104 Ave., Edmonton AB T5J 0K2, 403/421-6152
Operations (Montréal), Christine Skjerven, 514/399-3108
Operations (Toronto), Ian Thomson, 277 Front St., Toronto ON M5V 2X7, 416/217-2395
Public Affairs (Montréal), Louise Filion, 514/399-5916
Public Affairs (Toronto), Mark Hallman, 277 Front St., Toronto ON M5V 2X7, 416/217-2390

## CANADIAN PERMANENT COMMITTEE ON GEOGRAPHICAL NAMES/Comité permanent canadien des noms géographiques

#650, 615 Booth St., Ottawa ON K1A 0E9
613/992-3405; Fax: 613/943-8282; Email: geonames@NRCan.gc.ca; URL: http://NRCan.gc.ca/geonames
General Enquiries: 613/992-3892
**Chair**, E.A. Price
Executive Secretary, H. Kerfoot

## CANADIAN POLAR COMMISSION (CPC)/Commission canadienne des affaires polaires (CCAP)

Constitution Square, #1710, 360 Albert St., Ottawa ON K1R 7X7
613/943-8605; Fax: 613/943-8607; Email: mail@polarcom.gc.ca; URL: http://www.polarcom.gc.ca/
Canada's national advisory agency on polar affairs. The CPC monitors & promotes the development of knowledge in polar regions, with the view that social & scientific research involves all northern peoples & reflects their interests & concerns.
**Executive Officer**, Albert Haller
Executive Secretary, Sandra Bianchini
Chairman, Whit Fraser
Coordinator, Communications & Information, Alan Saunders
Research Assistant, Elaine Anderson
Northern Science Office, Jean-Marie Beaulieu

#### Regional Office

Yellowknife: #10, 4807 - 49 St., Yellowknife NT X1A 3TA – 867/920-7401; Fax: 867/920-7098, Northern Science Officer, André Légaré

## CANADIAN RADIO-TELEVISION & TELECOMMUNICATIONS COMMISSION (CRTC)/Conseil de la radiodiffusion et des télécommunications

1, Promenade du Portage, Terrasses de la Chaudière, Hull QC J8X 4B1
819/997-0313 (Public Affairs); Fax: 819/994-0218; URL: http://www.crtc.gc.ca/
TTY: 819/994-0423
Mailing Address: CRTC, Ottawa ON K1A ON2
The Commission is responsible for regulating all federally chartered telecommunication carriers, & regulating & supervising all aspects of the Canadian broadcasting system. Reports to government through the Minister of Canadian Heritage.
**Chair**, Françoise Bertrand, 819/997-3430
Vice-Chair, Charles Bélanger, 819/997-4126
Vice-Chair, David C. Colville, 819/997-8766
Secretary General & Chief Operarting Officer, Laura M. Talbot-Allan, 819/997-1027
Executive Director, Broadcasting, Susan Baldwin, 819/997-3749
Acting Executive Director, Telecommunications, Don Donovan, 819/997-4644
Director General, Broadcast Analysis, Diane Rhéaume, 819/997-5225
Director General, Broadcast Distribution & Technology, Wayne Charman, 819/997-5369
Director General, Broadcast Planning, Peter Fleming, 819/997-3643
Director General, Competition, Tariff & Convergence Policy, Malcolm Andrew, 819/997-2755
Director General, Decisions & Operations, Vacant, 819/994-0293
Director General, Finance & Management Services, Bill Weizenbach, 819/997-4009
Director General, Financial Services, Don Donovan, 819/997-4818
Director General, Secretariat Operations & Licensing, Rosemary Chisholm, 819/997-4427
Director, Public Affairs, Vacant
Acting General Counsel, John Keogh, 819/997-5533

## CANADIAN SPACE AGENCY (CSA)/Agence spatiale canadienne (ASC)

6767, rte de l'Aéroport, Saint-Hubert QC J3Y 8Y9
514/926-4351; Fax: 514/926-4352; Email: webmaster@radarsat.space.gc.ca; URL: http://www.space.gc.ca/
In partnership with the United States, nine Canadian provinces & the private sector, the CSA operates the Canadian RADARSAT Program. The program involves the development & operation of a remote sensing satellite, launched in 1995. Officially opened the Western Canadian RADARSAT tracking station in Saskatoon in late 1994.
The Canadian RADARSAT satellite observes the earth using a Sythetic Aperture Radar (SAR) sensor capable of obtaining detailed images in darkness & through clouds. Gathers essential data for more efficient resource management & environmental monitoring (including the survey of natural resources, & ice types & movements).
RADARSAT International Inc. (RSI) is a consortium of Canadian aerospace companies, incorporated to market & distribute RADARSAT data worldwide.
**President**, William MacDonald Evans
Executive Vice-President, Alain-F. Desfossés
Legal Counsel, Robert Lefebvre
Vice-President, Human Spaceflights, Karl Doetsch
Vice-President, Research & Applications, Garry Martin Lindberg
Acting Director General, Canadian Astronaut Program, Steven Glenwood MacLean
Director General, David Florida Laboratory, Rolf Mamen
Director General, RADARSAT Program, Joseph L. McNally
Acting Director General, Space Science Program, Barry Wetter
Director General, Space Technology Program, Jack Chambers
Acting Director, Communications, Alain Desfaris

## CANADIAN TRANSPORTATION AGENCY (CTA)/Office des transports du Canada (OTC)

Les Terrasses de la Chaudière, 15 Eddy St., Hull QC K1A 0N9
819/997-0344 (Communications); Fax: 819/953-8353; URL: http://www.cta-otc.gc.ca
Factsline: 819/997-5834; Air Complaints: 1-800-263-3027; Air & Accessible Complaints: 1-800-883-1813; TTY: 819/953-9705; 1-800-669-5575

Serves as economic regulator & decision-maker with respect to transportation services under federal jurisdiction. Responsibilities include issuing licences to air carriers & railways; dispute resolution over various air, rail & marine transportation rate & service matters; and determining the annual maximum rate scale for western grain movements. Also has powers to remove undue obstacles to the mobility of travellers with disabilities in the federally regulated transportation network.

#### ACTS ADMINISTERED

Canada Transportation Act
Coasting Trade Act
Pilotage Act
Railway Safety Act
St. Lawrence Seaway Authority Act
Shipping Conferences Exemption Act

**Chair**, Marian L. Robson, 819/997-9233
Vice-Chair, Jean Patenaude, 819/953-8921
Secretary & General Legal Counsel, Director General, Legal & Secretariat Branch, Marie-Paule Scott, Q.C., 819/953-6698
Director General, Air & Accessible Transportation Branch, Gavin Currie, 819/953-5074
Director General, Corporate Management Branch, Joan MacDonald, 819/997-6764
Director General, Rail & Marine Branch, Seymour Isenberg, 819/953-4657
Director, Communications, Daniel Lavoie, 819/953-7666

#### Field Investigation Offices

Atlantic: #9, 1045 Main St., Moncton NB E1C 1H1 – 506/851-6950; Fax: 506/851-2518, Senior Investigator, Brian Mercer
Central: 333 Main St., 21st Fl., Winnipeg MB R3C 0P6 – 204/984-6092; Fax: 204/984-6093, Senior Investigator, Mervyn Caldwell
Ontario: 7548 Bath Rd., Mississauga ON L4T 1L2 – 905/612-5792; Fax: 905/612-5794, Senior Investigator, Jeanette Anderson
Pacific: #250, 1095 West Pender St., Vancouver BC V6E 2M6 – 604/666-0620; Fax: 604/666-1267, Senior Investigator, Gordon King
Québec: #8023, 101, boul Rolland-Therrien, Longueuil QC J4H 4B9 – 514/928-4173; Fax: 514/928-4174, Senior Investigator, Richard Laliberté
Western: #1100, 9700 Jasper Ave., Edmonton AB T5J 4C3 – 403/495-6618; Fax: 403/495-5639, Senior Investigator, Linda Brooklyn

## CANADIAN WHEAT BOARD (CWB)/ Commission canadienne du blé

423 Main St., PO Box 816, Winnipeg MB R3C 2P5
204/983-0239, 3416; Fax: 204/983-3841; URL: http://canada.gc.ca/depts/agencies/cwbind_e.html
Telex: 07-57801; Cable: Wheatboard

Crown agency responsible for marketing Prairie-grown wheat, durum & barley. With sales of over $4.5 billion per year, it markets grain to more than 70 countries. The Wheat Board's operations are funded by Prairie grain producers.

**Minister Responsible**, Hon. Ralph Goodale
Chief Commissioner, Lorne F. Hehn
General Counsel & Corporate Secretary, Margaret Redmond
Executive Director, Finance & Treasurer, Donald E. Vernon
Executive Director, Human Resources, Patricia Wallace
Executive Director, Marketing, Adrian C. Measner
Executive Director, Planning, Brian T. Olsen

#### Overseas Offices

China: Tower B, Beijing COFCO Plaza, #708, 8 Jianguomen Nei St., Beijing 100005, China – 011-86-10-6526-3906; 6526-3908; Fax: 011-86-10-6526-3907
Japan: Kowa No. 9 Bldg., Annex 6-7, Akasaka 1-chome, 6th Fl., Tokyo 107, Japan – 011-81-33-583-4291; Fax: 011-81-33-587-1593

## CITIZENSHIP & IMMIGRATION CANADA/ Citoyenneté et Immigration Canada

Jean Edmonds Towers, 365 Laurier Ave. West, Ottawa ON K1A 1L1
613/954-9019; Fax: 613/954-2221; URL: http://cicnet.ingenia.com/english/index.html

The Department of Citizenship & Immigration administers Canada's citizenship & immigration policies, procedures & service. The department is responsible for the following:

- examining immigrants, visitors & people claiming refugee status at land borders, seaports & airports;
- processing applications for permanent residence, extensions of visitor status requests & sponsorships for relatives & refugees overseas;
- admitting students, temporary workers & qualified business immigrants;
- investigating & removing people who are in Canada illegally;
- working with & helping fund a network of settlement agencies & services to help immigrants adapt to & participate in day-to-day Canadian life;
- promoting the acceptance of immigrants by Canadians;
- cooperating with various levels of government on enforcement, program development & the delivery of services;
- accepting applications & verifying the eligibility & documentation of applicants;
- granting citizenship & administration of the Oath of Citizenship at ceremonies in Citizenship Courts & numerous community facilities across Canada;
- confirming Canadian citizenship status &;
- issuing proofs of citizenship to Canadians.

The Immigration & Refugee Board reports to Parliament through the minister.

#### ACTS ADMINISTERED

Citizenship Act
Immigration Act

**Minister**, Hon. Lucienne Robillard, 613/954-1064, Fax: 613/957-2688
Deputy Minister, Janice Cochrane, 613/954-3501
Asst. Deputy Minister, Operations, Gerry Campbell, 613/952-1770
Asst. Deputy Minister, Partnerships, Georges Tsaï, 613/957-3338, Fax: 613/957-3196
Asst. Deputy Minister, Policy, Greg Fyffe, 613/954-5335, Fax: 613/957-3196
Assoc. Deputy Minister, Marc Lafrenière, 613/957-0267, Fax: 613/954-3409
Director General, Finance & Administration, Jerry Robbins, 613/954-4443, Fax: 613/957-2775
Director General, Human Resources, Cathy Downes, 613/941-7788
Director General, Public Affairs, Maryse Brunet-Lalonde, 613/941-7077, Fax: 613/941-7099
Director, Legal Services, John Sims

#### CASE MANAGEMENT

613/957-3940; Fax: 613/957-7235
Director General, Bill Sheppit, 613/957-3941, Fax: 613/941-6754
Director, Case Review, Theresa Harvey, 613/957-1167
Director, Litigation, Joanne DesLauriers, 613/954-2508, Fax: 613/954-5896
Director, Organized Crime, Michel Gagné, 613/957-3515, Fax: 613/952-6319
Director, Security Review, Ian Taylor, 613/952-6336, Fax: 613/952-6825

#### DEPARTMENTAL DELIVERY NETWORK

613/941-9291; Fax: 613/941-0061
Director General, Tom Ryan, 613/941-8055
Director, Case Processing Centre - Vegreville, Brian Beaupré, #6212, 55 Ave., Vegreville AB T9C 1W5, 403/632-8000, Fax: 403/632-8100
Manager, Case Processing Centre, Frank Perriccioli, Mississauga ON, 905/803-7371, Fax: 905/803-7398
Manager, Case Processing Centre - Sydney, Bill White, PO Box 7000, Sydney NS B1P 6V6, 902/564-7825
Manager, Case Processing Centre, Phil Pirie, Vegreville AB, 403/632-8000, Fax: 403/632-8100
Manager, Citizenship Services, Danielle Charbonneau, 613/941-8405
Manager, Immigration Health Service, Dr. George Giovinazzo, 613/954-4470, Fax: 613/941-2179
Manager, Immigration Services, Susan Kramer, 613/941-1550, Fax: 613/952-6382
Manager, Immigration Warrant Response Centre, Chris McDonell, 613/954-2816, Fax: 613/954-9291
Manager, Interim Federal Health, Dr. Roland Fuca, 613/954-8210
Manager, Project Services, Brian Hudson, 613/941-0998
Manager, Query Response Centre, Jean-Yves Prevost, 613/957-4418, Fax: 613/957-4660
Manager, Support Services, Jim Trussler, 613/957-1090

#### ENFORCEMENT

613/954-4159; Fax: 613/954-6765
Director General, Pierre Bourget, 613/954-6132
Director, Case Presentation, Neil Cochrane, 613/957-4333, Fax: 613/954-5896
Director, Intelligence & Interdiction, Gary Blachford, 613/954-6061, Fax: 613/954-8571
Director, Investigation & Removal, Susan Leith, 613/954-5628, Fax: 613/954-5238
Director, Port of Entry Management, Brian McQuillan, 613/941-9026, Fax: 613/954-1673
Director, Program Development, Brian Grant, 613/954-2124, Fax: 613/954-6765

#### INFORMATION MANAGEMENT & TECHNOLOGY BRANCH

613/941-4873; Fax: 613/954-6209
Director General, Jill Velenosi, 613/954-2700
Director, Applications Development, Frank Brown, 613/954-5683, Fax: 613/954-2263
Director, Architecture & Database, Re-evaluation Governance, Chris McGee, 613/954-8043, Fax: 613/954-6510
Director, CIC Systems Modernization & Director, Project & Systems Integration, Al Bezanson, 613/941-4526, Fax: 613/954-2263
Director, Implementation & Roll-out, Re-evaluation Technology, Paul-André Laurin, 613/954-5866, Fax: 613/941-2620
Director, IMTB Project Office, Project Office & Client Relations, Christian Labelle, 613/952-7008
Director, Information Management, Roman Borowyk, 613/954-6067
Director, Operations, Re-evaluation Business, Peg Blair, 613/954-3895, Fax: 613/954-6510

#### INTEGRATION

613/957-4483; Fax: 613/957-0594
Director General, Agnes Jaouich, 613/957-3257
Director, Policy, Education & Promotion, Ingrid Hauck, 613/952-2301
Director, Registrar, Normand Sabourin, 613/952-7273, Fax: 613/957-2206

Director, Service Line Support, Helen Amundsen, 613/954-3355, Fax: 613/952-7416
Director, Settlement Operations, Marcia Shaw, 613/957-3433, Fax: 613/957-7673

### INTERNATIONAL REGION
613/957-5892; Fax: 613/957-5802
Director General, Jeff Lebane, 613/957-5893
Director, Africa & Middle East, Claire Lavoie, 613/957-5891
Director, Operational Coordination, Anne Arnott, 613/957-6891, Fax: 613/957-6991
Director, Pacific Operations, Brian O'Connor, 613/957-5813, Fax: 613/957-6985
Director, Personnel, Jim Versteegh, 613/941-1372, Fax: 613/957-6909
Director, Resource Management, Frank Andrews, 613/957-5890
Director, Western Hemisphere, Rodney Fields, 613/957-5820, Fax: 613/957-6988

### MINISTERIAL & EXECUTIVE SERVICES
613/952-5497; Fax: 613/952-5497
Director General, Claudette Deschênes, 613/954-9004, Fax: 613/952-5547
Director, Briefings & Parliamentary Affairs, Kathleen O'Connor, 613/952-5567
Director, Ministerial Enquiries Unit, Carrie Hunter, 613/957-1476
Director, Public Rights Administration, Janet Brooks, 613/957-6512, Fax: 613/957-6517

### REFUGEES
613/957-5873; Fax: 613/957-5869
Director General, Gerry VanKessel, 613/957-5874
Director, Asylum, Craig Goodes, 613/957-5867
Director, Refugee Resettlement, Rick Herringer, 613/957-9349, Fax: 613/957-5836
Director, Resettlement, Gilles Pelletier, 613/957-5951, Fax: 613/957-5946
Director, Service Line, John Kent, 613/957-5831
Senior Advisor, International Liaison, Sally Andrews, 613/957-5877

### SELECTION
613/941-8990; Fax: 613/941-9323
Director General, Joan Atkinson, 613/941-8989
Director, Business Immigration, Don Myatt, 613/941-8225, Fax: 613/941-9014
Director, Economic Policy, Dougall Aucoin, 613/954-4214
Director, Immigration Health Policy, Neil Heywood, 613/957-5939, Fax: 613/954-8653
Director, Service Line & Departmental Support, Chris McGee, 613/954-8043, Fax: 613/954-0924
Director, Social Policy & Programs, Nick Oosterveen, 613/941-8225

### STRATEGIC POLICY, PLANNING & RESEARCH
613/957-5953; Fax: 613/957-5955
Director General, Ann Radcliffe
Director, Collaboration, Carmen Hall, 613/957-5981, Fax: 613/597-5968
Director, Program Support, Elizabeth Ruddick, 613/957-5907, Fax: 613/957-5913
Director, Strategic Direction, Scott Heatherington, 613/957-5950
National Director, Settlement Renewal, David Neuman, 613/957-5910, Fax: 613/957-5913
Manager, Corporate Governance, Danielle Racette, 613/957-4166
Manager, Regulatory Process, Don MacKay, 613/957-5934
Manager, Scanning & Intelligence, Sheila Gariepy, 613/957-9803, Fax: 613/957-5940
Manager, Social Policy, Colette Arnal, 613/957-5915

### CANADA IMMIGRATION CENTRES & CITIZENSHIP OFFICES
Immigration visa offices are located in most Canadian Embassies and Consulates abroad, *see* Diplomats. Immigration centres are located at most ports of entry in Canada, and citizenship & immigration offices in major cities throughout the country. For specific addresses and other information contact the relevant regional Citizenship & Immigration Canada Communications Branch.

#### Regional Offices
Atlantic: 1875 Brunswick St., Halifax NS B3J 3L8 – 902/426-4241; Fax: 902/426-4241, Director, CIC Nova Scotia/PEI, Al Reardon, 902/426-3154, Regional Director, Atlantic, Darrel Mesheau, 902/426-2905, Regional Manager, Kathy Alexander, 709/772-5521, Fax: 709/772-2929
British Columbia & Yukon: Westar Bldg., #1800, 1188 West Georgia St., Vancouver BC V6E 4A2 – 604/666-0876; Fax: 604/666-1927, Director, Chris Taylor, 604/666-6301, Regional Manager, Lois Reimer, 604/666-8185
Ontario: 4900 Yonge St., North York ON M2N 6A8, Director General, Irene Bader, 416/954-7800, Fax: 416/954-7870, Regional Manager, Lucille Leblanc, 416/954-7849, Fax: 416/954-8018
Prairies - Northwest Territories: Johnston Terminal Bldg., #400, 25 Forks Market Rd., Winnipeg MB R3C 4S9, Regional Director, Robert Vineberg, 204/984-2013, Fax: 204/983-2867, Regional Manager, Ann Lawler, 204/984-7814, Fax: 204/983-2967
Québec: 715 Peel St., Succ A, Montréal QC H3C 4H6 – Fax: 514/496-2060, Director General, Monique Leclair, 514/283-4900, Regional Manager, Rose-Lise Arrelle, 514/283-5637

## Office of the CORRECTIONAL INVESTIGATOR/L'Enquêteur correctionnel Canada
#402, 275 Slater St., Ottawa ON K1P 5H9
613/990-2695; Fax: 613/990-9091; URL: http://canada.gc.ca/depts/agencies/ociind_e.html
Toll Free: 1-800-267-5982
Investigates complaints from inmates in Canadian institutions. Reports on problems inmates have that fall within the responsibility of the Solicitor General of Canada and meet the certain conditions. Reports to government through the Solicitor General of Canada.
**Correctional Investigator**, Ron L. Stewart

## CORRECTIONAL SERVICE CANADA/Service correctionnel Canada
340 Laurier Ave. West, Ottawa ON K1A 0P9
613/995-5364 (Communications); Fax: 613/947-0091; URL: http://www.csc-scc.gc.ca
An agency within the Department of the Solicitor General responsible for the administration of sentences with respect to convicted offenders sentenced to two or more years as decided by the federal courts, & certain provincial inmates who have been transferred to a federal institution. CSC is also responsible for the supervision of inmates who have been granted conditional release by the authority of the National Parole Board.
**Commissioner**, Ole Ingstrup, 613/995-5781, Fax: 613/995-3352
Senior Deputy Commissioner, Lucie McClung, 613/947-0643
Deputy Commissioner, Women, Nancy Stableforth, 613/992-6067
Asst. Commissioner, Communications, France Lagacé, 613/996-2609
Asst. Commissioner, Corporate Services, Louise St-Laurent, 613/992-0670
Asst. Commissioner, Performance Assurance, Gerry Hooper, 613/995-8977
Senior Financial Officer, Stan Fields, 613/992-0670
General Counsel, Legal Services, Carolyn Kobernick, 613/992-9009
Corporate Advisor, Aboriginal Programming, Millard Beane, 613/995-2557
Corporate Advisor, Chaplaincy, Pierre Allard, 613/996-0373
Corporate Advisor, Community Corrections, Gerry Minard, 613/992-4801
Corporate Advisor, Corporate Development, Brendan Reynolds, 613/995-2792
Corporate Advisor, Health Care, Robert Climie, 613/992-5713
Corporate Advisor, Personnel & Training, John Rama, 613/995-8899
Corporate Advisor, Sex Offender Programming, Sharon Williams, 613/545-8248

#### Regional Headquarters
Atlantic: #102, 1045 Main St., Moncton NB E1C 1H1 – 506/851-6313; Fax: 506/851-2418, Deputy Commissioner, Alphonse Cormier
Ontario: 440 King St. West, PO Box 1174, Kingston ON K7L 4Y8 – 613/545-8211; Fax: 613/545-8684, Deputy Commissioner, Irving Kulik
Pacific: 32560 Simon Ave., PO Box 4500, Abbotsford BC V2T 5L7 – 604/870-2501; Fax: 604/870-2430, Deputy Commissioner, Pieter De Vink
Prairies: 2313 Hanselman Pl., PO Box 9223, Saskatoon SK S7K 3X5 – 306/975-4850; Fax: 306/975-4435, Deputy Commissioner, Rémi Gobeil
Québec: 3 Pl. Laval, 2e étage, Laval QC H7N 1A2 – 514/967-3333; Fax: 514/967-3326, Deputy Commissioner, Jean-Claude Perron

#### District Parole Offices
Abbotsford-Fraser Valley: 33344 King Rd., PO Box 3333, Abbotsford BC V2S 5X7 – 604/870-2400; Fax: 604/870-2402, Director, B. Lang
Calgary: #311, 510 - 12 Ave. SW, Calgary AB T2R 0H3 – 403/292-5505; Fax: 403/292-5510, Director, Bernard Pitre
Edmonton-Alberta North, NWT: 9530 - 101 Av., 2nd Fl., Edmonton AB T5H 0B3 – 403/495-4900; Fax: 403/495-4975, Director, Don Kynoch
Guelph-Western Ontario: 42 Wyndham St. North, Guelph ON N1H 4E6 – 519/826-2144; Fax: 519/826-2143, Director, Craig Townson
Halifax/Dartmouth: 1888 Brunswick St., 7th Fl., Halifax NS B3J 3J8 – 902/426-3408; Fax: 902/426-8000, Director, Ron Lawlor
Hamilton: #411 - 150 Main St., Hamilton ON L8P 1H8 – 905/572-2695; Fax: 905/572-2072, Director, Marg Harlans
Kingston-Eastern Ontario: #203, 920 Princess St., Kingston ON K7L 1H1 – 613/545-8734; Fax: 613/545-8079, Director, Patrick Quinn
Moncton-New Brunswick & PEI: 1 Factory Lane, 1st Fl., Moncton NB E1C 9M3 – 506/851-6350; Fax: 506/851-2057, Director, Don Leblanc
Montréal-Métropolitan: Tour ouest, 200, boul René Lévesque ouest, 9e étage, Montréal QC H2Z 1X4 – 514/283-1776; Fax: 514/283-1783, Directeur, Gilles Thibault
Ottawa: 207 Queen St., 1st Fl., Ottawa ON K1P 6E5 – 613/996-7011; Fax: 613/954-1687, Director, Rosemary O'Brien
Prince George-Northern Interior: #201, 280 Victoria St., Prince George BC V2L 4X3 – 250/561-5314; Fax: 250/561-5537, Director, Lynne Hyatt
Regina-Saskatchewan: #200, 2550 - 15 Ave., Regina SK S4P 1A5 – 306/780-5050; Fax: 306/780-6935, Director, A. Rollo
St-Jérome-East & West Québec: #300, 222, rue St-Georges, St-Jérôme QC J7Z 4Z9 – 514/432-3737; Fax: 514/432-3221, Directeur, Normand Granger

Saint John-New Brunswick West: 61 Union St., 5th Fl., Saint John NB E2L 1A2 – 506/636-4795; Fax: 506/636-4870, Director, Marc Brideau

St. John's-Newfoundland & Area: 531 Charter Ave., St. John's NF A1A 1P7 – 709/772-6308; Fax: 709/772-6415, Director, B. Devine

Toronto-Central Ontario: 330 Keele St., Toronto ON M6P 2K7 – 416/604-4390; Fax: 416/973-9723, Director, Doug Orr

Truro/Kentville/Sydney: 14 Court St., Truro NS B2N 3H7 – 902/893-6760; Fax: 902/893-4961, Director, David Cail

Vancouver: New Westminster Federal Bldg., #417, 549 Columbia, New Westminster BC V3L 1B3 – 604/666-3731; Fax: 604/666-0161, Director, Wayne Oster

Victoria-Vancouver Island: #323, 816 Government St., Victoria BC V8W 1W9 – 250/363-3267; Fax: 250/363-3969, Director, Bob Brown

Winnipeg-Manitoba/Northwestern Ontario: 470 Notre-Dame Ave., 2nd Fl., Winnipeg MB R3B 1R5 – 204/983-4306; Fax: 204/983-5869, Director, Gord Holloway

## DEFENCE CONSTRUCTION CANADA/ Construction de Défense Canada

Place de Ville, Tower B, 112 Kent St., 17th Fl., Ottawa ON K1A 0K3

613/998-9548; Fax: 613/998-1061; URL: http://canada.gc.ca/depts/agencies/dccind_e.html

The Crown company that administers the major construction, building repair, maintenance programs & contracts for engineering consultant & architectural services for the Department of National Defence. The Company's legal title is "Defence Construction (1951) Limited". Reports to goverment through the Minister of Public Works & Government Services.

**President**, Ross Nicholls, P.Eng.

Vice-President, Finance & Administration & Sec.-Treas., Trevor Heavens

Vice-President, Operations & Chief Engineer, Russ Perrie, P.Eng.

## DEPARTMENT OF

These are listed in this book alphabetically by applied titles as follows:

Department of Agriculture & Agri-Food: AGRICULTURE & AGRI-FOOD CANADA

Department of Canadian Heritage: CANADIAN HERITAGE

Department of Citizenship & Immigration: CITIZENSHIP & IMMIGRATION CANADA

Department of Environment: ENVIRONMENT CANADA

Department of Finance: FINANCE CANADA (Department of)*

Department of Fisheries & Oceans: FISHERIES & OCEANS CANADA

Department of Foreign Affairs & International Trade: FOREIGN AFFAIRS & INTERNATIONAL TRADE CANADA

Department of Health: HEALTH CANADA

Department of Human Resources Development: HUMAN RESOURCES DEVELOPMENT CANADA

Department of Indian & Northern Affairs: INDIAN & NORTHERN AFFAIRS CANADA

Department of Industry: INDUSTRY CANADA

Department of Justice: JUSTICE CANADA (Department of)*

Department of National Defence: NATIONAL DEFENCE

Department of Natural Resources: NATURAL RESOURCES CANADA

Department of Public Works & Government Services: PUBLIC WORKS & GOVERNMENT SERVICES CANADA

Department of National Revenue: REVENUE CANADA

Department of the Solicitor General: SOLICITOR GENERAL CANADA

Department of Transport: TRANSPORT CANADA

Department of Veterans Affairs: VETERANS AFFAIRS CANADA

Department of Western Economic Diversification: WESTERN ECONOMIC DIVERSIFICATION CANADA

*Note that there are two departments that actually incorporate the words "Department of" in their applied titles; nevertheless departments are listed alphabetically in similar style to the rest of the departments.

## ELECTIONS CANADA/Élections Canada

The Jackson Bldg., 257 Slater St., Ottawa ON K1A 0M6

613/993-2975; Fax: 613/954-8584; Email: eleccan@magi.com; URL: http://www.elections.ca/

Toll Free: 1-800-463-6868, TDD: 1-800-361-8935

The Chief Electoral Officer of Canada is responsible for the conduct of federal elections & referendums in Canada & for ensuring that all provisions of the *Canada Elections Act* are complied with & enforced. Major activities include implementation of public education & information programs, the training of returning officers, the revision of polling division boundaries, the acquisition of election materials & supplies, the maintenance of a register of political parties, the compiling & publishing of statutory & statistical reports, the provision of advice & assistance to Parliament, as required, the production of lists of electors, & the certification of statutory payments to be made to auditors, political parties, & candidates under the election expenses provisions of the Act.

Following each decennial census, the Chief Electoral Officer must calculate the number of electoral districts to be assigned to each province according to rules contained in s. 51 of the *Constitution Act*, prepare population distribution maps for use by the eleven electoral boundaries commissions (ten provincial & one territorial) that are directly responsible for readjusting federal electoral district boundaries & publish their reports. Elections Canada also administers elections to the Legislative Assembly of the Northwest Territories, by agreement with the Commissioner of the Northwest Territories.

**Chief Electoral Officer**, Jean-Pierre Kingsley

Asst. Chief Electoral Officer, Ronald A. Gould

Commissioner of Canada Elections, Raymond Landry

Arbitrator, Broadcasting, Peter S. Grant

Director, Administration & Human Resources, Louise Gravel

Director, Communications, Marilyn Amondola

Director, Election Financing, Janice Vézina

Director, Information Technology, Wayne Donovan

Director, Legal Services & Registrar, Political Parties, Jacques Girard

Director, Operations, Jean-Claude Léger

Director, Strategic Planning, Judy Charles

## ENERGY SUPPLIES ALLOCATION BOARD/ Office de répartition des approvisionnements d'énergie

580 Booth St., 17th Fl., Ottawa ON K1A 0E4

613/995-5594; Fax: 613/992-8738

**Chair**, Jean C. McCloskey

Board Secretary, R. Lyman

## ENVIRONMENT CANADA (EC)/ Environnement Canada

Terrasses de la Chaudière, 10 Wellington St., Hull QC K1A 0H3

819/997-2800; Fax: 819/953-2225; Email: enviroinfo@cpgsv1.am.doe.ca; URL: http://www.ec.gc.ca

Toll Free: 1-800-668-6767

Environmental Emergencies (24-hour): 819/997-3742

Fosters a national capacity for sustainable development in cooperation with other governments, departments of government & the private sector that will result in a safe & healthy environment & a sound & prosperous economy by:

- undertaking & promoting programs to augment understanding of the environment;
- supporting environmentally responsible public & private decision-making;
- warning Canadians of risks to & from the environment;
- engaging Canadians as partners in measurably beneficial action to conserve, protect & restore the integrity of Canada's environment for the benefit of present & future generations.

#### ACTS ADMINISTERED

Canada Water Act (Part III is repealed)

Canada Wildlife Act

Canadian Environment Week Act

Canadian Environmental Assessment Act

Canadian Environmental Protection Act

Department of the Environment Act

Game Export Act

International River Improvements Act

Lac Seul Conservation Act

Lake of the Woods Control Board Act

Migratory Birds Convention Act

National Round Table on the Environment & the Economy Act

National Wildlife Week Act

Weather Modification Information Act

Wild Animal & Plant Protection & Regulation of International & Interprovincial Trade Act

#### Other Acts Administered by Environment Canada in Part:

Arctic Waters Pollution Prevention Act

Export & Import Permits Act

Fisheries Act

James Bay & Northern Québec Native Claims Settlement Act

Pest Control Products Act

Resources & Technical Surveys Act

Transportation of Dangerous Goods Act, 1992

#### Assistance to other Departments

Aeronautics Act

Agriculture & Rural Development Act

Canada Shipping Act

Energy Supplies Emergency Act

Hazardous Products Act

Health of Animals Act

International Boundary Waters Treaty Act

Motor Vehicle Safety Act

National Energy Board Act

National Housing Act

Territorial Lands Act

#### Major Legislation of General Application

Access to Information Act

Federal Real Property Act

Financial Administration Act

Privacy Act

**Minister**, Hon. Christine Stewart, 819/997-1441, Fax: 819/953-3457

Deputy Minister, Ian Glen, 819/997-4203, Fax: 819/953-6897

Assoc. Deputy Minister, Vacant, 819/953-7137

President, Canadian Environmental Agency, Sid Gershberg, 200, boul Sacré-Coeur, Hull QC K1A 0H3, 819/997-1006, Fax: 819/994-1469
Director General, Corporate Human Resources Directorate, Ginette Cloutier, 819/997-1845, Fax: 819/953-2757
Director General & Corporate Secretary, Corporate Secretariat, Jean-Claude Dumesnil, 819/953-9300, Fax: 819/953-0749
General Counsel, Legal Services, Ellen Fry, 819/953-1380, Fax: 819/953-9110

#### Environment Canada Regional Directors General

Atlantic: Queen Sq., 45 Alderney Dr., 5th Fl., Dartmouth NS B2Y 2N6 – 902/426-4824; Fax: 902/426-5168, Regional Director General, Garth Bangay
Ontario: 4905 Dufferin St., North York ON M3H 5T4 – 416/739-4666, Regional Director General, John Mills
Pacific & Yukon: #700, 1200 West 73 Ave., Vancouver BC V6P 6G5 – 604/664-9145; Fax: 604/664-9190, Regional Director General, Art Martell
Prairies & Northern: Twin Atria II, 4999 - 98 Ave., 2nd Fl., Edmonton AB T6B 2X3 – 403/951-8869, Regional Director General, Jim Vollmershausen
Québec: 1141, rte de l'Église, 6e étage, CP 10100, Ste-Foy QC G1V 4H5 – 418/648-4077; Fax: 418/649-6674, Regional Director General, François Guimont

### ATMOSPHERIC ENVIRONMENT SERVICE (AES)

4905 Dufferin St., Downsview ON M3H 5T4
416/739-4521
Asst. Deputy Minister, Dr. Gordon A. McBean, 416/739-4770, Fax: 416/739-4232, Hull: 819/997-2686
Acting Director General, Canadian Forces Weather Services, Rick Berry, Place Vincent Massey, 351, boul St-Joseph, Hull QC K1A 0H3, 613/995-4173, Fax: 613/995-4197
Director General, Canadian Meteorological Centre (Montréal), Hubert Allard, 514/421-4601, Fax: 514/421-4600
Director General, Climate & Atmospheric Research Directorate, Dr. Phil E. Merilees, 416/739-4995, Fax: 416/739-4265
Director General, National Weather Services Directorate, Nancy Cutler, 416/739-4938, Fax: 416/739-4967
Director General, Policy, Program & International Affairs, David Grimes, 416/739-4344, Ottawa: 819/997-0142; Fax: 819/994-8854

### CORPORATE SERVICES

Terrasses de la Chaudière, 10 Wellington St., Hull QC K1A 0H3
Asst. Deputy Minister, Laura Talbot-Allan, 819/953-7026, Fax: 819/953-4064
Director General, Administration, Jean Bilodeau, 819/997-2991, Fax: 819/997-1781
Director General, Corporate Management & Review, Cynthia Wright, 819/953-2091, Fax: 819/953-3388
Director General, Finance, Luc Desroches, 819/997-1561, Fax: 819/953-2459
Director General, Systems & Informatics, Jim Armstrong, 819/994-3634, Fax: 819/953-5995

### ENVIRONMENTAL CONSERVATION SERVICE (ECS)

Place Vincent-Massey, 351, boul St-Joseph, Hull QC K1A 0H3
Asst. Deputy Minister, Dr. Robert W. Slater, 819/997-2161, Fax: 819/997-1541
Director General, Biodiversity Directorate, Stephen McClellan, 819/994-2541, Fax: 819/997-1541
Director General, Canadian Wildlife Service, David B. Brackett, 819/997-1301, Fax: 819/953-7177
Director General, Ecosystem Conservation Directorate, Karen Brown, 819/953-9309, Fax: 819/953-0461
Director General, State of the Environment Reporting, Ian D. Rutherford, 613/994-9865, Fax: 613/994-6826

#### ECS Regional Offices

Atlantic: 17 Waterfowl Lane, PO Box 1590, Sackville NB E0A 3C0, Director, Dr. George Finney, 506/364-5011, Fax: 506/364-5062
Ontario: 4905 Dufferin St., Downsview ON M3H 5T4, Director, Simon Llewellyn, 416/739-5839, Fax: 416/739-4408
Pacific & Yukon: Environmental Conservation Branch, Airport Sqaure Bldg., #430, 1200 West 73 Ave., Vancouver BC V6P 6H9 – 604/664-4065; Fax: 604/664-4068, Director, J. Brian Wilson, Manager, Yukon District Office, Don Russell, Canadian Wildlife Service, Northern Conservation Division, Mile 917.6B Alaska Highway, Whitehorse YT Y1A 5X7, 867/393-6700, Fax: 867/667-7962
Prairie & Northern: #200, Twin Atria Bldg., 4999 - 98 Ave., 2nd Fl., Edmonton AB T6B 2X3, Director, Gerald McKeating, 403/951-8853, Fax: 403/495-2615
Québec: 1141, rte de l'Église, CP 10100, Ste-Foy QC G1V 4H5, Directeur, Michel Lamontagne, 418/648-7808, Fax: 418/649-6591

### ENVIRONMENTAL PROTECTION SERVICE (EPS)

Place Vincent-Massey, 351, boul St-Joseph, Hull QC K1A 0H3
Asst. Deputy Minister, Tony Clarke, 819/997-1575, Fax: 819/953-9452
Director General, Air Pollution Prevention Directorate, Vic Buxton, 819/997-1298, Fax: 819/953-9547
Director General, Environmental Technology Advancement Directorate, Ed Norrena, 819/953-3090, Fax: 819/953-9029
Director General, National Programs Directorate, David Egar, 819/997-2019, Fax: 819/997-0086
Acting Director General, Regulatory Affairs & Program Integration Directorate, Jennifer Moore, 819/997-5674, Fax: 819/953-5916
Director General, Toxics Pollution Prevention Directorate, Vic Shantora, 819/953-1114, Fax: 819/953-5371

### POLICY & COMMUNICATIONS (P&C)

Terrasses de la Chaudière, 10 Wellington St., Hull QC K1A 0H3
Asst. Deputy Minister, Avrim Lazar, 819/997-4882, Fax: 819/953-5981
Director General, Communications & Consultations Directorate, Anne Marie Smart, 819/997-6820, Fax: 819/953-6789
Director General, International & Economic Policy, Jim Wall, 613/994-5208
Director General, Strategic Directions & Policy Coordination, Yaprak Ballacioglu, 819/953-7634, Fax: 819/953-7632
Director, Federal-Provincial Relations Branch, Christine Guay, 819/994-1659, Fax: 819/953-5975
Director, International Affairs Branch, Brigita Gravitis-Beck, 819/953-9461, Fax: 819/953-7025

#### Regional Communications Offices

Atlantic: Queen Sq., 45 Alderney Dr., 15th Fl., Dartmouth NS B2Y 2N6 – 902/426-1930; Fax: 902/426-5340, Director, Wayne Eliuk
Ontario: 4905 Dufferin St., Toronto ON M3H 5T4 – 416/739-4848; Fax: 416/739-4776, Director, Claire Scrivens
Pacific & Yukon: 224 West Esplanade, North Vancouver BC V7M 3H7 – 604/666-9733; Fax: 604/666-4810, Director, Mary Beth Berube
Prairie & Northern: #1000, 266 Graham Ave., Winnipeg MB R3C 0J7 – 204/983-2110; Fax: 204/983-0964, Director, Tim Hibbard
Québec: 1141, rte de l'Église, 7e étage, CP 6060, Ste-Foy QC G1V 4H5 – 418/647-6510; Fax: 418/648-3859, Manager, Pierre Normand

#### Associated Agencies, Boards & Commissions

•Committee on the Status of Endangered Wildlife in Canada (COSEWIC): Ottawa ON K1A 0H3 – 819/997-4991; Fax: 819/953-6283
•Federal Water Policy Office: Place Vincent-Massey, 351, boul St-Joseph, Hull QC K1A 0H3 – 819/953-1513; Fax: 819/944-0237
•National Hydrology Research Institute (NHRI): 11 Innovation Blvd., Saskatoon SK S7N 3H5 – 306/975-5717; Fax: 306/975-5143
Director, Robert A. Halliday
•National Round Table on the Environment & Economy
Listed alphabetically in detail, this section.
•National Water Research Institute (NWRI): 867 Lakeshore Rd., PO Box 5050, Burlington ON L7R 4A6 – 905/336-4625; Fax: 905/336-4989; URL: http://www.cciw.ca/nwri/intro.html; Groundwater Remediation Project URL: http://gwrp.cciw.ca/
•National Wildlife Research Centre (NWRC): 100, boul Gamelin, Hull QC K1A 0H3 – 819/997-1092; Fax: 819/953-6612
Director, D. Bondy
•North American Waterfowl Management Plan (NAWMP): c/o Canadian Wildlife Service, Place Vincent-Massey, 351, boul St-Joseph, 3e étage, Hull QC K1A 0H3 – 819/997-2392; Fax: 819/994-4445; Email: sagik@cpits1.am.doe.ca
Communications Contact, Barbara Robinson, 819/953-9414
•North American Wetlands Conservation Council (Canada) (NAWCC)/Conseil nord-américain de conservation des terres humides: #200, 1750 Courtwood Cres., Ottawa ON K2C 2B5 – 613/228-2601; Fax: 613/228-0206; URL: http://www.wetlands.ca
Executive Secretary, Dr. Kenneth W. Cox, Email: kcox@igs.net
•St. Lawrence Centre: #700, 105, rue McGill, Montréal QC H2Y 2E7 – 514/283-7000; Fax: 514/283-9451
Director, Lynn Cleary, 514/283-5869

## EXPORT DEVELOPMENT CORPORATION (EDC)/Société pour l'expansion des exportations (SEE)

151 O'Connor St., Ottawa ON K1A 1K3
613/598-2500; Fax: 613/237-2690; Email: export@edc4.edc.ca; URL: http://www.edc.ca
Financial services corporation dedicated to helping Canadian business succeed & compete in the global marketplace. The EDC provides a wide range of flexible & innovative financial solutions to exporters across Canada & their customers around the world. Provides risk management services, including export-credit insurance, sales financing & guarantees. Represents a financially self-sustaining Crown corporation & operates on commercial principles, charging fees & premiums for its products & interest on its loans.
EDC is governed by a board of directors composed of representatives from both the private & public sectors, & reports to the Canadian Parliament through the Minister of International Trade.
**President & CEO**, V. Ian Gillespie
Chair, Alexander K. Stuart
Vice-President, Finance, Roger Pruneau
Vice-President, Market Management, Don Curtis
Vice-President, Medium- & Long-Term Financial Services, Eric Siegel
Vice-President, Secretariat & Legal Services, Gilles Ross

Vice-President, Short Term Financial Services, Rolfe Cooke

#### EDC Regional Offices

Calgary: #1030, 510 - 5 St. SW, Calgary AB T2P 3S2 – 403/292-6898; Fax: 403/292-6902

Halifax: Purdy's Wharf Tower II, #1410, 1969 Upper Water St., Halifax NS B3J 3R7 – 902/429-0426; Fax: 902/423-0881

London: #1512, 148 Fullarton St., London ON N6A 5P3 – 519/645-5828; Fax: 519/645-5580

Moncton: Centre du Commerce international, #103, 1045 Main St., 4th Fl., Moncton NB E1C 1H1 – 506/851-6066; Fax: 506/851-6406

Montréal: Tour de la Bourse, #4520, 800, Place Victoria, CP 124, Montréal QC H4Z 1C3 – 514/283-3013; Fax: 514/878-9891

Ottawa: 151 O'Connor St., Ottawa ON K1A 1K3 – 613/598-2500; Fax: 613/237-2690

Toronto: #810, 150 York St., Toronto ON M5H 3S5 – 416/973-6211; Fax: 416/862-1267

Vancouver: #1030, 505 Burrard St., Vancouver BC V7X 1M5 – 604/666-6234; Fax: 604/666-7550

Winnipeg: Commodity Exchange Tower, #2075, 360 Main St., Winnipeg MB R3C 323 – 204/983-5114; Fax: 204/984-0163

## FARM CREDIT CORPORATION CANADA/ Société du crédit agricole Canada

1800 Hamilton St., PO Box 4320, Regina SK S4P 4L3
306/780-8100; Fax: 306/780-5703; URL: http://www.fcc-sca.com
Toll Free: 1-800-387-3232

Provides Canadian farmers with a reliable source of long-term credit & personalized counselling services. Creates, administers & supervises farm loans, & carries out other duties required by the Governor in Council. Reports to government through the Minister of Agriculture & Agri-food.

**President & CEO**, John J. Ryan

Vice-President & Controller, Marie-Josée Bourassa

## Office of the Commissioner for FEDERAL JUDICIAL AFFAIRS/Bureau du Commissaire à la magistrature fédérale

110 O'Connor St., 11th Fl., Ottawa ON K1A 1E3
613/992-9175; Fax: 613/995-5615; Email: recep.info@fja-cmf.x400.gc.ca

**Commissioner**, Guy Y. Goulard, 613/992-9175, Email: guy.goulard@fja-cmf.x400.gc.ca

Deputy Commissioner, Denis Guay, 613/995-7438, Email: denis.guay@fja-cmf.x400.gc.ca

Director General, Policy & Corporate Services, André Gareau, 613/992-2930, Email: andre.gareau@fja-cmf.x400.gc.ca

Executive Editor, Federal Court Reports, William Rankin, 613/995-2706, Email: william.rankin@fja-cmf.x400.gc.ca

Secretary, Judicial Appointments Secretariat, Andre Millar, 613/992-9400, Email: andre.millar@fja-cmf.x400.gc.ca

Director, Judges' Language Training, Yolande Cloutier-Turcotte, 613/992-2990, Email: yolande.cloutier-turcotte@fja-cmf.x400.gc.ca

## FEDERAL OFFICE OF REGIONAL DEVELOPMENT (QUÉBEC)/Bureau fédéral de développement régional (Québec)

Tour de la Bourse, #3800, 800, Place Victoria, CP 247, Montréal QC H4Z 1E8
514/283-6412; Fax: 514/283-3302; URL: http://www.bfdrq-fordq.gc.ca
Ligne sans frais: 1-800-322-4636

Hull: Place du Portage II, 165, rue Hôtel de Ville, CP 1110, Succ B, Hull QC J8X 3X5 819/997-8249

FORDQ defines federal objectives relating to development opportunities in Québec. The agency delivers business assistance programs to small & medium-sized businesses in Québec for innovation, entrepreneurial & market development purposes. Provides support to programs for industry sector initiatives & fosters alliances among industry stakeholders (including small & medium-sized enterprises & industrial associations). Also, strengthens new & existing partnerships, improves access to government programs, & provides support for research & development for technology, demonstration, marketing & transfer programs.

**Minister Responsible**, Hon. John Manley, 613/995-9001, Fax: 613/992-0302

Secretary of State, Hon. Martin Cauchon, 514/496-1282, Fax: 514/496-5096

Deputy Minister, Renaud Caron, 514/283-4843, Fax: 514/283-7778

Director General, Communications, Jacques Cloutier, 514/283-8817

Director General, Finance, Administration & Corporate Services, Daniel McCraw, 514/283-4276

#### OPERATIONS

Asst. Deputy Minister, Guy McKenzie, 514/283-4766

Director General, Central Regions, Germain Simard, 514/283-3995, Fax: 514/283-3637

Director General, Montréal Region, Guy Bédard, 514/283-4766

Director General, Resources Regions, Robin D'Anjou, 514/283-6771, Fax: 514/283-3637

#### POLICY & LIAISON

Asst. Deputy Minister, Michel Cailloux, 819/997-7716

Director General, Liaison & Regional Advocacy, François Gauthier, 819/997-2476

Director General, Policy Analysis, Federal-Provincial Affairs, Micheline Côté, 514/283-2664

#### FORDQ Regional Business Offices

Abitibi-Témiscamingue: 906, av 5e, Val d'Or QC J9P 1B9 – 819/825-5260; Fax: 819/825-3245, Ligne sans frais: 1-800-567-6451, Directeur, Léo Couture

Bas St-Laurent - Gaspésie - Iles-de-la-Madeleine: #200, 212, rue Belzile, Rimouski QC G5L 3C3 – 418/722-3255; Fax: 418/722-3285, Ligne sans frais: 1-800-463-9073, Directeur, Robin D'Anjou

Côte Nord: #202B, 701, boul Laure, 2e étage, CP 698, Sept-Iles QC G4R 4K9 – 418/968-3426; Fax: 418/968-0806, Ligne sans frais: 1-800-463-1707, Directrice, Lorraine Bourillette

Estrie: #303, 1335, rue King ouest, Sherbrooke QC J1J 2B8 – 819/564-5904; Fax: 819/564-5912, Ligne sans frais: 1-800-567-6084, Directeur, Georges-Henri Goulet

Île de Montréal: #3800, 800 Place Victoria, CP 247, Montréal QC H4Z 1E8 – 514/283-2500; Fax: 514/283-3302, Directeur, Germain Paré

Laval - Laurentides - Lanaudière: #204, Tour du Triomphe II, Laval QC H7T 2SC – 514/973-6845; Fax: 514/973-6851, Ligne sans frais: 1-800-430-6844, Directrice, Lorraine Lussier

Mauricie - Bois-Francs (Drummondville): Place du Centre, #502, 150, rue Marchand, Drummondville QC J2C 4N1 – 819/478-4664; Fax: 819/478-4666, Ligne sans frais: 1-800-567-1418, Directeur, Claude Lortie

Mauricie - Bois-Francs (Trois Rivières): Le Bourg du Fleuve, #413, 25, rue des Forges, Trois-Rivières QC G9A 2G4 – 819/371-5182; Fax: 819/371-5186, Ligne sans frais: 1-800-567-8637, Directeur, Claude Lortie

Montérégie: Complexe Saint-Charles, #411, 1111, rue Saint-charles ouest, Longueuil QC J4K 5G4 – 514/928-4096; Fax: 514/928-4097, Ligne sans frais: 1-800-284-0335, Directeur, Robert Audet

Nord du Québec: – 514/283-5174; Fax: 514/283-3837, Ligne sans frais: 1-800-561-0633, Directrice (par intérim), Jocelyne Durand

Outaouais: #202, 259 boul Saint-Joseph, Hull QC J8Y 6T1 – 418/994-7442; Fax: 418/994-7846, Directeur, Guillaume Donati

Québec - Chaudière - Appalaches: 905, av Dufferin, 2e étage, Québec QC G1R 5M6 – 418/648-4451; Fax: 418/648-7291, Ligne sans frais: 1-800-463-5204, Directeur, Christian Audet

Saguenay - Lac Saint-Jean: #203, 170, rue Saint-Joseph, Alma QC G8B 3E8 – 418/668-3084; Fax: 418/668-7584, Ligne sans frais: 1-800-463-9808, Directrice, Rita Tremblay

## FINANCE CANADA/Finances Canada

Esplanade Laurier, 140 O'Connor St., Ottawa ON K1A 0G5
613/992-1573; Fax: 613/996-8404; URL: http://www.fin.gc.ca/fin-eng.html
TDD: 613/996-0035

Department responsible for providing the federal government with analysis & advice on financial & economic issues. Monitors & researches the performance of the Canadian economy's major factors (output, growth, employment, income, price stability, monetary policy, long-term change). Finance Canada interacts with various other federal departments to encourage coordination in all federal initiatives with an impact on the economy. The department places emphasis on consulting with the public regarding policy directions & options.

#### ACTS ADMINISTERED

Bank Act
Bank of Canada Act
Banks & Banking Law Revision Act
Bills of Exchange Act
Bretton Woods & Related Agreements Act
Canada Deposit Insurance Corporation Act
Canada Development Corporation Reorganization Act
Canada Mortgage & Housing Corporation Act
Canada-Newfoundland Atlantic Accord Implementation Act
Canada-Nova Scotia Offshore Petroleum Resources Accord Implementation Act
Canada Pension Plan Act
Canadian International Trade Tribunal Act
Canadian National Railways Capital Revision Act
Canadian National Railways Refunding Act
Canadian National Steamship (West Indies Service) Act
Co-operative Credit Association Act
Currency Act
Customs & Excise Offshore Application Act
Customs Tariff, Debt Servicing & Reduction Account Act
Diplomatic Service (Special) Superannuation Act
Excise Tax Act
Export Credit Insurance Act
Federal Provincial Fiscal Arrangements & Federal Post-Secondary Education & Health Contributions Act
Financial Administration Act
Garnishment Attachment & Pension Diversion Act
Governor General's Retiring Annuity Act
Halifax Relief Commission Pension Continuation Act
Income Tax Act
Income Tax Conventions Interpretation Act
Insurance Companies Canadian & British Act
Insurance Companies Foreign Act
Interest Act
International Development (Financial Institutions) Assistance Act
Investment Companies Act
Loan Companies Act

Members of Parliament Retiring Allowances Act
Newfoundland Additional Finance Assistance Act
Nova Scotia Offshore Retail Sales Tax Act
Office of the Superintendent of Financial Institutions Act
Oil Export Act
Pension Benefits Standards Act
Prairie Grain Loans Act
Prince Edward Island Subsidy Act
Provincial Subsidies Act
Public Service Superannuation Act
Québec Savings Bank Act
Residential Mortgage Financing Act
Small Business Loans Act
Special Import Measures Act
Tax Rental Agreements Act
Trust & Loans Companies Act
Winding Up Act

**Minister**, Hon. Paul Martin, 613/992-4284; 996-7861, Fax: 613/992-4291; 995-5176, Email: pmartin@fin.gc.ca
Secretary of State, International Financial Institutions, Hon. Jim Peterson, 613/996-3170, Fax: 613/995-2355
Deputy Minister, David Dodge, 613/992-4925, Fax: 613/952-9569
Assoc. Deputy Minister, C. Scott Clark, 613/996-1963, Fax: 613/952-9569
Chief of Staff, Terrie O'Leary
Departmental Secretary, Janice Elliott, 613/992-2580

### CONSULTATIONS & COMMUNICATIONS BRANCH

Asst. Deputy Minister, C. Peter Daniel, 613/995-5683, Fax: 613/943-0938
Director General, Alan Darisse, 613/992-9194
Acting Director, Communications Policy & Strategy Division, Amanda Maltby, 613/992-9195
Director, Public Affairs & Operations Division, Vacant, 613/943-2340

### CORPORATE SERVICES BRANCH

Provides joint services for the federal Treasury Board Secretariat & Finance Canada.
Asst. Deputy Minister, Joy Kane, 613/995-8487, Fax: 613/947-3643
Director, Administrative Services Division, Jim T. Eadie, 613/992-6650
Director, Business & Technology Integration Division, Sue MacGowan, 613/995-1755
Director, Financial Services Division, Larry Paquette, 613/992-0554
Director, Human Resources Division, Vacant, 613/992-1996
Director, Informatics Division, R. Brodeur, 613/992-4306
Director, Security Services Division, Tom Greenough, 613/995-5660

### CROWN CORPORATIONS & PRIVATIZATION BRANCH

Provides joint services for the federal Treasury Board Secretariat & Finance Canada.
Acting Asst. Secretary, Karen Mosners, 613/957-0163, Fax: 613/957-0151
Senior Director, Privatization, Dean McLean, 613/957-2658, Fax: 613/995-2355

### ECONOMIC & FISCAL POLICY BRANCH

Asst. Deputy Minister, Paul-Henri Lapointe, 613/995-6391, Fax: 613/992-5773
General Director, David Moloney, 613/996-0321
Executive Director, Economic Development Policy Secretariat, Anne Park, 613/992-1527
Director, Economic Analysis & Forecasting Division, Cliff Halliwell, 613/992-4321
Director, Economic Studies & Policy Analysis Division, Vacant, 613/992-4910
Director, Fiscal Policy Division, Peter DeVries, 613/996-7397

### FEDERAL PROVINCIAL RELATIONS & SOCIAL POLICY BRANCH

Asst. Deputy Minister, Susan Peterson, 613/996-0735, Fax: 613/992-7754
General Director, Andrew Treusch, 613/996-5083
Acting Director, Federal Provincial Relations Division, Peter Gusen, 613/943-0916
Director, Social Policy Division, Real Bouchard, 613/996-0533

### FINANCIAL SECTOR POLICY BRANCH

Asst. Deputy Minister, Bob Hamilton, 613/992-6843, Fax: 613/952-1596
General Director, David Tobin, 613/995-5798
Director, Financial Markets, Bill Mitchell, 613/992-9032
Director, Financial Sector Policy Division, F. Swedlove, 613/992-4679

### INTERNATIONAL TRADE & FINANCE BRANCH

Asst. Deputy Minister & Acting G-7 Deputy, James A.J. Judd, 613/992-6985, Fax: 613/992-7347
General Director, Bruce Montador, 613/996-8927
Director, International Finance & Economic Analysis Division & Director, International Trade Policy Division, Terry Collins-Williams, 613/992-6765

### LAW BRANCH

Acting Asst. Deputy Minister (Justice) & Counsel, Mark Jewett, L.Q.C., 613/996-4667, Fax: 613/995-7223
General Counsel, General Legislative Services Division, Vacant, Q.C., 613/995-8724
General Counsel, Tax Counsel Division, Gaston Jorré, 613/996-0941

### TAX POLICY BRANCH

Asst. Deputy Minister, Don Drummond, 613/992-1630, Fax: 613/996-0660
General Director, Analysis, Munir Sheikh, 613/992-2555
General Director, Legislation, Len Farber, 613/992-3024
Chair, Legislative Committee, Alan Short, 613/992-1785
Director, Business Income Tax Division, Paul Berg-Dick, 613/992-1008
Director, Personal Income Tax Division, Louis Levesque, 613/996-8267
Director, Sales Tax Division, Ruth Dantzer, 613/992-6298
Director, Tax Legislation Division, Vacant, 613/992-1916

#### Associated Agencies, Boards & Commissions

Listed alphabetically in detail, this Section.
Auditor General
Bank of Canada
Canada Deposit Insurance Corporation
Canadian International Trade Tribunal
Canada Investment & Savings
Revenue Canada
Office of the Superintendent of Financial Institutions
Treasury Board Secretariat

## Office of the Superintendent of FINANCIAL INSTITUTIONS (OSFI)/Bureau du surintendant des institutions financières Canada

Kent Square, 255 Albert St., Ottawa ON K1A 0H2
613/990-7788; Fax: 613/952-8219; URL: http://www.osfi-bsif.gc.ca/english.htm
Toll Free: 1-800-385-8647
Regulates all financial institutions & pension plans under federal jurisdiction. Included under federal jurisdiction are: banks, insurance companies, trust companies, loan companies, cooperative credit associations & fraternal benefit societies. Provides actuarial services & advice to the Government of Canada. Reports to government through the Minister of Finance.

**Superintendent**, John Palmer
Deputy Superintendent, Operations, John R. Thompson
Deputy Superintendent, Policy, Nick LePan
Asst. Superintendent, Corporate Services, Edna MacKenzie
Director General, Deposit Taking Institutions, Jack Heyes
Director General, Insurance, Michael Hale
Chief Actuary, Actuarial Services, Bernard Dussault
Manager, External Communications & Media Relations, André Gerard, 613/993-0577, Fax: 613/990-5591
Senior Officer, Complaints & Enquiries, Lyse Larameé, 613/990-7578

## FISHERIES & OCEANS CANADA (DFO)/ Pêches et Océans Canada (POC)

200 Kent St., Ottawa ON K1A 0E6
613/993-0999; Email: info@www.ncr.dfo.ca; URL: http://www.ncr.dfo.ca/home_e.htm
TDD: 1-800-668-5228
Coastal & Information Network URL: http://192.139.141.30
The only federal department with resource management & safety services responsibilities primarily focusing on water & the resources within it. DFO is responsible for all matters respecting oceans not by law assigned to any other department. Parliament's jurisdiction over sea-coast & inland fisheries & public harbours is established by the Constitution Act. DFO's merger with the Canadian Coast Guard (CCG) on April 1, 1995, consolidated the government's main civilian marine organizations. DFO's vision is to be a leader in ocean & marine resource management through the management of Canada's oceans & major waterways so that they are clean, safe, productive & accessible, to ensure sustainable use of fisheries resources & to facilitate marine trade & commerce.

#### ACTS ADMINISTERED

Atlantic Fisheries Restructuring Act
Coastal Fisheries Protection Act
Department of Fisheries & Oceans Act
Fish Inspection Act
Fisheries Act
Fisheries Development Act
Fisheries Improvement Loans Act
Fisheries Prices Support Act
Fisheries & Oceans Research Advisory Council Act
Fishing & Recreational Harbours Act
Freshwater Fish Marketing Act
Great Lakes Fisheries Convention Act
North Pacific Fisheries Convention Act
Northern Pacific Halibut Fisheries Convention Act
Saltfish Act
Territorial Sea & Fishing Zones Act

**Minister**, Hon. David Anderson, 613/992-3474, Fax: 613/990-7292
Secretary of State, Hon. Gilbert Normand, 613/947-4592, Fax: 613/947-4595
Deputy Minister, William A. Rowat, 613/993-2200, Fax: 613/993-2194
Executive Asst. to Deputy Minister, Darlene Elie, 613/993-2200
General Counsel, C. Beckton, 613/993-0966, Fax: 613/990-9385

### CANADIAN COAST GUARD (CCG)

Canada Bldg., 344 Slater St., Ottawa ON K1A 0N7
613/998-1574; Fax: 613/990-2780

Senior Asst. Deputy Minister & Commissioner, John F. Thomas, 613/993-0678
Deputy Commissioner, Michael A.H. Turner, 613/998-1570
Director General, Business Planning Development, Neil Tiessen, 613/993-5792
Director General, Marine Navigational Services, J. Lonquet, 613/990-5608
Director General, Marine Technical & Support Services, J. Clavelle, 613/998-1638
Director General, Program Planning & Coordination, J.R.F. Hodgson, 613/998-1439
Director General, Rescue & Environmental Response, J. Murray, 613/990-3110

### COMMUNICATIONS DIRECTORATE

Director General, Vacant, 613/993-0989
Director, Communications Operations, John Camp, 613/990-0211
Manager, Public Affairs, Lynda Cameron, 613/993-0996

### CORPORATE SERVICES

Fax: 613/990-9557
Asst. Deputy Minister, Martha Hynna, 613/993-0868
Director General, Finance & Administration Directorate, R. Ken Bond, 613/993-2670, Fax: 613/996-9055
Director General, Information Management & Technical Services, Bev Hopkins, 613/993-2051
Director General, Personnel Directorate, Pat Napoli, 613/990-0023, Fax: 613/990-0035

### FISHERIES MANAGEMENT

Asst. Deputy Minister, Pat Chamut, 613/990-9864, Fax: 613/990-9557
Director General, Aboriginal Affairs, Gerald Yaremchuk, 613/991-0181, Fax: 613/993-7651
Director General, Conservation & Protection, David Bevan, 613/990-6012
Director General, International, Earl Wiseman, 613/998-2644, Fax: 613/993-5995
Director General, Program Planning & Coordination, David Balfour, 613/993-2574
Director General, Resource Management, Jacques Robichaud, 613/990-0189

### INDUSTRY SERVICES

Acting Asst. Deputy Minister & Director General, Inspection, John Emberley, 613/990-0144, Fax: 613/993-4220
Director General, Small Craft Harbours, Mike Godin, 613/993-3012, Fax: 613/952-6788

### POLICY

Asst. Deputy Minister, Cheryl Fraser, 613/993-1808, Fax: 613/993-6958
Acting Director General, Economic & Policy Analysis, Les Burke, 613/993-1914, Fax: 613/991-3254
Director General, Industry Renewal, Karl Laubstein, 613/990-0140, Fax: 613/952-6802
Director General, International Directorate, Earl Wiseman, 613/993-1873, Fax: 613/993-5995
Acting Director General, Strategic Planning & Liaison, Susan Schultz, 613/998-5739, Fax: 613/990-2811

### SCIENCE

Asst. Deputy Minister, L. Scott Parsons, 613/993-0850, Fax: 613/990-2768
Director General, Canadian Hydrographic Service, S.B. MacPhee, 613/995-4413, Fax: 613/996-9053, Chart Distribution: 613/998-4931
Director General, Fisheries Science, Bill Doubleday, 613/990-0271, Fax: 613/954-0807
Director General, Habitat Management & Environmental Science, Gerry Swanson, 613/991-1280, Fax: 613/993-7493
Director General, Program Planning & Coordination, Mary Zamparo, 613/993-0802, Fax: 613/990-0313
Special Advisor to the ADM, Oceans Science, Geoff L. Holland, 613/990-0298, Fax: 613/990-5510

#### Regional Offices

Central & Arctic: 501 University Cr., Winnipeg MB R3T 2N6 – 204/983-5118; Fax: 204/984-2401, Regional Director General, Ray Pierce
Gulf: PO Box 5030, Moncton NB E1C 9B6 – 506/851-7750; Fax: 506/851-7732, Regional Director General, Bernard LeBlanc
Laurentian: CP 15500, Québec QC G1K 7Y7 – 418/648-4158; Fax: 418/648-4470, Regional Director General, Pierre Boisvert
Newfoundland: PO Box 5667, St. John's NF A1C 5X1 – 709/772-5150; Fax: 709/772-2156, Regional Director General, Lorne Humpries
Pacific: 555 West Hastings St., Vancouver BC V6B 5G3 – 604/666-6098; Fax: 604/666-3450, Regional Director General, L. Tousignant
Scotia-Fundy: PO Box 550, Halifax NS B3J 2S7 – 902/426-2581; Fax: 902/426-2256, Regional Director General, Neil Bellefontaine

#### Research Facilities

Bayfield Institute for Marine Science & Surveys: 867 Lakeshore Rd., PO Box 5050, Burlington ON L7R 4A6 – 905/336-4871; Fax: 905/336-6637; URL: http://www.cciw.ca/dfo/dfo-home.html
Bedford Institute of Oceanography: PO Box 1006, Dartmouth NS B2Y 4A2 – 902/426-2373; Fax: 902/426-7827; URL: http://biome.bio.dfo.ca
Freshwater Institute: 501 University Cr., Winnipeg MB R3T 2N6 – 204/983-5000; Fax: 204/983-6285
Gulf Fisheries Centre: PO Box 5030, Moncton NB E1C 9B6 – 506/851-6227; Fax: 506/851-7732
Halifax Fisheries Research Laboratory: 1707 Lower Water St., PO Box 550, Halifax NS B3J 2S7 – 902/426-7444; Fax: 902/426-2698
Institute of Ocean Sciences: 9860 West Saanich Rd., PO Box 6000, Sidney BC V8L 4B2 – 250/363-6517; Fax: 250/353-6807; URL: http://www.ios.bc.ca/
Maurice Lamontagne Institute: 850, Rte de le Mer, CP 1000, Mont-Joli QC G5H 3Z4 – 418/775-6553; Fax: 418/775-0542; URL: http://www.ncr.dfo.ca/communic/offices/iml/iml_e.htm
Northwest Atlantic Fisheries Centre: PO Box 5667, St. John's NF A1C 5X1 – 709/772-2020; Fax: 709/772-2156
Pacific Biological Station: Hammond Bay Rd., Nanaimo BC V9R 5K8 – 250/756-7000; Fax: 250/756-7053
Regional Fish Inspection Laboratory: 1721 Lower Water St., PO Box 550, Halifax NS B3J 2S7 – 902/426-2373
St. Andrews Biological Station: St. Andrews NB E0G 2X0 – 506/529-8854; Fax: 506/529-4274; URL: http://www.ncr.dro.ca/communic/office/st_andre/st_and-e.htm
West Vancouver Laboratory: 4160 Marine Dr., West Vancouver BC V7V 1N6 – 604/666-4813; Fax: 604/666-3497

#### Associated Agencies, Boards & Commissions

•Fisheries Resource Conservation Council (FRCC)/Le Conseil pour la conservation des ressources halieutiques (CCRH): PO Box 2001, Stn D, Ottawa ON K1A 5W3

Created in 1993 to form a partnership between scientific & academic expertise, & all sectors of the fishing industry. Council members make public recommendations to the Minister of Fisheries & Oceans on such issues as total allowable catches (TACs) & other conservation measures for the Atlantic fishery. The Council also provides advice in the areas of scientific research & assessment priorities.

Executive Director, David Rideout, 613/998-0433
•Freshwater Fish Marketing Corporation
Listed alphabetically in detail, this Section.
•Task Force on Incomes & Adjustment in the Atlantic Fishery: 200 Kent St., Ottawa ON K1A 0E6 – 613/941-6502
Chair, R. Cashin
Executive Director, K. Laubstein
•Northern Cod Research Program: PO Box 5667, St. John's NF A1C 5X1 – 709/772-2051; Fax: 709/772-6100
Director, Dr. J.S. Campbell

## FOREIGN AFFAIRS & INTERNATIONAL TRADE CANADA (DFAIT)/Affaires étrangères et du Commerce international (MAECI)

Lester B. Pearson Bldg., 125 Sussex Dr., Ottawa ON K1A 0G2
613/944-4000; Fax: 613/952-3904; Email: canadian@shell.portal.com; URL: http://www.dfait-maeci.gc.ca
Toll Free: 1-800-267-8376
Media Relations: 613/995-1874
Technology Inflow Program: 613/996-0971
Travel Advisory: 1-800-267-6788
FaxLink Service: 613/944-4500
International FaxLink Service: 613/944-6500
Consular Inquiries: 613/996-4376; TDD: 613/996-9136
Export Permits: 613/996-2387
Export Trade Information: 613/944-4000
Foreign Policy Information & Publications: 613/944-4000
Free Trade: 613/991-2014
Trade Information: 613/944-4000; 1-800-267-8376
Import Permits: Agriculture: 613/995-7762; Clothing & Textiles: 613/996-3711; Steel/Coffee: 613/995-2744
Passport Office: 613/994-3500
Protocol: 613/996-8683

The Department of Foreign Affairs & International Trade advises the government on foreign policy matters & implements the policy decisions the government takes. It is responsible for the promotion & protection of Canada's interests abroad & the conduct of Canada's external relations by:

- conducting all diplomatic & consular relations on behalf of Canada including assisting distressed Canadians abroad & ensuring that they are treated fairly under the laws of foreign countries;
- promoting the achievement of international peace and a safer world for the security of Canadians & the safe pursuit of their interests in all regions of the world;
- fostering the development of international law in order to defend & promote Canadian interests;
- coordinating the pursuit of Canada's interests through its international, political & economic relations;
- assisting Canadian businesses in expanding their sales to export markets;
- promoting foreign investment & technology inflow into Canada;
- delivering the Official Development Assistance and Immigration & Refugee programs abroad;
- conducting all official communications between the Government of Canada & all other countries' governments or international organizations;
- providing advice to the government on economic, political or other developments abroad likely to affect Canada's interests;
- ensuring that all domestic policy developments of other government departments are consistent with Canada's international obligations & foreign affairs interests;
- managing the foreign service including Canada's missions & delegations abroad.

Complete listings of "Canadian Diplomatic Representatives Abroad" and "Diplomatic & Consular

Representatives in Canada" may be found in this directory. Please consult the main/global Index.

#### ACTS ADMINISTERED

Asia-Pacific Foundation of Canada Act
Bretton Woods Agreements Act
Canadian Commercial Corporation Act
Canadian Institute for International Peace & Security Act
Cultural Property Export & Import Act
Diplomatic & Consular Privileges & Immunities Act
Export Development Act
Exports & Import Permits Act
Food & Agriculture Organization of the United Nations Act
Forgiveness of Certain Official Development Assistance Debts Act
Fort-Falls Bridge Authority Act
Geneva Conventions Act
High Commissioner of the United Kingdom Act
International Boundary Waters Treaty Act
International Centre for Ocean Development Act
International Development (Financial Institutions) Continuing Assistance Act
International Development Research Centre Act
Meat Import Act
Privileges & Immunities (International Organizations) Act
Privileges & Immunities (North Atlantic Treaty Organization) Act
Prohibition of International Air Services Act
Rainy Lake Watershed Emergency Control Act
Roosevelt-Campobello International Park Commission Act
Skagit River Valley Treaty Implementation Act
Softwood Lumber Products Charge Act
State Immunity Act
Territorial Sea & Fishing Zone Act
United Nations Act

**Minister, Foreign Affairs**, Hon. Lloyd Axworthy, 613/995-1851, Fax: 613/996-3546
**Minister, International Cooperation**, Hon. Diane Marleau, 819/953-6238, Fax: 819/953-2903
**Minister, International Trade**, Hon. Sergio Marchi, 613/992-7332, Fax: 613/996-8924
**Secretary of State, Asia-Pacific**, Hon. Raymond Chan, 613/995-1852, Fax: 613/996-1560
**Secretary of State, Latin America & Africa**, Hon. David Kilgour, 613/992-6560, Fax: 613/996-3443
Deputy Minister, Foreign Affairs, Donald Campbell, 613/993-4911, Fax: 613/944-0856
Deputy Minister, International Trade, Robert G. Wright, 613/944-5000, Fax: 613/944-8493
Ambassador, Circumpolar Affairs, Mary Simon, 613/992-6700, Fax: 613/944-1852
Ambassador, Environment & Sustainable Development, Hon. John A. Fraser, P.C., Q.C., 613/944-0886, Fax: 613/944-0892
Ambassador, Fisheries Conservation, Paul Lapointe, 613/995-6907, Fax: 613/995-2188
Chief Air Negotiator, Duane Van Beselaere, 613/944-4323, Fax: 613/944-0023
Ombudsman, David Stockwell, 613/944-1524, Fax: 613/944-1160
Head, Canadian Delegation to the Human Rights Commission, Anne Park
Advisor, Economics, John Curtis
Canadian Agent, Canada-France Maritime Boundary Arbitration, F.A. Mathys, 613/952-8653, Fax: 613/952-8663

#### AMERICAS & SECURITY INTELLIGENCE BRANCH

613/944-7877; Fax: 613/944-8493
Asst. Deputy Minister, Michael Kergin, 613/944-6183
Director General, United States Bureau, Michael Leir, 613/944-5900, Fax: 613/995-2603
Director General, Latin America & Caribbean Bureau, Paul Durand, 613/996-8435, Fax: 613/996-0677
Director, Caribbean & Central America Division, Alan Smith, 613/996-0676, Fax: 613/944-0760
Director, Mexico Division, Jon Allen, 613/996-5611, Fax: 613/996-6142
Director, South America & Inter-American Division, Peter Boehm, 613/992-2480, Fax: 613/943-8808
Director, US Business Development Division, Robert Mackenzie, 613/944-5725, Fax: 613/944-9119
Director, US General Relations Division, Glen Masters John Bailey, 613/944-7990, Fax: 613/944-8314
Director, US Transboundary Division, David Preston, 613/944-6909, Fax: 613/943-2423

#### ASIA PACIFIC & AFRICA BRANCH

613/996-7832; Fax: 613/996-4309
Asst. Deputy Minister, Leonard J. Edwards, 613/996-5095
Director General, Africa Bureau, Brian Buckley, 613/944-5989, Fax: 613/944-1199
Director General, North Asia & Pacific Branch, Roger Ferland, 613/995-1097, Fax: 613/943-8286
Director General, South & Southeast Asia Bureau, Ingrid Hall, 613/992-3372, Fax: 613/996-1248
Director, Asia Pacific Regional Coordination Division, John Klassen, 613/944-0462, Fax: 613/944-2732
Director, China Division, Colin Russel, 613/995-7575, Fax: 613/943-1068
Director, Eastern & Southern Africa Division, Aubrey Morantz, 613/944-6585
Director, Japan Division, Denis Comeau, 613/995-8985, Fax: 613/943-8286
Director, Korea & Oceania Division, Bruce Jutzi, 613/995-1186, Fax: 613/996-1248
Director, South Asia Division, Terry Colfer, 613/996-0910, Fax: 613/996-5897
Director, South Pacific Division, D. Buckley-Jones, 613/944-1830, Fax: 613/996-4309
Director, Southeast Asia Division, Marius Grinius, 613/992-6807, Fax: 613/944-1604
Director, West & Central Africa Division, Jacques Crête, 613/944-6578, Fax: 613/944-3566

#### EUROPE, MIDDLE EAST & NORTH AFRICA BRANCH

613/944-6329; Fax: 613/944-1180
Asst. Deputy Minister, Claude Laverdure, 613/944-6288
Director General, Central, East & Southern Europe Bureau, James Wright, 613/992-5303, Fax: 613/995-1277
Director General, European Union, North & West Europe Bureau, Paul Dubois, 613/992-8333, Fax: 613/995-5772
Director General, Middle East, North Africa & Gulf States Bureau, Paul Dingledine, 613/944-1144, Fax: 613/944-1200
Director, Central Europe Bureau, Robeert Noble, 613/996-6835, Fax: 613/995-8756
Director, Eastern Europe Division, Murray Fairweather, 613/992-7991, Fax: 613/995-1277
Director, European Union Division, David Hutton, 613/995-6115, Fax: 613/944-0034
Director, Maghreb & Arabian Peninsula Division, Mark Bailey, 613/944-6591, Fax: 613/944-7431
Director, Middle East Division, Bargara Gibson, 613/944-5991, Fax: 613/944-7975
Director, Southern Europe Division, Marie Gervais-Vidricaire, 613/992-2099, Fax: 613/958-8783
Director, Western Europe Division, Brian Northgrave, 613/992-0871, Fax: 613/995-5772
Special Coordinator, Mid-East Peace Process, Andrew Robinson, 613/944-6572, Fax: 613/944-1200
Special Coordinator, Reconstruction of Former Yugoslavia, Michael Berry, 613/992-6109, Fax: 613/944-1178
Analyst, Public Affairs & Communications, Carl Schwenger, 613/995-4595

#### COMMUNICATIONS BUREAU

613/995-6720; Fax: 613/992-2432, 992-6135
Director General, Peter Lloyd, 613/996-2213
Director, Communications Strategies & Planning Division, Pierre Pichette, 613/992-0760, Fax: 613/995-0667
Director, Corporate Communications Division, Wade Simon, 613/992-7005, Fax: 613/944-0684
Director, Media Relations Office, Malcolm McKechnie, 613/992-0956, Fax: 613/995-1405
Deputy Director, CanadExport Section, Amir Guindi, 613/992-6249
Deputy Director, International Marketing Section, Richard Bégin, 613/995-0780

##### Policy Staff

Head, Policy Staff, George Anderson, 613/944-1144, Fax: 613/944-0687
Director General, Federal-Provincial Relations, Ferry de Kerckhove, 613/944-0382, Fax: 613/944-0687
Director, Economic & Trade Policy, Keith Christie, 613/994-0367, Fax: 613/944-0375
Director, Federal-Provincial Relations Division, Jacques Crêtes, 613/992-3166, Fax: 613/995-6576
Director, Government Policy, Marie Gervais-Vidricaire, 613/944-0384, Fax: 613/944-067
Director, Political & Security Policy, Vacant, 613/944-6846, Fax: 613/995-8169
Coordinator, Coordination Unit, Marjorie Ravignat, 613/944-0378, Fax: 613/944-0687

#### CORPORATE SERVICES BRANCH

613/996-5370; Fax: 613/944-0442
Asst. Deputy Minister, Lucie Edwards, 613/996-5369
Dean, Canadian Foreign Service Institute, Graham Mitchell, 613/944-0010, Fax: 613/996-4381
Director General, Client Services Bureau, Michael Conway, 613/995-3549, Fax: 613/944-0884
Director General, Human Resources Development Bureau, Pierre Gosselin, 613/992-3548
Director General, Information Management & Technology Bureau, Richard Kohler, 613/943-1125, Fax: 613/944-0441
Director General, Physical Resources Branch, Ian Dawson, 613/952-8732, Fax: 613/952-8729
Director General, Resource Planning & Management Secretariat, Ron Halpin, 613/944-9097, Fax: 613/944-9021
Director, Administrative Services Division, Doug Woods, 613/992-9675, Fax: 613/944-0759
Director, Business Management Division, Thomas Miles, 613/943-0050, Fax: 613/944-0441
Director, Client Services Division, Douglas Rosenthal, 613/943-1127, Fax: 613/944-0441
Director, Compensation Services Division, Shirley Dupuis, 613/996-2803, Fax: 613/944-0884
Director, Data Management Division, Dave Gordon, 613/996-3175, Fax: 613/995-5933
Director, Direction & Planning Division, Greta Bossenmaier, 613/992-6032, Fax: 613/944-0441
Director, Distribution Service, Henri Meilleur, 613/996-1510, Fax: 613/992-5598
Director, Executive Pool & Heads of Mission Division, Jean White, 613/996-5595
Director, Financial Services Division, Francine Deschênes, 613/992-2609, Fax: 613/995-0725
Director, Financial Services & Travel Division, Normand Villeneuve, 613/996-2209, Fax: 613/992-2541
Director, Human Resources Policy & Operations Division, Denys Vermette, 613/996-2889, Fax: 613/944-0439
Director, Information Resources Division, Larry Hatt, 613/995-8387, Fax: 613/944-0441
Director, Infrastructure Technology, Art Barrett, 613/992-2854, Fax: 613/944-0044, 995-6067

Director, Language School, Renée Proulx-Dubé, Bison Campus, 15 Bison St., Hull QC J8Y 5M2, 613/994-7183, Fax: 613/953-3632
Director, Locally Engaged Staff Abroad Division, John Groves, 613/996-2456, Fax: 613/944-1448
Director, Management Services Division, David Dyet, Bison Campus, 15 Bison St., Hull QC J8Y 5M2, 613/992-9314, Fax: 613/997-7662
Director, Material Services Division, Ken Pearson, 613/954-4663, Fax: 613/952-8917
Director, Professional School, Michel Duval, 613/996-2095, Fax: 613/996-4381
Director, Project Implementation Division, Waine McQuinn, 613/957-4283, Fax: 613/957-4301
Director, Property Program Management Division, Frank Townson, Tower A, Place Vanier, 333 River Rd., 16th Fl., Vanier ON K1A 0G2, 613/952-8727, Fax: 613/952-4589
Director, Rotational Administrative Personnel Division, Marta Moszczenska, 613/992-3051, Fax: 613/944-0078
Director, Staff Relations Services, John McCann, 613/992-7732, Fax: 613/996-2479
Director, Trade & Political Personnel Division, Jean-Marc Duval, 613/995-1350, Fax: 613/995-0073, 995-9085

#### Office of the Inspector General

Tower A, Place Vanier, 333 River Rd., 18th Fl., Ottawa ON K1A 0G2
613/944-1933; Fax: 613/944-1930
Inspector General, Gen. André Simard, 613/944-1931
Deputy Inspector General, James D. Leach, 613/944-1932
Director, Audit Division, Al Whitla, 613/944-1934
Director, Planning & Practices Division, Ernest Chadler, 613/944-1935

### GLOBAL & SECURITY POLICY BRANCH

613/992-5072; Fax: 613/944-1121
Asst. Deputy Miniser, Paul Heinbecker, 613/944-4228
Secretary, Global & Human Issues Bureau, Bernice Brown, 613/944-1272
Director General, International Cultural Relation Bureau, Robin Higham, 613/996-0232, Fax: 613/992-5965
Director, Academic Relations Division, Brian Long, 613/996-4551, Fax: 613/992-5965
Director, Arts & Letters Division, Gerry Redmond, 613/992-9948, Fax: 613/992-5965
Director, Economic & Social Development Division, Jerry Kramer, 613/992-3979, Fax: 613/943-0605
Director, Environment Division, Richard Ballhorn, 613/992-6026, Fax: 613/944-0064
Director, Human Rights & Justice Division, Ross Hynes, 613/992-6356, Fax: 613/943-0606
Director, Migration, Population & Humanitarian Affairs Division, Ruth Archibald, 613/996-1231, Fax: 613/944-0758
Director, Peace-Building & Democratic Development Division, Gérald Cossette, 613/992-7993, Fax: 613/944-1226

### INTERNATIONAL BUSINESS & COMMUNICATIONS BRANCH

613/995-6877; Fax: 613/943-8819; URL: http://www.dfait-maeci.gc.ca/english/trade/winexp.htm
WIN Exports: 1-800-551-4946; WIN Exports Fax: 1-800-667-3802
Asst. Deputy Minister & Chief Trade Commissioner, Kathryn McCallion, 613/996-7065
Director General, International Business Operations Bureau, Peter Sutherland, 613/996-1799, Fax: 613/996-9265
Director General, International Business Planning Bureau, Bernard Giroux, 613/992-8785, Fax: 613/995-5773
Director, Export Financing Division, John Mundy, 613/996-6210, Fax: 613/943-1100
Director, Export Information Systems Division, Robert Lee, 613/996-3024, Fax: 613/992-3004
Director, Export Programs Division, Roger Chan, 613/944-0017, Fax: 613/995-5773
Director, International Business Opportunities Centre, Rick McElrea, 613/996-1816, Fax: 613/996-2635
Director, Investment & Technology Division, Robert Collette, 613/995-2224, Fax: 613/995-9604
Director, Market Intelligence Division, Kathryn Hewlett-Jobes, 613/996-0550
Director, Office of Forestry & Environment, Graham Lochhead, 613/996-3518
Director, Policy & Strategic Planning Division, Donald McLennan, 613/996-1775, Fax: 613/943-8819
Director, Team Canada Division, David Horley, 613/996-1430, Fax: 613/996-8688
Director, Trade Commissioner Services, Richard Lecoq, 613/996-2964, Fax: 613/996-8688
Director, Trade Coordination & Advisory Committees Secretariat, Maurice Hladik, 613/995-7667, Fax: 613/944-7981
Deputy Director, Investment Development, Vacant, 613/995-8400
Deputy Director, Partnering, Richard Lepage, 613/995-8956
Deputy Director, Program for Export Market Development (PEMD), Dennis Gibson, 613/996-1408
Deputy Director, Science & Technology Unit, Victor Bradley, 613/996-4819
Deputy Director, Trade Information, Anne Argyris, 613/996-1907
Coordinator, WIN Exports, Richard Gauthier, 613/996-5701

#### International Trade Centres

•Calgary: #300, 639 - 5 St. SW, Calgary AB T2P 0M9 – 403/292-4575; Fax: 403/292-4578
Trade Commissioner, Archie Campbell, Email: campbell.archie@ic.gc.ca
Trade Commissioner, Biotechnology/Environmental Equipment & Services, Claudie Vachon, Email: vachon.claudie@ic.gc.ca
Trade Commissioner, Oil & Gas Equipment/services, Energy & Power Equipment, Douglas Caston
•Charlottetown: 75 Fitzroy St., PO Box 1115, Charlottetown PE C1A 1R6 – 902/566-7426; Fax: 902/566-7450
Senior Trade Commissioner, Fraser Dickson
Trade Commissioner, Building, Forest Products, Agri-Food, Environment, Manufacturg, Bernard Postma
•Edmonton: Canada Place, #540, 9700 Jasper Ave., Edmonton AB T5J 4C3 – 403/495-3329; Fax: 403/495-4507
Senior Trade Commissioner, Ronald McLeod, Email: mcleod.ron@ic.gc.ca
Trade Commissioner, Forest Industries, Building Products, & Construction, Vacant
Coordinator, PEMD, Cathy Young, Email: young.cathy@ic.gc.ca
•Halifax: 1801 Hollis St., 5th Fl., PO Box 940, Stn M, Halifax NS B3J 2V9 – 902/426-7540; Fax: 902/426-2624
Senior Trade Commissioner, Barbara Giaconmin
Trade Commissioner, Environmental Technologies, Maryann Everett
Trade Commissioner, Forest Products & Manufacturing, Charles MacArthur
Coordinator, PEMD, Kim Lambert
•Moncton: #103, 1045 Main St., Moncton NB E1C 1H1 – 506/851-6440; Fax: 506/851-6429, Toll Free: 1-800-332-3801
Senior Trade Commissioner, Roger Léger
Trade Commissioner, Business/Commercial Services & Environment, Eric Anderson
Trade Commissioner, Forest Products, George Debbané
Coordinator, PEMD, Martha Wry
•Montréal: 5, Place Ville Marie, 7e étage, Montréal QC H3B 2G2 – 514/283-8797; Fax: 514/283-8794
Senior Trade Commissioner, Bruno Goulet
•Regina: 1919 Saskatchewan Dr., 6th Fl., PO Box 3750, Regina SK S4P 3N8 – 306/780-6124; Fax: 306/780-8797
Trade Commissioner, Lynne Tait, Email: tait.lynne@ic.gc.ca
•St. John's: #504, 215 Water St., PO Box 8950, St. John's NF A1B 3R9 – 709/772-6806; Fax: 709/772-2373
Senior Trade Commissioner, Patricia Hearn
Trade Commissioner, Culture, Forestry, Construction Products, Mining, Manufacturing, Leo Walsh
Trade Commissioner, Environment, Service Industry, Oil & Gas, CIDA Liaison, Keith Warren
Coordinator, PEMD, Pat Gale
•Saskatoon: 123 - 2 Ave. South, 7th Fl., Saskatoon SK S7K 7E6 – 306/975-5315; Fax: 306/975-5334
Senior Trade Commissioner, John Grantham, Email: grantham.john@ic.gc.ca
Trade Commissioner, Environmental, Equipment Services, Agri-biotechnology, Rana Pudifin, Email: pudifin.rana@ic.gc.ca
•Toronto: Dominion Public Bldg., 1 Front St. West, 4th Fl., Toronto ON M5J 1A5 – 416/973-5053; Fax: 416/973-8161
Senior Trade Commissioner & Director, International Business, Archie McArthur
•Vancouver: #2000, 300 West Georgia St., Vancouver BC V6B 6E1 – 604/666-5000; Fax: 604/666-8330
Senior Trade Commissioner, Robert Pedersen
Trade Commissioner, Consulting Engineers, Peter Bélanger
Trade Commissioner, Energy Industry, John Burbridge
Trade Commissioner, Environmental Industries, Ron Farris
Coordinator, PEMD, Jeanette Desmarais
•Winnipeg: 400 St. Mary's Ave., 4th Fl., PO Box 981, Winnipeg MB R3C 4K5 – 204/983-4540; Fax: 204/983-3182
Senior Trade Commissioner, Pierre-André Cusson, Email: cusson.pierreandre@ic.gc.ca
Trade Commissioner, Environment, Mining, Plastics, Transportation, Paul Brettle, Email: brettle.paul@ic.gc.ca
Trade Commissioner, Forest Products, Oil & Gas, Energy & Power, Construction & Coordinator, PEMD, Charle Hatzipanayis
Trade Commissioner, Agriculture Machinery, Computers/Software, Environment, Investment, Wanda Wiebe

### LEGAL & CONSULAR AFFAIRS BRANCH

613/996-1512; Fax: 613/944-0870
Asst. Deputy Minister, Vacant, 613/995-8901
Senior Advisor, Federal-Provincial Relations, Dilys Buckley-Jones, 613/996-1025
Director General, Bureau of Legal Affairs, Phillipe Kirsch, 613/992-2728
Director General, Consular Affairs Bureau, Pierre Giguère, 613/996-0639
Coordinator, Access to Information & Privacy Protection, Vacant, 613/992-1487
Coordinator, Environmental Assessment & Stewardship, D'Arcy Thorpe, 613/944-0428

#### Passport Office

Place du Centre, 200, Promenade du Portage, 6e étage, Hull QC K1A 0G3
819/994-3500; Fax: 819/953-5856; URL: http://www.dfait-maeci.gc.ca/passport/pass.htm

Ligne sans frais: 1-800-567-6868, TDD: 613/994-3560
Chief Executive Officer, M.J. Hutton, 613/994-3530

**Passport Information**

Toll Free (Canada): 1-800-567-6868
Toronto: 416/973-3251
Montréal: 514/283-2152
Vancouver: 604/586-2500
Mailed in Applications: Passport Office, Department of Foreign Affairs & International Trade, Ottawa ON K1A 0G3

**Passports:**

Canadian passports are issued only to Canadian citizens. The total life of a Canadian passport is five years. The passport is a valuable document, the loss of which must be reported to the local police & either to the Passport Office, Ottawa, one of the regional offices listed below, or to the nearest Canadian diplomatic mission (Embassy, High Commissioner's Office) or Consular Office abroad.

**Passport Requirements:**

All applicants (including children whose names will appear in a parent's passport) must submit original documentary evidence of Canadian Citizenship (not photocopies): (a) (Applicants born in Canada) Certificate of Birth; or Certificate of Canadian Citizenship (includes miniature certificate); large certificates issued after Feb. 14, 1977 are not acceptable. Applicants born in Québec prior to January 1994 may submit an original certificate issued by religious, municipal or judicial authorities, showing place & date of birth if it was issued prior to January 1, 1994; for individuals born after this date, only provincial birth certificates are accepted; (b) (Applicants born outside Canada) Certificate of Canadian Citizenship, or Certificate of Naturalization in Canada, or Certificate of Registration of Birth Abroad, or Certificate of Retention of Canadian Citizenship.

**Fee Schedule:**

Canadian passport....................................................$60.00
Name changes/additions to a passport....................$5.00

**Application for passport:**

Applications for a passport should be mailed to the Passport Office, Department of Foreign Affairs & International Trade Canada, Ottawa K1A 0G3, at least two weeks plus mailing time before the passport is required. Alternatively, they may be presented in person at any of the regional offices listed below, & persons who reside in a community where there is a passport office are requested to submit the applications in person. *Regional offices do not accept mailed-in applications.*
i.) Canadian citizens residing abroad should complete Form A (abroad) or Form B (abroad), available at the Canadian mission in their country of residence. Canadians living in the United States requiring a Canadian passport shoud apply by mail directly to Passport Office Headquarters in Ottawa. Application forms can be obtained from the Canadian Embassy in Washington DC, or at any consulate, or by calling 819/994-3500.
ii.) Regulations & instructions for persons applying for Canadian passports in Canada are contained in "Passport Application Form A (applicants 16 & over)", & "Passport Application Form B (for a child under 16)". Applications may be obtained from any travel agency in Canada, from the Passport Office, Ottawa, from the regional offices, or Northern Store Outlets.
iii.) Every application for a passport must be signed by a guarantor chosen from one of the eligible categories listed on the form, who must also certify the back of one of the applicant's photographs. In addition to being a member of one of the groups listed, the guarantor must be a Canadian citizen residing in Canada, who has known the applicant personally for at least two years. If there is no person available within the group of eligible guarantors who has known the applicant for the required two years, appropriate instructions will be found in the application form.

**Warning:**

The attention of applicants & guarantors is drawn to Section 57(2) of the Criminal Code covering passport fraud whereby: "Every one who, while in or out of Canada, for the purpose of procuring a passport for himself or any other person or for the purpose of procuring any material alteration or addition to any such passport, makes a written or oral statement that he knows is false or misleading (a) is guilty of an indictable offence & liable to imprisonment for a term not exceeding two years or (b) is guilty of an offence punishable on summary conviction."

**Children:**

The name of a child under 16 years of age may be included in the passport of one of the parents. Separate passports for children under 16 years may be obtained by using application Form B. A child's name may be added to a parent's existing passport by applying on Form B-1, which is available from any passport issuing office.

**Visas:**

A passport alone does not confer the right to enter any country. Travellers are advised to check with the embassy or consulate of the country they wish to visit to determine visa and entry/exit requirements, health certificates, customs, currency, etc., all of which are subject to change without notice.

**Work Permits:**

Most countries will not allow non-residents to accept gainful employment unless they have applied for & been granted work permits prior to their entry.
Chief Executive Officer, M.J. Hutton

**Regional Passport Offices**

Brampton: Brampton Civic Centre, #305, 150 Central Park Dr., Brampton ON
Calgary: #440, First St. Plaza, 138 - 4 Ave. SE, Calgary AB
Edmonton: #1630, Canada Place Building, 9700 Jasper Ave., Edmonton AB
Fredericton: Frederick Square, #470, 77 Westmorland St., Fredericton NB
Halifax: CIBC Building, #801, 1809 Barrington St., Halifax NS
Hamilton: Standard Life Bldg., #330, 120 King St. West, Hamilton ON
Jonquière: #302, Place St-Michel, 3885, boul Harvey, Jonquière QC
Kitchener: Canada Trust Centre, 55 King St. West, 5th Fl., Kitchener ON
Laval: #300, 2550, boul Daniel-Johnson, Laval QC
London: #803, 451 Talbot St., London ON
Montréal: Complexe Guy-Favreau, Tour Ouest, #215, 200, boul René-Lévesque ouest, Montréal QC
North York: Royal Bank Bldg., #421, 5001 Yonge St., North York ON
Ottawa: Level C-3, East Tower, C.D. Howe Bldg., 240 Sparks St., Ottawa ON
Québec (Ste-Foy): #2410, 2600, boul Laurier, 4e étage, Ste-Foy QC
Regina: #350, 1800 Hamilton St., Regina SK
St. Catharines: Landmark Bldg., 43 Church St., 6th Fl., St. Catharines ON
St. John's: TD Place, #702, 140 Water St., St. John's NF
St-Laurent: #112, 3300, ch Côte Vertu, St-Laurent QC
Saskatoon: #605, 101 - 22 St. East, Saskatoon SK
Scarborough: #828, 200 Town Centre Crt., Scarborough ON
Surrey: Guildford Landmark Bldg., #405, 15127 - 100 Ave., Surrey BC
Thunder Bay: Royal Insurance Bldg., #406, 28 North Cumberland St., Thunder Bay ON
Toronto: First Century Tower, #2200, 438 University Ave., Toronto ON
Vancouver: Sinclair Centre, #240, 757 West Hastings St., Vancouver BC
Victoria: Customs House, #228, 816 Government St., Victoria BC
Windsor: CIBC Building, #504, 100 Ouellette Ave., Windsor ON
Winnipeg: #910, 200 Graham Ave., Winnipeg MB

## MULTILATERAL TRADE NEGOTIATIONS BRANCH

Asst. Deputy Minister, Vacant, 613/995-8041
Senior Coordinator, Market Access, Kevin Gore, 613/992-7259
Senior Coordinator, Services & Investment, David P. Lee, 613/992-6700

## POLITICAL & INTERNATIONAL SECURITY AFFAIRS BRANCH

Asst. Deputy Minister, Michael Kergin, 613/944-4228
Acting Director General, Cultural Affairs & Higher Education Bureau, Derek Fraser, 613/996-0232
Director General, International Organizations Bureau, Vacant, 613/992-4341
Director General, International Security Bureau, Arms Control & CSCE Affairs, Vacant, 613/992-3402
Director General, Security & Intelligence Bureau, Vacant, 613/992-7400

## OFFICE OF PROTOCOL

613/996-8683; Fax: 613/943-1075
Chief, Lawrence D. Lederman, 613/992-2344
Deputy Chief of Protocol, Diplomatic Corps Services, William R. Bowden, 613/995-5185
Director, Management & Hospitality Services, Craig Bale, 613/996-9862, Fax: 613/944-0020
Director, Visits & Conferences, Heidi Bennet, 613/996-9740, Fax: 613/995-5661

## TRADE & ECONOMIC POLICY BRANCH

613/995-7972; Fax: 613/944-1471
Asst. Deputy Minister, Len Edwards, 613/995-7759
Director General, Economic Policy Bureau, Philip Somerville, 613/992-7825, Fax: 613/944-0076
Director General, Export & Import Controls Bureau, Margaret Huber, 613/992-3386, Fax: 613/996-0612
Director General, Trade Policy Bureau, John Gero, 613/944-2002, Fax: 613/996-1667
Director, Economic Relations With Developing Countries Division, Christopher Greenshields, 613/996-5638, Fax: 613/944-0076
Director, Export Controls Division, Lynda Watson, 613/992-9166, Fax: 613/996-9933
Director, Information & Technology Trade Policy Division, Jim Wall, 613/944-2014, Fax: 613/944-0066
Director, International Economic Relations & Summit Division, Laurette Glasgow, 613/992-9287, Fax: 613/943-2158
Acting Director, Investment Trade Policy Division, Stephen Brereton, 613/995-0990, Fax: 613/944-0679
Director, Services Trade Policy Division, Andrea Lyon, 613/944-2034
Director, Trade Controls Policy Division, Claudio Valle, 613/996-0640, Fax: 613/996-0612
Director, Trade & Economic Analysis Division, John Curtis, 613/992-7776, Fax: 613/992-4695
Deputy Director, Administration & Technology Services Division, Yvon Landry, 613/996-4143

**Associated Agencies, Boards & Commissions**

In addition to the Department, the Minister of Foreign Affairs is responsible to Parliament for the following

agencies, which are listed separatedly among the federal government listings.
Canadian Commercial Corporation
Canadian International Development Agency
Canadian International Grains Institute
Export Development Research Centre
International Joint Commission (Canadian Section)
International Boundary Commission (Canadian Section)
Roosevelt-Campobello International Park Commission

#### Other Associated Agencies, Boards & Commissions

• Arctic Council Secretariat: Place Vanier, Tower A, 18th Fl., 333 River Rd., Ottawa ON K1A 0G2 – 613/941-4011; Fax: 613/941-6490

The Arctic Council was founded in September 1996 by the governments of Canada, Denmark, Finland, Iceland, Norway, the Russian Federation, Sweden & the United States. The Council will provide a mechanism for addressing the common concerns & challenges faced by the governments & the people of the Arctic. It will provide for regular intergovernmental consideration of, & consultation on, Arctic issues ensuring the well-being of the inhabitants of the Arctic, sustainable development & protection of the environment. The main activities of the Council will focus on the existing programs established under the Arctic Environmental Protection Strategy (AEPS) & a new program dealing with economic, social & cultural issues.

Indigenous people are to be fully involved in Council operations and to this end various international organizations representing Arctic indigenous people have become permanent partcipants.

Executive Director, Mary E. Vandenhoff, Email: mary.vandenhoff@extvnier01.x400.gc.ca

## FRESHWATER FISH MARKETING CORPORATION/Office de commercialisation du poisson d'eau douce

1199 Plessis Rd., Winnipeg MB R2C 3L4
204/983-6600; Fax: 204/983-6497; URL: http://canada.gc.ca/depts/agencies/fwfind_e.html

The Corporation is a buyer, processor & international marketer of freshwater fish, harvested from over 400 lakes in Manitoba, Saskatchewan, Alberta, the Northwest Territories & Northwestern Ontario. Reports to the government through the Minister of Fisheries & Oceans.

**President**, J.T. Dunn
Chair, Sam Murdock
Vice-President, Marketing, Gerald F. Malone

## GREAT LAKES PILOTAGE AUTHORITY LTD./Administration de pilotage des Grands Lacs ltée

PO Box 95, Cornwall ON K6H 5R9
613/933-2995; Fax: 613/932-3793; Email: glpa@cnwl.igs.net; URL: http://canada.gc.ca/depts/agencies/glpind_e.html

The Authority provides pilotage services in the waters of the St. Lawrence River commencing at the northern entrance of St. Lambert Lock, the Great Lakes area & the Port of Churchill, Manitoba. Reports to government through the Minister of Transport.

**President**, R.G. Armstrong, 613/933-2991
Sec.-Treas., R. Lemire, C.A.

#### Regional Offices

Eastern: 202 Pitt St., 2nd Fl., Cornwall ON – 613/933-2991
Western: 345 Lakeshore Blvd., St.Catharines ON – 905/934-2921

## HEALTH CANADA/Santé Canada

Brooke Claxton Bldg., Tunney's Pasture, 120 Parkdale Ave., Ottawa ON K1A 0K9
613/957-2991; Fax: 613/941-5366; URL: http://www.hwc.ca/links/english.html
Pest Management Regulatory Agency (PMRA) URL: http://www.hwc.ca/pmra

Main federal government department focused on issues relating to the health & safety of Canadians. Provides the fundamental funding & policy in maintaining a high-quality, affordable health system in Canada. Responsibilities include:
• health protection & consumer product safety;
• delivery of health services to Indian bands & the Inuit;
• promotion of fitness;
• financial support to the provinces & territories for insured health care.

#### ACTS ADMINISTERED

Canada Health Act
Canada Medical Act
Canadian Centre on Substance Abuse Act
Canadian Environmental Protection Act
Department of Health Act
Federal-Provincial Fiscal Arrangements & Federal Post-Secondary Education & Health Contributions Act
Financial Administration Act
Fitness & Amateur Sport Act
Food & Drugs Act
Hazardous Materials Information Review Act
Hazardous Products Act
Health Resources Fund Act
Medical Research Council Act
Narcotic Control Act
Patent Act
Pest Control Products Act
Pesticide Residue Compensation Act
Quarantine Act
Queen Elizabeth II Canadian Research Fund Act
Radiation Emitting Devices Act
Tobacco Act

**Minister**, Hon. Allan Rock, Q.C., 913/957-0200, Fax: 913/952-1154
Deputy Minister, Michèle S. Jean, 613/957-0212, Fax: 613/952-8422
Assoc. Deputy Minister, Alan Nymark, 613/954-5904, Fax: 613/952-8422
Director General, Assets Management, M. Williams, 613/957-3375
Director General, Human Resources, R. Joubert, 613/957-3236

#### CORPORATE SERVICES BRANCH

Asst. Deputy Minister, R. Lafleur, 613/952-3984
Director General, Informatics, F. Bull, 613/954-8713
Director General, Planning & Financial Administration, O. Marquardt, 613/957-7762

#### HEALTH PROMOTIONS & PROGRAMS BRANCH

Asst. Deputy Minister, Ian Potter, 613/957-2953
Director General, Health Issues, Policy & Research, Diane Kirkpatrick, 613/954-8602
Director General, Population Health, Susan Fletcher, 613/957-7792
Director General, Research & Program Policy, Kathy Stewart, 613/954-8543
Director, HIV/Aids Policy Coordination & Program Division, Gweneth Gowanlock, 613/952-5258

#### Regional Offices

Alberta & Northwest Territories: #815, 9700 Jasper Ave. NW, Edmonton AB T5J 4C3, Regional Director, Don Onischak
Atlantic: #709, 1557 Hollis St., Halifax NS B3J 3V4 – 902/426-3931, Acting Regional Director, Kathy Coffin
Manitoba & Saskatchewan: #603, 213 Notre Dame Ave., Winnipeg MB R3B 1N3 – 204/983-2557; Fax: 204/983-8674, Regional Director, Gary Ledoux
Ontario: 55 St. Clair Ave. East, Toronto ON M4T 1M2 – 416/973-1804; Fax: 416/973-6409, A/Regional Director, Pegeen Walsh
Pacific: 750 Cambie St., 4th Fl., Vancouver BC V6B 4V5 – 604/666-7128; Fax: 604/666-8986, Acting Regional Director, Heather Fraser
Québec: #210, Tour Est, 200, boul René-Lévesque ouest, Montréal QC H2Z 1X4 – 514/283-1043; Fax: 514/283-3309, Regional Director, Yvette Mongeon

#### HEALTH PROTECTION BRANCH

Acting Asst. Deputy Minister, Dr. J.Z. Losos, 613/957-1804
Acting Director General, Environmental Health Directorate, Rod Raphael, 613/954-0291
Director General, Foods Directorate, Dr. George Paterson, 613/957-1821
Director General, Therapeutics Product Directorate, Dann Michols, 613/957-0369
Acting Director General, Laboratory Centre for Disease Control, Dr. F. Li, 613/957-0315
Director, Management & Program Services, W. Newton, 613/957-7984
Director, Scientific & Regulatory Affairs, J. Weiner, 613/952-3665

#### Regional Offices

Alberta/British Columbia/Yukon/NWT: 3155 Willingdon Green, Burnaby BC V5G 4P2 – 604/666-3359, Regional Director, Greg Smith
Atlantic: 1992 Baffin Blvd., PO Box 1060, Dartmouth NS B2Y 3Z7 – 902/426-2160, Acting Regional Director, Sharon Chard
Manitoba & Saskatchewan: 510 Lagimodière Blvd., Winnipeg MB R2J 3Y1 – 204/983-3004; Fax: 204/983-5547, Acting Regional Director, Donna-Mae Burgener
Ontario: 2301 Midland Ave., Scarborough ON M1P 4R7 – 416/973-1451; Fax: 416/291-1431, Regional Director, Dr. C. Broughton
Québec: 1001, rue St-Laurent ouest, Longueuil QC J4K 1C7 – 514/238-5488; Fax: 514/283-5471, Regional Director, Jean Lambert

#### MEDICAL SERVICES BRANCH

Asst. Deputy Minister, Paul Cochrane, 613/957-7701
Acting Director General, First Nations & Inuit Health Program, Paul Glover, 613/952-7177
Acting Director General, Non-Insured Health Benefits, Dr. J. Wortman, 613/954-8825
Director General, Occupational & Environmental Health Services, Dr. G.I. Lynch, 613/957-7699
Director General, Program, Policy, Transfer Secretariat & Planning, Judith A. Moses, 613/957-3402

#### Regional Offices

Alberta: Canada Place, #730, 9700 Jasper Ave., Edmonton AB T5J 4C3 – 403/495-2690, Regional Director, G. Corrigall
Atlantic: Park Lane Terrace, #301, 5657 Spring Garden Rd., Halifax NS B3J 1V6 – 902/426-3646, Regional Director, A. Garman
Manitoba: #500, Commissioners Bldg., 303 Main St., Winnipeg MB R3C 0H4 – 204/983-4172, Regional Director, Jerome Berthelette
Ontario: 1547 Merivale Rd., Ottawa ON K1A 0L3 – 613/952-0087, Regional Director, Moe Katt
Pacific: #540, 757 Hastings St. West, Vancouver BC V6C 3E6 – 604/666-3235, Regional Director, Larry McCafferty
Québec: #202, Tour Est, 200, boul René-Lévesque ouest, Montréal QC H2Z 1X4 – 514/283-4774, Regional Director, R. Legault

Saskatchewan: 1911 Broad St., Regina SK S4P 1Y1 – 306/780-5413, Regional Director, J. Roll
Yukon: Yukon Manor, No. 2 Hospital Rd., Whitehorse YT Y1A 3H8 – 867/668-6461, Regional Director, R. Dowdall

#### Federal Hospitals (of twenty beds or more)

Blood Indian Hospital: PO Box 490, Cardston AB T0K 0K0 – 403/653-3351
Fort Qu'Appelle Indian Hospital: Fort Qu'Appelle SK S0G 1S0 – 306/332-5611
Mayo General Hospital: Mayo YT Y0B 1M0 – 867/996-2345
Moose Factory General Hospital: Moose Factory ON P0L 1W0 – 705/658-4544
Percy E. Moore Hospital: Hodgson MB R0C 1N0 – 204/372-8444
Sioux Lookout Zone Hospital: Sioux Lookout ON P0V 2T0 – 807/737-3030
Whitehorse General Hospital: 5 Hospital Rd., Whitehorse YT Y1A 3H8 – 867/668-9444

### POLICY & CONSULTATION BRANCH

Asst. Deputy Minister, A. Juneau, 613/957-3059
Director General, Health Policy & Information Directorate, J. Ferguson, 613/957-3066
Director General, Intergovernmental Affairs, G. Bujold, 613/957-3081
Director General, Strategic Planning & Review, Carmelita Boivin-Cole, 613/954-8072
Director General, Women's Health Bureau, A. Hoffman, 613/957-1940

#### Communications Directorate

Director General, Carla Gilders, 613/957-2979, Fax: 613/952-7266
Director, Communications Services, Carole Peacock, 613/957-2987
Director, Communications Strategy & Planning, Denis Schuthe, 613/957-2981

#### Regional Communications Offices

Alberta: Canada Place, #710, 9700 Jasper Ave., Edmonton AB T5J 4C3 – 403/495-2651; Fax: 403/495-5551, Director, Lance Beswick
Atlantic: #750, 1557 Hollis St., Halifax NS B3J 3V4 – 902/426-2038; Fax: 902/426-3768, Director, Pat Brownlow
British Columbia: #405, Sinclair Centre, 757 West Hastings St., Vancouver BC V6C 1A1 – 604/666-2083; Fax: 604/666-2258, Director, Blair Parkhurst
Manitoba: #205, Eaton Place, 330 Graham Ave., Winnipeg MB R3C 4C8 – 204/983-2508; Fax: 204/983-3912, Director, Morgan Fontaine
Ontario: 25 St. Clair Ave. East, 4th Fl., Toronto ON M4T 1M2 – 416/954-9021; Fax: 416/973-1423, Director, Debbie Payne
Québec: Tour Est, #218, 200, boul René-Lévesque ouest, Montréal QC H2Z 1X4 – 514/283-2306; Fax: 514/283-6739, Director, Jean-Louis Caya

#### Associated Agencies, Boards & Commissions

•Hazardous Materials Information Review Commission (HMIRC): #9000, 200 Kent St., Ottawa ON K1A 0M1 – 613/993-4331; Fax: 613/993-4686; URL: http://canada.gc.ca/depts/agencies/hmiind_e.html

Independent agency that examines applications from suppliers & employers seeking exemptions from WHMIS disclosure requirements. The agency reviews product labels & material safety data sheets related to the claim &, if satisfied, keeps the actual ingredients on file & issues confidential numbers to safeguard the formulas. Fees are charged for the screening process & for administering appeals against the Commission's decisions.

President, Claude St-Pierre, 613/993-4441
Executive Assistant, Margaret Branch, 613/993-4429

•Pest Management Regulatory Agency: 2250 Riverside Dr., Ottawa ON K1A 0K9 – 613/763-3401; Fax: 613/736-3666 – Pesticides Information: 1-800-267-6315
Executive Director, Dr. Claire Franklin, 613/736-3708, Fax: 613/736-3707
Chief Registrar, W. Ormrod, 613/736-3704
Associate Director, Compliance & Regional Operations, J.B. Reid, 613/736-3500
Director, Management & Information, G. Flores, 613/736-3570, Fax: 613/736-3666
Director, Product Sustainability & Coordination, J. Taylor, 613/736-3780, Fax: 613/736-3770
Director, Regulatory Affairs & Innovation Division, Dr. R. Taylor, 613/736-3675, Fax: 613/736-3699

## HUMAN RESOURCES DEVELOPMENT CANADA (HRDC)/Développement des ressources humaines

Place du Portage, Phase IV, 140, Promenade du Portage, Hull QC K1A 0J9
819/994-6013 (Communications); URL: http://www.hrdc-drhc.gc.ca
Environmental Youth Internship Program: 403/233-0748; EYI Email: cchrei@netway.ab.ca

HRDC provides an integrated approach to Canada's national investment in people by bringing programs supporting the incomes of Canadians together with human resource programs linked to the requirements of the national economy & labour market. HRDC plays a leadership role in building the mobile, educated & skilled workforce needed to increase Canada's productivity, international competitiveness & the prosperity of its citizens. HRDC was formally established in July 1996. HRDC's programs & services are delivered through a network of Human Resource Centres of Canada, which are located in hundreds of communities across Canada.

The broad objectives of HRDC are:
• helping Canadians prepare for, find & keep work, thereby promoting economic growth & adjustment;
• assisting Canadians in their efforts to provide security for themselves & their families, thereby preventing or reducing poverty among Canadians;
• promoing a fair, safe, healthy, stable, cooperative & productive work environment that contributes to the social & economic well-being of all Canadians.

#### ACTS ADMINISTERED

Canada Assistance Plan Act
Canada Labour Code
Canada Pension Plan
Canada Student Financial Assistance Act
Canada Student Loans Act
Canadian Centre for Occupational Health & Safety Act
Corporations & Labour Unions Returns Act
Department of Human Resources Development Act
Employment Equity Act
Employment Insurance Act
Fair Wages & Hours of Labour Act
Family Orders & Agreements Enforcement Assistance Act
Federal-Provincial Fiscal Arrangements & Federal Post-Secondary Education & Health Contributions Act
Government Annuities Act
Government Annuities Improvement Act
Government Employees Compensation Act
Hudson Bay Mining & Smelting Company Ltd.
Labour Adjustment Benefits Act
Merchant Seamen Compensation Act
Non-smokers' Health Act
Old Age Security Act
Status of the Artist Act
Unemployment Assistance Act
Unemployment Insurance Act
Vocational Rehabilitation of Disabled Persons Act
Wages Liability Act

**Minister**, Hon. Pierre S. Pettigrew, 819/994-2482, Fax: 819/994-0448
**Minister, Labour**, Hon. Lawrence MacAulay, 819/953-5646, Fax: 819/994-5168
**Secretary of State, Children & Youth**, Hon. Ethel Blondin-Andrew, 613/953-8385, Fax: 613/953-0944
Deputy Minister & Chairperson, Mel Cappe, 819/994-4514, Fax: 819/953-5603
Commissioner, Employees, Fernand Boudreau, 819/994-6205, Fax: 819/994-7581
Commissioner, Employers, Peter S. Doyle, 819/994-6115, Fax: 819/953-8991
Director General, Ministerial & Corporate Affairs, Dave Cogliati, 819/994-9721, Fax: 819/994-4210
Executive Director, International Affairs, Stewart Goodings, 613/941-1044, Fax: 613/941-4576
Senior Asst. Deputy Minister, Legislative Review, Michael A. McDermott, 819/952-3799, Fax: 819/954-0899
Senior Asst. Deputy Minister, Service Delivery, Hy Braiter, 819/994-6686, Fax: 819/994-8126
Asst. Deputy Minister, Systems, David McNaughton, 819/994-1592, Fax: 819/997-8015
Senior General Counsel, Legal Services, Clare Beckton, 819/953-8301, Fax: 819/953-7317

#### COMMUNICATIONS

Director General, Monique Collette, 819/994-6013, Fax: 819/953-3981
Associate Director General, Corporate & Regional Communications, Peter Lantos, 819/953-1308, Fax: 819/953-4795
Director, Human Resources Investment, Sandra Souchotte, 819/994-4315, Fax: 819/997-9086
Director, Income Security Program, Ginette La Roche, 819/957-2807, Fax: 819/957-1602
Acting Director, Insurance, David Rutherford, 819/953-7250, Fax: 819/994-6296
Director, Labour, Sharron-Lee Kurtenbach, 819/997-2508, Fax: 819/953-6101
Director, Ministerial Services, Johanne Bélisle, 819/994-0162, Fax: 819/994-6097
Director, Strategic Policy, Peggy Binns, 819/997-2973, Fax: 819/994-1662
Chief, Management Services, Gillian Macdonnell, 819/994-4015, Fax: 819/994-4859

#### FINANCIAL & ADMINISTRATIVE SERVICES

Fax: 819/997-2407
Asst. Deputy Minister, Marcel Nouvet, 819/997-6481
Director General, Aboriginal Relations Office, Howard Green, 819/997-8551, Fax: 819/994-3297
Director General, Administrative Services, David Murray, 819/994-2580, Fax: 819/953-0790
Director General, FAS Policy & Systems, Ray Holland, 819/994-1714, Fax: 819/994-1450
Director General, Financial Services, Guy Tremblay, 819/994-2576, Fax: 819/953-0177
Director General, Internal Audit Bureau, James K. Martin, 819/953-0821, Fax: 819/953-0831
Director, Federal Provincial Programs, Ron Yzerman, 819/997-5564, Fax: 819/997-3415
Director, Learning Programs Policy, David Thornton, 819/953-5283, Fax: 819/953-4226
Director, Occupational & Career Development, Jo-Ann Sobkow, 819/953-7448, Fax: 819/997-0227
Director, Privacy & Security, Jean-Pierre Lecours, 819/994-3041, Fax: 819/994-2821

#### HUMAN RESOURCES

Asst. Deputy Minister, Monique Plante, 819/944-1791, Fax: 819/997-0699
Director General, Corporate Human Resources Services, Lois Pearce, 819/953-3092, Fax: 819/953-6215

Director General, Learning & Development, Andrée Verveille, 819/994-2329, Fax: 819/997-9194
Director, Executive Group Services, Sue Pettis, 819/953-1263, Fax: 819/997-6687
Director, National Headquarters Operations Directorate, Joanne O'Byrne, 819/997-3168, Fax: 819/953-1346
Director, Organizational Development, Ron Carr, 819/953-6420, Fax: 819/997-6687
Director, Planning & Information Management, Robert St-Jean, 819/994-5438, Fax: 819/994-2188

#### HUMAN RESOURCES INVESTMENT

Asst. Deputy Minister/Executive Director, David A. Good, 819/953-3729, Fax: 819/997-9715
Acting Director General, Human Resources Partnerships, Don DeJong, 819/994-3713, Fax: 819/953-3512
Acting Director General, Learning & Literacy, Tom Scrimger, 819/994-2377, Fax: 819/953-4226
Director General, Youth Initiatives Directorate, Suzanne Clément, 819/953-4662, Fax: 819/953-9354
Director, Office of Disabilities Issues, Cathy Chapman, 819/994-5692, Fax: 819/953-4797
Acting Director, Employability & Social Partnerships, Brian Chapman, 819/997-1647, Fax: 819/997-1359
Director, Older Worker Adjustment, Denis Côté, 819/994-8146, Fax: 819/953-8804
Executive Secretariat, National Literacy Secretariat & Office of Learning Technologies, Jim Page, 819/953-5460, Fax: 819/953-8076

#### INCOME SECURITY PROGRAMS

Place Vanier, 120 Parkdale Ave., Ottawa ON K1A 0L1
Asst. Deputy Minister, Serge Rainville, 613/957-3111, Fax: 613/957-1185
Director General, International Benefits, Ed Tamagno, 613/941-4776, Fax: 613/952-8901
Director General, Program Delivery Services, Dennis Kealy, 613/941-5075, Fax: 613/954-2578
Director General, Programs, Cathy Drummond, 613/957-2813, Fax: 613/957-2816
Project Manager, ISP Redesign, Wayne Ganim, 613/954-8401, Fax: 613/941-0711

#### INSURANCE

819/997-8662
Asst. Deputy Minister, Norine Smith, 819/994-1600, Fax: 819/953-5801
Director General, Control, Ron Stewart, 819/994-6868, Fax: 819/953-2633
Director General, Insurance Policies, John McWhinnie, 819/994-1880, Fax: 819/997-7851
Director General, Insurance Services, Doug Matheson, 819/994-6299, Fax: 819/953-4671
Chief Actuary, Actuarial Services, Michel Bedard, 819/994-4590, Fax: 819/953-8752

#### LABOUR

Inquiries: 819/994-6313
Asst. Deputy Minister, Nicole Senécal, 819/997-1493, Fax: 819/953-5685
Director General, Federal Mediation & Conciliation Service, Warren R. Edmondson, 819/997-3290, Fax: 819/953-3162
Director General, Operations, Gerry Blanchard, 819/997-2555, Fax: 819/953-8883
Director General, Strategic Policy & Partnerships, Yves Poisson, 819/953-7405, Fax: 819/953-8494
Director General, Workplace Information, Andrée Dubois, 819/994-4204, Fax: 819/953-9582

#### STRATEGIC POLICY

Fax: 819/997-7329
Asst. Deputy Minister, Jim Lahey, 819/994-4272
Director General, Applied Research Branch, Jean-Pierre Voyer, 819/994-1620, Fax: 819/953-8584
Director General, Federal/Provincial, David MacDonald, 819/994-4538, Fax: 819/953-4701
Director General, Labour Market Policy, Karen Jackson, 819/994-4989, Fax: 819/997-5856
Director General, Program Evaluation Branch, Bob Wilson, 613/954-2737, Fax: 613/952-4662
Director General, Social Policy Division, John Knubley, 819/994-2245, Fax: 819/953-9516
Acting Director General, Strategy & Coordination, Roger Scott-Douglas, 819/994-3737, Fax: 819/994-4533

##### Communications Regional Offices

Alberta & Northwest Territories: Canada Place, #1440, 9700 Jasper Ave., Edmonton AB T5J 4C1 – 403/495-2414; Fax: 403/495-5609, Regional Manager, Laurie Patterson
British Columbia & Yukon: Library Sq. Tower, 300 West Georgia St., 15th Fl., Vancouver BC V6B 6G3 – 604/666-0075; Fax: 604/666-7328, Regional Manager, Gill Eston
Manitoba: Paris Bldg., #500, 259 Portage Ave., Winnipeg MB R3B 3L4 – 204/983-3781; Fax: 204/984-2113, Acting Regional Manager, Sue Foley-Currie
New Brunswick: 615 Prospect St. West, PO Box 2600, Fredericton NB E3B 5V6 – 506/452-3012; Fax: 506/452-3518, Acting Regional Manager, Jacques Laprise
Newfoundland: 689 Topsail Rd., PO Box 12051, St. Johns NF A1B 3Z4 – 709/772-5346; Fax: 709/772-0444, Acting Regional Manager, Linda Bowering
Nova Scotia: Metropolitain Place, 99 Wyse Rd., PO Box 1350, Dartmouth NS B2Y 4B9 – 902/426-5383; Fax: 902/426-1840, Regional Manager, Kathy Moggridge
Ontario: #900, 4900 Yonge St., Willowdale ON M2N 6A8 – 416/954-7640; Fax: 416/954-7822, 7829, Regional Manager, Asoka Yapa
Prince Edward Island: 85 Fitzroy St., PO Box 8000, Charlottetown PE C1A 8K1 – 902/566-7653; Fax: 902/566-7580, Regional Manager, Catherine MacInnis-Gordon
Québec: 1441, rue St. Urbain, Montréal QC H3X 2M6 – 514/283-3180; Fax: 514/283-0123, Chef de cabinet, Léona Talbot
Saskatchewan: Financial Bldg., #814, 2101 Scarth St., Regina SK S4P 2H9 – 306/780-5939; Fax: 306/780-6221, Regional Manager, Brian Harris

##### Associated Agencies, Boards & Commissions

•Canada Labour Relations Board
Listed alphabetically in detail, this section.
•Canadian Centre for Occupational Health & Safety
Listed alphabetically in detail, this section.
•Canadian Labour Force Development Board (CLFDB): 66 Slater St., 23rd Fl., Ottawa ON K1P 5H1 – 613/230-6264; Fax: 613/230-7681

Provides a unique partnership between business, labour, the four designated equality groups & the training & education community. Advises the government on a broad range of labour force development policies & programs. Provides development of a coordinated training system for Canada.

Co-Chair, Jean Andréa Bernard
Co-Chair, Jean-Claude Parrot
•Labour Adjustment Review Board: Portage II, Place du Portage, 165 Hotel-de-ville St., Hull QC K1A 0J2 – 819/997-2555; Fax: 819/997-1664
Chair, Renée Godmer
•Merchant Seamen Compensation Board: Portage II, Place du Portage, 165 Hotel-de-Ville St., Ottawa ON K1A 0J2 – 819/997-2555; Fax: 819/997-1664
Chair, Renée Godmer
Vice-Chair, Capt. Barry F. McKay
•National Aboriginal Management Board (NAMB): Portage IV, #4F00, 140, Promenade du Portage, Hull QC K1A 0J9 – 819/994-2274

Determines human resouce development priorities regarding training & employment activities for aboriginal people.

Manager, Brian Chapman

### IMMIGRATION & REFUGEE BOARD (IRB)/ Commission de l'immigration et du statut de réfugié (CISR)

240 Bank St., Ottawa ON K1A 0K1
613/995-6486; Fax: 613/996-0543; URL: http://www.irb.gc.ca

The IRB is an independent statutory tribunal created by Parliament under Part IV of the Immigration Act. The Chairperson of the Board reports to Parliament through the Minister of Citizenship & Immigration. The Board's mission, on behalf of Canadians, is to make well-reasoned decisions on immigration & refugee matters efficiently, fairly & in accordance with the law.

The Board carries out three major functions: immigration inquiries & detention reviews; immigration appeals; & refugee determination.

• The *Adjudication Division* conducts detention reviews & immigration inquiries for certain categories of people believed to be inadmissable or removable from Canada.

• The *Convention Refugee Determination Division* (CRDD) deals exclusively with the determination of claims to Convention refugee status made within Canada. Claims to Convention refugee status are determined in accordance with the Immigration Act, the Canadian Charter of Rights & Freedoms, the 1951 Geneva Convention on the Status of Refugees & the 1967 Protocol of the Convention.

• The *Immigration Appeal Division* (IAD) hears appeals from permanent residents against removal orders & refusals of sponsored family class applications for permanent residence. The Division also hears appeals made by persons in possession of valid visitor visa, or returning resident permits, seeking admission to Canada, who have been detained, reported or ordered removed at ports of entry.

**Chair**, Nurjehan Mawani
Deputy Chairperson, Convention Refugee Determination Division, John Frecker
Deputy Chairperson, Immigration Appeal Division, Nancy Goodman
Executive Director, Paul Thibault
Director General, Adjudication & Director General, Renewal, Jennifer Benimahdu
Director General, Documentation, Information & Research, Graham Howell
Director General, Programs, Policy & Standards Development, Evelyn Levine
Director, Communications, Robert Desperrier
Director, Finance & Administration, Alain Séguin
Director, Information Systems, Sam Ho
Director, Personnel, Sharon Fleming
General Counsel, Legal Services, Philip Palmer

### INDIAN & NORTHERN AFFAIRS CANADA (INAC)/Affaires indiennes et du Nord Canada (AINC)

Tour Nord, Les Terrasses de la Chaudière, 10 Wellington St., Hull QC K1A 0H4
819/997-0380; Fax: 819/953-3017; Email: InfoPubs@inac.gc.ca; URL: http://www.inac.gc.ca/
Arctic Environmental Strategy: 819/994-7457
Environmental Action Program: 403/667-3180 (Yukon), 403/669-2589 (NWT)
Community Resource Mgmt. Programs: 403/669-2589
Indian Art Section: 819/994-1264
Inuit Art Section: 819/997-8307

Northern Information Network: 819/997-7281

The department fulfills the lawful obligations of the federal government to First nations & Inuit people arising from treaties, the Indian Act & other legislation. Has the primary federal mandate for providing basic services to registered Indians living on reserves, including the funding of First Nations for education, schools, housing, roads, water & sewage systems, & for the funding for social & family services. The Indian Act assigns specific trust responsibilities to the department with respect to Indian moneys, estates, & reserve lands, & creates responsibilities for elementary & secondary education & for band government. Negotiates & oversees the implementation of claims settlements, promotes economic development, & implements practical forms of self-government.

In the North, the department is responsible for assisting the development of political & economic institutions, managing sustainable development of natural resources, & protecting & rehabilitating the northern environment. INAC manages ongoing federal interests, including the administration of Crown land in the territories.

#### ACTS ADMINISTERED

Alberta Natural Resources Act
Arctic Waters Pollution Prevention Act
British Columbia Indian Cut-off Lands Settlement Act
British Columbia Indian Lands Settlement Act
British Columbia Indian Reserves Mineral Resources Act
British Columbia Treaty Commission Act
Canada Lands Surveys Act
Canada Oil & Gas Operations Act
Canada Petroleum Resources Act
Canadian Polar Commission Act
Caughnawaga Indian Reserve Act
Condominium Ordinance Validation Act
Cree-Naskapi (of Québec) Act
Department of Indian Affairs & Northern Development Act
Dominion Water Act
Fort Nelson Indian Reserve Minerals Revenue Sharing Act
Grassy Narrows & Islington Indian Bands Mercury Pollution Claims Settlement Act
Gwich'in Land Claim Settlement Act
Indian Act
Indian Lands Agreement (1986) Act
Indian Land Titles Act
Indian Land Titles Repeal Act
Indian Oil & Gas Act
Indian (Soldier Settlement) Act
James Bay & Northern Québec Native Claims Settlement Act
Manitoba Natural Resources Act
Manitoba Supplementary Provisions Act
Natural Resources Transfer (School Lands) Amendment Act
New Brunswick Indian Reserves Agreement Act
Northern Canada Power Commission (Share Issuance & Sale Authorization) Act
Northern Canada Power Commission Yukon Assets Disposal Authorization Act
Northwest Territories Act
Northwest Territories Waters Act
Nova Scotia Indian Reserves Agreement Act
Nunavut Act
Nunavut Land Claims Agreement Act
Pictou Landing Indian Band Agreement Act
Railway Belt Act
Railway Belt & Peace River Block Act
Railway Belt Water Act
St. Peters Indian Reserve Act
St. Regis Islands Act
Sahtu Dene & Metis Land Claim Settlement Act
Saskatchewan Natural Resources Act
Saskatchewan Treaty Land Entitlement Act
Sechelt Indian Band Self-Government Act
(An Act for the) settlement of certain questions between the Governments of Canada & Ontario respecting Indian Reserve Lands Act
Songhees Indian Reserve Act
Split Lake Cree First Nation Flooded Land Act
Territorial Lands Act
Western Arctic (Inuvialuit) Claims Settlement Act
Yukon Act
Yukon First Nations Land Claims Settlement Act
Yukon First Nations Self-Government Act
Yukon Placer Mining Act
Yukon Quartz Mining Act
Yukon Surface Rights Board Act
Yukon Waters Act

**Minister**, Hon. Jane Stewart, 819/997-0002, Fax: 819/953-4941
Deputy Minister, Scott Serson, 819/997-0133, Fax: 819/953-2251
Director, Indian Program & Funding Allocation Directorate, Al Horner, 819/953-9540

#### CLAIMS & INDIAN GOVERNMENT SECTOR

Asst. Deputy Minister, John Sinclair, 819/953-3180, Fax: 819/953-3246
Director General, Claims Implementation Branch, Terry Henderson, 819/994-3434, Fax: 819/953-6430
Director General, Comprehensive Claims Branch, Greg Gauld, 819/997-8145, Fax: 819/953-4366
Director General, Self Government Negotiations Branch, Barry Dewar
Director General, Specific Claims Branch, Michel Roy, 819/994-4924, Fax: 819/994-4924

##### Treaty Negotiation Offices

Vancouver: Comprehensive Claims Branch, #2700, 650 West Georgia St., PO Box 11576, Vancouver BC V6B 4N8 – 604/775-7114; Fax: 604/775-7149
Victoria: 535 Yates St., 2nd Fl., Victoria BC V8W 2Z6 – 250/363-6910; Fax: 250/363-6911

#### CORPORATE SERVICES SECTOR

Asst. Deputy Minister, Brent DiBartolo, 819/997-0020, Fax: 819/953-4094
Director General, Departmental Audit & Evaluation Branch, Marie-France D'Auray-Boult, 819/994-1323
Director General, Finance Branch, Bill Austin, 819/997-0640, Fax: 819/953-8475
Acting Director General, Human Resources Branch, Thomas R. Paul, 819/997-9646, Fax: 819/953-1311
Director General, Information Management Branch, James Phillips, 819/994-3334
Director General, Real Property Services, Jim Davison, 819/994-6456, Fax: 819/953-9395

#### LANDS & TRUSTS SERVICES SECTOR

Asst. Deputy Minister, Bob Watts, 819/953-5577
Director General, Lands & Environment Branch, Paul Cuillerier, 819/994-7551, Fax: 819/953-3201
Director General, Registration, Revenues & Band Governance Branch, Gregor MacIntosh, 819/994-0951, Fax: 819/953-3371

#### NORTHERN AFFAIRS SECTOR

Asst. Deputy Minister, Jim Moore, 819/953-3760, Fax: 819/953-6121
Director General, Sectoral Policy & Program Devolution Branch, John Berg, 819/997-9449, Fax: 819/997-0552
Director General, Natural Resources & Environment Branch, Hiram Beaubier, 819/997-9381, Fax: 819/953-8766

#### POLICY & STRATEGIC DIRECTION SECTOR

Asst. Deputy Minister, Gordon Shanks, 819/994-7555, Fax: 819/953-9465
Director General, Communications Branch, Jean-Pierre Villeneuve, 819/997-9885, Fax: 819/953-9465
Director General, Government Relations Branch, George Da Pont, 819/953-4968, Fax: 819/953-9027
Director General, Legislation Branch, John Graham, 819/997-8212
Director General, Strategic Policy Branch, Matthew King, 819/997-8359, Fax: 819/953-3320

##### Regional Offices

Alberta: #630, Canada Place, 9700 Jasper Ave., Edmonton AB T5J 4G2 – 403/495-2773; Fax: 403/495-4088, Associate Regional Director General, Jim Fleury
Atlantic: 40 Havelock St., PO Box 160, Amherst NS B4H 3Z3 – 902/661-6200; Fax: 902/661-6237, Acting Regional Director General, John Brown
British Columbia: #340, 1550 Alberni St., Vancouver BC V6G 3C5 – 604/666-7891; Fax: 604/666-2546, Regional Director General, John Watson
Manitoba: #1100, 275 Portage Ave., Winnipeg MB R3B 3A3 – 204/983-4928; Fax: 204/983-7820, Regional Director General, Brenda Kustra
Northwest Territories: PO Box 1500, Yellowknife NT X1A 2R3 – 867/669-2500; Fax: 867/669-2709, Associate Regional Director General, Lorne Tricoteux
Ontario: 25 St. Clair Ave. East, 5th Fl., Toronto ON M4T 1M2 – 416/973-6234; Fax: 416/954-6329, Acting Regional Director General, John Donnelly
Québec: 320, rue St-Joseph est, CP 51127, Succ Comptoir postal, Québec QC G1K 8Z7 – Fax: 418/648-4040, Ligne sans frais: 1-800-263-5592, Acting Regional Director General, Jérome Lapierre
Saskatchewan: 2221 Cornwall St., Regina SK S4P 4M2 – 306/780-5945; Fax: 306/780-5733, Regional Director General, Blair Carlson
Yukon: #345, 300 Main St., Whitehorse YT Y1A 2B5 – 867/667-3100; Fax: 867/667-3196, Regional Director General, Mike Ivanski

##### Associated Agencies, Boards & Commissions

•Beverly & Qamanirjuag Caribou Management Board: c/o 3565 Revelstoke Dr., Ottawa ON K1V 7B9 – 613/733-2007; Fax: 613/733-1304
Chairperson, Jerome Denechezhde
•British Columbia Treaty Commission: #203, 1155 West Pender St., Vancouver BC V6E 2P4 – 604/775-2075, Toll Free: 1-800-665-8330
Chief Commissioner, Alec Robertson, Q.C.
•Environmental Impact Review Board: PO Box 2120, Inuvik NT X0E 0T0 – 867/979-2828; Fax: 867/979-2610
•Environmental Impact Screening Committee Joint Secretariat: PO Box 2120, Inuvik NT X0E 0T0
•Indian Commission of Ontario: 14 Prince Arthur Ave., Toronto M5R 1A9 – 416/973-6390
Commissioner, Philip Goulet
•Indian Oil & Gas Canada (IOGC): #100, 9911 Chula Blvd., Tsuu T'ina (Sarcee) AB T2W 6H6 – 403/292-5625; Fax: 403/292-5618
CEO & Executive Director, W.J. Douglas, 403/292-5628, Fax: 403/292-4864
•Indian Taxation Advisory Board: 90 Elgin St., 2nd Fl., Ottawa ON K1A 0H4 – 613/954-9769; Fax: 613/954-2073; Email: admin-itab@itab.cactuscom.com; URL: http://itab.cactuscom.com/
•Nunavut Impact Review Board: PO Box 2264, Cambridge Bay NT X0E 0C0 – 867/983-2564; Fax: 867/983-2594
Contact, Larry Aknavigak
•Nunavut Implementation Commission: PO Box 1109, Iqaluit NT X0A 0H0 – 867/979-4199; Fax: 867/979-6862
Contact, John Amagoalik
•Nunavut Planning Commission: #1902, 130 Albert St., Ottawa ON K1P 5G4 – 613/238-1155; Fax: 613/238-5724

Contact, Bobby Lyall
•Nunavut Water Board: Gjoa Haven NT X0E 1J0
Contact, Thomas Kudlow
•Office of the Nunavut Environmental Scientist (NES): PO Box 1500, Yellowknife NT X1A 2R3 – 867/920-8200; Fax: 867/920-7809
Environmental Scientist, Lyn Hartley, 867/902-8238
•Porcupine Caribou Management Board: 35 Harbottle Rd., Whitehorse YT Y1A 5T2
Chair, Joe Tetlichi, 867/996-3930
Secretary Treasurer, Linda Hoffmann, 867/633-4780, Fax: 867/633-4780

## INDUSTRY CANADA/Industrie Canada

C.D. Howe Bldg., 235 Queen St., Ottawa ON K1A 0H5
613/941-0222; Fax: 613/954-6436; URL: http://info.ic.gc.ca; Strategis: http://strategis.ic.gc.ca
Publications: 613/947-7466; Fax: 613/954-6436
As Canada's flagship economic department, Industry Canada is now responsible for the majority of federal legislation & programs for business, science & consumer groups within a single federal department to better mobilize resources, merge complementary programs, & avoid duplication & overlap.
Responsible for national economic issues & provides policy advice, industry sector information & business services.
Industry Canada encourages international competitiveness & economic development, new technology development activities & formulates, integrates & coordinates regulations regarding industry & science. Provides strategic intelligence & helps industry develop & apply research & technology. Also provides reviews & updates of standards for the accurate measurement of products & services. Nationally administers & enforces consumer legislation for identification & safe usage of products. Provides access to federal trade development services & programs & has developed the Canadian Technology Network to provide access for small & medium-sized companies to support services, data, information & strategic intelligence.

#### ACTS ADMINISTERED

Bankruptcy & Insolvency Act
Bell Canada Act
Boards of Trade Act
British Columbia Telephone Company Act
Business Development Bank of Canada Act
Canada Business Corporations Act
Canada Co-operatieve Associations Act
Canada Corporations Act
Canadian Space Agency Act
Companies' Creditors Arrangement Act
Competition Act
Competition Tribunal Act
Consumer Packaging & Labelling Act
Copyright Act
Department of Industry Act
Electricity & Gas Inspection Act
Industrial Design Act
Integrated Circuit Topography Act
Investment Canada Act
Lobbyists Registration Act
National Research Council Act
Natural Sciences & Engineering Research Council Act
Patent Act
Precious Metals Marking Act
Public Servants Inventions Act
Radiocommunication Act
Small Business Investment Grants Act
Small Business Loans Act
Social Sciences & Humanities Research Council Act
Standards Council of Canada Act
Statistics Act
Telecommunications Act
Textile Labelling Act
Timber Marking Act
Trade-marks Act
Weights & Measures Act
**Minister**, Hon. John Manley, 613/995-9001, Fax: 613/992-0302, Email: minister.industry@ic.gc.ca
Secretary of State, Science, Research & Development & Western Economic Diversification Canada, Hon. Ronald J. Duhamel, 613/995-9001, Fax: 613/990-4056
Deputy Minister, Kevin Lynch, 613/992-4292, Fax: 613/954-3272
Asst. Deputy Minister, Shirley Serafini, 613/952-2296, Fax: 613/941-4205
Special Advisor to the DM, Robert Haack, 619/954-2873
Director General, Audit & Evaluation Branch, Owen Taylor, 613/954-5084, Fax: 613/954-5070
Director General, Communications Branch, Michelle d'Auray, 613/992-1120, Fax: 613/992-8562, Email: dauray.michelle@ic.gc.ca
Corporate Comptroller, Comptroller's Office, Mary Zamporo, 613/957-9288, Fax: 613/998-6950
Director General, Human Resources Branch, Tom Wright, 613/954-5474, Fax: 613/952-0239

#### Legal Services

General Counsel, F. Côté, 819/997-3325, Fax: 819/953-9267
General Counsel, Doug Lewis, 613/954-5340, Fax: 613/954-9536

#### Office of Consumer Affairs

Acting Director General, Derek Ireland, 613/952-6398, Fax: 613/952-6927
Director, Consumer Information & Coordination, Karen Ellis, 613/952-1971, Fax: 613/952-6927

#### Office of the Corporate Secretary

Corporate Secretary, Vacant, 613/943-7038, Fax: 613/952-0273
Manager, Corporate Briefing & Senior Executive, Marketing, Parliamentary Relations & Applied Procedures, Phillipe Bussy, 613/943-7040, Fax: 613/952-0273
Manager, Executive Correspondence & Records Centre, Cécile Langelier, 613/943-7072, Fax: 613/952-9073
Manager, Operations & Systems, Maureen Lamont, 613/943-7057, Fax: 613/952-0273
Senior Departmental Advisor, Information & Privacy Rights Administration, Pierre Trottier, 613/954-2752, Fax: 613/941-3085

#### Office of the Ethics Counsellor

66 Slater St., 22nd Fl., Ottawa ON K1A 0C9
613/995-0721; Fax: 613/995-7308
Ethics Counsellor, Howard Wilson, 613/995-6852
Director, Lobbyist Registration, Corinne MacLaurin, 613/957-2760, Fax: 613/957-3078
Director, Operations, Robert F. Benson, 613/995-7374

#### Technology Partnerships Canada (TPC)

613/954-0870; Fax: 613/954-9117
TPC, initiated in March 1996, is designed to enhance wealth creation by making Canadian firms more innovative by encouraging research & development & high technology projects in Canada. The fund's focus is on environmental technologies; on strategic enabling technologies, such as biotechnology (e.g. aquaculture), advanced materials (ceramics, composites), selected information technologies (telemedicine), & advanced manufacturing technologies (robotic); & on the aerospace & defence industries, including defence construction.
In partnership with the private sector, TPC invests in research, development, demonstration & market development of:
•environmental technologies, including pollution prevention & protection, water treatment, recycling technologies & clean car technologies;
•enabling technologies, such as advanced manufacturing technologies; advanced materials, biotechnology & selected information technologies;
•aerospace & defence industries, including avionics, flight simulators, aircraft communications, satellite remote sensing & surveillance, security systems & defence conversion.
Executive Director, Office of the Executive Director, Bruce Deacon, 613/941-6747
Director, Aerospace & Defence, Rick Thomas, 613/942-6738, Fax: 613/954-5654
Director, Enabling Technologies, Maureen Lofthouse, 613/954-2937, Fax: 613/954-5654
Director, Environmental Technologies, Nancy Bresolin, 613/941-7676
Acting Director, Program Services, John Brunet, 613/952-9254
Chief, Business & Business Case Analysis, Professional Practices, Economic Analysis, James Roberge, 613/954-0541
Senior Communications Advisor, Office of Communications Coordination, Bruce Stuart, 613/941-4671

#### COMPETITION BUREAU

Place du Portage, Phase I, 50, rue Victoria, 16e étage, Hull QC K1A 0C9
613/994-0798; Fax: 613/953-5013
Director, Konrad von Finckenstein, 819/997-3301
Head, Amendments Unit, Harry S. Chandler, 819/997-2868
Director General & Deputy Director, Compliance & Operations, Robert Morin, 819/953-7942, Fax: 819/997-0324
Director General, Consumer Products Directorate, Zane Brown, 613/953-3187, Fax: 613/953-2931, Email: brown.zane@ic.gc.ca
Director General & Deputy Director, Economics & International Affairs, Patricia Smith, 819/953-3318, Fax: 819/953-6400
Senior Deputy Director, Mergers, Francine Matte, 819/994-1860, Fax: 819/953-6169
Deputy Director, Civil Matters, André Lafond, 819/997-1209, Fax: 819/953-8546
Deputy Director, Criminal Matters, Harry S. Chandler, 819/997-1208, Fax: 819/997-3835
Deputy Director, Marketing Practices, Rachel Larabie-LeSieur, 819/997-1231, Fax: 819/953-2557

#### INDUSTRY & SCIENCE POLICY

Asst. Deputy Minister, Andrei Sulzenko, 613/995-9605, Fax: 613/995-2233
Acting Executive Director, Advisory Council on Science & Technology Secretariat, Farina Chummer, 613/993-6858
Director General, Corporate Governance Branch, Vinita Watson, 613/952-0211, Fax: 613/952-1980
Director General, Entrepreneurship & Small Business Office, Peter Sager, 613/954-5489, Fax: 613/954-5492
Director General, Innovation Policy, Ozzie Silverman, 613/991-9472, Fax: 613/996-7887
Director General, Internal Trade, Consultations & Federal-Provincial Relations, Tom Wallace, 613/954-9633, Fax: 613/954-8042
Director General, International Business, Ronald Watkins, 613/954-3508, Fax: 613/957-4454
Director Genera, Micro-Economic Policy Analysis, Denis Gauthier, 613/941-9224, Fax: 613/991-1261
Director General, Science Promotion & Academic Affairs, Doug Hull, 613/993-6857, Fax: 613/952-2307
Director General, Strategic Policy, Jerry Beausoleil, 613/954-3558, Fax: 613/952-8761
Director, Investment Review, Peter Caskey, 613/954-1887, Fax: 613/996-2515
Director, Operations, Vacant, 613/941-0624

### INDUSTRY SECTOR

Asst. Deputy Minister, John Banigan, 613/954-3798, Fax: 613/941-1134, Email: banigan.john@ic.gc.ca
Special Advisor to the ADM, Christopher Charette, 613/941-9216, Fax: 613/941-1134
Executive Director, Investment Partnerships Canada, Rocco Delvecchio, 613/941-2983, Fax: 613/941-3796
Executive Director, Canadian Biotechnology Strategy Task Force, Roy Atkinson, 613/946-8926, Fax: 613/941-5533
Director General & Manager, Aerospace & Defence, Catherine Kerr, 613/954-3343, Fax: 613/941-2379, Email: kerr.catherine@ic.gc.ca
Director General & Manager, Automotive & Transportation, Slawek Skorupinski, 613/954-3797, Fax: 613/952-8088, Email: skorupinski.slawek@ic.gc.ca
Director General & Manager, Coordination & Management Services, Emmy Verdun, 613/954-3801, Fax: 613/957-9955
Director General, Environmental Affairs, Lucien Bradet, 613/954-3080, Fax: 613/952-9564, Email: bradet.lucien@ic.gc.ca
Director General & Manager, Forest Industries & Building Products, Val Traversy, 613/957-0845, Fax: 613/952-8988, Email: traversy.val@ic.gc.ca
Director General & Manager, Manufacturing & Processing Technologies, Margaret McGuaig-Johnston, 613/954-3279, Fax: 613/941-2463, Email: mccuaig-johnston.margaret@ic.gc.ca
Director General & Manager, Service Industries & Capital Projects, Dennis De Melto, 613/954-2990, Fax: 613/952-9054, Email: demelto.dennis@ic.gc.ca
Director & Manager, Advanced Materials, Chemicals & Plastics, John Mihalus, 613/954-3064, Fax: 613/952-4209, Email: mihalus.john@ic.gc.ca
Director & Manager, Bio-Industries, George Michaliszyn, 613/954-3071, Fax: 613/952-4209, Email: michaliszyn.george@ic.gc.ca
Director & Manager, Consumer Products Industries, Frank Podruski, 613/954-3099, Fax: 613/954-3107
Director & Manager, Health Industries, David Hoye, 613/954-5258, Fax: 613/952-4209, Email: hoye.david@ic.gc.ca
Director & Manager, Metals & Minerals Processing, Charles Éthier, 613/954-3176, Fax: 613/954-3079, Email: ethier.charles@ic.gc.ca
Acting Director, International Business Opportunities Centre (IBOC), Dan Batista, 613/944-2010, Fax: 613/966-2635
Director, Women's Bureau, Monique Laurin, 613/954-3130, Fax: 613/945-4301

### OPERATIONS

Asst. Deputy Minister, Michelle Comeau, 613/954-3405, Fax: 613/954-4883

#### Aboriginal Business Canada

235 Queen St., Ottawa ON K1A 0H5
Executive Director, Bob Dickson, 613/957-5430, Fax: 613/957-7010
Director, East Region, David Elgie, 416/973-6870, Fax: 416/973-2255
Director, West Region, David McDougall, 904/666-0744, Fax: 904/666-1211
Manager, Finance & Operations, Suzanne Bourdage, 604/954-1826, Fax: 604/957-7010
Manager, Marketing & Program Relations, Joanne Spanton, 613/954-4061, Fax: 613/957-7010
Manager, Operations, Rob Ward, 613/954-8076, Fax: 613/957-7010
Manager, Policy, Tim Stupich, 613/954-4059, Fax: 613/957-7010

#### Canadian Intellectual Property Office (CIPO)

Place du Portage, Tour I, 50, rue Victoria, Hull QC K1A 0C9
EMail: CIPO.CONTACT@ic.gc.ca; URL: http://info.ic.ca/opengov/cipo/inq/inq_e.html
CEO & Commissioner, Patents & Registrar, Trademarks, Sheila Batchelor, 819/997-1057, Fax: 819/997-1890
Deputy Director, Automated Systems, Nabil Kraya, 819/997-2923, Fax: 819/953-5059
Executive Director, Jean Gariépy, 819/953-2990, Fax: 819/997-1890
Acting Chair, Patent Appeal Board, Peter Davies, 819/953-9067, Fax: 819/997-1890
Chair, Trade-Marks Opposition Board, Gary Partington, 819/994-4794, Fax: 819/997-1890
Special Advisor, Executive Office, Ray Taylor, 819/997-2186, Fax: 819/997-1890
Director & Registrar, Copyright & Industrial Design, Linda Steingarten, 819/997-1657, Fax: 819/953-6977
Director, Finance & Administration, Brenda Snarr, 819/997-3024, Fax: 819/994-0357
Director, Human Resources, Élise Morin, 819/997-2673, Fax: 819/997-2987
Director, Information, Ed Rymek, 819/997-2673, Fax: 819/953-7620
Director, Marketing, Chris McDermott, 819/953-6131, Fax: 819/953-6004
Director, Patents, Anthony McDonough, 819/953-5864, Fax: 819/994-1989
Director, Planning, International & Regulatory Affairs, Douglas Kuntze, 819/953-9090, Fax: 819/997-5052
Director, Trade-Marks, Barbara Bova, 819/997-2423, Fax: 819/997-1421

#### Communications Research Centre & Centre for Information Technologies Innovation

3701 Carling Ave., PO Box 11490, Stn H, Ottawa ON K2H 8S2
613/991-3313
President, Communications Research Centre, Gerry Turcotte, 613/990-3929, Fax: 613/990-7983
Interim Executive Vice-President, Communications Research Centre & Vice-President, Communications Systems Research, Robert Huck, 613/998-2768, Fax: 613/998-9875, 990-6339
President, Measurement Canada, Alan Johnston, 613/952-0655, Fax: 613/957-1265
Managing Partner, Management Consulting Centre, Radek Bandzierz, 613/954-2975, Fax: 613/954-0017
Vice-President, Engineering, Larry Fraser, 613/952-0635, Fax: 613/952-5404
Vice-President, Operations, Bob Bruce, 613/952-2626, Fax: 613/952-1736
Vice-President, Program Development, Sonia Roussy, 613/952-4285, Fax: 613/952-1736
Vice-President, Radio Communications & Broadcast Research, William Sawchuk, 613/998-2332, Fax: 613/990-7986
Director General, Corporations, Mary Walsh, 613/941-2837, Fax: 613/941-5783
Director General, FedNor, Louise Paquette, 705/671-0711, Fax: 705/670-6103
Director General, Management Services & Facilities Management, Yves Moisan, 613/954-3750, Fax: 613/957-4788
Director General, Programs & Services, Serge Croteau, 613/954-5533, Fax: 613/952-2635
Director General, Strategic Planning & Corporate Development, Michael Jenkin, 613/952-8075, Fax: 613/952-9026
Director General, Trade & Operations Integration & Management Consulting, Linda Keen, 613/954-5592, Fax: 613/954-0017
Director, Distribution, Mail & Records Services, Daniel Gagnon, 613/941-0904, Fax: 613/952-5592
Director, Facilities Management, Howard Dudley, 613/954-2823, Fax: 613/954-2303
Director, Incorporations & Disclosure Services, Elaine Collins, 613/941-8118, Fax: 613/941-0999
Director, Loan Insurance & Recoveries, George Hussey, 613/954-1832, Fax: 613/952-8779
Director, Operations Directorate, Robert A. Porter, 613/954-3449, Fax: 613/992-7499
Director, Small Business Loans Re-engineering Administration, Marie-Josée Thivierge, 613/952-7339, Fax: 613/952-0290
Director, Trade Integration Directorate, Warren Maybee, 613/941-3863, Fax: 613/992-7499
Program Manager, Technology & Society (TECSO), Catherine Geoffrey, 514/973-5779, Fax: 514/973-5757
Program Manager, Work & Technology, David Tippin, 514/993-5830, Fax: 514/993-5757
Manager, Administration, Hélène Bradbury, 613/952-6711, Fax: 613/952-5404
Manager, Administration, Finance & Personal Corporations, Hélène Revine, 613/941-2835, Fax: 613/941-5783
Manager, Business Competitiveness, Ron Cantin, 705/942-1327, Fax: 705/942-5434
Manager, Community Economic Development, Scott Merrifield, 705/671-0696, Fax: 705/671-0717
Manager, Compliance, Robert Weist, 613/941-5756, Fax: 613/941-5781
Manager, Corporate Services, Bill Pasiak, 705/942-1327, Fax: 705/942-5434
Manager, Informatics, Pierre Lapointe, 613/952-5870, Fax: 613/952-5404
Manager, Program Planning & Advocacy, Karen Streich, 705/942-1327, Fax: 705/942-5434
Senior Correspondence Officer, Coreespondence Unit, Josée Riopel, 613/954-2880, Fax: 613/954-4883

#### Office of the Chief Information Officer

235 Queen St., Ottawa ON K1A 0H5
Chief Information Officer, Tim Garrard, 613/954-3574, Fax: 613/941-1938
Executive Director, National Secretariat, Canadian Business Service Centres, Robert Smith, 613/954-3576, Fax: 613/954-5463
Director General, Strategic Information, David Waung, 613/952-6368, Fax: 613/990-4848
Director, Computing Development & Operations, Peter St-Germain, 613/941-3401, Fax: 613/941-8631
Director, Strategic Technology Direction, Samy Talbert, 613/954-2622, Fax: 613/941-1938
Director, Telecommunications Development & Operations, Jenny Steel, 613/954-2612, Fax: 613/941-4615
Manager, Electronic Commerce, Pierre Poirier, 613/954-2910, Fax: 613/941-1938
Manager, Operational Planning, Eileen Country, 613/954-2685, Fax: 613/941-1938

#### Office of the Superintendent of Bankruptcy

Journal Tower South, 365 Laurier St. West, 8th Fl., Ottawa ON K1A 0C8
613/941-1000; Fax: 613/941-2862
Superintendent, Marc Mayrand, 613/941-2691
Deputy Superintendent, J. Armstrong, 613/941-2605
Acting Deputy Superintendent, Ginette Trahan, 613/941-2854, Fax: 613/941-2892
Senior Legal Counsel, Richard Shaw, 613/942-2602, Fax: 613/941-2692

#### Regional Offices

•Atlantic: 1801 Hollis St., 5th Fl., PO Box 940, Stn M, Halifax NS B3J 2V9
Executive Director, Robert Russell, 902/426-3458, Fax: 902/426-6094
Provincial Director & Regional Director, NB/PEI Marketplace Services, George Richard, 506/851-6517, Fax: 506/851-6502
Provincial Director, Newfoundland, Patricia Hearn, 709/772-4866, Fax: 709/772-5093
Senior Trade Commissioner, Charlottetown, Fraser Dickson, 902/566-7443, Fax: 902/566-7450

Senior Trade Commissioner, Halifax, Barbara Giacomin, 902/426-6660, Fax: 902/426-2624
Senior Trade Commissioner, Moncton, Roger Léger, 506/851-6440, Fax: 506/851-6429
•Ontario: 1 Front St. West, 4th Fl., Toronto ON M5J 1A4
Executive Director, Brigette Hohn, 416/973-5001, Fax: 416/973-8714
Director, Canada/Ontario Business Call Centre, A. Anderson, 519/954-8593, Fax: 519/954-8597
Program Director, Computers for Schools, George Meek, 416/954-3674, Fax: 416/973-8714
Director, Consumer Products, Sharan Allan, 519/954-5453, Fax: 519/954-6654
Director, Finance, Administration & Informatics, Michael Jeanes, 416/954-8191, Fax: 416/973-8714
Director, Human Resources, Carolyn Rankin, 416/973-6235, Fax: 416/954-8836
Director, Industry Sectors & Infrastructure, Gerry Cooper, 519/973-5173, Fax: 519/973-5131
Director, International Business, A. MacArthur, 416/954-6326, Fax: 416/973-8161
Director, Planning, Analysis & Public Affairs, David Dallimore, 416/973-5036, Fax: 416/954-1385
Director, Spectrum Management, Vacant, 416/973-6280, Fax: 416/973-6272
•Pacific: #2000, 300 West Georgia St., Vancouver BC V6B 5E1
Executive Director, Bruce Drake, 604/666-1400, Fax: 604/666-8330
Team Leader, Canadian Buainess Service Centre, Linda Howe, 604/775-5573, Fax: 604/666-0277
Senior Trade Commissioner, International Trade Centre, Robert Pedersen, 604/666-8888, Fax: 604/666-0954
Acting Director, Corporate Services, Carol McGrath, 604/666-4663, Fax: 604/666-7981
Director, Industry, Brian Andersen, 604/666-1414, Fax: 604/666-8330
Acting Regional Director, Spectrum & Consumer Operations, Wayne Choi, 604/666-5207, Fax: 604/666-5471
•Prairies & NWT: Canada Place, #540, 9700 Jasper Ave., Edmonton AB T5J 4C3
Executive Director, Glenn Fields, 403/495-2951, Fax: 403/495-4582
Regional Director, Informatics, Patrick Nolan, 204/984-8047, Fax: 204/984-4205
Regional Manager & Coordinator, Industry Sector Officer, Bob Mckenzie, 306/975-4391, Fax: 306/975-5334
Director, Consumer Products, Dave McElheran, 204/983-2843, Fax: 204/983-5511
Director, Finance & Administration, Peter Hrymak, 204/983-3888, Fax: 204/984-4205
Director, Human Resources, Dawna Csatari, 204/983-2801, Fax: 204/983-8181
Director, International Trade, James Graham, 403/495-4415, Fax: 403/495-4507
Director, Regional Promotion & Marketing Division, Georgine Ulmer, 403/292-4576, Fax: 403/292-4578
Director, Spectrum Management & Telecommunications, Kevin Paterson, 204/983-4395, Fax: 204/983-4329
•Québec: 5, Place Ville Marie, 7e étage, Montréal QC H3B 2G2
Executive Director, Denise Boudrias, 514/283-1885, Fax: 514/496-7003
Regional Manager, Finance, Engineering & Administration, Christine Morier, 514/283-4324, Fax: 514/283-3096
Director, Canada-Québec Subsidiary Agreement on Industrial Development, Marcel Drouin, 514/283-4016, Fax: 514/283-4581
Director, Canada-Québec Subsidiary Agreement on Industrial Development, Benoît Raby, 514/283-4016, Fax: 514/283-4581
Director, Human Resources, Denis Cadotte, 514/293-1337, Fax: 514/496-8023
Director, Informatics & Technology Services, Diane Lemire, 514/496-2874, Fax: 514/283-3096
Director, International Trade Centre, Paul Delaney, 514/283-6796, Fax: 514/283-8794
Director, Public Affairs, Yvon Bureau, 514/283-2785, Fax: 514/283-2269
Director, Spectrum, Information Technologies & Consumer Products, Pierre Lemay, 514/283-7046, Fax: 514/283-5157
Director, Telehealth, Jocelyne Picot, 514/283-4236, Fax: 514/283-3096
Director, Tourism Industries, Antoine Samuelli, 514/283-4002, Fax: 514/496-7585
Coordinator, Strategic Information, Noël Bilodeau, 514/283-8874, Fax: 514/283-3096

#### SPECTRUM, INFORMATION TECHNOLOGIES & TELECOMMUNICATIONS

Journal Tower North, 300 Slater St., 20th Fl., Ottawa ON K1A 0C8
Asst. Deputy Minister, Michael Binder, 613/998-0368, Fax: 613/952-1203
Director General, Information & Communications Technologies: Manufacturing, Investment & Market Development Branch, David Mulcaster, 613/990-4294, Fax: 613/957-8839
Acting Director General, Information & Communications Technologies: Software, Advanced Networks, Keith Parsonage, 613/954-5598, Fax: 613/957-4076
Acting Director General, Information Policy & Planning, Helen McDonald, 613/990-4732, Fax: 613/941-0178
Director General, Radiocommunications & Broadcasting Regulatory, Jan Skora, 613/990-4817, Fax: 613/993-4433
Acting Director General, Spectrum Engineering, Robert McCaughern, 613/990-4820, Fax: 613/954-6091
Director General, Telecommunications Policy, Larry Shaw, 613/998-4241, Fax: 613/998-1256
Executive Director, Information Highway, Richard Simpson, 613/990-4292, Fax: 613/941-1164
Executive Director, Spectrum Telecommunications Program Renewal, Robert Chartrand, 613/991-3510, Fax: 613/993-4433

##### Associated Agencies, Boards & Commissions

•Canadian Tourism Commission (CTC)/Commission Canadienne du Tourisme (CCT): East Tower, 235 Queen St. E., 4th Fl., Ottawa ON K1A 0H6 – 613/954-3943; Fax: 613/954-3945; URL: http://xinfo.ic.gc.ca/Tourism/
Chair, Hon. J. Judd Buchanan, 604/631-2831
President, Douglas Fyfe, 613/954-3830, Fax: 613/952-9014
Vice-President, Marketing Overseas, Keith de Bellefeuille-Percy, 613/954-3975, Fax: 613/952-7906
Director, Corporate Services, Blair Stevens, 613/954-3882, Fax: 613/954-3826
Director, Special Initiatives, Michel Tremblay, 613/954-3838, Fax: 613/952-7906
Manager, Business Travel Marketing Americas, Joan Pollock, 613/954-1900, Fax: 613/954-3988
Manager, Information Services, Special Initiatives, Jim York, 613/954-3840, Fax: 613/952-7906
Manager, Japan Marketing Overseas, John Burcell, 613/954-3963, Fax: 613/952-7906
Manager, Leisure Travel Marketing Americas, Thomas Penny, 613/954-3874, Fax: 613/954-3988
Manager, Liaison, Industry Competitiveness, Carol Bruce, 613/954-3926, Fax: 613/952-9014
Manager, Operations & Research, Scott Meis, 613/954-3909, Fax: 613/954-3964
Manager, Operations Marketing Americas, Virginia Doucette, 613/954-3970, Fax: 613/954-3989
Manager, Primary Markets Marketing Overseas, Mary Pavich, 613/954-3821, Fax: 613/952-7906
Manager, Program Development & Special Initiatives, Sebastian Ieria, 613/954-3843, Fax: 613/952-7906
•Standards Council of Canada (SCC)/Conseil canadien des normes (CCN): #1200, 45 O'Connor St., Ottawa ON K1P 6N7 – 613/238-3222; Fax: 613/995-4564; URL: http://www.scc.ca/indexe.html – Sales Department: 1-800-267-8220

A non-regulatory body which administers the National Standards System, a federation of Canadian governments & organizations that develop standards & test products to specific standards.

President, Richard Lafontaine
Executive Director, Michael McSweeney
•National Advisory Council on Science & Technology (ACST)/Conseil consultatif national des sciences et de la technologie: 240 Sparks St., 8th Fl. West, Ottawa ON K1A 0H5 – 613/990-2007; Fax: 613/990-6260; Email: nabst@ic.gc.ca; URL: http://xinfo.ic.gc.ca/opengov/nabst/nabst.html

Newly formed Council, created with the mandate to review the nation's performance in science & technology innovation, identify emerging issues & provide advice on future developments.

Chair, Hon. John Manley, 613/995-9001

## INFORMATION COMMISSIONER OF CANADA/Commissaire à l'information du Canada

Tower B, Place de Ville, 112 Kent St., 3rd Fl., Ottawa ON K1A 1H3
613/995-2410; Fax: 613/995-1501; URL: http://infoweb.magi.com/ZXaccessca/index.html
Toll Free: 1-800-267-0441

The Commissioner investigates complaints that Federal Government departments & agencies have not complied with the Access to Information Act.

**Information Commissioner**, John W. Grace
Deputy Information Commissioner, Alan Leadbeater
Director General, Investigations, Dan Dupuis
Legal Counsel, Daniel Brunet

## Office of INTERGOVERNMENTAL AFFAIRS

c/o Privy Council Office, Langevin Block, 80 Wellington St., Ottawa ON K1A 0A3
URL: http://www.aia.gc.ca/

Federal government office responsible for the management of federal-provincial relations. The office supports the Prime Minister and the Minister of Intergovernmental Affairs & works closely with other federal and provincial departments & territorial governments to cover a variety of areas in which the federal government, the provinces & the territories are involved.

Operations of the office are divided into four secretariats: Policy and Research Secretariat, Intergovernmental Communications Secretariat, Federal-Provincial Relations Secretariat, Aboriginal Affairs Secretariat. The Office of Intergovernmental Affairs is a branch of the Privy Council Office.

**Minister Responsible**, Hon. Stéphane Dion, 613/943-1838, Fax: 613/943-8377
Deputy Minister, George Anderson, 613/947-7569, Fax: 613/947-7580
Information Contact, Gerard Simoneau, 613/957-5262, Fax: 613/957-5154

## INTERNATIONAL BOUNDARY COMMISSION/Commission de la frontière internationale

615 Booth St., Ottawa ON K1A 0E9
613/992-1294; Fax: 613/947-1337

This Commission has jurisdiction over regulation & maintenance of the Canada-US boundary in accordance with the Boundary Treaty of 1925, & the International Boundary Commission Act, RSC 1985, c. I-16.

**Commissioner, Canadian Section**, Mike O'Sullivan, 613/995-4341

Commissioner, United States Section, Thomas Baldini, 202/736-9007

## INTERNATIONAL DEVELOPMENT RESEARCH CENTRE (IDRC)/Centre de recherches pour le développement international (CRDI)

PO Box 8500, Ottawa ON K1G 3H9

613/236-6163; Fax: 613/238-7230; Email: info@idrc.ca; URL: http://www.idrc.ca; IDRC Report URL: http:www.idrc.ca/books/reports

Telnet: ddbs.idrc.ca

Through support for research, IDRC assists scientists in developing countries to identify long-term, practical solutions to pressing developmental problems.

**Chair**, Gordon F. Smith

President, Maureen O'Neil

Vice-President, Corporate Services Branch, Pierre Beemans

Vice-President & CEO, Finance & Administration, Ray Audet

Vice-President, Programs Branch, Caroline Pestieau

Information Officer, Public Affairs, Pauline Dole

#### MINISIS Systems Group

613/236-6163, ext.2335; Fax: 613/563-3858; URL: http://minisis.idrc.ca/minisis

A specialized unit within the IDRC, the group's mandate is to provide cost-effective solutions to organizations in & outside of Canada with respect to information management & technology. The goal of the MINISIS Systems Group is to provide a complete toolkit which facilitates & promotes the global sharing of knowledge. Its mission is to ensure organizations & countries have access to modern technological solutions to promote their growth from social, economical & environmental perspectives.

The MINISIS suite of software is entirely Canadian & includes a wide range of products.

Principal, World-wide Marketing, Christopher Burcsik, Email: cburcsik@idrc.ca

#### Regional Offices

Asia: IDRC, Tanglin, PO Box 101, Singapore 9124, Republic of Singapore – (011-65) 235-1344; Fax: (011-65) 235-1849; Telex: RS 61061;
Cable: IDRECENTRE SINGAPORE

Eastern & Southern Africa: IDRC, PO Box 62084, Nairobi, Kenya – (011-254-2) 7131603; Fax: (011-254-2) 711063

Latin America & the Caribbean: Centro Internacional de Investigaciones para el Desarrollo, Casilla de Correo 6379, Montevideo, Uruguay – (011-598-2) 92-20-31/34; Fax: (011-598-2) 92-02-23

Middle East & North Africa: PO Box 14, Orman, Giza, Cairo, Egypt – (011-20-2) 336-7051; Fax: (011-20-2) 336-7056

South Africa: IDRC, Braamfontein Centre, 23 Jorissen St., 9th Fl., Braamfontein, Johannesburg 2001, South Africa – (011-27-11) 403-3952; Fax: (011-27-11) 403-1417

South Asia: IDRC, 17 Jor Bagh, New Delhi 110 003, India – (011-91-11) 461-9411; Fax: (011-91-11) 462-2707; Telex: 3161536 IDRC IN

West & Central Africa: CRDI, CD Annexe, BP 11007, Dakar, Sénégal – (011-221) 24-42-31; Fax: (011-221) 25-32-55; Telex: 21674 RECENTRE SG;
Cable: RECENTRE DAKAR

## INTERNATIONAL JOINT COMMISSION (IJC)/Commission mixte internationale (CMI)

100 Metcalfe St., Ottawa ON K1P 5M1

613/995-2984; Fax: 613/993-5583

Great Lakes Water Quality Information: 519/257-6700

Under the Boundary Waters Treaty, this Commission has jurisdiction over certain questions arising between Canada & the United States, involving the use & regulation of waters forming or crossing the common boundary; it also has certain advisory responsibilities relating to transboundary air quality.

Chairman, Leonard H.J. Legault, Q.C.

Commissioner, Dr. Pierre Béland

Commissioner, C. Francis Murphy

Secretary, Dr. Murray Clamen

Adviser, Communications, Garwood Tripp, 613/995-0088, Email: trippg@ijc.achilles.net

#### United States Section

#100, 1250 - 23 St. NW, Washington DC 20440

202/736-9000; Fax: 202/736-9015

Chair, Thomas L. Baldini

Commissioner, Susan B. Bayh

Commissioner, Alice B. Chamberlin

Secretary, Vacant

#### Canada/United States-Great Lakes Regional Water Quality Agreement

Information: 519/257-6700

Director, Great Lakes Regional Office, Doug McTavish

## JUSTICE CANADA

Justice Bldg., 239 Wellington St., Ottawa ON K1A 0H8

613/957-4222; Fax: 613/954-0811; URL: http://canada.justice.gc.ca/

Toll Free Firearms Act Info: 1-800-731-4000

Federal Child Support Guidelines: 1-888-373-2222

Provides legal services to the Government of Canada, including its departments & agencies, & supervises the administration of justice in governmental affairs.

#### ACTS ADMINISTERED

Access to Information Act
Annulment of Marriages (Ontario) Act
Bills of Lading Act
Canada Evidence Act
Canada Prize Act
Canada-United Kingdom Civil & Commercial Judgements Convention Act
Canadian Bill of Rights
Canadian Human Rights Act
Canadian Laws Offshore Application Act
Commercial Arbitration Act (2nd Supp.)
Contraventions Act
Criminal Code
Crown Liability Proceedings Act
Department of Justice Act
Divorce Act (2nd Supp.)
Escheats Act
Extradition Act
Family Orders & Agreements Enforcement Assistance Act (2nd. Supp.)
Federal Court Act
Federal Real Property Act
Firearms Act
Foreign Enlistment Act
Foreign Extraterritorial Measures Act
Fugitive Offenders Act
Garnishment, Attachment & Pension Diversion Act
Identification of Criminals Act
International Sale of Goods Contracts Convention Act
Interpretation Act
Judges Act
Law Commission of Canada Act
Marriage (Prohibited Degrees) Act
Mutual Legal Assistance in Criminal Matters Act (2nd Supp.)
Narcotic Control Act
Official Languages Act (4th Supp.)
Official Secrets Act
Postal Services Interruption Relief Act
Privacy Act
Revised Statutes of Canada Act, 1985 (3rd Supp.)
Security Offences Act
State Immunity Act
Statute Revision Act
Statutory Instruments Act
Supreme Court Act
Tax Court of Canada Act
United Nations Foreign Arbitral Awards Convention Act (2nd Supp.)
Young Offenders Act

**Minister/Attorney General**, Hon. Anne McLellan, 613/992-4621, Fax: 613/990-7255

Deputy Minister & Deputy Attorney General, George M. Thomson, Q.C., 613/957-4997, Fax: 613/941-2279

Assoc. Deputy Minister, Canadian Unity, Mary Elizabeth Dawson, 613/957-4898, Fax: 613/952-4279

#### CIVIL LAW & CORPORATE MANAGEMENT SECTOR

Assoc. Deputy Minister, Mario Dion, 613/941-4073

Corporate Counsel, Deborah McNair, 613/952-1578

Director General, Corporate Management Policy, Systems & Services Directorate, Richard Asselin, 613/941-4095

Director General, Human Resources Directorate, Fiona Spencer, 613/941-1885

Acting Senior General Counsel, Civil Litigation & Real Property Law (Québec) Section, René LeBlanc, 613/957-4657

General Counsel, Civil Code Section, Louise Sabourin-Hébert, 613/941-0375

General Counsel, Commercial & Property Law (Québec), Michel Vermette, 613/957-4679

Acting Senior Counsel, Legal Education Division, Marie-Claude Turgeon, 613/952-2271

Director, Renewal Secretariat, Michel Valée, 613/991-8212

Coordinator, Francophonie & Visitors Program, Carole Johnson, 613/957-4391

#### COMMUNICATIONS & EXECUTIVE SERVICES BRANCH

Director General, Karen Laughlin, 613/957-4221, Fax: 613/941-2329

Director, Corporate Communications & Services, Marie-Claire Wallace, 613/957-4216

Director, Executive Services, David Merner, 613/952-8382

Director, Public Affairs, Wendy Sailman, 613/957-4211

Head, Media Relations, Irène Arsenault, 613/957-4207

Coordinator, Firearms, Hana Hruska, 613/952-6664

Senior Advisor, Conflict Resolution, Mathilde Gravelle-Bazinet, 613/941-1993, Fax: 613/952-8538

#### LEGAL OPERATIONS SECTOR

Assoc. Deputy Minister, Richard Thompson, Q.C., 613/957-4550

Asst. Deputy Attorney General, Aboriginal Affairs, Kathie MacCormick, 613/957-4626

Asst. Deputy Minister, Business Law & Counsel to Industry Canada, J. Edward Thompson, 613/954-3946

Asst. Deputy Minister, Central Agency Group, Mark Jewett, 613/996-4667

Asst. Deputy Attorney General, Citizenship & Immigration, John Sims

Acting Asst. Deputy Attorney General, Civil Litigation Branch, Edward Sojonky, Q.C., 613/957-4871

Asst. Deputy Attorney General, Criminal Law, Daniel Bellemare, Q.C., 613/957-4756

Asst. Deputy Attorney General, Tax Law Branch, Ian MacGregor, Q.C., 613/957-4811

Director General, Aboriginal Justice, Geoffrey Bickert, 613/957-4717
Chief General Counsel, General Counsel Group, Ivan Whitehall, Q.C., 613/957-4801
Senior General Counsel & Director, Criminal Law Sector, William Corbett, Q.C., 613/957-4765
Senior General Counsel, Indian & Northern Affairs Canada, William Elliott, 613/994-4141
Senior General Counsel, Maritime Law Secretariat, Alfred Popp, Q.C., 613/957-4666
Senior General Counsel, Strategic Prosecution Policy, Paul Kennedy, 613/952-7553
Senior Counsel, Work Profiling System Services, Bernie Shaffer, 613/941-4013
Head Counsel, Client Driven Services Secretariat, Donald Lemaire, 613/957-9586
General Counsel, Dispute Resolution Project, Myles Kirvan, 613/957-1235
Head, Business Portfolio, Michael Richard, 613/957-4646

#### LEGISLATIVE SERVICES BRANCH

Director, Legislative Services Branch, Lionel Levert, 613/941-4178
Chief Legislative Editor, Legislative Editing & Publishing Services, Robert DuPerron, 613/957-0005
Senior General Counsel, Regulations Section, Ginette Williams, 613/957-0065

#### POLICY SECTOR

Senior Asst. Deputy Minister, Thea Herman, 613/957-4781
Asst. Deputy Minister, Criminal Policy, Richard Mosley, 613/957-4725
Executive Director, National Crime Prevention Council Secretariat, Elaine Scott, 613/957-9639
Director General, Diversity, Equality & Access to Justice, Susan Campbell, 613/957-1524
Director General, Programs Directorate, Ajit Mehat, 613/957-4344
Coordinator, Conviction Review Group, Eugene Williams, 613/957-4784
Coordinator, Sentencing Team, David Daubney, 613/957-4755
Manager, Canadian Firearms Centre, Michael Plouffe, 613/952-3800
General Counsel, Child Support Team, Murielle Brazeau, 613/957-2788
General Counsel, Criminal Law Policy Section, Yvan Roy, 613/957-4728
General Consel, Family, Children & Youth Section, Glenn Rivard, 613/941-2339

#### Regional Offices

Edmonton: Bank of Montreal Tower, #211, 10199 - 101 St., Edmonton AB T5J 3Y4 – 403/495-2970; Fax: 403/495-2970, General Counsel, David Gates
Halifax: 5161 George St., 4th Fl., Halifax NS B3J 1M7 – 902/426-7592; Fax: 902/426-2329, General Counsel, Ted K. Tax
Montréal: Complexe Guy-Favreau, Tour Est, 200, boul René-Lévesque ouest, 9e étage, Montréal QC H2Z 1X4 – 514/283-4972; Fax: 514/283-9690, Senior General Counsel, Jacques Letellier, c.r.
Saskatoon: 229 - 4 Ave. South, 7th Fl., Saskatoon SK S7K 4K3 – 306/975-4761; Fax: 306/975-5013, General Counsel, Marilyn Doering
Calgary Sub Office: #308, 321 - 6 Ave. SW, Calgary AB T2P 3H2
403/299-3962, Fax: 403/299-3966
Toronto: #3400, First Canadian Place, PO Box 36, Stn First Canadian Place, Toronto ON M5X 1K6 – 416/973-3102; Fax: 416/983-3636, Senior General Counsel, Paul Evraire
Vancouver: #2800, Royal Centre, 1055 West Georgia St., PO Box 11118, Vancouver BC V6E 3P9 – 604/666-0131; Fax: 604/661-2760, General Counsel, J. Bissell, Q.C.
Whitehorse: #200, 300 Main St., Whitehorse YT Y1A 2B5 – 867/667-8103; Fax: 867/668-4809, General Counsel, Dennis Calxton
Winnipeg: #301, Centennial House, 310 Broadway, Winnipeg MB R3C 0S6 – 204/983-2252; Fax: 204/983-3636, General Counsel, Roger Lafreniere, Q.C.
Yellowknife: Joe Tobie Bldg., 5020 - 48 St., Yellowknife NT X1A 2N1 – 867/920-7711; Fax: 867/920-4022, General Counsel, Pierre Rousseau

#### Associated Agencies, Boards & Commissions

•National Crime Prevention Council
130 Albert St., Ottawa ON K1A 0H8
613/941-0505; Fax: 613/952-3515; Email: ncpc@crime-prevention.org; URL: http://crime-prevention.org/ncpc
An independent voluntary council with a mission to develop strategies to empower individuals & communities to improve safety & security. The council's goals are to: promote the safety of all individuals & their communities; to develop plans which look at the cause of crime, the opportunities to commit crime, & the conditions that leave people exposed to crime; to develop partnerships with communities to carry out crime prevention activities.

## LAURENTIAN PILOTAGE AUTHORITY CANADA/Administration de pilotage de Laurentides Canada

Tour de la Bourse, 715, Sq. Victoria, 6e étage, CP 680, Montréal QC H4Z 1J9
514/283-6320; Fax: 514/496-2409; Email: apl@apl.qc.ca; URL: http://canada.gc.ca/depts/agencies/lpaind_e.html
The Authority provides pilotage services in the province of Québec, north of St. Lambert Lock. Reports to government through the Minister of Transport.
**President**, Jean-Claude Michaud
Director, Operations, Clément Deschênes
Secretary, Guy P. Major
Treasurer, Yvon Martel

## LIBRARY OF PARLIAMENT/Bibliothèque du Parlement

111 Wellington St., Ottawa ON K1A 0A9
613/995-1166; Fax: 613/992-1269
The Library of Parliament is administered by the Parliamentary Librarian appointed by the Crown. The library maintains a basic collection of 616,000 books, documents, periodicals, microfilm, video tapes & a diversity of automated information retrieval services. Staff provides information, reference & research services to Parliament, its officers & personnel, Parliamentary committees & Parliamentary associations. The Library of Parliament also has responsibility over the Public Information Office (PIO).
**Parliamentary Librarian**, Richard Paré
Director General, Information & Documentation Branch, François LeMay
Director General, Parliamentary Research Branch, Hugh Finsten

## MARINE ATLANTIC INC.

100 Cameron St., Moncton NB E1C 5Y6
506/851-3600; Fax: 506/851-3615
Toll Free: 1-800-341-7981 (Reservations)
Marine Atlantic Inc. operates passenger, auto & freight ferry services in Atlantic Canada under contract to the federal government. The company reports to the Minister of Transport.
**Chairman**, Moya Cahill
**President & CEO**, Rod Morrison
Executive Vice-President, J. Laurie Brean
Vice-President, Finance & Administration, D.J. Weaver
Vice-President, Human Resources, Bud Harbidge
Vice-President, Public Affairs, Passenger Services & Marketing, D.G. Newman
Director, Public Relations, T.G. Bartlett

## MEDICAL RESEARCH COUNCIL OF CANADA/Conseil de recherches médicales du Canada

Tower B, Holland Cross, 1600 Scott St., 5th Fl., Ottawa ON K1A 0W9
613/941-2672; Fax: 613/954-1800; Email: mrcinfocrm@hpb.hwc.ca.; URL: http://wwwmrc.hwc.ca/
Queen Elizabeth II Canadian Research Fund: 613/954-1814
The primary function of the MRC is to assist & promote basic, applied, & clinical research in Canada in the health sciences. Research is carried out in universities, in the health sciences faculties, affiliated hospitals & institutions & other departments & faculties when the research projects are highly relevant to human health. University-Industry programs create the opportunity for collaboration between Canadian companies & researchers now conducting research in Canadian universities or affliated institutions. The Council also manages the health-related networks of centres of excellence.
**President**, Dr. Henry Friesen, 613/954-1809, Email: hfriesen@hpb.hwc.ca
Secretary to Council & Acting Executive Director, Carol Clemenhagen, 613/954-1813, Email: cclemenh@hpb.hwc.ca
Director, Business Development, Marc LePage, 613/941-2725, Email: mlepage@hpb.hwc.ca
Director, Communications, Marcel Chartrand, 613/954-1812, Email: mchartrand@hpb.hwc.ca
Director, Corporate Services, Guy D'Aloisio, 613/954-1946, Email: gdaloisi@hpb.hwc.ca
Director, Ethics & International Relations, Dr. Francis Rolleston, 613/954-1801, Email: frollest@hpb.hwc.ca
Director, MRC/PMAC Health Program, Robert Dugal, 613/941-6706, Email: rdugal@pmac-acim.org
Acting Director, Programs, Dr. Claude Roy, 613/954-1959, Email: clroy@hpb.hwc.ca

## NATIONAL ADVISORY COUNCIL ON AGING/Conseil consultatif national sur le troisième âge

Postal Locator 4203A, 473 Albert St., 3rd Fl., Ottawa ON K1A 0K9
613/957-1968; Fax: 613/957-7627; Email: seniors@inet.hwc.ca; URL: http://www.hc-sc.gc.ca/seniors-aines
The Council advises the Minister of Health on matters relating to the quality of Canada's aging population. It reviews the needs & problems of seniors & recommends remedial action; consults with institutions & groups involved in aging or representing seniors; publishes reports; disseminates information & stimulates public discussion on aging.
**Minister Responsible**, Hon. Allan Rock, Q.C., 613/957-0200
Chair, Patricia Raymaker
Communications Officer, Michelle Soulière

## NATIONAL ARCHIVES OF CANADA/Archives nationales du Canada

395 Wellington St., Ottawa ON K1A 0N3
613/995-5138; Fax: 613/995-6274; URL: http://www.archives.ca/
Reference Desk: 613/995-5138

The National Archives of Canada is a research institution responsible for acquiring archival material of "every kind, nature & description" concerning all aspects of Canadian life & the development of the country. It provides research services & facilities to make this material available to the public. In addition, as part of the federal government administration, it has broad responsibilities with regard to the promotion of efficiency & economy in the management of government records. The National Archives includes private papers, public records, machine-readable archives, maps, paintings, photographs, films, sound recordings & books on Canadian history & related subject fields. Reports to government through the Minister of Canadian Heritage.

**National Archivist**, J.-P. Wallot, 613/992-2473
Asst. National Archivist, M. Swift, 613/992-7445
Director General, Archives & Government Records Branch, L. McDonald, 613/995-3525
Director General, Public Programs Branch, F. Houle, 613/996-1241

#### Federal Records Centres:

Edmonton: 8707 - 51 Ave., Edmonton AB T6H 5H1 – 403/420-3120; Fax: 403/495-2259, Chief, Brian Sloan
Halifax: 270 Bluewater Rd., Bedford NS B4B 1J6 – 902/426-5940; Fax: 902/426-8970, Chief, Cindi Palmer
Montréal: 665A, Montée de Liesse, St-Laurent QC H4T 1P5 – 514/283-4044; Fax: 514/283-7347
Ottawa: Bldg. No. 15, Tunney's Pasture, Goldenrod St., Ottawa ON K1A 0N3 – 613/954-4175; Fax: 613/952-3972, Chief, Gilles Pommainville
Québec City: 75, de Hambourg, St-Augustin QC G3A 1S6 – 418/878-2825; Fax: 418/878-3123, Chief, Guy Ricard
Toronto: 190 Carrier Dr., Etobicoke ON M9W 5R1 – 416/739-2546; Fax: 416/675-2862, Chief, Charles Dwarka
Vancouver: Lake City Industrial Park, 2751 Production Way, Burnaby BC V5A 3G7 – 604/666-6539; Fax: 604/666-4990, Chief, Gord Fryer
Winnipeg: 201 Weston St., Winnipeg MB R3E 3H4 – 204/983-8845; Fax: 204/983-4649, Chief, Rick Weinholdt

## NATIONAL ARTS CENTRE (NAC)/Centre national des Arts (CNA)

53 Elgin St., PO Box 1534, Stn B, Ottawa ON K1P 5W1
613/996-5051, 947-7000; Fax: 613/996-9578

Dedicated to the development & promotion of the performing arts, the NAC produces, co-produces & presents a wide range of theatre, music & dance productions. Reports to government through the Minister of Canadian Heritage.

**Chair**, Jean Thérèse Riley
Director & CEO, John Cripton
Deputy CEO & Director, Planification & Communications, Denise M. Perrier
Senior Artistic Advisor, Brian Macdonald
Senior Director, Human Resources, Bernard Geneste
Senior Director, Operations, Gilles Landry
Director, Communications, Kelly Ann Beaton
Chief Financial Officer, Cy Cook

## NATIONAL BATTLEFIELDS COMMISSION/ Commission des champs de bataille nationaux

390, av de Bernières, Québec QC G1R 2L7
418/648-3506; Fax: 418/648-3638

Established to preserve, administer & enhance the Plains of Abraham battlefields park in Québec City (Plains of Abraham & des Braces Park). Reports to government through the Minister of Canadian Heritage.

**Chair**, André Juneau, Archit.
Secretary, Michel Leullier

## NATIONAL CAPITAL COMMISSION (NCC)/ Commission de la capitale nationale (CCN)

#202, 40 Elgin St., Ottawa ON K1P 1C7
613/239-5555; Fax: 613/239-5063; URL: http://canada.gc.ca/depts/agencies/nccind_e.html

Responsible for the planning, development, preservation & improvement of the National Capital Region, & for the support, organization, & promotion of public activities & events which enrich the Capital as a place representative of all Canadians & which reflect its special role as the seat of the Government of Canada. Reports to government through the Minister of Canadian Heritage.

**Chair**, Marcel Beaudry
Executive Vice-President & General Manager, Roger Légaré

## NATIONAL DEFENCE (CANADA)/Défense nationale

MGen. George R. Pearkes Bldg., 101 Colonel By Dr., Ottawa ON K1A 0K2
613/992-4581; URL: http://www.debbs.ndhq.dnd.ca/dnd.htm

The control & management of the Canadian forces, & all matters relating to national defence establishments & works for the defence of Canada, fall under the authority of the Minister of National Defence, who is responsible for presenting before the Cabinet those matters of major defence policy for which Cabinet direction is required.

The Deputy Minister is the senior public servant & principal civilian advisor to the Minister on all departmental affairs. The Deputy Minister is responsible for ensuring that all policy direction emanating from the government is reflected in the administration of the department.

The *Chief of Defence Staff*, the senior military adviser to the Minister, is charged with the control & administration of the Canadian Forces. He is responsible for the effective conduct of military operations & the readiness of the Canadian Forces to meet the commitments assigned to the department by the government.

In National Defence Headquarters, the Vice Chief of the Defence Staff, the Deputy Chief of the Defence Staff, six Asst. Deputy Ministers, as well as the Judge Advocate General, report to the Deputy Minister & the Chief of the Defence Staff. The Vice Chief of the Defence Staff is the principal assistant & adviser to the Deputy Minister & the Chief of Defence Staff, & acts for the latter during his absence. The Deputy Chief of the Defence Staff is responsible to the Chief of the Defence Staff for the effective & efficient performance of the operations of the Canadian Forces.

#### ACTS ADMINISTERED

Aeronautics Act, with respect to any matter relating to defence
Army Benevolent Act
Canadian Forces Superannuation Act
Defence Services Pension Continuation Act
Emergencies Act
Emergency Preparedness Act
Garnishment, Attachment & Pension Diversion Act, with respect to members & former members of the Canadian Forces
National Defence Act
Pension Benefits Division Act, with respect to members & former members of the Canadian Forces
Visiting Forces Act
In addition, the DND administers, under the general direction of the Chief Electoral Officer, the Special Voting Rules (Schedule II to the Canada Elections Act) as they relate Canadian Forces electors.

**Minister, National Defence**, Hon. Art Eggleton, 613/996-3100, Fax: 613/995-8189
Deputy Minister, Louise Fréchette, 613/992-4258, Fax: 613/995-2028
Chief of Defence, Lt.-Gen. Maurice Baril, 613/992-5054
Acting Vice-Chief of Defence Staff, M.Gen. L.C. Campbell, 613/992-6052
Acting Deputy Chief of the Defence Staff, M.Gen. R.R.J. Henault, 613/992-3355
Asst. Deputy Minister, Finance & Corporate Services, Robert M. Emond, 613/992-0359
Asst. Deputy Minister, Infrastructure & Environment, John L. Adams, 613/945-7545
Asst. Deputy Minister, Matieriel, Pierre L. Lagueux, 613/992-6622
Asst. Deputy Minister, Personnel, L.Gen David N. Kinsman, 613/992-7582
Asst. Deputy Minister, Policy, Dr. Ken J. Calder, 613/992-3458
Director General, Finance, R.Adm. G.E. Jarvis, 613/992-6907
Director General, International Security & Policy, R.Adm. J.A. King, 613/992-2769
Director General, Public Affairs, Col. R.C. Coleman, 613/996-8959, Fax: 613/995-2610
Assoc. Asst. Deputy Minister, Personnel, Monique Boudrias, 613/992-7443
Chairman, Defence Science Advisory Board, Dr. Dan Meneley, 613/992-4070
Chief, Reserves & Cadets, M.Gen. E.W. Linden, 613/995-9802
Chief, Review Services, M.Gen. K.W. Penney, 613/995-8561
Judge Advocate General, B.Gen. Pierre Boutet, 613/992-3019
Defence Chief Information Officer, Guy Thériault, 613/995-2017

#### EMERGENCY PREPAREDNESS CANADA (EPC)/Protection civile Canada (PCC)

Jackson Bldg., 122 Bank St., 2nd Fl., Ottawa ON K1A 0W6
613/991-7077; Fax: 613/998-9589; Email: cominfo@x400.gc.ca; URL: http://hoshi.cic.sfu.ca/epc
Emergency Coordination Centre: 613/991-7000

Under the Emergency Preparedness Act, the Minister of Defence is also responsible for advancing civil emergency preparedness in Canada for emergencies of all types, including war & other armed conflict, by facilitating & coordinating among government institutions & in cooperation with provincial governments, foreign governments & international organizations, the development of civil emergency plans.

Executive Director, Dr. Eric L. Shipley, 613/991-7031
Director, Communications, André Lamalice, 613/991-7034
Senior Communications Officer, Sharleen Bannon, 613/991-7038
Senior Communications Officer, Joan Borsu, 613/991-7039

#### COMMANDS

Commander, Air Command, L.Gen. A.M. DeQuetteville, C.M.M.,C.D.
Commander, Land Force Command, L.Gen. J.M. Baril, C.M.M., C.D.
Commander, Maritime Command, R.Adm. G.L. Garnett, C.M.M., C.D.
Commander, Northern Area, Col. P. Leblanc, C.D.
Commander, Canadian Forces Recruiting, Education & Training System, M.Gen. M. Caines, C.D.

#### Operations Groups

Land Force Atlantic Area Headquarters: Halifax NS – 902/427-7580, Commander, B.Gen. H.C. Ross

Land Force Central Area Headquarters: Toronto ON – 416/733-5305, Commander, M.Gen. B.E. Stephenson, C.D.
Land Force Western Area Headquarters: Edmonton AB – 403/973-4011, Commander, M.Gen. N.B. Jeffries, C.D.
Maritime Air Group: Halifax NS – 902/427-2141, Commander, B.Gen. Brian Cameron, O.M.M., C.D.
Maritime Forces Atlantic Headquarters: Halifax NS – 902/427-6355, Commander, R.Adm. G.R. Maddison, O.M.M., M.S.C., C.D.
Maritime Forces Pacific Headquarters: Victoria BC – 250/363-2800, Commander, R.Adm. R.D. Moore, C.D.
Secteur du Québec de la Force terrestre: Montréal QC – 514/846-4101, Commander, M.Gen. A.R. Forand, S.C., C.D.

#### Canadian Forces Bases (CFB) & Detachments

BFC Bagotville: Alouette QC G0C 1A0
CFB Borden: Borden ON L0M 1C0
CFB Cold Lake: Cold Lake AB T9M 2C6
CFB Comox: Lazo BC V0R 2K0
CFB Edmonton: PO Box 10500, Edmonton AB T5J 4J5
CFB Esquimalt: FMO, Victoria BC V9A 7N2
CFB Gagetown: Oromocto NB E2V 4J5
CFB Gander: PO Box 6000, Gander NF A1V 1X1
CFB Goose Bay: Goose Airport, Stn A, Goose Bay NF A0P 1S0
CFB Greenwood: Greenwood NS B0P 1N0
CFB Halifax: FMO Halifax NS B3K 5X5
CFB Kingston: Vimy Post Office, Kingston ON K7K 7B4
BFC Montréal: St-Hubert QC J3Y 5T4
CFB Moose Jaw: PO Box 5000, Moose Jaw SK S6H 7Z8
CFB North Bay: Hornell Heights ON P0H 1P0
CFB Petawawa: Petawawa ON K8H 2X3
CFB Shilo: Shilo MB R0K 2A0
CFB Suffield: PO Box 6000, Medicine Hat AB T1A 8K8
CFB Trenton: Astra ON K0K 3W0
BFC Valcartier: Courcelette QC G0A 4Z0
CFB Winnipeg: Westwin MB R3J 3Y5

#### Canadian Forces Stations

CFS Alert: Belleville ON K0K 3S0
CFS Leitrim: Ottawa ON K1A 0K5
CFS Masset: PO Box 2000, Masset BC V0T 1M0
CFS St. John's: PO Box 2028, St. John's NF A1C 6B5

#### Canadian Service Colleges

Canadian Forces College: Toronto ON – 416/482-6800, ext.6822, Commandant, B.Gen. E.H. Gosden, C.D.
Canadian Land Forces Command & Staff College: Kingston ON – 613/451-5818, Commandant, B.Gen. M.K. Jefferey, O.M.M., C.D.
Centre for National Security Studies: Kingston ON – 613/541-5010, ext.5840, Commanding Officer, Col. J. Roeterink, C.D.
Royal Military College: Kingston ON – 613/541-6000, Commandant, B.Gen. K.C. Hague, C.D.

#### Regional Public Affairs Office (National Defence)

Québec: Tour Ouest, Guy-Favreau Complex, #911, 200, boul René Lévesque, Montréal QC H2Z 1X4 – 514/283-5272

## NATIONAL ENERGY BOARD (NEB)/Office national de l'énergie (ONE)

311 - 6 Ave. SW, Calgary AB T2P 3H2
403/292-4800; Fax: 403/292-5503; URL: http://www.neb.gc.ca

The Board is a regulatory tribunal that reports to Parliament through the Minister of Natural Resources. It regulates specific areas of the oil, gas & electricity industries relating to: construction & operation of pipelines & international power lines; traffic, tolls & tariffs of pipelines; exports of natural gas, oil & electricity; imports of gas &; regulatory control of oil & gas resources on frontier lands, in all non-Accord areas.

**Minister Responsible**, Hon. Ralph Goodale, 613/996-2007
Chair, Roland Priddle
Executive Director, Gaétan Caron
Business Leader, Applications, Brenda Kenny
Business Leader, Commodities, Terrance Rochefort
Business Leader, Corporate Services, Sylvia Farrant
Business Leader, Information Management, Scott Richardson
Business Leader, Operations, John F. McCarthy

## NATIONAL FARM PRODUCTS COUNCIL (NFPC)/Conseil national des produits agricoles

Martel Bldg., 270 Albert, 13th Fl., PO Box 3430, Stn D, Ottawa ON K1P 6L4
613/995-6752; Fax: 613/995-2097; URL: http://www.aceis.agr.ca/./nfpce.html

Operates closely with non-government marketing agencies established by federal legislation & financed through levies. Reports to government through the Minister of Agriculture & Agri-food.

**Minister Responsible**, Hon. Lyle Vanclief, 613/759-1006
Chairperson, Cynthia Currie
Vice-Chairperson, Linda Boxall
Executive Director, Vacant
Director, Operations & Regulatory & Public Affairs, Carola McWade
Director, Policy & Programs, Dr. Keith Wilkinson

#### Marketing Agencies

Canadian Broiler Hatching Egg Marketing Agency: #1101, 75 Albert St., Ottawa ON K1P 5E7 – 613/232-3023; Fax: 613/232-5241, General Manager, Paul Jelley
Canadian Chicken Marketing Agency: #300, 377 Dalhousie St., Ottawa ON K1N 9N8 – 613/241-2800; Fax: 613/241-5999, Acting General Manager, Mike Dungate
Canadian Egg Marketing Agency: #1900, 320 Queen St., Ottawa ON K1R 5A3 – 613/238-2514; Fax: 613/238-1967, CEO, Neil Currie
Canadian Turkey Marketing Agency: #102, 960 Derry Rd., Mississauga ON L5T 2J7 – 905/564-3100; Fax: 905/564-9356, Executive Director, Phil Boyd

## NATIONAL FILM BOARD OF CANADA (NFB)/Office national du film du Canada

3155, rue Côte de Liesse, St-Laurent QC H4N 2N4
514/283-9000; Fax: 514/283-8971; URL: http://www.nfb.ca/

The Board is mandated to initiate & promote the production & distribution of films in the national interest, with the primary object of interpreting Canada to Canadians & to other nations. Reports to government through the Minister of Canadian Heritage.

**Minister Responsible**, Hon. Sheila Copps
Government Film Commissioner & Board Chair, Sandra Macdonald, 514/283-9244, 613/992-3615
Director General, Corporate Affairs, Vacant, 514/283-9247, Fax: 514/283-8971
Director General, English Program Branch, Barbara Janes, 514/283-9501
Director General, French Program Branch, Doris Girard, 514/283-9285
Director, Human Resources, Guy Gauthier, 514/283-9108
Director, Technical Services & Informatics, René Villeneuve, 514/283-9147
Advisory Director, Technological Development, Robert Forget, 514/283-9148

#### Regional Centres

Edmonton: #120, 9700 Jasper Ave., Edmonton AB T5J 4C3 – 403/495-3013; Fax: 403/495-6412, Chief, Graydon McCrea
Halifax: #201, 5475 Spring Garden Rd., Halifax NS B3J 1G2 – 902/426-6000; Fax: 902/426-8901, Chief, Vacant
Moncton: 1222 Main St., Moncton NB E1C 1H6 – 506/851-6104; Fax: 506/851-2246, Producer, Pierre Bernier
Montreal: 1564, rue St-Denis, Montréal QC H2X 3K2 – 514/496-6887; Fax: 514/283-0225
Toronto: 150 John St., Toronto ON M5V 3C3 – 416/973-2979; Fax: 416/973-7007, Chief, Louise Lore
Toronto (French Program): 150 John St., Toronto ON M5V 3C3 – 416/973-2226; Fax: 416/954-0775, Producer, Jacques Bisaillon
Vancouver: #300, 1045 Howe St., Vancouver BC V6Z 2B1 – 604/666-3838; Fax: 604/666-1569, Chief, Svend-Erik Eriksen
Winnipeg: 245 Main St., Winnipeg MB R3C 1A7 – 204/983-3160; Fax: 204/983-0742, Chief, Vacant

#### Offices Abroad

France: 5, rue de Constantine, Paris 75007, France – (011-33-1) 44-18-35-40; Fax: (011-33-1) 47-05-75-89
UK: 1 Grosvenor Sq., London W1X 0AB, UK – (011-44-171) 258-6481; Fax: (011-44-171) 258-6532, Representative, Ann Vautier
USA: 1251 Ave. of the Americas, 16th Fl., New York NY 10020, USA – 514/283-9441; Fax: 514/496-1895, Sales Manager, United States, Lynne Williams

## NATIONAL GALLERY OF CANADA/Musée des Beaux-Arts du Canada

Listed in Section 6; *see* Index.

## NATIONAL JOINT COUNCIL (NJC)/Conseil national mixte

C.D. Howe Bldg., 240 Sparks St. West, 7th Fl., PO Box 1525, Stn B, Ottawa ON K1P 5V2
613/990-1807

The NJC provides a forum for consultation on labour issues between the Government of Canada & the bargaining agents for it's employees.

**Chair & Employer Side**, c/o Human Resources Policy Branch, Treasury Board, 300 Laurier Ave. West, 4th Fl., Ottawa ON K1A 0R5, Vacant
Co-Chair & Bargaining Agent Side, G. Myers, c/o International Brotherhood of Electrical Workers, Local 2228, 1091 Wellington St., Ottawa ON K1Y 2Y4
General Secretary, F.M. Lalonde

## NATIONAL LIBRARY OF CANADA/Bibliothèque nationale du Canada

Listed in Section 6, *see* Index.

## NATIONAL MUSEUM OF SCIENCE & TECHNOLOGY/Musée national des sciences et de la technologie

Listed in Section 6; *see* Index

## NATIONAL PAROLE BOARD/Commission nationale des libérations conditionnelles

340 Laurier Ave. West, Ottawa ON K1A 0R1
613/954-7474; Fax: 613/995-4380; URL: http://canada.gc.ca/depts/agencies/npbind_e.html

The Board exercises authority for the conditional release of federal inmates & makes conditional release decisions on cases of those inmates in provinces & territories which do not have their own parole board. The Board also grants, issues, denies & revokes pardons & makes recommendations for the exercise of the royal prerogative of mercy.

**Minister Responsible**, Hon. Herb Gray, 613/991-2924
Chair, Willie Gibbs, 613/954-1150
Executive Vice-Chair, Renée Collette
Vice-Chair, Appeal Division, Catherine Ebbs-Lepage
Vice-Chair, Atlantic, Léonard J. LeBlanc
Vice-Chair, Ontario, Sheila P. Henriksen
Vice-Chair, Pacific, Kathy Louis
Vice-Chair, Prairies, Arthur Majkut
Vice-Chair, Québec, Serge Lavallée

#### Regional Offices

Atlantic: 1045 Main St., 1st Fl., Moncton NB E1C 1H1 – 506/851-6345; Fax: 506/851-6926, Regional Director, H. Chevalier
Ontario: #100, 516 O'Connor Dr., Kingston ON K7P 1N3 – 613/634-3857; Fax: 613/634-3861, Regional Director, S. Ferguson
Pacific: #305, 32315 South Fraser Way, Abbotsford BC V2T 1W6 – 604/854-2468; Fax: 604/854-2498, Regional Director, F. Simmons
Prairies: PO Box 9210, Saskatoon SK S7K 3X5 – 306/975-4228; Fax: 306/975-5892, Regional Director, N. Fagnou
Québec: 200, boul René-Lévesque ouest, 2e étage, Montréal QC H2Z 1X4 – 514/283-4584; Fax: 514/283-5484, Regional Director, Serge Lavallée

## NATIONAL RESEARCH COUNCIL CANADA (NRC)/Conseil national de recherches Canada (CNR)

Bldg. M-58, 1200 Montreal Rd., Ottawa ON K1A 0R6
613/993-9101; Fax: 613/952-7928; URL: http://www.nrc.ca/
IRAP Information: 613/993-1790
CISTI Information: 613/993-1600

Canada's leading national science & technology agency with laboratories & facilities coast to coast. NRC helps Canadian firms increase their technical competence, improve productivity, develop new products & solve technical problems in areas such as transportation, construction, biotechnology, manufacturing systems, industrial materials, information & telecommunication technologies, & aerospace research.

NRC carries out R&D in collaboration with, & maintains national facilities for, universities, other government departments & private sector organizations, through 16 research institutes.

In addition, the Canada Institute for Scientific & Technical Information (CISTI) maintains the largest S&T collection in the country & provides customized literature searches, & maintains highly specialized databanks. NRC's Industrial Research Assistance Program (IRAP) helps Canadian firms in the development or acquisition of technology.

**President**, Arthur J. Carty, 613/993-2024
Acting Vice-President, Research, Roy Van Koughnett, 613/993-9244
Vice-President, Technology & Industry Support, Jacques Lyrette, 613/998-3664
Secretary General, Lucie Lapointe
Director General, Canadian Institute for Scientific & Technical Information, Margot Montgomery
Director General, Industrial Research Assistance Program, David Ellis, 613/993-0695

#### IRAP Regional Offices

Alberta: Industrial Development Department, 250 Karl Clark Rd., PO Box 8330, Stn F, Edmonton AB T6H 5X2 – 403/495-6508; Fax: 403/495-6510, Manager, Andrew Gilliland
British Columbia: 3650 Wesbrook Mall, Vancouver BC V6S 2L2 – 604/221-3110; Fax: 604/221-3101, Manager, Desmond Mullan
Manitoba: 435 Ellice Rd., Winnipeg MB R3B 1Y6 – 204/984-6479; Fax: 204/983-8351, Acting Manager, Andrew Gilliland
New Brunswick: 921 College Hill Rd., Fredericton NB E3B 6C2 – 506/452-3831; Fax: 506/452-3827, Manager, David Healey
Newfoundland: Viking Bldg., 136 Crosbie Rd., St. John's NF A1B 3K3 – 709/772-5228; Fax: 709/772-5067, Manager, David Rideout
Nova Scotia: 1411 Oxford St., Halifax NS B3H 3Z1 – 902/426-6264; Fax: 902/426-1624, Manager, David Healey
Ontario: #1101, 200 Town Centre Ct., Scarborough ON M1P 5E9 – 416/973-4483; Fax: 416/973-9461, Manager, Roy Crew
Prince Edward Island: West Royalty Industrial Park, 35 First Ave., Charlottetown PE C1E 1B0 – 902/566-7642; Fax: 902/566-7641, Manager, David Healey
Québec: #P-101, 75, boul de Mortagne, Boucherville QC J4B 6Y4 – 514/641-5305; Fax: 514/641-5301, Manager, Jean-Pierre Lemieux
Saskatchewan: 110 Gymnasium Pl., Saskatoon SK S7N 0W9 – 306/975-4717; Fax: 306/975-4714, Acting Manager, Andrew Gilliland

#### Research & Technology Institutes

•Biotechnology Research Centre (BRC)/Institut de recherche en biotechnologie: 6100, av Royalmount, Montréal QC H4P 2R2 – 514/496-6100; Fax: 514/496-6388
Director General, Michel Desrochers
•Herzberg Institute of Astrophysics (HIA)/Institut Herzberg d'astrophysique: 5071 West Saanish Rd., Victoria BC V8X 4M6 – 613/363-0040; Fax: 613/363-8483
Director General, Don Morton
•Industrial Materials Institute (IMI)/Institut des matériaux industriels: 75, boul de Montagne, Boucherville QC J4B 6Y4 – 514/641-5050; Fax: 514/641-5101
Director General, Jacques Martel
•Institute for Advanced Manufacturing Technology (IME)/Institut des technologies de fabrication Intégrée: 1500 Montréal Rd., Ottawa ON K1A 0R6 – 613/993-5802; Fax: 613/952-6081
Director General, Walter Petryschuk
•Institute for Aerospace Research (IAR)/Institut de recherche aérospatiale: 1500 Montreal Rd., Ottawa ON K1A 0R6 – 613/993-0141; Fax: 613/952-7214
Acting Director General, Tom LeFeuvre
•Institute for Biodiagnostics/Institut du biodiagnostic: 435 Ellice Ave., Winnipeg MB R3B 1Y6 – 204/983-7526; Fax: 204/984-4722
Director General, Ian Smith
•Institute for Biological Sciences (IBS)/Institut des sciences biologiques: 1500 Montreal Rd., Ottawa ON K1A 0R6 – 613/993-7506; Fax: 613/957-7867
Director General, Gabrielle Adams
•Institute for Chemical Process & Environmental Technology (ICPET)/Institut de technologie des procédés chimiques et de l'environnement: 1500 Montreal Rd., Ottawa ON K1A 0R6 – 613/993-4041; Fax: 613/957-8231
Director General, Ed Capes
•Institute for Information Technology (IIT)/Institut de technologie de l'information: 1500 Montreal Rd., Ottawa ON K1A 0R6 – 613/993-2491; Fax: 613/952-0074
Acting Director General, M. Gentleman
•Institute for Marine Biosciences (IMB)/Institut des biosciences marines: 1411 Oxford St., Halifax NS B3H 3Z1 – 902/426-8332; Fax: 902/426-9413
Director General, Roger Foxall
•Institute for Marine Dynamics (IMD)/Institut de dynamique marine: Memorial University, Kerwin Pl. & Arctic Ave., PO Box 12093, Stn A, St. John's NF A1B 3T5 – 709/772-4939; Fax: 709/772-3101
Acting Director General, Roger Foxall
•Institute for Microstructural Sciences (IMS)/Institut des sciences des microstructures: 1500 Montreal Rd., Ottawa ON K1A 0R6 – 613/993-9369; Fax: 613/957-8734
Director General, Peter Dawson
•Institute for National Measurement Standards/Institut des étalons nationaux de mesure: 1500 Montreal Rd., Ottawa ON K1A 0R6 – 613/990-9326; Fax: 613/952-5113
Director General, Roy Van Koughnett
•Institute for Research in Construction (IRC)/Institut de recherche en construction: 1500 Montreal Rd., Ottawa ON K1A 0R6 – 613/993-3772; Fax: 613/941-0822
Director General, George Seaden
•Plant Biotechnology Institute (PBI)/Institut de biotechnologie des plantes: 110 Gymnasium Rd., Saskatoon SK S7N 0W9 – 306/975-5248; Fax: 306/975-4839
Director General, Kutty Kartha
•Steacie Institute for Molecular Sciences/Institut Steacie des sciences moléculaires: 100 Sussex Dr., Ottawa ON K1A 0R6 – 613/993-1053; Fax: 613/954-5242
Director General, Peter Hackett

#### Technology Centres

•Canadian Hydraulics Centre/Centre canadien d'hydraulique: Bldg M-32, Montreal Rd., Ottawa ON K1A 0R6 – 613/993-2417; Fax: 613/952-7679
Director, Bruce Pratte
•Centre for Fluid Power Technology/Centre de technologie des fluides puissants: Ottawa ON – 613/993-2731; Fax: 613/952-1395
Director, Mohan Vijay
•Centre for Surface Transportation Technology/Centre de technologie des transports de surface: U-89, 1500 Montreal Rd., Ottawa ON K1A 0R6 – 613/998-9639; Fax: 613/957-0831
Director, John Coleman
•Thermal Technology Centre/Centre de technologie thermique: M-17, Montreal Rd., Ottawa ON K1A 0R6 – 613/993-4892; Fax: 613/954-1235
Director, Keith Snelson

## NATIONAL ROUND TABLE ON THE ENVIRONMENT & ECONOMY (NRTEE)/Table ronde nationale sur l'environnement et l'économie (TRNEE)

Canada Bldg., #200, 344 Slater St., Ottawa ON K1R 7Y3
613/992-7189; Fax: 613/992-7385; Email: admin@nrtee-trnee.ca; URL: http://www.nrtee-trnee.ca

The NRTEE was created to play the role of catalyst in identifying, explaining & promoting, in all sectors of Canadian society & in all regions of Canada, principles & practices of sutainable development. Specifically, the agency identifies issues that have both environmental & economic implications, explores these implications, & attempts to identify actions that will balance economic prosperity with environmental preservation.

The NRTEE is composed of a Chair & up to 24 distinguished Canadians appointed by the federal government as opinion leaders representing a variety of regions & sectors of Canadian society including business, labour, academia, environmental organizations, & First Nations.

**Chair**, Dr. Stuart Smith
Executive Director & CEO, David McGuinty

Corporate Secretary & Director, Operations, Gene Nyberg
Manager, Communications, Moira Forrest
Office Manager & Coordinator, Conference/Meeting, Cathy Heroux

## NATIONAL SEARCH & RESCUE SECRETARIAT/Secrétariat national de recherches et sauvetage

Standard Life Bldg., 275 Slater St., 4th Fl., Ottawa ON K1A 0K2
Fax: 613/996-3746; URL: http://www.nss.gc.ca
Toll Free: 1-800-727-9414
The Secretariat provides a central managerial role in the overall coordination of search & rescue. It addresses program & policy issues related to the National Search & Rescue Program, & advises the lead minister for search & rescue.
**Minister Responsible**, Hon. Art Eggleton
Executive Director, R. William Slaughter, 613/992-0054

## NATURAL RESOURCES CANADA (NRCan)/ Ressources naturelles Canada (RNCan)

580 Booth St., Ottawa ON K1A 0E4
613/995-0947; Fax: 613/996-9094; URL: http://www.NRCan.gc.ca/
Emergency Operations Centre: 613/995-5555, 943-0000
The Minister of Natural Resources is responsible for coordinating, promoting & recommending national policies concerning energy, mines, minerals & other non-renewable resources & formulating plans for their conservation, development & use. In addition the Department is authorized to conduct research & technical surveys to assess mineral & energy resources, including a full & scientific examination & survey of Canada's geological structure & legal boundaries. NRCan also Prepares & provides public maps, conducts scientific & economic research relating to the energy, mining, & metallurgical industries, & establishes & operates scientific laboratories required for the conduct of these duties.

#### ACTS ADMINISTERED

Atomic Energy Act
Canadian Exploration & Development Incentives Program Act
Canadian Exploration & Incentives Program Act
Canadian Home Insulation Program Act
Co-operative Energy Act
Department of Energy, Mines & Resources Act
Energy Monitoring Act
Energy Supplies Emergency Act (Environment & Health have a role in respect of environmental considerations)
Explosives Act
Hibernia Development Project Act
Home Insulation (Nova Scotia & PEI) Program Act
International Boundary Act
Nuclear Liability Act
Oil Substitution & Conservation Act
Petro-Canada Act
Petroleum & Gas Revenue Tax Act
Petroleum Incentives Program Act

#### Administration of Acts re Changes in Provincial Boundaries

Alberta Act
Alberta/BC Boundary Act, 1974
Alberta/NWT Boundary Act,1958
BC-Yukon-NWT Boundary Act, 1967
Manitoba Boundaries Extension Act, 1912
Manitoba-NWT Boundary Act, 1966
Manitoba/Saskatchewan Boundary Act, 1966
Ontario Boundaries Extension Act, 1912
Ontario-Manitoba Boundary Act
Québec Boundaries Extension Act, 1912
Saskatchewan/NWT Boundary Act, 1966

#### Acts Administered in Part by Minister of Natural Resources

Access to Information Act
Arctic Waters Pollution Prevention Act (Transport/ Indian & Northern Affairs)
Canada Lands Survey Act (Indian & Northern Affairs)
Canada-Newfoundland Atlantic Accord Implementation Act (Finance/Revenue)
Canada-Nova Scotia Offshore Petroleum Resources Accord Implementation Act (Finance/Revenue)
Canada Oil & Gas Act (Indian & Northern Affairs)
Canada Petroleum Resources Act (Indian & Northern Affairs)
Canadian Ownership & Control Determination Act
Emergencies Act
Energy Administration Act (Environment/Fisheries & Oceans)
International Boundary Commission Act (Indian & Northern Affairs)
International Boundary Water Treatment Act
Motor Vehicle Fuel Consumption Standards Act (Transport)
National Energy Board Act (Transport)
Oil & Gas Production & Conservation Act (Indian & Northern Affairs)
Privacy Act
Resources & Technical Surveys Act (Fisheries & Oceans/Environment)
Transportation of Dangerous Goods Act
**Minister**, Hon. Ralph Goodale, 613/996-2007, Fax: 613/996-4516
**Secretary of State, Parks**, Hon. Andy Mitchell, 613/996-3434, Fax: 613/991-2147
Deputy Minister, Jean C. McCloskey, 613/992-3458, Fax: 613/992-3828

#### Communications Branch

613/992-0267; Fax: 613/996-9094
Director General, Denis St-Jean, 613/996-3355
Director, Client Services Division, Pierre Sauvé, 613/996-8070
Director, Strategic Analysis & Research, Mary O'Rourke, 613/992-9323

#### Legal Services

613/992-7795; Fax: 613/995-2598
General Counsel, S.K. Fraser, 613/992-0039
Senior Counsel, C. Scullion, Q.C., 613/992-0432

#### Canada Centre for Mineral & Energy Technology (CANMET)

580 Booth St., Ottawa ON K1A 0E4
As a key research & technology development arm of NRCan, CANMET works with the minerals, metals & energy industries to find safer, cleaner & more efficient methods to develop & use Canada's mineral & energy resources. In partnership with clients, the agency performs & sponsors commercial & cost-shared research & development, & technology transfer. The Energy Technology Branch & Mineral Technology Branch have recently been joined with policy groups of Energy Sector & Minerals & Metals Sector to ensure that policies & regulations are based on sound science.
Asst. Deputy Minister, Minerals & Metals Sector, Linda Keen, 613/992-2490, Fax: 613/996-7425
Asst. Deputy Minister, Energy Sector, Michael Cleland, 613/996-7848, Fax: 613/992-1405

#### Mineral Technology Branch

568 Booth St., Ottawa ON K1A 0G1
Director, Mining & Mineral Sciences Laboratory, R. Sage, 613/995-8248, Fax: 613/992-8735
Director, Western Research Centre, T.D. Brown, 1 Oil Patch Dr., Devon AB T0C 1E0, 403/987-8214, Fax: 403/987-8690

#### Mining & Mineral Sciences Laboratory

555 Booth St., Ottawa ON K1A 0G1
Director, R. Hargreaves, 613/947-6604, Fax: 613/992-8928

#### Policy, Planning & Services Branch

555 Booth St., Ottawa ON K1A 0G1
613/992-0593; Fax: 613/995-6881
Director, Johanne Desjardins, 613/996-1700, Fax: 613/952-7501
Director, Administrative & Informatics Services Division, Louis Marmen, 613/943-0273
Director, Corporate Planning & Communications Division, Keith Belinko, 613/995-4267, Fax: 613/995-3192
Director, Engineering & Technical Services Division, R. Webster, 613/996-5679
Director, Library & Documentation Services Division, M. Laurin, 562 Booth St., Ottawa ON K1A 0G1, 613/995-4059, Fax: 613/952-2587

### CANADIAN FOREST SERVICE (CFS)

580 Booth St., Ottawa ON K1A 0E4
613/947-7399; URL: http://mf.ncr.forestry.ca
Asst. Deputy Minister, Dr. Yvan Hardy, 819/947-7400

#### Industry, Economics & Programs Branch

Director General, Doug Ketcheson, 613/947-9052
Director, Economics & Statistics Division, D. Boulter, 613/947-9076
Director, Harvesting & Wood Products Division, M. Mes-Hartree, 613/947-9040
Director, Paper & Allied Industry Division, R. Glandon, 613/947-9051
Director, Programs Division, D. Welsh, 613/947-9053

#### Policy, Planning & International Affairs Branch

Director General, Jacques Carette, 613/947-9100
Director, International Affairs Division, D. Drake, 613/947-9078
Director, Policy Division, Vacant

#### Science Branch

Acting Director General, G. Miller, 819/947-8984
Director, Science Marketing & Business Opportunities Division, W. Cheliak, 613/947-9012
Director, Science Programs Division, G. Miller, 613/947-8984
Director, Science Relations Division, D. Winston, 613/947-8986

#### CFS Regional Offices

Edmonton: 5320 - 122 St., Edmonton AB T6H 3S5 – 403/435-7210; Fax: 403/435-7359, Director General, B. Case
Fredericton: Regent St. South, PO Box 4000, Fredericton NB E3B 5P7 – 506/452-3500; Fax: 506/452-3525, Director General, Hap Oldham
Québec: 1055, rue du PEPS, CP 3800, Ste-Foy QC G1V 4C7 – 418/648-5850; Fax: 418/648-5849, Director General, Normand Lafrenière
Sault Ste. Marie: 1219 Queen St. East, PO Box 490, Sault Ste. Marie ON P6A 5M7 – 705/949-9461; Fax: 705/759-5700, Director General, E. Kondo
Victoria: 506 West Burnside Rd., Victoria BC V8Z 1M5 – 250/363-0600; Fax: 250/363-0775, Director General, Carl H. Winget

### CORPORATE SERVICES SECTOR

613/995-4243; Fax: 613/922-8922
Asst. Deputy Minister, Richard B. Fadden, 613/995-4252
Acting Director General, Assets Management, Administrative Services Branch, Claude Menard, 613/996-0981
Director General, Financial Management Branch, Dave Bickerton, 613/943-8763

Director General, Human Resources Services, Vacant, 613/996-4008
Director, Accounting Policy & Systems Division, J. Klimczak
Director, Information Management Branch, Vacant, 613/996-8261
Director, Strategic Direction & Coordination Division, Vacant
Director, Technical Services Division, Vacant

### EARTH SCIENCES SECTOR
Asst. Deputy Minister, Dr. Marc Denis Everell, 613/992-9983
Chief Geoscientist, Dr. Jim. Franklin, 601 Booth St., Ottawa ON K1A 0E8, 613/995-4482
Executive Director, Business Development, David Carney, 615 Booth St., Ottawa ON K1A 0E9, 613/996-0441, Fax: 613/995-8737
Senior Communications Advisor, Communications Office, Dr. Robin Riddihough, 613/947-2789

#### Geological Survey of Canada (GSC)
601 Booth St., Ottawa ON K1A 0E8
613/996-3919; Fax: 613/996-9990;
Email: gsc_bookstore@gsc.nrcan.gc.ca; URL: http://www.emr.ca/gsc/; NAISMap GIS URL: http://www-nais.ccm.NRCan.gc.ca/wnaismap/naismap.html
Bookstore: 613/995-4342
Geoscience information is used to find & develop natural resources & understand the impact natural resource exploitations can have on the environment. Through environment-related activities, provides industry with the knowledge required to face environmental challenges, particularly in dealing with various land use issues, & the influence of activities on the environment & provides Canadian governments, at all levels, with scientifically sound data on which to base their policies & regulations.

#### Minerals & Regional Geoscience Branch
Director General, Dr. Murray Duke, 613/995-4093
Director, GSC Continental Geoscience, Dr. Janet King, 613/995-4314, Fax: 613/995-7322
Acting Director, Mineral Resources Division, C. Jefferson, 613/996-9223

#### Sedimentary & Marine Geoscience Branch
Also known as the Geophysics & Marine Geoscience Branch.
Director General, Sedimentary & Marine Geoscience Branch, Dr. Richard T. Haworth, 613/995-2340
Director, GSC Atlantic, Dr. Jacob Verhoef, Challenger Drive, PO Box 1006, Dartmouth NS B2Y 4A2, 902/426-3448
Director, GSC Calgary, Dr. Grant Mossop, #3303 - 33 St. NW, Calgary AB T2L 2A7, 403/292-7049
Director, GSC Québec, Aicha Achab, 2535, boul Laurier, CP 7500, Ste-Foy QC G1V 4C7, 418/654-2603
Director, Terrain Sciences, Dr. Jean-Serge Vincent, 613/995-4938
•Canada Centre for Remote Sensing
588 Booth St., Ottawa ON K1A 0Y7
613/947-1216; Fax: 613/947-3125; URL: http://www.ccrs.nrcan.gc.ca/
Director General, Dr. Edryd Shaw, 613/947-1222
Director, Applications Division, F.E. Guertin, 613/947-1356
Director, Data Acquisition Division, Dr. S. Till, 613/998-9060
Acting Director, Geographic Information Systems & Services, Dr. Mossad Allam
Director, Methods & Systems Division, Dr. R.A. O'Neil, 613/947-1245
Director, Technology Assessment Division, A.L. Whitney, 613/947-1211
•Centre for Topographic Information
#010, 2144, rue King ouest, Sherbrooke QC J1J 2E8
819/564-5600; Fax: 819/564-5698
Director, Yves Belzile, 819/564-5602
Acting Asst. Director, Data Standardization Section, D. DeGagne
•Geodetic Survey Division
615 Booth St., Ottawa ON K1A 0E9
613/995-4282
Acting Director, Mike Corey
Chief, Geodetic Networks, L.W. Nabe, 613/995-4341
•Legal Surveys Division
615 Booth St., Ottawa ON K1A 0E9
613/995-4356; URL: http://www.geocan.NRCan.gc.ca/lsd/
Surveyor General, Michael O'Sullivan
Acting Asst. Surveyor General, P. Sauvé
Commissioner, International Boundary Commission, S. Jacques

#### Geomatics Canada
580 Booth St., Ottawa ON K1A 0E4
613/995-4321; URL: http://www.geocan.nrcan.gc.ca/
Surveys Canadian lands & waters; prepares & distributes topographic, geographic, electoral & aeronautical maps & digital products, surveys federal-provincial boundaries; manages a national program for acquiring & using remote sensing data.

#### Mapping & Services Branch
615 Booth St., Ottawa ON K1A 0E9
613/995-4945; Fax: 613/995-8737
Canada Map Office: 1-800-465-6277 or 613/952-7009

#### Regional Offices/Surveys, Mapping & Remote Sensing
Alberta: #930, 9700 Jasper Ave., Edmonton AB T5J 4C3 – 403/420-2495; Fax: 403/495-4052, Regional Surveyor, G.E. Olsson
Atlantic: 136 Victoria St., Amherst NS B4H 1Y1 – 902/661-6766; Fax: 902/661-6769, Acting Regional Surveyor, G. Isaacs
British Columbia: #800, 1550 Alberni St., Vancouver BC V6G 3C6 – 604/666-5316; Fax: 604/666-0522, Regional Surveyor, D.K. Neilson
Manitoba: #501, 275 Portage Ave., Winnipeg MB R3B 2B3 – 204/983-4954; Fax: 204/983-0157, Regional Surveyor, G.W. Kitchen
Northwest Territories: Bellanca Bldg., 50th St., 8th Fl., PO Box 668, Yellowknife NT X1A 2N5 – 867/920-8295; Fax: 867/873-9949, Regional Surveyor, L. McNeice
Ontario: #606, 55 St. Clair Ave. East, Toronto ON M4T 1M2 – 416/973-7503; Fax: 416/973-6043, Regional Surveyor, Jim Hill
Québec: 2144, rue King ouest, Sherbrooke QC J1J 2E8 – 819/564-5781; Fax: 819/564-5775, Regional Surveyor, Jacques Sasseville
Saskatchewan: #304, 2110 Hamilton St., Regina SK S4P 2E3 – 306/780-5401; Fax: 306/780-5191, Regional Surveyor, D.A. Bouck
Yukon: #225, 300 Main St., Whitehorse YT Y1A 2B5 – 867/667-3950; Fax: 867/668-2382, Regional Surveyor, S.A. Hutchinson

#### Polar Continental Shelf Project
#6146, 615 Booth St., Ottawa ON K1A 0E4
613/947-1601; Fax: 613/947-1611
Resolute NWT Base: 403/252-3872; Fax: 403/252-3605
Tuktoyaktuk NWT Base: 403/997-2333; Fax: 403/977-2144
Director, Bonni Hrycyk, 613/947-1601, Email: bhrycyk@NRCan.gc.ca

#### Policy, Planning & Information Services Branch
Director General, P. Fisher, 819/996-9551, Fax: 819/953-8296
Director, Coordination & Planning Division, G. Kendall, 613/992-5032, Fax: 613/996-9670
Director, Geoscience Information Division, A.E. Bourgeois, 613/995-4089, Fax: 613/996-8748
Director, Planning & Administration Division, N.J. Corbett, 613/995-3665, Fax: 613/996-9670
Special Advisor, Policy, Planning & Information Services Branch, Dr. A.G. Plant, 613/995-9495, Fax: 613/996-9670

### ENERGY SECTOR
580 Booth St., Ottawa ON K1A 0E4
613/996-7432; Fax: 613/992-1405
Acting Asst. Deputy Minister, Michael Cleland, 613/996-7848
Director, Management Services Division, L. Marmen, 613/943-0273
Director, Operations & Research, M. Rodrigue, 613/996-5914
Manager, Deep River Disposal Project, P.A. Brown, 613/996-2395

#### Energy Efficiency Branch
Director General, Bill Jarvis, 613/995-0081,
Energy Efficiency Programs, 613/996-7512; Fax: 613/943-1590
Transportation Energy Division, 613/995-7300; Fax: 613/952-8169
Alternative Energy & Technology Division, 613/996-2873
Director, Demand Policy & Analysis Division, N.K. Marty
Director, Industrial, Commercial & Institutional Programs, R.A. McKenzie
Director, Residential, Regulatory & Information Programs Division, Vacant
Director, Transportation Energy Use Division, A.C. Taylor

#### Energy Policy Branch
Acting Director General, S. Kirby, 613/996-7669
Director, Economic & Fiscal Analysis Division, J.P. Campbell, 613/996-2663
Director, Energy Forecasting Division, N. McIlveen, 613/995-8762
Acting Director, Environment Division, B. Moore, 613/996-6474
Director, International Division, G. Winstanley, 613/996-2993
Director, Policy Analysis & Coordination Division, J.T. Lowe, 613/995-2821
Acting Director, Projects & Industrial Benefits Division, J.P. Campbell, 613/996-2663

#### Energy Resources Branch
Director General, D. Whelan
Director, Frontier Lands Management Division, D. Cioccio
Director, Natural Gas Division, J.S. Booth
Director, Oil Division, R. Lyman
Director, Renewable & Electrical Energy Division, D. Burpee

#### Energy Technology Branch (CANMET)
613/996-6220; Fax: 613/996-9416
Director General, B.D. Cook
Director, Energy Diversification Research Laboratory (Varennes QC), Gilles Jean, 514/652-6639, Fax: 514/652-5177
Acting Director, Energy Efficiency Centre, F.R. Campbell, 613/996-5419

#### Office of Energy Research & Development (OERD)
613/995-8860; Fax: 613/995-6146
Director General, Vacant
Senior Advisor, Science Policy & Planning Division, K.M. Cliffe

#### Uranium & Nuclear Energy Branch
Director General, R.W. Morrison

Director, Radioactive Waste Division, P.A. Brown, 613/996-2395

### MINERALS & METALS SECTOR
580 Booth St., Ottawa ON K1A 0E4

#### Economic & Financial Analysis Branch
613/995-4577; Fax: 613/943-8453
Director General, Keith J. Brewer, 613/992-2662
Director, Economic Analysis Division, D.L. Hull, 613/995-5301
Director, Financial & Corporate Analysis Division, R.K. Jones, 613/995-3422
Director, Fiscal Analysis Divsion, W.D. Kitts, 613/995-6351
Director, Tax Legislation Interpretation Division, R. Clark, 613/996-3286

#### Mineral & Metal Policy Branch
Director General, William J. McCann, 613/995-7029, Fax: 613/996-7425
Senior Policy Advisor, A. Ignatow
Director, Coal, Ferrous & Industrial Minerals Division, D.M. Lagacé, 613/992-2018
Director, International Division, B. McKean, 613/995-2661
Director, Nonferrous Division, R. Telewiak, 613/992-4481
Director, Regional & Intergovernmental Affairs Division, A. Clark, 613/995-8839
Director, Resource Management Division, D.W. Pasho, 613/992-7958

### STRATEGIC PLANNING & COORDINATION BRANCH
Coordinator, P. McLean
Director General, Audit & Evaluation Branch, Marcel Gibeault, 613/996-4940, Fax: 613/992-8799
Director, Corporate Secretariat, M. Macies, 613/947-8235
Director, Policy Coordination & Planning Division, L. Ree, 613/995-9263
Director, Science & Technology Policy Division, Vacant
Director, Sustainable Development & Environment Division, J. Forster, 613/992-4451

### SITING TASK FORCE SECRETARIAT
580 Booth St., 9th Fl., Ottawa ON K1A 0E4
613/995-5201; Fax: 613/996-6206
Project Manager, P.A. Brown, 613/996-2395
Chief, Technical Operations (North), Dr. D. Paktunc, 613/995-3236

#### Associated Agencies, Boards & Commissions
Listed alphabetically in detail, this section
Atomic Energy of Canada Ltd.
Atomic Energy Control Board
International Boundary Commission
National Energy Board

#### Other Associated Agencies, Boards & Commissions
- Energy Council of Canada: #400, 30 Colonnade Rd., Ottawa ON K2E 7J6 – 613/952-6469; Fax: 613/952-6470

Executive Director, Dr. E.P. Cockshutt

## NATURAL SCIENCES & ENGINEERING RESEARCH COUNCIL OF CANADA (NSERC)/ Conseil de recherches en sciences naturelles et en génie du Canada (CRSNG)
Constitution Square, 350 Albert St., Ottawa ON K1A 1H5
613/996-7235; Fax: 613/992-5337; Email: comm@nserc.ca; URL: http://www.nserc.ca
NSERC fosters the discovery & application of knowledge through the support of university research & the training of scientists & engineers. The Council promotes the use of this knowledge to build a strong national economy & improve the quality of life of all Canadians. NSERC fulfills its mission by awarding grants & scholarships through a competitive process & by building partnerships among universities, governments & the private sector.
**President**, Thomas A. Brzustowski, 613/995-5840
Secretary to Council, Marilyn Taylor, 613/995-5896
Director General, Common Administrative Services Directorate, Laurent Nador, 613/995-3914
Director General, Research Grants & Scholarships Directorate, Dr. Nigel Lloyd, 613/995-5833
Director General, Research Partnerships Directorate, Leo Derikx, 613/996-1545
Director, Policy & International Relations, Steve Shugar, 613/995-6449

## NORTH AMERICAN COMMISSION FOR ENVIRONMENTAL COOPERATION (NACEC)/ Commission Nord-Américaine de coopération environnementale
Secretariat, #200, 393, rue St-Jacques ouest, Montréal QC H2Y 1N9
514/350-4300; Fax: 514/350-4314
Established to improve environmental protection efforts in North America & complement the environmental provisions of the North American Free Trade Agreement (NAFTA). Comprises a Council of Ministers, Secretariat & Consultive Committee with representatives from Canadian, American & Mexican governments. Promotes sustainable development, provides trinational forum for the fight against pollution & advocates the observance of laws & regulations.
**Executive Director**, Victor Lichtinger
Director, G. Block
Manager, Communications, Rachel Vincent

## NORTH AMERICAN FREE TRADE AGREEMENT (NAFTA) SECRETARIAT/ Secrétariat de l'ALÉNA
Canadian Section, #705, 90 Sparks St., Ottawa ON K1P 5B4
613/992-9388; Fax: 613/992-9392
**Canadian Secretary**, Cathy Beehan
Deputy Secretary, Michael Eastman

## NORTHERN PIPELINE AGENCY CANADA (NPAC)/Administration du pipe-line du Nord Canada (APNC)
Lester B. Pearson Bldg., 125 Sussex Dr., Ottawa ON K1A 0G2
613/993-7466; Fax: 613/998-8787; URL: http://canada.gc.ca/depts/agencies/npaind_e.html
The Agency was established to oversee the planning & construction of the Canadian portion of the Alaska Highway Gas Pipeline to provide access to the Arctic natural gas reserves of both Canada & the United States.
**Commissioner**, Robert G. Wright
Special Advisor, Policy & Public Affairs, Bruce E. Macdonald

## Office of the Commissioner of OFFICIAL LANGUAGES/Commissariat aux langues officielles
110 O'Connor St., Ottawa ON K1A 0T8
613/996-6368; Fax: 613/993-5082; URL: http://ocol-clo.gc.ca
**Commissioner/Commissaire**, Dr. Victor C. Goldbloom, O.C., O.Q.
Director General, Investigations Branch, Michel Robichaud
Director General, Policy Branch, Gérard Finn
Executive Director, Corporate Secretariat & Regional Operations Branch, Monique Matza
Director, Corporate Services Branch, Marie Bergeron
Director, Legal Services Branch, Richard Tardif

## PACIFIC PILOTAGE AUTHORITY CANADA/ Administration de Pilotage du Pacifique Canada
#300, 1199 West Hastings St., Vancouver BC V6E 4G9
604/666-6771; Fax: 604/666-6093
The Authority operates pilotage services in Canadian waters in & around British Columbia. Reports to government through the Minister of Transportation.
**Chair**, Dennis B. Mclennan
Corporate Secretary & Office Manager, Eileen M. Hall
Controller, Bruce D. Chadwick
Director, Marine Operations, Capt. R.P. Heath

## PATENTED MEDICINE PRICES REVIEW BOARD/Conseil d'examen du prix des médicaments brevetés
Standard Life Centre, #1400, 333 Laurier Ave. West, PO Box L40, Ottawa ON K1P 1C1
613/952-7360; Fax: 613/952-7626; Email: pmprb@pmprb-cepmb.gc.ca; URL: http://www.pmprb-cepmb.gc.ca
**Chair**, Dr. R.G. Elgie, 613/952-7625
Vice-Chair, R. Sureau, 613/954-0454
Executive Director, W.D. Critchley, 613/952-7622
Secretary to the Board, S. Dupont Kirby, 613/954-8299

## PRIVACY COMMISSIONER OF CANADA/ Commissariat à la protection de la vie privée du Canada
Tower B, Place de Ville, 112 Kent St., Ottawa ON K1A 1H3
613/995-2410; Fax: 613/947-6850; URL: http://infoweb.magi.com/ZXprivcan/
Toll Free: 1-800-267-0441, TDD: 613/992-9190
The Privacy Commissioner investigates complaints from any persons present in Canada who consider that the federal government has wrongly denied them access to their personal records or refused to correct (or annotate) disputed information. The Commissioner may also investigate complaints the federal government is improperly collecting, using, disclosing or disposing of personal information which may be recorded in any form. The Commissioner may investigate government compliance with the Privacy Act on his own initiative.
**Privacy Commissioner**, Bruce Phillips
Executive Director, Julien Delisle
Legal Advisor, Holly Harris
Director, Investigations, Gerald Neary
Director, Issues Management & Assessment, Brian Foran
Director, Public Affairs, Sally Jackson

## PUBLIC SERVICE COMMISSION OF CANADA/Commission de la fonction publique du Canada
300 Laurier Ave. West, Ottawa ON K1A 0M7
613/992-9562; Fax: 613/954-7561; URL: http://www.psc-cfp.gc.ca
The Commission is responsible for staffing the public service according to the merit principle. Delegates its authority wherever practical, though not its responsibility to Parliament. Provides training & development services (including language training, for public servants), hears appeals on appointments & investigates complaints of questionable staffing practices. Reports to government through the Minister of Canadian Heritage.

**President**, Ruth Hubbard, 613/992-2788, Fax: 613/996-4337
Commissioner, Ginette Stewart
Commissioner, Mary Gusella
Director General, Appeals & Investigations Branch, L.M. Lalonde
Director General, Audit & Review Branch, R. Jelking
Director General, Human Resources Management Branch, Jacques Pelletier
Director General, Strategic Planning & Communications Directorate, Carole Jolicoeur
Executive Director, Corporate Management Branch & Secretary General, A. Armit
Executive Director, Executive Programs Branch, Margaret Amoroso
Acting Executive Director, Staffing Programs Branch, Len Slivinski
Executive Director, Training Programs Branch, M.J. Murphy

#### Regional & District Staffing Offices

Charlottetown: #420, 119 Kent St., Charlottetown PE C1A 1N3 – 902/566-7030; Fax: 902/566-7036
Edmonton: #830, 9700 Jasper Ave., Edmonton AB T5J 4G3 – 403/495-3144; Fax: 403/495-3145
Halifax: 1557 Hollis St., Halifax NS B3J 3V3 – 902/426-2990; Fax: 902/426-7455
Moncton: 777 Main St., 7th Fl., Moncton NB E1C 1E9 – 506/851-6616; Fax: 506/851-6618
Montréal: 200, boul René-Lévesque ouest, 8e étage, Montréal QC H2Z 1X4 – 514/283-5776; Fax: 514/283-6380
Ottawa: 66 Slater St., 3rd Fl., Ottawa ON K1A 0M7 – 613/996-8436; Fax: 613/996-8048
Regina: #400, 1975 Scarth St., Regina SK S4P 2H1 – 306/780-5720; Fax: 306/780-5723
St. John's: #302, 2 Steers Cove, St. John's NF A1C 5X8 – 709/772-4812; Fax: 709/772-4316
Sillery: 1126, ch St-Louis, 7e étage, Sillery QC G1S 1E5 – 418/648-3230; Fax: 418/648-4575
Toronto: 1 Front St. West, 3rd Fl., Toronto ON M5J 2R5 – 416/973-3131; Fax: 416/973-1883
Vancouver: 757 West Hastings St., 2nd Fl., Vancouver BC V6C 3M2 – 604/666-4829; Fax: 604/666-6808
Whitehorse: #400, 300 Main St., Whitehorse YT Y1A 2B5 – 867/667-3900; Fax: 867/668-5033
Winnipeg: #200, 344 Edmonton St., Winnipeg MB R3B 2L4 – 204/983-2486; Fax: 204/983-8188
Yellowknife: 4922 - 52 St., PO Box 2730, Yellowknife NT X1A 2R1 – 867/873-3545; Fax: 867/873-3601

## PUBLIC SERVICE STAFF RELATIONS BOARD (PSSRB)/Commission des relations de travail dans la fonction publique

240 Sparks St., PO Box 1525, Stn B, Ottawa ON K1P 5V2
613/990-1800; Fax: 613/990-1849
PSSRB reports to Parliament through the President of the Privy Council.
**Chairperson**, Yvon Tarte, 613/990-1777
Secretary & General Counsel, J.E. McCormick, 613/990-1830
Asst. Secretary, Corporate Services, Janet Dionne, 613/990-1669
Asst. Secretary, Operations, Gilles Brisson, 613/990-1820
Director, Mediation Services, N. Berstein, 613/990-1836

## PUBLIC WORKS & GOVERNMENT SERVICES CANADA (PWGSC)/Travaux publics et services gouvernementaux

Place du Portage, Phase III, 11, rue Laurier, Hull QC K1A 0S5
819/956-3115; URL: http://www.pwgsc.gc.ca
TDD: 819/994-5389
Sir Charles Tupper Bldg., 2250 Riverside Dr., Ottawa ON K1A 0M2
The Department serves as the purchasing & accounting arm of the Federal Government. It provides a number of major common services in the areas of procurement, supply & printing & in the areas of accounting, payment, audit & management advisory services. It manages real property for the Government & provides planning, design, construction & realty services to government departments & agencies.
Canadian Government Publications: Approximately 180 commercial & university bookstores in Canada are recognized by the Canadian Government Publishing Centre as Associated Bookstores for the sale of federal government priced publications.

#### ACTS ADMINISTERED

Bridges Act
Currency Act
Defence Production Act
Department of Supply & Services Act
Dry Docks Subsidies Act
Expropriation Act
Federal-Provincial Fiscal Arrangements & Federal Post-secondary Education & Health Contributions Act
Garnishment Attachment & Pension Diversion Act
Government Property Traffic Act
Government Works Toils Act
Municipal Grants Act
National Film Act
Ottawa River Act
Public Lands Grants Act
Public Works Act
Public Works Health Act
Publication of Statutes Act
Royal Canadian Mint Act
Surplus Crown Assets Act
Trading with the Enemy Act
Trans-Canada Highway Act
**Minister**, Hon. Alfonso Gagliano, 819/997-5421, Fax: 819/953-1908
Deputy Minister & Deputy Receiver General, Ranald A. Quail, 819/956-1706, Fax: 819/956-8280
Asst. Deputy Minister, Human Resources, Michael Cardinal, 613/736-2455
General Counsel, Frank Brodie, 819/956-0993, Fax: 819/953-6705
Director General, Communications, Carol Rutherford, 819/956-2304, Fax: 819/956-9062

#### CANADA COMMUNICATION GROUP INC. (QUEEN'S PRINTER FOR CANADA) (CCG)

URL: http://www.ccg-gcc.ca
Toll Free: 1-800-956-9111
The printing & distribution operations of the Canada Communication Group were sold to St. Joseph Corporation of Toronto in March 1997. The company's new name is Canada Communication Group Inc., a St. Joseph Corporation Company. The publishing operations (the Canada Gazette section, the Depository Services Program, the Electronic publishing & Licensing Centre, & the Publications Management Centre), formerly known as the Canada Communication Group - Publishing, were not included in this sale and have been transferred to Public Works & Government Services Canada.
CEO (Queen's Printer for Canada), René Guindon, 819/997-5321
Director General/Vice-President, Business Development, Kim McKinnon, 819/953-0991, Fax: 819/956-8794
Director General/Vice-President, Information Technology, Vacant, 819/994-7166
Director General/Vice-President, Operations Directorate, B.M. McLean, 819/956-8340
Director General/Vice-President, Professional Services, L. Saint-Pierre, 350 Albert St., Ottawa ON K1A 0S5, 613/990-8047

#### Enquiries Canada

47 Clarence St., 3rd Fl., Ottawa ON K1A 0S5
URL: http://canada.gc.ca
Toll Free: 1-800-667-3355
Index to Federal Royal Commissions URL: http:www.nlc-bnc.ca/ifrc
Director, Jean Brazeau, 613/941-3392
Asst. Director, 1-800 Services, Gerard Blais, 613/941-1826
Asst. Director, Reference Canada Program, Suzanne Beaudoin, 613/941-3382

#### CONSULTING & AUDIT CANADA

Tower B, Place de Ville, 112 Kent St., Ottawa ON K1A 0S5
613/996-0188
CEO, Jane Billings, 613/996-0231
Acting Director General, Audit, J. Shah, 613/996-5096
Director General, Client Services, N. McIntosh, 613/947-4972
Director General, Consulting, J. Kent, 613/947-2010

#### GOVERNMENT OPERATIONAL SERVICE BRANCH (GOS)

Asst. Deputy Minister, Jim Stobbe, 819/956-2871, Fax: 819/956-7853
Director General, Banking & Cash Management Sector, Ralph Sprague, 819/956-2942, Fax: 819/956-7585
Director General, Central Accounting & Reporting Sector, Guy Beaudry, 819/956-2875, Fax: 819/956-7583
Director General, Compensation Sector, Phil Charko, 819/956-1936, Fax: 819/956-2098
Director General, Departmental Products Sector, Joan Catterson, 819/956-2877, Fax: 819/956-5599

#### GOVERNMENT TELECOMMUNICATIONS & INFORMATICS SERVICES (GTIS)

819/956-4444; Fax: 819/956-4627
CEO, Philip McLellan, 819/956-2632
Chief Operating Officer, René Guindon, 819/956-2610
Vice-President, Application Management Services, John Riddle, 819/956-2354
Vice-President, Business & Departmental Support Services, Bruno Kierczak, 819/956-9492
Vice-President, Customer Services & Business Development Sector, Roger Bason, 613/956-9495
Vice-President, Network & Computer Services, Fred McCallum, 819/956-2348
Vice-President, Telecommunications, Paul Hayes, 613/990-2217, Fax: 613/998-9122

#### REAL PROPERTY SERVICES BRANCH

Asst. Deputy Minister, Michael G. Nurse, 613/736-2882
Director, Accommodation Management Directorate, M. Turcotte, 613/736-2162
Director, Asset & Investment Management - Capital Directorates, Laura Jackson, 613/736-2181
Director, Federal Facilities Directorate, Sue Axam, 613/736-2238
Director, Holdings Management, Marcia Carlyn, 613/736-2207
Director, Investment Management-Leasing Directorate, M. Ballantine, 613/736-3157
Director, Maintenance Management, Richard Marleau, 613/736-2655

Director, Operations, D. Sinclaire-Chenier, 613/736-2824
Director, Owner, Investor Office Accommodation Services, Barry Bragg, 613/736-2691
Director, Security & Emergency Preparedness, Robert Begin, 613/736-2520
Director, Technology & Environmental Services, Moe Cheung, 613/941-5581

### SUPPLY OPERATIONS SERVICE BRANCH

Canada's largest purchasing organization, purchasing contracts on behalf of over 100 federal government agencies. Responsible for the organization of the Open Bidding System (OBS), an entirely electronic procurement process which awards most federal government (& some provincial government) contracts. The OBS is the official distribution channel for all open bidding procurement notices & documents issued by PWGSC. Requirements are listed on an electronic board & are printed three times per week in "Government Business Opportunities".
Asst. Deputy Minister, Alan Williams, 819/956-1727, Fax: 819/953-1058
Director, European Region, Graeme J. Brown, MacDonald House, #1, Grosvenor Square, London, 011-44-71-258-6612, Fax: 011-44-71-258-6440
Director, Washington Region, Eleonor Lewicki, Canadian Embassy, 501 Pennsylvania Ave. NW, Washington DC 20001, 202/682-7604, Fax: 202/682-7613
Director General, Aerospace, Marine & Electronics Systems Sector, Harry T. Webster, 819/956-0010,
Aerospace & Electronics, 819/956-0236
Marine & Armament, 819/956-0684
Canadian Patrol Frigate Project, 613/996-6337
Canadian Airspace Systems Plan, 613/990-5755
Long Range Surveillance DRONE System Project, 819/952-9640
Director General, Industrial & Commercial Products Sector, Bob Spickett, 819/956-4056,
Food, Drug & Scientific Products, 819/956-3892
Special & Standard Vehicles, 819/956-3937
Security Safety & Industrial Products, 819/956-3553
Electronics, Electrical & Construction Products, 819/956-3940
Director General, Industrial & Commercial Products & Standardization Services Sector, Melvern B. Skinner, 819/956-4056, Fax: 819/956-5145
Director General, Science, Informatics & Professional Services Sector, Noel Bhumgara, 819/956-1782
Director General, Supply Program Management Sector, Barry Lipsett, 819/956-0930
Chief, Open Bidding Business Management, Luci Dove, 819/956-3435

#### Canadian General Standards Board (CGSB)

222 Queen St., Ottawa ON K1A 1G6
613/941-8709; URL: http://www.pwgsc.gc.ca/cgsb
One of seven standards-writing organizations accredited by the Standards Council. A major portion of federal government purchasing is done by reference to CGSB standards & accreditations.
Contact, Melvern B. Skinner, 613/956-0930
Director, Bernie Geiger, 613/941-8643, Fax: 613/954-2769

#### Open Bidding Service/MERX & Government Buiness Opportunities (OBS & GBO)

OBS, c/o Information Systems Management Corporation, PO Box 22011, Ottawa ON K1V 0W2
613/737-3374; Fax: 613/737-3643; URL: http://www.obs.ism.ca
Toll Free: 1-800-361-4637
GBO c/o Canada Communication Group, Publishing, Ottawa ON K1A 0S9
819/956-4802
URL: http://www.ccg-gcc.ca; Toll-free: 1-800-267-8480

The OBS is now the official distribution channel for all open bidding procurement notices & documents issued by PWGSC. Requirements are listed on an electronic board & are printed three times per week in "Government Business Opportunities". Provides suppliers with instant access to purchasing information via a computer & modem either directly to the service or through the internet. All Canadian firms, whether or not they are on a source list, can use the open bidding method. The OBS makes new markets instantly available to all companies through an open, fair, & cost-effective service. The service has expanded to include notices of other federal government departments (ie. Defence Construction Canada, CIDA, Environment Canada, National Resources Canada, etc.), provincial/territorial government procurement agencies (Alberta, Manitoba, New Brunswick, Ontario, Québec, & Saskatchewan), crown corporations, academic institutions & other public sector institutions. Informs 27,000 subscribers of business opportunities.

#### Public Relations & Print Contract Services Sector

350 Albert St., 4th Fl., Ottawa ON K1A 0S5
Director General, Liliane Saint Pierre, 613/990-8047
Manager, Publications Management, Donna Wood, 613/993-1193
Acting Manager, Requirements Definition, Antonella De Angelis, 613/990-9208

### TRANSLATION SERVICES BRANCH

Jules Léger Bldg., 15 Eddy St., Hull QC K1A 0M5
Provides translation, interpretation & terminology services to federal departments, organizations & Parliament. Translation services are optional & are provided on a fee-for-Parliament.
CEO, Diana Monnet
Director General, Management Services Sector, Christine O'Meara, 819/994-3653, Fax: 819/997-5686
Director General, Translation Operations Sector, Ginette Cloutier, 819/997-1719, Fax: 819/953-9585
Deputy Director General, Departmental Translation Services, Gabriel Huard, 819/997-7919, Fax: 819/953-5799

#### Regional Offices

Atlantic: 1713 Bedford Row, 7th Fl., PO Box 2247, Stn M, Halifax NS B3J 3C9 – 902/496-5133; Fax: 902/426-5041, Regional Director General, Bren McDonald
Ontario: 4900 Yonge St., North York ON M2N 6A6 – 416/512-5710; Fax: 416/512-5710, Regional Director General, Susanne Borup
Pacific: #1830, 800 Burrard St., Vancouver BC V6Z 2V8 – 604/666-1862; Fax: 604/666-6983, Regional Director General, Bonnie MacKenzie
Québec: Complexe Guy-Favreau, #702-14, 200, boul René-Lévesque ouest, Montréal QC H2Z 1X4 – 514/496-3739; Fax: 514/496-3744, Regional Director General, René Crête
Western: #1000, 9700 Jasper Ave., Edmonton AB T5J 4E2 – 403/497-3555; Fax: 403/497-3562, Regional Director General, Heather Peden

#### Associated Agencies, Boards & Commissions

Listed alphabetically in detail, this section.
Canada Lands Co. Ltd.
Canada Mortgage & Housing Corporation
Canada Post Corporation
Defence Construction Canada
Royal Canadian Mint

## REVENUE CANADA/Revenu Canada

875 Heron Rd., Ottawa ON K1A 0L8
613/952-0384; URL: http://www.rc.gc.ca
Customs Information: 613/993-0534
GST Information: 613/990-8584

#### ACTS ADMINISTERED

Canada Pension Plan Act, Part I
Customs Act
Customs & Excise Offshore Application Act
Customs Tariff Act
Department of National Revenue Act
Excise Act
Excise Tax Act
Exports & Imports Permits Act
Softwood Lumber Products Export Charge Act
Special Import Measures Act
Unemployment Insurance Act, Part III & VII
**Minister**, Hon. Harbance Singh Dhaliwal, 819/997-7788, Fax: 819/994-5987
Deputy Minister, Robert A. Wright, 613/957-3688, Fax: 613/941-4142
Asst. Deputy Minister, Human Resources Branch, Vacant, 613/954-8220
Senior General Counsel, Legal Services, Charles McNab, 613/957-2558
Director General, Communications Branch, Vacant
Director General, Corporate Affairs Branch, S. Rigby, 613/957-3708

### APPEALS BRANCH

Interim Asst. Deputy Minister, R.M. Beith, 613/957-2179
Director, Appeals Division, B. McGivern, 613/954-4817
Director, CPP/UI Division, L. Levasseur, 613/957-2237
Director, Income Tax Appeals Division, L.C. Tremblay, 613/957-2189
Director, Policy & Programs Division, P. Meerburg, 613/957-2225

### ASSESSMENT & COLLECTIONS BRANCH

Asst. Deputy Minister, K.M. Burpee, 613/954-6144
Director General, Business Returns & Payments Processing Directorate, Rod Quiney, 613/941-5007
Director General, Client Services Directorate, H. Beauchemin, 613/957-9362
Director General, Individual Returns & Payment Processing, G. Venner, 613/957-7497
Acting Director General, Revenue Collection Directorate, L. Gauvin, 613/954-1269
Director, Business Process Development Team, Marj Ogden, 613/952-9314

### CUSTOMS BORDER SERVICES

Asst. Deputy Minister, Allan Cocksedge, 613/954-7220
Director General, Commercial Services Directorate, E.D. Warren, 613/954-7190
Director General, Enforcement Directorate, W.E. LeDrew, 613/954-6431
Acting Director General, Program Planning & Analysis Directorate, B. McCauley, 613/954-7820
Director General, Travellers Directorate, R. Tait, 613/954-6368
Acting Director, Enforcement Operations, M. Connolly, 613/954-7620
Director, Inspection & Control, L. Noble, 613/954-7056
Director, Intelligence Services, F. Stefanelli, 613/954-7575
Acting Director, Operations & Policy, A. Lalonde, 613/952-6368
Director, Postal Courier & LVS, F. Light, 613/954-7130
Director, Program Development, G. Gulas, 613/952-3907
Acting Director, Project Management, G. Goatbe, 613/954-7501
Director, Systems Operations, L. Bratina, 613/954-6844
Director, Transportation Division, G. Rochon, 613/954-7191
Director, Travellers Assessment & Tax Policy Division, D. Cruikshank, 613/954-6360
Director, Travellers Services & Compliance, C. Collingridge, 613/954-7122

### FINANCE & ADMINISTRATION BRANCH

Asst. Deputy Minister, Vacant
Director General, Administration Directorate, R.C. Dudding, 613/957-9270
Director General, Finance Administration Directorate, William D. Boston, 613/954-6400
Director General, Laboratory & Scientific Services Directorate, Wayne Morris, 613/954-2200
Director General, Resource Management Directorate, John Kowalski, 613/952-3660
Director, Consolidation Administration, L. McElroy, 613/954-0248
Director, Facilites Management, S. Parent, 613/954-8330
Acitng Director, Publishing Services, R. Jones, 613/954-9302
Director, Security Directorate, Vacant, 613/957-2269

### INFORMATION TECHNOLOGY BRANCH

Asst. Deputy Minister, Richard Manicom, 613/954-8983
Director General, Client Identification & Returns Processing, Al Landsberg, 613/954-8995
Director General, Compliance & Information Systems Directorate, J. Patrick Beynon, 613/954-9039
Director General, Development Support Directorate, Dick Sansom, 613/954-9405
Director General, Revenue & Accounting Systems Directorate, Susan Brown, 613/994-1233
Director General, Strategic Planning & Management Services Directorate, G.A. Peters, 613/941-3505
Director General, Technology Operations & Client Support Directorate, Jill Velenosi, 613/941-2870

### POLICY & LEGISLATION BRANCH

123 Slater St., Ottawa ON K1A 0L8
Asst. Deputy Minister, Denis Lefebvre, 613/957-2041
Director General, Excise Act Review, R. O'Riordan, MacKenzie Ave., 7th Fl., Ottawa ON K1A 0L5, 613/941-3001
Director General, GST Rulings & Interpretations, W.K. McCloskey, Tower C, Vanier Towers, 25 McArthur Rd., Ottawa ON K1A 0L5, 613/952-9198
Acting Director General, Income Tax Rulings & Interpretations Directorate, Roy Shultis, 613/957-2132
Director General, Policy & Intergovernmental Affairs, W. Baker, 613/941-9964
Deputy Director General, Excise Duties & Taxes, Jean-Francois Apgrall, Tower C, Vanier Towers, 25 McArthur Rd., Ottawa ON K1A 0L5, 613/954-0111
Acting Associate Director General, GST Rulings & Interpretations Directorate, J. Daman, Tower C, Vanier Towers, 25 McArthur Rd., Ottawa ON K1A 0L5, 613/954-4291
Director, Business & General Division, Bryan Dath, 613/957-2089
Director, Charities Division, Ronald Davis, 613/954-0931
Director, Field Service & Administration Division, Keith Schinnour, Tower C, Vanier Towers, 25 McArthur Rd., Ottawa ON K1A 0L5, 613/952-9200
Director, Financial Industries Division, Brian Darling, 613/957-9767
Acting Director, Financial Institutions & Corporate Reorganizations Division, John Sitka, Tower C, Vanier Towers, 25 McArthur Rd., Ottawa ON K1A 0L5, 613/952-9248
Director, General Applications Division, L. Jones, Tower C, Vanier Towers, 25 McArthur Rd., Ottawa ON K1A 0L5, 613/954-7656
Director, International Relations Coordination Office, D. Meunier, 613/957-9776
Director, Legislative Policy Division, Robert D'Aurelio, 613/957-2061
Director, Manufacturing Industries, Partnerships & Trusts Division, Rick Biscaro, 613/957-8970
Director, Registered Plans Division, Stella Black, 613/954-0933
Director, Reorganization & Foreign Division, Michael Hiltz, 613/957-2113
Director, Special Sectors, A. Venne, Tower C, Vanier Towers, 25 McArthur Rd., Ottawa ON K1A 0L5, 613/954-7558

### TRADE ADMINISTRATION BRANCH

Interim Asst. Deputy Minister, A. Cocksedge, 613/954-7400
Director General, Anti-Dumping & Countervailing, B.W. Brimble, 613/954-7269
Director General, Tariff Programs, J. Shearer, 613/954-6990
Director, Adjudications, G. Greene, 613/954-7273
Acting Director, Management Systems & Services, P. Cork, 613/954-6970
Director, Valuation Division, M.R. Jordan, 613/954-7335

### VERIFICATION, ENFORCEMENT & COMPLIANCE RESEARCH BRANCH

Asst. Deputy Minister, Barry Lacombe, 613/957-3709
Director General, Audit Directorate, Ed Gauthier, 613/957-3585
Director General, Compliance Research Directorate, Vacant, 613/941-4621
Director General, International Tax, Carole Gouin, 613/952-7472
Director General, Special Investigations Directorate, Jeanne Flemming, 613/957-7780
Director, Compliance Enhancement & Services, Jean-Pierre Lavigne, 613/957-9390
Director, Enforcement Technology Support, Frank Fingust, 613/957-3649
Director, Large Business Division, Vacant, 613/957-3585
Director, Planning Division, A. Potvin, 613/957-3665
Director, Small & Medium Enterprises Division, Dick Courneyea, 613/954-5725

### ATLANTIC REGION

Cogswell Tower, #800, 2000 Barrington St., Halifax NS B3J 3K1
902/426-7994
Asst. Deputy Minister, Regional Operations, Dan Tucker, 902/426-6370

#### Customs/Border Services Office

Atlantic: 1809 Barrington St., PO Box 3080, Stn Park Lane Centre, Halifax NS B3J 3G6 – 902/426-2911, Interim Director, Dan Coffin, 902/426-2914

#### Trade Administration Services Office

Atlantic: Ralston Bldg., 1557 Hollis St., PO Box 3080, Stn Park Lane Centre, Halifax NS B3J 3G6 – 902/426-2911, Director, K. Larter, 902/426-6808

#### Tax Services Offices

Bathurst: 120 Harbourview Blvd., 4th Fl., PO Box 8888, Bathurst NB E2A 4L8 – 506/548-6744
Charlottetown: 94 Euston St., Charlottetown PE C1A 8L3 – 902/628-4200
Halifax: 1256 Barrington St., PO Box 638, Halifax NS B3J 2T5 – 902/426-2210
Moncton: #107, 1170 Main St., PO Box 1070, Moncton NB E1C 8P2 – 506/636-5999
Newfoundland & Labrador: Atlantic Place, 165 Duckworth St., PO Box 5968, St. John's NF A1C 5X6 – 709/772-2610
Saint John: 126 Prince William St., PO Box 6300, Saint John NB E2L 4H9 – 506/636-5999
St. John's: 290 Empire Ave., St. John's NF A1B 3Z1 – 709/772-2200
Summerside: 275 Pope Rd., Summerside PE C1N 5Z7 – 902/432-6000
Sydney: 47 Dorchester St., PO Box 1300, Sydney NS B1P 6K3 – 902/564-7080

### NORTHERN ONTARIO REGION

2265 St. Laurent Blvd., 2nd Fl., Ottawa ON K1G 4K3
613/991-0549
Asst. Deputy Minister, Regional Operations, Robin Glass, 613/952-1676

#### Customs/Border Services Office

Ottawa: 2265 St. Laurent Blvd., Ottawa ON K1K 4K3 – 613/991-0534, Acting Interim Director, Gary Gustafson, 613/993-0534

#### Trade Administration Services Office

Ottawa: 2265 St. Laurent Blvd., Ottawa ON K1K 4K3 – 613/993-0537, Director, Arthur Lawrence, 613/598-3946

#### International Taxation Office

Ottawa: 2204 Walkey Rd., Ottawa ON K1A 1A8 – 613/952-3741

#### Tax Services Offices

Belleville: 11 Station St., Belleville ON K8N 2S3 – 613/962-2887
Kingston: 385 Princess St., Kingston ON K7L 1C1 – 613/541-3607
Kirkland Lake: 145 Government Rd. West, PO Box 4500, Kirkland Lake ON P2N 3R5 – 705/568-4222
Ottawa: #9088B, 875 Heron Rd., Ottawa ON K1A 1A2 – 613/941-3333
Ottawa: 333 Laurier Ave. West, Ottawa ON K1A 0L9 – 613/598-2275
Peterborough: 185 King St. West, 5th Fl., Peterborough ON K9J 8M3 – 705/876-6420
Sault Ste. Marie: #301, 205 McNabb St., Sault Ste. Marie ON P6B 1Y3 – 705/941-5218
Sudbury: 1050 Notre Dame Ave., Sudbury ON P3A 6C1 – 705/671-0582
Thunder Bay: 130 Syndicate Ave. South, Thunder Bay ON P7E 1C7 – 807/623-1774

### SOUTHERN ONTARIO REGION

Ontario Regional Taxation Office, #909, 148 Fullarton St., London ON N6A 5P3
519/645-4360
Asst. Deputy Minister, Regional Operations, Ruby Howard

#### Customs/Border Services Offices

Mississauga: #604, 6725 Airport Rd., PO Box 6000, Mississauga ON L4V 1V2 – 905/676-3574, Director, Barbara Hébert
Windsor: 185 Ouellette Ave., 5th Fl., Stn Walkerville, Windsor ON N9A 5S8, Director, Dr. John Johnston

#### Trade Administration Services Office

Toronto: Dominion Public Bldg., #2538, 1 Front St. West, Toronto ON M5J 1A5 – 416/954-5623, Director, Alice Shields

#### Tax Services Offices

Hamilton: 150 Main St. West, PO Box 2220, Hamilton ON L8N 3E1 – 905/570-7125
Kitchener: 166 Frederick St., Kitchener ON N2G 4N1 – 519/579-2230
London: 451 Talbot St., London ON N6A 5E5 – 519/645-4211
St. Catharines: 32 Church St., St. Catharines ON L2R 3B9 – 905/688-5996
Toronto East: 200 Town Centre Court, Scarborough ON M1P 4Y3 – 905/973-5150
Toronto Centre: 36 Adelaide St. East, Toronto ON M5C 1J7 – 416/954-3500
Toronto North: 5001 Yonge St., 7th Fl., North York ON M2N 6P6 – 416/954-9303

Toronto West: 77 City Centre Dr., Mississauga ON L5B 1M5 – 905/566-6700

Windsor: 185 Ouellette Ave., Windsor ON N9A 5S8 – 519/973-7188

#### PACIFIC REGION

#708, 333 Dunsmuir St., Vancouver BC V6B 5R4

604/666-0456

Asst. Deputy Minister, Regional Operations, Barbara Fulton

##### Customs/Border Services Office

Vancouver: #709, 333 Dunsmuir St., Vancouver BC V6B 5R4 – 604/666-8633

##### Trade Administration Services Office

Vancouver: #501, 333 Dunsmuir St., Vancouver BC V6B 5R4 – 604/666-0545, Interim Director, Rita Barill

##### Tax Services Offices

Burnaby: #201, 4664 Lougheed Hwy., PO Box 02110, Burnaby BC V5C 6C2 – 604/689-5411

Kelowna: #200, 1835 Gordon Dr., PO Box 5181, Stn A, Kelowna BC V1Y 3H5 – 604/470-6670

Prince George: 280 Victoria St., PO Box 7500, Prince George BC V2L 5N8 – 250/561-7800

Penticton: 277 Winnipeg St., Penticton BC V2A 1N6 – 250/492-9393

Surrey Taxation Centre: 9755 King George Hwy., Surrey BC V3T 5E1 – 604/585-5200

Vancouver: 1166 West Pender St., Vancouver BC V6E 3H8 – 604/669-8376

Victoria: 910 Government St., Victoria BC V8W 1X8 – 250/363-0121

Whitehorse: 120 - 300 Main St., Whitehorse YT Y1A 2B5 – 867/667-8154

#### PRAIRIE REGION

391 York Ave., 4th Fl., PO Box 1022, Winnipeg MB R3C 0P5

204/983-1845

Asst. Deputy Minister, Regional Operations, Rodney Monette

##### Customs/Border Services Office

Winnipeg: Federal Bldg., 269 Main St., Winnipeg MB R3C 1B3 – 204/983-6004, Director, Mike Styre

##### Trade Administration Services

Winnipeg: Federal Bldg., 269 Main St., Winnipeg MB R3C 1B3 – 204/983-0004, Director, Arlene White

##### Tax Services Offices

Brandon: 153 - 11 St., PO Box 99, Brandon MB R7A 7K6 – 204/726-7800

Calgary: 220 - 4 Ave. SE, Calgary AB T2G 0L1 – 403/221-8919

Edmonton: #10, 9700 Jasper Ave., Edmonton AB T5J 4C8 – 403/495-5400

Lethbridge: #301, 704 - 4 Ave. South, PO Box 3009, Lethbridge AB T1J 4A9 – 403/382-3010

Red Deer: 4996 - 49 Ave., PO Box 5013, Red Deer AB T4N 6X2 – 403/341-7006

Regina: 1955 Smith St., Regina SK S4P 2N9 – 306/780-6015

Saskatoon: 340 - 3 Ave. North, Saskatoon SK S7K 0A8 – 306/975-4595

Winnipeg: 325 Broadway, Winnipeg MB R3C 4T4 – 204/983-3960

Winnipeg: 66 Stapon Rd., Winnipeg MB R3C 3M3 – 204/984-2470

Yellowknife: #902, 4920 - 52 St., Yellowknife NT X1A 3T1 – 867/920-6650

#### QUÉBEC REGION

400, Place d'Youville, 8e étage, Montréal QC H2Y 2C2

514/283-2464

Asst. Deputy Minister, Regional Operations, Danielle Vincent

##### Customs/Border Services Offices

Montréal: 400, Place d'Youville, Montréal QC H2Y 2C2 – 514/283-9900, Interim Director, Richard Watkins, 514/283-6201

##### Trade Administrion Services Office

Montréal: 400, Place d'Youville, Montréal QC H2Y 2C2 – 514/-283-9900, Director, Jacques Monette, 514/283-6332

##### Tax Services Offices

Chicoutimi: #211, 100, rue Lafontaine, Chicoutimi QC G7H 6X2 – 418/698-5580

Jonquière: 2251, boul Centrale, Jonquière QC G7S 5J1 – 418/699-0450

Laval: 3131, boul St-Martin ouest, Laval QC H7T 2A7 – 514/956-9101

Montérégie-Rive-Sud: 1000, rue de Serigny, Longueuil QC J4K 5J7 – 514/283-5300

Montréal: 305, boul René-Lévesque ouest, Montréal QC H2Z 1A6 – 514/283-5300

Outaoais: 15 Eddy St., Hull QC K1A 1L4 – 819/994-1995

Québec: 165, rue de la Pointe-aux-Lievres sud, Québec QC G1K 7L3 – 418/649-3180

Rimouski: 320, St-Germain est, Rimouski QC G5L 1C2 – 418/722-3104

Rouyn-Noranda: 44, av du Lac, Rouyn-Noranda QC J9X 6Z9 – 819/764-5171

Shawinigan-Sud: 4695, 12e av, Shawinigan-Sud QC G9N 7S6 – 819/537-5192

Sherbrooke: 50, Place de la Cité, CP 1300, Sherbrooke QC J1H 5L8 – 819/564-5888

Trois-Rivières: #111, 25, rue des Forges, Trois-Rivières QC G9A 2G4 – 819/373-2723

## ROOSEVELT CAMPOBELLO INTERNATIONAL PARK COMMISSION

Campobello Island, Campobello Is. NB E0G 3H0

506/752-2922; Fax: 506/752-6000

The Commission administers an international park on Campobello Island, New Brunswick, as a memorial to the late President of the United States, F.D. Roosevelt.

**Chair (American)**, Hon. Christopher du Pont Roosevelt

Vice-Chair (Canadian), Rowland C. Frazee

Executive Secretary & Superintendent, Henry W. Stevens

## ROYAL CANADIAN MINT/Monnaie royale canadienne

320 Sussex Dr., Ottawa ON K1A 0G8

613/993-3500; URL: http://www.rcmint.ca

The RCM has two plants located in Ottawa & Winnipeg. Foreign & domestic circulating coinage is manufactured in Winnipeg. The Ottawa facility is responsible for the production of foreign & domestic numismatic products, precious metals & the refining of gold. Reports to government through Public Works & Government Services.

**Chair**, Dr. Jose Blanco

Master, Danielle V. Wetherup

Vice-President, Manufacturing, Jean-Pierre Tremblay, 613/995-1975

Executive Director, Communications, Diane Plouffe Reardon, 613/993-2239, Fax: 613/998-5472

## ROYAL CANADIAN MOUNTED POLICE (RCMP)/Gendarmerie royale du Canada (GRC)

1200 Vanier Pkwy., Ottawa ON K1A OR2

613/993-1085; Fax: 613/993-5894; URL: http://www.rcmp-grc.gc.ca/html/rcmp2.htm

In 1873 the *North West Mounted Police* was constituted to provide Police protection in the unsettled portions of the North West. In 1904 the title "Royal" was given to the Force. In 1920 The *Dominion Police* was amalgamated with this Force & the name changed to "Royal Canadian Mounted Police". The headquarters was moved from Regina to Ottawa & the Force may be called upon to perform duties in any portion of the Dominion. In 1928 the RCMP absorbed the Saskatchewan Provincial Police & in 1932 the Provincial Police Forces of Alberta, Manitoba, New Brunswick, Nova Scotia & PEI were absorbed in like manner. During the year 1932, the Force also assumed the administration of the Preventive Service Branch of the Department of National Revenue. On August 1, 1950, the duties of the Newfoundland Rangers & certain members of the Newfoundland Constabulary were taken over by the RCMP, & on the 15th of the same month the BC Provincial Police were similarly absorbed. On November 24th, 1988, the New Brunswick Highway Patrol was absorbed. These arrangements were made by agreements between the respective Provincial Governments concerned & the Federal Government Recuits are trained at Regina, Saskatchewan.

##### ACTS ADMINISTERED

RCMP Act

**Commissioner**, J.P.R. Murray

Honorary Commissioner, Her Majesty Queen Elizabeth II

Deputy Commissioner, National Headquarters, C.G. Allen

Deputy Commissioner, Atlantic Region, J.T.G. Ryan

Deputy Commissioner, Central Region, J.R.H. Beaulac

Deputy Commissioner, North Western Region, C/Supt. R.V. Berlinquette

Deputy Commissioner, Pacific Region, Deputy Commr. L.R. Proke

Public Affairs & Information Directorate, C/Supt. P.D.D. Hovey

##### RCMP Divisions & Commanding Officers

"A" Division: 155 McArthur Ave., Vanier ON K1A 0R4 – 613/993-8860; Fax: 613/995-4677, A/Commr. R.L.J. Mercier

"B" Division: PO Box 9700, Stn B, St. John's NF A1A 3T5 – 709/772-5437; Fax: 709/772-6392, C/Supt. L. Warren

"C" Division: 4225, boul Dorchester ouest, CP 559, Westmount QC H3Z 1V5 – 514/939-8301; Fax: 514/939-8471, A/Commr. J.O.O. Emond

"D" Division: 1091 Portage Ave., Winnipeg MB R3C 3K2 – 204/983-5414; Fax: 204/984-2342P, A/Commr. E.F. Moodie

"E" Division: 657 West 37 St., Vancouver BC V5Z 1K6 – 604/264-2000; Fax: 604/264-3547, Deputy Commr. L.R. Proke

"F" Division: PO Box 2500, Regina SK S4P 3K7 – 306/780-5477; Fax: 306/780-5410, A/Commr. B.G. Watt

"G" Division: PO Box 5000, Yellowknife NT X1A 2R3 – 867/920-8322; Fax: 867/873-3633, C/Supt.. R.A. Grimmer

"H" Division: 3139 Oxford St., PO Box 2286, Halifax NS B3J 3E1 – 902/426-3940; Fax: 902/426-8845, A/Commr. D.L. Bishop

"J" Division: PO Box 3900, Fredericton NB E3B 4Z8 – 506/452-3419; Fax: 506/451-6053, C/Supt. G. Loeppky

"K" Division: 11140 - 109 St., PO Box 1320, Edmonton AB T5J 2N1 – 403/945-5444; Fax: 403/945-5601, A/Commr. D. McDermid
"L" Division: 450 University Ave., PO Box 1360, Charlottetown PE C1A 7N1 – 902/566-7132; Fax: 902/368-0357, C/Supt. A.E. Crosby
"M" Division: 4100 - 4 Ave., Whitehorse YT Y1A 1H5 – 867/667-5584; Fax: 867/667-2621, C/Supt. T. Egglestone
"O" Division: PO Box 3240, Stn B, London ON N6A 4K3 – 519/640-7309, A/Commr. G. Zaccardelli

#### Training Facilities

Canadian Police College: St. Laurent Blvd. & Sandridge Rd., PO Box 8900, Ottawa ON K1G 3J2 – 613/998-0883; Fax: 613/990-9738, C/Supt. R. Goulet
RCMP Training Academy: PO Box 650, Regina SK S4P 3J7 – 306/780-5760; Fax: 306/780-6337, C/Supt. J.R.A. Gauthier

## ROYAL CANADIAN MOUNTED POLICE EXTERNAL REVIEW COMMITTEE/Comité externe d'examen de la Gendarmerie royale du Canada

PO Box 1159, Stn B, Ottawa ON K1P 5R2
613/998-2134; Fax: 613/990-8969; Email: cloutierb@smtp.gc.ca; URL: http://canada.gc.ca/depts/agencies/ercind_e.html
**Acting Chair**, F. Jennifer Lynch, Q.C.
Executive Director, Bernard Cloutier

## ROYAL CANADIAN MOUNTED POLICE PUBLIC COMPLAINTS COMMISSION/Commission des plaintes du public contre la Gendarmerie royale

PO Box 3423, Stn D, Ottawa ON K1P 6L4
613/952-1471; Fax: 613/952-8045; URL: http://canada.gc.ca/depts/agencies/pccind_e.html
Toll Free: 1-800-267-6637
The Commission is responsible for the receipt of complaints from the public about the conduct of members of the RCMP. It is also responsible for the review of complaints when complainants are not satisfied with the disposition of their complaints by the RCMP. The Commission can inquire into complaints by means of public hearings & the chair of the Commission can investigate complaints. Annually, the chair reports to Parliament through the Solicitor General.
**Chair**, J.P. Beaulne
Executive Director, J.B. Giroux

#### Regional Offices

British Columbia & Yukon: #670, 840 Howe St., Vancouver BC V6Z 2L2 – 604/666-7363; Fax: 604/666-7362
Prairies & NWT: #1909, 10060 Jasper Avenue, Edmonton AB T5J 3R8 – 403/495-4201; Fax: 403/495-4200

## ROYAL SOCIETY OF CANADA/Société royale du Canada

Listed in Section 2; *see* Index.

## ST. LAWRENCE SEAWAY AUTHORITY (SLSA)/L'Administration de la voie maritime du Saint-Laurent

Place de Ville, Tower "B", 112 Kent St., 5th Fl., Ottawa ON K1P 5P2
613/598-4626; Fax: 613/598-4620; Email: marketing@seaway.ca; URL: http://www.seaway.ca
The SLSA is the federal government agency responsible for the safe and efficient movement of marine traffic through Canadian Seaway facilities. It shares operations with its American counterpart, the *Saint Lawrence Seaway Development Corporation*, in maintaining 13 locks between Montréal & Lake Erie. The authority reports to government through the Minister of Transportation.
**President & CEO**, G.R. Stewart, 613/598-4601
Vice-President, C. Côté
Vice-President, M. Fournier
Corporate Secretary, V.C. Durant

#### Regional Offices

Maisonneuve: PO Box 97, St. Lambert QC J4P 3N7, Vice-President, J.P. Patoine
Niagara: 508 Glendale Ave., St Catharines ON L2R 6V8, Vice-President, C.G. Trépanier

## SECURITY INTELLIGENCE REVIEW COMMITTEE (SIRC)/Comité de Surveillance des activités de renseignements de sécurité (CSARS)

PO Box 2430, Stn D, Ottawa ON K1P 5W5
613/990-8441; Fax: 613/990-5230; Email: sirc@synapse.net; URL: http://www.sirc-csars.gc.ca/main_e.html
Has as its mandate, under the Canadian Security Intelligence Service Act, to carry out the independent & external review of the Canadian Security Intelligence Service (CSIS) & to investigate complaints about CSIS activities. It is also required to investigate complaints from individuals who have had their employment prospects affected by the denial of a security clearance, & complaints referred to it by the Human Rights Commission. It is required to investigate reports made to it by, the Minister of Citizenship & Immigration, & the Solicitor General of Canada, which relate to national security or to an individual's involvement in organized crime. The Committee is required to report annually to Parliament through the Solicitor General on these matters.

#### ACTS ADMINISTERED

Canadian Security Intelligence Service Act
**Chair**, Hon. Paule Gauthier, P.C., Q.C.

## SOCIAL SCIENCES & HUMANITIES RESEARCH COUNCIL OF CANADA (SSHRC)/Conseil de recherches en sciences humaines du Canada (CRSH)

Constitution Sq., 350 Albert St., PO Box 1610, Ottawa ON K1P 6G4
613/992-0691; Fax: 613/992-1787; Email: z-info@sshrc.ca; URL: http://www.sshrc.ca
The key national research agency investing in the knowledge & skills Canada needs to build the quality of its social, cultural & economic life. SSHRC supports university-based research & training in the human sciences. It funds basic, applied & collaborative research, student training, research partnerships, knowledge transfer & the communication of research findings in all disciplines of the social sciences & humanities. Grants & fellowships are awarded through national competitions adjudicated by eminent researchers & scholars.
President, Dr. Lynn Penrod, 613/992-5488
Director General, Common Administrative Services, Laurent Nadon, 613/995-3914
Director General, Program Branch, Elaine Isabelle, 613/995-5455
Director, Communications, Pamela Wiggin, 613/992-4283
Director, Policy, Planning & International Relations, France Landriault, 613/992-5125

## SOLICITOR GENERAL CANADA/Solliciteur général Canada

Sir Wilfrid Laurier Bldg., 340 Laurier Ave. West, Ottawa ON K1A 0P8
613/991-3283; Fax: 613/993-7062; URL: http://www.sgc.gc.ca
The duties, powers & functions of the Solicitor General of Canada extend to & include all matters over which the Parliament of Canada has jurisdiction, not by law assigned to any other department, branch or agency of the Government of Canada, relating to (a) reformatories, prisons & penitentiaries; (b) parole & remissions; (c) The Royal Canadian Mounted Police; & (d) The Canadian Security Intelligence Service.

#### ACTS ADMINISTERED

Canadian Security Intelligence Act
Corrections & Conditional Release Act
Criminal Records Act
Department of the Solicitor General Act
Royal Canadian Mounted Police Act
Royal Canadian Mounted Police Pension Continuation Act
Royal Canadian Mounted Police Superannuation Act
Prisons & Reformatories Act
Security Offences Act
Transfer of Offenders Act
**Solicitor General**, Hon. Andy Scott, 613/991-2824, Fax: 613/952-2240
Deputy Solicitor General, Jean T. Fournier, 613/991-2895, Fax: 613/990-8312
Asst. Deputy Solicitor General, Horst Intscher, 613/991-2820, Fax: 613/990-8301
Director General, Aboriginal Policing, Christiane Ouimet, 613/993-4325, Fax: 613/991-0961
Director General, Communications Group, T.R.W. Farr, 613/991-2799, Fax: 613/993-7062
Director General, Corporate Services, Eva Plunkett, 613/990-2669, Fax: 613/990-8297
Director General, Corrections, Richard Zubrycki, 613/991-2821, Fax: 613/990-8295
Director General, National Security, Jim Harlick, 613/993-4136, Fax: 613/990-2632
Director General, Policing & Law Enforcement, Yvette Aloïsi, 613/990-2703, Fax: 613/993-5252
Director General, Policy, Planning & Coordination, Michelle Gosselin, 613/998-8934
Director, External Relations (Regional Affairs), Jane Johnston, 613/991-2952, Fax: 613/990-7023

#### CANADIAN SECURITY INTELLIGENCE SERVICE (CSIS)

PO Box 9732, Ottawa ON K1G 4G4
613/993-9620; URL: http://www.csis-scrs.gc.ca
Director, Ward Elcock, 613/231-0000
Director General, Communications Branch, Phil Gibson, 613/231-0100, Fax: 613/231-0612

#### CORRECTIONAL SERVICE OF CANADA

Listed alphabetically in detail, this section.

#### NATIONAL PAROLE BOARD

Listed alphabetically in detail, this section.

#### ROYAL CANADIAN MOUNTED POLICE (RCMP)

Listed alphabetically in detail, this section.

## STATISTICS CANADA/Statistique Canada

R.H. Coats Bldg., Tunney's Pasture, 120 Parkdale Ave., Ottawa ON K1A 0T6
613/951-8116; Fax: 613/951-0581; Email: infostats@statcan.ca; URL: http://www.statcan.ca
Toll Free: 1-800-263-1136, TDD: 1-800-363-7629
Agency of the federal government, headed by the Chief Statistician of Canada which reports to Parliament through the Minister of Industry. As Canada's central statistical agency, it has a mandate to "collect, compile, analyse, abstract and publish statistical information

relating to the commercial, industrial, financial, social, economic and general activities and condition of the people of Canada". Coordinates activities with its federal and provincial partners in the national statistical system to avoid duplication of effort and to ensure the consistency and usefulness of statistics.

The Agency provides information to governments at every level, to business, labour, academic and social institutions, to professional associations, to the international statistical community, and to the general public. The agency profiles and measures both social and economic changes in Canada. It presents a comprehensive picture of the national economy through statistics on manufacturing, agriculture, exports and imports, retail sales, services, prices, productivity changes, trade, transportation, employment and unemployment, and aggregate measures such as gross domestic product. It also presents a comprehensive picture of social conditions through statistics on demography, health, education, justice, culture, and household incomes and expenditures.

This information is produced at the national and provincial levels and, in some cases, for major population centres and other sub-provincial or "small" areas. Statistics Canada produces some 800 print publications, as well as computer tapes, printouts, microcomputer diskettes, CD-ROMs, microfilm and microfiche. All catalogued publications are distributed through the Depository Services Program, which includes some 700 libraries. The most popular titles are Canada Year Book; Canada: A Portrait; Canadian Economic Observer; Canadian Social Trends; Perspectives on Labour and Income; and Health Reports. The Statistics Canada Catalogue-available in print, on CD-ROM and on the Internet-contains information about the wide range of print and electronic information sources and services offered by Statistics Canada.

In addition, the Agency maintains an extensive online computerized database called *CANSIM* (Canadian Socio-economic Information Management System), which contains 700,000 time series collected from throughout Statistics Canada. Another important database is *TIERS* (Trade Information Enquiry and Retrieval System), which is a data and software package designed to facilitate the recovery of Canadian trade information. Published electronically every working day, *The Daily* is Statistics Canada's official release bulletin; it contains summary findings of statistical programs and major conclusions of analytical studies. Infomat is a weekly analytical summary of articles that appeared in The Daily.

Online access to Statistics Canada information is available through *StatsCan Online* and the Internet. Currently available on StatsCan Online are CANSIM, The Daily, and extensive databases containing international trade information and horticulture information. Currently available on Statistics Canada's growing Internet site are Canadian Dimensions (tables presenting basic economic and social data about Canada), CANSIM and other databases, The Daily, research papers, the Statistics Canada Catalogue and ordering information, and links to the web servers of other Government of Canada departments and other national statistical agencies.

Statistics Canada's national role is manifested by its regional presence. Household surveys, census operations, and, increasingly, business surveys are conducted from the regional offices located across Canada. The nine regional offices handle sales of print and electronic products and provide reference and consultative services. Each provides a professional staff to assist clients in the access and use of statistical information and to carry out research and custom work. Listings of Canadian Statistics may be found in this book. Please conuslt the main/global Index.

#### ACTS ADMINISTERED

Statistics Act

Corporations & Labour Unions Returns Act

**Chief Statistician of Canada**, Dr. Ivan P. Fellegi, 613/951-9757, Fax: 613/951-4842

#### BUSINESS & TRADE STATISTICS

Asst. Chief Statistician, J. Ryten, 613/951-8096, Fax: 613/951-3231

Director General, Industry, Trade & Prices Statistics, R. Ryan, 613/951-9493, Includes Industry; Prices; International Trade & Transportation.

Director General, Resources, Technology & Services Statistics, A. Meguerditchian, 613/951-3423, Includes Services; Science & Technology; Industrial Organization & Finance; Agriculture; Investment & Capital Stock; Small Business & Special Surveys.

Manager, Large Enterprise Statistics, P. Demmons, 613/951-4055

#### COMMUNICATIONS & OPERATIONS

Asst. Chief Statistician, Y. Goulet, 613/951-6088, Fax: 613/951-0556

Director General, Marketing & Information Services, D.J. Desjardins, 613/951-7614, Includes Communications; Dissemination; Library Services; & Marketing.

Director General, Regional Operations, M. Levine, 613/951-9750, Includes Survey Operations; & Advisory Services.

Director General, Surveys Branch, J.-P. Trudel, 613/951-9660, Includes Operations & Integration; Operations Research & Development; & Administrative Support Services.

#### INFORMATICS & METHODOLOGY

Asst. Chief Statistician & Acting Director General, Methodology, G.J. Brackstone, 613/951-9908, Fax: 613/951-4842, Includes Social Survey Methods; Small Area & Administrative Data; Business Survey Methods, Household Survey Methods.

Director General, Informatics, B. Slater, 613/951-9932, Includes Informatics User Services; Systems Development; & Main Computer Centre.

Director General, Classification Systems, R. Barnabé, 613/951-8096, Includes Business Register; Standards; & Geography.

Director, International & Professional Relations, B. Prigly, 613/951-8917

#### MANAGEMENT SERVICES

Asst. Chief Statistician, Y. Fortin, 613/951-9866, Fax: 613/951-5290

Director General, Human Resources, J.P. McLaughlin, 613/951-9955

Director, Data Access & Control Services, L. Desramaux, 613/951-9349

Director, Finance, Planning, Audit & Evaluation, J.W. Coombs, 613/951-3730

#### NATIONAL ACCOUNTS & ANALYTICAL STUDIES

Asst. Chief Statistician & Acting General Director, Analytical Studies, J.S. Wells, 613/951-9760, Fax: 613/951-5290, Includes Social & Economic Studies; Current Economic Analysis; Business & Labour Market Analysis; Micro Economic Studies & Analysis; & Family & Community Support Systems.

Director General, System of National Accounts, K. Lal, 613/951-9157, Includes Input-Output; Industry Measures & Analysis; National Accounts & Environment; Balance of Payments; & Public Institutions.

Senior Social Scientist, P. Reed, 613/951-8217

#### SOCIAL INSTITUTIONS & LABOUR STATISTICS

Asst. Chief Statistician, D.B. Petrie, 613/951-6155, Fax: 613/951-0556

Acting Director General, Census & Demographic Statistics, B. Laroche, 613/951-6537, Includes Census Management Office; Census Operations; Housing; Family & Social Statistics; & Demolinguistics.

Director General, Institutions & Social Statistics, M.C. Wolfson, 613/951-8216, Includes Education, Culture & Tourism; & Health Statistics.

Director General, Labour & Household Surveys, Vacant, 613/951-0053, Includes Household Surveys; Labour; Labour & Household Surveys Analysis; Post Censal Survey Program; & Special Surveys.

Executive Director, Canadian Centre for Justice Statistics, A. Kohut, 613/951-5858

Director, Integration & Development of Social Statistics, G.E. Priest, 613/951-9301

#### STATISTICS CANADA REGIONAL REFERENCE CENTRES

Toll Free: 1-800-263-1136, TDD: 1-800-363-7629

Toll Free Orders: 1-800-267-6677

Each centre provides a full range of the Agency's products and services. Each has a library and a sales counter where users can consult or purchase print and electronic publications, microcomputer diskettes, microfiche, maps and more. Each also has facilities to retrieve information from CANSIM and other databases, and most offer seminars and consultations.

##### Statistics Canada Regional Centres

Calgary: First Street Plaza, #401, 138 - 4 Ave. SE, Calgary AB T2G 4Z6 – 403/292-6717; Fax: 403/292-4958

Edmonton: Park Square, 10001 Bellamy Hill, 9th Fl., Edmonton AB T5J 3B6 – 403/495-3027; Fax: 403/495-5318

Halifax: North American Life Centre, 1770 Market St., Halifax NS B3J 3M3 – 902/426-5331; Fax: 902/426-9538

Montréal: Tour Est, Complexe Guy-Favreau, #412, 200, boul René-Lévesque ouest, Montréal QC H2Z 1X4 – 514/283-5725; Fax: 514/283-9350

Ottawa: R.H. Coats Bldg., Lobby, Tunney's Pasture, Ottawa ON K1A 0T6 – 613/951-8116; Fax: 613/951-0581

Regina: Avord Tower, 2002 Victoria Ave., 9th Fl., Regina SK S4P 0R7 – 306/780-5405; Fax: 306/780-5403

Toronto: Arthur Meighen Bldg., 25 St. Clair Ave. East, 10th Fl., Toronto ON M4T 1M4 – 416/973-6586; Fax: 416/973-7475

Vancouver: Library Square Tower, #600, 300 West Georgia St., Vancouver BC V6B 6C4 – 604/666-3691; Fax: 604/666-4863

Winnipeg: MacDonald Bldg., #300, 344 Edmonton St., Winnipeg MB R3B 3L9 – 204/983-4020; Fax: 204/983-7543

## STATUS OF WOMEN CANADA (SWC)/ Condition féminine Canada

#700, 360 Albert St., Ottawa ON K1A 1C3

613/995-7835; Fax: 613/957-3359; URL: http://canada.gc.ca/depts/agencies/swcind_e.html

SWC is the federal government department dedicated to women's equality. It is responsible for policy coordination, research, funding & technical assistance, & communications activities related to the promotion of women's equality in all spheres of Canadian life. SWC was the lead government department involved in the coordination of Canadian preparations for the Fourth United Nations World Conference on Women in Bejing, China (September 1995).

The Agency ensures that women's equality is integrated into all federal government legislation, policies, programs & initiatives. It provides financial & technical assistance to women's groups & other voluntary organizations which promote public understanding of women's equality issues. SWC also encourages action by key institutions to incorporate women's equality into their decision-making structures, policies & programs, & enables women's organizations working on women's equality issues to improve & develop their planning & organizational skills.

**Secretary of State**, Hon. Hedy Fry
Coordinator, Louise Bergeron-de Villiers
Director General, External Relations & Communications, Mary Glen
Director, Executive Secretariat, Marguerite Alexander
Director, Policy, Micheline Charlebois-McKinnon
Director, Research, Zeynep Karman
Director, Resource Management, Guylaine Metayer
Director, Women's Program, Jackie Claxton

## TELEFILM CANADA/Téléfilm Canada

Tour de la Banque Nationale, 600, De La Gauchetière ouest, 14e étage, Montréal QC H3B 4L8
514/283-6363; Fax: 514/283-8212; URL: http://www.telefilm.gc.ca

The Corporation supports & promotes private sector development of Canada's film, television & video industry. Reports to government through the Minister of Canadian Heritage.

**Chair**, Robert Dinan
Executive Director, François Macerola

**Offices in Canada**

Halifax: 5523 Spring Garden Rd., PO Box 27, Halifax NS B3J 3T1 – 902/426-8425; Fax: 902/426-4445
Toronto: 2 Bloor St. West, 22nd Fl., Toronto ON M4W 3E2 – 416/973-6436; Fax: 416/973-8606
Vancouver: #350, 375 Water St., Vancouver BC V6B 5C6 – 604/666-1566; Fax: 604/666-7754

**International Offices**

France: 5, rue de Constantine, Paris 75007, France – 011-33-1-44-18-35-30; Fax: 011-33-1-47-05-72-76

## TRANSPORT CANADA (TC)/Transports Canada

Transport Canada Building, 330 Sparks St., Ottawa ON K1A 0N5
613/990-2309; Fax: 613/954-4731; Email: MinTC@tc.gc.ca; URL: http://www.tc.gc.ca

Develops & administers policies, regulations & services for the best possible transportation system. Department consists of operational & support groups working at headquarters in Ottawa & at sites across Canada.

**ACTS ADMINISTERED**

Aeronautics Act
Act respecting regulations made pursuant to section 5 of the Aeronautics Act
Airport Transfer (Miscellaneous Matters) Act
Arctic Waters Pollution Prevention Act
Blue Water Bridge Authority Act
Buffalo & Fort Erie Public Bridge Company Act
Canada Shipping Act
Canada Transportation Act
Coasting Trade Act
Department of Transport Act
Hamilton Harbour Commissioners Act
Harbour Commissions Act
Intercolonial & PEI Railways Employees' Provident Fund Act
Marine & Aviation War Risks Act
Marine Insurance Act
Marine Transportation Security Act
Maritime Code Act
Meaford Harbour Act
Montréal Port Wardens Act
Motor Vehicle Fuel Consumption Standards Act
Motor Vehicle Safety Act
Navigable Waters Protection Act
Ontario Harbours Agreement Act
Pilotage Act
Public Harbours & Port Facilities Act
Québec Port Wardens Act
Railway Safety Act
Safe Containers Convention Act
Toronto Harbour Commissioners' Act
Toronto Harbour Commissioners' Act, 1985
Transportation of Dangerous Goods Act

**Acts Transport Canada is Responsible for, but does not Administer**

Bills of Lading Act
Canada Ports Corporation Act
Canadian National Commercialization Act
Canadian National Montréal Terminals Act
Canadian National Railways Act
Canadian National Railways Financing & Guarantee Act
Canadian National Toronto Terminals Act
Carriage by Air Act
Carriage of Goods by Water Act
Civil Air Navigation Services Commercialization Act
International Rapids Power Development Act
Marine Atlantic Inc. Acquisition Authorization Act
Motor Vehicle Transport Act
National Transcontinental Railway Act
Northern Transportation Company Ltd., Disposal Authorization
Railway Relocation & Crossing Act
St. Lawrence Seaway Authority Act
Shipping Conferences Exemption Act
Winnipeg Terminals Act

**Some Transport Implications**

Bridges Act
Canadian Environmental Assessment Act
Canadian Environmental Protection Act
Canadian Transportation Accident Investigation & Safety Board Act
Excise Tax Act
Government Property Traffic Act
National Energy Board Act
Non-smoker's Health Act
Public Works Act
Ste-Foy-St-Nicholas Bridge Act
United States Wreckers Act

**Minister**, Hon. David Collenette, 613/991-0700
Deputy Minister, Margaret Bloodworth, 613/990-7127, Fax: 613/991-0851
Director General, Communications, Rhoda Barrett, 613/990-6138, Fax: 613/995-0351
Departmental General Counsel, R.J. Green, 613/990-5768, Fax: 613/990-5777
Regional Director General, Atlantic, Gerry Berigan, 506/851-7315, Fax: 506/851-3099
Regional Director General, Ontario, Terence Gibson, 416/952-2170, Fax: 416/952-0170
Regional Director General, Pacific, Mark Duncan, 604/666-5849, Fax: 604/666-2961
Regional Director General, Prairie & Northern, J. Scott Broughton, 204/984-8105, Fax: 204/984-8119
Regional Director General, Québec, Suzanne Tining, 514/283-0084, Fax: 514/283-4661

**CORPORATE SERVICES GROUP**

Responsible for providing overall direction, management & services within the department in the areas of finance, human resources, information management & technology, audit & administration.

Asst. Deputy Minister, Micheline Desjardins, 613/991-6565, Fax: 613/991-0426
Director General, Executive Services, William J. McCullough, 613/993-7412, Fax: 613/954-1993
Director General, Finance, Jim Lynes, 613/993-5660, Fax: 613/991-4410
Director General, Human Resources, Lynette Cox, 613/991-6315, Fax: 613/991-0722
Director General, Informatics & Administrative Services, André Morency, 613/993-4307, Fax: 613/990-2469

**POLICY GROUP**

Responsible for setting policies relating to rail, marine, highways, motor carrier & air transportation, as well as setting departmental strategic policy & coordinating intergovernmental relations; assessing the performance of the overall transportation systems & its components, & developing supporting information; & supporting rail passenger services through payments to VIA Rail & three regional railways, & ferry services through payments to Marine Atlantic & to provincial & private operators.

Asst. Deputy Minister, Louis Ranger, 613/998-1880, Fax: 613/991-1440
Director General, Air Policy, Robert Mayes, 613/993-0054, Fax: 613/991-6445
Director General, Corporate Relations, Ted Cherrett, 613/991-6500, Fax: 613/991-6422
Director General, Economic Analysis, Roger Roy, 613/998-0684, Fax: 613/957-3280
Director General, Marine Policy, André Pageot, 613/998-1843, Fax: 613/998-1845
Director General, Program Evaluation, Jonathon Fisher, 613/993-4418, Fax: 613/991-1291
Director General, Surface Policy, Kristine Burr, 613/998-2689, Fax: 613/998-2686

**PROGRAMS & DIVESTITURE GROUP**

Responsible for negotiating transfers & leases of ports, harbours, airports & bridges; managing leases & real property; developing sustainable development & environment policy; administering departmental funded programs, such as Airports Capital Assistance Program, the Port Divestiture Fund, & federal-provincial highways & bridges; & operating facilites not yet divested.

Asst. Deputy Minister, Ronald R. Sully, 613/990-3001, Fax: 613/998-5008
Director General, Airport Programs & Divestiture, John Desmarais, 613/998-5172, Fax: 613/990-8630
Director General, Environmental Affairs, Victor Thom, 613/990-1401, Fax: 613/957-4260
Director General, Port Programs & Divestiture, Randy Morriss, 613/990-3014, Fax: 613/954-0838
Director General, Surface Programs & Divestiture, Dave Bell, 613/993-4464, Fax: 613/990-9639

**SAFETY & SECURITY GROUP**

Responsible for the development of regulations & national standards as well as the implementation of monitoring, testing, inspection, research & development, & subsidy programs to contribute to safety & security in the aviation, marine, rail & road modes of transport. Administers the delivery of aircraft services to government, department & certain other bodies. Also responsible for developing & enforcing regulations & standards under federal jurisdiction to protect public safety in the transportation of dangerous goods, & to prevent unlawful interference in the aviation, marine & railway modes of transport. Ensures that the department is prepard to respond to transportation & transportation-related emergencies.

Asst. Deputy Minister, Ronald Jackson, 613/990-3838, Fax: 613/990-2947
Director General, Aircraft Services, Ronald D. Armstrong, 613/998-3316, Fax: 613/991-0365
Director General, Civil Aviation, Don Spruston, 613/990-1322, Fax: 613/957-4208
Director General, Marine Safety, Bud Streeter, 613/998-0610, Fax: 613/954-1032
Director General, Railway Legislation, Colin J. Churcher, 613/993-7392, Fax: 613/990-7767

Director General, Railway Safety, Terry Burtch, 613/998-2984, Fax: 613/990-2924
Director General, Road Safety & Motor Vehicle Regulation, Nicole Pageot, 613/993-6735, Fax: 613/990-2914
Acting Director General, Safety Programs, Strategies & Co-ordination, Gaétan Boucher, 613/990-3797, Fax: 613/990-5058
Director General, Security & Emergency Planning, Hal Whiteman, 613/990-3651, Fax: 613/996-6381
Director General, Transport Dangerous Goods, Dr. J.A. Read, 613/990-1147, Fax: 613/993-5925

#### Associated Agencies, Boards & Commissions

•Civil Aviation Tribunal: 333 Laurier Ave. West, 12th Fl., Ottawa ON K1A 0N5 – 613/998-1275; Fax: 613/990-9153
Chair, Faye Helen Smith

#### Other Associated Agencies, Boards & Commissions

Listed alphabetically in detail, this section.
Atlantic Pilotage Authority
Canadian Transportation Agency
Great Lakes Pilotage Authority
Laurentian Pilotage Authority
Marine Atlantic Inc.
Pacific Pilotage Authority
St. Lawrence Seaway Authority
Via Rail Canada

## TRANSPORTATION SAFETY BOARD OF CANADA/Bureau de la sécurité des transports du Canada

200 Promenade du Portage, 4e étage, Hull QC K1A 1K8
819/994-3741; Fax: 819/997-2239; URL: http://bst-tsb.gc.ca
The Board is an independent agency reporting to Parliament through the President of the Queen's Privy Council. The formal name for the Board is the Canadian Transportation Accident Investigation & Safety Board. Its sole aim is the advancement of transportation safety in the marine, rail, commodity pipeline & air modes of transport. It conducts investigations of occurrences, makes findings, identifies safety deficiencies, conducts safety studies, & makes recommendations designed to prevent further occurrences. Because the Board is independent, its transportation accident investigations are completely separate from the regulatory agencies responsible for transportation. In making findings & recommendations it is not the function of the Board to assign fault or determine civil or criminal liability.
**Chair**, Hon. Benoît Bouchard
Executive Director, Ken Johnson
Chief, Communications, Jacques Babin, 819/994-8051, Email: Jacques.Babin@bst-tsb.x400.gc.ca

## TREASURY BOARD OF CANADA/Conseil du Trésor du Canada

140 O'Connor St., Ottawa ON K1A 0R5
613/957-2400; Fax: 613/952-3658; URL: http://www.tbs-sct.gc.ca
The Treasury Board is a Cabinet Committee of government headed by the President of the Treasury Board. The committee constituting the Treasury Board includes, in addition to the President, the Minister of Finance & four other ministers appointed by the Governor-in-Council. The main role of the Treasury Board is the management of the government's financial, personnel & administrative responsibilities. The Treasury Board derives its authority primarily from the Financial Administration Act & is supported by the Treasury Board Secretariat.
**President & Minister Responsible, Infrastructure**, Hon. Marcel Massé, 613/957-2666, Fax: 613/990-2806
Secretary & Comptroller General of Canada, V. Peter Harder, 613/952-1777, Fax: 613/952-6596
Deputy Minister, Corporate Services, Joy Kane, 613/995-8487, Fax: 613/947-3643
Deputy Secretary, Human Resources Policy Branch, Vacant, 613/952-3011, Fax: 613/954-1018
Deputy Secretary, Official Languages & Employment Equity Branch, Madeleine Ouellon, 613/952-2852, Fax: 613/941-4262
Acting Deputy Secretary, Program Branch, Paul Thibault, 613/957-0531, Fax: 613/957-0525
Special Advisor to the Secretary, John Edwards

#### OFFICE OF INFRASTRUCTURE

West Tower, 300 Laurier Ave. West, 3rd Fl., Ottawa ON K1A 0R5
613/952-3171; Fax: 613/952-7979; Email: infrastructure@tbs-sct.x400.gc.ca
Executive Director, Paul Thibault
Director, Policy & Coordination, Glynnis French

## VETERANS AFFAIRS CANADA/Anciens combattants Canada

Daniel J. MacDonald Bldg., 161 Grafton St., PO Box 7700, Charlottetown PE C1A 8M9
902/566-8195; Fax: 902/566-8508
Ottawa: 66 Slater St., Ottawa ON K1A 0P4
613/992-7467, Fax: 613/996-9969

#### ACTS ADMINISTERED

Army Benevolent Fund Act
Children of Deceased Veterans Education Assistance Act
Department of Veterans Affairs Act
Merchant Navy Veterans & Civilian War-related Benefits Act
Pension Act
The Returned Soldiers' Insurance Act
Soldier Settlement Act
Special Operators War Service Benefits Act
Supervisors War Service Benefits Act
Veterans Review & Appeal Board Act
Veterans Benefits Act
Veterans Insurance Act
Veterans' Land Act
War Service Grants Act
War Veterans Allowance Act
Women's Royal Naval Services & the South African Military Nursing Service (Benefits) Act

#### Related Acts

Halifax Relief Commission Pension Continuation Act
Royal Canadian Mounted Police Pension Continuation Act (in Part)
Royal Canadian Mounted Police Superannuation Act (in Part)
**Minister**, Hon. Fred J. Mifflin, 613/943-0362, Fax: 613/954-1054
Deputy Minister, J. David Nicholson, 902/566-8666, Fax: 902/566-7868, Ottawa: 613/996-6881; Fax: 613/952-7709
Director General, Communications, Sandra Lavigne, 902/566-8457
Director General, Corporate Planning, Keith Hillier, 902/566-8150
Director General, Portfolio Executive Services, B. Bowen, 613/992-3801
Project Manager, Benefits Redesign Project, Ron Herbert, 902/368-0530
Project Manager, Health Care Coordination Initiative, Mike Charles, 613/992-9003
Senior Advisor, Office of Conflict Resolution, Sue E. Campbell, 902/368-0435

#### CORPORATE SERVICES

Asst. Deputy Minister, Brian Ferguson, 902/566-8047, Fax: 902/566-8521
Director General, Audit & Evaluation, J.G. Harper, 902/566-8018
Director General, Finance, Marilyn MacPherson, 902/566-8320, Fax: 902/368-0411
Director General, Human Resources, Bob Mercer, 902/566-8408, Fax: 902/566-8781
Acting Director General, Information Technology Division, Howard Williams, 902/566-8236

#### VETERANS SERVICES

Asst. Deputy Minister, Dennis Wallace, 902/566-8100, Fax: 902/566-8780
Director General, Benefits, Doris Boulet, 613/566-8808, Fax: 613/566-8073
Director General, Commemoration, Al Puxley, 902/566-8148
Director General, Health Care, W.D. Mogan, 902/566-8302, Fax: 902/566-8039
Executive Director, Ste. Annes Hospital, R. Gravel, 514/457-8400

#### Regional Offices

Atlantic: 33 Alderney Dr., PO Box 1002, Dartmouth NS B2Y 2N4 – 902/426-6305; Fax: 902/426-7447, Director General, Ron Witt
Ontario: Bag Service 4000, 145 Government Rd. West, Kirkland Lake ON P2N 3P4 – 705/568-4132; Fax: 705/567-7971, Director General, Gisèle Toupin
Pacific: #400, 1185 West Georgia St., PO Box 5600, Vancouver BC V6B 5G4 – 604/666-3101; Fax: 604/666-2881, Director General, Bob Atkinson
Prairie: 234 Donald St., PO Box 6050, Winnipeg MB R3C 4G5 – 204/983-5316; Fax: 204/983-2563, Director General, Elaine Heinicke
Québec: 4545, rue Queen Mary, Montréal QC H3W 1W4 – 514/496-6412; Fax: 514/496-4339, Director General, Suzanne Lalonde

#### Associated Agencies, Boards & Commissions

•Bureau Of Pension Advocates: J. MacDonald Bldg., 2nd Fl., PO Box 7700, Charlottetown PE C1A 8M9 – 902/566-8640; Fax: 902/566-7804
Chief Pensions Advocate, Simon Coakeley
•Veterans Review & Appeal Board: Daniel J. MacDonald Bldg., PO Box 7700, Charlottetown PE C1A 8M9 – 902/566-8636; Fax: 902/566-7371
Chair, Brian Chambers

## VIA RAIL CANADA INC.

2, Place Ville-Marie, CP 8116, Succ A, Montréal QC H3C 3N3
514/871-6000; Fax: 514/861-6463
The Corporation manages Canada's national passenger rail network. Reports to government through the Minister of Transport.
**Chair**, Marc LeFrançois
President, Terry Ivany, 514/871-6161
Executive Vice-President & COO, James Roche
Vice-President & Chief of Transportation, Robert J. Guiney
Vice-President, Customer Service, Roy Arnold
Vice-President, Equipment Maintenance, Réjean Béchamp
Vice-President, Planning & Finance, Roger Paquette
Senior Vice-President, Human Resources & Administration, Jean-Roch Boivin
Treasurer, Rashid Maqsood
Vice-President, Marketing, Christena Keon Sirsly
General Manager, Public Affairs, Marc-André Charlebois
General Counsel, Jean Patenaude

## WESTERN ECONOMIC DIVERSIFICATION CANADA (WD)/Diversification de l'économie de l'Ouest Canada

Canada Place, #1500, 9700 Jasper Ave., Edmonton AB T5J 4H7
403/495-4164; Fax: 403/495-6223; URL: http://www.wd.gc.ca
Toll Free: 1-888-338-WEST (9378)
Promotes the development & diversification of the economy of Western Canada & advances the interests of Western Canada in national economic policy. Seeks new innovative partnerships with both the public & private sectors to address the information, business services & financing needs of small & medium-sized enterprises. By partnering with financial institutions, industry associations & the four western provinces, WD is satisfying the needs of small business by creating a positive business climate & by improving access to capital, information & business services. Resources are strategically targeted to industries having the greatest potential for growth in economic activity.
**Minister**, Hon. Ronald J. Duhamel, 613/995-9001, Fax: 613/990-4056
Deputy Minister, John McLure, 613/952-9382, Fax: 613/954-1044
Assoc. Deputy Minister, Oryssia Lennie, 403/495-5772, Fax: 403/495-6222
Director, Consultations, Marketing & Communications, Alec Jasen, 613/952-7101, Fax: 613/952-6775

#### Regional Offices

Alberta: Canada Place, #1500, 9700 Jasper Ave., Edmonton AB T5J 4H7 – 403/495-4164, Director, Vacant
British Columbia: Bentall Tower 4, #1200, 1055 Dunsmuir St., PO Box 49276, Vancouver BC V7X 1L3 – 604/666-6256, Director, Dan Genn
Manitoba: Cargill Bldg., #712, 240 Graham Ave., PO Box 777, Winnipeg MB R3C 2L4 – 204/983-0697, Director, Dave Boldt
Ottawa: 200 Kent St., 8th Fl., PO Box 2128, Stn D, Ottawa ON K1P 5W3 – 613/952-9378, Director, Onno Kremers
Saskatchewan: S.J. Cohen Bldg., #601, 119 - 4 Ave. South, PO Box 2025, Saskatoon SK S7K 3S7 – 306/975-4373, Director, Laura Small

# GOVERNMENT OF ALBERTA

**Seat of Government:** Legislative Assembly, 9718 - 107 St., Edmonton AB T5K 1E4
URL: http://www.gov.ab.ca/
The Province of Alberta entered Confederation September 1, 1905. It has an area of 638,232.66 km2, and the StatsCan census population in 1996 was 2,696,826.

## Office of the LIEUTENANT GOVERNOR

Legislature Bldg., 10800 - 97 Ave., 3rd Fl., Edmonton AB T5K 2B6
403/427-7243; Fax: 403/422-5134
**Lieutenant Governor**, Hon. Horace Andrew (Bud) Olson
Secretary, Astrid Casavant

## Office of the PREMIER

Legislature Bldg., #307, 10800 - 97 Ave., Edmonton AB T5K 2B6
403/427-2251; Fax: 403/427-1349; URL: http://www.gov.ab.ca/gov/prem/premier.html
**Premier**, Hon. Ralph Klein, Email: altatalk@censsw.gov.ab.ca
Deputy Minister, Executive Council, Vance MacNichol
Executive Director, Rod Love
Executive Asst., Sheryl Burns
Administrative Asst., Nargis Zaver
Director, Communications, Jim Dau, Fax: 403/422-3669
Director, Southern Alberta Office, Gordon Olsen, 403/297-6464, Fax: 403/297-4276

## EXECUTIVE COUNCIL

Legislature Bldg., 10800 - 97 Ave., Edmonton AB T5K 2B6
403/427-2251; Fax: 403/427-1349

#### ACTS ADMINISTERED

Alberta Bill of Rights
Family Day Act
Northern Alberta Development Council Act
Queen's Printer Act

Premier, President, Executive Council, Hon. Ralph Klein, 403/427-2251, Email: altatalk@censsw.gov.ab.ca
Minister, Economic Development & Tourism, Hon. Patricia Black, 403/427-3162
Minister without Portfolio, Hon. Pearl Calahasen, 403/427-2180
Provincial Treasurer, Hon. Stockwell Day, 403/427-8809
Minister, Advanced Education & Career Development, Hon. Clint Dunford, 403/427-2291
Minister, Municipal Affairs, Hon. Iris Evans, 403/427-3744
Minister, Federal & Intergovernmental Affairs, Hon. David Hancock, Q.C., 403/427-2585
Minister, Justice & Attorney General, Government House Leader, Hon. Jon Havelock, 403/427-2339
Minister, Health, Hon. Halvar Jonson, 403/427-3665
Minister, Environmental Protection, Hon. Ty Lund, 403/427-2391
Minister, Education, Hon. Gary G. Mar, 403/427-2025
Minister, Community Development, Hon. Shirley McClellan, 403/427-4928
Minister, Family & Social Services, Hon. Dr. Lyle Oberg, 403/427-2606
Minister, Transportation & Utilities, Hon. Walter Paszkowski, 403/427-2080
Minister, Labour, Hon. Murray Smith, 403/427-3664
Minister, Agriculture, Hon. Ed Stelmach, 403/427-2137
Minister, Science, Research & Information Technology, Hon. Dr. Lorne Taylor, 403/427-2294
Minister, Energy, Hon. Dr. Stephen C. West, 403/427-3740
Minister, Public Works, Supply & Services, Hon. Stan Woloshyn, 403/427-3666

#### Cabinet Office

Deputy Secretary, David Steeves
Director, Finance & Administration, Keray Henke, 403/427-1076
Coordinator, Cabinet Policy, Doris Porter
Coordinator, Cabinet Policy, Wendy Rogers

#### Cabinet Standing Committees

Agenda & Priorities
Agriculture & Rural Development
Community Resources
Education & Training
Financial Planning & Human Resources
Health Planning
Jobs & the Economy
Sustainable Development & Environmental Protection
Treasury Board

## LEGISLATIVE ASSEMBLY

c/o Clerk's Office, #801, Legislature Annex, 9718 - 107 St., Edmonton AB T5K 1E4
403/427-2478; Fax: 403/427-5688; URL: http://www.assembly.ab.ca/

#### ACTS ADMINISTERED

Auditor General Act
Conflict of Interest Act
Election Act
Election Finances & Contributions Disclosure Act
Electoral Boundaries Commission Act
Electoral Divisions Act
Legislative Assembly Act
Ombudsman Act

**Clerk:** W.J. David McNeil
**Speaker:** Hon. Ken Kowalski, 403/427-2464, Fax: 403/422-9553
**Hansard:** Gary Garrison, 403/427-1609, Fax: 403/427-1623
**Librarian:** Lorne Buhr, 403/427-0207, Fax: 403/427-6016
Clerk Asst., Louise Kamuchik
Speaker Asst., Moses Jung
Parliamentary Counsel, Shannon Dean
Parliamentary Counsel, Rob Reynolds
Manager, Financial Management & Administrative Services, Jacqueline Breault, 403/427-1359
Director, Human Resources, Cheryl Scarlett, 403/427-1368
Director, Public Information, Gary Garrison, 403/427-1609

#### Government Caucus Office (PC)

Legislature Annex, 9718 - 107 St., 7th Fl., Edmonton AB T5K 1E4
403/427-1800; Fax: 403/422-1671
Chief of Staff, Kathryn Dawson, #402, Legislature Bldg., Edmonton AB T5K 2B6

#### Official Opposition Office (Lib.)

Legislature Annex, #601, 9718 - 107 St., Edmonton AB T5K 1E4
403/427-2292; Fax: 403/427-3697
Leader, Grant Mitchell
Chief of Staff, Mary MacDonald
Senior Researcher, Mary Griffith
Deputy Leader, Debby Carlson

#### Standing Committees of the Legislature

Alberta Heritage Savings Trust Fund Act, Clerk, Diane Shumyla, 403/427-1350
Law & Regulations, Clerk, Corrine Dacyshyn, 403/427-1348
Legislative Offices, Clerk, Diane Shumyla, 403/427-1350
Members' Services, Clerk, David McNeil, 403/427-2478
Private Bills, Clerk, Florence Marston, 403/422-4837
Privileges & Election, Standing Orders & Printing, Clerk, Corinne Dacyshyn, 403/427-1348
Public Accounts, Clerk, Corrine Dacyshyn, 403/427-1348
Public Affairs, Clerk, Diane Shumlya, 403/427-1350

## TWENTY-FOURTH LEGISLATURE - ALBERTA

403/427-2478
Last General Election, March 11, 1997. Maximum Duration, 5 Years.
**Party Standings (June 9, 1997)**
Progressive Conservative (PC) 63
Liberal (Lib.) 18
New Democrat (NDP) 2
Total 83
**Salaries, Indemnities & Allowances**

March 1, 1993 frozen - Members' sessional indemnity $36,420 plus $18,210 tax-free expense allowance. In addition to this are the following:
Premier $56,865
Ministers $44,700 (with portfolio); $19,869 (without portfolio)
Leader of the Official Opposition $44,700
Speaker $44,700
Deputy Speaker; Chair of Committees $22,350
Leader of a recognized Opposition $19,869

**MEMBERS BY CONSTITUENCY**

Following is: constituency (number of eligible voters at 1993 election) member, party affiliation, Edmonton telephone number. (Address for all is Legislature Bldg., 10800 - 97 Ave., Edmonton AB T5K 2B6.)

Airdrie-Rocky View (23,081) Carol Haley, PC, 403/422-5372
Athabasca-Wabasca (11,591) Mike Cardinal, PC, 403/427-8098
Banff-Cochrane (23,740) Janice Tarchuk, PC, 403/415-0993
Barrhead-Westlock (16,915) Hon. Ken Kowalski, PC, 403/427-2464
Bonnyville-Cold Lake (16,465) Denis Ducharme, PC, 403/415-0995
Calgary-Bow (22,698) Bonny Laing, PC, 403/427-1811
Calgary-Buffalo (22,891) Gary Dickson, Lib., 403/427-2293
Calgary-Cross (21,803) Yvonne Fritz, PC, 403/422-5375
Calgary-Currie (22,851) Jocelyn Burgener, PC, 403/427-1837
Calgary-East (21,288) Moe Amery, PC, 403/422-5382
Calgary-Egmont (26,768) Denis Herard, PC, 403/422-5378
Calgary-Elbow (23,672) Hon. Ralph Klein, PC, 403/427-2251
Calgary-Fish Creek (22,671) Heather Forsyth, PC, 403/427-1851
Calgary-Foothills (28,493) Hon. Patricia Black, PC, 403/427-3740
Calgary-Fort (22,095) Wayne Cao, PC, 403/415-0984
Calgary-Glenmore (23,818) Ron Stevens, PC, 403/415-0966
Calgary-Lougheed (21,685) Marlene Graham, PC, 403/415-0991
Calgary-McCall (20,862) Shiraz Shariff, PC, 403/422-0685
Calgary-Montrose (19,623) Hung Pham, PC, 403/427-1865
Calgary-Mountain View (22,491) Mark Hlady, PC, 403/422-5380
Calgary-North Hill (22,029) Richard Magnus, PC, 403/427-3018
Calgary-North West (28,813) Greg Melchin, PC, 403/415-0972
Calgary-Nose Creek (26,446) Hon. Gary G. Mar, PC, 403/427-2025
Calgary-Shaw (32,938) Hon. Jon Havelock, PC, 403/422-5376
Calgary-Varsity (23,875) Hon. Murray Smith, PC, 403/427-3664
Calgary-West (27,181) Karen Kryczka, PC, 403/415-0983
Cardston-Taber-Warner (18,072) Ron Hierath, PC, 403/427-1864
Clover Bar-Fort Saskatchewan (23,297) Rob Lougheed, PC, 403/415-0990
Cypress-Medicine Hat (18,059) Hon. Dr. Lorne Taylor, PC, 403/427-1822
Drayton Valley-Calmar (17,236) Tom Thurber, PC, 403/415-0981
Drumheller Chinook (15,920) Hon. Shirley McClellan, PC, 403/427-4928
Dunvegan (16,054) Glen Clegg, PC, 403/427-1806
Edmonton-Beverly-Clareview (19,806) Julius Yankowsky, PC, 403/422-1357
Edmonton-Calder (22,083) Lance White, Lib., 403/427-2292
Edmonton-Castle Downs (21,345) Pamela Paul, Lib., 403/427-2292
Edmonton-Centre (19,463) Laurie Blakeman, Lib., 403/427-2292
Edmonton-Ellerslie (18,175) Debby Carlson, Lib., 403/427-2292
Edmonton-Glengarry (19,535) Bill Bonner, Lib., 403/427-2292
Edmonton-Glenora (21,230) Howard Sapers, Lib., 403/427-2292
Edmonton-Gold Bar (23,695) Hugh MacDonald, Lib., 403/427-2292
Edmonton-Highlands (18,533) Pam Barrett, NDP, 403/415-0944
Edmonton-Manning (24,368) Ed Gibbons, Lib., 403/427-2292
Edmonton-McLung (21,881) Grant Mitchell, Lib., 403/427-2292
Edmonton-Meadowlark (21,431) Karen Leibovici, Lib., 403/427-2292
Edmonton-Mill Creek (23,316) Gene Zwozdesky, Lib., 403/427-2292
Edmonton-Mill Woods (18,091) Dr. Don Massey, Lib., 403/427-2292
Edmonton-Norwood (18,008) Sue Olsen, Lib., 403/422-2292
Edmonton-Riverview (23,094) Linda Sloan, Lib., 403/427-2292
Edmonton-Rutherford (22,043) Percy Wickman, Lib., 403/427-2292
Edmonton-Strathcona (23,999) Raj Pannu, NDP, 403/415-0944
Edmonton-Whitemud (25,550) Hon. David Hancock, Q.C., PC, 403/427-2585
Fort McMurray (21,527) Guy Boutilier, PC, 403/415-0987
Grande Prairie-Smoky (18,831) Hon. Walter Paszkowski, PC, 403/427-2137
Grande Prairie-Wapiti (18,964) Wayne Jacques, PC, 403/427-1858
Highwood (24,173) Don Tannas, PC, 403/427-1826
Innisfail-Sylvan Lake (20,845) Gary Severtson, PC, 403/427-1857
Lac La Biche-St. Paul (14,434) Paul Langevin, PC, 403/422-5843
Lacombe-Stettler (19,231) Judy Gordon, PC, 403/427-1807
Leduc (22,263) Albert Klapstein, PC, 403/415-0989
Lesser Slave Lake (13,348) Hon. Pearl Calahasen, PC, 403/427-2180
Lethbridge-East (23,371) Dr. Ken Nicol, Lib., 403/427-2292
Lethbridge-West (22,291) Hon. Clint Dunford, PC, 403/427-1142
Little Bow (17,742) Barry McFarland, PC, 403/427-0879
Livingstone-MacLeod (24,292) David Coutts, PC, 403/427-1828
Medicine Hat (24,037) Rob Renner, PC, 403/427-1879
Olds-Didsbury-Three Hills (19,975) Richard Marz, PC, 403/415-0994
Peace River (16,102) Gary Friedel, PC, 403/422-5374
Ponoka-Rimbey (15,120) Hon. Halvar Jonson, PC, 403/427-3665
Red Deer-North (19,022) Hon. Stockwell Day, PC, 403/427-2606
Red Deer-South (21,090) Victor Doerksen, PC, 403/427-1145
Redwater (20,130) Dave Broda, PC, 403/415-0955
Rocky Mountain House (18,568) Hon. Ty Lund, PC, 403/427-2391
Sherwood Park (27,617) Hon. Iris Evans, PC
Spruce Grove-Sturgeon-St. Albert (21,087) Colleen Soetaert, Lib., 403/427-2292
St. Albert (25,583) Mary O'Neill, PC, 403/415-0975
Stony Plain (21,204) Hon. Stan Woloshyn, PC, 403/427-3666
Strathmore-Brooks (21,388) Hon. Dr. Lyle Oberg, PC, 403/427-2606
Vegreville-Viking (19,001) Hon. Ed Stelmach, PC, 403/427-1879
Vermillion-Lloydminster (19,339) Hon. Dr. Stephen C. West, PC, 403/427-3162
Wainwright (19,884) Robert (Butch) Fischer, PC, 403/427-3020
West Yellowhead (19,392) Ivan Strang, PC, 403/415-0986
Wetaskiwin-Camrose (22,065) LeRoy Johnson, PC, 403/415-0977
Whitecourt-St. Anne (18,986) Peter Trynchy, PC, 403/427-0495

**MEMBERS (ALPHABETICAL)**

Following is: member, constituency, (number of eligible voters at 1993 election) party affilitation, Edmonton telephone number. (Address for all is Legislature Bldg., 10800 - 97 Ave., Edmonton AB T5K 2B6.)

Moe Amery, Calgary-East (21,288) PC, 403/422-5382
Pam Barrett, Edmonton-Highlands (18,533) NDP, 403/415-0944
Hon. Patricia Black, Calgary-Foothills (28,493) PC, 403/427-3740
Laurie Blakeman, Edmonton-Centre (19,463) Lib., 403/427-2292
Bill Bonner, Edmonton-Glengarry (19,535) Lib., 403/427-2292
Guy Boutilier, Fort McMurray (21,527) PC, 403/415-0987
Dave Broda, Redwater (20,130) PC, 403/415-0955
Jocelyn Burgener, Calgary-Currie (22,851) PC, 403/427-1837
Hon. Pearl Calahasen, Lesser Slave Lake (13,348) PC, 403/427-2180
Wayne Cao, Calgary-Fort (22,095) PC, 403/415-0984
Mike Cardinal, Athabasca-Wabasca (11,591) PC, 403/427-8098
Debby Carlson, Edmonton-Ellerslie (18,175) Lib., 403/427-2292
Glen Clegg, Dunvegan (16,054) PC, 403/427-1806
David Coutts, Livingstone-MacLeod (24,292) PC, 403/427-1828
Hon. Stockwell Day, Red Deer-North (19,022) PC, 403/427-2606
Gary Dickson, Calgary-Buffalo (22,891) Lib., 403/427-2293
Victor Doerksen, Red Deer-South (21,090) PC, 403/427-1145
Denis Ducharme, Bonnyville-Cold Lake (16,465) PC, 403/415-0995
Hon. Clint Dunford, Lethbridge-West (22,291) PC, 403/427-1142
Hon. Iris Evans, Sherwood Park (27,617) PC
Robert (Butch) Fischer, Wainwright (19,884) PC, 403/427-3020
Heather Forsyth, Calgary-Fish Creek (22,671) PC, 403/427-1851
Gary Friedel, Peace River (16,102) PC, 403/422-5374
Yvonne Fritz, Calgary-Cross (21,803) PC, 403/422-5375
Ed Gibbons, Edmonton-Manning (24,368) Lib., 403/427-2292
Judy Gordon, Lacombe-Stettler (19,231) PC, 403/427-1807
Marlene Graham, Calgary-Lougheed (21,685) PC, 403/415-0991
Carol Haley, Airdrie-Rocky View (23,081) PC, 403/422-5372
Hon. David Hancock, Q.C., Edmonton-Whitemud (25,550) PC, 403/427-2585
Hon. Jon Havelock, Calgary-Shaw (32,938) PC, 403/422-5376

Denis Herard, Calgary-Egmont (26,768) PC, 403/422-5378
Ron Hierath, Cardston-Taber-Warner (18,072) PC, 403/427-1864
Mark Hlady, Calgary-Mountain View (22,491) PC, 403/422-5380
Wayne Jacques, Grande Prairie-Wapiti (18,964) PC, 403/427-1858
LeRoy Johnson, Wetaskiwin-Camrose (22,065) PC, 403/415-0977
Hon. Halvar Jonson, Ponoka-Rimbey (15,120) PC, 403/427-3665
Albert Klapstein, Leduc (22,263) PC, 403/415-0989
Hon. Ralph Klein, Calgary-Elbow (23,672) PC, 403/427-2251
Hon. Ken Kowalski, Barrhead-Westlock (16,915) PC, 403/427-2464
Karen Kryczka, Calgary-West (27,181) PC, 403/415-0983
Bonny Laing, Calgary-Bow (22,698) PC, 403/427-1811
Paul Langevin, Lac La Biche-St. Paul (14,434) PC, 403/422-5843
Karen Leibovici, Edmonton-Meadowlark (21,431) Lib., 403/427-2292
Rob Lougheed, Clover Bar-Fort Saskatchewan (23,297) PC, 403/415-0990
Hon. Ty Lund, Rocky Mountain House (18,568) PC, 403/427-2391
Hugh MacDonald, Edmonton-Gold Bar (23,695) Lib., 403/427-2292
Richard Magnus, Calgary-North Hill (22,029) PC, 403/427-3018
Hon. Gary G. Mar, Calgary-Nose Creek (26,446) PC, 403/427-2025
Richard Marz, Olds-Didsbury-Three Hills (19,975) PC, 403/415-0994
Dr. Don Massey, Edmonton-Mill Woods (18,091) Lib., 403/427-2292
Hon. Shirley McClellan, Drumheller Chinook (15,920) PC, 403/427-4928
Barry McFarland, Little Bow (17,742) PC, 403/427-0879
Greg Melchin, Calgary-North West (28,813) PC, 403/415-0972
Grant Mitchell, Edmonton-McLung (21,881) Lib., 403/427-2292
Dr. Ken Nicol, Lethbridge-East (23,371) Lib., 403/427-2292
Hon. Dr. Lyle Oberg, Strathmore-Brooks (21,388) PC, 403/427-2606
Sue Olsen, Edmonton-Norwood (18,008) Lib., 403/422-2292
Mary O'Neill, St. Albert (25,583) PC, 403/415-0975
Raj Pannu, Edmonton-Strathcona (23,999) NDP, 403/415-0944
Hon. Walter Paszkowski, Grande Prairie-Smoky (18,831) PC, 403/427-2137
Pamela Paul, Edmonton-Castle Downs (21,345) Lib., 403/427-2292
Hung Pham, Calgary-Montrose (19,623) PC, 403/427-1865
Rob Renner, Medicine Hat (24,037) PC, 403/427-1879
Howard Sapers, Edmonton-Glenora (21,230) Lib., 403/427-2292
Gary Severtson, Innisfail-Sylvan Lake (20,845) PC, 403/427-1857
Shiraz Shariff, Calgary-McCall (20,862) PC, 403/422-0685
Linda Sloan, Edmonton-Riverview (23,094) Lib., 403/427-2292
Hon. Murray Smith, Calgary-Varsity (23,875) PC, 403/427-3664
Colleen Soetaert, Spruce Grove-Sturgeon-St. Albert (21,087) Lib., 403/427-2292
Hon. Ed Stelmach, Vegreville-Viking (19,001) PC, 403/427-1879
Ron Stevens, Calgary-Glenmore (23,818) PC, 403/415-0966
Ivan Strang, West Yellowhead (19,392) PC, 403/415-0986
Don Tannas, Highwood (24,173) PC, 403/427-1826
Janice Tarchuk, Banff-Cochrane (23,740) PC, 403/415-0993
Hon. Dr. Lorne Taylor, Cypress-Medicine Hat (18,059) PC, 403/427-1822
Tom Thurber, Drayton Valley-Calmar (17,236) PC, 403/415-0981
Peter Trynchy, Whitecourt-St. Anne (18,986) PC, 403/427-0495
Hon. Dr. Stephen C. West, Vermillion-Lloydminster (19,339) PC, 403/427-3162
Lance White, Edmonton-Calder (22,083) Lib., 403/427-2292
Percy Wickman, Edmonton-Rutherford (22,043) Lib., 403/427-2292
Hon. Stan Woloshyn, Stony Plain (21,204) PC, 403/427-3666
Julius Yankowsky, Edmonton-Beverly-Clareview (19,806) PC, 403/422-1357
Gene Zwozdesky, Edmonton-Mill Creek (23,316) Lib., 403/427-2292

# ALBERTA GOVERNMENT DEPARTMENTS & AGENCIES

## Alberta ADVANCED EDUCATION & CAREER DEVELOPMENT

Commerce Place, 10155 - 102 St., 7th Fl., Edmonton AB T5J 4L5
403/422-4488; Fax: 403/422-5126; URL: http://www.gov.ab.ca/dept/aecd.html

### ACTS ADMINISTERED

Advanced Education Foundations Act
Alberta Heritage Scholarship Act
Banff Centre Act
Colleges Act
Private Vocational Schools Act
Student & Temporary Employment Act
Students Finance Act
Students Loan Act
Technical Institutes Act
Universities Act

**Minister**, Hon. Clint Dunford, 403/427-2291, Fax: 403/427-2610
Deputy Minister, Lynne Duncan, 403/427-3659, Fax: 403/427-1510
Director, Communications, Kathie Konarzewski, 403/422-4495, Fax: 403/422-1263
Director, Human Resources, John Bergin, 403/422-4493, Fax: 403/422-5362
Manager, Apprenticeship Operations, Tom Bodner, 403/427-6976, Fax: 403/427-0354

### APPRENTICESHIP & INDUSTRY TRAINING DIVISION

Fax: 403/422-7376
Executive Director, Shirley Dul, 403/422-1185
Director, Apprenticeship & Industry Training Board Secretariat, Don Ogaranko, 403/427-8765
Director, Policy, Promotion & Certification, Susan Johnston, 403/422-1193
Director, Program Development & Standards, Malcolm Cook, 403/427-0830

### FINANCE, ADMINISTRATION & AVC SUPPORT DIVISION

403/422-5126
Senior Director, Gerry Waisman, 403/427-5601
Director, Finance, Schubert Kwan, 403/422-1208

### INFORMATION & POLICY SERVICES DIVISION

Fax: 403/422-0408
Asst. Deputy Minister, Lois Hawkins, 403/427-3663
Director, Evaluation, Bill Wong, 403/427-4746, Fax: 403/422-0897
Acting Director, Federal/Provincial Activities & Acting Director, Learner Issues, Michelle Kirchner, 403/427-8501, Fax: 403/422-0880
Director, Information Technology Services, Grant Chaney, 403/422-1255, Fax: 403/422-5126
Director, Legislative Services, Linda Richardson, 403/427-3798, Fax: 403/427-0793
Director, Policy Development, Peter Hill, 403/422-4845, Fax: 403/422-0880
Director, Strategic Planning & Research, Archie Clark, 403/422-1281, Fax: 403/422-0880

### LEARNER ASSISTANCE DIVISION

Asst. Deputy Minister, Fred Hemingway, 403/422-0010
Executive Director, Operations, Steve MacDonald, 403/427-5551
Executive Director, Program Development & Evaluation, Ried Zittlau, 403/422-0010, Fax: 403/422-1651

#### Regional Offices

North: Seventh Street Plaza South, 10030 - 107 St., 8th Fl., Edmonton AB T5J 4X7 – 403/422-6991, Director, Joe-Anne Priel
South: Century Park Place, 855 - 8 Ave. SW, Calgary AB T2P 3P1 – 403/297-5318; Fax: 403/297-5183, Director, Alan Edser

### LEARNING SUPPORT & ACCOUNTABILITY DIVISION

Commerce Place, 10155 - 102 St., 11th Fl., Edmonton AB T5J 4L5
Asst. Deputy Minister, Phil Gougeon, 403/427-5607, Fax: 403/427-9430
Director, Business Planning & Evaluation, Wayne Shillington, 403/427-5634, Fax: 403/422-3688
Director, Private Institutions, Jean Sprague, 403/427-5609, Fax: 403/427-5920
Acting Director, Public Institutions, Ed Kozakewich, 403/427-5632, Fax: 403/427-4185
Director, System Information, Larry Orton, 403/427-5630, Fax: 403/427-4185

#### Associated Agencies, Boards & Commissions

•Alberta Apprenticeship & Industry Training Board: 10155 - 102 St., 10th Fl., Edmonton AB T5J 4L5 – 403/427-8765
Presiding Officer, Jake Thygesen
•Alberta Council on Admissions & Transfer: #430, 9942 - 108 St., Edmonton AB T5K 2J5
Chair, Terry Moore, 403/422-9021
•Private Colleges Accreditation Board: #430, 9942 - 108 St., Edmonton AB T5K 2J5
Chair, Dr. Peter J. Krueger, 403/427-8921
•Private Vocational Schools Advisory Council: Commerce Place, 10155 - 102 St., 10th Fl., Edmonton AB T5J 4L5 – 403/427-5609
Chair, Robert Graesser
•Students Finance Board: Baker Centre, 10025 - 106 St., 10th Fl., Edmonton AB T5J 1G7 – 403/427-2740; Fax: 403/422-4516
Chair, Fred Clarke
CEO, Fred Hemingway

## Alberta AGRICULTURE, FOOD & RURAL DEVELOPMENT

7000 - 113 St., Edmonton AB T6H 5T6
403/427-2727; Fax: 403/427-2861; URL: http://www.agric.gov.ab.ca/

### ACTS ADMINISTERED

Agricultural Operation Practices Act
Agricultural Pests Act
Agricultural Service Board Act
Agricultural Societies Act (& Agriculture Grants Amendment Regulation)

Agriculture Financial Services Act
Alberta Agricultural Research Institute Act
Animal Protection Act
Artificial Insemination of Domestic Animals Act
Bee Act
Brand Act
Crop Liens Priorities Act
Crop Payments Act
Dairy Board Act
Dairy Industry Act
Expropriation Act (jointly with Alberta Justice)
Farm Credit Stability Act
Farm Implement Act
Federal-Provincial Farm Assistance Act
Feeder Associations Guarantee Act
Fuel Tax Act (jointly with Alberta Treasury)
Fur Farms Act
Government Organization Act, Schedule 2
Horned Cattle Purchases Act
Irrigation Act Parts
Irrigation District Rehabilitation Act
Line Fence Act
Livery Stable Keepers Act
Livestock Diseases Act
Livestock Identification & Brand Inspection Act
Livestock Industry Diversification Act
Livestock & Livestock Products Act
Marketing of Agricultural Products Act
Meat Inspection Act
St. Mary & Milk Rivers Water Agreement (Termination) Act
Soil Conservation Act
Stray Animals Act
Surface Rights Act
Universities' Act
Vegetable Sales (Alberta) Act
Weed Control Act
Wheat Board Money Trust Act
Women's Institute Act

**Minister**, Hon. Ed Stelmach, 403/427-2137, Fax: 403/422-6035
Deputy Minister, C. Doug Radke, 403/427-2145, Fax: 403/422-6317
Farmers' Advocate, Wallace Daley, 403/427-2433, Fax: 403/422-9690
Director, Administration Division, Mike Mylod, 403/427-2151, Fax: 403/422-6529
Director, Communications Division, Brad Haddrell, 403/427-2127, Fax: 403/427-2861
Director, Internal Audit Division, Ralph Killips, 403/422-9183, Fax: 403/422-5220

### FIELD SERVICES SECTOR

Asst. Deputy Minister, Les Lyster, 403/427-2439, Fax: 403/422-6317
Director, Rural Development Division, John Tackaberry, 403/427-2409, Fax: 403/422-7755
Head, Agricultural Education & Community Services, Reg Kontz, 403/427-2171, Fax: 403/422-7755
Head, Engineering Services, Rick Atkins, 403/329-1212, Fax: 403/328-5562
Head, Public Land Management, Roger Marvin, 403/427-3595, Fax: 403/422-4244
Head, Rural Initiatives, Vacant, 403/427-4612, Fax: 403/422-7755
Head, 4H Branch, Malhon Weir, 403/427-4463, Fax: 403/422-7755

#### Field Service Offices

Central: Provincial Bldg., 3rd Fl., Red Deer AB T4N 6K8 – 403/340-5376; Fax: 403/340-4896, Regional Director, Alan W. Hall
Northeast: PO Box 24, Vermilion AB T9X IJ9 – 403/853-8109; Fax: 403/853-4776, Regional Director, Ralph F. Berkan
Northwest: PO Box 4560, Barrhead AB T7N 1A4 – 403/674-8264; Fax: 403/674-8309, Regional Director, John Knapp
Peace: PO Box 159, Fairview AB T0H 1L0 – 403/835-2291; Fax: 403/835-3600, Regional Director, Yvonne Grabowsky
Southern: Agriculture Centre, Lethbridge AB T1J 4C7 – 403/381-5130; Fax: 403/382-4526, Regional Director, Don Young

### PLANNING & DEVELOPMENT SECTOR

Asst. Deputy Minister, Ray Bassett, 403/427-1957, Fax: 403/427-6317
Director, Central Program Support Division, Ken Moholitny, 403/422-9167, Fax: 403/427-5921
Director, Economic Services Division, Glen Werner, 403/427-7311, Fax: 403/427-5220
Director, Irrigation & Resource Management Division, Brian Colgan, 403/422-4596, Fax: 403/422-0474
Director, Policy Secretariat, Joe Rasario, 403/422-2070, Fax: 403/422-6540

### PRODUCTION & MARKETING SECTOR

Director, Plant Industry Division, Don Macyk, 403/427-5341, Fax: 403/422-0783
Acting Director, Processing Industry Division, Lou Normand, 403/427-3166, Fax: 403/422-3655
Head, Food Processing Development Centre, Ron Pettitt, 403/427-4793, Fax: 403/986-5138
Head, Food Quality Branch, Dr. David Schroder, 403/427-4054, Fax: 403/436-9454
Acting Head, Industry Development Branch, Ron Popek, 403/427-7366, Fax: 403/422-3655
Program Leader, Pest Prevention & Management, W. Yarish, 403/427-5341, Fax: 403/422-0783

#### Plant Industry Offices

Agronomy Centre: 6903 - 116 St., Edmonton AB T6H 4P2 – 403/427-7098; Fax: 403/422-9745
Crop Diversification Centre North, Edmonton – 403/422-1789; Fax: 403/422-6096
Crop Diversification Centre South, Brooks – 403/362-1300; Fax: 403/362-2554
Field Crop Development Centre, Lacombe – 403/782-4641; Fax: 403/782-5514
Soil & Crop Diagnostic Centre: O.S. Longman Bldg., 6909 - 116 St., Edmonton AB T6H 4P2 – 403/427-6361; Fax: 403/427-1439

#### Associated Agencies, Boards & Commissions

•Agricultural Products Marketing Council: 7000 - 113 St., 3rd Fl., Edmonton AB T6H 5T6 – 403/427-2164; Fax: 403/422-9690
General Manager, Brian Rhiness
•Agriculture Financial Service Corporation (AFSC): 4910 - 52 St., PO Box 5000, Camrose AB T4V 4E8 – Lending: 403/679-1311; Fax: 403/679-1308 – Insurance: 403/782-8200; Fax: 403/782-5650
Chair, Bob Splane, 403/679-1300
President & Managing Director, Brian Manning, 403/782-8200
Vice-President, Finance & Administration, Lending Division, David Schurman, 403/782-8330, Fax: 403/782-7510
Vice-President, Insurance Operations, Ray Block, 5718 - 56 Ave., PO Box 16, Lacombe AB T0C 1S0, 403/782-8251, Fax: 403/782-4336
Vice-President, Lending Operations, Andrew Church, 403/679-1301, Fax: 403/679-1308
•Alberta Agricultural Research Institute (AARI): J.G. O'Donoghue Bldg., #300, 7000 - 113 St., Edmonton AB T6H 5T6 – 403/422-1072; Fax: 403/422-6317
Chair, Gary Severtson, 403/427-1857, Fax: 403/427-1835
Executive Director, Dr. Ralph G. Christian, Email: CHRISTI@agric.gov.ab.ca
Research Manager, Dr. Yilma Teklemariam, 403/427-1956, Fax: 403/427-3252
•Alberta Dairy Control Board: 5201 - 50 Ave., Wetaskiwin AB T9A 0S7 – 403/361-1231; Fax: 403/361-1236
Chair, James P. Heron
•Alberta Grain Commission: 7000 - 113 St., Edmonton AB T6H 5T6 – 403/427-7029; Fax: 403/422-9690
Chair, Ken Moholitny
•Irrigation Council: Provincial Bldg., #328, 200 - 5 Ave. S, PO Box 3014, Lethbridge AB T1J 4L1 – 403/381-5176; Fax: 403/382-4406
Chair, John Weing
Council Secretary, Len Ring, 403/381-5176, Fax: 403/382-4406
Administrative Officer, Laurie Hodge
•Land Compensation Board: Phipps-McKinnon Bldg., 10020 - 101A Ave., 18th Fl., Edmonton AB T5J 3G2 – 403/427-2444; Fax: 403/427-5798
Chair, C.J. Purves
•Surface Rights Board: Phipps-McKinnon Bldg., 10020 - 101A Ave., 18th Fl., Edmonton AB T5J 3G2 – 403/427-2444; Fax: 403/427-5798
Chair, C.J. Purves

#### Agricultural Marketing Boards & Commissions

•Alberta Canola Producers Commission: #170, 14315 - 118 Ave., Edmonton AB T5L 4S6 – 403/454-0844; Fax: 403/451-6933
•Alberta Cattle Commission: #216, 6715 - 8 St. NE, Calgary AB T2E 7H7 – 403/275-4400; Fax: 403/274-0007
Manager, Gary Sargent
•Alberta Chicken Producers' Marketing Board: #101, 11826 - 100 Ave., Edmonton AB T5K 0K3 – 403/488-2125; Fax: 403/488-3570
General Manager, Roger King
•Alberta Egg Producers Board: #15, 1915 - 32 Ave. NE, Calgary AB T2E 7C8 – 403/250-1197; Fax: 403/291-9216
General Manager, W.P. Chorney
•Alberta Fresh Vegetable Marketing Board: 220F - 12A St. North, Lethbridge AB T1H 2J1 – 403/327-0447; Fax: 403/327-0766
•Alberta Hatching Egg Marketing Board: 14815 - 119 Ave., Edmonton AB T5L 2N9 – 403/451-5837; Fax: 403/452-8726
General Manager, Neil Reid
•Alberta Pork Producers' Development Corporation: 10319 Princess Elizabeth Ave., Edmonton AB T5G 0Y5 – 403/474-8288; Fax: 403/471-8065
General Manager, Ed Schultz
•Alberta Pulse Growers Commission: 4301 - 50 St., Leduc AB T9E 7H3 – 403/986-9398; Fax: 403/986-9398
•Alberta Sheep & Wool Commission: #203, 2916 - 19 St. NE, Calgary AB T2E 6Y9 – 403/735-5111; Fax: 403/735-5113
Manager, Will Verboven
•Alberta Sugar Beet Growers' Marketing Board: 4900 - 50 St., Taber AB T1G 1T3 – 403/223-1110; Fax: 403/223-1022
Manager, Bruce Webster
•Alberta Turkey Growers Marketing Board: #212, 8711A - 50 St., Edmonton AB T6B 1E7 – 403/465-5755; Fax: 403/465-5528
Executive Director, Greg Smith
•Alberta Vegetable Growers Marketing Board: 5217 - 50 St., Taber AB TIG 1V4 – 403/223-4242; Fax: 403/223-4242
General Manager, Terry Cradduck
•Potato Growers of Alberta: Stockman's Centre, #6, 1323 - 44 Ave. NE, Calgary AB T2E 6L5 – 403/291-2430; Fax: 403/291-2641
Manager, Allen Stuart

## Alberta Office of the AUDITOR GENERAL

9925 - 109 St., 8th Fl., Edmonton AB T5K 2J8
403/427-4221; Fax: 403/422-9555; URL: http://www.assembly.ab.ca/auditor.gen/auditor.htm
**Auditor General**, Peter Valentine, F.C.A., Email: pvalentine@audg.gov.ab.ca
Asst. Auditor General, Ken Hoffman, C.A., Email: khoffman@audg.gov.ab.ca
Asst. Auditor General, Jim Hug, C.A., Email: jhug@audg.gov.ab.ca
Asst. Auditor General, Mike Morgan, C.A.
Asst. Auditor General, Don Neufeld, C.A., Email: dneufeld@audg.gov.ab.ca
Asst. Auditor General, Suzanne Nickerson, C.A., Email: snickerson@audg.gov.ab.ca
Asst. Auditor General, Merwan Saher, C.A., Email: msaher@audg.gov.ab.ca
Asst. Auditor General, Nick Shandro, C.A., Email: nshandro@audg.gov.ab.ca

## Alberta COMMUNITY DEVELOPMENT

Standard Life Centre, 10405 Jasper Ave., 7th Fl., Edmonton AB T5J 4R7
403/427-6530; Fax: 403/427-1496; URL: http://www.gov.ab.ca/ZXmcd/mcd.htm

### ACTS ADMINISTERED

Alberta Alcohol & Drug Abuse Act
Alberta Foundation for the Arts Act
Alberta Human Rights, Citizenship & Multiculturalism Act
Alberta Order of Excellence Act
Alberta Sport, Recreation, Parks & Wildlife Foundation Act
Amusements Act
Emblems of Alberta Act
Foreign Cultural Property Immunity Act
Glenbow-Alberta Institute Act
Government House Act
Historical Resources Act
Human Rights, Citizenship & Multiculturalism Act
Libraries Act
Protection for Persons in Care Act
Recreation Development Act
Seniors Advisory Council for Alberta Act
Seniors Benefit Act
Wild Rose Foundation Act
**Minister**, Hon. Shirley McClellan, 403/427-4928, Fax: 403/427-0188
Deputy Minister, Julian Nowicki, 403/427-2921, Fax: 403/427-5362, Email: julian j nowicki@mcd_dm_edm@comdev
Senior Director, Management Systems Branch, Dave Rehill, 403/427-6411, Fax: 403/427-0255
Director, Communications Branch, Gordon Turtle, 403/427-6530, Fax: 403/427-1496, Email: gordon turtle@mcd_com_edm@comdev

### ADMINISTRATIVE SERVICES DIVISION

Executive Director, Rai Batra, 403/427-2925, Fax: 403/427-0255, Email: rai f batra@exec_edm@comdev_asd
Director, Financial Services, Lothar Hellweg, 403/427-0221, Fax: 403/427-0255
Director, FOIP & Records Management Branch, Joe Forsyth, 403/431-2313, Fax: 403/422-1105
Director, Human Resources, Lynn Upshall, 403/427-2546, Fax: 403/422-3142, Email: lynn upshall@per_edm@comdev_asd

### COMMUNITY & CITIZENSHIP SERVICES DIVISION

Asst. Deputy Minister, Murray Finnerty, 403/427-5714, Fax: 403/422-2891, Email: murray finnerty@adm_edm@comdev_csd
Director, Arts & Libraries Branch, Dr. Clive Padfield, 403/427-6315, Fax: 403/422-9132, Email: clive padfield@arts_edm@comdev_csd
Director, Citizenship Services Branch, Marie Riddle, 403/427-2927, Fax: 403/422-6438, Email: marie riddle@wss_wpp_edm@comdev_irc
Director, Community Development Field Services Branch, Noni Heine, 403/427-9538, Fax: 403/421-0056, Email: Noni Heine@Exec.Edm@ComDev_CDFS
Director, Human Rights Secretariat, Manuel da Costa, 403/427-3116, Fax: 403/422-3563
Chair, Film Classification Board, Sharon McCann, 403/427-2006

### CULTURAL FACILITIES & HISTORICAL RESOURCES DIVISION

Old St. Stephen's College, 8820 - 112 St., Edmonton AB T6G 2P8
403/431-2300; Fax: 403/427-5598
Asst. Deputy Minister, Dr. Bill Byrne, 403/431-2309, Email: bill byrne@hr_adm_edm@culture
Director, Historic Sites Service, Frits Pannekoek, 403/431-2310, Email: frits pannekoek@hs_dir_edm@culture
Director, Planning, Marketing & Foundation Services, Mark Rasmussen, Email: mark rasmussen@hr_adm_edm@culture
Director, Provincial Archives, Dr. Sandra Thomson, 12845 - 102 Ave., Edmonton AB T5N 0H6, 403/427-1750, Fax: 403/427-4646
Director, Provincial Museum of Alberta, Dr. Philip H.R. Stepney, 12845 - 102 Ave., Edmonton AB T5N 0M6, 403/453-9102, Fax: 403/454-6629
Director, Royal Tyrrell Museum of Paleontology, Dr. Bruce Naylor, PO Box 7500, Drumheller AB T0J 0Y0, 403/823-7707, Fax: 403/823-7131

### SENIORS DIVISION

403/427-7876
Executive Director, Ken Wilson, 902/422-0122, Fax: 902/427-1132
Director, Customer Services, Dwight Ganske, 403/422-5417
Director, Operations, Chi Loo, 403/422-7259
Director, Seniors Policy & Special Needs, Dave Arsenault, 403/427-2705

#### Associated Agencies, Boards & Commissions

•AADAC Recovery Centre: 10302 - 107 St., Edmonton AB T5J 1K2 – 403/427-4291; Fax: 403/422-2881
Manager, Evelyn Kohlman
•Alberta Alcohol & Drug Abuse Commission (AADAC): Pacific Plaza Bldg., 10909 Jasper Ave., 6th Fl., Edmonton AB T5J 3M9 – 403/427-2837; Fax: 403/423-1419
CEO, Leonard Blumenthal, 403/415-0374
Chair, Jocelyn Burgener, 403/415-0372
Executive Director, Program Services, Brian Kearns, 403/427-6526, Fax: 403/423-1419
Director, Central Office, Louise Morose, Energy Square Bldg., #803, 10109 - 106 St., Edmonton AB T5J 3L7, 403/427-4263, Fax: 403/427-0456
Director, Northern Office, Corliss Burke, 11333 - 106 St., Grande Prairie AB T8V 6T7, 403/538-5216, Fax: 403/538-5256
Director, Southern Office, Dennis Jones, 1177 - 11 Ave. SW, Calgary AB T2R 0G5, 403/297-3038, Fax: 403/297-3041
•Henwood Treatment Centre: 18750 - 18 St., Edmonton AB T5B 4K3 – 403/422-9069; Fax: 403/422-5408
Manager, Betty Roline
Program Manager, Gordon Munro
•Lander Treatment Centre: 43 Ave. & 2 St. W, Claresholm AB T0L 0T0 – 403/625-1395; Fax: 403/625-1300
Manager, Rob Hale-Matthews
Renfrew Recovery Centre: 1611 Remington Rd. NE, Calgary AB T2E 5K6 – 403/276-8946; Fax: 403/297-4592, Manager, Alan Friesen
•Alberta Foundation for the Arts
Listed in Section 2, *see* Index.
•Alberta Human Rights & Citizenship Commission
Listed alphabetically in detail, this section.
•Alberta Human Rights, Citizenship & Multiculturalism Education Fund Advisory Committee: Standard Life Centre, #802, 10405 Jasper Ave., Edmonton AB T5J 4R7 – 403/427-2927; Fax: 403/422-6348
Chair, Yvonne Fritz
•Alberta Order of Excellence Council: Standard Life Centre, 10405 Jasper Ave., 7th Fl., Edmonton AB T5J 4R7 – 403/427-2925; Fax: 403/427-0255
•Alberta Sport, Recreation, Parks & Wildlife Foundation: Percy Page Centre, 11759 Groat Rd., Edmonton AB T5M 3K9 – 403/427-1976; Fax: 403/488-9755
Chair, Doug Fulford
•Glenbow-Alberta Institute Board of Governors: 130 - 9 Ave. SE, Calgary AB T2G 0P3 – 403/264-8300; Fax: 403/265-9769
•Government House Foundation: 12845 - 102 Ave., Edmonton AB T5N 0M6 – 403/431-2310; Fax: 403/422-1105
•Seniors' Advisory Council for Alberta: 10025 Jasper Ave., Main Fl., Edmonton AB T5J 2N3 – 403/422-2321; Fax: 403/422-3207
Chairman, Jocelyn Burgener
•Wild Rose Foundation
Listed in Section 2, *see* Index.

## Alberta ECONOMIC DEVELOPMENT & TOURISM

Commerce Place, 10155 - 102 St., Edmonton AB T5J 4L6
403/427-2280; URL: http://www.edt.gov.ab.ca
Business Line: 1-800-272-9675

### ACTS ADMINISTERED

Alberta Opportunity Fund Act
Department of Economic Development & Trade Act
Motion Picture Development Act
Small Business Equity Corporation Act
Vencap Equities Act
**Minister**, Hon. Patricia Black, 403/427-3162, Fax: 403/422-6338
Deputy Minister, Bob King, 403/427-0662, Fax: 403/427-2852
Minister's Executive Asst., Jim Kiss, 403/427-3162
Acting Director, Communications, Theresa Lumsdon, 403/427-0670, Fax: 403/427-1529

### BUSINESS FINANCE

403/427-3300; Fax: 403/422-9319
Asst. Deputy Minister, Brian Williams, 403/427-0667
Executive Director, Business Finance, Earl Nent
Executive Director, Financial Projects, Don Keech

### CORPORATE SERVICES

Asst. Deputy Minister, Peter Crerar, 403/427-1946
Executive Director, Finance & Administration, Robert H. Turner, 403/422-0188
Executive Director, Information Management, Neil Taylor, 416/422-1033
Executive Director, Strategic Planning & Policy, Vacant
Administrator, Administrative Services, Linda Gogal, 403/422-9092
Director, Business Policy, Duane Pyear, 403/427-0850
Director, Development Policy, Vacant, 403/427-3627
Director, Economic Scanning & Research Services, Vacant
Director, Human Resources, Gilbert Cleirbaut, 403/422-5498

Director, Policy Projects, Carole Shields, 403/427-4443
Director, Research Services, Fred McMullan, 403/422-1063
Manager, Business Planning, Colin Jeffares, 403/422-0531
Manager, Information & Data Retrieval, Greg Yaremko, 403/427-6302

**INDUSTRY DEVELOPMENT**

Executive Director, Mel Wong, 403/427-6476, Fax: 403/427-5924
Executive Director, Forestry Industry Development, Vacant, 403/422-7011, Fax: 403/427-5299
Senior Director & Film Commissioner, Lindsay Cherney, 403/427-6503
Senior Director, Chrys Dmytruk, 403/427-0816
Senior Director, Denny Ross-Smith, 403/427-6479

**INVESTMENT DEVELOPMENT**

Executive Director, Behrooz Sadrehashemi, 403/422-5197, Fax: 403/422-9127

**SMALL BUSINESS DEVELOPMENT**

Executive Director, Roger Jackson, 403/427-6634, Fax: 403/427-5926

**TOURISM, TRADE & INVESTMENT**

Fax: 403/427-1700
Asst. Deputy Minister, Murray Rasmusson, 403/422-2557
Managing Director, The Americas, Jerry Keller, 403/427-6291
Managing Director, Asia/Pacific, Dave Corbett, 403/427-6375
Managing Director, Eastern Region, Doug Lane, 403/427-1905
Managing Director, Europe, Erv Lack, 403/427-6326
Managing Director, Middle East/Africa/India, Bob Hunter, 403/422-2534
Managing Director, Western Region, Don Smithson, 403/427-6059
Acting Managing Director, Division Services, Behrooz Sadre-Hashemi, 403/422-5197
Director, Business Immigration, Peter Carsley, 403/427-6417
Director, Event Promotion, Drew Hutton, 403/427-6433
Director, Investment/IBIS, Joanne Miller, 403/427-6413
Director, Visitor Sales & Services, Barb Spencer, 403/427-4327

**Associated Agencies, Boards & Commissions**

•Alberta Economic Development Authority (AEDA): Commerce Place, 10155 - 102 St., 6th Fl., Edmonton AB T5J 4L6 – 403/427-2251; Fax: 403/427-5922
Executive Director, Hugh Tadman, 403/422-5404
•Alberta Gaming & Liquor Commission: 50 Corriveau Ave., St. Albert AB T8N 3T5 – 403/447-8600; Fax: 403/447-8916; URL: http://www.gov.ab.ca/gov/agency/galc.html
Minister Responsible, Hon. Patricia Black, 403/427-3162, Fax: 403/422-6338
Acting Chair, Norman Peterson, 403/447-8657
Chair's Secretary, Linda Zakowski
Acting CEO, Roy Bricker, 403/447-8820
•Alberta Motion Picture Development Corporation: #690, 10020 - 101A Ave., Edmonton AB T5J 3G2 – 403/424-8855; Fax: 403/424-7669
General Manager, Garry Toth
•Alberta Opportunity Company: 5110 - 49 Ave., PO Box 4040, Ponoka AB T4J 1R5 – 403/783-7011; Fax: 403/783-7032, Toll Free: 1-800-661-3811
•Alberta Racing Commission: Sloane Square, #507, 5920 - 1A St. SW, Calgary AB T2H 0G3 – 403/297-6551; Fax: 403/255-4078
Chair, Roy Farran
•Alberta Research Council (ARC)
Listed alphabetically in detail, this section.
•Alberta Science & Research Authority (ASRA): 250 Karl Clark Rd., Edmonton AB T6H 5X2 – 403/427-2294; URL: http://www.gov.ab.ca/ZXsra/
Chair, Dr. Robert B. Church
President, Dr. Robert Fessenden
Director, Communications, Ken Faulkner, 403/427-2294
Director, Secretaraiat, Barbara Nyland
•Alberta Tourism Education Council: Sterling Place, 9940 - 106 St., 12th Fl., Edmonton AB T5K 2P6 – 403/422-0781; Fax: 403/422-3430
Executive Director, Hon. Dr. Lorne Taylor
•Alberta Tourism Partnership (ATP): c/o Alberta Economic Development & Tourism, 10155 - 102 St., Edmonton ON T5J 4L6 – 403/531-4671
Provides an industry-led tourism organization to integrate the tourism industry. Created to simplify distribution & marketing systems, encourage private sector investment & make it easier for Alberta tourism businesses to participate.
Chair, Russ Tynan
Vice-Chair, Ted Kissane
President & CEO, Tom McCabe

## Alberta EDUCATION

Devonian Bldg., 11160 Jasper Ave., Edmonton AB T5K 0L2
403/427-7219; Fax: 403/427-0591; URL: http://ednet.edc.gov.ab.ca

**ACTS ADMINISTERED**

Alberta School Boards Association Act
Berry Creek School Division Act
Government Organization Act, Schedule 4
Northland School Division Act
Remembrance Day Act
School Act
Teachers' Pension Plans Act
Teaching Profession Act
**Minister**, Hon. Gary G. Mar, 403/427-2025, Fax: 403/427-5582
Deputy Minister, Dr. Leroy Sloan, 403/427-2889, Fax: 403/422-9735
Director, Communications, Carol Chawrun, 403/427-2285, Fax: 403/427-0591
Director, Human Resource Services, Terry Buck, 403/427-2058, Fax: 403/422-2114

**FINANCE & PLANNING**

Acting Executive Director & Director, Financial Operations, Gary Baron, 403/427-2051, Fax: 403/427-2147
Director, Planning, Sharon Campbell, 403/427-8217, Fax: 403/422-5255
Asst. Director, School Finance, Jeff Olson, 403/427-2055, Fax: 403/427-2147

**REGIONAL SERVICES DIVISION**

Acting Asst. Deputy Minister, Dr. Susan Lynch, 403/437-7484, Fax: 403/422-1400
Regional Manager, Calgary, Gerry Wilson, 403/297-6353, Fax: 403/297-3842
Director, Corporate Services & Information Access, Vacant, 403/427-2914, Fax: 403/422-3942
Director, National & International Education, Amelia Turnbull, 403/427-2035, Fax: 403/422-3014
Director, Native Education, Merv Kowalchuk, 403/427-2043, Fax: 403/422-5256
Director, Regional Offices, Ron Smith, 403/427-2952, Fax: 403/422-9682
Director, Special Education Branch, Harvey Finnestad, 403/422-6326, Fax: 403/422-2039
Director, Teacher Certification, Fred Burghardt, 403/427-2045, Fax: 403/422-4199
Asst. Director, School Facilities, Hoang Le, 403/427-2973, Fax: 403/427-5816
Asst. Director, School Operations, Steve Bemount, 403/427-7235, Fax: 403/427-5930

**STUDENT PROGRAMS & EVALUATION DIVISION**

Asst. Deputy Minister, Dr. Roger Palmer, 403/422-1608, Fax: 403/422-5129
Director, Curriculum Standards Branch, Keith Wagner, 403/427-2984, Fax: 403/422-3745
Director, Information Services, Ron Sohnle, 403/427-5739, Fax: 403/427-3201
Director, Language Services, Gerard Bissonnette, 403/427-2940, Fax: 403/422-1947
Director, Learning Resources Distributing Centre, Dr. John Myroon, 403/427-2767, Fax: 403/422-9750
Director, Learning Technologies Branch, Garry Popowich, 403/674-5333, Fax: 403/674-6561
Acting Director, Student Evaluation, Jim Brackenbury, 403/427-0010, Fax: 403/422-4200

**Associated Agencies, Boards & Commissions**

•Alberta Teachers' Retirement Fund Board: #600, 11010 - 142 St., Edmonton AB T5N 2R1
Contact, Dorothy E. Ungstad
•Council on Alberta Teaching Standards: Devonian Bldg., 11160 Jasper Ave., Edmonton AB T5K 0L2
Contact, Fred Burghardt
•School Buildings Board: Devonian Bldg., 11160 Jasper Ave., Edmonton AB T5K 0L2
Contact, Hoang Le

## Alberta Office of the Chief ELECTORAL OFFICER

#100, 11510 Kingsway Ave., Edmonton AB T5G 2Y5
403/427-7191; Fax: 403/422-2900;
Email: elections.alberta@gov.ab.ca
**Chief Electoral Officer**, Dermot F. Whelan
Deputy Chief, O. Brian Fjeldheim
Director, Registrations & Financial Operations, W.A. Sage

## Alberta ENERGY

Petroleum Plaza, North Tower, 9945 - 108 St., Edmonton AB T5K 2G6
403/427-7425; Fax: 403/427-3198; URL: http://www.energy.gov.ab.ca
Ensures that energy & mineral resource development & use occur in an effective, orderly & environmentally responsible manner. The department promotes the accelerated development of the oil sands, & encourages effective & responsible environmental safeguards. Also, reviews current land-use policies to address industry concerns relating to access & ensures economic conservation of resources & prevention of waste to maximize long-term revenue to the province. The agency consists of four divisions & a quasi-judicial regulatory agency called the Alberta Energy & Utilities Board (AEUB).

**ACTS ADMINISTERED**

Alberta Energy & Utilities Board Act
Coal Sales Act
Electric Utilities Act
Freehold Mineral Rights Tax Act
Gas Utilities Act
Land Surface Conservation & Reclamation Act
Mineral Titles Redemption Act
Mines & Minerals Act
Natural Gas Marketing Act
Natural Gas Price Administration Act
Natural Gas Pricing Agreement Act
Oil Sands Technology & Research Authority Act
Petroleum Incentives Program Act
Petroleum Marketing Act
Public Utilities Board Act

Small Power Research & Development Act
Take-or-pay Costs Sharing Act
Willmore Wilderness Park Act

**Acts Administered by the Energy Resources Conservation Board**

Coal Conservation Act
Coal Miners Rehabilitation Act
Energy Resources Conservation Act
Gas Resources Preservation Act
Hydro & Electric Energy Act
Oil & Gas Conservation Act
Oil Sands Conservation Act
Pipeline Act
Turner Valley Unit Operations Act

**Minister**, Hon. Dr. Stephen C. West, 403/427-3740, Fax: 403/422-0195
Deputy Minister, Richard Hyndman, 403/427-8032, Fax: 403/427-7737
Senior Solicitor, Legal Services, M. Kaga, 403/427-0940, Fax: 403/422-6068

#### CORPORATE SERVICES DIVISION

Asst. Deputy Minister, David Luff, 403/427-6342, Fax: 403/427-7737
Chief Financial Officer, Financial Services, Jim Vince, 403/427-3607, Fax: 403/422-4281
Executive Director, Human Resources, Margaret Munsch, 403/427-6768, Fax: 403/422-4299

#### MINERAL OPERATIONS DIVISION

Asst. Deputy Minister, David Smith, 403/427-8123, Fax: 403/427-7737
Head, Compliance & Assurance, Steve Slipp, 403/297-8782, Fax: 403/297-5199
Head, Gas Royalty & Mineral Tax, Clif Hetherington, 403/422-9231, Fax: 403/427-3334
Head, Internal Services, Stephen Pugh, 403/422-9135, Fax: 403/422-0382
Head, Mineral Access, Geology & Mapping, Diana Purdy, 403/422-9466
Head, Minerals Tenure, F. David Coombs, 403/422-9430, Fax: 403/422-1123
Head, Petroleum & Other Royalties, Linda White, 403/422-9119, Fax: 403/427-0865
Leader, MRIS Project Office, John McAllister, 403/422-5821, Fax: 403/427-4044

#### POLICY DIVISION

Asst. Deputy Minister, Larry Morrison, 403/427-0813, Fax: 403/427-7737
Executive Director, Environmental Affairs Branch, John Donner, 403/427-5200, Fax: 403/427-2278
Executive Director, Markets & Regulatory Policy Branch, Paul Precht, 403/427-8038, Fax: 403/422-2548
Executive Director, Royalty & Tenure Branch, Mike Ekelund, 403/427-8034, Fax: 403/422-2548
Senior Director, Electricity Branch, Larry Charach, 403/427-8177, Fax: 403/427-8065

#### RESEARCH & EXTERNAL RELATIONS DIVISION

Asst. Deputy Minister, Ken Bradley, 403/427-0815, Fax: 403/427-7737
Executive Director, External Relations, Elma Spady, 403/427-0226, Fax: 403/422-0800
Executive Director, Research & Technology, Roger Bailey, 403/297-5219, Fax: 403/297-3638
Director, Communications Branch, Sheila Munro, 403/422-3667, Fax: 403/422-0698
Coordinator, Freedom of Information & Privacy Office, Mary L. Penny, 403/427-0265, Fax: 403/422-0800

##### Associated Agencies, Boards & Commissions

•Alberta Energy & Utilities Board (AEUB): 640 - 5 Ave. SW, Calgary AB T2P 3G4 – 403/297-8311; Fax: 403/297-8398; URL: http://www.eub.gov.ab.ca
Chair, Celine Belanger
CEO, Lorne D. Fredlund

## Alberta ENVIRONMENTAL PROTECTION (AEP)

9915 - 108 St., Edmonton AB T5K 2G8
403/427-2739, 944-0313 (Information Centre); URL: http://www.gov.ab.ca/ZXenv/
Recycle Information Line: 1-800-463-6326
Pollution Emergency Response Team: 1-800-222-6514
Forest Fire Hotline: 403/427-FIRE (collect)
Department services & programs include:
•Environmental regulatory service-environmental assesment: pollution control; air & water approvals; chemical asessment & management; land reclamation; action on waste.
•Land & forest service-forest protection: forest management; program support; land administration.
•Natural resources services-water management: fish & wildlife; recreation & protected areas.

#### ACTS ADMINISTERED

Agricultural & Recreational Land Ownership Act
Alberta Environmental Research Trust Act
Bighorn Agreement Validating Act, 1969
Boundary Surveys Act
Brazeau River Development Act, 1960
Clean Air Act
Clean Water Act
Drainage Districts Act
Environment Council Act
Environmental Protection & Enhancement Act
Fish Marketing Act
Forest Reserves Act
Forests Act
Government Organization Act, Schedule 5
Land Agents Licensing Act
Land Surveyors Act
Natural Resources Conservation Board Act
Provincial Parks Act
Public Lands Act
Special Waste Management Corporation Act
Surveys Act (jointly with Alberta Municipal Affairs)
Water Resources Act (jointly with Alberta Public Works, Supply & Services)
Wilderness Areas, Ecological Reserves & Natural Areas Act
Wildlife Act
Willmore Wilderness Park Act (jointly with Alberta Energy)

**Minister**, Hon. Ty Lund, 403/427-2391
Deputy Minister, Peter Melnychuk, 403/427-6236, Fax: 403/422-6305
Director, Communications, Lee Funke, 403/427-8636

#### CORPORATE MANAGEMENT SERVICE

Asst. Deputy Minister, Ron Hicks, 403/427-8155, Fax: 403/422-6305
Director, Education Branch, Bev Yee, 403/427-6310
Director, Human Resources Division, Denis St. Arnaud, 403/427-6201, Fax: 403/427-2513
Director, Information Management Division, Paul Valentine, 403/422-6680, Fax: 403/422-3470
Director, Resource Data Division, Mike Toomey, 403/427-5719, Fax: 403/422-0712
Director, Strategic & Regional Support Division, Annette Trimbee, 403/427-1777, Fax: 403/422-5136

#### ENVIRONMENTAL REGULATORY SERVICE

Asst. Deputy Minister, Al Schulz, 403/427-6247, Fax: 403/427-1014
Director, Chemicals Assessment & Management, Jerry Lack, 403/427-5837, Fax: 403/422-5120
Director, Environmental Assessment, Bob Stone, 403/427-6270, Fax: 403/422-9714
Director, Land Reclamation, Larry Brocke, 403/427-6202, Fax: 403/422-0080
Director, Pollution Control, Fred Schulte, 403/427-6209, Fax: 403/427-3178

#### FINANCIAL SERVICES

Executive Director, Bill Simon, 403/427-5971
Senior Financial Manager, Budgets, Forecasts & Funds, Ray Duffy, 403/427-2002, Fax: 403/427-2512
Senior Financial Manager, Expenditures & Contracts Management, Eric Luczak, 403/427-9149, Fax: 403/427-2136
Senior Financial Manager, Financial Policies & Advisory Service, Larry Thachuk, 403/427-9929, Fax: 403/422-2862
Acting Senior Financial Manager, Revenue & Financial Systems, Lutaf Moloo, 403/427-9114, Fax: 403/422-0151

#### LAND & FOREST SERVICE

Asst. Deputy Minister, Cliff Henderson, 403/427-3542, Fax: 403/422-6068
Director, Forest Management Division, Dennis Quintilio, 403/427-4566
Director, Forest Protection Division, Kelly O'Shea, 403/427-6807
Director, Land Administration Division & Director, Program Support Division, Craig Quintilio, 403/422-4415

#### NATURAL RESOURCES SERVICE

Asst. Deputy Minister, J.R. Nichols, 403/427-6749, Fax: 403/427-8884
Director, Recreation & Protected Areas, Bruce Duffin, 403/427-7009, Fax: 403/427-8441
Director, Water Management, Doug Tupper, 403/427-8646

##### Fish & Wildlife

Director, Enforcement & Field Services Division, Ken Ambrock, 403/427-6735
Director, Fisheries Management Division, Morley Barrett, 403/427-6730
Director, Program Support Division, Deryl Empson, 403/427-6729
Director, Wildlife Management Division, Robert Andrews, 403/427-6750

##### Associated Agencies, Boards & Commissions

•Alberta Environmental Appeal Board (EAB): #400, 9925 - 109 St., Edmonton AB T5K 2J8 – 403/427-6207; Fax: 403/427-4693
Chair, William Tilleman
Executive Director, Joanne Taylor-Weir
•Natural Resources Conservation Board (NRCB): Pacific Plaza, 10909 Jasper Ave., Edmonton AB T5J 2L9 – 403/422-1977; URL: http://www.gov.ab.ca/ZXNRCB/index.html
Chair, Ken R. Smith
Executive Manager, Operations, J. Ingram
•Sustainable Development Coordinating Council (SDCC): South Petroleum Plaza, 9915 - 108 St., 10th Floor, Edmonton AB T5K 2G8 – 403/427-6236; Fax: 403/422-6305
Co-Chair, Al N. Craig, 403/427-0662
Co-Chair, Peter Melnychuk

## Alberta Office of the ETHICS COMMISSIONER

#410, 9925 - 109 St., Edmonton AB T5K 2J8
403/422-2273; Fax: 403/422-2261

#### ACTS ADMINISTERED

Alberta Conflicts of Interest Act

**Alberta Ethics Commissioner**, Robert Clark
General Counsel, Frank Work
Senior Administrator, Karen South

## Alberta FAMILY & SOCIAL SERVICES

Seventh St. Plaza, 10030 - 107 St., Edmonton AB T5J 3E4
403/427-2734; Fax: 403/422-9044; URL: http://www.gov.ab.ca/dept/fss.html

#### ACTS ADMINISTERED

Assured Income for the Severely Handicapped Act
Child Welfare Act
Department of Family & Social Services Act
Dependent Adults Act
Income Support Recovery Act
Parentage & Maintenance Act
Social Care Facilities Licensing Act
Social Care Facilities Review Committee Act
Social Development Act
Widows' Pension Act

**Minister**, Hon. Dr. Lyle Oberg, 403/427-2606, Fax: 403/427-0954
**Minister Responsible, Children's Services**, Hon. Pearl Calahasen
Deputy Minister, Don Fleming, 403/427-6448
Asst. Deputy Minister, Human Resources & Organizational Planning, Dave Banick, 403/427-7274
Director, Communications, Kathy Lazowski, 403/427-4801, Fax: 403/422-3071
Director, Media & Public Relations, Bob Scott, 403/422-3004
Children's Advocate, Jean Lafrance, 403/427-8934

#### ADULT SERVICES DIVISION

Asst. Deputy Minister, Patricia Boynton, 403/427-1245
Executive Director, Income & Employment Programs, Anne Ward Neville, 403/427-2635
Executive Director, Services to Persons with Disabilities, Norm McLeod, 403/422-0305
Director, Appeal & Advisory Secretariat, Gordon Thomas, 403/427-2709
Director, Quality Management & Family & Community Support Services (FCSS), Mic Farrell, 403/427-4420
Public Guardian, Gordon Cuff, 403/422-1868

#### CHILDREN'S SERVICES DIVISION

Asst. Deputy Minister, Mat Hanrahan, 403/427-6428
Executive Director, Child Welfare, Sharon Heron, 403/422-5187
Director, Day Care Programs, Neil Irvine, 403/427-4477
Acting Director, Family Violence Prevention, Jane Holliday, 403/422-5916
Director, Legislative Planning, Susan Rankin, 403/427-7267

#### RESOURCE MANAGEMENT SERVICES

Executive Director, Information Resource Services, Al Schut, 403/441-6814
Acting Executive Director, Resource Management Services, Duncan Campbell, 403/422-3719
Director, Administration Services, Jack McKendry, 403/427-4506

#### Associated Agencies, Boards & Commissions

- Office of the Commissioner of Services for Children & Families: c/o Alberta Family & Social Services, Seventh St. Plaza, 10030 - 107 St., Edmonton AB T5J 3E4 – 403/422-5011; Fax: 403/422-5036

Commissioner, John Lackey

## Alberta FEDERAL & INTERGOVERNMENTAL AFFAIRS

Commerce Place, 10155 - 102 St., 12th Fl., Edmonton AB T5J 4GB
403/427-2611; Fax: 403/423-6654; URL: http://www.gov.ab.ca/dept/figa.html

#### ACTS ADMINISTERED

Department of Federal & Intergovernmental Affairs Act

**Minister**, Hon. David Hancock, Q.C., 403/427-2585
Deputy Minister, Ron Hicks, 403/427-6644, Fax: 403/423-6654
Director, Communications, Donna Babchishin, 403/422-2465, Fax: 403/423-6654
Acting Information Resource Administrator, Information Resource Centre, Roxanne Harlton, 403/422-0267

#### ADMINISTRATIVE SERVICES CENTRE

1201, Legislature Annex, 9718 - 107 St., Edmonton AB T5K 1E4
403/427-1076; Fax: 403/427-0305
Director, Keray Henke, 403/422-4867, Fax: 403/427-5565, Email: khenke@exc.gov.ab.ca
Administrative & Payroll Services, Kathy Miller, 403/422-4091, Email: kmiller@exc.gov.ab.ca
Financial Services, Marilyn Johnston, 403/427-3839, Email: mjohnsto@exc.gov.ab.ca
Information & Technology Services, Carol Coroy, 403/422-2339, Email: coroy@exc.gov.ab.ca

#### ALBERTA OFFICE (IN OTTAWA)

Royal Bank Centre, #808, 90 Sparks St., Ottawa ON K1P 5B4
613/237-2615; Fax: 613/563-9934
Office Manager, Marcy Korchinski

#### CANADIAN FEDERALISM SECTION

Commerce Place, 10155 - 102 St., Edmonton AB T5J 4G8
Fax: 403/427-0939
Executive Director, Garry Pocock, 403/422-0453, Email: gpo@inter.gov.ab.ca
Director, Aboriginal Affairs, Paul Whittaker, 403/422-0964, Email: pdw@inter.gov.ab.ca
Director, Economics, Resources & Fiscal Relations Team, Randy Fischer, 403/422-0959, Email: raf@inter.gov.ab.ca
Director, Intergovernmental Relations/Coordinatiorn Team, Susan Cribbs, 403/422-1127, Email: sfc@inter.gov.ab.ca
Director, Federalism Constitution Team, Bruce Tait, 403/422-2300, Email: bta@inter.gov.ab.ca

#### INTERNATIONAL RELATIONS SECTION

Fax: 403/427-0699
Asst. Deputy Minister, Wayne Clifford, 403/422-2294
Director, Europe/Multilateral Relations, Rory Campbell, 403/422-2236
Director, Asia/Pacific, Marvin Schneider, 403/422-2332
Director, United States/Mexico/Latin America, Melanie McCallum, 403/422-2359

#### PROTOCOL OFFICE

Fax: 403/422-0786
Chief, Rory Campbell, 403/422-2236
Deputy Chief, Betty Spinks, 403/422-2235
Director, Operations, Judy Wilson Mahoney, 12845 - 102 Ave., Edmonton AB T5M 0M6, 403/427-2281, Fax: 403/422-6508

#### SOCIAL & FISCAL POLICY REFORM TEAM

Commerce Place, 10155 - 102 St., 12th Fl., Edmonton AB T5J 4GB
403/427-6706; Fax: 403/427-0939
Executive Officer, Francie Harle, 403/422-0452
Director, Sherry Thompson, 403/422-0224
Assoc. Director, Indira Roopnarine, 403/422-0199, Email: iro@inter.gov.ab.ca

#### TRADE POLICY TEAM

Commerce Place, 10155 - 102 St., 12th Fl., Edmonton AB T5J 4G8
Fax: 403/427-0699
Executive Director, Helmut Mach, 403/422-1128, Fax: 403/427-0699, Email: hem@inter.gov.ab.ca
Internal Director, Trade, Jim Ogilvy, 403/422-1129, Email: jao@inter.gov.ab.ca
International Trade Counsel, James Doherty, 403/422-1137, Fax: 403/427-0699, Email: jad@inter.gov.ab.ca
International Trade Counsel, Daryl Hanak, 403/422-1339, Fax: 403/427-0699, Email: dah@inter.gov.ab.ca
Associate Director, Internal Trade, Neil Kirkpatrick, 403/422-1130, Email: nrk@inter.gov.ab.ca

## Alberta GOVERNMENT REORGANIZATION SECRETARIAT

#404, Legislature Bldg., 10800 - 97 Ave., Edmonton AB T5K 2B6
403/427-2585
**Minister Responsible**, Hon. David Hancock, Q.C.

## Alberta HEALTH

PO Box 1360, Edmonton AB T5J 2N3
403/427-7164 (Communications); URL: http://www.health.gov.ab.ca/

#### ACTS ADMINISTERED

ABC Benefits Corporation Act
Alberta Health Care Insurance Act
Ambulance Services Act
Blind Persons' Rights Act
Cancer Programs Act
Dental Profession Act
Emergency Medical Aid Act
Government Organizaion Act, Schedule 7
Health Facilities Review Committee Act
Health Foundations Act
Health Insurance Premiums Act
Hospitals Act
Human Tissue Gift Act
Lloydminster Hospital Act
Medical Profession Act
Mental Health Act
M.S.I. Foundation Act
Nursing Homes Act
Nursing Profession Act
Optometry Profession Act
Physical Therapy Profession Act
Premier's Council on the Status of Persons with Disabilities Act
Provincial Health Authorities of Alberta Act
Public Health Act
Regional Health Authorities Act
Registered Dieticians Act

**Minister**, Hon. Halvar Jonson, 403/427-3665, Fax: 403/415-0961
Deputy Minister, Jack Davis, 403/422-0747, Fax: 403/427-1016
Executive Director, Health Workforce Services, Terry Chugg, 403/427-3274, Fax: 403/427-5597
Executive Director, Provincial Health Authorities, Mike Higgins, 403/426-8500
Director, Communications, Garth Norris, 403/427-7164, Fax: 403/427-1171

#### FINANCE & HEALTH PLAN ADMINISTRATION

Chief Financial Officer, Aslam Bhatti, 403/427-3601, Fax: 403/422-3631
Senior Team Leader, Claims, Jack Thackray, 403/427-1572, Fax: 403/427-1093
Senior Team Leader, Customer Services, Janet Skinner, 403/427-1490, Fax: 403/422-0102
Acting Senior Team Leader, Registration & Premiums Re-engineering, Dave Cathro, 403/427-1522, Fax: 403/422-0102

**HEALTH POLICY**

Asst. Deputy Minister, Don Ford, 403/427-5211, Fax: 403/422-3674

Senior Team Leader, Emergency Health Services, Elaine Stakiw, 403/422-9678, Fax: 403/422-0134

Senior Team Leader, Federal/Provincial Relations, Dave Alexander, 403/427-1421, Fax: 403/427-2511

Senior Team Leader, Health Resourcing, Tapan Chowdhury, 403/427-4938, Fax: 403/427-1577

Senior Team Leader, Issues Management, Anne Givens, 403/427-8029, Fax: 403/427-0738

Senior Team Leader, Legal & Legislative Services, Herb Schlotter, 403/415-0230, Fax: 403/427-2511

Senior Team Leader, Pharmacy Services, David Bougher, 403/427-1558, Fax: 403/427-0738

Senior Team Leader, Policy Development, Ron Dyck, 403/427-2653, Fax: 403/427-2511

**HEALTH STRATEGIES & RESEARCH**

Asst. Deputy Minister, Cecilie Lord, 403/427-8596, Fax: 403/422-3671

Provincial Health Officer, Disease Control & Prevention, Dr. John Waters, 403/427-5263, Fax: 403/422-6663

Senior Team Leader, Health Economics, Jon Brehaut, 403/415-0185, Fax: 403/427-0738

Senior Team Leader, Health Surveillance, Dr. Stephen Gabos, 403/427-4518, Fax: 403/427-6663

Senior Team Leader, Population Health, Denis Ostercamp, 403/427-2653, Fax: 403/427-2511

Senior Team Leader, Strategic & Business Planning, Evelyn Swanson, 403/422-4154, Fax: 403/427-7432

**Associated Agencies, Boards & Commissions**

•Alberta Cancer Board: PO Box 222, Edmonton AB T5J 2P4 – 403/482-9300

President & CEO, Jean-Michel Turc

•Alberta Provincial Mental Health Board: c/o Chair, PO Box 2739, Pincher Creek AB T0K 1W0 – 403/422-2233

Chair, Ron LaJeunesse

•Health Facilities Review Committee: Sterling Place, 9940 - 106 St., 8th Fl., Edmonton AB T5K 2N2 – 403/427-4924

Chair, Denis Herard

•Office of the Mental Health Patient Advocate: Centre West Bldg., 10035 - 108 St., 12th Fl., Edmonton AB T5J 3E1 – 403/422-1812

Director, Dr. Mervyn Hislop

•Premier's Council on the Status of Persons with Disabilities: #250, 11044 - 82 Ave., Edmonton AB T6G 0T2 – 403/422-1095; Fax: 403/422-9691; Email: pcspd@planet.eon.net

Chair, Gary McPherson

Executive Director, Fran Vargo

Director, Research & Policy Review, Diane Earl

## Alberta HUMAN RIGHTS & CITIZENSHIP COMMISSION

10405 Jasper Ave., 16th Fl., Edmonton AB T5J 4R7

403/427-7661; Fax: 403/422-3563

TTY: 403/427-1597

Southern Alberta Office, #102, 1333 - 8 St. SW, Calgary AB T2R 1M6

403/297-6571, Fax: 403/297-6567

TTY: 403/297-5639

**ACTS ADMINISTERED**

Alberta Human Rights, Citizenship & Multiculturalism Act

**Minister Responsible**, Hon. Shirley McClellan, 403/427-4928, Fax: 403/427-0188

Chief Commissioner, Charlach Mackintosh

Director, Communications, Carol Chawrun, 403/427-6530, Fax: 403/427-1496

## Alberta Office of the INFORMATION & PRIVACY COMMISSIONER

#410, 9925 - 109 St., Edmonton AB T5K 2J8

403/422-6860; Fax: 403/422-5682; Email: ipcab@planet.eon.net

**Information & Privacy Commissioner**, Robert Clark

Director & General Counsel, Frank Work

Administrative & Intake Officer, Leanne Levy

## Alberta JUSTICE

9833 - 109th St., Edmonton AB T5K 2E8

403/427-2745; Fax: 403/427-6821; URL: http://www.gov.ab.ca/dept/just.html

Legal Research & Analysis: 403/422-0500

**ACTS ADMINISTERED**

Administration of Estates Act
Administrative Procedures Act
Age of Majority Act
Alberta Evidence Act
Arbitration Act
Civil Enforcement Act
Commissioners for Oaths Act
Conflicts of Interest Act
Contributory Negligence Act
Corrections Act
Court of Appeal Act
Court of Queen's Bench Act
Criminal Injuries Compensation Act
Dangerous Dogs Act
Daylight Saving Time Act
Defamation Act
Devolution of Real Property Act
Domestic Relations Act
Expropriation Act (jointly with Alberta Agriculture, Food & Rural Development)
Extra-provincial Enforcement of Custody Orders Act
Factors Act
Family Relief Act
Fatal Accidents Act
Fatality Inquiries Act
Fraudulent Preferences Act
Frustrated Contracts Act
Government Organization Act, Schedule 9
Guarantees Acknowledgment Act
Innkeepers Act
International Child Abduction Act
International Commercial Arbitration Act
International Conventions Implementation Act
Interpretation Act
Interprovincial Subpoena Act
Intestate Succession Act
Judgement Interest Act
Judicature Act
Jury Act
Justice of the Peace Act
Landlord's Rights on Bankruptcy Act
Languages Act/Loi Linguistique
Legal Profession Act
Legitimacy Act
Limitation of Actions Act
Maintenance Enforcement Act
Maintenance Order Act
Married Women's Act
Masters & Servants Act
Matrimonial Property Act
Mechanical Recording of Evidence Act
Minors' Property Act
Motor Transport Act (jointly with Alberta Transportation & Utilities; Alberta Municipal Affairs)
Motor Vehicle Accident Claims Act (jointly with Alberta Municipal Affairs)
Notaries Public Act
Oaths of Office Act
Occupiers' Liability Act
Perpetuities Act
Personal Property Security Act (jointly with Alberta Municipal Affairs)
Petty Trespass Act
Police Act
Powers of Attorney Act
Private Investigators & Security Guards Act
Proceedings Against the Crown Act
Provincial Court Act
Provincial Court Judges Act
Provincial Offences Procedure Act
Public Inquiries Act
Public Trustee Act
Queen's Counsel Act
Reciprocal Enforcement of Judgements Act
Reciprocal Enforcement of Maintenance Orders Act
Regulations Act
Revised Statutes 1980 Act
Road Building Machinery Equipment Act
Sale of Goods Act
Surrogate Court Act
Survival of Actions Act
Survivorship Act
Tort-Feasors Act
Trustee Act
Ultimate Heir Act
Unconscionable Transactions Act
Victims' Programs Assistance Act
Warehouse Receipts Act
Wills Act
Young Offenders Act

**Minister & Attorney General**, Hon. Jon Havelock, 403/427-2339, Fax: 403/422-6621

Deputy Minister & Deputy Attorney General, Neil McCrank, 403/427-5032, Fax: 403/422-9639

Acting Executive Director, Human Resource Services, Sandra Hlus, 403/427-9617, Fax: 403/422-9639

Director, Aboriginal Justice Initiatives, Sylvia Novik, J.E. Brownlee Bldg., 10365 - 97 St., Edmonton AB T5J 3W7, 403/422-2779, Fax: 403/427-4670

Director, Staff College, Peter Nicholson, 16310 - 23 Ave. NW, Edmonton AB T6R 2H2, 403/422-6598, Fax: 403/422-2854

Chief Medical Examiner, Dr. Graeme P. Dowling, 7007 - 116 St. NW, Edmonton AB T6H 5R8, 403/427-4987, Fax: 403/422-1265

Deputy Chief Medical Examiner, Dr. Lloyd Denmark, 4070 Bowness Rd. NW, Calgary AB T3B 3R7, 403/297-8123, Fax: 403/297-3429

Asst. Chief Medical Examiner, Dr. Bernard G. Bannach, 7007 - 116 St. NW, Edmonton AB T6H 5R8, 403/427-4987, Fax: 403/422-1265

Chief Legislative Counsel, Peter J. Pagano, 403/427-2217, Fax: 403/422-7366

Public Trustee, Office of the Public Trustee, Jack E. Klinck, Q.C., #400S, 10365 - 97 St., Edmonton AB T5J 3Z8, 403/427-2744, Fax: 403/422-9136

Asst. Public Trustee, William D. Polglase, 403/427-2744

Asst. Public Trustee, Brian M. Smith, #2100, 411 - 1 St. SE, Calgary AB T2G 4Y5, 403/297-6541, Fax: 403/297-2823

**For list of Courts & other Legal Officers, including Judicial Officials & Judges *see* Section 10 of this book.**

**ADMINISTRATION DIVISION**

Fax: 403/422-9639

Executive Director, Dan Mercer, 403/427-3301

Acting Director, Administrative Services, Robert Remmer, 403/427-0060

Director, Communications, Lesley Gronow, 403/427-8530, Fax: 403/422-7363

Director, Corporate Support Services, Randy Petruk, 10365 - 97 St., Edmonton AB T5J 3W7, 403/422-5969, Fax: 403/427-6002

Director, Finance, D. Ian Hope, 403/427-4997, Fax: 403/422-1648

Director, Internal Audit, Mike Brown, 10365 - 97 St., Edmonton AB T5J 3W7, 403/422-1189, Fax: 403/427-6002

Acting Director, Maintenance Enforcement Program, Dennis P. Medwid, PO Box 2404, Edmonton AB T5J 3Z7, 403/422-5554, Fax: 403/422-1215
Acting Director, Systems & Information Services, Don Mottershead, 10365 - 97 St., Edmonton AB T5J 3W7, 403/422-5964, Fax: 403/422-2829

#### CIVIL LAW DIVISION

403/427-0940; Fax: 403/427-1871 (Energy)
403/427-3496; Fax: 403/427-4343 (Environmental Law); 403/427-8045; Fax: 403/427-0996 (Municipal Affairs); 403/427-2097; Fax: 403/422-2664 (Transportation)
Asst. Deputy Minister, Doug Rae, 403/427-0912
Executive Director, Civil Law Branch, R. Neil Dunne, Q.C., 403/422-8787, Fax: 403/425-0307
Director, Civil & Family Legal Services, Peggy Hartman, 403/422-9175, Fax: 403/425-0307
Director, Constitutional Law, Nolan Steed, 403/422-9653, Fax: 403/425-0307
Director, Legal Research & Analysis, Clark Dalton, 403/422-8989, Fax: 403/425-0307

#### CORRECTIONAL SERVICES DIVISION

Fax: 403/427-5905
Asst. Deputy Minister, Hank O'Handley, 403/427-3440
Executive Director, Adult Centre Operations Branch, Dave Forbes, J.E. Brownlee Bldg., 10365 - 97 St., Edmonton AB T5J 3W7, 403/427-4703, Fax: 403/427-1904
Executive Director, Community Corrections & Release Programs Branch, Arnold Galet, 10365 - 97 St., Edmonton AB T5J 3W7, 403/422-5757, Fax: 403/422-3098
Executive Director, Young Offender Branch, Patricia Meade, 10365 - 97 St., Edmonton AB T5J 3W7, 403/422-5019, Fax: 403/422-0732

#### COURT SERVICES DIVISION

Fax: 403/422-9639
Asst. Deputy Minister, Rod Wacowich, 403/427-9620
Director, Corporate Services, Andrzej Nowacki, 403/422-6428, Fax: 403/422-6613
Manager, Provincial Court Library, Sandra Perry, Law Courts Bldg., 5th Fl., North, 1A Sir Winston Churchill Square, 2nd Fl. South, Edmonton AB T5J 0R2, 403/427-5579, 5580, Fax: 403/427-0481

#### CRIMINAL JUSTICE DIVISION

Fax: 403/422-9639
Asst. Deputy Minister, Michael Allen, 403/427-5046
Director, Appeals & Criminal Law Policy, Ken Tjosvold, 403/422-5402, Fax: 403/422-1106
Director, Special Prosecutions Branch, Terry Matchett, 10365 - 97 St., Edmonton AB T5J 3W7, 403/422-0640, Fax: 403/422-1217

#### PUBLIC SECURITY DIVISION

10365 - 97 St., Edmonton AB T5J 3W7
Fax: 403/427-1194
Asst. Deputy Minister, Robert B. Dunster, 403/427-3457
Acting Director, Policing Services Branch, Judy Mackay, 403/427-3457, Fax: 403/427-5916
Director, Regulatory & Administrative Support Branch, Neil Warner, 403/427-3457, Fax: 403/427-5916
Director, Security Operations Branch, Al Palmer, 403/422-3791, Fax: 403/427-0476
Director, Serious & Violent Crime Initiatives, Gary Hutnan, Bowker Bldg., 9833 - 109 St., Edmonton AB T5K 2E8, 403/427-9030, Fax: 403/422-1330
Manager, Victims' Programs, Barb Pratt, 403/427-3460, Fax: 403/427-5916
Chief Officer, Provincial Firearms, George Reid, 403/427-0437, Fax: 403/427-1100

##### Associated Agencies, Boards & Commissions

•Access to Information & Protection of Privacy Panel: #420, Legislature Bldg., Edmonton AB T5K 2B6 – 403/427-3666
Chair, Robert (Butch) Fischer
•Alberta Law Foundation: #300, 407 - 8 Ave. SW, Calgary AB T2P 1E5 – 403/264-4701; Fax: 403/294-9238
Executive Director, O.G. Snider
•Alberta Legal Aid Society: Revlon Bldg., #300, 10320 - 102 Ave., Edmonton AB T5J 4A1 – 403/427-7575; Fax: 403/427-5909
•Alberta Review Board: J.E. Brownlee Bldg., 10365 - 97 St., 5th Fl., Edmonton AB T5J 3W7 – 403/422-5994; Fax: 403/427-1762
Chair, Michael Stevens-Guille, Q.C.
Administrator, Lorraine Russell
•Crimes Compensation Board: J.E. Brownlee Bldg., 10365 - 97 St., 10th Fl., Edmonton AB T5J 3W7 – 403/427-7217; Fax: 403/422-4213
Chair, Dr. B.A. Nahornick
Secretary to the Board, Linda Unger
•Fatality Review Board: 4070 Bowness Rd. NW, Calgary AB T3B 3R7 – 403/297-8123; Fax: 403/297-3429
Chairperson, Margaret Gowlland
•Law Enforcement Review Board: 10365 - 97 St. 10th Fl., Edmonton AB T5J 3W7 – 403/422-9376; Fax: 403/422-4782
Chair, Patrick Knoll
Secretary to the Board, Barbara Newton

## Alberta LABOUR

10808 - 99 Ave., Edmonton AB T5K 0G5
403/427-2723; URL: http://www.gov.ab.ca/dept/lbr.html

#### ACTS ADMINISTERED

Agrologists Act
Blind Workers' Compensation Act
Burial of the Dead Act
Certified General Accountants Act
Certified Management Accountants Act
Chartered Accountants Act
Chiropractic Profession Act
Dental Disciplines Act
Dental Mechanics Act
Employment Pension Plans Act
Employment Standards Code
Forestry Profession Act
Government Organization Act, Schedule 10
Health Disciplines Act
Labour Relations Code
Land Surveyors Act
Managerial Exclusion Act
M.L.A. Compensation Act
Occupational Health & Safety Act
Occupational Therapy Profession Act
Opticians Act
Pharmaceutical Profession Act
Podiatry Act
Police Officers Collective Bargaining Act
Professional & Occupational Associations Registration Act
Psychology Profession Act
Public Service Employee Relations Act
Radiation Protection Act
Safety Codes Act
Social Work Profession Act
Veterinary Profession Act
Workers' Compensation Act
**Minister**, Hon. Murray Smith, 403/427-3664, Fax: 403/422-9556
Deputy Minister, Peter Kruselnicki, 403/427-8305, Fax: 403/422-9205
Director, Communications, Charlotte Moran, 403/427-5585, Fax: 403/427-5988
Director, Personnel, Denis St. Arnaud, 403/427-8391, Fax: 403/422-6615

#### ISSUES & REGIONAL MANAGEMENT DIVISION

403/427-8301; Fax: 403/427-6327
Asst. Deputy Minister, Shelley Ewart-Johnson, 403/422-3041, Fax: 403/422-9205
Commissioner, Office of the Provincial Fire Commissioner, Tom Makey, 403/427-8392, Fax: 403/422-3562
Superintendent, Pensions, Gail Armitage, 403/427-8322, Fax: 403/422-4283
Coordinator, Training Services, Linda Fields, 403/427-1173, Fax: 403/422-3091
Director, Information Services, Alec Campbell, 403/427-8531, Fax: 403/422-5070
Director, Work Standards, Mike Kolmatycki, 403/427-8541, Fax: 403/422-3562

#### PROFESSIONAL & TECHNICAL SERVICES DIVISION

10011 - 109 St., 5th Fl., Edmonton AB T5J 3S8
403/427-2655; Fax: 403/422-9734
Asst. Deputy Minister, Don Woytowich, 403/427-8387, Fax: 403/422-9205
Senior Technical Advisor, Building & Fire Safety, Chris Tye, 403/427-8265, Fax: 403/422-3562
Senior Technical Adviser, Plumbing & Gas, Ken Fenning, 403/427-8256, Fax: 403/422-0308
Chief Electrical Inspector, Ken McLennan, 403/427-8260, Fax: 403/427-0380
Chief Elevator Inspector, Al Griffin, 403/427-8260, Fax: 403/427-0380

##### Occupational Health & Safety

403/427-6724; Fax: 403/427-5698
Acting Director, John MacPherson
Manager, Legislation Standards & Technical Service, Dan Clarke, 403/427-2687

##### Associated Agencies, Boards & Commissions

•Labour Relations Board/Public Service Employee Relations Board: #503, 10808 - 99 Ave., Edmonton AB T5K 0G5 – 403/427-8547; Fax: 403/422-0970, Toll Free: 1-800-463-2572
Chair, Bob Blair
•Occupational Health & Safety Council: 10808 - 99 Ave., Edmonton AB T5K 0G5 – 403/427-8305; Fax: 403/422-9205
Chair, Wayne Cameron

## Alberta MUNICIPAL AFFAIRS (AMA)

Commerce Place, 10155 - 102 St., Edmonton AB T5J 4L4
403/427-2732; Fax: 403/422-9105; URL: http://www.gov.ab.ca/dept/ma.html
Communications: 403/427-8862; Fax: 403/422-1419
Provides administrative, financial & planning services to municipalities, sets & enforces marketplace standards, licenses businesses & trades, & offers consumer information & advice.

#### ACTS ADMINISTERED

Alberta Educational Communications Corporation Act
Alberta Housing Act
Bankruptcy & Insolvency Act (Canada)
Border Areas Act
Builders' Lien Act
Business Corporations Act
Calgary-Canadian Pacific Transit Agreement Act
Calgary (City of) & Calgary Power Agreement Act
Calgary (City of) & Calgary Power Authorization Agreement Act
Calgary Exhibition Stampede Limited - Calgary Lease Authorization Act
Cemeteries Act
Cemetery Companies Act

Change of Name Act
Charitable Fund-raising Act
Collection Practices Act
Companies Act
Condominium Property Act
Consumer Credit Transactions Act
Co-operative Associations Act
Debtors' Assistance Act
Direct Sales Cancellation Act
Dower Act
Edmonton (City of) & Calgary Power Ltd. Agreement Validation Act
Edmonton - Meadowview Agreement Act
Franchises Act
Fuel Oil Licensing Act
Garagemen's Lien Act
Land Titles Act
Law of Property Act
Licensing of Trades & Businesses Act
Lloydminster Municipal Amalgamation Act
Local Authorities Election Act
Marriage Act
Mewata Park Enabling Act
Mobile Homes Sites Tenancies Act
Municipal Government Act
Park Towns Act
Partnership Act
Personal Property Security Act
Possessory Liens Act
Prearranged Funeral Services Act
Public Auctions Act
Real Estate Act
Religious Societies' Land Act
Residential Tenancies Act
Smoky Lake (Town of) Gas Utility Act
Societies Act
Special Areas Act
Spirit River Agreement O.C.
Surveys Act
Unfair Trade Practices Act
Vital Statistics Act
Warehousemen's Lien Act
Woodmen's Lien Act
**Minister**, Hon. Iris Evans, 403/427-3744
Deputy Minister, John McGowan, 403/427-9660, Fax: 403/427-0453

#### FINANCE & ADMINISTRATION DIVISION
Asst. Deputy Minister, Vacant, 403/427-1898, Fax: 403/422-9561
Executive Director, Financial Services, Bruce Perry, 403/427-1899, Fax: 403/422-5840
Director, Accounting Services, Bryan Huygen, 403/427-4245, Fax: 403/422-3109
Director, Administrative Services, Ron Todoruk, 403/427-4878
Director, Agencies & Funds, Perry Twaits, 403/427-5942, Fax: 403/427-0453
Director, Budgets & Reporting, Lothar Hellweg, 403/427-4158, Fax: 403/422-5840
Director, Communications, Laurie Collins, 403/427-8882, Fax: 403/422-1419
Director, Corporate Services, Tom Hong, 403/427-3181, Fax: 403/422-4923

#### HOUSING & CONSUMER AFFAIRS DIVISION
403/427-3917; Fax: 403/427-0418
Asst. Deputy Minister, R.S. Leitch
Executive Director, Field Services, Reegan McCullough, 403/427-3919
Executive Director, Major Projects, Rick Beaupre, 403/422-9528
Executive Director, Program Services, Vacant, 403/427-4517
Director, Divisional Support Services, Penny Stinson
Manager, Grants, Subsidies & Recoveries, Wayne Wendell, 403/427-6897, Fax: 403/427-4315

#### LOCAL GOVERNMENT SERVICES DIVISION
Asst. Deputy Minister, Eric McGhan, 403/427-9660, Fax: 403/427-0453
Acting Executive Director, Local Government Advisory, Larry Austman, 403/427-6534, Fax: 403/422-9133
Executive Director, Local Government Development, Brian Quickfall, 403/427-2523, Fax: 403/420-1016
Director, Assessment Standard & Equalizations, Harold Williams, 403/422-1377, Fax: 403/422-3110
Director, Special Services & Management Support, Theresa Ostrum, 403/427-5642, Fax: 403/427-0453

#### REGISTRIES DIVISION
John E. Brownlee Bldg., 10365 - 97 St., Edmonton AB T5J 3W7
403/422-2362 (Edmonton), 403/297-8980 (Calgary)
Toll Free: 1-800-465-5009 (in Alberta)
Responsible for motor vehicles, corporate registry, vital statistics & personal property registry. $20.00 each for birth, marriage & death certificates.
Acting Asst. Deputy Minister, Bill Campion, 403/427-4095, Fax: 403/422-0818
Business Development & Private Agent Support, David Howden, 403/427-0937, Fax: 403/422-0665
Acting Officer, Registration Services, Rae Runge, 403/427-5166, Fax: 403/422-3105
Research & Program Development, Laurie Beveridge, 403/427-8250, Fax: 403/422-5018

##### Associated Agencies, Boards & Commissions
- Alberta Municipal Government Board: 10155 - 102 St., 18th Fl., Edmonton AB T5J 4L4 – 403/427-4864; Fax: 403/427-0986

Executive Director, Gerald Thomas
- Alberta Social Housing Corporation: 10155 - 102 St., 14th Fl., Edmonton AB T5J 4L4 – 403/422-9222; Fax: 403/427-0961
- Alberta Special Areas Board: PO Box 820, Hanna AB T0J 1P0 – 403/854-5600; Fax: 403/854-5527

Chair, J.J. Stemp

## NORTHERN ALBERTA DEVELOPMENT COUNCIL (NADC)
#206, Provincial Bldg., 9621 - 96 Ave., PO Bag 900-14, Peace River AB T8S 1T4
403/624-6274; Fax: 403/624-6184; URL: http://www.nadc.gov.ab.ca
**Minister Responsible**, Hon. Ralph Klein, 403/427-2251, Fax: 403/427-1349, Email: altatalk@censsw.gov.ab.ca
Chair, Mike Cardinal, 403/427-3643, Fax: 403/422-0351

#### NORTHERN DEVELOPMENT BRANCH
403/624-6277; Fax: 403/624-6184; Email: council@nadc.gov.ab.ca
Executive Director, Rick Sloan
Director, Economic Development, Brian Pountney, 403/624-6276
Senior Officer, Northern Development, Audrey Dewit
Senior Officer, Northern Development, Allen Geary
Senior Officer, Northern Development, Kelly Kincaid
Senior Officer, Northern Development, Colin Needham
Manager, Finance & Administration, Kathy Miller, Legislature Annex, #1201, 9718 - 107 St., Edmonton AB T5K 1E4, 403/422-9176, Fax: 403/427-5880

## Alberta Office of the OMBUDSMAN
Phipps-McKinnon Bldg., #1630, 10020 - 101A Ave., Edmonton AB T5J 3G2
403/427-2756; Fax: 403/427-2759
Calgary Office: #850, Ford Tower, 633 - 6 Ave. SW, Calgary AB T2P 2Y5
403/297-6185, Fax: 403/297-5121
**Ombudsman**, Harley Johnson

## Alberta PUBLIC AFFAIRS BUREAU
Park Plaza, 10611 - 98 Ave., 6th Fl., Edmonton AB T5K 2P7
403/427-2754; Fax: 403/422-4168
**Minister Responsible**, Hon. Ralph Klein, 403/427-2251, Fax: 403/427-1349, Email: altatalk@gov.ab.ca
Managing Director, Gerry Bourdeau, 403/427-4350, Fax: 403/427-1010, Email: gerry.bourdeau@gov.ab.ca
Executive Director, Communications Support Services, Dick Steiner, 403/427-4366, Fax: 403/422-4665, Email: dick.steiner@gov.ab.ca
Coordinator, Alberta Communications Network (ACN), Allen MacDonald, 403/427-4374, Fax: 403/422-4665, Email: allen.macdonald@gov.ab.ca
Director, Government Communications Group & Advertising, Dona Miller, 403/427-4805, Fax: 403/427-7464, Email: dona.miller@gov.ab.ca
Director, Print & Graphic Design Services, Marvin Luethe, 403/427-2698, Fax: 403/422-4650, 4651, Email: marvin.luethe@gov.ab.ca
Director, Publication Services & Queen's Printer, Annie Re, 11510 Kingsway Ave., 2nd Fl., Edmonton AB T5G 2Y5, 403/422-2787, Fax: 403/452-0668, Email: reanni@censsw.gov.ab.ca
Director, Regional Information Telephone Enquiries (RITE) & Director, Human Resources/Administration, Elaine Dougan, 403/422-4097, Fax: 403/422-4168, Email: elaine.dougan@gov.ab.ca

## Alberta PUBLIC WORKS, SUPPLY & SERVICES (APWSS)
6950 - 113 St., 3rd Fl., Edmonton AB T6H 5V7
403/427-7988; Fax: 403/427-0812; URL: http://www.gov.ab.ca/ZXpwss/

#### ACTS ADMINISTERED
Architects Act
Builders' Lien Act
Consulting Engineers of Alberta Act
Engineering Geological & Geophysical Professions Act
Health Care Facility Construction Legislation
Major Surface Water Management Legislation
Public Works Act (jointly with Alberta Transportation & Utilities)

##### Legislation used by the department in the delivery of programs & services
Balanced Budget & Debt Retirement Act
Deficit Elimination Act
Financial Administration Act
Government Accountability Act
Government Organization Act
Individual Rights Protection Act
Occupational Health & Safety Act
Public Service Act
Public Service Employee Relations Act
**Minister**, Hon. Stan Woloshyn, 403/427-3666, Fax: 403/427-3649
Deputy Minister, Dan Bader, P.Eng., 403/427-3921, Fax: 403/422-0186
Executive Director, Finance, Paul Pellis, 403/427-1990, Fax: 403/422-5141
Executive Director, Human Resources, Gordon Shopland, 403/427-3986, Fax: 403/422-5138
Director, Communications, Jan Berkowski, 403/422-0326, Fax: 403/427-0812

#### INFORMATION TECHNOLOGY & SUPPLY
Asst. Deputy Minister, Gregg Hook, 403/427-8894, Fax: 403/422-1801, Email: gregg.hook@gov.ab.ca

Acting Executive Director, Information Technology Division, Roger Roberts, 403/427-4203, Fax: 403/427-1449
Acting Executive Director, Telecommunications, Doug Sigler, 403/422-1140, Fax: 403/427-0238
Director, Air Transportation Services, John Tenzer, 11940 - 109 St., Edmonton AB T5G 2T8, 403/427-7341, Fax: 403/422-1232
Director, Contracted Services, Ron Caruk, 12360 - 142 St., Edmonton AB T5L 2H1, 403/427-3222 ext.266, Fax: 403/427-0834
Director, Purchasing Branch, Mike Long, 403/427-3222 ext.223
Director, Supplier Development Branch, Wayne Kenny, 403/427-3222 ext.272

**PROPERTY DEVELOPMENT DIVISION**
Asst. Deputy Minister, Casey Skakun, 403/427-3835, Fax: 403/427-3873
Executive Director, Capital Projects Division, Malcolm Johnson, 403/422-1659, Fax: 403/422-5832
Executive Director, Civil Projects Division, John Ruttan, 403/422-7649, Fax: 403/422-9594
Executive Director, Health Facility Projects Division, John Bennett, 403/422-7531, Fax: 403/422-9749
Executive Director, Strategic Planning Division, Larry James, 403/422-7490, Fax: 403/422-9043
Executive Director, Technical Resources & Standards Division, Tom O'Neill, 403/427-7458, Fax: 403/422-7479

**PROPERTY MANAGEMENT DIVISION**
Asst. Deputy Minister, Bob Smith, 403/427-3875, Fax: 403/422-0284
Director, Land Acquisition Branch, Garry Summers, 403/422-1384, Fax: 403/422-5419
Director, Leasing Branch, Bill Hunt, 403/422-0601, Fax: 403/422-2113
Manager, Maintenance & Energy Support Group, John Gibson, 403/422-0106, Fax: 403/427-1129
Manager, Transportation Utility Corridor Management, Dave Bentley, 403/422-1135, Fax: 403/422-2661

## Alberta RESEARCH COUNCIL (ARC)
250 Karl Clark Rd., PO Box 8330, Edmonton AB T6H 5X2
403/450-5111; Fax: 403/461-2651; URL: http://www.arc.ab.ca
Calgary Office: Digital Bldg., 6815 - 8 St. NE, 3rd Fl., Calgary AB T2E 7H7
Calgary Tel.: 403/297-2600, Fax: 403/297-2607
A provincial technology corporation commited to advancing the economy of Alberta through science & technology applications in agriculture, biotechnology, environment, information technologies, manufacturing & natural resources.
**Minister Responsible**, Hon. Dr. Lorne Taylor
President & CEO, Dr. George B. Miller, 403/450-5200, Fax: 403/450-1490
Director, Corporate Relations, Karen D. Beliveau, 403/450-5203, Fax: 403/450-1490, Email: beliveau@arc.ab.ca

**ADVANCED TECHNOLOGIES DIVISION**
Head, Advanced Computing & Engineering, K.I. Gamble, 403/297-7580
Head, Biotechnology, Dr. W.T. Leps, 403/450-5319
Head, Manufacturing Technologies, C.C. Lumb, 403/450-5401
Director, Information Systems, W.J. Neilson, 403/450-5188

**DEVELOPMENT & PLANNING DIVISION**
Director, Corporate Marketing, Dr. T.R. Heidrick, 403/450-5218
Manager, Technology Management/Joint Research Venture, R.J. Hipkin, 403/297-2682

**RESOURCE TECHNOLOGIES DIVISION**
Vice-President, Dr. M.P. du Plessis, 403/297-2604
Head, Breakthrough Technologies, Heavy Oil & Oil Sands, Dr. E.E. Isaacs, 403/472-4249
Head, Energy Technologies, Dr. D.M. Nguyen, 403/987-8119
Head, Environmental Technologies, Dr. G.W. Bird, 403/472-4400
Head, Forest Products, R.W.F. Wellwood, 403/450-5419

## Alberta SUCCESSION DUTY OFFICE
J.E. Brownlee Bldg., #400 South, 10365 - 97 St., Edmonton AB T5J 3Z8
403/422-2824; Fax: 403/422-9136
**Collector, Succession Duties**, Georgette A. Dawes

## Alberta TRANSPORTATION & UTILITIES
Twin Atria, 4999 - 98 Ave., Edmonton AB T6B 2X3
403/427-2731; URL: http://www.gov.ab.ca/ZXtu/ext.htm
Dangerous Goods Transportation: 1-800-272-9600

**ACTS ADMINISTERED**
Alberta Resources Railway Corporation Act
Canadian Airlines Corporation Act
Central Western Railway Act
City Transportation Act
Department of Transportation & Utilities Act
Highway Traffic Act
Motor Transport Act
Natural Gas Rebates Act
Off-Highway Vehicle Act
Public Highways Development Act
Public Safety Services Act
Railway Act
Regional Airports Authorities Act
Rural Electrification Long Term Financing Act
Rural Electrification Revolving Fund Act
Rural Gas Act
Rural Utilities Act
Transportation of Dangerous Goods Act
Water, Gas, Electric & Telephone Companies Act
**Minister**, Hon. Walter Paszkowski, 403/427-2080, Fax: 403/422-2722
Deputy Minister, Ed McLellan, P.Eng., 403/427-2081, Fax: 403/465-1135
Director, Communications, Philip Mulder, 403/427-7674
Acting Executive Director, Personnel, Brigitte Fulgham, 403/427-7602

**CONTRACTS & COMPLIANCE**
Fax: 403/422-2822
Senior Advisor to the Deputy Minister, Dave Shillabeer, 403/424-0141
Executive Director, Contracts & Compliance, Tim Hawnt, 403/427-3642
Director, Internal Audit Services, Ralph Timleck, 403/415-1086

**FINANCE & ADMINISTRATION**
Fax: 403/465-1135
Asst. Deputy Minister, Ray Reshke, 403/427-0142
Executive Director, Finance & Facility Services, Bob James, 403/422-1063
Acting Executive Director, Policy & Coordination, Rod Thompson, 403/427-7944
Director, Finance Planning & Analysis, Sheena Sheppy, 403/427-7396
Director, Performance Measures, Les Hempsey, 403/422-3992
Director, Revenue & Expenditure Services, Don Tworowski, 403/427-8604
Solicitor, Legal Services, Jim McFadzen, 403/415-0699

**PLANNING, PROGRAMMING & TECHNICAL SERVICES**
Fax: 403/422-6515
Asst. Deputy Minister, Jim Sawchuk, 403/427-7379
Executive Director, Planning & Programming, Brian Marcotte, 403/415-1386
Executive Director, Project Management, J. Ramotar, 403/427-6912
Executive Director, Rural Utilities, Wayne Brown, 403/427-3030
Executive Director, Technical Standards, Allan G. Kwan, 403/427-2087

**REGIONAL SERVICES**
Fax: 403/415-1268
Asst. Deputy Minister, Lyle O'Neill, 403/427-7215
Regional Director, Central Region - Red Deer, Rob Penny, 403/340-5166
Regional Director, North Central Regiona - Barrhead, John Schroder, 403/674-8221
Regional Director, Peace Region - Peace River, Bruno Zutautas, 403/624-6280
Regional Director, Southern Region - Lethbridge, Alec Waters, 403/381-5426

**TRAFFIC SAFETY SERVICES**
Fax: 403/415-0782
Asst. Deputy Minister, Gary Boddez, 403/415-1146
Executive Director, Disaster Services, Ron Wolsey, 403/422-9000
Executive Director, Driver Services, Sherri Thorsen, 403/422-2672
Executive Director, Vehicle Safety & Carrier Services, Roger Clarke, 403/340-5033
Director, Dangerous Goods Control, Shaun Hammond, 403/422-9600
Director, Transport Engineering, Vacant, 403/340-5189

**Associated Agencies, Boards & Commissions**
•Traffic Safety Board: Twin Atria Bldg., 4999 - 98 Ave., 1st Fl., Edmonton AB T6B 2X3 – 403/427-7178; Fax: 403/427-1740
Chair, George Pedersen

## Alberta TREASURY
Terrace Bldg., 9515 - 107 St., Edmonton AB T5K 2C3
403/427-3035; Fax: 403/422-2463

**ACTS ADMINISTERED**
Alberta Corporate Tax Act
Alberta Heritage Savings Trust Fund Act
Alberta Income Tax Act
Alberta Municipal Financing Corporation Act
Alberta Securities Commission Reorganization Act
Alberta Stock Savings Plan Act
Alberta Taxpayers Protection Act
Appropriation Acts
Balanced Budget & Debt Retirement Act
Civil Services Garnishee Act
Credit Union Act
Deficit Elimination Act
Farm Credit Stability Fund Act
Financial Administration Act
Financial Consumers Act
Fuel Tax Act
Government Accountability Act
Government Emergency Guarantee Act
Hotel Room Tax Act
Insurance Act
Loan & Trust Corporations Act
Lottery Fund Transfer Act
Members of the Legislative Assembly Pension Plan Act
Municipal Debentures Act

Pari Mutuel Tax Act
Pension Fund Act
Public Sector Pension Plans Act
Securities Act
Small Business Term Assistance Fund Act
Statistics Bureau Act
Tobacco Tax Act
Treasury Branches Act
Trust Companies Act
Utility Companies Income Tax Rebates Act

**Provincial Treasurer**, Hon. Stockwell Day, 403/427-8809, Fax: 403/428-1341
Executive Asst., Greg Moffatt, 403/427-8809, Fax: 403/428-1341
Deputy Provincial Treasurer, Budget & Management, Al O'Brien, 403/427-4106, Fax: 403/427-0178
Asst. Deputy Provincial Treasurer, Revenue, Len Rokosh, 403/427-3052, Fax: 403/427-0178
Asst. Deputy Provincial Treasurer, Treasury Operations, Robert Bhatia, 403/427-3052, Fax: 403/427-0178
Controller, Jim Peters, 403/427-3052, Fax: 403/427-0178
Ministerial Projects & Liaison, Alex Fowlie, 403/427-3052, Fax: 403/427-1147

#### ADMINISTRATION
Corporate Secretary, Michael Faulkner, 403/422-2858, Fax: 403/422-7235

#### BANKING & CASH MANAGEMENT
Director, Mike B. Neuman, 403/427-9766 ext.226, Fax: 403/427-0473
Acting Senior Manager, Securities Administration, Doug de Brujin, 403/427-3041 ext.271
Senior Manager, Securities Systems, J. Allan Benbow, 403/427-9920 ext.247

#### BUDGET & MANAGEMENT OFFICE
Group Leader, Budget Planning, Agriculture & Rural Development, Ann Hammond, 403/427-8741, Fax: 403/426-3951
Group Leader, Budget Planning, Community Services, Bonnie Lovelace, 403/427-8703, Fax: 403/426-4564
Group Leader, Budget Planning, Education, Training & Finance, Bob Stothart, 403/427-7699, Fax: 403/422-2164
Group Leader, Budget Planning, Health, Larry Bailer, 403/427-8701, Fax: 403/426-4564
Group Leader, Budget Planning, Natural Resources & Sustainable Development, Susan Williams, 403/427-8710, Fax: 403/426-4564
Financial & Reporting Standards, Tim Wiles, 403/427-7320, Fax: 403/422-2164
Pensions Policy, Virendra Gupta, 403/427-8730, Fax: 403/426-4564

#### COMMUNICATIONS
Director, Trish Filevich, 403/427-5364, Fax: 403/427-1147

#### FINANCIAL INSTITUTIONS
Director, Terry Stroich, 403/427-5064 ext.268, Fax: 403/422-2175

#### INSURANCE
Superintendent of Insurance, Bernie Rodrigues, 403/422-1592 ext.225, Fax: 403/420-0752
Deputy Superintendent of Insurance, Arthur Hagan, 403/422-1592 ext.226

#### INVESTMENT MANAGEMENT
Chief Investment Officer, Stan J. Susinski, 403/427-3087, Fax: 403/425-9153
Director, Debt Securities, J. Maurice Husken, 403/427-7981
Director, Equities, Vida Grace, 403/427-7983
Director, Liability Management, Jai Parihar, 403/427-3088
Director, Structured Investment & Portfolio Research, Rocco Klein, 403/427-3093

#### LOANS & GUARANTEES
Director, Peter McNeil, 403/427-9722 ext.254, Fax: 403/422-0981
Senior Manager, Financing & Administration, Stan Bebenek, 403/427-9722 ext.264

#### RISK MANAGEMENT & INSURANCE
Director, Richard Whitehouse, 403/427-4134, Fax: 403/422-5271
Senior Manager, Risk Management Operations, Dick Ewert, 403/427-4134

#### TAX & REVENUE ADMINISTRATION
Director, Compliance, Terry Burns, 403/427-0540, Fax: 403/422-3770
Director, Internal Support, John Parton, 403/427-9416, Fax: 403/427-5074
Director, Revenue Operations, Rick Callaway, 403/427-3244, Fax: 403/427-0348
Director, Strategic Management & Integration, Peter Tsang, 403/427-9403, Fax: 403/427-9631
Director, Tax Services, Lukas Huisman, 403/427-9425, Fax: 403/427-5074

##### Alberta Heritage Savings Trust Fund
403/427-3076
The fund manages the province's resource tax revenues & has a mandate to diversify the Alberta economy for the general good of the population. The Deputy Provincial Treasurer, Finance & Revenue has over-all responsibility.

##### Associated Agencies, Boards & Commissions
•Alberta Municipal Financing Corporation: Terrace Bldg., #403, 9515 - 107 St., Edmonton AB T5K 2C3 – 403/427-9711; Fax: 403/422-2175
President, Robert Splane
•Alberta Pensions Administration: Park Plaza, 3rd Fl., 10611 - 98 Ave., Edmonton AB T5K 2P7 – 403/427-2782; Fax: 403/427-1621; Email: apaco@ibm.net
Responsible for the administration of the Public Sector Pension Plans Act.
Chief Operating Officer, George Buse
Chair, Board of Directors, Jack H. McMahon
Chair, Local Authorities Pension Plan Board of Trustees, Sandra Weidner
Chair, Management Employees Pension Board, Dianne Keefe
Chair, Public Service Pension Board, Tim Wiles
Chair, Special Forces Pension Board, Michael Dungey
Chair, Universities Academic Pension Board, Dr. Ron Bercov
Corporate Secretary, D. Jill Wlosek
•Alberta Securities Commission: 10025 Jasper Ave., 19th Fl., Edmonton AB T5J 3Z5 – 403/427-5201; Fax: 403/422-0777
Calgary Office: 300 - 5 Ave., S.W., 4th Fl., Calgary AB T2P 3C4 – 403/297-6454, Fax: 403/297-6156
An industry funded corporation responsible for the regulation of Alberta's capital market. The Commission performs its responsibilities under the Securities Act.
Chair, William L. Hess, Q.C., 403/297-4280
Executive Director, R.D. Sczinski, C.A., 403/422-1490
Director, Capital Markets, Darrell Bartlett, C.A., 403/422-1505
Director, Market Standards, H. Charles Blakey, 403/297-4221
Director, Securities Analysis, Kenneth Parker, C.A., 403/422-0145
•Automobile Insurance Board: #407, Terrace Bldg., 9515 - 107 St., Edmonton AB T5K 2C3 – 403/427-5428; Fax: 403/422-2175
Administrator, S. Steeves

## Alberta WORKERS' COMPENSATION BOARD
9912 - 107 St., PO Box 2415, Edmonton AB T5J 2S5
403/498-4000; Fax: 403/422-0972
**Minister Responsible**, Hon. Murray Smith, 403/427-3664, Fax: 403/422-9556
President & CEO, Dr. John Cowell, 403/498-4901
Vice-President, Claimant & Health Care Services, John Quince, 403/498-4250
Vice-President, Employer Services, Dieter Brunsch, 403/498-4909
Vice-President, Finance & Administrative Services, David Renwick, 403/498-4188
Chair, Appeals Commission, George Pheasey, 403/422-9539
Chair, Assessment Review Committee, Kenneth Ogston, 403/498-7830
Chair, Claims Services Review Committee, Dirk Smith, 403/498-4441

# GOVERNMENT OF BRITISH COLUMBIA

**Seat of Government:** Legislative Assembly, Parliament Bldgs., Victoria BC V8V 1X4
URL: http://www.gov.bc.ca/
The Province of British Columbia entered Confederation July 20, 1871. It has an area of 892,677 km2, & the StatsCan census population in 1996 was 3,724,500.

## Office of the LIEUTENANT GOVERNOR
Government House, 1401 Rockland Ave., Victoria BC V8S 1V9
250/387-2080; Fax: 250/387-2077
**Lieutenant Governor**, Hon. Garde B. Gardom, Q.C.
Secretary, J. Michael Roberts, L.V.O.

## Office of the PREMIER
#156, West Annex, Legislative Bldgs., 1150 McKenzie Ave., Victoria BC V8V 1X4
250/387-1715; Fax: 250/387-0087
**Premier & President, Executive Council**, Hon. Glen Clark
Deputy Premier, Hon. Dan Miller
Executive Director, Ron Wickstrom
Principal Secretary, Adrian Dix
Director, Communications, Geoff Meggs
Ministerial Asst., Cindy Lowe
Press Secretary, Trish Webb

#### BRITISH COLUMBIA HOUSE OTTAWA
World Exchange Plaza, #880, 45 O'Connor St., Ottawa ON K1P 1A4
613/237-1966; Fax: 613/237-1636
Senior Representative, Vacant
Intergovernmental Relations Officer, Heather Sheffield, 250/387-0752
Executive Asst. & Office Administrator, Jeanette Gasparini

#### BRITISH COLUMBIA TRADE DEVELOPMENT CORPORATION (BC TRADE)
#730, 999 Canada Place, Vancouver BC V6C 3E1
604/844-1900; Fax: 604/660-2457
Vice-President, Trade Intelligence Division, Vacant, 604/844-1969
Vice-President, Trade Operations Division, Steve Mostardi, 604/844-1936

## EXECUTIVE COUNCIL

#156, Parliament Bldgs., 1150 McKenzie Ave., Victoria BC V8V 1X4

Premier & Minister Responsible, Youth, Hon. Glen Clark, 250/387-1715, Fax: 250/387-0087

Minister, Transportation & Highways, Hon. Lois Boone

Minister, Aboriginal Affairs & Minister, Labour, Hon. John Cashore, 250/387-0886, Fax: 250/356-1124

Attorney General & Minister Responsible, Multiculturalism, Human Rights & Immigration, Hon. Ujjal Dosanjh, 250/356-3027

Minister, Agriculture, Fisheries & Food, Hon. Corky Evans, 250/387-1023, Fax: 250/387-1522

Minister, Women's Equality, Hon. Sue Hammell, 250/387-1223, Fax: 250/387-4312

Minister, Environment, Lands & Parks, Hon. Cathy McGregor, 250/387-1187, Fax: 250/387-1356

Minister, Health & Minister Responsible, Seniors, Hon. Joy K. MacPhail, 250/387-5394, Fax: 250/387-3696

Minister, Employment & Investment & Minister, Municipal Affairs & Housing; Deputy Premier, Hon. Dan Miller, 250/356-7020, Fax: 250/356-5587

Minister, Finance & Corporate Relations & Minister Responsible, Intergovernmental Relations, Hon. Andrew Petter, 250/387-3751, Fax: 250/387-5594

Minister, Children & Families, Hon. Penny Priddy, 250/387-9699, Fax: 250/387-9722

Minister, Small Business, Tourism & Culture, Hon. Jan Pullinger, 250/387-1683, Fax: 250/387-4348

Minister, Education, Hon. Paul Ramsey, 250/387-1977, Fax: 250/387-3200

Minister, Social Services, Hon. Dennis Streifel, 250/387-3180, Fax: 250/387-5720

Minister, Forests, Hon. David Zirnhelt, 250/387-6240, Fax: 250/387-1040

#### Cabinet Operations

#272, West Annex, Legislative Bldgs., Victoria BC V8V 1X4

250/387-0986; Fax: 250/356-7258

Deputy Minister & Secretary to the Executive Council, Douglas McArthur, 250/387-0986, Fax: 250/356-7258

Deputy Minister's Executive Asst., Julie Turner

Asst. Deputy Minister, Intergovernmental Relations, Robin Ciceri, 250/387-0752, Fax: 250/387-1920

Director, Government Operations, Shelley Canitz

#### Cabinet Committees

Aboriginal Affairs Working Group of Planning Board

Government Priorities

Land Use Planning Working Group of Planning Board

Planning Board

Planning Board Working Group on Income Security Review

Planning Board Working Group on Legislation

Regulations & Orders in Council

Treasury Board

## LEGISLATIVE ASSEMBLY

c/o Clerk's Office, #221 Parliament Bldgs., Victoria BC V8V 1X4

250/387-3785; Fax: 250/387-0942; URL: http://www.legis.gov.bc.ca/

**Clerk:** E. George MacMinn, Q.C.

**Speaker:** Hon. Dale Lovick, 250/387-3952, Fax: 250/387-2813

**Sergeant-at-Arms:** Anthony A. Humphreys, 250/356-6966

**Chief, Hansard:** Peter Robbins, 250/387-3681, Fax: 250/356-5095

**Director, Library Administration:** Joan Barton, 250/387-6500, Fax: 250/356-1373

#### Government Caucus Office (NDP)

#166, East Annex, Parliament Bldgs., Victoria BC V8V 1X4

250/387-3655; Fax: 250/356-7156; URL: http://www.bc.ndp.ca

Executive Director, John McInnis

#### Office of the Official Opposition (Lib.)

#201, Parliament Bldgs., Victoria BC V8V 1X4

250/356-6171; Fax: 250/356-6176

Leader, Gordon Campbell

Director, Caucus Services, Adam J. Leary

Director, Research, Vacant

#### Office of the Reform BC Party (Ref.)

Parliament Bldgs., Victoria BC V8V 1X4

250/356-6707; Fax: 250/356-6705

Leader, Jack Weisgerber

Research & Communications, Sarah Bonner

#### Office of the Progressive Democratic Alliance Party (PDA)

Parliament Bldgs., Victoria BC V8V 1X4

250/356-8176; Fax: 250/387-4088; URL: http://www.xmission.com/ZXseer/pda/pda.html

Leader, Gordon Wilson

#### Legislative Committees

#224, Parliament Bldgs., Victoria BC V8V 1X4

250/356-2933; Fax: 250/356-8172

Clerk of Committees, C.H. James

Aboriginal Affairs

Agriculture & Fisheries

Crown Corporations

Economic Development, Science, Labour, Training & Technology

Education, Culture & Multiculturalism

Environment & Tourism

Finance & Government Services

Forests, Energy, Mines & Petroleum Resources

Health & Social Services

Justice, Consitutional Affairs & Intergovernmental Relations

Legislative Initiatives

Parliamentary Reform, Ethical Conduct, Standing Orders & Private Bills

Public Accounts

Transportation, Municipal Affairs & Housing

Women's Equality

## THIRTY-SIXTH LEGISLATURE - BRITISH COLUMBIA

250/387-3785

Last General Election, May 28, 1996. Maximum Duration, 5 Years

**Party Standings (June 1996)**

New Democratic Party (NDP) 39

Liberal (Lib.) 33

BC Reform (Ref.) 2

Progressive Democratic Alliance (PDA) 1

Total 75

**Salaries, Indemnities & Allowances**

Effective April 1, 1997. Basic Compensation $69,900 for Members. In addition to the Basic Compensation as a Member of the Legislative Assembly are the following:

Premier $45,000

Ministers with Portfolio $39,000

Ministers without Portfolio $25,000

Parliamentary Secretaries $6,000

Speaker $39,000

Leader of the Official Opposition $39,000

Leader of the Third Party $19,500

Deputy Speaker $19,500

Deputy Chair, Committee of the Whole House $9,000

Government Whip $9,000

Deputy Government Whip $6,000

Official Opposition Whip $9,000

Third Party Whip $6,000

Official Opposition House Leader $9,000

Third Party House Leader $6,000

Government Caucus Chair $9,000

Official Opposition Caucus Chair $9,000

Third Party Caucus Chair $9,000

Chair of Select Standing or Special Committees $6,000

#### MEMBERS BY CONSTITUENCY

Following is: constituency (number of eligible voters in 1996 election) member, party affiliation, Victoria Telephone & Fax numbers. (Address for all is Parliament Bldgs., Victoria, BC V8V 1X4.)

Abbotsford (31,712) John Van Dongen, Lib., 250/356-3074, Fax: 250/356-6176

Alberni (19,516) Gerard A. Janssen, NDP, 250/387-0967, Fax: 250/356-0596

Bulkley Valley-Stikine (18,241) Bill Goodacre, NDP, 250/387-2312, Fax: 250/387-0827

Burnaby North (27,250) Pietro Calendino, NDP, 250/387-2347, Fax: 250/387-0827

Burnaby-Edmonds (30,460) Fred G. Randall, NDP, 250/356-3011, Fax: 250/387-0827

Burnaby-Willingdon (32,406) Joan Sawicki, NDP, 250/356-9172, Fax: 250/387-0827

Cariboo North (19,418) John Wilson, Lib., 250/356-6171, Fax: 250/356-6176

Cariboo South (21,785) Hon. David Zirnhelt, NDP, 250/387-6240, Fax: 250/387-1040

Chilliwack (35,838) Barry Penner, Lib., 250/381-2794, Fax: 250/356-7109

Columbia River-Revelstoke (20,843) Jim Doyle, NDP, 250/356-3015, Fax: 250/387-0827

Comox Valley (42,619) Evelyn Gillespie, NDP, 250/387-3655, Fax: 250/356-7156

Coquitlam-Maillardville (32,719) Hon. John Cashore, NDP, 250/387-0886, Fax: 250/356-1124

Cowichan-Ladysmith (33,375) Hon. Jan Pullinger, NDP, 250/387-7165, Fax: 250/356-7156

Delta North (27,470) Reni Masi, Lib., 250/356-6171, Fax: 250/356-6176

Delta South (30,717) Fred Gingell, Lib., 250/356-6587, Fax: 250/356-6176

Esquimalt-Metchosin (34,220) Moe Sihota, NDP, 250/387-1977, Fax: 250/387-3200

Fort Langley-Aldergrove (33,522) Rich Coleman, Lib., 250/356-6171, Fax: 250/356-6176

Kamloops (33,137) Hon. Cathy McGregor, NDP, 250/387-3655, Fax: 250/356-7156

Kamloops-North Thompson (23,339) Kevin Krueger, Lib., 250/356-6171, Fax: 250/356-6176

Kootenay (24,422) Erda Walsh, NDP, 250/387-3655, Fax: 250/356-7156

Langley (27,360) Lynn Stephens, Lib., 250/356-3086, Fax: 250/356-6176

Malahat-Juan de Fuca (30,284) Rick Kasper, NDP, 250/387-0855, Fax: 250/387-0827

Maple Ridge-Pitt Meadows (38,522) Bill Hartley, NDP, 250/356-3033, Fax: 250/356-7156

Matsqui (31,594) Mike de Jong, Lib., 250/356-3082, Fax: 250/356-6176

Mission-Kent (26,424) Hon. Dennis Streifel, NDP, 250/387-3180, Fax: 250/387-5720

Nanaimo (33,207) Hon. Dale Lovick, NDP, 250/387-5426, Fax: 250/356-0596

Nelson-Creston (27,293) Hon. Corky Evans, NDP, 250/387-1023, Fax: 250/387-1522

New Westminster (31,879) Graeme Bowbrick, NDP, 250/387-3655, Fax: 250/356-7156

North Coast (17,912) Hon. Dan Miller, NDP, 250/356-7020, Fax: 250/356-5587

North Island (26,446) Glenn Robertson, NDP, 250/387-3655, Fax: 250/356-7156

North Vancouver-Lonsdale (28,574) Katherine Whittred, Lib., 250/356-6171, Fax: 250/356-6176

North Vancouver-Seymour (32,798) Daniel Jarvis, Lib., 250/356-3078, Fax: 250/356-6176

Oak Bay-Gordon Head (33,476) Ida Chong, Lib., 250/356-6171, Fax: 250/356-6176
Okanagan East (34,968) John Weisbeck, Lib., 250/356-6171, Fax: 250/356-6176
Okanagan West (47,909) Sindi Hawkins, Lib., 250/356-6171, Fax: 250/356-6176
Okanagan-Boundary (24,471) Bill Barisoff, Lib., 250/356-6171, Fax: 250/356-6176
Okanagan-Penticton (33,856) Rick Thorpe, Lib., 250/356-6171, Fax: 250/356-6176
Okanagan-Vernon (35,354) April Sanders, Lib., 250/356-6171, Fax: 250/356-6176
Parksville-Qualicum (42,549) Paul Reitsma, Lib., 250/356-6171, Fax: 250/356-6176
Peace River North (18,165) Richard Neufeld, Ref., 250/356-6707, Fax: 250/356-6705
Peace River South (19,619) Jack Weisgerber, Ref., 250/356-6707, Fax: 250/356-6705
Port Coquitlam (43,544) Hon. Mike Farnworth, NDP, 250/356-1019, Fax: 250/356-7156
Port Moody-Burnaby Mountain (31,552) Christy Clark, Lib., 250/356-6171, Fax: 250/356-6176
Powell River-Sunshine Coast (29,389) Gordon Wilson, PDA, 250/387-2788, Fax: 250/356-5224
Prince George North (22,271) Hon. Paul Ramsey, NDP, 250/387-1187, Fax: 250/387-1356
Prince George-Mount Robson (18,290) Hon. Lois Boone, NDP, 250/387-1978, Fax: 250/356-2290
Prince George-Omineca (22,229) Paul Nettleton, Lib., 250/356-6171, Fax: 250/356-6176
Richmond Centre (26,241) Douglas Symons, Lib., 250/356-3066, Fax: 250/356-6176
Richmond East (25,822) Linda Reid, Lib., 250/356-3056, Fax: 250/356-6176
Richmond Steveston (23,006) Geoff Plant, Lib., 250/356-6171, Fax: 250/356-6176
Rossland-Trail (22,784) Ed Conroy, NDP, 250/356-3052, Fax: 250/356-7156
Saanich North & the Islands (36,247) Murray Robert Coell, Lib., 250/356-6171, Fax: 250/356-6176
Saanich South (32,204) Hon. Andrew Petter, NDP, 250/387-3751, Fax: 250/387-5594
Shuswap (34,454) George Abbott, Lib., 250/356-6171, Fax: 250/356-6176
Skeena (18,894) Helmut Giesbrecht, NDP, 250/356-3029, Fax: 250/387-0827
Surrey-Cloverdale (39,904) Bonnie McKinnon, Lib., 250/356-6171, Fax: 250/356-6176
Surrey-Green Timbers (29,922) Hon. Sue Hammell, NDP, 250/387-1223, Fax: 250/387-4312
Surrey-Newton (39,876) Hon. Penny Priddy, NDP, 250/356-6348, Fax: 250/356-6595
Surrey-Whalley (22,787) Joan Smallwood, NDP, 250/356-9496, Fax: 250/387-0827
Surrey-White Rock (41,109) Gordon Hogg, Lib.
Vancouver-Burrard (34,585) Tim Stevenson, NDP, 250/387-3655, Fax: 250/356-7156
Vancouver-Fraserview (26,726) Ian Waddell, NDP, 250/387-3655, Fax: 250/356-7156
Vancouver-Hastings (27,260) Hon. Joy K. MacPhail, NDP, 250/387-5394, Fax: 250/387-3696
Vancouver-Kensington (26,954) Hon. Ujjal Dosanjh, NDP, 250/387-1866, Fax: 250/387-6411
Vancouver-Kingsway (27,063) Hon. Glen Clark, NDP, 250/387-1715, Fax: 250/387-0087
Vancouver-Langara (26,965) Val Anderson, Lib., 250/356-3072, Fax: 250/356-6176
Vancouver-Little Mountain (35,332) Gary Farrell-Collins, Lib., 250/356-3060, Fax: 250/356-6176
Vancouver-Mount Pleasant (29,255) Jenny Wai Ching Kwan, NDP, 250/387-3655, Fax: 250/356-7156
Vancouver-Point Grey (36,608) Gordon Campbell, Lib., 250/356-3090, Fax: 250/356-6176
Vancouver-Quilchena (29,973) Colin Hansen, Lib., 250/356-6171, Fax: 250/356-6176
Victoria-Beacon Hill (33,697) Gretchen Brewin, NDP, 250/356-3031, Fax: 250/387-0827
Victoria-Hillside (32,382) Steve Orcherton, NDP, 250/387-3655, Fax: 250/356-7156
West Vancouver-Capilano (30,782) Jeremy Dalton, Lib., 250/356-3070, Fax: 250/356-6176
West Vancouver-Garibaldi (29,666) Ted Nebbeling, Lib., 250/356-6171, Fax: 250/356-6176
Yale-Lillooet (23,982) Harry Lali, NDP, 250/356-3017, Fax: 250/387-0827

**MEMBERS (ALPHABETICAL)**

Following is: member, constituency (number of eligible voters in 1996 election) party affiliation, Victoria Telephone & Fax numbers. (Address for all is Parliament Bldgs., Victoria, BC V8V 1X4.)

George Abbott, Shuswap (34,454) Lib., 250/356-6171, Fax: 250/356-6176
Val Anderson, Vancouver-Langara (26,965) Lib., 250/356-3072, Fax: 250/356-6176
Bill Barisoff, Okanagan-Boundary (24,471) Lib., 250/356-6171, Fax: 250/356-6176
Hon. Lois Boone, Prince George-Mount Robson (18,290) NDP, 250/387-1978, Fax: 250/356-2290
Graeme Bowbrick, New Westminster (31,879) NDP, 250/387-3655, Fax: 250/356-7156
Gretchen Brewin, Victoria-Beacon Hill (33,697) NDP, 250/356-3031, Fax: 250/387-0827
Pietro Calendino, Burnaby North (27,250) NDP, 250/387-2347, Fax: 250/387-0827
Gordon Campbell, Vancouver-Point Grey (36,608) Lib., 250/356-3090, Fax: 250/356-6176
Hon. John Cashore, Coquitlam-Maillardville (32,719) NDP, 250/387-0886, Fax: 250/356-1124
Ida Chong, Oak Bay-Gordon Head (33,476) Lib., 250/356-6171, Fax: 250/356-6176
Christy Clark, Port Moody-Burnaby Mountain (31,552) Lib., 250/356-6171, Fax: 250/356-6176
Hon. Glen Clark, Vancouver-Kingsway (27,063) NDP, 250/387-1715, Fax: 250/387-0087
Murray Robert Coell, Saanich North & the Islands (36,247) Lib., 250/356-6171, Fax: 250/356-6176
Rich Coleman, Fort Langley-Aldergrove (33,522) Lib., 250/356-6171, Fax: 250/356-6176
Ed Conroy, Rossland-Trail (22,784) NDP, 250/356-3052, Fax: 250/356-7156
Jeremy Dalton, West Vancouver-Capilano (30,782) Lib., 250/356-3070, Fax: 250/356-6176
Mike de Jong, Matsqui (31,594) Lib., 250/356-3082, Fax: 250/356-6176
Hon. Ujjal Dosanjh, Vancouver-Kensington (26,954) NDP, 250/387-1866, Fax: 250/387-6411
Jim Doyle, Columbia River-Revelstoke (20,843) NDP, 250/356-3015, Fax: 250/387-0827
Hon. Corky Evans, Nelson-Creston (27,293) NDP, 250/387-1023, Fax: 250/387-1522
Hon. Mike Farnworth, Port Coquitlam (43,544) NDP, 250/356-1019, Fax: 250/356-7156
Gary Farrell-Collins, Vancouver-Little Mountain (35,332) Lib., 250/356-3060, Fax: 250/356-6176
Helmut Giesbrecht, Skeena (18,894) NDP, 250/356-3029, Fax: 250/387-0827
Evelyn Gillespie, Comox Valley (42,619) NDP, 250/387-3655, Fax: 250/356-7156
Fred Gingell, Delta South (30,717) Lib., 250/356-6587, Fax: 250/356-6176
Bill Goodacre, Bulkley Valley-Stikine (18,241) NDP, 250/387-2312, Fax: 250/387-0827
Hon. Sue Hammell, Surrey-Green Timbers (29,922) NDP, 250/387-1223, Fax: 250/387-4312
Colin Hansen, Vancouver-Quilchena (29,973) Lib., 250/356-6171, Fax: 250/356-6176
Bill Hartley, Maple Ridge-Pitt Meadows (38,522) NDP, 250/356-3033, Fax: 250/356-7156
Sindi Hawkins, Okanagan West (47,909) Lib., 250/356-6171, Fax: 250/356-6176
Gordon Hogg, Surrey-White Rock (41,109) Lib.
Gerard A. Janssen, Alberni (19,516) NDP, 250/387-0967, Fax: 250/356-0596
Daniel Jarvis, North Vancouver-Seymour (32,798) Lib., 250/356-3078, Fax: 250/356-6176
Rick Kasper, Malahat-Juan de Fuca (30,284) NDP, 250/387-0855, Fax: 250/387-0827
Kevin Krueger, Kamloops-North Thompson (23,339) Lib., 250/356-6171, Fax: 250/356-6176
Jenny Wai Ching Kwan, Vancouver-Mount Pleasant (29,255) NDP, 250/387-3655, Fax: 250/356-7156
Harry Lali, Yale-Lillooet (23,982) NDP, 250/356-3017, Fax: 250/387-0827
Hon. Dale Lovick, Nanaimo (33,207) NDP, 250/387-5426, Fax: 250/356-0596
Hon. Joy K. MacPhail, Vancouver-Hastings (27,260) NDP, 250/387-5394, Fax: 250/387-3696
Reni Masi, Delta North (27,470) Lib., 250/356-6171, Fax: 250/356-6176
Hon. Cathy McGregor, Kamloops (33,137) NDP, 250/387-3655, Fax: 250/356-7156
Bonnie McKinnon, Surrey-Cloverdale (39,904) Lib., 250/356-6171, Fax: 250/356-6176
Hon. Dan Miller, North Coast (17,912) NDP, 250/356-7020, Fax: 250/356-5587
Ted Nebbeling, West Vancouver-Garibaldi (29,666) Lib., 250/356-6171, Fax: 250/356-6176
Paul Nettleton, Prince George-Omineca (22,229) Lib., 250/356-6171, Fax: 250/356-6176
Richard Neufeld, Peace River North (18,165) Ref., 250/356-6707, Fax: 250/356-6705
Steve Orcherton, Victoria-Hillside (32,382) NDP, 250/387-3655, Fax: 250/356-7156
Barry Penner, Chilliwack (35,838) Lib., 250/381-2794, Fax: 250/356-7109
Hon. Andrew Petter, Saanich South (32,204) NDP, 250/387-3751, Fax: 250/387-5594
Geoff Plant, Richmond Steveston (23,006) Lib., 250/356-6171, Fax: 250/356-6176
Hon. Penny Priddy, Surrey-Newton (39,876) NDP, 250/356-6348, Fax: 250/356-6595
Hon. Jan Pullinger, Cowichan-Ladysmith (33,375) NDP, 250/387-7165, Fax: 250/356-7156
Hon. Paul Ramsey, Prince George North (22,271) NDP, 250/387-1187, Fax: 250/387-1356
Fred G. Randall, Burnaby-Edmonds (30,460) NDP, 250/356-3011, Fax: 250/387-0827
Linda Reid, Richmond East (25,822) Lib., 250/356-3056, Fax: 250/356-6176
Paul Reitsma, Parksville-Qualicum (42,549) Lib., 250/356-6171, Fax: 250/356-6176
Glenn Robertson, North Island (26,446) NDP, 250/387-3655, Fax: 250/356-7156
April Sanders, Okanagan-Vernon (35,354) Lib., 250/356-6171, Fax: 250/356-6176
Joan Sawicki, Burnaby-Willingdon (32,406) NDP, 250/356-9172, Fax: 250/387-0827
Moe Sihota, Esquimalt-Metchosin (34,220) NDP, 250/387-1977, Fax: 250/387-3200
Joan Smallwood, Surrey-Whalley (22,787) NDP, 250/356-9496, Fax: 250/387-0827
Lynn Stephens, Langley (27,360) Lib., 250/356-3086, Fax: 250/356-6176
Tim Stevenson, Vancouver-Burrard (34,585) NDP, 250/387-3655, Fax: 250/356-7156
Hon. Dennis Streifel, Mission-Kent (26,424) NDP, 250/387-3180, Fax: 250/387-5720
Douglas Symons, Richmond Centre (26,241) Lib., 250/356-3066, Fax: 250/356-6176
Rick Thorpe, Okanagan-Penticton (33,856) Lib., 250/356-6171, Fax: 250/356-6176
John Van Dongen, Abbotsford (31,712) Lib., 250/356-3074, Fax: 250/356-6176
Ian Waddell, Vancouver-Fraserview (26,726) NDP, 250/387-3655, Fax: 250/356-7156
Erda Walsh, Kootenay (24,422) NDP, 250/387-3655, Fax: 250/356-7156
John Weisbeck, Okanagan East (34,968) Lib., 250/356-6171, Fax: 250/356-6176
Jack Weisgerber, Peace River South (19,619) Ref., 250/356-6707, Fax: 250/356-6705

Katherine Whittred, North Vancouver-Lonsdale (28,574) Lib., 250/356-6171, Fax: 250/356-6176
Gordon Wilson, Powell River-Sunshine Coast (29,389) PDA, 250/387-2788, Fax: 250/356-5224
John Wilson, Cariboo North (19,418) Lib., 250/356-6171, Fax: 250/356-6176
Hon. David Zirnhelt, Cariboo South (21,785) NDP, 250/387-6240, Fax: 250/387-1040

# BRITISH COLUMBIA GOVERNMENT DEPARTMENTS & AGENCIES

## Ministry of ABORIGINAL AFFAIRS

PO Box 9100, Stn Prov. Gov't, Victoria BC V8W 9B1
250/356-8281; Fax: 250/387-1785; URL: http://www.aaf.gov.bc.ca/aaf/

### ACTS ADMINISTERED

British Columbia Treaty Commission Act
First Peoples' Heritage, Language & Culture Act
Indian Cut-off Land Disputes Act
Indian Self Government Enabling Act
Sechelt Indian Government Enabling Act
Special Accounts Appropriation & Control Act
**Minister**, Hon. John Cashore, 250/387-0886, Fax: 250/356-1124
Deputy Minister, Jack Ebbels, 250/387-6338, Fax: 250/387-6073
Asst. Deputy Minister, Treaty Negotiations, Angus Robertson, 250/356-9516, Fax: 250/387-8195
Executive Coordinator, Ingrid Fee, 250/356-6804

### ABORIGINAL RELATIONS DIVISION

Fax: 604/356-6662
Asst. Deputy Minister, Randy Brant, 250/387-5210
Director, Lands & Resources Branch, Linda Martin, 250/356-8282
Director, Social & Economic Incentives Branch, Robert Botterel, 250/356-6599

### MANAGEMENT SERVICES

Fax: 604/387-6073
Executive Director, Anne Kirkaldy, 250/356-8699
Director, Finance & Administration Branch, Brian Price, 250/356-1799, Fax: 250/356-0783
Director, Human Resources, Bill Montgomery, 250/356-6247
Director, Information Management Branch, Randy Prokop, 250/356-9518

### POLICY, PLANNING & RESEARCH DIVISION

Fax: 604/356-0215
Asst. Deputy Minister, Joy Illington, 250/356-0226
Executive Director, Aboriginal Policy Branch, Deborah McNevin
Executive Director, Treaty Mandates Branch, Nerys Poole, 250/356-2207

### PUBLIC AFFAIRS DIVISION

Director, Communications Branch, Tim Myers, 250/356-9090, Fax: 250/387-1785
Director, Public Consultation Branch, Judy Birch, 250/356-8283

## Ministry of AGRICULTURE, FISHERIES & FOOD

808 Douglas St., Victoria BC V8W 2Z7
250/387-5121; Fax: 250/387-5130; URL: http://www.agf.gov.bc.ca/

### ACTS ADMINISTERED

Agricultural Credit Act
Agricultural Land Commission Act
Agricultural Produce Grading Act
Agricultural & Rural Development (BC) Act
Agrologists Act
Animal Disease Control Act
Bee Act
British Columbia Wine Act
Cattle (Horned) Act
Columbia Basin Trust Act
Farm Distress Assistance Act
Farm Income Insurance Act
Farm Practices Protection (Right to Farm) Act
Farm Product Industry Act
Farmers' & Womens' Institutes Act
Farming & Fishing Industries Development Act
Fish Inspection Act
Fisheries Act
Food Choice & Disclosure Act
Food Products Standards Act
Fur Farm Act
Game Farm Act
Grains & Oilseeds Revenue Protection Plan Trust Fund Act
Grasshopper Control Act
Grazing Enhancement Special Account Act
Insurance for Crops Act
Livestock Act
Livestock Brand Act
Livestock Lien Act
Livestock Protection Act
Livestock Public Sale Act
Meat Inspection Act
Milk Industry Act
Ministry of Agriculture & Food Act
Municipal Act (Sections 916-9)
Natural Products Marketing (BC) Act
Okanagan Valley Tree Fruit Authority Act
Pharmacists, Pharmacy Operations & Drug Scheduling Act (Sections 65-71 only)
Plant Protection Act
Prevention of Cruelty to Animals Act
Seed Grower Act
Seed Potato Act
Soil Conservation Act
Veterinarians Act
Veterinary Laboratory Act
Weed Control Act
**Minister**, Hon. Corky Evans, 250/387-1023, Fax: 250/387-1522
Deputy Minister, Catharine Read, 250/356-1800, Fax: 250/356-7279
Director, Communications Branch, Laura Stringer, 250/356-2862, Fax: 250/387-9105

#### Policy & Legislation

Executive Director, D.M. Matviw, 250/356-1816

### AGRICULTURE DIVISION

Asst. Deputy Minister, Gord Macatee, 250/356-1821
Executive Officer, Ron Sera, 250/356-1821
Chief Veterinarian, Abbotsford, Dr. P. Hewitt, 604/854-4400
Director, Industry Organizations Development, H. Sasaki, 250/356-1828
Director, Risk Management Branch, R. Jarvin, 250/356-1615
Director, Soils & Engineering, Abbotsford, R. Bertrand, 604/852-5363
Director, North Central Region, Prince George, T. Dever, 250/565-6466
Director, South Coastal Region, Abbotsford, D. Sands, 604/852-5222
Director, Southern Interior Region, Kelowna, B. Baehr, 250/861-7211

### CORPORATE SERVICES

Acting Executive Financial Officer, D. Davies, 250/356-1810
Director, Information Technology, Hugh Westwood, 250/356-1668
Acting Director, Personnel, Duff McCaghey, 250/356-1860

### FISHERIES & FOOD DIVISION

Asst. Deputy Minister, Vacant, 250/356-1608
Director, Aquaculture & Commercial Fisheries, Jim Anderson, 250/356-1608, Fax: 250/356-7280
Acting Director, Food Industry, Al Helmerson, 250/356-2946
Director, Trade Competition, John Schildroth, 250/387-7183

#### Associated Agencies, Boards & Commissions

•Animal Health Centre: Abbotsford Agriculture Centre, 1767 Angus Campbell Road, Abbotsford BC V3G 2M3 – 604/556-3003; Fax: 604/556-3010; URL: http://www.agf.gov.bc.ca/agric/ahcweb/ahcweb.htm, Toll Free: 1-800-661-9903 (BC Only)

A full-service veterinary diagnostic laboratory with a mandate to diagnose, monitor and assist in controlling & preventing animal disease in BC. Provides diagnostic testing, including pathology, bacteriology, virology, & toxicology. Involved in research and in development of new diagnostic tests.

Manager & Asst. Chief Veterinarian, Dr. R. Lewis, Email: rlewis@galaxy.gov.bc.ca
Supervisor, Monitoring Laboratory, L. Curley, Email: lcurley@galaxy.gov.bc.ca

•Fisheries Renewal British Columbia: (no address available at time of printing) – 250/387-4250

Established in April 1997, priorities of this new agency will be habitat protection & enhancement projects; commercial & recreational fisheries development & diversification; skills training for fisheries workers; community-based fisheries job creation strategies; & a long-term strategy to coordinate government's fisheries programs.

Director, Jim Anderson

•Provincial Agricultural Land Commission: #133, 4940 Canada Way, Burnaby BC V5G 4K6 – 604/660-7000; Fax: 604/660-7033

General Manager & Chair, K. Miller

#### Agricultural Marketing Boards & Commissions

•British Columbia Marketing Board: Hartwig Ct., #107, 1208 Wharf St., Victoria BC V8W 3B9 – 250/356-8946; Fax: 250/356-5131

Chair, R. Husdon
General Manager, James Sandever

•British Columbia Broiler Hatching Egg Commission: 464 Riverside Rd. South, RR#2, Abbotsford BC V2S 4N2 – 604/850-1854; Fax: 604/853-8419

Secretary Manager, John Durham

•British Columbia Chicken Marketing Board: #203, 5752 - 176 St., Surrey BC V3S 4C8 – 604/576-2855; Fax: 604/576-6729

General Manager, R.A. Stafford

•British Columbia Cranberry Marketing Board: c/o RSW Professional Centre, #200, 8811 Cooney Rd., Richmond BC V6X 3J6 – 250/923-6096; Fax: 250/923-7905

Chair, Ron May

•British Columbia Egg Marketing Board: 34470 Fraser Way South, PO Box 310, Abbotsford BC V2S 4P2 – 604/853-3348; Fax: 604/853-8714

Chair, Gerry Zaph

•British Columbia Grape Marketing Board: #5, 1864 Spall Rd., Kelowna BC V1Y 4R1 – 250/762-4652

Chair, Gerald Moore

•British Columbia Hog Marketing Commission: 2010 Abbotsford Way, Abbotsford BC V2S 6X8 – 604/853-9461; Fax: 604/853-0764

General Manager, Glen Lucas

•British Columbia Milk Marketing Board: #105, 4664 Lougheed Hwy., Burnaby BC V5C 5T5 – 604/294-6454; Fax: 604/294-4566

General Manager, Tom Demma
•British Columbia Mushroom Marketing Board: #302, 34252 Marshall Rd., Abbotsford BC V25 5E4 – 604/853-7575; Fax: 604/853-3556
General Manager, Jack Sharp
•British Columbia Tree Fruit Marketing Board: PO Box 24023, Penticton BC V2A 8L9 – 250/492-0663
Chair, Brian Karrer
•British Columbia Turkey Marketing Board: #106, 19329 Enterprise Way, Surrey BC V3S 6J8 – 604/534-5644; Fax: 604/534-3651
Manager, Colyn Welsh
•British Columbia Vegetable Marketing Commission: #201, 7560 Vantage Way, Delta BC V4G 1H1 – 604/940-0188; Fax: 604/940-0661, Toll Free: 1-800-663-1461
General Manager, Rodger Hughes
•Council of Marketing Boards of British Columbia: 846 Broughton St., Victoria BC V8W 1E4 – 250/383-7171; Fax: 250/383-5031
Secretary, Andy Dolberg
•Farm Practices Board: Hartwig Ct., #107, 1208 Wharf St., Victoria BC V8W 3B9 – 250/356-8946; Fax: 250/356-5131
Chair, R. Husdon
General Manager, James Sandever

## Ministry of the ATTORNEY GENERAL

PO Box 9282, Stn Prov. Gov't, Victoria BC V8W 9J7
250/356-9596 (Policy & Education); Fax: 250/356-9037
Location Address, 1001 Douglas St., 11th Fl., Victoria BC

### ACTS ADMINISTERED

Accountants (Management) Act
Adult Guardianship Act
Age of Majority Act
Attorney General Act
Builders Lien Act
Cabinet Appeals Abolition Act
Civil Rights Protection Act
Commercial Appeals Commission Act
Commercial Arbitration Act
Commercial Tenancy Act
Commissioner on Resources & Environment Act
Company Act
Condominium Act
Conflict of Laws Rules for Trusts Act
Constitution Act
Constitutional Question Act
Coroners Act
Correction Act
County Boundary Act
Court Agent Act
Court of Appeal Act
Court Order Enforcement Act
Court Order Interest Act
Court Rules Act
Criminal Injury Compensation Act
Crown Counsel Act
Crown Franchise Act
Crown Proceeding Act
Curfew Act
Disciplinary Authority Protection Act
Election Act
Electoral Boundaries Commission Act
Electoral Districts Act
Emergency Program Act
Enforcement of Canadian Judgments Act
Escheat Act
Estate Administration Act
Estates of Missing Persons Act
Evidence Act
Expropriation Act
Family Compensation Act
Family Maintenance Enforcement Act
Family Relations Act
Federal Courts Jurisdiction Act
Financial Disclosure Act
Firearm Act
Flood Relief Act
Foreign Arbitral Awards Act
Foreign Money Claims Act
Foresters Act
Fraudulent Conveyance Act
Fraudulent Preference Act
Frustrated Contract Act
Good Samaritan Act
Holiday Shopping Regulation Act
Homestead Act
Horse Racing Act
Infants Act
Inquiry Act
International Sale of Goods Act
International Trusts Act
Interpretation Act
Judicial Review Procedure Act
Jury Act
Justice Administration Act
Land (Spouse Protection) Act
Land Title Act
Land Title Inquiry Act
Land Transfer Form Act
Law & Equity Act
Law Reform Commission Act
Legal Profession Act
Legal Services Society Act
Libel & Slander Act
Limitation Act
Liquor Control & Licensing Act
Liquor Distribution Act
Members' Conflict of Interest Act
Ministry of Provincial Secretary & Government Services Act
Motion Picture Act
Motor Carrier Act
Municipal Act
National Cablevision Limited Transfer of Jurisdiction Act
Negligence Act
Notaries Act
Occupiers Liability Act
Offence Act
Ombudsman Act
Pacific Racing Association Act
Parole Act
Partition of Property Act
Patients Property Act
Pawnbrokers Act
Perpetuity Act
Police Act
Power of Appointment Act
Power of Attorney Act
Privacy Act
Private Investigators & Security Agencies Act
Probate Recognition Act
Property Law Act
Provincial Court Act
Public Guardian & Trustee Act
Public Trustee Act
Queen's Counsel Act
Referendum Act
Regulations Act
Rent Distress Act
Representation Agreement Act
Sales on Consignment Act
Senatorial Selection Act
Senior Citizen Automobile Insurance Grant Act
Sheriff Act
Small Claims Act
Statute Revision Act
Statute Uniformity Act
Subpoena (Interprovincial) Act
Supreme Court Act
Survivorship & Presumption of Death Act
Teaching Profession Act
Traffic Victims Indemnity Fund Repeal Act
Transport of Dangerous Goods Act
Trespass Act
Trust & Settlement Variation Act
Trustee Act
Trustee (Church Property) Act
Victims' Rights & Services Act
Wills Act
Wills Variation Act
Young Offenders (British Columbia) Act

**Attorney General**, Hon. Ujjal Dosanjh, 250/356-3027
Deputy Minister, Maureen A. Maloney, 250/356-0149, Fax: 250/387-6224

### COMMUNITY JUSTICE BRANCH

Fax: 604/356-1092
Asst. Deputy Minister, Alison MacPhail
Executive Director, Gene Errington, 250/953-3180
Director, Family Justice Reform, Wendy Galloway, 250/387-1111
Program Manager, Victim Services, Kay Charbonneau, 250/387-6848

#### Consumer Service Division

1019 Wharf St., Victoria BC V8V 1X4
URL: http://www.lcs.gov.bc.ca/
Director, Consumer Operations Branch & Registrar, Motor Dealers, Terry Barnett, 250/387-9112, Fax: 250/953-3533
Director, Debtor Assistance Branch, Harry Atkinson, 250/387-1747, Fax: 250/353-4782
Director, Financial Administration Branch, John Dowler, 250/387-1719, Fax: 250/387-6574
Director, Human Resources Branch, Ernie Kirchgesner, 250/387-3790, Fax: 250/387-6008
Director, Residential Tenancy Branch, Leah Bailey, 250/356-3413, Fax: 250/387-0271
Director, Support Services Branch, Terry Barnett, 250/387-3909, Fax: 250/387-1615
Registrar, Cemeteries, Paul Snickars, 250/387-9114, Fax: 250/953-3533
Registrar, Credit Reporting Agencies, Harry Atkinson, 250/387-1747, Fax: 250/953-4782
Registrar, Travel Services, Chris Saunders, 604/660-3540, Fax: 604/660-3521
Manager, Freedom of Information & Privacy, Mark Grady, 250/387-1736

### CORRECTIONS BRANCH

250/387-5059; Fax: 250/387-5698
Asst. Deputy Minister, Don Demers, 250/387-5354
Executive Director, Management Services, Brian Mason, 250/356-7930
Director, Program Analysis & Evaluation, Alan Markwart, 250/387-1564
Director, Resource Analysis, Carol MacKillop, 250/378-6366

### COURT SERVICES BRANCH

Asst. Deputy Attorney General, Malcolm McAvity, 250/356-1527, Fax: 250/356-8152
Director, Inspections Unit, Doris St. Germain, 250/356-1528

**For list of Courts & other Legal Offices, including Judicial Officials & Judges *see* Section 10 of this book.**

### CRIMINAL JUSTICE BRANCH

Asst. Deputy Attorney General, Ernie Quantz, Q.C., 250/387-5174, Fax: 250/387-0090

### LAND TITLE BRANCH

910 Government St., 1st Fl., Victoria BC V8V 1X4
250/387-1903; Fax: 250/387-1763
Director, Linda O'Shea, 250/387-6900
Registrar, Kamloops, Ian Smith, #114, 455 Columbia St., Kamloops BC V2C 6K4, 250/828-4455

Acting Registrar, Nelson, Beverly Stevens, 310 Ward St., Nelson BC V1L 5S4, 250/851-1777
Registrar, Prince George, Brian Bigras, #401, 299 Victoria St., Prince George BC V2L 5B8, 250/565-6200
Registrar, Prince Rupert, Kenneth D. Jacques, 730 Second Ave. West, Prince Rupert BC V8J 1H3, 250/627-0530
Registrar, Vancouver/New Westminster, Linda O'Shea, 88 - 6 St., New Westminster BC V3L 5B3, 604/660-2595
Manager, Victoria, Kenneth D. Jacques, Law Courts, 850 Burdett Ave., Victoria BC V8W 1B4, 250/387-6331

#### LEGAL SERVICES BRANCH

Asst. Deputy Attorney General, Gillian Wallace
Chief Legislative Counsel, Brian Greer, Q.C., 250/356-5751
Senior Counsel, Barristers Division, William Pearce, Q.C., 250/356-8866
Director, Library Services, Jane Taylor, 250/356-8495, Fax: 250/387-5758

#### LIQUOR CONTROL & LICENSING BRANCH

1019 Wharf St., Victoria BC V8V 1X4
250/387-1254; Fax: 250/387-9184
Responsible for: issuing, renewing & transferring licenses for the sale of liquor; licensing breweries, distilleries, wineries & their agents; inspecting licensed premises; approving & monitoring advertising of beer, wine & liquor; enforcing the Liquor Control & Licensing Act & Regulations.
General Manager, Robert C. Simson

#### LIQUOR DISTRIBUTION BRANCH

2625 Rupert St., Vancouver BC V5M 3T5
604/252-3021; Fax: 604/252-3026
TLX 04-53470
Solely responsible for the selection, purchasing, pricing & distribution of all alcoholic beverages (wines, spirits & beer) throughout British Columbia in a retail store system of more than 200 government liquor stores & over 70 agency stores.
General Manager, John Nieuwenburg

#### MANAGEMENT SERVICES BRANCH

Fax: 604/387-0081
Asst. Deputy Minister, Rick McCandless, 250/387-5929
Acting Executive Director, Human Resources Division, Bill White, 530 Fort St., 2nd Fl., Victoria BC V8V 1X4, 250/387-5303, Fax: 250/387-7909
Acting Executive Director, Information Technology Division, Scott Andison, 250/356-8787, Fax: 250/356-7699
Executive Director, Policy & Communications, Mary Beeching, 250/387-8030, Fax: 250/387-3719
Director, Communications Division, Christine McKnight, 250/387-0601, Fax: 250/356-9037

#### MULTICULTURALISM & IMMIGRATION BRANCH

#309, 703 Broughton St., Victoria BC V8W 1E2
250/387-7970; Fax: 250/356-5316
Executive Director, Ann Bozoian
Director, Business Immigration, John Gray, 250/844-1801, Fax: 250/660-4092
Director, Immigration Policy, Gordon Whitehead, 250/387-7951, Fax: 250/356-5316
Director, Multiculturalism BC, Ed Eduljee, 250/660-2395, Fax: 250/660-1150

#### PUBLIC SAFETY & REGULATORY BRANCH

Asst. Deputy Minister, Patti Stockton, 250/387-1292, Fax: 250/356-7747
Executive Director, Coordinated Law Enforcement Unit, Peter Engstad, 250/387-0287
Director, Investigation, Inspection & Standards, Allan Anderson
Director, Police Services, Kevin Begg, 250/356-5483, Fax: 250/356-7747
Director, Provincial Emergency Program, A.J. (Tony) Heemskerk, 250/387-5956, Fax: 250/387-9900
Acting Director, Security Programs, Henry C. Mathias, 250/356-1504, Fax: 250/387-5697

#### Associated Agencies, Boards & Commissions

•British Columbia Board of Parole: #301, 10090 - 152 St., Surrey BC V3R 8X8 – 604/660-8846; Fax: 604/660-8877
Chair, Helen M. Joe
Executive Director, D. Bell
•British Columbia Coroner's Service: 4595 Canada Way, 2nd Fl., Burnaby BC V5G 4L9 – 604/660-7739; Fax: 604/660-7776
Chief Coroner, J.V. Cain
•British Columbia Council of Human Rights: 844 Courtney St., 2nd. Fl., Victoria BC V8V 1X4 – 250/387-3710; Fax: 250/387-3643
Acting Chairman, Harinder Mahil
Manager, Administrative Services, Shyrl Desjardins
•British Columbia Police Commission: #405, 815 Hornby St., Vancouver BC V6Z 2E6 – 604/660-2385; Fax: 604/660-1223
Chair, J.D.N. Edgar
•British Columbia Review Board: #310, 435 Columbia St., New Westminster BC V3L 5N8 – 604/669-8789; Fax: 604/660-8809
Chair, Norman J. Prelypchan
•Commercial Appeals Commission: #1304, 865 Hornby St., Vancouver BC V6Z 2H4 – 604/660-2987; Fax: 604/660-3372
Chair, Wallace I. Auerbach
•Elections British Columbia
Listed alphabetically in detail, this Section.
•Expropriation Compensation Board: 514 Government St., Victoria BC V8V 2L7 – 250/387-4321; Fax: 250/387-0711
Chair, Jeanne Harvey
•Judicial Council of British Columbia: Pacific Centre, Box 10287, #501, 700 West Georgia St., Vancouver BC V7Y 1E8 – 604/660-2864; Fax: 604/660-1108
Chief Judge, Provincial Court of B.C., Hon. Robert W. Metzger
•Law Courts Education Society of British Columbia: #221, 800 Smithe St., Vancouver BC V6Z 2E1 – 604/660-9870; Fax: 604/660-2420
Executive Director, Rick Craig
•Law Reform Commission: #601, 865 Hornby St., Vancouver BC V6Z 2G3 – 604/660-2366; Fax: 604/660-2378
Chair, Arthur L. Close, Q.C.
Commissioner, Thomas G. Anderson
•Legal Services Society: #1500, 1140 West Pender St., PO Box 3, Vancouver BC V6E 4G1 – 604/601-6000; Fax: 604/682-7967
CEO, David S. Duncan
•Liquor Appeal Board: #1304, 865 Hornby St., Vancouver BC V6Z 2H4 – 604/660-2987; Fax: 604/660-3372
Chair, Wallace I. Auerbach
•Motion Picture Appeal Board: #310, 435 Columbia St., New Westminster BC V3L 5N8 – 604/660-8789; Fax: 604/660-8809
Chair, Wallace I. Auerbach
•Office of the Public Trustee: #600, 808 West Hastings St., Vancouver BC V6C 3L3 – 604/660-4444; Fax: 604/660-4456
Public Trustee, Dorothy Ewen, 604/660-4489
•Workers' Compensation Board
Listed alphabetically in detail, this Section.

## Office of the AUDITOR GENERAL

8 Bastion Sq., Victoria BC V8V 1X4
250/387-6803; Fax: 250/387-1230; URL: http://www.aud.gov.bc.ca/
**Auditor General**, George Morfitt
Asst. Auditor General, Compliance & Special Projects, Gordon Dawson, 250/356-2636
Asst. Auditor General, Financial Statement Attest, Frank Barr, 250/356-2667
Asst. Auditor General, Value-for-Money Audit, J. Peter Gregory, 250/356-2638

## Ministry of CHILDREN & FAMILIES (CFAM)

1022 Government St., 3rd Fl., Victoria BC V8V 1X4
250/356-3004; Fax: 250/356-3007 (Communications); URL: http://www.ssrv.gov.bc.ca/
BC Children's Commission: 250/356-0831; Fax: 250/356-0837
Website: http://www.childservices.gov.bc.ca
This ministry was created in September 1996 to streamline child & family services & strengthen BC's child protection system. Four goals form the basis for all ministry planning & services delivery: promoting the healthy development & functioning of children, youth, adults & families; protecting children & youth from abuse, neglect & harm; supporting adults with developmental & multiple disabilities to live successfully & participate in the community; ensuring public safety.

**Programs & Services**

•Children: child protection, including foster care, group homes, services for children in care & support for women who witness abuse; services for children with special needs including summer program for deaf/blind students & the Jericho residential program for students attending the provincial school for the deaf; school-based social equity programs, including school meals, community schools & early academic intervention; public & community health services, including child development centres; dental & optical care for children in lower-income families; mental health services
•Youth: support for youth at risk including alternate schools, emergency shelters & outreach to street youth; youth corrections including counseling, therapy, & probation programs; alcohol & drug services; mental health services; public & community health services; youth forensic psychiatric services, including the Maples residential program.
•Families: family support, including parent training, homemaker services & respite care programs; adoption services; child care programs, including daycare subsidies & daycare support for teen parents; alcohol & drug services for adults.
•Adults: with developmental & multiple disabilites: residential care; health services; training & support services.

#### ACTS ADMINISTERED

Adoption Act
Child, Family & Community Service Act
Child, Youth & Family Advocacy Act
Community Resource Board Act
Family & Child Service Act
Guaranteed Available Income for Need Act
Human Resource Facility Act
Social Workers Act
**Minister**, Hon. Penny Priddy, 250/387-9699, Fax: 250/387-9722
Deputy Minister, Robert Plecas, 604/387-2000, Fax: 604/387-2558

#### CHILD, FAMILY & COMMUNITY SERVICE

Asst. Deputy Minister, Chris Haynes, 250/387-6905, Fax: 250/387-2418
Asst. Deputy Director, Rita Maybin, 250/387-7091, Fax: 250/387-7914

Director, Audit & Review Division, Judy Hayes, 604/660-1828, Fax: 604/660-2383
Director, Child, Family & Community Services Division, Jeremy Berland, 250/387-7060, Fax: 250/356-7862
Deputy Director, Aboriginal Services, Mavis Henry, 250/387-7091, Fax: 250/387-7914
Acting Manager, Adoption Programs, Trudy Usher, 250/387-3660, Fax: 250/356-7862

#### COMMUNITY SUPPORT SERVICES

Asst. Deputy Minister, Theresa Kerin, 250/387-3159, Fax: 250/387-2418
Director, Community Placement Project (Coquitlam), Gillian Chetty, 604/660-8477, Fax: 604/660-8810
Director, Community Support Services Division, Paula Grant, 250/387-1275, Fax: 250/356-6534
Director, Information & Privacy Division, Al Boyd, 250/387-0820, Fax: 250/387-0817
Director, Services for Community Living, Peter Melhuish, 250/952-2722, Fax: 250/952-2723
Manager, Adult Residential Care, Frank Van Zandwijk, 250/387-1275, Fax: 250/356-6534
Manager, Children with Special Needs, Kate Irving, 250/387-1275, Fax: 250/356-6534
Manager, Day Care Subsidies/Community Projects, Pieta Van Dyke, 250/387-1275, Fax: 250/356-6534
Manager, Day Programs (adults with mental handicaps), Randi Mjolsness, 250/387-1275, Fax: 250/356-6534
Coordinator, Senior Citizen Counsellors, Barb Wilson, 250/387-1275, Fax: 250/356-6534

## Office of the CONFLICT OF INTEREST COMMISSIONER

#101, 431 Menzies St., Victoria BC V8V 1X4
250/356-9283; Fax: 250/356-6580
**Commissioner**, Vacant

## Ministry of EDUCATION, SKILLS & TRAINING

PO Box 9150, Stn Prov Govt, Victoria BC V8W 9H1
250/356-2500; Fax: 250/356-5945; URL: http://www.est.gov.bc.ca/

#### ACTS ADMINISTERED

Accountants (Certified General) Act
Accountants (General) Act
Accountants (Management) Act
Applied Science Technologists & Technicians Act
Architects Act
Architects (Landscape) Act
Barbers Act
College & Institute Act
Engineers & Geoscientists Act
Hairdressers Act
Independent School Act
Institute of Technology Act
Music Teachers (Registered) Act
Open Learning Agency Act
Privated Post-Secondary Education Act
Royal Roads University Act
School Act
Teaching Profession Act
University Act
University Foundations Act
University of Northern British Columbia Act
Workers Compensation Act
**Minister**, Hon. Paul Ramsey, 250/387-1977, Fax: 250/387-3200
Deputy Minister, Don Wright, PO Box 9594, Stn Prov Govt, Victoria BC V8W 9K4, 250/356-2026, Fax: 250/387-8322

#### EDUCATION PROGRAMS DIVISION

Asst. Deputy Minister, Dr. Sam Lim, 250/356-2499, Fax: 250/356-6063
Acting Director, Career Programs Branch, John Fitzgibbon, 250/387-7044, Fax: 250/387-1418
Director, Curriculum & Resources Branch, Jerry Mussio, 250/356-2317, Fax: 250/356-2316
Director, Examinations & Assessment Branch, Becky Matthews, 250/356-7269, Fax: 250/387-3682
Director, Field Services Team (K-12), Jerry Mussio, 250/356-2575, Fax: 250/356-8267
Director, Technology & Distance Education Branch, Dr. Barry Carbol, 250/356-2326, Fax: 250/387-5515

#### MANAGEMENT SERVICES DIVISION

Asst. Deputy Minister, Jim Crone, 250/387-2046, Fax: 250/356-8322
Director, Finance & Administrative Services Branch, Neil Matheson, 250/356-2470, Fax: 250/387-9695
Director, Freedom of Information & Privacy Branch, Rob Langridge, 250/356-7508, Fax: 250/387-6315
Director, Human Resources Branch, Lorie Hunchak, 250/356-2351, Fax: 250/356-1520
Director, Information Management Branch, Dorothy Drislane, 250/387-6155, Fax: 250/356-0033

#### POLICY, PLANNING & SPECIAL PROGRAMS DIVISION

Asst. Deputy Minister, Paul Pallan, 250/356-2487, Fax: 250/356-2604
Executive Director, Planning & Accountability Section, Derek Sturko, 250/356-7347, Fax: 250/356-9121
Executive Director, Policy, Legislation & Corporate Services Section, Allyson McKay, 250/356-5406, Fax: 250/387-3750
Executive Director, Special Programs Section, Peter Owen, 250/356-0522, Fax: 250/953-4908
Director, Aboriginal Education Branch (K-12), Brian Domney, 250/387-1544, Fax: 250/387-1470
Director, Accountability Branch, Barry Anderson, 250/356-7693, Fax: 250/356-2504
Director, Office for Disability Issues, Frank Jonasen, 250/387-3813, Fax: 250/387-3114, TDD: 250/387-3555
Director, Evaluation & Reporting Branch, Gerald Morton, 250/356-1233, Fax: 250/356-0407
Director, Federal/Provincial Relations & International Education Branch, Gail Thomas, 250/356-7250, Fax: 250/387-0878
Acting Director, French Programs Branch, Raymond Ouimet, 250/356-2524, Fax: 250/387-1470
Acting Director, Legislation Branch, Stella Bailey, 250/356-9734, Fax: 250/387-3750
Director, Planning Branch, Mike Hoebel, 250/356-2332, Fax: 250/356-2504
Acting Director, Policy Branch, Sharon Russell, 250/356-1404, Fax: 250/356-2504
Director, Research & Analysis Branch, Jim Howie, 250/356-7248, Fax: 250/387-0878
Director, School Facilities Branch, Rick Connolly, 250/356-2368, Fax: 250/387-1451
Director, School Finance & Data Management Branch, Joan Axford, 250/356-2586, Fax: 250/387-1451
Director, Social Equity Branch, Robin Syme, 250/356-2565, Fax: 250/356-0580
Director, Special Education Branch, Dr. Shirley McBride, 250/356-2333, Fax: 250/356-7631, TDD: 250/356-7632
Inspector, Independent Schools Branch, Gerry Ensing, 250/356-2508, Fax: 250/953-4908

#### POST SECONDARY EDUCATION DIVISION

Asst. Deputy Minister, Shell Harvey, 250/387-0893, Fax: 250/356-8322
Director, Access & Health Programs Branch, Devron Gaber, 250/387-6198, Fax: 250/356-8851
Director, Business & Technical Programs Branch, Duncan MacRae, 250/387-6191, Fax: 250/356-8131
Director, Facilities Services & Capital Innovations Branch, Jim Parker, 250/387-6450, Fax: 250/387-5259
Director, Innovation & Continuing Education Branch, Jim Soles, 250/356-7740, Fax: 250/387-5259
Director, Post Secondary Finance & Student Assistance, Tom Austin, 250/387-6169, Fax: 250/356-8131
Director, Student Services Branch, Jim Vanstone, 250/387-6100, Fax: 250/356-9455
Director, Universities & Aboriginal Programs Branch, Robin Ciceri, 250/387-6166, Fax: 250/356-8851

#### SKILLS DEVELOPMENT DIVISION

Asst. Deputy Minister, Betty Notar, 250/356-1379, Fax: 250/387-3296
Executive Director, BC Benefits Transition Team, Heather Dickson, 250/387-4280, Fax: 250/356-8082
Director, Corporate Services Branch, Scott Browning, 634/387-1515, Fax: 634/356-8082
Acting Director, Field Services Branch, Michael Woodcock, 250/387-6012, Fax: 250/356-8082
Director, Program Operations Branch, Kerry Jothen, 250/387-4287, Fax: 250/387-2069
Director, Program Planning & Development Branch, Franki Craig, 250/356-5991, Fax: 250/387-0262

#### Associated Agencies, Boards & Commissions

•Open Learning Agency: 4355 Mathissi Pl., Burnaby BC V5G 4S8 – 604/431-3000; Fax: 604/431-3333
Chair, Reva Dexter
President, Dr. Glen M. Farrell

## ELECTIONS BRITISH COLUMBIA

1075 Pendergast St., Victoria BC V8V 1X4
250/387-5305; Fax: 250/387-3578; URL: http://vvv.com/ZXelectionsbc/
**Chief Electoral Officer**, Robert A. Patterson

## Ministry of EMPLOYMENT & INVESTMENT

712 Yates St., Victoria BC V8W 9N1
250/356-8702; Email: webmaster@eivic.ei.gov.bc.ca; URL: http://www.ei.gov.bc.ca/

The lead provincial agency for creating & protecting jobs across British Columbia. The ministry:
•develops sectoral trade opportunities;
•fosters international & domestic private sector investments;
•facilitates & coordinates strategic public sector capital investments;
•works with the public sector in its economic development responsibilities;
•facilitates the development of the science & technology sector;
•ensures that the province's energy & mineral resources are managed for the benefit of British Columbians;
•encourages the revitalization of traditional industries; &
•collects revenues generated by petroleum & mining activities in the province.

#### ACTS ADMINISTERED

British Columbia Buildings Corporation Act
British Columbia Enterprise Corporation Act (other than in relation to the BC Pavilion Corporation)
Build BC Act
Coal Act
Community Financial Services Act
Development Corporation Act
Document Disposal Act
Economic Development Electricity Rate Act
Energy Efficiency Act
Expo 86 Corporation Act
Ferry Corporation Act

Fort Nelson Indian Reserve Minerals Revenue Sharing Act
Freedom of Information & Protection of Privacy Act
Gas Utility Act
Geothermal Resources Act
Hydro & Power Authority Act
Hydro & Power Authority Privatization Act
Hydro Power Measures Act
Indian Reserve Mineral Resource Act
Industrial Development Incentive Act (other than in relation to the Small Business Incentive Program)
Insurance Corporation Act
International Commercial Arbitration Act
Job Protection Act
Mineral Land Tax Act
Mineral Tax Act
Mineral Tenure Act
Mines Act
Mining Right of Way Act
Ministry of Energy, Mines & Petroleum Resources Act
Ministry of Industry & Small Business Development Act (other than in relation to small business & tourism)
Ministry of International Business & Immigration Act (other than in relation to immigration)
Ministry of International Trade, Science & Investment (other than in relation to small business & tourism)
Ministry of Transportation & Highways Act (Sections 61-67, pertaining to the Victoria Line Ltd.)
Natural Gas Price Act
Natural Resource Community Fund Act
Petroleum & Natural Gas Act
Petroleum & Natural Gas (Vancouver Island Railway Lands) Act
Petroleum Corporation Repeal Act
Pipeline Act (Part 7 only)
Science Council Act
Science & Technology Fund Act
Special Enterprise Zone & Tax Relief Act
Telephone (Rural) Act
Trade Development Corporation Act
Vancouver Island Natural Gas Pipeline Act
**Minister**, Hon. Dan Miller
Deputy Minister, Charles Kang, 250/952-0102, Fax: 250/952-0600
Acting Executive Director, Communications Division, Don Zadravec, 250/952-0607, Fax: 250/952-0625
Director, Corporate Relations Branch, Suzanne Christiansen, 250/952-0628, Fax: 250/952-0600

### BRITISH COLUMBIA TRADE & INVESTMENT OFFICE (BCTIO)

#730, 999 Canada Place, Vancouver BC V6C 3E1
Fax: 604/660-4048; Email: jburnes@eivic.ei.gov.bc.ca
Victoria Fax: 250/952-0637
1810 Blanshard St., 7th Fl., PO Box 9307, Victoria BC V8W 9N3
Asst. Deputy Minister, Chris Nelson, 250/952-0635
Director, Financial Services Branch, Mark Lofthouse, 250/952-0638
Director, International Services Branch, Harold Middleton, 604/844-1835
Acting Director, Investment Facilitation Branch, John Gray, 250/952-0648
Director, Strategic Industries Branch, Allan Collier, 250/952-0661

### ECONOMIC DEVELOPMENT DIVISION

Asst. Deputy Minister, Cheryl Brooks, 250/952-0115, Fax: 250/952-0111
Director, Economic Partnerships Branch, Jacqui Morgan, 250/952-0677, Fax: 250/952-0688
Director, Economics Branch, Louise Wilson, 250/952-0698, Fax: 250/952-0705
Director, International Branch, Noel Schacter, 250/952-0708, Fax: 250/952-0716
Director, Resource Policy Branch, Brian Parrott, 250/952-0502, Fax: 250/952-0501

### ENERGY & MINERALS DIVISION (EMD)

1810 Blanshard St., 5th Fl., PO Box 9324, Victoria BC V8W 9N3
Asst. Deputy Minister, Peter Ostergaard, 250/952-0132, Fax: 250/952-0121
Chief Geologist, Geological Survey Branch, Ron Smyth, 250/952-0429, Fax: 250/952-0371
Director, Engineering & Operations Branch, Bou van Oort, 250/952-0302, Fax: 250/952-0291
Director, Mineral Titles Branch, Denis Lieutard, 250/952-0542, Fax: 250/952-0541
Director, Petroleum Geology Branch, John MacRae, 250/952-0352, Fax: 250/952-0291
Director, Regional Operations Health & Safety, Fred Hermann, 250/952-0494, Fax: 250/952-0491
Commissioner, Petroleum Titles Branch, Gerald German, 250/952-0334, Fax: 250/952-0331

### REVENUE & MANAGEMENT SERVICES DIVISION

1810 Blanshard St., 8th Fl., Victoria BC V8W 9N3
Asst. Deputy Minister, Joan Hesketh, 250/952-0122, Fax: 250/952-0101
Coordinator, Community Development Unit, Jim Green, 604/775-1695, Fax: 604/775-1184

#### Associated Agencies, Boards & Commissions

•Asia Pacific Foundation: #666, 999 Canada Place, Vancouver BC V6C 3E1 – 604/684-5986; Fax: 604/681-1370
President & CEO, Bill Saywell
•BC Rail Ltd.: PO Box 8770, Vancouver BC V6B 4X6 – 604/984-5001; Fax: 604/984-5201; URL: http://www.bcrail.com
Chair, Edmond E. Price, 604/986-2012
President & CEO, Paul McElligott
Corporate Secretary, Carol A. Lee, 604/984-5222
Vice-President, Finance & Information Technology, J. Roger Clarke, 604/984-5235
Vice-President, Human Resources & Strategic Planning, Eric Lush, 604/984-5158
Vice-President, Rail Support Services, J. Chuck Trainor, 604/984-5238
Vice-President, Sales & Customer Service Delivery, Wayne C. Banks, 604/984-5056
•British Columbia Advisory Council on Mining: 1810 Blanshard St., Victoria BC V8V 1X4 – 250/952-0152
•British Columbia Buildings Corporation: 3350 Douglas St., PO Box 1112, Victoria BC V8W 2T4 – 250/387-7211; Fax: 250/387-0024; URL: http://www.bcbc.gov.bc.ca
President & CEO, Dennis Truss, 250/387-7344, Fax: 250/356-2919
Vice-President, Human Resources & Corporate Services, Sharon Halkett
Director, Corporate Communications, Denis Racine
•British Columbia Ferry Corporation: 1112 Fort St., Victoria BC V8V 4V2 – 250/381-1401; Fax: 250/381-5452; URL: http://vvv.com/ferries/index.html
President & CEO, Frank Rhodes
•British Columbia Gaming Commission: 848 Courtney St., 2nd Fl., Victoria BC V8V 1X4 – 250/356-2992; Fax: 250/356-7949
Chair, Vacant
•British Columbia Hydro & Power Authority
Listed alphabetically in detail, this Section.
•British Columbia Mediation & Arbitration Board: 10142 - 101 Ave., Fort St. John BC V1J 2B3 – 250/787-3403; Fax: 250/787-3228
Chair, Ewart Loucks
•British Columbia Racing Commission: Metro Tower 11, #2003, 4720 Kingsway, Burnaby BC V5H 4N2 – 604/660-7400; Fax: 604/660-7414
Chair, Lorna Romilly
•Crown Corporations Secretariat: 848 Courtney St., 4th Fl., PO Box 9300, Victoria BC V8W 9N2
Deputy Minister, Lawrie McFarlane, 250/387-8456
Director, Energy, Insurance Crowns, Bruce Duncan, 250/356-6723
Director, Transportation Crowns, Frank Blasetti, 250/356-6721
•Information, Science & Technology Agency (ISTA): 563 Superior St., 3rd Fl., PO Box 9441, Victoria BC V8V 1X4 – 250/387-0811; Fax: 250/356-9287

The Information and Technology Access Office (ITAO) was created by Cabinet Order in August 1995 under government obligation to the Electronic Highway Accord. In February 1996, the British Columbia Archives & Records Services, the Information & Privacy Branch, & Enquiry BC joined ITAO. In November 1996, the mandate of the ITAO was broadened to include responsibility for the development & growth of all aspects of science & technology in B.C. The agency was renamed the Information Science and Technology Agency (ISTA).

Deputy Minister/Chief Information Officer, Philip Halkett
•International Commercial Arbitration Centre: #670, 999 Canada Place, Vancouver BC V6C 2E2 – 604/684-2821; Fax: 604/641-1250
Governing Trustee, Graham Clarke
•International Finance Centre - Vancouver Society (IFC): World Trade Centre, #658, 999 Canada Place, Vancouver BC V6C 3E1 – 604/683-6626; Fax: 604/683-6646
Executive Director, Liam Hopkins
•International Maritime Centre: Harbour Centre, #1550, 555 West Hastings St., PO Box 12118, Vancouver BC V6B 4N6 – 604/681-9515; Fax: 604/683-2435
Chair & Director, Graham Clarke
•Job Protection Commission: #369, 1177 West Hastings St., Vancouver BC V6E 2K3 – 604/775-0162; Fax: 604/775-0228, Toll Free: 1-800-665-4605
Commissioner, Doug Kerley
•Lotteries Advisory Committee: 712 Yates St., 3rd Fl., PO Box 9311, Victoria BC V8W 9N1 – 250/387-0219; Fax: 250/356-1910
Chair, Peter Clark
•Premiers' Advisory Council on Science & Technology: #501, 168 Chadwick Ct., North Vancouver BC V7M 3L4 – 604/987-8477; Fax: 604/987-5617
Chair, Julia Levy
•Science Council of British Columbia (SCBC): #800, 4710 Kingsway, Burnaby BC V5H 4M2 – 604/438-2752; Fax: 604/438-6564; URL: http://www.scbc.org/, Toll Free: 1-800-665-7222
President, Dr. Jim Reichert

## Ministry of ENVIRONMENT, LANDS & PARKS (ELP)

810 Blanshard St., Victoria BC V8V 1X5
250/387-9419; Fax: 250/356-6464; Email: wwwmail@pubaffair.env.gov.bc.ca; URL: http://www.env.gov.bc.ca/
General Inquiries: 250/387-1161; Environmental Statutes URL: http://www.env.gov.bc.ca/epd/cpr/admin/cpr.html

Provincial Department responsible for providing a naturally diverse & healthy environment.

•BC Environment has management responsibility over air, water, wildlife & wild freshwater fish & sport fish resources. In addition BC Environment regulates waste disposal & pesticide use, assesses major development proposals, enforces environmental legislation & protects resources, property & the public from human & natural hazards.

•BC Lands manages & allocates public land to ensure access for industry, commerce, settlement, recreation & conservation uses that are sensitive to both environmental needs & sustainable development.

•BC Parks is responsible for the management of parks, recreation areas & ecological reserves with a commitment to the conservation & management of natural features & diverse environments in the province.

#### ACTS ADMINISTERED

Beaver Lodge Lands Trust Renewal Act
Boundary Act
Commercial River Rafting Safety Act
Creston Valley Wildlife Act
Dogwood, Rhododendron & Trillium Protection Act
Drainage & Dyking Adjustment & Repeal Act, 1965
Drainage, Ditch & Dyke Act
Dyke Maintenance Act
Dyking Authority Act
Ecological Reserve Act
Environment & Land Use Act
Environment Management Act
Environmental Assessment Act
Financial Administration Act (in part)
Greenbelt Act
Industrial Development Act
Industrial Operation Compensation Act
Kootenay Canal Land Acquisition Act
Land Act
Land Survey Act
Land Surveyors Act
Land Title Act
Land (Veterans) Act
Libby Dam Reservoir Act
Litter Act
Ministry of Environment Act
Ministry of Lands, Parks & Housing Act
Park Act
Park (Regional) Act
Pesticide Control Act
Railway Act (in part)
Skagit Environmental Enhancement Act
Sustainable Environment Fund Act
Universities Real Estate Development Corporation Act (in part)
University Endowment Land Act (in part)
University Endowment Land Park Act
Waste Management Act
Water Act
Water Protection Act
Water Utility Act
Weather Modification Act
West Coast National Park Act
Wildlife Act (1982)

**Minister**, Hon. Cathy McGregor
Deputy Minister, Cassie Doyle
Director, Forest Practices Code, Dr. Don A. Kasianchuk, 965 Broughton St., 6th Fl., Victoria BC V8V 1X4, 250/387-6989, Fax: 250/953-5170

#### CORPORATE SERVICES DIVISION

810 Blanshard St., 4th Fl., Victoria BC V8V 1X4
250/387-9878; Fax: 250/387-5669
Asst. Deputy Minister, Greg Koyl, 250/387-9888
Director, Central Services Branch, Wilda F. Dirks, 250/356-9228
Acting Director, Corporate Policy Branch, Linda Hannah, 250/387-9670, Fax: 250/387-8894
Acting Director, Financial Services, Kathy Bryce, 250/356-1377, Fax: 250/356-9239
Director, Human Resources Branch, Ken J. Gower, 250/387-9819, Fax: 250/356-7286
Director, Systems Services Branch, John Roche, 737 Courtney St. 3rd Fl., Victoria BC V8V 1X4, 250/387-9605, Fax: 250/356-7297

#### CROWN LAND REGISTRY SERVICES BRANCH

3400 Davidson Ave., Victoria BC V8V 1X4
250/387-4461; Fax: 250/387-1830; URL: http://www.env.gov.bc.ca/ZXclrsweb/
Director & Surveyor General, Crown Land Registry Services Branch, Greg Roberts
Director, Geographic Data BC, Gary T. Sawayama, 1802 Douglas St., 4th Fl., 250/387-6316, Fax: 250/356-7831
Director, Hydrology Branch, Jim S. Mattison, 250/387-1112, Fax: 250/356-5496
Director, Real Estate Services Branch, Brian Clarke, 1802 Douglas St., 3rd Fl., 250/387-1934
Director, Tenure Management Branch, Lynn Kennedy
Director, Water Resources Branch, Jack E. Farrell, 250/387-6945, Fax: 250/356-8298

#### ENVIRONMENT & LANDS HEADQUARTERS DIVISION

777 Broughton St., Victoria BC V8V 1X4
250/387-9990; Fax: 250/356-9836
Asst. Deputy Minister, Don A. Fast, 250/387-1280
Acting Director, Air Resources Branch, Prad Khare, 250/387-9987
Director, Industrial Waste & Hazardous Contaminants Branch, Lanny T. Hubbard, 250/387-9992, Fax: 250/387-9935
Director, Municipal Waste Reduction Branch, Ron J. Driedger, 250/387-9974, Fax: 250/356-9974
Director, Pollution Prevention Section, Tom J. Galimberti, 250/356-6027, Fax: 250/356-9836
Acting Director, Water Quality Branch, Shelley Forrester, 250/387-9500, Fax: 250/356-8298
Manager, Laboratory Services & Systems Management Section, Larry Keith, 250/953-3080

#### ENVIRONMENT & LANDS REGIONS DIVISION

Fax: 250/357-5669
Asst. Deputy Minister, Dr. Jon O'Riordan, 250/387-9877

#### FISHERIES, WILDLIFE & HABITAT PROTECTION DEPARTMENT

250/356-0121; Fax: 250/387-5669
Asst. Deputy Minister, Jim H.C. Walker, 250/356-0139
Director, Fisheries Branch, Dr. Harvey Andrusak, 780 Blanshard St., 2nd Fl., Victoria BC V8V 1X4, 250/387-9711, Fax: 250/387-9750
Director, Forest Renewal Coordination Branch, Al Martin
Director, Habitat Protection Branch, Nancy Wilkin, 780 Blanshard St., 3rd Fl., Victoria BC V8V 1X4, 250/387-9555, Fax: 250/356-5104
Acting Director, Wildlife Branch, D. Ray Halladay, 780 Blanshard St., Victoria BC V8V 1X4, 250/387-9731, Fax: 250/357-6750

#### PARKS DIVISION (BC PARKS)

800 Johnson St., 2nd Fl., Victoria BC V8V 1X4
250/387 5002; Fax: 250/387-5757; URL: http://www.env.gv.bc.ca/land/parks.html
Parks Reservations: 1-800-689-9025
Asst. Deputy Minister, Denis O'Gorman, 250/387-9997
Director, District Operations Branch, Jack Hall, 250/387-3987
Director, Parks Department Services, Lynn Kennedy, 250/387-3943
Acting Director, Parks & Ecological Reserves Management Branch, Bob Dalziel
Director, Parks & Ecological Reserves Planning, Colin Campbell

#### POLICY, PLANNING & LEGISLATION DEPARTMENT

250/356-7223; Fax: 250/387-5669
Asst. Deputy Minister, Toby Vigod
Director, Aboriginal Affairs Branch, Ingrid James, 250/387-9730, Fax: 250/387-8897
Director, Enforcement & Environmental Emergencies Branch, Donna Humphries, 250/387-9401, Fax: 250/387-1041
Director, Environmental Assessment Branch, Doug W. Dryden, 250/387-9678, Fax: 250/356-7183
Director, Evaluation & Economics Branch, Ray Payne, 250/356-0204, Fax: 250/356-9836
Director, Land Use Branch, David Johns, 250/387-1850, Fax: 250/356-1916
Director, Strategic Planning, Policy & Legislation Branch, Cindy Brown, 250/356-1907, Fax: 250/387-8894

#### PUBLIC AFFAIRS & COMMUNICATIONS BRANCH

250/387-9422; Fax: 250/356-6464
Ministry News Releases URL: http://www.env.gov.bc.ca/main/news_releases.html
Executive Director, Mark Stefanson, 250/387-9422
Manager, Communications Services, Jennifer Smyth, 250/387-9418
Manager, Corporate Services, Monica Collins, 250/356-6799
Librarian, Ministry Library, Kathy Neer, 250/387-9745
Executive Coordinator, Public Affairs & Communications, Kellie Paterson, 250/387-3755
Senior Coordinator, Communications, Liz Bicknell, 250/356-7045
Senior Coordinator, Communications, Joanne McGachie, 250/387-5704
Coordinator, Public Affairs, Jennifer Ireland, 250/387-9417
Coordinator, Public Information, Annette Juch, 250/953-3902

##### Associated Agencies, Boards & Commissions

- British Columbia-Alberta Boundary Commission: 3400 Davidson Ave., Victoria BC V8V 1X4 – 250/387-4461; Fax: 250/387-1830

Commissioner, Don Duffy

- British Columbia-Yukon-Northwest Territories Boundary Commission: 3400 Davidson Ave., Victoria BC V8V 1X4 – 250/387-4461; Fax: 250/387-1830

Commissioner, Don Duffy

- Environmental Appeal Board: #125, 911 Yates St., Victoria BC V8V 1X5 – 250/387-3464; Fax: 250/356-9923

Chair, Linda Michaluk

## British Columbia ENVIRONMENTAL ASSESSMENT OFFICE

836 Yates St., 2nd Fl., Victoria BC V8V 1X4
250/356-7475; Fax: 250/356-7477; Email: eaoinfo@galaxy.gov.bc.ca; URL: http://www.eao.gov.bc.ca/
**Deputy Minister & Executive Director**, Sheila Wynn
Director, Aboriginal Affairs, Martyn Glassman, 250/387-2206
Director, Corporate Services, Patty Shelton, 250/356-7476
Director, Destination Resorts & Transportation, Ray Crook, 250/356-7492
Director, Energy & Hydro Electric, Derek Griffin, 250/387-1543
Director, Mining, Mike Kent, 604/356-0312
Director, Mining, Norm Ringstad, 250/356-7481
Director, Petroleum & Natural Gas, Marcia Farquhar, 250/356-7484
Director, Waste Management, Jackie Hamilton, 250/387-1624
Director, Waste Management, Lislie Hildebrant, 250/387-1624
Director, Water, Impoundments & Reservoirs, Daphne Stancil, 250/356-7483

## Ministry of FINANCE & CORPORATE RELATIONS (FCR)

617 Government St., Victoria BC V8V 1X4
250/387-9278; URL: http://www.fin.gov.bc.ca/
ENQUIRY BC: 250/387-6121

#### ACTS ADMINISTERED

Auditor General Act
Bankruptcy & Insolvency Act (in part)

Bonding Act
British Columbia Endowment Fund Act
British Columbia Enterprise Corporation Loan Privatization Act
British Columbia Payment to Canada of Federal Income Tax on Behalf of Natural Gas Producers Act
British Columbia Railway Finance Act
British Columbia Statistics Act, 1979
Budget Measures Implementation Act
Capital Commission Act
Commodity Contract Act
Company Act, except s. 348
Company Clauses Act
Compensation Fairness Act
Condominium Act, except all matters affecting the powers & duties of the Registrar of Titles
Cooperative Association Act
Corporation Capital Tax Act
Credit Reporting Act
Credit Union Act
Credit Union Incorporation Act
Creditor Assistance Act
Debt Collection Act
Debtor Assistance Act
Document Disposal Act
Educational Institution Capital Finance Act
Esquimalt & Nanaimo Railway Belt Tax Act
Financial Administration Act
Financial Information Act
Financial Institutions Act
Home Acquisition Act
Home Conversion & Leasehold Loan Act
Home Mortgage Assistance Program Act
Home Purchase Assistance Act
Homeowner Interest Assistance Act
Horse Racing Tax Act
Hospital District Finance Act
Hotel Room Tax Act
Housing Construction (Elderly Citizens) Act
Housing & Employment Development Act
Income Tax Act
Insurance Act
Insurance (Captive Company) Act
Insurance (Marine) Act
Insurance Premium Tax Act
International Financial Business Act
International Financial Business (Tax Refund) Act
Land Tax Deferment Act
Legislative Assembly Allowances & Pension Act
Logging Tax Act
Lottery Act
Lottery Corporation Act
Lottery Tax Act
Manufactured Home Act
Mining Tax Act
Miscellaneous Registrations Act, 1992
Ministry of Provincial Secretary & Government Services Act, Ss. 1, 2(3), 4, 8
Mobile Home Act
Mortgage Brokers Act
Motor Dealer Act
Motor Fuel Tax Act
Multilevel Marketing Act
Mutual Fire Insurance Companies Act
Pacific North Coast Native Cooperative Act
Partnership Act
Pension (College) Act
Pension (Municipal) Act
Pension (Public Service) Act
Pension (Teachers) Act
Pension Agreement Act
Pension Society Act
Pension Statutes (Transitional Arrangement) Act
Personal Property Security Act
Privatization Benefits Fund Act
Property Purchase Tax Act
Provincial Municipal Partnership (Taxation Measures) Act
Public Sector Employment Act
Public Service Act. S.B.C., 1985, c. 15
Public Service Act. S.B.C., 1993, c. 66
Public Service Benefit Plan Act
Public Service Bonding Act
Public Service Labour Relations Act
Purchasing Commission Act
Queen's Printer Act
Rate Increase Restraint Act
Real Estate Act
Repairers Lien Act
Residential Tenancy Act
Sale of Goods Act
School District Capital Finance Act
Securities Act, except s. 142
Securities (Forged Transfer) Act
Social Service Tax Act
Society Act
Special Accounts Appropriation & Control Act
Special Appropriation Act
Supply Act (Annual)
Taxation (Rural Area) Act
Taxpayer Protection Act
Tobacco Tax Act
Tourist Accommodation (Assessment Relief) Act
Trade Practice Act
Tugboat Worker's Lien Act
Unclaimed Money Act
Vancouver Stock Exchange Act
Warehouse Lien Act
Warehouse Receipt Act
Woodworker Lien Act

**Minister**, Hon. Andrew Petter, 250/387-3751
Deputy Minister, Vacant, 250/387-3184
Comptroller General, Alan J. Barnard, 250/387-8543, Fax: 250/356-2001
Executive Director, Communications Branch, Shawn Thomas, 250/356-8712, Fax: 250/356-7042
Director, Communications, Tom Workman, 250/387-9286
Acting Director, Federal-Provincial Relations & Research, Michael Butler, 250/387-9018
Director, Protocol & Events Branch, Dianne Lawson, 250/387-4304, Fax: 250/356-2814
Program Manager, Enquiry BC, Susan Park, 525 Superior St., 1st Fl., Victoria BC V8V 1X4, 250/387-9273, Fax: 250/953-4302
Provincial Archivist, BC Archives & Records Services, John A. Bovey, 655 Belleville St., Victoria BC V8V 1X4, 250/387-5885, Fax: 250/387-2072
Deputy Provincial Archivist, BC Archives & Records Services, Gary A. Mitchell, 655 Belleville St., Victoria BC V8V 1X4, 250/387-2992

#### BRITISH COLUMBIA PURCHASING COMMISSION (BCPC)

#102, 1962 Canso Rd., PO Box 2190, Sidney BC V8L 3S8
250/655-2400; Fax: 250/356-5851
Provides purchasing, warehousing, asset disposal, printing, postal, vehicle management & air services to government ministries & other public agencies. Assists British Columbia firms in becoming "sales ready" & stimulates investment in the province by promoting joint ventures, cooperative sourcing & opportunity matching. Maintains comprehensive purchasing information, including all tenders, at the BCPC Internet Web Site.
Asst. Deputy Minister, Bob de Faye, 250/356-5846
Executive Director, Queen's Printer & Product Sales & Services, Vern Burkhardt, 250/356-5849
Executive Director, Supply Management Division, Dave Collisson, 4000 Seymour Place, Victoria BC V8X 4Y3, 250/655-2401, Fax: 250/655-2409
Manager, Customer Service & Purchasing, Ken Carpenter, 4234 Glanford Ave., Victoria BC V8V 1X4, 250/953-3406, Fax: 250/953-3121
Manager, Queen's Printer Financial & Administrative Services, Ian Bashford, 250/387-4180, Fax: 250/387-0388
Director, BC Mail Plus, Bob Beazley, Postal & Distribution Services, 1150 Mckenzie Ave., Victoria BC V8V 1X4, 250/727-3611, Fax: 250/727-6735

#### B.C. STATS

EMail: bcstats@fincc04.fin.gov.bc.ca
Acting Director, D. McRae, 250/356-2119, Fax: 250/387-9145
Manager, Business & Economic Statistics, Steve Miller, 250/387-0365, Fax: 250/387-0380
Manager, Data Services, Paul Gosh, 250/387-9221, Fax: 250/387-0329
Manager, Labour & Social Statistics, Anne Kitredge, 250/387-0374, Fax: 250/387-0380
Acting Manager, Population Statistics, Ruth McDougall, 250/387-0337, Fax: 250/387-0380

#### INFORMATION TECHNOLOGY SERVICES DIVISION

250/389-3916; Fax: 250/389-3101
Head, Chris Boulsbee

#### PROVINCIAL TREASURY

620 Superior St., Victoria BC V8V 1X4
Asst. Deputy Minister, Chris Trumpy, 250/387-9295, Fax: 250/387-9099
Chief Investment Officer, Doug Pearce, 250/387-7161
Director, Banking & Cash Management, Arn van Iersel, 250/387-9295, Fax: 250/387-3024
Director, Corporate Operations, Janet Fraser, #208, 553 Superior St., Victoria BC V8V 1X4, 250/387-8986, Fax: 250/387-6577
Director, Debt Management, Bruce Sampson, 250/387-6210
Director, Loan Administration, Sheila Ausman, 1312 Blanshard St., Victoria BC V8W 2J1, 250/387-7161, Fax: 250/387-3078
Director, Risk Management Branch, Phil Grewar, 716 Courtney St., 4th Fl., Victoria BC V8V 1X4, 250/387-0521

##### Treasury Board Staff

Executive Director, Analysis & Evaluation, Har Singh, 250/356-8910
Director, Economic Development Policy, Tony Stark, 250/387-9047
Director, Estimates & Capital Budget, Murray Crowther, 250/387-9052
Director, Fiscal & Economic Analysis, Lois McNabb, 250/387-9023
Acting Director, Program Review, Jim Weir, 250/387-9071
Director, Social Policy, Tom Vincent, 250/387-9038
Director, Tax Policy, Andy Robinson, 250/387-9011

#### REGISTRIES & MINISTRY SUPPORT SERVICES

Executive Director, Bill Bell, 250/387-3989
Registrar, Corporate & Personal Property, John Powell, 250/356-8658, Corporate Registry Hotline: 604/387-7848; Fax: 604/356-0206
Director, Corporate Development Services, Heather Daynard, 250/387-2719
Director, Financial Services & Administration, Brian Mann, 250/387-8139
Director, Human Resource Services, Grant Price, 250/387-8156
Chief Information Officer, Information Technology Management, Tom Dagg, 250/387-8961, Fax: 250/387-3634

#### REVENUE DIVISION

Asst. Deputy Minister, E. Lloyd Munro, 250/387-6207
Executive Director, Consumer Taxation, Greg Reimer, 250/387-0666, Fax: 250/387-6218

Director, Income Taxation, Alan Carver, 250/387-3320, Fax: 250/953-3094
Director, Real Property Taxation, Dan Johnstone, 250/387-0352, Fax: 250/356-5347
Director, Revenue Administration, Harold Hilton, 250/387-1667, Fax: 250/356-1090

#### Associated Agencies, Boards & Commissions

•Auditor Certification Board: 940 Blanshard St., 2nd Fl., Victoria BC V8W 3E6 – 250/356-8658; Fax: 250/387-3055
•British Columbia Educational Institutions Capital Financing Authority: c/o Provincial Treasury, 620 Superior St., Victoria BC V8V 1X4 – 250/387-7132; Fax: 250/387-3024
Contact, Bill Newburg
•British Columbia Housing & Employment Development Financing Authority: c/o Provincial Treasury, 620 Superior St., Victoria BC V8V 1X4 – 250/387-7132; Fax: 250/387-3024
Contact, Bill Newburg
•British Columbia Lottery Corporation: 74 West Seymour St., Kamloops BC V2C 1E2 – 604/270-0649; Fax: 604/828-5637
President, Guy Simonis
•British Columbia Regional Hospital Districts Financing Authority: c/o Provincial Treasury, 620 Superior St., Victoria BC V8V 1X4 – 250/387-7132; Fax: 250/387-3024
Contact, Bill Newburg
•British Columbia School Districts Capital Financing Authority: c/o Provincial Treasury, 620 Superior St., Victoria BC V8V 1X4 – 250/387-7132; Fax: 250/387-3024
Contact, Bill Newburg
•British Columbia Securities Commission: #1100, 865 Hornby St., Vancouver BC V6Z 2H4 – 604/660-4800; Fax: 604/660-2688; Email: inquiries@email.bcsc.gov.bc.ca; URL: http://www.bcsc.bc.ca/, Toll Free: 1-800-373-6393 (outside Vancouver area)
Chair, Doug Hyndman, 604/660-4881
Vice-Chair, Joyce Maykut, 604/660-4886
•Credit Union Deposit Insurance Corporation of British Columbia (CUDIC): #1900, 1050 West Pender St., Vancouver BC V6E 4K8 – 604/660-2947; Fax: 604/660-3170; Email: ficom@bcsc02.gov.bc.ca; URL: http://www.fic.gov.bc.ca

Guarantees deposits & non-equity shares of depositors of BC credit unions up to the limits prescribed by the Financial Institutions Act (FIA).

Director, Michael Costelle
Director, J. Stewart Cunningham
Director, Ian Downie
Director, Maureen E. Howe
Director, Dale G. Parker
•Financial Institutions Commission (FICOM): #1900, 1050 West Pender St., Vancouver BC V6E 3S7 – 604/660-2947; Fax: 604/660-3170; Email: ficom@bcsc02.gov.bc.ca; URL: http://www.fic.gov.bc.ca/

Protects the public & serves the financial sector through the delivery of clear impartial judgements, based on legislation, that enable the financial sector to earn customer confidence.

Chair, J. Stewart Cunningham
Vice-Chair, Maureen E. Howe
CEO & Superintendent, Financial Institutions & Superintendent, Real Estate, Registrar, Mortgage Brokers, Robert J. Hobart, 604/660-2923
Deputy Superintendent, Credit Unions & Trust Companies, Joseph B. Corsbie
Deputy Superintendent, Insurance & IFBs, Larry Neilsen, 604/660-4825
Deputy Superintendent, Real Estate & Deputy Registrar, Mortgage Brokers, Adrienne M. Murray
•Insurance Council of British Columbia: #300, 1040 West Georgia St., PO Box 7, Vancouver BC V6E 4H1 – 604/688-0321; Fax: 604/662-7767
General Manager, Jerry Matier
•Provincial Capital Commission (PCC): 613 Pandora Ave., Victoria BC V8W 1N8 – 250/386-1356; Fax: 250/386-1303
Chair, Pamela Charlesworth
Executive Director, Larry Beres
•Public Service Commission: 3301 Douglas St., 5th Fl., Victoria BC V8V 1X4 – 250/387-8085; Fax: 250/356-1488
Chair, Graeme Roberts
•Public Service Employee Relations Commission
Commissioner, John Mochrie, 250/387-0512, Fax: 250/356-7074
Director, Corporate Personnel Services, Wayne Scale, 250/387-6323
Director, Labour Relations, Ron McEachern, 250/387-6323, Fax: 250/387-0527
•Real Estate Council of British Columbia: #900, 750 West Pender St., Vancouver BC V6C 2T8 – 604/683-9664; Fax: 604/683-9017
Chair, Allan Terry, 604/543-7211
•Superannuation Commission: 548 Michigan St., Victoria BC V8V 4R5 – 250/387-1002; Fax: 250/387-4199
Commissioner, John W. Cook, 205/387-8201
Deputy Commissioner, Jerry Woytack, 250/387-0410

## Ministry of FORESTS

PO Box 9517, Stn Prov Govt, Victoria BC V8W 9C2
250/387-5255; Fax: 250/387-8485; URL: http://www.for.gov.bc.ca
Forest Practices Code Information: 1-800-565-4838
Physical Address: #300, 1675 Douglas St., Victoria BC

#### ACTS ADMINISTERED

Boom Chain Brand Act
Carmanah Pacific Park Act
Forest Act
Forest Land Reserve Act
Forest Practices Code of British Columbia Act
Forest Renewal Act
Forest Stand Management Fund Act
Foresters Act
Ministry of Forests Act
Range Act
South Moresby Implementation Account Act
**Minister**, Hon. David Zirnhelt
Deputy Minister, John Allan, 250/387-4809, Fax: 250/387-7065
Acting Director, Public Affairs Branch, Eileen Harper, 250/387-5255, Fax: 250/387-8485

#### FORESTRY DIVISION

Chief Forester, Larry Pedersen, 250/387-1296, Fax: 250/356-9499
Director, Forestry Division Services Branch, Tom Lester, 250/387-2517, Fax: 250/387-2513
Director, Forest Practices Branch, Henry Benskin, 250/387-6656, Fax: 250/387-6751
Director, Inventory Branch, Dave Gilbert, 250/387-1314, Fax: 250/387-5999
Director, Research Branch, Ted Baker, 250/387-6721, Fax: 250/387-0046
Director, Timber Supply Branch, Gary Townsend, 250/356-5947, Fax: 250/953-3838

#### OPERATIONS DIVISION

Asst. Deputy Minister, Janna Kumi, 250/387-1236, Fax: 250/953-3687
Director, Business Design Branch, Shelley Sullivan, 250/356-1592, Fax: 250/356-5355
Director, Compliance & Enforcement Branch, Roberta Reader, 250/356-9841, Fax: 250/387-2539
Director, Nursery & Seed Operations Branch, Drew Brazier, 250/387-8955, Fax: 250/387-1467
Director, Protection Branch, Jim Dunlop, 250/387-5965, Fax: 250/387-5685
Director, Resource Tenures & Engineering Branch, Jim Langridge, 250/387-5291, Fax: 250/387-6445

#### Regional Forestry Offices

Cariboo: #200, 640 Borland St., Williams Lake BC V2G 1R8 – 250/398-4345; Fax: 250/398-4380, Regional Manager, Mike Carlson
Kamloops: 515 Columbia St., Kamloops BC V2C 2T7 – 250/828-4131; Fax: 250/828-4154, Regional Manager, Fred Baxter
Nelson: 518 Lake St., Nelson BC V1L 4C6 – 250/354-6200; Fax: 250/354-6250, Regional Manager, Ross Tozer
Prince George: 1011 - 4 Ave., Prince George BC V2L 3H9 – 250/565-6100; Fax: 250/565-6396, Regional Manager, Al Gorley
Prince Rupert: 3726 Alfred Ave., Bag 5000, Smithers BC V0J 2N0 – 250/847-7500; Fax: 250/847-7217, Regional Manager, Jim Snetsinger
Vancouver: 2100 Labieux Rd., Nanaimo BC V9T 6E9 – 250/751-7001; Fax: 250/751-7190, Regional Manager, Ken Collingwood

#### POLICY & PLANNING DIVISION

Executive Director, Hartley Lewis, 250/387-3656, Fax: 250/387-6267
Director, Aboriginal Affairs Branch, Christie Brown, 250/356-6083, Fax: 250/356-6076
Director, Corporate Policy & Planning Branch, Sue Stephen, 250/356-7880, Fax: 250/356-7903
Director, Economics & Trade Branch, Lois McNabb, 250/356-8610, Fax: 250/387-5050

#### REVENUE & CORPORATE SERVICES DIVISION

Asst. Deputy Minister, Harry Powell, 250/387-1300, Fax: 250/387-6267
Director, Audit Services Branch, Ian Birch, 250/387-8671, Fax: 250/356-2085
Director, Financial Management Branch, Bob A. Battles, 250/387-1421, Fax: 250/387-5795
Director, Human Resources Branch, Brian Mader, 250/387-1102, Fax: 250/387-6424
Director, Information Systems Branch, John Ellis, 250/387-8400, Fax: 250/387-5132
Director, Revenue Branch, Bill Howard, 250/387-1701, Fax: 250/387-5670

#### Associated Agencies, Boards & Commissions

•Forest Renewal BC: 727 Fisgard St., Victoria BC V8V 1X4 – 250/387-2500
CEO, Colin Smith
•Timber Export Advisory Committee: 1450 Government St., 1st Fl., Victoria BC V8W 3E7 – 250/387-8359
Recording Chairman, Don Ruhl

## British Columbia GOVERNMENT COMMUNICATIONS OFFICE

612 Government St., Victoria BC V8V 1X4
250/387-1337; Fax: 250/387-3534
This office reports to the Ministry of Finance & Corporate Relations.
**Assoc. Deputy Minister**, Evan Lloyd, 250/387-1886
Asst. Deputy Minister, Public Issues & Consultation, John Heaney, 614 Government St., Victoria BC V8V 1X4, 250/387-1027, Fax: 250/387-6070
Acting Director, Public & Corporate Relations, Noelle Reeve, 250/387-4315, Fax: 250/387-1399
Executive Director, John Usher

## Ministry of HEALTH

1515 Blanshard St., 7th Fl., Victoria BC V8W 3C8
250/952-3456; URL: http://www.hlth.gov.bc.ca
Toll Free: AIDS Hotline 1-800-661-3886
Alcohol & Drug Information: 1-800-663-1441
Cancer Information Line: 1-800-663-4242

Food & Nutrition Information: 1-800-667-DIET
Medical Services Plan Subscriber Information: 1-800-663-7100
Screening Mammography Information Line: 1-800-663-9203, 604/660-3639 (Vancouver)
Travel Assistance Program: 1-800-661-2668
Vital Statistics Hotline: 1-800-663-8328
Ensures that health system promotes & provides for the physical, mental, & social well-being of all residents.

**ACTS ADMINISTERED**

Access to Abortion Services Act
Anatomy Act
British Columbia Health Research Foundation Act
Chiropractors Act
Community Care Facility Act
Continuing Care Act
Dental Technicians & Denturists Act
Dentists Act
Emergency Medical Assistants Act
Forensic Psychiatry Act
Health Act
Health Authorities Act
Health Care (Consent) & Care Facility (Admission) Act (not in force)
Health Emergency Act
Health Professions Act
Hearing Aid Act
Hospital Act
Hospital (Auxiliary) Act
Hospital District Act
Hospital Insurance Act
Human Tissue Gift Act
Marriage Act
Meat Inspection Act
Medical & Health Care Services Act
Medical Practitioners Act
Medicare Protection Act
Mental Health Act
Ministry of Health Act
Name Act
Naturopaths Act
Nurses (Licensed Practical) Act
Nurses (Registered Psychiatric) Act
Optometrists Act
Pharmacists Act
Pharmacists, Pharmacy Operations & Drug Scheduling Act (not in force)
Physiotherapists Act
Podiatrists Act
Psychologists Act
Public Toilet Act
Seniors Advisory Council Act
Tobacco Product Act
Tobacco Sales Act
Venereal Disease Act
Vital Statistics Act
Wills Act (Part II)

**Minister & Minister Responsible, Seniors**, Hon. Joy K. MacPhail
Deputy Minister, David S. Kelly, 250/952-2609, Fax: 250/952-1909

**CORPORATE SERVICES**

Asst. Deputy Minister, Robert F. Cronin, 250/952-2601, Fax: 250/952-2205
Chair, Medical Services Commission, John Mochrie, 250/952-3465, Fax: 250/952-3131
Executive Director, BC Ambulance Service, Val Pattee, 1810 Blanshard St., Victoria BC V8V 1X4, 250/952-0885, Fax: 250/952-0905
Executive Director, Communications & Public Affairs, Garth Cramer, 250/952-1889, Fax: 250/952-1883
Executive Director, Design & Construction, Roald Anderson, 1520 Blanshard St., Victoria BC V8W 3C8, 250/952-1204, Fax: 250/952-1202
Executive Director, Finance & Management Services, John D. Herbert, 250/952-2066, Fax: 250/952-1940
Executive Director, Legislation & Professional Regulation, Alan Moyes, 250/952-2281, Fax: 250/952-2205
Executive Director, Pharmacare, Mike Corbeil, 250/952-1706, Fax: 250/952-2235
Executive Director, Policy, Planning & Economics, Vacant
Executive Director, Systems Division, Barry H. Gray, 250/952-2440, Fax: 250/952-2235

**Vital Statistics**

818 Fort St., Victoria BC V8W 1H8
250/952-2681; Fax: 250/952-2576
Kelowna: 604/868-7798; Fax: 604/868-7799
Prince George: 604/565-7105; Fax: 604/565-7106
Vancouver: 604/660-2937; Fax: 604/660-2645
For a certificate of a registration or record: $25.00 per copy. For each search for one registration or record for each three-year period or fraction thereof overwhich the search is conducted: $25.00.
Director, Ron J. Danderfer, 250/952-2563, Fax: 250/952-2587

**REGIONAL PROGRAMS**

Associate Deputy Minister, Thea Vakil, 250/952-1297, Fax: 250/952-1052
Executive Director, Acute Care Programs, Leah Hollins, 250/952-1237, Fax: 250/952-1282
Executive Director, Community Health Programs, Diane Johnston, 250/952-1544, Fax: 250/952-1426
Executive Director, Continuing Care Programs, Rod MacDonald, 250/952-1097, Fax: 250/952-1132
Executive Director, Health Protection & Safety, Andrew G. Hazlewood, 250/952-1731, Fax: 250/952-1486
Executive Director, Mental Health Programs, Brian Copley, 250/952-1608, Fax: 250/952-1589
Executive Director, Program Standards & Information Management, Dr. Doug Bigelow, 1810 Blanshard St., Victoria BC B8B 1X4, 250/952-0937, Fax: 250/952-0942
Executive Director, Provincial Programs, David Babiuk, 250/952-2329, Fax: 250/952-1282
Executive Director, Regional Coordination, Christine Kline, #402 - 1245 West Broadway, Vancouver BC V6H 1G7, 604/775-0661, Fax: 604/775-0596
Executive Director, Regional Funding & Support, Manjit Sidhu, 250/952-1646, Fax: 250/952-1649
Director, Women's Health Bureau, Phyllis Chuly, 250/952-1231, Fax: 250/952-1282

**STRATEGIC SERVICES**

Asst. Deputy Minister, John Greschener, 250/952-2164, Fax: 250/952-2109
Executive Director, Human Resources, B. White, 250/952-2127, Fax: 250/952-2125
Executive Director, Medical Services Plan Operations, Janet McGregor, 250/952-3187, Fax: 250/952-3131
Executive Director, Medical Services Plan Resource Management, Deborah Shera, 250/952-3122, Fax: 250/952-3131
Executive Director, New Directions Development, Sue Rothwell, 250/952-0980, Fax: 250/952-0985
Director, Information & Privacy Program, Vel Clark, 1810 Blanshard St., Victoria BC V8V 1X4, 250/952-0887, Fax: 250/952-0874
Director, Office for Seniors, Geri Hinton, 250/952-1238, Fax: 250/952-1159
Director, Strategic Labour Services, Rick Fell, 250/952-2245, Fax: 250/952-1795
Director, Strategic Management Services, Deborah Morrow, 250/952-2241, Fax: 250/952-2235
Secretary, Medical Services Commissions, Brenda Stewart, 250/952-3163, Fax: 250/952-3131
Provincial Nurses Advisor, Andrea Henning, 250/952-1111, Fax: 250/952-2235

## Ministry of HUMAN RESOURCES

Parliament Bldgs., Victoria BC V8V 1X4
URL: http://www.mhr.gov.bc.ca
Note: This Ministry was still undergoing organization at the time of publishing. Names & numbers of individuals listed below may change and it may be necessary to contact the Deputy Minister's office for more information.
The Ministry was created from the former Ministry of Social Services in September 1996 to streamline welfare services.

**ACTS ADMINISTERED**

BC Benefits (Appeals) Act
BC Benefits (Income Assistance) Act
Disability Benefits Program Act
Ministry of Social Services & Housing Act
Residence & Responsibility Act

**Minister**, Hon. Dennis Streifel, 250/387-3180, Fax: 250/387-5720
Deputy Minister, Dr. Sharon Manson Singer, 250/387-3121, Fax: 250/387-5775
Director, Communications Division, Carol Carman, 250/387-6485, Fax: 250/356-7801
Director, Corporate Services, Tom Greene, 250/387-7030, Fax: 250/387-5775
Manager, Information & Privacy Branch, Susan Irvine, 250/387-3128, Fax: 250/387-3311

**FINANCE & MANAGEMENT SERVICES**

Asst. Deputy Minister, Cynthia Lukaitis, 250/387-3124, Fax: 250/387-2418
Director, Administrative Services Division, Ann Cameron, 250/387-3411, Fax: 250/356-7346
Director, Financial Planning Division, Mary-Ethel Audley, 250/387-5035, Fax: 250/356-9799
Director, Financial Services Division, Stew Churlish, 250/387-3947, Fax: 250/356-9637
Director, Personnel Services, Judith McDonald, 250/387-4511, Fax: 250/387-1610
Director, Systems Business Consulting Division, Sandy Logan, 604/660-1650, Fax: 604/660-1821

**INCOME SUPPORT**

Asst. Deputy Minister, Judy Cavanagh, 250/387-3122, Fax: 250/387-2418
Director, Health Services Division, Susan Doyle, 250/387-5664, Fax: 250/356-7290
Director, Income Assistance Division, Mariann Burka, 250/387-1486, Fax: 250/387-8164
Acting Director, Intergovernmental Relations Division, Su-Lin Shum, 250/387-4552, Fax: 250/356-8182
Director, Prevention, Compliance & Enforcement Division, Mervin Harrower, 250/387-8200, Fax: 250/356-8182

**PLANNING & PERFORMANCE MEASUREMENT**

Executive Director, Vacant, 250/387-7036, Fax: 250/387-2418
Director, Performance Measurement & Management Information, Heather Daynard, 250/387-6448, Fax: 250/387-2364
Director, Planning Branch, Michele McBride, 250/387-6448, Fax: 250/387-2364
Manager, Emergency Social Services, Ivan Carlson, 250/387-0030, Fax: 250/387-2364

**REGIONAL OPERATIONS**

Asst. Deputy Minister, Chris Haynes, 250/387-6905, Fax: 250/387-1400
Regional Manager, Fraser North, Fred Taylor, 604/527-1216, Fax: 604/524-1255
Regional Manager, Fraser South, Thelma Barkley, 604/576-0753, Fax: 604/576-0759
Regional Manager, North Vancouver Island, Alison Meredith, 250/390-5450, Fax: 250/390-5477

Regional Manager, Okanagan/Kootenays, Ann Horan, 250/470-0888, Fax: 250/470-0890
Regional Manager, Prince George & North, Cam Millar, 250/565-6220, Fax: 250/565-6366
Regional Manager, Richmond/Burnaby/North Shore/ Howe Sound, Leslie Wilson, 604/660-0202, Fax: 604/ 660-5049
Regional Manager, South Central Interior, Bruce Smith, 250/828-4600, Fax: 250/828-4756
Regional Manager, South Vancouver Island, Lori Mist, 250/952-4337, Fax: 250/952-4346
Regional Manager, Vancouver, Fred Milowsky, 604/ 660-3224, Fax: 604/660-2503

## British Columbia HYDRO & POWER AUTHORITY

6911 Southpoint Dr., Burnaby BC V3N 4X8
604/528-1600; Fax: 604/623-3901; Email: info.serv@ bchydro.bc.ca; URL: http://www.bchydro.bc.ca
Provincial Crown corporation established in 1962 to generate, transmit & distribute electricity. B.C. Hydro's Board of Directors is appointed by the Lieutenant-Governor in Council & is responsible for the overall direction of the corporation. The corporation's activities are subject to regulation by the British Columbia Utilities Commission. The third largest electricity utility in Canada, B.C. Hydro serves more than 1.3 million customers in an area containing over 92 percent of British Columbia's population.
**Chair**, Brian R.D. Smith, 604/623-4480
Vice-Chair, Dr. Sharon Manson Singer, 604/623-4466
President & CEO, Michael Costello, 604/623-4490
Vice-President, General Counsel & Corporate Secretary, Darlene M. Barnett, 333 Dunsmuir St., 18th Fl., Vancouver BC V6B 5R3, 604/623-3600
Senior Vice-President, Corporate & Financial Affairs & CFO, David A. Harrison, 604/623-4129
Senior Vice-President, Customer Services, Gail Sexsmith, 604/528-3373
Acting Senior Vice-President, Human Resources, Aboriginal Relations & Environment, Roy G. Staveley, 604/528-1590
Senior Vice-President, Power Supply, P. Donald Swoboda, 604/528-3218
Senior Vice-President, Transmission & Distribution, Ronald J. Threlkeld, 604/528-2224

## Office of the INFORMATION & PRIVACY COMMISSIONER

1675 Douglas St., 4th Fl., Victoria BC V8V 1X4
250/387-5629; Fax: 250/387-1696; Email: oipc@ gems5.gov.bc.ca; URL: http://www.oipcbc.org
Toll Free: 1-800-663-7867 (within BC)
250/660-2421 (Vancouver)
**Commissioner**, David Flaherty
Librarian, Ellinore Barker, Email: ecbarker@ galaxy.gov.bc.ca

## INSURANCE CORPORATION OF BC (AUTOPLAN)

151 West Esplanade, North Vancouver BC V7M 3H9
604/661-2800; Fax: 604/661-2244
**President & CEO**, Thom Thompson
Senior Vice-President, Insurance & Licensing, H. Graham Reid
Senior Vice-President, Operations, Neil D. Weatherston
Vice-President, Finance & Chief Financial Officer, I. Meharry
Vice-President, Human Resources & General Counsel, Linda K.Y Robertson
Vice-President, Information Services, Richard R. Nelson
Acting Vice-President, Insurance Operations, Terry M. Condon
Vice-President, Public Affairs & Road Safety, Darlene K. Hyde
Government & Corporate Relations Executive, Greg D. Basham
Corporate Secretary, M. Claire Carr

## Ministry of LABOUR

825 Fort St., 2nd Fl., PO Box 9570, Stn Prov. Gov't, Victoria BC V8W 9K1
250/356-1487; Fax: 250/356-1653; URL: http:// www.labour.gov.bc.ca/welcome.htm

### ACTS ADMINISTERED

Accountants (Certified General) Act
Accountants (Chartered) Act
Accountants (Management) Act (except s. II-3)
Applied Science Technologists & Technicians Act
Apprenticeship Act
Architects Act (except s. 24-1)
Architects (Landscape) Act
Barbers Act
College & Institute Act
Educational Programs Continuation Act
Employment Standards Act
Engineers & Geoscientists Act (except s. 8-2)
Fire Department Act
Fishers' Collective Bargaining Act
Hairdressers Act
Institute of Technology Act
Labour Education Centre of British Columbia Act
Labour Regulation Act
Labour Relations Code
Ministry of Labour Act (except in relation to gas, electrical, elevating devices, boiler & pressure vessel safety)
Open Learning Agency Act
Pension Benefits Standards Act
Private Post-Secondary Education Act
Skills Development & Fair Wage Act
University Act
University Foundations Act
University of Northern British Columbia Act
Workers' Compensation Act
Workplace Act
**Minister**, #124, Parliament Bldgs., Victoria BC V8V 1X4, Hon. John Cashore
Deputy Minister, Margaret Arthur, 818 Broughton St., Victoria BC V8W 9K4, 250/387-3154, Fax: 250/356-5186
Director, Communications Branch, Mike Hughes, 250/ 387-2699, Fax: 250/356-1653
Office Manager, Communications Branch, Colleen Davis, 250/356-1487

### APPRENTICESHIP INITATIVES DIVISION

URL: http://www.labour.gov.bc.ca/apprent/ welcome.htm
Executive Director, Stuart Clark, 250/387-6151, Fax: 250/387-1193
Director, Apprenticeship Branch, Vacant, #220, 4946 Canada Way, Burnaby BC V5G 4J6, 604/660-1197

### LABOUR PROGRAMS

818 Broughton St., 3rd Fl., Victoria BC V8W 9K4
Asst. Deputy Minister, Gary Martin, 250/387-3914, Fax: 250/356-5186
Superintendent of Pensions, Pension Benefits Standards, Sherallyn Miller, #210, 4946 Canada Way, Burnaby BC V5G 4J6, 604/775-1349, Fax: 604/ 660-6517, URL: http://labour.gov.bc.ca/psb
Director, Collective Agreement Arbitration Bureau, Geoffrey Crampton, #800, 360 West Georgia St., Vancouver BC V6B 6B2, 604/775-1351, Fax: 604/ 775-1356
Director, Employers' Advisor, Ray Bozzer, #4003, 8171 Ackroyd Rd., Richmond BC V6X 3K1, 604/ 660-7253, Fax: 604/660-7486
Director, Employment Standards Headquarters, Jill Walker, 825 Fort St., 2nd Fl., Victoria BC V8W 9K1, 250/387-3300, Fax: 250/356-1886, URL: http:// labour.gov.bc.ca/esb
Director, Labour Policy & Program Development Branch, Jan Rossley, 250/356-0677, Fax: 250/356-5335
Director, Workers' Advisor, Blake Williams, #3000, 8171 Ackroyd Rd., Richmond BC V6X 3K1, 604/ 660-7888, Fax: 604/660-5284, Toll Free: 1-800-663-4261

### LABOUR RELATIONS

818 Broughton St., 3rd Fl., Victoria BC V8W 9K4
Acting Asst. Deputy Minister, Don Cott, 250/387-3161, Fax: 250/356-5186

#### Associated Agencies, Boards & Commissions

•Employment Standards Tribunal: #800, 360 West Georgia St., Vancouver BC V6B 6B2 – 604/775-3512; Fax: 604/775-3372
Chair, Geoffrey Crampton
•Labour Relations Board: 1125 Howe St., Vancouver BC V6Z 2K8 – 604/660-1300; Fax: 604/ 660-1892
Commissioner, Stan Lanyon
Registrar, Lisa Hansen
•Workers' Compensation Board
Listed alphabetically in detail, this section
•Workers' Compensation Review Board: #200, 1700 West 75 Ave., Vancouver BC V6P 6G2 – 604/664-7800; Fax: 604/664-7898
Chair, P. Michael O'Brien

## Ministry of MUNICIPAL AFFAIRS & HOUSING (MAFF)

Municipal Affairs, PO Box 9490, Victoria BC V8W 9N7
Housing, PO Box 9491, Victoria BC V8W 9N7
250/387-4089; Fax: 250/356-1070; URL: http:// www.marh.gov.bc.ca/

### ACTS ADMINISTERED

Assessment Act
Assessment Authority Act
Building Safety Standards Act
Cultus Lake Park Act
Electrical Safety Act
Elevating Devices Safety Act
Fire Services Act
Fireworks Act
Gas Safety Act
Greater Nanaimo Water District Act
Greater Vancouver Sewerage & Drainage District Act
Greater Vancouver Water District Act
Home Owner Grant Act
Islands Trust Act
Library Act
Library Foundation of British Columbia Act
Local Government Grants Act
Local Services Act
Manufactured Home Tax Act
Ministry of Labour Act
Ministry of Lands, Parks & Housing Act (sections 5 (c) and 10)
Ministry of Municipal Affairs Act
Mountain Resort Associations Act
Municipal Act (except part 20)
Municipal Aid Act
Municipal Expenditure Restraint Act
Municipal Finance Authority Act
Municipal Improvements Assistance Enabling Act
Municipalities Assistance Act
Municipalities Enabling & Validating Act
Municipalities Enabling & Validaing Act (No.2)
New Westminster Redevelopment Act

Power Engineers & Boiler & Pressure Vessel Safety Act
Provincial-Municipal Partnership Act
Railway Act
Resort Municipality of Whistler Act
Sechelt Indian Government District Enabling Act
Sechelt Indian Government District Home Owner Grant Act
Shelter Aid for Elderly Renters Act
Tourist Accomodation Act
University Endowment Act
Vancouver Charter (not a public act)
**Minister**, Hon. Dan Miller, 250/387-3602, Fax: 250/387-1334
Deputy Minister, Suzanne Veit, 250/387-4104, Fax: 250/387-7973
Asst. Deputy Minister & Inspector, Office of the Inspector of Municipalities, Ken MacLeod, 205/356-6575, Fax: 205/387-7973
Executive Director, Human & Corporate Development, Lorne Bulmer, 250/387-9193
Executive Director, Safety Systems Review, Harry Diemer, 250/387-4095, Email: ssr@hq.marh.gov.bc.ca

#### LOCAL GOVERNMENT SERVICES

Executive Director, David G. Morris, 250/356-7377, Fax: 250/387-4048
Program Administrator, Downtown Revitalization, Martin Thomas, 250/387-4090
Director, Library Services, Barbara Greeniaus, 250/356-1795, Fax: 250/387-4048
Director, Municipal Administrative Services, Norm McCrimmon, 250/387-4022
Director, Municipal Financial Services, Al Tamblin, 250/387-4067
Director, Municipal Investigations, Fred Thompson, 250/387-4098
Director, Planning Branch, Erik Karlsen, 250/387-4039
Director, Policy & Research, Brian Walisser, 250/387-4050

#### SAFETY & STANDARDS DEPARTMENT

Asst. Deputy Minister, Gary Harkness, 250/387-4095, Fax: 250/387-7973
Commissioner, Office of the Fire Commissioner, Rick Dumala, 250/356-9000, Fax: 250/356-9019, Email: firecomm@hq.marh.gov.bc.ca
Director, Boiler & Pressure Vessel Safety, Allan Pringle, 604/660-6251
Director, Building Standards, Jack Robertson, 250/387-4011, Fax: 250/356-9019
Director, Elevating Devices, Allan Pringle, 604/660-6204
Director, Electrical Safety, Rick Porcina, 604/660-6261, Fax: 604/660-6661
Director, Engineering & Inspection, Vacant, #245, 4299 Canada Way, Burnaby BC V5G 1H9, 604/660-5960, Fax: 604/660-5997
Director, Gas Safety, Suzana Katz, #300, 750 Pacific Blvd. South, Vancouver BC V6B 5E7, 604/660-6233, Fax: 604/660-3460
Director, Management Services, Vicky Barr-Humphries, 604/775-0940, Fax: 604/660-6215
Director, Safety Engineering Services, Harry Diemer, 250/387-4095

##### Associated Agencies, Boards & Commissions

•Assessment Appeal Board: #101, 22356 McIntosh Ave., Maple Ridge BC V2X 3C1 – 604/463-9300; Fax: 604/467-3892
•Board of Examiners: 800 Johnson St., Victoria BC V8V 1X4 – 250/387-4053
Secretary, Mary Harkness
•British Columbia Assessment: 1537 Hillside Ave., Victoria BC V8T 4Y2 – 250/595-6211; Fax: 250/595-6222
Chair, David Driscoll
Assessment Commissioner & CEO, Thomas Johnstone
Director, Communications, Nigel Atkin
•British Columbia Housing Management Commission/BC Housing (BCHMC): #1701, 4330 Kingsway, Burnaby BC V5H 4G7 – 604/433-1711; Fax: 604/439-4722
General Manager, Richard Peddie, 604/439-4903
Acting Supervisor, Shelter Aid for Elderly Renters, Debbie Richie, 1175 Douglas St., 4th Fl., Victoria BC V8W 2E1, 250/387-3461, Fax: 250/387-4264
Director, Corporate Services Branch, Peter Stobie, 604/439-4732
Director, Development Services & Director, Housing & Community Services, Jim Woodward, 604/439-4721
•Islands Trust: 1627 Fort St., 2nd. Fl., Victoria BC V8R 1H8 – 250/387-4000; Fax: 250/387-4047
Chair, Graeme Dinsdale
Executive Director, Gordon McIntosh

## Office of the OMBUDSMAN

931 Fort St., Victoria BC V8V 3K3
250/387-5855; Fax: 250/387-0198; URL: http://www.ombud.gov.bc.ca/
Toll Free: 1-800-567-3247
1111 Melville St., Vancouver BC V6E 3V6
Fax: 604/660-1691
**Ombudsman**, S. Dulcie McCallum
Deputy Ombudsman, D. Brent Parfitt
Librarian, Caroline Daniels, 604/660-1391, Email: cdaniels@dgvic2.ombd.gov.bc.ca

## BC PAVILION CORPORATION

#600, 375 Water St., Vancouver BC V6B 5C6
604/482-2200; Fax: 604/681-9017; Email: info@bcpavco.com; URL: http://www.bcpavco.com
**President & CEO**, Warren Buckley
Vice-President & General Manager, BC Place Stadium, Neil Campbell
General Manager, Bridge Studios, Susan Groome
General Manager, Robson Square Conference Centre, Tracey Short
General Manager, Tradex, Lauren Thomas
Acting General Manager, Vancouver Trade & Convention Centre, Catherine Wong

## British Columbia PROVINCIAL EMERGENCY PROGRAM (PEP)

455 Boleskine Rd., Victoria BC V8Z 1E7
250/387-5956; Fax: 250/952-4888; URL: http://hoshi.cic.sfu.ca/ZXpep/
Emergency Coordination Centre (24-hour): 1-800-663-3456
Mailing address:, PO Box 9201, Stn Prov. Government, Victoria BC V8W 9J1
Operations administered by the British Columbia Ministry of Attorney General.

#### ACTS ADMINISTERED

Emergency Program Act & Regulations 1993
**Director**, A.J. (Tony) Heemskerk, Email: theemske@pep.bc.ca
Manager, Operations, Geoff Amy, Email: gamy@pep.bc.ca

## Ministry of SMALL BUSINESS, TOURISM & CULTURE (SBTC)

1405 Douglas St., Victoria BC V8W 3C1
URL: http://www.tbc.gov.bc.ca/homepage.html

#### ACTS ADMINISTERED

Cultural Foundation of British Columbia Act
Heritage Conservation Act
Employee Investment Act
Hotel Guest Registration Act
Hotel Keepers Act
Industrial Development Incentive Act (in relation to the Small Business Incentive Program)
Ministry of Industry & Small Business Development Act (in relation to small business)
Ministry of International Trade, Science & Investment Act (portions)
Ministry of Tourism Act
Museum Act
Pacific National Exhibition Incorporation Act
Small Business Venture Capital Act
Travel Regulation Act
**Minister**, Hon. Jan Pullinger
Deputy Minister, Lyn Tait, 250/356-2175, Fax: 250/387-1420
Asst. Deputy Minister, Management Services, Rhonda Hunter, 250/387-0111, Fax: 250/387-1420
Director, Communications, Dale Weston, 250/356-6305, Fax: 250/387-3798

#### COMMUNITY & REGIONAL DEVELOPMENT DIVISION

250/356-7363; Fax: 250/387-5633
Asst. Deputy Minister, David Richardson, 250/356-2124
Director, Business Equity Branch, Bob Kennedy, 250/387-0225, 844-1823 (Vancouver), Fax: 250/387-1080
Director, Client Ministries & Regional Support Services, A. Paxton Mann, 250/356-2038, Fax: 250/387-5633
Director, Small Business Development Branch, Greg Goodwin, 250/356-2034, Fax: 250/356-8948

##### Business Information Centres

Vancouver: 601 Cordova St. West, Vancouver BC V6B 1G1 – 604/660-3900; Fax: 604/660-4166, Marcis Esmits
Victoria: 1001 Douglas St., Victoria BC V8V 1X4 – 250/356-5777; Fax: 250/356-5951, Chuck Dary

#### CULTURE DIVISION

URL: http://www.tbc.gov.bc.ca/culture/culturehome.html
Asst. Deputy Minister, Rob Egan, 250/387-0106, Fax: 250/387-4099
Director, Archaeology Branch, Brian Apland, 250/356-1049, Fax: 250/387-4420
Director, BC Film Commission, Peter Mitchell, 604/660-2732, Fax: 604/660-4790
Director, Cultural Services Branch, Richard Brownsey, 250/356-1721, Fax: 250/387-4420
Director, Heritage Branch, Wayne Carter, 250/356-1434, Fax: 250/356-7796
Director, Recreation & Sport Branch, Charles Parkinson, 250/356-1160, Fax: 250/387-4253
Executive Director, BC Games Society, Roger Skillings, #200, 990 Fort St., Victoria BC V8V 3K2, 250/387-4684, Fax: 250/387-4489

#### TOURISM DIVISION

URL: http://www.tbc.gov.bc.ca/tourism/tourismhome.html
Asst. Deputy Minister, Rod Harris, 250/356-2026, Fax: 250/356-6988
Executive Director, Tourism Services, Rick Lemon, 250/387-0130, Fax: 250/356-6988
Director, Industry Development, Denise Hayes, 250/387-6929, Fax: 250/387-2305
Director, Marketing, Don Foxgord, 604/660-3754, Fax: 604/660-3383

##### Associated Agencies, Boards & Commissions

•British Columbia Arts Council: 800 Johnson St., 5th Fl., Victoria BC V8V 1X4 – 250/356-1718
Chair, Mavor Moore
•British Columbia Festival of the Arts Society: 3577 Douglas St., Victoria BC V8Z 3L6 – 250/383-4214

•British Columbia Heritage Trust: 800 Johnson St., 5th Fl., Victoria BC V8V 1X4 – 250/356-1433; Fax: 250/356-7796
Executive Officer, Wayne Carter

## Ministry of TRANSPORTATION & HIGHWAYS

940 Blanshard St., Victoria BC V8W 3E6
250/387-3198; Fax: 250/387-6431

#### ACTS ADMINISTERED

British Columbia Railway Act
Coquihalla Highway Construction Acceleration Act
Ferry Act
Highway Act
Highway (Industrial) Act
Highways Scenic Improvements Act
Insurance Corporation Act
Insurance (Motor Vehicle) Act
Motor Carrier Act
Motor Vehicle Act
Railway Act
Riverbank Protection Act
**Minister**, Hon. Lois Boone
Acting Deputy Minister, Dan Doyle, 250/387-3280

#### ADMINISTRATIVE SERVICES DEPARTMENT

Asst. Deputy Minister, Vacant
Director, Finance & Administration Branch, Bob Buckingham, 250/387-3100
Director, Information Services Branch, Floyd A. Mailhot, 250/387-1457
Director, Personnel Services Branch, Barry T. Wilton, 250/387-5539
Director, Public Affairs Branch, Jerry Colman, 250/387-7788

#### HIGHWAY OPERATIONS DEPARTMENT

Asst. Deputy Minister, Dan Doyle, 250/387-3260
Chief Highway Engineer, Professional Services Division, Earl A. Lund, 250/387-6772
Director, Aboriginal Issues Project, Mary Koyl, 250/387-5925
Director, Bridge Engineering Branch, Peter H. Brett, 250/387-3267
Director, Geotechnical & Materials Engineering Branch, Orlando Tisot, 250/387-1881
Director, Highway Engineering Branch, Merv Clark, 250/356-7747
Director, Highway Safety Branch, Lorne Holowachuk, P.Eng., 250/387-5838
Director, Maintenance Services Branch, W.C. Bedford, 250/387-8626
Director, Properties Branch, Stewart N. Logan, 250/387-1838

#### MOTOR VEHICLE BRANCH

2631 Douglas St., Victoria BC V8T 5A3
250/387-3140; Fax: 250/387-1169
Asst. Deputy Minister/Superintendent, Vicki Farrally, 250/387-5692
Executive Director, Operations Division/Deputy Superintendent, Craig Morris, 250/387-6278
Executive Director, Policy & Program Development Division, Mark Medgyesi, 250/387-1752
Director, Information Technology Division, Karen Dellert, 250/356-1274
Director, Inspection & Carrier Safety, Vacant, 250/387-6634, Fax: 250/356-8986
Director, Management Services Division, Brian Sibley, 250/356-6197
Director, Planning & Corporate Development Division, Drew Ritchie, 250/387-1869

#### PLANNING & MAJOR PROJECTS DEPARTMENT

Asst. Deputy Minister, Bruce McKeown, 250/387-6742
Director, Highway Planning Branch, Tim Stevens, 250/387-7540
Director, Planning Services Branch, Richard H. Dixon, 250/356-5156
Senior Policy Advisor, Policy Branch, Sam Brand, 250/387-5997
Asst. Senior Manager, Major Projects Branch, Dave Ferguson, 250/387-7560

#### Associated Agencies, Boards & Commissions

•British Columbia Transit: 13401 - 108 Ave., Surrey BC V3T 5T4 – 604/264-5000; Fax: 604/264-5029
President & CEO, Michael O'Connor
General Manager, Victoria Office, Rogert Lingwood, 250/385-2551
•British Columbia Transportation Financing Authority: 2250 Granville Square, Vancouver BC V6C 1S4 – 604/775-1174; Fax: 604/775-2792
President & CEO, Blair Redlin
•Motor Carrier Commission: #200, 703 Broughton St., Victoria BC V8W 1E2 – 250/953-3777; Fax: 250/953-3788
Chair, Doug Allen

## TREASURY BOARD STAFF

#248, Legislative Bldgs., 1150 McKenzie Ave., Victoria BC V8V 1X4
250/387-6210; Fax: 250/387-9099
**Chair**, Hon. Andrew Petter, 250/387-3751, Fax: 250/387-5594
Secretary, Don Wright, 250/953-4364, Fax: 250/387-9099

## British Columbia UTILITIES COMMISSION

900 Howe St., 6th Fl., PO Box 250, Vancouver BC V6Z 2N3
604/660-4700; Fax: 604/660-1102; Email: bcuc@pop.gov.bc.ca
Toll Free: 1-800-663-1385 (B.C. only)
**Chair & CEO**, Dr. Mark K. Jaccard, 604/660-4757
Deputy Chair, Lorna R. Barr, 604/660-4722
Asst. to Chair & Deputy Chair, Marilyn E. Donn, 604/660-4719, Email: medonn@pop.gov.bc.ca
Executive Director, William J. Grant
Commission Secretary, Robert J. Pellatt, 604/660-4727

## Ministry of WOMEN'S EQUALITY

756 Fort St., Victoria BC V8V 1X4
250/387-3600; Fax: 250/356-1396; URL: http:www.weq.gov.bc.ca
**Minister**, Hon. Sue Hammell, 250/387-1223, Fax: 250/387-4312
Deputy Minister, Valerie Mitchell, 250/387-0413, Fax: 250/356-9377
Deputy Minister, Eloise Spitzer, 250/387-0413, Fax: 250/356-9377
Acting Asst. Deputy Minister, Linda Martin, 250/953-3466, Fax: 250/356-6072, Email: Linda.Martin@gems9.gov.bc.ca
Director, Communications, Sharlene Smith, 250/953-4570, Email: sfsmith@galaxy.gov.bc.ca

## WORKERS' COMPENSATION BOARD OF BRITISH COLUMBIA

6951 Westminster Hwy., Richmond BC V7C 1C6
604/273-2266; Fax: 604/276-3151; URL: http://www.wcb.bc.ca/
Toll Free: 1-800-661-2112
**Minister Responsible**, Hon. John Cashore
President/CEO, Dale Parker, 604/276-3190
Vice-President, Compensation Division, Ron Buchhorn
Vice-President, Finance & Information Services, Sid Fattedad
Vice-President, Human Resources & Corporate Development, David Anderson
Vice-President, Prevention Division, Ralph McGinn

# GOVERNMENT OF MANITOBA

**Seat of Government:** Legislative Bldg., Winnipeg MB R3C 0V8
URL: http://www.gov.mb.ca/
The Province of Manitoba entered Confederation July 15, 1870. It has an area of 547,703.85 km2, and the StatsCan census population in 1996 was 1,113,898.

## Office of the LIEUTENANT GOVERNOR

Legislative Bldg., #235, 450 Broadway, Winnipeg MB R3C 0V8
204/945-2753; Fax: 204/945-4329
**Lieutenant Governor**, Hon. W. Yvon Dumont
Executive Asst., Georgina Buddick

## Office of the PREMIER

Legislative Bldg., #204, 450 Broadway, Winnipeg MB R3C 0V8
204/945-3714; Fax: 204/949-1484; Email: premier@leg.gov.mb.ca; URL: http://www.gov.mb.ca/text/quotepg1.html
**Premier**, Hon. Gary Filmon, Email: premier@leg.gov.mb.ca
Deputy Premier, Hon. James Downey
Clerk of the Executive Council & Deputy Minister, Donald A. Leitch, 204/945-5640, Fax: 204/945-8390
Executive Asst. to the Premier, Lizanne Lachance-Mann, 204/945-2113
Director, Cabinet Communications Secretariat, Bonnie Staples-Lyon, 204/945-1494
Acting Director, Policy Management Secretariat, John Meldrum, 204/945-0723
Chief of Staff, Taras Sokolyk, 204/945-5642
Secretary, Bonnie Barley, 204/945-3714
Secretary to Cabinet for Intergovernmental Relations, Jim Eldridge, 204/945-5343

#### MANITOBA GOVERNMENT OFFICE - OTTAWA

#512, 90 Sparks St., Ottawa ON K1P 5B4
613/233-4228; Fax: 613/233-3509
Reports to the Clerk of the Executive Council on Federal-Provincial issues & to the Minister of Industry, Trade & Tourism on business & procurement issues.
Senior Representative, John Blackwood

## EXECUTIVE COUNCIL

Legislative Bldg., 450 Broadway, Winnipeg MB R3C 0V8
Premier, President, Executive Council & Minister, Federal-Provincial Relations, Hon. Gary Filmon, 204/945-3714, Fax: 204/949-1484, Email: premier@leg.gov.mb.ca
Deputy Premier & Minister, Industry, Trade & Tourism, Hon. James Downey, 204/945-0067, Fax: 204/945-4882, Email: minitt@leg.gov.mb.ca
Minister, Natural Resources, Hon. J. Glen Cummings, 204/945-3730, Fax: 204/945-3586, Email: minnr@leg.gov.mb.ca
Minister, Rural Development, Hon. Leonard Derkach, 204/945-3788, Fax: 204/945-1383, Email: minrd@leg.gov.mb.ca

Minister, Agriculture, Hon. Harry Enns, 204/945-3722, Fax: 204/945-3470, Email: minagr@leg.gov.mb.ca
Minister, Highways & Transportation, Hon. Glen Findlay, 204/945-3723, Fax: 204/945-7610, Email: minhwy@leg.gov.mb.ca
Minister, Labour, Hon. Harold Gilleshammer, 204/945-4079, Fax: 204/945-8312, Email: minlab@leg.gov.mb.ca
Minister, Environment, Hon. James C. McCrae, 204/945-3522, Fax: 204/945-1127, Email: minenv@leg.gov.mb.ca
Minister, Education & Training, Hon. Linda G. McIntosh, 204/945-3720, Fax: 204/945-1291, Email: minedu@leg.gov.mb.ca
Minister, Family Services, Hon. Bonnie E. Mitchelson, 204/945-4173, Fax: 204/945-5149, Email: minfam@leg.gov.mb.ca
Minister, Energy & Mines & Minister, Northern Affairs, Minister responsible, Native Affairs, Hon. David G. Newman, 204/945-3719, Fax: 204/945-8374, Email: minem@leg.gov.mb.ca
Minister, Government Services, Hon. Franklin P. Pitura, 204/945-2979, Fax: 204/945-7331, Email: mings@leg.gov.mb.ca
Minister, Health & Minister responsible, French Language Services, Hon. Darren T. Praznik, 204/945-3731, Fax: 204/945-0441, Email: minhlt@leg.gov.mb.ca
Minister, Consumer & Corporate Affairs, Hon. Michael Radcliffe, Q.C., 204/945-4256, Fax: 204/945-4009, Email: mincca@leg.gov.mb.ca
Minister, Urban Affairs & Minister, Housing, Minister responsible, Seniors, Hon. Jack F. Reimer, 204/945-0074, Fax: 204/945-1299, Email: minhou@leg.gov.mb.ca, Email: minua@leg.gov.mb.ca
Minister, Finance & Minister responsible, Sport, Hon. Eric Stefanson, 204/945-3952, Fax: 204/945-6057, Email: minfin@leg.gov.mb.ca
Minister, Justice & Attorney General, Minister responsible, Constitutional Affairs, Hon. Victor E. Toews, Q.C., 204/945-3728, Fax: 204/945-2517, Email: minjus@leg.gov.mb.ca
Minister, Culture, Heritage & Citizenship & Minister responsible, Multiculturalism, Hon. Rosemary Vodrey, 204/945-3729, Fax: 204/945-5223

#### Cabinet Office

Clerk, Executive Council, Donald A. Leitch, 204/945-5640, Fax: 204/945-8390
Legislative Asst., Agriculture, Hon. Franklin P. Pitura, 204/945-4519, Fax: 204/948-2092
Legislative Asst., Culture, Heritage & Citizenship, Hon. Michael Radcliffe, Q.C., 204/945-4609, Fax: 204/945-1284
Legislative Asst., Education & Training, Peter George Dyck, 204/945-4469, Fax: 204/948-2092
Legislative Asst., Industry, Trade & Tourism, Gerry McAlpine, 204/945-1583, Fax: 204/948-2092
Legislative Asst., Justice, Hon. David G. Newman, 204/945-3871, Fax: 204/945-5921
Legislative Asst., Rural Development, Mervin Tweed, 204/945-4198, Fax: 204/948-2092

#### Cabinet Committees

Assessment Reform
Economic Development Board
Joint Council
Multicultural Affairs
Native Affairs
Provincial Land Use
Regulatory Review
Sustainable Development
Treasure Board Committee
Urban Affairs

## LEGISLATIVE ASSEMBLY

c/o Clerk's Office, Legislative Bldg., #237, 450 Broadway Ave., Winnipeg MB R3C 0V8
204/945-3636; Fax: 204/948-2507; URL: http://www.gov.mb.ca/leg-asmb/index1.html; Hansard URL: http://www.gov.mb.ca/leg-asmb/hansard/index.
**Clerk:** W.H. Remnant
**Speaker:** Hon. Louise M. Dacquay
**Sergeant-at-Arms:** Dennis Gray
**Manager, Hansard:** Edith McLure
**Law Officer:** Shirley Strutt
**Deputy Clerk:** B. Bosiak

#### Government Caucus Office (PC)

Legislative Bldg., #227, 450 Broadway Ave., Winnipeg MB R3C 0V8
204/945-3709; Fax: 204/945-1284; Email: filmonteam@manpc.mb.ca
Chief of Staff, Ed Greenberg

#### Official Opposition Office (NDP)

Legislative Bldg., #234, 450 Broadway Ave., Winnipeg MB R3C 0V8
204/945-3710; Fax: 204/948-2005; Email: ndpmb@mbnet.mb.ca
Leader, Gary Doer, 204/945-4484
Chief of Staff & Director, Research, Paul Vogt
Acting Executive Asst., Glen Holmes, 204/945-4482
Deputy Leader, Jean Friesen
Administrative Secretary, Jeannette Lanthier, 204/945-4484

#### Office of the Liberal Party (Lib.)

Legislative Bldg., #151, 450 Broadway Ave., Winnipeg MB R3C 0V8
204/945-1793; Fax: 204/945-0874; Email: liberal@freenet.mb.ca
Leader, Jenny Hasselfield

#### Legislative Committees

Legislative Bldg., #249, 450 Broadway Ave., Winnipeg MB R3C 0V8
Fax: 204/945-0038
Committee Contact, Patricia Chaychuk, 204/945-0796
Committee Contact, Shabnam Datta, 204/945-4729
Agriculture
Economic Development
Industrial Relations
Law Amendments
Municipal Affairs
Private Bills
Privileges & Elections
Public Accounts
Public Utilities & Natural Resources
Rules of the House
Statutory Regulations & Orders

## THIRTY-SIXTH LEGISLATURE - MANITOBA

204/945-3707
Last General Election, April 25, 1995. Legal Duration, 5 Years.
**Party Standings (October 1, 1997)**
Progressive Conservative (PC) 31
New Democratic Party (NDP) 23
Liberal (Lib.) 2
Independent (Ind.) 1
Total 57
**Salaries, Indemnities & Allowances**
Members' annual indemnity $57,065. In addition to this are the following:
Premier $41,249
Ministers (with portfolio); Leader of the Opposition $25,781
Ministers (without portfolio); Leader of the Second Opposition $20,625
Speaker $21,656
Manitoba has a cost of living indexing system as prescribed by Sec. 53(3) of the Legislative Assembly Act.

#### MEMBERS BY CONSTITUENCY

Following is: constituency (number of eligible voters at 1995 election) member, party affiliation, Winnipeg Telephone number. (Address for all is Legislative Bldg., Winnipeg, MB R3C 0V8).
Refer to Cabinet List, Caucus Offices, for Fax numbers.

Arthur-Virden (12,045) Hon. James Downey, PC, 204/945-0067
Assiniboia (11,545) Hon. Linda G. McIntosh, PC, 204/945-3720
Brandon East (13,037) Leonard S. Evans, NDP, 204/945-8793
Brandon West (13,407) Hon. James C. McCrae, PC, 204/945-3522
Broadway (10,883) Conrad Santos, NDP, 204/945-4918
Burrows (11,103) Doug Martindale, NDP, 204/945-2645
Charleswood (13,296) James A. Ernst, PC, 204/945-3280
Concordia (11,401) Gary Doer, NDP, 204/945-4484
Crescentwood (14,202) Tim Sale, Lib., 204/945-3981
Dauphin (12,460) Stan Struthers, NDP, 204/945-1464
Elmwood (11,734) Jim Maloway, NDP, 204/945-2175
Emerson (11,958) Jack Penner, PC, 204/945-5639
Flin Flon (9,225) Gerard Jennissen, NDP, 204/945-2936
Fort Garry (17,418) Hon. Rosemary Vodrey, PC, 204/945-3729
Gimli (14,758) Ed Helwer, PC, 204/945-1790
Gladstone (12,136) Denis Rocan, PC, 204/945-0079
Inkster (12,989) Kevin Lamoureux, Lib., 204/945-4472
Interlake (11,602) Clif Evans, NDP, 204/945-4966
Kildonan (15,106) Dave Chomiak, NDP, 204/945-3965
Kirkfield Park (13,202) Hon. Eric Stefanson, PC, 204/945-3952
La Verendrye (12,777) Ben Sveinson, PC, 204/945-4046
Lac du Bonnet (13,846) Hon. Darren Praznik, PC, 204/945-3731
Lakeside (11,877) Hon. Harry Enns, PC, 204/945-3722
Minnedosa (12,593) Hon. Harold Gilleshammer, PC, 204/945-4079
Morris (13,104) Hon. Franklin P. Pitura, PC, 204/945-2979
Niakwa (15,089) Hon. Jack F. Reimer, PC, 204/945-0074
Osborne (13,917) Diane McGifford, NDP, 204/945-3969
Pembina (13,287) Peter George Dyck, PC, 204/945-4469
Point Douglas (8,569) George Hickes, NDP, 204/945-4323
Portage la Prairie (11,792) David Faurschou, PC
Radisson (14,183) Marianne Cerilli, NDP, 204/945-1567
Riel (12,415) Hon. David G. Newman, PC, 204/945-3719
River East (13,593) Hon. Bonnie E. Mitchelson, PC, 204/945-4173
River Heights (13,893) Hon. Michael Radcliffe, Q.C., PC, 204/945-4256
Roblin-Russell (12,394) Hon. Leonard Derkach, PC, 204/945-3788
Rossmere (12,234) Hon. Victor E. Toews, Q.C., PC, 204/945-3728
Rupertsland (9,924) Eric Robinson, NDP, 204/945-1370
Seine River (17,525) Hon. Louise M. Dacquay, PC, 204/945-3706
Selkirk (14,123) Gregory Dewar, NDP, 204/945-0143
Springfield (15,809) Hon. Glen Findlay, PC, 204/945-3723
St. Boniface (12,459) Neil Gaudry, Lib., 204/945-8073
St. James (11,895) Mary Ann Mihychuk, NDP, 204/945-4026

St. Johns (11,482) Gord Mackintosh, NDP, 204/945-3485
St. Norbert (14,971) Marcel Laurendeau, PC, 204/945-1689
St. Vital (13,037) Shirley Render, PC, 204/945-0301
Ste. Rose (11,532) Hon. J. Glen Cummings, PC, 204/945-3730
Steinbach (13,710) Albert Driedger, PC, 204/945-0231
Sturgeon Creek (13,710) Gerry McAlpine, PC, 204/945-1583
Swan River (11,643) Rosann Wowchuk, NDP, 204/945-7328
The Maples (13,402) Gary Kowalski, Ind., 204/945-8075
The Pas (12,056) Oscar Lathlin, NDP, 204/945-6487
Thompson (10,724) Steve Ashton, NDP, 204/945-4067
Transcona (13,003) Daryl Reid, NDP, 204/945-0774
Turtle Mountain (11,800) Mervin Tweed, PC, 204/945-4198
Tuxedo (18,019) Hon. Gary Filmon, PC, 204/945-3714
Wellington (10,537) Becky Barrett, NDP, 204/945-2698
Wolseley (10,670) Jean Friesen, NDP, 204/945-0009

#### MEMBERS (ALPHABETICAL)

Following is: member, constituency (number of eligible voters at 1995 election) party affiliation, Winnipeg Telephone number. (Address for all is Legislative Bldg., Winnipeg, MB R3C 0V8).
Refer to Cabinet List, Caucus Offices, for Fax numbers.

Steve Ashton, Thompson (10,724) NDP, 204/945-4067
Becky Barrett, Wellington (10,537) NDP, 204/945-2698
Marianne Cerilli, Radisson (14,183) NDP, 204/945-1567
Dave Chomiak, Kildonan (15,106) NDP, 204/945-3965
Hon. J. Glen Cummings, Ste. Rose (11,532) PC, 204/945-3730
Hon. Louise M. Dacquay, Seine River (17,525) PC, 204/945-3706
Hon. Leonard Derkach, Roblin-Russell (12,394) PC, 204/945-3788
Gregory Dewar, Selkirk (14,123) NDP, 204/945-0143
Gary Doer, Concordia (11,401) NDP, 204/945-4484
Hon. James Downey, Arthur-Virden (12,045) PC, 204/945-0067
Albert Driedger, Steinbach (13,710) PC, 204/945-0231
Peter George Dyck, Pembina (13,287) PC, 204/945-4469
Hon. Harry Enns, Lakeside (11,877) PC, 204/945-3722
James A. Ernst, Charleswood (13,296) PC, 204/945-3280
Clif Evans, Interlake (11,602) NDP, 204/945-4966
Leonard S. Evans, Brandon East (13,037) NDP, 204/945-8793
David Faurschou, Portage la Prairie (11,792) PC
Hon. Gary Filmon, Tuxedo (18,019) PC, 204/945-3714
Hon. Glen Findlay, Springfield (15,809) PC, 204/945-3723
Jean Friesen, Wolseley (10,670) NDP, 204/945-0009
Neil Gaudry, St. Boniface (12,459) Lib., 204/945-8073
Hon. Harold Gilleshammer, Minnedosa (12,593) PC, 204/945-4079
Ed Helwer, Gimli (14,758) PC, 204/945-1790
George Hickes, Point Douglas (8,569) NDP, 204/945-4323
Gerard Jennissen, Flin Flon (9,225) NDP, 204/945-2936
Gary Kowalski, The Maples (13,402) Ind., 204/945-8075
Kevin Lamoureux, Inkster (12,989) Lib., 204/945-4472
Oscar Lathlin, The Pas (12,056) NDP, 204/945-6487
Marcel Laurendeau, St. Norbert (14,971) PC, 204/945-1689
Gord Mackintosh, St. Johns (11,482) NDP, 204/945-3485
Jim Maloway, Elmwood (11,734) NDP, 204/945-2175
Doug Martindale, Burrows (11,103) NDP, 204/945-2645
Gerry McAlpine, Sturgeon Creek (13,710) PC, 204/945-1583
Hon. James C. McCrae, Brandon West (13,407) PC, 204/945-3522
Diane McGifford, Osborne (13,917) NDP, 204/945-3969
Hon. Linda G. McIntosh, Assiniboia (11,545) PC, 204/945-3720
Mary Ann Mihychuk, St. James (11,895) NDP, 204/945-4026
Hon. Bonnie E. Mitchelson, River East (13,593) PC, 204/945-4173
Hon. David G. Newman, Riel (12,415) PC, 204/945-3719
Jack Penner, Emerson (11,958) PC, 204/945-5639
Hon. Franklin P. Pitura, Morris (13,104) PC, 204/945-2979
Hon. Darren Praznik, Lac du Bonnet (13,846) PC, 204/945-3731
Hon. Michael Radcliffe, Q.C., River Heights (13,893) PC, 204/945-4256
Daryl Reid, Transcona (13,003) NDP, 204/945-0774
Hon. Jack F. Reimer, Niakwa (15,089) PC, 204/945-0074
Shirley Render, St. Vital (13,037) PC, 204/945-0301
Eric Robinson, Rupertsland (9,924) NDP, 204/945-1370
Denis Rocan, Gladstone (12,136) PC, 204/945-0079
Tim Sale, Crescentwood (14,202) Lib., 204/945-3981
Conrad Santos, Broadway (10,883) NDP, 204/945-4918
Hon. Eric Stefanson, Kirkfield Park (13,202) PC, 204/945-3952
Stan Struthers, Dauphin (12,460) NDP, 204/945-1464
Ben Sveinson, La Verendrye (12,777) PC, 204/945-4046
Hon. Victor E. Toews, Q.C., Rossmere (12,234) PC, 204/945-3728
Mervin Tweed, Turtle Mountain (11,800) PC, 204/945-4198
Hon. Rosemary Vodrey, Fort Garry (17,418) PC, 204/945-3729
Rosann Wowchuk, Swan River (11,643) NDP, 204/945-7328

# MANITOBA GOVERNMENT DEPARTMENTS & AGENCIES

## Manitoba AGRICULTURE

Norquay Bldg., #809, 401 York Ave., Winnipeg MB R3C 0P8
204/945-3433 (Administration); Fax: 204/945-5024; Email: minagr@leg.gov.mb.ca; URL: http://www.gov.mb.ca/agriculture/

#### ACTS ADMINISTERED

Agricultural Credit Corporation Act
Agricultural Societies Act
Agricultural Productivity Council Act
Agriculture Producers' Organization Funding Act
Department of Agriculture Act
Agrologists Act
Animal Diseases Act
Animal Husbandry Act
Bee Act
Cattle Producers' Association Act
Coarse Grain Marketing Control Act
Crop Insurance Act
Crown Lands Act, (in part) Sections 6, 7, 10, 12(1), 14, 16, 17, 18, 21, 23, 24 to 28 both inclusive
Dairy Act
Family Farm Protection Act
Farm Income Assurance Plans Act
Farm Lands Ownership Act
Farm Machinery & Equipment Act
Farm Practices Protection Act
Fruit & Vegetable Sales Act
Horse Racing Regulation Act
Horticultural Society Act
Land Rehabilitation Act
Livestock & Livestock Products Act
Margarine Act
Milk Prices Review Act
Natural Products Marketing Act
Noxious Weeds Act
Pesticides & Fertilizers Control Act
Plant Pests & Diseases Act
Seed & Fodder Relief Act
Veterinary Medical Act
Veterinary Science Scholarship Fund Act
Veterinary Services Act
Wildlife Act, (in part) Section 89(e)
Women's Institute Act

**Minister**, Hon. Harry Enns, 204/945-3722
Deputy Minister, Don Zasada, 204/945-3734, Fax: 204/948-2095

#### AGRICULTURAL DEVELOPMENT & MARKETING DIVISION

Asst. Deputy Minister, D.I. Donaghy, 204/945-3736
Director, Animal Industry Branch, Agricultural Services Complex, Univ. of Manitoba, Dr. John Taylor, 204/945-7690, Fax: 204/945-4327
Director, Marketing & Farm Business Management Branch, D. Gingera, 204/945-4521
Director, Soils & Crops Branch, Dr. Barry Todd, 65 - 3 Ave., PO Box 1149, Carman MB R0G 0J0, 204/745-2040, Fax: 204/745-2299
Director, Veterinary Services Branch, Agricultural Services Complex, Univ. of Manitoba, Vacant, 204/945-7647, Fax: 204/945-8062

#### MANAGEMENT & OPERATIONS DIVISION

Asst. Deputy Minister, R.L. Baseraba, 204/945-3735
Director, Administrative & Accounting Services & Director, Human Resources, M. Robinson
Acting Director, Program & Policy Analysis, G.A. Fearn, 204/945-3979
Manager, Computer Services, R. Takeuchi, 204/945-3435
Manager, Financial Administration, M. Richter, 204/945-3306

#### POLICY & ECONOMICS DIVISION

Asst. Deputy Minister, C. Lee, 204/945-3910

#### REGIONAL AGRICULTURAL SERVICES DIVISON

Asst. Deputy Minister, R.L. Baseraba, 204/945-3735
Acting Director, Agricultural Crown Lands Branch, R. Chychota, 36 Centre Ave. West, PO Box 1286, Minnedosa MB R0J 1E0, 204/867-3419, Fax: 204/867-5696
Principal, Agricultural Extension Centre, Keith Levenick, 1129 Queens Ave., Brandon MB R7A 1L9, 204/726-6348, Fax: 204/728-8260

#### Associated Agencies, Boards & Commissions

•Agricultural Societies Advisory Board: Norquay Bldg., #810, 401 York Ave., Winnipeg MB R3C 0P8 – 204/945-4522; Fax: 204/945-5024
Superintendent, R. Collins
•Farm Lands Ownership Board: #915 Norquay Bldg., 401 York Ave., Winnipeg MB R3C 0P8 – 204/945-3149; Fax: 204/945-6134
Executive Director, H. Nelson
•Farm Machinery Board: Norquay Bldg., #915, 401 York Ave., Winnipeg MB R3C 0P8 – 204/945-3856; Fax: 204/945-6134
Acting Secretary Manager, R. Ozunko
•Manitoba Agricultural Credit Corporation: #100, 1525 - 1 St., Brandon MB R7A 7A1 – 204/726-6850; Fax: 204/726-6849
General Manager, Gill Shaw
•Manitoba Broiler Hatching Egg Commission: #200, 666 St. James St., Winnipeg MB R3G 3J6 – 204/488-3075; Fax: 204/783-8598

Chair, R.W. Scott
•Manitoba Crop Insurance Corporation: #400, 50 - 24 St. NW, Portage la Prairie MB R1N 3V9 – 204/239-3246; Fax: 204/239-3401
General Manager, B. Manning
•Manitoba Farm Mediation Board: #600, 491 Portage Ave., Winnipeg MB R3B 2E4 – 204/945-0358; Fax: 204/945-1489
Executive Director, H. Nelson
•Manitoba Natural Products Marketing Council: #915 Norquay Bldg., 401 York Ave., Winnipeg MB R3C 0P8 – 204/945-4495; Fax: 204/945-6134
Secretary, G. MacKenzie
•Milk Prices Review Commission: #915 Norquay Bldg., 401 York Ave., Winnipeg MB R3C 0P8 – 204/945-0629; Fax: 204/945-6134
Acting Secretary, A. Khan
•National Tripartite Stabilization Program: #300, 50 - 24 St. NW, Portage la Prairie MB R1N 3V8 – 204/239-3232; Fax: 204/857-6597
Manager, Craig Thomson

**Agricultural Marketing Boards**
•Manitoba Chicken Producer Board: 430-A Dovercourt Dr., Winnipeg MB R3Y 1N4 – 204/489-4603; Fax: 204/489-4907
General Manager, K.L. Dexter
•Manitoba Egg Producers' Marketing Board: #18, Waverley Sq., 5 Scurfield Blvd., Winnipeg MB R3Y 1G3 – 204/488-4888; Fax: 204/488-3544
General Manager, P. Kelly
•Manitoba Honey Producers' Marketing Board: #201, 545 University Cres., Winnipeg MB R3T 5S6 – 204/945-3861; Fax: 204/945-3427
Provincial Apiarist, D. Dixon
•Manitoba Milk Producers' Marketing Board: 36 Scurfield Blvd., Winnipeg MB R3T 3N5 – 204/488-6455; Fax: 204/488-4772
•Manitoba Pork: 750 Marion St., Winnipeg MB R2J 0K4 – 204/233-4991; Fax: 204/233-0049
General Manager, R.L. Sedgwick
•Manitoba Turkey Producers' Marketing Board: 430A Dovercourt Dr., Winnipeg MB R3Y 1N4 – 204/489-4635; Fax: 204/489-4907
General Manager, B.F. Waters
•Manitoba Vegetable Producers' Marketing Board: 1200 King Edward St., Winnipeg MB R3H 0R5 – 204/633-7926; Fax: 204/697-0088
General Manager, T.A. Young

## Office of the Provincial AUDITOR
405 Broadway, 12th Fl., Winnipeg MB R3C 3L6
204/945-3790; Fax: 204/945-2169
**Provincial Auditor**, J.W. Singleton
Asst. Provincial Auditor, W.A. Johnson, 204/945-3791

## Manitoba CONSUMER & CORPORATE AFFAIRS (MCCA)
#317, 450 Broadway, Winnipeg MB R3C 0V8
204/945-1718; Email: mincca@leg.gov.mb.ca

### ACTS ADMINISTERED
**Administration**
Manitoba Evidence Act, Parts II & III
**Cooperative, Credit Union Regulation**
Cooperatives Act
Credit Unions & Caisses Populaires Act
**Consumers' Bureau**
Bedding, Upholstered & Stuffed Articles Regulation (of the Public Health Act)
Business Practices Act
Charities Endorsement Act
Consumer Protection Act
Hearing Aid Act & Regulation
Personal Investigations Act
**Residential Tenancies**
Condominium Act
Landlord & Tenant Act
Residential Tenancies Act
**Companies Office**
Business Names Registration Act
Corporations Act
Partnership Act
Religious Societies' Lands Act
**Deputy Minister**
Embalmers' & Funeral Directors' Act
Trade Practices Inquiry Act
**Insurance**
Insurance Act
Insurance Corporations Tax Act
Marine Insurance Act
**Manitoba Securities Commission**
Commodity Futures Act
Mortgage Dealers Act
Real Estate Brokers Act
Securities Act
**Property Rights**
Hudson's Bay Company Land Register Act
Personal Property Security Act
Real Property Act
Registry Act
Revenue Act (part III)
Special Survey Act
Surveys Act
Title to Certain Lands Act
**Public Utilities Board**
Cemeteries Act
Prearranged Funeral Services Act
Public Utilities Board Act
**Residential Tenancies**
Condominium Act
Landlord & Tenant Act
Residential Tenancies Act
**Trusts & Loans**
Part XXIV Corporations Act
**Vital Statistics**
Change of Name Act
Marriage Act
Vital Statistics Act

**Minister**, Hon. Michael Radcliffe, Q.C., 204/945-4256, Fax: 204/945-4009
Deputy Minister, A. Morton, 204/945-3742, Fax: 204/945-4009, Email: dmcca@leg.gov.mb.ca
Acting Superintendent, Insurance, L. Couture, #1142, 405 Broadway, Winnipeg MB R3C 3L6, 204/945-2542, Fax: 204/948-2268
Commissioner, Residential Tenancies Commission, A. Zivot, 204/945-4242, Fax: 204/945-5453
Director, Administration Office, Fred D. Bryans, 204/945-2653, Fax: 204/945-0430
Director, Companies Office, M. Pawlowsky, 204/945-4206, Fax: 204/945-1459
Director, Consumers' Bureau, Denis Robidoux, #302, 258 Portage Ave., Winnipeg MB R3C 0B6, 204/945-3800, Fax: 204/945-0728
Director, Cooperative & Credit Union Regulations & Director, Trust & Loan, R. Pozernick, 204/945-2771, Fax: 204/945-0864
Director, Research & Planning, I. Anderson, #1105, 405 Broadway, Winnipeg MB R3C 3L6, 204/945-7892, Fax: 204/948-2268
Director, Residential Tenancies Branch, R. Barsy, 204/945-4069, Fax: 204/945-6273

### PROPERTY RIGHTS DIVISION
405 Broadway, 10th Fl., Winnipeg MB R3C 3L6
Registrar General & COO, Property Registration, Rick Wilson, Q.C., 204/945-2243, Fax: 204/948-3276

**Land Titles & Personal Property**
Registrar, Personal Property, D. Crockatt, 204/945-2656
Examiner of Surveys, G. Fraser, 204/945-2281
Deputy Examiner of Surveys, G. Lund, 204/945-2282

**Land Titles Offices**
Brandon: 705 Princess Ave., Brandon MB R7A 0P4 – 204/726-6279, District Registrar, J.S. Grewal
Dauphin: 308 Main St. South, Dauphin MB R7N 1K7 – 204/622-2084, District Registrar, Vacant
Morden: 351 Stephen St., Morden MB R0G 1J0 – 204/822-4436, District Registrar, R.E. James
Neepawa: 329 Hamilton St., Neepawa MB R0J 1H0 – 204/476-2106, District Registrar, E. Sims
Portage la Prairie: 25 Tupper St. North, Portage la Prairie MB R1N 3K1 – 204/239-3306, District Registrar, J. Kushniruk
Winnipeg: 405 Broadway, Lower Lobby, Winnipeg MB R3C 3L6 – 204/945-2042, 2043, District Registrar/Deputy Registrar General, Barry Effler, 204/945-2242, Senior Deputy District Registrar, H. Armstrong, 204/945-2251, Deputy District Registrar, A. Brown, 204/945-2250, Deputy District Registrar, V. Patel, 204/945-5560

### VITAL STATISTICS
254 Portage Ave., Winnipeg MB R3C 0B8
204/945-2034, 8177; Fax: 204/945-0777
Toll Free: Fax Certificate Requests: 204/948-3128
Provincial agency responsible for the issuance of birth, death, change of name & marriage certificates. Written or faxed requests must be submitted. Fee for each certificate is $25.00.
Director, C. Kaus, 204/945-3701
Manager, Customer Services, D. Whittaker
Supervisor, Application Processing, L. Turzak
Supervisor, Registration Information Systems, F. Beer

**Associated Agencies, Boards & Commissions**
•Automobile Injury Compensation Appeal Commission: #106, 167 Lombard Ave., Winnipeg MB R3Z 3Z5 – 204/945-4155
Chief Commissioner, R. Taylor, 204/945-4353
•Credit Union Deposit Guarantee Corporation: #100, 233 Portage Ave., Winnipeg MB R3B 2A7 – 204/942-8480; Fax: 204/947-1723
General Manager, George A. Keter
•Hearing Aid Board: 114 Garry St., Winnipeg MB R3C 1G1 – 204/956-2040; Fax: 204/945-0728
Secretary, Denis Robidoux
•Manitoba Securities Commission: #1128, 405 Broadway, Winnipeg MB R3C 3L6 – 204/945-2548; Fax: 204/945-0330
Chair, Jocelyn Samson
Counsel, David Cheop
Deputy Director, Corporate Finance, Robert Bouchard
•Public Utilities Board: 280 Smith St., 2nd Fl., Winnipeg MB R3C 1K2 – 204/945-2638; Fax: 204/945-2643
Chair, Gerry D. Forrest, 204/945-2640
Executive Director, G.O. Barron

## Manitoba CULTURE, HERITAGE & CITIZENSHIP
213 Notre Dame., Winnipeg MB R3B 1N3
204/945-3729; Email: minchc@leg.gov.mb.ca;
URL: http://www.gov.mb.ca/manitoba/chc/immsettl/citz_hom.html

### ACTS ADMINISTERED
Amusements Act, Parts I, III to X
Arts Council Act
Centennial Centre Corporation Act
Le Centre Culturel Franco-Manitobain Act
Coat of Arms, Emblems & The Manitoba Tartan Act
Department of Labour Act (in part)
Fitness & Amateur Sport Act
Foreign Cultural Objects Immunity from Seizure Act

Freedom of Information Act
Heritage Manitoba Act
Heritage Resources Act
Legislative Library Act
Manitoba Multiculturalism Act
Manitoba Museum Act
Museums & Miscellaneous Grants Act
Public Libraries Act
Public Printing Act
**Minister**, Hon. Rosemary Vodrey, Fax: 204/945-5223
Deputy Minister, Roxy Freedman, 204/945-4136, Fax: 204/948-3102

#### ADMINISTRATION & FINANCE DIVISION

Fax: 204/945-5760
Executive Director, Dave Paton, 204/945-2233
Acting Manager, Financial Administration, Lenore Ireland, 204/945-4096
Manager, Grants Administration, Pauline Rosmus, 204/945-4580
Manager, Information Systems, Rosemary Unrau, 204/945-4436
Manager, Management Services, Kerry O'Shaughnessy, 204/945-4215
Director, Community Places Program, Wayne Blackburn, 204/945-1368, Fax: 204/945-2086
Director, Human Resource Services, Art Proulx, 405 Broadway, 9th Fl., Winnipeg MB R3C 3L6, 204/945-2885, Fax: 204/945-6692

#### CITIZENSHIP DIVISION

Asst. Deputy Minister, Gerald L. Clement, 204/945-8174, Fax: 204/948-2256
Director, Immigrant Credentials & Labour Market Branch, Vacant
Director, Immigration/Settlement Policy & Planning Branch, Vacant
Director, Settlement & Adult Language Training Branch, M. Kenny, 204/945-8081, Fax: 204/948-2148
Manager, Citizenship Support Services Branch, N. Kostyshyn-Bailey, 204/945-1649, Fax: 204/948-2148

#### CULTURE, HERITAGE & RECREATION PROGRAMS DIVISION

Asst. Deputy Minister, Lou-Anne Buhr, 204/945-4078, Fax: 204/945-2739
Acting Director, Arts Branch, Terrence Welsh, 204/945-4579, Fax: 204/945-1684
Director, Historic Resources, Donna Dul, 204/945-4389, Fax: 204/948-2384
Director, Public Library Services, Sylvia Nicholson, #200, 1595 - 1 St., Brandon MB R7A 7A1, 204/726-6864, Fax: 204/726-6868
Director, Recreation & Wellness Promotion, Jim Hamilton, 204/945-0487, Fax: 204/945-1684
Director, Regional Services, Roberta de Pencier, 204/945-4396, Fax: 204/945-1684

#### INFORMATION RESOURCES DIVISION

155 Carlton St., 10th Fl., Winnipeg MB R3C 3H8
Acting Executive Director, Cindy Stevens, 204/945-4271, Fax: 204/948-2219
Acting Director, Communication Services, Gail Granger, 204/945-4971, Fax: 204/948-2147
Director, Information Services, Dwight MacAulay, 204/945-3746, Fax: 204/945-3988
Acting Associate Director, Advertising Services, Lori Yarchuk, 204/945-5164, Fax: 204/948-2147
Manager, Business Services, Mike Baudic, 204/945-4392, Fax: 204/948-2219
Manager, Production Services, Heather Coleman, 204/945-7121, Fax: 204/948-2332
Supervisor, Citizens' Inquiry, Liliana Romanowski, 204/945-3744, Fax: 204/945-4261
Supervisor, Statutory Publications, Keith Holness, 204/945-3101, Fax: 204/945-7172

#### PROVINCIAL SERVICES DIVISION

200 Vaughan St., Winnipeg MB R3C 1T5
Fax: 204/948-2008
Executive Director & Legislative Librarian, Legislative Library, S. Bishop, 204/945-3968
Provincial Archivist, Provincial Archives, Peter Bower, 204/945-4233
Director, Translation Services, M. Freynet, 213 Notre Dame Ave., 2nd Fl., Winnipeg MB R3B 1N3, 204/945-3095, Fax: 204/945-5879

##### Associated Agencies, Boards & Commissions

•Le Centre Culturel franco-manitobain/Franco-Manitoban Cultural Centre: 340, boul Provencher, St. Boniface MB R2H 0G7 – 204/233-8972; Fax: 204/233-3324
Director, Alain Boucher
•Film Classification Board (& Film Classification Appeal Board): #216, 301 Weston St., Winnipeg MB R3E 3H4 – 204/945-8962; Fax: 204/945-0890
Director, George Rooswinkel
•Heritage Grants Advisory Council: 213 Notre Dame Ave., 3rd Fl., Winnipeg MB R3B 1N3 – 204/945-4580; Fax: 204/945-5760
Executive Director, P. Rosmus
•Manitoba Arts Council: #525, 93 Lombard Ave., Winnipeg MB R3B 3B1 – 204/945-2239; Fax: 204/945-5925
Executive Director, Victor Jerrett-Enns
•Manitoba Centennial Centre Corporation: #117, 555 Main St., Winnipeg MB R3B 1C3 – 204/956-1360; Fax: 204/944-1390
Executive Director, John Walton
•Manitoba Heritage Council: 213 Notre Dame Ave., Main Fl., Winnipeg MB R3B 1N3 – 204/945-4389; Fax: 204/948-2384
Chair, Bill Neville
•Manitoba Liquor Control Commission: 1555 Buffalo Place, PO Box 1023, Winnipeg MB R3C 2X1 – 204/284-2501; URL: http://www.mlcc.mb.ca
President & CEO, Ian G. Wright
•Manitoba Museum
Listed in Section 1; *see* Index.
•Multicultural Grants Advisory Council: 213 Notre Dame Ave., 4th Fl., Winnipeg MB R3B 1N3 – 204/945-4458; Fax: 204/945-1675
Executive Director, R. Taruc
•Multiculturalism Secretariat: 213 Notre Dame Ave., 5th Fl., Winnipeg MB R3B 1N3 – 204/945-6300; Fax: 204/948-2256

## Manitoba DEVELOPMENT CORPORATION (MDC)

#555, 155 Carlton St., Winnipeg MB R3C 3H8
204/945-7626; Fax: 204/957-1793
**Minister Responsible**, Hon. James Downey, 204/945-0067, Fax: 204/945-4882
General Manager, Ian Robertson, 204/945-2472
Corporate Secretary, Jim Kilgour

## Manitoba EDUCATION & TRAINING

#168, Legislative Bldg., 401 York Ave., Winnipeg MB R3C 0P8
204/945-4325; Fax: 204/945-1291; Email: minedu@leg.gov.mb.ca; URL: http://www.gov.mb.ca/educate/index.html

##### ACTS ADMINISTERED

Blind Persons' & Deaf Persons' Maintenance & Education Act
Education Administration Act
Licensed Practical Nurses Act, ss. 14, 15
Private Vocational Schools Act
Public Schools Act
Public Schools Finance Board Act
Teachers' Pension Act
Teachers' Society Act
Universities Establishment Act
Universities Grants Commission Act
University of Manitoba Act
**Minister**, Hon. Linda G. McIntosh, 204/945-3720
Deputy Minister, Education, J. Carlyle, 204/945-3752, Fax: 204/945-8330
Deputy Minister, Training & Advanced Education, Tom Carson, 204/945-8528, Fax: 204/948-2490

#### ADMINISTRATION & FINANCE DIVISION

1181 Portage Ave., Winnipeg MB R3G 0T3
Asst. Deputy Minister, Jim Glen, 204/945-6904, Fax: 204/945-8303
Director, Administration & Professional Certification, Brian Hanson, 204/945-7391, Fax: 204/948-2154
Director, Finance, T. Thompson, 204/945-6908, Fax: 204/948-2193
Director, Schools Finance, Gerald Farthing, 204/945-0515, Fax: 204/948-2000

#### BUREAU DE L'EDUCATION FRANÇAISE/French Language Education Office

#509. 1181 Portage Ave., Winnipeg MB R3C 0T3
Sous-ministre adjoint, Guy Roy, 204/945-6928, Fax: 204/945-1625

#### PLANNING & POLICY DEVELOPMENT BRANCH

#409, 1181 Portage Ave., Winnipeg MB R3G 0T3
204/945-6171; Fax: 204/945-0194
Executive Director, John Didyk
Project Coordinator, Distance Education Implementation, Dr. Beth Cruikshank, 204/945-2811

#### SCHOOL PROGRAMS DIVISION

1181 Portage Ave., Winnipeg MB R3G 0T3
Asst. Deputy Minister, Carolyn Loeppky, 204/945-7935, Fax: 204/945-8303
Director, Instructional Resources, John Tooth, 204/945-7833, Fax: 204/945-8756
Director, Native Education, Juliette Sabot, 204/945-7883, Fax: 204/948-2010
Director, Program Development Branch, Pat MacDonald, #W120, 1970 Ness Ave., Winnipeg MB R3J 0Y9, 204/945-0926, Fax: 204/945-5060
Acting Director, Program Implementation Branch, Erika Kreis, #W130, 1970 Ness Ave., Winnipeg MB R3J 0Y9, 204/945-1033, Fax: 204/945-5060
Director, Student Support Services, N.J. Cenerini, 204/945-7911, Fax: 204/945-7914
Coordinator, Assessment & Evaluation Unit, Norman Mayer, 204/945-6157, Fax: 204/945-8303
Acting Manager, Manitoba Textbook Bureau, Lanny Kingerski, 130 - 1 Ave. West, Souris MB R0K 2C0
Program Manager, Independent Study Program, Gerry Gros, Main Plaza, 555 Main St., Winkler MB R6W 1C4, 204/325-2306, Fax: 204/325-4212

#### TRAINING & ADVANCED EDUCATION

185 Carlton St., 4th Fl., Winnipeg MB R3C 3J1
Asst. Deputy Minister, Tom Carson, 204/945-8528, Fax: 204/948-2490
Director, Apprenticeship, Harvey Miller, 204/945-3339, Fax: 204/948-2346
Acting Director, Employment Development Programs, Pam McConnell, 209 Notre Dame Ave., 4th Fl., Winnipeg MB R3B 1M9, 204/945-6997, Fax: 204/945-0221
Director, Labour Market Support Services, Earl McArthur, 204/945-0608, Fax: 204/945-1792
Acting Director, Manitoba Literacy & Continuing Education, Louise Gordon, 204/945-8571, Fax: 204/945-1792
Acting Director, Workforce 2000 & Youth Programs, B. Knight, 204/945-6195, Fax: 204/945-1792

Acting Manager, Student Financial Assistance Program, Kim Huebner, Box 6, 693 Taylor Ave., Winnipeg MB R3M 3T9, 204/945-8729, Fax: 204/477-5596

## ELECTIONS MANITOBA

200 Vaughan St., Main Fl., Winnipeg MB R3C 1T5
204/945-3225; Fax: 204/945-6011; Email: election@access.mbnet.mb.ca
**Chief Electoral Officer**, Richard D. Balasko

## Manitoba EMERGENCY MANAGEMENT ORGANIZATION (MEMO)

#1510, 405 Broadway, Winnipeg MB R3C 3L6
204/945-4772; Fax: 204/945-4620
**Executive Coordinator**, Harold Clayton, 204/945-4789
MEMO is a division of Manitoba Government Services, listed separately in this section.

## Manitoba ENERGY & MINES

#360, 1395 Ellice Ave., Winnipeg MB R3G 3P2
204/945-4154; Fax: 204/945-0586, 1406; Email: minem@leg.gov.mb.ca; URL: http://www.gov.mb.ca/em/index.html
Ordering Publications: 204/945-4154; Fax: 204/945-8427; Email: publications@em.gov.mb.ca
Develops & administers policies & legislation that foster & promote environmentally sustainable economic development of Manitoba's mineral resources & the development & efficient use of energy resources available to the province.

### ACTS ADMINISTERED

Energy Act
Gas Allocation Act
Gas Pipe Line Act
Greater Winnipeg Gas Distribution Act (SM 1988, c. 40)
Homeowners Tax & Insulation Assistance Act (in Part)
Manitoba Natural Resources Development Act (as it applies to Manitoba Resources Ltd.)
Mineral Exploration Incentive Program Act
Mines & Minerals Act
Mining & Metallurgy Compensation Act
Natural Gas Supply Act
Oil & Gas Act
Oil & Gas Production Tax Act
**Minister**, Hon. David G. Newman, 204/945-6429
Deputy Minister, Michael Fine, 204/945-4172

### GEOLOGICAL SERVICES BRANCH

204/945-6567
Director, W.D. McRitchie, 204/945-6559

### MARKETING BRANCH

204/945-8093
Director, Jim Crone, 204/945-1874

### MINES BRANCH

204/945-6522
Director, A. Ball, 204/945-6505

### PETROLEUM & ENERGY BRANCH

204/945-6577; Fax: 204/945-0586; Email: htisdale@em.gov.mb.ca; URL: http://www.gov.mb.ca/em/petroleum/index.html
Toll Free: 1-800-282-8069 (Energy)
Petroleum Information: 204/748-1557
Energy Information: 204/945-3760
Director, L.R. Dubreuil, 204/945-6573
Officer, Building Codes, Ken Klassen, 204/945-2792
Officer, Commercial Energy Use & Renewable Alternate Energy, Terry Silcox, 204/945-0757
Officer, Crown Land Sales, Carol Martiniuk, 204/945-6570
Officer, Drilling Licences, Dan Surzyshyn, 204/945-8102
Officer, Geological Information, Harry Klassen, 204/945-6571
Officer, Maps, Reports & Publications, Barb Johnston, 204/748-1557
Officer, Pipelines & Surface Rights, John Fox, 204/945-6574
Officer, Residential Energy Use, Randy Romas, 204/945-4335
Officer, Transportation, Marc Arbez, 204/945-0757

#### Associated Agencies, Boards & Commissions

•Manitoba Mining Board (MMB): #360, 1395 Ellice Ave., Winnipeg MB R3G 3P2 – 204/943-6740
Presiding Member, Doug Abra

## Manitoba ENVIRONMENT

#160, 123 Main St., Winnipeg MB R3C 1A5
204/945-7100; Email: minenv@leg.gov.mb.ca; URL: http://www.gov.mb.ca/environ/index.html

### ACTS ADMINISTERED

Contaminated Sites Remediation Act
Dangerous Goods Handling & Transportation Act
Environment Act
High Level Radioactive Waste Act
Manitoba Hazardous Waste Management Corporation Act
Ozone Depleting Substances Act
Public Health Act
Waste Reduction & Prevention (WRAP) Act
**Minister**, Hon. James C. McCrae, 204/945-3522, Fax: 204/942-1127
Deputy Minister, Norman Brandson, 204/945-8807, Fax: 204/945-1256
Director, Administration, Wolf Boehm, 204/945-7006, Fax: 204/948-2338
Director, Legislation & Intergovernmental Affairs, Richard Stephens, 204/945-8152

### ENVIRONMENTAL MANAGEMENT DIVISION

204/945-7107; Fax: 204/945-5229
Asst. Deputy Minister, Serge Scrafield
Director, Environmental Approvals Branch, Larry Strachan, 204/945-7071
Director, Environmental Quality Standards Branch, Max Morelli, 204/945-7032
Director, Pollution Prevention Branch, Jerry Spiegel, 204/945-7083

### ENVIRONMENTAL OPERATIONS DIVISION

204/945-7008; Fax: 204/945-5229
Environmental Accidents Information: 204/945-7039
Emergency Reporting (24-hour): 204/944-4888
Asst. Deputy Minister, Dave Wotton
Supervisor, Transportation & Handling of Dangerous Goods, Dave Ediger, 204/945-7039
Senior Operations Consultant, Regional Operations, K. Hawkins, 204/945-7009

#### Regional Operations

Brandon: Scotia Towers, 1011 Rosser Ave., Brandon MB R7A 0L5 – 204/726-6565, Regional Director, Bernie Chrisp
Steinbach: Town Square, 284 Reimer Ave., Steinbach MB R0A 2A0 – 204/326-3468, Regional Director, Dennis Brown
The Pas: Provincial Bldg., 3rd & Ross Ave., PO Box 2550, The Pas MB R9A 1M4 – 204/627-8362, Regional Director, Steve Davis
Winkler: Main Plaza, 555 Main St., Winkler MB R6W 1C4 – 204/325-2291, Regional Director, Leslie MacCallum
Winnipeg: #160, 123 Main St., Winnipeg MB R3C 1A5 – 204/945-7081, Regional Director, Vacant

#### Manitoba Round Table on the Environment & Economy (MRTEE)

Secretariat: Sustainable Development Coordination Unit, #305, 155 Carlton St., Winnipeg MB R3C 3H8
204/945-1124; Fax: 204/945-0090
Acting Executive Director, Bryan R. Gray

#### Associated Agencies, Boards & Commissions

•Clean Environment Commission: Town Square, PO Box 21420, Steinbach MB R0A 2T3 – 204/326-2395; Fax: 204/326-2472
Chair, Dale Stewart

## Manitoba FAMILY SERVICES

#219, 114 Garry St., Winnipeg MB R3C 4V6
204/945-2324 (Policy & Planning); Fax: 204/945-2156; Email: minfam@leg.gov.mb.ca; URL: http://www.gov.mb.ca/fs/first/ffindex.html

### ACTS ADMINISTERED

Child & Family Services Act
Community Child Day Care Standards Act
Department of Labour Act (as it applies to Family Services)
Mental Health Act (in Part)
Parents' Maintenance Act, s. 10
Social Allowances Act
Social Services Administration Act
**Minister**, Hon. Bonnie E. Mitchelson, 204/945-4173, Fax: 204/945-5149, Email: minfam@leg.gov.mb.ca
Deputy Minister, Tannis Mindell, 204/945-6700, Fax: 204/945-1896
Children's Advocate, Office of the Children's Advocate, Wayne Govereau, 204/945-1427, Fax: 204/948-2278
Director, Human Resources Services, Audrey Clifford, 204/945-3165, Fax: 204/945-0601

### CHILD & FAMILY SERVICES DIVISION

Asst. Deputy Minister, David Langtry, 204/945-3257, Fax: 204/945-0291
Executive Director, Child Welfare & Family Support, Phil Goodman, 204/945-6948, Fax: 204/945-6717
Director, Child Day Care, Gisella Rempel, 204/945-2668, Fax: 204/948-2143
Director, Children's Special Services, Eleanor Chornoboy, 204/945-3251, Fax: 204/945-2669
Director, Compliance, Bev Ann Murray, 204/945-4272, Fax: 204/945-6717
Director, Family Conciliation, Sandra Dean, 204/945-7235, Fax: 204/948-2142
Director, Family Dispute Services, Marlene Bertrand, 204/945-7259
Director, Seven Oaks Youth Centre, Duncan Michie, 204/339-1934

### COMMUNITY LIVING DIVISION

Asst. Deputy Minister, Martin Billinkoff, 204/945-2204, Fax: 204/945-5029
Executive Director, Adult Services, Wes Henderson, 204/945-0172, Fax: 204/945-5668
Executive Director, Regional Operations, Ron Fenwick, 204/945-2120, Fax: 204/945-0082
Director, Residential Care Licensing, Mike McKenzie, 204/945-3576, Fax: 204/944-0254
Chief Executive Officer, Manitoba Developmental Centre, Steve Bergson, 204/856-4237, Fax: 204/856-4258
Commissioner, Vulnerable Persons' Commission Office, Dr. Allen Hansen, 204/945-5039, Fax: 204/948-2603

### EMPLOYMENT & INCOME ASSISTANCE DIVISION

Associate Deputy Minister, Doug Sexsmith, 204/945-2692, Fax: 204/948-2153
Executive Director, Administration & Finance, Kim Sharman, 204/945-5600, Fax: 204/948-2153

Executive Director, Client Services, Gerry Schmidt, 204/945-2685, Fax: 204/945-0082
Director, Finance & Administration, Gerry Bosma, 204/945-3080, Fax: 204/945-2760
Director, Income Supplement Programs, Ellen Coates, 204/523-4499
Director, Information Systems, Ken Mason, 204/945-2206, Fax: 204/945-1697
Director, Investigations & Recoveries, Don Feener, 204/945-8627, Fax: 204/945-0082
Director, Municipal Cost-Sharing & Regulation, Sue Bentley, 204/945-2996, Fax: 204/945-0082
Director, Policy & Planning, Drew Perry, 204/945-2324, Fax: 204/945-2156
Director, Welfare Reform, Dan Haughey, 204/945-5795, Fax: 204/945-0082

## Manitoba FINANCE

#109, Legislative Bldg., Winnipeg MB R3C 0V8
204/945-3754; Fax: 204/945-8316; Email: minfin@leg.gov.mb.ca; URL: http://www.gov.mb.ca/finance/
Telex: 0636700391

Established in 1969 under authority of the Financial Administration Act. Responsible for central accounting, payroll & financial reporting services for the government, & central financial control of cost-shared agreements. The ministry manages government borrowing programs & is responsible for federal-provincial relations.

#### ACTS ADMINISTERED

Corporation Capital Tax Act
Crown Corporations Public Review & Accountability Act
Energy Rate Stabilization Act
Financial Administration Act
Fire Insurance Reserve Fund Act
Fiscal Stabilization Fund Act
Gasoline Tax Act
Health & Post Secondary Education Tax Levy Act
Homeowners Tax & Insulation Assistance Act (Parts I & II)
Hospital Capital Financing Authority Act
Income Tax Act (Manitoba)
Mining Claim Tax Act
Mining Tax Act
Motive Fuel Tax Act
Pari-Mutual Tax Act
Provincial-Municipal Tax Sharing Act
Public Officers Act
Retail Sales Tax Act
Revenue Act, 1964
Succession Duty Act
Suitors' Moneys Act
Tobacco Tax Act
Treasury Branches Act

**Minister**, Hon. Eric Stefanson, 249/945-3952, Fax: 249/945-6057
Deputy Minister, J. Patrick Gannon, 204/945-3754, Fax: 204/945-8316
Secretary, Treasury Board, J.D. Benson, #300, 333 Broadway, Winnipeg MB R3C 0S9, 204/945-1100, Fax: 204/945-4878
Assoc. Secretary, Treasury Board, Don Potter, 204/945-1088, Fax: 204/945-4878

#### COMPTROLLER'S DIVISION

#709, 401 York Ave., Winnipeg MB R3C 0P8
Asst. Deputy Minister, E.H. Rosenhek, 204/945-4920, Fax: 204/945-0896
Director, Disbursements & Accounting, Gerry Gaudreau

#### FEDERAL-PROVINCIAL RELATIONS & RESEARCH DIVISION

#203, 333 Broadway Ave., Winnipeg MB R3C 0S9
Asst. Deputy Minister, E. Boschmann, 204/945-3962, Fax: 204/945-5051

#### TAXATION DIVISION

401 York Ave., 4th Fl., Winnipeg MB R3C 0P8
Asst. Deputy Minister, S.J. Puchniak, 204/945-3758, Fax: 204/945-0896
Director, Audit Branch, Leon Ballegeer
Director, Tax Administration Branch, Brian Forbes
Director, Taxation Management & Research Branch, Barry Draward

#### TREASURY DIVISION

Asst. Deputy Minister, Neil S. Benditt, 204/945-3756, Fax: 204/945-1361
Director, Capital Finance, Donald Delisle
Director, Money Management & Banking, William J. Cessford
Director, Treasury Services, Donald Wood

##### Associated Agencies, Boards & Commissions

•Crown Corporations Council: #320, 530 Kenaston Blvd., Winnipeg MB R3N 1Z4 – 204/949-5270; Fax: 204/949-5283; Email: crowncc@mb.sympatico.ca
Chair, W. Mauro
President & CEO, J. Douglas Sherwood

## Manitoba GOVERNMENT SERVICES (MGS)

1700 Portage Ave., Main Fl., Winnipeg MB R3J 0E1
204/945-4800 (Administration)

The Department provides support services to all Manitoba government departments & some agencies, boards & commissions. Services include: planning, design, acquisition, construction & management of government-owned and leased properties; & acquisition, supply and management of common commodities & services such as fleet vehicles, purchasing, office equipment, inventory management, telecommunications & postal services.

#### ACTS ADMINISTERED

Emergency Measures Act
Expropriation Act
Government Air Services Act
Government House Act
Government Purchases Act
Land Acquisition Act
Public Works Act

**Minister**, Hon. Franklin P. Pitura, 204/945-2979
Deputy Minister, H.G. Eliasson, 204/945-4414, Fax: 204/945-1857
Executive Coordinator, Manitoba Emergency Management Organization, Harold Clayton, 204/945-4789, Fax: 204/945-4620, Emergencies (24 hour): 204/945-5555

#### ACCOMMODATION DEVELOPMENT DIVISION

1700 Portage Ave., 2nd Fl., Winnipeg MB R3J 0E1
Asst. Deputy Minister, Ian Robertson, 204/945-7552, Fax: 204/945-0908
Director, Corporate Accommodation Planning Branch, F. LeClair
Director, Leasing & Contracts, M. Shewchuk
Director, Technical Resources Branch, A. Lorimer

#### ADMINISTRATION & FINANCE DIVISION

Fax: 204/948-2016
Director, Finance, Vacant
Director, Human Resources, M. Brownscombe, 405 Broadway Ave., 15th Fl., Winnipeg MB R3C 3L6, 204/945-3001
Acting Manager, Information Technology Services, D. Bolger

#### PROPERTY MANAGEMENT DIVISION

Asst. Deputy Minister, Hugh Swan, 204/945-7535, Fax: 204/945-5933
Director, Physical Plant, B. Lightly

#### SUPPLY & SERVICES DIVISION

270 Osborne St. North, Winnipeg MB R3C 1V7
Asst. Deputy Minister, G.W. Berezuk, 204/945-6340, Fax: 204/945-1455
Director, Fleet Vehicles Agency, D. Ducharme, 626 Henry Ave., Winnipeg MB R3A 1P7
Director, Land Management Agency, D. Parnell, 25 Tupper St. North, Portage la Prairie MB R1N 3K1
Director, Materials Distribution, T. Danowski, 1680 Church Ave., Winnipeg MB R2X 2W9
Director, Office Equipment Services, Vacant
Director, Purchasing, E.F. Baranet, 204/945-6380, Fax: 204/245-1455
Director, Telecommunications, Vacant

##### Associated Agencies, Boards & Commissions

•Manitoba Disaster Appeals Board: 405 Broadway Ave., 15th Fl., Winnipeg MB R3C 3L6 – 204/945-3050; Fax: 204/945-4620
Chair, Sydney Reimer
•Manitoba Land Value Appraisal Commission: 800 Portage Ave., Winnipeg MB R3G 0N4 – Fax: 204/948-2235

Determines & certifies compensation for the acquisition of land by a designated authority with a power of purchase or expropriation under The Expropriation Act.

Chair, C. Harvey

## Manitoba HEALTH

599 Empress St., PO Box 925, Winnipeg MB R3C 2T6
204/786-7191 (Finance & Administration Branch); Email: minhlt@leg.gov.mb.ca; URL: http://www.gov.mb.ca/health/index.html

#### ACTS ADMINISTERED

Addictions Foundation Act
Ambulance Services Act
Anatomy Act
Cancer Treatment & Research Foundation Act
Chiropodists Act
Chiropractic Act
Dental Association Act
Dental Health Services Act
Dental Health Workers Act
Denturists Act
Department of Health Act
District Health & Social Services Act
Elderly & Infirm Persons' Housing Act (with respect to elderly persons housing units as defined in the Act)
Health Care Directives Act
(Manitoba) Health Research Council Act
Health Sciences Centre Act, 1988-89
Health Services Act
Health Services Insurance Act
Hearing Aid Act
Hospitals Act
Human Tissue Act
Licensed Practical Nurses Act
Medical Act
Mental Health Act (Except Parts II, III, & IV)
Minors Intoxicating Substances Act
Naturopathic Act
Non-Smokers Health Protection Act
Occupational Therapists Act
Ophthalmic Dispensers Act
Optometry Act
Pharmaceutical Act
Physiotherapists Act
Prescription Drugs Cost Assistance Act
Private Hospitals Act
Psychologists Registration Act

Public Health Act
Registered Dieticians Act
Registered Nurses Act
Registered Psychiatric Nurses Act
Registered Respiratory Therapists Act
Sanitorium Board of Manitoba Act
**Minister**, Hon. Darren Praznik, 204/945-3731, Fax: 204/945-0441
Deputy Minister, Frank DeCock, 204/945-3771, Fax: 204/945-4564
CEO, Children & Youth Secretariat, Doris Mae Oulton, 447 Portage Ave., 12th Fl., Winnipeg MB R3B 3H5, 204/945-6707, Fax: 204/948-2258

#### COMMUNITY & MENTAL HEALTH SERVICES DIVISION

Assoc. Deputy Minister, Sue Hicks, 204/786-7360, Fax: 204/775-3412
Chief Medical Officer, Dr. John Guilfoyle, #301, 800 Portage Ave., Winnipeg MB R3G 0N4, 204/945-6839
Registrar, Emergency Services, Lorne Charbonneau, 800 Portage Ave., Winnipeg MB R3G 0N4, 204/945-0711
Executive Director, Winnipeg Operations - Hospital Services, Sean Drain, 204/786-7138
Laboratory Director, Cadham Provincial Laboratory, Dr. Trevor Williams, 750 William Ave., PO Box 8450, Winnipeg MB R3C 3Y1, 204/946-2507
Director, Finance & Administration, Peter Todman, 800 Portage Ave., Winnipeg MB R3G 0N4, 204/945-6690, Fax: 204/948-2040
Interim Director, Home Care, Carol Renner, #205, 800 Portage Ave., Winnipeg MB R3G 0N4, 204/945-6736
Acting Director, Long Term Care, M. Redston, 800 Portage Ave., 2nd Fl., Winnipeg MB R3C 0N4, 204/945-7493, Fax: 204/948-2040
Director, Program Development, Laurie Thompson, 204/786-7312
Director, Public Health, Dr. Greg Hammond, #301, 800 Portage Ave., Winnipeg MB R3G 0N4, 204/945-6720, Fax: 204/948-2190
Acting Director, Winnipeg Region, Peter Dubienski, #5, 189 Evanson St., Winnipeg MB R3G 0N9, 204/945-3302, Fax: 204/945-1735

#### FINANCE & ADMINISTRATION DIVISION

Fax: 204/774-1325
Assoc. Deputy Minister, Don Potter, 204/786-7263, Fax: 204/775-3412
Director, Finance & Administration Branch, Susan Murphy, 204/788-2508
Director, Health Information Systems Branch, G.K. Neill, 204/786-7347
Director, Human Resources Branch, J. Morris, #602, 330 Graham Ave., Winnipeg MB R3C 4C8, 204/945-5900, Fax: 204/945-1999

#### HEALTH SERVICES INSURANCE FUND

447 Portage Ave., 12th Fl., Winnipeg MB R3B 3H5
Secretary, Manitoba Health Board, Don B. Nelson, 204/945-8875

#### MANAGEMENT & PROGRAM SUPPORT SERVICES DIVISION

Fax: 204/783-2171
Executive Director, Insured Benefits, R.H. Harvey, 204/786-7215
Director, Facilities Development Branch, L. Bakken, 800 Portage Ave., Winnipeg MB R3G 0N4, 204/945-3997
Director, Funded Accountability, W. Campbell, 599 Empress St., Winnipeg MB R3G 3H2, 204/786-7149, Fax: 204/775-3412

##### Associated Agencies, Boards & Commissions

•Drug Standards/Therapeutics Committee: #128, 599 Empress St., PO Box 925, Winnipeg MB R3C 2T6 – 204/786-7233; Fax: 204/783-2171
Secretary, Ken Brown

## Manitoba HIGHWAYS & TRANSPORTATION

215 Garry St., Winnipeg MB R3C 3Z1
204/945-3888; Fax: 204/945-7610; Email: minhwy@leg.gov.mb.ca

#### ACTS ADMINISTERED

Highways & Transportation Construction Contracts Disbursements Act
Highways & Transportation Department Act
Highway Protection Act
Highway Traffic Act
Off-Road Vehicles Act
Taxicab Act
Trans-Canada Highway Act
**Minister**, Hon. Glen Findlay, 204/945-3723
Deputy Minister, Andrew Horosko, 204/945-3768, Fax: 204/945-4766

#### ADMINISTRATIVE SERVICES DIVISION

215 Garry St., 17th Fl., Winnipeg MB R3C 3Z1
Fax: 204/945-5115
Executive Director, Paul Rochon, 204/945-3887
Director, Financial Services, F. Schnerch, 204/945-5869
Budget Coordinator, Financial Services, P. LaRue, 204/945-1996
Manager, Occupational Health & Safety, G. Mortimer, 204/945-5819

#### CONSTRUCTION & MAINTENANCE DIVISION

215 Garry St., 16th Fl., Winnipeg MB R3C 3Z1
Fax: 204/945-3841
Acting Asst. Deputy Minister, B. Tinkler, 204/945-3733
Director, Bridges & Structures, W. Saltzberg, 204/945-5058
Acting Director, Operational Services, R. Mckay, 204/945-3778
Engineer, Maintenance Management, V. Weselak, 204/945-3896
Contract Engineer, Operational Services, G. Tencha, 204/945-3776

#### DRIVER & VEHICLE LICENSING DIVISION

1075 Portage Ave., Winnipeg MB R3G 0S1
Fax: 204/948-2018
Acting Asst. Deputy Minister/Registrar, M. Zyluk, 204/945-7370
Director/Deputy Registrar, Safety, B. MacMartin, 204/945-8195
Director, Transport Safety & Regulation, D. Nelson, 204/945-8925
Acting Manager, Administration & Finance, D. Puls, 204/945-7362
Manager, Systems, A. Fulsher, 204/945-7374

#### ENGINEERING & TECHNICAL SERVICES DIVISION

215 Garry St., 14th Fl., Winnipeg MB R3C 3Z1
Fax: 204/945-5539
Asst. Deputy Minister, J. Hosang, 204/945-3772
Director, Materials & Research, R. Van Cauwenberghe, 204/945-8982, Fax: 204/945-2229
Director, Mechanical Equipment Services, C. DeBlonde, 215 Garry St., 17th Fl., Winnipeg MB R3C 3Z1, 204/945-8567, Fax: 204/945-4930
Director, Northern Airports & Marine, D. Selby, 204/945-3421
Director, Traffic Engineering, Ben Rogers, 204/945-3781
Senior Design Engineer, Highway Planning & Design, Vacant, 204/945-4089
Highway Programming Engineer, Programming, T. Curtis, 204/945-3679

#### TRANSPORTATION POLICY, PLANNING & DEVELOPMENT DIVISION

215 Garry St., 15th Fl., Winnipeg MB R3C 3Z1
Fax: 204/945-5539
Asst. Deputy Minister, Donald Norquay, 204/945-1967
Director, Corporate Services, L. Gibson, 204/945-2886
Director, Policy & Service Development, J. Spacek, 204/945-8617
Director, Systems Planning & Development, A. Chadha, 204/945-2269

#### REGIONAL OPERATIONS DIVISION

##### Region 1 (Eastern)

Steinbach Office: #316, 323 Main St., Steinbach MB R0A 2A0 – 204/326-4434; Fax: 204/326-4852, Director, B. Prentice
Selkirk: #203, 446 Main St., Selkirk MB R1A 1V7 – 204/785-5248; Fax: 204/785-5249, Maintenance Manager, R. Farrell
Winnipeg: #1, 35 Lakewood Blvd., Winnipeg MB R2J 2M8 – 204/945-8955; Fax: 204/945-6270, Construction Engineer, G. Cooper

##### Region 2 (South Central)

Portage La Prairie Office: 25 Tupper St. North, Portage La Prairie MB R1N 3K1 – 204/239-3292; Fax: 204/239-3301, Director, B. Petzold, Construction Engineer, R. McKibbin
Carman: 49 Main St., Carman MB R0G 0J0 – 204/745-2086; Fax: 204/745-3439, Maintenance Manager, A. Schollenberg

##### Region 3 (South Western)

Brandon Office: #1525, 1 St. North, Brandon MB R7C 1B5 – 204/726-6807; Fax: 204/726-6836, Director, R. Scrase
Minnedosa: 36 Center Ave. NW, 2nd Fl., Minnedosa MB R0J 1E0 – 204/867-2744; Fax: 204/867-5096, Construction Engineer, M. Robinson
Boissevain: PO Box 959, Boissevain MB R0K 0E0 – 204/534-2481; Fax: 204/534-6894, Maintenance Manager, K. Dern

##### Region 4 (West Central)

Dauphin Office: Industrial Rd., Dauphin MB R7N 3B3 – 204/622-2261; Fax: 204/638-6696, Director, A. Safronetz
Swan River: 201 - 4 Ave. South, Swan River MB R0L 1Z0 – 204/734-3413; Fax: 204/734-3886, Construction Engineer, J. Gottfried

##### Region 5 (Northern)

Thompson Office: 11 Nelson Rd., Thompson MB R8N 0B3 – 204/677-6540; Fax: 204/677-6354, Director, G. Swaine
The Pas: Otineka Mall, 2nd Fl., The Pas MB R9A 1M4 – 204/623-3803; Fax: 204/623-2893, Construction/Maintenance Engineer, R. Meisters

##### Associated Agencies, Boards & Commissions

•Highway Traffic Board: #200, 301 Weston St., Winnipeg MB R3E 3H4 – 204/945-6529; Fax: 204/783-6529
Chair, E. Penner, 204/945-8912
Secretary, H.C. Moster, 204/945-8912
•Licence Suspension Appeal Board: #206, 1075 Portage Ave., Winnipeg MB R3G 0S1 – 204/945-7350; Fax: 204/945-0653
Chair, E.R. Guenther
Secretary, D. Hallson
•Manitoba Motor Transport Board: #200, 301 Weston St., Winnipeg MB R3E 3H4 – 204/945-5915; Fax: 204/783-6529
Chair, E. Penner, 204/945-1967
Secretary, H.C. Moster, 204/945-0944
•Taxicab Board: #206, 301 Weston St., Winnipeg MB R3E 3H4 – Fax: 204/948-2315

Secretary, S. Champagne
Chair, G. Orle

## Manitoba HOUSING

#201, 280 Broadway Ave., Winnipeg MB R3C 0R8
204/945-4692; Email: minhou@leg.gov.mb.ca

#### ACTS ADMINISTERED

Elderly & Infirm Persons' Housing Act (in part)
Housing & Renewal Corporation Act
**Minister**, Hon. Jack F. Reimer, 204/945-0074
Deputy Minister, W.J. Kinnear, 204/945-4756
Director, Financial Services, H. Bos, 204/945-4703
Director, Personnel Services, S. Gaska, 204/945-4692
Manager, Client Services, P. Sanderson, 204/945-4693
Manager, Research & Planning, L. McFadyen, 204/945-4650

#### Associated Agencies, Boards & Commissions

•Manitoba Housing Authority: #303, 280 Broadway Ave., Winnipeg MB R3C 0R8 – 204/945-3935; Fax: 204/945-0546
Executive Director, R. Fallis
•Manitoba Housing & Renewal Corporation: 280 Broadway, Winnipeg MB R3C 0R8 – 204/945-4748; Fax: 204/945-1249

## Manitoba HYDRO

820 Taylor Ave., PO Box 815, Winnipeg MB R3C 2P4
204/474-3311; Fax: 204/475-9044; Email: publicaffairs@hydro.mb.ca; URL: http://www.hydro.mb.ca
**Minister Responsible**, Hon. David G. Newman, 204/945-6429
President & CEO, Bob B. Brennan, 204/474-3600
Vice-President, Customer Service & Marketing, Vince A. Warden
Vice-President, Power Supply, Al M. Snyder
Vice-President, Transmission & Distribution, F. Al Macatavish
General Counsel & Corporate Secretary, K. Doug Munro
Manager, Public Affairs, Glenn P. Schneider

## Manitoba INDUSTRY, TRADE & TOURISM (MITT)

155 Carlton St., 6th Fl., Winnipeg MB R3C 3H8
204/945-2066; Fax: 204/945-1354; Email: minitt@leg.gov.mb.ca

#### ACTS ADMINISTERED

Convention Centre Corporation Act
Cooperative Association Loans & Loans Guarantee Act
Cooperative Promotion Trust Act
Design Institute Act
Development Corporation Act
Economic Innovation & Technology Council Act
Horse Racing Commission Act
Manitoba Employee Ownership Fund Corporation & Consequential Amendments Act (Crocus Investment Fund)
Manitoba Trade & Investment Corporation Act
Statistics Act
Tourism & Recreation Act
**Minister**, Hon. James Downey, 204/945-0067, Fax: 204/945-4882
Deputy Minister, Murray Cormack, 204/945-4076, Fax: 204/945-1561
Asst. Deputy Minister, Manitoba Trade, Rod Sprange, 204/945-2420, Fax: 204/957-1793
Asst. Deputy Minister, Tourism & Business Development, Loretta Clarke, 204/945-7731, Fax: 204/945-2804
Director, Finance & Administration, Jack Dalgliesh

#### BUSINESS DEVELOPMENT BRANCH

204/945-7719; Fax: 204/945-2804
Manager, Business Services, Tony Romero, 204/945-2019
Manager, Brandon Office, George Ranson, 204/726-6253
Manager, Information Services, Gord Kraemer, 204/945-7734
Consultant, Aboriginal Projects, Janet Fontaine, 204/945-2449
Business Start-up Officer, Mary Fox, 204/945-7720
Cooperative Development Officer, Al Charr, 204/945-4451
Mobile Business Services Officer, Roland Lavalle, 204/945-4025
Women's Entrepreneurship Officer, Marilyn Gault, 204/945-6942

#### BUSINESS LIBRARY

Fax: 204/945-2804
Manager, John Giesbrecht, 204/945-2036
Records Officer, Jane Bullied, 204/945-2057

#### ECONOMIC INITIATIVE PAN AMERICAN GAMES

Fax: 204/943-0031
Executive Director, Hubert Mesman, 204/945-4204

#### FINANCIAL SERVICES

204/945-2770; Fax: 204/945-1193
Director, Ian Robertson, 204/945-2472
Asst. Director, Jim Kilgour, 204/945-7626

#### INDUSTRY DEVELOPMENT

204/945-7206; Fax: 204/945-3977
Director, Consulting Services, Nigel Lilley, 204/945-7343
Manager, Steve Davidge, 204/945-1056
Manager, David Sprange, 204/945-7938

#### MANITOBA BUREAU OF STATISTICS

#333, 260 St. Mary Ave., Winnipeg MB R3C 0M6
204/945-2999; Fax: 204/945-0695
Director, Wilf Falk, 204/945-2988
Head, Statistical Services, D. Greenwood, 204/945-2989

#### MANITOBA CALL CENTRE TEAM

204/945-6507; Fax: 204/943-0031
Executive Vice-President, Stephen Demmings, 204/945-0701

#### MANITOBA TRADE/MANITOBA TRADING CORPORATION

155 Carlton St., 4th Fl., Winnipeg MB R3C 3H8
204/945-2466; Fax: 204/957-1793
Manager, Operations, Carol Cowles, 204/945-2445
Director, Bob Dilay, 204/945-8695
Director, Garry Hastings, 204/945-1454

#### RESEARCH & ECONOMIC SERVICES

204/945-8836; Fax: 204/945-1354
Director, A. Barber, 204/945-8714

#### TOURISM

204/945-3796; Fax: 204/945-2302; URL: http://www.gov.mb.ca/manitoba/itt/travel/explore/
Toll Free: 1-800-665-0040
Manager, Tourism Development, Henry Goy, 204/945-2307
Manager, Tourism Marketing & Promotion, Danita Schmidtke, 204/945-2392
Manager, Tourism Services, Ken Hildebrand, 204/945-8773
Clerk, Master Angler Program, J. Kosie, 204/945-4254

#### Associated Agencies, Boards & Commissions

•Economic Development Board Secretariat: #648, 155 Carlton St., Winnipeg MB R3C 3H8 – 204/945-8221; Fax: 204/945-8229; URL: http://www.gov.mb.ca/manitoba/board/board.html
Secretary, Vacant, 204/945-1116
•Economic Innovation & Technology Council: #648, 155 Carlton St., Winnipeg MB R3C 3H8 – 204/945-5940; Fax: 204/945-8229; URL: http://www.eitc.mb.ca/eitc.html
Vice-President, John Clarkson
•Manitoba Development Corporation
Listed alphabetically in detail, this Section.
•Manitoba Horse Racing Commission: PO Box 46086, Winnipeg MB R3R 3S3
Chair, Wayne Anderson, 204/885-7770
Office Supervisor, Helen Penner, 204/885-7770

## Manitoba INFORMATION SERVICES

#29, Legislative Bldg., 450 Broadway, Winnipeg MB R3C 0V8
204/945-3746; Fax: 204/945-3988
Provides news releases & television & radio news items.
**Minister Responsible**, Hon. Rosemary Vodrey, 204/945-3729, Fax: 204/945-5223
Director, Dwight MacAulay
Media Specialist, Carla McLeod
Television Editor, T. Proveda

#### CITIZENS' INQUIRY SERVICE

#511, 401 York Ave., Winnipeg MB R3C 0P8
204/945-3744; Fax: 204/945-4261
Toll Free: 1-800-282-8060, TDD: 204/945-4796
Answers queries regarding Manitoba's provincial & federal government departments & agencies.
Manager, Liliana Romanowski

## Manitoba Public INSURANCE

234 Donald St., 9th Fl., PO Box 6300, Winnipeg MB R3C 4A4
204/985-7000; Fax: 204/943-9851
Administers Manitoba's Public Automobile Insurance Program & sells extension auto coverage on a competitive basis.
**President & General Manager**, J.W. Zacharias
Vice-President, Claims, W.L. Bedard
Manager, Corporate Communications, J.W. Kingdon, 204/985-8247, Fax: 204/942-2216
Vice-President, Corporate Resources, R.B. Best
Vice-President, Customer Relations, K.M. McCulloch
Vice-President, Finance & Corporate Information Systems, B.W. Galenzoski
Vice-President, Insurance Operations, D.R. Kidd

## Manitoba JUSTICE

405 Broadway, 5th Fl., Winnipeg MB R3C 3L6
204/945-2852; Email: minjus@leg.gov.mb.ca

#### ACTS ADMINISTERED

Canada-United Kingdom Judgements Enforcement Act
Condominium Act (Sections 2 & 3 - with respect to the division of land, Sections 4 & 5 with respect to registration requirements, Section 6 & subsection 7[1])
Constitutional Questions Act
Corrections Act
Court of Appeal Act
Court of Queens' Bench Act
Crime Prevention Foundation Act
Criminal Injuries Compensation Act
Crown Attorneys Act
Child Custody Enforcement Act
Department of Justice Act
Discriminatory Business Practices Act
Escheats Act
Executive Government Organization Act (Subsection 12(2), only, as Keeper of the Great Seal)

Expropriation Act
Fatality Inquiries Act
Hudson's Bay Company Land Register Act
Human Rights Code
International Commercial Arbitration Act
International Sale of Goods Act
Interprovincial Subpoena Act
Intoxicated Persons Detention Act
Jury Act
Justice for Victims of Crime Act
Law Enforcement Review Act
Law Fees Act
Manitoba Women's Advisory Council Act
Mental Health Act (Part IV)
Minors Intoxicating Substances Control Act
Personal Property Security Act
Privacy Act
Private Investigators & Security Guards Act
Proceeding Against in the Crown Act
Provincial Court Act
Provincial Police Act
Public Trustee Act
Real Property Act
Reciprocal Enforcement of Judgement Act
Registry Act
Regulations Act
Sheriffs Act
Special Survey Act
Summary Convictions Act
Surveys Act (Part I)
Transboundary Pollution Reciprocal Access Act
Uniform Law Conference Commissioners Act
Vacant Property Act

**Minister & Attorney General**, Hon. Victor E. Toews, Q.C., 204/945-3728, Fax: 204/945-2517
Deputy Minister & Deputy Attorney General, Bruce MacFarlane, 204/945-3739, Fax: 204/945-4133, Email: dmjus@leg.gov.mb.ca
Executive Director, Administration & Finance Division, P. Sinnott, 204/945-2880

#### CORRECTIONS DIVISION

405 Broadway, 8th Fl., Winnipeg MB R3C 3L6
Asst. Deputy Minister, G. Graceffo, 204/945-7291, Fax: 204/945-5537
Executive Director, Adult Correctional Services, Jim Wolfe, 204/945-7307
Executive Director, Community & Youth Correctional Services, L. Goulet, 204/945-7891, Fax: 204/948-2166
Manager, Fine Option Program, Tom Jennings, 204/945-7894, Fax: 204/488-4173

#### COURTS DIVISION

405 Broadway, 2nd Fl., Winnipeg MB R3C 3L6
Asst. Deputy Minister, M.W.G. Bruce, 204/945-2049

#### JUSTICE DIVISION

405 Broadway, 7th Fl., Winnipeg MB R3C 3L6
204/945-2832
Associate Deputy Attorney General, R. Perozzo, 204/945-2847
Director, Civil Legal Services, T. Hague, 204/945-2846
Deputy Director, Civil Legal Services, N.D. Shende, 204/945-2837
Director, Constitutional Law Branch, Donna Miller, 204/945-0716
Director, Family Law Branch, Joan MacPhail, 204/945-2841
Public Trustee, Office of the Public Trustee, Irene Hamilton, 204/945-2703

#### LEGISLATIVE COUNSEL & LEGAL TRANSLATION DIVISION

405 Broadway, 4th Fl., Winnipeg MB R3C 3L6
204/945-5758
Legislative Counsel & Asst. Deputy Attorney General, Shirley Strutt, 204/945-3708
Director, Legal Translation, Michel Nantel, 204/945-4597

#### PUBLIC PROSECUTIONS DIVISION

[illegible]
Asst. Deputy Attorney General, A. [illegible], 204/945-2873
Director, Prosecutions, Rob Finlayson, 204/945-2860
General Counsel, Gregg Lawlor, 204/945-2870
General Counsel, Rick Saull, 204/945-2863
Coordinator, Victim/Witness Assistance Program, Margaret Bilash, 408 York Ave., 4th Fl., Winnipeg MB R3C 0P9, 204/945-2303
Chief Medical Examiner, Dr. Peter Markesteyn, Office of the Chief Medical Examiner, #210, 1 Wesley Ave., Winnipeg MB R3C 4A5, 204/945-0571

**For list of Courts & other Legal Offices, including Judicial Officials & Judges *see* Section 10 of this book.**

##### Associated Agencies, Boards & Commissions

•Board of Review: 408 York St., 2nd Fl., Winnipeg MB R3C 3L6 – 204/945-4438; Fax: 204/945-1260
Secretary, M.A. Ewatski
•Criminal Injuries Compensation Board: 763 Portage Ave., Winnipeg MB R3G 3N2 – 204/775-7821; Fax: 204/784-1452
Executive Director, A. Lovell
•Human Rights Commission: #301, 259 Portage Ave., Winnipeg MB R3B 2A9 – 204/945-3007; Fax: 204/945-1292, TDD: 945-3442
Executive Director, Diane Scarth, 204/945-3020
•Law Enforcement Review Agency: 405 Broadway, 14th Fl., Winnipeg MB R3C 3L6 – 204/945-8667; Fax: 204/945-6692
Commissioner, Norm Ralph, 204/945-8696
•Legal Aid Manitoba: #402, 294 Portage Ave., Winnipeg MB R3C 0B9 – 204/985-8505; Fax: 204/944-8582
Executive Director, R. Klassen, 204/945-8510

## Manitoba LABOUR

#156, Legislative Bldg., 450 Broadway, Winnipeg MB R3C 0V8
204/945-4039 (Deputy Minister); URL: http://www.gov.mb.ca/labour/

#### ACTS ADMINISTERED

Amusements Act (Part II)
Buildings & Mobile Homes Act
Construction Industry Wages Act
Department of Labour Act
Electricians' Licence Act
Elevator Act
Employment Services Act
Employment Standards Act
Fire Departments Arbitration Act
Fires Prevention Act (Part II)
Gas & Oil Burner Act
Labour Relations Act
Municipal Act (sections 301-314)
Pay Equity Act
Payment of Wages Act
Pension Benefits Act
Power Engineers Act
Remembrance Day Act
Retail Business Holiday Closing Act
Steam & Pressure Plants Act
Vacations with Pay Act
Workers Compensation Act (as it relates to Worker Advisors, s 108)
Workplace Safety & Health Act

**Minister**, Hon. Harold Gilleshammer, 204/945-4079, Fax: 204/945-8312, Email: minlab@leg.gov.mb.ca
Deputy Minister, Tom Farrell, 204/945-4039, Fax: 204/945-8312, Email: tfarrell@labour.gov.mb.ca

#### EMPLOYMENT STANDARDS DIVISION

URL: http://www.gov.mb.ca/labour/standards/index.html
Executive Director, Jim McFarlane, 204/945-3354, Fax: [illegible]
Manager, Worker Advisor Office, Terry Hampson, 204/945-4211, Fax: 204/948-2020

#### LABOUR/MANAGEMENT SERVICES DIVISION

Asst. Deputy Minister, Jim Nykoluk, 204/945-8446, Fax: 204/948-2085
Director, Conciliation & Mediation Services, Al Fleury, 204/945-3360, Email: afleury@labour.gov.mb.ca
Director, Financial Services, J. Wood, 204/945-3409
Director, Human Resources & Acting Director, Information Systems, Ken Kowalski, 204/945-3316, Fax: 204/948-2085, Email: kkowalski@labour.gov.mb.ca
Director, Legislation & Policy Coordination, P. Bonin, 204/945-2352
Manager, Research Branch, Glenda Segal, 204/945-4889, Fax: 204/948-2085, Email: gsegal@labour.gov.mb.ca

#### WORKPLACE SAFETY & HEALTH DIVISION

#200, 401 York Ave., Winnipeg MB R3C 0P8
204/945-3446; Fax: 204/945-4556; URL: http://www.gov.mb.ca/labour/safety/index.html
Executive Director, Geoff Bawden, 204/945-3605, Email: gbawden@labour.gov.mb.ca
Director, Mechanical & Engineering, Wayne Mault, 204/945-3507, Fax: 204/948-2309, Email: wmault@labour.gov.mb.ca
Director, Mines Inspection Branch, J.E. (Ted) Hewitt, 204/682-1621, Email: ehewitt@mb.sympatico.ca
Director, Mining Special Projects & Approvals, Kesari Reddy, 204/945-0848, Email: kreddy@labour.gov.mb.ca
Director, Workplace Safety & Health Branch, Garry Hildebrand, 204/945-3602, Email: ghildebrand@labour.gov.mb.ca
Chief Medical Officer, Occupational Health Branch, Dr. Ted Redekop, 204/945-3608, Email: tredekop@labour.gov.mb.ca

##### Associated Agencies, Boards & Commissions

•Advisory Council on Workplace Safety & Health: #200, 401 York Ave., Winnipeg MB R3C 0P8 – 204/945-3446; Fax: 204/945-4556
Chair, W.N. Fox-Decent
•Manitoba Civil Service Commission: #935, 155 Carlton St., Winnipeg MB R3C 3H8 – 204/945-4088; Fax: 204/945-1486; Email: rdilts@csc.gov.mb.ca
Commissioner, Paul Hart
•Manitoba Labour Board: A.A. Heaps Bldg., #402, 254-258 Portage Ave., Winnipeg MB R3C 0B6 – 204/945-5873; Fax: 204/945-1296
Chair, John Korpesho, Email: korpesho@labour.gov.mb.ca
•Office of the Fire Commissioner
Fax: 204/948-2089
Commissioner, Doug Popowich, 204/945-3328, Email: dpopowic@labour.gov.mb.ca
Deputy Fire Commissioner, Chuck Sanderson, 204/945-0453, Email: csanderson@labour.gov.mb.ca
•Pension Commission
Superintendent, Pension Commission, Guy Gordon, 204/945-2742, Fax: 204/945-2375, Email: ggordon@labour.gov.mb.ca

## Manitoba NATURAL RESOURCES

#327, Legislative Bldg., Winnipeg MB R3C 0V8
204/945-4071; Fax: 204/945-3586; Email: minnr@leg.gov.mb.ca; URL: http://www.gov.mb.ca/natres/index.html

#### ACTS ADMINISTERED

Crown Lands Act
Dutch Elm Disease Act

Dyking Authority Act
Ecological Reserves Act
Endangered Species Act
Fires Prevention Act (Part I)
Fisheries Act (Part III)
Fisherman's Assistance & Polluters' Liability Act
Forest Act
Ground Water & Water Well Act
International Peace Garden Act
Lake of the Woods Control Board Act
Manitoba Fishery Regulations (Section 34 of the Fisheries Act, Canada)
Manitoba Habitat Heritage Act
Manitoba Natural Resources Development Act
Manitoba Natural Resources Transfer Act
Natural Resources Agreement Amendment Act, 1938
Provincial Park Lands Act
Provincial Parks Act
Rivers & Streams Act
Surveys Act (Part II)
Tourism & Recreation Act
Water Commission Act
Water Power Act
Water Resources Administration Act
Water Rights Act
Water Supply Commissions Act
Wildlife Act
Wild Rice Act
**Minister**, Hon. J. Glen Cummings
Deputy Minister, David Tomasson, 204/945-3785, Fax: 204/948-2403

#### HEADQUARTERS OPERATIONS
200 Salteaux Cr., Winnipeg MB R3J 3W3
Asst. Deputy Minister, Harvey J. Boyle, 204/945-4842, Fax: 204/945-3125
Director, Wayne Fisher, 204/945-6647, Fax: 204/945-7782

#### LAND INFORMATION CENTRE
1007 Century St., Winnipeg MB R3H 0W4
Executive Director, Jack Schreuder, 204/945-6613, Fax: 204/945-1365
Director, Surveys Branch, Wayne Leeman, 204/945-0011, Fax: 204/945-1365

#### MANAGEMENT SERVICES DIVISION
1577 Dublin Ave., Winnipeg MB R3E 3J5
Executive Director, W.J. Podolsky, 204/945-4056, Fax: 204/945-2385
Director, Financial Services, Peter J. Lockett, 204/945-4187, Fax: 204/945-2385
Director, Human Resource Services, Lorraine Metz, 204/945-2810, Fax: 204/948-2159
Director, Resource Information Systems, Kerry Poole, 200 Saulteaux Crescent, PO Box 90, Winnipeg MB R3J 3W3, 204/945-2929, Fax: 204/945-4232

#### RESOURCES DIVISION
200 Saulteaux Cres., PO Box 20, Winnipeg MB R3J 3W3
Fisheries URL: http://www.gov.mb.ca/natres/fish/fish.html; Forestry URL: http://www.gov.mb.ca/natres/forestry/forestry.html; Parks URL: http://www.gov.mb.ca/natres/parks/homepage.html;
Asst. Deputy Minister, Dr. Merlin Shoesmith, 204/945-6829, Fax: 204/945-3125
Director, Fisheries Branch, Joe O'Connor, 204/945-7814, Fax: 204/945-2308
Director, Forestry Branch, Arthur Hoole, 200 Saulteaux Crescent, PO Box 70, Winnipeg MB R3J 3W3, 204/945-7998, Fax: 204/948-2671
Acting Director, Lands Branch, Bryan Sheridan, 204/476-3441, Fax: 204/476-2097
Director, Parks & Natural Areas Branch, Gordon Prouse, 200 Saulteaux Cr., PO Box 50, Winnipeg MB R3J 3W3, 204/945-4362, Fax: 204/945-0012
Director, Policy Coordination Branch, Grant Baker, 200 Saulteaux Cr., PO Box 38, Winnipeg MB R3J 3W3, 204/945-6658, Fax: 204/945-4552
Director, Water Resources Branch, Steven Topping, 1577 Dublin Ave., Winnipeg MB R3E 3J5, 204/945-7488, Fax: 204/945-7419
Director, Wildlife Branch, Brian Gillespie, 200 Saulteaux Cr., PO Box 24, Winnipeg MB R3J 3W3, 204/945-7761, Fax: 204/945-3077

##### Associated Agencies, Boards & Commissions
•Assiniboine River Management Advisory Board: 200 Saulteaux Cr., PO Box 70, Winnipeg MB R3J 3W3 – 204/945-7950
Chair, Vacant
•Ecological Reserves Advisory Committee: PO Box 355, Stn St. Vital, Winnipeg MB R2M 5C8 – 204/942-6617
Chair, David Hatch
•Endangered Species Advisory Committee: 200 Saulteaux Cr., PO Box 80, Winnipeg MB R3J 3W3 – 204/945-6829
Chair, Dr. Merlin Shoesmith
•Lake of the Woods Control Board: c/o Ontario Hydro, 700 University Ave., Toronto ON M5G 1X6
Chair, Joan Eaton
•Lower Red River Valley Water Commission: PO Box 1180, Altona MB R0G 0B0 – 204/324-8365
Chair, R. Martel
•Manitoba Habitat Heritage Board: #200, 1555 St. James St., Winnipeg MB R3H 1B5 – 204/784-4350
Chair, Ted Poyser
•Prairie Provinces Water Board: #201, 2050 Cornwall St., Regina SK S4P 2K5 – 306/522-6671
Chair, Jim Vollmershausen
•Saskeram Wildlife Management Area Advisory Committee: PO Box 2550, The Pas MB R9A 1M4 – 204/627-8266
Chair, R.C. Uchtmann
•Souris River Water Commission: PO Box 399, Hartney MB R0M 0X0 – 204/858-2590
Chair, Wayne Drummond

## Manitoba NORTHERN AFFAIRS
59 Elizabeth Dr., PO Box 37, Thompson MB R8N 1X4
204/677-6607; Fax: 204/677-6753; Email: sfrank@norcom.mb.ca

#### ACTS ADMINISTERED
Communities Economic Development Act
Manitoba Natural Resources Development Act
Northern Affairs Act
Planning Act
**Minister**, #314, Legislative Bldg., 450 Broadway Ave., Winnipeg MB R3C 0V8, Hon. David G. Newman, 204/945-6429, Fax: 204/945-8374
Deputy Minister, Michael Fine, #314, Legislative Bldg., 450 Broadway Ave., Winnipeg MB R3C 0V8, 204/945-4172, Fax: 204/945-8374, Email: dmem@leg.gov.mb.ca
Executive Director, Administration & Finance, Rene Gagnon, 204/677-6609, Email: rgagnon@norcom.mb.ca

#### LOCAL GOVERNMENT DEVELOPMENT DIVISION
Asst. Deputy Minister, Oliver Boulette, 204/677-6795, Fax: 204/677-6525, Email: oboulette@norcom.mb.ca
Director, Inter Regional Services, M. Duval, 204/677-6829, Fax: 204/677-6525
Director, Technical Services, C. Boyd, 204/677-6683, Fax: 204/677-6525

##### Regional Offices
Dauphin: Provincial Bldg., 27 Second Ave. SW, Dauphin MB R7N 3E5 – 204/622-2152; Fax: 204/622-2305, Regional Director, J. Perchaluk
Selkirk: Rami Bldg., 339A Main St., Selkirk MB R1A 1T3 – 204/785-5089; Fax: 204/785-5218, Regional Director, J. Gordon
Thompson: Provincial Bldg., 59 Elizabeth Dr., PO Box 27, Thompson MB R8N 1X4 – 204/677-6737; Fax: 204/677-6753, Regional Director, K. Barker

##### Agreements Management & Coordination
#200, 500 Portage Ave., Winnipeg MB R3C 3X1
Director, Jeff Polakoff, 204/945-2507, Fax: 204/945-3689, Email: jpolakof@gov.mb.ca
Provincial Coordinator, Northern Flood, B. Ketcheson, 204/945-2511, Fax: 204/945-3689

##### Native Affairs Secretariat
Director, Harvey Bostrom, 204/945-0572, Fax: 204/945-3689, Email: hbostrom@na.gov.mb.ca

##### Associated Agencies, Boards & Commissions
•Communities Economic Development Fund: 23 Station Rd., Thompson MB R8N 0N6 – 204/778-4138; Fax: 204/778-4313, Toll Free: 1-800-561-4315
General Manager, G. Wakeling
Administrative Asst., M. Beckmann

## Manitoba Office of the OMBUDSMAN
#750, 500 Portage Ave., Winnipeg MB R3C 3X1
204/786-6483; Fax: 204/942-7803
Toll Free: 1-800-665-0531
**Provincial Ombudsman**, Barry E. Tuckett
Officer Manager, Laura Foster

## Manitoba RURAL DEVELOPMENT
#301, 450 Broadway, Winnipeg MB R3C 0V8
Fax: 204/945-1383; Email: mnrd@leg.gov.mb.ca

#### ACTS ADMINISTERED
Conservation Districts Act
Local Authorities Election Act
Local Government Districts Act
Municipal Act
Municipal Affairs Administration Act
Municipal Assessment Act
Municipal Board Act
Municipal Council Conflict of Interest Act
Municipal Debt Adjustment Act
Municipal Works Assistance Act
Official Time Act
Planning Act
Soldiers' Taxation Relief Act
Surface Rights Act
Unconditional Grants Act
Water Services Board Act
**Minister**, Hon. Len Derkach, 204/945-3788, Fax: 204/945-1383
Deputy Minister, Winston Hodgins, 204/945-3787, Fax: 204/945-5255
Chief, Financial Services, Brian Johnston, 204/945-2199
Administrator, Personnel, Zinovia Solomon, 204/945-2147

#### LOCAL GOVERNMENT SERVICES DIVISION
#609, 800 Portage Ave., Winnipeg MB R3G ON4
Asst. Deputy Minister, Marie Elliott, 204/945-2533, Fax: 204/945-0673
Executive Director, Local Government Support Services, Roger Dennis, 204/945-2567, Fax: 204/948-2780
Provincial Municipal Assessor, Assessment Branch, K. Graham, 204/945-2605, Fax: 204/945-1994
Director, Information Systems, Larry Phillips, 204/945-2585, Fax: 204/945-1994
Coordinator, Municipal Services, Fred Butler, 204/945-2570, Fax: 204/945-1994

#### RURAL ECONOMIC DEVELOPMENT DIVISION
204/945-6258
Asst. Deputy Minister, Larry Martin, 204/945-3089, Fax: 204/945-0673
General Manager, Infrastructure Services (Manitoba Water Services Board), Dick Menon, 2022 Currie Blvd., PO Box 22080, Brandon MB R7A 6Y9, 204/726-6073, Fax: 204/726-6290
Director, Community Economic Development Branch, Peter Mah, 204/945-2192, Fax: 204/945-5059
Director, Corporate Planning & Business Development, Ron Riopka, 204/945-2595, Fax: 204/945-5059
Director, Rural Economic Development Initiative (REDI), John Melymick, 204/945-2165, Fax: 204/945-5059
Director, Small Business & Community Support Branch, Paul Staats, 204/945-4236, Fax: 204/945-3769

#### Manitoba Conservation Districts Commission
Legislative Bldg., #309, 450 Broadway Ave., Winnipeg MB R3C 0V8
204/945-7496; Fax: 204/945-5059
Chair, Winston Hodgins, 204/945-3787
Secretary, Lyle Duguay

#### Conservation Districts
Alonsa: PO Box 33, Alonsa MB R0H 0A0 – 204/767-2044; Fax: 204/767-2301, Manager, Harry Harris
Cooks Creek: 530 Main St., PO Box 100, Oakbank MB R0E 1J0 – 204/444-3652; Fax: 204/444-3652, Manager, B. Lussier
Pembina Valley: 261 Main St., PO Box 659, Manitou MB R0G 1G0 – 204/242-3267; Fax: 204/242-3281, Manager, C. Greenfield
Turtle Mountain: 129 Broadway North, PO Box 508, Deloraine MB R0M 0M0 – 204/747-2530; Fax: 204/747-2956, Manager, Gary Davis
Turtle River Watershed: PO Box 449, Ste. Rose du Lac MB R0L 1S0 – 204/447-2139; Fax: 204/447-2837, Manager, M. Boychuk
Upper Assiniboine River: PO Box 223, Miniota MB R0M 1M0 – 204/567-3554; Fax: 204/567-3587, Manager, M. Kopytko
West Souris River: PO Box 339, Reston MB R0M 1X0 – 204/877-3020; Fax: 204/877-3090, Manager, Glen Campbell
Whitemud Watershed: PO Box 130, Neepawa MB R0J 1H0 – 204/476-5019; Fax: 204/476-2811, Manager, S.W. Hildebrand

#### Associated Agencies, Boards & Commissions
•Manitoba Municipal Board: #408, 800 Portage Ave., Winnipeg MB R3G 0N4 – 204/945-1789; Fax: 204/948-2235
Chair, Robert Smellie, Q.C.
•Manitoba Surface Rights Board (MSRB): 2022 Currie Blvd., PO Box 22080, Brandon MB R7A 6Y9 – 204/726-7026; Fax: 204/726-6290
Presiding Member, Thomas A. Cowan
•Manitoba Water Services Board: 2022 Currie Blvd., PO Box 1059, Brandon MB R7A 6A3 – 204/726-6076; Fax: 204/726-6290

## Manitoba SENIORS DIRECTORATE
#822, 155 Carlton St., Winnipeg MB R3C 3H8
204/945-2127; Fax: 204/948-2514
**Minister Responsible**, Hon. Jack F. Reimer, 204/945-0074, Fax: 204/945-1299
Executive Director, Kathy Yurkowski

#### Associated Agencies, Boards & Commissions
•Manitoba Council on Aging:Program Consultant, Gerontology, B. Kyle, 204/945-8731

## Manitoba TELECOM SERVICES (MTS)
489 Empress St., Winnipeg MB R3C 3V6
204/941-4111; Fax: 204/772-6391; URL: http://www.mts.mb.ca/
**Chair**, Tom Stefanson
President & CEO, Bill Fraser
Executive Vice-President, Roger Ballance
Vice-President, Finance, Cheryl Barker
Director, Communications, June Kirby

## Manitoba TREASURY BOARD
#200, 386 Broadway, 3rd Fl., Winnipeg MB R3C 3R6
204/945-1101; Fax: 204/948-2358
**Chair**, Hon. Eric Stefanson
Secretary, Julian Benson

## Manitoba URBAN AFFAIRS
#203, 280 Broadway Ave., Winnipeg MB R3C 0R8
Fax: 204/945-1249; Email: minua@leg.gov.mb.ca

#### ACTS ADMINISTERED
City of Winnipeg Act
**Minister**, Hon. Jack F. Reimer, 204/945-0074, Fax: 204/945-1299
Deputy Minister, W.J. Kinnear, 204/945-4278, Fax: 204/948-2555
Asst. Deputy Minister, Heather MacKnight, 204/945-3872
Director, Urban Government & Finance, Marianne Farag, 204/945-4690
Senior Coordinator, Urban Finance, Jon Gunn, 204/945-3864
Senior Urban Policy Coordinator, Ray Klassen, 204/945-3866

## Manitoba WORKERS' COMPENSATION BOARD
333 Maryland St., Winnipeg MB R3G 1M2
204/786-5471; Fax: 204/786-3704
Toll Free: 1-800-362-3340 (Manitoba)
**Chair & CEO**, Prof. Wally Fox-Decent

# COUNCIL OF MARITIME PREMIERS (CMP)

Council Secretariat, #1006, 5161 George St., PO Box 2044, Halifax NS B3J 2Z1
902/424-7590; Fax: 902/424-8976; Email: premiers@fox.nstn.ns.ca
**Council Secretary**, Keith Wornell
Information Officer, Kim Thomson

The Premiers of New Brunswick, Nova Scotia & Prince Edward Island constitute the Council. It was established by identical legislation in the three provinces to: promote unity of purpose among their respective Governments; ensure maximum coordination of the activities of the Governments & their agencies &; establish a framework for joint action & undertakings. The Council meets at least four times annually to discuss matters of mutual interest or concern to the three Maritime governments. A Secretariat acts as the focal point for coordinating the efforts of the three Governments in identifying potential benefits that could result from a regional approach to policy formulation & program development.

#### ATLANTIC PROVINCES EDUCATION FOUNDATION
PO Box 2044, Halifax NS B3J 2Z1
902/424-5352; Fax: 902/424-8976; Email: premiers@fox.nstn.ns.ca
Secretary, Barbara Murray

Coordinates efforts of the four provincial Departments of Education in the development of common curriculum & educational materials for the Atlantic region with a view to increasing the effectiveness & efficiency of the four systems.

#### MARITIME MUNICIPAL TRAINING & DEVELOPMENT BOARD
6100 University Ave., Halifax NS B3H 3J5
902/494-3712, 494-1463; URL: http://ccn.cs.dal.ca/Government/MMTDB/mmtdb-intro.html
Executive Director, A. Donald Smeltzer

In cooperation with municipal associations & local governments, this agency is dedicated to upgrading the administrative capability of municipal employees by encouraging the coordination of efforts & assisting in the establishment of new programs & initiatives.

#### MARITIME PROVINCES HARNESS RACING COMMISSION
Harbour Quay Bldg., #7, 263 Harbour Dr., Summerside PE C1N 5P1
902/888-3489; Fax: 902/888-2762
Director, Ted Andrews

To govern & regulate harness racing in the Maritime provinces.

#### MARITIME PROVINCES HIGHER EDUCATION COMMISSION (MPHEC)
PO Box 6000, Fredericton NB E3B 5H1
506/453-2844; Fax: 506/453-2106
Acting Chair, Barbara Murray

An advisory body which assists the provinces & the post-secondary institutions in attaining a more efficient & effective utilization & allocation of resources in the field of higher education.

# GOVERNMENT OF NEW BRUNSWICK

**Seat of Government:** Legislative Bldg., Legislative Bldg., PO Box 6000, Fredericton NB E3B 5H1
URL: http://www.gov.nb.ca/
The Province of New Brunswick entered Confederation July 1, 1867. It has an area of 71,569.23 km2, and the StatsCan census population in 1996 was 738,133.

## Office of the LIEUTENANT GOVERNOR
736 King St., PO Box 6000, Fredericton NB E3B 5H1
506/453-2505; Fax: 506/444-5280
**Lieutenant Governor**, Hon. Marilyn Trenholme Counsell
Principal Secretary, Corinne Norrad

## Office of the PREMIER
Centennial Bldg., 670 King St., PO Box 6000, Fredericton NB E3B 5H1
506/453-2144; Fax: 506/453-7407; Email: premier@gov.nb.ca
**Premier**, Hon. J. Raymond Frenette
Deputy Minister, Georgio Gaudet
Executive Asst. to the Premier, Ruth McCrea
Director, Communications, Maurice Robichaud

## EXECUTIVE COUNCIL
Centennial Bldg., PO Box 6000, Fredericton NB E3B 5H1
Premier, President, Executive Council & Government House Leader, Hon. J. Raymond Frenette, 506/457-6757, Fax: 506/453-2266
Solicitor General, Hon. Jane Barry, 506/453-7414, Fax: 506/453-3870, Email: jbarry@gov.nb.ca

Minister, Finance & Minister of State for Quality, Hon. Edmond Blanchard, Q.C., 506/453-2451, Fax: 506/457-4989, Email: blanchard@gov.nb.ca
Minister, Municipalities, Culture & Housing, Hon. Ann Breault, 506/457-7866, Fax: 506/453-7478, Email: annb@gov.nb.ca
Minister of State, Mines & Energy, Hon. Greg Byrne
Minister of State, Literacy & Adult Education & Minister of State, Youth, Hon. Georgie Day, 506/457-6734, Fax: 506/444-5245, Email: gday@gov.nb.ca
Minister, Fisheries & Aquaculture, Hon. Danny Gay, 506/453-2662, Fax: 506/453-5210
Minister, Natural Resources & Energy, Hon. Alan Graham, 506/453-2510, Fax: 506/453-2930
Minister of State, Rural Development, Hon. Stuart Jamieson, 506/453-2448, Email: jamieson@gov.nb.ca
Minister, Health & Community Services, Hon. Russell H.T. King, M.D., 506/453-2581, Fax: 506/453-5243
Minister, Environment, Hon. Joan Kingston, 506/453-2558, Fax: 506/453-3777
Minister, Supply & Services, Hon. Peter LeBlanc
Minister, Transportation, Hon. Sheldon Lee, 506/453-2559, Fax: 506/457-3596
Minister, Justice & Attorney General, Hon. James Lockyer, Q.C., 506/453-2523, Fax: 506/457-4810, Email: jamesl@gov.nb.ca
Minister, Advanced Education & Labour, Hon. Roland MacIntyre, 506/453-2342
Minister, Human Resources Development & Minister Responsible, Status of Women, Hon. Marcelle Mersereau, 506/457-7866, Fax: 506/453-2164, Email: marcellm@gov.nb.ca
Minister, Education, Hon. Bernard Richard, 506/444-5077, Fax: 506/444-5420, Email: bernardr@gov.nb.ca
Minister Responsible, Regional Development Corporation & Northern Development, Hon. Jean Paul Savoie, 506/453-8521, Fax: 506/453-7988, Email: jeanps@gov.nb.ca
Minister, Intergovernmental & Aboriginal Affairs, Hon. Bernard Thériault, 506/453-2662, Fax: 506/453-3402, Email: bernart@gov.nb.ca
Minister, Economic Development & Tourism & Minister Responsible, Information Highway Secretariat, Hon. Camille Thériault, 506/453-3009, Email: cth@gov.nb.ca
Minister, Agriculture & Rural Development & Deputy Government House Leader, Hon. Doug Tyler, 506/453-2448, Fax: 506/444-5022

#### Executive Council Office

Fax: 506/453-2266
Clerk, Executive Council & Secretary, Cabinet, Claire Morris, 506/453-2718
Asst. Clerk, Executive Council & Asst. Secretary, Cabinet, Judith E. Nicholls, 506/453-2985

## LEGISLATIVE ASSEMBLY

c/o Clerk's Office, Legislative Bldg., PO Box 6000, Fredericton NB E3B 5H1
506/453-2506; Fax: 506/453-7154; URL: http://www.gov.nb.ca/legis/index.htm
**Clerk:** Loredana Catalli Sonier
**Speaker:** Vacant
**Sergeant-at-Arms:** Phyllis A. LeBlanc, 506/453-2527
**Director, Hansard & Debates Translation:** Valmond LeBlanc, 506/453-2689
**Legislative Librarian:** Eric Swanick, 506/453-2338
Clerk's Asst., Donald J. Forestell

#### Government Caucus Office (Lib.)

506/453-2548; Fax: 506/453-3956
Director, Steven MacKinnon
Officer, Administrative Services, Gabriella Marchetti-Mockler

#### Office of the Official Opposition (PC)

PO Box 6000, Fredericton NB E3B 5H1
506/453-7494; Fax: 506/453-3461
Leader, Hon. Bernard Valcourt
Executive Asst., Marie-France Pelletier
Director, Administration, Bradley Green

#### Office of the New Democratic Party (NDP)

PO Box 6000, Fredericton NB E3B 5H1
506/453-3305; Fax: 506/453-3688
Leader, Elizabeth Weir
Legislative Asst., Joan Weinman
Provincial Secretary, Roger Couvrette

#### Standing Committees of the House

Crown Corporations
Law Amendments
Legislative Administration
Ombudsmen
Private Bills
Privileges
Procedure
Public Accounts

#### Select Committees of the House

Demographics
Electoral Reform
Gasoline Pricing

## FIFTY-THIRD LEGISLATURE - NEW BRUNSWICK

506/453-2506
Last General Election, September 11, 1995. Maximum Duration, 5 years.
**Party Standings (October, 1997)**
Liberal (Lib.) 45
Progressive Conservatives (PC) 6
New Democratic Party (NDP) 1
Vacant 3
Total 55
**Salaries, Indemnities & Allowances (1997)**
Members' annual indemnity $36,594.97, plus $14,637.99 for expenses. In addition to this are the following:
Premier $49,012.77
Ministers $32,675.86 (with portfolio); $24,507.92 (without portfolio)
Leader of the Opposition $32,675.86
Speaker $24,507.92

#### MEMBERS BY CONSTITUENCY

Following is: constituency (number of eligible voters at 1995 election) member, party affiliation. (Address for all is PO Box 6000, Fredericton NB E3B 5H1.)
Refer to Cabinet List, Government Caucus Office, & the Party Listings, for Telephone & Fax numbers.

Albert (8,289) Harry Doyle, Lib.
Bathurst (9,634) Hon. Marcelle Mersereau, Lib.
Campbellton (8,755) Hon. Edmond Blanchard, Q.C., Lib.
Caraquet (9,357) Hon. Bernard Thériault, Lib.
Carleton (10,029) Dale Graham, PC
Centre-Péninsule (7,673) Denis Landry, Lib.
Charlotte (7,613) Hon. Sheldon Lee, Lib.
Dalhousie-Restigouche East (9,481) Carolle de Ste-Croix, Lib.
Dieppe-Memramcook (12,467) Greg O'Donnell, Lib.
Edmundston (8,391) Hon. Bernard Valcourt, PC
Fredericton North (11,973) Jim Wilson, Lib.
Fredericton South (10,827) Hon. Russell H.T. King, M.D., Lib.
Fredericton-Fort Nashwaak (8,732) Hon. Greg Byrne, Lib.
Fundy Isles (3,418) Eric Allaby, Lib.
Grand Bay-Westfield (7,987) Milton Sherwood, PC
Grand Falls Region/Région de Grand-Sault (8,614) Hon. Paul E. Duffie, Q.C., Lib.
Grand Lake (9,277) Hon. Doug Tyler, Lib.
Hampton-Belleisle (10,477) Hon. Georgie Day, Lib.
Kennebecasis (10,580) Hon. Peter LeBlanc, Lib.
Kent (8,419) Hon. Alan Graham, Lib.
Kent South (10,982) Hon. Camille Thériault, Lib.
Kings East (9,524) Le Roy Armstrong, Lib.
Lamèque-Shippagan-Miscou (9,637) Jean-Camille DeGrâce, Lib.
Mactaquac (10,049) David Olmstead, Lib.
Madawaska-la-Vallée (8,138) Percy Mockler, PC
Madawaska-les-Lacs (8,618) Jeannot Volpé, PC
Miramichi Bay (8,739) Hon. Danny Gay, Lib.
Miramichi Centre (10,090) John McKay, Lib.
Miramichi-Bay du Vin (9,604) Vacant,
Moncton Crescent (10,315) Ken MacLeod, Lib.
Moncton East (11,208) Hon. J. Raymond Frenette, Lib.
Moncton North (11,353) Gene Devereux, Lib.
Moncton South (11,054) Hon. James Lockyer, Q.C., Lib.
Nepisiguit (9,226) Alban Landry, Lib.
New Maryland (10,537) Hon. Joan Kingston, Lib.
Nigadoo-Chaleur (9,814) Albert Doucet, Lib.
Oromocto-Gagetown (10,313) Hon. Vaughn Blaney, Lib.
Petitcodiac (8,131) Hollis Steeves, Lib.
Restigouche West (8,131) Hon. Jean Paul Savoie, Lib.
Riverview (10,425) Al Kavanaugh, Lib.
Rogersville-Kouchibouguac (7,738) Kenneth Johnson, Lib.
Saint John Champlain (9,830) Hon. Roland MacIntyre, Lib.
Saint John Harbour (9,221) Elizabeth Weir, NDP
Saint John Lancaster (10,075) Hon. Jane Barry, Lib.
Saint John Portland (10,090) Leo A. McAdam, Lib.
Saint John-Fundy (8,495) Hon. Stuart Jamieson, Lib.
Saint John-Kings (10,221) Laureen Jarrett, Lib.
Shediac-Cap-Pelé (10,986) Hon. Bernard Richard, Lib.
Southwest Miramichi (8,659) Reg MacDonald, Lib.
Tantramar (7,559) Vacant, Lib.
Tracadie-Sheila (9,432) Elvy Robichaud, PC
Victoria-Tobique (8,429) Vacant, Lib.
Western Charlotte (8,663) Hon. Ann Breault, Lib.
Woodstock (9,739) Hon. Bruce A. Smith, Lib.
York (9,828) John Flynn, Lib.

#### MEMBERS (ALPHABETICAL)

Following is: member, constituency (number of eligible voters at 1995 election) party affiliation. (Address for all is PO Box 6000, Fredericton NB E3B 5H1.)
Refer to Cabinet List, Government Caucus Office, & the Party Listings, for Telephone & Fax numbers.

Eric Allaby, Fundy Isles (3,418) Lib.
Le Roy Armstrong, Kings East (9,524) Lib.
Hon. Jane Barry, Saint John Lancaster (10,075) Lib.
Hon. Edmond Blanchard, Q.C., Campbellton (8,755) Lib.
Hon. Vaughn Blaney, Oromocto-Gagetown (10,313) Lib.
Hon. Ann Breault, Western Charlotte (8,663) Lib.
Hon. Greg Byrne, Fredericton-Fort Nashwaak (8,732) Lib.
Hon. Georgie Day, Hampton-Belleisle (10,477) Lib.
Jean-Camille DeGrâce, Lamèque-Shippagan-Miscou (9,637) Lib.
Gene Devereux, Moncton North (11,353) Lib.
Albert Doucet, Nigadoo-Chaleur (9,814) Lib.
Harry Doyle, Albert (8,289) Lib.
Hon. Paul E. Duffie, Q.C., Grand Falls Region/Région de Grand-Sault (8,614) Lib.
John Flynn, York (9,828) Lib.
Hon. J. Raymond Frenette, Moncton East (11,208) Lib.
Hon. Danny Gay, Miramichi Bay (8,739) Lib.
Hon. Alan Graham, Kent (8,419) Lib.
Dale Graham, Carleton (10,029) PC
Hon. Stuart Jamieson, Saint John-Fundy (8,495) Lib.

Laureen Jarrett, Saint John-Kings (10,221) Lib.
Kenneth Johnson, Rogersville-Kouchibouguac (7,738) Lib.
Al Kavanaugh, Riverview (10,425) Lib.
Hon. Russell H.T. King, M.D., Fredericton South (10,827) Lib.
Hon. Joan Kingston, New Maryland (10,537) Lib.
Alban Landry, Nepisiguit (9,226) Lib.
Denis Landry, Centre-Péninsule (7,673) Lib.
Hon. Peter LeBlanc, Kennebecasis (10,580) Lib.
Hon. Sheldon Lee, Charlotte (7,613) Lib.
Hon. James Lockyer, Q.C., Moncton South (11,054) Lib.
Reg MacDonald, Southwest Miramichi (8,659) Lib.
Hon. Roland MacIntyre, Saint John Champlain (9,830) Lib.
Ken MacLeod, Moncton Crescent (10,315) Lib.
Leo A. McAdam, Saint John Portland (10,090) Lib.
John McKay, Miramichi Centre (10,090) Lib.
Hon. Marcelle Mersereau, Bathurst (9,634) Lib.
Percy Mockler, Madawaska-la-Vallée (8,138) PC
Greg O'Donnell, Dieppe-Memramcook (12,467) Lib.
David Olmstead, Mactaquac (10,049) Lib.
Hon. Bernard Richard, Shediac-Cap-Pelé (10,986) Lib.
Elvy Robichaud, Tracadie-Sheila (9,432) PC
Hon. Jean Paul Savoie, Restigouche West (8,131) Lib.
Milton Sherwood, Grand Bay-Westfield (7,987) PC
Hon. Bruce A. Smith, Woodstock (9,739) Lib.
Carolle de Ste-Croix, Dalhousie-Restigouche East (9,481) Lib.
Hollis Steeves, Petitcodiac (8,131) Lib.
Hon. Bernard Thériault, Caraquet (9,357) Lib.
Hon. Camille Thériault, Kent South (10,982) Lib.
Hon. Doug Tyler, Grand Lake (9,277) Lib.
Hon. Bernard Valcourt, Edmundston (8,391) PC
Jeannot Volpé, Madawaska-les-Lacs (8,618) PC
Elizabeth Weir, Saint John Harbour (9,221) NDP
Jim Wilson, Fredericton North (11,973) Lib.

#### Vacancies

Miramichi-Bay du Vin (9,604)
Tantramar (7,559)
Victoria-Tobique (8,429)

## NEW BRUNSWICK GOVERNMENT DEPARTMENTS & AGENCIES

### Department of ADVANCED EDUCATION & LABOUR/Enseignement Supérieur et travail

Chestnut Complex, 470 York St., PO Box 6000, Fredericton NB E3B 5H1
Fax: 506/453-3806; URL: http://www.gov.nb.ca/ael/index.htm

#### ACTS ADMINISTERED

Adult Education & Training Act
Apprenticeship & Occupational Certification Act
Boiler & Pressure Vessel Act
Electrical Installation & Inspection Act
Elevators & Lifts Act
Employment Development Act
Employment Standards Act
Fisheries Bargaining Act
Higher Education Foundation Act
Hospital Services Act
Human Rights Act
Industrial Relations Act
Labour & Employment Board Act
Labour Market Research Act
Occupational Health & Safety Act
Pension Benefits Act
Plumbing Installation & Inspection Act
Public Service Labour Relations Act
Silicosis Compensation Act
Trade Schools Act
Workers' Compensation Act (administered by Workplace Health, Safety & Compensation Commission)
Workplace Health, Safety & Compensation Commission Act
Youth Assistance Act

**Minister**, Hon. Roland MacIntyre, 506/453-2342, Fax: 506/453-3038
**Minister of State, Literacy & Adult Education & Minister of State, Youth**, Hon. Georgie Day, 506/457-6734, Fax: 506/444-5425
Deputy Minister, W. David Ferguson, 506/453-2343, Fax: 506/453-3038
Director, Corporate Communications, Vacant, 506/444-5335, Fax: 506/444-4314
Director, Human Resource Services, Roger Arseneau, 506/453-8209, Fax: 506/453-7913

#### CORPORATE PROGRAMS DIVISION

Asst. Deputy Minister, Wm. H. Smith, 506/453-8262, Fax: 506/444-4314
Executive Director, Advocacy Services, Maryanne Bourgeois, 506/453-3298, Fax: 506/453-3300
Director, Human Rights Commission, Janet Cullinan, 506/453-2301, Fax: 506/453-2653
Director, Student Services, Don Chevarie, 506/453-3358, Fax: 506/444-4333
Senior Advocate, Office of the Workers' Advocate, Rick Clark, 506/658-2472, Fax: 506/658-3075
Advocate, Office of the Employers' Advocate, Richard Fitzgerald, 506/457-3510

#### DEPARTMENTAL SERVICES DIVISION

Executive Director, Patrick Doherty, 506/453-2587, Fax: 506/444-4314
Acting Director, Finance, Luc Paulin, 506/453-2519, Fax: 506/453-7913
Director, Information Technology Services, Ken Fitzpatrick, 506/453-2588
Acting Manager, Administration, Bev Bishop
Manager, Facilities Management, Ron LeBlanc, 506/453-8244, Fax: 506/453-7913
Manager, Trade Schools, Gerald Stillwell, 506/453-8214, Fax: 506/453-7913

#### DIVISION DES SERVICES ÉDUCATIFS (FRANCOPHONE)

Sous-ministre adjoint, Bernard Paulin, 506/444-5732, Fax: 506/444-4314
Directeur éxecutif, TéléÉducation, Rory McGreal, 506/444-4230, Fax: 506/444-4232
Directeur, Services éducatifs, Laurent McLaughlin, 506/453-8237, Fax: 506/444-4960

#### EDUCATIONAL SERVICES DIVISION (ANGLOPHONE)

Asst. Deputy Minister, Mike McIntosh, 506/453-8202, Fax: 506/444-4314
Director, Apprenticeship & Occupational Certification, André Ferlatte, 506/453-2260, Fax: 506/453-3806

#### LABOUR & EMPLOYMENT DIVISION

Asst. Deputy Minister, John P. Chenier, 506/453-2091, Fax: 506/453-3038
Acting Executive Asst., Employment, Michel Thériault, 506/453-3041, Fax: 506/453-7969
Executive Director, Planning & Policy Development, Dave Easby, 506/453-2889
Director, Employment Administration, Karla Ploude, 506/444-4226, Fax: 506/453-7967
Director, Employment Programs, Michel Thériault, 506/453-3818, Fax: 506/453-7967
Director, Employment Services, Roger Lévesque, 506/444-4046, Fax: 506/453-7967
Director, Employment Standards Branch, Maurice Boucher, 506/453-3902
Director, Industrial Relations Branch, J. Armand Thomas, 506/453-2261, Fax: 506/453-3806
Director, Technical Inspections, Calvin Duncan, 506/453-2336, Fax: 506/457-7394
Chief, Boiler Inspector, Dale Ross, 506/453-4493, Fax: 506/457-7394
Chief, Elevator Inspector, Lee Boudreau, 506/453-2336
Chief, Plumbing Inspector, Fred Holland, 506/453-2336
Director, Labour Market Analysis, Dehorah Burns, 506/457-4859
Director, Planning, Vacant, 506/453-3940
Superintendent, Pensions Branch, Danielle Métivier, 506/453-2055

#### Associated Agencies, Boards & Commissions

- Apprenticeship & Occupational Certification Board: PO Box 6000, Fredericton NB E3B 5H1 – 506/453-2260; Fax: 506/453-3806

Secretary, Dianne Robinson-Hansen, 506/457-7299
Chair, Darrel LeBlanc, 506/453-2912

- Board of Examiners for Compressed Gas: PO Box 6000, Fredericton NB E3B 5H1 – 506/453-2336; Fax: 506/457-7394

Chair, Michael O'Hearn

- Board of Examiners for Stationary Engineers: PO Box 6000, Fredericton NB E3B 5H1 – 506/453-2336; Fax: 506/457-7394

Chair, Dale Ross

- Ministerial Advisory Committee on Multiculturalism: PO Box 6000, Fredericton NB E3B 5H1 – 506/444-4331; Fax: 506/453-3300

Secretary, Beverly Woznow

- New Brunswick Human Rights Commission: 751 Brunswick St., PO Box 6000, Fredericton NB E3B 5H1 – 506/453-2301; Fax: 506/453-2653

Chair, Prof. Constantine Passaris
Director, Janet Cullinan

- New Brunswick Labour & Employment Board: 191 Prospect St., PO Box 908, Fredericton NB E3B 1B0 – 506/453-2881; Fax: 506/453-3892

This agency replaces the former Industrial Relations Board, Public Services Labour Relations Board, Employment Standards Tribunal, & Pensions Tribunal.
Chair, Paul Lordon, Q.C.

- Workplace Health, Safety & Compensation Commission of New Brunswick (WHSCC): 1 Portland St., PO Box 160, Saint John NB E2L 3X9 – 506/632-2200; Fax: 506/632-2226, Toll Free: 1-800-222-9775; URL: http://www.gov.nb.ca/whscc/index.htm

Listed alphabetically in detail, this section.

### Department of AGRICULTURE & RURAL DEVELOPMENT (ARD)/Agriculture et Aménagement rural (AAR)

PO Box 6000, Fredericton NB E3B 5H1
506/453-2666; Fax: 506/453-7978; URL: http//www.gov.nb.ca/agricult/index.htm

#### ACTS ADMINISTERED

Agricultural Associations Act
Agricultural Commodity Price Stabilization Act
Agricultural Development Act
Agricultural Operation Practices Act
Agricultural Rehabilitation & Development Act
Agricultural Schools Act
Apiary Inspection Act
Artificial Insemination Act
Branding Act
Crop Insurance Act
Dairy Industry Act
Dairy Products Act
Diseases of Animals Act
Drainage of Farm Lands Act
Encouragement of Seed Growing Act
Farm Credit Corporation Assistance Act
Farm Improvement Assistance Loans Act
Farm Income Assurance Act

Farm Machinery Loans Act
Farm Products Boards and Marketing Agencies Act
Farm Products Marketing Act
Fences Act
Harness Racing Commission Act
Imitation Dairy Products Act
Injurious Insect and Pest Act
Keswick Islands Act
Livestock Incentives Act
Livestock Yard Sales Act
Marshland Reclamation Act
Natural Products Grades Act
New Brunswick Grain Act
Oleomargarine Act
Plant Diseases Act
Potato Development and Marketing Council Act
Potato Disease Eradication Act
Poultry Health Protection Act
Pounds Act
Sheep Protection Act
Society for the Prevention of Cruelty Act
Weed Control Act
Women's Institute Act

**Minister**, Hon. Doug Tyler, 506/453-2448, Fax: 506/444-5022
Deputy Minister, Jack Syroid, 506/453-2450, Fax: 506/444-5022
Executive Director, Planning & Development, Dr. Ibrahim Ghanem, 506/453-2406

#### MARKETING & RURAL DEVELOPMENT

Asst. Deputy Minister, Claire LePage, 506/453-3886
Director, Administrative Services Branch, Roger B. Hunter, 506/453-2521
Director, Communications & Education Branch, John White, 506/453-5451
Director, Farm Business & Risk Management Branch, D. McQuade, 506/453-2185
Director, Marketing & Business Development Branch, Dr. Brian Dykeman, 506/453-2214
Director, Rural Development Branch, Janet Gagnon, 506/444-5967

#### TECHNICAL & FIELD SERVICES

Asst. Deputy Minister, E.T. Pratt, 506/453-2366
Director, Land Resources Branch, Paul Smith, 506/453-2109
Director, Livestock & Livestock Feed Branch, Dr. Mike Maloney, 506/453-2457
Director, Land Resources Branch, Paul Smith, 506/453-2109
Director, Potato & Horticulture Branch, Clair Gartley, 506/453-2172
Chief, Veterinary Section, Dr. M.F. Maloney, 506/453-2210

##### Regional Offices

Central: Chatham NB – 506/778-6030; Fax: 506/773-4076, Acting Regional Manager, Brian DuPlessis
East: Bathurst NB – 506/547-2088; Fax: 506/547-2064, Regional Manager, V. Taylor
Northeast: Bathurst NB – 506/547-2088; Fax: 506/547-2064, Regional Manager, I. Breau
Northwest: Grand Falls NB – 506/476-5515; Fax: 506/473-6641, Regional Manager, L. Arsenault
South: Sussex NB – 506/432-2000; Fax: 506/432-2044, Regional Manager, J. Herod
Southeast: Moncton NB – 506/856-2277; Fax: 506/856-2669, Regional Manager, P. Jensen
West: Wicklow NB, Regional Manager, C. Gartley

##### Associated Agencies, Boards & Commissions

- Agricultural Development Board: c/o Department of Agriculture & Rural Development, PO Box 6000, Fredericton NB E3B 5H1 – 506/453-2185; Fax: 506/453-7406

Secretary Manager, Paul Cooper
- Farm Products Marketing Commission: c/o Department of Agriculture & Rural Development, PO Box 6000, Fredericton NB E3B 5H1 – 506/453-3647; Fax: 506/453-7406

Chair, Robert Shannon
Executive Director, Wayne J. Buffett
- Livestock Incentives Act, & Farm Machinery Loans Act: c/o Department of Agriculture & Rural Development, PO Box 6000, Fredericton NB E3B 5H1 – 506/453-2524; Fax: 506/453-7170

Manager, Paul Cooper
- New Brunswick Crop Insurance Commission: c/o Department of Agriculture & Rural Development, PO Box 6000, Fredericton NB E3B 5H1 – 506/453-2185; Fax: 506/453-7406

General Manager, Paul Smith
- New Brunswick Grain Commission: c/o Department of Agriculture & Rural Development, PO Box 6000, Fredericton NB E3B 5H1 – 506/453-2172; Fax: 506/453-7978

Secretary Manager, Dave Walker
- New Brunswick Potato Development & Marketing Council: c/o Incutech Complex, Bag Service 69000, Fredericton NB E3B 6C2 – 506/453-3562

Chair, Don Keenan

##### Agricultural Marketing Boards & Commissions

- Agence de la pomme de terre du N.B.: CP 2140, Grand-Sault NB E3Z 1E2 – 506/473-3036; Fax: 506/473-4647

Chair, Lionel Poitras
- New Brunswick Apple Marketing Board: #206, 1115 Regent St., Fredericton NB E3B 3Z2 – 506/452-8100; Fax: 506/452-1625

Secretary-Manager, Bruce Thompson
- New Brunswick Cattle Marketing Agency: RR#4, Perth - Andover NB E0J 1V0 – 506/273-6729

Secretary Manager, Neville Delong
- New Brunswick Chicken Marketing Board: #103, 1115 Regent St., Fredericton NB E3B 3Z2 – 506/452-8085; Fax: 506/451-2121

Secretary Manager, Louis Martin
- New Brunswick Cream Marketing Board: RR#5, Sussex NB E0E 1P0 – 506/433-5051

President, Albert Scott
- New Brunswick Egg Marketing Board: 181 Westmorland St., PO Box 126, Stn A, Fredericton NB E3B 4Y2 – 506/458-8885; Fax: 506/453-0645

Secretary Manager, April Sexsmith
- New Brunswick Flue-Cured Tobacco Marketing Board: RR#1, PO Box 516, Bouctouche NB E0A 1G0

President, Normand Poirier
- New Brunswick Greenhouse Products Marketing Board: #206, 1115 Regent St., Fredericton NB E3B 3Z2 – 506/452-8100; Fax: 506/452-1625

Secretary Manager, Bruce Thompson
- New Brunswick Hog Marketing Board: 830 Hanwell Rd., Fredericton NB E3B 6A2 – 506/458-8051; Fax: 506/453-1985

Secretary-Manager, Susan Fox
- New Brunswick Milk Marketing Board: Rochville Rd., PO Box 490, Sussex NB E0E 1P0 – 506/432-9120; Fax: 506/432-9130

Chair, John Robinson
- New Brunswick Potato Agency: PO Box 238, Florenceville NB E0J 1K0 – 506/392-6022; Fax: 506/392-8164

Chair, Pat MacDonald
- New Brunswick Turkey Marketing Board: #103, 1115 Regent St., Fredericton NB E3B 3Z2 – 506/452-8103; Fax: 506/452-1625

President, Bruce Thompson

## Office of the AUDITOR GENERAL/Bureau du Vérificateur général

PO Box 758, Fredericton NB E3B 5B4
506/453-2243; Fax: 506/453-3067
**Auditor General**, Daryl Wilson, F.C.A.
Deputy Auditor General, Kenneth D. Robinson, C.A., 506/453-2243, Email: kdr@gov.nb.ca
Executive Secretary, Darlene Wield

## COMMUNICATIONS NEW BRUNSWICK/ Communications Nouveau-Brunswick

225 King St., PO Box 6000, Fredericton NB E3B 5H1
506/453-2240; Fax: 506/453-5329
**General Manager**, Howie Trainor, Email: htrainor@gov.nb.ca
Director, Audio-Visual Services Branch, Vacant, 506/453-3042, Fax: 506/457-3556
Director, Edit Services, Jim McCarthy, Email: mccarthy@gov.nb.ca
Director, Design Services Branch, Michel Cote, 506/453-3037

## Office of the COMPTROLLER/Bureau du Contrôleur

Centennial Bldg., 670 King St., Fredericton NB E3B 5H1
506/453-2565; Fax: 506/453-2917; URL: http://www.gov.nb.ca/ooc
**Comptroller**, Edward L. Mehan, CMA
Director, Accounting Services, Michael Ferguson, CA
Director, Audit & Consulting Services, Stephen Thompson, CMA
Secretary, Jocelyne Macfarlane

## Premier's Council on the Status of DISABLED PERSONS/Conseil du Première ministre sur la condition des personnes handicapées

#648, 440 King St., Fredericton NB E3B 5H8
506/444-3000; Fax: 506/444-3001; Email: pcsdp@gov.nb.ca; URL: http://www.gov.nb.ca/pcsdp/english/index.htm

Advises the Minister on matters relating to the status of persons with disabilities & presents to government the public matters of interest & concern to persons with disabilities. The council promotes the prevention of disabling conditions, promotes employment opportunities for persons with disabilities & promotes access by persons with disabilites to all services offered to the citizens of the province.

**Executive Director**, Randy Dickinson

## Department of ECONOMIC DEVELOPMENT & TOURISM/Développement économique et Tourisme

Centennial Bldg., 670 King St., 5th Fl., PO Box 6000, Fredericton NB E3B 5H1
506/453-2850 (Communications & Promotion); Fax: 506/444-4586; URL: http://www.gov.nb.ca/edt/index.htm

Provincial Department responsible for the following:
- the development & marketing of investment opportunities, job creation & the tourism industry;
- encourages the growth of small & medium-sized businesses in New Brunswick;
- improves competitiveness in the global marketplace &;
- assists companies in increasing sales & business in domestic & foreign markets & establishing new markets & export opportunities.

##### ACTS ADMINISTERED

Economic Development Act
Stock Savings Plan Act

Tourism Development Act

**Minister**, Hon. Camille Thériault, 506/453-3009, Email: camillet@gov.nb.ca

Deputy Minister, Francis McGuire, 506/453-2795, Email: francism@gov.nb.ca

Director, Corporate Services, Paul R. LeBlanc, 506/453-2482, Fax: 506/453-5428, Email: paulleb@gov.nb.ca

#### FINANCE INFRASTRUCTURE & POLICY

Asst. Deputy Minister, Richard Burgess, 506/453-2111, Fax: 506/453-5428, Email: dickb@gov.nb.ca

Director, Financial Programs, Doug Holt, 506/453-2474, Fax: 506/453-7904, Email: dough@gov.nb.ca

Director, Planning & Research, Gary Jochelman, 506/453-2629, Fax: 506/444-5299, Email: garyj@gov.nb.ca

#### INDUSTRIAL DEVELOPMENT

Asst. Deputy Minister, Paul Aucoin, 506/453-2794, Fax: 506/453-5428, Email: paula@gov.nb.ca

Director, Industry Services, John Adams, 506/453-2298, Fax: 506/457-7282, Email: johna@gov.nb.ca

Director, Small Business Directorate, Denis Caron, 506/453-3890, Fax: 506/444-4182, Email: kenh@gov.nb.ca

Director, Trade & Investment, Michael MacBride, 506/453-2876, Fax: 506/453-3783, Email: michaelm@gov.nb.ca

Executive Director, Tourism & Parks, Harvey Sawler, 506/453-4283, Fax: 506/444-4586, Email: harveys@gov.nb.ca, URL: http://www.gov.nb.ca/tourism/index.htm

#### INFORMATION HIGHWAY SECRETARIAT

URL: http://www.gov.nb.ca/edt/infohigh/index.htm

Asst. Deputy Minister, Jerrie Fowler, 506/453-3707, Email: jerrief@gov.nb.ca

Director, Brian Freeman, 506/444-4296, Fax: 506/453-3993, Email: brianf@gov.nb.ca

Executive Director, Connect NB, David Roberts, 506/444-4703, Fax: 506/444-4058, Email: droberts@nbnet.nb.ca

##### Associated Agencies, Boards & Commissions

•Canada/New Brunswick Business Service Centre: 570 Queen St., Fredericton NB E3B 6Z6 – 506/444-6158, Toll Free: 1-800-668-1010

Information Agent, Paulianne McLellan

•New Brunswick Industrial Development Board: PO Box 6000, Fredericton NB E3B 5H1 – 506/453-2474; Fax: 506/453-7904

•Provincial Holdings Ltd.: PO Box 6000, Fredericton NB E3B 5H1 – 506/453-2474; Fax: 506/453-7904

Secretary-Treasurer, Jim Lovett, Email: jiml@gov.nb.ca

## Department of EDUCATION/Éducation

PO Box 6000, Fredericton NB E3B 5H1

506/453-3678; Fax: 506/453-3325; URL: http://www.gov.nb.ca/education/index.htm

#### ACTS ADMINISTERED

Education Act

**Minister**, Hon. Bernard Richard, 506/453-2523, Fax: 506/444-4400

Deputy Minister, Carol Loughrey, 506/453-2529, Email: cloughHRE@gov.nb.ca

Deputy Minister, Normand Martin, 506/453-2409, Email: helenef@gov.nb.ca

Director, Communications, Margaret Smith, 506/444-4714, Email: margares@gov.nb.ca

Director, Research & Planning, Vacant, 506/453-3090

#### EDUCATIONAL SERVICES DIVISION (ANGLOPHONE)

Asst. Deputy Minister, Byron James, 506/453-3326, Email: byronj@gov.nb.ca

Director, Curriculum Development, Barry Lydon, 506/453-2155, Email: barryl@gov.nb.ca

Director, Evaluation, Cary Grobe, 506/453-2744, Email: caryg@gov.nb.ca

#### SECTEUR DES SERVICES FRANCOPHONES D'ÉDUCATION

Sous-ministre adjoint, Raymond Daigle, 506/453-2086, Email: rdaigle@gov.nb.ca

Directeur, Mesures et évaluation, Guy Léveillé, 506/453-2157, Email: guyl@gov.nb.ca

Directrice, Services Pédagogiques, Donata Thériault, 506/453-2743, Email: donatat@gov.nb.ca

#### SUPPORT SERVICES DIVISION

Asst. Deputy Minister, Jolène LeBlanc, 506/453-2085, Email: jolenel@gov.nb.ca

Director, Computer Support Services, Elizabeth Abraham, 506/453-7158, Email: abrahaml@gov.nb.ca

Director, Educational Facilities, Ronald Breau, 506/453-2242, Email: ronaldb@gov.nb.ca

Director, Finance & Services, Etienne Leboeuf, 506/453-2085, Email: etiennel@gov.nb.ca

Director, Human Resources, Mary Jane Richards, 506/453-2030, Email: maryjr@gov.nb.ca

Director, Instructional Resources, Gérald Breau, 505/453-2319, Email: gbreau@gov.nb.ca

## Office of the Chief ELECTORAL OFFICER/ Bureau de la directrice générale des élections

PO Box 6000, Fredericton NB E3B 5H1

506/453-2218; Fax: 506/457-4926

Toll Free: 1-800-308-2922

#### ACTS ADMINISTERED

Controverted Elections Act

Elections Act

Municipal Elections Act

**Chief Electoral Officer**, Barbara J. Landry, Email: barbarl@gov.nb.ca

Elections Coordinator, Annise Hollies, Email: holliesa@gov.nb.ca

Research & Planning Officer, Mapping, Ron Armitage, Email: armitagr@gov.nb.ca

Election Analyst, Carrie Bartlett

Senior Policy Analyst, David Strang

Project Leader, Diane Nadeau

System Analyst, Janet Burrows

## Department of the ENVIRONMENT/ Environnement

364 Argyle St., PO Box 6000, Fredericton NB E3B 5H1

506/453-3700; Fax: 506/453-3843; URL: http://www.gov.nb.ca/environ/index.htm

#### ACTS ADMINISTERED

Beverage Containers Act

Clean Air Act

Clean Environment Act

Clean Water Act

Environmental Trust Fund Act

Pesticides Control Act

Unsightly Premises Act

**Minister**, Hon. Joan Kingston, 506/453-2523

Deputy Minister, Donald Dennison, 506/453-3095

#### ASSESSMENT & APPROVALS

Fax: 506/453-2390

Director, Dr. Nabil D. Elhadi, 506/457-4848

Manager, Industrial Approvals, Cheryl Heathwood, 506/457-4848

Manager, Municipal Services, Perry E. Haines, 506/444-4599, Fax: 506/457-7805

Manager, Project Assessment, Kirk Gordon, 506/444-5382

Manager, Technical Approvals, Dr. James Shaffner, P.Eng., 506/453-7945, Fax: 506/453-2893

#### CORPORATE SERVICES

506/453-3703

Executive Director, Dr. David I. Besner

Director, Communications & Policy, Gerald N. Hill, 506/453-3700

Director, Finance & Administration, Simon Caron

Manager, Communications & Environmental Education, Elizabeth Hayward, 506/453-3700

Manager, Finance & Administration, Byron Jeffrey

Manager, Human Resources, Brian Cross

Manager, Policy & Intergovernmental Affairs, Paul Monti

#### ENVIRONMENTAL QUALITY

506/457-4844; Fax: 506/453-2265

Director, James F.L. Knight

Manager, Analytical Services, David Schellenberg, 506/453-2477, Fax: 506/453-3269

Manager, Environmental Evaluation, Claire MacInnis

Manager, Environmental Planning, William C. Ayer, 506/457-4846, Fax: 506/457-7823

Manager, Information Management, Grant MacLeod, 506/453-2862

#### REGIONAL SERVICES & ENFORCEMENT

506/457-4850; Fax: 506/453-2893

Director, K. Bradford Marshall

Manager, Compliance & Enforcement, Stanley V. Wadden

Manager, Regional Services, Michael Sprague

##### Associated Agencies, Boards & Commissions

•New Brunswick Pesticides Advisory Council: c/o Department of the Environment, PO Box 6000, Fredericton NB E3B 5H1 – 506/457-4848; Fax: 506/453-2893

Coordinator, Pesticides Management Unit, Ken Browne

•New Brunswick Round Table on Environment & Economy/Table Ronde sur Environnement & Economie: c/o Department of the Environment, PO Box 6000, Fredericton NB E3B 5H1 – 506/453-3703; Fax: 506/457-7800

Executive Secretary, Dr. David I. Besner

## Department of FINANCE/Finances

PO Box 6000, Fredericton NB E3B 5H1

506/453-2286; Fax: 506/457-4989; URL: http://www.gov.nb.ca/finance/index.htm

#### ACTS ADMINISTERED

Appropriation Act

Arts Development Trust Fund

Auditor General Act

Balanced Budget Act

Beaverbrook Art Gallery Act (in part)

Beaverbrook Auditorium Act (in part)

Civil Service Act

Crown Construction Contracts Act

Environmental Trust Fund (administration of fund)

Expenditure Management Act, 1991 & 1992

Financial Administration Act

Financial Corporation Capital Tax Act

Gasoline & Motive Fuel Tax Act

Harmonized Sales Tax Act

Income Tax Act

Liquor Control Act

Loan Act

Lotteries Act

Maritime Provinces Harness Racing Commission

Members' Pension Act
Members' Superannuation Act
Municipalities Act (in part)
New Brunswick Investment Management Corporation Act
New Brunswick Liquor Corporation Act
New Brunswick Municipal Finance Corporation Act
Northumberland Strait Crossing Act
Ombudsman Act (in part)
Pari-Mutual Tax Act
Pay Equity Act
Provincial Court Act
Provincial Loans Act
Public Service Labour Relations Act (in part)
Public-Service Superannuation Act
Real Property Tax Act (except sections 3 & 4)
Real Property Transfer Tax Act
Restricted Beverages Act
Retirement Plan Benificiaries Act
Revenue Administration Act
Social Services & Education Tax Act
Special Appropriations Act
Special Retirement Program Act
Sport Development Trust Fund Act (administration of fund)
Statistics Act
Teachers' Pension Act
Tobacco Tax Act
**Minister**, Hon. Edmond Blanchard, Q.C., 506/453-2451, Email: blanchard@gov.nb.ca
Deputy Minister, John Mallory, 506/453-2534

#### BUDGET PLANNING & FINANCIAL SERVICES
Fax: 506/444-4499
Executive Director, John Campbell, 506/453-3051
Asst. Secretary to the Board of Management, John St. Pierre, 506/453-2808
Director, Financial Management Services, Terry Christie, 506/453-3075

#### DEPARTMENT & MANAGEMENT SERVICES
Executive Director, Chris Aiton, 506/453-2962, Fax: 506/444-5311
Director, Financial Services, Rick Phillips, 506/453-6904, Fax: 506/444-4724
Director, Human Resources, Geneva Hirsch, 506/453-8093, Fax: 506/444-4724
Director, Information Technology, Jean Lee, 506/454-5411, Fax: 506/444-3471
Director, Management Services, Leona Hurley, 506/453-2962, Fax: 506/444-5311

#### HUMAN RESOURCES MANAGEMENT
Executive Director, Ellen Barry, 506/453-2799
Director, Human Resources Information, Frank Camm, 506/453-2543
Director, Labour Relations, Andrew Kitchen, 506/453-2699
Acting Director, Program Services, Jean Stewart, 506/453-7191
Director, Public Service Employee Benefits, Cyril Thériault, 506/453-2296
Director, Strategic Services, Vacant, 506/444-5008

#### REVENUE DIVISION
Fax: 506/457-7335
Acting Provincial Tax Commissioner, David Morrison, 506/453-2401
Director, Account Management, Larry Bennett, 506/453-2709
Director, Accounting, Audit & Central Services, Rick McCullough, 506/453-2138
Director, Policy & Communications, Vacant, 506/453-2401
Director, System Development & Support, Dayle Riva, 506/454-4793

#### TAXATION & FISCAL POLICY
Fax: 506/453-2281
Executive Director, Norm Campbell, 506/453-2096
Acting Director, Budget Policy & Fiscal Relations, Peter Kieley, 506/453-2097
Director, New Brunswick Statistics Agency, Vacant, 506/453-2381, Fax: 506/453-7970
Director, Tax Policy, James Turgeon, 506/453-2097

#### TREASURY & DEBT MANAGEMENT
Fax: 506/453-2053
Executive Director, Bryan MacDonald, 506/453-3952
Director, Financial Policy & Debt Management, Ann Flewelling, 506/453-2515
Director, Treasury Management, James Carr, 506/453-3859

##### Associated Agencies, Boards & Commissions
•Atlantic Lottery Corporation (ALC): 770 St. George Blvd., PO Box 5500, Moncton NB E1C 8W6 – 506/867-5800; Fax: 506/388-4246
Chair, Ernest MacKinnon
President, Cluny Macpherson
Vice-President, Information Technology, Vincent Brunet
Vice-President, Sales & Promotion, Bert McWade
•Civil Service Commission of New Brunswick: c/o Office of the Ombudsman, 767 Brunswick St., PO Box 6000, Fredericton NB E3B 5H1 – 506/453-3733; Fax: 506/453-3733
Ombudsman responsible for the CSC, Ellen E. King
•New Brunswick Investment Management Corporation: PO Box 6000, Fredericton NB E3B 5H1 – 506/444-5800
President, Ernest MacKinnon

## Department of FISHERIES & AQUACULTURE/Pêches et Aquaculture
York Tower, King's Place, 6th Fl., PO Box 6000, Fredericton NB E3B 5H1
506/453-2251; Fax: 506/453-5210; URL: http://www.gov.nb.ca/dfa/index.htm

#### ACTS ADMINISTERED
Aquaculture Act
Fish Inspection Act
Fish Processing Act
Fisheries Bargaining Act
Fisheries Development Act
Inshore Fisheries Representation Act
Irish Moss Act
**Minister**, Hon. Danny Gay, 506/453-2662
Deputy Minister, Robert Gamble, 506/453-2766, Email: rwg@gov.nb.ca

#### CORPORATE SERVICES
Asst. Deputy Minister, Alfred Losier, 506/457-7303, Email: losiera@gov.nb.ca
Executive Director, Finance & Administration, Maurice Bernier, 506/453-2302, Email: mauriceb@gov.nb.ca
Director, School of Fisheries (Caraquet), Hédard Albert, 506/726-2500, Fax: 506/726-2408, Email: hedarda@gov.nb.ca

#### PROCESSING & AQUACULTURE
Asst. Deputy Minister, David MacMinn, 506/453-2047, Email: macminnd@gov.nb.ca
Director, Aquaculture, John Kershaw, 506/453-2253, Email: johnk@gov.nb.ca
Director, Aquarium & Marine Centre (Shippagan), Clarence LeBreton, 506/336-3013, Fax: 506/336-3057, Email: clarencel@gov.nb.ca
Director, Licensing & Inspection, Kerry Wilson, 506/453-2048, Email: kerryw@gov.nb.ca
Acting Director, Market Development, Louis Arsenault, 506/453-2438, Email: louisa@gov.nb.ca
Coordinator, Environmental Services, Barry Jones, 506/453-2047, Email: barryj@gov.nb.ca

#### RESOURCE POLICY & PLANNING
Executive Director, Linda Haché, 506/453-2252, Email: hachel@gov.nb.ca

##### Associated Agencies, Boards & Commissions
•Fisheries Development Board: PO Box 6000, Fredericton NB E3B 5H1 – 506/453-2302; Fax: 506/453-5210
Executive Director, Maurice Bernier, Email: mauriceb@gov.nb.ca

## New Brunswick GEOGRAPHIC INFORMATION CORPORATION/ Corporation d'information géographique du Nouveau-Brunswick
985 College Hill Rd., PO Box 6000, Fredericton NB E3B 5H1
506/457-3581; Fax: 506/453-3898; Email: nbgic@gov.nb.ca; URL: http://www.gov.nb.ca/nbgic/
**Chair**, Thomas O'Neil
President, Mavis Hurley, Email: mmh@gov.nb.ca
Vice-President, Legal, & Chief Registrar of Deeds, Roderick W. MacKenzie, Q.C., 506/457-7374, Email: rwm@gov.nb.ca
Vice-President, Operations, Fraser Nicholson, 506/444-5945, Fax: 506/453-3043, Email: fln@gov.nb.ca
Chief Financial Officer, Carol Macdonald, 506/453-3916, Fax: 506/453-3043, Email: cmm@gov.nb.ca
Manager, Public Relations, Arnold Kearney, 506/453-3804, Email: adk@gov.nb.ca

##### Regional Offices
Bathurst: 161 Main St., Bathurst NB E2A 1A6 – 506/547-2090; Fax: 506/547-2925, Regional Director, Operations, Alfred Losier
Campbellton: City Centre, #306, 157 Water St., Campbellton NB E3N 3H5 – 506/789-2305; Fax: 506/789-2582, Regional Director, Operations, Ronnie Arseneau
Edmundston: #219, 121, rue de l'Église, Edmundston NB E3V 3L3 – 506/735-2036; Fax: 506/735-4894, Director, Vincent Violette
Fredericton: Frederick Square, #250, 77 Westmorland St., Fredericton NB E3B 5G4 – 506/453-3390; Fax: 506/444-5030, Regional Director, Operations, Paul Scullion
Hampton: 9 Centennial Dr., Hampton NB E0G 1Z0 – 506/832-6060; Fax: 506/832-6008, Director, George Schurman, Email: schurman@nbnet.nb.ca
Miramichi: 360 Pleasant St., Miramichi NB E1V 3X1 – 506/627-4028; Fax: 506/627-4448, Regional Director, Operations, Joe Cormier, Email: cormierj@nbnet.nb.ca
Moncton: 633 Main St., Moncton NB E1C 8R3 – 506/856-3303; Fax: 506/856-2609
Richibucto: 26 Main St., Richibucto NB E0A 2M0 – 506/523-7725; Fax: 506/523-7629, Director, Michelle Dunn
Saint John: 15 King Square North, 2nd Fl., Saint John NB E2L 4Y9 – 506/643-6200; Fax: 506/658-2156, Regional Director, Operations, George Gregory, Email: ggregory@nbnet.nb.ca
St. Stephen: 73 Milltown Blvd., St. Stephen NB E3L 1G5 – 506/466-7335; Fax: 506/466-7358, Director, Ken Reid
Woodstock: Bicentennial Place, 200 King St., Woodstock NB E0J 2B0 – 506/325-4410; Fax: 506/325-4475, Director, Ron Smith

##### Service New Brunswick Offices
Caraquet: Place Caraquet, 25, boul St-Pierre ouest, Caraquet NB E1W 1B8 – 506/727-7013; Fax: 506/727-7016, Director, Aurelien Lanteigne

Moncton: Assomption Bldg., 770 Main St., Moncton NB E2C 1E7 – 506/856-2204; Fax: 506/856-2987, Director, Ron Gallagher
Saint John: 15 King's Sq. North, Saint John NB E2L 4L4 – 506/658-2500; Fax: 506/658-3995, Director, Gary Bard
Woodstock: 200 King St., Woodstock NB E0J 2B0 – 506/325-4476; Fax: 506/325-4482, Director, Sandra Bourque

## Department of HEALTH & COMMUNITY SERVICES/Santé et Services communautaires

PO Box 5100, Fredericton NB E3B 5G8
506/453-2536; Fax: 506/444-4697; URL: http://www.gov.nb.ca/hcs/

#### ACTS ADMINISTERED

Advanced Life Support Services Act
Ambulance Services Act
Anatomy Act
Cemetery Companies Act
Change of Name Act
Family Services Act
Health Act
Hospital Act
Hospital Services Act
Human Tissues Act
Jordan Memorial Home Act
Marriage Act
Medical Consent of Minors Act
Medical Services Payment Act
Mental Health Act
Mental Health Commission of New Brunswick Act
Nursing Homes Act
Prescription Drug Payment Act
Radiological Health Protection Act
Tobacco Sales Act
Treatment of Intoxicated Persons Act
Venereal Disease Act
Vital Statistics Act
**Minister**, Hon. Russell H.T. King, M.D., 506/453-2581
Deputy Minister, Jean Guy Finn, 506/453-2542
Director, Communications, Gerald Weseen, 506/453-2536

#### ADMINISTRATION & FINANCE DIVISION

Asst. Deputy Minister, Laura Freeman, 506/453-2775
Director, Administrative Support Services, David Gibbs, 506/453-2745
Director, Construction Services, Gérard LeBlanc, 506/444-4804
Director, Financial Services, Ron Durelle, 506/453-2117
Director, Human Resources, Marc Leger, 506/453-7961
Director, Information Systems, Jean-Claude Haché, 506/453-2279

#### Vital Statistics

Fax: 506/453-3245
Administers the Vital Statistics Act, the Change of Name Act & the Marriage Act. For certified Birth, Marriage & Death Certificates, remit $25.00 for each copy required. The fee for wallet size birth certificate or marriage certificate is $20.00. A search costs $10.00.
Registrar General, Alice Garner, 506/453-2714

#### FAMILY & COMMUNITY SOCIAL SERVICES DIVISION

Asst. Deputy Minister, Gérard Doucet, 506/453-2181
Executive Director, Bob Steele, 506/444-4726
Acting Director, Access/Assessment, Protection & Post Adoption Services, Dick Quigg, 506/453-2040
Director, Executive & Program Support Services, Joy Haines-Bacon, 506/453-2955
Director, Family & Protection Services Office, Edith Doucet, 506/453-2950, Fax: 506/453-2082

#### INSTITUTIONAL SERVICES DIVISION

Asst. Deputy Minister, James Carter, 506/453-4238
Executive Director, Hospital Services, Jean Castonguay, 506/453-2283
Acting Director, Ambulance Services, Andrew Easton, 506/453-2220
Director, Nursing Homes, Etienne Theriault, 506/453-3821
Acting Director, Program Support Services, Vacant, 506/453-3724

#### MENTAL HEALTH SERVICES DIVISION

Asst. Deputy Minister, Ken Ross, 506/453-3888
Executive Director, Programs, Rachel Bard, 506/444-4442
Director, Quality Management & Executive Support, Claude Allard, 506/444-4442

#### PLANNING & EVALUATION DIVISION

Executive Director, Bonny Hoyt-Hallett, 506/453-2582
Director, Strategic Planning, Bill Leonard, 506/444-4049
Coordinator, Federal-Provincial Relations, Stephen Chase, 506/453-4050
Coordinator, Legislation Development, Marilyn Born, 506/453-4050

#### PUBLIC HEALTH & MEDICAL SERVICES DIVISION

Asst. Deputy Minister, John Dicaire, 506/453-2321
Chief Public Health Officer, Dr. Denis Allard, 506/453-2323
Provincial Epidemologist, Dr. B. Christofer Balram, 506/453-3092
Acting Director, Medicare/Prescription Drug Program, Fay Mackie, 506/453-2415
Director, Prescription Drug Program, Vacant, 506/453-2415

## Department of HUMAN RESOURCES DEVELOPMENT/Développement des ressources humaines

520 King St., 5th Fl., PO Box 6000, Fredericton NB E3B 5H1
506/453-2001; Fax: 506/453-7478; Email: wwwhrdnb@gov.nb.ca; URL: http://inter.gov.nb.ca/hrd/

#### ACTS ADMINISTERED

Family Income Security Act
Health Services Act
Vocational Rehabilitation for Disabled Persons Act
**Minister**, Hon. Marcelle Mersereau, 506/453-2558, Email: marcellm@gov.nb.ca
Deputy Minister, Ernest MacKinnon, 506/453-2590

#### CORPORATE SERVICES DIVISION

Executive Director, Michael O'Rourke, 506/453-2712
Director, Audit Services, James Church, 506/453-2941
Director, Human Resource Services, Jean Finn, 506/453-2940
Director, Information Systems, Joan Ramsay, 506/453-2866

#### INCOME SECURITY DIVISION

Asst. Deputy Minister, Karen Mann, 506/453-2379
Director, Income Support, Roger Bourgeois, 506/453-2039

#### PLANNING & EVALUATION DIVISION

Executive Director, Norma Dubé, 506/453-2460
Director, Programs, Donald Ferguson, 506/453-2379

#### Associated Agencies, Boards & Commissions

•Social Welfare Appeals Board: PO Box 12999, Fredericton NB E3B 6C2 – 506/525-4007
Chair, Maurice Harquail

## Department of INTERGOVERNMENTAL & ABORIGINAL AFFAIRS/Affaires intergouvernementales et autochtones

PO Box 6000, Fredericton NB E3B 5H1
506/453-2384; Fax: 506/453-2995; URL: http://www.gov.nb.ca/iga/home1_e.htm
**Minister**, Hon. Bernard Thériault
Acting Deputy Minister, Frank Swift, 506/453-7454
Asst. Deputy Minister, Federal-Provincial Affairs, Kevin Malone, 506/457-7275
Asst. Deputy Minister, Intergovernmental Cooperation, François Rioux, 506/453-2976
Director, Aboriginal Affairs, Dan Horsman, 506/453-2671
Protocol Officer, Office of Protocol, Anne Reynolds, 506/453-2671

## Department of JUSTICE/Justice

#412, Centennial Bldg., PO Box 6000, Fredericton NB E3B 5H1
506/453-2719 (Administration); Fax: 506/453-8718; URL: http://www.gov.nb.ca/justice/index.htm

#### ACTS ADMINISTERED

Absconding Debtors Act
Age of Majority Act
Arbitration Act
Arrest & Examinations Act
Assignments & Preferences Act
Attorney General Act
Auctioneers Licence Act
Bulk Sales Act
Business Corporations Act
Charter Compliance Act
Collection Agencies Act
Commissioners for Taking Affidavits Act
Companies Act
Conflict of Laws Rules for Trusts Act
Consumer Product Warranty & Liability Act
Contributory Negligence Act
Controverted Elections Act
Cooperative Associations Act
Corporations Act
Corrupt Practices Inquiries Act
Cost of Credit Disclosure Act
Court Reporters Act
Credit Unions Act
Creditors Relief Act
Criminal Prosecution Expenses Act
Crown Debts Act
Crown Prosecutors Act
Defamation Act
Demise of the Crown Act
Devolution of Estates Act
Direct Sellers Act
Divorce Court Act
Easements Act
Entry Warrants Act
Escheats & Forfeitures Act
Evidence Act
Executors & Trustees Act
Expropriation Act
Factors & Agents Act
Family Services Act (Part VII)
Fatal Accidents Act
Federal Courts Jurisdiction Act
Foreign Judgments Act
Foreign Resident Corporations Act
Frustrated Contracts Act
Garnishee Act
Great Seal Act
Guardianship of Children Act
Habeas Corpus Act
Infirm Persons Act
Innkeepers Act
Inquiries Act
Insurance Act

International Child Abduction Act
International Commercial Arbitration Act
International Sale of Goods Act
International Trusts Act
International Wills Act
Interpretation Act
Interprovincial Subpoena Act
Judges Disqualification Removal Act
Judicature Act
Jury Act
Landlord & Tenant Act
Law Reform Act
Legal Aid Act
Liens on Goods & Chattels Act
Limitation of Actions Act
Limited Partnership Act
Loan & Trust Companies Act
Marine Insurance Act
Marital Property Act
Married Woman's Property Act
Mechanics' Lien Act
Memorials & Executions Act
Merger of Supreme & County Courts of New Brunswick Act
Notaries Public Act
Nova Scotia Grants Act
Partnership Act
Partnerships & Business Names Registration Act
Postal Services Interruption Act
Pre-arranged Funeral Services Act
Premium Tax Act
Presumption of Death Act
Probate Court Act
Proceedings Against the Crown Act
Property Act
Protection of Persons Acting Under Statute Act
Provincial Court Act
Provincial Offences Procedure Act
Provincial Offences Procedure for Young Persons Act
Provision for Dependants Act
Public Records Act
Queen's Counsel & Precedence Act
Queen's Printer Act
Quieting of Titles Act
Real Estate Agents Act
Reciprocal Enforcement of Judgments Act
Reciprocal Enforcement of Maintenance Orders Act
(An Act respecting the Convention Between Canada & the United Kingdom of Great Britain & Northern Ireland & Providing for the) Reciprocal Recognition & Enforcement of Judgments in Civil & Commercial Matters
Recording of Evidence by Sound Recording Machine Act
Regulations Act
(An Act Respecting the) Removal of Archaic Terminology from the Acts of New Brunswick
Residential Tenancies Act
Sale of Goods Act
Sale of Lands Publication Act
Security Frauds Prevention Act
Small Claims Act
Special Insurance Companies Act
Statute Law Amendment Act
Statute of Frauds Act
Succession Law Amendment Act
Surety Bonds Act
Survival of Actions Act
Survivorship Act
Tortfeasors Act
Trespass Act
Trustees Act
Unconscionable Transactions Relief Act
Wage-Earners Protection Act
Warehouse Receipts Act
Warehouseman's Lien Act
Wills Act
Winding-up Act
Woodmen's Lien Act

**Minister & Attorney General**, Hon. James Lockyer, Q.C., 506/453-2583, Fax: 506/453-3651
Deputy Minister, Paul M. LeBreton, Q.C., 506/453-2208, Fax: 506/453-3651
Asst. Deputy Minister, Suzanne Bonnell-Burley, 506/453-2458, Fax: 506/453-3651
Director, Research & Planning, Pauline Desrosier-Hickey, 506/453-3693, Fax: 506/453-7483

**For list of Courts & other Legal Officers, including Judicial Officials & Judges *see* Section 10 of this book.**

### ADMINISTRATIVE SERVICES

Executive Director & Director, Human Resources Services, Neil Foreman
Director, Financial Services, Raymond McLaughlin
Provincial Director, Legal Aid New Brunswick, David Potter, 506/451-1424, Fax: 506/451-1429
Director, Legal Services, Richard Burns, Q.C., 506/453-2222, Fax: 506/453-3275
Director, Legislative Services, Elaine Gunter, 506/453-2544, Fax: 506/457-7342
Director, Public Legal Education & Information Service, Deborah Doherty, 506/453-5369, Fax: 506/457-7342
Director, Public Prosecutions, Glen Abbott, Q.C., 506/453-2784, Fax: 506/453-5364

#### Office of the Queen's Printer

PO Box 6000, Fredericton NB E3B 5H1
506/453-2520; Fax: 506/457-7899
Queen's Printer, Marie-Ange Lévesque

### COURT SERVICES

Executive Director & Director, Operations Court Services, Carolyn Lovely, 506/453-2935, Fax: 506/453-3651
Registrar, Court of Appeal & Court of Queen's Bench, A. DiGiacinto, 506/453-2452, Fax: 506/453-7921
Director, Program Support Court Services, Lynda Richard, 506/453-2452, Fax: 506/453-7921

### JUSTICE SERVICES

Director, Consumer Affairs & Chief Rentalsman, Judy Budovitch, 506/453-2682, Fax: 506/444-4494
Director, Corporate Affairs, Charles McAllister, 506/453-3860, Fax: 506/453-2613
Director, Credit Unions, Cooperatives & Trust Companies & Director, Examinations Branch, Pierre LeBlanc, 506/457-4852, Fax: 506/453-7474
Director, Securities Administration, Donne Smith Jr., 506/658-3060, Fax: 506/658-3059
Superintendent, Insurance, Reginald Richard, 506/453-2512, Fax: 506/453-2613

#### Associated Agencies, Boards & Commissions

•Expropriations Advisory Office: 295 boul St-Pierre ouest, CP 297, Caraquet NB E0B 1K0 – 506/727-3481; Fax: 506/727-2783
Officer, Reginald Leger
•New Brunswick Real Estate Council: PO Box 785, Fredericton NB E3B 5B4 – 506/455-9733; Fax: 506/450-8719
Chair, Carl Sherwood
•Office of the Administrator of Securities: #606, 133 Prince William St., PO Box 5001, Saint John NB E2L 4Y9 – 506/658-3060; Fax: 506/658-3059
Administrator, Donne W. Smith Jr.
Deputy Administrator, Enforcement & Compliance, Edouard LeBlanc

## New Brunswick LIQUOR CORPORATION/ Société des alcools du Nouveau-Brunswick

PO Box 20787, Fredericton NB E3B 5B8
506/452-6826; Fax: 506/452-9890
**Chair**, Wallace Deschenes
President & CEO, Roger J.E. Landry
Executive Vice-President, D. Jack Dorcas
Secretary, Elizabeth Fairley

### LIQUOR LICENSING BRANCH

PO Box 3000, Fredericton NB E3B 5G5
506/453-3732; Fax: 506/457-7335
Policy Advisor, Brian Steeves

## Department of MUNICIPALITIES, CULTURE & HOUSING/Municipalités, culture et habitation

Marysville Place, 20 McGloin St., PO Box 6000, Fredericton NB E3B 5H1
506/453-2690; Fax: 506/457-4991; URL: http://www.gov.nb.ca/mch/index.htm

#### ACTS ADMINISTERED

Arts Development Trust Fund Act
Assessment Act
Business Improvement Areas Act
Cemetery Companies Act (as it pertains to Non-incorporated Areas)
Closing of Retail Establishments Act
Community Planning Act
Condominium Property Act, s. 7(11)
Control of Municipalities Act
Controverted Elections Act
Days of Rest Act
Elections Act (Provincial)
Emergency Measures Act
Film & Video Act
Fire Prevention Act
Flood & Storm Damage Act
Historic Sites Protection Act
Kings Landing Corporation Act
Le Centre Communautaire Sainte-Anne Act
Legislative Assembly Act, ss. 23/24
Libraries Act
Metric Conversion Act
Municipal Assistance Act
Municipal Capital Borrowing Act
Municipal Debenture Act
Municipal Elections Act
Municipal Heritage Preservation Act
Municipal Thoroughfare Easements Act
Municipalities Act
New Brunswick Arts Board Act
New Brunswick Housing Act
New Brunswick Museum Act
Real Property Tax Act (as it pertains to Assessment)
Registry Act (as it pertains to Affidavits)
Residential Property Tax Relief Act
Sport Development Trust Funds Act
Theatres Cinematographs & Amusements Act
Youth Assistance Act (in part)

**Minister**, Hon. Ann Breault, 506/453-3001, Email: annb@gov.nb.ca
Deputy Minister, Julian H. Walker, 506/453-2522, Email: JulianW@gov.nb.ca

### CORPORATE SERVICES DIVISION

Executive Director, Michael McKendy, 506/453-3925, Email: MikeMcK@gov.nb.ca
Director, Budget Services & Acting Director, Financial Services, James Murphy, 506/454-4160, Email: JPMurphy@gov.nb.ca
Director, Communications Services, Susan Morell, 506/457-7843, Fax: 506/453-3676, Email: SMorrell@gov.nb.ca
Director, Information Management Services, Louise Lemon, 506/444-4742, Email: LouiseL@gov.nb.ca
Director, Policy & Planning, Michael Merritt, 506/457-7811, Email: MikeJM@gov.nb.ca

#### COMMUNITY SERVICES DIVISION
Fax: 506/453-2416
Asst. Deputy Minister, Pauline Rivard, 506/453-3259, Email: PaulineR@gov.nb.ca
Director, Housing, Charles Boulay, 506/453-7450, Email: CharlesB@gov.nb.ca
Director, Regional Services, Aline Saintonge, 506/444-5813, Email: ALINESA@gov.nb.ca
Director, Sport, Recreation & Active Living, Suzanne Mason, 506/453-2928, Email: SNMason&gov.nb.ca
Executive Asst., NB Sports Hall of Fame, Deborah Williams, 506/453-3747, Email: DeborahW@gov.nb.ca

#### CULTURAL AFFAIRS DIVISION
Fax: 506/453-2416
Asst. Deputy Minister, Louise Boudreau Gillis, 506/453-5135, Email: LouiseG@gov.nb.ca
Director, Archaeology, Dr. Christopher Turnbull, 506/453-2738, Email: turnbull@gov.nb.ca
Director, Arts Branch, Yolande Bourgeois, 506/453-2555, Email: YolandeB@gov.nb.ca
Director, Heritage Branch, Wayne Burley, 506/453-2324, Email: WayneB@gov.nb.ca
Director, Kings Landing Historical Settlement, Robert Dallison, 506/363-4999, Email: KingsLan@gov.nb.ca
Director, New Brunswick Museum (Saint John), Dr. Frank Milligan, 506/643-2336
Directeur, Village historique acadien, Jean-Yves Thériault, 506/727-3467, Email: villhis1@nbnet.nb.ca

#### HUMAN RESOURCE SERVICES & ADMINISTRATION DIVISION
Executive Director, Sylvie Levesque-Finn, 506/453-5239, Email: SylvieLF@gov.nb.ca

#### LIBRARIES DIVISION
Asst. Deputy Minister, James (Jim) Morell, 506/453-2550, Email: MorrellJ@gov.nb.ca
Executive Director, Jocelyne LeBel, 506/453-2354, Email: JLeBel@gov.nb.ca

#### MUNICIPAL SERVICES DIVISION
Fax: 506/457-4991
Asst. Deputy Minister, Paul O'Connell, 506/453-3256, Email: PaulOc@gov.nb.ca
Chief Electoral Officer, Elections Branch, Barbara J. Landry, 506/453-2218, Email: BarbaraL@gov.nb.ca
Manager, Downtown Development Branch, Walter Waite, 506/457-4947, Fax: 506/458-9369, Email: WalterW@gov.nb.ca
Director, Land Use Planning Branch, Gérard Belliveau, 506/453-2171, Email: GerardB@gov.nb.ca
Director, Municipal Government Services, Paul Blackmore, 506/453-2434, Email: BlackmoreP@gov.nb.ca
Secretary, Municipal Capital Borrowing Board, Dan Rae, 506/453-2154, Email: DanRae@gov.nb.ca

#### PUBLIC SAFETY SERVICES DIVISION
Executive Director & Provincial Fire Marshal, James Stith, 506/453-2072

##### New Brunswick Emergency Measures Organization (EMO)
65 Brunswick St., PO Box 6000, Fredericton NB E3B 5H1
506/453-2133; Fax: 506/453-5513; URL: http://www.gov.nb.ca/pss/emo.htm
Deputy Director, Art Skaling, 506/453-5507

##### Office of the Fire Marshall
PO Box 6000, Fredericton NB E3B 5H1
506/453-2004; Fax: 506/457-4899; URL: http://www.gov.nb.ca/pss/fmo.htm
Deputy Fire Marshal, Philippa Gourley, 506/453-2004
Acting Office Manager, Lisa Munn, 506/453-2284

##### Associated Agencies, Boards & Commissions
•Film NB: – 506/453-2553; Email: FilmNB@gov.nb.ca; URL: http://www.gov.nb.ca/filmnb/index.htm
Responsible for fostering New Brunswick's film industry.
Executive Director, Sam Grana
•New Brunswick Film Classification Board: c/o Dept. of Municipalities, Culture & Housing, 20 McGloin St., PO Box 6000, Fredericton NB E3B 5H1 – 506/454-5475
Chair & Director, Vacant
Secretary, Janice Morgan, Email: MorganJA@gov.nb.ca
•Regional Assessment Review Board: PO Box 6000, Fredericton NB E3B 5H1 – 506/453-2126
Chair, Lawrence Garvie

### Department of NATURAL RESOURCES & ENERGY (NRE)/Ressources naturelles et énergie (RNE)
PO Box 6000, Fredericton NB E3B 5H1
506/453-3826; Fax: 506/444-4367; URL: http://www.gov.nb.ca/dnre/index.htm
Manages all natural resources within the province including fish & wildlife, timber, minerals, energy, Crown lands & water resources. Responsible for the development, protection, allocation & utilization of resources in a way that is considered economically, environmentally & socially acceptable.

#### ACTS ADMINISTERED
Bituminous Shale Act
Crown Lands & Forests Act
Ecological Reserves Act
Endangered Species Act
Energy Efficiency Act
Fish & Wildlife Act
Forest Fires Act
Forest Products Act
Gas Distribution Act
Gasoline, Diesel Oil & Home Heating Oil Pricing Act
Maritime Forestry Complex Corporation Act
Metallic Minerals Tax Act
Mining Act
Oil & Natural Gas Act
Ownership of Minerals Act
Oyster Fisheries Act
Parks Act
Pipe Line Act
Quarriable Substances Act
Scalers Act
Surveys Act
Territorial Division Act
Underground Storage Act
**Minister**, Hon. Alan Graham, 506/453-2510, Fax: 506/453-2930
Deputy Minister, George Bouchard, 506/453-2501, Fax: 506/453-2930

#### CORPORATE SERVICES
Asst. Deputy Minister, Pam Breau, 506/453-2207, Fax: 506/453-2930
Executive Director, Regional Operations, Tom Reid, 506/453-2207, Fax: 506/453-2930
Director, Communications, Louella Woods, 506/453-2614, Fax: 506/457-4881
Director, Financial Services, Keith Burgess, 506/453-2468, Fax: 506/453-4279
Director, Information System Services, Peter Andrews, 506/453-5598, Fax: 506/453-6889
Director, Parks & Natural Areas, Don Boudreau, 506/453-2730, Fax: 506/453-6630
Director, Policy & Planning, Humphrey Sheenan, 506/453-2684, Fax: 506/453-2930
Director, Regional Support Services, Richard Monroe, 506/453-2488, Fax: 506/453-2412

#### MINERAL RESOURCES & ENERGY
Asst. Deputy Minister, Don Barnett, 506/453-3862, Fax: 506/453-2930, Email: dbarnett@gov.nb.ca
Commissioner, Mining, Michael Quinn, 506/450-0980, Fax: 506/450-7824
Director, Geological Surveys Branch, Vacant, 506/453-2206, Fax: 506/453-3671
Director, Mines & Energy Branch, Darwin Curtis, 506/444-5005, Fax: 506/453-3671, Email: dcurtis@gov.nb.ca

#### RENEWABLE RESOURCES
Asst. Deputy Minister, M. David MacFarlane, 506/453-3063, Fax: 506/453-2930
Director, Crown Lands, Jean Paul Robichaud, 506/453-2437, Fax: 506/457-4802
Director, Fish & Wildlife, Dr. Arnold H. Boer, 506/453-2440, Fax: 506/453-6699
Director, Forest Management, Thomas L. Spinney, 506/453-2432, Fax: 506/453-6689

##### Associated Agencies, Boards & Commissions
•Board of Examiners under the Scaler's Act: PO Box 6000, Fredericton NB E3B 5H1 – 506/453-2441; Fax: 506/453-6689
•Forest Protection Limited: Comp 5, Site 24, RR#1, Fredericton NB E3B 4X2 – 506/446-6930; Fax: 506/446-6934
•New Brunswick Forest Products Commission: PO Box 6000, Fredericton NB E3B 5H1 – 506/453-2196; Fax: 506/457-4966
Chair, Richard N. Renouf
Executive Director, Linda D. Gould

### Office of the OMBUDSMAN/Bureau de l'ombudsman
767 Brunswick St., PO Box 6000, Fredericton NB E3B 5H1
506/453-2789; Fax: 506/453-5599; Email: nbombud@gov.nb.ca
**Ombudsman**, Ellen E. King
Asst. Ombudsman & Legal Counsel, Claire Pitre
Secretary, Marielle Goggin

### New Brunswick POLICE COMMISSION (NBPC)/Commission de police du Nouveau-Brunswick
#103, 191 Prospect St. West, Fredericton NB E3B 2T7
506/453-2069; Fax: 506/457-3542
The Commission investigates & determines complaints alleging misconduct by municipal & regional police officers; investigates any matter relating to any aspect of policing in any area of the province; determines the adequacy of municipal, regional and RCMP police forces within the province.
**Chair**, Hon. Stuart G. Stratton, Q.C.
Executive Director, Clem Bolduc

### New Brunswick POWER CORPORATION (NBPC)/La société d'énergie du Nouveau-Brunswick
515 King St., PO Box 2000, Fredericton NB E3B 4X1
506/458-3166
**President & CEO**, James Hannkinson
Senior Vice-President, Chuck Baird
Director, Environmental Affairs, Glen Wilson
Manager, Environmental Assessment & Assurance, Charles Hickman

## REGIONAL DEVELOPMENT CORPORATION (RDC)/Société d'aménagement régional (SAR)

836 Churchill Row, PO Box 428, Fredericton NB E3B 5R4
Fredericton: 506/453-2277; Fax: 506/453-7988; URL: http://www.gov.nb.ca/rdc/home_e.htm
Bathurst: 506/547-2094, Fax: 506/547-2797
Head agency for the negotiation & planning processes associated to federal & provincial economic development agreements & arrangements. The RDC makes recommendations to the provincial Cabinet concerning economic development opportunities & priorities.
Provides ongoing financial & administrative management services for federal & provincial agreements. The delivery of programs & projects is primarily the responsibility of provincial departments. Staff work cooperatively with other federal & provincial personnel to in various activities. The RDC also works with the Atlantic Canada Opportunities Agency on many regional economic development projects & issues in New Brunsiwck. The Corporation is responsible for the implementation of the Development Assistance Program (DAP), the Action North Initiative (ANI).
**Minister Responsible**, Hon. Jean Paul Savoie
General Manager, Frank Swift
Asst. General Manager, Development, Roland Cormier
Asst. General Manager, Finance & Administration, Gordon Gilman
Program Administrator, Develpment Assistance Program, Elsie Gardner, 506/453-8534, Email: elsieg@gov.nb.ca
Manager, Corporate Secretariat, Oscar Paulin, 506/453-8533, Email: oscarp@gov.nb.ca
Manager, Financial & Administrative Services, Duska Geldart, 506/453-8527, Email: duskag@gov.nb.ca
Manager, Northern Development, Charles-Édouard Landry, 506/457-2094, Fax: 506/547-2797, Email: celandry@gov.nb.ca
Manager, Planning & Analysis, Michel Gauvin, 506/453-8537, Email: michelg@gov.nb.ca
Project Executive, Rocky Landry, 506/453-8495, Email: rockyl@gov.nb.ca
Project Executive, Jocelyne Mills, 506/453-8539, Email: jmills@gov.nb.ca
Project Executive, Ray Wilson, 506/453-8540, Email: rayw@gov.nb.ca
Project Officer, Ronald Pitre, 506/547-2094, Email: rpitre@gov.nb.ca

## New Brunswick RESEARCH & PRODUCTIVITY COUNCIL (RPC)/Conseil de la recherche et de la productivité du Nouveau-Brunswick (CRP)

921 College Hill Rd., Fredericton NB E3B 6Z9
506/452-8994; Fax: 506/452-1395; Email: vjackson@rpc.unb.ca; URL: http://www.rpc.unb.ca
**Executive Director**, Dr. P. Lewell, 506/452-0585, Email: plewell@rpc.unb.ca
Head, Administration & Finance, Stephen Fox, 506/452-1380, Email: sfox@rpc.unb.ca
Head, Chemical & Biotechnical Services, Dr. Peter Silk, 506/452-1369, Email: psilk@rpc.unb.ca
Head, Engineering Materials & Diagnostics, Jarek Goszczynski, 506/452-1396, Email: jgoszczy@rpc.unb.ca
Head, Food, Fisheries & Aquaculture, Dr. Bev Bacon, 506/452-1368, Email: bbacon@rpc.unb.ca
Head, IRAP, Dr. P. Lewell, 506/452-1385, Email: plewell@rpc.unb.ca
Head, Process & Environmental Technology, Dr. P. Lewell, 506/460-5653, Email: plewell@rpc.unb.ca
Head, Product Innovation, Mike Carr, 506/452-0590, Email: mcarr@rpc.unb.ca
Coordinator, Information Centre, Virginia Jackson, 506/452-1381, Email: vjackson@rpc.unb.ca

## Department of the SOLICITOR GENERAL/ Solliciteur général

Barker House, 4th Fl., PO Box 6000, Fredericton NB E3B 5H1
506/453-7414; Fax: 506/453-3870; URL: http://www.gov.nb.ca/solgen/index.htm

#### ACTS ADMINISTERED

Coroners Act
Corrections Act
Criminal Code
Custody & Detention of Young Persons Act
Intoxicated Persons Detention Act
Police Act
Private Investigators & Security Services Act
Salvage Dealers Licensing Act
Sheriffs Act
Training School Act
Victim Services Act
Young Offenders Act
**Minister**, Hon. Jane Barry
Deputy Solicitor General, Ronald Murray, 506/453-7412
Chief Coroner, Peter Dickens, 506/453-3604
Chief Sheriff, Eric Howatt, 506/453-3604
Asst. Deputy Minister, Corporate Services, Grant Garneau, 506/453-7142

#### CORRECTIONAL SERVICES

Asst. Deputy Minister, Nora Kelly, 506/444-4028
Director, Adults Institutional Services, Brian Mackin, 506/453-2846
Acting Director, Institutional & Young Offender Services, Bob Ecktein, 506/453-2846, Fax: 506/453-2307
Director, Victim & Community Services, Doug Naish, 506/453-2846

#### LAW ENFORCEMENT

Executive Director, Brian Alexander, 506/453-3603, Fax: 506/457-4957
Director, Commercial Vehicle Enforcement, B. Doyle, 506/453-7157
Coordinator, Transportation of Dangerous Goods, Wayne Hennigar, 506/856-2860
Chief, Provincial Firearms Office, Dianne Kelly, 506/453-3775

## DEPARTMENT OF SUPPLY & SERVICES

PO Box 6000, Fredericton NB E3B 5H1
506/453-3742; Fax: 506/444-4400; URL: http://www.gov.nb.ca/supply/index.htm

#### ACTS ADMINISTERED

Archives Act
Public Purchasing Act
Public Works Act
**Minister**, Hon. Peter LeBlanc
Deputy Minister, G. Stephenson Wheatley, P.Eng.
Chief Information Officer, Corporate Information Management Services, Lori MacMullen, 506/457-6849, Fax: 506/453-2270

#### ADMINISTRATION

Director, Corporate Services, Richard Burnett, 506/453-6060
Director, Human Resources & Administration, Eric White, 506/453-5952
Communications Officer, Donald MacPherson, 506/444-3281

#### BUILDINGS GROUP

Asst. Deputy Minister, Vacant, 506/453-2228
Executive Director, Design & Construction, Ashley Cummings, 506/453-2228
Executive Director, Facilities Management, Greg Cook, 506/444-4530
Director, Property Management, Preston Hawkins, 506/453-2221

#### SERVICES GROUP

URL: http://www.gov.nb.ca/supply/sgs/index.htm (Purchasing)
Asst. Deputy Minister, Vacant
Executive Director, Supply & General Services, Richard Dunphy, 506/453-8727, Fax: 506/444-4200
Director, Provincial Archives of New Brunswick, Marion Beyea, 506/453-3811, Fax: 506/453-3288
Director, Translation Bureau, Jean-Eudes Levesque, 506/453-2920, Fax: 506/459-7911

## Department of TRANSPORTATION/ Transports

King Tower, Kings Pl., 2nd Fl., PO Box 6000, Fredericton NB E3B 5H1
506/453-3626
Motor Vehicles: 506/453-2810

#### ACTS ADMINISTERED

All-Terrain Vehicle Act
Highway Act
Motor Vehicle Act
New Brunswick Highway Corporation Act
New Brunswick Transportation Authority Act
Public Utilities Act
**Minister**, Hon. Sheldon Lee, 506/453-2559
Deputy Minister, Donald J. McCrea, 506/453-2549, Email: dot007@gov.nb.ca
Asst. Deputy Minister & Chief Highway Engineer, David J. Johnstone, 506/453-2351, Email: dot006@gov.nb.ca
Executive Director, Administration, Dale Wilson, 506/453-2552, Email: dalew@gov.nb.ca
Executive Director, Engineering Services, D.W. Manuel, 506/453-2849, Email: dot005@gov.nb.ca
Executive Director, Motor Vehicles & Policy, Walter W. Steeves, 506/453-2552, Email: dot008@gov.nb.ca
Executive Director, Operations, George Haines, 506/453-2849, Email: dot018@gov.nb.ca
Director, Administrative Services, S.C. Andrews-Caron, 506/453-2663, Email: adm046@gov.nb.ca
Director, Construction, K. Lawson, 506/453-2673, Email: con004@gov.nb.ca
Director, Design, C.H. Page, 506/453-2608, Email: des040@gov.nb.ca
Director, Human Resources, Marguerite Levesque, 506/453-2332, Email: hrb004@gov.nb.ca
Director, Information Systems, Kenneth Connell, 506/453-2990, Email: connellk@gov.nb.ca
Director, Maintenance & Traffic, Emilia Rodrigues, 506/453-2600, Email: tec021@gov.nb.ca
Director & Registrar, Motor Vehicles & Officer Responsible, Dangerous/Hazardous Substances Transport, James Morrison, 506/453-2407, Email: dmv022@gov.nb.ca
Director, Planning & Land Management, G.A. Goguen, 506/453-2754, Email: tra007@gov.nb.ca
Director, Quality Initiatives, G.H. Keenan, 506/453-7955, Email: dot012@gov.nb.ca
Director, Structures, Frederick Blaney, 506/453-2674, Email: str031@gov.nb.ca
Acting Director, Transportation Policy, John Palmer, 506/453-2802, Email: pol006@gov.nb.ca
Supervisor, Safety Promotion, Michael Crowther, 506/453-3645

#### Associated Agencies, Boards & Commissions

•Board of Commissioners of Public Utilities: 110 Charlotte St., PO Box 5001, Saint John NB E2L 4Y9 – 506/658-2504; Fax: 506/633-0163

Chair, D.C. Nicholson

Secretary, Lorraine Legere

•Motor Vehicle Dealer Licensing Board: PO Box 6000, Fredericton NB E3B 5H1 – 506/453-2443

The New Brunswick Motor Carrier Board was abolished on May 15, 1995. Questions concerning public motor bus requirements may be directed to 506/658-2504; transport-related questions may be directed to 506/453-3939.

Officer, T.C. Walton

•New Brunswick Transportation Agency: Kings Place, PO Box 6000, Fredericton NB E3B 5H1 – 506/453-2802; Fax: 506/453-2900

Chair, Donald J. McCrea, 506/453-2549

Vice-Chair, W.W. Steeves, 506/453-2552

## WORKPLACE HEALTH, SAFETY & COMPENSATION COMMISSION OF NEW BRUNSWICK (WHSCC)/Santé, securité et indemnisation des accidents au travail du Nouveau-Brunswick

1 Portland St., PO Box 160, Saint John NB E2L 3X9

506/632-2200; Fax: 506/632-2226; URL: http://www.gov.nb.ca/whscc/index.htm

Toll Free: 1-800-222-9775

Fredericton: 500 Beaverbrook Ct., 4th Fl., Fredericton NB E3B 5X4

506/453-2467, Fax: 506/453-7982

Toll Free: 1-800-442-9776

#### ACTS ADMINISTERED

Occupational Health & Safety Act

Workers' Compensation Act

**President & CEO**, Vacant

Executive Vice-President & Vice-President, Technology & Planning, David Greason

Chair, Médard Collette

Chair, Appeals Tribunal, Léonard Arsenault

Vice-President, Finance & Administration, Frank Chevrier

Vice-President, Operations, Brian Connell

Vice-President, Prevention & Rehabilitation, Dow Dorcas

Manager, Public Affairs, France Haché

Director, Workers' Rehabilitation Centre, Barb Keir

## YOUTH COUNCIL OF NEW BRUNSWICK (YCNB)/Conseil de la jeunesse du Nouveau-Brunswick

736 King St., PO Box 6000, Fredericton NB E3B 5H1

506/453-3271; Fax: 506/444-4413

**Chair**, Corinne Godbout

Executive Director, Beverley J. Barnes

# GOVERNMENT OF NEWFOUNDLAND & LABRADOR

**Seat of Government:** Legislative Assembly, Confederation Bldg., St. John's NF A1B 4J6

URL: http://www.gov.nf.ca/

The Province of Newfoundland entered Confederation March 31, 1949. It has an area of 371,634.56 km2, and the StatsCan census population in 1996 was 551,792.

## Office of the LIEUTENANT GOVERNOR

Government House, Military Rd., PO Box 5517, St. John's NF A1C 5W4

709/729-4494; Fax: 709/729-2234

**Lieutenant Governor**, Hon. A.M. (Max) House

Private Secretary, D. Wayne Mitchell

## Office of the PREMIER

Confederation Bldg., 8th Fl., PO Box 8700, St. John's NF A1B 4J6

Fax: 709/729-5875; URL: http://www.gov.nf.ca/exec/premier/premier.htm

**Premier**, Hon. Brian Tobin, 709/729-3570

Acting Chief of Staff, Alphonsus E. Faour, 709/729-3558

Parliamentary Asst., Oliver Langdon, 709/729-2328

Executive Asst., Ed Joyce, 709/637-2462

Executive Asst., Paul D. Sparkes, 709/729-3961

Personal Asst., Margot Brown, 709/729-3972

Director, Communications, Cathy Coady, 709/729-3960

Legislative Asst., Heidi Bonnell, 709/729-0499

Special Asst., Ed Hollett

Special Asst., Gail V. Joy, 709/729-2578

Administrative Officer, Olive White, 709/729-3566

## EXECUTIVE COUNCIL

Confederation Bldg., PO Box 8700, St. John's NF A1B 4J6

709/729-5645; URL: http://www.gov.nf.ca/exec/start.htm

Premier & President, Executive Council, Minister, Energy & Mines, Minister Responsible, Intergovernmental Affairs, Hon. Brian Tobin, 709/729-3570, Fax: 709/729-5875

Minister, Health, Hon. Joan Marie Aylward, 709/729-3124, Fax: 709/729-0121

Minister, Environment, Hon. Kevin Aylward, M.H.A., 709/729-2574, Fax: 709/729-0112

Minister, Human Resources & Minister Responsible, Status of Women, Hon. Julie Bettney, 709/729-3580, Fax: 709/729-6996

Minister, Justice & Attorney General, Hon. Chris D. Decker, 709/729-2869, Fax: 709/729-0469

Minister, Finance & President, Treasury Board, Hon. Paul D. Dicks, Q.C., 709/729-2858, Fax: 709/729-2232

Minister, Fisheries & Aquaculture, Hon. R. John Efford, 709/729-3705, Fax: 709/729-0360

Minister, Development & Rural Renewal, Hon. Judy Foote, 709/729-4729, Fax: 709/729-0654

Minister, Industry, Trade & Technology, Hon. Charles J. Furey, 709/729-2791, Fax: 709/729-2828

Minister, Education, Hon. Roger D. Grimes, 709/729-5040, Fax: 709/729-0414

Minister, Tourism, Culture & Recreation, Hon. Sandra Kelly, 709/729-0659, Fax: 709/729-0662

Minister, Government Services & Lands, Hon. Ernest McLean, 709/729-4713, Fax: 709/729-4754

Minister, Works, Service & Transportation, Hon. Lloyd Matthews, 709/729-3678, Fax: 709/729-4285

Minister, Municipal & Provincial Affairs, Hon. Arthur D. Reid, 709/729-3048, Fax: 709/729-0943

Minister, Forest Resources & Agrifoods & Government House Leader, Hon. Beaton Tulk, 709/729-4716, Fax: 709/729-2076

#### Cabinet Secretariat

709/729-5218

Clerk, Executive Council & Secretary to Cabinet, Malcolm Rowe, Q.C., 709/729-2853, Fax: 709/729-5218

Deputy Clerk, Executive Council & Asst. Secretary to Cabinet, Alphonsus E. Faour, 780/729-2844, Fax: 780/729-5218

Asst. Secretary, Economic Policy, Andrew Noseworthy, 709/729-2845, Fax: 709/729-5218

Asst. Secretary, Social Policy, Florence Delaney, 709/729-2850, Fax: 709/729-5218

Executive Director, Communications & Consultations, John Downton, 709/729-4164, Fax: 709/729-0584

Director, Financial Administration, Douglas Heffernan, 709/729-1984, Fax: 709/729-0435

#### Cabinet Committees

Economic Policy Committee

Planning & Priorities Committee

Social Policy Committee

Treasury Board Committee

Cabinet Committee on Routine Matters & Appointments

Cabinet Committee on Rural Revitalization

#### Government Programs Office

Fax: 709/729-5038

Director, Resource & Economic Policy, Tim Murphy, 709/729-2980

Director, Social & Fiscal Policy, Bruce Hollett, 709/729-3954

#### Intergovernmental Affairs Secretariat

Fax: 709/729-5038

Minister Responsible, Hon. Brian Tobin, 709/729-3570, Fax: 709/729-5875

Secretary, Intergovernmental Affairs, Barbara Knight, 709/729-2134

Asst. Secretary, Intergovernmental Affairs, Brian Bursey, 709/729-3164

#### Labrador & Aboriginal Affairs Secretariat

Fax: 709/729-4900

Secretary, Harold Marshall, 709/729-4814

Asst. Secretary, Aboriginal Affairs, Raymond Hawco, 709/729-6062

#### Treasury Board Secretariat

709/729-2156; URL: http://www.gov.nf.ca/exec/Presiden/presiden.htm

President, Hon. Paul D. Dicks, Q.C., 709/729-2858, Fax: 709/729-2232

Secretary, Peter Kennedy, 709/729-3559

Asst. Secretary, Human Resources & Budgeting, Robert Smart, 709/729-2633

## HOUSE OF ASSEMBLY

c/o Clerk's Office, Confederation Bldg., PO Box 8700, St.John's NF A1B 4J6

709/729-3405; Fax: 709/729-4820; URL: http://www.gov.nf.ca/house/hoa_ovr.htm

Legislative Library: 709/729-3604

**Clerk & Law Clerk:** A. John Noel

**Speaker:** Hon. Lloyd Snow, 709/729-3403

**Sergeant-at-Arms:** Elizabeth Gallagher

**Manager of Hansard:** Irene Tapper, 709/729-0960

Deputy Speaker & Chair, Committees, Percy Barrett

Deputy Chair, Committees, Melvin Penney

Clerk Asst., Elizabeth Murphy

#### Government Caucus Office (Lib.)

PO Box 8700, St. John's NF A1B 4J6

709/729-3400; Fax: 709/729-5774

#### Office of the Official Opposition (PC)

Confederation Bldg., 5th Fl., PO Box 8700, St. John's NF A1B 4J6

709/729-3391; Fax: 709/729-5202

Leader, Loyola Sullivan

Opposition House Leader, Harvey Hodder

#### Office of the New Democratic Party (NDP)

PO Box 8700, St. John's NF A1B 4J6

709/729-0270; Fax: 709/576-1443

Leader, Jack Harris

#### House Committees

Clerk of Committees, Elizabeth Murphy, 709/729-3434

Government Services Committee
Resource Committee
Select Committee on Insurance
Social Service Committee
Standing Committee on Privileges & Elections
Standing Committee on Public Accounts
Standing Orders Committee
Striking Committee

## FORTY-THIRD ASSEMBLY - NEWFOUNDLAND & LABRADOR

709/729-3405
Last General Election, February 22, 1996. Maximum Duration, 5 years.
**Party Standings (June 12, 1997)**
Liberal (Lib.) 36
Progressive Conservative (PC) 9
New Democratic Party (NDP) 1
Independent 1
Vacancy 1
Total 48
**Salaries, Indemnities & Allowances (1996)**
Members' sessional indemnity $38,028. In addition to this are the following:
Premier $54,843
Ministers; Speaker; Leader of the Opposition $39,834
Government Whip & Opposition Whip $6,000
Chair of Committees (Deputy Speaker) $19,917
Deputy Chair of Committees $9,958
Opposition House Leader $19,917

#### MEMBERS BY CONSTITUENCY

Following is: constituency (number of eligible voters at 1996 election) member, party affiliation, St. John's Telephone number. (Address for all is Confederation Bldg., PO Box 8700, St. John's NF A1B 4J6.)
Refer to Cabinet List, Government Caucus Office, and Opposition Office, for Fax numbers.

Baie Verte (7,461) Paul Shelley, PC, 709/729-4841
Bay of Islands (8,041) Hon. Brian Tobin, Lib., 709/729-3570
Bellevue (8,207) Percy Barrett, Lib., 709/729-5204
Bonavista North (8,613) Hon. Beaton Tulk, Lib., 709/729-4715
Bonavista South (9,277) Roger Fitzgerald, PC, 709/729-6131
Burgeo & La Poile (8,864) William Ramsay, Lib., 709/729-5207
Burin-Placentia West (8,609) Mary Hodder, Lib., 709/729-0739
Cape St. Francis (7,860) Jack Byrne, PC, 709/729-6979
Carbonear-Harbour Grace (9,069) Hon. Arthur D. Reid, Lib., 709/729-3048
Cartwright-L'Anse au Clair (3,396) Yvonne Jones, Ind., 709/729-3573
Conception Bay East & Bell Island (8,170) James Walsh, Lib., 709/729-5209
Conception Bay South (8,023) Bob French, PC, 709/729-5907
Exploits (8,269) Hon. Roger D. Grimes, Lib., 709/729-0659
Ferryland (8,302) Loyola Sullivan, PC, 709/729-4884
Fortune Bay-Cape la Hune (8,142) Oliver Langdon, Lib., 709/729-2328
Gander (8,237) Hon. Sandra Kelly, Lib., 709/729-0657
Grand Bank (8,695) Hon. Judy Foote, Lib., 709/729-4729
Grand Falls-Buchans (8,700) Anna Thistle, Lib., 709/729-4726
Harbour Main-Whitbourne (8,434) Don Whelan, Lib., 709/729-0140
Humber East (8,514) Robert Mercer, Lib., 709/729-3424
Humber Valley (7,728) Rick Woodford, Lib., 709/729-4864
Humber West (7,916) Hon. Paul D. Dicks, Q.C., Lib., 709/729-2858
Kilbride (8,635) Edward Byrne, PC, 709/729-3758
Labrador West (6,803) Perry Canning, Lib., 709/729-0264
Lake Melville (6,009) Hon. Ernest McLean, Lib., 709/729-4712
Lewisporte (8,397) Melvin Penney, Lib., 709/729-5274
Mount Pearl (8,520) Hon. Julie Bettney, Lib., 709/729-3580
Placentia & St. Mary's (8,101) Anthony Sparrow, Lib., 709/729-3841
Port au Port (8,334) Gerald Smith, Lib., 709/729-5045
Port de Grave (8,862) Hon. R. John Efford, Lib., 709/729-3678
Signal Hill-Quidi Vidi (6,886) Jack Harris, NDP, 709/729-0270
St. Barbe (7,720) Hon. Charles J. Furey, Lib., 709/729-2791
St. George's-Stephenville East (8,630) Hon. Kevin Aylward, M.H.A., Lib., 709/729-2722
St. John's Centre (8,109) Hon. Joan Marie Aylward, Lib., 709/729-3124
St. John's East (7,747) John Ottenheimer, PC, 709/729-3651
St. John's North (6,703) Hon. Lloyd Matthews, Lib., 709/729-3678
St. John's South (8,452) Tom Osborne, PC, 709/729-4882
St. John's West (8,642) Vacant,
Terra Nova (8,777) Tom Lush, Lib., 709/729-4649
The Straits & White Bay South (8,310) Hon. Chris D. Decker, Lib., 709/729-2869
Topsail (8,143) Ralph Wiseman, Lib., 709/729-4853
Torngat Mountains (1,233) Wally Anderson, Lib., 709/729-0990
Trinity North (8,982) Doug Oldford, Lib., 709/729-0138
Trinity-Bay de Verde (9,136) Hon. Lloyd Snow, Lib., 709/729-3403
Twillingate & Fogo (9,040) Gerry Reid, Lib., 709/729-4717
Virginia Waters (8,592) Walter Noel, Lib., 709/729-5208
Waterford Valley (9,361) Harvey Hodder, PC, 709/729-4234
Windsor-Springdale (8,962) Graham R. Flight, Lib., 709/729-1948

#### MEMBERS (ALPHABETICAL)

Following is: member, constituency (number of eligible voters at 1996 election) party affiliation, St. John's Telephone number. (Address for all is Confederation Bldg., PO Box 8700, St. John's NF A1B 4J6.)
Refer to Cabinet List, Government Caucus Office, and Opposition Office, for Fax numbers.

Wally Anderson, Torngat Mountains (1,233) Lib., 709/729-0990
Hon. Joan Marie Aylward, St. John's Centre (8,109) Lib., 709/729-3124
Hon. Kevin Aylward, M.H.A., St. George's-Stephenville East (8,630) Lib., 709/729-2722
Percy Barrett, Bellevue (8,207) Lib., 709/729-5204
Hon. Julie Bettney, Mount Pearl (8,520) Lib., 709/729-3580
Edward Byrne, Kilbride (8,635) PC, 709/729-3758
Jack Byrne, Cape St. Francis (7,860) PC, 709/729-6979
Perry Canning, Labrador West (6,803) Lib., 709/729-0264
Hon. Chris D. Decker, The Straits & White Bay South (8,310) Lib., 709/729-2869
Hon. Paul D. Dicks, Q.C., Humber West (7,916) Lib., 709/729-2858
Hon. R. John Efford, Port de Grave (8,862) Lib., 709/729-3678
Roger Fitzgerald, Bonavista South (9,277) PC, 709/729-6131
Graham R. Flight, Windsor-Springdale (8,962) Lib., 709/729-1948
Hon. Judy Foote, Grand Bank (8,695) Lib., 709/729-4729
Bob French, Conception Bay South (8,023) PC, 709/729-5907
Hon. Charles J. Furey, St. Barbe (7,720) Lib., 709/729-2791
Hon. Roger D. Grimes, Exploits (8,269) Lib., 709/729-0659
Jack Harris, Signal Hill-Quidi Vidi (6,886) NDP, 709/729-0270
Harvey Hodder, Waterford Valley (9,361) PC, 709/729-4234
Mary Hodder, Burin-Placentia West (8,609) Lib., 709/729-0739
Yvonne Jones, Cartwright-L'Anse au Clair (3,396) Ind., 709/729-3573
Hon. Sandra Kelly, Gander (8,237) Lib., 709/729-0657
Oliver Langdon, Fortune Bay-Cape la Hune (8,142) Lib., 709/729-2328
Tom Lush, Terra Nova (8,777) Lib., 709/729-4649
Hon. Lloyd Matthews, St. John's North (6,703) Lib., 709/729-3678
Hon. Ernest McLean, Lake Melville (6,009) Lib., 709/729-4712
Robert Mercer, Humber East (8,514) Lib., 709/729-3424
Walter Noel, Virginia Waters (8,592) Lib., 709/729-5208
Doug Oldford, Trinity North (8,982) Lib., 709/729-0138
Tom Osborne, St. John's South (8,452) PC, 709/729-4882
John Ottenheimer, St. John's East (7,747) PC, 709/729-3651
Melvin Penney, Lewisporte (8,397) Lib., 709/729-5274
William Ramsay, Burgeo & La Poile (8,864) Lib., 709/729-5207
Hon. Arthur D. Reid, Carbonear-Harbour Grace (9,069) Lib., 709/729-3048
Gerry Reid, Twillingate & Fogo (9,040) Lib., 709/729-4717
Paul Shelley, Baie Verte (7,461) PC, 709/729-4841
Gerald Smith, Port au Port (8,334) Lib., 709/729-5045
Hon. Lloyd Snow, Trinity-Bay de Verde (9,136) Lib., 709/729-3403
Anthony Sparrow, Placentia & St. Mary's (8,101) Lib., 709/729-3841
Loyola Sullivan, Ferryland (8,302) PC, 709/729-4884
Anna Thistle, Grand Falls-Buchans (8,700) Lib., 709/729-4726
Hon. Brian Tobin, Bay of Islands (8,041) Lib., 709/729-3570
Hon. Beaton Tulk, Bonavista North (8,613) Lib., 709/729-4715
James Walsh, Conception Bay East & Bell Island (8,170) Lib., 709/729-5209
Don Whelan, Harbour Main-Whitbourne (8,434) Lib., 709/729-0140
Ralph Wiseman, Topsail (8,143) Lib., 709/729-4853
Rick Woodford, Humber Valley (7,728) Lib., 709/729-4864

#### Vacancies:

St. John's West (8,642)

## NEWFOUNDLAND & LABRADOR GOVERNMENT DEPARTMENTS & AGENCIES

### Office of the AUDITOR GENERAL

Confederation Bldg., PO Box 8700, St. John's NF A1B 4J6
709/729-2700; Fax: 709/729-5970
**Auditor General**, Elizabeth Marshall, C.A.

## CHURCHILL FALLS (LABRADOR) CORPORATION LIMITED

PO Box 12500, St. John's NF A1B 3T5
709/737-1450; Fax: 709/737-1782
**CEO**, William E. Wells, 709/737-1291
President, T. David Collett, 709/737-1372
Vice-President, Finance & Chief Financial Officer, D.W. Osmond, 709/737-1389
Vice-President, Human Resources, General Counsel & Secretary, Maureen Greene, 709/737-1465
General Manager, J.R. Haynes, 709/925-8231
Manager, Corporate Affairs, Donald J. Barrett, 709/737-1370, Fax: 709/737-1816

## Department of DEVELOPMENT & RURAL RENEWAL

PO Box 8700, St. John's NF A1B 4J6
URL: http://www.gov.nf.ca/dev.htm
The department has a mandate to create jobs & growth in rural areas. It has three core business lines:
Regional economic development assitance is provided through assistance to the province's 20 economic zones operated by locally elected boards.
Small enterprise development is provided through business opportunity identificaion & business development services from the department's 15 offices. Services include business information, counselling, networking & mentoring together with small loans targeted at strategic growth sectors & the seeding of small business start-ups.
Employment Development is provided through employment programs delivered in partnership with government agencies, private sector sponsors & not-for-profit organizations that stimulate job creation & assist employers to find employees.
**Minister**, Hon. Judy Foote, 709/729-4729
Deputy Minister, John Scott, 709/729-4732
Asst. Deputy Minister, Enterprise Services/Avalon Region, Bruce Saunders, 709/729-7101
Asst. Deputy Minister, Central Region, William MacKenzie, 709/256-5000
Asst. Deputy Minister, Labrador Region, Harold Marshall, 709/896-2400
Asst. Deputy Minister, Western Region, Vacant, 709/639-9691
Director, Craft Development, Jim Callahan, 709/729-7182, Fax: 709/729-7160
Director, Policy & Strategic Planning, Rob Greenwood, 709/729-4817
Director, Public Relations, Susan Laite, 709/729-4750
Director, Regional Economic Development, Gary Cake, 709/729-7260

#### EMPLOYMENT & REGIONAL ECONOMIC DEVELOPMENT

Asst. Deputy Minister, Sam Kean
Acting Director, Employment Services, Clayton Johnson, 709/729-5675

## Department of EDUCATION

Confederation Bldg., PO Box 8700, St. John's NF A1B 4J6
709/729-5097; Fax: 709/729-5896; URL: http://www.gov.nf.ca/edu/startedu.htm

#### ACTS ADMINISTERED

Bay St. George Community College Act
College of Fisheries Act
College of Trades & Technology Act
Department of Education Act
Education Apportionment Act
Education (Public Examinations) Act
Education (Teacher Training) Act
Education (Teachers' Pensions) Act
Local School Tax Act
Memorial University Act
Memorial University (Pensions) Act
Memorial University (Property) Act
Newfoundland Teachers' Association Act
Newfoundland Teachers' Collective Bargaining Act
Polytechnical Institute Act
Post Secondary & Vocational Education Act
Regulation of Trade Schools Act
School Attendance Act
Schools Act
Teachers' Loan Act
Technical & Vocational Training Act
University Fees & Allowances Act
**Minister**, Hon. Roger D. Grimes
Deputy Minister, Deborah E. Fry, 709/729-2723
Director, Public Relations, Carl Cooper, 709/729-0048

#### ADVANCED STUDIES BRANCH

Asst. Deputy Minister, Dr. Frank Marsh, 709/729-3026
Director, Institutional & Industrial Education Division, Barry Roberts, 709/729-2350
Director, Student Aid Division, Norman Snelgrove, 709/729-5849
Manager, Human Resource Development Secretariat, Hayward Harris, 709/729-4090

#### DENOMINATIONAL EDUCATION COUNCILS

133 Crosbie Rd., St. John's NF A1B 1H3
Fax: 709/579-8222
Executive Director, Integrated Education Council, Hubert Norman, 709/753-7260
Executive Director, Pentecostal Education Council, Pastor A.E. Batstone, 709/753-7263
Executive Director, Roman Catholic Education Council, Gerald Fallon, 709/753-4741

#### FINANCE & ADMINISTRATION BRANCH

Asst. Deputy Minister, Florence Delaney, 709/729-3025
Director, Evaluation, Research & Planning Division, Lenora Perry-Fagan, 709/729-3000
Director, External Financial Relations Division, Jack Thompson, 709/729-3013
Director, Human Resources Division, Glenn Saunders, 709/729-5750
Director, Information Technology Division, Ian Munn, 709/729-5590
Director, Youth Services Division, William J. Wilson, 709/729-3503, Fax: 709/729-3669

#### PRIMARY, ELEMENTARY & SECONDARY EDUCATION BRANCH

Asst. Deputy Minister, Dr. Wayne Oakley, 709/729-5720
Director, Program Development Division, Dr. Glen Loveless, 709/729-3004
Director, School Services & Professional Development Division, Gary Hatcher, 709/729-3034
Director, Student Support Services Division, Edward Mackey, 709/729-3023

##### Associated Agencies, Boards & Commissions

•Literacy Development Council: 238 Blackmarsh Rd., PO Box 8700, St. John's NF A1E 1T2 – 709/738-7323
Executive Director, Wayne Taylor

## Office of the Chief ELECTORAL OFFICER

39 Hallett Cr., St. John's NF A1B 4C4
709/729-0712; Fax: 709/729-0679
**Chief Electoral Officer**, D. Wayne Mitchell

## Department of ENVIRONMENT & LABOUR

Confederation Bldg., PO Box 8700, St. John's NF A1B 4J6
Fax: 709/729-1930; URL: http://www.gov.nf.ca/envlab.htm

#### ACTS ADMINISTERED

**Environment**
Act to Amend the Waste Material (Disposal) Act
Act to Amend the Waste Material (Disposal) Act (No. 2)
Environment Act
Environmental Assessment Act
Packaging Materials Act
Pesticides Control Act
Waste Material Disposal Act
Well Drilling Act
**Labour**
Department of Employment & Labour Relations Act
Fishing Industry Collective Bargaining Act
Human Rights Code
Industrial Standards Act
Interns & Residents Collective Bargaining Act
Labour Relations Act
Public Service Collective Bargaining Act
Shops' Closing Act
Teachers Collective Bargaining Act
**Occupational Health & Safety**
Amusement Rides Act & Regulations
(The) Asbestos Abatement Code of Practice
Boiler & Pressure Vessels Act & Regulations
Building Accessibility Act & Regulations
Electrical Inspection Fees Regulations
Electrical Regulations
Elevators Act & Regulations
Mines Act & Mines (Safety of Workman) Regulations
Occupational Health & Safety Act & Regulations
Radiation Health & Safety Act & Regulations
Workplace Hazardous Materials Inspection System (WHMIS) Regulations
**Minister**, Hon. Kevin Aylward, M.H.A., 709/729-2577
Deputy Minister, Leslie Grattan, 709/729-2572
Director, Financial & General Operations, Rick Hayward, 709/729-0939
Director, Human Resources, Kay Mullins, 709/729-0936
Director, Public Relations, Sean Kelly, 709/729-2575

#### ENVIRONMENT BRANCH

Spill Reporting (24-hours): 709/772-2083
Asst. Deputy Minister, Gary Norris, 709/729-5732
Director, Environmental Assessment, Phil Graham, 709/729-2562
Director, Policy & Planning, Thomas R. Graham, 709/729-0030
Director, Pollution Prevention, Kenneth Dominie, 709/729-2556
Director, Water Resource Division, Martin Goebel, 709/729-2563

#### LABOUR RELATIONS BRANCH

Asst. Deputy Minister, Joseph P. O'Neill, 709/729-2715
Executive Director, Occupational Health & Safety, David Clark, P.Eng., 709/729-2721
Director, Labour Standards, Vacant, 709/729-2743

##### Associated Agencies, Boards & Commissions

•Human Rights Commission
Listed alphabetically in detail, this Section.
•Labour Relations Board: Beothuck Bldg., 20 Crosbie Rd., 3rd Fl., PO Box 8700, St. John's NF A1B 4J6 – 709/729-2707; Fax: 709/729-5736
CEO, Joe M. Noel
•Labour Standards Board: Confederation Bldg., West Block, PO Box 8700, St. John's NF A1B 4J6 – 709/729-2742; Fax: 709/729-6639
Chair, Frank Tilley
•Workers' Compensation Review Division: St. John's NF A1B 4J6 – 709/729-5542; Fax: 709/729-6956
Administrator, Marlene Norman
•Workers' Compensation Commission
Listed alphabetically in detail, this Section.

## Department of FINANCE & TREASURY BOARD

Confederation Bldg., PO Box 8700, St. John's NF A1B 4J6
709/729-2858; URL: http://www.gov.nf.ca/fin/
Tax Inquiries: 709/729-3831
The Treasury Board Secretariat is listed with the Executive Council at the beginning of the Newfoundland & Labrador government listings.

#### ACTS ADMINISTERED

Co-operative Societies Act
Chiropractors Act
Communicable Diseases Act
Control of Foods Distribution Act
Daycare & Homemaker Services Act
Death Duties Act
Dental Act
Denturists Act
Department of Finance Act
Department of Health Act
Dieticians Act
Dispensing Opticians Act
Embalmers & Funeral Directors Act
Emergency Medical Aid Act
Exhumation Act
Food & Drug Act
General Hospital Management Act
Generic Dispensing of Prescription Drugs Act
Grand Falls Hospital (Management) Act
Health & Public Welfare Act
Hearing Aid Dealers Act
Homes for Special Care Act, 1973
Hospital Insurance (Agreement) Act
Hospital & Nursing Home Association Act
Hospitals Act, 1971
Human Tissues Act, 1971
Medical Act, 1974
Medical Care Insurance Act
Mental Health Act, 1971
Mentally Incompetent Persons Act
Midwifery Act
Nurses Training School Building Act
Nursing Assistants Act
Occupational Therapists Act
Old Age Assistance Act
Optometry Act
Pharmaceutical Association Act
Physiotherapy Act
Private Homes for Special Care (Allowances) Act, 1973
Psycologists Act
Registered Nurses Act
Rehabilitation Act
St. Clare's Mercy Hospital Act
Senior Citizens Housing Act
Smoke Free Environment Act
Solemnization of Marriage Act, 1974
Tobacco Control Act
Venereal Disease Prevention Act
Vital Statistics Act
Western Memorial Hospital Corporation Act

**Minister**, Hon. Paul D. Dicks, Q.C., 709/729-2942, Fax: 709/729-2232
Deputy Minister, Finance, Philip Wall, 709/729-2946
Asst. Deputy Minister, Debt Management & Pensions, John Bennett, 709/729-2949, Fax: 709/729-2070
Asst. Deputy Minister, Economics & Statistics, Beverley Carter, 709/729-2906, Fax: 709/729-0393
Asst. Deputy Minister, Fiscal & Tax Policy, Robert Vardy, 709/729-2944, Fax: 709/729-2070
Asst. Deputy Minister, Taxation, Robert Clarke, 709/729-2966, Fax: 709/729-2856
Director, Administration, Maureen McCarthy, 709/729-5993
Director, Audit & Compliance, Bernard Cook, 709/729-2952, Fax: 709/729-2856
Director, Debt Management, Earl Saunders, 709/729-6848
Director, Economic Research & Analysis, John Rideout, 709/729-2951, Fax: 709/729-0393
Director, Fiscal Policy, Christopher Butt, 709/729-6714, Fax: 709/729-2070
Director, Newfoundland Statistics Agency, Alton Hollett, 709/729-0158, Fax: 709/729-0393
Director, Strategic & Human Resource Policy, Noreen Holden, 709/729-6435, Fax: 709/729-2156
Director, Tax Policy, Terry Paddon, 709/729-6847, Fax: 709/729-2070
Administrator, Provincial School Tax, Flora Pennell, 709/729-4092, Fax: 709/729-2856
Manager, Tax Audit, Collections, Donna O'Brien, 709/729-6406, Fax: 709/729-2856
Program Co-ordinator, Data Processing, Beverley Lester, 709/729-5914

#### Associated Agencies, Boards & Commissions

•Newfoundland Liquor Corporation: Kenmount Rd., PO Box 8750, Stn A, St. John's NF A1B 3V1 – 709/754-1100; Fax: 709/754-0321
Acting President & Vice-President, Finance, G. . Adams
Vice-President, Operations, M. Clarke
•Newfoundland Municipal Financing Corporation (NMFC): Confederation Bldg., PO Box 8700, St. John's NF A1B 4J6 – 709/729-6686; Fax: 709/729-2070
Financial Officer, Cynthia LeGrow

## Department of FISHERIES & AQUACULTURE

Fisheries Bldg., 30 Strawberry Marsh Rd., PO Box 8700, St. John's NF A1B 4J6
709/729-3723; Fax: 709/729-6082; URL: http://www.gov.nf.ca/fishaq.htm
Provides financial assistance & management advice on commercial fisheries & seafood processors; research & development & data dissemination in harvesting & processing methods; market development studies & promotion.
Committed to federal-provincial-industry cooperation to ensure that groundfish & other ocean resources are protected, rebuilt & sustainably harvested; promotes a diverse, multi-species approach to fisheries development (such as the successful harvest of crab, scallops, shrimp & surf clams); establishing a joint industry-government-union task force to develop proposals for solving processing capacity/resource capacity problems.
Provides financial & marketing assistance to new & existing aquaculture enterprises; supports coastal area aquaculture planning; provides aquaculture technology transfer, research & development.

#### ACTS ADMINISTERED

Aquaculture Act
Fish Inspection Act

**Minister**, Hon. R. John Efford, 709/729-3705
Deputy Minister, Leslie Dean, 709/729-3707
Director, Planning Services, Mike Warren, 709/729-3712
Director, Public Relations, Josephine Cheeseman, 709/729-3733

#### AQUACULTURE BRANCH

Fax: 709/729-0360
Asst. Deputy Minister, Jerry Ward, 709/729-3710
Director, Finfish Aquaculture Development, Brian Meaney, 709/729-3711
Director, Shellfish Aquaculture Development, Ron Scaplen, 709/729-3724
Manager, Licensing & Administration, Vacant

#### FISHERIES BRANCH

Fax: 709/729-6082
Acting Asst. Deputy Minister, Glenn Blackwood, 709/729-3713
Senior Director, Fisheries Development, Frank Pinhorn, 709/729-3736
Manager, Licensing & Inspection, Ian Burford, 709/729-2450
Manager, Processing & Marketing, Mike Handrigan, 709/729-3390

#### Regional Offices

Avalon - St. John's: – 709/729-3717; Fax: 709/729-6082, Regional Director, Brett Wareham
Central - Gander: – 709/256-1030; Fax: 709/256-1032, Regional Director, Nelson Higdon
Eastern - Grand Bank: – 709/832-2860; Fax: 709/832-1669, Regional Director, Rex Matthews
Labrador - Goose Bay: – 709/896-3412; Fax: 709/896-3483, Regional Director, Harvey Best
Western - Port Saunders: – 709/861-3537; Fax: 709/861-3536, Regional Director, Joseph Kennedy

## Department of FOREST RESOURCES & AGRIFOODS

PO Box 8700, St. John's NF A1B 4J6
709/729-4716; URL: http://www.gov.nf.ca/forest.htm
Responsible for the management of the province's mineral, energy, land, forest & wildlife resources in a manner that will ensure optimum benefits for the people of the province.

#### ACTS ADMINISTERED

Agriculture Societies Act
Agrologists Act
Animal Protection Act
Animal and Poultry Feed Mill Act
Bowater's Newfoundland Act, 1938
Canada-Newfoundland Atlantic Accord Implementation (Newfoundland) Act, 1986
Crop Insurance Act
Department of Forestry and Agriculture Act, 1989
Dog Act
Farm Development Act
Forest Protection Act
Government-Kruger Agreements Act
Hardwood Veneers Act
Industrial Developmnent (Incentives) Act
Labrador Linerboard Limited Agreemnt Act, 1979
Lands Act - Agricultural Development Regulations
Livestock Act
Livestock Community Sales Act
Livestock Health Act
Livestock Insurance Act
Meat Inspection Act
Miscellaneous Financial Provisions Act
Natural Products Marketing Act
Newfoundland Farm Products Corporation Act
Parks Act
Plant Protection Act
Pulp & Paper, An Act to Encourage the manufacture of, 1905, c.10
Poultry and Poultry Products Act
Salt Fish Marketing Act and Regulations
Transportation of Timber over Streams & Lakes Act, 1904-05, as amended
Vegetable Grading Act
Veterinary Medical Act

**Minister**, Hon. Beaton Tulk
Deputy Minister, Hal Stanley, 709/729-4720
Director, Financial Operations Division, Leonard Clarke, 709/729-5054
Director, Human Resources Division, Margaret Power, 709/729-6559
Director, Information Technology Division, Mark Brown, 709/729-2201

**AGRIFOODS BRANCH**

Provincial Agriculture Bldg., Brookfield Rd., PO Box 8700, St. John's NF A1B 4J6

Asst. Deputy Minister, Martin Howlett, 709/729-3787, Fax: 709/729-0973

Director, Animal Health Division, Dr. Hugh Whitney, 709/729-0055

Director, Farm Business & Evaluation Division, Donna Kelland, 709/729-5090

Director, Production & Marketing Division, David Mackey, 709/729-6758

Director, Soil & Land Management Division, Hazen Scarth, 709/729-6587

Director, Special Projects Division, Philip McCarthy, 709/729-0831

**FORESTRY & WILDLIFE BRANCH**

Confederation Complex, PO Box 8700, St. John's NF A1B 4J6

Asst. Deputy Minister, Dr. M. Nazir, 709/729-2704, Fax: 709/729-6782

**Forestry Branch (Newfoundland Forest Service) (NFS)**

Herald Bldg., PO Box 2006, Corner Brook NF A2H 6J8

Director, Forest Management Division, James Taylor, 709/637-2344

Director, Forest Policy & Planning Coordination, Gary Young, 709/729-0023, Fax: 709/729-3374

Director, Forest Products Development Division, Barry Garland, 709/637-2247

Director, Forest Protection & Access Roads Division, G.J. Fleming, 709/637-2349

Director, Forest Regulations & Law Enforcement Division, R.M. Carroll, Forest Protection Centre, PO Box 2222, Gander NF A1V 1N9, 709/256-2892, Fax: 709/256-8869

Director, Silviculture & Research Division, Ivan N. Downton, 709/637-2284

**Wildlife Branch**

709/729-2815

Director, Jim Hancock, 709/729-2817, Fax: 709/729-4989

Acting Chief, Conservation & Habitat, Mike Cahill, 709/729-2548

Chief, Inland Fisheries & Biodiversity, Ken Curnew, 709/729-2540

Chief, Research & Inventories, Shane Mahoney, 709/729-2542

Chief, Wildlife Conservation, Robert Whitten, 709/729-2647

**Agricultural Marketing Boards & Commissions**

•Agricultural Products Marketing Board: Provincial Agriculture Bldg., Brookfield Rd., PO Box 8700, St. John's NF A1B 4J6 – 709/729-3799; Fax: 709/729-6040

Chair, Scott Simmons

•Livestock Owners' Compensation Board: Provincial Agriculture Bldg., Brookfield Rd., PO Box 634, St. John's NF A1N 2X1 – 709/729-5090; Fax: 709/729-6046

Chair, Donna Kelland

•Newfoundland Chicken Marketing Board: Donovans Industrial Park, 51 Clyde Ave., St. John's NF A1N 4R8 – 709/747-1493; Fax: 709/747-0544

Manager, A.R. Garland

•Newfoundland Crop Insurance Agency: 35 Hallett Cres., PO Box 634, St. John's NF A1N 2X1 – 709/729-5090; Fax: 709/729-6046

Chair, Donna Kelland

•Newfoundland Egg Marketing Board: PO Box 8453, St. John's NF A1B 3N9 – 709/722-2953; Fax: 709/722-6204

Manager, Ruth Noseworthy

•Newfoundland Farm Products Corporation: Bldg. 902, PO Box 9457, Stn B, St. John's NF A1A 2Y4 – 709/722-3751; Fax: 709/722-7813

President & CEO, Vacant

•Newfoundland Hog Marketing Board: Donovans Industrial Park, 51 Clyde Ave., St. John's NF A1N 4R8 – 709/747-1493; Fax: 709/747-0544

Manager, Rosalind Dyke

•Newfoundland Milk Marketing Board: 655 Topsail Rd., St. John's NF A1E 2E3 – 709/364-6634; Fax: 709/364-8364

Manager, Martin J. Hammond

## Department of GOVERNMENT SERVICES & LANDS

PO Box 8700, St. John's NF A1B 4J6

URL: http://www.gov.nf.ca/gsl/startgsl.htm

Since its creation in March 1996, this department has taken significant steps to improve services to the public & the business community in Newfoundland & Labrador, to increase consumer protection & to promote efficient & effective use of Crown land resources. Some of the department's responsibilities are: Crown lands administration, motor vehicle registration, government service centres, consumer protection, trade practices, vital statistics, lotteries, registries, building accessibility, residential tenancies services, regulation of financial institutions, permits, licences, approvals & inspections.

**ACTS ADMINISTERED**

Accident & Sickness Insurance Act
Adoption of Children Act (shared with Social Services)
Amusement Rides Act
Architects Act
Assignment of Book Debts Act
Automobile Dealers Act
Automobile Insurance Act
Bills of Sale Act
Boiler, Pressure Vessel & Compressed Gas Act
Building Supplies Act
Bulk Sales Act
Certified General Accountants Act
Certified Public Accountants Act
Change of Name Act (shared with Justice)
Chartered Accountants Act
Chartered Accountants & Certified Public Accountants Merger Act
Children's Law Act (shared with Justice)
Collections Act
Conditional Sales Act
Condominium Act
Consumer Protection Act
Consumer Reporting Agencies Act
Conveyancing Act
Co-operative Societies Act
Corporations Act
Corporations Guarantees Act
Credit Union Act
Dangerous Goods Transportation Act
Direct Sellers Act
Elevators Act
Engineers & Geoscientists Act
Environment Act (shared with Environment & Labour)
Fire Insurance Act
Fire Prevention Act, 1991 (shared with Municipal & Provincial Affairs)
Food & Drug Act (shared with Health)
Fraudulent Conveyances Act (shared with Justice)
Geographical Name Board Act
Highway Traffic Act
Income Tax Savings Plan Act
Innkeepers Act
Insurance Adjusters, Agencies & Brokers Act
Insurance Companies Act
Insurance Contracts Act
Investment Contracts Act
Judgement Recovery (Newfoundland) Ltd. Act
Land Surveyors Act, 1991
Landlords' Taxes Act
Lands Act
Life Insurance Act
Limited Partnership Act
Lodgers' Goods Protection Act
Management Accountants Act
Mechanics Act
Mortgage Brokers Act
Motor Carrier Act (shared with Works, Services & Transportation)
Motorized Snow Vehicles & All-Terrain Vehicles Act
Newfoundland Liquor Control Act
Packaging Material Act (shared with Environment & Labour)
Pension Benefits Act
Pension Plans Designation of Beneficiaries Act
Perpetuities & Accumulations Act
Pesticides Control Act (shared with Environment & Labour)
Private Investigation & Security Services Act
Public Accounting Act
Public Health Act (shared with Health)
Public Safety Act
Real Estate Trading Act
Registration of Deeds Act
Residential Tenancies Act
Sale of Goods Act
Salvage Dealers Licensing Act
Securities Act
Security Interest Registration Act
Smoke-free Environment Act (shared with Health)
Trade Practices Act
Unconscionable Transactions Act
Unsolicited Goods & Credit Cards Act
Urban & Rural Planning Act (shared with Municipal & Provincial Affairs
Vital Statistics Act
Warehouse Receipts Act
Warehouser's Lien Act
Waste Material Disposal Act (shared with Environment & Labour)
Works, Services & Transportation Act (shared with Works, Services & Transportation)

**Minister**, Hon. Ernest McLean, 709/729-4712, Fax: 709/729-4754

Deputy Minister, Wayne Green, 709/729-4752, Fax: 709/729-4754

Director, Financial & General Operations, Garland Mouland, 709/729-5292, Fax: 709/729-2609

Manager, Financial Operations, Felix Croke, 709/720-2041, Fax: 709/729-2609

Manager, General Operations, Clar Simmons, 709/729-5427, Fax: 709/729-2609

Director, Human Resources, David Butler, 709/729-3643, Fax: 709/729-2609

Manager, Human Resources, Doug Redmond, 709/729-4385, Fax: 709/729-2609

**COMMERCIAL & CORPORATE AFFAIRS**

Promotes economic development by assisting businesses & protecting consumers. The branch is responsible for regulating the insurance industry, the trust & loan industry, the credit union industry, the real estate industry, collection agencies, mortgage brokers, automobile dealers, provincial lotteries, private investigation agencies, firearms acquistition & registration, & landlord-tenant relations.

Asst. Deputy Minister, Winston Morris, 709/729-2570, Fax: 709/729-4151

Acting Director/Registrar, Commercial Registrations, Gerald Stone, 709/729-3316, Fax: 709/729-0232

Director, Deposit Taking Institutions, Doug Laing, Terrace on the Square, PO Box 8863, Stn A, St. John's NF A1B 3T2, 709/753-6405, Fax: 709/753-0133

Acting Director, Insurance & Pensions, Doug Connolly, C.A., 709/729-2594, Fax: 709/729-3205
Director, Residential Tenancies, Robert LeGrow, 709/729-2608, Fax: 709/729-6998
Acting Director, Securities Administration, Susan Churchill, 709/729-4189, Fax: 709/729-6187
Acting Director, Trade Practices & Licensing, Anthony Patey, 709/729-2600, Fax: 709/729-3205

### GOVERNMENT SERVICES BRANCH

Provides a one-stop service to the public & business community & is committed to reducing red tape. It processes various permits, licences, & approvals, carries out inspections & investigations on behalf of various departments & conducts on highway enforcement of the motor carrier industry. Also administers the Highway Traffic Act & registers vital events such as births, marriages, deaths & name changes.

Asst. Deputy Minister, Michael Dwyer, P.Eng., 709/729-3056, Fax: 709/729-4151

#### Government Service Centre

5 Mews Pl., PO Box 8700, St. John's NF A1B 4J6

A regionally-based network which provides service to the general public & the business community in their day to day dealings with government. The GSC was designed to eliminate inefficiencies & duplications of services by providing a more streamlined "one-stop" approval process for clients. It processes various permits, licences, inspections & approvals & carries out inspections & investigations on behalf of various line departments.

Director, Operations, Roy Layden, 709/729-3084, Fax: 709/729-3980
Director, Support Services, Weldon Moores, P.Eng., 709/729-3084, Fax: 709/729-3980
Manager, Bay Roberts, Sandy Hounsell, Government Bldg., Water St., PO Box 300, Bay Roberts NF A0A 1G0, 709/786-5032, Fax: 709/786-5032
Director, Clarenville, Guy Perry, 2 Masonic Terrace, PO Box 1148, Clarneville NF A0E 1J0, 709/466-4060, Fax: 709/466-4070
Director, Corner Brook, Shawn Tetford, Norton Bldg., 1 Riverside Dr., PO Box 2006, Corner Brook NF A2H 6J8, 709/637-2680, Fax: 709/637-2905, 2905
Director, Gander, Roger LeDrew, McCurdy Complex, PO Box 2222, Gander NF A1V 2N9, 709/256-1420, Fax: 709/256-1438
Manager, Grand Falls-Windsor, Rick Conway, Provincial Bldg., 3 Cromer Ave., Grand Falls-Windsor NF A2A 1W9, 709/292-4347, Fax: 709/292-4528
Acting Director, Happy Valley-Goose Bay, Darryl Johnson, Thomas Bldg., 13 Churchill St., PO Box 3014, Stn B, Happy Valley-Goose Bay NF A0P 1E0, 709/896-2661, Fax: 709/896-4340

#### GSC Offices

Bay Roberts: Government Bldg., Water St., PO Box 300, Bay Roberts NF A0A 1G0 – 709/786-5032; Fax: 709/786-5039
Clarenville: 2 Masonic Terrace, PO Box 1148, Clarenville NF A0E 1J0 – 709/466-4060; Fax: 709/466-4070
Corner Brook: Noton Bldg., 1 Riverside Dr., PO Box 2006, Corner Brook NF A2H 6J8 – 709/637-2680; Fax: 709/637-2681; 637-2905
Gander: McMurdy Complex, PO Box 2222, Gander NF A1V 2N9 – 709/256-1420; Fax: 709/256-1438
Grand Falls-Windsor: Provincial Bldg., 3 Cromer Ave., Grand Falls-Windsor NF A2A 1W9 – 709/292-4347; Fax: 709/292-4528
Happy Valley-Goose Bay: Thomas Bldg., 13 Churchill St., PO Box 3014, Stn B, Happy Valley-Goose Bay NF A0P 1E0 – 709/896-2661; Fax: 709/896-4340

#### Motor Registration Division

149 Smallwood Dr., PO Box 8710, Mount Pearl NF A1B 4J5

Provides services based on the operation of vehicles in Newfoundland.

Registrar, Motor Vehicles, Max Hussey, 709/729-2521, Fax: 709/729-6955
Deputy Registrar, George Barbour, 709/729-4517, Fax: 709/729-6955
Deputy Registrar, Corner Brook, Kieran Griffin, Sir Richard Squires Bldg., Corner Brook NF A2H 6J8, 709/637-2212, Fax: 709/637-2615
Deputy Registrar, Grand Falls-Windsor, Verdon Young, Provincial Bldg., 3 Cromer Ave., Grand Falls-Windsor NF A2A 1W9, 709/292-4352, Fax: 709/292-4387

#### Vital Statistics Division

5 Mews Pl., PO Box 8700, St. John's NF A1B 4J6
Fax: 709/729-2071

Registers births, marriages & deaths in the province. In addition, the division registers adoptions & legal name changes & certifies clergy who are authorized to solemnize marriages. From this division, the public may obtain a birth, marriage, death, or change of name certificate, or a marriage licence. Vital Statistics services are available from GSC offices.

Registrar, Brenda Andrews
Deputy Registrar, Rose Evans

### LANDS BRANCH

Crown holdings, covering about 95 percent of the province, provide much of its forest, mineral, wildlife, agriculture & recreational area, & includes major water resources. The branch helps to create a competitive economy by undertaking the development of policies & programs to protect, enhance & ensure the wise use of Crown lands.

Asst. Deputy Minister, Wilson Barfoot, 709/729-3236, Fax: 709/729-4151
Director, Land Management Division, John Power, 709/729-3227, Fax: 709/729-0690
Director, Surveys & Mapping Division, Neil MacNaughton, 709/729-0602, Fax: 709/729-0690

#### Crown Land Administration Division

Director, Bill Parrott, 709/729-3174, Fax: 709/729-4361
Manager, Crown Lands Administration, Wayne Boggan, 709/729-3149, Fax: 709/729-4361
Lands Manager, Central Region, Joe Blanchard, McCurdy Complex, PO Box 2222, Gander NF A1V 2N9, 709/256-1401, Fax: 709/256-1095
Lands Manager, Eastern Region, Walter Milley, 709/729-0345, Fax: 709/729-0726
Lands Manager, Labrador Region, Paul Aylward, Thomas Bldg., PO Box 3014, Stn B, Happy Valley-Goose Bay NF A0P 1E0, 709/896-2488, Fax: 709/896-9566
Lands Manager, Western Region, Don Winsor, Noton Bldg., 1 Riverside Dr., PO Box 2006, Corner Brook NF A2H 6J8, 709/637-2393, Fax: 709/637-2905

#### Associated Agencies, Boards & Commissions

•Credit Union Deposit Guarantee Corporation: PO Box 8700, St. John's NF A1B 4J6 – 709/753-6498
Executive Director, Doug Laing
Manager, Operations, William Langthorne
Supervisor, Examinations, Julian McCarthy, 709/753-6496
Examiner, John Perry, 709/753-6414
Administrative Asst., Jocelyn Walsh, 709/753-6405
•Newfoundland & Labrador Geographical Names Board: PO Box 8700, St. John's NF A1B 4J6
Secretary, Gary Fry, 709/729-3250

## Department of HEALTH

West Block, Confederation Bldg., PO Box 8700, St. John's NF A1B 4J6
709/729-5021; Fax: 709/729-5824; URL: http://www.gov.nf.ca/health/starthel.htm

#### ACTS ADMINISTERED

Cancer Treatment & Research Foundation Act
Chiropractors Act
Communicable Diseases Act
Dental Act
Denturists Act
Department of Health Act
Dieticians Act
Dispensing Opticians Act
Embalmers & Funeral Directors Act
Emergency Medical Aid Act
Food & Drug Act
Generic Dispensing of Prescription Drugs Act
Health & Public Welfare Act (except part XII)
Health & Social Agencies Act
Hearing Aid Dealers Act
Hospital Insurance Agreement Act
Hospital & Nursing Home Association Act
Hospitals Act
Human Tissue Act
Medical Act
Medical Care Insurance Act
Mental Health Act
Mentally Incompetent Persons Act
Midwifery Act
Nursing Assistants Act
Occupational Therapists Act
Optometry Act
Pharmaceutical Association Act
Pharmaceutical Association Act, 1994
Physiotherapy Act
Psychologists Act
Registered Nurses Act
Smoke-free Environment Act
Solemnization of Marriage Act
Tobacco Control Act
Venereal Disease Prevention Act
Vital Statistics Act
Welfare Institutions Act

**Minister**, Hon. Joan Marie Aylward, 709/729-3124
Deputy Minister, Dr. R.J. Williams, 709/729-3125

### ADMINISTRATIVE SERVICES & PROGRAMS

Asst. Deputy Minister, Finance & Administration, Christopher Hart, 709/729-0620
Director, Human Resources, Cecil Templeman, 709/729-3141
Director, Institutional Financial Services, David Saunders, 709/729-5277
Director, Public Relations, Jill Sooley, 709/729-1377
Acting Financial Manager, Max Osmond, 709/729-3054
Financial Manager, Cost Shared Programs, Gordon Nash, 709/729-3054

### COMMUNITY HEALTH

Asst. Deputy Minister, Gerry White, 709/729-3103
Director, Continuing Care, Eleanor Gardner, 709/729-3658
Director, Disease Control & Epidemiology, Dr. Faith Stratton, 709/729-3430
Director, Drug Dependency Services, Beverley Clarke, 709/729-0623
Director, Environmental Health, Reginald L. Coates, 709/729-3422
Director, Health Promotion, Eleanor Swanson, 709/729-3940
Director, Mental Health Services, Debbie Sue Martin, 709/729-3658
Director, Parent & Child Health, Lynn Vivian-Book, 709/729-3110

Director, Public Health Laboratories, Dr. Sam Ratnam, 709/737-6565
Director, Public Health Nursing, Helen Lawlor, 709/729-3110

**INSTITUTIONS**
Asst. Deputy Minister, Roy Manuel, 709/729-3127
Acting Director, Facilities Planning, Roy Dawe, 709/729-3123
Acting Director, Hospital Services, Moira Hennessey, 709/729-3105
Director, Personal Care Home Program, Nancy Knight, 709/772-3553
Acting Director, Welfare Institutions Licensing & Inspections, Tom Power, 709/729-3257

**POLICY & PROGRAMS**
Asst. Deputy Minister, Gerald White, 709/729-3103
Director, Drug Programs & Services, John Downton, 709/729-6507
Director, Health Human Resources, Jeff Young, 709/729-3531
Director, Health Research & Statistics, Catherine Ryan, 709/729-3130
Director, Policy, John Houser, 709/729-3157
Director, Transportation & Special Assistance Programs, Edward Hollett, 709/729-3145

**Associated Agencies, Boards & Commissions**
•Newfoundland Cancer Treatment & Research Foundation
Listed in Section 2; *see* Index.
•Newfoundland Medical Care Commission: Elizabeth Towers, 100 Elizabeth Ave., St. John's NF A1C 5J3 – 709/722-6980; Fax: 709/722-0718
Executive Director, Robert Peddigrew
Director, Dental, Bruce Bowden, B.Sc., D.D.S.
Director, Medical, Dr. Gregory Russell

## Newfoundland & Labrador HOUSING CORPORATION (NLHC)
2 Canada Dr., PO Box 220, St. John's NF A1C 5J2
709/724-3000; Fax: 709/724-3250; Email: cirincon@nlhc.nf.ca; URL: http://www.gov.nf.ca/nlhc/nlhc.htm
**Minister Responsible**, Hon. Arthur D. Reid
Chair & CEO, Clyde C. Granter
Vice-President, Business Development & Corporate Services, Peter Honeygold
Vice-President, Finance & Executive Services, Edward L. Heath
Vice-President, Human Resources & Information Systems, Mary Marshall
Vice-President, Programs & Regional Operations, Steve McLean

## Department of HUMAN RESOURCES & EMPLOYMENT
Confederation Bldg., PO Box 8700, St. John's NF A1B 4J6
709/729-2478; Fax: 709/729-6996; URL: http://www.gov.nf.ca/hre/startdos.htm

**ACTS ADMINISTERED**
Adoption of Children Act
Child Welfare Act
Day Care Homemaker Services Act
Rehabilitation Act
Social Assistance Act
Social Workers Registration Act
Young Persons Offences Act
**Minister**, Hon. Julie Bettney, 709/729-3580
Deputy Minister, Joan Dawe, 709/729-3582
Director, Communications, Jill Sooley, 709/729-4062

**FINANCIAL, EMPLOYMENT & SUPPORT SERVICES**
Asst. Deputy Minister, Dave Roberts, 709/729-3594
Director, Finance & General Operations, Jim Strong, 709/729-3584
Director, Human Resources, Rebecca Roome, 709/729-2457
Director, Income Support, David Lewis, 709/729-3243
Director, Information Technology, Glenn Stokes, 709/729-5101
Director, Internal Audit, Robert Clouter, 709/729-3589
Director, Labour Market Services, Ray Franey, 709/729-5701

**PROGRAM DEVELOPMENT**
Asst. Deputy Minister, George W.N. Skinner, 709/729-0217
Director, Child Welfare & Community Corrections, Elizabeth Crawford, 709/729-2668
Director, Family & Rehabilitative Services, Don Gallant, 709/729-2436
Director, Planning & Policy, Vivian Randell, 709/729-0494
Enquiries Division, Elaine Cleary, 709/729-2478

**Associated Agencies, Boards & Commissions**
•Day Care & Homemaker Services Licensing Board: Confederation Bldg., PO Box 8700, St. John's NF A1B 4J6
•Social Services Appeal Board: Confederation Bldg., PO Box 8700, St. John's NF A1B 4J6
Executive Secretary, Barbara McKim, 709/729-2479

## Newfoundland & Labrador HUMAN RIGHTS COMMISSION
PO Box 8700, St. John's NF A1B 4J6
709/729-2709; Fax: 709/729-0790
**Executive Director**, Gladys Vivian

## Newfoundland & Labrador HYDRO
PO Box 12400, St. John's NF A1B 4K7
709/737-1400; Fax: 709/737-1231
**President & CEO**, William E. Wells
Executive Vice-President, Power Production, T.D. Collett
Vice-President, Finance, D.W. Osmond
Vice-President, Human Resources, General Counsel & Corporate Secretary, Maureen P. Greene
Vice-President, Transmission & Rural Operations, David Reeves
Manager, Corporate Affairs, Donald J. Barrett, 709/737-1370, Fax: 709/737-1816

## Department of INDUSTRY, TRADE & TECHNOLOGY
Confederation Annex, 4th Fl., PO Box 8700, St. John's NF A1B 4J6
709/729-5600; Fax: 709/729-5936; Email: info@ditt.gov.nf.ca; URL: http://www.gov.nf.ca/itt/startitt.htm
Toll Free: 1-800-563-2299
Responsible for expanding & diversifying the provincial economy by creating a business environment favorable to private sector expansion & growth. Offers financial support, business analysis, educational opportunities & other assistance to business clients; Monitors & promotes opportunities for investment, assesses & promotes local competitiveness in the wider marketplace, markets the province as an investment location & assists local companies in identifying markets & market requirements, & promotes partnerships between business, goverment & education.

**ACTS ADMINISTERED**
Economic Diversification & Growth Enterprises (EDGE) Act
Industries Act
Research Council Act
**Minister**, Hon. Charles J. Furey, 709/729-2791
Deputy Minister, Max Ruelokke, 709/729-2787
Asst. Deputy Minister, Advanced Technology & Industry, Sid Blundon, 709/729-0882
Asst. Deputy Minister, Industry, Trade & Investment, David French, 709/729-2788
Asst. Deputy Minister, Policy, Planning & Business Analysis, Lorne Spracklin, 709/729-3613
Director, Public Relations, John Doody, 709/729-0050

**ADMINISTRATION**
Director, David Butler, 709/729-2790
Manager, Financial Operations, Randy Snelgrove, 709/729-2786
Manager, Human Resources, Charlie Phillips, 709/729-3943
Manager, Systems & Methods, Vacant
Compliance Officer, Ed Janes, 709/729-1919
Registrar, Maureen Bursey, 709/729-5982

**ADVANCED TECHNOLOGY**
Director, Linda Cooper, 709/729-5592
Manager, Industrial Technology & Information Industries, Terry Johnstone, 709/729-5592
Manager, Strategic Technologies, Robert Robinson, 709/729-5652

**BUSINESS ANALYSIS**
Director, Brian Condon, 709/729-5066
Manager, Business Support Programs, Pierre Tobin, 709/729-6223
Senior Industrial Development Officer, Vacant

**BUSINESS DEVELOPMENT**
Director, Harry Bishop, 709/729-2781
Manager, Business Development, Kirk Tilley, 709/729-4205
Manager, Business Model Development, Jim Cardwell, 709/729-3648

**INDUSTRIAL BENEFITS**
Director, Fred Murrin, 709/729-5064
Senior Development Officer, Special Projects, David Hallett, 709/729-1044
Industrial Development Officer, Valerie Hillier, 709/729-5641

**INDUSTRIAL SUPPORT**
Director, Hunter Rowe, 709/729-3296

**MARKETING**
Director, Geoff Tooton, 709/729-2800
Manager, Marketing Research & Development, Paul Morris, 709/729-2369

**POLICY & STRATEGIC PLANNING**
Director, Margaret Allan, 709/729-2798
Senior Policy Planning Officer, Vacant, 709/729-5727

**PROJECT & PROGRAM ANALYSIS**
Director, Brian Hurley, 709/729-3664
Manager, Economic Impact Analysis, Charles Brown, 709/729-4797
Manager, Economic Research, Bryon Hynes, 709/729-6427
Manager, Financial Analysis, Bill Mullaly, 709/729-4363

**STRATEGIC PROCUREMENT**
Director, Anthony Patey, 709/729-2796
Manager, Trade Policy & Agreements, Dan Fallon, 709/729-2797
Policy & Planning Officer, Tom Fleming, 709/729-5859

Senior Development Officer, Special Projects, Donovan Arnaud

**Associated Agencies, Boards & Commissions**

•Operation ONLINE: PO Box 8700, St. John's NF A1B 4J6 – 709/729-0050

Established in early 1995 to oversee the implementation of Operation ONLINE (Opportunities for Newfoundland & Labrador in the New Economy), a comprehensive five-year strategy to develop the province's information technology sector.

Co-Chair, David Oake

Co-Chair, Dennis Young

Head, Operational Support, Frank Davis, 709/729-5600

## INTERGOVERNMENTAL AFFAIRS SECRETARIAT

Listed with the Executive Council, this section.

## Department of JUSTICE & ATTORNEY GENERAL

Confederation Bldg., PO Box 8700, St. John's NF A1B 4J6

709/729-5942; Fax: 709/729-2129; URL: http://www.gov.nf.ca/just/startjus.htm

**ACTS ADMINISTERED**

Adult Corrections Act
Advance Health Care Directives Act
Age of Majority Act
Agreement for Policing the Province Act
American Bases Act, 1941
Apportionment Act
Arbitration Act
Attachment of Wages Act
Bankers' Books Act
Blind Persons' Rights Act
Canada & United Kingdom Reciprocal Recognition & Enforcement of Judgments Act
Change of Name Act (with Government Services & Lands)
Chattels Real Act
Children's Law Act (with Government Services & Lands)
Commissioners for Oaths Act
Contributory Negligence Act
Criminal Code
Defamation Act
Detention of Intoxicated Persons Act
Divorce Act, 1985 (Canada)
Election Act
Electoral Boundaries Act
Enduring Powers of Attorney Act
Evidence Act
Exhumation Act
Family Law Act
Family Relief Act
Fatal Accidents Act
Fatalities Investigations Act
Federal Courts Jurisdiction Act
Fraudulent Conveyances Act (with Government Services & Lands)
Freedom of Information Act
Frustrated Contracts Act
International Commercial Arbitration Act
International Sale of Goods Act
International Trusts Act
Interpretation Act
Interprovincial Subpoena Act
Intestate Succession Act
Judgment Debts Instalments Act
Judgment Interest Act
Judicature Act
Jury Act, 1991
Justices Act
Justices & Other Public Authorities Protection Act
Law Reform Commission Act
Law Society Act
Leaseholds in St. John's Act
Legal Aid Act
Limitations Act
Mentally Disabled Persons' Estates Act
Notaries Public Act
Oaths Act
Oaths of Office Act
Partnership Act
Penitentiary Act (Canada)
Petty Trespass Act
Presumption of Death Act
Prisons Act
Prisons & Reformatories Act (Canada)
Privacy Act
Proceedings Against the Crown Act
Proof of Death (Members of Armed Forces) Act
Provincial Court Act
Provincial Offences Act
Public Inquiries Act
Public Investigations Evidence Act
Public Trustee Act
Public Utilities Act
Public Utilities Acquisition of Lands Act
Queen's Counsel Act
Quieting of Titles Act
Reciprocal Enforcement of Judgments Act
Reciprocal Enforcement of Support Orders Act
Recording of Evidence Act
Revised Statutes, 1990 Act
Royal Newfoundland Constabulary Act, 1992
Sheriff's Act, 1991
Small Claims Act
Statutes Act
Statutes Amendment Act
Statutes & Subordinate Legislation Act
Subordinate Legislation Revision & Consolidation Act
Support Orders Enforcement Act (with Social Services)
Survival of Actions Act
Survivorship Act
Unified Family Court Act
Victims of Crime Services Act
Wills Act
Young Offenders Act (Canada - with Social Services)
Young Persons Offences Act(with Social Services)

**Minister & Attorney General**, Hon. Chris D. Decker, 709/729-2869

Deputy Minister & Deputy Attorney General, Lynn E. Spracklin, Q.C., 709/729-2872

Director, Finance & General Operations Division, George White, 709/729-2890

Director, Human Resources Division, David Hickey, 709/729-4256

Director, Information Technology Division, Joan McCarthy-Wiseman, 709/729-3617

Chief, Forensic Pathology, Dr. Simon Avis, Health Sciences Complex, 300 Prince Philip Dr., St. John's NF A1B 3V6, 709/737-6402

**For list of Courts & other Legal Officers, including Judicial Officials & Judges *see* Section 10 of this book.**

**CIVIL LAW & RELATED SERVICES**

Asst. Deputy Minister, John R. Cummings, 709/729-2880

Director, Civil Law Division, John McCarthy, 709/729-2893

Director, Legal Information Services, Mona Pearce, 709/729-2861

Director, Support Enforcement Division, Cy Simmons, 709/729-2658

**PUBLIC PROTECTION & SUPPORT SERVICES**

Asst. Deputy Minister, Ralph Alcock, 709/729-4896

Superintendent, Prisons, Donald Saunders, 709/729-0356

Chief Probation Officer, Community Corrections, Wanda Lundrigan, 709/729-0407

Chief, Royal Newfoundland Constabulary, L.P. Power, 709/729-8151, Inquiries: 709/729-8000

Director, Adult Corrections Division, Marvin McNutt, 709/729-3880, Fax: 709/729-0416

Manager, Victim Services, Jacqueline Lake, 709/729-0885

**SENIOR LEGISLATIVE COUNSEL**

Asst. Deputy Minister, Calvin Lake, 709/729-2881

Secretary, Gerry Ryan, 709/729-1162

**Associated Agencies, Boards & Commissions**

•Atlantic Lottery Corporation

*See* listing under New Brunswick Finance, this Section.

•Newfoundland Legal Aid Commission: Centre Bldg., 21 Church Hill St., St. John's NF A1C 3Z8 – 709/753-7860; Fax: 709/753-6226

Provincial Director, N. Petten

•Newfoundland & Labrador Public Utilities Commission

Listed alphabetically in detail, this section.

•Royal Newfoundland Constabulary Public Complaints Commission: PO Box 21128, St. John's NF A1A 5B2 – 709/729-0950

Commissioner, Dr. Leslie Harris

## LOWER CHURCHILL DEVELOPMENT CORPORATION LIMITED

PO Box 12700, St. John's NF A1B 3T5

709/737-1288; Fax: 709/737-1782

**President & CEO**, William E. Wells

Manager, Corporate Affairs, Donald J. Barrett, 709/737-1370

## Department of MINES & ENERGY

PO Box 8700, St. John's NF A1B 4J6

709/729-2301; URL: http://www.gov.nf.ca/mines.htm

**ACTS ADMINISTERED**

Buildings Accessibility Act & Regulations
Canada-Newfoundland Atlantic Accord Implementation (Newfoundland) Act, 1986
Crown Lands Act
Department of Mines & Energy Act
Electrical Power Control Act
Elevators Act
Emergency Measures Act (Petroleum related emergencies)
Federal-Provincial Power Act, 1962
Industrial Development (Incentives) Act, 1970
Lands Act, 1991
Lower Churchill Development Act, 1979
Mineral Act, 1976
Mineral Holdings Impost Act
Mineral Lands (Certain) Act
Mineral Vesting in the Crown Act
Mines Act & Mines (Safety of Workmen) Regulations
Miscellaneous Financial Provisions Act, 1975
Natural Products Marketing Act
Newfoundland & Labrador Hydro Act, 1975
Newfoundland & Labrador Power Commission (Water Power) Act, 1970
Newfoundland & Labrador Rural Electricity Act
Parks Act
Occupational Health & Safety Act
Petroleum Corporation Act, 1980
Petroleum & Natural Gas Act, 1970
Quarry Materials Act, 1976
Radiation Health & Safety Act
Regulations of Mines Act
Rural Electrification Act, 1970
Undeveloped Minerals Areas Act
Workplace Hazardous Materials Inspection System (WHMIS) Regulations, 1989

**Minister**, Hon. Brian Tobin, 709/729-2920
Deputy Minister, Frederick G. Way, 709/729-2356
Director, Financial Operations Division, Leonard Clarke, 709/729-5054
Director, Human Resources Division, Margaret Power, 709/729-6559
Director, Information Technology Division, Mark Brown, 709/729-2201

#### ENERGY BRANCH
Asst. Deputy Minister, Martin Sheppard, 709/729-2315
Director, Energy Policy Analysis, Barry Rodgers, 709/729-3674
Director, Petroleum Projects Monitoring, Brian Maynard, 709/729-0021
Director, Petroleum Resource Development, David Hawkins, 709/729-2323
Director, Policy, Planning & Coordination, Charles Lester, 709/729-2339

#### MINES BRANCH
Fax: 709/729-6782
Asst. Deputy Minister, Paul Dean, 709/729-2768
Director, Mineral Lands Division, Ken Andrews, 709/729-6425
Director, Project Management, Wayne Ryder, 709/729-2063
Manager, Engineering Analysis, Fred Morrissey, 709/729-6449
Manager, Prospectors Assistance, M.J. Collins, 709/729-2358

#### Geological Survey
Fax: 709/729-3493
Director, Vacant, 709/729-2763
Senior Geochemist, Geochemistry/Geophysical & Terrain Sciences, Peter Davenport, 709/729-2171
Senior Geologist, Labrador Mapping, Richard Wardle, 709/729-2107
Senior Geologist, Mineral Deposits, Baxter Kean, 709/729-5946
Senior Geologist, Newfoundland Mapping, Stephen Colman-Sadd, 709/729-3574
Senior Geologist, Publications & Information, Frank Blackwood, 709/729-6541

#### Associated Agencies, Boards & Commissions
•Canada-Newfoundland Offshore Petroleum Board: TD Place, #500, 140 Water St., St. John's NF A1C 6H6 – 709/778-1400; Fax: 709/778-1473; Email: cnopb@nfld.com; URL: http://canada.gc.ca/depts/agencies/cnpind_e.html
Acting Chair & CEO, John Fitzgerald

## Department of MUNICIPAL & PROVINCIAL AFFAIRS
West Block, Confederation Bldg., PO Box 8700, St. John's NF A1B 4J6
709/729-3053; URL: http://www.gov.nf.ca/mpa/startmpa.htm

#### ACTS ADMINISTERED
Assessment Act
Avian Emblem Act
Building Standards Act
City of Corner Brook Act
City of Mount Pearl Act
City of St. John's Act
Coat of Arms Act
Commemoration Day Act
Crown Corporations Local Taxation Act
Emergency Measures Act
Evacuated Communities Act
Family Homes Expropriation Act
Fire Prevention Act, 1991 (with Government Services & Lands)
Floral Emblem Act
Housing Act
Housing Association Loans Act
Housing Corporation Act
Labrador Act
Mineral Emblem Act
Municipal Affairs Act
Municipalities Act
Provincial Anthem Act
Provincial Flag Act
Rememberence Day Act
Regional Services Boards Act
St. John's Assessment Act
St. John's Centennial Foundation Act
St. John's Municipal Council Parks Act
St. John's Municipal Elections Act
Standard Time Act
Taxation of Utilities & Cable Television Companies Act
Urban & Rural Planning Act (with Government Services & Lands)
Water & Sewerage Corporation of Greater Corner Brook Act, 1951

**Minister**, Hon. Arthur D. Reid, 709/729-3048
Deputy Minister, Robert Noseworthy, 709/729-3049
Director, Emergency Measures Division, Elizabeth Munn, 709/729-3703, Fax: 709/729-3857, 24-hour Emergencies: 709/722-7107
Director, Public Relations, Gary Callahan, 709/729-3142
Coordinator, Canada/Newfoundland Infrastructure Program, Erik Seaward, 709/729-5411

#### MUNICIPAL SUPPORT SERVICES
Asst. Deputy Minister, Ramona Cole, 709/729-3051
Director, Finance & General Operations, Garland L. Mouland, 709/729-5292
Director, Human Resources, Dave Butler, 709/729-3643
Director, Local Government, John Moore, 709/729-3066
Director, Municipal Engineering Services, Wayne Churchill, 709/729-5328
Director, Municipal Finance, C. Goodland, 709/729-3057
Director, Urban & Rural Planning, Stan Clinton, 709/729-3090
Manager, Finance & General Operations, Felix Croke, 709/729-3096

#### Associated Agencies, Boards & Commissions
•Newfoundland & Labrador Housing Corporation
Listed alphabetically in detail, this Section.
•Office of the Fire Commissioner: Bldg. 9001, Pleasantville, PO Box 8700, St. John's NF A1B 4J6 – 709/726-1050; Fax: 709/729-2524
Fire Commissioner, Fred Hollett

## Newfoundland & Labrador PUBLIC SERVICE COMMISSION
#146, 148 Forest Rd., St. John's NF A1A 1E6
709/729-2751; URL: http://www.gov.nf.ca/psc/psc.htm

#### ACTS ADMINISTERED
Conflict of Interest Act & Regulations
Public Inquiries Act
Public Investigations Evidence Act
Public Service Commission Act, 1973
**Chair & Deputy Minister**, Robert Olivero, 709/729-2650, Email: rolivero@psc.gov.nf.ca
Vice-Chair, Grant Chalker, 709/729-2659, Email: gchalker@psc.gov.nf.ca
Commissioner, Sheila Devine, 709/729-2651, Email: sdevine@psc.gov.nf.ca

## Newfoundland & Labrador PUBLIC UTILITIES COMMISSION
PO Box 21040, St. John's NF A1A 5B2
709/726-0955; Fax: 709/726-9604
**Chair**, David Vardy
Vice-Chair, Leslie E. Galway, C.A., M.B.A.
Clerk, Chery P. Blundon, 709/726-8600

## Provincial Advisory Council on the STATUS OF WOMEN
131 Le Marchant Rd., St. John's NF A1C 2H3
709/753-7270; Fax: 709/753-2606; Email: pacsw@thezone.net; URL: http://www.thezone.net/pocsw
**Minister Responsible**, Hon. Julie Bettney
President, Joyce Hancock
Office Administrator, Linda Williams
Community Liaison/Communications Coordinator, Rebecca Woodrow
Community Liaison, Provincial Strategy to Address Violence, Jennifer Mercer

## Department of TOURISM, CULTURE & RECREATION
Confederation Bldg., PO Box 8700, St. John's NF A1B 4J6
709/729-0928; Fax: 709/729-0662; URL: http://public.gov.nf.ca/tcr/

#### ACTS ADMINISTERED
Arts Council Act
Books (Preservation of Copies) Act
Innkeepers Act
Tourist Establishments Act
**Minister**, Hon. Sandra Kelly
Acting Deputy Minister, Mike Buist
Director, Financial & General Operations, Rick Hayward, 709/729-0851, Fax: 709/729-0870
Director, Human Resources, Kay Mullins, 709/729-0936, Fax: 709/729-0870
Director, Public Relations, Laura Cochrane, 709/729-0928
Director, Systems & Methods, Ray Piercy, 709/729-0315

#### CULTURAL AFFAIRS BRANCH
Asst. Deputy Minister, Elizabeth Batstone, 709/729-3609, Fax: 709/729-0870
Acting Director, Cultural Affairs, E.A. Channing, 709/729-3650, Fax: 709/729-5952
Director, Historic Resources, David Mills, 709/729-2460, Fax: 709/729-0870
Director, Provincial Archives, David Davis, 709/729-3065, Fax: 709/729-0578
Resource Archaeologist, Martha Drake, 709/729-2462, Fax: 709/729-0870

#### PARKS & RECREATION BRANCH
Asst. Deputy Minister, Mike Buist, 709/729-0865, Fax: 709/729-0870
Director, Community Recreation, Sport & Fitness, Vic Janes, 709/729-5261, Fax: 709/729-5293
Director, Parks, Donald Hustins, 709/729-2424, Fax: 709/729-1100

#### TOURISM & CRAFTS BRANCH
Asst. Deputy Minister, Susan Sherk, 709/729-2821, Fax: 709/729-0870
Director, Tourism Development, Mike Joy, 709/729-2822, Fax: 709/729-0474
Director, Tourism Marketing, Marilyn Butland, 709/729-2831, Fax: 709/729-0057
Director, Tourism Planning & Research, Juanita Keel-Ryan, 709/729-2974, Fax: 709/729-0870

## TWIN FALLS POWER CORPORATION

PO Box 12500, St. John's NF A1B 3T5
709/737-1450; Fax: 709/737-1782
**President**, T. David Collett, P.Eng.
Manager, Corporate Affairs, Donald J. Barrett, 709/737-1370, Fax: 709/737-1816

## Newfoundland & Labrador WORKERS' COMPENSATION COMMISSION

#146, 148 Forest Rd., PO Box 9000, St. John's NF A1A 3B8
709/778-1000; Fax: 709/738-1714
**CEO**, Barbara Stark

## Department of WORKS, SERVICES & TRANSPORTATION

Confederation Bldg., PO Box 8700, St. John's NF A1B 4J6
709/729-3676; Fax: 709/729-4285; URL: http://public.gov.nf.ca/wst/

#### ACTS ADMINISTERED

Department of Works, Services & Transportation Act
Expropriation Act
Family Homes Expropriation Act
Local Roads Boards Act
Pippy Park Commission Act
Provincial Preference Act
Public Tender Act
Railways Act
**Minister**, Hon. Lloyd Matthews, 709/729-3678
Deputy Minister, Barbara B. Wakeham, 709/729-3676
Registrar, J. Anthony, 709/729-3284
Chief, Safety & Security, J. Clarke, 709/729-3443
Director, Public Relations, Doug Burgess, 709/729-1968

#### CORPORATE SERVICES

Asst. Deputy Minister, Don Osmond, 709/729-5672
Director, Highway Design & Construction, Keith White, 709/729-3796
Director, Human Resources & Financial Operations, Gordon Murphy, 709/729-3292
Director, Maintenance, Neil Campbell, 709/729-3636
Director, Policy & Planning, Tom Beckett, 709/729-5344
Director, Transportation Services, Tom Prim, P.Eng., 709/729-3278

#### WORKS BRANCH

Asst. Deputy Minister, George Greenland, 709/729-3999
Director, Design & Construction, Gunar Leja, 709/729-3355
Director, Engineering Support Services, Keith Noel, 709/729-3019
Director, Government Purchasing Agency, Larry Cahill, 709/729-3343
Director, Information Systems/Communications, David Penney, 709/729-3367
Acting Director, Printing Services & Queen's Printer, Earl Tucker, 709/729-3210
Director, Realty Services & Accommodations, Martin Balodis, 709/729-3690

#### Associated Agencies, Boards & Commissions

•C.A. Pippy Park Commission: PO Box 8861, Stn A, St. John's NF A1B 3T2 – 709/737-3655; Fax: 709/737-3303
Chair & CEO, Dr. Phillip Warren
Director, Administration & General Operations, T. Hopkins

# GOVERNMENT OF THE NORTHEST TERRITORIES

**Seat of Government:** Legislative Assembly, PO Box 1320, Yellowknife NT X1A 2L9
URL: http://www.ssmicro.com/ZXxpsognwt/Net/index.html

The Northwest Territories was reconstituted September 1, 1905. It has an area of 3,246,389.46 km2, and the StatsCan population in 1996 was 64,402.

The Northwest Territories comprises: 1) all of Canada north of the 60th Parallel of North Latitude, except the portions within the Yukon Territory & the Provinces of Québec & Newfoundland; & 2) the islands of Hudson Bay, James Bay & Ungava Bay, except those islands within the provinces of Manitoba, Ontario & Québec.

The Northwest Territories is governed by a fully elected Legislative Assembly of 24 members elected for a four-year term. Government is by consensus rather than party politics. The Legislature elects the Premier & a seven-member Executive Council, which is charged with the operation of government & the establishment of program & spending priorities.

The Commissioner of the Northwest Territories is appointed by the Federal Government, & serves a role similar to that of a Lieutenant Governor in provincial jurisdictions.

## Office of the COMMISSIONER

Courthouse Bldg., 4903 - 49 St., PO Box 1320, Yellowknife NT X1A 2L9
867/873-7210; Fax: 867/873-0223
**Commissioner**, Hon. Helen Maksagak, 867/873-7400
Deputy Commissioner, Daniel J. Marion
Executive Secretary, Doris Franceschi

## Office of the PREMIER

Legislative Assembly Bldg., PO Box 1320, Yellowknife NT X1A 2L9
867/669-2311; 2322; Fax: 867/873-0385
**Premier**, Hon. Don Morin, 867/669-2311
Deputy Premier, Hon. Goo Arlooktoo, 867/669-2399
Executive Asst., Delilah St. Arneault, 867/669-2306
Principal Secretary, Ferne Babiuk, 867/669-2325
Correspondence Secretary, Catherine McLean
Press Secretary, Val Mellesmoen, 867/669-2302
Executive Secretary, Hilda Camirand

## EXECUTIVE COUNCIL

PO Box 1320, Yellowknife NT X1A 2L9
Premier & Minister, Executive, Minister Responsible, Intergovernmental Affairs, Hon. Don Morin, 867/689-2311, Fax: 867/873-0385
Minister, Transportation & Minister Responsible, Aboriginal Affairs, Hon. James Antoine, 867/669-2333, Fax: 867/873-0169
Deputy Premier, Minister Responsible, NWT Housing Corporation & Minister, Public Works & Services, Hon. Goo Arlooktoo, 867/669-2355, Fax: 867/873-0169
Minister, Education, Culture & Employment, Minister Responsible, Youth & Minister Responsible, NWT Power Corporation, Hon. Charles Dent, 867/669-2355, Fax: 867/873-0169
Minister, Resources, Wildlife & Economic Development & Minister, National Constitutional Affairs, Hon. Stephen Kakfwi, 867/669-2366, Fax: 867/873-0169, Email: stephen_kakfwi@gov.nt.ca
Minister, Health & Social Services & Minister, Justice, Hon. Kelvin Ng, 867/669-2388, Fax: 867/873-0169
Minister, Municipal & Community Affairs & Minister Responsible, Women's Directorate, Hon. Manitok Thompson, 867/669-2344, Fax: 867/873-0169
Government House Leader, Minister, Finance & Minister Responsible, Financial Management Board Secretariat, Workers' Compensation Board, Public Utilities Board, Hon. John Todd, 867/669-2377, Fax: 867/873-0169

#### Cabinet Office

Fax: 867/873-0122
Secretary to Cabinet, J.G. Gilmour, 867/873-7100, Fax: 867/873-0279
Deputy Secretary to Cabinet, David Colpitts, 867/873-7240
Director, Executive Corporate Services, David Waddell, 867/873-7148, Fax: 867/873-0110
Advisor, Status of Women, Bertha Norwegian, 867/920-3106
Policy Advisor, Karen Bergman-Illnik, 867/873-7242
Policy Advisor, Alan Cash, 867/873-7652
Policy Advisor, Catherine Cushman-Biddle, 867/873-7137
Policy Advisor, Marie Doyle, 867/873-7242
Policy Advisor, Michael Kalnay, 867/920-8678

#### Financial Management Board Secretariat

Chair, Hon. John Todd, 403/669-2377
Secretary to the FMB, Lew Voytilla, 403/873-7211, Fax: 403/873-0122
Deputy Secretary, Audit & Evaluation, Gordon Robinson, 403/873-7338, Fax: 403/873-0258
Director, Audit Bureau, Doug Hill, 403/873-7106, Fax: 403/873-0209
Director, Budgeting & Evaluation, Debbie DeLancey, 403/920-6196, Fax: 403/873-0258
Director, Compensation Services & Labour Relations, Herb Hunt, 403/873-7970, Fax: 403/873-0105
Director, Government Accounting, John Carter, 403/920-3401, Fax: 403/873-0296
Director, Information Management, Keith Rogers, 403/920-8962, Fax: 403/873-0128
Director, Job Evaluation, Vacant, 403/920-6983, Fax: 403/873-0175

#### Legislation & House Planning

Legislative Coordinator, Kevin O'Keefe, 403/669-2239, Fax: 403/873-0139

#### Office of Official Languages

Asst. Deputy Minister, Elizabeth Biscaye, 867/920-6960, Fax: 867/873-0122
Official Languages Advisor, Denise Canuel, 867/920-6962

#### Division Secretariat

Fax: 867/873-0104
Asst. Deputy Minister, Tom Isaac, 867/920-3319
Secretariat Administrator, Tony Weir, 867/920-6213
Director, John Borkovic, 867/873-7064
Senior Policy Advisor, April Taylor, 867/920-3340

#### Personnel Secretariat

Fax: 867/873-0235
Asst. Deputy Minister, Darryl Bohnet, 867/920-3398
Manager, Corporate Services, Mike Cluderay, 867/920-3312

#### Regulatory Reform Secretariat

Fax: 867/873-0599
Executive Director, Alan Downe, 867/873-7365
Project Specialist, Lorraine Whiteman, 867/920-3252

#### Intergovernmental Affairs - Ottawa

613/234-6525; Fax: 613/234-9667
Asst. Deputy Minister, Elizabeth Snider
Office Manager, Sandi Briscoe

## LEGISLATIVE ASSEMBLY

c/o Clerk's Office, PO Box 1320, Yellowknife NT X1A 2L9
867/669-2299, 669-2200; Fax: 867/920-4735; URL: http://www.ssimicro.com/ZXepsognwt/Net/departments/assembly/Gov.html
Toll Free: 1-800-661-0784
**Clerk:** David M. Hamilton
**Speaker:** Hon. Samuel Gargan, 867/669-2233
**Deputy Speaker:** John Ningark
**Librarian, Legislative Library:** Vera Raschke, 867/669-2203
Clerk of Committees, Doug Schauerte
Director, Research & Information Services, Lynn Elkin, 867/669-2213
Coordinator, Public Information, Ronna Bremer, 867/669-2230

#### Elections NWT/Plebiscite Office

PO Box 1320, Yellowknife NT X1A 2L9
867/920-6999
Deputy Chief, Glen McLean, 867/920-6140

#### Office of the Languages Commissioner

PO Box 1320, Yellowknife NT X1A 2L9
867/873-7034
Languages Commissioner, Judi Tutcho

#### Standing Committees of the Legislature

URL: http://www.ssimicro.com/ZXxpsognwt/Net//assembly/committees.html
Government Operations
Infrastructure
Management & Services Board
Resource Management & Development
Rules & Procedures
Social Programs

## THIRTEENTH LEGISLATURE - NORTHWEST TERRITORIES

Last General election, October 16, 1995. Maximum Duration, four years.
**Salaries, Indemnities & Allowances**
Basic indemnity $36,748; Ordinary members' constituency indemnity $18,665; Ministers'/Speaker's consituency indemnity $6,222. Ordinary members are entitled to $207 for each day they attend a meeting of a Standing or Special Committee of the Legislative Assembly when the Assembly is not in session. Members are entitled to a living allowance while attending sittings of the Legislature, committee meetings or performing constituency duties. Members are provided with a set operating budget to defray the expenses of travel & administration while undertaking work on behalf of their constituents.
In addition are the following remunerations:
Premier $62,975
Minister with Portfolio $57,916
Speaker $57,916
Deputy Speaker $5,580
Deputy Chairperson of Committee of the Whole $3,255
Chairperson of a Standing Committee $2,790
Chairperson of Caucus $1,860

#### MEMBERS BY CONSTITUENCY

Following is: constituency (unofficial number of eligible voters in 1995 election) member, constituency Telephone number - if available. (Address for all is PO Box 1320, Yellowknife NT X1A 2L9.)

Aivilik (599) Hon. Manitok Thompson, 819/645-2322
Amittuq (1,976) Mark Evaloarjuk
Baffin Central (967) Tommy Enuaraq
Baffin South (768) Hon. Goo Arlooktoo
Deh Cho, (608) Hon. Samuel Gargan, 867/874-3230
Hay River (1,740) Jane Groenewegen
High Arctic (392) Levi Barnabas
Inuvik (1,175) Floyd K. Roland,
Iqaluit (1,428) Edward Picco
Keewatin Central (1,148) Hon. John Todd, 819/645-3241
Kitikmeot (1,114) Hon. Kelvin Ng, 867/983-2835
Kivallivik (1,291) Kevin J. O'Brien
Mackenzie Delta (772) David Krutko
Nahendeh, Hon. James Antoine, 403/695-3403
Natilikmiot (704) John Ningark, 867/769-6031
North Slave (1,132) James Rabesca
Nunakput (635) Vince Steen
Sahtu (1,571) Hon. Stephen Kakfwi, 867/598-2130
Thebacha (1,393) J. Michael Miltenberger
Tu Nedhe (536) Hon. Don Morin, 867/394-3172
Yellowknife Centre (1,263) Jake Ootes
Yellowknife Frame Lake (752) Hon. Charles Dent, 867/920-3337
Yellowknife North (1,621) Roy Erasmus
Yellowknife South (2,339) Seamus Henry

#### MEMBERS (ALPHABETICAL)

Following is: member, constituency (unofficial number of eligible voters in 1995 election) constituency Telephone number - if available. (Address for all is PO Box 1320, Yellowknife NT X1A 2L9.)

Mark Evaloarjuk, Amittuq (1,976)
Hon. James Antoine, Nahendeh, 867/695-3403
Kevin J. O'Brien, Kivallivik (1,291)
Roy Erasmus, Yellowknife North (1,621)
Vince Steen, Nunakput (635)
Hon. Charles Dent, Yellowknife Frame Lake (752) 867/920-3337
Hon. Samuel Gargan, Deh Cho (608) 867/874-3230
Hon. Stephen Kakfwi, Sahtu (1,571) 867/598-2130
Floyd K. Roland, Inuvik (1,175)
Jake Ootes, Yellowknife Centre (1,263)
J. Michael Miltenberger, Thebacha (1,393)
Tommy Enuaraq, Baffin Central (967)
Hon. Don Morin, Tu Nedhe (536) 867/394-3172
David Krutko, Mackenzie Delta (772)
Hon. Kelvin Ng, Kitikmeot (1,114) 867/983-2835
John Ningark, Natilikmiot (704) 867/769-6031
Edward Picco, Iqaluit (1,428)
Jane Groenewegen, Hay River (1,740)
Hon. Goo Arlooktoo, Baffin South (768)
Levi Barnabas, High Arctic (392)
Hon. Manitok Thompson, Aivilik (599) 867/645-2322
Hon. John Todd, Keewatin Central (1,148) 867/645-3241
Seamus Henry, Yellowknife South (2,339)
James Rabesca, North Slave (1,132)

## NORTHWEST TERRITORIES GOVERNMENT DEPARTMENTS & AGENCIES

## Ministry of ABORIGINAL AFFAIRS

Precambrian Bldg., 7th Fl., PO Box 1320, Yellowknife NT X1A 2L9
867/873-7143; Fax: 867/873-0233
**Minister**, Hon. James Antoine, 867/669-2333, Fax: 867/669-0399
Deputy Minister, Bob Overvold, 867/873-7143
Executive Secretary, Kathy Green, 867/920-8045

## AURORA RESEARCH INSTITUTE (ARI)

c/o Aurora College, PO Box 1450, Inuvik NT X0E 0T0
EMail: davidm@inuvik.net
ARI is an arms-length agency of the Territorial Government & a division of Aurora College. Operations were merged with Aurora College in January 1995. The Institute administers the research licensing provisions of the Northwest Territories Scientists Act & provides for seasonal & continuous research projects to be carried out
**Minister Responsible**, Hon. Charles Dent, 867/669-2355
Director, David Malcolm, 867/979-3298, Fax: 867/979-4264
Director, Scientific Services, Gary White, 867/920-6180
Administrator, Yellowknife & Coordinator, NRC IRAP Program, Craig D'Entremont, #500, 5022 - 49 St., Yellowknife NT X1A 3R7, 867/873-7592, Fax: 867/873-0227
Manager, Technology Development, Dr. S.Y. Ahmad, 867/920-3073

## Department of EDUCATION, CULTURE & EMPLOYMENT

PO Box 1320, Yellowknife NT X1A 2L9
867/920-6222 (Policy & Planning); Email: info@ece.learnnet.nt.ca; URL: http://siksik.learnnet.nt.ca
**Minister**, Hon. Charles Dent, 867/669-2355, Fax: 867/873-0169
Deputy Minister, Mark Cleveland, 867/873-0456
Director, Financial & Management Services, Paul Devitt, 867/873-7739
Director, Policy & Planning, Bronwyn Watters, 867/920-6221
Coordinator, Public Affairs, Cathy Jewison, 867/920-6222, Fax: 867/873-0155

#### CULTURE & CAREERS BRANCH

867/873-7252; Fax: 867/873-0155
Acting Asst. Deputy Minister, Lesley Allen
Director, Career Development, David Gilday, 867/873-7146
Acting Director, Colleges & Continuing Education, Robert Galipeau, 867/920-8827
Director, Culture & Heritage, Charles Arnold, 867/873-7551
Director, Income Support Programs, Dana Heide, 867/920-8922, Fax: 867/873-0443
Territorial Archivist, Richard Valpy, 867/873-7657

#### EDUCATIONAL DEVELOPMENT BRANCH

867/920-8061; Fax: 867/873-0155
Asst. Deputy Minister, Pauline Gordon
Director, Board Operations, Malcolm Farrow, 867/920-8990
Director, Early Childhood & School Services, Fiona O'Donoghue, 867/920-3491
Director, Information Networks, Peter Crass, 867/873-7251
Acting Territorial Librarian, NWT Public Library Services, Suliang Feng, PO Box 1100, Hay River NT X0E 0R0, 867/874-6531

#### INCOME SECURITY BRANCH

867/920-6160; Fax: 867/920-0443
Asst. Deputy Minister, Conrad Pilon

#### Associated Agencies, Boards & Commissions

•Northwest Territories Apprenticeship & Trade Certification Board: PO Box 1192, Yellowknife NT X1A 2N8 – 867/873-7357
Chair, Richard Edjericon
Acting Manager, Apprenticeship & Occupational Certification, Bryan Johnson, 867/873-7553
•Northwest Territories Arts Council: PO Box 1320, Stn Main, Yellowknife NT X1A 2L9
Contact, Evelyn D'hont, 867/920-3103

## Department of the EXECUTIVE

PO Box 1320, Yellowknife NT X1A 2L9
867/920-3398; Fax: 867/873-0235

#### ACTS ADMINISTERED

Financial Administration Act
Legislative Assembly & Executive Council Act
Public Service Act

**Minister**, Hon. Don Morin, 867/669-2311, Fax: 867/873-0385
Asst. Deputy Minister, Darryl Bohnet, 867/920-3398
Director, Staffing Services, Tom Williams, 867/920-8932

## Department of FINANCE

PO Box 1320, Yellowknife NT X1A 2L9
URL: http://www.fin.gov.nt.ca
The department is responsible for obtaining the financial resources to carry on the functions of government & for intergovernmental fiscal negotiating & arrangements. The territorial government has a budget of over $1 billion (including federal government transfers of $876 million).

### ACTS ADMINISTERED

Borrowing Authorization Act
Income Tax Act
Income Tax Collection Agreement Questions Act
Liquor Act
Loan Authorization Act
Payroll Tax Act, 1993
Petroleum Products Tax Act
Property & Assessment Taxation Act
Tobacco Tax Act
**Minister**, Hon. John Todd, 867/669-2377, Fax: 867/873-0169
Acting Deputy Minister, Margaret M. Melhorn, 867/873-7117, Fax: 867/873-0414
Senior Policy & Planning Analyst, Joseph La Ferla, 867/920-6364, Fax: 867/873-0414, Email: jlafe@fin.gov.nt.ca

### BUREAU OF STATISTICS

Fax: 867/873-0275
Territorial Statistician, David Stewart, 867/873-7147
Statistician, Valerie Watt, 867/920-3147
Statistics Asst., Carmelita Hiebert, 867/873-7147, Email: lita@stats.gov.nt.ca

### FINANCE & ADMINISTRATION

Fax: 867/873-0325
Director, William Setchell, 867/873-7158, Email: wsetchell@fin.gov.nt.ca
Administrative Asst., Dodi Cargill, 867/873-7293, Email: dodi_cargill@gov.nt.ca
Officer, Systems & Administration, David Mah, 867/920-3238, Email: dmah@fin.gov.nt.ca

### FISCAL POLICY

Fax: 867/873-0381
Responsible for the development & analysis of expenditures & taxation strategies for the executive branch of government. The branch is also responsible for intergovernmental fiscal relations.
Acting Director, Fiscal Policy, Kathleen LeClair, 867/873-7303, Email: mmelhorn@fin.gov.nt.ca
Manager, Tax Policy, John Monroe, 867/873-7171, Email: jmonroe@fin.gov.nt.ca
Specialist, Tax Policy, Vacant, 867/920-3240
Analyst, Tax Policy, Francis Parfitt, 867/920-6329
Analyst, Fiscal Policy, Graham Monroe, 867/920-3261

### TREASURY

Fax: 867/873-0325
The Treasury collects tax revenues & provides expertise on technical management of governmental financial assets. The division manages the government's cash position; conducts banking, borrowing & investment activities for the government; provides related advisory & cash management services; & protects government activities/assets from risk of loss through insurance coverage & risk management activities. The division also administers legislated tax programs & responds to taxpayer inquiries. Other services include: analysis of administrative & taxation revenue; maintenance of a database of taxpayer information; & participation in interjurisdictional exchange agreements to control tax evasion. Additionally, activities include funding for interest expenses on funds borrowed by the government, including interest on the bonds issued for the purchase of the NWT Power Corporation.
Director, Tony Dawson, 867/873-7308, Email: tony_dawson@gov.nt.ca
Manager, Banking & Investment, Wally Peterson, 867/873-7496, Email: wally_peterson@gov.nt.ca
Officer, Risk Management, Lois Grabke, 867/873-7307, Email: lois_grabke@gov.nt.ca
Secretary, Taxation, Kim Cederland, 867/920-3470, Email: kcederland@fin.gov.nt.ca
Tax Auditor II, Gerry Gagnon, 867/873-7294, Email: gmg0@fin.gov.nt.ca
Clerk, Insurance Registry, Pedro Tolentino, 867/920-8056, Email: pedro_tolentino@gov.nt.ca

#### Associated Agencies, Boards & Commissions

•Northwest Territories Liquor Commission: Hay River NT X0E 0R0 – 867/874-2100; Fax: 867/874-2180
General Manager, Ron Courtorielle
Manager, Finance & Administration, Kyle Reid
•Northwest Territories Liquor Licensing Board: Hay River NT X0E 0R0 – 867/874-2906; Fax: 867/874-6011
Chair, Rosemary Cairns
Acting Manager, Licensing & Enforcement, John Ruggles

## Department of HEALTH & SOCIAL SERVICES

Centre Square Tower, 8th Fl., PO Box 1320, Yellowknife NT X1A 2L9
867/920-6173; Fax: 867/873-0266; URL: http://www.hlthss.gov.nt.ca/

### ACTS ADMINISTERED

Aboriginal Custom Adoption Recognition Act (assent given, not yet proclaimed)
Adoption Act
Certified Nursing Assistants Act
Child & Family Services Act
Child Welfare Act, Guardianship & Trustee Act (assent given, not yet proclaimed)
Dental Auxiliaries Act
Dental Mechanics Act
Dental Professions Act
Disease Registries Act
Emergency Medical Aid Act
Guardianship & Trusteeship Act
Human Tissue Act
Medical Care Act
Medical Profession Act
Mental Health Act
Nursing Profession Act
Ophthalmic Medical Assistants Act
Optometry Act
Pharmacy Act
Psychologists Act
Public Health Act
Territorial Hospital Insurance Services Act
**Minister**, Hon. Kelvin Ng, 867/669-2388, Fax: 867/873-0169
Deputy Minister, David Ramsden, Email: dave_ramsden@gov.nt.ca
Asst. Deputy Minister, Don Ellis, 867/873-7646, Email: don_ellis@gov.nt.ca
Director, Financial & Management Services, Warren St. Germaine, 867/920-8931, Fax: 867/920-4969, Email: warren_st.germaine@gov.nt.ca
Director, Policy, Planning & Evaluation, Bronwyn Watters, 867/873-7155, Fax: 867/873-0484, Email: bronwyn_watters@inukshuk.gov.nt.ca

### HEALTH SERVICES DEVELOPMENT

Chief Medical Health Director, Dr. Ian Gilchrist, 867/920-8946, Fax: 867/873-0266, Email: ian_gilchrist@gov.nt.ca
Director, Health Services Administration, Darrell Bower, 867/873-7714, Fax: 867/873-0280, Email: darrell_bower@gov.nt.ca
Director, Population Health & Board Development, Norman Hatlevik, 867/920-8945, Fax: 867/873-0280, Email: norm_hatlevik@gov.nt.ca

### COMMUNITY PROGRAMS & SERVICES

URL: http://siksik.learnnet.nt.ca/HIV-Aids/index.html (HIV/Aids Strategy Info)
Director, Community Health, Cathy Praamsma, 867/873-7738, Fax: 867/873-7706, Email: cathy_praamsma@gov.nt.ca
Director, Family Support & Child Protection, Andrew Langford, 867/920-6255, Fax: 867/873-0444, Email: andrew_langford@gov.nt.ca

## Northwest Territories HOUSING CORPORATION

Scotia Centre, PO Box 2100, Yellowknife NT X1A 2P6
**Minister Responsible**, Hon. Goo Arlooktoo, 867/669-2399, Fax: 867/873-0274
President, D.J. (Dave) Murray, 867/873-7853, Fax: 867/873-9426
Vice-President, Finance & Administration, Jim Nelson, 867/873-7873, Fax: 867/873-9426
Vice-President, Operations, Tom Beaulieu, 867/873-7898, Fax: 867/669-7010
Comptroller, Finance, Jeff Anderson, 867/873-7897, Fax: 867/920-8024
Director, Human Resources & Administration, Jalal Toeg, 867/873-7895, Fax: 867/669-7115
Director, Operations East, Jim Fennell, 867/920-6502, Fax: 867/669-7010
Director, Operations West, Marsh Wilson, 867/873-7861, Fax: 867/669-7010
Director, Policy, Gary McLellan, 867/920-6533, Fax: 867/669-7901

## Department of JUSTICE

PO Box 1320, Yellowknife NT X1A 2L9
867/920-6197; URL: http://pingo.gov.nt.ca/Phone/Dept/dep0013.htm#Il
**Minister**, Hon. Kelvin Ng, 867/669-2388
Deputy Minister, Donald Cooper, Q.C.
Asst. Deputy Minister, Solicitor General Branch, Nora Sanders, 867/873-7005
Acting Chief Coroner, Coroner's Office, Larry Pontus, 867/873-7460
Chief Territorial Firearms Officer, Firearms Office, Emily Overbo, 867/920-8714
Public Trustee, Public Trustee's Office, Larry Pontus, 867/873-7464
Sheriff, Sheriff's Office, Colin McCluskie, 867/920-6301
Executive Director, Legal Services Board, Bruce McKay, 867/873-7485
Director, Corrections, Midge Ravensdale, 867/920-8922
Director, Court Services Administration, Cayley Thomas, 867/873-7488
Director, Financial & Management Services, Louise Dundas-Matthews, 867/873-7641
Director, Legal Division, Reg Tolton, 867/920-8003
Director, Legal Registries/Land Titles, Gary MacDougall, 867/873-7490
Director, Legislation Division, Mark Aitken, Q.C., 867/873-7462
Director, Policy & Planning, Gerald Sutton, 867/920-6418
Coordinator, Victims Services, Lawrence Norbert, 867/920-6911

Coordinator, Young Offenders, Doug Friesen, 867/920-8823

**For list of Courts & other Legal Officers, including Judicial Officials & Judges *see* Section 10 of this book.**

#### Associated Agencies, Boards & Commissions

•Judicial Council: PO Box 188, Yellowknife YT X1A 2P1 – 867/873-7105; Fax: 867/873-0287

Chair, Hon. Mr. Justice J.E. Richard

•Legal Services Board of the Northwest Territories: PO Box 1320, Yellowknife NT X1A 2L9 – 867/873-7450; Fax: 867/873-5320

Executive Director, Bruce Mckay

Solictor, Gregory Nearing

•Victims Assistance Committee: c/o Community Justice Division, PO Box 1320, Yellowknife NT X1A 2L9 – 867/920-6911; Fax: 867/873-0299

Chair, Gail Cyr, 867/920-8893

Coordinator, Dawn McCinnes

## Department of MUNICIPAL & COMMUNITY AFFAIRS

#600, 5201 - 50 Ave., PO Box 1310, Yellowknife NT X1A 2L9

867/873-7118; Fax: 867/873-0309; URL: http://www.maca.gov.nt.ca

#### ACTS ADMINISTERED

Area Development Act
Charter Communities Act
Cities, Towns & Villages Act
Civil Emergency Measures Act
Commissioner's Land Act
Community Employees Benefits Act
Hamlets Act
Local Authorities Elections Act
Planning Act
Property Assessment & Taxation Act
Senior Citizens' & Disabled Persons' Property Tax Relief Act
Settlements Act
Western Canada Lotteries Act

**Minister**, Hon. Manitok Thompson, 867/669-2344, Fax: 867/873-0169

Deputy Minister, Penny Ballantyne, Email: pballant@maca.gov.nt.ca

Asst. Deputy Minister, Community Development/Empowerment, Graham Murchie, 867/873-7997

Asst. Deputy Minister, Programs & Services, Vern Christensen, 867/873-6355, Email: vchriste@maca.gov.nt.ca

Director, Corporate Affairs, Chris Keeley, 867/873-7613, Fax: 867/873-0152, Email: ckeeley@maca.gov.nt.ca

Director, Community Development, Ian Legaree, 867/873-7245, Fax: 867/920-6467, Email: ilegaree@maca.gov.nt.ca

#### COMMUNITY OPERATIONS

Director, Dennis Adams, 867/920-3144, Fax: 867/920-6156, Email: dadams@maca.gov.nt.ca

Senior Engineer, Municipal Planning, Terry Brookes, 867/920-8601

Senior Engineer, Municipal Planning, Siva Sutendra, 867/920-3262

Manager, Capital Projects, Al Shevkenek, 867/873-7135

Manager, Operations & Administration, Brenda Becker, 867/873-7573

#### EMERGENCY SERVICES DIVISION

867/873-7554; Fax: 867/873-8193

Director, Eric Bussey, 867/920-6133, Fax: 867/873-8193, Email: ebussey@maca.gov.nt.ca

Coordinator, Max Rispin, 867/873-7083

Fire Marshall, Don Gillis, 867/873-7469

Administration Asst., Debbie Decker, 867/873-7892

#### Associated Agencies, Boards & Commissions

•Assessment Appeal Tribunal of the Northwest Territories: PO Box 1320, Yellowknife NT X1A 2L9 – 867/920-6208; Fax: 867/920-6467

Senior Industrial Assessor, Terry Kozak, Email: tkozak@maca.gov.nt.ca

•Territorial Board of Revision: PO Box 1320, Yellowknife NT X1A 2L9 – 867/873-7997; Fax: 867/920-3159

Senior Officer, Terry Kozak, Email: tkozak@maca.gov.nt.ca

Administrator, Assessment Appeals, Kim Hjelmeland, Email: khjelmel@maca.gov.nt.ca

## NUNAVUT RESEARCH INSTITUTE (NRI)

Aeroplex Bldg., PO Box 1720, Iqualuit NT X0A 0H0

867/979-4115; Fax: 867/979-4681

Responsible for science & technology in the Nunavut region. The Institute operates in cooperation with the Nunavut Arctic College & conducts & supports research projects in the Eastern Arctic.

Executive Director, Bruce Rigby

Manager, Igloolik Research Centre, Leah Otak

Manager, Iqualuit Research Centre, Lynn Peplinski

Manager, Science & Technology Services, Richard Isnor, 819/979-4105

## Northwest Territories POWER CORPORATION

4 Capital Drive, Hay River NT X0E 1G2

867/874-5200; Fax: 867/874-5251

**Minister Responsible**, Hon. Charles Dent, 867/669-2355, Fax: 867/873-0169

Chair & CEO, Pierre R. Alvarez, 867/669-3390, Fax: 867/669-3395

President & Chief Operating Officer, Leon Courneya, 867/874-5245, Fax: 867/874-5229

Director, Engineering, Gerd Sandrock

## Department of PUBLIC WORKS & SERVICES

Bldg. YK, 7th Fl., PO Box 1320, Yellowknife NT X1A 2L9

867/873-7114; Fax: 867/873-0264; URL: http://www.gov.nt.ca/pws

Designs, constructs, maintains & operates all territorial buildings, equipment & operations; implements energy efficiency projects; provides essential petroleum products to the public where they are not available from the private sector.

**Minister**, Hon. Goo Arlooktoo, 867/669-2399, Fax: 867/873-0169

Deputy Minister, Ken Lovely

Director, Computer Services & Communications, Peter Dunn, 867/873-7017

Director, Corporate Services, Gay Kennedy, 867/920-8668

Director, Project Management Division, Joe Auge, 867/873-7829

Director, Petroleum Products Division, Brian Austin, 867/645-5178, Fax: 867/645-3554

Director, Regional Support Services Division, Sue Bevington, 867/873-7517

#### REGIONAL OFFICES

Regional Superintendent, Baffin, Ross Mrazek, 867/979-5150, Fax: 867/979-4748

Regional Superintendent, Fort Smith, Ralph Shelton, 867/872-7260, Fax: 867/872-2830

Regional Superintendent, Inuvik, Brian Lemax, 867/979-7140, Fax: 867/979-7347

Regional Superintendent, Keewatin, Greg Pilgrim, 867/645-5050, Fax: 867/645-2242

Regional Superintendent, Kitikmeot, Brent Boddy, 867/983-7285, Fax: 867/983-2158

Regional Superintendent, Yellowknife, Vince Dixon, 867/873-7650, Fax: 867/873-0257

#### Associated Agencies, Boards & Commissions

•Public Utilities Board of the Northwest Territories: PO Box 5006, Hay River NT X0E 0R0 – 867/874-3944

Chair, John Hill

## Department of RESOURCES, WILDLIFE & ECONOMIC DEVELOPMENT (RWED)

PO Box 1320, Yellowknife NT X1A 2L9

URL: http://www.edt.gov.nt.ca/

Spill Report Line: 403/920-8130

The department promotes self-sufficiency & growth through the sustainable development of natural resources & enhances the creation of new opportunities in the traditional & wage economy. Aims to protect the condition, quality, diversity & abundance of resources, & the condition & quality of the environment.

#### ACTS ADMINISTERED

Co-operative Associations Act
Credit Union Act
Environmental Protection Act
Environmental Rights Act
Flood Damage Reduction Agreements Act
Forest Management Act
Forest Protection Act
Freshwater Fish Marketing Act
Herd & Fencing Act
Natural Resources Conservation Trust Act
Norman Wells Natural Gas Distribution Act
NWT Business Credit Corporation Act
NWT Development Corporation Act
Pesticide Act
Territorial Parks Act
Travel & Tourism Act
Water Resources Agreement Act
Wildlife Act

**Minister**, Hon. Stephen Kakfwi, 867/669-2366, Fax: 867/873-0169, Email: stephen_kakfwi@gov.nt.ca

Deputy Minister, Andrew Gamble, 867/920-8694, Fax: 867/873-0563, Email: andrew_gamble@gov.nt.ca

Asst. Deputy Minister, East, Katherine Trumper, W.G. Browne Bldg., PO Box 1000, Iqaluit NT X0A 0H0, 867/979-5071, Fax: 867/979-6026, Email: katherine_trumper@gov.nt.ca

Asst. Deputy Minister, West, Robert McLeod, 867/873-7420, Fax: 867/873-0114, Email: bob_mcleod@gov.nt.ca

Executive Director, Resources & Economic Development, Doug Doan, 867/873-7115, Fax: 867/920-2756

Director, Corporate Services, Jim Kennedy, 867/920-8920, Fax: 867/873-0563, Email: jim_kennedy@gov.nt.ca

Director, Environmental Protection, Emery Paquin, 867/873-7654, Fax: 867/873-0221, Email: emery_paquin@gov.nt.ca

Director, Forest Management, Bob Bailey, 867/872-7700, Fax: 867/872-2077, Email: bob_bailey@gov.nt.ca

Acting Director, Minerals, Oil & Gas, Doug Matthews, 867/920-3214, Fax: 867/873-0254, Email: doug_matthews@gov.nt.ca

Director, Parks & Tourism, Robin Reilly, 867/873-7903, Fax: 867/873-0163, Email: robin_reilly@gov.nt.ca

Director, Policy, Legislation & Communications, Kathryn Emmett, 867/920-8046, Fax: 867/873-0114, Email: kathryn_emmett@gov.nt.ca

Director, Strategic Planning, Garry Singer, 867/873-7318, Fax: 867/873-0434

Director, Trade & Investment, Otto Olah, 867/873-7361, Fax: 867/920-2756, Email: otto_olah@gov.nt.ca
Director, Wildlife & Fisheries, Doug Stewart, 867/920-8716, Fax: 867/873-0221, Email: doug_stewart@gov.nt.ca
Manager, Northwest Territories Remote Sensing Centre, Helmut Epp, 867/920-3329, Fax: 867/873-0221, Email: hemlut_epp@gov.nt.ca

#### Regional Offices

Baffin: W.G. Browne Bldg., PO Box 1000, Iqaluit NT X0A 0H0 – 867/979-5072; Fax: 867/979-6026, Regional Superintendent, Clay Buchanan
Deh Cho: Milton Bldg., 2nd Fl., PO Box 240, Fort Simpson NT X0E 0NO – 867/695-2231; Fax: 867/695-2442, Regional Superintendent, Paul Kraft
Inuvik: Semmler Bldg., 2nd Fl., Bag Service #1, Inuvik NT X0E 0T0 – 867/979-7230; Fax: 867/979-7321, Acting Regional Superintendent, Ron Morrison
Keewatin: Government of the NWT Office, Arviat NT X0C 0E0 – 867/857-2828; Fax: 867/857-2900, Acting Regional Superintendent, Tim Devine
Kitikmeot: PO Bag 200, Cambridge Bay NT X0E 0C0 – 867/982-7241; Fax: 867/982-3701, Regional Superintendent, John Stevenson
North Slave: Tapwe Bldg., 5017 - 49 St., PO Box 1320, Yellowknife NT X1A 2L9 – 867/920-8966; Fax: 867/873-6109, Regional Superintendent, Larry Adamson
Sahtu: Norman Wells NT – 867/587-2310; Fax: 867/587-2204, Regional Superintendent, Gerry LePrieur
South Slave: Sweetgrass Bldg., PO Box 390, Fort Smith NT X0E 0P0 – 867/872-4242; Fax: 867/872-4250, Regional Superintendent, Lloyd Jones

#### Associated Agencies, Boards & Commissions

•Northwest Territories Business Credit Corporation: Northern United Place, 5004 - 54 St., PO Box 1320, Yellowknife NT X1A 2L9 – 867/920-6454; Fax: 867/873-0308
CEO & Manager, Loan Funds, Afzal Currimbhoy, Email: afzal_currimbhoy@gov.nt.ca
•Northwest Territories Development Corporation (DEVCORP): Tower 7, PO Box 1437, Yellowknife NT X1A 2P1 – 867/920-7700; Fax: 867/920-7701
Chair, Robert Leonard
President, Glenn Soloy
•Northwest Territories Workers' Compensation Board
Listed alphabetically in detail, this Section.

## Department of TRANSPORTATION

Lahm Ridge Bldg., PO Box 1320, Yellowknife NT X1A 2L9
867/920-3460; Fax: 867/873-0363; URL: http://www.gov.nt.ca/Transportation

#### ACTS ADMINISTERED

Motor Vehicles Act
Public Highways Act
Public Service Vehicles Act
Transportation of Dangerous Goods Act(s)
**Minister**, Hon. James Antoine, 867/669-2333, Fax: 867/873-0169
Deputy Minister, Joseph Handley
Asst. Deputy Minister, Bruce Rattray, 867/920-3461
Asst. Deputy Minister, Nunavut, Jason Brown, 867/645-5087
Director, Finance & Administration, Raj Downe, 867/920-3459
Director, Policy & Coordination, Doug Howard, 867/920-3461

#### ARCTIC AIRPORTS

Director, Jim Winsor, 867/873-7725
Asst. Director, Facilities, Marvin Zaorziny, 867/873-7695
Asst. Director, Nunavut, Richard Mackenzie, 867/645-5120
Asst. Director, Programs & Standards, Daniel Auger, 867/873-7822

#### HIGHWAYS & ENGINEERING

867/920-8771; Fax: 867/873-0288
Director, Peter Vician, 867/873-7800
Manager, Contracts, Dennis Malloy, 867/920-3434
Manager, Technical Services, Larry Purcka, 867/873-7647
Project Manager, John Bowen, 867/920-6473
Project Manager, Lyle Dewar, 867/920-8023
Project Manager, Airports Section, Rob Nelson, 867/873-7809
Head, Structures, Jivko Jivkov, 867/873-7564

#### MOTOR VEHICLES

867/920-8915
Director, Richard MacDonald
Asst. Director, Compliance, Mark Schauerte, 867/874-5007
Asst. Director, Safety & Regulations, Gary Walsh, 867/920-8633
Manager, Registration & Licensing, Dave Buchan, 867/873-7418

#### TRANSPORTATION PLANNING

867/873-7666; Fax: 867/920-2565
Director, Masood Hassan, 867/873-7934
Manager, Environmental Affairs, Leslie Green, 867/873-7063, Email: greenl@internorth.com
Senior Planner, Transportation, Russell Neudorf, 867/920-3366

## Northwest Territories WATER BOARD

PO Box 1500, Yellowknife NT X1A 2R3
867/669-2772; Fax: 867/669-2719
**Chair**, Gordon Wray

## STATUS OF WOMEN OF THE NORTHWEST TERRITORIES

PO Box 1320, Yellowknife NT X1A 2L9
867/920-6177
Reports directly to the Executive Council on matters concerning women in the Northwest Territories.
**Minister Responsible**, Hon. Manitok Thompson, 867/669-2344, Fax: 867/873-0169
President, Rita Arey, PO Box 183, Aklavik NT X0E 0A0
Vice-President (Baker Lake), Rebecca Kudloo
Vice-President (Fort Smith), Sister Agnes Sutherland

## Northwest Territories WORKERS' COMPENSATION BOARD

PO Box 8888, Yellowknife NT X1A 2R3
867/920-3888; Fax: 867/873-4596
**Minister Responsible**, Hon. John Todd, 867/669-2377, Fax: 867/873-0169
Chair, Fred Koe, 867/920-5898, Fax: 867/920-3892
President, Gerry Meier, 867/920-3887
Director, Client Services, Carl Malmsten, 867/920-3817
Director, Corporate Services, Trevor Alexander, 867/920-3815
Director, Finance Services, John Doyle, 867/920-3850
Director, Prevention Services, Joan Perry, 867/669-4407

# GOVERNMENT OF NOVA SCOTIA

**Seat of Government:** Legislative Assembly, Province House, Halifax NS B3J 2T3
URL: http://www.gov.ns.ca/
The Province of Nova Scotia entered Confederation July 1, 1867. It has an area of 52,840.83 km2, and the StatsCan census population in 1996 was 909,282.

## Office of the LIEUTENANT GOVERNOR

Government House, 1451 Barrington St., Halifax NS B3J 1Z2
902/425-6300; Fax: 902/424-0537
**Lieutenant Governor**, Hon. John James Kinley, C.D., S.M., D.Eng., P.Eng., FEIC
Executive Asst., Mary M. McGrath

## Office of the PREMIER

One Government Place, 1700 Granville St., PO Box 726, Halifax NS B3J 1X5
902/424-6600; Fax: 902/424-7648; Email: premier@gov.ns.ca; URL: http://www.gov.ns.ca/govt/prem/
Premier, Hon. Russell MacLellan, Q.C., Email: premier@gov.ns.ca
Deputy Premier, Hon. J. William Gillis, Ph.D., 902/424-5720
Deputy Minister, Robert A. Mackay, 902/424-8940
Principal Asst., Suzan Maclean, 902/424-4135
Executive Asst., David Cowan, 902/424-2588
Senior Advisor, Jeanne Wilson Clarke, 902/424-4092
Director, Communications, David Harrigan, 902/424-3750
Coordinator, Administrative Affairs, Arlene D'Eon, 902/424-6604
Coordinator, Scheduling, Stephanie Bennett, 902/424-6601
Media Relations, Ann Graham Walker, 902/424-2590

## EXECUTIVE COUNCIL

One Government Place, PO Box 2125, Halifax NS B3J 3B7
902/424-5970; Fax: 902/424-0667
Premier & President, Executive Council, Minister, Intergovernmental Affairs, Hon. Russell MacLellan, Q.C.
Deputy Premier, Deputy President, Executive Council & Minister, Finance, Hon. J. William Gillis, Ph.D., 902/424-5720, Fax: 902/424-0635
Minister, Environment, Hon. F. Wayne Adams, 902/424-2358, Fax: 902/424-0644
Minister, Fisheries & Aquaculture, Hon. James A. Barkhouse, 902/424-8953, Fax: 902/424-4671
Minister, Housing & Municipal Affairs, Hon. Guy Brown, 902/424-4388, Fax: 902/424-3948
Minister, Community Services, Hon. Francene Cosman
Minister, Transportation & Public Works, Hon. Donald R. Downe, 902/424-5875, Fax: 902/424-0532
Minister, Business & Consumer Services, Hon. Wayne J. Gaudet, 902/424-4484, Fax: 902/424-0698
Minister, Education & Culture, Hon. Robert S. Harrison, 902/424-4236, Fax: 902/424-0680
Minister Responsible, Technology & Science Secretariat, Hon. Bruce Holland
Minister, Agriculture & Marketing, Hon. Edward F. Lorraine
Minister, Natural Resources, Hon. Kenneth MacAskill
Minister, Justice & Attorney General, Hon. Alan Mitchell, 902/424-4044
Minister, Labour, Hon. Gerald J. O'Malley, 902/424-2900, Fax: 902/424-0500
Minister, Health, Hon. James A. Smith, M.D., 902/424-5550, Fax: 902/424-0581

Minister, Human Resources & Minister Responsible, Acadian Affairs, Hon. Allister Surrette, 902/424-5465, Fax: 902/424-0555

#### Cabinet Office

Secretary to the Executive Council, Robert A. MacKay, 902/424-6611, Fax: 902/424-7638
Acting Clerk, James G. Spurr, 902/424-5970, Fax: 902/424-0667, Email: spurrj@gov.ns.ca
Executive Director, Acadian Affairs, Paul J. Gaudet, 902/424-0497, Fax: 902/424-0555
Director, Intergovernmental Affairs, Dr. Alastair Saunders, 902/424-4899, Fax: 902/424-0728
Chief of Protocol, Colleen MacDonald, 902/424-4463, Fax: 902/424-4309

## LEGISLATIVE HOUSE OF ASSEMBLY

c/o Clerk's Office, Province House, 2nd Fl., PO Box 1617, Halifax NS B3J 2Y3
902/424-5978; Fax: 902/424-0574; URL: http://www.gov.ns.ca/legi/house.htm
**Clerk of Assembly:** R.K. MacArthur
**Speaker:** Hon. Wayne J. Gaudet, Q.C., 902/424-5707, Fax: 902/424-0526
**Sergeant-at-Arms (Interim):** Douglas Giles, 902/424-6603
**Legislative Librarian:** Margaret Murphy, 902/424-5932
Acting Clerk, Arthur Fordham, Q.C.
Director, Administration, Dale Robbins, 902/424-4403
Director, Legislative T.V., Donald Ledger, 902/424-7992
Editor, Hansard, Rodney Caley, 902/424-5706
Chief Legislative Counsel, Gordon D. Hebb

#### Government Caucus Office (Lib.)

Centennial Bldg., 1660 Hollis St., 10th Fl., PO Box 1617, Halifax NS B3J 2Y3
902/424-8637; Fax: 902/424-0539
Executive Director, George Doucet

#### Office of the Official Opposition (PC)

Centennial Bldg., 1645 Granville Ave., 8th Fl., PO Box 1617, Halifax NS B3J 2Y3
902/424-2731; Fax: 902/424-7484
Opposition Leader, John F. Hamm
Caucus Chairman, Donald P. McInnes
Chief of Staff, Debi Forsyth-Smith
Administrative Asst., Susan Millard

#### Office of the New Democratic Party

Roy Bldg., 1657 Barrington St., PO Box 1617, Halifax NS B3J 2Y3
902/424-4134; Fax: 902/424-0504
Leader, Robert Chisholm
Chief of Staff & Director, Richard Starr
Principal Secretary, Bernard Butler

#### Standing Committees of the House

Committees Office, 1740 Granville St., 3rd Fl., PO Box 2630, Stn M, Halifax NS B3J 3N5
902/424-4432; Fax: 902/424-0513
Chief Clerk, Legislative Committees, Mora Stevens, 902/424-4494
Clerk, Legislative Committees, Darlene Henry, 902/424-5241
Assembly Matters, Nancy Kinsman, 902/424-5707
Community Services Committee, Darlene Henry, 902/424-5241
Economic Development, Darlene Henry, 902/424-5241
Human Resources, Mora Stevens, 902/424-4494
Internal Affairs, Mora Stevens, 902/424-4494
Law Amendments, Gordon Hebb, 902/424-8941
Private & Local Bills, Arthur Fordham, 902/424-8941
Public Accounts, Mora Stevens, 902/424-4494
Resources, Darlene Henry, 902/424-5241
Veterans Affairs, Mora Stevens, 902/424-4491

## FIFTY-SIXTH ASSEMBLY - NOVA SCOTIA

902/424-5978
Last General Election, May 25, 1993. Maximum Duration, 5 years.
**Party Standings (June 17, 1997)**
Liberals (Lib.) 39
Progressive Conservative (PC) 8
New Democratic Party (NDP) 3
Vacant 2
Total, 52.
**Salaries, Indemnities & Allowances**
Members' sessional indemnity $30,130 plus a $15,065 expense allowance. In addition to this are the following:
Premier $52,012
Ministers $37,055
Leader of the Opposition $37,055
Leader of a recognized Party $17,650
Speaker $37,055
Deputy Speaker $18,533

#### MEMBERS BY CONSTITUENCY

Following is: constituency (number of eligible voters at 1993 election) member, party affiliation. (Address for all is c/o House of Assembly, Province House, Halifax NS B3J 2Y3.)
Refer to Cabinet List, Government Caucus Office, the Offices of the Official Opposition & of the New Democratic Party, for Telephone & Fax numbers.

Annapolis (7,136) Earle Rayfuse, Lib.
Antigonish (7,292) Hon. J. William Gillis, Ph.D., Lib.
Argyle (3,090) Hon. Allister Surrette, Lib.
Bedford-Fall River (4,754) Hon. Francene Cosman, Lib.
Cape Breton Centre (5,643) Russell MacNeil, Lib.
Cape Breton East (7,566) John MacEachern, Lib.
Cape Breton North (5,540) Ronald D. Stewart, O.C., M.D., Lib.
Cape Breton Nova (6,524) Paul W. MacEwan, Lib.
Cape Breton South (5,667) Hon. Manning MacDonald, Lib.
Cape Breton The Lakes (6,591) J. Bernard Boudreau, Q.C., Lib.
Cape Breton West (7,355) Alfie MacLeod, PC
Chester-St. Margarets (5,014) Hon. James A. Barkhouse, Lib.
Clare (3,491) Hon. Wayne J. Gaudet, Lib.
Colchester North (4,984) Hon. Edward F. Lorraine, Lib.
Colchester-Musquodoboit Valley (4,130) Brooke Taylor, PC
Cole Harbour-Eastern Passage (4,734) Dennis Richards, Lib.
Cumberland North (5,676) Vacant, Lib.
Cumberland South (6,714) Hon. Guy Brown, Lib.
Dartmouth East (4,912) Hon. James A. Smith, M.D., Lib.
Dartmouth North (3,301) Sandra L. Jolly, Lib.
Dartmouth South (4,346) John P. Savage, Lib.
Dartmouth-Cole Harbour (4,097) Hon. Alan Mitchell, Lib.
Digby-Annapolis (5,805) Joe Casey, Lib.
Eastern Shore (3,760) Keith Colwell, Lib.
Guysborough-Port Hawkesbury (5,487) Raymond White, Lib.
Halifax Atlantic (4,069) Robert Chisholm, NDP
Halifax Chebucto (3,905) Jay F. Abbass, Lib.
Halifax Citadel (4,608) Vacant, Q.C., PC
Halifax Fairview (13,702) Eileen O'Connell, NDP
Halifax Needham (4,527) Hon. Gerald J. O'Malley, Lib.
Halifax-Bedford Basin (4,667) Gerry Fogerty, Lib.
Hants East (4,295) Bob Carruthers, Lib.
Hants West (4,152) Ron Russell, PC
Inverness (5,806) Charles MacArthur, Lib.
Kings North (4,137) George Archibald, PC
Kings South (3,069) Hon. Robert S. Harrison, Lib.
Kings West (4,895) George Moody, PC
Lunenburg (3,982) Lila O'Connor, Lib.
Lunenburg West (6,266) Hon. Donald R. Downe, Lib.
Pictou Centre (4,841) John F. Hamm, PC
Pictou East (10,228) Wayne Fraser, Lib.
Pictou West (4,032) Don McInnis, PC
Preston (1,846) Hon. F. Wayne Adams, Lib.
Queens (3,526) John Leefe, PC
Richmond (5,440) Richard W. Mann, Lib.
Sackville-Beaverbank (3,620) Bill MacDonald, Lib.
Sackville-Cobequid (5,032) John Holm, NDP
Shelburne (5,437) Clifford Huskilson, Lib.
Timberlea-Prospect (3,470) Hon. Bruce Holland, Lib.
Truro-Bible Hill (4,357) Eleanor E. Norrie, Lib.
Victoria (3,119) Hon. Kenneth MacAskill, Lib.
Yarmouth (5,197) W. Richard Hubbard, Lib.

#### MEMBERS (ALPHABETICAL)

Following is: member, constituency (number of eligible voters at 1993 election) party affiliation. (Address for all is c/o House of Assembly, Province House, Halifax NS B3J 2Y3.)
Refer to Cabinet List, Government Caucus Office, the Offices of the Official Opposition & of the New Democratic Party, for Telephone & Fax numbers.

Jay F. Abbass, Halifax Chebucto (3,905) Lib.
Hon. F. Wayne Adams, Preston (1,846) Lib.
George Archibald, Kings North (4,137) PC
Hon. James A. Barkhouse, Chester-St. Margarets (5,014) Lib.
J. Bernard Boudreau, Q.C., Cape Breton The Lakes (6,591) Lib.
Hon. Guy Brown, Cumberland South (6,714) Lib.
Bob Carruthers, Hants East (4,295) Lib.
Joe Casey, Digby-Annapolis (5,805) Lib.
Robert Chisholm, Halifax Atlantic (4,069) NDP
Keith Colwell, Eastern Shore (3,760) Lib.
Hon. Francene Cosman, Bedford-Fall River (4,754) Lib.
Hon. Donald R. Downe, Lunenburg West (6,266) Lib.
Gerry Fogerty, Halifax-Bedford Basin (4,667) Lib.
Wayne Fraser, Pictou East (10,228) Lib.
Hon. Wayne J. Gaudet, Clare (3,491) Lib.
Hon. J. William Gillis, Ph.D., Antigonish (7,292) Lib.
John F. Hamm, Pictou Centre (4,841) PC
Hon. Robert S. Harrison, Kings South (3,069) Lib.
Hon. Bruce Holland, Timberlea-Prospect (3,470) Lib.
John Holm, Sackville-Cobequid (5,032) NDP
W. Richard Hubbard, Yarmouth (5,197) Lib.
Clifford Huskilson, Shelburne (5,437) Lib.
Sandra L. Jolly, Dartmouth North (3,301) Lib.
John Leefe, Queens (3,526) PC
Hon. Edward F. Lorraine, Colchester North (4,984) Lib.
Charles MacArthur, Inverness (5,806) Lib.
Hon. Kenneth MacAskill, Victoria (3,119) Lib.
Bill MacDonald, Sackville-Beaverbank (3,620) Lib.
Hon. Manning MacDonald, Cape Breton South (5,667) Lib.
John MacEachern, Cape Breton East (7,566) Lib.
Paul W. MacEwan, Cape Breton Nova (6,524) Lib.
Alfie MacLeod, Cape Breton West (7,355) PC
Russell MacNeil, Cape Breton Centre (5,643) Lib.
Richard W. Mann, Richmond (5,440) Lib.
Don McInnis, Pictou West (4,032) PC
Hon. Alan Mitchell, Dartmouth-Cole Harbour (4,097) Lib.
George Moody, Kings West (4,895) PC
Eleanor E. Norrie, Truro-Bible Hill (4,357) Lib.
Eileen O'Connell, Halifax Fairview (13,702) NDP
Lila O'Connor, Lunenburg (3,982) Lib.
Hon. Gerald J. O'Malley, Halifax Needham (4,527) Lib.
Earle Rayfuse, Annapolis (7,136) Lib.
Dennis Richards, Cole Harbour-Eastern Passage (4,734) Lib.
Ron Russell, Hants West (4,152) PC
John P. Savage, Dartmouth South (4,346) Lib.

Hon. James A. Smith, M.D., Dartmouth East (4,912) Lib.
Ronald D. Stewart, O.C., M.D., Cape Breton North (5,540) Lib.
Hon. Allister Surrette, Argyle (3,090) Lib.
Brooke Taylor, Colchester-Musquodoboit Valley (4,130) PC
Raymond White, Guysborough-Port Hawkesbury (5,487) Lib.

#### Vacancies

Cumberland North (5,676)
Halifax Citadel (4,608)

## NOVA SCOTIA GOVERNMENT DEPARTMENTS & AGENCIES

### Department of AGRICULTURE & MARKETING

Joseph Howe Bldg., #700, 1690 Hollis St., PO Box 190, Halifax NS B3J 2M4
902/424-6734; Fax: 902/424-3948; URL: http://www.nsac.ns.ca/nsdam/
Truro:, PO Box 550, Truro NS B2N 5E3
Responsible for assisting the agriculture industry in its role as a significant contributor to the economy of Nova Scotia. The department's three core business functions are: agri-business development; resource stewardship; & education & lifelong learning.

#### ACTS ADMINISTERED

Agricultural Operations Protection Act
Agriculture & Marketing Act
Agriculture & Rural Credit Act
Agrologists Act
Animal Cruelty Prevention Act
Animal Health & Protection Act
Baby Chick Protection Act
Bee Industry Act
Beef Commission Act
Brucellosis Control Act
Cattle Pests Control Act
Cold Storage Plants Loan Act
Crop & Livestock Insurance Act
Dairy Commission Act
Farm Registration Act
Federations of Agriculture Act
Fences & Detention of Stray Livestock Act
Fencing & Impounding of Animals Act
Grain & Forage Commission Act
Imitation Dairy Products Act
Livestock Brands Act
Livestock Health Services Act
Livestock Loans Guarantee Act
Margarine Act
Maritime Provinces Harness Racing Commission Act
Marshland Reclamation Act
Meat Inspection Act
Natural Products Act
Potato Industry Act
Provincial Berry Act
Sheep Protection Act
Stray Animals Act
Weed Control Act
Wildlife Act
Women's Institute of Nova Scotia Act

**Minister**, Hon. Edward F. Lorraine, 902/424-4389
Deputy Minister, Dr. L.E. Haley, 902/424-3244, Email: Les.Haley@nsac.ns.ca
Principal, N.S. Agricultural College, Dr. Garth Coffin, 902/893-6720, Fax: 902/897-9399, Email: gcoffin@cadmin.nsac.ns.ca

#### BUSINESS DEVELOPMENT BRANCH

902/893-6510; Fax: 902/895-7693; Email: BDinfo@nsac.ns.ca
Provides advice in business management, delivery of safety net programs, administration of development programs, & land & credit services.
Acting Director, George Burris, 902/893-6511, Email: gburris@es.nsac.ns.ca
Senior Farm Management Specialist, Kentville, Gary Morton, 902/679-6007, Email: gmorton@kent.nsac.ns.ca
Senior Loan Officer, Kentville, Robb MacMillan, 902/679-6008, Email: rmacmillan@kent.nsac.ns.ca

#### MARKETING & FOOD INDUSTRY DEVELOPMENT BRANCH

902/893-6380; Email: MSinfo@nsac.ns.ca
Administration Fax: 902/895-9403; Research & Information Fax: 902/895-4464
Responsible for marketing programs & services, developing sustainable marketing management opportunities, market research & information, & providing advice, training & leadership in agri-food marketing.
Director, Linda MacDonald, 902/893-6388, Email: l.macdonald@nsac.ns.ca
Marketing Specialist, Market Development & Administrator, Nova Scotia Milk Program, Raymond Foote, 902/893-6382, Email: ray.foote@nsac.ns.ca
Marketing Specialist, Product & Quality Development, Laurie Sandeson, 902/893-6387, Email: l.sandeson@nsac.ns.ca
Marketing Specialist, Research & Information, Claire Hanlon Smith, 902/893-4491, Email: c.hanlonsmith@nsac.ns.ca

#### PRODUCTION TECHNOLOGY BRANCH

902/893-6642; Fax: 902/893-0244; Email: PTinfo@nsac.ns.ca
Integrates all crop & livestock services, & related support.
Director, David Sangster, 902/893-6555, Email: DSangster@gov.ns.ca
Manager, Agronomy, Dwane Mellish, 902/893-6556, Email: DMellish@gov.ns.ca
Manager, Engineering, Peter Swinkels, 902/893-6570, Email: PSwinkels@gov.ns.ca
Manager, Horticulture, Dr. Rick Whitman, 902/679-6039, Email: RWhitman@gov.ns.ca
Manager, Livestock, George Chant, 902/893-6515, Email: GChant@gov.ns.ca

#### QUALITY EVALUATION BRANCH

902/893-6530; Fax: 902/893-6531; Email: QEinfo@nsac.ns.ca
Supports the administration of the provincial meat inspection program, livestock health services program, & provides laboratory services in the areas of veterinary pathology, dairy, soils, water, & livestock feeds.
Director, George C. Smith, 902/893-6363, Email: GSmith@cadmin.nsac.ns.ca
Manager, Food Inspection, Mike Horwich, 902/893-6541

#### RESOURCE STEWARDSHIP BRANCH

Provides advice, training, research & technology adaptation in sustainable resource management & environmental standards for agriculture.
Director, Michael Langman, 902/893-6557, Fax: 902/893-0335

#### RURAL LEADERSHIP BRANCH

Coordinates the delivery of extension & training programs, leadership development, agricultural awareness, & distance education.
Director, Jim B. Goit, 902/893-7950, Email: JGoit@pam.nsac.ns.ca
Asst. Director, Field Services, George MacKenzie, 902/893-6589, Email: GMackenzie@es.nsac.ns.ca
Supervisor, 4-H & Rural Organizations, Liz Crouse, 902/893-6587, Email: ECrouse@nsdam.gov.ns.ca

#### Associated Agencies, Boards & Commissions

•Nova Scotia Beef Commission: PO Box 550, Truro NS B2N 5E3 – 902/893-6514; Fax: 902/897-9768
Manager, Vacant
•Nova Scotia Crop & Livestock Insurance Commission: MacRae Library Bldg., PO Box 1092, Truro NS B2N 5G9 – 902/893-6370; Fax: 902/895-4622; Email: nsclic info@nsac.ns.ca
Manager, Brian M. Mahoney
•Nova Scotia Dairy Commission: PO Box 782, Truro NS B2N 5E8 – 902/893-6379; Fax: 902/897-9768
Manager, Gabriel Comeau, Email: GComeau@cadmin.nsac.ns.ca
•Nova Scotia Farm Loan Board: PO Box 550, Truro NS B2N 5E3 – 902/893-6506; Fax: 902/895-7693
Director, R.G. Adams, 902/893-6500, Email: RAdams@lcs.nsac.ns.ca
Senior Loan Officer, Wayne MacLeod, 902/893-6507
•Nova Scotia Grain & Forage Commission: Kentville Agricultural Centre, 32 Main St., Kentville NS B4N 1J5 – 902/893-6556; Fax: 902/893-0244
Contact, Dwane Mellish

#### Agricultural Marketing Boards & Commissions

•Natural Products Marketing Council: PO Box 550, Truro NS B2N 5E3 – 902/893-6380; Fax: 902/895-9403
Chair, S.F. Allaby
Acting Secretary, Linda MacDonald
•Nova Scotia Chicken Producers Board: PO Box 338, Canning NS B0P 1H0 – 902/582-7400; Fax: 902/582-7066
Secretary, Robert French
•Nova Scotia Egg & Pullet Producers Marketing Board: PO Box 1096, Truro NS B2N 5G9 – 902/895-6341; Fax: 902/895-6343
Secretary, James Bragg
•Nova Scotia Flue-Cured Tobacco Growers' Marketing Board: Blair House, Kentville Agricultural Centre, PO Box 154, Kentville NS B4N 3W4 – 902/678-0533; Fax: 902/679-1074
Secretary-Manager, Sonya D. MacKillop
•Nova Scotia Grain Marketing Board: PO Box 308, Kentville NS B4N 3X1 – 902/678-5512; Fax: 902/678-1215
Secretary Manager, A. Findlay MacRae
•Nova Scotia Greenhouse Vegetable Marketing Board: PO Box 1422, Truro NS B2N 5V2 – 902/893-3966; Fax: 902/897-9019
Manager, Marie Brody
•Nova Scotia Potato Marketing Board: Blair House, Kentville Agricultural Centre, Kentville NS B4N 1J5 – 902/678-0533; Fax: 902/679-1074
Secretary-Manager, Sonya D. MacKillop
•Nova Scotia Processing Pea & Bean Growers Marketing Board: Blair House, Kentville Agricultural Centre, Kentville NS B4N 1J5 – 902/678-0533; Fax: 902/679-1074
Secretary-Manager, Sonya D. MacKillop
•Nova Scotia Turkey Marketing Board: Blair House, Kentville Agricultural Centre, PO Box 130, Kentville NS B4N 3W4 – 902/678-5836; Fax: 902/679-1074
Operations Manager, Sonya Adams
•Nova Scotia Wool Marketing Board: PO Box 550, Truro NS B2N 5E3 – 902/893-6517; Fax: 902/893-6531
Secretary, Roy MacKenzie

•Pork Nova Scotia: PO Box 1341, Truro NS B2N 5N2 – 902/895-0581; Fax: 902/893-4236
Secretary, John Miller

## Office of the AUDITOR GENERAL

#302, 1888 Brunswick St., Halifax NS B3J 3J8
902/424-5907; Fax: 902/424-4350; URL: http://www.gov.ns.ca/legi/audg/
**Auditor General**, Roy Salmon, F.C.A., 902/424-4046, Email: salmoner@gov.ns.ca
Senior Audit Director, Claude D. Carter, C.A., 902/424-4396, Email: cartercd@gov.ns.ca
Executive Secretary, Darleen Langille, 902/424-4108, Email: langildm@gov.ns.ca

## Department of BUSINESS & CONSUMER SERVICES (DBCS)

South Maritime Centre, #8, 1505 Barrington St., Halifax NS B3J 2X1
902/424-7777; Fax: 902/424-7434; Email: bcs@gov.ns.ca; URL: http://www.gov.ns.ca/bacs/
Announced in March 1996, the development of the new Department of Business & Consumer Services. The new department combines the following: consumer & commercial relations & financial institutions divisions from the former Department of Housing & Consumer Affairs; vital statistics from the Department of Health; registry of motor vehicles from the former Department of Transortation; provincial tax commission; certain aspects of the Economic Renewal Agency; & the public inquiries service.

#### ACTS ADMINISTERED

Business & Electronic Filing Act
Cemetary & Funeral Services Act
Change of Name Act
Collection Agenices Act
Companies Act
Condominium Act
Consumer Creditors' Conduct Act
Consumer Protection Act
Consumer Reporting Act
Consumer Services Act
Corporations Registration Act
Corporations Securities Registration Act
Credit Union Act
Dangerous Goods Transportation Act
Direct Sellers' Licensing & Regulation Act
Embalmers & Funeral Directors Act
Future Services Act
Gaming Control Act
Gasoline & Diesel Oil Tax Act
Government Records Act
Health Services Tax Act
Homeowners' Incentive Grants Act
Insurance Act
Insurance Premiums Tax Act
Limited Partnerships Act
Liquor Control Act
Loan Companies Inspection Act
Mortgage Brokers' & Lenders' Registration Act
Motor Carrier Act
Motor Vehicle Act
Mutual Insurance Act
Off-Highway Vehicles Act
Partnerships & Business Names Registration Act
Private Investment Holding Companies Act
Public Accountants Act
Public Highways Act
Real Estate Broker's Licensing Act
Rental Property Conversion Act
Rent Review Act
Residential Tenancies Act
Revenue Act
Societies Act
Solemnization of Marriage Act
Summary Proceedings Act
Theatre & Amusements Act
Trust & Loans Companies Act
Unconscionable Transactions Relief Act
Vital Statistics Act
**Minister**, Hon. Wayne J. Gaudet, Q.C., 902/424-7579, Fax: 902/424-0754
Deputy Minister, A.A. Rovers, 902/424-7788

#### ACCESS NOVA SCOTIA

902/424-7009; Fax: 902/424-2633; Email: access@gov.ns.ca
Toll Free: 1-800-225-8227
Provincial agency responsible for providing government, community & business information as it pertains to current programs & services.

#### COMMUNICATIONS SERVICES/PUBLIC INQUIRIES OFFICE

One Government Place, 1700 Granville St., Ground Fl., PO Box 608, Halifax NS B3J 2R7
902/424-5200; Fax: 902/425-3026; Email: burnsca@gov.ns.ca
Toll Free: 1-800-670-4357
Acting Executive Director, Jim Vibert, 902/424-4886
Acting Coordinator, Carla Burns, 902/424-2876

#### FINANCIAL INSTITUTIONS DIVISION/SUPERINTENDENT OF INSURANCE

902/424-6331; Fax: 902/424-5327
Regulates the operations of credit unions, trust & loan companies & insurance companies, agents, brokers & adjusters in Nova Scotia; provides a public enquiry & complaint service relating to financial insitutions & the insurance industry; administers the collection of insurance premiums tax.
Director, Paul LeBlanc

#### PROVINCIAL TAX COMMISSION

PO Box 755, Halifax NS B3J 2V4
902/424-4411; Fax: 902/424-0523; Email: keefeg@gov.ns.ca
Toll Free: 1-800-565-2336
Commissioner, Thelma Costello, Email: Costello@gov.ns.ca

#### REGISTRY OF JOINT STOCK COMPANIES

PO Box 1529, Halifax NS B3J 2Y4
902/424-7742; Fax: 902/424-4633; Email: jstocks@ra.isisnet.com; URL: http://www.gov.ns.ca/bacs/rjsc/
Registrar, Catherine Smith

#### REGISTRY OF MOTOR VEHICLES

PO Box 1652, Halifax NS B3J 2Z3
902/424-5851; Fax: 902/424-0544; Email: rmv@gov.ns.ca; URL: http://www.gov.ns.ca/bacs/rmv/
Toll Free: 1-800-898-7668
Executive Director, Marie Mullally, 902/424-0544

#### VITAL STATISTICS

Halifax NS B3J 2M9
902/424-4381; Fax: 902/424-0678; Email: Vstat@gov.ns.ca; URL: http://www.gov.ns.ca/bacs/vstat/
Responsible for the registration & supply of vital statistics information for the province. Official Birth, Marriage & Death certificates may be obtained through the service. Fee for each ordinary certificate is $20.00.
Deputy Registrar General, Vital Statistics, Betty Etter, 902/424-8907
Administrator, Information Systems & Vital Statistics, Dan Rice

##### Associated Agencies, Boards & Commissions

•Atlantic Lottery Corporation
*See* listing under New Brunswick Finance, this Section.
•Nova Scotia Liquor Commission: 93 Chainlake Dr., PO Box 8720, Stn A, Halifax NS B3K 5M4 – 902/450-6752; Fax: 902/453-1153
Chief Commissioner, Douglas A. Caldwell, 902/450-5803, Fax: 902/450-5243
General Manager, G.D. Findlay, 902/450-5802, Fax: 902/450-5225
Executive Director, Retail Services, B.E. Rogers, 902/450-5903, Fax: 902/450-5265
•Nova Scotia Liquor Licence Board: PO Box 545, Dartmouth NS B2Y 3Y8 – 902/424-3660; Fax: 902/424-8987
Chair & CEO, Margaret A.M. Shears
•Nova Scotia Residential Tenancies Board: PO Box 998, Halifax NS B3J 2X3 – 902/424-4690
Acting Director, Barbara Jones-Gordon

## Department of COMMUNITY SERVICES

Johnston Bldg., 5182 Prince St., 5th Fl., PO Box 696, Halifax NS B3J 2T7
902/424-4326; Fax: 902/424-0502

#### ACTS ADMINISTERED

Adoption Information Act
Adult Protection Act
Children & Family Services Act
Day Care Act
Disabled Persons' Commission Act
Family Benefits Act
Homes for Special Care Act
Senior Citizens' Financial Aid Act
Senior Citizens' Secretariat Act
Social Assistance Act
Social Services Councils Act
**Minister**, Hon. Francene Cosman, 902/424-4304, Fax: 902/424-0549
Acting Deputy Minister, Ron L'Esperance, 902/424-4325
Administrator, Finance & Administration, George Hudson, 902/424-2750
Director, Audit Services, Colleen Cooper, 902/424-4147
Director, Communications, Cathy Shaw, 902/424-4326

#### FAMILY & CHILDREN'S SERVICES

Fax: 902/424-0708
Administrator, Jane Fitzgerald, 902/424-4279
Director, Child Welfare, George Savoury, 902/424-3202
Director, Community Outreach Services, Judy Jackson, 902/424-5863
Acting Director, Prevention Services, Goranka Vukelich, 902/424-3204
Project Manager, Welfare Reform Initiative, Peter Barteaux, 902/424-2498
Coordinator, Mentally & Physically Challenged Children, Lorna MacPherson, 902/424-5863

#### INCOME & EMPLOYMENT SUPPORT

Fax: 902/424-0721
Acting Administrator, Barbara Burles, 902/424-6762
Acting Director, Community Support for Adults, Janet Bray, 902/424-0930
Director, Employment Evaluation Support Services, Tracey Williams, 902/424-4329
Acting Director, Income Assistance, Mary Lou Griswald, 902/424-4262

#### STRATEGIC PLANNING & POLICY

Fax: 902/424-0502
Administrator, Shulamith Medjuck, 902/424-4039
Coordinator, Family Violence Prevention Initiative, Vacant, 902/424-2079
Director, Program Evaluation Review & Research, Elizabeth McNaughton, 902/424-7900
Director, Staff & Management Support Services, Greg Gammon, 902/424-3960

#### Regional Offices

Eastern: Sydney – 902/563-3302, Administrator, Frank Capstick
Halifax: Metro One Bldg., 6061 Young St., Halifax NS B3K 2A3 – 902/424-4755, Administrator, William Campbell
Northern: New Glasgow – 902/755-7023, Administrator, Nina Clark
Western: Kentville – 902/679-6715, Administrator, Phillip Warren

#### Associated Agencies, Boards & Commissions

•Nova Scotia Disabled Persons Commission: #203, 2695 Dutch Village Rd., Halifax NS B3L 4T9 – 902/424-8280; Fax: 902/424-0592, Toll Free: 1-800-565-8280 (within Nova Scotia)
Chair, Reid Nicholson
Executive Director, Charles Macdonald
•Senior Citizens Secretariat: 1740 Granville St., 4th Fl., PO Box 2065, Halifax NS B3J 2Z1 – 902/424-6322; Fax: 902/424-0561
Director, Brian Vandervaart

## Nova Scotia ECONOMIC RENEWAL AGENCY

1800 Argyle St., PO Box 519, Halifax NS B3J 2R7
902/424-8920; Fax: 902/424-0582; Email: econ.era@gov.ns.ca; URL: http://www.gov.ns.ca/ecor/

#### ACTS ADMINISTERED

Bedford Waterfront Development Act
Business Development Corporation Act
Camping Establishments Regulation Act
Cooperative Associations Act
Economic Renewal Agency Act
Hotel Regulations Act
Industrial Development Act
Industrial Estates Limited Act
Industrial Loan Act
Industry Closing Act
Innovation Corporation Act
Nova Scotia Film Development Corporation Act
Research Foundation Corporation Act
Small Business Development Act
Sydney Waterfront Development Corporation Act
Tartan Act
Trade Development Authority Act
Venture Corporation Act
Voluntary Planning Act
**Minister Responsible**, Hon. Manning MacDonald, 902/424-5680, Fax: 902/424-0514
Deputy Minister, C.H. (Bert) Loveless, C.A., 902/424-3231, Email: econ.deputy@gov.ns.ca
Special Asst. to Deputy Minister, David Oxner, 902/424-6632
Senior Policy Coordinator, Policy & Coordination, Robert Doherty, 902/424-6624
Senior Advisor, Communications & Public Relations, Steve Warburton, 902/424-0927

### COMMUNITY ECONOMIC DEVELOPMENT

EMail: econ.ced@gov.ns.ca
Executive Director, Chris Bryant, 902/424-3545
Director, Regional Operations, Neal Conrad, 902/424-6014
Acting Coordinator, Provincial Employment Program, Brian Watson, 902/424-2106

#### Canada Nova Scotia Business Service Centre

1575 Brunswick St., Halifax NS B3J 2G1
902/426-8604; Fax: 902/426-6530; Email: halifax@cbsc.ic.gc.ca
Toll Free: 1-800-668-1010
Faxback: 902/426-3201

### CORPORATE SERVICES

Executive Director, Brian McDonough, 902/424-7444
Director, Human Resources, Janet Lee, 902/424-7439
Manager, Accounting, David MacKay, 902/424-7446

### INVESTMENT & TRADE

EMail: econ.iat@gov.ns.ca
Trade Development Centre: 902/424-5448; Fax: 902/424-5739
Executive Director, Roy Sherwood, 902/424-3656
Director, Trade, Andy Hare, 902/424-3672
Officer, Investment, Tab Borden, 902/424-3821
Officer, Investment, Marilyn Mullett, 902/424-8282
Officer, Investment, Tom Mulrooney, 902/424-6142
Officer, Investment, Craig Stanfield, 902/424-6140

### LENDING & FINANCIAL SERVICES

Executive Director, Donald A. Leet, 902/424-8958
Director, Lending, Doug Giannou, 902/424-6867

### NOVA SCOTIA MARKETING AGENCY

Executive Director, Dan Brennan, 902/424-4554
Director, Marketing Policy & Creative Services, Rae Owen, 902/424-0664
Specialist, Attractions & Events, Patricia Lynch, 902/424-4678
Specialist, Market Development, Minto Stewart, 902/424-4646
Specialist, Travel Trade, Rick Young, 902/424-4182

### TOURISM NOVA SCOTIA

Executive Director, Michele McKenzie, 902/424-2989
Coordinator, Enquiries, Robert Boyd, 902/424-2906
Supervisor, Tourist Information Centre, Kathryn Malone, 902/424-4576

#### Foreign Office

United States: 4 Copley Sq., Boston MA 02116, USA – 617/262-7677; Fax: 617/262-7689, Director of Nova Scotia in New England, Gary MacPherson

#### Associated Agencies, Boards & Commissions

•Nova Scotia Innovation Corporation (InNOVAcorp): Woodside Industrial Park, 101 Research Dr., PO Box 790, Dartmouth NS B2Y 3Z7 – 902/424-8670; Fax: 902/424-8679; URL: http://www.innovacorp.ns.ca, Toll Free: 1-800-565-7051 – Email: ticentre@ra.isisnet.com (Tech. Innov. Centre)

A technology commercialization corporation formed in 1995 to promote relationships that enable Nova Scotia firms to compete internationally. Offers scientific, engineering & business extension services to assist in developing new technology-based products & services, then helps Nova Scotia companies develop trade ties for these products. Works in cooperation with universities, research institutions & the private sector.
CEO, Ross McCurdy
Chief Operating Officer, Laszlo Mayer
CFO, Bob MacNeil
Executive Director, Corporate Affairs, Kimberly MacDonald-Vibert
Executive Director, Business Development, Randolf Harrold
General Manager, Nova Magnetics Ltd., Jeffrey Knapp, Email: nml@innovacorp.ns.ca
Manager, Analytical & Environmental Chemistry Group, Mike Robicheau
Manager, Environmental Simulation Lab, Neil Richter
Manager, International Development, Ray Roberts
Manager, Microbiology Group, Dr. Austin Reade
Manager, Quality & Productivity Initiatives, Gerry Archibald, Email: garchibald@innovacorp.ns.ca
Manager, Technology Commercialization, David Roach
Manager, Technological People in Industry, Ian Glass
•Nova Scotia Business Development Corporation: World Trade & Convention Centre, 1800 Argyle St., 6th Fl., Halifax NS B3J 2R7 – 902/424-6488; Fax: 902/424-6823

Encourages business development & promotes employment opportunities in the province. Offers secured business project financing to companies qualifying for assistance.
•Nova Scotia Film Development Corporation: 1724 Granville St., Halifax NS B3J 1X5 – 902/424-7177, 7185; Email: nsfdc@fox.nstn.ca; URL: http://fox.nstn.ca/ZXnsfdc/
Chair, Vacant
•Waterfront Development Corporation Ltd.: 1751 Lower Water St., Halifax NS B3J 1S5 – 902/422-6591; Fax: 902/422-7582; URL: http://www.gov.ns.ca/ecor/cpr/aagagi.htm#wdc
President & CEO, Fred Were
•World Trade & Convention Centre: 1800 Argyle St., PO Box 955, Halifax NS B3J 2V9 – 902/421-8686; Fax: 902/422-2922
President & CEO, Fred MacGillivray

## Department of EDUCATION & CULTURE

2021 Brunswick St., PO Box 578, Halifax NS B3J 2S9
902/424-5168; Fax: 902/424-0511; URL: http://www.ednet.ns.ca/

#### ACTS ADMINISTERED

Apprenticeship & Trades Qualifications Act
Art Gallery Act
Arts Council Act
Cosmetology Act
Cultural Foundation Act
Degree Granting Act
Education Act & Regulations
Education Assistance Act
Education of the Blind Act
Educational Communications Agency Act
Gaelic College Foundation Act
Government Records Act
Handicapped Persons' Education Act & Regulations
Hospital Education Assistance Act
Libraries Act & Regulations
Maritime Provinces Higher Education (Nova Scotia) Act
Multiculturalism Act
Nova Scotia Community College Act
Nova Scotia Museum Act
Nova Scotia School Boards Association Act
Public Archives of Nova Scotia Act
Sherbrooke Restoration Commission Act
Shubenacadie Canal Commission Act
Special Places Protection Act
Student Aid Act
Tartan Act
Teachers' Collective Bargaining Act
Teaching Profession Act
Trade Schools Regulation Act
Universities Assistance Act
Universities Foundation Act
**Minister**, Hon. Robert S. Harrison, 902/424-4236, Fax: 902/424-0680
Deputy Minister, Marilyn Gaudet, 902/424-5643, Email: gaudetm@gov.ns.ca
Communications Officer, Donna MacDonald, 902/424-2615, Fax: 902/424-0680, Email: macdondc@gov.ns.ca
Director, Human Resources, Susan Crandall, 902/424-5766, Fax: 902/424-0657, Email: crandase@gov.ns.ca

### ACADIAN & FRENCH LANGUAGE SERVICES BRANCH

Executive Director, Charles Gaudet, 902/424-6097, Fax: 902/424-0613, Email: gaudetcj@gov.ns.ca
Director, Programs Division, Margelaine Holding, 902/424-6327, Email: holdinms@gov.ns.ca

### COMMUNITY COLLEGE BRANCH

Acting Executive Director, Rick Butler, 902/424-4060, Fax: 902/424-0643, Email: butlerrm@gov.ns.ca

Director, Adult Learning & Innovation, Nancy Hyland, 902/424-8880, Fax: 902/424-0666, Email: hylandnm@gov.ns.ca

Director, Apprenticeship Training Division, Vacant, 902/424-8903, Fax: 902/424-0717

Director, Student Assistance Office, Kathleen Thompson, 902/424-8433, Fax: 902/424-0540, Email: thompski@gov.ns.ca

#### FINANCE & OPERATIONS BRANCH

Executive Director, Douglas Nauss, 902/424-3646, Fax: 902/424-0732, Email: naussde@gov.ns.ca

Acting Director, Facilities, Planning & Equipment Division, Charles Clattenburg, 902/424-4386, Email: clattecd@gov.ns.ca

Director, Financial Management Division, Reg Clayton, 902/424-5698, Email: claytowr@gov.ns.ca

Director, Grants & Audit Division, Richard Morris, 902/424-3956, Email: morrisre@gov.ns.ca

#### HERITAGE & CULTURE BRANCH (NOVA SCOTIA MUSEUM)

Executive Director, Candace Stevenson, 902/424-6472, Fax: 902/424-0560, Email: stevencj@gov.ns.ca

Director, Cultural Affairs Division, Peggy Walt, 902/424-5929, Fax: 902/424-0710

Acting Director, Maritime Museum of the Atlantic, Marven Moore, 902/424-6440, Fax: 902/424-0612, Email: mooreme@gov.ns.ca

Director, Museum Services Division, Robert Frame, 902/424-6478, Fax: 902/424-0560, Email: framerw@gov.ns.ca

Director, Nova Scotia Museum of Natural History, Debra Burleson, 902/424-7353, Fax: 902/424-0560

Acting Director, Planning & Communications Division, Debra Burleson, 902/424-6471, Fax: 902/424-0560

#### POLICY BRANCH

Executive Director, Wayne Doggett, 902/424-4377, Fax: 902/424-0626, Email: doggetwf@gov.ns.ca

Director, Information Technology Services Division, Andrew Cornwall, 902/424-4167, Fax: 902/424-0874, Email: cornwaab@gov.ns.ca

Director, Planning & Research Division, Maryann Ricketts, 902/424-5631, Fax: 902/424-0626, Email: ricketmh@gov.ns.ca

Director, Publishing & Document Management Services, Rusty McClelland, 902/424-7747, Fax: 902/424-0519, Email: mcclelrs@gov.ns.ca

Director, Regional Education, Michael Sweeney, 902/424-5829, Fax: 902/424-0519, Email: sweenemd@gov.ns.ca

Director, Testing & Evaluation Division, Vincent Warner, 902/424-7746, Fax: 902/424-0614, Email: warnerhv@gov.ns.ca

Provincial Librarian, Provincial Library, Marion Pape, 902/424-2457, Fax: 902/424-0633

#### PROGRAM BRANCH

Executive Director, Tom Rich, 902/424-5799, Fax: 902/424-0749, Email: richt@gov.ns.ca

Director, African Canadian Services Division, Robert Upshaw, 902/424-2515, Fax: 902/424-7210, Email: upshawrt@gov.ns.ca

Director, English Program Services Division, Robert LeBlanc, 902/424-5745, Fax: 902/424-0613, Email: leblanrm@gov.ns.ca

Director, Learning Resources & Technology, Michael Jeffrey, 902/424-2462, Fax: 902/424-0633

Acting Director, Mi'Kmaq Services Division, Sr. Dorothy Moore, 902/424-7378, Fax: 902/424-0749, Email: mooredg@gov.ns.ca

Director, Student Services Division, Anne Power, 902/424-7454, Fax: 902/424-0749, Email: powerda@gov.ns.ca

##### Associated Agencies, Boards & Commissions

•Nova Scotia Arts Council: PO Box 1559, Halifax NS B3J 2Y3 – 902/422-1123

Executive Director, Russell Kelly

•Nova Scotia Council on Higher Education: 2021 Burnswick St., PO Box 2086, Stn M, Halifax NS B3J 3B7 – 902/424-6992; Fax: 902/424-0651

Executive Director, Vacant

•Nova Scotia Provincial Apprenticeship Board: PO Box 578, Halifax NS B3J 2S9 – 902/424-0872; Fax: 902/424-0717; Email: hlfxtrad.educ.youngsl@gov.ns.ca; URL: http://www.ednet.ns.ca/educ/abc/apprent/apprenhp.htm

Executive Secretary, Bernie Mac Donald

## Nova Scotia ELECTIONS OFFICE

Joseph Howe Bldg., 9th Fl., PO Box 2246, Halifax NS B3J 3C8

902/424-8584; Fax: 902/424-6622

Election Supply Centre, 2543 Barrington St., Halifax NS B3K 2X2

902/424-4375

**Acting Chief Electoral Officer**, Janet Willwerth

## Nova Scotia EMERGENCY MEASURES ORGANIZATION (EMO)

PO Box 2107, Halifax NS B3J 3B7

902/424-5620; Fax: 902/424-5376; Email: emo@gov.ns.ca; URL: http://www.gov.ns.ca/envi/dept/emo

#### ACTS ADMINISTERED

Emergency Measures Act
Emergency 911 Act

**Minister Responsible**, Hon. F. Wayne Adams, 902/424-2358, Fax: 902/424-0644

Director, Michael R. Lester

Program Administration Officer, Michael Myette

Training Officer, Tanya Crawford

##### Zone Offices

Cape Breton: PO Box 714, Sydney NS B1P 6J7 – 902/563-2093; Fax: 902/563-2319, Controller, Winston Musgrave

Central: PO Box 824, Truro NS B2N 5G6 – 902/893-5880; Fax: 902/893-1648, Controller, William A. Weagle

Western: PO Box 1240, Middleton NS B0S 1P0 – 902/825-2181; Fax: 902/825-4471, Controller, Vacant

## Department of the ENVIRONMENT

5151 Terminal Rd., 5th Fl., PO Box 2107, Halifax NS B3J 3B7

902/424-5300; Fax: 902/424-0503; URL: http://www.gov.ns.ca/envi/

#### ACTS ADMINISTERED

Clean Nova Scotia Foundation Act
Dangerous Goods & Hazardous Wastes Management Act
Derelict Vehicles Removal Act
Emergency "911" Act
Emergency Measures Act
Environmental Assessment Act
Environmental Protection Act
Environmental Trust Act
Litter Abatement Act
Ozone Layer Protection Act
Pest Control Products (Nova Scotia) Act
Recycling Act
Salvage Yards Licensing Act
Water Act
Well Drilling Act
Youth Conservation Corps Act

**Minister**, Hon. F. Wayne Adams, 902/424-2358

Deputy Minister, Peter Underwood, 902/424-2359

Director, Finance, Scott Nicholson, 902/424-2362, Fax: 902/424-0503

Public Relations, Margaret Murphy, 902/424-2575

#### ENVIRONMENTAL INDUSTRIES & TECHNOLOGIES DIVISION

902/424-7025; URL: http://www.gov.ns.ca/envi/infoserv/eit/home.htm

Asst. Deputy Minister, Lin Chang, 902/424-3617

Director, Robert Langdon, P.Eng., 902/424-2386, Email: hlfxterm.envi.langdobe@gov.ns.ca

Executive Manager, Trade & Investment, Mauritz Erhard, 902/424-5205, Email: hlfxterm.envi.erhardmx@gov.ns.ca

Manager, Regional Development, Kim MacNeil, 902/424-6304, Email: hlfxterm.envi.macneijk@gov.ns.ca

#### ENVIRONMENTAL SUPPORT SERVICES DIVISION

902/424-6305; Fax: 902/424-0501

Acting Director, William Smith, 902/424-5071

Manager, Enforcement Branch, Derek White, 902/424-6341

Acting Manager, Environmental Review Branch, Andrew Kendall, 902/424-6343

Manager, Training & Education Services Branch, Lee Lewis, 902/424-6304

#### POLICY PLANNING & COORDINATION DIVISION

902/424-4944; Fax: 902/424-0501

Director, Frances Martin, 902/424-5695

Director, Research, Statistics & Studies Branch, Vacant

Asst. Director, Policy & Planning Branch, Frances Martin, 902/424-8695

#### REGIONAL OFFICES DIVISION

902/424-2547; Fax: 902/424-0569

Director, Creighton Brisco, 902/424-2548

#### RESOURCE MANAGEMENT & ENVIRONMENTAL PROTECTION DIVISION

902/424-2375; Fax: 902/424-0503

Director, Clive Oldreive, 902/424-2385

Manager, Air Quality Branch, Creighton Brisco, 902/424-2550

Manager, Industrial Pollution Control Branch, Dan E. Hiltz, 902/424-2284

Manager, Water Resources Branch, Andrew Cameron, 902/424-2554

Asst. Manager, Pesticide Management Branch, Craig Morrison, 902/424-2541

#### UTILITIES DIVISION

Fax: 902/424-0503

Director, George Searle, 902/424-2581

Supervisor, Construction, Robert Anderson, 902/424-2580

##### Nova Scotia Round Table on Environment & Economy

c/o Department of Environment, PO Box 2107, Halifax NS B3J 3B7

902/424-6346; Fax: 902/424-0501

Chair, Hon. F. Wayne Adams

Provincial Coordinator, Brenda MacNeil

##### Associated Agencies, Boards & Commissions

•Nova Scotia Emergency Measures Organization

Listed alphabetically in detail, this section.

•Nova Scotia Environmental Assessment Board: PO Box 2107, Halifax NS B3J 3B7 – 902/424-2574; Fax: 902/424-0503

CEO, Shirley L. Nicholson

•Nova Scotia Environmental Trust Fund: PO Box 2107, Halifax NS B3J 3B7 – 902/424-6346; Fax: 902/424-0501

Secretariat, Jeanne Bourque

•Nova Scotia Resource Recovery Fund Board: PO Box 2107, Halifax NS B3J 3B7 – 902/424-2577; Fax: 902/424-0503
Administrator, Vacant

## Department of FINANCE

PO Box 187, Halifax NS B3J 2N3
902/424-5554; Fax: 902/424-0635; URL: http://www.gov.ns.ca/fina/

#### ACTS ADMINISTERED

Appropriations Act
Corporations Capital Tax Act
Equity Tax Act
Expenditure Control Act
Income Tax Act
Members' Retiring Allowances Act
Nova Scotia Stock Savings Plan Act
Pension Benefits Act
Provincial Finance Act
Public Service Superannuation Act
Succession Duty Act
Teachers' Plan Act & Regulations
**Minister**, Hon. J. William Gillis, Ph.D., 902/424-5720, Fax: 902/424-0635
Deputy Minister, Robert P. Moody, 902/424-5553, Email: moodyrp@gov.ns.ca
Acting Controller, Glenn Hynes, C.A., 902/424-5944, Email: HynesG@gov.ns.ca
Director, Accounting Services, R. Noble, C.M.A., 902/424-5761
Director, Administration, Ivan Richardson, C.M.A., 902/424-2430
Director, Budget, Lynne Burrell, C.A., 902/424-5029
Director, Internal Audit, Vicki Dimick, 902/424-2407
Director, Management Information Systems, Holly Fancy, 902/424-3993
Director, Payroll Services, S. MacDonald, 902/424-5902

#### FISCAL & ECONOMIC POLICY BRANCH

Acting Executive Director, Elizabeth Cody, 902/424-4160, Email: codye@gov.ns.ca
Director, Economic Policy Division, Charlie Pye
Acting Director, Fiscal Policy, Bruce Hennebury, 902/424-4168, Fax: 902/424-0590, Email: hennebub@gov.ns.ca
Director, Statistics Division, Paul Dober, 902/424-5691, Fax: 902/424-0714, Email: doberp@gov.ns.ca

#### INVESTMENTS, PENSIONS & TREASURY SERVICES BRANCH

Executive Director, Richard W. McAloney, CA, CFA, CIA, 902/424-5557, Email: mcaloner@gov.ns.ca
Superintendent, Pension Registration, Nancy MacNeill, 902/424-8915, Email: hlfxprov.fina.macneiln@gov.ns.ca
Director, Investments, Peter Vanloon, 902/424-4140
Director, Liability Management & Treasury Services Division, Douglas Stratton, 902/424-4475, Fax: 902/429-0257, Email: strattod@gov.ns.ca
Director, Pensions, Robert Jack, 902/424-5911

#### GOVERNMENT PURCHASING AGENCY/PUBLIC TENDERS OFFICE

Central Services Bldg., 6176 Young St., Suite 120, Halifax NS B3K 2A6
902/424-5520; Fax: 902/463-5732; URL: http://www.gov.ns.ca/fina/ptns/index.htm
Director, George Murphy, Email: ssvsgpa.murphyg@gov.ns.ca

## Department of FISHERIES

Bank of Montreal Bldg., 5151 George St., 7th Fl., PO Box 2223, Halifax NS B3J 3C4
902/424-4560; Fax: 902/424-4671; URL: http://www.gov.ns.ca/fish/
Pictou Office: 902/485-8031

#### ACTS ADMINISTERED

Aquaculture Act
Fisheries Act
Fisheries Development Act
Irish Moss Act
Sea Plant Harvesting Act
**Minister**, Hon. James A. Barkhouse, 902/424-8953
Deputy Minister, Alan Steel, 902/424-0300
Director, Financal Services Division, Frank Dunn
Director, Human Resources Division, Frank MacLean
Director, Training Division, Barbara Riley, 902/424-0328

#### AQUACULTURE DIVISION

Acting Director, Alan Chandler, 902/424-3644
Manager, Aquaculture Development, I. Judson, 902/424-3644
Supervisor, Development Unit, C. Reardon, 902/424-0324
Supervisor, Licensing Unit, C. Morrison, 902/424-0354

#### INLAND FISHERIES DIVISION

Director, Murray Hill, 902/485-7021
Asst. Director, Don A. MacLean, RR#3, St. Andrews NS B0H 1X0, 902/485-7022
Manager, Fraser's Mill Trout Hatchery, D.D. Murrant, RR#3, St. Andrews NS B0H 1X0, 902/783-2926
Manager, Mcgowan Lake Trout Hatchery, Michael MacNeil, PO Box 141, Caledonia NS B0T 1B0, 902/682-2576

#### MARKETING DIVISION

902/424-0333
Director, Janis Raymond, 902/424-0330
Seafood Consultant, A. Estelle Bryant, 902/424-0331

#### POLICY, PLANNING DIVISION

902/424-0350
Director, A.A. Longard, 902/424-0347
Advisor, Marine Resources (Groundfish), C. F. MacKinnon, 902/424-0349
Advisor, Marine Resources (Invertebrates), S. Gregory Roach, 902/424-0348
Advisor, Marine Resources (Pelagics), Dr. Robert Crawford, 902/424-0351

#### TECHNOLOGY & INSPECTION DIVISION

902/424-0343
Director, David Hansen, 902/424-0337
Manager, Technology Development, Marshall Giles, 902/424-0336

##### Associated Agencies, Boards & Commissions

•Fisheries Loan Board: Bank of Montreal Bldg., 5151 George St., 7th Fl., Halifax NS B3J 3C4 – 902/424-0312; Fax: 902/424-4671
Chair, J.A. Marsters
Director, J.P. Sarty

## Department of HEALTH

Joseph Howe Bldg., 1690 Hollis St., PO Box 488, Halifax NS B3J 2R8
902/424-4310; Fax: 902/424-0559; Email: heal.webmaster@gov.ns.ca; URL: http://www.gov.ns.ca/heal
Toll Free: 1-800-387-6665

#### ACTS ADMINISTERED

Adult Protection Act
AIDS Advisory Commission Act
An Act to Restrict the Privatization of Medical Services
Anatomy Act
Camp Hill Hospital Act
Cancer Treatment & Research Foundation Act
Cape Breton Regional Hospital Act
Children & Family Services Act
Chiropractic Act
Cobequid Multi-Service Centre Act
Dental Act
Dental Technicians Act
Denturist Act
Disabled Persons' Commission Act
Dispensing Opticians Act
Drug Dependency Act
Emergency Health Services Act
Fatality Inquiries Act
Halifax Infirmary Act
Health Act
Health Services & Insurance Act
Homes for Special Care Act
Hospital Services Planning Commission Act
Hospital Trusts Act
Hospitals Act
Human Tissue Gift Act
Incompetent Persons Act
Individual Hospital Acts of Incorporation
Medical Act
Medical Consent Act
Medical Radiation Technologists Act
Medical Services Act
Municipal Hospitals Loan Act
Narcotic Drug Addicts Act
N.S. Hospital Foundation Act
N.S. Sanatorium Act
Nursing Assistants Act
Occupational Therapists Act
Optometry Act
Pharmacy Act
Physiotherapy Act
Professional Dietitians Act
Psychologists Act
Regional Health Boards Act
Registered Nurses Association Act
Tobacco Access Act
Victoria General Hospital Act
**Minister**, Hon. James A. Smith, M.D., 902/424-3377
Deputy Minister, Ed Cramm, 902/424-7570
Director, Communications, Alan Jeffers, 902/424-5925
Legal Counsel, Wayne Cochrane, 902/424-7729

#### CORPORATE SERVICES

Fax: 902/424-0615
Services include: accounting; regional funding; revenue/recovery; information technology & computer services; administrative services & human resources management.
Executive Director, Pam McCormick, 902/424-5948

#### EMERGENCY HEALTH SERVICES BRANCH

902/424-3928; Fax: 902/424-0647
Jurisdictional responsibilities for all prehospital emergency health services delivery, including ambulance services, first responder & trauma programs, public access & routine critical care inter-hospital transfers.
Executive Director, Dr. Mike Murphy

#### INSURED PROGRAMS MANAGEMENT & CLINICAL RATIONALIZATION BRANCH

Services include insured programs, pharmaceutical services, ambulance services & administrative services.
Executive Director, Dr. Rick LeMoine, 902/424-7998
Senior Director, Insured Programs, Derek Dinham, 902/424-6880, Fax: 902/424-0605

#### OPERATIONS & REGIONAL SUPPORT BRANCH

Fax: 902/424-0550; 424-5769
Responsible for the delivery of facility, public health, drug dependency & home care services consistent with a regional model.
Executive Director, Bob Fowler

Senior Director, Community Health Services, Dennis Holland, 902/424-3749
Senior Director, Operations & Regional Support, Bob St. Laurent, 902/424-7233

**STRATEGIC PLANNING & POLICY DEVELOPMENT BRANCH**
Fax: 902/424-0730
Offers program planning, policy development, research statistics & evaluation & AIDS advisory assistance.
Executive Director, Mary Jane Hampton, 902/424-3732
Senior Director, Strategic Planning & Intergovernmental Relations, Richard O'Brien, 902/424-3218

**Associated Agencies, Boards & Commissions**
•Cancer Treatment & Research Foundation of Nova Scotia
Listed in Section 2, *see* Index.
•Nova Scotia Advisory Commission on AIDS: Dennis Bldg., 1740 Granville St., 6th Fl., Halifax NS B3J 1X5 – 902/424-5730; Fax: 902/424-4727
Chair, Dr. W.C. Hart, Ph.D.

## Department of HOUSING & MUNICIPAL AFFAIRS
PO Box 216, Halifax NS B3J 2M4
902/424-4141; Fax: 902/424-0531; URL: http://www.gov.ns.ca/homa/
Physical Address: Summit Place, 1601 Lower Water St., 4th Fl., Halifax NS
Provides leadership in the achievement of effective local government, adequate, affordable housing, & an integrated land information managment system to meet the needs of local and provincial agencies & residents of Nova Scotia.

**ACTS ADMINISTERED**
Assessment Act
Building Access Act
Building Code Act
Cape Breton Regional Municipality Act
Deed Transfer Tax Act
Ditches & Water Courses Act
Fences & Detention of Stray Livestock Act
Fences & Impounding of Animals Act
Heritage Property Act
Housing Act
Housing Development Corporation Act
Industrial Commissions Act
Louisbourg District Planning & Development Commission Act
Metropolitan Authority Act
Municipal Act
Municipal Affairs Act
Municipal Boundaries & Representation Act
Municipal Conflict of Interest Act
Municipal Elections Act
Municipal Finance Corporation Act
Municipal Grants Act
Municipal Housing Corporations Act
Municipal Loan & Building Fund Act
Planning Act
Regional Transit Authority Act
Registry Act
Rural Fire District Act
Sheep Protection & Dog Regulation Act
Shopping Centre Development Act
Stray Animals Act
Time Definition Act
Towns Act
Village Service Act
**Minister**, Hon. Guy Brown, 902/424-5550, Fax: 902/424-0581
Deputy Minister, Dr. Patricia Ripley, 902/424-4100
Executive Director, Assessment Services Division, John MacKay, 902/424-5671
Executive Director, Municipal Services Division, David Darrow, 902/424-7415
Director, Land Information Management Services, Kevin Aucoin, 902/424-7136
Director, Policy Development & Research, Laurel Russell, 902/424-4988
Departmental Solicitor, Cathleen O'Grady, 902/424-7716
Information Officer, Michelle Whelan, 902/424-6336

**NOVA SCOTIA GEOMATICS CENTRE**
16 Station St., Amherst NS B4H 3E3
902/667-7231; Fax: 902/667-6008; Email: info@nsgc.gov.ns.ca; URL: http://www.nsgc.gov.ns.ca
Toll Free: 1-800-798-0706
Director, Rob Doiron, Email: rdoiron@fox.nstn.ns.ca
Manager, Client Services, Curt Speight
Manager, Database Development, Bert Seely

**REGISTRY OF DEEDS**
PO Box 2205, Halifax NS B3J 3C4
902/424-8571
Registrar, Conrad Doucette

**Associated Agencies, Boards & Commissions**
•Nova Scotia Municipal Finance Corporation: 1601 Lower Water St., PO Box 850, Stn M, Halifax NS B3J 2V2 – 902/424-4590; Fax: 902/424-0525
Chair, Dr. Patricia Ripley
Secretary, G. Harding
CEO & Treasurer, Mark Gilbert

## Department of HUMAN RESOURCES
One Government Place, 1700 Granville St., PO Box 943, Halifax NS B3J 2V9
902/424-7660; Fax: 902/424-0611;
Email: humr.webmaster@gov.ns.ca; URL: http://www.gov.ns.ca/humr/
TDD: 424-3966
Lead government human resources agency responsible for providing leadership in the development & implementation of human resource policies & practices applicable to civil servants in all agencies of government. The department also provides advisory services to government & the public sector, & is responsible for negotiating & directing the negotiations for specific employee groups paid from public funds.
**Minister**, Hon. Allister Surrette, 902/424-5465, Fax: 902/424-0555
Deputy Minister, Mildred M. Royer, 902/424-6617, Fax: 902/424-0555
Director, Client Services, Judith Sullivan-Corney, 902/424-5633
Director, Corporate Services, William Lahey, 902/424-4086, Fax: 902/424-0956

**Associated Agencies, Boards & Commissions**
•Advisory Council on the Status of Women
Listed alphabetically in detail, this Section.
•Nova Scotia Sport & Recreation Commission: 5516 Spring Garden Rd., 2nd Fl., PO Box 864, Halifax NS B3J 2V2 – 902/424-7512; Fax: 902/424-0520
Executive Director, Vacant
Manager, Recreation Policy, Michael Arthur, 902/424-7629
•Nova Scotia Youth Secretariat: One Government Place, 1700 Granville St., 5th Fl., PO Box 1617, Halifax NS B3J 2Y3 – 902/424-3780; Fax: 902/424-7638
Executive Director, Richard Gilbert

## Nova Scotia HUMAN RIGHTS COMMISSION
Lord Nelson Arcade, 5675 Spring Garden Rd., 7th Fl., PO Box 2221, Halifax NS B3J 3C4
902/424-4111; Fax: 902/424-0596; URL: http://www.gov.ns.ca/just/humanrts/
TYY: 902/424-3139

**ACTS ADMINISTERED**
Human Rights Act
**Chair**, Mary MacLennan
Executive Director, Wayne Mackay
Public Education Officer, May Lui

**Regional Offices**
Digby: Basin Place, 68 Water St., PO Box 1029, Digby NS B0V 1A0 – 902/245-4791; Fax: 902/245-5011
New Glasgow: Bridgeview Sq., 115 Maclean St., PO Box 728, New Glasgow NS B2H 4M5 – 902/752-3086; Fax: 902/755-7239
Sydney: Provincial Bldg., Prince St., Sydney NS B1P 5L1 – 902/563-2140; Fax: 902/563-5613

## Department of JUSTICE
5151 Terminal Rd., PO Box 7, Halifax NS B3J 2L6
902/424-7125; Fax: 902/424-0510;
Email: hlfxterm.just.wilsonfi@gov.ns.ca;
URL: http://www.gov.ns.ca/just/

**ACTS ADMINISTERED**
Accountant General of the Supreme Court Act
Age of Majority Act
Alimony Act
Alternative Penalty Act
Anatomy Act
Angling Act
Apportionment Act
Arbitration Act
Architects Act
Assignment of Book Debts Act
Assignments & Preferences Act
Barristers & Solicitors Act
Beneficiaries Designation Act
Bills of Landing Act
Bills of Sale Act
Bulk Sales Act
Canada & the United Kingdom Reciprocal Recognition & Enforcement of Judgments Act
Cape Breton Barristers' Society Act
Child Abduction Act
Collection Act
Companies Act
Companies Winding Up Act
Conditional Sales Act
Constables Act
Constables' Protection Act
Constitutional Questions Act
Contributory Negligence Act
Controverted Elections Act
Conveyancing Act
Corporations Miscellaneous Provisions Act
Corporations Securities Registration Act
Corrections Act
Costs & Fees Act
Court for Divorce & Matrimonial Causes Act
Court Houses & Lockups Act
Court Reporters Act
Court Security Act
Creditors' Relief Act
Defamation Act
Demise of the Crown Act
Ditches & Water Courses Act
Elections Act
Engineering Profession Act
Escheats Act
Estate Actions Act
Estreats Act
Evidence Act
Expropriation Act, 1973

Family Orders Information Release Act
Fatal Injuries Act
Fatal Inquiries Act
Fences & Detention of Stray Livestock Act
Fences & Impounding of Animals Act
Floral Emblem Act
Forcible Entry & Detainer Act
Freedom of Information & Protection of Privacy Act
Gasoline & Fuel Oil Licensing Act
Guardianship Act
Hairdressers Act
Halifax-Dartmouth Bridge Commission Act
House of Assembly Act
Human Tissue Gift Act
Incompetent Persons Act
Indian Lands Act
Indigent Debtors Act
Inebriates' Guardianship Act
Interest on Judgements Act
International Commercial Arbitration Act
Interpretation Act
Intestate Succession Act
Judicature Act
Judicial Disqualifications Removal Act
Juries Act
Justices' & Judges' Protection Act
Justices of the Peace Act
Land Actions Venue Act
Land Holdings Disclosure Act
Land Titles Act
Law Reform Commission Act
Legal Aid Act
Liberty of the Subject Act
Lieutenant Governor & Great Seal Act
Limitation of Actions Act
Limited Partnerships Act
Maintenance Orders Enforcement Act
Margarine Act
Married Women's Deed Act
Married Women's Property Act
Marsh Act
Matrimonial Property Act
Mechanics' Lien Act
Members & Public Employees Disclosure Act
Municipal Conflict of Interest Act
Night Courts Act
Notaries & Commissioners Act
Nova Scotia Tartan Act
Occupiers of Land Liability Act
Official Tree Act
Overholding Tenants Act
Partition Act
Partnership Act
Partnerships & Business Names Registration Act
Payment into Court Act
Pledging of Service Emblems Act
Police Act
Police Services Act
Powers of Attorney Act
Presumption of Death Act
Private Investigators & Private Guards Act
Private Investment Holding Companies Act
Private Ways Act
Probate Act
Proceedings Against the Crown Act
Protection of Property Act
Prothonotaries & Clerks of the Crown Act
Provincial Court Act
Public Accountants Act
Public Archives Act
Public Inquiries Act
Public Offices & Officers Act
Public Prosecutions Act
Public Records Act
Public Records Disposal Act
Public Services Act
Public Subscriptions Act
Public Trustee Act
Quieting Titles Act
Real Property Act
Real Property Transfer Validation Act
Reciprocal Enforcement of Custody Orders Act
Reciprocal Enforcement of Judgments Act
Registered Barbers Act
Registered Nurses' Association Act
Registry Act
Regulations Act
Religious & Charitable Corporations Property Act
Religious Congregations & Societies Act
Remembrance Day Act
Remission of Penalties Act
Residential Tenancies Act
Retail Business Uniform Closing Day Act
Sale of Goods Act
Sale of Land under Execution Act
Salvage Yards Licensing Act
Securities Act
Settlement Act
Sheep Protection & Dog Regulation Act
Sheriffs Act
Slot Machine Act
Small Claims Court Act
Statute of Frauds
Statute Revision Act
Stray Animals Act
Summary Proceedings Act
Supreme Court & Exchequer Court of Canada Act
Sureties Act
Survival of Actions Act
Survivorship Act
Taxing Masters Act
Tenancies & Distress for Rent Act
Testators' Family Maintenance Act
Ticket of Leave Act
Time Definition Act
Tortfeasors Act
Trustee Act
Unclaimed Articles Act
Unconscionable Transactions Relief Act
Uniform Law Act
Unsightly Premises Act
Variation of Trusts Act
Vendors & Purchasers Act
Victims Rights & Services Act
Volunteer Services Act
Warehouse Receipts Act
Warehousemen's Lien Act
Wills Act
Woodmen's Lien Act
Young Persons Summary Proceedings Act

**Minister**, Hon. Alan Mitchell, 902/424-4044
Deputy Minister, Gordon Ginnis, Q.C., 902/424-4223
Director, Policy Planning & Research, Kit Waters, 902/424-5341, Fax: 902/424-0546, Email: hlfxterm.just.pauls@gov.ns.ca
Director, Communications, Michele McKinnon

**For list of Courts & other Legal Officers, including Judicial Officials & Judges *see* Section 10 of this book.**

#### CORRECTIONAL SERVICES DIVISION
PO Box 968, Stn M, Halifax NS
902/424-6290; Fax: 902/424-0692
Acting Director, Fred Honsberger
Administrator, Northern Regional Office, R.G. Parsons, #214, 500 George Place, Sydney NS B1P 1K6, 902/563-2360, Fax: 902/563-3639
Administrator, Southern Regional Office, A.J. Pottier, Lord Nelson Arcade, #800, 5675 Spring Garden Rd., Halifax NS B3J 1H1, 902/424-5776, Fax: 902/424-0693

#### COURTS & REGISTRIES DIVISION
902/424-7125; Fax: 902/424-0252
Executive Director, Marion Tyson, 902/424-4025

#### LEGAL SERVICES DIVISION
902/424-8990; Fax: 902/424-0252
Executive Director, Douglas J. Keefe, 902/424-3236
Director, Civil Litigation, Reinhold Endres, 902/424-4024
Director, Solicitor Services, Bruce Davidson, Q.C., 902/424-4023

#### POLICING SERVICES DIVISION
902/424-2504; Fax: 902/424-0700
Executive Director, Robert A. Barss, 902/424-7795
Chief Officer, Licensing & Gun Control, M. Kramers, 902/424-6689

#### VICTIMS' SERVICES DIVISION
902/424-8785; Fax: 902/424-0252
Acting Director, J. Mariott-Thorne

#### OFFICE OF THE CHIEF MEDICAL EXAMINER
5788 University Ave., Halifax NS B3H 1V8
902/428-4052; Fax: 902/424-0607
Chief Medical Examiner, Dr. John Butt

##### Associated Agencies, Boards & Commissions
•Alcohol & Driving Countermeasures Office: 1690 Hollis St., PO Box 217, Stn M, Halifax NS B3J 2M4 – 902/424-4673; Fax: 902/424-0700
Coordinator, Richard James
•Human Rights Commission
Listed alphabetically in detail, this Section.
•Expropriations Compensation Board: 1601 Lower Water St., PO Box 1692, Stn M, Halifax NS B3J 3S3 – 902/424-4448; Fax: 902/424-3919
Chair, S. David Bryson, Q.C.
•Nova Scotia Legal Aid Commission: #401, 5475 Spring Garden Rd., Halifax NS B3J 3T2 – 902/420-6584; Fax: 902/420-3471; URL: http://www.gov.ns.ca/just/lega/
Chair, J. Mark McCrea, 902/420-6584
Executive Director, William Digby, 902/420-6565
•Nova Scotia Police Commission: #300, 1601 Lower Water St., Halifax NS B3J 2Y3 – 902/424-3246; Fax: 902/424-3919; Email: uarb.polcom@gov.ns.ca
Chair, M. Jean Beeler
•Nova Scotia Securities Commission: PO Box 458, Halifax NS B3J 2P8 – 902/424-7768; Fax: 902/424-4625
Chair, Robert B. MacLellan
Vice Chair, Daniel F. Gallivan, Q.C.
Commission Member, Kiki Kachafanas
Director, Securities, Nicholas A. Pittas
Deputy Director, Capital Markets, Elaine Anne MacGregor
Deputy Director, Compliance & Enforcement, Nigel M. Green
Deputy Director, Corporate Finance, J. William Slattery, C.A.
•Public Prosecution Service
902/424-8931
Director, Public Prosecutions, Jerry Pitzul, 902/424-8931
Registrar, Probate, Vacant, 902/424-7421, Fax: 902/424-0595

## Department of LABOUR
5151 Terminal Rd., PO Box 697, Halifax NS B3J 2T8
902/424-4125; Fax: 902/424-3239; URL: http://www.gov.ns.ca/labr/

#### ACTS ADMINISTERED
Act to Provide for Pay Equity
Amusement Devices Safety Act
Coal Mines Regulation Act
Electrical Installation Act
Elevators & Lifts Act
Fire Prevention Act
Fireworks Act

Labour Standards Code
Lightning Rod Act
Metalliferous Mines & Quarries Act
Occupational Health & Safety Act
Standard Hose Coupling Act
Stationary Engineers Act
Steam Boiler & Pressure Vessel Act
Trade Union Act
**Minister**, Hon. Gerald J. O'Malley
Deputy Minister, George Fox, 902/424-4148
Fire Marshall, Fire Marshall's Office, Robert Cormier, 902/424-4553, Email: cormierr@gov.ns.ca
Director, Administration & Accounting, Peter Horne, 902/424-3967
Solicitor, Pat Clahane, 902/424-5928
Communications Officer, Jennifer McIsaac, 902/424-4680, Email: macisjen@gov.ns.ca

#### CONCILIATION SERVICES

902/424-4156
Director, Laurie Rantala
Conciliator, J.D. Hood, 902/424-8470
Conciliator, Jack O'Brien, 902/424-8469

#### LABOUR STANDARDS

902/424-4311; Fax: 902/424-0648
Director, Hon. Ross Mitchell, 902/424-5404, Email: mitchelr@gov.ns.ca

#### PUBLIC SAFETY

Fax: 902/424-3239
Director, Eugene Chown, 902/424-8479
Acting Chief Inspector, Boiler Safety, Chuck Castle, 902/424-8493
Chief Inspector, Elevators, Lifts & Amusement Devices, Mario Liberatore, 902/424-8487
Inspector, Power Engineers & Crane Operators, Dave Steele, 902/424-8491

#### RESEARCH

Director, John Patterson, 902/424-4313, Email: pattersj@gov.ns.ca

##### Associated Agencies, Boards & Commissions

•Construction Industry Panel: PO Box 697, Halifax NS B3J 2T8 – 902/424-6730; Fax: 902/424-3239
Chair, P.E. Darby
CEO, Gary Ross
•Labour Relations Board: PO Box 697, Halifax NS B3J 2T8 – 902/424-6730; Fax: 902/424-3239
Chair, P.E. Darby
CEO, Gary Ross
•Labour Standards Tribunal: PO Box 697, Halifax NS B3J 2T8 – 902/424-6730; Fax: 902/424-3239
Chair, Susan Ashley
Executive Officer, Mary Lou Stewart
•Pay Equity Commission: PO Box 697, Halifax NS B3J 1T8 – 902/424-8595; Fax: 902/424-3239; URL: http://www.gov.ns.ca/labr/pequity.htm
Chair, Patricia Paul
Acting Executive Director, Pat Sherwood
•Stationary Engineers Act, Board of Examiners: PO Box 697, Halifax NS B3J 2T8 – 902/424-7521; Fax: 902/424-3239
Chair, C.W. Purcell
•Workers' Advisers Program: c/o Dept. of Labour, 5151 Terminal Rd., PO Box 697, Halifax NS B3J 2T8
Chief Workers' Adviser, Anne Clarke
•Workers' Compensation Appeal Tribunal: c/o Workers' Compensation Board, PO Box 1150, Halifax NS B3J 2Y2 – 902/424-2257
Chief Appeals Commissioner, Judith Ferguson
•Workers' Compensation Board
Listed alphabetically in detail, this section.

## Department of NATURAL RESOURCES

Founder's Square, 1701 Hollis St., PO Box 698, Halifax NS B3J 2T9
902/424-5935; Fax: 902/424-7735; URL: http://www.gov.ns.ca/natr/
Responsible for the administration & management of provincial Crown lands, development of mineral & energy resources, protection & sustainable development of forest resources & operation & maintenance of parks system.

#### ACTS ADMINISTERED

Act to Confer Certain Powers upon the Lieutenant Governor in Council & to amend the Mines Act
Act to Protect Georges Bank
Beaches Act
Beaches & Foreshores Act
Blueberry Association Act
Bowater Mersey Agreement Act
Canada-Nova Scotia Offshore Petroleum Resources Accord Implementation (Nova Scotia) Act
Coal Mines Regulation Act
Conservation Easements Act
Crown Lands Act
Energy & Mines Resources Conservation Act
Energy-Efficient Appliances Act
Forest Enhancement Act
Forests Act
Gas Storage Exploration Act
Gas Utilities Act
Gypsum Mining Income Tax Act
Halifax Power & Pulp Company Limited Agreement Act, 1962
Indian Lands Act
Kedgemakooge National Park Act
Land Holdings Disclosure Act
Land Surveyors Act
Land Titles Clarification Act
Metalliferous Mines & Quarries Regulation Act
Mineral Resources Act
Natural Resources Advisory Council Act
Offshore Petroleum Royalties Act
Parks Development Act
Petroleum Resources Act
Pipeline Act
Provincial Parks Act
Primary Forest Products Marketing Act
Scalers Act
Scott Maritimes Limited Agreement (1965) Act
Stora Forest Industries Agreement Act
Trails Act
Treasure Trove Act
Wildlife Act
**Minister**, Hon. Kenneth MacAskill, 902/424-4037, Fax: 902/424-0594
Deputy Minister, William D. Hogg, C.A., 902/424-4121, Email: wdhogg@gov.ns.ca.
Public Information Officer, Blain Henshaw, 902/424-5252

#### CORPORATE SERVICES BRANCH

Executive Director, Gary Rix, 902/424-6694, Email: gerix@gov.ns.ca
Director, Financial Services, Jim Morrison, 902/424-5990, Email: j_morris@gov.ns.ca
Acting Director, Fleet Management (Shubenacadie), Colin Gillis, 902/758-3438, Fax: 902/758-3355
Director, Human Resources, Paul Edwards, 902/424-8134, Email: pdedward@gov.ns.ca
Director, Information Services, Graham Gagne, 902/424-3947, Email: gagagne@gov.ns.ca
Director, Land Administration, Rosalind Penfound, 902/424-4267, Fax: 902/424-3173
Manager, Education & Publication Services (Truro), Emily Gratton, 902/893-5643, Fax: 902/893-6102

#### MINERALS & ENERGY BRANCH

902/424-5346
Executive Director, Pat Phelan, 902/424-7943, Email: pwphalen@gov.ns.ca
Director, Mineral & Energy Resources, Scott Swinden, 902/424-2525
Director, Mines & Energy Development, Don Jones, Ph.D., P.Eng., 902/424-5618, Email: dsjones@gov.ns.ca

#### PETROLEUM DEVELOPMENT AGENCY

Chief Operating Officer, P. Carey Ryan, 902/424-8203, Email: pcryan@gov.ns.ca
Director, Planning Secretariat, Vicki Harnish, 902/424-8161, Email: vlharnis@gov.ns.ca

#### REGIONAL SERVICES BRANCH

Executive Director, Dan Graham, 902/424-3949, Email: djgraham@gov.ns.ca
Director, Crown Lands Management, Dan Eidt, 902/424-7594
Director, Extension Services, Gerald Joudrey, 902/424-4445, Email: gtjoudre@gov.ns.ca
Director, Private Lands Management, Arden Whidden, 902/424-5703
Director, Surveys Division, Keith AuCoin, 902/424-3145
Manager, Enforcement & Hunter Safety, John Mombourquette, 902/424-5254
Manager, Provincial Crown Lands Record Centre, Don Parker, 902/424-8681

#### RENEWABLE RESOURCES BRANCH

Executive Director, John Smith, 902/424-4103, Email: jdsmith@gov.ns.ca
Director, Forestry, Ed MacAulay, 902/893-5749, Fax: 902/893-6102
Director, Parks & Recreation (Belmont), Barry Diamond, 902/662-3030, Fax: 902/662-2160
Director, Wildlife Division, Barry Sabean, PO Box 516, Kentville NS B4N 3X3, 902/678-6091, Fax: 902/679-6176
Manager, Program Development & Evaluation, G. Peter MacQuarrie, 902/424-7708, Email: gpmacqua@gov.ns.ca.

##### Associated Agencies, Boards & Commissions

•Canada-Nova Scotia Offshore Petroleum Board: TD Centre, 1791 Barrington St., 6th Fl., Halifax NS B3J 3K9 – 902/422-5588; Fax: 902/422-1799; URL: http://Fox.nstn.ca/ZXcnsopb/
Acting CEO, J.E. (Jim) Dickey
•Primary Forest Products Marketing Board: Metropolitan Place, #470, 99 Wyse Rd., Dartmouth NS B3A 4S5 – 902/424-7598; Fax: 902/463-0159
Chair, Lee Nauss

## Office of the OMBUDSMAN

Lord Nelson Arcade, #300, 5675 Spring Garden Rd., PO Box 2152, Halifax NS B3J 3B7
902/424-6780; Fax: 902/424-6675; URL: http://www.gov.ns.ca/govt/ombu/
Toll Free: 1-800-670-1111 (In Nova Scotia only)
**Ombudsman**, Douglas G. Ruck
Secretary, Muriel Mappin

## Nova Scotia PRIORITIES & PLANNING SECRETARIAT

1700 Granville St., 5th Fl., PO Box 1617, Halifax NS B3J 2Y3
902/424-8910; Fax: 902/424-7638
The Secretariat advances the priorities of government, aligns government policies & plans with these priorities, & promotes accountability.
**Chair**, J. Bernard Boudreau, Q.C.
Deputy Minister, Robert A. MacKay
Director, Aboriginal Affairs, Alan Clark

## Nova Scotia RESOURCES LIMITED (NSRL)
#600, 1718 Argyle St., PO Box 2111, Stn M, Halifax NS B3J 3B7
902/420-8800; Fax: 902/425-2195
**President & CEO**, Donald A. Leet
General Manager, James G. MacDonald
Secretary, Elizabeth Cuddihy
Treasurer, C.H. (Bert) Loveless, C.A.

## SYDNEY STEEL CORPORATION
PO Box 1450, Sydney NS B1P 6K5
902/564-7900; Fax: 902/564-7903
**Minister Responsible**, Hon. Manning MacDonald, 902/424-6647
Acting President & Vice-President & Corporate Secretary, Finance, J.A. Rudderham, 902/564-7920
Vice-President, Marketing, S.H. Didyk, 902/564-7910

## Nova Scotia TECHNOLOGY & SCIENCE SECRETARIAT (TSS)
Maritime Centre, 1505 Barrington St., 14th Fl., PO Box 2311, Halifax NS B3T 3C8
902/424-0377; Fax: 902/424-0129; URL: http://www.gov.ns.ca/tss/
Helps the province define a new framework for developing & instituting technological information transfer within the province. Major emphasis is placed on information technology.
**Minister**, Hon. Bruce Holland, 902/424-2908
Acting Deputy Minister, R.P. MacDonald, 902/424-2902
Acting Executive Director, Kevin Hall, 902/424-2888

## TIDAL POWER CORPORATION
1701 Hollis St., PO Box 698, Halifax NS B3J 2T9
902/424-7680; Fax: 902/424-7735
**Minister Responsible**, Hon. Manning MacDonald
Corporate Secretary, Allan Parker, 902/424-8175, Email: alparker@gov.ns.ca

## Department of TRANSPORTATION & PUBLIC WORKS (TPW)
1969 Upper Water St., PO Box 186, Halifax NS B3J 2N2
902/424-5837
The department is responsible for highway construction & maintenance services, ferry services, & the coordination of provincial programs relating to the transportation of dangerous goods. Provides common services for all government departments & agencies, including real estate services, information & communications, publishing & postal services, & the Provincial Data Centre.

#### ACTS ADMINISTERED
Highway 104: Western Alignment Act
Motor Vehicle Act (signage & traffic sections)
Public Highways Act
Railways Act
Surplus Crown Property Disposal Act
**Minister**, Hon. Donald R. Downe, 902/424-5875, Fax: 902/424-0171
Deputy Minister, Bruce Atwell, P.Eng., 902/424-4036, Fax: 902/424-2014
Acting Director, Finance, Pam McCormick, 902/424-4126, Fax: 902/424-0722.
Director, Human Resources Division, Patrick Hartling, 902/424-4407, Fax: 902/425-4579
Director, Information Technology, Don Crawley, 902/424-6999, Fax: 902/424-0570
Acting Director, Internal Audit, Jeannie Chow, 902/424-3630, Fax: 902/424-0571
Director, Policy & Planning, Brian Gallivan, 902/424-2907
Director, Public Affairs & Communications, Chris Welner, 902/424-8687, Fax: 902/424-0532, Email: welnerch@gov.ns.ca

#### HIGHWAY PROGRAMS
Executive Director, Martin Delaney, 902/424-4059, Fax: 902/424-2014
Director, Equipment, Vacant, 902/861-1911, Fax: 902/861-1152
District Director, Central, Jim Talbot, 902/424-5328, Fax: 902/424-0568
District Director, Eastern, Tom Hackett, 902/563-2250, Fax: 902/563-0540, Email: thackett@gov.ns.ca
District Director, Northern, John Archibald, 902/893-5780, Fax: 902/893-8175
District Director, Western, Vic Coldwell, 902/453-4121, Fax: 902/543-5596, Email: vcoldwell@gov.ns.ca

#### REAL PROPERTY SERVICES
Acting Executive Director, John McLean, 902/424-2808
Acting Director, Accomodation Services, Don Sheppard, 902/424-2808
Director, Enterprise Development, Gary Campbell, 902/424-2800
Director, Fleet Management, Doug Smith, 902/861-1911
Director, Transition Planning & Implementation, Calvin Archibald, 902/861-1911
Manager, Enterprise Operations, Andrew Miller, 902/424-2952

#### SPECIALIZED SUPPORT
Executive Director, Al MacRae, 902/424-5687, Email: amacrae@gov.ns.ca
Director, Building Design, Alan North, 902/424-2952
Director, Engineering & Design, John O'Connor, 902/424-2756
Director, Infrastructure, Ralph Spares, 902/424-4193, Email: rwspares@gov.ns.ca
Acting Director, Right-of-Way Claims, Frank Harland, 902/424-5563, Fax: 902/424-0583
Manager, Environmental Services, Denis Rushton, 902/424-4082
Manager, Highway & Bridge Design, Mark Pertus, 902/424-3362
Manager, Needs & Programs, Phil Corkum, 902/424-3508
Manager, Network Information, Ralph Hessian, 902/424-3270

## Nova Scotia UTILITY & REVIEW BOARD
#300, 1601 Lower Water St., PO Box 1692, Stn M, Halifax NS B3J 3S3
902/424-4448; Fax: 902/424-3919
Excercises authority over all public utilities in Nova Scotia, including water, electricity & transportation.

#### ACTS ADMINISTERED
The Assessment Act
The Deed Transfer Tax Act
Expropriation Act
Gas Utilities Act
Gasoline & Diesel Oil Tax Act
Halifax-Dartmouth Bridge Commission Act
Health Services Tax Act
Heritage Property Act
Insurance Act (automobile insurance only)
Metropolitan Authority Act
Motor Carrier Act (public passenger only)
Motor Vehicle Transport Act of Canada, 1987 (Federal)
Municipal Boundaries & Representation Act
Nova Scotia Power Corporation Act
Nova Scotia Power Privatization Act
Planning Act
Public Utilities Act
Regional Transit Authority Act
Revenue Act
Rural Telephone Act
School Board Act
Shopping Centre Development Act
Tobacco Tax Act
Utility & Review Board Act
Village Services Act
**Chair**, M. Heather Robertson, Q.C.
Vice-Chair, John A. Morash, C.A., F.C.M.A., C.B.V.
Administrator, Paul G. Allen, C.A.
Senior Advisor, Regulation & Finance, John Murphy, P.Eng.

## Nova Scotia Advisory Council on the STATUS OF WOMEN
PO Box 745, Halifax NS B3J 2T3
902/424-8662; Fax: 902/424-0573; URL: http://www.gov.ns.ca/govt/staw/
The agency advocates for improved legislation, policies & programs for women, & provides research & policy advice to government on ways in which public policies & programs could better serve women.
**Minister Responsible**, Eleanor E. Norrie, 902/424-4037
Chair, Patricia Doyle-Bedwell, 902/424-8662

## WORKERS' COMPENSATION BOARD OF NOVA SCOTIA
5668 South St., PO Box 1150, Halifax NS B3J 2Y2
902/424-8440; Fax: 902/424-0509; Email: info@wcb.gov.ns.ca; URL: http://www.pixelmotion.ns.ca/wcb/home.html
**Chair**, Dr. Innis Christie
CEO, David Stuewe
Director, Communications, donalee Moulton, 902/424-8339

# GOVERNMENT OF ONTARIO

**Seat of Government:** Legislative Bldgs., Queen's Park, Toronto ON M7A 1A2
URL: http://www.gov.on.ca/
The Province of Ontario entered Confederation July 1, 1867. It has an area of 916,733.7 km2, and the StatsCan census population in 1996 was 10,753,573.

## Office of the LIEUTENANT GOVERNOR
#131, Legislative Bldg., Queen's Park, Toronto ON M7A 1A1
416/325-7780; Fax: 416/325-7787; URL: http://ontla.on.ca/assemsrv/lg.htm
**Lieutenant Governor**, Hon. Hilary Weston
Executive Asst., Bryn MacPherson-White
Chief Aide-de-Camp, Col. Roy Beckett
Deputy Chief Aide-de-Camp, LCol. Sandy Cameron
Deputy Chief Aide-de-Camp, Chief Supt. Ken Turriff
Deputy Chief Aide-de-Camp, Cdr. Tony Pitts

## Office of the PREMIER
Legislative Bldg., #281, 1 Queen's Park Cres. South, Toronto ON M7A 1A1
416/325-1941; Fax: 416/325-7578; Email: premier@gov.on.ca; URL: http://www.gov.on.ca/premier/office/html
TDD: 416/325-7702

#### ACTS ADMINISTERED
Executive Council Act
Lieutenant Governor Act
Policy & Priorities Board of Cabinet Act
Representation Act, 1986
Social Contract Act

Premier, Hon. Michael D. Harris, 416/325-1941, Fax: 416/325-3745, Email: premier@gov.on.ca
Deputy Premier & Government House Leader, Hon. Ernie Eves, Frost Bldg. South, 416/325-0405
Chief of Staff, Ron McLaughlin, 416/325-9255, Fax: 416/326-1687
Executive Asst., Caucus Liaison, Bill King, 416/325-1692, Fax: 416/325-7578
Director, Communications, Ab Campion, 416/325-3847, Fax: 416/325-0803
Director, Issues Management & Tour, Debbie Hutton, 416/325-7804, Fax: 416/325-0060
Director, Outreach, Stuart Braddick, 416/325-2133, Fax: 416/326-1687
Director, Policy & Planning, Guy Giorno, 416/325-9257, Fax: 416/325-0803
Press Secretary, Bob Reid, 416/325-7808, Fax: 416/325-7571
Deputy Principal Secretary, Mitch Patten, 416/325-9255
Premier's Secretary, Kitty Knight, 416/325-7796
Manager, Correspondence, Liz Hickey, 416/325-7798

#### THE PREMIER'S COUNCIL

1 Dundas St. West, 25th Fl., Toronto ON M7A 1Y7
416/326-6756; Fax: 416/326-6769
Deputy Minister, Dr. Thomas A. Brzustowski
Administrative Asst., Jane Grier

## EXECUTIVE COUNCIL

Whitney Block, Queen's Park, 99 Wellesley St. West, 6th Fl., Toronto ON M7A 1A1
416/325-7641; URL: http://ontla.on.ca/members/exec.htm
Premier & President of the Executive Council, Hon. Michael D. Harris, #281, Legislative Bldg., Queen's Park, Toronto ON M7A 1A1, 416/325-1941, Fax: 416/325-3745, Email: premier@gov.on.ca
Deputy Premier, Government House Leader & Minister, Finance, Hon. Ernie Eves, Frost Bldg. South, 7 Queen's Park Cres., 7th Fl., Toronto ON M7A 1Y7, 416/325-0400, Fax: 416/325-0374
Minister, Citizenship, Culture & Recreation, Hon. Isabel Bassett, 416/325-6200, Fax: 416/325-6195
Minister, Transportation, Hon. Tony Clement, 416/327-9200
Minister, Intergovernmental Affairs & Minister Responsible, Women's Issues, Hon. Dianne Cunningham, Mowat Block, 900 Bay St., 6th Fl., Toronto ON M7A 1C2, 416/326-1600, Fax: 416/326-1638
Minister, Community & Social Services, Hon. Janet Ecker, Hebburn Block, 80 Grosvenor, 6th Fl., Toronto ON M7A 1E8, 416/325-5225, Fax: 416/325-5221
Minister, Labour, Hon. Jim Flaherty, 416/326-7000, Fax: 416/326-1449
Minister, Attorney General & Minister Responsible, Native Affairs, Hon. Charles Harnick, 720 Bay St., 11th Fl., Toronto ON M5G 2K1, 416/326-4000, Fax: 416/326-4016
Chairman, Management Board of Cabinet & Minister, Northern Development & Mines, Hon. Chris Hodgson, 416/314-2301, Fax: 416/314-2216
Minister without Portfolio & Minister Responsible, Senior Citizens, Hon. Cameron Jackson, Mowat Block, 3rd Fl., 900 Bay St., Toronto ON M7A 1L2, 416/326-9326, Fax: 416/326-9338
Minister, Education, Hon. David Johnson, 416/327-2333, Fax: 416/327-3790
Minister, Municipal Affairs & Housing, Hon. Allan Leach, 777 Bay St., 17th Fl., Toronto ON M5G 2E5, 416/585-7000, Fax: 416/585-6470
Minister, Economic Development, Trade & Tourism, Hon. Al Palladini, 416/327-9200, Fax: 416/327-9188
Minister, Solicitor General & Correctional Services, Hon. Robert W. Runciman, #400, 175 Bloor St. East, Toronto ON M4W 3R8, 416/326-5075, Fax: 416/326-5085
Minister without Portfolio & Minister Responsible, Privatization, Hon. Rob Sampson, 175 Bloor St. East, 4th Fl., Toronto ON M4W 3R8, 416/325-0408, Fax: 416/325-6067
Minister, Natural Resources, Hon. John Snobelen, 416/325-2600, Fax: 416/325-2608
Minister, Environment, Hon. Norman W. Sterling, 135 St. Clair Ave. West, 15th Fl., Toronto TO M4V 1P5, 416/323-4360, Fax: 416/323-4682
Minister, Consumer & Commercial Relations, Hon. David H. Tsubouchi, 250 Yonge St., 35th Fl., Toronto ON M5B 2N5, 416/326-8500, Fax: 416/326-8520
Minister, Agriculture, Food & Rural Affairs & Minister Responsible, Francophone Affairs, Hon. Noble Villeneuve, 801 Bay St., 11th Fl., Toronto ON M7A 2B2, 416/326-3067, Fax: 416/326-3083
Minister, Energy, Hon. Jim Wilson, 416/327-4300, Fax: 416/326-1571
Minister, Health, Hon. Elizabeth Witmer, 416/326-7600, Fax: 416/326-1449
Minister Responsible, Children's Issues, Hon. Margaret Marland

#### Cabinet Office

Whitney Block, Queen's Park, 99 Wellesley St. West, 6th Fl., Toronto ON M7A 1A1
416/325-7641; Fax: 416/314-8980
TDD: 416/314-5721
Secretary of Cabinet & Clerk of Executive Council, Rita Burak, 416/325-7641
Associate Secretary, Linda Stevens, 416/325-1607
Executive Asst. to Associate Secretary, Scott Bolton, 416/325-1609
Executive Asst., Bohodar Rubashewsky, 416/325-4400
Personal Secretary to the Secretary of the Cabinet, Sue Stafford, 416/325-7618
Executive Secretary (Bilingual), Louise Beaupré, 416/314-4687
Acting Executive Coordinator, Gord Evans, 416/325-7693, Fax: 416/327-9505
Acting Director, Communications, Brian LeGrow, 416/325-3729, Fax: 416/325-7627
Director, Corporate Issues, Kevin Finnerty, 416/325-3772, Fax: 416/325-3781
Director, Information Technology Systems & Services, Ginnie Nelson-Turner, 416/325-7670, Fax: 416/314-8962
Director, Resources Management, Marysia Chmiel, 416/325-4745, Fax: 416/325-7646
Manager, Executive Council Support, Suzanne Wilson, 416/325-7691, Fax: 416/327-9505
Manager, Premier's Correspondence Unit, Aine Scully, 416/325-3736, Fax: 416/325-3745

#### Cabinet Committees

•Legislation/Regulation Committee
Secretary, Suzanne Wilson, 416/325-7691, Fax: 416/327-9505
•Management Board
Asst. Deputy Minister, Kathy Bouey, 416/327-3155, Fax: 416/325-4993
•Policy & Priorities Board
Policy Advisor, Karen Tilford, 416/325-7619, Fax: 416/327-9505
•Privatization Committee
Manager, John Taylor, 416/325-1143, Fax: 416/325-9224

## LEGISLATIVE ASSEMBLY

c/o Clerk's Office, #104, Legislative Bldg., Queen's Park, Toronto ON M7A 1A2
416/325-7340; Fax: 416/325-7344; Email: assembly@ontla.ola.org.; URL: http://www.ontla.on.ca
Note: On December 9, 1996, royal assent was given to Bill 81, the short title of which is the Fewer Politicians Act. This Bill provides for the adoption of federal electoral district boundaries for provincial elections, reducing the number of members in the Legislative Assembly from 130 to 103. These boundaries will take effect at an election when the Legislature is dissolved after January 1, 1998. Until that time, the current boundaries would be used for a general election & the boundaries of the current provincial electoral districts are in effect for any by-election which occurs during the life of the present Legislative Assembly.

#### ACTS ADMINISTERED

Election Act
Election Finances Act
Fewer Politicians Act, 1996
Freedom of Information & Protection of Privacy Act
Legislative Assembly Act
Legislative Assembly Retirement Allowances Act
Members' Integrity Act
Ombudsman Act
**Speaker:** #180, Legislative Bldg., Queen's Park, Toronto ON M7A 1A8, Chris Stockwell, 416/325-7435, Fax: 416/325-7483
**Clerk:** Claude L. DesRosiers, 416/325-7341, URL: http://ontla.on.ca/assemsrv/clerk.htm
**Controller, Finance & Administration:** #2503, Whitney Block, Queen's Park, Toronto ON M7A 1A2, William Ponick, 416/325-3568, Fax: 416/314-5995
**Executive Director, Assembly Services:** #411, North Wing, Legislative Bldg., Queen's Park, Toronto ON M7A 1A2, Barbara Speakman, 416/325-3579, Fax: 416/325-3969
**Executive Director, Legislative Library:** #409, North Wing, Legislative Bldg., Queen's Park, Toronto ON M7A 1A9, Mary E. Dickerson, 416/325-3939, Fax: 416/325-3909, Reference Inquiries: 416/325-3900
**Executive Director:** #1405, Whitney Block, Queen's Park, Toronto ON M7A 1A2, Deborah Deller, 416/325-3502, Fax: 416/325-3505, Inquiries: 416/325-3500
**Sergeant-at-Arms:** #414, North Wing, Legislative Bldg., Queen's Park, Toronto ON M7A 1A2, Dennis Clark, 416/325-7445, Fax: 416/325-7154, Emergency: 416/325-1111

#### Officers of the Legislative Assembly

Chief Election Officer, W.R. Bailie, 51 Rolark Dr., Scarborough ON M1R 3B1, 416/321-3000, Fax: 416/320-6853
Integrity Commissioner, Hon. G.T. Evans, LL.D., Ph.D., K.C.S.G., 101 Bloor St. West, 4th Fl., Toronto ON M5S 2Z7, 416/314-8983, Fax: 416/314-8987
Election Finances Commissioner, Jack Murray, #1110, 151 Bloor St. West, Toronto ON M5S 1S4, 416/325-9451, Fax: 416/325-9466
Environmental Commissioner, Eva Ligeti, #605, 1075 Bay St., Toronto ON M5S 2W5, 416/325-3377, Fax: 416/325-3370
Information & Privacy Commissioner, Dr. Ann Cavoukian, #1700, 80 Bloor St. West, Toronto ON M5S 2V1, 416/326-3333, Fax: 416/325-9195, Toll Free: 1-800-387-0073

#### Officers of the Legislative Assembly

Ombudsman, Roberta Jamieson, 125, Queen's Park, Toronto ON M5S 2C7, 416/586-3300, Fax: 416/586-3485
Provincial Auditor, Erik Peters, 1530, 20 Dundas St. West, PO Box 105, Toronto ON M5G 2C2, 416/974-9866, Fax: 416/324-7012

#### Government Caucus Services

#124, North Wing, Legislative Bldg., Queen's Park, 7 Queen's Park Circle, Toronto ON M7A 1A8

416/325-7736; Fax: 416/325-3810; URL: http://ontariopc.on.ca

#249, Legislative Bldg., Queen's Park, Toronto ON M7A 1A8

Deputy Premier, Hon. Ernie Eves, 416/325-0400

Government House Leader, Hon. Norman W. Sterling, 416/323-4360, Fax: 416/323-4682

Chief Government Whip, David Turnbull

Chair, Government Caucus, Hon. Margaret Marland

Executive Coordinator, Research & Communications, Jerry Redmond

Director, Administration, Barbara Cowieson, 416/325-7272

#### Office of the Official Opposition (Lib.)

#349, Legislative Bldg., Queen's Park, Toronto ON M7A 1A4

416/325-7200; Fax: 416/325-9898; Email: liberal@io.org; URL: http://www.io.org/ZXliberal

Leader, Dalton J.P. McGuinty, 416/325-7155, Fax: 416/325-9895

Deputy Leader, Gerry Phillips, #470, Legislative Bldg., Queen's Park, Toronto ON M7A 1A4, 416/325-3619, Fax: 416/325-9590

Chief Opposition Whip, John Gerretsen, 416/325-9210, Fax: 416/325-9214

Executive Director, Liberal Caucus Service Bureau, Peter Curtis, #1603, Whitney Block, Queen's Park, Toronto ON M7A 1A4, 416/325-7202

Principal Secretary, Michael Cochrane, 416/325-7163

Official Opposition House Leader, Hon. James Bradley, #331, Legislative Bldg., Queen's Park, Toronto ON M7A 1A4, 416/325-7194, Fax: 416/325-9696

Official Opposition Caucus Chair, Bruce Crozier, #1304, Whitney Block, Queen's Park, Toronto ON M7A 1A4, 416/325-7298, Fax: 416/325-9003

Senior Advisor, Issues Management, Bob Lopinski, #1640, Whitney Block, Queen's Park, Toronto ON M7A 1A4, 416/325-7253, Fax: 416/325-9894

#### Office of the New Democratic Party

#381, Legislative Bldg., Queen's Park, Toronto ON M7A 1A5

416/325-7530; Fax: 416/325-8222; Email: ondp@io.org; URL: http://www.ndp.on.ca

Leader, Howard Hampton

Deputy Leader, Tony Silipo, 416/325-6311, Fax: 416/325-7111

New Democratic Party House Leader, Bud Wildman, 416/325-6800, Fax: 416/325-7029

New Democratic Party Chief Whip, Frances Lankin, 416/325-6904, Fax: 416/325-3336

New Democratic Party Caucus Chair, David Christopherson, 416/325-3188, Fax: 416/325-7111

Chief of Staff, Jill Marzetti, 416/325-8648

Director, Communications, Rosemary Hnatiuk, 416/325-7307, Fax: 416/325-7126

#### Standing Committees of the Legislative Assembly

Administration of Justice Committee: Clerk, Douglas Arnott, 416/325-3506

Estimates Committee: Clerk, Rosemarie Singh, 416/325-3522

Finance & Economic Affairs Committee: Clerk, Franco Carrozza, 416/325-3514

General Government Committee: Clerk, Tom Prins, 416/325-3509

Legislative Assembly Committee: Clerk, Peter Sibenik, 416/325-3531

Ombudsman Committee: Clerk, Franco Carrozza, 416/325-3514

Public Accounts Committee: Clerk, Donna Bryce, 416/325-3525

Regulations & Private Bills Committee: Clerk, Rosemarie Singh, 416/325-3522

Resources Development Committee: Clerk, Donna Bryce, 416/325-3525

Social Development Committee: Clerk, Tonia Grannum, 416/325-3519

## THIRTY-SIXTH PARLIAMENT - ONTARIO

416/325-7341; URL: http://ontla.on.ca/members/members.htm

Last General Election, June 8, 1995. Maximum Duration, 5 years.

**Party Standings (May 27, 1997)**

Progressive Conservative (PC) 82

Liberal (Lib.) 30

New Democratic Party (NDP) 15

Independent (Ind.) 1

Vacant 2

Total 130

**Salaries**

Each Member is entitled to an annual base salary of $78,007. Additional salary is paid to the following office holders:

Premier $61,680

Ministers $32,997 (with portfolio); Ministers $14,977 (without portfolio)

Leader of the Opposition $43,060

Leaders of Parties with recognized membership of 12 or more in the Assembly $27,848

Speaker $24,338

#### MEMBERS BY CONSTITUENCY

Following is: constituency (number of eligible voters at 1995 election) member, party affiliation, Toronto office Telephone number.

Refer to Cabinet List, Government Caucus Services Office, Liberal Caucus Services Office, & Office of the Progressive Conservative Party, for Fax numbers.

Email addresses for all MPPs are formatted as follows - firstname_lastname-mpp@ontla.ola.org.

Algoma (21,864) Bud Wildman, NDP, 416/325-6800

Algoma-Manitoulin (26,128) Mike Brown, Lib., 416/325-3601

Beaches-Woodbine (38,523) Frances Lankin, NDP, 416/325-6904

Brampton North (69,435) Joe Spina, PC, 416/327-0616

Brampton South (74,364) Hon. Tony Clement, PC, 416/314-5741

Brant-Haldimand (48,807) Peter L. Preston, PC, 416/325-8216

Brantford (55,445) Ron Johnson, PC, 416/325-7027

Bruce (46,559) Barb Fisher, PC, 416/326-3058

Burlington South (49,821) Hon. Cameron Jackson, PC, 416/326-9326

Cambridge (62,324) Gerry Martiniuk, PC, 416/325-8451

Carleton (70,780) Hon. Norman W. Sterling, PC, 416/323-4360

Carleton East (61,643) Gilles E. Morin, Lib., 416/325-7216

Chatham-Kent (49,769) Jack Carroll, PC, 416/325-5246

Cochrane North (26,037) Len Wood, NDP, 416/325-7040

Cochrane South (38,584) Gilles Bisson, NDP, 416/325-7122

Cornwall (44,191) John Cleary, Lib., 416/325-3642

Don Mills (42,758) Hon. David Johnson, PC, 416/325-7754

Dovercourt (30,963) Tony Silipo, NDP, 416/325-6311

Downsview (36,926) Annamarie Castrilli, Lib., 416/325-8688

Dufferin-Peel (54,176) David Tilson, PC, 416/325-4154

Durham Centre (66,818) Hon. Jim Flaherty, PC, 416/326-2485

Durham East (62,205) John O'Toole, PC, 416/325-6745

Durham West (84,476) Hon. Janet Ecker, PC, 416/325-5225

Durham-York (65,909) Julia Munro, PC, 416/325-3392

Eglinton (48965) Hon. William Saunderson, PC, 416/325-6900

Elgin (54,155) Peter North, Ind., 416/325-7271

Essex South (53,088) Bruce Crozier, Lib., 416/325-7298

Essex-Kent (47,000) Pat Hoy, NDP, 416/325-9099

Etobicoke West (47,256) Chris Stockwell, PC, 416/325-7435

Etobicoke-Humber (48,706) Douglas B. Ford, PC, 416/325-6578

Etobicoke-Lakeshore (50,083) Morley Kells, PC, 416/325-8230

Etobicoke-Rexdale (44,393) John Hastings, PC, 416/325-6001

Fort William (43,643) Lyn McLeod, Lib., 416/325-0293

Fort York (41,147) Rosario Marchese, NDP, 416/325-9092

Frontenac-Addington (51,066) Bill Vankoughnet, Ind., 416/325-8662

Grey-Owen Sound (61,048) Bill Murdoch, PC, 416/325-6242

Guelph (61,691) Brenda Elliott, PC, 416/323-2780

Halton Centre (47,738) Terrence Young, PC, 416/325-2274

Halton North (47,738) Ted Chudleigh, PC, 416/314-2195

Hamilton Centre (40,459) David Christopherson, NDP, 416/325-3188

Hamilton East (44,757) Domonic Agostino, Lib., 416/325-8711

Hamilton Mountain (59,371) Trevor Pettit, PC, 416/325-3715

Hamilton West (49,673) Lillian Ross, PC, 416/326-8506

Hastings-Peterborough (44,719) Harry Danford, PC, 416/326-3063

High Park-Swansea (39,294) Derwyn Shea, PC, 416/314-7782

Huron (41,549) Helen Johns, PC, 416/323-4617

Kenora (33,061) Frank Miclash, Lib., 416/325-3639

Kingston & The Islands (42,165) John Gerretsen, Lib., 416/325-9210

Kitchener (56,066) Wayne Wettlaufer, PC, 416/325-8220

Kitchener-Wilmot (65,102) Gary Leadston, PC, 416/325-8644

Lake Nipigon (21,708) Gilles Pouliot, NDP, 416/325-4075

Lambton (43,019) Marcel Beaubien, PC, 416/325-1209

Lanark-Renfrew (60,270) Leo Jordan, PC, 416/325-7520

Lawrence (40,099) Joseph Cordiano, Lib., 416/325-3619

Leeds-Grenville (54,953) Hon. Robert W. Runciman, PC, 416/326-5075

Lincoln (54,677) Frank Sheehan, PC, 416/325-8640

London Centre (56,666) Marion Boyd, NDP, 416/325-3170

London North (68,675) Hon. Dianne Cunningham, PC, 416/326-1600

London South (66,875) Bob Wood, PC, 416/325-4925

Markham, Hon. David H. Tsubouchi, PC, 416/326-8500

Middlesex (59,061) Bruce Smith, PC, 416/325-2505

Mississauga East (53,159) Carl DeFaria, PC, 416/325-8502

Mississauga North (81,425) Hon. John Snobelen, PC, 416/325-2600

Mississauga South (51,180) Hon. Margaret Marland, PC, 416/325-7731

Mississauga West (96,475) Hon. Rob Sampson, PC, 416/325-0408

Muskoka-Georgian Bay (53,179) Bill Grimmett, PC, 416/325-6673

Nepean (54,832) John Baird, PC, 416/325-6351

Niagara Falls (47,729) Bart Maves, PC, 416/326-1463

Niagara South (38,787) Tim Hudak, PC, 416/325-8454

Nickel Belt (26,850) Floyd Laughren, NDP, 416/325-4060
Nipissing (49,020) Hon. Michael D. Harris, PC, 416/325-1941
Norfolk (56,118) Toby Barrett, PC, 416/325-8404
Northumberland (55,696) Doug Galt, PC, 416/323-4364
Oakville South (48,544) Gary Carr, PC, 416/325-6271
Oakwood (31,493) Mike Colle, Lib., 416/325-8707
Oriole (37,687) David Caplan, Lib.
Oshawa (54,110) Jerry J. Ouellette, PC, 416/325-8489
Ottawa Centre (44,958) Richard Patten, Lib., 416/325-1628
Ottawa East (48,272) Bernard C. Grandmaître, Lib., 416/325-3610
Ottawa South (43,793) Dalton J.P. McGuinty, Lib., 416/325-7155
Ottawa West (50,027) Alex Cullen, Lib., 416/325-3654
Ottawa-Rideau (53,961) Garry J. Guzzo, PC, 416/325-8177
Oxford (55,914) Ernie Hardeman, PC, 416/585-7285
Parkdale (27,999) Tony Ruprecht, Lib., 416/325-7777
Parry Sound (37,484) Hon. Ernie Eves, PC, 416/325-0400
Perth (49,097) Bert Johnson, PC, 416/325-5609
Peterborough (65,678) R. Gary Stewart, PC, 416/325-6639
Port Arthur (47,672) Michael Gravelle, NDP, 416/325-1559
Prescott & Russell (79,574) Jean-Marc Lalonde, Lib., 416/325-7289
Prince Edward-Lennox-South Hastings (47,891) Gary Fox, PC, 416/325-1725
Quinte (50,783) E.J. Douglas Rollins, PC, 416/325-8209
Rainy River (19,406) Howard Hampton, NDP, 416/325-8300
Renfrew North (49,678) Sean Conway, Lib., 416/325-7197
Riverdale (36,682) Marilyn Churley, NDP, 416/325-3250
S.D.G. & East Grenville (46,086) Hon. Noble Villeneuve, PC, 416/326-3074
Sarnia (45,210) Dave Boushy, PC, 416/325-8373
Sault Ste. Marie (57,581) Tony Martin, NDP, 416/325-4014
Scarborough Centre (44,325) Dan Newman, PC, 416/327-9829
Scarborough East (53,750) Steve Gilchrist, PC, 416/585-6940
Scarborough West (42,890) Jim Brown, PC, 416/325-8636
Scarborough-Agincourt (48,203) Gerry Phillips, Lib., 416/325-3628
Scarborough-Ellesmere (43,252) Marilyn Mushinski, PC, 416/325-6200
Scarborough-North (57,970) Alvin Curling, Lib., 416/325-7277
Simcoe Centre (81,753) Joseph N. Tascona, PC, 416/325-4579
Simcoe East (58,477) Allan K. McLean, PC, 416/325-3855
Simcoe West (56,980) James Wilson, PC, 416/327-4300
St. Andrew-St. Patrick (48,709) Hon. Isabel Bassett, PC, 416/326-9092
St. Catharines (46,146) Hon. James Bradley, Lib., 416/325-7194
St. Catharines-Brock (41,047) Tom Froese, PC, 416/325-8227
St. George-St. David (46,174) Hon. Allan Leach, PC, 416/585-7000
Sudbury (49,582) Rick Bartolucci, Lib., 416/325-8716
Sudbury East (49,123) Shelley Martel, NDP, 416/325-9203
Timiskaming (29,037) David Ramsay, Lib., 416/325-7137
Victoria-Haliburton (56,217) Hon. Chris Hodgson, PC, 416/314-2301
Waterloo North (70,170) Hon. Elizabeth Witmer, PC, 416/326-7600
Welland-Thorold (46,713) Peter Kormos, NDP, 416/325-7106
Wellington (50,529) Ted Arnott, PC, 416/325-6913
Wentworth East (56,023) Ed Doyle, PC, 416/325-8411
Wentworth North (54,022) Tony Skarica, PC, 416/325-6178
Willowdale (51,149) Hon. Charles Harnick, PC, 416/326-4016
Wilson Heights (45,228) Monte Kwinter, Lib., 416/325-7208
Windsor-Riverside (50,573) Wayne Lessard, NDP, 416/325-8116
Windsor-Sandwich (51,421) Sandra Pupatello, Lib., 416/325-1496
Windsor-Walkerville (48,141) Dwight Duncan, Lib., 416/325-1398
York Centre (129,108) Hon. Al Palladini, PC, 416/327-9200
York East (44,733) John L. Parker, PC, 416/325-5548, Voice & TTY: 416/425-2329
York Mills (43,180) David Turnbull, PC, 416/325-3877
York South (37,192) Gerard Kennedy, Lib., 416/325-2884
York-Mackenzie (66,558) Frank Klees, PC, 416/325-8934
Yorkview (32,827) Mario Sergio, Lib., 416/325-1404

**MEMBERS (ALPHABETICAL)**

Following is: member, constituency (number of eligible voters at 1995 election) party affiliation, Toronto office Telephone number.
Refer to Cabinet List, Government Caucus Services Office, Liberal Caucus Services Office, & Office of the Progressive Conservative Party, for Fax numbers.
Email addresses for all MPPs are formatted as follows - firstname_lastname-mpp@ontla.ola.org.

Domonic Agostino, Hamilton East (44,757) Lib., 416/325-8711
Ted Arnott, Wellington (50,529) PC, 416/325-6913
John Baird, Nepean (54,832) PC, 416/325-6351
Toby Barrett, Norfolk (56,118) PC, 416/325-8404
Rick Bartolucci, Sudbury (49,582) Lib., 416/325-8716
Hon. Isabel Bassett, St. Andrew-St. Patrick (48,709) PC, 416/326-9092
Marcel Beaubien, Lambton (43,019) PC, 416/325-1209
Gilles Bisson, Cochrane South (38,584) NDP, 416/325-7122
Dave Boushy, Sarnia (45,210) PC, 416/325-8373
Marion Boyd, London Centre (56,666) NDP, 416/325-3170
Hon. James Bradley, St. Catharines (46,146) Lib., 416/325-7194
Jim Brown, Scarborough West (42,890) PC, 416/325-8636
Mike Brown, Algoma-Manitoulin (26,128) Lib., 416/325-3601
David Caplan, Oriole (37,687) Lib.
Gary Carr, Oakville South (48,544) PC, 416/325-6271
Jack Carroll, Chatham-Kent (49,769) PC, 416/325-5246
Annamarie Castrilli, Downsview (36,926) Lib., 416/325-8688
David Christopherson, Hamilton Centre (40,459) NDP, 416/325-3188
Ted Chudleigh, Halton North (47,738) PC, 416/314-2195
Marilyn Churley, Riverdale (36,682) NDP, 416/325-3250
John Cleary, Cornwall (44,191) Lib., 416/325-3642
Hon. Tony Clement, Brampton South (74,364) PC, 416/314-5741
Mike Colle, Oakwood (31,493) Lib., 416/325-8707
Sean Conway, Renfrew North (49,678) Lib., 416/325-7197
Joseph Cordiano, Lawrence (40,099) Lib., 416/325-3619
Bruce Crozier, Essex South (53,088) Lib., 416/325-7298
Alex Cullen, Ottawa West (50,027) Lib., 416/325-3654
Hon. Dianne Cunningham, London North (68,675) PC, 416/326-1600
Alvin Curling, Scarborough-North (57,970) Lib., 416/325-7277
Harry Danford, Hastings-Peterborough (44,719) PC, 416/326-3063
Carl DeFaria, Mississauga East (53,159) PC, 416/325-8502
Ed Doyle, Wentworth East (56,023) PC, 416/325-8411
Dwight Duncan, Windsor-Walkerville (48,141) Lib., 416/325-1398
Hon. Janet Ecker, Durham West (84,476) PC, 416/325-5225
Brenda Elliott, Guelph (61,691) PC, 416/323-2780
Hon. Ernie Eves, Parry Sound (37,484) PC, 416/325-0400
Barb Fisher, Bruce (46,559) PC, 416/326-3058
Hon. Jim Flaherty, Durham Centre (66,818) PC, 416/326-2485
Douglas B. Ford, Etobicoke-Humber (48,706) PC, 416/325-6578
Gary Fox, Prince Edward-Lennox-South Hastings (47,891) PC, 416/325-1725
Tom Froese, St. Catharines-Brock (41,047) PC, 416/325-8227
Doug Galt, Northumberland (55,696) PC, 416/323-4364
John Gerretsen, Kingston & The Islands (42,165) Lib., 416/325-9210
Steve Gilchrist, Scarborough East (53,750) PC, 416/585-6940
Bernard C. Grandmaître, Ottawa East (48,272) Lib., 416/325-3610
Michael Gravelle, Port Arthur (47,672) NDP, 416/325-1559
Bill Grimmett, Muskoka-Georgian Bay (53,179) PC, 416/325-6673
Garry J. Guzzo, Ottawa-Rideau (53,961) PC, 416/325-8177
Howard Hampton, Rainy River (19,406) NDP, 416/325-8300
Ernie Hardeman, Oxford (55,914) PC, 416/585-7285
Hon. Charles Harnick, Willowdale (51,149) PC, 416/326-4016
Hon. Michael D. Harris, Nipissing (49,020) PC, 416/325-1941
John Hastings, Etobicoke-Rexdale (44,393) PC, 416/325-6001
Hon. Chris Hodgson, Victoria-Haliburton (56,217) PC, 416/314-2301
Pat Hoy, Essex-Kent (47,000) NDP, 416/325-9099
Tim Hudak, Niagara South (38,787) PC, 416/325-8454
Hon. Cameron Jackson, Burlington South (49,821) PC, 416/326-9326
Helen Johns, Huron (41,549) PC, 416/323-4617
Bert Johnson, Perth (49,097) PC, 416/325-5609
Hon. David Johnson, Don Mills (42,758) PC, 416/325-7754
Ron Johnson, Brantford (55,445) PC, 416/325-7027
Leo Jordan, Lanark-Renfrew (60,270) PC, 416/325-7520
Morley Kells, Etobicoke-Lakeshore (50,083) PC, 416/325-8230
Gerard Kennedy, York South (37,192) Lib., 416/325-2884
Frank Klees, York-Mackenzie (66,558) PC, 416/325-8934
Peter Kormos, Welland-Thorold (46,713) NDP, 416/325-7106
Monte Kwinter, Wilson Heights (45,228) Lib., 416/325-7208
Jean-Marc Lalonde, Prescott & Russell (79,574) Lib., 416/325-7289
Frances Lankin, Beaches-Woodbine (38,523) NDP, 416/325-6904
Floyd Laughren, Nickel Belt (26,850) NDP, 416/325-4060
Hon. Allan Leach, St. George-St. David (46,174) PC, 416/585-7000

Gary Leadston, Kitchener-Wilmot (65,102) PC, 416/325-8644
Wayne Lessard, Windsor-Riverside (50,573) NDP, 416/325-8116
Rosario Marchese, Fort York (41,147) NDP, 416/325-9092
Hon. Margaret Marland, Mississauga South (51,180) PC, 416/325-7731
Shelley Martel, Sudbury East (49,123) NDP, 416/325-9203
Tony Martin, Sault Ste. Marie (57,581) NDP, 416/325-4014
Gerry Martiniuk, Cambridge (62,324) PC, 416/325-8451
Bart Maves, Niagara Falls (47,729) PC, 416/326-1463
Dalton J.P. McGuinty, Ottawa South (43,793) Lib., 416/325-7155
Allan K. McLean, Simcoe East (58,477) PC, 416/325-3855
Lyn McLeod, Fort William (43,643) Lib., 416/325-0293
Frank Miclash, Kenora (33,061) Lib., 416/325-3639
Gilles E. Morin, Carleton East (61,643) Lib., 416/325-7216
Julia Munro, Durham-York (65,909) PC, 416/325-3392
Bill Murdoch, Grey-Owen Sound (61,048) PC, 416/325-6242
Marilyn Mushinski, Scarborough-Ellesmere (43,252) PC, 416/325-6200
Dan Newman, Scarborough Centre (44,325) PC, 416/327-9829
Peter North, Elgin (54,155) Ind., 416/325-7271
John O'Toole, Durham East (62,205) PC, 416/325-6745
Jerry J. Ouellette, Oshawa (54,110) PC, 416/325-8489
Hon. Al Palladini, York Centre (129,108) PC, 416/327-9200
John L. Parker, York East (44,733) PC, 416/325-5548, Voice & TTY: 416/425-2329
Richard Patten, Ottawa Centre (44,958) Lib., 416/325-1628
Trevor Pettit, Hamilton Mountain (59,371) PC, 416/325-3715
Gerry Phillips, Scarborough-Agincourt (48,203) Lib., 416/325-3628
Gilles Pouliot, Lake Nipigon (21,708) NDP, 416/325-4075
Peter L. Preston, Brant-Haldimand (48,807) PC, 416/325-8216
Sandra Pupatello, Windsor-Sandwich (51,421) Lib., 416/325-1496
David Ramsay, Timiskaming (29,037) Lib., 416/325-7137
E.J. Douglas Rollins, Quinte (50,783) PC, 416/325-8209
Lillian Ross, Hamilton West (49,673) PC, 416/326-8506
Hon. Robert W. Runciman, Leeds-Grenville (54,953) PC, 416/326-5075
Tony Ruprecht, Parkdale (27,999) Lib., 416/325-7777
Hon. Rob Sampson, Mississauga West (96,475) PC, 416/325-0408
Hon. William Saunderson, Eglinton (48965) PC, 416/325-6900
Mario Sergio, Yorkview (32,827) Lib., 416/325-1404
Derwyn Shea, High Park-Swansea (39,294) PC, 416/314-7782
Frank Sheehan, Lincoln (54,677) PC, 416/325-8640
Tony Silipo, Dovercourt (30,963) NDP, 416/325-6311
Tony Skarica, Wentworth North (54,022) PC, 416/325-6178
Bruce Smith, Middlesex (59,061) PC, 416/325-2505
Hon. John Snobelen, Mississauga North (81,425) PC, 416/325-2600
Joe Spina, Brampton North (69,435) PC, 416/327-0616
Hon. Norman W. Sterling, Carleton (70,780) PC, 416/323-4360
R. Gary Stewart, Peterborough (65,678) PC, 416/325-6639
Chris Stockwell, Etobicoke West (47,256) PC, 416/325-7435
Joseph N. Tascona, Simcoe Centre (81,753) PC, 416/325-4579
David Tilson, Dufferin-Peel (54,176) PC, 416/325-4154
Hon. David H. Tsubouchi, Markham PC, 416/326-8500
David Turnbull, York Mills (43,180) PC, 416/325-3877
Bill Vankoughnet, Frontenac-Addington (51,066) Ind., 416/325-8662
Hon. Noble Villeneuve, S.D.G. & East Grenville (46,086) PC, 416/326-3074
Wayne Wettlaufer, Kitchener (56,066) PC, 416/325-8220
Bud Wildman, Algoma (21,864) NDP, 416/325-6800
James Wilson, Simcoe West (56,980) PC, 416/327-4300
Hon. Elizabeth Witmer, Waterloo North (70,170) PC, 416/326-7600
Bob Wood, London South (66,875) PC, 416/325-4925
Len Wood, Cochrane North (26,037) NDP, 416/325-7040
Terrence Young, Halton Centre (47,738) PC, 416/325-2274

## ONTARIO GOVERNMENT DEPARTMENTS & AGENCIES

### Ministry of AGRICULTURE, FOOD & RURAL AFFAIRS (OMAFRA)

Communications Branch, 1 Stone Rd. West, Guelph ON N1G 4Y2
519/826-4240; Fax: 519/826-3262; URL: http://www.gov.on.ca/OMAFRA/english/ag.html
Toll Free: 1-888-466-2372

**ACTS ADMINISTERED**

Abandoned Orchards Act
Agricultural & Horticultural Organizations Act
Agricultural Committees Act
Agricultural Rehabilitation & Development Act (Ontario)
Agricultural Representatives Act
Agricultural Research Institute of Ontario Act
Agricultural Tile Drainage Installation Act
Animals for Research Act
Artificial Insemination of Livestock Act
Beef Cattle Marketing Act
Bees Act
Bull Owners Liability Act
Commodity Board Members Act
Commodity Boards & Marketing Agencies Act
Cooperative Loans Act
Crop Insurance Act (Ontario)
Dead Animal Disposal Act
Drainage Act
Edible Oil Products Act
Farm Implements Act
Farm Income Stabilization Act
Farm Practices Protection Act
Farm Products Containers Act
Farm Products Grades & Sales Act
Farm Products Marketing Act
Farm Products Payments Act
Farm Registration & Farm Organizations Funding Act
Fur Farms Act
Grain Corn Marketing Act
Grain Elevator Storage Act
Hunter Damage Compensation Act
Junior Farmer Establishment Act
Livestock & Livestock Products Act
Livestock Branding Act
Livestock Community Sales Act
Livestock Medicines Act
Livestock, Poultry & Honey Bee Protection Act
Meat Inspection Act (Ontario)
Milk Act
Ministry of Agriculture & Food Act
Non-resident Agricultural Interests Registration Act
Oleomargarine Act
Ontario Agricultural Museum Act
Ontario Food Terminal Act
Plant Diseases Act
Pounds Act
Provincial Auctioneers Act
Riding Horse Establishments Act
Seed Potatoes Act
Sheep & Wool Marketing Act
Stock Yards Act
Tile Drainage Act
Topsoil Preservation Act
Veterinarians Act
Weed Control Act

**Minister**, Hon. Noble Villeneuve, 416/326-3067, Fax: 416/326-3083
Deputy Minister, Kenneth W. Knox, 416/326-3101, Fax: 416/326-3106

**Communications Branch**

1 Stone Rd. West, Guelph ON N1G 4Y2
519/826-4240; Fax: 519/826-3262
Toll Free: 1-888-466-2372
Director, Vacant
Manager, Broadcast Services, Graham Howe, 519/826-3163
Manager, Media & Editorial Services, Tom Rekstis, 519/826-3174

**Legal Services Branch**

801 Bay St., 10th Fl., Toronto ON M7A 2B2
416/326-3384; Fax: 416/326-3385
Guelph: 519/826-4250; Fax: 519/826-3385
Director, Stephen Stepinac, 416/326-3378

**AGRICULTURE & RURAL DIVISION**

519/826-3506; Fax: 519/826-3259
Asst. Deputy Minister, Dr. Frank Ingratta, 519/826-3525
Director, Business Development & Central Region, Gwen Zellen, 519/826-3138
Acting Director, Farm Business Management & Western Region, Rod Stork, 416/767-3151, Fax: 416/837-3049
Director, Livestock Technology & Field Services East Region, Don Taylor, 519/767-3112, Fax: 519/826-3254
Director, Resources & Regulations Branch, David Thomson, Guelph Agriculture Centre, PO Box 1030, Guelph ON N1H 1G3, 519/767-3561, Fax: 519/824-6941
Director, Rural Development & North Region, Kathy Biondi, 519/826-3419

**CORPORATE SERVICES DIVISION**

416/326-3097; Fax: 416/326-3390
Asst. Deputy Minister, Barb Miller, 416/326-3095
Acting Director, Audit Services, Walter Kent, 416/326-3777, Fax: 416/326-3793
Director, Financial Operations, Pauline Moeller, 416/326-3186, Fax: 416/326-3329
Director, Financial Planning Secretariat, Richard Kirsh, 416/326-3191, Fax: 416/326-3264
Director, Human Resources Branch, Nancy Navkar, 416/326-3717, Fax: 416/326-3128
Director, Management Systems Branch, John Birss, 416/326-3599, Fax: 416/326-3447
Director, Relocation & Administrative Services, Michael Keith, 416/325-1179, Fax: 416/326-6575

**EDUCATION, RESEARCH & LABORATORIES DIVISION**

519/826-3388; Fax: 519/826-4211
Safety response Unit: 519/826-4175
Asst. Deputy Minister, Norris Hoag, 519/826-4166, Fax: 519/826-4222
Director, Agriculture & Food Laboratory Services Centre, Dr. Jim Pettit, 519/767-5013, Fax: 519/767-0060

Director, Horticultural Research Institute of Ontario, Dr. Frank Eady, PO Box 7000, Vineland Station ON L0R 2E0, 905/562-4141, Fax: 905/562-3413

Director, Veterinary Laboratory Services, Dr. Deb Stark, 519/837-5081, Fax: 519/767-0015

## FOOD INDUSTRY DIVISION

416/326-3759; Fax: 416/326-3747

Asst. Deputy Minister, James Farrar, 416/326-3757

Director, Dairy, Fruit & Vegetable Industry Inspection Branch, Diane Coates Milne, 519/837-5045, Fax: 519/767-0336

Director, Food Industry Competitiveness Branch, James Farrar, 416/326-3047, Fax: 416/326-3094

Acting Director, Market Development Branch, Bill Allen, 416/326-3510, Fax: 416/326-7630

Director, Meat Industry Inspection Branch, Charles Lalonde, 519/837-5060, Fax: 519/767-0305

## POLICY & FARM FINANCE DIVISION

519/826-3205; Fax: 519/826-3492

Asst. Deputy Minister, Robert Seguin, 416/326-3204

Acting Director, Policy Analysis, Dave Hope, 519/826-3244

Director, Policy & Program Coordination, Len Roozen, 416/326-3252

### Crop Insurance & Stabilization

Director, Agricorp, Greg Brown, 416/326-3300, Fax: 416/326-3133

### Associated Agencies, Boards & Commissions

•Agricultural Research Institute of Ontario (ARIO): 1 Stone Rd. West, Guelph ON N1G 4Y2 – 519/826-4166; Fax: 519/826-4211

Director, Norris Hoag

•Cooperative Loans Board of Ontario: #100, 10 Alcorn Ave., Toronto ON M4V 3B3 – 416/326-3493

Chair, Rolly Stroeter

•Council of the College of Veterinarians of Ontario: Guelph Agriculture Centre, 259 Grange Rd., PO Box 1030, Guelph ON N1H 6N1 – 519/767-3116

Contact, Dr. Deb Stark

•Crop Insurance Commission of Ontario: 801 Bay St., 5th Fl., Toronto ON M7A 2B2 – 416/326-3276; Fax: 416/326-3133

Chair, Greg Brown

•Ontario Agricultural Licensing & Registration Review Board: Guelph Agriculture Centre, PO Box 1030, Guelph ON N1H 1G3 – 519/767-3547

Contact, David Thomson

•Ontario Agricultural Museum Advisory Board: PO Box 38, Milton ON L9T 2Y3 – 905/878-8151

Chair, John Wiley

•Ontario Agricultural Rehabilitation & Development Directorate: 1 Stone Rd. West, 2nd Fl., Guelph ON N1G 4Y2

Chair, Rolly Stroeter

•Ontario Beginning Farmer Assistance Program Review Committee: #100, 10 Alcorn Ave., Toronto ON M4V 3B3 – 416/326-3492

Chair, Rolly Stroeter

•Ontario Crop Insurance Arbitration Board: 801 Bay St., 5th Fl., Toronto ON M7A 2B2 – 416/326-3276; Fax: 416/326-3133

Chair, Greg Brown

•Ontario Drainage Tribunal: Cooperators Bldg., 130 Macdonell St., #303A, Guelph ON N1H 2Z6 – 519/763-3430; Fax: 519/763-0351

•Ontario Egg Fund Board: #800, 33 Yonge St., Toronto ON M5E 1X2 – 416/326-7486

Contact, Gloria Marco Borys

•Ontario Farm Family Advisor Program Board: Guelph Agricultural Centre, 52 Royal Rd., PO Box 1030, Guelph ON N1H 6N1 – 519/767-3151

Contact, Rod Stork

•Ontario Farm Implements Board: Guelph Agriculture Centre, 52 Royal Rd., PO Box 1030, Guelph ON N1H 1G3 – 519/767-3547; Fax: 519/824-6941

Chair, David Thomson

•Ontario Farm Income Stabilization Commission: 801 Bay St., 5th Fl., Toronto ON M7A 2B2 – 416/326-3300

Contact, Greg Brown

•Ontario Farm Organizations Accreditation Tribunal: #100, 10 Alcorn Ave., Toronto ON M4V 3B3 – 416/326-3493

Chair, Rolly Stroeter

•Ontario Farm Practices Protection Board: Guelph Agriculture Centre, 1 Stone Rd. West, Guelph ON N1H 4Y2 – 519/826-3577

Chair, Edward Oldfield

•Ontario Farm Products Appeal Tribunal: Cooperators Bldg., #303A, 130 Macdonell St., Guelph ON N1H 2Z6 – 519/763-3430; Fax: 519/763-0351

Chair, John Johnston

•Ontario Farm Products Marketing Commission: #800, 33 Yonge St., Toronto ON M5E 1X2 – 416/326-7490; Fax: 416/326-7630 – TELEX: 06-22546

Chair, Jim Wheeler, 519/326-7087

General Manager, David K. Alles, 416/326-7003

•Ontario Farm Tax Rebate Appeal Board: #100, 10 Alcorn Ave., Toronto ON M4V 3B3 – 416/326-3492; Fax: 416/326-3501

Chair, Rolly Stroeter

•Ontario Food Terminal Board: 165 The Queensway, Toronto ON M8Y 1H8 – 416/259-5479; Fax: 416/259-4303

General Manager, C.E. Carsley

•Ontario Grain Financial Protection Board: #800, 33 Yonge St., PO Box 1030, Toronto ON M5E 1X2 – 416/326-7547

Chair, Bill Moore

•Ontario Junior Farmers Establishment Loan Corporation: #100, 10 Alcorn Ave., Toronto ON M4V 3B3 – 416/326-3493; Fax: 416/326-3133

Chair, Rolly Stroeter

•Ontario Livestock Financial Protection Board: #800, 33 Yonge St., Toronto ON M5E 1X2 – 416/326-7547

Chair, Bill Moore

•Ontario Livestock Medicines Advisory Committee: Guelph Agriculture Centre, 52 Royal Rd., PO Box 1030, Guelph ON N1H 1G3 – 519/767-3547

Chair, David Thomson

•Ontario Produce Arbitration Board: Guelph Agriculture Centre, 259 Grange Rd., PO Box 1030, Guelph ON N1H 6N1 – 519/837-5044

Chair, Diane Coates Milne

•Ontario Provincial Decision Committee (Private Mortgage Guarantee Program): #100, 10 Alcorn Ave., Toronto ON M4V 3B3 – 416/326-3492

Contact, Rolly Stroeter

•Ontario Stock Yards Board: 801 Bay St., 4th Fl., Toronto ON M7A 2B2 – 416/326-3015

Chair, Robert Seguin

•Ontario Wolf Damage Assessment Board: #100, 10 Alcorn Ave., Toronto ON M4V 3B3 – 416/326-3492

Contact, Rolly Stroeter

### Agricultural Marketing Boards & Commissions

•Ontario Apple Marketing Commission: 7195B Millcreek Dr., Mississauga ON L5A 3R3 – 905/858-1060; Fax: 905/858-3299

•Ontario Asparagus Growers' Marketing Board: 71C Front St. West., Strathroy ON N7G 1X6 – 519/246-1640; Fax: 519/246-1634

Chair, John Jacques

•Ontario Bean Producers' Marketing Board: 140 Raney Cres., London ON N6L 1C3 – 519/652-3566; Fax: 519/652-9607

General Manager, Charles E. Broadwell

•Ontario Broiler Hatching Egg & Chick Commission: 291 Woodlawn Rd. West, Unit 9B, Guelph ON N1H 7L6 – 519/837-0005; Fax: 519/837-0464

General Manager, Roger J. Bennett

•Ontario Chicken Producers' Marketing Board: 3380 South Service Rd., PO Box 5035, Burlington ON L7R 3Y8 – 905/637-0025; Fax: 905/637-3464

General Manager, William V. Doyle

•Ontario Cream Producers' Marketing Board: 6780 Campobello Rd., Mississauga ON L5N 2L8 – 905/821-8970; Fax: 905/821-3160

Secretary Manager, J. Bilyea

•Ontario Egg Producers' Marketing Board: 7195 Millcreek Dr., Mississauga ON L5N 4H1 – 905/858-9790; Fax: 905/821-3160

General Manager, B. Ellsworth

•Ontario Flue-Cured Tobacco Growers' Marketing Board: PO Box 70, Tillsonburg ON N4G 4H4 – 519/842-3661; Fax: 519/842-7813

Secretary, M.E. Lepage

•Ontario Grape Growers' (Fresh & Processing) Marketing Board: PO Box 100, Vineland Stn, Vineland ON L0R 2E0 – 905/688-0990; Fax: 905/688-3211 – (Grapes for Processing)

Secretary, J.R. Rainforth

•Ontario Greenhouse Vegetable Producers' Marketing Board: PO Box 417, Leamington ON N8H 3W5 – 519/326-2604; Fax: 519/326-7842

Secretary, William K. Power

•Ontario Milk Marketing Board: 6780 Campobello Rd., Mississauga ON L5N 2L8 – 905/821-8970; Fax: 905/821-3160

Secretary, H. Parker

•Ontario Pork Producers' Marketing Board: PO Box 740, Etobicoke ON M9C 5H3 – 416/621-1874; Fax: 416/621-6869

Secretary, G. Agnew

•Ontario Potato Growers' (Fresh & Processing) Marketing Board: 570 Brant St., Burlington ON L7R 2G8 – 905/637-5609; Fax: 905/637-7653

Secretary Manager, W.L. Armstrong

•Ontario Processing Tomato Seedling Plant Growers' Marketing Board: PO Box 157, Leamington ON N8H 3W2 – 519/326-4481; Fax: 519/326-3413

Secretary, G. Woodsit

•Ontario Seed Corn Growers' Marketing Board: 785 St. Clair St., RR#7, Chatham ON N7M 5J7 – 519/352-6710; Fax: 519/352-0526

Secretary Manager, Brad Caughy

•Ontario Sheep Marketing Agency: 50 Dovercliffe Rd., Unit 13, Guelph ON N1G 3A6 – 519/836-0043; Fax: 519/824-9101

Secretary Manager, F.E. Winger

•Ontario Soybean Growers' Marketing Board: PO Box 1199, Chatham ON N7M 5L8 – 519/352-7730; Fax: 519/352-8983

Secretary Manager, Fred Brandenburg

•Ontario Tender Fruit Producers' Marketing Board: PO Box 100, Vineland Stn, Vineland ON L0R 2E0 – 905/688-0990; Fax: 905/688-3211

Secretary Manager, J.R. Rainforth

•Ontario Turkey Producers' Marketing Board: 60 New Dundee Rd., RR#2, Kitchener ON N2G 3W5 – 519/748-9636; Fax: 519/748-2742

General Manager, JoAnn White

•Ontario Vegetable Growers' Marketing Board: 435 Consortium Ct., London ON N6E 2S8 – 519/681-1875; Fax: 519/685-5719

Chair, Leonard Harwood

Secretary Manager, John Mumford

•Ontario Wheat Producers' Marketing Board: 880 Richmond St., PO Box 668, Chatham ON N7M 5K8 – 519/354-4430; Fax: 519/354-0675

Secretary Manager, William McClounie

## Ministry of the ATTORNEY GENERAL
720 Bay St., 11th Fl., Toronto ON M5G 2K1
416/326-2220; Fax: 416/326-4088

**ACTS ADMINISTERED**
Absconding Debtors Act
Absentees Act
Accidental Fires Act
Accumulations Act
Administration of Justice Act
Age of Majority & Accountability Act
Aliens' Real Property Act
Anglican Church of Canada
Arbitrations Act
Architects Act
Assessment Review Board Act
Bail Act
Barristers Act
Blind Persons' Rights Act
Bulk Sales Act
Business Records Protection Act
Canada-United Kingdom Convention
Canadian Citizenship & British Status Act
Change of Name Act
Charitable Gifts Act
Charities Accounting Act
Children's Law Reform Act
Commissioners for Taking Affidavits Act
Compensation for Victims of Crime Act
Construction Lien Act
Consultants Act
Conveyance & Law of Property Act
Costs of Distress Act
Court Reform Statute Law Amendment Act
Courts of Justice Act
Creditors' Relief Act
Crown Administration of Estates Act
Crown Agency Act
Crown Attorneys Act
Crown Witnesses Act
Disorderly Houses Act
Dog Owners' Liability Act
English & Wahigoon River Systems Mercury Contamination Settlement Agreement Act
Equality Rights Statute Law Amendment Act
Escheats Act
Estates Act
Estates Administration Act
Evidence Act
Execution Act
Expropriation Act
Family Law Act
Fines & Forfeitures Act
Foreign Arbitral Awards Act
Fraudulent Conveyances Act
Fraudulent Debtors Arrest Act
Frustrated Contracts Act
Gaming Act
Group Defamation Act
Habeas Corpus Act
Hague Convention on Child Abduction
Hague Convention on Service of Documents Abroad
Hospitals & Charitable Institutions Inquiries Act
Hotel Registration of Guests Act
Human Artificial Reproduction Act
Innkeepers Act
International Commercial Arbitration Act
International Sale of Goods Act
Interpretation Act
Interprovincial Subpoenas Act
Intervenor Funding Project Act
Judicial Review Procedure Act
Juries Act
Justices of the Peace Act
Landlord & Tenant Act
Law Society Act
Legal Aid Act
Legal Profession Statute Law Amendment Act
Libel & Slander Act
Limitations Act
Mandatory Retirement Act
Master & Servant Act
Mechanics' Lien Act
Members' Conflict of Interest Act
Mental Incompetency Act
Ministry of the Attorney General Act
Minors' Protection Act
Mortgages Act
Negligence Act
Notaries Act
Occupiers' Liability Act
Ombudsman Act
Ontario Law Reform Commission Act
Ontario Municipal Board Act
Ontario Native Justice of Peace Program Act
Ontario Québec Exchange of Judges Act
Partition Act
Pawnbrokers Act
Perpetuities Act
Police Services Act
Powers of Attorney Act
Proceedings Against the Crown Act
Professional Engineers Act
Profits of Crime Act
Property & Civil Rights Act
Provincial Offences Act
Provincial Residence Mobility Rights Act
Public Accountancy Act
Public Authorities' Protection Act
Public Halls Act
Public Inquiries Act
Public Institutions Inspection Act
Public Officers Act
Public Trustee Act
Race Relations Issues Act
Reciprocal Enforcement of Judgements Act
Reciprocal Enforcement of Judgements (U.K.) Act
Reciprocal Enforcement of Maintenance Orders Act
Regulations Act
Regulations Revision Act
Religious Freedom Act
Religious Organizations' Lands Act
Revised Statutes Confirmation Act
Sale of Goods Act
Search & Seizure Act
Settled Estates Act
Short Forms of Conveyances Act
Short Forms of Leases Act
Short Forms of Mortgages Act
Solicitors Act
South African Trust Investments Act
Statute of Frauds
Statutes Act
Statutes Revision Act
Statutory Powers Procedure Act
Succession Law Reform Act
Support & Custody Orders Enforcement Act
Ticket Speculation Act
Time Act
Transboundary Pollution Reciprocal Access Act
Trespass to Property Act
Trustee Act
Unconscionable Transactions Relief Act
University Expropriation Powers Act
Variation of Trusts Act
Vendors & Purchasers Act
Vienna Sales Convention
Wages Act
Warehouse Receipts Act
Warehousemen's Lien Act

**Minister**, Hon. Charles Harnick, 416/326-4000, Fax: 416/326-4016
Deputy Minister, Timothy Millard
Director, Communications Branch, Anji Husain, 416/326-2205; Fax: 416/326-4007
Manager, Drinking/Driving Countermeasures, John Lefebvre, 416/326-4408; Fax: 416/326-4007

**Special Investigations Unit**
320 Front St. West, 10th Fl., Toronto ON M5V 3V5
416/314-2915; Fax: 416/314-2925
Director, Graham Reynolds
Communications & Outreach Officer, Sarah Persaud

**FINANCE & ADMINISTRATION**
Asst. Deputy Attorney General, Richard Monzon, 416/326-2610, Fax: 416/326-2326
Director, Audit Services Branch, Anton M. Odeh, 416/326-4224, Fax: 416/326-4219
Director, Computer & Telecommunications Services Branch, Kalman Brettler, 416/326-2001, Fax: 416/326-4797
Director, Financial & Administrative Services Branch, Helen Hayward, 416/326-4372, Fax: 416/326-4312
Director, Human Resources Branch, Peter W. Clendinneng, 416/326-2700, Fax: 416/326-4009
Coordinator, Freedom of Information & Privacy, Ruth Mallard, 416/326-4300, Fax: 416/326-4307

**Justice Review Project**
#205, 101 Bloor St. West, Toronto ON M5S 1P7
416/325-4910; Fax: 416/326-6298
Director, Dick Barnhorst

**LEGISLATIVE COUNSEL**
Whitney Block, #3600, 99 Wellesley St. West, Toronto ON M7A 1A2
416/326-2841; Fax: 416/326-2806
Chief Legislative Counsel, Donald L. Revell, 416/326-2770
Deputy Chief Legislative Counsel, Administration & Statutes Revision, Sidney Tucker, Q.C., 416/326-2777
Deputy Chief Legislative Counsel, French Language Services, Michael J.B. Wood, 416/326-2766
Deputy Chief Legislative Counsel, Legislative Counsel Services, Corneila Schuh, 416/326-2741
Registrar, Regulations, Lucinda Mifsud, 416/326-2748, Fax: 416/326-2805

**COURTS ADMINISTRATION PROGRAM**
Asst. Deputy Attorney General, Sandra Lang, 416/326-2609, Fax: 416/326-2652
Director, Facilities & Special Court Services Branch, Matt Veskimets, 416/326-4033, Fax: 416/326-4029
Acting Director, Family Support Plan, Harvey Brownstone, 416/326-4710, Fax: 416/326-4735
Acting Director, Program Development Branch, Axel Frandsen, 416/326-4264, Fax: 416/326-4289
**For list of Courts & other Legal Offices, including Judicial Officials & Judges *see* Section 10 of this book.**

**CIVIL LAW DIVISION**
416/326-2607; Fax: 416/326-4014
Asst. Deputy Attorney General, Leslie H. Macleod, 416/326-2608
Executive Coordinator, Seconded Legal Services, Brock Grant, 416/326-4020, Fax: 416/326-4019
Acting Public Trustee, Office of the Public Trustee, Susan Himel, 416/314-2690, Fax: 416/314-2716, General Inquiry: 416/314-2800
Official Guardian, Office of the Official Guardian, Willson McTavish, 393 University Ave., 14th Fl., Toronto ON M5G 1W9, 416/314-8011, Fax: 416/314-8000
Associate Director, Advisory Services, Corey Simpson, 416/326-4098
Associate Director, Litigation, Leah Price, 416/326-4478
Director, Civil Crown Law Office, Heather Cooper, 416/326-4008, Fax: 416/326-4181

#### CONSTITUTIONAL LAW & POLICY
Director & Chief Counsel, Bonnie J. Wein, 416/326-2584
Deputy Director & General Counsel, Carol Creighton, 416/326-4476
Acting Director, Constitutional Law, Elizabeth C. Goldberg, 416/326-2624
Office Administrator, Clita J. Saldanha
Acting Coordinator, Constitutional Information, Michel Y. Hélie, 416/326-4454
Constitutional Information Asst., Heather Janack, 416/326-4474
Criminal Counsel, Susan Chapman, 416/326-4590

#### CRIMINAL LAW DIVISION
Asst. Deputy Attorney General, Michael Code, 416/326-2616, Fax: 416/326-2063
Provincial Coordinator, Victim-Witness Services, Susan Lee, 416/326-2429
Director, Criminal Crown Law Office, Murray Segal, 416/326-2300, Fax: 416/326-4619
Director, Criminal Prosecutions, Brian Trafford, 416/326-2618, Fax: 416/326-2423
Director, Divisional Planning & Administration, Marnie D. Brown, 416/326-2405

#### POLICY DEVELOPMENT DIVISION
416/326-2500; Fax: 416/326-2699
Director, J. Douglas Ewart, 416/326-2620
Acting Deputy Director, Ann Merritt, 416/326-2509
Deputy Director, Equality Rights Branch, Lori Newton, 416/326-2513

##### Associated Agencies, Boards & Commissions
•Assessment Review Board: 121 Bloor St. East, 3rd Fl., Toronto ON M4W 3H5 – 416/314-6900; Fax: 416/314-6906, Toll Free: 1-800-263-3237
Registrar, Deborah Guild
Assessment Contact, Theresa E. Camacho
Assessment Contact, Marilyn Gamble
Assessment Contact, Annette Robinson
•Board of Negotiation: 720 Bay St., 4th Fl., Toronto ON M5G 2K1 – 416/326-4700
Chair, G.W. Swayze
•Criminal Injuries Compensation Board: 439 University Ave., 4th Fl., Toronto ON M5G 1Y8 – 416/326-2900; Fax: 416/326-2883
Chair, Wendy Calder
Manager, Administration, Dina Alexis
•Office of the Police Complaints Commissioner: 595 Bay St., 9th Fl., PO Box 23, Toronto ON M5G 2C2 – 416/325-4700; Fax: 416/325-4704
Police Complaints Commissioner, Clare E. Lewis
Executive Director, Mark Conacher
•Ontario Criminal Code Review Board: 700 Bay St., 23rd Fl., Toronto ON M5G 1Z6 – 416/327-8868; Fax: 416/327-8867
•Ontario Law Reform Commission: 720 Bay St., 11th Fl., Toronto ON M5G 1L9 – 416/326-4200; Fax: 416/326-4693
Chair, John McCamus
Vice Chair, Richard E.B. Simeon
•Royal Commissions & Inquiries: 180 Dundas St. West, 22nd Fl., Toronto ON M5G 1Z8 – 416/598-0411; Fax: 416/325-8739
Coordinator, Inge Sardy

## Office of the Provincial AUDITOR
#1530, 20 Dundas St. West, PO Box 105, Toronto ON M5G 2C2
416/327-2381; Fax: 416/327-9862
**Provincial Auditor**, Erik Peters, 416/327-1325
Asst. Provincial Auditor, Ken W. Leishman, 416/327-1326
Executive Director, Finance, Public Accounts & General Government Portfolio, Jim McCarter
Director, Community & Social Services Portfolio, Walter Bordne
Director, Crown Agencies, Boards & Commissions Portfolio, John McDowell
Director, Economic Development Portfolio, Gerard Fitzmaurice
Director, Education & Training, Housing & Municipal Affairs Portfolio, Gary Peall
Director, Health Portfolio, Nick Mishchenko
Director, Justice & Regulatory Portfolio, Andrew Cheung

## Ministry of CITIZENSHIP, CULTURE & RECREATION (MCCR)
77 Bloor St. West, 6th Fl., Toronto ON M7A 2R9
416/327-2422

#### ACTS ADMINISTERED
Advocacy Act
Archives Act
Art Gallery of Ontario Act
Arts Council Act
Centennial Centre of Science & Technology Act
Community Recreation Centres Act
Foreign Cultural Objects Immunity from Seizure Act
George R. Gardiner Museum of Ceramic Art Act
McMichael Canadian Collection Act
Ministry of Citizenship & Culture Act
Ministry of Tourism & Recreation Act
Ontario Heritage Act
Ontario Human Rights Code
Parks Assistance
Public Libraries Act
Royal Ontario Museum Act
Science North Act
**Minister**, Hon. Isabel Bassett, 416/325-6200, Fax: 416/325-6195
Deputy Minister, Naomi Alboim, 416/325-6220, Fax: 416/325-6196
Director, Communications Branch (Citizenship), Bernadette Sulgit, 416/325-7725, Fax: 416/314-4965
Acting Team Leader, Corporate Affairs Branch (Culture & Recreation), André Quenneville, 416/314-7379, Fax: 416/314-4965

#### CORPORATE SERVICES & ORGANIZATIONAL PLANNING DIVISION
Asst. Deputy Minister, Fran Grant, 416/314-7311
Coordinator, French Language Services, Jeanne Drouillard, 416/325-6214, Fax: 416/314-7277
Includes: Audit & Evaluation Services, Financial & Administrative Services, Human Resources, Information Technology, Legal Services, Organizational Planning, Relocation Project, Budget Planning & Analysis.

#### CULTURE DIVISION
77 Bloor St. West, 6th Fl., Toronto ON M7A 2R9
416/314-7265; Fax: 416/314-7313
Asst. Deputy Minister, Jane Marlatt, 416/314-7262
Director, Cultural Liaison Branch, Linda Loving, 416/314-7342
Director, Cultural Program Branch, Lyn Hamilton, 416/314-7081
Director, Heritage, Arts & Cultural Industries Policy Branch, Robert Montgomery, 416/314-7115
Acting Director, Libraries & Community Information Branch, Stan Squires

##### Native Community Branch
Director, Allan Chrisjohn, 416/314-7414, Fax: 416/314-7428

##### Regional Offices
Fort Frances: 283 Church St., Fort Frances ON P9A 1C9 – 807/274-9732; Fax: 807/274-0671
Geraldton: 303 Main St. East, PO Box 778, Geraldton ON P0T 1M0 – 807/854-0169; Fax: 807/854-2465
Kenora: 227 - 2 St. South, 3rd Fl., Kenora ON P9N 1G1 – 807/468-2864; Fax: 807/468-2788
London: #601, 255 Dufferin Ave., London ON N6A 5K6 – 519/679-7146; Fax: 519/679-7032
Orillia: 15 Matchedash St. North, Orillia ON L3V 4T4 – 705/325-9561; Fax: 705/329-6024
Sault Ste. Marie: 390 Bay St., 3rd Fl., Sault Ste. Marie ON P6A 1X2 – 705/942-0419; Fax: 705/945-6912
Sioux Lookout: 34 Front St. East, Sioux Lookout ON P8T 1A3 – 807/737-1018; Fax: 807/737-3379
Sudbury: 10 Elm St., 4th Fl., Sudbury ON P3C 5N3 – 705/675-4349; Fax: 705/675-4439
Thunder Bay: 1825 East Arthur St., Thunder Bay ON P7E 5N7 – 807/475-1683; Fax: 807/623-6629
Timmins: 22 Wilcox St., 2nd Fl., Timmins ON P4N 3K6 – 705/267-8018; Fax: 705/360-2013
Toronto: 77 Bloor St. West, 20th Fl., Toronto ON M7A 2R9 – 416/314-7429

#### ONTARIO ANTI-RACISM SECRETARIAT
Asst. Deputy Minister, Ann-Marie Stewart, 416/326-9723, Fax: 416/326-9725
Director, Community Relations Branch, Daniele D'Ignazio, 416/314-6786, Fax: 416/326-9725
Director, Public Sector Support Branch, Selwyn McSween, 416/326-9704, Fax: 416/326-9725

#### POLICY & PLANNING DIVISION
Asst. Deputy Minister, Karen Cohl, 416/314-6046, Fax: 416/314-7599
Director, Corporate Planning Branch, Sharon Cohen, 416/314-4497, Fax: 416/314-7599
Director, Policy & Research Branch, Andrea Maurice, 416/314-7290, Fax: 416/314-7307
Senior Coordinator, Disability Issues Group, Sandra Carpenter, 700 Bay St., 3rd Fl., Toronto ON M5G 1Z6, 416/326-0201, Fax: 416/327-4080, Disability Issues Inquiry/Voice & TDD: 1-800-387-4456; 416/326-0111

#### PROGRAM MANAGEMENT DIVISION
Asst. Deputy Minister, Clive Joakim, 416/314-7495, Fax: 416/314-7518
Director, Client Services Branch, Edna Rigby, 416/314-7732, Fax: 416/314-7743
Director, Program Development Branch, John DeMarco, 416/326-6214, Fax: 416/326-6265
Senior Manager, Ontario Welcome House Network, Nancy Newton, 132 St. Patrick St., Toronto ON M5T 1V1, 416/314-5747, Fax: 416/314-6707
Senior Coordinator, Seniors' Issues Group, Peter Murchison, 76 College St., 6th Fl., Toronto ON M7A 1N3, 416/327-2441, Fax: 416/327-2425, Toll Free: 1-800-267-7329, TDD: 416/327-2488

##### Field Offices
Hamilton: 119 King St. West, 8th Fl., Hamilton ON L8N 3Z9 – 905/521-7517; Fax: 905/521-7613
London: 255 Dufferin St., 6th Fl., London ON N6A 5K6 – 519/679-7146; Fax: 519/679-7032
Ottawa: #612, One Nicholas St., Ottawa ON K1N 7B7 – 613/566-3728; Fax: 613/566-2703
Sault Ste. Marie: 390 Bay St., 3rd Fl., Sault Ste. Marie ON P6A 1X2 – 705/759-8652; Fax: 705/945-6912
Thunder Bay: 1825 East Arthur St., Thunder Bay ON P7E 5N7 – 807/475-1683; Fax: 807/475-1286
Toronto: 35 McCaul St., 4th Fl., Toronto ON M5T 1V7 – 416/314-6793; Fax: 416/314-6646
Windsor: 221 Mill St., Windsor ON N9C 2R1 – 519/256-5486; Fax: 519/256-1637

**RECREATION DIVISION**

Asst. Deputy Minister, Gillian Platt, 416/314-1547, Fax: 416/314-7461

Includes: Recreation Policy, Recreation Programs, Regional Services

**Regional Offices**

Central/East: #400, 10 Rideau St., Ottawa ON K1N 9J1 – 613/787-4000; Fax: 613/787-4020

Central/West: 35 McCaul St., 4th Fl., Toronto ON M5T 1V7 – 416/314-6685; Fax: 416/314-6686

Northern: West Arthur Pl., #302, 1265 East Arthur St., Thunder Bay ON P7E 6E7 – Fax: 807/475-1297, Toll Free: 1-800-465-6861

**Associated Agencies, Boards & Commissions**

•Archives of Ontario: 77 Grenville St., Toronto ON M5S 1B3 – 416/327-1600; Fax: 416/327-1999, Toll Free: 1-800-668-9933

Provincial Archivist, Ian E. Wilson

Deputy Archivist, Melanie Goldhar, 416/327-1577

•Art Gallery of Ontario: 317 Dundas St. West, Toronto ON M5T 1G4 – 416/977-0414; Fax: 416/979-6646; URL: http://www.ago.on.ca/

President, Joseph Rotman

Director, Maxwell Anderson

•Conservation Review Board: 77 Bloor St. West, 2nd Fl., Toronto ON M7A 2R9 – 416/314-7125; Fax: 416/314-7175

Chair, Robert Bowes

Secretary, Nancy Smith

•McMichael Canadian Art Collection: 10365 Islington Ave., Kleinburg ON L0J 1C0 – 905/893-1121; Fax: 905/893-2588; URL: http://www.mcmichael.com/

Chair, Joan Goldfarb

Director/CEO, Barbara A. Tyler

Curator, Megan Bice

•Northern Ontario Library Service: 334 Regent St., Sudbury ON P3C 4E2 – 705/675-6467; Fax: 705/675-6108

Chief Executive Officer, Alan Pepper

•Ontario Advisory Council on Disability Issues: 35 McCaul St., 3rd Fl., Toronto ON M5T 1V7 – 416/314-6650 (Voice & TDD); Fax: 416/314-6658

Chair, Dr. Shirley Van Hoof

Executive Officer, Catherine Chandler, 416/314-6654

•Ontario Advisory Council on Multiculturalism & Citizenship: 35 McCaul St., 3rd Fl., Toronto ON M5T 1V7 – 416/314-6650 (Voice & TDD); Fax: 416/314-6658

Chair, Hanny Hassan

Executive Officer, Catherine Chandler, 416/314-6654

•Ontario Advisory Council on Senior Citizens: 35 McCaul St., 3rd Fl., Toronto ON M5T 1V7 – 416/314-6650 (Voice & TDD); Fax: 416/314-6658

Chair, William A. Hughes

Executive Officer, Catherine Chandler, 416/314-6654

•Ontario Arts Council: 151 Bloor St. West, 5th Fl., Toronto ON M5S 1T6 – 416/961-1660; Fax: 416/969-7447; URL: http://www.ffa.ucalgary.ca/oac/index.html

Chair, Paul Hoffert

Executive Director, Gwenlyn Setterfield

•Ontario Film Development Corporation: North Tower, #300, 175 Bloor St. East, Toronto ON M4W 3R8 – 416/314-6858; Fax: 416/314-6876; URL: http://www.to-ontfilm.com/

Chair, Diane Chabot

Chief Executive Director, Alexandra Raffé

•Ontario Heritage Foundation (OHF): 10 Adelaide St. East, Toronto ON M5C 1J3 – 416/325-5000; Fax: 416/325-5071; Email: natural@heritage.gov.on.ca

Chair, Joanna Bedard

Executive Director, Lesley Lewis

Director, Heritage Programs, Richard Moorhouse

Manager, Heritage Community Services, Brian Rogers

Manager, Marketing & Communications, John Ecker

•Ontario Human Rights Commission: 400 University Ave., 12th Fl., Toronto ON M7A 2R9 – 416/314-4500; Fax: 416/314-4533

Chief Commissioner, Rosemary Brown

Executive Director, Remy Beauregard, 416/314-4539

Director, Communication & Education, Pearl Eliadis, 416/314-4522

•Ontario Science Centre: 770 Don Mills Rd., Toronto ON M3C 1T3 – 416/696-2000; Fax: 416/696-3135; URL: http://www.osc.on.ca/

Chair, Phyllis Yaffe

Director General, Emlyn H. Koster

•Ontario Trillium Foundation: 23 Bedford Rd., 3rd Fl., Toronto ON M5R 2J9 – 416/961-0194; Fax: 416/961-9599

Chair, Ron Crawford

Executive Director, Julie White

•Royal Botanical Gardens: PO Box 399, Hamilton ON L8N 3H8 – 905/527-1158; Fax: 905/529-5040

President, Joseph Pigott

Director, Dr. Garry R. Watson

•Royal Ontario Museum (ROM): 100 Queen's Park Cres., Toronto ON M5S 2C6 – 416/586-5549; Fax: 416/586-5863; URL: http://www.rom.on.ca/

Chair, Ken Harrigan

Director, Dr. John McNeill

•Science North: 100 Ramsey Lake Rd., Sudbury ON P3E 5S9 – 705/522-3701; Fax: 705/522-4954

Chair, Lloyd Douglas Reed

CEO, James Marchbank

•Southern Ontario Library Service: #50, 55 West Beaver Creek, Richmond Hill ON L4B 1K5 – 905/771-1522; Fax: 905/771-1526

CEO, Laurie Levine

•Thunder Bay Ski Jumps Ltd.: 11 Little Norway Rd., Site 3, RR#3, Thunder Bay ON P7C 4V2 – 807/475-4402; Fax: 807/475-8315

Chair, John Hatton

General Manager, Lindsay Durno

•TV Ontario: 2180 Yonge St., 5th Fl., Toronto ON M4S 2C1 – 416/484-2600; Fax: 416/484-4234; URL: http://www.tvo.org/

Chair & CEO, Peter Herrndorf

## Ministry of COMMUNITY & SOCIAL SERVICES (MCSS)

Hepburn Block, 80 Grosvenor St., 6th Fl., Toronto ON M7A 1E9

416/325-5666; Fax: 416/325-5172, 5171; URL: http://www.gov.on.ca/CSS/

Welfare Fraud Hotline: 1-800-394-7867

**ACTS ADMINISTERED**

Charitable Institutions Act

Child & Family Services Act

Day Nurseries Act

Developmental Services Act

District Welfare Administration Boards Act

Family Benefits Act

General Welfare Assistance Act

Homes for Retarded Persons Act

Indian Welfare Services Act

Jewish Family & Child Service of Metro Toronto Act

Ministry of Community & Social Services Act

Soldiers' Aid Commission Act

Vocational Rehabilitation Services Act

**Minister**, Hon. Janet Ecker

Deputy Minister, Vacant

Director, Communications & Marketing, Sara Clodman, 416/325-5203, Fax: 416/325-5191

Director, Legal Services, Andrea Walker, 416/327-4917

**CHILDREN, FAMILY & COMMUNITY SERVICES DIVISION**

Asst. Deputy Minister, Lucille Roch, 416/325-5605, Fax: 416/525-5615

Director, Child Care Branch, Ron Bakker, Hepburn Block, 4th Fl., Toronto ON M7A 1E9, 416/327-4864, Fax: 416/327-0570

Director, Children's Services Branch, Nicole Lafrenière-Davis, 416/325-5325, Fax: 416/325-5349

Senior Manager, Community Services Unit, Brad Archer, 416/327-4958, Fax: 416/327-0570

Manager, Aboriginal Healing & Wellness, Carrie Hayward, 416/326-6907, Fax: 416/326-7934

**CORPORATE SERVICES DIVISION**

Asst. Deputy Minister, Lynn Macdonald, 416/325-5588, Fax: 416/325-5615

Director, Comprehensive Audit & Investigations Branch, Richard Bradley, 2195 Yonge St., 3rd Fl., Toronto ON M4S 2B1, 416/314-6921, Fax: 416/314-3605

Director, Financial & Administrative Services Branch, Jim Tighe, 880 Bay St., 6th Fl., Toronto ON M7A 2B6, 416/326-8202, Fax: 416/326-8192

Director, Financial & Capital Planning Branch, Alfred Carr, 416/325-5105, Fax: 416/325-5125

Director, Human Resources Branch, Donna Marafioti, 2 Bloor St. West, 23rd Fl., Toronto ON M7A 1E9, 416/327-4753, Fax: 416/327-0595

Director, Information Systems, Angela Forest, 5140 Yonge St., 12th Fl., Toronto ON M2N 6L7, 416/327-1111, Fax: 416/327-1848

**PROGRAM MANAGEMENT DIVISION**

Client Information & Support Services: 416/325-5766; 1-800-665-6129

Responsible for the operation of 12 regional offices.

Asst. Deputy Minister, Suzanne Herbert, 416/325-5579, Fax: 416/325-5432

Director, Development Services Branch, Brian Low, 416/325-5826, Fax: 416/325-5554

Director, Management Support Branch, Doug Hayman, 416/325-5446, Fax: 416/325-5500

Manager, Adoption Operational Services, Collette Kent, 2 Bloor St. West, 24th Fl., Toronto ON M7A 1E9, 416/327-4930

Manager, Office of Child & Family Service Advocacy, Judy Finlay, 416/325-5669, Fax: 416/325-5681

**SOCIAL ASSISTANCE & EMPLOYMENT OPPORTUNITIES DIVISION**

Asst. Deputy Minister, Kevin Costante, 416/325-5570, Fax: 416/325-5424

Director, Automating Social Assistance Project, Janet Faas, 416/327-4975, Fax: 416/327-1404

Director, Employment Programs Branch, Cliodhna McMullin, 416/326-8171, Fax: 416/326-9777

Director, Social Assistance Programs Branch, Mary Kardos-Burton, 416/325-5260, Fax: 416/325-5266

**Associated Agencies, Boards & Commissions**

•Child & Family Services Review Board: 2 Bloor St. West, 24th Fl., Toronto ON M7A 1E9 – 416/327-4671

Chair, Dr. Herbert Sohn

•Custody Review Board: 2 Bloor St. West, 24th Fl., Toronto ON M7A 1E9 – 416/327-4673; Fax: 416/327-0558

Chair, Keith Quigg

•Social Assistance Review Board (SARB): 1075 Bay St., 7th Fl., Toronto ON M5S 2B1 – 416/326-5104; Fax: 416/326-5135, Toll Free: 1-800-387-5655

Chair, Laura Bradbury

•Soldiers Aid Commission: 2 Bloor St. West, 24th Fl., Toronto ON M7A 1E9 – 416/327-4674

Chair, Dr. T. Divinec

## Ministry of CONSUMER & COMMERCIAL RELATIONS (MCCR)

250 Yonge St., Toronto ON M5B 2N5
416/326-8555; URL: http://www.ccr.gov.on.ca/mccr/welcome.htm
Toll Free: 1-800-268-1142
Communications: 416/326-8525; Fax: 416/326-8543

#### ACTS ADMINISTERED

Amusement Devices Act
Apportionment Act
Assignments & Preferences Act
Athletic Control Act
Bailiffs Act
Boilers & Pressure Vessels Act
Boundaries Act
Bread Sales Act
Business Corporations Act
Business Information Statute Law Amendment Act
Business Names Act
Business Practices Act
Cemeteries Act
Certification of Titles Act
Change of Name Act
Collection Agencies Act
Condominium Act
Consumer Protection Act
Consumer Protection Bureau Act
Consumer Reporting Act
Corporations Act
Corporations Information Act
Debt Collectors Act
Discriminatory Business Practices Act
Elevating Devices Act
Energy Act
Extra-Provincial Corporations Act
Factors Act
Funeral Directors & Establishments Act
Gasoline Handling Act
Land Registration Reform Act
Land Titles Act
Limited Partnerships Act
Liquor Control Act
Liquor Licence Act
Marriage Act
Ministry of Consumer & Commercial Relations Act
Motor Vehicle Dealers Act
Motor Vehicle Repair Act
Ontario New Home Warranties Plan Act
Operating Engineers Act
Paperback & Periodical Distributors Act
Partnerships Act
Partnerships Registration Act
Personal Property Security Act
Prearranged Funeral Services Act
Prepaid Services Act
Racing Commission Act
Real Estate & Business Brokers Act
Registry Act
Repair & Storage Liens Act
Residential Complex Sales Representation Act
Theatres Act
Travel Industry Act
Upholstered & Stuffed Articles Act
Vital Statistics Act
Wine Content Act
and
Criminal Code (Canada), s. 190 (administration dealing with lottery licences issued to charitable & religious organizations to raise money for charitable or religious purposes)

**Minister**, Hon. David H. Tsubouchi, 416/326-8500, Fax: 416/326-8520
Deputy Minister, Stien K. Lal, 416/326-8480, Fax: 416/326-8409
Director, Legal Services, Teri Kirk, 416/326-8448, Fax: 416/314-5179

#### GENERAL INQUIRY UNIT

416/326-8555; Fax: 416/326-8543
Toll Free: 1-800-268-1142
TTY/TTD: 416/326-8566
Manager, B. Darby

##### Entertainment Standards

1075 Millwood Rd., Toronto ON M4G 1X6
416/314-3626; Fax: 416/314-3632
Senior Manager & Director, Theatres Act, David Scriven
Officer, Policy & Program Development, Molly Acton

##### Office of the Athletic Commissioner

1075 Millwood Rd., Toronto ON M4G 1X6
416/314-3630; Fax: 416/314-3623
Athletics Commissioner, Ken Hzyzshi

#### BUSINESS DIVISION

416/326-8575; Fax: 416/325-6192
Asst. Deputy Minister, Art Daniels

##### Business Affairs Branch

416/326-8835; Fax: 416/326-8859
Director, Angela Longo
Registrar, Bailiffs, Collection Agencies, Reports, Paperbacks & Periodicals, Michael Pepper, 416/326-8805
Registrar, Cemeteries Regulation Branch, Stewart Smith, 416/326-8394
Registrar, Motor Vehicle Dealers, Stewart Smith, 416/326-8670
Registrar, Real Estate & Business Brokers, Gordon Randall, 416/326-8679
Registrar, Travel Industry, R. McKenna, 416/326-8741

##### Companies Branch

393 University Ave., 2nd Fl., Toronto ON M7A 2H6
416/596-3725; Fax: 416/596-0438
Director, Carol Kirsh, 416/596-3729
Deputy Director, Bev Hawton, 416/314-5150
Manager, Compliance, Ron Hartlen, 416/314-0845
Manager, Corporate Search & BNLP Services, S.K. Lambe, 416/314-0097
Manager, Corporate Services, Robert McLeod, 416/314-0084
Manager, Document Processing, Rita Maio, 416/314-4809

##### Consumer Affairs Branch

416/326-8600; Fax: 416/326-8665
Director, Brent Gibbs
Supervisor, Compliance Section, Marilyn Gurevsky, 416/326-8639
Acting Manager, Consumer Services Bureau, Vishnu Kangalee, 416/326-8641
Manager, Forensic Accountant, Mike Mouncey, 416/326-8638
Manager, Investigation Section, Brenda Cowley, 416/326-8598
Manager, Resources & Administration, Deborah McCrae, 416/326-8640

#### REGISTRATION DIVISION

393 University Ave., 4th Fl., Toronto ON M7A 2H6
416/596-3600; Fax: 416/596-3802
Asst. Deputy Minister, Despina Georges
Director, Personal Property Security Registration, Katharine Smith, 416/596-3771
Director, Real Property Registration, Tony Sharpe, 416/596-3643

##### Registrar General Branch

189 Red River Rd., PO Box 4600, Thunder Bay ON P7B 6L8
807/343-7414; Fax: 807/343-7411
Toll Free: 1-800-461-2156
Fees are: Birth Certificate, $11; Marriage Certificate, $11; Death Certificate, $11; Certified Copies, $22; Genealogical Extracts, $22.
Deputy Registrar General, Ted Kelly

##### Registrations against Personal Property

Security agreements involving personal property - such as chattel mortgages, conditional sales, debentures - are governed by the *Personal Property Security Act, 1989.* Registrations under the *Personal Property Security Act, 1989* may be submitted by mail to the central office or in person at any branch office of the personal property security registration system. Registration periods are variable. Registrations made under the *Repair & Storage Liens Act, 1989* are also registered in the personal property registration system & may be submitted by mail to the central office or in person to a branch registry office. A central registry has been established for searches.

The *Personal Property Security Act* provides that where collateral is or includes fixtures or goods that may become fixtures, or crops, or oil, gas or other minerals to be extracted, or timber to be cut, a Notice of Security interest may be registered in the proper land registry office.

#### TECHNICAL STANDARDS DIVISION

West Tower, 3300 Bloor St. West, 4th Fl., Toronto ON M8X 2X4
Fax: 416/325-2000
Asst. Deputy Minister, John Walter, 416/325-0104
Director, Engineering & Standards Branch, Michael Philip, 416/325-9605
Director, Inspection & Enforcement, E. Stephan, 416/235-0125
Manager, Licensing & Administration Branch, Susan Allain, 416/325-2490

##### Associated Agencies, Boards & Commissions

•Commercial Registration Appeal Tribunal: 1 St. Clair Ave. West, 12th Fl., Toronto ON M4V 1K6 – 416/965-7798; Fax: 416/965-0429
Chair, Judith A. Killoran, Q.C.
Registrar, F. Blais
•Gaming Control Commission: 1099 Bay St., 2nd Fl., Toronto ON M5S 2B3 – 416/326-8880; Fax: 416/326-8711
Chair, Clare Lewis
Executive Director, Duncan Brown
Director, Investigations, Gary Wood, 416/326-8355
Director, Legal, Jerry Cooper, 416/326-8935
Director, Operations, Linda Monzon, 416/326-8703
Counsel, Casino Operations, Jacquie Castel, 416/325-0427
Senior Manager, Native Liaison, Cy Wood, 416/326-8594
•Liquor Control Board of Ontario: 55 Lake Shore Blvd. East, Toronto ON M7A 2H6 – 416/864-2570; Fax: 416/864-2476; URL: http://www.lcbo.com/
Chair, Andrew S. Brandt
Executive Vice-President, Larry Gee
•Liquor Licence Board of Ontario: 55 Lake Shore Blvd. East, Toronto ON M5E 1A4 – Fax: 416/326-0308
Chair & CEO, Andromache Karakatsanis, 416/326-0375
Executive Director, B. Tocher, 416/326-0381
Director, Inspection, Tom Bolton, 416/326-0330
Director, Licensing, Katherine Donnelly, 416/326-0350
•Ontario Film Review Board: 1075 Millwood Rd., Toronto ON M4G 1X6 – 416/314-3626
Chair, Leslie Ann Adams
Office Manager, Linda Sullivan
•Ontario New Home Warranty Program: North East Tower, 6th Fl., 5160 Yonge St., Toronto ON M2N 6L9 – 416/229-9200; Fax: 416/229-3800

•Ontario Racing Commission: #1400, 180 Dundas St. West, Toronto ON M5G 1Z8 – 416/327-0520; Fax: 416/325-3478
Chair, Stan Sandinsky
Director, Jean Major

## Ministry of ECONOMIC DEVELOPMENT, TRADE & TOURISM (MEDTT)

Hearst Block, 900 Bay St., Toronto ON M7A 2E1
416/325-6666; Fax: 416/325-6688; URL: http://www.gov.on.ca

#### ACTS ADMINISTERED

Acts respecting Development Corporations in Ontario
Historical Parks Act
Metropolitan Toronto Convention Centre Corporation Act
Ministry of Industry & Trade Act
Niagara Parks Act
Ontario International Corporation Act
Ontario Lottery Corporation Act
Ontario Place Corporation Act
Ontario Research Foundation Act
Ottawa Congress Centre Act
St. Clair Parkway Commission Act
St. Lawrence Parks Commission Act
Sheridan Park Corporation Act
Technology Centres Act
Tourism Act
**Minister**, Hon. Al Palladini, 416/325-6900, Fax: 416/325-6918
Deputy Minister, Patrick Draper, 416/325-6927, Fax: 416/325-6999
Director, Communications Branch, George Hutchinson, 416/325-8521, Fax: 416/325-6688
Director, Legal Services Branch, Ingrid Peters, 416/326-1001, Fax: 416/326-1021

#### BUSINESS DEVELOPMENT & TOURISM DIVISION

Asst. Deputy Minister, Jean Lam, 416/325-6961
General Manager, Business Development Branch, Peter Friedman, 416/325-6485
Director, Investment, Saad Rafi, 416/325-6758
Director, Tourism, Ruth Cornish, 416/314-7105
Executive Director, Niagara Gateway Project, Roberta Veley

#### CORPORATE RESOURCES & AGENCY RELATIONS DIVISION

416/325-6997; Fax: 416/325-6999
Asst. Deputy Minister, Brian K. Wood, 416/325-6929
Manager, Agency Relations Branch, Carol Hancock
Director, Audit Services Branch, Gordon H. Aue, 416/326-1702, Fax: 416/326-1712
Director, Finance & Administration Branch, Valerie Wilson, 416/325-6420, Fax: 416/325-6449
Director, Human Resources Branch, Tom Clark, 416/325-6605, Fax: 416/325-6715
Director, Information & Technology Systems Branch, Uma Ganesan, 416/325-6590, Fax: 416/325-6635

#### MARKETING & TRADE DIVISION

Asst. Deputy Minister, Grahame Richards
Director, International Relations & Chief of Protocol, Ernesto Feu, 416/325-8545, Fax: 416/325-8550
Director, Market Ontario Branch, Geoff Hare, 416/325-6758

#### STRATEGIC ANALYSIS, SECTORS & TECHNOLOGY DIVISION

Asst. Deputy Minister, Peter Sadlier-Brown, 416/325-6962, Fax: 416/325-6985
Acting Director, Capital Goods & Technology Sectors Branch, Phil Baker, 416/326-9621
Director, Economic Development, Coordination & Analysis Branch, Philip D. Howell, 416/325-6806
Director, Manufacturing Sectors Branch, Penny Dutton, 416/325-6849
Director, Service Sectors Branch, Ann Whalen, 416/325-6751, Fax: 416/325-6757
Director, Technology & Training Development Branch, Dr. Chris Riddle, 416/314-8205, Fax: 416/314-8224
Director, Trade Policy Branch, Katherine McGuire, 416/325-6930, Fax: 416/325-6949

#### Regional Offices

Central - Barrie: 449 Dunlop St. West, Barrie ON L4N 1C3 – 705/725-7612; Fax: 705/725-7296
Central - Hamilton: Bank of Montreal Tower, #200, 1 James St. North, Hamilton ON L8R 2K3 – 905/521-7783; Fax: 905/521-7398
Central - Huntsville: 42 King William St., Huntsville ON P0A 1K0 – 705/789-4448; Fax: 705/789-9533
Central - Peel: #370, 4 Robert Speck Pkwy., Mississauga ON L4Z 1S1 – 905/279-7771; Fax: 905/279-7193
Central - St. Catharines: 301 St. Paul St., 9th Fl., St. Catharines ON L2R 7R4 – 416/704-3940; Fax: 416/704-3955
Central - Toronto: #520, 5 Park Home Ave., North York ON M2N 6L4 – 416/325-1240; Fax: 416/325-1262
Eastern - Kingston: #202, 1055 Princess St., Kingston ON K7L 5T3 – 613/545-4444; Fax: 613/545-4466, Toll Free: 1-800-267-7848
Eastern - Ottawa: #612, 1 Nicholas St., Ottawa ON K1N 7B7 – 613/241-3841; Fax: 613/241-2545, Toll Free: 1-800-267-6592
Eastern - Peterborough: #190, 380 Armour Rd., Peterborough ON K9H 7L7 – 705/742-1468; Fax: 705/748-4306
Northern - Dryden: Ontario Government Bldg., 479 Government Rd., PO Box 3000, Dryden ON P8N 3B3 – 807/223-7601; Fax: 807/223-6942, Toll Free: 1-800-465-7208
Northern - Kenora: 227 - 2 St. South, 3rd Fl., Kenora ON P9N 1G1 – 807/468-2450; Fax: 807/468-2788, Toll Free: 1-800-465-1108
Northern - North Bay: 147 McIntyre St., 1st Fl., North Bay ON P1B 2Y5 – 705/494-4163; Fax: 705/474-4946
Northern - Sault Ste. Marie: Egan Tower, 747 Queen St. East., Sault Ste. Marie ON P6A 2A8 – 705/942-3751; Fax: 705/942-8043, Toll Free: 1-800-461-2409
Northern - Sudbury: 159 Cedar St., 6th Fl., Sudbury ON P3E 6A5 – 705/670-7034; Fax: 705/670-7063
Northern - Thunder Bay: #332, 435 South James St., Thunder Bay ON P7E 6S7 – 807/475-1450; Fax: 807/475-1765, Toll Free: 1-800-561-3399
Northern - Timmins: Ontario Government Office, Hwy. 101 East, PO Box 3065, South Porcupine ON P0N 1H0 – 705/235-1420; Fax: 705/235-1421
Southwestern - Hanover: 399 - 18 Ave., Hanover ON N4N 3S5 – 519/364-1626; Fax: 519/364-2500
Southwestern - Kitchener: #906, 30 Duke St. West, Kitchener ON N2H 3W5 – 519/744-6391; Fax: 519/571-6104, Toll Free: 1-800-265-2428
Southwestern - London: #607, 195 Dufferin Ave., London ON N6A 1K7 – 519/433-8105; Fax: 519/661-6625, Toll Free: 1-800-265-4743
Southwestern - Windsor: Ontario Government Bldg., #627, 250 Windsor Ave., Windsor ON N9A 6V9 – 519/252-3475; Fax: 519/973-1378, Toll Free: 1-800-265-1345

#### Associated Agencies, Boards & Commissions

•Huronia Historical Advisory Council: PO Box 160, Midland ON L4R 4K8 – 705/526-7838; Fax: 705/526-9193
•Innovation Ontario Corporation: 56 Wellesley St. West, 7th Fl., Toronto ON M7A 2E7 – 416/326-1164; Fax: 416/326-1109
President & Managing Director, Vacant
•Metro Toronto Convention Centre Corporation: 255 Front St. West, Toronto ON M5V 2W6 – 416/585-8000; Fax: 416/585-8224
•Niagara Parks Commission (NPC): 7400 Portage Rd. South, PO Box 150, Niagara Falls ON L2E 6T2 – 905/356-2241; Fax: 905/354-6041
Chair, Gary F. Burroughs
General Manager, Robert W. Tytaneck
•Old Fort William Advisory Committee: Vickers Heights Post Office, Thunder Bay ON P0T 2Z0 – 807/577-8461; Fax: 807/473-2327
•Ontario Development Corporation: 56 Wellesley St. West, 6th Fl., Toronto ON M7A 2E7 – 416/326-1070; Fax: 416/326-1073
•Ontario Lottery Corporation (OLC): #800, 70 Foster Dr., Sault Ste. Marie ON P6A 6V2 – 705/946-6400; Fax: 705/946-6846
President, Garth Manness
•Ontario Place Corporation: 955 Lake Shore Blvd. West, Toronto ON M6K 3B9 – 416/314-9817; Fax: 416/314-9993; URL: http://www.inforamp.net/op/ – General Information: 416/314-9900
General Manager, Maxwell Beck
•Ottawa Congress Centre: 55 Colonel By Dr., Ottawa ON K1N 9J2 – 613/787-5707; Fax: 613/563-7646
•St. Clair Parkway Commission: PO Box 700, Corunna ON N0N 1G0 – 519/862-2291; Fax: 519/862-2294
Chair, Jon Shimizu
General Manager, David Cram
•St. Lawrence Parks Commission: RR#1, Morrisburg ON K0C 1X0 – 613/543-3704; Fax: 613/543-2847
Chair, Gary Clarke
General Manager, Frank G. Shaw

## Ministry of EDUCATION & TRAINING

Mowat Block, 900 Bay St., Toronto ON M7A 1L2
416/325-2929; Fax: 416/325-2934;
Email: public.inquiries@edu.gov.on.ca; URL: http://www.edu.gov.on.ca
Toll Free: 1-800-387-5514
Youth Employment Hotline: 1-800-387-0777
Training Hotline: 1-800-387-5656

#### ACTS ADMINISTERED

Colleges Collective Bargaining Act
Degree Granting Act
Development Charges Act, Part III
Education Act
Essex County French-language Secondary School Act
Lake Superior Board of Education Act
Lambton County Board of Education & Training Dispute Resolution Act
Metropolitan Separate School Board Act
Ministry of Colleges & Universities Act
Municipal & School Board Payments Adjustment Act
Ontario Institute for Studies in Education Act
Ontario School Trustees' Council Act
Ontario Training & Adjustment Board Act
Ottawa-Carleton French Language School Board Transferred Employees Act
Private Vocational Schools Act
Provincial Schools Negotiations Act
School Boards & Teachers Collective Negotiations Act
School Trust Conveyances Act
Teachers Pension Act
Teaching Profession Act
Trades Qualification & Apprenticeship Act
University Foundations Act
**Minister**, Hon. David Johnson, 416/325-2600, Fax: 416/325-2608

Deputy Minister, Veronica Lacey, 416/325-2180, Fax: 416/327-9063
Director, Communications, Suzanna Birchwood, 416/325-2947

#### ELEMENTARY/SECONDARY OPERATIONS & FRENCH-LANGUAGE EDUCATION

Asst. Deputy Minister, Mariette Carrier-Fraser, 416/325-2132, Fax: 416/327-1182
Director, Capital & Operating Grants Administration, Drew Nameth, 416/325-4030
Director, French-Language Education Policy & Programs, Richard Gauthier, 416/325-2127
Director, Independent Learning Centre, Russ Garrett, 416/325-4243
Director, Operations & Field Services, Teresa Gonzalez, 416/325-2470
Director, Provincial Schools Branch, Ruth Taber, 416/325-2507

##### District Offices

Barrie: 20 Rose St., 2nd Fl., Barrie ON L4M 2T2 – 705/725-7625, Toll Free: 1-800-470-1147, Manager, Michel Robineau
Greater Toronto Area (GTA): #360, 700 Lawrence Ave. West, 3rd Fl., Toronto ON M6A 1B4 – 416/256-2903; Fax: 416/256-2904, Acting Manager, Richard Adams
Kingston: 1580 Merivale Rd., 4th Fl., Nepean ON K2G 4B5 – 613/225-9210; Fax: 613/225-2881, Acting Manager, Maurice Poirier
Kitchener-Waterloo: 30 Duke St., 9th Fl., Kitchener ON N2H 3W5 – 519/571-6134; Fax: 519/571-6148, Toll Free: 1-800-909-6550, Manager, Norah Franklin
London: 759 Hyde Park Rd., London ON N6H 3S6 – 519/472-1440; Fax: 519/472-6178, Manager, Terry Boucher
Metro Toronto: Mowat Block, 900 Bay St., 5th Fl., Toronto ON M7A 1L2 – 416/314-8679; Fax: 416/325-6793, Manager, Denese Belchetz
North Bay/Sudbury: 447 McKeown Ave., 2nd Fl., PO Box 3020, North Bay ON P1B 8K7 – 705/474-7210; Fax: 705/494-4075, Manager, Lise Presseault
Ottawa: 1580 Merivale Rd., 4th Fl., Nepean ON K2G 4B5 – 613/225-9210; Fax: 613/225-2881, Manager, Maurice Poirier
Thunder Bay: 435 James St. South, PO Box 5000, Thunder Bay ON P7C 5G6 – 807/475-1571; Fax: 807/475-1571, Manager, Jackie Dojack

#### ELEMENTARY/SECONDARY POLICY DIVISION

416/325-2132; Fax: 416/325-1182
Acting Asst. Deputy Minister, Mariette Carrier-Fraser
Acting Director, Curriculum, Learning, & Teaching Branch, Pauline Laing, 416/325-4138
Director, Education Finance Branch, Peter Wright, 416/325-2828
Director, Policy Branch, Marjorie Mercer, 416/325-2659
Director, Secondary School Project, A. Gitterman, 416/325-2538
Acting Director, School Governance Branch, Brian Fleming, 416/327-9057
Manager, Differentiated Staffing Project, Julie Lindhout, 416/325-2390

#### ORGANIZATION DEVELOPMENT & SERVICES DIVISION

416/325-2772; Fax: 416/325-2778
Asst. Deputy Minister, Garth Jackson, 416/325-2773
Director, Audit, Compliance, & Evaluation & Director, Information Technology Systems, Patrick Madden, 416/325-2140
Director, Finance & Administration Services, Doug Holder, 416/327-9091
Director, Human Resources Planning & Services, Maureen Edgar, 416/327-9003
Director, Legal Services Unit, Alan Wolfish, 416/325-2399
Manager, Corporate Planning Unit, Carol Lawson, 416/325-1818
Project Director, Technology Incentive Partnership Program Project, Bob Kennedy, 416/326-5665

#### POSTSECONDARY EDUCATION DIVISION

Asst. Deputy Minister, David Trick, 416/325-2116, Fax: 416/326-3256
Director, Colleges Branch, Catriona King, 416/325-1815
Director, Postsecondary Education Policy Branch, Vacant
Director, Student Support Branch, Helmut Zisser, 416/325-4181
Director, Universities Branch, B. James Mackay, 416/325-1952

#### TRAINING DIVISION

Asst. Deputy Minister, Joan Andrew, 416/325-2989, Fax: 416/325-2995
Manager, Adult Education Project, Kay Eastham, 416/325-2577
Director, Apprenticeship Reform Project, Leah Myers, 416/314-5166
Director, Labour Market Policy, Planning, & Research, Bruce Baldwin, 416/967-8349
Director, Workplace Preparation, Sante Mauti, 416/326-5883
Director, Workplace Support Services, Judith Robertson, 416/326-5608

##### Associated Agencies, Boards & Commissions

•College Relations Commission: #400, 111 Avenue Rd., Toronto ON M5R 3J8 – 416/922-7679; Fax: 416/325-4134
CEO, Fred Long
•Education Relations Commission: #400, 111 Avenue Rd., Toronto ON M5R 3J8 – 416/922-7679; Fax: 416/325-4134
Chair, Paula Knopf
•Languages of Instruction Commission of Ontario: 56 Wellesley St. West, 11th Fl., Toronto ON M7A 2B7 – 416/314-3500; Fax: 416/314-3502
Chair, Keith Reilly
•Ontario Council of Regents for Colleges of Applied Arts & Technology: 790 Bay St., 10th Fl., Toronto ON M5G 1N8 – 416/325-1780; Fax: 416/325-1792
Chair, H. Noble
•Ontario Parent Council: 56 Wellesley St. West, 16th Fl., Toronto ON M7A 2B7 – 416/314-0426; Fax: 416/314-0425, Toll Free: 1-800-361-6483
Chair, William Robson
Executive Secretary, Monique Guibert
Bilingual Secretary, Pascale Demers
•Ontario Teachers' Pension Plan Board: #400, 5650 Yonge St., Toronto ON M2M 4H5 – 416/226-2700; Fax: 416/730-5349
Chair, C.E. Medland

## ELECTIONS ONTARIO

51 Rolark Dr., Scarborough ON M1R 3B1
416/321-3000; Fax: 416/321-6853
Toll Free: 1-800-668-2727

#### ACTS ADMINISTERED

Election Act
**Chief Election Officer**, W.R. Bailie
Acting Asst. Chief Election Officer, Loren A. Wells
Manager, Operations Section, Alison Carpenter

## Ministry of ENVIRONMENT & ENERGY (MOEE)

135 St. Clair Ave. West, Toronto ON M4V 1P5
416/325-4000 (Public Information Centre); Fax: 416/323-4564; URL: http://www.ene.gov.on.ca/
Toll Free: 1-800-565-4923

#### ACTS ADMINISTERED

Consolidated Hearings Act
Energy Act
Energy Efficiency Act
Environment Statute Law Amendment Act
Environmental Assessment Act
Environmental Protection Act
Ministry of Energy Act
Ministry of the Environment Act
Ontario Energy Board Act
Ontario Energy Corporation Act
Ontario Waste Management Corporation Act
Ontario Water Resources Act
Pesticides Act
Power Corporation Act
Waste Management Act
**Minister, Energy**, Hon. Jim Wilson
**Minister, Environment**, Hon. Norman W. Sterling
Deputy Minister, Linda Stevens, 416/323-4271, Fax: 416/323-4513

#### CONSERVATION & PREVENTION DIVISION

416/323-4320; Fax: 416/323-4481
Asst. Deputy Minister, Judith Wright, 416/323-4319
Director, Environmental Assessment Branch, Chuck Pautler, 250 Davisville Ave., 5th Fl., Toronto ON M4S 1H2, 416/440-3480, Fax: 416/440-3771
Director, Environmental Planning & Analysis Branch, Brian Nixon, 250 Davisville Ave., 3rd Fl., Toronto ON M4S 1H2, 416/440-3772, Fax: 416/440-7039
Director, Industry Conservation Branch, Linda Ploeger, 416/327-1457
Director, Waste Reduction Branch, Bob Breeze, 40 St. Clair Ave. West, 7th Fl., Toronto ON M4V 1M2, 416/325-4440

##### Green Industry Office

416/323-4578; Fax: 416/323-4436
Manager, Jacquie Maund, 416/323-4688
Senior Business Development Advisor, Brad Defoe, 416/323-4688
Senior Business Development Officers: Nora Gurland, 416/323-4452; Rebecca McKenzie, 416/323-4219; Deborah McKeown, 416/323-4657

#### CORPORATE MANAGEMENT DIVISION

416/323-4382; Fax: 416/323-4645
Asst. Deputy Minister, André Castel, 416/323-4356
Director, Finance & Administration Branch, Margaret LaPierre, 416/314-4095
Director, Fiscal Planning & Information Management Branch, Carl Griffith, 416/323-4558, Fax: 416/323-4322, General Inquiry: 416/323-4554
Director, Human Resources Branch, MaryEtta Cheney, 416/314-9305, Fax: 416/314-9313

#### ENVIRONMENTAL SCIENCES & STANDARDS DIVISION

416/323-4512; Fax: 416/323-4396
Acting Asst. Deputy Minister, Ivy Wile, 416/323-4384
Director, Environmental Bill of Rights Office, Helle Tosine, 416/314-3920, Fax: 416/323-5031
Director, Environmental Monitoring & Reporting Branch, Ed Piché, 416/235-6160, Fax: 416/235-6235
Director, Laboratory Services Branch, Dr. Bern Schnyder, 416/235-5747, Fax: 416/235-5744
Director, Program Development & Support Branch, Helle Tosine, 416/314-3920, Fax: 416/314-4128
Director, Science & Technology Branch, Helle Tosine, 416/323-5222, Fax: 416/323-5031

Director, Standards Development Branch, Ivy Wile, 416/323-5096, Fax: 416/323-5166

#### OPERATIONS DIVISION

416/323-4380; Fax: 416/323-4615; 4501

Asst. Deputy Minister, Sheila Willis, 416/323-4354

Director, Approvals Branch, Wilfred Ng, 250 Davisville Ave., Toronto ON M4S 1H2, 416/440-3546, Fax: 416/440-6973

Director, Investigations & Enforcement Branch, Patricia Hollett, 250 Davisville Ave., 5th Fl., Toronto ON M4S 1H2, 416/440-3510, Fax: 416/440-3539

Head, Spills Action Centre, Gary Zikovitz, 5775 Yonge St., 10th Fl., Toronto ON M2M 4S1, 416/325-3000, Fax: 416/325-3011, Toll Free: 1-800-268-6060

##### Regional Offices

Central Region: Toronto Regional & Metro Toronto District Offices, 5775 Yonge St., 8th Fl., North York ON M2M 4J1 – 416/326-6700; Fax: 416/325-6345, Director, David Crump, 416/326-1825

Eastern Region: Kingston Regional & District Office, 133 Dalton Ave., Kingston ON K7K 6C2 – 613/549-4000; Fax: 613/548-6908, Director, Brian Ward

Northern Region: Thunder Bay Regional & District Office, #331, 435 James St. South, Thunder Bay ON P7E 6E3 – 807/475-1205; Fax: 807/475-1754, Director, Wayne Scott, 807/475-1714

Southwestern Region: London Regional Office, 985 Adelaide St. South, London ON N6E 1V3 – 519/661-2200; Fax: 519/661-1742, Director, Jim Janse, 519/661-2270

West Central Region: Hamilton Regional & District Office, 119 King St. West, 12th Fl., PO Box 2112, Hamilton ON L8N 3Z9 – 905/521-7640; Fax: 905/521-7820, Director, Hardy Wong, 905/521-7652

#### POLICY DIVISION

416/323-4255; Fax: 416/323-4410

Asst. Deputy Minister, Les Horswill, 416/323-4352

Director, Economic Services Branch, Rick Jennings, 416/327-1400, Fax: 416/327-1511

Director, Energy Conservation & Liaison, Tony Rockingham, 416/323-5626, Fax: 416/323-5636

Executive Coordinator, Intergovernmental Relations Office, Ken J. Richards, 416/323-4652, Fax: 416/323-4442

Manager, Aboriginal Affairs Office, Daniel Cayen, 416/323-4260, Fax: 416/323-4442

##### Associated Agencies, Boards & Commissions

•Environmental Appeal Board: #502, 112 St. Clair Ave. West, Toronto ON M4V 1N3 – 416/314-3300; Fax: 416/314-3299

Chair, John Swaigen

•Environmental Assessment Board: #1201, 2300 Yonge St., PO Box 2382, Toronto ON M4P 1E4 – 416/484-7800

Chair, Grace Patterson, 416/323-4809

•Ontario Clean Water Agency (OCWA): #700, 20 Bay St., Toronto ON M5J 2N8 – 416/314-5600; Fax: 416/314-8300

CEO & President, Jeff Marshall, 416/314-0757

Director, International Projects, Nick Markettos

•Ontario Energy Board: 2300 Yonge St., 26th Fl., Toronto ON M4P 1E4 – 416/481-1967; Fax: 416/440-7656

Chair, Marie C. Rounding, 416/440-7601

•Ontario Energy Corporation (OEC): South Tower, #905, 175 Bloor St. East, Toronto ON M4W 3R8 – 416/926-4200; Fax: 416/926-9641

Chair, President & CEO, Vacant

•Ontario Hydro

Listed alphabetically in detail, this section.

•Ontario Pesticides Advisory Committee: 40 St. Clair Ave. West, 4th Fl., Toronto ON M4V 1M2 – 416/314-9230; Fax: 416/314-9237

Chair, Dr. C.M. Switzer, 416/314-9233

## ENVIRONMENTAL COMMISSIONER OF ONTARIO (ECO)

#605, 1075 Bay St., Toronto ON M5S 2B1

416/325-3377; Fax: 416/325-3370; Email: webmaster@gov.on.ca

Toll Free: 1-800-701-6454

**Commissioner**, Eva Ligeti

Coordinator, Communications & Public Affairs, Adrienne Jackson

## Ministry of FINANCE

Frost Bldg. South, 7 Queen's Park Cres., Toronto ON M7A 1Y7

416/325-0333 (Communications); Fax: 416/325-0339; URL: http://www.gov.ca/FIN/hmpage.html

Oshawa Office: 33 King St. West, PO Box 627, Oshawa ON L1H 8H5

905/433-6096 (Customer Service Centre), Fax: 905/433-6777

Toll Free: 1-800-263-7965

Ligne sans frais: 1-800-668-5821

TTY: 1-800-263-7776

#### ACTS ADMINISTERED

Assessment Act
Audit Act
Canadian Insurance Exchange Act
Central Trust Company Act
Commercial Concentration Tax Act
Commodity Futures Act
Compulsory Automobile Insurance Act
Cooperative Corporations Act
Corporations Tax Act
Credit Unions & Caisses Populaires Act
Crown Trust Company Act
Deposits Regulation Act
Employee Share Ownership Plan Act
Employer Health Tax Act
Financial Administration Act
Fuel Tax Act
Gasoline Tax Act
Guarantee Companies Securities Act
Income Tax Act
Insurance Act
Investment Contracts Act
Labour Sponsored Venture Capital Corporations Act
Land Transfer Tax Act
Loan & Trust Corporations Act
Marine Insurance Act
Mining Tax Act
Ministry of Revenue Act
Ministry of Treasury & Economics Act
Mortgage Brokers Act
Motor Vehicle Accident Claims Act
Ontario Credit Union League Limited Act
Ontario Deposit Insurance Corporation Act
Ontario Economic Council Act
Ontario Guaranteed Annual Income Act
Ontario Home Ownership Savings Plan Act
Ontario Loan Act
Ontario Municipal Improvement Corporation Act
Ontario Pensioners Property Tax Assistance Act
Pension Benefits Act
Prepaid Hospital & Medical Services Act
Province of Ontario Savings Office Act
Provincial Land Tax Act
Race Tracks Tax Act
Registered Insurance Brokers Act
Retail Sales Tax Act
Securities Act
Small Business Development Corporations Act
Social Contract Act
Statistics Act
Succession Duty Act
Succession Duty Supplementary Provisions Act
Supply Act
Tobacco Tax Act
Toronto Futures Exchange Act
Toronto Stock Exchange Act
Treasury Board Act

**Minister**, Hon. Ernie Eves

Minister without Portfolio, Hon. Rob Sampson, 416/325-0413

Parliamentary Asst., Isabel Bassett, 416/326-9092, Fax: 416/325-1584

Parliamentary Asst., Bill Grimmett, 416/325-0408, Fax: 416/325-1584

Deputy Minister, Finance, Michael L. Gourley, 416/325-1590, Fax: 416/325-1595

Deputy Minister, Revenue & Financial Institutions, Dina Palozzi, 416/325-3300, Fax: 416/325-3295

Asst. Deputy Minister, Office of the Treasury, Tony Salerno, 416/325-8001, Fax: 416/325-8005

Director, Communications & Corporate Affairs Branch, Don Black, 416/325-0333, Fax: 416/325-0339

Director, Audit Services Branch, Larry Lindberg, 905/433-6479, Fax: 905/433-5222 (Oshawa), 416/325-8323, Fax: 416/325-5096 (Toronto)

Acting Director, Financial Services Policy Branch, Roman Zydownyk, 250 Yonge St., 30th Fl., Toronto ON M5B 2N7, 416/326-0936, Fax: 416/327-0941

Director, Office of Legal Services, G. Stoodley, 416/325-1450, Fax: 416/325-1460

#### CORPORATE SERVICES DIVISION

Asst. Deputy Minister, Vacant, 905/433-6994, Fax: 905/433-6688

Director, Administration & Facilities Branch, Jim Ireland, 905/433-5905

Director, Corporate Planning & Finance Branch, Dave Roote, 905/433-5661

Director, Human Resources Branch, Ed Farragher, 905/433-6049

Director, Information Technology Branch, Alan Wilson, 905/433-6823

Director, Taxation Data Centre & Customer Service Centre, Bob Thompson, 905/433-5880

#### OFFICE OF THE BUDGET & TAXATION

Asst. Deputy Minister, Bob Christie, 416/327-0223, Fax: 416/327-0160

Director, Intergovernmental Finance Policy Branch, Bruce MacNaughton, 416/327-0140, Fax: 416/327-0160

Director, Taxation Policy Branch, Tom Sweeting, 416/327-0228, Fax: 416/327-0260

Director, Tax Design & Legislation Branch, Vacant, 416/327-0222, Fax: 416/325-0438

#### OFFICE OF ECONOMIC POLICY

Asst. Deputy Minister, Steve Dorey, 416/325-0850, Fax: 416/325-9224

Director, Labour Economics Branch, Anne Martin, 416/325-0801, Fax: 416/325-0841

Director, Macroeconomics Analysis & Policy Branch, Pat Deutscher, 416/325-0754, Fax: 416/325-0796

Director, Structural Economics Branch, Karen Sadlier-Brown, 416/325-0902, Fax: 416/325-1187

#### FISCAL & FINANCIAL POLICY DIVISION

Job Security Fund: 416/325-1651, Fax: 416/325-8235

Controller/ADM, Anne Evans, 416/325-0290, Fax: 416/327-2136

Director, Controllership Branch, Robert Siddall, 416/325-8084, Fax: 416/325-8028

Director, Fiscal Planning Branch, Colin Anderson, 416/327-0165, Fax: 416/327-0160

Director, Accounts Receivable Project, Vacant, 416/325-8006, Fax: 416/325-8442

#### DEPOSIT INSTITUTIONS DIVISION

The new Financial Services Commission of Ontario will combine the administration & operations of the Ontario Insurance Commission, the Pension Commission of Ontario & the Deposit Institutions Division of the Ministry of Finance. Structural alterations to the three former organizations will begin with support services amalgamation & is not expected to effect day-to-day operations until early 1998.

Asst. Deputy Minister, Ross Peebles, 416/314-0626, Fax: 416/326-9267

Asst. Superintendent & Registrar, Mortgage Brokers Act, Bill Vasiliou, 416/326-9038, Fax: 416/326-9004

Director, Credit Unions & Co-operatives Branch, John Harper, 416/326-9271, Fax: 416/326-9313

Acting Director, Investigations Branch, Robert Barbour, 416/326-9368, Fax: 416/326-9392

Director, Loan & Trust Corporations Branch, Erich Beifuss, 416/326-9002, Fax: 416/326-9004

#### PROPERTY ASSESSMENT DIVISION

Asst. Deputy Minister, Elizabeth Patterson, 905/433-5772, Fax: 905/436-4513

Director, Appraisal Services Branch, Larry Hummel, 905/433-5701, Fax: 905/433-6020

Director, Central & Western Regional Branch, Carl Isenberg, 905/433-5804, Fax: 905/433-6658

Director, Data Services & Development Branch, Chis Lopes, 905/433-5677, Fax: 905/436-4473

Director, Eastern & Northern Regional Operations Branch, Michael O'Dowd, 905/433-6263, Fax: 905/433-5162

#### TAX DIVISION

Asst. Deputy Minister, Roy Lawrie, 905/433-5614, Fax: 905/433-6686

Acting Director, Business Services Branch, Tony Ming, 905/433-6592

Director, Collections Branch, John Godden, 905/433-5640

Director, Corporations Tax Branch, Richard Gruchala, 905/436-4590

Director, Employer Health Tax Branch, Claude Dagenais, 905/433-6495

Director, Motor Fuels & Tobacco Tax Branch, Pauline Goral, 905/433-6329

Director, Retail Sales Tax Branch, Jay Young, 905/433-6156

Director, Special Investigations Branch, Dario Savio, 905/433-6905

Director, Tax Appeals Branch, Nicole Anidjar, 905/435-2040

Director, Tax Credits & Grants Branch, Marion Crane, 905/433-6941

##### Associated Agencies, Boards & Commissions

•Deposit Insurance Corporation of Ontario: #700, 4711 Yonge St., Toronto ON M2N 6K8

Chair, Lili-Ann Renaud-Foster, 416/325-9444, Fax: 416/325-9568

President & CEO, Andrew Poprawa, 416/325-9580, Fax: 416/325-9568

•Financial Services Commission of Ontario (FSCO) c/o Ministry of Finance, Frost Bldg. South, 7 Queen's Park Cres., Toronto ON M7A 1Y7

The new Financial Services Commission of Ontario will combine the administration & operations of the Ontario Insurance Commission, the Pension Commission of Ontario & the Deposit Institutions Division of the Ministry of Finance. A bill was introduced & received first reading in June 1997 & is expected to be passed in the 1997 fall session, prior to publishing of this book. Structural alterations to the three former organizations will begin with support services amalgamation & is not expected to effect day-to-day operations until early 1998. For more information contact the Policy Coordinator, Jeffrey Stutz, 416/327-0940.

•Ontario Financing Authority (OFA): #1400, 1 Dundas St. West, Toronto ON M7A 1Y7

Chair/Deputy Minister, Michael L. Gourley, 416/325-1592, Fax: 416/325-1595

Vice-Chair & CEO, Tony Salerno, 416/325-8001, Fax: 416/325-8005

Executive Director, Capital Markets, Gadi Mayman, 416/325-8131, Fax: 416/325-8111

Director, Capital Markets Treasury Division, Christine Moszynski, 416/325-8085, Fax: 416/325-8118

Director, Corporate Finance, Bill Ralph, 416/325-8057

Director, Province of Ontario Savings Office, David Brand, 416/325-8101, Fax: 416/325-8005

Director, Risk Management, Mike Manning, 416/325-8930

Acting Director, Risk Policy, David Brand, 416/325-9816, Fax: 416/325-8140

•Ontario Insurance Commission: 5160 Yonge St., PO Box 85, Toronto ON M2N 6L9 – 416/250-7250; Fax: 416/590-7070, Toll Free: 1-800-668-0128

The new Financial Services Commission of Ontario will combine the administration & operations of the Ontario Insurance Commission, the Pension Commission of Ontario & the Deposit Institutions Division of the Ministry of Finance. Structural alterations to the three former organizations will begin with support services amalgamation & is not expected to effect day-to-day operations until early 1998.

Commissioner, Dina Palozzi, 416/590-7000

Acting Superintendent of Insurance, Grant Swanson, 416/590-7200

Director, Arbitration, Dispute Resolution, Elisabeth Sachs, 416/590-7060

Director, Corporate Licensing & Examinations, Grant Swanson

Director, Corporate Operations, Malcolm Campbell, 416/590-7157

Acting Director, Legal Services, Cheryl Cottle, 416/590-7102

Director, Office of the Insurance Ombudsman, Lea Algar, 416/590-7063

Director, Motor Vehicle Accident Claims Fund, Barbara Dudzinski, 416/590-7080, Fax: 416/590-7076

Director, Rates & Classification, Charles Anderson, 416/590-7061

•Ontario Securities Commission: #1800, 20 Queen St. West, Toronto ON M5H 3S8 – 416/597-0681; Fax: 416/593-8240

Chair, Jack Geller, 416/593-8200, Fax: 416/593-8241

Executive Director, Vacant

Vice-Chair, Morley Carscallen, 416/593-8081, Fax: 416/593-8241

Secretary to the Commission, Daniel Iggers, 416/593-8212, Fax: 416/593-8122

Acting Deputy Director, Corporate Services & Information Technology, Robert Burner, 416/593-8198, Fax: 416/593-8188

•Pension Commission of Ontario: 250 Younge St., 29th Fl., Toronto ON M5B 2N7 – 416/314-0660; Fax: 416/314-0620

The new Financial Services Commission of Ontario will combine the administration & operations of the Ontario Insurance Commission, the Pension Commission of Ontario & the Deposit Institutions Division of the Ministry of Finance. Structural alterations to the three former organizations will begin with support services amalgamation & is not expected to effect day-to-day operations until early 1998.

Chair, C.S. Moore, 416/314-0630, Fax: 416/314-1798

Superintendent, Pensions, Ross Peebles, 416/314-0626, Fax: 416/314-1798

Director, Pensions Plans, Nurez Jiwani, 416/314-0588

Director, Policy & Research, Pauline Dawson, 416/314-0599

## Office of FRANCOPHONE AFFAIRS

Mowat Block, 900 Bay St., 4th Fl., Toronto ON M7A 1C2

416/325-4949; Fax: 416/325-4980; Email: ofa@inforamp.net

Toll Free: 1-800-268-7507

A central agency that assists the Government of Ontario in its delivery of services in French, & in the development of policies & programs that meet the needs of the province's francophones.

#### ACTS ADMINISTERED

French Language Services Act

**Minister Responsible**, Hon. Noble A. Villeneuve

Executive Director, Denis Fortin

Director, Policy & Ministry Services & Community Relations Branch, Jacqueline Frank, 416/325-4943

Manager, Communications, Vacant, 416/325-4938

## Ministry of HEALTH

Hepburn Block, 8th Fl., Queen's Park, #1400, 80 Grosvenor St., Toronto ON M7A 1S2

416/327-4327 (Health Information Centre); Fax: 416/327-4389; URL: http://www.gov.on.ca/health

Toll Free: 1-800-268-1153

#### ACTS ADMINISTERED

Alcoholism & Drug Addiction [Research Foundation] Act
Ambulance Act
Cancer Act
Cancer Remedies Act
Chiropody Act
Chiropractic Act
Community Psychiatric Hospitals Act
Consent to Treatment Act, 1992
Dental Hygiene Act, 1991
Dental Technicians Act
Dental Technology Act, 1991
Dentistry Act, 1991
Denturism Act, 1991
Developmental Services Act (long-term care programs & services)
Dietetics Act, 1991
Drug & Pharmacies Regulation Act
Drugless Practitioners Act
Elderly Persons Centres Act
Expenditure Control Plan Statute Law Amendment Act, 1993
Fluoridation Act
Healing Arts Radiation Protection Act
Health Cards & Numbers Control Act, 1991
Health Care Accessibility Act
Health Facilities Special Orders Act
Health Insurance Act
Health Protection & Promotion Act
Homemakers & Nurses Services Act
Homes for the Aged & Rest Homes Act
Homes for Retarded Persons Act (long-term care programs & services)
Homes for Special Care Act
Human Tissue Gift Act
Hypnosis Act
Immunization of School Pupils Act
Independent Health Facilities Act
Laboratory & Specimen Collection Centre Licensing Act
Long Term Care Statute Law Amendment Act, 1993
Massage Therapy Act
Medical Laboratory Technology Act, 1991
Medical Radiation Technology Act, 1991
Medicine Act, 1991
Mental Health Act
Mental Hospitals Act
Midwifery Act
Ministry of Health Act
Municipal Health Services Act

Nursing Act, 1991
Nursing Homes Act
Occupational Therapy Act
Ontario Drug Benefit Act
Ontario Medical Association Dues Act, 1991
Ontario Mental Health Foundation Act
Opticianary Act, 1991
Optometry Act, 1991
Pharmacy Act, 1991
Physiotherapy Act, 1991
Prescription Drug Cost Regulation Act
Private Hospitals Act
Psychology Act, 1991
Public Hospitals Act
Regulated Health Professions Act, 1991
Respiratory Therapy Act, 1991
Tobacco Control Act, 1994
Toronto Hospital Act, 1986
War Veterans Burial Act

**Minister**, Hon. Elizabeth Witmer, 416/327-4300, Fax: 416/326-1571
**Minister Responsible for Seniors**, Hon. Cameron Jackson, 416/326-9326
Deputy Minister, Sandra Lang
Director, Communications & Information Branch, Claude Decelles, 416/327-4352, Fax: 416/327-8791
Director, Legal Services Branch, G. Sharpe, 416/327-8591, Fax: 416/327-8605
Coordinator, Health Information Centre, Susan Furino, 416/314-8337, Fax: 416/314-8721

#### Health Economic Development

Head, A. Szénde, 416/327-4531

### CORPORATE SERVICES

Asst. Deputy Minister, B. Gibbs, 416/327-0985
Acting Director, Audit Branch, V. Liu, 416/327-7786
Director, Fiscal Strategies Branch, L. Steele, 416/327-8674
Director, Human Resources Branch, D. Ferenc, 416/327-8747
Director, Supply & Financial Services Branch, G. Dadd, 416/327-7160
Acting Director, Systems Development Branch, B. McKee, 416/327-8234
Director, Systems Support Branch, Robert Cavanaugh, 613/548-6486
Acting Director, User Support Branch, M. Kerr, 613/548-6566

### HEALTH INSURANCE & RELATED PROGRAMS

Asst. Deputy Minister, M.C. Lindberg, 416/327-4266
Director, Drug Programs Branch, L. Tennant, 416/327-8109
Director, Laboratory Services Branch, Dr. Helen Demshar, 416/235-5941
Acting Director, Negotiations Secretariat, N. Ho, 416/327-4490
Director, Provider Services Branch, Marsha Barnes, 613/548-6716 (Kingston)
Director, Registration & Claims Branch, D. Segal, 613/548-6650 (Kingston)

### INSTITUTIONAL HEALTH & COMMUNITY SERVICES

Acting Asst. Deputy Minister, Ron Sapsford, 416/314-5923
Acting Director, Institutional Services Branch, L. Pisko-Bezruchko, 416/327-7050
Acting Regional Director, Central Hospital Region, A. Garland, 416/327-7115
Regional Director, North/East Hospital Region, G. Monaghan, 416/327-7117
Regional Director, South/West Hospital Region, M. McEwen, 416/327-7156

### INTEGRATED POLICY & PLANNING

Acting Asst. Deputy Minister, Charlie A. Bigenwald, 416/327-0859
Acting Executive Director, Health Human Resources Planning Division, J. Bertram, 416/327-8643
Director, Health Policy Branch, R. Bamhorst, 416/327-8533
Acting Director, Information Planning & Evaluation Branch, M.B. Valentine, 416/327-7482
Director, Northern Health Programs & Planning Branch, E. Mahood, 705/670-7248
Director, Professional Relations Branch, A.R. Burrows, 416/327-8888
Regional Director, Central, B. Sulzenko-Laurie, 416/327-7494
Regional Director, South & Central West, M.B. Valentine, 416/327-7487

### POPULATION HEALTH & COMMUNITY SERVICES SYSTEM GROUP

Toll Free: 1-800-668-2437 (AIDS Bureau)
AIDS Information: 416/392-2437
Asst. Deputy Minister, S. Campbell, 416/327-4537, Fax: 416/327-4409
Chief Medical Officer & Director, Health, Dr. R. Schabas, 416/327-7392
Executive Director, Community Health Division, Celia Denov, 416/327-7225, Fax: 416/327-7230
Executive Director, Long-term Care Division, Geoffrey Quirt, 416/327-8370
Director, Community Health Branch, Dorothy Loranger, 416/327-7535
Director, Emergency Health Services Branch, Graham Brand, 416/327-7907
Director, Assistive Devices Branch, Mark Cox, 416/327-8135
Acting Director, Health Promotion Branch, G. Pasut, 416/314-5484
Director, In-Home Services Branch, Tim Young, 416/326-9750
Director, Policy Branch, Patrick T. Laverty, 416/326-9755

#### Health Boards Secretariat

151 Bloor St. West, 9th Fl., Toronto ON M5S 2T5
416/327-8510; Fax: 416/327-8524
The following Boards can be reached through the Health Boards Secretariat:
Consent & Capality Board
Health Facilities Appeal Board
Health Professions Board
Health Protection Appeal Board
Health Services Appeal Board
Hospital Appeal Board
Laboratory Review Board
Nursing Homes Review Board

#### Associated Agencies, Boards & Commissions

•Addiction Research Foundation (ARF)
Listed in Section 2, *see* Index.
•Board of Directors of Drugless Therapy-Naturopathy: 4195 Dundas St. West, Etobicoke ON M8X 1V4 – 416/236-4593; Fax: 416/236-4387
Chair, James W. Spring, N.D.
Sec.-Treas., Robert L. Gatis, N.D.
•Chaplaincy Services Ontario: #200, 35 McCaul St., Toronto ON M5T 1V7 – 416/326-6860; Fax: 416/326-6867
Provincial Coordinator, Rev. Michael Steeves
•Healing Arts Radiation Protection Commission (HARP): 5700 Yonge St., 3rd Fl., North York ON M2M 4K5 – 416/327-7952; Fax: 416/327-8805
•Health Services Restructuring Commission: 56 Wellesley St. West, 12th Fl., Toronto ON M5S 2S3 – 416/327-5919
•Ontario Cancer Institute: Princess Margaret Hospital, 610 University Ave., Toronto ON M5G 2M9 – 416/924-2000
Chair, Ed King
•Ontario Cancer Treatment & Research Foundation: 620 University Ave., 16th Fl., Toronto ON M5G 2L7 – 416/971-9800; Fax: 416/971-6888
•Ontario Mental Health Foundation: #1708, 365 Bloor St. East, Toronto ON M4W 3L4 – 416/920-7721; Fax: 416/920-0026
Executive Director, Dr. Howard Cappell
•Psychiatric Patient Advocate Office: 56 Wellesley St. West, 8th Fl., Toronto ON M5S 2S3 – 416/327-7000; Fax: 416/327-7008
Acting Director, Brock Grant

## INFORMATION & PRIVACY COMMISSIONER OF ONTARIO

#1700, 80 Bloor St. West, Toronto ON M5S 2V1
416/326-3333; Fax: 416/325-9195; URL: http://www.ipc.on.ca
Toll Free: 1-800-387-0073
TTY: 416/325-7539

The Office has two main responsibilities: ensuring the public's right of access to information held by provincial & local government organizations; & protecting the individual's right of privacy, as it relates to personal information held by provincial & local government organizations. Anyone not satisfied with a government decision about access to information may ask the Commissioner to review the government's decision. In addition, the Commissioner investigates complaints from individuals who feel the government has wrongfully collected, used or disclosed their personal information. The Commissioner reports directly to the Legislative Assembly.

#### ACTS ADMINISTERED

Freedom of Information & Protection of Privacy Act
Municipal Freedom of Information & Protection of Privacy Act

**Acting Commissioner & Asst. Commissioner, Privacy**, Dr. Ann Cavoukian, 416/326-3948
Acting Asst. Commissioner, Access, Ken Anderson, 416/326-0012
Executive Director, Judy Hubert, 416/326-3938
Director, Legal Services, Ken Anderson, 416/326-3922

## Office of the INTEGRITY COMMISSIONER

#1301, 101 Bloor St. West, Toronto ON M5S 2Z7
416/314-8983; Fax: 416/314-8987

The Commissioner administers the Members' Integrity Act, 1994, as it applies to members of the Legislative Assembly & Executive Council in Ontario.

**Commissioner**, Hon. G.T. Evans, LL.D., Ph.D., K.C.S.G.

## Ministry of INTERGOVERNMENTAL AFFAIRS

900 Bay St., 6th Fl., Toronto ON M7A 1C2
416/325-4760 (Communications); Fax: 416/325-4759

#### ACTS ADMINISTERED

Ministry of Intergovernmental Affairs Act

**Minister**, Hon. Dianne Cunningham, 416/326-1600, Fax: 416/326-1656
Deputy Minister, Judith Wolfson, 416/325-4785, Fax: 416/325-4787
Asst. Deputy Minister, Constitutional Affairs, Michal Ben-Gera, 416/325-4804
Asst. Deputy Minister, Ottawa Office, Vacant, 613/239-1682, Fax: 613/239-1688
Asst. Deputy Minister, Québec Office, Stephen Bornstein, 418/692-1366, Fax: 418/692-1037, Ontario: 416/325-4800
Executive Coordinator, Communications, Laurie Spephens, 416/325-4810, Fax: 416/325-4759
Manager, Finance & Administration Services Branch, Inez Pinder, 416/325-4766

## Ministry of LABOUR

400 University Ave., 14th Fl., Toronto ON M7A 1T7
416/326-7565; Fax: 416/326-7406; URL: http://www.gov.on.ca/LAB/main.htm
Toll Free: 1-800-267-9517

#### ACTS ADMINISTERED

Blind Workmen's Compensation Act
Crown Employees Collective Bargaining Act
Employment Agencies Act
Employment Standards Act
Government Contracts Hours & Wages Act
Hospital Labour Disputes Arbitration Act
Industrial Standards Act
Labour Relations Act
Ministry of Labour Act
Occupational Health & Safety Act
One Day's Rest in Seven Act
Pay Equity Act
Rights of Labour Act
Smoking in the Workplace Act
Workers' Compensation Act
Workmen's Compensation Insurance Act

**Minister**, Hon. Jim Flaherty, 416/326-7000, Fax: 416/326-1449
Deputy Minister, Vacant
Director, Communications & Marketing Branch, Tim Nau, 416/326-7400
Director, Legal Services Branch, Nancy Austin, 416/326-7953

#### BUSINESS & ORGANIZATION SERVICES DIVISION

416/326-7586; Fax: 416/326-7599
Asst. Deputy Minister, Carola Lane, 416/326-7585
Director, Business Management & Accountability Branch, Peter Inokai, 416/326-7271, Fax: 416/326-7274
Acting Director, Client Support Services Branch, Val James, 416/326-7225, Fax: 416/326-7241
Director, Information & Technology Services Branch, Arjun Krishnan, 416/326-7131, Fax: 416/326-7138
Team Leader, Integrated Planning Secretariat, Bruce Stewart, 416/326-1354, Fax: 416/326-7599
Director, Organizational Learning & Effectiveness Branch, Ron Brittain, 416/326-7685, Fax: 416/326-7745
Coordinator, Freedom of Information, Privacy & Records Management Office, Christopher Berzins, 416/326-7786, Fax: 416/314-8749
Coordinator, Occupational Health & Safety, Monica Harding, 416/326-7247, Fax: 416/314-5203

#### LABOUR MANAGEMENT SERVICES

416/326-7606; Fax: 416/314-8755
Deputy Minister, Vacant, 416/326-7574
Director, Office of Arbitration, Jean M. Read, 416/326-1300, Fax: 416/326-1329
Director, Office of Mediation, Paul G. Gardner, 416/326-7358, Fax: 416/326-7367

#### OPERATIONS DIVISION

416/326-7668; Fax: 416/326-7599
Acting Asst. Deputy Minister, Lynn Binette, 416/326-7665
Director, Employment Practices Branch, Pat Coursey, 416/326-7000, Fax: 416/326-7061
Director, Occupational Health & Safety Branch, Ed McCloskey, 416/326-1359, Fax: 416/326-7761
Manager, Information & Administrative Services, Marg Fraser, 416/326-7732, Fax: 416/326-7745
Provincial Coordinator, Construction Health & Safety Program, Ian Carruthers, 416/326-7776
Provincial Coordinator, Industrial Health & Safety Program, John Vander Doelen, 416/326-7904, Fax: 416/326-7761
Provincial Coordinator, Mining Health & Safety Program, Ian Plummer, 705/670-5703, Fax: 705/670-5698
Provincial Coordinator, Professional & Specialized Services, Dr. Om Malik, 416/326-1404
Chief, Materials Testing Laboratory, Marcel D'Jivre, 705/670-5711
Chief, Occupational Health Laboratory Service & Radiation Protection Service, John Tai-Pow, 416/235-5913

#### POLICY & COMMUNICATIONS DIVISION

416/326-7558; Fax: 416/326-7599
Asst. Deputy Minister, Tony Dean, 416/326-7555
Director, Communications & Marketing, Valery Chavossy, 416/326-7404
Director, Employment & Labour Policy, Ron Saunders, 416/326-7623
Director, Prevention & Compensation Policy, Marguerite Rappolt, 416/326-7628
Acting Coordinator, Policy & Information Coordination Unit, Tracy Mill, 416/326-7652

##### Associated Agencies, Boards & Commissions

•Industrial Disease Standards Panel: #1004, 69 Yonge St., Toronto ON M5E 1K3 – 416/327-4156; Fax: 416/327-4166
Chair, Nicolette Carlan
•Office of the Employer Advisor: #501, 101 Bloor St. West, Toronto ON M5S 1P5 – 416/327-0020; Fax: 416/327-0726
Director, Jeffrey Stutz
•Office of the Worker Advisor: #1300, 123 Edward St., Toronto ON M5G 1E2 – 416/325-8570; Fax: 416/325-4830
Director, Alec Farquhar
•Ontario Labour Relations Board: 400 University Ave., 4th Fl., Toronto ON M7A 1T7 – 416/326-7500; Fax: 416/326-7531
Chair, Judith McCormack
•Pay Equity Commission: 150 Eglinton Ave. East, 5th Fl., Toronto ON M4P 1E8 – 416/481-4464; Fax: 416/314-8741
Commissioner, Brigid O'Reilly
•Workers' Compensation Board
Listed alphabetically in detail, this section.
•Workplace Health & Safety Agency: #900, 121 Bloor St. East, Toronto ON M4W 3M5 – 416/975-9728; Fax: 416/975-9775
Chair, Bruce Stanton

## MANAGEMENT BOARD OF CABINET

Ferguson Block, 77 Wellesley St. West, 12th Fl., Toronto ON M7A 1N3
416/325-1688 (Employment Services); Fax: 416/327-3790
Management Board: 416/326-1234
Queen's Printer: 416/326-5316

#### ACTS ADMINISTERED

Management Board of Cabinet Act
Public Service Act

**Chair**, Hon. Chris Hodgson, 416/327-2333
Executive Director, Ontario Public Service Social Contract Implementation, Richard Lundeen, 416/325-1392
Director, Legal Services Branch, Heather Cooper, 416/325-9391, Fax: 416/325-9404
Chief of Staff, Mac Penney, 416/327-0942
Special Asst., Communications, Rita Smith, 416/326-9091
Special Asst., Outreach Constituency, Val Fogarty, 416/327-2944
Special Asst., Policy, Jordan Berger, 416/327-2559
Special Asst., Policy, Andrew Lee, 416/327-4249
Special Asst., Press Secretary, David McCully, 416/327-0948

#### MANAGEMENT BOARD SECRETARIAT

Secretary, Management Board of Cabinet & Deputy Minister, Management Board Secretariat, Michele M. Noble, 416/327-3805, Fax: 416/327-3809

##### Communications Services Branch

416/327-2789; Fax: 416/327-2817
Director, Linda Leighton, 416/327-2790
Manager, Customer Accounts Unit, Angela Coke, 416/327-2794
Manager, Issues Management, Corporate Priorities & Media Relations, Vacant, 416/327-2793, Fax: 416/327-2718
Manager, Publishing Inc. & Acting Manager, Operational Planning, Production, External Recruitment Advertising, Margaret Cassidy, 416/325-1353, Fax: 416/325-1367
Manager, Strategic Communication Planning & Policy, Elizabeth Lea, 416/325-1363

#### CORPORATE SERVICES DIVISION

Asst. Deputy Minister, Harold Wu, 416/327-2862, Fax: 416/327-2866
Acting Director, Audit Branch, Marie Davis, 416/314-3448, Fax: 416/314-3467
Director, Finance & Office Services Branch, Ralph Grant, 416/327-2900
Director, Information Technology Services Branch, George Radford, 416/327-2828, Fax: 416/327-2530, Helpline: 416/327-2700
Asst. Director, Human Resources, Jane Corbet, 416/327-3814
Coordinator, Library & Information Services, Marilyn MacKellar, 416/327-2533

#### INFORMATION & TECHNOLOGY DIVISION

155 University Ave., 8th Fl., Toronto ON M5H 3B7
416/327-3442; Fax: 416/327-3264
Asst. Deputy Minister, David Girvin, 416/327-9696
Director, Customer Service & Support Branch, Bryan Izatt, 416/327-3440, Fax: 416/327-3256
Director, Information & Technology Policy Branch, Trevor Moon, 56 Wellesley St. West, Toronto ON M7A 1Z6, 416/327-3250, Fax: 416/327-3274
Director, Processing Services Branch, Ernie Dark, 1201 Wilson Ave., Toronto ON M3M 1J8, 416/235-4584
Director, Telecommunications Services Branch, Terry Ham, 416/327-3026, Fax: 416/327-3281

#### OPERATIONS & MINISTRY SUPPORT DIVISION

#1104, 790 Bay St., Toronto ON M7A 1Y7
416/325-1610; Fax: 416/325-1612
Asst. Deputy Minister, Susan Waterfield, 416/325-1607
Director, Freedom of Information & Privacy Branch, Frank White, 101 Bloor St. West, Toronto ON M5S 1P7, 416/327-2084, Fax: 416/327-2190
Director, Operational Policy & Program Development Branch, Linda Kahn, 416/325-1617, Fax: 416/325-1753
Director, Ministry Support Branch, Morag Dion, 416/325-1777, Fax: 416/325-1605
Director, Special Programs & Services Branch, Angela Forest, 416/325-0222, Fax: 416/325-0251

#### PROJECT RENEWAL DIVISION

416/327-9698; Fax: 416/327-3772
Acting Asst. Deputy Minister, Rob Lowry, 416/327-9699
Project Director, Peter Crabtree, 416/327-9729

#### PROPERTY MANAGEMENT DIVISION

77 Wellesley St. West, 5th Fl., Toronto ON M7A 1N3
416/327-2779; Fax: 416/327-2785
Executive Director, Julie Leggatt, 416/327-2778
Director, Central Operations Branch, Mike Lukacko, 416/327-2660, Fax: 416/327-2695

Director, Client Services & Portfolio Management Branch, Barbara Hewett, 416/327-3722, Fax: 416/327-3772
Director, Contract Management Branch, Vacant, 416/327-2619, Fax: 416/327-2606
Director, Corporate Management & Mortgage Branch, Vern M. Chaves, 77 Grenville St., 9th Fl., Toronto ON M5S 1B3, 416/327-3748, Fax: 416/314-3677
Director, Leasing Services Branch, Del Jackson, 416/327-3943, Fax: 416/327-2694

**REAL ESTATE SERVICES DIVISION**

777 Bay St., 16th Fl., Toronto ON M5G 2E5
416/585-6777; Fax: 416/585-7577
Executive Director, Kathy Bouey, 416/585-6730
Director, Central Branch, Gordon Laschinger, 416/585-4212, Fax: 416/585-4263
Acting Director, Northern & Eastern Branch, Marie Cardno, 416/585-6742, Fax: 416/585-5263
Director, Western Branch, Peter B. Johansen, 416/585-6770, Fax: 416/585-4005

**REALTY GROUP**

77 Wellesley St. West, 11th Fl., Toronto ON M7A 1N3
416/327-3937; Fax: 416/327-3942
Asst. Deputy Minister, Tim Casey, 416/327-3933
Acting Director, Design Services Branch, Ann Gabriel, 416/327-1900, Fax: 416/327-1852
Director, Ontario Realty Corporation Transition Team, Ian Veitch, 416/327-2754, Fax: 416/327-4194
Director, Project Management Branch, David McHugh, 720 Bay St., 4th Fl., Toronto ON M5G 2K1, 416/326-4856, Fax: 416/326-4871
Director, Special Projects, Larry Loop, 416/327-2883

**STRATEGIC POLICY DIVISION**

416/325-1534; Fax: 416/325-1393
Asst. Deputy Minister, Phyllis Clark, 416/325-1531
Executive Director, Agency Reform, Pam Bryant, 416/327-2030, Fax: 416/327-2186
Chief Actuary, Actuarial Services, Clare Pitcher, 416/327-8384, Fax: 416/327-8402
Acting Director, Compensation & Labour Relations Policy Branch, Murray Lapp, 416/325-1488, Fax: 416/327-8402
Director, Data Support Branch, Sheree Davis, 56 Wellesley St. West, 4th Fl., Toronto ON M7A 1Z6, 416/327-2090, Fax: 416/327-1682
Director, Management Structure & Workforce Planning, Wendy Noble, 416/327-2044, Fax: 416/327-2186
Director, Strategic Direction & Planning Branch, Valerie Cook-Jackson, 416/327-3623, Fax: 416/327-2593
Chief Negotiator, Negotiations Secretariat, Angelo Pesce, 416/325-1476, Fax: 416/325-1483

**SUPPLY & SERVICE DIVISION**

416/327-3515; Fax: 416/327-3517
Asst. Deputy Minister, David McGeown, 416/327-3511
Acting Director, Employee Health & Safety Services Branch, Judith Berg, 416/327-1080, Fax: 416/327-1115
Acting Director, General Services Branch, Gary Vamplew, 416/314-3434, Fax: 416/314-3411
Director, (The) Green Workplace & Project Director, Strategic Procurement Project, Pat Werner, 416/327-4185, Fax: 416/327-4193, Recycling Hotline: 416/327-3777
Director, Human Resource Information Services Branch, David Ritcey, 416/327-9210, Fax: 416/327-9254
Director, Information Services Branch, Eric Steeves, 416/327-2890, Fax: 416/327-3652
Director, Public Appointments Secretariat, Marilyn Roycroft, 416/327-2640, Fax: 416/327-2640
Director, Purchasing Services Branch, Dan Kusel, 416/327-3518, Fax: 416/327-3573
Manager, Access & Inquiry Services, Mary LeFeuvre, 416/325-3444, Fax: 416/325-3407
Acting Manager, Occupational Health Service, Brenda Brautigam, 416/327-1131
Manager, Policy & Program Development Section, Gulbaz Khan, 416/327-3580, Environmental Procurement: 416/327-3581
Manager, Queen's Printer (Publications Ontario), Ruth Hawkins, 416/326-5316
Manager, Supplier Information Service, Brendan Power, 416/327-3552
Manager, Travel Program, Kathy Tortell, 416/327-2568
General Manager, Corporate Contracting Services, Robert Farnley, 416/327-3536
General Manager, Office Products Centre, Bob Hogg, 4375 Chesswood Dr., Toronto ON M3J 2C2, 416/327-3319, General Inquiry: 416/327-3004

**Citizens' Inquiry Bureau**

416/326-1234 (Ontario collect)
TDD: 416/325-3408
Supervisor, Bertha Beniusis

**Associated Agencies, Boards & Commissions**

•Civil Service Commission: #803, 101 Bloor St. West, Toronto ON M5S 1P7 – 416/325-6314; Fax: 416/325-6317
Chair, Valerie A. Gibbons
Executive Officer & Secretary, Cynthia Bedborough
•Ontario Land Corporation: Ferguson Block, 77 Wellesley St. West, 13th Fl., Toronto ON M7A 1N3 – 416/327-3937
CEO, Tim Casey, 416/327-3933
•Ontario Mortgage Corporation: 62 Wellesley St. West, Toronto ON M5S 2X3 – 416/314-3650
CEO, Tim Casey, 416/327-3933
•Ontario Pension Board: #1200, 1 Adelaide St. East, Toronto ON M5C 2X6 – 416/364-8558; Fax: 416/364-7578, Toll Free: 1-800-668-6203
President, J.J. Wilbee
Chair, W.H. Somerville

## Ministry of MUNICIPAL AFFAIRS & HOUSING

777 Bay St., 17th Fl., Toronto ON M5G 2E5
416/585-7041 (Communications Branch); Fax: 416/585-6227; URL: http://nrserv.mmah.gov.on.ca/

**ACTS ADMINISTERED**

Barrie Innisfil Annexation Act
Barrie-Vespra Annexation Act
Brantford-Brant Annexation Act
Building Code Act
City of Cornwall Annexation Act
City of Gloucester Act
City of Hamilton Act
City of Hazeldean-March Act
City of London Act
City of Nepean Act
City of Ottawa Road Closing & Conveyance Validation Act
City of Port Colborne Act
City of Sudbury Hydro-Electric Service Act
City of Thorold Act
City of Thunder Bay Act
City of Timmins-Porcupine Act
City of Toronto Act
Community Economic Development Act
County of Haliburton Act
County of Oxford Act
County of Simcoe Act
Development Charges Act
District Municipality of Muskoka Act
District of Parry Sound Local Government Act
Geographic Township of Hansen Act
Housing Development Act
International Bridges Municipal Payments Act
Line Fences Act
Local Improvement Act
London-Middlesex Act
Ministry of Municipal Affairs & Housing Act
Moosonee Development Area Board Act
Municipal Act
Municipal Affairs Act
Municipal Arbitrations Act
Municipal Boundary Negotiations Act
Municipal Conflict of Interest Act
Municipal Corporations Quieting Orders Act
Municipal Elderly Residents' Assistance Act
Municipal Elections Act
Municipal Extra Territorial Tax Act
Municipal Franchises Act
Municipal Interest & Discount Rates Act
Municipal Payments in Lieu of Taxes Statute Law Amendment Act
Municipal Private Acts Repeal Act
Municipal & School Tax Credit Assistance Acts
Municipal Subsidies Adjustment Repeal Act
Municipal Tax Assistance Act
Municipal Tax Sales Act
Municipal Unemployment Relief Act
Municipal Works Assistance Act
Municipality of Metropolitan Toronto Act
Municipality of Shuniah Act
Niagara Escarpment Planning & Development Act
Ontario Housing Corporation Act
Ontario Municipal Board Act
Ontario Municipal Employees Retirement System Act
Ontario Planning & Development Act
Ontario Unconditional Grants Act
Ontario Water Resources Act (Clauses 44(2) a, b & c Sec.48)
Ottawa-Carleton Amalgamations & Elections Act
Parkway Belt Planning & Development Act
Planning Act
Police Village of St. George Act
Public Parks Act
Public Utilities Act
Public Utilities Corporations Act
Regional Municipalities Act
Regional Municipality of Durham Act
Regional Municipality of Haldimand-Norfolk Act
Regional Municipality of Halton Act
Regional Municipality of Hamilton-Wentworth Act
Regional Municipality of Niagara Act
Regional Municipality of Ottawa-Carleton Act
Regional Municipality of Ottawa-Carleton Land Acquisition Act
Regional Municipality of Peel Act
Regional Municipality of Sudbury Act
Regional Municipality of Waterloo Act
Regional Municipality of York Act
Rent Control Act
Residential Complexes Financing Costs Restraint Act
Residential Rent Regulation Act
Residential Tenancies Act
Road Access Act
Rural Housing Assistance Act
Sarnia-Lambton Act
Shoreline Property Assistance Act
Snow Roads & Fences Act
Statute Labour Act
Tax Sales Confirmation Act
Territorial Division Act
Tom Longboat Act
Toronto District Heating Corporation Act
Toronto Islands Act
Toronto Islands Residential Community Stewardship Act
Town of Wasaga Beach Act
Township of North Plantagenet Act
Township of South Dumfries Act
Waterfront Regeneration Trust Agency Act

Wharfs & Harbours Act
**Minister**, Hon. Allan Leach, 416/585-7000, Fax: 416/585-6470
Deputy Minister, Daniel Burns, 416/585-7100, Fax: 416/585-7211
Chair, Board of Negotiation, Gordon Swayze, 416/326-4700
Faciltator, Urban Economic Development, Dale Martin, 416/585-7474
Director, Communications Branch, Sally Sheppard, 416/585-6900

#### CORPORATE MANAGEMENT SERVICES
Asst. Deputy Minister, Larry Close, 416/585-6262
Director, Information Management Branch, Les Fincham, 416/585-7223
Director, Subsidies Management Branch, Vacant, 416/585-6193
Manager, Government Liaison Unit, Bruce McLeod, 416/585-6236
Manager, Office of Francophone Municipal Relations & Ministry Correspondence, Joyce Irvine, 416/585-7556
Manager, Resources Planning Unit, Harvey Regush, 416/585-7193

#### CORPORATE RESOURCES MANAGEMENT DIVISION
Asst. Deputy Minister, Arnie Temple, 416/585-6670
Director, Administrative Services Branch, Nadia Vakharia, 416/585-7437
Acting Director, Audit Services Branch, Andy Glendenning, 416/585-6550
Director, Financial Controller & Treasurer, Ontario Housing Corporation, Victor Augustine, 416/585-6659
Director, Human Resources Branch, Jim Parker, 416/585-7570
Director, Information & Technology Services Branch, Kurtis Bishop, 416/585-6830
Director, Legal Branch, Andrea Baston, 416/585-6701

#### HOUSING OPERATIONS DIVISION
Asst. Deputy Minister, Shirley Hoy, 416/585-6373
Chair, Ontario Housing Corporation, William Carson, 416/585-6518, Fax: 416/585-7617
Registrar, Rent Registry, David Braund, 415 Yonge St., 19th Fl., Toronto ON M5B 2E7, 416/326-0923, Fax: 416/326-0930
Acting Executive Director, Housing Field Operations, Peter Schafft, 416/585-6400, Fax: 416/585-7610
Acting Director, Management & Operational Support Branch, Marsha Goldford, 416/585-6847
Director, Program Development & Support Branch, Philip Schwartz, 416/585-7637, Fax: 416/585-4004

#### HOUSING PLANNING & POLICY DIVISION
Asst. Deputy Minister, Anne Beaumont, 416/585-7482
Director, Housing Development & Buildings Branch, Ann Borooah, 416/585-4238
Director, Housing Policy Branch, Scott Harcourt, 416/585-7019
Director, Strategic Planning & Research Branch, Crom Sparling, 416/585-6360

#### MUNICIPAL OPERATIONS DIVSION
Asst. Deputy Minister, Brian Riddell, 416/585-6600
Executive Coordinator, Field Management, Peter Boles, 416/585-7251
Director, Community Development Branch, Tania Melnyk, 416/585-6264
Acting Director, Municipal Boundaries Branch, D. Taylor, 416/585-7275
Director, Plans Administration Branch (Central & Southwest), Diana Jardine, 416/585-6025
Director, Plans Administration Branch (North & East), Bryan Hill, 416/585-6093

#### MUNICIPAL POLICY DEVELOPMENT DIVISION
Asst. Deputy Minister, Dana Richardson, 416/585-6321
Director, Canada-Ontario Infrastructure Works, Myra Wiener, 416/585-6296
Director, Local Government Policy Branch, Doug Bonnes, 416/585-7270
Director, Municipal Finance Branch, Nancy Bardecki, 416/585-6951
Acting Director, Municipal Planning Policy Branch, Philip McKinstry, 416/585-6225
Director, Provincial Planning Branch, Meredith Beresford, 416/585-7177

#### OFFICE FOR THE GREATER TORONTO AREA
Waterpark Pl., #300, 10 Bay St., Toronto ON M5J 2R8
416/314-6400; Fax: 416/314-6440
Asst. Deputy Minister, Elizabeth A. McLaren, 416/314-6417

##### Associated Agencies, Boards & Commissions
•Office of the Provincial Facilitator: 777 Bay St., 12th Fl., Toronto ON M5G 2E5 – 416/585-6736; Fax: 416/585-7411
Provincial Facilitator, Dale Martin, 416/585-7474
•Ontario Municipal Board (OMB): 655 Bay St., 15th Fl., Toronto ON M5G 1E5 – 416/326-6255; Fax: 416/326-5370
Chair, Helen Cooper, 416/326-6246
Secretary & Chief Operating Officer, Diana Macri, 416/326-6249
•Ontario Municipal Employees Retirement Board: #100, One University Ave., Toronto ON M5J 2P1 – 416/369-2400; Fax: 416/360-0217
Chair, Gary Mugford
•Rent Review Hearings Board: 77 Bloor St. West, 10th Fl., Toronto ON M5S 1M2 – 416/314-0051; Fax: 416/314-0061
Chair, Brian Goodman
•Waterfront Regeneration Trust: #580, 207 Queen's Quay West, Toronto ON M5J 1A7 – 416/314-9490; Fax: 416/314-9497; Email: info@wrtrust.com
Commissioner, Hon. David Crombie, 416/314-9468
Deputy Commissioner, David Carter, 416/314-9470
Director, Lake Ontario Program, Suzanne Barrett, 416/314-9471
Information Services Specialist, Janet Hollingsworth, 416/314-4660

## Ontario NATIVE AFFAIRS SECRETARIAT
#1009, 595 Bay St., Toronto ON M5G 2C2
416/326-4740; Fax: 416/326-4017
**Minister Responsible**, Hon. Charles Harnick
Secretary, Murray Coolican, 416/326-4741
Special Advisor, Corporate Negotiations, Ted Wilson, 416/326-4771
Director, Communications, Sandy Hunter, 416/326-4763
Director, Negotiations Support & Community Relations, Wallis Smith, 416/326-4762
Director, Policy Coordination Branch, Tim Eger, 416/326-4744

## Ministry of NATURAL RESOURCES (MNR)
Whitney Block, 99 Wellesley St. West, Toronto ON M7A 1W3
416/314-2000; Fax: 416/314-2051; URL: http://www.mnr.gov.on.ca/mnr/

#### ACTS ADMINISTERED
Aggregate Resources Act
Algonquin Forestry Authority Act
Algonquin Provincial Park Extension Act
An Act to Confirm the title of the Government of Canada to certain Lands & Indian Lands
An Act for the Settlement of certain Questions between the Governments of Canada and Ontario respecting Indian Reserve Lands
Arboreal Emblem Act
Beds of Navigable Waters Act
Canada Company's Lands Act
Conservation Authorities Act
Conservation Land Act
Crown Forest Sustainability Act
Endangered Species Act
Fish Inspection Act
Fisheries Act (Canada) - Ontario Fishery Regulations
Fisheries Development Act (Canada)
Fisheries Loans Act
Forest Fires Prevention Act
Forest Tree Pest Control Act
Forestry Act
Forestry Workers Employment Act
Forestry Workers Lien for Wages Act
Freshwater Fish Marketing Act (Ontario)
Game & Fish Act
Gananoque Lands Act
Gas & Oil Leases Act
Indian Lands Agreement Confirmation Act
Indian Lands Act
Industrial and Mining Lands Compensation Act
Lac Seul Conservation Act
Lake of the Woods Control Board Act
Lakes & Rivers Improvement Act
Manitoba-Ontario Lake St. Joseph Diversion Agreement Authorization Act
Migratory Birds Convention Act (Canada)
Mineral Emblem Act
Mining Act (Certain Sections)
Ministry of Natural Resources Act
National Radio Observatory Act
North Georgian Bay Recreational Reserve Act
Ontario Geographic Names Board Act
Ontario Harbours Agreement Act
Ottawa River Water Powers Act
Petroleum Resources Act
Provincial Parks Act
Public Lands Act
Seine River Diversion Act
Settlers' Pulpwood Protection Act
Spruce Pulpwood Exportation Act
Steep Rock Iron Ore Development Act
Surveyors Act
Surveys Act
Trees Act
Water Transfer Control Act
Wild Rice Harvesting Act
Wilderness Areas Act
Woodlands Improvement Act
**Minister**, Hon. John Snobelen, 416/314-2301, Fax: 416/314-2216
Deputy Minister, Ron J. Vrancart, 416/314-2150, Fax: 416/314-2159
Director, Communications Services Branch, Sean Krantzberg, 416/314-2119
Acting Director, Organizational Development Branch, Michael Williams, 416/314-2306

#### CORPORATE SERVICES DIVISION (CSD)
416/314-1900; Fax: 416/314-1901
Asst. Deputy Minister, Patricia Malcolmson, 416/314-1897
Director, Corporate Affairs Branch, Larry Douglas, 416/314-1923
Director, Finance & Administration Branch, John Kenrick, 416/314-1893
Director, Human Resources Branch, Gabriella Zillmer, 416/314-1752
Director, Legal Services, Barry G. Jones, 416/314-2025

#### FIELD SERVICES DIVISION
Ontario Government Bldg., #224, 435 James St. South, Thunder Bay ON P7E 6E3

807/475-1271; Fax: 807/475-1503
Asst. Deputy Minister, Cam Clark, 807/475-1438
Director, Aviation, Flood & Fire Management, Karan Aquino, #400, 70 Foster Dr., Sault Ste. Marie ON P6A 6V5, 705/945-5937
Manager, Provincial Enforcement Section, Guy Winterton, 705/755-1750
Regional Director, Northeast Region, Dick Hunter, 705/272-7014
Regional Director, Northwest Region, Mike Willick, 807/475-1264
Regional Director, Southcentral Region, Al Stewart, 705/789-9611

### NATURAL RESOURCE MANAGEMENT DIVISION

Whitney Block, #6540, 99 Wellesley St. West, Toronto ON M7A 1W3
416/314-6132; Fax: 416/314-1994
Asst. Deputy Minister, Gail Beggs, 416/314-6131
Director, Fish & Wildlife Branch, Andy Houser
Director, Forest Management Branch, Bill Thornton, 705/945-6660
Director, Lands & Natural Heritage Branch, Bob Beecher, 705/755-1212
Director, Land Use Planning Branch, Dave Walton, 705/789-9611
Managing Director, Ontario Parks, Norm Richards, 705/740-1224
Acting Manager, Native Affairs Unit, Monika Turner, 416/314-1188

### SCIENCE & INFORMATION RESOURCES DIVISION

Fax: /314-1531
Asst. Deputy Minister, Dr. David Balsillie, 416/314-1528
Director, Information Technology Services Branch, Mike Roach, 416/314-1401
Acting Director, Natural Resources Information, Glenn Holder, 416/314-1219
Director, Science Development & Transfer Branch, Jim Maclean, 905/832-7133, Fax: 905/832-7149
Acting Director, Systems Development, Mike Connolly, 416/314-1518

### ASSOCIATION OF CONSERVATION AUTHORITIES OF ONTARIO

418A Sheridan St., Peterborough ON K9H 3S9
705/749-9131; Fax: 705/749-9345

#### Conservation Authorities

Ausable Bayfield: RR#3, Exeter ON NOM 1S5 – 519/235-2610; Fax: 519/235-1963, General Manager, Tom Prout
Cataraqui Region: 1641 Perth Rd., PO Box 160, Glenburnie ON K0H 1S0 – 613/546-4228; Fax: 613/547-6474, General Manager, William Warwick
Catfish Creek: RR#5, Aylmer ON N5H 2R4 – 519/773-9037; Fax: 519/765-1489, General Manager, Kim Smale
Central Lake Ontario: 100 Whiting Ave., Oshawa ON L1H 3T3 – 905/579-0411; Fax: 905/579-0994, Chair, Irv Harrell
Credit Valley: 1255 Derry Rd. West, Meadowvale ON L5N 6R4 – 905/670-1615; Fax: 905/670-2210, General Manager, Vicki Barron
Crowe Valley: PO Box 416, Marmora ON K0K 2M0 – 613/472-3137; Fax: 613/472-5516, General Manager, Kelly Pender
Essex Region: 360 Fairview Ave. West, Essex ON N8M 1Y6 – 519/776-5209; Fax: 519/776-8688, General Manager, Ken Schmidt
Ganaraska Region: PO Box 328, Port Hope ON L1A 3W4 – 905/885-8173; Fax: 905/885-9824, General Manager, Gayle Wood
Grand River: 400 Clyde Rd., PO Box 729, Cambridge ON N1R 5W6 – 519/621-2761; Fax: 519/621-4844, General Manager, Allan Holmes
Grey Sauble: RR#4, Inglis Falls Rd., Owen Sound ON N4K 5N6 – 519/376-3076; Fax: 519/371-0437, General Manager, James Manicom
Halton Region: 2596 Britannia Rd. West, RR#2, Milton ON L9T 2X6 – 905/336-1158; Fax: 905/336-7014, General Manager, Murray Stephen
Hamilton Region: 833 Mineral Springs Rd., PO Box 7099, Ancaster ON L9G 3L3 – 905/525-2181, 648-4427; Fax: 905/525-2214, General Manager, Ben W. Vanderbrug
Kawartha Region: Kenrei Park Rd., RR#1, Lindsay ON K9V 4R1 – 705/328-2271; Fax: 705/328-2286, General Manager, Ian MacNab
Kettle Creek: RR#8, St. Thomas ON N5P 3T3 – 519/631-1270; Fax: 519/631-5026, General Manager, Bryan Hall
Lakehead Region: 1136 Oliver Rd., PO Box 3476, Thunder Bay ON P7B 5J9 – 807/344-5857; Fax: 807/345-9156, General Manager, Mervi Henttonen
Lake Simcoe Region: 120 Bayview Ave., PO Box 282, Newmarket ON L3Y 4X1 – 905/895-1281; Fax: 905/853-5881, Chief, Marilyn Pearce
Long Point Region: RR#3, Simcoe ON N3Y 4K2 – 519/428-4623; Fax: 519/428-1520, General Manager, James Oliver
Lower Thames Valley: 100 Thomas St., Chatham ON N7L 2Y8 – 519/354-7310; Fax: 519/352-3435, General Manager, Jerry Campbell
Lower Trent Region: 441 Front St., Trenton ON K8V 6C1 – 613/394-4829; Fax: 613/394-5226, Acting General Manager, Kelly Pender
Maitland Valley: Marietta St., PO Box 127, Wroxeter ON N0G 2X0 – 519/335-3557; Fax: 519/335-3516, General Manager, Ross Duncan
Mattagami Region: 100 Lakeshore Rd., Timmins ON P4N 8R5 – 705/264-5309; Fax: 705/268-6544, General Manager, Brian Tees
Metro Toronto & Region: 5 Shoreham Dr., North York ON M3N 1S4 – 416/661-6600; Fax: 416/661-6898, General Manager, Craig Mather
Mississippi Valley: Hwy. 511, PO Box 268, Lanark ON K0G 1K0 – 613/259-2491; Fax: 613/259-3468, General Manager, Paul Lehman
Moira River: Wallbridge-Loyalist Rd. & Hwy. 2, PO Box 698, Belleville ON K8N 5B3 – 613/968-3434; Fax: 613/968-8240, General Manager, Terry Murphy
Napanee Region: 25 Ontario St. West, Napanee ON K7R 3S6 – 613/354-3312; Fax: 613/354-5930, General Manager, Terry Murphy
Niagara Peninsula: 2358 Centre St., Allanburg ON L0S 1A0 – 905/227-1013; Fax: 905/227-2998, General Manager, A.L. Burt
Nickel District: 200 Brady St., Sudbury ON P3E 5K3 – 705/674-5249; Fax: 705/674-7939, General Manager, Allen Bonnis
North Bay-Mattawa: RR#5, Site 12, Comp. 5, 233 Birchs Rd., North Bay ON P1B 8Z4 – 705/474-5420; Fax: 705/474-9793, Secretary-Manager, William Beckett
Nottawasaga Valley: RR#1, Hwy. 90, Angus ON L0M 1B0 – 705/424-1479; Fax: 705/424-2115, General Manager, Wayne Wilson
Otanabee Region: Time Sq., #200, 380 Armour Rd., Peterborough ON K9H 7L7 – 705/745-5791; Fax: 705/745-7488, General Manager, Dan White
Prince Edward Region: Union St., PO Box 310, Picton ON K0K 2T0 – 613/476-7408; Fax: 613/476-7146, General Manager, Keith Taylor
Raison Region: County Rd. 18, PO Box 10, Martintown ON K0C 1S0 – 613/528-4823; Fax: 613/528-4825, General Manager, Michel Lalonde
Rideau Valley: Mill St., PO Box 599, Manotick ON K4M 1A5 – 613/692-3571; Fax: 613/692-0831, Toll Free: 1-800-267-3504, General Manager, Dell Hallett
Saugeen Valley: RR#1, Hanover ON N4N 3B8 – 519/364-1255; Fax: 519/364-6990, General Manager, James H. Coffey
Sault Ste. Marie Region: 1100 - 5 Line East, RR#2, Sault Ste. Marie ON P6A 5K7 – 705/946-8530; Fax: 705/946-8533, General Manager, Ralph Yanni
South Nation River: 15 Union St., PO Box 69, Berwick ON K0C 1G0 – 613/984-2948; Fax: 613/984-2872, General Manager, Dennis O'Grady
St. Clair Region: 205 Mill Pond Cres., Strathroy ON N7G 3P9 – 519/245-3710; Fax: 519/245-3348, General Manager, John King
Upper Thames River: RR#6, London ON N6A 4C1 – 519/451-2800; Fax: 519/451-1188, General Manager, Donald Pearson

#### Associated Agencies, Boards & Commissions

•Algonquin Forestry Authority - Huntsville: 222 Main St. West, PO Box 1198, Huntsville ON P0A 1K0 – 705/789-9647; Fax: 705/789-3353
General Manager, W.J. Brown
•Algonquin Forestry Authority - Pembroke: #84, 6 Isabella St., Pembroke ON K8A 5S5 – 613/735-0173; Fax: 613/735-4192
Manager, Operations, B.A. Connelly
•Centre for Northern Forest Ecosystem Research (CNFER): Lakehead University, 955 Oliver Rd., Thunder Bay ON P7B 5E1 – 807/343-4016; Fax: 807/343-4001; URL: http://www.cnfer.on.ca

Research unit of the Ontario Ministry of Natural Resources, located at Lakehead University in Thunder Bay. CNFER maintains close links with the Faculty of Forestry & Department of Biology at Lakehead University, & many CNFER scientists have adjunct status at the University to supervise Graduate students. CNFER is multi-disciplinary research unit, with a mandate to study the effects of forestry practices on boreal aquatic & terrestrial ecosystems.

Manager, Kim Armstrong
Administration Officer, Marvin Koski
•Leslie M. Frost Natural Resources Centre: RR#2, Minden ON K0M 2K0 – 705/766-2451; Fax: 705/766-9677
•Mining & Lands Commissioner: 700 Bay St., 24th Fl., Box 330, Toronto ON M5G 1Z6 – 416/314-2320; Fax: 416/314-2327
Commissioner, Linda Kamerman
•Office of the Surveyor General: 90 Sheppard Ave. East, 4th Fl., North York ON M2N 3A1 – 416/314-1286; Fax: 416/223-6215
Surveyor General, Pier L. Finos
•Ontario Geographic Names Board: 90 Sheppard Ave. East, Toronto ON M2N 3A1 – 416/314-1278; Fax: 416/314-1338
Executive Secretary, Michael Smart
•Provincial Parks Council: 2450 McDougall St., Windsor ON N8X 3N6 – 519/255-6731; Fax: 519/255-7990
Chair, L.O.W. Burridge

## NIAGARA FALLS BRIDGE COMMISSION

PO Box 395, Niagara Falls ON L2E 6T8
905/354-5641; Fax: 905/354-3256
**General Manager & Sec.-Treas.**, Allen Gandell

## Ministry of NORTHERN DEVELOPMENT & MINES (MNDM)

Whitney Block, Room 5630, 5th Fl., Queen's Park, 99 Wellesley St. West, Toronto ON M7A 1W3
416/327-0633; Fax: 416/327-0634; URL: http://www.gov.on.ca/MNDM
159 Cedar St., 7th Fl., Sudbury ON P3E 6A5
705/670-7107, Fax: 705/670-7108 (Communications)

#### ACTS ADMINISTERED

Local Services Boards Act

Mining Act
Ministry of Northern Affairs Act
Northern Ontario Heritage Fund Act
Ontario Mineral Exploration Program Act
Ontario Northland Transportation Commission Act
**Minister**, Hon. Chris Hodgson, 416/327-0661, Fax: 416/327-0665
Manager, Editorial Services & Events Planning, Communications, Ronald J. St. Louis, 416/327-0620

#### BUSINESS PLANNING SECRETARIAT

159 Cedar St., 7th Fl., Sudbury ON P3E 6A5
705/670-7050; Fax: 705/670-7057
Director, Don Ignacy, 705/670-7004

#### MINES & MINERALS DIVISION

Willet Green Miller Centre, 933 Ramsey Lake Rd., 6th Fl., Sudbury ON P3E 6B5
Asst. Deputy Minister, Dr. John B. Gammon, 705/670-5877, Fax: 705/670-5818
Senior Manager, Data Services Section, Gianfranco Merlino, 705/670-5750, Fax: 705/670-5754
Senior Manager, Information Services Section, Marc Couse, 705/670-5839, Fax: 705/670-5807
Senior Manager, Mines Group, Dick Cowan, 933 Ramsey Lake Rd., Sudbury ON P3E 6B5, 705/670-5784, Fax: 705/670-5803
Senior Manager, Mining Lands Section, Ron Gashinski, 705/670-5840, Fax: 705/670-5863
Acting Senior Manager, Ontario Geological Survey, PreCambrian Geoscience Section, Andy Fyon, 705/670-5992, Fax: 705/670-5928
Senior Manager, Ontario Geological Survey, Resident Geologists Section, Hial Newsome, 705/670-5955, Fax: 705/670-5953
Senior Manager, Ontario Geological Survey, Sedimentary Geoscience Section, C.L. (Cam) Baker, 705/670-5902, Fax: 705/670-5904

#### NORTHERN DEVELOPMENT DIVISION

#200, 70 Foster Dr., Sault Ste. Marie ON P6A 6V8
705/945-5900; Fax: 705/945-5931
Asst. Deputy Minister, Jim McClure, 705/945-5901
Director, Regional Coordination Branch, Royal Poulin, 159 Cedar St., 6th Fl., Sudbury ON P3E 6A5, 705/670-7003, Fax: 705/670-7031
Director, Trade & Investment Marketing Branch, Russ Sawchuk, 705/945-5903
Senior Manager, Program & Service Delivery, Fred Lalonde, Ontario Government Complex, Hwy. 101 East, PO Box 3060, South Porcupine ON P0N 1H0, 705/235-1654, Fax: 705/235-1660
Senior Manager, Regional Economic Development, Cal McDonald, 705/670-7139, Fax: 705/670-7155
Senior Manager, Special Projects, Aime Dimatteo, 159 Cedar St., 6th Fl., Sudbury ON P3E 6A5, 705/670-7135, Fax: 705/670-7313
Acting Senior Manager, Transportation Unit, Tom Marcolini, 705/945-5836, Fax: 705/945-5931

##### Area Offices

Kenora: 12 Main St. South, PO Box 5050, Kenora ON P9N 3X9 – 807/468-2938; Fax: 807/468-2942, Senior Economist, Don Cameron
Thunder Bay: 435 James St. South, PO Box 435, Thunder Bay ON P7E 6L3 – 807/475-1518; Fax: 807/475-1589, Co-ordinator, Dale Ashbee
Timmins: 60 Wilson Ave., Timmins ON P4N 2S7 – 705/267-8455; Fax: 705/360-2000, Manager, Fred Lalonde

##### Associated Agencies, Boards & Commissions

•Northern Ontario Heritage Fund Corporation: Roberta Bondar Place, #150, 70 Foster Dr., Sault Ste. Marie ON P6A 6V8 – 705/945-6700; Fax: 705/945-6701
General Manager, Royal Poulin
•Ontario Northland: 555 Oak St. East, North Bay ON P1B 8L3 – 705/472-4500; Fax: 705/476-5598
President, John Wallace

## Office of the OMBUDSMAN

125 Queen's Park, Toronto ON M5S 2C7
416/586-3300; Fax: 416/586-3485; Email: info@ombudsman.on.ca; URL: http://www.ombudsman.on.ca
Toll Free: 1-800-263-1830 (English), TDD: 416/586-3510
Ligne sans frais: 1-800-387-2620 (Français)
**Ombudsman**, Roberta Jamieson
Executive Director, Fiona Crean, 416/586-3438
Director, Investigations & Legal Services, Murray Lapp, 416/586-3358
Coordinator, Communications, Gene Long, 416/586-3402

## Ontario HYDRO

700 University Ave., Toronto ON M5G 1X6
416/592-5111; URL: http://www.hydro.on.ca
Toll Free: 1-800-263-9000
**Chairman**, Bill Farlinger, 416/592-2115, Fax: 416/971-3691
President & CEO, Vacant, 416/592-2121, Fax: 416/592-4171
Senior Vice-President, Central Market Operations, Dave Goulding, 416/592-3277, Fax: 416/592-7508
Senior Vice-President, Corporate General Counsel & Secretary, Larry Leonoff, 416/592-2755, Fax: 416/592-1480
Vice-President, Corporate Affairs, Mary McLaughlin, 416/592-2113, Fax: 416/592-2174
Vice-President, Corporate Human Resources, Susan Wright, 416/592-3009, Fax: 416/592-9257
Vice-President, Corporate Services, Eric Preston, 416/592-3079, Fax: 416/592-4891
Vice-President, Corporate Strategies, Rod Taylor, 416/592-3333, Fax: 416/592-3205

#### CORPORATE BUSINESS DEVELOPMENT

Executive Vice-President, Chief Financial Officer & CEO, Eleanor Clitheroe, 416/592-3452, Fax: 416/592-3190
Senior Vice-President, Commercial Analysis & Venture Development, Ian London, 416/506-4920, Fax: 416/506-4688
Vice-President, Corporate Finance, Malen Ng, 416/592-9436, Fax: 416/592-1864
Vice-President, Technology Services & New Product Development Group, Jim Brown, 416/231-6152, Fax: 416/237-9053
Vice-President, Venture Development, Carol Lawrence, 416/506-2014, Fax: 416/506-4684
Treasurer, John Mulligan, 416/592-7654, Fax: 416/592-3903

#### GENERATION COMPANY

Executive Vice-President & Managing Director, John Fox, 416/592-3321, Fax: 416/592-8490
Acting General Manager, Fossil, Brian MacFarlane, 416/592-5130, Fax: 416/592-5136
General Manager, Hydroelectric, Larry Doran, 416/592-1999, Fax: 416/592-6552, 3927
Vice-President, Strategic & Investment Planning, Patrick McNeil, 416/592-1670, Fax: 416/592-1650

#### RETAIL COMPANY

Executive Vice President & Management Director, Ron Stewart, 416/592-2936, Fax: 416/592-4044
General Manager, Distribution Network, Tom Rusnov, 905/946-6770, Fax: 905/946-6772
General Manager, Network Services, Vipin Suri, 416/592-3505, Fax: 416/592-8434
Vice-President, Customer Care Services, Chris Bieber, 905/946-3330
Vice-President, Retail Merchant, Vacant

#### TRANSMISSION COMPANY

Executive Vice President & Managing Director, Karen Robinson, 416/592-3514, Fax: 416/592-3526
General Manager, Land Management Business, Vacant
General Manager, Network Management Business, Doug Shelton, 416/592-5895, Fax: 416/592-6396
General Manager, Network Services Business, Vacant

#### NUCLEAR

Executive Vice President & Chief Nuclear Officer, Carl Andognini, 416/592-2094, Fax: 416/592-2828
Site Vice-President, Bruce Nuclear, Jim Ryder, 519/361-5495, Fax: 519/361-5496
Site Vice-President, Darlington Nuclear, Bob Strickert, 905/697-7497, Fax: 905/697-7540
Site Vice-President, Pickering Nuclear, Ken Talbot, 905/839-3500, Fax: 905/839-4788
Vice-President, Management Systems & Operational Performance Assessments, Richard Machon, 416/592-8224, Fax: 416/592-8085
Vice-President, Nuclear Training, Pierre Trembley, 905/428-4141, Fax: 905/428-0911
Vice-President, Nuclear Waste, Ken Nash, 416/592-7537, Fax: 416/592-7051
Vice-President, Operations & Maintenance, Gene Preston, 416/592-8225, Fax: 416/592-8129
Vice-President, Quality, Robert Ferguson, 416/592-8227, Fax: 416/592-8218
Vice-President, Regulatory Affairs, Brian Debs, 416/592-8229, Fax: 416/592-8221
Vice-President, Regulatory Affairs & Nuclear Assurance, Walter Lee, 416/592-4283, Fax: 416/592-3226
Vice-President, Station Engineering & Support, Warren Peabody, 416/592-8226, Fax: 416/592-8090

## Ministry of the SOLICITOR GENERAL & CORRECTIONAL SERVICES

200 - 1 Ave. West, North Bay ON P1B 9M3
705/497-9500
Corporate Office: North Tower, 25 Grosvenor St., 18th Fl., Toronto ON
416/326-5000, Fax: 416/326-0498

##### ACTS ADMINISTERED

Anatomy Act
Coroners Act
Egress from Public Buildings Act
Emergency Plans Act
Fire Accidents Act
Fire Departments Act
Fire Fighters' Exemption Act
Fire Marshals Act
Hotel Fire Safety Act
Lightning Rod Act
Ministry of Correctional Services Act
Ministry of the Solicitor General Act
Ontario Society for the Prevention of Cruelty to Animals Act
Police Services Act
Private Investigators & Security Guards Act
Public Works Protection Act
Retail Business Holidays Act
**Solicitor General & Minister**, Hon. Robert W. Runciman, 416/326-5075, Fax: 416/326-5085, Email: runciman@epo.gov.on.ca
Deputy Minister, Elaine Todres, 416/326-5060 (Toronto), Fax: 416/327-0469, 705/494-3001 (North Bay)
Director, Communications Branch, Kirk C. Smith, 416/326-5010

Director, Legal Services, Denise Bellamy, 416/326-5044
Director, Race Relations & Policing Unit, Winston Tinglin, 416/326-9333
Acting Manager, Independent Investigations Unit, Brian Scott, 905/826-7335

#### Strategic Policy & Planning Division

25 Grosvenor St., 10th Fl., Toronto ON M7A 1Y6
416/314-3355; Fax: 416/325-3465
Executive Director, Dan McIntyre
Director, Corporate Policy, Bev Ward

### CORPORATE SERVICES DIVISION

200, First Ave. West, PO Box 4100, North Bay ON P1B 9M3
Asst. Deputy Minister, Michael Jordan, 705/494-3003, Fax: 705/494-3004
Director, Bell Cairn Staff Development Centre, Greg Simmons, 905/548-5000, Fax: 905/548-5001
Director, Finance & Administrative Services Branch, Gord Jamieson, 705/494-3103
Director, Human Resources Branch, Nancy Carey, 705/494-3074 (North Bay); 705/329-6604 (Orillia)
Director, Operational Review, Audit & Investigation Branch, Trinela Cane, 705/494-3429

### CORRECTIONAL SERVICES DIVISION

101 Bloor St. West, 7th Fl., Toronto ON M5S 2Z7
Asst. Deputy Minister, Neil McKerrell, 416/327-9911
Director, Operational Support & Coordination Branch, Paul Fleury, 705/494-3339

#### Regional Operations

Eastern: #404, 1055 Princess St., Kingston ON K7L 1H3 – 613/545-4580; Fax: 613/545-1698, Regional Director, John O'Brien
Northern: 957 Cambrian Heights Dr., 2nd Fl., Sudbury ON P3C 5M6 – 705/675-4321; Fax: 705/524-9413, Asst. Regional Director, André Clement
Southern: #220, 300 The East Mall, Toronto ON M9B 6B7 – 416/314-0520; Fax: 416/314-0527, Regional Director, David Parker
Western: 80 Dundas St., 1st Fl., PO Box 5600, Stn A, London ON N6A 2P3 – 519/675-7757; Fax: 519/679-0699, Regional Director, Pauline Radley

### INFORMATION RESOURCES DIVISION

25 Grosvenor St., 11th Fl., Toronto ON M7A 1Y6
416/326-6950; Fax: 416/326-1104
Asst. Deputy Minister, John A. Rollock, 416/326-6952
Director, Computer Operations & Telecommunications Branch, Moy Nahon, 416/326-6967
Director, Information Technology Customer Services Branch, W.D. Gray, 705/494-3230 (North Bay)
Director, Information Technology Development Branch, Ailsa Hamilton, 416/326-6946
Asst. Director, Information Management Services Branch, Kevin Griffin, 416/314-0168, Fax: 416/314-0216
Director, Integrated Justice Project, Kalman Brettler, 416/326-6390
Director, Integrated Safety Project, Frank White, 416/327-6697, Fax: 416/327-6699

### ONTARIO PROVINCIAL POLICE (OPP)

50 Andrew St. South, 3rd Fl., Orillia ON L3V 7T5
URL: http://www.gov.on.ca/opp/
Commissioner, Thomas B. O'Grady, 705/329-6190
Mr. O'Grady will be retiring on or before May 31st, 1998.
Deputy Commissioner, Corporate Support, Diane S. Nagel, 416/314-9376, Fax: 416/314-9433
Deputy Commissioner, Operations, Gerald Boose, 705/329-6300, Fax: 705/329-6304
Chief Superintendent, Administrative Services Division, R.W. Chandler, 705/329-6170
Division Commander & Chief Superintendent, Support Services, E.F. Gibson, 416/314-9174
Chief Superintendent, Investigation Division, G.A. Hawke, 705/329-6310

### POLICING SERVICES DIVISION

25 Grosvenor St., 9th Fl., Toronto ON M7A 2H3
Asst. Deputy Minister, Fred Peters, 416/314-3379, Fax: 416/314-3388
Director, Criminal Intelligence Service Ontario, Insp. Roy Teeft, 416/314-3049
Director, Police Support & Programs Branch, Michael Mitchell, 416/314-3015
Director, Standards & New Programs Branch, L.S. Griffiths, 416/314-3072
Coordinator, Public Appointments Unit, Jane Eeles, 416/314-3344

#### Ontario Police College

County Rd. #32, PO Box 1190, Aylmer ON N5H 2T2
519/773-5361; Fax: 519/773-5762
Director, Noreen Alleyne

### PUBLIC SAFETY DIVISION

416/314-3382; Fax: 416/314-3388
Asst. Deputy Minister, James Young, 416/314-3381

#### Centre of Forensic Sciences

25 Grosvenor St., 2nd Fl., Toronto ON M7A 2G8
416/325-3200; Fax: 416/314-3225
Acting Director, George Cimbura

#### Emergency Measures Ontario (EMO)

25 Grosvenor St., 19th Fl., Toronto ON M7A 1Y6
416/314-3723; Fax: 416/314-3758
Director, Jim Ellard, 416/314-8621
Manager, Administration, Shirley Chen, 416/314-8610

#### Office of the Chief Coroner

26 Grenville St., 2nd Fl., Toronto ON M7A 2G9
416/314-4000; Fax: 416/314-4030
Chief Coroner, J.G. Young, M.D.

#### Office of the Fire Marshal

5775 Yonge St., North York ON M2M 4J1
416/325-3100; Fax: 416/325-3119; URL: http://www.gov.on.ca/OFM/
Fire Marshal, Bernard Moyle, 416/325-3101

#### Ontario Fire College

PO Box 850, Gravenhurst ON P0C 1G0
705/687-2294; Fax: 705/687-7911
Principal, G.E. Schenk

#### Associated Agencies, Boards & Commissions

•Ontario Board of Parole: #201, 2195 Yonge St., Toronto ON M4S 2B1 – 416/325-4480; Fax: 416/325-4485
Chair, Ken S. Sandhu
•Ontario Civilian Commission on Police Services (OCCPS): 25 Grosvenor St., 9th Fl., Toronto ON M7A 2H3 – 416/314-3004; Fax: 416/314-0198
Chair, Murray Chitra
Information Contact, Gordon Hampson, 416/314-3013
•Ontario Police Arbitration Commission: 25 Grosvenor St., 1st Fl., Toronto ON M7A 1Y6 – 416/314-3520; Fax: 416/314-3522
Chair, Cindy Dymond

## Ministry of TRANSPORTATION (MTO)

301 St. Paul St., St. Catharines ON L2R 1W6
EMail: mtoinfo1@epo.gov.on.ca; URL: http://www.gov.on.ca/MTO/
Toll Free: 1-800-268-4686
MTO INFO: 905/704-2000; Fax: 905/704-2002

#### ACTS ADMINISTERED

Airports Act
Bluewater Bridge Act
Bridges Act
Commuter Services Act
Dangerous Goods Transportation Act
Ferries Act
Highway Traffic Act
Local Roads Boards Act
Ministry of Transportation Act
Motorized Snow Vehicles Act
Off-Road Vehicles Act
Ontario Highway Transport Board Act
Ontario Transportation Development Corporation Act
Public Service Works on Highways Act
Public Transportation and Highway Improvement Act
Public Vehicles Act
Railways Act
Rainbow Bridge Act
Statute Labour Act (part)
Toll Bridges Act
Toronto Area Transit Operating Authority Act
Township of Pelee Act
Truck Transportation Act
Urban Transportation Development Corporation Ltd. Act

**Minister**, Hon. Tony Clement, 416/327-9200
Deputy Minister, Janet Rush
Executive Assistant, Lynn Betzner, 416/235-4451
Director, Communications & Public Education, Marj Welch, 416/235-3904, Fax: 416/235-4841
Director, Customer Service Branch, Wil Vanderelst, 416/235-3908, Fax: 416/235-5072
Director, Internal Audit, Ian Nethercot, 416/235-4316
Director, Legal Services Branch, Anne Marie Gutierrez, 416/235-4404

### CORPORATE SERVICES DIVISION

Asst. Deputy Minister, Mary Proc, 905/704-2701, Fax: 905/704-2575
Director, Facilities & Operation Services Branch, John Thorne, 905/704-2893, Fax: 905/704-2833
Director, Financial Planning & Administration Branch, David Aranoff, 416/235-4219, Fax: 416/235-5277
Director, Human Resources Branch, Tatiana Benzaquen, 416/235-3846, Fax: 416/235-4842
Director, Information Systems Branch, Blair Smith, 416/235-3926, Fax: 416/235-4833
Manager, Corporate Operations, John Holland, 905/704-2906
Manager, Greater Toronto Area/Downsview Corporate Services, Joan Crowther, 416/235-5370, Fax: 416/235-4847

### OPERATIONS DIVISION

Asst. Deputy Minister, Vacant, 416/235-4457, Fax: 416/235-4950
Director, Operations (Central Region), Denise Evans, 416/235-5185
Director, Planning & Engineering (Central Region), Kevin Pask, 416/235-5400
Director, Resources Management Branch, Ian Oliver, 416/235-4152, Fax: 416/235-4255

### POLICY & PLANNING DIVISION

Asst. Deputy Minister, David Guscott, 416/327-2619, Fax: 416/327-8746
Director, Corporate Policy, Linda Clifford, 416/235-4437, Fax: 416/235-5243
Director, Freight Transportation Policy, Rob Bergevin, 416/235-4039
Director, Investment Strategies, Tony Salerno, 416/235-4042

Director, Passenger Transportation Policy, Frank D'Onofrio, 416/235-4050
Director, Strategic Transportation Research Branch, Susan Crawford, 416/235-5070
Director, Transportation Systems Planning, Ravi Girdhar, 416/235-3976

#### QUALITY & STANDARDS DIVISION

Asst. Deputy Minister, Stephen C.J. Radbone, 416/327-8788, Fax: 416/327-9229
Director, Acquisition Standards, Carol Hennum, 416/235-5205
Director, Hwy. 407 Engineering, David Garner, 905/709-2715
Director, Program Development, Bert Vervenne, 416/235-4008
Director, Research & Development, George Gera, 416/235-4707
Director, Transportation Engineering Standards Branch, Stephen C.J. Radbone, 416/235-4402
Director, Transportation Operations Branch, Colin Rayman, 416/235-3811, Fax: 416/235-4427

#### RELOCATION DIVISION

Asst. Deputy Minister, Margaret Kelch, 416/235-5312, Fax: 416/235-5368

#### SAFETY & REGULATION DIVISION

Acting Asst. Deputy Minister, Rudi Wycliffe, 416/235-4453, Fax: 416/235-4153
Director, Business Technology Integration Group, David Mee, 416/235-3589
Director, Compliance Branch, Mike Weir, 905/704-2507
Director, Licensing & Control Branch, Jennifer D'Angelo, 416/235-4793
Director, Road Safety Business Services Group, Blake Forrest, 416/235-3845
Director, Safety Information Technology Branch, Doug Farrar, 416/235-5315
Director, Safety Policy Branch, John Hughes, 416/235-3591

#### Associated Agencies, Boards & Commissions

•GO Transit: 1120 Finch Ave. West, Toronto ON M3J 3J8 – 416/869-3600; Fax: 416/869-1755
Chair, David Hobbs
Managing Director, Richard Ducharme
•Licence Suspension Appeal Board: 700 Bay St., 24th Fl., PO Box 329, Toronto ON M5G 1Z6 – 416/325-0209
Secretary, Donna Bodok
•Ontario Highway Transport Board: 151 Bloor St. West, 10th Fl., Toronto ON M5S 2T5 – 416/326-6739; Fax: 416/326-6728
Chair, George Samis
Secretary, Marquita McKenzie

### Ontario WOMENS DIRECTORATE

900 Bay St., 6th Fl., Toronto ON M7A 1L2
416/314-0300; Fax: 416/314-0247; URL: http://www.gov.on.ca/owd
**Minister Responsible**, Hon. Dianne Cunningham, 416/326-1600, Fax: 416/326-1656
Asst. Deputy Minister, Mayann Francis

### WORKERS' COMPENSATION BOARD

2 Bloor St. East, 20th Fl., Toronto ON M4W 3C3
416/927-4135; Fax: 416/927-5141; URL: http://www.wcb.on.ca/
**Minister Responsible**, Hon. Cameron Jackson, 416/326-1460
Chair, Edoardo Di Santo

## GOVERNMENT OF PRINCE EDWARD ISLAND

**Seat of Government:** Legislative Assembly, Province House, PO Box 487, Charlottetown PE C1A 7L1
URL: http://www.gov.pe.ca/
The Province of Prince Edward Island entered Confederation July 1, 1873. It has an area of 5,660.38 km2, and the StatsCan census population in 1996 was 134,557.

### Office of the LIEUTENANT GOVERNOR

Government House, PO Box 846, Charlottetown PE C1A 7L9
902/368-5480; Fax: 902/368-5481; URL: http://www.gov.pe.ca/lg/index.html
**Lieutenant Governor**, Hon. Gilbert Clements
Private Secretary, Judy Burke

### Office of the PREMIER

Shaw Bldg., 95 Rochford St., 5th Fl. South, PO Box 2000, Charlottetown PE C1A 7N8
902/368-4400; Fax: 902/368-4416; URL: http://www.gov.pe.ca/premier/index.html
**Premier**, Hon. Patrick Binns
Chief of Staff, Maurice Rogerson
Private Secretary, Gayle Roberts
Principal Secretary, Peter McQuaid
Officer, Protocol, Maurice Rogerson

### EXECUTIVE COUNCIL

Shaw Bldg., PO Box 2000, Charlottetown PE C1A 7N8
URL: http://www.gov.pe.ca/ec/index.html
Premier & President, Executive Council, Hon. Patrick Binns, 902/368-4400, Fax: 902/368-4416, Email: pgbinns@gov.pe.ca
Minister, Transportation & Public Works, Hon. Michael F. Currie, 902/368-5120, Fax: 902/368-5385, Email: mfcurrie@gov.pe.ca
Minister, Health & Social Services, Hon. Mildred A. Dover, 902/368-4930, Fax: 902/368-4974, Email: madover@gov.pe.ca
Minister, Education, Hon. J. Chester Gillan, 902/368-4610, Fax: 902/368-4699, Email: jcgillan@gov.pe.ca
Minister, Agriculture & Forestry, Hon. Eric Hammill, 902/368-4820, Fax: 902/368-4846, Email: jehammill@gov.pe.ca
Minister, Fisheries & Environment, Hon. Kevin MacAdam, 902/368-6410, Fax: 902/368-6488
Minister, Economic Development & Tourism, Hon. J.W. (Wes) MacAleer, 902/368-4230, Fax: 902/368-4242
Provincial Treasurer, Hon. Patricia J. Mella, 902/368-4050, Fax: 902/368-6575, Email: pjmella@gov.pe.ca
Minister, Community Affairs & Attorney General, Hon. P. Mitchell Murphy, 902/368-5250, Fax: 902/368-4121, Email: pmmurphy@gov.pe.ca
**Minister Responsible**, Hon. Francene Cosman, 902/424-4037

#### Executive Council Office

Clerk & Secretary to Cabinet, Verna Bruce, 902/368-4502, Fax: 902/368-6118, Email: vebruce@gov.pe.ca
Clerk Asst., Lynn E. Ellsworth, 902/368-4300, Fax: 902/368-6118, Email: leellsworth@gov.pe.ca
Director, Labour Force Development, Jake Baird, 902/368-4506, Fax: 902/368-6118, Email: jsbaird@gov.pe.ca
Trade Advisor, Sandy Stewart, 902/368-4504, Fax: 902/368-6118, Email: wastewart@gov.pe.ca

#### Standing Committees of Cabinet

Management Board: PO Box 2000, Charlottetown PE C1A 7N8, Acting Secretary, Bill Harper, 902/368-4053, Fax: 902/368-6575, Email: wgharper@gov.pe.ca
Policy Board: PO Box 2000, Charlottetown PE C1A 7N8, Secretary, Verna Bruce, 902/368-4502, Fax: 902/368-6118, Email: vebruce@gov.pe.ca

### LEGISLATIVE ASSEMBLY

c/o Clerk's Office, Province House, PO Box 2000, Charlottetown PE C1A 7N8
902/368-5970; Fax: 902/368-5175; URL: http://www.gov.pe.ca/leg.index.html
**Clerk:** Verna Bruce, 902/368-5970
**Speaker:** Hon. Wilbur MacDonald, 902/368-4310, Fax: 902/368-5175
**Sergeant-at-Arms:** Ivan Kerry
Clerk Asst. & Clerk of Committees, Charles MacKay, Email: cmackay@peinet.pe.ca

#### Government Members' Office (Lib.)

Coles Bldg., 100 Richmond St., 3rd Fl., PO Box 338, Charlottetown PE CIA 8C5
902/368-4360; Fax: 902/368-4377
Government Caucus Chair, Elmer Macfadyen
Administrative Asst., Colleen Chipman

#### Office of the Official Opposition (Lib.)

Coles Bldg., 100 Richmond St., 2nd Fl., PO Box 2890, Charlottetown PE C1A 8C5
902/368-4330; Fax: 902/368-4348; URL: http://www.gov.pe.ca/leg/govmem.html
Executive Asst., Myrtle Jenkins-Smith

### FIFTY-NINTH GENERAL ASSEMBLY - PRINCE EDWARD ISLAND

URL: http://www.gov.pe.ca/leg/index.html
Last General Election, November 18, 1996. Legal Duration, 5 Years.
**Party Standings (November 19, 1996)**
Progressive Conservative (PC) 18
Liberal (Lib.) 8
New Democratic Party (NDP) 1
Total 27
**Salaries, Indemnities & Allowances**
Effective 1 April, 1997 members' sessional indemnity $30,645 plus a $9,287 tax-free expense & travelling allowance. In addition to this are the following:
Premier $50,158
Ministers $35,433
Speaker $17,549
Deputy Speaker $7,755
Leader of the Opposition, $35,433
Prince Edward Island made major changes to the Election Act on May 2, 1996. The most significant change was the elimination of former 16 dual member ridings (Assemblymen & Councillors) & the re-drawing of the electoral map to constitute 27 new member ridings. Each new riding will elect just one member to the legislature, thus reducing the number of MLAs from 32
to 27.

#### MEMBERS BY CONSTITUENCY

Following is: constituency (unofficial number of voters at 1996 election) member, party affiliation. (Address for all is PO Box 2000, Charlottetown PE C1A 7N8.) Refer to Cabinet List, Government Members Office, & to Office of the Opposition, for Fax numbers.

1st (2,500) Andy Mooney, PC
2nd (2,656) Hon. Kevin MacAdam, PC
3rd (2,688) Hon. Michael F. Currie, PC
4th (2,294) Jim Bagnall, PC
5th (2,443) Hon. Patrick Binns, PC

6th (2,616) Hon. Wilbur MacDonald, PC
7th (3,417) Hon. Pat Mella, PC
8th (2,881) Hon. Mildred A. Dover, PC
9th (3,194) Jamie Ballem, PC
10th (3,004) Elmer MacFayden, PC
11th (2,761) Hon. J. Chester Gillan, PC
12th (2,783) Provincial by-election held on Nov. 17, 1997, results not known at time of printing.
13th (2,866) Paul Connolly, Lib., 902/892-5615
14th (3,462) Hon. J.W. (Wes) MacAleer, PC
15th (3,516) Don MacKinnon, PC
16th (3,788) Ron MacKinley, Lib., 902/566-3963
17th (3,525) Norman MacPhee, PC
18th (3,663) Beth MacKenzie, PC
19th (3,025) Hon. Eric Hammill, PC
20th (3,559) Hon. P. Mitchell Murphy, PC
21st (3,392) Greg Deighan, PC
22nd (3,168) Nancy Guptill, Lib., 902/436-4488
23rd (2,694) Hon. Keith W. Milligan, Lib., 902/831-2105
24th (2,443) Robert Maddix, Lib., 902/436-5076
25th (2,399) Dr. Herb Dickieson, NDP
26th (2.733) Hector MacLeod, Lib., 902/853-2796
27th (2,618) Robert J. Morrissey, Lib., 902/882-3238

#### MEMBERS (ALPHABETICAL)

Following is: MEMBER, constituency (unofficial number of voters at 1996 election), party affiliation. (Address for all is PO Box 2000, Charlottetown PE C1A 7N8.)
Refer to Cabinet List, Government Members Office, & to Office of the Opposition, for Fax numbers.

Jim Bagnall, 4th (2,294) PC
Jamie Ballem, 9th (3,194) PC
Hon. Patrick Binns, 5th (2,443) PC
Wayne D. Cheverie, Q.C., 12th (2,783) Lib., (by-election to replace Mr. Cheverie, Nov. 12, 1997)
Paul Connolly, 13th (2,866) Lib., 902/892-5615
Hon. Michael F. Currie, 3rd (2,688) PC
Greg Deighan, 21st (3,392) PC
Dr. Herb Dickieson, 25th (2,399) NDP
Hon. Mildred A. Dover, 8th (2,881) PC
Hon. J. Chester Gillan, 11th (2,761) PC
Nancy Guptill, 22nd (3,168) Lib., 902/436-4488
Hon. Eric Hammill, 19th (3,025) PC
Hon. Kevin MacAdam, 2nd (2,656) PC
Hon. J.W. (Wes) MacAleer, 14th (3,462) PC
Hon. Wilbur MacDonald, 6th (2,616) PC
Elmer MacFayden, 10th (3,004) PC
Beth MacKenzie, 18th (3,663) PC
Ron MacKinley, 16th (3,788) Lib., 902/566-3963
Don MacKinnon, 15th (3,516) PC
Hector MacLeod, 26th (2.733) Lib., 902/853-2796
Norman MacPhee, 17th (3,525) PC
Robert Maddix, 24th (2,443) Lib., 902/436-5076
Hon. Pat Mella, 7th (3,417) PC
Hon. Keith W. Milligan, 23rd (2,694) Lib., 902/831-2105
Andy Mooney, 1st (2,500) PC
Robert J. Morrissey, 27th (2,618) Lib., 902/882-3238
Hon. P. Mitchell Murphy, 20th (3,559) PC

# PRINCE EDWARD ISLAND GOVERNMENT DEPARTMENTS & AGENCIES

## Department of AGRICULTURE & FORESTRY

Jones Bldg., 11 Kent St., PO Box 2000, Charlottetown PE C1A 7N8
902/368-4880; Fax: 902/368-4857; URL: http://www.gov.pe.ca/daff/index.html
Pest Information Line: 902/368-5658

#### ACTS ADMINISTERED

Agricultural Insurance Act
Agricultural Products Standards Act
Agrologists Act
Animal Health & Protection Act
Apiary Inspection Act
Artificial Insemination Act
Dairy Industry Act
Dairy Producers Act
Dog Act
Farm Implement Act
Fences & Detention of Stray Livestock Act
Fish Inspection Act
Forest Management Act
Grain Elevators Corporation Act
Livestock Community Auction Sales Act
Maritime Provinces Harness Racing Commission Act
Natural Products Marketing Act
Pesticides Control Act
Plant Health Act
Potato Crop Mortgage Act
Poultry & Poultry Products Act
Sea Plants Act
Veterinary Profession Act
Weed Control Act
Women's Institute Act

**Minister**, Hon. Eric Hammill, 902/368-4820, Fax: 902/368-4846, Email: JEHammill@gov.pe.ca
Deputy Minister, Rory Francis, 902/368-4830, Fax: 902/368-4846, Email: rmfrancis@gov.pe.ca
Director, Administration & Income Support Division, Vacant
Director, Communications, Wayne MacKinnon, 902/368-4888, Email: wemackinnon@gov.pe.ca

#### AGRICULTURE DIVISION

Research Station, PO Box 1600, Stn University, Charlottetown PE C1A 7N3
902/368-5600; Fax: 902/368-5661
Director, Dr. Wendell Grasse, 902/368-5645, Email: wegrasse@gov.pe.ca
Supervisor, Dairy Lab, Boyce MacIsaac, 16 Walker Dr., Charolottetown PE C1A 8S6, 902/368-4480, Fax: 902/368-4486
Manager, Farm Business Management, Jim Newson, 902/368-5613, Email: jfnewson@gov.pe.ca
Manager, Livestock, Feed & Feeding Section, Teresa Mellish, Fax: 902/368-5729
Manager, Research, Resources & Laboratories & Officer Responsible, The Pesticides Act, Richard Veinot, PO Box 306, Kensington PE C0B 1M0, 902/368-5646
Inspector, Pesticides Act, Thane Clarke, 902/836-5450

##### District Agricultural Offices

Charlottetown: Agricultural Research & Extension Bldg., University Ave., PO Box 1600, Charlottetown PE C1A 7N3 – Fax: 902/368-5729, Farm Management Consultant, Frank Duguay
Montague: Southern Kings Regional Service Centre, PO Box 1500, Montague PE C0A 1R0 – Fax: 902/838-2922, Farm Management Consultant, Colleen Younie
O'Leary: West Prince Regional Services Centre, PO Box 8, O'Leary PE C0B 1V0 – Fax: 902/859-8709, Farm Management Consultant, James Harris
Souris: Johnny Ross Young Regional Services Centre, PO Box 550, Souris PE C0A 2B0 – Fax: 902/687-2026, Farm Management Consultant, Don Sutherland
Summerside: East Prince Regional Services Centre, 109 Water St., Summerside PE C1N 1A9 – Fax: 902/888-8023, Farm Management Consultant, John Coldwill

#### FORESTRY DIVISION

J. Frank Gaudet Tree Nursery, Upton Rd., West Royalty, PO Box 2000, Charlottetown PE C1A 7N8
902/368-4700; Fax: 902/368-4713
Forest Fire Emergencies: 1-800-237-5053
Director, Jerry Gavin, 902/368-4705, Email: jpgavin@gov.pe.ca
Manager, Production Development, Bill Butler, 902/368-4711
Manager, Silviculture Development, Bill Glen, 902/368-4703

##### District Operations

Central: Beach Grove Rd., PO Box 2000, Charlottetown PE C1A 7N8 – 902/368-4800; Fax: 902/368-4806, Manager, Dan McAskill
Eastern: PO Box 29, St. Peter's Bay PE C0A 2A0 – 902/961-2172; Fax: 902/961-3005, Manager, Brian Brown
Western: RR#1, Wellington Station PE C0B 2E0 – 902/854-2155; Fax: 902/888-8402, Manager, Herbert Isherwood

#### PLANNING & DEVELOPMENT DIVISION

902/368-4840; Fax: 902/368-4857
Director, John MacQuarrie, 902/368-6451, Email: jamacquarrie@gov.pe.ca
Officer, Primary Resource Development Agreement Administration, Sandra MacKinnon, 902/368-5593, Email: sjmackinnon@gov.pe.ca
Officer, Trade Relations, Dr. Robert Morrison, 902/368-5087, Email: wrmorrison@gov.pe.ca

##### Associated Agencies, Boards & Commissions

•Agricultural Development Corporation: PO Box 2000, Charlottetown PE C1A 7N8 – 902/368-4830; Fax: 902/368-5743
General Manager, Rory Francis
•Grain Elevator Corporation: PO Box 250, Kensington PE COB 1M0 – 902/836-3605; Fax: 902/836-3716
President, Allan Ling

##### Agricultural Marketing Boards & Commissions

•Prince Edward Island Egg Commodity Marketing Board: Farm Centre, 420 University Ave., Charlottetown PE C1A 7Z5 – 902/892-8401
Manager, Murray Myles
•Prince Edward Island Hog Commodity Marketing Board: Farm Centre, 420 University Ave., Charlottetown PE C1A 7Z5 – 902/892-4201
Manager, Bob Harding
•Prince Edward Island Marketing Council: PO Box 2000, Charlottetown PE C1A 7N8 – 902/368-4816; Fax: 902/368-4846
General Manager, Bob Morrison
•Prince Edward Island Pedigreed Seed Commodity Marketing Board: PO Box 1600, Charlottetown PE C1A 7N3 – 902/368-5633; Fax: 902/368-5661
Secretary, Winston Cousins
•Prince Edward Island Potato Board: Farm Centre, 420 University Ave., Charlottetown PE C1A 7Z5 – 902/892-6551; Fax: 902/566-4914
Manager, Ivan Noonan
•Prince Edward Island Poultry Marketing Board: Baldwin's Rd., RR#6, Cardigan PE C0A 1G0 – 902/838-4108; Fax: 902/838-4108
Manager, Janet Murphy

## PEI Public ARCHIVES & RECORDS OFFICE

PO Box 1000, Charlottetown PE C1A 7M4
902/368-4290; Fax: 902/368-6327; Email: htholman@gov.pe.ca
**Provincial Archivist**, Harry T. Holman

## Office of the AUDITOR GENERAL

PO Box 2000, Charlottetown PE C1A 7N8
902/368-4520; Fax: 902/368-4598
**Auditor General**, J. Wayne Murphy, F.C.A.

## Department of COMMUNITY AFFAIRS & ATTORNEY GENERAL

PO Box 2000, Charlottetown PE C1A 7N8
902/368-5250; Fax: 902/368-5283; 5355; URL: http://www.gov.pe.ca/paag/index.html

#### ACTS ADMINISTERED

Affidavits Act
Age of Majority Act
Ancient Burial Grounds Act
Appeals Act
Apportionment Act
Arbitration Act
Assignment of Book Debts Act
Auctioneers Act
Bailable Proceedings Act
Bills of Sale Act
Bulk Sales Act
Business Practices Act
Canada-United Kingdom Judgements Recognition Act
Cemeteries Act
Charities Act
Child Status Act
Collection Agencies Act
Commorientes Act
Companies Act
Conditional Sales Act
Condominium Act
Consumer Protection Act
Consumer Reporting Act
Contributory Negligence Act
Controverted Elections (Provincial) Act
Cooperative Associations Act
Coroners Act
Corporation Securities Registration Act
Court Security Act
Court Stenographers Act
Credit Unions Act
Crown Proceedings Act
Custody Jurisdiction & Enforcement Act
Defamation Act
Dependents of a Deceased Person Relief Act
Designation of Beneficiaries under Benefit Plans, An Act Respecting
Direct Sellers Act
Escheats Act, (jointly with Dept. of Transportation & Public Works)
Evidence Act
Factors Act
Family Law Act
Fatal Accidents Act
Films Act
Fire Prevention Act
Foreign Resident Corporations Act
Frauds on Creditors Act
Frustrated Contracts Act
Garage Keeper's Lien Act
Garnishee Act
Habeas Corpus Act
Insurance Act
International Commercial Arbitration Act
International Sale of Goods Act
International Trusts Act
Interpretation Act
Interprovincial Subpoena Act
Investigation of Titles Act
Island Regulatory & Appeals Commission Act
Judgement & Execution Act
Judicial Review Act
Jury Act
Lands Protection Act
Licencing Act
Limited Partnerships Act
Maintenance Enforcement Act
Mechanics' Lien Act
Occupiers' Liability Act
Partnership Act
Pension Benefits Act
Perpetuities Act
Police Act
Powers of Attorney Act
Prearranged Funeral Services Act
Premium Tax Act
Private Investigators & Security Guards Act
Probate Act
Provincial Administrator of Estates Act
Provincial Court Act
Public Trustee Act
Quieting Titles Act
Real Estate Trading Act
Real Property Act
Reciprocal Enforcement of Judgements Act
Reciprocal Enforcement of Maintenance Orders Act
Sale of Goods Act
Securities Act
Sheriffs Act
Statute of Frauds
Statute of Limitations
Statute Revision Act
Store Hours Act
Summary Proceedings Act
Supreme Court Act
Survival of Actions Act
Time in Public Offices Act
Transboundary Pollution (Reciprocal Access) Act
Trespass to Property Act
Trustee Act
Unclaimed Articles Act
Unconscionable Transactions Relief Act
Uniformity Commissioners Act
Variation of Trusts Act
Warehousemen's Liens Act
Water & Sewerage Act
Winding Up Act

**Attorney General & Minister**, Hon. Mitch Murphy, Fax: 902/368-4121
Deputy Minister, Dave Riley, Fax: 902/368-4121
Chief Coroner, Office of the Chief Coroner, Dr. Charles Trainer, 902/566-4100

#### CONSUMER, CORPORATE & INSURANCE DIVISION

Shaw Building, 95 Rochford St., 4th Fl., PO Box 2000, Charlottetown PE C1A 7N8
902/368-4550

The Consumer Affairs section is responsible for administering Orderly Payment of debts (OPD), lottery schemes, gun control & film clasification, & for handling consumer complaints & inquiries.

The Corporations section is responsible for registering business names, incorporating companies, cooperatives & credit unions, & licensing out-of-province companies, brokers, security salespeople & securities sold to the public.

The insurance, real estate & public trustee section operates under the supervision of the Superintendent of Insurance & is responsible for real estate licenses, insurance legislation, insurance complaints, & collecting premium & fire prevention taxes.

Director, Edison J. Shea, 902/368-4551, Fax: 902/368-5283
Registrar/Corporations Officer, Securities & Consumer, Corporate & Insurance Services, Ruth Demone, 902/368-4552
Superintendent, Insurance & Real Estate Division & Public Trustee, W. Bennett Campbell, 902/368-4564
Manager, Consumer Services, Eric Goodwin, 902/368-4580, Fax: 902/368-5355

#### CROWN ATTORNEYS DIVISION

Acting Director, Darrell Coombs, Q.C., 902/368-4595, Fax: 902/368-5812

#### FRANCOPHONE AFFAIRS

Director, Claudette Theriault, 902/368-4509

#### LABOUR & INDUSTRIAL RELATIONS DIVISION

Director, Barry Curley, 902/368-5565, Fax: 902/368-5526
Manager, Employment Standards, Wayne S. MacKinnon, 902/368-5550
Officer, Industrial Relations Council, Marlene Clark, 902/368-5553

#### LEGAL & JUDICIAL SERVICES DIVISION

Director, Charles Thompson, 902/368-4594, Fax: 902/368-4563
Manager, Legal Aid, Kent Brown, 902/368-6042
Legislative Counsel, Raymond Moore, 902/368-4291
Officer, Maintenance Enforcement, Deborah Conway, 902/368-6010

**For a list of Courts & other Legal Officers, including Judicial Officials & Judges *see* Section 10 of this book.**

#### PLANNING & INSPECTION SERVICES DIVISION

902/368-5582; Fax: 902/368-5526
Director, Albert MacDonald, 902/368-4229
Chief Fire Marshal, Office of the Fire Marshal, David Blacquiere, 902/368-4869
Manager, Building & Development Services, Don Walters, 902/368-4874
Manager, Inspection Services, Gerry MacDonald, 902/368-4884, Fax: 902/368-5544
Manager, Provincial Planning, Kingsley Lewis, 902/368-4871, Fax: 902/368-5544
Chief Officer, Boiler & Pressure Vessel, Plumbing & Propane Inspection, Ken Hynes
Municipal Affairs Officer, John Berry, 902/368-4876, Fax: 902/368-5544

##### Regional Service Centres

East Prince: Summerside PE – 902/888-8000; Fax: 902/888-8023, Administrator, Mary Lynn Arsenault, Email: mlarsenault@gov.pe.ca
Evangeline: Wellington PE – 902/854-7250; Fax: 902/854-7255, Administrator, Armand Arsenault, Email: ajasenault@gov.pe.ca
Johnny Ross Young: Souris PE – 902/687-7000; Fax: 902/687-2026, Administrator, Eleanor Avery, Email: emavery@gov.pe.ca
Southern Kings/Queens: Montague PE – 902/838-0600; Fax: 902/838-0610, Administrator, Jim Kinnee, Email: jmkinnee@gov.pe.ca
Tignish & Area: Tignish PE – 902/882-7351; Fax: 902/882-2414, Bilingual Information Secretary, Claudette LeClair
West Prince: O'Leary PE – 902/859-8800; Fax: 902/859-8709, Acting Administrator, Martha Dawson

#### POLICY & ADMINISTRATION DIVISION

Director, George Likely, 902/368-4233
Manager, Administration, Don Gorveatt, 902/368-4810
Director, Francophone Affairs Secretariat, Claudette Theriault, 902/368-4509
Coordinator, Infrastructure Program, Dennis Friesen, 902/368-4882

##### Associated Agencies, Boards & Commissions

•Atlantic Lottery Corporation
*See* listing under New Brunswick Finance, this Section.
•Employment Standards Board: PO Box 2000, Charlottetown PE C1A 7N8 – 902/368-5550; Fax: 902/368-5526
Chair, Michael F. Hennessey
Secretary, Wayne S. MacKinnon
•Labour Relations Board: PO Box 2000, Charlottetown PE C1A 7N8 – 902/368-5550; Fax: 902/368-5526
Chair, George Lyle
CEO, Roy J. Doucette
•Prince Edward Island Emergency Measures Organization
Listed alphabetically in detail, this section.

## Department of ECONOMIC DEVELOPMENT & TOURISM

Shaw Bldg., 95 Rochford St., 5th Fl., PO Box 2000, Charlottetown PE C1A 7N8
902/368-4476; Fax: 902/368-4242; URL: http://www.gov.pe.ca/edt/index.html
Provides leadership & support in the advancement & implementation of business & tourism strategies on PEI. The department is responsible for the creation of jobs for Islanders; wealth creation for Island operations; promoting entrepreneurial growth & risk sharing; promoting community economic development; providing effective, efficient & economic management of the overall operations; & aggressively promoting & positioning PEI as a competitive place to live, work, do business & vacation.

#### ACTS ADMINISTERED

Area Industrial Commission Act
Confederation Birthplace Act
Employment Development Agency Act
Energy Corporation Act
Energy-efficient Appliances Act (when proclaimed)
Enterprise P.E.I. Act
Fathers of Confederation Buildings Act
Highways Advertisements Act (until repealed)
Institute of Man & Resources Act
Island Investment Development Act
Maritime Economic Cooperation Act
Mineral Resources Act
National Park Act
Oil & Natural Gas Act
Recreation Development Act
Roadside Signs Act (when proclaimed)
Tourism Industry Act
Trails Act
**Minister**, Hon. J.W. (Wes) MacAleer, 902/368-4230
Deputy Minister, Leo J. Walsh, 902/368-4250
Coordinator, Cooperation Agreements, Gary Petitpas, 902/368-4246, Canada/PEI Cooperation Agreement on Industrial Development contact.
Manager, Program Coordination, Susan MacKenzie, 902/368-5079
Coordinator, Public Relations, Ann Stanley, 902/368-6322

#### ADMINISTRATION & FINANCE

Shaw Bldg., 95 Rochford St., 4th Fl., Charlottetown PE C1A 7N8
902/368-4240; Fax: 902/368-4224
Director, Karen Fisher

#### COMMUNITY DEVELOPMENT SECTION

Shaw Bldg., 95 Rochford St., 4th Fl., Charlottetown PE C1A 7N8
Manager, Birt MacKinnon, 902/368-4244, Fax: 902/368-4224, Email: bmackinnon@gov.pe.ca

#### DEVELOPMENT DIVISION

Chief Operating Officer, Brian Thompson, 902/360-6306, Email: blthomps@gov.pe.ca
Director, Aerospace & Food, Lennie Kelly, 902/368-5957
Director, Information & Communications Technology, Dave McLane, 902/368-6388
Director, Manufacturing, Lori Pendleton, 902/368-5963
Director, Marketing & Communications, Sheri Coles, 902/368-6326
Director, Public Sector Development, John Hughes
Director, Technological Partnering, Colin Marr, 902/368-5859
Director, Trade Development, Steve Murray, 902/368-0051
Manager, Information Technology Development, Lee Brammer
Manager, Research, Dave Bryanton, 902/368-6342
Supervisor, Business Support Programs, Alex Rogers
Representative, Telecommunications Investment, Elmer Stavert, 902/368-5966
Representative, Trade Development, Shelley Clark, 902/368-6307
Sector Specialist, Agri-food, Patricia Manning
Sector Specialist, Fisheries, Phyllis Duffy
Film Commissioner, Berni Wood, 902/368-6329

#### ENERGY & MINERALS DIVISION

Holman Bldg., 25 University Ave, 3rd & 4th Fls., PO Box 910, Charlottetown PE C1A 7L9
Manager, Virginia Bulger, 902/368-5018
Advisor, Ronald Estabrooks, 902/368-5011
Officer, Mike Proud, 902/368-5019

#### ENTERPRISE PEI

Holman Bldg., 25 University Ave., 3rd & 4th Fls., PO Box 910, Charlottetown PE C1A 7L9
902/368-6300; Fax: 902/368-6301; Email: invest@gov.pe.ca; URL: http://www.gov.pe.ca/edt/epei.html
Toll Free: 1-800-563-3734
Promotes new economic development for the province & solicits & supports investment. Supports small business & encourages entrepreneurship & investment risk-sharing. The division also develops energy & technology strategies, conducts market research & promotes PEI as a competitive place to do business.
CEO, Leo J. Walsh, 902/368-4250

#### LENDING SERVICES DIVISION

Confederation Court Office Bldg., #201, 134 Kent St., PO Box 1420, Charlottetown PE C1A 7N1
902/368-6200; Fax: 902/368-6201
Acting Executive Director, Peter Wilson
Account Manager, Agriculture, G.F. Gahan
Account Manager, Agriculture, Hugh Campbell
Account Manager, Agriculture, Edgar Coffin
Account Manager, Fisheries & Aquaculture, Dan Smith
Account Manager, Small Business, Anne Wood
Account Manager, Tourism, Gerry Soy
Asst., Resource Lending, Lauraine Simpson
Chair, Credit Review Committee, Tom Cullen

#### POLICY & PLANNING DIVISION

Shaw Bldg., 95 Rochford St., 4th Fl., PO Box 2000, Charlottetown PE C1A 7N8
Provides policy & planning assistance for all divisions throughout the ministry & collects & develops research meterials which are central to overall economic development initiatives. The division also is also mandated to carry out labour market & economic analysis; provide computer support for staff; develop computer systems; develop the province's Internet Information Centre; represent the department on various interdepartmental policy initiatives; provide policy assistance with respect to federal/provincial agreements; & coordinate annual reports & briefing books.
Director, Carol Mayne, 902/368-4264, Email: camayne@gov.pe.ca
Manager, Research, Planning & Evaluation, Charlotte Gorrill, 902/368-4266, Email: clgorrill@gov.pe.ca

#### TOURISM PEI

Annex 1, West Royalty Industrial Park, 1 Watts Ave., Charlottetown PE C1E 1B0
902/368-5540; Fax: 902/368-4438; Email: tourpei@gov.pe.ca; URL: http://www.gov.pe.ca
Toll Free: 1-800-465-4734
Chief Operating Officer, Frank Butler, 902/368-5956
Director, Development, Ron MacNeill, 902/368-5505, Email: rnmacnei@gov.pe.ca
Director, Marketing, Rob McCloskey, 902/368-5951
Director, Sales & Trade, Lori Lawless
Manager, Advertising & Promotions, Greg Arsenault
Manager, Golf, Jack Kane, 902/368-4238
Manager, Provincial Parks, Greg McKee, 902/368-4404
Manager, Quality Services, Brenda Gallant
Officer, Project Development, Doug Murray
Officer, Project Development, Burce Garrity
Officer, Quality Standards, Peter McCrady
Chair, Tourism Marketing Authority, Dale Larkin

#### Associated Agencies, Boards & Commissions

•East Isle Shipyards Inc.: PO Box 220, Georgetown PE C0A 1L0 – 902/652-2275
Director, Operations, Jim Theriault
•Food Technology Centre: University of PEI Campus, 550 University Ave., Charlottetown PE C1A 4P3 – 902/566-1725; Fax: 902/566-5627; Email: peiftc@peinet.pe.ca; URL: http://www.gov.pe.ca/ftc/index.html
Executive Director, Dr. Richard Ablett
Director, Operations, Brenda Tremere
Director, Research & Development Technology, Jim Smith
Manager, Information & Promotion, Mary Jane Grant

## Department of EDUCATION

Sullivan Bldg., 16 Fitzroy St., PO Box 2000, Charlottetown PE C1A 7N8
902/368-4600; Fax: 902/368-4663; Email: education@gov.pe.ca; URL: http://www.gov.pe.ca/educ/
Management Information: 902/368-4602

#### ACTS ADMINISTERED

Archeological Sites Protection Act
Archives Act
Fathers of Confederation Buildings Act
Heritage Places Protection Act
Island Regulatory & Appeals Commission Act
Lucy Maud Montgomery Foundation Act
Museum Act
Public Libraries Act
School Act
Sports Commission Act
Teachers' Superannuation Act
**Minister**, Hon. J. Chester Gillan, 902/368-4610, Fax: 902/368-4699, Email: jcgillan@gov.pe.ca
Deputy Minister, M. Elaine Noonan, 902/368-4662, Fax: 902/368-4699, Email: menoonan@gov.pe.ca
Director, Administration & Finance, Gar Andrew, 902/368-4605, Email: agandrew@gov.pe.ca
Director, Adult Learning & Literacy, Faye Martin, 902/368-4517, Email: fmmartin@gov.pe.ca
Director, Culture, Heritage & Recreation, Don LeClair, 902/368-4789, Email: dfleclair@gov.pe.ca
Director, English Programs & Services, Eldon Rogerson, 902/368-6070, Fax: 902/368-4622, Email: eerogers@gov.pe.ca
Director, French Programs & Services, Tilmon Gallant, 902/368-4671, Fax: 902/368-4622, Email: tjgallan@gov.pe.ca
Director, Higher Education & Training, Mike Clow, 902/368-4615, Email: gmclow@gov.pe.ca
Director, Policy & Evaluation, Dr. Parnell Garland, 902/368-4282, Email: pjgarlan@gov.pe.ca
Director, Provincial Libraries & Archives, Harry T. Holman, 902/368-4227, Fax: 902/368-6327, Email: hthlolman@gov.pe.ca
Registrar, Teacher Certification & Pensions, Ronald F. Rice, 902/368-4651, Email: rfrice@gov.pe.ca
Officer, Francophone Cultural Affairs, Donald DesRoches, 902/368-4788, Email: djdesroches@gov.pe.ca
Coordinator, Professional Development, Lloyd Mallard, 902/368-4283, Email: lfmallar@gov.pe.ca

## ELECTIONS PRINCE EDWARD ISLAND

180 Richmond St., 2nd Fl., PO Box 2000, Charlottetown PE C1A 7N8

902/368-5895; Fax: 902/368-6500; URL: http://www.gov.pe.ca/election/
**Chief Electoral Officer**, Merrill H. Wigginton

## Prince Edward Island EMERGENCY MEASURES ORGANIZATION

East Prince Regional Service Centre, PO Box 2063, Summerside PE C1N 5L2
902/888-8050; Fax: 902/888-8054
**Minister responsible**, Hon. P. Mitchell Murphy, 902/368-5250, Fax: 902/368-4121
Acting Director, Albert MacDonald, 902/368-5582, Fax: 902/368-5526
Manager, Michael A. Francis, 902/368-5549, Fax: 902/368-5526, Email: mafrancis@gov.pe.ca

## Department of FISHERIES & ENVIRONMENT

Jones Bldg., 11 Kent St., 4th Fl., PO Box 2000, Charlottetown PE CIA 7N8
902/368-5000; Fax: 902/368-5830; URL: http://www.gov.pe.ca/env/index.html
Environmental Emergencies: 1-800-565-1633

### ACTS ADMINISTERED

Automobile Junkyards Act
Environmental Protection Act
Fish & Game Protection Act
Natural Areas Protection Act
Unsightly Property Act
**Minister**, Hon. Kevin MacAdam, 902/368-6410, Fax: 902/368-6488
Deputy Minister, Diane Griffin, 902/368-5340, Email: dfgriffin@gov.pe.ca

### Cooperation Agreement for Sustainable Economic Development

902/368-6080
Director, H. Arthur Smith, 902/368-4684
Program Planner, Bruce Smith, 902/368-6081

### ENVIRONMENTAL PROTECTION DIVISION

902/368-5024
Director, Don Jardine, 902/368-5035, Email: dejardine@gov.pe.ca
Manager, Air Quality & Hazardous Materials Section & Manager, Enforcement Section, Mark Victor, 902/368-5037
Manager, Solid Waste Section, Gerry Stewart, 902/368-5029, Email: gbstewart@gov.pe.ca

### FISH & WILDLIFE DIVISION

902/368-4683
Director, H. Arthur Smith, 902/368-6083, Email: hasmith@gov.pe.ca
Chief Officer, Conservation, Walter Stewart, 902/368-4808
Manager, Habitat & Natural Areas Section, Rosemary Curley, 902/368-4807
Manager, Waterfowl & Furbearers Section, Randy Dibblee, 902/368-4666

### FISHERIES & AQUACULTURE DIVISION

902/368-5251; Fax: 902/368-5542
Director, Lewie Creed, 902/368-5241, Email: lpcreed@gov.pe.ca
Biologist, Marine Fisheries, Dave Gillis, 902/368-5261, Email: djgillis@gov.pe.ca
Biologist, Shellfish, Richard Gallant, 902/368-5524, Email: rkgallant@gov.pe.ca

### PLANNING & ADMINISTRATION DIVISION

902/368-5320
Director, Andre Lavoie, 902/368-5032, Email: ajlavoie@gov.pe.ca
Coordinator, Environmental Impact Assessment, Alan Godfrey, 902/368-5274, Email: apgodfrey@gov.pe.ca
Coordinator, MIS, Gordon Jenkins, Email: gbjenkins@gov.pe.ca
Coordinator, Policy & Planning, Christine MacKinnon, 902/368-5031, Email: cgmackinnon@gov.pe.ca
Head, Investigations & Enforcement, Gerald MacDougall, 902/368-4808, Email: dgmacdougall@gov.pe.ca
Officer, Communications, Lee Bartley, 902/368-5286, Email: elbartley@gov.pe.ca

### WATER RESOURCES DIVISION

902/368-5028
Director, Clair Murphy, 902/368-5036, Email: ccmurphy@gov.pe.ca
Manager, Engineering & Utilities Section, Jim Young, 902/368-5034, Email: jjyoung@gov.pe.ca
Manager, Groundwater Section, George Somers, 902/368-5046, Email: ghsomers@gov.pe.ca
Manager, Rivers & Estuaries Section, Bruce Raymond, 902/368-5054, Email: bgraymond@gov.pe.ca
Coordinator, Water Analysis, Cheryl Burke, 902/368-5044, Email: ceburke@gov.pe.ca

## Department of HEALTH & SOCIAL SERVICES

Jones Bldg., 11 Kent St., 2nd Fl., PO Box 2000, Charlottetown PE C1A 7N8
902/368-4900; Fax: 902/368-4969; URL: http://www.gov.pe.ca/hss/index.html
Note: This department was undergoing major restructuring at the time of publication. Names and numbers may no longer be current. If necessary contact the department's main line or Deputy Minister for further information.
The former Council on Health & Community Service Policy, & the Health & Community Service Agency have been disbanded.

### ACTS ADMINISTERED

Adoption Act
Adult Protection Act
Change of Name Act
Child Care Facilities Act
Chiropractic Act
Community Care Facilities & Nursing Homes Act
Consent to Treatment & Health Care Directives Act
Dental Profession Act
Dietitians Act
Dispensing Opticians Act
Donation of Food Act
Drug Cost Assistance Act
Family & Child Services Act
Health & Community Services Act
Health Services Payment Act
Hospital & Diagnostic Services Insurance Act
Hospitals Act
Housing Corporation Act
Human Tissue Donation Act
Licensed Nursing Assistants Act
Marriage Act
Medical Act
Mental Health Act
Nurses Act
Occupational Therapists Act
Optometry Act
Pharmacy Act
Physiotherapy Act
Premarital Health Examination Act
Provincial Health Number Act
Psychologists Act
Public Health Act
Rehabilitation of Disabled Persons Act
Social Work Act
Supported Decision Making & Adult Guardianship Act
Tobacco Sales to Minors Act
Vital Statistics Act
Welfare Assistance Act
White Cane Act
**Minister**, Hon. Mildred A. Dover, 902/368-4930, Fax: 902/368-4974, Email: healthmin@gov.pe.ca
Deputy Minister, Verna Bruce, Email: vxbruce@gov.pe.ca

### ADMINISTRATION & FEDERAL-PROVINCIAL RELATIONS

Director, George Mason, 902/368-4926
Officer, Federal Claims, Sandra Howard
Officer, Federal-Provincial Relations & Special Projects, Rick Callaghan
Auditor, Canada Assistance Plan, Belinda Rogers

### HEALTH POLICY RESEARCH & DEVELOPMENT

Acting Director, Jo-Anne MacDonald, 902/368-4985
Research & Administrative Asst., Judy Morrison
Officer, Public Policy Liaison, Laraine Poole

### PUBLIC HEALTH

Chief Health Officer, Lamont Sweet, M.D., 902/368-4996
Epidemiologist, Linda Van Til
Officer, Research & Administrative Support, Connie Cheverie
Research Nurse, Arlenn Walsh

### STRATEGIC PLANNING & EVALUATION

Director, Danny Gallant, 902/368-4945
Legislative Specialist, Rob Thomson
Policy Analyst, Dan Pridmore
Research & Evaluation Specialist, Paul Chaulk
Research & Evaluation Specialist, Joanne Ross Keizer

## Prince Edward Island HUMAN RIGHTS COMMISSION

3 Queen St., PO Box 2000, Charlottetown PE C1A 7N8
902/368-4180; Fax: 902/368-4236; Email: jwyatt@peinet.ca
**Executive Director**, James Wyatt

## Prince Edward Island LIQUOR CONTROL COMMISSION

PO Box 967, Charlottetown PE C1A 7M4
902/368-5710; Fax: 902/368-5735
**Chair**, W.J.R. (Mac) Macdonald
**CEO**, Wayne A. MacDougall

## Department of the PROVINCIAL TREASURY

PO Box 2000, Charlottetown PE C1A 7N8
902/368-4000; Fax: 902/368-5544; URL: http://www.gov.pe.ca/pt/index.html

### ACTS ADMINISTERED

Advisory Council on the Status of Women Act
Appropriation Act
Civil Service Act
Civil Service Superannuation Act
Deposit Receipt Act
Environment Tax Act
Financial Administration Act
Financial Corporation Capital Tax Act
Gasoline Tax Act
Health Tax Act
Income Tax Act
Liquor Control Act
Loan Act
Lotteries Commission Act
Northumberland Strait Crossing Act
Public Accounting & Auditing Act
Public Purchasing Act

Public Sector Pay Reduction Act
Queen's Printer Act
Real Property Assessment Act
Real Property Tax Act
Revenue Administration Act
Registry Act
Revenue Tax Act
Supplementary Appropriation Act
**Minister**, Hon. Patricia J. Mella, 902/368-4050, Fax: 902/368-6575
Acting Deputy Provincial Treasurer, Bill Harper, 902/368-4053, Fax: 902/368-6575
Coordinator, Administration, Millie Morrison, 902/368-6215
Director, Policy & Evaluation Division, Bill Harper, 902/368-4202, Fax: 902/368-6575
Manager, Interministerial Womens' Secretariat, Sandra Bentley, 902/368-4710, Fax: 902/368-6144

#### Office of the Comptroller

Comptroller, K. Scott Stevens, 902/368-4020, Fax: 902/368-4077

### FISCAL MANAGEMENT

Fax: 902/368-4034
Investments: 902/368-4173; Fax: 902/368-4077
Director, Roy Spence, 902/368-5802

### HUMAN RESOURCES

Director, Marie MacDonald, 902/368-4207, Fax: 902/368-6622
Manager, Employee Assistance - Harbourside, Frank MacAulay, 902/368-5736, Fax: 902/368-5737
Manager, Employee Benefits, Bob Ramsay, 902/368-4002, Fax: 902/368-4383
Manager, Human Resources Development Centre, Craig McDowall, 180 Richmond St., Charlottetown PE C1A 1J2, 902/368-4164, Fax: 902/368-4382
Manager, Occupational Health & Safety, Sheila MacLure, 902/368-4200, Fax: 902/368-6622
Manager, Personnel Services, Colleen Malone, 902/368-4254, Fax: 902/368-6622

### SUPPLY & SERVICES

Fax: 902/368-5444
Director, Des Lecky, 902/368-4129
Manager, Communications & Support Services & Acting Manager, Payment Processing, Daryl Montgomery, 902/368-5080, Fax: 902/368-6243
Manager, Computer Support Services, Lorne Gaudet, 902/368-4124, Help Desk: 902/368-5815
Manager, Information Systems Delivery, Beth Gaudet, 902/368-4126
Manager, Procurement Services, Phil O'Neill, 902/368-4040, Fax: 902/368-5171
Manager, Risk Management & Insurance, Brian Gallant, 902/368-6170, Fax: 902/368-6243
Supervisor, Audio & Text Support Services, Irwin Campbell, 902/368-5078, Fax: 902/368-6243
Provincial Photographer, Brian Simpson, 902/368-4019, Fax: 902/368-6243
Queen's Printer & Supervisor, Postal Services, Beryl Bujosevich, 902/368-5190, 5084, Fax: 902/368-5168

#### Island Information Service

11 Kent St., PO Box 2000, Charlottetown PE C1A 7N8
902/368-4000; Fax: 902/368-5544; Email: island@gov.pe.ca
Supervisor, Florine Proud

### TAXATION & PROPERTY RECORDS

Provincial Tax Commissioner, James B. Ramsay, 902/368-4070, Fax: 902/368-6164
Registrar, Deeds, Kathy Toole, 902/368-4591, Fax: 902/368-4399
Manager, Client Services, Robert F. Kenny, 902/368-4070, Fax: 902/368-6164
Manager, Commercial & Special Purpose Assessments, William Found, 902/368-4073, Fax: 902/368-6164
Manager, Geomatics Information Centre, Brenda Campbell-Perry, 902/368-5165, Fax: 902/368-4399
Manager, Residential & Farm Assessments, Kevin Dingwell, 902/368-4078, Fax: 902/368-6164
Manager, Tax Administration, Blair White, 902/368-4146, Fax: 902/368-6164
Acting Manager, Tax Audit, Mary Hennessey, 902/368-4174, Fax: 902/368-6164

#### Associated Agencies, Boards & Commissions

- Advisory Council on the Status of Women: PO Box 2000, Charlottetown PE C1A 7N8 – 902/368-4510; Fax: 902/368-4516; Email: peiacsw@isn.net

Executive Director, Lisa Murphy
Chair, Sharon O'Brien

- Prince Edward Island Lotteries Commission: Office of the Deputy Provincial Treasurer, PO Box 2000, Charlottetown PE C1A 7N8 – 902/368-4053; Fax: 902/368-6575

Sec.-Treas., Mike Kelly

## Island REGULATORY & APPEALS COMMISSION

#501, 134 Kent St., PO Box 577, Charlottetown PE C1A 7L1
902/892-3501; Fax: 902/566-4076; Email: irac@irac.pe.ca
Toll Free: 1-800-501-6268

### ACTS ADMINISTERED

Electric Power & Telephone Act
Lands Protection Act
Planning Act
Real Property Assessment Act
Real Property Tax Act
Rental of Residential Properties Act
Revenue Administration Act
Revenue Tax Act
Roads Act
Unsightly Property Act
Water & Sewerage Act
**Chair & CEO**, Wayne D. Cheverie, Q.C.
Vice-Chair, Stirling (Ginger) Breedon
Director, Land & Property Division, Chris Jones
Director, Petroleum Division, H. Doris Pursey
Director, Rental Division, Boyde White
Director, Technical Services Division, Donald G. Sutherland

## Prince Edward Island STAFFING & CLASSIFICATION BOARD

PO Box 2000, Charlottetown PE C1A 7N8
902/368-4080; Fax: 902/368-4383
**CEO**, Ron Lewis

## Department of TRANSPORTATION & PUBLIC WORKS

Jones Bldg., PO Box 2000, Charlottetown PE C1A 7N8
902/368-5100; Fax: 902/368-5395; URL: http://www.gov.pe.ca/tpw/index.html

### ACTS ADMINISTERED

Access to Public Buildings Act
Architects Act
Crown Building Corporation Act
Dangerous Goods (Transportation) Act
Engineering Profession Act
Expropriation Act
Georgetown Common Land Act
Highway Traffic Act
Land Survey Act. 1971 (& 1951)
Land Surveyors Act
Motor Carrier Act
Off Highway Vehicle Act
Public Works Act
Roads Act
Vehicle Dealers & Salesmen Act
**Minister**, Hon. Michael F. Currie, 902/368-5120
Deputy Minister, W. Philip MacDougall, 902/368-5130, Fax: 902/368-5385, Email: wpmacdougall@gov.pe.ca
Director, Administration, P.J. Murphy, 902/368-5125

### BUILDINGS DIVISION

Director, Joe Caswell, 902/368-5145
Engineer, Building Construction Section, Foster Millar
Manager, Operations & Maintenance Section, Frank Chiaisson, 902/368-5113
Manager, Properties & Surveys Section, Paul Knox, 902/368-5131
Officer, Surveys, Serge Bernard

### HIGHWAY OPERATIONS DIVISION

Chief Engineer, Wayne MacQuarrie, 902/368-6969
Director, Design Section, Allan Bartlett, 902/368-5105
Director, Engineering Services, George Trainor, 902/368-5095
Senior Manager, Materials Laboratory, Terry Kelly, 902/368-4740, Fax: 902/368-5537
Senior Manager, Mechanical, Mark Belfry, 902/368-4750, Fax: 902/368-5537
Manager, Central Region, Gary McLure, 902/368-5182
Manager, East Region, Rick Smith, 902/368-5183
Manager, West Region, Foch McNally, 902/368-5181

### HIGHWAY SAFETY DIVISION

17 Haviland St., 1st Fl., Charlottetown PE C1A 3S7
Director, Glen Beaton, 902/368-5200, Fax: 902/368-5236
Registrar, Motor Vehicles, John B. MacDonald, 902/368-5200, Fax: 902/368-5236
Coordinator, Safety, Wilfred MacDonald
Supervisor, Inspection, Charles Easter

## Prince Edward Island WORKERS' COMPENSATION BOARD

PO Box 757, Charlottetown PE C1A 7L7
902/368-5680; Fax: 902/368-5696
**Chair**, Arthur MacDonald
CEO, A.B. Wells
Chief Officer, George Stewart, 902/368-5470
Safety Officer, Wayne Corrigan
Safety Officer, Chris Keefe
Safety Officer, Roger Walsh

# GOVERNMENT OF QUÉBEC

**Seat of Government:** Assemblée Nationale, Hôtel du Parlement, Québec QC G1A 1A4
URL: http://www.gouv.qc.ca/
The Province of Québec entered Confederation July 1, 1867. It has an area of 1,357,811.73 km2, and the StatsCan census population in 1996 was 7,138,795.

## Cabinet du LIEUTENANT GOUVERNEUR/ Office of the Lieutenant Governor

Édifice André-Laurendeau, 1050, rue des Parlementaires, Québec QC G1A 1A1
418/643-5385; Fax: 418/644-4677
**Lieutenant Gouverneur**, Lise Thibault
Chef du Cabinet & Aide-de-Camp, Jean-François Provençal

## Cabinet du PREMIER MINISTRE/Office of the Premier

Édifice J, 885, Grande-Allée est, 3e étage, Québec QC G1A 1A2

418/643-5321; Fax: 418/643-3924; URL: http://www.premier.gouv.qc.ca

75, boul René-Lévesque ouest, 12e étage, Montréal QC H2Z 1A4

514/873-3411, Fax: 514/873-6769

**Premier ministre/Premier**, Hon. Lucien Bouchard, Email: premier.ministre@gouv.qc.ca

Vice premier ministre/Deputy Premier, Bernard Landry

Chef de Cabinet/Chief of Staff, Hubert Thibault

Chef de Cabinet adjoint/Deputy Chief of Staff, François Leblanc

Conseiller spécial/Special Advisor, Jean-Roch Boivin

Attachée de presse/Press Attaché, Marthe Lawrence

Adjointe de l'attachée de presse/Deputy Press Attaché, Isabelle Rondeau

## CONSEIL EXÉCUTIF/Executive Council

Hôtel du Parlement, Québec QC G1A 1A4

URL: http://www.cex.gouv.qc.ca

Premier ministre, Hon. Lucien Bouchard, Édifice J, 885, Grande Allée est, 3ème étage, Québec QC G1A 1A2, 418/643-5321, Fax: 418/643-3924, Email: premier.ministre@gouv.qc.ca, (Premier)

Ministre, Culture et Communications & Ministre responsable, Charte de la langue française, Louise Beaudoin, 225, Grande Allée est, Bloc 1A, Québec QC G1R 5G5, 418/643-2110, Fax: 418/643-9164, (Minister Culture & Communications & Minister Resp., French Language Charter)

Ministre, Environnement et Faune & Ministre responsable, Région Côte-Nord, Paul Bégin, 1200, rte de l'Eglise, 9e étage, Ste-Foy QC G1V 4M1, 418/643-4210, Fax: 418/646-0027, (Minister, Environment & Wildlife & Minister Resp., Côte-Nord Region)

Ministre, Sécurité publique, Pierre Bélanger, #1.39, Édifice Pamphile-Lemay, Québec QC G1A 1A5, 418/643-3804, Fax: 418/643-2514, (Minister, Public Security)

Ministre délégué, Industrie et Commerce, Roger Bertrand, 3800, rue Marly, 6e étage, Ste-Foy QC G1X 4A5, 418/652-6835, Fax: 418/643-7379, (Minister Resp., Industry & Trade)

Ministre délégué, Relations avec les citoyens et Immigration, André Boisclair, #336, 900, boul René-Lévesque est, Québec QC G1R 2B5, 418/644-2128, Fax: 418/528-0829, (Minister, Relations with Citizens & Immigration)

Ministre, Transports & Ministre responsable, Affaires intergouvernementales canadiennes et Région Saguenay Lac-Saint-Jean, Jacques Brassard, Place Haute-Ville, 700, boul René-Lévesque est, 29e étage, Québec QC G1R 5H1, 418/643-6980, Fax: 418/643-2033, (Minister, Transportation, Minister Resp., Canadian Intergovernmental Affairs & Minister Resp., Saguenay Lac-Saint-Jean Region)

Ministre déléguée, Mines, Terres et Forêts & Ministre responsable, Région Chaudière-Appalaches, Denise Carrier-Perreault, Édifice de l'Atrium, #A308, 5700, 4e av. ouest, Charlesbourg QC G1H 6R1, 418/643-7295, Fax: 418/643-4872, (Minister Resp., Mines, Lands & Forests & Minister Resp., Chaudière-Appalaches Region)

Ministre d'État, Ressources naturelles & Ministre responsable, Développement des régions et Réforme électorale et parlementaire et de la Région de Lanaudière, Guy Chevrette, Édifice de l'Atrium, #A308, 5700, 4e av ouest, Charlesbourg QC G1H 6R1, 418/643-7295, Fax: 418/643-4318, (Minister of State, Natural Resources, Minister Resp., Regional Development, Minister Resp., Electoral & Parliamentary Reform & Minister Resp., Lanaudière Region & Northern Québec)

Ministre délégué, Tourisme & Ministre responsable, Région de Laval, David Cliche, Édifice Marie-Guyart, 675, boul René-Lévesque est, 30e étage, Québec QC G1R 5V7, 418/643-8259, Fax: 418/643-4143, (Minister, Tourism & Minister Resp., Laval Region)

Ministre d'État, Revenu, Rita Dionne-Marsolais, 710, Place D'Youville, 6e étage, Québec QC G1R 4Y4, 418/691-5650, Fax: 418/643-8553, (Minister of State, Revenue)

Ministre, Emploi et Solidarité & Ministre responsable, Condition féminine et Action communautaire autonome, Louise Harel, 425, rue Saint-Amable, 4e étage, Québec QC G1R 4Z1, 418/643-4810, Fax: 418/643-2802, (Minister of State, Employment & Solidarity, Minister Resp., Status of Women & Community Groups)

Leader parlementaire du gouvernement & Ministre délégué, Réforme électorale, Jean-Pierre Jolivet, (Government House Leader & Minister Resp., Electoral & Parliamentary Reform)

Ministre, Agriculture, Pêcheries et Alimentation & Ministre responsable, Région Mauricie Bois-Francs, Guy Julien, 200-A, ch Sainte-Foy, 12e étage, Québec QC G1R 4X6, 418/643-2525, Fax: 418/643-8422, (Minister, Agriculture, Fisheries & Food & Minister Resp., Mauricie Bois-Francs Region)

Vice-premier ministre & Ministre d'État, Économie et Finances et Ministre responsable, Région de l'Estrie, Bernard Landry, 12, rue Saint-Louis, 1er étage, Québec QC G1R 5L3, 418/643-5270, Fax: 418/643-6626, (Deputy Premier, Minister of Finance, Minister of Industry, Trade, Science & Technology, Minister of Revenue, Minister of State, Finance & Economy & Minister Resp., Estrie Region)

Président, Conseil du trésor & Ministre délégué, Administration à la Fonction publique et Ministre responsable, Région des Laurentides, Jacques Léonard, #4.17, 875, Grande Allée est, Québec QC G1R 5R8, 418/643-5926, Fax: 418/643-7824, (Chairman, Treasury Board, Minister Resp., Public Service & Administration & Minister Resp., Laurentides Region)

Ministre, Éducation & Ministre responsable de la Famille, Ministre responsable de la Région de la Montérégie, Pauline Marois, Édifice Marie-Guyart, 1035, rue de la Chevrotière, 16e étage, Québec QC G1R 5A5, 418/644-0664, Fax: 418/646-7551, (Minister, Education & Minister Resp., Family Policy, Minister Resp., Montérégie Region)

Ministre, Justice, Serge Ménard, Édifice H, #2.600, 875, Grande Allée est, Québec QC G1R 4Y8, 418/646-3018, Fax: 418/643-6377, (Minister, Justice)

Ministre, Métropole & Ministre Responsable, Région de Montréal, Robert Perreault, 2525, boul Laurier, 5e étage, Ste-Foy QC G1V 2L2, 418/643-2112, Fax: 418/646-6168, (Minister of State, Greater Montréal & Minister Resp., Montréal Region)

Ministre, Travail & Ministre responsable, Région du Bas-Saint-Laurent-Gaspésie-Îles-de-la-Madeleine, Matthias Rioux, 200, ch Sainte-Foy, 6e étage, Québec QC G1R 5S1, 418/643-5297, Fax: 418/644-0003, (Minister, Labour & Minister Resp., Bas-Saint-Laurent-Gaspésie-Îles-de-la-Madeleine Region)

Ministre, Santé et Services sociaux & Ministre responsable, Région de Québec, Jean Rochon, 1075, ch Sainte-Foy, 15e étage, Québec QC G1S 2M1, 418/643-3160, Fax: 418/644-4534, (Minister, Health & Social Services & Minister Resp., Québec Region)

Ministre, Relations internationales & Ministre responsable, Francophonie et Région de l'Outaouais, Sylvain Simard, 525, boul René-Lévesque est, 4e étage, Québec QC G1R 5R9, 418/649-2319, Fax: 418/643-4804, (Minister, International Relations, Minister Resp., for Relations with French Speaking Communities, Minister Resp., Outaouais Region)

Ministre, Affaires municipales & Ministre responsable, Région Abitibi-Témiscamingue, Rémy Trudel, Édifice Cook-Chauveau, Secteur B, 20, rue Chauveau, 3e étage, Québec QC G1R 4J3, 418/691-2050, Fax: 418/643-1795, (Minister of Municipal Affairs, Minister Resp., Abitibi-Temiskaming Region)

#### Cabinet Office

885, Grande Allée est, Québec QC G1A 1A2

Secrétaire général et greffier, Michel Carpentier, 418/643-7355, Fax: 418/646-0866

#### Cabinet Committees

Secrétariat général, Edifice J, 885, Grande Allée est, 2e étage, Québec QC G1A 1A2

418/643-7355; Fax: 418/646-0866

Repondant, Colette Gauthier

Comité ministerial des affaires régionales et territoriales (Regional & Territorial Affairs Committee)

Comité ministérial du développement social (Social Development Committee)

Comité ministérial de l'éducation et de la culture (Education & Culture Committee)

Comité ministérial de l'emploi et du développement économique (Employment & Economic Development Committee)

Comité de législation - Secrétariat à la législation (Legislation Committee)

Comité des priorités (Priorities Committee)

## ASSEMBLÉE NATIONALE/National Assembly

c/o Secrétariat général, Édifice Honoré-Mercier, #3.57, 1025, rue St-Augustin, Québec QC G1A 1A3

418/643-2724; Fax: 418/643-5062; URL: http://www.assnat.qc.ca

**Secrétaire Général/Secretary General:** Pierre Duchesne

**Président/Speaker:** Jean-Pierre Charbonneau, 418/646-2820, Fax: 418/643-3423

**Adjoint Sergeant-at-Arms:** Roger Gagnon, 418/643-2793

**Directeur, Bibliothèque et Études documentaires:** Gaston Bernier, 418/643-4032, Fax: 418/646-4873

**Directeur, Secrétariat des commissions/Clerk of Committees:** Vacant, 418/643-2722, Fax: 418/634-0249

Directeur général, Affaires juridiques et législatives/Law Clerk, René Chrétien

Vice-président/Deputy Speaker, Raymond Brouillet

Vice-président/Deputy Speaker, Claude Pinard

Whip en chef du gouvernement, Jocelyne Caron, 418/643-6018, Fax: 418/643-5462

#### Bureaux de l'opposition/Office of the Official Opposition (Lib.)

#2.83, Hôtel du Parlement, 1160 rue Honoré Mercier, Québec QC G1A 1A4

418/643-2301; Fax: 418/643-1905

Chef/Leader, Daniel Johnson, 418/643-2743, Fax: 418/643-2957

Chef du Cabinet/Chief of Staff, Martial Fillion

Whip de l'opposition/Opposition Whip, Georges Farrah

Coordonnateur, Recherche et Communications/Director, Research & Communications, Christian Barrette

## THIRTY-FIFTH LEGISLATURE - QUÉBEC

Hôtel du Parlement, Québec QC G1A 1A4
418/643-2726

Last General Election, September 12, 1994. Maximum Duration, 5 Years.

**Party Standings (May 7, 1997)**
Parti québécois (PQ) 74
Libéral (Lib.) 44
Action démocratique du Québec (ADQ) 1
Independant (Ind.) 2
Vacant 4
Total 125

**Salaries, Indemnities & Allowances (1997)**
Members' annual indemnity $63,469 plus $11,869 expense allowance. In addition to this are the following:
Premier $66,642
Ministers $47,602
Speaker $47,602
Leader of the Opposition $47,602

### MEMBERS BY CONSTITUENCY

Following is: constituency (number of eligible voters in 1994 election, or subsequent by-election) member, party affiliation, Québec Telephone number. (Address for all is Hôtel du Parlement, Québec, PQ G1A 1A4.) Refer to Cabinet List, Government Caucus Office, & the Office of the Opposition for Fax numbers.

Abitibi-Est (30,462) André Pelletier, PQ, 418/644-4869
Abitibi-Ouest (32,416) François Gendron, PQ, 418/646-8741
Acadie (40,487) Yvan Bordeleau, Lib., 418/644-5990
Anjou (31,878) Pierre Bélanger, PQ, 418/643-3804
Argenteuil (44,509) Régent L. Beaudet, Lib., 418/528-1960
Arthabaska (42,142) Jacques Baril, PQ, 418/644-5905
Beauce-Nord (30,668) Normand Poulin, Lib., 418/528-2847
Beauce-Sud (41,284) Diane Leblanc, Lib., 418/528-2935
Beauharnois-Huntingdon (39,163) André Chenail, Lib., 418/644-5992
Bellechasse (29,607) Claude Lachance, PQ, 418/528-1215
Berthier (44,574) Gilles Baril, PQ, 418/528-1282
Bertrand (38,854) Denis Chalifoux, Lib.
Blainville (36,530) Céline Signori, PQ, 418/528-1349
Bonaventure (29,626) Marcel Landry, PQ, 418/646-0505
Borduas (33,126) Jean-Pierre Charbonneau, PQ, 418/643-2820
Bourassa (31,793) Michèle Lamquin-Ethier, Lib.
Bourget (33,761) Camille Laurin, PQ, 418/528-1657
Brome-Missisquoi (36,354) Pierre Paradis, Lib., 418/643-1275
Châteauguay (39,950) Jean-Marc Fournier, Lib., 418/528-9478
Chambly (47,620) Louise Beaudoin, PQ, 418/643-2110
Champlain (42,908) Yves Beaumier, PQ, 418/528-0555
Chapleau (54,005) Claire Vaive, Lib., 418/528-0759
Charlesbourg (45,931) Jean Rochon, PQ, 418/643-3160
Charlevoix (30,604) Rosaire Bertrand, PQ, 418/528-0986
Chauveau (54,351) Raymond Brouillet, PQ, 418/643-2750
Chicoutimi (44,767) Jeanne L. Blackburn, PQ, 418/646-6362
Chomedey (47,051) Thomas J. Mulcair, Lib., 418/528-2381
Chutes-de-la-Chaudière (49,902) Denise Carrier-Perreault, PQ, 418/643-7295
Crémazie (36,637) Jean Campeau, PQ, 418/646-2619
D'Arcy-McGee (38,868) Lawrence Bergman, Lib., 418/528-2210
Deux-Montagnes (52,644) Hélène Robert, PQ, 418/528-0765
Drummond (45,476) Normand Jutras, PQ, 418/528-1285
Dubuc (34,450) Gérard-R. Morin, PQ, 418/644-5901
Duplessis (36,402) Normand Duguay, PQ
Fabre (46,899) Joseph Facal, PQ, 418/528-0309
Frontenac (34,353) Roger Lefebvre, Lib., 418/644-6236
Gaspé (29,448) Guy Lelièvre, PQ, 418/528-5818
Gatineau (37,878) Réjean Lafrenière, Lib., 418/644-5980
Gouin (39,276) André Boisclair, PQ, 418/644-2128
Groulx (39,898) Robert Kieffer, PQ, 418/528-2445
Hochelaga-Maisonneuve (31,087) Louise Harel, PQ, 418/643-4810
Hull (43,670) Robert LeSage, Lib., 418/644-9954
Îles-de-la-Madeleine (10,682) Georges Farrah, Lib., 418/643-2301
Iberville (44,299) Richard Le Hir, Ind., 418/643-8474
Jacques-Cartier (44,842) Geoffrey Kelley, Lib., 418/646-6342
Jean-Talon (31,938) Margaret F. Delisle, Lib., 418/646-6349
Jeanne-Mance (36,038) Michel Bissonnet, Lib., 418/528-1488
Johnson (33,877) Claude Boucher, PQ, 418/646-6451
Joliette (41,557) Guy Chevrette, PQ, 418/643-7295
Jonquière (43,614) Hon. Lucien Bouchard, PQ, 418/643-5321
Kamouraska-Témiscouata (33,639) Claude Béchard, Lib.
L'Assomption (48,626) Jean-Claude St-André, PQ, 418/528-5474
La Peltrie (49,607) Michel Côté, PQ, 418/646-6506
La Pinière (42,307) Fatima Houda-Pepin, Lib., 418/646-7385
La Prairie (53,079) Monique Simard, PQ, 418/646-4325
Labelle (34,980) Jacques Léonard, PQ, 418/643-5926
Lac-Saint-Jean (37,557) Jacques Brassard, PQ, 418/643-6980
LaFontaine (45,521) Jean-Claude Gobé, Lib., 418/643-4019
Laporte (44,101) André Bourbeau, Lib., 418/644-0093
Laurier-Dorion (41,718) Christos Sirros, Lib., 418/644-0520
Laval-des-Rapides (37,451) Serge Ménard, PQ, 418/646-3018
Laviolette (33,886) Jean-Pierre Jolivet, PQ, 418/643-6018
Lévis (36,866) Jean Garon, PQ, 418/646-3766
Limoilou (43,877) Michel Rivard, PQ, 418/646-0650
Lotbinière (28,906) Jean-Guy Paré, PQ, 418/646-8085
Louis-Hébert (38,649) Paul Bégin, PQ, 418/643-4210
Marguerite-Bourgeoys (40,182) Liza Frulla, Lib., 418/644-7196
Marguerite-D'Youville (41,008) François Beaulne, PQ, 418/644-5965
Marie-Victorin (40,023) Cécile Vermette, PQ, 418/643-5611
Marquette (36,992) François Ouimet, Lib., 418/646-3202
Maskinongé (42,095) Rémy Désilets, PQ, 418/646-5756
Masson (41,397) Yves Blais, PQ, 418/643-5771
Matane (28,055) Matthias Rioux, PQ, 418/643-5297
Matapédia (29,857) Danielle Doyer, PQ, 418/646-6147
Mégantic-Compton (29,896) Madeleine Bélanger, Lib., 418/643-7640
Mercier (39,636) Robert Perreault, PQ, 418/643-2112
Mille-Îles (44,549) Lyse Leduc, PQ, 418/646-1402
Mont-Royal (36,101) John Ciaccia, Lib., 418/643-8695
Montmagny-L'Islet (31,722) Réal Gauvin, Lib., 418/643-9503
Montmorency (51,684) Jean Filion, Ind., 418/528-2272
Nelligan (51,444) Russell Williams, Lib., 418/644-5986
Nicolet-Yamaska (32,530) Michel Morin, PQ, 418/646-3967
Notre-Dame-de-Grâce (36,019) Russell Copeman, Lib., 418/646-5752
Orford (45,802) Robert Benoit, Lib., 418/644-5988
Outremont (42,354) Pierre-Étienne Laporte, Lib., 418/528-5976
Papineau (35,003) Norman MacMillan, Lib., 418/644-6940
Pointe-aux-Trembles (38,313) Nicole Léger, PQ, 418/528-2755
Pontiac (35,797) Robert Middlemiss, Lib., 418/644-2666
Portneuf (38 312) Roger Bertrand, PQ, 418/652-6835
Prévost (46,261) Lucie Papineau, PQ, 418/646-0245
Richelieu (38,688) Sylvain Simard, PQ, 418/649-2319
Richmond (31,371) Yvon Vallières, Lib., 418/643-8092
Rimouski (37,584) Solange Charest, PQ, 418/646-0999
Rivière-du-Loup (29,252) Mario Dumont, ADQ, 418/644-4560
Robert-Baldwin (42,600) Pierre Marsan, Lib., 418/646-5554
Roberval (41,215) Benoît Laprise, PQ, 418/646-7697
Rosemont (36,518) Rita Dionne-Marsolais, PQ, 418/691-5650
Rousseau (40,316) Lévis Brien, PQ, 418/646-9124
Rouyn-Noranda-Témiscamingue (40,695) Rémy Trudel, PQ, 418/691-2050
Saguenay (35,344) Gabriel-Yvan Gagnon, PQ, 418/646-9851
Saint-François (39,844) Monique Gagnon-Tremblay, Lib., 418/644-2817, Fax: 418/646-6640
Saint-Henri-Sainte-Anne (39,197) Nicole Loiselle, Lib., 418/644-5976
Saint-Hyacinthe (44,389) Léandre Dion, PQ, 418/644-5283
Saint-Jean (47,426) Roger Paquin, PQ, 418/644-5604
Saint-Laurent (41,530) Normand Cherry, Lib., 418/644-7058
Saint-Maurice (33,780) Claude Pinard, PQ, 418/643-2810
Sainte-Marie-Saint-Jacques (41,452) André Boulerice, PQ, 418/643-2327
Salaberry-Soulanges (48,520) Serge Deslières, PQ, 418/644-7844
Sauvé (31,792) Marcel Parent, Lib., 418/643-3067
Shefford (47,958) Bernard Brodeur, Lib., 418/646-4622
Sherbrooke (38,615) Marie Malavoy, PQ, 418/528-2655
Taillon (48,478) Pauline Marois, PQ, 418/644-0664
Taschereau (30,849) André Gaulin, PQ, 418/644-0981
Terrebonne (39,981) Jocelyne Caron, PQ, 418/644-5920
Trois-Rivières (36,391) Guy Julien, PQ, 418/643-2525
Ungava (26,483) Michel Létourneau, PQ, 418/528-1683
Vachon (39,122) David Payne, PQ, 418/644-5195
Vanier (46,924) Diane Barbeau, PQ, 418/644-2640
Vaudreuil (48,829) Daniel Johnson, Lib., 418/643-2743, Fax: 418/643-2957
Verchères (34,854) Bernard Landry, PQ, 418/643-5270
Verdun (41,967) Henri-François Gautrin, Lib., 418/644-5959
Viau (36,378) William Cusano, Lib., 418/643-1874
Viger (35,299) Cosmo Maciocia, Lib., 418/643-7913
Vimont (49,729) David Cliche, PQ, 418/643-8259
Westmount-Saint-Louis (43,275) Jacques Chagnon, Lib., 418/643-4313

### MEMBERS (ALPHABETICAL)

Following is: member, constituency (number of eligible voters in 1994 election, or subsequent by-election) party affiliation, Québec Telephone number. (Address for all is Hôtel du Parlement, Québec, PQ G1A 1A4.) Refer to Cabinet List, Government Caucus Office, & the Office of the Opposition for Fax numbers.

Diane Barbeau, Vanier (46,924) PQ, 418/644-2640
Gilles Baril, Berthier (44,574) PQ, 418/528-1282
Jacques Baril, Arthabaska (42,142) PQ, 418/644-5905
Régent L. Beaudet, Argenteuil (44,509) Lib., 418/528-1960
Louise Beaudoin, Chambly (47,620) PQ, 418/643-2110
François Beaulne, Marguerite-D'Youville (41,008) PQ, 418/644-5965
Yves Beaumier, Champlain (42,908) PQ, 418/528-0555

Claude Béchard, Kamouraska-Témiscouata (33,639) Lib.
Paul Bégin, Louis-Hébert (38,649) PQ, 418/643-4210
Madeleine Bélanger, Mégantic-Compton (29,896) Lib., 418/643-7640
Pierre Bélanger, Anjou (31,878) PQ, 418/643-3804
Robert Benoit, Orford (45,802) Lib., 418/644-5988
Lawrence Bergman, D'Arcy-McGee (38,868) Lib., 418/528-2210
Roger Bertrand, Portneuf (38 312) PQ, 418/652-6835
Rosaire Bertrand, Charlevoix (30,604) PQ, 418/528-0986
Michel Bissonnet, Jeanne-Mance (36,038) Lib., 418/528-1488
Jeanne L. Blackburn, Chicoutimi (44,767) PQ, 418/646-6362
Yves Blais, Masson (41,397) PQ, 418/643-5771
André Boisclair, Gouin (39,276) PQ, 418/644-2128
Yvan Bordeleau, Acadie (40,487) Lib., 418/644-5990
Hon. Lucien Bouchard, Jonquière (43,614) PQ, 418/643-5321
Claude Boucher, Johnson (33,877) PQ, 418/646-6451
André Boulerice, Sainte-Marie-Saint-Jacques (41,452) PQ, 418/643-2327
André Bourbeau, Laporte (44,101) Lib., 418/644-0093
Jacques Brassard, Lac-Saint-Jean (37,557) PQ, 418/643-6980
Lévis Brien, Rousseau (40,316) PQ, 418/646-9124
Bernard Brodeur, Shefford (47,958) Lib., 418/646-4622
Raymond Brouillet, Chauveau (54,351) PQ, 418/643-2750
Jean Campeau, Crémazie (36,637) PQ, 418/646-2619
Jocelyne Caron, Terrebonne (39,981) PQ, 418/644-5920
Denise Carrier-Perreault, Chutes-de-la-Chaudière (49,902) PQ, 418/643-7295
Jacques Chagnon, Westmount-Saint-Louis (43,275) Lib., 418/643-4313
Denis Chalifoux, Bertrand (38,854) Lib.
Jean-Pierre Charbonneau, Borduas (33,126) PQ, 418/643-2820
Solange Charest, Rimouski (37,584) PQ, 418/646-0999
André Chenail, Beauharnois-Huntingdon (39,163) Lib., 418/644-5992
Normand Cherry, Saint-Laurent (41,530) Lib., 418/644-7058
Guy Chevrette, Joliette (41,557) PQ, 418/643-7295
John Ciaccia, Mont-Royal (36,101) Lib., 418/643-8695
David Cliche, Vimont (49,729) PQ, 418/643-8259
Russell Copeman, Notre-Dame-de-Grâce (36,019) Lib., 418/646-5752
Michel Côté, La Peltrie (49,607) PQ, 418/646-6506
William Cusano, Viau (36,378) Lib., 418/643-1874
Margaret F. Delisle, Jean-Talon (31,938) Lib., 418/646-6349
Rémy Désilets, Maskinongé (42,095) PQ, 418/646-5756
Serge Deslières, Salaberry-Soulanges (48,520) PQ, 418/644-7844
Léandre Dion, Saint-Hyacinthe (44,389) PQ, 418/644-5283
Rita Dionne-Marsolais, Rosemont (36,518) PQ, 418/691-5650
Danielle Doyer, Matapédia (29,857) PQ, 418/646-6147
Normand Duguay, Duplessis (36,402) PQ
Mario Dumont, Rivière-du-Loup (29,252) ADQ, 418/644-4560
Joseph Facal, Fabre (46,899) PQ, 418/528-0309
Georges Farrah, Îles-de-la-Madeleine (10,682) Lib., 418/643-2301
Jean Filion, Montmorency (51,684) Ind., 418/528-2272
Jean-Marc Fournier, Châteauguay (39,950) Lib., 418/528-9478
Liza Frulla, Marguerite-Bourgeoys (40,182) Lib., 418/644-7196
Gabriel-Yvan Gagnon, Saguenay (35,344) PQ, 418/646-9851
Monique Gagnon-Tremblay, Saint-François (39,844) Lib., 418/644-2817, Fax: 418/646-6640
Jean Garon, Lévis (36,866) PQ, 418/646-3766
André Gaulin, Taschereau (30,849) PQ, 418/644-0981
Henri-François Gautrin, Verdun (41,967) Lib., 418/644-5959
Réal Gauvin, Montmagny-L'Islet (31,722) Lib., 418/643-9503
François Gendron, Abitibi-Ouest (32,416) PQ, 418/646-8741
Jean-Claude Gobé, LaFontaine (45,521) Lib., 418/643-4019
Louise Harel, Hochelaga-Maisonneuve (31,087) PQ, 418/643-4810
Fatima Houda-Pepin, La Pinière (42,307) Lib., 418/646-7385
Daniel Johnson, Vaudreuil (48,829) Lib., 418/643-2743, Fax: 418/643-2957
Jean-Pierre Jolivet, Laviolette (33,886) PQ, 418/643-6018
Guy Julien, Trois-Rivières (36,391) PQ, 418/643-2525
Normand Jutras, Drummond (45,476) PQ, 418/528-1285
Geoffrey Kelley, Jacques-Cartier (44,842) Lib., 418/646-6342
Robert Kieffer, Groulx (39,898) PQ, 418/528-2445
Claude Lachance, Bellechasse (29,607) PQ, 418/528-1215
Réjean Lafrenière, Gatineau (37,878) Lib., 418/644-5980
Michèle Lamquin-Ethier, Bourassa (31,793) Lib.
Bernard Landry, Verchères (34,854) PQ, 418/643-5270
Marcel Landry, Bonaventure (29,626) PQ, 418/646-0505
Pierre-Étienne Laporte, Outremont (42,354) Lib., 418/528-5976
Benoît Laprise, Roberval (41,215) PQ, 418/646-7697
Camille Laurin, Bourget (33,761) PQ, 418/528-1657
Richard Le Hir, Iberville (44,299) Ind., 418/643-8474
Diane Leblanc, Beauce-Sud (41,284) Lib., 418/528-2935
Lyse Leduc, Mille-Îles (44,549) PQ, 418/646-1402
Roger Lefebvre, Frontenac (34,353) Lib., 418/644-6236
Nicole Léger, Pointe-aux-Trembles (38,313) PQ, 418/528-2755
Guy Lelièvre, Gaspé (29,448) PQ, 418/528-5818
Jacques Léonard, Labelle (34,980) PQ, 418/643-5926
Robert LeSage, Hull (43,670) Lib., 418/644-9954
Michel Létourneau, Ungava (26,483) PQ, 418/528-1683
Nicole Loiselle, Saint-Henri-Sainte-Anne (39,197) Lib., 418/644-5976
Cosmo Maciocia, Viger (35,299) Lib., 418/643-7913
Norman MacMillan, Papineau (35,003) Lib., 418/644-6940
Marie Malavoy, Sherbrooke (38,615) PQ, 418/528-2655
Pauline Marois, Taillon (48,478) PQ, 418/644-0664
Pierre Marsan, Robert-Baldwin (42,600) Lib., 418/646-5554
Serge Ménard, Laval-des-Rapides (37,451) PQ, 418/646-3018
Robert Middlemiss, Pontiac (35,797) Lib., 418/644-2666
Gérard-R. Morin, Dubuc (34,450) PQ, 418/644-5901
Michel Morin, Nicolet-Yamaska (32,530) PQ, 418/646-3967
Thomas J. Mulcair, Chomedey (47,051) Lib., 418/528-2381
François Ouimet, Marquette (36,992) Lib., 418/646-3202
Lucie Papineau, Prévost (46,261) PQ, 418/646-0245
Roger Paquin, Saint-Jean (47,426) PQ, 418/644-5604
Pierre Paradis, Brome-Missisquoi (36,354) Lib., 418/643-1275
Jean-Guy Paré, Lotbinière (28,906) PQ, 418/646-8085
Marcel Parent, Sauvé (31,792) Lib., 418/643-3067
David Payne, Vachon (39,122) PQ, 418/644-5195
André Pelletier, Abitibi-Est (30,462) PQ, 418/644-4869
Robert Perreault, Mercier (39,636) PQ, 418/643-2112
Claude Pinard, Saint-Maurice (33,780) PQ, 418/643-2810
Normand Poulin, Beauce-Nord (30,668) Lib., 418/528-2847
Matthias Rioux, Matane (28,055) PQ, 418/643-5297
Michel Rivard, Limoilou (43,877) PQ, 418/646-0650
Hélène Robert, Deux-Montagnes (52,644) PQ, 418/528-0765
Jean Rochon, Charlesbourg (45,931) PQ, 418/643-3160
Céline Signori, Blainville (36,530) PQ, 418/528-1349
Monique Simard, La Prairie (53,079) PQ, 418/646-4325
Sylvain Simard, Richelieu (38,688) PQ, 418/649-2319
Christos Sirros, Laurier-Dorion (41,718) Lib., 418/644-0520
Jean-Claude St-André, L'Assomption (48,626) PQ, 418/528-5474
Rémy Trudel, Rouyn-Noranda-Témiscamingue (40,695) PQ, 418/691-2050
Claire Vaive, Chapleau (54,005) Lib., 418/528-0759
Yvon Vallières, Richmond (31,371) Lib., 418/643-8092
Cécile Vermette, Marie-Victorin (40,023) PQ, 418/643-5611
Russell Williams, Nelligan (51,444) Lib., 418/644-5986

## QUÉBEC GOVERNMENT DEPARTMENTS & AGENCIES

### Secrétariat aux AFFAIRES AUTOCHTONES/ Native Affairs

Edifice H, 875, Grande-Allée est, 2e étage, Québec QC G1R 4Y8
419/644-3166; Fax: 419/646-4918; URL: http://www.gouv.qc.ca/gouv/francais/minorg/saa/index.html
**Ministre responsable**, Guy Chevrette, 418/643-7295, Fax: 418/643-4318
Sous-ministre associé, André Magny

### Secrétariat aux AFFAIRES INTERGOUVERNEMENTALES CANADIENNES/Intergovernmental Affairs

Edifice H, 3e étage, 875, Grande Allée est, Québec QC G1R 4Y8
418/643-4011; Fax: 418/643-8730; URL: http://www.gouv.qc.ca/francais/minorg/maig/maig_intro.html
**Ministre responsable**, Jacques Brassard, 418/646-5950
Secrétaire général associé, Michel Boivin
Secrétaire adjoint, Gilbert Charland
Secrétaire adjointe, Line Gagné
Directeur, Affaires économiques, culturelles et sociales, Paul Vécès
Directeur, Bureaux coopération et francophonie, Yves Castonguay

#### Directions régionales/Regional Offices

Moncton: Bureau du Québec, Place l'Assomption, 770, rue Main, Moncton NB E1C 1E7 – 506/857-9851; Fax: 506/857-9883
Ottawa: Bureau du Québec, Place de Ville, Tour B, #700, 112, rue Kent, Ottawa ON K1P 5P2 – 613/238-5322; Fax: 613/563-9137
Toronto: Bureau du Québec, #1504, 20 Queen St. West, PO Box 13, Toronto ON M5H 3S3 – 416/977-6060; Fax: 416/596-1407
Vancouver: Bureau du Québec, World Trade Centre, #640, 999 Canada Place, Vancouver BC V6C 3E1 – 604/844-2833; Fax: 604/844-2834

### Ministère des AFFAIRES MUNICIPALES/ Municipal Affairs

Édifice Cook-Chauveau, 20, rue Pierre-Olivier-Chauveau, Québec QC G1R 4J3
418/691-2015; Fax: 418/643-7385; URL: http://www.mam.gouv.qc.ca

**ACTS ADMINISTERED**

Code municipal du Québec
Loi sur les cités et les villes
Loi sur la Commission municipale
Loi sur le Ministère des Affaires municipales

**Municipal Organization**

Loi sur la Communauté urbaine de l'Outaouais
Loi sur la Communauté urbaine de Montréal
Loi sur la Communauté urbaine de Québec
Loi sur le Conseil régional de zone de la Baie-James
Loi sur les conseils intermunicipaux de transport dans la région de Montréal
Loi sur les corporations municipales & intermunicipales de transport
Loi sur l'entraide municipale contre les incendies
Loi sur les villages cris & le village Naskapi
Loi sur les villages Nordiques & l'Administration régionale Kativik
Loi sur l'organisation territoriale municipale

**Fiscal & Financial**

Loi sur les dettes & les emprunts municipaux
Loi concernant les droits sur les divertissements
Loi sur la fiscalité municipale
Loi sur les immeubles industriels municipaux
Loi sur l'interdiction de subventions municipales
Loi concernant les droits sur les mutations immobilières

**Municipal Administration**

Loi sur cours municipales
Loi sur les régimes de retraite des maires & des conseillers des municipalités
Loi sur le traitement des élus municipaux
Loi sur le régime de retraite des élus municipaux
Loi sur la Société québécoise d'assainissement des eaux

**Municipal Democracy**

Loi sur les élections & les référendums dans les municipalités
Loi sur le ministère de l'Habitation & de la Protection du consommateur
Loi sur le parc de la Mauricie & ses environs
Loi sur la Régie du logement
Loi sur la Société d'habitation du Québec
Loi sur la Société du parc industriel & commercial aéroportuaire de Mirabel

**Planning & Development**

Loi sur l'aménagement & l'urbanisme
Loi sur le développement de la région de la Baie-James

**Municipal Services**

Loi sur l'aide municipale à la protection de public aux traverses de chemin de fer
Loi sur les concessions municipales
Loi sur la contribution municipale à la construction de chemins
Loi sur la Régie de la securité dans le sport
Loi sur les rues publiques
Loi sur les travaux municipaux
Loi sur la vente des services publics municipaux

**Miscellaneous Acts**

Loi sur les abus préjudiciables à l'agriculture
Loi sur les colporteurs

**Ministre**, Rémy Trudel, 418/691-2050, Fax: 418/643-1795
Sous-ministre, Alain Gauthier, 418/691-2040, Fax: 418/644-9863
Sous-ministre adjoint, Affaires juridiques et législatives, Marcel Blanchet, 418/691-2040, Fax: 418/644-9863
Sous-ministre adjoint, Développement des politiques et des programmes, Georges Felli, 418/691-2040, Fax: 418/644-9863
Sous-ministre adjointe, Loisir et sports, Diane Lavallée, 418/691-2096, Fax: 418/644-4517
Directrice générale, Gestion, Louise Milhomme, 418/691-2000, Fax: 418/646-0779
Directeur général, Politiques et fiscalité, Réjean Carrier, 418/691-2043, Fax: 418/643-3204
Directeur, Bureau de coordination des Affaires autochones, Jean-Guy Blouin, 418/691-2031, Fax: 418/643-8611
Directeur, Bureau de vérification interne, Jean-Guy Morel, 418/691-2029
Directeur, Communications, Philippe Gagnon, 418/691-2019, Fax: 418/643-7385
Secrétaire, Bureaux regionaux, Mario St-Germain, 418/691-2032, Fax: 418/644-6725

**Regional Offices**

Abitibi-Témiscamingue: #105, 170, av Principale, Rouyn-Noranda QC J9X 4P7 – 819/764-9581; Fax: 819/797-6803
Bas-Saint-Laurent: 337, rue Moreault, 2e étage, Rimouski QC G5L 1P4 – 418/727-3629; Fax: 418/727-3537
Chaudière-Appalaches: R.C. #34, 1200, route de l'Eglise, Ste-Foy QC G1V 4K9 – 418/643-1343; Fax: 418/643-4086
Côte-Nord: #1.801, 625, boul Laflèche, Baie-Comeau QC G5C 1C5 – 418/589-7241; Fax: 418/589-1955
Estrie: #4.04, 200 rue Belvédère Nord, Sherbrooke QC J1H 4A9 – 819/820-3244; Fax: 819/820-3979
Gaspésie-Îles-de-la-Madeleine: 220, rue Commerciale est, CP 310, Chandler QC G0C 1K0 – 418/689-5024; Fax: 418/689-4823
Mauricie-Bois-Francs: #313, 100, rue Laviolette, Trois-Rivières QC G9A 5S9 – 819/371-6653; Fax: 819/371-6953
Montréal: 3, Complexe Desjardins, 26e étage, CP 185, Montréal QC H5B 1B3 – 514/873-5487; Fax: 514/873-3057
Outaouais: #6.380, 170 rue de l'Hôtel-de-Ville, Hull QC J8X 4C2 – 819/772-3006; Fax: 819/772-3989
Sageunay-Lac-Saint-Jean: #306, 227, rue Racine est, Chicoutimi QC G7H 7B4 – 418/698-3523; Fax: 418/698-3526

**Associated Agencies, Boards & Commissions**

•Bureau de révision de l'évaluation foncière du Québec/Québec Real Estate Assessment Review Board: #RC10, 575, rue St-Amable, Québec QC G1R 5R4 – 418/643-3355; Fax: 418/646-0846
Président, Christian Beaudoin, 418/643-6786
•Commission municipale du Québec/Québec Municipal Commission: 20, rue Pierre-Olivier-Chauveau, 5e étage, Québec QC G1R 4J3 – 418/691-2014; Fax: 418/644-4676
Président, Jacques O'Bready
514/873-3031, Fax: 514/873-3764
•Régie du logement/Québec Rental Board: #11.65, 1, rue Notre-Dame est, Montréal QC H2Y 1B6 – 514/873-6575; Fax: 514/873-6805
Présidente, Louise Thibault
514/643-1697, Fax: 514/646-3570
•Société d'aménagement de l'Outaouais/Outaouais Development: Maison du Citoyen, 25, rue Laurier, CP 1666, Hull QC J8X 3Y5 – 819/770-1500; Fax: 819/770-3213
•Société d'habitation du Québec/Québec Housing: Bloc 2, 1054, Conroy, 4e étage, Québec QC G1R 5E7 – 418/643-7676; Fax: 418/643-2166
Président, Jean-Paul Arsenault
514/873-8130, Fax: 514/873-8340
•Société québécoise d'assainissement des eaux (SQAE)/Québec Wastewater Treatment: 1055, boul René-Lévesque est, 10e étage, Montréal QC H2L 4S5 – 514/873-7411; Fax: 514/873-7879 – Québec: 418/643-2616; Fax: 418/643-0991
Président et Directeur général, Jean-Yves Babin

## Ministère de l'AGRICULTURE, des PÊCHERIES et de l'ALIMENTATION (MAPAQ)/Agriculture, Fisheries & Food

200, ch Sainte-Foy, Québec QC G1R 4X6
418/643-2673; Fax: 418/646-0829; Email: info@agr.gouv.qc.ca; URL: http://www.agr.gouv.qc.ca/mapaq/

**ACTS ADMINISTERED**

Agricultural Abuses Act
Agricultural Merit Act
Agricultural Societies Act
Animal Health Protection Act
An Act respecting commercial fisheries & aquaculture
An Act respecting farmers' & dairymen's associations
An Act respecting municipal taxation (certain sections)
An Act respecting prevention of disease in potatoes
An Act respecting public agricultural lands in the public domain
An Act respecting the bread trade
An Act respecting the École de laiterie & intermediate agricultural schools
An Act respecting the lands in the public domain (certain sections)
An Act respecting the Ministère de l'Agriculture, des Pêcheries & de l'Alimentation
Bees Act
Butter & Cheese Societies Act
Dairy Products & Dairy Products Substitutes Act (certain sections)
Horticultural Societies Act
Maritime Fisheries Credit Act
Mining Act (in part)
Plant Protection Act
Restaurant Merit Act
Stock Breeding Syndicates Act
Thoroughbred Cattle Act
Tourist Establishments Act (certain sections)

**Administered by the Société de financement agricole du Québec**

An Act respecting farm financing
An Act respecting farm-loan insurance & forestry-loan insurance
An Act respecting the conservation & development of wildlife
An Act respecting the Communauté urbaine de Montréal (certain sections)
An Act respecting the marketing of marine products
An Act to promote forest credit by private institutions
Cities & Towns Act (certain sections)
Farm Credit Act
Farmers' Clubs Act
Forestry Credit Act
Municipal Code of Québec (certain sections)
Fishermen's Merit Act
The Charter of the City of Québec (certain sections)
The Charter of the City of Sherbrooke (certain sections)
The Charter of the City of Trois-Rivières (certain sections)
The Marine Products Processing Act

**Administered by the Commission de protection du territoire agricole du Québec**

An Act governing the acquisition of farm land by non-residents
An Act to preserve agricultural land

**Administered by the Régie des assurances agricoles du Québec**

An Act respecting farm income stabilization insurance
Crop Insurance Act

**Administered by the Régie des marchés agricoles**

An Act respecting the sale price of pulpwood sold by farmers
Dairy Products & Dairy Products Substitutes Act (certain sections)
Farm, Food & Fishery Products Marketing Act
Farm Producers Act
Grain Act

**Administered by the Société québécoise d'initiatives agro-alimentaires**

An Act respecting the Société québécoise d'initiatives agro-alimentaires

**Administered by the Raffinerie de sucre du Québec**

An Act respecting the Raffinerie de sucre du Québec

An Act respecting the sale of the Raffinerie de sucre du Québec

**Ministre**, Guy Julien, 418/643-2525, Fax: 418/643-8422

Sous-ministre, André Vézina, 418/643-2336, Fax: 418/646-7747

Secrétaire du ministère, Yvon Bougie, 418/643-2336, Fax: 418/646-7747

Directrice, Affaires juridiques, Huguette Pagé, 418/643-2355, Fax: 418/643-1676

Directeur (par intérim), Planification, Gilles Turcotte, 418/528-1419, Fax: 418/646-7747

### AFFAIRES ÉCONOMIQUES/Economic Affairs

418/643-2460; Fax: 418/646-6564

Sous-ministre adjoint, Marc Dion, 418/643-2336, Fax: 418/646-7747

Directeur, Analyse de l'information économique, Pascal Van Nieuwenhuyse

Directeur, Appui aux enterprises, Gilles Hains

Directeur, Développement des marchés, Zénon Bergeron, 201, boul Crémazie est, 4e étage, Montréal QC H2L 1M4, 514/873-4410, Fax: 514/873-2364

Directeur, Politiques commerciales, Gaétan Busque

Directeur, Relations intergouvernementales, Louis Vallée

Directeur, Securité du revenu agricole, Daniel Roy

### PÊCHES, FORMATION ET RECHERCHE/Fisheries, Research & Development

Sous-ministre adjointe, Hélène Tremblay, 418/643-2336, Fax: 418/646-7747

Directeur, Analyses et politiques, Laval Poulin, 418/528-2877, Fax: 418/643-8820

Directrice, Formation et main-d'oeuvre en bioalimentaire, Nadine Girardville, 418/644-1315, Fax: 418/644-3049

Directeur, Innovation et technologies, Lucien Poirier, 96, montée Sandy Beach, PO Box 1070, Gaspé QC G0C 1R0, 418/368-7637, Fax: 418/368-1275

Directeur, Recherche, Daniel Chez, 418/644-1653, Fax: 418/646-0832

Directeur, Centre de recherche et d'expérimentation agricole de St-Hyacinthe, Bernard Aurouze, 3300, rue Sicotte, PO Box 480, St-Hyacinthe QC J2S 7B8, 514/778-6522, Fax: 514/778-6539

Directrice, Centre de recherche et d'expérimentation de Deschambault, Suzanne Pilote, 120-A, ch du Roy, Deschambault QC G0A 1S0, 418/286-3351, Fax: 418/286-3597

Directeur, Centre de recherche et d'expérimentation en régie et protection de, Jean-François Bertrand, 2700, rue Einstein, Ste-Foy QC G1P 3W8, 418/643-2380, Fax: 418/646-0832

Directeur, Centre de recherche et d'expérimentation Les Buissons, Jean-François Bertrand, 358, ch. Principal, PO Box 455, Les Buissons QC G0H 1H0, 418/567-2235, Fax: 418/567-8791

Directeur, Centre de recherche en téchnologie alimentaire, Bernard Aurouze, 3600, boul. Casavant ouest, St-Hyacinthe QC J2S 8E3, 514/773-1105, Fax: 514/773-8461

Directeur, Institut de technologie agroalimentaire de La Pocatière, André Simard, 401, rue Poiré, La Pocatière QC G0R 1Z0, 418/856-1110, Fax: 418/856-1719

Directeur, Institut de technologie agroalimentaire de Saint-Hyacinthe, Gilles Vézina, 3230, rue Sicotte, CP 70, Sainy-Hyacinthe QC J2S 7B3, 514/778-6504, Fax: 514/778-6536

Directeur régional (par intérim), Côte-Nord, Michel Lanouette, 466, rue Arnaud, Sept-Iles QC G4R 3B1, 418/962-5521, Fax: 418/962-0744

Directeur régional, Estuaire et Eaux intérieures, Michel Lanouette, 460, boul Louis-Fréchette, Nicolet QC J3T 1Y2, 819/293-5677, Fax: 819/293-8519

Directeur régional (par intérim), Gaspésie, Danielle Bouchard, 96, montée Sandy Beach, CP 1070, Gaspé QC G0C 1R0, 418/368-7630, Fax: 418/368-5851

Directeur régional, Iles-de-la-Madeleine, Réjean Richard, 125, rue du Parc, CP 338, Cap-aux-Meules QC G0B 1B0, 418/986-2098, Fax: 418/986-4421

### PRODUCTION ET AFFAIRES RÉGIONALES/Regional Operations

Sous-ministre adjoint, Jacques Landry, 418/643-2336, Fax: 418/646-7747

Directeur (par intérim), Analyse et coordination, Alain Pouliot, 418/646-9681, Fax: 418/644-3049

Directeur, Environnement et développement durable, Denis Sanfaçon, 418/643-3029, Fax: 418/528-0485

Directeur associé, Services technologiques, Yvan Savoie, 418/644-4686, Fax: 418/643-6680

### QUALITÉ DES ALIMENTS ET SANTÉ ANIMALE/Food Quality & Animal Health

Sous-ministre adjointe, Jocelyne Dagenais, 418/643-2336, Fax: 418/644-7747

Directeur, Laboratoires d'expertises et d'analyses alimentaires, Jacques Boulanger, 2700, rue Einstein, Ste-Foy QC G1P 3W8, 418/644-5226, Fax: 418/643-0131

Directeur, Normes et programmes, Vacant, 418/646-8083, Fax: 418/644-3049

Directeur, Soutien aux opérations et de la coordination de l'information, Michel Lemay, 418/646-8322, Fax: 418/644-3049

Directeur régional, Bas-Saint-Laurent - Gaspésie - Iles-de-la-Madeleine, Claude Beauregard, 298 boul Thériault, 3e étage, Rivière-du-Loup QC G5R 4C2, 418/862-6341, Fax: 418/867-4126

Directeur régional, Laurentides - Outaouais - Abitibi-Témiscamingue, Laval Tremblay, #110, 1065, boul de la Carrière, Hull QC J8Y 6V5, 819/772-3009, Fax: 819/772-3541

Directeur régional, Mauricie - Bois-Francs - Estrie, Serge Robert, 460, boul Louis-Fréchette, Nicolet QC J3T 1Y2, 819/-293-8509, Fax: 819/293-2971

Directeur régional, Montérégie, Pierre Chartier, 3220, rue Sicotte, PO Box 3500, Saint-Hyacinthe QC J2S 7X9, 514/778-6542, Fax: 514/778-6535

Directeur régional, Montréal - Laval - Lanaudière, Yves Proulx, 867, boul l'Ange-Gardien, L'Assomption QC J5W 4M9, 514/589-5745, Fax: 514/589-0648

Directeur régional, Québec - Chaudière - Appalaches - Saguenay - Lac-Saint-Jean - Côte-Nord, Robert Clermont, 2700, rue Einstein, Ste-Foy QC G1P 3W8, 418/644-6140, Fax: 418/644-6327

### SERVICES À LA GESTION/Management Services

Directrice, Évaluation de programmes, Mishèle Bérubé, 418/643-7209, Fax: 418/644-4533

Directeur, Ressources financières et matérielles, André Abgral, 418/643-2420, Fax: 418/646-0869

Directeur, Ressources humaines, Jean Hébert, 418/643-7830, Fax: 418/644-4533

Directeur, Ressources informationnelles, André Roy, 418/643-0752, Fax: 418/646-0869

Directrice, Services en communication, Colombe Cliche, 418/643-2517, Fax: 418/643-8307

**Associated Agencies, Boards & Commissions**

•Commission de protection du territoire agricole/Agricultural Land Preservation: 200, ch Ste-Foy, 2e étage, Québec QC G1R 4X6 – 418/643-3314; Fax: 418/643-2261

Président, Bernard Ouimet

•Fonds d'Assurance-Préts Agricoles & Forestiers/Agriculture & Forest Insurance Fund: 1020, rte de l'Eglise, 8e étage, Ste-Foy QC G1V 4P2 – 418/643-2610; Fax: 418/646-9712

Président, Michel R. St-Pierre

•Régie des assurances agricoles du Québec/Québec Agricultural Insurance Board: 5825, rue St-Georges, Lévis QC G6V 4L2 – 418/833-5363; Fax: 418/833-6145

Président & Directeur général, Luc Roy

•Régie des marchés agricoles & alimentaires du Québec/Québec Agriculture & Food Marketing Board: 201, boul Crémazie est, Montréal QC H2M 1L3 – 514/873-4024; Fax: 514/873-3984

Président, Jean-Yves Lavoie

•Société de financement agricole du Québec/Québec Agricultural Finance: 1020, rte de l'Église, 8e étage, Ste-Foy QC G1V 4P2 – 418/643-2610; Fax: 418/646-9712

Président, Michel R. St-Pierre

•Société de promotion de l'industrie des courses de chevaux/Québec Horse Racing: 5400, boul des Galeries, 2e étage, Québec QC G2K 2B4 – 418/646-1632; Fax: 418/646-2528

Directeur-général, André St-Jean

Montréal Office: #302, 7881, boul Décarie, Montréal QC H4P 2H2
514/873-5000, Fax: 514/873-0296

•Société québécoise d'initiatives agro-alimentaires (SOQUIA)/Québec Food & Fishing Industries Venture Capital Investment: #284, 1275, ch Ste-Foy, Québec QC G1S 4S5 – 418/643-2238; Fax: 418/643-2553 – Telex: 051-3023

Président, Lucien Biron

•Tribunal d'Appel en Matière de Protection du Territoire Agricole: 200, ch Ste-Foy, 4e étage, Québec QC G1R 4X6 – 418/646-3047; Fax: 418/643-0022

Présidente, Rita Bédard

**Agricultural Marketing Boards & Commissions**

•Centre de développement du porc inc.: 200, ch Ste-Foy, 1er étage, Québec QC G1R 4X6 – 418/649-5070; Fax: 418/649-5077

Directrice générale, Odile Comeau

•Conseil des productions animales du Québec inc (CPAQ)/Québec Animal Products Council: 200, ch Sainte-Foy, 12e étage, Québec QC G1R 4X6 – 418/646-5781; Fax: 418/646-1830, Directeur exécutif, Claude Martin

•Conseil des productions végétales du Québec inc/Québec Vegetable Products Council: 200 ch Sainte-Foy, 12e étage, Québec QC GIR 4X6 – 418/646-5766; Fax: 418/646-1830

Directrice générale, Claudine Martel

•Groupe Gestion & économie agricoles inc. (GEAGRI): 200, ch Ste-Foy, 12e étage, Québec QC G1R 4X6 – 418/646-5772; Fax: 418/646-1830

Directeur exécutif, Claude Tremblay

•L'Union des Producteurs Agricoles: 555, boul Roland-Therrien, Longueuil QC J4H 3Y9 – 514/679-0530; Fax: 514/679-5436

Président général, Laurent Pellerin

•Office des producteurs de tabac à cigare & à pipe du Québec/Québec Cigar & Pipe Tobacco Producers: 60, rue Vennes, St-Jacques QC J0K 2R0 – 514/839-3641; Fax: 514/839-2874

Secrétaire, Gaétan Laporte

•Office des producteurs de tabac jaune du Québec: 813, rue Principale, St-Thomas-de-Joliette QC J0K 3L0 – 514/756-2640

Secrétaire, Jean-Pierre Labyt

## Ministère des Relations avec les CITOYENS et de l'IMMIGRATION

360, rue McGill, 4e étage, Montréal QC H2Y 2E9
514/873-9940; Fax: 514/864-2899; URL: http://www.immq.gouv.qc.ca/
Québec: #336, 900 boul René-Lévesque est, Québec QC G1R 2B5
418/644-2428, Fax: 418/528-0829

#### ACTS ADMINISTERED

Department of Immigration Act

**Ministre**, Louise Harel, 514/873-9450, Fax: 514/873-1810
**Ministre délégué, Immigration**, André Boisclair, 418/643-6322, Fax: 418/643-8936, Email: andre.boisclair/depute/pq@assnat.qa
Sous-ministre, Nicole Fontaine, 514/873-9450, Fax: 514/873-1810
Sous-ministre associée, Nicole Brodeur, 514/873-9447, Fax: 514/864-1930
Secrétaire générale, Secteur immigration et communautés culturelles, Francine Émond, 514/499-2199, Fax: 514/873-1810

#### Communication-Québec

1500-C, boul Charest Ouest, 1er étage, Ste-Foy QC G1N 2E5
418/643-1430; Fax: 418/643-5190
This office is the general information service of the provincial government.
Directrice générale, Marcelle Girard
Directrice, Services centraux, Lise Monette, 418/644-0382

#### Information gouvernementale/Communication Services

Directrice générale, Marcelle Girard, 418/644-7789, Fax: 418/643-6177
Directeur, Distribution, Roger Hakim, 418/643-1804, Fax: 418/643-6177
Directeur, Edition gouvernementale, Jean-Pierre Lemonde, 418/644-3228, Fax: 418/644-7813
Directeur, Information documentaire, François C. Reny, 418/643-1515, Fax: 418/646-8132
Directeur, Moyens de communication, Maurice Arguin, 418/644-2866, Fax: 418/643-7432

#### Associated Agencies, Boards & Commissions

•Bureau de révision en immigration: 2055, rue Peel, Montréal QC H3A 1V4 – 514/864-3010; Fax: 514/864-3181
Directeur, Chahé-Philippe Arslanian
•Conseil des communautés culturelles & de l'immigration/Cultural Communities & Immigration Council: #418, Tour de la Place-Victoria, CP 158, Montréal QC H4Z 1C3 – 514/873-8501; Fax: 514/873-3469
Président, Vacant
Vice-président, Immigration, Jacques Johnson, 514/873-8502
Vice-président, Immigration, Raymond Paquin, 514/873-4802

## Secrétariat à la CONDITION FÉMININE/Québec Women's Secretariat

#2.700, 875, Grande-Allée est, Québec QC G1R 5W5
418/643-9052; Fax: 418/643-4991
**Ministre responsable**, Louise Harel, 418/643-4810, Fax: 418/643-2802
Sous-ministre associée, Léa Cousineau
Directrice générale, Michèle Laberge

#### CONSEIL DU STATUT DE LA FEMME/Status of Women Council

#300, 8, rue Cook, Québec QC G1R 5J7
418/643-4326; Fax: 418/643-8926
Présidente, Diane Lemieux

## Ministère de la CULTURE et des COMMUNICATIONS/Culture & Communications

225, Grand-Allée est, Québec QC G1R 5G5
418/643-2183; Fax: 418/643-4457; URL: http://www.mcc.gouv.qc.ca
Bureau de Montréal, 480, boul St-Laurent, Montréal QC H2Y 3Y7
514/873-2255, Fax: 514/864-2448

#### ACTS ADMINISTERED

Loi sur les archives
Loi sur la Bibliothèque nationale du Québec
Loi sur les biens culturels
Charte de la langue française
Loi sur le cinéma
Loi sur les concours artistiques, littéraires et scientifiques
Loi sur le Conseil des arts et des lettres du Québec
Loi sur le Conservatoire
Loi sur le Conservatoire de musique et d'art dramatique du Québec
Loi sur le développement des entreprises québécoises dans le domaine du livre
Loi sur le ministère de la Culture et des Communications
Loi sur le Musée des beaux-arts de Montréal
Loi sur les musées nationaux
Loi sur la programmation éducative
Loi sur la Régie des télécommunications
Loi sur la Société de développement des entreprises culturelles
Loi sur la Société de la Place des Arts de Montréal
Loi sur la Société de télédiffusion du Québec
Loi sur la Société du Grand Théâtre de Québec
Loi sur le statut professionnel des artistes des arts visuels, des métiers d'art et de la littérature et sur leurs contrats avec les diffuseurs
Loi sur le statut professionnel et les conditions d'engagement des artistes de la scène, du disque et du cinéma

**Ministre**, Louise Beaudoin, 418/643-2110, Fax: 418/643-9164
Sous-ministre, Martine Tremblay, 418/643-3310, Fax: 418/643-4023
Sous-ministre adjoint, Action Culturelle et Partenariat, Pierre Lafleur, 418/643-3310, Fax: 418/643-4023
Directrice, Affaires juridiques, Julie Gosselin, 418/643-3747, Fax: 418/646-6849
Directeur, Communications, André Dorval, 418/643-6300, Fax: 418/643-4457
Directeur, Secrétariat à la politique linguistique, Guy Dumas, 418/643-4248, Fax: 418/646-7832
Directeur, Secrétariat de l'autotroute de l'information, Vacant, 418/528-2640, Fax: 418/528-0339

#### ADMINISTRATION ET SERVICES MINISTÉRIELS/Administration & Ministerial services

Directeur général, Pierre-Denis Cantin, 418/643-7293, Fax: 418/643-4023
Directeur, Personnel et organisation du travail, Jean Cossette, 418/643-6529, Fax: 418/646-6440
Directrice (par intérim), Ressources financières et matérielles, Élisabeth Verge, 418/643-2101, Fax: 418/646-5448
Directeur (par intérim), Ressources informationnelles, Jean-Pierre Lorenger, 418/644-6314, Fax: 418/644-9014
Directrice, Service de l'information de gestion, évaluation, et développement, Élisabeth Verge, 418/643-7293, Fax: 418/643-5448

#### ACTION RÉGIONALE/Regional Operations

Directrice, Murielle Doyle, 418/644-4789, Fax: 418/644-4776

#### Directions

Montréal: 480, boul St-Laurent, 6e étage, Montréal QC H2Y 3Y7 – 514/873-2255; Fax: 514/864-2448, Directrice, Monique Barriault
Québec: Bloc C, R.C., 225, Grande-Allée est, Québec QC G1R 5G5 – 418/643-6246; Fax: 418/644-9014, Directeur, François Paquette, 418/643-6246, Fax: 418/644-9014

#### ARCHIVES NATIONALES/National Archives

Pavillon Louis-Jacques Casault, 1210 av du Séminaire, Ste-Foy QC G1N 4V1
Directeur général, Robert Garon, 418/643-4376
Directeur, Centre d'archives de Québec, Jean-Pierre Therrien, 418/644-4787
Responsable, Centre des documents semi-actifs, Marie Phoenix, 2750, rue Dalton, Ste-Foy QC G1P 3S4, 418/646-7696

#### COMMUNICATIONS ET ACTION STRATÉGIQUE/Communications & Strategic planning

Sous-ministre adjoint, Adélard Guillemette, Québec QC G1R 5G5, 418/646-3310, Fax: 418/643-4023
Directeur, Centre de conservation du Québec, Michel Cauchon, 1825, rue Semple, Québec QC G1N 4B7, 418/643-7001, Fax: 418/646-5419
Directeur, Inforoutes et multimédia, André Duplessis, 418/643-8096, Fax: 418/528-0874
Directrice, Médias et télécommunications, Louise Gingras, 418/643-1887, Fax: 418/643-7853
Directrice, Recherche, Hélène Cantin, 418/643-8824, Fax: 418/643-6214

#### CONSERVATOIRES DE MUSIQUE ET D'ART DRAMATIQUE DU QUÉBEC/Conservatories of Music and Drama

225, Grande-Allée est, 3e étage-bloc C, Québec QC G1R 5G5
Directeur général (par intérim), Gilles Simard, 418/643-7427, Fax: 418/646-0175
Directeur, Études, Gilles Simard, 418/643-4796, Fax: 418/646-0175

#### DÉVELOPPEMENT INTERNATIONAL ET PROSPECTIVE/International development

Fax: 418/643-6214
Directeur général, Jacques Vallée, 418/646-4273
Directrice, Action stratégique, Micheline Boivin, 418/643-1363
Responsable, Développement international, Louise Bourassa, 418/643-3560

#### PRIORITÉS GOUVERNEMENTALES ET PROJETS SPÉCIAUX/Government priorities & Special projects

Directrice, Odette Duplessis, 418/644-7215, Fax: 418/644-4776

#### SOCIÉTÉS D'ÉTAT ET PROGRAMMATION

Fax: 418/643-4080
Directrice générale & Directrice (par intérim), Sociétés d'État, Marie-Claire Lévesque, 418/643-4211
Directeur, Formation et éducation, André Couture, 418/644-7198, Fax: 418/644-4776
Responsable, Intégration des arts à l'architecture, Nicole Genêt, 418/644-2109, Fax: 418/644-9014
Directeur, Interventions réseau, Claude Roy, 418/644-8923, Fax: 418/643-8457
Directrice, Loisir culturel, Claudette Bolduc, 418/646-4095, Fax: 418/643-4023
Directeur, Politiques et coordination des programmes, Denis Delangie, 418/644-0485, Fax: 418/643-0380
Directeur, Secrétariat de la propriété intellectuelle, Vacant, 418/644-7194

#### Associated Agencies, Boards & Commissions

•Bibliothèque nationale du Québec/Québec National Library
Listed in Section 1 of this book; *see* Index.

•Commission des biens culturels du Québec/Québec Cultural Property Commission: 12, rue Ste-Anne, 2e étage, Québec QC G1R 3X2 – 418/643-8378; Fax: 418/643-8591
Président, Cyril Simard, 418/643-8380
•Commission de reconnaissance des associations d'artistes: #750, 425, boul de Maisonneuve ouest, Montréal QC H3A 3G5 – 514/873-6012; Fax: 514/873-6267
Président, Me Denis Hardy
•Conseil des arts et des lettres du Québec: #320, 79, boul René-Lévesque est, Québec QC G1R 5N5 – 418/643-1707; Fax: 418/643-4558
Présidente et Directrice générale, Marie Lavigne, 514/864-3351, Fax: 514/873-7885
Directeur général, Programmes, André Leclerc, Fax: 514/864-4160
Directeur adjoint, Programmes, Germain Breton, 418/643-2364
500, Place d'Armes, 15e étage, Montréal QC H2Y 2W2
514/864-3350
Ligne sans frais: 1-800-608-3350
•Musée d'art contemporain de Montréal/Montréal Museum of Contemporary Art
Listed in Section 6 of this book; *see* Index.
•Musée de la civilisation/Museum of Civilisation
Listed in Section 6 of this book; *see* Index.
•Musée du Québec/Museum of Québec
Listed in Section 6 of this book; *see* Index.
•Régie du Cinéma/Cinema Board: 455, rue Ste-Hélène, Montréal QC H2Y 2L3 – 514/873-2491; Fax: 514/873-8874
Président, Claude Benjamin
•Régie des télécommunications du Québec: #5.00, 900 place d'Youville, Québec QC G1R 3P7 – 418/643-5560; Fax: 418/643-2960
Vice président & Régisseur, Richard Labrie
•Société de développement des enterprises culturelles (SODEC)/Arts & Cultural Enterprise Development Commission: #200, 1755, boul René-Lévesque est, Montréal QC H2K 4P6 – 514/873-7768; Fax: 514/873-4388, Ligne sans frais: 1-800-363-0401
Président, Pierre Lampron, Fax: 514/873-8213
Secrétaire & Directeur général, Administration, Michel Fortier
36 1/2, rue St-Pierre, Québec QC G1K 3Z6
418/643-2581, Fax: 418/643-8918
•Société du Grand Théâtre de Québec: 269, boul René-Lévesque est, Québec QC G1R 2B3 – 418/644-8921; Fax: 418/646-7670
Président, Pierre-Michel Bouchard
Directrice générale, Francine Grégoire
•Société de la Place des Arts de Montréal: 260, boul de Maisonneuve ouest, Montréal QC H2X 1Y9 – 514/285-4210; Fax: 514/285-1968
Président, Clément Richard
Directrice générale, France Fortin
•Société de télédiffusion du Québec/Radio-Québec: 1000, rue Fullum, Montréal QC H2K 3L7 – 514/521-2424; Fax: 514/873-7739, Ligne sans frais: 1-800-361-4301
Président-Directeur général (par intérim), Robert Normand
Vice-président, Affaires corporatives & Secrétaire général, Me Luc Audet

**Associated Agencies, Boards & Commissions (under the French Language Charter)**

•Commission de toponymie/Geographical Names: Édifice Marie-Guyart, Aile René-Lévesque, 1060, rue Louis-Alexandre-Taschereau, 4e étage, Québec QC G1R 5V8 – Fax: 418/644-9466
Président (par intérim), Alain Vallières, 418/644-2392
•Conseil de la langue française/French Language Council: 800, Place d'Youville, 13e étage, Québec QC G1R 3P4 – 418/643-2814; Fax: 418/644-7654
Présidente, Nadia Brédimas-Assimopoulos
1200, av McGill Collège, 22e étage, Montréal QC H3B 4J8
514/873-2285, Fax: 514/873-7863
•Office de la langue française/French Language Board: Tour de la Place-Victoria, 16e étage, CP 316, Montréal QC H4Z 1G8 – 514/873-0797; Fax: 514/873-3488
Président, Nicole René
200, ch Ste-Foy, 4e étage, Québec QC G1R 5S4
418/643-2145, Fax: 418/643-3210
•Secrétariat à la politique linguistique: RC-A, 225 Grande Allée est, Québec QC G1R 5G5 – 418/643-4248; Fax: 418/646-7832
Directeur, Guy Dumas

## CURATEUR PUBLIC du QUÉBEC/Québec Public Trustee

#500, 600, boul René-Lévesque ouest, Montréal QC H3B 4W9
514/873-4074; Fax: 514/873-4972
Directeur, Marjolaine Loiselle

## Secrétariat au DÉVELOPPEMENT des RÉGIONS/Regional Affairs Secretariat

Édifice H, #3.600, 875, Grande Allée est, Québec QC G1R 5W5
418/528-0930; Fax: 418/644-5610
**Ministre d'État**, Guy Chevrette, 418/644-5846, Fax: 418/528-0372
Sous-ministre associée, Monique Bégin, 418/528-0930
Ententes gouvernementales, Serge Doyon
Opérations et services, Lawrence Desrosiers
Politiques gouvernementales, Serge Doyon

**Sous-ministries adjoints/Asst. Deputy Ministers**

Abitibi-Témiscamingue: #1.03, 180, boul Rideau, Rouyn-Noranda QC J9X 1N9 – 819/762-3561; Fax: 819/797-1462, Sous-ministre adjoint, Denise Voynaud
Bas-Saint-Laurent: 337, rue Moreault, Rimouski QC G5L 1P4 – 418/727-3566; Fax: 418/727-3576, Sous-ministre adjoint, Simon Chabot
Chaudière-Appalaches: 700, av Notre-Dame nord, Suite D, Sainte-Marie-de-Beauce QC G6E 2K9 – 418/386-8677; Fax: 418/386-8037, Sous-ministre adjoint, Richard Bellemare
Côte-Nord: #1.802, 625, boul Laflèche, Baie-Comeau QC G5C 1C5, Sous-ministre adjointe, Lyse Lévesque, 418/589-4345, Fax: 418/589-5199
Estrie: #405, 200, rue Belvedère nord, Sherbrooke QC J1H 4A9 – 819/820-3155; Fax: 819/820-3929, Sous-ministre adjoint, Pierre Deland
Gaspésie-Îles-de-la-Madeleine: 220, rue Commerciale est, CP 1360, Chandler QC G0C 1K0 – 418/689-2019; Fax: 418/689-4108, Sous-ministre adjoint, Claude Rioux
Lanaudière: 138, rue Saint-Paul, Joliette QC J6E 5G3 – 514/752-6866; Fax: 514/752-6877, Sous-ministre adjointe (par intérim), Monique Savinau
Laurentides: #215, 85, rue De Martigny ouest, Saint-Jérôme QC J7Y 3R8 – 514/569-3126; Fax: 514/569-3131, Sous-ministre adjoint, Jean-Guy Tremblay
Laval: #210, 1555, boul Chomedey, Laval QC H7V 3Z1 – 514/686-1428; Fax: 514/686-9106, Sous-ministre adjointe, Micheline Larrivée
Mauricie-Bois-Francs: #114, 100, rue Laviolette, Trois-Rivières QC G9A 5S9 – 819/371-6617; Fax: 819/371-6960, Sous-ministre adjoint, Robert Verreault
Montérégie: #4.05, 201, Place Charles-Lemoyne, Longueuil QC J4K 2T5 – 514/928-7643; Fax: 514/928-7650, Sous-ministre adjoint, Yvon Richer
Montréal: Édifice Mercantile, 770, rue Sherbrooke ouest, 4e étage, Montréal QC H3A 1G1 – 514/873-5845; Fax: 514/873-3224, Sous-ministre adjoint, Jean-Pierre Nepveu
Nord-du-Québec: #3.600, 875 Grande-Allée est, Québec QC G1R 5W5 – 418/528-0930; Fax: 418/644-5610, Sous-ministre adjoint, Langevin Gagnon
Outaouais: #7120, 170, rue Hôtel-de Ville, Hull QC J8X 4C2 – 819/772-3038; Fax: 819/772-3968, Sous-ministre adjoint, Paul-André David
Québec: #RC01, 875, Grande Allée est, Québec QC G1R 5W5 – 418/643-4957; Fax: 418/528-1410, Sous-ministre adjointe, France Boucher
Saguenay-Lac-Saint-Jean: 3950, boul Harvey, 2e étage, Jonquière QC G7X 8L6 – 418/695-7970; Fax: 418/695-7975, Sous-ministre adjointe (par intérim), Ginette Dim

## Ministère de l'ÉDUCATION/Education

1035, rue De La Chevrotière, 11e étage, Québec QC G1R 5A5
418/643-7095; Fax: 418/646-6561; 528-2080; Email: Dircom@meq.gouv.qc.ca; URL: http://www.gouv.qc.ca/francais/minorg/medu/medu_intro.html

**ACTS ADMINISTERED**

Loi sur l'accréditation et le financement des associations d'élèves ou d'étudiants
Loi sur l'aide financière aux étudiants
Charte de la langue française Chap. VIII, La langue de l'enseignement
Loi sur le Collège militaire royal de Saint-Jean
Loi sur les collèges d'enseignement général et professionnel
Loi sur la Commission d'évaluation de l'enseignement collégial et modifiant certaines dispositions législatives
Loi concernant l'Institut Armand-Frappier
Loi sur les concours artistiques, littéraires et scientifiques
Loi sur le Conseil supérieur de l'Éducation
Loi sur les élections scolaires
Loi sur l'enseignement privé
Loi sur les établissements d'enseignement de niveau universitaire
Loi favorisant le développement scientifique et technologique du Québec
Loi sur l'Institut québécois de recherche sur la culture
Loi sur l'instruction publique
Loi sur l'instruction publique pour les autochtones cris, inuit et naskapis
Loi sur les investissements universitaires
Loi sur le Ministère de l'Éducation
Loi sur la Société de la maison des sciences et des techniques
Loi sur l'Université du Québec
**Ministre**, Pauline Marois, 418/644-0664, Fax: 418/646-7551
Sous-ministre, Pauline Champoux-Lesage, 418/643-3810, Fax: 418/644-4591
Sous-ministre adjoint, Foi catholique, Christine Cadrin-Pelletier, 418/643-3810, Fax: 418/644-4591
Sous-ministre adjoint, Foi protestante, C. Grant Hawley, 418/643-3810, Fax: 418/644-4591

**COMMUNAUTÉ ANGLOPHONE/Anglophone Services**

600, rue Fullum, Montréal QC H2K 4L1
514/873-4630; Fax: 514/873-1082
Sous-ministre adjointe & Directrice (par intérim), Politiques et projets, Élaine Freeland, 514/873-3772
Présidente, Commission de l'éducation en langue anglaise, Gretta Chambers, 514/873-5656
Directrice, Production en langue anglaise, Phyllis Koper-Naggiar, 514/873-6073

**ÉDUCATION PRÉSCOLAIRE, ENSEIGNEMENT PRIMAIRE ET SECONDAIRE/Preschool education, Elementary & secondary school education**

Sous-ministre adjoint, Robert Bisaillon, 418/643-3810

Directeur (par intérim), Adaption scolaire et services complémentaires, Normand Gagné, 418/646-7000
Directrice, Communautés culturelles, Marie-France Benes, 514/873-6029
Directeur, Formation générale des adultes & Directeur (par intérim), Formation générale des jeunes, Alain Mercier, 418/643-5287
Directrice, Recherche, Marie Giroux, 418/643-1723
Directeur, Ressources didactiques, Roger Vézina, 514/873-7681
Directeur, Sanction des études, Jacques Tardif, 418/644-0905
Directrice, Titularisation et formation du personnel scolaire, Diane Gagnon, 418/643-8610

#### ENSEIGNEMENT SUPÉRIEUR/Higher Education
Sous-ministre adjoint, Jacques Babin, 418/643-3810
Directrice, Affaires éducatives collégiales, Claire Prévost-Fournier, 418/643-6671
Directeur, Aide financière aux études, Pierre-Paul Allaire, 418/646-5313
Directeur, Enseignement collégial privé et coordination interne, Jean-Yves Marquis, 418/646-1328
Directeur, Enseignement et recherche universitaires, Louis Gendreau, 418/644-9806
Directeur, Financement et équipement, Pierre Malouin, 418/646-4533
Directeur, Relations du travail, Gilles Pouliot, 418/646-1572

#### RÉSEAUX/Networks
Sous-ministre adjoint, Henri-Paul Chaput, 418/643-3810
Directeur général, Financement et équipement, Réjean Morel, 418/643-3108
Directeur, Affaires autochtones, Paul Rémillard, 418/644-4011
Directeur, Coordination régionale, Jeannot Bordeleau, 418/643-5357
Directeur, Enseignement privé, Robert Dépatie, 418/646-3939
Directeur, Relations du travail, Claude Pagé, 418/643-8610

#### SERVICES À LA GESTION/Management Services
Directeur général, Yvan Dussault, 418/643-0220
Directeur, Développement des systèmes, Denis Tremblay, 418/643-5292
Directeur, Édition, Jacques Caron, 418/643-3790
Directeur, Gestion des systèmes de collecte, Gaston Mongeau, 418/643-7528
Directeur, Organisation des données et des systèmes, Guy Morneau, 418/644-3880
Directeur, Ressources financières, Mario Laliberté, 418/644-1122
Directeur, Ressources humaines, Régis A. Malenfant, 418/643-0090
Directeur, Ressources matérielles, Daniel Caron, 418/646-9848
Directeur, Statistiques et études quantitatives, Robert Maheu, 418/644-0383
Directeur, Traitement et bureautique, Constant Gravel, 418/643-4256

##### Associated Agencies, Boards & Commissions
•Centre québécois de valorisation des biomasses et des biotechnologies (CQVB)/Promotion of biomass & biotechnology: #620, 2875, boul Laurier, Ste-Foy QC G1V 2M2 – 418/657-3853; Fax: 418/657-7934; Email: cqvb@cqvb.qc.ca; URL: http://www.cqvb.qc.ca
Président, Marcel Risi, Email: Marcel.Risi@cqvb.qc.ca
•Commission consultative de l'enseignement privé/Advisory Committee on Private Education: 1035, rue De La Chevrotière, 9e étage, Québec QC G1R 5A5 – 418/646-1249; Fax: 418/528-2661
Président, Jean Poulin
•Commission d'evaluation de l'enseignement collégial: 905, Dufferin-Montmorency, 3e étage, Québec QC G1R 3M6 – 418/646-5811; Fax: 418/643-9019
Président, Jacques L'Écuyer
•Conseil supérieur de l'Éducation/Education Council: 2050, boul René-Lévesque ouest, 4e étage, Ste-Foy QC G1V 2K8 – 418/643-3850; Fax: 418/644-2530
Vice-Président, Judith Newman
•Fonds pour la formation de chercheurs et l'aide à la recherche/Researcher Training & Research Assistance Fund: #102, 3700, rue du Campanile, Ste-Foy QC G1X 4G6 – 418/643-8560; Fax: 418/643-1451
Président (par intérim), Yves Rousseau

## ÉLECTIONS DU QUÉBEC/Elections Office
3460, rue de La Pérade, Ste-Foy QC G1X 3Y5
418/643-5380; Fax: 418/643-7291; Email: dgeq@dgeq.qc.ca
#325, 1575, boul Henri-Bourassa ouest, Montréal QC H3M 3A9
514/956-5475
**Directeur général des élections**, Vacant

## Ministère de l'EMPLOI ET de la SOLIDARITÉ/Income Security
425, rue St-Amable, 2e étage, Québec QC G1R 4Z1
418/643-9818; Fax: 418/646-5426; URL: http://www.msr.gouv.qc.ca/
Toll Free: 1-800-361-4743
Montréal: 255, boul Crémazie est, Montréal QC H2M 1L5

#### ACTS ADMINISTERED
An Act respecting family benefits
An Act respecting income security
An Act respecting income security for Cree hunters & trappers who are beneficiaries under the Agreement concerning James Bay & Northern Québec
An Act respecting supplementary pension plans
An Act respecting the Commission des affaires sociales
An Act respecting the Ministère de l'Emploi et de la Solidarité & establishing the Commission des partenaires du marchédu travail
An Act respecting the Québec Pension Plan
Supplemental Pension Plans Act
**Ministre**, Louise Harel, 418/643-4810, Fax: 418/643-2802
Sous-ministre, Michel Noël de Tilly, 418/643-4820, Fax: 418/643-1226
Sous-ministre adjoint, Planification stratégique et operationnelle, Alain Deroy, 418/643-5568, Fax: 418/646-6436
Sous-ministre adjointe, Politiques et programmes (emploi), Hélène Simard, 418/643-7006, Fax: 418/643-0019
Sous-ministre adjointe, Politiques et des programmes de securité du revenu, Suzanne Lévesque, 416/643-9483, Fax: 416/643-0019
Sous-ministre adjoint, Réseau travail-Québec, Claude B. Simard, 418/643-3390, Fax: 418/644-4599

##### Associated Agencies, Boards & Commissions
•Office de la sécurité de revenu des chasseurs et piégeurs Cris/Cree Hunters & Trappers Income Security Board: Tour Frontenac, #703, 2700, boul Laurier, Ste-Foy QC G1V 2L8 – 418/643-7300; Fax: 418/643-6803
Président, Marcel Lesyk
•Régie des rentes/Québec Pension Board: 2600, boul Laurier, Ste-Foy QC G1V 4T3 – 418/643-8302; Fax: 418/643-9586
Président, Claude Legault

## Ministère de l'ENVIRONNEMENT et de la FAUNE/Ministry of Environment & Wildlife
Édifice Marie-Guyart, 675, boul René-Lévesque est, Québec QC G1R 5V7
418/643-3127; Fax: 418/646-5974; Email: info@mef.gouv.qc.ca; URL: http://www.mef.gouv.qc.ca
Ligne sans frais: 1-800-561-1616

#### ACTS ADMINISTERED
Act respecting the Agreement concerning James Bay & Northern Québec
Act respecting acid rain
Act respecting the assistance program for Inuit beneficiaries of the James Bay & Northern Québec Agreement (with respect to hunting, fishing & trapping activities)
Act respecting the Conseil de la conservation et de l'environnement
Act respecting the conservation & development of wildlife
Act respecting Cree Villages & the Naskapi Village
Act respecting hunting, fishing rights in James Bay & Northern Québec Territory
Act respecting the Forillon Park & its surroundings
Act respecting the Mauricie Park & its surroundings
Act respecting the Ministère de l'Environnement
Act respecting the Ministère du Loisir, de la Chasse et de la Pêche
Act respecting the protection of non-smokers in certain public places
Act respecting the Société québecoise de récupération et de recyclage
Act respecting threatened or vulnerable species
Ecological Reserves Act
Environment Quality Act
Fisheries Act (federal)
Migratory Birds Convention Act (federal)
Parks Act
Pesticides Act
Tree Protection Act
Watercourses Act
**Ministre**, Paul Bégin
Sous-ministre, Diane Gaudet, 418/643-7860, Fax: 418/643-3619
Secrétaire du ministère, Hervé Bolduc, 418/643-7860, Fax: 418/643-3619
Directeur, Affaires institutionelles et des communications, Lucien Beaumont, 418/521-3823, Fax: 418/646-4762
Directeur, Affaires juridiques, Michel Lalande, 418/643-2691, Fax: 418/646-0908

#### DIRECTION GÉNÉRALE DU DÉVELOPPEMENT DURABLE/Sustainable Development
Fax: 418/643-7812
Sous-ministre adjointe, Suzanne Giguère, 418/643-7860
Directeur, Affaires intergouvernemenatales et des relations avec les autochtones, Georges Goulet, 418/521-3828, Fax: 418/644-4598
Directeur, Éducation et promotion du développement durable, Michel Damphousse, 418/643-4115, Fax: 418/643-3754
Directeur, Évaluation environnementale des projets en milieu terrestre, Pierre Lefebvre, 418/521-3900, Fax: 418/644-8222
Directeur, Évaluation environnementale des projets industriels et en milieu hydrique, Gilles R. Plante, 418/521-3933, Fax: 418/644-8222
Directrice, Information et de la coordination de la recherche, Clémence Veillette, 418/643-2073, Fax: 418/646-9262

#### DIRECTION GÉNÉRALE DE L'ENVIRONNEMENT/Environment
Fax: 418/643-7812
Sous-ministre adjoint, Denys Jean, 418/643-7860
Directrice, Écosystèmes aquatiques, Denyse Gouin, 418/521-3820, Fax: 418/646-8483

Directeur, Milieu atmosphérique, Raynald Brulotte, 418/643-4588, Fax: 418/643-9591
Directeur, Politiques des secteurs agricole et naturel, Guy Demers, 418/646-0753, Fax: 418/528-1035
Directeur, Politiques du secteur industriel, Jean Rivet, 418/528-2363, Fax: 418/644-8562
Directeur (par intérim), Politiques du secteur municipal, Jean-Maurice Latulippe, 418/644-7434, Fax: 418/644-2003

#### DIRECTION GÉNÉRALE DES OPÉRATIONS/Operations

Fax: 418/643-4747
Sous-ministre adjoint, Normand Carrier, 418/643-7860, Fax: 418/643-3619
Directeur, Affaires régionales, Philippe Bussières, 418/644-3987
Directeur, Enquêtes, Eric-Yves Harvey, 418/643-6185, Fax: 418/643-8923
Directeur, Hydraulique, Yvon Gosselin, 418/644-3556, Fax: 418/643-6900

#### DIRECTION GÉNÉRALE DU PATRIMOINE FAUNIQUE ET NATUREL/Wildlife & Natural Heritage

Fax: 418/643-3619
Sous-ministre adjoint, George Arsenault, 418/643-7860
Directeur, Conservation et patrimoine écologique, Léopold Gaudreau, 418/643-5397, Fax: 418/646-6169
Directeur, Faune et habitats, Richard Chatelain, 418/644-2823, Fax: 418/646-6863
Directeur, Milieu hydrique, Normand R. Trempe, 418/643-4553, Fax: 418/646-2367
Directeur, Parcs québécois, Luc Berthiaume, 418/644-9393, Fax: 418/644-8932
Directrice, Territoires fauniques, Claudette Blais, 418/643-7674

##### Associated Agencies, Boards & Commissions

•Bureau d'audiences publiques sur l'environnement (BAPE)/Environmental Public Hearing Board: 625 rue St-Amable, 2e étage, Québec QC G1R 2G5 – 418/643-7447; Fax: 418/643-9474, Toll Free: 1-800-463-4732 – Montréal: 514/873-7790; Fax: 514/873-5024
Président, André Harvey
•Comité conjoint de chasse, de pêche et de piégeage/Hunting, Fishing & Trapping Joint Committee: #369, 393, rue Saint-Jacques, Montréal QC H2Y 1N9 – 514/224-2151; Fax: 514/224-0039
Président, Denis Vandal
•Comité consultatif de l'environnement Kativik/Katavik Environmental Advisory Committee: c/o Administration régionale Kativik, CP 75, Kuujjuaq QC J0M 1C0 – 418/521-3895; Fax: 418/646-0266
Présidente, Louise Filion
•Comité consultatif pour l'environnement de la Baie-James (CCEBJ)/James Bay Advisory Committee on the Environment: Direction Régionale du Nord-du-Québec, 150, boul René-Lévesque est, 8e étage, Québec QC G1R 4Y1 – 418/528-7354; Fax: 418/646-0266
Président, Diom Roméo Saganash
Executive Secretary, Denis Bernatchez
•Fondation de la faune du Québec/Québec Wildlife Foundation: Place Iberville II, #420, 1175, rue Lavigerie, Sainte-Foy QC G1V 4P1 – 418/644-7926; Fax: 418/643-7655
Président et Directeur général, Bernard Beaudin
•Société québécoise de récupération et de recyclage (RECYC-QUÉBEC)/Québec Re-Use & Recycling Council: #500, 7171 rue Jean-Talon est, Anjou QC H1M 3N2 – 514/352-5002; Fax: 514/873-6542
Québec: #210, 900 Place d'Youville, Qúebec QC G1R 3P7
418/643-0394, Fax: 418/643-6507

## Secrétariat à la FAMILLE/Family Secretariat

#3.300, 875, Grande-Allée est, Québec QC G1R 4Y8
418/643-6414; Fax: 418/528-2009; Email: famille@cex.gouv.qc.ca; URL: http://www.gouv.qc.ca/gouv/francais/minorg/sfamille/const.html
**Ministre responsable**, André Boisclair
Secrétaire général associé, Jean-Louis Bazin, 418/646-7963

## Ministère des FINANCES/Ministry of Finance

12, rue St-Louis, Québec QC G1R 5L3
418/691-2233; Fax: 418/646-5643, 1631; URL: http://www.finances.gouv.qc.ca/

#### ACTS ADMINISTERED

Charter of the Québec Deposit & Investment Fund Deposit Act
Financial Administration Act
Lotteries & Races Act (Part IV)
**Ministre**, Bernard Landry, 418/643-5321, Fax: 418/643-3924
Sous-ministre, Gilles Godbout, 418/643-5738, Fax: 418/646-0923
Sous-ministre adjoint, Financement, Jean Laflamme, 418/691-2243, Fax: 418/643-4700
Sous-ministre adjoint, Politiques économiques, Jean-Guy Turcotte, 418/691-2225, Fax: 418/646-6163
Sous-ministre adjoint, Politiques fiscales et budgétaires, Jean St-Gelais, 418/643-5738, Fax: 418/646-0923
Sous-ministre adjoint, Politiques et institutions financières, Bernard Turgeon, 418/691-2237, Fax: 418/646-6217
Contrôleur des finances, André Fiset, 418/643-6488, Fax: 418/643-0976
Directeur général, Gestion de l'encaisse et de la dette publique, Bob McCollough
Directeur général, Politiques financières et comptables, Jacques Poirer
Directeur, Administration, André Montminy, 418/691-2200
Directeur, Analyse et prévision économique, Abraham Assayag
Directeur, Développement des politiques économiques, M-F. Germain
Directeur, Marchés de capitaux, Michel Gosselin
Directeur adjoint, Marchés de capitaux, Gaston Simoneau
Directrice, Politiques-Institutions Financières, Leandre Nadeau

##### Associated Agencies, Boards & Commissions

•Bureau de la statistique du Québec (BSQ)/Québec Statistics Office: 200, ch Ste-Foy, 5e étage, Québec QC G1R 5T4 – 418/691-2401; Fax: 418/643-4129, Toll Free: 1-800-463-4090

The Statistics office gathers, compiles, analyses & publishes statistical information on any matter under provincial jurisdiction & carries out statistical research. The office complements & coordinates the activities of the various stakeholders in the production of statistics on Québec. In 1985, the legislator broadened the BSQ's mandate to include gathering, compiling & preserving (for statistical and demographic purposes), data on births, marriages, divorces, marriage annulments & deaths in the province.

Directeur général, Luc Bessette
Directeur général, Statistiques et enquêtes, Guy Savard, 418/691-2407
Directeur général, Statistiques et informatique, Denis Baribeau, 418/691-2407
•Caisse de dépôt et placement du Québec: 1981, av McGill College, Montréal QC H3A 3C7 – 514/842-3261; Fax: 514/842-4833
Président et chef de la Direction, Jean-Claude Scraire
Premier vice-président, Planification des investissements, Michel Nadeau
•Commission des valeurs mobilières du Québec/Securities Commission: Tour de la Bourse, 800, Place Victoria, 17e étage, Montréal QC H4Z 1G3 – 514/873-5326; Fax: 514/873-0711
Président, Jean Martel, Q.C.
Secrétaire général, Jacques Labelle
Directrice, Affaires publiques, Louise Lebel-Chevalier
Directeur, Contentieux, Jean-Pierre Dupont
Directeur, Encadrement du marché, Pierre Lizé
•Société des loteries du Québec/Québec Lotteries: #2000, 500, rue Sherbrooke ouest, Montréal QC H3A 3G6 – 514/282-8000; Fax: 514/873-8999
Président, Michel Crète

## Commission de la FONCTION PUBLIQUE du QUÉBEC/Public Service Commission

8, rue Cook, 4e étage, Québec QC G1R 5J8
418/648-3977; Fax: 418/643-7264
**Président**, Jean-Noël Poulin
Secrétaire, Michel Poirier, 418/643-1425
Commissaire, Juliette Barcelo
Commissaire, Jean-Paul Roberge
Commissaire, Gilles R. Tremblay

## HYDRO-QUÉBEC

75, boul René-Lévesque ouest, Montréal QC H2Z 1A4
514/289-2211; Fax: 514/843-3163
Centre d'information & de documentation: 514/289-4919; Fax: 514/289-4932
**Ministre responsable**, Guy Chevrette
Président et Directeur général, André Caillé
Vice-Présidente executive, Distribution et Service à la clientale, Lucie Bertrand
Vice-Président, Planning & Strategic Development, Thierry Vandal
Vice-Président executif, Power Generation, Ghislain Ouellet
Vice-président exécutif, Projets et Affaires Internationales, Michel Clair
Vice-Président, Qualité, Jean-Marie Gonthier
Vice-Président executif, Services energetiques, Michel Gourdeau
Vice-Président executif, Transmission, Jacques Régis

##### Subsidiaries

•Hydro-Québec International: 800, boul de Maisonneuve est, 23e étage, Montréal QC H2L 4L8 – 514/985-4200; Fax: 514/985-3076
Président-directeur général, Michel Clair
•Nouveler: #1400, 1000, rue de la Gauchetière ouest, Montréal QC H3B 4W5 – 514/879-1938; Fax: 514/862-6303
Président-directeur général, Claude Bolduc
•Société d'Énergie de la Baie-James (SEBJ)/James Bay Energy: 500, boul René-Lévesque ouest, 26e étage, Montréal QC H2Z 1Z9 – 514/879-8010; Fax: 514/879-8013
Directeur général, Jean-Guy René

## Ministère de l'INDUSTRIE, du COMMERCE, de la SCIENCE et de la TECHNOLOGIE/Industry, Commerce, Science & Technology

710, Place d'Youville, 9e étage, Québec QC G1R 4Y4
418/691-5950 (Renseignements); Fax: 418/644-0118; URL: http://www.gouv.qc.ca/francais/minorg/micst/micst_intro.html
Montréal: 770, rue Sherbrooke ouest, 10e étage, Montréal QC H3A 1G1
514/982-3000, Fax: 514/873-9913

**ACTS ADMINISTERED**

Act respecting the Ministère de l'Industrie & du Commerce
Act respecting the Société de développement industriel du Québec
Act respecting the Centre de recherche industrielle du Québec
Act respecting the Société des alcools du Québec
Act respecting the establishment of an integrated steel complex by Sidbec
Act respecting the Société du parc industriel du centre du Québec
Act respecting the Société générale de financement du Québec
Act respecting commercial establishment business hours
Act respecting stuffing & upholstered & stuffed articles
Act respecting the Société de développment des coopératives
Act respecting municipal industrial immovables
Act respecting assistance for tourist development
Act respecting beer & soft drink distributors' permits
Cooperatives Act
Cooperatives Syndicates Act
Act respecting Québec business investment companies
**Ministre délégué**, Roger Bertrand
Sous-ministre, Jacques Brind'Amour, 418/691-5656, Fax: 418/646-6497
Secrétaire générale, Christine Ellefsen, 418/691-5656
Directeur général, Administration, Michel Gauthier
Directeur général, Ressources humaines, Michel Gagnon
Directrice, Communications, Josée Turcotte

**COMMERCE EXTÉRIEUR ET INVESTISSEMENTS ÉTRANGERS**

Sous-ministre adjoint, André Dorr
Directeur général, Amériques, François Boullhac
Directeur général (par intérim), Investissements étrangers, Marc St-Onge
Directeur général, Marchés outre-mer, Harold Mailhot
Directrice, Développement des réseaux commerciaux, Lorraine Goyette

**INDUSTRIE ET DÉVELOPPEMENT TECHNOLOGIQUE**

Sous-ministre adjoint & Directeur général (par intérim), Industries des biens d'équipement, André-P. Caron
Directeur général, Chimie, matériaux, santé, mode et textiles, Michel Chevrier
Directeur général, Technologie et promotion de la science, Georges Archambault

**OPÉRATIONS RÉGIONALES, SERVICES AUX ENTREPRISES ET AUX COOPÉRATIVES**

Sous-ministre adjointe, Micheline Fortin
Directeur général, Opérations régionales, Pierre Giard
Directeur général, Services aux entreprises et aux coopératives, François Paradis
Directeur, Activités commerciales, Jacques Ouimet
Directeur (par intérim), Entrepreneurship et gestion d'entreprises, Robert Cossette
Directeur (par intérim), Promotion des exportations, Pierre A. Guénette

**POLITIQUES ET SOCIÉTÉS D'ÉTAT**

Sous-ministre adjoint, Carl Grenier
Directeur général, Analyse économique, Yvon Pomerleau
Directeur général, Politique commerciale, Gérald Audet
Directeur général, Politiques industrielles, scientifiques et technologiques, Marc Jean
Directeur général, Relations avec les sociétés d'état, Gilbert Delage

**Directions régionales/Regional Offices**

Abitibi-Témiscamingue: 180, boul Rideau, Rouyn-Noranda QC J9X 1N9 – 819/762-0865; Fax: 819/762-6496, Directeur, Claude Lecours
Bas-St-Laurent: 92, 2e rue ouest, Rimouski QC G5L 8B3 – 418/727-3577; Fax: 418/727-3640, Directeur, Réjean Dion
Chaudière/Appalaches: 800, Place D'Youville, 4e étage, Québec QC G1R 3P4 – 418/643-8993; Fax: 418/643-4099, Directrice, Jacques Drolet
Côte-Nord et Nord-du-Québec: 625, boul Laflèche, Baie Comeau QC G5C 1C5 – 418/589-5715; Fax: 418/589-4885, Directeur, Pierre Hébert
Estrie: 200, rue Belvédère nord, Sherbrooke QC J1H 4A9 – 819/820-3205; Fax: 819/820-3966, Directrice, Diane Lamothe
Gaspèsie/Îles-de-la-Madeleine: 224, rue Principale, New Carlisle QC G0C 1Z0 – 418/752-2229; Fax: 418/752-2902, Directeur (par intérim), Roger Cyr
Lauentides-Lanaudière: 85, rue De Martigny ouest, Saint-Jérôme QC J7Y 3R8 – 514/569-3031; Fax: 514/569-3039, Directeur, Jacques-A. Gagnon
Mauricie-Bois-Francs: 100, rue Laviolette, Trois-Rivières QC G9A 5S9 – 519/371-6776; Fax: 519/371-6962, Directeur, Roger Leclerc
Montérégie: #101, 201, Place Charles Lemoyne, Longueuil QC – 514/928-7456; Fax: 514/928-7465, Directeur, Jacques Quérillon
Montréal: 770, Sherbrooke ouest, 10e étage, Montréal QC H3A 1G1 – 514/982-3000; Fax: 514/873-9913, Directeur, André Labrie
Outaouais: 170, rue de l'Hôtel-de-Ville, Hull QC J8X 4C2 – 819/772-3131; Fax: 819/772-3981, Directeur, Richard Picard
Saguenay/Lac-Saint-Jean: 3950, boul Harvey, Jonquière QC G7X 8L6 – 418/695-7862; Fax: 418/695-7870, Directeur, Denys Masson

**Associated Agencies, Boards & Commissions**

•Centre de recherche industrielle du Québec (CRIQ)/ Industrial Research Centre: Parc technologique du Québec métro, 333, rue Franquet, CP 9038, Ste-Foy QC G1V 4C7 – 418/659-1550; Fax: 418/652-2251, Ligne sans frais: 1-800-667-2386
Président et Directeur général, Serge Guérin
•Conseil de la science et de la technologie/Science & Technology Council: 2050, boul René-Lévesque, 5e étage, Ste-Foy QC G1V 2K8 – 418/644-1165; Fax: 418/646-0920; Email: Camil.Guy@cst.gouv.qc.ca; URL: http://www.cst.gouv.qc.ca/cst/cst_mandatE.html
Président, Camille Limoges
•Groupe Société générale de financement - Québec (SGF)/General Investment Corp.: #1700, 600, rue de la Gauchetière ouest, Montréal QC H3B 4L8 – 514/876-9290; Fax: 514/395-8055
Président et Chef de la direction, Marc G. Fortier
•Service de placement étudiant/Student Placement Service: 2700, boul Laurier, 3e étage, Sainte-Foy QC G1V 2L8 – 418/643-6965; Fax: 418/643-7901
Directeur (par intérim), Louis Durand
•Parc technologique du Québec Métropolitain: #390, 2750, rue Einstein, CP 8743, Ste-Foy QC G1P 4R1
Directeur général, Pierre Prémont
•Société des alcools du Québec (SAQ)/Québec Liquor Corp.: 905, rue de Lorimier, Montréal QC H2K 3V9 – 514/873-2020; Fax: 514/873-6788
Présidente et Directrice générale, Jocelyn Tremblay
•Société de développement industriel du Québec (SDI)/Québec Industrial Development: Place Sillery, 1126, ch St-Louis, 5e étage, Québec QC G1S 1E5 – 418/643-5172
Président et Directeur général, Louis Roquet
•Société du parc industriel & portuaire de Bécancour (SPIPB)/Bécancour Waterfront Industrial Park: 1000, boul Arthur-Sicard, Bécancour QC G0X 1B0 – 819/294-6656; Fax: 819/294-9020
Président et Directeur général, Pierre Clouâtre
•Société du parc industriel & portuaire Québec-Sud/ South Québec Waterfront Industrial Park: 12, rue St-Louis, Lévis QC G6V 4E2 – 418/833-5925
Président, Deny Grenier

## L'Inspecteur général des INSTITUTIONS FINANCIÈRES/Inspector General of Financial Institutions

800, place D'Youville, Québec QC G1R 4Y5
418/694-5018 (Communications); Fax: 418/643-3336; Email: igif@igif.gouv.qc.ca; URL: http://www.igif.gouv.qc.ca/
Montréal: 800, Tour de la Place-Victoria, Montréal QC H4Z 1H9
514/873-4495, Fax: 514/873-2366

**ACTS ADMINISTERED**

Loi sur les assurances (Insurance)
Loi sur les caisses d'entraide économique (Mutual Aid; Economic Assistance)
Loi concernant certaines caisses d'entraide économique (Economic Assistance)
Loi sur les caisses d'épargne et de crédit (Savings & Loan)
Loi sur les compagnies (Companies) Loi sur les compagnies minières (Mining Companies)
Loi sur les corporations de fonds de sécurité (Security Funds)
Loi sur le courtage immobilier (Real Estate Brokerage)
Loi sur les intermédiaires de marché (Market-place Intermediaries)
Loi sur la liquidation des compagnies (Bankruptcy)
Loi sur les pouvoirs spéciaux des corporations (Special Powers of Corporations)
Loi sur la publicité légale des entreprises individuelles, des sociétés et des personnes morales (Legal Publicity of Sole Proprietorships, Partnerships & Legal Persons) Loi sur les sociétés d'entraide économique (Mutual Aid; Assistance Societies)
Loi sur les sociétés de fiducie et les sociétés d'épargne (Trust & Loan Companies)
Loi sur les sociétés de prêts et de placements (Loans & Investments) Loi remplaçant la Loi concernant la Confédération des caisses populaires et d'économie Desjardins
Loi concernant certains placements des compagnies d'assurance (Investments of Insurance Companies)

**Acts Administered in Part or Jointly with Other Ministries**

Code du travail (Labour Code)
Code municipal du Québec (Municipal Code)
Loi sur l'assurance automobile (Auto Insurance)
Loi sur l'assurance-dépôts (Deposit Insurance)
Loi sur les cercles agricoles
Loi sur les cités et villes (Cities & Towns)
Loi sur les clubs de chasse et de pêche (Hunting & Fishing Clubs)
Loi sur les clubs de récréation, (Recreational Clubs)
Loi sur la communauté régionale de l'Outaouais
Loi sur la communauté urbaine de Montréal
Loi sur la communauté urbaine de Québec
Loi sur les compagnies de cimetière (Cemeteries)
Loi sur les compagnies de flottage
Loi sur les compagnies de gaz, d'eau et d'électricité (Gas, Water & Electric Companies)
Loi sur les compagnies de télégraphe et de téléphone
Loi sur la constitution de certaines églises
Loi sur les coopératives Loi sur les corporations de cimetières catholiques romains (Roman Catholic Cemeteries)
Loi sur les corporations religieuses (Religious Organizations)
Loi sur les évêques catholiques romains (Roman Catholic Bishops)
Loi sur les fabriques (Manufacturing Companies)
Loi constituant le Fonds de solidarité des travailleurs du Québec(F.T.Q.)

Loi sur l'Inspecteur général des institutions financières
Loie modifiant la Loi sur l'Inspecteur général des institutions financières
Loi sur l'instruction publique (Public Education) Loi sur les produits laitiers et leurs succédanés
Loi sur les services de santé et les services sociaux (Health & Social Services)
Loi sur les sociétés agricoles et laitières (Dairy & Agriculture)
Loi sur les sociétés d'agriculture (Agriculture)
Loi sur les sociétés d'horticulture (Horticulture)
Loi sur les sociétés de fabrication de beurre et de fromage (Butter & Cheese)
Loi sur les sociétés nationales de bienfaisance (Charities)
Loi sur les sociétés préventives de cruauté envers les animaux (Associations for prevention of cruelty to animals)
Loi sur les syndicats coopératifs (Cooperatives)
Loi sur les syndicats d'élevage (Breeding)
Loi sur les syndicats professionels (Professional Trade Unions)
**Ministre responsable**, Bernard Landry, 416/643-5270, Fax: 416/643-6626
Inspecteur général, Institutions financières, Jacques Dumont, 418/694-5015
Inspecteur général adjoint, Richard Boivin, 418/694-5011, Fax: 418/528-0835
Surintendant, Intermédiaires de marché et courtage immobilier, Alain Samson, 418/694-5020

#### Associated Agencies, Boards & Commissions

•Régie de l'assurance-dépôts du Québec: 800, place D'Youville, Québec QC G1R 4Y5 – 418/694-5014; Fax: 418/643-3336
Président-directeur général, Jacques Dumont

## Ministère de la JUSTICE/Justice

1200, rte de l'Église, Ste-Foy QC G1V 4M1
418/643-5140 (Communications); Fax: 418/646-4449; URL: http://www.gouv.qc.ca/francais/minorg/mjust/mjust_intro.html

#### ACTS ADMINISTERED

An Act respecting Adoptions of children domiciled in the People's Republic of China
An Act respecting Assistance for victims of crime
An Act respecting Attorney General's prosecutors
An Act respecting Municipal courts
An Act respecting Public inquiry commissions
An Act respecting Reciprocal enforcement of Maintenance Orders
An Act respecting Registry offices
An Act respecting the Barreau du Québec (in part)
An Act respecting the Civil aspects of international & interprovincial child abduction
An Act respecting the Class action
An Act respecting the Collection of certain debts
An Act respecting the Consolidation of the statutes & regulations
An Act respecting the Constitution Act
An Act respecting the Floral emblem
An Act respecting the Implementation of the reform of the Civil Code
An Act respecting the Industrial accidents & occupational diseases (in part)
An Act respecting the Judgements rendered in the Supreme Court of Canada on the language of statutes & other instruments of a legislative nature
An Act respecting the Ministère de la Justice
An Act respecting the Official flag
An Act respecting the Payment of certain Crown witnesses
An Act respecting the Payment of certain fines
An Act respecting the Practice of midwifery within the framework of pilot projects
An Act respecting the Public curator
An Act to promote the Reform of the cadastre in Québec (in part)
An Act respecting the Salaries of officers of Justice
An Act respecting the Société québécoise d'information juridique
An Act respecting the United Nations Convention on Contracts for the International Sale of Goods
An Act to secure the carrying out of the Entente between France & Québec respecting mutual aid in in judicial matters
Charter of Human Rights & Freedoms
Chartered Accountants Act
Chiropractic Act
Civil Code of Québec
Code of Civil Procedure
Code of Penal Procedure
Court of Appeal Reference Act
Courts of Justice Act
Crime Victims Compensation Act
Crown Payments Prescription Act
Dental Act
Denturologists Act
Disorderly Houses Act
Dispensing Opticians Act
Engineers Act
Expropriation Act (in part)
Forest Engineers Act
Freedom of Worship Act
Hearing-aid Accousticians Act
Highway Safety Code (in part)
Interpretation Act
Jurors Act
Labour Code (in part)
Land Surveyors Act
Legal Aid Act
Magistrate's Privileges Act
Medical Act
Newspaper Declaration Act
Notarial Act
Nurses Act
Official Time Act
Optometry Act
Pharmacy Act
Podiatry Act
Press Act
Professional Chemists Act
Professional Code
Public Officers Act
Radiology Technicians Act
Regulations Act (in part)
Sheriffs' Act
Special Procedure Act
Stenographers' Act
Territorial Division Act (in part)
Veterinary Surgeons Act
Youth Protection Act (in part)
**Ministre**, Serge Ménard
Sous-ministre & Sous-procureur général, Michel Bouchard, 418/643-4090, Fax: 418/643-3877
Sous-ministre associé, Services de gestion, Rodrigue Desmeules, 418/643-4314, Fax: 418/646-3899
**For list of Courts & other Legal Officers, including Judicial Officials & Judges *see* Section 10 of this book.**

#### Direction de l'Etat Civil/Civil Status Records Office

418/643-3900; Fax: 418/646-3255
Montreal Fax: 514/864-4563
Fax: 514/864-4563
This office is responsible for issuing birth, death & marriage certificates in the province of Québec. Fee for each certificate is $15.00 & is available within ten days. Emergency orders are available for a fee of $35.00.

#### DIRECTION GÉNÉRALE DES AFFAIRES CRIMINELLES ET PÉNALES/Criminal & Penal Affairs

Sous-ministre associé, Mario Bilodeau, 418/643-4085
Directeur, Direction des affaires criminelles, Paul Monty
Directeur, Direction du droit de la jeunesse, Jean Turmel

#### DIRECTION GÉNÉRALE DES AFFAIRES JURIDIQUES ET LÉGISLATIVES/Judicial & Legislative Affairs

Sous-ministre associé, Jean K. Samson, 418/643-4228
Directeur général adjoint, Direction des affaires juridiques, Jean-Paul Dupré
Directeur, Direction des affaires contentieuses, Jean-Yves Bernard
Directrice, Direction des affaires législatives, Marie José Longtin
Directeur, Direction du droit administratif et privé, Serge Lafontaine
Directrice, Direction du droit autochtone et constitutionnel, Dominique Langis

#### DIRECTION GÉNÉALE DES SERVICES DE JUSTICE/Justice Services

Sous-ministre associé, Gaétan Lemoyne, 418/643-7595
Directrice, Bureau d'aide aux victimes d'actes criminels, Christine Viens
Directeur, Direction des services administratifs, Jean Gauvin
Directeur (par intérim), Mission de la publicité des droits, Gilles Harvey
Directeur (par intérim), Mission des services judiciaires, Simon Marcotte
Directrice, Registre des droits personnels et réels mobiliers, Suzanne Potvin-Plamondon

#### Associated Agencies, Boards & Commissions

•Chambre de la jeunesse: 410, rue Bellechasse est, Montréal QC H2S 1X3 – 514/495-5817; Fax: 514/873-8938
Juge en chef adjoint, Michel Jasmin
•Commission d'appel en matière de lésions professionelles: #700, 900, Place d'Youville, Québec QC G1R 3P7 – 418/644-8205
Président, Freddy Henderson
•Commission des affaires sociales/Social Affairs Commission: Edifice 55 Q, 2525, boul Laurier, 2e étage, Ste-Foy QC – 418/643-3400; Fax: 418/643-5335
Présidente, Lise Morency
•Commission des services juridiques/Legal Services Commission: Tour de l'Est, #1404, 2, Complexe Desjardins, Montréal QC H5B 1B3 – 514/873-3562; Fax: 514/873-8762
Président, Pierre Lorrain
Secrétaire, Jacques Lemaître-Auger
•Conseil de la Magistrature: #RG 08, 300, boul Jean-Lesage, Québec QC G1K 8K6 – 418/649-3577
Présidente, Hugette St-Louis
Secrétaire, Bernard Tellier
•Fonds d'Aide aux Recours Collectifs: #1201, 360, rue St-Jacques ouest, Montréal QC H2Y 1P5 – 514/864-2750; Fax: 514/864-2998
Président, Jean Bernier
•Société québécoise d'information juridique: 715, Square Victoria, 8e étage, Montréal QC H2Y 2H7 – 514/842-8741; Fax: 514/844-8984
Président, Jean-Paul Gagné

## Ministère de la MÉTROPOLE/Ministry of Metropolitan Affairs

Édifice H, #2.600, 875, Grande Allée Est, Québec QC G1R 4Y8
418/646-3018; Fax: 418/643-6377; URL: http://www.metropole.gouv.qc.ca
**Ministre**, Robert Perreault
Sous-ministre, Jacques-Yves Therrien
Sous-ministre adjointe, Affaires publiques, Laurette Laurin, #2.50, 800, Tour Place Victoria, CP 83, Montréal QC H4Z 1B7, 514/873-6710, Fax: 514/864-4080

## Office des PROFESSIONS du QUÉBEC/ Occupations Board

Complexe de la Place Jacques-Cartier, 320, rue St-Joseph est, 1er étage, Québec QC G1K 8G5

418/643-6912; Fax: 418/643-0973

**Président**, Robert Diamant

Directrice, Recherche, Sylvie de Grandmont

Directeur, Secrétariat général et communications, Michel Sparer

## PROTECTEUR du CITOYEN/Ombudsman

2875, boul Laurier, 4e étage, Ste-Foy QC G1V 2M2

418/643-2688; Fax: 418/643-8759; URL: http://www.ombuds.gouv.qc.ca

Email Correspondence: Protecteur.citoyen@ombuds.gouv.qc.ca

#11.40, 1 Notre-Dame est, Montréal QC H2Y 1B6

514/873-2032, Fax: 514/873-4640

**Protecteur du citoyen**, Daniel Jacoby

## Secrétariat à la RÉFORME ÉLECTORALE et PARLEMENTAIRE/Electoral & Parliamentary Reform

875, Grande Allée est, Québec QC G1R 4Y8

418/643-2483; Fax: 418/643-5612

**Ministre délégué**, Pierre Bélanger, 418/643-3804, Fax: 418/643-2514

Secrétaire, Michel Mercier

## Ministère des RELATIONS INTERNATIONALES/International Relations

Édifice Hector-Fabre, 525, boul Réne-Levesque est, Québec QC G1R 5R9

418/649-2300; Fax: 418/649-2656; Email: communications@mri.gouv.qc.ca; URL: http://www.mri.gouv.qc.ca

Montréal: 380, rue St-Antoine ouest, Montréal QC H2Y 3X7

514/499-2171, Fax: 514/873-7468

**Ministre**, Sylvain Simard

Sous-ministre, Michelle Bussières, 418/649-2335, Fax: 418/643-4047

Sous-ministre adjoint, Affaires bilatérales et multilatérales, Denis Gervais, 418/649-2335, Fax: 418/643-4047

Sous-ministre adjointe, Politiques et services à la gestion, Vacant, 418/649-2335, Fax: 418/643-4047

Sous-ministre adjointe & Chef du protocole, Lucie Latulippe, 418/649-2346, Fax: 418/649-2657

### DIRECTIONS BILATÉRALES; INSTITUTIONS FRANCOPHONES ET MULTILATÉRALES/Bilateral Divisions & Branches; Francophone & Multilateral Institutions

Directeur, Afrique et Moyen-Orient, Jean Clavet, 418/649-2318, Fax: 418/649-2406

Directeur, Amérique latine et Antilles, Lucien Vallières, 418/649-2315, Fax: 418/649-2659

Directeur général, Asie-Pacifique, Vacant, 418/649-2342, Fax: 418/649-2427

Directrice générale, États-Unis, Raymonde Saint-Germain, 418/649-2312, Fax: 418/649-2418

Directeur général, Europe, Jean-Marc Blondeau, 418/649-2306, Fax: 418/649-2421

Directeur général, France, Vacant, 418/649-2329, Fax: 418/649-2654

Directeur général, Institutions francophones et multilatérales, Paul-André Boisclair, 418/649-2341, Fax: 418/649-2664

## Ministère des RESSOURCES NATURELLES/ Natural Resources

#B-302, 5700 - 4 av ouest, 3e étage, Charlesbourg QC G1H 6R1

418/627-8600 (Renseignements); Fax: 418/644-7160; Email: drp@mrn.gouv.qc.ca; URL: http://www.mrn.gouv.qc.ca

Ligne sans frais: 1-800-463-4558

### ACTS ADMINISTERED

Loi sur l'Administration régionale Crie
Loi sur les arpentages
Loi sur le cadastre
Loi sur les compagnies de flottage
Loi approuvant la Convention de la Baie James et Nord Québécois
Loi approuvant la Convention du Nord-Est Québécois
Loi favorisant le crédit forestier par les institutions privées
Loi sur le crédit forestier
Loi sur le développement de la région de la Baie James
Loi concernant les droits sur les mines
Loi sur l'efficicacité énérgétique d'appareils fonctionnant à l'éléciticité ou hydrocarbures
Loi sur l'exportation de l'énergie électrique
Loi sur les forêts
Loi sur Hydro-Québec
Loi sur l'utilisation des produits petroliers
Loi sur les mesureurs de bois
Loi sur les mines
Loi sur le Ministère des Ressources Naturelles
Loi sur le mode de paiement des services d'électricité et de gaz dans certains immeubles
Loi favorisant la réforme du cadastre Québécois
Loi sur la Régie de l'énergie
Loi sur la régie du gaz naturel
L'article 3 de la section VIII de la loi sur le régime des eaux
Loi concernant le régime des terres dans les territoires de la Baie James et du Nouveau-Québec
Loi sur la Société de Développement Autochtone de la Baie James
Loi sur la Société Eeyou de la Baie James
Loi sur la Société Nationale de l'Amiante
Loi sur la Société Québécoise d'Exploration Minière
Loi sur la Société Québécoise d'Initiatives Pétrolières
Loi sur la Société de Récupération, d'exploitation et de développement Forestiers du Québec
Loi sur les systèmes municipaux et les systèmes privés d'électricité
Loi sur les terres du domaine public
Loi sur les titres de propriété dans certains districts électoraux

**Ministre d'État**, Guy Chevrette, 418/643-7295, Fax: 418/643-4318

**Ministre déléguée, Mines, Terres et Forêts**, Denise Carrier-Perreault, 418/643-7295, Fax: 418/643-4872

Sous-ministre, Jean-Paul Beaulieu, 418/627-6370 poste 3570, Fax: 418/643-1443

Secrétariat du Ministère, Cécile St-Pierre, 418/627-6370 poste 3561, Fax: 418/643-1443

Directeur (par intérim), Relations publiques, Raymond Moisan, 418/627-8609 poste 3001

Directeur générale (par intérim), Services à la gestion, Louis-Gilles Picard, 418/627-6270 poste 3661

### ÉNERGIE/Energy

Fax: 418/643-0701

Sous-ministre associé, Jacques Lebuis, 418/627-6377 poste 8000

Directeur, Droits hydrauliques et tarifs, René Paquette, 418/627-6386 poste 8351

Directeur, Efficacité énergétique, Gaby Polisois, 418/627-6379 poste 8021

Directeur, Électricité, Florent Côté, 418/627-6389 poste 8301

Directeur, Gaz et pétrole, Alain Lefebvre, 418/627-6390 poste 8251

Directeur, Politiques, Études et Recherche, Claude Desjarlais, 418/627-6380 poste 8111

Directeur, Produits pétroliers, Pierre Lavallée, 418/627-6385 poste 8171

### FORÊTS/Forests

880, ch Ste-Foy, Québec QC G1S 4X4

Sous-ministre associé, Jacques Robitaille, 418/643-3987, Fax: 418/646-4335

Directeur, Conservation des forêts, Jean-Claude Delarosbil, 418/643-7735, Fax: 418/643-2368

Directeur, Développement de l'Industrie des Produits Forestiers, Jean-P. Gilbert, 418/644-4364, Fax: 418/643-9534

Directeur, Environnement Forestier, Gilles Gaboury, 418/643-8587, Fax: 418/643-5651

Directeur, Gestion des stocks forestiers, Jean Brunet, 418/646-3381

Directeur, Programmes forestiers, Marc Ledoux, 418/646-8945, Fax: 418/646-9245

Directeur, Recherche forestière, Jacques St-Cyr, 418/643-7994, Fax: 418/643-2165

### MINES

Sous-minstre associé, Duc Vu, 418/627-6273 poste 5000, Fax: 418/644-7617

Directeur, Centre de recherche minérale, Bruno Duchesne, 418/643-4540, Fax: 418/643-6706

Directeur, Géologie, Jean-L. Caty, 418/627-6274 poste 5021, Fax: 418/643-2816

Directeur, Industrie minérale, Gilles Mahoney, 418/627-6294 poste 5511, Fax: 418/643-3803

Directeur, Redevances et titres miniers, Raymond Boutin, 418/627-6372 poste 5455, Fax: 418/643-9297, Toll Free: 1-800-363-7233

### SERVICES RÉGIONAUX/Regional services

880, ch Ste-Foy, Québec QC G1S 4X4

Sous-ministre associé, Maurice Boisvert, 418/643-3987, Fax: 418/528-1278

Directeur, Assistance technique, Guy Boulianne, 418/643-3987

Directeur, Production des semences et des plants, Guy Boulianne, 418/644-4484

### TERRES/Lands

Sous-ministre associé, Rémy Girard, 418/627-6353 poste 2361, Fax: 418/644-7617

Directrice, Politiques territoriales, coordination et diffusion, Francine Beaulieu, 418/627-6353 poste 2362

Directeur, Relevés techniques, Réal St-Laurent, 418/627-6285 poste 2161

Directrice générale, Cadastre, Jocelyne Lefort, 418/644-6224

Directeur général, Opérations régionales, Jean-Yves Dupéré, 418/627-6367 poste 2801, Fax: 418/528-2075

### Associated Agencies, Boards & Commissions

•Bureau des examinateurs des mesureurs de bois: 880 ch Ste-Foy, 9e étage, Ste-Foy QC G1S 4X4 – 418/656-5828; Fax: 418/646-9267

•Hydro Québec

Listed alphabetically in detail, this Section.

•Régie du gaz naturel/Natural Gas: Tour de la Bourse, #255, 800, Place Victoria, CP 001, Montréal QC H4Z 1A2 – 514/873-2452; Fax: 514/873-2070

Président, Jean Giroux

•Société de développement de la Baie-James (SDBJ)/James Bay Development: #110, boul Matagami, CP 970, Matagami QC J0Y 2A0 – 819/739-4717; Fax: 819/739-4329

Président du conseil, J. Yvon Goyette

Président, Donald Murphy

•Société nationale de l'Amiante (SNA)/Asbestos: 615, Monfette nord, Thetford Mines QC G6G 7H4 – 418/338-0131; Fax: 418/338-3856

Président, Benoît Cartier

•Société québécoise d'exploration minière (SOQUEM)/Québec Mineral Exploration: Place Belle Cour, #2500, 2600, boul Laurier, Ste-Foy QC G1V 4M6 – 418/658-5400; Fax: 418/658-5459
Président et Directeur général, Yves Harvey
•Société québécoise d'initiatives pétrolières (SOQUIP)/Québec Oil & Gas Exploration: #180, 1175, ave de Lavigerie, Ste-Foy QC G1V 4P1 – 418/651-9543; Fax: 418/651-2292
Président et chef, Yves Rhéault
•Société de récupération, d'exploitation et de développement forestier (REXFOR)/Québec Forestry Development: 1195, ave de Lavigerie, Ste-Foy QC G1V 4N3 – 418/659-4530; Fax: 418/643-4037
Président, André L'Ecuyer

## Ministère du REVENU/Revenue

3800, rue De Marly, Ste-Foy QC G1X 4A5
Montréal: 3, Complexe Desjardins, CP 3000, Succ Desjardins, Montréal QC H5B 1A4
TVQ/TPS: 514/873-4692; 1-800-567-4692
Retenues à la source: 514/873-6995; 418/659-7313; 1-800-567-4692
Impôt des corporations: 514/864-4155; 1-800-450-4155
Impôt des particuliers: 514/864-6299; 1-800-267-6299

#### ACTS ADMINISTERED

Act respecting fiscal incentives to industrial development (in part)
Act respecting income security (in part)
Act respecting labour standards (in part)
Act respecting municipal taxation (in part)
Act respecting real estate tax refund
Act respecting the application of the Taxation Act
Act respecting the Ministère du Revenu
Act respecting the Payment of a Allowances to certain self-employed workers
Act respecting the Québec Pension Plan (in part)
Act respecting the Québec Sales Tax
Act respecting the Régie de l'assurance-maladie du Québec (in part)
Act to facilitate the payment of support
Act to foster the development of man power training
Act to promote industrial development by means of fiscal advantages
Fuel Tax Act
Land Transfer Duties Act
Licenses Act
Meals & Hotels Tax Act (abrogated)
Taxation Act
Telecommunications Tax Act
Tobacco Tax Act
**Ministre**, Rita Dionne-Marsolais
**Ministre d'État, Économie et Finances**, Bernard Landry, 418/643-5270, Fax: 418/643-6266
Sous-ministre, Nicole Malo, F.C.A., 418/652-6833, Fax: 418/643-4962, 514/287-8288; Fax: 514/873-7502

#### BUREAU DU SOUS-MINISTRE/Deputy Minister

Directeur général, Rénald Dion, 418/652-6868
Directrice, Secrétariat du Ministère, Micheline S. Gravel, 418/652-6834
Directeur, Bureau des plaintes, Gaétan Hallé, 418/652-6159
Directeur, Coordination ministérielle, Bruno Boudreault, 418/652-6864
Directeur, Sécurité et Enquètes, Claude Gauthier, 418/652-6808
Directeur, Services administratifs, techniques et liaison, Pierre Sarto Blanchard, 418/652-5576

#### CENTRE DE PERCEPTION FISCALE/Tax Collection

3800 rue De Marly, Secteur 6-4-9, Ste-Foy QC G1X 4A5
Responsible for collecting income tax & consumption taxes that are payable under the provincial laws the ministry administers. Implements, for other provincial government departments & agencies, specific social & economic-related programs developed to balance public funds. Relies on the cooperation of agents (to collect & remit consumption taxes) & taxpayers.
Directeur général, Gabriel Cayer, 418/577-0011, Fax: 418/646-8269
Directeur général adjoint, Montréal, Alain Lambert, 514/287-4431, Fax: 514/873-7346
Directeur général adjoint, Montréal, Pierre Leclerc, 514/287-6875, Fax: 514/864-3265
Directeur général adjoint (par intérim), Québec, Claude Rivard, 418/684-2801, Fax: 418/646-0986

#### DIRECTION GÉNÉRALE DE L'ADMINISTRATION/ Administration

Sous-ministre adjoint et directeur général, Onil Roy, 418/652-6884, Fax: 418/643-8482
Directeur, Administration - Montréal, Gilbert Chapleau, 514/287-6841
Directrice, Communications, Michèle Lasanté, 418/652-4935
Directeur, Études et contróle des revenus, Michel Bordeleau, 418/652-5100
Directeur, Ressources humaines, Yves Cantin, 418/652-6820
Directeur, Ressources matérielles, Pierre Veilleux, 418/652-6801

#### DIRECTION GÉNÉRALE DES CONTRIBUABLES/Taxpayers

Directeur général (par intérim), Michel Vaillancourt, 418/652-6872, Fax: 418/646-8499
Directeur général adjoint, Montréal, Réjean Beaulieu, 514/287-8051
Directeur général adjoint, Québec, Michel Vaillancourt, 418/652-6629
Directeur, Perception automatique des pensions alimentaires, Claude Aubin, 418/643-7040, Fax: 418/646-8270

#### DIRECTION GÉNÉRALE DE LA LÉGISLATION/Legislation

Sous-ministre adjoint et directeur général, André Brochu, 418/652-6844, Fax: 418/643-9381
Directeur, Affaires juridiques, Jacques Pinsonnault, 418/652-6843
Directeur, Contentieux, Paul Veillette, 514/287-8213, Fax: 514/873-8992
Directeur, Lois sur les impôts, François T. Tremblay, 418/652-6836
Directeur, Lois sur les taxes, Serge Bouchard, 418/652-6837
Directeur, Oppositions - Montréal, Luc R. Gervais, 514/287-8322
Directeur, Oppositions - Québec, Hubert Gaudry, 418/652-6268
Responsable, Service du Contentieux - Montréal, Michel Desrosiers, 514/287-8215
Responsable, Service de Contentieux - Québec, Claude Deamarais, 418/652-6842

#### DIRECTION GÉNÉRALE DES MANDATAIRES

Sous-ministre adjoint et Directeur général, Denis Rheault, 418/652-6876, Fax: 418/646-9965
Directeur général adjoint, Montréal, Roger Pelletier, 514/864-9722
Directeur général adjoint, Québec, Michel Charbonneau, 418/652-4896
Groupe responsable des relations avec Revenu Canada, Pierre Boisvert, 418/652-2795
Groupe responsable des relations avec Revenu Canada, Rodrigue Lachance, 418/652-2794

#### DIRECTION GÉNÉRALE DES TECHNOLOGIES DE L'INFORMATION/Information Technology

Directeur général, André Gariepy, 418/652-5117, Fax: 418/646-0987
Directeur, Infrastructure systémique, Ghislain Guérin, 418/652-6958
Directeur, Systèmes des entreprises, Jean-Guy Parent, 418/652-5738
Directeur, Systèmes des particuliers, Pierre Bouchard, 418/652-5985

#### DIRECTION GÉNÉRALE DU TRAITEMENT ET DES TECHNOLOGIES

Sous-ministre adjoint, Pierre Boisvert, 418/652-4959, Fax: 418/646-4944
Directrice générale adjointe, Montréal, Renée Méthot, 514/287-3079
Directeur général adjoint, Québec, Guy Morel, 418/652-4726
Directeur, Traitement informatique, Yves Saint-Jacques, 418/652-4901

#### DIRECTION GÉNÉRALE DE LA VÉRIFICATION ET DES ENQUÊTES

Sous-ministre adjoint et directeur général, Bertrand Croteau, 418/652-6870, Fax: 418/646-0985
Directeur général adjoint, Enquêtes, Alain Dufour, 418/652-5903, Fax: 418/528-2049
Directeur général adjoint, Laval, Assaad Rizk, 705, ch du Trait-Carré, Laval QC H7N 1B3, 514/975-3301, Fax: 514/669-4707
Directeur général adjoint, Montréal, Michel Lussier, 514/287-8400, Fax: 514/864-1961
Directeur général adjoint, Québec, André Gingras, 418/652-6811

## Ministère de la SANTÉ ET des SERVICES SOCIAUX/Health & Social Services

1075, ch Ste-Foy, Québec QC G1S 2M1
URL: http://www.msss.gouv.qc.ca
Renseignements généraux, 1088, rue Raymond-Casgrain, Québec QC G1S 2E4
418/643-3380, Fax: 418/643-3177

#### ACTS ADMINISTERED

Act respecting the Conseil médical du Québec
Act respecting the Ministère de la Santé et des services sociaux
Act respecting the Ministère des Affaires sociales
Act respecting Health Services & Social Services
Health Insurance Act
Act respecting the Régie de l'assurance maladie du Québec
Hospital Insurance Act
Public Health Act
Act respecting health services for Cree & Inuit native persons
Act respecting the practice of midwifery within the framework of pilot projects
Youth Protection Act
Mental Patients Protection Act
Public Health Protection Act
Act to secure the handicapped in the exercise of their rights
Act respecting the Commission des affaires sociales
Non-Catholic Cemeteries Act
Act respecting the Conseil de la santé et du bien-être
Act respecting the Conseil des ainés
**Ministre**, Jean Rochon, 418/643-3160, Fax: 418/644-4534
Sous-ministre, Pierre-André Paré, 418/643-6462, Fax: 418/643-9217
Sous-ministre adjointe, Administration et des immobilisations, Cécile Cléroux, 418/643-3224, Fax: 418/643-0596
Sous-ministre adjointe, Planification et à l'évaluation, Sylvie Dillard, 418/644-7304, Fax: 418/646-1956
Sous-ministre adjoint, Relations professionnelles, Hubert Gauthier, 418/643-7463, Fax: 418/643-7472
Sous-ministre adjointe, Santé publique, Christine Colin, 418/646-3487, Fax: 418/528-2651
Directeur, Protection de la santé publique et du centre québécois de coordination sur le sida, Maurice

Poulin, 418/643-6390, Fax: 418/528-2651, Email: maurice.poulin@msss.gouv.qc.ca

#### Associated Agencies, Councils & Commissions

•Bureau des personnes handicapées du Québec/Office for Handicapped Persons: 309, rue Brock, CP 820, Drummondville QC J2B 6X1 – 819/477-7100; Fax: 819/477-8493

Président et Directeur général, Gaston J. Perreault

•Comité de la santé mentale du Québec: 1075, ch Ste-Foy, Québec QC G1S 2M1 – 418/643-9210; Fax: 418/646-1956

Président, Robert Paquet

•Commissaire aux plaintes: 5199, rue Sherbrooke est, Québec QC H1T 3X3 – 418/873-3205; Fax: 418/873-5665

Commissaire, Jean Francoeur

•Commission d'appel pour les Autochtones du Québec/Native Appeals: 2, av du Palais, Rouyn QC J9X 2N9 – 819/762-2838

Président, Jean-Charles Coutu

•Commission québécoise d'examen (troubles mentaux): 785, av De Salaberry, Québec QC G1R 2T8 – 418/643-2613; Fax: 418/644-7180

Président, Roch Rioux

•Conseil Consultatif de Pharmacologie/Advisory Council on Pharmacology: 1125, ch St-Louis, 8e étage, Sillery QC G1S 1E7 – 418/643-3140; Fax: 418/646-8349

Président, Dr. Jacques Le Lorier

•Conseil Consultatif sur les aides technologiques: 845, av Joffre, Québec QC G1S 4N4 – 418/643-1213; Fax: 418/646-2134

Président, J.-Auguste Mockle

•Conseil de la santé et du bien-être/Health & Welfare Council: 1126, ch St-Louis, Sillery QC G1S 1E5 – 418/643-3040; Fax: 418/644-0654

Président, Norbert Rodrigue

•Conseil d'évaluation des technologies de la Santé/Health Technology Council: #4205, 800, Place Victoria, CP 215, Montréal QC H4Z 1E3 – 514/873-2563; Fax: 514/873-1369

Président, Renaldo N. Batiste

•Conseil des aînés/Seniors: 1005, ch Ste-Foy, Québec QC G1S 4N4 – 418/643-6720; Fax: 418/646-9895

Présidente, Nicole Dumont-Larouche

•Conseil médical du québec: 1005, ch Ste-Foy, Québec QC G1S 4N4 – 418/646-4379; Fax: 418/646-9895

Président, Juan Roberto Iglesias

•Conseil québécois de la recherche sociale/Québec Social Research Council: 1088, rue Raymond-Casgrain, 1er étage, Québec QC G1S 2E4 – 418/643-7582; Fax: 418/643-4768

Président, Marc Renaud

•Corporation d'Hébergement du Québec/Québec Social Care Facilities: 2050, boul René-Lévesque Ouest, Ste-Foy QC G1V 2K8 – 418/643-6112; Fax: 418/644-0563

Président et Directeur général, Conrad Dubuc

•Fonds de la Recherche en Santé du Québec/Québec Health Research Fund: #1950, 550, rue Sherbrooke ouest, Montréal QC H3A 1B9 – 514/873-2114; Fax: 514/873-8768

Président, Fernand Labrie

•Régie de l'Assurance-maladie du Québec/Québec Health Insurance Board: 1125, ch St-Louis, Québec QC G1K 7T3 – 418/682-5111

Président et Directeur général par intérim, Denis Morency, 418/682-5162

Adjoint au président et directeur général, Pierre Boucher, 418/682-5162

•Service Ambulancier du Québec/Québec Ambulance Service: 1005, ch Ste-Foy, 5e étage, Québec QC G1S 4N4 – 418/643-3700

Directeur intérim, Martin Soucy

## Ministère de la SÉCURITÉ PUBLIQUE/ Public Security

Tour des Laurentides, 2525, boul Laurier, 5e étage, Ste-Foy QC G1V 2L2

418/643-3500; Fax: 418/643-0275; Email: Infocom@secpub.gouv.qc.ca; URL: http://www.secpub.gouv.qc.ca/

Montréal Office: 3, Complexe Desjardins, Tour nord, 26e étage, Montréal QC H5B 1E9

514/873-2112, Fax: 514/873-6597

#### ACTS ADMINISTERED

Bicycle ownership Act

An Act respecting the Communauté urbaine de Montréal

An Act respecting correctional services

An Act respecting detectives or security agencies

An Act respecting the determination of the causes & circumstances of death

An Act respecting explosives

Fire Investigations Act

Fire Prevention Act

Highway Safety Code (partially administred by the MSP)

An Act respecting liquor permits

An Act respecting lotteries, publicity, contests & amusement machines

An Act respecting the Ministère de la Sécurité publique

An Act respecting Northern Villages & the Kativik regional Government (partially administered by the MSP)

An Act respecting offences relating to Alcoholic Beverages

An Act respecting police organization

Police Act

An Act to promote the parole of inmates

An Act respecting the protection of persons & property in the event of disaster

An Act respecting racing

An Act respecting the Régie des alcools, des courses et des jeux

Safe-Deposit Boxes Act

An Act respecting the Société des alcools du Québec (partially administered by MSP)

An Act respecting the Société des loteries du Québec (partially administered by the MSP)

An Act respecting the Syndical Plan of the Sûreté du Québec

An Act respecting tear bombs

Temperance Act

**Ministre**, Pierre Bélanger

Sous-ministre, Florent Gagné

### ADMINISTRATION

Sous-ministre associé, Jean-Louis Lapointe, 418/643-8498, Fax: 418/528-1713

Directrice, Informatique et systèmes, Ann Chamberland, 418/644-0795, Fax: 418/644-4593

Directeur, Organisation et ressources humaines, Jean Demers, 418/528-1431, Fax: 418/528-6878

Directrice, Ressources matérielles et financières, Micheline Blache, 418/528-2897, Fax: 418/528-1713

### DIRECTION GÉNÉRALE DE LA SÉCURITÉ ET DE LA PRÉVENTION/Security & Prevention

2525, boul Laurier, 6e étage, Ste-Foy QC G1V 2L2

418/646-8523; Fax: 418/646-5427

Sous-ministre associé, Charles Côté

Directeur, Direction des affaires policières et de la sécurité incendie, Daniel St-Onge, 418/644-9774, Fax: 418/646-3564

Directrice (par intérim), Direction de la sécurité civile et des régions, Louise Jacob, 418/646-7950, Fax: 418/528-5503

Directeur, Laboratoire de sciences judiciaires et de médécine légale/Forensic Science, Yves Ste-Marie, 1701, rue Parthenais, 5e étage, PO Box 1500, Stn Succ. C, Montréal QC H2L 4K6, 514/873-2704, Fax: 514/873-4847

Directeur, Services de sécurité et de protection, François Côté, 418/643-9353, Fax: 418/646-9265

Responsable, Service général d'inspection, Marc Lizotte, 418/643-3575; 514/864-1900, Fax: 418/644-0132; 514/873-2656

### SERVICES CORRECTIONNELS/Correctional Services

Sous-ministre associé, Louise Pagé, 418/643-3612, Fax: 418/644-7159

Directeur (par intérim), Centre d'expertise et de coordination en sécurité, Gilles Soucy, 418/643-5141, Fax: 418/644-5645

Directeur, Partenariat et conseil en services correctionnels, Michel Roberge, 418/644-7887, Fax: 418/644-5645

Directeur, Services administratifs, Gilles Soucy, 418/644-3821, Fax: 418/643-3426

#### Associated Agencies, Boards & Commissions

•Bureau du coroner/Office of the Coroner: 1200, route de l'Église, 5e étage, Ste Foy QC G1V 4Z7 – 418/643-1845; Fax: 418/643-6174

Coroner en chef, Pierre Morin

Coroner en chef adjoint, Dr. Serge Turmel

•Comité de déontologie policière/Police Ethics Committee: Edifice SSQ, Tour du Saint-Laurent, #A-200, 2525, boul Laurier, 2e étage, Ste-Foy QC G1V 4Z6 – 418/646-1936; Fax: 418/528-0987

Président, Me Claude Brazeau

•Commissaire à la déontologie policière: 1200, Route de l'Église, R-C 20, Sainte-Foy QC G1V 4Y9 – 418/643-7897; Fax: 418/528-9473

Commissaire, Me Denis Racicot

•Commissariat aux incendies/Fire Commissioner: 455, rue Dupont, Québec QC G1K 6N2 – 418/529-5706; Fax: 418/529-9922

Commissaire, Cyrille Delâge

•Commission québécoise des libérations conditionnelles/Parole Board: #200, 2055, rue Peel, Montréal QC H3A 1V4 – 514/873-2230; Fax: 514/873-7580

Présidente, Isabelle Demers

Montréal: #200, 2055, rue Peel, Montréal QC H3A 1V4

514/873-2230, Fax: 514/873-7580

•Institut de police du Québec: 350, rue Marguerite d'Youville, Nicolet QC J3T 1X4 – 819/293-8631; Fax: 819/293-4018

Directrice, Louise Gagnon-Gaudreault

•Régie des alcools, des courses et des jeux/Liquor, Gaming & Racing Board: 1, rue Notre-Dame est, Montréal QC H2Y 1B6 – 514/873-3577; Fax: 514/864-9664

Président, Ghislain K. Laflamme

•Sûreté du Québec/Provincial Police: 1701, rue Parthenais, Montréal QC H2L 4K7 – 514/598-4488; Fax: 514/598-4957

Directeur général (par intérim), Guy Coulombe

Directeur général adjoint, Affaires corporatives, Georges Boilard, 514/598-4545

Directeur général (par intérim), Enquêtes criminelles, Jean Bourdeau, 514/598-4422, Fax: 514/596-3688

Directeur générale adjoint (par intérim), Supports opérationnels, Normand Proulx, 514/598-4411, Fax: 514/596-3026

Directeur général adjoint, Surveillance du territoire, Gilles Falardeau, 514/598-4747

Directeur, Affaires internes, Insp.-chef Paul Quirion, 514/598-4900, Fax: 514/598-4886

Directeur, Communications, Capt. Denis Fiset, 514/598-4848, Fax: 514/598-4917

Directeur, Vérification et contrôle de gestion, Cpt. Maurice Sénécal, 514/598-3545, Fax: 514/598-4911

## TOURISME QUÉBEC/Tourism Québec

#412, 900, boul René-Lévesque est, Québec QC G1R 2B5
418/643-5959; Fax: 418/646-8723; URL: http://www.tourisme.gouv.qc.ca
Toll Free: 1-800-363-7777 (Tourism Information)
CP 979, Montréal QC H3C 2W3
514/873-2015, Fax: 514/864-3838

### ACTS ADMINISTERED

Loi sur les établissements touristiques (Tourism Establishments)

**Ministre délégué, Industrie et Commerce**, David Cliche
Sous-ministre associée, Tourisme, Lucillee Daoust, 418/643-9141, Fax: 418/643-8499
Directeur, Relations publiques, André Lachapelle, 418/643-5959, Fax: 418/646-8723

Note: Tourism representatives are also located in Brussels, London, New York, Paris, Tokyo, & Toronto. *See* listings for the Ministère des Relations Internationales & the Secrétariat aux Affaires Intergouvernementales Canadiennes.

### Associated Agencies, Boards & Commissions

•Société du Centre des congrès de Québec/Québec Convention Centre: #214, 900 boul René-Lévesque est, Québec QC G1R 2B5 – 418/644-4000; Fax: 418/644-6455
Président et Directeur général (par intérim), François Noël

## Ministère des TRANSPORTS (MTQ)/ Transportation

700, boul René-Lévesque est, 28e étage, Québec QC G1R 5H1
418/643-6740; URL: http://www.gouv.qc.ca/francais/minorg/mtrans/mtrans_intro.html

### ACTS ADMINISTERED

Loi sur l'assurance automobile
Loi sur les autoroutes
Loi sur les chemins de colonisation
Loi sur les chemins de fer
Code de la sécurité routière
Loi sur les conseils intermunicipaux de transport dans la région de Montréal
Loi sur les corporations municipales & intermunicipales de transport
Loi sur l'expropriation
Loi sur l'indemnisation des victimes d'accidents d'automobiles
Loi sur le Ministère des Transports
Loi sur la Société de l'assurance automobile du Québec
Loi sur la Société des traversiers du Québec
Loi sur la Société québécoise des transports
Loi sur le transport par taxi
Loi sur les transports
Loi sur la voirie
Loi sur l'instruction publique (transport des écoliers)
Loi sur la Société de transport de la ville de Laval
Loi sur la Société de transport de la rive Sud de Montréal
Loi sur le camionnage
Loi sur la publicité de long des routes

**Ministre**, Jacques Brassard, 418/643-6980, Fax: 418/643-2033
Secrétaire du ministère, Pierre Perron
Sous-ministre, Yvan Demers, Fax: 418/643-9836
Sous-ministre adjoint, Planification et technologie, Liguori Hinse, 418/528-0808, Fax: 418/643-9836
Sous-ministre adjoint, Services à la gestion, Alain Vallières, 418/528-0808, Fax: 418/643-9836
Sous-ministre adjoint, Montréal, Yvon Tourigny, 35, rue de Port Royal est, 5e étage, Montréal QC H3L 3T1, 514/873-4172, Fax: 514/864-2836
Sous-ministre adjoint, Ouest, Luc Crépeault, 35, rue de Port Royal est, 5e étage, Montréal QC H3L 3T1, 514/873-4172, Fax: 514/864-2836
Chef de service, Vérification interne, Marcel Plante, 418/643-6591, Fax: 418/643-1269
Directeur, Affaires juridiques, Michel Lalande, 418/643-6937, Fax: 418/643-3980

### Associated Agencies, Boards & Commissions

•Commission des Transports du Québec/Transport Commission: 200, ch Ste-Foy, 7e étage, Québec QC G1R 5V5 – 418/644-6041; Fax: 418/643-7404
Président, Louis Gravel
•Conseil de la Recherche et du développement en transport/Transportation Research & Development: #1000, 545, boul Crémazie est, 9e étage, Montréal QC H2M 2V1 – 514/523-3232; Fax: 514/523-2666
Président, Gérard Laganière
Secrétaire général, Vacant
•Société de l'assurance automobile du Québec/Québec Auto Insurance: 333, boul Jean-Lesage, CP 19600, Québec QC G1K 8J6 – 418/528-3100; Fax: 418/644-0339
Président et Directeur général, Jean-Yves Gagnon
•Société du port ferroviaire Baie-Comeau-Hauterive/Baie-Comeau-Hauterive Railway Station: 28, Place La Salle, CP 135, Baie-Comeau QC G4Z 2G9 – 418/296-6785
Président, Jean-Guy Rousseau
•Société québécoise des transports du Québec/Québec Transportation Board: 35, rue de Port-Royal est, Montréal QC H3L 3T1 – 514/864-1664; Fax: 514/873-7389
Directeur général, Yvan Demers
•Société traversiers du Québec/Ferries Québec: 109, rue Dalhousie, Québec QC G1K 9A1 – 418/643-2019; Fax: 418/643-7308
Président et Directeur général, Yvan Demers

## Ministère du TRAVAIL/Employment

200, ch Ste-Foy, 6e étage, Québec QC G1R 5S1
418/643-4817; Fax: 418/644-6969; URL: http://www.travail.gouv.qc.ca/

### ACTS ADMINISTERED

Act Respecting Collective Agreement Decrees
Act respecting the Ministère du travail
Act respecting the process of negotiating of the collective agreements in the public & parapublic sectors

**Acts Administered by Labour Agencies**

Act respecting building contractors vocational qualifications
Act respecting complementary social benefits plans in the construction industry
Act respecting electrical installations
Act respecting indemnities for victims of asbestosis or silicosis in mines & quarries
Act respecting industrial accidents & occupational diseases
Act respecting labour relations vocational training & manpower management in the construction industry
Act respecting labour standards
Act respecting manpower vocational training & qualification
Act respecting occupational health & safety
Act respecting piping installations
Act respecting pressure vessels
Act respecting the Conseil consultatif du travail et de la main d'oeuvre
Act respecting the conservation of energy in buildings
Building Act
Master Electricians Act
Master Pipe Mechanics Act
National Holiday Act
Public Buildings Safety Act
Stationary Enginemen Act
Workmen's Compensation Act

**Ministre**, Matthias Rioux, 418/643-5297, Fax: 418/644-0003
Sous-ministre, Jean-Marc Boily, 418/643-2902, Fax: 418/643-3069
Sous-ministre adjoint, Administration, Pierre Boisvert, 418/643-2902, Fax: 418/643-3069
Sous-ministre adjoint, Planification, recherches et construction, Jacques Henry, 418/643-2902, Fax: 418/643-3069
Sous-ministre adjoint, Relations de travail, Normand Gauthier, 514/873-4678, Fax: 514/873-6253
Secrétaire du Ministère, Christine Barbe, 418/643-2902

### Associated Agencies, Boards & Commissions

•Commission de la Construction du Québec/Construction Commission: 3530, Jean-Talon ouest, Montréal QC H3R 2G3 – 514/341-7740; Fax: 514/341-6354
Président, André Ménard
•Commission des normes du travail/Labour Standards Commission: 400, boul Jean-Lesage, Québec QC G1K 8W1 – Fax: 514/864-4711, Toll Free: 1-800-265-1414
Président, Jean-Guy Rivard
•Commission de la santé et de la sécurité du travail du Québec (CSST)/Occupational Health & Safety Commission: 1199, rue de Bleury, CP 6056, Succ Centre-Ville, Montréal QC H3C 4E1 – 514/873-7183; Fax: 514/873-7007; Email: lbeaudoi@riq.qc.ca
Président, Conseil d'administration & Chef de la direction, Trefflé Lacombe, 514/873-3503
Président et chef des opérations, Pierre Gabrièle, 418/873-3503
Secrétaire général adjoint, Michel Brunet
Vice-président, Finances, Roland Longchamps, 418/646-3171
Vice-président, Opérations & Directeur (par intérim), Services médicaux, Gérard Bibeau, 418/646-3171
Vice-président, Programmation et expertise-conseil, Alain Albert, 514/873-3503
Vice-président, Relations avec les clientèles et les partenaires, Donald Brisson, 418/646-3171
Vice-présidente, Services, Vacant, 514/873-3503
Responsable, Affaires publiques, Jacques Millette, 514/873-5828
•Conseil consultatif du travail & de la main d'oeuvre/Advisory Council on Labour & Manpower: #2026, 800, Tour de la Place Victoria, CP 87, Montréal QC H4Z 1B7 – 514/873-2880; Fax: 514/873-1129
Président, Yves Dulude
•Conseil des services essentiels/Essential Services Council: #2771, 5199, rue Sherbrooke est, Montréal QC H1T 3X1 – 514/873-7246; Fax: 514/873-3839
Présidente, Madeleine Lemieux
•Institut de recherche & d'information sur la rémunération: #1220, 500, rue Sherbrooke ouest, Montréal QC H3A 3C6 – 514/288-1394; Fax: 514/288-3536
Présidente, Nicole P. Poupart
•Régie du bâtiment du Québec/Québec Construction Companies Board: 545, boul Crémazie est, Montréal QC H2M 2V2 – 514/873-0976; Fax: 514/873-7667, Toll Free: 1-800-361-0761
Président, Jean-Claude Riendeau
•Société québécoise de développement de la main-d'oeuvre/Québec Manpower Development: 425, rue St-Amable, Québec QC G1R 2C5 – 418/643-1892; Fax: 418/643-1714
Présidente, Diane Bellemare

## Conseil du TRÉSOR/Treasury Board

Edifice H, 4e étage, 875, Grande Allée est, Québec QC G1R 5R8
418/643-5926; Fax: 418/643-7824; URL: http://www.riq.qc.ca/scthtml/sct.htm
Renseignements généraux: 418/643-1529; Fax: 418/643-9226
Secrétariat du conseil du trésor: 418/643-1977; Fax: 418/643-6494

#### ACTS ADMINISTERED

Loi sur la fonction publique
Loi sur l'administration financière
Loi sur les services gouvernementaux aux ministères et organismes publics et modifiant diverses dispositions légales (ministries & government organizations)
Loi sur le Services des achats du gouvernement (government purchasing)
**Président**, Jacques Léonard
Secrétaire, Pierre Roy, 418/643-1977, Fax: 418/643-6494
Secrétaire associé, Services gouvernementaux, Byrne Amyot
Directeur général, Politiques de rénumération, Yvan Cossette, 418/528-6401, Fax: 418/646-8102
Directeur, Communications, Démosthène Blasi, 418/643-1529, Fax: 418/643-9226
Directeur, Fichier, Louis A. Hemel, 418/644-6249, Fax: 418/643-7544
Directeur (par intérim), Verification interne, Alain Chasse, 418/646-7954, Fax: 418/644-8528
Greffier (par intérim), Greffe, Robert Cavanagh, 418/528-6110
Responsable, Secretariat de Centraide secteur public, Yvan Daigle, 418/528-6771, Fax: 418/646-4638

#### ADMINISTRATION

575, rue St-Amable, Québec QC G1R 5N9
Directeur général, Roland Guérin, 418/643-8760, Fax: 418/646-1089
Directeur, Ressources financières, Yvan Bouchard, 418/643-8760, Fax: 418/646-1089
Directeur, Ressources humaines, Jean-Louis Laberge, 418/644-0495, Fax: 418/643-5881
Directeur, Ressources informationnelles, Richard Sirois, 418/646-0651, Fax: 418/646-9880
Directeur, Ressources matérielles, Roland Cloutier, 418/644-6615, Fax: 418/643-6006

#### APPROVISIONNEMENTS/Purchasing

Édifice Cyrille-Duquet, 1500-H, rue Jean-Talon nord, Ste-Foy QC G1N 4T5
Secrétaire adjoint, Michel Gagnon, 418/643-3395, Fax: 418/646-5457
Directeur, Acquisitions, Vacant
Directeur, Equipements informatiques, Jacques Darveau, 418/643-3592, Fax: 418/644-6797
Directeur, Fournitures et de l'ameublement, Claude Denis, 418/643-7577, Fax: 418/643-4076
Directeur, Reprographie gouvernementale, Michel C. Tanguay, 418/643-5038, Fax: 418/646-7507

#### MARCHÉS PUBLICS ET TECHNOLOGIES DE L'INFORMATION/Public Markets & Information Technology

Secrétaire associé, Jacques Lafrance, 418/643-9383, Fax: 418/528-6877
Directeur, Coordination gouvernementale en technologies de l'information, Pierre A. Bélanger, 418/528-6197, Fax: 418/528-6877
Directeur, Développement, Michel Brown, 418/644-6276, Fax: 418/643-2987
Directeur, Gestion des biens et services, Denis Corriveau, 418/528-6166, Fax: 418/528-6877
Directeur, Marchés publics, Claude Tremblay, 418/644-3456, Fax: 418/646-9880

#### PERSONNEL DE LA FONCTION PUBLIQUE

Secrétaire adjoint, Jean Larochelle, 418/528-6195, Fax: 418/643-4877
Directeur, Dotation et des activitiés régionales, Richard Tanguay, 418/528-6611, Fax: 418/643-8083
Directeur, Formation et développement, Gilbert Fournier, 418/528-6701, Fax: 418/643-7500
Directeur, Politiques de personnel, Johanne St-Cyr, 418/528-6450, Fax: 418/646-8131
Directeur, Relations professionnelles, Pierre Boudreault, 418/528-6225, Fax: 418/643-0865

#### POLITIQUES BUDGÉTAIRES ET PROGRAMMES/Budget Policies & Programs

Secrétaire associée, Diane Jean, 418/643-1977, Fax: 418/646-4294
Directeur, Paul-Émile Arseneault, 418/528-6301, Fax: 418/643-7288
Directrice, Programmes administratifs, sociaux et de santé, Mireille Fillion, 418/528-6512, Fax: 418/643-6569
Directeur, Programmes économiques, éducatifs et culturels, Yves Lessard, 418/528-6252, Fax: 418/643-7288

#### RESSOURCES HUMAINES/Human Resources

Secrétaire associé, Maurice Charlebois, 418/528-6180, Fax: 418/644-8528
Directeur, Affaires juridiques, Luc Crevier, 1500-H, rue Jean-Talon nord, 1er étage, Ste-Foy QC G1N 4T5, 418/528-6666, Fax: 418/528-2338

##### Services aériens et postaux/Postal Services

Directeur général & Directeur, Service aérien gouvernemental, Gaston Couillard, 418/877-8383, Fax: 418/871-5313
Directeur, Service gouvernemental de courrier, Pierre-André Dupont, 418/644-0018, Fax: 418/646-3660

##### Services informatiques gouvernementaux/Information Services

Directeur général, Bernard Beauchemin, 418/644-6108, Fax: 418/646-0988
Directeur, Connexité et gestion des plates-formes mini et réseaux, Paul Lessard, 418/643-5800, Fax: 418/646-0988
Directeur, Opérations, Jean Pellerin, 418/644-4913, Fax: 418/646-0988
Directeur, Planification et gestion, Michel Rochette, 418/644-6468, Fax: 418/646-0988
Directrice, Services à la clientèle, Danielle Ferland, 418/644-7588, Fax: 418/646-0988
Directeur, Services conseils en informatique, Jacques Proulx, 418/644-1866, Fax: 418/646-0988
Directeur, Soutien technique, Paul Lessard, 418/643-5800, Fax: 418/646-0988
Directeur, Systèmes de gestion en ressources humaines, Léo Ferland, 418/528-6540, Fax: 418/646-5453

##### Télécommunications/Telecommunications

Directeur général, Raynald Brulotte, 418/643-7774, Fax: 418/646-3566
Directeur, Communications informatiques, Marcel W. Landry, 418/644-6111, Fax: 418/646-3566
Directeur, Communications mobiles, Jacques A. Bilodeau, 418/646-7606, Fax: 418/646-3566
Directeur, Communications téléphoniques, Gilbert Coutu, 418/644-9490, Fax: 418/946-3566
Directeur, Inforoute gouvernementale, Gilbert Labonté, 418/644-2694, Fax: 418/646-3566
Directeur, Promotion et marketing, Laval Girard, 418/643-2196, Fax: 418/646-3566

##### Associated Agencies, Boards & Commissions

•Commission administrative des régimes de retraite et d'assurances (Québec): 2875, boul Laurier, 2e étage, Ste-Foy QC G1V 4J8 – 418/644-8661; Fax: 418/646-8721
Président, Michel Sanschagrin
•Commission de la fonction publique (Québec): 8, rue Cook, Québec QC G1R 5J8 – 418/643-3977; Fax: 418/643-7264
Président, Michel Paquet
•Société immobilière du Québec/Québec Buildings Corp.: 475, rue St-Amable, Québec QC G1R 4X9 – 418/646-1766 poste 3470; Fax: 418/643-7932
Président et Directeur général, Jean P. Vézina

## VÉRIFICATEUR GÉNÉRAL du QUÉBEC/ Auditor General

#6.00, 900, Place d'Youville, Québec QC G1R 3P7
418/691-5900; Fax: 418/646-1307; URL: http://www.sgo.gouv.qc.ca/vgq
**Vérificateur général**, Guy Breton, 418/691-5901, Email: gbreton@vqg.gouv.qc.ca
Vérificateur général adjoint, Gilles Bédard, 418/691-5903
Vérificateur général adjoint, Jacques Henrichon, 418/691-5904
Directeur, Administration, Louis-Philippe Fiset, 418/691-5930

# GOVERNMENT OF SASKATCHEWAN

**Seat of Government:** Legislative Bldg., Regina SK S4S 0B3
306/781-0222; URL: http://www.gov.sk.ca/
Toll Free: 1-800-667-0666
The Province of Saskatchewan entered Confederation on September 1, 1905. It has an area of 570,113.47 km2, and the StatsCan census population in 1996 was 990,237.

## Office of the LIEUTENANT GOVERNOR

Government House, 4607 Dewdney Ave., Regina SK S4P 3V7
306/787-4070; Fax: 306/787-7716
**Lieutenant Governor**, Hon. J.E.N. Wiebe
Private Secretary, Irene White

## Office of the PREMIER

2405 Legislative Dr., Regina SK S4S 0B3
306/787-9433; Fax: 306/787-0885; URL: http://www.sasknet.sk.ca
**Premier**, Hon. Roy Romanow, Q.C., Email: premier@sasknet.sk.ca
Acting Chief of Staff, Judy Samuelson, 306/787-1902
Special Advisor, Carlo Binda
Director, Correspondence, Donna Easto, 306/787-1914
Deputy Premier, Hon. Dwain Lingenfelter

## EXECUTIVE COUNCIL

Legislative Bldg., 2405 Legislative Dr., Regina SK S4S 0B3
URL: http://www.gov.sk.ca/execcoun/cabinet.htm#nillson
Premier & President, Executive Council, Hon. Roy Romanow, Q.C., 306/787-0958, Fax: 306/787-0885
Minister, Education, Hon. Pat Atkinson, 306/787-1684, Fax: 306/787-0237
Minister, Highways & Transportation & Minister Responsible, Status of Women, Hon. Judy Bradley, 306/787-0369, Fax: 306/787-6499
Minister, Social Services & Minister Responsible, Seniors & Disabilities Directorate, Hon. Lorne Calvert, 306/787-7363, Fax: 306/787-0656

Minister, Finance, Hon. Eric Cline, 306/787-6059, Fax: 306/787-6055
Minister, Post-Secondary Education & Skills Training & Minister Responsible, Gaming, Hon. Joanne Crofford, 306/787-0354, Fax: 306/787-2202
Minister, Northern Affairs, Hon. Keith N. Goulet, 306/787-1885, Fax: 306/787-0399
Minister, Energy & Mines, Hon. Eldon Lautermilch, 306/787-0605, Fax: 306/787-8100
Deputy Premier & Minister, Crown Investments Corp., Hon. Dwain Lingenfelter, 306/787-6944, Fax: 306/787-8487
Government House Leader & Minister, Economic & Cooperative Development, Hon. Janice MacKinnon, 306/787-7347, Fax: 306/787-9135
Minister, Labour, Hon. Robert W. Mitchell, Q.C., 306/787-0659, Fax: 306/787-6946
Minister, Justice & Attorney General, Hon. John Nilson, Q.C., 306/787-0613, Fax: 306/787-1232
Minister, Environment & Resource Management, Hon. Lorne Scott, 306/787-8824, Fax: 306/787-0395
Minister, Health, Hon. Clay Serby, 306/787-7387, Fax: 306/787-8677
Provincial Secretary & Deputy Government House Leader, Hon. Ned Shillington, 306/787-0365, Fax: 306/787-1100
Minister Responsible, Saskatchewan Property Management Corp., Hon. Maynard Sonntag, 306/787-6478, Fax: 306/787-8747
Minister, Municipal Government, Hon. Carol Teichrob, 306/787-0623, Fax: 306/787-0630
Minister, Agriculture & Food, Hon. Eric Upshall, 306/787-0338, Fax: 306/787-1094
Minister, Intergovernmental & Aboriginal Affairs, Hon. Bernhard Wiens, 306/787-0394, Fax: 306/787-1669

#### Department of Executive Council

#135, Legislative Bldg., Regina SK S4S OB3
Fax: 306/787-8338
Cabinet Secretary & Deputy Minister to the Premier, Gregory Marchildon, 306/787-6338, Fax: 306/787-8338

#### Cabinet Secretariat

#32, Legislative Bldg., 2405 Legislative Dr., Regina SK S4S 0B3
Fax: 306/787-8299
Clerk, Executive Council & Asst. Cabinet Secretary, Lois Thacyk

#### Chief of Staff's Office

#110, Legislative Bldg., 2405 Legislative Dr., Regina SK S4S 0B3
306/787-1910; Fax: 306/787-0883
Chief of Staff, Judy Samuelson

#### Policy & Planning Secretariat

#37, Legislative Bldg., 2405 Legislative Dr., Regina SK S4S 0B3
306/787-6339; Fax: 306/787-0012
Associate Deputy Minister to the Premier, Marianne Weston

#### Cabinet Standing Committees

Cabinet Committee on Economic Development, Secretary, Clare Kirkland
Legislative Review, Secretary, Lois Thacyk
Order in Council Review, Secretary, Lois Thacyk
Planning & Priorities, Secretary, Marianne Weston
Public Sector Bargaining Compensation, Secretary, Wynne Young
Regulations Review, Secretary, Lois Thacyk
Treasury Board, Secretary, Bill Jones

## LEGISLATIVE ASSEMBLY

c/o Clerk's Office, #239, Legislative Bldg., 2405 Legislative Dr., Regina SK S4S 0B3
306/787-2279; Fax: 306/787-0408; URL: http://www.legassembly.sk.ca/
**Clerk:** Gwenn Ronyk, 306/787-2374
**Speaker:** Hon. Glenn Hagel, 306/787-2282
**Sergeant-at-Arms:** Patrick Shaw, 306/787-2184
**Director, Hansard:** Susan Hope, 306/787-2290
**Librarian, Legislative Library:** Marian Powell, 306/787-2277
Director, Personnel & Administrative Services, Linda Kaminski, 306/787-2338
Director, Broadcast Services, H. Gary Ward, 306/787-2181
Clerk Asst. (Journals), Rose Zerr, 306/787-3992
Legislative Counsel & Law Clerk, Robert Cosman, 306/787-8984

#### Government Caucus Office (NDP)

#203, Legislative Bldg., 2405 Legislative Dr., Regina SK S4S 0B3
306/787-7388; Fax: 306/787-6247; URL: http://www.sasknet.com/ZXndpmla/
Chief of Staff, Jim Fodey
Director, Administration, Gail Fehr

#### Office of the Official Opposition (SP)

#265, Legislative Bldg., 2405 Legislative Dr., Regina SK S4S 0B3
306/787-4300; Fax: 306/787-3174; Email: skcaucus@sk.sypatico.ca; URL: http://www.skcaucus.domhost.com
Leader, Ken Krawetz
Deputy Leader, Dan D'Autremont

#### Office of the Third Party (Lib.)

#140, Legislative Bldg., 2405 Legislative Dr., Regina SK S4S 0B3
306/787-0860; Fax: 306/787-0250; URL: http://www.lights.com/sklibcaucus/
Leader, Bill Boyd, Email: billboyd@sk.sypatico.ca
Chief of Staff, Reg Downs
Deputy Leader, Ron Osika
Director, Communications, Kathy Peter
Researcher, Lyle Hewitt

#### Standing Committees of the Legislature

Agriculture
Communication
Constitutional Affairs
Continuing Select
Crown Corporations
Education
Environment
Estimates
Municipal Law
Non-Controversial Bills
Private Members' Bills
Privileges & Elections
Public Accounts

#### Special Committees of the Legislature

Nominating
Regulations
Rules & Procedures

## TWENTY-SECOND LEGISLATURE - SASKATCHEWAN

306/787-2279
Last General Election, June 21, 1995. Maximum Duration 5 Years.
**Party Standings (September 12, 1997)**
New Democratic Party (NDP) 41
Saskatchewan Party (SP) 8
Liberal (Lib.) 6
Independent (Ind.) 3
Total 58
**Salaries, Indemnities & Allowances**
Members' indemnity & expense allowance $59,500. In addition to this are the following:
Premier $49,680
Deputy Premier $39,744
Ministers $34,776
Leader of the Opposition $34,776
Leader of the third Party $17,390
Speaker $29,808
Deputy Speaker $9,936

#### MEMBERS BY CONSTITUENCY

Following is: constituency, member, party affiliation, Regina Telephone & Fax numbers. (Address for all is 2405 Legislature Dr., Regina SK S4S 0B3.)

Arm River, Harvey McLane, Lib., 306/787-7530, Fax: 306/787-0250
Athabasca, Buckley Belanger, Lib., 306/787-7585, Fax: 306/787-0250
Battleford-Cut Knife, Sharon Murrell, NDP, 306/787-1837, Fax: 306/787-6247
Cannington, Dan D'Autremont, SP, 306/787-4300, Fax: 306/787-3174
Canora-Pelly, Ken Krawetz, SP, 306/787-4300, Fax: 306/787-3174
Carrot River Valley, Hon. Andy Renaud, NDP, 306/787-9311, Fax: 306/787-7905
Cumberland, Hon. Keith N. Goulet, NDP, 306/787-1885, Fax: 306/787-0399
Cypress Hills, Jack Goohsen, Ind., 306/787-0871, Fax: 306/787-5303
Estevan, Larry Ward, NDP, 306/787-1833, Fax: 306/787-6247
Humboldt, Arlene Julé, Ind., 306/787-7583, Fax: 306/787-0983
Indian Head-Milestone, Hon. Lorne Scott, NDP, 306/787-0393, Fax: 306/787-0395
Kelvington-Wadena, June Draude, SP, 306/787-4300, Fax: 306/787-3174
Kindersley, Bill Boyd, SP, 306/787-4300, Fax: 306/787-3174
Last Mountain-Touchwood, Dale Flavel, NDP, 306/787-0935, Fax: 306/787-7905
Lloydminster, Violet Stanger, NDP, 306/787-0898, Fax: 306/787-6247
Meadow Lake, Hon. Maynard Sonntag, NDP, 306/787-1889, Fax: 306/787-8747
Melfort-Tisdale, Rod Gantefoer, SP, 306/787-4300, Fax: 306/787-3174
Melville, Ron Osika, Lib., 306/787-0860, Fax: 306/787-0250
Moose Jaw North, Hon. Glenn Hagel, NDP, 306/787-2282, Fax: 306/787-2283
Moose Jaw Wakamow, Hon. Lorne Calvert, NDP, 306/787-3661, Fax: 306/787-0656
Moosomin, Donald J. Toth, SP, 306/787-4300, Fax: 306/787-3174
North Battleford, Jack Hillson, Lib., 306/787-0879, Fax: 306/787-0250
Prince Albert Carlton, Myron Kowalsky, NDP, 306/787-1888, Fax: 306/787-6247
Prince Albert Northcote, Hon. Eldon Lautermilch, NDP, 306/787-0615, Fax: 306/787-8100
Redberry Lake, Walter Jess, NDP, 306/787-0937, Fax: 306/787-7905
Regina Centre, Hon. Joanne Crofford, NDP, 306/787-6662, Fax: 306/787-2202
Regina Coronation Park, Kim Trew, NDP, 306/787-1898, Fax: 306/787-7905
Regina Dewdney, Ed Tchorzewski, NDP, 306/787-7979, Fax: 306/787-6247
Regina Elphinstone, Hon. Dwain Lingenfelter, NDP, 306/787-2396, Fax: 306/787-8487
Regina Lakeview, Hon. John Nilson, Q.C., NDP, 306/787-5353, Fax: 306/787-1232

Regina Northeast, Hon. Ned Shillington, NDP, 306/787-0365, Fax: 306/787-1100
Regina Qu'Appelle Valley, Suzanne Murray, NDP, 306/787-0899, Fax: 306/787-6247
Regina Sherwood, Lindy Kasperski, NDP, 306/787-1802, Fax: 306/787-7905
Regina South, Andrew Thomson, NDP, 306/787-1827, Fax: 306/787-6247
Regina Victoria, Harry Van Mulligen, NDP, 306/787-1900, Fax: 306/787-7905
Regina Wascana Plains, Doreen Hamilton, NDP, 306/787-0891, Fax: 306/787-6247
Rosetown-Biggar, Hon. Bernhard Wiens, NDP, 306/787-0394, Fax: 306/787-1669
Rosthern, Ben Heppner, SP, 306/787-4300, Fax: 306/787-3174
Saltcoats, Bob Bjornerud, SP, 306/787-4300, Fax: 306/787-3174
Saskatchewan Rivers, Jack Langford, NDP, 306/787-0985, Fax: 306/787-7905
Saskatoon Eastview, Bob Pringle, NDP, 306/787-8802, Fax: 306/787-7905
Saskatoon Fairview, Hon. Robert W. Mitchell, Q.C., NDP, 306/787-1117, Fax: 306/787-6946
Saskatoon Greystone, Lynda Haverstock, Ind., 306/787-7731, Fax: 306/787-4232
Saskatoon Idylwyld, Hon. Janice MacKinnon, NDP, 306/787-9124, Fax: 306/787-9135
Saskatoon Meewasin, Hon. Carol Teichrob, NDP, 306/787-6100, Fax: 306/787-0630
Saskatoon Mount Royal, Hon. Eric Cline, NDP, 306/787-6059, Fax: 306/787-6055
Saskatoon Northwest, Grant Whitmore, NDP, 306/787-0766, Fax: 306/787-6247
Saskatoon Nutana, Hon. Pat Atkinson, NDP, 306/787-7360, Fax: 306/787-0237
Saskatoon Riversdale, Hon. Roy Romanow, Q.C., NDP, 306/787-9433, Fax: 306/787-0885
Saskatoon Southeast, Pat Lorje, NDP, 306/787-0895, Fax: 306/787-7905
Saskatoon Sutherland, Mark Koenker, NDP, 306/787-1887, Fax: 306/787-7905
Shellbrook-Spiritwood, Lloyd Johnson, NDP, 306/787-0931, Fax: 306/787-7905
Swift Current, John Wall, NDP, 306/787-0936, Fax: 306/787-7905
Thunder Creek, Gerard Aldridge, Lib., 306/787-7518, Fax: 306/787-0250
Watrous, Hon. Eric Upshall, NDP, 306/787-0338, Fax: 306/787-1094
Weyburn-Big Muddy, Hon. Judy Bradley, NDP, 306/787-6447, Fax: 306/787-6499
Wood River, Glen McPherson, Lib., 306/787-0896, Fax: 306/787-0250
Yorkton, Hon. Clay Serby, NDP, 306/787-7345, Fax: 306/787-8677

**MEMBERS (ALPHABETICAL)**

Following is: constituency, member, party affiliation, Regina Telephone & Fax numbers. (Address for all is 2405 Legislature Dr., Regina SK S4S 0B3.)

Gerard Aldridge, Thunder Creek Lib., 306/787-7518, Fax: 306/787-0250
Hon. Pat Atkinson, Saskatoon Nutana NDP, 306/787-7360, Fax: 306/787-0237
Buckley Belanger, Athabasca Lib., 306/787-7585, Fax: 306/787-0250
Bob Bjornerud, Saltcoats SP, 306/787-4300, Fax: 306/787-3174
Bill Boyd, Kindersley SP, 306/787-4300, Fax: 306/787-3174
Hon. Judy Bradley, Weyburn-Big Muddy NDP, 306/787-6447, Fax: 306/787-6499
Hon. Lorne Calvert, Moose Jaw Wakamow NDP, 306/787-3661, Fax: 306/787-0656
Hon. Eric Cline, Saskatoon Mount Royal NDP, 306/787-6059, Fax: 306/787-6055
Hon. Joanne Crofford, Regina Centre NDP, 306/787-6662, Fax: 306/787-2202
Dan D'Autremont, Cannington SP, 306/787-4300, Fax: 306/787-3174
June Draude, Kelvington-Wadena SP, 306/787-4300, Fax: 306/787-3174
Dale Flavel, Last Mountain-Touchwood NDP, 306/787-0935, Fax: 306/787-7905
Rod Gantefoer, Melfort-Tisdale SP, 306/787-4300, Fax: 306/787-3174
Jack Goohsen, Cypress Hills Ind., 306/787-0871, Fax: 306/787-5303
Hon. Keith N. Goulet, Cumberland NDP, 306/787-1885, Fax: 306/787-0399
Hon. Glenn Hagel, Moose Jaw North NDP, 306/787-2282, Fax: 306/787-2283
Doreen Hamilton, Regina Wascana Plains NDP, 306/787-0891, Fax: 306/787-6247
Lynda Haverstock, Saskatoon Greystone Ind., 306/787-7731, Fax: 306/787-4232
Ben Heppner, Rosthern SP, 306/787-4300, Fax: 306/787-3174
Jack Hillson, North Battleford Lib., 306/787-0879, Fax: 306/787-0250
Walter Jess, Redberry Lake NDP, 306/787-0937, Fax: 306/787-7905
Lloyd Johnson, Shellbrook-Spiritwood NDP, 306/787-0931, Fax: 306/787-7905
Arlene Julé, Humboldt Ind., 306/787-7583, Fax: 306/787-0983
Lindy Kasperski, Regina Sherwood NDP, 306/787-1802, Fax: 306/787-7905
Mark Koenker, Saskatoon Sutherland NDP, 306/787-1887, Fax: 306/787-7905
Myron Kowalsky, Prince Albert Carlton NDP, 306/787-1888, Fax: 306/787-6247
Ken Krawetz, Canora-Pelly SP, 306/787-4300, Fax: 306/787-3174
Jack Langford, Saskatchewan Rivers NDP, 306/787-0985, Fax: 306/787-7905
Hon. Eldon Lautermilch, Prince Albert Northcote NDP, 306/787-0615, Fax: 306/787-8100
Hon. Dwain Lingenfelter, Regina Elphinstone NDP, 306/787-2396, Fax: 306/787-8487
Pat Lorje, Saskatoon Southeast NDP, 306/787-0895, Fax: 306/787-7905
Hon. Janice MacKinnon, Saskatoon Idylwyld NDP, 306/787-9124, Fax: 306/787-9135
Harvey McLane, Arm River Lib., 306/787-7530, Fax: 306/787-0250
Glen McPherson, Wood River Lib., 306/787-0896, Fax: 306/787-0250
Hon. Robert W. Mitchell, Q.C., Saskatoon Fairview NDP, 306/787-1117, Fax: 306/787-6946
Suzanne Murray, Regina Qu'Appelle Valley NDP, 306/787-0899, Fax: 306/787-6247
Sharon Murrell, Battleford-Cut Knife NDP, 306/787-1837, Fax: 306/787-6247
Hon. John Nilson, Q.C., Regina Lakeview NDP, 306/787-5353, Fax: 306/787-1232
Ron Osika, Melville Lib., 306/787-0860, Fax: 306/787-0250
Bob Pringle, Saskatoon Eastview NDP, 306/787-8802, Fax: 306/787-7905
Hon. Andy Renaud, Carrot River Valley NDP, 306/787-9311, Fax: 306/787-7905
Hon. Roy Romanow, Q.C., Saskatoon Riversdale NDP, 306/787-9433, Fax: 306/787-0885
Hon. Lorne Scott, Indian Head-Milestone NDP, 306/787-0393, Fax: 306/787-0395
Hon. Clay Serby, Yorkton NDP, 306/787-7345, Fax: 306/787-8677
Hon. Ned Shillington, Regina Northeast NDP, 306/787-0365, Fax: 306/787-1100
Hon. Maynard Sonntag, Meadow Lake NDP, 306/787-1889, Fax: 306/787-8747
Violet Stanger, Lloydminster NDP, 306/787-0898, Fax: 306/787-6247
Ed Tchorzewski, Regina Dewdney NDP, 306/787-7979, Fax: 306/787-6247
Hon. Carol Teichrob, Saskatoon Meewasin NDP, 306/787-6100, Fax: 306/787-0630
Andrew Thomson, Regina South NDP, 306/787-1827, Fax: 306/787-6247
Donald J. Toth, Moosomin SP, 306/787-4300, Fax: 306/787-3174
Kim Trew, Regina Coronation Park NDP, 306/787-1898, Fax: 306/787-7905
Hon. Eric Upshall, Watrous NDP, 306/787-0338, Fax: 306/787-1094
Harry Van Mulligen, Regina Victoria NDP, 306/787-1900, Fax: 306/787-7905
John Wall, Swift Current NDP, 306/787-0936, Fax: 306/787-7905
Larry Ward, Estevan NDP, 306/787-1833, Fax: 306/787-6247
Grant Whitmore, Saskatoon Northwest NDP, 306/787-0766, Fax: 306/787-6247
Hon. Bernhard Wiens, Rosetown-Biggar NDP, 306/787-0394, Fax: 306/787-1669

## SASKATCHEWAN GOVERNMENT DEPARTMENTS & AGENCIES

### Saskatchewan AGRICULTURE & FOOD

Walter Scott Bldg., 3085 Albert St., Regina SK S4S 0B1
306/787-5140; Fax: 306/787-0216; URL: http://www.gov.sk.ca/agfood/
SaskAgInfoNet Inc.: http://www.aginfonet.sk.ca

**ACTS ADMINISTERED**

Agri-Food Act
Agri-Food Innovation Act
Agricultural Credit Corporation of Saskatchewan Act
Agricultural Development & Adjustment Act
Agricultural Operations Act
Agricultural Safety Net Act
Agricultural Societies Act
Agriculture Development Fund Act
Agrologists Act
Animal Identification Act
Animal Products Act
Animal Protection Act
Apiaries Act
Cattle Marketing Deductions Act
Crop Insurance Act
Crop Payment Act
Department of Agriculture Act
Diseases of Animals Act
Drainage Act
Expropriation Act
Expropriation (Rehabilitation Projects) Act
Farm Financial Stability Act
Farmers' Counselling & Assistance Act
Farming Communities Land Act
Grain Charges Limitation Act
Grain & Fodder Conservation Act
Horned Cattle Purchases Act
Horticultural Societies Act
Land Bank Repeal & Temporary Provisions Act
Leafcutting Beekeepers Registration Act
Line Fence Act
Livestock Facilities Tax Credit Act
Livestock Investment Tax Credit Act
Milk Control Act, 1992
Noxious Weeds Act, 1984
Pest Control Act
Pest Control Products (Saskatchewan) Act
Pollution (by Livestock) Control Act, 1984
Prairie Agricultural Machinery Institute Act
Provincial Lands Act
Sale or Lease of Certain Lands Act
Saskatchewan 4-H Foundation Act

Saskatchewan Farm Security Act
Seed Grain Advances Act
Soil Drifting Control Act
Stray Animals Act
Vegetable, Fruit & Honey Sales Act
Veterinarians Act, 1987
Veterinary Services Act
Wildlife Act (subject to Provisions of O.C. 469/94)
**Minister**, Hon. Eric Upshall, 306/787-0338, Fax: 306/787-1094
Acting Deputy Minister & Asst. Deputy Minister, Policy & Planning, Terrence Scott, 306/787-5171, Email: tscott@agr.gov.sk.ca
Asst. Deputy Minister, Financial Support & Program Management, Dale Sigurdson, 306/787-5245, Fax: 306/787-2393, Email: dsigurd1@agr.gov.sk.ca
Asst. Deputy Minister, Research, Development & Finance Division, Susie Miller, 306/787-5171, Email: smiller@agr.gov.sk.ca
Director, Extension Services, Vacant, 306/787-8524, Fax: 306/787-9623

#### ADMINISTRATIVE SERVICES BRANCH
Fax: 306/787-0600
Director, Jack Zepp, 306/787-5131, Email: jzepp@agr.gov.sk.ca
Manager, Financial Services, Ken Petruic, 306/787-5142
Manager, Operations, Ross Johnson, 306/787-5141

#### AGRI-FOOD EQUITY FUND
Fax: 306/787-0852
Executive Director, Carl Neggers, 306/787-0816, Email: cneggers@agr.gov.sk.ca

#### AGRICULTURE RESEARCH BRANCH
Fax: 306/787-2654
Agri-Food Innovation Fund: 1-800-242-8369
Director, Martin Wrubleski, 306/787-5960, Email: mwrubleski@agr.gov.sk.ca
Program Coordinator, Engineering, Environment & Economics, Ron Kehrig, 306/933-5094
Program Coordinator, Livestock, Hamid Javed, 306/787-5924
Program Coordinator, Bruce Baumann, 306/787-5107
Program Coordinator, Abdul Jalil, 306/787-8076

#### COMMUNICATIONS BRANCH
Director, Harvey Johnson, 306/787-6395, Email: hjohnson@agr.gov.sk.ca
Asst. Director, Janet Peters, 306/787-5389
Media Relations, Colleen Slater-Smith, 306/787-5155

#### EXTENSION SERVICE BRANCH
Fax: 306/787-9623
Director, Louise Greenberg, 306/787-5018, Email: lgreenberg@agr.gov.sk.ca

#### HUMAN RESOURCES BRANCH
Fax: 306/787-5919
Director, Erna Stinnen, 306/787-5211, Email: estinnen@agr.gov.sk.ca

#### INDUSTRY DEVELOPMENT BRANCH
Fax: 306/787-0271
Director, Maryellen Carlson, 306/787-8526, Email: mcarlson@agr.gov.sk.ca
Marketing Manager, Consumer Products, Ken Evans, 306/787-8537

#### LANDS BRANCH
306/787-5180
Director, Greg Haase, 306/787-5154, Email: ghaase@agr.gov.sk.ca

#### LIVESTOCK & VETERINARY OPERATIONS BRANCH
Fax: 306/787-5180
Director, Ernie Spencer, 306/787-5087, Email: espencer@agr.gov.sk.ca
Manager, Intensive Livestock Operations, Donn Farrer, 306/787-5465

#### PASTURES BRANCH
Fax: 306/787-5180
Director, Peter Rempel, 306/787-5191, Email: prempel@agr.gov.sk.ca

#### POLICY & PROGRAM DEVELOPMENT BRANCH
Fax: 306/787-5134
Director, Hal Cushon, 306/787-5961, Email: hcushon@agr.gov.sk.ca
Coordinator, Land Policy Section, Gloria Parisien, 306/787-5207

#### PORK CENTRAL
Fax: 306/787-9297
Director, Jacquie Gibney, 306/787-5190, Email: jgibney@agr.gov.sk.ca

#### STATISTICS BRANCH
Fax: 306/787-0276
Director, David Boehm, 306/787-5204, Email: dboehm@agr.gov.sk.ca

#### SUSTAINABLE PRODUCTION BRANCH
Fax: 306/787-0428
Director, J.A. Buchan, 306/787-4661, Email: jbuchan@agr.gov.sk.ca
Supervisor, Crop Protection Laboratory, Grant Holzgang, 306/787-8130
Manager, Crop Industry Development Section, Mike McAvoy, 306/787-4668
Manager, Economics & Business Development, Don Barber, 306/787-5962
Manager, Production Technology Section, Doug Billett, 306/787-8061

##### Associated Agencies, Boards & Commissions
•Agricultural Credit Corporation of Saskatchewan: 350 Cheadle St. West, PO Box 820, Swift Current SK S9H 4Y7 – 306/778-8480; Fax: 306/778-8459
General Manager, Norm Ballagh
•Agri-Food Council: #329, 3085 Albert St., Regina SK S4S 0B1 – 306/787-5952; Fax: 306/787-0271
Secretary, Roy White
•Farm Stress Unit: #329, 3085 Albert St., Regina SK S4S 0B1 – 306/787-5196; Fax: 306/787-9623, Toll Free: 1-800-667-4442
Manager, Ken Imhoff
•Milk Control Board: #1210, 2500 Victoria Ave., Regina SK S4P 3X2 – 306/787-5319; Fax: 306/787-1988
CEO, S.H. Barber
•Prairie Agricultural Machinery Institute: PO Box 1900, Humboldt SK S0K 2A0 – 306/682-2555; Fax: 306/682-5080
Director, Barrie Broad
•Saskatchewan Crop Insurance Corporation: 484 Prince William Dr., PO Box 3000, Melville SK S0A 2P0 – Fax: 306/728-7260
General Manager, Doug Matthies, 306/728-7205
•Saskatchewan Land Allocations Appeal Board: #302, 3085 Albert St., Regina SK S4S 0B1 – 306/787-5955; Fax: 306/787-5134
Administrative Officer, Joe Novak

##### Agricultural Marketing Boards & Commissions
•Saskatchewan Broiler Hatching Egg Producers Marketing Board: PO Box 130, Unity SK S0K 4L0 – 306/834-5140; Fax: 306/834-5140
Sec.-Manager, Ronalda Kleinsaser
•Saskatchewan Canola Development Commission: #212, 111 Research Dr., Saskatoon SK S7N 3R2 – 306/975-6621; Fax: 306/975-0136
Administrator, Arlaine Moe
•Saskatchewan Chicken Marketing Board: 1810 - 9 Ave. North, PO Box 1637, Regina SK S4P 3C4 – 306/775-1677; Fax: 306/949-1353
Secretary Manager, Van Stewart
•Saskatchewan Commercial Egg Producers' Marketing Board: 1810 - 9 Ave. North, PO Box 1637, Regina SK S4P 3C4 – 306/924-1505; Fax: 306/924-1515
Secretary Manager, Dave Mackie
•Saskatchewan Flax Development Corporation 306/776-2439; Fax: 306/776-2573
Chair, Chris Hale
•Saskatchewan Pork International Marketing Group (SPI): 502 - 45 St. West, Saskatoon SK S7L 6H2 – 306/653-3014; Fax: 306/244-2918, Toll Free: 1-800-667-2003
General Manager, D. Hrapchak
•Saskatchewan Poultry Council: 502 - 45 St. West, 2nd Fl., Saskatoon SK S7L 6H2 – 306/931-1050; Fax: 306/931-2825
Sec.-Manager, Rose Olsen
•Saskatchewan Pulse Crop Development Board: PO Box 516, Regina SK S4P 3A2 – 306/781-7475; Fax: 306/525-4173
Administrator, Vacant
•Saskatchewan Sheep Development Board: 2910 - 11 St. West, PO Box 5025, Saskatoon SK S7K 4E3 – 306/933-5200
Manager, Alesa Verreaut
•Saskatchewan Turkey Producers Marketing Board: 502 - 45 St. West, 2nd Fl., Saskatoon SK S7L 6H2 – 306/931-1050; Fax: 306/931-2825
Secretary Manager, Rose Olsen
•Saskatchewan Vegetable Marketing & Development Board: #101, 2515 Victoria Ave., Regina SK S4P 0T2 – 306/247-2086; Fax: 306/525-4173
Secretary Manager, Tom Hyland

## Saskatchewan ARCHIVES BOARD
University of Regina, 3737 Wascana Pkwy., Regina SK S4S 0A2
306/787-4068; Fax: 306/787-1975
University of Saskatchewan, Murray Bldg., 3 Campus Dr., Saskatoon SK S7N 5A4
306/933-5832, Fax: 306/933-7305
**Provincial Archivist**, Trevor J.D. Powell
Chair, Dr. B. Zagorin, 306/586-4267
Director, Government Records Branch, Don Herperger, 306/787-3864
Director, Historical Records Branch, D'Arcy Hande, 306/933-5833

## Saskatchewan ASSESSMENT MANAGEMENT AGENCY (SAMA)
#1600, 1920 Broad St., Regina SK S4P 3V2
306/924-8000; Fax: 306/924-8070
Toll Free: 1-800-667-7262
Independent agency responsible for the design & administration of the property assessment system in Saskatchewan.
Chair, Mark Thompson
CEO, Bryan Hebb

## Provincial AUDITOR SASKATCHEWAN
#1500, 1920 Broad St., Regina SK S4P 3V7
306/787-6398; Fax: 306/787-6383;
Email: prov.auditor.pas@govmail.gov.sk.ca;
URL: http://www.legassembly.sk.ca/ProvAud/default.htm
**Provincial Auditor**, Wayne K. Strelioff, 306/787-6360
Asst. Provincial Auditor, Fred Wendel, 306/787-6366
Executive Secretary, Linda Kuntz, 306/787-6361
Executive Director, Brian Atkinson, 306/787-6384
Executive Director, Judy Ferguson, 306/787-6372

Executive Director, Mike Heffernan, 306/787-6364
General Director, Mobashar Ahmad, 306/787-6387
Director, Bob Black, 306/787-6369
Director, Ray Bohn, 306/787-6363
Director, Phil Creaser, 306/787-6388
Director, Ed Montgomery, 306/787-6389
Principal, Jane Knox, 306/787-6368
Manager, Angèle Borys, 306/787-6326
Manager, Lorianne Earis, 306/787-6313
Manager, Rod Grabarczyk, 306/787-6373
Manager, Bill Harasymchuk, 306/787-6453
Manager, Rodd Jersak, 306/787-6316
Manager, Shelley Lipon, 306/787-6305
Manager, Dale Markewich, 306/787-6320
Manager, Andrew Martens, 306/787-6374
Manager, Glen Nyhus, 306/787-6385
Manager, Karim Pradhan, 306/787-6386
Manager, Victor Schwab, 306/787-6375
Manager, Rosemarie Volk, 306/787-6380
Manager, Leslie Wendel, 306/787-6370

## Saskatchewan COMMUNICATIONS NETWORK (SCN)

North Block, 2440 Broad St., Regina SK S4P 3V7
306/787-0490; Fax: 306/787-0496; Email: scn@uregina.ca; URL: http://www.scn.sk.ca
**Minister Responsible**, Hon. Joanne Crofford, 306/787-0354
President & CEO, James Benning, 306/787-2390
Executive Director, Operations, Paul Fudge, 306/787-0447
Executive Director, Programming, Richard Gustin, 306/787-0446
Director, Public Affairs, Iain MacDonald, 306/787-0497

## Saskatchewan CROWN INVESTMENTS CORPORATION (CIC)

#400, 2400 College Ave., Regina SK S4P 1C8
306/787-6851; Fax: 306/787-8125; URL: http://www.gov.sk.ca/govt/crowninv/
Acts as a financial holding company & oversees the operations of commercial Crown corporations. Sponsor for the Capital Pension Plan administering pension & benefit services to 37 organizations.
**Minister Responsible**, Hon. Dwain Lingenfelter
President, John Wright
Vice-President, Corporate Services, Don Axtell, 306/787-5841
Vice-President, Finance & Accounting Services, Patti Beatch, 306/787-9309
Vice-President, Human Resources, Bill Hyde, 306/787-1504
Vice-President, Projects, David Hughes, 306/787-5908
Director, Communications, John Miller, 306/787-9039

## Saskatchewan ECONOMIC & CO-OPERATIVE DEVELOPMENT

1919 Saskatchewan Dr., Regina SK S4P 3V7
306/787-2232; URL: http://www.gov.sk.ca/econdev/
The Business Line: 1-800-265-2001
Promotes & administers programs to develop & serve small business in the province. The department provides assistance & guidance to all stages of development & planning of cooperative enterprises & provides support services to new & existing enterprises. Provides financial assistance to the province's Regional Economic Development Authorities (REDAs), under which municipal governments, cooperatives, development organizations, communities & businesses can coordinate their professional, organizational & financial resources to develop new jobs & create investment.

### ACTS ADMINISTERED

Department of Economic Development Act, 1993
**Minister**, Hon. Janice MacKinnon, 306/787-4864, Fax: 306/787-9135
Deputy Minister, Clare Kirkland, 306/787-9580, Fax: 306/787-2159
Director, Communications Branch, Debbie Wilkie, 306/787-7982

### COOPERATIVES DIRECTORATE

Asst. Deputy Minister, Tom Marwick, 306/787-0192, Fax: 306/787-2198

### DIVERSIFICATION DIVISION

Asst. Deputy Minister, Vacant, 306/787-8178, Fax: 306/787-3989
Director, Development Services Branch, Lorne Bryden, 306/787-2227, Fax: 306/787-1620
Director, Market Development, Iain Hollier, 306/787-0927
Director, Sector Development, Bryce Baron, 306/787-2246

### POLICY & COORDINATION DIVISION

Acting Executive Director, Policy, Dave McQuinn, 306/787-7983
Director, Business Policy, Laverne Moskal, 306/787-9553

### PROGRAMS & CORPORATE SERVICES DIVISION

Asst. Deputy Minister, Janis Rathwell, 306/787-5775
Acting Director, Administrative Services, Donna Johnson, 306/787-1612
Director, Investment Programs, Denise Haas, 306/787-3524

### REGIONAL ECONOMIC DEVELOPMENT SERVICES DIVISION

306/787-1605; Fax: 306/787-1620
Asst. Deputy Minister, Special Projects, Brian Hansen, #206, 15 Innovation Pl., Saskatoon SK S7N 2X8, 306/933-7200, Fax: 306/933-8244

#### Regional Offices

Estevan: 1106 - 6 St., Estevan SK S4A 1A8 – 306/657-4505; Fax: 306/637-4510, Regional Manager, John Slatnik
Moose Jaw: 45 Thatcher Dr. East, Moose Jaw SK S6H 6V2 – 306/694-3623; Fax: 306/694-3500, Regional Manager, Grant McWilliams
North Battleford: 509 Pioneer Ave., North Battleford SK S9A 1E9 – 306/446-7444; Fax: 306/446-7442, Regional Manager, Jan Swanson
Prince Albert: 800 Central Ave., Prince Albert SK S6V 6G1 – 306/953-2775; Fax: 306/922-6499, Regional Manager, Wayne Phillip
Swift Current: 885 - 6 Ave. NE, Swift Current SK S9H 2M9 – 306/778-8415; Fax: 306/778-8526, Regional Manager, Doug Howorko
Yorkton: 38 - 5 Ave. North, Yorkton SK S3N 0Y8 – 306/786-1415; Fax: 306/786-1417, Regional Manager, Wayne Clarke

#### Outside Offices

Ottawa: #1306, 155 Queen St., Ottawa ON K1A 1K2 – 613/232-6544; Fax: 613/232-4472
New York: #2107, 630 - 5th Ave., New York NY 10111, U.S.A. – 212/969-9100; Fax: 212/969-9549

#### Associated Agencies, Boards & Commissions

•Saskatchewan Opportunities Corporation: Grenfell Tower, 1945 Hamilton St., 6th Fl., Regina SK S4P 3V7 – 306/787-8595; Fax: 306/787-8515; URL: http://www.gov.sk.ca/soco/
President, Zach Douglas
Vice-President, Moyez Somani
•Saskatchewan Tourism Authority (STA): #500, 1900 Albert St., Regina SK S4P 4L9 – 306/787-9600; Fax: 306/787-0715, Toll Free: 1-800-667-7191
CEO, Randall Williams, 306/787-2218
Vice President, Marketing & Programs, Stephen Pearce, 306/787-9575
Director, Administration, Neil Brotheridge, 306/787-1535
Director, Education & Training (Saskatchewan Tourism Education Council Division), Carol Lumb, 306/933-5905
Director, Membership & Visitor Services, Neil Sawatzky, 306/787-2320
•Saskatchewan Trade & Export Partnership (STEP): 1919 Saskatchewan Dr., Regina SK S4P 3V7 – 306/787-9210; Fax: 306/787-6666
Chairman & CEO, Milton Fair, 306/787-1550

## Saskatchewan EDUCATION

2220 College Ave., Regina SK S4P 3V7
306/787-2010; Fax: 306/787-1300; URL: http://www.sasked.gov.sk.ca

### ACTS ADMINISTERED

Education Act, 1995
League of Educational Administrators, Directors & Superintendents Act
Saskatchewan Association of School Business Officials Act
Teachers' Dental Plan Act
Teachers' Federation Act
Teachers' Life Insurance (Government Contributory) Act
Teachers' Superannuation & Disability Benefits Act
Teachers' 1990-91 Collective Agreement Implementation Act
**Minister**, Hon. Pat Atkinson, 306/787-7360, Fax: 306/787-0237
Deputy Minister, Craig Dotson, 306/787-7071
Executive Director, Teachers' Superannuation Commission, John McLaughlin, 1870 Albert St., 3rd Fl., Regina SK S4P 3V7, 306/787-9188, Fax: 306/787-1939

### EDUCATION DIVISION (K-12)

Asst. Deputy Minister, Ken Horsman, 306/787-6068
Executive Director, Communications Branch, Susan Hogarth, 306/787-5271
Executive Director, Curriculum & Instruction Branch, Margaret Lipp, 306/787-6032
Executive Director, Educational Services Branch, Ernie Cychmistruk, 306/787-5592
Executive Director, Finance & Operations Branch, Mae Boa, 306/787-6066
Executive Director, Human Resources Branch, Don Trew, 306/787-5654
Executive Director, Official Minority Language Office Branch, Rene Archambault, 306/787-6089
Executive Director, Planning & Evaluation Branch, Gillian McCreary, 306/787-5863
Director, Third Party Funding Unit, Michael Littlewood, 306/787-1185

## Office of the Chief ELECTORAL OFFICER

1702 Park St., Regina SK S4N 6B2
306/787-4000; Fax: 306/787-4052; Email: elecoff@sk.sympatico.ca
**Chief Electoral Officer**, Vacant
**Acting Chief Electoral Officer**, Jan Baker

## Saskatchewan ENERGY & MINES (SEM)

1914 Hamilton St., Regina SK S4P 4V4
306/787-2526; Fax: 306/787-7338; URL: http://www.gov.sk.ca/enermine/
Saskatchewan Energy Conservation: 1-800-668-4636

Provincial Department charged with the responsibility to achieve full & responsible development of Saskatchewan's energy & mineral resources. Delivers services & programs in a manner promoting job creation & developing economic activity in the Province. The department provides valuable revenues to fund government programs and services in all sectors. Produces, promotes, markets, and distributes information on Saskatchewan's resources to the resource industries and the general public.

#### ACTS ADMINISTERED

Crown Minerals Act, 1985
Department of Energy & Mines Act
Freehold Oil & Gas Production Tax Act
Mineral Resources Act, 1985
Mineral Taxation Act, 1983
Oil & Gas Conservation Act
Pipelines Act
Potash Resources Act
**Minister**, Hon. Eldon Lautermilch, 306/787-0605
Deputy Minister, Ray Clayton, 306/787-2496, Fax: 306/787-5718

#### FINANCE & ADMINISTRATION DIVISION

Asst. Deputy Minister, Donald Koop, 306/787-3624, Fax: 306/787-5718
Director, Communications, Marg Moran McQuinn, 306/787-2567, Fax: 306/787-2527
Acting Director, Mineral Revenue Branch, Hal Sanders, 306/787-2832
Director, Personnel & Administration Branch, Lynn Jacobson, 306/787-2525, Fax: 306/787-5718
Director, System Services Branch, Adeline Skwara, 306/787-2548, Fax: 306/787-2333
Supervisor, Accounts, Doug Koepke, 306/787-2505
Supervisor, Purchasing, Ron Robinson, 306/787-2545

#### EXPLORATION & GEOLOGICAL SERVICES DIVISION

Executive Director, George Patterson, 306/787-2560, Fax: 306/787-2488
Director, Northern Survey Branch, Dr. T.I.I. Sibbald, 306/787-2568, Fax: 306/787-2488
Director, Petroleum Geology Branch, Dr. D.F. Paterson, 201 Dewdney Ave. East, Regina SK S4N 4G3, 306/787-2625, Fax: 306/787-4608
Director, Sedimentary Geodata Branch, Paul Guilov, 306/787-2583, Fax: 306/787-2488
Supervisor & Geological Editor, Support Services, Dr. Charlie T. Harper, 306/787-2578, Fax: 306/787-2488

#### PETROLEUM & NATURAL GAS DIVISION

Fax: 306/787-2478
Executive Director, Bruce W. Wilson, 306/787-2591
Director, Economic & Fiscal Analysis Branch, Dale Fletcher, 306/787-2605
Director, Engineering Services Branch, Myron Sereda, 306/787-2318
Director, Geology & Petroleum Lands Branch, Gordon Hutch, 306/787-2606
Director, Petroleum Development Branch, Brian Mathieson, 306/787-2593
Director, Petroleum Statistics Branch, Joe Dang, 306/787-2607, Fax: 306/787-8236

#### RESOURCE POLICY & ECONOMICS DIVISION

Asst. Deputy Minister, Dan McFadyen, 306/787-2523, Fax: 306/787-5718
Director, Energy Development Branch, Malcolm Wilson, 306/787-2618, Fax: 306/787-2333
Director, Energy Economics Branch, Trevor Dark, 306/787-2469, Fax: 306/787-2333
Director, Industrial Minerals Branch, Maurice Hall, 306/787-2521, Fax: 306/787-2333
Director, Metallic Minerals Branch, Jane Forster, 306/787-2501, Fax: 306/787-2333

## Saskatchewan ENVIRONMENT & RESOURCE MANAGEMENT

3211 Albert St., Regina SK S4S 5W6
306/787-2700; Fax: 306/787-3941; URL: http://www.gov.sk.ca/govt/environ/
Toll Free: 1-800-667-2757
Environment Resource Network: 1-800-567-4224
Provincial Forest Fires: 1-800-667-9660
Saskatchewan provincial department responsible for the following:
• manages, protects & enhances the province's natural & environmental resources;
• monitors & regulates mining & milling operations & the reclamation & decommissioning of mine sites;
• administers resource conservation services, enforces resource & environmental legislation;
• manages parks & recreation areas;
• maintains & constructs facilities & assists in forest fire management;
• maintains a database of forest resources;
• allocates & manages Crown lands & integrated land resource management &;
• monitors industrial & municipal waste & landfill sites.

#### ACTS ADMINISTERED

Clean Air Act
Conservation Easements Act
Ecological Reserves Act
Environmental Management & Protection Act (subject to OC 518/87)
Fisheries Act (Saskatchewan), 1994
Forest Act
Forest Resources Management Act
Grasslands National Park Act
Litter Control Act
Natural Resources Act
Ozone-depleting Substances Control Act
Parks Act
Prairie & Forest Fires Act
Provincial Lands Act
Regional Parks Act
Renewable Resources, Recreation & Culture Act (subject to OC 177/93)
Sale or Lease of Certain Lands Act
State of the Environment Report Act
Water Appeal Board Act
Wildlife Act
Wildlife Habitat Protection Act
**Minister**, Hon. Lorne Scott, Fax: 306/787-0395
Deputy Minister, Stuart Kramer, 306/787-2930, Fax: 306/787-2947, Email: stuart.kramer.erm@govmail.gov.sk.ca
Executive Director, Environmental Assessment Branch, Ron Zukowsky, 306/787-6132, Fax: 306/787-0930, Email: zukowsky.ron@sasknet.sk.ca
Director, Communication Services Branch, Jocelyn Souliere, 306/787-9637, Fax: 306/787-3941, Email: jocelyn.s@sasknet.sk.ca

#### CORPORATE SERVICES DIVISION

Executive Director, Shelly Vandermey, 306/787-5482, Fax: 306/787-2947, Email: vanderme@mailhost.sasktel.sk.ca
Director, Information Management Branch, Vacant, 306/787-3194, Fax: 306/787-3913
Director, Service Bureaus, Donna Kellsey, 306/787-6121, Fax: 306/787-8441, Email: donna.kellsey.erm@govmail.gov.sk.ca

#### OPERATIONS DIVISION

Asst. Deputy Minister, Ross MacLennan, 306/787-9079, Fax: 306/787-0219, EMail ross.maclennan.erm@govmail.gov.sk.ca
Director, Enforcement & Compliance, Dave Harvey, 306/953-2993, Fax: 306/953-2502, Email: enf@sasknet.sk.ca
Director, Forest Fire Management, Gus MacAuley, 306/953-2206, Fax: 306/953-2502
Director, Parks & Facilities, Don MacAulay, 306/787-2846, Fax: 306/787-7000, Email: don.macaulay.erm@govmail.gov.sk.ca
Director, Regional Services, Dave Phillips, 306/787-9117, Fax: 306/787-0598

#### POLICY & PROGRAMS DIVISION

Assoc. Deputy Minister, Les Cooke, 306/787-5419, Fax: 306/787-2947, Email: les.cooke@sasknet.sk.ca
Director, Environmental Protection Branch, Bob Ruggles, 306/787-6178, Fax: 306/787-0197, Email: bob.ruggles.erm@govmail.gov.sk.ca
Director, Fish & Wildlife Branch, Dennis Sherratt, 306/787-2309, Fax: 306/787-9544, Email: dennis.sherratt.erm@govmail.gov.sk.ca
Acting Director, Fisheries Branch, Ed Dean, 306/787-2884, Fax: 306/787-0737, Email: ed.dean.erm@govmail.gov.sk.ca
Director, Forestry Ecosystems, Allan Willcocks, 306/953-2486, Fax: 306/953-2360
Acting Director, Policy & Legislation Branch, Ross Barclay, 306/787-7034, Fax: 306/787-0024
Director, Sustainable Land Management, Doug Mazur, 306/787-7024, Fax: 306/787-1349, Email: doug.mazur.erm@govmail.gov.sk.ca
Senior Manager, Ecosystem Management, Lynda Langford, 306/787-6868, Fax: 306/787-0024
Senior Manager, Integrated Water Management Strategy, Ed Dean, 306/787-7812, Fax: 306/787-0737, Email: ed.dean.erm@govmail.gov.sk.ca
Senior Manager, Public Involvement & Aboriginal Affairs, Joe Muldoon, 306/787-7803, Fax: 306/787-0024
Senior Manager, Sustainable Economic Development, Hugh Hunt, 306/787-7572, Fax: 306/787-0024

#### Associated Agencies, Boards & Commissions

•Saskatchewan Conservation Data Centre: #326, 3211 Albert St., Regina SK S4S 5W6 – 306/787-5021; Fax: 306/787-1349
Contact, Marlon Killaby
•Saskatchewan Wetland Conservation Corporation: #202, 2050 Cornwall St., Regina SK S4P 2K5 – 306/787-0726; Fax: 306/787-0780; URL: http://www.wetland.sk.ca/
General Manager, Bob Carles
•Wascana Centre Authority: 2900 Wascana Dr., PO Box 7111, Regina SK S4P 3S7 – 306/522-3661; Fax: 306/565-2742
Park Naturalist, Robert Ewart

## Saskatchewan FINANCE

2350 Albert St., Regina SK S4P 4A6
306/787-6768; Fax: 306/787-6544; URL: http://www.gov.sk.ca/govt/finance/

#### ACTS ADMINISTERED

Balanced Budget Act
Certified General Accountants Act, 1994
Chartered Accountants Act, 1986
Cooperation Income Tax Collection Agreement Act, 1947
Corporation Capital Tax Act
Crown Foundations Act
Crown Foundations for District Health Boards Act
Education & Health Tax Act
Estate Tax Rebate Act, 1969
Estate Tax Rebates Reciprocal Arrangements Act, 1970
Federal-Provincial Agreements Act
Financial Administration Act
Fuel Tax Act, 1987
Gift Tax Act, 1972
Home Energy Loan Act
Hospital Revenue Act (jointly with Saskatchewan Health)
Income Tax Act

Insurance Premiums Tax Act
Labour-sponsored Venture Capital Corporations Act
Liquor Consumption Tax Act
Management Accountants Act
Members of the Legislative Assembly Superannuation Act, 1979
Mortgage Interest Reduction Act
Mortgage Protection Act
Motor Vehicle Insurance Premiums Tax Act
Municipal Employees' Superannuation Act
Municipal Financing Corporation Act
Pioneer Trust Company Depositors Assistance Act
Provincial Auditor Act
Public Employees Pension Plan Act
Public Service Superannuation Act
Revenue & Financial Services Act
Saskatchewan Development Fund Act
Saskatchewan Pension Annuity Fund Act
Saskatchewan Pension Plan Act
Statistics Act
Stock Savings Tax Credit Act
Superannuation (Supplementary Provisions) Act
Tobacco Tax Act

**Minister**, Hon. Eric Cline, 306/787-6060, Fax: 306/787-6055

Deputy Minister, Bill Jones, 306/787-6621, Fax: 306/787-7155

Provincial Comptroller, Terry Paton, 306/787-9254, Fax: 306/787-9720

Executive Director, Public Employees Benefits Agency, Brian L. Smith, 306/787-6757, Fax: 306/787-0244

General Manager, Saskatchewan Pension Plan, Kathy Strutt, 306/463-5412, Fax: 306/463-3500

#### ADMINISTRATION DIVISION

Executive Director, Bill Van Sickle, 306/787-6530

Director, Financial Services Branch, Bill Hoover, 306/787-6529

Director, Human Resources Branch, Jim Graham, 306/787-6535

Manager, Administrative Services Branch, Cathy O'Byrne, 306/787-6532, Fax: 306/787-6576

Manager, System Support Branch, Jennifer Hogan, 306/787-7692

#### BUDGET ANALYSIS DIVISION

Asst. Deputy Minister, Economic & Fiscal Policy Branch, Jim Marshall, 306/787-6724

Asst. Deputy Minister, Taxation & Intergovernmental Affairs Branch, Kirk McGregor, 306/787-6731

Executive Director, Treasury Board Branch, Larry Spannier, 306/787-6780, Fax: 306/787-3482

Director, Bureau of Statistics, Ron McMahon, 306/787-6328

Director, Intergovernmental Affairs, Glen Veikle, 306/787-6735

Director, Planning, Joel Prager, 306/787-6626

Senior Economist, Economics, Fred Young, 306/787-6792

Manager, Fiscal Policy, Joanne Brockman, 306/787-6743

#### REVENUE DIVISION

Asst. Deputy Minister, Len Rog, 306/787-6685, Fax: 306/787-0241

#### TREASURY & DEBT MANAGEMENT DIVISION

Asst. Deputy Minister & Registrar, Securities, Sheldon Schwartz, 306/787-6751, Fax: 306/787-8493

Executive Director, Capital Markets Branch, Rae Haverstock, 306/787-6773

Executive Director, Cash & Debt Management Branch, Dennis Polowyk, 306/787-3923

Executive Director, Investment & Liability Management Branch, Vacant, 306/787-9474

##### Associated Agencies, Boards & Commissions

•Board of Revenue Commissioners: #480, 2151 Scarth St., Regina SK S4P 3V7 – 306/787-6227

Chair, B.G. McNamee

Secretary, Marilyn Turanich

•Saskatchewan Development Fund Corporation: #300, 2400 College Ave., Regina SK S4P 1C8 – 306/787-1645; Fax: 306/787-8125

Chair, Ed Tchorzewski

General Manager, Don Axtel

## Saskatchewan HEALTH

3475 Albert St., Regina SK S4S 6X6
306/787-8332; Fax: 306/787-8310; URL: http://www.gov.sk.ca/govt/health/

#### ACTS ADMINISTERED

Abandoned Refrigerator Act
Ambulance Act
Anatomy Act
Change of Name Act
Dental Care Act
Department of Health Act
Health Districts Act
Health Services Utilization & Research Commission Act
Health Statutes Amendment Act, 1993
Hearing Aid Act
Home Care Act
Hospital Revenue Act
Hospital Standards Act
Housing & Special-care Homes Act
Medical & Hospitalization Tax Repeal Act
Medical Laboratory Licensing Act
Medical Scholarships & Bursaries Act
Mental Health Services Act
Mutual Medical & Hospital Benefit Associations Act
Personal Care Homes Act
Prescription Drugs Act
Public Health Act
Saskatchewan Hospitalization Act
Saskatchewan Medical Care Insurance Act
Union Hospital Act
Venereal Disease Prevention Act
Vital Statistics Act

**Acts in which Saskatchewan Health has a Direct Interest**

Cancer Foundation Act
Chiropody Profession Act
Chiropractic Act, 1994
Community Health Unit Act
Dental Professions Act
Dental Technicians Act
Dental Therapists Act
Denturists Act
Emergency Medical Aid Act
Human Tissue Gift Act
Licensed Practical Nurses Act
Lloydminster Hospital Act, 1948
Medical Care Insurance Supplementary Provisions Act
Medical Profession Act, 1981
Medical Radiation Technologists Act
Medical Scholarships & Bursaries Act
Naturopathy Act
Opthalmic Dispensers Act
Optometry Act, 1985
Osteopathic Practice Act
Pharmacy Act
Physical Therapists Act, 1984
Professional Dietitians Act
Registered Psychiatric Nurses Act
Registered Nurses Act, 1988
Registered Occupational Therapists Act
Registered Psychologists Act
Residential Services Act
Saskatchewan Embalmers Act
Speech Language Pathologists & Audiologists Act
White Cane Act

**Minister**, Hon. Clay Serby, 306/787-7345, Fax: 306/787-8677

Deputy Minister, N. Duane Adams, 306/787-3041, Fax: 306/787-4533

#### INSURED SERVICES DIVISION

Responsible for the issuance of provincial birth, marriage & death certificates. Fee for each certificate is $15.00.

Associate Deputy Minister, Glenda Yeates, 416/787-4695

Executive Director, Medical Care Insurance Branch, Lawrence Krahn, 306/787-3423, Fax: 306/787-3761

Executive Director, Prescription Drug Services Branch, Barb Shea, 306/787-3301, Fax: 306/787-8679

Executive Director, Provincial Laboratory Services, George Peters, 306/787-3629, Fax: 306/787-3112

Director, Vital Statistics & Health Insurance Registration Branch, Ronn Wallace, 1919 Rose St., Regina SK S4P 3V7, 306/787-1167

#### INTEGRATED HEALTH SERVICES DIVISION

Associate Deputy Minister, Steve Petz, 306/787-4595

Executive Director, District Support Branch, Lois Borden, 306/787-3359

Executive Director, Programs Branch, Danni Boyd, 306/787-6092

Director, Capital & Special Policy Unit, Jim Simmons, 306/787-3235

Service Area Coordinator, Dr. Gary Bell, 306/787-3325

#### INTERNATIONAL DIVISION

Vice-President, Cy Scheske, 306/787-8339

Executive Director, Communications & Public Information Branch, Mark Seland, 306/787-3825

Executive Director, Finance & Management Services Branch, Kathy Langlois, 306/787-3051

Executive Director, Human Resources & Fee Negotiations Branch, Kelly Kummerfield, 306/787-3070

#### STRATEGIC SERVICES DIVISION

Senior Associate Deputy Minister, Lorraine Hill, 306/787-3047

Asst. to the Senior Associate Deputy Minister, Dale Bloom, 306/787-3088

Provincial Epidemiologist, Dr. William Osei, 306/787-1580

Executive Director, Corporate Information & Technology Branch, Neil R. Gardner, 306/787-3043, Fax: 306/787-7589

Executive Director, Health Planning & Policy Development Branch, Maureen Yeske, 306/787-3144

Executive Director, Northern Health Services, Kathy Chisholm, 306/425-4517

Executive Director, Provincial Information Network, Bill Morton, 306/787-4635

Executive Director, Strategic Programs Branch, Carol Klassen, 306/787-3200, Fax: 306/787-6113

Director, Wellness & Health Promotion Branch, Pat Bell, 306/787-3083

##### Associated Agencies, Boards & Commissions

•Provincial Health Council: Faculty of Physical Activity Studies, University of Regina, #100, 3737 Wascana Pkwy., Regina SK S4S 0A2 – 306/585-4876; Fax: 306/585-4854

Chair, Ralph Nilson

•Saskatchewan Health Services Utilization & Research Commission: PO Box 46, Stn 41, Saskatoon SK S7N 0X0 – 306/966-1500; Fax: 306/966-1462

## Saskatchewan HIGHWAYS & TRANSPORTATION

1855 Victoria Ave., Regina SK S4P 3V5
306/787-4804; Fax: 306/787-9777; URL: http://www.gov.sk.ca/govt/highways/

#### ACTS ADMINISTERED

Dangerous Goods Transportation Act
Department of Highways & Transportation Act
Engineering Profession Act
Highways & Transportation Act
Railway Act
Sand & Gravel Act

**Minister**, Hon. Judy Bradley, 306/787-6447, Fax: 306/787-6499
Deputy Minister, Brian King, 306/787-4950, Email: brian.king.hi0@govmail.gov.sk.ca
Director, Communications & Public Relations, Mike Woods, 306/787-4804, Email: mike.woods.hi0@govmail.gov.sk.ca
Director, Human Resources, Dave Atkinson, 306/787-4757, Email: dave.atkinson.hi0@govmail.gov.sk.ca
Senior Supervisor, Public Relations, John Charlton, 306/787-4805

#### CORPORATE INFORMATION SERVICES DIVISION

Executive Director, Lynn Tullock, 306/787-4734
Director, Geographic Information Services, Roy Chursinoff, 306/787-4857
Director, Property Services, Jeff Grigg, 306/787-4885

#### ENGINEERING SERVICES

Executive Director, Barry Martin, 306/787-4859

#### LOGISTICS, PLANNING & COMPLIANCE DIVISION

Executive Director, Bernie Churko, 306/787-4866, Email: bernie.churko.hi0@govmail.gov.sk.ca
Director, Business Support, Greg Gilks, 306/787-4851
Director, Compliance, Peter Hurst, 306/787-4072
Director, Grain & Rail Logistics, Harold Hugg, 306/787-5311
Director, Project Management Team, Mike Hossack, 306/787-4776

## Saskatchewan INDIAN & METIS AFFAIRS SECRETARIAT

2151 Scarth St., 4th Fl., Regina SK S4P 3V7
306/787-6250; Fax: 306/787-6336; URL: http://www.gov.sk.ca/govt/indmet/

#### ACTS ADMINISTERED

Government Organization Act
Indian & Native Affairs Secretariat Act

**Minister Responsible**, Hon. Joanne Crofford, 306/787-2207, Fax: 306/787-2202
Acting Secretary, Ernie Lawton, 306/787-5738
Asst. Deputy Minister, Indian Affairs Branch, Vacant, 306/787-5738
Asst. Deputy Minister, Metis Affairs Branch, Donovan Young, 306/787-6253
Executive Director, Indian Lands & Resources, Glen Benedict, 306/787-6681
Executive Director, Planning, John Reid, 306/787-6678
Manager, Aboriginal Employment Development, Vacant, 306/787-5176
Senior Policy Analyst, Mary Tkach, 306/787-5725
Senior Policy Analyst, Indian Affairs Branch, Loree Buchanan, 306/787-2634
Senior Policy Analyst, Indian Lands & Resources, Kay Lerat, 306/787-2634
Senior Policy Analyst, Treaty Land Entitlement, Archana Jaiswal, 306/787-0064
Senior Advisor, Inter-Jurisdictional Affairs, John Hill, 306/787-5752
Policy Analyst, Metis Affairs Branch, Doreen Bradshaw, 306/787-6265
Policy Analyst, Metis Affairs Branch, Giselle Marcotte, 306/787-0098
Policy Analyst, Treaty Land Entitlement, Ross Burrows, 306/787-5752
Policy Analyst, Treaty Land Entitlement, Susan Shalapata, 306/787-9706
Contact, Policy & Communication, Rob Cunningham, 306/787-6683

## INFORMATION & PRIVACY COMMISSIONER OF SASKATCHEWAN

#500, 2220 - 12 Ave., Regina SK S4P 0M8
306/787-8350; Fax: 306/757-4858
**Commissioner**, Derril McLeod, Q.C.
Secretary, Elizabeth Susa

## Saskatchewan Government INSURANCE (SGI)

2260 - 11 Ave., Regina SK S4P 0J9
306/751-1200; Fax: 306/787-7477
**Minister Responsible**, Hon. Clay Serby, 306/787-7387
President, Larry Fogg
Vice-President, Auto Fund, Alan Cookman
Vice-President, Claims, Earl Cameron
Vice-President, Finance & Administration, John Dobie
Vice-President, Systems, Margaret Anderson
Vice-President, Underwriting, Randy Heise
Manager, Driver Licensing, Bill McCallum
Manager, Vehicle Standards & Inspection, Brian Kline
Secretary to the President, Elsie E. Beshara, 306/751-1683

## Saskatchewan INTERGOVERNMENTAL AFFAIRS

1919 Saskatchewan Dr., Regina SK S4P 3V7
306/787-1643; Fax: 306/787-1987; URL: http://www.gov.sk.ca/govt/intergov/
**Minister**, Hon. Bernhard Wiens
Deputy Minister, Gregory Marchildon, 306/787-1925
Chief, Protocol Office, Michael Jackson, 306/787-3109, Fax: 306/787-1269
General Manager, Information Technology & Telecommunications, Vacant, 306/787-8276, Fax: 306/787-8577
Acting Director, Constitutional Relations, Ian Peach, 306/787-8006
Director, Federal/Provincial Affairs, Alan Hilton, 306/787-7962
Director, Office of French Language Coordination, Vacant, 306/787-2028, Fax: 306/787-6352

## Saskatchewan JUSTICE

1874 Scarth St., Regina SK S4P 3V7
306/787-7872 (Communications); Fax: 306/787-3874; URL: http://www.gov.sk.ca/govt/justice/

#### ACTS ADMINISTERED

##### Justice Related Acts

Aboriginal Courtworkers Commission Act
Absconding Debtors Act
Absentee Act
Age of Majority Act
Agreements of Sale Cancellation Act
Agricultural Leaseholds Act
Arbitration Act, 1992
Assignment of Wages Act
Attachment of Debts Act
Builders' Lien Act
Canada-United Kingdom Judgments Enforcement Act
Canadian Institute of Management (Saskatchewan Division) Act
Children's Law Act
Choses in Action Act
Closing-out Sales Act
Commissioners for Oaths Act
Condominium Property Act, 1993
Constitutional Questions Act
Contributory Negligence Act
Coroners Act
Correctional Services Act
Court Officials Act, 1984
Court of Appeal Act
Creditors' Relief Act
Crown Administration of Estates Act
Crown Employment Contracts Act
Crown Suits (Costs) Act
Department of Justice Act
Dependants' Relief Act, 1996
Dependent Adults Act
Devolution of Real Property Act
Distress Act
Enforcement of Foreign Arbitral Awards Act
Enforcement of Maintenance Orders Act
Equality of Status of Married Persons Act
Escheats Act
Executions Act
Exemptions Act
Expropriation Procedures Act
Factors Act
Family Maintenance Act
Fatal Accidents Act
Federal Courts Act
Foreign Judgements Act
Fraudulent Preferences Act
Freedom of Information & Protection of Privacy Act
Frustrated Contracts Act
Garage Keepers Act
Homesteads Act, 1989
Hotel Keepers Act
Improvements under Mistake of Title Act
International Child Abduction Act, 1996
International Commercial Arbitration Act
International Sale of Goods Act
Interpretation Act, 1995
Interprovincial Subpoena Act
Intestate Succession Act, 1996
Judgments Extension Act
Judges' Orders Enforcement Act
Jury Act, 1981
Justice of the Peace Act, 1988
Land Contracts (Actions) Act
Land Titles Act
Landlord & Tenant Act
Language Act
Law Reform Commission Act
Laws Declaratory Act
Legal Aid Act
Legal Profession Act, 1990
Libel & Slander Act
Limitation of Actions Act
Limitation of Civil Rights Act
Local Authority Freedom of Information & Protection of Privacy Act
Lord's Day (Saskatchewan) Act
Marriage Act, 1995
Marriage Settlement Act
Matrimonial Property Act
Mechanics' Lien Act
Member Conflict of Interest Act
Mentally Disordered Persons Act
Minors Tobacco Act
Notaries Public Act
Ombudsman & Children's Advocate Act
Parents' Maintenance Act
Partnership Act
Penalties & Forfeitures Act
Pension Benefits Act, 1992
Personal Property Security Act, 1993
Police Act, 1990
Powers of Attorney Act, 1996
Pre-judgement Interest Act

Privacy Act
Private Investigators & Security Guards Act
Proceedings Against the Crown Act
Provincial Court Act
Provincial Mediation Board Act
Public Inquiries Act
Public Officers' Protection Act
Public Trustee Act
Public Utilities Easements Act
Queen's Bench Act
Queen's Counsel Act
Queen's Printer's Act
Reciprocal Enforcement of Judgments Act, 1996
Reciprocal Enforcement of Maintenance Orders Act, 1993 & 1996
Recording of Evidence by Sound Recording Machine Act
Recovery of Possession of Land Act
Referendum & Plebiscite Act
Regulations Act, 1989
Residential Tenancies Act
Revised Statutes Act, 1979
Sale of Goods Act
Sales on Consignment Act
Saskatchewan Evidence Act
Saskatchewan Farm Security Act
Saskatchewan Human Rights Code
Saskatchewan Insurance Act
Securities Act, 1988
Slot Machine Act
Small Claims Act
Summary Offences Procedure Act, 1990
Surface Rights Acquisition & Compensation Act
Survival of Actions Act
Survivorship Act, 1993
Tabling of Documents Act, 1991
Thresher Employees Act
Thresher's Lien Act
Trading Stamp Act
Traffic Safety Council of Saskatchewan Act, 1988
Trustee Act
Trusts Convention Implementation Act
Unconscionable Transactions Relief Act
Variation of Trusts Act
Victims of Crime Act, 1995
Victims of Domestic Violence Act
Warehousemen's Lien Act
Wills Act
Wills Act, 1996
Woodmen's Lien Act

**Consumer Related Acts**

Agricultural Implements Act
Auctioneers Act
Business Corporations Act
Business Names Registration Act
Cemeteries Act
Collection Agents Act
Companies Act
Companies Winding Up Act
Consumer & Commercial Affairs Act
Cooperatives Act, 1989 (except Part XIX)
Cost of Credit Disclosure Act
Credit Reporting Agencies Act
Credit Union Act, 1985 (except Part XVIII)
Direct Sellers Act
Family Farm Credit Act
Film & Video Classification Act
Guarantee Companies Securities Act
Home Owners' Protection Act
Mortgage Brokers Act
Motor Dealers Act
Municipal Hail Insurance Act
Names of Homes Act
Non-profit Corporations Act, 1995
Partnership Act
Prepaid Funeral Services Act
Pyramid Franchises Act
Real Estate Act
Religious Societies Land Act
Sale of Training Courses Act
Saskatchewan Embalmers Act
Saskatchewan Insurance Act
Trust & Loan Corporations Act

**Minister & Attorney General**, Hon. John T. Nilson, Q.C., 306/787-0613
Deputy Minister & Deputy Attorney General, John Whyte, Q.C., 306/787-5351
Assoc. Deputy Minister, Finance & Administration, Keith Laxdal, 306/787-7869
Registrar of Licensing & Investigations, Consumer Protection Branch, Al Dwyer, 306/787-2952, Fax: 306/787-5550
Deputy Registrar, Consumer Protection Branch, Larry Wilson, 306/787-5712
Superintendent, Insurance & Registrar, Credit Unions, J.M. Hall, 306/787-7881, Fax: 306/787-9779
Deputy Superintendent, Insurance & Deputy Registrar, Credit Unions, Linda Zarzeczny, 306/787-2958, Fax: 306/787-9779
Superintendent, Pensions, Dave Wild, 306/787-2458, Fax: 306/787-9779
Director, Administrative Services Branch, Elizabeth Smith, 306/787-5472
Director, Communications, Lisa Ann Wood, 306/787-7872
Director, Human Resources, Barry Sockett, 306/787-5475, Fax: 306/787-2084

**For list of Courts & other Legal Officers, including Judicial Officials & Judges *see* Section 10 of this book.**

### CIVIL LAW DIVISION

Executive Director, Darryl Bogdasavich, Q.C., 306/787-6602, Fax: 306/787-0581

### COMMUNITY JUSTICE DIVISION

Fax: 306/787-9111
Executive Director, Doug Moen, Q.C., 306/787-5360
Chief, Provincial Firearms Office, Mitch Crumley, 306/787-9713
Chief Coroner, Coroner's Branch, Dr. John Nyssen, 306/787-5541
Executive Director, Law Enforcement Services & Executive Director, Saskatchewan Police Commission, John Baker, 306/787-0400, Fax: 306/787-8084
Director, Community Services Branch, Jan Turner, 306/787-5112, Fax: 306/787-3874
Director, Victims Services, Katrine McKenzie, 306/787-0418, Fax: 306/787-0081

### CORRECTIONS DIVISION

Fax: 306/787-8084
Executive Director, Dick Till, 306/787-3573
Director, Regina Correctional Centre, Robert Smerchinski, PO Box 617, Regina SK S4P 3A6, 306/924-9022

### PUBLIC LAW & POLICY DIVISION

Fax: 306/787-9111
Executive Director, Doug Moen, Q.C., 306/787-5360
Chief Crown Counsel, Legislative Drafting, Ian Brown, 306/787-9346
Director, Constitutional Law Branch, Graeme Mitchell, 306/787-8385
Director, Legislative Services Branch, Susan Amrud, 306/787-8990
Director, Policy, Planning & Evaluation Branch, Betty Ann Pottruff, Q.C., 306/787-8954
Director, Victims Services, Katrine Macaulay, 306/787-0418
Manager, Queen's Printer, Marilyn Lustig-McEwen, 306/787-9345
Asst. Chief, Provincial Firearms Office, Alan Terry

### PUBLIC PROSECUTIONS DIVISION

Executive Director, C. Richard Quinney, Q.C., 306/787-5490

### REGISTRY SERVICES DIVISION

Asst. Deputy Minister, Ron Hewitt, Q.C., 306/787-5333, Fax: 306/787-8737
Executive Director, Court Services, Barb Hookenson, 306/787-5680, Fax: 306/787-8737
Executive Director, Property Registration Branch, Beverley Bradshaw, 306/787-5504, Fax: 306/787-8737
Public Trustee, Public Trustees' Office, Ron Kruzeniski, Q.C., 306/787-5427
Director, Corporations Branch, Phil Flory, 306/787-2970, Fax: 306/787-8999
Director, Maintenance Enforcement Office, Lionel McNabb, 306/787-1650, Fax: 306/787-1420
Director, Mediation Services, Ken W. Acton, 306/787-5749, Fax: 306/787-0088

**Associated Agencies, Boards & Commissions**

•Agricultural Implements Board: 1871 Smith St., Regina SK S4P 3V7 – 306/787-3550; Fax: 306/787-9779
•Law Reform Commission of Saskatchewan: c/o University of Saskatchewan, College of Law, Saskatoon SK S7N 0W0 – 306/966-2699; Fax: 306/966-5574
Director, Research, K.P.R. Hodges
Legal Research Officer, M.J.W. Finley
•Provincial Mediation Board/Office of the Rentalsman: 2103 - 11 Ave., 5th Fl., Regina SK S4P 3V7 – 306/787-2699; Fax: 306/787-5574
Chair, Terry Chin
•Public & Private Rights Board: 2151 Scarth St., Regina SK S4P 3V7 – 306/787-4071; Fax: 306/787-0088
Chair, Kenneth W. Acton
•Saskatchewan Farm Land Security Board: #207, 3988 Albert St., Regina SK S4S 3R1 – 306/787-5147; Fax: 306/787-8599
Chair, George Lee
General Manager, Dan Patterson
Farm Foreclosure Section, Jim Chernick
Home Quarter Protection, Dick Wellman
•Saskatchewan Farm Security Programs: 122 - 3 Ave. North, Saskatoon SK S7K 2H6 – 306/933-5105; Fax: 306/933-5009
General Manager, Dan Patterson
•Saskatchewan Farm Tenure Arbitration Board: 1871 Smith St., Regina SK SHP 3V7 – 306/787-2101
Manager, Melissa Wallace
•Saskatchewan Film Classification Board: 1871 Smith St., Regina SK S4P 3V7 – 306/787-5884; Fax: 306/787-9779
Chair, Elizabeth Pederson
•Saskatchewan Film Classification Appeal Commission: 1871 Smith St., Regina SK S4P 3V7 – 306/787-5884; Fax: 306/787-9779
Chair, Betsy Bury
•Saskatchewan Human Rights Commission: 122 - 3 Ave. North, 8th Fl., Saskatoon SK S7K 2H6 – 306/933-5952; Fax: 306/933-7863; URL: http://www.gov.sk.ca/govt/hrc/
Chief Commissioner, Donna Scott
Executive Director, Donalda Ford
•Saskatchewan Police Commission: 1874 Scarth St., 7th Fl., Regina SK S4P 3V7 – 306/787-6534
Director, Tom Savage
•Saskatchewan Police Complaints Investigator: 2151 Scarth St., 3rd Fl., Regina SK S4P 3V7 – 306/787-6519; Fax: 306/787-6528
Investigator, Elton Gritzfeld, Q.C.
Director, Gary Treble
•Saskatchewan Securities Commission: Toronto Dominion Bank Bldg., 1920 Broad St., 8th Fl.,

Regina SK S4P 3V7 – 306/787-5645; Fax: 306/787-5899
Chair, Marcel de la Gorgendière, Q.C., 306/787-5630
Vice-Chair, Arthur T. Wakabayashi, 3234 Mountbatten Cres., Regina SK S4V 0Z4
Director, Barbara L. Shourounis, 306/787-5842
Deputy Director, Corporate Finance, Ian McIntosh, 306/787-5867
Deputy Director, Enforcement, Vic Pankratz, 306/787-5850
Deputy Director, Legal, Dean Murrison, 306/787-5879
Acting Deputy Director, Registration, Terry Ford, 306/787-5876
•Saskatoon Child Centre: c/o Saskatchewan Justice, 1874 Scarth St., Regina SK S4P 3V7 – 306/975-8250
A new innovative facility which provides an integrated, coordinated response to child abuse.
Chair, Norm Doell
•Surface Rights Board of Arbitration: 113 - 2 Ave., PO Box 1597, Kindersley SK S0L 1S0 – 306/463-5447; Fax: 306/463-5449
Chair, Richard Gibbons

## Saskatchewan LABOUR

1870 Albert St., Regina SK S4P 3V7
306/787-4496; Fax: 306/787-2208; URL: http://www.gov.sk.ca/govt/labour/
TDD: 306/787-2429

#### ACTS ADMINISTERED

Building Trades Protection Act
Construction Industry Labour Relations Act, 1992
Employment Agencies Act
Fire Departments Platoon Act
Human Resources, Labour and Employment Act
Labour-Management Disputes (Temporary Provisions) Act
Labour Standards Act
Occupational Health and Safety Act, 1993
Radiation Health and Safety Act, 1985
Trade Union Act
Victims of Workplace Injuries Day of Mourning Act
Wages Recovery Act
**Minister**, Hon. Robert W. Mitchell, Q.C., 306/787-6662, Fax: 306/787-6946
Deputy Minister, Sandra Morgan, 306/787-2399, Fax: 306/787-2315
Special Advisor, Ted Boyle, 306/787-4156
Asst. Deputy Minister, Cheryl Hanson, 306/787-8414

#### LABOUR RELATIONS, MEDIATION & CONCILIATION SERVICES DIVISION

Executive Director, Terry Stevens, 306/787-5050, Fax: 306/787-5804

#### LABOUR SERVICES DIVISION

Executive Director, Graham Mitchell, 306/787-2471, Fax: 306/787-4780

#### LABOUR SUPPORT DIVISION

Executive Director, Vacant, Fax: 306/787-7229
Director, Human Resources & Administrative Services, Dawn McKibben, Fax: 306/787-4038
Director, Planning Policy & Communications, John Boyd, 306/787-3370
Acting Manager, Budget & Operations, S. Little, 306/787-4527, Fax: 306/787-1064

#### OCCUPATIONAL HEALTH & SAFETY DIVISION

Toll Free: 1-800-567-7233 (Saskatchewan)
Executive Director, Jeff Parr, Email: sklab2@sasknet.sk.ca
Director, Safety Services, F. Kelada, 306/787-4485
Manager, Hygiene, Risk Assessment & Standards Services, Herb Wooley, 306/787-4506
Acting Manager, Mine & Radiation Safety, Ernie Becker, 306/787-5055
Manager, Workplace Safety, Bob Ross, 306/787-4134
Acting Manager, Workplace Safety, Norm Fengstad

#### Associated Agencies, Boards & Commissions

•Labour Relations Board: 1914 Hamilton St., Regina SK S4P 4V4 – 306/787-2406; Fax: 306/787-2664
Chair, Beth Bilson
Vice-Chair, Gwen Gray
•Minimum Wage Board: 1870 Albert St., Regina SK S4P 3V7 – 306/787-2474; Fax: 306/787-4780
Chair, Murray Cheyne
•Office of the Worker's Advocate: 1870 Albert St., Regina SK S4P 3V7 – 306/787-2456
Acting Director, Wendy Dean
•Saskatchewan Workers' Compensation Board: – Listed alphabetically in detail, this section.

## Saskatchewan LIQUOR & GAMING AUTHORITY

2500 Victoria Ave., PO Box 5054, Regina SK S4P 3M3
306/787-4213; Fax: 306/787-8468; URL: http://www.gov.sk.ca/govt/lga/
**Minister Responsible**, Hon. Joanne Crofford, 306/787-0354
President & CEO, Gordon Nystuen, 306/787-1737
Manager, Public Education & Communications, Lisa Thomson, 306/787-1721

## Saskatchewan Government MEDIA SERVICES

#3, Legislative Bldg., Regina SK S4S 0B3
306/787-6281
The central information arm of the government (Executive Council), acting as the coordinating unit for the information sections of the departments.
**Director**, Vacant

## Saskatchewan MUNICIPAL GOVERNMENT

1855 Victoria Ave., Regina SK S4P 3V7
306/787-8282; Fax: 306/787-4181; URL: http://www.gov.sk.ca/govt/munigov/

#### ACTS ADMINISTERED

Amusement Ride Safety Act
Archives Act
Arts Board Act
Assessment Management Agency Act
Boiler & Pressure Vessel Act
Border Areas Act
Community Planning Profession Act
Controverted Municipal Elections Act
Culture & Recreation Act, 1993
Cutknife Reference Act
Department of Rural Development Act
Department of Urban Affairs Act
Doukhobors of Canada C.C.U.B. Trust Fund Act
Electrical Licensing Act
Emergency Planning Act
Emergency 911 System Act
Fire Prevention Act, 1992
Flin Flon Extension of Boundaries Act, 1952
Gas Licensing Act
Heritage Property Act
House Building Assistance Act
Industrial Towns Act
Interprovincial Lotteries Act, 1984
Jean-Louis Legare Act/Loi sur Jean-Louis Legare
Libraries Cooperation Act
Lloydminster Municipal Amalgamation Act, 1930
Local Government Election Act
Local Improvements Act, 1993
Meewasin Valley Authority Act
Municipal Board Act
Municipal Debentures Repayment Act
Municipal Development & Loan Act
Municipal Expropriation Act
Municipal Improvements Assistance (Sask) Act
Municipal Industrial Development Corporation Act
Municipal Reference Act
Municipal Revenue Sharing Program Act
Municipal Tax Sharing (Potash) Act
Northern Municipalities Act
Passenger & Freight Elevator Act
Planning & Development Act, 1983
Public Libraries Act, 1984
Rural Development Act
Rural Municipal Administrators Act
Rural Municipality Act, 1989
Saskatchewan Centre of the Arts Act
Saskatchewan Heritage Foundation Act
Saskatchewan Housing Corporation Act
Saskatchewan Multicultural Act
Senior Citizens Home Repair Assistance Act, 1984
Subdivisions Act
Tartan Day Act
Tax Enforcement Act
Time Act
Uniform Building & Accessibility Standards Act
Urban Municipal Administrators Act
Urban Municipality Act, 1984
Wakamow Valley Authority Act
Wascana Centre Act
Western Development Museum Act
**Minister**, Hon. Carol Teichrob, 306/787-6100, Fax: 306/787-0630
Deputy Minister, Ken Pontikes, 306/787-2630, Fax: 306/787-1530
Director, Finance & Administration, Larry Chaykowski, 306/787-2011, Fax: 306/787-4161
Director, Human Resources, Don Harazny, 306/787-2831, Fax: 306/787-4181
Manager, Communications, Maureen Boyle, 306/787-5959, 8282, Fax: 306/787-4181

#### CULTURE & RECREATION DIVISION

URL: http://www.gov.sk.ca/govt/munigov/cult&rec/
Assoc. Deputy Minister, Brij Mathur, 306/787-5765, Fax: 306/787-1530
Director, Heritage Branch, Dean Clark, 306/787-2809, Fax: 306/787-0069
Director, Sport, Recreation & Lotteries, Bill Werry, 306/787-5737, Fax: 306/787-8560
Manager, Government House Heritage Property, Peggy Brunsdon, 4607 Dewdney Ave., Regina SK S4P 3V7, 306/787-5720, Fax: 306/787-5714
Manager, Heritage Foundation, Garth Pugh, 306/787-4188
Acting Manager, Royal Saskatchewan Museum, David Baron, College Ave. & Albert St., Regina SK S4P 3V7, 306/787-2813, Fax: 306/787-2820

#### HOUSING DIVISION

URL: http://www.gov.sk.ca/govt/munigov/housing/
Toll Free: 1-800-667-7567 (Saskatchewan)
Associate Deputy Minister, Ron Styles, 306/787-4200, Fax: 306/787-1530
Executive Director, Program Operations, Darrell Jones, 306/787-7311, Fax: 306/787-5166
Director, Financial Operations, Peter Hoffman, 306/787-4174, Fax: 306/787-8571
Director, Intergovernmental Affairs & Northern Housing, Tom Young, 306/787-1791, Fax: 306/787-5166
Director, Property Management, Craig Marchinko, 306/787-8569

#### MUNICIPAL SERVICES DIVISION

Executive Director, Protection Services Branch, Nick Surtees, 306/787-4509, Fax: 306/787-9273
Director, Emergency Planning, Wayne Marr, 306/787-9567, Fax: 306/787-1694

Director, Municipal Development, Paul Raths, 306/787-2710
Director, Municipal Policy, Legislative Services & Finance, John Edwards, 306/787-2665
Director, Saskatchewan Infrastructure Program, Russ Krywulak, 306/787-8887, Fax: 306/787-3641
Chief Building Official, Building Standards Branch, Margaret Miller, 306/787-4517, Fax: 306/787-9273
Commissioner, Office of the Fire Commissioner, Rick McCullough, 306/787-4516, Fax: 306/787-9273
Chair, Board of Examiners, Jean Lazar, 306/787-2643

#### Associated Agencies, Boards & Commissions

•Saskatchewan Arts Board: T.C. Douglas Bldg., 3475 Albert St., 3rd Fl., Regina SK S4S 6X6 – 306/787-4056; Fax: 306/787-4199, Toll Free: 1-800-667-7526 (Saskatchewan)
Chair, Cheryl Kloppenburg
Vice-Chair, Paul Rezansoff
Executive Director, Valerie Creighton
Director, Operations, Peter Sametz
•Saskatchewan Municipal Board (SMB): 2151 Scarth St., 4th Fl., Regina SK S4P 3V7 – 306/787-6221; Fax: 306/787-1610; URL: http://www.citt.gc.ca
Chair, B.G. McNamee, 306/787-6223
Vice-Chair, J.S. Pass, 306/787-6163
Member, W.R. Armstrong, 306/787-7989
Member, J.D. Robinson, 306/787-6228
Secretary, Assessment Appeals & Condominium Property Act Apportionment Committees, Cindy Schwindt, 306/787-2644
Secretary, Board, Local Government & Property Maintenance Appeals Committee, Marilyn Turanich, 306/787-6227
Secretary, Municipal Boundary & Planning & Fire Prevention Appeals Committees, Barry Fry, 306/787-6244

## Saskatchewan NORTHERN AFFAIRS

PO Box 5000, La Ronge SK S0J 1L0
306/425-4200; Fax: 306/425-4349
1919 Saskatchewan Dr., Regina SK S4P 3V7
306/787-2906, Fax: 306/787-2909
**Minister**, Hon. Keith N. Goulet, 306/787-1885, Fax: 306/787-0399
Deputy Minister, Ray McKay, 306/425-4207
Executive Director, Resource Development Division, Alison Stickland, 1919 Saskatchewan Dr., Regina SK S4P 3V7, 306/787-2908

## Saskatchewan OMBUDSMAN

#150, 2401 Saskatchewan Dr., Regina SK S4P 3V7
306/787-6211; Fax: 306/787-9090
Saskatoon: 344 - 3 Ave. North, Saskatoon SK
306/933-5500, Fax: 306/933-8406
**Ombudsman**, Barbara Tomkins
Asst. Ombudsman, Murray Knoll, 306/787-6210
Asst. Ombudsman, Saskatoon Sub-Office, Glenda Cooney

## Saskatchewan POST-SECONDARY EDUCATION & SKILLS TRAINING

2220 College Ave., Regina SK S4P 3V7
306/787-2010; URL: http://www.gov.sk.ca
New Careers: 306/787-0106

#### ACTS ADMINISTERED

Ancillary Dental Personnel Education Act
Apprenticeship & Trade Certification Act
Education Act, 1995 s. 3,4,8,9
Private Vocational Schools Regulation Act
Regional Colleges Act
Registered Music Teachers Act
Saskatchewan Association of School Business Officials Act
Saskatchewan Institute of Applied Science & Technology (SIAST) Act
Student Assistance & Student Aid Fund Act, 1985
University of Regina Act
University of Saskatchewan Act
University of Saskatchewan Foundation Act
**Minister**, Hon. Joanne Crofford, 306/787-6662, Fax: 306/787-6946
Deputy Minister, Dan Perrins, 306/787-5586, Fax: 306/787-1300
Asst. Deputy Minister, Lily Stonehouse, 306/787-5676
Assoc. Deputy Minister, Ken Alecxe, 306/787-6056, Fax: 306/787-1300
Executive Director, Communications Branch, Susan Hogarth, 306/787-5271
Executive Director, Finance & Operations Branch, Mae Boa, 306/787-6066
Executive Director, Human Resources Branch, Don Trew, 306/787-5654
Executive Director, Institutions Branch, Shelley Hoover, 306/787-0530
Executive Director, Policy & Evaluation Branch, Donna Krawetz, 306/787-7213
Executive Director, Training Programs Branch, Wayne McElree, 306/787-2093
Executive Director, University Services Branch, John Biss, 306/787-5900
Director, Intergovernmental Relations Branch, Barbara MacLean, 306/787-5746
Director, Student Financial Assistance Unit, Brady Salloum, 306/787-0106
Coordinator, Training Strategy, Ken Sagal, 306/787-7027

## Saskatchewan POWER CORPORATION (SaskPower)

2025 Victoria Ave., Regina SK S4P 0S1
306/566-2121; Fax: 306/566-2330
**Minister Responsible**, Hon. Eldon Lautermilch, 306/787-0605, Fax: 306/787-8100
President & CEO, John R. Messer, 306/566-3103
Executive Vice-President, Corporate & Business Services, Carole Bryant, 306/566-3515
Vice-President & General Manager, Customer Service, Kelly Staudt, C.M.A., 306/566-2161
Vice-President, Finance & Information Systems, Ken Christensen, 306/566-2620
Vice-President, Human Resources & Government Relations, Bill Hyde, 306/566-2410
Vice-President & General Manager, Power Production, Rick Patrick, 306/566-2955
Vice-President & General Manager, System Operations & Decision Support, Tony Harras, 306/566-2102
Vice-President & General Manager, Transmission & Distribution, Roy Yeske, 306/566-3271

## Saskatchewan PROPERTY MANAGEMENT CORPORATION (SPMC)

1840 Lorne St., Regina SK S4P 3V7
306/787-6911; Fax: 306/787-1061

#### ACTS ADMINISTERED

Alberta-Saskatchewan Boundary Act, 1939
Architects Act
Geographic Names Board Act
Interior Designers Act
Land Surveys Act
Manitoba-Saskatchewan Boundary Acts, 1937, 1942, 1966, 1978
Purchasing Act
Saskatchewan Land Surveyors Act
Saskatchewan-Northwest Territories Act, 1966
Saskatchewan Property Management Corporation Act
**Minister Responsible**, Hon. Maynard Sonntag, 306/787-7387
President, John Law, 306/787-6520, Fax: 306/787-6547
Vice-President, Accommodation, Garth Rusconi, 306/787-6863
Vice-President, Commercial Services, Al Moffat, 306/787-9909
Vice-President, Finance & Corporate Services, Debbie Koshman, 306/787-1071

#### Associated Agencies, Boards & Commissions

•SaskGeomatics: 2151 Scarth St., Regina SK S4P 3V7 – 306/787-2800
Secretary, David Arthur

## Saskatchewan PUBLIC SERVICE COMMISSION

2103 - 11 Ave., Regina SK S4P 3V7
Fax: 306/787-7533; URL: http://www.gov.sk.ca/psc/
Saskatoon Fax: 306/933-8248
**Minister**, Hon. Lorne Calvert, 306/787-7363
Chair, Wynne Young, 306/787-7551, Fax: 306/787-4074
Executive Director, Employee Relations, Rick McKillop, 306/787-7606
Executive Director, Staffing & Development, Ron Wight, 306/787-8478
Director, Administrative & Information Services, Sharon Roulston, 306/787-7507
Manager, Communications, Don Black, 306/787-7506

## Saskatchewan RESEARCH COUNCIL (SRC)

15 Innovation Blvd., Saskatoon SK S7N 2X8
306/933-5400; Fax: 306/933-7446; URL: http://www.src.sk.ca
**Minister Responsible**, Hon. Eldon Lautermilch, 306/787-0615
Chair, John Cross, #318, 111 Research Dr., Saskatoon SK S7N 3R2, 306/668-8220
President, Ron Woodward, 306/933-5402, Email: woodward@src.sk.ca
Vice-President, Agricultural Biotechnology Group/Small Industry Services Branch, Rick Tofani, 306/933-5490, Email: tofani@src.sk.ca
Vice-President, Resources & Environment Group, Jim Hutchinson, 306/933-7717, Email: hutchinson@src.sk.ca, Regina: 306/787-9401
Controller, Financial Services & Manager, Staff Resource Services, Crystal Smudy, 306/933-8111, Email: smudy@src.sk.ca
Manager, Corporate Administrative Services, Ken Owens, 306/933-5422, Email: owens@src.sk.ca

## SASKENERGY INCORPORATED

#1100, 1945 Hamilton St., Regina SK S4P 2C7
306/777-9426; Fax: 306/777-9889
**Minister Responsible**, Hon. Eldon Lautermilch, 306/787-0605, Fax: 306/787-8100
President & CEO, Ronald S. Clark
Executive Vice-President, TransGas Ltd., Jullian Olenick
Vice-President, Distribution Utility, Doug Kelln
Vice-President, Finance & Administration, Elaine Bourassa
Vice-President, Gas Supply, Ken From
Vice-President, Human Resources, Robert Haynes
Acting Director, Corporate Affairs, Ron Podbielski
General Counsel & Corporate Secretary, Mark Guillet

#### Bayhurst Gas Ltd.

President, Ronald S. Clark
General Counsel & Corporate Secretary, Mark Guillet

#### Many Islands Pipe Lines (Canada) Ltd. (MIPL)

President, Ronald S. Clark
General Counsel & Corporate Secretary, Mark Guillet

**TransGas Ltd.**
President, Ronald S. Clark
Executive Vice-President, Jullian Olenick
Vice-President, Business Development & Marketing, Dean Reeve

## Saskatchewan SOCIAL SERVICES
1920 Broad St., Regina SK S4P 3V6
306/787-3494; Fax: 306/787-1032; Email: ENVOY 100:cosask.soc.services; URL: http://www.gov.sk.ca/govt/socserv/

#### ACTS ADMINISTERED
Adoption Act
Child Care Act
Child & Family Services Act
Department of Social Services Act
Family Services Act
Housing & Special-care Homes Act (in part)
Legal Aid Act
Rehabilitation Act
Residential Services Act
Registered Social Workers Act
Saskatchewan Assistance Plan Act
**Minister**, Hon. Lorne Calvert, 306/787-7363
Deputy Minister, Con Hnatiuk, 306/787-3491
Assoc. Deputy Minister, Neil Yeates, 306/787-4909
Asst. Deputy Minister, Vic Taylor, 306/787-7357
Executive Director, Policy & Planning, Brenda Righetti, 306/787-3621
Director, Communications & Public Education, Virginia Wilkinson, 306/787-0916
Acting Director, Research & Evaluation, David Rosenbluth, 306/787-7354

#### COMMUNITY LIVING DIVISION
Central Office, #216, 110 Ominica St. West, Moose Jaw SK S6H 6V2
306/694-3800; Fax: 306/694-3842
Executive Director, Larry Moffatt, 306/787-2705
Manager, Income Security, Tony Coughlan, 2151 Scarth St., 1st Fl., Regina SK S4P 3V7, 306/787-3536
Manager, Protection & Children's Services, Dorothea Warren, 2240 Albert St., Regina SK S4P 3V7, 306/787-2928
Manager, Young Offenders, Bob Kary, 306/787-9165

#### FAMILY & YOUTH SERVICES DIVISION
306/787-7010; Fax: 306/787-0925
Executive Director, Richard Hazel, 306/787-3652
Director, Child & Youth Family Services Programs, Dave Hedlund, 306/787-3647
Director, Community Youth Services, Vacant, 306/787-4702
Director, Residential, Custodial & Therapeutic Services, Ron Lisk, 306/787-4701
Director, Dales House, Ken Cameron, 160 McIntosh St., Regina SK S4R 4Z4, 306/787-3617, Fax: 306/787-1750
Director, Kenosee Youth Camp, Tony Yanick, PO Box 699, Carlyle SK S0C 0R0, 306/577-2300
Director, Paul Dojack Youth Centre, Ron Simpson, Ritter & Toothill St., Regina SK S4P 3V7, 306/787-3561, Fax: 306/787-7546

#### HUMAN RESOURCES DIVISION
306/787-9070; Fax: 306/787-3441
Executive Director, Dave Atkinson, 306/787-3597
Director, Child Day Care Division, Deborah Bryck, 306/787-3855
Director, Federal/Provincial Arrangements, Don Fairbairn, 306/787-3627

#### INCOME SECURITY PROGRAMS DIVISION
306/787-7469
Executive Director, Phil Walsh, 306/787-9239
Manager, Central Operations, Jan Yaworski, 306/787-3389
Manager, Child Day Care Subsidy Unit, Lorraine Snell, 306/787-3885, Toll Free: 1-800-667-7155
Manager, Family Income Plan (FIP), Lorraine Snell, 306/787-3885, Toll Free: 1-800-667-7552
Manager, Saskatchewan Income Plan (SIP), Jan Yaworski, 306/787-3389, Toll Free: 1-800-667-7161

#### SUPPORT SERVICES DIVISION
306/787-8667; Fax: 306/787-1600
Executive Director, Wes Mazer, 306/787-8666
Director, Budget Branch, Bob Wihlidal, 306/787-8669
Director, Departmental Services Branch, Joe Makan, 306/787-3106
Director, Financial Services Branch, Bill Duncan, 306/787-3575
Director, Information & Technology Services, Ron Naidu, 306/787-9200

#### Associated Agencies, Boards & Commissions
•Saskatchewan Legal Aid Commission: #820, 410 - 22 St. East, Saskatoon SK S7K 2H6 – 306/933-5300; Fax: 306/933-6764
Chair, Jane L. Lancaster, Q.C.

## Saskatchewan TELECOMMUNICATIONS (SaskTel)
2121 Saskatchewan Dr., Regina SK S4P 3Y2
306/777-3737; Fax: 306/565-8717; URL: http://www.sasktel.com/
Provides telecommunication services throughout Saskatchewan & throughout the world through SaskTel International; provides a full range of national & worldwide long distance communication services.
**Minister Responsible**, Hon. Carol Teichrob
President & CEO, Don Ching
President, SaskTel International, Dale Bassen, C.M.A.
Senior Vice-President, Strategic Business Development & Marketing, Dan Baldwin
Group Vice-President, Customer Services, Garry Simons
Vice-President, Corporate Counsel & Regulatory Affairs, John Meldrum
Vice-President, Human Resources/Industrial Relations, Vacant
Vice-President, Mobility, D. Milenkovic
Vice-President, Sales & Service, Gord Farmer
Chief Financial Officer, Randy Stephanson
Chief Technology Officer, Kelvin Shepherd
General Manager, Corporate Affairs, Sean Caragata, 306/777-4105, Fax: 306/359-0305

## Saskatchewan WATER CORPORATION (Sask Water)
Victoria Place, 111 Fairford St. East, Moose Jaw SK S6H 7X9
306/694-3900; Fax: 306/694-3944; Email: saskwater.cd@sasknet.sk.ca
Northern Operations Office, 800 Central Ave., PO Box 3003, Prince Albert SK S6V 6G1
306/953-2250, Fax: 306/953-2200
Provincial Crown corporation which manages, protects & develops the province's water & land related resources for the economic & social benefit of the province.
**Minister Responsible**, Hon. Eldon Lautermilch, 306/787-0605, Fax: 306/787-8100
President, Brian Kaukinen, 306/694-3903
Vice-President, Finance & Corporate Services, Wayne Phillips, 306/694-3909
Vice-President, Irrigation & Agricultural Services, Harvey Fjeld, 306/694-3943
Vice-President, Water Resources Management, Wayne Dybvig, 306/694-3950
Vice-President, Water Supply & Transmission, Al Veroba, 306/694-3905

## Saskatchewan WOMEN'S SECRETARIAT
1855 Victoria Ave., 7th Fl., Regina SK S4P 3V5
306/787-2329; Fax: 306/787-2058
**Minister Responsible**, Hon. Joanne Crofford, 306/787-2207
Executive Coordinator, Faye Rafter

## Saskatchewan WORKERS' COMPENSATION BOARD
#200, 1881 Scarth St., Regina SK S4P 4L1
306/787-4370; Fax: 306/787-0213
**Minister Responsible**, Hon. Robert W. Mitchell, Q.C., 306/787-6662, Fax: 306/787-6946
Chair, Stan Cameron, 306/787-4378
Director, Planning, Research & Communication, Janice Siekawitch, 303/787-4386

# GOVERNMENT OF THE YUKON TERRITORY

**Seat of Government:** Legislative Assembly, PO Box 2703, Whitehorse YT Y1A 2C6
The Yukon was created as a separate territory June 13, 1898. It has an area of 531,843.62 km2, and the StatsCan census population in 1996 was 30,766.
A federally appointed commissioner (similar to a provincial lieutenant-governor) oversees federal interests in the territory, but the day-to-day operation of the government rests with the wholly elected executive council (cabinet). The territorial legislature has power to make acts on generally all matters of a local nature in the territory, including the imposition of local taxes, property & civil rights & the administration of justice, education & health & social services. Legislative powers vested in the provinces but not available to the territory include control of unoccupied Crown land, renewable & non-renewable resources (except wildlife & sport fisheries) & the power to amend the Yukon Act, a federal statute.

## Office of the COMMISSIONER
211 Hawkins St., Whitehorse YT Y1A 1X3
867/667-5121; Fax: 867/393-6201
The Yukon Territory is governed by a commissioner appointed to an indefinite term by the federal government, a government leader, an executive council which functions as a cabinet, & a legislative assembly. The Yukon Act provides for the establishment of a commissioner & the elected legislative assembly.
**Commissioner**, Hon. Judy Gingell
Executive Secretary, Eileen Fry

## Office of the GOVERNMENT LEADER
PO Box 2703, Whitehorse YT Y1A 2C6
867/667-5885; Fax: 867/667-8424
**Leader**, Hon. Piers McDonald

## EXECUTIVE COUNCIL
PO Box 2703, Whitehorse YT Y1A 2C6
867/667-5812; Fax: 867/667-8424

#### ACTS ADMINISTERED
Cabinet & Caucus Employees Act
Flag Act
Floral Emblem Act
Intergovernmental Agreements Act
Languages Act

Public Inquiries Act
Yukon Tartan Act

Leader & Minister, Finance, Hon. Piers McDonald
Minister, Renewable Resources & Minister Responsible, Yukon Housing Corporation & Yukon Liquor Corporation, Hon. Eric Fairclough
Government House Leader & Minister, Economic Development, Minister Responsible Public Service Commission, Yukon Energy Corp., Yukon Workers' Compensation Health & Safety Board, Hon. Trevor Harding
Minister, Community & Transportation Services & Minister, Tourism, Hon. Dave Keenan
Minister, Education & Minister, Justice, Hon. Lois Moorcroft
Minister, Health & Social Services & Minister, Government Services, Hon. David Sloan

#### Cabinet Office

Deputy Minister & Cabinet Secretary, John Lawson, 867/667-5866, Fax: 867/393-6214
Deputy Cabinet Secretary, Janet Moodie, 867/667-5866
Asst. Deputy Minister, Federal Relations Office, Glenn Grant, #707, 350 Sparks St., Ottawa ON K1R 7S8, 613/234-3206, Fax: 613/563-9602
Chief Negotiator, Land Claims, Self Government & Devolution, Tim McTiernan, 867/667-5908, Fax: 867/393-6214
Protocol Officer, Pamela Bangart, 867/667-5875
Director, Aboriginal Language Services, Mike Smith, 867/667-3737, Fax: 867/393-6229
Director, Bureau of French Language Services, Harley Trudeau, 867/667-3775, Fax: 867/393-6226
Acting Director, Bureau of Management Improvement, Karen Johnson, 867/667-5316
Director, Bureau of Statistics, Gerry Ewert, 867/667-5640, Fax: 867/393-6203
Director, Finance & Management Services, Bonnie Love, 867/667-3539
Director, Policy & Communications, Kimberley Bain, 867/667-5854, 5393, 5939, Fax: 867/393-6202

#### Associated Agencies, Boards & Commissions

- Yukon Council on the Economy & the Environment: A-8E, PO Box 2703, Whitehorse YT Y1A 2C6 – 867/667-5939; Fax: 867/668-4936
  Combines operations with Economic Development, & Renewable Resources.
  Chair, Tim Preston
- Yukon Health & Social Services Council: c/o Executive Council Office, PO Box 2703, Whitehorse YT Y1A 2C6 – 867/668-4421
  Combines operations with Health, Social Services & Justice.
  Chair, Dave Buchan

## LEGISLATIVE ASSEMBLY

c/o Clerk's Office, PO Box 2703, Whitehorse YT Y1A 2C6
867/667-5498; Fax: 867/393-6280

#### ACTS ADMINISTERED

Controverted Elections Act
Elections Act
Electoral District Boundaries Act
Legislative Assembly Act
Legislative Assembly Retirement Allowances Act
**Clerk & Chief Electoral Officer:** Patrick L. Michael, 867/667-5498
**Speaker:** Robert Bruce, 867/667-5662
**Sergeant-at-Arms:** Emery Shilleto
Deputy Clerk, Missy Follwell, 867/667-5499

#### Office of the Leader of the Opposition

Fax: 867/393-6252

The official opposition party had not been determined by the time of publication. The opposition will be known after the Yukon Legislative Assembly sits in the fall of 1996. Contact the Legislative Assembly for further information.
**Leader**, Hon. John Ostashek, 867/667-5603

#### Standing Committees of the Legislature

Members' Services Board Committee
Public Accounts Committee
Rules, Elections & Privileges Committee
Statutory Instruments Committee

## TWENTY-EIGHTH LEGISLATURE - YUKON TERRITORY

867/667-5498
Last General Election, September 30, 1996. Maximum Duration, 4 years.
**Party Standings (October 1996)**
New Democratic Party (NDP) 11
Yukon Party (YP) 3
Liberal (Lib.) 3
Total 17
**Salaries, Indemnities & Allowances**
1994 - Members' indemnity $30,832 plus a $15,416 expense allowance (Whitehorse members receive $13,460). In addition to this are the following:
Premier $28,971
Ministers $21,147
Leader of the Official Opposition $21,147
Leader of the Third Party $4,229
Speaker $7,049
Deputy Speaker $5,287

#### MEMBERS BY CONSTITUENCY

Following is: constituency (total number of ballots cast in September 1996 election) member, party affiliation, Telephone number. (Address for all is PO Box 2703, Whitehorse YT Y1A 2C6.)

Faro (562) Hon. Trevor Harding, NDP, 867/667-8416
Klondike (1,099) Peter Jenkins, YP, 867/667-5806
Kluane (751) Gary McRobb, NDP, 867/667-8892
Lake Laberge (1,120) Doug Livingston, NDP, 867/667-8661
Mayo-Tatchun (641) Hon. Eric Fairclough, NDP, 867/667-8416
McIntyre-Takhini (900) Hon. Piers McDonald, NDP, 867/667-8415
Mount Lorne (1,227) Hon. Lois Moorcroft, NDP, 867/667-8417
Porter Creek North (979) Hon. John Ostashek, YP, 867/667-5603
Porter Creek South (1,017) Pat Duncan, Lib., 867/667-8879
Riverdale North (945) Doug Phillips, YP, 867/667-5716
Riverdale South (852) Sue Edelman, Lib., 867/667-8878
Riverside (692) Jack Cable, Lib., 867/667-8422
Ross River-Southern Lakes (857) Hon. Dave Keenan, NDP, 867/667-8262
Vuntut Gwitchin (164) Robert Bruce, NDP, 867/667-8262
Watson Lake (842) Dennis Fentie, NDP, 867/667-8626
Whitehorse Centre (716) Todd Hardy, NDP, 867/667-8650
Whitehorse West (1,195) Hon. David Sloan, NDP, 867/667-8417

#### MEMBERS (ALPHABETICAL)

Following is: constituency (total number of ballots cast in September 1996 election) member, party affiliation, Telephone number. (Address for all is PO Box 2703, Whitehorse YT Y1A 2C6.)

Robert Bruce, Vuntut Gwitchin (164) NDP, 867/667-8262
Jack Cable, Riverside (692) Lib., 867/667-8422
Pat Duncan, Porter Creek South (1,017) Lib., 867/667-8879
Sue Edelman, Riverdale South (852) Lib., 867/667-8878
Hon. Eric Fairclough, Mayo-Tatchun (641) NDP, 867/667-8416
Dennis Fentie, Watson Lake (842) NDP, 867/667-8626
Hon. Trevor Harding, Faro (562) NDP, 867/667-8416
Todd Hardy, Whitehorse Centre (716) NDP, 867/667-8650
Peter Jenkins, Klondike (1,099) YP, 867/667-5806
Hon. Dave Keenan, Ross River-Southern Lakes (857) NDP, 867/667-8262
Doug Livingston, Lake Laberge (1,120) NDP, 867/667-8661
Hon. Piers McDonald, McIntyre-Takhini (900) NDP, 867/667-8415
Gary McRobb, Kluane (751) NDP, 867/667-8892
Hon. Lois Moorcroft, Mount Lorne (1,227) NDP, 867/667-8417
Hon. John Ostashek, Porter Creek North (979) YP, 867/667-5603
Doug Phillips, Riverdale North (945) YP, 867/667-5716
Hon. David Sloan, Whitehorse West (1,195) NDP, 867/667-8417

## YUKON TERRITORY GOVERNMENT DEPARTMENTS & AGENCIES

## Yukon COMMUNITY & TRANSPORTATION SERVICES

PO Box 2703, Whitehorse YT Y1A 2C6
867/667-5144; Fax: 867/393-6404

#### ACTS ADMINISTERED

Area Development Act
Assessment & Taxation Act
Boiler & Pressure Vessels Act
Building Standards Act
Cemeteries & Burial Sites Act
Civil Emergency Measures Act
Dangerous Goods Transportation Act
Electrical Protection Act
Elevator & Fixed Conveyances Act
Fire Prevention Act
Gas Burning Devices Act
Gasoline Handling Act
Highways Act
Home Owner's Grant Act
Lands Act
Motor Transport Act
Motor Vehicles Act
Municipal Act
Municipal Finance & Community Grants Act
Municipal General Purposes Loan Act
Public Government Act
Public Lotteries Act
Public Service Act
Recreation Act
Subdivision Act
**Minister**, Hon. Dave Keenan, 867/667-8262, Fax: 867/667-8424
Deputy Minister, John Cormie, 867/667-5155
Director, Communications, Telecommunications & Broadcasting Branch, Dan McArthur, 867/667-5804
Director, Emergency Measures Organization, Eric Magnuson, 867/667-5220, Fax: 867/393-6266
Director, Finance, Systems & Administration, Temes Cherinet, 867/667-5311, Fax: 867/393-6264
Director, Human Resources, Jean Dell, 867/667-5156, Fax: 867/667-3685
Director, Policy, Planning & Evaluation, Dale Kozmeniuk, 867/667-5941

#### MUNICIPAL & COMMUNITY AFFAIRS DIVISION

Asst. Deputy Minister, Virginia Labelle, 867/667-5636, Fax: 867/393-6258, Email: VLabelle@gov.yk.ca
Director, Community Services Branch, Bill Forsythe, 867/667-5299
Director, Engineering & Development, Jim Mayoh, 867/667-5707, Fax: 867/393-6216
Director, Lands & Property Assessment Branch, Lyle Henderson, 867/667-5218, Fax: 867/667-6258
Director, Public Safety Branch, Walter Brennan, 867/667-5824, Fax: 867/393-6249
Director, Sport & Recreation Branch, Peter Milner, 867/667-5608, Fax: 867/393-6416
Fire Marshal, Office of the Fire Marshal, John Holesworth, 867/667-5217

#### TRANSPORTATION DIVISION

Acting Director, Aviation & Marine Branch, Jim Logan, PO Box 2129, Haines Junction YT Y0B 1L0, 867/634-2035, Fax: 867/634-2131
Director, Transportation Engineering, Robin Walsh, 867/633-7928, Fax: 867/393-6447
Director, Transportation Maintenance, Robert Magnuson, 867/667-5761, Fax: 867/667-3608
Manager, Transport Services Branch, Lynn Alcock, 867/667-5833
Deputy Registrar, Motor Vehicles, Fred Jennex, 867/667-5315

#### Associated Agencies, Boards & Commissions

•Yukon Assessment Appeal Board: PO Box 2703, Whitehorse YT Y1A 2C6 – 867/667-5234
Chair, Ann King
•Yukon Driver Control Board: PO Box 2703, Whitehorse YT Y1A 2C6 – 867/667-3638
Chair, Tom Fairman
•Yukon Lottery Commission: PO Box 2703, Whitehorse YT Y1A 2C6 – 867/633-7890
Chair, Doug Beaumont
•Yukon Motor Transport Board: PO Box 2703, Whitehorse YT Y1A 2C6 – 867/667-5782
Chair, Jean Murphy
•Yukon Municipal Board: PO Box 2703, Whitehorse YT Y1A 2C6 – 867/667-3546
Chair, Craig Tuton

## Yukon ECONOMIC DEVELOPMENT

211 Main St., PO Box 2703, Whitehorse YT Y1A 2C6
867/667-5466; Fax: 867/668-8601

#### ACTS ADMINISTERED

Business Development Assistance Act
Economic Development & Regional Development Agreement Act
Economic Development Act
Energy Conservation Act
Energy Conservation Agreement Act
Energy Conservation Assistance Act
Loan Guarantee Act
**Minister**, Hon. Trevor Harding, 867/667-8942
Deputy Minister, Maurice Albert, 867/667-5417
Mining Facilitator, Jesse Duke, 867/667-3422

#### FINANCE & ADMINISTRATION

Director, Val Mather, 867/667-5016
Manager, Financial Operations, Miko Miyahara, 867/667-3755
Financial Clerk, Barbara Milward, 867/667-3637
Financial Clerk, Paula Nugent, 867/667-5382

#### INDUSTRY TRADE & INVESTMENT

Coorinator, Economic Development, Glenn Hart, 867/667-3013
Coordinator, Economic Development, Mike Kenny, 867/667-5027
Marketing Promotion Officer, Bert Perry, 867/667-3566
Marketing Promotion Officer, John Pert, 867/667-3565
Trade Promotion Officer, Bob Snyder, 867/667-3014

#### MINES & RESOURCE DEVELOPMENT

Senior Director, Robert Holmes, 867/667-5462
Analyst, Mineral Policy, Shirley Abercrombie, 867/667-3438
Director, Energy Resources Branch, Brian Love, #209, 212 Main St., Whitehorse YT Y1A 2B1, 867/667-5014, Fax: 867/393-6262
Acting Director, Mineral Resources Development, Rod Hill, 867/667-8085
Coordinator, Energy Unit, Chris Dray, 867/667-8085
Senior Project Geologist, Geological Surveys, Don Murphy, 867/667-8516

#### STRATEGIC MANAGEMENT/INDUSTRY TRADE & INVESTMENT

Asst. Deputy Minister, Terry Sewell, 867/667-5461
Senior Economist, Economic Research, Paul Kishchuk, 867/667-5946
Economist, Economic Research, Derrick Hynes
Resources Development, Christian Pekarik
Senior Planner, Renewable Resources, Lawrie Crawford, 867/667-8011
Senior Planner, Renewable Resources, Suzzanne Green, 867/667-5809
Senior Planner, Renewable Resources, Scott Milton, 867/667-3432

#### Associated Agencies, Boards & Commissions

•Business Development Advisory Board: PO Box 2703, Whitehorse YT Y1A 2C6 – 867/667-5470
Chair, Jose Janssen

## Yukon EDUCATION

PO Box 2703, Whitehorse YT Y1A 2C6
867/667-5141; Fax: 867/393-6254

The Yukon has 28 public schools (14 in Whitehorse, 14 in other communities) & two private schools. The public schools are administered directly by the Department of Education, although elected school council officials are gradually assuming more powers under the 1990 Education Act, & may evolve into school boards in the near future. In 1996, the Yukon Francophone School Board was created, becoming Yukon's first school board.

Curriculum is largely based on that of British Columbia, with flexibility for locally developed courses, particularly from a First Nations perspective (one quarter of the Yukon's 5977 students are of native ancestry). Seven different native languages are taught in various Yukon schools, as well as French immersion.

#### ACTS ADMINISTERED

Access to Information Act
Apprentice Training Act
Archives Act
Canada Student Loans Act (federal)
College Act
Education Act
Employment Expansion & Development Act
Occupational Training Act
Public Libraries Act
Students' Financial Assistance Act
Teaching Profession Act
Trade Schools Regulation Act
**Minister**, Hon. Lois Moorcroft
Minister, Wolf Riedl

#### ADVANCED EDUCATION BRANCH

Fax: 867/667-8555
Asst. Deputy Minister, Gordon McDevitt, 867/667-5131
Director, Training Programs, Ken Smith, 867/667-5140, Email: klsmith@gov.yk.ca
Student Financial Officer, Carol Theriault, 867/667-5929, Email: edassist@gov.yk.ca
Student Financial Officer, Judy Thrower, 867/667-5929, Email: jthrower@gov.yk.ca
President, Yukon College, Sally Ross, PO Box 2799, Whitehorse YT Y1A 5K4, 867/668-8704, Fax: 867/668-8896

#### EDUCATION SUPPORT SERVICES

Acting Deputy Minister, George Gartner
Director, Communications, Policy & Legislative Support, Sheila Rose, 867/667-5605, Fax: 867/393-6339, Email: srose@gov.yk.ca
Acting Director, Finance & Systems, Annette Hartnoll, Email: ahartnol@gov.yk.ca
Director, Libraries & Archives, Linda Johnson, 867/667-5309
Manager, Facilities & Transportation, Gordon deBruyn

#### PUBLIC SCHOOLS BRANCH

Fax: 867/393-6339
Acting Asst. Deputy Minister, Wally Seipp, 867/667-8658, Email: wseipp@gov.yk.ca
Acting Superintendent, Schools Area 1, Chris Gonnet, Email: chris.gonnet@gov.yk.ca
Acting Superintendent, Schools Area 2, Pat Berrel
Superintendent, Schools Area 3, Carol McCauley, 867/393-5723
Superintendent, Curriculum, French Programs, Special Programs, Mavis Fisher, 867/667-8238, Email: mfisher@gov.yk.ca

## Yukon EMERGENCY MEASURES ORGANIZATION (YEMO)

PO Box 2703, Whitehorse YT Y1A 2C6
867/667-5220; Fax: 867/393-6266
**Director**, Eric Magnuson

## Yukon ENERGY CORPORATION (YEC)

PO Box 5920, Whitehorse YT Y1A 5L7
867/667-5028; Fax: 867/393-6327
**Minister Responsible**, Hon. Trevor Harding, 867/667-8416
Chair, B. Ernewein
President, Rob McWilliam, Q.C., 867/667-8121
Vice-President & CFO, Oliver P. O'Rourke, P.Eng.
Vice-President, Policy & Regulatory Affairs, Duncan Sinclair, 867/667-8852
Senior Utility Engineer, John F. Maissan, P.Eng., 867/667-8119

## Yukon FINANCE

PO Box 2703, Whitehorse YT Y1A 2C6
867/667-5343; Fax: 867/393-6217

#### ACTS ADMINISTERED

Banking Agency Guarantee Act
Faro Mine Loan Act
Financial Administration Act
Fuel Oil Tax Act
Income Tax Act
Insurance Premium Tax Act
Liquor Tax Act
Loan Agreement Act
Public Sector Compensation Restraint Act
Public Servants Superannuation Act
Tobacco Tax Act
Yukon Development Corporation Loan Guarantee Act
**Minister**, Hon. Piers McDonald, 867/667-3767
Deputy Minister, Charles Sanderson, 867/667-3571

#### FINANCIAL OPERATIONS & REVENUE SERVICES
Acting Asst. Deputy Minister & Director, Accounting Services, Dave Hrycan, 867/667-5279; 5375
Director, Financial Systems, Mederic Tremblay, 867/667-5278
Director, Investments & Debt Services, Jeff Frketich, 867/667-5346
Director, Revenue Services, Norm McIntyre, 867/667-3074

#### FISCAL RELATIONS & MANAGEMENT BOARD SECRETARIAT
Asst. Deputy Minister, Fiscal Relations & Management Board Secretariat, Leo Chassé, 403/667-5821
Director, Budgets, Joanna Reynolds, 867/667-5344
Director, Fiscal Relations, Tim Shoniker, 867/667-5303
Director, Management Board Secretariat, Helen Bebak, 867/667-5277

## Yukon GOVERNMENT SERVICES
PO Box 2703, Whitehorse YT Y1A 2C6
867/667-5436; Fax: 867/393-6218

#### ACTS ADMINISTERED
Public Printing Act
**Minister**, Hon. David Sloan, 867/667-8894, Fax: 867/667-8424
Deputy Minister, D.P. Odin, 867/667-3732
Acting Asst. Deputy Minister, Corporate Services, Peter Laight, 867/667-3732
Director, Finance & Administration, Christine Mahar, 867/667-5410
Director, Human Resources, Derek Holmes, 867/667-3748
Director, Policy & Planning, Siegfried Fuchsbichler
Officer, Business Incentive Office, Rita MacKenzie-Grieve, 867/667-3505

#### INFORMATION SERVICES
Fax: 867/667-5304
Director, Jim Hill, 867/667-3712
Manager, Administration & Communications, Ian Burnett, 867/667-5827
Manager, Production & Network Services, Peter Dielissen, 867/667-5600
Supervisor, Network Support, Gaile Trafford, 867/667-5034, Fax: 867/393-6200
Manager, Client Services, Bob Chambers, 867/667-8018
Acting Manager, Production Services, Bob Forward, 867/667-3044, Fax: 867/393-6200

#### PROPERTY MANAGEMENT
Acting Asst. Deputy Minister, Dave Parfitt, 867/667-8191, Fax: 867/393-6319
Acting Director, Building Development, Pat Molloy, 867/667-3064
Director, Facilities Management, Mike Bartsch, 867/667-5966, Fax: 867/393-6319
Director, Realty & Regional Services, Vacant, 867/667-5916, Fax: 867/393-6319
Accounting Supervisor, Elly Lohmann, 867/667-3706, Fax: 867/393-6319
Acting Manager, Project Management, Peter Blum, 867/667-5138
Acting Manager, Realty Services, Helen Fitzsimmons, 867/667-5104
Acting Manager, Technical Support, Al Fromme, 867/667-3589
Facilities Manager, Jack Robinson, 867/667-3654
Facilities Manager, Jim Tessier, 867/667-8882

#### SUPPLY SERVICES
Fax: 867/393-6299
Acting Director, Roland McCaffrey, 867/667-5289
Manager, Purchasing, Al Alcock, 867/667-5459
Manager, Queen's Printer, Frank Wilps, 867/667-3585, Fax: 867/668-3585
Manager, Transportation & Communications, Ray Pilloud, 867/667-5793
Manager, Warehouse, John Debrecini, 867/667-5732

#### Regional Offices
Eastern: PO Box 2500, Watson Lake YT Y0A 1C0 – 867/536-7494; Fax: 867/536-2784, Regional Manager, Darrell W. Peters
Northern: PO Box 4030, Dawson City YT Y0B 1G0 – 867/993-5499; Fax: 867/993-6814, Regional Manager, Pat Hogan
Western: PO Box 2068, Haines Junction YT Y0B 1L0 – 867/634-2219; Fax: 867/634-2932, Regional Manager, John Farynowski

## Yukon HEALTH & SOCIAL SERVICES
PO Box 2703, Whitehorse YT Y1A 2C6
867/667-3673 (Communications); Fax: 867/667-3096

#### ACTS ADMINISTERED
Change of Name Act
Child Care Act
Children's Act
Dependants' Relief Act
Disabled Persons' Allowance Act
Health Act
Health Care Insurance Plan Act
Hospital Act
Hospital Insurance Services Act
Marriage Act
Mental Health Act
Pioneer Utility Grant Act
Public Health Act
Rehabilitation Services Act
Seniors' Income Supplement Act
Social Assistance Act
Travel for Medical Treatment Act
Vital Statistics Act
Young Offenders Agreement Act
Young Persons Offences Act
**Minister**, Hon. David Sloan, 867/667-3769, Fax: 867/667-3035
Deputy Minister, Bruce McLennan, 867/667-5770, Email: mclennan@yknet.yk.ca
Coordinator, Communications, Patricia Living, 867/667-3673, Fax: 867/667-3096, Email: pliving@gov.yk.ca

#### HEALTH SERVICES BRANCH
Asst. Deputy Minister, Malcolm Maxwell, 867/667-5686
Director, Health Care Insurance Services, Joanne Fairlie, 867/667-5202, Fax: 867/668-3786
Deputy Registrar, Vital Statistics, Sylvia Kitching, 867/667-5207, Fee for each birth, marriage or death certificate: $10.00.

#### SOCIAL SERVICES BRANCH
Asst. Deputy Minister, Bonnie Clark, 867/667-5684
Director, Family/Children's Services, Anne Sheffield, 867/667-8117, Fax: 867/668-4613

## Yukon HOUSING CORPORATION
410A Jarvis St., PO Box 2703, Whitehorse YT Y1A 2C6
867/667-5759; Fax: 867/667-3664
**Minister Responsible**, Hon. Eric Fairclough, 867/667-8899
President, Sandie Romanczak
Director, Program Administration, Donald Flinn, 867/667-3549
Director, Program Delivery, Al Lyon, 867/667-3773
Director, Corporate Relations, Don Routledge, 867/667-8093
Director, Finance & Administration, Louise Girard, 867/667-5760

## Yukon JUSTICE
PO Box 2703, Whitehorse YT Y1A 2C6
867/667-8292 (Communications); Fax: 867/393-6272

#### ACTS ADMINISTERED
Age of Majority Act
Animal Protection Act
Business Corporations Act
Business Licence Act
Canada & the United Kingdom Reciprocal Recognition & Enforcement of Judgements Act
Central Trust Company & Crown Trust Company Act
Certified General Accountants Act
Chartered Accountants Act
Chiropractors Act
Choses in Action Act
Collection Act
Compensation of Victims of Crime Act
Condominium Act
Conflict of Laws (Traffic Accidents) Act
Constitutional Questions Act
Consumer Protection Act
Contributory Negligence Act
Cooperative Associations Act
Coroners Act
Corrections Act
Court of Appeal Act
Creditor's Relief Act
Criminal Code of Canada (federal)
Day of Mourning for Victims of Workplace Injury Act
Defamation Act
Dental Profession Act
Dental Technicians Act
Devolution of Real Property Act
Distress Act
Divorce Act (federal)
Electronic Registration Act
Employment Agencies Act
Employment Standards Act
Enhancement Republication Act, 1993
Enduring Power of Attorney Act
Engineering Profession Act
Evidence Act
Executions Act
Exemptions Act
Expropriation Act
Factors Act
Family Property & Support Act
Fatal Accidents Act
Fine Option Act
Foreign Arbitral Awards Act
Fraudulent Preferences & Conveyances Act
Frustrated Contracts Act
Funeral Directors Act
Gaols Act
Garage Keepers' Lien Act
Garnishee Act
Human Rights Act
Human Tissue Gift Act
Insurance Act
International Commercial Arbitration Act
International Sale of Goods Act
Interpretation Act
Interprovincial Subpoena Act
Intestate Succession Act
Judicature Act
Jury Act
Landlord & Tenant Act
Land Titles Act
Legal Profession Act
Legal Services Society Act
Limitation of Actions Act
Lottery Licensing Act
Maintenance & Custody Orders Enforcement Act

Married Women's Property Act
Mechanic's Lien Act
Medical Profession Act
Miner's Lien Act
Noise Prevention Act
Notaries Act
Nursing Assistants Registration Act
Occupational Health & Safety Act
Optometrists Act
Partnership Act
Pawnbrokers & Second-hand Dealers Act
Perpetuities Act
Personal Property & Security Act
Pharmacists Act
Presumption of Death Act
Private Investigators & Security Guards Act
Public Utilities Act
Real Estate Agent's Act
Reciprocal Enforcement of Judgements Act
Reciprocal Enforcement of Maintenance Orders Act
Recording of Evidence Act
Registered Nurses Profession Act
Regulations Act
Retirement Plan Beneficiaries Act
Revised Statutes Act
Sale of Goods Act
School Tresspass Act
Securities Act
Small Claims Court Act
Societies Act
Society of Management Accountants Act
Summary Convictions Act
Supreme Court Act
Survivorship Act
Tenants in Common Act
Territorial Court Act
Torture Prohibition Act
Trustee Act
Variation of Trusts Act
Victim Services Act
Warehousemen's Lien Act
Warehouse Receipts Act
Wills Act
Woodmen's Lien Act
Young Offenders Act (federal)
Young Offenders Agreement Act (federal)
Young Offenders Welfare Agreement Act (federal)
Yukon Surface Rights Board Act (Canada - federal)

**Minister**, Hon. Lois Moorcroft, 867/667-8417, Fax: 867/667-8424
Deputy Minister, Stuart Whitley, Q.C., 867/667-5959, Fax: 867/393-6272
Director, Finance & Administration, Susan Ryan, 867/667-5446, Fax: 867/667-5790, Email: susan.ryan@gov.yk.ca

**For list of Courts & other Legal Officers, including Judicial Officials & Judges *see* Section 10 of this book.**

#### COMMUNITY & CORRECTIONAL SERVICES BRANCH

Director, Joy Waters, 867/667-8294, Fax: 867/393-6326, Email: joy.waters@gov.yk.ca
Manager, Adult Probation Unit, Jon. Gaudry, 867/667-3586, Fax: 867/667-3446, Email: jon.gaudry@gov.yk.ca
Manager, Teslin Community Correctional Centre, Bill Watson, 867/390-2032, Fax: 867/390-2921
Manager, Victim Services/Family Violence Prevention Unit, Michael Hanson, 867/667-3023, Fax: 867/393-6240, Email: michael.hanson@gov.yk.ca
Superintendent, Whitehorse Correctional Centre, Don Head, 867/393-6208, Email: don.head@gov.yk.ca
Chief Territorial Firearms Officer, Ron Daniels, 867/667-3088, Fax: 867/393-6209

#### COMMUNITY DEVELOPMENT & POLICING BRANCH

Director, Robert Cole, 867/667-5962, Fax: 867/667-6826

#### COURT SERVICES BRANCH

Director, Linda Adams, 867/667-5942, Fax: 867/393-6212, Email: linda.adams@gov.yk.ca
Manager, Court Operations, Edna Delisle-Jackson, 867/667-3440
Trial Coordinator, Iris Warde, 867/667-3442
Sheriff, Sheriff's Office, Paul Cowan, 867/667-5365

#### CONSUMER & COMMERCIAL SERVICES BRANCH

Asst. Deputy Minister, Noreen McGowan, 867/667-5256
Chief Coroner, Coroner's Service, R. Kent Stewart, 867/667-5317
Registrar, Land Titles, Dianne Gau, 867/667-5612
Official Guardian & Public Administrator, Official Guardian's Office, Judith Suley, 867/667-5366
Manager, Consumer Services & Registrar, Medical Practitioners, Superintendent, Insurance, Elsie Bagan, 867/667-5257
Manager, Corporate Affairs & Registrar of Securities, Richard Roberts, 867/667-5225
Acting Manager, Labour Services, Brian Werlin, 867/667-5944

#### LEGAL SERVICES BRANCH

Director, Howard Kushner, 867/667-3469, Fax: 867/393-6379
Acting Executive Director, Legal Aid, Karen Ruddy, 867/667-5210
Chief, Legislative Counsel, Steven Horn, 867/667-5776

##### Associated Agencies, Boards & Commissions

•Employment Standards Board: PO Box 2703, Whitehorse YT Y1A 2C6
Chair, Glenis Allen, 867/667-5944
•Yukon Human Rights Commission: 205 Rogers St., Whitehorse YT Y1A 1X1 – 867/667-6226
Chair, Geraldine Hutchings
•Yukon Human Rights Panel of Adjudicators: #202, 208 Main St., Whitehorse YT Y1A 2B2 – 867/667-7667
Chief Adjudicator, Monica Leask
•Yukon Judicial Council: PO Box 4010, Whitehorse YT Y1A 3S9 – 867/667-3524
Chair, Mr. Justice R.E. Hudson
•Yukon Law Foundation: PO Box 5330, Whitehorse YT Y1A 4Z2 – 867/668-4231
Chair, Brian Morris
•Law Society of Yukon - Executive: #201, 302 Steele St., Whitehorse YT Y1A 2C5 – 867/668-4231
President, Kenneth A. Oyler
•Law Society of Yukon - Lawyers' Discipline Committee: #201, 302 Steele St., Whitehorse YT Y1A 2C5 – 867/668-4231
•Yukon Legal Services Society/Legal Aid: 207 Strickland St., Whitehorse YT Y1A 2J7 – 867/667-5210
Executive Director, Karen Ruddy
•Yukon Lottery Appeal Board: c/o Consumer Services, PO Box 2703, Whitehorse YT Y1A 2C6 – 867/667-5257
•Yukon Medical Council: PO Box 2703, Whitehorse YT Y1A 2C6 – 867/667-5257
Chair, Dr. Lis Densmore
•Nursing Assistants Advisory Committee: Registrar's Office, PO Box 2703, Whitehorse YT Y1A 2C6 – 867/667-5257
Registrar, Elsie Bagan
•Yukon Utilities Board: PO Box 6070, Whitehorse YT Y1A 5L7 – 867/667-5058
Chair, Brian Morris

## Yukon LIQUOR CORPORATION

PO Box 2703, Whitehorse YT Y1A 2C6
867/667-5245; Fax: 867/668-7806
**Minister Responsible**, Hon. Eric Fairclough, 867/667-5651
President & CEO, Jean Besier, 867/667-8923
Chief Liquor Inspector, Jeannine McGregor, 867/667-8926
Director, Corporate Services, David Steele, 867/667-8924
Director, Operations & Purchasing, Bob Morris, 867/667-5244

## Yukon PUBLIC SERVICE COMMISSION

PO Box 2703, Whitehorse YT Y1A 2C6
867/667-5252; Fax: 867/667-6705
**Minister Responsible**, Hon. Trevor Harding, 867/667-8416
Commissioner, Patricia N. Cumming
Acting Director, Administration Branch, Lucy Coulthard, 867/667-5861
Director, Benefits Management, Terry Kinney, 867/667-5251
Director, Corporate Human Resource Services, Mal Malloch, 867/667-5250
Director, Planning & Research Branch, Pat Byers, 867/667-3537
Director, Staff Development Branch, Cheryl Van Blaricom, 867/667-8267
Director, Staffing Relations Branch, Megan Slobodin, 867/667-5201

## Yukon RENEWABLE RESOURCES (YRR)

PO Box 2703, Whitehorse YT Y1A 2C6
867/667-5237
Toll Free: 1-800-661-0408 (Yukon)

#### ACTS ADMINISTERED

Agricultural Products Act
Agriculture Development Act
Brands Act
Environment Act
Fisheries Act (Canada) -Administrative agreement for freshwater fisheries
Forest Protection Act
Freshwater Fisheries Agreement Act
Mackenzie River Basin Agreements Act
Parks Act
Pounds Act
Wildlife Act
Yukon River Basin & Alsek River Basin Agreements Act
Yukon River Basin Study Agreement Act

**Minister**, Hon. Eric Fairclough, 867/667-8899
Deputy Minister, William Oppen, 867/667-5460
Asst. Deputy Minister, Mark Hoffman, 867/667-8955
Coordinator, Communications, Dennis Senger

#### AGRICULTURE BRANCH

Fax: 867/393-6222
Director, Dave Beckman, 867/667-5838

#### ENVIRONMENT PROTECTION & ASSESSMENT BRANCH

Fax: 867/393-6213
Director, Joe Ballantyne, 867/667-8177
Manager, Environmental Assessment, Kelvin Leary, 867/667-5409
Manager, Standards & Approvals, Bengt Pettersson, 867/667-5610

#### FIELD SERVICES BRANCH

Fax: 867/393-6206
Director, Ross Leef, 867/667-8005
Manager, Enforcement & Compliance, Dan Lindsey, 867/667-8936
Regional Resource Manager, North, John Russell, 867/993-6951
Regional Resource Manager, South, Tony Grabowski, 867/667-5115

**FINANCE & ADMINISTRATION BRANCH**
Director, Stan Marinoske, 867/667-5197, Fax: 867/393-6219
Manager, Financial Services, Darrel March, 867/667-5160
Manager, Information Services & Economic Programs, Steve Smyth, 867/667-5160
Manager, Personnel Services, Nonie Mikeli, 867/667-8659

**FISH & WILDLIFE BRANCH**
Fax: 867/393-6213
Acting Director, Don Toews, 867/667-5715
Chief, Fisheries, Don Toews, 867/667-5117
Chief, Habitat Management, Manfred Hoefs, 867/667-5671
Chief, Regional Management, Brian Pelchat, 867/667-5720
Chief, Wildlife Management, Doug Larsen, 867/667-5177

**PARKS & OUTDOOR RECREATION BRANCH**
Fax: 867/668-7823
Director, Jim McIntyre, 867/667-5261
Project Manager, Peter Frankish, 867/667-3057
Regional Superintendent, Klondike, Sandy Sippola, 867/993-6850
Regional Superintendent, Kluane, George Nassiopoulos, 867/634-2026
Regional Superintendent, Liard, Ray Wotton, 867/821-4609

**POLICY & PLANNING BRANCH**
Fax: 867/667-3641
Director, Jim Connell, 867/667-5634
Manager, Geographic Information Section, Lauren Crooks, 867/667-8137
Manager, Geographic Information Section, Beth Hawkings, 867/667-8137
Manager, Land Claims Coordination Unit, Allan Koprowsky
Manager, Policy Analysis & Development, Vacant

**Associated Agencies, Boards & Commissions**
•Alsek Renewable Resources Council: PO Box 2077, Haines Junction YT Y0B 1L0
Chair, Mike Crawshay, 867/634-2524
•Mayo Renewable Resources Council: PO Box 249, Mayo YT Y0B 1M0
Chair, Dan McDiarmid, 867/996-2942
•Teslin Renewable Resources Council: PO Box 186, Teslin YT Y0A 1B0
Chair, Denny Denison, 867/390-2323
•Vuntut Gwitchin Renewable Resources Council: PO Box 80, Old Crow YT Y0B 1N0
Chair, Roy Moses, 867/996-3034
•Yukon Fish & Wildlife Management Board: PO Box 5954, Whitehorse YT Y1A 5L7 – 867/667-3754; Fax: 867/667-2099
Chair, Mike Smith, 867/667-3754, Fax: 867/667-2099

## Yukon TOURISM
PO Box 2703, Whitehorse YT Y1A 2C6
867/667-5430; Fax: 867/667-8844

**ACTS ADMINISTERED**
Historic Resources Act
Historic Sites & Monuments Act
Hotels & Tourist Establishments Act
Scientists & Explorers Act
**Minister**, Hon. Dave Keenan, 867/667-8262
Deputy Minister, Vicki Hancock, 867/667-5430
Director, Arts Branch, Rick Lemaire, 867/667-8592
Director, Corporate Services, Cynthia Jenkins, 867/667-3009
Director, Heritage Branch, Jeff Hunston, 867/667-5363
Director, Industry Services Branch, John Spicer, 867/667-5633
Director, Marketing Branch, Klaus W. Roth, 867/667-5390
Coordinator, Historic Sites, Doug Olynyk, 867/667-5295
Yukon Archaeologist, Ruth Gotthardt, 867/667-5983

## Yukon WOMEN'S DIRECTORATE
PO Box 2703, Whitehorse YT Y1A 2C6
867/667-3030; Fax: 867/393-6270
**Minister Responsible**, Hon. Lois Moorcroft
Director, Elda Ward, 867/667-5182, Email: eward@gov.yk.ca

## Yukon WORKERS' COMPENSATION HEALTH & SAFETY BOARD (YWCHSB)
401 Strickland St., Whitehorse YT Y1A 5N8
867/667-5645; Fax: 867/393-6279
Toll Free: 1-800-661-0443

**ACTS ADMINISTERED**
Workers' Compensation Act
Occupational Health & Safety Act
**Minister Responsible**, Hon. Trevor Harding, 867/667-8416
President & CEO, Dr. Barry Davidson, 867/667-5224
Director, Claimant Services, Sheila Lillies, 867/667-3776
Director, Occupational Health & Safety, Mike Tischer, 867/667-8616
Director, Corporate Services, Tony Armstrong, 867/667-8186
Chief Financial Officer, David Tyler, 867/667-5624
Medical Advisor, Dr. Allon Reddoch, 867/667-8981
Communications Officer, Bonnie King, 867/667-8983

# FOREIGN GOVERNMENT EQUIVALENCY TABLE

## CANADIAN GOVERNMENT COMPARISONS WITH MAJOR TRADING PARTNERS

| Canada | Australia | Belgium | China | France | Germany | Italy | Japan |
|---|---|---|---|---|---|---|---|
| **Office of the Prime Minister** | Office of the Prime Minister | Office of the Prime Minister | Office of the Premier | Office of the Prime Minister | Office of the Fed. Chancellor | Office of the Prime Minister | Office of the Prime Minister |
| **House of Commons** | House of Representatives | Chamber of Representatives | Ntl. People's Congress | Ntl. Assembly | Fed. Assembly | Chamber of Deputies | House of Representatives |
| **Agriculture & Agri-food** | Dept. of Primary Industries & Energy | Min. of Agriculture & Small- & Medium-Sized Business | Min. of Agriculture | Min. of Agriculture & Fisheries | Min. of Food, Agriculture & Forestry | Min. of Agriculture | Min. of Agriculture, Forestry & Fisheries |
| **Canadian Heritage** | Dept. of Immigration & Multicultural Affairs | Min. of the Interior/ Min. of Telecommunications | Min. of Culture/ State Physical Culture & Sports Comm. | Min. of Culture & Communications/ Min. of Youth & Sport | --- | Min. of Cultural Heritage & Sport | Min. of Home Affairs |
| **Citizenship & Immigration Canada** | Dept. of Immigration & Multicultural Affairs | Min. of Foreign Affairs/Min. of Justice | Min. of Civil Affairs/ State Nationalities Affairs Commn. | Min. of Culture & Communications/ Min. of Foreign Affairs, European Sec. | Min. of Justice | Min. of the Interior/ Min. of Foreign Affairs | Min. of Justice |
| **Environment Canada** | Dept. of Environment, Sport & Territories | Min. of the Interior/ Min. of Pensions & Public Health, Sec. for Social Integration & Environment | Min. of Forestry/ Min. of Water Resources/State Bureau of Environmental Protection | Min. of Town & Country Planning & the Environment | Min. for the Environment, Nature Conservation & Nuclear Safety | Min. of Environment/Energy, Environment & New Technology Agency | Min. of Agriculture, Forestry & Fisheries/ Japan Environmental Agency |
| **Finance Canada** | Dept. of Finance & Admin. | Min. of the Budget/ Min. of Finance | Min. of Finance | Min. of Economy, Finance & Industry | Min. of Economic Affairs/Min. of Finance | Min. of Finance | Min. of Finance/ Economic Planning Agency |
| **Fisheries & Oceans Canada** | Dept. of Primary Industries & Energy | --- | --- | Min. of Agriculture & Fisheries | Min. for the Environment, Nature Conservation & Nuclear Safety | --- | Min. of Agriculture, Forestry & Fisheries/ Japanese Fisheries Agency |
| **Foreign Affairs & International Trade Canada** | Dept. of Foreign Affairs & Trade | Min. of Foreign Affairs/Min. of Foreign Trade | Min. of Foreign Affairs/Min. of Foreign Trade & Economic Co-op./ Chinese Council for the Promotion of Intl. Trade/Beijing Foreign Trade Corp. | Min. of Foreign Affairs/Min. of the Interior, Overseas Development Sec. | Min. of Foreign Affairs/Fed. Office for Foreign Trade Information | Min. of Foreign Affairs/Min. of Foreign Trade/Ntl. Inst. for Foreign Trade | Min. of Foreign Affairs/Min. of Intl. Trade & Industry/ Japan External Trade Organization |
| **Health Canada** | Dept. of Health & Family Services | Min. of Pensions & Public Health | Min. of Public Health/State Family Planning Commn. | Min. of Employment & Solidarity, Health Sec. | Min. of Health | Min. of Health | Min. of Health & Welfare/Japan Food Agency |
| **Human Resources Development Canada** | Dept. of Employment, Education, Training & Youth Affairs/Dept. of Social Security | Min. of Employment, Labour & Equal Opportunity/ Min. of Pensions & Public Health | Min. of Labour/Min. of Public Security | Min. of Employment & Solidarity/Min. of Ntl. Education, Research & Technology | Min. of Labour & Social Affairs/Min. of Education, Science, Research & Tech./Min. of Family & Senior Citizens | Min. of Employment & Social Welfare/ Min. of Family & Social Affairs/Min. of Education & Research | Min. of Health & Welfare/Min. of Labour |
| **Indian & Northern Affairs Canada** | Aboriginal & Torres Strait Islander Commn./Dept. of the Transport & Regional Development | --- | --- | --- | Min. of Regional Planning, Building & Urban Development | Dept. of Public Admin. & Regional Affairs | --- |
| **Justice Canada** | Dept. of the Attorney General & Justice | Min. of Justice | Min. of Justice | Min. of Justice | Min. of Justice | Min. of Justice | Min. of Justice |
| **National Defence Canada** | Dept. of Defence | Min. of Ntl. Defence | Min. of Ntl. Defence | Min. of Defence | Min. of Defence | Min. of Defence | Japanese Defence Agency |

## FOREIGN GOVERNMENT EQUIVALENCY TABLE

### CANADIAN GOVERNMENT COMPARISONS WITH MAJOR TRADING PARTNERS

| Malaysia | México | Netherlands | Norway | South Korea | Taiwan | United Kingdom | United States |
|---|---|---|---|---|---|---|---|
| Office of the Prime Minister | Office of the President | Office of the Prime Minister | Office of the Prime Minister | Office of the Prime Minister | Office of the Premier | Office of the Prime Minister | Office of the President |
| House of Representatives | Chamber of Deputies | Second Chamber | Odelsting | Ntl. Assembly | Ntl. Assembly | House of Commons | House of Representatives |
| Min. of Agriculture | Sec. of Agriculture & Water Resources/ Sec. of Agrarian Reform | Min. of Agriculture, Nature Management & Fisheries | Min. of Agriculture | Min. of Agriculture & Forestry | Council for Agriculture | Min. of Agriculture, Fisheries & Food | Dept. of Agriculture |
| Min. of Culture, Arts & Tourism/Min. of Ntl. Unity & Community Development | Sec. of Social Development/Sec. of Tourism | Min. of Education, Cultural Affairs & Science | Min. of Cultural Affairs | Min. of Culture & Sports | Council for Cultural Planning & Development | Dept. of Ntl. Heritage/Northern Ireland Office/Scottish Office/Welsh Office | Dept. of State/Ntl. Park Service/Smithsonian Institution |
| Min. of Ntl. Unity & Community Development/Min. of Youth & Sports | Sec. of the Interior | Min. of Home Affairs | Min. of Justice | Min. of Home Affairs/Min. of Justice | Min. of Justice | Home Office | Dept. of Justice, Immigration & Naturalization Service |
| Min. of Science, Technology & the Environment | Sec. of Environment, Natural Resources & Fisheries | Min. of Agriculture, Nature Management & Fisheries | Min. of Environment | Min. of the Environment/Environment Mgmt. Corp./ Korean Environmental Preservation Association | Central Weather Bureau/Environment Protection Admin. | Dept. of the Environment, Transport & the Regions, Environment | Dept. of the Interior/ Environmental Protection Agency |
| Min. of Finance | Sec. of Finance & Public Credit | Min. of Finance | Min. of Finance | Min.of Finance & the Economy/ Economic Planning Board | Min. of Finance/ Budget, Accounting & Statistics Office | Her Majesty's Treasury | Dept. of Commerce |
| Min. of Primary Industries | Sec. of Environment, Natural Resources & Fisheries, Fisheries Development | Min. of Agriculture, Nature Management & Fisheries | Min. of Fisheries | Min. of Maritime Affairs & Fisheries/ Korean Maritime Inst./Korean Ocean Research & Development Inst. | --- | Min. of Agriculture, Fisheries & Food | Dept. of Commerce, Oceans & Atmosphere Office/Dept. of the Interior, U.S. Fish & Wildlife Service |
| Min. of Foreign Affairs/Min. of Intl. Trade & Industry | Sec. of Foreign Affairs/Ntl. Commercial Exports Council/Ntl. Foreign Investment Commn. | Min. of Foreign Affairs | Min. of Foreign Affairs/Min. of Trade & Shipping | Min. of Foreign Affairs/Min. of Justice, Korean Customs Service/Inst. for Intl. Economics & Trade | Min. of Foreign Affairs/Overseas Chinese Affairs Commn./Fair Trade Commn. | Foreign & Commonwealth Office/Dept. of Intl. Development/Dept. of Trade & Industry/HM Treasury, Customs & Excise | Dept. of Commerce/ Dept. of State, Foreign Service/Intl. Trade Admin./U.S. Intl. Trade Commn./ Adv. Committee for Trade & Policy Negotiations/Office of the U.S. Trade Representative |
| Min. of Health | Sec. of Health | Min. of Health, Welfare & Sports | Min. of Health & Social Affairs | Min. of Health & Welfare/Korean Inst. for Health & Social Affairs | Dept. of Health | Dept. of Health | Dept. of Health & Human Services |
| Min. of Education/ Min. of Human Resources | Sec. of Labour & Social Welfare/Sec. of Social Development | Min. of Social Affairs & Employment | Min. of Health & Social Services/Min. of Local Government & Labour | Min. of Labour | Council of Labour Affairs | Dept. of Education & Employment/ Dept. of Social Security | Dept. of Health & Human Services, Social Security Admin./Dept. of Labour |
| Min. of Rural Development | --- | --- | Min. of Development Co-op. | --- | --- | Dept. of the Environment, Transport & the Regions | Dept. of the Interior, Bur. of Indian Affairs |
| Min. of Home Affairs | Office of the Attorney General | Min. of Justice | Min. of Justice | Min. of Justice | Min. of Justice | Lord Chancellor's Dept./Lord Advocate's Dept. | Dept. of Justice |
| Min. of Defence | Sec. of Ntl. Defence/ Sec. of the Navy | Min. of Defence | Min. of Defence | Min. of Ntl. Defence | Min. of Ntl. Defence | Min. of Defence | Dept. of Defence/ Ntl. Security Council |

# FOREIGN GOVERNMENT EQUIVALENCY TABLE

## CANADIAN GOVERNMENT COMPARISONS WITH MAJOR TRADING PARTNERS

| Canada | Australia | Belgium | China | France | Germany | Italy | Japan |
|---|---|---|---|---|---|---|---|
| **Industry Canada** | Dept. of Industry, Science & Technology/Dept. of Workplace Relations & Small Business | Min. of Agriculture & Small & Medium Size Business/Min. of Economic Affairs | Min. of: the Chemical Industry; the Coal Industry; the Electronics Industry; the Machine Building Industry; the Metallurgical Industry/All-China Fedn. of Industry & Commerce | Min. of Economy, Finance & Industry/ France Development Fund | Min. of Economic Co-op. & Development/Fed. Patent Office/Fed. Export Office | Min. of Industry & Tourism/Manufacturing Industries Investment & Financing Authority | Min. of Intl. Trade & Industry/Small- & Medium-sized Businesses Agency/ Hokkaido & Okinawa Development Agency |
| **Natural Resources Canada** | Dept. of Primary Industries & Energy | Min. of the Interior | Min. of the Power Industry/Min. of Forestry/Min. of Geology & Mineral Resources/Min. of Water Resources | Min. of Town & Country Planning & the Environment | Min. for the Environment, Nature Conservation & Nuclear Safety/Min. of Food, Agriculture & Forestry | Min. of Agriculture/ Min. of the Interior/ Energy Environment & New Technology Agency | Min. of Agriculture, Forestry & Fisheries/ Japan Environmental Agency/Ntl. Land Agency |
| **Public Works & Govt. Services Canada** | Dept. of Finance & Admin. | Min. of Justice | Min. of Communications/Min. of Construction/Min. of Water Resources/ State Planning Comm. | Min. of Capital Works, Transport & Housing | Min. of Regional Planning, Building & Urban Development | Min. of Public Works | Min. of Construction |
| **Revenue Canada** | Dept. of the Treasury | Min. of Finance/Min. of Pensions & Public Health/Min. of Social Affairs | Bureau of Taxation | Min. of Economy, Finance & Industry | Min. of Finance/Min. of Economic Affairs | Min. of Finance/Min. of Treasury & the Budget | Min. of Finance |
| **Solicitor General Canada** | Dept. of the Attorney General & Justice | Min. of the Interior | Min. of Public Security/Min. of State Security | Min. of the Interior/ Min. of Justice | Min. of the Interior/ Fed. Office for Public Security | Min. of the Interior/ Min. of Justice | Min. of Home Affairs/Min. of Justice |
| **Statistics Canada** | --- | --- | --- | Min. of Ntl. Education, Research & Technology | Fed. Statistics Office | --- | --- |
| **Status of Women Canada** | Dept. of Health & Family Services | Min. of Employment, Labour & Equal Opportunity/ Min. of Social Affairs | --- | Min. of Employment & Solidarity | Min. for Family, Senior Citizens, Women & Youth | Dept. of Family & Social Affairs | --- |
| **Transport Canada** | Dept. of Transport & Regional Development | Min. of Transportation | Min. of Communications/Min. of Railways/Civil Aviation Admin. | Min. of Capital Works, Transport & Housing | Min. of Transport/ Fed. Aviation Office | Min. of Transport | Min. of Transport |
| **Treasury Board of Canada** | Dept. of the Treasury | Min. of the Budget/ Min. of Finance | Min. of Finance | Min. of Economy, Finance & Industry | Min. of Economic Affairs/Min. of Finance | Min. of Treasury & the Budget | Min. of Finance |
| **Veterans Affairs Canada** | Dept. of Veterans' Affairs | --- | --- | Min. of Defence, Veterans Affairs | Min. for Family, Senior Citizens, Women & Youth | --- | --- |
| **Associated Agencies** | | | | | | | |
| **Atomic Energy of Canada Ltd.** | --- | --- | China Nuclear Energy Industry Corp. | France Electricity | Min. for the Environment, Nature Conservation & Nuclear Energy | Ntl. Nuclear Energy Committee | Japan Atomic Energy Commn. |
| **Bank of Canada** | --- | Ntl. Bank of Belgium | Bank of China/People's Bank of China | Bank of France | Bank of the Fed. Republic of Germany | Bank of Italy | Bank of Japan |
| **Canada Post Corp.** | --- | Inst. of Posts & Telecommunications | Min. of Posts & Telecommunications | Min. of Economy, Finance & Industry, Industry Sec. | Min. of Posts & Telecommunications | Min. of Posts & Telecommunications | Min. of Posts & Telecommunications |

## FOREIGN GOVERNMENT EQUIVALENCY TABLE

**CANADIAN GOVERNMENT COMPARISONS WITH MAJOR TRADING PARTNERS**

| Malaysia | México | Netherlands | Norway | South Korea | Taiwan | United Kingdom | United States |
|---|---|---|---|---|---|---|---|
| Min. of Domestic Trade & Consumer Affairs/Min. of Entrepreneurial Development/Min. of Intl. Trade & Industry/Min. of Science, Technology & the Environment | Sec. of Trade & Industrial Promotion | Min. of Economic Affairs & Foreign Trade | Min. of Development Coordination/ Min. of Industry & Energy/Fedn. of Commercial & Service Enterprises | Min. of Trade & Industry/Korean Development Inst./ Korean Inst. of Industry & Technology | Min. of Economic Affairs/Council for Economic Planning & Development | Dept. of Intl. Development/Dept. of Trade & Industry | Small Business Admin./U.S. Trade & Development Agency |
| Min. of Energy, Telecommunications & Posts/Min. of Land & Co-operative Development | Sec. of Environment, Natural Resources & Fisheries/Mining Sector Development Agency/Council of Mineral Resources Development/Ntl. Water Commn. | Min. of Agriculture, Nature Management & Fisheries | Min. of the Environment/Min. of Industry & Energy/Ntl. Energy Inst./Norwegian Petroleum Directorate | Min. of Agriculture, Forestry/Min. of the Environment/Min. of Maritime Affairs & Fisheries/Inst. for Energy Research/ Inst. of Geology, Mining & Materials | Min. of the Interior/ Environment Protection Admin. | Dept. of the Environment, Transport & the Regions/Dept. of Ntl. Heritage, Royal Parks/HM Land Registry | Dept. of Agriculture, Forest Service/Dept. of Energy/Dept. of the Interior, Bureau of Mines, Bureau of Land Management, Ntl. Parks Service |
| Min. of Works | Sec. of the Interior | Min. of Transport & Public Works | Min. of Administrative Affairs | Min. of Government Admin./Min. of Transportation & Construction | Council for Economic Planning & Development | Cabinet Office, Buying Agency/Office of Public Services/ Office of Water Services | Dept. of Housing & Urban Development General Services Admin./ |
| --- | Sec. of Finance & Public Credit | Min. of Finance | Min. of Finance | Min. of Finance & Economy | Budget, Accounting & Statistics Office | Board of Inland Revenue/Ntl. Audit Office | Dept. of the Treasury, Internal Revenue Service/U.S. Customs Service |
| Min. of Home Affairs | Sec. of the Interior | Min. of Home Affairs/Min. of Justice | Min. of Justice | Min. of Home Affairs/Min. of Justice | Min. of the Interior | Home Office/Law Officer's Dept. | Dept. of Justice/Ntl. Security Council/ Central Intelligence Agency |
| --- | Sec. of the Interior, Population & Migration | --- | --- | Min. of Data & Communications | Budget, Accounting & Statistics Office | Office for Ntl. Statistics/Home Office, Research & Statistics Directorate | Dept. of Commerce, Economic & Statistics Admin., Bureau of Census |
| --- | Sec. of Social Development | Min. of Home Affairs/Min. of Health, Welfare & Sports | Min. of Children & Family Affairs | Inst. of Health & Social Affairs | --- | Dept. of Social Security, Women | Dept. of Labor, Women's Bureau |
| Min. of Transport | Sec. of Transportation & Communications/Ntl. Railways of México | Min. of Transport & Public Works | Min. of Transportation & Communications/Norwegian State Railway | Min. of Transportation & Construction/ Korean Maritime Inst./Korean Transport Inst. | Min. of Transportation & Communications | Dept. of Environment, Transport & the Regions/Associated British Ports/ British Railways Board | Dept. of Transportation/Ntl. Transportation Safety Board |
| Min. of Finance | Sec. of Finance & Public Credit | Min. of Finance | Min. of Finance | Min. of Government Admin./Economic Planning Board | Min. of Finance | HM Treasury | Dept. of Commerce/ Dept. of the Treasury |
| --- | --- | --- | Min. of Health & Social Services | Min. of Patriots & Veterans Affairs | Vocational Assistance Commn. for Retired Servicemen | Min. of Defence | Dept. of Veterans Affairs |
| | | | | | | | |
| --- | Ntl. Nuclear Development Standards Commn. | --- | --- | Korean Atomic Energy Research Institute/Korean Nuclear Society | Atomic Energy Council | UK Atomic Energy Authority | Nuclear Regulatory Commn. |
| --- | Bank of México | Bank of the Netherlands | --- | Bank of Korea | Bank of China | Bank of England | Fed. Reserve System |
| Min. of Energy, Telecommunications & Posts | Sec. of Transportation & Communications | --- | Min. of Transportation & Communications | Min. of Data & Communications | Min. of Transportation & Communications | The Post Office | U.S. Postal Service |

## FOREIGN GOVERNMENT EQUIVALENCY TABLE
### CANADIAN GOVERNMENT COMPARISONS WITH MAJOR TRADING PARTNERS

| Canada | Australia | Belgium | China | France | Germany | Italy | Japan |
|---|---|---|---|---|---|---|---|
| **Canadian Broadcasting Corp.** | --- | Min. of Telecommunications/Inst. of Posts & Telecommunications | Min. of Posts & Telecommunications/ Min. of Television, Radio & Cinema | France Radio-telephone Company/ France Telecom | Min. of Posts & Telecommunications | Min. of Posts & Telecommunications | Min. of Posts & Telecommunications |
| **Canadian National Railway Co.** | --- | --- | Min. of Railways | --- | --- | --- | --- |
| **Canadian Radio-Television & Telecommunications Commn.** | --- | Min. of Telecommunications/Inst. of Posts & Telecommunications | Min. of Posts & Telecommunications/ Min. of Television, Radio & Cinema | Min. of Economy, Finance & Industry, Industry Sec. | Min. of Posts & Telecommunications | Min. of Posts & Telecommunications | Min. of Posts & Telecommunications |
| **Canadian Space Agency** | --- | --- | --- | Aerospace Industries | --- | --- | Inst. of Space & Astronautical Science |
| **Correctional Service Canada** | Dept. of the Attorney General & Justice | Min. of Justice | Min. of Justice | Min. of Justice | Min. of Justice | Min. of Justice | Min. of Justice |
| **Export Development Corp.** | Dept. of Foreign Affairs & Trade | Min. of Foreign Trade | Min. of Foreign Trade & Economic Co-op./Beijing Foreign Trade Corp. | Min. of Economy, Finance & Industry | Fed. Export Office/ Fed. Office for Foreign Trade Information | Min. of Foreign Trade/Ntl. Inst. for Foreign Trade | Japan External Trade Organization |
| **National Energy Board** | --- | --- | Min. of the Power Industry/China Intl. Water & Electric Corp./China Ntl. Petroleum & Natural Gas Corp./ China Nuclear Energy Corp. | France Electricity/ France Gas Co. | --- | Energy, Environment & New Technology Agency/ Ntl. Nuclear Energy Committee | --- |
| **National Research Council** | --- | Min. of Scientific Policy | Chinese Academy of Sciences/State Science & Technology Commn. | Min. of Ntl. Education, Research & Technology | Min. of Education, Science, Research & Technology | Min. of Universities, Scientific & Technological Research/ Min. of Education & Research | Japan Science & Technology Agency |
| **Public Service Commn. of Canada** | --- | --- | Min. of Personnel | Min. of Civil Service, Administrative Reform & Decentralization | --- | Min. of Public Admin. & Regional Affairs | --- |
| **Royal Canadian Mounted Police** | --- | --- | Min. of Public Security/Min. of Supervision | --- | Min. of the Interior, Academy of State Police/Office of Criminal Investigation | --- | --- |

# FOREIGN GOVERNMENTS

Following is a listing of government information for those countries which constitute Canada's major trading partners. According to Statistics Canada trade information (*see* "Principal Trading Partners in 1996", page 1-52) Canada's major trading partners include: Australia, Belgium, China, France, Germany, Hong Kong, Italy, Japan, Malaysia, Mexico, the Netherlands, Norway, South Korea, Taiwan, the United Kingdom and the United States.

Major trading countries are listed alphabetically and contain information about major government ministries and departments followed by main federal government agencies and corporations. For information about foreign government diplomatic and consular offices in Canada, *see* "Diplomatic & Consular Representatives in Canada" in the main/general Index.

## GOVERNMENT OF AUSTRALIA (AS)

URL: http://www.nla.gov.au/oz/gov/
Capital: Canberra
Major Political Parties: Liberal-National Coalition; Australian Labour Party; Australian Democratic Party
Currency: Australian Dollar
Total Area: 7,686,850 km2
Population: 18,260,863 (1996 est.)
Language(s): English

### OFFICE OF THE GOVERNOR-GENERAL

Governor-General, Sir William Deane

### OFFICE OF THE PRIME MINISTER

3-5 National Circuit, Barton, Canberra ACT 2600, Australia
(011-61-6) 271-5111, Fax: (011-61-6) 271-5415
Prime Minister, John Howard
Deputy Prime Minister, Tim Fischer
Special Minister of State, Nick Minchin
Minister, Customs & Consumer Affairs, Warren Truss
Minister, Status of Women, Judi Moylan

### SENATE

Canberra ACT 2600, Australia
President, Michael Bearhan

### HOUSE OF REPRESENTATIVES

Canberra ACT 2600, Australia
(011-61-6) 277-7111, Fax: (011-61-6) 277-3387
URL: http://www.aph.gov.au/house/
Speaker, Bob Halverson

### ABORIGINAL & TORRES STRAIT ISLANDER COMMISSION

MLC Tower, Woden Town Centre, Phillip, Canberra ACT 2606, Australia
(011-61-6) 289-1222, Fax: (011-61-6) 281-0772
Minister, John Herron

### DEPARTMENT OF THE ATTORNEY GENERAL & JUSTICE

Robert Garran Offices, Barton, Canberra ACT 2600, Australia

## FOREIGN GOVERNMENT EQUIVALENCY TABLE
### CANADIAN GOVERNMENT COMPARISONS WITH MAJOR TRADING PARTNERS

| Malaysia | México | Netherlands | Norway | South Korea | Taiwan | United Kingdom | United States |
|---|---|---|---|---|---|---|---|
| Min. of Energy, Telecommunications & Posts | Telecommunications México | --- | Norwegian Telecommunications Authority | Min. of Data & Communications | Min. of Transportation & Communications | British Broadcasting Corp. | Ntl. Telecommunications & Information Admin. |
| --- | Ntl. Railways of México | --- | Min. of Transportation & Construction, Ntl. Railroad | Korean Ntl. Railroad | --- | British Railways Board | Dept. of Transportation, Fed. Railway Admin. |
| --- | Sec. of Transportation & CommunicationsTelecommunic ations México | --- | Min. of Transportation & Communications/Norwegian Telecommunications Authority | Min. of Data & Communications/ Electronics & Telecommunications Research Inst. | Min. of Transportation & Communications | British Telecom Intl./British Telecommunications PLC/Wireless PLC/ Radiotelecommunications Agency | Fed. Communications Commn./Ntl. Telecommunications & Information Admin. |
| --- | --- | --- | --- | Korean Aerospace Research Inst. | Civil Aeronautics Admin. | British Aerospace | Ntl. Aeronautics & Space Admin. |
| Sec. of the Interior | --- | Min. of Justice | Min. of Justice | Min. of Justice | Min. of Justice | Home Office, HM Prison Service | Dept. of Justice, Bureau of Prisons |
| --- | Ntl. Commercial Exports Council | Min. of Economic Affairs & Foreign Trade | Min. of Trade & Shipping | Korean Inst. for Intl. Economics & Trade | Min. of Economic Affairs, Board of Foreign Trade/Fair Trade Commn. | Dept. of Trade & Industry/Export Credits Guarantee Dept. | Fed. Trade Commn./ US Trade & Development Agency |
| Min. of Science, Technology & Industry | Ntl. Council of Mineral Resources Development/Ntl. Electricity Commn. | --- | Ntl. Energy Inst. | Korean Energy Economic Inst./Korean Inst. of Energy Research | Taiwan Power Co. | Office of Electricity Regulation/Oil & Pipelines Agency | Fed. Energy Regulatory Commn. |
| Min. of Science, Technology & Industry | --- | Min. of Education, Cultural Affairs & Science | Min. of Education, Research & Church Affairs | Min. of Science & Technology/Korean Inst. of Advanced Science & Technology | Ntl. Science Council/ Research, Development & Evaluation Commn. | Office of Science & Technology | Ntl. Science Fdn./ Smithsonian Institution |
| --- | Sec. of the Interior | --- | Min. of Administrative Affairs | Min. of Government Admin. | Central Personnel Admin. | Office of Public Service, Civil Service | Office of Personnel Management |
| --- | Sec. of the Interior, Civil Protection | --- | --- | Min. of Home Affairs, Ntl. Police Headquarters | Min. of the Interior, Ntl. Police Admin. | Home Office/UK Police Service/Ntl. Criminal Intelligence Service | Fed. Bureau of Investigation/Dept. of the Treasury, US Secret Service |

(011-61-6) 250-6666, Fax: (011-61-6) 250-5900

Attorney General & Minister, Daryl Williams, A.M., Q.C.

Minister, Justice, Amanda Vanstone

**DEPARTMENT OF DEFENCE**

Russell Offices, Canberra ACT 2600

(011-61-6) 265-9111

Minister, Ian McLachlan

Minister, Defence Industry, Science & Personnel, Bronwyn Bishop

**DEPARTMENT OF EMPLOYMENT, EDUCATION, TRAINING & YOUTH AFFAIRS**

POB 9880, Canberra ACT 2601

(011-61-6) 240-8848, Fax: (011-61-6) 240-8861

Minister, David Kemp

Minister, Schools, Vocational Education & Training, Christopher Ellison

**DEPARTMENT OF THE ENVIRONMENT, SPORT & TERRITORIES**

POB 787, Canberra ACT 2601, Australia

(011-61-6) 274-1111, Fax: (011-61-6) 274-1123

Minister, Robert Hill

Minister, Sport & Tourism & Minister Assisting the Prime Minister, Sydney 2000 Games, Andrew Thomson

**DEPARTMENT OF FINANCE & ADMINISTRATION**

Newlands St., Parkes, Canberra ACT 2600, Australia

(011-61-6) 263-2222, Fax: (011-61-6) 273-3021

Minister, John Fahey

**DEPARTMENT OF FOREIGN AFFAIRS & TRADE**

Locked Bag 40, QVT, Canberra ACT 2600

(011-61-6) 261-9111, Fax: (011-61-6) 261-3111

Minister, Foreign Affairs, Alexander Downer

Minister, Trade, Rim Fischer

**DEPARTMENT OF HEALTH & FAMILY SERVICES**

POB 9848, Canberra ACT 2601, Australia

(011-61-6) 286-1555, Fax: (011-61-6) 281-6946

Minister, Dr. Michael Wooldridge

Minister, Family Services, Warwick Smith

**DEPARTMENT OF IMMIGRATION & MULTICULTURAL AFFAIRS**

Benjamin Offices, Chan St., Belconnen, Canberra ACT 2617

(011-61-6) 264-1111, Fax: (011-61-6) 264-2670

Minister, Phillip Ruddock

**DEPARTMENT OF INDUSTRY, SCIENCE & TECHNOLOGY**

20 Allara St., Canberra ACT 2601, Australia

(011-61-6) 213-6000, Fax: (011-61-6) 213-7000

Minister, John Moore

**DEPARTMENT OF PRIMARY INDUSTRIES & ENERGY**

POB 858, Canberra ACT 2601, Australia

(011-61-6) 272-3933, Fax: (011-61-6) 272-5161

Minister, John Anderson

Minister, Resources & Energy, Warwick Parer

**DEPARTMENT OF SOCIAL SECURITY**
POB 7788, Canberra Mail Centre, Canberra ACT 2610, Australia
(011-61-6) 244-7788, Fax: (011-61-6) 244-5900
Minister, Jocelyn Newman

**DEPARTMENT OF TRANSPORT & REGIONAL DEVELOPMENT**
POB 594, Canberra ACT 2601, Australia
(011-61-6) 274-7111, Fax: (011-61-6) 257-2505
Minister, Mark Vaile
Minister, Regional Development, Territories & Local Government, Alex Somlyay

**DEPARTMENT OF THE TREASURY**
Parkes Place, Parkes, Canberra ACT 2600, Australia
(011-61-6) 263-2111, Fax: (011-61-6) 273-2614
Minister, Peter Costello
Asst. Treasurer, Rod Kemp

**DEPARTMENT OF VETERANS' AFFAIRS**
POB 21, Woden, Canberra ACT 2606, Australia
(011-61-6) 289-1111, Fax: (011-61-6) 289-6025
Minister, Bruce Scott

**DEPARTMENT OF WORKPLACE RELATIONS & SMALL BUSINESS**
GPO 9879, Canberra ACT 2601, Australia
(011-61-6) 243-7904, Fax: (011-61-6) 243-7542
Minister, Peter Reith

## GOVERNMENT OF BELGIUM/Belgique (BE)
Capital: Brussels
Major Political Parties: Flemish Social Christian (CVP); Francophone Socialist (PS); Flemish Socialist (SP); Flemish Liberals & Democrats (VLD)
Currency: Belgian Franc
Total Area: 30,528 km2
Population: 10,131,000 (1994)
Language(s): Dutch, French, German

**OFFICE OF THE KING**
Palais Royal, Rue de Brèderode, 1000, Brussels, Belgium
(011-32-2) 551-2020
King, H.M. King Albert II
Marshal of the Court, G. Jacques

**OFFICE OF THE PRIME MINISTER**
16, rue de La Loi, 1000, Brussels, Belgium
(011-32-2) 501-02-11, Fax: (011-32-2) 512-69-53
Prime Minister, Jean-Luc Dehaene
Chief of Cabinet, Paul Maertens
Secretary, Council of Ministers, Steve Dubois

**SENATE OF BELGIUM**
Palais de la Nation, 1009, Brussels, Belgium
(011-32-2) 515-82-11, Fax: (011-32-2) 574-06-85
President, Frank Swaelen

**CHAMBER OF REPRESENTATIVES**
Palais de la Nation, 1008, Brussels, Belgium
(011-32-2) 419-80-91, Fax: (011-32-2) 519-83-02
President, Charles-Ferdinand Nothomb

**MINISTRY OF AGRICULTURE & SMALL- & MEDIUM-SIZED BUSINESS**
Rue Marie-Thérese 1, 1040, Brussels, Belgium
(011-32-2)211-06-11, Fax: (011-32-2) 219-61-30
Minister, Karel Pinxten

**MINISTRY OF THE BUDGET**
7, Place Quetelet, 1030, Brussels, Belgium
(011-32-2) 219-01-19, Fax: (011-32-2) 219-09-14
Minister, Herman Van Rompuy

**DEPARTMENT OF DEVELOPMENT CO-OPERATION**
5, av Galilée, 1030, Brussels, Belgium
(011-32-2) 210-19-11, Fax: (011-32-2) 217-33-28
Secretary of State, Réginald Moreels

**MINISTRY OF ECONOMIC AFFAIRS**
23, Square de Meeûs, 1040, Brussels, Belgium
(011-32-2) 506-51-11, Fax: (011-32-2) 514-46-83
Minister, Elio Di Rupo

**MINISTRY OF EMPLOYMENT, LABOUR & EQUAL OPPORTUNITY**
51-53, rue Bélliard, 1040, Brussels, Belgium
(011-32-2) 233-51-11, Fax: (011-32-2) 230-1067
Minister, Miet Smet

**MINISTRY OF FINANCE**
12, rue de la Loi, 1000, Brussels, Belgium
(011-32-2) 233-81-11, Fax: (011-32-2) 233-80-03
Minister, Philippe Maystadt

**MINISTRY OF FOREIGN AFFAIRS**
2, rue des Quatre Bras, 1000, Brussels, Belgium
(011-32-2) 516-81-11, Fax: (011-32-2) 511-63-85
Minister, Erik Derycke

**MINISTRY OF FOREIGN TRADE**
2, rue des Quatre Bras, 1000, Brussels, Belgium
(011-32-2) 516-83-11, Fax: (011-32-2) 512-72-21
Minister, Philippe Maystadt

**MINISTRY OF THE INTERIOR**
60, rue Royale, 1000, Brussels, Belgium
(011-32-2) 227-0700, Fax: (011-32-2) 219-7930
Minister, Johan Van de Lanotte
State Secretary, Security Secretariat, Jan Peeters, 5, rue Gallilée, 10ème étage, 1030, Brussels, (011-32-2) 210-19-11

**MINISTRY OF JUSTICE**
115, boul de Waterloo, 1000, Brussels, Belgium
(011-32-2) 542-79-11, Fax: (011-32-2) 538-07-67
Minister, Stefaan De Clerck

**MINISTRY OF NATIONAL DEFENCE**
Rue Lambermont 8, 1000, Brussels, Belgium
(011-32-2) 516-8211, Fax: (011-32-2) 550-2919
Minister, Jean-Pol Poncelet
Chief of Staff, Air Force, Lt. Gen. Guido Van Hecke, (011-32-2) 243-31-11
Chief of Joint Staff, Armed Forces, V. Adm. Willy Herteleer, (011-32-2) 701-31-11
Chief of Staff, Army, Vacant, (011-32-2) 243-31-11
Chief of Staff, Navy, R. Adm. M. Verhulst, (011-32-2) 701-31-19

**MINISTRY OF PENSIONS & PUBLIC HEALTH**
Bâtiment Amazone, 33, boul Bischoffsheim, 1000, Brussels, Belgium
(011-32-2) 220-20-11, Fax: (011-32-2) 220-20-67
Minister, Marcel Colla
State Secretary, Secretariat for Social Integration & Environment, Jan Peeters, 5, rue Gallilée, 10ème étage, 1030, Brussels, (011-32-2) 210-19-11

**MINISTRY OF PUBLIC AFFAIRS**
Résidence Palace, 9ème étage, Rue de la Loi 155, 1040, Brussels, Belgium
(011-32-2) 233-05-11, Fax: (011-32-2) 233-05-90
Minister, André Flahaut

**MINISTRY OF SCIENTIFIC POLICY**
66, rue de la Loi, 1040, Brussels, Belgium
(011-32-2) 238-28-11, Fax: (011-32-2) 230-38-62
Minister, Yvan Ylieff

**MINISTRY OF SOCIAL AFFAIRS**
66, rue de la Loi, 1040, Brussels, Belgium
(011-32-2) 238-28-11, Fax: (011-32-2) 230-38-95
Minister, Magda de Galan

**MINISTRY OF TELECOMMUNICATIONS**
65, rue de la Loi, 1040, Brussels, Belgium
(011-32-2) 237-67-11, Fax: (011-32-2) 230-18-24
Minister, Elio Di Rupo

**MINISTRY OF TRANSPORTATION**
65, rue de la Loi, 1040, Brussels, Belgium
(011-32-2) 237-67-11, Fax: (011-32-2) 230-18-24
Minister, Michel Daerden

**Associated Agencies**
•Belgian Business Federation
4, rue Ravenstein, 1000, Brussels, Belgium
(011-32-2) 515-0811, Fax: (011-32-2) 515-09-99
President, Urbain Devoldere
•Institute of Posts & Telecommunications
5, rue Van Orlay, 1210, Brussels, Belgium
(011-32-2) 213-46-02
•National Bank of Belgium
14, boul de Berlaimont, 1000, Brussels, Belgium
(011-32-2) 221-21-11, Fax: (011-21-2) 221-31-00
Governor, Alfonse Verplaetse

## GOVERNMENT OF CHINA/Zhong Guo (CH)
Capital: Beijing
Major Political Parties: Chinese Communist Party (CCP)
Currency: Yuan
Total Area: 9,596,960 km2
Population: 1,210,004,956 (1996 est.)
Language(s): Chinese (Mandarin), Yue (Cantonese), Wu (Shanghainese), Minbei (Fuzhou), Minnan (Hokkien-Taiwanese), Xiang, Gan, Hakka

**OFFICE OF THE PRESIDENT**
c/o State Council Secretariat, Zhong Nan Hai, Beijing, China
(011-86-10) 3098375
President, Jiang Zemin
Vice-President, Rong Yiren

**OFFICE OF THE PREMIER**
c/o State Council Secretariat, Zhong Nan Hai, Beijing, China
(011-86-10) 666453
Premier, Li Peng
Vice-Premier, Wu Bangguo
Vice-Premier, Jiang Chunyun
Vice-Premier, Zou Jiahua
Vice-Premier, Li Lanqing
Vice-Premier, Quan Qichen

**THE POLITBURO**
Zhong Nan Hai, Beijing, China
(011-86-10) 335987
General Secretary, Jiang Zemin

**NATIONAL PEOPLE'S CONGRESS/Quango Renmin Diabiao Dahui**
Standing Committee, Great Hall of the People, Beijing, China
(011-86-10) 667380
Chair, Qiao Shi
Vice-Chair, Tian Jiyun

**MINISTRY OF AGRICULTURE**
11 Nong Zhan Nan Li, East District, Beijing 100017, China
(011-86-10) 64193366, Fax: (011-86-10) 64192468
Minister, Liu Jiang

**MINISTRY OF THE CHEMICAL INDUSTRY**
Bldg. #16, 7th Zone, He Ping Li, East District, Beijing 100013, China

(011-86-10) 64914455, Fax: (011-86-10) 64215982
Minister, Gu Xiulian

**MINISTRY OF CIVIL AFFAIRS**
9 Xi Huang Cheng Gen Nen Jie, West District, Beijing 100032, China
(011-86-10) 65135544
Minister, Doje Cering

**MINISTRY OF THE COAL INDUSTRY**
21 Hepinglibei Jie, Dongcheng Qu, Beijing 100713, China
(011-86-10) 64214117, Fax: (011-86-10) 64215627
Minister, Wang Senhao

**MINISTRY OF COMMUNICATIONS**
11 Jianguomennei Dajie, Beijing 100736, China
(011-86-10) 65292114
Minister, Huang Zhendong

**MINISTRY OF CONSTRUCTION**
9 Shan Li He Rd., Hai Dian District, Beijing 100835, China
(011-86-10) 68394114
Minister, Hou Jie

**MINISTRY OF CULTURE**
Jia 83 Dong An Men Bei Jie, Beijing 100722, China
(011-86-10) 64012255
Minister, Liu Zhongde

**MINISTRY OF THE ELECTRONICS INDUSTRY**
27 Wan Shou Lu, Hai Dian District, Beijing 100846, China
(011-86-10) 68212233, Fax: (011-86-10) 68221838
Minister, Hu Qili

**MINISTRY OF FINANCE**
3 San Li He Nan Jie, Fu Xing Men Wai, West District, Beijing 100820, China
(011-86-10) 68526612, Fax: (011-86-10) 68513428
Minister, Liu Zhongli

**MINISTRY OF FOREIGN AFFAIRS**
225 Chao Yang Men Nei Da Jie, Dong Si, East District, Beijing 100701, China
(011-86-10) 65135586
Minister, Qian Qichen

**MINISTRY OF FOREIGN TRADE & ECONOMIC CO-OPERATION**
2 Chang An Blvd. East, Beijing 100731, China
(011-86-10) 65126644, Fax: (011-86-10) 65129214
Minister, Wu Yi

**MINISTRY OF FORESTRY**
18 He Ping Li Dong Jie, East District, Beijing 100714, China
(011-86-10) 64214909, Fax: (011-86-10) 64219149
Minister, Xu Youfang

**MINISTRY OF GEOLOGY & MINERAL RESOURCES**
64 Fu Chen Men Nei Jie, Beijing 100812, China
(011-86-10) 66031144, Fax: (011-86-10) 66017791
Minister, Song Ruixiang

**MINISTRY OF INTERNAL TRADE**
25 Yuetanbei Jie, Xicheng Qu, Beijing 100834, China
(011-86-10) 68392000
Minister, Chen Bangzhu

**MINISTRY OF JUSTICE**
11 Xia Guang Li, San Yuan Qiao, Chaoyang District, Beijing 100016, China
(011-86-10) 64677144
Minister, Xiao Yang

**MINISTRY OF LABOUR**
12 He Ping Li Zhong Jie, East District, Beijing 100716, China
(011-86-10) 64213431, Fax: (011-86-10) 64219310
Minister, Li Boyong

**MINISTRY OF MACHINE BUILDING INDUSTRY**
46 San Li He, West District, Beijing 100823, China
(011-86-10) 68594711, Fax: (011-86-10) 68522644
Minister, Bao Xuding

**MINISTRY OF METALLURGICAL INDUSTRY**
46 Xi Dong Si Jie, Beijing 100020, China
(011-86-10) 65131942, Fax: (011-86-10) 65130074
Minister, Liu Qi

**MINISTRY OF NATIONAL DEFENCE**
25 Huang Si Da Jie, De Sheng Men Wai, East District, Beijing 100011, China
(011-86-10) 66370000
Minister, Gen. Chi Haotian
Chief of Staff, Department of the People's Liberation Army, Gen. Fu Quanyou
Director, Eastern District, Gen. Yu Yongbo
Director, General Logistics Department, Gen. Wang Ke
Commander, Air Force, Lt. Gen. Yu Zhengwu
Commander, Navy, Adm. Zhang Lianzhong

**MINISTRY OF PERSONNEL**
12 He Ping Li Zhong Jie, East District, Beijing 100716, China
(011-86-10) 464213431, Fax: (011-86-10) 64218719
Minister, Song Defu

**MINISTRY OF POSTS & TELECOMMUNICATIONS**
13 Xichangan Jie, Beijing 100804, China
(011-86-10) 66010540, Fax: (011-86-10) 66011250
Minister, Wu Jichuan

**MINISTRY OF THE POWER INDUSTRY (ENERGY)**
137 Fu Yu Jie, Beijing 100031, China
(011-86-10) 66054131, Fax: (011-86-10) 68016077
Minister, Shi Dazhen

**MINISTRY OF PUBLIC HEALTH**
44 Hou Hai Bei Yan, West District, Beijing 100725, China
(011-86-10) 64034433, Fax: (011-86-10) 64014331
Minister, Chen Minzhang

**MINISTRY OF PUBLIC SECURITY**
14 Dong Chang An Jie, East District, Beijing 100741, China
(011-86-10) 65122831, Fax: (011-86-10) 65136577
Minister, Tao Siju

**MINISTRY OF RAILWAYS**
10 Fuxing Lu, Haidian Qu, Beijing 100844, China
(011-86-10) 63240114
Minister, Han Zhubin

**MINISTRY OF STATE SECURITY**
14 Dong Chang An Jie, East District, Beijing 100741, China
(011-86-10) 65244702
Minister, Jia Chunwang

**MINISTRY OF SUPERVISION**
4 Chao Jun Miao, Hai Dian District, Beijing 100081, China
(011-86-10) 62566688, Fax: (011-86-10) 62254258
Minister, Cao Qingze

**MINISTRY OF TELEVISION, RADIO & CINEMA**
2 Fu Xing Men Wai Jie, PO Box 4501, Beijing 100866, China
(011-86-10) 6862753, Fax: (011-86-10) 682122174
Minister, Sun Juazheng

**MINISTRY OF WATER RESOURCES**
1 Bai Guang Lu Ertiao, Guang An Men, Xuan Wu District, Beijing 100761, China
(011-86-10) 63260495, Fax: (011-86-10) 63260365
Minister, Niu Maosheng

**Associated Agencies**
•All-China Federation of Industry & Commerce
93 Bei He Yan Da Jie, Beijing 100006, China
(011-86-10) 6554231
Chair, Wang Zhongfu
•Bank of China
410 Fu Cheng Men Nei Da Jie, Beijing, China
(011-86-10) 66016688
President, Wang Xuebing
•Beijing Foreign Trade Corporation
#12, Yong An Dong Li, Jian Guo Men Wai, Beijing 100022, China
(011-86-10) 65001843
Director, Yu Xiaosong
•Bureau of Environmental Protection
115 Xi Zhi Men Nei, Xiao Jie, East District, Beijing 100035, China
(011-86-10) 66011199
Director, Xie Zhenhua
•Bureau of Taxation
68 Cao Lin Qing Jie, Xuan Wu District, Beijing 100063, China
(011-86-10) 63266836
Director, Liu Zhongli
•China International Water & Electric Corporation
Block 1, Liu Pu Kang, Beijing, 100011
(011-86-10) 64015511
President, Zhu Jingde
•China National Offshore Oil Corporation
23-F Jing Xin Bldg., Jia 2, North Dong San Huan Rd., Chao Yang District, Beijing 100027, China
(011-86-10) 64663696
President, Wang Yan
•China National Petro-Chemical Corporation
Jia 6, Hui Xin Don Jie, Chao Yang District, Beijing 100013, China
(011-86-10) 64216731
President, Sheng Hauren
•China National Petroleum & Natural Gas Corporation
Liu Pu Kang, Beijing, China
(011-86-10) 62015544
President, Wang Tao
•China Nuclear Energy Industry Corporation
Jia 1, Dong Kou, Yuetan Bei Jie, Beijing, China
(011-86-10) 6867717
President, Zhang Xinduo
Chinese Academy of Sciences
52 Shan Li He Lu, West District, Beijing, China
(011-86-10) 6863972
President, Zhou Guangzhao
•Chinese Council for the Promotion of International Trade
1 Fu Xing Men Wai Do Jie, PO Box 4509, Beijing 100860, China
(011-86-10) 8513344
Chair, Zheng Hongye
•Civil Aviation Administration
165 Dong So Zo Da Jie, East District, Beijing 100710, China
(011-86-10) 64012233
Director, Chen Guangyi
•People's Bank of China
32 Cheng Fang St., West District, Beijing 100800, China
(011-86-10) 66016705
Governor, Dai Xianglong
•State Commission for Economic Restructuring
22 Xi An Men St., Beijing 100017, China
(011-86-10) 63096437

Minister of State, Li Tieying
•State Commission of Science & Technology & Industry for National Defence
Dong Guan Fang, Dianmenxi Dajie, Xicheng Qu, Beijing 100035, China
(011-86-10) 66738080
Minister of State, Cao Gangchuan
•State Economic & Trade Commission
26 Xuan Wu Men West Ave., Beijing 100053, China
(011-86-10) 63045336
Minister of State, Wang Zhongyu
•State Education Commission
37 Da Mu Cang Hu Tong, West District, Beijing 100816, China
(011-86-10) 66011049
Minister of State, Zhu Kaixuan
•State Family Planning Commission
14 Zhichun Lu, Haidian Qu, Beijing 100088, China
(011-86-10) 62046622, Fax: (011-86-10) 62051865
Minister of State, Peng Peiyun
•State Nationalities Affairs Commission
252 Taipingqiao Dajie, Xicheng Qu, Beijing 100800, China
(011-86-10) 66016611
Minister of State, Iamail Amat
•State Physical Culture & Sports Commission
9 Tiyuguan Lu, Chong Wen Qu, Beijing 100763, China
(011-86-10) 67012233, Fax: (011-86-10) 67015858
Minister of State, We Shaozu
•State Planning Commission
38 Yuetannan Jie, Xicheng Qu, Beijing 100824, China
(011-86-10) 68501240
Minister of State, Chen Jinhua
•State Science & Technology Commission
54 San Li He, West District, Beijing 100862, China
(011-86-10) 68515544
Minister of State, Song Jian

## GOVERNMENT OF FRANCE (FR)

Capital: Paris
Major Political Parties: Rally for the Republic (RPR); Socialist Party (PS); Union for French Democracy (UDF); Community Party (PCF)
Currency: French Franc
Total Area: 632,841 km2 with French Overseas Territories
Population: 58,317,450 (1996 est.)
Language(s): French

### OFFICE OF THE PRESIDENT

Palais de l'Elysée, #55, 57, rue du Faubourg-Saint Honoré, 75008, Paris, France
(011-33-1) 42-92-81-00, Fax: (011-33-1) 47-42-24-65
President, H.E. Jacques Chirac

### OFFICE OF THE PRIME MINISTER

Hôtel Matignon, 57, rue de Varenne, 75700, Paris 07 SP, France
(011-33-1) 42-75-80-00, Fax: (011-33-1) 45-44-15-72
URL: http://www.premier-ministre.gouv.fr
Prime Minister, Lionel Jospin
President, Social & Economic Council, Jean Mattéoli, Palais d'Iéna, 1, av d'Iéna, 75775, Paris CEDEX 16, (011-33-1) 44-43-60-00

### SENATE

Palais de Luxembourg, 15, rue de Vaugirard, 75291, Paris CEDEX 06, France
(011-33-1) 42-34-20-00, Fax: (011-33-1) 42-14-26-77
URL: http://www.senat.fr/
President, René Monory

### NATIONAL ASSEMBLY

Au Palais-Bourbon, 126, rue de l'Université, 75007, Paris, France
(011-33-1) 40-63-60-00, Fax: (011-331) 42-60-99-03
URL: http://www.assemblee-nat.fr/
President, Philippe Séguin

### MINISTRY OF AGRICULTURE & FISHERIES

78, rue de Varenne, 75007, Paris 07 SP, France
(011-33-1) 49-55-49-55
URL: http://www.agriculture.gouv.fr
Minister, Louis Le Pensec

### MINISTRY OF CAPITAL WORKS, TRANSPORT & HOUSING

246, boul Saint-Germain, 75700, Paris 07 SP, France
(011-33-1) 40-81-21-22, Fax: (011-33-1) 40-81-30-99
Minister, Jean-Claude Gayssot
Secretary of State, Housing, Louis Besson, 3, place de Fontenoy, 75007, Paris, (011-33-1) 44-49-80-00
Secretary of State, Tourism, Michelle Demessine, 40, rue de Bac, 75007, Paris, (011-33-1) 40-81-21-22, URL: http://www.equipement.gouv.fr

### MINISTRY OF CIVIL SERVICE, ADMINISTRATIVE REFORM & DECENTRALIZATION

72, rue de Varenne, 75700, Paris 07 SP, France
(011-33-1) 42-75-80-00
URL: http://www.fonction-publique.gouv.fr
Minister, Emile Zuccarelli

### MINISTRY OF CULTURE & COMMUNICATIONS

3, rue de Valois, 75042, Paris CEDEX 01, France
(011-33-1) 40-15-80-00, Fax: (011-33-1) 42-61-35-77
URL: http://www.culture.fr/
Minister, Catherine Trautmann

### MINISTRY OF DEFENCE

14, rue Saint-Dominique, 75700, CP 00452, Succ Armées, Paris, France
(011-33-1) 42-19-30-11, Fax: (011-33-1) 47-05-40-91
Minister, Alain Richard
Secretary of State, Veterans Affairs, Jean-Pierre Masseret, 37, rue de Bellechasse, 75007, Paris, (011-33-1) 44-42-10-00
Chief of Staff, Armed Forces, Gen. Jean-P. Douin, (011-33-1) 40-65-30-11
Chief of Staff, Air Force, Gen. Jean Rannou, (011-33-1) 45-52-34-56
Chief of Staff, Army, Gen. Mercier, (011-33-1) 42-19-30-11
Chief of Staff, Navy, Adm. Jean Charles Lefebvre, (011-33-1) 42-92-10-00

### MINISTRY OF ECONOMY, FINANCE & INDUSTRY

139, rue de Bercy, 75572, Paris CEDEX 12, France
(011-33-1) 40-04-04-04, Fax: (011-33-1) 43-45-73-89
URL: http://www.finances.gouv.fr; http://www.industrie.gouv.fr; http://www.pme-commerce-artisanat.gouv.fr
Minister, Dominique Strauss-Kahn
Secretary of State, Small- & Medium-sized Business & Artisan Activities, Marylise Lebranchu, 80, rue de Lille, 75353, Paris 07 SP, (011-33-1) 46-19-24-24
Secretary of State, Budget, Christian Sautter
Secretary of State, Exterior Commerce, Jacques Dondoux
Secretary of State, Industry, Christian Pierret, (011-33-1) 43-19-36-36

### MINISTRY OF EMPLOYMENT & SOLIDARITY

127, rue de Grenelle, 75007, Paris, France
(011-33-1) 44-38-38-38
Minister, Martine Aubry
Secretary of State, Health, Bernard Kouchner, 8, av de Ségur, 75350, Paris 07 SP, (011-33-1) 40-56-60-00

### MINISTRY OF FOREIGN AFFAIRS

37, qaui d'Orsay, 75351, Paris CEDEX 07, France
(011-33-1) 43-17-53-53, Fax: (011-33-1) 45-51-60-12
URL: http://www.diplomatie.fr/
Minister, Hubert Vedrine
Minister Delegate, Cooperation, Charles Josselin, 20, rue Monsieur, 75700, Paris 07 SP, (011-33-1) 47-83-10-10
Minister Delegate, European Affairs, Pierre Moscovici

### MINISTRY OF INTERIOR

Place Beauvau, 75800, Paris, France
(011-33-1) 49-27-49-27, Fax: (011-33-1) 43-59-89-50
URL: http://www.interieur.gouv.fr; http://www.outremer.gouv.fr
Minister, Jean-Pierre Chevenement
Secretary of State, Overseas Developments, Jean-Jack Queyranne, 27, rue Oudinot, 75358, Paris 07 SP, (011-33-1) 47-83-01-23

### MINISTRY OF JUSTICE

13, place Vendôme, 75042, Paris CEDEX 01, France
(011-33-1) 44-77-60-60, Fax: (011-33-1) 42-60-69-38
URL: http://www.justice.gouv.fr
Minister of State & Keeper of the Seals, Elisabeth Guigou

### MINISTRY OF NATIONAL EDUCATION, RESEARCH & TECHNOLOGY

110, rue de Grenelle, 75357, Paris 07 SP, France
(011-33-1) 49-55-10-10
URL: http://www.education.gouv.fr; http://www.recherche.gouv.fr
Minister, Claude Allegre
Minister Delegate, School Education, Ségolène Royal, 101, rue Grenelle, 75007, Paris, (011-33-1) 49-55-10-10

### MINISTRY OF RELATIONS WITH THE PARLIAMENT

69, rue de Varenne, 75700, Paris 07 SP, France
(011-33-1) 42-75-80-00
Minister, Daniel Vaillant

### MINISTRY OF TOWN & COUNTRY PLANNING & THE ENVIRONMENT

20, av de Ségur, 75302, Paris 07 SP, France
(011-33-1) 42-19-20-21, Fax: (011-33-1) 42-19-11-23
URL: http://www.environnement.gouv.fr/
Minister, Dominique Voynet

### MINISTRY OF YOUTH & SPORT

78, rue Olivier de Serres, 75015, Paris, France
(011-33-1) 40-45-90-00, Fax: (011-33-1) 42-50-42-49
Minister, Marie-George Buffet

#### Associated Agencies

•Aerospace Industies
37, boul de Montmorency, 75781, Paris CEDEX 16, France
(011-33-1) 42-24-24-24
President, Yves Michot
•Bank of France
1, rue La Vrilière, 75001, Paris, France
(011-33-1) 42-92-42-92, Fax: (011-33-1) 42-96-04-23
Governor, Jean-Claude Trichet
•France Development Fund
35, rue Boissy-d'Anglas, 75379, Paris CEDEX 08, France
(011-33-1) 40-06-31-31, Fax: (011-33-1) 47-42-75-14
Director General, Antoine Pouillieute
•France Electricity
2, rue Louis Murat, 75384, Paris CEDEX 08, France
(011-33-1) 40-42-22-22, Fax: (011-33-1) 40-42-31-83
Chair, Gilles Ménage
•France Gas Company
23, rue Philibert Delorme, 75840, Paris CEDEX 17, France
(011-33-1) 47-54-24-17, Fax: (011-33-1) 47-54-24-85
Director General, Pierre Gadonneix
•France Radio-Telephone Company
116, av du President Kennedy, 75786, Paris CEDEX 16, France
(011-33-1) 42-30-22-22, Fax: (011-33-1) 42-30-14-88

President, Jean Maheu
•France Telecom
6, Place d'Alleray, 75505, Paris CEDEX 15, France
(011-33-1) 44-44-22-22
President, Marcel Roulet

## GOVERNMENT OF GERMANY/Deutschland (GM)

URL: http://www.bundesregierung.de/
Capital: Berlin
Major Political Parties: Christian Democratic Union (CDU); Social Democratic Party (SPD); Free Democratic Party (FDP); Christian Social Union (CSU); Party of Democratic Socialism (PDS)
Currency: Deutsche Mark
Land Area: 356,910 km2
Population: 81,337,541 (1995)
Language(s): German

### OFFICE OF THE PRESIDENT

Sch. Bellevue, Spreeweg 1, 10557, Berlin, Germany
(011-49-30) 39-08-40, Fax: (011-49-30) 200-0
URL: http://www.bundespraesident.de/
President, Prof. Dr. Roman Herzog
State, Secretary, Wilhelm Staudacher

### OFFICE OF THE FEDERAL CHANCELLOR

Adenauerallee 141, 53113, Bonn, Germany
(011-49-228) 560, Fax: (011-49-228) 562357
Chancellor, Dr. Helmut Kohl
Vice-Chancellor, Dr. Klaus Kinkel
Minister of State, Anton Pfeifer
Minister of State, Intelligence Coordination, Bernd Schmidbauer
Minister, Special Tasks & Head of Federal Chancellery, Friedrich Bohl

#### Press & Information Office of the Federal Government

Welckerstr. 11, 53113, Bonn, Germany
(011-49-228) 2080, Fax: (011-49-228) 2082555
Director, Peter Hausmann
Deputy Director, Wolfgang G. Gibowski

#### Federal Intelligence Service

Heilmanstr. 30, 82049, Pullach, Germany
(011-49-89) 7931567
President, Dr. Hansjörg Geiger

### FEDERAL COUNCIL/Bundesrat

Bendeshaus, Görresstr. 15, 53113, Bonn, Germany
(011-49-228) 9100, Fax: (011-49-228) 9100400
President, Erwin Teufel

### FEDERAL ASSEMBLY/Bundestag

Reichstagsgebäude, Scheidemannstr. 2, 10557, Berlin, Germany
(011-49-30) 39770, Fax: (011-49-30) 394751
URL: http://www.bundestag.de/
President, Prof. Dr. Rita Süssmuth

### MINISTRY OF DEFENCE

Hardthöhe, Postfach 13 28, 53123, Bonn, Germany
(011-49-228) 1200, Fax: (011-49-228) 125357
URL: http://www.bmvg.government.de/
Minister, Volker Rühe
Inspector General, Air Force, Lt. Gen Bernhard Mende, (011-49-228) 12-4600
Inspector General, Armed Forces, Gen. Hartmut Bagger, (011-49-228) 12-9200
Inspector General, Army, Lt. Gen. Helmut Willmann, (011-49-228) 12-4500
Inspector General, Navy, V. Adm. Hans-Rudolf Böhmer, (011-49-228) 12-4700

### MINISTRY OF ECONOMIC AFFAIRS

Villemomblerstr. 76, 53123, Bonn, Germany
(011-49-228) 615-0, Fax: (011-49-228) 6154436
URL: http://www.bmwi.de/
Minister, Dr. Günter Rexrodt

### MINISTRY OF ECONOMIC COOPERATION & DEVELOPMENT

Friedrich-Ebert Allee 40, 53113, Bonn, Germany
(011-49-228) 5350, Fax: (011-49-228) 535-3500
Minister, Carl-Dieter Spranger

### MINISTRY OF EDUCATION, SCIENCE, RESEARCH & TECHNOLOGY

Heinemannstr. 2, 53175, Bonn, Germany
(011-49-228) 570, Fax: (011-49-228) 573601
URL: http://www.bmbf.de/
Minister, Dr. Jürgen Rüttgers

### MINISTRY FOR THE ENVIRONMENT, NATURE CONSERVATION & NUCLEAR SAFETY

Kennedyallee 5, 53175, Bonn, Germany
(011-49-228) 3050, Fax: (011-49-228) 3053225
URL: http://www.bmu.de/
Minister, Dr. Angela Merkel

### MINISTRY FOR THE FAMILY, SENIOR CITIZENS, WOMEN & YOUTH

Rochusstr. 8 - 10, 53123, Bonn, Germany
(011-49-228) 9300, Fax: (011-49-228) 930-2221
Minister, Claudia Nolte

### MINISTRY OF FINANCE

Graurheindorferstr. 108, 53117, Bonn, Germany
(011-49-228) 6820, Fax: (011-49-228) 6824420
Minister, Dr. Theodor Waigel

### MINISTRY OF FOOD, AGRICULTURE & FORESTRY

Rochusstr. 1, 53123, Bonn, Germany
(011-49-228) 5290, Fax: (011-49-228) 5294262
URL: http://www.dainet.de/BML/home.htm
Minister, Jochen Borchert

### MINISTRY OF FOREIGN AFFAIRS

Adenauerallee 99-103, 53113, Bonn, Germany
(011-49-228) 170, Fax: (011-49-228) 173402
URL: http://www.auswaertiges-amt.government.de/
Minister, Dr. Klaus Kinkel
Minister of State, Europe, Dr. Werner Hoyer
Minister of State, Helmut Schäfer

### MINISTRY OF HEALTH

Am Probsthof 78a, 53121, Bonn, Germany
(011-49-228) 9410, Fax: (011-49-228) 9414900
URL: http://www.bmgesundheit.de/bmg.html
Minister, Horst Seehofer

### MINISTRY OF THE INTERIOR

Graurheindorferstr. 198, 53117, Bonn, Germany
(011-49-228) 6810, Fax: (011-49-228) 6814665
Minister, Manfred Kanther
President, Office of Criminal Investigation, Dr. Ulrich Kersten, Thaerstr. 11, P.F. 18 20, 65193, Wiesbaden
President, Office for the Protection of the Constitution, Dr. Peter Frisch, Merianstr. 100, P.F. 100553, 50765, Köln
President, Academy of State Police, Dieter Wellershoff, Rosenburgweg, 53115, Bonn

### MINISTRY OF JUSTICE

Heinemannstr. 6, 53175, Bonn, Germany
(011-49-228) 580, Fax: (011-49-228) 584525
Minister, Prof. Dr. Edzard Schmidt-Jortzig

### MINISTRY OF LABOUR & SOCIAL AFFAIRS

Postfach 140280, Rochusstr. 1, 53123, Bonn, Germany
(011-49-228) 5270, Fax: (011-49-228) 5272965
Minister, Dr. Norbert Blüm
President, Office of Employment, Bernhard Jagoda, Regensburgerstr. 104, 90478, Nürnberg

### MINISTRY OF POSTS & TELECOMMUNICATIONS

Heinrich von Stephan Str. 1, Postfach 8001, 53175, Bonn, Germany
(011-49-228) 140, Fax: (011-49-228) 148872
Minister, Dr. Wolfgang Bötsch

### MINISTRY OF REGIONAL PLANNING, BUILDING & URBAN DEVELOPMENT

Deichmanns Aue 31-37, 53179, Bonn, Germany
(011-49-228) 3370, Fax: (011-49-228) 3373060
Minister, Prof. Dr. Klaus Töpfer

### MINISTRY OF TRANSPORT

Robert-Schuman Pl. 1, 53175, Bonn, Germany
(011-49-228) 3000, Fax: (011-49-228) 3003428
Minister, Matthias Wissman

#### Associated Agencies

•Bank of the Federal Republic of Germany
Wilhelm-Epstein Str. 14, 60431, Frankfurt am Main, Germany
(011-49-69) 95661, Fax: (011-49-69) 5601071
President, Dr. Hans Tietmeyer
•Federal Archives
Postadamer Str. 1, 56075, Koblenz, Germany
(011-49-261) 5050, Fax: (011-49-261) 505-226
President, Dr. Friedrich Kahlenberg
•Federal Aviation Office
Lilienthalpl. 6, 38108, Braunschweig, Germany
(011-49-531) 23550, Fax: (011-49-531) 2355254
Director, Dieter Horst
•Federal Export Office
Frankfurter Str. 29-35, 65760, Eschborn, Germany
(011-49-6196) 9080, Fax: (011-49-6196) 908800
President, Dr. Wolfgang Danner
•Federal Office for Foreign Trade Information
Agrippastr. 87-93, 50676, Köln, Germany
(011-49-221) 20570, Fax: (011-49-221) 2057212
Director, Hans Diether Dammann
•Federal Office for Public Security
Deutschherrenstr, 93, 53177, Bonn, Germany
(011-49-228) 9400, Fax: (011-49-228) 9401424
President, Helmut Schuch
•Federal Patent Office
Zweibrückenstr. 12, 80331, Munich, Germany
(001-49-89) 21950, Fax: (001-49-89) 21952221
President, Norbert Haugg
•Federal Statistics Office
Gustav-Stresemann-Ring 11, 65189, Wiesbaden, Germany
(011-49-611) 751, Fax: (011-49-611) 724000
President, Johann Hahlen

## GOVERNMENT OF ITALY/Italia (IT)

Capital: Rome
Major Political Parties: Northern League; Democratic Party of the Left; Forza Italia; National Alliance; Communist Refoundation Party; Christian Democratic Center; Popular Party
Currency: Italian Lira
Total Area: 301,230 km2
Population: 57,460,279 (1996 est.)
Language(s): Italian, German, French, Slovenian

### OFFICE OF THE PRESIDENT

Palazzo del Quirinale, 00187, Rome, Italy
(011-39-6) 46991, Fax: (011-39-6) 46992384
President & Chair, Supreme Defense Council, H.E. Oscar Luigi Scalfaro

### OFFICE OF THE PRIME MINISTER

Piazza Colonna, 370, 00187, Rome, Italy
(011-39-6) 67791, Fax: (011-39-6) 6796894
Prime Minister, Prof. Romano Prodi
Deputy Prime Minister, Walter Veltroni
Minister without Portfolio, Equal Opportunities, Anna Finocchiaro

Director, Executive Committee for Intelligence & Security, Gen. Giuseppe Tavormina

**SENATE/Senato della Repubblica**
Palazzo Madama, 00186, Rome, Italy
(011-39-6) 67061
President & Speaker, Nicola Mancino

**CHAMBER OF DEPUTIES/Camera dei Deputati**
Piazza Montecitorio, 00186, Rome, Italy
(011-39-6) 67601
President, Luciano Violante

**MINISTRY OF AGRICULTURE**
Via XX Settembre, 20, 00187, Rome, Italy
(011-39-6) 4665, Fax: (011-39-6) 4746178
Minister, Michele Pinto

**MINISTRY OF CULTURAL HERITAGE & SPORT**
Via de Collegio Romano, 27, 00186, Rome, Italy
(011-39-6) 67231
Minister, Walter Veltroni

**MINISTRY OF DEFENCE**
Palazzo Baracchini, Via XX Settembre, 8, 00187, Rome, Italy
(011-39-6) 4882126, Fax: (011-39-6) 4747775
Minister, Beniamino Andreatta
Chief of Staff, Defence General Staff, Adm. Franco Venturoni, (011-39-6) 46911
Chief of Staff, Air Force, Gen. Adelchi Pillinini, (011-39-6) 49861
Chief of Staff, Army, Lt. Gen. Bonifazio Incisa di Camerana, (011-39-6) 47351
Chief of Staff, Navy, Adm Angelo Mariani, (011-39-6) 36801

**MINISTRY OF EDUCATION & RESEARCH**
Viale Trastevere, 76a, 00153, Rome, Italy
(011-39-6) 58491, Fax: (011-39-6) 5813515
Minister, Luigi Berlinguer

**MINISTRY OF EMPLOYMENT & SOCIAL WELFARE**
Via Flavia, 6, 00187, Rome, Italy
(011-39-6) 4683
Minister, Tiziano Treu
Director General, Industrial Relations, Dr. Giuseppe Cacopardi

**MINISTRY OF ENVIRONMENT**
Piazza Venezia 11, 00186, Rome, Italy
(011-39-6) 70361, Fax: (011-39-6) 6790130
Minister, Edo Ronchi
State Secretary, Paolo Gerelli
Director General, Air & Noise Pollution, Dr. Dorrado Clini
Director General, Evaluation of Impact Assessment, Education & Information, Costanza Pera
Director General, Nature Preservation, Bruno Agricola
Director General, Water, Waste & Soil, Gianfranco Mascazzini

**MINISTRY OF FAMILY & SOCIAL AFFAIRS**
Via Veneto 46, 00187, Rome, Italy
(011-39-6) 4820172, Fax: (011-39-6) 4821207
Minister, Livia Turco

**MINISTRY OF FINANCE**
Viale America 242, Rome, Italy
(011-39-6) 59648826, Fax: (011-39-6) 5910993
Minister, Vincenzo Visco

**MINISTRY OF FOREIGN AFFAIRS**
Palazzo le Farnesina, I, Foro Italico, 00194, Rome, Italy
(011-39-6) 3691, Fax: (011-39-6) 3222850
Minister, Prof. Romano Prodi

**MINISTRY OF FOREIGN TRADE**
Viale America, 341, 00144, Rome, Italy
(011-39-6) 59931, Fax: (011-39-6) 5921573
Minister, Augusto Fantozzi

**MINISTRY OF HEALTH**
Viale Dell'Industria, 20, 00144, Rome, Italy
(011-39-6) 59931, Fax: (011-39-6) 5921573
Minister, Rosi Bindi

**MINISTRY OF INDUSTRY & TOURISM**
Via Vittorio Veneto 33, 00187, Rome, Italy
(011-39-6) 47051, Fax: (011-39-6) 47053117
Minister, Pierluigi Bersani
Chief of Staff, Commerce, Guiseppe Mazza
Chief of Staff, Industry & Crafts, Guiseppe Barbagallo

**MINISTRY OF THE INTERIOR**
Palazzo Viminale, Via A. Depretis, 00184, Rome, Italy
(011-39-6) 65101, Fax: (011-39-6) 68802034
Minister, Georgio Napolitano

**MINISTRY OF JUSTICE**
Via Arenula, 70, Rome 00186, Italy
(011-39-6) 65101, Fax: (011-39-6) 68802034
Minister, Giovanni Maria Flick

**MINISTRY OF POSTS & TELECOMMUNICATIONS**
Viale America, 00144, Rome, Italy
(011-39-6) 59581, Fax: (011-39-6) 5942274
Minister, Antonio Maccanico

**MINISTRY OF PUBLIC ADMINISTRATION & REGIONAL AFFAIRS**
Via Vidoni, Corso Vittorio Emanuele 116, 00186, Rome, Italy
(011-39-6) 680031, Fax: (011-39-6) 68003238
Minister, Franco Bassanini

**MINISTRY OF PUBLIC WORKS**
Piazza dei porti pia, 1, 00198, Rome, Italy
(011-39-6) 44121, Fax: (011-39-6) 442-67275
Minister, Paulo Costa

**MINISTRY OF TRANSPORT**
Piazza della Croce Rossa, 1, 00161, Rome, Italy
(011-39-6) 84901, Fax: (011-39-6) 8417268
Minister, Claudio Burlando

**MINISTRY OF THE TREASURY & THE BUDGET**
Via XX Settembre, 97, 00187, Rome, Italy
(011-39-6) 59931, Fax: (011-39-6) 5913751
Acting Minister, Carlo Azeglio Ciampi

**MINISTRY OF UNIVERSITIES, SCIENTIFIC & TECHNOLOGICAL RESEARCH**
Piazzale J.F. Kennedy, 20, 00144, Rome, Italy
(011-39-6) 59991
Minister, Luigi Berlinguer

**Associated Agencies**
•Bank of Italy/Banca d'Italia
CP 2484, Via Nazionale, 91, 00184, Rome, Italy
(011-39-6) 47921, Fax: (011-39-6) 47922253
Governor, Antonio Fazio
•Energy, Environment & New Technology Agency
Viale Regina Margherita, 125, 00198, Rome, Italy
(011-39-6) 85281, Fax: (011-39-6) 8528277
President, Nicola Cabibbo
•Manufacturing Industries Investment & Financing Agency
Via XXIV Maggio, 43-45, 00187, Rome, Italy
(011-39-6) 47101, Fax: (011-39-6) 476527
President, Gaetano Mancini
•National Airline Company (Alitalia)
Via della Magliana, 886, 00148, Rome, Italy
(011-39-6) 62621, Fax: (011-39-6) 5920089
CEO & Managing Director, Giovanni Bisignani
•National Institute for Foreign Trade
EUR-Via Liszt, 00100, Rome, Italy
(011-39-6) 599121, Fax: (011-39-6) 5910508
President, Marcello Inghilesi
•National Nuclear Energy Committee
Viale Regina Margherita, 125, 00198, Rome, Italy
(011-39-6) 85281
President, Vacant
•State Oil Company
Piassale Enrico Mattei, 1, 00144, Rome, Italy
(011-39-6) 59821, Fax: (011-39-6) 59822141
President, Luigi Meanti

## GOVERNMENT OF JAPAN/Nippon (JA)

Capital: Tokyo
Major Political Parties: Liberal Democratic Party (LDP); Shinshinto (New Frontier) Party; Democratic Party; Japan Communist Party (JCP)
Currency: Yen
Total Area: 377,835 km2
Population: 125,960,000 (1996 est.)
Language(s): Japanese

**IMPERIAL HOUSEHOLD AGENCY**
1-1 Chiyoda, Chiyada-ku, Tokyo 100, Japan
(011-81-3) 3213-1111
Emperor, H.I.M. Akihito
Grand Master, Ceremonies, Kiyoshi Sumiya

**OFFICE OF THE PRIME MINISTER**
1-7-1 Nagata-cho, Chiyada-ku, Tokyo 100, Japan
(011-81-3) 3581-2361
URL: http://www.kantei.go.jp/
Prime Minister, Ryutaro Hashimoto

**HOUSE OF COUNCILLORS/Sang-in**
1-7-1 Nagata-cho, Chiyada-ku, Tokyo 100, Japan
(011-81-3) 3581-3111, Fax: (011-81-3) 3581-2900
President, Bunbei Hara
Speaker, Misao Akagiri

**HOUSE OF REPRESENTATIVES/Shugi-in**
1-7-1 Nagata-cho, Chiyada-ku, Tokyo 100, Japan
(011-81-3) 3581-5111
Speaker, Takako Doi
Deputy Speaker, Hyosuke Kujiraoka

**MINISTRY OF AGRICULTURE, FORESTRY & FISHERIES**
1-2-1 Kasumigaseki, Chiyada-ku, Tokyo 100, Japan
(011-81-3) 3502-8111, Fax: (011-81-3) 3592-7697
URL: http://www.maff.go.jp/eindex.html
Minister, Takao Fujimoto

**MINISTRY OF CONSTRUCTION**
2-1-3 Kasumigaseki, Chiyada-ku, Tokyo 100, Japan
(011-81-3) 3580-4311, Fax: (011-81-3) 3502-3955
Minister, Shizuka Kamei

**MINISTRY OF EDUCATION**
3-2-2 Kasumigaseki, Chiyada-ku, Tokyo 100, Japan
(011-81-3) 3581-4211, Fax: (011-81-3) 3591-8072
Minister, Takashi Kosugi

**MINISTRY OF FINANCE**
3-1-1 Kasumigaseki, Chiyada-ku, Tokyo 100, Japan
(011-81-3) 3581-4111, Fax: (011-81-3) 3592-1025
Minister, Hiroshi Mitsuzuka

**MINISTRY OF FOREIGN AFFAIRS**
2-2-1 Kasumigaseki, Chiyada-ku, Tokyo 100, Japan
(011-81-3) 3580-3311, Fax: (011-81-3) 3581-9675
URL: http://www.mofa.go.jp/
Minister, Yukihiko Ikeda
Director General, International Economic Relations, Choe Yong-Chin

**MINISTRY OF HEALTH & WELFARE**
1-2-2 Kasumigaseki, Chiyada-ku, Tokyo 100, Japan
(011-81-3) 3503-1711, Fax: (011-81-3) 3501-4853
URL: http://www.ncc.go.jp/mhw/index.html
Minister, Junichiro Koizumi

**MINISTRY OF HOME AFFAIRS**
2-1-2 Kasumigaseki, Chiyada-ku, Tokyo 100, Japan
(011-81-3) 3581-5311, Fax: (011-81-3) 3593-3758
Minister, Katsuhiko Shirakawa

**MINISTRY OF INTERNATIONAL TRADE & INDUSTRY**
1-3-1 Kasumigaseki, Chiyada-ku, Tokyo 100, Japan
(011-81-3) 3501-1511, Fax: (011-81-3) 3501-1337
URL: http://www.miti.go.jp/index-e.html
Minister, Shinji Sato

**MINISTRY OF JUSTICE**
1-1-1 Kasumigaseki, Chiyada-ku, Tokyo 100, Japan
(011-81-3) 3580-4111, Fax: (011-81-3) 3592-7011
Minister, Isao Matsuura

**MINISTRY OF LABOUR**
1-2-2 Kasumigaseki, Chiyada-ku, Tokyo 100, Japan
(011-81-3) 3593-1211, Fax: (011-81-3) 3502-6711
Minister, Yutaka Okano

**MINISTRY OF POSTS & TELECOMMUNICATIONS**
1-3-2 Kasumigaseki, Chiyada-ku, Tokyo 100, Japan
(011-81-3) 3504-4411, Fax: (011-81-3) 3504-0265
URL: http://www.mpt.go.jp
Minister, Hisao Horinouchi

**MINISTRY OF TRANSPORT**
2-1-3 Kasumigaseki, Chiyada-ku, Tokyo 100, Japan
(011-81-3) 3580-3111, Fax: (011-81-3) 3593-0474
Minister, Makoto Koga

**Associated Agencies**
•Bank of Japan/Nippon Ginko
2-1-1 Hongoku-cho, 2 Chome, Nihonbashi, Chuo-ku, Tokyo 103, Japan
(011-81-3) 3279-1111, Fax: (011-81-3) 3245-0358
Governor, Yasuo Matsushita
•Economic Planning Agency
3-1-1 Kasumigaseki, Chiyada-ku, Tokyo 100, Japan
(011-81-3) 3581-0261, Fax: (011-81-3) 3581-3907
Minister of State & Director General, Taro Aso
Deputy Director General, Tsutomu Tanaka
•Hokkaido & Okinawa Development Agency
Hokkaido Development Agency, 3-1-1 Kasumigaseki, Chiyada-ku, Tokyo 100, Japan
(011-81-3) 3581-9111, Fax: (011-81-3) 3581-1208
Minister of State & Director General, Jitsuo Inagaki
•Institute of Space & Astronautical Science
3-1-1 Yoshinodai, Sagamihara, Kanagawa 229, Japan
(011-81-3) 2751-3911, Fax: (011-81-3) 2759-4255
Director General, Ryojiro Akiba
•Japan Atomic Energy Commission
2-2-1 Kasumigaseki, Chiyada-ku, Tokyo 100, Japan
(011-81-3) 3581-2585, Fax: (011-81-3) 3581-5198
Chair, Makiko Tanaka
•Japan Environmental Agency
3-1-1 Kasumigaseki, Chiyada-ku, Tokyo 100, Japan
(011-81-3) 3581-3351, Fax: (011-81-3) 3504-1634
Minister of State & Director General, Michiko Ishii
•Japan External Trade Organization
2-5 Toranomon, Minato-ku, Tokyo 105, Japan
(011-81-3) 3582-5511, Fax: (011-81-3) 3587-0219
President, Noboru Hatekeyama
•Japan Fisheries Agency
1-2-1 Kasumigaseki, Chiyada-ku, Tokyo 100, Japan
(011-81-3) 3502-8111
Director General, Michio Chinzei
•Japan Food Agency
1-2-1 Kasumigaseki, Chiyada-ku, Tokyo 100, Japan
(011-81-3) 3502-8111
Director General, Hirofuji Ueno
•Japan Management & Co-ordination Agency
3-1-1, Kasumigaseki, Chiyoda-ku, Tokyo 100, Japan
(011-81-3) 3581-6361
Minister of State & Director General, Kabun Muto
•Japan Science & Technology Agency
2-2-1 Kasumigaseki, Chiyada-ku, Tokyo 100, Japan
(011-81-3) 3581-5271
Minister of State & Director General, Riichiro Chikaoka
•Japanese Defence Agency
9-7-45 Akasaka, Minato-ku, Tokyo 107, Japan
(011-81-3) 3408-5211, Fax: (011-81-3) 3408-5211
Minister of State & Director General, Fumio Kyuma
Chair, Joint Staff Council, Self Defence Forces, Gen. Tetsuya Nishimoto, (011-81-3) 33408-5211
Chief of Staff, Air Self Defence Forces, Gen. Isao Ishizuka, (011-81-3) 33408-5211
Chief of Staff, Ground Self Defence Forces, Gen. Hikary Tomizawa, (011-81-3) 33408-5211
Chief of Staff, Maritime Self Defence Forces, Adm. Takeo Fukuchi, (011-81-3) 33408-5211
•National Land Agency
1-2-2 Kasumigaseki, Chiyada-ku, Tokyo 100, Japan
(011-81-3) 3593-3311
Minister of State & Director General, Kosuke Ito
•National Space Development Agency of Japan
World Trade Centre Bldg., 2-4-1 Hamamatsu-cho, Minato-ku, Tokyo 105-60, Japan
(011-81-3) 5470-4111, Fax: (011-81-3) 3436-2928
President, Masato Yamano
•Small- & Medium-Sized Business Agency
1-3-1 Kasumigaseki, Chiyada-ku, Tokyo 100, Japan
(011-81-3) 3581-1511

## GOVERNMENT OF MALAYSIA (MY)
Capital: Kuala Lumpur
Major Political Parties: National Front; Democratic Action Party; Parti Bersaty Sabah; Parti Islam Sa-Malaysia
Currency: Ringgit
Total Area: 329,744 km2
Population: 19,962,893 (1996 est.)
Language(s): Malay, English, Hokkien

**SUPREME HEAD OF STATE**
Supreme Head of State, H.M. Yang di-Pertuan Agong
Deputy Supreme Head of State, H.R.H. Timbalan Yang di-Pertuan Agong

**OFFICE OF THE PRIME MINISTER**
Jabatan Perdana Menteri, Kuala Lumpur, Malaysia
(011-60-3) 232-1957, Fax: (011-60-3) 232-9227
Prime Minister, Dato Seri Dr. Mahathir Mohamad
Deputy Prime Minister, Dato Seri Anwar Ibrahim

**SENATE/Dewan Negara**
Speaker, Tan Sri Benedict Stephens

**HOUSE OF REPRESENTATIVES/Dewan Rakyat**
Speaker, Tan Sri Muhammad Zahir Ismail
Deputy Speaker, Ong Tee Keat

**MINISTRY OF AGRICULTURE**
Wisma Tani, Jalan Sultan Salahuddin, 50624, Kuala Lumpur, Malaysia
(011-60-3) 298-2011, Fax: (011-60-3) 291-3758
Minister, Datuk Amar Dr. Sulaiman Daud

**MINISTRY OF CULTURE, ARTS & TOURISM**
Putra World Trade Centre, Meanara Dato Onn, 34-36 Fl., POB 5-7, 45 Jalan Tun Ismail, 50694, Kuala Lumpur, Malaysia
(011-60-3) 293-7111, Fax: (011-60-3) 291-0951
Minister, Dato Sabbaruddin Chik

**MINISTRY OF DEFENCE**
Jalan Padang Tembak, 50634, Kuala Lumpur, Malaysia
(011-60-3) 292-1333, Fax: (011-60-3) 298-4662
Minister, Dato Syed Hamid bin Syed Jaafar Albar

**MINISTRY OF DOMESTIC TRADE & CONSUMER AFFAIRS**
Tinghat 19, 22-24, 40, Menara Maybank, 100 Jalan Tun Perak, 50050, Kuala Lumpur, Malaysia
(011-60-3) 232-9955, Fax: (011-60-3) 238-9558
Minister, Dato Megat Junid Megat Ayob

**MINISTRY OF EDUCATION**
Block J, Pusat Level 7, Bandar Damansara, 50604, Kuala Lumpur, Malaysia
(011-60-3) 255-6900
Minister, Dato Seri Najib Razak

**MINISTRY OF ENERGY, TELECOMMUNICATIONS & POSTS**
Wisma Damansara, 3rd Fl., Jalan Semantan, 50668, Kuala Lumpur, Malaysia
(011-60-3) 256-2222, Fax: (011-60-3) 255-7901
Minister, Dato Leo Moggie anak Irok

**MINISTRY OF ENTREPRENEURIAL DEVELOPMENT**
Tinghat 24, Medan Mara, Jalan Raja Laut, 50652, Kuala Lumpur, Malaysia
(011-60-3) 298-5022, Fax: (011-60-3) 291-7623
Minister, Dato Mustapha Mohamad

**MINISTRY OF FINANCE**
#9, Pejabat Kerajaan Complex, Jalan Duta, 50592, Kuala Lumpur, Malaysia
(011-60-3) 258-2000, Fax: (011-60-3) 255-6264
Minister, Dato Seri Anwar Ibrahim

**MINISTRY OF FOREIGN AFFAIRS**
Wisma Putra, Jalan Wisma Putra, 50602, Kuala Lumpur, Malaysia
(011-60-3) 248-8088, Fax: (011-60-3) 242-4551
Minister, Dato Abdullah Ahmad Badawi

**MINISTRY OF HEALTH**
Jalan Cenderasari, 50590, Kuala Lumpur, Malaysia
(011-60-3) 298-5077, Fax: (011-60-3) 298-5964
Minister, Dato Chua Jui Meng

**MINISTRY OF HOME AFFAIRS**
Jalan Dato Onn, 50546, Kuala Lumpur, Malaysia
(011-60-3) 230-9344, Fax: (011-60-3) 230-1051
Minister, Dato Seri Dr. Mahathir Mohamad

**MINISTRY OF HOUSING & LOCAL GOVERNMENT**
Paras 4-5, Block K, Pusat Bandar Damansara, 50782, Kuala Lumpur, Malaysia
(011-60-3) 254-7033, Fax: (011-60-3) 254-7380
Minister, Dato Dr. Ting Chew Peh

**MINISTRY OF HUMAN RESOURCES**
Pusat Bandar Damansara, Block B Utara, Jalan Damanlela, 50530, Kuala Lumpur, Malaysia
(011-60-3) 255-7200, Fax: (011-60-3) 255-4700
Minister, Dato Lim Ah Lek

**MINISTRY OF INFORMATION**
Angkasapuri, Bukit Putra, 50610, Kuala Lumpur, Malaysia
(011-60-3) 282-5333, Fax: (011-60-3) 282-1255
Minister, Dato Mahamad bin Rahmat

**MINISTRY OF INTERNATIONAL TRADE & INDUSTRY**
Complex Pejabat Kerajaan, Block 10, Jalan Duta, 50622, Kuala Lumpur, Malaysia
(011-60-3) 651-0033, Fax: (011-60-3) 651-2306
Minister, Dato Seri Paduka Rafidah Aziz

**MINISTRY OF LAND & CO-OPERATIVE DEVELOPMENT**
Wisma Keramat, 13 Fl., Jalan Semarak, 50574, Kuala Lumpur, Malaysia
(011-60-3) 292-1566, Fax: (011-60-3) 291-8641
Minister, Datuk Osu bin Haji Sukam

### MINISTRY OF NATIONAL UNITY & COMMUNITY DEVELOPMENT

Tinghat 20, Wisma Bumi Raya, Jalan Semarak, 50574, Kuala Lumpur, Malaysia
(011-60-3) 292-5022, Fax: (011-60-3) 293-7353
Minister, Datin Paduka Zaleha Ismail

### MINISTRY OF PRIMARY INDUSTRIES

Menara Daya Bumi, 6th Fl., Jalan Sultan Hishamuddin, 50654, Kuala Lumpur, Malaysia
(011-60-3) 274-7511, Fax: (011-60-3) 274-5014
Minister, Dato Seri Dr. Lim Keng Yaik

### MINISTRY OF RURAL DEVELOPMENT

Kewangan Complex, 5th Fl., Jalan Raja Chulan, 50606, Kuala Lumpur, Malaysia
(011-60-3) 261-2622, Fax: (011-60-3) 261-1339
Minister, Dato Haji Annuar bin Musa

### MINISTRY OF SCIENCE, TECHNOLOGY & ENVIRONMENT

Wisma Sime Darby, 14th Fl., Jalan Raja Laut, 50662, Kuala Lumpur, Malaysia
(011-60-3) 293-8955, Fax: (011-60-3) 293-6006
Minister, Datuk Law Hieng Ding

### MINISTRY OF TRANSPORT

Wisma Perdana, 5th Fl., Jalan Dungun, 50616, Kuala Lumpur, Malaysia
(011-60-3) 254-8122, Fax: (011-60-3) 255-7041
Minister, Datuk Seri Dr. Ling Liong Sik

### MINISTRY OF WORKS

Jalan Sultan Salahuddin, 50580, Kuala Lumpur, Malaysia
(011-60-3) 291-9011, Fax: (011-60-3) 298-6612
Minister, Dato Seri S. Samy Vellu

### MINISTRY OF YOUTH & SPORTS

Pusat Bandar Damansara, Block K, 7th Fl., Bukit Damansara, 50570, Kuala Lumpur, Malaysia
(011-60-3) 255-2255, Fax: (011-60-3) 255-6521
Minister, Tan Sri Haji Muhyiddin Yassin

## GOVERNMENT OF MÉXICO (MX)

Capital: Mexico City
Major Political Parties: Institutional Revolutionary Party (PRI); National Action Party (PAN); Democratic Revolutionary Party (PRD)
Currency: Mexican Peso
Total Area: 1,972,550 km2
Population: 95,772,462 (1996 est.)
Language(s): Spanish

### OFFICE OF THE PRESIDENT

Los Pinos, Puierta 1, Col. San Miguel, Chapultepec, 11850, México DF, México
(011-52-5) 515-3717, Fax: (011-52-5) 510-8713
President, H.E. Ernesto Zedillo Ponce de León

### SENATE/Congreso de la Unión

Xicoténcatl #9, Ava. Zaragoza y Calle Corregidora, 06018, México DF, México
(011-52-5) 521-0020
President, Emilio González

### CHAMBER OF DEPUTIES/Cámara Federal de Diputados

Palacio Legislativo, Ava. Congreso de la Unión, Colonia del Parque, 15969, México, D.F., México
(011-52-5) 794-7044
President, Guillermo Jiminéz Morales

### SECRETARIAT OF STATE FOR AGRARIAN REFORM

Torre B, #15, Calzada de la Viga 1174, Col. Apatlaco, 09430, México DF, México
(011-52-5) 650-6311, Fax: (011-52-5) 650-6100
Secretary, Arturo Warman Gryj

### SECRETARIAT OF STATE FOR AGRICULTURE & WATER RESOURCES

Ava. Insurgentes Sur #476, 13 Piso, 06760, México DF, México
(011-52-5) 584-0096, Fax: (001-52-5) 584-0652
Secretary, Francisco Labastida Ochoa

### SECRETARIAT OF STATE FOR ENERGY

Colonia Roma Sur, Deleg. Cuauhtémoc, Ava. Insurgentes Sur #552, 3 Piso, Colonia Roma Sur, 06769, México DF, México
(011-52-5) 564-9789, Fax: (011-52-5) 564-9769
Secretary, Jesús Reyes Heroles

### SECRETARIAT OF STATE FOR THE ENVIRONMENT, NATURAL RESOURCES & FISHERIES

Ava. Alvaro Obregón #269, 6 Piso, Col. Roma Sur, 06700, México DF, México
(011-52-5) 208-1291, Fax: (011-52-5) 208-1834
Secretary, Julia Carabias Lillo
Undersecretary, Coordination & Development, Carlos Camacho Gaos
Undersecretary, Fisheries Development, Carlos Camacho Gaos
Undersecretary, Natural Resources, Dr. Oscar González Rodríguez
Undersecretary, Planning, Enrique Provencio Durazo

### SECRETARIAT OF STATE FOR FINANCE & PUBLIC CREDIT

Palacio Nacional, Patio Central, 3 Piso, #3025, Col. Centro, Deleg. Cuahtémoc, 06066, México DF, México
(011-52-5) 518-5420, Fax: (011-52-5) 542-221
Secretary, Dr. Guillermo Ortiz Martínez
Comptroller General, Norma Sanamiego, (011-52-5) 575-3983

### SECRETARIAT OF STATE FOR FOREIGN AFFAIRS

Ava. Ricardo Flores Magón #1, 19 Piso, 06995, México DF, México
(011-52-5) 782-3594, Fax: (011-52-5) 254-5549
Secretary, José Angel Gurría Trevino

### SECRETARIAT OF STATE FOR HEALTH

Lieja #7, Colonia Juárez, 1 Piso, 06696, México DF, México
(011-52-5) 553-6967
Secretary, Juan Ramón de la Fuente Ramírez

### SECRETARIAT OF STATE FOR THE INTERIOR

Bucareli #99, 1 Piso, 06699, México DF, México
(011-52-5) 566-0245
Secretary, Emilio Chuayffet Chemor
Undersecretary, Civil Protection, Humberto Lira Mora
Undersecretary, Government, Arturo Nunez Jimenez
Undersecretary, Political Development, Luis Fernando Aguilar
Undersecretary, Population & Migration, Manuel Rodriguez Arriaga

### SECRETARIAT OF STATE FOR LABOUR & SOCIAL WELFARE

Periférico Sur. #4271, Edificio A, Nivel 9, Col. Fuentes del Pedregal, Tlalpan, 14149, México DF, México
(011-52-5) 645-5591, Fax: (011-52-5) 645-2345
Minister, Javier Bonilla

### SECRETARIAT OF STATE FOR NATIONAL DEFENCE

Avila Camacho e Industria Militar, Lomas de Sotelo, 11640, México DF, México
(011-52-5) 557-4500, Fax: (011-52-5) 395-6766
Secretary, Gen. Enrique Cervantes Aguirre
Undersecretary, Gen. Jaime Contreras Cuerrero
Chief of Staff, Army, Brig. Gen. Enrique Salgado Cordero, (011-52-5) 557-4500
Chief of Staff, Navy, Adm. Alejandro Maldonado Mendoza, (011-52-5) 679-6411
Commander, Air Force, Div. Gen. Humberto Lucero Nevárez, (011-52-5) 557-3310

### SECRETARIAT OF STATE FOR THE NAVY

Eje 2 Oriente Trama Heróica, Escuela Naval 861, 04830, México DF, México
(011-52-5) 679-6411, Fax: (011-52-5) 685-4266
Secretary, Adm. José Ramón Lorenzo Franco

### SECRETARIAT OF STATE FOR PUBLIC EDUCATION

Ava. República de Argentina y González, Obregón #28, 06029, México DF, México
(011-52-5) 328-1000
Secretary, Miguel Limón Rojas

### SECRETARIAT OF STATE FOR SOCIAL DEVELOPMENT

Ava. Constituyentes #947, Edificio B.P.A., Colonia Belén de las Flores, 01110, México DF, México
(011-52-5) 271-8521, Fax: (011-52-5) 271-6614
Secretary, Carlos Rojas Gutiérrez

### SECRETARIAT OF STATE FOR TOURISM

Ava. Presidente Masarik #172, 11587, México DF, México
(011-52-5) 250-8206
Secreatary, Silvia Hernández Enriquez

### SECRETARIAT OF STATE FOR TRADE & INDUSTRIAL PROMOTION

Alfonso Reyes #30, 10 Piso, Col Hipódromo Condesa, 06140, México DF, México
(011-52-5) 286-1823, Fax: (011-52-5) 286-0804
Secretary, Herminio Blanco
Undersecretary, Domestic Trade, Eugenio Carrión Rodríguez
Undersecretary, Foreign Trade & Investigation, Decio de Maria Serrano
Undersecretary, Industries, Raúl Ramos Tercero
Undersecretary, International Trade Negotiations, Jaime Zabludovsky

### SECRETARIAT OF STATE FOR TRANSPORT & COMMUNICATIONS

Ava. Univeridad - Xola, Cuerpo C, 2 Piso, Colonia Navarte, 03028, México DF, México
(011-52-5) 519-7456, Fax: (011-52-5) 519-9748
Secretary, Carlos Ruiz Sacristán

#### Associated Agencies

•Bank of México
Ava. 5 de Mayo #2, Apartado 98, 06059, México DF, México
(011-52-5) 237-2000, Fax: (011-52-5) 237-2150
Director General, Miguel Mancera Aguayo
•Energy Policy & Planning Commission
Francisco Márquez 160, Colonia Condesa, México DF, México
Chair, Fernando Hiriart Valderrama
•Fruit Industry Commission
Allende 8 Sur., 76007, Querétaro, México
(011-52-463) 570-2499
Director, Francisoco merino Rabago
•Mexican Oil Company (PEMEX)
Ava. Marina Nacional 319, 44 Piso, Colonia Anáhuac, 11311, México DF, México
(011-52-5) 531-6239
Director General, Adrián Lajous Vargas
•Mining Sector Development Agency
Puente de Tecamachalco 26, Lomas de Chapultepec, 11000, México DF, México
(011-52-5) 540-2906
Director, Luis de Pablo Serno
•National Commercial Exports Council
Edificio de las Instituciones, 7 Piso, O'campo 250, Apartado 2674, Monterrey, México
(011-52-83) 42-2143
President, José Trevito Salinas
•National Council of Mineral Resources Development

Ava. Ninos Heroes, 139, 06720, México DF, México
(011-52-5) 568-6112
Director, Renando Castillo Nieto
•National Electricity Commission
Río Ródano 14, 6 Piso, Colonia Cuauhtémoc, 06568, México DF, México
(011-52-5) 553-6400
Director, Rogelio Gasca Neri
•National Railways of México
Edificio Administrativo, Ava. Jusús Garcia Corona, #140, Colonia Buenavista, 06358, México DF, México
(011-52-5) 327-3600
Director General, Luis de Pable Serna
•National Foreign Investment Commission
Blvd. Avila Camacho, #1, 11 Piso, 11000, México DF, México
(011-52-5) 540-1426
Executive Secretary, Dr. Carlos Camacho Gaos
•National Nuclear Development Standards Commission
Dr. Barragán 779, Col. Narvarte, Del. Benito Juárez, 03020, México DF, México
(011-52-5) 590-1481
Director General, Miguel Medina Vaillard
•National Water Commission
Insurgentes Sur. 2140, 2 Piso, Co. Ermita, 01070, México DF, México
(011-52-5) 661-3806
Director General, Guillermo Guerrero Villalobos
•Office of the Attorney General
Ref.#75 esq., Violeta y Soto, PO Box 06200, Stn Col. Guerrero, México DF, México
(011-52-5) 626-4000, Fax: (011-52-5) 626-4419
Attorney General, Jorge Madrazo Cúellar
•Telecommunications México
Torre Central de Telecomunicaciones, Eje Central Lázaro Cardenas 567, 11 Piso, Col. Navarte, 03020, México DF, México
(011-52-5) 519-4049
Director General, Carlos Minteran Ordiales

## GOVERNMENT OF THE NETHERLANDS/ Nederland (NL)

Capital: Amsterdam
Seat of Government: The Hague
Major Political Parties: Labour Party (PvdA); People's Party for Freedom & Democracy (VVD); Democrats '66 (D'66)
Currency: Netherlands guilder
Total Area: 37,330 km2
Population: 15,568,034 (1996 est.)
Language(s): Dutch

### OFFICE OF THE QUEEN

Paleis Noordeinde, PO Box 30412, 2500 GK, The Hague, Netherlands
(011-31-70) 362-4701, Fax: (011-31-70) 361-5214
H.M. Queen Beatrix Wilhelmina Armgard

### OFFICE OF THE PRIME MINISTER

Binnenhof 20, Postbus 20001, 2500 EA, The Hague, Netherlands
(011-31-70) 356-4100, Fax: (011-31-70) 356-4683
Prime Minister, Wim Kok
Vice Prime Minister, H.F. Dijkstal
Vice Prime Minister, Hans Van Mierlo

### FIRST CHAMBER/Eerste Kamer

Binnenhof 22, PO Box 20017, 2500 AA, s'Gravenhage, Netherlands
(011-31-70) 362-4571, Fax: (011-31-70) 365-3868
Chair, F. Korthals Altes

### SECOND CHAMBER/Tweede Kamer

Plein 2, PO Box 20018, 2500 EA, s'Gravenhage, Netherlands
(011-31-70) 318-2211, Fax: (011-31-70) 365-4122
Chair, P. Buckman

### MINISTRY OF AGRICULTURE, NATURE MANAGEMENT & FISHERIES

Bezuidenhoutsweg 73, 2594 AC, The Hague, Netherlands
(011-31-70) 379-3911, Fax: (011-31-70) 381-5153
Minister, Jozias van Aartsen

### MINISTRY OF DEFENCE

Bezuidenhoutseweg 30, Postbus 20701, 2500 ES, The Hague, Netherlands
(011-31-70) 318-8188, Fax: (011-31-70) 318-7888
Minister of Defence, Dr. Jon's Voohoeve
Chief of Staff, Defence Staff, Lt. Gen. Henk G.B. van den Breemen, (011-31-70) 318-7331
Commander-in-Chief, Royal Netherlands Air Force & Chief of Staff, Lt. Gen. Ben Droste, (011-31-70) 349-3591
Commander-in-Chief, Royal Netherlands Army, Lt. Gen. J. Schouten
Commander-in-Chief, Royal Netherlands Navy & Chief of Staff, V. Adm. L. Kroon

### MINISTRY OF ECONOMIC AFFAIRS & FOREIGN TRADE

Bezuidenhoutseweg 30, 2594 AV, The Hague, Netherlands
(011-31-70) 379-8911, Fax: (011-31-70) 347-4081
Minister, Economic Affairs, Gerardus J. Wijers
Minister, Foreign Trade, Anneke van Dok-van Weele

### MINISTRY OF EDUCATION, CULTURAL AFFAIRS & SCIENCE

Europaweg 4, Postbus 25000, 2700 LZ, Zoetermeer, Netherlands
(011-31-79) 323-2323, Fax: (011-31-79) 323-2320
Minister, Dr. Jozef M.M. Ritzen

### MINISTRY OF FINANCE

Korte Voorhout 7, Postbus 20201, 2500 EE, The Hague, Netherlands
(011-31-70) 342-8000, Fax: (011-31-70) 342-7905
Minister, Gerrit Zalm

### MINISTRY OF FOREIGN AFFAIRS

Bezuidenhoutseweg 67, Postbus 20061, 2500 EB, The Hague, Netherlands
(011-31-70) 348-6486, Fax: (011-31-70) 348-4848
Minister, Hans Van Mierlo
Minister, Development Cooperation, Jan Pronk

### MINISTRY OF HEALTH, WELFARE & SPORTS

Sir Winston Churchillaan 362, Postbus 5406, 2280 HK, Rijswijk, Netherlands
(011-31-70) 340-7911, Fax: (011-31-70) 340-7834
Minister, Else Borst-Eilers

### MINISTRY OF HOME AFFAIRS

Schedeldoekshaven 200, Postbus 20011, 2500 EA, The Hague, Netherlands
(011-31-70) 302-6302, Fax: (011-31-70) 363-9153
Minister, Hans F. Dijkstal

### MINISTRY HOUSING, PLANNING & ENVIRONMENT

Rijnstraat 8, Postbus 20951, 2500 EZ, The Hague, Netherlands
(011-31-70) 339-3939, Fax: (011-31-70) 339-1352
Minister, Margreeth de Boer

### MINISTRY OF JUSTICE

Schedeldoekshaven 100, Postbus 20301, 2500 EH, The Hague, Netherlands
(011-31-70) 370-7911, Fax: (011-31-70) 370-7900
Minister, Winnifred Sorgdrager

### MINISTRY FOR NETHERLANDS ANTILLEAN & ARUBAN AFFAIRS

Herengracht 19A, Postbus 20051, 2500 EB, The Hague, Netherlands
(011-31-70) 312-3232, Fax: (011-31-70) 365-2679
Minister Plenipotentiary, Joris Voorhoeve
Minister Plenipotentiary, Aruba, A.G. Croes, Paleisstraat 6, 2514 JA, The Hague, (011-31-70) 365-9824, Fax: (011-38-70) 345-1446
Minister Plenipotentiary, Netherlands Antilles, C.P. de Haseth, Badhuisweg 175, 2597 JP, The Hague, (011-31-70) 351-2811, Fax: (011-31-70) 351-2722

### MINISTRY OF SOCIAL AFFAIRS & EMPLOYMENT

Anna Van Hannoverstraat 4, Postbus 90801, 2509 LV, The Hague, Netherlands
(011-31-70) 333-4444, Fax: (011-31-70) 333-4040
Minister, A.P.W. Melkert

### MINISTRY OF TRANSPORT & PUBLIC WORKS

Plesmanweg 1, Postbus 20901, 2500 EX, The Hague, Netherlands
(011-31-70) 351-6171, Fax: (011-31-70) 351-7895
Minister, Annemaria Jorritsma-Lebbink

#### Associated Agencies

•Bank of the Netherlands/Nederlandsche Bank
Westeinde 1, PO Box 98, 1000 AB, Amsterdam, Netherlands
(011-31-20) 524-9111, Fax: (011-31-20) 524-2500
President, Dr. A.H.E.M. Wellink

## GOVERNMENT OF NORWAY/Norge (NO)

Capital: Oslo
Major Political Parties: Labour Party; Conservative Party; Center Party
Currency: Norwegian Krone
Total Area: 324,220 km2
Population: 4,314,604 (1994)
Language(s): Norwegian, Lapp, Finnish
*Note: A general election was held in Norway on September 15, 1997. Changes to ministries were still taking place at time of publishing. Post-election information was obtained concerning the legislative (the Storting), the executive (The King & his Council) & the ministers.

### OFFICE OF THE KING

Ket. Kgl. Slott, 0010, Oslo 1, Norway
(011-47-22) 44-19-20, Fax: (011-47-22) 55-08-80
H.M.King Harald V
Queen Sonja

### OFFICE OF THE PRIME MINISTER

Akersgaten 42, PO Box 8001 Dep., 0030, Oslo, Norway
(011-47-22) 34-90-00, Fax: (011-47-22) 34-95-00
Prime Minister, Kjell Magne Bondevik

### STORTING/Stortinget

Karl Johansgt. 22, 0026, Oslo 1, Norway
(011-47-22) 31-30-50, Fax: (011-47-22) 31-38-50
President, Kiristi Kolle Grondahl
Vice-President, Hans J. Rosjorde

### LAGTING

Karl Johans Gate 22, 0032, Oslo, Norway
(011-47-22) 31-30-50
President, Odd Holten
Vice-President, Svein Ludvigsen

### ODELSTING

Karl Johansgt 22, 0032, Oslo 1, Norway
(011-47-22) 31-30-50, Fax: (011-47-22) 31-38-38
President, Gunnar Skaug
Vice-President, Jorunn Ringstad

### MINISTRY OF AGRICULTURE
Akersgaten 42, PO Box 8007 Dep., 0030, Oslo 1, Norway
(011-47-22) 34-90-90, Fax: (011-47-22) 34-95-55
Minister, Kare Gjonnes, (011-47-22) 24-91-00

### MINISTRY OF CHILDREN & FAMILY AFFAIRS
Ploensgate 8, PO Box 8036 Dep., 0030, Oslo 1, Norway
(011-47-22) 34-90-90, Fax: (011-47-22) 34-95-15
Minister, Valgerd Svarstad Haugland, (011-47-22) 24-24-00

### MINISTRY OF CULTURAL AFFAIRS
PO Box 8030 Dep., 0030, Oslo 1, Norway
(011-47-22) 34-90-90, Fax: (011-47-22) 34-95-50
Minister, Anne Enger Lahnstein, (011-47-22) 24-78-00

### MINISTRY OF DEFENCE
Myntgaten 1, PO Box 8126 Dep., 0032, Oslo, Norway
(011-47-22) 40-20-03, Fax: (011-47-22) 40-23-02
Minister, Dag Jostein Fjaervoll, (011-47-22) 40-20-01
Chief of Defence Staff, Armed Forces, Gen. Arne Solli
Chief of Staff, Air Force, Maj. Gen. Elinar K. Smedsvig
Chief of Staff, Army, Maj. Gen. Sven A. Sved
Chief of Staff, Home Guard, Maj. Gen. Per Mathisen
Chief of Staff, Navy, R. Adm. Hans K. Svensholt

### MINISTRY OF DEVELOPMENT COOPERATION
7, Juniplass 1, PO Box 8114 Dep., 0032, Oslo 1, Norway
(011-47-22) 34-36-00, Fax: (011-47-22) 34-95-80
Minister, Hilde Frafjord Johnson, (011-47-22) 24-39-00

### MINISTRY OF EDUCATION, RESEARCH & CHURCH AFFAIRS
Akersgaten 42, PO Box 8119 Dep., 0032, Oslo 1, Norway
(011-47-22) 34-90-90, Fax: (011-47-22) 34-95-40
Minister, Jon Lilletun, (011-47-22) 24-74-00

### MINISTRY OF THE ENVIRONMENT
Myntgaten 2, PO Box 8013 Dep., 0030, Oslo 1, Norway
(011-47-22) 34-90-90, Fax: (011-47-22) 34-95-60
Minister, Guro Fjellanger, (011-47-22) 24-57-00

### MINISTRY OF FINANCE & CUSTOMS
Akersgaten 42, PO Box 8008 Dep., 0030, Oslo 1, Norway
(011-47-22) 34-90-90, Fax: (011-47-22) 34-95-05
Minister, Gudmund Restad, (011-47-22) 24-41-00

### MINISTRY OF FISHERIES
Ovre Slottsgate 2, PO Box 8118 Dep., 0032, Oslo 1, Norway
(011-47-22) 34-90-90, Fax: (011-47-22) 34-95-85
Minister, Peter Angelsen, (011-47-22) 24-64-00

### MINISTRY OF FOREIGN AFFAIRS
7, Juniplass 1, PO Box 8114 Dep., 0032, Oslo 1, Norway
(011-47-22) 34-36-00, Fax: (011-47-22) 34-95-80
Minister, Knut Vollebaek, (011-47-22) 24-30-00

### MINISTRY OF HEALTH & SOCIAL AFFAIRS
Gruggegaten 10, PO Box 8011 Dep., 0030, Oslo 1, Norway
(011-47-22) 34-90-90, Fax: (011-47-22) 34-95-75
Minister, Health, Dagfinn Hoybraten, (011-47-22) 24-84-02
Minister, Social Affairs, Magnhild Meltveit Kleppa, (011-47-22) 24-84-00

### MINISTRY OF JUSTICE & THE POLICE
Akersgaten 42, PO Box 8005 Dep., 0030, Oslo 1, Norway
(011-47-22) 34-90-90, Fax: (011-47-22) 34-95-30
Minister, Aud Inger Aure, (011-47-22) 24-51-00

### MINISTRY OF LOCAL GOVERNMENT & LABOUR
PO Box 8112 Dep., 0032, Oslo, Norway
(011-47-22) 34-90-90, Fax: (011-47-22) 34-95-45
Minister, Ragnhild Queseth Haarstad, (011-47-22) 24-68-00

### MINISTRY OF NATIONAL PLANNING & COORDINATION
Plesensgate 8, PO Box 8004 Dep., 0030, Oslo 1, Norway
(011-47-22) 34-90-90, Fax: (011-47-22) 27-14-37
As of January 1, 1998 this ministry is planning to reorganize & form the new Ministry of Labour & Government Administration.
Minister, Eldbjorg Lower, (011-47-22) 24-46-00

### MINISTRY OF PETROLEUM & ENERGY
Grubbegata 8, PO Box 8148 Dep., 0033, Oslo 1, Norway
(011-47-22) 34-90-90, Fax: (011-47-22) 34-95-25
Minister, Marit Arnstad, (011-47-22) 24-61-00

### MINISTRY OF TRADE & INDUSTRY
7, Juniplass 1, PO Box 8114 Dep., 0032, Oslo 1, Norway
(011-47-22) 34-36-00, Fax: (011-47-22) 34-95-80
Minister, Lars Sponheim, (011-47-22) 24-37-00

### MINISTRY OF TRANSPORTATION & COMMUNICATIONS
Mollergaten 1-3, PO Box 8010 Dep., 0030, Oslo 1, Norway
(011-47-22) 34-90-90, Fax: (011-47-22) 34-95-70
Minister, Odd Einar Dorum, (011-47-22) 24-81-00

#### Associated Agencies
•Central Bank of Norway/Norges Bank
Bankplassen 2, PO Box 1179 Sentrum, 0107, Oslo 1, Norway
(011-47-22) 31-60-00, Fax: (011-47-22) 41-31-05
Governor & Chair, Torstein Moland
•Federation of Commercial & Service Enterprises
Drammensveien 30, PO Box 2483, 0202, Oslo 2, Norway
(011-47-22) 55-82-20
President, Vacant
•National Energy Institute
PO Box 40, 2007, Kjeller, Norway
(011-47-6) 80-60-00
Chair, Henrik Ager-Hanssen
•Norwegian Petroleum Directorate
Prof. Olav Hanssensvei 10, PO Box 600, 4001, Stavanger, Norway
(011-47-51) 87-60-00
Director General, Fredrik Hagemann
•Norwegian State Railway
Prinsensgt. 7-9, 0107, Oslo, Norway
(011-47-22) 36-80-00
•Norwegian Telecommunications Authority
PO Box 447 Sentrum, 0104, Oslo, Norway
(011-47-22) 82-46-06
Director General, Roald Ekholdt

## GOVERNMENT OF SOUTH KOREA/Taehan-min'guk (KS)
Capital: Seoul
Major Political Parties: Democratic Party (DP); National Congress for New Politics (NCNP); New Korea Party (NKP); United Liberal Democrates (UID)
Currency: South Korean Won
Total Area: 98,480 km2
Population: 45,482,291 (1996 est.)
Language(s): Korean, English

### OFFICE OF THE PRESIDENT
Chong Wa Dae, 1 Sejong-no, Chongno-ku, Seoul, South Korea
(011-82-2) 770-0011, Fax: (011-82-2) 770-0344
President, H.E. Kim Yong-sam
Chief Secretary, Kim Kwang-II
Director, Presidential Security Service, Kim Kwang-suk, 70 Sejong-no, Chongno-ku, Seoul, (011-82-2) 720-2201

### OFFICE OF THE PRIME MINISTER
77 Sejong-no, Chongno-gu, Seoul, South Korea
(011-82-2) 720-2006, Fax: (011-82-2) 720-2005
Prime Minister, Koh Kon
Deputy Prime Minister, Kang Kyong-sik
Deputy Prime Minister, Kwon O-kie
First Minister of State, Political Affairs, Choo Don-shik

### NATIONAL ASSEMBLY
1-1 Youido-dong, Yongdungpo-gu, Seoul, South Korea
(011-82-2) 784-0911
Speaker, Hwang Nak-joo

### MINISTRY OF AGRICULTURE & FORESTRY
1 Jungang-dong, Kyonggi Prov., Gwachon City, South Korea
(011-82-2) 503-7208, Fax: (011-82-2) 503-7249
Minister, Chong Si-chae
Administrator, Fisheries Administration, Yi Hui-su
Administrator, Forestry Administration, Kwak Mahn-sup
Administrator, Rural Development Administration, Kim Kwang-hui

### MINISTRY OF CULTURE & SPORTS
82-1 Sejongno, Chongno-ku, 110-703, Seoul, South Korea
(011-82-2) 734-5833, Fax: (011-82-2) 736-8513
Minister, Song Tae-hoe

### MINISTRY OF DATA & COMMUNICATIONS
100 Sejong-no, Chongno-ku, Seoul 110-777, South Korea
(011-82-2) 750-2222, Fax: (011-82-2) 750-2915
Minister, Kang Bong-kyun

### MINISTRY OF EDUCATION
77 Sejong-no, Chongno-ku, 110-760, Seoul, South Korea
(011-82-2) 720-3053, Fax: (011-82-2) 736-3402
Minister, Ahn Byung-young

### MINISTRY OF THE ENVIRONMENT
7-16 Shinchon-dong, Songpa-ku, Seoul, South Korea
(011-82-2) 421-0220, Fax: (011-82-2) 421-0280
Minister, Kang Hyon-uk

### MINISTRY OF FINANCE & THE ECONOMY
1 Jungang-dong, Kyonggi Prov., Gwachon City, South Korea
(011-82-2)503-7171, Fax: (011-82-2) 503-9033
Minister, Kang Kyong-sik

### MINISTRY OF FOREIGN AFFAIRS
77 Sejong-no, Chongno-ku, Seoul, South Korea
(011-82-2) 720-2301, Fax: (011-82-2) 724-8291
Minister, Yu Chong-ha
Director, Agency for National Security Planning, Kwon Young-hae

### MINISTRY OF GOVERNMENT ADMINISTRATION
77-6 Sejong-no, Chongno-ku, Seoul, South Korea
(011-82-2) 720-4351, Fax: (011-82-2) 720-8681
Minister, Kim Han-kyu

### MINISTRY OF HEALTH & WELFARE
1 Jungang-dong, 427-760, Kyonggi Prov., Gwachon City, South Korea
(011-82-2) 503-7524, Fax: (011-82-2) 504-6418
Minister, Son Hyak-kyul

### MINISTRY OF HOME AFFAIRS
77 Sejong-no, Chongno-ku, Seoul, South Korea
(011-82-2) 731-2121, Fax: (011-82-2) 733-2755
Minister, Kang Oon-tae
Director General, National Police Headquarters, Kim Hwa-nam, 77 Sejong-no, Chongno-ku, Seoul, (011-82-2) 213-2241

Director General, Office of Administrative Control, Kim Si-hyong, (011-82-2) 731-2170

**MINISTRY OF INFORMATION**
77 Sejong-no, Chongno-ku, 732-050, Seoul, South Korea
(011-82-2) 720-1456, Fax: 011-82-2) 732-8221
Minister, Oh In-whan
Director General, Korean Overseas Information Service, Yi Chang-yong, 82-1 Sejong-no, Chongno-ku, 1101-050, Seoul, (011-82-2) 720-4817

**MINISTRY OF JUSTICE**
1 Jungang-dong, Kyonggi, Gwachon City, South Korea
(011-82-2) 503-7011, Fax: (011-82-2) 504-3337
Minister, Choe Chang-yop
Commissioner, Korean Customs Service, Lee Hwan-kywu, 71 Nonhyun-dong, Kangram-gu, Seoul, (011-82-2) 512-0011

**MINISTRY OF LABOUR**
Government Compex II, 1 Jungang-dong, Kyonggi Prov., Gwachon City, South Korea
(011-82-2) 503-9714, Fax: (011-82-2) 503-9771
Minister, Jin Nyum

**MINISTRY OF LEGISLATION**
77 Sejong-no, Chongno-ku, Seoul 110-760, South Korea
(011-82-2) 720-4484, Fax: (011-82-2) 738-2649
Minister, Kim Ki-suk

**MINISTRY OF MARITIME AFFAIRS & FISHERIES**
Jinsol Bldg., #826-14, Yoksam-dong, Kyonggi Prov., Gwachon City, South Korea
(011-82-2) 554-2022, Fax: (011-82-2) 554-2023
Minister, Shin Sang-woo

**MINISTRY OF NATIONAL DEFENCE**
1 Yonsan-dong, 3-ka, Yongsan-ku, Seoul, South Korea
(011-82-2) 795-0071, Fax: (011-82-2) 748-7056
Chair, Joint Chiefs of Staff, Armed Forces, Gen. Kim Tong-chin, Yongsan-ku, Seoul, (011-82-2) 792-6081
Chief of Staff, Air Force, Gen. Kim Hong-rae, 320-919, PO Box 301, Poonam-ri, Doom-myun, Nonsan-kun, Choongnam
Chief of Staff, Army, Gen. Yun Yong-nam, Bunam-ri, Duma-myun, Nonsan-gun, Choongram
Chief of Naval Operations, Navy, Adm. An Pyong-tae, Bunam-ri, Duma-myun, Nonsan-gun, Choongnam, (011-82-42) 551-3005

**MINISTRY OF NATIONAL UNIFICATION**
#77-6, Sejong-no, Chongno-ku, 110-760, Seoul, South Korea
(011-82-2) 720-2104
Minister, Kwon O-kie
Secretary General, Council for Democratic & Peaceful Unification, Chong Ho-kun

**MINISTRY OF PATRIOTS & VETERANS AFFAIRS**
17-23 Yoido-dong, Yongdungpo-ku, Seoul, South Korea
(011-82-2) 780-9607, Fax: (011-82-2) 784-1087
Minister, Hwang Chang-pyong

**MINISTRY FOR POLITICAL AFFAIRS**
77 Sejong-no, Chongno-ku, Seoul, South Korea
(011-82-2) 720-2271, Fax: (011-82-2) 737-4648
Minister, Sin Kyong-sik
Minister, Kim Yoon-duk

**MINISTRY OF SCIENCE & TECHNOLOGY**
Government Complex Bldg. II, 1 Jungang-dong, Kyonggi Prov., Gwachon City, South Korea
(011-82-2) 503-7608, Fax: (011-82-2) 503-7673
Minister, Kwon Suk-il

**MINISTRY OF TRADE & INDUSTRY**
1 Jungang-dong, Kyonggi Prov., Gwachon City, South Korea
(011-82-2) 503-9404, Fax: (011-82-2) 503-9649
Minister, Lim Chang-yul
Administrator, Industrial Advancement Administration, Pak Sam-yyu, (011-82-2) 503-7950
Commissioner, Industrial Property Administration, Park Hong-sik, (011-82-2) 568-5830

**MINISTRY OF TRANSPORTATION & CONSTRUCTION**
1 Jungang-dong, Kyonggi Prov., Gwachon City, South Korea
(011-82-2) 503-7312, Fax: (011-82-2) 503-7409
Minister, Lee Hwan-kyun
Deputy Minister, Construction, Yu Sang-yol
Deputy Minister, Transportation, Ku Pon-yong
Administrator, Maritime & Port, Kim Chol-yong, (011-82-2) 745-7321
Administrator, National Railroad, Dhoe Pyong-uk, (011-82-2) 392-0078

**Associated Agencies**
•Bank of Korea
110, 3ka Namdaemun-no, Chung-ku, PO Box 26, Seoul 100-794, South Korea
(011-82-2) 759-4114, Fax: (011-82-2) 759-4037
Governor, Kim Myong-ho
•Economic Planning Board
1 Chungang-dong, Kwach'on, Kyonggi, South Korea
(011-82-2) 503-9020, Fax: (011-82-2) 503-9033
Minister, Hong Chae-hyung
•Electronics & Telecommunications Research Institute
PO Box 8, Taedok Science Town, Taejon 305-606, South Korea
(011-82-2) 587-7001
President, Yang Seung-taik
•Environment Management Corporation
Kangwon Bldg., 1024-4 Daechi-dong, Kangnam-ku, Seoul, South Korea
(011-82-42) 563-7211
President, Lee Chang-ki
•Korean Aerospace Reseach Institute
PO Box 15, Daeduk Science Town, Taejon 305-606, South Korea
(011-82-42) 860-2140
President, Hong Jae-hak
•Korean Atomic Energy Research Institute
150 Duckjin-dong, Yusong-ku, Taejon, South Korea
(011-82-42) 868-2121
President, Shin Jae-in
•Korean Development Institute
207-41, Cheongryangri-dong, Dongdaemoon-ku, Seoul 131-101, South Korea
(011-82-2) 960-0080
President, Whang In-joung
•Korean Energy Economic Institute
665-1, Naeson-dong, Uiwang City, Kyunggi-do 437-082, South Korea
(011-82-62) 34321-0681
President, Lee Hoe-sung
•Korean Environmental Preservation Association
Korea Chamber of Commerce Bldg. 45, Namdaemoonro, 4-ka, Chung-ku, Seoul, South Korea
(011-82-2) 753-7641
President, Chung Soo-chang
•Korean Institute of Advanced Science & Technology
373-1, Koosung-dong, Yusong-ku, Taejon 305-701, South Korea
(011-82-2) 958-3222
President, Chun Soung-soon
•Korean Institute of Energy Research
71-2, Jang-dong, Yusong-ku, Taejon, South Korea
(011-82-42) 860-3000
President, Auh Chung-moo
•Korean Institute of Geology, Mining & Materials
30 Kajeong-dong, Yusong-ku, Taejon 305-350, South Korea
(011-82-42) 868-3270
President, Kim Dong-hak
•Korean Institute for Health & Social Affairs
San 42-14, Bulkwang-dong, Eunpyung-ku, Seoul 122-040, South Korea
(011-82-2) 355-8001
President, Lee Sung-woo
•Korean Institute of Industry & Technology
206-9, Cheongryangri-dong, Dongdaemoon-ku, Seoul, South Korea
(011-82-2) 962-6211
President, Park Hong-shik
•Korean Institute for International Economics & Trade
206-9, Cheongryangri-dong, Dongdaemoon-ku, Seoul 131-010, South Korea
(011-82-2) 962-6211
President, Cha Dong-se
•Korean Maritime Institute
112-2 Inui-dong, Chongro-gu, Seoul, South Korea
(011-82-2) 745-7521
President, Bai Byung-tsi
•Korean Nuclear Society
B-109, Keco Nam Seoul Bldg., 21, Yoido-dong, Youngdungpo-ku, Seoul, South Korea
(011-82-2) 782-0141
President, Yoon Yong-ku
•Korean Ocean Research & Development Institute
PO Box 29, Ansan, Kyunggi-do, Seoul, South Korea
(011-82-2) 863-4770
President, Kwak Hee-sang
•Korean Rural Economic Institute
4-102, Hoegi-dong, Dongdaemoon-ku, Seoul 131-050, South Korea
(011-82-2) 962-7312
President, Chung Young-il
•Korean Transport Institute
Ildong Bldg., 968-5, Daechi-dong, Kangnam-ku, Seoul 135-280
(011-82-2) 860-1200
•National Unification Board
77 Sejong-no, Chongno-gu, Seoul, South Korea
(011-82-2) 720-2104, Fax: (011-82-2) 720-2432
Deputy Prime Minister, Rha Woong-bae

## GOVERNMENT OF TAIWAN/T'ai-wan (TW)
Capital: Taipei
Major Political Parties: Kuomintang (KMT); Democratic Progressive Party (DPP); New Party (NP)
Currency: New Taiwan Dollar
Total Area: 35,980 km2
Population: 21,500,583 (1995)
Language(s): Mandarin, Taiwanese

**OFFICE OF THE PRESIDENT**
Chiehshou Hall, 122, Chungking S. Rd., Sec. 1, Taipei, Taiwan
(011-886-2) 311-3731, Fax: (011-886-2) 314-0746
President & Chair, National Security Council, H.E. Li Teng-hui
Vice-President, Lien Chan
Secretary General, Huang Kun-huei

**OFFICE OF THE PREMIER**
1, Chunghsiao E. Rd., Sec. 1, Taipei, Taiwan
(011-886-2) 365-1500, Fax: (011-886-2) 394-8727
Premier, Lien Chan
Vice-Premier, Hsu Li-teh

**LEGISLATIVE YÜAN/Li-Fa Yüan**
1, Chungshan S. Rd., Taipei, Taiwan
(011-886-2) 321-1531, Fax: (011-886-2) 322-3557
President, Liu Sung-pan
Vice-President, Wang Chin-p'ing

**NATIONAL ASSEMBLY/Kwo-Min Ta-Hui**
1, Sui Shan St., Taipei, Taiwan
(011-886-2) 331-1986, Fax: (011-886-2) 361-2515
Speaker, Frederick Chien

**COUNCIL FOR AGRICULTURE**
37, Nanhai Rd., Taipei, Taiwan
(011-886-2) 381-2997, Fax: (011-886-2) 331-0341
Chair, Tjiu Mau-ying

**COUNCIL FOR CULTURAL PLANNING & DEVELOPMENT**
102 Ai Kwo East Rd., Taipei, Taiwan
(011-886-2) 522-5300, Fax: (011-886-2) 551-9011
Chair, Lin Cheng-chih

**MINISTRY OF ECONOMIC AFFAIRS**
15, Foo chow St., Taipei, Taiwan
(011-886-2) 321-2200, Fax: (011-886-2) 391-9398
Minister, Wang Chih-kang
Director General, Board of Foreign Trade, Lin Yi-fu, (011-886-2) 351-0271
Director, Industrial Development Bureau, Yiin Cheih-min, (011-886-2) 754-1255
Director, Industrial Development & Investment Centre, Chen Yung-hsiang, (011-886-2) 398-2111
Director, International Cooperation Department, Lei Dao-yu, (011-886-2) 391-8198
Director General, National Bureau of Standards, Chen Zso-chen, (011-886-2) 738-0007
Chair, Investment Commission, Shen Ke-sheng, (011-886-2) 351-3151

**COUNCIL FOR ECONOMIC PLANNING & DEVELOPMENT**
87, Nanking East Rd., Sec. 2, Taipei, Taiwan
(011-886-2) 552-5300, Fax: (011-886-2) 551-9011
Director General, Chiang Pin-kung

**MINISTRY OF EDUCATION**
5, Chung shan South Rd., 10040, Taipei, Taiwan
(011-886-2) 389-8820, Fax: (011-886-2) 395-2073
Minister, Wu Jin

**MINISTRY OF FINANCE**
2, Ai kuo West Rd., Taipei, Taiwan
(011-886-2) 322-8000, Fax: (011-886-2) 321-1205
Minister, Paul Cheng-hsiung chiu

**MINISTRY OF FOREIGN AFFAIRS**
2, Chiehshou Rd., Taipei, Taiwan
(011-886-2) 311-9292, Fax: (011-886-2) 314-4972
Minister, John H. Chang

**DEPARTMENT OF HEALTH**
100, Ai kuo East Rd., Taipei, Taiwan
(011-886-2) 321-0151, Fax: (011-886-2) 312-2907
Director General, Chang Po-ya

**MINISTRY OF THE INTERIOR**
5, Hsu chow Rd., Taipei, Taiwan
(011-886-2) 356-5000, Fax: (011-886-2) 397-6850
Minister, Lin Fong-cheng
Director, National Police Administration, Lu Yu-chun, (011-886-2) 321-9011

**MINISTRY OF JUSTICE**
130, Chungking South Rd., Sec. 1, Taipei, Taiwan
(011-886-2) 314-6871, Fax: (011-886-2) 389-6274
Minister, Liao Cheng-hao

**COUNCIL OF LABOUR AFFAIRS**
132, Men sheng East Rd., Sec. 3, Taipei, Taiwan
(011-886-2) 718-2512, Fax: (011-886-2) 514-9240
Chair, Hsieh Shen-shan

**MINISTRY OF NATIONAL DEFENCE**
Chiehshou Hall, Chungking South Rd., Taipei 10016, Taiwan
(011-886-2) 311-6117
Minister, Gen. Chiang Chung-ling
Commander-in-Chief, General Staff, Gen. Wang Wen-hsiem
Commander-in-Chief, Air Force, Gen. Huang Hsien-jung
Commander-in-Chief, Army, Gen. Li Chen-lin
Commander-in-Chief, Navy, Adm. Ku Chung-lien

**MINISTRY OF TRANSPORTATION & COMMUNICATIONS**
2, Chang sha St., Sec. 1, Taipei, Taiwan
(011-886-2) 349-2900, Fax: (011-886-2) 381-2260
Minister, Tsay Jaw-yang
Director General, Civil Aeronautics Administration, Mao Chi-kuo, (011-886-2) 514-2400
Director General, Telecommunications Directorate, Steven Chen, (011-886-2) 344-3691

**Associated Agencies**
•Atomic Energy Council
67 Lane, 144, Keelung Rd., Sec. 4, Taipei, Taiwan
(011-886-2) 363-4180, Fax: (011-886-2) 363-5377
Chair, Hu Ching-piao
•Budget, Accounting & Statistics Office
1 Chung Hsiao East Rd., Sec. 1, Taipei, Taiwan
(011-886-2) 381-4910, Fax: (011-886-2) 331-9925
Director General, Wei Duan
•Central Bank of China
2, Roosevelt Rd. Sec. 1, Taipei, Taiwan
(011-886-2) 393-6161, Fax: (011-886-2) 322-3223
Governor, Y.D. Sheu
•Central Personnel Administration
109 Huai Ning St., Taipei, Taiwan
(011-886-2) 311-1720, Fax: (011-886-2) 371-5252
Director General, Chen Keng-chin
•Central Weather Bureau
64, Kungyuan Rd., Taipei, Taiwan
(011-886-2) 371-3181, Fax: (011-886-2) 391-8971
Director, Shieh Shinn-liang
•Environmental Protection Administration
41, Chung hua Rd., Sec. 1, Taipei, Taiwan
(011-866-2) 311-7722, Fax: (011-866-2) 321-2491
Administrator, Tsai Hsung-hsiung
•Fair Trade Commission
Taipei, Taiwan
(011-886-2) 545-5501, Fax: (011-886-2) 545-0107
Chair, Chao Yang-ching
•Government Information Office
2, Tientsin St., Taipei, Taiwan
(011-886-2) 322-8888, Fax: (011-886-2) 341-6252
Director General, Su Chi
•Mainland Affairs Council
4 Chung Hsiao West Rd., 14-17th Fl., Taipei, Taiwan
(011-886-2) 314-6969, Fax: (011-886-2) 331-5083
Chair, Chang King-yuh
•Mongolian & Tibetan Affairs Commission
5 Hsu Chou Rd., 4th Fl., Sec. 1, Taipei, Taiwan
(011-886-2) 356-6166, Fax: (011-886-2) 356-6432
Chair, Lee Hou-kao
•National Science Council
106, Hoping East Rd., Sec. 2, Taipei, Taiwan
(011-886-2) 737-7500, Fax: (011-886-2) 737-7668
Chair, Liu Chao-shiuan
•National Youth Commission
5 Hsu Chou Rd., 14th Fl., Taipei, Taiwan
(011-886-2) 356-6271, Fax: (011-886-2) 356-690
Chair, Wu Wan-lan
•Overseas Chinese Affairs Commission
5 Hsu Chou Rd., 4th Fl., Sec. 1, Taipei, Taiwan
(011-886-2) 356-6166, Fax: (011-886-2) 356-6323
Chair, James C.Y. Chu
•Research, Development & Evaluation Commission
4, Chunghsiao W. Rd., Sec. 1, Taipei, Taiwan
(011-886-2) 388-0833, Fax: (011-886-2) 392-8133
Chair, Huang Ta-chou
•Taiwan Power Company
242, Roosevelt Rd., Sec. 3, Taipei, Taiwan
(011-886-2) 365-1234, Fax: (011-886-2) 367-8593
President, S.C. Hsi
•Vocational Assistance Commission for Retired Servicemen
222, Chung hsiao East Rd., Sec. 5, Taipei, Taiwan
(011-886-2) 725-5700, Fax: (011-886-2) 723-0170
Chair, Gen. Yang Ting-yun

## GOVERNMENT OF THE UNITED KINGDOM (UK)

Capital: London
Major Political Parties: Conservative & Unionist Party; Labour Party; Liberal Democratic Party
Currency: British Pound
Total Area: 244,820 km2
Population: 58,295,119 (1995)
Language(s): English, Welsh, Scottish

**HER MAJESTY'S HOUSEHOLD**
Buckingham Palace, London SW1A 1AA, United Kingdom
(011-44-171) 930-4832, Fax: (011-44-171) 321-0380
Queen, United Kingdom of Great Britain & Northern Ireland, H.M. Queen Elizabeth II
Lord Chamberlain, Earl of Airlie, K.T., G.C.V.O.
Private Secretary, The Rt. Hon. Sir Robert Fellowes, K.C.V.O., K.C.B., (011-44-171) 930-4832
Prince of Wales, H.R.H. Prince Charles, St. James's Palace, London SW1 1BS, (011-44-171) 930-4832

**OFFICE OF THE PRIME MINISTER**
10 Downing St., London SW1 2AA, United Kingdom
(011-44-171) 270-3000, Fax: (011-44-171) 930-2831
URL: http://www.number-10/gov.uk/
Prime Minister, Rt. Hon. Tony Blair
First Secretary & Deputy Prime Minister, John Prescott

**HOUSE OF COMMONS**
Westminster, London SW1A 0AA, United Kingdom
(011-44-171) 219-3000, Fax: (011-44-171) 219-5839
URL: http://www.parliament.uk/
Lord President of the Council & Leader of the House, Ann Taylor
Speaker, Betty Boothroyd

**HOUSE OF LORDS**
Parliament Office, Westminister SW1A 0PW, United Kingdom
(011-44-171) 219-3000
Leader of the House, Lord Richard
Lord High Chancellor, Lord Irvine of Lairg
Lord Chair of Committees, Lord Boston of Faversham

**MINISTRY OF AGRICULTURE, FISHERIES & FOOD**
Whitehall Place, London SW1A 2HH, United Kingdom
(011-44-171) 270-3000, Fax: (011-44-171) 270-8125
URL: http://www.open.gov.uk/maff/maffhome.htm
Minister, Dr. John Cunningham
Minister of State, Agriculture, Fisheries & Food, Jeffrey Rooker

**MINISTRY OF DEFENCE**
Main Bldg., Whitehall, London SW1A 2HB, United Kingdom
(011-44-171) 218-9000
URL: http://www.mod.uk/
Secretary of State, George Robertson
Minister, Armed Forces, Dr. John Reid
Minister, Defence Procurement, Lord Gilbert
Chair & Chief of Staff, Armed Forces, Gen. Sir Peter Inge
Chief of Staff, Air Force, ACM Sir Michael Graydon
Chief of Staff, Army, Gen. Sir Charles H. Guthrie
Chief of Staff, Navy, Adm. Sir Benjamin Bathurst

**DEPARTMENT OF EDUCATION & EMPLOYMENT**
Sanctuary Bldg., Great Smith St., London SW1P 3BT, United Kingdom
(011-44-171) 925-5000, Fax: (011-44-171) 925-6000
URL: http://www.open.gov.uk/dfee/dfeehome.htm
Secretary of State, David Blunkett
Minister, Education & Employment (Lords), Baroness Blackstone
Minister, Employment & Disability Rights, Andrew Smith
Minister, School Standards, Stephen Byers

**DEPARTMENT OF THE ENVIRONMENT, TRANSPORT & THE REGIONS**
Bressenden Place, London SW1E 5DU, United Kingdom
(011-44-171) 890-3000, Fax: (011-44-171) 276-0818
URL: http://www.open.gov.uk/doe/doehome.htm
Secretary of State, John Prescott
Minister, Environment, Michael Meacher
Minister, Transport, Gavin Strang
Minister of State, Local Government & Housing, Hilary Armstrong
Minister of State, Regions, Regeneration & Planning, Richard Caborn

**FOREIGN & COMMONWEALTH AFFAIRS OFFICE**
Whitehall, London SW1A 2AH, United Kingdom
(011-44-171) 270-3000, Fax: (011-44-171) 270-3094
URL: http://www.fco.gov.uk/
Secretary of State, Robert Cook, Q.C.
Minister of State, Derek Fatchett
Minister of State, Douglas Henderson
Minister of State, Tony Lloyd

**DEPARTMENT OF HEALTH**
Richmond House, 79 Whitehall, London SW1A 2NS
(011-44-171) 210-3000, Fax: (011-44-171) 210-5523
URL: http://www.open.gov.uk/doh/dhhome.htm
Secretary of State, Frank Dobson
Minister, Public Health, Tessa Jowell
Minister of State, Baroness Jay of Paddington
Minister of State, Alan Milburn

**HOME OFFICE**
50 Queen Anne's Gate, London SW1H 9AT, United Kingdom
(011-44-171) 273-3000, Fax: (011-44-171) 273-2190
URL: http://www.open.gov.uk/home_off/hofront.htm
Secretary of State, John Straw, Q.C.
Minister of State, Alun Michael
Minister of State, Joyce Quin

**DEPARTMENT OF INTERNATIONAL DEVELOPMENT**
94 Victoria St., London SW1E 5JL, United Kingdom
(011-44-171) 917-7000
Secretary of State, Clare Short

**LAW OFFICER'S DEPARTMENT**
Attorney General's Chambers, 9 Buckingham Gate, London SW1E 6JP, United Kingdom
(011-44-171) 828-7155
Attorney General, John Morris, Q.C.
Solicitor General, Lord Falconer of Thronton, Q.C.

**LORD ADVOCATE'S DEPARTMENT**
2 Carlton Gardens, London SW1Y 5AA, United Kingdom
(011-44-171) 210-1010, Fax: (011-44-171) 210-1025
Lord Advocate, Lord Advocate of Hardie, Q.C.
Solicitor General, Scotland, Colin Boyd, Q.C.

**LORD CHANCELLOR'S DEPARTMENT**
House of Lords, London SW1A OPW, United Kingdom
(011-44-171) 219-6790, Fax: (011-44-171) 219-4711
Lord Chancellor, Lord Irvine of Lairg

**DEPARTMENT OF NATIONAL HERITAGE**
Horse Guard's Rd., London SW1P 3AL, United Kingdom
(011-44-171) 211-6000, Fax: (011-44-171) 211-6032
URL: http://www.heritage.gov.uk/
Secretary of State, Christopher Smith
Minister, Film & Tourism, Thomas Clarke

**NORTHERN IRELAND OFFICE**
Whitehall, London SW1A 2AZ, United Kingdom
(011-44-171) 210-3000, Fax: (011-44-171) 210-6549
URL: http://www.nics.gov.uk/nio/
Secretary of State, Dr. Marjorie Mowlam
Minister of State, Adam Ingram
Minister of State, Paul Murphy

**OFFICE OF PUBLIC SERVICE**
70 Whitehall, London SW1A 2AS, United Kingdom
(011-44-171) 270-3000, Fax: 270-0196
Minister, Civil Service & Prime Minister, Tony Blair

**SCOTTISH OFFICE**
Dover House, Whitehall, London SW1A 2AU, United Kingdom
(011-44-171) 270-3000, Fax: (011-44-171) 270-6730
URL: http://www.open.gov.uk/scotoff/scofhom.htm
Secretary of State, Donald Dewar
Minister, Education & Industry, Brian Wilson
Minister, Home Affairs & Devolution, Henry McLeish

**DEPARTMENT OF SOCIAL SECURITY**
Richmond House, 79 Whitehall, London SW1A 2NS, United Kingdom
(011-44-171) 238-0800, Fax: (011-44-171) 210-5523
URL: http://www.open.gov.uk/dss/dsshome1.htm
Secretary of State & Minister, Women, Harriet Harman
Minister of State, Welfare Reform, Frank Field

**DEPARTMENT OF TRADE & INDUSTRY**
1 Victoria St., London SW1H 0ET, United Kingdom
(011-44-171) 215-5000, Fax: (011-44-171) 828-3258
URL: http://www.dti.gov.uk/
Secretary of State & President, Board of Trade, Margaret Beckett
Minister, Trade, Lord Clinton-Davis
Minister, Trade & Competitiveness in Europe, Lord Simpson of Highbury
Minister of State, John Battle
Minister of State, Ian McCartney

**HER MAJESTY'S TREASURY**
Treasury Chambers, Parliament St., London SW1P 3AG, United Kingdom
(011-44-171) 270-3000, Fax: (011-44-171) 270-5653
URL: http://www.hm-treasury.gov.uk/
First Lord of the Treasury, Rt. Hon. Tony Blair
Chancellor of the Exchequer, Gordon Brown, Q.C.
Chief Secretary, Treasury, Alisdair Darling
Financial Secretary, Treasury, Dawn Primarolo

**Customs & Excise**
New King's Bean House, 22 Upper Ground Rd., London, United Kingdom
(011-44-171) 620-1313

**Board of Inland Revenue**
Somerset House, Strand, London WC2R 1LB, United Kingdom
(011-44-171) 438-6622
Chancellor of the Exchequer, Kenneth Clarke

**WELSH OFFICE**
Gwydyr House, Whitehall, London SW1A 2ER, United Kingdom
(011-44-171) 270-3000, Fax: (011-44-171) 270-0586
URL: http://www.open.gov.uk/woffice/whome.htm
Secretary of State, Ronald Davies

**Associated Agencies**
•Associated British Ports
150 Holborn St., London EC1N 2LR, United Kingdom
(011-44-171) 486-6621
Chair, J.K. Stuart
•Bank of England
Threadneedle St., London EC2R 8AH, United Kingdom
(011-44-171) 601-4444
URL: http://www.bankofengland.co.uk/
Governor, Edward George
•British Aerospace
Warwick House, Farnborough Aerospace Centre, Farnborough, Hants GU14 6YU, United Kingdom
(011-44-1252) 373-232
Chair, R.P. Bauman
•British Airways PLC
Speedbird House, PO Box 10, Heathrow Airport, Hounslow, Middlesex TW6 2JA, United Kingdom
(011-44-181) 759-5511
Chair, Lord King of Wartnaby
•British Broadcasting Corporation
Broadcasting House, London W1A 1AA, United Kingdom
(011-44-171) 580-4468
Chair, Marmaduke Hussey
•British Gas PLC
Rivermill House, 152 Grosvenor Rd., London SW1V 3JL, United Kingdom
(011-44-171) 821-1444
Chair, Sir Dennis Rooke
•British Railways Board
Euston House, 24 Eversholt St., PO Box 100, London NW1 1DZ, United Kingdom
(011-44-171) 922-6545
Chair, Sir Bob Reid
•British Telecom International
#820, Holburn Centre, 120 Holburn St., London EC1N 2TE, United Kingdom
(011-44-171) 492-2000
Director, Tom Edwards
•British Telecommunications PLC
British Telecom Centre, 81 Newgate St., London EC1A 7AJ, United Kingdom
(011-44-171) 356-5000
Chair, Sir Ian Vallance
•Cable & Wireless PLC
124 Theobalds Rd., London VC1X 8RX, United Kingdom
(011-44-171) 315-4000
CEO, J. Ross
•Central Office of Information
Hercules Rd., London SE1 7DU, United Kingdom
(011-44-171) 928-2345
CEO, G.M. Devereau
•Civil Aviation Authority
CAA House, 4-12 Queen Anne's Gate, London SW1H 9AZ, United Kingdom
(011-44-171) 379-7311
Chair, Christopher Chataway
•Export Credits Guarantee Department
2 Exchange Tower, Harbour Exchange Square, London E14 9GS
(011-44-171) 512-7887, Fax: (011-44-171) 512-7649
•HM Land Registry
Lincoln's Inn Fields, London WC2A 3PH, United Kingdom
(011-44-171) 405-3488
Chief Land Registrar & CEO, E.J. Pryer
•National Audit Office
197 Buckingham Palace Rd., Victoria, London SW1W 9SP, United Kingdom
(011-44-171) 798-7000
URL: http://www.open.gov.uk/nao/home.htm
Comptroller & Auditor General, John Bourn
•Office of Electricity Regulation
Hagley House, Hagley Rd., Birmingham B16 8QG, United Kingdom

(011-44-121) 456-2100
Director General, Prof. S.C. Littlechild
•Office for National Statistics (ONS)
General Register Office, Trafalgar Rd., Southport PR8 2HH, United Kingdom
(011-44-151) 471-4801
Director, Dr. Tim Holt
•Office of Science & Technology (OST)
1 Victoria St., UG.A.35, London SW1 HEOT, United Kingdom
(011-44-171) 215-0053, Fax: (011-44-171) 215-0054
•Office of Telecommunications
Export House, Ludgate Hill, London EC4M 7JJ, United Kingdom
(011-44-171) 822-1600
URL: http://www.open.gov.uk/oftel/oftelhm.htm
Director General, Sir Brian Carsberg
•Office of Water Services
Centre City Tower, 7 Hill St., Birmingham B5 4UA, United Kingdom
Director General, I.C.R. Byatt
•Oil & Pipelines Agency
35-38 Portman Square, London W1H 0EU, United Kingdom
Director General, Geoffrey Richards
•The Post Office
148 Old St., 4th Fl., London EC1 9HQ, United Kingdom
(011-44-171) 490-2888
Chair, Michael Heron
•Radiotelecommunications Agency
Waterloo Bridge House, Waterloo Rd., London SE1 8UA, United Kingdom
(011-44-171) 215-5000
CEO, M.J. Mitchell
•Royal Mint
Llantrisant, Pontyclun, Mid-Clamorgan CF7 8YT, United Kingdom
(011-44-1433) 222-111
CEO, A.D. Garrett
•UK Atomic Energy Authority
Harwell Laboratory, Oxfordshire 0X11 0RA, United Kingdom
(011-44-1325) 821-111
Chair, Sir Anthony Cleaver

## GOVERNMENT OF THE UNITED STATES OF AMERICA/United States (US)

Capital: Washington
Major Political Parties: Republican Party; Democratic Party
Currency: United States Dollar
Total Area: 9,372,610 km2
Population: 263,814,032 (1995)
Languages: English, Spanish

### OFFICE OF THE PRESIDENT

1600 Pennsylvania Ave. NW, Washington DC 20500, USA
202/456-2883, Fax: 202/456-2883
President, William J. Clinton
First Lady, Hillary Rodham Clinton
Chief of Staff, Erskine B. Bowles
Whitehouse Spokesperson, Michael McCurry

### OFFICE OF THE VICE-PRESIDENT

1600 Pennsylvania Ave. NW, Washington DC 20500, USA
202/456-1414, Fax: 202/456-7044
Vice President, Albert Gore Jr.
National Security Advisor, Leon S. Fuerth

### SENATE

Capitol Bldg., Washington DC, USA
202/224-3121
President of the Senate, Albert Gore Jr.
Majority Leader, Trent Lott
Minority Leader, Tom Dashle

### HOUSE OF REPRESENTATIVES

Capitol Bldg., Washington DC, USA
202/225-3121
Speaker, Hon. Newt Gingrich
Majority Leader, Richard Armey
Minority Leader, Richard Gephardt

#### Special Agencies

##### Advisory Committee for Trade Policy & Negotiations

Windsor Bldg., 600 - 17th St. NW, Washington DC 20506
202/395-3204, Fax: 202/395-6224
Chair, Susan Hammer

##### Central Intelligence Agency

Old Executive Office Bldg., 17th St. & Pennsylvania Ave. NW, Washington DC 20500, USA
703/482-1100, Fax: 703/527-5040
Director, John Deutch

##### Foreign Intelligence Advisory Board

Old Executive Office Bldg., 17th St. & Pennsylvania Ave. NW, Washington DC 20500, USA
202/456-2352, Fax: 202/395-3403
Chair, Vacant

##### National Security Council

1600 Pennsylvania Ave. NW, Washington DC 20500, USA
202/456-2255, Fax: 202/456-1414
Asst. to the President, Samuel Berger

##### Office of Science & Technology Policy

17th St. & Pennsylvania Ave. NW, Washington DC 20500, USA
202/456-7116, Fax: 202/395-3719
Asst. to the President & Director, OSTP, John Gibbons

##### Office of the United States Trade Representative

600 - 17th St. NW, Washington DC 20508, USA
202/395-3204, Fax: 202/395-3719
U.S. Trade Representative, Charlene Barshefsky

### DEPARTMENT OF AGRICULTURE

Administration Bldg., 14th St. & Independence Ave. SW, Washington DC 20250, USA
202/720-3631
Secretary, Daniel Glickman

##### Forest Service

Auditors Bldg., 201 - 14th St. SW, Washington DC 20090, USA
202/205-1661, Fax: 202/205-1765
Chief, Michael P. Dombeck

### DEPARTMENT OF COMMERCE

Herbert C. Hoover Bldg., 14th St. & Constitution Ave. NW, Washington DC 20230, USA
202/482-2000
Secretary, William Daley
Deputy Secretary, David J. Barrum
Undersecretary, Economic & Statistics Administration, Evertt M. Ehrilich
Undersecretary, Export Administration, William A. Reinsch
Undersecretary, Oceans & Atmosphere, Donald J. Baker
Undersecretary, Technology Administration, Mary L. Good

##### International Trade Administration

Herbert C. Hoover Bldg., 14th St. & Constitution Ave. NW, Washington DC 20230, USA
202/482-2867, Fax: 202/482-4821
Undersecretary, Stuart Eizenstat

### DEPARTMENT OF DEFENSE

The Pentagon, Washington DC 20301, USA
703/545-6700
Secretary, William S. Cohen
Office of the Deputy Secretary, John M. Deutch
Chair, Joint Chiefs of Staff, Gen. John M. Shalikashvili, 703/695-3337
Secretary, Air Force, Sheila E. Widnall, 703/697-7376
Secretary, Army, Togo D. West, 703/695-3211
Secretary, Navy, John H. Dalton, 703/695-3131
Commandant, United States Coast Guard, V. Adm. Robert E. Kramek, 202/267-2390

##### Defense Intelligence Agency

7400 Defense Pentagon, Washington DC 20301-7400, USA
703/695-7353
Director, Lt. Col. James R. Clapper

### DEPARTMENT OF EDUCATION

Federal Office Bldg. 6, 400 Maryland Ave. SW, Washington DC 20202-0101
202/401-3000
Secretary, Richard W. Riley
Deputy Secretary, Madeleine M. Kunin

### DEPARTMENT OF ENERGY

Forrestal Bldg., 1000 Independence Ave. SW, Washington DC 20585, USA
202/586-6210, Fax: 202/586-8134
Secretary, Federico Pena
Deputy Secretary, William H. White

##### Federal Energy Regulatory Commission (FERC)

825 North Capital St. NE, Washington DC 20426, USA
202/208-0000, Fax: 202/208-2106
Chair, Elizabeth Moler

### DEPARTMENT OF HEALTH & HUMAN SERVICES

Hubert H. Humphrey Bldg., 200 Independence Ave. SW, Washington DC 20201, USA
202/690-7000, Fax: 202/245-3380
Secretary, Donna Shalala
Deputy Secretary, Walter D. Broadnax

##### Centre for Disease Control & Prevention

1600 Clifton Rd. NE, Atlanta GA 30333, USA
404/639-3291
Director, David Satcher

##### Food & Drug Administration (FDA)

Parklawn Bldg., 5600 Fishers Lane, Rockville MD 20857, USA
301/827-2410, Fax: 301/443-3100
Acting Commissioner, Dr. Michael Friedman

##### Social Security Administration

Altmeyer Bldg., 6401 Security Blvd., Baltimore MD 21235, USA
410/965-3120, Fax: 410/966-1463
Commissioner, Shirley Chater

### DEPARTMENT OF HOUSING & URBAN DEVELOPMENT

HUD Bldg., 451 - 7th St. SW, Washington DC 20410-1047, USA
202/708-0417
Secretary, Andrew Cuomo
Deputy Secretary, Terrence R. Duvernay Sr.

### DEPARTMENT OF THE INTERIOR

Interior Bldg., 1849 C St. NW, Washington DC 20240, USA
202/208-7351, Fax: 202/208-5048
Secretary, Bruce Babbitt
Deputy Secretary, John Garamendi

**Bureau of Indian Affairs**
c/o Dept. of the Interior, Interior Bldg., 1849 C St. SW, Washington DC 20240, USA
202/208-3710
Asst. Secretary, Ada Deer

**Bureau of Land Management**
c/o Dept. of the Interior, Interior Bldg., 1849 C St. NW, Washington DC 20240
202/208-3435
Director, Vacant

**National Park Service**
1100 Ohio Dr. SW, Washington DC 20242, USA
202/619-7005
Director, Roger Kennedy

**United States Bureau of Mines**
810 Seventh St. NW, Washington DC 20241, USA
202/501-9649
Director, Rhea Graham

**United States Fish & Wildlife Service**
Arlington Square, 4401 North Fairfax Dr., Arlington VA 22203, USA
202/208-4717
Director, Mollie Beattie

## DEPARTMENT OF JUSTICE
Main Justice Bldg., 10th St. & Constitution Ave. NW, Washington DC 20530, USA
202/514-2001, Fax: 202/633-4371
Attorney General, Janet Reno
Deputy Attorney General, Philip B. Heymann

**Bureau of Prisons**
320 First St. NW, Washington DC 20534, USA
202/307-3198
Director, Kathleen Hawk

**Drug Enforcement Administration (DEA)**
600 - 700 Army Navy Dr., Arlington VA 22202, USA
202/307-1000, Fax: 202/367-1000
Administrator, Thomas Consantine

**Federal Burau of Investigation (FBI)**
J. Edgar Hoover FBI Bldg., 9th St. & Pennsylvania Ave. NW, Washington DC 20535, USA
202/324-3444, Fax: 202/324-4705
Director, Louis J. Freeh
Deputy Director, David Binney

**Immigration & Naturalization Service**
Chester Arthur Bldg., 425 Eye St. NW, Washington DC 20536, USA
202/514-1900
Commissioner, Doris Meissner

**United States Marshals Service**
Airport Plaza 2, 2611 Jefferson Davis Highway, Arlington VA 22202, USA
202/307-9001, Fax: 202/557-9788
Director, Eduardo Gonzalez

## DEPARTMENT OF LABOR
Frances Perkins Bldg., 200 Constitution Ave. NW, Washington DC 20210, USA
202/219-8274
Secretary, Alexis Herman
Deputy Secretary, Thomas Glynn

## DEPARTMENT OF STATE
Main State Dept. Bldg., 2201 C St. NW, Washington DC 20520, USA
202/647-4910
URL: http://dosfan.lib.uic.edu/
Secretary, Madeleine Albright
Deputy Secretary, Strobe Talbott

## DEPARTMENT OF TRANSPORTATION
Nassif Bldg., 400 - 7th St. SW, Washington DC 20590, USA
202/366-1111, Fax: 202/366-7256
Secretary, Rodney Slater
Deputy Secretary, Mortimer L. Downey

**Federal Aviation Administration (FAA)**
800 Independence Ave. SW, Washington DC 20591, USA
202/267-3111, Fax: 202/267-3505
Acting Administrator, Barry Valentine

**Federal Highway Administration**
Nassif Bldg., 400 - 7th St. SW, Washington DC 20590, USA
202/366-0650, Fax: 202/366-3244
Administrator, Vacant

**Federal Railroad Administration**
Nassif Bldg., 400 - 7th St. SW, Washington DC 20590, USA
202/366-0710, Fax: 202/366-3055
Administrator, Jolene Molitoris

**Federal Transit Administration**
Nassif Bldg., 400 - 7th St. SW, Washington DC 20590, USA
202/366-4040, Fax: 202/366-3472
Administation, Gordon Linton

## DEPARTMENT OF THE TREASURY
Main Treasury, 1500 Pennsylvania Ave. NW, Washington DC 20220, USA
202/622-1100
Secretary, Robert E. Rubin
Deputy Secretary, Lawrence H. Summers

**Internal Revenue Service (IRS)**
1111 Constitutional Ave. NW, Washington DC 20224, USA
202/622-4115
Commissioner, Margaret Milner Richardson

**Bureau of Alcohol, Tobacco & Firearms**
650 Massachusetts Ave. NW, Washington DC 20226, USA
202/927-8700, Fax: 202/927-8876
Director, John Magaw

**United States Secret Service**
1800 G St. NW, Washington DC 20223, USA
202/435-5700, Fax: 202/435-5246
Director, Eljay Brown

**United States Customs Service**
1301 Constitution Ave. NW, Washington DC 20229, USA
202/927-1000
Commissioner, George Weise

## DEPARTMENT OF VETERANS AFFAIRS
TechWorld Bldg., 801 - 1 St. NW, Washington DC 20001, USA
202/273-4800
Secretary, Jesse Brown
Deputy Secretary, Hershel Gober

**Associated Agencies**
•Environmental Protection Agency
Waterside Mall, 401 M St. SW, Washington DC 20460, USA
202/260-4700, Fax: 202/260-0279
Administrator, Carol M. Browner
•Federal Communications Commission (FCC)
1919 M St. NW, Washington DC 20554-0001, USA
202/418-1000, Fax: 202/632-0942
Chair, Marsha Martin
•Federal Election Commission
PEPCO Bldg., 999 E St. NW, Washington DC 20463-0001, USA
202/219-4100, Fax: 202/219-3880
Chair, Lee Ann Elliott
•Federal Emergency Management Agency
Federal Center Plaza, 500 C St. SW, Washington DC 20472, USA
202/-646-3923, Fax: 202/646-4086
Director, James Witt
•Federal Reserve System
Federal Reserve Board Bldg., 20th St. & C St. NW, Washington DC 20551, USA
202/452-3201, Fax: 202/452-3819
Chair, Alan Greenspan
•Federal Trade Commission
6th St. & Pennsylvania Ave. NW, Washington DC 20580-0001, USA
202/326-2100, Fax: 202/326-2050
Chair, J.D. Steiger
•General Services Administration
General Services Bldg., Eighteenth & F Sts. NW, Washington DC 20405, USA
202/708-5082
Administrator, Roger W. Johnson
•National Aeronautics & Space Administration (NASA)
Independence Square, 300 E St. SW, Washington DC 20546, USA
202/358-0000, Fax: 202/358-2810
Administrator, Daniel Goldin
•National Science Foundation
4201 Wilson Blvd., Arlington VA 22230, USA
703/306-1234
Director, Neal Lane
•National Telecommunications & Information Administration
Herbert C. Hoover Bldg., 14th St. & Constitution Ave. NW, Washington DC 20230
202/482-1840
Asst. Secretary, Clarence Irving
•National Transportation Safety Board
490 L'Enfant Plaza East SW, Washington DC 20594, USA
202/382-6506, Fax: 202/382-6715
Chair, Jim Hall
•Nuclear Regulatory Commission
1717 H St. NW, Washington DC 20555
202/492-7000
Chair, Shirley Ann Jackson
•Office of Personnel Management
1900 E St. NW, Washington DC 20415-0001, USA
202/606-1800
Director, James King
•Peace Corps
Esplande Mall, 1990 K St. NW, Washington DC 20526-0001, USA
202/606-3970, Fax: 202/606-4458
Director, Mark Gearan
•Small Business Administration
Washington Office Center, 409 - 3rd St. SW, Washington DC 20416, USA
202/205-6605, Fax: 202/205-7064
Administrator, Aida Alvarez
•Smithsonian Institution
1000 Jefferson Dr. SW, Washington DC 20560, USA
202/357-1300
Secretary, Michael Heyman
Inspector General, Thomas Blair
•United States Arms Control & Disarmament Agency
State Department Bldg., 320 - 21st St. NW, Washington DC 20451-0001, USA
202/647-9610, Fax: 202/647-6928
Director, John Holum
•United States Information Agency (USIA)
USIA Bldg., 301 - 4th St. SW, Washington DC 20547, USA
202/619-4742, Fax: 202/619-6988

URL: http://www.usia.gov/
Director, Joseph Duffy
•United States International Trade Commission (USITC)
500 E St. SW, Washington DC 20436-0001
202/205-2781, Fax: 202/205-2798
Chair, Peter Watson
•United States Postal Service
475 L'Enfant Plaza SW, Washington DC 20260-0001, USA
202/268-4800
Chair, Sam Winters
•United States Trade & Development Agency
#309, State Annex 16, Washington DC 20523-1602, USA
703/875-4357
Director, Joseph Grandmaison

# THE QUEEN & ROYAL FAMILY

## THE HOUSE OF WINDSOR

In 1917 the late King George V, by Proclamation, changed the House name of the Royal Family from Saxe-Coburg-Gotha to the House of Windsor.

THE QUEEN. - Elizabeth the Second, (Elizabeth Alexandra Mary, of Windsor) by the Grace of God, of the United Kingdom, Canada and Her other Realms and Territories Queen; Head of the Commonwealth, Defender of the Faith, Succeeded to the throne February 6th, 1952, and was crowned June 2nd, 1953, at Westminster Abbey. Her Majesty, the elder daughter of the late King George VI and Queen Elizabeth The Queen Mother, was born at 17 Bruton St., London, W.1, on April 21st, 1926, married November 20th, 1947, H.R.H. The Prince Philip, Duke of Edinburgh, K.G., K.T., O.M., G.B.E., A.C., Q.S.O.

THE CHILDREN of Queen Elizabeth and H.R.H. The Prince Philip, Duke of Edinburgh are:

H.R.H. Prince Charles Philip Arthur George, Prince of Wales and Earl of Chester, Duke of Cornwall and Duke of Rothesay, Earl of Carrick and Baron Renfrew, Lord of the Isles, and Great Steward of Scotland, K.G., K.T., G.C.B., A.K., Q.S.O., A.D.C., born November 14th, 1948. Married July 29th, 1981, The Lady Diana Spencer (died August 31st, 1997) and has issue. Prince William of Wales, born June 21st, 1982 and Prince Henry of Wales, born September 15th, 1984. Marriage dissolved 1996.

H.R.H. The Princess Royal, Anne Elizabeth Alice Louise, K.G., G.C.V.O., Q.S.O., born August 15th, 1950. Married 1st November 14th, 1973 Captain Mark Anthony Peter Phillips, C.V.O., A.D.C. and has issue. Peter Phillips born November 15th, 1977 and Zara Phillips born May 15th, 1981. Marriage dissolved 1992. Married 2nd December 12th, 1993 Captain Timothy James Hamilton Laurence, M.V.O., R.N.

H.R.H. The Prince Andrew Albert Christian Edward, C.V.O., A.D.C., Duke of York, Earl of Inverness and Baron Killyleagh, born February 19th, 1960, married July 23rd, 1986 Miss Sarah Margaret Ferguson and has issue, Princess Beatrice of York, born August 8th, 1988, and Princess Eugenie of York, born March 23rd, 1990. Marriage dissolved 1996.

H.R.H. The Prince Edward Antony Richard Louis, C.V.O., born March 10th, 1964.

THE LATE GEORGE VI. -- George VI succeeded to the Throne December 11th, 1936; and was crowned at Westminster Abbey, May 12th, 1937. Second son of King George V and Queen Mary, he was born at York Cottage, Sandringham, on December 14th, 1895, married, April 26th, 1923, Lady Elizabeth Bowes-Lyon, daughter of the Earl and Countess of Strathmore and Kinghorne. As Heir Presumptive succeeded to the Throne on the abdication of Edward VIII.

QUEEN ELIZABETH, THE QUEEN MOTHER -- born August 4th, 1900, daughter of the 14th Earl of Strathmore and Kinghorne; married, April 26th, 1923.

THE ISSUE of the late King George VI and Queen Elizabeth are:

The reigning Sovereign, Elizabeth the Second (elder daughter).

The Princess Margaret (Rose), Countess of Snowdon, C.I., G.C.V.O., born August 21st, 1930, married Antony Charles Robert Armstrong-Jones, G.C.V.O., (since created Earl of Snowdon) May 6th, 1960, and has issue, Viscount Linley, born November 3rd, 1961 and the Lady Sarah Frances Elizabeth Armstrong-Jones, born May 1st, 1964. Marriage dissolved 1978.

SUCCESSION--The order stands:
The Prince of Wales
Prince William of Wales
Prince Henry of Wales
The Duke of York
Princess Beatrice of York
Princess Eugenie of York
The Prince Edward
The Princess Royal
Mr. Peter Phillips
Miss Zara Phillips
The Princess Margaret, Countess of Snowdon
Viscount Linley
The Lady Sarah Chatto
Master Samuel Chatto
The Duke of Gloucester
Earl of Ulster
The Lady Davina Windsor
The Lady Rose Windsor
The Duke of Kent
Lord Downpatrick
The Lady Marina Charlotte Windsor
The Lady Amelia Windsor
The Lord Nicholas Windsor
The Lady Helen Taylor
Master Columbus Taylor
Master Cassius Taylor
The Lord Frederick Windsor
The Lady Gabriella Windsor
Princess Alexandra, The Hon. Lady Ogilvy
Mr. James Ogilvy
Miss Flora Ogilvy
Mr. Paul Mowatt
Master Christian Mowatt
Miss Zeuonska Mowatt
The Earl of Harewood

### HER MAJESTY'S HOUSEHOLD

Lord Chamberlain, The Earl of Airlie, K.T., G.C.V.O.
Lord Steward, The Viscount Ridley, K.G., G.C.V.O., T.D.
Master of the Horse, The Lord Somerleyton, K.C.V.O.
Private Secretary to The Queen, The Rt. Hon. Sir Robert Fellowes, G.C.V.O., K.C.B.
Keeper of the Privy Purse & Treasurer to The Queen, Mr. Michael Peat, Esq., C.V.O.
Master of the Household, Major General Sir Simon Cooper, K.C.V.O.
Crown Equerry, Lt.-Col. Seymour Gilbart-Denham, C.V.O.
Press Secretary, Geoffrey Crawford, Esq., L.V.O.
The Lord Chamberlain has the general supervision of the Royal Household.

# THE COMMONWEALTH

## (COMMONWEALTH OF NATIONS)

The Commonwealth is a voluntary association of 53 independent member countries representing 1.5 billion people around the world -- in Africa, the Americas, Asia, the Caribbean, Europe & the Pacific. It promotes good governance, democracy, sustainable economic & social development, the rule of law & human rights. These & other principles are enshrined in the Harare Commonwealth Declaration of 1991.

There are three principal international organizations of the Commonwealth:

### THE COMMONWEALTH SECRETARIAT

Marlborough House, Pall Mall, London SW1Y 5HX, +44 (0)171-839 3411; Fax: +44 (0)171-930 0827
HE Chief Emeka Anyaoku, CON (Nigeria), Commonwealth Secretary-General
Sir Humphrey Maud (Britain), Deputy Commonwealth Secretary-General (Economic & Social Affairs)
Nick Hare (Canada), Deputy Commonwealth Secretary-General (Development Co-operation)
Krishnan Srinivasan (India), Deputy Commonwealth Secretary-General (Political Affairs)
Michael Fathers (New Zealand), Director, Information & Public Affairs

### THE COMMONWEALTH FOUNDATION

Marlborough House, Pall Mall, London SW1Y 5HY, +44 (0)171-930 3783; Fax: +44 (0)171-839 8157
Dr. Humayun Khan (Pakistan), Director

### THE COMMONWEALTH OF LEARNING (COL)

#1700-777 Dunsmuir St., PO Box 10428, Pacific Centre, Vancouver BC V7Y 1K4, 604/775-8200; Fax: 604/775-8210, Email: info@col.org, URL: http://www.col.org

For information pertaining to the Commonwealth write to: The Director, Information Division, Commonwealth Secretariat, Marlborough House, Pall Mall, London SW1Y 5HX, U.K.

## MEMBER STATES

(showing Capital, Population (1993) & Date of Membership. Dates for Australia, Canada & New Zealand are those on which Dominion Status was acquired):

Antigua & Barbuda - St. John's; 67,000; Nov. 1, 1981
Australia - Canberra; 17,707,000; Jan. 1, 1901
- External territories: Norfolk Island, Coral Sea Islands Territory, Australian Antarctic Territory, Heard Island & McDonald Islands, Cocos (Keeling) Islands, Christmas Island, Territory of Ashmore & Cartier Islands
The Bahamas - Nassau; 266,000; July 10, 1973
Bangladesh - Dhaka; 116,702,000; Apr. 18, 1972
Barbados - Bridgetown; 260,000; Nov. 30, 1966
Belize - Belmopan; 205,000; Sept. 21, 1981
Botswana - Gaborone; 1,402,000; Sept. 30, 1966
Britain - London; 58,040,000
- Dependent territories: Anguilla, Bermuda, British Antarctic Territory, British Indian Ocean Territory, British Virgin Islands, Cayman Islands, Falkland Islands, Gibraltar, Montserrat, Pitcairn, Henderson, Ducie & Oeno Islands, St. Helena & St. Helena Dependencies (Ascension & Tristan da Cunha), South Georgia & the South Sandwich Islands, & Turks & Caicos Islands
Brunei Darussalam - Bandar Seri Begawan; 281,000; Jan. 1, 1984
Cameroon - Yaoundé; 12,611,000; Nov., 1995
Canada - Ottawa; 27,814,000; July 1, 1867
Cyprus - Nicosia; 726,000; Mar. 13, 1961
Dominica - Roseau; 72,000; Nov. 3, 1978
The Gambia - Banjul; 1,019,000; Feb. 18, 1965
Ghana - Accra; 16,261,000; Mar. 6, 1957
Grenada - Grenada; 91,000; Feb. 7, 1974
Guyana - Georgetown; 812,000; May 26, 1966
India - New Delhi; 900,543,000; Aug. 15, 1947
Jamaica - Kingston; 2,415,000; Aug. 6, 1962
Kenya - Nairobi; 25,376,000; Dec. 12, 1963
Kiribati - Tarawa; 76,000; July 12, 1979
Lesotho - Maseru; 1,899,000; Oct. 4, 1966
Malawi - Lilongwe; 9,303,000; July 6, 1964

Malaysia - Kuala Lumpur; 19,032,000; Aug. 31, 1957
Maldives - Malé; 236,000; July 9, 1982
Malta - Valletta; 362,000; Sept. 21, 1964
Mauritius - Port Louis; 1,111,000; Mar. 12, 1968
Mozambique - Maputo; 16,916,000; Nov., 1995
Namibia - Windhoek; 1,565,000; Mar. 21, 1990
Nauru - Nauru; 8,000; Jan. 31, 1968
New Zealand - Wellington; 3,462,000; Sept. 26, 1907
- Includes the territories of Tokelau & the Ross Dependency (Antarctic). Self-governing countries in free association with New Zealand: Cook Islands & Niue.
Nigeria - Abuja; 104,893,000; Oct. 1, 1960 N.B. Under suspension since Nov., 1995.
Pakistan - Islamabad; 122,829,000; Mar. 23, 1989 (previously member 1947-1972)
Papua New Guinea - Port Moresby; 4,148,000; Sept. 16, 1975
St. Kitts & Nevis - Basseterre; 41,000; Sept. 19, 1983
St. Lucia - Castries; 158,000; Feb. 22, 1979
St. Vincent & The Grenadines - Kingstown; 110,000; Oct. 27, 1979
Samoa - Apia; 163,000; Aug. 28, 1970
Seychelles - Mahé; 70,000; June 29, 1976
Sierra Leone - Freetown; 4,468,000; Apr. 27, 1961
Singapore - Singapore; 2,867,000; Oct. 16, 1965
Solomon Islands - Honiara; 346,000; July 7, 1978
Sri Lanka - Colombo; 17,622,000; Feb. 4, 1948
Swaziland - Mbabane; 888,000; Sept. 6, 1968
Tanzania - Dar es Salaam; 26,743,000; Dec. 9, 1961
Tonga - Nuku'alofa; 93,000; June 4, 1970
Trinidad & Tobago - Port of Spain; 1,282,000; Aug. 31, 1962
Tuvalu - Funafuti; 9,000; Oct. 1, 1978
Uganda - Kampala; 18,026,000; Oct. 9, 1962
Vanuatu - Port Vila; 161,000; July 30, 1980
Zambia - Lusaka; 8,527,000; Oct. 24, 1964
Zimbabwe - Harare; 10,638,000; Apr. 18, 1981

# LA FRANCOPHONIE

**Member Name, population, national holiday**

Belgique (La Royaume de), 10,01 M, 21 juillet
Bénin (République du), 5,215 M, 1er août
Bularie (République de), 8,469 M, 3 mars
Bukina Faso, 9,682, 4 aôut
Burundi (République du), 5,958, 1er juillet
Cambodgne, 9,308, 25 juin
Cameroun (République du), 12,547, 20 mai
Canada, 29,248 M, 1er juillet
Canada - Nouveau-Brunswick (Province du), 0,759 M, 15 aôut
Canada - Québec (Province du), 7,208 M, 24 juin
Cap-Vert (République du), 0,395 M, 5 juillet
Centrafrique (République), 3,258 M, 1er décembre
Communauté française de Belgique (Wallonie-Bruxelles), 4,5 M, 27 septembre
Comores (République féderale islamique des), 0,607 M, 6 juillet
Congo (République du), 2,441 M, 15 août
Côte d'Ivoire (République de), 13,397 M, 7 décembre
Djibouti (République de), 0,481 M, 27 juin
Dominique (Commonwealth de), 0,072 M, 27 février
Égypte (République arabe d'), 56,488 M, 23 juillet
France (République française), 57,660 M, 14 juillet
Gabon (République gabonaise), 1,012 M, 17 août
Guinée (République de), 6,306 M, 2 octobre
Guinée-Bissau (République de Guine'e-Bissao), 1,028 M, 24 septembre
Guinée équatoriale (République de), 0,379 M, 12 octobre
Haiti (République d'), 6,903 M, 1er janvier
Laos (République démocratique populaire lao), 4,605 M, 2 décembre
Liban (République libanaise), 2,901 M,, 22 novembre
Luxembourg (Grande-Duché de), 0,380 M, 23 juin
Madagascar (République de), 13,259 M, 26 juin
Mali (République de), 10,137 M, 22 septembre
Maroc (Royaume de), 26,069 M, 3 mars
Maurice (République de), 1,098 M, 12 mars
Mauritanie (République islamique de), 2,206 M, 28 novembre
Monaco (Principauté de), 0,028 M, 19 novembre
Niger (République du), 8,361 M, 18 décembre
Roumanie, 22,755 M, 1er décembre
Rwanda (République rwandaise), 7,789 M, 1er juillet
Sainte-Lucie, 0,139 M, 22 février
Sénégal (République du), 7,736 M, 4 avril
Seychelles (République des), 0,072 M, 5 juin
Suisse (Confédération), 6,938 M, 1er aôut
Tchad (République du), 6,098 M, 11 janvier
Togo (République togolaise), 3,885 M, 27 avril
Tunisie (République tunisienne), 8,579 M, 20 mars
Vanuatu (République de), 0,156 M, 30 juillet
Viêtnam (République socialiste du), 70,902 M, 2 septembre
Zaïre (République du), 41,166 M, 30 juin

# INTERNATIONAL ORGANIZATIONS IN CANADA

**INTERNATIONAL ATOMIC ENERGY AGENCY**
#1702, 365 Bloor St. East, Toronto ON M4W 3L4
416/928-9149; Fax: 416/928-0046
Head, Mr. Godswill Ch. Madueme

**INTERNATIONAL CIVIL AVIATION ORGANIZATION**
1000 Sherbrooke St. West, Montréal PQ H3A 2R2
514/285-8219; Fax: 514/288-4772
President, Dr Assad Kotaite
Secretary General, Dr. Philippe H.P. Rochat

**INTERNATIONAL LABOUR ORGANIZATION**
#202, 75 Albert St., Ottawa ON K1P 5E7
613/233-1114; Fax: 613/233-6255
Director, Robert Nadeau

**INTERNATIONAL NORTH PACIFIC FISHERIES COMMISSON**
6640 North West Marine Dr., Vancouver BC V6T 1X2
604/228-1128; Fax: 604/228-1135
Executive Director, Shigeto Hase

**NORTHWEST ATLANTIC FISHERIES ORGANIZATION**
PO Box 638, Dartmouth NS B2Y 3Y9
902/469-9105; Fax: 902/469-5729
Executive Secretary, Leonard I. Chepel

**PERMANENT JOINT BOARD ON DEFENCE (CANADA-U.S.A.)**
International Security & Defence Relations, DFAIT, 125 Sussex Dr., Ottawa ON K1A 0G2
613/992-5457; Fax: 613/992-2482
Secretary, Mervin Meadows

**UNITED NATIONS ASSOCIATION IN CANADA**
#808, 63 Sparks St., Ottawa ON K1P 5A6
613/232-5751; Fax: 613/563-2455
Executive Director, Angus Archer

**UNITED NATIONS CENTRE FOR HUMAN SETTLEMENTS (HABITAT)**
Information Office for North America and the Caribbean, #417, 130 Albert St., Ottawa ON K1P 5G4
613/235-6400; Fax: 613/235-6226
Head, Information Office for North America & the Caribbean, Selman Erguden

**UNITED NATIONS HIGH COMMISSIONER FOR REFUGEES**
#401, 280 Albert St., Ottawa ON K1P 5G8
613/232-0909; Fax: 613/230-1855
Representative, Gary G. Troeller

**UNITED NATIONS EDUCATIONAL, SCIENTIFIC & CULTURAL ORGANIZATION (UNESCO)**
#400, 56, rue St-Pierre, 4e étage, Québec PQ G1K 4A1
418/692-3333; Fax: 418/692-2562
Representative, Agustin Larrauri

**UNITED NATIONS ENVIRONMENT PROGRAMME (UNEP)**
Montréal Trust Bldg., 27th Fl., 1800 McGill College Ave., Montréal PQ H3A 3J6
514/282-1122; Fax: 514/282-0068
Chief Officer, Dr. Omar El-Sayed El-Arini

**CANADIAN UNICEF COMMITTEE**
443 Mount Pleasant Rd., Toronto ON M4S 2L8
416/482-4444; Fax: 416/482-8035
Executive Director, Harry S. Black

# CANADIAN PERMANENT MISSIONS & DELEGATIONS ABROAD

**MISSION OF CANADA TO THE EUROPEAN COMMUNITIES**
2, av de Tervuren, 1040 Brussels, Belgium
(011-32-2) 735-9125; Fax: (011-32-2) 735-3383
Head of Mission, Ambassador, Gordon S. Smith
Deputy Head of Mission & Minister-Counsellor, W.H. Dowswell
Counsellor, Trade Policy, S. Brereton

**NORAD (NORTH AMERICAN AEROSPACE DEFENSE COMMAND)**
DNDPA NORAD Headquarters, NORAD PA, Peterson AFB, Colorado Springs, CO USA 80914-5002
719/554-3714; Fax: 719/554-3165

**NORTH ATLANTIC COUNCIL**
Léopold III Blvd., 1110 Brussels, Belgium
(011-32-2) 216-0346; Fax: (011-32-2) 245-2462
Permanent Representative & Ambassador, James K. Bartleman
Responsible for all NATO (North American Treaty Organization) correspondence.

**ORGANIZATION FOR ECONOMIC COOPERATION & DEVELOPMENT**
15 bis, rue de Franqueville, 75116 Paris, France
(011-33-1) 40-67-18-45; Fax: (011-33-1) 45-20-30-08
Ambassador & Permanent Representative, Anne Marie Doyle

**ORGANIZATION OF AMERICAN STATES**
501 Pennsylvania Ave. NW, Washington DC 20001 USA
202/682-1768; Fax: 202/682-7624
Ambassador, Permanent Representative, Brian Dickson, Q.C.

**UNITED NATIONS**
- Permanent Mission of Canada to the United Nations, One Dag Hammarkjold Plaza, 885 Second Ave., 14th Fl., New York NY 10017-1897 USA. (212) 751-5600; Fax: (212) 486-1295

Ambassador & Permanent Representative, Robert R. Fowler
- Permanent Mission of Canada to the Office of the United Nations at Geneva, 1, rue du Pré-de-la-Bichette, 1202 Geneve, Switzerland – (011-41-22) 733-9000; Fax: (011-41-22) 734-7919
  *Also at this address:*
  - Permanent Mission of Canada to the Secretariat of the General Agreement on Tariffs & Trade (GATT)

  Permanent Representative & Ambassador, Gerald E. Shannon
- Permanent Mission of Canada to the International Civil Aviation Organization (ICAO), #876, 1000

Sherbrooke St. West, Montréal PQ H3A 3G4 – (514) 285-8320; Fax: (514) 283-3256
Representative, G.H. Duguay
•Permanent Mission of Canada to the United Nations Centre for Human Settlements (Habitat), Comcraft House, Hailé Sélassie Ave., PO Box 30481, Nairobi – (011-254-2) 33-40-33; Fax: (011-254-2) 33-40-90
*Also at this address:*
•Permanent Mission of Canada to the United Nations Environment Program (UNEP)
Representative, Lucie Edwards
•Permanent Mission of Canada to the United Nations Educational, Scientific & Cultural Organization (UNESCO), 1, rue Miollis, 75015 Paris, France – (011-33-1) 45-68-35-17; Fax: (011-33-1) 43-06-87-27
Ambassador & Permanent Delegate, Jacques Demers
•Permanent Mission of Canada to the Food & Agriculture Organization (FAO), Via Zara 30, 00198 Rome, Italy – (011-39-6) 440-3028; Fax: (011-39-6) 440-3063
Permanent Representative, Robert Andrigo
•Permanent Mission of Canada to the International Organizations in Vienna, Dr. Karl Lueger Ring 10, A-1010 Vienna, Austria – (011-43-222) 533-3691; Fax: (011-43-222) 664-4731
Permanent Representative & Ambassador, Peter F. Walker

## INTERNATIONAL FISHERIES ORGANIZATIONS

These Commissions are non-governmental organizations whose members are governments or associations of governments.

#### GREAT LAKES FISHERY COMMISSION

2100 Commonwealth Blvd., #209, Ann Arbor, MI 48105-1563 USA
313/662-3209; Fax: 313/668-2531
Executive Secretary, R.W. Beecher
Canadian Commissioners, F.W.H. Beamish, G. Beggs, P. Sutherland, C. Fraser

#### INTERNATIONAL COMMISSION FOR THE CONSERVATION OF ATLANTIC TUNAS

Principe de Vergara 17, 7th Fl., Madrid 28001, Spain (011-34-1) 431-0329; Fax: (011-34-1) 57-6968
Executive Secretary, Dr. Antonio Fernandez

#### INTERNATIONAL PACIFIC HALIBUT COMMISSION

PO Box 95009, Seattle WA USA 98145
206/634-1838; Fax: 206/632-2983
Director, Investigation, D.A. McCaughran
Canadian Commissioners, L. Alexander, A. Sheppard, R. Beamish

#### INTERNATIONAL WHALING COMMISSION

The Red House, 135 Station Rd., Histon, Cambridge, England CB4 4NP
(011-44-223) 233971; Fax: (011-44-223) 232876
Secretary, Dr. R. Gambell

#### NORTH ATLANTIC SALMON CONSERVATION ORGANIZATION

11 Rutland Sq., Edinburgh, Scotland EH1 2AS
(011-44-31) 228-2551; Fax: (011-44-31) 228-4384
Executive Secretary, Dr. Malcolm Windsor
Canadian Commissioners: J.E. Haché, Dr. W.M. Carter, Jean-Paul Duguay

#### NORTHWEST ATLANTIC FISHERIES ORGANIZATION

PO Box 638, Dartmouth NS B2Y 3Y9
902/469-9105; Fax: 902/469-5729
Executive Secretary, Dr L.I. Chepel

#### PACIFIC SALMON COMMISSION

#600, 1155 Robson St., Vancouver BC V6E 1B5
604/684-8081; Fax: 604/666-8707
Executive Secretary, Ian Todd
Canadian Commissioners: B. Buchanan, P.S. Chamut, J. Gosnell, R. Wright

# DIPLOMATIC & CONSULAR REPRESENTATIVES IN CANADA

Commonwealth countries are designated by 'High Commissioner'. Foreign countries are designated by 'Ambassador'. It is Almanac editorial style to list Consulates in alphabetical order according to the city of location. Occasionally we have deviated from this style at the special request of the embassy of a particular country and listed their Consulates and Honorary Consulates.

## Republic of Albania

Embassy of Albania (to Canada): #1000, 1511 K St. NW, Washington DC 20005
202/222-4942; Fax: 202/628-7342
Ambassador, USA & Canada, His Excellency Lublin Dilja
Counsellor, Genc Miloja

## People's Democratic Republic of Algeria

Embassy of Algeria: 435 Daly Ave., Ottawa ON K1N 6H3
613/789-8505; Fax: 613/789-1406
Ambassador, His Excellency Abdesslam Bedrane
Counsellor, Naceur Boucherit

## Antigua & Barbuda *c/o* Organization of the Eastern Caribbean States

Dartmouth: Hon. Consul, Castor Williams, 13 Oathill Cr., NS B2Y 4C3, 902/465-8127
Toronto: Consul, Madeline Blackman, #304, 60 St. Clair Ave. East, ON M4T 1N5, 416/961-3143; Fax: 416/961-7218

## Argentine Republic

Embassy of the Argentine Republic: #910, 90 Sparks St., Ottawa ON K1P 5B4
613/236-2351; Fax: 613/235-2659
Commercial Office Fax: 613/563-7925
Ambassador, Her Excellency Lillian O'Connell de Alurralde
Minister, Economic & Commercial Affairs, Guillermo Azrak
Montréal: Consul General, Ernesto Santiago Martinez Gondra, #710, 2000, rue Peel, QC H3A 2W5, 514/842-6582; Fax: 514/842-5797
Toronto: Consul General, Jorge Stok-Capella, #5840, 1 First Canadian Place, ON M5X 1K2, 416/955-0232; Fax: 416/955-0868

## Commonwealth of Australia

Australian High Commission: #710, 50 O'Connor St., Ottawa ON K1P 6L2
613/236-0841; Fax: 613/236-4376
Email: ahc1.otwa@sympatico.ca
High Commissioner, His Excellency Greg Wood
Deputy High Commissioner, Pat Hardy
Counsellor, Andrew Engel
Toronto: Consul General, P. Kane, #314, 175 Bloor St. East, ON M4W 3R8, 416/323-1155; Fax: 416/323-3910
Vancouver: Consul, Graeme South, World Trade Centre Office Complex, #602, 999 Canada Place, BC V6C 3E1, 604/684-1177; Fax: 604/684-1856

## Republic of Austria

Embassy of Austria: 445 Wilbrod St., Ottawa ON K1N 6M7
613/789-1444; Fax: 613/789-3431
Ambassador, His Excellency Dr. W. Lichem
Calgary: Hon. Consul General, Hans Ockermueller, 1131 Kensington Rd. NW, AB T2N 3P4, 403/283-6526; Fax: 403/283-1512
Halifax: Hon. Consul, Michael Novac, #620, 1718 Argyle St., NS B3J 3N6, 902/429-8200; Fax: 902/425-0581
Montréal: Hon. Consul General, Ulrike Billard-Florian, #1030, 1350, rue Sherbrooke ouest, QC H3G 1J1, 514/845-8661; Fax: 514/845-9397
Montréal: Trade Commissioner, Peter Paul Schwartz, #1410, 1010, rue Sherbrooke ouest, QC H3A 2R7, 514/849-3708; Fax: 514/849-9577
Regina: Hon. Consul, E.F. Anthony Merchant, #100, 2401 Saskatchewan Dr. Plaza, SK S4P 4H9, 306/359-7777; Fax: 306/522-3299
Toronto: Hon. Consul General, Frank Stronach, #1010, 360 Bay St., ON M5H 2Y6, 416/863-0649; Fax: 416/863-1459
Toronto: Consul (Commercial Affairs), Gerhard Müller, #3330, 2 Bloor St. East, ON M4W 1A8, 416/967-3348; Fax: 416/967-4101
Vancouver: Hon. Consul General, Graham P. Clarke, #206, 1810 Alberni St., BC V6G 1B3, 604/687-3338; Fax: 604/681-3578
Vancouver: Trade Commissioner, Michael Poetscher, #1380, 200 Granville St., BC V6C 1S4, 604/683-5808; Fax: 604/662-8528
Winnipeg: Hon. Consul, John Klassen, 330 Saulteaux Cr., MB R3C 3T2, 204/885-2882; Fax: 204/885-7557

## Republic of Azerbaijan

Embassy of Azerbaijan (to Canada): #700, 927 - 15th St. NW, Washington DC 20005
202/842-0001; Fax: 202/842-0004
Email: azerbaijan@mcimail.com; URL: http://ourworld.compuserve.com/homepages/azerbaijan
Ambassador Designate, His Excellency Hafiz Mir-Jalal Oglu Pashayev

## Commonwealth of the Bahamas

High Commission for the Bahamas: #1020, 360 Albert St., Ottawa ON K1R 7X7
613/232-1724; Fax: 613/232-0097
High Commissioner, His Excellency Luther E. Smith
Second Secretary & Vice-Consul, Freddie C. Tucker

## State of Bahrain

Embassy of Bahrain (to Canada): 3502 International Dr. NW, Washington DC 20008
202/342-0741; Fax: 202/362-2192
Ambassador, His Excellency Muhammad Abdul-Ghaffar
Montréal: Consul, Abdulnabi Mussayab Mohamed, 1869, boul René-Lévesque ouest, QC H3H 1R4, 514/931-7000; Fax: 514/931-5988

## People's Republic of Bangladesh

Bangladesh High Commission: #302, 275 Bank St., Ottawa ON K2P 2L6
613/236-0138; Fax: 613/567-3213
Email: bdootcanada@iosphere.net
Acting High Commissioner, Anwar ul-Alam

## Barbados

High Commission for Barbados: #302, 130 Albert St., Ottawa ON K1P 5G4
613/236-9517; Fax: 613/230-4362
Email: barhcott@travel-net.com
High Commissioner, Her Excellency June Clarke
First Secretary, Juliette Babb-Riley

Toronto: Consul General, Errol Humphrey, #1010, 105 Adelaide St. West, ON M5H 1P9, 416/214-9805; Fax: 416/214-9815

Vancouver: Hon. Consul, Annette Goodridge, #401, 2020 Haro St., BC V6G 1J3, 604/872-4444; Fax: 604/681-0740

Westmount: Consul, Jennifer V. Barrow, #523, 4800, de Maisonneuve ouest, QC H3Z 1M2, 514/932-3206; Fax: 514/932-3775

## Kingdom of Belgium

80 Elgin St., 4th Fl., Ottawa ON K1P 1B7

613/236-7267; Fax: 613/236-7882

Ambassador, His Excellency Christian Fellens

Minister-Counsellor, Edgard De Vleeshouwer

Calgary: Hon. Consul, Bernard Callebut, 1313 - 1st St. SE, AB T2G 5L1, 403/265-5777; Fax: 403/265-7738

Edmonton: Hon. Consul, George de Rappard, #107, 4990 - 92 Ave., AB T6B 2W1, 403/496-9565; Fax: 403/463-5280

Montréal: Consul General, Louis Engelen, #850, 999, boul de Maisonneuve ouest, QC H3A 3L4, 514/849-7394; Fax: 514/844-3170

Toronto: Consul General, Jean Mineur, #2006, 2 Bloor St. West, PO Box 88, ON M4W 3E2, 416/944-1422; Fax: 416/944-1421

Vancouver: Hon. Consul, Monique Poncelet-Gheleyns, Birks Place, #570, 688 West Hastings St., BC V6B 1P1, 604/684-6838; Fax: 604/684-0371

Winnipeg: Hon. Consul, Paul Deprez, 15 Acadia Bay, MB R3T 3J1, 204/261-1415

## Belize

High Commission for Belize: 2535 Massachusetts Ave. NW, Washington DC 20008

202/332-9636; Fax: 202/332-6888

High Commissioner, His Excellency James Schofield Murphy

Montréal: Hon. Consul General, Harry J.F. Bloomfield, Q.C., 1080, Côte du Beaver Hall, QC H2Z 1S8, 514/871-4741; Fax: 514/397-0816

## Republic of Benin

Embassy of Benin: 58 Glebe Ave., Ottawa ON K1S 2C3

613/233-4429; Fax: 613/233-8952

Ambassador, His Excellency Leopold David-Gnahoui

Calgary: Hon. Consul, Dale M. Simmons, #700, 1207 - 11th Ave. SW, AB T3C 0M5, 403/245-8405

Montréal: Hon. Consul, Marie B. Archambault, 429, av Viger est, QC H2L 2N9, 514/287-1583; Fax: 514/769-6088

## Republic of Bolivia

Embassy of Bolivia: #504, 130 Albert St., Ottawa ON K1P 5G4

613/236-5730; Fax: 613/236-8237

Email: bolcan@iosphere.net

Ambassador, Vacant

Minister-Counsellor & Chargé d'Affaires, Myriam Paz Cerruto

Edmonton: Consul General, Carlos Pechtel, 11231 Jasper Ave., AB T5K 0L5, 403/488-1525; Fax: 403/488-0350

Montréal: Hon. Consul, Pilar Ramos de Arto, 18, av Severn, QC H3Y 2C7, 514/989-5132; Fax: 514/989-5177

Vancouver: Hon. Consul, Dr. A.S. Andree, #680, 789 West Pender St., BC V6E 4H1, 604/685-8121; Fax: 604/685-8120

## Republic of Botswana

High Commission for Botswana (to Canada): c/o Republic of Botswana: #7M, Intelsat Bldg., 3400 International Dr. NW, Washngton DC 20008

202/244-4990; Fax: 202/244-4164

High Commissioner, His Excellency Archibald M. Mogwe

Toronto: Hon. Consul, Douglas G. Hartle, 14 South Dr., ON M4W 1R1, 416/324-8239

## Federative Republic of Brazil

Embassy of Brazil: 450 Wilbrod St., Ottawa ON K1N 6M8

613/237-1090; Fax: 613/237-6144

Email: brasemb@ottawa.net

Ambassador, His Excellency Carlos Augusto R. Santos Neves

Minister-Counsellor, Eduardo M.B. Roxo

Edmonton: Hon. Consul, Peter Elzinga, 8619 Strathearn Dr., AB T6C 4C6, 403/466-3130; Fax: 403/465-0247

Halifax: Hon. Consul, Raymond W. Ferguson, 3630 Kempt Rd., PO Box 8870, Stn A, NS B3K 3Y4, 902/455-9638

Montréal: Consul General, Antonino Marques Portoe Santos, #1700, 2000, rue Mansfield, QC H3A 3A5, 514/499-0968; Fax: 514/499-9363

Toronto: Consul General, Luiz Fernando Gouvea de Athayde, #1109, 77 Bloor St. West, ON M5S 1M2, 416/922-2503; Fax: 416/922-1832

Vancouver: Consul General, Isnard Penha Brasil Jr., #1300, 1140 West Pender St., BC V6E 4G1, 604/687-4589; Fax: 604/681-6534

## Brunei Darussalam

High Commission of Brunei Darussalam: 395 Laurier Ave. East, Ottawa ON K1N 6R4

613/234-5656; Fax: 613/234-4397

High Commissioner, Pengiran Abdul Momin

First Secretary, Magdalene Teo Chee Siong

## Republic of Bulgaria

Embassy of the Republic of Bulgaria: 325 Stewart St., Ottawa ON K1N 6K5

613/789-3215; Fax: 613/789-3524

Ambassador, His Excellency Slav Danev

Counsellor & Deputy Head of Mission, Svilen Iliev

Counsellor, Economic & Commercial, Nikolay Babev

Toronto: Consul General, Dimitar Filipov Serafimov, #406, 65 Overlea Blvd., ON M4H 1P1, 416/696-2420; Fax: 416/696-8019

## Burkina-Faso

Embassy of Burkina-Faso: 48 Range Rd., Ottawa ON K1N 8J4

613/238-4796; Fax: 613/238-3812

URL: http://www.multiservices.com/burkina

Ambassador, Mouhoussine Nacro

Counsellor, Eric Tiare

Magog: Hon. Consul, Pierre Bastien, 1718, ch Alfred-Desrochers, RR#2, QC J1X 3W3, 819/847-1747

Toronto: Hon. Consul, Peter K. Large, #610, 372 Bay St., ON M5H 2W9, 416/867-8669

Vancouver: Hon. Consul, Chunilal Roy, #1417, 750 West Broadway Ave., BC V5Z 1J4, 604/872-8719

## Republic of Burundi

Embassy of Burundi: 50 Kaymar St., Rothwell Heights, Gloucester ON K1J 7C7

613/741-8828; Fax: 613/741-2424

Ambassador, Frédéric Ndayegamiye

Counsellor, Hermenegilde Nkurabagaya

Montréal: Hon. Consul, Jean-Guy Laurendeau, 4017 Lacombe St., QC H3T 1M7, 514/739-5204

Toronto: Hon. Consul, David Wright, 5 Dewbourne Ave., ON M5P 1Z1, 416/932-8212; Fax: 416/922-3667

## Republic of Cameroon

Embassy of Cameroon: 170 Clemow Ave., Ottawa ON K1S 2B4

613/236-1522; Fax: 613/236-3885

Ambassador, His Excellency Philémon Y. Yang

Counsellor, Economic Affairs, Célestin Ngassam

## Republic of Cape Verde

Embassy of Cape Verde (to Canada): 3415 Massachusetts Ave. NW, Washington DC 20007

202/965-6820; Fax: 202/965-1207

Ambassador, His Excellency Corentino Virgilio Santos

Attaché, Amelia Silva

Toronto: Hon. Consul, Alfredo Luis Evora, ON

## Central African Republic

Embassy of Central African Republic (to Canada): 1618 - 22nd St. NW, Washington DC 20008

202/462-2517

Ambassador, His Excellency Henry Koba

Counsellor, Ndinga Gaba

Montréal: Hon. Consul General, Jean-François Boisvert, #1703, 500, Place d'Armes, QC H2Y 2W2, 514/849-8381

Ottawa: Hon. Consul, Stuart E. Hendin, 726, 50 O'Connor St., ON K1P 6L2, 613/563-4804; Fax: 613/563-3878

Québec: Hon. Consul, Marc Dorion, #201, 112 Dalhousie St., QC G1K 4C1, 418/692-1532; Fax: 418/692-5091

## Republic of Chad

Embassy of Chad (to Canada): 2002 R St. NW, Washington DC 20009

202/462-4009; Fax: 202/265-1937

Ambassador, Ahmat Mahat-Saleh

Counsellor, Lémaye Favitsou-Boulandi

## Republic of Chile

Embassy of Chile: #1413, 50 O'Connor St., Ottawa ON K1N 6L2

613/235-4402; Fax: 613/235-1176

Email: echileca@istar.ca

Ambassador, His Excellency José Tomas Letelier

Minister-Counsellor, Fernando Urrutia

Edmonton: Hon. Consul, Domingo Chavez, Letourneau Centre, 4612 - 99 St., AB T6E 4C8, 403/439-9839; Fax: 403/433-2376

Montréal: Consul General, Alejandro Carvajal, #710, 1010, rue Sherbrooke ouest, QC H3A 2R7, 514/499-0405; Fax: 514/499-8914

Toronto: Consul General, Milenko Skoknic, #800, 170 Bloor St. W., ON M5R 3L9, 416/924-0106; Fax: 416/924-2627

Vancouver: Consul General, Dennis J. Biggs, #1250, 1185 West Georgia St., BC V6E 4E6, 604/681-9162; Fax: 604/682-2445

Winnipeg: Hon. Consul, Dr. Fernardo Guijon, #403, 810 Sherbrooke St., MB R3A 1R8, 204/787-4259; Fax: 204/889-4410

## People's Republic of China

Embassy of China: 515 St. Patrick St., Ottawa ON K1N 5H3

613/789-3434; Fax: 613/789-1911

Ambassador, His Excellency Zhang Yijun

Minister-Counsellor, Political Affairs, Wang Yongqiu

Minister-Counsellor, Commercial Affairs, Chen Shibiao

Counsellor, Science & Technology, Lu Jicai

Toronto: Consul General, Chen Wenzhao, 240 St George St., ON M5R 2P4, 416/964-7260; Fax: 416/324-6468

Vancouver: Consul General, Yang Zongliang, 3380 Granville St., BC V6H 3K3, 604/734-7492; Fax: 604/737-0154

## Republic of Colombia

Embassy of Colombia: #1002, 360 Albert St., Ottawa ON K1R 7X7

613/230-3760; Fax: 613/230-4416

Ambassador, His Excellency Alfonso Lopez Caballero

Minister-Counsellor, Hèctor Cacères

Calgary: Hon. Consul, Lois Mitchell, #1510, 335 - 8th Ave. SW, AB T2P 1C9, 403/266-1881; Fax: 403/237-6799

Montréal: Consul, Eufracio Morales, #420, 1010, rue Sherbrooke ouest, QC H3A 2R7, 514/849-4852; Fax: 514/849-4324

Toronto: Consul General, Clara Maria Leon, #2108, One Dundas St. West, ON M5G 1Z3, 416/977-0098; Fax: 416/977-1025

Vancouver: Hon. Consul, William Bush, 890, 789 West Pender St., BC V6C 1H2, 604/685-6435; Fax: 604/685-6485

## Republic of the Congo

Embassy of the Congo (to Canada): 4891 Colorado Ave. NW, Washington DC 20011

202/726-5500; Fax: 202/726-1860

Ambassador, His Excellency Dieudonné Antoine-Ganga

First Counsellor, Political Affairs, Daniel Mouellet

Second Counsellor, Cultural, Technical, Scientific Affairs, Jean-Alain Backoulas

First Secretary, Financial Affairs, Auguste Biyo

Pointe-Claire: Hon. Consul, Marcel P. Rigny, 2 Cedar Ave., QC H9S 4Y1, 514/697-3781; Fax: 514/697-9860

## Republic of Costa Rica

Embassy of Costa Rica: #208, 135 York St., Ottawa ON K1N 5T4

613/562-2855; Fax: 613/562-2582

Ambassador, His Excellency Carlos Miranda

Minister-Counsellor, Francisco Gonzalez

Montréal: Consul General, Patricia Gudino, 1425, boul René Lévesque ouest, QC H3G 1T7, 514/393-1057; Fax: 514/393-1624

Toronto: Hon. Consul General, Peter A. Kircher, 164 Avenue Rd., ON M5R 2H9, 416/961-6773; Fax: 416/961-6771

Vancouver: Consul General, Jorge A. Soto, #430, 789 West Pender St., BC V6C 1H2, 604/681-2152; Fax: 604/688-2152

## Republic of Côte d'Ivoire

Embassy of Côte d'Ivoire: 9 Marlborough Ave., Ottawa ON K1N 8E6

613/236-9919; Fax: 613/563-8287

Ambassador, His Excellency Julien Kacou

Montréal: Hon. Consul, André Vannerum, #602, 417, rue St-Pierre, QC H2Y 2N4, 514/845-8121; Fax: 514/688-7473

Toronto: Hon. Consul, Peter J. Dawes, 260 Adelaide St. East, PO Box 110, ON M5A 1N1, 416/366-8490; Fax: 416/947-1534

Vancouver: Hon. Consul, Jim O'Hara, 1531 Haywood Ave. West, BC V7W 1W4, 604/291-5182; Fax: 604/291-5225

## Republic of Croatia

Embassy of Croatia: #1700, 130 Albert St., Ottawa ON K1P 5G4

613/230-7351; Fax: 613/230-7388

Ambassador, His Excellency Zeljko Urban

Counsellor, Economic, Vesela Mrdjen

First Secretary & Consul, Hrvoje Sagrak

Counsellor, Politics, Culture & Media, Kolinda Grabar-Kitarovic

Mississauga: Consul General, Ivan Picukaric, #302, 918 Dundas St. East, ON L4Y 2B8, 905/277-9051; Fax: 905/277-5432

## Republic of Cuba

Embassy of Cuba: 388 Main St., Ottawa ON K1S 1E3

613/563-0141; Fax: 613/563-0068

Email: cuba@iosphere.net; URL: http://www.cubaweb.cu

Ambassador, His Excellency Bienvenido Garcia Negrin

Minister Counsellor, Jorge Lamadrid Mascaro

Third Secretary, Yuri Gala Lopez

Montréal: Consul General, Gabriel Tiel, 1415, av Pine ouest, QC H3G 2B2, 514/843-8897; Fax: 514/845-1063

Toronto: Consul General, Jose Garcia Menendez, #401, 5353 Dundas St. West, ON M9B 6H8, 416/234-8181; Fax: 416/234-2754

## Republic of Cyprus

High Commission for Cyprus (to Canada): c/o Republic of Cyprus: 2211 R St. NW, Washington DC 20008

202/462-5772; Fax: 202/483-6710

High Commisioner, His Excellency Andreas J. Jacovides

Counsellor, Leonidas Markides

Montréal: Hon. Consul General, Dr. Michael P. Paidoussis, #PH2, 2930, boul Édouard Montpetit, QC H3T 1J7, 514/735-7233; Fax: 514/398-7365

Ottawa: Hon. Consul, John M. Scott, #1400, 155 Queen St., ON K1P 6L1, 613/238-2229; Fax: 613/238-2371

Toronto: Consul General, Achilleas Antoniades, Cyprus Consulate, 365 Bloor St. East, 10th Fl., ON M4W 3L4, 413/944-0998; Fax: 416/944-9149

Winnipeg: Hon. Consul, Costas P. Ataliotis, 1430 Ellice Ave., MB R3G 0G4, 204/774-6724; Fax: 204/774-2002

## Czech Republic

Embassy of the Czech Republic: 541 Sussex Dr., Ottawa ON K1N 6Z6

613/562-3875; Fax: 613/562-3878

Email: ottawa@embassy.mzv.cz

Ambassador, His Excellency Stanislav Chylek

Counsellor, Martin Kosatka

First Secretary, Economic & Trade Affairs, Jaroslav Zeman

Second Secretary, Culture & Press Affairs, Radka Calábková

Attaché, Consular Affairs, Eva Hendrychová

Calgary: Hon. Consul, Lubos Pesta, Market Mall Professional Centre, #226, 4935 - 40th Ave NW, AB T3A 2N1, 403/288-6500; Fax: 403/288-6510

Montréal: Consul-General, Petr Dokladal, 1305, av Pine ouest, QC H3G 1B2, 514/849-4495; Fax: 849-4117

Vancouver: Hon. Consul, Miroslav F.M. Hermann, #2100, 1111 West Georgia St., PO Box 48800, BC V7X 1K9, 604/661-7530; Fax: 688-0829

## Kingdom of Denmark

Embassy of Denmark: #450, 47 Clarence St., Ottawa ON K1N 9K1

613/562-1811; Fax: 613/562-1812

Email: danem@cyberus.ca

Ambassador, His Excellency Jorgen M. Behnke

First Secretary, Susanne Shine

Calgary: Hon. Consul, Kai Mortensen, 1235 - 11 Ave. SW, AB T3C 0M5, 403/245-5755; Fax: 403/228-6739

Edmonton: Hon. Consul, Donn Larsen, Oxford Tower, #1112, 10235 - 101 St., AB T5J 1G1, 403/426-1457; Fax: 403/420-0005

Halifax: Hon. Consul of Denmark, H.I. Mathers, 1525 Birmingham St., PO Box 3550 South, NS B3J 3J3, 902/429-5680; Fax: 902/429-5221

Montréal: Hon. Consul, Michel Blouin, 1, Place Ville Marie, 35e étage, QC H3B 4M4, 514/877-3060; Fax: 514/871-8977

Regina: Consul, Inge Ryan, c/o MacPherson, Leslie & Tyerman, 1919 Saskatchewan Dr., 6th Fl., SK S4P 3V7, 306/787-4750; Fax: 306/787-3989

St. John's: Hon. Consul, Peter Norman Outerbridge, 92 Elizabeth Ave., PO Box 6150, NF A1C 5X8, 709/726-0020; Fax: 709/726-6013

Toronto: Consul General, Poul Laursen, #310, 151 Bloor St. West, ON M5S 1S4, 416/962-5661; Fax: 416/962-3668

Vancouver: Hon. Consul, Jorn Bjodstrup Petersen, #755, 777 Hornby St., BC V6Z 1S4, 604/684-5171; Fax: 604/684-8054

Winnipeg: Hon. Consul, Anders Bruun, 239 Aubert St., MB R2H 3G8, 204/233-8541; Fax: 204/942-0570

## Republic of Djibouti

c/o Embassy of the Republic of Djibouti: #515, 1156 - 15th St. NW, Washington DC 20005

202/331-0270; Fax: 202/331-0302

Ambassador, His Excellency Roble Olhaye

Counsellor, Dysane Dorani

### Commonwealth of Dominica *c/o* Organization of the Eastern Caribbean States

## Dominican Republic

Montréal: Consul-General, Grecia Fiordalicia Pichardo Polanco, Central Tower, #241, 1055, St-Mathieu, QC H3H 2S3, 514/933-9008; Fax: 514/933-2070

Saint John: Hon. Consul, John Driscoll, 59 Broad St., NB E2L 1Y3

St. John's: Hon. Consul, M.G. Renouf, 10 Forest Ave., NF A1C 3J9

Vancouver: Hon. Vice-Consul, Andrew H.S. Leung, #616, 1155 West Georgia St., BC V6E 3H4, 604/683-8688; Fax: 683-8033

## Organization of the Eastern Caribbean States

High Commission for the Countries of the Eastern Caribbean States: #1610, 112 Kent St., Ottawa ON K1P 5P2

613/236-8952; Fax: 613/236-3042

High Commissioner, His Excellency George R.E. Bullen

Minister-Counsellor, Jean-François Michel

First Secretary, Political & Consular, C.O. Dasent

Includes: Antigua & Barbuda, Commonwealth of Dominica, Grenada, Montserrat, Saint Christopher (Saint Kitts) & Nevis, Saint Lucia, Saint Vincent & the Grenadines

## Republic of Ecuador

Embassy of Ecuador: #1311, 50 O'Connor St., Ottawa ON K1P 6L2
613/563-8206; Fax: 613/235-5776
Email: mecua_can@inasec.ca
Counsellor & Chargé d'Affaires, Rafael Paredes
Montréal: Consul, Maria de Lourdes Rodriguez, #440, 1010, rue Ste-Catherine ouest, QC H3B 3R3, 514/874-4071; Fax: 514/874-4071
Richmond: Hon. Consul, Etienne Walter, #802, 7100 Gilbert Rd., BC V7C 5C3, 604/273-8577; Fax: 604/273-8576
Toronto: Consul General, Francisco Martinez, #470, 151 Bloor St. West, ON M5S 1S4, 416/968-2077; Fax: 416/968-3348

## Arab Republic of Egypt

Embassy of Egypt: 454 Laurier Ave. East, Ottawa ON K1N 6R3
613/234-4931; Fax: 613/234-9347
Commercial Office: #207, 85 Range Rd., Ottawa ON K1N 8J6, 613/238-6263; Fax: 613/238-2578
Ambassador, His Excellency Mahmoud Mahmoud Farghal
Counsellor & Deputy Chief of Mission, Mohamed Badreldin Zayed
Montréal: Consul General, Dr. Mohamed Ismail, #2617, 1, Place Ville Marie, QC H3B 4S3, 514/866-8455; Fax: 514/866-0835

## Republic of El Salvador

Embassy of El Salvador: #504, 209 Kent St., Ottawa ON K2P 1Z8
613/238-2939; Fax: 613/238-6940
Email: 103234.607@compuserve.com
Ambassador, Mauricio Rosales Rivera
Minister-Counsellor, Carolina Calderon
First Secretary & Consul General, Ricardo A. Cisneros
Montréal: #1604, 1080, Cote du Beaver Hall, QC H2Z 1S8, 514/861-6515; Fax: 861-6513
Toronto: Consul, Guillermo Antonio Guevara Lacayo, #320, 151 Bloor St. West, ON M5S 1T6, 416/975-0812; Fax: 416/975-0283
Vancouver: Hon. Consul, Jeffery Rodd Moore, Sinclair Centre, PO Box 649, Stn A, BC V6C 2N5, 604/732-8142

## Eritrea

Embassy of Eritrea (to Canada): 1708 New Hampshire Ave., Washington DC 20006
202/319-1991; Fax: 202/319-1304
Ambassador, His Excellency Amdemicael Kahsai

## Republic of Estonia

Embassy of Estonia (to Canada): 2131 Massachusetts Ave. NW, Washington DC 20008
202/588-0101; Fax: 202/588-0108
Email: info@estemb.org; URL: http://www.estemb.org
Ambassador, His Excellency Kalev G. Stoicescu
Toronto: Hon. Consul General, Ilmar Heinsoo, #202, 958 Broadview Ave., ON M4K 2R6, 416/461-0764; Fax: 416/461-0448

## Democratic Republic of Ethiopia

Embassy of Federal Democratic Republic of Ethiopia: #210, 151 Slater St., Ottawa ON K1P 5H3
613/235-6637; Fax: 613/235-4638
Email: infoethi@magi.com
Ambassador, His Excellency Dr. Fecadu Gadamu
Counsellor, Wahide Belay
Third Secretary, Beleyou Kifelew

## European Union

Delegation of the European Commission: #1110, 350 Sparks St., Ottawa ON K1R 7S8
613/238-6464; Fax: 613/238-5191
Ambassador & Head of Delegation, His Excellency John R. Beck
Attaché, David Tyson
Counsellor, Economic and Commercial Affairs, Carlos Freitas da Silva

## Fiji

Embassy of Fiji (to Canada): 630 Third Ave., 7th Fl., New York NY 10017
212/687-4130; Fax: 212/687-3963
Email: fjiun@undp.org
Ambassador, His Excellency Poseci W. Bune
Ottawa: Hon. Consul, Dr. D. Elaine Pressman, #750, 130 Slater St., ON, 613/233-9252; Fax: 613/594-8705
Vancouver: Hon. Vice-Consul, Jerome Schneider, #900, 1285 West Pender St., BC V6E 4B1, 604/687-7668; Fax: 604/687-7608

## Republic of Finland

Embassy of Finland: #850, 55 Metcalfe St., Ottawa ON K1P 6L5
613/236-2389; Fax: 613/238-1474
Email: finembott@synapse.net; URL: http://www.finemb.com
Ambassador, His Excellency Veijo Sampovaara
First Secretary (Deputy Head of Mission), Roy Eriksson
Calgary: Hon. Consul, Judith M. Romanchuk, Bow Valley Square 4, #1070, 250 - 6th Ave. SW, AB T2P 3H7, 403/299-9805; Fax: 403/299-9850
Edmonton: Hon. Consul, Christian Graefe, Alberta Word 1 Trade Centre, #502, 10303 Jasper Ave., AB T5J 2N5, 403/420-1155; Fax: 403/424-3091
Halifax: Hon. Consul, Frank Metcalf, Benjamin Wier House, 1459 Hollis St., NS B3J 1V1, 902/420-1990; Fax: 902/429-1171
Montréal: Hon. Consul, James G. Wright, Stock Exchange Tower, #3400, 800 Place Victoria, PO Box 242, QC H4Z 1E9, 514/397-7437; Fax: 514/397-7600
Québec: Hon. Consul, Henri Grondin, Edifice Mérci, #200, 801, ch St-Louis, QC G1S 1C1, 418/683-3000; Fax: 418/683-8784
Regina: Hon. Consul, Gordon J. Kuski, Royal Bank Bldg., #700, 2010 - 11th Ave., SK S4P 0J3, 306/757-1641; Fax: 306/359-0785
Saint John: Hon. Consul, Thomas L. McGloan, PO Box 7174, Stn A, NB E2L 4S6, 506/634-7450; Fax: 506/634-3612
Sault Ste. Marie: Hon. Consul, Raimo Viitala, 29 Pageant Dr., ON P6B 5J7, 705/942-6196
Sudbury: Hon. Consul, R. Hannu Piironen, 176 McNaughton St., ON B3E 1V3, 705/675-0067; Fax: 705/675-0067
Thunder Bay: Hon. Consul, Seppo K. Paivalainen, c/o Gordon, Vauthier, Paivalainen, 275 Bay St., ON P7B 1R7, 807/343-9394; Fax: 807/344-1562
Timmins: Hon. Consul, Margaret Kangas, 128 Queens St., ON P4N 4L6, 705/267-6175
Toronto: Consul, Helena Lappalainen, #604, 1200 Bay St., ON M5R 2A5, 416/964-0066; Fax: 416/964-1524
Vancouver: Hon. Consul General, Lars-Henrik Wrede, #1100, 1188 Georgia St. West, BC V6E 4A2, 604/688-4483; Fax: 604/687-8237
Winnipeg: Hon. Consul, Vacant, #127, 167 Lombard Ave., MB R3B 0T6, 204/942-7457; Fax: 204/942-7458

## France

Embassy of France: 42 Sussex Dr., Ottawa ON K1M 2C9
613/789-1795; Fax: 613/789-3484
Ambassador, His Excellency Alfred Siefer-Gaillardin
Minister-Counsellor, Jean-François Vallette
Counsellor, Cultural Affairs, Francois Trécourt
Counsellor, Economic & Commercial Affairs, Pierre Letocart
Calgary: Hon. Consular Agent, Marie-Odette Littmann, 1408 Windsor St. NW, AB T2N 3X3, 403/284-4928
Chicoutimi: Hon. Consul, François Brochet, 1596, Bégin, QC G7H 5T6, 418/545-7098
Halifax: Hon. Consul, Ghislaine Laguens, 5523A Young St., NS B3K 1Z7, 902/455-4411; Fax: 902/455-4149
Moncton: Consul General, Olivier Arribe, 250 Lutz St., PO Box 1109, NB E1C 8P6, 506/857-4191; Fax: 506/858-8169
Montréal: Consul General, Gérard Leroux, #2601, 1, Place Ville Marie, QC H3B 4S3, 514/878-4385; Fax: 514/878-3981
- Commercial Section: #2710, 1000, rue de la Gauchetière ouest, 27e étage, Montréal, PQ, H3B 4W5, 514/878-9851; Fax: 514/878-3677

North Sydney: Hon. Vice Consul, Thérèse Goora, North Sydney Consulate, 190 Brook St., PO Box 308, NS B2A 3M4, 902/794-3676
Québec: Consul General, Dominique de Combles de Nayves, Kent House, 25, rue St-Louis, QC G1R 3Y8, 418/694-2294; Fax: 418/694-2297
- Cultural & Scientific Affairs: 25, rue St-Louis, Québec PQ G1R 3Y8, 418/688-0430

Saskatoon: Hon. Consul, Bernard M. Michel, Saskatoon Consulate, Cameco Corporation, 2121 - 11th St. West, SK S7M 1J3, 306/956-6305; Fax: 306/956-6200
St. John's: Hon. Vice Consul, Pierre Morin, St. John's Consulate, 19 Diefenbaker St., NF A1A 2M2, 709/737-8924
Sudbury: Hon. Consul, Onésime Tremblay, Sudbury Consulate, 1101 Ramsey Lake Rd., Site 3, PO Box 18, ON P3E 5J2, 705/674-8503
Toronto: Consul General, Pierre-Jean Vandoorne, #400, 130 Bloor St. West, ON M5S 1N5, 416/925-8233; Fax: 416/925-3076; Visa Section: 416/925-8233
Vancouver: Consul General and Cultural Affairs, Maryse Berniau, The Vancouver Bldg., #1201, 736 Granville St., BC V6Z 1H9, 604/681-4345; Fax: 604/681-4287
- Commercial Section:, 604/684-1271; Fax: 604/684-2359

Victoria: Hon. Consul, Gordon Denford, 1162 Fort St., BC V8V 3K8, 250/385-1505; Fax: 250/385-9851
Whitehorse: Hon. Consul, Rolf Hougen, 305 Main St., YT Y1A 2B4, 403/667-4222; Fax: 403/668-6328
Winnipeg: Hon. Consul, Frédéric Granger, Winnipeg Consulate, 64 Athlone Dr., MB R3J 3L2, 204/837-9583

## Gabonese Republic

Embassy of Gabon: 4 Range Rd., Ottawa ON K1N 8J3
613/232-5301; Fax: 613/232-6916
Ambassador, His Excellency Alphonse Oyabi-Gnala
Counsellor, Economic & Financial Affairs, Lucien Moubouyi
Montréal: Hon. Consul, Luc Benoît, 85, rue Ste-Catherine ouest, QC H2X 3P4, 514/287-8500; Fax: 514/287-8643

## Republic of the Gambia

High Commission for Gambia (to Canada): c/o Gambia Embassy: #1000, 1155 - 15th St., NW, Washington DC 20005
202/785-1399; Fax: 202/785-1430
Email: gamembdc@gambia.com; URL: http://www.gambia.com
High Commissioner, H.E. Crispin Grey-Johnson
Montréal: Hon. Consul, Victor Podd, 255, av Beverley, QC H3P 1K8, 514/731-5775; Fax: 514/731-4374

Vancouver: Hon. Consul of Gambia, U. Gary Charlwood, #900, 1199 West Pender St., BC V6E 2R1, 604/662-3800; Fax: 604/662-3878

## Federal Republic of Germany

Embassy of Germany: 1 Waverley St., Ottawa ON K2P 0T8
613/232-1101; Fax: 613/594-9330
Email: 100566.2620@compuserve.com
Postal Address: PO Box 379, Stn A, Ottawa ON K1N 8V4
Ambassador, His Excellency Dr. Hans-Guenter Sulimma
Minister-Counsellor, Ruediger Lemp
Counsellor, Cultural Affairs, Charlotte Schwarzer
Counsellor, Economic & Commercial Affairs, Ulrich Grau
Counsellor, Press & Information Office, Ulrich Koehn
Defence Attaché, Lt. Col. Christian Ibrom
Calgary: Hon. Consul, Osmar Beltzner, #970, 700 - 4th Ave. SW, AB T2P 3J4, 403/269-5900; Fax: 403/269-5901
Fort St. John: Hon. Consul, Friedrich von Ilberg, #9832, 98 A Avenue, BC V1J 1S2, 250/785-4300; Fax: 250/785-5028
Halifax: Hon. Consul, Prof. Edgar Gold, Bank of Commerce Bldg., #708, 1809 Barrington St., NS B3J 3K8, 902/420-1599; Fax: 902/422-4713
Kitchener: Hon. Consul, Peter D. Kruse, 385 Frederick St., ON N2H 2P2, 519/745-6149; Fax: 519/576-0591
London: Hon. Consul, Barbara Weis, 71 Wharncliff Rd. South, ON N6J 2J8, 519/432-4133; Fax: 519/667-5187
Montréal: Consul General, Fritz von Rottenburg, 1250, boul René-Lévesque ouest, QC H3B 4W8, 514/931-2277; Fax: 514/931-7239
Regina: Consul, Guenter Kocks, 3534 Argyle Rd., SK S4S 2B8, 306/586-8762; Fax: 306/586-8762
St. John's: Hon. Consul, Gunter Sann, 22 Poplar Ave., NF A1B 1C8, 709/753-7777; Fax: 709/739-6666
Toronto: Consul General, Wiprecht von Treskow, 77 Admiral Rd., ON M5R 2L4, 416/925-2813; Fax: 416/925-2818
Vancouver: Consul General, Peter Maier-Oswald, World Trade Centre, #704, 999 Canada Place, BC V6C 3E1, 604/684-8377, 684-4258 (Visas); Fax: 604/684-8334
Winnipeg: Hon. Consul, Gerhard Spindler, #101, 1200 Pembina Hwy., MB R3T 2A7, 204/475-3088; Fax: 204/475-3089

## Republic of Ghana

High Commission for Ghana: 1 Clemow Ave., Ottawa ON K1S 2A9
613/236-0871/3; Fax: 613/236-0874
High Commissioner, His Excellency Annan Arkyin Cato
Counsellor, C.K. de Souza
Montréal: Hon. Consul-General, Joachim Normand, #900, 1420, rue Sherbrooke ouest, QC H3G 1K3, 514/849-1417; Fax: 514/849-2643
North Vancouver: Hon. Consul-General, Dr. William Herbert Lawrence Allsopp, 2919 Eddystone Cr., BC V7H 1B8, 604/929-1496; Fax: 604/929-1860

## Hellenic Republic

Embassy of Greece: 76-80 MacLaren St., Ottawa ON K2P 0K6
613/238-6271; Fax: 613/238-5676
Email: grnews@sympatico.ca
Ambassador, His Excellency John Thomoglou
Counsellor, Constantine Giovas
Montréal: Consul General, Nicholas Vamvounakis, 1170, Place du Frère André, 3e étage, QC H3B 3C6, 514/875-2119; Fax: 514/875-8781
Toronto: Consul General, Alexandra Papadopoulou, #1800, 365 Bloor St. East, ON M4W 3L4, 416/515-0133; Fax: 416/515-0209
Vancouver: Consul, Nicolaos Plexidas, #500, 688 West Hastings St., BC V6B 1P1, 604/681-1381; Fax: 604/681-6656

## Grenada c/o Organization of the Eastern Caribbean States

Toronto: Consul General, Adrian C.A. Hayes, #820, 439 University Ave., ON M5G 1Y8, 416/595-1343; Fax: 416/595-8278
Winnipeg: Hon. Consul, Caspar A. Shade, 10 Rice Rd., MB R3T 3N4, 204/269-4788; Fax: 204/452-8491

## Republic of Guatemala

Embassy of Guatemala: #1010, 130 Albert St., Ottawa ON K1P 5G4
613/233-7237; Fax: 613/233-0135
Consular Section: 613/233-7188
Ambassador, His Excellency Francisco Villagran de Leon
Minister-Counsellor, Carmen Aida Aguilera
Norval: Hon. Consul, Roberto Sierra, PO Box 319, ON L0P 1K0, 416/604-0655
Québec: Hon. Consul, Paul Bouchard, 50, rue Aberdeen, QC G1R 2C7, 418/523-0426
Vancouver: Consul General, Vacant, #760, 777 Hornby St., BC V6Z 1S4, 604/688-5209; Fax: 688-5210

## Republic of Guinea

Embassy of Guinea: 483 Wilbrod St., Ottawa ON K1N 6N1
613/789-8444; Fax: 613/789-7560
Ambassador, His Excellency Thierno Habib Diallo
First Secretary, Jeanne Bangoura
Calgary: Hon. Consul, Giovanni De Maria, Alberta Consulate, 79 Willamette Dr. SE, AB T2J 2A3, 403/225-2956; Fax: 403/225-2957
Toronto: Hon. Consul, Charles Arthur Downes, 1 St. John's Rd., ON M6P 4C7, 416/656-4812; Fax: 416/767-6070

## Republic of Guinea-Bissau

Embassy of Guinea-Bissau (to Canada): 918 - 16th St. NW, Mezzanine Suite, Washington DC 20006
202/872-4222
Montréal: Hon. Consul, Nicolas M. Matte, 1100, boul René-Lévesque ouest, 25e étage, QC, 514/397-6905; Fax: 514/397-8515

## Co-operative Republic of Guyana

Burnside Building: #309, 151 Slater St., Ottawa ON K1P 5H3
613/235-7249; Fax: 613/235-1447
High Commissioner, His Excellency Brindley H. Benn
First Secretary, Jennifer Wills
Willowdale: Hon. Consul, Geoffrey Da Silva, #206, 505 Consumers Rd., ON M2J 4V8, 416/494-6040; Fax: 416/494-1530

## Republic of Haiti

Embassy of Haiti, Tour B, Place de Ville: #205, 112 Kent St., Ottawa ON K1P 5P2
613/238-1628; Fax: 613/238-2986
Ambassador, His Excellency Emmanuel Ambroise
Minister/Counsellor, Lhande J. Henriquez
Montréal: Consul, Lyonel Laviolette, #1335, 1801 av McGill College, 13e étage, QC H3A 2N4, 514/499-1919; Fax: 514/499-1818

## Republic of Honduras

Embassy of Honduras: #805, 151 Slater St., Ottawa ON K1P 5H3
613/233-8900; Fax: 613/232-0193
Email: scastell@magmacom.com; breina@magmacom.com
Ambassador, Her Excellency Salomé Casstellanos Delgado
Counsellor, Commercial, Bertha M. Reina
Third Secretary & Consular Affairs, Maria Eugenia Naranio
Attaché, Cultural, Nora Bueso
Attaché, Press, Patricia Osorio
Montréal: Consul, Amparo Arita, #306, 1650, boul de Maisonneuve ouest, QC H3H 2P3, 514/937-1138
Québec: Hon. Consul, Thérèse Lacroix, 1334 Maréchal Foch, QC G1S 2C4, 418/681-5070
Toronto: Hon. Consul, Jeffrey Howard Burns, 488 Huron St., 3rd Fl., ON M5R 2R3, 416/960-1907; Fax: 416/960-1381
Vancouver: Hon. Consul, Enrique Gonzalez-Calvo, #1026, 510 West Hasting St., BC V6B 1L8, 604/685-7711

## Republic of Hungary

Embassy of Hungary: 299 Waverley St., Ottawa ON K2P 0V9
613/230-2717; Fax: 613/230-7560
URL: http://www.docuweb.ca/hungary/
Ambassador, His Excellency Károly Gedai
Minister Plenipotentiary, István Torzsa
Head, Consular Section, Norbert Konkoly
Calgary: Hon. Consul General, Béla Balázs, 1700 - 96 Ave. SW, AB T2V 5E5, 403/258-0052; Fax: 403/262-8343
Montréal: Consul, Istvan Szepes, #2040, 1200, av McGill Collège, QC H3B 4G7, 514/393-1048; Fax: 514/393-8226
Toronto: Consul General, Gabor Menczel, #1115, 121 Bloor St. East, ON M4W 3M5, 416/923-8981; Fax: 416/923-2732
Vancouver: Hon. Consul, André Molnár, 1650 West 2nd Ave., BC V6J 4R3, 604/734-6698
Vancouver: Hon. Vice-Consul, Brigitte A. Farkas, #201, 1039 Richards St., BC V6B 3E4, 604/681-5936; Fax: 604/681-5930

## Republic of Iceland

Embassy of Iceland (to Canada): #1200, 1156 - 15 St. NW, Washington DC 20005
202/265-6653; Fax: 202/265-6656
Email: idemb.wash@utn.stjr.is; URL: http://www.iceland.org
Ambassador, His Excellency Einar Benediktsson
Minister-Counsellor, Sveinn Bjornsson
Edmonton: Hon. Consul, Gudmundur A. Arnason, 14434 McQueen Rd., AB T5N 3L6, 403/455-7946
Montréal: Hon. Consul General, William I.M. Turner Jr., #575, 1981, av McGill College, QC H3A 2X1, 514/982-0188; Fax: 514/982-0190
Ottawa: Hon. Consul General, E.T. Lahey, 485 Broadview Ave., ON K2A 2L2, 613/724-5982; Fax: 613/724-1209
Regina: Hon. Consul, Jon Orn Jonsson, 4705 Castle Rd., SK S4S 4W9, 306/586-7737; Fax: 306/359-1885
St. John's: Hon. Consul, Avalon M. Goodridge, 20 Glasgow Place, NF A1B 2B4, 709/753-2787; Fax: 709/753-2787
Timberlea: Hon. Consul, Lawrence J. Cooke, 14 Bay Ct., NS B3T 1C4, 902/876-0657; Fax: 902/876-0657
Toronto: Hon. Consul, J. Ragnar Johnson, #2400, 250 Yonge St., ON M5B 2M6, 416/979-6740; Fax: 416/979-1234
West Vancouver: Hon. Consul, Heather Alda Ireland, 940 Younette Dr., BC V7T 1S9, 604/922-0854; Fax: 604/925-2524

Winnipeg: Hon. Consul General, Neil Bardal, 984 Portage Ave., MB R3G 0R6, 204/949-2200; Fax: 204/783-5916

## Republic of India

High Commission of India: 10 Springfield Rd., Ottawa ON K1M 1C9

613/744-3751; Fax: 613/744-0913

Email: hicomind@ottawa.net; URL: http://www.docuweb.ca/india

High Commissioner, His Excellency Prem Kumar Budhwar

Deputy High Commissioner & Minister, A.K. Banerjee

Toronto: Consul General, Rajiv Kumar Bhatia, #500, 2 Bloor St. West, ON M4W 3E2, 416/960-0751; Fax: 416/960-9812; Email: cgindia@pathcom.com

Vancouver: Consul General, Jawahar Lal, 325 Howe St., 2nd Fl., BC V6C 1Z7, 604/662-8811; Fax: 604/682-2471; Email: indiaadm@axionet.com

## Republic of Indonesia

55 Parkdale Ave., Ottawa ON K1Y 1E5

613/724-1100; Fax: 613/724-1105

Email: kbri@prica.org; URL: http://www.prica.org

Ambassador, His Excellency Benjamin Parwoto

Counsellor, Economic, Chaidir Siregar

Toronto: Consul, Titiek S.A. Suyono, 129 Jarvis St., ON M5C 2H6, 416/360-4020; Fax: 416/360-4295

Vancouver: Consul, Jacky D. Wahyu, 1455 West Georgia St., 2nd Fl., BC V6G 2T3, 604/682-8855; Fax: 604/662-8396

## Islamic Republic of Iran

Embassy of the Islamic Republic of Iran: 245 Metcalfe St., Ottawa ON K2P 2K2

613/235-4726, 233-4726; Fax: 613/232-5712

Email: iranemb@sonetis.com

Ambassador, His Excellency Seyed Mohammed Hoddein Adeli

Deputy Chief of Mission, Parvis Afshari

## Republic of Iraq

Embassy of Iraq: 215 McLeod St., Ottawa ON K2P 0Z8

613/236-9177; Fax: 613/567-1101

Ambassador, Vacant

Chargé d'Affaires, Haitham Taufiq Al-Najjar

Attaché, Mohammed Fakhri

## Ireland

Embassy of Ireland: #1105, 130 Albert St., Ottawa ON K1P 5G4

613/233-6281; Fax: 613/233-5835

Ambassador, His Excellency Paul Dempsey

First Secretary, Maeve Collins

Third Secretary, Christopher McCamley

## State of Israel

Embassy of Israel: #1005, 50 O'Connor St., Ottawa ON K1P 6L2

613/567-6450; Fax: 613/237-8865

Email: embisrott@cyberus.ca

http://www.israelca.org

Ambassador, David Sultan

Montréal: Consul General, Daniel Gal, #2620, 1155, boul René-Lévesque ouest, QC H3B 4S5, 514/393-9372; Fax: 514/393-8795

Toronto: Consul General, Yehudi Kinar, #700, 180 Bloor St. West, ON M5S 2V6, 416/961-1126; Fax: 416/961-7737

## Italian Republic

Embassy of Italy: 275 Slater St., 21st Fl., Ottawa ON K1P 5H9

613/232-2401; Fax: 613/233-1484

Ambassador, His Excellency Andrea Negrotto

Minister-Counsellor, Sandro de Bernardin

Brantford: Hon. Vice Consul, Arcangelo Martino, 288 Murray St., ON N3S 5T1, 519/753-0404

Calgary: Hon. Consular Agent, Augusto Ambrosino, 326 - 27 Ave. NE, AB T2E 2A2, 403/276-9389

Edmonton: Vice Consul, Pierfrancesco De Cerchio, #1900, Midland Walwyn Tower, Edmonton Centre, AB T5J 2Z2, 403/423-5153; Fax: 403/423-5214

Guelph: Hon. Vice-Consul, Imelda Porcellato, 127 Ferguson St., ON N1E 2Y9, 519/763-2228

Halifax: Hon. Vice Consul, Rodolfo Meloni, #7, 1574 Argyle St., PO Box 12, NS B3J 2B3, 902/422-0066

Hamilton: Vice Consul, Salvatore Di Venezia, #509, 105 Main St. East, ON L8N 1G6, 905/529-5030; Fax: 905/529-7028

Kingston: Hon. Vice Consul, Nicla A. d'Anna Sivilotti, 165 Ontario St., ON K7L 2Y6, 613/548-4380

London: Hon. Vice Consul, Luigi Rossetti, 344 Richmond St. 2nd Fl., ON N6A 3C3, 519/438-6740

Montréal: Consul General, Carlo Selvaggi, 3489, av Drummond ouest, 2e étage, QC H3G 1X6, 514/849-8351; Fax: 514/499-9471

Niagara-on-the-Lake: Hon. Vice Consul, Caloge Puma, 907 Line N.1, ON L0S 1J0, 905/468-3092

Prince Rupert: Hon. Consular Agent, Mario Giovanni Marogna, PO Box 640, BC V8T 3S1, 250/624-6282; Fax: 250/624-6613

Québec: Hon. Consul, Riccardo Rossini, 355, 23e rue, QC G1L 1W8, 418/529-9801; Fax: 418/529-2996

Regina: Hon. Vice Consul, Lucia Papini, 82 Lowry Place, SK S4S 4P5, 306/586-6832; Fax: 306/585-4894

Sarnia: Hon. Vice Consul, Antonio Domenichini, #210, 785 Exmouth St., ON N7T 5P7, 519/336-0101

Sault Ste. Marie: Hon. Vice Consul, Rudolph C. Peres, Professional Place, #201, 212 Queen St. East, ON P6A 5X8, 705/949-0704

St. John's: Hon. Consular Agent, Guido Del Rizzo, PO Box 5993, NF A1B 2J9, 709/368-8800

Sudbury: Hon. Vice Consul, Dr. Roberto Grosso, 96 Larch St., ON P3E 1C1, 705/674-4922

Sydney: Hon. Consular Agent, Leonardo D'Addario, NS

Thunder Bay: Hon. Vice Consul, Giovanna Pirotta Zovatto, #205, 105 May St. North, ON P7C 3N9, 807/622-9052

Timmins: Hon. Vice Consul, Rino Charles Bragagnolo, #131, 101 Mall, 38 Pine St. South, ON P4N 6K6, 705/264-1285

Toronto: Consul General, Leonardo Sampoli, 136 Beverley St., ON M5T 1Y5, 416/977-1566; Fax: 416/977-1119

Trail: Hon. Consular Agent, Gemma Merlo, 128 Colley St., BC V1R 2M2, 250/364-1826

Vancouver: Consul General, Arnaldo Abeti, #705, 1200 Burrard St., BC V6Z 2C7, 604/684-7288; Fax: 604/685-4263

Victoria: Hon. Vice Consul, Yolanda Pagnotta McKimmie, #207, 1050 Park Blvd., BC V8V 2T4, 250/386-3277; Fax: 250/595-5812

Windsor: Hon. Vice Consul, Liliana Scotti Busi, 1145 Erie St. East, ON N9A 3Z6, 519/256-0092

Winnipeg: Hon. Vice Consul, Bruno Esposito, #309, 283 Portage Ave., MB R3B 2B5, 204/943-7637

## Ivory Coast *c/o* Republic of Côte d'Ivoire

## Jamaica

Jamaican High Commission: #800, 275 Slater St., Ottawa ON K1P 5H9

613/233-9311; Fax: 613/233-0611

High Commissioner, Her Excellency Maxine Eleanor Roberts

Counsellor, Ann Scott

First-Secretary, Caroline Blake

New Westminster: Hon. Consul, Dr. Astley E. Smith, #604, 534 Sixth St., BC V3L 5K7, 604/515-0443

St. Albert: Hon. Consul, Dolli Booth, 36 Windermere Cres., AB T8N 3S5, 403/459-8440

Toronto: Consul General, Herman LaMont, #402, 214 King St. West, ON M5H 3S6, 416/598-3008

Winnipeg: Hon. Consul, Prof. D.K. Gordon, 11 Wadham Bay, MB R3T 3K2, 204/269-5319

## Japan

Embassy of Japan: 255 Sussex Dr., Ottawa ON K1N 9E6

613/241-8541; Fax: 613/241-2232

Email: emb@japan.magi.com; URL: http://www.emb-japan.can.org

Ambassador, His Excellency Takashi Tajima

Minister, Takashi Koezuka

Minister, Tsutomu Hiraoka

Counsellor, Tsuneyoshi Tatsuoka

Edmonton: Consul General, Shigeru Ise, ManuLife Place, #2480, 10180 - 101 St., AB T5J 3S4, 403/422-3752; Fax: 403/424-1635

Halifax: Hon. Consul General, Bruce S.C. Oland, Lindwood Holdings Ltd., Keith Hall, 1475 Hollis St., PO Box 2066, NS B3J 2Z1, 902/429-6530

Montréal: Consul General, Tadanori Inomata, #2120, 600, rue de La Gauchetière ouest, QC H3B 4L8, 514/866-3429; Fax: 514/395-6000

Regina: Hon. Consul General, Arthur Tsuneo Wakabayashi, 3234 Mountbatten Cres., SK S4V 0Z4, 306/789-3221; Fax: 306/761-0766

St. John's: Hon. Consul General, Aidan Maloney, 2 Laughlin Cres., NF A1A 2G2, 709/722-3016

Toronto: Consul General, Hajime Tsujimoto, #2702, Toronto Dominion Bank Tower, Toronto Dominion Centre, PO Box 10, ON M5K 1A1, 416/363-7038; Fax: 416/367-9392

Vancouver: Consul General, Shuji Shimokoji, #900, 1177 Hastings St. West, BC V6E 2K9, 604/684-5868; Fax: 604/684-6939

Winnipeg: Hon. Consul General, Otto Lang, 680 Wellington Cres., MB R3M 0C2, 204/284-0478

## Hashemite Kingdom of Jordan

Embassy of Jordan: #701, 100 Bronson Ave., Ottawa ON K1R 6G8

613/238-8090; Fax: 613/232-3341

Ambassador, His Excellency Samir Khalifeh

Minister Plenipotentiary, Sami Lash

Counsellor, Mohammad Homoud

## Republic of Kazakhstan

Consulate General of Kazakhstan: #1014, 200 Queen St. West, Toronto ON M5H 3R3

416/593-4043; Fax: 416/593-4037

Hon. Consul, Roza Kassenova

## Republic of Kenya

High Commission for Kenya: 415 Laurier Ave. East, Ottawa ON K1N 6R4

613/563-1773; Fax: 613/233-6599

High Commissioner, His Excellency Mwanyengela Ngali

Counsellor, Danielo Mayaka

## Republic of Korea

Embassy of Korea: 150 Boteler St., Ottawa ON K1A 5A6

613/232-1715; Fax: 613/232-0928

Ambassador, His Excellency Hang Kyung Kim

Minister, Young-Jo Jung

Montréal: Consul General, Tae Kyu Yang, #2500, 1002, rue Sherbrooke ouest, QC H3A 3G4, 514/845-3243; Fax: 514/845-8517
Toronto: Consul General, Kyoung-Bo Shim, 555 Avenue Rd., ON M4V 2J7, 416/920-3809; Fax: 416/924-7305
Vancouver: Consul General, Wung Sik Kang, #830, 1066 Hastings St. West, BC V6E 3X1, 604/681-9581; Fax: 604/681-4864

## State of Kuwait
Embassy of Kuwait: 80 Elgin St., Ottawa ON K1P 1C6
613/780-9999; Fax: 613/780-9905
Ambassador, His Excellency Abdulmoshin Yousef Al-Duaij
Counsellor, Abdullatif A. Al-Mawwash

## Kyrgyz Republic
Embassy of Kyrgyzstan (to Canada): 1732 Wisconsin Ave. NW, Washington DC 20007
202/338-5141; Fax: 202/338-5139
Email: embassy@kyrgyzstan.org; URL: http://www.kyrgyzstan.org
Ambassador Extraordinary and Plenipotentiary, Baktybek Abdrisaev

## Lao People's Democratic Republic
Embassy of Laos (to Canada): 2222 - S St. NW, Washington DC 20008
202/332-6416; Fax: 202/332-4923
Ambassador, Hiem Phommachanh
Counsellor, Seng Soukhathivong

## Republic of Latvia
Embassy of Latvia, Tower B: #208, 112 Kent St., Ottawa ON K1P 5P2
613/238-6014; Fax: 613/238-7044
Email: latvia-embassy@magmacom.com; URL: http://www2.magmacom.com//~latemb
Consular Division: 613/238-6868
Ambassador, His Excellency Georgs Andrejevs
Counsellor & Deputy Head of Mission, Martins Lacis

## Lebanese Republic
Embassy of Lebanon: 640 Lyon St., Ottawa ON K1S 3Z5
613/236-5825; Fax: 613/232-1609
Ambassador, His Excellency Dr. Assem Salman Jaber
First Secretary, Mansour Abdallah
Edmonton: Hon. Consul, Samir Ghosein, 7708 - 190 St., AB T5J 4A1, 403/421-7907; Fax: 403/424-2138
Halifax: Hon. Consul, Wadih Maurice Fares, #201, 117 Kearney Lake Rd., NS B3M 4N9, 902/457-6676; Fax: 902/457-4686
Outremont: Consul General, Charbel Wehbi, 40, ch Côte Ste Catherine, QC H2V 2A2, 514/276-2638; Fax: 514/276-0090

## Kingdom of Lesotho
Montréal: Hon. Consul General, Louis D. Burke, 4750, The Boulevard, QC H3Y 1V3, 514/482-1946; Fax: 514/483-6595
Vancouver: Hon. Consul, Kenneth L. Burke, 2046 - 14 Ave. West, BC V6J 2K4, 604/734-2729; Fax: 604/734-0627

## Republic of Liberia
Ottawa Embassy closed temporarily.
Burlington: Hon. Consul, Edward A. Collis, 1441 Ontario St., ON L7S 1G5, 905/333-4000; Fax: 905/632-4000

Montréal: Hon. Consul General, H.J.F. Bloomfield, #1720, 1080, Côte du Beaver Hall, QC H2Z 1S8, 514/871-4741; Fax: 514/397-0816
Ste-Foy: Hon. Consul, Philip Berlach, 400, rue Morse, QC G1N 4L4
Toronto: Hon. Consul General, Erwin Singer, 24 Hazelton Ave., ON M5R 2E2, 416/920-2599; Fax: 416/920-0815
Vancouver: Hon. Consul General, Philip Garratt, #502, 815 Hornby St., BC V6Z 2E6, 604/684-5988; Fax: 604/684-0367

## Socialist People's Libyan Arab Jamahiriya
c/o Permanent Mission of Libya to the U.N.: #309, 315 East 48th St., New York NY 10017
212/752-5775; Fax: 212/593-4787
Ambassador, His Excellency Mohamed Azwai
Chargé d'Affaires, Ibrahim A. Omar

## Liechtenstein *c/o* Swiss Confederation

## Republic of Lithuania
Embassy of Lithuania: #204, 130 Albert St., Ottawa ON K1P 5G4
613/567-5458; Fax: 613/567-5315
Ambassador, Dr. Alfonsas Eidintas
Chargé d'Affaires ai, Jonas Paslauskas

## Grand Duchy of Luxembourg
Embassy of Luxembourg (to Canada): 2200 Massachusetts Ave. NW, Washington DC 20008
202/265-4171; Fax: 202/328-8270
Ambassador, His Excellency Alphonse Berns
Minister-Counsellor, Carlo Krieger
Calgary: Hon. Consul, Z.G. (Dan) Havlena, PO Box 6990, Stn D, AB T2P 2G2, 403/262-5576; Fax: 403/262-3556
Montréal: Hon. Consul General, Marie-Claire Lefort, 3877, av Draper, QC H4A 2N9, 514/489-6052
Vancouver: Hon. Consul, Klaus Priebe, #300, 1111 Melville St., BC V6E 4H7, 604/682-3664; Fax: 604/688-3830

## Republic of Madagascar
Embassy of Madagascar: 649 Blair Rd., Gloucester ON K1J 7M4
613/744-2530; Fax: 613/744-2530
Ambassador, His Excellency René Fidèle Rajaonah
Brossard: Hon. Vice Consul, Julien Randrianarivony, 8530, rue Saguenay, QC J4X 1M6, 514/672-0353; Fax: 514/466-1552
Calgary: Hon. Consul, Zdenek Geoffrey Havlena, c/o Cec Papke Sales & Rentals Ltd., #216, 816 - 7 Ave. SW, AB T2P 1A1, 403/262-5576; Fax: 403/262-3556

## Republic of Malawi
High Commission for Malawi: 7 Clemow Ave., Ottawa ON K1S 2A9
613/236-8931; Fax: 613/236-1054
High Commissioner, His Excellency Bright McBin. Msaka
First Secretary, Gusto Mabvuto
Montréal: Hon. Consul, Yvon Maloney, #200, 6, Place du Commerce, Brassard, QC J4W 3J9, 514/466-9543
Toronto: Hon. Consul, Robert A. Elek, #544, 21 Dale Ave., ON M4W 1K3, 416/234-9333

## Malaysia
High Commission of Malaysia: 60 Boteler St., Ottawa ON K1N 8Y7
613/241-5182; Fax: 613/241-5214
Email: malott@istar.ca

High Commissioner, His Excellency Dato Abdullah Zawawi Bin Haji Mohamed
Counsellor, Jaafar Bin Abdul Manaf
North York: Consul, Sahban Bin Haji Muksan, #460, 100 Sheppard Ave. East, 4th Fl., ON M2N 6N5, 416/224-2202; Fax: 416/224-2204
Vancouver: Consul General, Ali Bin Abdullah, #1900, 925 West Georgia St., BC V6C 3L2, 604/685-9550; Fax: 604/685-9520

## Republic of Mali
Embassy of Mali: 50 Goulburn Ave., Ottawa ON K1N 8C8
613/232-1501; Fax: 613/232-7429
Ambassador, His Excellency Diakité Manassa Danioko
Counsellor, Mohamed Maiga
Montréal: Hon. Consul, Paul Fortin, #1810, 1 Westmount Sq., QC H3Z 2P9, 514/939-1267; Fax: 514/939-1296
Toronto: Hon. General Consul, Paul John Tuz, 519 Spadina Rd., ON M5P 2W6, 416/489-4849; Fax: 416/489-0379

## Malta
High Commission for Malta (to Canada); c/o Embassy of Malta: 2017 Connecticut Ave. NW, Washington DC 20008
202/462-3611; Fax: 202/387-5470
Email: malta_embassy@compuserve.com; URL: http://www.magnet.mt
High Commissioner, His Excellency Dr. Mark Anthony Micallef
Etobicoke: Hon. Consul General, Alfred Dalli, West Tower, Mutual Group Centre, #730, 3300 Bloor St. West, ON M8X 2X2, 416/207-0922; Fax: 416/207-0986
St. John's: Hon. Consul General, Charles E. Puglisevich, #1, 611 Torbay Rd., NF A1A 5J1, 709/222-2744; Fax: 709/722-3208
Vancouver: Hon. Consul General, Joachim Grubner, #310, 1001 Broadway West, BC V6H 4B1, 604/732-4453; Fax: 604/738-4796

## Islamic Republic of Mauritania
Embassy of Mauritania: 249 McLeod St., Ottawa ON K2P 1A1
613/237-3283; Fax: 613/237-3287
Ambassador, His Excellency Abdel Majid Kamil
Counsellor, Sidi Ould Mohamed Lagdhaf

## Republic of Mauritius
High Commission for Mauritius (to Canada): c/o Embassy of Mauritius: #441, 4301 Connecticut Ave. NW, Washington DC 20008
202/244-1491; Fax: 202/966-0983
High Commissioner, His Excellency Chitmansing Jesseramsing
Second Secretary, M. Nagub Soomauroo
Montréal: Hon. Consul, Richard Gervais, #200, 606, rue Cathcart, QC H3B 1K9, 514/393-9500; Fax: 514/393-9324

## United Mexican States
Embassy of Mexico: #1500, 45 O'Connor St., Ottawa ON K1P 1A4
613/233-8988, 9272; Fax: 613/235-9123
Email: info@embamexcan.com; URL: http://www.docuweb.ca/Mexico
Commercial Section, 613/235-7782; Fax: 613/235-1129
Ambassador, Her Excellency Sandra Fuentes-Berain
Minister & Deputy Head of Mission, Hector Romero Barraza

Minister, Commercial Affairs, Jose Poblano
Calgary: Hon. Consul, Bernardo Vergara, The Devenish Building, #312, 908 - 17 Ave. SW, AB T2T 0A3, 403/209-2007; Fax: 403/209-2017
Dartmouth: Hon. Consul, Galo Carrera, 53 Hawthorne St., NS B2Y 2Y7, 902/466-3678
Montréal: Consul General, Celso H. Delgado Ramirez, #1015, 2000, rue Mansfield, QC H3A 2Z7, 514/288-2502; Fax: 514/288-8287; Tourist section: 514/871-1052
Commercial Section: #1540, 1501 McGill College, Montréal, PQ, H3H 2T5, 514/287-1669; Fax: 514/287-1844
Sillery: Hon. Consul, Madeleine Therrien, #1407, 380, rue Saint-Louis, QC G1S 4M1, 418/681-3192
St. John's: Hon. Consul, John Crosbie, The Hon., Scotia Centre, 235 Water St., PO Box 610, NF A1C 5L3, 709/726-6124; Fax: 709/722-0483
Toronto: Consul General, Ramon Gonzalez Jameson, #4440, 99 Bay St., PO Box 266, ON M5L 1E9, 416/368-2875; Fax: 416/368-1672
Vancouver: Consul General, Gabriel Rosales Vega, #810, 1130 Pender St. West, BC V6E 4A4, 604/684-3547; Fax: 604/684-2485

## Principality of Monaco
Montréal: Hon. Consul General, Michel Pasquin, #1500, 1155 Sherbrooke St. West, QC H3A 2W1, 514/849-0589; Fax: 514/631-2771

## Mongolia
Embassy of Mongolia (to Canada): c/o U.S. Embassy of Mongolia: 2833 M St. NW, Washington DC 20007
202/333-7117; Fax: 202/298-9227
Email: monemb@aol.com
Ambassador, His Excellency Jalbuu Choinhor

### Montserrat *c/o* Organization of the Eastern Caribbean States

## Kingdom of Morocco
Embassy of Morocco: 38 Range Rd., Ottawa ON K1N 8J4
613/236-7391; Fax: 613/236-6164
Ambassador, His Excellency Tajeddine Baddou
Counsellor, El Houcine Fardani
Montréal: Consul General, Elyazid El Kadiri, #1510, 1010, rue Sherbrooke ouest, QC H3A 2R7, 514/288-8750; Fax: 514/288-4859
Vancouver: Hon. Consul, Percy Von Lipinsky, 3357 Pt. Grey Rd., BC V6K 1A4, 604/738-3357; Fax: 604/689-9132

## Republic of Mozambique
Embassy of Mozambique (to Canada): #570, 1990 M St. NW, Washington DC 20036
202/293-7146; Fax: 202/835-0245
Acting High Commissioner, Esperanca Alfredo Machavel

## Union of Myanmar
Embassy of Myanmar: #902, 85 Range Rd., Ottawa ON K1N 8J6
613/232-6434; Fax: 613/232-6435
Ambassador, His Excellency Dr. Kyaw Win

## Republic of Namibia
High Commission for Namibia (to Canada): 1605 New Hampshire Ave. NW, Washington DC 20009
202/986-0540; Fax: 202/986-0443
Email: embnamibia@aol.com
High Commissioner, His Excellency Veiccoh K. Nghiwete
Waterloo: Hon. Consul, Walter McLean, 122 Avondale Ave. South, ON N2L 2G3, 519/578-5932; Fax: 519/578-7799

## Kingdom of Nepal
Royal Nepalese Embassy (to Canada): c/o Embassy of Nepal: 2131 Leroy Place NW, Washington DC 20008
202/667-4550; Fax: 202/667-5534
Ambassador, His Excellency Dr. Bhekh Thapa
Minister, Lava Kumar Devacota
Toronto: Hon. Consul General, Kunjar Sharma, 2 Sheppard Ave. East, ON M2N 5Y7, 416/226-8722; Fax: 416/224-9070

## Kingdom of the Netherlands
Royal Netherlands Embassy: #2020, 350 Albert St., Ottawa ON K1R 1A4
613/237-5030; Fax: 613/237-6471
Counsellor, Economic & Commercial Affairs, Fred Olthof
Counsellor & Deputy Head of Mission, Henk Revis
Ambassador, His Excellency Dirk Jan van Houten
Calgary: Hon. Consul, I.M. Bakker, Lancaster Building, #708, 304 - 8th Ave. SW, AB, 403/265-0599
Edmonton: Hon. Consul, R. Dootjes, 10214 - 112 St., AB T5K 1M5, 403/428-7513; Fax: 403/424-2053
Halifax: Hon. Consul, Gavin Joseph Rainnie, Purdy's Wharf, #1306, 1959 Upper Water St., NS B3J 3N2, 902/422-1485; Fax: 902/420-1787
Kingston: Hon. Vice Consul, Dr. H. Westenberg, 115 Lower Union St., ON K7L 2N3, 613/542-7095
London: Hon. Vice Consul, Dr. R.D. ter-Vrugt, 650 Colborne St., ON N5W 5A1, 519/551-0453; Fax: 519/663-1834
Montréal: Consul General, Hans van Dam, #2201, 1002, rue Sherbrooke ouest, QC H3A 3L6, 514/849-4247; Fax: 514/849-8260
Québec: Hon. Consul, W. Blanchet, 174 Grande Allée Ouest, QC G1R 2G9, 418/525-8344; Fax: 418/522-4398
Regina: Hon. Consul, W.B.C. de Lint, 2432-14 Ave., SK S4P 0Y3, 306/522-8081; Fax: 306/522-7794
Saint John: Hon. Consul, C.D. Whelly, #1600, 1 Brunswick Sq., PO Box 1324, Stn A, NB E2L 4H8, 506/632-8900; Fax: 506/632-8809
St. John's: Hon. Consul, A.A. Bruneau, The Fortis Building, 139 Water St., NF A1B 3T2, 709/737-5616; Fax: 709/737-5307
Thunder Bay: Hon. Vice Consul, R.P. Welter, 179 South Algoma St., ON P7B 3C1, 807/345-1551; Fax: 807/625-9630
Toronto: Consul General, P.W.A. Schellekeus, #2106, 1 Dundas St. West, ON M5G 1Z3, 416/598-2520; Fax: 416/598-8064
Vancouver: Consul General, Baron K.H. Birkman, Crown Trust Bldg., #821, 475 Howe St., BC V6C 2B3, 604/684-6448; Fax: 604/684-3549
Winnipeg: Hon. Consul, Hans Hasenack, 69 Shorecrest Dr., MB R3P 1N9, 204/487-1211; Fax: 204/489-4219

## New Zealand
New Zealand High Commission: #727, 99 Bank St., Ottawa ON K1P 6G3
613/238-5991; Fax: 613/238-5707
Email: nzhcott@istar.ca; URL: http://www.nzhcottawa.org
Immigration/Visas: 613/238-6097
High Commissioner, Jim Gerard
Deputy High Commissioner, Stephen Jacobi
First Secretary, Barbara Bridge
Vancouver: Consul General & Trade Commissioner, Stephen Bryant, #1200, 888 Dunsmuir St., BC V6C 3K4, 604/684-7388; Fax: 604/684-7333

## Republic of Nicaragua
Embassy of Nicaragua: #407, 130 Albert St., Ottawa ON K1P 5G4
613/234-9631; Fax: 613/238-7666
Consular Section: 613/238-7677
Ambassador, Vacant
Minister-Counsellor Chargé d'affaires, A.I., Susan Grigsby de Fonseca
First Secretary, Consular Affairs, Juan Manuel Siero Cantarero
Mississauga: Hon. Consul, Ilse Mendieta de McGrath, 2351 Poplar Cr., ON L5J 4H2, 905/855-3960; Fax: 905/855-1513
Montréal: Hon. Consul, Noel Lacayo Barreto, 4870 Doherty, QC H4V 2V2, 514/484-8250; Fax: 514/484-7928

## Republic of Niger
Embassy of Niger: 38 Blackburn Ave., Ottawa ON K1N 8A2
613/232-4291; Fax: 613/230-9808
Ambassador, His Excellency Aboubacar Abdou
Counsellor, Boubacar Adarnor
Second Secretary, M. Saley Brah
Montréal: Hon. Consul, Pierre Thomas, #850, 231, rue St-Jacques ouest, QC H2Y 1M6, 514/844-4428
Toronto: Hon. Consul, Jean Michel Beck, ON
Vancouver: Hon. Consul, John Akerley, BC

## Kingdom of Norway
Royal Norwegian Embassy: #532, 90 Sparks St., Ottawa ON K1P 5B4
613/238-6571; Fax: 613/238-2765
Ambassador, His Excellency Johan Lovald
Attaché, Elna Verheyleweghen
Calgary: Hon. Consul, L.E. Bjornsen, North Tower, Western Canadian Place, #1753, 707 - 8th Ave. SW, PO Box 6525, Stn D, AB T2P 3G7, 403/263-2270; Fax: 403/298-6081
Dartmouth: Hon. Consul, Steinar J. Engeset, #206, 11 Morris Dr., NS B3B 1M2, 902/468-1330; Fax: 902/468-7200
Edmonton: Hon. Consul, Roar Tungland, 2310 - 80 Ave., AB T6P 1N2, 403/440-2292; Fax: 403/440-1241
Mississauga: Hon. Consul General, Trygve Husebye, 2600 South Sheridan Way, ON L5J 2M4, 905/822-2339; Fax: 905/855-1450
Montréal: Hon. Consul General, Richard Pound, #3900, 1155, boul René Lévesque ouest, QC H3B 3V2, 514/874-9087; Fax: 514/397-3063
Québec: Hon. Consul, Gaétan Thivierge, 2 Nouvelle France, Wolves Crove, PO Box 40, Stn B, QC G1K 7A2, 418/525-8171; Fax: 418/525-9940
Saint John: Hon. Consul, Donald F. MacGowan, Q.C., 40 Wellington Row, PO Box 6850, Stn A, NB E2L 4S3, 506/633-3800; Fax: 506/633-3811
St. John's: Hon. Consul, Robert I. Collingwood, Baine Johnston Centre, #800, 10 Fort William Place, PO Box 5367, NF A1C 5W2, 709/576-1780; Fax: 709/576-1273
Vancouver: Hon. Consul General, Bjorn Hareid, Waterfront Centre, #1200, 200 Burrard St., BC V6C 3L6, 604/682-7977; Fax: 604/682-8376
Victoria: Consul, Cecil P. Ridout, Hartwig Court, #401, 1208 Wharf St., PO Box 577, BC V8W 2P5, 250/384-1174; Fax: 250/382-3231
Winnipeg: Hon. Consul, Astrid Walker, 336 Lindenwood Dr. East, MB R3P 2H1, 204/489-1626

## Sultanate of Oman
Embassy of Oman (to Canada): 2342 Massachusetts Ave. NW, Washington DC 20008
202/387-1980; Fax: 202/745-4933
Ambassador, His Excellency Abdulla bin Mohamed Al-Dhahab

## Islamic Republic of Pakistan

High Commission for Pakistan: #608, 151 Slater St., Ottawa ON K1P 5H3

613/238-7881; Fax: 613/238-7296

Email: hcpak@magi.com

High Commissioner, Farouk A. Rana

First Secretary, Muhammad Sarfraz A. Khanzada

Montréal: Consul General, Muhammad Ashraf, 3421, rue Peel, QC H3A 1W7, 514/845-2297; Fax: 514/845-1354

Willowdale: Consul General, Yusuf Shah, #810, 4881 Yonge St., ON M2N 5X3, 416/250-1255; Fax: 416/250-1321

## Republic of Panama

Embassy of Panama: #300, 130 Albert St., Ottawa ON K1P 5G4

613/236-7177; Fax: 613/236-5775

Ambassador, His Excellency Carlos Ozores Typaldos

Montréal: Consul General, Luis E. Uribe, #904, 1425, boul René-Lévesque ouest, QC H3G 1T7, 514/874-1929

Toronto: Consul General, Vilma Diaz de Dorado, 879 St. Clair Ave. West, ON M6C 1C4, 416/651-2350; Fax: 416/651-3141

Vancouver: Hon. Consul, Esteban Diaz Jaen, #700, 555 West Hastings St., BC V6B 4N5, 604/893-7033; Fax: 604/687-2043

## Papua New Guinea

High Commission of Papua New Guinea (to Canada): #300, 1615 New Hampshire Ave., Washington DC 20009

202/745-3680; Fax: 202/745-3679

High Commissioner, His Excellency Nagora Bogan

Toronto: Hon. Consul, David Beatty, Old Canada Investment Corp. Ltd., #2700, 145 King St. West, ON M5H 1J8, 416/865-0470

## Republic of Paraguay

Embassy of Paraguay: #401, 151 Slater St., Ottawa ON K1P 5H3

613/567-1283; Fax: 613/567-1679

Email: embapar@magmacom.com; URL: http://www.magmacom.com/~embapar

First Secretary, Chargé d'Affaires, Raul Cano Ricciardi

## Republic of Peru

Embassy of Peru: #1901, 130 Albert St., Ottawa ON K1P 5G4

613/238-1777; Fax: 613/232-3062

Email: emperuca@magi.com

Ambassador, His Excellency Hernan Couturier Mariategui

Montréal: Consul General, Raul A. Rivera Maravi, La Tour Ouest, #970, 550, rue Sherbrooke ouest, QC H3A 1B9, 514/844-5123; Fax: 514/843-8425

Toronto: Consul General, Luis Hernandez, #301, 10 Saint Mary St., ON M4Y 1P9, 416/963-9696; Fax: 416/963-9074

Vancouver: Consul General, Amador Velasquez, #260, 505 Burrard St., BC V7X 1M3, 604/662-8880; Fax: 604/662-3564

## Republic of the Philippines

Embassy of the Philippines: #606-608, 130 Albert St., Ottawa ON K1P 5G4

613/233-1121; Fax: 613/233-4165

Email: ottawape@istar.ca

Ambassador, His Excellency Raul Ilustre Goco

Minister-Counsellor & Consul General, Pedro O. Chan

Edmonton: Hon. Consul, Victoriano K. Cui, 15012 - 116 St., AB T5X 1L1, 403/444-0086; Fax: 403/414-1305

Montréal: Hon. Consul, Erlinda V. Quintos, 1418, rue Notre-Dame ouest, QC H3C 1K8, 514/938-3849; Fax: 514/934-2346

Regina: Gerardo Gilongos, Hon. Consul, 1401 King St., SK S4T 4G5, 306/757-9571; Fax: 306/565-2399

Toronto: Consul General, Francisco Santos, #365, 151 Bloor St. West, ON M5S 1S4, 416/922-7181; Fax: 416/922-2638

Trade Section: #409, 60 Bloor St. West, Toronto, ON, M4W 3B8, 416/967-1788; Fax: 416/967-6236

Vancouver: Consul General, Lourdes G. Morales, #301-308, 470 Granville St., BC V6C 1V5, 604/685-7645; Fax: 604/685-9945

Winnipeg: Consul General, Dr. Rolando D. Guzman, Philippine Center, 88 Juno St., MB R3A 1G1, 204/774-6065; Fax: 204/889-4638

## Republic of Poland

Embassy of Poland: 443 Daly Ave., Ottawa ON K1N 6H3

613/789-0468; Fax: 613/789-1218

Email: aj201@freenet.carleton.ca

Ambassador, His Excellency Tadeusz Diem

Counsellor, Maksymilian Podstawski

Montréal: Consul General, Dobromir Dziewulak, 1500, av Pine ouest, QC H3G 1B4, 514/937-9481; Fax: 514/937-7272

Commercial Section: 3501, av Musée, Montréal, PQ, H3G 2C8, 514/937-9481; Fax: 514/937-7272

Toronto: Consul General, Wojciech Tycinski, 2603 Lake Shore Blvd. West, ON M8V 1G5, 416/252-5471; Fax: 416/252-0509

Commercial Section: #2860, 3300 Bloor St. West, Centre Tower, Toronto, ON, M8X 2W8, 416/233-6571; Fax: 416/233-9578

Vancouver: Consul General, Krzysztof Smyk, #1600, 1177 Hastings St. West, BC V6E 2K3, 604/688-3530; Fax: 604/688-3537

## Portugal

Embassy of Portugal: 645 Island Park Dr., Ottawa ON K1Y 0B8

613/729-0883; Fax: 613/729-4236

Consular Section: Tel: 613/729-2270

Ambassador, His Excellency Fernando Manuel da Silva Marques

Counsellor, Vera Maria Fernandes

Edmonton: Hon. Consul, Luis Filipe da Rocha Rodrigues Freire, 398 Clearview Rd., AB T5A 4G6, 403/473-1005; Fax: 403/473-2985

Halifax: Hon. Consul, Arthur R. Moreira, 1646 Barrington St., PO Box 355, NS B3J 2N7, 902/423-7211

Montréal: Consul General, Antonio Jorge Jacob de Carvalho, #1725, 2020, rue University, QC H3A 2A5, 514/499-0359; Fax: 514/499-0366

Commercial Section: #940, 500, rue Sherbrooke ouest, Montréal PQ H3A 3C6, 514/282-1264; Fax: 514/499-1450

Québec: Hon. Consul, Fernao Mendonça Perestrelo, #710, 775, av Murray, QC G1S 4T2, 418/681-8650

St. John's: Hon. Consul, Hernani Eurico da Silva Martins, 40 Mansfield Cres., PO Box 5249, NF A1E 5A8, 709/726-2440, 745-2271

Toronto: Consul General, Antonio Augusto Montenegro Vieria Cardoso, 121 Richmond St. West, 7th Fl., ON M5H 2K1, 416/360-8260; Fax: 416/360-0350

Commercial & Tourism Sections: #1005, 60 Bloor St. West, Toronto, ON, M4W 3B8, 416/921-4925; Fax: 416/921-1353

Vancouver: Consul, Walid Maciel Chaves Saad, #904, 700 West Pender St., BC V6C 1G8, 604/688-6514; Fax: 604/685-7042

Winnipeg: Consul, Gustavo Uriel da Roza, Jr., #908, 167 Lombard Ave., MB R3B 1N7, 204/943-8941

## State of Qatar

Embassy of Qatar (to Canada), c/o Mission to the United Nations: 4200 Wisconsin Ave., Washington DC 20016

202/274-1603; Fax: 202/237-0061

Ambassador, His Excellency Saad Mohamed Al-Kobaisi

## Republic of Romania

Embassy of Romania: 655 Rideau St., Ottawa ON K1N 6A3

613/789-3709; Fax: 613/789-4365

Ambassador, His Excellency Tudorel Postolache

Minister-Counsellor, Ioan Sebastian Anastasescu

Montréal: Acting Consul General, Nicolae Liute, #M01.04, 1111, rue St. Urbain, QC H2Z 1X6, 514/876-1792; Fax: 514/876-1797

Toronto: Consul General, Ilie Puscas, #530, 111 Peter St., ON M5V 2H1, 416/585-5802; Fax: 416/585-4798

## Russian Federation

Embassy of the Russian Federation: 285 Charlotte St., Ottawa ON K1N 8L5

613/235-4341; Fax: 613/236-6342

Consular Section: 52 Range Rd., Ottawa K1N 8J5, 613/236-7220; Fax: 613/238-6158

Ambassador, His Excellency Alexander M. Belonogov

Minister-Counsellor, Mikhail Lyssenko

Counsellor, Commercial, Valeri Makharadze

Counsellor, Consular, Iouri Kouteinikov

Montréal: Consul General, Nikoli Smirnov, 3685, av du Musée, QC H3G 2E1, 514/843-5901; Fax: 514/842-2012

Trade Section: 95 Wurtemburg St., Ottawa ON K1N 8Z7, 613/236-1222; Fax: 613/238-2951

## Rwandese Republic

121 Sherwood Dr., Ottawa ON K1Y 3V1

613/722-5835; Fax: 613/722-4052

Ambassador, His Excellency Valens Munyabagisha

Counsellor, Augustin Mukama

North York: Hon. Consul, Ronald Heynneman, #102, 211 Consumers St., ON M2J 4G8, 416/493-5474; Fax: 416/493-8171

## Saint Kitts & Nevis *c/o* Organization of the Eastern Caribbean States

Halifax: Hon. Consul, E. Anthony Ross, CLL Group Building, #602, 2695 Dutch Village Rd., NS B3L 4T9, 902/455-9090

## Saint Lucia *c/o* Organization of the Eastern Caribbean States

Markham: Consul, Dunstan Fontenelle, 3 Dewberry Dr., ON L3S 2R7, 416/472-1423; Fax: 416/472-6379

## Saint Vincent & the Grenadines *c/o* Organization of the Eastern Caribbean States

North York: Consul for Saint Vincent & the Grenadines, Burns Bonadie, 210 Sheppard Ave. East, Ground Fl., ON M2N 3A9, 416/222-0745; Fax: 416/222-3830

## San Marino

Toronto: Hon. Consul, Germano Valle, #1104, 15 McMurrich St., ON M5R 3M6, 416/971-4848; Fax: 416/971-4849

## Democratic Republic of Sao Tomé & Principe

c/o Permanent Mission of Sao Tomé & Principe to the U.N.: #1604, 122 East 42nd St., New York NY 10168

212/697-4211; Fax: 212/687-8389

Ambassador, Vacant

First Secretary, Domingos Ferreira

Montréal: Hon. Consul, Alain Berranger, 4068, av Beaconsfield, QC H4A 2H3, 514/484-2706

## Kingdom of Saudi Arabia

Royal Embassy of Saudi Arabia: #901, 99 Bank St., Ottawa ON K1P 6B9

613/237-4100; Fax: 613/237-0567

Consular Section: 613/237-4104

First Secretary, Hassan Attar

Ambassador, Vacant

## Republic of Senegal

Embassy of Senegal: 57 Marlborough Ave., Ottawa ON K1N 8E8

613/238-6392; Fax: 613/238-2695

Ambassador, His Excellency Pierre Diouf

Minister-Counsellor, César Coly

Toronto: Hon. Consul, Leila Joy MacKenzie, 97 Old Forest Hill Rd., ON M5P 2R8, 416/282-4676

**Serbia *c/o* Federal Republic of Yugoslavia**

## Republic of Seychelles

High Commission for Seychelles (to Canada): #900F, 820 Second Ave., New York NY 10017

212/687-9766; Fax: 212/922-9177

High Commissioner, Vacant

Montréal: Hon. Consul, Gerard Le Chêne, #403, 417, rue St-Pierre, QC H2Y 2M4, 514/284-2199

## Republic of Singapore

c/o Permanent Mission of the Republic of Singapore to the U.N.: 231 East 51st St., New York NY 10022

212/826-0840; Fax: 212/826-2964

High Commissioner, Bilahari Kausikan

Vancouver: Hon. Consul General, Hon. N.T. Nemetz, C.C., Q.C., #1305, 999 Hastings St. West, BC V6C 2W2, 604/669-5115; Fax: 604/669-5153

## Slovak Republic

Embassy of the Slovak Republic: 50 Rideau Terrace, Ottawa ON K1M 2A1

613/749-4442; Fax: 613/749-4989

Email: slovak@pccs.ca; URL: http://www.slovak.com/can_embassy/

Chargé d'Affaires, a.i. Stanislav Opiela

First Secretary, Economic & Commercial Affairs, Stanislav Polonsky

Second Secretary, Milan Kollár

Calgary: Hon. Consul, Ludovit Zanzotto, 208 Scenic Glen Place NW, AB T3L 1K3, 403/239-3543

Dollard des Ormeaux: Hon. Consul, Mark Kmec, 36 Paddington, QC H9G 2S4, 514/626-9779; Fax: 514/626-9779

Toronto: Hon. Consul, John Stephens, #407, 1280 Finch Ave. West, ON M3J 3K6, 416/665-1499; Fax: 416/665-7488

Vancouver: Hon. Consul, Stanislav Lisiak, 5646 Eagle Court, BC V7R 4V4, 604/732-4439; Fax: 604/904-0301

Winnipeg: Hon. Consul, Jozef Kiska, 99 Grace St., MB R3B 0E4, 204/947-1728

## Republic of Slovenia

Embassy of Slovenia: #2101, 150 Metcalfe St., Ottawa ON K2P 1P1

613/565-5781; Fax: 613/565-5783

Minister-Plenipotentiary, Mitja Strukelj

Second Secretary, Goran Kriz

## Solomon Islands

High Commission c/o Permanent Mission to the U.N.: #800B, 820 - 2 Ave., New York NY 10017

212/599-6194

High Commissioner Designate, His Excellency Rex Stephen Horoi

## Republic of South Africa

High Commission for South Africa: 15 Sussex Dr., Ottawa ON K1M 1M8

613/744-0330; Fax: 613/741-1639

Email: safrica@ottawa.net; URL: http://www.docuweb.ca/SouthAfrica/

High Commissioner, His Excellency B.l.L. Modise

Montréal: Consul, Heyn van Rooyen, #2615, 1, Place Ville Marie, QC H3B 4S3, 514/878-9217; Fax: 514/878-4751

Toronto: Consul General, Patrick Evans, #2300, 2 First Canadian Place, PO Box 424, ON M5X 1E3, 416/364-0314; Fax: 416/364-1737

## Kingdom of Spain

Embassy of Spain: 74 Stanley Ave., Ottawa ON K1M 1P4

613/747-2252, 7293; Fax: 613/744-1224

Email: spain@ott.hookup.net

Ambassador, His Excellency Fernando M. Valenzuela

Minister-Counsellor, Luis F. de Segovia

Defence Attaché, Col. Antonio Diaz Rojas

Counsellor, Cultural, Enrique Viguera

Counsellor, Commercial, Alfonso Carbajo

Counsellor, Labour, José Antonio Bocanegra

Attaché, Education, José Félix Barrio

Burnaby: Hon. Consul, Joaquin Ayala, 3736 Parker St., BC V5C 3B1, 604/299-7760; Fax: 604/255-2532

Calgary: Hon. Consul, Steve Jaksi, #2402, 835 - 6th Ave. SW, AB T2P 0V4, 403/237-5975

Halifax: Hon. Vice Consul, Louis Holmes, 82 Bedford Hills Rd., NS B4A IJ9, 902/835-4900; Fax: 902/835-9439

Montréal: Consul General, José Maria Castroviejo, #1456, 1 Westmount Sq., QC H3Z 2P9, 514/935-5235; Fax: 514/935-4655

Montréal: Consul, Commercial, Fernando Baiget, Place Bonaventure, Mart E, CP 1137, QC H5A 1G4, 514/866-4914

Québec: Hon. Vice Consul, François Robitaille St-Cyr, 1085, av Bougainville, QC G1S 3B1, 418/688-9872

St. John's: Hon. Vice Consul, Nathaniel J. Cooper, 87 Water St., PO Box 5128, NF A1C 5V6, 709/726-8000; Fax: 709/726-9891

Toronto: Consul General, Mariano Alonso-Burón, #400, 1200 Bay St., ON M5R 2A5, 416/967-4949; Fax: 416/925-4949

Toronto: Consul, Commercial, Arturo Pina, #1204, 55 Bloor St. West, ON M4W 1A5, 416/967-0488; Fax: 416/968-9547

Toronto: Consul, Tourism, Fernando Villalba, 2 Bloor St. West, 34th Fl., ON M4W 3E2, 416/961-3131; Fax: 416/961-1992

Toronto: Hon. Vice-Consul, Pedro Arenas, 199 McAllister Rd., ON M3H 2P1, 416/630-4673

Winnipeg: Hon. Vice Consul, Donald Allan Green, 1025 Buchanan Blvd., MB R2Y 1N7, 204/831-6033

## Democratic Socialist Republic of Sri Lanka

High Commission of the Democratic Socialist Republic of Sri Lanka: #1204, 333 Laurier Ave. West, Ottawa ON K1P 1C1

613/233-8449; Fax: 613/238-8448

Email: lankacom@magi.com; URL: http://www.magi.com/~lankacom

High Commissioner, His Excellency A.C. Goonasekera

Minister-Counsellor, S.B. Weragama

Counsellor, Information, Mohan Samarasinghe

First Secretary, Commercial, Sonali Wijeratne

Third Secretary, Sweenie de Silva

Attaché, L.G. Silva

Vancouver: Hon. Consul, Mir Ihor Huculak, #807, 938 Howe St., BC V6Z 1N9, 604/331-2505; Fax: 604/331-2515

## Republic of The Sudan

Embassy of The Sudan: #507, 85 Range Rd., Ottawa ON K1N 8J6

613/235-4000, 4999; Fax: 613/235-6880

Minister-Counsellor, Elfadil O.M. Ahmed

## Republic of Suriname

Embassy of Suriname (to Canada): #108, 4301 Connecticut Ave. NW, Washington DC 20008

202/244-7488; Fax: 202/244-5878

Ambassador, Willem A. Udenhout

Toronto: Hon. Consul, William A. Basztyk, #210, 260 Adelaide St. East, ON M5A 1N0, 416/492-0006; Fax: 416/492-0722

## Kingdom of Swaziland

High Commission for Swaziland: #1204, 130 Albert St., Ottawa ON K1P 5G4

613/567-1480; Fax: 613/567-1058

High Commissioner, His Excellency Bremer M. Nxumalo

First Secretary, S. Ntshangase

Third Secretary, Ambrose H. Maziya

Administrative Attaché, Khetsiwe V. Maseko

## Kingdom of Sweden

Embassy of Sweden: 377 Dalhousie St., Ottawa ON K1N 9N8

613/241-8553; Fax: 613/241-2277

Email: sweden@cyberus.ca

Ambassador, His Excellency Jan Stahl

Counsellor, Ulf Lindell

Calgary: Consul, Gunilla Mungan, 1039 Durham Ave. SW, AB T2T 0P8, 403/541-0354; Fax: 403/244-7728

Edmonton: Consul, Donald G. Bishop, c/o Bishop & McKenzie, #2500, 10104 - 103 Ave., AB T5J 1V3, 403/426-5550; Fax: 403/426-1305

Fredericton: Consul, Allen M. Ruben, c/o Ruben & Kingston, #301, 259 Brunswick St., NB E3B 5C2, 506/458-0000; Fax: 506/451-8766

Halifax: Consul, Kaj Nielsen, c/o Volvo Canada, PO Box 2027, NS B3J 2Z1, 902/450-5252; Fax: 902/450-5272

Montréal: Consul, Lionel Hurtubise, c/o Ericsson Communications Inc., 8400, boul Decarie, QC H4P 2N2, 514/345-2727; Fax: 514/345-7972

Québec: Consul General, Paule Gauthier, c/o Desjardins Ducharme Stein Monast Le St-Amable, #300, 1150 Claire Fontaine, QC G1R 5G4, 418/640-4437; Fax: 418/523-5391

Regina: Consul, Ronald E. Shirkey, #325, 2550 - 15 Ave., SK S4P 1A5, 306/359-1000; Fax: 306/359-3300

St. John's: Consul, Albert Hickman, 85 Kenmount Rd., PO Box 8340, Stn A, NF A1B 3N7, 709/726-6990; Fax: 709/726-4003

Toronto: Consul General, Robert Stocks, #1504, 2 Bloor St. West, ON M4W 3E2, 416/963-8768; Fax: 416/923-8809

Vancouver: Consul General, Magnus Ericson, #1100, 1188 West Georgia St., BC V6E 4A2, 604/683-5838; Fax: 604/687-8237

Winnipeg: Consul, Neil E. Carlson, 1035 Mission St., MB R2J 0A4, 204/233-3373; Fax: 204/233-6938

## Swiss Confederation

Embassy of Switzerland: 5 Marlborough Ave., Ottawa ON K1N 8E6

613/235-1837; Fax: 613/563-1394

Email: 106335.3143@compuserve.com

Ambassador, His Excellency Daniel Dayer

Ministre, Betrand Louis

Calgary: Hon. Consul, Klaus D. Zahnd, Sun Life Plaza West Tower, 1220, 144 - 4th Ave. SW, AB T2P 3N4, 403/233-8919; Fax: 403/269-3048

Edmonton: Hon. Consul, Bruno Dobler, 4926 - 89 St., AB T6E 5K1, 403/462-9221; Fax: 403/463-6319

Montréal: Consul General, Albert Mehr, 1572, av Dr. Penfield, QC H3G 1C4, 514/932-7181; Fax: 514/932-9028

Québec: Hon. Consul, Jean-Pierre Beltrami, 3293, 1ere av, QC G1L 3R2, 418/623-9864; Fax: 418/623-6644

Toronto: Consul General, Claude Duboulet, #601, 154 University Ave., ON M5H 3Y9, 416/593-5371; Fax: 416/593-5083

Vancouver: Consul General, Robert Wenger, World Trade Centre, #790, 999 Canada Place, BC V6C 3E1, 604/684-2231; Fax: 604/684-2806

## Syrian Arab Republic

Embassy of Syria (to Canada): 2215 Wyoming Ave. NW, Washington DC 20008

202/232-6313; Fax: 202/234-9548

Ambassador, His Excellency Walid Al-Moualem

Montréal: Hon. Consul General, Fares M. Attar, #109-110, 111 St. Urbain, QC H2Z 1Y6, 514/397-9595; Fax: 514/397-6801

## United Republic of Tanzania

High Commission for Tanzania: 50 Range Rd., Ottawa ON K1N 8J4

613/232-1500; Fax: 613/232-5184

High Commissioner, His Excellency Fadhil D. Mbaga

## Kingdom of Thailand

Royal Thai Embassy: 180 Island Park Dr., Ottawa ON K1Y 0A2

613/722-4444; Fax: 613/722-6624

Email: thai_ott@cyberus.ca

Commercial Section: 1801, 275 Slater St., Ottawa ON K1P 5H9, 613/238-4002; Fax: 613/238-6226

Ambassador, His Excellency Virasakdi Futrakul

Minister, Cholchineepan Chiranond

Minister-Counsellor, Commercial, Prasit Lisawad

Edmonton: Hon. Consul, Kurt Beier, 8625 - 112 St., AB T6G 1K8, 403/469-3576; Fax: 403/432-1387

Montréal: Hon. Consul General, Marc J. Besso, #224, 759, Victoria Sq., QC H2Y 2J7, 514/985-0666; Fax: 514/985-3237

Toronto: Hon. Consul General, Richard C. Meech, Q.C., 44th Fl., Scotia Plaza, 40 King St. West, ON M5H 3Y4, 416/367-6750; Fax: 416/367-6749

Vancouver: Consul General, Chamni Ridthiprasart, #501, 700 West Pender St., BC V6C 1G8, 604/687-1143; Fax: 604/687-6775

## Republic of Togo

Embassy of Togo: 12 Range Rd., Ottawa ON K1N 8J3

613/238-5916,5917; Fax: 613/235-6425

Ambassador, Vacant

Minister-Counsellor, Biam Bidinabé Hodjo

Calgary: Hon. Consul, Garry Tarrant, #700, 1207 - 11 Ave., AB T3C 0M5, 403/229-0103; Fax: 403/245-5156

Toronto: Hon. Consul, Paul John Tuz, 519 Spadina Rd., ON M5P 2W6, 416/489-4849

Verdun: Hon. Consul, Gérard Shanks, Verdun Consulate, 484 - 5 Ave., QC H4G 2K1, 514/769-4888

## Republic of Trinidad & Tobago

High Commission for Trinidad & Tobago: #508, 75 Albert St., Ottawa ON K1P 5E7

613/232-2418; Fax: 613/232-4349

Email: tthcotta@travel-net.com; URL: http://www.travel-net.com-ttcotta

High Commissioner, His Excellency Robert Sabga

Deputy High Commissioner, Stephen Kangal

First Secretary, Dennison Webster

North York: Consul General, Cyril Blanchfield, #303, 2005 Sheppard Ave. East, ON M2J 5B4, 416/495-9442; Fax: 416/495-6934

## Republic of Tunisia

Embassy of Tunisia: 515 O'Connor St., Ottawa ON K1S 3P8

613/237-0330; Fax: 613/237-7939

Ambassador, His Excellency Habib Lazreg

Montréal: Hon. Consul, Emile Colas, #501, 511, Place d'Armes, QC H2Y 2W7, 514/289-8633; Fax: 514/288-6469

North York: Hon. Consul, Carl Stockman, #200, 2 Sheppard Ave. East, ON M2N 5Y7, 416/226-6565; Fax: 416/226-6576

Vancouver: Hon. Consul, Lyall Knott, #800, 885 West Georgia St., BC V6C 3H1, 604/687-5700

## Republic of Turkey

Embassy of Turkey: 197 Wurtemburg St., Ottawa ON K1N 8L9

613/789-4044; Fax: 613/789-3442

Ambassador, His Excellency Omer Ersun

Counsellor, Osman Getintas

Counsellor, Commercial, Deger Berkol

Counsellor, Economic, Mehmet B. Tutuncu

Montréal: Hon. Consul General, Ali T. Argun, #2500, 1100, boul René-Lévesque ouest, QC H3B 5C9, 514/397-6903; Fax: 514/397-8515

## Republic of Uganda

High Commission for Uganda: 231 Cobourg St., Ottawa ON K1N 8J2

613/789-7797; Fax: 613/789-8909

Minister-Counsellor, James H.O. Okullo

High Commissioner, His Excellency William Weasa Wamimbi

Vancouver: Hon. Consul, John Halani, 1361 Robson St., BC V6E 1C6, 604/687-6631; Fax: 604/687-5724

## Republic of Ukraine

Embassy of Ukraine: 310 Somerset St. West, Ottawa ON K2P 0J9

613/230-2961; Fax: 613/230-2400

Consular Section: 613/230-8015

Consular Section: 331 Metcalfe St., Ottawa ON K2P 1S3, 613/230-8015; Fax: 613/230-2655

Ambassador, His Excellency Volodymyz Furkalo

Commissioner, Trade, Igor Sanin

## United Arab Emirates

c/o Permanent Mission of the United Arab Emirates to the U.N.: 747 Third Ave., 36th Fl., New York NY 10017

212/371-0480; Fax: 212/371-4923

Ambassador, His Excellency Mohammed J. Samhan

Counsellor, Khalid K. Al-Mualla

First Secretary, Yacub Y. Al-Hosani

## United Kingdom of Great Britain & Northern Ireland

British High Commission: 80 Elgin St., Ottawa ON K1P 5K7

613/237-1530; Fax: 613/237-7980

High Commissioner, His Excellency Sir Anthony M. Goodenough, K.C.M.G.

Deputy High Commissioner, Linda Duffield

Counsellor, Economic & Commercial, Martin Uden

Counsellor, Robert M.F. Kelly

Dartmouth: Hon. Consul, A.A. Smithers, 1 Canal St., PO Box 605, NS B2Y 3YB, 902/461-1381; Fax: 902/463-7678

Montréal: Consul General, I. Rawlinson, #4200, 1000, rue De La Gauchetière ouest, QC H3B 4W5, 514/866-5863; Fax: 514/866-0202

St. John's: Hon. Consul, Frank D. Smith, 113 Topsail Rd., NF A1E 2A9, 709/579-2002; Fax: 709/579-0475

Toronto: Consul General, Terrence Curran, College Park, #2800, 777 Bay St., ON M5G 2G2, 416/593-1290; Fax: 416/593-1229

Vancouver: Consul General, B.P. Austin, #800, 1111 Melville St., BC V6E 3V6, 604/683-4421; Fax: 604/681-0693

Winnipeg: Hon. Consul, R.E.M. Hill, 229 Athlone Dr., MB R3J 3L6, 204/896-1380; Fax: 204/269-3025

## United States of America

Embassy of U.S.A.: 100 Wellington St., PO Box 866, Stn B, Ottawa ON K1P 5T1

613/238-5335; Fax: 613/238-8750

Consular Section: 85 Albert St., Ottawa ON K1P 6A4, 613/238-5335

Ambassador, Gordon D. Giffin

Minister, The Hon. Thomas G. Weston

Minister-Counsellor, Foreign Commercial Affairs, Dale V. Slaght

Minister-Counsellor, Environment, Science & Technological Affairs, Susan M. Lysyshyn

Calgary: Consul General, Richard V. Fisher, #1050, 615 Macleod Trail SE, AB T2G 4T8, 403/266-8962

Halifax: Consul General, R. Bruce Erhnman, Scotia Sq., 910 Cogswell Tower, NS B3J 3K1, 902/429-2480; Fax: 902/423-6861

Montréal: Consul General, Eleanor Savage, 455, boul René-Lévesque, PO Box 65, Stn Desjardins, QC H2Z 1Z2, 514/398-9695; Fax: 514/398-0973

Québec: Consul General, Stephen. Kelly, 2, Place Terrasse Dufferin, PO Box 939, QC G1R 4T9, 418/692-2095; Fax: 418/692-4640

Toronto: Consul General, Gregory L. Johnson, 360 University Ave., ON M5G 1S4, 416/595-1700

Vancouver: Consul General, Judson L. Bruns, 1095 West Pender St., BC V6E 4E9, 604/685-4311; Fax: 604/685-5285

## Eastern Republic of Uruguay

Embassy of Uruguay: #1905, 130 Albert St., Ottawa ON K1P 5G4

613/234-2727; Fax: 613/233-4670

Email: urott@iosphere.net; URL: http://www.sonetis.com/~urott

Consular Section: 234-2937

Ambassador, Elbio Rosselli

First Secretary, Eduardo Anon

Second Secretary, Carlos Gitto

North York: Hon. Consul, Carlos Garcia, #1610, 2 Sheppard Ave. East, ON M2N 5Y7, 416/221-7799; Fax: 416/221-7199
Vancouver: Hon. Consul, Conrado Beckerman, 827 West Pender St., BC V6C 3G8, 604/681-1377; Fax: 604/731-6775

## Holy See (Vatican)
Apostolic Nunciature: 724 Manor Ave., Rockcliffe Park, Ottawa ON K1M 0E3
613/746-4914; Fax: 613/746-4786
Apolistic Nuncio, His Excellency The Most Rev. Carlo Curis
First Secretary, The Right Rev. Vito Rallo

## Republic of Venezuela
Embassy of Venezuela: 32 Range Rd., Ottawa ON K1N 8J4
613/235-5151; Fax: 613/235-3205
Email: embaven@ottawa.net; URL: http://www.ottawa.net/~embaven/
Ambassador, His Excellency José Ignacio Moreno Léon
Minister-Counsellor, Velia M. Villegas
Counsellor, Marisol Black
Montréal: Consul General, Nelly Pulido de Tagliaferro, #400, 2055, rue Peel, QC H3A 1V4, 514/842-3417; Fax: 514/287-7101
Toronto: Consul General, Hilda Hernandez, #1904, 365 Bloor St. East, ON M4W 3L4, 416/960-6070; Fax: 416/960-6077

## Socialist Republic of Vietnam
Embassy of Vietnam: 226 MacLaren St., Ottawa ON K2P 0L6
613/236-0772; Consular Section 236-1398; Fax: 613/236-2704; Consular Section 236-0819
Ambassador, His Excellency Dinh Thi Minh Huyen
Counsellor, Commercial, Tran Ve

## Western Samoa
High Commission for Western Samoa (to Canada): #800D, 820 Second Ave., New York NY 10017
212/599-6196; Fax: 212/599-0797
URL: http://www.interwebinc.com/samoa/
High Commissioner, His Excellency Tuiloma Neroni Slade

## Republic of Yemen
Embassy of the Republic of Yemen: 788 Island Park Dr., Ottawa ON K1Y 0C2
613/729-6627; Fax: 613/729-8915
Ambassador, His Excellency Dr. Mohamed Hazza Mohamed
Minister-Plenipotentiary, Abdulmalek Saleh

## Federal Republic of Yugoslavia
Embassy of Yugoslavia: 17 Blackburn Ave., Ottawa ON K1N 8A2
613/233-6289; Fax: 613/233-7850
First Secretary & Chargé d'Affaires, A. Mitic
Ambassador, Vacant
Montréal: Hon. Consul, Kalman Samuels, 1200, rue du Fort, QC H3H 2B3, 514/939-1200

## Republic of Zambia
High Commission for Zambia (to Canada): 2419 Massachusetts Ave. NW, Washington DC 20008
202/265-9717; Fax: 202/332-0826
Email: zambia@tmn.com
High Commissioner, His Excellency Dunstan W. Kamana

## Republic of Zimbabwe
High Commission for the Republic of Zimbabwe: 332 Somerset St. West, Ottawa ON K2P 0J9
613/237-4388; Fax: 613/563-8269
Email: zim.highcomm@sympatico.ca; URL: http://www.docuweb.ca/zimbabwe
High Commissioner, Her Excellency Lillie Chitauro
Counsellor, Commercial, Wilbert C.T.T. Dumba
Counsellor, Reward Marufu

# CANADIAN DIPLOMATIC REPRESENTATIVES ABROAD

### Republic of Albania *c/o* Republic of Hungary

## People's Democratic Republic of Algeria
Canadian Embassy: 27 bis, rue des Frères Benhafid, Hydra
(011-213-2) 69-16-11; Fax: (011-213-2) 69-39-20
Email: alger@paris03.x400.gc.ca
Postal Address: PO Box 225, Alger-Gare, Algeria
Ambassador, Franco D. Pillarella
Counsellor, Commercial, W.A. McKenzie
Commercial Officer, Zahra Bensalah, Email: zahra.bensalah@paris03.x400.gc.ca

### Principality of Andorra *c/o* Kingdom of Spain

## People's Republic of Angola *c/o* Republic of Zimbabwe
Luanda: Hon. Consul, Allan Cain, Honourary Consulate of Canada, Rua Rei Katyavala #113, Angola, (011-244-2) 348-371; Fax: (011-244-2) 343-754 (2100-0800hrs Angola time)

### Anguilla *c/o* Barbados

### Antigua & Barbuda *c/o* Barbados

## Argentine Republic
Canadian Embassy: Tagle 2828, 1425, Buenos Aires
(011-54-1) 805-3032; Fax: (011-54-1) 806-1209
Email: commerce@bairs01.x400.gc.ca
Postal Address: Casilla de Correo 1598, Buenos Aires, Argentina
Ambassador, Robert G. Clark
First Secretary, Commercial & Economic, S. Harper
Ambassador, Uruguay, Roland Goulet
Commercial Officer, Elena Masciarelli, Email: elena.masciarelli@bairs01.x400.gc.ca

### Republic of Armenia *c/o* Russian Federation

### Aruba *c/o* Republic of Venezuela

## Commonwealth of Australia
Canadian High Commission: Commonwealth Ave., Canberra ACT 2600
(011-61-6) 273-3844; Fax: (011-61-2) 273-3285
Email: cnbra.td@cnbra01.x400.gc.ca
High Commissioner, Brian Schumacher
Deputy High Commissioner, G.J. Wilson
Counsellor, Commercial, J.F. Donaghy
Commercial Officer (Sydney), Robert G. Gow, (011-61-2) 364-3000; Fax: (011-61-2) 364-3098; Email: Bob.Gow@sydny01.x400.gc.ca
Melbourne: Hon. Consul, T. Moore, Honorary Consulate of Canada, 123 Camberwell Rd., East Hawthorn, VIC 3123, Australia, (011-61-03) 9811-9999; Fax: (011-61-03) 9811-9969
Perth: Hon. Consul, R.B. Blake, Honorary Consulate of Canada, 267 St. George's Terrace, 3rd Fl., WA 6000, Australia, (011-61-09) 322-7930
Sydney: Consul General, Alan Virtue, Canadian Consulate General, Quay West Bldg, Level 5, 111 Harrington St., NSW 2000, Australia, (011-61-2) 364-3000; Fax: (011-61-2) 364-3098

## Republic of Austria
Canadian Embassy: Laurenzerber 2, A - 1010, Vienna
(011-43-1) 531-38-3000; Fax: (011-43-1) 531-38-3321
Email: commerce@vienn02.x400.gc.ca
Ambassador, Peter F. Walker
Counsellor, Commercial, T. Marr
Minister-Counsellor, P. McKellar
Commercial Officer, Roland J. Rossi, Email: roland.rossi@vienn02.x400.gc.ca

### Republic of Azerbaijan *c/o* Republic of Turkey

### Azores *c/o* Portuguese Republic

## Commonwealth of the Bahamas *c/o* Jamaica
Nassau: Hon. Consul, H.A. Jacobsen, Honorary Consulate of Canada, Shirley Street Plaza, PO Box SS-6371, Bahamas, 809/393-2123; Fax: 809/393-1305

### State of Bahrain *c/o* State of Kuwait

## People's Republic of Bangladesh
Canadian High Commission: House CWN 16/A, Rd. 48, Gulshan Ave., Dhaka
(011-880-2) 88-70-91; Fax: (011-88-2) 88-30-43
Postal Address: GPO Box 569, 1000 Dhaka, Bangladesh
High Commissioner, Nicholas Etheridge
Counsellor, Development, J. Deyell
Senior Commercial Officer, Syed Shamimur Rahman, Email: syed.rahman@dhaka01.x400.gc.ca

## Barbados
Canadian High Commission: Bishop's Court Hill, PO Box 404, St. Michael
809/429-3550; Fax: 809/437-3780
High Commissioner, Colleen Swords
Counsellor, K. Harley
Trade Commissioner, Peter Hermant
Counsellor, Development, N. Norcott

### Republic of Belarus *c/o* Russian Federation

## Kingdom of Belgium
Canadian Embassy: 2, av de Tervuren, B - 1040, Brussels
(011-32-2) 741-0611; Fax: (011-32-2) 741-0606
Email: commerce@bru03.x400.gc.ca
Ambassador, Jean-Paul Hubert
Minister/Counsellor, G. Béchard
Counsellor, Commercial/Economic, S. Doyon
Commercial Officer, Fabienne Dekimpe, Email: fabienne.dekimpe@bur03.x400.gc.ca

## Belize *c/o* Jamaica
Belize City: Lester Young, Hon. Consul, Honorary Consulate of Canada, 85 North Front St., PO Box

610, Belize, (011-501-02) 33-722; Fax: (011-501-02) 30-060

### Republic of Benin *c/o* Republic of Côte d'Ivoire

### Bermuda *c/o* United States of America

## Republic of Bolivia *c/o* Republic of Peru
La Paz: Hon. Consul, Hector Arduz, Honorary Consulate of Canada, Av 20 de octubre 2475, Plaza Avaroa, Sopocachi, PO Box 13045, Bolivia, (011-591-2) 431-215; Fax: (011-591-2) 432-330

## Bosnia & Herzegovina
The Canadian Embassy: Logavina 7, 71000, Sarajevo
(011-387-71) 447-900; Fax: (011-387-71) 447-901
Ambassador, Serge Marcoux

## Republic of Botswana *c/o* Republic of Zimbabwe
Gaborone: Hon. Consul, D. Leonard, Honorary Consulate of Canada, PO Box 1009, Botswana, (011-267) 30-44-11

## Federative Republic of Brazil
Canadian Embassy: Setor de Embaixadas Sul, #803, Ava das Naçcoes, lote 16, 70410-900, Brasilia, D.F.
(011-55-61) 321-2171; Fax: (011-55-61) 321-4529
Postal Address: Caixa Postal 00961, 70359-900 Brasilia D.F., Brazil
Ambassador, Nancy M. Stiles
Counsellor & Consul, B. Wilkin
Counsellor, Commercial/Economic, P. Williams
Commercial Officer (Sao Paulo), Mariangela Olivieri de Lima
Rio de Janeiro: Hon. Consul, Jack Delmar, Honourary Consulate of Canada, Rua Lauro Muller 166, #2707, Torre Rio Sul, Botafogo, 22290-160, Brazil, (011-55-21) 542-7593; Fax: (011-55-21) 275-2195
Sao Paulo: Consul General, Michael C. Spencer, Canadian Consulate General, Edificio Top Centre, Ava Paulista 1106, 1st Floor, 01310-100, Brazil, (011-55-11) 287-2122; Fax: (011-55-11) 251-5057; Email: spalo.td@spalo01.x400.gc.ca

### British Virgin Islands *c/o* Barbados

## Brunei
Canadian High Commission: #51, Britannia House, Jalan Cator, Bandar Seri Begawn
(011-673-2) 22-00-43; Fax: (011-673-2) 22-00-40
Postal Address: PO Box 2808, Bandar Seri Begawan 1928, Brunei
High Commissioner, Gardiner James Wilson
Counsellor, Development, M. Archambault
Counsellor, Development, T. Broughton

## Republic of Bulgaria *c/o* Republic of Romania
Sofia: Hon. Consul, L. Hampartzoumian, Honourary Consulate of Canada, Coopers & Lybrand (Sofia), 3, Positano St., 1000, Bulgaria, (011-359-2) 81-55-76; Fax: (011-359-2) 80-32-20

## Burkina-Faso
Canadian Embassy: Agostino Neto St., PO Box 548, Ouagaougou
(011-226) 31-18-94; Fax: (011-226) 31-19-00
Postal Address: PO Box 548, Ouagadougou 01, Kadiogo, Burkina-Faso

Ambassador, Jules Savaria
First Secretary, Development, S. Ostiguy

## Republic of Burundi *c/o* Republic of Kenya
Bujumbura: Hon Consul, J.M.A. Persoons, Honorary Consulate of Canada, boul du 28 novembre, CP 5, Burundi, (011-257) 22-16-32; Fax: (011-257) 22-28-16

## Kingdom of Cambodia
Canadian Embassy: Villa 9, Senei Vinnavaut Oum, Sangkat Chaktamouk, Khand Daun Penh, Phnom Penh
(011-855-23) 426-000; Fax: (011-855-23) 211-389
Ambassador, Gordon Longmuir

## Republic of Cameroon
Canadian Embassy: Immeuble Stamatiades, Place de l'Hôtel de Ville, Yaoundé
(011-237) 22-19-36; Fax: (011-237) 22-10-90
Email: MITNET: 317-0000
Cable: DOMCAN YAOUNDÉ
Postal Address: PO Box 572, Yaoundé, Cameroon
Ambassador, Pierre Siguère
Counsellor, Development, P. Marion
Douala: Hon. Consul, L. LeGuerrier, The Consulate of Canada, Avenue de Gaulle 1726, P.B. 2373, Bonanjo,, (011-237) 42-31-03; Fax: (011-237) 42-31-09

### Republic of Cape Verde *c/o* Republic of Senegal

### Cayman Islands *c/o* Jamaica

## Central African Republic *c/o* Republic of Cameroon
Quartier Sissongo Bangui: Hon. Consul, Lyne Godmaire, Honorary Consulate of Canada, PO Box 973, Central African Republic

### Republic of Chad *c/o* Republic of Cameroon

## Republic of Chile
Canadian Embassy: Nueva Tajamar 481, 12th Fl., Santiago
(011-56-2) 362-9660; Fax: (011-56-2) 362-9663
Email: stago.td@stago01.x400.gc.ca
Postal Address: Casilla 139, Correo 10, Santiago, Chile
Ambassador, David Lederman
Counsellor, Commercial, P. Furesz
Commercial Officer, Margot Edwards
Conception: Hon. Consul, F. Trucco, Honorary Consulate of Canada, a/s Isapre Mas Vida, Caupolican III, PO Box 425, Chile, (011-56-41) 235-650

## People's Republic of China
Canadian Embassy: 19 Dong Zhi Men Wai St., Chao Yang Dist., Beijing 100600
(011-86-10) 6532-3536; Fax: (011-86-10) 6532-4311
Email: bejing.td@bejing03.x400.gc.ca
Ambassador, Howard Balloch
Minister, Commercial, K. Sunquist
Minister-Counsellor & Consul, G. Saint-Jacques
Third Secretary (Commercial), Ping Kitnikone
Commercial Officer/Interpreter, Q. Chen, Email: qi.chen@bejing03.x400.gc.ca
Guangzhou: Consul, M.C. Boyd, Consulate of Canada, China Hotel Office Tower, #1563-4, Liu Hua Lu, 510015, China, (011-86-20) 666-0569; Fax: (011-86-20) 667-2401
Hong Kong: Consul General, Colin Russel, Hong Kong, Tower 1, Exchange Square, 8 Connaught Place, 11th Fl., China, (011-852) 2810-4321; Fax: (011-852) 2810-6736; Email: td.hkong@hkong02-x400.gc.ca; Website: http://www.canada.org.hk
Shanghai: Consul General, Ted Lipman, Canadian Consulate General, American International Centre, Shanghai Centre, West Tower, #604, 1376 Nanjing Xi Lu, 200040, China, (011-86-21) 6279-8400; Fax: (011-1-86-21) 6279-8401

## Republic of Colombia
Canadian Embassy: Calle 76, No. 11-52, Bogota (011-57-1) 313-1355; Fax: (011-57-1) 316-3046
Email: bgota@bgota01.x400.gc.ca
Postal Address: Apartado Aéreo 53531, Bogota 2, Colombia
Ambassador, Archibald McArthur
Counsellor, Commercial, Z.W. Burianyk
Counsellor & Consul, D. Gillett
Commercial Officer, Carlos E. Rivera, Email: carlos.rivera@bgota01.x400.gc.ca
Cartagena: Hon. Consul, Verona Edelstein, Honourary Consulate of Canada, Edificio Punta Gigante, Apt. 301, Bocagrande Carrera 4, #6-106, Colombia, (011-95) 6658-096; Fax: (011-95) 6650-207

### Islamic Federal Republic of the Comoros *c/o* United Republic of Tanzania

## Democratic Republic of Congo
Canadian Office c/o Embassy of the USA: 310, av des Aviateurs, Kinshasa
(011-243-12) 21-532; Fax: (011-243-88) 43-805
Cable: AMEMBASSY KINSHASA
Head, Canadian Office, Counsellor & Consul, Denis Grégoire-de-Blois

## Republic of Costa Rica
Canadian Embassy: Oficentro Ejecutivo La Sabana - detras de la Contraloria, Sabana Sur, San José
(011-506) 296-4149; Fax: (011-506) 296-4270
Email: canadacr@sol.racsa.co.cr
Apertado Postal 351 - 1077 Centre Colon, San José, Costa Rica
Ambassador, Dan Goodleaf
Counsellor & Consul, G. Lapointe
First Secretary & Consul, Commercial, M. Lebleu
Commercial Officer, Adolfo Quesada V., Email: adolfo.quesada@sjose01.x400.gc.ca

## Republic of Côte d'Ivoire
Canadian Embassy, Immeuble Trade Centre: 23, av Nogùes, Le Plateau, Abidjan
(011-225) 21-20-09; Fax: (011-225) 22-05-30
Email: commerce@abdjn01.x400.gc.ca
Postal Address: PO Box 4104, Abidjan 01, Côte d'Ivoire.
Ambassador, Suzanne Laporte
Counsellor & Consul, G. Paquet
First Secretary, Commercial, P. Veilleux
Commercial Officer, Ousmane Somali

## Republic of Croatia
Canadian Embassy, Hotel Esplanade: Mihanoviceva 1, 10000, Zagreb
(011-385-1) 457-7885; Fax: (011-385-1) 457-7913
Ambassador, Donald W. Smith
Counsellor & Consul, Commercial, R. Lecoq

## Republic of Cuba
Canadian Embassy: Calle 30, No. 518, Esquina a 7a, Miramar, Havana

(011-53-7) 33-25-16; Fax: (011-53-7) 33-20-44
Email: MITNET: 389-0000
Ambassador, Keith H. Christie
Counsellor & Consul, Commercial, R. Mailhot
Varadero: Hon. Consul, Y. des Hayes, Honorary Consulate of Canada, Granma Hotel, Bloque 18, apt. 210, Cuba, (011-56) 64-177; Fax: (011-56) 33-7149

## Republic of Cyprus *c/o* State of Israel
Nicosia: Hon. Consul, M. G. Ioannides, Honorary Consulate of Canada, Margarita House, #403, 15 Themistocles Dervis St., Cyprus, (011-357-2) 45-16-30; Fax: (011-357-2) 45-90-96
Postal Address: PO Box 2125, Nicosia, Cyprus

## Czech Republic
Canadian Embassy: Mickiewiczova 6, 125 33, 6, Prague
(011-42-2) 2431-1108; Fax: (011-42-2) 2431-0294
Ambassador, Ronald Halpin
Counsellor & Consul, Y. Jobin
Counsellor, Commercial, R. Bélanger
Commercial Officer, Pavel Szappanos, Email: pavel.szappanos@prgue01.x400.gc.ca

## Kingdom of Denmark
Canadian Embassy: Kr. Bernikowsgade 1, 1105, Copenhagen
(011-45-33) 12-22-99; Fax: (011-45-33) 14-05-85
Email: copen.td@copen.01x400.gc.ca; MITNET: 460-0000
Ambassador, Brian Baker
R.C.D., Looye, Counsellor & Consul
Counsellor, Commercial, G. Cadieux
Commercial Officer, David Horup
Nuuk: Hon. Consul, L.P. Danielsen, The Consulate of Canada, Groenlandsfly, A/S 3900, Greenland, (011-299) 28-888; Fax: (011-299) 27-288
Postal Address: PO Box 1012, 3900 Nuuk, Greenland

## Republic of Djibouti *c/o* Democratic Republic of Ethiopia
Djibouti: Hon. Consul, R. Arsenault, Honorary Consulate of Canada, c/o SNC-Lavalin, House No. 233, Kampala St., PO Box 914, Djibouti, (011-253) 35-11-59; Fax: (011- 253) 35-44-23

### Commonwealth of Dominica *c/o* Barbados

## Dominican Republic
Canadian Embassy: Maximo Gomez 30, Santo Domingo
809/689-0002; Fax: 809/682-2691
Postal Address: PO Box 2054, Santo Domingo 1, Dominican Republic
Ambassador (resident in Caracas, Venezuela), Yves Gagnon
Counsellor & Consul, Commercial (Caracus, Venezuela), P. Giroux
First Secretary & Consul, Commercial (Caracus, Venezuela), G. Lemieux
Puerto Plata: Hon. Consul, T. Hall, Honorary Consulate of Canada, #3, Beller 51, Dominican Republic, 809/586-5761; Fax: 809/586-5762

## Republic of Ecuador
Edificio Josueth Gonzalez, 4th Fl.: Ava. 6 de Diciembre, 2816, Quito
(011-593-2) 564-795; Fax: (011-593-2) 503-108
Postal Address: PO Box 17-11-6512, Quito, Ecuador
Ambassador, David Adam
Third Secretary & Consul, Administration, M. Felisiak
Guayaquil: Hon. Consul, F. Costa, Honorary Consulate of Canada, General Cordova No. 800 & Victor Manuel Rendon, 21st Fl., Office 6, Ecuador, (011-593-4) 566-747; Fax: (011-593-4) 314-562

## Arab Republic of Egypt
Canadian Embassy: 5 Midan El Saraya el Kobra St., Garden City, Cairo
(011-20-2) 354-3110; Fax: (011-20-2) 354-7659
Postal Address: PO Box 1667, Cairo, Egypt
Ambassador, Michael D. Bell
Counsellor & Consul, Commercial/Economic, D. Paterson
Counsellor, Development, J. Sinclair
Commercial Officer, Hany W. Ibrahim, Email: hany.h.w.i.ibrahim@cairo01.x400.gc.ca
Alexandria: Hon. Consul, A.M.M. Khairy, Honorary Consulate of Canada, Arab Express Shipping Co., 59 El Horria St., Egypt, (011-203) 493-9142; Fax: (011-203) 490-9696

## Republic of El Salvador
Canadian Embassy: Ava Las Palmas no. 111, Colonia San Benito, San Salvador
(011-503-2) 794-655; Fax: (011-503-2) 790-765
Postal Address: Apartado Postal 3078, Centro de Gobierno, San Salvador, El Salvador
Ambassador (Resident in Guatamala City), Daniel Livermore
Hon. Consul, J.D. Hunter
Counsellor, Development (located in Guatamala City), E.W.E. Doe
Counsellor, Development (located in Tegulcigalpa, Honduras), J. Touzel
San Salvador: Hon. Consul, James D. Hunter, Canadian Consulate, 111 Av. Las Palmas, Colonia San Benito, El Salvador, (011-503) 241-648; Fax: (011-503) 790-765
Postal Address: Apartado Postal 3078, Centro de Gobierno, San Salvador

### England *c/o* United Kingdom of Great Britain & Northern Ireland

### Republic of Equatorial Guinea *c/o* Gabonese Republic

### Eritrea *c/o* Democratic Republic of Ethiopia

## Republic of Estonia
Canadian Embassy: Toom Kooli 13, 2nd Fl., 0100, Tallinn
(011-372) 631-3570; Fax: (011-372) 631-3573
Ambassador (located in Stockholm, Sweden), William L. Clarke
Minister-Counsellor (located in Riga, Latvia), G.R. Skinner
First Secretary, Commercial (located in Latvia), H.J. Kunzer

## Democratic Republic of Ethiopia
Canadian Embassy: Old Airport Area, Higher 23, Kebele 12, #122, Addis Ababa
(011-251-1) 71-30-22; Fax: (011-251-1) 71-30-33
Postal Address: PO Box 1130, Addis Ababa, Ethiopia
Ambassador, Gabriel M. Lessard
Counsellor & Consul, Development, P. Hitschfeld
First Secretary & Consul, T. Martin

## European Union
The Mission of Canada to the European Union: av de Tervuren 2, 1040, Brussels
(011-32-2) 741-0660; Fax: (011-32-2) 741-0629
Email: MITNET: 448-3274
Head of Mission, Ambassador, Jean-Pierre Juneau
Deputy Head of Mission & Minister-Counsellor, R. Hage
Counsellor, Economic Affairs, R. Stewart
Counsellor, Science & Technology, W. Coderre
Counsellor, Trade Policy, S. Brereton

### Falkland Islands *c/o* Argentine Republic

### Faroe Islands *c/o* Kingdom of Denmark

## Fiji *c/o* New Zealand
Nadi Airport: Hon. Consul, R. Sharp, Honorary Consulate of Canada, PO Box 10690, Fiji, (011-679) 72-19-36

## Republic of Finland
Canadian Embassy: P. Esplanadi 25B, 00100, Helsinki
(011-358-0) 171-141; Fax: (011-358-0) 601-060
Email: hsnki.td@paris03.x400.gc.ca
Postal Address: PO Box 779, 00101 Helsinki, Finland
Ambassador, Craig T. MacDonald
Counsellor & Consul, J. Pearce
Second Secretary, Administration, R. Flanagan

## French Republic
Canadian Embassy: 35, av Montaigne, 75008, Paris
(011-33-1) 44-43-29-00; Fax: (011-33-1) 44-43-29-98
Email: paris.td@paris02.x400.gc.ca
Ambassador, Jacques Roy
Minister, Noble, J.J. Noble
Minister-Counsellor, Commercial & Economic, B. Côté
Commercial Officer, Linda Bernard, Email: linda.bernard@paris.02.x400.gc.ca
La Wantzenau: Hon. Consul, Jean-Jacques Hetzel, Honorary Consulate of Canada, Polysar France, rue de Ried, France, (011-33-3) 88-96-65-02; Fax: (011-33-3) 88-96-25-17
Postal Address: CP 7, 67610 La Wantzenau, France
Lyon: Consul, M.M. Dubois, Consulate of Canada, Insitut Marcel Mérieux, 17-21 rue Bourgelat, 69002, France, (011-33) 72-73-79-20; Fax: (011-33) 72-73-79-93
Nice: Hon. Consul, M. Felizzola, Honorary Consulate of Canada, c/o Agence de Voyages French Med'Tours, 64, av Jean Médecin, 06000, France, (011-33-4) 93-92-93-22; Fax: (011-33-4) 93-92-55-51
St. Pierre: Hon. Consul, F. Park, Honorary Consulate of Canada, Institut Frecher, CP 470, F-97500, St. Pierre et Miquelon, (011-33-5) 08-41-55-10; Fax: (011-33-5) 08-41-55-01
Toulouse: Hon. Consul, Jacques Guibert, Honorary Consulate of Canada, 30, boul de Strasbourg, 31014, France, (011-33-5) 61-99-30-16; Fax: (011-33-5) 61-63-43-37
Postal Address: CP 138, Toulouse, France

### French Polynesia *c/o* French Republic

## Gabonese Republic
Canadian Embassy, PO Box 4037, Libreville
(011-241) 74-34-64; Fax: (011-241) 74-34-66
Email: MITNET: 326-0000
Ambassador, Robert Noble
Counsellor & Consul, D. Gregoire de Blois

### Republic of the Gambia *c/o* Republic of Senegal

### Republic of Georgia *c/o* Republic of Turkey

## Federal Republic of Germany

Canadian Embassy: Friedrich-Wilhelm-Strasse 18, 53113, Bonn
(011-49-228) 968-0; Fax: (011-49-228) 968-3900
Email: bonn.td@bonn01.x400.gc.ca; URL: http://www.dfait-maeci.gc.ca/~bonn/menu.html
Ambassador, Gaétan Lavertu
Minister, L. Friedlaender
Counsellor, Commercial, D. Butler
Counsellor, Science & Technology, H. Martin
Berlin: Minister, Fredericka Gregory, Canadian Embassy Office, Friedrich-Strasse 95, 10117, Germany, (011-49-30) 261-1161; Fax: (011-49-30) 262-9206
Düsseldorf: Consul, R.M. Bollman, Canadian Consulate, Prinz-Georg-Strasse 126, 40479, Germany, (011-49-211) 17-21-70; Fax: (011-49-211) 35-91-65
Hamburg: Consul & Senior Trade Commissioner, D. Baker, Canadian Consulate, ABC Strasse, 45, 20534, Germany, (011-49-40) 355-56290; Fax: (011-49-40) 355-66294
Munich: Consul & Senior Trade Commissioner, T. Williams, Canadian Consulate, Tal 29, 80331, Germany, (011-49-89) 219 9570; Fax: (011-49-89) 219 9575

## Republic of Ghana

Canadian High Commission: 42 Independence Ave., Accra
(011-233-21) 77-37-91; Fax: (011-233-21) 77-37-92
Email: MITNET: 313-0000
Postal Address: PO Box 1639, Accra, Ghana
High Commissioner, John Schram
First Secretary, Development, A. Lavender
First Secretary, Development, C. Thiruchittampalamj

**Gibraltar *c/o* United Kingdom of Great Britain & Northern Ireland**

## Hellenic Republic

Canadian Embassy: 4 Ioannou Ghennadiou St., Athens 115 21
(011-30-1) 725-4011; Fax: (011-30-1) 725-3994
Email: commerce@athns01.x400.gc.ca
Ambassador, Derek Fraser
Counsellor, Commercial, D. Cohen
Commercial Officer, Marianna Saropoulous, Email: marianna.saropoulos@athns01.x400.gc.ca

## Greenland *c/o* Kingdom of Denmark

Nuuk: Hon. Consul, Lars Peter Danielsen, Canadian Honorary Consulate, Groenlandsfly A/S, 3900, Greenland, (011-299) 28888; Fax: (011-299) 27288
Postal Address: PO Box 1012, 3900 Nuuk, Greenland

**Grenada *c/o* Barbados**

**Saint Vincent & the Grenadines *c/o* Barbados**

**Guadeloupe *c/o* Barbados**

**Guam *c/o* Japan**

## Republic of Guatemala

Canadian Embassy: 13 Calle 8 - 44, Zona 10, Edyma Plaza, Guatemala City
(011-50-2) 333-6104; Fax: (011-50-2) 333-6189
Postal Address: PO Box 400 Guatemala City, Guatemala
Ambassador, Daniel Livermore
Counsellor & Consul, Commercial, R. Shaw-Wood
Counsellor & Consul, Development, E.W.E. Doe
Commercial Assistant, Margo Dannemiller, Email: margo.dannemiller@gtmla01.x400.gc.ca

## Republic of Guinea

Canadian Embassy, PO Box 99, Conakry
(011-224) 41-23-95; Fax: (011-224) 41-42-36
Email: MITNET: 311-3000
Ambassador, Denis Briand
First Secretary & Consul, Development, S. Marchand

**Republic of Guinea-Bissau *c/o* Republic of Senegal**

## Co-operative Republic of Guyana

Canadian High Commission: High & Young Sts., Georgetown
(011-592-2) 72081; Fax: (011-592-2) 58380
Email: MITNET: 398-0000
Cable: DOMCAN GEORGETOWN
Postal Address: PO Box 10880, Georgetown, Guyana
High Commissioner, Alan Bowker
First Secretary, Development, S. Greaves

## Republic of Haiti

Canadian Embassy, Édifice Banque de Nova Scotia: rte de Delmas, Port-au-Prince
(011-509) 23-2358; Fax: (011-509) 23-8720
Email: MITNET: 310-0000
Postal Address: CP 826, Port-au-Prince, Haiti
Ambassador, Gilles Bernier
Counsellor & Consul, L.-R. Daigle
Counsellor, Development, S. Fortin

## Republic of Honduras

Canadian Embassy, Edificio Commercial Los Castatnos: 60 piso, Blvd. Morazán, Tegucigalpa
(011-504) 31-45-51; Fax: (011-504) 31-57-93
Postal Address: Apartado Postal 351-1007, Centro Colon, San José, Costa Rica
Ambassador (located in San José, Costa Rica), Dan Goodleaf
Counsellor (located in Costa Rica), G. Soroka
Counsellor, Development (located in Costa Rica), J. Melanson

## Republic of Hungary

Canadian Embassy: Budakeszi út 32, 1121, XII, Budapest
(011-36-1) 275-1200; Fax: (011-36-1) 275-1215
Email: bpest.td@bpest01.x400.gc.ca
Ambassador, Susan M.W. Cartwright
Counsellor, S. Marcoux
Counsellor & Consul, Commercial, R. Lecoq
Commercial Officer, Ilona Csete-Horvath, Email: ilona.csete-horvath@bpestanx01.400.gc.ca

## Republic of Iceland *c/o* Kingdom of Norway

Reykjavik: Hon. Consul General, J.H. Bergs, Honorary Consulate General of Canada, Suourlandsbraut 10, 108, Iceland, (011-354-5) 680-820; Fax: (011-354-5) 680-899
Postal Address: PO Box 8094, 128 Reykjavik, Iceland

## Republic of India

Canadian High Commission: 7/8 Shantipath, Chanakyapuri, New Delhi 110021
(011-91-11) 687-6500; Fax: (011-91-11) 687-6579
Postal Address: PO Box 5207, New Delhi 110021, India
High Commissioner, Stanley E. Gooch
Deputy High Commissioner, D. Waterfall
Counsellor, Commercial, D. Summers
Counsellor, Development, S. Gibbons
Counsellor, Immigration, J. Roberge
Commercial Officer, Viney Gupta, Email: viney.gupta@delhi01.x400.gc.ca
Commercial Officer (Bombay), Apurva Mehta, (011-91-22) 287-5479; Fax: (011-91-22) 287-5514; Email: consulate.canada@coc.sprintrpg.sprint.com
Bangalore: Sr. Advisor, D.P. Vittal Nath, Canadian Trade Office, 103 Prestige Meridien 1, 29 M.G. Rd., 560001, India, (011-91-80) 559-9418; Fax: (011-91-80) 559-9424
Bombay: Consul & Trade Commissioner, A. Vary, Canadian Consulate, 41/42 Maker Chambers VI, 6 Jamnalal Bajaj Marg, Nariman Point, 400021, India, (011-91-22) 287-6027; Fax: (011-91-22) 287-5514
Chandigarh: Canadian High Commission, S.C.O. No. 33-34-35, Sector 17A, India
Madras: Hon. Consul, V. Srinivasan, Honorary Consulate of Canada, c/o W.S. Industries Limited, Karumuttu Centre, 498 Anna Salai, 2nd Fl., Nandanam, 600035, India, (011-91-44) 434-9295; Fax: (011-91-44) 434-0847

## Republic of Indonesia

Canadian Embassy: Wisma Metropolitan 1, Jalan Jendral Sudirman Kav 29, 5th Fl., Jakarta 12920
(011-62-21) 525-0709; Fax: (011-62-21) 571-2251
Postal Address: PO Box 8324/JKS.MP, Jakarta 12084, Indonesia
Ambassador, Gary J. Smith
Counsellor, Development, N. Macdonnell
Consul & Counsellor, Commercial, M. Moszczenska
Commercial Officer, Husni Djaelani, Email: djaelani.husni@jkrta02.x400.gc.ca
Surabaya: A. Markus, Hon. Consul, Honorary Consulate of Canada, c/o P.T. Maspion, Head Office, JL. Kembang Jepun, No. 38-40, 60162, Indonesia, (011-62-31) 344-330; Fax: (011-62-31) 344-331

## Islamic Republic of Iran

Canadian Embassy: 57 Shahid Sarafraz, Ostad-Motahari Ave., Tehran 15868
(011-98-21) 873-2623; Fax: (011-98-21) 873-3202
Postal Address: PO Box 11365 - 4647, Tehran, Iran
Ambassador, Michel de Salaberry
Counsellor & Consul, G. Jacoby
Counsellor, Commercial, G. Rassman
Third Secretary (Commercial), Emmanuel Kamarianakis, Email: emmanuel.kamarianakis@teran01.x400.gc.ca

**Republic of Iraq *c/o* Hashemite Kingdom of Jordan**

## Republic of Ireland

Canadian Embassy, Canada House: 65 St. Stephen's Green, Dublin 2
(011-353-1) 478-1988; Fax: (011-353-1) 478-1285
Email: cdnembsy@iol.ie
Ambassador, Michael B. Phillips
Counsellor, Commercial, M. Heron
First Secretary & Consul, P. Pinnington
Commercial Officer, John Sullivan

## State of Israel

Canadian Embassy: 3 Nirim, Tel Aviv 67060
(011-972-03) 636-3300; Fax: (011-972-03) 636-3380
Postal Address: PO Box 6410, Tel Aviv 63405, Israel
Ambassador, David Berger
Counsellor & Consul, D. Viveash
Counsellor, Commercial, R. Zeisler
Canadian Forces Attaché, Col. J. Bender
Commercial Officer, Atalia Kahan, Email: atalia.kahan@taviv.01.x400.gc.ca

## Italian Republic
Canadian Embassy: Via G.B. de Rossi 27, 00161, Rome
(011-39-6) 44598-1; Fax: (011-39-6) 4459-8750
Email: rome@rome01.x400.gc.ca
Ambassador, Jeremy K.B. Kinsman
Minister-Counsellor, J. Junke
Minister-Counsellor, Economic/Commercial, N. Kalisch
Counsellor, Development, G. Saint Cyr
Counsellor, Development, R. Rose
Counsellor, Public Affairs, M. Cousineau
Commercial Officer, Alex L. Jones, Email: alex.jones@rome01.x400.gc.ca
Commercial Officer (Milan), Umberto Corazzi, Email: umberto.corazzi@milan01.x400.gc.ca
Milan: Consul General, Ian McLean, Canadian Consulate General, Via Vittor Pisani 19, 20124, Italy, (011-39-2) 6758-1; Fax: (011-39-2) 6758-3900; URL: http://www.agora.stm.it/canaca/homepage.htm; Email: milan@milan01x400.gc.ca

## Jamaica
Canadian High Commission, Mutual Security Bank Bldg.: 30-36 Knutsford Blvd., Kingston 5
809/926-1500; Fax: 809/926-1702
Email: MITNET: 333-0000
Postal Address: PO Box 1500, Kingston 10, Jamaica
High Commissioner, Gavin Stewert
Counsellor, Commercial, W.P. Molson
Montego Bay: Hon. Consul, L.J. Crichton, Consulate of Canada, 29 Gloucester Ave., Jamaica, 809/952-6198; Fax: 809/979-1086

## Japan
Canadian Embassy: 3 - 38 Akasaka 7-chrome, Minato-ku, Tokyo 107
(011-81-3) 3408-2101; Fax: (011-81-3) 3479-5320
Trade & Investment Section, (011-81-3) 3470-7280
Ambassador, Donald W. Campbell
Minister, Economic/Commercial, J. Tennant
Counsellor, Commercial, R. Brocklebank
Counsellor, Commercial, S. Gawreletz
Counsellor, Commercial, R. Davidson
Counsellor, Commercial, M. Clugston
Minister-Counsellor, Commercial, M.M. MadConald
Counsellor, Investment, L. Boisvert
Commercial Officer, Noboru Aoki, Email: noboru.aoki@tokyo04.x400.gc.ca
Fukuoka: Consul & Trade Commissioner, B. Préfontaine, Consulate of Canada, FT Bldg., 9F, 4-8-28 Watanabe-Dori, Chuo-Ku, 810, Japan, (011-81-92) 752-6055; Fax: (011-81-92) 752-6077
Hiroshima: Hon. Consul, K. Tada, Consulate of Canada, c/o Chugoku Electric Power Co. Inc., 4-33 Komachi, Naka-ku, 730, Japan, (011-81-82) 246-0057
Nagoya: Consul & Trade Commissioner, Robert Mason, Consulate of Canada, Nakato Marunouchi Bldg., 6F, 3-7-16 Marunouchi, Naka-Ku, Japan, (011-81-52) 972-0450; Fax: (011-81-52) 972-0453
Osaka: Consul General, Peter G. Campbell, Consulate General of Canada, Daisan Shoho Bldg., 12th Fl., 2-2-3, Nishi-Shinsaibashi, Chuo-ku, 542, Japan, (011-81-6) 212-4910; Fax: (011-81-6) 212-4914
Postal Address: PO Box 150, Osaka Minami 542-91, Japan
Sapporo City: Hon. Consul, T. Morihana, Consulate of Canada, c/o The Hokkaido Bank Ltd., 1-banchi, Nishi 4-chrome, Oldori, Chuo-ku, 060, Japan, (011-81-510) 219-0617
Sendai City: Hon. Consul, T. Akema, Consulate of Canada, c/o Tohoku Electric Power Co. Inc., 3-7-1 Ichibancho, Aoba-ku, 980, Japan, (011-81-22) 268-5030

## Hashemite Kingdom of Jordan
Canadian Embassy, Pearl of Shmeisani Bldg.: Shmeisani, Amman
(011-962-6) 66-61-24; Fax: (011-962-6) 68-92-27
Postal Address: PO Box 815403, Amman 11180, Jordan
Ambassador, Michael J. Molloy
First Secretary & Consul, S.L. Bennett
First Secretary, Development, D. Joly
Counsellor, Commercial (located in Syria), T. Greenwood
Commercial Officer, Hala Helou

## Republic of Kazakhstan
Canadian Embassy: 34 Vinagradova St., Almaty
(011-7-327) 250-11-51; Fax: (011-7-327) 581-14-93
Ambassador, Richard Mann
Consul & First Secretary, Commercial, D. MacLeod
Minister-Counsellor, Commercial (located in Russia), J. DiGangi

## Republic of Kenya
Canadian High Commission, Comcraft House: Hailé Sélassie Ave., Nairobi
(011-254-2) 21-48-04; Fax: (011-254-2) 22-69-87
Email: nrobi.gr@nrobi01.x400.gc.ca
Postal Address: PO Box 30481, Nairobi, Kenya
High Commissioner, Bernard Dussault
Counsellor, P. Haddow
Counsellor, Development, J. Lobsinger
Senior Commercial Assistant, Thelma R. Staussi

### Republic of Kiribati *c/o* New Zealand

## Republic of Korea
Canadian Embassy, Kolon Bldg., 10th Fl.: 45 Mugyo-Dong, Jung-Ku, 100 - 170, Seoul
(011-82-2) 753-2605; Fax: (011-82-2) 755-0686
Email: seoul.td@seoul01.x400.gc.ca
Postal Address: PO Box 6299, Seoul 100-662, Korea
Ambassador, Michel E. Perrault
Minister-Counsellor & Consul, Commercial, D.B. Collins
Counsellor, Commercial, K. Panday
Counsellor & Consul, L. De Lorimier
Third Secretary, Commercial, Jean-Dominique Ieraci, Email: jean-dominique.j.d.i.ieraci@seoul02.x400.gc.ca
Commercial Officer, Y.H. Choi
Pusan: Hon. Consul, H.-W. Koo, Honorary Consulate of Canada, c/o Bumin Mutual Savings & Finance Corporation, #32-1, 2-GA, Daecheung-Dong, Chung-Ku, Korea, (011-8251) 246-7024; Fax: (011-8251) 247-8443

## State of Kuwait
Canadian Embassy: Villa 24, Area 4, Plot 121, Al-Mutawakel, Da'aiyah, Kuwait City
(001 965) 256-3025; Fax: (001-965) 256-4167
Email: kwait.td@paris03.x400.gc.ca
Postal Address: PO Box 25281, Safat 13113, Kuwait City, Kuwait
Ambassador, Terry W. Colfer
Counsellor & Consul, Commercial, J.N. Guérin
Commercial Officer, Ibtissam Hajj, Email: ibtissam.hajj@paris03.x400.gc.ca

### Republic of Kyrgyzstan *c/o* Republic of Kazakhstan

### Lao People's Democratic Republic *c/o* Kingdom of Thailand

## Republic of Latvia
Canadian Embassy: Doma laukums 4, 4th Fl., Riga LV-1977
(011-371) 783-0141; Fax: (011-371) 783-0140
Ambassador (located in Sweden), William L. Clarke
Minister-Counsellor, G.R. Skinner
First Secretary, Commercial, H.J. Kunzer

## Lebanese Republic
Canadian Embassy: Coolrite Bldg., 434 Autostrade Jal-El-Dib, 1st Fl., Beirut
(011-961-1) 521-163; Fax: (011-961-1) 521-167
Email: berut@paris03.x400.gc.ca
Postal Address: PO Box 60163, Jal-El-Dib, Beirut, Lebanon
Ambassador, Daniel Marchand
Second Secretary & Vice Consul, Commercial, M. Poirier
Counsellor, Commercial, M. Abou Guendia

## Kingdom of Lesotho *c/o* Republic of South Africa
Maseru: Hon. Consul, Z.M. Bam, Honorary Consulate of Canada, Canadian Consulate, Maseru Book Centre Kingsway, 1st Fl., PO Box 1165, Lesotho, (011-266) 325-632; Fax: (011-266) 316-462

### Republic of Liberia *c/o* Republic of Ghana

### Socialist People's Libyan Arab Jamahiriya *c/o* Republic of Tunisia

### Principality Liechtenstein *c/o* Swiss Confederation

## Republic of Lithuania
Canadian Embassy: Gedimino pr. 64, 2001, Vilnius
(011-370-2) 220-898; Fax: (011-370-2) 220-884
Ambassador (located in Sweden), William L. Clarke
Minister-Counsellor (located in Latvia), G.R. Skinner
First Secretary, Commercial (located in Latvia), J.H. Kunzer

## Grand Duchy of Luxembourg *c/o* Kingdom of Belgium
Luxembourg: Hon. Consul, P. Krier, Honorary Consulate of Canada, c/o Price-Waterhouse & Co., 24-26, av de la Liberté, L-1930, Luxembourg, (011-35-2) 40-24-20; Fax: (011-35-2) 40-24-55

### Macao *c/o* People's Republic of China

### Republic of Macedonia *c/o* Federal Republic of Yugoslavia

## Democratic Republic of Madagascar *c/o* United Republic of Tanzania
Antananarivo: Hon. Consul, Serge P. Lachapelle, Honorary Consulate of Canada, c/o QIT-Madagascar Minerals, Villa Paula Androhibe, Lot II-J-169, 101, Madagascar, (011-261-2) 425-59; Fax: (011-261-2) 425-06
Postal Address: Canadian Consulate, CP 4003, Antananarivo 101, Madagascar

### Madeira *c/o* Portuguese Republic

## Republic of Malawi *c/o* Republic of Zambia
Blantyre-Limbe: Hon. Consul, K. Okhai, Honorary Consulate of Canada, c/o Comet Ltd., PO Box

51146, Malawi, (011-265) 645-441; Fax: (011-265) 645-004

## Malaysia

Canadian High Commission: Plaza MBF, 172 Jalan Ampang, 7th Fl., 50450, Kuala Lumpur

(011-60-3) 261-2000; Fax: (011-60-3) 261-3248

Email: tradcan@po.jaring.my

Postal Address: PO Box 10990, 50732, Kuala Lumpur, Malaysia

High Commissioner, André Simard

Counsellor, Commercial, P.S. Lau

Counsellor, Commercial, B. Reid

Third Secretary, Commercial, Pamela O'Donnell

### Republic of Maldives *c/o* Democratic Socialist Republic of Sri Lanka

## Republic of Mali

Canadian Embassy, PO Box 198, Bamako

(011-223) 22-22-36; Fax: (011-223) 22-42-62

Ambassador, Yves Boulanger

## Republic of Malta *c/o* Italian Republic

Valletta: Hon. Consul, J.M. Demajo, Honorary Consulate of Canada, Demajo House, 103 Archbishop St., Malta, (011-356) 233-121; Fax: (011-356) 235-147

### Marshall Islands *c/o* Republic of the Philippines

### Martinique *c/o* Barbados

## Islamic Republic of Mauritania *c/o* Republic of Senegal

Nouakchott: Hon. Consul, J. Chauvin, Honorary Consulate of Canada, PO Box 428, Mauritania, (011-222-2) 534-48; Fax: (011-222-2) 540-09

## Republic of Mauritius *c/o* Republic of South Africa

Port Louis: Hon. Consul, P.M. Birger, Canadian Consulate, 18 Jules Koenig St., Mauritius, (011-230) 208-0821; Fax: (011-230) 208-3391

Postal Address: PO Box 209, Port Louis, Mauritius

## United Mexican States

Canadian Embassy: Calle Schiller No. 529, Colonia Polanco, 11560, Mexico City

(011-52-5) 724-7900; Fax: (011-52-5) 724-7982

Postal Address: Apartado Postal 105-05, 11580 Mexico City, D.F. Mexico

Ambassador, Stanley Gooch

Minister-Counsellor, Economic/Commercial, D. Thibault

Counsellor, Commercial, B. Hood

Counsellor, Commercial, C. Rockburne

Canadian Forces Attaché, L.Col. J.J.G. Tremblay

Second Secretary, Commercial, Sophie Legendre, Email: sophie.legendre@mxico02.x400.gc.ca

Acapulco: Hon. Consul, Diane McLean de Huert, Honorary Consulate of Canada, Centro Commercial Marbella, Local 23 esq Prolongacion Farallon y Miguel Aleman, Mexico, (011-52-74) 84-1305; Fax: (011-52-74) 94-1306

Ajijic: Hon. Consul, A.C. Rose, Honorary Consulate of Canada, Hotel Real de Chapala, Paseo del Prado 20, Mexico, (011-52-376) 62-288; Fax: (011-52-376) 62-420

Cancun: Hon. Consul, Daniel Lavoie, Honorary Consulate of Canada, Plaza Caracol II, Local 330, Blvd, Kukulcan km 8.5, 77500, Mexico, (011-52-98) 83-3360; Fax: (011-52-98) 83-3232

Guadalajara: Consul & Trade Commissioner, J. Daubeny, Canadian Consulate, Hotel Fiesta Americana, Local 31, Aurelio Aceves 225, Col. Vallarta Poniente, 44100, Mexico, (011-52-3) 616-56-42; Fax: (011-52-3) 615-86-65

Mazatlan: Hon. Consul, F. Balcarcel, Honorary Consulate of Canada, Hotel Playa Mazatlan, Zona Dorada, 202 Rodolfo Loaiza St., 82110, Mexico, (011-52-69) 13-73-20; Fax: (011-52-69) 14-66-55

Postal Address: Apartado Postal 614, 82210, Mazatlan, Sinaloa, Mexico

Monterrey: Consul & Trade Commissioner, T.G. Cullen, Canadian Consulate, Edificio Kalos, Piso C-1, Local 108-A, Zaragoza 1300 Sur y Constitucion, 6400, Mexico, (011-52-83) 44-27-53; Fax: (011-52-83) 44-30-48

Oaxaca: Hon. Consul, Frances May, Honorary Consulate of Canada, 119 Dr. Liceaga #8, 68000, Mexico, (011-52-95) 13-37-77; Fax: (011-52-95) 15-21-47

Postal Address: Apartado Postal 29 Sucursal C, Col. Reforma, 68050 Oaxaco, Mexico

Puerto Vallarta: Hon. Consul, L. Benoit, Honorary Consulate of Canada, Calle Hidalgo 226, 160 Zaragoza, Interior 10, Col. Centro, 48300, Mexico, (011-52-32) 22-53-98; Fax: (011-52-32) 22-35-17

San Miguel de Allende: Hon. Consul, G. Bisaillon, Honorary Consulate of Canada, Mesones 38, Interior 15, 37700, Mexico, (011-52-41) 52-30-25; Fax: (011-52-41) 52-68-56

Tijuana: Hon. Consul, R.E. Ripa, Honorary Consulate of Canada, German Gedovius 10411-101, Condominio del Parque, Zona Rio, 22320, Mexico, (011-52-66) 84-04-61; Fax: (011-52-66) 84-03-01

### Republic of Moldova *c/o* Republic of Romania

### Principality of Monaco *c/o* French Republic

### Mongolian People's Republic *c/o* People's Republic of China

### Montenegro *c/o* Federal Republic of Yugoslavia

### Montserrat *c/o* Barbados

## Kingdom of Morocco

Canadian Embassy: 13 bis, rue Jaafar As-Sadik, Rabat-Agdal

(011-212-7) 67-28-80; Fax: (011-212-7) 67-21-87

Postal Address: CP 709, Rabat-Agdal, Morocco

Ambassador, Jean-Guy St-Martin

Counsellor & Consul, D. Laliberté

First Secretary, Development, G. Lachance

First Secretary, Commercial, H. Guillot

Commercial Officer, Najat Benyahia, Email: majat.benyahia@rabat01.x400.gc.ca

## Republic of Mozambique

Canadian Embassy: 1345, rue Thomas Nduda, Maputo

(011-258-1) 492-623; Fax: (011-258-1) 492-667

Postal Address: CP 1578, Maputo, Mozambique

Ambassador (located in Zimbabwe), Art Wright

Counsellor & Consul, Development (located in Zimbabwe), J. Copland

Counsellor, Development (located in Kenya), R. Benoit

### Union of Myanmar *c/o* Kingdom of Thailand

## Republic of Namibia *c/o* Republic of South Africa

Windhoek: Hon. Consul, I. Swanepoel, Honorary Consulate of Canada, PO Box 9704, Namibia, (011-27) 235-841; Fax: (011-27) 235-841

### Nauru *c/o* Commonwealth of Australia

### Kingdom of Nepal *c/o* Republic of India

## Kingdom of the Netherlands

Canadian Embassy: Sophialaan 7, 2514 JP, The Hague

(011-31-70) 311-1600; Fax: (011-31-70) 442-3220

Ambassador, Marie Bernard-Meunier

Minister-Counsellor, Commercial/Economic, C. Fontaine

Technology Development Officer, Prisce Haemers, Email: prisce.haemers@hague01.x400.gc.ca

Curaçao: Hon. Consul, W.H.L. Fabro, The Consulate of Canada, Maduro and Curiels Bank, N.V. 2-4 Plaza JoJo Correa, Netherlands Antilles, (011-599-9) 66-11-15; Fax: (011-599-9) 66-11-22

Postal Address: PO Box 305, Curaçao, Netherlands Antilles

## Netherlands Antilles *c/o* Republic of Venezuela

Curaçao: Hon. Consul, L.K. Lynch, Canadian Consulate, Maduro and Curiels Bank N.V., Plaza JoJo Correa 2-4, Willemstad,, (011-599-9) 66-11-15; Fax: (011-599-9) 66-11-22

### New Caledonia *c/o* Commonwealth of Australia

## New Zealand

Canadian High Commission: 61 Molesworth St., 3rd Fl., Thorndon, Wellington

(011-64-4) 473-9577; Fax: (011-64-4) 471-2082

Postal Address: PO Box 12-049, Thorndon, Wellington, New Zealand

High Commissioner, Valerie Raymond

Commercial Officer (Auckland), Brian Emsley, (011-64-9) 309-3690; Fax: (011-64-9) 307-3111

Auckland: Consul & Trade Commissioner, J. Hill, Canadian Consulate, Jetset Centre, 44 - 48 Emily Place, 9th Fl., 1, New Zealand, (011-64-9) 309-3690; Fax: (011-64-9) 307-3111

Postal Address: PO Box 6186, Wellesley Street, Auckland, New Zealand

## Republic of Nicaragua *c/o* Republic of Costa Rica

Managua: Counsellor, M. Gagnon, Honorary Consulate of Canada, 2 cuadras al oeste, Calle Nogal 25, Bolonia, Managua, Nicaragua, (011-505-2) 68-0433; Fax: (011-505-2) 68-0437

Postal Address: PO Box 25, Managua, Nicaragua

## Republic of Niger

Canadian Embassy, Édifice Sonara II.: av du Premier Pont, Niamey

(011-227) 73-36-86; Fax: (011-227) 75-31-01

Postal Address: CP 362, Niamey, Niger

Ambassador (located in Côte d'Ivoire), Suzanne Laporte

Counsellor & Consul, Development, J.G. Lépine

Counsellor & Consul, G. Paquet

## Federal Republic of Nigeria
Canadian High Commission, Committee of Vice-Chancellors Bldg.: Plot 8A, 4 Idowa-Taylor St., Victoria Island, Lagos
(011-234-1) 262-2512; Fax: (011-234-1) 262-2517
Postal Address: PO Box 54506, Ikoyi Station, Lagos, Nigeria
High Commissioner, Vacant
Counsellor, G.L. Ohlsen
Abuja: Liaison Officer, J. Frik, Canadian High Commission, Liaison Office, Plot 622, Gana St., Zone A5, Maitama, Nigeria, (011-234-090) 803-249; Fax: (011-234-090) 803-249
Postal Address: PO Box 6924 WUSE, Abuja, FCT, Nigeria

**Niue *c/o* New Zealand**

**Northern Ireland *c/o* United Kingdom of Great Britain & Northern Ireland**

**Northern Marianas *c/o* Republic of the Philippines**

## Kingdom of Norway
Canadian Embassy: Wergelandsveien 7, N-0244, Oslo
(011-47) 22-99-53-00; Fax: (011-47) 22-99-53-01
Ambassador, Marie-Lucie Morin
Counsellor & Consul, G. Gingras
Counsellor & Consul, Commercial, C. Dickson
Commercial Asst., Commercial, Jill Ringiua

## Sultanate of Oman *c/o* State of Kuwait
Muscat: Hon. Consul, M.A. Moosa, Honourary Consulate of Canada, Flat #310, Bldg. 477, Moosa Abdul Rahman Hassan Bldg., Way 2907, A'Noor St., Ruwi, Oman, (011-968) 791-566; Fax: (011-968) 709-091
Postal Address: PO Box 1275, Muttrah 114, Sultanate of Oman

## Islamic Republic of Pakistan
Canadian High Commission: Diplomatic Enclave, Sector G-5, Islamabad
(011-92-51) 279-100; Fax: (011-92-51) 279-110
Postal Address: GPO Box 1042, Islamabad, Pakistan
High Commissioner, Marie-Andrée Beauchemin
Counsellor, D.K. Hallman
Counsellor, Development, T. Brophy
Commercial Officer, Ali Khan
Karachi: Hon. Consul, B. Avari, Honourary Consulate of Canada, Beach Luxury Hotel, 3rd Fl., Moulvi Tamiz Uddin Khan Rd., 0227, Pakistan, (011-92-21) 561-1031; Fax: (011-92-21) 561-0673
Lahore: Hon. Consul, A.M. Saleem, Honourary Consulate of Canada, PAAF Bldg., 5th Fl., 7D Kashmire/Egerton Rd., Pakistan, (011-92-42) 636-6230; Fax: (011-92-42) 636-5086

## Republic of Panama
Edificio Banco Central Hispano: Ava. Samuel Lewis, 4th Fl., Panama City
(011-507) 264-9731; Fax: (011-507) 263-8083
Postal Address: Apartado 3658, Balboa Ancon, Panama City, Panama
Ambassador, Louise Léger
Third Secretary & Vice-Consul, A. Baldwin
First Secretary, Commercial, J. Blackstock
Panama City: Hon. Consul, Ruth Lister de Denton, Canadian Consulate, Edificio Proconsa, Aero Peru, Piso 5B, Calle Manuel y Caza, Campo Alegre, Panama, (011-507) 64-70-14; Fax: (011-507) 23-54-70
Postal Address: Apartado Postal 3658, Balboa, Panama

## Papua New Guinea *c/o* Commonwealth of Australia
Port Moresby: Hon. Consul, R. Hiatt, Honourary Consulate of Canada, The Lodge, Brampton St., 2nd Fl., Papua New Guinea, (011-675) 213-559; Fax: (011-675) 213-098
Postal Address: PO Box 851, Port Moresby, Papua New Guinea

## Republic of Paraguay *c/o* Republic of Chile
Asunción: Hon. Consul, B. Wiebe, Honourary Consulate of Canada, El Paraguayo Independiente 995, Mezzanine, Oficinas 1 y 2, Paraguay, (011-595-21) 449-505; Fax: (011-595-21) 449-506
Postal Address: Casilla 2577, Asunción, Paraguay

## Republic of Peru
Canadian Embassy: Federico Gerdes 130 (antes Calle Libertad), Miraflores, Lima
(011-51-1) 444-4015; Fax: (011-51-1) 444-4347
Postal Address: Casilla 18 - 1126, Correo Miraflores, 18, Lima, Peru
Ambassador, Graeme C.. Clark
Counsellor & Consul, D. Bickford
Counsellor & Consul, Development, G. Rivard
First Secretary & Consul, Commercial, D. Ayotte

## Republic of the Philippines
Canadian Embassy, Allied Bank Centre, 9th & 11th Fls.: 6754 Ayala Ave., Makati, Manila
(011-63-2) 810-0001; Fax: (011-63-2) 810-8839
Postal Address: PO Box 2168, Makati Central Post Office, 1261 Makati, Manila, Philippines
Ambassador, John Treleaven
Counsellor, Commercial, A. Fraser
Counsellor, Commercial, J. St-George

## Republic of Poland
Canadian Embassy: ul. Matejki 1/5, Warsaw 00-481
(011-48-22) 629-80-51; Fax: (011-48-22) 629-64-57
Ambassador, Serge April
Counsellor & Consul, Commercial, L. McDonald

## Portuguese Republic
Canadian Embassy: 144/56 Av. da Liberdade, 4th Fl., 1250, Lisbon
(011-351-1) 347-4892; Fax: (011-351-1) 347-6466
Ambassador, Patricia Marsden-Dole
Counsellor & Consul, Commercial, L.M. Gaetan
Commercial Officer, Carlos Lindo da Silva
Faro: Hon. Consul, L. Filipe Afonso, Honourary Consulate of Canada, Rua Frei Lourenço de Sta Maria No. 1, 1st Fl., Apt. 79, 8001, Portugal, (011-351-89) 80-37-57; Fax: (011-351-89) 80-47-77
Postal Address: PO Box 79, 8001 Faro, Portugal

**Principe *c/o* Gabonese Republic**

**Puerto Rico *c/o* United States of America**

**State of Qatar *c/o* State of Kuwait**

## Republic of Romania
Canadian Embassy: 36 Nicolae Iorga, 71118, Bucharest
(011-40-1) 222-9845; Fax: (011-40-1) 312-0366
Postal Address: PO Box 117, Post Office No. 22, Bucharest, Romania
Ambassador, Gilles Duguay
Counsellor & Consul, Commercial, M.R. Vlad
Commercial Officer, Octavian Bonea

## Russian Federation
Canadian Embassy: 23 Starokonyushenny Pereulok, 12100, Moscow
(011-7-095) 956-6666; Fax: (011-7-095) 232-9948
Email: mosco.td@mosco01.x400.gc.ca
Ambassador, Anne Leahy
Minister-Counsellor, Commercial, M.L. Morin
Minister-Counsellor, J. DiGangi
Counsellor, L. Heuckroth
Counsellor, Commercial, G. Jones
Commercial Officer, Lilya Panova, Email: lilya.panova@mosco01.x400.gc.ca
St. Petersburg: Consul General, Ann Collins, Canadian Consulate, 32 Malodetskoselsky Pkt., 198013, Russia, (011-7-812) 325-84-48; Fax: (011-7-812) 325-83-93

## Rwandese Republic
Canadian Embassy: rue Akagera, Kigali
(011-250) 73210; Fax: (011-250) 72719
Postal Address: PO Box 1117, Kigali, Rwanda
Ambassador (located in Kenya), Bernard Dussault
Counsellor, Development (located in Kenya), G. Ohlsen
Counsellor, P. Haddow

**Saint Kitts and Nevis *c/o* Barbados**

**Saint Lucia *c/o* Barbados**

**Republic of San Marino *c/o* Italian Republic**

**Democratic Republic of Sao Tomé & Principe *c/o* Gabonese Republic**

## Kingdom of Saudi Arabia
Canadian Embassy: Diplomatic Quarter, Riyadh
(011-966-1) 488-2288; Fax: (011-966-1) 488-1997
Email: ryadh.td@ryadh01.x400.gc.ca
Postal Address: PO Box 94321, 11693, Riyadh, Saudi Arabia
Ambassador, Edward D. Hobson
Minister-Counsellor, Commercial, R. Craig
Counsellor, Commercial, G. Debbané
Second Secretary (Commercial), David McGregor, Email: david.d.m.mcgregor@ryadh01.X400.gc.ca
Counsellor, Commercial, J. Clapp
Jeddah: Hon. Consul, S.T.Y. Zahid, Honourary Consulate of Canada, Headquarters Bldg., Zahid Corporate Group, 21492, Saudi Arabia, (011-966-2) 667-1156; Fax: (011-966-2) 669-0727
Postal Address: PO Box 8928, Jeddah 21492, Saudi Arabia

**Scotland *c/o* United Kingdom of Great Britain & Northern Ireland**

## Republic of Senegal
Canadian Embassy: 45, av de la République, Dakar
(011-221) 23-92-90; Fax: (011-221) 23-87-49
Postal Address: PO Box 3373, Dakar, Senegal
Ambassador, Wilfrid-Guy Licari
Counsellor, Development, P. Lachance
Counsellor & Consul, Development, R. Pelletier

**Serbia *c/o* Federal Republic of Yugoslavia**

**Republic of Seychelles *c/o* United Republic of Tanzania**

**Republic of Sierra Leone *c/o* Republic of Ghana**

## Republic of Singapore
Canadian High Commission, IBM Towers: 80 Anson Rd., 14th & 15th Fls., 079907, Singapore
(011-65) 325-3200; Fax: (011-65) 325-3297
Email: cdatanjs@signet.com.sg
Postal Address: Robinson Rd., PO Box 845, 90165, Singapore, Singapore
High Commissioner, Barry Carin
Counsellor, Commercial, W. Roberts
Counsellor, Development, M. Archambault
Counsellor, Development, A. Heuchan
Second Secretary, Commercial, Alain Gendron

## Slovak Republic *c/o* Czech Republic
Bratislava: Hon. Consul, P. Erben, Honourary Consulate of Canada, Blaha & Erben & Novak & Werner Advokatska Kancelaria, 47 Stefanikova St., 811-04, Slovakia, (011-42-07) 361-277; Fax: (011-42-07) 361-220

## Republic of Slovenia *c/o* Republic of Hungary
Ljubljana: Hon. Consul, J. Obersnel, The Canadian Consulate, Triglav Insurance Company Ltd., Miklosiceva 19, 61000, Slovenia, (011-386-61) 131-10-20; Fax: (011-386-61) 316-456

### Solomon Islands *c/o* Commonwealth of Australia

### Somali Democratic Republic *c/o* Republic of Kenya

## Republic of South Africa
Canadian High Commission: 1103 Arcadia St., Hatfield 0083, Pretoria
(011-27-12) 422-3000; Fax: (011-27-12) 422-3052
Postal Address: Private Bag X13, Hatfield 0028, Pretoria, South Africa
High Commissioner, Arthur Perron
Minister-Counsellor, C. McMaster
Counsellor, Economic, R. Sandor
Counsellor, Development, R. Benoit
Counsellor, Development, G. Hawes
First Secretary, Commercial, G. Graham
Commercial Officer (Johannesburg), Ronelle de Wet, Email: ronelle.r.d.dewet@pret01.x400.gc.ca
Capetown: Canadian High Commission, Reserve Bank Bldg., 360 St. George's Mall St., 8001, South Africa, (011-27-21) 23-5240; Fax: (011-27-21) 23-4893
Postal Address: PO Box 683, Capetown 8000, South Africa
Durban: Hon. Consul, R.B. McElligott, Honourary Consulate of Canada, c/o Farm-ag Ltd., South Africa, (011-322) 334-061; Fax: (011-322) 336-293
Postal Address: PO Box 5448, Durban 4000, South Africa
Johannesburg: Canadian High Commission Trade Office, Cradock Place, 10 Arnold St., 1st Fl., Rosebank, South Africa, (011-27-11) 442-3130; Fax: (011-27-11) 442-3325; Email: jburg@pret01.x400.gc.ca
Postal Address: Canadian High Commission Trade Office, PO Box 1394, Parklands 2121, Johannesburg, South Africa

## Kingdom of Spain
Canadian Embassy, Edificio Goya: Calle Nunez de Balboa 35, 28001, Madrid
(011-34-1) 431-4300; Fax: (011-34-1) 431-3893
Email: canem@mad.servicom.es; URL: http://www.jrnet.com/canada
Postal Address: Apartado 587, 28080, Madrid, Spain
Ambassador, Anthony G. Vincent
Counsellor, Commercial, G. Bruneau
Counsellor & Consul, P. Wilcox
Commerical Officer, Isidro Garcia, Email: isidro.garcia@mdrid01.X400.gc.ca
Barcelona: Hon. Consul, B. Masoliver, Canadian Consulate, Passeig de Gracia, 77, 30-08008, Spain, (011-34-3) 215-07-04; Fax: (011-34-3) 487-91-17
Bilbao: Hon. Consul, S. Gardiner, Honourary Consulate of Canada, Ava. Juan Antonio Zunzunegui, 2, 1, 48013, Spain, (011-34-4) 427-69-22; Fax: (011-34-4) 427-15-78
Malaga: Hon. Consul, John Schwarzmann, Honourary Consulate of Canada, Horizonte Bldg., Plaza de la Malagueta 3, 29016, Spain, (011-34-52) 22-33-46; Fax: (011-34-52) 22-40-23
Postal Address: PO Box 99, 29080 Malaga, Spain
Seville: Hon. Consul, Julian Garcia-Hidalgo, Honourary Consulate of Canada, Ava. de la Constitución 30, 2nd Fl., local 4-41001, Spain, (011-34-54) 22-94-13

## Democratic Socialist Republic of Sri Lanka
Canadian High Commission: 6 Gregory's Rd., Cinnamon Gardens, Colombo 7
(011-94-1) 69-58-41; Fax: (011-94-1) 68-70-49
Cable: DOMCANADA COLOMBO
Postal Address: PO Box 1006, Colombo 7, Sri Lanka
High Commissioner, Konrad Sigurdson
Counsellor, Development, M. Girvan
Counsellor, Commercial, D. Summers

### St. Martin/St-Marten *c/o* Barbados

### Republic of The Sudan *c/o* Democratic Republic of Ethiopia

## Republic of Suriname *c/o* Co-operative Republic of Guyana
Paramaribo: Hon. Consul, A.F. Smit, Honourary Consulate of Canada, Waterkant 90-94, Suriname, (011-597) 471-222; Fax: (011-597) 475-718
Postal Address: PO Box 1849-1850, Paramaribo, Suriname

### Kingdom of Swaziland *c/o* Republic of South Africa

## Kingdom of Sweden
Canadian Embassy: Tegelbacken 4, 7th Fl., Stockholm
(011-46-8) 453-3000; Fax: (011-46-8) 242-491
Email: stlkm@stklm01.X400.gc.ca
Postal Address: PO Box 16129, 10323, Stockholm, Sweden
Ambassador, William L. Clarke
Counsellor, Commercial, J. Sotvedt
Commercial Officer, Inga-Lill Olsson, Email: inga.olsson@stkhm01.x400.gc.ca
Göteborg: Hon. Consul, K.S.U. Granander, Honorary Consulate of Canada, c/o ACL Sweden AB, Sydathlanten, Skandiahammen, PO Box 403 36, Sweden (011) 46-31-64-55-80; Fax: (011) 46-31-64-55-75

## Swiss Confederation
Canadian Embassy: Kirchenfeldstr. 88, 3005, Berne
(011-41-31) 357-3200; Fax: (011-41-31) 357-3210
Email: bern.cda@ping.ch
Postal Address: PO Box 3000, Berne 6, Switzerland
Ambassador, Réjean Frenette
Counsellor & Consul, P. Ducharme
Counsellor & Consul, Commercial, J. Schwartzburg
Senior Commercial Officer, Werner Naef, Email: werner.naef@bern01.x400.gc.ca

## Syrian Arab Republic
Canadian Embassy: Lot 12, Mezzeh Autostr., Damascus
(011-963-11) 611-6692; Fax: (011-963-11) 611-4000
Postal Address: PO Box 3394, Damascus, Syria
Ambassador, Alexandra Bugailiskis
Counsellor & Consul, C. Sheck
Counsellor, Commercial, T. Greenwood

## Taiwan
Canadian Trade Office: 365 Fu Hsing North Rd., 13th Fl., 10483, Taipei
(011-886-2) 547-9500; Fax: (011-886-2) 712-7244
Director, Hugh Stevens, Email: hugh.stephens@tapei01.x400.gc.ca
Executive Deputy Director & Senior Trade Commissioner, Stewart Beck, Email: stewart.beck@tapei01.x400.gc.ca
Asst. Trade Commissioner, Handol Kim, Email: handol.kim@tapei01.x400.gc.ca

### Republic of Tajikistan *c/o* Republic of Kazakhstan

## United Republic of Tanzania
Canadian High Commission: 38 Mirambo St., Dar-es-Salaam
(011-255-51) 112 832; Fax: (011-255-51) 116 897
Postal Address: PO Box 1022, Dar-es-Salaam, Tanzania
High Commissioner, Wayne Hammond
Counsellor, Political & Public Affairs, F.X.E. Loignon
Counsellor, Development, A. Poplawski
First Secretary, Development, D. Foxall

## Kingdom of Thailand
Canadian Embassy, Boonmitr Bldg.: 138 Silom Rd., 11th Fl., 10500, Bangkok
(011-66-2) 237-4125; Fax: (011-66-2) 236-6463
Email: bngkk.td@bngkk02.x400.gc.ca
Postal Address: PO Box 2090, 10500, Bangkok, Thailand
Ambassador, Bernard Giroux
Counsellor & Consul, Commercial, K. Lewis
Counsellor & Consul, Commercial, D. Cameron
Counsellor, Development, I. Thomson
Chiang Mai: Hon. Consul, N. Wangviwat, Honorary Canadian Consulate, c/o Raming Tea Co. Ltd., 151 Moo 3 Super Hwy., Tasala, 5000, Thailand, (011-66-53) 24-22-92; Fax: (011-66-53) 24-26-16

## Republic of Togo *c/o* Republic of Ghana
Lomé: Hon. Consul, R. Gemmell, The Consulate of Canada, Societé des chemins de fer du Togo, PO Box 340, Togo, (011-228) 21 22 11; Fax: (011-228) 21 22 19

### Kingdom of Tonga *c/o* New Zealand

## Republic of Trinidad & Tobago
Canadian High Commission, Maple House: 3-3A Sweet Briad Rd., St. Clair, Port-of-Spain
809/623-6232; Fax: 809/628-2581
Cable: Canadian Port of Spain
Postal Address: PO Box 1246, Port-of-Spain, Trinidad
High Commissioner, Peter M. Lloyd

## Republic of Tunisia
Canadian Embassy: 3, rue du Sénégal, Place d'Afrique, Tunis
(011-216-1) 796-577; Fax: (011-216-1) 792-371
Email: tunis.td@paris03.x400.gc.ca

Postal Address: PO Box 31, Belvédère, 1002, Tunis, Tunisia
Ambassador, Arsène Després
First Secretary & Consul, Commercial, Jean-Pierre Hamel
Counsellor, Development, G. Barchechat

## Republic of Turkey
Canadian Embassy: Nenehatun Caddesi No. 75, Gaziosmanpasa, 06700, Ankara
(011-90-312) 436-1275; Fax: (011-90-312) 446-4437
Ambassador, Michael Mace
Counsellor, Commercial, B. Desjardins
Second Secretary (Commercial), David Usher, Email: david.usher@ankra.01.x400.gc.ca
Istanbul: Hon. Consul, Z.B. Tesal, Honourary Consulate of Canada, Büyükdere Cad. 107/3, Begün Han, 80300 Gayrettepe, Turkey, (011-90-1) 271-5174; Fax: (011-90-1) 272-3427

### Turkmenistan *c/o* Republic of Turkey

### Turks & Caicos Islands *c/o* Jamaica

### Republic of Tuvalu *c/o* New Zealand

### U.S. Virgin Islands *c/o* United States of America

## Republic of Uganda *c/o* Republic of Kenya
Kampala: Hon. Consul, D. Campbell, Honourary Consulate of Canada, The Consulate of Canada, 4 Ternan Ave., Nakasero, Uganda, (011-256-041) 25-81-41; Fax: (011-256-041) 24-15-18
Postal Address: c/o Uganda Bata, PO Box 20115, Kampala, Uganda

## Republic of Ukraine
Canadian Embassy: 31 Yaroslaviv Val St., 252034, Kiev
(011-38-044) 212-2112; Fax: (011-380-44) 212-2339
Ambassador, Christopher W. Westdal
Counsellor, Commercial, L. Duffield
Senior Commercial Officer, George Grushchenko

## United Arab Emirates
The Canadian Embassy, Tawam Tower 1: 1st Floor, Suite 00-1 (between Khalifa St. and The Corniche), Abu Dhabi
(011-971) 2-263655; Fax: (011-971) 2-263424
Email: mcdowasb@emirates.net.ae
Postal Address: P.O. Box 6970, Abu Dhabi, United Arab Emirates
Ambassador, Stuart B. McDowall
Commercial Officer, Nicole AbiAad Zaroubi
Bur Dubai: Consul & Senior Trade Commissioner, Richard J. Winter, Canadian Consulate, Juma Al Majid Bldg.,, #708, Khalid Ibn Al Waleed St., United Arab Emirates, (011-971-4) 52-17-17; Fax: (011-971-4) 51-77-22
Postal Address: PO Box 52472, Dubai, United Arab Emirates

## United Kingdom of Great Britain & Northern Ireland
Canadian High Commission, Macdonald House: One Grosvenor Sq., London W1X OAB
(011-44-171) 258-6600; Fax: (011-44-171) 258-6333
Email: ldn.td@ldn02.x400.gc.ca
High Commissioner, The Hon. Roy MacLaren
Minister, Commercial/Economic, R. Burchill
Minister, Political/Public Affairs, J. Wright
Counsellor, Commercial/Economic, J.-M. Roy
Commercial Officer, Partick Stratton
Belfast: Hon. Consul, J.M. Rankin, Honourary Consulate of Canada, 378 Strandmillis Rd., BT9 5EU, United Kingdom, (011-353-1232) 331-532; Fax: (011-353-1232) 312-093
Birmingham: Hon. Consul, D. Birch, Honorary Consulate of Canada, 55 Colmore Row, B3 2AS, United Kingdom, (011-44) 121-236-6474
Edinburgh: Hon. Consul, A.S. Bell, Honorary Consulate of Canada, 3 George St.,, (011-32) 220-4333

## United States of America
Canadian Embassy: 501 Pennsylvannia Ave. NW, Washington DC 20001
202/682-1740; Fax: 202/682-7726
URL: http://www.nstn.ca/wshdc
Ambassador, Raymond A.J. Chrétien
Minister, Deputy Head of Mission, Douglas G. Waddell
Counsellor, Commercial, D. Brown
Counsellor, Commercial, D. Horton
Counsellor, Commercial Agriculture & Fisheries, D. Plunkett
Counsellor, Science & Technology, D. Strange
First Secretary, Commercial, Katherine Aleong, Email: kathryn.aleong@wshdc01.x400.gc.ca
First Secretary, Commercial, R. Cairns
First Secretary, Commercial, R. Rutherford
Commercial Officer (Atlanta), John F. Alexander
Commercial Officer (Boston), Martin Robichaud, Email: martin.robichaud@bostn01.x400.gc.ca
Commercial Officer (Buffalo), Jay Mileham, Email: jay.mileham@bfalo01.x400.gc.ca
Commercial Officer (Chicago), Matthew E. Share, Email: matthew.share@chcgo01.x400.gc.ca
Commercial Officer (Dallas), Joanne E. Kirby
Commercial Officer (Detroit), Anne Cascadden, Email: anne.cascadden@dtrot01.x400.gc.ca
Commercial Officer (Los Angeles), Michael Pascal, Email: michael.pascal@lngls02.x400.gc.ca
Commercial Officer (Minneapolis), Lisa L. Swanson, Email: lisa.swanson@mnpls01.x400.gc.ca
Investment/Trade Officer (New York), Antonio Raposo, 212/596-1657
Marketing Officer (Seattle), M. Jane Hardessen-Shaw, Email: mary.hardessen-shaw@seatl01.x400.gc.ca
Atlanta: Consul General, Allan J. Stewart, Canadian Consulate General, 100, Colony Square, #1700, 1175 Peachetree St. NE, GA 30361, USA, 404/532-2000; Fax: 404/532-2050
Boston: Consul General, Mary Clancy, Canadian Consulate General, #400, 3 Copley Place, MA 02116, USA, 617/262-3760; Fax: 617/262-3415
Buffalo: Consul General, Mark Romoff, Canadian Consulate General, #3000, 1 Marine Midland Center, NY 14203-2884, USA, 716/858-9500; Fax: 716/852-4340
Chicago: Consul General, J. Christopher Poole, Canadian Consulate General, 2 Prudential Plaza, #2400, 180 North Stetson Ave., IL 60601, USA, 312/616-1860; Fax: 312/616-1877
Dallas: Consul General, Jon Swanson, Canadian Consulate General, St. Paul Place, #1700, 750 North St. Paul St., TX 75201, USA, 214/922-9806; Fax: 214/922-9815
Detroit: Consul General, Donald Wismer, Canadian Consulate General, #1100, 600 Renaissance Center, MI 48243-1798, USA, 313/567-2340; Fax: 313/567-2164; URL: http://www.bizserve.com/canadian-detroit; MITNET: 473-0000
Los Angeles: Consul General, Kim Campbell, Rt. Hon., Canadian Consulate General, California Plaza, 300 Grand Ave., 10th Fl., CA 90071, USA, 213/346-2700; Fax: 213/346-2767; Email: congen@ic.netcom.com
Miami: Consul & Trade Commissioner, D. Campbell, Canadian Consulate General, #1600, 200 South Biscayne Blvd., FL 33131, USA, 305/579-1600; Fax: 305/368-3900
Minneapolis: Consul General, Robert Déry, Canadian Consulate General, #900, 701 - 4th Ave. South, MN 55415-1899, USA, 612/333-4641; Fax: 612/332-4061; MITNET: 474-0000
New York: Consul General, George. Haynal, Canadian Consulate General, 1251 Ave. of the Americas, 16th Fl., NY 10020-1175, USA, 212/596-1600; Fax: 212/596-1790; Email: cngny@cngny01.x400.gc.ca ; URL: http://www.canada-ny.org
Princeton: Consul & Trade Commissioner, Donald Marsan, Canadian Government Trade Office, 90 Westcott Rd., NJ 08540, USA, 609/252-0777; Fax: 609/252-0792
San Juan: Hon. Consul, R.D.K. Seymour, Honourary Consulate of Canada, 107 Cereipo St., Alt. de Santa Maria, Guaynabo, Puerto Rico, 809/790-2210; Fax: 809/790-2205
Seattle: Consul General, J. Thomas Boehm, Canadian Consulate General, 412 Plaza 600, Sixth & Stewart Sts., WA 98101-1286, USA, 206/443-1777; Fax: 206/443-1782; MITNET: 477-0000

## Eastern Republic of Uruguay
Edifio Torre Libertad: Plaza Cagangha 1335, off. 1105, 11100, Montevideo
(011-598-2) 92-20-30; Fax: (011-598-2) 92-20-29
Ambassador, Roland Goulet

### Republic of Uzbekistan *c/o* Russian Federation

### Republic of Vanuatu *c/o* Commonwealth of Australia

## Holy See (Vatican)
Canadian Embassy: Via della Conciliazione 4/D, 00193, Rome
(011-39-6) 6830-7316; Fax: (011-39-6) 6880-6283
Email: MITNET: 464-0000
Ambassador, J. Fernand Tanguay
Counsellor, Y. Saint-Hilaire

## Republic of Venezuela
Canadian Embassy, Edificio Torre Europa: Ava. Francisco de Miranda, Piso 7, Campo Alegre, 1060, Caracas
(011-58-2) 951-6166; Fax: (011-58-2) 951-4950
Email: crcas@crcas01.x400.gc.ca
Postal Address: Apt. 62302, Caracas 1060A, Venezuela
Ambassador, Yves Gagnon
First Secretary & Consul, Commercial, G. Lemieux
Third Secretary & Vice Consul, Peter Lundy, Email: peter.lundy@crcas01.x400.gc.ca
Porlamar: Hon. Consul, R.B. Todd, Porlamar (Island Margarita), The Consulate of Canada, Calle Charaima, Quinta Tres Pinos, Los Bucaneros, Venezuela, (011-58-95) 613-475

## Socialist Republic of Vietnam
Canadian Embassy: 31 Hung Vuong St., Hanoi
(011-844) 823-5500; Fax: (011-844) 823-5351
Ambassador, Marius Grinius
Counsellor, Commercial, D. Dix
Counsellor, Development, P. Hoffman
Third Secretary, Commercial, Nathalie Dubé, Email: natalie.n.d.dube@paris03.x400.gc.ca
Ho Chi Minh City: Consul General, Sara S. Hradecky, Canadian Consulate, #102, 203 Dong Khoi St., Dist. 1, Vietnam, (011-84-8) 824-2000; Fax: (011-84-8) 829-4528

**Wales *c/o* United Kingdom of Great Britain & Northern Ireland**

**Independent State of Western Samoa *c/o* New Zealand**

## Republic of Yemen *c/o* Kingdom of Saudi Arabia
Sanaa: Hon. Consul, A.A. Zabarah, Honourary Consulate of Canada, c/o Yemen Computer Co., Ltd., Bldg 4, Street 11 (near Haddah St.), Yemen, (011-967-1) 20-88-14; Fax: (011-967-1) 20-95-23
Postal Address: PO Box 340, Sanaa, Yemen

## Federal Republic of Yugoslavia
Canadian Embassy: Kneza Milosa 75, 11000, Belgrade
(011-381-11) 64-46-66; Fax: (011-381-11) 64-14-80
Ambassador, Raphael Girard

## Republic of Zambia
Canadian High Commission: 5199 United Nation Ave., Lusaka
(011-260-1) 25-08-33; Fax: (011-260-1) 25-41-76
Postal Address: PO Box 31313, Lusaka, Zambia
High Commissioner, Dilys Buckley Jones

## Republic of Zimbabwe
Canadian High Commission: 45 Baines Ave., Harare
(011-263-4) 733 881; Fax: (011-263-4) 732 917
Postal Address: PO Box 1430, Harare, Zimbabwe
High Commissioner, Anne M. Charles
Counsellor, Development, J. Copland
Commercial Officer, Josée Lanctôt

# SECTION 4

## MUNICIPALITIES DIRECTORY



**See ADDENDA at the back of this book for late changes & additional information.**

## MUNICIPAL GOVERNMENT

The Municipal Section of the Almanac is in three parts. *Part 1* is a list of local municipalities in Canada, arranged by provinces, and including population and electoral districts. Each provincial list is preceded by notes about local municipal organization and elections. *Part 2* includes in-depth listings for major municipalities in Canada, listed alphabetically. *Part 3* includes regional governments in large population areas, in British Columbia, Ontario, and Québec. Please note that Federal Electoral Districts have been updated to the new Federal Electoral Districts established in the 1996 Representation Order and which went into effect in 1997. The 1996 census population is reflected in the population figures.

## Part 1 (Cities, Towns Villages, etc., with Officials, listed by Province)

### ALBERTA

The major legislation concerning municipal government in Alberta is the Municipal Government Act.

Municipal government in Alberta is either rural or urban. Rural municipal governments are organized into Municipal Districts, with Specialized Municipalities created to meet the unique needs of a specific municipality. Elected councils are responsible for all municipal functions and the levying of taxes. Two other rural categories are Improvement Districts and Special Areas, which are geographically large, sparsely populated areas for which the provincial government levies and collects all taxes and provides services.

Urban municipalities include Summer Villages, Villages, Towns and Cities. These are fully autonomous municipal units, each with an elected council. They are responsible for providing all municipal services within their corporate limits and for levying taxes and rates.

In addition to the above forms of municipal government there are eight Metis Settlements established under the Metis Settlements Act.

Types of Municipalities that may be formed:

Municipal District: A majority of the buildings used as dwellings are on parcels of land with an area of at least 1,850 square metres and there is a population of 1,000 or more.

Summer Village: There are at least sixty parcels of land that have buildings used as dwellings located on them; a majority of the persons who would be electors of the proposed summer village do not reside in the area; there is a population of less than 300.

Village: A majority of the buildings are on parcels of land smaller than 1,850 square metres and there is a population of 1,000 or more.

Town: A majority of the buildings are on parcels of land smaller than 1,850 square metres and there is a population of 1,000 or more.

City: A majority of the buildings are on parcels of land smaller than 1,850 square metres and there is a population of 10,000 or more.

Specialized Municipality: An area in which the Minister is satisfied that a type of municipality (as listed above) does not meet the needs of the proposed municipality; to provide for a form of local government that, in the opinion of the Minister, will provide for the orderly development of the municipality to a type of municipality (as listed above), or to another form of specialized municipality; an area in which the Minister is satisfied for any other reason that it is appropriate in the circumstances to form a specialized municipality.

Incorporation and changes in status are determined by the Lieutenant Governor in Council (Provincial Cabinet) on the recommendation of the Minister of Municipal Affairs. It is not necessary to change status by reason of population change.

Cities in CAPITALS; Towns marked †; Villages marked (V); Summer Villages marked (SV). Alberta Counties & Municipal Districts, Specialized Municipalities and Improvement Districts follow this list. An in-depth listing for municipalities marked with * appears in Part 2 (check Index for page numbers).

| MUNICIPALITY | 1996 POP. | FEDERAL ELECTORAL DISTRICT | PROVINCIAL ELECTORAL DISTRICT | CONTACT PERSON WITH ADDRESS, PHONE & FAX |
|---|---|---|---|---|
| Acme (V) | 600 | Wild Rose | Three Hills-Airdrie | Joanne Weller, Adm., PO Box 299, Acme T0M 0A0 – 403/546-3783, Fax: 403/546-3014 |
| AIRDRIE | 15,946 | Wild Rose | Three Hills-Airdrie | Sharon Pollyck, City Clerk, PO Box 5, Airdrie T4B 2C9 – 403/948-8800, Fax: 403/948-6567 |

Cities in CAPITALS; Towns marked †; Villages marked (V); Summer Villages marked (SV). Alberta Counties & Municipal Districts, Specialized Municipalities and Improvement Districts follow this list. An in-depth listing for municipalities marked with * appears in Part 2 (check Index for page numbers).

| MUNICIPALITY | 1996 POP. | FEDERAL ELECTORAL DISTRICT | PROVINCIAL ELECTORAL DISTRICT | CONTACT PERSON WITH ADDRESS, PHONE & FAX |
|---|---|---|---|---|
| Alberta Beach (SV) | 640 | Yellowhead | Whitecourt-Ste. Anne | Lori Donner, CAO, PO Box 278, Alberta Beach T0E 0A0 – 403/924-3181, Fax: 403/924-3313 |
| Alix (V) | 765 | Crowfoot | Lacombe-Stettler | Karen G. Mack, Adm., PO Box 87, Alix T0C 0B0 – 403/747-2495, Fax: 403/747-3663 |
| Alliance (V) | 220 | Crowfoot | Wainright | Tamina Miller, Adm., PO Box 149, Alliance T0B 0A0 – 403/879-3911, Fax: 403/879-2235 |
| Amisk (V) | 214 | Crowfoot | Wainwright | Joyce DeBord, Adm., PO Box 72, Amisk T0B 0B0 – 403/856-3980, Fax: 403/856-3980 |
| Andrew (V) | 484 | Lakeland | Vegreville-Viking | John K. Woychuk, Adm., PO Box 180, Andrew T0B 0C0 – 403/365-3687, Fax: 403/365-2061 |
| Argentia Beach (SV) | 4 | Wetaskiwin | Drayton Valley-Calmar | Ken D. Armstrong, Adm., 9322 - 73 Ave., Edmonton T6E 1A7 – 403/433-4969, Fax: 403/433-4969 |
| Arrowwood (V) | 163 | Macleod | Little Bow | Denise Kuntz, Sec.-Treas., PO Box 36, Arrowwood T0L 0B0 – 403/534-3821, Fax: 403/534-3821 |
| Athabasca † | 2,313 | Athabasca | Athabasca-Wabasca | Cliff Sawatzky, Mgr., 4705 - 49 Ave., Athabasca T9S 1B7 – 403/675-2063, Fax: 403/675-4242 |
| Banff † | 6,098 | Wild Rose | Banff-Cochrane | James Bennett, Mgr., PO Box 1260, Banff T0L 0C0 – 403/762-1200, Fax: 403/762-1260 |
| Barnwell (V) | 552 | Medicine Hat | Taber-Warner | Wendy Bateman, Adm., PO Box 159, Barnwell T0K 0B0 – 403/223-4018, Fax: 403/223-2373 |
| Barons (V) | 285 | Macleod | Little Bow | Darrell Garceau, Adm., PO Box 129, Barons T0L 0G0 – 403/757-3633, Fax: 403/757-3633 |
| Barrhead † | 4,239 | Yellowhead | Barrhead-Westlock | John M. MacLean, Municipal Sec., PO Box 4189, Barrhead T7N 1A2 – 403/674-3301, Fax: 403/674-5648 |
| Bashaw † | 774 | Crowfoot | Ponoka-Rimbey | Orlene Wigglesworth, Mgr., PO Box 510, Bashaw T0B 0H0 – 403/372-3911, Fax: 403/372-2335 |
| Bassano † | 1,272 | Medicine Hat | Bow Valley | Gerry Neighbour, Adm., PO Box 299, Bassano T0J 0B0 – 403/641-3788, Fax: 403/641-2585 |
| Bawlf (V) | 351 | Crowfoot | Ponoka-Rimbey | Myrna Schapansky, Adm., PO Box 40, Bawlf T0B 0J0 – 403/373-3797 |
| Beaumont † | 5,810 | Wetaskiwin | Leduc | Connie McKinney, Sec., 5600 - 49 St., Beaumont T4X 1A1 – 403/929-8782, Fax: 403/929-8729 |
| Beaverlodge † | 1,997 | Peace River | Grande Prairie-Wapiti | Ivan Hegland, Mgr., PO Box 30, Beaverlodge T0H 0C0 – 403/354-2202, Fax: 403/354-2207 |
| Beiseker (V) | 708 | Wild Rose | Three Hills-Airdrie | Wendy Ramberg, Adm., PO Box 349, Beiseker T0M 0G0 – 403/947-3774, Fax: 403/947-2146 |
| Bentley (V) | 987 | Wetaskiwin | Rocky Mountain House | Elizabeth Smart, CAO, PO Box 179, Bentley T0C 0J0 – 403/748-4044, Fax: 403/748-3213 |
| Berwyn (V) | 606 | Peace River | Dunvegan | Harry Aspin, Adm., PO Box 250, Berwyn T0H 0E0 – 403/338-3922, Fax: 403/338-2224 |
| Betula Beach (SV) | 6 | Yellowhead | Stony Plain | Jeanette Killips, Sec.-Treas., 10544 - 55 Ave., Edmonton T6H 0W7 – 403/434-9975 |
| Big Valley (V) | 308 | Crowfoot | Lacombe-Stettler | Yvette Cassidy, Adm., PO Box 236, Big Valley T0J 0G0 – 403/876-2269, Fax: 403/876-2223 |
| Birch Cove (SV) | 23 | Yellowhead | Whitecourt-Ste Anne | Wes Romanchuk, Adm., 5312 - 56 St., Barrhead T7N 1C3 – 403/674-6638, Fax: 403/674-5648 |
| Birchcliff (SV) | 102 | Red Deer | Rocky Mountain House | Marianne Whitehead, Adm., #104, 4505 - 50 Av.., Sylvan Lake T4S 1V9 – 403/887-2822, Fax: 403/887-2897 |
| Bittern Lake (V) | 193 | Crowfoot | Wetaskiwin-Camrose | Anne Hoyme, Sec.-Treas., General Delivery, Bittern Lake T0C 0L0 – 403/672-7373, Fax: 403/672-7373 |
| Black Diamond † | 1,811 | Macleod | Highwood | Dianne Kreh, Mgr., PO Box 10, Black Diamond T0L 0H0 – 403/933-4348, Fax: 403/933-5865 |
| Blackfalds † | 2,001 | Red Deer | Lacombe-Stettler | Jerry Bagozzi, CAO, PO Box 220, Blackfalds T0M 0J0 – 403/885-4677, Fax: 403/885-4610 |
| Blackie (V) | 301 | Macleod | Highwood? | Sharlene Shaw, Adm., PO Box 220, Blackie T0L 0J0 – 403/684-3688, Fax: 403/684-3308 |
| Bon Accord † | 1,493 | Elk Island | Redwater | Leo Ludwig, CAO, PO Box 100, Bon Accord T0A 0K0 – 403/921-3550, Fax: 403/921-3585 |
| Bondiss (SV) | 86 | Athabasca | Athabasca-Wabasca | John H. Crowston, Adm., 16411 - 79A Ave., Edmonton T5R 3J2 – 403/483-8817 |
| Bonnyville † | 5,100 | Lakeland | Bonnyville | Barry J. Temple, CAO, PO Box 1006, Bonnyville T9N 2J7 – 403/826-3496, Fax: 403/826-4806 |
| Bonnyville Beach (SV) | 64 | Lakeland | Bonnyville | Dollard L. Demers, Adm., PO Box 6439, Bonnyville T9N 2G3 – 403/826-2925, Fax: 403/826-3734 |
| Botha (V) | 194 | Crowfoot | Lacombe-Stettler | Josie Hunter, Adm., PO Box 160, Botha T0C 0N0 – 403/742-5079, Fax: 403/742-6586 |
| Bow Island † | 1,688 | Medicine Hat | Cypress-Medicine Hat | Kenneth Hollinger, Adm., PO Box 100, Bow Island T0K 0G0 – 403/545-2522, Fax: 403/545-6642 |
| Bowden † | 1,014 | Wild Rose | Innisfail-Sylvan Lake | Frances Berggren, Clerk, PO Box 338, Bowden T0M 0K0 – 403/224-3395, 2133, Fax: 403/224-2244 |
| Boyle (V) | 802 | Athabasca | Athabasca-Wabasca | Darryll White, Adm., PO Box 9, Boyle T0A 0M0 – 403/689-3642, 3643, Fax: 403/689-3998 |

Cities in CAPITALS; Towns marked †; Villages marked (V); Summer Villages marked (SV). Alberta Counties & Municipal Districts, Specialized Municipalities and Improvement Districts follow this list. An in-depth listing for municipalities marked with * appears in Part 2 (check Index for page numbers).

| MUNICIPALITY | 1996 POP. | FEDERAL ELECTORAL DISTRICT | PROVINCIAL ELECTORAL DISTRICT | CONTACT PERSON WITH ADDRESS, PHONE & FAX |
|---|---|---|---|---|
| Breton (V) | 521 | Wetaskiwin | Drayton Valley-Calmar | Charlene Freeson, Adm., PO Box 480, Breton T0C 0P0 – 403/696-3636, Fax: 403/696-3590 |
| Brooks † | 10,093 | Medicine Hat | Bow Valley | Kevin Bridges, Mgr., PO Box 880, Brooks T1R 1B7 – 403/362-3333, Fax: 403/362-4787 |
| Bruderheim † | 1,198 | Elk Island | Vegreville-Viking | Paul Ross, CAO, PO Box 280, Bruderheim T0B 0S0 – 403/796-3731, Fax: 403/796-3037 |
| Burdett (V) | 286 | Medicine Hat | Cypress-Medicine Hat | Roselyn Pahl, Adm., PO Box 37, Burdett T0K 0J0 – 403/833-3794, Fax: 403/833-3794 |
| Burnstick Lake (SV) | 4 | Red Deer | Rocky Mountain House | Sharon Plett, Adm., PO Box 5754, High River T1V 1P3 – 403/652-4636, Fax: 403/652-3125 |
| *CALGARY | 768,082 | Calgary Centre; Calgary Northeast; Calgary East; Calgary Southeast; Calgary Southwest; Calgary West; Calgary-Nosehill | Cal.-Bow; Cal.-Buffalo; Cal.-Currie; Cal.-Egmont; Cal.-Elbow; Cal.-Fish Creek; Cal.-Cross; Cal.-East.; Cal.-Foothills; Cal.-Forest Lawn; Cal.-Glenmore; Cal.-Lougheed; Cal.-McCall; Cal.-McKnight; Cal.-Millican; Cal.-Montrose; Cal.-Mountain View; Cal.-North Hill; Cal.-Nose Creek; Cal.-NW.; Cal.-Shaw; Cal.-Varsity; Cal. W. | D. L. Garner, Clerk, PO Box 2100, Calgary T2P 2M5 – 403/268-2111, Fax: 403/268-2633, URL: http//www.gov.calgary.ab.ca/ |
| Calmar † | 1,797 | Wetaskiwin | Drayton Valley-Calmar | Shirley Melnikel, CEO, PO Box 750, Calmar T0C 0V0 – 403/985-3604, Fax: 403/985-3039 |
| CAMROSE | 13,728 | Crowfoot | Wetaskiwin-Camrose | J. Neil Brodie, Clerk, City Hall, 5204 - 50 Ave., Camrose T4V 0S8 – 403/672-4426, Fax: 403/672-2469, URL: http://www.camrose.com/ |
| Canmore † | 8,354 | Wild Rose | Banff-Cochrane | Glenn Pitman, CAO, 600 - 9 St., Canmore T1W 2T2 – 403/678-1500, 1501, Fax: 403/678-1534 |
| Carbon (V) | 450 | Crowfoot | Drumheller | Wendy J. Sowerby, Adm., PO Box 249, Carbon T0M 0L0 – 403/572-3244, Fax: 403/572-3778 |
| Cardston † | 3,417 | Lethbridge | Cardston-Chief Mountain | Gregory D. Burt, Adm., PO Box 280, Cardston T0K 0K0 – 403/653-3366, Fax: 403/653-2499 |
| Carmangay (V) | 258 | Macleod | Little Bow | Audrey Wilcox, Adm., PO Box 130, Carmangay T0L 0N0 – 403/643-3595, Fax: 403/643-2007 |
| Caroline (V) | 472 | Red Deer | Rocky Mountain House | Edna Topp, Adm., PO Box 148, Caroline T0M 0M0 – 403/722-3781, Fax: 403/722-4050 |
| Carstairs † | 1,887 | Wild Rose | Olds-Didsbury | Daphne Turner, CAO, PO Box 370, Carstairs T0M 0N0 – 403/337-3341, Fax: 403/337-3343 |
| Castle Island (SV) | 19 | Yellowhead | Whitecourt-Ste Anne | Patricia Ludwig, Adm., PO Box 638, Bon Accord T0A 0K0 – 403/483-5637, Fax: 403/483-5637 |
| Castor † | 970 | Crowfoot | Chinook | Michael Yakielashek, CAO, PO Box 479, Castor T0C 0X0 – 403/882-3215,3454, Fax: 403/882-2700 |
| Cereal (V) | 211 | Crowfoot | Chinook | Carol Hok, Adm., PO Box 160, Cereal T0J 0N0 – 403/326-3823, Fax: 403/326-3823 |
| Champion (V) | 362 | Macleod | Little Bow | Marjorie Robinson, Adm., PO Box 367, Champion T0L 0R0 – 403/897-3833, Fax: 403/897-2250 |
| Chauvin (V) | 400 | Crowfoot | Wainwright | Betty Swanson, Adm., PO Box 160, Chauvin T0B 0V0 – 403/858-3881, Fax: 403/858-2125 |
| Chestermere † | 1,911 | Wild Rose | Drumheller | Frank Kosa, CAO, 156 East Chestermere Dr., Chestermere T1X 1C1 – 403/272-9744,9745, Fax: 403/569-0512 |
| Chipman (V) | 230 | Elk Island | Vegreville-Viking | Pat Tomkow, Adm., PO Box 176, Chipman T0B 0W0 – 403/363-3982, Fax: 403/363-3766 |
| Claresholm † | 3,427 | Macleod | Pincher Creek-MacLeod | Larry Flexhaug, Town Coordinator, PO Box 1000, Claresholm T0L 0T0 – 403/625-3381, Fax: 403/625-3869 |
| Clive (V) | 517 | Wetaskiwin | Lacombe-Stettler | Karen Kane, Adm., PO Box 90, Clive T0C 0Y0 – 403/784-3366, Fax: 403/784-2012 |
| Clyde (V) | 410 | Athabasca | Barrhead-Westlock | Wyatt Glebe, Adm., PO Box 190, Clyde T0G 0P0 – 403/348-5356, Fax: 403/348-5356 |
| Coaldale † | 5,731 | Lethbridge | Taber-Warner | Sheldon Steinke, Mgr., 1920 - 17 St., Coaldale T1M 1M1 – 403/345-1300, Fax: 403/345-1311 |
| Coalhurst † | 1,439 | Lethbridge | Little Bow | Marge Williams, Adm., PO Box 456, Coalhurst T0L 0V0 – 403/381-3033, Fax: 403/381-2924 |
| Cochrane † | 7,424 | Wild Rose | Banff-Cochrane | Julian deCocq, CAO, PO Box 10, Cochrane T0L 0W0 – 403/932-2075, Fax: 403/932-6032 |
| Cold Lake † | 4,089 | Lakeland | Bonnyville | Mark Power, Interim CAO, 5319 - 48 Ave., Cold Lake T9M 1A1 – 403/594-4494, Fax: 403/594-3480 |
| Consort (V) | 794 | Crowfoot | Chinook | Allan Harvey, Adm., PO Box 490, Consort T0C 1B0 – 403/577-3623, Fax: 403/577-2024 |
| Coronation † | 1,166 | Crowfoot | Chinook | Terrence Schneider, Adm., PO Box 219, Coronation T0C 1C0 – 403/578-3679, Fax: 403/578-3020 |

Cities in CAPITALS; Towns marked †; Villages marked (V); Summer Villages marked (SV). Alberta Counties & Municipal Districts, Specialized Municipalities and Improvement Districts follow this list. An in-depth listing for municipalities marked with * appears in Part 2 (check Index for page numbers).

| MUNICIPALITY | 1996 POP. | FEDERAL ELECTORAL DISTRICT | PROVINCIAL ELECTORAL DISTRICT | CONTACT PERSON WITH ADDRESS, PHONE & FAX |
|---|---|---|---|---|
| Coutts (V) | 386 | Lethbridge | Taber-Warner | Shirley A. Heather-Kalau, CAO, PO Box 202, Coutts T0K 0N0 – 403/344-3848, Fax: 403/344-4360 |
| Cowley (V) | 273 | Macleod | Pincher Creek-MacLeod | Laurie Wilgosh, Adm., PO Box 40, Cowley T0K 0P0 – 403/628-3808, Fax: 403/628-3808 |
| Cremona (V) | 380 | Wild Rose | Olds-Didsbury | Penny Fox, CAO, PO Box 10, Cremona T0M 0R0 – 403/637-3762, Fax: 403/637-2101 |
| Crossfield † | 1,899 | Wild Rose | Olds-Didsbury | Brian L. Irvine, CAO, PO Box 500, Crossfield T0M 0S0 – 403/946-5565, Fax: 403/946-4523 |
| Crowsnest Pass † | 6,356 | Macleod | Pincher Creek-MacLeod | Pat Lyster, Acting Adm., PO Box 600, Blairmore T0K 0E0 – 403/562-8833, Fax: 403/563-5474 |
| Crystal Springs (SV) | 55 | Wetaskiwin | Drayton Valley-Calmar | Bernie Bawol, Adm., 46 Mission St., Sherwood Park T8A 0V7 – 403/464-2346, Fax: 403/464-2346 |
| Czar (V) | 199 | Crowfoot | Wainwright | Tricia Strang, Adm., PO Box 30, Czar T0B 0Z0 – 403/857-3740, Fax: 403/857-2353 |
| Daysland † | 679 | Crowfoot | Wainwright | Avril Crossley, Adm., PO Box 610, Daysland T0B 1A0 – 403/374-3767, Fax: 403/374-2455 |
| Delburne (V) | 641 | Crowfoot | Innisfail-Sylvan Lake | Larry Baran, Adm., PO Box 341, Delburne T0M 0V0 – 403/749-3606, Fax: 403/749-2800 |
| Delia (V) | 208 | Crowfoot | Drumheller | Velma V. Kalhs, Sec.-Treas., PO Box 206, Delia T0J 0W0 – 403/364-3787, Fax: 403/364-2089 |
| Derwent (V) | 110 | Lakeland | Vermillion-Lloydminster | Shirley Crabbe, Sec.-Treas., PO Box 102, Derwent T0B 1C0 – 403/741-3792, Fax: 403/741-3792 |
| Devon † | 4,496 | Wetaskiwin | Leduc | Gerald Rhodes, CAO, PO Box 400, Devon T0C 1E0 – 403/987-3366, Fax: 403/987-4778 |
| Dewberry (V) | 185 | Lakeland | Vermillion-Lloydminster | Anne Elliott, Sec.-Treas., PO Box 30, Dewberry T0B 1G0 – 403/847-3053 |
| Didsbury † | 3,553 | Wild Rose | Olds-Didsbury | Evan Parliament, CAO, PO Box 790, Didsbury T0M 0W0 – 403/335-3391, Fax: 403/335-9794 |
| Donalda (V) | 235 | Crowfoot | Lacombe-Stettler | Robin O. Cosgrove, CAO, PO Box 160, Donalda T0B 1H0 – 403/883-2345, Fax: 403/883-2022 |
| Donnelly (V) | 375 | Peace River | Dunvegan | Helene Hausler, Sec., PO Box 200, Donnelly T0H 1G0 – 403/925-3835, Fax: 403/925-2100 |
| Drayton Valley † | 5,883 | Yellowhead | Drayton Valley-Calmar | Manny Deol, Mgr., PO Box 6837, Drayton Valley T7A 1A1 – 403/542-5327, Fax: 403/542-5753 |
| DRUMHELLER | 6,587 | Crowfoot | Drumheller | Raymond Romanetz, Mgr., 703 - 2 Ave. West, Drumheller T0J 0Y3 – 403/823-1339, Fax: 403/823-7739 |
| Duchess (V) | 693 | Medicine Hat | Bow Valley | Karen Grove, Sec.-Treas., PO Box 158, Duchess T0J 0Z0 – 403/378-4452, Fax: 403/378-3860 |
| Eckville † | 901 | Red Deer | Rocky Mountain House | Therese Kleeberger, Adm., PO Box 578, Eckville T0M 0X0 – 403/746-2171, Fax: 403/746-2900 |
| Edberg (V) | 137 | Crowfoot | Ponoka-Rimbey | Bernice McAmmond, Adm., PO Box 160, Edberg T0B 1J0 – 403/877-3959, Fax: 403/877-2562 |
| Edgerton (V) | 372 | Crowfoot | Wainwright | Mary Trefiak, CAO, PO Box 57, Edgerton T0B 1K0 – 403/755-3933, Fax: 403/755-3750 |
| *EDMONTON | 616,306 | Edmonton East; Edmonton North; Edmonton Northwest; Edmonton Southeast; Edmonton Southwest; Edmonton-Strathcona | Edmonton-Avonmore; Ed.-Beverly-Belmont; Ed.-Centre; Ed.-Ellerslie; Ed.-Glengarry; Ed.-Glenora; Ed.-Gold Bar; Ed.-Highlands-Beverly; Ed.-Manning; Ed.-Mayfield; Ed.-McClung; Ed.-Meadowlark; Ed.-Mill Woods; Ed.-Norwood; Ed.-Roper; Ed.-Rutherford; Ed.-Strathcona; Ed.-Whitemud | David Edey, City Clerk, City Hall, 1 Sir Winston Churchill Sq., Edmonton T5J 2R7 – 403/496-8222, Fax: 403/496-8220, URL: http://www.gov.edmonton.ab.ca/ |
| Edmonton Beach (SV) | 425 | St. Albert | Stony Plain | Lynn Kibblewhite, CAO, Box 77, Site 3, RR#4, Stony Plain T7Z 1X4 – 403/963-4211, Fax: 403/963-4260 |
| Edson † | 7,399 | Yellowhead | West Yellowhead | Clarence Joly, Mgr., PO Box 6300, Edson T7E 1T7 – 403/723-4401, Fax: 403/723-3508 |
| Elk Point † | 1,403 | Lakeland | Lac La Biche-St Paul | J. Curt Svendsen, Mgr., PO Box 448, Elk Point T0A 1A0 – 403/724-3810, Fax: 403/724-2762 |
| Elnora (V) | 247 | Crowfoot | Innisfail-Sylvan Lake | Gwen Renouf, Adm., PO Box 629, Elnora T0M 0Y0 – 403/773-3922, Fax: 403/773-3922 |
| Empress (V) | 186 | Medicine Hat | Bow Valley | Wendi Miller, Sec., PO Box 159, Empress T0J 1E0 – 403/565-3938, Fax: 403/565-2010 |
| Entwistle (V) | 453 | Yellowhead | Stony Plain | Elsie Patterson, Adm., PO Box 270, Entwistle T0E 0S0 – 403/727-3652, Fax: 403/727-2168 |
| Evansburg (V) | 740 | Yellowhead | Whitecourt-Ste Anne | Rhonda Stoneouse, Adm., PO Box 39, Evansburg T0E 0T0 – 403/727-3583, Fax: 403/727-2384 |
| Fairview † | 3,316 | Peace River | Dunvegan | Larry Chorney, Mgr., PO Box 730, Fairview T0H 1L0 – 403/835-5461, Fax: 403/835-3576 |

Cities in CAPITALS; Towns marked †; Villages marked (V); Summer Villages marked (SV). Alberta Counties & Municipal Districts, Specialized Municipalities and Improvement Districts follow this list. An in-depth listing for municipalities marked with * appears in Part 2 (check Index for page numbers).

| MUNICIPALITY | 1996 POP. | FEDERAL ELECTORAL DISTRICT | PROVINCIAL ELECTORAL DISTRICT | CONTACT PERSON WITH ADDRESS, PHONE & FAX |
|---|---|---|---|---|
| Falher † | 1,149 | Peace River | Dunvegan | Gerard A. Nicolet, Adm., PO Box 155, Falher T0H 1M0 – 403/837-2247, Fax: 403/837-2647 |
| Ferintosh (V) | 130 | Crowfoot | Ponoka-Rimbey | Myrna Fankhanel, Adm., PO Box 160, Ferintosh T0B 1M0 – 403/877-3767, Fax: 403/877-3767 |
| Foremost (V) | 556 | Medicine Hat | Cypress-Medicine Hat | Kelly Calhoun, Adm., PO Box 159, Foremost T0K 0X0 – 403/867-3733, Fax: 403/867-2031 |
| Forestburg (V) | 930 | Crowfoot | Wainwright | Marion Oberg Riise, Adm., PO Box 210, Forestburg T0B 1N0 – 403/582-3668, Fax: 403/582-2233 |
| Fort Macleod † | 3,034 | Macleod | Pincher Creek-MacLeod | Lane McLaren, Mgr., PO Box 1420, Fort Macleod T0L 0Z0 – 403/553-4425, Fax: 403/553-2426 |
| FORT SASKATCHEWAN | 12,408 | Elk Island | Clover Bar-Fort Saskatchewan | Laurine Gunness, Clerk, 10005 - 102 St., Fort Saskatchewan T8L 2C5 – 403/992-6200, Fax: 403/998-4774 |
| Fox Creek † | 2,321 | Yellowhead | Grande Prairie-Smoky | Blaine Alexander, Mgr., PO Box 149, Fox Creek T0H 1P0 – 403/622-3896, Fax: 403/622-4247 |
| Gadsby (V) | 40 | Crowfoot | Lacombe-Stettler | Lavone Smith, Sec.-Treas., PO Box 80, Gadsby T0C 1K0 – 403/574-3793 |
| Galahad (V) | 175 | Crowfoot | Wainwright | Donna Schroeder, Adm., PO Box 66, Galahad T0B 1R0 – 403/583-3741, Fax: 403/583-2230 |
| Ghost Lake (SV) | 63 | Wild Rose | Banff-Cochrane | Ernest Janzen, Adm., PO Box 207, Carseland T0J 0M0 – 403/934-5008, Fax: 403/934-5008 |
| Gibbons † | 2,748 | Elk Island | Redwater | Maisie Metrunec, Mgr., PO Box 68, Gibbons T0A 1N0 – 403/923-3331, Fax: 403/923-3691 |
| Girouxville (V) | 332 | Peace River | Dunvegan | Estelle Girard, Adm., PO Box 276, Girouxville T0H 1S0 – 403/323-4270, Fax: 403/323-4110 |
| Gleichen † | 335 | Wild Rose | Little Bow | Phyllis Allen, Adm., PO Box 159, Gleichen T0J 1N0 – 403/734-3732, Fax: 403/734-2660 |
| Glendon (V) | 418 | Lakeland | Bonnyville | Tammy Hellum, CAO, PO Box 177, Glendon T0A 1P0 – 403/635-3807, Fax: 403/635-2100 |
| Glenwood (V) | 295 | Macleod | Cardston-Chief Mountain | Gordon Burt, Adm., PO Box 1084, Glenwood T0K 2R0 – 403/626-3233, Fax: 403/626-3233 |
| Golden Days (SV) | 92 | Wetaskiwin | Drayton Valley-Calmar | Ray Pratt, Administrataor, 16815 - 117 Ave., Edmonton T5M 3V6 – 403/483-4129, Fax: 403/451-0221 |
| Grande Cache † | 4,441 | Yellowhead | West Yellowhead | Duane J. Dukart, Adm., PO Box 300, Grande Cache T0E 0Y0 – 403/827-3362, 3363, Fax: 403/827-2406 |
| GRANDE PRAIRIE | 31,140 | Peace River | Grande Prairie-Smoky; Grande Prairie-Wapiti | Janette Ferguson, City Clerk, City Hall, PO Bag 4000, Grande Prairie T8V 6V3 – 403/538-0300, Fax: 403/539-1056, URL: http://www.ccinet.ab.ca/city-of-gp/homepage.htm |
| Grandview (SV) | 64 | Wetaskiwin | Drayton Valley-Calmar | Kathy Graber, Adm., PO Box 99, Ma Me O Beach T0C 1X0 – 403/586-2251, Fax: 403/586-3615 |
| Granum † | 337 | Macleod | Pincher Creek-MacLeod | Kevin Moore, Adm., PO Box 88, Granum T0L 1A0 – 403/687-3822, Fax: 403/687-2285 |
| Grimshaw † | 2,661 | Peace River | Dunvegan | Jenny Cole, Sec., PO Box 377, Grimshaw T0H 1W0 – 403/332-4626, Fax: 403/332-1250 |
| Gull Lake (SV) | 149 | Wetaskiwin | Rocky Mountain House | Larry E. Waud, Adm., #2, 22 Bruns Rd., Lacombe T4L 1N9 – 403/782-2510, Fax: 403/782-2510 |
| Hairy Hill (V) | 46 | Lakeland | Vegreville-Viking | Don Laing, Adm., PO Box 83, Hairy Hill T0B 1S0 – 403/768-3840, Fax: 403/768-3840 |
| Half Moon Bay (SV) | 53 | Red Deer | Rocky Mountain House | Marianne Whitehead, Adm., #104, 4505 - 50 Av., Sylvan Lake T4S 1V9 – 403/887-2822, Fax: 403/887-2897 |
| Halkirk (V) | 131 | Crowfoot | Chinook | H. Jean Anderson, Sec.-Treas., PO Box 126, Halkirk T0C 1M0 – 403/884-2464, Fax: 403/884-2113 |
| Hanna † | 3,001 | Crowfoot | Chinook | J. Duff Carroll, Mgr., PO Box 430, Hanna T0J 1P0 – 403/854-4433, Fax: 403/854-2772 |
| Hardisty † | 808 | Crowfoot | Wainwright | Debbie Johannesson, Adm., PO Box 10, Hardisty T0B 1V0 – 403/888-3623, Fax: 403/888-2200 |
| Hay Lakes (V) | 352 | Crowfoot | Leduc | Jennifer Grahn, Adm., PO Box 40, Hay Lakes T0B 1W0 – 403/878-3200, Fax: 403/878-3200 |
| Heisler (V) | 195 | Crowfoot | Wainwright | Bonnie Bendfeld, Adm., PO Box 60, Heisler T0B 2A0 – 403/889-3774, Fax: 403/889-2280 |
| High Level † | 3,093 | Peace River | Peace River | Anna Neustaeter, Municipal Sec., PO Box 485, High Level T0H 1Z0 – 403/926-2201, Fax: 403/926-2899 |
| High Prairie † | 2,907 | Athabasca | Lesser Slave Lake | Kevin Greig, Mgr., PO Box 179, High Prairie T0G 1E0 – 403/523-3388, Fax: 403/523-5930 |
| High River † | 7,359 | Macleod | Highwood | Gary Hudson, Mgr., 129 - 3 Ave. West, High River T1V 1M9 – 403/652-2110, Fax: 403/652-2396 |
| Hill Spring (V) | 220 | Macleod | Cardston-Chief Mountain | Michael D. Merill, Adm., PO Box 40, Hill Spring T0K 1E0 – 403/626-3876, Fax: 403/626-3876 |
| Hines Creek (V) | 437 | Peace River | Dunvegan | Hazel Reintjes, Mgr., PO Box 421, Hines Creek T0H 2A0 – 403/494-3690, Fax: 403/494-3605 |
| Hinton † | 9,961 | Yellowhead | West Yellowhead | Bernie Kreiner, Mgr., 813 Switzer Dr., Hinton T7V 1V1 – 403/865-6016, Fax: 403/865-5706 |

Cities in CAPITALS; Towns marked †; Villages marked (V); Summer Villages marked (SV). Alberta Counties & Municipal Districts, Specialized Municipalities and Improvement Districts follow this list. An in-depth listing for municipalities marked with * appears in Part 2 (check Index for page numbers).

| MUNICIPALITY | 1996 POP. | FEDERAL ELECTORAL DISTRICT | PROVINCIAL ELECTORAL DISTRICT | CONTACT PERSON WITH ADDRESS, PHONE & FAX |
|---|---|---|---|---|
| Holden (V) | 397 | Lakeland | Vegreville-Viking | Christine B. Mackay, CAO, PO Box 357, Holden T0B 2C0 – 403/688-3928, Fax: 403/688-2091 |
| Horseshoe Bay (SV) | 37 | Lakeland | Lac La Biche-St Paul | Ken Parsons, Adm., 15035 - 80 St., Edmonton T5C 1M4 – 403/475-2407 |
| Hughenden (V) | 258 | Crowfoot | Wainwright | Trudy Pelsey, Adm., PO Box 26, Hughenden T0B 2E0 – 403/856-3830, Fax: 403/856-2034 |
| Hussar (V) | 157 | Wild Rose | Drumheller | Valerie Allan, Adm., PO Box 100, Hussar T0J 1S0 – 403/787-3766 |
| Hythe (V) | 712 | Peace River | Grande Prairie-Wapiti | Christene Livingstone, Adm., PO Box 219, Hythe T0H 2C0 – 403/356-3888, Fax: 403/356-2009 |
| Innisfail † | 6,116 | Red Deer | Innisfail-Sylvan Lake | Dale P. Mather, CAO, 4945 - 53 St., Innisfail T4G 1A1 – 403/227-3376, Fax: 403/227-4045 |
| Innisfree (V) | 238 | Lakeland | Vermilion-Lloydminster | Andrea Stepanik, Adm., PO Box 69, Innisfree T0B 2G0 – 403/592-3886, Fax: 403/592-3729 |
| Irma (V) | 472 | Crowfoot | Wainwright | Evelyn Mark, CAO, PO Box 241, Irma T0B 2H0 – 403/754-3665, Fax: 403/754-3668 |
| Irricana (V) | 823 | Wild Rose | Three Hills-Airdrie | Rosemary Wittevrongel, CAO, PO Box 100, Irricana T0M 1B0 – 403/935-4672, Fax: 403/935-4270 |
| Island Lake (SV) | 187 | Athabasca | Athabasca-Wabasca | Shelley Bowles, Adm., PO Box 119, Legal T0J 1L0 – 403/961-2487, Fax: 403/961-2024 |
| Island Lake South (SV) | 76 | Athabasca | Athabasca-Wabasca | Ken Parsons, Adm., 15035 - 80 St., Edmonton T5C 1M4 – 403/475-2407 |
| Itaska Beach (SV) | 8 | Wetaskiwin | Drayton Valley-Calmar | John F. Tyler, CAO, PO Box 420, Breton T0C 0P0 – 403/696-3880, Fax: 403/696-3880 |
| Jarvis Bay (SV) | 83 | Red Deer | Rocky Mountain House | Marianne Whitehead, Adm., #104, 4505 - 50 Ave., Sylvan Lake T4S 1V9 – 403/887-2822, Fax: 403/887-2897 |
| Kapasiwin (SV) | 10 | Yellowhead | Stony Plain | Jolly Drever, Adm., PO Box 3, Kapasiwin T0E 2Y0 – 403/892-2879 |
| Killam † | 1,048 | Vegreville | Wainwright | Russell Warderope, Adm., PO Box 189, Killam T0B 2L0 – 403/385-3977, Fax: 403/385-2120 |
| Kinuso (V) | 258 | Athabasca | Lesser Slave Lake | June Roe, Adm., PO Box 57, Kinuso T0G 1K0 – 403/775-3570, Fax: 403/775-3910 |
| Kitscoty (V) | 643 | Lakeland | Vermilion-Lloydminster | Jean E. Buha, Adm., PO Box 128, Kitscoty T0B 2P0 – 403/846-2221, Fax: 403/846-2221 |
| Lac La Biche † | 2,611 | Lakeland | Lac la Biche-St Paul | Richard Persson, Sec., PO Box 387, Lac La Biche T0A 2C0 – 403/623-4323, Fax: 403/623-3510 |
| Lacombe † | 8,018 | Wetaskiwin | Lacombe-Stettler | Robert Jenkins, CAO, 5034 - 52 St., Lacombe T4L 1A1 – 403/782-6666, Fax: 403/782-5655 |
| Lakeview (SV) | 15 | Yellowhead | Stony Plain | Jeanette Killips, Sec.-Treas., 10544 - 55 Ave., Edmonton T6H 0W7 – 403/434-9975 |
| Lamont † | 1,581 | Elk Island | Vegreville-Viking | Dean Pickering, CAO, PO Box 330, Lamont T0B 2R0 – 403/895-2010, Fax: 403/895-2595 |
| Larkspur (SV) | 11 | Athabasca | Barrhead-Westlock | Don Baillie, Adm., PO Box 339, Boyle T0A 0M0 – 403/689-2080, Fax: 403/689-3998 |
| Lavoy (V) | 122 | Lakeland | Vegreville-Viking | Shirley Rattray, Sec.-Treas., PO Box 179, Lavoy T0B 2S0 |
| LEDUC | 14,305 | Wetaskiwin | Leduc | Coral Callioux, City Clerk, 1 Alexandra Park, Leduc T9E 4C4 – 403/980-7177, Fax: 403/980-7127 |
| Legal (V) | 1,095 | St. Albert | Redwater | Wilma Weiss, Adm., PO Box 390, Legal T0G 1L0 – 403/961-3773, Fax: 403/961-4133 |
| *LETHBRIDGE | 63,053 | Lethbridge | Lethbridge-East; Lethbridge-West | Dianne Nemeth, City Clerk, City Hall, 910 - 4 Ave. South, Lethbridge T1J 0P6 – 403/320-3900, Fax: 403/320-9369, URL: http://www.city.lethbridge.ab.ca |
| Linden (V) | 565 | Wild Rose | Three Hills-Airdrie | Bernice Eitzen, Acting Adm., PO Box 213, Linden T0M 1J0 – 403/546-3888, Fax: 403/546-2112 |
| LLOYDMINSTER | 7,636[1] | Lakeland | Vermillion-Lloydminster | Tom Lysyk, Clerk, City Hall, 5011 - 49 Ave., Lloydminster S9V 0T8 – 306/825-6184, Fax: 306/825-7170 |
| Lomond (V) | 170 | Macleod | Little Bow | Tracy Doram, CAO, PO Box 268, Lomond T0L 1G0 – 403/792-3611, Fax: 403/792-3782 |
| Longview (V) | 303 | Macleod | Highwood | Judy Wiebe, Adm., PO Box 147, Longview T0L 1H0 – 403/558-3922, Fax: 403/558-3743 |
| Lougheed (V) | 253 | Crowfoot | Wainwright | Stan Towers, Sec.-Treas., PO Box 5, Lougheed T0B 2V0 – 403/386-3970, Fax: 403/386-2136 |
| Ma Me O Beach (SV) | 65 | Wetaskiwin | Drayton Valley-Calmar | Kathy Graber, Adm., PO Box 99, Ma Me O Beach T0C 1X0 – 403/586-2251, Fax: 403/586-3615 |
| Magrath † | 1,867 | Lethbridge | Cardston-Chief Mountain | Rodney Bly, Adm., PO Box 520, Magrath T0K 1J0 – 403/758-3212, Fax: 403/758-6333 |
| Manning † | 1,295 | Peace River | Peace River | Penny Kary, Adm., PO Box 125, Manning T0H 2M0 – 403/836-3606, 3728, Fax: 403/836-3570 |
| Mannville (V) | 758 | Lakeland | Vermilion-Lloydminster | Kent Staden, Adm., PO Box 180, Mannville T0B 2W0 – 403/763-3500, Fax: 403/763-3643 |
| Marwayne (V) | 449 | Lakeland | Vermilion-Lloydminster | G.T. Horton, CAO, PO Box 113, Marwayne T0B 2X0 – 403/847-3962, Fax: 403/847-3896 |

Cities in CAPITALS; Towns marked †; Villages marked (V); Summer Villages marked (SV). Alberta Counties & Municipal Districts, Specialized Municipalities and Improvement Districts follow this list. An in-depth listing for municipalities marked with * appears in Part 2 (check Index for page numbers).

| MUNICIPALITY | 1996 POP. | FEDERAL ELECTORAL DISTRICT | PROVINCIAL ELECTORAL DISTRICT | CONTACT PERSON WITH ADDRESS, PHONE & FAX |
|---|---|---|---|---|
| Mayerthorpe † | 1,669 | Yellowhead | Whitecourt-Ste Anne | Ed Mitchell, Mgr., PO Box 420, Mayerthorpe T0E 1N0 – 403/786-2416, Fax: 403/786-4590 |
| McLennan † | 867 | Peace River | Dunvegan | Richard Duncan, Mgr., PO Box 356, McLennan T0H 2L0 – 403/324-3065, Fax: 403/324-2288 |
| MEDICINE HAT | 46,783 | Medicine Hat | Cypress-Medicine Hat; Medicine Hat | Larry P. Godin, Clerk, City Hall, 580 - 1 St. SE, Medicine Hat T1A 8E6 – 403/529-8220, Fax: 403/529-8182 |
| Mewatha Beach (SV) | 76 | Athabasca | Athabasca-Wabasca | Don Baillie, Adm., PO Box 339, Boyle T0A 0M0 – 403/689-2080, Fax: 403/689-3998 |
| Milk River † | 929 | Lethbridge | Taber-Warner | Lavinia Henderson, CAO, PO Box 270, Milk River T0K 1M0 – 403/647-3773, Fax: 403/647-3772 |
| Millet † | 1,894 | Wetaskiwin | Wetaskiwin-Camrose | Michael E. (Mike) Storey, CAO, PO Box 270, Millet T0C 1Z0 – 403/387-4554, Fax: 403/387-4459 |
| Milo (V) | 117 | Macleod | Little Bow | Colleen Deitz, Adm., PO Box 65, Milo T0L 1L0 – 403/599-3883, Fax: 403/599-2201 |
| Minburn (V) | 95 | Lakeland | Vermilion-Lloydminster | Shari-Anne Doolaege, Sec.-Treas., PO Box 65, Minburn T0B 3B0 – 403/593-3939 |
| Mirror (V) | 487 | Crowfoot | Lacombe-Stettler | Lavern Clark, Adm., PO Box 130, Mirror T0B 3C0 – 403/788-3011, Fax: 403/788-2345 |
| Morinville † | 6,226 | St. Albert | Spruce Grove-Sturgeon-St Albert | Bryce S.D. Walt, Mgr., 10125 - 100 Ave., Morinville T8R 1L6 – 403/939-4361, Fax: 403/939-5633 |
| Morrin (V) | 275 | Crowfoot | Drumheller | Annette Plachner, Sec.-Treas., PO Box 149, Morrin T0J 2B0 – 403/772-3870, Fax: 403/772-2123 |
| Mundare † | 578 | Lakeland | Vegreville-Viking | Peter Polischuk, Adm., PO Box 348, Mundare T0B 3H0 – 403/764-3929, Fax: 403/764-2003 |
| Munson (V) | 201 | Crowfoot | Drumheller | Ken Raduenz, Adm., PO Box 10, Munson T0J 2C0 – 403/823-6987, Fax: 403/823-6987 |
| Myrnam (V) | 294 | Lakeland | Vermillion-Lloydminster | Gloria Yaremchuk, Sec.-Treas., PO Box 278, Myrnam T0B 3K0 – 403/366-3910, Fax: 403/366-3910 |
| Nakamun Park (SV) | 14 | Yellowhead | Whitecourt-Ste Anne | Shelley Bowles, Sec.-Treas., Site 1, RR#1, Onoway T0E 1V0 – 403/961-2024, Fax: 403/961-2024 |
| Nampa (V) | 427 | Peace River | Peace River | Sharon Unrau, Adm., PO Box 69, Nampa T0H 2R0 – 403/322-3852, Fax: 403/322-2100 |
| Nanton † | 1,665 | Macleod | Little Bow | Karen G. Harty, Adm., PO Box 609, Nanton T0L 1R0 – 403/646-2029, Fax: 403/646-2653 |
| New Norway (V) | 270 | Crowfoot | Ponoka-Rimbey | Anne Flynn, Adm., PO Box 60, New Norway T0B 3L0 – 403/855-3915, Fax: 403/855-3915 |
| New Sarepta (V) | 359 | Wetaskiwin | Leduc | Orville Borys, Adm., PO Box 278, New Sarepta T0B 3M0 – 403/941-3929, Fax: 403/941-3929 |
| Nobleford (V) | 558 | Lethbridge | Little Bow | Darrell Garceau, Adm., PO Box 67, Nobleford T0L 1S0 – 403/824-3555, Fax: 403/824-3555 |
| Norglenwold (SV) | 281 | Red Deer | Rocky Mountain House | Marianne Whitehead, Adm., #104, 4505 - 50 Av., Sylvan Lake T4S 1V9 – 403/887-2822, Fax: 403/887-2897 |
| Norris Beach (SV) | 23 | Wetaskiwin | Drayton Valley-Calmar | John B. Ludwig, Adm., 9615 - 152 St., Edmonton T5P 1W7 – 403/484-4213, Fax: 403/481-2887 |
| Okotoks † | 8,510 | Macleod | Highwood | Will Pearce, Mgr., PO Box 220, Okotoks T0L 1T0 – 403/938-4404, Fax: 403/938-7387 |
| Olds † | 5,815 | Wild Rose | Olds-Didsbury | Garry Gelech, CAO, 4911 - 51 Ave., Olds T4H 1R5 – 403/556-6981, Fax: 403/556-6537 |
| Onoway (V) | 788 | Yellowhead | Whitecourt-Ste Anne | Catherine Dunn, Director of Municipal Operations, PO Box 540, Onoway T0E 1V0 – 403/967-5338, Fax: 403/967-3226 |
| Oyen † | 1,009 | Crowfoot | Chinook | Debbie Kovitch, Adm., PO Box 360, Oyen T0J 2J0 – 403/664-3511, 3585, Fax: 403/664-3712 |
| Paradise Valley (V) | 141 | Lakeland | Vermillion-Lloydminster | Connie Wilkinson, Adm., PO Box 24, Paradise Valley T0B 3R0 – 403/745-2287, Fax: 403/745-2287 |
| Parkland Beach (SV) | 97 | Macleod | Wetaskiwin | Susan Koots, Adm., PO Box 130, Rimbey T0C 2J0 – 403/843-2055, Fax: 403/843-6499 |
| Peace River † | 6,536 | Peace River | Peace River | Gordon Lundy, Mgr., PO Box 6600, Peace River T8S 1S4 – 403/624-2574, Fax: 403/624-4664 |
| Pelican Narrows (SV) | 106 | Lakeland | Bonnyville | Padey Lapointe, Adm., PO Box 7878, Bonnyville T9N 2J2 – 403/826-5907 |
| Penhold † | 1,625 | Red Deer | Innisfail-Sylvan Lake | Linda See, Adm., PO Box 10, Penhold T0M 1R0 – 403/886-4567, Fax: 403/886-4039 |
| Picture Butte † | 1,669 | Lethbridge | Little Bow | Nona C. Housenga, Adm., PO Box 670, Picture Butte T0K 1V0 – 403/732-4555, 4482, Fax: 403/732-4334 |
| Pincher Creek † | 3,659 | Macleod | Pincher Creek-MacLeod | Sandy Chrapko, Mgr., PO Box 159, Pincher Creek T0K 1W0 – 403/627-3156, Fax: 403/627-4784 |
| Plamondon (V) | 256 | Lakeland | Lac la Biche-St Paul | Collette Borgen, Adm., PO Box 98, Plamondon T0A 2T0 – 403/798-3883, Fax: 403/789-2400 |
| Point Alison (SV) | 6 | Yellowhead | Stony Plain | Birch Nero, Adm., 112 Langholm Dr., St. Albert T8N 3N9 – 403/458-0285 |
| Ponoka † | 6,149 | Wetaskiwin | Ponoka-Rimbey | Dave Dmytryshyn, Mgr., 5102 - 48 Ave., Ponoka T4J 1P7 – 403/783-4431, Fax: 403/783-6745 |

Cities in CAPITALS; Towns marked †; Villages marked (V); Summer Villages marked (SV). Alberta Counties & Municipal Districts, Specialized Municipalities and Improvement Districts follow this list. An in-depth listing for municipalities marked with * appears in Part 2 (check Index for page numbers).

| MUNICIPALITY | 1996 POP. | FEDERAL ELECTORAL DISTRICT | PROVINCIAL ELECTORAL DISTRICT | CONTACT PERSON WITH ADDRESS, PHONE & FAX |
|---|---|---|---|---|
| Poplar Bay (SV) | 66 | Wetaskiwin | Drayton Valley-Calmar | John B. Ludwig, Adm., 9615 - 152 St., Edmonton T5P 1W7 – 403/484-4213, Fax: 403/481-2887 |
| Provost † | 1,904 | Crowfoot | Wainwright | Lynda P. Berry, Adm., PO Box 449, Provost T0B 3S0 – 403/753-2261, Fax: 403/753-6889 |
| Rainbow Lake † | 1,138 | Peace River | Peace River | J. Melville Burge, Mgr., PO Box 149, Rainbow Lake T0H 2Y0 – 403/956-3934, Fax: 403/956-3570 |
| Raymond † | 3,056 | Lethbridge | Cardston-Chief Mountain | Scott Barton, CAO, PO Box 629, Raymond T0K 2S0 – 403/752-3322, Fax: 403/752-4379 |
| *RED DEER | 60,075 | Red Deer | Red Deer-North; Red Deer-South | Kelly Kloss, Clerk, City Hall, PO Box 5008, Red Deer T4N 3T4 – 403/342-8111, 8132, Fax: 403/346-6195, URL: http://www.city.red-deer.ab.ca/ |
| Redcliff † | 4,104 | Medicine Hat | Bow Valley | Randy Giesbrecht, Mgr., PO Box 40, Redcliff T0J 2P0 – 403/548-3618, Fax: 403/548-6623 |
| Redwater † | 2,053 | Elk Island | Redwater | Don McLeod, Mgr., PO Box 397, Redwater T0A 2W0 – 403/942-3519, Fax: 403/942-4321 |
| Rimbey † | 2,106 | Wetaskiwin | Ponoka-Rimbey | Greg Gayton, Mgr., PO Box 350, Rimbey T0C 2J0 – 403/843-2113, Fax: 403/843-6599 |
| Rochon Sands (SV) | 86 | Crowfoot | Lacombe-Stettler | Delmar Tweit, Adm., PO Box 1746, Stettler T0C 2L0 – 403/742-4717, 3841, Fax: 403/742-2766 |
| Rocky Mountain House † | 5,805 | Red Deer | Rocky Mountain House | Larry Holstead, Mgr., PO Box 1509, Rocky Mountain House T0M 1T0 – 403/845-2866, Fax: 403/845-3230 |
| Rockyford (V) | 346 | Wild Rose | Drumheller | Lois Mountjoy, Adm., PO Box 294, Rockyford T0J 2R0 – 403/533-3950, Fax: 403/533-3950 |
| Rosalind (V) | 195 | Crowfoot | Ponoka-Rimbey | Maxine King, Adm., General Delivery, Rosalind T0B 3Y0 – 403/375-3996, Fax: 403/375-3996 |
| Rosemary (V) | 332 | Medicine Hat | Bow Valley | Verna Plett, Sec.-Treas., PO Box 128, Rosemary T0J 2W0 – 403/378-4246, Fax: 403/378-3144 |
| Ross Haven (SV) | 108 | Yellowhead | Whitecourt-Ste Anne | Dennis Evans, Adm., 16, 26213 Township Rd. 512, Spruce Grove T7Y 1C6 – 403/987-3204, Fax: 403/987-3204 |
| Rycroft (V) | 667 | Peace River | Dunvegan | Sandra Isaac, Adm., PO Box 360, Rycroft T0H 3A0 – 403/765-3652, Fax: 403/765-2002 |
| Ryley (V) | 465 | Lakeland | Vegreville-Viking | Bob Luross, Adm., PO Box 230, Ryley T0B 4A0 – 403/663-3653, Fax: 403/663-3541 |
| ST. ALBERT | 46,888 | St. Albert | Spruce Grove-Sturgeon-St Albert; St Albert | Norbert Van Wyk, Clerk, 5 St. Anne St., St. Albert T8N 3Z9 – 403/459-1500, Fax: 403/460-2394, URL: http://www.city.st-albert.ab.ca |
| St. Paul † | 4,861 | Lakeland | Lac La Biche-St Paul | Wayne C. Horner, Adm., PO Box 1480, St. Paul T0A 3A0 – 403/645-4481, Fax: 403/645-5076 |
| Sandy Beach (SV) | 171 | St-Albert | Whitecourt-Ste Anne | Shelley Bowles, Adm., Site 1, RR#1, PO Box 63, Onoway T0E 1V0 – 403/967-2873, Fax: 403/967-2873 |
| Sangudo (V) | 398 | Yellowhead | Whitecourt-Ste Anne | Pamela Nelson, CAO, PO Box 190, Sangudo T0E 2A0 – 403/785-2258, Fax: 403/785-3393 |
| Seba Beach (SV) | 124 | Yellowhead | Stony Plain | Susan Dzus, Adm., PO Box 190, Seba Beach T0E 2B0 – 403/797-3863, Fax: 403/797-3800 |
| Sedgewick † | 937 | Crowfoot | Wainwright | Thelma Harris, Acting Adm., PO Box 129, Sedgewick T0B 4C0 – 403/384-3504, Fax: 403/384-3545 |
| Sexsmith † | 1,481 | Peace River | Grande Prairie-Smoky | Carolyn Gaunt, Mgr., PO Box 420, Sexsmith T0H 3C0 – 403/568-3681, Fax: 403/568-2200 |
| Silver Beach (SV) | 47 | Wetaskiwin | Drayton Valley-Calmar | Ray Pratt, Adm., 16815 - 117th Ave., Edmonton T5M 3V6 – 403/483-4129, Fax: 403/451-0221 |
| Silver Sands (SV) | 105 | Yellowhead | Whitecourt-Ste Anne | Mark T. Anker, Adm., 14403 - 110A Ave., Edmonton T5N 1J7 – 403/454-9414, Fax: 403/452-5238 |
| Slave Lake † | 6,553 | Athabasca | Lesser Slave Lake | Pat Vincent, Mgr., PO Box 1030, Slave Lake T0G 2A0 – 403/849-8000, Fax: 403/849-2633 |
| Smoky Lake † | 1,087 | Lakeland | Redwater | David Sarsfield, Adm., PO Box 460, Smoky Lake T0A 3C0 – 403/656-3674, Fax: 403/656-3675 |
| South Baptiste (SV) | 66 | Athabaska | Athabasca-Wabasca | Don Baillie, Adm., PO Box 339, Boyle T0A 0M0 – 403/689-2080, Fax: 403/689-3998 |
| South View (SV) | 60 | Yellowhead | Whitecourt-Ste Anne | Mark T. Anker, Adm., 14403 - 110A Ave., Edmonton T5N 1J7 – 403/454-9414, Fax: 403/452-5238 |
| Spirit River † | 1,112 | Peace River | Dunvegan | Ron Thompson, Mgr., PO Box 130, Spirit River T0H 3G0 – 403/864-3998, Fax: 403/864-3433 |
| SPRUCE GROVE | 14,271 | St. Albert | Spruce Grove-Sturgeon-St Albert | Diane Roy, Clerk, 315 Jespersen Ave., Spruce Grove T7X 3E8 – 403/962-2611, Fax: 403/962-2526 |
| Standard (V) | 366 | Wild Rose | Drumheller | Evelyn Larsen, CAO, PO Box 249, Standard T0J 3G0 – 403/644-3968, Fax: 403/644-2284 |
| Stavely † | 453 | Macleod | Little Bow | Sheryl Fath, Adm., PO Box 249, Stavely T0L 1Z0 – 403/549-3761, Fax: 403/549-3743 |
| Stettler † | 5,220 | Crowfoot | Lacombe-Stettler | Robert Stoutenberg, Mgr., PO Box 280, Stettler T0C 2L0 – 403/742-8305, Fax: 403/742-1404 |
| Stirling (V) | 874 | Lethbridge | Taber-Warner | J. Scott Barton, Adm., PO Box 360, Stirling T0K 2E0 – 403/756-3379, Fax: 403/756-2262 |

Cities in CAPITALS; Towns marked †; Villages marked (V); Summer Villages marked (SV). Alberta Counties & Municipal Districts, Specialized Municipalities and Improvement Districts follow this list. An in-depth listing for municipalities marked with * appears in Part 2 (check Index for page numbers).

| MUNICIPALITY | 1996 POP. | FEDERAL ELECTORAL DISTRICT | PROVINCIAL ELECTORAL DISTRICT | CONTACT PERSON WITH ADDRESS, PHONE & FAX |
|---|---|---|---|---|
| Stony Plain † | 8,274 | St. Albert | Stony Plain | Phil Hamel, Mgr., 4905 - 51 Ave., Stony Plain T7Z 1Y1 – 403/963-2151, Fax: 403/963-0935 |
| Strathmore † | 5,282 | Wild Rose | Drumheller | Dwight Stanford, Mgr., 680 Westchester Rd., Strathmore T1P 1J1 – 403/934-3133, Fax: 403/934-4713 |
| Strome (V) | 269 | Crowfoot | Wainwright | Betty Mohler, Adm., PO Box 51, Strome T0B 4H0 – 403/376-3558, Fax: 403/376-3558 |
| Sunbreaker Cove (SV) | 86 | Red Deer | Rocky Mountain House | Marianne Whitehead, Adm., #104, 4505 - 50 Av., Sylvan Lake T4S 1V9 – 403/887-2822, Fax: 403/887-2897 |
| Sundance Beach (SV) | 35 | Wetaskiwin | Drayton Valley-Calmar | Ken Armstrong, Adm., 9322 - 73 Ave., Edmonton T6E 1A7 – 403/433-4969, Fax: 403/433-4969 |
| Sundre † | 2,028 | Wild Rose | Olds-Didsbury | Harvey Doering, Adm., PO Box 420, Sundre T0M 1X0 – 403/638-3551, Fax: 403/638-2100 |
| Sunrise Beach (SV) | 84 | Lakeland | Whitecourt-Ste Anne | Shelley Bowles, Adm., Site 1, RR#1, PO Box 18, Onoway T0E 1V0 – 403/967-5473, Fax: 403/967-2873 |
| Sunset Beach (SV) | 33 | Athabasca | Athabasca-Wabasca | Jim Pollock, Adm., Site 1, RR#1, PO Box 39, Onoway T0E 1V0 – 403/967-5473, Fax: 403/967-5473 |
| Sunset Point (SV) | 125 | Yellowhead | Whitecourt-Ste Anne | Robert L. Tessier, CAO, 120 Country Club Place, Edmonton T6M 2H7 – 403/481-5017 |
| Swan Hills † | 2,030 | Yellowhead | Barrhead-Westlock | Brad Watson, Mgr., PO Box 149, Swan Hills T0G 2C0 – 403/333-4477, Fax: 403/333-4547 |
| Sylvan Lake † | 5,178 | Red Deer | Innisfail-Sylvan Lake | Lyle Wack, Mgr., 4926 - 50 Ave., Sylvan Lake T4S 1A1 – 403/887-2141, Fax: 403/887-3660 |
| Taber † | 7,214 | Medicine Hat | Taber-Warner | Bevin Keith, Mgr., 4900A - 50 St., Taber T1G 1T1 – 403/223-5500, Fax: 403/223-5530 |
| Thorhild (V) | 486 | Elk Island | Redwater | Debbie Hamilton, Adm., PO Box 310, Thorhild T0A 3J0 – 403/398-3688, Fax: 403/398-2100 |
| Thorsby (V) | 725 | Wetaskiwin | Drayton Valley-Calmar | Jo-Anne Lambert, CAO, PO Box 297, Thorsby T0C 2P0 – 403/789-3935, Fax: 403/789-3779 |
| Three Hills † | 3,022 | Crowfoot | Three Hills-Airdrie | Jack Ramsden, Mgr., PO Box 610, Three Hills T0M 2A0 – 403/443-5822, Fax: 403/443-2616 |
| Tilley (V) | 368 | Medicine Hat | Bow Valley | Teresa Fillingham, Adm., PO Box 155, Tilley T0J 3K0 – 403/377-2203, Fax: 403/377-2203 |
| Tofield † | 1,726 | Lakeland | Vegreville-Viking | Cindy Neufeld, Adm., PO Box 30, Tofield T0B 4J0 – 403/662-3269, Fax: 403/662-3929 |
| Torrington (V) | 177 | Wild Rose | Three Hills-Airdrie | Irene Wilson, Adm., PO Box 10, Torrington T0M 2B0 – 403/631-3866, Fax: 403/631-2140 |
| Trochu † | 958 | Crowfoot | Three Hills-Airdrie | Maureen Malaka, Adm., PO Box 340, Trochu T0M 2C0 – 403/442-3085, Fax: 403/442-2528 |
| Turner Valley † | 1,527 | Macleod | Highwood | Sharon Plett, Mgr., PO Box 330, Turner Valley T0L 2A0 – 403/933-4944, Fax: 403/933-5377 |
| Two Hills † | 1,040 | Lakeland | Vegreville-Viking | Myron J. Goyan, CAO, PO Box 630, Two Hills T0B 4K0 – 403/657-3395, Fax: 403/657-2158 |
| Val Quentin (SV) | 123 | Yellowhead | Whitecourt Ste-Anne | Lori Donner, CAO, PO Box 128, Alberta Beach T0E 0A0 – 403/924-3085, Fax: 403/963-4260 |
| Valleyview † | 1,906 | Peace River | Grande Prairie-Smoky | Doug Topinka, Mgr., PO Box 270, Valleyview T0H 3N0 – 403/524-5150, Fax: 403/524-2727 |
| Vauxhall † | 1,011 | Medicine Hat | Little Bow | Brian Schnarr, Acting Adm., PO Box 509, Vauxhall T0K 2K0 – 403/654-2174, Fax: 403/654-4110 |
| Vegreville † | 5,337 | Lakeland | Vegreville-Viking | Richard Binnendyk, Mgr., PO Box 640, Vegreville T9C 1R7 – 403/632-2606, Fax: 403/632-3088 |
| Vermilion † | 3,744 | Lakeland | Vermilion-Lloydminster | Robert Watt, Mgr., PO Box 328, Vermilion T0B 4M0 – 403/853-5358, Fax: 403/853-4910 |
| Veteran (V) | 317 | Crowfoot | Chinook | Betty A. Christianson, Adm., PO Box 439, Veteran T0C 2S0 – 403/575-3954, Fax: 403/575-3954 |
| Viking † | 1,081 | Lakeland | Vegreville-Viking | Lydia Hanson, CAO, PO Box 369, Viking T0B 4N0 – 403/336-3466, Fax: 403/336-2660 |
| Vilna (V) | 274 | Lakeland | Lac La Biche-St Paul | Debbie Bobocel, Adm., PO Box 10, Vilna T0A 3L0 – 403/636-3620 |
| Vulcan † | 1,537 | Macleod | Little Bow | Wally Sholdice, Adm., PO Box 360, Vulcan T0L 2B0 – 403/485-2417, Fax: 403/485-2914 |
| Wabamun (V) | 645 | Yellowhead | Stony Plain | Leagh Randle, Adm., PO Box 240, Wabamun T0E 2K0 – 403/892-2699, Fax: 403/892-2669 |
| Wainwright † | 5,079 | Crowfoot | Wainwright | Ray Poulin, Adm., 1018 - 2 Ave, Wainwright T9W 1R1 – 403/842-3381, Fax: 403/842-2898 |
| Waiparous (SV) | 47 | Wild Rose | Banff-Cochrane | Sharon Plett, Adm., PO Box 5754, High River T1V 1P3 – 403/652-4636, Fax: 403/652-3125 |
| Wanham (V) | 167 | Peace River | Dunvegan | Tara L. Foote, Adm., PO Box 189, Wanham T0H 3P0 – 403/694-3946, Fax: 403/694-2647 |
| Warburg (V) | 549 | Wetaskiwin | Drayton Valley-Calmar | Chris Pankewitz, Adm., PO Box 29, Warburg T0C 2T0 – 403/848-2841, Fax: 403/848-2296 |
| Warner (V) | 421 | Lethbridge | Taber-Warner | Arlene B. Gerard, Adm., PO Box 88, Warner T0K 2L0 – 403/642-3877, Fax: 403/642-2011 |

Cities in CAPITALS; Towns marked †; Villages marked (V); Summer Villages marked (SV). Alberta Counties & Municipal Districts, Specialized Municipalities and Improvement Districts follow this list. An in-depth listing for municipalities marked with * appears in Part 2 (check Index for page numbers).

| MUNICIPALITY | 1996 POP. | FEDERAL ELECTORAL DISTRICT | PROVINCIAL ELECTORAL DISTRICT | CONTACT PERSON WITH ADDRESS, PHONE & FAX |
|---|---|---|---|---|
| Warspite (V) | 79 | Elk Island | Redwater | Joan Prusak, Sec.-Treas., PO Box 96, Warspite T0A 3N0 – 403/383-3838 |
| Waskatenau (V) | 237 | Elk Island | Redwater | Bernice Macyk, Adm., PO Box 99, Waskatenau T0A 3P0 – 403/358-2208, Fax: 403/358-2208 |
| Wembley † | 1,441 | Peace River | Grande Prairie-Wapiti | Karen Steinke, Adm., PO Box 89, Wembley T0H 3S0 – 403/766-2269, Fax: 403/766-2868 |
| West Baptiste (SV) | 51 | Athabasca | Athabasca-Wabasca | Ken Parsons, Adm., 15035 - 80 St., Edmonton T5C 1M4 – 403/475-2407 |
| West Cove (SV) | 85 | Yellowhead | Whitecourt-Ste Anne | Mark T. Anker, Adm., 14403 - 110A Ave., Edmonton T5N 1J7 – 403/454-9414, Fax: 403/452-5238 |
| Westlock † | 4,817 | Athabasca | Barrhead-Westlock | Garth Bancroft, Adm., PO Box 2220, Westlock T0G 2L0 – 403/349-4444, 428-1025, Fax: 403/349-4436 |
| WETASKIWIN | 10,959 | Wetaskiwin | Wetaskiwin-Camrose | Shelley Klinger, Clerk, 4904 - 51 St., Wetaskiwin T9A 1L2 – 403/352-3344, 421-0953, Fax: 403/352-0930 |
| Whispering Hills (SV) | 79 | Athabasca | Athabasca-Wabasca | Norm Milke, Adm., #1502, 12319 Jasper Ave., Edmonton T5N 4A7 – 403/488-5603 |
| White Gull (SV) | 24 | Athabasca | Athabasca-Wabasca | Don Baillie, Adm., PO Box 339, Boyle T0A 0M0 – 403/689-2080, Fax: 403/689-3998 |
| White Sands (SV) | 49 | Crowfoot | Lacombe-Stettler | Robert J. Krejci, Sec.-Tres., PO Box 460, Stettler T0C 2L0 – 403/742-4431, Fax: 403/742-1266 |
| Whitecourt † | 7,783 | Yellowhead | Whitecourt-Ste Anne | W.L. (Bud) Winger, Mgr., PO Box 509, Whitecourt T7S 1N6 – 403/778-2273, Fax: 403/778-4166 |
| Willingdon (V) | 309 | Lakeland | Vegreville-Viking | Olivia Walcheske, Adm., PO Box 210, Willingdon T0B 4R0 – 403/367-2337, Fax: 403/367-2167 |
| Wood Buffalo Reg. Mun. | 35,213 | Athabasca | Fort McMurray | Glen Laubenstein, Mgr., 9909 Franklin Ave., Fort McMurray T9H 2K4 – 403/743-7000, Fax: 403/743-7028 |
| Yellowstone (SV) | 97 | Yellowhead | Whitecourt-Ste Anne | Mark T. Anker, Adm., 14403 - 110A Ave., Edmonton T5N 1J7 – 403/454-9414, Fax: 403/452-5238 |
| Youngstown (V) | 239 | Crowfoot | Chinook | Evelyn Blagen, Adm., PO Box 99, Youngstown T0J 3P0 – 403/779-3873, Fax: 403/779-2279 |

1. Population figure incorporates Alberta & Saskatchewan populations.

## ALBERTA MUNICIPAL DISTRICTS

| MUNICIPAL DISTRICTS | 1996 POP. | CONTACT PERSON WITH ADDRESS, PHONE & FAX |
|---|---|---|
| Acadia No. 34 | 533 | Murray Peers, Sec.-Treas., PO Box 30, Acadia Valley T0J 0A0 – 403/972-3808, Fax: 403/972-3833 |
| Athabasca County No. 12 | 7,415 | Jim Woodward, Mgr., 3602 - 48 Ave., Athabasca T9S 1M8 – 403/675-2273, 423-0592, Fax: 403/675-5512 |
| Badlands No. 7 | 1,246 | Kay Brink, Adm., PO Box 1588, Drumheller T0J 0Y0 – 403/823-1200, Fax: 403/823-2550 |
| Barrhead County No. 11 | 5,870 | Dale Uhrbach, Mgr., 5306 - 49 St., Barrhead T7N 1N5 – 403/674-3331, Fax: 403/674-2777 |
| Beaver County No. 9 | 5,659 | Ron Pepper, CAO, PO Box 140, Ryley T0B 4A0 – 403/663-3730, 421-4058, Fax: 403/663-3602 |
| Big Lakes No. 125 | 5,830 | John Eriksson, CAO, Provincial Bldg., PO Box 239, High Prairie T0G 1E0 – 403/523-5955, Fax: 403/523-6566 |
| Bighorn No.8 | 1,269 | D. Sam Hall, Mgr., PO Box 310, Exshaw T0L 2C0 – 403/673-3611, 233-7678, Fax: 403/673-3895 |
| Birch Hills No. 19 | 1,356 | Don Spink, Mgr., Birch Hills Service Centre, PO Box 157, Wanham T0H 3P0 – 403/694-3793, Fax: 403/694-3788 |
| Bonnyville No. 87 | 17,352 | R.A. (Roy) Doonanco, Mgr., PO Box 1010, Bonnyville T9N 2J7 – 403/826-3171, Fax: 403/826-4524 |
| Brazeau No. 77 | 6,589 | Ken Porter, Mgr., PO Box 77, Drayton Valley T7A 1R1 – 403/542-7777, Fax: 403/542-7770 |
| Camrose County No. 22 | 7,613 | Brian D. Austrom, Adm., 3755 - 43 Ave., Camrose T4V 3S8 – 403/672-4446, 424-1239, Fax: 403/672-1008 |
| Cardston No. 6 | 4,565 | M. Vern Quinton, Adm., PO Box 580, Cardston T0K 0K0 – 403/653-4977, 328-4062, Fax: 403/653-1126 |
| Clear Hills No. 21 | 2,886 | Faye Kary, Sec.-Treas., PO Box 240, Worsley T0H 3W0 – 403/685-3925, Fax: 403/685-3960 |
| Clearwater No. 99 | 10,915 | Brian Irmen, Mgr., PO Box 550, Rocky Mountain House T0M 1T0 – 403/845-4444, Fax: 403/845-7330 |
| Cypress No. 1 | 5,353 | Lutz Perschon, Mgr., PO Box 108, Dunmore T0J 1A0 – 403/526-2888, Fax: 403/526-8958 |
| East Peace No. 131 | 2,264 | Kelly Bunn, CAO, Kit Business Ctr., 2nd Fl., PO Box 1300, Peace River T8S 1Y9 – 403/624-6580, Fax: 403/624-6595 |
| Fairview No. 136 | 1,829 | Lloyd Brattly, Sec.-Treas., PO Box 189, Fairview T0H 1L0 – 403/835-4903, Fax: 403/835-3131 |
| Flagstaff County No. 29 | 4,015 | Shelly Armstrong, Mgr., PO Box 358, Sedgewick T0B 4C0 – 403/384-3537, Fax: 403/384-3635 |
| Foothills No. 31 | 13,714 | Harry Riva Cambrin, Mgr., PO Box 5605, High River T1V 1M7 – 403/652-2341, Fax: 403/652-7880 |
| Forty Mile County No. 8 | 3,230 | Shirley R. Leverton, Adm., PO Box 160, Foremost T0K 0X0 – 403/867-3530, Fax: 403/867-2242 |
| Greenview No. 16 | 5,433 | Gordon Frank, Mgr., PO Box 1079, Valleyview T0H 3N0 – 403/524-3193, Fax: 403/524-4307 |
| Kneehill No. 48 | 4,887 | John C. Jeffery, Adm., PO Box 400, Three Hills T0M 2A0 – 403/443-5541, 263-8118, Fax: 403/443-5115 |
| Lac Ste. Anne County No. 28 | 8,737 | Len Szybunka, Adm., PO Box 219, Sangudo T0E 2A0 – 403/785-3411, 459-1900, Fax: 403/785-2359 |
| Lacombe County No. 14 | 10,081 | Edwin E. Koberstein, Commr., 5432 - 56 Ave., Lacombe T4L 1E9 – 403/782-6601, Fax: 403/782-3820 |
| Lamont County No. 30 | 4,212 | Helen Patterson, Mgr., General Delivery, Lamont T0B 2R0 – 403/895-2233, Fax: 403/895-7404 |
| Leduc County No. 25 | 12,361 | Larry R. Majeski, Mgr., #101, 1101 - 5 St., Nisku T9E 2X3 – 403/955-3555, 986-2251, Fax: 403/955-3444 |
| Lesser Slave River No. 124 | 2,716 | Jack Ramme, Mgr., PO Box 722, Slave Lake T0G 2A0 – 403/849-7130, Fax: 403/849-4939 |
| Lethbridge County No. 26 | 9,290 | Layne Johnson, Mgr., 904 - 4 Ave. South, Lethbridge T1J 4E4 – 403/328-5525, Fax: 403/328-5602 |
| Mackenzie No. 23 | 7,980 | Dennis Litke, CAO, PO Box 640, Fort Vermillion T0H 1N0 – 403/927-3717, Fax: 403/927-4266 |
| Minburn County No. 27 | 3,405 | David Marynowich, Mgr., PO Box 550, Vegreville T9C 1R6 – 403/632-2082, Fax: 403/632-6296 |
| Mountain View County No.17 | 11,277 | Herman Epp, Commr., PO Box 100, Didsbury T0M 0W0 – 403/335-3311, Fax: 403/335-9207 |
| Newell County No. 4 | 6,421 | Marlene Bowen, Adm., PO Box 130, Brooks T1R 1B2 – 403/362-3266, Fax: 403/362-8681 |
| Northern Lights No. 22 | 4,462 | Ian Becker, CAO, PO Box 200, Peace River T8S 1Z1 – 403/624-6121, Fax: 403/624-6494 |
| Opportunity No. 17 | | Harvey Prokiw, Manger, PO Box 60, Wabasca T0G 2K0 – 403/891-3778, Fax: 403/891-3772 |
| Paintearth County No. 18 | 2,316 | W. Tim Peterson, Adm., PO Box 509, Castor T0C 0X0 – 403/882-3211, Fax: 403/882-3560 |
| Parkland County | 24,769 | James V. Simpson, Commr., 4601 - 48 St., Stony Plain T7Z 1R1 – 403/963-2231, Fax: 403/963-2980 |
| Peace No. 135 | 1,562 | Joyce Sydnes, Adm., PO Box 34, Berwyn T0H 0E0 – 403/338-3845, Fax: 403/338-2222 |

| MUNICIPAL DISTRICTS | 1996 POP. | CONTACT PERSON WITH ADDRESS, PHONE & FAX |
|---|---|---|
| Pincher Creek No. 9 | 3,172 | Ron Leaf, CAO, PO Box 279, Pincher Creek T0K 1W0 – 403/627-3130, Fax: 403/627-5070 |
| Ponoka County No. 3 | 8,313 | Charlie Cutforth, Adm., 6000 Hwy. 2A, Ponoka T4J 1P6 – 403/783-3333, Fax: 403/783-6965 |
| Provost No. 52 | 2,705 | Rod Hawken, Adm., PO Box 300, Provost T0B 3S0 – 403/753-2434, Fax: 403/753-6432 |
| Ranchland No. 66 | | Twyla Cyr, Adm., PO Box 906, Nanton T0L 1R0 – 403/646-3131, Fax: 403/646-3141 |
| Red Deer County No.23 | 17,126 | Lorne McLeod, Commr., 4758 - 32 St., Red Deer T4N 0M8 – 403/350-2150, Fax: 403/346-9840 |
| Rocky View No. 44 | 23,326 | Peter Kivisto, Mgr., PO Box 3009, Calgary T2M 4L6 – 403/230-1401, Fax: 403/277-5977 |
| Saddle Hills No. 20 | 2,724 | Don Spink, Mgr., PO Box 69, Spirit River T0H 3G0 – 403/864-3760, Fax: 403/864-3904 |
| St. Paul County No. 19 | 6,335 | Robert Krawchuk, Adm., 5015 - 49 Ave., St. Paul T0A 3A4 – 403/645-3301, Fax: 403/645-3104 |
| Smoky Lake County No. 13 | 2,689 | Cary Smigerowsky, Mgr., PO Box 310, Smoky Lake T0A 3C0 – 403/656-3730, 424-7103, Fax: 403/656-3768 |
| Smoky River No. 130 | 2,491 | Lucien G. Turcotte, Adm., PO Box 210, Falher T0H 1M0 – 403/837-2221, Fax: 403/837-2453 |
| Spirit River No. 133 | 809 | Veronica Andruchiw, Adm., PO Box 389, Spirit River T0H 3G0 – 403/864-3500, Fax: 403/864-4303 |
| Starland No. 47 | 2,075 | Ross D. Rawlusyk, Adm., PO Box 249, Morrin T0J 2B0 – 403/772-3793, Fax: 403/772-3807 |
| Stettler County No. 6 | 5,278 | Tim Timmons, Commr., PO Box 1270, Stettler T0C 2L0 – 403/742-4441, Fax: 403/742-1277 |
| Strathcona County | 64,176 | Rick Powell, Acting Commr., 2001 Sherwood Dr., Sherwood Park T8A 3W7 – 403/464-8111, Fax: 403/464-8050 |
| Sturgeon County | 15,945 | Gilbert J. Boddez, Adm., 9601 - 100 St., Morinville T8R 1L9 – 403/939-4321, Fax: 403/939-3003 |
| Taber No. 14 | 5,644 | Clarence F. Schile, Adm., 4900B - 50 St., Taber T1G 1T2 – 403/223-3541, Fax: 403/223-1799 |
| Thorhild County No. 7 | 2,901 | Bill Kostiw, Adm., PO Box 10, Thorhild T0A 3J0 – 403/398-3741, 429-3928, Fax: 403/398-3748 |
| Two Hills County No. 21 | 2,707 | Gary Popowich, Adm., PO Box 490, Two Hills T0B 4K0 – 403/657-3358, Fax: 403/657-3504 |
| Vermilion River County No. 24 | 7,553 | Karen Gartner, Adm., PO Box 69, Kitscoty T0B 2P0 – 403/846-2244, Fax: 403/846-2716 |
| Vulcan County No. 2 | 3,829 | Robert Strauss, Adm., PO Box 180, Vulcan T0L 2B0 – 403/485-2241, Fax: 403/485-2920 |
| Wainwright No. 61 | 4,044 | Kelly Buchinski, Adm., 717 - 14 Ave., Wainwright T9W 1B3 – 403/842-4454, Fax: 403/842-2463 |
| Warner County No. 5 | 3,561 | Allan K. Romeril, Adm., PO Box 90, Warner T0K 2L0 – 403/642-3635, Fax: 403/642-3631 |
| Westlock No. 92 | 6,958 | Wyatt Glebe, Adm., PO Box 219, Westlock T0G 2L0 – 403/349-3346, 429-1135, Fax: 403/349-2012 |
| Wetaskiwin County No. 10 | 10,467 | Frank Coutney, Adm., PO Box 6960, Wetaskiwin T9A 2G5 – 403/352-3321, Fax: 403/352-3486 |
| Wheatland County | 6,714 | Ernie Maser, Mgr., 435B Hwy#1, Strathmore T1P 1J4 – 403/934-3321, Fax: 403/934-4889 |
| Willow Creek No. 26 | 5,113 | Cindy Zabolotney, Adm., PO Box 550, Claresholm T0L 0T0 – 403/625-3351, Fax: 403/625-3886 |
| Woodlands No. 15 | 3,699 | Norm Kjemhus, Adm., Provincial Bldg., #210, 5020 - 52 Ave., Whitecourt T7S 1N2 – 403/778-7102, Fax: 403/778-7209 |
| Yellowhead No. 94 | 9,352 | Terry Broome, Mgr., 2716 - 1st Ave., Edson T7E 1N9 – 403/325-3782, Fax: 403/723-5066 |

## ALBERTA IMPROVEMENT DISTRICTS AND NATIVE SERVICES DIVISON

Rural & Improvement Districts Association of Alberta, Shirley Mercier, Sec-T., Box 36, Site 206, RR#2, St. Alberta AB T8N 1M9; 403/973-6762

| DISTRICTS | CONTACT PERSON WITH ADDRESS, PHONE & FAX |
|---|---|
| Districts 4 (Waterton), 6, 9 (Banff), 12 (Jasper), 13 (Elk Island), 24 | Rick Grimson, ID Mgr., Local Government Advisory Branch, 10155-102 St., 15th Fl., Edmonton T5J 4L4 – 403/427-2225, Fax: 403/422-9133 |
| Jasper Improvement District | George Krefting, Mgr., PO Box 520, Jasper T0E 1E0 – 403/852-3356, Fax: 403/852-4019 |
| Kananaskis Country | Dave Nielsen, Mgr., PO Box 70, Kananaskis T0L 2H0 – 403/673-2344, Fax: 403/673-3587 |

## ALBERTA METIS SETTLEMENTS

Metis Settlements General Council, Thomas Droege, Executive Director, 649, Princeton Place, 10339 - 124 St., Edmonton AB T5N 1R1; 403/488-6500, Fax: 403/488-5700

| SETTLEMENT | 1996 POP. | CONTACT PERSON WITH ADDRESS, PHONE & FAX |
|---|---|---|
| Buffalo Lake | 620 | Maria Hawke, Interim Adm., PO Box 20, Caslan T0A 0R0 – 403/689-2170, Fax: 403/689-2024 |
| East Prairie | 431 | Judy Hopkins, Adm., PO Box 1289, High Prairie T0G 1E0 – 403/523-2594, Fax: 403/523-2777 |
| Elizabeth | 551 | Karen Collins, Adm., PO Box 420, Grand Centre T0A 1T0 – 403/594-5026, Fax: 403/594-5452 |
| Fishing Lake | | Ryck Chalifoux, Adm., General Delivery, Sputinow T0A 3G0 – 403/943-2202, Fax: 403/943-2575 |
| Gift Lake | 535 | Gerry Peardon, Adm., PO Box 60, Gift Lake T0G 1B0 – 403/767-3894, Fax: 403/767-3888 |
| Kikino | | Roger Littlechilds, Adm., General Delivery, Kikino T0A 2B0 – 403/623-7001, Fax: 403/623-7080 |
| Paddle Prairie | 242 | Barbara Auger, Adm., General Delivery, Paddle Prairie T0H 2W0 – 403/981-2227, Fax: 403/981-3737 |
| Peavine | 431 | Sherry Cunningham, Acting Adm., PO Box 238, High Prairie T0G 1E0 – 403/523-2557, Fax: 403/523-5616 |

## BRITISH COLUMBIA

Incorporated municipalities in British Columbia include Villages, Towns, Cities, and District Municipalities as well as one Indian Government District. Twenty-seven regional districts provide local government services to the unincorporated areas and, in many cases, co-ordinate service delivery between such areas and the incorporated municipalities included within the regional district boundaries.

Municipal elections in all municipalities are held on the third Saturday of November. Terms of office are three years (1996, 1999, etc.).

Legislation: The Municipal Act, excluding the City of Vancouver, which is regulated under the provisions of the Vancouver Charter.

Cities in CAPITALS; Districts marked D; District municipalities marked DM; Towns marked †; Villages marked (V). British Columbia Regional Districts follow this list. An in-depth listing for municipalities marked with * appears in Part 2 (check Index for page numbers).

| MUNICIPALITY | 1996 POP. | COUNTY OR DISTRICT | FEDERAL ELECTORAL DISTRICT | PROVINCIAL ELECTORAL DISTRICT | CONTACT PERSON WITH ADDRESS, PHONE & FAX |
|---|---|---|---|---|---|
| *ABBOTSFORD | 105,403 | Central Fraser Valley | Fraser Valley | Abbotsford; Matsqui | Toiressa O. Strong, City Clerk, 32315 South Fraser Way, Abbotsford V2T 1W7 – 604/853-2281, Fax: 604/853-1934, URL: http://www.city.abby.bc.ca.abby |
| Alert Bay (V) | 612 | Mount Waddington | Vancouver Island North | North Island | John Rowell, Clerk, PO Box 28, Alert Bay V0N 1A0 – 250/974-5213, Fax: 250/974-5470 |
| Anmore (V) | 961 | Greater Vancouver | Port Moody-Coquitlam | Port Moody-Burnaby Mountain | Howard Carley, Clerk, 2697 Sunnyside Rd., Port Moody V3H 3C8 – 604/469-9877, Fax: 604/469-0537 |
| ARMSTRONG | 3,906 | North Okanagan | Okanagan-Shuswap | Shuswap | Barry Gagnon, Clerk-Treas., PO Box 40, Armstrong V0E 1B0 – 250/546-3023, Fax: 250/546-3710 |

Cities in CAPITALS; Districts marked D; District municipalities marked DM; Towns marked †; Villages marked (V). British Columbia Regional Districts follow this list. An in-depth listing for municipalities marked with * appears in Part 2 (check Index for page numbers).

| MUNICIPALITY | 1996 POP. | COUNTY OR DISTRICT | FEDERAL ELECTORAL DISTRICT | PROVINCIAL ELECTORAL DISTRICT | CONTACT PERSON WITH ADDRESS, PHONE & FAX |
|---|---|---|---|---|---|
| Ashcroft (V) | 1,858 | Thompson-Nicola | Cariboo-Chilcotin | Yale-Lillooet | Al Benson, Sec.-Treas., PO Box 129, Ashcroft V0K 1A0 – 250/453-9161, Fax: 250/453-9664 |
| Belcarra (V) | 665 | Greater Vancouver | Port Moody-Coquitlam | Port Moody-Burnaby Mountain | Moira McGregor, Sec.-Treas., 4084 Bedwell Bay Rd., Belcarra V3H 4P8 – 604/939-4100, Fax: 604/939-5034 |
| *BURNABY | 179,209 | Greater Vancouver | Burnaby-Douglas; Vancouver South-Burnaby; New Westminster-Coquitlam-Burnaby | Burnaby-Edmonds; Burnaby North; Burnaby-Willingdon | Chad Turpin, City Clerk, 4949 Canada Way, Burnaby V5G 1M2 – 604/294-7944, Fax: 604/294-7537 |
| Burns Lake (V) | 1,793 | Bulkley-Nechako | Prince George-Bulkley Valley | Bulkley Valley-Stikine | Lonny Miller, Sec.-Treas., PO Box 570, Burns Lake V0J 1E0 – 250/692-7587, Fax: 250/692-3059 |
| Cache Creek (V) | 1,115 | Thompson-Nicola | Cariboo-Chilcotin | Yale-Lillooet | Gordon Daily, Clerk, PO Box 7, Cache Creek V0K 1H0 – 250/457-6237, Fax: 250/457-9192 |
| Campbell River (DM) | 28,851 | Comox-Strathcona | Vancouver Island North | North Island | William Halstead, Clerk, 301 St. Ann's Rd., Campbell River V9W 4C7 – 250/286-5700, Fax: 250/286-5760 |
| CASTLEGAR | 7,027 | Central Kootenay | West Kootenay-Okanagan | Rossland-Trail | Dianne Hunter, Clerk, 460 Columbia Ave., Castlegar V1N 1G7 – 250/365-7227, Fax: 250/365-4810 |
| Central Saanich (DM) | 14,611 | Capital | Saanich-Gulf Islands | Saanich North & the Islands | G. Nason, Clerk-Adm., 1903 Mt. Newton Cross Rd., Saanichton V8M 2A9 – 250/652-4444, Fax: 250/652-0135, 250/652-4737 |
| Chase (V) | 2,460 | Thompson-Nicola | Kamloops | Shuswap | Christopher Coates, Acting Sec.-Treas., PO Box 440, Chase V0E 1M0 – 250/679-3238, Fax: 250/679-3070 |
| Chetwynd (DM) | 2,980 | Peace River | Prince George-Peace River | Peace River South | Jannene Disher, Clerk, PO Box 357, Chetwynd V0C 1J0 – 250/788-2281, Fax: 250/788-2299 |
| Chilliwack (DM) | 60,186 | Fraser-Cheam | Fraser Valley | Chilliwack | David W. Hampson, Clerk, 8550 Young Rd. South, Chilliwack V2P 4P1 – 604/792-9311, Fax: 604/795-8443, URL: http://www.gov.chilliwack.bc.ca/ |
| Clinton (V) | 729 | Thompson-Nicola | Cariboo-Chilcotin | Cariboo South | Isabell Hadford, Sec.-Treas., PO Box 309, Clinton V0K 1K0 – 250/459-2261, Fax: 250/459-2227 |
| Coldstream (DM) | 8,975 | North Okanagan | Okanagan-Shuswap | Okanagan-Vernon | Greg Betts, Clerk, 9901 Kalamalka Rd., Vernon V1B 1L6 – 250/545-5304, Fax: 250/545-4733 |
| COLWOOD | 13,848 | Capital | Esquimalt-Juan de Fuca | Esquimalt-Metchosin | Barry Bennett, Clerk, 3300 Wishart Rd., Victoria V9C 1R1 – 250/478-5541, Fax: 250/478-7516 |
| Comox † | 11,069 | Comox-Strathcona | Vancouver Island North | Comox Valley | Helen M. Dale, Clerk, 1809 Beaufort Ave., Comox V9M 1R9 – 250/339-2202, Fax: 250/339-7110 |
| *COQUITLAM | 101,820 | Greater Vancouver | Port Moody-Coquitlam | Mission-Coquitlam; Port Coquitlam | Warren Jones, Clerk, 1111 Brunette Ave., Coquitlam V3K 1E9 – 604/664-1400, Fax: 604/664-1650, URL: http://www.gov.coquitlam.bc.ca/ |
| COURTENAY | 17,335 | Comox-Strathcona | Vancouver Island North | Comox Valley | Dora Pelletier, Clerk, 750 Cliffe Ave., Courtenay V9N 2J7 – 250/334-4441, Fax: 250/334-4241 |
| CRANBROOK | 18,131 | East Kootenay | Kootenay-Columbia | Kootenay | Carmen Biafore, Adm., 40 - 10 Ave. South, Cranbrook V1C 2M8 – 250/426-4211, Fax: 250/426-4026, URL: http://city.cranbrook.bc.ca/~cityhall/index.htm |
| Creston † | 4,816 | 400 Central Kootenay | Kootenay-Columbia | Nelson-Creston | Bill Hutchinson, Sec.-Treas., PO Box 1339, Creston V0B 1G0 – 250/428-2214, Fax: 250/428-9164 |
| Cumberland (V) | 2,548 | Comox-Strathcona | Vancouver Island North | Comox Valley | Terry Kelly, Sec.-Treas., PO Box 340, Cumberland V0R 1S0 – 250/336-2291, Fax: 250/336-2321 |
| DAWSON CREEK | 11,125 | Peace River | Prince George-Peace River | Peace River South | Jim Noble, Clerk, PO Box 150, Dawson Creek V1G 4G4 – 250/784-3600, Fax: 250/782-3352 |
| *Delta (Corporation) | 95,930 | Greater Vancouver | Delta-South Richmond | Delta North; Delta South | Tanalee Hesse, Clerk, 4500 Clarence Taylor Cres., Delta V4K 3E2 – 604/946-4141, Fax: 604/946-3390 |
| DUNCAN | 4,583 | Cowichan Valley | Nanaimo-Cowichan | Cowichan-Ladysmith | Paul Douville, Clerk, PO Box 820, Duncan V9L 3Y2 – 250/746-6126, Fax: 250/746-6129 |
| Elkford (DM) | 2,729 | East Kootenay | Kootenay-Columbia | Kootenay | Betty-Lou Wyatt, Clerk-Treas., PO Box 340, Elkford V0B 1H0 – 250/865-2241, Fax: 250/865-2429 |
| ENDERBY | 2,754 | North Okanagan | Okanagan-Shuswap | Shuswap | Robert W. Watson, Clerk-Treas., PO Box 400, Enderby V0E 1V0 – 250/838-7230, Fax: 250/838-6007 |

Cities in CAPITALS; Districts marked D; District municipalities marked DM; Towns marked †; Villages marked (V). British Columbia Regional Districts follow this list. An in-depth listing for municipalities marked with * appears in Part 2 (check Index for page numbers).

| MUNICIPALITY | 1996 POP. | COUNTY OR DISTRICT | FEDERAL ELECTORAL DISTRICT | PROVINCIAL ELECTORAL DISTRICT | CONTACT PERSON WITH ADDRESS, PHONE & FAX |
|---|---|---|---|---|---|
| Esquimalt † | 16,151 | Capital | Esquimalt-Juan de Fuca | Esquimalt-Metchosin | Robert Seright, Clerk, 1229 Esquimalt Rd., Victoria V9A 3P1 – 250/385-2461, Fax: 250/385-6668 |
| FERNIE | 4,877 | East Kootenay | Kootenay-Columbia | Kootenay | Jennifer Bridarolli, Clerk, PO Box 190, Fernie V0B 1M0 – 250/423-6817, Fax: 250/423-3034 |
| Fort Nelson † | 4,401 | Fort Nelson-Liard | Prince George-Peace River | Peace River North | Patricia A. Bailey, Clerk, PO Box 399, Fort Nelson V0C 1R0 – 250/774-2541, Fax: 250/774-6794 |
| Fort St. James (D) | 2,046 | Bulkley-Nechako | Prince George-Bulkley Valley | Prince George-Omineca | Dan Zabinsky, Clerk-Treas., PO Box 640, Fort St. James V0J 1P0 – 250/996-8233, Fax: 250/996-2248 |
| FORT ST. JOHN | 15,021 | Peace River | Prince George-Peace River | Peace River North | Barb Jackman, Acting Clerk, 10631 - 100 St., Fort St. John V1J 3Z5 – 250/787-8150, Fax: 250/787-8181 |
| Fraser Lake (V) | 1,344 | Bulkley-Nechako | Prince George-Bulkley Valley | Prince George-Omineca | Angus Davis, Clerk, PO Box 430, Fraser Lake V0J 1S0 – 250/699-6257, Fax: 250/699-6469 |
| Fruitvale (V) | 2,117 | Kootenay Boundary | West Kootenay-Okanagan | Rossland-Trail | Vince Morelli, Clerk, PO Box 370, Fruitvale V0G 1L0 – 250/367-7551, Fax: 250/367-9267 |
| Gibsons † | 3,732 | Sunshine Coast | West Vancouver-Sunshine Coast | Powell River-Sunshine Coast | Terry Lester, Acting Clerk, PO Box 340, Gibsons V0N 1V0 – 604/886-2274, Fax: 604/886-9735 |
| Gold River (V) | 2,041 | Comox-Strathcona | Vancouver Island North | North Island | Larry Plourde, Acting Clerk, PO Box 610, Gold River V0P 1G0 – 250/283-2202, Fax: 250/283-7500 |
| Golden † | 3,968 | Columbia-Shuswap | Kootenay-Columbia | Columbia River-Revelstoke | Ian Fremantle, Clerk, PO Box 350, Golden V0A 1H0 – 250/344-2271, Fax: 250/344-6577 |
| GRAND FORKS | 3,994 | Kootenay Boundary | West Kootenay-Okanagan | Okanagan-Boundary | Lynne Burch, Clerk, PO Box 220, Grand Forks V0H 1H0 – 250/442-8266, Fax: 250/442-8000 |
| Granisle (V) | 446 | Bulkley-Nechako | Prince George-Bulkley Valley | Bulkley Valley-Stikine | Elizabeth Moysir, Sec.-Treas., PO Box 128, Granisle V0J 1W0 – 250/697-2248, Fax: 250/697-2306 |
| GREENWOOD | 784 | Kootenay Boundary | West Kootenay-Okanagan | Okanagan-Boundary | Monique Beaudry, Clerk-Treas., PO Box 129, Greenwood V0H 1J0 – 250/445-6644, Fax: 250/445-6441 |
| Harrison Hot Springs (V) | 898 | Fraser-Cheam | Dewdney-Alouette | Mission-Kent | Mark Brennan, Sec.-Treas., PO Box 160, Harrison Hot Springs V0M 1K0 – 604/796-2171, Fax: 604/796-2192 |
| Hazelton (V) | 347 | Kitimat-Stikine | Skeena | Bulkley Valley-Stikine | Joy Fleming, Sec.-Treas., PO Box 40, Hazelton V0J 1Y0 – 250/842-5991, Fax: 250/842-5152 |
| Highlands (DM) | 1,423 | Capital | Esquimalt-Juan de Fuca | Malahat-Juan de Fuca, Saanich South | Bruce Woodbury, Clerk-Treas., 1564 Millstream Rd., Victoria V9B 5T9 – 250/474-1773, Fax: 250/474-3677 |
| Hope (DM) | 6,247 | Fraser-Cheam | Okanagan-Coquihalla | Yale-Lillooet | Eric McMurran, Clerk, PO Box 609, Hope V0X 1L0 – 604/869-5671, Fax: 604/869-2275 |
| Houston (DM) | 3,934 | Bulkley-Nechako | Prince George-Bulkley Valley | Bulkley Valley-Stikine | Bill Beamish, Clerk, PO Box 370, Houston V0J 1Z0 – 250/845-2238, Fax: 250/845-3429 |
| Hudson's Hope (DM) | 1,122 | Peace River | Prince George-Peace River | Peace River North | Fay Lavallee, Clerk-Treas., PO Box 330, Hudson's Hope V0C 1V0 – 250/783-9901, Fax: 250/783-5741 |
| Invermere (DM) | 2,687 | East Kootenay | Kootenay-Columbia | Columbia River-Revelstoke | Bill Lindsay, Clerk, PO Box 339, Invermere V0A 1K0 – 250/342-9281, Fax: 250/342-2934 |
| *KAMLOOPS | 76,394 | Thompson-Nicola | Kamloops | Kamloops; Kamloops-North Thompson | Wayne Vollrath, City Clerk-Asst. Adm., 7 Victoria St. West, Kamloops V2C 1A2 – 250/828-3311, Fax: 250/828-3578 |
| Kaslo (V) | 1,063 | Central Kootenay | West Kootenay-Okanagan | Nelson-Creston | Rae Sawyer, Sec.-Treas., PO Box 576, Kaslo V0G 1M0 – 250/353-2311, Fax: 250/353-7767 |
| *KELOWNA | 89,442 | Central Okanagan | Kelowna | Okanagan East; Okanagan West | David L. Shipclark, Clerk, City Hall, 1435 Water St., Kelowna V1Y 1J4 – 250/763-6011, Fax: 250/862-3399 |
| Kent (DM) | 4,844 | Fraser-Cheam | Dewdney-Alouette | Mission-Kent | Anthony C. Lewis, Clerk-Treas., PO Box 70, Agassiz V0M 1A0 – 604/796-2235, Fax: 604/796-9854 |
| Keremeos (V) | 1,167 | Okanagan-Similkameen | Okanagan-Coquihalla | Okanagan-Boundary | Andrew Verigin, Sec.-Treas., PO Box 160, Keremeos V0X 1N0 – 250/499-2711, Fax: 250/499-5477 |
| KIMBERLEY | 6,738 | East Kootenay | Kootenay-Columbia | Columbia River-Revelstoke | George Stratton, Clerk, 340 Spokane St., Kimberley V1A 2E8 – 250/427-5311, Fax: 250/427-5252 |
| Kitimat (DM) | 11,136 | Kitimat-Stikine | Skeena | Skeena | Walter McLellan, Clerk, 270 City Centre, Kitimat V8C 2H7 – 250/632-2161, Fax: 250/632-4995 |
| Ladysmith † | 6,456 | Cowichan Valley | Nanaimo-Cowichan | Cowichan-Ladysmith | Patrick Durban, Clerk, Town Hall, PO Box 220, Ladysmith V0R 2E0 – 250/245-6400, Fax: 250/245-6411 |

Cities in CAPITALS; Districts marked D; District municipalities marked DM; Towns marked †; Villages marked (V). British Columbia Regional Districts follow this list. An in-depth listing for municipalities marked with * appears in Part 2 (check Index for page numbers).

| MUNICIPALITY | 1996 POP. | COUNTY OR DISTRICT | FEDERAL ELECTORAL DISTRICT | PROVINCIAL ELECTORAL DISTRICT | CONTACT PERSON WITH ADDRESS, PHONE & FAX |
|---|---|---|---|---|---|
| Lake Country (D) | | | Kelowna | Okanagan East | Randy Rose, Clerk, #17, 11852 Hwy. 97, Lake Country V4V 1E3 – 250/766-5650, Fax: 250/766-0116 |
| Lake Cowichan † | 2,856 | Cowichan Valley | Nanaimo-Cowichan | Cowichan-Ladysmith | Ed Gilman, Sec.-Treas., PO Box 860, Lake Cowichan V0R 2G0 – 250/749-6681, Fax: 250/749-3900 |
| Langford (D) | | | Esquimalt-Juan de Fuca | Equimalt-Metchasin Malahat-Juan de Fuca | Geoff Pearce, Clerk, 2805 Carlow Rd., Victoria V9B 5V9 – 250/478-7882, Fax: 250/478-7864 |
| LANGLEY | 22,523 | Central Fraser Valley | Langley-Abbotsford | Langley | Robert Wilson, Clerk, 5549 - 204 St., Langley V3A 1Z4 – 604/530-3131, Fax: 604/530-4371 |
| *Langley (DM) | 80,179 | Central Fraser Valley, Langley, Surrey-White Horse | South Surrey-White Rock-Langley | Fort Langley-Aldergrove | Rodney T. Edwards, Municipal Clerk, 4914 - 221 St., Langley V3A 3Z8 – 604/534-3211, Fax: 604/533-6098 |
| Lillooet (D) | 1,988 | Squamish-Lillooet | Cariboo-Chilcotin | Yale-Lillooet | Hedley Crowther, Clerk, PO Box 610, Lillooet V0K 1V0 – 250/256-4289, Fax: 250/256-4288 |
| Lions Bay (V) | 1,347 | Greater Vancouver | West Vancouver-Sunshine Coast | West Vancouver-Garibaldi | Bernice Pullen, Sec.-Treas., PO Box 141, Lions Bay V0N 2E0 – 604/921-9333, Fax: 604/921-6643 |
| Logan Lake (DM) | 2,492 | Thompson-Nicola | Kamloops | Yale-Lillooet | Doug Fleming, Clerk-Treas., PO Box 190, Logan Lake V0K 1W0 – 250/523-6225, Fax: 250/523-6678 |
| Lumby (V) | 1,689 | North Okanagan | Okanagan-Shuswap | Okanagan-Vernon | Robert Jackman, Sec.-Treas., PO Box 430, Lumby V0E 2G0 – 250/547-2171, Fax: 250/547-6894 |
| Lytton (V) | 322 | Thompson-Nicola | Cariboo-Chilcotin | Yale-Lillooet | Joyce Madigan, Sec.-Treas., PO Box 100, Lytton V0K 1Z0 – 250/455-2355, Fax: 250/455-2142 |
| Mackenzie (DM) | 5,997 | Fraser-Fort George | Prince George-Peace River | Peace River South | Brian Ritchie, Clerk, PO Box 340, Mackenzie V0J 2C0 – 250/997-3221, Fax: 250/997-5186 |
| Maple Ridge (DM) | 56,173 | Dewdney-Alouette | Dewdney-Alouette | Maple Ridge-Pitt Meadows | Jim McBride, Clerk, 11995 Haney Place, Maple Ridge V2X 6A9 – 604/463-5221, Fax: 604/467-7329, URL: http://district.maple-ridge.bc.ca |
| Masset (V) | 1,293 | Skeena-Queen Charlotte | Skeena | North Coast | Alfred Brockley, Sec.-Treas., PO Box 68, Masset V0T 1M0 – 250/626-3995, Fax: 250/626-3968 |
| McBride (V) | 740 | Fraser-Fort George | Prince George-Bulkley Valley | Prince George-Mount Robson | Ronald V. Brown, Sec.-Treas., PO Box 519, McBride V0J 2E0 – 250/569-2229, Fax: 250/569-3276 |
| MERRITT | 7,631 | Thompson-Nicola | Okanagan-Coquihalla | Yale-Lillooet | Yvonne Porada, Clerk, PO Box 189, Merritt V0K 2B0 – 250/378-4224, Fax: 250/378-2600 |
| Metchosin (DM) | 4,709 | Capital | Esquimalt-Juan de Fuca | Esquimalt-Metchosin | Gerald Mellott, Clerk-Treas., 4450 Happy Valley Rd., RR#4, Victoria V9B 5T6 – 250/474-3167, Fax: 250/474-6298 |
| Midway (V) | 686 | Kootenay Boundary | West Kootenay-Okanagan | Okanagan-Boundary | Robert J. Hatton, Sec.-Treas., PO Box 160, Midway V0H 1M0 – 250/449-2222, Fax: 250/449-2258 |
| Mission (DM) | 30,519 | Dewdney-Alouette | Dewdney-Alouette | Mission-Kent | Jacqueline Fennellow, Clerk, PO Box 20, Mission V2V 4L9 – 604/820-3700, Fax: 604/826-1363, URL: http://www.city.mission.bc |
| Montrose (V) | 1,137 | Kootenay Boundary | West Kootenay-Okanagan | Rossland-Trail | Gerry A. Henke, Sec.-Treas., PO Box 510, Montrose V0G 1P0 – 250/367-7234, Fax: 250/367-7288 |
| Nakusp (V) | 1,736 | Central Kootenay | West Kootenay-Okanagan | Nelson-Creston | Malcolm Buckley, Clerk, PO Box 280, Nakusp V0G 1R0 – 250/265-3689, Fax: 250/265-3788 |
| *NANAIMO | 70,130 | Nanaimo | Nanaimo-Cowichan; Nanaimo-Alberni | Nanaimo; Parksville-Qualicum | Jim Bowden, City Clerk, 455 Wallace St., Nanaimo V9R 5J6 – 250/754-4251, Fax: 250/755-4436, URL: http://www.city.nanaimo.bc.ca/ |
| NELSON | 9,585 | Central Kootenay | West Kootenay-Okanagan | Nelson-Creston | Marla Olson, Clerk, 502 Vernon St., Nelson V1L 4E8 – 250/352-5511, Fax: 250/352-2131 |
| New Denver (V) | 579 | Central Kootenay | West Kootenay-Okanagan | Nelson-Creston | Carol Gordon, Sec.-Treas., PO Box 40, New Denver V0G 1S0 – 250/358-2316, Fax: 250/358-7251 |
| New Hazelton (DM) | 822 | Kitimat-Stikine | Skeena | Bulkley Valley-Stikine | Brian Fassnidge, Clerk-Treas., PO Box 340, New Hazelton V0J 2J0 – 250/842-6571, Fax: 250/842-6077 |
| NEW WESTMINSTER | 49,350 | Greater Vancouver | New Westminster-Coquitlam-Burnaby | New Westminster | Susan Brown, Clerk, 511 Royal Ave., New Westminster V3L 1H9 – 604/521-3711, Fax: 604/521-3895 |
| North Cowichan (DM) | 25,305 | Cowichan Valley | Nanaimo-Cowichan | Cowichan-Ladysmith | Mark Ruttan, Clerk, PO Box 278, Duncan V9L 3X4 – 250/746-3100, Fax: 250/746-3133 |
| North Saanich (DM) | 10,411 | Capital | Saanich-Gulf Islands | Saanich North & the Islands | Pam Hilchie, Clerk, PO Box 2639, Sidney V8L 4C1 – 250/656-0781, Fax: 250/656-3155 |

Cities in CAPITALS; Districts marked D; District municipalities marked DM; Towns marked †; Villages marked (V). British Columbia Regional Districts follow this list. An in-depth listing for municipalities marked with * appears in Part 2 (check Index for page numbers).

| MUNICIPALITY | 1996 POP. | COUNTY OR DISTRICT | FEDERAL ELECTORAL DISTRICT | PROVINCIAL ELECTORAL DISTRICT | CONTACT PERSON WITH ADDRESS, PHONE & FAX |
|---|---|---|---|---|---|
| *North Vancouver (DM) | 80,418 | Greater Vancouver | North Vancouver | N. Vancouver-Lonsdale; N. Vancouver-Seymour; W. Vancouver-Capilano | Dennis Back, Municipal Clerk, PO Box 86218, North Vancouver V7L 4K1 – 604/987-7131, Fax: 604/984-9637, URL: http://www.district.north-van.bc.ca/ |
| NORTH VANCOUVER | 41,475 | Greater Vancouver | North Vancouver | N. Vancouver-Lonsdale; N. Vancouver-Seymour; W. Vancouver-Capilano | Bruce Hawkshaw, Clerk, 141 - 14 St. West, North Vancouver V7M 1H9 – 604/985-7761, Fax: 604/985-9417 |
| Oak Bay (DM) | 17,865 | Capital | Victoria | Oak Bay-Gordon Head | Tom MacDonald, Clerk, 2167 Oak Bay Ave., Victoria V8R 1G2 – 250/598-3311, Fax: 250/598-9108 |
| Oliver † | 4,285 | Okanagan-Similkameen | West Kootenay-Okanagan | Okanagan-Boundary | Debbie McGinn, Clerk, PO Box 638, Oliver V0H 1T0 – 250/498-3404, Fax: 250/498-4466 |
| 100 Mile House (DM) | 1,850 | Cariboo | Cariboo-Chilcotin | Cariboo South | Ronald Haggstrom, Clerk-Treas., PO Box 340, 100 Mile House V0K 2E0 – 250/395-2434, Fax: 250/395-3625 |
| Osoyoos † | 4,021 | Okanagan-Similkameen | West Kootenay-Okanagan | Okanagan-Boundary | Brad Elenko, Acting Clerk, PO Box 3010, Osoyoos V0H 1V0 – 250/495-6515, Fax: 250/495-2400 |
| PARKSVILLE | 9,472 | Nanaimo | Nanaimo-Alberni | Parksville-Qualicum | Shirley E. Hine, Clerk, PO Box 1390, Parksville V9P 2H3 – 250/248-6144, Fax: 250/248-6650 |
| Peachland (DM) | 4,524 | Central Okanagan | Okanagan-Coquihalla | Okanagan-Penticton | Bill Brown, Clerk, PO Box 390, Peachland V0H 1X0 – 250/767-2647, Fax: 250/767-3433 |
| Pemberton (V) | 855 | Squamish-Lillooet | West Vancouver-Sunshine Coast | West Vancouver-Garibaldi | Bryan Kirk, Sec.-Treas., PO Box 100, Pemberton V0N 2L0 – 604/894-6135, Fax: 604/894-5708 |
| PENTICTON | 30,987 | Okanagan-Similkameen | Okanagan-Coquihalla | Okanagan-Penticton | Leo den Boer, Clerk, 171 Main St., Penticton V2A 5A9 – 250/490-2400, Fax: 250/490-2402 |
| Pitt Meadows (DM) | 13,436 | Dewdney-Alouette | Dewdney-Alouette | Maple Ridge-Pitt Meadows | Brian E. Strong, Clerk, 12007 Harris Rd., Pitt Meadows V3Y 2B5 – 604/465-5454, Fax: 604/465-2404 |
| PORT ALBERNI | 18,468 | Alberni-Clayoquot | Nanaimo-Alberni | Alberni | George Wiley, Clerk, 4850 Argyle St., Port Alberni V9Y 1V8 – 250/723-2146, Fax: 250/723-1003 |
| Port Alice (V) | 1,331 | Mount Waddington | Vancouver Island North | North Island | James Thackray, Clerk, PO Box 130, Port Alice V0N 2N0 – 250/284-3391, Fax: 250/284-3416 |
| Port Clements (V) | 558 | Skeena-Queen Charlotte | Skeena | North Coast | Jukka Efraimsson, Sec.-Treas., PO Box 198, Port Clements V0T 1R0 – 250/557-4295, Fax: 250/557-4568 |
| PORT COQUITLAM | 46,682 | Greater Vancouver | Port Moody-Coquitlam | Port Coquitlam | Susan Rauh, Clerk, 2580 Shaughnessy St., Port Coquitlam V3C 2A8 – 604/944-5411, Fax: 604/944-5402 |
| Port Edward (DM) | 700 | Skeena-Queen Charlotte | Skeena | North Coast | Robert Earl, Clerk-Treas., 770 Pacific Av., Port Edward V0V 1G0 – 250/628-3667, Fax: 250/628-9225 |
| Port Hardy (DM) | 5,283 | Mount Waddington | Vancouver Island North | North Island | Joseph A. Fernandez, Clerk-Treas., PO Box 68, Port Hardy V0N 2P0 – 250/949-6665, Fax: 250/949-7433 |
| Port McNeill † | 2,925 | Mount Waddington | Vancouver Island North | North Island | Margaret Page, Clerk, PO Box 728, Port McNeill V0N 2R0 – 250/956-3111, Fax: 250/956-4300 |
| PORT MOODY | 20,847 | Greater Vancouver | Port Moody-Coquitlam | Port Moody-Burnaby Mountain | Colleen Rohde, Clerk, PO Box 36, Port Moody V3H 3E1 – 604/469-4500, Fax: 604/469-4550 |
| Pouce Coupé (V) | 894 | Peace River | Prince George-Peace River | Peace River South | Diana Chorney, Sec.-Treas., PO Box 190, Pouce Coupé V0C 2C0 – 250/786-5794, Fax: 250/786-5257 |
| Powell River (DM) | 13,131 | Powell River | West Vancouver-Sunshine Coast | Powell River-Sunshine Coast | Victor Petersen, Clerk, 6910 Duncan St., Powell River V8A 1V4 – 604/485-6291, Fax: 604/485-2913 |
| *PRINCE GEORGE | 75,150 | Fraser-Fort George | Prince George-Bulkley Valley; Prince George-Peace River | Pr. George-Mt. Robson; Pr. George N.; Pr. George-Omineca | Allan Chabot, City Clerk, City Hall, 1100 Patricia Blvd., Prince George V2L 3V9 – 250/561-7600, Fax: 250/561-0183 |
| PRINCE RUPERT | 16,714 | Skeena-Queen Charlotte | Skeena | North Coast | Patti Sawka, Clerk, 424 West Third Ave., Prince Rupert V8J 1L7 – 250/627-0934, Fax: 250/627-0999 |
| Princeton † | 2,826 | Okanagan-Similkameen | Okanagan-Coquihalla | Yale-Lillooet | Cornelius Froese, Clerk, PO Box 670, Princeton V0X 1W0 – 250/295-3135, Fax: 250/295-3477 |
| Qualicum Beach † | 6,728 | Nanaimo | Nanaimo-Alberni | Parksville-Qualicum | Mark D. Brown, Clerk, PO Box 130, Qualicum Beach V9K 1S7 – 250/752-6921, Fax: 250/752-1243 |
| QUESNEL | 8,468 | Cariboo | Cariboo-Chilcotin | Cariboo North | Doug Ruttan, Clerk, 405 Barlow Ave., Quesnel V2J 2C3 – 250/992-2111, Fax: 250/992-2206 |

Cities in CAPITALS; Districts marked D; District municipalities marked DM; Towns marked †; Villages marked (V). British Columbia Regional Districts follow this list. An in-depth listing for municipalities marked with * appears in Part 2 (check Index for page numbers).

| MUNICIPALITY | 1996 POP. | COUNTY OR DISTRICT | FEDERAL ELECTORAL DISTRICT | PROVINCIAL ELECTORAL DISTRICT | CONTACT PERSON WITH ADDRESS, PHONE & FAX |
|---|---|---|---|---|---|
| Radium Hot Springs (V) | 530 | East Kootenay | Kootenay Columbia | Columbia River-Revelstoke | Laura Green, Sec.-Treas., PO Box 340, Radium Hot Springs V0A 1M0 – 250/347-6455, Fax: 250/347-9068 |
| REVELSTOKE | 8,047 | Columbia-Shuswap | Kootenay-Columbia | Columbia River-Revelstoke | Rick Butler, Clerk, PO Box 170, Revelstoke V0E 2S0 – 250/837-2161, Fax: 250/837-4930 |
| *RICHMOND | 148,867 | Greater Vancouver | Richmond; Delta-South Richmond | Richmond-Centre; Richmond E.; Richmond-Steveston | Richard McKenna, City Clerk, 6911 - No. 3 Rd., Richmond V6Y 2C1 – 604/276-4000, Fax: 604/278-5139, URL: http://www.city.richmond.bc.ca |
| ROSSLAND | 3,802 | Kootenay Boundary | West Kootenay-Okanagan | Rossland-Trail | Andre Carrel, Clerk, PO Box 1179, Rossland V0G 1Y0 – 250/362-7396, Fax: 250/362-5451 |
| *Saanich | 101,388 | Capital | Esquimalt-Juan de Fuca; Saanich-Gulf Islands; Victoria | Oak Bay-Gordon Head; Saanich N. & the Islands; Saanich S. | Terry R. Kirk, Municipal Clerk, 770 Vernon Ave., Victoria V8X 2W7 – 250/475-1775, Fax: 250/475-5400 |
| Salmo (V) | 1,202 | Central Kootenay | West Kootenay-Okanagan | Rossland-Trail | Brian Ryder, Sec.-Treas., PO Box 1000, Salmo V0G 1Z0 – 250/357-9433, Fax: 250/357-9633 |
| Salmon Arm (DM) | 14,664 | Columbia-Shuswap | Okanagan-Shuswap | Shuswap | Wayne Buchanan, Clerk, PO Box 40, Salmon Arm V1E 4N2 – 250/832-6021, Fax: 250/832-5584 |
| Sayward (V) | 440 | Comox-Strathcona | Vancouver Island North | North Island | Jean Phye, Sec.-Treas., PO Box 29, Sayward V0P 1R0 – 250/282-5512, Fax: 250/282-5511 |
| Sechelt (DM) | 7,343 | Sunshine Coast | West Vancouver-Sunshine Coast | Powell River-Sunshine Coast | Michael P. Vaughn, Clerk, PO Box 129, Sechelt V0N 3A0 – 604/885-1986, Fax: 604/885-7591 |
| Sicamous (DM) | 2,827 | Columbia-Shuswap | Okanagan-Shuswap | Shuswap | Karen Smith, Clerk-Treas., PO Box 219, Sicamous V0E 2V0 – 250/836-2477, Fax: 250/836-4314 |
| Sidney † | 10,701 | Capital | Saanich-Gulf Islands | Saanich N. & the Islands | Alan Cameron, Clerk, 2440 Sidney Ave., Sidney V8L 1Y7 – 250/656-1184, Fax: 250/655-4508 |
| Silverton (V) | 241 | Central Kootenay | West Kootenay-Okanagan | Nelson-Creston | Dorothy Mellen, Sec.-Treas., PO Box 14, Silverton V0G 2B0 – 250/358-2472, Fax: 250/358-2321 |
| Slocan (V) | 335 | Central Kootenay | West Kootenay-Okanagan | Nelson-Creston | Bonnie St. Thomas, Sec.-Treas., PO Box 50, Slocan V0G 2C0 – 250/355-2277, Fax: 250/355-2666 |
| Smithers † | 5,624 | Bulkley-Nechako | Skeena | Bulkley Valley-Stikine | Terri-Anne Barge, Clerk, PO Box 879, Smithers V0J 2N0 – 250/847-1600, Fax: 250/847-1601 |
| Spallumcheen (DM) | 5,322 | North Okanagan | Okanagan-Shuswap | Shuswap | George Sawada, Clerk-Treas., PO Box 100, Armstrong V0E 1B0 – 250/546-3013, Fax: 250/546-8878 |
| Sparwood (DM) | 3,982 | East Kootenay | Kootenay-Columbia | Kootenay | Sandy Hansen, Clerk, PO Box 520, Sparwood V0B 2G0 – 250/425-6271, Fax: 250/425-7277 |
| Squamish (DM) | 13,994 | Squamish-Lillooet | West Vancouver-Sunshine Coast | West Vancouver-Garibaldi | Joe Barry, Clerk, PO Box 310, Squamish V0N 3G0 – 604/892-5217, Fax: 604/892-1083 |
| Stewart (DM) | 858 | Kitimat-Stikine | Skeena | North Coast | Brian Woodward, Clerk-Treas., PO Box 460, Stewart V0T 1W0 – 250/636-2251, Fax: 250/636-2417 |
| Summerland (DM) | 10,584 | Okanagan-Similkameen | Okanagan-Coquihalla | Okanagan-Penticton | George Redlich, Clerk, PO Box 159, Summerland V0H 1Z0 – 250/494-6451, Fax: 250/494-1415 |
| *SURREY | 304,477 | Greater Vancouver | Surrey North; South Surrey-White Rock-Langley; Surrey Central | Surrey-Cloverdale; Surrey-Green Timbers; Surrey-Newton; Surrey-Whalley; Surrey-White Rock | Donna Kenny, City Clerk & General Mgr., Legislative Services, 14245 - 56 Ave., Surrey V3X 3A2 – 604/591-4011, Fax: 604/591-4357, URL: http://www.city.surrey.bc.ca/ |
| Tahsis (V) | 940 | Comox-Strathcona | Vancouver Island North | North Island | Paul R. Edgington, Sec.-Treas., PO Box 519, Tahsis V0P 1X0 – 250/934-6344, Fax: 250/934-6622 |
| Taylor (DM) | 1,031 | Peace River | Prince George-Peace River | Peace River North | Terry Johnston, Clerk-Treas., PO Box 300, Taylor V0C 2K0 – 250/789-3392, Fax: 250/789-3543 |
| Telkwa (V) | 1,194 | Bulkley-Nechako | Skeena | Bulkley Valley-Stikine | Arlene de Gelder, Sec.-Treas., PO Box 220, Telkwa V0J 2X0 – 250/846-5212, Fax: 250/846-9572 |
| TERRACE | 12,779 | Kitimat-Stikine | Skeena | Skeena | Robert Hallsor, Clerk, 3215 Eby St., Terrace V8G 2X8 – 250/635-6311, Fax: 250/638-4777 |
| Tofino (DM) | 1,170 | Alberni-Clayoquot | Nanaimo-Alberni | Alberni | Charles Hamilton, Clerk, PO Box 9, Tofino V0R 2Z0 – 250/725-3229, Fax: 250/725-3775 |
| TRAIL | 7,696 | Kootenay Boundary | West Kootenay-Okanagan | Rossland-Trail | James D. Forbes, Clerk, 1394 Pine Ave., Trail V1R 4E6 – 250/364-1262, Fax: 250/364-0830 |
| Tumbler Ridge (DM) | 3,775 | Peace River | Prince George-Peace River | Peace River South | Norma Everett, Clerk, PO Box 100, Tumbler Ridge V0C 2W0 – 250/242-4242, Fax: 250/242-3993 |

Cities in CAPITALS; Districts marked D; District municipalities marked DM; Towns marked †; Villages marked (V). British Columbia Regional Districts follow this list. An in-depth listing for municipalities marked with * appears in Part 2 (check Index for page numbers).

| MUNICIPALITY | 1996 POP. | COUNTY OR DISTRICT | FEDERAL ELECTORAL DISTRICT | PROVINCIAL ELECTORAL DISTRICT | CONTACT PERSON WITH ADDRESS, PHONE & FAX |
|---|---|---|---|---|---|
| Ucluelet (D) | 1,658 | Alberni-Clayoquot | Nanaimo-Alberni | Alberni | Jack Copland, Clerk, PO Box 999, Ucluelet V0R 3A0 – 250/726-7744, Fax: 250/726-7335 |
| Valemount (V) | 1,303 | Fraser-Fort George | Prince George-Bulkley Valley | Prince George-Mount Robson | Dennis Goddard, Clerk, PO Box 168, Valemount V0E 2Z0 – 250/566-4435, Fax: 250/566-4249 |
| *VANCOUVER | 514,008 | Greater Vancouver | Vancouver Centre; Vancouver East; Vancouver-Kingsway; Vancouver Quadra; Vancouver South-Burnaby | Vancouver Burrard; Vanc.-Fraserview; Vanc.-Hastings; Vanc.-Kensington; Vanc.-Kingsway; Vanc.-Langara; Vanc.-Little Mtn.; Vanc.-Mt. Pleasant; Vanc.-Point Grey; Vanc.-Quilchena | Maria Kinsella, Clerk, 453 West 12 Ave., Vancouver V5Y 1V4 – 604/873-7011, Fax: 604/873-7419, URL: http://www.city.vancouver.bc.ca/ |
| Vanderhoof (DM) | 4,401 | Bulkley-Nechako | Prince George-Bulkley Valley | Prince George-Omineca | Mike Redfearn, Clerk, PO Box 900, Vanderhoof V0J 3A0 – 250/567-4711, Fax: 250/567-9169 |
| VERNON | 31,817 | North Okanagan | Okanagan-Shuswap | Okanagan-Vernon | Marg Bailey, Clerk, 3400 - 30 St., Vernon V1T 5E6 – 250/545-1361, Fax: 250/545-7876 |
| *VICTORIA | 73,504 | Capital | Victoria | Esquimalt-Metchosin; Oak Bay-Gordon Head; Victoria-Beacon Hill; Victoria-Hillside | Mark Johnston, Clerk & Director, Corporate Services, One Centennial Sq., Victoria V8W 1P6 – 250/385-5711, Fax: 250/361-0348, URL: http://www.city.victoria.bc.ca/ |
| View Royal † | 6,441 | Capital | Esquimalt-Juan de Fuca | Esquimalt-Metchosin | Heinz Burki, Clerk, 45 View Royal Ave., Victoria V9B 1A6 – 250/479-6800, Fax: 250/727-9551 |
| Warfield (V) | 1,788 | Kootenay Boundary | West Kootenay-Okanagan | Rossland-Trail | Shirley A. Tognotti, Sec.-Treas., 555 Schofield Hwy., Trail V1R 2G7 – 250/368-8202, Fax: 250/368-9354 |
| West Vancouver (DM) | 40,882 | Greater Vancouver | West Vancouver-Sunshine Coast | N. Vancouver-Lonsdale; W. Vancouver-Capilano; W. Vancouver-Garibaldi | Margaret K. Warwick, Clerk, 750 - 17 St., West Vancouver V7V 3T3 – 604/925-7000, Fax: 604/925-7006 |
| Whistler (DM) | 7,172 | Squamish-Lillooet | West Vancouver-Sunshine Coast | West Vancouver-Garibaldi | Brenda M. Sims, Clerk, 4325 Blackcomb Way, Whistler V0N 1B4 – 604/932-5535, Fax: 604/932-6636 |
| WHITE ROCK | 17,210 | Greater Vancouver | South Surrey-White Rock-Langley | Surrey-White Rock | Diane A. Middler, Clerk, 15322 Buena Vista Ave., White Rock V4B 1Y6 – 604/531-9111, Fax: 604/541-2118 |
| WILLIAMS LAKE | 10,472 | Cariboo | Cariboo-Chilcotin | Cariboo North; Cariboo South | Wayne Thiessen, Clerk, 450 Mart St., Williams Lake V2G 1N3 – 250/392-2311, Fax: 250/392-4408 |
| Zeballos (V) | 232 | Comox-Strathcona | Vancouver Island North | North Island | Holli Bellavie, Sec.-Treas., PO Box 127, Zeballos V0P 2A0 – 250/761-4229, Fax: 250/761-4331 |

## BRITISH COLUMBIA REGIONAL DISTRICTS

| REG. DISTRICTS | 1996 POP. | CONTACT PERSON WITH ADDRESS, PHONE & FAX |
|---|---|---|
| Alberni-Clayoquot | 31,652 | Bob Harper, Sec., 3008 - 5 Ave., Port Alberni V9Y 2E3 - 250/720-2700, Fax: 250/723-1327 |
| Bulkley-Nechako | 41,642 | J. Jay Simons, Adm., PO Box 820, Burns Lake V0J 1E0 – 250/692-3195, Fax: 250/692-3305 |
| Capital | 317,989 | William Jordan, Executive Director, 524 Yates St., PO Box 1000, Victoria V8W 2S6 – 250/360-3000, Fax: 250/360-3130, URL: http://vvv.com/crd/ |
| Cariboo | 66,475 | Bob Long, Sec., 525 Borland St., Williams Lake V2G 1R9 – 250/392-3351, Fax: 250/392-2812 |
| Central Coast | 3,921 | Donna Mikkelson, Sec.-Treas., PO Box 186, Bella Coola V0T 1C0 – 250/799-5291, Fax: 250/799-5750 |
| Central Kootenay | 58,099 | Barry Baldigara, Sec.-Asst. Adm., 601 Vernon St., Nelson V1L 4E9 – 250/352-6665, Fax: 250/352-9300 |
| Central Okanagan | 136,541 | Wayne d'Easum, Sec., 1450 KLO Rd., Kelowna V1W 3Z4 – 250/763-4918, Fax: 250/763-0606 |
| Columbia-Shuswap | 48,116 | Al Kuroyama, Sec., PO Box 978, Salmon Arm V1E 4P1 – 250/832-8194, Fax: 250/832-3375 |
| Comox-Strathcona | 97,666 | Barbra Whitehead, Sec., PO Box 3370, Courtenay V9N 5N5 – 250/334-6000, Fax: 250/334-4358 |
| Cowichan Valley | 70,978 | Jennifer Forrest, Sec., 137 Evans St., Duncan V9L 1P5 – 250/746-2500, Fax: 250/746-5612 |
| East Kootenay | 59,366 | Wayne McNamar, Sec., 19 - 24 Ave. South, Cranbrook V1C 3H8 – 250/489-2791, Fax: 250/489-3498 |
| Fort Nelson-Liard | 5,856 | Patricia A. Bailey, Sec., PO Box 399, Fort Nelson V0C 1R0 – 250/774-2541, Fax: 250/774-6794 |
| Fraser-Fort George | 98,974 | Anne Hogan, Sec., 987 - 4 Ave., Prince George V2L 3H7 – 250/960-4400, Fax: 250/563-7520 |
| Fraser Valley | 222,397 | Robert Moore, Clerk-Sec., 8430 Cessna Drive, Chilliwack V2P 7K4 – 604/702-5000, Fax: 604/792-9684 |
| Greater Vancouver | 1,831,665 | Paulette Vetleson, Sec., 4330 Kingsway, Burnaby V5H 4G8 – 604/432-6200, Fax: 604/432-6248, URL: http://www.gvrd.bc.ca/index.html |
| Kitimat-Stikine | 43,618 | Bob Marcellin, Sec., #300, 4545 Lazelle Ave., Terrace V8G 4E1 – 250/635-7251, Fax: 250/635-9222 |
| Kootenay Boundary | 32,906 | Larry Robinson, Sec., #202, 843 Rossland Ave., Trail V1R 4S8 – 250/368-9148, Fax: 250/368-3990, URL: http://www.rdkb.com |
| Mount Waddington | 14,601 | Joe Mackenzie, Sec., PO Box 729, Port McNeill V0N 2R0 – 250/956-3161, Fax: 250/956-3232 |
| Nanaimo | 121,783 | Carol Mason, Sec., PO Box 40, Lantzville V0R 2H0 – 250/390-4111, Fax: 250/390-4163 |
| North Okanagan | 71,607 | Barry Gagnon, Sec.-Treas., 9848 Aberdeen Rd., Vernon V1B 2K9 – 250/545-5368, Fax: 250/545-1445 |
| Okanagan-Similkameen | 75,933 | Vanessa Sutton, Adm.-Sec., 101 Martin St., Penticton V2A 5J9 – 250/492-0237, Fax: 250/492-0063 |
| Peace River | 56,477 | Moray Stewart, Sec., PO Box 810, Dawson Creek V1G 4H8 – 250/784-3200, Fax: 250/784-3201 |
| Powell River | 19,936 | Frances Ladret, Sec., 5776 Marine Ave., Powell River V8A 2M4 – 604/483-3231, Fax: 604/483-2229 |

| REG. DISTRICTS | 1996 POP. | CONTACT PERSON WITH ADDRESS, PHONE & FAX |
|---|---|---|
| Skeena-Queen Charlotte | 24,795 | Bryce Barnewall, Sec., #115 West 1st Av., Prince Rupert V8J 4K8 – 250/624-2002, Fax: 250/627-8493 |
| Squamish-Lillooet | 29,401 | Rick Beauchamp, Sec., PO Box 219, Pemberton V0N 2L0 – 604/894-6371, Fax: 604/894-6526 |
| Sunshine Coast | 24,914 | Larry Jardine, Sec., PO Box 800, Sechelt V0N 3A0 – 604/885-2261, Fax: 604/885-7909 |
| Thompson-Nicola | 118,801 | Eric Shishido, Sec., 2079 Falcon Rd., Kamloops V2C 4J2 – 250/372-9336, Fax: 250/372-5048 |

## MANITOBA

All municipalities in Manitoba (except Winnipeg, which is governed by the City of Winnipeg Act) come under authority of the Manitoba Municipal Act.

In Manitoba there are no counties or regional governments; there are only urban & rural municipalities. Incorporation of a new municipality requires a population of at least 1,000 residents & a population density of at least 400 residents per square kilometre for an urban municipality & a population density of less than 400 residents per square kilometre for a rural municipality. Urban municipalities may be called cities, towns, villages & urban municipalities. The population requirement for a city is at least 7,500 residents.

Effective, January 1, 1997, with the proclamation of the new Manitoba Municipal Act, 15 local government districts have been transferred to full municipal status. Four will be continued as towns & 11 as rural municipalities. Only Mystery Lake & Pinawa will remain as local government districts.

All municipal elections are held every three years; thus, October 1998, October 2001 etc.

Cities in CAPITALS; Towns marked †; Villages marked (V); Rural Municipalities marked (RM). An in-depth listing for municipalities marked with * appears in Part 2 (check Index for page numbers).

| MUNICIPALITY | 1996 POP. | FEDERAL ELECTORAL DISTRICT | PROVINCIAL ELECTORAL DISTRICT | CONTACT PERSON WITH ADDRESS, PHONE & FAX |
|---|---|---|---|---|
| Albert (RM) | 475 | Brandon-Souris | Arthur-Virden | Rick Branston, CAO, PO Box 70, Tilston R0M 2B0 – 204/686-2271, Fax: 204/686-2335 |
| Alexander (RM) | 2,555 | | | Rose-Marie Beaudry, CAO, PO Box 100, St. Georges R0E 1V0 – 204/367-2235, Fax: 204/367-2257 |
| Alonsa (RM) | 1,769 | | | Pamela Sul, CAO, PO Box 127, Alonsa R0H 0A0 – 204/767-2054, Fax: 204/767-2044 |
| Altona † | 3,286 | Provencher | Emerson | Jim Spencer, CAO, 111 Centre Av. East, PO Box 163, Altona R0G 0B0 – 204/324-6468, Fax: 204/324-1550 |
| Arborg (V) | 1,012 | Selkirk-Interlake | Interlake | Roger Huel, CAO, 337 River Rd., PO Box 159, Arborg R0C 0A0 – 204/376-2647, Fax: 204/376-5379 |
| Archie (RM) | 441 | Dauphin-Swan River | Roblin-Russell | Dawna Jamieson, CAO, Qu'Appelle St., PO Box 67, McAuley R0M 1H0 – 204/722-2053, Fax: 204/722-2027 |
| Argyle (RM) | 1,220 | Portage-Lisgar | Turtle Mountain | Gord Dearsley, CAO, 132 Second St., PO Box 40, Baldur R0K 0B0 – 204/535-2176, Fax: 204/535-2176 |
| Armstrong (RM) | 1,866 | | | Don Rybachuk, CAO, PO Box 69, Inwood R0C 1P0 – 204/278-3377, Fax: 204/278-3437 |
| Arthur (RM) | 528 | Brandon-Souris | Arthur-Virden | Joan Cooper, CAO, 138 Main St., PO Box 429, Melita R0M 1L0 – 204/522-3263, Fax: 204/522-8706 |
| Beauséjour † | 2,712 | Selkirk-Interlake | Lac du Bonnet | Jack Douglas, CAO, 639 Park Av., PO Box 1028, Beauséjour R0E 0C0 – 204/268-2008, Fax: 204/268-3107 |
| Benito (V) | 460 | Dauphin-Swan River | Swan River | Karon Harness, CAO, 126 Main St., PO Box 369, Benito R0L 0C0 – 204/539-2634, Fax: 204/539-2221 |
| Bifrost (RM) | 2,851 | Selkirk-Interlake | Interlake | L. Grant Thorsteinson, CAO, 329 River Rd., PO Box 70, Arborg R0C 0A0 – 204/376-2391, Fax: 204/376-2742 |
| Binscarth (V) | 463 | Dauphin-Swan River | Roblin-Russell | Bonnie Cozens, CAO, 116 Russell St., PO Box 54, Binscarth R0J OG0 – 204/532-2223, Fax: 204/532-2153 |
| Birtle † | 720 | Dauphin-Swan River | Roblin-Russell | Joan E. Taylor, CAO, PO Box 57, Birtle R0M 0C0 – 204/842-3234, Fax: 204/842-3496 |
| Birtle (RM) | 862 | Dauphin-Swan River | Roblin-Russell | Debbie Jensen, CAO, 678 Main St., PO Box 70, Birtle R0M 0C0 – 204/842-3403, Fax: 204/842-3622 |
| Blanshard (RM) | 655 | Dauphin-Swan River | Minnedosa | Diane Kuculym, CAO, 10 Cochrane St., PO Box 179, Oak River R0K 1T0 – 204/566-2146, Fax: 204/566-2126 |
| Boissevain † | 1,544 | Brandon-Souris | Turtle Mountain | Lloyd Leganchuk, CAO, 420 South Railway, PO Box 490, Boissevain R0K 0E0 – 204/534-2433, Fax: 204/534-3710 |
| Boulton (RM) | 341 | Dauphin-Swan River | Roblin-Russell | Raymond G. Bomback, CAO, PO Box 110, Inglis R0J 0X0 – 204/564-2589, Fax: 204/564-2643 |
| Bowsman (V) | 358 | Dauphin-Swan River | Swan River | Laurie-Ann Maidy, CAO, 105 - 2 St., PO Box 244, Bowsman R0L 0H0 – 204/238-4351, Fax: 204/238-4351 |
| *BRANDON | 39,175 | Brandon-Souris | Brandon East; Brandon West | W. Ian Ford, Clerk, 410 - 9 St., Brandon R7A 6A2 – 204/729-2186, Fax: 204/729-8244 |
| Brenda (RM) | 726 | Brandon-Souris | Arthur-Virden | Ron Bertholet, CAO, Second St., PO Box 40, Waskada R0M 2E0 – 204/673-2401, Fax: 204/673-2663 |
| Brokenhead (RM) | 3,495 | Selkirk-Interlake | Lac du Bonnet | Wayne Omichinski, CAO, PO Box 490, Beauséjour R0E 0C0 – 204/268-1624, Fax: 204/268-1504 |
| Cameron (RM) | 537 | Brandon-Souris | Arthur-Virden | Brad Coe, CAO, 315 East Railway St., PO Box 399, Hartney R0M 0X0 – 204/858-2590, Fax: 204/858-2681 |
| Carberry † | 1,493 | Portage-Lisgar | Gladstone | Myrtle McMillan, CAO, 122 Main St., PO Box 130, Carberry R0K 0H0 – 204/834-2195, Fax: 204/834-2795 |
| Carman † | 2,704 | Portage-Lisgar | Morris | Cheryl Young, CAO, 12 - 2 Ave. SW, PO Box 160, Carman R0G 0J0 – 204/745-2443, 1-800-207-2721, Fax: 204/745-2903 |
| Cartier (RM) | 3,009 | Portage-Lisgar | Lakeside | Andre C. Carriere, CAO, PO Box 117, Elie R0H 0H0 – 204/353-2214, Fax: 204/353-2335 |
| Cartwright (V) | 345 | Portage-Lisgar | Turtle Mountain | Colleen Mullin, CAO, 485 Curwen, PO Box 9, Cartwright R0K 0L0 – 204/529-2363, Fax: 204/529-2288 |
| Churchill † | 1,089 | | | Rod McKenzie, CAO, 180 La Verendrye Ave., PO Box 459, Churchill R0B 0E0 – 204/675-8871, Fax: 204/675-2934 |

Cities in CAPITALS; Towns marked †; Villages marked (V); Rural Municipalities marked (RM). An in-depth listing for municipalities marked with * appears in Part 2 (check Index for page numbers).

| MUNICIPALITY | 1996 POP. | FEDERAL ELECTORAL DISTRICT | PROVINCIAL ELECTORAL DISTRICT | CONTACT PERSON WITH ADDRESS, PHONE & FAX |
|---|---|---|---|---|
| Clanwilliam (RM) | 470 | Dauphin-Swan River | Minnedosa | Colleen Synchyshyn, CAO, 44 Main St., PO Box 40, Erickson R0J 0P0 – 204/636-2431, Fax: 204/636-2516 |
| Coldwell (RM) | 1,399 | Selkirk-Interlake | Lakeside | Diane Jacobs, CAO, 35 Main St., PO Box 90, Lundar R0C 1Y0 – 204/762-5421, Fax: 204/762-5177 |
| Consol (RM) | | | | Leona Axcell, CAO, 264 Fischer Ave., PO Box 578, The Pas R9A 1K6 – 204/623-7474, Fax: 204/623-4546 |
| Cornwallis (RM) | 4,279 | Brandon-Souris | Minnedosa | R.L. (Bob) Wallis, CAO, Site 500, RR#5, PO Box 10, Brandon R7A 5Y5 – 204/725-8686, Fax: 204/725-3659 |
| Crystal City (V) | 433 | Portage-Lisgar | Turtle Mountain | Douglas E. Cavers, CAO, 26 South Railway Ave. East, PO Box 310, Crystal City R0K 0N0 – 204/873-2591, Fax: 204/873-2459 |
| Daly (RM) | 895 | Brandon-Souris | Minnedosa | John B. MacLellan, CAO, 615 - 2 Ave., PO Box 538, Rivers R0K 1X0 – 204/328-7410, Fax: 204/328-7410 |
| Dauphin † | 8,266 | Dauphin-Swan River | Dauphin | Jim Puffalt, CAO, 21 - 2 Ave. NW, Dauphin R7N 1H1 – 204/638-3938, Fax: 204/638-5790 |
| Dauphin (RM) | 2,488 | Dauphin-Swan River | Dauphin | Gail Anderson, CAO, Hwy. 20A East, PO Box 574, Dauphin R7N 2V4 – 204/638-4531, Fax: 204/638-7598 |
| De Salaberry (RM) | 3,067 | Provencher | Emerson; Morris | Ron Musick, CAO, 466 Sabourin St., PO Box 40, St. Pierre Jolys R0A 1V0 – 204/433-7406, Fax: 204/433-7063 |
| Deloraine † | 1,041 | Brandon-Souris | Arthur-Virden | Ronald H. Amey, CAO, 102 Broadway St. South, PO Box 510, Deloraine R0M 0M0 – 204/747-2655, Fax: 204/747-2927 |
| Dufferin (RM) | 2,408 | Portage-Lisgar | Morris | Linda C. Baleja, CAO, 12 - 2 Av. SW, PO Box 100, Carman R0G 0J0 – 204/745-2301, Fax: 204/745-6348 |
| Dunnottar (V) | 392 | Selkirk-Interlake | Gimli | Nora L. Rentz, CAO, #210, 1839 Main St., Winnipeg R2V 2A4 – 204/339-1639, Fax: 204/339-1630 |
| East St. Paul (RM) | 6,437 | Selkirk-Red River | Springfield | Janet Nylen, CAO, 3021 Birds Hill Rd., East St. Paul R2E 1A7 – 204/668-8112, Fax: 204/668-1987 |
| Edward (RM) | 759 | Brandon-Souris | Arthur-Virden | Rob Trott, CAO, PO Box 100, Pierson R0M 1S0 – 204/634-2231, Fax: 204/634-2479 |
| Elkhorn (V) | 514 | Brandon-Souris | Arthur-Virden | Garth Mitchell, CAO, 10 Grange St., PO Box 280, Elkhorn R0M 0N0 – 204/845-2161, Fax: 204/845-2312 |
| Ellice (RM) | 526 | Dauphin-Swan River | Roblin-Russell | J. C. Chartier, CAO, Main St. North, PO Box 100, St. Lazare R0M 1Y0 – 204/683-2241, Fax: 204/683-2317 |
| Elton (RM) | 1,406 | Brandon-Souris | Minnedosa | Kathleen E.I. Steele, CAO, Forrest R0K 0W0 – 204/728-7834, Fax: 204/725-1865 |
| Emerson † | 737 | Provencher | Emerson | Pat Ihme, CAO, 104 Church, PO Box 340, Emerson R0A 0L0 – 204/373-2002, Fax: 204/373-2486 |
| Erickson (V) | 507 | Dauphin-Swan River | Minnedosa | Colleen Synchyshyn, CAO, 44 Main St., PO Box 40, Erickson R0J 0P0 – 204/636-2431, Fax: 204/636-2516 |
| Eriksdale (RM) | 942 | Selkirk-Interlake | Lakeside | Debra Surgenor, CAO, 16 Main St., PO Box 10, Eriksdale R0C 0W0 – 204/739-2666, Fax: 204/739-2073 |
| Ethelbert (V) | 315 | Dauphin-Swan River | Swan River | Eleanor Kuzyk, CAO, PO Box 185, Ethelbert R0L 0T0 – 204/742-3301, Fax: 204/742-3228 |
| Ethelbert (RM) | 514 | Dauphin-Swan River | Swan River | Dennis Puchailo, CAO, PO Box 115, Ethelbert R0L 0T0 – 204/742-3212, Fax: 204/742-3642 |
| Fisher (RM) | 2,154 | | | Linda Podaima, CAO, PO Box 280, Fisher Branch R0C 0Z0 – 204/372-6393, Fax: 204/372-8470 |
| FLIN FLON | 6,572 | Churchill | Flin Flon | Ken Shoemaker, CAO, 20 - 1 Ave., PO Box 100, Flin Flon R8A 1M6 – 204/687-7511, Fax: 204/687-5133 |
| Franklin (RM) | 1,724 | Lisgar-Marquette | Emerson | Helen I. Robbins, CAO, 115 Waddell Ave., PO Box 66, Dominion City R0A 0H0 – 204/427-2557, Fax: 204/427-2224 |
| Garson (V) | 339 | Selkirk-Interlake | Lac du Bonnet | Eileen Boonstra, CAO, 13 Thompson Ave., PO Box 97, Garson R0E 0R0 – 204/268-2382 |
| Gilbert Plains (V) | 748 | Dauphin-Swan River | Dauphin | Ernie Mouck, CAO, 114 Main St. North, PO Box 39, Gilbert Plains R0L 0X0 – 204/548-2761 |
| Gilbert Plains (RM) | 976 | Dauphin-Swan River | Dauphin | Joan E. Priest, CAO, 115 Main St. North, PO Box 220, Gilbert Plains R0L 0X0 – 204/548-2326, Fax: 204/548-2564 |
| Gillam (RM) | 1,534 | | | Hilda M. Price, CAO, 323 Railway Ave., PO Box 100, Gillam R0B 0L0 – 204/652-2121, Fax: 204/652-2338 |
| Gimli † | 1,574 | Selkirk-Interlake | Gimli | Danny Jo Sigmundson, CAO, 64 - 2 Ave., PO Box 88, Gimli R0C 1B0 – 204/642-5210, Fax: 204/642-7151 |
| Gimli (RM) | 3,124 | Selkirk-Interlake | Gimli | Christopher Fulsher, CAO, Centre St. West, PO Box 1246, Gimli R0C 1B0 – 204/642-8593, Fax: 204/642-8149 |
| Gladstone † | 927 | Portage-Lisgar | Gladstone | Louise Blaire, CAO, 48 Dennis St. West, PO Box 25, Gladstone R0J 0T0 – 204/385-2332, Fax: 204/385-2391 |
| Glenboro (V) | 663 | Brandon-Souris | Gladstone | Donald E. Foster, CAO, 109 Broadway St., PO Box 190, Glenboro R0K 0X0 – 204/827-2083, Fax: 204/827-2553 |
| Glenella (RM) | 555 | Dauphin-Swan River | Ste. Rose | Aaren Robertson, CAO, 50 Main St. North, PO Box 10, Glenella R0J 0V0 – 204/352-4281, Fax: 204/352-4281 |
| Glenwood (RM) | 710 | Brandon-Souris | Turtle Mountain | Dennis Bauldic, CAO, 100 - 2 St. South, PO Box 487, Souris R0K 2C0 – 204/483-2822, Fax: 204/483-2062 |
| Grahamdale (RM) | 1,625 | | | Beverley Yaworsky, CAO, 23 Government Rd., PO Box 160, Moosehorn R0C 2E0 – 204/768-2858, Fax: 204/768-3374 |

Cities in CAPITALS; Towns marked †; Villages marked (V); Rural Municipalities marked (RM). An in-depth listing for municipalities marked with * appears in Part 2 (check Index for page numbers).

| MUNICIPALITY | 1996 POP. | FEDERAL ELECTORAL DISTRICT | PROVINCIAL ELECTORAL DISTRICT | CONTACT PERSON WITH ADDRESS, PHONE & FAX |
|---|---|---|---|---|
| Grand Rapids † | 404 | | | Lillian Turner, CAO, PO Box 301, Grand Rapids R0C 1E0 – 204/639-2260, Fax: 204/639-2475 |
| Grandview † | 856 | Dauphin-Swan River | Dauphin | James W. Wilson, CAO, 436 Main St., PO Box 219, Grandview R0L 0Y0 – 204/546-2792, Fax: 204/546-2589 |
| Grandview (RM) | 904 | Dauphin-Swan River | Dauphin | Joan Scott, CAO, 414 Main St., PO Box 340, Grandview R0L 0Y0 – 204/546-2564, Fax: 204/546-3019 |
| Gretna (V) | 538 | Provencher | Emerson | Mary Harder, CAO, 568 Hespeler Ave., PO Box 280, Gretna R0G 0V0 – 204/327-5578, Fax: 204/327-5458 |
| Grey (RM) | 2,201 | Portage-Lisgar | Lakeside | Ronald D. Hayward, CAO, 34 Main St. North, PO Box 99, Elm Creek R0G 0N0 – 204/436-2014, Fax: 204/436-2543 |
| Hamiota (V) | 847 | Dauphin-Swan River | Roblin-Russell | Ernest G. Buhler, CAO, 44 Maple Ave. East, PO Box 100, Hamiota R0M 0T0 – 204/764-2779, Fax: 204/764-2671 |
| Hamiota (RM) | 515 | Dauphin-Swan River | Roblin-Russell | Ernest G. Buhler, CAO, 44 Maple Ave. East, PO Box 100, Hamiota R0M 0T0 – 204/764-2779, Fax: 204/764-2671 |
| Hanover (RM) | 9,833 | Provencher | Steinbach | Charles Teetaert, CAO, 216 Main St., PO Box 1720, Steinbach R0A 2A0 – 204/326-4488, Fax: 204/326-4830 |
| Harrison (RM) | 894 | Dauphin-Swan River | Minnedosa | Shelley Glenn, CAO, 106 Main St., PO Box 220, Newdale R0J 1J0 – 204/849-2107, Fax: 204/849-2107 |
| Hartney † | 462 | Brandon-Souris | Arthur-Virden | Brad Coe, CAO, 237 East Railway, PO Box 339, Hartney R0M 0X0 – 204/858-2429, Fax: 204/858-2429 |
| Headingley (RM) | 1,587 | Charleswood-Assiniboine | Charleswood | Lorne F. Erb, CAO, #1, 126 Bridge Rd., Headingley R4H 1G9 – 204/837-5766, Fax: 204/831-7207 |
| Hillsburg (RM) | 559 | Dauphin-Swan River | Roblin-Russell | Eleanor Nykolaishyn, CAO, 130 - 2 Ave. NW, PO Box 1180, Roblin R0L 1P0 – 204/937-2155 |
| Killarney † | 2,208 | Brandon-Souris | Turtle Mountain | Harold A. Lamb, CAO, 415 Broadway Ave., PO Box 10, Killarney R0K 1G0 – 204/523-7120, Fax: 204/523-4637 |
| La Broquerie (RM) | 2,493 | Provencher | Steinbach | Laurent Tétrault, CAO, 94 Principale St., PO Box 130, La Broquerie R0A 0W0 – 204/424-5251, Fax: 204/424-5193 |
| Lac du Bonnet (V) | 1,070 | Provencher | Lac du Bonnet | Colleen L. Johnson, CAO, 84 - 2 St., PO Box 339, Lac du Bonnet R0E 1A0 – 204/345-8693, Fax: 204/345-8694 |
| Lac du Bonnet (RM) | 2,280 | Provencher | Lac du Bonnet | vacant , CAO, PO Box 100, Lac du Bonnet R0E 1A0 – 204/345-2619, Fax: 204/345-6716 |
| Lakeview (RM) | 407 | Portage-Lisgar | Ste. Rose | Viola K. Wild, CAO, 103 Main St., PO Box 100, Langruth R0H 0N0 – 204/445-2243, Fax: 204/445-2162 |
| Langford (RM) | 722 | Dauphin-Swan River | Ste. Rose | Vinetta Hannaburg, CAO, 282 Hamilton St., PO Box 280, Neepawa R0J 1H0 – 204/476-5775, Fax: 204/476-5431 |
| Lansdowne (RM) | 966 | Dauphin-Swan River | Ste. Rose | Carol Henderson, CAO, PO Box 141, Arden R0J 0B0 – 204/368-2202, Fax: 204/368-2202 |
| Lawrence (RM) | 608 | Dauphin-Swan River | Dauphin | Elizabeth Tymchuk, CAO, PO Box 220, Rorketon R0L 1R0 – 204/732-2333, Fax: 204/732-2557 |
| Leaf Rapids † | 1,504 | Churchill | Flin Flon | Ernie Epp, CAO, Town Centre, PO Box 340, Leaf Rapids R0B 1W0 – 204/473-2436, Fax: 204/473-2566 |
| Lorne (RM) | 2,167 | Portage-Lisgar | Gladstone | Val Turner, CAO, PO Box 10, Somerset R0G 2L0 – 204/744-2133, Fax: 204/744-2349 |
| Louise (RM) | 1,090 | Portage-Lisgar | Turtle Mountain | Douglas E. Cavers, CAO, 26 South Railway Ave. East, PO Box 310, Crystal City R0K 0N0 – 204/873-2591, Fax: 204/873-2459 |
| Lynn Lake † | 1,038 | | | Fred Salter, CAO, 503 Sherrit Ave., PO Box 100, Lynn Lake R0B 0W0 – 204/356-2418, Fax: 204/356-8297 |
| Macdonald (RM) | 4,900 | Portage-Lisgar | Morris | W. Tom Raine, CAO, 161 Mandan Dr., PO Box 100, Sanford R0G 2J0 – 204/736-2255, Fax: 204/736-4335 |
| MacGregor (V) | 898 | Portage-Lisgar | Gladstone | Lawrence Hart, CAO, 27 Hampton St. East, PO Box 190, MacGregor R0H 0R0 – 204/685-2211, Fax: 204/685-2616 |
| Manitou (V) | 781 | Portage-Lisgar | Pembina | Jacalyn Clayton, CAO, 418 Main St., PO Box 280, Manitou R0G 1G0 – 204/242-2515, Fax: 204/242-2599 |
| McCreary (V) | 537 | Dauphin-Swan River | Ste. Rose | Wendy L. Turko, CAO, 436 Second Ave., PO Box 267, McCreary R0J 1B0 – 204/835-2341, Fax: 204/835-2658 |
| McCreary (RM) | 582 | Dauphin-Swan River | Ste. Rose | Linda Cripps, CAO, 432 - 1st Ave., PO Box 338, McCreary R0J 1B0 – 204/835-2309, Fax: 204/835-2649 |
| Melita † | 1,152 | Brandon-Souris | Arthur-Virden | Scott Spicer, CAO, 79 Main St., PO Box 364, Melita R0M 1L0 – 204/522-3413, Fax: 204/522-3587 |
| Miniota (RM) | 1,027 | Dauphin-Swan River | Roblin-Russell | Doug McAulay, CAO, Sarah Ave., PO Box 70, Miniota R0M 1M0 – 204/567-3683, Fax: 204/567-3807 |
| Minitonas (V) | 598 | Dauphin-Swan River | Swan River | Brent J. Fowler, CAO, 305 Main St., PO Box 9, Minitonas R0L 1G0 – 204/525-4461, Fax: 204/525-4857 |
| Minitonas (RM) | 1,193 | Dauphin-Swan River | Swan River | Brent J. Fowler, CAO, 305 Main St., PO Box 9, Minitonas R0L 1G0 – 204/525-4461, Fax: 204/525-4857 |
| Minnedosa † | 2,443 | Dauphin-Swan River | Minnedosa | Gail V. Graves, CAO, 103 Main St. South, PO Box 426, Minnedosa R0J 1E0 – 204/867-2727, Fax: 204/867-2686 |
| Minto (RM) | 661 | Brandon-Souris | Minnedosa | Susan Hoglund, CAO, 49 Main St., PO Box 247, Minnedosa R0J 1E0 – 204/867-3865, Fax: 204/867-1937 |
| Montcalm (RM) | 1,567 | Provencher | Emerson | Michel Duval, CAO, 46 First St. East, PO Box 300, Letellier R0G 1C0 – 204/737-2271, Fax: 204/737-2032 |

Cities in CAPITALS; Towns marked †; Villages marked (V); Rural Municipalities marked (RM). An in-depth listing for municipalities marked with * appears in Part 2 (check Index for page numbers).

| MUNICIPALITY | 1996 POP. | FEDERAL ELECTORAL DISTRICT | PROVINCIAL ELECTORAL DISTRICT | CONTACT PERSON WITH ADDRESS, PHONE & FAX |
|---|---|---|---|---|
| Morden † | 5,689 | Lisgar-Portage | Pembina | Abe Bergmann, CAO, #100, 195 Stephen St., Morden R6M 1V3 – 204/822-4434, Fax: 204/822-6494 |
| Morris † | 1,645 | Provencher | Morris | Conrad Nicholson, CAO, 233 Main St. North, PO Box 28, Morris R0G 1K0 – 204/746-2531, Fax: 204/746-6009 |
| Morris (RM) | 2,816 | Provencher | Morris; Emerson | Grant MacAulay, CAO, 207 Main St. North, PO Box 518, Morris R0G 1K0 – 204/746-2642, Fax: 204/746-8801 |
| Morton (RM) | 832 | Brandon-Souris | Turtle Mountain | Lloyd Leganchuk, CAO, 420 South Railway, PO Box 490, Boissevain R0K 0E0 – 204/534-2433, Fax: 204/534-3710 |
| Mossey River (RM) | 752 | Dauphin-Swan River | Swan River | John E. Pascal, CAO, PO Box 80, Fork River R0L 0V0 – 204/657-2331, Fax: 204/657-2202 |
| Mountain (RM) | 1,142 | | | Christine Playfoot, CAO, PO Box 155, Birch River R0L 0E0 – 204/236-4222, Fax: 204/236-4773 |
| Neepawa † | 3,301 | Dauphin-Swan River | Ste. Rose | Ken Jenkins, CAO, 282 Hamilton St., PO Box 339, Neepawa R0J 1H0 – 204/476-2317, Fax: 204/476-5431 |
| Niverville † | 1,615 | Provencher | Steinbach | G. Jim Buys, CAO, 86 Main St., PO Box 267, Niverville R0A 1E0 – 204/388-4600, Fax: 204/388-6110 |
| North Cypress (RM) | 1,900 | Portage-Lisgar | Gladstone | Myrtle J.W. McMillan, CAO, 122 Main St., PO Box 130, Carberry R0K 0H0 – 204/834-2195, Fax: 204/834-2795 |
| North Norfolk (RM) | 3,024 | Portage-Lisgar | Gladstone | Lawrence Hart, CAO, 27 Hampton St. East, PO Box 190, MacGregor R0H 0R0 – 204/685-2211, Fax: 204/685-2616 |
| Notre Dame de Lourdes (V) | 620 | Portage-Lisgar | Gladstone | Roger Fouasse, CAO, 55 Rodgers St., PO Box 89, Notre Dame de Lourdes R0G 1M0 – 204/248-2348, Fax: 204/248-2348 |
| Oak Lake † | 369 | Brandon-Souris | Arthur-Virden | Mary Smith, CAO, 293 - 2 Ave. West, PO Box 100, Oak Lake R0M 1P0 – 204/855-2423, Fax: 204/855-2836 |
| Oakland (RM) | 1,086 | Brandon-Souris | Turtle Mountain | Doug Boake, CAO, PO Box 28, Nesbitt R0K 1P0 – 204/824-2374, Fax: 204/824-2374 |
| Ochre River (RM) | 980 | Selkirk-Interlake | Dauphin | Ilene Mayne, CAO, 206 MacKenzie Ave., PO Box 40, Ochre River R0L 1K0 – 204/733-2423, Fax: 204/733-2259 |
| Odanah (RM) | 553 | Dauphin-Swan River | Minnedosa | Susan Hoglund, CAO, 49 Main St., PO Box 1197, Minnedosa R0J 1E0 – 204/867-3282, Fax: 204/867-1937 |
| Park (RM) | 1,362 | | | Sylvester Yakielashek, CAO, PO Box 190, Onanole R0J 1N0 – 204/848-7614, Fax: 204/848-2082 |
| Pembina (RM) | 1,850 | Portage-Lisgar | Pembina | Judy D. Young, CAO, 315 Main St., PO Box 189, Manitou R0G 1G0 – 204/242-2838, Fax: 204/242-2798 |
| Pilot Mound (V) | 716 | Portage-Lisgar | Turtle Mountain | Tannis Stevenson, CAO, 219 Broadway Ave., PO Box 39, Pilot Mound R0G 1P0 – 204/825-2587, Fax: 204/825-2362 |
| Piney (RM) | 1,604 | | | Reynald Preteau, CAO, PO Box 48, Vassar R0A 2J0 – 204/437-2060, Fax: 204/437-2556 |
| Pipestone (RM) | 1,710 | Brandon-Souris | Arthur-Virden | William W. Busby, CAO, 401 - 3rd Ave., PO Box 99, Reston R0M 1X0 – 204/877-3327, Fax: 204/877-3999 |
| Plum Coulee (V) | 729 | Provencher | Emerson | Ron Wm. Wiebe, CAO, 253 Main Ave., PO Box 36, Plum Coulee R0G 1R0 – 204/829-3419, Fax: 204/829-3436 |
| PORTAGE LA PRAIRIE | 13,077 | Portage-Lisgar | Portage la Prairie | Dale Lyle, City Mgr., 97 Saskatchewan Ave. East, Portage la Prairie R1N 0L8 – 204/239-8337, Fax: 204/239-1532 |
| Portage la Prairie (RM) | 6,627 | Portage-Lisgar;Selkirk-Interlake | Portage la Prairie; Lakeside | Richard C. Locke, CAO, 35 Tupper St. South, Portage la Prairie R1N 1W7 – 204/857-3821, Fax: 204/239-0069 |
| Powerview (V) | 759 | Churchill | Lac du Bonnet | Janice Thevenot, CAO, PO Box 220, Powerview R0E 1P0 – 204/367-8483, Fax: 204/367-4747 |
| Rapid City † | 408 | Dauphin-Swan River | Minnedosa | Valerie P. Irving, CAO, 410 - 3 Ave., PO Box 146, Rapid City R0K 1W0 – 204/826-2679, Fax: 204/826-2679 |
| Reynolds (RM) | 1,314 | | | Jeanne Kozak, CAO, General Delivery, Hadashville R0E 0X0 – 204/426-5305, Fax: 204/426-5552 |
| Rhineland (RM) | 4,204 | Provencher | Emerson | Jake Bergen, CAO, 72 - 2nd St. NE, PO Box 270, Altona R0G 0B0 – 204/324-5357, Fax: 204/324-1516 |
| Ritchot (RM) | 5,364 | St. Boniface | La Verendrye; Morris | Yves Sabourin, CAO, 352 Main St., St. Adolphe R5A 1B9 – 204/883-2293, Fax: 204/883-2674 |
| Rivers † | 1,117 | Brandon-Souris | Minnedosa | Shirley Warkentin, CAO, 670 - 2 Ave., PO Box 520, Rivers R0K 1X0 – 204/328-5250, Fax: 204/328-5374 |
| Riverside (RM) | 827 | Lisgar-Marquette | Turtle Mountain | Susan Lamont, CAO, 123 Dunlop St., PO Box 126, Dunrea R0K 0S0 – 204/776-2113, Fax: 204/776-2228 |
| Riverton (V) | 566 | Selkirk-Interlake | Interlake | Nadine Eyjolfson, CAO, 56 Laura St., PO Box 250, Riverton R0C 2R0 – 204/378-2281, Fax: 204/378-5616 |
| Roblin † | 1,885 | Dauphin-Swan River | Roblin-Russell | Marna J. Ellwood, CAO, 125 - 1 Ave. NW, PO Box 730, Roblin R0L 1P0 – 204/937-8333, Fax: 204/937-4382 |
| Roblin (RM) | 968 | Portage-Lisgar | Turtle Mountain | Colleen Mullin, CAO, 485 Curwen, PO Box 9, Cartwright R0K 0L0 – 204/529-2363, Fax: 204/529-2288 |
| Rockwood (RM) | 7,504 | Selkirk-Interlake | Gimli | Janis L. Gluchi, CAO, 33 Main St., PO Box 902, Stonewall R0C 2Z0 – 204/467-2272, Fax: 204/467-5329 |
| Roland (RM) | 984 | Portage-Lisgar | Morris | Dianne R. Toews, CAO, 45 Third St., PO Box 119, Roland R0G 1T0 – 204/343-2061, Fax: 204/343-2001 |
| Rosedale (RM) | 1,644 | Dauphin-Swan River | Ste. Rose | Harold McConnell, CAO, 282 Hamilton St., PO Box 100, Neepawa R0J 1H0 – 204/476-5414, Fax: 204/476-5431 |

Cities in CAPITALS; Towns marked †; Villages marked (V); Rural Municipalities marked (RM). An in-depth listing for municipalities marked with * appears in Part 2 (check Index for page numbers).

| MUNICIPALITY | 1996 POP. | FEDERAL ELECTORAL DISTRICT | PROVINCIAL ELECTORAL DISTRICT | CONTACT PERSON WITH ADDRESS, PHONE & FAX |
|---|---|---|---|---|
| Rossburn (V) | 580 | Dauphin-Swan River | Roblin-Russell | Leonard A. Mackedenski, CAO, 43 Main St. North, PO Box 70, Rossburn R0J 1V0 – 204/859-2762, Fax: 204/859-2959 |
| Rossburn (RM) | 626 | Dauphin-Swan River | Roblin-Russell | Ernie Antonow, CAO, 39 Main St. North, PO Box 100, Rossburn R0J 1V0 – 204/859-2779, Fax: 204/859-2959 |
| Rosser (RM) | 1,349 | Selkirk-Interlake | Lakeside | Linda Van De Walle, CAO, Rosser R0H 1E0 – 204/467-5711, Fax: 204/467-5958 |
| Russell † | 1,605 | Dauphin-Swan River | Roblin-Russell | Wally R. Melnyk, CAO, 135 Pelly Ave. North, PO Box 10, Russell R0J 1W0 – 204/773-2253, Fax: 204/773-3370 |
| Russell (RM) | 553 | Dauphin-Swan River | Roblin-Russell | Louise Ewankiw, CAO, 362 Main St. North, PO Box 220, Russell R0J 1W0 – 204/773-2294, Fax: 204/773-2294 |
| St. Andrews (RM) | 10,144 | Selkirk-Interlake | Selkirk; Gimli | Marilyn S. Regiec, CAO, General Delivery, Clandeboye R0C 0P0 – 204/738-2264, 453-8198, Fax: 204/738-2500 |
| Ste. Anne (V) | 1,511 | Provencher | La Verendrye | J. Guy Levesque, CAO, 181 Central Ave., Ste. Anne R5H 1G3 – 204/422-5293, Fax: 204/422-5459 |
| Ste. Anne (RM) | 4,213 | Provencher | La Verendrye | Alice De Baets, CAO, 141 Central Ave., Ste. Anne R5H 1C3 – 204/422-5929, Fax: 204/422-9723 |
| St. Claude (V) | 609 | Portage-Lisgar | Lakeside | Simone Dupasquier, CAO, 12 First St., PO Box 249, St. Claude R0G 1Z0 – 204/379-2382, Fax: 204/379-2072 |
| St. Clements (RM) | 8,516 | Selkirk-Interlake | Lac du Bonnet; Springfield | Tom Mollard, CAO, Grp. 35, RR#1, PO Box 2, East Selkirk R0E 0M0 – 204/482-3300, 474-2642, Fax: 204/482-3098 |
| St. François Xavier (RM) | 992 | Selkirk-Interlake | Lakeside | Colleen Atamanchuk, CAO, 1060, Hwy 26, St. François Xavier R4L 1A5 – 204/864-2092, Fax: 204/864-2390 |
| St. Laurent (RM) | 1,020 | Selkirk-Interlake | Lakeside | Lisa Wurm, CAO, I St. Laurent Dr., General Delivery, St. Laurent R0C 2S0 – 204/646-2259, Fax: 204/646-2705 |
| St. Lazare (V) | 289 | Dauphin-Swan River | Roblin-Russell | Claude Chartier, CAO, Main St. North, PO Box 100, St. Lazare R0M 1Y0 – 204/683-2241, Fax: 204/683-2317 |
| St. Pierre-Jolys (V) | 925 | Provencher | Morris | Rita I. Bazin, CAO, 466 Sabourin St., PO Box 218, St. Pierre-Jolys R0A 1V0 – 204/433-7832, Fax: 204/433-7053 |
| Ste. Rose (RM) | 944 | Dauphin-Swan River | Ste. Rose | Michelle Denys, CAO, 630 Central Ave., PO Box 30, Ste. Rose du Lac R0L 1S0 – 204/447-2633, Fax: 204/447-2278 |
| Ste. Rose du Lac (V) | 1,047 | Dauphin-Swan River | Ste. Rose | Marlene M. Bouchard, CAO, 580 Central Ave., PO Box 445, Ste. Rose du Lac R0L 1S0 – 204/447-2229, Fax: 204/447-2875 |
| Saskatchewan (RM) | 661 | Dauphin-Swan River | Minnedosa | Dorinda Watson, CAO, 435 - 3rd Ave., PO Box 9, Rapid City R0K 1W0 – 204/826-2515, Fax: 204/826-2515 |
| Selkirk † | 9,881 | Selkirk-Interlake | Selkirk | James Fenske, Mgr., 200 Eaton Ave., Selkirk R1A 0W6 – 204/785-4900, Fax: 204/482-5448 |
| Shell River (RM) | 1,050 | Dauphin-Swan River | Roblin-Russell | Twyla Ludwig, CAO, 213 - 2nd Ave. NW, PO Box 998, Roblin R0L 1P0 – 204/937-4430, Fax: 204/937-8496 |
| Shellmouth (RM) | 733 | Dauphin-Swan River | Roblin-Russell | Raymond G. Bomback, CAO, PO Box 62, Inglis R0J 0X0 – 204/564-2589, Fax: 204/564-2643 |
| Shoal Lake (V) | 801 | Dauphin-Swan River | Roblin-Russell | Beverley Wells, CAO, 438 Station Rd., PO Box 342, Shoal Lake R0J 1Z0 – 204/759-2270, Fax: 204/759-2690 |
| Shoal Lake (RM) | 621 | Dauphin-Swan River | Roblin-Russell | Thelma Chegwin, CAO, 306 Elm St., PO Box 278, Shoal Lake R0J 1Z0 – 204/759-2565, Fax: 204/759-2740 |
| Sifton (RM) | 759 | Dauphin-Swan River | Arthur-Virden | Mary Smith, CAO, 293 - 2nd Ave. West, PO Box 100, Oak Lake R0M 1P0 – 204/855-2423, Fax: 204/855-2836 |
| Siglunes (RM) | 1,585 | Portage-Interlake | Interlake | Mel Bullerwell, CAO, 38 Main St., PO Box 370, Ashern R0C 0E0 – 204/768-2641, Fax: 204/768-2301 |
| Silver Creek (RM) | 567 | Dauphin-Swan River | Roblin-Russell | Sophia Smith, CAO, PO Box 130, Angusville R0J 0A0 – 204/773-2449, Fax: 204/773-2449 |
| Snow Lake † | 1,310 | Churchill | Flin Flon | E.C. (Chuck) Dunning, CAO, 113 Elm St., PO Box 40, Snow Lake R0B 1M0 – 204/358-2551, Fax: 204/358-2112 |
| Somerset (V) | 471 | Portage-Lisgar | Gladstone | Linda L. Talbot, CAO, 291 Carlton Ave., PO Box 187, Somerset R0G 2L0 – 204/744-2171, Fax: 204/744-2171 |
| Souris † | 1,613 | Brandon-Souris | Turtle Mountain | Elwin W. Swan, CAO, 100 - 2nd St. South, PO Box 518, Souris R0K 2C0 – 204/483-2169, Fax: 204/483-2129 |
| South Cypress (RM) | 862 | Brandon-Souris | Gladstone | Eric Plaetinck, CAO, 618 Railway Ave., PO Box 219, Glenboro R0K 0X0 – 204/827-2252, Fax: 204/827-2553 |
| South Norfolk (RM) | 1,282 | Portage-Lisgar | Gladstone | Sheila Mowatt, CAO, 180 Broadway, PO Box 30, Treherne R0G 2V0 – 204/723-2044, Fax: 204/723-2719 |
| Springfield (RM) | 12,162 | Provencher; Selkirk-Interlake | Springfield | Eric Towler, CAO, 628 Main St., PO Box 219, Oakbank R0E 1J0 – 204/444-3321, Fax: 204/444-2137 |
| Stanley (RM) | 4,616 | Portage-Lisgar | Pembina | Rick Klippenstein, CAO, #100, 379 Stephen St., Morden R6M 1V1 – 204/822-6251, Fax: 204/822-3596 |
| Steinbach † | 8,478 | Provencher | Steinbach | Jack Kehler, Mgr., 225 Reimer Ave., PO Box 1090, Steinbach R0A 2A0 – 204/326-9877, Fax: 204/326-4171 |
| Stonewall † | 3,689 | Selkirk-Interlake | Gimli | Robert J. Potter, CAO, 377 Main St., PO Box 250, Stonewall R0C 2Z0 – 204/467-5561, Fax: 204/467-9129 |
| Strathclair (RM) | 1,026 | Dauphin-Swan River | Minnedosa | E. Jo-Ann McKerchar, CAO, 127 Minnedosa Ave., PO Box 160, Strathclair R0J 2C0 – 204/365-2196, Fax: 204/365-2056 |
| Strathcona (RM) | 817 | Brandon-Souris | Turtle Mountain | Barrie McGill, CAO, 3rd St., PO Box 100, Belmont R0K 0C0 – 204/537-2241, Fax: 204/537-2364 |

Cities in CAPITALS; Towns marked †; Villages marked (V); Rural Municipalities marked (RM). An in-depth listing for municipalities marked with * appears in Part 2 (check Index for page numbers).

| MUNICIPALITY | 1996 POP. | FEDERAL ELECTORAL DISTRICT | PROVINCIAL ELECTORAL DISTRICT | CONTACT PERSON WITH ADDRESS, PHONE & FAX |
|---|---|---|---|---|
| Stuartburn (RM) | 1,563 | | | Judy Reimer, CAO, 108 Main St. North, PO Box 59, Vita R0A 2K0 – 204/425-3218, Fax: 204/425-3513 |
| Swan River † | 3,986 | Dauphin-Swan River | Swan River | Harry Showdra, CAO, 135 - 5 Ave. North, PO Box 879, Swan River R0L 1Z0 – 204/734-4586, Fax: 204/734-5166 |
| Swan River (RM) | 2,907 | Dauphin-Swan River | Swan River | Betty Nemetchek, CAO, 216 Main St. West, PO Box 610, Swan River R0L 1Z0 – 204/734-3344, Fax: 204/734-3701 |
| Taché (RM) | 8,273 | Provencher | La Verendrye | Ernest A. Lajoie, CAO, 450 Dawson Rd., PO Box 100, Lorette R0A 0Y0 – 204/878-3321, Fax: 204/878-9977 |
| Teulon (V) | 1,055 | Selkirk-Interlake | Gimli | Laura L. Humbert, CAO, 44 - 4 Ave. SE, PO Box 69, Teulon R0C 3B0 – 204/886-2314, Fax: 204/886-3918 |
| The Pas † | 5,945 | Churchill | The Pas | John F. Marnock, CAO, 81 Edwards Ave., PO Box 870, The Pas R9A 1K8 – 204/623-6481, Fax: 204/623-5506 |
| THOMPSON | 14,385 | Churchill | Thompson | Lynn Taylor, City Mgr., City Hall, 226 Mystery Lake Rd., Thompson R8N 1S6 – 204/677-7910, Fax: 204/677-7981 |
| Thompson (RM) | 1,321 | Portage-Lisgar | Morris | Mary Riddell, CAO, 531 Norton Ave., PO Box 190, Miami R0G 1H0 – 204/435-2114, Fax: 204/435-2067 |
| Treherne (V) | 675 | Portage-Lisgar | Gladstone | Sheila Mowatt, CAO, 180 Broadway Ave., PO Box 30, Treherne R0G 2V0 – 204/723-2044, Fax: 204/723-2719 |
| Turtle Mountain (RM) | 1,179 | Brandon-Souris | Turtle Mountain | Harold A. Lamb, CAO, 415 Broadway Ave., PO Box 160, Killarney R0K 1G0 – 204/523-7058, Fax: 204/523-4637 |
| Victoria (RM) | 1,275 | Portage-Lisgar | Gladstone | Yvon P. L. Bruneau, CAO, 130 Broadway St., PO Box 40, Holland R0G 0X0 – 204/526-2423, Fax: 204/526-2028 |
| Victoria Beach (RM) | 227 | Selkirk-Interlake | Lac du Bonnet | Raymond Moreau, CAO, #303, 960 Portage Ave., Winnipeg R3G 0R4 – 204/774-4263, Fax: 204/774-9834 |
| Virden † | 2,956 | Brandon-Souris | Arthur-Virden | Robert Eslinger, CAO, 236 Wellington St. West, PO Box 310, Virden R0M 2C0 – 204/748-2440, Fax: 204/748-2501 |
| Wallace (RM) | 1,835 | Brandon-Souris | Arthur-Virden | Don Stephenson, CAO, 304 Nelson St. West, PO Box 2200, Virden R0M 2C0 – 204/748-1239, Fax: 204/748-3450 |
| Waskada (V) | 288 | Brandon-Souris | Arthur-Virden | Ron Bertholet, CAO, Second St., PO Box 40, Waskada R0M 2E0 – 204/673-2401, Fax: 204/673-2663 |
| Wawanesa (V) | 485 | Brandon-Souris | Turtle Mountain | Barbara Roney, CAO, 106 Fourth St., PO Box 278, Wawanesa R0K 2G0 – 204/824-2244, Fax: 204/824-2244 |
| West St. Paul (RM) | 3,720 | Winnipeg-St-Paul | Selkirk | Mel Didyk, CAO, 3550 Main St., West St. Paul R4A 5A3 – 204/338-0306, Fax: 204/338-3539 |
| Westbourne (RM) | 2,035 | Portage-Lisgar | Gladstone; Ste. Rose | Patricia Pugh, CAO, PO Box 150, Gladstone R0J 0T0 – 204/385-2388, Fax: 204/385-2388 |
| Whitehead (RM) | 1,535 | Brandon-Souris | Minnedosa | James F. Madder, CAO, 517 Second Ave., PO Box 107, Alexander R0K 0A0 – 204/752-2261, Fax: 204/752-2129 |
| Whitemouth (RM) | 1,639 | Provencher | La Verendrye | Rita E. Bell, CAO, Railway Ave., PO Box 248, Whitemouth R0E 2G0 – 204/348-2221, Fax: 204/348-2576 |
| Whitewater (RM) | 766 | Brandon-Souris | Turtle Mountain | Murray R. Jackson, CAO, PO Box 53, Minto R0K 1M0 – 204/776-2172, Fax: 204/776-2252 |
| Winchester (RM) | 625 | Brandon-Souris | Arthur-Virden | Leona Williams, CAO, 129 Broadway St. North, PO Box 387, Deloraine R0M 0M0 – 204/747-2572, Fax: 204/747-2883 |
| Winkler † | 7,241 | Portage-Lisgar | Pembina | Vince Anderson, CAO, 185 Main St., Winkler R6W 1B4 – 204/325-9524, Fax: 204/325-9515 |
| *WINNIPEG | 618,477 | Charleswood-Asiniboine; Saint Boniface; Winnipeg Centre; Winnipeg North Centre; Winnipeg North-St. Paul; Winnipeg South; Winnipeg South Centre; Winnipeg Transcona | Assiniboia; Broadway; Burrows; Charleswood; Concordia; Crescentwood; Elmwood; Fort Garry; Inkster; Kildonan; Kirkfield Park; Niakwa; Osborne; Point Douglas; Radisson; Riel; River East; River Heights; Rossmere; St. Boniface; St. James; St. Johns; St. Norbert; St. Vital; Seine River; Sturgeon Creek; The Maples; Transcona; Tuxedo; Wellington; Wolseley | Dorothy E. Browton, City Clerk, Council Building, Civic Centre, 510 Main St., Winnipeg R3B 1B9 – 204/986-2196, Fax: 204/949-0566, URL: http://www.city.winnipeg.mb.ca/city |
| Winnipeg Beach † | 746 | Selkirk-Interlake | Gimli | Valerie D. Moore, CAO, 29 Robinson Ave., PO Box 160, Winnipeg Beach R0C 3G0 – 204/389-2698, Fax: 204/389-2019 |
| Winnipegosis † | 730 | Dauphin-Swan River | Swan River | Terry Tomlinson, CAO, 130 - 2nd St., PO Box 370, Winnipegosis R0L 2G0 – 204/656-4791, Fax: 204/656-4751 |
| Woodlands (RM) | 3,457 | Selkirk-Interlake | Lakeside | A. Eilene Myskiw, CAO, PO Box 10, Woodlands R0C 3H0 – 204/383-5679, Fax: 204/383-5169 |
| Woodworth (RM) | 1,047 | Brandon-Souris | Arthur-Virden | Howard J. Norek, CAO, PO Box 148, Kenton R0M 0Z0 – 204/838-2317, Fax: 204/838-2000 |

## MANITOBA LOCAL GOVERNMENT DISTRICTS

Incorporated under "The Local Government Districts Act," January 1st, 1945. Local Government Districts have basically the same powers, functions and purposes as regular municipalities except that although they have an elected council, they are ultimately responsible to the Minister of Rural Development. Effective January 1, 1997 a change to legislation transfered most of the Local Government Districts to full municipal status. Roger Dennis, Executive Director, Local Government Support Services Branch, #508 800 Portage Ave., Winnipeg; 204/945-2572

| DISTRICTS | 1996 POP. | CONTACT PERSON WITH ADDRESS, PHONE & FAX |
|---|---|---|
| Mystery Lake | 5 | Don C. Taylor, Resident Adm., PO Box 189, Thompson R8N 1N1 – 204/677-4075, Fax: 204/778-7642 |
| Pinawa | 1,672 | Gary Hanna, Resident Adm., 36 Burrows Rd., PO Box 100, Pinawa R0E 1L0 – 204/753-2331, Fax: 204/753-2770 |

## NEW BRUNSWICK

The provincial government of New Brunswick provides all services of a municipal nature for the rural area of the province while municipalities provide these services to their residents. For the rural area, an advisory committee may be elected at public meetings biennially to assist and advise the Minister. Municipal councils are elected to look after the affairs of the municipalities.

Acts of the legislature governing municipalities are the Municipalities Act, the Municipal Assistance Act, the Community Planning Act, the Assessment Act, the Municipal Capital Borrowing Act, the Municipal Elections Act, and the Control of Municipalities Act.

Population requirements for incorporation of municipalities are 10,000 for cities and 1,500 for towns. There are no specified requirements for villages.

Municipal elections are held every three years on the second Monday in May; thus, May 1998, May 2001 etc.

Cities in CAPITALS; Towns marked †; Villages marked (V). An in-depth listing for municipalities marked with * appears in Part 2 (check Index for page numbers).

| MUNICIPALITY | 1996 POP. | COUNTY | FEDERAL ELECTORAL DISTRICT | PROVINCIAL ELECTORAL DISTRICT | CONTACT PERSON WITH ADDRESS, PHONE & FAX |
|---|---|---|---|---|---|
| Alma (V) | 312 | Albert | Beauséjour-Petitcodiac | Albert | Louise Butland, Clerk-Treas., Main St., PO Box 38, Alma E0A 1B0 – 506/887-6123, Fax: 506/887-6124 |
| Aroostook (V) | 397 | Victoria | Tobique-Mactaquac | Victoria-Tobique | Darlene Francoeur, Clerk, PO Box 90, Aroostook E0J 1B0 – 506/273-6443, Fax: 506/273-3025 |
| Atholville (V) | 1,376 | Restigouche | Madawaska-Restigouche | Campbellton | Jeannette Gould, Gref, 247, rue Notre-Dame, CP 10, Atholville E0K 1A0 – 506/789-1213, Fax: 506/789-0290 |
| Baker Brook (V) | 629 | Madawaska | Madawaska-Restigouche | Madawaska-les-Lacs | Gertrude Albert, Gref., 3677, rue Principale, pièce A, Baker Brook E7A 1V3 – 506/258-3250, Fax: 506/258-1023 |
| Balmoral (V) | 1,975 | Restigouche | Madawaska-Restigouche | Dalhousie-Restigouche-East | Marco Pitre, Gref., 625, av des Pionniers, CP 60, Balmoral E0B 1C0 – 506/826-2826, Fax: 506/826-1180 |
| Bas-Caraquet (V) | 1,775 | Gloucester | Acadie-Bathurst | Caraquet | Richard Frigault, Adm., 8185, rue St-Paul, CP 60, Bas-Caraquet E0B 1E0 – 506/726-2776, Fax: 506/726-2770 |
| Bath (V) | 629 | Carleton | Tobique-Mactaquac | Carleton | Christa Walton, Clerk, 161 School St., PO Box 38, Bath E0J 1E0 – 506/278-5293, Fax: 506/278-5932 |
| BATHURST | 13,815 | Gloucester | Acadie-Bathurst | Bathurst | Louise C. Wafer, Clerk, 256 St. Andrew St., PO Box 116, Bathurst E2A 2Z1 – 506/548-0400, Fax: 506/548-0435 |
| Belledune (V) | 2,060 | Gloucester | Madawaska-Restigouche | Nigadoo-Chaleur | Brenda Cromier, Clerk-Treas., 931 Main St., Belledune E0B 1G0 – 506/522-5613, Fax: 506/522-9804 |
| Beresford † | 4,720 | Gloucester | Acadie-Bathurst | Nigadoo-Chaleur | Norval Godin, Adm.-Gref., 855, rue Principale, CP 600, Beresford E0B 1H0 – 506/542-2000, Fax: 506/542-1880 |
| Bertrand (V) | 1,379 | Gloucester | Acadie-Bathurst | Caraquet | M.J. Léonel Thériault, Adm., 651, boul des Acadiens, CP 119, Bertrand E0B 1J0 – 506/726-2442, Fax: 506/726-2449 |
| Blacks Harbour (V) | 1,148 | Charlotte | Charlotte | Charlotte | Deanna Hunter, Clerk-Mgr., #2, 881 Main St., Blacks Harbour E5H 1E5 – 506/456-4870, Fax: 506/456-4872 |
| Blackville (V) | 957 | Northumberland | Miramichi | Southwest Miramichi | Kurt Marks, Adm., PO Box 17, Blackville E0C 1C0 – 506/843-6337, Fax: 506/843-6043 |
| Bouctouche † | 2,459 | Kent | Beauséjour-Petitcodiac | Kent South | Jean-Clovis Collette, Gref., 211, boul Irving, CP 370, Bouctouche E0A 1G0 – 506/743-1480, Fax: 506/743-1481 |
| Bristol (V) | 707 | Carleton | Tobique-Mactaquac | Carleton | Nancy Shaw, Clerk, 104 Juniper Rd., PO Box 57, Bristol E0J 1G0 – 506/392-6013, Fax: 506/392-5211 |
| Cambridge-Narrows (V) | 634 | Queens | Fundy-Royal | Oromocto-Gagetown | Shelley Poirier, Clerk, Municipal Bldg., Cambridge-Narrows E0E 1B0 – 506/488-3155, Fax: 506/488-1018 |
| CAMPBELLTON | 8,404 | Restigouche | Madawaska-Restigouche | Campbellton | Ronald F. Mahoney, Clerk-Adm., Campbellton City Centre, PO Box 100, Campbellton E3N 3G1 – 506/789-2700, Fax: 506/759-7403 |
| Canterbury (V) | 415 | York | Charlotte | Woodstock | Eva Mott, Clerk, 95 Main St., PO Box 90, Canterbury E0H 1C0 – 506/279-2048, Fax: 506/325-1014 |
| Cap Pelé (V) | 2,242 | Westmorland | Beauséjour-Petitcodiac | Shediac-Cap-Pelé | Michel Mélanson, Gref.-Adm., 31, ch St-André, CP 540, Cap-Pelé E0A 1J0 – 506/577-4157, Fax: 506/577-2602 |

Cities in CAPITALS; Towns marked †; Villages marked (V). An in-depth listing for municipalities marked with * appears in Part 2 (check Index for page numbers).

| MUNICIPALITY | 1996 POP. | COUNTY | FEDERAL ELECTORAL DISTRICT | PROVINCIAL ELECTORAL DISTRICT | CONTACT PERSON WITH ADDRESS, PHONE & FAX |
|---|---|---|---|---|---|
| Caraquet † | 4,653 | Gloucester | Acadie-Bathurst | Caraquet | Pierre Doiron, Gref., 50, rue Du Colisée, CP 420, Caraquet E0B 1K0 – 506/727-1717, Fax: 506/727-1726 |
| Centreville (V) | 559 | Carleton | Tobique-Mactaquac | Carleton | Cynthia R. Geldart, Clerk, 836 Central St., PO Box 117, Centreville E0J 1H0 – 506/276-3671, Fax: 506/276-9891 |
| Charlo (V) | 1,610 | Restigouche | Madawaska-Restigouche | Dalhousie-Restigouche-East | Adolphe Goulette, Gref.-Adm., 616, rue Chaleur, CP 62, Charlo E0B 1M0 – 506/684-3597, Fax: 506/684-4481 |
| Chipman (V) | 1,518 | Queens | Fundy-Royal | Grand Lake | Brenda Barton, Clerk, 2 Civic Ct., PO Box 149, Chipman E0E 1C0 – 506/339-6601, Fax: 506/339-6197 |
| Clair (V) | 905 | Madawaska | Madawaska-Restigouche | Madawaska-les-Lacs | Nicole Michaud, Gref., 809E, rue Principale, Clair E7A 2H7 – 506/992-6030, Fax: 506/992-0021 |
| Dalhousie † | 4,500 | Restigouche | Madawaska-Restigouche | Dalhousie-Restigouche East | Michael Allain, Clerk-Adm., 111 Hall St., PO Box 250, Dalhousie E0K 1B0 – 506/684-7600, Fax: 506/684-7613 |
| Dieppe † | 12,497 | Westmorland | Moncton | Dieppe-Memramcook | Rolande Gallant, Gref., 333 Acadia Ave., Dieppe E1A 1G9 – 506/877-7900, Fax: 506/877-7910 |
| Doaktown (V) | 986 | Northumberland | Miramichi | Southwest Miramichi | Marilyn Price, Clerk, 328 Main St., PO Box 97, Doaktown E0C 1G0 – 506/365-7970, Fax: 506/365-7111 |
| Dorchester (V) | 1,179 | Westmorland | Beauséjour-Petitcodiac | Tantramar | Simonne Malenfant-Edgett, Clerk-Treas., 4984 Main St., Dorchester E0A 1M0 – 506/379-3030, Fax: 506/379-3033 |
| Drummond (V) | 983 | Victoria | Tobique-Mactaquac | Grand Falls Region; Region de Grand-Sault | Chantal McCarthy, Gref., Site 59, Bôite 6, 1412 ch Tobique, Drummond E0J 1M0 – 506/473-2660, Fax: 506/473-4543 |
| EDMUNDSTON [1] | 11,033 | Madawaska | Madawaska-Restigouche | Edmundston | Paul Lavoie, Secrétaire municipal, 7, ch Canada, Edmundston E3V 1T7 – 506/739-2115, Fax: 506/737-6820 |
| Eel River Crossing (V) | 1,446 | Restigouche | Madawaska-Restigouche | Dalhousie-Restigouche East | Kim Bujold, Clerk, 20, rue Savoie, CP 159, Eel River Crossing E0B 1P0 – 506/826-2490, Fax: 506/826-3912 |
| Florenceville (V) | 707 | Carleton | Tobique-Mactaquac | Carleton | Bernice Snowden, Clerk, PO Box 152, Florenceville E0J 1K0 – 506/392-5249, Fax: 506/392-6143 |
| *FREDERICTON | 46,507 | York | Fredericton | Fredericton North; Fredericton South; Fredericton-Fort Nashwaak | Donna Lavigne, City Clerk, PO Box 130, Fredericton E3B 4Y7 – 506/460-2020, Fax: 506/460-2042, URL: http://www.city.fredericton.nb.ca |
| Fredericton Junction (V) | 736 | Sunbury | Charlotte | New Maryland | Jocelyn Nason, Clerk, 102 Wilsey Rd., Fredericton Junction E0G 1T0 – 506/368-2628, Fax: 506/368-1900 |
| Gagetown (V) | 660 | Queens | Charlotte | Oromocto-Gagetown | Allison Blair, Clerk, Front St., PO Box 189, Gagetown E0G 1V0 – 506/488-3567, Fax: 506/488-3543 |
| Grand Bay-Westfield † [2] | 3,713 | Kings | Charlotte | Grand Bay-Westfield | Sandra M. Gautreau, Clerk-Mgr., 77 River Valley Dr., PO Box 180, Grand Bay E0G 1W0 – 506/738-8457, Fax: 506/738-1824, URL: http://www.town.grandbay.nb.ca/ |
| Grand Falls-Grand-Sault † | 6,133 | Victoria | Tobique-Mactaquac | Grand Falls Region; Région de Grand-Sault | Joseph L. Côté, Adm.-Gref., 142 Court St., PO Box 800, Grand Falls E3Z 1C3 – 506/475-7777, Fax: 506/475-7779 |
| Grand Manan (V) | 2,577 | Charlotte | Charlotte | Fundy Isles | Geraldine Ingalls, Clerk, Grand Harbour, Grand Manan E0G 1X0 – 506/662-8109, Fax: 506/662-8737 |
| Grande-Anse (V) | 965 | Gloucester | Acadie-Bathurst | Nepisiguit | Thérèse Haché, Adm., 19, rue Acadie, CP 147, Grande Anse E0B 1R0 – 506/732-5411, Fax: 506/732-5267 |
| Hampton † | 4,081 | Kings | Fundy-Royal | Hampton-Belleisle | Margaret Clarke, Clerk, 10 DeMille Ct., PO Box 370, Hampton E0G 1Z0 – 506/832-6065, Fax: 506/832-6098 |
| Hartland † | 892 | Carleton | Tobique-Mactaquac | Carleton | Judy Dee, Clerk, Orser St., PO Box 358, Hartland E0J 1N0 – 506/375-4357, Fax: 506/375-8265 |
| Harvey (V) | 383 | York | Beauséjour-Petitcodiac | York | Ellen Bransfield, Clerk, PO Box 125, Harvey Station E0H 1H0 – 506/366-6240, Fax: 506/366-6242 |
| Hillsborough (V) | 1,272 | Albert | Beauséjour-Petitcodiac | Albert | Danny Jonah, Adm.-Clerk, 197 Main St., PO Box 100, Hillsborough E0A 1X0 – 506/734-3733, Fax: 506/734-3711 |

Cities in CAPITALS; Towns marked †; Villages marked (V). An in-depth listing for municipalities marked with * appears in Part 2 (check Index for page numbers).

| MUNICIPALITY | 1996 POP. | COUNTY | FEDERAL ELECTORAL DISTRICT | PROVINCIAL ELECTORAL DISTRICT | CONTACT PERSON WITH ADDRESS, PHONE & FAX |
|---|---|---|---|---|---|
| Kedgwick (V) | 1,221 | Restigouche | Madawaska-Restigouche | Restigouche West | Diane Thompson, Gref., 12, rue Notre-Dame, CP 267, Kedgwick E0K 1C0 – 506/284-2160, Fax: 506/284-2859 |
| Lac Baker (V) | 226 | Madawaska | Madawaska-Restigouche | Madawaska-les-Lacs | Paul Ouellette, Gref., 69, rue de la Pointe, Lac Baker E7A 1J1 – 506/992-2531, Fax: 506/992-3045 |
| Lamèque † | 1,671 | Gloucester | Acadie-Bathurst | Lamèque-Shippagan-Miscou | Henri-Paul Guignard, Adm.-Gref., 28, rue De L'Hôpital, CP 58, Lamèque E0B 1V0 – 506/344-3222, Fax: 506/344-3266 |
| Le Goulet (V) | 1,029 | Gloucester | Acadie-Bathurst | Lamèque-Shippagan-Miscou | Alvine Bulger, Gref.-Trés., 917, rue Principale, CP 300, Le Goulet E0B 1W0 – 506/336-9711, Fax: 506/336-2499 |
| Maisonnette (V) | 675 | Gloucester | Acadie-Bathurst | Caraquet | Nicole Boudreau, Gref.-Trés., CP 248, Maisonnette E0B 1X0 – 506/727-6888, Fax: 506/727-4290 |
| McAdam (V) | 1,570 | York | Charlotte | York | Ann Donahue, Clerk, 146 Saunders Rd., PO Box 299, McAdam E0H 1K0 – 506/784-2293, Fax: 506/784-1402 |
| Meductic (V) | 236 | York | Charlotte | Woodstock | Reta Cummings, Clerk, PO Box 27, Meductic E0H 1L0 – 506/272-2106 |
| Memramcook (V) | 4,904 | Westmorland | Beasèjour | Dieppe-Memramcook | Louis Arthur Gaudet, Adm.-Gref., 612, rue Centrale, CP 300, Saint Joseph E0A 2Y0 – 506/758-4078, Fax: 506/758-4079 |
| Millville (V) | 321 | York | Tobique-Mactaquac | York | Christine Myshrall, Clerk, PO Box 39, Millville E0H 1M0 – 506/463-8251, Fax: 506/463-8262 |
| Minto (V) | 3,056 | Sunbury-Queens | Fundy-Royal | Grand Lake | Rose Collette, Clerk, 19 Maple St., PO Box 7, Minto E0E 1J0 – 506/327-3383, Fax: 506/327-3041 |
| MIRAMICHI | 19,241 | Northcumberland | Miramichi | Miramichi Bay; Miramichi-Bay Duvin; Miramichi-Centre | James F. Lamkey, Clerk, 141 Henry St., Miramichi E1V 2N5 – 506/623-2201, Fax: 506/623-2200 |
| *MONCTON | 59,313 | Westmorland | Moncton | Moncton E.; Monc. N.; Monc. S.; Monc. Crescent | Elizabeth Reade, Clerk, 655 Main St., Moncton E1C 1E8 – 506/853-3333, Fax: 506/859-4225 |
| Nackawic † | 1,167 | York | Tobique-Mactaquac | York | William MacLean, Clerk, 115 Otis Dr., PO Box 638, Nackawic E0H 1P0 – 506/575-2241, Fax: 506/575-2035 |
| Néguac (V) | 1,735 | Northumberland | Miramichi | Miramichi Bay | Pascal Robichaud, Adm., 1175, rue Principale, CP 106, Néguac E0C 1S0 – 506/776-8328, Fax: 506/776-3500 |
| New Maryland (V) | 4,284 | York | Fredericton | New Maryland | Connie Saulnier, Clerk, #202, 429 New Maryland Hwy., New Maryland E3C 2H6 – 506/451-8508, Fax: 506/450-1605 |
| Nigadoo (V) | 961 | Gloucester | Acadie-Bathurst | Nigadoo-Chaleur | Nancy Martin-Nadeau, Gref., 385, rue Principale, CP 190, Nigadoo E0B 2A0 – 506/783-2488, Fax: 506/783-2989 |
| Norton (V) | 1,390 | Kings | Fundy-Royal | Hampton-Belleisle | Bev Wilcox, Clerk, Route 124, PO Box 240, Norton E0G 2N0 – 506/839-2373, Fax: 506/839-5560 |
| Oromocto † | 9,194 | Sunbury | Fredericton | Oromocto-Gagetown | A. Wayne Carnell, Adm., 137 MacDonald Ave., Oromocto E2V 1A6 – 506/357-4400, Fax: 506/357-6723 |
| Paquetville (V) | 731 | Gloucester | Acadie-Bathurst | Centre-Péninsule | Muriel Gallien, Adm., 1094, rue du Parc, CP 159, Paquetville E0B 2B0 – 506/764-5493, Fax: 506/764-1353 |
| Perth-Andover (V) | 1,861 | Victoria | Tobique-Mactaquac | Victoria-Tobique | Murray Watters, Clerk-Adm., 344 East Riverside Dr., PO Box 219, Perth-Andover E0J 1V0 – 506/273-2235, Fax: 506/273-6351 |
| Petit-Rocher (V) | 2,078 | Gloucester | Acadie-Bathurst | Nigadoo-Chaleur | Guy Clavette, Gref., 582, rue Principale, CP 270, Petit-Rocher E0B 2E0 – 506/783-0820, Fax: 506/783-0839 |
| Petitcodiac (V) | 1,425 | Westmorland | Beauséjour-Petitcodiac | Petitcodiac | Pam Cochrane, Clerk, 63 Main St., PO Box 479, Petitcodiac E0A 2H0 – 506/756-3140, 3141, Fax: 506/756-3142 |
| Plaster Rock (V) | 1,220 | Victoria | Tobique-Mactaquac | Victoria-Tobique | Barbara Wishart-Fawcett, Adm., 81 Ridgewell, PO Box 129, Plaster Rock E0J 1W0 – 506/356-6070, Fax: 506/356-6081 |
| Pointe-Verte (V) | 1,122 | Gloucester | Acadie-Bathurst | Nigadoo-Chaleur | Donald Hammond, Gref.-Adm., 375, rue Principale, CP 89, Pointe-Verte E0B 2H0 – 506/783-7973, Fax: 506/783-8950 |
| Port Elgin (V) | 445 | Westmorland | Beauséjour-Petitcodiac | Tantramar | Sonia M. Wells, Clerk-Treas., PO Box 180, Port Elgin E0A 2K0 – 506/538-2120, Fax: 506/538-2110 |

Cities in CAPITALS; Towns marked †; Villages marked (V). An in-depth listing for municipalities marked with * appears in Part 2 (check Index for page numbers).

| MUNICIPALITY | 1996 POP. | COUNTY | FEDERAL ELECTORAL DISTRICT | PROVINCIAL ELECTORAL DISTRICT | CONTACT PERSON WITH ADDRESS, PHONE & FAX |
|---|---|---|---|---|---|
| Quispamsis † [3] | 8,839 | Kings | Fundy-Royal | Kennebecasis | Catherine Snow, Clerk, Municipal Dr., PO Box 21085, Quispamsis E2E 4Z4 – 506/847-8878, Fax: 506/849-5025 |
| Rexton (V) | 908 | Kent | Beauséjour-Petitcodiac | Kent | Barry Glencross, Clerk-Admin., 96 Main St., PO Box 100, Rexton E0A 2L0 – 506/523-6921, Fax: 506/523-7383 |
| Richibucto † | 1,414 | Kent | Beauséjour-Petitcodiac | Rogersville-Kouchibouguac | Jean-Paul Mazerolle, Gérant, 31, rue Principale, CP 337, Richibucto E0A 2M0 – 506/523-4467, Fax: 506/523-1826 |
| Riverside-Albert (V) | 415 | Albert | Beauséjour-Petitcodiac | Albert | Deborah Murray, Clerk-Treas., PO Box 59, Riverside-Albert E0A 1A0 – 506/882-3022, 3023, Fax: 506/882-2038 |
| Riverview † | 16,653 | Albert | Moncton | Riverview | David Muir, Clerk-Mgr., 30 Honour House Ct., Riverview E1B 3Y9 – 506/387-2020, Fax: 506/387-2033 |
| Rivière-Verte (V) | 929 | Madawaska | Madawaska-Restigouche | Madawaska-la-Vallée | Evelyn Therrien, Gref., 78, rue Principale, CP 100, Rivière-Verte E0L 1E0 – 506/263-1060, Fax: 506/263-1065 |
| Rogersville (V) | 1,336 | Kent | Miramichi | Rogersville-Kouchibouguac | Hélène LeBlanc, Adm.-Gref., 4, rue de l'École, CP 70, Rogersville E0A 2T0 – 506/775-1200, Fax: 506/775-6544 |
| Rothesay † [4] | 1,695 | Kings | Fundy-Royal | Saint-John-Kings | Tom Newcombe, Clerk-Mgr., PO Box 4699, Rothesay E2E 5L5 – 506/847-7132, Fax: 506/847-9367 |
| Sackville † | 5,393 | Westmorland | Beauséjour-Petitcodiac | Tantramar | Bob Cooling, CAO, 2 Main St. East, PO Box 660, Sackville E0A 3C0 – 506/364-4930, Fax: 506/364-4976 |
| Saint-André (V) | 438 | Madawaska | Tobique-Mactaquac | Grand Falls Region; Région de Grand-Sault | Giselle Ouellette, Secrétaire-Gref., Boîte 1, Site 155, RR#4, Grand-Sault E0J 1M0 – 506/473-7580, Fax: 506/473-7159 |
| St. Andrews † | 1,752 | Charlotte | Charlotte | Western Charlotte | Bill Mallory, Mgr., 212 Water St., PO Box 160, St. Andrews E0G 2X0 – 506/529-1820, Fax: 506/529-3383 |
| Sainte-Anne-de-Madawaska (V) | 1,273 | Madawaska | Madawaska-Restigouche | Madawaska-la-Vallée | Jocelyn Roy, Gref., 75, rue Principale, Sainte-Anne-de-Madawaska E0L 1G0 – 506/445-2449, Fax: 506/445-2405 |
| Saint-Antoine (V) | 1,463 | Kent | Beauséjour-Petitcodiac | Kent South | Bernadine Maillet, Gref., 51, rue Principale, CP 180, Saint-Antoine E0A 2X0 – 506/525-2212, Fax: 506/525-9531 |
| Saint-François-de-Madawaska (V) | 631 | Madawaska | Madawaska-Restigouche | Madawaska-les-Lacs | Colette Lévesque, Gref., 2033, rue Commerciale, Saint-François-de-Madawaska E7A 1B3 – 506/992-6050, Fax: 506/992-6049 |
| St. George † | 2,357 | Charlotte | Charlotte | Charlotte | Ross Norman, Mgr., 1 School St., PO Box 148, St. George E0G 2Y0 – 506/755-1020, Fax: 506/755-1029 |
| Saint-Hilaire (V) | 255 | Madawaska | Madawaska-Restigouche | Madawaska-les-Lacs | Jacqueline Ouellet, Gref., 2167, rue Centrale, St. Hilaire E3V 3K3 – 506/258-3307, Fax: 506/258-1802 |
| Saint-Isidore (V) | 912 | | Acadie-Bathurst | Centre-Péninsule | Louis LeBouthillier, Gref, CP 145, Saint-Isidore E0B 2L0 – 506/358-6356, Fax: 506/358-2020 |
| *SAINT JOHN | 72,494 | Saint John | Saint John | S. John-Fundy; S. John-Kings; S. John-Champlain; S. John-Harbour; S. John-Portland; S. John-Lancaster; Grand Bay-Westfield | Mary L. Munford, Common Clerk, City Hall, Market Sq., PO Box 1971, Saint John E2L 4L1 – 506/658-2800, Fax: 506/658-2802, URL: http://www.city.saint-john.nb.ca |
| Saint-Léolin (V) | 858 | Gloucester | Acadie-Bathurst | Caraquet | Gérard Battah, Gref., CP 8, Saint-Léolin E0B 2M0 – 506/732-5367, Fax: 506/732-3177 |
| Saint Léonard † | 1,450 | Madawaska | Madawaska-Restigouche | Madawaska-la-Vallée | Julie Pelletier, Gref.-Trés., 108, rue du Pont, CP 390, Saint Léonard E0L 1M0 – 506/423-3111, Fax: 506/423-3115 |
| Saint-Louis-de-Kent (V) | 1,015 | Kent | Miramichi | Rogersville-Kouchibouguac | Léo-Paul Frigault, Gref., 33, rue Beauséjour, CP 220, Saint-Louis-de-Kent E0A 2Z0 – 506/876-2441, Fax: 506/876-4530 |
| Sainte-Marie-Saint-Raphaël (V) | 1,185 | Gloucester | Acadie-Bathurst | Lamèque-Shippagan-Miscou | Denis Ducharme, Adm., 1541, boul De La Mer, CP 91, Sainte-Marie-Saint-Raphaël E0B 2N0 – 506/344-3210, Fax: 506/344-3213 |
| St. Martins (V) | 386 | Saint John | Fundy-Royal | Saint John-Fundy | Sandra Roy, Clerk, St. Martins E0G 2Z0 – 506/833-4430, Fax: 506/833-2008 |

Cities in CAPITALS; Towns marked †; Villages marked (V). An in-depth listing for municipalities marked with * appears in Part 2 (check Index for page numbers).

| MUNICIPALITY | 1996 POP. | COUNTY | FEDERAL ELECTORAL DISTRICT | PROVINCIAL ELECTORAL DISTRICT | CONTACT PERSON WITH ADDRESS, PHONE & FAX |
|---|---|---|---|---|---|
| Saint-Quentin (V) | 2,424 | Restigouche | Madawaska-Restigouche | Restigouche West | Roger Cyr, Gref., 10, rue Deschênes, CP 489, Saint-Quentin E0K 1J0 – 506/235-2425, Fax: 506/235-1952 |
| St. Stephen † | 4,961 | Charlotte | Charlotte | Western Charlotte | Wayne Tallon, Mgr., 34 Milltown Blvd., St. Stephen E3L 1G3 – 506/466-7000, Fax: 506/466-7001 |
| Salisbury (V) | 1,878 | Westmorland | Beauséjour-Petitcodiac | Petitcodiac | Carol Wortman, Clerk-Admin., 56, rue Douglas, PO Box 270, Salisbury E0A 3E0 – 506/372-3230, Fax: 506/372-3225 |
| Shediac † | 4,664 | Westmorland | Beauséjour-Petitcodiac | Shediac-Cap-Pelé | Jeannette Bourque, Gref., 170, rue Main, CP 969, Shediac E0A 3G0 – 506/532-7000, Fax: 506/532-6156 |
| Shippagan † | 2,862 | Gloucester | Acadie-Bathurst | Lamèque-Shippagan-Miscou | Éloi Haché, Gref., 200, av Hôtel de Ville, CP 280, Shippagan E0B 2P0 – 506/336-3900, Fax: 506/336-3901 |
| Stanley (V) | 426 | York | Tobique-Mactaquac | Mataquac | Lorna Pinnock, Clerk, 17 Glen Rd., PO Box 149, Stanley E0H 1T0 – 506/367-3245, Fax: 506/367-0006 |
| Sussex † | 4,293 | Kings | Fundy-Royal | Kings East | Paul Maguire, Clerk, 22 Maple Ave., PO Box 1057, Sussex E0E 1P0 – 506/433-7200, Fax: 506/432-6116 |
| Sussex Corner (V) | 1,337 | Kings | Fundy-Royal | Kings East | Sandra Daigle, Clerk, 179 Post Rd., Sussex Corner E0E 1R0 – 506/433-5184, Fax: 506/433-3785 |
| Tide Head (V) | 1,170 | Restigouche | Madawaska-Restigouche | Campbellton | Christine Babcock, Clerk, 4 Mountain St., PO Box 60, Tide Head E0K 1K0 – 506/753-5738, Fax: 506/753-7347 |
| Tracadie-Sheila † | 4,773 | Gloucester | Acadie-Bathurst | Tracadie-Sheila | Cécile Rousselle, Gref., 4293, rue Beauregard, CP 3600, Tracadie-Sheila E1X 1G5 – 506/394-4020, Fax: 506/394-4025 |
| Tracy (V) | 605 | Sunbury | Charlotte | New Maryland | Geraldine Harris, Clerk, Tracy E0G 3C0 – 506/368-2878, Fax: 506/368-1014 |
| Woodstock † | 5,092 | Carleton | Charlotte; Tobique-Mactaquac | Woodstock | Ken Harding, CAO, 824 Main St., PO Box 1059, Woodstock E0J 2B0 – 506/328-3307, Fax: 506/328-8344 |

1. Effective January 1, 1998 the new city of Edmundston will be created through the amalgamation of the villages of Verret, Saint-Jacques & Saint-Basile.
2. Effective January 1, 1998 the new town of Grand Bay-Westfield will be created through the amalgamation of the town of Grand Bay & the village of Westfield.
3. Effective January 1, 1998 the new town of Quispamsis will be created through the amalgamation of the town of Quispamsis & the village of Gondola Point.
4. Effective January 1, 1998 the new town of Rothesay will be created through the amalagamation of the town of Rothesay & the villages of Renforth, Fairvale & East Riverside-Kingshurst.

## NEWFOUNDLAND

The provincial government of Newfoundland and Labrador exercises control over the activities of all municipalities in accordance with the Executive Council Act and the Municipal Affairs Act. Under the provisions of the Municipalities Act, the Department exercises a certain degree of financial and administrative control over all municipalities with the exception of the Cities of St. John's, Corner Brook and Mount Pearl. The towns incorporated under the Municipalities Act do not require ministerial approval of their annual budgets, but the Department employs Municipal Analysts to oversee municipal activities. The province assumes responsibility for public health, welfare and law enforcement which are elsewhere generally considered to be municipal functions.

The cities and towns incorporated in Newfoundland are authorized to levy taxes and to provide a wide range of municipal services and to make appropriate bylaws or regulations for the implementation and administration of these services.

City and town councils in Newfoundland are elected on the last Tuesday in September every four years (1997, 2001, etc.).

Cities in CAPITALS; Towns marked †; Communities marked ‡. An in-depth listing for municipalities marked with * appears in Part 2 (check Index for page numbers).

| MUNICIPALITY | 1996 POP. | FEDERAL ELECTORAL DISTRICT | PROVINCIAL ELECTORAL DISTRICT | CONTACT PERSON WITH ADDRESS, PHONE & FAX |
|---|---|---|---|---|
| Admiral's Beach ‡ | 255 | St. John's West | Placentia & St. Mary's | Vacant, Clerk, PO Box 196, Admiral's Beach A0B 3A0 – 709/521-2671, Fax: 709/521-2671 |
| Anchor Point ‡ | 350 | Humber-St. Barbe-Baie Verte | St. Barbe | Elizabeth Genge, Clerk, PO Box 117, Anchor Point A0K 1A0 – 709/456-2337, Fax: 709/456-2011 |
| Appleton † | 572 | Gander-Grand Falls | Gander | Mavis Simms, Clerk, Site 4, RR#1, PO Box 31, Appleton A0G 2K0 – 709/679-2289, Fax: 709/679-5552 |
| Aquaforte ‡ | 172 | St. John's West | Ferryland | Darlene George, Clerk, Aquaforte A0A 1A0 – 709/363-2253 |
| Arnold's Cove † | 1,115 | Bonavista-Trinity-Conception | Bellevue | Wayne Slade, Clerk, PO Box 70, Arnold's Cove A0B 1A0 – 709/463-2323, Fax: 709/463-2323 |
| Avondale † | 765 | St. John's East | Harbour Main-Whitbourne | Carol Ann Cantwell, Clerk, PO Box 59, Avondale A0A 1B0 – 709/229-4201, Fax: 709/229-4446 |
| Badger † | 997 | Gander-Grand Falls | Grand Falls-Buchans | Pansy Hurley, Clerk, PO Box 130, Badger A0H 1A0 – 709/539-2406, Fax: 709/539-5262 |
| Baie Verte † | 1,708 | Humber-St. Barbe-Baie Verte | Baie Verte | Ruth Burton, Clerk, PO Box 218, Baie Verte A0K 1B0 – 709/532-8222, Fax: 709/532-4134 |
| Baine Harbour ‡ | 170 | Burin-St. George's | Burin-Placentia West | Vacant, Clerk, General Delivery, Baine Harbour A0E 1A0 – 709/532-8222 |

Cities in CAPITALS; Towns marked †; Communities marked ‡. An in-depth listing for municipalities marked with * appears in Part 2 (check Index for page numbers).

| MUNICIPALITY | 1996 POP. | FEDERAL ELECTORAL DISTRICT | PROVINCIAL ELECTORAL DISTRICT | CONTACT PERSON WITH ADDRESS, PHONE & FAX |
|---|---|---|---|---|
| Bauline † | 380 | St. John's East | Cape St. Francis | Gail Tobin, Clerk, 2 Brook Path, Bauline A1K 1E9 – 709/335-2483, Fax: 709/335-2053 |
| Bay Bulls † | 1,063 | St. John's West | Ferryland | Andrea Norman, Clerk, PO Box 70, Bay Bulls A0A 1C0 – 709/334-3454, Fax: 709/334-3454 |
| Bay de Verde † | 594 | Bonavista-Trinity-Conception | Trinity-Bay de Verde | Molly Walsh, Clerk, PO Box 10, Bay de Verde A0A 1E0 – 709/587-2260, Fax: 709/587-2049 |
| Bay L'Argent † | 377 | Burin-St. George's | Bellevue | Wanda Stewart, Clerk, PO Box 29, Bay L'Argent A0E 1B0 – 709/461-2606, Fax: 709/461-2608 |
| Bay Roberts † | 5,472 | Bonavista-Trinity-Conception | Port de Grave | Daphne Earle, Clerk, PO Box 114, Bay Roberts A0A 1G0 – 709/786-2126, Fax: 709/786-2128 |
| Baytona ‡ | 363 | Gander-Grand Falls | Lewisporte | Linda Budden, Clerk, PO Box 29, Baytona A0G 2J0 – 709/659-6101 |
| Beachside ‡ | 239 | Gander-Grand Falls | Baie Verte | Mary Bennett, Clerk, 112 Bayview Rd., Beachside A0J 1T0 – 709/267-5251, Fax: 709/267-5251 |
| Bellburns ‡ | 114 | Humber-St. Barbe-Baie Verte | St. Barbe | Miriam House, Clerk, Bellburns A0K 1H0 – 709/898-2468 |
| Belleoram † | 564 | Burin-St. George's | Fortune Bay-Cape La Hune | Hilda Gould, Clerk, PO Box 29, Belleoram A0H 1B0 – 709/881-6161, Fax: 709/881-6161 |
| Bide Arm ‡ | 269 | Humber-St. Barbe-Baie Verte | The Straits & White Bay North | Phyllis Randell, Clerk, Bide Arm A0K 1J0 – 709/457-2811, Fax: 709/457-2253 |
| Birchy Bay † | 735 | Gander-Grand Falls | Lewisporte | Ruby Pollard, Clerk, PO Box 40, Birchy Bay A0G 1E0 – 709/659-3221, Fax: 709/659-2121 |
| Bird Cove ‡ | 333 | Humber-St. Barbe-Baie Verte | St. Barbe | Sharon Pittman, Clerk, 67 Michaels Dr., Bird Cove A0K 1L0 – 709/247-2256, Fax: 709/247-2128 |
| Biscay Bay ‡ | 66 | St. John's West | Ferryland | Fred White, Clerk, Site 10, PO Box 14, Trepassey A0A 4B0 – 709/438-2425 |
| Bishop's Cove ‡ | 282 | Bonavista-Trinity-Conception | Port de Grave | Joan Smith, Clerk, PO Box 141, Bishop's Cove A0A 3X0 – 709/589-2194 |
| Bishop's Falls † | 4,048 | Gander-Grand Falls | Exploits | Josephine Budgell, Clerk, PO Box 310, Bishop's Falls A0H 1C0 – 709/258-6581, Fax: 709/258-6346 |
| Bonavista † | 4,526 | Bonavista-Trinity-Conception | Bonavista South | David Hiscock, Clerk, PO Box 279, Bonavista A0C 1B0 – 709/468-7816, Fax: 709/468-2495 |
| Botwood † | 3,613 | Gander-Grand Falls | Exploits | Audrey Rowsell, Clerk, PO Box 490, Botwood A0H 1E0 – 709/257-2839, Fax: 709/257-3330 |
| Branch ‡ | 351 | St. John's West | Placentia & St. Mary's | Augustine Power, Clerk, PO Box 129, Branch A0B 1E0 – 709/338-2920, Fax: 709/338-2921 |
| Brent's Cove ‡ | 283 | Humber-St. Barbe-Baie Verte | Baie Verte | Ellen Butler, Clerk, Brent's Cove A0K 1R0 – 709/661-5301 |
| Brighton ‡ | 272 | Gander-Grand Falls | Windsor-Springdale | Donna Ince, Clerk, Brighton A0J 1B0 – 709/263-7391, Fax: 709/263-2595 |
| Brigus † | 902 | Bonavista-Trinity-Conception | Harbour Main-Whitbourne | Wayne Rose, Clerk, PO Box 220, Brigus A0A 1K0 – 709/528-4588, Fax: 709/528-4588 |
| Bryant's Cove ‡ | 449 | Bonavista-Trinity-Conception | Port de Grave | Louise Noseworthy, Clerk, PO Box 5, Bryant's Cove A0A 3P0 – 709/596-2291, Fax: 709/596-0015 |
| Buchans † | 1,056 | Gander-Grand Falls | Grand Falls-Buchans | Margaret Hamilton, Clerk, PO Box 190, Buchans A0H 1G0 – 709/672-3972, Fax: 709/672-3702 |
| Burgeo † | 2,098 | Burin-St. George's | Burgeo & La Poile | Stanley Cossar, Clerk, PO Box 220, Burgeo A0M 1A0 – 709/886-2250, Fax: 709/886-2166 |
| Burin † | 2,682 | Burin-St. George's | Burin-Placentia West | Beth Hanrahan, Clerk, PO Box 370, Burin A0E 1E0 – 709/891-1760, Fax: 709/891-2069 |
| Burlington ‡ | 432 | Humber-St. Barbe-Baie Verte | Baie Verte | Velma Young, Clerk, Burlington A0K 1S0 – 709/252-2607, Fax: 709/252-2161 |
| Burnt Islands † | 919 | Burin-St. George's | Burgeo & La Poile | Rosetta Glover, Clerk, PO Box 39, Burnt Islands A0M 1B0 – 709/698-3512, Fax: 709/698-3515 |
| Campbellton † | 642 | Gander-Grand Falls | Lewisporte | Elaine Hart, Clerk, PO Box 70, Campbellton A0G 1L0 – 709/261-2300, Fax: 709/261-2300 |
| Cape Broyle ‡ | 633 | St. John's West | Ferryland | Andrew O'Brien, Clerk, Cape Broyle A0A 1P0 – 709/432-2288, Fax: 709/432-2288 |
| Cape St. George ‡ | 1,095 | Burin-St. George's | Port au Port | Sandra Jesso, Clerk, PO Box 130, Cape St. George A0N 1E0 – 709/644-2290, Fax: 709/644-2291 |
| Carbonear † | 5,168 | Bonavista-Trinity-Conception | Carbonear-Harbour Grace | Bruce Foote, Clerk, PO Box 999, Carbonear A1Y 1C5 – 709/596-3831, Fax: 709/596-5021 |
| Carmanville † | 913 | Gander-Grand Falls | Bonavista North | Mary Sheppard, Clerk, PO Box 239, Carmanville A0G 1N0 – 709/534-2814, Fax: 709/534-2425 |
| Cartwright ‡ | 628 | Labrador | Cartwright-L'Anse au Clair | Charlotte Dyson, Clerk, PO Box 129, Cartwright A0K 1V0 – 709/938-7259, Fax: 709/938-7454 |
| Catalina † | 1,155 | Bonavista-Trinity-Conception | Bonavista South | Valerie Rogers, Clerk, PO Box 2, Catalina A0C 1J0 – 709/469-2615, Fax: 709/469-2772 |
| Centreville et al † | 1,328 | Bonavista-Trinity-Conception | Bonavista North | Selena Brown, Clerk, PO Box 130, Centreville A0G 4P0 – 709/678-2840, Fax: 709/678-2536 |
| Chance Cove † | 394 | Bonavista-Trinity-Conception | Bellevue | Debbie Collett, Clerk, Chance Cove A0B 1K0 – 709/460-4151 |

Cities in CAPITALS; Towns marked †; Communities marked ‡. An in-depth listing for municipalities marked with * appears in Part 2 (check Index for page numbers).

| MUNICIPALITY | 1996 POP. | FEDERAL ELECTORAL DISTRICT | PROVINCIAL ELECTORAL DISTRICT | CONTACT PERSON WITH ADDRESS, PHONE & FAX |
|---|---|---|---|---|
| Change Islands † | 460 | Gander-Grand Falls | Twillingate & Fogo | Doris Hoffe, Clerk, PO Box 67, Change Islands A0G 1R0 – 709/621-4181, Fax: 709/621-4181 |
| Channel-Port aux Basques † | 5,243 | Burin-St. George's | Burgeo & La Poile | Donna Bragg, Clerk, PO Box 70, Port aux Basques A0M 1C0 – 709/695-2214, Fax: 709/695-9852 |
| Chapel Arm † | 575 | Bonavista-Trinity-Conception | Bellevue | Phyllis Pretty, Clerk, Chapel Arm A0B 1L0 – 709/592-2720, Fax: 709/592-2800 |
| Charlottetown ‡ | 330 | Labrador | Cartwright-L'Anse au Clair | Dale Burt, Clerk, Charlottetown A0K 5Y0 – 709/949-0229, Fax: 709/949-0377 |
| Clarenville † | 5,335 | Bonavista-Trinity-Conception | Trinity North | Marie Blackmore, Clerk, PO Box 66, Clarenville A0E 1J0 – 709/466-7937, Fax: 709/466-2276 |
| Clarke's Beach † | 1,244 | Bonavista-Trinity-Conception | Harbour Main-Whitbourne | Joan Wilcox, Clerk, PO Box 159, Clarke's Beach A0A 1W0 – 709/786-3993, Fax: 709/786-3993 |
| Coachman's Cove ‡ | 182 | Humber-St. Barbe-Baie Verte | Baie Verte | Marina Bryan, Clerk, Coachman's Cove A0K 1X0 – 709/253-2142 |
| Colinet ‡ | 208 | St. John's West | Placentia & St. Mary's | Maureen Didham, Clerk, Colinet A0B 1M0 – 709/521-2300 |
| Colliers † | 774 | St. John's East | Harbour Main-Whitbourne | Vacant, Clerk, PO Box 84, Colliers A0A 1Y0 – 709/229-4333, Fax: 709/229-4333 |
| Come By Chance † | 300 | Bonavista-Trinity-Conception | Bellevue | Patsy Smith, Clerk, PO Box 89, Come By Chance A0B 1N0 – 709/542-3240, Fax: 709/542-3121 |
| Comfort Cove-Newstead ‡ | 597 | Gander-Grand Falls | Lewisporte | Mary Lou Ginn, Clerk, PO Box 10, Comfort Cove-Newstead A0G 3K0 – 709/244-4121, Fax: 709/244-4122 |
| Conception Bay South † | 19,265 | St. John's East | Conception Bay South; Topsail | Maureen Harvey, Clerk, PO Box 280, Manuels A0A 2Y0 – 709/834-6500, Fax: 709/834-8337 |
| Conception Harbour † | 888 | St. John's East | Harbour Main-Whitbourne | Colleen Wade, Clerk, Conception Harbour A0A 1Z0 – 709/229-4781 |
| Conche ‡ | 345 | Humber-St. Barbe-Baie Verte | The Straits & White Bay North | Laboura Whelan, Clerk, PO Box 59, Conche A0K 1Y0 – 709/622-4531, Fax: 709/622-4491 |
| Cook's Harbour † | 260 | Humber-St. Barbe-Baie Verte | The Straits & White Bay North | Margaret Elliott, Clerk, Cook's Harbour A0K 1Z0 – 709/249-3111, Fax: 709/249-4125 |
| Cormack ‡ | 767 | Humber-St.Barbe-Baie Verte | Humber Valley | Cynthia Fry, Clerk, Site 26, RR#2, PO Box 4, Deer Lake A0K 2E0 – 709/635-7025, Fax: 709/635-7363 |
| CORNER BROOK | 21,893 | Humber-St. Barbe-Baie Verte | Humber East; Humber West; Bay of Islands | James Kennedy, City Clerk, City Hall, PO Box 1080, Corner Brook A2H 6E1 – 709/637-1500, Fax: 709/637-1543 |
| Cottlesville † | 351 | Gander-Grand Falls | Twillingate & Fogo | Shelly Philpott, Clerk, PO Box 10, Cottlesville A0G 1S0 – 709/629-3505, Fax: 709/629-7411 |
| Cow Head † | 665 | Humber-St. Barbe-Baie Verte | St. Barbe | Eura Curtis, Clerk, PO Box 40, Cow Head A0K 2A0 – 709/243-2446, Fax: 709/243-2446 |
| Cox's Cove ‡ | 898 | Humber-St. Barbe-Baie Verte | Bay of Islands | Sandra Warren, Clerk, PO Box 100, Cox's Cove A0L 1C0 – 709/688-2900 |
| Crow Head ‡ | 267 | Gander-Grand Falls | Twillingate & Fogo | Meta J. Hamlyn, Clerk, PO Box 250, Crow Head A0G 4M0 – 709/884-5651, Fax: 709/884-2344 |
| Cupids † | 891 | Bonavista-Trinity-Conception | Harbour Main-Whitbourne | Linda Noseworthy, Clerk, PO Box 99, Cupids A0A 2B0 – 709/528-4428, Fax: 709/528-4428 |
| Daniel's Harbour ‡ | 430 | Humber-St. Barbe-Baie Verte | St. Barbe | Melda House, Clerk, PO Box 68, Daniel's Harbour A0K 2C0 – 709/898-2300, Fax: 709/898-2593 |
| Deer Lake † | 5,222 | Humber-St. Barbe-Baie Verte | Humber Valley | Maxine Hayden, Clerk, PO Box 940, Deer Lake A0K 2E0 – 709/635-2451, Fax: 709/635-5857 |
| Dover † | 821 | Bonavista-Trinity-Conception | Terra Nova | Larry Rogers, Clerk, PO Box 10, Dover A0G 1X0 – 709/537-2139, Fax: 709/537-2018 |
| Duntara ‡ | 85 | Bonavista-Trinity-Conception | Bonavista South | Dorothy Power, Clerk, Duntara A0C 1M0 – 709/447-3190 |
| Eastport † | 557 | Bonavista-Trinity-Conception | Terra Nova | Cynthia Lane, Clerk, PO Box 119, Eastport A0G 1Z0 – 709/677-2161, Fax: 709/677-2144 |
| Elliston † | 461 | Bonavista-Trinity-Conception | Bonavista South | Bonnie Critch, Clerk, PO Box 115, Elliston A0C 1N0 – 709/468-2649, Fax: 709/468-2867 |
| Embree † | 819 | Gander-Grand Falls | Lewisporte | Maxine Lane, Clerk, Embree A0G 2A0 – 709/535-8712, Fax: 709/535-8716 |
| Englee † | 827 | Humber-St. Barbe-Baie Verte | The Straits & White Bay North | Doris Randell, Clerk, PO Box 160, Englee A0K 2J0 – 709/866-2711, Fax: 709/866-2357 |
| English Harbour East ‡ | 253 | Burin-St. George's | Bellevue | Daphne Hynes, Clerk, PO Box 21, English Harbour East A0E 1M0 – 709/245-4271, Fax: 709/245-4306 |
| Fermeuse ‡ | 446 | St. John's West | Ferryland | Patrick Walsh, Clerk, Fermeuse A0A 2G0 – 709/363-2400, Fax: 709/363-2308 |
| Ferryland ‡ | 667 | St. John's West | Ferryland | Doris Kavanagh, Clerk, PO Box 75, Ferryland A0A 2H0 – 709/432-2127, Fax: 709/432-2209 |
| Flatrock † | 1,087 | St. John's East | Cape St. Francis | Rita Farrell, Clerk, 663 Wind Gap Rd., Flatrock A1K 1C7 – 709/437-6312 |
| Fleur de Lys † | 375 | Humber-St. Barbe-Baie Verte | Baie Verte | Judy Traverse, Clerk, Fleur de Lys A0K 2M0 – 709/253-3131, Fax: 709/253-2146 |
| Flower's Cove † | 354 | Humber-St. Barbe-Baie Verte | The Straits & White Bay North | Bruce Way, Clerk, PO Box 149, Flower's Cove A0K 2N0 – 709/456-2124, Fax: 709/456-2055 |

Cities in CAPITALS; Towns marked †; Communities marked ‡. An in-depth listing for municipalities marked with * appears in Part 2 (check Index for page numbers).

| MUNICIPALITY | 1996 POP. | FEDERAL ELECTORAL DISTRICT | PROVINCIAL ELECTORAL DISTRICT | CONTACT PERSON WITH ADDRESS, PHONE & FAX |
|---|---|---|---|---|
| Fogo † | 982 | Gander-Grand Falls | Twillingate & Fogo | Bruce Pomeroy, Clerk, PO Box 57, Fogo A0G 2B0 – 709/266-2237, Fax: 709/266-2972 |
| Fogo Island Region Reg. Mun. | | | | Sandra Cull, Clerk, PO Box 159, Joe Batt's Arm A0G 2X0 – 709/266-1212 |
| Forteau ‡ | 505 | Labrador | Cartwright-L'Anse au Clair | Gail Flynn, Clerk, PO Box 99, Forteau A0K 2P0 – 709/931-2241, Fax: 709/931-2037 |
| Fortune † | 1,969 | Burin-St. George's | Grand Bank | Basil Collier, Clerk, PO Box 159, Fortune A0E 1P0 – 709/832-2810, Fax: 709/832-2210 |
| Fox Cove-Mortier † | 442 | Burin-St. George's | Burin-Placentia West | Gladys Kavanagh, Clerk, Site 25, PO Box 17, Burin A0E 1E0 – 709/891-1500, Fax: 709/891-1500 |
| Fox Harbour ‡ | 394 | St. John's West | Placentia & St. Mary's | Patricia Quilty, Clerk, PO Box 64, Fox Harbour A0B 1V0 – 709/227-2271 |
| Frenchman's Cove ‡ | 220 | Burin-St. George's | Grand Bank | Miriam Power, Clerk, Frenchman's Cove A0E 1R0 – 709/826-2190 |
| Gallants ‡ | 65 | Burin-St. George's | Humber West | Beverley Hickey, Clerk, Gallants A0L 1G0 – 709/646-2912 |
| Gambo † | 2,339 | Bonavista-Trinity-Conception | Terra Nova | Scott Pritchett, Clerk, PO Box 250, Gambo A0G 1T0 – 709/674-4476, Fax: 709/674-5399 |
| Gander † | 10,364 | Gander-Grand Falls | Gander | James Butler, Clerk, PO Box 280, Gander A1V 1W6 – 709/651-2949, Fax: 709/256-2124 |
| Garnish † | 691 | Burin-St. George's | Grand Bank | Steven Grandy, Clerk, PO Box 70, Garnish A0E 1T0 – 709/826-2330, Fax: 709/826-2330 |
| Gaskiers-Point La Haye ‡ | 432 | St. John's West | Placentia & St. Mary's | Gertrude Kielley, Clerk, RR#1, PO Box 122, St. Mary's A0B 3B0 – 709/525-2430 |
| Gaultois † | 423 | Burin-St. George's | Fortune Bay-Cape La Hune | Sylvin Rose, Clerk, PO Box 101, Gaultois A0H 1N0 – 709/841-6546, Fax: 709/841-3521 |
| Gillams ‡ | 465 | Humber-St. Barbe-Baie Verte | Bay of Islands | Lois Blanchard, Clerk, RR#2, PO Box 3968, Corner Brook A2H 6B9 – 709/783-2800, Fax: 709/783-2671 |
| Glenburnie-Birchy Head-Shoal Brook ‡ | 321 | Humber-St. Barbe-Baie Verte | Humber Valley | Eulah Raike, Clerk, Birchy Head A0K 1K0 – 709/453-7220, Fax: 709/453-2594 |
| Glenwood † | 893 | Gander-Grand Falls | Gander | Cynthia Davis, Clerk, PO Box 130, Glenwood A0G 2K0 – 709/679-2159, Fax: 709/679-5470 |
| Glovertown † | 2,292 | Bonavista-Trinity-Conception | Terra Nova | Joanne Perry, Clerk, PO Box 224, Glovertown A0G 2L0 – 709/533-2351, Fax: 709/533-2225 |
| Goose Cove East ‡ | 315 | Humber-St. Barbe-Baie Verte | The Straits & White Bay North | Gertrude Troy, Clerk, PO Box 208, St. Anthony A0K 4S0 – 709/454-8393 |
| Grand Bank † | 3,328 | Burin-St. George's | Grand Bank | Cathy Trimm, Clerk, PO Box 640, Grand Bank A0E 1W0 – 709/832-1600, Fax: 709/832-1636 |
| Grand Falls-Windsor † | 14,160 | Gander-Grand Falls | Grand Falls-Buchans; Windsor-Springdale | Rod French, Clerk, PO Box 439, Grand Falls-Windsor A2A 2J8 – 709/489-0412, Fax: 709/489-0465 |
| Grand Le Pierre ‡ | 327 | Burin-St. George's | Bellevue | Martha Bolt, Clerk, PO Box 35, Grand La Pierre A0E 1Y0 – 709/662-2702, Fax: 709/662-2076 |
| Great Harbour Deep ‡ | 196 | Humber-St. Barbe-Baie Verte | Humber Valley | Gaye Newman, Clerk, Great Harbour Deep A0K 2Z0 – 709/843-3481, Fax: 709/843-3113 |
| Greenspond † | 425 | Bonavista-Trinity-Conception | Bonavista North | Derrick Bragg, Clerk, PO Box 100, Greenspond A0G 2N0 – 709/269-3111, Fax: 709/269-3191 |
| Hampden ‡ | 651 | Humber-St. Barbe-Baie Verte | Humber Valley | Ruth Jenkins, Clerk, PO Box 9, Hampden A0K 2Y0 – 709/455-4212, Fax: 709/455-2117 |
| Hant's Harbour † | 519 | Bonavista-Trinity-Conception | Trinity-Bay de Verde | Doris J. Short, Clerk, PO Box 40, Hant's Harbour A0B 1Y0 – 709/586-2741, Fax: 709/586-2888 |
| Happy Adventure ‡ | 285 | Bonavista-Trinity-Conception | Terra Nova | Kim Holloway, Clerk, PO Box 106, Eastport A0G 1Z0 – 709/677-2593, Fax: 709/677-2058 |
| Happy Valley-Goose Bay † | 8,655 | Labrador | Lake Melville | Valerie Sheppard, Clerk, PO Box 40, Happy Valley-Goose Bay A0P 1E0 – 709/896-3321, Fax: 709/896-9454 |
| Harbour Breton † | 2,290 | Burin-St. George's | Fortune Bay-Cape La Hune | Bernice Herritt, Clerk, PO Box 130, Harbour Breton A0H 1P0 – 709/885-2354, Fax: 709/885-2095 |
| Harbour Grace † | 3,740 | Bonavista-Trinity-Conception | Carbonear-Harbour Grace | Sean O'Brien, Clerk, PO Box 310, Harbour Grace A0A 2M0 – 709/596-3631, Fax: 709/596-1991 |
| Harbour Main-Chapel's Cove-Lakeview † | 1,244 | St. John's East | Harbour Main-Whitbourne | Gloria Brazil, Clerk, PO Box 40, Harbour Main A0A 2P0 – 709/229-6822, Fax: 709/229-6234 |
| Hare Bay † | 1,224 | Bonavista-Trinity-Conception | Terra Nova | George R. Collins, Clerk, PO Box 130, Hare Bay A0G 2P0 – 709/537-2187 |
| Hawke's Bay † | 514 | Humber-St. Barbe-Baie Verte | St. Barbe | Yvonne House, Clerk, Hawkes Bay A0K 3B0 – 709/248-5216, Fax: 709/248-5201 |
| Heart's Content † | 538 | Bonavista-Trinity-Conception | Trinity-Bay de Verde | Alice Cumby, Clerk, PO Box 31, Heart's Content A0B 1Z0 – 709/583-2491, Fax: 709/583-2226 |
| Heart's Delight-Islington † | 841 | Bonavista-Trinity-Conception | Trinity-Bay de Verde | Sherry Chislett, Clerk, PO Box 129, Heart's Delight A0B 2A0 – 709/588-2708, Fax: 709/588-2235 |
| Heart's Desire † | 339 | Bonavista-Trinity-Conception | Trinity-Bay de Verde | Eleanor Andrews, Clerk, Heart's Desire A0B 2B0 – 709/588-2280, Fax: 709/588-2280 |
| Hermitage-Sandyville ‡ | 687 | Burin-St. George's | Fortune Bay-Cape La Hune | Myrtle Kendall, Clerk, PO Box 126, Hermitage A0H 1S0 – 709/883-2343, Fax: 709/883-2150 |
| Holyrood † | 2,090 | St. John's East | Concession Bay South; Harbour Main-Whitbourne | Germaine Crawley, Clerk, PO Box 100, Holyrood A0A 2R0 – 709/834-7600, Fax: 709/834-7600 |

Cities in CAPITALS; Towns marked †; Communities marked ‡. An in-depth listing for municipalities marked with * appears in Part 2 (check Index for page numbers).

| MUNICIPALITY | 1996 POP. | FEDERAL ELECTORAL DISTRICT | PROVINCIAL ELECTORAL DISTRICT | CONTACT PERSON WITH ADDRESS, PHONE & FAX |
|---|---|---|---|---|
| Hopedale ‡ | 591 | Labrador | Torngat Mountains | Judy Dicker, Clerk, Hopedale A0P 1G0 – 709/933-3864, Fax: 709/933-3800 |
| Howley † | 336 | Humber-St. Barbe-Baie Verte | Humber Valley | Blanche Gilley, Clerk, PO Box 40, Howley A0K 3E0 – 709/635-5555, Fax: 709/635-5555 |
| Hughes Brook ‡ | 181 | Humber-St. Barbe-Baie Verte | Bay of Islands | Debbie White, Clerk, RR#2, PO Box 2527, Corner Brook A2H 6B9 – 709/783-2921 |
| Humber Arm South † | 1,991 | Humber-St. Barbe-Baie Verte | Bay of Islands | Marion Evoy, Clerk, Benoit's Cove A0L 1A0 – 709/789-2981, Fax: 709/789-2981 |
| Indian Bay ‡ | 217 | Bonavista-Trinity-Conception | Bonavista North | Jackie Cook, Clerk, Indian Bay A0G 2V0 – 709/678-2727 |
| Irishtown-Summerside † | 1,424 | Humber-St. Barbe-Baie Verte | Bay of Islands | Geraldine Wheeler, Clerk, RR#2, PO Box 2795, Corner Brook A2H 6B9 – 709/783-2146 |
| Isle aux Morts † | 988 | Burin-St. George's | Burgeo & La Poile | Richard Lillington, Clerk, PO Box 110, Isle aux Morts A0M 1J0 – 709/698-3441, Fax: 709/698-3449 |
| Jackson's Arm ‡ | 470 | Humber-St. Barbe-Baie Verte | Humber Valley | Alfreda Osmond, Clerk, PO Box 10, Jackson's Arm A0K 3H0 – 709/459-3122, Fax: 709/459-3173 |
| Joe Batt's Arm-Barr'd Islands-Shoal Bay † | 1,028 | Gander-Grand Falls | Twillingate & Fogo | Elaine Penton, Clerk, PO Box 28, Joe Batt's Arm A0G 2X0 – 709/658-3490, Fax: 709/658-3408 |
| Keels ‡ | 101 | Bonavista-Trinity-Conception | Bonavista South | Glenys Byrne, Clerk, PO Box 20, Keels A0C 1R0 – 709/447-3126 |
| King's Cove ‡ | 175 | Bonavista-Trinity-Conception | Bonavista South | Gerald Barron, Clerk, King's Cove A0C 1S0 – 709/477-4361 |
| King's Point † | 845 | Gander-Grand Falls | Baie Verte | Andrea Budgell, Clerk, King's Point A0J 1H0 – 709/268-3838, Fax: 709/269-3838 |
| Kippens † | 1,887 | Burin-St. George's | Port au Port | Norma Childs, Clerk, Kippens A2N 3H8 – 709/643-5281, Fax: 709/643-9773 |
| La Scie † | 1,254 | Humber-St. Barbe-Baie Verte | Baie Verte | Vida Short, Clerk, PO Box 130, La Scie A0K 3M0 – 709/675-2266, Fax: 709/675-2168 |
| Labrador City † | 8,455 | Labrador | Labrador West | Joyce Narduzzi, Clerk, PO Box 280, Labrador City A2V 2K5 – 709/944-2621, Fax: 709/944-6353 |
| Lamaline † | 440 | Burin-St. George's | Grand Bank | Shelley Lovell, Clerk, PO Box 40, Lamaline A0E 2C0 – 709/857-2341, Fax: 709/857-2021 |
| L'Anse au Clair ‡ | 264 | Labrador | Cartwright-L'Anse au Clair | Loretta Griffin, Clerk, L'Anse au Clair A0K 3K0 – 709/931-2481, Fax: 709/931-2481 |
| L'Anse au Loup ‡ | 621 | Labrador | Cartwright-L'Anse au Clair | Doreen Belbin, Clerk, PO Box 101, L'Anse au Loup A0K 3L0 – 709/927-5573, Fax: 709/927-5263 |
| Lark Harbour ‡ | 681 | Humber-St. Barbe-Baie Verte | Bay of Islands | Debra Park, Clerk, PO Box 40, Lark Harbour A0L 1H0 – 709/681-2270, Fax: 709/681-2900 |
| Lawn † | 957 | Burin-St. George's | Grand Bank | Ruth M. Bennett, Clerk, PO Box 29, Lawn A0E 2E0 – 709/873-2439, Fax: 709/873-3006 |
| Leading Tickles West ‡ | 513 | Gander-Grand Falls | Exploits | Kimberly Newman, Clerk, PO Box 39, Leading Tickles West A0H 1T0 – 709/483-2180 |
| Lewin's Cove ‡ | 604 | Burin-St. George's | Grand Bank | Linda Inkpen, Clerk, PO Box 40, Lewin's Cove A0E 2G0 – 709/894-4777, Fax: 709/894-4952 |
| Lewisporte † | 3,709 | Gander-Grand Falls | Lewisporte | Helen Combden, Clerk, PO Box 219, Lewisporte A0G 3A0 – 709/535-2737, Fax: 709/535-2695 |
| Little Bay ‡ | 150 | Gander-Grand Falls | Baie Verte | Stella Simms, Clerk, PO Box 39, Little Bay A0J 1J0 – 709/267-5257 |
| Little Bay East ‡ | 180 | Burin-St. George's | Bellevue | Gail Clarke, Clerk, Little Bay East A0E 2J0 – 709/461-2724 |
| Little Bay Islands ‡ | 244 | Gander-Grand Falls | Baie Verte | Betty Tucker, Clerk, PO Box 64, Little Bay Islands A0J 1K0 – 709/626-3511, Fax: 709/626-3512 |
| Little Burnt Bay † | 412 | Burin-St.George's | Lewisporte | Maisie Wells, Clerk, PO Box 40, Little Burnt Bay A0G 3B0 – 709/535-6415, Fax: 709/535-6490 |
| Little Catalina † | 630 | Bonavista-Trinity-Conception | Bonavista South | Marilyn Reid, Clerk, PO Box 59, Little Catalina A0C 1W0 – 709/469-2795 |
| Logy Bay-Middle Cove-Outer Cove † | 1,881 | St. John's East | Cape St. Francis | Barbara Power, Clerk, SS#3, PO Box 51428, St. John's A1B 4M2 – 709/726-7930, Fax: 709/726-2178 |
| Long Harbour-Mount Arlington Heights † | 472 | St. John's West | Bellevue | Loretta Keating, Clerk, PO Box 40, Long Harbour A0B 2J0 – 709/228-2920, Fax: 709/228-2900 |
| Lord's Cove ‡ | 302 | Burin-St. George's | Grand Bank | Christina Lundrigan, Clerk, Lord's Cove A0E 2C0 – 709/857-2316 |
| Lourdes ‡ | 758 | Burin-St. George's | Port au Port | Loretta Snook, Clerk, PO Box 29, Lourdes A0N 1R0 – 709/642-5812, Fax: 709/642-5812 |
| Lumsden † | 653 | Bonavista-Trinity-Conception | Bonavista North | Edison Goodyear, Clerk, PO Box 100, Lumsden A0G 3E0 – 709/530-2309, Fax: 709/530-2144 |
| Lushes Bight-Beaumont-Beaumont North ‡ | 348 | Gander-Grand Falls | Windsor-Springdale | Madeline Burton, Clerk, Beaumont A0J 1A0 – 709/264-3271, Fax: 709/264-3191 |
| Main Brook † | 424 | Humber-St. Barbe-Baie Verte | The Straits & White Bay North | Ella R. Pilgrim, Clerk, PO Box 28, Main Brook A0K 3N0 – 709/865-6561, Fax: 709/865-3279 |
| Makkovik ‡ | 367 | Labrador | Torngat Mountains | David Dyson, Clerk, PO Box 68, Makkovik A0P 1J0 – 709/923-2221, Fax: 709/923-2126 |
| Mary's Harbour ‡ | 474 | Labrador | Cartwright-L'Anse au Clair | Glenys Rumbolt, Clerk, Mary's Harbour A0K 3P0 – 709/921-6281, Fax: 709/921-6255 |

Cities in CAPITALS; Towns marked †; Communities marked ‡. An in-depth listing for municipalities marked with * appears in Part 2 (check Index for page numbers).

| MUNICIPALITY | 1996 POP. | FEDERAL ELECTORAL DISTRICT | PROVINCIAL ELECTORAL DISTRICT | CONTACT PERSON WITH ADDRESS, PHONE & FAX |
|---|---|---|---|---|
| Marystown † | 6,742 | Burin-St. George's | Burin-Placentia West | Dennis P. Kelly, Clerk, PO Box 918, Marystown A0E 2M0 – 709/279-1661, Fax: 709/279-2862 |
| Massey Drive † | 736 | Humber-St. Barbe-Baie Verte | Humber East | Phyllis Stratton, Clerk, Massey Dr., Massey Drive A2H 7A2 – 709/634-2742, Fax: 709/634-2899 |
| McIvers ‡ | 725 | Humber-St. Barbe-Baie Verte | Bay of Islands | Bernice E. Parsons, Clerk, RR#2, PO Box 4375, Corner Brook A2H 6B9 – 709/688-2603 |
| Meadows ‡ | 737 | Humber-St. Barbe-Baie Verte | Bay of Islands | Phyllis Brake, Clerk, RR#2, PO Box 3529, Corner Brook A2H 6B9 – 709/783-2339, Fax: 709/783-2501 |
| Melrose ‡ | 366 | Bonavista-Trinity-Conception | Bonavista South | Rosemary Donovan, Clerk, Melrose A0C 1Y0 – 709/469-2882 |
| Middle Arm ‡ | 640 | Humber-St. Barbe-Baie Verte | Baie Verte | Neta Mitchell, Clerk, PO Box 51, Middle Arm A0K 3R0 – 709/252-2521, Fax: 709/252-2521 |
| Miles Cove ‡ | 204 | Gander-Grand Falls | Windsor-Springdale | Nellie Reid, Clerk, Miles Cove A0J 1L0 – 709/652-3505 |
| Millertown ‡ | 134 | Gander-Grand Falls | Grand Falls-Buchans | Judy Menchenton, Clerk, PO Box 56, Millertown A0H 1V0 – 709/852-6216, Fax: 709/852-5431 |
| Milltown-Head of Bay D'Espoir † | 1,124 | Burin-St. George's | Fortune Bay-Cape La Hune | Kimberly King, Clerk, PO Box 70, Milltown A0H 1W0 – 709/882-2232, Fax: 709/882-2636 |
| Ming's Bight ‡ | 435 | Humber-St. Barbe-Baie Verte | Baie Verte | Glenda Regular, Clerk, PO Box 59, Ming's Bight A0K 3S0 – 709/254-6516, Fax: 709/254-6516 |
| Morrisville ‡ | 194 | Burin-St. George's | Fortune Bay-Cape La Hune | Derrick McDonald, Clerk, PO Box 19, Morrisville A0H 1W0 – 709/882-2322, Fax: 709/882-2564 |
| Mount Carmel et al. † | 534 | St. John's West | Placentia & St. Mary's | Bernadette Didham, Clerk, Mount Carmel A0B 2M0 – 709/521-2040, Fax: 709/521-2258 |
| Mount Moriah † | 748 | Humber-St. Barbe-Baie Verte | Bay of Islands | Carol Hussey, Clerk, PO Box 31, Mount Moriah A0L 1J0 – 709/785-5232, Fax: 709/785-5232 |
| MOUNT PEARL | 25,519 | St. John's West | Mount Pearl; Waterford Valley | Gerard Lewis, City Clerk, 3 Centennial St., Mount Pearl A1N 1G4 – 709/748-1006, Fax: 709/364-8935 |
| Musgrave Harbour † | 1,386 | Gander-Grand Falls | Bonavista North | Sophie Mercer, Clerk, PO Box 159, Musgrave Harbour A0G 3J0 – 709/655-2119, Fax: 709/655-2064 |
| Musgravetown † | 687 | Bonavista-Trinity-Conception | Terra Nova | Charlotte Wiseman, Clerk, PO Box 129, Musgravetown A0C 1Z0 – 709/467-2726, Fax: 709/467-2109 |
| Nain † | 996 | Labrador | Torngat Mountains | Dasi Ikkusek, Clerk, PO Box 59, Nain A0P 1L0 – 709/922-2842, Fax: 709/922-2295 |
| New Perlican † | 252 | Bonavista-Trinity-Conception | Trinity-Bay de Verde | Denyce Peddle, Clerk, PO Box 39, New Perlican A0B 2S0 – 709/583-2500, Fax: 709/583-2085 |
| New Wes-Valley † | | Bonavista-Trinity-Conception | Bonavista North | Harry Winter, Clerk, PO Box 64, Badger's Quay A0G 1B0 – 709/536-2010, Fax: 709/536-3481 |
| Nipper's Harbour ‡ | 226 | Humber-St. Barbe-Baie Verte | Baie Verte | Beth Prole, Clerk, PO Box 10, Nipper's Harbour A0K 3T0 – 709/255-3151, Fax: 709/255-3151 |
| Norman's Cove-Long Cove † | 988 | Bonavista-Trinity-Conception | Bellevue | Diane Hudson, Clerk, PO Box 70, Norman's Cove A0B 2T0 – 709/592-2490, Fax: 709/592-2106 |
| Norris Arm † | 1,007 | Gander-Grand Falls | Lewisporte | Betty Saunders, Clerk, PO Box 70, Norris Arm A0G 3M0 – 709/653-2519, Fax: 709/653-2163 |
| Norris Point ‡ | 850 | Humber-St. Barbe-Baie Verte | St. Barbe | Regina Organ, Clerk, PO Box 119, Norris Point A0K 3V0 – 709/458-2207, Fax: 709/458-2883 |
| North River ‡ | 589 | Bonavista-Trinity-Conception | Harbour Main-Whitbourne | Beverly Sparkes, Clerk, PO Box 104, North River A0A 3C0 – 709/786-6216, Fax: 709/786-6216 |
| North West River † | 567 | Labrador | Lake Melville | Melinda Baikie, Clerk, PO Box 100, North West River A0P 1M0 – 709/497-8533, Fax: 709/497-8228 |
| Northern Arm † | 422 | Gander-Grand Falls | Exploits | Ella Humphries, Clerk, PO Box 2006, Northern Arm A0H 1E0 – 709/257-3482, Fax: 709/257-3482 |
| Old Perlican † | 747 | Bonavista-Trinity-Conception | Trinity-Bay de Verde | Judi Barter, Clerk, PO Box 39, Old Perlican A0A 3G0 – 709/587-2266, Fax: 709/587-2261 |
| Pacquet ‡ | 291 | Humber-St. Barbe-Baie Verte | Baie Verte | Janet Sacrey, Clerk, Pacquet A0K 3X0 – 709/251-5496, Fax: 709/251-5497 |
| Paradise † | 7,960 | Gander-Grand Falls | Conception Bay East & Bell Island; Topsail | Joyce Moss, Clerk, PO Box 100, Paradise A1L 1C4 – 709/782-1400, Fax: 709/782-3601 |
| Parkers Cove ‡ | 427 | Burin-St. George's | Burin-Placentia West | Bernadette Synard, Clerk, Parker's Cove A0E 1H0 – 709/443-2216 |
| Parson's Pond ‡ | 530 | Humber-St. Barbe-Baie Verte | St. Barbe | Joan Parsons, Clerk, PO Box 39, Parson's Pond A0K 3Z0 – 709/243-2564 |
| Pasadena † | 3,445 | Humber-St. Barbe-Baie Verte | Humber East | Melvina Tracey, Clerk, 18 Tenth Ave., Pasadena A0L 1K0 – 709/686-2075, Fax: 709/686-2507 |
| Peterview † | 862 | Gander-Grand Falls | Exploits | Venus Samson, Clerk, PO Box 10, Peterview A0H 1Y0 – 709/257-2926, Fax: 709/257-2926 |
| Petty Harbour-Maddox Cove † | 954 | St. John's West | Ferryland | Noreen Hearn, Clerk, PO Box 70, Petty Harbour A0A 3H0 – 709/368-3959, Fax: 709/368-3994 |
| Pilley's Island ‡ | 432 | Gander-Grand Falls | Windsor-Springdale | Betty Traverse, Clerk, PO Box 70, Pilley's Island A0J 1M0 – 709/652-3555, Fax: 709/652-3555 |
| Pinware ‡ | 144 | Labrador | Cartwright-L'Anse au Clair | Vacant, Clerk, Pinware A0K 5S0 – 709/927-5588 |
| Placentia † | 5,013 | St. John's West | Placentia & St. Mary's | Margie Hatfield, Clerk, PO Box 99, Placentia A0B 2Y0 – 709/227-2151, Fax: 709/227-2048 |

Cities in CAPITALS; Towns marked †; Communities marked ‡. An in-depth listing for municipalities marked with * appears in Part 2 (check Index for page numbers).

| MUNICIPALITY | 1996 POP. | FEDERAL ELECTORAL DISTRICT | PROVINCIAL ELECTORAL DISTRICT | CONTACT PERSON WITH ADDRESS, PHONE & FAX |
|---|---|---|---|---|
| Plate Cove East ‡ | 144 | Bonavista-Trinity-Conception | Bonavista South | Barry Mavin, Adm., Plate Cove East A0C 2C0 – 709/227-2151 |
| Plate Cove West ‡ | 210 | Bonavista-Trinity-Conception | Bonavista South | Barry Mavin, Adm., Plate Cove West A0C 2E0 – 709/227-2151 |
| Point au Gaul ‡ | 112 | Burin-St. George's | Grand Bank | Peter M. Lockyer, Clerk, PO Box 20, Point au Gaul A0E 2C0 – 709/857-2514 |
| Point Lance ‡ | 141 | St. John's West | Placentia & St. Mary's | Bernadette Careen, Clerk, PO Box 23, Point Lance A0B 1E0 – 709/337-2355 |
| Point Leamington † | 783 | Gander-Grand Falls | Exploits | Patricia Earle, Clerk, PO Box 39, Point Leamington A0H 1Z0 – 709/484-3421, Fax: 709/484-3556 |
| Point May ‡ | 377 | Burin-St. George's | Grand Bank | Darlene Hewitt, Clerk, Site 5, PO Box 19, Point May A0E 2C0 – 709/857-2640 |
| Point of Bay ‡ | 183 | Gander-Grand Falls | Exploits | Sybil Boone, Clerk, Point of Bay A0H 2A0 – 709/257-3171 |
| Pool's Cove ‡ | 241 | Burin-St. George's | Fortune Bay-Cape La Hune | Lloyd Spurrell, Clerk, PO Box 10, Pool's Cove A0H 2B0 – 709/665-3371 |
| Port Anson ‡ | 185 | Gander-Grand Falls | Windsor-Springdale | Daphne Hewlett, Clerk, Port Anson A0J 1N0 – 709/652-3656 |
| Port au Bras ‡ | 268 | Burin-St. George's | Burin-Placentia West | Beatrice Abbott, Clerk, RR#1, PO Box 359, Burin A0E 1E0 – 709/891-1195, Fax: 709/891-1195 |
| Port au Choix † | 1,146 | Humber-St. Barbe-Baie Verte | St. Barbe | Maurice Kelly, Clerk, PO Box 89, Port au Choix A0K 4C0 – 709/861-3406, 3409, Fax: 709/861-3061 |
| Port au Port East ‡ | 707 | Burin-St. George's | Port au Port | Theresa Hann, Clerk, PO Box 39, Port au Port East A0N 1T0 – 709/648-2731, Fax: 709/648-9481 |
| Port au Port West-Aguathuna-Felix Cove † | 619 | Burin-St. George's | Port au Port | Daniel McCann, Clerk, PO Box 89, Aguathuna A0N 1A0 – 709/648-2891 |
| Port Blandford † | 603 | Bonavista-Trinity-Conception | Terra Nova | Vida Greening, Clerk, PO Box 70, Port Blandford A0C 2G0 – 709/543-2170, Fax: 709/543-2153 |
| Port Hope Simpson ‡ | 577 | Labrador | Cartwright-L'Anse au Clair | Betty Sampson, Clerk, Port Hope Simpson A0K 4E0 – 709/960-0236, Fax: 709/960-0387 |
| Port Kirwan ‡ | 94 | St. John's West | Ferryland | Lucy Bosch, Clerk, Site 2, PO Box 40, Port Kirwan A0A 2G0 – 709/363-2417 |
| Port Rexton ‡ | 439 | Bonavista-Trinity-Conception | Trinity North | Lois Long, Clerk, PO Box 55, Port Rexton A0C 2H0 – 709/464-2006, Fax: 709/464-2006 |
| Port Saunders † | 876 | Humber-St. Barbe-Baie Verte | St. Barbe | Judy Quinlan, Clerk, PO Box 39, Port Saunders A0K 4H0 – 709/861-3105, Fax: 709/861-2137 |
| Port Union † | 542 | Bonavista-Trinity-Conception | Bonavista South | Thomas Sutton, Clerk, PO Box 91, Port Union A0C 2J0 – 709/469-2571, Fax: 709/469-3444 |
| Portugal Cove-St Philip's † | 5,773 | St. John's East | Conception Bay East & Bell Island | Loretta Tucker, Clerk, PO Box 144, Portugal Cove A0A 3K0 – 709/895-6594, Fax: 709/895-3780 |
| Portugal Cove South ‡ | 322 | St. John's West | Ferryland | Mary O'Leary, Clerk, Site 11, PO Box 8, Trepassey A0A 4B0 – 709/438-2092 |
| Postville ‡ | 223 | Labrador | Torngat Mountains | Shirley Goudie, Clerk, Postville A0P 1N0 – 709/479-9830, Fax: 709/479-9888 |
| Pouch Cove † | 1,885 | St. John's East | Cape St. Francis | Lillian Moran, Clerk, PO Box 59, Pouch Cove A0A 3L0 – 709/335-2848, Fax: 709/335-2840 |
| Raleigh ‡ | 366 | Humber-St. Barbe-Baie Verte | The Straits & White Bay North | Helen Greene, Clerk, PO Box 119, Raleigh A0K 4J0 – 709/452-4461, Fax: 709/452-2135 |
| Ramea † | 1,080 | Burin-St. George's | Fortune Bay-Cape La Hune | Wilfred Cutler, Clerk, PO Box 69, Ramea A0M 1N0 – 709/625-2280, Fax: 709/625-2010 |
| Red Bay ‡ | 275 | Labrador | Cartwright-L'Anse au Clair | Josie Moores, Clerk, Red Bay A0K 4K0 – 709/920-2197, Fax: 709/920-2197 |
| Red Harbour ‡ | 248 | Burin-St. George's | Burin-Placentia West | Walter Kenway, Clerk, Red Harbour A0E 2R0 – 709/443-2599 |
| Reidville ‡ | 496 | Humber-St. Barbe-Baie Verte | Humber Valley | Gail King, Clerk, Site 14, RR#2, PO Box 5, Deer Lake A0K 2E0 – 709/635-5232 |
| Rencontre East ‡ | 215 | Burin-St. George's | Fortune Bay-Cape La Hune | Barbara Caines, Clerk, Rencontre East A0H 2C0 – 709/848-3171, Fax: 709/848-3231 |
| Renews-Cappahayden ‡ | 503 | St. John's West | Ferryland | Doris Moriarty, Clerk, PO Box 40, Renews A0A 3N0 – 709/363-2500, Fax: 709/363-2143 |
| Rigolet ‡ | 259 | Labrador | Torngat Mountains | Paula Flowers, Clerk, Rigolet A0P 1L0 – 709/947-3382, Fax: 709/947-3360 |
| River of Ponds ‡ | 308 | Humber-St. Barbe-Baie Verte | St. Barbe | Margaret House-Hoddinott, Clerk, River of Ponds A0K 4M0 – 709/225-3161 |
| Riverhead ‡ | 311 | St. John's West | Placentia & St. Mary's | Ann Lee, Clerk, Riverhead A0B 3B0 – 709/525-2106 |
| Robert's Arm † | 963 | Gander-Grand Falls | Windsor-Springdale | Ada Rowsell, Clerk, PO Box 10, Robert's Arm A0J 1R0 – 709/652-3331, Fax: 709/652-3079 |
| Rocky Harbour ‡ | 1,066 | Humber-St. Barbe-Baie Verte | St. Barbe | Colleen Hutchings, Acting Clerk, PO Box 24, Rocky Harbour A0K 4N0 – 709/458-2376, Fax: 709/458-2293 |
| Roddickton † | 1,103 | Humber-St. Barbe-Baie Verte | The Straits & White Bay North | Arthur Locke, Clerk, PO Box 10, Roddickton A0K 4P0 – 709/457-2413, Fax: 709/457-2663 |
| Rose Blanche-Harbour Le Cou † | 814 | Burin-St. George's | Burgeo & La Poile | Ivy Cokes, Clerk, PO Box 159, Rose Blanche A0M 1P0 – 709/956-2540, Fax: 709/956-2541 |

Cities in CAPITALS; Towns marked †; Communities marked ‡. An in-depth listing for municipalities marked with * appears in Part 2 (check Index for page numbers).

| MUNICIPALITY | 1996 POP. | FEDERAL ELECTORAL DISTRICT | PROVINCIAL ELECTORAL DISTRICT | CONTACT PERSON WITH ADDRESS, PHONE & FAX |
|---|---|---|---|---|
| Rushoon ‡ | 442 | Burin-St. George's | Burin-Placentia West | Jacqueline Gaulton, Clerk, Rushoon A0E 2S0 – 709/443-2572 |
| St. Alban's † | 1,563 | Burin-St. George's | Fortune Bay-Cape La Hune | Genevieve Tremblett, Clerk, PO Box 10, St. Alban's A0H 2E0 – 709/538-3132, Fax: 709/538-3683 |
| St. Anthony † | 2,996 | Humber-St. Barbe-Baie Verte | The Straits & White Bay North | Wallace Green, Clerk, PO Box 430, St. Anthony A0K 4S0 – 709/454-3454, Fax: 709/454-4154 |
| St. Bernard's-Jacques Fontaine † | 751 | Burin-St. George's | Bellevue | Marie McCarthy, Clerk, PO Box 70, St. Bernard's A0E 2T0 – 709/461-2257, Fax: 709/461-2179 |
| St. Brendan's ‡ | 321 | Bonavista-Trinity-Conception | Terra Nova | Rita White, Clerk, PO Box 43, St. Brendan's A0G 3V0 – 709/669-4271 |
| St. Bride's ‡ | 542 | St. John's West | Placentia & St. Mary's | Joan McGrath, Clerk, St. Bride's A0B 2Z0 – 709/337-2160 |
| St. George's † | 1,536 | Burin-St. George's | St. George's-Stephenville East | Francis Alexander, Clerk, PO Box 250, St. George's A0N 1Z0 – 709/647-3283, Fax: 709/647-3180 |
| St. Jacques-Coomb's Cove † | 827 | Burin-St. George's | Fortune Bay-Cape La Hune | Francis Courtney, Clerk, PO Box 102, English Harbour W. A0M 1M0 – 709/888-6141, Fax: 709/888-6102 |
| *ST. JOHN'S | 101,936 | St. John's East; St. John's West | Kilbride; Signal Hill-Quidi Vidi; St. J. Centre; St. J. East; St. J. North; St. J. South; St. J. West; Virginia Waters; Waterford Valley | Damien Ryan, City Clerk & Director, Administrative Services, City Hall, PO Box 908, St. John's A1C 5M2 – 709/576-8600, Fax: 709/576-8474 |
| St. Joseph's ‡ | 176 | St. John's West | Placentia & St. Mary's | Joseph Dobbin, Clerk, PO Box 9, St. Joseph's A0B 3A0 – 709/521-2486 |
| St. Lawrence † | 1,697 | Burin-St. George's | Grand Bank | Gregory Quirke, Clerk, PO Box 128, St. Lawrence A0E 2V0 – 709/873-2222, Fax: 709/873-3352 |
| St. Lewis ‡ | 312 | Labrador | Cartwright-L'Anse au Clair | Ruby Poole, Clerk, St. Lewis A0K 4W0 – 709/920-2197, Fax: 709/920-2197 |
| St. Lunaire-Griquet † | 929 | Humber-St. Barbe-Baie Verte | The Straits & White Bay North | Glenda Burden, Clerk, PO Box 9, St. Lunaire-Griquet A0K 2X0 – 709/623-2323, Fax: 709/623-2170 |
| St. Mary's ‡ | 617 | St. John's West | Placentia & St. Mary's | Theresa Power, Clerk, PO Box 15, St. Mary's A0B 3B0 – 709/525-2586, Fax: 709/525-2641 |
| St. Pauls ‡ | 384 | Humber-St. Barbe-Baie Verte | St. Barbe | Verna Legge, Clerk, PO Box 9, St. Pauls A0K 4Y0 – 709/243-2279, Fax: 709/243-2299 |
| St. Shotts ‡ | 209 | St. John's West | Placentia & St. Mary's | Raymond Molloy, Clerk, St. Shotts A0A 3R0 – 709/438-2454 |
| St. Vincent's-St. Stephen's-Peter's River † | 589 | St. John's West | Placentia & St. Mary's | Madonna Stamp, Clerk, PO Box 39, St. Vincent's A0B 3C0 – 709/525-2540, Fax: 709/525-2110 |
| Sally's Cove ‡ | 53 | Humber-St. Barbe-Baie Verte | St. Barbe | Inez Roberts, Clerk, PO Box 14, Sally's Cove A0K 4Z0 – 709/458-2529 |
| Salmon Cove † | 786 | Bonavista-Trinity-Conception | Carbonear-Harbour Grace | Jacqueline Deering, Clerk, General Delivery, Salmon Cove A0A 3S0 – 709/596-2101, Fax: 709/596-2101 |
| Salvage † | 240 | Bonavista-Trinity-Conception | Terra Nova | Cynthia Burden, Clerk, Salvage A0G 3X0 – 709/677-3535 |
| Sandringham ‡ | 291 | Bonavista-Trinity-Conception | Terra Nova | Audrey Penney, Clerk, Sandringham A0G 3Y0 – 709/677-2317, Fax: 709/677-2317 |
| Sandy Cove ‡ | 160 | Bonavista-Trinity-Conception | Terra Nova | Anne Benger, Clerk, Site 8, PO Box 37, Eastport A0G 1Z0 – 709/677-2731 |
| Seal Cove (Fortune Bay) ‡ | 419 | Burin-St. George's | Fortune Bay-Cape La Hune | Emily Loveless, Clerk, PO Box 69, Seal Cove A0H 2G0 – 709/851-4431, Fax: 709/851-2104 |
| Seal Cove (White Bay) † | 560 | Humber-St. Barbe-Baie Verte | Baie Verte | Lily Miller, Clerk, PO Box 119, Seal Cove A0K 5E0 – 709/531-2550, Fax: 709/531-2551 |
| Seldom-Little Seldom † | 533 | Gander-Grand Falls | Twillingate & Fogo | Shirley Penney, Clerk, PO Box 100, Seldom A0G 3Z0 – 709/627-3246, Fax: 709/627-3489 |
| Small Point-Broad Cove-Blackhead-Adam's Cove † | 492 | Bonavista-Trinity-Conception | Carbonear-Harbour Grace | Loretta Diamond, Clerk, Site 6, PO Box 24, Adam's Cove A0A 1T0 – 709/598-2610, Fax: 709/598-2610 |
| South Brook † | 639 | Gander-Grand Falls | Windsor-Springdale | Hope Rowsell, Clerk, PO Box 63, South Brook A0J 1S0 – 709/657-2206, Fax: 709/657-2206 |
| South River † | 761 | Bonavista-Trinity-Conception | Harbour Main-Whitbourne | Sheila Bowering, Clerk, PO Box 40, South River A0A 3W0 – 709/786-6761, Fax: 709/786-6761 |
| Southern Harbour † | 635 | Bonavista-Trinity-Conception | Bellevue | Linda Ryan, Clerk, PO Box 10, Southern Harbour A0B 3H0 – 709/463-2329, Fax: 709/463-2208 |
| Spaniard's Bay † | 2,771 | Bonavista-Trinity-Conception | Port de Grave | Wayne Smith, Clerk, PO Box 190, Spaniard's Bay A0A 3X0 – 709/786-3568, Fax: 709/786-7273 |
| Springdale † | 3,381 | Gander-Grand Falls | Windsor-Springdale | Fabian Connors, Clerk, PO Box 57, Springdale A0J 1T0 – 709/673-3439, Fax: 709/673-4969 |
| Steady Brook † | 416 | Humber-St. Barbe-Baie Verte | Humber East | Wanda Baggs, Clerk, PO Box 117, Steady Brook A2H 2N2 – 709/634-7601, Fax: 709/634-7547 |
| Stephenville † | 7,764 | Burin-St. George's | St. George's-Stephenville East; Port au Port | Barry Coates, Clerk, PO Box 420, Stephenville A2N 2Z5 – 709/643-8360, Fax: 709/643-2770 |
| Stephenville Crossing † | 2,283 | Burin-St. George's | St. George's-Stephenville East | Yvonne Young, Clerk, PO Box 68, Stephenville Crossing A0N 2C0 – 709/646-2600, Fax: 709/646-2605 |

Cities in CAPITALS; Towns marked †; Communities marked ‡. An in-depth listing for municipalities marked with * appears in Part 2 (check Index for page numbers).

| MUNICIPALITY | 1996 POP. | FEDERAL ELECTORAL DISTRICT | PROVINCIAL ELECTORAL DISTRICT | CONTACT PERSON WITH ADDRESS, PHONE & FAX |
|---|---|---|---|---|
| Summerford † | 1,137 | Gander-Grand Falls | Twillingate & Fogo | Vicky Anstey, Clerk, PO Box 59, Summerford A0G 4E0 – 709/629-3419, Fax: 709/629-7532 |
| Sunnyside † | 621 | Bonavista-Trinity-Conception | Bellevue | Wanda Holloway, Clerk, PO Box 89, Sunnyside A0B 3J0 – 709/472-4506, Fax: 709/472-4182 |
| Terra Nova ‡ | 28 | Bonavista-Trinity-Conception | Terra Nova | Walter Calloway, Sec., Site 1, PO Box 8, Terra Nova A0C 1L0 – 709/265-6311 |
| Terrenceville † | 737 | Burin-St. George's | Bellevue | Lucy Hickey, Clerk, PO Box 54, Terrenceville A0E 2X0 – 709/662-2204 |
| Tilt Cove ‡ | 13 | Humber-St. Barbe-Baie Verte | Baie Verte | Margaret Collins, Clerk, PO Box 22, Tilt Cove A0K 3M0 – 709/675-2641 |
| Tilting ‡ | 339 | Gander-Grand Falls | Twillingate & Fogo | Mary O'Keefe, Clerk, PO Box 40, Tilting A0G 4H0 – 709/658-7236, Fax: 709/658-7239 |
| Torbay † | 5,230 | St. John's East | Cape St. Francis | Mary Thorne, Clerk, PO Box 190, Torbay A1K 1E3 – 709/437-6532, Fax: 709/437-1309 |
| Traytown ‡ | 333 | Bonavista-Trinity-Conception | Terra Nova | Elizabeth Carter, Clerk, Traytown A0G 4K0 – 709/533-2156, Fax: 709/533-2156 |
| Trepassey † | 1,084 | St. John's West | Ferryland | Yvonne Power, Clerk, PO Box 129, Trepassey A0A 4B0 – 709/438-2641, Fax: 709/438-2749 |
| Trinity ‡ | 277 | Bonavista-Trinity-Conception | Trinity North | Joanne Mackey, Clerk, PO Box 42, Trinity A0C 2S0 – 709/464-3836 |
| Triton-Jim's Cove-Cord's Harbour † | 1,249 | Gander-Grand Falls | Windsor-Springdale | Astrid Fudge, Clerk, PO Box 10, Triton A0J 1V0 – 709/263-2264, Fax: 709/263-2381 |
| Trout River ‡ | 688 | Humber-St. Barbe-Baie Verte | Humber Valley | Vacant, Clerk, PO Box 89, Trout River A0K 5P0 – 709/451-5376, Fax: 709/451-2127 |
| Twillingate † | 2,954 | Gander-Grand Falls | Twillingate & Fogo | David Burton, Clerk, PO Box 220, Twillingate A0G 4M0 – 709/884-2438, Fax: 709/884-5278 |
| Upper Island Cove † | 2,034 | Bonavista-Trinity-Conception | Port de Grave | Baxter Drover, Clerk, PO Box 149, Upper Island Cove A0A 4E0 – 709/589-2503, Fax: 709/589-2522 |
| Victoria † | 1,849 | Bonavista-Trinity-Conception | Carbonear-Harbour Grace | Sharon Snooks, Clerk, PO Box 130, Victoria A0A 4G0 – 709/596-3783, Fax: 709/596-5020 |
| Wabana † | 3,136 | St. John's East | Conception Bay East & Bell Island | Diane Butler, Clerk, PO Box 1229, Bell Island A0A 4H0 – 709/488-2990, Fax: 709/488-3181 |
| Wabush † | 2,018 | Labrador | Labrador West | Florence Harnett, Clerk, PO Box 190, Wabush A0R 1B0 – 709/282-5696, Fax: 709/282-5142 |
| West St. Modeste ‡ | 170 | Labrador | Cartwright-L'Anse au Clair | Robin O'Dell, Clerk, West St. Modeste A0K 5S0 – 709/927-5583, Fax: 709/927-5898 |
| Westport ‡ | 412 | Humber-St. Barbe-Baie Verte | Baie Verte | Peggy Randell, Clerk, PO Box 29, Westport A0K 5R0 – 709/224-5501, Fax: 709/224-5501 |
| Whitbourne † | 988 | Bonavista-Trinity-Conception | Harbour Main-Whitbourne | Wanda Lynch, Clerk, General Delivery, Whitbourne A0B 3K0 – 709/759-2780, Fax: 709/759-2016 |
| Whiteway ‡ | 360 | Bonavista-Trinity-Conception | Trinity-Bay de Verde | Lori Harnum, Clerk, Whiteway A0B 3L0 – 709/588-2948, Fax: 709/588-2837 |
| Winterland ‡ | 318 | Burin-St. George's | Grand Bank | Marlyese Simms, Clerk, Winterland A0E 2Y0 – 709/279-3701, Fax: 709/583-2010 |
| Winterton † | 622 | Bonavista-Trinity-Conception | Trinity-Bay de Verde | Joan Hiscock, Clerk, PO Box 59, Winterton A0B 3M0 – 709/583-2010, Fax: 709/583-2099 |
| Witless Bay † | 1,118 | St. John's West | Ferryland | Joan Yard, Clerk, PO Box 147, Witless Bay A0A 4K0 – 709/334-3407, Fax: 709/334-2377 |
| Woodstock ‡ | 289 | Humber-St. Barbe-Baie Verte | Baie Verte | Cora-Lee Decker, Clerk, Woodstock A0K 5X0 – 709/251-3176, Fax: 709/251-4111 |
| Woody Point ‡ | 400 | Humber-St. Barbe-Baie Verte | Humber Valley | Judy Goosney, Clerk, PO Box 76, Bonne Bay A0K 1P0 – 709/453-2273 |
| York Harbour ‡ | 416 | Humber-St. Barbe-Baie Verte | Bay of Islands | Marina Kendall, Clerk, York Harbour A0L 1L0 – 709/681-2280 |

## THE ROYAL ARMS OF CANADA BY PROCLAMATION OF KING GEORGE V IN 1921

The Royal Arms of Canada were established by proclamation of King George V on 21 November, 1921. On the advice of the Prime Minister of Canada, Her Majesty the Queen approved, on 12 July, 1994, that the arms be augmented with a ribbon bearing the motto of the Order of Canada, DESIDERANTES MELIOREM PATRIAM – "They desire a better country".

This coat of arms was developed by a special committee appointed by Order in Council and is substantially based on a version of the Royal Arms of the United Kingdom, featuring the historic arms of England and Scotland. To this were added the old arms of Royal France and the historic emblem of Ireland, the harp of Tara, thus honouring many of the founding European peoples of modern Canada. To mark these arms as Canadian, the three red maple leaves on a field of white were added.

The supporters, and the crest, above the helmet, are also versions of elements of the Royal Arms of the United Kingdom, including the lion of England and unicorn of Scotland. The lion holds the Union Jack and the unicorn, the banner of Royal France. The crowned lion holding the maple leaf, which is the Royal Crest of Canada, has, since 1981, also been the official symbol of the Governor General of Canada, the Sovereign's representative.

At the base of the Royal Arms are the floral emblems of the founding nations of Canada, the English Rose, the Scottish Thistle, the French Lily and the Irish Shamrock.

The motto — A MARI USQUE AD MARE — "From sea to sea" — is an extract from the Latin version of verse 8 of the 72nd Psalm — "He shall have dominion also from sea to sea, and from the river unto the ends of the earth."

## THE NATIONAL FLAG

The National Flag of Canada, otherwise known as the Canadian Flag, was approved by Parliament and proclaimed by Her Majesty Queen Elizabeth II to be in force as of February 15, 1965. It is described as a red flag of the proportions two by length and one by width, containing in its centre a white square the width of the flag, bearing a single red maple leaf. Red and white are the official colours of Canada, as approved by the proclamation of King George V appointing Arms for Canada in 1921. The Flag is flown on land at all federal government buildings, airports, and military bases within and outside Canada, and may appropriately be flown or displayed by individuals and organizations. The Flag is the proper national colours for all Canadian ships and boats; and it is the flag flown on Canadian Naval vessels.

The Flag is flown daily from sunrise to sunset. However, it is not contrary to etiquette to have the Flag flying at night. No flag, banner or pennant should be flown or displayed above the Canadian Flag. Flags flown together should be approximately the same size and flown from separate staffs at the same height. When flown on a speaker's platform, it should be to the right of the speaker. When used in the body of an auditorium; it should be to the right of the audience. When two or more than three flags are flown together, the Flag should be on the left as seen by spectators in front of the flags. When three flags are flown together, the Canadian Flag should occupy the central position.

A complete set of rules for flying the Canadian Flag can be obtained from the Department of Canadian Heritage.

## THE ROYAL UNION FLAG

The Royal Union Flag, generally known as the Union Jack, was approved by Parliament on December 18, 1964 for continued use in Canada as a symbol of Canada's membership in the Commonwealth of Nations and of her allegiance to the Crown. It will, where physical arrangements make it possible, be flown along with the National Flag at federal buildings, airports, and military bases and establishments within Canada on the date of the official observance of the Queen's birthday, the Anniversary of the Statute of Westminster (December 11th), Commonwealth Day (second Monday in March), and on the occasions of Royal Visits and certain Commonwealth gatherings in Canada.

## QUEEN'S PERSONAL CANADIAN FLAG

In 1962, Her Majesty The Queen adopted a personal flag specifically for use in Canada. The design comprises the Arms of Canada with The Queen's own device in the centre. The device – the initial "E" surmounted by the St. Edward's Crown within a chaplet of roses – is gold on a blue background.

When the Queen is in Canada, this flag is flown, day and night, at any building in which She is in residence. Generally, the flag is also flown behind the saluting base when She conducts troop inspections, on all vehicles in which She travels, and on Her Majesty's Canadian ships (HMCS) when the Queen is aboard.

## FLAG OF THE GOVERNOR GENERAL

The Governor General's standard is a blue flag with the crest of the Arms of Canada in its centre. A symbol of the Sovereignty of Canada, the crest is made of a gold lion passant imperially crowned, on a wreath of the official colours of Canada, holding in its right paw a red maple leaf. The standard was approved by Her Majesty The Queen on February 23, 1981. The Governor General's personal standard flies whenever the incumbent is in residence, and takes precedence over all other flags in Canada, except The Queen's.

## CANADIAN ARMED FORCES BADGE

The Canadian Armed Forces Badge was sanctioned by Her Majesty Queen Elizabeth II in May 1967. The description is as follows:

Within a wreath of ten stylized maple leaves Red, a cartouche medium Blue edge Gold, charged with a foul anchor Gold, surmounted by Crusader's Swords in Saltire Silver and blue, pommelled and hilted Gold; and in front an eagle volant affront head to the sinister Gold, the whole ensigned with a Royal Crown proper.

The Canadian Forces Badge replaces the badges of the Royal Canadian Navy, the Canadian Army, and the Royal Canadian Air Force.

## ALBERTA

The Arms of the Province of Alberta were granted by Royal Warrant on May 30, 1907. On July 30th, 1980, the Arms were augmented as follows: Crest: Upon a Helm with a Wreath Argent and Gules a Beaver couchant upholding on its back the Royal Crown both proper; Supporters: On the dexter side a Lion Or armed and langued Gules and on the sinister side a Pronghorn Antelope (Antilocapra americana) proper; the Compartment comprising a grassy mount with the Floral Emblem of the said Province of Alberta the Wild Rose (Rosa acicularis) growing therefrom proper; Motto: FORTIS ET LIBER (Strong and Free) to be borne and used together with the Arms upon Seals, Shields, Banners, Flags or otherwise according to the Laws of Arms.

In 1958 the Government of Alberta authorized the design and use of an offical flag. A flag bearing the Armorial Ensign on a royal ultramarine blue background was adopted and the Flag Act proclaimed June 1st, 1968. Proportions of the flag are two by length and one by width with the Armorial Ensign seven-elevenths of the width of the flag carried in the centre. The flag may be used by citizens of the Province and others in a manner befitting its dignity and importance but no other banner or flag that includes the Armorial Ensign may be assumed or used.

**Floral Emblem:** Wild Rose (Rosa Acicularis). Chosen in the Floral Emblem Act of 1930.

**Provincial Bird:** Great horned owl (budo virginianus). Adopted May 3, 1977.

## BRITISH COLUMBIA

The shield of British Columbia was granted by Royal Warrant on March 31, 1906. On October 15th, 1987, the shield was augmented by Her Majesty Queen Elizabeth II. The crest and supporters have become part of the provincial Arms through usage. The heraldic description is as follows: Crest: Upon a Helm with a Wreath Argent and Gules the Royal Crest of general purpose of Our Royal Predecessor Queen Victoria differenced for Us and Our Successors in right of British Columbia with the Lion thereof garlanded about the neck with the Provincial Flower that is to say the Pacific Dogwood (Cornus nuttallii) with leaves all proper Mantled Gules doubled Argent; Supporters: On the dexter side a Wapiti Stag (Cervus canadensis) proper and on the sinister side a Bighorn Sheep Ram (Oviscanadensis) Argent armed and unguled Or; Compartment: Beneath the Shield a Scroll entwined with Pacific Dogwood flowers slipped and leaved proper inscribed with the Motto assigned by the said Warrant of Our Royal Predecessor King Edward VII that is to say SPLENDOR SINE OCCASU, (splendour without diminishment).

The flag of British Columbia was authorized by an Order-in-Council of June 27, 1960. The Union Jack symbolizes the province's origins as a British colony, and the crown at its centre represents the sovereign power linking the nations of the Commonwealth. The sun sets over the Pacific Ocean. The original design of the flag was located in 1960 by Hon. W. A. C. Bennett at the College of Arms in London.

**Floral Emblem:** Pacific Dogwood (Cornus Nuttallii, Audubon). Adopted under the Floral Emblem Act, 1956.

**Provincial Bird:** Steller's jay. Adopted November 19, 1987.

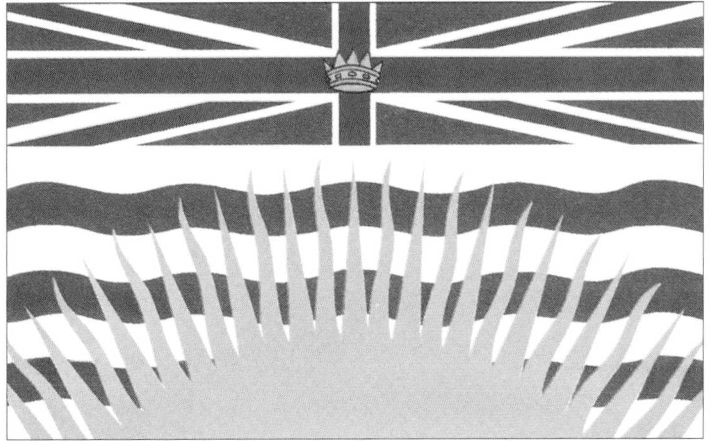

## MANITOBA

The Arms of the Province of Manitoba were granted by Royal Warrant on May 10, 1905, augmented by warrant of the Governor General on October 23, 1992. The description is as follows: above the familiar shield of 1905 is a helmet and mantling; above the helmet is the Crest, including the beaver holding a prairie crocus, the province's floral emblem. On the beaver's back is the royal crown. The left supporter is a unicorn wearing a collar bearing a decorative frieze of maple leaves, the collar representing Manitoba's position as Canada's "keystone" province. Hanging from the collar is a wheel of a Red River cart. The right supporter is a white horse, and its collar of bead and bone honours First Peoples. The supporters and the shield rest on a compartment representing the province's rivers and lakes, grain fields and forests, composed of the provincial tree, the white spruce, and seven prairie crocuses. At the base is a Latin translation of the phrase "Glorious and Free."

The flag of the Province of Manitoba was adopted under The Provincial Flag Act, assented to May 11, 1965, and proclaimed into force on May 12, 1966. It incorporates parts of the Royal Armorial Ensigns, namely the Union and Red Ensign; the badge in the fly of the flag is the shield of the arms of the province.

Description: A flag of the proportions two by length and one by width with the Union Jack occupying the upper quarter next the staff and with the shield of the armorial bearings of the province centred in the half farthest from the staff.

**Floral Emblem:** Pasque Flower, known locally as Prairie Crocus (Anemone Patens). Adopted 1906.

**Provincial Bird:** Great gray owl. Adopted July 16, 1987.

## NEW BRUNSWICK

The Arms of New Brunswick were granted by Royal Warrant on May 26, 1868. The motto SPEM REDUXIT (hope restored) was added by Order-in-Council in 1966. The description is as follows: The upper third of the shield is red and features a gold lion, symbolizing New Brunswicks' ties to Britain. The lion is also found in the arms of the Duchy of Brunswick in Germany, the ancestral home of King George III. The lower part of the shield displays an ancient galley with oars in action. It could be interpreted as a reference to the importance of both shipbuilding and seafaring to New Brunswick in those days. It is also based on the design of the province's original great seal which featured a sailing ship on water. The shield is supported by two white-tailed deer wearing collars of Indian wampum. From one is suspended the Royal Union Flag (the Union Jack), from the other the fleur-de-lis to indicate the province's British and French background. The crest consists of an Atlantic Salmon leaping from a coronet of gold maple leaves and bearing St. Edward's Crown on its back. The base, or compartment, is a grassy mound with fiddleheads as well as purple violets, the provincial floral emblem. The motto: "Spem Reduxit" is taken from the first great seal of the province.

The flag of New Brunswick, adopted by Proclamation on February 24, 1965, is based on the Arms of the province. The chief and charge occupy the upper one-third of the flag, and the remainder of the armorial bearings occupy the lower two-thirds. The proportion is four by length and two and one half by width.

**Floral Emblem:** Purple Violet (Viola Cuculata). Adopted by Order-in-Council, December 1, 1936, at the request of the New Brunswick Women's Institute.

**Provincial Bird:** Black-capped chickadee. Adopted August 1983.

## NEWFOUNDLAND

The Arms of Newfoundland were granted by Royal Letters Patent dated January 1, 1637 by King Charles I. The heraldic description is as follows: Gules, a Cross Argent, in the first and fourth quarters a Lion passant guardant crowned Or, in the second and third quarters an Unicorn passant Argent armed and crined Or, gorged with a Coronet and a Chain affixed thereto reflexed of the last. Crest: on a wreath Or and Gules a Moose passant proper. Supporters: two Savages of the clime armed and apparelled according to their guise when they go to war. The motto reads QUAERITE PRIMEREGNUM DEI (seek ye first the kingdom of God).

The official flag of Newfoundland, adopted in 1980, has primary colours of Red, Gold and Blue, against a White background. The Blue section on the left represents Newfoundland's Commonwealth heritage and the Red and Gold section on the right represents the hopes for the future with the arrow pointing the way. The two triangles represent the mainland and island parts of the province.

**Floral Emblem:** Pitcher Plant (Sarracenia Purpurea). Adopted June 1954.

**Provincial Bird:** Atlantic puffin. Proposed, but not officially adopted.

## NOVA SCOTIA

The Arms of the Province of Nova Scotia were granted to the Royal Province in 1625 by King Charles I. The complete Armorial Achievement includes the Arms, surmounted by a royal helm with a blue and silver scroll or mantling representing the Royal cloak. Above is the crest of heraldic symbols: two joined hands, one armoured and the other bare, supporting a spray of laurel for peace and thistle for Scotland. On the left is the mythical royal unicorn and on the right a 17th century representation of the North American Indian. The motto reads MUNIT HAEC ET ALTERA VINCIT (one defends and the other conquers). Entwined with the thistle of Scotland at the base is the mayflower, added in 1929, as the floral emblem of Nova Scotia.

The flag of the Province of Nova Scotia is a blue St. Andrew's Cross on a white field, with the Royal Arms of Scotland mounted thereon. The width of the flag is three-quarters of the length.

The flag was originally authorized by Charles I in 1625. In 1929, on petition of Nova Scotia, a Royal Warrant of King George V was issued, revoking the modern Arms and ordering that the original Arms granted by Charles I be borne upon (seals) shields, banners, and otherwise according to the laws of Arms.

**Floral Emblem:** Trailing Arbutus, also known as Mayflower (Epigaea Repens). Adopted April 1901.

**Provincial Bird:** Osprey. Adopted Spring, 1994.

## ONTARIO

The Arms of the Province of Ontario were granted by Royal Warrants on May 26, 1868 (shield), and February 27, 1909 (crest and supporters). The heraldic description is as follows: Vert, a Sprig of three leaves of Maple slipped Or on a Chief Argent the Cross of St. George. Crest: upon a wreath Vert and Or a Bear passant Sable. The supporters are on the dexter side, a Moose, and on the sinister side a Canadian Deer, both proper. The motto reads: UT INCEPIT FIDELIS SIC PERMANET (loyal in the beginning, so it remained).

The flag of the Province of Ontario was adopted under the Flag Act of May 21, 1965. It incorporates parts of the Royal Armorial Ensigns, namely the Union and Red Ensign; the badge in the fly of the flag is the shield of the Arms of the province. The flag is of the proportions two by length and one by width, with the Union Jack occupying the upper quarter next the staff and the shield of the armorial bearings of the province centred in the half farthest from the staff.

**Floral Emblem:** White Trillium (Trillium Grandiflorum). Adopted March 25, 1937.

**Provincial Bird:** Common loon. Proposed, but not officially adopted.

## PRINCE EDWARD ISLAND

The Arms of the Province of Prince Edward Island were granted by Royal Warrant, May 30, 1905. The heraldic description is as follows: Argent on an Island Vert, to the sinister an Oak Tree fructed, to the dexter thereof three Oak saplings sprouting all proper, on a Chief Gules a Lion passant guardant Or. The motto reads: PARVA SUB INGENTI (the small under the protection of the great).

The flag of the Province of Prince Edward Island was authorized by an Act of the Legislative Assembly, March 24, 1964. The design of the flag is that part of the Arms contained within the shield, but is of rectangular shape, with a fringe of alternating red and white. The chief and charge of the Arms occupies the upper one-third of the flag, and the remainder of the Arms occupies the lower two-thirds. The proportions of the flag are six, four, and one-quarter in relation to the fly, the hoist, and the depth of the fringe.

**Floral Emblem:** Lady's Slipper (Cypripedium Acaule). Designated as the province's floral emblem by the Legislative Assembly in 1947. A more precise botanical name was included in an amendment to the Floral Emblem Act in 1965.

**Provincial Bird:** Blue Jay (cyanocitta cristata) was designated as avian emblem by the Provincial Emblems Acts, May 13, 1977.

## QUÉBEC

The Arms of the Province of Québec were granted by Queen Victoria, May 26, 1868, and revised by a Provincial Order-in-Council on December 9, 1939. The heraldic description is as follows: Tierced in fess: Azure, three Fleurs-de-lis Or; Gules, a Lion passant guardant Or armed and langued Azure; Or, a Sugar Maple sprig with three leaves Vert veined Or. Surmounted with the Royal Crown. Below the shield a scroll argent, surrounded by a bordure Azure, inscribed with the motto JE ME SOUVIENS Azure.

The official flag of the Province of Québec was adopted by a Provincial Order-in-Council of January 21, 1948. It is a white cross on a sky blue ground, with the fleur-de-lis in an upright position on the blue ground in each of the four quarters. The proportion is six units wide by four units deep.

**Floral Emblem:** White Garden (Madonna) Lily (Lilium Candidum). Adopted under the Floral Emblem Act, 1963.

**Provincial Bird:** Snowy owl. Adopted December 17, 1987.

## SASKATCHEWAN

The complete armorial bearings of the Province of Saskatchewan were granted by Royal Warrant on September 16, 1986, through augmentation of the original shield of arms granted by King Edward VII on August 25, 1906. The heraldic description is as follows: Shield: Vert three Garbs in fesse Or, on a Chief of the last a Lion passant guardant Gules. Crest: Upon a Helm with a Wreath Argent and Gules a Beaver upholding with its back Our Royal Crown and holding in the dexter fore-claws a Western Red Lily (Lilium philadelphicumandinum) slipped all proper Mantled Gules doubled Argent. Supporters: On the dexter side a Lion Or gorged with a Collar of Prairie Indian beadwork proper and dependent therefrom a six-pointed Mullet faceted Argent fimbriated and garnished Or charged with a Maple Leaf Gules and on the sinister side a White tailed deer (Odocoileus virginianus) proper gorged with a like Collar and dependent therefrom a like Mullet charged with a Western Red Lily slipped and leaved proper. Motto: Beneath the Shield a Scroll entwined with Western Red Lilies slipped and leaved proper inscribed with the Motto MULTIS E GENTIBUS VIRES.

The official flag was dedicated on September 22, 1969, and features the Arms of the province in the upper quarter nearest the staff, with the Western Red Lily, in the half farthest from the staff. The upper green portion represents forests, while the gold symbolizes prairie wheat fields. The basic design was adopted from the prize-winning entry of Anthony Drake of Hodgeville from a province-wide flag design competition.

**Floral Emblem:** Western Red Lily (Lilium philadelphicum var. andinum). Adopted April 8, 1941.

**Provincial Bird:** Prairie sharp-tailed grouse. Adopted March 30, 1945.

## NORTHWEST TERRITORIES

The Arms of the Northwest Territories were approved by Her Majesty Queen Elizabeth II on February 24, 1956. The crest consists of two gold narwhals guarding a compass rose, symbolic of the magnetic north pole. The white upper third of the shield represents the polar ice pack and is crossed by a wavy blue line portraying the Northwest Passage. The tree line is reflected by the diagonal line separating the red and green segments of the lower portion of the shield: the green symbolizing the forested areas south of the tree line, and the red standing for the barren lands north of it. The important bases of northern wealth, minerals and fur, are represented by gold billets in the green portion and the mask of a white fox in the red.

The official flag of the Northwest Territories was adopted by the Territorial Council on January 1, 1969. Blue panels at either side of the flag represent the lakes and waters of the Territories. The white centre panel, equal in width to the two blue panels combined, symbolizes the ice and snow of the North. In the centre of the white portion is the shield from the Arms of the Territories.

**Floral Emblem:** Mountain Avens (Dryas Integrifolia). Adopted by the Council on June 7, 1957.

**Provincial Bird:** Gyrfalcon. Adopted June 1990.

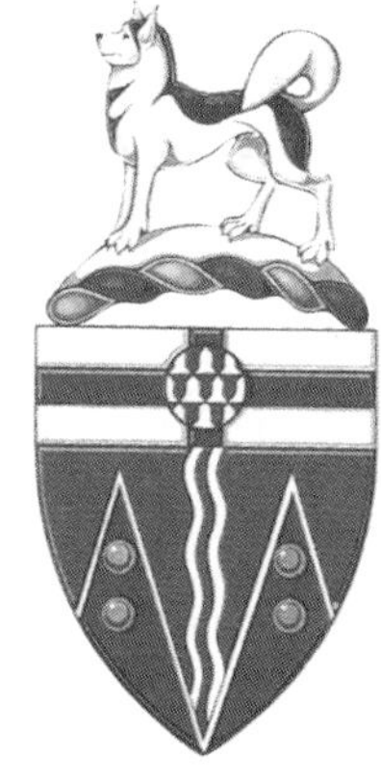

## YUKON

The Arms of the Yukon, granted by Queen Elizabeth II on February 24, 1956, have the following explanation: The wavy white and blue vertical stripe represents the Yukon River and refers also to the rivers and creeks where gold was discovered. The red spire-like forms represent the mountainous country, and the gold discs the mineral resources. The St. George's Cross is in reference to the early explorers and fur traders from Great Britain, and the roundel in vair in the centre of the cross is a symbol for the fur trade. The crest displays a Malamute dog, an animal which has played an important part in the early history of the Yukon.

The Yukon flag, designed by Lynn Lambert, a Haines Junction student, was adopted by Council in 1967. It is divided into thirds: green for forests, white for snow, and blue for water.

The flag consists of three vertical panels, the centre panel being one and one-half times the width of each of the other two panels. The panel adjacent to the mast is coloured green, the centre panel is coloured white and has the Yukon Crest disposed above a symbolic representation of thefloral emblem of the territory, epilobium augustifolium, (fireweed), and the panel on the fly is coloured blue. The stem and leaves of the floral emblem are coloured green, and the flowers thereof are coloured red. The Yukon Crest is coloured red and blue, with the Malamute dog coloured black.

**Floral Emblem:** Fireweed (Epilobium Angustifolium). Adopted November 16, 1957.

**Provincial Bird:** Common raven. Adopted October 28, 1985.

## ORDER OF CANADA

Companions of the Order of Canada

Members of the Order of Canada

Officers of the Order of Canada

## ORDER OF MILITARY MERIT

Officers of the the Order of Military Merit

Commanders of the Order of Military Merit

Members of the Order of Military Merit

## CANADIAN BRAVERY DECORATIONS

Star of Courage

Cross of Valour

Medal of Bravery

## MERITORIOUS SERVICE DECORATIONS

Meritorious Service Cross
Obverse (Military Version)

Meritorious Service Medal
Reverse (Civil Version)

# NORTHWEST TERRITORIES

LEGISLATION: The Cities, Towns and Villages Act/ Hamlets Act; Charter Communities Act; Property Assessment and Taxation Act; Local Authorities Elections Act.

Incorporation as a city, town or village is determined by assessed value of all assessable land. In order to incorporate as a village, a community requires total assessed value of more than $10 million; as a town an assessed value of more than $50 million; and as a city an assessed value of more than $200 million.

Municipal elections in cities, towns and villages are held on the third Monday of October; in hamlets, elections are held on the second Monday of December; in charter communities, election dates vary, depending on what has been established in the community's charter.

The term of office for a mayor and councillor in a city, town or village is three years, unless a by-law has been enacted to reduce the term to two years; in a hamlet, the term of office for a mayor is two years, unless a by-law has been enacted to establish the term at three years, and for councillors the term of office is two years and terms are staggered. In charter communities the term of office for members of council are established in the community's charter. The term of office for council members of a settlement is two years and may be staggered. The chairperson of a settlement council is chosen by the members of the council.

In cities, towns and villages members of council commence their term of office at 12 noon on the first Monday in November following their election; in hamlets the term of office commences at 12 noon on the first Monday in January; and in charter communities the commencement of terms is established in the community's charter.

Band Councils, under GWNT policy and Memorandum of Understanding may be designated as the local "governing authority" for the purposes of contracting certain municipal services i.e. water & sewage services.

Cities in CAPITALS; Towns marked †; Hamlets marked (H). An in-depth listing for municipalities marked with * appears in Part 2 (check Index for page numbers).

| MUNICIPALITY | 1996 POP. | FEDERAL ELECTORAL DISTRICT | TERRITORIAL ELECTORAL DISTRICT | CONTACT PERSON WITH ADDRESS, PHONE & FAX |
|---|---|---|---|---|
| Aklavik (H) | 727 | Western Arctic | Mackenzie Delta | Nellie Gruben, Sr. Admin. Officer, PO Box 88, Aklavik X0E 0A0 – 867/978-2361, 978-2351 (Band Office), Fax: 867/978-2434 |
| Arctic Bay (H) | 639 | Nunavut | High Arctic | Cecil Marshall, Sr. Admin. Officer, PO Box 150, Arctic Bay X0A 0A0 – 867/439-9917, 9918, Fax: 867/439-8767 |
| Arviat (H) | 1,559 | Nunavut | Kivallivik | Darren Flynn, Sr. Admin. Officer, General Delivery, Arviat X0C 0E0 – 867/857-2841, Fax: 867/857-2519 |
| Baker Lake (H) | 1,385 | Nunavut | Kivallivik | Dennis Zettler, Sr. Admin. Officer, PO Box 149, Baker Lake X0C 0A0 – 867/793-2874, Fax: 867/793-2509 |
| Broughton Island (H) | 488 | Nunavut | Baffin Central | Don Pickle, Sr. Admin. Officer, General Delivery, Broughton Island X0A 0B0 – 867/927-8832, 8117, Fax: 867/927-8120 |
| Cambridge Bay (H) | 1,351 | Nunavut | Kitikmeot | Henry Brown, Sr. Admin. Officer, PO Box 16, Cambridge Bay X0E 0C0 – 867/983-2337, Fax: 867/983-2193 |
| Cape Dorset (H) | 1,118 | Nunavut | Baffin South | Timoon Toonoo, Sr. Admin. Officer, PO Box 30, Cape Dorset X0A 0C0 – 867/897-8943, 8981, Fax: 867/897-8030 |
| Chesterfield Inlet (H) | 337 | Nunavut | Aivilik | Roy Mullins, Sr. Admin. Officer, General Delivery, Chesterfield Inlet X0E 0B0 – 867/898-9951, Fax: 867/898-9108 |
| Clyde River (H) | 708 | Nunavut | Baffin Central | Jonathon Palluq, Sr. Admin. Officer, General Delivery, Clyde River X0A 0E0 – 867/924-6220, 6301, Fax: 867/924-6293 |
| Coral Harbour (H) | 669 | Nunavut | Aivilik | Louis Primeau, Sr. Admin. Officer, General Delivery, Coral Harbour X0C 0C0 – 867/925-8867, Fax: 867/925-8233 |
| Fort Liard (H) | 512 | Western Arctic | Nahendeh | John McKee, Sr. Admin. Officer, General Delivery, Fort Liard X0G 0A0 – 867/770-4104, Fax: 867/770-4004 |
| Fort McPherson (H) | 878 | Western Arctic | Mackenzie Delta | Paul Fraser, Sr. Admin. Officer, PO Box 57, Fort McPherson X0E 0J0 – 867/952-2428, Fax: 867/952-2725 |
| Fort Providence (H) | 748 | Western Arctic | Deh Cho | Albert Lafferty, Sr. Admin. Officer, General Delivery, Fort Providence X0E 0L0 – 867/699-3441, Fax: 867/699-3210 |
| Fort Simpson (V) | 1,257 | Western Arctic | Nahendeh | John Crisp, Sr. Admin. Officer, PO Box 438, Fort Simpson X0E 0N0 – 867/695-2253, 2254, Fax: 867/695-2005 |
| Fort Smith † | 2,441 | Western Arctic | Thebacha | Roy Scot, Sr. Admin. Officer, PO Box 147, Fort Smith X0E 0P0 – 867/872-2014, 2045, Fax: 867/872-4345 |
| Gjoa Haven (H) | 879 | Nunavut | Natilikmiot | Greg Morash, Sr. Admin. Officer, General Delivery, Gjoa Haven X0E 1J0 – 867/360-7141, Fax: 867/360-6309 |
| Grise Fiord (H) | 148 | Nunavut | High Arctic | Lizzie Pallituq, Sr. Admin. Officer, General Delivery, Grise Fiord X0A 0J0 – 867/980-9959, 9060, Fax: 867/980-9052 |
| Hall Beach (H) | 543 | Nunavut | Amittuq | Marie Kringuk, Sr. Admin. Officer, General Delivery, Hall Beach X0A 0K0 – 867/928-8829, 8945, Fax: 867/928-8871 |
| Hay River † | 3,611 | Bras d'Or | Hay River | Charles Scarborough, Sr. Admin. Officer, 73 Woodland Dr., Hay River X0E 1G1 – 867/874-6522, Fax: 867/874-3237 |
| Holman (H) | 423 | Western Arctic | Nunakput | Eleanor Young, Sr. Admin. Officer, General Delivery, Holman X0E 0S0 – 867/396-3511, Fax: 867/396-3256 |
| Igloolik (H) | 1,174 | Nunavut | Amittuq | Henry Boychuk, Sr. Admin. Officer, General Delivery, Igloolik X0A 0L0 – 867/934-8940, 8830, Fax: 867/934-8757 |
| Inuvik † | 3,296 | Western Arctic | Inuvik | Don Howden, Sr. Admin. Officer, PO Box 1160, Inuvik X0E 0T0 – 867/979-2607, Fax: 867/979-2071 |
| Iqaluit † | 4,220 | Nunavut | Iqaluit | Sara Brown, Sr. Admin. Officer, PO Box 460, Iqaluit X0A 0H0 – 867/979-5600, Fax: 867/979-5922 |
| Kimmirut (H) | 397 | Nunavut | Baffin South | Raymond Kaslak, Sr. Admin. Officer, General Delivery, Kimmirut X0A 0N0 – 867/939-2247, 2002, Fax: 867/939-2045 |
| Kugluktuk (H) | 1,201 | Nunavut | Kitikmeot | PO Box 271, Kugluktuk X0E 0E0 – 867/982-4461, 4471, Fax: 867/982-3060 |
| Norman Wells † | 798 | Western Arctic | Sahtu | Alec Simpson, Sr. Admin. Officer, PO Box 5, Norman Wells X0E 0V0 – 867/587-2238, 2205, Fax: 867/587-2678 |
| Pangnirtung (H) | 1,243 | Nunavut | Baffin Central | Rita Mike, Sr. Admin. Officer, PO Box 253, Pangnirtung X0A 0R0 – 867/473-8953, 8831, Fax: 867/473-8832 |
| Paulatuk (H) | 277 | Western Arctic | Nunakput | Ken Thompson, Sr. Admin. Officer, General Delivery, Paulatuk X0E 1N0 – 867/580-3531, Fax: 867/580-3703 |
| Pelly Bay (H) | 496 | Nunavut | Natilikmiot | Marla Limousin, Sr. Admin. Officer, General Delivery, Pelly Bay X0E 1K0 – 867/769-6281, Fax: 867/769-6069 |

Cities in CAPITALS; Towns marked †; Hamlets marked (H). An in-depth listing for municipalities marked with * appears in Part 2 (check Index for page numbers).

| MUNICIPALITY | 1996 POP. | FEDERAL ELECTORAL DISTRICT | TERRITORIAL ELECTORAL DISTRICT | CONTACT PERSON WITH ADDRESS, PHONE & FAX |
|---|---|---|---|---|
| Pond Inlet (H) | 1,154 | Nunavut | Amittuq | Jake Anaviapik, Sr. Admin. Officer, General Delivery, Pond Inlet X0A 0S0 – 867/899-8934, 8935, Fax: 867/899-8940 |
| Rae-Edzo (H) | 1,662 | Western Arctic | North Slave | Ralph Butterworth, Sr. Admin. Officer, PO Box 68, Rae X0E 0Y0 – 867/392-6500, 6561, Fax: 867/392-6139 |
| Rankin Inlet (H) | 2,058 | Nunavut | Keewatin Central | Antonio Masone, Sr. Admin. Officer, PO Box 310, Rankin Inlet X0C 0G0 – 867/645-2953, Fax: 867/645-2146 |
| Repulse Bay (H) | 559 | Nunavut | Aivilik | Sheldon Dorey, Sr. Admin. Officer, General Delivery, Repulse Bay X0C 0H0 – 867/462-9952, Fax: 867/462-4144 |
| Resolute (H) | | Nunavut | High Arctic | Daniel M. Leaman, Sr. Admin. Officer, General Delivery, Resolute Bay X0A 0V0 – 867/252-3616, 3689, Fax: 867/252-3749 |
| Sachs Harbour (H) | 135 | Western Arctic | Nunakput | Jackie Kuptana, Sr. Admin. Officer, General Delivery, Sachs Harbour X0E 0Z0 – 867/690-4351, Fax: 867/690-4802 |
| Sanikiluaq (H) | 631 | Nunavut | Baffin South | Brian Fleming, Sr. Admin. Officer, General Delivery, Sanikiluaq X0A 0W0 – 867/266-8874, 8996, Fax: 867/266-8903 |
| Taloyoak (H) | 648 | Nunavut | Natilikmiot | Elwood Johnson, Sr. Admin. Officer, General Delivery, Taloyoak X0E 1B0 – 867/561-6341, Fax: 867/561-5057 |
| Tuktoyaktuk (H) | 943 | Western Arctic | Nunakput | Lucy Kuptana, Sr. Admin. Officer, PO Box 120, Tuktoyaktuk X0E 1C0 – 867/977-2286, Fax: 867/977-2110 |
| Tulita (H) | 450 | Western Arctic | | John Smith, Sr. Admin. Officer, General Delivery, Tulita X0E 0K0 – 867/588-4471, Fax: 867/588-4908 |
| Wha Ti (H) | 418 | Western Arctic | North Slave | Thomas Matus, Sr. Admin. Officer, General Delivery, Wha Ti X0E 1P0 – 867/573-3401, Fax: 867/573-3018 |
| Whale Cove (H) | 301 | Nunavut | Keewatin Central | Terry Rogers, Sr. Admin. Officer, General Delivery, Whale Cove X0C 0J0 – 867/896-9961, Fax: 867/896-9109 |
| *YELLOWKNIFE | 17,275 | Western Arctic | Yellowknife South; Yellowknife North; Yellowknife Centre; Yellowknife Frame Lake | Douglas Lagore, Sr. Administration Officer, PO Box 580, Yellowknife X1A 2N4 – 867/920-5600, Fax: 867/920-5649, URL: http://www.city.yellowknife.nt.ca |

## NOVA SCOTIA

Nova Scotia is geographically divided into 18 counties. Twelve of these constitute separate municipalities. The remaining six are each divided into two districts and each of these constitutes a separate municipality. Thus there are 24 rural municipalities. Within these areas are autonomous incorporated towns and the new regional municipalities (Cape Breton, Halifax and Queens), and other local organizations with limited jurisdiction, including school boards, boards of school trustees, village commissions, local service commissions, rural fire districts and other special purpose forms.

Incorporation of a town is governed by the Municipal Boundaries & Representation Act.

The organization of towns is specified in the Towns Act and that of rural municipalities in the Municipal Act. Villages are governed by the Village Service Act. Additional regulation is provided by the Municipal Affairs Act, the Municipal Boundaries & Representation Act, the Municipal Finance Corporation Act, and the Planning Act.

All general and special municipal elections, including elections for school board members, are governed by the Municipal Elections Act, 1979. The term of office for mayors, councillors, aldermen, and elective school board members is three years. Elections take place on the third Saturday in October, every third year, thus: October 1997, October 2000, October 2003.

Cities in CAPITALS; Regional Municipalities marked (Reg. Mun.); Towns marked †; Villages marked (V); Rural Municipalities marked (RM). An in-depth listing for municipalities marked with * appears in Part 2 (check Index for page numbers).

| MUNICIPALITY | 1996 POP. | COUNTY | FEDERAL ELECTORAL DISTRICT | PROVINCIAL ELECTORAL DISTRICT | CONTACT PERSON WITH ADDRESS, PHONE & FAX |
|---|---|---|---|---|---|
| Amherst † | 9,669 | Cumberland | Cumberland-Colchester | Cumberland North | Ed Childs, Town Mgr., Ratchford St., PO Box 516, Amherst B4H 4A1 – 902/667-3352, Fax: 902/667-3356 |
| Annapolis County (Mun.) | 22,324 | Annapolis; South West Nova | Annapolis East | Annapolis; Digby-Annapolis Royal | Jacquie Lawrence, Municipal Clerk, 752 George St., PO Box 100, Annapolis Royal B0S 1A0 – 902/532-2331, Fax: 902/532-2096, URL: http://www.tartannet.ns.ca/~munofann/ |
| Annapolis Royal † | 583 | Annapolis | West Nova | Digby-Annapolis Royal | Sherman Hudson, Clerk-Treas., 285 St. George St., PO Box 310, Annapolis Royal B0S 1A0 – 902/532-2043, Fax: 902/532-7443 |
| Antigonish † | 4,860 | Antigonish | Pictou-Antigonish-Guysborough | Antigonish | Brian MacNeil, Clerk-Treas., 274 Main St., Antigonish B2G 2C4 – 902/863-1312, Fax: 902/863-9201 |
| Antigonish County (RM) | 19,554 | Antigonish | Cape Breton Highlands-Canso | Antigonish | Alan Bond, Clerk-Treas., 42 West St., Antigonish B2G 2H5 – 902/863-1117, Fax: 902/863-5751 |
| Argyle District (RM) | 8,947 | Yarmouth | West Nova | Argyle | Robert Thibault, Clerk-Treas., 27 Courthouse St., PO Box 10, Tusket B0W 3M0 – 902/648-2311, Fax: 902/648-0367 |
| Aylesford (V) | 766 | Kings | Kings-Hants | Kings West | Dianne Steele, Clerk-Treas., PO Box 91, Aylesford B0P 1C0 – 902/847-9876 |
| Baddeck (V) | 937 | Victoria | Sydney-Victoria | Victoria | Brian Trask, Clerk-Treas., PO Box 370, Baddeck B0E 1B0 – 902/295-3231, Fax: 902/295-3331 |
| Barrington District (RM) | 7,883 | Shelburne | South Shore | Shelburne | Brian Holland, Clerk-Treas., PO Box 100, Barrington B0W 1E0 – 902/637-2015, Fax: 902/637-2075 |
| Berwick † | 2,195 | Kings | Kings-Hants | Kings West | Judith Mitchell, Clerk-Treas., 236 Commercial St., PO Box 130, Berwick B0P 1E0 – 902/538-8068, Fax: 902/538-3724 |

Cities in CAPITALS; Regional Municipalities marked (Reg. Mun.); Towns marked †; Villages marked (V); Rural Municipalities marked (RM). An in-depth listing for municipalities marked with * appears in Part 2 (check Index for page numbers).

| MUNICIPALITY | 1996 POP. | COUNTY | FEDERAL ELECTORAL DISTRICT | PROVINCIAL ELECTORAL DISTRICT | CONTACT PERSON WITH ADDRESS, PHONE & FAX |
|---|---|---|---|---|---|
| Bible Hill (V) | | Colchester | Cumberland-Colchester | Truro-Bible Hill | Robert Christianson, Clerk-Treas., 39 Pictou Rd., Bible Hill B2N 2R9 – 902/893-8083, Fax: 902/897-0430 |
| Bridgetown † | 994 | Annapolis | West Nova | Annapolis | William F. Hamilton, Clerk-Treas., 271 Granville St., PO Box 609, Bridgetown B0S 1C0 – 902/665-4637, Fax: 902/665-4039 |
| Bridgewater † | 7,351 | Lunenburg | South Shore | Lunenburg West | Lisa Rhuland, Clerk, 60 Pleasant St., PO Box 9, Bridgewater B4V 2W7 – 902/543-4651, Fax: 902/543-6876 |
| Canning (V) | 745 | Kings | Kings-Hants | Kings North | Gloria Porter, Clerk-Treas., PO Box 9, Canning B0P 1H0 – 902/582-3768 |
| Canso † | 1,127 | Guysborough | Pictou-Antigonish-Guysborough | Guysborough-Port Hawkesbury | Scott Conrod, Clerk-Treas., 2 Telegraph St., PO Box 189, Canso B0H 1H0 – 902/366-2525, Fax: 902/366-3093 |
| *Cape Breton Reg. Mun. | | Cape Breton | Sydney-Victoria; Bras d'Or | Cape Breton Centre; Cape Breton East; Cape Breton North; Cape Breton Nova; Cape Breton South; Cape Breton-The Lakes | Bernie White, Clerk, 320 Esplanade, Sydney B1P 1A7 – 902/563-5005, Fax: 902/564-0481 |
| Chester (V) | 1,590 | Lunenburg | South Shore | Lunenburg East | Annette Collicutt, Clerk-Treas., RR#1, Chester B0J 1J0 – 902/275-2118 |
| Chester District (RM) | 10,602 | Lunenburg | South Shore | Chester-St. Margaret's | Barry Lenihan, Clerk-Treas., 151 King St., PO Box 369, Chester B0J 1J0 – 902/275-3554, Fax: 902/275-4771 |
| Clare District (RM) | 9,298 | Digby | West Nova | Clare | Delphis J. Comeau, Clerk-Treas., PO Box 458, Little Brook B0W 1Z0 – 902/769-2031, Fax: 902/769-3773 |
| Clark's Harbour † | 980 | Shelburne | South Shore | Shelburne | Brian Crowell, Clerk-Treas., 2648 Main St., PO Box 160, Clark's Harbour B0W 1P0 – 902/745-2390, Fax: 902/745-1772 |
| Colchester County (RM) | 49,262 | Colchester | Cumberland-Colchester | Colchester-Musqudoboit Valley; Colchester North; Truro-Bible Hill | Andrew Beckett, Executive Director, PO Box 697, Truro B2N 5E7 – 902/897-3160, Fax: 902/895-9983 |
| Cornwallis Square (V) | | Kings | Kings-Hants | Kings West | Robyn Peterson, Clerk-Treas., PO Box 129, Waterville B0P 1V0 – 902/679-0632, Fax: 902/678-9543 |
| Cumberland County (RM) | 33,804 | Cumberland | Cumberland-Colchester | Cumberland North; Cumberland South | Rennie Bugley, CAO, PO Box 428, Amherst B4H 3Z5 – 902/667-2313, Fax: 902/667-1352 |
| Digby † | 2,199 | Digby | West Nova | Digby-Annapolis Royal | Mike Ireland, Clerk-Treas., 147 First Ave., PO Box 579, Digby B0V 1A0 – 902/245-4769, Fax: 902/245-2121 |
| Digby District (RM) | 8,926 | Digby | South West Nova | Digby-Annapolis Royal | Brian Cullen, Clerk-Treas., PO Box 429, Digby B0V 1A0 – 902/245-4777, Fax: 902/245-5748 |
| Dover (V) | | Halifax | Pictou-Antigonish-Guysborough | Guysborough-Port Hawkesbury | Leslie Boudreau Jr., Chairman, Little Dover B0H 1V0 |
| Freeport (V) | 367 | Digby | West Nova | Digby-Annapolis | Dale Tibert, Clerk-Treas., PO Box 31, Freeport B0V 1B0 – 902/839-2144 |
| Greenwood (V) | | Kings | Kings-Hants | Kings West | Marian Elsworth, Clerk-Treas., 904 Central Ave., PO Box 1068, Greenwood B0P 1N0 – 902/765-8788 |
| Guysborough District (RM) | 5,942 | Guysborough | Pictou-Antigonish-Guysborough | Guysborough-Port Hawkesbury | Shirley Nixon, Clerk-Treas., Municipal Bldg., 33 Pleasant St., PO Box 79, Guysborough B0H 1N0 – 902/533-3705, Fax: 902/533-2749 |
| *Halifax Reg. Mun. | 332,518 | | Halifax; Halifax West | Bedford-Fall River; Chester-St. Margaret's; Colchester-Musquidoboit Valley; Cole Harbour-Eastern Passage; Dartmouth Cole Harbour; Dartmouth East; Dartmouth North; Dartmouth South; Eastern Shore; Halifax Atlantic; Halifax Bedford Basin; Halifax Chebucto; Halifax Citadel; Halifax Fairview; Halifax Needham; Preston; Sackville Beaverbank; Sackville Cobequid; Timberlea-Prospect | Kenneth R. Meech, Chief Administrative Officer, 1841 Argyle St., PO Box 1749, Halifax B3J 3A5 – 902/490-4000, Fax: 902/490-4208, URL: http://www.region.halifax.ns.ca/ |
| Hants East District (RM) | 19,767 | Hants | Annapolis Valley-Hants | Hants East | Ian Glasgow, Clerk, PO Box 190, Shubenacadie B0N 2H0 – 902/758-2299, Fax: 902/758-3497 |
| Hants West District (RM) | 13,792 | Hants | Annapolis Valley-Hants | Hants West | Dwight Bennett, Clerk-Treas., Industrial Mall, 76 Morrison Dr., PO Box 3000, Windsor B0N 2T0 – 902/798-8391, Fax: 902/798-8553 |

Cities in CAPITALS; Regional Municipalities marked (Reg. Mun.); Towns marked †; Villages marked (V); Rural Municipalities marked (RM). An in-depth listing for municipalities marked with * appears in Part 2 (check Index for page numbers).

| MUNICIPALITY | 1996 POP. | COUNTY | FEDERAL ELECTORAL DISTRICT | PROVINCIAL ELECTORAL DISTRICT | CONTACT PERSON WITH ADDRESS, PHONE & FAX |
|---|---|---|---|---|---|
| Hantsport † | 1,252 | Hants | Kings-Hants | Hants West | Jeff Lawrence, Clerk-Treas., 3 Oak St., PO Box 399, Hantsport B0P 1P0 – 902/684-3211, Fax: 902/684-3417 |
| Havre Boucher (V) | 431 | Antigonish | Pictou-Antigonish-Guysborough | Antigonish | Raymond Carpenter, Clerk-Treas., Havre Boucher B0P 1P0 – 902/232-3088 |
| Hebbville (V) | 952 | Lunenburg | South Shore | Lunenburg West | Murray Jodrie, Clerk-Treas., RR#4, Bridgewater B4V 2W3 – 902/543-8181, Fax: 902/543-7123 |
| Inverness County (RM) | 20,918 | Inverness | Bras d'Or | Guysborough-Port Hawkesbury; Inverness; Victoria | Kate Beaton, Clerk-Treas., PO Box 179, Port Hood B0E 2W0 – 902/787-2274, Fax: 902/787-3110 |
| Kentville † | 5,551 | Kings | Kings-Hants | Kings North | William Boyd, Clerk-Treas., 354 Main St., PO Box 218, Kentville B4N 3W4 – 902/679-2500, Fax: 902/679-2375 |
| Kings County (RM) | 59,193 | Kings | Annapolis Valley-Hants | Kings North; Kings South; Kings West | R.G. Ramsay, CAO, 87 Cornwallis St., PO Box 100, Kentville B4N 3W3 – 902/678-6141, Fax: 902/679-2820 |
| Kingston (V) | | Kings | Kings-Hants | Kings West | Pat Fleury, Clerk-Treas., 522 Victoria Dr., PO Box 254, Kingston B0P 1R0 – 902/765-2800, Fax: 902/765-2800 |
| Lawrencetown (V) | 678 | Annapolis | West Nova | Annapolis | Dene Marshall, Clerk-Treas., 83 Lawrencetown Lane, PO Box 38, Lawrencetown B0S 1M0 – 902/584-3559, Fax: 902/584-3559 |
| Lockeport † | 692 | Shelburne | South Shore | Shelburne | Maureen Lewis, Clerk-Treas., 26 North St., PO Box 189, Lockeport B0T 1L0 – 902/656-2216, Fax: 902/656-2935 |
| Lunenburg † | 2,599 | Lunenburg | South Shore | Lunenburg | Beatrice Renton, Town Mgr., 119 Cumberland St., PO Box 129, Lunenburg B0J 2C0 – 902/634-4410, Fax: 902/634-4416 |
| Lunenburg District (RM) | 25,949 | Lunenburg | South Shore | Cheester-St. Margaret's Lunenburg; Lunenburg West | D.E. Steele, CAO, 210 Aberdeen Rd., PO Box 200, Bridgewater B4V 2W8 – 902/543-8181, Fax: 902/543-7123 |
| Mahone Bay † | 1,017 | Lunenburg | South Shore | Lunenburg | Kyle Hiltz, Clerk-Treas., 493 Main St., PO Box 530, Mahone Bay B0J 2E0 – 902/624-8327, Fax: 902/624-8069 |
| Middleton † | 1,800 | Annapolis | West Nova | Annapolis | E.L. Bennett, Clerk-Treas., 131 Commercial St., PO Box 340, Middleton B0S 1P0 – 902/825-4841, Fax: 902/825-6460 |
| Mulgrave † | 896 | Guysborough | Pictou-Antigonish-Guysborough | Guysborough-Port Hawkesbury | Nathan Gorall, Clerk-Treas., 457 MacLeod St., PO Box 129, Mulgrave B0E 2G0 – 902/747-2243, Fax: 902/747-2585 |
| New Glasgow † | 9,812 | Pictou | Pictou-Antigonish-Guysborough | Pictou Centre | Jim Langille, Clerk-Treas., 111 Provost St., PO Box 7, New Glasgow B2H 5E1 – 902/755-7788, Fax: 902/755-6242 |
| New Minas (V) | | Kings | Kings-Hants | Kings South | Linda Lockhart, Clerk-Treas., 9209 Commercial St., New Minas B4N 3G1 – 902/681-6972, Fax: 902/681-0779 |
| Oxford † | 1,352 | Cumberland | Cumberland-Colchester | Cumberland South | H.M. McCormack, Clerk-Treas., PO Box 338, Oxford B0M 1P0 – 902/447-2170, Fax: 902/447-2485 |
| Parrsboro † | 1,617 | Cumberland | Cumberland-Colchester | Cumberland South | Ashley Brown, Clerk-Treas., 1 Eastern Ave., PO Box 400, Parrsboro B0M 1S0 – 902/254-2036, Fax: 902/254-2313 |
| Pictou † | 4,022 | Pictou | Pictou-Antigonish-Guysborough | Pictou West | David L. Steele, Clerk-Treas., PO Box 640, Pictou B0K 1H0 – 902/485-4372, Fax: 902/485-8110 |
| Pictou County (RM) | 48,718 | Pictou | Central Nova | Pictou Centre; Pictou East; Pictou West | Clyde A. Purvis, Clerk, 28 Willow St., PO Box 910, Pictou B0K 1H0 – 902/485-4311, Fax: 902/485-6475 |
| Port Hawkesbury † | 3,809 | Inverness | Bras d'Or | Guysborough-Port Hawkesbury | Colin J. MacDonald, Clerk-Treas., Provincial Bldg., MacSween St., PO Box 10, Port Hawkesbury B0E 2V0 – 902/625-2746, Fax: 902/625-0040 |
| Port Williams (V) | 3,151 | Kings | Kings-Hants | Kings North | Glenda Clark, Clerk-Treas., 1045 Main St., PO Box 153, Port Williams B0P 1T0 – 902/542-4411 |
| Pugwash (V) | 897 | Cumberland | Cumberland-Colchester | Cumberland North | Katheryne Langille, Clerk-Treas., 124 Water St., PO Box 220, Pugwash B0K 1L0 – 902/243-2946, Fax: 902/243-2126 |
| *Queens Reg. Mun. | | Queens | South Shore | Queens | Clerk, PO Box 1264, Liverpool B0T 1K0 – 902/354-3453, Fax: 902/354-7473 |
| Richmond County (RM) | 11,022 | Richmond | Cumberland-Colchester | Richmond | Louis Digout, CAO, PO Box 120, Arichat B0E 1A0 – 902/226-2400, Fax: 902/226-1510 |
| River Hebert (V) | 669 | Cumberland | Cumberland-Colchester | Cumberland South | Judy Jollymore, Clerk-Treas., River Hebert B0L 1G0 – 902/251-2368 |
| St. Mary's District (RM) | 2,952 | Guysborough | Pictou-Antigonish-Guysborough | Guysborough-Port Hawkesbury | Helen MacDonald, Clerk-Treas., PO Box 296, Sherbrooke B0J 3C0 – 902/522-2049, Fax: 902/522-2309 |

Cities in CAPITALS; Regional Municipalities marked (Reg. Mun.); Towns marked †; Villages marked (V); Rural Municipalities marked (RM). An in-depth listing for municipalities marked with * appears in Part 2 (check Index for page numbers).

| MUNICIPALITY | 1996 POP. | COUNTY | FEDERAL ELECTORAL DISTRICT | PROVINCIAL ELECTORAL DISTRICT | CONTACT PERSON WITH ADDRESS, PHONE & FAX |
|---|---|---|---|---|---|
| St. Peter's (V) | | Richmond | Bras d'Or | Richmond | Rena Burke, Clerk-Treas., PO Box 452, St. Peter's B0E 3B0 |
| Shelburne † | 2,132 | Shelburne | South Shore | Shelburne | Wilmont Hardy, Clerk-Treas., 168 Water St., PO Box 670, Shelburne B0T 1W0 – 902/875-2991, Fax: 902/875-3932 |
| Shelburne District (RM) | 5,315 | Shelburne | South Shore | Shelburne | Alan Merritt, Clerk-Treas., 136 Hammond Rd., PO Box 280, Shelburne B0T 1W0 – 902/875-3083, Fax: 902/875-1278 |
| Springhill † | 4,193 | Cumberland | Cumberland-Colchester | Cumberland South | Donald Tabor, Clerk-Treas., 29 Main St., PO Box 1000, Springhill B0M 1X0 – 902/597-3751, Fax: 902/597-3637 |
| Stellarton † | 4,968 | Pictou | Pictou-Antigonish-Guysborough | Pictou Centre | A.A. Pearson, Clerk-Treas., 250 Ford St., PO Box 2200, Stellarton B0K 1S0 – 902/752-2114, Fax: 902/755-4105 |
| Stewiacke † | 1,405 | Colchester | Cumberland-Colchester | Colchester-Musqodoboit Valley | Lillian Smith, Clerk-Treas., PO Box 8, Stewiacke B0N 2J0 – 902/639-2231, Fax: 902/639-2221 |
| Tatamagouche (V) | 722 | Colchester | Cumberland-Colchester | Colchester North | Marilyn Ebsary, Clerk-Treas., Tatamagouche B0K 1V0 – 902/657-3696 |
| Tiverton (V) | | Digby | West Nova | Digby-Annapolis | Mary Cossaboom, Clerk-Treas., PO Box 16, Tiverton B0V 1G0 – 902/839-2369 |
| Trenton † | 2,952 | Pictou | Pictou-Antigonish-Guysborough | Pictou Centre | Robin Campbell, Clerk-Treas., 120 Main St., PO Box 328, Trenton B0K 1X0 – 902/752-5311, Fax: 902/752-0090 |
| Truro † | 11,938 | Colchester | Cumberland-Colchester | Truro-Bible Hill | D.G. Gilroy, Clerk-Treas., 730 Prince St., PO Box 427, Truro B2N 5C5 – 902/895-4484, Fax: 902/893-0501 |
| Victoria County (RM) | 8,482 | Victoria | Cumberland-Colchester | Victoria | Brian Trask, Clerk-Treas., Chebucto St., PO Box 370, Baddeck B0E 1B0 – 902/295-3231, Fax: 902/295-3331 |
| Westport (V) | 310 | Digby | West Nova | Digby-Annapolis | Caroline Norwood, Clerk-Treas., Bedfprd St., PO Box 1192, Westport B0V 1H0 – 902/839-2219 |
| Westville † | 3,976 | Pictou | Pictou-Antigonish-Guysborough | Pictou East | Jim Langille, Clerk-Treas., 111 Provost St., PO Box 7, New Glasgow B2H 5E1 – 902/752-4245, Fax: 902/755-6242 |
| Weymouth (V) | | Digby | West Nova | Digby-Annapolis | Clyde Cossman, Clerk-Treas., PO Box 121, Weymouth B0W 3T0 – 902/837-5257 |
| Windsor † | 3,726 | Hants | Kings-Hants | Hants West | Lawrence Armstrong, Clerk-Treas., 100 King St., PO Box 158, Windsor B0N 2T0 – 902/798-2275, Fax: 902/798-5679 |
| Wolfville † | 3,833 | Kings | Kings-Hants | Kings South | Roy Brideau, Town Mgr., 195 Main St., PO Box 1030, Wolfville B0P 1X0 – 902/542-5767, Fax: 902/542-4789 |
| Yarmouth † | 7,568 | Elgin | West Nova | Yarmouth | Raymond Gallant, CAO, 400 Main St., Yarmouth B5A 1G2 – 902/742-8565, Fax: 902/742-6244 |
| Yarmouth District (RM) | 10,722 | Yarmouth | Elgin-Middlesex-London | Yarmouth | Ken Moses, Clerk-Treas., 403 Main St., PO Box 152, Yarmouth B5A 4B2 – 902/742-7159, Fax: 902/742-3164 |

# ONTARIO

Southern Ontario is divided into upper-tier municipal units including the counties, the regional municipalities, the Municipality of Metropolitan Toronto, the District Municipality of Muskoka and the Restructured County of Oxford.

The cities, except for the City of Sarnia in the County of Lambton, and separated towns located within the counties do not come within the jurisdiction of the county councils. The municipalities within the other areas have been restructured and are all included in the upper-tier system.

County councils consist of the reeves of all the local municipalities and, in the cases of larger communities, the deputy reeves. Restructured upper-tier councils have representation established by individual statute based generally on representation by population.

Restructured units, which contain about two-thirds of the Provincial population, generally have fewer and larger local municipalities within them than do the counties. The functions of the upper-tier councils of restructured areas are more extensive than those of the counties (i.e. water supply, sewage treatment, waste management, regional planning, social services, long term financing and, in most areas, policing).

Northern Ontario consists of one regional municipality (Sudbury) and a number of local municipalities (cities, towns, villages, townships and improvement districts). The north is divided into 10 territorial districts which do not serve any municipal purpose. A large part of Northern Ontario is unorganized for municipal purposes.

Under the Municipal Elections Act, local government elections in Ontario are normally held on the second Monday in November. A standard three-year term of office is provided for all municipal councils, school boards and other local boards. Regional Chairs in Ottawa-Carleton and Hamilton-Wentworth are directly elected as well.

The preliminary list of electors is based on information obtained through triennial enumeration by mail-out questionnaire by provincial assessment commissioners during the month of May.

A mandatory advance poll is held by all municipalities on the Saturday, nine days before polling day and the Wednesday immediately before polling day. Additional advance polls may be held as provided by a by-law passed by the council of a municipality before Nomination Day. Contact the Local Government Policy Branch for any further information (Local Government Policy Branch, Ministry of Municipal Affairs, 777 Bay St., Toronto ON M5G 2E5, 416/585-7266).

NOTE: Province-wide municipal restructuring has resulted in a number of amalgamations that were in effect for the November 1997 elections or which are scheduled to take place in 1998 and 1999. Listed below are the municipalities as they existed prior to amalgamation; a footnote (following the table) explains the municipality's structure following amalgamation. Effective date of Amalgamation is January 1, 1998, unless otherwise noted. *See* Addenda for amalgamations currently under review.

Cities in CAPITALS; Towns marked †; Villages marked (V); Townships marked Twp; Municipalities marked (Mun.); Separated Towns marked (SE); Development Areas marked (DA). An in-depth listing for municipalities marked with * appears in Part 2 (check Index for page numbers).

| MUNICIPALITY | 1996 POP. | COUNTY OR DISTRICT | FEDERAL ELECTORAL DISTRICT | PROVINCIAL ELECTORAL DISTRICT | CONTACT PERSON WITH ADDRESS, PHONE & FAX |
|---|---|---|---|---|---|
| Adelaide Twp | 1,901 | Middlesex | Lambton-Kent-Middlesex | Middlesex | Sylvia E. Hammer, Clerk, RR#5, Strathroy N7G 3H6 – 519/247-3687, Fax: 519/247-3411 |
| Adjala-Tosorontio Twp | 9,361 | Simcoe | Simcoe-Grey | Simcoe West | William B. Fox, Mgr.-Clerk-Treas., PO Box 94, Loretto L0G 1L0 – 905/936-3471, Fax: 905/936-3041 |
| Admaston Twp | 1,648 | Renfrew | Renfrew-Nipissing-Pembroke | Lanark-Renfrew | Beverly Briscoe, Clerk-Treas., RR#2, Renfrew K7V 3Z5 – 613/432-2885, Fax: 613/432-4052 |
| Adolphustown Twp [1] | 946 | Lennox & Addington | Hastings-Frontenac-Lennox & Addington | Prince Edward-Lennox-South Hastings | Kathy Purcell, Clerk-Treas., RR#1, Bath K0H 1G0 – 613/373-2859, Fax: 613/373-2110 |
| Ailsa Craig (V) | 1,044 | Middlesex | Perth-Middlesex | Middlesex | Tanya Gregory, Clerk-Treas., PO Box 29, Ailsa Craig N0M 1A0 – 519/293-3401, Fax: 519/293-3475 |
| Airy Twp | 774 | Nipissing District | Renfrew-Nipissing-Pembroke | Renfrew North | Harold Luckasavitch, Adm.-Clerk-Treas., Post St., Whitney K0J 2M0 – 613/637-2650, Fax: 613/637-5368 |
| *Ajax † | 64,430 | Durham Reg. Mun. | Pickering-Ajax-Uxbridge | Durham West | Martin J. de Rond, Clerk, 65 Harwood Ave. South, Ajax L1S 2H9 – 905/683-4550, Fax: 905/683-1061 |
| Albemarle Twp | 1,217 | Bruce | Bruce-Grey | Bruce | Rhonda J. Cook, Clerk-Treas., RR#6, Wiarton N0H 2T0 – 519/534-2668, Fax: 519/534-4941 |
| Alberton Twp | 1,027 | Rainy River District | Kenora-Rainy River | Rainy River | Faye Flatt, Clerk-Treas., RR#1 - B2, PO Box 759, Fort Frances P9A 3M2 – 807/274-6053, Fax: 807/274-8449 |
| Aldborough Twp [2] | 4,042 | Elgin | Elgin-Middlesex-London | Elgin | Joanne Groch, Clerk-Treas., RR#1, PO Box 490, Rodney N0L 2C0 – 519/785-0560, Fax: 519/785-0644 |
| Alexandria † [3] | 3,531 | Stormont, Dundas & Glengarry | Glengarry-Prescott | Dundas & Glengarry | Leo Poirier, Clerk-Adm., 90 Main St. South, PO Box 700, Alexandria K0C 1A0 – 613/525-1110, Fax: 613/525-1649 |
| Alfred (V) [4] | 1,228 | Prescott & Russell | Glengarry-Prescott-Russell | Prescott & Russell | Pierre Lemay, Clerk-Treas., 265 St. Philippe St., PO Box 70, Alfred K0B 1A0 – 613/679-2292, Fax: 613/679-4939 |
| Alfred & Plantagenet Twp [4] | 2,387 | Prescott & Russell | Glengarry-Prescott | Prescott & Russell | Diane Thauvette, Clerk-Treas., 205 Old Hwy. 17, PO Box 271, Plantagenet K0B 1L0 – 613/679-2292, Fax: 613/679-1156 |
| Alice & Fraser Twp | 4,124 | Renfrew | Renfrew-Nipissing-Pembroke | Renfrew North | Bruce Lloyd, Clerk-Treas., RR#4, Pembroke K8A 6W5 – 613/735-6291, Fax: 613/735-5820 |
| Almonte † [5] | 4,611 | Lanark | Lanark-Carleton | Lanark-Renfrew | J. Des Houston, Adm.-Clerk-Treas., 14 Bridge St., PO Box 400, Almonte K0A 1A0 – 613/256-1685, Fax: 613/256-5759 |
| Alnwick Twp | 1,078 | Northumberland | Northumberland | Northumberland | Michael Rutter, Clerk-Treas., PO Box 70, Roseneath K0K 2X0 – 905/352-2841, Fax: 905/352-2032 |
| Alvinston (V) | 1,037 | Lambton | Lambton-Kent-Middlesex | Lambton | Robert G. Alderman, Clerk-Treas., 3236 River St., PO Box 28, Alvinston N0N 1A0 – 519/898-2173, Fax: 519/898-5653 |
| Amabel Twp | 3,917 | Bruce | Bruce-Grey | Bruce | William E. Johnston, Clerk-Adm., RR#1, Sauble Beach N0H 2G0 – 519/422-1551, Fax: 519/422-2844 |

Cities in CAPITALS; Towns marked †; Villages marked (V); Townships marked Twp; Municipalities marked (Mun.); Separated Towns marked (SE); Development Areas marked (DA). An in-depth listing for municipalities marked with * appears in Part 2 (check Index for page numbers).

| MUNICIPALITY | 1996 POP. | COUNTY OR DISTRICT | FEDERAL ELECTORAL DISTRICT | PROVINCIAL ELECTORAL DISTRICT | CONTACT PERSON WITH ADDRESS, PHONE & FAX |
|---|---|---|---|---|---|
| Amaranth Twp | 3,450 | Dufferin | Dufferin-Peel-Wellington-Grey | Dufferin-Peel | William Bospoort, Clerk-Treas., RR#7, Orangeville L9W 2Z3 – 519/941-1007, Fax: 519/941-1802 |
| Ameliasburgh Twp | 5,571 | Prince Edward | Prince Edward-Hastings | Prince Edward-Lennox-South Hastings | Richard L. Woodley, Clerk-Treas., PO Box 66, Ameliasburgh K0K 1A0 – 613/962-2551, Fax: 613/962-1514 |
| Amherst Island Twp [6] | 399 | Lennox & Addington | Hastings-Frontenac-Lennox & Addington | Kingston & the Islands | Diane Pearce, Clerk-Treas., Stella K0H 2S0 – 613/389-3393, Fax: 613/389-0040 |
| Amherstburg † [7] | 10,245 | Essex | Essex | Essex South | Thomas C. Kilgallin, Clerk-Adm., 271 Sandwich St. South, PO Box 159, Amherstburg N9V 2Z3 – 519/736-0012, Fax: 519/736-5403 |
| Ancaster † | 23,403 | Hamilton-Wentworth Reg. Mun. | Wentworth-Burlington | Wentworth North | Trish Sweeney, Clerk-Treas., 300 Wilson St. East, Ancaster L9G 2B9 – 905/648-4475, Fax: 905/648-3557 |
| Anderdon Twp [7] | 5,730 | Essex | Essex | Essex South | David Mailloux, CAO & Clerk., 3400 Middle Side Rd., RR#4, Amherstburg N9V 2Y9 – 519/736-5495, Fax: 519/736-8445 |
| Anson, Hindon & Minden Twp | 3,459 | Haliburton | Victoria-Haliberton | Victoria-Haliburton | Tammy McKelvey, Clerk-Treas., 7 Milne St., PO Box 359, Minden K0M 2K0 – 705/286-1260, Fax: 705/286-4917 |
| The Archipelago Twp | 555 | Parry Sound District | Parry Sound-Muskoka | Parry Sound | Billee Hurd, Deputy Clerk, 9 James St., Parry Sound P2A 1T4 – 705/746-4243, Fax: 705/746-7301 |
| Arkona (V) | 560 | Lambton | Lambton-Kent-Middlesex | Lambton | Robert Jefferson, Clerk-Treas., 16 Smith St., PO Box 95, Arkona N0M 1B0 – 519/828-3947, Fax: 519/828-3268 |
| Armour Twp | 1,464 | Parry Sound District | Parry Sound-Muskoka | Parry Sound | Laura Rowley, Clerk-Treas., PO Box 533, Burk's Falls P0A 1C0 – 705/382-3332, Fax: 705/382-2068 |
| Armstrong Twp | 1,398 | Timiskaming District | Timiskaming-Cochrane | Timiskaming | Gilles Richard, Adm.-Clerk-Treas., 35 - 10th St., PO Box 546, Earlton P0J 1E0 – 705/563-2375, Fax: 705/563-2093 |
| Arnprior † | 7,113 | Renfrew | Renfrew-Nipissing-Pembroke | Lanark-Renfrew | Diane Labelle, Clerk-Adm., 105 Elgin St. West, PO Box 130, Arnprior K7S 3H4 – 613/623-4231, Fax: 613/623-8091 |
| Arran Twp | 1,707 | Bruce | Bruce-Grey | Bruce | Stan Dolphin, Clerk-Treas., RR#2, Tara N0H 2N0 – 519/934-2051, Fax: 519/934-3595 |
| Artemesia Twp [8] | 2,881 | Grey | Simcoe-Grey | Grey | Margaret Russell, Clerk-Treas., RR#2, Flesherton N0C 1E0 – 519/924-2208, 924-3019, Fax: 519/924-3806 |
| Arthur (V) | 2,139 | Wellington | Dufferin-Peel-Wellington-Grey | Wellington | Marlene M. Ternan, Clerk-Treas., 146 George St., PO Box 490, Arthur N0G 1A0 – 519/848-2120, Fax: 519/848-3551 |
| Arthur Twp | 2,529 | Wellington | Waterloo-Wellington | Wellington | Cathy More, Clerk-Treas., General Delivery, Kenilworth N0G 2E0 – 519/848-3620, Fax: 519/848-3228 |
| Ashfield Twp | 1,885 | Huron | Huron-Bruce | Huron | Linda Andrew, Clerk-Treas., RR#7, Lucknow N0G 2H0 – 519/529-7383, Fax: 519/529-1024 |
| Asphodel Twp [9] | 2,611 | Peterborough | Peterborough | Hastings-Peterborough | John M. Duchene, Clerk-Treas., RR#3, Hastings K0L 1Y0 – 705/696-2161, Fax: 705/696-3783 |
| Assiginack Twp | 926 | Manitoulin District | Algoma-Manitoulin | Algoma-Manitoulin | Sheila M. Keys, Clerk-Treas., Spragge St., PO Box 238, Manitowaning P0P 1N0 – 705/859-3196, Fax: 705/859-3010 |
| Athens (V) | 997 | Leeds & Grenville | Leeds-Grenville | Leeds-Grenville | Betty-Ann Hayes, Clerk-Treas., 1 Main St. West, PO Box 159, Athens K0E 1B0 – 613/924-2044, Fax: 613/924-2091 |
| Athol Twp | 1,383 | Prince Edward | Prince Edward-Hastings | Prince Edward-Lennox-South Hastings | Beverly Williams, Clerk-Treas., PO Box 124, Cherry Valley K0K 1P0 – 613/476-6709, Fax: 613/476-6709 |
| Atikokan Twp | 4,043 | Rainy River District | Thunder Bay-Atikokan | Rainy River | Susan Bryk, Clerk-Treas., 120 Mark St., PO Box 1330, Atikokan P0T 1C0 – 807/597-2738, Fax: 807/597-6186 |
| Augusta Twp | 7,626 | Leeds & Grenville | Leeds-Grenville | Leeds-Grenville | Ray Gilmour, Adm.-Clerk-Treas., RR#2, Prescott K0E 1T0 – 613/925-4231, Fax: 613/925-3499 |
| Aurora † | 34,857 | York Reg. Mun. | Vaughan-King-Aurora | York North | Lawrence Allison, Clerk, 100 John West Way, PO Box 1000, Aurora L4G 6J1 – 905/727-1375, Fax: 905/841-3483 |
| Aylmer † | 7,018 | Elgin | Elgin-Middlesex-London | Elgin | Phyllis Ketchabaw, Clerk, 46 Talbot St. West, Aylmer N5H 1J7 – 519/773-3164, Fax: 519/765-1446 |
| Bagot & Blythfield Twp [10] | 1,371 | Renfrew | Renfrew-Nipissing-Pembroke | Lanark-Renfrew | Cathy Reddy, Clerk-Treas., PO Box 180, Calabogie K0J 1H0 – 613/752-2222, Fax: 613/752-2617 |

Cities in CAPITALS; Towns marked †; Villages marked (V); Townships marked Twp; Municipalities marked (Mun.); Separated Towns marked (SE); Development Areas marked (DA). An in-depth listing for municipalities marked with * appears in Part 2 (check Index for page numbers).

| MUNICIPALITY | 1996 POP. | COUNTY OR DISTRICT | FEDERAL ELECTORAL DISTRICT | PROVINCIAL ELECTORAL DISTRICT | CONTACT PERSON WITH ADDRESS, PHONE & FAX |
|---|---|---|---|---|---|
| Baldwin Twp | 694 | Sudbury District | Algoma-Manitoulin | Nickel Belt | Joan Seidel, Clerk-Treas., PO Box 7095, McKerrow P0P 1M0 – 705/869-0225, Fax: 705/869-5049 |
| Bancroft † | 2,554 | Hastings | Hastings-Frontenac-Lennox & Addington | Hastings-Peterborough | Barry Wannamaker, Clerk-Treas., 24 Flint St., PO Box 790, Bancroft K0L 1C0 – 613/332-3331, Fax: 613/332-0384 |
| Bangor, Wicklow & McClure Twp | 1,154 | Hastings | Hastings-Frontenac-Lennox & Addington | Hastings-Peterborough | Donald C. Bloom, Clerk-Treas., PO Box 130, Maynooth K0L 2S0 – 613/338-2811, Fax: 613/338-3292 |
| Barclay Twp [11] | 1,578 | Kenora | Kenora-Rainy River | Rainy River | Mabel A. Korkola, Clerk-Treas., Site 108, RR#1, PO Box 75, Dryden P8N 2Y4 – 807/937-6200, Fax: 807/937-2045 |
| *BARRIE | 79,191 | Simcoe | Barrie-Simcoe-Bradford | Simcoe Centre | John E. Craig, City Clerk, 70 Collier St., PO Box 400, Barrie L4M 4T5 – 705/726-4242, Fax: 705/739-4243, URL: http://www.city.barrie.on.ca/citymin.htm |
| Barrie Twp [12] | 822 | Frontenac | Hastings-Frontenac-Lennox & Addington | Frontenac-Addington | Lynne Dodds, Clerk-Treas., PO Box 250, Cloyne K0H 1K0 – 613/336-8633, Fax: 613/336-9840 |
| Barrie Island Twp | 60 | Manitoulin District | Algoma-Manitoulin | Algoma-Manitoulin | Pam Bond, Clerk-Treas., PO Box 30, Gore Bay P0P 1H0 – 705/282-2991 |
| Barry's Bay (V) | 1,086 | Renfrew | Renfrew-Nipissing-Pembroke | Renfrew North | Robert J. Norlock, Clerk-Treas., 10 Bay St. South, PO Box 940, Barry's Bay K0J 1B0 – 613/756-2747, Fax: 613/756-0553 |
| Bastard & S. Burgess Twp [13] | 2,692 | Leeds & Grenville | Leeds-Grenville | Leeds-Grenville | Troy J. McHarg, Clerk, PO Box 500, Delta K0E 1G0 – 613/928-2251, Fax: 613/928-3097 |
| Bath (V) [6] | 1,389 | Lennox & Addington | Hastings-Frontenac-Lennox & Addington | Prince Edward-Lennox-South Hastings | Sandra E. McNamee, Adm.-Clerk-Treas., 352 Academy St., PO Box 100, Bath K0H 1G0 – 613/352-3361, Fax: 613/352-5726 |
| Bathurst Twp [14] | 3,179 | Lanark | Lanark-Carleton | Lanark-Renfrew | Cathie Ritchie, Clerk-Treas., RR#4, Perth K7H 3C6 – 613/267-5353, Fax: 613/264-8516 |
| Bayfield (V) | 833 | Huron | Huron-Bruce | Huron | Glen R, Knox, Clerk-Treas., PO Box 99, Bayfield N0M 1G0 – 519/565-2455, Fax: 519/565-2333 |
| Bayham Twp [15] | 4,721 | Elgin | Elgin-Middlesex-London | Elgin | Maureen Beatty, Clerk, PO Box 160, Straffordville N0J 1Y0 – 519/866-5521, Fax: 519/866-3884 |
| Beachburg (V) | 902 | Renfrew | Renfrew-Nipissing-Pembroke | Renfrew North | Phyllis McLeese, Clerk-Treas., 181 Main St., PO Box 100, Beachburg K0J 1C0 – 613/582-3625, Fax: 613/582-7046 |
| Beardmore Twp [16] | 418 | Thunder Bay District | Thunder Bay-Nipigon | Lake Nipigon | Margaret E. Dupuis, Clerk-Treas., 226 Main St., PO Box 270, Beardmore P0T 1G0 – 807/875-2639, Fax: 807/875-2726 |
| Beckwith Twp | 5,495 | Lanark | Lanark-Carlton | Lanark Renfrew | Yvonne L. Robert, Clerk-Treas., RR#2, Carleton Place K7C 3P2 – 613/257-1539, Fax: 613/257-8996 |
| Bedford Twp [17] | 1,112 | Frontenac | Hastings-Frontenac-Lennox & Addington | Frontenac-Addington | M.Micheline Grondin, Clerk, RR#2, Godfrey K0H 1T0 – 613/374-2066, Fax: 613/374-1584 |
| Belle River † [18] | 4,531 | Essex | Essex | Essex-Kent | Austin L. Mousseau, Clerk-Treas., 419 Notre Dame St., PO Box 580, Belle River N0R 1A0 – 519/728-2700, Fax: 519/728-4577 |
| BELLEVILLE [19] | 37,083 | Hastings | Prince Edward-Hastings | Quinte | William C. Moreton, City Clerk, City Hall, 169 Front St., Belleville K8N 2Y8 – 613/968-6481, Fax: 613/968-9534, URL: http://www.city.belleville.on.ca/ |
| Belmont (V) [20] | 1,632 | Elgin | Elgin-Middlesex-London | Elgin | Allan Hovi, Clerk-Treas., 189 Main St., Belmont N0L 1B0 – 519/644-1071, Fax: 519/644-0766 |
| Belmont & Methuen Twp [21] | 2,975 | Peterborough | Peterborough | Hastings-Peterborough | Stephen Kaegi, Clerk-Treas., RR#3, PO Box 10, Havelock K0L 1Z0 – 705/778-2308, Fax: 705/778-5248 |
| Bentinck Twp | 3,597 | Grey | Bruce-Grey | Grey | Mark Turner, Clerk-Deputy Treas., RR#1, Elmwood N0G 1S0 – 519/364-1909, Fax: 519/364-3785 |
| Bexley Twp | 1,306 | Victoria | Victoria-Haliburton | Victoria-Haliburton | Helen A. Russell, Clerk-Treas., Grandy Rd., PO Box 90, Coboconk K0M 1K0 – 705/454-3322, Fax: 705/454-2392 |
| Bicroft Twp | 634 | Haliburton | Victoria-Haliburton | Victoria-Haliburton | Frances A. Clark, Clerk-Treas., Monck Rd., PO Box 160, Cardiff K0L 1M0 – 613/339-2442, Fax: 613/339-2442 |
| Biddulph Twp | 2,208 | Middlesex | Perth-Middlesex | Middlesex | Lawrence G. Hotson, Clerk-Treas., PO Box 190, Lucan N0M 2J0 – 519/227-4491, Fax: 519/227-4998 |
| Billings Twp | 538 | Manitoulin District | Algoma-Manitoulin | Algoma-Manitoulin | Jessie M. Graham, Clerk-Treas., PO Box 34, Kagawong P0P 1J0 – 705/282-2611, Fax: 705/282-3199 |

Cities in CAPITALS; Towns marked †; Villages marked (V); Townships marked Twp; Municipalities marked (Mun.); Separated Towns marked (SE); Development Areas marked (DA). An in-depth listing for municipalities marked with * appears in Part 2 (check Index for page numbers).

| MUNICIPALITY | 1996 POP. | COUNTY OR DISTRICT | FEDERAL ELECTORAL DISTRICT | PROVINCIAL ELECTORAL DISTRICT | CONTACT PERSON WITH ADDRESS, PHONE & FAX |
|---|---|---|---|---|---|
| Black River-Matheson Twp | 3,220 | Cochrane District | Timiskaming-Cochrane | Cochrane South | Thomas E. Monahan, Clerk, 429 Park Lane, PO Box 601, Matheson P0K 1N0 – 705/273-2313, Fax: 705/273-2140 |
| Blandford-Blenheim Twp | 7,455 | Oxford | Oxford | Oxford | Keith I. Reibling, Clerk-Treas., 47 Wilmot St. South, PO Box 100, Drumbo N0J 1G0 – 519/463-5347, Fax: 519/463-5881 |
| Blanshard Twp [22] | 1,988 | Perth | Perth-Middlesex | Perth | Anthony Serpa, Clerk-Treas., RR#6, St Marys N4X 1C8 – 519/229-8707, Fax: 519/229-8928 |
| Blenheim † | 4,873 | Kent | Kent-Essex | Essex-Kent | Elinor Mifflin, Clerk-Treas., 35 Talbot St. West, PO Box 2128, Blenheim N0P 1A0 – 519/676-5405, Fax: 519/676-0244 |
| Blind River † | 3,152 | Algoma District | Algoma-Manitoulin | Algoma | Ken Corbiere, Clerk-Adm., 11 Hudson St., PO Box 640, Blind River P0R 1B0 – 705/356-2251, Fax: 705/356-7343 |
| Bloomfield (V) | 687 | Prince Edward | Prince Edward-Hastings | Prince Edward-Lennox-South Hastings | Kim White, Clerk-Treas., 289 Main St., PO Box 19, Bloomfield K0K 1G0 – 613/393-2424, Fax: 613/393-1323 |
| Blyth (V) | 991 | Huron | Huron-Bruce | Huron | John Stewart, Clerk-Treas., 103 Queen St. South, PO Box 393, Blyth N0M 1H0 – 519/523-4545, Fax: 519/523-9895 |
| Bobcaygeon (V) | 2,753 | Victoria | Victoria-Haliburton | Victoria-Haliburton | M. Mardelle Braine, Clerk-Treas., 123 East St. South, PO Box 250, Bobcaygeon K0M 1A0 – 705/738-2363, Fax: 705/738-5623 |
| Bonfield Twp | 1,765 | Nipissing District | Nipissing | Parry Sound | Lise I. McMillan, Adm.-Clerk-Treas., 365 Hwy 531, Bonfield P0H 1E0 – 705/776-2641, Fax: 705/776-1154 |
| Bosanquet † | 5,356 | Lambton | Lambton-Kent-Middlesex | Lambton | Carol P. McKenzie, Clerk, Louisa St., PO Box 269, Thedford N0M 2N0 – 519/296-4953, Fax: 519/296-5666 |
| Bothwell † | 990 | Kent | Lambton-Kent-Middlesex | Chatham-Kent | Attie Dewit, Clerk-Treas., 320 Main St., PO Box 400, Bothwell N0P 1C0 – 519/695-2722, Fax: 519/695-5079 |
| Bracebridge † | 13,223 | Muskoka Dist. Mun. | Parry Sound-Muskoka | Muskoka-Georgian Bay | R.M. Clarke, CAO, 23 Dominion St., Bracebridge P1L 1R6 – 705/645-5264, Fax: 705/645-7525 |
| Bradford West Gwillimbury † | 20,213 | Simcoe | Barrie-Simcoe-Bradford | Simcoe Centre | Juanita Dempster-Evans, Clerk-Adm., 61 Holland St. East, PO Box 160, Bradford L3Z 2A8 – 905/775-5303, Fax: 905/775-0153 |
| Braeside (V) [23] | 715 | Renfrew | Renfrew-Nipissing-Pembroke | Lanark-Renfrew | Noreen C. Mellema, Clerk-Treas., Centre St., PO Box 40, Braeside K0A 1G0 – 613/623-5433, Fax: 613/623-9423 |
| *BRAMPTON | 268,251 | Peel Reg. Mun. | Brampton Centre; Brampton West-Mississauga; Bramalea-Gore-Malton | Brampton North; Brampton South | Leonard Mikulich, City Clerk & Director, Administration, 2 Wellington St. West, Brampton L6Y 4R2 – 905/874-2000, Fax: 905/874-2119, URL: http://www.city.brampton.on.ca/ |
| Brant Twp | 3,455 | Bruce | Bruce-Grey | Bruce | Gary Napper, Clerk-Treas., RR#1, Elmwood N0G 1S0 – 519/881-0188 |
| *BRANTFORD | 84,764 | Brant | Brant | Brantford | Vacant, City Clerk, City Hall, 100 Wellington Sq., Brantford N3T 2M3 – 519/759-4150, Fax: 519/759-7840, URL: http://207.61.52.13:80/brantford/ |
| Brantford Twp | 6,487 | Brant | Brant | Brant-Haldimand | Margaret E. Kiernan, Clerk, 80 Chatham St., PO Box 1295, Brantford N3T 5T6 – 519/756-7470, Fax: 519/756-0662 |
| Brethour Twp | 181 | Timiskaming District | Timiskaming-Cochrane | Timiskaming | Roland Lachapelle, Clerk-Treas., Belle Vallée P0J 1A0 – 705/647-7632, Fax: 705/647-7632 |
| Brighton † | 4,584 | Northumberland | Northumberland | Northumberland | Christine Boutilier, Clerk-Treas., 36 Alice St., PO Box 189, Brighton K0K 1H0 – 613/475-0670, Fax: 613/475-3453 |
| Brighton Twp | 4,438 | Northumberland | Northumberland | Northumberland | Donald J. O'Neil, Clerk-Treas., 50 Chatten Rd., RR#7, Brighton K0K 1H0 – 613/475-2894, Fax: 613/475-2599 |
| Brock Twp | 11,705 | Durham Reg. Mun. | Victoria-Haliburton | Durham York | George S. Graham, Clerk, 1 Cameron St. East, PO Box 10, Cannington L0E 1E0 – 705/432-2681, Fax: 705/432-3487 |
| BROCKVILLE | 21,752 | Leeds & Grenville | Leeds-Grenville | Leeds-Grenville | Brian C. Switzer, CAO-Clerk, Victoria Bldg., 1 King St. West, PO Box 5000, Brockville K6V 7A5 – 613/342-8772, Fax: 613/342-8720, URL: http://www.brockville.com |
| Bromley Twp | 1,189 | Renfrew | Renfrew-Nipissing-Pembroke | Renfrew North | Lauretta Rice, Clerk-Treas., RR#1, Douglas K0J 1S0 – 613/649-2342, Fax: 613/649-2770 |

Cities in CAPITALS; Towns marked †; Villages marked (V); Townships marked Twp; Municipalities marked (Mun.); Separated Towns marked (SE); Development Areas marked (DA). An in-depth listing for municipalities marked with * appears in Part 2 (check Index for page numbers).

| MUNICIPALITY | 1996 POP. | COUNTY OR DISTRICT | FEDERAL ELECTORAL DISTRICT | PROVINCIAL ELECTORAL DISTRICT | CONTACT PERSON WITH ADDRESS, PHONE & FAX |
|---|---|---|---|---|---|
| Brooke Twp | 1,857 | Lambton | Lambton-Kent-Middlesex | Lambton | Gloria Ruth Bedford, Clerk-Treas., RR#7, Alvinston N0N 1A0 – 519/847-5566, Fax: 519/847-5468 |
| Brougham Twp [10] | 262 | Renfrew | Renfrew-Nipissing-Pembroke | Renfrew North | Murray Hanes, Clerk-Treas., Dacre K0J 1N0 – 613/649-2379, Fax: 613/649-2744 |
| Bruce Twp [24] | 1,510 | Bruce | Huron Bruce | Bruce | Bob Waram, Clerk-Treas., RR#3, Tiverton N0G 2T0 – 519/368-7066, Fax: 519/368-5196 |
| Bruce Mines † | 653 | Algoma District | Algoma-Manitoulin | Algoma | Kerry Vasey, Clerk-Treas., 56 Taylor St., PO Box 220, Bruce Mines P0R 1C0 – 705/785-3493, Fax: 705/785-3170 |
| Brudenell & Lyndoch Twp | 791 | Renfrew | Renfrew-Nipissing-Pembroke | Renfrew North | Corinna Frew, Clerk-Treas., PO Box 91, Quadeville K0J 2G0 – 613/758-2651, Fax: 613/758-2192 |
| Brussels (V) | 1,131 | Huron | Huron-Bruce | Huron | Donna M. White, Clerk-Treas., 399 Turnberry St., PO Box 119, Brussels N0G 1H0 – 519/887-6572, Fax: 519/887-6572 |
| Burford Twp | 5,858 | Brant | Haldimand-Norfolk-Brant | Brant Haldimand | John R. Innes, Clerk-Treas., 116 King St. East, PO Box 249, Burford N0E 1A0 – 519/449-2434, Fax: 519/449-1380 |
| Burk's Falls (V) | 986 | Parry Sound District | Parry Sound-Muskoka | Parry Sound | Jarvis W. Osborne, Clerk-Treas., 172 Ontario St., PO Box 160, Burk's Falls P0A 1C0 – 705/382-3138, Fax: 705/382-2273 |
| Burleigh & Anstruther Twp [25] | 1,451 | Peterborough | Victoria-Haliburton | Hastings-Peterborough | Patricia R. Hall, Acting Clerk, PO Box 128, Apsley K0L 1A0 – 705/656-4445, Fax: 705/656-4446 |
| *BURLINGTON | 136,976 | Halton Reg. Mun. | Burlington; Halton; Wentworth-Burlington | Burlington South-Halton Centre | Ronald C. Lathan, City Clerk, City Hall, 426 Brant St., PO Box 5013, Burlington L7R 3Z6 – 905/335-7777, Fax: 905/335-7881, URL: http://worldchat.com/cob |
| Burpee Twp [26] | 228 | Manitoulin District | Algoma-Manitoulin | Algoma-Manitoulin | M. Jeanette Clark, Clerk-Treas., General Delivery, Evansville P0P 1E0 – 705/282-3099 |
| Cache Bay † [27] | 648 | Nipissing District | Timiskaming-Cochrane | Nipissing | Pauline Pinkas, Clerk-Adm., 55 Cache St., PO Box 40, Cache Bay P0H 1G0 – 705/753-1220, Fax: 705/753-5100 |
| Caldwell Twp [27] | 1,625 | Nipissing District | Timiskaming-Cochrane | Nipissing | Marcelin L. Tellier, Clerk-Treas., 20 Hwy 64, PO Box 12, Verner P0H 2M0 – 705/594-2318, Fax: 705/594-9153 |
| Caledon † | 39,893 | Peel Reg. Mun. | Dufferin-Peel-Wellington-Grey | Dufferin-Peel | Marjory Morden, Clerk, 6311 Old Church Rd., PO Box 1000, Caledon East L0N 1E0 – 905/584-2272, Fax: 905/857-7217 |
| Caledonia Twp [28] | 1,474 | Prescott & Russell | Glengarry-Prescott-Russell | Prescott & Russell | Joanne Bougie-Normand, Clerk-Treas., 6950 County Rd. #22, RR#1, St. Bernardin K0B 1N0 – 613/678-2100, Fax: 613/678-2990 |
| Calvin Twp | 562 | Nipissing District | Nipissing | Parry Sound | Kathleen Moore, Clerk-Treas., RR#2, Mattawa P0H 1V0 – 705/744-2700, Fax: 705/744-0309 |
| *CAMBRIDGE | 101,429 | Waterloo Reg. Mun. | Cambridge | Cambridge | James Anderson, Commissioner (City Clerk), Public Access and Council Services, 73 Water St. North, PO Box 669, Cambridge N1R 5W8 – 519/623-1340, Fax: 519/740-3011 |
| Cambridge Twp [28] | 6,403 | Prescott & Russell | Glengarry-Prescott-Russell | Prescott & Russell | Roger Brunette, Clerk-Adm., 985 Hwy. 500 West, RR#3, Casselman K0A 1M0 – 613/764-5444, Fax: 613/764-3310 |
| Camden Twp | 2,142 | Kent | Lambton-Kent-Middlesex | Chatham-Kent | Shelley Wilkins, Clerk-Adm.-Treas., 25367 Kent Bridge Rd., RR#6, Dresden N0P 1M0 – 519/683-4921, Fax: 519/683-2438 |
| Camden East Twp [29] | 4,928 | Lennox & Addington | Hastings-Frontenac-Lennox & Addington | Frontenac-Addington | Dorothy Wilson, Clerk-Adm., General Delivery, Centreville K0K 1N0 – 613/378-2475, Fax: 613/378-0033 |
| Campbellford † [30] | 3,647 | Northumberland | Northumberland | Northumberland | James Timlin, Adm.-Clerk-Treas., 36 Front St. South, PO Box 1056, Campbellford K0L 1L0 – 705/653-1900, Fax: 705/653-5203 |
| Capreol † | 3,817 | Sudbury Reg. Mun. | Nickel Belt | Sudbury East | Edgar Bérubé, Clerk-Treas., 9 Morin St., PO Box 700, Capreol P0M 1H0 – 705/858-1212, Fax: 705/858-1085 |
| Caradoc Twp | 6,248 | Middlesex | Lambton-Kent-Middlesex | Middlesex | Marion Loker, Clerk-Treas., 22501 Adelaide Rd., PO Box 190, Mt. Brydges N0L 1W0 – 519/264-1001, Fax: 519/264-9634 |
| Carden Twp | 887 | Victoria | Victoria-Haliburton | Victoria-Haliburton | Jean M. Jones, Clerk-Treas., RR#1, Sebright L0K 1W0 – 705/833-2811, Fax: 705/833-2815 |
| Cardiff Twp | 733 | Haliburton | Victoria-Haliburton | Victoria-Haliburton | Roger J. Hogan, Clerk, RR#3, Bancroft K0L 1C0 – 613/339-2323, Fax: 613/339-3098 |
| Cardinal (V) | 1,777 | Leeds & Grenville | Leeds-Grenville | SDG & East Grenville | John Walsh, Acting Clerk-Treas., 618 King's 2 Hwy., PO Box 400, Cardinal K0E 1E0 – 613/657-3266, Fax: 613/657-3001 |

Cities in CAPITALS; Towns marked †; Villages marked (V); Townships marked Twp; Municipalities marked (Mun.); Separated Towns marked (SE); Development Areas marked (DA). An in-depth listing for municipalities marked with * appears in Part 2 (check Index for page numbers).

| MUNICIPALITY | 1996 POP. | COUNTY OR DISTRICT | FEDERAL ELECTORAL DISTRICT | PROVINCIAL ELECTORAL DISTRICT | CONTACT PERSON WITH ADDRESS, PHONE & FAX |
|---|---|---|---|---|---|
| Carleton Place † | 8,450 | Lanark | Lanark-Carleton | Lanark-Renfrew | Duncan H. Rogers, Clerk, 175 Bridge St., Carleton Place K7C 2V8 – 613/257-3101, Fax: 613/257-8170 |
| Carling Twp | 952 | Parry Sound District | Parry Sound-Muskoka | Parry Sound | Susan Murphy, Clerk-Adm., RR#1, Nobel P0G 1G0 – 705/342-5856, Fax: 705/342-9527 |
| Carlow Twp | 430 | Hastings | Hastings-Frontenac-Lennox & Addington | Hastings-Peterborough | Arlene Douglas, Clerk-Treas., Boulter K0L 1G0 – 613/332-1760, Fax: 613/332-2175 |
| Carnarvon Twp | 1,118 | Manitoulin District | Algoma-Manitoulin | Algoma-Manitoulin | Mary-Ann McCutcheon, Clerk-Treas., PO Box 187, Mindemoya P0P 1S0 – 705/377-5726, Fax: 705/377-5585 |
| Carrick Twp [31] | 2,431 | Bruce | Bruce-Grey | Bruce | Alex T. Mitchell, Clerk-Treas., PO Box 400, Mildmay N0G 2J0 – 519/367-5330, Fax: 519/367-5252 |
| Casey Twp | 421 | Timiskaming District | Timiskaming-Cochrane | Timiskaming | Michel Lachapelle, Clerk-Treas., PO Box 460, Belle Vallée P0J 1A0 – 705/647-7257, Fax: 705/647-7257 |
| Casimir, Jennings & Appleby Twp | 1,131 | Sudbury District | Timiskaming-Cochrane | Sudbury East | Gaétane D. Lemieux, CAO & Clerk-Treas., PO Box 70, St. Charles P0M 2W0 – 705/867-2032, Fax: 705/867-5789 |
| Casselman (V) | 2,877 | Prescott & Russell | Glengarry-Prescott-Russell | Prescott & Russell | Gilles R. Lortie, Clerk, 751 St. Jean St., PO Box 710, Casselman K0A 1M0 – 613/764-3139, Fax: 613/764-5709 |
| Cavan Twp [32] | 5,730 | Peterborough | Victoria-Haliburton | Peterborough | Nancy Davis, Clerk, 1 King St. East, PO Box 189, Millbrook L0A 1G0 – 705/932-2929, Fax: 705/932-3458 |
| Chalk River (V) | 974 | Renfrew | Renfrew-Nipissing-Pembroke | Renfrew North | Pauline G. Rantz, Clerk-Treas., 15 Main St., PO Box 59, Chalk River K0J 1J0 – 613/589-2985, Fax: 613/589-2015 |
| Chamberlain Twp | 361 | Timiskaming District | Timiskaming-Cochrane | Timiskaming | Susan Renaud, Clerk-Treas., RR#3, Englehart P0J 1H0 – 705/544-8088, Fax: 705/544-8088 |
| Chandos Twp [25] | 653 | Peterborough | Victoria-Haliburton | Hastings-Peterborough | Dorothy Walke, CAO, RR#1, Apsley K0L 1A0 – 705/656-4936, Fax: 705/656-1557 |
| Chapleau Twp | 2,934 | Sudbury District | Algoma-Manitoulin | Nickel Belt | Allan D. Pellow, Clerk & CAO, 20 Pine St., PO Box 129, Chapleau P0M 1K0 – 705/864-1330, Fax: 705/864-1824 |
| Chapman Twp [33] | 645 | Parry Sound District | Parry Sound-Muskoka | Parry Sound | Linda Saunders, Clerk-Treas., PO Box 70, Magnetawan P0A 1P0 – 705/387-4680, Fax: 705/387-4875 |
| Chapple Twp | 909 | Rainy River District | Kenora-Rainy River | Rainy River | Doris I. Dyson, Clerk-Treas., PO Box 4, Barwick P0W 1A0 – 807/487-2354, Fax: 807/487-2406 |
| Charlottenburgh Twp [34] | 7,983 | Stormont, Dundas & Glengarry | Stormont-Dundas | Cornwall | Marcel J. Lapierre, Adm.-Clerk, 19687 William St., PO Box 40, Williamstown K0C 2J0 – 613/347-2444, Fax: 613/347-3411 |
| Charlton † | 297 | Timiskaming District | Timiskaming-Cochrane | Timiskaming | Carolyn M. Ryan, Clerk-Treas., PO Box 50, Charlton P0J 1B0 – 705/544-2363, Fax: 705/544-8188 |
| CHATHAM [35] | 43,409 | Kent | Kent-Essex | Chatham-Kent | Brian W. Knott, Solicitor-Clerk, Civic Centre, 315 King St. West, PO Box 640, Chatham N7M 5K8 – 519/352-4500, Fax: 519/436-3237, URL: http://www.wincom.net/CHATHAM/ |
| Chatham Twp | 6,321 | Kent | Lambton-Kent-Middlesex | Chatham-Kent | Nelson J. Praill, Adm.-Clerk-Treas., 785 St. Clair St. Ext., Chatham N7M 5J7 – 519/352-8260, Fax: 519/352-4188 |
| Chatsworth (V) | 522 | Grey | Bruce-Grey | Grey | Elizabeth Thompson, Clerk-Treas., 184 Garafraxa St., PO Box 150, Chatsworth N0H 1G0 – 519/794-3232, Fax: 519/794-4654 |
| Chesley † | 1,904 | Bruce | Bruce-Grey | Bruce | Joan Albright, Clerk-Treas., 112 First Ave. South, PO Box 70, Chesley N0G 1L0 – 519/363-2524 |
| Chesterville (V) [36] | 1,497 | Stormont | Stormont-Dundas | Stormont-Dundas | Howard F. Smith, Clerk-Treas., 1 Mill St., Chesterville K0C 1H0 – 613/448-2342, Fax: 613/448-1232 |
| Chisholm Twp | 1,197 | Nipissing District | Nipissing | Parry Sound | Linda M. Ringler, Clerk-Treas., 2847 Chiswick Line, RR#4, Powassan P0H 1Z0 – 705/724-3526, Fax: 705/724-5099 |
| Christie Twp [37] | 537 | Parry Sound District | Parry Sound-Muskoka | Parry Sound | Craig Jeffery, Clerk, RR#3, Parry Sound P2A 2W9 – 705/732-2355, Fax: 705/732-1274 |
| Clarence Twp [38] | 10,563 | Prescott & Russell | Glengarry-Prescott-Russell | Prescott & Russell | Lynn (Leonie) Richard, Municipal Clerk, 415 Lemay St., CP 70, Clarence Creek K0A 1N0 – 613/488-2570, Fax: 613/488-2324 |
| Clarendon & Miller Twp [12] | 545 | Frontenac | Hastings-Frontenac-Lennox & Addington | Frontenac-Addington | Donna Gemmill, Clerk-Treas., PO Box 97, Plevna K0H 2M0 – 613/479-2231, Fax: 613/479-2352 |

Cities in CAPITALS; Towns marked †; Villages marked (V); Townships marked Twp; Municipalities marked (Mun.); Separated Towns marked (SE); Development Areas marked (DA). An in-depth listing for municipalities marked with * appears in Part 2 (check Index for page numbers).

| MUNICIPALITY | 1996 POP. | COUNTY OR DISTRICT | FEDERAL ELECTORAL DISTRICT | PROVINCIAL ELECTORAL DISTRICT | CONTACT PERSON WITH ADDRESS, PHONE & FAX |
|---|---|---|---|---|---|
| *Clarington (Mun.) | 60,615 | Durham Reg. Mun. | Durham | Durham East | Patti Barrie, Clerk, 40 Temperance St., Bowmanville L1C 3A6 – 905/623-3379, Fax: 905/623-4169, URL: http://www.municipality.clarington.on.ca |
| Clearview Twp | 12,407 | Simcoe | Wellington-Grey-Dufferin-Simcoe | Simcoe West | Robert Campbell, Clerk, 217 Gideon St., PO Box 200, Stayner L0M 1S0 – 705/428-6230, Fax: 705/428-0288 |
| Clifford (V) | 775 | Wellington | Waterloo-Wellington | Wellington | Dianne Epworth, Clerk-Treas., PO Box 29, Clifford N0G 1M0 – 519/327-8141, Fax: 519/327-8148 |
| Clinton † | 3,216 | Huron | Huron-Bruce | Huron | C. Marie Jefferson, Clerk-Treas., 23 Albert St., PO Box 400, Clinton N0M 1L0 – 519/482-3997, Fax: 519/482-9183 |
| Cobalt † | 1,401 | Timiskaming District | Timiskaming-Cochrane | Timiskaming | Bill Rayburn, CAO-Clerk-Treas., 18 Silver St., PO Box 70, Cobalt P0J 1C0 – 705/679-8877, Fax: 705/679-5050 |
| Cobden (V) | 1,020 | Renfrew | Renfrew-Nipissing-Pembroke | Renfrew North | Dean Sauriol, Clerk-Treas., 44 Main St., PO Box 40, Cobden K0J 1K0 – 613/646-2282, Fax: 613/646-2283 |
| Cobourg † | 16,027 | Northumberland | Northumberland | Northumberland | Richard G. Stinson, Clerk, 55 King St. West, Cobourg K9A 2M2 – 905/372-4301, Fax: 905/372-1533 |
| Cochrane † | 4,443 | Cochrane District | Timiskaming-Cochrane | Cochrane North | Pierre Demers, Clerk & CAO, 171 - 4 Ave., PO Box 490, Cochrane P0L 1C0 – 705/272-4361, Fax: 705/272-6068 |
| Cockburn Island Twp | 2 | Manitoulin District | Algoma-Manitoulin | Algoma-Manitoulin | Austin Clipperton, Clerk-Treas., Walford P0P 2E0 – 705/844-2289 |
| Colborne (V) | 2,054 | Northumberland | Northumberland | Northumberland | Jean Kernaghan, Clerk-Treas., 1 Toronto St., PO Box 357, Colborne K0K 1S0 – 905/355-2821, Fax: 905/355-3430 |
| Colborne Twp | 2,182 | Huron | Huron-Bruce | Huron | Helen R. Grubb, Deputy Treas., RR#5, Goderich N7A 3Y2 – 519/524-4669, Fax: 519/524-1951 |
| Colchester North Twp | 4,000 | Essex | Essex | Essex-South | Norma F. Meloche, Clerk-Treas., 2610 City Road #12, RR#2, Essex N8M 2X6 – 519/776-6476, Fax: 519/776-7171 |
| Colchester South Twp | 5,846 | Essex | Essex | Essex-South | Michael W. Girard, Clerk-Adm., 44 King St. East, PO Box 449, Harrow N0R 1G0 – 519/738-2282, Fax: 519/738-3404 |
| Coleman Twp | 499 | Timiskaming District | Timiskaming-Cochrane | Timiskaming | Claire Bigelow, Clerk-Treas., 10 Prospect Ave., PO Box 40, Cobalt P0J 1C0 – 705/679-8833, Fax: 705/679-8300 |
| Collingwood † | 15,596 | Simcoe | Simcoe-Grey | Simcoe West | Carman K. Morrison, Clerk-Adm., 97 Hurontario St., PO Box 157, Collingwood L9Y 3Z5 – 705/445-1030, Fax: 705/445-2448 |
| Collingwood Twp [39] | 3,904 | Grey | Simcoe-Grey | Grey | Chris Fawcett, Clerk-Mgr., Hillcrest Dr., PO Box 40, Clarksburg N0H 1J0 – 519/599-3070, Fax: 519/599-2474 |
| Conmee Twp | 729 | Thunder Bay District | Thunder Bay-Atikokan | Port Arthur | Karen Bazilewich, Clerk-Treas., RR#1, Kakabeka Falls P0T 1W0 – 807/475-5229, Fax: 807/475-5229 |
| CORNWALL | 47,403 | Stormont, Dundas & Glengarry | Stormont-Dundas | Cornwall | Richard Allaire, Clerk & CAO, 360 Pitt St., PO Box 877, Cornwall K6H 5T9 – 613/932-6252, Fax: 613/932-8145, URL: http://www.city.cornwall.on.ca |
| Cornwall Twp [40] | 6,797 | Stormont, Dundas & Glengarry | Stormont-Dundas | Cornwall | Bernard J. Chisholm, Clerk-Treas., RR#1, Long Sault K0C 1P0 – 613/933-1162, Fax: 613/933-7876 |
| Cosby, Mason & Martland Twp | 1,578 | Sudbury District | Timiskaming-Cochrane | Sudbury East | Jody E. Lundy, CAO-Clerk, 17 Dollard St., PO Box 156, Noelville P0M 2N0 – 705/898-2294, Fax: 705/898-2181 |
| Cramahe Twp | 3,420 | Northumberland | Northumberland | Northumberland | Trudy Merrill, Clerk, PO Box 39, Castleton K0K 1M0 – 905/344-7352, Fax: 905/344-5040 |
| Culross Twp [41] | 1,638 | Bruce | Huron-Bruce | Bruce | G. Elizabeth Stobo, Clerk-Treas., Gordon St., PO Box 10, Teeswater N0G 2S0 – 519/392-6623, Fax: 519/392-6266 |
| Cumberland Twp | 47,367 | Ottawa-Carleton Reg. Mun. | Carleton-Gloucester | Prescott & Russell | Carmelle Bédard, Clerk, #100, 255 Centrum Blvd., Orleans K1E 3V8 – 613/830-6200, Fax: 613/830-8741, URL: http://www.municipality.cumberland.on.ca |
| Dack Twp | 478 | Timiskaming District | Timiskaming-Cochrane | Timiskaming | Louise Williams, Clerk-Treas., RR#2, Englehart P0J 1H0 – 705/544-7525 |

Cities in CAPITALS; Towns marked †; Villages marked (V); Townships marked Twp; Municipalities marked (Mun.); Separated Towns marked (SE); Development Areas marked (DA). An in-depth listing for municipalities marked with * appears in Part 2 (check Index for page numbers).

| MUNICIPALITY | 1996 POP. | COUNTY OR DISTRICT | FEDERAL ELECTORAL DISTRICT | PROVINCIAL ELECTORAL DISTRICT | CONTACT PERSON WITH ADDRESS, PHONE & FAX |
|---|---|---|---|---|---|
| Dalton Twp | 442 | Victoria | Algoma-Manitoulin | Victoria-Haliburton | Jean M. Jones, Clerk-Treas., RR#1, Sebright L0K 1W0 – 705/833-2011 |
| Darling Twp [42] | 527 | Lanark | Lanark-Carleton | Lanark-Renfrew | Della Ranger, Clerk-Treas., RR#4, Lanark K0G 1K0 – 613/259-5263, Fax: 613/259-2694 |
| Dawn Twp [43] | 1,595 | Lambton | Lambton-Kent-Middlesex | Lambton | Donna MacDougall, Clerk-Treas., 4591 Lambton Line, RR#4, Dresden N0P 1M0 – 519/692-5148, Fax: 519/692-5511 |
| Dawson Twp [44] | | Rainy River District | Kenora-Rainy River | Rainy River | Patrick W. Giles, Clerk-Treas., PO Box 427, Rainy River P0W 1L0 – 807/852-3529, Fax: 807/852-3529 |
| Day & Bright Add'l. Twp | 217 | Algoma District | Algoma-Manitoulin | Algoma | Deborah Tonelli, Clerk-Treas., RR#2, Thessalon P0R 1L0 – 705/842-5102, Fax: 705/842-5102 |
| Deep River † | 4,491 | Renfrew | Renfrew-Nipissing-Pembroke | Renfrew North | Larry Simmons, Clerk-Treas., 100 Deep River Rd., PO Box 400, Deep River K0J 1P0 – 613/584-2000, Fax: 613/584-3237 |
| Delaware Twp [45] | 2,436 | Middlesex | Elgin-Middlesex-London | Middlesex | Marilyn Loeb, Clerk, 2652 Gideon Dr., PO Box 70, Delaware N0L 1E0 – 519/652-5441, Fax: 519/652-0412 |
| Delhi Twp | 16,521 | Haldimand-Norfolk Reg. Mun. | Haldimand-Norfolk-Brant | Norfolk | Betteanne M. Cadman, Clerk, 183 Main St., PO Box 182, Delhi N4B 2W9 – 519/582-2100, Fax: 519/582-4571 |
| Deloro (V) [46] | 183 | Hastings | Hastings-Frontenac-Lennox & Addington | Hastings-Peterborough | Frank Mills, Clerk-Treas., PO Box 459, Marmora K0K 2M0 – 613/472-2629 |
| Denbigh Abinger & Ashby Twp [47] | 717 | Lennox & Addington | Hastings-Frontenac-Lennox & Addington | Frontenac-Addington | Jack Pauhl, Clerk-Treas., Denbigh K0H 1L0 – 613/333-2736, Fax: 613/333-2736 |
| Derby Twp | 2,891 | Grey | Bruce-Grey | Grey | Bruce Hoffman, Clerk-Treas., RR#3, Owen Sound N4K 5N5 – 519/376-2672, Fax: 519/376-5284 |
| Deseronto † | 1,811 | Hastings | Prince Edward-Hastings | Prince Edward-Lennox-South Hastings | Richard J. Beare, Clerk-Adm., 331 Main St., PO Box 310, Deseronto K0K 1X0 – 613/396-2440, Fax: 613/396-3141 |
| Dorion Twp | 472 | Thunder Bay District | Thunder Bay-Nipigon | Lake Nipigon | Helena Tamminen, Clerk-Treas., Dorion Loop Rd., RR#1, Dorion P0T 1K0 – 807/857-2289, Fax: 807/857-2203 |
| Douro Twp [48] | 3,671 | Peterborough | Peterborough | Hastings-Peterborough | Robert C. Allen, Clerk-Treas. & CAO, Douro K0L 1S0 – 705/652-3374, Fax: 705/652-5061 |
| Dover Twp | 4,040 | Kent | Lambton-Kent-Middlesex | Chatham-Kent | M. Dianne Caryn, CAO & Clerk, 515 Grand Ave. West, Chatham N7L 1C5 – 519/354-3350, Fax: 519/354-1664 |
| Downie Twp [22] | 2,355 | Perth | Perth-Middlesex | Perth | Muriel King, Clerk-Treas., PO Box 181, St. Pauls Station N0K 1V0 – 519/271-0619, Fax: 519/271-0647 |
| Drayton (V) [49] | 1,427 | Wellington | Waterloo-Wellington | Wellington | Deborah Lucas Switzer, Clerk-Treas., 22 John St., PO Box 160, Drayton N0G 1P0 – 519/638-3097, Fax: 519/638-5102 |
| Dresden † | 2,589 | Kent | Lambton-Kent-Middlesex | Chatham-Kent | James L. Babcock, Adm.-Clerk-Treas., 485 St. George St., PO Box 730, Dresden N0P 1M0 – 519/683-4306, Fax: 519/683-6623 |
| Drummond Twp [50] | 3,185 | Lanark | Lanark-Carleton | Lanark-Renfrew | Linda Van Alstine, Clerk-Treas., RR#6, Perth K7H 3C8 – 613/267-5444, Fax: 613/267-3911 |
| Dryden † [11] | 6,711 | Kenora District | Kenora-Rainy River | Kenora | Linda R. Lemieux, Clerk, 30 Van Horne Ave., Dryden P8N 2A7 – 807/223-2225, Fax: 807/223-3999 |
| Dubreuilville Twp | 990 | Algoma District | Algoma-Manitoulin | Algoma | Monique Ouellet, Deputy Clerk, 23 Pine St., PO Box 149, Dubreuilville P0S 1B0 – 705/884-2340, Fax: 705/884-2626 |
| Dummer Twp [48] | 3,053 | Peterborough | Peterborough | Hastings-Peterborough | David Clifford, Adm.-Clerk-Treas., 894 South St., PO Box 92, Warsaw K0L 3A0 – 705/652-8392, Fax: 705/652-5044 |
| Dundalk (V) | 1,776 | Grey | Dufferin-Peel-Wellington-Grey | Grey | Bonnie Riddell, Clerk-Adm., 80 Main St. East, PO Box 249, Dundalk N0C 1B0 – 519/923-2144, Fax: 519/923-2685 |
| Dundas † | 23,125 | Hamilton-Wentworth Reg. Mun. | Wentworth-Burlington | Wentworth North | Susan Steele, Clerk, 60 Main St., PO Box 8584, Dundas L9H 5E7 – 905/628-6327, Fax: 905/628-5077 |
| Dungannon Twp | 1,526 | Hastings | Hastings-Frontenac-Lennox & Addington | Hastings-Peterborough | Peter Degeer, Clerk-Treas., L'Amable K0L 2L0 – 613/332-3711, Fax: 613/332-3154 |
| Dunnville † | 12,471 | Haldimand-Norfolk Reg. Mun. | Erie-Lincoln | Brant-Haldimand | Ronald T. Sparks, Clerk-Adm., 111 Broad St. East, PO Box 187, Dunnville N1A 2X5 – 905/774-7595, Fax: 905/774-4294 |
| Dunwich Twp [51] | 2,288 | Elgin | Elgin-Middlesex-London | Elgin | Ken Loveland, Clerk-Treas., 156 Main St., PO Box 329, Dutton N0L 1J0 – 519/762-2204, Fax: 519/762-2278 |

Cities in CAPITALS; Towns marked †; Villages marked (V); Townships marked Twp; Municipalities marked (Mun.); Separated Towns marked (SE); Development Areas marked (DA). An in-depth listing for municipalities marked with * appears in Part 2 (check Index for page numbers).

| MUNICIPALITY | 1996 POP. | COUNTY OR DISTRICT | FEDERAL ELECTORAL DISTRICT | PROVINCIAL ELECTORAL DISTRICT | CONTACT PERSON WITH ADDRESS, PHONE & FAX |
|---|---|---|---|---|---|
| Durham † | 2,641 | Grey | Bruce-Grey | Grey | Dan Sullivan, Clerk-Treas., 137 Garafraxa St. North, PO Box 639, Durham N0G 1R0 – 519/369-2200, Fax: 519/369-5962 |
| Dutton (V) [51] | 1,315 | Elgin | Elgin-Middlesex-London | Elgin | Kim V.H. Watson, Clerk-Treas., 199 Main St., PO Box 59, Dutton N0L 1J0 – 519/762-2736, Fax: 519/762-3739 |
| Dymond Twp | 1,270 | Timiskaming District | Timiskaming-Cochrane | Timiskaming | John A. Telfer, Clerk-Treas., PO Box 5030, New Liskeard P0J 1P0 – 705/647-6044, Fax: 705/647-6686 |
| Dysart et al Twp | 5,380 | Haliburton | Parry Sound-Muskoka | Victoria-Haliburton | Donna L. McCallum, Adm.-Clerk-Treas., Maple Ave., PO Box 389, Haliburton K0M 1S0 – 705/457-1740, Fax: 705/457-1964 |
| Ear Falls Twp | 1,170 | Kenora District | Kenora-Rainy River | Kenora | Dennis Kristjanson, Clerk-Treas., 15 Spruce St., PO Box 309, Ear Falls P0V 1T0 – 807/222-3624, Fax: 807/222-2384 |
| East Ferris Twp | 4,139 | Nipissing District | Nipissing | Parry Sound | F. Brad Claridge, Adm.-Clerk-Treas., RR#1, Corbeil P0H 1K0 – 705/752-2740, Fax: 705/752-2452 |
| East Garafraxa Twp | 2,084 | Dufferin | Dufferin-Peel-Wellington-Grey | Dufferin-Peel | Susan M. Stone, Clerk-Treas., RR#3, Orton L0N 1N0 – 519/928-5298; 855-9833, Fax: 519/928-2345 |
| East Gwillimbury † | 19,770 | York Reg. Mun. | York North | Durham-York | Beth A. McKay, Clerk-Adm., 19000 Leslie St., Sharon L0G 1V0 – 905/478-4282, Fax: 905/478-2808 |
| East Hawkesbury Twp | 3,296 | Prescott & Russell | Glengarry-Prescott-Russell | Prescott & Russell | Réjeanne Clermont, Clerk-Treas., PO Box 340, St. Eugene K0B 1P0 – 613/674-2170, Fax: 613/674-2989 |
| East Luther Grand Valley Twp | 2,773 | Dufferin | Dufferin-Peel-Wellington-Grey | Dufferin-Peel | Jane M. Wilson, Clerk-Treas., 5 Main St. North, PO Box 249, Grand Valley L0N 1G0 – 519/928-5652, Fax: 519/928-2275 |
| East Wawanosh Twp | 1,167 | Huron | Huron-Bruce | Huron | Winona E. Thompson, Clerk-Treas., PO Box 160, Belgrave N0G 1E0 – 519/357-2880, Fax: 519/357-4214 |
| East Williams Twp | 1,366 | Middlesex | Perth-Middlesex | Middlesex | Linda Groke, Clerk-Treas., 4427 Queen St., RR#1, Ailsa Craig N0M 1A0 – 519/232-4506, Fax: 519/232-9095 |
| *East York (Borough) [52] | 107,822 | Metro Mun. | Beaches-East York; Broadview-Greenwood; Don Valley West | Don Mills; York East | William Alexander, Borough Clerk, 850 Coxwell Ave., East York M4C 5R1 – 416/778-2000, Fax: 416/778-9134 |
| East Zorra-Tavistock Twp | 7,348 | Oxford | Oxford | Oxford | Jeff Carswell, Clerk & Dep. Treas., 90 Loveys St. East, PO Box 100, Hickson N0J 1L0 – 519/462-2697, Fax: 519/462-2961 |
| Eastnor Twp | 1,443 | Bruce | Bruce-Grey | Bruce | Kelly Thompson, Clerk-Treas., RR#2, PO Box 40, Lion's Head N0H 1W0 – 519/793-3227, Fax: 519/793-3725 |
| Edwardsburgh Twp | 4,938 | Leeds & Grenville | Leeds-Grenville | SDG & East Grenville | Richard Bennett, Clerk-Treas., 18 Centre St., PO Box 129, Spencerville K0E 1X0 – 613/658-3055, Fax: 613/658-3445 |
| Eganville (V) | 1,319 | Renfrew | Renfrew-Nipissing-Pembroke | Renfrew North | Vivian Rosien, Clerk-Treas., 85 Bonnechere St., PO Box 249, Eganville K0J 1T0 – 613/628-3101, Fax: 613/628-1336 |
| Egremont Twp | 2,679 | Grey | Dufferin-Peel-Wellington-Grey | Grey | Brenda Anderson, Clerk-Treas., General Delivery, County Rd. 109, Holstein N0G 2A0 – 519/334-3480, Fax: 519/334-3388 |
| Ekfrid Twp | 2,318 | Middlesex | Lambton-Kent-Middlesex | Middlesex | Janneke Newitt, Clerk-Treas., 48 Wellington St., PO Box 276, Appin N0L 1A0 – 519/289-2016, Fax: 519/289-2331 |
| Elderslie Twp | 1,231 | Bruce | Bruce-Grey | Bruce | Connie McKinnon, Clerk-Treas., PO Box 57, Chesley N0G 1L0 – 519/363-3039, Fax: 519/363-2604 |
| Eldon Twp | 2,956 | Victoria | Victoria-Haliburton | Victoria-Haliburton | Donald A. Grant, Adm.-Clerk-Treas., PO Box 247, Kirkfield K0M 2B0 – 705/438-3141, Fax: 705/438-5212 |
| Elizabethtown Twp | 7,761 | Leeds & Grenville | Leeds-Grenville | Leeds-Grenville | Stephen McDonald, Adm. & Clerk-Treas., 6544 New Dublin Rd., RR#2, Addison K0E 1A0 – 613/345-7480, Fax: 613/345-7235 |
| Ellice Twp [53] | 3,137 | Perth | Perth-Middlesex | Perth | Arnold Siroen, Clerk-Treas., General Delivery, Rostock N0K 1T0 – 519/393-6237, Fax: 519/593-5445 |
| ELLIOT LAKE | 13,588 | Algoma District | Algoma-Manitoulin | Algoma-Manitoulin | Larry E. Burling, Clerk, 45 Hillside Dr. North, Elliot Lake P5A 1X5 – 705/848-2287, Fax: 705/461-7244, URL: http://www.cityofelliotlake.com/ |

Cities in CAPITALS; Towns marked †; Villages marked (V); Townships marked Twp; Municipalities marked (Mun.); Separated Towns marked (SE); Development Areas marked (DA). An in-depth listing for municipalities marked with * appears in Part 2 (check Index for page numbers).

| MUNICIPALITY | 1996 POP. | COUNTY OR DISTRICT | FEDERAL ELECTORAL DISTRICT | PROVINCIAL ELECTORAL DISTRICT | CONTACT PERSON WITH ADDRESS, PHONE & FAX |
|---|---|---|---|---|---|
| Elma Twp [54] | 3,991 | Perth | Perth-Middlesex | Perth | George S. Tucker, Clerk-Treas., 194 King St., Atwood N0G 1B0 – 519/356-2231, Fax: 519/356-2161 |
| Elora (V) | 3,346 | Wellington | Waterloo-Wellington | Wellington | Donald D. Wilson, Adm.-Clerk-Treas., 1 MacDonald Sq., PO Box 508, Elora N0B 1S0 – 519/846-9691, Fax: 519/846-2074 |
| Elzevir & Grimsthorpe Twp [55] | 854 | Hastings | Hastings-Frontenac-Lennox & Addington | Hastings-Peterborough | Patricia Bergeron, Clerk-Treas., RR#3, PO Box 63, Tweed K0K 3J0 – 613/478-5818, Fax: 613/478-5818 |
| Emily Twp | 6,724 | Victoria | Victoria-Haliburton | Victoria-Haliburton | Nancy Paish, Clerk-Treas., RR#4, Omemee K0L 2W0 – 705/799-5254, Fax: 705/799-5957 |
| Emo Twp | 1,366 | Rainy River District | Kenora-Rainy River | Rainy River | Brenda J. Cooke, Clerk-Adm., 39 Queen St., PO Box 358, Emo P0W 1E0 – 807/482-2378, Fax: 807/482-2741 |
| Englehart † | 1,703 | Timiskaming District | Timiskaming-Cochrane | Timiskaming | Brian Koski, Adm.-Clerk-Treas., 61 Fifth Ave., PO Box 399, Englehart P0J 1H0 – 705/544-2244, Fax: 705/544-8737 |
| Enniskillen Twp | 3,288 | Lambton | Lambton-Kent-Middlesex | Lambton | Duncan McTavish, Clerk-Adm., 4465 Rokeby Line, RR#1, Petrolia N0N 1R0 – 519/882-2490, Fax: 519/882-3335 |
| Ennismore Twp [56] | 4,465 | Peterborough | Peterborough | Peterborough | Norman K. Kyle, Adm.-Clerk-Treas., 549 Ennis Rd., Ennismore K0L 1T0 – 705/292-8903, Fax: 705/292-8964 |
| Eramosa Twp | 6,317 | Wellington | Guelph-Wellington | Wellington | Virginia Sinnott, Clerk & CAO, RR#1, Rockwood N0B 2K0 – 519/856-9951, Fax: 519/856-2240 |
| Erie Beach (V) | 251 | Kent | Essex-Kent | Essex-Kent | Lisa Enid Docherty, Clerk, PO Box 100, Erieau N0P 1N0 – 519/676-3681, Fax: 519/676-1050 |
| Erieau (V) | 499 | Kent | Essex-Kent | Essex-Kent | Jane Blonde, Clerk-Treas., 780 Ross Lane, PO Box 121, Erieau N0P 1N0 – 519/676-3681, Fax: 519/676-1050 |
| Erin (V) [57] | 2,633 | Wellington | Dufferin-Peel-Wellington-Grey | Wellington | Kathryn Ironmonger, Clerk-Adm., 109 Main St., PO Box 149, Erin N0B 1T0 – 519/833-2604, Fax: 519/833-7458 |
| Erin Twp [57] | 8,024 | Wellington | Dufferin-Peel-Wellington-Grey | Wellington | Lisa Hass, Clerk, 5684 Hwy.25, PO Box 250, Hillsburgh N0B 1Z0 – 519/855-4407, Fax: 519/855-4821 |
| Ernestown Twp [6] | 12,763 | Lennox & Addington | Hastings-Frontenac-Lennox & Addington | Prince Edward-Lennox-South Hastings | Michael G. Wade, CAO-Clerk, 263 Main St., PO Box 70, Odessa K0H 2H0 – 613/386-7351, Fax: 613/386-3833 |
| Escott, Front of Twp | 1,383 | Leeds & Grenville | Leeds-Grenville | Leeds-Grenville | Marilyn Noseworthy, Clerk-Treas., 1367 County Rd. 2, Mallorytown K0E 1R0 – 613/659-3455 |
| Espanola † | 5,454 | Sudbury District | Algoma-Manitoulin | Algoma-Manitoulin | Merwyn P. Sheppard, Clerk-Treas.-Adm., #2, 100 Tudhope St., PO Box 638, Espanola P5E 1S6 – 705/869-1540, Fax: 705/869-0083 |
| Essa Twp | 16,363 | Simcoe | Simcoe-Grey | Simcoe West | Brenda Sigouin, Clerk-Adm., PO Box 10, Angus L0M 1B0 – 705/424-9770, Fax: 705/424-2367 |
| Essex † | 6,785 | Essex | Essex | Essex-South | Wayne Miller, Clerk-Adm., 33 Talbot St. South, Essex N8M 1A8 – 519/776-7336, Fax: 519/776-8811 |
| *ETOBICOKE [52] | 328,718 | Metro Mun. | Etobicoke Centre; Etobicoke-Lakeshore; Etobicoke North | Etobicoke-Rexdale; Etobicoke West; Etobicoke-Lakeshore; Etobicoke-Humber | Brenda Glover, Clerk-Treas. & Commissioner, Administrative Services, City Hall, 399 The West Mall, Etobicoke M9C 2Y2 – 416/394-8000, Fax: 416/394-8895, URL: http://www.busdev.city.etobicoke.on.ca |
| Euphemia Twp [43] | 982 | Lambton | Elgin-Middlesex-London | Lambton | Joan Webster, Clerk-Treas., RR#2, Bothwell N0P 1C0 – 519/695-2312, Fax: 519/695-3705 |
| Euphrasia Twp | 1,513 | Grey | Bruce-Grey | Grey | Debbie Robertson, Clerk-Treas., RR#2, Meaford N4L 1W6 – 519/538-2030, Fax: 519/538-5651 |
| Evanturel Twp | 493 | Timiskaming District | Timiskaming-Cochrane | Timiskaming | Lorne A. LaCarte, Clerk-Treas., PO Box 209, Englehart P0J 1H0 – 705/544-8200, Fax: 705/544-8200 |
| Exeter † | 4,472 | Huron | Huron-Bruce | Huron | Elizabeth Bell, Clerk-Treas., PO Box 759, Exeter N0M 1S6 – 519/235-0310, Fax: 519/235-3304 |
| Faraday Twp | 1,638 | Hastings | Hastings-Frontenac-Lennox & Addington | Hastings-Peterborough | Elizabeth Mackey, Clerk-Treas., PO Box 929, Bancroft K0L 1C0 – 613/332-3638, Fax: 613/332-3006 |
| Fauquier-Strickland Twp | 684 | Cochrane District | Timmins-James Bay | Cochrane North | Louisette Morin, Deputy Clerk-Treas., 25 Grzela Rd., PO Box 40, Fauquier P0L 1G0 – 705/339-2521, Fax: 705/339-2421 |
| Fenelon Twp | 5,931 | Victoria | Victoria-Haliburton | Victoria-Haliburton | Nancy Wright-Laking, Clerk, RR#1, Cameron K0M 1G0 – 705/887-3880, 3946 |

Cities in CAPITALS; Towns marked †; Villages marked (V); Townships marked Twp; Municipalities marked (Mun.); Separated Towns marked (SE); Development Areas marked (DA). An in-depth listing for municipalities marked with * appears in Part 2 (check Index for page numbers).

| MUNICIPALITY | 1996 POP. | COUNTY OR DISTRICT | FEDERAL ELECTORAL DISTRICT | PROVINCIAL ELECTORAL DISTRICT | CONTACT PERSON WITH ADDRESS, PHONE & FAX |
|---|---|---|---|---|---|
| Fenelon Falls (V) | 2,040 | Victoria | Victoria-Haliburton | Victoria-Haliburton | Joanne Young, Clerk, 21 Market St., PO Box 179, Fenelon Falls K0M 1N0 – 705/887-3133, Fax: 705/887-4337 |
| Fergus † | 8,884 | Wellington | Waterloo-Wellington | Wellington | William J. Tigert, Clerk-Treas. & CAO, 198 St. Andrew St. West, PO Box 10, Fergus N1M 2W7 – 519/843-3250, Fax: 519/843-7601 |
| Field Twp [27] | 636 | Nipissing District | Timiskaming-Cochrane | Nipissing | Robert Courchesne, Clerk-Treas., 110 Morin St., PO Box 70, Field P0H 1M0 – 705/758-6659, Fax: 705/758-9529 |
| Finch (V) [58] | 458 | Stormont, Dundas & Glengarry | Stormont-Dundas | SDG & East Grenville | Madeleine Brown, Clerk-Treas., PO Box 200, Finch K0C 1K0 – 613/984-2525, Fax: 613/984-0168 |
| Finch Twp [58] | 2,903 | Stormont, Dundas & Glengarry | Stormont-Dundas | SDG & East Grenville | Arnott V. Empey, Clerk-Treas., 2 Victoria St., PO Box 99, Berwick K0C 1G0 – 613/984-2821, Fax: 613/984-2908 |
| Flamborough † | 34,037 | Hamilton-Wentworth Reg. Mun. | Wentworth-Burlington | Wentworth North | M. Jane Lee, Clerk, 163 Dundas St. East, PO Box 50, Waterdown L0R 2H0 – 905/689-7351, Fax: 905/689-3310 or 689-9379, URL: http://www.town.flamborough.on.ca |
| Flesherton (V)[8] | 625 | Grey | Simcoe-Grey | Grey | Christine C. Kinsman, Clerk-Treas., 4 Elizabeth St., PO Box 99, Flesherton N0C 1E0 – 519/924-2609, Fax: 519/924-2938 |
| Foley Twp [37] | 1,627 | Parry Sound District | Parry Sound-Muskoka | Parry Sound | Tom Miller, Treasurer-Tax Collector, RR#2, Parry Sound P2A 2W8 – 705/378-2485, Fax: 705/378-5121 |
| Forest † | 3,020 | Lambton | Hastings-Frontenac-Lennox-Addington | Lambton | John Byrne, Clerk-Adm., 40 King St. West, PO Box 610, Forest N0N 1J0 – 519/786-2335, Fax: 519/786-2135 |
| Fort Erie † | 27,183 | Niagara Reg. Mun. | Erie-Lincoln | Niagara South | Carolyn Booth, Clerk, 1 Municipal Centre, Fort Erie L2A 2S6 – 905/871-1600, Fax: 905/871-4022 |
| Fort Frances † | 8,790 | Rainy River District | Kenora-Rainy River | Rainy River | Glenn W. Treftlin, Clerk, 320 Portage Ave., PO Box 38, Fort Frances P9A 3M5 – 807/274-5323, Fax: 807/274-8479, URL: http://www.ff.lakeheadu.ca/rrfdc/ff-title |
| Frankford (V) [59] | 2,096 | Hastings | Prince Edward-Hastings | Quinte | David Pearson, Clerk-Treas., 12 Trent St. North, PO Box 388, Frankford K0K 2C0 – 613/398-6200, Fax: 613/398-8826 |
| Fullarton Twp [60] | 1,662 | Perth | Perth-Middlesex | Perth | Donald Feeney, Clerk-Treas., Fullarton N0K 1H0 – 519/229-8828, Fax: 519/229-8914 |
| Galway & Cavendish Twp [61] | 765 | Peterborough | Victoria-Haliburton | Hastings-Peterborough | Joan McCausland, Clerk-Treas., Kinmount K0M 2A0 – 705/488-2981, Fax: 705/488-2993 |
| Gananoque (SE) | 5,219 | Leeds & Grenville | Leeds-Grenville | Leeds-Grenville | Corinne Wendt, Clerk-Treas., 30 King St. East, PO Box 100, Gananoque K7G 2T6 – 613/382-2149, Fax: 613/382-8587 |
| Gauthier Twp | 152 | Timiskaming District | Timiskaming-Cochrane | Timiskaming | Dianne Quinn, Clerk-Treas., 82 McPherson St., PO Box 65, Dobie P0K 1B0 – 705/568-8951, Fax: 705/568-8951 |
| Georgian Bay Twp | 2,230 | Muskoka Dist. Mun. | Parry Sound-Muskoka | Muskoka-Georgian Bay | Winanne Grant, Clerk-Adm., RR#1, Hwy. 69, Port Severn L0K 1S0 – 705/538-2337, Fax: 705/538-1850 |
| Georgina † | 34,777 | York Reg. Mun. | York North | Durham-York | Larry R. Simpson, Clerk, 26557 Civic Centre, RR#2, Keswick L4P 3G1 – 905/476-4301, Fax: 905/476-8100 |
| Geraldton † [16] | 2,627 | Thunder Bay District | Thunder Bay-Nipigon | Lake Nipigon | Roy T. Sinclair, Clerk & CAO, 301 East St., PO Box 70, Geraldton P0T 1M0 – 807/854-1100, Fax: 807/854-1947 |
| Gillies Twp | 497 | Thunder Bay District | Thunder Bay-Atikokan | Fort William | Orma Kempe, Clerk-Treas., South Gillies P0T 2V0 – 807/475-3185, Fax: 807/473-0767 |
| Glackmeyer Twp | 1,092 | Cochrane District | Timiskaming-Cochrane | Cochrane North | Jean-Pierre Ouellette, Clerk-Treas.-CAO, PO Box 1867, Cochrane P0L 1C0 – 705/272-4313, Fax: 705/272-2885 |
| Glamorgan Twp | 632 | Haliburton | Victoria-Haliburton | Victoria-Haliburton | Glen Madill, Clerk-Treas., PO Box 70, Gooderham K0M 1R0 – 705/447-2410, Fax: 705/447-3180 |
| Glanbrook Twp | 10,564 | Hamilton-Wentworth Reg. Mun. | Stoney Creek | Wentworth East | Harry Kooyman, Clerk-Chief Bldg. Official, 4280 Binbrook Rd., RR#1, Binbrook L0R 1C0 – 905/692-9225, Fax: 905/692-9199 |
| Glencoe (V) | 2,178 | Middlesex | Lambton-Kent-Middlesex | Middlesex | William Black, Clerk-Treas., 153 McKellar St., PO Box 218, Glencoe N0L 1M0 – 519/287-2015, Fax: 519/287-2359 |

Cities in CAPITALS; Towns marked †; Villages marked (V); Townships marked Twp; Municipalities marked (Mun.); Separated Towns marked (SE); Development Areas marked (DA). An in-depth listing for municipalities marked with * appears in Part 2 (check Index for page numbers).

| MUNICIPALITY | 1996 POP. | COUNTY OR DISTRICT | FEDERAL ELECTORAL DISTRICT | PROVINCIAL ELECTORAL DISTRICT | CONTACT PERSON WITH ADDRESS, PHONE & FAX |
|---|---|---|---|---|---|
| Glenelg Twp | 2,136 | Grey | Bruce-Grey | Grey | Susan Shannon, Clerk-Treas., PO Box 434, Markdale N0C 1H0 – 519/369-5131 |
| *GLOUCESTER | 104,022 | Ottawa-Carleton Reg. Mun. | Carleton-Gloucester; Ottawa South; Ottawa-Vanier | Carleton East; Ottawa East; Ottawa-Rideau | Michèle Giroux, Clerk, 1595 Telesat Court, PO Box 8333, Gloucester K1G 3V5 – 613/748-4100, Fax: 613/748-0235, URL: http://www.city.gloucester.on.ca/ |
| Goderich † | 7,553 | Huron | Huron-Bruce | Huron | Larry J. McCabe, Clerk-Adm., 57 West St., Goderich N7A 2K5 – 519/524-8344, Fax: 519/524-7209 |
| Goderich Twp | 2,768 | Huron | Huron-Bruce | Huron | Linda M. Cranston, Clerk-Treas., RR#3, Clinton N0M 1L0 – 519/482-9804, Fax: 519/482-9516 |
| Golden Twp | 2,248 | Kenora District | Kenora-Rainy River | Kenora | Sten Lif, CAO & Clerk, PO Box 190, Balmertown P0V 1C0 – 807/735-2096, Fax: 807/735-2286 |
| Gordon Twp | 473 | Manitoulin District | Algoma-Manitoulin | Algoma-Manitoulin | Susan Slamke, Clerk-Treas., PO Box 120, Gore Bay P0P 1H0 – 705/282-2702, Fax: 705/282-2702 |
| Gore Bay † | 907 | Manitoulin District | Algoma-Manitoulin | Algoma-Manitoulin | Joyce Foster, Clerk-Treas. & CAO, 15 Water St., PO Box 298, Gore Bay P0P 1H0 – 705/282-2420, Fax: 705/282-3076 |
| Gosfield North Twp | 4,768 | Essex | Essex | Essex-South | Brian Weaver, Clerk-Adm., 122 Fox St., PO Box 130, Cottam N0R 1B0 – 519/839-4844, Fax: 519/839-5566 |
| Gosfield South Twp | 7,650 | Essex | Essex | Essex-South | Dan M. DiGiovanni, Clerk-Adm., 2021 Division Rd. North, Kingsville N9Y 2Y9 – 519/733-2305, Fax: 519/733-8108 |
| Goulbourn Twp | 19,267 | Ottawa-Carleton Reg. Mun. | Nepean-Carleton | Carleton | Moira A. Winch, Clerk, 2135 Huntley Rd., PO Box 189, Stittsville K2S 1A3 – 613/836-2832, Fax: 613/831-2279, URL: http://www.twp.goulbourn.on.ca/welcome.htm |
| Grand Bend (V) | 1,027 | Lambton | Lambton-Kent-Middlesex | Lambton | Paul Turnbull, Clerk-Treas., 4 Ontario St. North, PO Box 340, Grand Bend N0M 1T0 – 519/238-8461, Fax: 519/238-8577 |
| Grattan Twp | 1,328 | Renfrew | Renfrew-Nipissing-Pembroke | Renfrew North | Thomas J. Gallagher, Clerk-Treas., RR#2, Eganville K0J 1T0 – 613/628-2728, Fax: 613/628-2855 |
| Gravenhurst † | 10,030 | Muskoka Dist. Mun. | Parry Sound-Muskoka | Muskoka-Georgian Bay | William E. Winegard, CAO-Clerk, 190 Harvie St., Gravenhurst P1P 1S9 – 705/687-3412, Fax: 705/687-7016 |
| Greenock Twp | 1,672 | Bruce | Huron-Bruce | Bruce | Audrey E. Wells, Clerk-Treas., RR#1, Cargill N0G 1J0 – 519/366-2226, Fax: 519/366-2484 |
| Grey Twp | 2,036 | Huron | Huron-Bruce | Huron | Brad Knight, Clerk-Treas., RR#3, Brussels N0G 1H0 – 519/887-6268, Fax: 519/887-6231 |
| Griffith & Matawatchan Twp | 400 | Renfrew | Renfrew-Nipissing-Pembroke | Renfrew North | Audrey Youmans, Clerk-Treas., Hwy. 41, Griffith K0J 2R0 – 613/333-2789, Fax: 613/333-5213 |
| Grimsby † | 19,585 | Niagara Reg. Mun. | Lincoln | Lincoln | Kathryn Vout, Clerk, 160 Livingston Ave., PO Box 159, Grimsby L3M 4G3 – 905/945-9634, Fax: 905/945-5010 |
| *GUELPH | 95,821 | Wellington | Guelph-Wellington | Guelph | Lois A. Giles, Clerk & Director, Information Services, 59 Carden St., Guelph N1H 3A1 – 519/822-1260, Fax: 519/763-1269 |
| Guelph Twp | 3,282 | Wellington | Guelph-Wellington | Wellington | Janice Sheppard, Clerk-Adm., PO Box 20030, Guelph N1H 6H6 – 519/822-4661, Fax: 519/822-4044 |
| Hagar Twp | 903 | Sudbury District | Timiskaming-Cochrane | Sudbury East | Lorraine Demore, Clerk-Treas., 21 Main St. South, PO Box 79, Markstay P0M 2G0 – 705/853-4536, Fax: 705/853-4964 |
| Hagarty & Richards Twp | 2 | Renfrew | Renfrew-Nipissing-Pembroke | Renfrew North | Lorna Hudder, Clerk-Treas., RR#2, Killaloe K0J 2A0 – 613/757-2344, Fax: 613/757-2927 |
| Hagerman Twp | 489 | Parry Sound District | Parry Sound-Muskoka | Parry Sound | Muriel Junck, Clerk-Treas., General Delivery, Hwy. 124, Dunchurch P0A 1C0 – 705/389-2466, Fax: 705/389-1855 |
| Haileybury † | 4,875 | Timiskaming District | Timiskaming-Cochrane | Timiskaming | James D. Smyth, Clerk-Admn., 451 Meridian Ave., Bag D, Haileybury P0J 1K0 – 705/672-3363, Fax: 705/672-3200 |
| Haldimand † | 22,128 | Haldimand-Norfolk Reg. Mun. | Haldimand-Norfolk-Brant | Brant-Haldimand | Janis Lankester, Clerk, 45 Munsee St. North, PO Box 400, Cayuga N0A 1E0 – 905/772-3324, Fax: 905/772-3542 |
| Haldimand Twp | 4,450 | Northumberland | Northumberland | Northumberland | Terrence J. Korotki, Clerk-Treas. & CAO, PO Box 70, Grafton K0K 2G0 – 905/349-2822, Fax: 905/349-3259 |
| Hallowell Twp | 4,577 | Prince Edward | Prince Edward-Hastings | Prince Edward-Lennox-South Hastings | Malcolm G. (Mac) MacDonald, Clerk-Treas., RR#1, Picton K0K 2T0 – 613/393-2011, Fax: 613/393-5792 |

Cities in CAPITALS; Towns marked †; Villages marked (V); Townships marked Twp; Municipalities marked (Mun.); Separated Towns marked (SE); Development Areas marked (DA). An in-depth listing for municipalities marked with * appears in Part 2 (check Index for page numbers).

| MUNICIPALITY | 1996 POP. | COUNTY OR DISTRICT | FEDERAL ELECTORAL DISTRICT | PROVINCIAL ELECTORAL DISTRICT | CONTACT PERSON WITH ADDRESS, PHONE & FAX |
|---|---|---|---|---|---|
| Halton Hills † | 42,390 | Halton Reg. Mun. | Halton | Halton North | Janet Lunn Stewart, Clerk, 1 Halton Hills Dr., PO Box 128, Georgetown L7G 5G2 – 905/873-2601 or 877-3524, Fax: 905/873-2347 |
| *HAMILTON | 322,352 | Hamilton-Wentworth Reg. Mun. | Hamilton East; Hamilton Mountain; Hamilton West; Stoney Creek | Ham. Centre; Ham. East; Ham. West; Ham. Mountain; Wentworth East | Joseph J. Schatz, City Clerk, City Hall, 71 Main St. West, Hamilton L8P 4Y5 – 905/546-2700, Fax: 905/546-2095 |
| Hamilton Twp | 10,140 | Northumberland | Northumberland | Northumberland | Peggy Cramp, Clerk & CAO, PO Box 1060, Cobourg K9A 4W5 – 905/342-2810, Fax: 905/342-2818 |
| Hanover † | 6,844 | Grey | Bruce-Grey | Grey | Robert Casselman, Clerk-Adm., 341 - 10 St., Hanover N4N 2P1 – 519/364-2780, Fax: 519/364-6456 |
| Harley Twp | 608 | Timiskaming District | Timiskaming-Cochrane | Timiskaming | Michel Lachapelle, Clerk-Treas., RR#2, New Liskeard P0J 1P0 – 705/647-5439, Fax: 705/647-5439 |
| Harris Twp | 553 | Timiskaming District | Timiskaming-Cochrane | Timiskaming | Wilda A. Gibson, Clerk-Treas., RR#3, Site 4-96, New Liskeard P0J 1P0 – 705/647-5094 |
| Harriston † | 2,008 | Wellington | Waterloo-Wellington | Wellington | Dianne Friesen, Clerk-Treas., 68 Elora St., PO Box 10, Harriston N0G 1Z0 – 519/338-3444, Fax: 519/338-2359 |
| Harrow † | 2,806 | Essex | Essex | Essex-South | Jerome E. Marion, Adm. & Clerk-Treas., 44 King St. East, PO Box 129, Harrow N0R 1G0 – 519/738-2523, Fax: 519/738-9040 |
| Harvey Twp [61] | 3,635 | Peterborough | Victoria-Haliburton | Hastings-Peterborough | John W. Millage, Adm.-Clerk-Treas., PO Box 130, Buckhorn K0L 1J0 – 705/657-8883, Fax: 705/657-9077 |
| Harwich Twp | 6,594 | Kent | Kent-Essex | Essex-Kent | W. Michael Phipps, Adm.-Clerk, 21633 Communication Rd., PO Box 2022, Chatham N7M 5L9 – 519/436-1122, Fax: 519/436-1127 |
| Hastings (V) | 1,140 | Northumberland | Northumberland | Northumberland | Margaret Montgomery, Clerk-Treas., 6 Albert St. East, PO Box 250, Hastings K0L 1Y0 – 705/696-2351, Fax: 705/696-2323 |
| Havelock (V) [21] | 1,352 | Peterborough | Peterborough | Hastings-Peterborough | Donald L. Kelloway, Adm.-Clerk-Treas., 1 Oak St., PO Box 190, Havelock K0L 1Z0 – 705/778-2282, Fax: 705/778-5129 |
| Hawkesbury † [62] | 10,162 | Prescott & Russell | Glengarry-Prescott-Russell | Prescott & Russell | Gilbert Heroux, CAO-Clerk, 600 Higginson St., Hawkesbury K6A 1H1 – 613/632-4888, Fax: 613/632-2463 |
| Hay Twp | 2,254 | Huron | Huron-Bruce | Huron | Janisse Zimmerman, Clerk-Treas., Mill St., PO Box 250, Zurich N0M 2T0 – 519/236-4351, Fax: 519/236-4329 |
| Head, Clara & Maria Twp | 294 | Renfrew | Renfrew-Nipissing-Pembroke | Renfrew North | Diane Beauchamp, Clerk-Treas., Stonecliffe K0J 2K0 – 613/586-2526, Fax: 613/586-2596 |
| Hearst † | 6,049 | Cochrane District | Timmins-James Bay | Cochrane North | Claude J. Laflamme, Clerk, 925 Alexandra St., PO Bag 5000, Hearst P0L 1N0 – 705/362-4341, Fax: 705/362-5902 |
| Hensall (V) | 1,187 | Huron | Huron-Bruce | Huron | Luanne F. Phair, Clerk-Treas., 108 King St., PO Box 279, Hensall N0M 1X0 – 519/262-2812, Fax: 519/262-2821 |
| Hepworth (V) | 470 | Bruce | Bruce-Grey | Bruce | William Johnston, Clerk, PO Box 69, Hepworth N0H 1P0 – 519/935-2911, Fax: 519/935-2911 |
| Herschel Twp | 1,407 | Hastings | Hastings-Frontenac-Lennox & Addington | Hastings-Peterborough | Erma Dafoe, Clerk-Treas., RR#2, Bancroft K0L 1C0 – 613/332-3757, Fax: 613/332-5609 |
| Hibbert Twp [60] | 1,348 | Perth | Perth-Middlesex | Perth | Patricia Taylor, Clerk-Treas., PO Box 129, Dublin N0K 1E0 – 519/345-2931, Fax: 519/345-2901 |
| Highgate (V) | 446 | Kent | Kent-Essex | Essex-Kent | Rita Jackson, Clerk-Treas., 291 King St., PO Box 198, Highgate N0P 1T0 – 519/678-3936, Fax: 519/678-3936 |
| Hilliard Twp | 253 | Timiskaming District | Timiskaming-Cochrane | Timiskaming | Janet Gore, Clerk-Treas., RR#3, PO Box 12, Thornloe P0J 1S0 – 705/563-2593, Fax: 705/563-2593 |
| Hillier Twp | 1,851 | Prince Edward | Prince Edward-Hastings | Prince Edward-Lennox-South Hastings | Brian M Quibell, Clerk-Treas., PO Box 20, Hillier K0K 2J0 – 613/399-3377 |
| Hilton Twp | 255 | Algoma District | Algoma-Manitoulin | Algoma | E. Ann Langer, Clerk-Treas., PO Box 205, Hilton Beach P0R 1G0 – 705/246-2472, Fax: 705/246-0132 |
| Hilton Beach (V) | 213 | Algoma District | Algoma-Manitoulin | Algoma | Gloria Fischer, Clerk-Treas., PO Box 25, Hilton Beach P0R 1G0 – 705/246-2242, Fax: 705/246-2913 |

Cities in CAPITALS; Towns marked †; Villages marked (V); Townships marked Twp; Municipalities marked (Mun.); Separated Towns marked (SE); Development Areas marked (DA). An in-depth listing for municipalities marked with * appears in Part 2 (check Index for page numbers).

| MUNICIPALITY | 1996 POP. | COUNTY OR DISTRICT | FEDERAL ELECTORAL DISTRICT | PROVINCIAL ELECTORAL DISTRICT | CONTACT PERSON WITH ADDRESS, PHONE & FAX |
|---|---|---|---|---|---|
| Himsworth North Twp | 3,168 | Parry Sound District | Parry Sound-Muskoka | Parry Sound | Virginia Onley, Clerk, 280 Main St. North, PO Box 100, Callander P0H 1H0 – 705/752-1410, Fax: 705/752-3116 |
| Himsworth South Twp | 1,572 | Parry Sound District | Parry Sound-Muskoka | Parry Sound | Judith Gauthier, Clerk-Treas., 70 King St. West, PO Box 159, Powassan P0H 1Z0 – 705/724-2740, Fax: 705/724-3872 |
| Hinchinbrooke Twp [63] | 1,328 | Frontenac | Hastings-Frontenac-Lennox & Addington | Frontenac-Addington | Heather J. Fox, Clerk-Treas., RR#2, Godfrey K0H 1T0 – 613/374-2619, Fax: 613/374-1399 |
| Holland Twp | 2,904 | Grey | Bruce-Grey | Grey | Arnold Rosenburg, Clerk-Treas., RR#3, Holland Centre N0H 1R0 – 519/794-2307 |
| Hope Twp | 3,748 | Northumberland | Northumberland | Northumberland | Frances (Fran) Aird, Adm.-Clerk-Treas., 5325 County Road 10, PO Box 85, Port Hope L1A 3V9 – 905/753-2230, Fax: 905/753-2434 |
| Hornepayne Twp | 1,480 | Algoma District | Algoma-Manitoulin | Algoma | Susan Smith, Clerk, 68 Front St., PO Box 370, Hornepayne P0M 1Z0 – 807/868-2020, Fax: 807/868-2787 |
| Horton Twp | 2,515 | Renfrew | Renfrew-Nipissing-Pembroke | Lanark-Renfrew | Mackie J. McLaren, Clerk-Treas., RR#5, Renfrew K7V 3Z8 – 613/432-6271, Fax: 613/432-7298 |
| Howard Twp | 2,449 | Kent | Kent-Essex | Essex-Kent | James A. Campbell, Clerk-Treas., 57 Main St. East, PO Box 369, Ridgetown N0P 2C0 – 519/674-3315, Fax: 519/674-5108 |
| Howe Island Twp [64] | 481 | Frontenac | Kingston & the Islands | Kingston & the Islands | Carol Dwyre, Clerk-Treas., 50 Baseline Rd., RR#4, Gananoque K7G 2V6 – 613/544-6348, Fax: 613/548-7545 |
| Howick Twp | 3,685 | Huron | Huron-Bruce | Huron | Mary Ellen Greb, Clerk-Treas., RR#1, PO Box 89, Gorrie N0G 1X0 – 519/335-3208, Fax: 519/335-6208 |
| Howland Twp [65] | 990 | Manitoulin District | Algoma-Manitoulin | Algoma-Manitoulin | E.O. (Ned) Martin, Clerk-Treas., Sheguiandah P0P 1W0 – 705/368-2009, Fax: 705/368-3017 |
| Hudson Twp | 501 | Timiskaming District | Timiskaming-Cochrane | Timiskaming | Stephan Palmateer, Clerk-Treas., RR#1, New Liskeard P0J 1P0 – 705/647-5568, Fax: 705/647-6373 |
| Hullett Twp | 1,878 | Huron | Huron-Bruce | Huron | Beverly M. Shaddick, Clerk-Treas., PO Box 226, Londesboro N0M 2H0 – 519/523-4340, Fax: 519/523-9787 |
| Humphrey Twp [37] | 1,194 | Parry Sound District | Parry Sound-Muskoka | Parry Sound | Donna L. Besman, CAO, RR#2, Parry Sound P2A 2W8 – 705/732-4300, Fax: 705/732-6347 |
| Hungerford Twp [55] | 3,280 | Hastings | Hastings-Frontenac-Lennox-Addington | Hastings-Peterborough | Gary P. Thompson, Clerk-Treas., 63 Victoria St. North, PO Box 568, Tweed K0K 3J0 – 613/478-3035, Fax: 613/478-1145 |
| Huntingdon Twp [66] | 2,639 | Hastings | Hastings-Frontenac-Lennox & Addington | Hastings-Peterborough | Bonnie E. Jones, Clerk-Treas., RR#5, Madoc K0K 2K0 – 613/473-4030, Fax: 613/473-5444 |
| Huntsville † | 15,918 | Muskoka Dist. Mun. | Parry Sound-Muskoka | Muskoka-Georgian Bay | Robert W. Small, Clerk-Adm., 37 Main St. East, Huntsville P1H 1A1 – 705/789-1751, Fax: 705/789-6689 |
| Huron Twp | 3,792 | Bruce | Huron-Bruce | Bruce | Laura Haight, Clerk, PO Box 130, Ripley N0G 2R0 – 519/395-3735, Fax: 519/395-4107 |
| Ignace Twp | 1,782 | Kenora District | Kenora-Rainy River | Rainy River | Chris Wray, CAO-Clerk-Treas., 200 Beaver St., PO Box 248, Ignace P0T 1T0 – 807/934-2202, Fax: 807/934-2864 |
| Ingersoll † | 9,849 | Oxford | Oxford | Oxford | Edward Hunt, Clerk-Adm., PO Box 340, Ingersoll N5C 3V3 – 519/485-0120, Fax: 519/485-3543 |
| Innisfil † | 24,711 | Simcoe | Barrie-Simcoe-Bradford | Simcoe Centre | Paul G. Landry, Clerk, 2147 Innisfil Beach Rd., PO Box 5000, Stroud L0L 2M0 – 705/436-3710, Fax: 705/436-7120 |
| Iron Bridge (V) | 777 | Algoma District | Algoma-Manitoulin | Algoma | Noella Brown, Clerk-Treas., 10 John St., PO Box 460, Iron Bridge P0R 1H0 – 705/843-2033, Fax: 705/843-2035 |
| Iroquois (V) [67] | 1,278 | Stormont, Dundas & Glengarry | Stormont-Dundas | SDG & East Grenville | Lorna D. Seibert, Clerk-Treas., PO Box 249, Iroquois K0E 1K0 – 613/652-4422, Fax: 613/652-4636 |
| Iroquois Falls † | 5,714 | Cochrane District | Timiskaming-Cochrane | Cochrane South | John J. Buchan, Clerk-Adm., 235 Main St., PO Box 230, Iroquois Falls P0K 1G0 – 705/232-5700, Fax: 705/232-4241 |
| Jaffray Melick † | 4,012 | Kenora District | Kenora-Rainy River | Kenora | Gordon R. Meads, Clerk & CAO, 243 Rabbit Lake Rd., RR#2, Kenora P9N 3W8 – 807/548-4234, Fax: 807/548-1728 |
| James Twp | 483 | Timiskaming District | Timiskaming-Cochrane | Timiskaming | Myrna J. Hayes, Clerk-Treas., Pine St., PO Box 10, Elk Lake P0J 1G0 – 705/678-2237, Fax: 705/678-2495 |

Cities in CAPITALS; Towns marked †; Villages marked (V); Townships marked Twp; Municipalities marked (Mun.); Separated Towns marked (SE); Development Areas marked (DA). An in-depth listing for municipalities marked with * appears in Part 2 (check Index for page numbers).

| MUNICIPALITY | 1996 POP. | COUNTY OR DISTRICT | FEDERAL ELECTORAL DISTRICT | PROVINCIAL ELECTORAL DISTRICT | CONTACT PERSON WITH ADDRESS, PHONE & FAX |
|---|---|---|---|---|---|
| Jocelyn Twp | 294 | Algoma District | Algoma-Manitoulin | Algoma | Janet Boucher, Clerk-Treas., RR#1, Richards Landing P0R 1J0 – 705/246-2025, Fax: 705/246-3282 |
| Johnson Twp | 729 | Algoma District | Algoma-Manitoulin | Algoma | Jo-Ann McDiarmid, Clerk-Treas., Canadian Pacific Ave., PO Box 160, Desbarats P0R 1E0 – 705/782-6601, Fax: 705/782-6780 |
| Joly Twp | 311 | Parry Sound District | Parry Sound-Muskoka | Parry Sound | Susan Webster, Clerk-Treas., PO Box 519, Sundridge P0A 1Z0 – 705/384-5428, Fax: 705/384-5428 |
| Kaladar, Anglesea & Effingham Twp [47] | 1,712 | Lennox & Addington | Hastings-Frontenac-Lennox & Addington | Frontenac-Addington | Margaret Wood, Clerk-Treas., PO Box 89, Flinton K0H 1P0 – 613/336-2286, Fax: 613/336-2847 |
| KANATA | 47,909 | Ottawa-Carleton Reg. Mun. | Lanark-Carleton | Carleton | Anna Lapointe, Clerk, 580 Terry Fox Dr., Kanata K2L 4C2 – 613/592-4281, Fax: 613/592-8183 |
| Kapuskasing † | 10,036 | Cochrane District | Timmins-James Bay | Cochrane North | Nancy Montpellier, Clerk-Treas., 88 Riverside Dr., Kapuskasing P5N 1B3 – 705/335-2341, Fax: 705/337-1741 |
| Kearney † | 837 | Parry Sound District | Parry Sound-Muskoka | Parry Sound | Elwood Varty, Clerk-Treas. & CAO, Monteith Rd., PO Box 38, Kearney P0A 1M0 – 705/636-7752, Fax: 705/636-0527 |
| Keewatin † | 2,058 | Kenora District | Kenora-Rainy River | Kenora | Warren D. Spencer, Clerk & CAO, 221 Main St., PO Box 139, Keewatin P0X 1C0 – 807/547-2881, Fax: 807/547-2284 |
| Kemptville † [68] | 3,272 | Leeds & Grenville | Leeds-Grenville | SDG & East Grenville | Cahl Pominville, Clerk, 15 Water St., PO Box 130, Kemptville K0G 1J0 – 613/258-3483, Fax: 613/258-4322 |
| Kennebec Twp [63] | 968 | Frontenac | Hastings-Frontenac-Lennox & Addington | Frontenac-Addington | Shirley Conner, Clerk-Treas., PO Box 70, Arden K0H 1B0 – 613/335-2000, Fax: 613/335-2922 |
| Kenora † | 10,063 | Kenora District | Kenora-Rainy River | Kenora | William E. Preisentanz, Clerk & CAO, 1 Main St. South, Kenora P9N 3X2 – 807/467-2000, Fax: 807/467-2045 |
| Kenyon Twp [3] | 3,447 | Stormont, Dundas & Glengarry | Glengarry-Prescott-Russell | SDG & East Grenville | Johanna (Annie) Levac, Clerk-Treas., RR#5, PO Box 11, Alexandria K0C 1A0 – 613/527-2090, Fax: 613/527-2019 |
| Keppel Twp [69] | 4,042 | Grey | Bruce-Grey | Grey | Robert A. Hewines, CAO-Clerk, RR#1, Wiarton N0H 2T0 – 519/534-2247, Fax: 519/534-4970 |
| Kerns Twp | 400 | Timiskaming District | Timiskaming-Cochrane | Timiskaming | Stephan Palmateer, Clerk-Treas., RR#1, New Liskeard P0J 1P0 – 705/647-5568, Fax: 705/647-6373 |
| Killaloe (V) | 669 | Renfrew | Renfrew-Nipissing-Pembroke | Renfrew North | Susan Sheridan, Clerk-Treas., 1 John St., PO Box 39, Killaloe K0J 2A0 – 613/757-2300, Fax: 613/757-3634 |
| Kincardine † | 6,620 | Bruce | Huron-Bruce | Bruce | Maureen A. Couture, Clerk-Adm., 707 Queen St., Kincardine N2Z 1Z9 – 519/396-3468, Fax: 519/396-8288, URL: http://www.town.kincardine.on.ca/ |
| Kincardine Twp | 2,954 | Bruce | Huron-Bruce | Bruce | Muriel P. Eskrick, Clerk-Treas., RR#5, PO Box 14, Kincardine N2Z 2X6 – 519/396-8100, Fax: 519/396-8432 |
| King Twp | 18,223 | York Reg. Mun. | Vaughan-King-Aurora | York North | Cameron H. Duncan, Clerk, 3565 King Rd., King City L7B 1A1 – 905/833-5321, Fax: 905/833-2300 |
| *KINGSTON [70] | 55,947 | Frontenac | Kingston & the Islands | Kingston & the Islands | Sheila Birrell, City Clerk, City Hall, 216 Ontario St., Kingston K7L 2Z3 – 613/546-4291, Fax: 613/546-5232, URL: http://www.city.kingston.on.ca |
| Kingston Twp [70] | 43,756 | Frontenac | Kingston & the Islands | Frontenac-Addington | Susan A. McLean-Snow, Clerk, 1425 Midland Ave., Kingston K7L 5L8 – 613/384-1770, Fax: 613/384-7106 |
| Kingsville † | 5,991 | Essex | Essex | Essex-South | Victoria Sim, Clerk-Adm., 41 Division St. South, Kingsville N9Y 1P4 – 519/733-2315, Fax: 519/733-5588 |
| Kinloss Twp | 1,277 | Bruce | Huron-Bruce | Bruce | Mark Becker, Clerk-Treas., Holyrood N0G 2B0 – 519/395-3575, Fax: 519/395-4920 |
| Kirkland Lake † | 9,905 | Timiskaming District | Timiskaming-Cochrane | Timiskaming | Gary D. Shay, Clerk, 3 Kirkland St. West, PO Box 1757, Kirkland Lake P2N 3K3 – 705/567-9361, Fax: 705/567-3535 |
| *KITCHENER | 178,420 | Waterloo Reg. Mun. | Cambridge; Kitchener Centre; Kitchener-Waterloo; Waterloo-Wellington | Kitchener; Kitchener-Wilmot | Robert W. Pritchard, City Clerk & Commissioner, General Services, City Hall, 200 King St. West, PO Box 1118, Kitchener N2G 4G7 – 519/741-2286, Fax: 519/741-2705, URL: http://www.oceta.on.ca/city.kitchener |
| Kitley Twp | 2,461 | Leeds & Grenville | Leeds-Grenville | Leeds-Grenville | Atty Jones, Clerk-Treas., 424 Hwy. 29, Toledo K0E 1Y0 – 613/275-2277, Fax: 613/275-2093 |

Cities in CAPITALS; Towns marked †; Villages marked (V); Townships marked Twp; Municipalities marked (Mun.); Separated Towns marked (SE); Development Areas marked (DA). An in-depth listing for municipalities marked with * appears in Part 2 (check Index for page numbers).

| MUNICIPALITY | 1996 POP. | COUNTY OR DISTRICT | FEDERAL ELECTORAL DISTRICT | PROVINCIAL ELECTORAL DISTRICT | CONTACT PERSON WITH ADDRESS, PHONE & FAX |
|---|---|---|---|---|---|
| La Vallée Twp | 1,130 | Rainy River District | Kenora-Rainy River | Rainy River | Laurie A. Witherspoon, Clerk-Treas., Main St., PO Box 99, Devlin P0W 1C0 – 807/486-3452, Fax: 807/486-3863 |
| Laird Twp | 1,073 | Algoma District | Algoma-Manitoulin | Algoma | Phyllis L. MacKay, Clerk-Treas., RR#4, Echo Bay P0S 1C0 – 705/248-2395, Fax: 705/248-1138 |
| Lake of Bays Twp | 2,850 | Muskoka Dist. Mun. | Parry Sound-Muskoka | Muskoka-Georgian Bay | S. Faye Tibbel, CAO-Clerk, 3 Dwight Bay Rd., Dwight P0A 1H0 – 705/635-2272, Fax: 705/635-2132 |
| Lakefield (V) | 2,444 | Peterborough | Peterborough | Hastings-Peterborough | R. Lane Vance, Clerk-Treas., 1 Bridge St., PO Box 400, Lakefield K0L 2H0 – 705/652-3381, Fax: 705/652-3995 |
| Lanark (V) [71] | 865 | Lanark | Lanark-Carleton | Lanark-Renfrew | Laurie Cordick, Clerk-Treas., 75 George St., PO Box 20, Lanark K0G 1K0 – 613/259-2398, Fax: 613/259-2291 |
| Lanark Twp [71] | 1,722 | Lanark | Lanark-Carleton | Lanark-Renfrew | Paul Snider, Clerk-Treas., RR#2, Lanark K0G 1K0 – 613/259-5686, Fax: 613/259-2583 |
| Lancaster (V) [34] | 825 | Stormont, Dundas & Glengarry | Glengarry-Prescott-Russell | SDG & East Grenville | Marilyn LeBrun, Clerk-Treas., Pine St., PO Box 220, Lancaster K0C 1N0 – 613/347-2023, Fax: 613/347-1146 |
| Lancaster Twp [34] | 3,841 | Stormont, Dundas & Glengarry | Glengarry-Prscsott-Russell | SDG & East Grenville | Michel J. Samson, Clerk-Treas., 21138 Conc. 5 Rd., North Lancaster K0C 1Z0 – 613/347-2476, Fax: 613/347-2477 |
| Larder Lake Twp | 982 | Timiskaming District | Timiskaming-Cochrane | Timiskaming | Robert E. Emmell, Clerk-Treas., 13 Godfrey St., PO Box 40, Larder Lake P0K 1L0 – 705/643-2158, Fax: 705/643-2311 |
| LaSalle † | 20,566 | Essex | Essex | Windsor-Sandwich | Kenneth M. Antaya, Clerk-Adm., 5950 Malden Rd., LaSalle N9H 1S4 – 519/969-7770, Fax: 519/969-4469 |
| Latchford † | 338 | Timiskaming District | Timiskaming-Cochrane | Timiskaming | Lynn M. Godden, Adm.-Clerk-Treas., 10 Main St., PO Box 10, Latchford P0J 1N0 – 705/676-2416, Fax: 705/676-2121 |
| Lavant, Dalhousie & N. Sherbrooke Twp [71] | 1,515 | Lanark | Lanark-Carleton | Lanark-Renfrew | Mary L. Kirkham, Clerk-Treas., Bag Service, McDonald's Corners K0G 1M0 – 613/278-2694, Fax: 613/278-2694 |
| Laxton, Digby & Longford Twp | 1,114 | Victoria | Victoria-Haliburton | Victoria-Haliburton | Brenda A. Greer, Clerk-Treas., PO Box 70, Norland K0M 2L0 – 705/454-3418, Fax: 705/454-3209 |
| Leamington † | 16,188 | Essex | Essex-Kent | Essex South | Brian R. Sweet, Clerk-Solicitor, 38 Erie St. North, Leamington N8H 2Z3 – 519/326-5761, Fax: 519/326-2481 |
| Leeds & Lansdowne, Front of Twp | 4,897 | Leeds & Grenville | Leeds-Grenville | Leeds-Grenville | John A. Trudgen, Clerk-Adm., 129 Jessie St., PO Box 129, Lansdowne K0E 1L0 – 613/659-2415, Fax: 613/659-3619 |
| Leeds & Lansdowne, Rear of Twp | 2,895 | Leeds & Grenville | Leeds-Grenville | Leeds-Grenville | Eileen Watson, Clerk-Treas., PO Box 160, Lyndhurst K0E 1N0 – 613/928-2423, Fax: 613/928-3116 |
| Limerick Twp | 396 | Hastings | Hastings-Frontenac-Lennox & Addington | Hastings-Peterborough | Carlene Baker, Clerk-Treas., RR#2, Gilmour K0L 1W0 – 613/474-2863, Fax: 613/474-0478 |
| Lincoln † | 18,801 | Niagara Reg. Mun. | Erie-Lincoln | Lincoln | Kyle S. Kruger, Clerk-Treas., 4800 South Service Rd., Beamsville L0R 1B1 – 905/563-8205, Fax: 905/563-6566 |
| Lindsay † | 17,638 | Victoria | Victoria-Haliburton | Victoria-Haliburton | Percy Luther, Clerk, 180 Kent St. West, Lindsay K9V 2Y6 – 705/324-6171, Fax: 705/324-2051 |
| Lindsay Twp | 500 | Bruce | Bruce-Grey | Bruce | Norma Brinkman, Clerk-Treas., RR#2, Lion's Head N0H 1W0 – 519/793-3522, Fax: 519/793-3823 |
| Lion's Head (V) | 550 | Bruce | Bruce-Grey | Bruce | Janet Morrow, Clerk-Treas., 90 Main St., PO Box 310, Lion's Head N0H 1W0 – 519/793-3731, Fax: 519/793-4222 |
| Listowel † [54] | 5,467 | Perth | Perth-Middlesex | Perth | R. Les Tervit, Adm.-Clerk-Treas., 330 Wallace Ave. North, Listowel N4W 1L3 – 519/291-2950, Fax: 519/291-5611, URL: http://www.micro-man.com/listowel |
| Little Current † [65] | 1,575 | Manitoulin District | Algoma-Manitoulin | Algoma-Manitoulin | Edwin Bond, Clerk-Treas., 50 Meredith St. West, Little Current P0P 1K0 – 705/368-2277, Fax: 705/368-2245 |
| Lobo Twp [45] | 5,553 | Middlesex | Perth-Middlesex | Middlesex | Sharon A. McMillan, Clerk-Adm., 10227 Ilderton Rd., RR#2, Ilderton N0M 2A0 – 519/666-0190, Fax: 519/666-0271 |
| Lochiel Twp [3] | 2,938 | Stormont, Dundas & Glengarry | Glengarry-Prescott-Russell | SDG & East Grenville | Rhéal M. (Ray) Charbonneau, Clerk-Treas., RR#1, Alexandria K0C 1A0 – 613/525-3283, Fax: 613/525-5052 |

Cities in CAPITALS; Towns marked †; Villages marked (V); Townships marked Twp; Municipalities marked (Mun.); Separated Towns marked (SE); Development Areas marked (DA). An in-depth listing for municipalities marked with * appears in Part 2 (check Index for page numbers).

| MUNICIPALITY | 1996 POP. | COUNTY OR DISTRICT | FEDERAL ELECTORAL DISTRICT | PROVINCIAL ELECTORAL DISTRICT | CONTACT PERSON WITH ADDRESS, PHONE & FAX |
|---|---|---|---|---|---|
| Logan Twp [60] | 2,227 | Perth | Perth-Middlesex | Perth | Karen McLagan, Clerk-Treas., RR#1, Bornholm N0K 1A0 – 519/347-2404, Fax: 519/347-2939 |
| *LONDON | 325,646 | Middlesex | London Fanshawe; Elgin-Middlesex-London; London North Centre; London West | London Centre; London North; London South; Middlesex | Jeffrey A. Malpass, City Clerk, City Hall, 300 Dufferin Ave., PO Box 5035, London N6A 4L9 – 519/661-4500, Fax: 519/661-4892, URL: http://www.city.london.on.ca |
| London Twp [45] | 4,996 | Middlesex | Perth-Middlesex | Middlesex | Albert F. Bannister, Clerk-Adm., 14361 Medway Rd., Arva N0M 1C0 – 519/660-0092, Fax: 519/660-3653 |
| Longlac † [16] | 2,074 | Thunder Bay District | Thunder Bay-Nipigon | Lake Nipigon | Jane Jantunen, Clerk-Treas., 105 Hamel Ave., PO Box 640, Longlac P0T 2A0 – 807/876-2316, Fax: 807/876-2396 |
| Longueuil Twp [62] | 1,368 | Prescott & Russell | Glengarry-Prescott-Russell | Prescott & Russell | Jeanne Charlebois, Clerk-Treas., 925 Hwy 17, PO Box 343, L'Orignal K0B 1K0 – 613/675-4727, Fax: 613/675-1050 |
| L'Orignal (V) [62] | 1,999 | Prescott & Russell | Glengarry-Prescott-Russell | Prescott & Russell | Diane Lalonde, Clerk-Treas., 36 Court St., PO Box 271, L'Orignal K0B 1K0 – 613/675-2294, Fax: 613/675-2830 |
| Loughborough Twp [17] | 5,046 | Frontenac | Hastings-Frontenac-Lennox & Addington | Frontenac-Addington | Carolyn Holland, Clerk., PO Box 100, Sydenham K0H 2T0 – 613/376-3027, Fax: 613/376-6657 |
| Lucan (V) | 1,958 | Middlesex | Perth-Middlesex | Middlesex | Ronald J. Reymer, Clerk, 161 Main St., PO Box 449, Lucan N0M 2J0 – 519/227-4253, Fax: 519/227-1755 |
| Lucknow (V) | 1,215 | Bruce | Huron-Bruce | Bruce | Bertha M. Whitcroft, Clerk-Treas., 526 Campbell St., PO Box 40, Lucknow N0G 2H0 – 519/528-3539, Fax: 519/528-3630 |
| Lutterworth Twp | 927 | Haliburton | Victoria-Haliburton | Victoria-Haliburton | Mary Jane Irwin, Clerk-Treas., PO Box 850, Minden K0M 2K0 – 705/286-1541, Fax: 705/286-6005 |
| MacDonald, Meredith & Aberdeen; Add'l Twp | 1,521 | Algoma District | Algoma-Manitoulin | Algoma | Jean V. Robbins, Clerk-Treas., 208 Church St., PO Box 10, Echo Bay P0S 1C0 – 705/248-2441, Fax: 705/248-3091 |
| Machar Twp | 835 | Parry Sound District | Parry Sound-Muskoka | Parry Sound | Brenda Sinclair Paul, Clerk-Treas., Municipal Rd. North, PO Box 70, South River P0A 1X0 – 705/386-7741, Fax: 705/386-0765 |
| Machin Twp | 1,117 | Kenora District | Kenora-Rainy River | Kenora | D. Marie Wiebe, Adm.-Clerk-Treas., PO Box 249, Vermilion Bay P0V 2V0 – 807/227-2633, Fax: 807/227-5443 |
| Madoc (V) [65] | 1,464 | Hastings | Hastings-Frontenac-Lennox & Addington | Hastings-Peterborough | Doug Parks, Clerk-Treas., 107 St. Lawrence St. West, PO Box 310, Madoc K0K 2K0 – 613/473-5211, Fax: 613/473-5446 |
| Madoc Twp | 2,031 | Hastings | Hastings-Frontenac-Lennox & Addington | Hastings-Peterborough | Bill G. Lebow, Clerk-Treas., PO Box 503, Madoc K0K 2K0 – 613/473-2677, Fax: 613/473-5580 |
| Magnetawan (V) [33] | 241 | Parry Sound District | Parry Sound-Muskoka | Parry Sound | Sharon Sohm, Clerk-Treas., PO Box 70, Magnetawan P0A 1P0 – 705/387-3947, Fax: 705/387-3947 |
| Maidstone Twp [18] | 11,770 | Essex | Essex | Essex-Kent | Csop Toth, Clerk, 1089 Puce Rd., RR#3, Essex N8M 2X7 – 519/727-6668, Fax: 519/727-3757 |
| Malahide Twp [72] | 6,255 | Elgin | Elgin-Middlesex-London | Elgin | Randall R. Millard, Clerk-Adm., 87 John St. South, Aylmer N5H 2C3 – 519/773-5344, Fax: 519/773-5334 |
| Malden Twp [7] | 3,298 | Essex | Essex | Essex-South | Richard Beachey, Adm.-Clerk-Treas., 6744 Concession #6, RR#2, Amherstburg N9V 2Y8 – 519/736-3141, Fax: 519/736-7787 |
| Manitouwadge Twp | 3,395 | Thunder Bay District | Algoma-Manitoulin | Lake Nipigon | Sally Saudners, Clerk, 1 Mississauga Dr., Manitouwadge P0T 2C0 – 807/826-3227, Fax: 807/826-4592 |
| Manvers Twp | 5,624 | Victoria | Victoria-Haliburton | Durham East | D.M. Peggy Whitteker, Clerk-Treas., PO Box 210, Bethany L0A 1A0 – 705/277-2321, Fax: 705/277-1580 |
| Marathon † | 4,791 | Thunder Bay District | Thunder Bay-Nipigon | Lake Nipigon | Kathy Dallaire, Clerk, 4 Hemlo Dr., PO Box TM, Marathon P0T 2E0 – 807/229-1340, Fax: 807/229-1999 |
| Mariposa Twp | 7,456 | Victoria | Victoria-Haliburton | Victoria-Haliburton | Sandra Lloyd, Clerk, Hwy. 7, PO Box 70, Oakwood K0M 2M0 – 705/953-9900, Fax: 705/953-9184 |
| Markdale (V) | 1,354 | Grey | Simcoe-Grey | Grey | Geoffrey A. Barlow, Clerk-Treas., 50 Lorne St., PO Box 439, Markdale N0C 1H0 – 519/986-2811, Fax: 519/986-3643 |
| *Markham † | 173,383 | York Reg. Mun. | Markham; Oak Ridges; Thornhill | Markham | Bob Panizza, Clerk, 101 Town Centre Blvd., Markham L3R 9W3 – 905/477-7000, Fax: 905/479-7771, URL: http://www.city.markham.on.ca |

Cities in CAPITALS; Towns marked †; Villages marked (V); Townships marked Twp; Municipalities marked (Mun.); Separated Towns marked (SE); Development Areas marked (DA). An in-depth listing for municipalities marked with * appears in Part 2 (check Index for page numbers).

| MUNICIPALITY | 1996 POP. | COUNTY OR DISTRICT | FEDERAL ELECTORAL DISTRICT | PROVINCIAL ELECTORAL DISTRICT | CONTACT PERSON WITH ADDRESS, PHONE & FAX |
|---|---|---|---|---|---|
| Marmora (V) | 1,483 | Hastings | Hastings-Frontenac-Lennox & Addington | Hastings-Peterborough | Carol D. Church, Adm.-Clerk-Treas., 12 Bursthall St., PO Box 417, Marmora K0K 2M0 – 613/472-2533, Fax: 613/472-3015 |
| Marmora & Lake Twp [46] | 2,208 | Hastings | Hastings-Frontenac-Lennox & Addington | Hastings-Peterborough | Frank Mills, Clerk & CAO, Hwy. 7 West, PO Box 459, Marmora K0K 2M0 – 613/472-2629, Fax: 613/472-5330 |
| Maryborough Twp | 2,882 | Wellington | Waterloo-Wellington | Wellington | Robert Skeoch, Clerk-Treas., 1 Hilwood Dr., PO Box 39, Moorefield N0G 2K0 – 519/638-3043, Fax: 519/638-2200 |
| Massey † | 1,171 | Sudbury District | Algoma-Manitoulin | Algoma-Manitoulin | Ellen Jordan, Clerk-Treas., 205 Sable St., PO Box 490, Massey P0P 1P0 – 705/865-2181, Fax: 705/865-2514 |
| Matachewan Twp | 402 | Timiskaming District | Timiskaming-Cochrane | Timiskaming | Jacqueline Walkingshaw, Clerk-Treas., PO Box 177, Matachewan P0K 1M0 – 705/565-2274, Fax: 705/565-2564 |
| Matilda Twp [67] | 3,520 | Stormont, Dundas & Glengarry | Stormont-Dundas | SDG & East Grenville | Wilmont E. (Bill) Horner, Clerk-Treas., Brinston K0E 1C0 – 613/652-4403, Fax: 613/652-2279 |
| Mattawa † | 2,281 | Nipissing District | Nipissing | Parry Sound | Wayne P. Belter, Clerk & CAO, 160 Water St., PO Box 390, Mattawa P0H 1V0 – 705/744-5611, Fax: 705/744-0104 |
| Mattawan Twp | 115 | Nipissing District | Nipissing | Parry Sound | Irvine J. Burke, Clerk-Treas., PO Box 610, Mattawa P0H 1V0 – 705/744-5737 |
| Mattice-Val Côté Twp | 935 | Cochrane District | Timmins-James Bay | Cochrane North | Gilbert Brisson, Clerk-Adm., 500 Hwy.11, PO Box 129, Mattice P0L 1T0 – 705/364-6511, Fax: 705/364-6431 |
| Maxville (V) [3] | 885 | Stormont, Dundas & Glengarry | Glengarry-Prescott-Russell | SDG & East Grenville | Connie A. Charbonneau, Clerk-Treas., 2 Spring St., PO Box 277, Maxville K0C 1T0 – 613/527-2705, Fax: 613/527-2066 |
| Mayo Twp | 461 | Hastings | Hastings-Frontenac-Lennox & Addington | Hastings-Peterborough | Lois Ward, Clerk-Treas., RR#4, Bancroft K0L 1C0 – 613/332-2637, Fax: 613/332-2637 |
| McCrosson & Tovell Twp | 240 | Rainy River District | Kenora-Rainy River | Rainy River | Patrick W. Giles, Clerk-Treas., 211 - 4 St., PO Box 427, Rainy River P0W 1L0 – 807/852-3529, Fax: 807/852-3529 |
| McDougall Twp | 2,299 | Parry Sound District | Parry Sound-Muskoka | Parry Sound | Norma Bryant, Clerk-Adm., RR#3, Parry Sound P2A 2W9 – 705/342-5252, Fax: 705/342-5573 |
| McGarry Twp | 1,015 | Timiskaming District | Timiskaming-Cochrane | Timiskaming | Ardene Lefebvre, Clerk-Treas., 27 Webster St., PO Box 99, Virginiatown P0K 1X0 – 705/634-2145, Fax: 705/634-2700 |
| McGillivray Twp | 1,861 | Middlesex | Perth-Middlesex | Middlesex | Shirley Scott, Clerk-Treas., RR#3, Ailsa Craig N0M 1A0 – 519/293-3686, Fax: 519/293-3878 |
| McKellar Twp | 939 | Parry Sound District | Parry Sound-Muskoka | Parry Sound | Shawn Boggs, Clerk-Treas., PO Box 69, McKellar P0G 1C0 – 705/389-2842, Fax: 705/389-1244 |
| McKillop Twp | 1,363 | Huron | Huron-Bruce | Huron | Marion McClure, Clerk-Treas., RR#1, Seaforth N0K 1W0 – 519/527-1916, Fax: 519/527-1916 |
| McMurrich Twp [73] | 632 | Parry Sound District | Parry Sound-Muskoka | Parry Sound | Richard Gibb, Clerk-Treas., PO Box 70, Sprucedale P0A 1Y0 – 705/685-7901, Fax: 705/685-7393 |
| McNab Twp [23] | 5,765 | Renfrew | Renfrew-Nipissing-Pembroke | Lanark-Renfrew | Murray Yantha, Clerk-Treas., RR#2, Arnprior K7S 3G8 – 613/623-5756, Fax: 613/623-9138 |
| Meaford † | 4,681 | Grey | Bruce-Grey | Grey | Graham D. Shaw, Clerk-Treas., 12 Nelson St. East, Meaford N4L 1A1 – 519/538-1060, Fax: 519/538-5240 |
| Melancthon Twp | 2,607 | Dufferin | Dufferin-Peel-Wellington-Grey | Dufferin-Peel | Marion A. Hunter, Clerk-Treas., RR#6, Shelburne L0N 1S9 – 519/925-5525, Fax: 519/925-1110 |
| Merrickville (V) [74] | 1,027 | Leeds & Grenville | Leeds-Grenville | Leeds-Grenville | Wayne T. Kirby, Clerk-Treas., 317 Brock St. West, PO Box 340, Merrickville K0G 1N0 – 613/269-4791, Fax: 613/269-4793 |
| Mersea Twp | 9,201 | Essex | Essex-Kent | Essex-South | Lynn Foster, Clerk-Adm., 38 Erie St. North, Leamington N8H 2Z3 – 519/326-5725, Fax: 519/322-1441 |
| Metcalfe Twp | 1,057 | Middlesex | Lambton-Kent-Middlesex | Middlesex | Raymond G. Wilson, Clerk-Treas., RR#3, Strathroy N7G 3H5 – 519/247-3868, Fax: 519/247-3868 |
| Michipicoten Twp | 4,145 | Algoma District | Algoma-Manitoulin | Algoma | Grant E. Southwell, CAO-Clerk, 40 Broadway Ave., PO Box 500, Wawa P0S 1K0 – 705/856-2244, Fax: 705/856-2120 |
| Midland † | 15,035 | Simcoe | Simcoe North | Muskoka-Georgian Bay | Fred G. Flood, Adm.-Clerk, 575 Dominion Ave., Midland L4R 1R2 – 705/526-4275, Fax: 705/526-9971 |
| Mildmay (V) [31] | 1,110 | Bruce | Bruce-Grey | Bruce | David H. Johnston, Clerk-Treas., 16 Peter St., PO Box 128, Mildmay N0G 2J0 – 519/367-2617, Fax: 519/367-2155 |

Cities in CAPITALS; Towns marked †; Villages marked (V); Townships marked Twp; Municipalities marked (Mun.); Separated Towns marked (SE); Development Areas marked (DA). An in-depth listing for municipalities marked with * appears in Part 2 (check Index for page numbers).

| MUNICIPALITY | 1996 POP. | COUNTY OR DISTRICT | FEDERAL ELECTORAL DISTRICT | PROVINCIAL ELECTORAL DISTRICT | CONTACT PERSON WITH ADDRESS, PHONE & FAX |
|---|---|---|---|---|---|
| Millbrook (V) [32] | 1,312 | Peterborough | Victoria-Haliburton | Peterborough | Gail A. Empey, Adm.-Clerk-Treas., 7 King St. East, PO Box 58, Millbrook L0A 1G0 – 705/932-2780, Fax: 705/932-2595 |
| Milton † | 32,104 | Halton Reg. Mun. | Halton | Halton North; Halton Centre | William Roberts, Clerk, Victoria Park Square, PO Box 1005, Milton L9T 4B6 – 905/878-7211, Fax: 905/878-6995 |
| Milverton (V) [53] | 1,618 | Perth | Perth-Middlesex | Perth | Arthur J. Brubacher, Clerk-Treas., 25 Mill St. East, Milverton N0K 1M0 – 519/595-8321, Fax: 519/595-8765 |
| Minto Twp | 2,603 | Wellington | Waterloo-Wellington | Wellington | Frances Hale, Clerk-Treas., 5941 Hwy.89, PO Box 160, Harriston N0G 1Z0 – 519/338-2511, Fax: 519/338-2005 |
| *MISSISSAUGA | 544,382 | Peel Reg. Mun. | Bramalea-Gore-Malton; Brampton West-Mississauga; Mississauga Centre; Mississauga East; Mississauga South; Mississauga West | Mississauga East; Mississauga North; Mississauga South; Mississauga West | Arthur Grannum, Deputy City Clerk, 300 City Centre Dr., Mississauga L5B 3C1 – 905/896-5000, Fax: 905/896-5220, URL: http://www.city.mississauga.on.ca |
| Mitchell † [60] | 3,670 | Perth | Perth-Middlesex | Perth | Donald J. Eplett, Clerk-Treas., 169 St. David St., Mitchell N0K 1N0 – 519/348-8429, Fax: 519/348-4155 |
| Monmouth Twp | 919 | Haliburton | Victoria-Haliburton | Victoria-Haliburton | Sharon Stoughton-Craig, Clerk-Treas., PO Box 10, Wilberforce K0L 3C0 – 705/448-2981, Fax: 705/448-2532 |
| Mono Twp | 6,552 | Dufferin | Dufferin-Peel-Wellington-Grey | Dufferin-Peel | Keith H. McNenly, Clerk-Adm., RR#1, Orangeville L9W 2Y8 – 519/941-3599, Fax: 519/941-9490 |
| Montague Twp | 3,802 | Lanark | Lanark-Carleton | Lanark-Renfrew | Judy Nesbitt, Clerk-Adm., Roger Stevens Rd., PO Box 755, Smiths Falls K7A 4W6 – 613/283-7478, Fax: 613/283-3112 |
| Monteagle Twp | 1,268 | Hastings | Hastings-Frontenac-Lennox & Addington | Hastings-Peterborough | Eleanor N. Tully, Clerk-Treas., Township Garage, RR#5, Bancroft K0L 1C0 – 613/338-3193, Fax: 613/338-2752 |
| Moonbeam Twp | 1,322 | Cochrane District | Timmins-James Bay | Cochrane North | Carole Gendron, Clerk-Treas., 53 St. Aubin Ave., PO Box 330, Moonbeam P0L 1V0 – 705/367-2244, Fax: 705/367-2610 |
| Moore Twp | 10,864 | Lambton | Sarnia-Lambton | Lambton | Ron H. Whitman, Clerk, 1155 Emily St., Mooretown N0N 1M0 – 519/867-2021, Fax: 519/867-5509 |
| Moosonee (DA) | 1,939 | | | Cochrane North | Laurie McGoldrick, Clerk, PO Box 127, Moosonee P0L 1Y0 – 705/336-2993, Fax: 705/336-2426 |
| Morley Twp | 478 | Rainy River District | Kenora-Rainy River | Rainy River | Anna H.M. Boily, Clerk-Treas., PO Box 40, Stratton P0W 1N0 – 807/483-5455, Fax: 807/483-5882 |
| Mornington Twp [53] | 3,332 | Perth | Perth-Middlesex | Perth | Constance Flanagan, Clerk-Treas., PO Box 70, Newton N0K 1R0 – 519/595-8917, Fax: 519/595-8778 |
| Morris Twp | 1,732 | Huron | Huron-Bruce | Huron | Nancy Michie, Clerk-Treas., RR#4, Brussels N0G 1H0 – 519/887-6137, Fax: 519/887-6424 |
| Morrisburg (V) [67] | 2,538 | Stormont, Dundas & Glengarry | Stormont-Dundas | SDG & East Grenville | Cheryl V. Tynski, Clerk-Treas., 6 - 5th St. West, PO Box 737, Morrisburg K0C 1X0 – 613/543-2504, Fax: 613/543-4430 |
| Morson Twp | 192 | Rainy River District | Kenora-Rainy River | Rainy River | Patrick M. Giles, Clerk-Treas., 211 - 4 St., PO Box 427, Rainy River P0W 1L0 – 807/852-3529, Fax: 807/852-3529 |
| Mosa Twp | 1,268 | Middlesex | Lambton-Kent-Middlesex | Middlesex | Betty Ann MacKinnon, Clerk-Treas., RR#1, Glencoe N0L 1M0 – 519/693-4403, Fax: 519/693-4404 |
| Mount Forest † | 4,530 | Wellington | Dufferin-Peel-Wellington-Grey | Wellington | E.C. (Al) Brubacher, Adm.-Clerk-Treas., 102 Main St. South, PO Box 188, Mount Forest N0G 2L0 – 519/323-2150, Fax: 519/323-2930 |
| Mountain Twp [36] | 3,617 | Stormont, Dundas & Glengarry | Stormont-Dundas | SDG & East Grenville | Glenna A. MacIntosh, Clerk-Treas., PO Box 9, Mountain K0E 1S0 – 613/989-2915, Fax: 613/989-3294 |
| Mulmur Twp | 2,903 | Dufferin | Dufferin-Peel-Wellington-Grey | Dufferin-Peel | Terry M. Horner, Clerk-Treas., RR#2, Lisle L0M 1M0 – 705/466-3341, Fax: 705/466-2922 |
| Murray Twp [59] | 7,355 | Northumberland | Northumberland | Northumberland | C. Ken Rose, Clerk & CAO, RR#1, Trenton K8V 5P4 – 613/392-4435, Fax: 613/392-7151 |
| Muskoka Lakes Twp | 6,061 | Muskoka Dist. Mun. | Parry Sound-Muskoka | Muskoka-Georgian Bay | James W. McDivitt, Clerk-Adm., PO Box 129, Port Carling P0B 1J0 – 705/765-3156, Fax: 705/765-6755 |

Cities in CAPITALS; Towns marked †; Villages marked (V); Townships marked Twp; Municipalities marked (Mun.); Separated Towns marked (SE); Development Areas marked (DA). An in-depth listing for municipalities marked with * appears in Part 2 (check Index for page numbers).

| MUNICIPALITY | 1996 POP. | COUNTY OR DISTRICT | FEDERAL ELECTORAL DISTRICT | PROVINCIAL ELECTORAL DISTRICT | CONTACT PERSON WITH ADDRESS, PHONE & FAX |
|---|---|---|---|---|---|
| Nairn Twp [75] | 419 | Sudbury District | Algoma-Manitoulin | Nickel Belt | Robert Deschene, Clerk-Treas., 64 McIntyre St., PO Box 159, Nairn Centre P0M 2L0 – 705/869-4232, Fax: 705/869-5248 |
| Nakina Twp [16] | 566 | Thunder Bay District | Thunder Bay-Nipigon | Lake Nipigon | W. Terrance Dowhaniuk, Adm.-Clerk-Treas., 168 Centre Ave., PO Box 210, Nakina P0T 2H0 – 807/329-5361, Fax: 807/329-5982 |
| NANTICOKE | 23,485 | Haldimand-Norfolk Reg. Mun. | Haldimand-Norfolk-Brant | Norfolk | B. Hugh Hanly, Adm.-Clerk, 230 Main St., Port Dover N0A 1N0 – 519/583-0890, Fax: 519/583-1431 |
| Napanee † [1] | 5,450 | Lennox & Addington | Hastings-Frontenac-Lennox & Addington | Prince Edward-Lennox-South Hastings | John C. (Jack) McNamee, Adm.-Clerk-Treas., 124 John St., PO Box 97, Napanee K7R 3L4 – 613/354-3351, Fax: 613/354-6545 |
| Neebing Twp | 1,021 | Thunder Bay District | Thunder Bay-Atikokan | Fort William | Glen R. Mills, Clerk-Treas., RR#7, Thunder Bay P7C 5V5 – 807/964-2092, Fax: 807/964-2076 |
| *NEPEAN | 115,100 | Ottawa-Carleton Reg. Mun. | Nepean-Carleton; Ottawa West-Nepean | Nepean; Ottawa-Rideau | John LeMaistre, Commissioner & City Clerk, Administrative Services, Nepean Civic Square, 101 Centrepointe Dr., Nepean K2G 5K7 – 613/727-6600, Fax: 613/727-6701, URL: http://www.city.nepean.on.ca |
| Neustadt (V) | 568 | Grey | Bruce-Grey | Grey | Janice M. Hallahan, Clerk-Treas., 449 Mill St., PO Box 66, Neustadt N0G 2M0 – 519/799-5758, Fax: 519/799-5353 |
| New Liskeard † | 5,112 | Timiskaming District | Timiskaming-Cochrane | Timiskaming | Kenneth D.N. Boal, CAO & Clerk, 90 Whitewood Ave., PO Box 730, New Liskeard P0J 1P0 – 705/647-4367, Fax: 705/647-4442 |
| New Tecumseth † | 22,902 | Simcoe | Simcoe-Grey | Simcoe West | Sterling W. Zeran, Clerk, 10 Wellington St. East, PO Box 910, Alliston L9R 1A1 – 705/435-6219, Fax: 705/435-2873 |
| Newboro (V) [13] | 291 | Leeds & Grenville | Leeds-Grenville | Leeds-Grenville | Dianne G. Bresee, Clerk-Treas., PO Box 10, Newboro K0G 1P0 – 613/272-2265, Fax: 613/272-3299 |
| Newburgh (V) [29] | 729 | Lennox & Addington | Hastings-Frontenac-Lennox & Addington | Frontenac-Addington | Darlene Plumley, Clerk-Treas., PO Box 189, Newburgh K0K 2S0 – 613/378-6617, Fax: 613/378-6617 |
| Newbury (V) | 430 | Middlesex | Lambton-Kent-Middlesex | Middlesex | Betty D. Gordon, Clerk-Treas., Hagerty Rd., PO Box 130, Newbury N0L 1Z0 – 519/693-4941, Fax: 519/693-4902 |
| Newmarket † | 57,125 | York Reg. Mun. | York North | York North | Robert M. Prentice, Clerk, 465 Davis Dr., PO Box 328, Newmarket L3Y 4X7 – 905/895-5193, Fax: 905/895-6004 |
| *NIAGARA FALLS | 76,917 | Niagara Reg. Mun. | Niagara Falls | Niagara Falls; Niagara South | Elwood Wagg, City Clerk, City Hall, 4310 Queen St., PO Box 1023, Niagara Falls L2E 6X5 – 905/356-7521, Fax: 905/356-9083, URL: http://www.niagara.com/city.niagara-falls |
| Niagara on the Lake † | 13,238 | Niagara Reg. Mun. | Niagara Falls | St. Catharines-Brock | Robert Howse, Clerk, PO Box 100, Virgil L0S 1T0 – 905/468-3266, Fax: 905/468-2959 |
| Nichol Twp | 4,223 | Wellington | Waterloo-Wellington | Wellington | Barbara Hodsman, Clerk-Treas., 485 Washington St., Site 1, PO Box 23, Elora N0B 1S0 – 519/846-5317, Fax: 519/846-9553 |
| Nickel Centre † | 13,017 | Sudbury Reg. Mun. | Nickel Belt | Sudbury East | Sandra Olson, Clerk, 190 Church St., Garson P3L 1T8 – 705/693-2771, Fax: 705/693-2710 |
| Nipigon Twp | 2,210 | Thunder Bay District | Thunder Bay-Nipigon | Lake Nipigon | Ronald J. Lanigan, Adm.-Clerk-Treas., 25 - 2nd St., PO Box 160, Nipigon P0T 2J0 – 807/887-3135, Fax: 807/887-3564 |
| Nipissing Twp | 1,524 | Parry Sound District | Nipissing | Parry Sound | Charles H. Barton, Clerk-Treas., Nipissing P0H 1W0 – 705/724-2144, Fax: 705/724-5385 |
| Norfolk Twp | 12,590 | Haldimand-Norfolk Reg. Mun. | Haldimand-Norfolk-Brant | Norfolk | Merlin House, Clerk-Adm., PO Box 128, Langton N0E 1P0 – 519/875-4485, Fax: 519/875-4789 |
| Normanby Twp | 2,678 | Grey | Bruce-Grey | Grey | Susan Shannon, Clerk-Treas., PO Box 60, Ayton N0G 1C0 – 519/665-7550, Fax: 519/665-2284 |
| North Algona Twp | 664 | Renfrew | Renfrew-Nipissing-Pembroke | Renfrew North | Edith Frew, Clerk-Treas., PO Box 99, Golden Lake K0J 1X0 – 613/625-2561, Fax: 613/625-2561 |
| *NORTH BAY | 54,332 | Nipissing District | Nipissing | Nipissing | Bonny Harrison, City Clerk, City Hall, 200 McIntyre St. East, PO Box 360, North Bay P1B 8H8 – 705/474-0400, Fax: 705/495-4353, URL: http://www.city.north-bay.on.ca/northbay.htm |
| North Burgess Twp [14] | 1,269 | Lanark | Lanark-Carleton | Lanark-Renfrew | Verna Poole, Clerk-Treas., RR#3, Perth K7H 3C5 – 613/267-7922, Fax: 613/267-7922 |
| North Crosby Twp [13] | 1,097 | Leeds & Grenville | Leeds-Greenville | Leeds-Grenville | Alison Fath, Clerk-Treas., RR#2, Westport K0G 1X0 – 613/273-2097, Fax: 613/273-2794 |

Cities in CAPITALS; Towns marked †; Villages marked (V); Townships marked Twp; Municipalities marked (Mun.); Separated Towns marked (SE); Development Areas marked (DA). An in-depth listing for municipalities marked with * appears in Part 2 (check Index for page numbers).

| MUNICIPALITY | 1996 POP. | COUNTY OR DISTRICT | FEDERAL ELECTORAL DISTRICT | PROVINCIAL ELECTORAL DISTRICT | CONTACT PERSON WITH ADDRESS, PHONE & FAX |
|---|---|---|---|---|---|
| North Dorchester Twp | 8,665 | Middlesex | Elgin-Middlesex-London | Middlesex | Robert G. Lacroix, Clerk-Adm., 4305 Hamilton Rd., PO Box 209, Dorchester N0L 1G0 – 519/268-7334, Fax: 519/268-3928 |
| North Dumfries Twp | 7,817 | Waterloo Reg. Mun. | Cambridge | Brant-Haldimand | Marvin Bosetti, Clerk-Treas., RR#4, Cambridge N1R 5S5 – 519/621-0340, Fax: 519/623-7641 |
| North Easthope Twp [53] | 2,169 | Perth | Perth-Middlesex | Perth | William R. Hoffard, Clerk-Treas., RR#1, Stratford N5A 6S2 – 519/625-8726 |
| North Elmsley Twp [50] | 3,018 | Lanark | Lanark-Carleton | Lanark-Renfrew | Judy M. Carroll, Clerk, RR#5, Perth K7H 3C7 – 613/267-6500, Fax: 613/267-2083 |
| North Fredericksburgh Twp [1] | 3,258 | Lennox & Addington | Hastings-Frontenac-Lennox & Addington | Prince Edward-Lennox-South Hastings | Dianne B. Young, Clerk-Treas., RR#2, Napanee K7R 3K7 – 613/354-2186, Fax: 613/354-2750 |
| North Marysburgh Twp | 1,312 | Prince Edward | Prince Edward-Hastings | Prince Edward-Lennox-South Hastings | Wanda C. Thissen, Clerk-Treas., RR#4, Picton K0K 2T0 – 613/476-4436, Fax: 613/476-2635 |
| North Monaghan Twp [32] | 1,210 | Peterborough | Peterborough | Peterborough | Linda Levitt, Clerk-Treas., 2199 Davis Rd., RR#3, Peterborough K9J 6X4 – 705/749-1688, Fax: 705/749-1787 |
| North Plantagenet Twp | 3,733 | Prescott & Russell | Glengarry-Prescott-Russell | Prescott & Russell | Elise Campbell, Clerk-Treas., PO Box 271, Plantagenet K0B 1L0 – 613/673-4797, Fax: 613/673-4812 |
| The North Shore Twp | 678 | Algoma District | Algoma-Manitoulin | Algoma-Manitoulin | Dugal G. McQuarrie, Clerk-Treas., PO Box 108, Algoma Mills P0R 1A0 – 705/849-2213, Fax: 705/849-2428 |
| *NORTH YORK [52] | 589,653 | Metro Mun. | Don Valley East; Don Valley West; Eglinton-Lawrence; Willowdale; York Centre; York South-Weston; York West | Don Mills; Downsview; Lawrence; Oriole; Willowdale; Wilson Heights; York Mills; Yorkview | Denis G. Kelly, City Clerk, 5100 Yonge St., North York M2N 5V7 – 068/395-6910, Fax: 068/395-6920 |
| Norwich Twp | 10,611 | Oxford | Oxford | Oxford | Robert C. Watkins, Clerk-Adm., 10 Main St. East, PO Box 100, Otterville N0J 1R0 – 519/879-6568, Fax: 519/879-6385, URL: http://www.oxford.net/~twpnor/ns2/ |
| Norwood (V) [9] | 1,469 | Peterborough | Peterborough | Hastings-Peterborough | Glenn Girven, Adm.-Clerk-Treas., 78 Colborne St., PO Box 29, Norwood K0L 2V0 – 705/639-5343, Fax: 705/639-1880 |
| Oakland Twp | 1,377 | Brant | Haldimand-Norfolk-Brant | Brant-Haldimand | David Brenneman, Clerk-Treas., General Delivery, Oakland N0E 1L0 – 519/446-2924, Fax: 519/446-2924 |
| *Oakville † | 128,405 | Halton Reg. Mun. | Halton; Oakville | Halton Centre; Oakville South | Judith Muncaster, Town Clerk, 1225 Trafalgar Rd., PO Box 310, Oakville L6J 5A6 – 905/845-6601, Fax: 905/815-2025 |
| O'Connor Twp | 739 | Thunder Bay District | Thunder Bay-Atikokan | Fort William | Ruby Delyea, Clerk-Treas., RR#1, Kakabeka Falls P0T 1W0 – 807/475-4761, Fax: 807/473-0891 |
| Oil Springs (V) | 773 | Lambton | Lambton-Kent-Middlesex | Lambton | Marilyn G. Sanderson, Clerk-Treas., 4596 Oil Springs Line, PO Box 22, Oil Springs N0N 1P0 – 519/834-2939, Fax: 519/834-2333 |
| Olden Twp [63] | 906 | Frontenac | Hastings-Frontenac-Lennox & Addington | Frontenac-Addington | Judy C. Gray, Clerk-Treas., RR#1, PO Box 74, Mountain Grove K0H 2E0 – 613/335-5539, Fax: 613/335-2480 |
| Oliver Twp [76] | 2,711 | Thunder Bay District | Thunder Bay-Atikokan | Port Arthur | Sharron Martyn, Clerk-Treas., Municipal Office, PO Box 10, Murillo P0T 2G0 – 807/935-2613, Fax: 807/935-2161 |
| Omemee (V) | 1,271 | Victoria | Victoria-Haliburton | Victoria-Haliburton | Judy Currins, Clerk-Treas., 1 King St. West, PO Box 1000, Omemee K0L 2W0 – 705/799-5032, Fax: 705/799-2020 |
| Onaping Falls † | 5,277 | Sudbury Reg. Mun. | Nickel Belt | Nickel Belt | Colin Van Wallegham, Clerk-Treas.-Adm., 53 Hwy. 144, PO Box 400, Dowling P0M 1R0 – 705/855-4583, Fax: 705/855-2591 |
| Onondaga Twp | 1,650 | Brant | Haldimand-Norfolk-Brant | Brant-Haldimand | Arlene Jackson, Clerk-Treas., 734 Hwy#54, RR#7, Brantford N3T 5L9 – 519/758-1143, Fax: 519/758-1619 |
| Opasatika Twp | 349 | Cochrane District | Timmins-James Bay | Cochrane North | Benoit Sigouin, Clerk-Treas. & CAO, 50 Government Rd., PO Box 100, Opasatika P0L 1Z0 – 705/369-4531, Fax: 705/369-2002 |
| Ops Twp | 4,311 | Victoria | Victoria-Haliburton | Victoria-Haliburton | Sandra Richardson, Clerk-Treas., RR#5, PO Box 337, Lindsay K9V 4S3 – 705/324-5132, Fax: 705/328-2086 |
| Orangeville † | 21,498 | Dufferin | Dufferin-Peel-Wellington-Grey | Dufferin-Peel | Linda J. Dean, Clerk, 87 Broadway St., Orangeville L9W 1K1 – 519/941-0439, Fax: 519/941-9033, URL: http://www.headwaters.com/orangeville/ |

Cities in CAPITALS; Towns marked †; Villages marked (V); Townships marked Twp; Municipalities marked (Mun.); Separated Towns marked (SE); Development Areas marked (DA). An in-depth listing for municipalities marked with * appears in Part 2 (check Index for page numbers).

| MUNICIPALITY | 1996 POP. | COUNTY OR DISTRICT | FEDERAL ELECTORAL DISTRICT | PROVINCIAL ELECTORAL DISTRICT | CONTACT PERSON WITH ADDRESS, PHONE & FAX |
|---|---|---|---|---|---|
| Orford Twp | 1,359 | Kent | Kent-Essex | Essex-Kent | Jane Smith, Clerk-Treas., Main St., PO Box 196, Highgate N0P 1T0 – 519/678-3961, Fax: 519/678-3694 |
| ORILLIA | 27,846 | Simcoe | Simcoe North | Simcoe East | Ronald Ellett, City Clerk, 35 West St. North, PO Box 340, Orillia L3V 6J1 – 705/325-1311, Fax: 705/325-5178, URL: http://www.city.orillia.on.ca/ |
| Oro-Medonte Twp | 16,698 | Simcoe | Simcoe North | Simcoe East | Lynda Aiken, Clerk, PO Box 100, Oro L0L 2X0 – 705/487-2171, Fax: 705/487-0133 |
| Osgoode Twp | 15,904 | Ottawa-Carleton Reg. Mun. | Nepean-Carleton | Carleton | Wayne Robinson, Clerk, 8243 Victoria St., PO Box 130, Metcalfe K0A 2P0 – 613/821-1107, Fax: 613/821-4359 |
| *OSHAWA | 134,364 | Durham Reg. Mun. | Durham; Oshawa | Durham East; Oshawa; Durham Centre | Brian Suter, City Clerk, City Hall, 50 Centre St. South, Oshawa L1H 3Z7 – 905/725-7351, Fax: 905/436-5697 |
| Osnabruck Twp [40] | 4,787 | Stormont, Dundas & Glengarry | Stormont-Dundas | SDG & East Grenville | Betty de Haan, Clerk-Treas., PO Box 340, Ingleside K0C 1M0 – 613/537-2362, Fax: 613/537-8113 |
| Oso Twp [63] | 1,413 | Frontenac | Hasting-Frontenac-Lennox & Addington | Frontenac-Addington | Cathy MacMunn, Clerk-Treas., PO Box 89, Sharbot Lake K0H 2P0 – 613/279-2935, Fax: 613/279-2422 |
| Osprey Twp | 2,247 | Grey | Simcoe-Grey | Grey | Linda Fry, Clerk-Treas., Maxwell N0C 1J0 – 519/922-2551, Fax: 519/922-2502 |
| Otonabee Twp [77] | 5,447 | Peterborough | Peterborough | Hastings-Peterborough | Christine A. Wright, Adm.-Clerk-Treas., Third St., PO Box 70, Keene K0L 2G0 – 705/295-6852, Fax: 705/295-6405 |
| *OTTAWA | 323,340 | Ottawa-Carleton Reg. Mun. | Ottawa Centre; Ottawa South; Ottawa-Vanier; Ottawa West-Nepean | Carleton East; Ottawa-Rideau; Ottawa Centre; Ottawa East; Ottawa South; Ottawa West | Pierre Pagé, City Clerk, City Hall, 111 Sussex Dr., Ottawa K1N 5A1 – 613/244-5300, Fax: 613/244-5396, URL: http://city.ottawa.on.ca |
| OWEN SOUND | 21,390 | Grey | Bruce-Grey | Grey | Glen E. Henry, City Clerk, City Hall, 808 - 2nd Ave. East, Owen Sound N4K 2H4 – 519/376-1440, Fax: 519/371-0511 |
| Oxford-on-Rideau Twp [68] | 6,876 | Leeds & Grenville | Leeds-Grenville | SDG & East Grenville | Martha Sladek, Clerk-Treas., PO Box 2010, Oxford Mills K0G 1S0 – 613/258-3995, Fax: 613/258-9366 |
| Paipoonge Twp [76] | 3,196 | Thunder Bay District | Thunder Bay-Atikokan | Fort William | Linda Hamilton, Clerk-Treas., RR#6, Thunder Bay P7C 5N5 – 807/939-1543, Fax: 807/939-1550 |
| Paisley (V) | 1,106 | Bruce | Huron-Bruce | Bruce | Joanne Marklewitz, Clerk-Treas., 338 Goldie St., PO Box 460, Paisley N0G 2N0 – 519/353-5609, Fax: 519/353-7145 |
| Pakenham Twp [5] | 2,007 | Lanark | Lanark-Carleton | Lanark-Renfrew | Diane Smithson, Clerk-Treas., Municipal Office, PO Box 40, Pakenham K0A 2X0 – 613/624-5430, Fax: 613/624-5646 |
| Palmerston † | 2,468 | Wellington | Waterloo-Wellington | Wellington | Larry C. Adams, Clerk-Treas., 250 Daly St., PO Box 190, Palmerston N0G 2P0 – 519/343-2340, Fax: 519/343-2278 |
| Palmerston & N. & S. Canonto Twp [12] | 406 | Frontenac | Lanark-Carleton | Frontenac-Addington | Heather Gemmill, Clerk-Treas., RR#1, Ompah K0H 2J0 – 613/479-2811, Fax: 613/479-2364 |
| Papineau-Cameron Twp | 973 | Nipissing District | Nipissing | Parry Sound | Sandra J. Morin, Clerk-Treas., PO Box 630, Mattawa P0H 1V0 – 705/744-5610, Fax: 705/744-0434 |
| Paris † | 8,987 | Brant | Brant | Brant-Haldimand | Gloria Taylor, Clerk-Adm., 66 Grand River St. North, Paris N3L 2M2 – 519/442-6324, Fax: 519/442-3461 |
| Parkhill † | 1,765 | Middlesex | Lambton-Kent-Middlesex | Middlesex | Vivian L. Gunness, Adm.-Clerk-Treas., 229 Main St., PO Box 9, Parkhill N0M 2K0 – 519/294-6244, Fax: 519/294-0573 |
| Parry Sound † | 6,326 | Parry Sound District | Parry Sound-Muskoka | Parry Sound | Ian Mollett, CAO, 52 Seguin St., Parry Sound P2A 1B4 – 705/746-2101, Fax: 705/746-7461 |
| Peel Twp [48] | 4,499 | Wellington | Waterloo-Wellington | Wellington | Christine Oosterveld, Clerk-Treas., PO Box 119, Drayton N0G 1P0 – 519/638-3314, Fax: 519/638-5113 |
| Pelee Twp | 283 | Essex | Essex | Essex-South | Daphne B. Rae, Clerk-Treas., Pelee Island N0R 1M0 – 519/724-2931, Fax: 519/724-2470 |
| Pelham † | 14,343 | Niagara Reg. Mun. | Niagara Centre | Lincoln | Murray Hackett, Clerk-Adm., 20 Pelham Town Square, PO Box 400, Fonthill L0S 1E0 – 905/892-2607, Fax: 905/892-5055 |
| PEMBROKE | 14,177 | Renfrew | Renfrew-Nipissing-Pembroke | Renfrew North | Raymond J. Brazeau, CAO, 1 Pembroke St. East, PO Box 277, Pembroke K8A 6X3 – 613/735-6821, Fax: 613/735-3660 |

Cities in CAPITALS; Towns marked †; Villages marked (V); Townships marked Twp; Municipalities marked (Mun.); Separated Towns marked (SE); Development Areas marked (DA). An in-depth listing for municipalities marked with * appears in Part 2 (check Index for page numbers).

| MUNICIPALITY | 1996 POP. | COUNTY OR DISTRICT | FEDERAL ELECTORAL DISTRICT | PROVINCIAL ELECTORAL DISTRICT | CONTACT PERSON WITH ADDRESS, PHONE & FAX |
|---|---|---|---|---|---|
| Pembroke Twp | 2,017 | Renfrew | Renfrew-Nipissing-Pembroke | Renfrew North | Darrel J. Ryan, Adm.-Clerk-Treas., RR#4, Pembroke K8A 6W5 – 613/735-2319, Fax: 613/735-6614 |
| Penetanguishene † | 7,291 | Simcoe | Simcoe North | Simcoe East | George N. Vadeboncoeur, CAO-Clerk, 10 Robert St. West, PO Box 580, Penetanguishene L9M 2E4 – 705/549-7453, Fax: 705/549-3743 |
| Percy Twp | 3,208 | Northumberland | Northumberland | Northumberland | Ria Colquhoun, Clerk & CAO, 40 Main St., PO Box 129, Warkworth K0K 3K0 – 705/924-2931, Fax: 705/924-3139 |
| Perry Twp | 2,215 | Parry Sound District | Parry Sound-Muskoka | Parry Sound | Alton Hobbs, CAO-Clerk, Old Government Rd., PO Box 70, Emsdale P0A 1J0 – 705/636-5941, Fax: 705/636-5759 |
| Perth † | 5,886 | Lanark | Lanark-Carleton | Lanark-Renfrew | Stephen J. Fournier, Clerk-Adm., 80 Gore St. East, Perth K7H 1H9 – 613/267-3311, Fax: 613/267-5635 |
| Petawawa (V) [78] | 6,540 | Renfrew | Renfrew-Nipissing-Pembroke | Renfrew North | Robert W. Rantz, Clerk-Treas., 30 Victoria St., PO Box 69, Petawawa K8H 2X1 – 613/687-5536, Fax: 613/687-5973 |
| Petawawa Twp [78] | 8,764 | Renfrew | Renfrew-Nipissing-Pembroke | Renfrew North | Mitchell W. (Mitch) Stillman, Adm.-Clerk-Treas., 680 Hwy. 17 West, Pembroke K8A 7H5 – 613/735-2591, Fax: 613/735-7335 |
| *PETERBOROUGH | 69,535 | Peterborough | Peterborough | Peterborough | Steven F. Brickell, City Clerk, 500 George St. North, Peterborough K9H 3R9 – 705/742-7771, Fax: 705/743-7825 |
| Petrolia † | 4,908 | Lambton | Lambton-Kent-Middlesex | Lambton | Brad Loosley, Adm.-Clerk-Treas., 4201 Petrolia St., PO Box 1270, Petrolia N0N 1R0 – 519/882-2350, Fax: 519/882-3373 |
| *Pickering † | 78,989 | Durham Reg. Mun. | Pickering-Ajax-Uxbridge | Durham West | Bruce J. Taylor, Town Clerk, Pickering Civic Complex, One The Esplanade, Pickering L1V 6K7 – 905/420-2222, Fax: 905/420-0515, URL: http://www.town.pickering.on.ca |
| Pickle Lake Twp | 544 | Kenora District | Kenora-Rainy River | Lake Nipigon | Heather B. Brown, Clerk-Treas., PO Box 340, Pickle Lake P0V 3A0 – 807/928-2034, Fax: 807/928-2708 |
| Picton † | 4,673 | Prince Edward | Prince Edward-Hastings | Prince Edward-Lennox-South Hastings | Sterling P. Johnston, Clerk-Treas., 74 King St., PO Box 1670, Picton K0K 2T0 – 613/476-5966, Fax: 613/476-8144 |
| Pilkington Twp | 2,577 | Wellington | Waterloo-Wellington | Wellington | Caroline Hacking, Clerk-Treas., RR#2, Elora N0B 1S0 – 519/846-9801, Fax: 519/846-9858 |
| Pittsburgh Twp [70] | 12,902 | Frontenac | Hastings-Frontenac-Lennox & Addington; Kingston & the Islands | Frontenac-Addington; Kingston & the Islands | Beulah N. Webb, Clerk, 900 McLean Crt., PO Box 966, Kingston K7L 4X8 – 613/546-3283, Fax: 613/546-0908 |
| Plantagenet (V) [4] | 967 | Prescott & Russell | Glengarry-Prescott-Russell | Prescott & Russell | Sylvio Simard, Clerk-Treas., 220 Main St., PO Box 350, Plantagenet K0B 1L0 – 613/673-4859, Fax: 613/673-1021 |
| Plummer, Add'l Twp | 693 | Algoma District | Algoma-Manitoulin | Algoma | Caroline Hart, Clerk-Treas., RR#1, Bruce Mines P0R 1C0 – 705/785-3479, Fax: 705/785-3135 |
| Plympton Twp | 5,247 | Lambton | Lambton-Kent-Middlesex | Lambton | Archie W. McKinlay, Clerk, PO Box 400, Wyoming N0N 1T0 – 519/845-3939, Fax: 519/845-0597 |
| Point Edward (V) | 2,257 | Lambton | Sarnia-Lambton | Sarnia | Joe Simon, Clerk-Treas., 36 St. Clair St., Point Edward N7V 4G8 – 519/337-3021, Fax: 519/337-5963 |
| Port Burwell (V) [15] | 1,023 | Elgin | Elgin-Middlesex-London | Elgin | David Free, Clerk-Adm., 21 Pitt St., PO Box 10, Port Burwell N0J 1T0 – 519/874-4343, Fax: 519/874-4948, URL: http://www.kanservu.ca/burwell/ |
| PORT COLBORNE | 18,451 | Niagara Reg. Mun. | Erie-Lincoln | Niagara South | Len C. Hunt, Clerk-Treas., 66 Charlotte St., Port Colborne L3K 3C8 – 905/835-2900, Fax: 905/835-2939 |
| Port Elgin † | 7,041 | Bruce | Huron-Bruce | Bruce | Martin Parker, Clerk, 515 Goderich St., Port Elgin N0H 2C4 – 519/832-2008, Fax: 519/832-2140 |
| Port Hope † | 11,698 | Northumberland | Northumberland | Northumberland | Mike Rostetter, Clerk & CAO, 56 Queen St., PO Box 117, Port Hope L1A 3V9 – 905/885-4544, Fax: 905/885-7698 |
| Port Stanley (V) [20] | 2,499 | Elgin | Elgin-Middlesex-London | Elgin | Donald N. Leitch, Clerk-Adm., 302 Bridge St., Port Stanley N5L 1J7 – 519/782-3383, Fax: 519/782-5142 |
| Portland Twp [17] | 5,085 | Frontenac | Hastings-Frontenac-Lennox & Addington | Frontenac-Addington | Deborah Bracken, Clerk-Treas., PO Box 1000, Hartington K0H 1W0 – 613/372-2743, Fax: 613/372-1108 |

Cities in CAPITALS; Towns marked †; Villages marked (V); Townships marked Twp; Municipalities marked (Mun.); Separated Towns marked (SE); Development Areas marked (DA). An in-depth listing for municipalities marked with * appears in Part 2 (check Index for page numbers).

| MUNICIPALITY | 1996 POP. | COUNTY OR DISTRICT | FEDERAL ELECTORAL DISTRICT | PROVINCIAL ELECTORAL DISTRICT | CONTACT PERSON WITH ADDRESS, PHONE & FAX |
|---|---|---|---|---|---|
| Powassan † | 1,125 | Parry Sound District | Nipissing | Parry Sound | Traven D. Reed, Adm., 270 King St., PO Box 250, Powassan P0H 1Z0 – 705/724-2813, Fax: 705/724-5533 |
| Prescott (SE) | 4,480 | Leeds & Grenville | Leeds-Grenville | Leeds-Grenville | Andrew Brown, Clerk & CAO, 360 Dibble St. West, PO Box 160, Prescott K0E 1T0 – 613/925-2812, Fax: 613/925-4381 |
| Prince Twp | 971 | Algoma District | Algoma-Manitoulin | Algoma | Rachel Tyczinski, Adm.-Clerk-Treas., 3042 2nd Line West, RR#6, Sault Ste. Marie P6A 6K4 – 705/779-2992, Fax: 705/779-2725 |
| Proton Twp | 2,005 | Grey | Dufferin-Peel-Wellington-Grey | Grey | Helgi Scott, Clerk, RR#1, Dundalk N0C 1B0 – 519/923-2110, Fax: 519/923-9262 |
| Puslinch Twp | 5,416 | Wellington | Guelph-Wellington | Wellington | Brenda Law, Clerk-Treas., RR#3, Guelph N1H 6H9 – 519/763-1226, Fax: 519/763-5846 |
| Radcliffe Twp | 1,116 | Renfrew | Renfrew-Nipissing-Pembroke | Renfrew North | Pat E. Pilgrim, Clerk-Treas., Farmer Rd., PO Box 70, Combermere K0J 1L0 – 613/756-3704, Fax: 613/756-3704 |
| Raglan Twp | 820 | Renfrew | Renfrew-Nipissing-Pembroke | Renfrew North | Evaliene Krieger, Clerk-Treas., Palmer Rapids K0J 2E0 – 613/758-2061, Fax: 613/758-2235 |
| Rainy River † | 1,008 | Rainy River District | Kenora-Rainy River | Rainy River | Irwin E. Johnston, Clerk-Treas., 200 Atwood Ave., PO Box 488, Rainy River P0W 1L0 – 807/852-3978, Fax: 807/852-3553 |
| Raleigh Twp | 5,566 | Kent | Essex-Kent | Essex-Kent | Stu Cuthbert, Adm.-Clerk-Treas., RR#5, Merlin N0P 1W0 – 519/689-4206, Fax: 519/689-4870 |
| Ramara Twp | 7,812 | Simcoe | Simcoe North | Simcoe East | Richard Bates, Adm., PO Box 130, Brechin L0K 1B0 – 705/484-5374, Fax: 705/484-0441 |
| Ramsay Twp [5] | 4,451 | Lanark | Lanark-Carleton | Lanark-Renfrew | Ross E. Trimble, Adm.-Clerk-Treas., RR#2, Almonte K0A 1A0 – 613/256-2064, Fax: 613/256-4887, URL: http://www.ott.igs.net/~pakenham/ramsay |
| Ratter & Dunnet Twp | 1,291 | Sudbury District | Timiskaming-Cochrane | Sudbury East | Katherine McCauley, Clerk-Treas., 38 Rutland Ave., PO Box 250, Warren P0H 2N0 – 705/967-2174, Fax: 705/967-2177 |
| Rawdon Twp [79] | 2,732 | Hastings | Hastings-Frontenac-Lennox & Addington | Hastings-Peterborough | Cheryl Robson, Clerk-Treas. & Adm., General Delivery, Springbrook K0K 3C0 – 613/395-3962, Fax: 613/395-0672 |
| Rayside-Balfour † | 16,050 | Sudbury Reg. Mun. | Nickel Belt | Nickel Belt | Gary J. Michalak, Clerk, 3400 Hwy. 144, PO Box 639, Chelmsford P0M 1L0 – 705/855-9061, Fax: 705/855-5737 |
| Red Lake Twp | 2,277 | Kenora District | Kenora-Rainy River | Kenora | Arthur Osborne, CAO-Clerk, 117 Howey St., PO Box 308, Red Lake P0V 2M0 – 807/727-2311, Fax: 807/727-3980 |
| Red Rock Twp | 1,258 | Thunder Bay District | Thunder Bay-Nipigon | Lake Nipigon | Michael W. Groulx, Adm. & Clerk-Treas., 42 Salls St., PO Box 447, Red Rock P0T 2P0 – 807/886-2245, Fax: 807/886-2793 |
| Renfrew † | 8,125 | Renfrew | Renfrew-Nipissing-Pembroke | Lanark-Renfrew | Dorion Laurier, Clerk, 127 Raglan St. South, PO Box 2000, Renfrew K7V 4G7 – 613/432-4848, Fax: 613/432-8265 |
| Richmond Twp [1] | 4,143 | Lennox & Addington | Hastings-Frontenac-Lennox & Addington | Prince Edward-Lennox-South Hastings | Jane E. Sopha, Clerk-Treas., PO Box 100, Selby K0K 2Z0 – 613/388-2603, Fax: 613/388-2790 |
| *Richmond Hill † | 101,725 | York Reg. Mun. | Oak Ridges | York Centre | Robert Douglas, Town Clerk, 225 East Beaver Creek Rd., PO Box 300, Richmond Hill L4C 4Y5 – 905/771-8800, Fax: 905/771-2502 |
| Rideau Twp | 12,444 | Ottawa-Carleton Reg. Mun. | Nepean-Carleton | Carleton | J. David Ball, Clerk, 2155 Roger Stevens Dr., North Gower K0A 2T0 – 613/489-3314, Fax: 613/489-2880 |
| Ridgetown † | 3,454 | Kent | Kent-Essex | Essex-Kent | Gerald P. Secord, Adm.-Clerk-Treas., 45 Main St. East, PO Box 550, Ridgetown N0P 2C0 – 519/674-5583, Fax: 519/674-0660, URL: http://www.ciaccess.com/chatll/rcat.ridge.ridge.htm |
| Rochester Twp | 4,458 | Essex | Essex | Essex-Kent | Annette Drouillard, Clerk-Adm., 958 Hwy#2, St. Joachim N0R 1S0 – 519/728-2213, Fax: 519/728-4614 |
| Rockcliffe Park (V) | 1,995 | Ottawa-Carleton Reg. Mun. | Ottawa-Vanier | Carleton East | Murray MacLean, CAO-Clerk, 350 Springfield Rd., Rockcliffe Park K1M 0K7 – 613/749-9791, Fax: 613/749-0127 |
| Rockland † [38] | 8,070 | Prescott & Russell | Glengarry-Prescott-Russell | Prescott & Russell | Daniel Gatien, CAO-Clerk, 1560 Laurier St., PO Box 909, Rockland K4K 1P7 – 613/446-6022, Fax: 613/446-7320 |
| Rolph, Buchanan, Wylie & McKay Twp | 1,810 | Renfrew | Renfrew-Nipissing-Pembroke | Renfrew North | Mary Mysyk, Clerk-Treas. & CAO, RR#1, Deep River K0J 1P0 – 613/584-3114, Fax: 613/584-3285 |

Cities in CAPITALS; Towns marked †; Villages marked (V); Townships marked Twp; Municipalities marked (Mun.); Separated Towns marked (SE); Development Areas marked (DA). An in-depth listing for municipalities marked with * appears in Part 2 (check Index for page numbers).

| MUNICIPALITY | 1996 POP. | COUNTY OR DISTRICT | FEDERAL ELECTORAL DISTRICT | PROVINCIAL ELECTORAL DISTRICT | CONTACT PERSON WITH ADDRESS, PHONE & FAX |
|---|---|---|---|---|---|
| Romney Twp | 2,176 | Kent | Essex-Kent | Essex-Kent | Earl R. Waites, Clerk-Treas., 994 Talbot Trail, RR#1, Wheatley N0P 2P0 – 519/825-4618, Fax: 519/825-4619 |
| Ross Twp | 1,968 | Renfrew | Renfrew-Nipissing-Pembroke | Renfrew North | Eleanor Tabbert, Clerk-Treas., PO Box 1, Forester's Falls K0J 1V0 – 613/646-7428, Fax: 613/646-7332 |
| Rosseau (V) [37] | 280 | Parry Sound District | Parry Sound-Muskoka | Parry Sound | Yvonne Mullen, Clerk-Treas., Victoria St., PO Box 8, Rosseau P0C 1J0 – 705/732-4231, Fax: 705/732-1817 |
| Roxborough Twp [58] | 3,539 | Stormont, Dundas & Glengarry | Stormont-Dundas | SDG & East Grenville | Mary J. McCuaig, Clerk-Treas., 2594 Tolmies Corners Rd., PO Box 189, Moose Creek K0C 1W0 – 613/538-2531, Fax: 613/538-2650 |
| Russell Twp | 11,877 | Prescott & Russell | Glengarry-Prescott-Russell | Prescott & Russell | Ginette Bertrand, Acting Clerk, 717 Notre Dame St., Embrun K0A 1W1 – 613/443-3066, Fax: 613/443-1042 |
| Rutherford & George Island Twp | 401 | Manitoulin District | Algoma-Manitoulin | Algoma-Manitoulin | Jeannette Roque, Clerk-Treas., 32 Commissioner St., Killarney P0M 2A0 – 705/287-2424, Fax: 705/287-2660 |
| Ryerson Twp | 676 | Parry Sound District | Parry Sound-Muskoka | Moosomin | Judy McCarty, Clerk-Treas., RR#1, Burk's Falls P0A 1C0 – 705/382-3232, Fax: 705/382-3286 |
| *ST CATHARINES | 130,926 | Niagara Reg. Mun. | St. Catharines; Niagara Centre | St. Catharines-Brock; St. Catharines; Lincoln | Kenneth R. Todd, City Clerk & Director, Corporate Support Services, City Hall, 50 Church St., PO Box 3012, St. Catharines L2R 7C2 – 905/688-5600, Fax: 905/641-4450 |
| St. Clair Beach (V) | 3,705 | Essex | Windsor-St. Clair | Windsor-Riverside | Andre M. Barrette, Clerk-Treas., 13677 St. Gregory's Rd., Windsor N8N 3E4 – 519/735-6261, Fax: 519/735-8388 |
| St. Edmunds Twp | 1,007 | Bruce | Bruce-Grey | Bruce | Cathy Robins, Clerk-Adm., PO Box 70, Tobermory N0H 2R0 – 519/596-2430, Fax: 519/596-2536 |
| St. Isidore (V) [28] | 766 | Prescott & Russell | Glengarry-Prescott-Russell | Prescott & Russell | Norman Bonneville, Clerk-Treas., 25 rue de l'Église, PO Box 10, St. Isidore K0C 2B0 – 613/524-2155, Fax: 613/524-3406 |
| St. Joseph Twp | 1,235 | Algoma District | Algoma-Manitoulin | Algoma | A. Michael Jagger, Clerk-Treas., 1511 - 10 Side Rd., PO Box 187, Richards Landing P0R 1J0 – 705/246-2625, Fax: 705/246-3142 |
| St. Marys (SE) | 5,952 | Perth | Perth-Middlesex | Perth | Kenneth G. Storey, Adm.-Clerk-Treas., 175 Queen St. East, PO Box 998, St. Marys N4X 1B6 – 519/284-2340, Fax: 519/284-2881 |
| ST. THOMAS | 32,275 | Elgin | Elgin-Middlesex-London | Elgin | Peter Leack, Clerk, City Hall, 545 Talbot St., PO Box 520, St. Thomas N5P 3V7 – 519/631-1680, Fax: 519/633-9019 |
| St. Vincent Twp | 2,610 | Grey | Bruce-Grey | Grey | Jim Foster, Clerk-Treas., RR#1, Meaford N4L 1W5 – 519/538-2421, Fax: 519/538-5599 |
| Sandfield Twp | 284 | Manitoulin District | Algoma-Manitoulin | Algoma-Manitoulin | Ruth F. Legge, Clerk-Treas., RR#1, Mindemoya P0P 1C0 – 705/377-5621, Fax: 705/377-5621 |
| Sandwich South Twp | 6,618 | Essex | Essex | Essex-Kent | Gerald Sykes, Clerk-Adm., 3455 North Talbot Rd., Oldcastle N0R 1L0 – 519/737-6971, Fax: 519/737-1975 |
| Sarawak Twp | 2,832 | Grey | Bruce-Grey | Grey | Kenneth J. Clarke, Adm. & Clerk-Treas., RR#2, Owen Sound N4K 5N4 – 519/376-2729, Fax: 519/372-1620 |
| *SARNIA | 72,738 | Lambton | Sarnia-Lambton | Sarnia | Ann Tuplin, City Clerk, City Hall, 255 North Christina St., PO Box 3018, Sarnia N7T 7N2 – 519/332-0330, Fax: 519/332-3995 |
| Saugeen Twp | 1,892 | Bruce | Huron-Bruce | Bruce | Linda White, Clerk-Dep. Treas., PO Box 249, Port Elgin N0H 2C0 – 519/389-5550, Fax: 519/389-4305 |
| *SAULT STE. MARIE | 80,054 | Algoma District | Sault Ste. Marie | Sault Ste. Marie | Donna P. Irving, City Clerk, Civic Centre, 99 Foster Dr., PO Box 580, Sault Ste Marie P6A 5N1 – 705/759-2500, Fax: 705/759-2310, URL: http://www.sault-canada.com |
| *SCARBOROUGH [52] | 558,960 | Metro Mun. | Scarborough-Agincourt; Scarborough Centre; Scarborough East; Scarborough-Rouge River; Scarborough Southwest | Scarborough-Agincourt; Scarborough Centre; Scarborough East; Scarborough-Ellesmere; Scarborough North; Scarborough West | W. Drew Westwater, City Clerk, Civic Centre, 150 Borough Dr., Scarborough M1P 4N7 – 416/396-7111, Fax: 416/396-6920, URL: http://www.city.scarborough.on.ca/ |
| Schreiber Twp | 1,788 | Thunder Bay District | Thunder Bay-Nipigon | Lake Nipigon | Dawn Halcrow, Clerk-Treas.-Adm., 608 Winnipeg St., Schreiber P0T 2S0 – 807/824-2711, Fax: 807/824-3231 |

Cities in CAPITALS; Towns marked †; Villages marked (V); Townships marked Twp; Municipalities marked (Mun.); Separated Towns marked (SE); Development Areas marked (DA). An in-depth listing for municipalities marked with * appears in Part 2 (check Index for page numbers).

| MUNICIPALITY | 1996 POP. | COUNTY OR DISTRICT | FEDERAL ELECTORAL DISTRICT | PROVINCIAL ELECTORAL DISTRICT | CONTACT PERSON WITH ADDRESS, PHONE & FAX |
|---|---|---|---|---|---|
| Scugog Twp | 18,837 | Durham Reg. Mun. | Durham | Durham East | Earl S. Cuddie, Adm.-Clerk, 181 Perry St., PO Box 780, Port Perry L9L 1A7 – 905/985-7346, Fax: 905/985-1931 |
| Seaforth † | 2,302 | Huron | Huron-Bruce | Huron | James D. Crocker, CAO & Clerk-Treas., 72 Main St. South, PO Box 610, Seaforth N0K 1W0 – 519/527-0160, Fax: 519/527-2561 |
| Sebastopol Twp | 589 | Renfrew | Renfrew-Nipissing-Pembroke | Renfrew North | Sandra Yonin, Clerk-Treas., Municipal Hall, Foymount K0J 1W0 – 613/754-2825, Fax: 613/754-2825 |
| Severn Twp | 10,257 | Simcoe | Simcoe North | Simcoe East | James B. Mather, Clerk & CAO, PO Box 159, Orillia L3V 6J3 – 705/325-2315, Fax: 705/327-5818 |
| Seymour Twp [30] | 4,442 | Northumberland | Northumberland | Northumberland | Shirley M. Preston, Clerk-Treas., 66 Front St. South, PO Box 1027, Campbellford K0L 1L0 – 705/653-2330, Fax: 705/653-5413 |
| Shallow Lake (V) [69] | 491 | Grey | Bruce-Grey | Grey | Rosemary Buchanan, Clerk-Treas., 12 Cruickshank St., Shallow Lake N0H 2K0 – 519/935-3164, Fax: 519/935-3164 |
| Shedden Twp | 899 | Algoma District | Elgin-Middlesex-London | Algoma-Manitoulin | Mary Bray, Clerk-Treas.-Adm., 8 Trunk Rd., PO Box 70, Spanish P0P 2A0 – 705/844-2300, Fax: 705/844-2622 |
| Sheffield Twp [29] | 1,572 | Lennox & Addington | Hastings-Frontenac-Lennox & Addington | Frontenac-Addington | Susan Beckel, Clerk, Ottawa St., PO Box 3, Tamworth K0K 3G0 – 613/379-2923, Fax: 613/379-2789 |
| Shelburne † | 3,790 | Dufferin | Dufferin-Peel-Wellington-Grey | Dufferin-Peel | Susan McKenzie, Clerk-Treas., 203 Main St. East, PO Box 69, Shelburne L0N 1S0 – 519/925-2600, Fax: 519/925-6134 |
| Sherborne et al Twp | 487 | Haliburton | Parry Sound-Muskoka | Victoria-Haliburton | Diane J. Griffin, Adm.-Clerk-Treas., PO Box 99, Dorset P0A 1E0 – 705/766-2211, Fax: 705/766-9688 |
| Sherwood, Jones & Burns Twp | 2,140 | Renfrew | Renfrew-Nipissing-Pembroke | Renfrew North | Valerie R. Jahn, Clerk-Treas., RR#2, Barry's Bay K0J 1B0 – 613/756-2741, Fax: 613/756-0251 |
| Shuniah Twp | 2,346 | Thunder Bay District | Thunder Bay-Nipigon | Port Arthur | Ken Taniwa, Clerk, 420 Leslie Ave., Thunder Bay P7A 1X8 – 807/683-3611, Fax: 807/683-6982 |
| Sidney Twp [59] | 16,172 | Hastings | Prince Edward-Hastings | Quinte | James R. (Jim) Pine, CAO, RR#5, Belleville K8N 4Z5 – 613/966-8330, Fax: 613/966-4973 |
| Simcoe † | 15,380 | Haldimand-Norfolk Reg. Mun. | Haldimand-Norfolk-Brant | Norfolk | Lori Heinbuch, Clerk, 50 Colborne St. South, PO Box 545, Simcoe N3Y 4N5 – 519/426-5870, Fax: 519/426-8573 |
| Sioux Lookout † | 3,469 | Kenora District | Kenora-Rainy River | Kenora | Mary L. MacKenzie, Clerk, 25 - 5 Ave., PO Box 158, Sioux Lookout P8T 1A4 – 807/737-2700, Fax: 807/737-3436 |
| Sioux Narrows Twp | 430 | Kenora District | Kenora-Rainy River | Kenora | Debbie Sinclair, Clerk-Treas., PO Box 417, Sioux Narrows P0X 1N0 – 807/226-5241, Fax: 807/226-5712 |
| Smith Twp [56] | 9,200 | Peterborough | Peterborough | Peterborough | Derick A. Holyoake, Adm.-Clerk-Treas., PO Box 270, Bridgenorth K0L 1H0 – 705/292-9507, Fax: 705/292-6491 |
| Smiths Falls | 9,131 | Lanark | Lanark-Carleton | Lanark-Renfrew | Kathy L. Coulthart-Dewey, Clerk, 77 Beckwith St. North, PO Box 695, Smiths Falls K7A 4T6 – 613/283-4124, Fax: 613/283-4764 |
| Smooth Rock Falls † | 1,982 | Cochrane District | Timmins-James Bay | Cochrane North | Roger Labelle, Clerk & CAO, 142 - 1st St., PO Box 249, Smooth Rock Falls P0L 2B0 – 705/338-2717, Fax: 705/338-2584 |
| Snowdon Twp | 950 | Halburton | Victoria-Haliburton | Victoria-Haliburton | Ernest A. Hills, Clerk-Treas., RR#1, Minden K0M 2K0 – 705/286-2657, Fax: 705/286-1685 |
| Sombra Twp | 4,217 | Lambton | Sarnia-Lambton | Lambton | John De Mars, Clerk-Adm., PO Box 40, Sombra N0P 2H0 – 519/892-3637, Fax: 519/892-3543 |
| Somerville Twp | 2,238 | Victoria | Victoria-Haliburton | Victoria-Haliburton | Elinor Burke, Clerk-Treas., Hwy. 121, PO Box 59, Kinmount K0M 2A0 – 705/488-2571, Fax: 705/488-2576 |
| Sophiasburgh Twp | 2,283 | Prince Edward | Prince Edward-Hastings | Prince Edward-Lennox-South Hastings | Bryson Bates, Clerk-Treas., Demorestville K0K 1W0 – 613/476-2209, Fax: 613/476-2220 |
| South Algona Twp | 386 | Renfrew | Renfrew-Nipissing-Pembroke | Renfrew North | Brenda Jolicoeur, Clerk-Treas., RR#4, Killaloe K0J 2A0 – 613/625-2323, Fax: 613/625-2323 |
| South Crosby Twp [13] | 1,910 | Leeds & Grenville | Leeds-Grenville | Leeds-Grenville | Myrna Stearry, Clerk-Treas., RR#1, Elgin K0G 1E0 – 613/359-5830, Fax: 613/359-5849 |
| South Dorchester Twp [72] | 1,899 | Elgin | Elgin-Middlesex-London | Elgin | Jane Knapp, Clerk-Treas., RR#2, Springfield N0L 2J0 – 519/765-4175 |
| South Dumfries Twp | 5,441 | Brant | Brant | Brant-Haldimand | James G. Wilson, Clerk-Treas., 13 Main St. South, PO Box 40, St. George N0E 1N0 – 519/448-1432, Fax: 519/448-3105 |

Cities in CAPITALS; Towns marked †; Villages marked (V); Townships marked Twp; Municipalities marked (Mun.); Separated Towns marked (SE); Development Areas marked (DA). An in-depth listing for municipalities marked with * appears in Part 2 (check Index for page numbers).

| MUNICIPALITY | 1996 POP. | COUNTY OR DISTRICT | FEDERAL ELECTORAL DISTRICT | PROVINCIAL ELECTORAL DISTRICT | CONTACT PERSON WITH ADDRESS, PHONE & FAX |
|---|---|---|---|---|---|
| South Easthope Twp [53] | 1,853 | Perth | Perth-Middlesex | Perth | Margaret Hislop, Clerk-Treas., 37 William St. West, PO Box 269, Shakespeare N0B 2P0 – 519/625-8372, Fax: 519/625-8498 |
| South Elmsley Twp [13] | 3,574 | Leeds & Grenville | Leeds-Grenville | Leeds-Grenville | Sharon Seward, Clerk-Treas., 441 Hwy. 15, RR#1, Smiths Falls K7A 5B8 – 613/283-5427, Fax: 613/283-5918 |
| South Fredericksburgh Twp [1] | 1,197 | Lennox & Addington | Hastings-Frontenac-Lennox & Addington | Prince Edward-Lennox-South Hastings | Lorraine Patterson, Clerk-Treas., RR#2, Napanee K7R 3K7 – 613/354-2420, Fax: 613/354-7682 |
| South Gower Twp [68] | 2,500 | Leeds-Grenville | Leeds & Grenville | SDG & East Grenville | Dorothy McCargar, Clerk-Treas., RR#3, Kemptville K0G 1J0 – 613/258-2781, Fax: 613/258-5574 |
| South Marysburgh Twp | 1,018 | Prince Edward | Prince Edward-Hastings | Prince Edward-Lennox-South Hastings | Clifford Walker, Clerk-Treas., PO Box 12, Milford K0K 2P0 – 613/476-6771, Fax: 613/476-6771 |
| South Monaghan Twp [77] | 1,302 | Peterborough | Peterborough | Peterborough | June M. Buettner, Clerk-Treas., 199 Highway 28, Bailieboro K0L 1B0 – 705/939-6079, Fax: 705/939-1096 |
| South Plantagenet Twp [28] | 1,835 | Prescott & Russell | Glengarry-Prescott-Russell | Prescott & Russell | Calista Nicholas, Clerk-Treas., 3248 County Rd. #9, RR#1, Fournier K0B 1G0 – 613/524-2932, Fax: 613/524-3351 |
| South River (V) | 1,098 | Parry Sound District | Parry Sound-Muskoka | Parry Sound | Richard V. Clouthier, Clerk-Adm., 209 Ottawa Ave., PO Box 310, South River P0A 1X0 – 705/386-2573, Fax: 705/386-0702 |
| South Sherbrooke Twp [14] | 732 | Lanark | Lanark-Carleton | Lanark-Renfrew | Allan Burn, Clerk-Treas., RR#1, Maberly K0H 2B0 – 613/268-2194, Fax: 613/268-2478 |
| South-West Oxford Twp | 8,441 | Oxford | Oxford | Oxford | Allen Forrester, Clerk-Treas.-Adm., RR#1, Mount Elgin N0J 1N0 – 519/485-0477, Fax: 519/485-2932 |
| Southampton † | 3,151 | Bruce | Huron-Bruce | Bruce | Ronald G. Brown, Clerk-Adm., 201 High St., PO Box 340, Southampton N0H 2L0 – 519/797-2015, Fax: 519/797-3088 |
| Southwold Twp | 4,282 | Elgin | Elgin-Middlesex-London | Elgin | R. Alex Pow, Clerk, General Delivery, Fingal N0L 1K0 – 519/769-2010, Fax: 519/769-2837 |
| The Spanish River Twp | 1,598 | Sudbury District | Algoma-Manitoulin | Algoma-Manitoulin | Austin H. Clipperton, Clerk-Treas., Site 1, RR#3, PO Box 5, Massey P0P 1P0 – 705/865-2646, Fax: 705/865-2736 |
| Springer Twp [27] | 2,433 | Nipissing District | Timiskaming-Cochrane | Nipissing | Normand Roberge, Clerk-Treas. & CAO, 245 Hwy 17 East, PO Box 1390, Sturgeon Falls P0H 2G0 – 705/753-0570, Fax: 705/753-1034 |
| Springfield (V) [72] | 741 | Elgin | Elgin-Middlesex-London | Elgin | Catherine Bearss, Clerk-Treas., 106 Main St., PO Box 29, Springfield N0L 2J0 – 519/765-4222, Fax: 519/765-4222 |
| Springwater Twp | 14,793 | Simcoe | Simcoe-Grey | Simcoe Centre | Eleanor Rath, Clerk, County of Simcoe Administrative Centre, Midhurst L0L 1X0 – 705/728-4784, Fax: 705/728-6957 |
| Stafford & Pembroke Twp [80] | 2,837 | Renfrew | Renfrew-Nipissing-Pembroke | Renfrew North | Darryl J. Ryan, Adm.-Clerk-Treas., RR#4, Pembroke K8A 6W5 – 613/735-3955, Fax: 613/735-6614 |
| Stanhope Twp | 1,200 | Haliburton | Victoria-Haliburton | Victoria-Haliburton | Gerald C. Bain, Adm.-Clerk-Treas., RR#2, Minden K0M 2K0 – 705/489-2379, Fax: 705/489-3491 |
| Stanley Twp | 1,714 | Huron | Huron-Bruce | Huron | E. Ansberth Willert, Clerk-Treas., RR#1, Varna N0M 2R0 – 519/233-7907, Fax: 519/233-3111 |
| Stephen Twp | 4,222 | Huron | Huron-Bruce | Huron | Laurence R. Brown, CAO & Clerk-Treas., 38 Victoria St. East, Crediton N0M 1M0 – 519/234-6331, Fax: 519/234-6301 |
| Stirling (V) [79] | 2,173 | Hastings | Hastings-Frontenac-Lennox & Addington | Hastings-Peterborough | Kathy Reid, Adm.-Clerk-Treas., 98 Front St. East, PO Box 40, Stirling K0K 3E0 – 613/395-3380, Fax: 613/395-0864 |
| *STONEY CREEK | 54,318 | Hamilton-Wentworth Reg. Mun. | Stoney Creek | Wentworth East | Rose Caterini, City Clerk, 777 Hwy. 8, PO Box 9940, Stoney Creek L8G 4N9 – 905/643-1261, Fax: 905/643-6161 |
| Storrington Twp [17] | 4,468 | Frontenac | Hastings-Frontenac-Lennox & Addington | Frontenac-Addington | David Bass, Adm. & Clerk-Treas., RR#1, Battersea K0H 1H0 – 613/353-2222, Fax: 613/353-1225 |
| STRATFORD | 28,987 | Perth | Perth-Middlesex | Perth | Ron Shaw, Clerk-Adm., City Hall, One Wellington St., PO Box 818, Stratford N5A 6W1 – 519/271-0250, Fax: 519/273-5041 |
| Strathroy † | 11,852 | Middlesex | Lambton-Kent-Middlesex | Middlesex | Angela Toth, Acting Clerk, 52 Frank St., Strathroy N7G 2R4 – 519/245-1070, Fax: 519/245-6353 |
| Strong Twp | 1,393 | Parry Sound District | Parry Sound-Muskoka | Parry Sound | Diana Georgie, Clerk-Treas., Hwy 11 South, PO Box 420, Sundridge P0A 1Z0 – 705/384-5819, Fax: 705/384-5892 |

Cities in CAPITALS; Towns marked †; Villages marked (V); Townships marked Twp; Municipalities marked (Mun.); Separated Towns marked (SE); Development Areas marked (DA). An in-depth listing for municipalities marked with * appears in Part 2 (check Index for page numbers).

| MUNICIPALITY | 1996 POP. | COUNTY OR DISTRICT | FEDERAL ELECTORAL DISTRICT | PROVINCIAL ELECTORAL DISTRICT | CONTACT PERSON WITH ADDRESS, PHONE & FAX |
|---|---|---|---|---|---|
| Sturgeon Falls † [27] | 6,162 | Nipissing District | Timiskaming-Cochrane | Nipissing | Guy Savage, Adm.-Clerk-Treas., 225 Holditch St., PO Box 270, Sturgeon Falls P0H 2G0 – 705/753-2250, Fax: 705/753-3950 |
| Sturgeon Point (V) | 111 | Victoria | Victoria-Haliburton | Victoria-Haliburton | Marlyn Beggs, Clerk-Treas., RR#3, Fenelon Falls K0M 1N0 – 705/887-2343, Fax: 705/887-9340 |
| *SUDBURY | 92,059 | Sudbury Reg. Mun. | Nickel Belt; Sudbury | Sudbury; Sudbury East | Thom M. Mowry, Clerk, City Hall, Civic Square, 200 Brady St., PO Box 5000, Sudbury P3A 5P3 – 705/674-3141, Fax: 705/673-3096, URL: http://www.city.sudbury.on.ca |
| Sullivan Twp | 2,852 | Grey | Bruce-Grey | Grey | Will Moore, Clerk-Treas., PO Box 92, Desboro N0H 1K0 – 519/794-3024, Fax: 519/794-4499 |
| Sundridge (V) | 1,019 | Parry Sound District | Parry Sound-Muskoka | Parry Sound | Lillian S. Fowler, Clerk-Treas., 110 Main St., PO Box 129, Sundridge P0A 1Z0 – 705/384-5316, Fax: 705/384-7874 |
| Sydenham Twp | 3,206 | Grey | Bruce-Grey | Grey | Richard Holland, Clerk-Treas., RR#8, Owen Sound N4K 5W4 – 519/376-8487, Fax: 519/376-8090 |
| Tara (V) | 903 | Bruce | Bruce-Grey | Bruce | Holly M. MacArthur, Clerk-Treas., 39 Yonge St., PO Box 238, Tara N0H 2N0 – 519/934-2544, Fax: 519/934-2651 |
| Tarbutt & Tarbutt Add'l Twp | 432 | Algoma District | Algoma-Manitoulin | Algoma | Ruth Kelso, Clerk-Treas., RR#1, Desbarats P0R 1E0 – 705/782-6776, Fax: 705/782-4274 |
| Tay Twp | 10,965 | Simcoe | Simcoe North | Muskoka-Georgian Bay | Ted Walker, Clerk & CAO, Park St., PO Box 100, Victoria Harbour L0K 2A0 – 705/534-7248, Fax: 705/534-4493 |
| Tecumseh † | 12,828 | Essex | Windsor-St. Clair | Windsor-Riverside | Leo A. Lessard, Clerk-Treas., 917 Lesperance Rd., Tecumseh N8N 1W9 – 519/735-2184, Fax: 519/735-6712 |
| Teeswater (V) [41] | 1,069 | Bruce | Huron-Bruce | Bruce | Kendra J. Reinhart, Clerk-Treas., 2 Clinton St. South, PO Box 369, Teeswater N0G 2S0 – 519/392-6818, Fax: 519/392-6819 |
| Tehkummah Twp | 371 | Manitoulin District | Algoma-Manitoulin | Algoma-Manitoulin | Shirley Pyette, Clerk-Treas., Municipal Bldg., Tehkummah P0P 2C0 – 705/859-3293, Fax: 705/859-2605 |
| Temagami Twp [81] | 871 | Nipissing District | Timiskaming-Cochrane | Timiskaming | John Hodgson, Clerk-Treas. & CAO, PO Box 220, Temagami P0H 2H0 – 705/569-3421, Fax: 705/569-2834 |
| Terrace Bay Twp | 2,324 | Thunder Bay District | Thunder Bay-Nipigon | Lake Nipigon | M. Heather Adams, Clerk & CAO, 12 Simcoe Plaza, PO Box 40, Terrace Bay P0T 2W0 – 807/825-3315, Fax: 807/825-9576 |
| Thamesville (V) | 972 | Kent | Lambton-Kent-Middlesex | Essex-Kent | Violet Harry, Clerk-Treas., London Rd., PO Box 280, Thamesville N0P 2K0 – 519/692-3991, Fax: 519/692-5915 |
| Thedford (V) | 831 | Lambton | Lambton-Kent-Middlesex | Lambton | Jackie Mason, Clerk-Treas., 89 Main St., PO Box 70, Thedford N0M 2N0 – 519/296-4980, Fax: 519/296-4648 |
| Thessalon † | 1,485 | Algoma District | Algoma-Manitoulin | Algoma | Robert MacLean, Clerk-Treas., 169 Main St., PO Box 220, Thessalon P0R 1L0 – 705/842-2217, Fax: 705/842-2572 |
| Thessalon Twp | 758 | Algoma District | Algoma-Manitoulin | Algoma | Beverly Eagleson, Adm.-Clerk-Treas., RR#1, Thessalon P0R 1L0 – 705/842-3800, Fax: 705/842-3800 |
| Thompson Twp | 125 | Algoma District | Algoma-Manitoulin | Algoma | Sandra Leach, Clerk-Treas., RR#1, Blind River P0R 1B0 – 705/356-7393, Fax: 705/356-7393 |
| Thornbury † [39] | 1,763 | Grey | Simcoe-Grey | Grey | Janette Scott, Clerk, 26 Bridge St., PO Box 310, Thornbury N0H 2P0 – 519/599-3250, Fax: 519/599-7723 |
| Thornloe (V) | 132 | Timiskaming District | Timiskaming-Cochrane | Timiskaming | Gordon Edwards, Clerk-Treas., Main St., PO Box 30, Thornloe P0J 1S0 – 705/563-8303, Fax: 705/563-8192 |
| THOROLD | 17,883 | Niagara Reg. Mun. | Niagara Centre; Niagara Falls | Welland-Thorold | John K. Bice, City Clerk, 8 Carleton St. South, PO Box 1044, Thorold L2V 4A7 – 905/227-6613, Fax: 905/227-5590, URL: http://www.thorold.com/mayor.html |
| *THUNDER BAY | 113,662 | Thunder Bay District | Thunder Bay-Atikokan; Thunder Bay-Nipigon | Fort William; Port Arthur | M. Elaine Bahlieda, City Clerk, City Hall, 500 Donald St. East, Thunder Bay P7E 5V3 – 807/625-2230, Fax: 807/623-5468 |
| Thurlow Twp [19] | 7,986 | Hastings | Prince Edward-Hastings | Prince Edward-Lennox-South Hastings | Gary King, Clerk-Adm., General Delivery, River Road South, RR#1, Corbyville K0K 1K0 – 613/968-5553, Fax: 613/968-2930 |

Cities in CAPITALS; Towns marked †; Villages marked (V); Townships marked Twp; Municipalities marked (Mun.); Separated Towns marked (SE); Development Areas marked (DA). An in-depth listing for municipalities marked with * appears in Part 2 (check Index for page numbers).

| MUNICIPALITY | 1996 POP. | COUNTY OR DISTRICT | FEDERAL ELECTORAL DISTRICT | PROVINCIAL ELECTORAL DISTRICT | CONTACT PERSON WITH ADDRESS, PHONE & FAX |
|---|---|---|---|---|---|
| Tilbury † | 4,448 | Kent | Essex-Kent | Essex-Kent | Robert J. Bourassa, Clerk-Adm., 17 Superior St., PO Box 1299, Tilbury N0P 2L0 – 519/682-2583, Fax: 519/682-3123 |
| Tilbury East Twp | 2,304 | Kent | Essex-Kent | Essex-Kent | George Darnley, Clerk-Treas., RR#1, Merlin N0P 1W0 – 519/682-0803, Fax: 519/682-1611 |
| Tilbury North Twp | 3,591 | Essex | Essex | Essex-Kent | M. Daniel Perdu, Clerk-Treas., 6690 Tecumseh Rd., PO Box 70, Stoney Point N0R 1N0 – 519/798-3115, Fax: 519/798-5976 |
| Tilbury West Twp | 1,777 | Essex | Essex | Essex-Kent | Donald H. McMillan, Clerk-Treas., 6400 Main St., PO Box 158, Comber N0P 1J0 – 519/687-2240, Fax: 519/687-2911 |
| Tillsonburg † | 13,211 | Oxford | Oxford | Norfolk | David C. Morris, Clerk-Adm., 200 Broadway St., 2nd Fl., Tillsonburg N4G 5A7 – 519/842-6428, Fax: 519/842-9431, URL: http://oxford.net/~tburg |
| TIMMINS | 47,499 | Cochrane District | Timmins-James Bay | Cochrane South | R. Jack Watson, City Clerk, 220 Algonquin Blvd. East, Timmins P4N 1B3 – 705/264-1331, Fax: 705/360-1392 |
| Tiny Twp | 8,644 | Simcoe | Simcoe North | Simcoe East | Vicki Robertson, Clerk-Adm., 130 Balm Beach, RR#1, Perkinsfield L0L 2J0 – 705/526-4204, Fax: 705/526-2372 |
| Tiverton (V) [24] | 824 | Bruce | Huron-Bruce | Bruce | Sharon Mooser, Clerk-Treas., PO Box 130, Tiverton N0G 2T0 – 519/368-7860, Fax: 519/368-5535 |
| *TORONTO [52] | 653,734 | Metro Mun. | Beaches-East York; Broadview-Greenwood; Davenport; Don Valley West; Eglinton-Lawrence; Parkdale-High Park; Toronto Centre-Rosedale; St. Paul's; Trinity-Spadina; York South-Weston | Beaches-Woodbine; Dovercourt; Eglinton; Fort York; High Park-Swansea; Oakwood; Parkdale; Riverdale; St. Andrew-St. Patrick; St. George-St. David | Sydney Baxter, City Clerk, City Hall, 100 Queen St. West, Toronto M5H 2N2 – 416/392-9111, Fax: 416/392-6990, URL: http://www.city.toronto.on.ca/ |
| TRENTON [59] | 17,179 | Hastings | Northumberland | Quinte | Cheryl J. Vandervoort, City Clerk, 65 Dundas St. West, PO Box 490, Trenton K8V 5R6 – 613/392-2841, Fax: 613/392-0714 |
| Trout Creek † | 614 | Parry Sound District | Nipissing | Parry Sound | Betty Young, Clerk-Treas., Main St. West, PO Box 99, Trout Creek P0H 2L0 – 705/723-5253, Fax: 705/723-1034 |
| Tuckersmith Twp | 3,105 | Huron | Huron-Bruce | Huron | John R. McLachlan, Clerk-Treas., 42 - 1 Ave., Vanastra N0M 1L0 – 519/482-9523, Fax: 519/482-7621 |
| Tudor & Cashel Twp | 696 | Hastings | Hastings-Frontenac-Lennox & Addington | Hastings-Peterborough | Andrew J. McMurray, Clerk-Treas., RR#1, Gilmour K0L 1W0 – 613/474-2583 |
| Turnberry Twp | 1,772 | Huron | Huron-Bruce | Huron | Dorothy R. Kelly, Clerk-Treas., 100 Queen St., Bluevale N0G 1G0 – 519/357-2991, Fax: 519/357-4106 |
| Tweed (V) [55] | 1,572 | Hastings | Hastings-Frontenac-Lennox-Addington | Hastings-Peterborough | Martha Murphy, Clerk-Treas., 320 Colborne St., PO Box 729, Tweed K0K 3J0 – 613/478-2535, Fax: 613/478-6457 |
| Tyendinaga Twp | 3,549 | Hastings | Prince Edward-Hastings | Prince Edward-Lennox-South Hastings | Carman J. Milligan, Clerk-Treas., RR#1, Shannonville K0K 3A0 – 613/396-1944, Fax: 613/396-2080 |
| Usborne Twp | 1,535 | Huron | Huron-Bruce | Huron | Sandra J. Strang, Clerk-Treas., RR#3, Exeter N0M 1S5 – 519/235-2900 |
| Uxbridge Twp | 15,882 | Durham Reg. Mun. | Pickering-Ajax-Uxbridge | Durham | Walter E. Taylor, Clerk, 51 Toronto St. South, PO Box 190, Uxbridge L9P 1T1 – 905/852-9181, Fax: 905/852-9674 |
| Val Rita-Harty Twp | 1,112 | Cochrane District | Timmins-James Bay | Cochrane North | Christiane Potvin, Clerk-Treas., 2, avenue de l'Église, PO Box 100, Val Rita P0L 2G0 – 705/335-6146, Fax: 705/337-6292 |
| Valley East † | 23,537 | Sudbury Reg. Mun. | Nickel Belt | Sudbury East | Roland O. Chenier, Town Adm. & Clerk, 1679 Main St., PO Box 430, Val Caron P3N 1P6 – 705/897-4938, Fax: 705/897-2667 |
| VANIER | 17,247 | Ottawa-Carleton Reg. Mun. | Ottawa-Vanier | Ottawa East | Daniel J.P. Ouimet, CAO-Clerk, 300 des Pères-blancs Ave., Vanier K1L 7L5 – 613/746-8105, Fax: 613/745-2985 |
| Vankleek Hill † [62] | 2,030 | Prescott & Russell | Glengarry-Prescott-Russell | Prescott & Russell | Gerard Sauvé, Clerk-Treas., 11 Queen St., PO Box 40, Vankleek Hill K0B 1R0 – 613/678-2206, Fax: 613/678-2988 |

Cities in CAPITALS; Towns marked †; Villages marked (V); Townships marked Twp; Municipalities marked (Mun.); Separated Towns marked (SE); Development Areas marked (DA). An in-depth listing for municipalities marked with * appears in Part 2 (check Index for page numbers).

| MUNICIPALITY | 1996 POP. | COUNTY OR DISTRICT | FEDERAL ELECTORAL DISTRICT | PROVINCIAL ELECTORAL DISTRICT | CONTACT PERSON WITH ADDRESS, PHONE & FAX |
|---|---|---|---|---|---|
| *VAUGHAN | 132,549 | York Reg. Mun. | Thornhill; Vaughan-King-Aurora | York Centre | J.D. Leach, City Clerk, 2141 Major Mackenzie Dr., Vaughan L6A 1T1 – 905/832-2281, Fax: 905/832-8535, URL: http://www.city.vaughan.on.ca |
| Verulam Twp | 4,373 | Victoria | Victoria-Haliburton | Victoria-Haliburton | Barbara Meacham, Clerk-Treas., 21 Canal St. East, PO Box 820, Bobcaygeon K0M 1A0 – 705/738-2431, Fax: 705/738-6026 |
| Vienna (V) [15] | 490 | Elgin | Elgin-Middlesex-London | Elgin | Lynda Millard, Clerk-Treas., PO Box 133, Vienna N0J 1Z0 – 519/874-4225, Fax: 519/874-4225 |
| Wainfleet Twp | 6,253 | Niagara Reg. Mun. | Erie-Lincoln | Niagara South | Albert Guiler, Clerk-Treas., Hwy. 3, PO Box 40, Wainfleet L0S 1V0 – 905/899-3463, Fax: 905/899-2340 |
| Walden † | 10,292 | Sudbury Reg. Mun. | Nickel Belt | Nickel Belt | Donna Kennedy, Clerk, 25 Black Lake Rd., PO Box 910, Walden P3Y 1J3 – 705/692-3613, Fax: 705/692-3225 |
| Walkerton † | 5,036 | Bruce | Bruce-Grey | Bruce | Richard Radford, Clerk, 111 Jackson St., PO Box 68, Walkerton N0G 2V0 – 519/881-2223, Fax: 519/881-2991 |
| Wallace Twp [54] | 2,350 | Perth | Perth-Middlesex | Perth | Gordon M. Burns, Clerk-Treas., Gowanstown N0G 1Y0 – 519/291-2760, Fax: 519/291-1902 |
| Wallaceburg † | 11,772 | Kent | Lambton-Kent-Middlesex | Chatham-Kent | Sheldon W. Parsons, Clerk, 786 Dufferin Ave., Wallaceburg N8A 2V3 – 519/627-1603, Fax: 519/627-1212, URL: http://www/kent.net/wallaceburg |
| Wardsville (V) | 440 | Middlesex | Lambton-Kent-Middlesex | Middlesex | Janet Salliss, Clerk-Treas., 156 Hagerty Rd., PO Box 64, Wardsville N0L 2N0 – 519/693-4962, Fax: 519/693-4962 |
| Warwick Twp [82] | 2,481 | Lambton | Lambton-Kent-Middlesex | Lambton | Donald I. Craig, Clerk-Treas., 6332 Nauvoo Rd., RR#8, Watford N0M 2S0 – 519/849-3926, Fax: 519/849-6136 |
| Wasaga Beach † | 8,698 | Simcoe | Simcoe-Grey | Simcoe West | Eric E. Collingwood, Clerk-Treas.-Adm., 30 Lewis St., PO Box 110, Wasaga Beach L0L 2P0 – 705/429-3844, Fax: 705/429-6732 |
| *WATERLOO | 77,949 | Waterloo Reg. Mun. | Kitchener-Waterloo | Waterloo North | Lew Ayers, City Clerk, City Hall, 100 Regina St. South, PO Box 337, Waterloo N2J 4A8 – 519/886-1550, Fax: 519/747-8760, URL: http://www.city.waterloo.on.ca |
| Watford (V) [82] | 1,660 | Lambton | Lambton-Kent-Middlesex | Lambton | Frances Woods, Clerk-Treas., 5288 Nauvoo Rd., PO Box 10, Watford N0M 2S0 – 519/876-2740, Fax: 519/876-3531 |
| Webbwood † | 563 | Sudbury District | Algoma-Manitoulin | Algoma-Manitoulin | Judy Van Norman, Clerk-Treas., 16 Main St., PO Box 10, Webbwood P0P 2G0 – 705/869-3861, Fax: 705/869-1394 |
| WELLAND | 48,411 | Niagara Reg. Mun. | Niagara Centre | Welland-Thorold | Craig A. Stirtzinger, City Clerk, 411 East Main St., Welland L3B 3K4 – 905/735-1700, Fax: 905/732-1919 |
| Wellesley Twp | 8,664 | Waterloo Reg. Mun. | Waterloo-Wellington | Waterloo North | Gordon Ludington, Clerk-Treas., RR#1, Clements N0B 2M0 – 519/699-4611, Fax: 519/699-4540 |
| Wellington (V) | 1,691 | Prince Edward | Prince Edward-Hastings | Prince Edward-Lennox-South Hastings | Doreen Kendall, Clerk-Treas., 28 East St., PO Box 160, Wellington K0K 3L0 – 613/399-3424, Fax: 613/399-1802 |
| West Carleton Twp | 16,541 | Ottawa-Carleton Reg. Mun. | Lanark-Carleton | Carleton | Monica Ceschia, Clerk, 5670 Carp Rd., Kinburn K0A 2H0 – 613/832-5644, Fax: 613/832-3341 |
| West Garafraxa Twp | 3,777 | Wellington | Waterloo-Wellington | Wellington | Dianne Smith, Clerk-Treas., Belwood N0B 1J0 – 519/843-2259, Fax: 519/843-6614 |
| West Hawkesbury Twp | 2,978 | Prescott & Russell | Glengarry-Prescott-Russell | Prescott & Russell | Robert Lefebvre, Clerk-Treas., 948 Pleasant Corners Rd. East, Vankleek Hill K0B 1R0 – 613/678-3003, Fax: 613/678-3363 |
| West Lincoln Twp | 11,513 | Niagara Reg. Mun. | Erie-Lincoln | Lincoln | Salter Hayden, Clerk-Director of Corporate Servs., 318 Canborough St., PO Box 400, Smithville L0R 2A0 – 905/957-3346, Fax: 905/957-3219 |
| West Lorne (V) [2] | 1,531 | Elgin | Elgin-Middlesex-London | Elgin | Diane Van Dyk, Acting Clerk, 223 Graham St., PO Box 309, West Lorne N0L 2P0 – 519/768-1234, Fax: 519/768-2783 |
| West Luther Twp | 1,235 | Wellington | Dufferin-Peel-Wellington-Grey | Wellington | Dea Baker-Pearce, Clerk-Treas., RR#4, Kenilworth N0G 2E0 – 519/848-3451, Fax: 519/848-9350 |
| West Nissouri Twp | 3,484 | Middlesex | Perth-Middlesex | Middlesex | Stewart M. Findlater, Clerk-Adm., 160 King St., Thorndale N0M 2P0 – 519/461-0750, Fax: 519/461-1427, URL: http://www.twp.est-nissouri-on.ca |

Cities in CAPITALS; Towns marked †; Villages marked (V); Townships marked Twp; Municipalities marked (Mun.); Separated Towns marked (SE); Development Areas marked (DA). An in-depth listing for municipalities marked with * appears in Part 2 (check Index for page numbers).

| MUNICIPALITY | 1996 POP. | COUNTY OR DISTRICT | FEDERAL ELECTORAL DISTRICT | PROVINCIAL ELECTORAL DISTRICT | CONTACT PERSON WITH ADDRESS, PHONE & FAX |
|---|---|---|---|---|---|
| West Wawanosh Twp | 1,410 | Huron | Huron-Bruce | Huron | Liliane Nolan, Clerk-Treas., RR#2, Lucknow N0G 2H0 – 519/528-2903, Fax: 519/528-3327 |
| West Williams Twp | 942 | Middlesex | Lambton-Kent-Middlesex | Middlesex | Beverley LeCouteur, Clerk-Treas., RR#2, Parkhill N0M 2K0 – 519/294-0001, Fax: 519/294-0021 |
| Westmeath Twp | 2,686 | Renfrew | Renfrew-Nipissing-Pembroke | Renfrew North | Randi Keith, Clerk-Treas., General Delivery, Westmeath K0J 2L0 – 613/587-4464, Fax: 613/587-4229 |
| Westport (V) | 683 | Leeds & Grenville | Leeds-Grenville | Leeds-Grenville | Scott Bryce, Clerk-Treas., PO Box 68, Westport K0G 1X0 – 613/273-2191, Fax: 613/273-3460 |
| Wheatley (V) | 1,657 | Kent | Essex-Kent | Essex-Kent | W. Tim Jackson, Clerk-Treas., 25 Erie St. South, PO Box 530, Wheatley N0P 2P0 – 519/825-4819, Fax: 519/825-4045 |
| *Whitby † | 73,794 | Durham Reg. Mun. | Whitby-Ajax | Durham East; Durham Centre | Donald G. McKay, Town Clerk, 575 Rossland Rd. East, Whitby L1N 2M8 – 905/668-5803, Fax: 905/686-7005, URL: http://town.whitby.on.ca |
| Whitchurch-Stouffville † | 19,835 | York Reg. Mun. | Oak Ridges | Durham-York | Michele Kennedy, Clerk, 19 Civic Ave., PO Box 419, Stouffville L4A 7Z6 – 905/640-1900, Fax: 905/640-7957 |
| White River Twp | 1,022 | Algoma District | Algoma-Manitoulin | Algoma | Marilyn Parent Lethbridge, Clerk-Adm., 102 Durham St., PO Box 307, White River P0M 3G0 – 807/822-2450, Fax: 807/822-2719 |
| Wiarton † | 2,400 | Bruce | Bruce-Grey | Bruce | R. Ruthann Carson, Clerk, 315 George St., PO Box 310, Wiarton N0H 2T0 – 519/534-1400, Fax: 519/534-4862 |
| Wilberforce Twp | 1,931 | Renfrew | Renfrew-Nipissing-Pembroke | Renfrew North | Marilyn Schruder, Clerk-Treas., RR#1, Eganville K0J 1T0 – 613/628-2080, Fax: 613/628-3341 |
| Williamsburgh Twp [67] | 3,564 | Stormont, Dundas & Glengarry | Stormont-Dundas | SDG & East Grenville | Michael S. Waddell, Adm.-Clerk-Treas., PO Box 160, Williamsburgh K0C 2H0 – 613/535-2673, Fax: 613/535-2099 |
| Wilmot Twp | 13,831 | Waterloo Reg. Mun. | Waterloo-Wellington | Kitchener-Wilmot | Jane M. Steller, Clerk, 60 Snyder's Rd. West, Baden N0B 1G0 – 519/634-8444, Fax: 519/634-5522 |
| Winchester (V) [36] | 2,334 | Stormont, Dundas & Glengarry | Stormont-Dundas | SDG & East Grenville | Bonnie Dingwall, Adm. & Clerk-Treas., 547 St. Lawrence St., PO Box 489, Winchester K0C 2K0 – 613/774-2105, Fax: 613/774-5699 |
| Winchester Twp [36] | 3,616 | Stormont, Dundas & Glengarry | Stormont-Dundas | SDG & East Grenville | Nancy Krisjanis, Clerk-Treas., RR#4, Winchester K0C 2K0 – 613/448-2772, Fax: 613/448-1470 |
| *WINDSOR | 197,694 | Essex | Windsor-St. Clair; Windsor-West | Windsor-Riverside; Windsor-Sandwich; Windsor-Walkerville | Thomas W. Lynd, City Clerk, City Hall, 350 City Hall Sq., PO Box 1607, Windsor N9A 6S1 – 519/255-6500, Fax: 519/255-6868, URL: http://www.city.windsor.on.ca/ |
| Wingham † | 2,941 | Huron | Huron-Bruce | Huron | J. Byron Adams, Clerk-Treas., 274 Josephine St., PO Box 90, Wingham N0G 2W0 – 519/357-3550, Fax: 519/357-1110 |
| Wolfe Island Twp [64] | 1,180 | Frontenac | Kingston & the Islands | Kingston & the Islands | Terry J. O'Shea, Clerk-Treas., PO Box 130, Wolfe Island K0H 2Y0 – 613/385-2216, Fax: 613/385-1032 |
| Wolford Twp [74] | 1,603 | Leeds & Grenville | Leeds-Grenville | Leeds-Grenville | Angie M. McLean, Acting Clerk-Treas., RR#3, PO Box 1, Jasper K0G 1G0 – 613/283-8683, Fax: 613/283-6087 |
| Wollaston Twp | 719 | Hastings | Hastings-Frontenac-Lennox & Addington | Hastings-Peterborough | Jacqueline Dalby, Clerk-Treas., PO Box 99, Coe Hill K0L 1P0 – 613/337-5731, Fax: 613/337-5789 |
| WOODSTOCK | 32,086 | Oxford | Oxford | Oxford | Louise Gartshore, City Clerk, 500 Dundas St., PO Box 40, Woodstock N4S 7W5 – 519/539-1291, Fax: 519/539-7705 |
| Woodville (V) | 751 | Victoria | Victoria-Haliburton | Victoria-Haliburton | Heather Muir, Clerk, 78 King St., PO Box 9, Woodville K0M 2T0 – 705/439-2505, Fax: 705/439-2319 |
| Woolwich Twp | 17,325 | Waterloo Reg. Mun. | Waterloo-Wellington | Waterloo North | Bob Byron, Chief Administrative Officer, 69 Arthur St. South, PO Box 158, Elmira N3B 2Z6 – 519/669-1647, Fax: 519/669-1820 |
| Wyoming (V) | 2,131 | Lambton | Lambton-Kent-Middlesex | Lambton | Caroline DeSchutter, Clerk-Treas., 546 Niagara St., PO Box 250, Wyoming N0N 1T0 – 519/845-3351, Fax: 519/845-0730 |
| Yarmouth Twp [20] | 7,148 | Elgin | Elgin-Middlesex-London | Elgin | Ken G. Sloan, Clerk-Adm., 1229 Talbot St., St. Thomas N5P 1G8 – 519/631-4860, Fax: 519/631-4036 |
| Yonge & Escott, Rear of Twp | 1,868 | Leeds & Grenville | Leeds-Grenville | Leeds-Grenville | Darlene Noonan, Clerk-Treas., 5 Central St., PO Box 189, Athens K0E 1B0 – 613/924-9049, Fax: 613/924-1958 |

Cities in CAPITALS; Towns marked †; Villages marked (V); Townships marked Twp; Municipalities marked (Mun.); Separated Towns marked (SE); Development Areas marked (DA). An in-depth listing for municipalities marked with * appears in Part 2 (check Index for page numbers).

| MUNICIPALITY | 1996 POP. | COUNTY OR DISTRICT | FEDERAL ELECTORAL DISTRICT | PROVINCIAL ELECTORAL DISTRICT | CONTACT PERSON WITH ADDRESS, PHONE & FAX |
|---|---|---|---|---|---|
| Yonge, Front of Twp | 2,530 | Leeds & Grenville | Leeds-Grenville | Leeds-Grenville | Nancy A. Petri, Clerk-Treas., 1514 County Road #2, PO Box 130, Mallorytown K0E 1R0 – 613/923-2251, Fax: 613/923-2421, URL: http://www.mulberry.com/~fofyonge/ |
| *YORK [52] | 146,534 | Metro Mun. | Davenport; Eglinton-Lawrence; Parkdale-High Park; St. Paul's; York South-Weston | Oakwood; St. Andrew-St. Patrick; York South | Ron W. Maurice, City Clerk, Legislative & Administrative Services, 2700 Eglinton Ave. West, Toronto M6M 1V1 – 416/394-2507, Fax: 416/394-2681, URL: http://www.city.york.on.ca |
| Zone Twp | 1,039 | Kent | Lambton-Kent-Middlesex | Chatham-Kent | Wynnona Revell, Clerk-Treas., RR#3, Bothwell N0P 1C0 – 519/695-2307, Fax: 519/695-2307 |
| Zorra Twp | 8,141 | Oxford | Oxford | Oxford | Donald W. MacLeod, Clerk-Adm., 274620 - 27th Line, PO Box 306, Ingersoll N5C 3K5 – 519/485-2490, Fax: 519/485-2520 |
| Zurich (V) | 886 | Huron | Huron-Bruce | Huron | Maureen Simmons, Clerk-Treas., 22 Main St. West, PO Box 280, Zurich N0M 2T0 – 519/236-4974, Fax: 519/236-7687 |

1. Amalgamation of the townships of Adolphustown, North Fredericksburgh, South Fredericksburgh & Richmond, & the town of Napanee to form the town of Greater Napanee.
2. Amalgamation of the township of Aldborough & the village of West Lorne to form the township of West Elgin.
3. Amalgamation of the townships of Kenyon & Lochiel, the town of Alexandria & the village of Maxville to form the township of North Glengarry.
4. Amalgamation of the township of Alfred & Plantagenet & the villages of Alfred & Plantagenet to form the township of Alfred & Plantagenet (effective Jan 1./97).
5. Amalgamation of the town of Almonte, townships of Pakenham & Ramsay to form the town of Mississippi Mills.
6. Amalgamation of the townships of Amherst Island & Ernestown, & the village of Bath to form Loyalist township.
7. Amalgamation of the town of Amherstburg, the townships of Anderdon & Malden to form the new town of Amherstburg.
8. Amalgamation of the township of Artemesia & the village of Flesherton to form the new township of Artemesia.
9. Amalgamation of the township of Asphodel & the village of Norwood to form the township of Asphodel-Norwood.
10. Amalgamation of the townships of Bagot & Blythfield, & Brougham to form the township of Bagot & Blythfield & Brougham.
11. Amalgamation of the township of Barclay & the town of Dryden to form the city of Dryden.
12. Amalgamation of the townships of Barrie, Clarendon & Miller, Palmerston, North & South Canonto to form the township of North Frontenac.
13. Amalgamation of the townships of Bastard & South Burgess, North & South Crosby, South Elmsley & the village of Newboro to form the township of Rideau Lakes.
14. Amalgamation of the townships of Bathurst, North Burgess & South Sherbrooke to form the township of Bathurst, North Burgess & South Sherbrooke.
15. Amalgamation of the township of Bayham & the villages of Port Burwell & Vienna to form the township of Bayham-Port Burwell-Vienna.
16. Amalgamation of the townships of of Beardmore & Nakina & the towns of Geraldton & Longlac to form the town of Greenstone.
17. Amalgamation of the townships of Bedford, Loughborough, Portland & Storrington to form the township of South Frontenac.
18. Amalgamation of the town of Belle River & the township of Maidstone to form Lakeshore township.
19. Amalgamation of the city of Belleville & the township of Thurlow to form the new city of Belleville.
20. Amalgamation of the villages of Belmont & Port Stanley & the township of Yarmouth to form the township of Central Elgin.
21. Amalgamation of the township of Belmont & Methuen & the village of Havelock to form the township of Havelock-Belmont-Methuen.
22. Amalgamation of the townships of Blanshard & Downie to form the township of Perth South.
23. Amalgamation of the village of Braeside & the township of McNab to form the township of McNab-Braeside.
24. Amalgamation of the village of Tiverton & Bruce township to form the new township of Bruce.
25. Amalgamation of the township of Burleigh & Anstruther, & Chandos to form the township of Burleigh-Anstruther-Chandos.
26. Annexation of the unorganized township of Mills to the township of Burpee to form the township of Burpee & Mills.
27. Amalgamation of the towns of Cache Bay & Sturgeon Falls, the townships of Caldwell, Field & Springer, & unorganized areas to form the town of West Nipissing (effective Jan. 1/99).
28. Amalgamation of the townships of Caledonia, Cambridge, St. Isidore & South Plantagenet to form the township of the Township of the Nation.
29. Amalgation of the townships of Camden East & Sheffield & the village of Newburgh to form the township of Stone Mills.
30. Amalgation of the towns of Campbellford & the township of Seymour to form the town of Campbellford-Seymour.
31. Amalgamation of the village of Mildmay & the township of Carrick to form the township of Mildmay-Carrick.
32. Amalgamation of the townships of Cavan & North Monaghan, & the village of Millbrook to form the township of Cavan-Millbrook-North Monaghan.
33. Amalgamation of the township of Chapman & the village of Magnetawan & the unorganized township of Croft to form the township of Magnetawan.
34. Amalgamation of the townships of Charlottenburgh & Lancaster, & the village of Lancaster to form the township of South Glengarry.
35. Amalgamation of the city of Chatham & the county of Kent to form the City of Chatham-Kent.
36. Amalgamation of the villages of Chesterville & Winchester & the townships of Mountain & Winchester to form the township of North Dundas.
37. Amalgamation of the townships of Christie, Humphrey & Foley, the village of Rosseau & the unorganized township of Monteith to form the township of Seguin.
38. Amalgamation of the township of Clarence & the town of Rockland to form the city of Clarence-Rockland.
39. Amalgamation of the township of Collingwood & the town of Thornbury to form the town of Thornbury-Collingwood.
40. Amalgamation of the townships of Cornwall & Osnabruck to form the township of South Stormont.
41. Amalgamation of the village of Teeswater & township of Culross to form the township of Teeswater-Culross.
42. Amalgamation of the townships of Darling & North West Lanark to form the corporation of the township of North West Lanark; see also note 71 below.
43. Amalgamation of the townships of Dawn & Euphemia to form the township of Dawn-Euphemia.
44. Amalgamation of the township of Atwood & unorganized areas to form the township of Dawson (effective Jan. 1/97).
45. Amalgamation of the townships of Delaware, Lobo & London to form the township of Middlesex Centre.
46. Amalgamation of the village of Deloro & the township of Marmora & Lake to form the township of Marmora & Lake.
47. Amalgamation of the townships of Denbigh, Abinger & Ashby, & Kaladar, Anglesea & Effingham to form the township of Addington Highlands.
48. Amalgamation of the townships of Douro & Dummer to form the township of Douro-Dummer.
49. Amalgamation of the village of Drayton & the township of Peel to form the township of Mapleton.
50. Amalgamation of the townships of Drummond & N. Elmsley to form the township of Drummond-North Elmsley.
51. Amalgamation of the township of Dunwich & the village of Dutton to form the township of Dutton-Dunwich.
52. In April 1997, the Government of Ontario passed the City of Toronto Act whereby the six constituent municipalities (Toronto, Etobicoke, North York, York, Scarborough, East York) of Metropolitan Toronto will be amalgamated into a single City of Toronto. The present City of Toronto & Metropolitan Toronto will cease to exist & the new City of Toronto will assume responsibility for providing all municipal services.

53. Amalgamation of the townships of Ellice, Mornington, North & South Easthope, & the village of Milverton to form the township of Perth East.
54. Amalgamation of the townships of Elma & Wallace, & the town of Listowel to form the town of North Perth.
55. Amalgamation of the townships of Elzevir & Grimsthorpe, & Hungerford & the village of Tweed to form the township of Tweed.
56. Amalgamation of the townships of Ennismore & Smith to form the township of Smith-Ennismore.
57. Amalgamation of the village & township of Erin to form the town of Erin.
58. Amalgamation of the village of Finch, & the townships of Finch & Roxborough to form the township of North Stormont.
59. Amalgamation of the village of Frankford, the city of Trenton & the townships of Sidney & Murray to form the city of Quinte West.
60. Amalgamation o f the townships of Fullarton, Hibbert & Logan, & the town of Mitchell to form the township of West Perth.
61. Amalgamation of the townships of Harvey, & Galway & Cavendish to form the township of Galway-Cavendish & Harvey.
62. Amalgamation of the townships of Hawkesbury, L'Orignal, Longueuil & Vankleek Hill to form the township of Champlain.
63. Amalgamation of the townships of Hinchinbrooke, Kennebec, Olden & Oso to form the township of United Municipality of Central Frontenac.
64. Amalgamation of the townships of Howe Island & Wolfe Island to form the township of Frontenac Islands.
65. Amalgamation of the township of Howland & the town of Little Current & unorganized areas of the Islands in the District of Manitoulin to form the town of Northeastern Manitoulin & the Islands.
66. Amalgamation of the township of Huntingdon & the village of Madoc to form the township of Centre Hastings.
67. Amalgamation of the villages of Iroquois & Morrisburg, & the townships of Matilda & Williamsburg to form the township of South Dundas.
68. Amalgamation of the town of Kemptville & the townships of Oxford-on-Rideau & South Gower to form the township of North Grenville.
69. Amalgamation of the village of Shallow Lake & the township of Keppel to form the new township of Keppel.
70. Amalgamation of the city of Kingston, & the townships of Kingston & Pittsburgh to form the new city of Kingston.
71. Amalgamation of the village of Lanark, & the townships of Lanark & Lavant, Dalhousie & N. Sherbrooke to form the corporation of the township of Lanark-Highlands (May 15/97 effective date).
72. Amalgamation of the townships of Malahide & South Dorchester, & the village of Springfield to form the township of Malahide-South Dorchester-Springfield.
73. Annexation of the unorganized township of Monteith to the township of McMurrich to form the township of McMurrich-Monteith.
74. Amalgamation of the village of Merrickville & the township of Wolford to form the village of Merrickville-Wolford.
75. Annexation of the unorganized township of Hyman to the township of Nairn to form the township of Nairn & Hyman.
76. Amalgamation of the townships of of Oliver & Paipoonge to form the township of Oliver & Paipoonge.
77. Amalgamation of the townships of Otonabee & South Monaghan to form the township of Otonabee-South Monaghan.
78. Amalgamation of the village & township of Petawawa formed the town of Petawawa (effective July 1/97).
79. Amalgamation of the township of Rawdon & the village of Stirling to form the township of Stirling-Rawdon.
80. Amalgamation of the townships of Pembroke & Stafford to form the township of Stafford & Pembroke (effective Jan. 1/97).
81. Annexation of unorganized areas to the township of Temagami to form the town of Temagami.
82. Amalgamation of the township of Warwick & the village of Watford to form the new township of Warwick.

## ONTARIO COUNTIES

| COUNTY | 1996 POP. | CONTACT PERSON WITH ADDRESS, PHONE & FAX |
|---|---|---|
| Brant | 114,564 | Dan Ciona, Clerk-Treas., 1249 Colborne St. West, PO Box 160, Burford N0E 1A0 – 519/449-2451, Fax: 519/449-2454, URL: http://www.bfree.on.ca/comdir/brantcounty/brantco.htm |
| Bruce | 65,680 | Bettyanne Bray, Clerk-Treas., 30 Park St., PO Box 70, Walkerton N0G 2V0 – 519/881-1291, Fax: 519/881-1619 |
| Dufferin | 45,657 | Scott A. Wilson, Clerk-Adm., 51 Zina St., Orangeville L9W 1E5 – 519/941-2816, Fax: 519/941-4565 |
| Elgin | 79,159 | Mark G. McDonald, Clerk, 450 Sunset Dr., St. Thomas N5R 5V1 – 519/631-1460, Fax: 519/633-7661 |
| Essex | 350,329 | John H. Curran, CAO & Clerk, 360 Fairview Ave. West, Essex N8M 1Y6 – 519/776-6441, Fax: 519/776-4455 |
| Frontenac | 136,365 | Sylvia G. Coburn, Clerk, Court House, Court St., Kingston K7L 2N4 – 613/548-4202, Fax: 613/548-8193 |
| Grey | 87,632 | Sharon Vokes, Clerk-Treas., County Bldg., 595 Ninth Ave. East, Owen Sound N4K 3E3 – 519/376-2205, Fax: 519/376-7970 |
| Haliburton | 15,321 | Les Shepherd, Acting CAO, 11 Newcastle St., PO Box 399, Minden K0M 2K0 – 705/286-1333, Fax: 705/286-4829 |
| Hastings | 118,744 | Bill Bouma, CAO & Clerk, 235 Pinnacle St., PO Box 4400, Belleville K8N 3A9 – 613/966-1311, Fax: 613/966-2574 |
| Huron | 60,220 | Lynn Murray, Clerk-Adm., Court House Sq., Goderich N7A 1M2 – 519/524-8394, Fax: 519/524-2044 |
| Kent [1] | 109,650 | Chuck L. Knapp, Clerk-Adm., 435 Grand Ave. West, PO Box 1230, Chatham N7M 5L8 – 519/351-1010, Fax: 519/351-9669 |
| Lambton | 128,975 | H. Wayne Kloske, CAO, 789 Broadway St., PO Box 3000, Wyoming N0N 1T0 – 519/845-0801, Fax: 519/845-3160 |
| Lanark | 59,845 | Cynthia Moyle, Treas. & Dep. Clerk, County Admin. Bldg., Sunset Blvd., PO Box 37, Perth K7H 3E2 – 613/267-4200, Fax: 613/267-2964, URL: http://www.county.lanark.on.ca |
| Leeds & Grenville | 96,284 | Fred W. Dollman, Adm.-Clerk-Treas., Court House, PO Box 729, Brockville K6V 5V8 – 613/342-3840, Fax: 613/342-2101 |
| Lennox & Addington | 39,203 | Larry Keech, Clerk & CAO, 97 Thomas St. East, PO Box 1000, Napanee K7R 3S9 – 613/354-4883, Fax: 613/354-3112 |
| Middlesex | 389,616 | Donald Hudson, Clerk-Treas., 399 Ridout St. North, London N6A 2P1 – 519/434-7321, Fax: 519/434-0638 |
| Northumberland | 81,792 | Lynda Mitchell, CAO-Clerk-Treas., 860 William St., Cobourg K9A 3A9 – 905/372-0141, Fax: 905/372-3046 |
| Oxford | 97,142 | Kenneth J. Whiteford, CAO-Clerk, Court House, 415 Hunter St., PO Box 397, Woodstock N4S 7Y3 – 519/539-5688, Fax: 519/537-3024, URL: http://www.hometown.on.ca |
| Perth | 72,106 | James A. Bell, Clerk-Treas., Court House, 1 Huron St., Stratford N5A 5S4 – 519/271-0531, Fax: 519/271-6265 |
| Peterborough | 123,448 | Joseph W. Tierney, Adm., County Court House, 470 Water St., Peterborough K9H 3M3 – 705/743-0380, Fax: 705/876-1730 |
| Prescott & Russell | 74,013 | Jean-Pierre Pitre, Clerk-Treas. & CAO, 59 Court St., PO Box 304, L'Orignal K0B 1K0 – 613/675-4661, Fax: 613/675-2519 |
| Prince Edward [2] | 25,046 | Donald Ward, Clerk-Treas., 332 Main St., PO Box 1550, Picton K0K 2T0 – 613/476-2148, Fax: 613/476-8356 |
| Renfrew | 96,224 | James D. Kutschke, Treas.-Deputy Clerk, 9 International Dr., Pembroke K8A 6W5 – 613/735-7288, Fax: 613/735-2081 |
| Simcoe | 329,865 | Al F. Pelletier, Clerk, Admin Centre, Midhurst L0L 1X0 – 705/726-9300, Fax: 705/726-3991 |
| Stormont, Dundas & Glengarry | 111,301 | Raymond J. Lapointe, Co-ordinator-Clerk-Treas., 20 Pitt St., Cornwall K6J 3P2 – 613/932-4302, Fax: 613/936-2913 |
| Victoria | 67,926 | George Brown, Clerk, 26 Francis St., PO Box 9000, Lindsay K9V 5R8 – 705/324-9450, Fax: 705/324-1750 |
| Wellington | 171,395 | James C. Andrews, Clerk & CAO, 74 Woolwich St., Guelph N1H 3T9 – 519/837-2600, Fax: 519/837-1909 |

1. Amalgamation of the city of Chatham & the county of Kent to form the City of Chatham-Kent (effective Jan. 1/98).
2. Prince Edward County amalgamated to form the city of the County of Prince Edward (effective Jan. 1/98).

## ONTARIO DISTRICTS

| DISTRICTS | 1996 POP. | LOCATION |
|---|---|---|
| Algoma | 125,455 | Sault Ste. Marie |
| Cochrane | 93,240 | Cochrane |
| Kenora | 63,335 | Kenora |
| Manitoulin | 11,413 | Gore Bay |
| Nipissing | 84,832 | North Bay |
| Parry Sound | 39,906 | Parry Sound |

| DISTRICTS | 1996 POP. | LOCATION |
|---|---|---|
| Rainy River | 23,163 | Fort Frances |
| Sudbury | 25,457 | Espanola |
| Thunder Bay | 157,619 | Thunder Bay |
| Timiskaming | 37,807 | Haileybury |

## ONTARIO REGIONAL MUNICIPALITIES

An in-depth listing for the regional districts appears in Part 3 (check Index for page numbers).

| MUNICIPALITY | 1996 POP. | CONTACT PERSON WITH ADDRESS, PHONE & FAX |
|---|---|---|
| Durham | 458,616 | Patricia M. Madill, Clerk, 605 Rossland Rd. East, PO Box 623, Whitby L1N 6A3 – 905/668-7711, Fax: 905/668-9963 |
| Haldimand-Norfolk | 102,575 | Gerald van der Wolf, Regional Clerk, 70 Town Centre Dr., Townsend N0A 1S0 – 519/587-4911, Fax: 519/587-5554 |
| Halton | 339,875 | Joan A. Eaglesham, Regional Clerk, 1151 Bronte Rd., Oakville L6M 3L1 – 905/825-6000, Fax: 905/825-8838, URL: http://www.region.halton.on.ca |
| Hamilton-Wentworth | 467,799 | Robert C. Prowse, Regional Clerk, 119 King St. West, PO Box 910, Hamilton L8N 3V9 – 905/546-4111, Fax: 905/546-2546 |
| Metropolitan Toronto | 2,385,421 | *See* City of Toronto |
| Muskoka | 50,463 | William C. (Bill) Calvert, Clerk & Chief Administrative Officer, 70 Pine St., Bracebridge P1L 1N3 – 705/645-2231, Fax: 705/645-5319 |
| Niagara | 403,504 | Thomas R. Hollick, Regional Clerk, 2201 St. David's Rd., PO Box 1042, Thorold L2V 4T7 – 905/685-1571, Fax: 905/687-4977, URL: http://www.regional.niagara.on.ca |
| Ottawa-Carleton | 721,136 | Mary Jo Woollam, Regional Clerk, Cartier Sq., 111 Lisgar St., Ottawa K2P 2L7 – 613/560-1337, Fax: 613/560-6017, URL: http://www.rmoc.on.ca (English) http://www.rmoc.on.ca/Bienvenue.html (French) |

## PRINCE EDWARD ISLAND

Enabling legislation in P.E.I. includes the Charlottetown Area Municipalities Act, the City of Summerside Incorporation Act, and the Municipalities Act (replaces the former Village Service Act, the Town Act, and the Community Improvement Act).There are no population considerations for incorporation of a municipality, but a petition must be made by at least 25 residents of an area indicating their desire to incorporate; stating the boundaries of the area, whether it is to be a town or a community, and the services which are to be provided.

Municipal Elections are held every three years in November.

Cities in CAPITALS; Towns marked †; Communities marked ‡. An in-depth listing for municipalities marked with * appears in Part 2 (check Index for page numbers).

| MUNICIPALITY | 1996 POP. | FEDERAL ELECTORAL DISTRICT | PROVINCIAL ELECTORAL DISTRICT | CONTACT PERSON WITH ADDRESS, PHONE & FAX |
|---|---|---|---|---|
| Abram's Village ‡ | 328 | Egmont | Evangeline-Miscouche | Desmond Arsenault, CAO, PO Box 104, Abram's Village C0B 2E0 – 902/854-2501 |
| Afton ‡ | 1,595 | Malpeque | Tracadie-Fort Augustus | Joseph Clow, CAO, RR#2, Cornwall C0A 1H0 – 902/675-3515 |
| Alberton † | 1,084 | Egmont | Alberton-Miminegash | Susan Wallace, CAO, PO Box 153, Alberton C0B 1B0 – 902/853-2720, Fax: 902/853-2720 |
| Alexandra ‡ | 1,073 | Cardigan | Belfast-Pownal Bay | Sheila White, CAO, PO Box 2683, Charlottetown C1A 8C3 – 902/569-4760 |
| Annandale--Little Pond--Howe Bay ‡ | 507 | Cardigan | Georgetown-Baldwin's Road | Jim Mills, CAO, Annandale-Little Pond, RR#4, Souris C0A 2B0 – 902/583-2492 |
| Bedeque ‡ | 148 | Malpeque | Borden-Kinkora | Clara Lockhart, CAO, PO Box 4007, Bedeque C0B 1C0 – 902/887-2244 |
| Belfast ‡ | 1,410 | Cardigan | Belfast-Pownal Bay | Janice MacDonald, CAO, RR#3, Belle River C0A 1B0 – 902/659-2813, Fax: 902/659-2813 |
| Bonshaw ‡ | 755 | Malpeque | Crapaud-Hazel Grove | Elizabeth Glen, CAO, RR#1, Bonshaw C1E 1Z3 – 902/675-4715, Fax: 902/675-2640 |
| Borden-Carleton ‡ | | Malpeque | Borden-Kinkora | Paul Arsenault, CAO, 244 Borden Ave., PO Box 89, Borden C0B 1X0 – 902/437-2225, Fax: 902/437-2610 |
| Brackley ‡ | 367 | Malpeque | Stanhope-East Royalty | Leo MacLeod, CAO, 1 Cudmore Lane, Brackley C0A 2H0 – 902/368-8283 |
| Breadalbane ‡ | 171 | Malpeque | Crapaud-Hazel Grove | Sandy MacKay, CAO, Breadalbane C0A 1E0 – 902/964-2500 |
| Brudenell ‡ | 944 | Cardigan | Montague-Kilmuir | Gordon Nixon, CAO, PO Box 836, Montague C0A 1R0 – 902/838-4044, Fax: 902/838-4069 |
| Cardigan ‡ | 371 | Cardigan | Georgetown-Baldwin's Road | Margaret Forgarty, CAO, Cardigan C0A 1G0 – 902/583-2198, Fax: 902/583-2198 |
| Central Bedeque ‡ | 182 | Malpeque | Borden-Kinkora | Doug MacMurdo, CAO, PO Box 3964, Central Bedeque C0B 1G0 – 902/888-2097 |
| Central Kings ‡ | 488 | Cardigan | | Marion Trowbridge, CAO, RR#5, Cardigan C0A 1G0 – 902/583-2084 |
| *CHARLOTTETOWN | 32,531 | Hillsborough | Sherwood-Hillsborough; Parkdale-Belvedere; Charlottetown-Kings Square; Charlottetown-Rochefort Square; Charlottetown-Spring Park | Harry Gaudet, CAO, PO Box 98, Charlottetown C1A 7K2 – 902/566-5548, Fax: 902/566-4701, URL: http://www.munisource.org/charlottetown/welcome.html |
| Clyde River ‡ | 601 | Malpeque | Crapaud-Hazel Grove | Janice McAlduff, CAO, PO Box 644, Cornwall C0A 1H0 – 902/628-1550 |
| Cornwall † | 4,291 | Malpeque | North River-Rice Point | Eldon Sentner, CAO, PO Box 430, Cornwall C0A 1H0 – 902/566-2354, Fax: 902/566-5228 |
| Crapaud ‡ | 378 | Malpeque | Crapaud-Hazel Grove; Borden-Kinkora | Susan Williams, CAO, Crapaud C0A 1J0 – 902/658-2297 |
| Darlington ‡ | 1,617 | Malpeque | Crapaud-Hazel Grove | Doreen MacPherson, CAO, Darlington, North Wiltshire C0A 1Y0 – 902/621-0555 |
| Eastern Kings ‡ | 631 | Cardigan | | Kay Sweeny, CAO, RR#1, Elmira C0A 1K0 – 902/357-2534 |

Cities in CAPITALS; Towns marked †; Communities marked ‡. An in-depth listing for municipalities marked with * appears in Part 2 (check Index for page numbers).

| MUNICIPALITY | 1996 POP. | FEDERAL ELECTORAL DISTRICT | PROVINCIAL ELECTORAL DISTRICT | CONTACT PERSON WITH ADDRESS, PHONE & FAX |
|---|---|---|---|---|
| Ellerslie-Bideford ‡ | 898 | Egmont | Cascumpec-Grand River | Linda MacKinnon, CAO, PO Box 13, Ellerslie C0B 1C0 – 902/831-3476 |
| Georgetown † | 732 | Cardigan | Georgetown-Baldwin's Road | Patsy Gotell, CAO, PO Box 89, Georgetown C0A 1L0 – 902/652-2924, Fax: 902/652-2701 |
| Grand Tracadie ‡ | | Cardigan | Tracadie-Fort Augustus | Patsy McKinnon, Adm., Grand Tracadie, Little York C0A 1P0 – 902/672-3429 |
| Greenmount-Montrose ‡ | | Egmont | Tignish-DeBlois | June Pridham, CAO, RR#2, Alberton C0B 1B0 – 902/853-2583 |
| Hampshire ‡ | | Malpeque | North River-Rice Point; Crapaud-Hazel Grove | Gail Stewart, CAO, RR#2, North Wiltshire C0A 1Y0 – 902/368-1144, Fax: 902/368-1144 |
| Hazelbrooke ‡ | | Cardigan | Belfast-Pownal Bay; Tracadie-Fort Augustus | Bill Power, CAO, RR#1, Charlottetown C1A 7J6 – 902/569-4197 |
| Hunter River ‡ | 354 | Malpeque | Crapaud-Hazel Grove; Park Corner-Oyster Bed | Desi Nantes, CAO, PO Box 74, Hunter River C0A 1N0 – 902/964-2417 |
| Kensington † | 1,383 | Malpeque | Kensington-Malpeque | Frances Salsman, CAO, PO Box 418, Kensington C0B 1M0 – 902/836-3781, Fax: 902/836-3781 |
| Kingston ‡ | | Malpeque | Noth River-Rice Point; Crapaud-Hazel Grove | Teresa Hughes, CAO, RR#3, Cornwall C0A 1H0 – 902/675-3711 |
| Kinkora ‡ | 321 | Malpeque | Borden-Kinkora | Leonard Keefe, CAO, PO Box 38, Kinkora C0B 1N0 – 902/887-2868, Fax: 902/887-3514 |
| Lady Slipper ‡ | 898 | Egmont | | Douglas MacLeod, CAO, RR#2, Tyne Valley C0B 1J0 – 902/831-3496, Fax: 902/887-3514 |
| Linkletter ‡ | 304 | Egmont | St. Eleanors-Summerside | Gary Linkletter, CAO, 250 Glenn Dr., Linkletter C1N 5N2 – 902/436-6922 |
| Lorne Valley ‡ | | Cardigan | Georgetown-Baldwin's Road | Louise Sheppard, CAO, PO Box 81, Cardigan C0A 1G0 – 902/583-2926 |
| Lot 11 and Area ‡ | 586 | Egmont | Cascumpec-Grand River | Mary Williams, CAO, RR#2, Ellerslie C0B 1J0 – 902/831-2787 |
| Lower Montague ‡ | | Cardigan | Montague-Kilmuir | Elizabeth Nicholson, CAO, PO Box 821, Montague C0A 1R0 – 902/838-3359 |
| Malpeque Bay ‡ | | Malpeque | Kensington-Malpeque | Joanne. McGarvill, CAO, RR#5, Kensington C0B 1M0 – 902/836-5029 |
| Meadowbank ‡ | 354 | Malpeque | North River-Rice Point | Lawson Drake, CAO, Meadowbank, RR#2, Cornwall C0A 1H0 – 902/836-5029 |
| Miltonvale Park ‡ | 1,242 | Malpeque | | Judy K. MacDonald, CAO, PO Box 38, Winsloe C1E 1Z4 – 902/368-3090 |
| Miminegash ‡ | 210 | Egmont | Alberton-Miminegash | Shirley Perry, CAO, Miminegash C0B 1S0 – 902/882-3237 |
| Miscouche ‡ | 679 | Egmont | Evangeline-Miscouche | Judy Gallant, CAO, PO Box 70, Miscouche C0B 1T0 – 902/436-4962, Fax: 902/436-4692 |
| Montague † | 1,995 | Cardigan | Montague-kilmuir | Laurel Halstrum, CAO, PO Box 546, Montague C0A 1R0 – 902/838-2528, Fax: 902/838-3392 |
| Morell ‡ | 336 | Cardigan | Morell-Fortune Bay | George Morrison, CAO, PO Box 173, Morell C0A 1S0 – 902/961-2420 |
| Mount Stewart ‡ | 310 | Cardigan | Tracadie-Fort Augustus | Muriel Jay Matheson, CAO, PO Box 143, Mount Stewart C0A 1T0 – 902/676-2881, Fax: 902/676-2881 |
| Murray Harbour ‡ | 356 | Cardigan | Murray River-Gaspereaux | Jill Harris, CAO, PO Box 119, Murray Harbour C0A 1V0 – 902/962-3835, Fax: 902/962-3835 |
| Murray River ‡ | 420 | Cardigan | Murray River-Gaspereaux | Doris White, CAO, Murray River C0A 1W0 – 902/962-2633 |
| New Haven-Riverdale ‡ | | Malpeque | Crapaud-Hazel Grove | Diane Dowling, CAO, RR#3, Bonshaw C0A 1C0 – 902/675-3670, Fax: 902/675-4115 |
| North Rustico ‡ | 650 | Malpeque | Park Corner-Oyster Bed | Freda Pineau, CAO, PO Box 38, North Rustico C0A 1X0 – 902/963-3211 |
| North Shore ‡ | | Malpeque | | Wanda Myers, CAO, RR#1, York C0A 1P0 – 902/672-2363 |
| North Wiltshire ‡ | | Malpeque | Crapaud-Hazel Grove | Wendell Clark, CAO, North Wiltshire C0A 1Y0 – 902/621-0397, Fax: 902/621-0239 |
| Northport ‡ | | Egmont | Alberton-Miminegash | Paula Foley, CAO, RR#2, Alberton C0A 1B0 – 902/853-2551 |
| O'Leary ‡ | 877 | Egmont | West Point-Bloomfield | Beverley Coughlin, CAO, PO Box 130, O'Leary C0B 1V0 – 902/859-3311, Fax: 902/859-3311 |
| Pleasant Grove ‡ | | Malpeque | Stanhope-East Royalty | David Cairns, CAO, Pleasant Grove, RR#1, Little York C0A 1P0 – 902/672-3472 |
| Richmond ‡ | | Egmont | Cascumpec-Grand River; Evangeline-Miscouche | May McNeill, CAO, Richmond C0B 1Y0 – 902/854-2011 |
| St. Felix ‡ | | Egmont | Tignish-DeBlois | Barb Pitre, CAO, PO Box 22, Tignish C0B 2B0 – 902/882-3443, 3363, Fax: 902/882-2168 |
| St. Louis ‡ | 100 | Egmont | Alberton-Miminegash; Tignish-DeBlois | Dorothy Doucette, Adm., PO Box 40, St. Louis C0B 1Z0 – 902/882-3305, Fax: 902/882-2093 |
| St. Nicholas ‡ | | Egmont | Evangeline-Miscouche | Yvonne Poirier, CAO, RR#2, Miscouche C0B 1T0 – 902/854-2731 |
| St. Peter's Bay ‡ | 283 | Cardigan | Morell-Fortune Bay | Mary Burge, CAO, PO Box 51, St. Peters Bay C0A 2A0 – 902/961-2268, Fax: 902/961-3148 |
| Sherebrooke ‡ | 160 | Egmont | Kensington-Malpeque | Peggy L. Kilbride, CAO, PO Box 1344, Summerside C1N 4K2 – 902/436-7005, Fax: 902/436-7005 |
| Souris † | 1,293 | Cardigan | Souris-Elmira | Mildred Ehler, CAO, 75 Main St., Souris C0A 2B0 – 902/687-2157, Fax: 902/687-4426 |
| Souris West ‡ | | Cardigan | Souris-Elmira | Margaret MacDonald, CAO, PO Box 680, Souris C0A 2B0 – 902/687-2251 |
| Southport ‡ | | Hillsborough | | Carol Lowther, Adm., 13 Glenn Stewart Dr., Charlottetown C1A 8X9 – 902/569-3914, Fax: 902/569-3331 |

Cities in CAPITALS; Towns marked †; Communities marked ‡. An in-depth listing for municipalities marked with * appears in Part 2 (check Index for page numbers).

| MUNICIPALITY | 1996 POP. | FEDERAL ELECTORAL DISTRICT | PROVINCIAL ELECTORAL DISTRICT | CONTACT PERSON WITH ADDRESS, PHONE & FAX |
|---|---|---|---|---|
| Stanley Bridge et al | | Malpeque | Park Corner-Oyster Bed | Brenda Larter, Adm., PO Box 157, Hunter River C0A 1N0 – 902/963-2698, Fax: 902/963-2698 |
| Stratford † | 5,869 | Hillsborough | Glen Stewart-Bellevue Cove | Carol Lowther, CAO, 110 Mason Rd., Stratford C1A 7J7 |
| SUMMERSIDE | 14,525 | Egmont | Wilmot-Summerside; St. Eleanors-Summerside | Terry Murphy, CAO, PO Box 1510, Summerside C1N 4K4 – 902/436-4222, Fax: 902/436-9296 |
| Tignish ‡ | 839 | Egmont | Tignish-DeBlois | Karen Buote, CAO, PO Box 57, Tignish C0B 2B0 – 902/882-2600, Fax: 902/882-2414 |
| Tignish Shore ‡ | | Egmont | | Donna Pitre, CAO, Kildare Cape, Tignish C0B 2B0 – 902/882-3811, 853-3931 |
| Tyne Valley ‡ | 231 | Egmont | Cascumpec-Grand River | Marie Barlow, CAO, PO Box 39, Tyne Valley C0B 2C0 – 902/831-2938 |
| Union Road ‡ | 218 | Malpeque | Georgetown-Baldwin's Road | Ian MacArthur, CAO, Union Road, RR#3, Charlottetown C1A 7J7 – 902/368-8213 |
| Valleyfield ‡ | | Cardigan | Georgetown-Baldwin's Road; Montague-Kilmuir; Belfast-Pownal Bay | Donald Nicholson, CAO, PO Box 39, Tyne Valley C0B 2C0 – 902/831-2938 |
| Victoria ‡ | 158 | Malpeque | Crapaud-Hazel Grove | Kaye MacVittie, CAO, PO Box 39, Victoria C0A 1R0 – 902/658-2085 |
| Warren Grove ‡ | 295 | Malpeque | North River-Rice Point | Gail Sanderson, CAO, Warren Grove, RR#4, Cornwall C0A 1H0 – 902/566-3655 |
| Wellington ‡ | 427 | Egmont | Cascumpec-Grand River; Evangeline-Miscouche | Sharon MacNeill, CAO, PO Box 26, Wellington C0B 2E0 – 902/854-3028, Fax: 902/854-2920 |
| West River ‡ | | Malpeque | | Billy Grant, CAO, PO Box 1008, Charlottetown C1A 8C3 – 902/675-3675 |
| Winsloe ‡ | | Malpeque | Winsloe-West Royalty | Betty Pryor, Adm., PO Box 121, Winsloe C0A 2H0 – 902/628-1598 |
| Winsloe South ‡ | 207 | Malpeque | Winsloe-West Royalty | Joanne Turner, CAO, RR#9, Winsloe C1E 1Z3 – 902/368-1444 |
| York ‡ | | Malpeque | Stanhope-East Royalty | Sharon MacKinnon, CAO, PO Box 8819, York C0A 1P0 – 902/629-1313 |

## QUÉBEC

(Source: Ministère des Affaires municipales)

Québec municipalities are governed either by the Municipal Code, by the Cities and Towns Act, by special legislation or specific charter.

Local municipalities divide into three broad categories, each comprising different types of municipalities. Rural municipalities come under the Municipal Code. Urban municipalities are ruled by the Cities and Towns Act. In spite of the double designation in the Act, cities and towns have the same powers. Municipalities governed by special legislation include the Cree and Northern villages created following the 1975 James Bay Agreement, as well as the cities of Montréal and Québec, which are governed almost exclusively by their own Pre-Confederation charters. There are also 110 unorganized areas which are included in the territory of regional county municipalities and are directly administered by them.

Each municipality is administered by a Council including a Mayor and at least six councillors. The term of each individual Council member is four years. In a rural municipality, all members of council are generally elected at large but may adopt a by-law providing for the rotation of half of its councillors every two years. Urban municipalities are usually divided into wards.

In addition to local municipalities, there are three types of second-tier or regional municipalities, and every local municipality is a member of a second-tier municipality.

Urban communities exist since 1970. There are three of them, one including all 29 municipalities on Montréal Island, one for Québec City metropolitan area, and one for Hull-Gatineau metropolitan area. Each urban community has been established by a separate Act.

Regional county municipalities (RCM) constitute another type of second-tier municipality. They have been established by letters patent since 1980, by virtue of the 1979 Act respecting land use planning and development. The whole settled part of the province is covered by 96 such regional county municipalities, except for the municipalities included in the urban communities. The council of an RCM or an urban community is composed of members of all the municipalities included in the territory.

The third type of regional municipality is represented by the Kativik Regional Administration established in 1980. It provides local services to 14 Inuit villages scattered along the extreme northern shore of Québec.

Urban Centres (Villes) in CAPITALS; Villages marked (V); Townships/Cantons marked (Canton);United townships/Cantons unis marked (Cantons); Parishes marked (P); Municipalities marked (Mun.).; Northern villages/Villages nordiques marked (NV); Cree Villages/Villages Cris marked (VC); Naskapi Villages/Villages Naskapi marked (VN); In the third column, Urban Community/Communauté Urbaine marked Urb. Com. An in-depth listing for municipalities marked with * appears in Part 2 (check Index for page numbers).

| MUNICIPALITY | 1996 POP. | REGIONAL COUNTY MUN. | FEDERAL ELECTORAL DISTRICT | PROVINCIAL ELECTORAL DISTRICT | CONTACT PERSON WITH ADDRESS, PHONE & FAX |
|---|---|---|---|---|---|
| Abercorn (V) | 344 | Brome-Missisquoi | Brome-Missisquoi | Brome-Missisquoi | Lyne Vaillancourt, Sec.-Trés., 10, ch des Églises ouest, Abercorn J0E 1B0 – 514/538-2664, Fax: 514/538-6295 |
| ACTON-VALE | 4,685 | Acton | St-Hyacinthe-Bagot | Johnson | Rita Parent, Gref., 1025, rue Boulay, CP 640, Acton-Vale J0H 1A0 – 514/546-2703, Fax: 514/546-4865 |
| Aguanish (Mun.) | 380 | Minganie | Manicouagan | Duplessis | Marie-Paule Chevarie, Sec.-Trés., 106, rte Jacques-Cartier, CP 47, Aguanish G0G 1A0 – 418/533-2323, Fax: 418/533-2205 |
| Akulivik (NV) | 411 | Kativik | Abitibi | Ungava | Larry Hubert, Sec.-Trés., Akulivik J0M 1V0 – 819/496-2073, Fax: 819/496-2200 |
| Albanel (Mun.) | 2,540 | Maria-Chapdelaine | Roberval | Roberval | Gilles Lambert, Sec.-Trés., 160, rue Principale, Albanel G8M 3J5 – 418/279-5250, Fax: 418/279-3147 |
| Alleyn-et-Cawood (Cantons) | 185 | Pontiac | Pontiac-Gatineau-Labelle | Gatineau | Lynn Gagenais, Sec.-Trés., ch Harrison, CP 75, Danford Lake J0X 1P0 – 819/467-2941, Fax: 819/467-2941 |
| ALMA | 26,127 | Lac-St-Jean-Est | Lac-St-Jean | Lac-St-Jean | Jean Paradis, Gref., Hôtel de Ville, 140, rue St-Joseph sud, Alma G8B 3R1 – 418/669-5000, Fax: 418/669-5019 |

Urban Centres (Villes) in CAPITALS; Villages marked (V); Townships/Cantons marked (Canton);United townships/Cantons unis marked (Cantons); Parishes marked (P); Municipalities marked (Mun.).; Northern villages/Villages nordiques marked (NV); Cree Villages/Villages Cris marked (VC); Naskapi Villages/Villages Naskapi marked (VN); In the third column, Urban Community/Communauté Urbaine marked Urb. Com. An in-depth listing for municipalities marked with * appears in Part 2 (check Index for page numbers).

| MUNICIPALITY | 1996 POP. | REGIONAL COUNTY MUN. | FEDERAL ELECTORAL DISTRICT | PROVINCIAL ELECTORAL DISTRICT | CONTACT PERSON WITH ADDRESS, PHONE & FAX |
|---|---|---|---|---|---|
| Amherst (Canton) | 1,145 | Les Laurentides | Argenteuil-Papineau | Labelle; Papineau | Bernard Davidson, Sec.-Trés., 124, rue St-Louis, CP 30, St-Rémi-d'Amherst J0T 2L0 – 819/687-3355, Fax: 819/687-8430 |
| AMOS | 13,632 | Abitibi | Abitibi | Abitibi-Ouest | France Beaulieu, Gref., Hôtel de Ville, 182, 1e rue est, Amos J9T 2G1 – 819/732-3254, Fax: 819/727-9792 |
| AMQUI | 6,800 | La Matapédia | Matapédia-Matane | Matapédia | Mario Lavoie, Gref., 20, promenade de l'Hôtel-de-Ville, CP 1030, Amqui G0J 1B0 – 418/629-4242, Fax: 418/629-4090 |
| Angliers (V) | 306 | Témiscamingue | Rouyn-Noranda-Témiscamingue | Rouyn-Noranda-Témiscamingue | Aline Arsenault, Sec.-Trés., 14, de la Baie-Miller, CP 9, Angliers J0Z 1A0 – 819/949-4351, Fax: 819/949-4431 |
| ANJOU | 37,308 | Montréal (Urb. Com.) | Anjou-Rivière-des-Prairies | Anjou | Robert Ménard, Gref., 7701, boul Louis-H.-Lafontaine, Anjou H1K 4B9 – 514/493-8000, Fax: 514/493-8009 |
| Armagh (Mun.) | 1,604 | Bellechasse | Bellechasse-Montmagny-L'Islet | Bellechasse | Christian Noël, Sec.-Trés., 5, rue de la Salle, CP 87, Armagh G0R 1A0 – 418/466-2916, Fax: 418/466-2409 |
| Arntfield (Mun.) | 433 | Rouyn-Noranda | Rouyn-Noranda-Témiscamingue | Rouyn-Noranda-Témiscamingue | Sylvain Munger, Sec.-Trés., 15, av Fugère, CP 46, Arntfield J0Z 1B0 – 819/279-2241, Fax: 819/279-2481 |
| Arundel (Canton) | 533 | Les Laurentides | Argenteuil-Papineau | Argenteuil | Bernice Goulet, Sec.-Trés., 2, rue du Village, CP 40, Arundel J0T 1A0 – 819/687-3991, Fax: 819/687-8760 |
| ASBESTOS | 6,271 | Asbestos | Richmond-Arthabaska | Richmond | Yvan Provencher, Gref., 185, rue du Roi, Asbestos J1T 1S4 – 819/879-7171, Fax: 819/879-2343 |
| Ascot (Mun.) | 8,663 | Sherbrooke | Compton-Stanstead | Orford; St-François | Mario Boily, Sec.-Trés., 600, rue Thibault, Ascot J1H 6G7 – 819/563-3993, Fax: 819/563-3203 |
| Ascot-Corner (Mun.) | 2,280 | Le Haut-St-François | Compton-Stanstead | Mégantic-Compton | Suzanne B.-Jacques, Sec.-Trés., 5655, route 112, CP 209, Ascot-Corner J0B 1A0 – 819/566-5436, Fax: 819/566-8526 |
| Aston-Jonction (V) | 214 | Nicolet-Yamaska | Richelieu | Nicolet-Yamaska | Line Camiré, Sec.-Trés., 235, rue Vigneault, CP 27, Aston-Jonction G0Z 1A0 – 819/226-3459, Fax: 819/226-3459 |
| Aubert-Gallion (Mun.) | 2,209 | Beauce-Sartigan | Beauce | Beauce-Sud | Claude Dutil, Sec.-Trés., #335, 15e rue, St-Georges-Ouest G5Y 4X2 – 418/227-0383, Fax: 418/227-0383 |
| Auclair (Mun.) | 546 | Témiscouata | Kamouraska-Rivière-du-Loup-Témiscouata | Kamouraska-Témiscouata | Ginette Levasseur, Sec.-Trés., 49, rue des Pionniers, Auclair G0L 1A0 – 418/899-2834, Fax: 418/899-6958 |
| Audet (Mun.) | 732 | Le Granit | Frontenac-Mégantic | Mégantic-Compton | Jean-Louis Boucher, Sec.-Trés., 251, rue Principale, CP 27, Audet G0Y 1A0 – 819/583-1596, Fax: 819/583-1596 |
| Aumond (Canton) | 592 | La Vallée-de-la-Gatineau | Pontiac-Gatineau-Labelle | Gatineau | Johanne Grondin, Sec.-Trés., 679, rte Principale, Aumond J0W 1W0 – 819/449-4006, Fax: 819/449-7448 |
| Aupaluk (NV) | 159 | Kativik | Abitibi | Ungava | Lazarussie Angutinguak, Sec.-Trés., Aupaluk J0M 1X0 – 819/491-7070, Fax: 819/491-7035 |
| Austin (Mun.) | 1,083 | Memphrémagog | Brome-Missisquoi | Brome-Missisquoi | Anne-Marie Ménard, Sec.-Trés., 21, ch Millington, CP 10, Austin J0B 1B0 – 819/843-2388, Fax: 819/843-8211 |
| Authier (Mun.) | 324 | Abitibi-Ouest | Rouyn-Noranda-Témiscamingue | Abitibi Ouest | Louise Lambert, Sec.-Trés., 605, av Principale, CP 90, Authier J0Z 1C0 – 819/782-3093, Fax: 819/782-3203 |
| Authier-Nord (Mun.) | 374 | Abitibi-Ouest | Rouyn-Noranda-Témiscamingue | Abitibi-Ouest | Carole Lefebvre, Sec.-Trés., 452A, 9e Rang, Authier-Nord J0Z 1E0 – 819/782-3914, Fax: 819/782-3009 |
| Ayer's Cliff (V) | 986 | Memphrémagog | Compton-Stanstead | Orford | Ginette Savard-Gauvin, Sec.-Trés., 958, rue Main, CP 36, Ayer's Cliff J0B 1C0 – 819/838-5006, Fax: 819/838-4411 |
| AYLMER | 34,901 | Outaouais (Urb. Com.) | Hull-Aylmer | Pontiac | Suzanne Ouellet, Gref.,Hôtel de Ville, 115, rue Principale, Aylmer J9H 3M2 – 819/685-5005, Fax: 819/685-5019 |
| BAIE-COMEAU | 25,554 | Manicouagan | Charlevoix | Saguenay | Sylvain Ouellet, Gref., 19, av Marquette, Baie-Comeau G4Z 1K5 – 418/296-4931, Fax: 418/296-3759 |
| Baie-de-Shawinigan (V) | 265 | Le Centre-de-la-Mauricie | St-Maurice | St-Maurice | Réjeanne Jacob, Sec.-Trés., 2, rue de l'Édifice-Municipal, Baie-de-Shawinigan G9N 1Z3 – 819/536-2217, Fax: 819/536-3449 |
| Baie-des-Sables (Mun.) | 657 | Matane | Matapédia-Matane | Matane | Myriam Mercier, Sec.-Trés., 20, rue du Couvent, CP 39, Baie-des-Sables G0J 1C0 – 418/772-6218, Fax: 418/772-6218 |
| Baie-du-Febvre (Mun.) | 1,196 | Nicolet-Yamaska | Richelieu | Nicolet-Yamaska | Maryse Baril, Sec.-Trés., 420A, rte Marie-Victorin, Baie-du-Febvre J0G 1A0 – 514/783-6422, Fax: 514/783-6423 |
| BAIE-D'URFÉ | 3,774 | Montréal (Urb. Com.) | Lac-Saint-Louis | Nelligan | Françoise Lange, Gref., 20410, ch Lakeshore, Baie d'Urfé H9X 1P7 – 514/457-5324, Fax: 514/457-5671 |
| Baie-James (Mun.) | 1,978 | Terr. du Nouveau-Québec | Abitibi | Abitibi-Ouest; Ungava | Robert L'Africain, Gref., 110, boul de Matagami, CP 500, Matagami J0Y 2A0 – 819/739-2030, Fax: 819/739-2713 |

Urban Centres (Villes) in CAPITALS; Villages marked (V); Townships/Cantons marked (Canton);United townships/Cantons unis marked (Cantons); Parishes marked (P); Municipalities marked (Mun.).; Northern villages/Villages nordiques marked (NV); Cree Villages/Villages Cris marked (VC); Naskapi Villages/Villages Naskapi marked (VN); In the third column, Urban Community/Communauté Urbaine marked Urb. Com. An in-depth listing for municipalities marked with * appears in Part 2 (check Index for page numbers).

| MUNICIPALITY | 1996 POP. | REGIONAL COUNTY MUN. | FEDERAL ELECTORAL DISTRICT | PROVINCIAL ELECTORAL DISTRICT | CONTACT PERSON WITH ADDRESS, PHONE & FAX |
|---|---|---|---|---|---|
| Baie-Johan-Beetz (Mun.) | 85 | Minganie | Manicouagan | Duplessis | Jean Devost, Sec.-Trés., 20, rue Johan Beetz, Baie-Johan-Beetz G0G 1B0 – 418/539-0125 |
| Baie-Ste-Catherine (Mun.) | 295 | Charlevoix-Est | Charlevoix | Charlevoix | Ève Savard, Sec.-Trés., 308, rue Leclerc, CP 10, Baie-Ste-Catherine G0T 1A0 – 418/237-4241, Fax: 418/237-4223 |
| BAIE-ST-PAUL [1] | 3,569 | Charlevoix | Charlevoix | Charlevoix | Maurice Lavoie, Sec.-Trés., 6, rue St-Jean-Baptiste, CP 220, Baie-St-Paul G0A 1B0 – 418/435-2205, Fax: 418/435-2688 |
| Baie-Trinité (V) | 646 | Manicouagan | Manicouagan | Saguenay | Monique C.-Chouinard, Sec.-Trés., 51, route 138 ouest, CP 100, Baie-Trinité G0H 1A0 – 418/939-2231, Fax: 418/939-2616 |
| Barford (Canton) | 656 | Coaticook | Compton-Stanstead | Mégantic-Compton | Solange Dupont, Sec.-Trés., 10, rte 147 sud, CP 200, Coaticook J1A 2T7 – 819/849-4853, Fax: 819/849-4854 |
| BARKMERE | 53 | Les Laurentides | Argenteuil-Papineau | Argenteuil | Robert Mearns, Sec.-Trés., 182, ch de Barkmere, CP 11, Barkmere J0T 1A0 – 819/687-3373, Fax: 819/687-3373 |
| Barnston (Canton) | 1,500 | Coaticook | Compton-Stanstead | Orford | Marie Dagenais, Sec.-Trés., 1525, ch Riendeau, Barnston J1A 2S5 – 819/849-9186, Fax: 819/849-3952 |
| Barnston-Ouest (Mun.) | 598 | Coaticook | Compton-Stanstead | Orford | Wanda Rozynska, Sec.-Trés., 2133, ch de Ways Mills, RR#1, Ayer's Cliff J0B 1C0 – 819/838-4321 |
| Barraute (Mun.) | 2,134 | Abitibi | Abitibi | Abitibi-Est | Richard Nantel, Sec.-Trés., 481, 8e av, CP 299, Barraute J0Y 1A0 – 819/734-6574, Fax: 819/734-5186 |
| Batiscan (Mun.) | 891 | Francheville | Champlain | Champlain | Sylvie Brousseau, Sec.-Trés., 395, rue Principale, Batiscan G0X 1A0 – 418/362-2421, Fax: 418/362-3174 |
| BEACONSFIELD | 19,414 | Montréal (Urb. Com.) | Lac-St-Louis | Jacques-Cartier | Johanne Legault, Gref., 303, boul Beaconsfield, Beaconsfield H9W 4A7 – 514/428-4400, Fax: 514/428-4424 |
| Béarn (Mun.) | 973 | Témiscamingue | Témiscamingue | Rouyn-Noranda-Témiscamingue | Lynda Gaudet, Sec.-Trés., 28, 2e rue nord, CP 369, Béarn J0Z 1G0 – 819/726-4121, Fax: 819/726-4121 |
| BEAUCEVILLE | 3,751 | Robert-Cliche | Beauce | Beauce-Nord | Roger Longchamps, Sec.-Trés., 540, 1re av Renault, CP 579, Beauceville G0S 1A0 – 418/774-9137, Fax: 418/774-9141 |
| Beaudry (Mun.) | 1,139 | Rouyn-Noranda | Rouyn-Noranda-Témiscamingue | Rouyn-Noranda-Témiscamingue | Fleurette Lefebvre, Sec.-Trés., 667, rue Principale, CP 10, Beaudry J0Z 1J0 – 819/797-5333, Fax: 819/797-2108 |
| BEAUHARNOIS | 6,435 | Beauharnois-Salaberry | Beauharnois-Salaberry | Beauharnois-Huntingdon | Jean Beaulieu, Gref., #400, 600, rue Ellice, Beauharnois J6N 3P7 – 514/429-3546, Fax: 514/429-6663 |
| Beaulac (V) | 397 | L'Amiante | Frontenac-Mégantic | Richmond | Claude Jacques, Sec.-Trés., 22B, rue St-Jacques, CP 40, Beaulac G0Y 1B0 – 418/458-2375, Fax: 418/458-2375 |
| *BEAUPORT | 72,920 | Québec (Urb. Com.) | Beauport-Montmorency-Orléans | Montmorency; Limoilou | Josette Tessier, Gref., 10, rue de l'Hôtel-de-Ville, CP 5187, Beauport G1E 6P4 – 418/666-2121, Fax: 418/666-6124 |
| BEAUPRÉ | 2,799 | La Côte-de-Beaupré | Beauport-Montmorency-Orléans | Charlevoix | Jean-Paul Paré, Sec.-Trés., 216, rue Prévost, Beaupré G0A 1E0 – 418/827-4541, Fax: 418/827-3818 |
| Beaux-Rivages (Mun.) | 1,104 | Antoine-Labelle | Pontiac-Gatineau-Labelle | Labelle | Nicole Sarrasin, Sec.-Trés., 330, rte 117 est, CP 30, Lac-des-Écorces J0W 1H0 – 819/585-4600, Fax: 819/585-4610 |
| BÉCANCOUR | 11,489 | Bécancour | Richelieu | Nicolet-Yamaska | France Leclerc, Gref.,1295, av Nicolas-Perrot, Bécancour G0X 1B0 – 819/294-6500, Fax: 819/294-6535 |
| Bedford (Canton) | 799 | Brome-Missisquoi | Brome-Missisquoi | Brome-Missisquoi | Claire Capistran, Sec.-Trés., 86, rue des Cèdres, Bedford J0J 1A0 – 514/248-7576, Fax: 514/248-4678 |
| BEDFORD | 2,748 | Brome-Missisquoi | Brome-Missisquoi | Brome-Missisquoi | Bertrand Déry, Sec.-Trés., 14, rue Philippe-Côté, CP 420, Bedford J0J 1A0 – 514/248-2440, Fax: 514/248-3220 |
| Bégin (Mun.) | 920 | Le Fjord-du-Saguenay | Lac-St-Jean | Dubuc | Alain Coudé, Sec.-Trés., 126, rue Brassard, Bégin G0V 1B0 – 418/672-4270, Fax: 418/672-6161 |
| Belcourt (Mun.) | 285 | Vallée-de-l'Or | Abitibi | Abitibi-Est | Nathalie Lizotte, Sec.-Trés., 219, rue Communautaire, CP 22, Belcourt J0Y 2M0 – 819/737-8894, Fax: 819/737-8894 |
| Bellecombe (Mun.) | 755 | Rouyn-Noranda | Rouyn-Noranda-Témiscamingue | Rouyn-Noranda-Témiscamingue | Lise Plourde, Sec.-Trés., 1161, rte des Pionniers, CP 55, Bellecombe J0Z 1K0 – 819/797-8302, Fax: 819/797-6585 |
| Bellefeuille (P) | 12,803 | La Rivière-du-Nord | Laurentides | Prévost | Claudette Pion, Sec.-Trés., 999, rue de l'Église, Bellefeuille J0R 1A0 – 514/436-7447, Fax: 514/436-8422 |
| BELLETERRE | 395 | Témiscamingue | Rouyn-Noranda-Témiscamingue | Rouyn-Noranda-Témiscamingue | Liliane Rochon, Sec.-Trés., 265, 1re av, CP 130, Belleterre J0Z 1L0 – 819/722-2122, Fax: 819/722-2527 |

Urban Centres (Villes) in CAPITALS; Villages marked (V); Townships/Cantons marked (Canton);United townships/Cantons unis marked (Cantons); Parishes marked (P); Municipalities marked (Mun.).; Northern villages/Villages nordiques marked (NV); Cree Villages/Villages Cris marked (VC); Naskapi Villages/Villages Naskapi marked (VN); In the third column, Urban Community/Communauté Urbaine marked Urb. Com. An in-depth listing for municipalities marked with * appears in Part 2 (check Index for page numbers).

| MUNICIPALITY | 1996 POP. | REGIONAL COUNTY MUN. | FEDERAL ELECTORAL DISTRICT | PROVINCIAL ELECTORAL DISTRICT | CONTACT PERSON WITH ADDRESS, PHONE & FAX |
|---|---|---|---|---|---|
| BELOEIL | 19,294 | La Vallée-du-Richelieu | Chambly | Borduas | Sylvie Piérard, Gref., 777, rue Laurier, Beloeil J3G 4S9 – 514/467-2835, Fax: 514/464-5445 |
| Bergeronnes (Canton) | 212 | La Haute Côte-Nord | Charlevoix | Saguenay | Louise Gauthier, Sec.-Trés., 424, rue de la Mer, CP 189, Grandes-Bergeronnes G0T 1G0 – 418/232-6735, Fax: 418/232-6671 |
| Bernierville (V) | 1,871 | L'Érable | Lotbinière | Frontenac | Sylvie Tardif, Sec.-Trés., 821, rue Principale, CP 340, St-Ferdinand G0N 1N0 – 418/428-9404, Fax: 418/428-9724 |
| Berry (Mun.) | 501 | Abitibi | Abitibi | Abitibi-Ouest | Annie Todd, Sec.-Trés., 271, rte 399, St-Nazaire-de-Berry J0Y 2G0 – 819/732-1815, Fax: 819/732-1815 |
| Berthier-sur-Mer (P) | 1,227 | Montmagny | Bellechasse-Montmagny-L'Islet | Montmagny-L'Islet | Suzanne Blais, Sec.-Trés., 5, rue du Couvent, Berthier-sur-Mer G0R 1E0 – 418/259-7343, Fax: 418/259-2038 |
| BERTHIERVILLE | 3,952 | D'Autray | Berthier-Montcalm | Berthier | Céline Lahaie, Gref., 588, rue De Montcalm, CP 269, Berthierville J0K 1A0 – 514/836-7035, Fax: 514/836-1446 |
| Béthanie (Mun.) | 354 | Acton | St-Hyacinthe-Bagot | Johnson | Claire Petit, Sec.-Trés., 745, ch du Dixième-Rang, Valcourt J0E 2L0 – 514/548-2826, Fax: 514/548-5693 |
| Biencourt (Mun.) | 675 | Témiscouata | Kamouraska-Rivière-du-Loup-Témiscouata | Rimouski | Lucette Viel, Sec.-Trés., 2, rue St-Marc, CP 70, Biencourt G0K 1T0 – 418/499-2423, Fax: 418/499-2708 |
| BLACK LAKE | 4,408 | L'Amiante | Frontenac-Mégantic | Frontenac | Réjean Martin, Sec.-Trés., 350, rue St-Hubert, Black Lake G6H 1R5 – 418/423-2773, Fax: 418/423-4707 |
| BLAINVILLE | 29,603 | Thérèse-de-Blainville | Terrebonne-Blainville | Blainville | Gisèle Gauvreau, Gref.,1001, ch du Camp-Bouchard, Blainville J7C 4N4 – 514/434-5200, Fax: 514/434-5229 |
| Blanc-Sablon (Mun.) | 1,248 | | Manicouagan | Duplessis | Rollande Russell, Sec.-Trés., 1149, boul Dr.-Camille-Marcoux, CP 400, Lourdes-de-Blanc-Sablon G0G 1W0 – 418/461-2707, Fax: 418/461-2529 |
| Blue-Sea (Mun.) | 595 | La Vallée-de-la-Gatineau | Pontiac-Gatineau-Labelle | Gatineau | France Carpentier, Sec.-Trés., 7, rue Principale, CP 99, Blue Sea Lake J0X 1C0 – 819/463-2261, Fax: 819/463-4345 |
| Boileau (Mun.) | 228 | Papineau | Argenteuil-Papineau | Papineau | Nicole Bourret, Sec.-Trés., 702, ch de Boileau, RR#1, Namur J0V 1N0 – 819/687-3436, Fax: 819/687-3745 |
| BOIS-DES-FILION | 7,124 | Thérèse-de-Blainville | Terrebonne-Blainville | Blainville | Martin Nadon, Gref.,60, 36e av sud, Bois-des-Filion J6Z 2G6 – 514/621-1460, Fax: 514/621-8483 |
| Bois-Franc (Mun.) | 425 | La Vallée-de-la-Gatineau | Pontiac-Gatineau-Labelle | Gatineau | Johanne Villeneuve, Sec.-Trés., 466, rte 105, Bois-Franc J9E 3A9 – 819/449-2252, Fax: 819/449-4407 |
| BOISBRIAND | 25,227 | Thérèse-de-Blainville | St-Eustache-Ste-Thérèse | Groulx | Lucie Mongeau, Gref.,940, boul de la Grande-Allée, Boisbriand J7G 2J7 – 514/435-1954, Fax: 514/435-6398 |
| Boischatel (Mun.) | 4,152 | La Cote de Beaupré | Beauport-Montmorency-Orléans | Montmorency | Michel Lefebvre, Sec.-Trés., 9, côte de l'Église, Boischatel G0A 1H0 – 418/822-0721, Fax: 418/822-2373 |
| Bolton-Est (Mun.) | 651 | Memphrémagog | Brome-Missisquoi | Brome-Missisquoi | Michael Merovitz, Sec.-Trés., 858, rue Missisquoi, Bolton-Centre J0E 1G0 – 514/292-3444, Fax: 514/292-4224 |
| Bolton-Ouest (Mun.) | 575 | Brome-Missisquoi | Brome-Missisquoi | Brome-Missisquoi | Carrol Kralik, Sec.-Trés., 9, ch Town Hall, CP 711, Knowlton J0E 1V0 – 514/242-2704, Fax: 514/242-2705 |
| Bonaventure (Mun.) | 2,884 | Bonaventure | Bonaventure-Gaspé-Îles-de-la-Madeleine-Pabok | Bonaventure | Gilles Malouin, Sec.-Trés., 127, av Louisbourg, CP 428, Bonaventure G0C 1E0 – 418/534-2313, Fax: 418/534-4336 |
| Bonne-Espérance (Mun.) | 906 | | Manicouagan | Duplessis | René Fequet, Sec.-Trés., CP 40, Rivière St-Paul G0G 2P0 – 418/379-2911, Fax: 418/379-2959 |
| Bonsecours (Mun.) | 503 | Le Val-St-François | Shefford | Brome-Missisquoi | Carole Lévesque, Sec.-Trés., 605, rue du Couvent, CP 119, Bonsecours J0E 1H0 – 514/532-3139, Fax: 514/532-3953 |
| Boucher (Mun.) | 454 | Mékinac | Champlain | Laviolette | Nicole Léveillé, Sec.-Trés., 610, rte Principale, St-Joseph-de-Mékinac G0X 2E0 – 819/646-5686, Fax: 819/646-5686 |
| BOUCHERVILLE | 34,989 | Lajemmerais | Verchères | Marguerite-D'Youville | Claude Caron, Gref., 500, rue de la Rivière-aux-Pins, Boucherville J4B 2Z7 – 514/449-3131, Fax: 514/655-0086 |
| Bouchette (Mun.) | 722 | La Vallée-de-la-Gatineau | Pontiac-Gatineau-Labelle | Gatineau | Christine Lacroix, Sec.-Trés., 36, rue Principale, CP 59, Bouchette J0X 1E0 – 819/465-2555, Fax: 819/465-2318 |
| Bowman (Mun.) | 516 | Papineau | Argenteuil-Papineau | Papineau | Denise Wilson, Sec.-Trés., 214, rte 307, CP 29, Val-des-Bois J0X 3C0 – 819/454-2421, Fax: 819/454-2133 |

Urban Centres (Villes) in CAPITALS; Villages marked (V); Townships/Cantons marked (Canton);United townships/Cantons unis marked (Cantons); Parishes marked (P); Municipalities marked (Mun.).; Northern villages/Villages nordiques marked (NV); Cree Villages/Villages Cris marked (VC); Naskapi Villages/Villages Naskapi marked (VN); In the third column, Urban Community/Communauté Urbaine marked Urb. Com. An in-depth listing for municipalities marked with * appears in Part 2 (check Index for page numbers).

| MUNICIPALITY | 1996 POP. | REGIONAL COUNTY MUN. | FEDERAL ELECTORAL DISTRICT | PROVINCIAL ELECTORAL DISTRICT | CONTACT PERSON WITH ADDRESS, PHONE & FAX |
|---|---|---|---|---|---|
| Brébeuf (P) | 695 | Les Laurentides | Laurentides | Labelle | Lynda Foisy, Sec.-Trés., 217, rte 323, Brébeuf J0T 1B0 – 819/425-9833, Fax: 819/425-6611 |
| Brigham (Mun.) | 2,290 | Brome-Missisquoi | Brome-Missisquoi | Brome-Missisquoi | Johanne Lapointe, Sec.-Trés., 118, av des Cèdres, CP 70, Brigham J2K 4K4 – 514/263-5942, Fax: 514/263-8380 |
| Bristol (Canton) | 1,129 | Pontiac | Pontiac-Gatineau-Labelle | Pontiac | Keith R. Emmerson, Sec.-Trés., RR#1, Bristol J0X 1G0 – 819/647-5555, Fax: 819/647-2424 |
| Brome (V) | 287 | Brome-Missisquoi | Brome-Missisquoi | Brome-Missisquoi | Linda Flanagan, Sec.-Trés., 330, ch Stage Coach, CP 2, Brome J0E 1K0 – 514/243-0489, Fax: 514/243-1091 |
| BROMONT | 4,290 | La Haute-Yamaska | Brome-Missisquoi | Brome-Missisquoi | Danielle Rioux, Gref., 88, boul de Bromont, Bromont J0E 1L0 – 514/534-2021, Fax: 514/534-1025 |
| Brompton (Canton) | 2,157 | Le Val-St-François | Richmond-Arthabasca | Johnson | Réjeanne Gagnon, Sec.-Trés., 30, rue du Couvent, CP 900, Bromptonville J0B 1H0 – 819/846-6811, Fax: 819/846-6812 |
| BROMPTONVILLE | 3,426 | Le Val-St-François | Richmond-Arthabasca | Johnson | Michel Dupont, Sec.-Trés., 133, rue Laval, CP 610, Bromptonville J0B 1H0 – 819/846-2757, Fax: 819/846-6621 |
| *BROSSARD | 65,927 | Champlain | Brossard-La Prairie | La Pinière | Daniel Carrier, Gref., 2001, boul de Rome, Brossard J4W 3K5 – 514/923-7000, Fax: 514/923-7016, URL: http://www.ville.brossard.qc.ca |
| Brownsburg (V) | 2,583 | Argenteuil | Argenteuil-Papineau | Argenteuil | Line Ross, Sec.-Trés., 300, rue de l'Hôtel de Ville, CP 40, Brownsburg J0V 1A0 – 514/533-6687, Fax: 514/533-5795 |
| Bryson (V) | 753 | Pontiac | Pontiac-Gatineau-Labelle | Pontiac | Lucille Lanoix, Sec.-Trés., 770, rue Centrale, CP 190, Bryson J0X 1H0 – 819/648-5940, Fax: 819/648-5297 |
| BUCKINGHAM | 11,678 | Outaouais (Urb. Com.) | Gatineau | Papineau | Carole St-Arnaud-Gaboury, Sec.-Trés., 515, rue Charles, Buckingham J8L 2K4 – 819/986-3351, Fax: 819/986-8336 |
| Bury (Mun.) | 1,151 | Le Haut-St-François | Compton-Stanstead | Mégantic-Compton | Marilyn Matheson, Sec.-Trés., 563, rue Main, CP 179, Bury J0B 1J0 – 819/872-3692 |
| CABANO | 3,086 | Témiscouata | Kamouraska-Rivière-du-Loup-Témiscouata | Kamouraska-Témiscouata | Gilles Ruest, Sec.-Trés., 79, rue Commerciale, CP 188, Cabano G0L 1E0 – 418/854-2116, Fax: 418/854-0118 |
| CADILLAC | 930 | Rouyn-Noranda | Rouyn-Noranda-Témiscamingue | Abitibi-Est | Réal Maranda, Sec.-Trés., 2, rue Dumont est, CP 185, Cadillac J0Y 1C0 – 819/759-3606, Fax: 819/759-3607 |
| Calixa-Lavallée (P) | 467 | Lajemmerais | Verchères | Verchères | Monique Pigeon, Sec.-Trés., 771, ch de la Beauce, Calixa-Lavallée J0L 1A0 – 514/583-6470, Fax: 514/583-5508 |
| Calumet (V) | 602 | Argenteuil | Argenteuil-Papineau | Argenteuil | Carole Constantineau, Sec.-Trés., 105, rue des Érables, CP 10, Calumet J0V 1B0 – 819/242-4966, Fax: 819/242-1232 |
| Campbell's Bay (V) | 874 | Pontiac | Pontiac-Gatineau-Labelle | Pontiac | Colleen Larivière, Sec.-Trés., 59, rue Leslie, CP 157, Campbell's Bay J0X 1K0 – 819/648-5811, Fax: 819/648-2045 |
| CANDIAC | 11,805 | Roussillon | Brossard-La Prairie | La Prairie | Carole Lemaire, Gref., 100, boul Montcalm nord, Candiac J5R 3L8 – 514/444-6000, Fax: 514/444-6009 |
| Cantley (Mun.) | 5,425 | Les Collines-de-l'Outaouais | Pontiac-Gatineau-Labelle | Gatineau | Vacant, Sec.-Trés., 8, ch River, Cantley J8V 2Z9 – 819/827-3434, Fax: 819/827-4328 |
| Cap-à-l'Aigle (V) | 713 | Charlevoix-Est | Charlevoix | Charlevoix | Robert Lapointe, Sec.-Trés., 760, rue St-Raphaël, CP 10, Cap-à-l'Aigle G0T 1B0 – 418/665-7596, Fax: 418/665-7597 |
| Cap-aux-Meules (V) | 1,661 | Les Îles-de-la-Madeleine | Bonaventure-Gaspé-Îles-de-la-Madeleine-Pabok | Îles-de-la-Madeleine | Hubert Poirier, Sec.-Trés., 460, ch Principal, CP 309, Cap-aux-Meules G0B 1B0 – 418/986-2460, Fax: 418/986-6962 |
| CAP-CHAT | 2,847 | Denis-Riverin | Matapédia-Matane | Matane | Claudette Lemieux-Soucy, Gref.,53, rue Notre-Dame, CP 279, Cap-Chat G0J 1E0 – 418/786-5537, Fax: 418/786-5540 |
| CAP-DE-LA-MADELEINE | 33,438 | Francheville | Champlain | Champlain | Yolaine Tremblay, Gref., 10, rue de l'Hôtel-de-Ville, CP 220, Cap-de-la-Madeleine G8T 7W4 – 819/375-1661, Fax: 819/375-3101 |
| CAP-ROUGE | 14,163 | Québec (Urb. Com.) | Louis-Hébert | La Peltrie | Marcel Laroche, Gref., 4473, rue St-Félix, Cap-Rouge G1Y 3A6 – 418/650-7777, Fax: 418/651-9528 |
| Cap-St-Ignace (Mun.) | 3,078 | Montmagny | Bellechasse-Montmagny-L'Islet | Montmagny-L'Islet | Donald Bernier, Sec.-Trés., 850, rte du Souvenir, Cap-St-Ignace G0R 1H0 – 418/246-5631, Fax: 418/246-5663 |
| Cap-Santé (Mun.) | 2,615 | Portneuf | Portneuf | Portneuf | Jacques Blais, Sec.-Trés., 194, rte 138, Cap-Santé G0A 1L0 – 418/285-1207, Fax: 418/285-0009 |
| Caplan (Mun.) | 2,145 | Bonaventure | Bonaventure-Gaspé-Îles-de-la-Madeleine-Pabok | Bonaventure | Argée Garant, Sec.-Trés., 17, boul Perron est, CP 360, Caplan G0C 1H0 – 418/388-2075, Fax: 418/388-2429 |

Urban Centres (Villes) in CAPITALS; Villages marked (V); Townships/Cantons marked (Canton);United townships/Cantons unis marked (Cantons); Parishes marked (P); Municipalities marked (Mun.).; Northern villages/Villages nordiques marked (NV); Cree Villages/Villages Cris marked (VC); Naskapi Villages/Villages Naskapi marked (VN); In the third column, Urban Community/Communauté Urbaine marked Urb. Com. An in-depth listing for municipalities marked with * appears in Part 2 (check Index for page numbers).

| MUNICIPALITY | 1996 POP. | REGIONAL COUNTY MUN. | FEDERAL ELECTORAL DISTRICT | PROVINCIAL ELECTORAL DISTRICT | CONTACT PERSON WITH ADDRESS, PHONE & FAX |
|---|---|---|---|---|---|
| Capucins (Mun.) | 280 | Denis-Riverin | Matapédia-Matane | Matane | Maryse Lavoie, Sec.-Trés., 294, rue du Village, Capucins G0J 1H0 – 418/786-5021, Fax: 418/786-5517 |
| CARIGNAN | 5,614 | La Vallée-du-Richelieu | Champlain | Chambly | Jean Lacroix, Gref., 2555, ch Bellevue, Carignan J3L 6G8 – 514/658-1066, Fax: 514/658-6079 |
| Carillon (V) | 258 | Argenteuil | Argenteuil-Papineau | Argenteuil | Danielle Jacques-Roy, Sec.-Trés., 21, rue Kelly, Carillon J0V 1C0 – 514/537-8400, Fax: 514/537-8400 |
| CARLETON | 2,886 | Avignon | Matapédia-Matane | Bonaventure | André Allard, Sec.-Trés., CP 237, Carleton G0C 1J0 – 418/364-7073, Fax: 418/364-7314 |
| CAUSAPSCAL | 2,080 | La Matapédia | Matapédia-Matane | Matapédia | Jean-Noël Barriault, Gref., 1, rue Saint-Jacques nord, Causapscal G0J 1J0 – 418/756-5588, Fax: 418/756-3344 |
| Cayamant (Mun.) | 706 | La Vallée-de-la-Gatineau | Pontiac-Gatineau-Labelle | Gatineau | Suzanne Vallières, Sec.-Trés., 6, che Lachapelle, Lac-Cayamant J0X 1Y0 – 819/463-3587, Fax: 819/463-4020 |
| CHAMBLY | 19,716 | La Vallée-du-Richelieu | Chambly | Chambly | Louise Bouvier, Greffe., 1, pl de la Mairie, Chambly J3L 4X1 – 514/658-8788, Fax: 514/658-4214 |
| Chambord (Mun.) | 1,784 | Le Domaine-du-Roy | Roberval | Roberval | Steve Gagnon, Sec.-Trés., 104, rue Principale, CP 70, Chambord G0W 1G0 – 418/342-6274, Fax: 418/342-8438 |
| Champlain (Mun.) | 1,608 | Francheville | Champlain | Champlain | Jean Houde, Sec.-Trés., 819, rue Notre-Dame, CP 250, Champlain G0X 1C0 – 819/295-3979, Fax: 819/295-3032 |
| Champneuf (Mun.) | 169 | Abitibi | Abitibi | Abitibi-Ouest | Diane Fleurent, Sec.-Trés., 12, 6e av nord, Champneuf J0Y 1E0 – 819/754-2053, Fax: 819/754-2053 |
| CHANDLER | 3,358 | Pabok | Gaspé-Bonaventure-Îles-de-la-Madaleine | Gaspé | Léandre Savoie, Gref., 35, rue Commerciale ouest, CP 459, Chandler G0C 1K0 – 418/689-2221, Fax: 418/689-4963 |
| CHAPAIS | 2,030 | Terr. du Nouveau-Québec | Roberval | Ungava | Daniel Dufour, Sec.-Trés., 145, boul Springer, CP 380, Chapais G0W 1H0 – 418/745-2511, Fax: 418/745-3871 |
| Chapeau (V) | 442 | Pontiac | Pontiac-Gatineau-Labelle | Pontiac | Richard Vaillancourt, Sec.-Trés., 37, rue St-Joseph, CP 100, Chapeau J0X 1M0 – 819/689-2266, Fax: 819/689-5619 |
| Charette (Mun.) | 962 | Le Centre-de-la-Mauricie | St-Maurice | Maskinongé | Claire Gélinas, Sec.-Trés., 390, rue St-Édouard, Charette G0X 1E0 – 819/221-2095, Fax: 819/221-3493 |
| CHARLEMAGNE | 5,739 | L'Assomption | Repentigny | Masson | Léo M. Lepage, Gref., 84, rue du Sacré-Coeur, Charlemagne J5Z 1W8 – 514/581-2541, Fax: 514/581-0597 |
| *CHARLES-BOURG | 70,942 | Québec (Urb. Com.) | Charlesbourg | Charlesbourg; Chauveau | Jacques Dorais, Gref., 160, 76e rue est, Charlesbourg G1H 7H5 – 418/624-7500, Fax: 418/624-7525 |
| CHARNY | 10,661 | Les Chutes-de-la-Chaudière | Lévis | Les Chutes-de-la-Chaudière | Michel Hallé, Gref., 5333, rue de la Symphonie, Charny G6X 3B6 – 418/832-4695, Fax: 418/832-4978 |
| Chartierville (Mun.) | 328 | Le Haut-St-François | Frontenac-Mégantic | Mégantic-Compton | Monique Bissonnette, Sec.-Trés., 27, rue St-Jean-Baptiste, Chartierville J0B 1K0 – 819/656-2323 |
| CHÂTEAU-RICHER | 3,579 | La Côte-de-Beaupré | Beauport-Montmorency-Orléans | Montmorency | Vacant, Sec.-Trés., 8006, av Royale, Château-Richer G0A 1N0 – 418/824-4294, Fax: 418/824-3277 |
| CHÂTEAUGUAY | 41,423 | Roussillon | Châteauguay | Châteauguay | Vacant, Gref., 5, boul d'Youville, Châteauguay J6J 2P8 – 514/698-3000, Fax: 514/698-3019 |
| Chatham (Canton) | 4,100 | Argenteuil | Argenteuil-Papineau | Argenteuil | Jackline Williams, Sec.-Trés., 270, rte du Canton, Chatham J8G 1R4 – 514/562-9121, Fax: 514/562-1482 |
| Chazel (Mun.) | 388 | Abitibi-Ouest | Témiscamingue | Abitibi-Ouest | Florianne Trépanier, Sec.-Trés., 335, rue Principale, Chazel J0Z 1N0 – 819/333-4758, Fax: 819/333-4758 |
| Chelsea (Mun.) | 5,925 | Les Collines-de-l'Outaouais | Pontiac-Gatineau-Labelle | Gatineau | Alcide Cloutier, Sec.-Trés., 100, ch d'Old Chelsea, CP 330, Chelsea J0X 1N0 – 819/827-1124, Fax: 819/827-2672 |
| Chénéville (Mun.) [2] | 646 | Papineau | Argenteuil-Papineau | Papineau | Claire Blais, Sec.-Trés., 63, rue de l'Hôtel-de-Ville, CP 70, Chénéville J0V 1E0 – 819/428-3583, Fax: 819/428-3583 |
| Chertsey (Mun.) | 3,853 | Matawinie | Berthier-Montcalm | Bertrand | Pierre Mercier, Sec.-Trés., 333, av de l'Amitié, CP 120, Chertsey J0K 3K0 – 514/882-2920, Fax: 514/882-3333 |
| Chester-Est (Canton) | 333 | Arthabaska | Richmond-Arthabaska | Arthabaska | Jeanne-d'Arc Guillemette, Sec.-Trés., 130, rue Guillemette, RR#1, Ste-Hélène-de-Chester G0P 1H0 – 819/382-2650, Fax: 819/382-9933 |
| Chesterville (Mun.) | 784 | Arthabaska | Richmond-Arthabaska | Arthabaska | Lyse Côté, Sec.-Trés., 261, rue de l'Accueil, Chesterville G0P 1J0 – 819/382-2059, Fax: 819/382-2059 |
| CHIBOUGAMAU | 8,664 | Terr. du Nouveau-Québec | Roberval | Ungava | Luc Mongeau, Gref., 650, 3e rue, Chibougamau G8P 1P1 – 418/748-2688, Fax: 418/748-6562 |

Urban Centres (Villes) in CAPITALS; Villages marked (V); Townships/Cantons marked (Canton);United townships/Cantons unis marked (Cantons); Parishes marked (P); Municipalities marked (Mun.).; Northern villages/Villages nordiques marked (NV); Cree Villages/Villages Cris marked (VC); Naskapi Villages/Villages Naskapi marked (VN); In the third column, Urban Community/Communauté Urbaine marked Urb. Com. An in-depth listing for municipalities marked with * appears in Part 2 (check Index for page numbers).

| MUNICIPALITY | 1996 POP. | REGIONAL COUNTY MUN. | FEDERAL ELECTORAL DISTRICT | PROVINCIAL ELECTORAL DISTRICT | CONTACT PERSON WITH ADDRESS, PHONE & FAX |
|---|---|---|---|---|---|
| Chichester (Canton) | 462 | Pontiac | Pontiac-Gatineau-Labelle | Pontiac | Richard Vaillancourt, Sec.-Trés., 37, rue St-Joseph, CP 158, Chapeau J0X 1M0 – 819/689-2266, Fax: 819/689-5619 |
| *CHICOUTIMI | 63,061 | Le Fjord-du-Saguenay | Chicoutimi; Jonquière | Chicoutimi | Hélène Savard, Gref.,Services juridiques, 201, rue Racine est, CP 129, Chicoutimi G7H 5B8 – 418/698-3000, Fax: 418/698-3019 |
| Chisasibi (VC) | | | Abitibi | Ungava | Christopher Napash, Sec.-Trés., CP 150, Chisasibi J0M 1E0 – 819/855-2878, Fax: 819/855-2875 |
| Chute-aux-Outardes (V) | 2,155 | Manicouagan | Charlevoix | Saguenay | Gilles Lavoie, Sec.-Trés., 44, rue Jean, CP 490, Chute-aux-Outardes G0H 1C0 – 418/567-2144, Fax: 418/567-4478 |
| Chute-St-Philippe (Mun.) | 778 | Antoine-Labelle | Pontiac-Gatineau-Labelle | Labelle | Marie-Andrée Bouchard, Sec.-Trés., 592, ch du Progrès, Chute-St-Philippe J0W 1A0 – 819/585-3397, Fax: 819/585-4949 |
| Clarendon (Canton) | 1,474 | Pontiac | Pontiac-Gatineau-Labelle | Pontiac | Lorna Younge, Sec.-Trés., C427, rte 148, CP 777, Shawville J0X 2Y0 – 819/647-3862, Fax: 819/647-3862 |
| Clermont (Canton) | 539 | Abitibi-Ouest | Rouyn-Noranda-Témiscamingue | Abitibi-Ouest | Yvette Portelance, Sec.-Trés., 722, 4e rang, St-Vital-de-Clermont J0Z 3M0 – 819/333-6129, Fax: 819/333-3811 |
| CLERMONT | 3,225 | Charlevoix-Est | Charlevoix | Charlevoix | Guy-Raymond Savard, Sec.-Trés., 2, rue des Maisons-Neuves, Clermont G4A 1G6 – 418/439-3931, Fax: 418/439-4889 |
| Clerval (Mun.) | 356 | Abitibi-Ouest | Rouyn-Noranda-Témiscamingue | Abitibi-Ouest | Lise Roy, Sec.-Trés., 579, 2e rang, Clerval J0Z 1R0 – 819/783-2640, Fax: 819/783-2640 |
| Cleveland (Canton) | 1,581 | Le Val-St-François | Richmond-Arthabaska | Richmond | Jacques St-Jean, Sec.-Trés., 292, ch de la Rivière, Richmond J0B 2H0 – 819/826-3546, Fax: 819/826-2827 |
| Clifton-Est (Canton) | 364 | Le Haut-St-François | Compton-Stanstead | Mégantic-Compton | Adèle Madore, Sec.-Trés., 207, rte 253, St-Isidore-d'Auckland J0B 2X0 – 819/889-2706, Fax: 819/889-2706 |
| Cloridorme (Canton) | 1,084 | La Côte-de-Gaspé | Bonaventure-Gaspé-Îles-de-la-Madeleine-Pabok | Gaspé | Marie Dufresne, Sec.-Trés., 472, rte 132, CP 100, Cloridorme G0E 1G0 – 418/395-2808, Fax: 418/395-2228 |
| Cloutier (Mun.) | 356 | Rouyn-Noranda | Rouyn-Noranda-Témiscamingue | Rouyn-Noranda-Témiscamingue | Denis Grenier, Sec.-Trés., CP 100, Cloutier J0Z 1S0 – 819/797-5598, Fax: 819/797-5598 |
| COATICOOK | 6,653 | Coaticook | Compton-Stanstead | Orford | Roma Fluet, Gref.,150, rue Child, Coaticook J1A 2B3 – 819/849-2721, Fax: 819/849-9669 |
| Colombier (Mun.) | 947 | La Haute-Côte-Nord | Charlevoix | Saguenay | Max Brisson, Sec.-Trés., 568, rue Principale, CP 69, Colombier G0H 1P0 – 418/565-3343, Fax: 418/565-3289 |
| Colombourg (Mun.) | 780 | Abitibi-Ouest | Rouyn-Noranda-Témiscamingue | Abitibi-Ouest | Nicole Bouffard, Sec.-Trés., 705, rang 3, CP 27, Colombourg J0Z 1T0 – 819/333-5783, Fax: 819/333-1075 |
| Compton (Mun.) | 2,185 | Coaticook | Compton-Stanstead | St-François | Sylvie Dolbec, Sec.-Trés., #201, 3, ch de Hatley, Compton J0B 1L0 – 819/835-5584, Fax: 819/835-5750 |
| Compton Station (Mun.) | 858 | Coaticook | Compton-Stanstead | St-François | Réginald Rémillard, Sec.-Trés., #202, 3, ch de Hatley, CP 190, Compton J0B 1L0 – 819/835-5345, Fax: 819/835-0015 |
| Contrecoeur (Mun.) | 5,331 | Lajemmerais | Verchères | Verchères | Yves Beaulieu, Sec.-Trés., 5000, rte Marie-Victorin, Contrecoeur J0L 1C0 – 514/587-5901, Fax: 514/587-5855 |
| COOKSHIRE | 1,532 | Le Haut-St-François | Compton-Stanstead | Mégantic-Compton | André Croisetière, Sec.-Trés., 220, rue Principale est, CP 430, Cookshire J0B 1M0 – 819/875-3165, Fax: 819/875-5311 |
| Côte-Nord-du-Golfe-du-St-Laurent (Mun.) | 1,214 | | Manicouagan | Duplessis | Monger Richmond, Adm., Chevery G0G 1G0 – 419/787-2244, Fax: 419/787-2241 |
| Côte-St-Luc | 29,705 | Montréal (Urb. Com.) | Mont-Royal | D'Arcy McGee | Jocelyne Habra, Gref., 5801, boul Cavendish, Côte-St-Luc H4W 3C3 – 514/485-6800, Fax: 514/485-6963 |
| Coteau-du-Lac (Mun.) | 4,559 | Vaudreuil-Soulanges | Vaudreuil-Soulanges | Salaberry-Soulanges | Guy Lauzon, Sec.-Trés., 191, rte 338, Coteau-du-Lac J0P 1B0 – 514/763-5822, Fax: 514/763-0938 |
| Courcelles (P) | 988 | Le Granit | Frontenac-Mégantic | Beauce-Sud | Renée Mathieu, Sec.-Trés., 116, av du Domaine, CP 160, Courcelles G0M 1C0 – 418/483-5540, Fax: 418/483-5540 |
| COWANSVILLE | 12,051 | Brome-Missisquoi | Brome-Missisquoi | Brome-Missisquoi | Claude Deschênes, Gref., 220, place Municipale, Cowansville J2K 1T4 – 514/263-0141, Fax: 514/263-9357 |
| Crabtree (Mun.) [3] | 2,339 | Joliette | Joliette | Joliette | Sylvie Malo, Sec.-Trés., 412, 1re av, CP 660, Crabtree J0K 1B0 – 514/754-3434, Fax: 514/754-2172 |
| D'Alembert (Mun.) | 810 | Rouyn-Noranda | Rouyn-Noranda-Témiscamingue | Rouyn-Noranda-Témiscamingue | Diane Pépin, Sec.-Trés., 1007, ch des Pins, D'Alembert J9X 5A3 – 819/797-0007, Fax: 819/797-2136 |

Urban Centres (Villes) in CAPITALS; Villages marked (V); Townships/Cantons marked (Canton);United townships/Cantons unis marked (Cantons); Parishes marked (P); Municipalities marked (Mun.).; Northern villages/Villages nordiques marked (NV); Cree Villages/Villages Cris marked (VC); Naskapi Villages/Villages Naskapi marked (VN); In the third column, Urban Community/Communauté Urbaine marked Urb. Com. An in-depth listing for municipalities marked with * appears in Part 2 (check Index for page numbers).

| MUNICIPALITY | 1996 POP. | REGIONAL COUNTY MUN. | FEDERAL ELECTORAL DISTRICT | PROVINCIAL ELECTORAL DISTRICT | CONTACT PERSON WITH ADDRESS, PHONE & FAX |
|---|---|---|---|---|---|
| DANVILLE | 1,796 | Asbestos | Richmond-Arthabaska | Richmond | René Allard, Sec.-Trés., 52, rue Daniel-Johnson, CP 310, Danville J0A 1A0 – 819/839-2966, Fax: 819/839-3734 |
| Daveluyville (Mun.) | 1,038 | Arthabaska | Lotbinière | Nicolet-Yamaska | Gaston Bélanger, Sec.-Trés., 337, rue Principale, CP 187, Daveluyville G0Z 1C0 – 819/367-3395, Fax: 819/367-3395 |
| Deauville (V) | 2,599 | Sherbrooke | Compton-Stanstead | Orford | Armand Comeau, Sec.-Trés., 7894, boul Bourque, Deauville J1N 3L1 – 819/864-4213, Fax: 819/864-6266 |
| DÉGELIS | 3,437 | Témiscouata | Kamouraska-Rivière-du-Loup-Témiscouata | Kamouraska-Témiscouata | Claire Bérubé, Gref., 369, av Principale, Dégelis G5T 2G3 – 418/853-2332, Fax: 418/853-3464 |
| Déléage (Mun.) | 2,036 | La Vallée-de-la-Gatineau | Pontiac-Gatineau-Labelle | Gatineau | Jacinthe St-Amour-Labelle, Sec.-Trés., 175, route 107, RR#1, Maniwaki J9E 3A8 – 819/449-1979, Fax: 819/449-7441 |
| Delisle (Mun.) | 4,256 | Lac-St-Jean-Est | Lac-St-Jean | Lac-St-Jean | Florent Côté, Sec.-Trés., 4800, av de la Grande-Décharge, CP 158, Delisle G0W 1L0 – 418/347-3307, Fax: 418/347-3967 |
| DELSON | 6,703 | Roussillon | Châteauguay | La Prairie | Nicole Lafontaine, Gref., 50, rue Ste-Thérèse, Delson J0L 1G0 – 514/632-1050, Fax: 514/632-1571 |
| Denholm (Canton) | 493 | La Vallée-de-la-Gatineau | Pontiac-Gatineau-Labelle | Gatineau | Lorraine Paquette, Sec.-Trés., 419, ch du Poisson-Blanc, Denholm J0X 2S0 – 819/457-2992, Fax: 819/457-9862 |
| Des Ruisseaux (Mun.) | 5,139 | Antoine-Labelle | Pontiac-Gatineau-Labelle | Labelle | Normand Bélanger, Sec.-Trés., 1269, boul des Ruisseaux, Des Ruisseaux J9L 3G6 – 819/623-5451, Fax: 819/623-6810 |
| DESBIENS | 1,202 | Lac-St-Jean-Est | Lac-St-Jean | Lac-St-Jean | Fernand Lapointe, Sec.-Trés., 925, rue Hébert, CP 9, Desbiens G0W 1N0 – 418/346-5571, Fax: 418/346-5422 |
| Deschaillons-sur-St-Laurent (Mun.) | 1,060 | Bécancour | Lotbinière | Lotbinière | Sylvie Dubois, Sec.-Trés., 1056, rte Marie-Victorin, CP 176, Deschaillons-sur-Saint-Laurent G0S 1G0 – 819/292-2085, Fax: 819/292-3194 |
| Deschambault (Mun.) | 1,240 | Portneuf | Portneuf | Portneuf | Claire St-Arnaud, Sec.-Trés., 120, rue St-Joseph, CP 220, Deschambault G0A 1S0 – 418/286-4511, Fax: 418/286-6511 |
| Destor (Mun.) | 445 | Rouyn-Noranda | Rouyn-Noranda-Témiscamingue | Rouyn-Noranda-Témiscamingue | Brigitte Drapeau, Sec.-Trés., 921, ch du Parc, CP 13, Destor J9X 5A3 – 819/637-2073, Fax: 819/637-5512 |
| DEUX-MONTAGNES | 15,953 | Deux-Montagnes | St-Eustache-Ste-Thérèse | Deux-Montagnes | Gilles Chamberland, Sec.-Trés., 803, ch d'Oka, CP 55, Deux-Montagnes J7R 1L8 – 514/473-2796, Fax: 514/473-3412 |
| Disraëli (P) | 1,069 | L'Amiante | Frontenac-Mégantic | Frontenac | Magda Matteau, Sec.-Trés., 8306, route 112, CP 760, Disraëli G0N 1E0 – 418/449-5329, Fax: 418/449-5329 |
| DISRAËLI | 2,657 | L'Amiante | Frontenac-Mégantic | Frontenac | Jocelyn Turcotte, Sec.-Trés., 550, av Jacques-Cartier, CP 2050, Disraëli G0N 1E0 – 418/449-2771, Fax: 418/449-4299 |
| Ditton (Canton) | 519 | Le Haut-St-François | Frontenac-Mégantic | Mégantic-Compton | Lucie Lortitch, Sec.-Trés., 18, rue Chartier, CP 90, La Patrie J0B 1Y0 – 819/888-2691, Fax: 819/888-2691 |
| Dixville (Mun.) | 751 | Coaticook | Compton-Stanstead | Mégantic-Compton | Mary Brus, Sec.-Trés., 251, ch Parker, Dixville J0B 1P0 – 819/849-3037, Fax: 819/849-3037 |
| DOLBEAU | 8,310 | Maria-Chapdelaine | Roberval | Roberval | André Côté, Gref., 1100, boul Wallberg, Dolbeau G8L 1G7 – 418/276-0160, Fax: 418/276-8312 |
| DOLLARD-DES-ORMEAUX | 47,826 | Montréal (Urb. Com.) | Pierrefonds-Dollard | Robert-Baldwin | Louise Pinault, Gref., 12001, boul de Salaberry, Dollard-des-Ormeaux H9B 2A7 – 514/684-1010, Fax: 514/684-1273 |
| DONNACONA | 5,739 | Portneuf | Portneuf | Portneuf | Bernard Naud, Gref., 138, av Pleau, CP 609, Donnacona G0A 1T0 – 418/285-0110, Fax: 418/285-0020 |
| DORVAL | 17,572 | Montréal (Urb. Com.) | Lac-St-Louis | Jacques Cartier | Marcel Guérin, Gref., 60, av Martin, Dorval H9S 3R4 – 514/633-4040, Fax: 514/633-4138 |
| Dosquet (P) | 908 | Lotbinière | Lotbinière | Lotbinière | Louisette Chartrand, Sec.-Trés., 179, rue St-Joseph sud, Dosquet G0S 1H0 – 418/728-3653, Fax: 418/728-3338 |
| DRUMMOND-VILLE | 44,882 | Drummond | Drummond | Drummond | Thérèse Cajolet, Gref., 413, rue Lindsay, CP 398, Drummondville J2B 1G8 – 819/478-6554, Fax: 819/478-3363 |
| Dubuisson (Mun.) | 1,655 | Vallée-de-l'Or | Abitibi | Abitibi-Est | Robert Cadieux, Sec.-Trés., 128, rue Marguerite-Bourgeoys, Dubuisson J9P 4N7 – 819/738-4892, Fax: 819/738-4017 |
| Dudswell (Mun.) | 1,607 | Le Haut-St-François | Compton-Stanstead | Mégantic-Compton | Hélène Leroux, Sec.-Trés., 76, rue Principale, CP 180, Bishopton J0B 1G0 – 819/884-5926 |

Urban Centres (Villes) in CAPITALS; Villages marked (V); Townships/Cantons marked (Canton);United townships/Cantons unis marked (Cantons); Parishes marked (P); Municipalities marked (Mun.).; Northern villages/Villages nordiques marked (NV); Cree Villages/Villages Cris marked (VC); Naskapi Villages/Villages Naskapi marked (VN); In the third column, Urban Community/Communauté Urbaine marked Urb. Com. An in-depth listing for municipalities marked with * appears in Part 2 (check Index for page numbers).

| MUNICIPALITY | 1996 POP. | REGIONAL COUNTY MUN. | FEDERAL ELECTORAL DISTRICT | PROVINCIAL ELECTORAL DISTRICT | CONTACT PERSON WITH ADDRESS, PHONE & FAX |
|---|---|---|---|---|---|
| Duhamel (Mun.) | 321 | Papineau | Argenteuil-Papineau | Papineau | Claire Dinel, Sec.-Trés., 1899, rue Principale, CP 117, Duhamel J0V 1G0 – 819/428-7100, Fax: 819/428-1941 |
| Duhamel-Ouest (Mun.) | 671 | Témiscamingue | Rouyn-Noranda-Témiscamingue | Rouyn-Noranda-Témiscamingue | Lise Gosselin, Sec.-Trés., 9, rue Notre-Dame-de-Lourdes, CP 1499, Ville-Marie J0Z 3W0 – 819/629-2522, Fax: 819/629-2522 |
| Dundee (Canton) | 392 | Le Haut-St-Laurent | Beauharnois-Salaberry | Beauharnois-Huntingdon | Jacinthe Deschambault, Sec.-Trés., 3296, montée Smallman, Dundee J0S 1L0 – 514/264-4674, Fax: 514/264-4674 |
| DUNHAM | 3,370 | Brome-Missisquoi | Brome-Missisquoi | Brome-Missisquoi | Pierre Loiselle, Gref., 3777, rue Principale, CP 70, Dunham J0E 1M0 – 514/295-2418, Fax: 514/295-2182 |
| DUPARQUET | 738 | Abitibi-Ouest | Rouyn-Noranda-Témiscamingue | Abitibi-Ouest | Andrée Cloutier, Sec.-Trés., 86, rue Principale, CP 190, Duparquet J0Z 1W0 – 819/948-2266, Fax: 819/948-2466 |
| Dupuy (Mun.) | 1,100 | Abitibi-Ouest | Rouyn-Noranda-Témiscamingue | Abitibi-Ouest | Hélène Ayotte, Sec.-Trés., 2 av du Chemin-de-Fer, CP 59, Dupuy J0Z 1X0 – 819/783-2595, Fax: 819/783-2595 |
| Durham-Sud (Mun.) | 988 | Drummond | Drummond | Johnson | France Gagon-Noël, Sec.-Trés., 70, rue de l'Hôtel-de-Ville, CP 70, Durham-Sud J0H 2C0 – 819/858-2044, Fax: 819/858-2044 |
| EAST-ANGUS | 3,642 | Le Haut-St-François | Compton-Stanstead | Mégantic-Compton | Michel Roy, Sec.-Trés., 146, rue Angus nord, CP 400, East Angus J0B 1R0 – 819/832-2868, Fax: 819/832-2938 |
| East Broughton (Mun.) | 2,489 | L'Amiante | Frontenac-Mégantic | Frontenac | Marc-André Grondin, Sec.-Trés., 600, 10e av sud, East Broughton G0N 1H0 – 418/427-2608, Fax: 418/427-3414 |
| East Farnham (V) | 518 | Brome-Missisquoi | Brome-Missisquoi | Brome-Missisquoi | Ginette B.-Lafrance, Sec.-Trés., 228, rue Principale, East Farnham J0E 1N0 – 514/263-4252, Fax: 514/263-9405 |
| East Hereford (Mun.) | 317 | Coaticook | Compton-Stanstead | Mégantic-Compton | Diane Lauzon-Rioux, Sec.-Trés., 15, rue de l'Église, East Hereford J0B 1S0 – 819/844-2463, Fax: 819/844-2463 |
| Eastmain (VC) | | | Abitibi | Ungava | Norman Cheezo, Sec.-Trés., 147, Shabow Meskino, Baie-James J0M 1W0 – 819/977-0211, Fax: 819/977-0281 |
| Eastman (V) | 711 | Memphrémagog | Brome-Missisquoi | Brome-Missisquoi | Bénédict Fortin, Sec.-Trés., 395, rue Principale, CP 150, Eastman J0E 1P0 – 514/297-2114, Fax: 514/297-2398 |
| Eaton (Canton) | 2,819 | Le Haut-St-François | Compton-Stanstead | Mégantic-Compton | Jean Hivert, Sec.-Trés., 375, rte 253, RR#3, Cookshire J0B 1M0 – 819/875-3554, Fax: 819/875-5646 |
| Egan-Sud (Mun.) | 578 | La Vallée-de-la-Gatineau | Pontiac-Gatineau-Labelle | Gatineau | Louise Saint-Amour, Sec.-Trés., 95, rte 105, Egan-Sud J9E 3A9 – 819/449-1702, Fax: 819/449-7423 |
| Elgin (Canton) | 448 | Le Haut-St-Laurent | Beauharnois-Salaberry | Beauharnois-Huntingdon | Diane L'Écuyer, Sec.-Trés., 933, 2e Concession, Athelstan J0S 1A0 – 514/264-2320, Fax: 514/264-2320 |
| Entrelacs (Mun.) | 732 | Matawinie | Berthier-Montcalm | Bertrand | Jean-François René, Sec.-Trés., 2351, ch d'Entrelacs, Entrelacs J0T 2E0 – 514/228-2529, Fax: 514/228-4866 |
| Escuminac (Mun.) | 661 | Avignon | Matapédia-Matane | Bonaventure | Barbara Borris, Sec.-Trés., 83, rue de l'Eglise, CP 5, Pointe-à-la-Garde G0C 2M0 – 418/788-5644, Fax: 418/788-2613 |
| Esprit-Saint (Mun.) | 472 | Rimouski-Neigette | Rimouski-Mitis | Rimouski | Diane Ouellet, Sec.-Trés., 121, rue Principale, Esprit-Saint G0K 1A0 – 418/779-2716, Fax: 418/779-2716 |
| ESTÉREL | 108 | Les Pays-d'en-Haut | Laurentides | Bertrand | Richard Gagné, Sec.-Trés., 115, ch Dupuis, CP 8, Estérel J0T 1E0 – 514/228-2501, Fax: 514/228-3268 |
| Évain (Mun.) | 3,892 | Rouyn-Noranda | Rouyn-Noranda-Témiscamingue | Rouyn-Noranda-Témiscamingue | Michèle Morel, Sec.-Trés., 200, rue Côté ouest, CP 330, Évain J0Z 1Y0 – 819/768-5818, Fax: 819/768-5040 |
| FARNHAM | 6,044 | Brome-Missisquoi | Brome-Missisquoi | Iberville | Jean-Bernard Luneau, Gref., 477, rue de l'Hôtel-de-Ville, Farnham J2N 2H3 – 514/293-3178, Fax: 514/293-2989 |
| Fassett (Mun.) | 500 | Papineau | Argenteuil-Papineau | Papineau | Hélène Larente, Sec.-Trés., 19, rue Gendron, CP 70, Fassett J0V 1H0 – 819/423-6943, Fax: 819/423-5388 |
| Fatima (Mun.) | 2,966 | Îles-de-la-Madeleine | Bonaventure-Gaspé-Îles-de-la-Madeleine-Pabok | Îles-de-la-Madeleine | Jacques Arseneault, Sec.-Trés., 395, ch de l'Hôpital, CP 610, Fatima G0B 1G0 – 418/986-3341, Fax: 418/986-3803 |
| Ferland-et-Boilleau (Mun.) | 652 | Le Fjord-du-Saguenay | Chicoutimi | Dubuc | Sylvie Gagnon, Sec.-Trés., 462, rte 381, Ferland-et-Boilleau G0V 1H0 – 418/676-2282, Fax: 418/676-2681 |
| Ferme-Neuve (P) | 913 | Antoine-Labelle | Pontiac-Gatineau-Labelle | Labelle | Thérèse Boivin, Sec.-Trés., 53, rte 309, CP 179, Ferme-Neuve J0W 1C0 – 819/587-4115, Fax: 819/587-3049 |

Urban Centres (Villes) in CAPITALS; Villages marked (V); Townships/Cantons marked (Canton);United townships/Cantons unis marked (Cantons); Parishes marked (P); Municipalities marked (Mun.).; Northern villages/Villages nordiques marked (NV); Cree Villages/Villages Cris marked (VC); Naskapi Villages/Villages Naskapi marked (VN); In the third column, Urban Community/Communauté Urbaine marked Urb. Com. An in-depth listing for municipalities marked with * appears in Part 2 (check Index for page numbers).

| MUNICIPALITY | 1996 POP. | REGIONAL COUNTY MUN. | FEDERAL ELECTORAL DISTRICT | PROVINCIAL ELECTORAL DISTRICT | CONTACT PERSON WITH ADDRESS, PHONE & FAX |
|---|---|---|---|---|---|
| Ferme-Neuve (V) | 2,178 | Antoine-Labelle | Pontiac-Gatineau-Labelle | Labelle | Claude Campeau, Sec.-Trés., 280, 6e av, CP 370, Ferme-Neuve J0W 1C0 – 819/587-3400, Fax: 819/587-4733 |
| FERMONT | 3,234 | Caniapiscau | Manicouagan | Duplessis | Gervais Boucher, Sec.-Trés., 100, Place Daviault, CP 520, Fermont G0G 1J0 – 418/287-5411, Fax: 418/287-5413 |
| FLEURIMONT | 16,262 | Sherbrooke | Sherbrooke | St-François | Thérèse Beaubien, Gref., 1735, ch Galvin, Fleurimont J1G 3E7 – 819/565-9954, Fax: 819/565-5476 |
| Fontainebleau (Mun.) | 137 | Le Haut-St-François | Frontenac-Mégantic | Mégantic-Compton | Sonia Poulin, Sec.-Trés., 34, ch de la Mine, Fontainebleau J0B 3J0 – 819/877-2723 |
| FORESTVILLE | 3,894 | La Haute Côte-Nord | Charlevoix | Saguenay | Jacques Beaulieu, Sec.-Trés., 1, 2e av, CP 70, Forestville G0T 1E0 – 418/587-2285, Fax: 418/587-6212 |
| Fort-Coulonge (V) | 1,716 | Pontiac | Pontiac-Gatineau-Labelle | Pontiac | Ken Rose, Sec.-Trés., 134, rue Principale, CP 640, Fort Coulonge J0X 1V0 – 819/683-2259, Fax: 819/683-3627 |
| Fortierville (V) | 419 | Bécancour | Lotbinière | Lotbinière | Nicole Laveaux, Sec.-Trés., 198, rue de la Fabrique, Fortierville G0S 1J0 – 819/287-5922, Fax: 819/287-5922 |
| FOSSAMBAULT-SUR-LE-LAC | 921 | La Jacques-Cartier | Portneuf | Portneuf | Johanne Bédard, Sec.-Trés., 145, rue Gingras, Fossambault-sur-le-Lac G0A 3M0 – 418/875-3133, Fax: 418/875-3544 |
| Franklin (Mun.) | 1,640 | Le Haut-St-Laurent | Beauharnois-Salaberry | Beauharnois-Huntingdon | Carole Boutin, Sec.-Trés., 1670, rte 202, CP 84, Franklin Centre J0S 1E0 – 514/827-2538, Fax: 514/827-2640 |
| Franquelin (Mun.) | 391 | Manicouagan | Manicouagan | Saguenay | Ginette Plante, Sec.-Trés., 27, rue des Érables, CP 10, Franquelin G0H 1E0 – 418/296-1406, Fax: 418/296-1406 |
| Frelighsburg (Mun.) | 1,048 | Brome-Missisquoi | Brome-Missisquoi | Brome-Missisquoi | Anne Pouleur, Sec.-Trés., 2, pl. de l'Hôtel-de-Ville, Frelighsburg J0J 1C0 – 514/298-5133, Fax: 514/298-5557 |
| Frontenac (Mun.) | 1,402 | Le Granit | Frontenac-Mégantic | Mégantic-Compton | Bruno Turmel, Sec.-Trés., 2430, rue St-Jean, Frontenac G6B 2S1 – 819/583-3295, Fax: 819/583-0855 |
| Fugèreville (Mun.) | 376 | Témiscamingue | Rouyn-Noranda-Témiscamingue | Rouyn-Noranda-Témiscamingue | Marlène L'Heureux, Sec.-Trés., 43, rue Principale, CP 831, Fugèreville J0Z 2A0 – 819/748-3241, Fax: 819/748-2114 |
| Gallichan (Mun.) | 478 | Abitibi-Ouest | Rouyn-Noranda-Témiscamigue | Abitibi-Ouest | Yvette Fournier-Boutin, Sec.-Trés., 219, ch de la Rivière ouest, CP 38, Gallichan J0Z 2B0 – 819/787-6092, Fax: 819/787-6092 |
| Gallix (Mun.) | 616 | Sept-Rivières | Manicouagan | Duplessis | Lise Chiasson, Sec.-Trés., 524, rue Lapierre, Gallix G0G 1L0 – 418/766-3161, Fax: 418/766-3264 |
| Garthby (Canton) | 399 | L'Amiante | Frontenac-Mégantic | Richmond | Marcel Bilodeau, Sec.-Trés., 6599, rte 112, Garthby G0Y 1B0 – 418/458-2363, Fax: 418/458-2363 |
| GASPÉ | 16,517 | La Côte-de-Gaspé | Bonaventure-Gaspé-Îles-de-la-Madeleine-Pabok | Gaspé | Judith Desmeules, Gref., 25, rue de l'Hôtel-de-Ville, CP 618, Gaspé G0C 1R0 – 418/368-2104, Fax: 418/368-4871 |
| *GATINEAU | 100,702 | Outaouais (Urb. Com.) | Gatineau | Gatineau; Chapleau | J.C. Laurin, Gref., 144, boul de l'Hôpital, Gatineau J8T 7S7 – 819/243-2345, Fax: 819/243-2338, URL: http://gamma.omnimage.ca/clients/gatineau/ |
| Gayhurst-Partie-Sud-Est (Canton) | 187 | Le Granit | Frontenac-Mégantic | Beauce-Sud | Yvette Roy, Sec.-Trés., 234, 2e rang sud, St-Ludger G0M 1W0 – 819/548-5145, Fax: 819/548-5145 |
| Girardville (Mun.) | 1,350 | Maria-Chapdelaine | Roberval | Roberval | Denis Desmeules, Sec.-Trés., 180, rue Principale, CP 340, Girardville G0W 1R0 – 418/258-3293, Fax: 418/258-3473 |
| Godbout (V) | 390 | Manicouagan | Manicouagan | Saguenay | Carolle Vallée, Sec.-Trés., 144, rue Pascal-Comeau, CP 248, Godbout G0H 1G0 – 418/568-7581, Fax: 418/568-7401 |
| Godmanchester (Canton) | 1,550 | Le Haut-St-Laurent | Beauharnois-Salaberry | Beauharnois-Huntingdon | Élaine Duhème, Sec.-Trés., 2282, ch Ridge, Godmanchester J0S 1H0 – 514/264-4116, Fax: 514/264-9749 |
| Gore (Canton) | 1,133 | Argenteuil | Argenteuil-Papineau | Argenteuil | Louise Rochon-McGarr, Sec.-Trés., 9, ch Cambria, Lakefield J0V 1K0 – 514/562-2025, Fax: 514/562-5424 |
| Gracefield (V) | 713 | La Vallée-de-la-Gatineau | Pontiac-Gatineau-Labelle | Gatineau | Sylvain Bertrand, Sec.-Trés., 3, rue de la Polyvalente, CP 329, Gracefield J0X 1W0 – 819/463-3458, Fax: 819/463-4236 |
| Granby (Canton) | 11,266 | La Haute-Yamaska | Shefford | Shefford | Réal Paré, Sec.-Trés., 735, rue Dufferin, CP 579, Granby J2G 8E9 – 514/372-3442, Fax: 514/372-7345 |
| GRANBY | 43,316 | La Haute-Yamaska | Shefford | Shefford | Michel Pinault, Gref., 87, rue Principale, Granby J2G 2T8 – 514/776-8282, Fax: 514/776-8211 |

Urban Centres (Villes) in CAPITALS; Villages marked (V); Townships/Cantons marked (Canton);United townships/Cantons unis marked (Cantons); Parishes marked (P); Municipalities marked (Mun.).; Northern villages/Villages nordiques marked (NV); Cree Villages/Villages Cris marked (VC); Naskapi Villages/Villages Naskapi marked (VN); In the third column, Urban Community/Communauté Urbaine marked Urb. Com. An in-depth listing for municipalities marked with * appears in Part 2 (check Index for page numbers).

| MUNICIPALITY | 1996 POP. | REGIONAL COUNTY MUN. | FEDERAL ELECTORAL DISTRICT | PROVINCIAL ELECTORAL DISTRICT | CONTACT PERSON WITH ADDRESS, PHONE & FAX |
|---|---|---|---|---|---|
| Grand-Calumet (Canton) | 774 | Pontiac | Pontiac-Gatineau-Labelle | Pontiac | Jacques Mantha, Sec.-Trés., 8, rue Brizard, CP 130, L'Île-du-Grand-Calumet J0X 1J0 – 819/648-5965, Fax: 819/648-2659 |
| GRAND-MÈRE | 14,223 | Le Centre-de-la-Mauricie | St-Maurice | Laviolette | Christiane Houle, Gref., 333 - 5e av, CP 350, Grand-Mère G9T 5L1 – 819/538-9543, Fax: 819/538-7244 |
| Grand-Métis (Mun.) | 276 | La Mitis | Rimouski-Mitis | Matane | Claudette Michaud, Sec.-Trés., 155, 2e rang ouest, Grand-Métis G0J 1Z0 – 418/775-2860 |
| Grand-Remous (Canton) | 1,257 | La Vallée-de-la-Gatineau | Pontiac-Gatineau-Labelle | Gatineau | Betty McCarthy, Sec.-Trés., 1567, rte Transcanadienne, Grand-Remous J0W 1E0 – 819/438-2877, Fax: 819/438-2364 |
| Grand-St-Esprit (Mun.) | 499 | Nicolet-Yamaska | Richelieu | Nicolet-Yamaska | Nicole Larochelle, Sec.-Trés., 5410, route Principale, Grand-St-Esprit J0G 1B0 – 819/289-2410, Fax: 819/289-2410 |
| Grande-Cascapédia (Mun.) | 261 | Bonaventure | Bonaventure-Gaspé-Îles-de-la-Madeleine-Pabok | Bonaventure | Heather Woodman, Sec.-Trés., 161A, rte 299, CP 70, Grande-Cascapédia G0C 1T0 – 418/392-4338 |
| Grande-Entrée (Mun.) | 692 | Îles-de-la-Madeleine | Bonaventure-Gaspé-Îles-de-la-Madeleine-Pabok | Îles-de-la-Madeleine | Roméo Bénard, Sec.-Trés., CP 58, Grande-Entrée G0B 1H0 – 418/985-2277, Fax: 418/985-2149 |
| Grande-Île (Mun.) | 4,468 | Beauharnois-Salaberry | Beauharnois-Salaberry | Salaberry-Soulanges | Alain Gagnon, Sec.-Trés., 1155, boul. Mgr-Langlois, Grande-Ile J6S 1B9 – 514/373-8860, Fax: 514/373-1630 |
| GRANDE-RIVIÈRE | 3,888 | Pabok | Bonaventure-Gaspé-Îles-de-la-Madeleine-Pabok | Gaspé | Éliane Hotton-Beaulieu, Gref., 108, rue de l'Hôtel de Ville, CP 188, Grande-Rivière G0C 1V0 – 418/385-2282, Fax: 418/385-2290 |
| Grande-Vallée (P) | 1,431 | La Côte-de-Gaspé | Bonaventure-Gaspé-Îles-de-la-Madeleine-Pabok | Gaspé | Diane Côté, Sec.-Trés., 3, rue St-François-Xavier est, CP 98, Grande-Vallée G0E 1K0 – 418/393-2161, Fax: 418/393-2274 |
| Grandes-Bergeronnes (V) | 601 | La Haute Côte-Nord | Charlevoix | Saguenay | Hélène Hervieux, Sec.-Trés., 424, rue de la Mer, CP 158, Grandes-Bergeronnes G0T 1G0 – 418/232-6244, Fax: 418/232-6602 |
| Grandes-Piles (V) | 371 | Mékinac | St-Maurice | Laviolette | Pierrette Fontaine, Sec.-Trés., 620, 5e av, Grandes-Piles G0X 1H0 – 819/538-9708, Fax: 819/538-6947 |
| GREENFIELD PARK | 17,337 | Champlain | St-Lambert | Laporte | Carole Leroux, Gref., 156, boul Churchill, Greenfield Park J4V 2M3 – 514/466-8100, Fax: 514/466-8129 |
| Grenville (Canton) | 1,964 | Argenteuil | Argenteuil-Papineau | Argenteuil | Christine Groulx, Sec.-Trés., 40, ch Maple, Grenville J0V 1J0 – 819/242-8762, Fax: 819/242-9341 |
| Grenville (V) | 1,443 | Argenteuil | Argenteuil-Papineau | Argenteuil | Alain Léveillé, Sec.-Trés., 21, rue Tri-Jean, CP 220, Grenville J0V 1J0 – 819/242-2146, Fax: 819/242-5891 |
| Grondines (Mun.) | 718 | Portneuf | Portneuf | Portneuf | Jean Gravel, Sec.-Trés., 220, rue Principale, Grondines G0A 1W0 – 418/268-8583, Fax: 418/268-5553 |
| Gros-Mécatina (Mun.) | 622 | | Manicouagan | Duplessis | Rita Collier, Sec.-Trés., La Tabatière G0G 1T0 – 418/773-2263, Fax: 418/773-2696 |
| Grosse-Île (Mun.) | 567 | Les Îles-de-la-Madeleine | Bonaventure-Gaspé-Îles-de-la-Madeleine-Pabok | Îles-de-la-Madeleine | Charles Taker, Sec.-Trés., 246, rte Principale, CP 30, Leslie G0B 1M0 – 418/985-2510, Fax: 418/985-2297 |
| Grosses-Roches (Mun.) | 493 | Matane | Matapédia-Matane | Matane | Linda Imbeault, Sec.-Trés., 122, rue de la Mer, CP 69, Grosses-Roches G0J 1K0 – 418/733-4273, Fax: 418/733-4273 |
| Guérin (Canton) | 297 | Témiscamingue | Rouyn-Noranda-Témiscamingue | Rouyn-Noranda-Témiscamingue | Jacqueline Arbour, Sec.-Trés., 516A, rue St-Gabriel, CP 1040, Guérin J0Z 2E0 – 819/784-7011, Fax: 819/784-7011 |
| Halifax-Nord (Canton) | 345 | L'Érable | Lotbinière | Frontenac | Doris Turgeon, Sec.-Trés., 10, rue de l'Église, Ste-Sophie-de-Mégantic G0P 1L0 – 819/362-2225 |
| Ham-Nord (Canton) | 959 | Arthabaska | Richmond-Arthabaska | Richmond | Sombeleine Martel, Sec.-Trés., 474, rue Principale, CP 29, Ham-Nord G0P 1A0 – 819/344-2424, Fax: 819/344-2805 |
| Hampden (Canton) | 153 | Le Haut-St-François | Frontenac-Mégantic | Mégantic-Compton | Germaine Lapointe, Sec.-Trés., 863, ch Ditton, route 257, CP 212, Scotstown J0B 3B0 – 819/657-4942, Fax: 819/657-4942 |
| HAMPSTEAD | 6,986 | Montréal (Urb. Com.) | Mont-Royal | D'Arcy McGee | Maurice Guay, Gref., 5569, ch Queen-Mary, Hampstead H3X 1W5 – 514/369-8200, Fax: 514/369-8229 |
| Harrington (Canton) | 730 | Argenteuil | Argenteuil-Papineau | Argenteuil | Luc Lafontaine, Sec.-Trés., 2811, rte 327, Arundel J0T 1A0 – 819/687-2122, Fax: 819/687-8610 |
| Hatley (Canton) | 777 | Memphrémagog | Compton-Stanstead | Orford | France Boisvert, Sec.-Trés., 135, rue Main, CP 570, North Hatley J0B 2C0 – 819/842-2977, Fax: 819/842-2639 |
| Hatley (Mun.) | 642 | Memphrémagog | Compton-Stanstead | Orford | Emile Royer, Sec.-Trés., 810, rte 208 ouest, CP 360, Ayer's Cliff J0B 1C0 – 819/838-4646 |

Urban Centres (Villes) in CAPITALS; Villages marked (V); Townships/Cantons marked (Canton);United townships/Cantons unis marked (Cantons); Parishes marked (P); Municipalities marked (Mun.).; Northern villages/Villages nordiques marked (NV); Cree Villages/Villages Cris marked (VC); Naskapi Villages/Villages Naskapi marked (VN); In the third column, Urban Community/Communauté Urbaine marked Urb. Com. An in-depth listing for municipalities marked with * appears in Part 2 (check Index for page numbers).

| MUNICIPALITY | 1996 POP. | REGIONAL COUNTY MUN. | FEDERAL ELECTORAL DISTRICT | PROVINCIAL ELECTORAL DISTRICT | CONTACT PERSON WITH ADDRESS, PHONE & FAX |
|---|---|---|---|---|---|
| Havelock (Canton) | 811 | Le Haut-St-Laurent | Beauharnois-Salaberry | Beauharnois-Huntingdon | Linda Hébert, Sec.-Trés., 481, rte 203, Havelock J0S 2C0 – 514/826-4741, Fax: 514/826-4800 |
| Havre-aux-Maisons (Mun.) | 2,211 | Les Îles-de-la-Madeleine | Bonaventure-Gaspé-Îles-de-la-Madeleine-Pabok | Îles-de-la-Madeleine | Jean Richard, Sec.-Trés., 37, ch Central, CP 128, Havre-aux-Maisons G0B 1K0 – 418/969-2222, Fax: 418/969-2872 |
| Havre-St-Pierre (Mun.) | 3,450 | Minganie | Manicouagan | Duplessis | André Cyr, Sec.-Trés., 1081, rue de la Digue, CP 910, Havre-St-Pierre G0G 1P0 – 418/538-2717, Fax: 418/538-3439 |
| Hébertville (Mun.) | 2,438 | Lac-St-Jean-Est | Lac-St-Jean | Lac-St-Jean | Sabin Larouche, Sec.-Trés., 351, rue Turgeon, Hébertville G8N 1S8 – 418/344-1302, Fax: 418/344-4618 |
| Hébertville-Station (V) | 1,393 | Lac-St-Jean-Est | Lac-St-Jean | Lac-St-Jean | Yvon Baril, Sec.-Trés., 6, rue Tremblay, CP 69, Hébertville-Station G0W 1T0 – 418/343-3961, Fax: 418/343-2349 |
| Hemmingford (Canton) | 1,748 | Les Jardins-de-Napierville | Beauharnois-Salaberry | Beauharnois-Huntingdon | Margaret Hess, Sec.-Trés., #3, 505, rue Frontière, CP 576, Hemmingford J0L 1H0 – 514/247-2050, Fax: 514/247-3283 |
| Hemmingford (V) | 751 | Les Jardins-de-Napierville | Beauharnois-Salaberry | Beauharnois-Huntingdon | Diane Lawrence, Sec.-Trés., #5, 505, rue Frontière, Hemmingford J0L 1H0 – 514/247-3310, Fax: 514/247-2389 |
| Henryville (Mun.) | 857 | Le Haut-Richelieu | Brome-Missisquoi | Iberville | Christiane Veilleux, Sec.-Trés., 133, rue St-Georges, Henryville J0J 1E0 – 514/299-2655, Fax: 514/299-2655 |
| Henryville (V) | 701 | Le Haut-Richelieu | Brome-Missisquoi | Iberville | Sonia Côté, Sec.-Trés., 165, rue de l'Église, CP 120, Henryville J0J 1E0 – 514/299-2833, Fax: 514/299-2833 |
| Hérouxville (P) | 1,314 | Mékinac | Champlain | Laviolette | Denise Cossette, Sec.-Trés., 1060, rue St-Pierre, CP 10, Hérouxville G0X 1J0 – 418/365-7135, Fax: 418/365-7041 |
| Hinchinbrooke (Canton) | 2,407 | Le Haut-St-Laurent | Beauharnois-Salaberry | Beauharnois-Huntingdon | Kevin Neal, Sec.-Trés., 1056, ch Brook, Athelstan J0S 1A0 – 514/264-5353, Fax: 514/264-3787 |
| Honfleur (Mun.) | 836 | Bellechasse | Bellechasse-Montmagny-L'Islet | Bellechasse | Jérôme Fortier, Sec.-Trés., 320, rue St-Jean, Honfleur G0R 1N0 – 418/885-9195, Fax: 418/885-9195 |
| Hope (Canton) | 822 | Bonaventure | Bonaventure-Gaspé-Îles-de-la-Madeleine-Pabok | Bonaventure | Louise Delarosbil, Sec.-Trés., 330, rte 132, Hope G0C 2K0 – 418/752-3212, Fax: 418/752-6986 |
| Hope Town (Mun.) | 371 | Bonaventure | Bonaventure-Gaspé-Îles-de-la-Madeleine-Pabok | Bonaventure | Cynthia Major, Sec.-Trés., 209, rte 132 ouest, CP 146, St-Godefroi G0C 3C0 – 418/752-2137, Fax: 418/752-2137 |
| Howick (V) | 617 | Le Haut-St-Laurent | Beauharnois-Salaberry | Beauharnois-Huntingdon | Claudette Provost, Sec.-Trés., 51, rue Colville, CP 40, Howick J0S 1G0 – 514/825-2032, Fax: 514/825-0026 |
| Huberdeau (Mun.) | 942 | Les Laurentides | Argenteuil-Papineau | Argenteuil | Mona St-Georges, Sec.-Trés., 101, rue du Pont, Huberdeau J0T 1G0 – 819/687-8321, Fax: 819/687-8808 |
| HUDSON | 4,796 | Vaudreuil-Soulanges | Vaudreuil-Soulanges | Vaudreuil | Louise L.-Villandré, Sec.-Trés., 481, rue Principale, CP 550, Hudson J0P 1H0 – 514/458-5348, Fax: 514/458-4922 |
| *HULL | 62,339 | Outaouais (Urb. Com.) | Hull-Aylmer | Hull | Jean-Pierre Chabot, Directeur général adjoint, 25, rue Laurier, CP 1970, Hull J8X 3Y9 – 819/595-7180, Fax: 819/595-7192 |
| HUNTINGDON | 2,746 | Le Haut-St-Laurent | Beauharnois-Salaberry | Beauharnois-Huntingdon | Diane Taillon, Sec.-Trés., 16, rue Prince, Huntingdon J0S 1H0 – 514/264-5389, Fax: 514/264-6826 |
| IBERVILLE | 9,635 | Le Haut-Richelieu | St-Jean | Iberville | François Lapointe, Gref., 855, 1re rue, Iberville J2X 3C7 – 514/347-2318, Fax: 514/347-7550 |
| Inukjuak (NV) | 1,184 | Kativik | Abitibi | Ungava | Caroline Naktialuk, Sec.-Trés., Inukjuak J0M 1M0 – 819/254-8845, Fax: 819/254-8779 |
| Inverness (Canton) | 602 | L'Érable | Lotbinière | Lotbinière | Marie Turcotte, Sec.-Trés., 1799, route Dublin, CP 129, Inverness G0S 1K0 – 418/453-2512, Fax: 418/453-2554 |
| Inverness (V) | 253 | L'Érable | Lotbinière | Lotbinière | Johanne Tardif, Sec.-Trés., 1831, rue Dublin, CP 128, Inverness G0S 1K0 – 418/453-2108 |
| Irlande (Mun.) | 1,011 | L'Amiante | Frontenac-Mégantic | Frontenac | Céline Roy, Sec.-Trés., 157, ch Gosford, Irlande G0N 1N0 – 418/428-9216, Fax: 418/428-9216 |
| Ivry-sur-le-Lac (Mun.) | 346 | Les Laurentides | Laurentides | Bertrand | Chantale Marion, Sec.-Trés., 601, ch de la Gare, Ivry-sur-le-Lac J8C 2Z8 – 819/326-0554, Fax: 819/326-8618 |
| Ivujivik (NV) | 274 | Kativik | Abitibi | Ungava | Adamie Kalingo, Sec.-Trés., Ivujivik J0M 1H0 – 819/922-9940, Fax: 819/922-3045 |
| JOLIETTE | 17,541 | Joliette | Joliette | Joliette | Louis-André Garceau, Gref., 614, boul Manseau, Joliette J6E 3A4 – 514/753-8000, Fax: 514/753-8199 |

Urban Centres (Villes) in CAPITALS; Villages marked (V); Townships/Cantons marked (Canton);United townships/Cantons unis marked (Cantons); Parishes marked (P); Municipalities marked (Mun.).; Northern villages/Villages nordiques marked (NV); Cree Villages/Villages Cris marked (VC); Naskapi Villages/Villages Naskapi marked (VN); In the third column, Urban Community/Communauté Urbaine marked Urb. Com. An in-depth listing for municipalities marked with * appears in Part 2 (check Index for page numbers).

| MUNICIPALITY | 1996 POP. | REGIONAL COUNTY MUN. | FEDERAL ELECTORAL DISTRICT | PROVINCIAL ELECTORAL DISTRICT | CONTACT PERSON WITH ADDRESS, PHONE & FAX |
|---|---|---|---|---|---|
| *JONQUIÈRE | 56,503 | Le Fjord-du-Saguenay | Jonquière | Jonquière | Pierre Brassard, Gref., Hôtel de Ville, 2890, Place Davis, CP 2000, Jonquière G7X 7W7 – 418/546-2222, Fax: 418/699-6018, URL: http://ville.jonquiere.qc.ca |
| Kamouraska (Mun.) | 707 | Kamouraska | Kamouraska-Rivière-du-Loup-Témiscouata | Kamouraska-Témiscouata | Michèle Lévesque, Sec.-Trés., 67, av Morel, CP 130, Kamouraska G0L 1M0 – 418/492-6523, Fax: 418/492-6523 |
| Kangiqsualujjuaq (NV) | 648 | Kativik | Abitibi | Ungava | Tommy Annanack, Sec.-Trés., Kangiqsualujjuaq J0M 1N0 – 819/337-5271, Fax: 819/337-5200 |
| Kangiqsujuaq (NV) | 479 | Kativik | Abitibi | Ungava | Mary Arngak, Sec.-Trés., Kangiqsujuaq J0M 1K0 – 819/338-3342, Fax: 819/338-3237 |
| Kangirsuk (NV) | 394 | Kativik | Abitibi | Ungava | Marc Carrier, Sec.-Trés., Kangirsuk J0M 1A0 – 819/935-4388, Fax: 819/935-4287 |
| Kawawachikamach (VN) | | | | Duplessis | CP 970, Schefferville G0G 2T0 – 418/585-2686, Fax: 418/418/585-3130 |
| Kazabazua (Mun.) | 759 | La Vallée-de-la-Gatineau | Pontiac-Gatineau-Labelle | Gatineau | Eleonore Wilson, Sec.-Trés., 30, ch Begley, CP 10, Kazabazua J0X 1X0 – 819/467-2852, Fax: 819/467-3872 |
| Kiamika (Mun.) | 722 | Antoine-Labelle | Pontiac-Gatineau-Labelle | Labelle | Josée Lacasse, Sec.-Trés., 3, ch Valiquette, Kiamika J0W 1G0 – 819/585-3225, Fax: 819/585-3992 |
| Kingsbury (V) | 157 | Le Val-St-François | Richmond-Arthabaska | Johnson | Marie-Manon Bergeron, Sec.-Trés., 370, rue du Moulin, Kingsbury J0B 1X0 – 819/826-2527 |
| Kingsey (Canton) | 1,439 | Drummond | Drummond | Richmond | Marie-Sylvie Janelle, Sec.-Trés., 1205, rue de l'Église, CP 29, St-Félix-de-Kingsey J0B 2T0 – 819/848-2321, Fax: 819/848-2202 |
| Kingsey Falls (Mun.) | 539 | Arthabaska | Richmond-Arthabaska | Richmond | Nicole Henrichon, Sec.-Trés., 57, boul Kingsey, CP 59, Kingsey Falls J0A 1B0 – 819/363-2480, Fax: 819/363-2480 |
| Kingsey Falls (V) | 1,329 | Arthabaska | Richmond-Arthabaska | Richmond | Hélène Laroche, Sec.-Trés., 15, rue Caron, CP 270, Kingsey Falls J0A 1B0 – 819/363-3810, Fax: 819/363-3819 |
| Kinnear's Mills (Mun.) | 358 | L'Amiante | Frontenac-Mégantic | Frontenac | Lucien Trépanier, Sec.-Trés., 120, rue des Églises, Kinnear's Mills G0N 1K0 – 418/424-3377, Fax: 418/424-3015 |
| Kipawa (Mun.) | 549 | Témiscamingue | Rouyn-Noranda-Témiscamingue | Rouyn-Noranda-Témiscamingue | Marie-Rose Tremblay, Sec.-Trés., 15, rue Principale, Tee Lake J0Z 3P0 – 819/627-3500, Fax: 819/627-1067 |
| KIRKLAND | 18,678 | Montréal (Urb. Com.) | Lac-Saint-Louis | Nelligan | Lise Labrosse, Gref., 17200, boul Hymus, Kirkland H9J 3Y8 – 514/694-4100, Fax: 514/630-2711 |
| Kuujjuaq (NV) | 1,729 | Kativik | Abitibi | Ungava | Ian Robertson, Sec.-Trés., CP 58, Kuujjuaq J0M 1C0 – 819/964-2943, Fax: 819/964-2980 |
| Kuujjuarapik (NV) | 579 | Kativik | Abitibi | Ungava | Myva Niviaxie, Sec.-Trés., Kuujjuarapik J0M 1G0 – 819/929-3360, Fax: 819/929-3453 |
| LA BAIE | 21,057 | Le Fjord-du-Saguenay | Chicoutimi | Dubuc | Dominique Tremblay, Gref., 422, rue Victoria, La Baie G7B 3M4 – 418/697-5000, Fax: 418/697-5059 |
| La Baleine (Mun.) | 279 | Charlevoix | Charlevoix | Charlevoix | Kathia Parent, Sec.-Trés., 145, ch Principale, La Baleine G0A 2A0 – 418/438-2878, Fax: 418/438-2878 |
| La Bostonnais (Mun.) | 524 | Le Haut-St-Maurice | Champlain | Laviolette | Estelle Giguère, Sec.-Trés., 506, rte 155 nord, CP 2, La Tuque G9X 3N6 – 819/523-6091, Fax: 819/523-6091 |
| La Conception (Mun.) | 917 | Les Laurentides | Laurentides | Labelle | Jean-Denis Larocque, Sec.-Trés., 1371, boul. du Centenaire, La Conception J0T 1M0 – 819/686-3016, Fax: 819/686-5808 |
| La Corne (Mun.) | 621 | Abitibi | Abitibi | Abitibi-Ouest | Suzan McLaughlin, Sec.-Trés., 324, route 111, La Corne J0Y 1R0 – 819/799-3571, Fax: 819/799-3571 |
| La Doré (P) | 1,624 | Le Domaine-du-Roy | Roberval | Roberval | Laurent-Paul Dallaire, Sec.-Trés., 5000, rue des Peupliers, La Doré G8J 1E8 – 418/256-3545, Fax: 418/256-3496 |
| La Durantaye (P) | 721 | Bellechasse | Bellechasse-Montmagny-L'Islet | Bellechasse | Rachel Lamontagne, Sec.-Trés., 539, rue Piémont, La Durantaye G0R 1W0 – 418/884-3465, Fax: 418/884-3048 |
| La Guadeloupe (V) | 1,772 | Beauce-Sartigan | Beauce | Beauce-Sud | Marc-André Doyle, Sec.-Trés., 483 - 9e rue est, CP 279, La Guadeloupe G0M 1G0 – 418/459-3342, Fax: 418/459-3507 |
| La Macaza (Mun.) | 1,020 | Antoine-Labelle | Pontiac-Gatineau-Labelle | Labelle | Guy Goudreau, Sec.-Trés., 53, rue des Pionniers, CP 28, La Macaza J0T 1R0 – 819/275-2077, Fax: 819/275-3429 |
| LA MALBAIE-POINTE-AU-PIC | 4,918 | Charlevoix-Est | Charlevoix | Charlevoix | Roger Arpin, Sec.-Trés., 280, rue Nairn, La Malbaie-Pointe-au-Pic G5A 1L9 – 418/665-3747, Fax: 418/665-4935 |

Urban Centres (Villes) in CAPITALS; Villages marked (V); Townships/Cantons marked (Canton);United townships/Cantons unis marked (Cantons); Parishes marked (P); Municipalities marked (Mun.).; Northern villages/Villages nordiques marked (NV); Cree Villages/Villages Cris marked (VC); Naskapi Villages/Villages Naskapi marked (VN); In the third column, Urban Community/Communauté Urbaine marked Urb. Com. An in-depth listing for municipalities marked with * appears in Part 2 (check Index for page numbers).

| MUNICIPALITY | 1996 POP. | REGIONAL COUNTY MUN. | FEDERAL ELECTORAL DISTRICT | PROVINCIAL ELECTORAL DISTRICT | CONTACT PERSON WITH ADDRESS, PHONE & FAX |
|---|---|---|---|---|---|
| La Martre (Mun.) | 315 | Denis-Riverin | Matapédia-Matane | Matane | Marielle Cloutier-Gagnon, Sec.-Trés., 10, av du Phare, La Martre G0E 2H0 – 418/288-5605, Fax: 418/288-5144 |
| La Minerve (Canton) | 927 | Les Laurentides | Laurentides | Labelle | Robert Charette, Sec.-Trés., 6, rue Mailloux, La Minerve J0T 1S0 – 819/274-2364, Fax: 819/274-2031 |
| La Morandière (Mun.) | 295 | Abitibi | Abitibi | Abitibi-Ouest | Sandra Hardy, Sec.-Trés., 204, rte 397, La Morandière J0Y 1S0 – 819/734-6143, Fax: 819/734-6143 |
| La Motte (Mun.) | 409 | Abitibi | Abitibi | Abitibi-Ouest | Lyne Daigle, Sec.-Trés., 349, ch St-Luc, CP 644, La Motte J0Y 1T0 – 819/732-2878, Fax: 819/732-2878 |
| La Patrie (V) | 297 | Le Haut-St-François | Frontenac-Mégantic | Mégantic-Compton | Ghislaine Giard, Sec.-Trés., 44, rue Garneau, CP 180, La Patrie J0B 1Y0 – 819/888-2514, Fax: 819/888-2514 |
| La Pêche (Mun.) | 6,160 | Les Collines-de-l'Outaouais | Pontiac-Gatineau-Labelle | Gatineau | Charles Ricard, Sec.-Trés., 1, rue Principale ouest, La Pêche J0X 2W0 – 819/456-2161, Fax: 819/456-4534 |
| LA PLAINE | 14,413 | Les Moulins | Repentigny | Masson | Louise Langlois, Sec.-Trés., 3630, de l'Hôtel-de-Ville, La Plaine J7M 1A1 – 514/478-2555, Fax: 514/478-3860 |
| LA POCATIÈRE | 4,887 | Kamouraska | Kamouraska-Rivière-du-Loup-Témiscouata | Kamouraska-Témiscouata | Claude Crête, Sec.-Trés., 412, 9e rue, CP 668, La Pocatière G0R 1Z0 – 418/856-3394, Fax: 418/856-5465 |
| LA PRAIRIE | 17,128 | Roussillon | Brossard-La Prairie | La Prairie | Bernard Blain, Gref., #400, 170, boul Taschereau, La Prairie J5R 5H6 – 514/444-0540, Fax: 514/444-0548 |
| La Présentation (P) | 1,851 | Les Maskoutains | St-Hyacinthe-Bagot | Verchères | André Charron, Sec.-Trés., 772, rue Principale, La Présentation J0H 1B0 – 514/796-2317, Fax: 514/796-1707 |
| La Rédemption (P) | 562 | La Mitis | Rimouski-Mitis | Matapédia | Gaétane Viens, Sec.-Trés., 68, rue Soucy, CP 39, La Rédemption G0J 1P0 – 418/776-5311, Fax: 418/776-5711 |
| La Reine (Mun.) | 437 | Abitibi-Ouest | Rouyn-Noranda-Témiscamingue | Abitibi-Ouest | Diane Sévigny-East, Sec.-Trés., 1, 3e av ouest, CP 40, La Reine J0Z 2L0 – 819/947-5271, Fax: 819/947-5271 |
| LA SARRE | 8,345 | Abitibi-Ouest | Rouyn-Noranda-Témiscamingue | Abitibi-Ouest | François Casaubon, Sec.-Trés., 6, 4e av est, La Sarre J9Z 1J9 – 819/333-2282, Fax: 819/333-3090 |
| La Trinité-des-Monts (P) | 283 | Rimouski-Neigette | Rimouski-Mitis | Rimouski | Thérèse Dumont, Sec.-Trés., 12, rue Principale ouest, CP 9, La Trinité-des-Monts G0K 1B0 – 418/779-2421, Fax: 418/779-2421 |
| LA TUQUE | 12,102 | Le Haut-St-Maurice | Champlain | Laviolette | Yves Tousignant, Gref., 558, rue Commerciale, La Tuque G9X 3A9 – 819/523-5110, Fax: 819/523-5419 |
| La Visitation-de-l'Île-Dupas (Mun.) | 564 | D'Autray | Berthier-Montcalm | Berthier | Claire Hérard, Sec.-Trés., 113, rue de l'Église, La Visitation-de-l'Île-Dupas J0K 2P0 – 514/836-6019, Fax: 514/836-6019 |
| La Visitation-de-Yamaska (Mun.) | 400 | Nicolet-Yamaska | Richelieu | Nicolet-Yamaska | Nancy Vouligny, Sec.-Trés., 21, rue Principale, La Visitation J0G 1C0 – 514/564-2818, Fax: 514/564-2818 |
| Labelle (Mun.) | 2,256 | Les Laurentides | Laurentides | Labelle | Pierre Delage, Sec.-Trés., 1, rue du Pont, CP 390, Labelle J0T 1H0 – 819/686-2144, Fax: 819/686-3820 |
| Labrecque (Mun.) | 1,224 | Lac-St-Jean-Est | Lac-St-Jean | Lac-St-Jean | Suzanne Couture, Sec.-Trés., 3425, rue Ambroise, CP 9, St-Léon G0W 2S0 – 418/481-2022, Fax: 418/481-1210 |
| Lac-à-la-Croix (Mun.) | 1,013 | Lac-St-Jean-Est | Lac-St-Jean | Lac-St-Jean | Marie-Hélène Boily, Sec.-Trés., 353, rue St-Jean, Lac-à-la-Croix G0W 1W0 – 418/349-2892, Fax: 418/349-8724 |
| Lac-à-la-Tortue (Mun.) | 3,050 | Le Centre-de-la-Mauricie | St-Maurice | St-Maurice | Madeleine Lahaie, Sec.-Trés., 1082, 37e av, Lac-à-la-Tortue G0X 1L0 – 819/538-5882, Fax: 819/538-5340 |
| Lac-au-Saumon (V) | 1,314 | La Matapédia | Matapédia-Matane | Matapédia | Nadia Saint-Pierre, Sec.-Trés., 24, Place de la Municipalité, CP 98, Lac-au-Saumon G0J 1M0 – 418/778-3378, Fax: 418/778-3706 |
| Lac-aux-Sables (P) | 1,441 | Mékinac | Champlain | Portneuf | Benoit Beaupré, Sec.-Trés., 820, rue St-Alphonse, Lac-aux-Sables G0X 1M0 – 418/336-2331, Fax: 418/336-2500 |
| Lac-Beauport (Mun.) | 5,008 | La Jacques-Cartier | Charlesbourg | Chauveau | Jean-François Parent, Sec.-Trés., 65, ch du Tour-du-Lac, CP 159, Lac-Beauport G0A 2C0 – 418/849-7141, Fax: 418/849-0361 |
| Lac-Bouchette (Mun.) | 1,445 | Le Domaine-du-Roy | Roberval | Roberval | Serge Martel, Sec.-Trés., 186, rue Principale, CP 40, Lac-Bouchette G0W 1V0 – 418/348-6306, Fax: 418/348-9477 |
| LAC-BROME | 5,073 | Brome-Missisquoi | Brome-Missisquoi | Brome-Missisquoi | Catherine Bouchard, Gref., 122, ch Lakeside, CP 60, Knowlton J0E 1V0 – 514/243-6111, Fax: 514/243-5300 |
| LAC-DELAGE | 368 | La Jacques-Cartier | Charlesbourg | Chauveau | Guylaine Thibault, Sec.-Trés., 24, rue Pied-des-Pentes, Lac-Delage G0A 4P0 – 418/848-2417, Fax: 418/848-2417 |

Urban Centres (Villes) in CAPITALS; Villages marked (V); Townships/Cantons marked (Canton);United townships/Cantons unis marked (Cantons); Parishes marked (P); Municipalities marked (Mun.).; Northern villages/Villages nordiques marked (NV); Cree Villages/Villages Cris marked (VC); Naskapi Villages/Villages Naskapi marked (VN); In the third column, Urban Community/Communauté Urbaine marked Urb. Com. An in-depth listing for municipalities marked with * appears in Part 2 (check Index for page numbers).

| MUNICIPALITY | 1996 POP. | REGIONAL COUNTY MUN. | FEDERAL ELECTORAL DISTRICT | PROVINCIAL ELECTORAL DISTRICT | CONTACT PERSON WITH ADDRESS, PHONE & FAX |
|---|---|---|---|---|---|
| Lac-des-Aigles (Mun.) | 644 | Témiscouata | Kamouraska-Rivière-du-Loup-Témiscouata | Rimouski | Sylvie Samson, Sec.-Trés., 75, rue Principale, CP 70, Lac-des-Aigles G0K 1V0 – 418/779-2300, Fax: 418/779-3024 |
| Lac-des-Écorces (V) | 989 | Antoine-Labelle | Pontiac-Gatineau-Labelle | Labelle | Guy Legault, Sec.-Trés., 111, boul St-François sud, Lac-des-Écorces J0W 1H0 – 819/585-2555, Fax: 819/585-9155 |
| Lac-des-Plages (Mun.) | 380 | Papineau | Argenteuil-Papineau | Papineau | Denis Dagenais, Sec.-Trés., 2053, ch Tour-du-Lac, Lac-des-Plages J0T 1K0 – 819/426-2391, Fax: 819/426-2391 |
| Lac-des-Seize-Îles (Mun.) | 184 | Les Pays-d'en-Haut | Argenteuil-Papineau | Argenteuil | Luce Bergeron, Sec.-Trés., 47, rue de l'Église, CP 360, Lac-des-Seize-Iles J0T 2M0 – 514/226-3117, Fax: 514/226-3117 |
| Lac-Drolet (Mun.) | 1,133 | Le Granit | Frontenac-Mégantic | Mégantic-Compton | Ronald Leclerc, Sec.-Trés., 685, rue Principale, CP 148, Lac-Drolet G0Y 1C0 – 819/549-2332 |
| Lac-du-Cerf (Mun.) | 425 | Antoine-Labelle | Pontiac-Gatineau-Labelle | Labelle | Jacinthe Valiquette, Sec.-Trés., 15, rue Émard, Lac-du-Cerf J0W 1S0 – 819/597-2424, Fax: 819/597-4036 |
| Lac-Dufault (Mun.) | 978 | Rouyn-Noranda | Rouyn-Noranda-Témiscamingue | Rouyn-Noranda-Témiscamingue | Lise Bélair, Sec.-Trés., 34, rue Principale, Lac-Dufault J9X 5A3 – 819/797-3068, Fax: 819/797-5236 |
| Lac-Édouard (Mun.) | 155 | Le Haut-St-Maurice | Champlain | Laviolette | Lise Côté, Sec.-Trés., 195, rue Principale, CP 4049, Lac-Édouard G0X 3N0 – 819/653-2238, Fax: 819/653-2017 |
| LAC-ETCHEMIN | 2,488 | Les Etchemins | Bellechasse-Montmagny-L'Islet | Bellechasse | Marcel Lachance, Sec.-Trés., 208, 2e av, CP 370, Lac-Etchemin G0R 1S0 – 418/625-4521, Fax: 418/625-3175 |
| Lac-Frontière (Mun.) | 174 | Montmagny | Bellechasse-Montmagny-L'Islet | Montmagny-L'Islet | Dany Robert, Sec.-Trés., 22, rue de l'Église, Lac-Frontière G0R 1T0 – 418/245-3553 |
| Lac-Kénogami (Mun.) | 1,517 | Le Fjord-du-Saguenay | Jonquière | Jonquière | Germain Girard, Sec.-Trés., 3000, ch de l'Église, Lac-Kénogami G7X 7V6 – 418/547-8869, Fax: 418/547-6158 |
| LAC-MÉGANTIC | 5,864 | Le Granit | Frontenac-Mégantic | Mégantic-Compton | Jean Perreault, Gref., #200, 5527, rue Frontenac, Lac-Mégantic G6B 1H6 – 819/583-2441, Fax: 819/583-5920 |
| Lac-Nominingue (Mun.) | 1,930 | Antoine-Labelle | Pontiac-Gatineau-Labelle | Labelle | Louise Boivin, Sec.-Trés., 2110, ch Tour-du-Lac, CP 390, Lac-Nominingue J0W 1R0 – 819/278-3384, Fax: 819/278-4967 |
| Lac-Poulin (V) | 63 | Beauce-Sartigan | Beauce | Beauce-Sud | Paul Poulin, Sec.-Trés., 1855, 127e rue, CP 186, St-Georges G5Y 5C7 – 418/228-6115 |
| Lac-Saguay (V) | 318 | Antoine-Labelle | Pontiac-Gatineau-Labelle | Labelle | Richard Gagnon, Sec.-Trés., 257A, rte 117, Lac-Saguay J0W 1L0 – 819/278-3972, Fax: 819/278-0260 |
| LAC-ST-CHARLES | 8,540 | Québec (Urb. Com.) | Charlesbourg | Chauveau | Jacques Lacombe, Sec.-Trés., 510, rue Delage, CP 8, Lac-St-Charles G0A 2H0 – 418/849-2811, Fax: 418/849-2849 |
| LAC-ST-JOSEPH | 83 | La Jacques-Cartier | Portneuf | Portneuf | Armand Létourneau, Sec.-Trés., 4417, rue des Lierres, Charlesbourg G1G 1S2 – 418/626-3598, Fax: 418/624-0997 |
| Lac-Ste-Marie (Mun.) | 492 | La Vallée-de-la-Gatineau | Pontiac-Gatineau-Labelle | Gatineau | Johanne D'Amour, Sec.-Trés., 106, ch de Lac-Ste-Marie, CP 97, Lac-Ste-Marie J0X 1Z0 – 819/467-5437, Fax: 819/467-3691 |
| Lac-St-Paul (Mun.) | 415 | Antoine-Labelle | Pontiac-Gatineau-Labelle | Labelle | Francine Bélec, Sec.-Trés., 388, rue Principale, Lac-St-Paul J0W 1K0 – 819/587-4283, Fax: 819/587-4892 |
| LAC-SERGENT | 198 | Portneuf | Portneuf | Portneuf | Nicole Lacasse, Sec.-Trés., 1149, ch Tour-du-Lac nord, Lac-Sergent G0A 2J0 – 418/875-4854, Fax: 418/875-4854 |
| Lac-Simon (Mun.) | 667 | Papineau | Argenteuil-Papineau | Papineau | Gisèle Prévost, Sec.-Trés., 849, ch du Tour-du-Lac, CP 220, Chénéville J0V 1E0 – 819/428-3906, Fax: 819/428-3455 |
| Lac-Supérieur (Mun.) | 1,199 | Les Laurentides | Laurentides | Labelle | Clarisse Daoust, Sec.-Trés., 1281, ch du lac-Supérieur, Lac-Supérieur J0T 1J0 – 819/688-2208, Fax: 819/688-3010 |
| Lac-Tremblant-Nord (Mun.) | | Labelle | Laurentides | Labelle | Michèle Dutrisac-Kilburn, Sec.-Trés., 328, av Wood, Westmount H3Z 1Z2 – 514/937-3528, Fax: 514/938-9274 |
| L'Acadie (Mun.) | 5,474 | Le Haut-Richelieu | St-Jean | St-Jean | Denis L'Heureux, Sec.-Trés., 1161, ch du Clocher, L'Acadie J2Y 1A1 – 514/347-8221, Fax: 514/347-6642 |
| LACHENAIE | 18,489 | Les Moulins | Repentigny | Terrebonne | Judith Viens, Gref., 3060, boul St-Charles, Lachenaie J6V 1A1 – 514/471-2424, Fax: 514/471-9872 |
| LACHINE | 35,171 | Montréal (Urb. Com.) | Notre-Dame-de-Grâce-Lachine | Marquette | Sylvie Aubin, Gref., 1800, boul St-Joseph, Lachine H8S 2N4 – 514/634-3471, Fax: 514/634-8164, URL: http://sun2.cum.qc.ca/LACHINE/ |

Urban Centres (Villes) in CAPITALS; Villages marked (V); Townships/Cantons marked (Canton);United townships/Cantons unis marked (Cantons); Parishes marked (P); Municipalities marked (Mun.).; Northern villages/Villages nordiques marked (NV); Cree Villages/Villages Cris marked (VC); Naskapi Villages/Villages Naskapi marked (VN); In the third column, Urban Community/Communauté Urbaine marked Urb. Com. An in-depth listing for municipalities marked with * appears in Part 2 (check Index for page numbers).

| MUNICIPALITY | 1996 POP. | REGIONAL COUNTY MUN. | FEDERAL ELECTORAL DISTRICT | PROVINCIAL ELECTORAL DISTRICT | CONTACT PERSON WITH ADDRESS, PHONE & FAX |
|---|---|---|---|---|---|
| LACHUTE | 11,493 | Argenteuil | Argenteuil-Papineau | Argenteuil | Isabelle Grenier, Gref., 380, rue Principale, Lachute J8H 1Y2 – 514/562-3781, Fax: 514/562-1431 |
| Lacolle (V) | 1,554 | Le Haut-Richelieu | St-Jean | St-Jean | Georgette Chevrefils, Sec.-Trés., 1, rue de l'Église sud, CP 400, Lacolle J0J 1J0 – 514/246-3201, Fax: 514/246-4412 |
| Lafontaine (V) | 9,008 | La Rivière-du-Nord | Laurentides | Prévost | Fernand Campbell, Sec.-Trés., 70, 106e av, Lafontaine J7Y 1G5 – 514/438-2264, Fax: 514/438-4355 |
| Laforce (Mun.) | 295 | Témiscamingue | Rouyn-Noranda-Témiscamingue | Rouyn-Noranda-Témiscamingue | Yves Nolet, Sec.-Trés., 703, che du Village, CP 25, Laforce J0Z 2J0 – 819/722-2461, Fax: 819/722-2461 |
| Lamarche (Mun.) | 564 | Lac-St-Jean-Est | Lac-St-Jean | Lac-St-Jean | Aline Perron, Sec.-Trés., 100, rue Principale, Lamarche G0W 1X0 – 418/481-2861, Fax: 418/481-1412 |
| Lambton (Mun.) | 1,517 | Le Granit | Frontenac-Mégantic | Mégantic-Compton | Claire Bédard, Sec.-Trés., 230, rue du Collège, CP 206, Lambton G0M 1H0 – 418/486-7438, Fax: 418/486-7440 |
| L'ANCIENNE-LORETTE | 15,895 | Québec (Urb. Com.) | Québec-Est | La Peltrie | Serge Morin, Gref., 1575, rue Turmel, L'Ancienne-Lorette G2E 3J5 – 418/872-9811, Fax: 418/872-1962 |
| Landrienne (Canton) | 1,007 | Abitibi | Abitibi | Abitibi-Ouest | Jacques Perron, Sec.-Trés., 158, av Principale est, Landrienne J0Y 1V0 – 819/732-4357, Fax: 819/732-3866 |
| L'Ange-Gardien (Mun.) | 3,521 | Les Collines-de-l'Outaouais | Pontiac-Gatineau-Labelle | Papineau | Paul St-Louis, Sec.-Trés., 870, ch Donaldson, L'Ange-Gardien J8L 2W7 – 819/986-7470, Fax: 819/986-8349 |
| L'Ange-Gardien (P) | 2,841 | La Côte-de-Beaupré | Beauport-Montmorency-Orléans | Montmorency | Jacques Villeneuve, Sec.-Trés., 6405, av Royale, L'Ange-Gardien G0A 2K0 – 418/822-1555, Fax: 418/822-2526 |
| L'Ange-Gardien (V) | 599 | Rouville | Shefford | Iberville | André Parent, Sec.-Trés., 249, rue St-Joseph, CP 120, L'Ange-Gardien J0E 1E0 – 514/293-7575, Fax: 514/293-6635 |
| Langelier (Canton) | 539 | Le Haut-St-Maurice | Champlain | Laviolette | Manon Shallow, Sec.-Trés., 47, rue Principale, CP 2010, La Croche G0X 1R0 – 819/523-2061, Fax: 819/523-2061 |
| L'Annonciation (V) | 2,085 | Antoine-Labelle | Pontiac-Gatineau-Labelle | Labelle | Lise Cadieux, Sec.-Trés., 25, rue Principale sud, CP 398, L'Annonciation J0T 1T0 – 819/275-2929, Fax: 819/275-3676 |
| Lanoraie-d'Autray (Mun.) | 1,904 | D'Autray | Berthier-Montcalm | Berthier | Robert Coolidge, Sec.-Trés., 57, rue Laroche, CP 308, Lanoraie J0K 1E0 – 514/887-2364, Fax: 514/887-2077 |
| L'Anse-St-Jean (Mun.) | 1,250 | Le Fjord-du-Saguenay | Chicoutimi | Dubuc | Lolita Boudreault, Sec.-Trés., 3, rue du Couvent, L'Anse-St-Jean G0V 1J0 – 418/272-2633, Fax: 418/272-3148 |
| Lantier (Mun.) | 631 | Les Laurentides | Laurentides | Bertrand | Lise Loiseau, Sec.-Trés., 118, 29e av, CP 39, Lantier J0T 1V0 – 819/326-2674, Fax: 819/326-5204 |
| Larouche (P) | 1,049 | Le Fjord-du-Saguenay | Jonquière | Lac-St-Jean | Paul-Henri Munger, Sec.-Trés., 709, rue Gauthier, Larouche G0W 1Z0 – 418/695-2201, Fax: 418/695-4989 |
| *LASALLE | 72,029 | Montréal (Urb. Com.) | LaSalle-Émard | Marguerite-Bourgeoys; Marquette | Nicole Herby, Gref., 55, av Dupras, LaSalle H8R 4A8 – 514/367-1000, Fax: 514/367-6600 |
| L'Ascension (Mun.) | 755 | Antoine-Labelle | Pontiac-Gatineau-Labelle | Labelle | Sylvain Michaudville, Sec.-Trés., 59, rue de l'Hôtel-de-Ville, CP 30, L'Ascension J0T 1W0 – 819/275-3027, Fax: 819/275-3489 |
| L'Ascension-de-Notre-Seigneur (P) | 1,867 | Lac-St-Jean-Est | Lac-St-Jean | Lac-St-Jean | Roger Boily, Sec.-Trés., 51, 4e av est, L'Ascension-de-Notre-Seigneur G0W 1Y0 – 418/347-3482, Fax: 418/347-4253 |
| L'Ascension-de-Patapédia (Mun.) | 267 | Avignon | Matapédia-Matane | Bonaventure | Nancy Gagné, Sec.-Trés., 82, rue Principale, CP 9, L'Ascension-de-Patapédia G0J 1R0 – 418/299-2024, Fax: 418/299-2024 |
| L'ASSOMPTION | 11,366 | L'Assomption | Joliette | L'Assomption | Suzanne Dubé, Gref., 399, rue Dorval, L'Assomption J5W 1A1 – 514/589-5671, Fax: 514/589-4512 |
| LATERRIÈRE | 4,815 | Le Fjord-du-Saguenay | Jonquière | Dubuc | Normand Girard, Gref., 6166, rue Notre-Dame, CP 69, Laterrière G0V 1K0 – 418/678-2216, Fax: 418/678-2647 |
| Latulipe-et-Gaboury (Cantons) | 351 | Témiscamingue | Rouyn-Noranda-Témiscamingue | Rouyn-Noranda-Témiscamingue | Gisèle Gauthier, Sec.-Trés., 1, rue Principale est, CP 9, Latulipe J0Z 2N0 – 819/747-4281, Fax: 819/747-2194 |
| Launay (Canton) | 260 | Abitibi | Abitibi | Abitibi-Ouest | Claudette Laroche, Sec.-Trés., 843, rue des Pionniers, Launay J0Y 1W0 – 819/796-2545 |
| LAURENTIDES | 2,703 | Montcalm | Berthier-Montcalm | Rousseau | Jean-Guy Champoux, Sec.-Tres., 250, 12e av, CP 128, Laurentides J0R 1C0 – 514/439-2539, Fax: 514/439-6384 |
| Laurier-Station (V) | 2,399 | Lotbinière | Lotbinière | Lotbinière | Réjean Tousignant, Sec.-Trés., 137, rue de la Station, Laurier Station G0S 1N0 – 418/728-3852, Fax: 418/728-4801 |

Urban Centres (Villes) in CAPITALS; Villages marked (V); Townships/Cantons marked (Canton);United townships/Cantons unis marked (Cantons); Parishes marked (P); Municipalities marked (Mun.).; Northern villages/Villages nordiques marked (NV); Cree Villages/Villages Cris marked (VC); Naskapi Villages/Villages Naskapi marked (VN); In the third column, Urban Community/Communauté Urbaine marked Urb. Com. An in-depth listing for municipalities marked with * appears in Part 2 (check Index for page numbers).

| MUNICIPALITY | 1996 POP. | REGIONAL COUNTY MUN. | FEDERAL ELECTORAL DISTRICT | PROVINCIAL ELECTORAL DISTRICT | CONTACT PERSON WITH ADDRESS, PHONE & FAX |
|---|---|---|---|---|---|
| Laurierville (V) | 915 | L'Érable | Lotbinière | Lotbinière | Réjean Gingras, Sec.-Trés., 140, rue Grenier, CP 159, Laurierville G0S 1P0 – 819/365-4646, Fax: 819/365-4200 |
| *LAVAL | 330,393 | Laval | Laval-Centre; Laval-Est; Laval-Ouest | Chomedey; Fabre; Laval-des-Rapides; Mille-Îles; Vimont | Guy Collard, Gref., Hôtel de Ville, 1, Place du Souvenir, CP 422, Laval H7V 1W7 – 514/978-8000, Fax: 514/978-5943, URL: http://www.ville.laval.qc.ca/ |
| Lavaltrie (V) | 5,821 | D'Autray | Berthier-Montcalm | Berthier | Réjean Nantais, Sec.-Trés., 1370, rue Notre-Dame, Lavaltrie J0K 1H0 – 514/586-2921, Fax: 514/586-3939 |
| L'Avenir (Mun.) | 1,274 | Drummond | Drummond | Johnson | Andrée Béland, Sec.-Trés., 575, rue Principle, CP 112, L'Avenir J0C 1B0 – 819/394-2422, Fax: 819/394-2222 |
| Laverlochère (P) | 813 | Témiscamingue | Rouyn-Noranda-Témiscamingue | Rouyn-Noranda-Témiscamingue | Monique Rivest, Sec.-Trés., 11, rue St-Isidore ouest, CP 159, Laverlochère J0Z 2P0 – 819/765-5111, Fax: 819/765-5111 |
| Lawrenceville (V) | 666 | Le Val-St-François | Shefford | Brome-Missisquoi | René Majella, Sec.-Trés., 2100, rue Dandenault, CP 60, Lawrenceville J0E 1W0 – 514/535-6398, Fax: 514/535-6398 |
| Le Bic (Mun.) | 2,999 | Rimouski-Neigette | Rimouski-Mitis-Mitis | Rimouski | Camille Roussel, Sec.-Trés., 149, rue Ste-Cécile, CP 99, Le Bic G0L 1B0 – 418/736-5833, Fax: 418/736-4834 |
| LE GARDEUR | 16,853 | L'Assomption | Joliette | Masson | Céline Girard, Gref., 1, Montée des Arsenaux, Le Gardeur J5Z 2C1 – 514/585-1140, Fax: 514/585-7679 |
| LEBEL-SUR-QUÉVILLON | 3,416 | Terr. du Nouveau-Québec | Abitibi | Ungava | Serge Woods, Gref., 500, Place Quévillon, CP 430, Lebel-sur-Quévillon J0Y 1X0 – 819/755-4826, Fax: 819/755-8124 |
| Leclercville (V) | 295 | Lotbinière | Lotbinière | Lotbinière | Rachel Héroux, Sec.-Trés., 182, rue St-Jean-Baptiste, Leclercville G0S 2K0 – 819/292-2769, Fax: 819/292-2736 |
| Lefebvre (Mun.) | 792 | Drummond | Drummond | Johnson | Carole Côté, Sec.-Trés., 186, 10e rang, Lefebvre J0H 2C0 – 819/394-2782, Fax: 819/394-2782 |
| Lejeune (Mun.) | 371 | Témiscouata | Kamouraska-Rivière-du-Loup-Témiscouata | Kamouraska-Témiscouata | Lynda Caron-Damboise, Sec.-Trés., 69, rue de la Grande-Coulée, CP 40, Lejeune G0L 1S0 – 418/855-2428, Fax: 418/855-2428 |
| Lemieux (Mun.) | 347 | Bécancour | Lotbinière | Lotbinière | France Hénault, Sec.-Trés., 530, rue de l'Église, Lemieux G0X 1S0 – 819/283-2506, Fax: 819/283-2506 |
| LEMOYNE | 5,052 | Champlain | St-Lambert | Laporte | André Bellefeuille, Sec.-Trés., 2205, rue St-Georges, Lemoyne J4R 1V7 – 514/671-5940, Fax: 514/671-1578 |
| LENNOXVILLE | 4,036 | Sherbrooke | Sherbrooke | St-François | Johanne Henson, Gref., 150, rue Queen, Lennoxville J1M 1J6 – 819/569-9388, Fax: 819/563-3705 |
| L'Épiphanie (P) | 2,739 | L'Assomption | Joliette | Rousseau | Nicole Renaud, Sec.-Trés., 331, rang du Bas-de-l'Achigan, L'Épiphanie J5X 1E1 – 514/588-5547, Fax: 514/588-6050 |
| L'ÉPIPHANIE | 4,153 | L'Assomption | Joliette | Rousseau | Johane Ducharme, Gref., 66, rue Notre-Dame, L'Épiphanie J0K 1J0 – 514/588-5515, Fax: 514/588-6171 |
| LÉRY | 2,410 | Roussillon | Châteauguay | Châteauguay | Rose-Hélène Langlais, Sec.-Trés., 1, rue de l'Hôtel-de-Ville, Léry J6N 1E8 – 514/692-6861, Fax: 514/692-6881 |
| Les Boules (Mun.) | 410 | La Mitis | Rimouski-Mitis-Mitis | Matane | Yolande Marcheterre, Sec.-Trés., 41A, du Couvent, Les Boules G0J 1S0 – 418/936-3255, Fax: 418/936-3117 |
| Les Cèdres (Mun.) | 4,641 | Vaudreuil-Soulanges | Vaudreuil-Soulanges | Salaberry-Soulanges | Normand Meilleur, Sec.-Trés., 1060, ch du Fleuve, Les Cèdres J7T 1A1 – 514/452-4340, Fax: 514/452-4605 |
| Les Coteaux (Mun.) | 2,843 | Vaudreuil-Soulanges | Vaudreuil-Soulanges | Salaberry-Soulanges | Claude Madore, Sec.-Trés., 65, route 338, Les Coteaux J0P 1C0 – 514/267-3531, Fax: 514/267-3532 |
| Les Éboulements (Mun.) | 1,013 | Charlevoix | Charlevoix | Charlevoix | André Girard, Sec.-Trés., 248, rue du Village, CP 130, Les Éboulements G0A 2M0 – 418/635-2755, Fax: 418/635-2520 |
| Les Escoumins (Mun.) | 2,136 | La Haute-Côte-Nord | Charlevoix | Saguenay | Micheline Savard, Sec.-Trés., 2, rue Sirois, CP 160, Les Escoumins G0T 1K0 – 418/233-2766, Fax: 418/233-3273 |
| Les Hauteurs (Mun.) | 636 | La Mitis | Rimouski-Mitis-Mitis | Matapédia | Diane Bernier, Sec.-Trés., 50, rue de l'Église, CP 69, Les Hauteurs G0K 1C0 – 418/798-8266, Fax: 418/798-8266 |
| Les Méchins (Mun.) | 1,280 | Matane | Matapédia-Matane | Matane | Lyne Fortin, Sec.-Trés., 108, rte des Fonds, Les Méchins G0J 1T0 – 418/729-3952, Fax: 418/729-3952 |
| Leslie-Clapham-et-Huddersfield (Cantons) | 1,002 | Pontiac | Pontiac-Gatineau-Labelle | Pontiac | Anita Lafleur, Sec.-Trés., 15, av Palmer, CP 70, Otter Lake J0X 2P0 – 819/453-7049, Fax: 819/453-7311 |

Urban Centres (Villes) in CAPITALS; Villages marked (V); Townships/Cantons marked (Canton);United townships/Cantons unis marked (Cantons); Parishes marked (P); Municipalities marked (Mun.).; Northern villages/Villages nordiques marked (NV); Cree Villages/Villages Cris marked (VC); Naskapi Villages/Villages Naskapi marked (VN); In the third column, Urban Community/Communauté Urbaine marked Urb. Com. An in-depth listing for municipalities marked with * appears in Part 2 (check Index for page numbers).

| MUNICIPALITY | 1996 POP. | REGIONAL COUNTY MUN. | FEDERAL ELECTORAL DISTRICT | PROVINCIAL ELECTORAL DISTRICT | CONTACT PERSON WITH ADDRESS, PHONE & FAX |
|---|---|---|---|---|---|
| L'Étang-du-Nord (Mun.) | 3,087 | Les Îles-de-la-Madeleine | Bonaventure-Gaspé-Îles-de-la-Madeleine-Pabok | Îles-de-la-Madeleine | Dominique Delaney, Sec.-Trés., 1589, ch Étang-du-Nord, CP 689, L'Étang-du-Nord G0B 1E0 – 418/986-3321, Fax: 418/986-6231 |
| LÉVIS | 40,407 | Desjardins | Lévis | Lévis | Sylvie Dionne, Gref., 225, côte du Passage, Lévis G6V 5T4 – 418/838-4000, Fax: 418/838-4051 |
| L'Île-aux-Coudres (Mun.) | 1,066 | Charlevoix | Charlevoix | Charlevoix | Marcelle Pedneault, Sec.-Trés., 23, rue Royale ouest, L'Île-aux-Coudres G0A 3J0 – 418/438-2583, Fax: 418/438-2750 |
| L'Île-Bizard (V) | 13,038 | Montréal (Urb. Com.) | Pierrefonds-Dollard | Nelligan | Danielle Ruest, Sec.-Trés., 350, rue de l'Église, L'île-Bizard H9C 1G9 – 514/620-6331, Fax: 514/620-2189 |
| L'ÎLE-CADIEUX | 121 | Vaudreuil-Soulanges | Vaudreuil-Soulanges | Vaudreuil | Annie Herrbach, Sec.-Trés., 50, ch de l'Île, L'Ile-Cadieux J7V 8P3 – 514/424-4273, Fax: 514/424-6327 |
| L'Île-d'Anticosti (Mun.) | 263 | Minganie | Manicouagan | Duplessis | Alain Descarreaux, Sec.-Trés., 38, ch des Forestiers, CP 119, Port-Menier G0G 2Y0 – 418/535-0311, Fax: 418/535-0381 |
| L'Île-d'Entrée (V) | 175 | Les Îles-de-la-Madeleine | Bonaventure-Gaspé-Îles-de-la-Madeleine-Pabok | Îles-de-la-Madeleine | Clara Chenell, Sec.-Trés., L'Ile-d'Entrée G0B 1C0 – 418/986-4179, Fax: 418/986-3764 |
| L'ÎLE-DORVAL | 2 | Montréal (Urb. Com.) | Lac-St-Louis | Jacques-Cartier | Claire Robinson, Sec.-Trés., CP 53061, Dorval H9S 5W4 – 514/633-0182, Fax: 514/344-2615 |
| L'Île-du-Havre-Aubert (Mun.) | 2,443 | Les Îles-de-la-Madeleine | Bonaventure-Gaspé-Îles-de-la-Madeleine-Pabok | Îles-de-la-Madeleine | Jean-Yves Lebreux, Sec.-Trés., 280, ch du Bassin, CP 37, L'île-du-Havre-Aubert G0B 1J0 – 418/937-5205, Fax: 418/937-5558 |
| L'ÎLE-PERROT | 9,178 | Vaudreuil-Soulanges | Vaudreuil-Soulanges | Vaudreuil | Lucie Coallier, Gref., 110, boul Perrot, L'Île-Perrot J7V 3G1 – 514/453-1751, Fax: 514/453-2432 |
| Lingwick (Canton) | 425 | Le Haut-St-François | Frontenac-Mégantic | Mégantic-Compton | Suzane Beaudoin, Sec.-Trés., 72, rte 108, Lingwick J0B 2Z0 – 819/877-3311, Fax: 819/877-3311 |
| L'Isle-aux-Allumettes (Canton) | 590 | Pontiac | Pointe-Gatineau-Labelle | Pontiac | Richard Vaillancourt, Sec.-Trés., 37, rue St-Joseph, CP 100, Chapeau J0X 1M0 – 819/689-2266, Fax: 819/689-5619 |
| L'Isle-aux-Allumettes Est (Canton) | 450 | Pontiac | Pontiac-Gatineau-Labelle | Pontiac | Dennis Czmielewski, Sec.-Trés., RR#4, Chapeau J0X 1M0 – 819/689-2586, Fax: 819/689-2586 |
| L'Isle-Verte (V) | 971 | Rivière-du-Loup | Kamouraska-Rivière-du-Loup-Témiscouata | Rivière-du-Loup | Guy Bérubé, Sec.-Trés., 141, rue St-Jean-Baptiste, CP 159, Isle-Verte G0L 1K0 – 418/898-2812, Fax: 418/898-2788 |
| L'ISLET | 934 | L'Islet | Bellechasse-Etchemins-Montmagny-L'Islet | Montmagny-L'Islet | Marie-Josée Bernier, Sec.-Trés., 92, 7e rue, CP 68, L'Islet G0R 2C0 – 418/247-5345, Fax: 418/247-5345 |
| L'Islet-sur-Mer (Mun.) | 1,786 | L'Islet | Bellechasse-Montmagny-L'Islet | Montmagny-L'Islet | Colette Lord, Sec.-Trés., 130, rue Notre-Dame, CP 99, L'Islet-sur-Mer G0R 2B0 – 418/247-3060, Fax: 418/247-5009 |
| Litchfield (Canton) | 484 | Pontiac | Pontiac-Gatineau-Labelle | Pontiac | Claire Romain, Sec.-Trés., 201, route 148, CP 340, Campbell's Bay J0X 1K0 – 819/648-5511, Fax: 819/648-5575 |
| Lochaber (Canton) | 510 | Papineau | Argenteuil-Papineau | Papineau | Marthe Thibaudeau, Sec.-Trés., 164, rte 148 est, Thurso J0X 3B0 – 819/985-3291 |
| Lochaber-Partie-Ouest (Canton) | 477 | Papineau | Argenteuil-Papineau | Papineau | Mario Bélisle, Sec.-Trés., 1021, rue de Liesse, Masson-Angers J8M 1H7 – 819/986-3321, Fax: 819/986-1516 |
| Longue-Pointe (Mun.) | 537 | Minganie | Manicouagan | Duplessis | Célyne B.-Loiselle, Sec.-Trés., 20, ch du Roi ouest, Longue-Pointe G0G 1V0 – 418/949-2053, Fax: 418/949-2166 |
| *LONGUEUIL | 127,977 | Champlain | Longueuil; Saint-Lambert | Marie-Victorin; Taillon | Claude Comtois, Gref., 350, rue Saint-Charles, CP 5000, Longueuil J4K 4Y7 – 514/646-8218, Fax: 514/646-8080 |
| LORETTEVILLE | 14,168 | Québec (Urb. Com.) | Québec-Est | Chauveau | Gilles Martel, Gref., 305, rue Racine, Loretteville G2B 1E7 – 418/842-1921, Fax: 418/842-2585 |
| LORRAINE | 8,876 | Thérèse-de-Blainville | Terrebonne-Blainville | Blainville | Brenda Bernard, Gref., 33, boul De Gaulle, Lorraine J6Z 3W9 – 514/621-8550, Fax: 514/621-4763 |
| Lorrainville (Mun.) | 1,507 | Témiscamingue | Rouyn-Noranda-Témiscamingue | Rouyn-Noranda-Témiscamingue | Monique Bastien, Sec.-Trés., 2, rue St-Jean-Baptiste est, CP 218, Lorrainville J0Z 2R0 – 819/625-2167, Fax: 819/625-2380 |
| Lotbinière (Mun.) | 1,008 | Lotbinière | Lotbinière | Lotbinière | Bernard Lepage, Sec.-Trés., 7523, route Marie-Victorin, CP 70, Lotbinière G0S 1S0 – 418/796-2103, Fax: 418/796-2103 |
| LOUISEVILLE | 7,911 | Maskinongé | Trois-Rivières | Maskinongé | Aline Corriveau-Lambert, Gref., 105, rue Saint-Laurent, Louiseville J5V 1J6 – 819/228-9437, Fax: 819/228-2263 |
| Low (Canton) | 807 | La Vallée-de-la-Gatineau | Pontiac-Gatineau-Labelle | Gatineau | Liette Hickey, Sec.-Trés., 4A, ch d'Amour, Low J0X 2C0 – 819/422-3528, Fax: 819/422-3796 |

Urban Centres (Villes) in CAPITALS; Villages marked (V); Townships/Cantons marked (Canton);United townships/Cantons unis marked (Cantons); Parishes marked (P); Municipalities marked (Mun.).; Northern villages/Villages nordiques marked (NV); Cree Villages/Villages Cris marked (VC); Naskapi Villages/Villages Naskapi marked (VN); In the third column, Urban Community/Communauté Urbaine marked Urb. Com. An in-depth listing for municipalities marked with * appears in Part 2 (check Index for page numbers).

| MUNICIPALITY | 1996 POP. | REGIONAL COUNTY MUN. | FEDERAL ELECTORAL DISTRICT | PROVINCIAL ELECTORAL DISTRICT | CONTACT PERSON WITH ADDRESS, PHONE & FAX |
|---|---|---|---|---|---|
| Luceville (V) | 1,421 | La Mitis | Rimouski-Mitis-Mitis | Matapedia | Marie-Andrée Jeffrey, Sec.-Trés., 67, boul St-Pierre, CP 310, Luceville G0K 1E0 – 418/739-3566, Fax: 418/739-3566 |
| Lyster (Mun.) | 1,715 | L'Érable | Lotbinière | Lotbinière | Pierre Dubois, Sec.-Trés., 2375, rue Bécancour, CP 220, Lyster G0S 1V0 – 819/389-5787, Fax: 819/389-5981 |
| Lytton (Canton) | 252 | La Vallée-de-la-Gatineau | Pontiac-Gatineau-Labelle | Gatineau | Marthe Joanisse, Sec.-Trés., 189, ch Montcerf, Lytton J0W 1N0 – 819/449-5205, Fax: 819/449-5205 |
| Macamic (P) | 549 | Abitibi-Ouest | Rouyn-Noranda-Témiscamingue | Abitibi-Ouest | Joëlle Rancourt, Sec.-Trés., 6, 7e av est, CP 277, Macamic J0Z 2S0 – 819/782-4867, Fax: 819/782-4886 |
| MACAMIC | 1,711 | Abitibi-Ouest | Rouyn-Noranda-Témiscamingue | Abitibi-Ouest | Denis Bédard, Sec.-Trés., 1, 7e av ouest, CP 128, Macamic J0Z 2S0 – 819/782-4604, Fax: 819/782-4283 |
| Maddington (Canton) | 428 | Arthabaska | Lotbinière | Nicolet-Yamaska | Robert Desaulniers, Sec.-Trés., 572, rue Principale, CP 339, Daveluyville G0Z 1C0 – 819/367-2818, Fax: 819/367-2143 |
| Magog (Canton) | 5,216 | Memphrémagog | Brome-Missisquoi | Orford | Gilbert Cyr, Sec.-Trés., 61, ch Southière, Magog J1X 5R9 – 819/843-3339, Fax: 819/843-9840 |
| MAGOG | 14,050 | Memphrémagog | Brome-Missisquoi | Orford | Michel Pinault, Gref., 7, rue Principale est, Magog J1X 1Y4 – 819/843-6501, Fax: 819/843-1091 |
| MALARTIC | 4,154 | Vallée-de-l'Or | Abitibi | Abitibi-Est | Vacant, Gref., 901, rue Royale, CP 3090, Malartic J0Y 1Z0 – 819/757-3611, Fax: 819/757-3084 |
| MANIWAKI | 4,527 | La Vallée-de-la-Gatineau | Pontiac-Gatineau-Labelle | Gatineau | Claire Prud'homme, Gref., 186, rue Principale sud, Maniwaki J9E 1Z9 – 819/449-2800, Fax: 819/449-7078 |
| Manseau (V) | 559 | Bécancour | Lotbinière | Lotbinière | Mario Geoffroy, Sec.-Trés., 200, rue Roux, CP 200, Manseau G0X 1V0 – 819/356-2450, Fax: 819/356-2721 |
| Mansfield-et-Pontefract (Cantons) | 2,115 | Pontiac | Pontiac-Gatineau-Labelle | Pontiac | Donald Marion, Sec.-Trés., 300, rue Principale, CP 880, Mansfield J0X 1V0 – 819/683-2944, Fax: 819/683-3590 |
| MAPLE GROVE | 2,606 | Beauharnois-Salaberry | Beauharnois-Salaberry | Châteauguay | Guylaine Côté, Gref., 149, rue St-Laurent, Maple Grove J6N 1K2 – 514/225-5061, Fax: 514/429-6540 |
| Marchand (Mun.) | 1,430 | Antoine-Labelle | Pontiac-Gatineau-Labelle | Labelle | Claire Coulombe, Sec.-Trés., 106, rue Principale sud, CP 695, L'Annonciation J0T 1T0 – 819/275-3202, Fax: 819/275-1318 |
| Maria (Mun.) | 2,581 | Avignon | Matapédia-Matane | Bonaventure | Gilbert Leblanc, Sec.-Trés., 26, route des Geais, Maria G0C 1Y0 – 418/759-3883, Fax: 418/759-3059 |
| Maricourt (Mun.) | 458 | Le Val-St-François | Shefford | Johnson | Lucille Boissonneault, Sec.-Trés., RR#1, Racine J0E 1Y0 – 514/532-2243, Fax: 514/532-2243 |
| MARIEVILLE | 5,510 | Rouville | Chambly | Iberville | Marie-Claude Thibault, Gref., 682, rue St-Charles, Marieville J3M 1P9 – 514/460-4444, Fax: 514/460-2770 |
| Marsoui (V) | 440 | Denis-Riverin | Matapédia-Matane | Matane | Nancy Leclerc, Sec.-Trés., 1, rue du Quai, CP 130, Marsoui G0E 1S0 – 418/288-5552, Fax: 418/288-5104 |
| Marston (Canton) | 595 | Le Granit | Frontenac-Mégantic | Mégantic-Compton | Jeanne-Mance Roy, Sec.-Trés., 344, rte 263 sud, RR#1, Nantes G0Y 1G0 – 819/583-0435 |
| Martinville (Mun.) | 476 | Coaticook | Compton-Stanstead | Mégantic-Compton | Roland Gascon, Sec.-Trés., 233, rue Principale est, Martinville J0B 2A0 – 819/835-5390, Fax: 819/835-5390 |
| MASCOUCHE | 28,097 | Les Moulins | Repentigny | Masson | Danielle Lord, Gref., 3034, ch Ste-Marie, Mascouche J7K 1P1 – 514/474-4133, Fax: 514/474-6401 |
| Maskinongé (V) | 1,052 | Maskinongé | Trois-Rivières | Maskinongé | Marie-Josée Cournoyer, Sec.-Trés., 36B, rue St-Denis, Maskinongé J0K 1N0 – 819/227-2515, Fax: 819/227-2061 |
| MASSON-ANGERS | 7,989 | Outaouais (Urb. Com.) | Gatineau | Papineau | Pierre Hayes, Sec.-Trés., 57, ch de Montréal est, CP 670, Masson-Angers J8M 1K7 – 819/986-1250, Fax: 819/986-9539 |
| Massueville (V) | 592 | Le Bas-Richelieu | Richelieu | Richelieu | Bernard Choquette, Sec.-Trés., 973, rue Royale, CP 90, Massueville J0G 1K0 – 514/788-2957, Fax: 514/788-2843 |
| MATAGAMI | 2,243 | Terr. du Nouveau-Québec | Abitibi | Ungava | Jean-Robert Gagnon, Gref., 195, boul de Matagami, CP 160, Matagami J0Y 2A0 – 819/739-2541, Fax: 819/739-4278 |
| MATANE | 12,364 | Matane | Matapédia-Matane | Matane | André Lavoie, Gref., 230, av St-Jérôme, Matane G4W 3A2 – 418/562-2333, Fax: 418/562-4869 |
| Matapédia (P) | 749 | Avignon | Matapédia-Matane | Bonaventure | Aimée Firth, Sec.-Trés., 1, rue de l'Hôtel-de-Ville, CP 207, Matapédia G0J 1V0 – 418/865-2917, Fax: 418/865-2828 |
| Mayo (Mun.) | 401 | Papineau | Argenteuil-Papineau | Papineau | Michel Vézina, Sec.-Trés., 140, rue Joseph, CP 300, Buckingham J8L 2X5 – 819/986-2586, Fax: 819/986-2586 |

Urban Centres (Villes) in CAPITALS; Villages marked (V); Townships/Cantons marked (Canton);United townships/Cantons unis marked (Cantons); Parishes marked (P); Municipalities marked (Mun.).; Northern villages/Villages nordiques marked (NV); Cree Villages/Villages Cris marked (VC); Naskapi Villages/Villages Naskapi marked (VN); In the third column, Urban Community/Communauté Urbaine marked Urb. Com. An in-depth listing for municipalities marked with * appears in Part 2 (check Index for page numbers).

| MUNICIPALITY | 1996 POP. | REGIONAL COUNTY MUN. | FEDERAL ELECTORAL DISTRICT | PROVINCIAL ELECTORAL DISTRICT | CONTACT PERSON WITH ADDRESS, PHONE & FAX |
|---|---|---|---|---|---|
| McMasterville (Mun.) | 3,813 | La Vallée-du-Richelieu | Chambly | Borduas | Pierre Landry, Sec.-Trés., 255, boul Constable, McMasterville J3G 6N9 – 514/467-3580, Fax: 514/467-2493 |
| McWatters (Mun.) | 1,914 | Rouyn-Noranda | Rouyn-Noranda-Témiscamingue | Rouyn-Noranda-Témiscamingue | Lise Paquet, Sec.-Trés., 200, rue de l'Eglise, McWatters J9X 5B7 – 819/762-2725, Fax: 819/762-1842 |
| Melbourne (Canton) | 977 | Le Val-St-François | Johnson | Johnson | John Barley, Sec.-Trés., 1257, route 243, CP 4, Melbourne J0B 2B0 – 819/826-3555, Fax: 819/826-3981 |
| Melbourne (V) | 531 | Le Val-St-François | Richmond-Arthabaska | Johnson | Donna Smith, Sec.-Trés., 22, rue Principale, CP 70, Melbourne J0B 2B0 – 819/826-6200, Fax: 819/826-6200 |
| Melocheville (V) | 2,486 | Beauharnois-Salaberry | Beauharnois-Salaberry | Salaberry-Soulanges | Normand Charette, Sec.-Trés., 380, boul Edgar-Hébert, Melocheville J0S 1J0 – 514/429-6426, Fax: 514/429-2346 |
| MERCIER | 9,059 | Roussillon | Châteauguay | Châteauguay | Chantal Bergeron, Gref., 794, boul St-Jean-Baptiste, Mercier J6R 2L3 – 514/691-6090, Fax: 514/691-6529 |
| Messines (Mun.) | 1,517 | La Vallée-de-la-Gatineau | Pontiac-Gatineau-Labelle | Gatineau | Paul Beaudoin, Sec.-Trés., 3, ch de la Ferme, CP 69, Messines J0X 2J0 – 819/465-2323, Fax: 819/465-2943 |
| MÉTABETCH-OUAN | 3,474 | Lac-St-Jean-Est | Lac-St-Jean | Lac-St-Jean | Laurent Rheault, Gref., 81, rue St-André, CP 99, Métabetchouan G0W 2A0 – 418/349-2060, Fax: 418/349-2395 |
| Métis-sur-Mer (V) | 211 | La Mitis | Rimouski-Mitis-Mitis | Matane | Karen Turriff, Sec.-Trés., 31, rue de la Station, CP 44, Métis-sur-Mer G0J 1W0 – 418/936-3420, Fax: 418/936-3838 |
| Milan (Mun.) | 281 | Le Granit | Frontenac-Mégantic | Mégantic-Compton | Suzanne Durivage, Sec.-Trés., 403, rang Ste-Marie, CP 54, Milan G0Y 1E0 – 819/657-4527, Fax: 819/657-4527 |
| Mille-Isles (Mun.) | 1,157 | Argenteuil | Argenteuil-Papineau | Argenteuil | Chantal St-Pierre, Sec.-Trés., 1262, ch de Mille-Isles, Mille-Isles J0R 1A0 – 514/438-2958, Fax: 514/438-6157 |
| MIRABEL | 22,689 | Mirabel | Argenteuil-Papineau | Argenteuil | Suzanne Mireault, Gref., 14111, rue St-Jean, Mirabel J0N 1R0 – 514/476-0360, Fax: 514/475-7195 |
| MISTASSINI | 6,904 | Roberval | Roberval | Roberval | Christian Painchaud, Gref., 173, boul St-Michel, Mistassini G8M 1E9 – 418/276-3685, Fax: 418/276-8164 |
| Mistissini (VC) | | | Abitibi | Ungava | Thomas Neeposh, Sec.-Trés., 187, rue Main, Mistissini G0W 1C0 – 418/923-3253, Fax: 418/923-3115 |
| Moffet (Mun.) | 226 | Témiscamingue | Rouyn-Noranda-Témiscamingue | Rouyn-Noranda-Témiscamingue | Linda Roy, Sec.-Trés., 14D, rue Principale, CP 89, Moffet J0Z 2W0 – 819/747-6116 |
| MOISIE | 897 | Sept-Rivières | Manicouagan | Duplessis | Ronald Bernatchez, Sec.-Trés., 1085, rue Lamothe, CP 340, Moisie G0G 2B0 – 418/927-2122, Fax: 418/927-2653 |
| Mont-Carmel (Mun.) | 1,287 | Kamouraska | Kamouraska-Rivière-du-Loup-Témiscouata | Kamouraska-Témiscouata | Léa Lévesque, Sec.-Trés., 22, rue de la Fabrique, Mont-Carmel G0L 1W0 – 418/498-2050, Fax: 418/489-2522 |
| MONT-JOLI | 6,267 | La Mitis | Rimouski-Mitis-Mitis | Matapédia | Roger Boudreau, Gref., 40, av de l'Hôtel-de-Ville, Mont-Joli G5H 1W8 – 418/775-7285, Fax: 418/775-6320 |
| MONT-LAURIER | 8,007 | Antoine-Labelle | Pontiac-Gatineau-Labelle | Labelle | Blandine Boulianne, Gref., 485, rue Mercier, Mont-Laurier J9L 3N8 – 819/623-1221, Fax: 819/623-4840 |
| Mont-Lebel (Mun.) | 355 | Rimouski-Neigette | Rimouski-Mitis-Mitis | Rimouski | Denise Pelletier, Sec.-Trés., 63, rang 3 & 4 ouest, Mont-Lebel G0K 1J0 – 418/735-5772, Fax: 418/735-5772 |
| Mont-Rolland (V) | 2,882 | Les Pays-d'en-Haut | Laurentides | Bertrand | Yves Desmarais, Sec.-Trés., 1425, rue Morin, CP 280, Mont-Rolland J0R 1G0 – 514/229-2200, Fax: 514/229-6842 |
| MONT-ROYAL | 18,282 | Montréal (Urb. Com.) | Mont-Royal | Mont-Royal | Josée C.-Katz, Gref., 90, av Roosevelt, Mont-Royal H3R 1Z5 – 514/734-2900, Fax: 514/734-3084 |
| Mont-St-Grégoire (Mun.) | 3,112 | Le Haut-Richelieu | St-Jean | Iberville | Christianne Pouliot, Sec.-Trés., 225, rue St-Joseph sud, CP 120, Mont-St-Grégoire J0J 1K0 – 514/347-5376, Fax: 514/347-9200 |
| MONT-ST-HILAIRE | 13,064 | La Vallée-du-Richelieu | Chambly | Borduas | Estelle Simard, Gref., 100, rue du Centre-Civique, Mont-St-Hilaire J3H 3M8 – 514/467-2854, Fax: 514/467-6460 |
| Mont-St-Michel (Mun.) | 616 | Antoine-Labelle | Pontiac-Gatineau-Labelle | Labelle | Lucie Gagnon, Sec.-Trés., 94, rue de l'Église, Mont-St-Michel J0W 1P0 – 819/587-3093, Fax: 819/587-3781 |
| Mont-St-Pierre (V) | 288 | Denis-Riverin | Matapédia-Matane | Gaspé | Marianne Ouellet, Sec.-Trés., 102, rue Cloutier, CP 9, Mont-St-Pierre G0E 1V0 – 418/797-2898, Fax: 418/797-2307 |
| Mont-Tremblant (Mun.) | 977 | Les Laurentides | Laurentides | Labelle | Daniel-G. Décarie, Sec.-Trés., 1875, ch Principal, CP 179, Mont-Tremblant J0T 1Z0 – 819/425-8671, Fax: 819/425-5091 |

Urban Centres (Villes) in CAPITALS; Villages marked (V); Townships/Cantons marked (Canton);United townships/Cantons unis marked (Cantons); Parishes marked (P); Municipalities marked (Mun.).; Northern villages/Villages nordiques marked (NV); Cree Villages/Villages Cris marked (VC); Naskapi Villages/Villages Naskapi marked (VN); In the third column, Urban Community/Communauté Urbaine marked Urb. Com. An in-depth listing for municipalities marked with * appears in Part 2 (check Index for page numbers).

| MUNICIPALITY | 1996 POP. | REGIONAL COUNTY MUN. | FEDERAL ELECTORAL DISTRICT | PROVINCIAL ELECTORAL DISTRICT | CONTACT PERSON WITH ADDRESS, PHONE & FAX |
|---|---|---|---|---|---|
| Montbeillard (Mun.) | 677 | Rouyn-Noranda | Rouyn-Noranda-Témiscamingue | Rouyn-Noranda-Témiscamingue | Claude Hachey, Sec.-Trés., 551, rue du Village, CP 10, Montbeillard J0Z 2X0 – 819/797-2985, Fax: 819/797-2390 |
| Montcalm (Mun.) | 449 | Les Laurentides | Argenteuil-Papineau | Argenteuil | Lucie Tremblay-Côté, Sec.-Trés., 10, rue de l'Hôtel-de-Ville, Weir J0T 2V0 – 819/687-2836, Fax: 819/687-2836 |
| Montcerf (Mun.) | 474 | La Vallée-de-la-Gatineau | Pontiac-Gatineau-Labelle | Gatineau | Liliane Crytes, Sec.-Trés., 18, rue Principale nord, Montcerf J0W 1N0 – 819/449-4578, Fax: 819/449-7310 |
| Montebello (V) | 1,066 | Papineau | Argenteuil-Papineau | Papineau | Charles-Guy Beauchamp, Sec.-Trés., 550, rue Notre-Dame, CP 190, Montebello J0V 1L0 – 819/423-5123, Fax: 819/423-5703 |
| MONTMAGNY | 11,885 | Montmagny | Bellechasse-Montmagny-L'Islet | Montmagny-L'Islet | Louise Bhérer, Gref., 134, rue St-Jean-Baptiste est, Montmagny G5V 1K6 – 418/248-3361, Fax: 418/248-0923 |
| Montpellier (Mun.) | 835 | Papineau | Argenteuil-Papineau | Papineau | Henriette Dupuis, Sec.-Trés., 4, rue du Bosquet, Montpellier J0V 1M0 – 819/428-3663, Fax: 819/428-1221 |
| *MONTRÉAL | 1,016,376 | Montréal (Urb. Com.) | Ahuntsic; Anjou-Rivière-des-Prairies; Bourassa; Hochelaga-Maisonneuve; LaSalle-Émard; Laurier-Ste-Marie; Mercier; Mont-Royal; Notre-Dame-de-Grâce-Lachine; Outremont; Papineau-St-Denis; Rosemont; Westmount-Ville-Marie; St-Laurent-Cartierville; St-Léonard-St-Michel; Verdun-St Henri | Acadie; Anjou; Bourassa; Bourget; Crémazie; D'Arcy McGee; Gouin; Hochelaga-Maisonneuve; Jeanne-Mance; LaFontaine; Laurier-Dorion; Mercier; Mont-Royal; Notre-Dame de Grâce; Outremont; Pointe-aux-Trembles; Rosemont; St-Henri-Ste-Anne; St-Laurent; Ste-Marie-St-Jacques; Viau; Viger; Westmount-St-Louis | Léon Laberge, Directeur, Service du greffe, Hôtel de Ville, 275, rue Notre-Dame est, Montréal H2Y 1C6 – 514/872-1111, Fax: 514/872-5655, URL: http://www.ville.montreal.qc.ca/ |
| MONTRÉAL-EST | 3,523 | Montréal (Urb. Com.) | Mercier | Pointe-aux-Trembles | André Lesage, Gref., 11370, rue Notre-Dame est, Montréal-Est H1B 2W6 – 514/645-7431, Fax: 514/645-0107 |
| *MONTRÉAL-NORD | 81,581 | Montréal (Urb. Com.) | Bourassa | Bourassa; Sauvé | Hélène Simoneau, Gref., 4242, Place de l'Hôtel-de-Ville, Montréal-Nord H1H 1S5 – 514/328-4000, Fax: 514/328-4299 |
| MONTRÉAL-OUEST | 5,254 | Montréal (Urb. Com.) | Notre-Dame-de-Grâce-Lachine | Notre-Dame-de-Grâce | Georgina Mastromonaco, Gref., 50, av Westminster sud, Montréal-Ouest H4X 1Y7 – 514/481-8125, Fax: 514/481-4554 |
| Morin-Heights (Mun.) | 2,332 | Les Pays-d'en-Haut | Argenteuil-Papineau | Argenteuil | Dominique Valiquette, Sec.-Trés., 823, rue du Village, Morin-Heights J0R 1H0 – 514/226-3232, Fax: 514/226-8786 |
| Mulgrave-et-Derry (Cantons) | 250 | Papineau | Argenteuil-Papineau | Papineau | Michel-A. Vézina, Sec.-Trés., 140, rue Joseph, CP 300, Buckingham J8L 2X5 – 819/986-2586, Fax: 819/986-2586 |
| MURDOCHVILLE | 1,595 | La Côte-de-Gaspé | Bonaventure-Gaspé-Îles-de-la-Madeleine-Pabok | Gaspé | Daniel Bujold, Sec.-Trés., 635, 5e rue, CP 1120, Murdochville G0E 1W0 – 418/784-2536, Fax: 418/784-2607 |
| Namur (Mun.) | 543 | Papineau | Argenteuil-Papineau | Papineau | Sharon Besson, Sec.-Trés., 331, rue de l'Hôtel-de-Ville, Namur J0V 1N0 – 819/426-2457, Fax: 819/426-3074 |
| Nantes (Mun.) | 1,361 | Le Granit | Frontenac-Mégantic | Mégantic-Compton | Robert Busque, Sec.-Trés., 1244, rue Principale, CP 60, Nantes G0Y 1G0 – 819/547-3655 |
| Napierville (V) | 3,004 | Les Jardins-de-Napierville | Beauharnois-Salaberry | Beauharnois-Huntingdon | Ginette Leblanc-Pruneau, Sec.-Trés., 260, rue de l'Église, CP 1120, Napierville J0J 1L0 – 514/245-7210, Fax: 514/245-7691 |
| Natashquan (Canton) | 356 | Minganie | Manicouagan | Duplessis | Lorraine Hounsell, Sec.-Trés., 29, ch d'en-Haut, CP 99, Natashquan G0G 2E0 – 418/726-3362, Fax: 418/726-3698 |
| Nédélec (Canton) | 474 | Témiscamingue | Rouyn-Noranda-Témiscamingue | Rouyn-Noranda-Témiscamingue | Anny Cloutier, Sec.-Trés., 33, rue Principale, CP 70, Nédélec J0Z 2Z0 – 819/784-3311, Fax: 819/784-2126 |
| Nemiscau (VC) | | | Abitibi | Ungava | Lawrence Jimiken, Gref., 2, rue Lakeshore, Nemiscau J0M 3B0 – 819/673-2512, Fax: 819/673-2542 |
| Neuville (V) | 1,013 | Portneuf | Portneuf | Portneuf | Ysa Brochu, Sec.-Trés., 230, rue du Père-Rhéaume, Neuville G0A 2R0 – 418/876-2280, Fax: 418/876-3349 |

Urban Centres (Villes) in CAPITALS; Villages marked (V); Townships/Cantons marked (Canton);United townships/Cantons unis marked (Cantons); Parishes marked (P); Municipalities marked (Mun.).; Northern villages/Villages nordiques marked (NV); Cree Villages/Villages Cris marked (VC); Naskapi Villages/Villages Naskapi marked (VN); In the third column, Urban Community/Communauté Urbaine marked Urb. Com. An in-depth listing for municipalities marked with * appears in Part 2 (check Index for page numbers).

| MUNICIPALITY | 1996 POP. | REGIONAL COUNTY MUN. | FEDERAL ELECTORAL DISTRICT | PROVINCIAL ELECTORAL DISTRICT | CONTACT PERSON WITH ADDRESS, PHONE & FAX |
|---|---|---|---|---|---|
| New Carlisle (Mun.) | 1,538 | Bonaventure | Bonaventure-Gaspé-Îles-de-la-Madeleine-Pabok | Bonaventure | Donald Kerr, Sec.-Trés., 138, rue Main, CP 40, New Carlisle G0C 1Z0 – 418/752-3141, Fax: 418/752-3140 |
| New Glasgow (V) | 157 | La Rivière-du-Nord | Berthier-Montcalm | Rousseau | France Massé, Sec.-Trés., 819, rue Raby, CP 35, New Glasgow J0R 1J0 – 514/436-2894, Fax: 514/436-2894 |
| NEW RICHMOND | 3,941 | Bonaventure | Bonaventure-Gaspé-Îles-de-la-Madeleine-Pabok | Bonaventure | Line Cormier, Gref., 99, Place Suzanne-Guité, CP 338, New Richmond G0C 2B0 – 418/392-7001, Fax: 418/392-5331 |
| Newport (Canton) | 729 | Le Haut-St-François | Compton-Stanstead | Mégantic-Compton | Andrée Gagnon, Sec.-Trés., 1452, rte 212, CP 730, Cookshire J0B 1M0 – 819/875-5475, Fax: 819/875-5884 |
| Newport (Mun.) | 2,029 | Pabok | Bonaventure-Gaspé-Îles-de-la-Madeleine-Pabok | Bonaventure | Georges-Walter Smith, Sec.-Trés., 300, rte 132, CP 7, Newport G0C 2A0 – 418/777-2281, Fax: 418/777-2865 |
| NICOLET | 4,352 | Nicolet-Yamaska | Richelieu | Nicolet-Yamaska | Monique Corriveau, Gref., 180, rue de Mgr-Panet, Nicolet J3T 1S6 – 819/293-6901, Fax: 819/293-6767 |
| Nicolet-Sud (Mun.) | 367 | Nicolet-Yamaska | Richelieu | Nicolet-Yamaska | Claude Bouchard, Sec.-Trés., 420, rue Houde, St-Célestin J0C 1G0 – 819/229-3642, Fax: 819/229-1149 |
| Norbertville (V) | 255 | Arthabaska | Richmond-Arthabaska | Arthabaska | Gilles Gauvreau, Sec.-Trés., 17, rue Landry, Norbertville G0P 1B0 – 819/369-9294 |
| NORMANDIN | 3,873 | Maria-Chapdelaine | Roberval | Roberval | Florian Girard, Gref., 1048, rue St-Cyrille, Normandin G8M 4R9 – 418/274-2004, Fax: 418/274-7171 |
| Normétal (Mun.) | 1,129 | Abitibi-Ouest | Rouyn-Noranda-Témiscamingue | Abitibi-Ouest | Gaétan Petit, Sec.-Trés., 59, 1re rue, CP 308, Normétal J0Z 3A0 – 819/788-2550, Fax: 819/788-2730 |
| North-Hatley (V) | 737 | Memphrémagog | Compton-Stanstead | Orford | Solange Morisette, Sec.-Trés., 210, rue Main, CP 30, North Hatley J0B 2C0 – 819/842-2754, Fax: 819/842-4501 |
| Northfield (Mun.) | 516 | La Vallée-de-la-Gatineau | Pontiac-Gatineau-Labelle | Gatineau | Yvon Blanchard, Sec.-Trés., RR#1, Gracefield J0X 1W0 – 819/463-2182, Fax: 819/463-2757 |
| Notre-Dame-Auxiliatrice-de-Buckland (P) | 844 | Bellechasse | Bellechasse-Montmagny-L'Islet | Bellechasse | Jocelyne Nadeau, Sec.-Trés., 4340, rue Principale, CP 40, Buckland G0R 1G0 – 418/789-3119, Fax: 418/789-3535 |
| Notre-Dame-de-Bon-Secours (Mun.) | 1,516 | Rouville | Chambly | Chambly | Lucie Sabourin, Sec.-Trés., 387, ch Marieville, Notre-Dame-De-Bon-Secours J3L 4A7 – 514/658-2662, Fax: 514/658-5954 |
| Notre-Dame-de-Bon-Secours Nord (P) | 273 | Papineau | Argenteuil-Papineau | Papineau | Gilles Gignac, Sec.-Trés., 550, rue Notre-Dame, CP 310, Montebello J0V 1L0 – 819/423-5575, Fax: 819/423-5575 |
| Notre-Dame-de-Ham (Mun.) | 343 | Arthabaska | Richmond-Arthabaska | Richmond | Christiane Leblanc, Sec.-Trés., 25, rue de l'Église, Notre-Dame-de-Ham G0P 1C0 – 819/344-5806, Fax: 819/344-5806 |
| Notre-Dame-de-la-Merci (Mun.) | 726 | Matawinie | Berthier-Montcalm | Bertrand | Jean-Maurice Gadoury, Sec.-Trés., 1900, montée de la Réserve, Notre-Dame-de-la-Merci J0T 2A0 – 819/424-2113, Fax: 819/424-7347 |
| Notre-Dame-de-la-Paix (P) | 688 | Papineau | Argenteuil-Papineau | Papineau | Hugues Servant, Sec.-Trés., 283, rue Notre-Dame, CP 10, Notre-Dame-de-la-Paix J0V 1P0 – 819/522-6610, Fax: 819/522-6610 |
| Notre-Dame-de-la-Salette (Mun.) | 678 | Les Collines-de-l'Outaouais | Pontiac-Gatineau-Labelle | Papineau | Jean-Pierre Valiquette, Sec.-Trés., 2, rue Rollin, CP 59, Notre-Dame-de-la-Salette J0X 2L0 – 819/766-2533, Fax: 819/766-2533 |
| Notre-Dame-de-l'Île-Perrot (P) | 7,059 | Vaudreuil-Soulanges | Vaudreuil-Soulanges | Vaudreuil | Serge Jolin, Sec.-Trés., 21, rue de l'Église, Notre-Dame-de-l'Île-Perrot J7V 8P4 – 514/453-4128, Fax: 514/453-8961 |
| Notre-Dame-de-Lorette (Mun.) | 234 | Maria-Chapdelaine | Roberval | Roberval | Michèle Tremblay, Sec.-Trés., 54, rue Principale, Notre-Dame-de-Lorette G0W 1B0 – 418/276-1934, Fax: 418/276-1934 |
| Notre-Dame-de-Lourdes (P) | 752 | L'Érable | Lotbiniére | Lotbinière | Gervaise Côté, Sec.-Trés., 830, rue Principale, Lourdes G0S 1T0 – 819/385-4315, Fax: 819/385-4315 |
| Notre-Dame-de-Lourdes (P) | 2,087 | Joliette | Joliette | Joliette | François Hétu, Sec.-Trés., 4050, rue Principale, Notre-Dame-de-Lourdes J0K 1K0 – 514/759-2277, Fax: 514/759-2055 |
| Notre-Dame-de-Montauban (Mun.) | 909 | Mékinac | Champlain | Portneuf | Manon Frenette, Sec.-Trés., 555, av des Loisirs, CP 69, Montauban G0X 1W0 – 418/336-2640, Fax: 418/336-2353 |
| Notre-Dame-de-Pierreville (P) | 813 | Nicolet-Yamaska | Richelieu | Nicolet-Yamaska | Micheline Bénard, Sec.-Trés., 48, rue Principale, Notre-Dame-de-Pierreville J0G 1G0 – 514/568-2087, Fax: 514/568-6059 |
| Notre-Dame-de-Pontmain (Mun.) | 581 | Antoine-Labelle | Pontiac-Gatineau-Labelle | Labelle | Micheline Grenier, Sec.-Trés., 1027, rue Principale, Notre-Dame-de-Pontmain J0W 1S0 – 819/597-2382, Fax: 819/597-2382 |

Urban Centres (Villes) in CAPITALS; Villages marked (V); Townships/Cantons marked (Canton);United townships/Cantons unis marked (Cantons); Parishes marked (P); Municipalities marked (Mun.).; Northern villages/Villages nordiques marked (NV); Cree Villages/Villages Cris marked (VC); Naskapi Villages/Villages Naskapi marked (VN); In the third column, Urban Community/Communauté Urbaine marked Urb. Com. An in-depth listing for municipalities marked with * appears in Part 2 (check Index for page numbers).

| MUNICIPALITY | 1996 POP. | REGIONAL COUNTY MUN. | FEDERAL ELECTORAL DISTRICT | PROVINCIAL ELECTORAL DISTRICT | CONTACT PERSON WITH ADDRESS, PHONE & FAX |
|---|---|---|---|---|---|
| Notre-Dame-de-Portneuf (P) | 1,727 | Portneuf | Portneuf | Portneuf | Jacques Chevalier, Sec.-Trés., 500, rue Notre-Dame, CP 218, Notre-Dame-de-Portneuf G0A 2Z0 – 418/286-6641, Fax: 418/286-4493 |
| Notre-Dame-de-St-Hyacinthe (P) | 866 | Les Maskoutains | St-Hyacinthe-Bagot | St-Hyacinthe | Jean-Luc Giard, Sec.-Trés., 4740, rue Gouin, St-Hyacinthe J2S 1E1 – 514/773-3720, Fax: 514/773-5611 |
| Notre-Dame-de-Stanbridge (P) | 814 | Brome-Missisquoi | Brome-Missisquoi | Brome-Missisquoi | Gaétan Lanoue, Sec.-Trés., 900, rue Principale, CP 40, Notre-Dame-de-Stanbridge J0J 1M0 – 514/296-4710, Fax: 514/296-4710 |
| Notre-Dame-des-Anges (P) | 370 | Portneuf | Champlain | Taschereau | Colette Huot, Sec.-Trés., 260, boul Langelier, Québec G1K 5N1 – 418/529-0931, Fax: 418/529-0813 |
| Notre-Dame-des-Bois (Mun.) | 654 | Le Granit | Frontenac-Mégantic | Mégantic-Compton | Guylaine Blais, Sec.-Trés., 35, côte de l'Église, Notre-Dame-des-Bois J0B 2E0 – 819/888-2724, Fax: 819/888-2904 |
| Notre-Dame-des-Monts (Mun.) | 913 | Charlevoix-Est | Charlevoix | Charlevoix | Nicole Williams, Sec.-Trés., 15, rue Principale, Notre-Dame-des-Monts G0T 1L0 – 418/439-3452, Fax: 418/439-3452 |
| Notre-Dame-des-Neiges des Trois-Pistoles (P) | 1,318 | Les Basques | Kamouraska-Rivière-du-Loup-Témiscouata-Les Basques-Les Basques | Rivière-du-Loup | Danielle Ouellet, Sec.-Trés., 4, 2e rang Centre, CP 729, Trois-Pistoles G0L 4K0 – 418/851-3009, Fax: 418/851-3169 |
| Notre-Dame-des-Pins (P) | 1,025 | Beauce-Sartigan | Beauce | Beauce-Sud | Claude Poulin, Sec.-Trés., 2790, 1re av, Notre-Dame-des-Pins G0M 1K0 – 418/774-9718, Fax: 418/774-9718 |
| Notre-Dame-des-Prairies (Mun.) | 6,837 | Joliette | Joliette | Joliette | Carol Henri, Sec.-Trés., 225, boul Antonio-Barrette, Notre-Dame-des-Prairies J6E 1E7 – 514/759-7741, Fax: 514/759-6255 |
| Notre-Dame-des-Sept-Douleurs (P) | 42 | Rivière-du-Loup | Kamouraska-Rivière-du-Loup-Témiscouata-Les Basques-Les Basques | Rivière-du-Loup | Gérald Dionne Jr., Sec.-Trés., École Fraser, Île-Verte G0L 1K0 – 418/898-3451, Fax: 418/898-3492 |
| Notre-Dame-du-Bon-Conseil (P) | 956 | Drummond | Drummond | Richmond | Pierrette Bourgeois-Richard, Sec.-Trés., 1428, route 122, Notre-Dame-du-Bon-Conseil J0C 1A0 – 819/336-5374, Fax: 819/336-2389 |
| Notre-Dame-du-Bon-Conseil (V) | 1,343 | Drummond | Drummond | Richmond | Vacant, Sec.-Trés., 541, rue Notre-Dame, CP 128, Notre-Dame-du-Bon-Conseil J0C 1A0 – 819/336-2744, Fax: 819/336-2030 |
| NOTRE-DAME-DU-LAC | 2,193 | Témiscouata | Kamouraska-Rivière-du-Loup-Témiscouata-Les Basques-Les Basques | Kamouraska-Témiscouata | Hermel Roussel, Gref., 5, rue de l'Hôtel-de-Ville, CP 158, Notre-Dame-du-Lac G0L 1X0 – 418/899-6743, Fax: 418/899-2041 |
| Notre-Dame-du-Laus (Mun.) | 1,378 | Antoine-Labelle | Pontiac-Gatineau-Labelle | Labelle | Yves Larocque, Sec.-Trés., 66, rue Principale, CP 10, Notre-Dame-du-Laus J0X 2M0 – 819/767-2247, Fax: 819/767-3102 |
| Notre-Dame-du-Mont-Carmel (P) | 4,835 | Le Centre-de-la-Mauricie | St-Maurice | St-Maurice | Jean Lachance, Sec.-Trés., 3860, rue de l' Hôtel de Ville, Notre-Dame-du-Mont-Carmel G0X 3J0 – 819/375-9856, Fax: 819/373-4045 |
| Notre-Dame-du-Mont-Carmel (P) | 940 | Le Haut-Richelieu | St-Jean | St-Jean | Sylvie Larose-Asselin, Sec.-Trés., 82, rte 202, Notre-Dame-du-Mont-Carmel J0J 1J0 – 514/246-2692, Fax: 514/246-2692 |
| Notre-Dame-du-Nord (Mun.) | 1,250 | Témiscamingue | Témiscamingue | Rouyn-Noranda-Témiscamingue | Lucien Beauregard, Sec.-Trés., 71, rue Principale, CP 160, Notre-Dame-du-Nord J0Z 3B0 – 819/723-2294, Fax: 819/723-2483 |
| Notre-Dame-du-Portage (P) | 1,209 | Rivière-du-Loup | Kamouraska-Rivière-du-Loup-Témiscouata-Les Basques-Les Basques | Rivière-du-Loup | Eric Bérubé, Sec.-Trés., 560, route de la Montagne, CP 69, Notre-Dame-du-Portage G0L 1Y0 – 418/862-9163, Fax: 418/862-9163 |
| Notre-Dame-du-Rosaire (Mun.) | 394 | Montmagny | Lac-St-Jean | Montmagny-L'Islet | Maryse Bernard, Sec.-Trés., 22, rue Jolicoeur, Notre-Dame-du-Rosaire G0R 2H0 – 418/469-2802, Fax: 418/469-2802 |
| Notre-Dame-du-Sacré-Coeur-d'Issoudun (P) | 759 | Lotbinière | Lotbinière | Lotbinière | Suzanne Therrien-Croteau, Sec.-Trés., 455, route de l'Église, Issoudun G0S 1L0 – 418/728-2006, Fax: 418/728-2303 |
| Nouvelle (Mun.) | 2,009 | Avignon | Matapédia-Matane | Bonaventure | Lise Castilloux, Sec.-Trés., 470, rue Francoeur, CP 68, Nouvelle G0C 2E0 – 418/794-2253, Fax: 418/794-2076 |
| Noyan (Mun.) | 1,012 | Le Haut-Richelieu | Brome-Missisquoi | Iberville | Brenda McDonald, Sec.-Trés., 1312, ch de la Petite-France, CP 8, Noyan J0J 1B0 – 514/294-2689, Fax: 514/294-2175 |
| Ogden (Mun.) | 769 | Memphrémagog | Compton-Stanstead | Orford | Faye Dustin, Sec.-Trés., 70, ch Ogden, Beebe J0B 1E0 – 819/876-7117, Fax: 819/876-2121 |

Urban Centres (Villes) in CAPITALS; Villages marked (V); Townships/Cantons marked (Canton);United townships/Cantons unis marked (Cantons); Parishes marked (P); Municipalities marked (Mun.).; Northern villages/Villages nordiques marked (NV); Cree Villages/Villages Cris marked (VC); Naskapi Villages/Villages Naskapi marked (VN); In the third column, Urban Community/Communauté Urbaine marked Urb. Com. An in-depth listing for municipalities marked with * appears in Part 2 (check Index for page numbers).

| MUNICIPALITY | 1996 POP. | REGIONAL COUNTY MUN. | FEDERAL ELECTORAL DISTRICT | PROVINCIAL ELECTORAL DISTRICT | CONTACT PERSON WITH ADDRESS, PHONE & FAX |
|---|---|---|---|---|---|
| Oka (Mun.) | 1,514 | Deux-Montagnes | Argenteuil-Papineau | Deux-Montagnes | Marie Daoust, Sec.-Trés., 183, rue des Anges, CP 369, Oka J0N 1E0 – 514/479-8388, Fax: 514/479-1886 |
| Oka (P) | 1,498 | Deux-Montagnes | Argenteuil-Papineau | Deux-Montagnes | Jacques Fournier, Sec.-Trés., 2017, ch Oka, CP 38, Oka J0N 1E0 – 514/479-8333, Fax: 514/479-6869 |
| Omerville (V) | 2,068 | Memphrémagog | Brome-Missisquoi | Orford | Jean-Paul Bergeron, Sec.-Trés., 51, rue St-Jacques ouest, Omerville J1X 4H4 – 819/843-5744, Fax: 819/843-5303 |
| Orford (Canton) | 1,427 | Memphrémagog | Brome-Missisquoi | Orford | Jean-Marie Beaupré, Sec.-Trés., 2530, ch du Parc, Orford J1X 3W3 – 819/843-3111, Fax: 819/843-2707 |
| Ormstown (V) | 1,604 | Le Haut-St-Laurent | Beauharnois-Salaberry | Beauharnois-Huntingdon | Jean-Claude Marcil, Sec.-Trés., 81, rue Lambton, Ormstown J0S 1K0 – 514/829-2625, Fax: 514/829-4162 |
| OTTERBURN-PARK | 6,402 | La Vallée-du-Richelieu | Chambly | Borduas | Jean Tremblay, Sec.-Trés., 472, av Prince-Edward, Otterburn Park J3H 1W4 – 514/536-0303, Fax: 514/467-8260 |
| OUTREMONT | 22,571 | Montréal (Urb. Com.) | Outremont | Outremont | Mario Gerbeau, Gref., 543, ch Côte-Ste-Catherine, Outremont H2V 4R2 – 514/495-6200, Fax: 514/495-6290 |
| Pabos (Mun.) | 1,488 | Pabok | Bonaventure-Gaspé-Îles-de-la-Madeleine-Pabok | Gaspé | Marcel Moreau, Sec.-Trés., 440, boul Pabos, CP 39, Pabos G0C 2H0 – 418/689-4920, Fax: 418/689-5644 |
| Pabos Mills (Mun.) | 1,578 | Pabok | Bonaventure-Gaspé-Îles-de-la-Madeleine-Pabok | Gaspé | Raymond Cyr, Sec.-Trés., 151, rte 132, Pabos Mills G0C 2J0 – 418/689-3523, Fax: 418/689-4664 |
| Packington (P) | 637 | Témiscouata | Kamouraska-Rivière-du-Loup-Témiscouata-Les Basques-Les Basques | Kamouraska-Témiscouata | Denis Moreau, Sec.-Trés., 35A, rue Principale, Packington G0L 1Z0 – 418/853-2269, Fax: 418/853-2269 |
| Padoue (Mun.) | 296 | La Mitis | Rimouski-Mitis-Mitis | Matane | Marc-André Lavoie, Sec.-Trés., 215, rue Beaulieu, CP 15, Padoue G0J 1X0 – 418/775-8188, Fax: 418/775-8177 |
| Palmarolle (Mun.) | 1,561 | Abitibi-Ouest | Témiscamingue | Abitibi-Ouest | Hélène Larivière, Sec.-Trés., 499, route 393, CP 309, Palmarolle J0Z 3C0 – 819/787-2303, Fax: 819/787-2303 |
| Papineauville (V) | 1,628 | Papineau | Argenteuil-Papineau | Papineau | Paula Pagé, Sec.-Trés., 266, rue Viger, CP 248, Papineauville J0V 1R0 – 819/427-5511, Fax: 819/427-5590 |
| Parent (V) | 387 | Le Haut-St-Maurice | Champlain | Laviolette | Sylvie Ruel, Sec.-Trés., 2, rue de l'Hôtel-de-Ville, CP 8, Parent G0X 3P0 – 819/667-2323, Fax: 819/667-2542 |
| Parisville (P) | 553 | Bécancour | Lotbinière | Lotbinière | Ginette C.-Bisaillon, Sec.-Trés., 1260, rue St-Jacques, Parisville G0S 1X0 – 819/292-2222, Fax: 819/292-2222 |
| Paspébiac (Mun.) | 2,945 | Bonaventure | Bonaventure-Gaspé-Îles-de-la-Madeleine-Pabok | Bonaventure | Jean-Guy Duguay, Sec.-Trés., 178, 9e rue, CP 130, Paspébiac G0C 2K0 – 418/752-2277, Fax: 418/752-6566 |
| Paspébiac-Ouest (Mun.) | 709 | Bonaventure | Bonaventure-Gaspé-Îles-de-la-Madeleine-Pabok | Bonaventure | Céline Poirier-Berthelot, Sec.-Trés., 11, route Scott, CP 99, Paspébiac-Ouest G0C 2K0 – 418/752-6777, Fax: 418/752-5670 |
| PERCÉ | 3,993 | Pabok | Bonaventure-Gaspé-Îles-de-la-Madeleine-Pabok | Gaspé | Bruno Cloutier, Sec.-Trés., 137, rte 132 ouest, CP 99, Percé G0C 2L0 – 418/782-2933, Fax: 418/782-5487 |
| Péribonka (Mun.) | 588 | Maria-Chapdelaine | Roberval | Roberval | Normand Fortin, Sec.-Trés., 312, rue Édouard-Niquet, Péribonka G0W 2G0 – 418/374-2967, Fax: 418/374-2355 |
| Petit-Matane (Mun.) | 1,360 | Matane | Matapédia-Matane | Matane | Lise Gauthier, Sec.-Trés., 676, ch de la Grève, Petit-Matane G0J 1Y0 – 418/566-2135 |
| Petit-Saguenay (Mun.) | 918 | Le Fjord-du-Saguenay | Chicoutimi | Dubuc | Alexis Lavoie, Sec.-Trés., 35, ch du Quai, CP 40, Petit-Saguenay G0V 1N0 – 418/272-2323, Fax: 418/272-2346 |
| Petite-Rivière-St-François (Mun.) | 753 | Charlevoix | Charlevoix | Charlevoix | Francine Dufour, Sec.-Trés., 1067, rue Principale, CP 10, Petite-Rivière-St-François G0A 2L0 – 418/632-5831, Fax: 418/632-5886 |
| Petite-Vallée (Mun.) | 224 | La Côte-de-Gaspé | Bonaventure-Gaspé-Îles-de-la-Madeleine-Pabok | Gaspé | Simon Côté, Sec.-Trés., 45, rue Principale, CP 1067, Petite-Vallée G0E 1Y0 – 418/393-2949, Fax: 418/393-2592 |
| Philipsburg (V) | 245 | Brome-Missisquoi | Brome-Missisquoi | Brome-Missisquoi | Michèle Bertrand, Sec.-Trés., 203, rue Philips, CP 360, Philipsburg J0J 1N0 – 514/248-2124, Fax: 514/248-2124 |
| Piedmont (Mun.) | 1,862 | Les Pays-d'en-Haut | Laurentides | Bertrand | Gilbert Aubin, Sec.-Trés., 670, rue Principale, Piedmont J0R 1K0 – 514/227-1888, Fax: 514/227-6716 |

Urban Centres (Villes) in CAPITALS; Villages marked (V); Townships/Cantons marked (Canton);United townships/Cantons unis marked (Cantons); Parishes marked (P); Municipalities marked (Mun.).; Northern villages/Villages nordiques marked (NV); Cree Villages/Villages Cris marked (VC); Naskapi Villages/Villages Naskapi marked (VN); In the third column, Urban Community/Communauté Urbaine marked Urb. Com. An in-depth listing for municipalities marked with * appears in Part 2 (check Index for page numbers).

| MUNICIPALITY | 1996 POP. | REGIONAL COUNTY MUN. | FEDERAL ELECTORAL DISTRICT | PROVINCIAL ELECTORAL DISTRICT | CONTACT PERSON WITH ADDRESS, PHONE & FAX |
|---|---|---|---|---|---|
| PIERREFONDS | 52,986 | Montréal (Urb. Com.) | Pierrefonds-Dollard; Lac-St-Louis | Nelligan; Robert Baldwin | Chantal Gauvreau, Gref., 13665, boul Pierrefonds, CP 2500, Pierrefonds H9H 4N2 – 514/624-1124, Fax: 514/624-1300 |
| Pierreville (V) | 976 | Nicolet-Yamaska | Richelieu | Nicolet-Yamaska | Michel Gagnon, Sec.-Trés., 26, rue Ally, CP 300, Pierreville J0G 1J0 – 514/568-2139, Fax: 514/568-0689 |
| PINCOURT | 10,023 | Vaudreuil-Soulanges | Vaudreuil-Soulanges | Vaudreuil | Hélène Boudreau, Sec.-Trés., 919, ch Duhamel, Pincourt J7V 4G8 – 514/453-8981, Fax: 514/453-0934 |
| Pintendre (Mun.) | 6,035 | Desjardins | Lévis | Lévis | Hervé Tremblay, Sec.-Trés., 344, 10e av, Pintendre G6C 1G7 – 418/838-6070, Fax: 418/838-6085 |
| Piopolis (Mun.) | 300 | Le Granit | Frontenac-Mégantic | Mégantic-Compton | Julie Cloutier, Sec.-Trés., 433, rue Principale, Piopolis G0Y 1H0 – 819/583-3953, Fax: 819/583-3953 |
| Plaisance (Mun.) | 992 | Papineau | Argenteuil-Papineau | Papineau | Benoit Hébert, Sec.-Trés., 281, rue Desjardins, Plaisance J0V 1S0 – 819/427-5363, Fax: 819/427-5015 |
| Plessisville (P) | 2,728 | L'Érable | Lotbinière | Arthabaska | Roger Chandonnet, Sec.-Trés., 290, route 165 sud, CP 245, Plessisville G6L 2Y7 – 819/362-2712, Fax: 819/362-9185 |
| PLESSISVILLE | 6,810 | L'Érable | Lotbinière | Arthabaska | René Turcotte, Sec.-Trés., 1700, rue St-Calixte, Plessisville G6L 1R3 – 819/362-3284, Fax: 819/362-6421 |
| POHÉNÉGAMOOK | 3,259 | Témiscouata | Kamouraska-Rivière-du-Loup-Témiscouata-Les Basques-Les Basques | Kamouraska-Témiscouata | Georges Comeau, Sec.-Trés., 1309, rue Principale, Pohénégamook G0L 1J0 – 418/859-2533, Fax: 418/859-3465 |
| Pointe-à-la-Croix (Mun.) | 1,607 | Avignon | Matapédia-Matane | Bonaventure | Claude Audet, Sec.-Trés., 30, rue Chouinard, CP 159, Pointe-à-la-Croix G0C 1L0 – 418/788-2011, Fax: 418/788-2916 |
| POINTE-AU-PÈRE | 4,145 | Rimouski-Neigette | Rimouski-Mitis-Mitis | Matapédia | Luc Babin, Sec.-Trés., 315, av Dionne, Pointe-au-Père G5M 1M8 – 418/724-7723, Fax: 418/724-6112 |
| Pointe-aux-Outardes (V) | 1,339 | Manicouagan | Charlevoix | Saguenay | Dania Hovington, Sec.-Trés., 471, ch Principal, Les Buissons G0H 1H0 – 418/567-2203, Fax: 418/567-4409 |
| Pointe-aux-Trembles (P) | 2,248 | Portneuf | Portneuf | Portneuf | Yves Raymond, Sec.-Trés., 230, rue Père-Rhéaume, CP 158, Neuville G0A 2R0 – 418/876-2233, Fax: 418/876-3349 |
| Pointe-Calumet (Mun.) | 5,443 | Deux-Montagnes | Argenteuil-Papineau | Deux-Montagnes | Chantal Pilon, Sec.-Trés., 300, av Basile-Routhier, Pointe-Calumet J0N 1G2 – 514/473-5930, Fax: 514/473-6571 |
| POINTE-CLAIRE | 28,435 | Montréal (Urb. Com.) | Lac-St-Louis | Jacques-Cartier | Jean-Denis Jacob, Gref., 451, boul St-Jean, Pointe-Claire H9R 3J3 – 514/630-1200, Fax: 514/630-1227 |
| Pointe-des-Cascades (V) | 910 | Vaudreuil-Soulanges | Vaudreuil-Soulanges | Salaberry-Soulanges | Christiane Cyr, Sec.-Trés., 52, ch du Fleuve, Pointe-des-Cascades J0P 1M0 – 514/455-3414, Fax: 514/455-9671 |
| Pointe-du-Lac (Mun.) | 6,197 | Francheville | Trois-Rivières | Maskinongé | Martial Beaudry, Trés., 1597, ch Ste-Marguerite, Pointe-du-Lac G0X 1Z0 – 819/377-1121, Fax: 819/377-2415 |
| Pointe-Fortune (V) | 451 | Vaudreuil-Soulanges | Argenteuil-Papineau | Vaudreuil | Hélène Therrien, Sec.-Trés., 694, rue du Tisseur, CP 60, Pointe-Fortune J0P 1N0 – 514/451-5178, Fax: 514/451-5178 |
| Pointe-Lebel (V) | 2,011 | Manicouagan | Charlevoix | Saguenay | Patricia Huet, Sec.-Trés., 365, rue Granier, Pointe-Lebel G0H 1N0 – 418/589-8073, Fax: 418/589-6154 |
| PONT-ROUGE [4] | 4,676 | Portneuf | Portneuf | Portneuf | Line Morasse, Sec.-Trés., 212, rue Dupont est, CP 1240, Pont-Rouge G0A 2X0 – 418/873-4481, Fax: 418/873-3494 |
| Pontbriand (Mun.) | 858 | L'Amiante | Frontenac-Mégantic | Frontenac | Aline Turmel, Sec.-Trés., 1279, rue de l'Église, Pontbriand G0N 1K0 – 418/338-0432, Fax: 418/338-6008 |
| Pontiac (Mun.) | 4,722 | Les Collines-de-l'Outaouais | Pontiac-Gatineau-Labelle | Pontiac | Germain Clairoux, Sec.-Trés., 2024, rte 148, Pontiac J0X 2G0 – 819/455-2401, Fax: 819/455-9756 |
| PORT-CARTIER | 7,070 | Sept-Rivières | Manicouagan | Duplessis | Guylaine Morissette, Gref., 40, av Parent, Port-Cartier G5B 2G5 – 418/766-2343, Fax: 418/766-6236 |
| Port-Daniel (Mun.) | 1,755 | Pabok | Bonaventure-Gaspé-Îles-de-la-Madeleine-Pabok | Bonaventure | Conrad Jones, Sec.-Trés., 490, route 132, CP 130, Port-Daniel G0C 2N0 – 418/396-5225, Fax: 418/396-5588 |
| Portage-du-Fort (V) | 289 | Pontiac | Pontiac-Gatineau-Labelle | Pontiac | Fernand Roy, Sec.-Trés., CP 59, Portage-du-Fort J0X 2T0 – 819/683-3027, Fax: 819/683-2694 |
| PORTNEUF | 1,470 | Portneuf | Portneuf | Portneuf | Dominique Lavallée, Sec.-Trés., 100, rue Paquin, CP 100, Portneuf G0A 2Y0 – 418/286-3844, Fax: 418/286-4304 |
| Potton (Canton) | 1,690 | Memphrémagog | Brome-Missisquoi | Brome-Missisquoi | Jacques Hébert, Sec.-Trés., 2, rue de Vale Perkins, CP 330, Mansonville J0E 1X0 – 514/292-3313, Fax: 514/292-5555 |

Urban Centres (Villes) in CAPITALS; Villages marked (V); Townships/Cantons marked (Canton);United townships/Cantons unis marked (Cantons); Parishes marked (P); Municipalities marked (Mun.).; Northern villages/Villages nordiques marked (NV); Cree Villages/Villages Cris marked (VC); Naskapi Villages/Villages Naskapi marked (VN); In the third column, Urban Community/Communauté Urbaine marked Urb. Com. An in-depth listing for municipalities marked with * appears in Part 2 (check Index for page numbers).

| MUNICIPALITY | 1996 POP. | REGIONAL COUNTY MUN. | FEDERAL ELECTORAL DISTRICT | PROVINCIAL ELECTORAL DISTRICT | CONTACT PERSON WITH ADDRESS, PHONE & FAX |
|---|---|---|---|---|---|
| Poularies (Mun.) | 838 | Abitibi-Ouest | Témiscamingue | Abitibi-Ouest | Hélène Richer, Sec.-Trés., 990, rue Principale, CP 58, Poularies J0Z 3E0 – 819/782-5159, Fax: 819/782-5063 |
| Preissac (Mun.) | 619 | Abitibi | Abitibi | Abitibi-Ouest | François Roch, Sec.-Trés., 6, rue des Rapides, Preissac J0Y 2E0 – 819/732-4938, Fax: 819/732-4938 |
| Prévost (Mun.) | 7,308 | La Rivière-du-Nord | Laurentides | Prévost | Diane Paquin, Greffie@re, 2870, boul du Curé-Labelle, Prévost J0R 1T0 – 514/224-2981, Fax: 514/224-8323 |
| Price (V) | 1,916 | La Mitis | Rimouski-Mitis | Matapédia | Louise Furlong, Sec.-Trés., 18, rue Fournier, CP 340, Price G0J 1Z0 – 418/775-2144, Fax: 418/775-2459 |
| Princeville (P) | 1,753 | L'Érable | Lotbinière | Arthabaska | Jean-Marc Bédard, Sec.-Trés., 101, rue Demers est, Princeville G6L 4E8 – 819/364-3092, Fax: 819/364-3970 |
| PRINCEVILLE | 3,997 | L'Érable | Lotbinière | Arthabaska | Mario Juaire, Sec.-Trés., 50, av St-Jacques ouest, Princeville G6L 4Y5 – 819/364-5179, Fax: 819/364-5198 |
| Puvirnituq (NV) | 1,169 | Kativik | Abitibi | Ungava | Mary Angiyou, Sec.-Trés., Puvirnituq J0M 1P0 – 819/964-2825, Fax: 819/988-2751 |
| Quaqtaq (NV) | 257 | Terr. du Nouveau Québec | Abitibi | Ungava | Sammy Tukkiapik, Sec.-Trés., Quaqtaq J0M 1J0 – 819/492-9912, Fax: 819/492-9935 |
| *QUÉBEC | 167,264 | Québec (Urb. Com.) | Québec; Québec-Est | Chauveau; Jean-Talon; La Peltrie; Limoilou; Taschereau; Vanier | Antoine Carrier, Gref., Hôtel de ville, 2, rue des Jardins, CP 700, Québec G1R 4S9 – 418/691-4636, Fax: 418/691-2346, URL: http://www.megatoon.com/web-quebec |
| Racine (Mun.) | 1,036 | Le Val-St-François | Shefford | Johnson | André Courtemanche, Sec.-Trés., 136, rte 222, CP 120, Racine J0E 1Y0 – 514/532-2876, Fax: 514/532-2865 |
| Ragueneau (P) | 1,684 | Manicouagan | Charlevoix | Saguenay | Alain Landry, Sec.-Trés., 523, rte 138, CP 190, Ragueneau G0H 1S0 – 418/567-2345, Fax: 418/567-2344 |
| Rainville (Mun.) | 1,855 | Brome-Missisquoi | Brome-Missisquoi | Iberville | Marie-Josée Lepage, Sec.-Trés., 1810, rue Principale est, Rainville J2N 1N4 – 514/293-3326, Fax: 514/293-4341 |
| Rapide-Danseur (Mun.) | 247 | Abitibi-Ouest | Témiscamingue | Abitibi-Ouest | Yvette Fournier-Boutin, Sec.-Trés., 535, route du Village, CP 459, Rapide-Danseur J0Z 3G0 – 819/948-2152, Fax: 819/948-2152 |
| Rapides-des-Joachims (Mun.) | 185 | Pontiac | Pontiac-Gatineau-Labelle | Pontiac | Fernand Roy, Sec.-Trés., RR#1, CP 92, Rapides-des-Joachims J0X 3M0 – 819/683-3027, Fax: 819/683-2694 |
| Rawdon (Canton) | 4,399 | Matawinie | Berthier-Montcalm | Rousseau | Ginette Filion, Sec.-Trés., 3647, rue Queen, CP 730, Rawdon J0K 1S0 – 514/834-2587, Fax: 514/834-3031 |
| Rawdon (V) | 3,855 | Matawinie | Berthier-Montcalm | Rousseau | Jean-Guy Charest, Sec.-Trés., 3647, rue Queen, CP 550, Rawdon J0K 1S0 – 514/834-2596, Fax: 514/834-2329 |
| Rémigny (Mun.) | 364 | Témiscamingue | Témiscamingue | Rouyn-Noranda-Témiscamingue | Paquerette Roy, Sec.-Trés., 1304, ch de l'Église, Rémigny J0Z 3H0 – 819/761-2421, Fax: 819/761-2421 |
| *RÉPENTIGNY | 53,824 | L'Assomption | Répentigny | L'Assomption | Jean Fafard, Gref., 435, boul Iberville, Répentigny J6A 2B6 – 514/654-2323, Fax: 514/654-2421 |
| RICHELIEU | 3,195 | Rouville | Chambly | Chambly | Richard Blouin, Gref., 200, boul Richelieu, Richelieu J3L 3R4 – 514/658-1157, Fax: 514/658-5096 |
| RICHMOND | 3,053 | Le Val-St-François | Richmond-Arthabaska | Richmond | Martin Lafleur, Sec.-Trés., 745, rue Gouin, CP 1250, Richmond J0B 2H0 – 819/826-3789, Fax: 819/826-6281 |
| Rigaud (Mun.) | 6,057 | Vaudreuil-Soulanges | Vaudreuil-Soulanges | Vaudreuil | Diane Desjardins, Sec.-Trés., 391, ch de la Mairie, CP 580, Rigaud J0P 1P0 – 514/451-0869, Fax: 514/451-4227 |
| RIMOUSKI | 31,773 | Rimouski-Neigette | Rimouski-Mitis-Mitis | Rimouski | Marc Doucet, Gref., 205, av de la Cathédrale, CP 710, Rimouski G5L 7C7 – 418/723-3313, Fax: 418/724-3180 |
| Rimouski-Est (V) | 2,119 | Rimouski-Neigette | Rimouski-Mitis-Mitis | Rimouski | Denis Ouellet, Sec.-Trés., 540, rue St-Germain est, Rimouski-Est G5L 1E9 – 418/723-8388, Fax: 418/722-0226 |
| Ripon (Canton) | 714 | Papineau | Argentenuil-Papineau | Papineau | Danièle Migneault, Sec.-Trés., 31, rue Coursol, CP 40, Ripon J0V 1V0 – 819/983-2000, Fax: 819/983-1327 |
| Ripon (V) | 657 | Papineau | Argenteuil-Papineau | Papineau | Lorraine Sabourin, Sec.-Trés., 31, rue Coursol, CP 100, Ripon J0V 1V0 – 819/983-6685, Fax: 819/983-1327 |
| Risborough (Mun.) | 942 | Le Granit | Beauce | Beauce-Sud | Pierrette Morin, Sec.-Trés., 212, rue La Salle, CP 129, St-Ludger G0M 1W0 – 819/548-5408, Fax: 819/548-5408 |
| Ristigouche Sud-Est (Canton) | 155 | Avignon | Matapédia-Matane | Bonaventure | Suzanne Bourdages, Sec.-Trés., 35, ch Kempt, RR#2, Matapédia G0J 1V0 – 418/788-5769, Fax: 418/788-2598 |

Urban Centres (Villes) in CAPITALS; Villages marked (V); Townships/Cantons marked (Canton);United townships/Cantons unis marked (Cantons); Parishes marked (P); Municipalities marked (Mun.).; Northern villages/Villages nordiques marked (NV); Cree Villages/Villages Cris marked (VC); Naskapi Villages/Villages Naskapi marked (VN); In the third column, Urban Community/Communauté Urbaine marked Urb. Com. An in-depth listing for municipalities marked with * appears in Part 2 (check Index for page numbers).

| MUNICIPALITY | 1996 POP. | REGIONAL COUNTY MUN. | FEDERAL ELECTORAL DISTRICT | PROVINCIAL ELECTORAL DISTRICT | CONTACT PERSON WITH ADDRESS, PHONE & FAX |
|---|---|---|---|---|---|
| Rivière-à-Claude (Mun.) | 192 | Denis-Riverin | Matapédia-Matane | Matane | Claudine Auclair, Sec.-Trés., 520, rue Principale est, Rivière-à-Claude G0E 1Z0 – 418/797-2422, Fax: 418/797-2455 |
| Rivière-à-Pierre (Mun.) | 694 | Portneuf | Portneuf | Portneuf | Yolande Gauvreau, Sec.-Trés., 830, rue Principale, Rivière-à-Pierre G0A 3A0 – 418/323-2112, Fax: 418/323-2111 |
| Rivière-au-Tonnerre (Mun.) | 476 | Minganie | Manicouagan | Duplessis | Carmelle Anglehart, Sec.-Trés., 473, rue Jacques Cartier, CP 129, Rivière-au-Tonnerre G0G 2L0 – 418/465-2255, Fax: 418/465-2956 |
| Rivière-Beaudette (Mun.) | 1,381 | Vaudreuil-Soulanges | Vaudreuil-Soulanges | Salaberry-Soulanges | Céline Chayer, Sec.-Trés., 663, ch de la Frontière, Rivière-Beaudette J0P 1R0 – 514/269-2931, Fax: 514/269-2815 |
| Rivière-Bleue (Mun.) | 1,517 | Témiscouata | Kamouraska-Rivière-du-Loup-Témiscouata-Les Basques | Kamouraska-Témiscouata | Claude A. Dubé, Sec.-Trés., 32, rue des Pins est, CP 98, Rivière-Bleue G0L 2B0 – 418/893-5559, Fax: 418/893-5530 |
| RIVIÈRE-DU-LOUP | 14,721 | Rivière-du-Loup | Kamouraska-Rivière-du-Loup-Témiscouata-Les Basques | Rivière-du-Loup | Georges Deschênes, Gref., 65, rue de l'Hôtel-de-Ville, CP 37, Rivière-du-Loup G5R 3Y7 – 418/862-9810, Fax: 418/862-2817 |
| Rivière-Éternité (Mun.) | 572 | Le Fjord-du-Saguenay | Chicoutimi | Dubuc | Denis Houde, Sec.-Trés., 418, rte Principale, Rivière-Éternité G0V 1P0 – 418/272-2860, Fax: 418/272-3454 |
| Rivière-Héva (Mun.) | 1,096 | Vallée-de-l'Or | Abitibi | Abitibi-Est | Chantal Côté, Sec.-Trés., 740, route St-Paul nord, CP 60, Rivière-Héva J0Y 2H0 – 819/735-3521, Fax: 819/735-4251 |
| Rivière-Malbaie (Mun.) | 2,022 | Charlevoix-Est | Charlevoix | Charlevoix | Daniel Lavoie, Sec.-Trés., 250, ch de la Vallée, Rivière-Malbaie G5A 1V4 – 418/665-3218, Fax: 418/665-7353 |
| Rivière-Ouelle (Mun.) | 1,257 | Kamouraska | Kamouraska-Rivière-du-Loup-Témiscouata-Les Basques | Kamouraska-Témiscouata | André Lacombe, Sec.-Trés., 106, rue de l'Église, CP 99, Rivière-Ouelle G0L 2C0 – 418/856-3829, Fax: 418/856-1790 |
| Rivière-Pentecôte (Mun.) | 640 | Sept-Rivières | Manicouagan | Duplessis | Maryse Dugas, Sec.-Trés., 4344, route Jacques-Cartier, CP 3, Rivière-Pentecôte G0H 1R0 – 418/799-2262, Fax: 418/799-2263 |
| Rivière-St-Jean (Mun.) | 319 | Minganie | Manicouagan | Duplessis | Josée Beaudoin, Sec.-Trés., 116, rue du Quai, Rivière-St-Jean G0G 2N0 – 418/949-2464, Fax: 418/949-2489 |
| Robertsonville (V) | 1,829 | L'Amiante | Frontenac-Mégantic | Frontenac | Robert Perreault, Sec.-Trés., 184, rue Notre Dame sud, Robertsonville G0N 1L0 – 418/338-6177, Fax: 418/338-5553 |
| ROBERVAL | 11,640 | Le Domaine-du-Roy | Roberval | Roberval | Jean-Guy Tardif, Gref., 851, boul St-Joseph, Roberval G8H 2L6 – 418/275-0202, Fax: 418/275-5031 |
| Rochebaucourt (Mun.) | 227 | Abitibi | Abitibi | Abitibi-Ouest | Louise C. Noël, Sec.-Trés., 20, rue Chanoine-Girard, Rochebaucourt J0Y 2J0 – 819/754-2083, Fax: 819/754-2083 |
| ROCK FOREST | 16,604 | Sherbrooke | Compton-Stanstead | Orford | Pierre Ménard, Gref., 1000, av du Haut-Bois, Rock Forest J1N 3V4 – 819/564-7444, Fax: 819/564-8144 |
| Rollet (Mun.) | 408 | Rouyn-Noranda | Témiscamingue | Rouyn-Noranda-Témiscamingue | Paulette Lemay, Sec.-Trés., 761, rue Principale, CP 10, Rollet J0Z 3J0 – 819/493-4141, Fax: 819/493-4141 |
| Roquemaure (Mun.) | 459 | Abitibi-Ouest | Témiscamingue | Abitibi-Ouest | Lise Roy, Sec.-Trés., 15, rue Raymond est, CP 40, Roquemaure J0Z 3K0 – 819/787-6311, Fax: 819/787-6311 |
| ROSEMÈRE | 12,025 | Thérèse-de-Blainville | Terrebonne-Blainville | Groulx | Sylvie Trahan, Gref., 100, rue Charbonneau, Rosemère J7A 3W1 – 514/621-3500, Fax: 514/621-7601 |
| Rougemont (V) | 1,237 | Rouville | Shefford | Iberville | Louise Berthiaume, Sec.-Trés., 839, rue Principale, Rougemont J0L 1M0 – 514/469-3484, Fax: 514/469-5232 |
| ROUYN-NORANDA | 28,819 | Rouyn-Noranda | Témiscamingue | Rouyn-Noranda-Témiscamingue | Daniel Samson, Gref., 100, rue Taschereau est, CP 220, Rouyn-Noranda J9X 5C3 – 819/797-7111, Fax: 819/797-7120 |
| ROXBORO | 5,950 | Montréal (Urb. Com.) | Pierrefonds-Dollard | Robert-Baldwin | Sophie Valois, Gref., 13, rue du Centre-Commercial, Roxboro H8Y 2N9 – 514/684-0555, Fax: 514/684-0705 |
| Roxton (Canton) | 1,116 | Acton | St-Hyacinthe-Bagot | Johnson | Denise Audet, Sec.-Trés., 216, rang Ste-Geneviève, CP 278, Roxton Falls J0H 1E0 – 514/548-2500, Fax: 514/548-2412 |
| Roxton Falls (V) | 1,371 | Acton | St-Hyacinthe-Bagot | Johnson | Hélène Lussier, Sec.-Trés., 189, rue Notre-Dame, CP 180, Roxton Falls J0H 1E0 – 514/548-5790, Fax: 514/548-5881 |
| Roxton Pond (P) | 2,357 | La Haute-Yamaska | Shefford | Shefford | Raymond Loignon, Sec.-Trés., 901, rue St-Jean, CP 60, Roxton Pond J0E 1Z0 – 514/372-6875, Fax: 514/372-1205 |

Urban Centres (Villes) in CAPITALS; Villages marked (V); Townships/Cantons marked (Canton);United townships/Cantons unis marked (Cantons); Parishes marked (P); Municipalities marked (Mun.).; Northern villages/Villages nordiques marked (NV); Cree Villages/Villages Cris marked (VC); Naskapi Villages/Villages Naskapi marked (VN); In the third column, Urban Community/Communauté Urbaine marked Urb. Com. An in-depth listing for municipalities marked with * appears in Part 2 (check Index for page numbers).

| MUNICIPALITY | 1996 POP. | REGIONAL COUNTY MUN. | FEDERAL ELECTORAL DISTRICT | PROVINCIAL ELECTORAL DISTRICT | CONTACT PERSON WITH ADDRESS, PHONE & FAX |
|---|---|---|---|---|---|
| Roxton Pond (V) | 991 | La Haute-Yamaska | Shefford | Shefford | Raymond Loignon, Sec.-Trés., 901, rue St-Jean, CP 60, Roxton Pond J0E 1Z0 – 514/372-6875, Fax: 514/372-1205 |
| Sacré-Coeur (Mun.) | 2,081 | La Haute-Côte-Nord | Rimouski-Mitis | Saguenay | Sarto Simard, Sec.-Trés., 88, rue Principale nord, CP 159, Sacré-Coeur G0T 1Y0 – 418/236-4621, Fax: 418/236-9144 |
| Sacré-Coeur-de-Jésus (P) | 604 | L'Amiante | Frontenac-Mégantic | Frontenac | Marie-France Létourneau, Sec.-Trés., 4118, rte 112, Sacré-Coeur-de-Jésus G0N 1G0 – 418/427-3447, Fax: 418/427-3447 |
| Sacré-Coeur-de-Marie-Sud (P) | 668 | L'Amiante | Frontenac-Mégantic | Frontenac | Jean-Rock Turgeon, Sec.-Trés., 11, 8e rang, Sacré-Coeur-de-Marie G0N 1W0 – 418/335-3968, Fax: 418/335-2667 |
| St-Adalbert (Mun.) | 708 | L'Islet | Bellechasse-Etchemins-Montmagny-L'Islet | Montmagny-L'Islet | Normande Chouinard, Sec.-Trés., 55, rue Principale, St-Adalbert G0R 2M0 – 418/356-5271, Fax: 418/356-5271 |
| STE-ADÈLE | 5,837 | Les Pays-d'en-Haut | Laurentides | Bertrand | Michel Rousseau, Gref., 1381, boul de Ste-Adèle, Ste-Adèle J0R 1L0 – 514/229-2921, Fax: 514/229-4179 |
| St-Adelme (P) | 543 | Matane | Matapédia-Matane | Matane | Rita Bernier, Sec.-Trés., 231, rue Principale, CP 39, St-Adelme G0J 2B0 – 418/733-4044, Fax: 418/733-4111 |
| St-Adelphe (P) | 1,014 | Mékinac | Champlain | Laviolette | Daniel Bacon, Sec.-Trés., 150, rue Baillargeon, St-Adelphe G0X 2G0 – 418/322-5721, Fax: 418/322-5434 |
| St-Adolphe-d'Howard (Mun.) | 2,632 | Les Pays-d'en-Haut | Argenteuil-Papineau | Argenteuil | Lise B.-Villeneuve, Sec.-Trés., 1881, ch du Village, CP 180, St-Adolphe-d'Howard J0T 2B0 – 819/327-2044, Fax: 819/327-2282 |
| St-Adrien (Mun.) | 534 | Asbestos | Richmond-Arthabaska | Richmond | Henriette Giguère, Sec.-Trés., 1589, rue Principale, St-Adrien J0A 1C0 – 819/828-2872, Fax: 819/828-0442 |
| St-Adrien-d'Irlande (Mun.) | 375 | L'Amiante | Frontenac-Mégantic | Frontenac | Doris Lessard, Sec.-Trés., 152, rue Municipale, St-Adrien-d'Irlande G0N 1M0 – 418/335-2585, Fax: 418/335-2585 |
| St-Agapit (Mun.) | 2,913 | Lotbinière | Lotbinière | Lotbinière | Denis Pelletier, Sec.-Trés., 1186, rue Principale, St-Agapit G0S 1Z0 – 418/888-4620, Fax: 418/888-4791 |
| Ste-Agathe (P) | 561 | Lotbinière | Lotbinière | Lotbinière | Ghislaine Gravel, Sec.-Trés., 254, rue St-Pierre, CP 159, St-Agathe G0S 2A0 – 418/599-2605, Fax: 418/599-2605 |
| Ste-Agathe (V) | 675 | Lotbinière | Lotbinière | Lotbinière | Rolande Viger, Sec.-Trés., 46, rue St-Jacques, CP 125, Ste-Agathe G0S 2A0 – 418/599-2548, Fax: 418/599-2548 |
| STE-AGATHE-DES-MONTS | 5,669 | Les Laurentides | Laurentides | Bertrand | Maurice Hews, Sec.-Trés., 50, rue St-Joseph, Ste-Agathe-des-Monts J8C 1M9 – 819/326-4595, Fax: 819/326-5784 |
| Ste-Agathe-Nord (Mun.) | 1,454 | Les Laurentides | Laurentides | Bertrand | Monique Carmel, Sec.-Trés., 1155, route 329 nord, Ste-Agathe-Nord J8C 2Z8 – 819/326-3187, Fax: 819/326-1578 |
| Ste-Agathe-Sud (V) | 2,209 | Les Laurentides | Laurentides | Bertrand | Benoît Fugère, Sec.-Trés., 1700, rue Principale est, Ste-Agathe-Sud J8C 1M2 – 819/326-3920, Fax: 819/326-9157 |
| Ste-Agnès (P) | 675 | Charlevoix-Est | Charlevoix | Charlevoix | Micheline Murray, Sec.-Trés., 11, rue Principale, Ste-Agnès G0T 1R0 – 418/439-4155, Fax: 418/439-4155 |
| St-Aimé (P) | 560 | Le Bas-Richelieu | Richelieu | Richelieu | Claire Lassonde, Sec.-Trés., 285, rue Bonsecours, CP 240, Massueville J0G 1K0 – 514/788-2737, Fax: 514/788-2737 |
| St-Aimé-des-Lacs (Mun.) | 900 | Charlevoix-Est | Charlevoix | Charlevoix | Suzanne Gaudreault, Sec.-Trés., 119, rue Principale, St-Aimé des Lacs G0T 1S0 – 418/439-2229, Fax: 418/439-2229 |
| St-Aimé-du-Lac-des-Îles (Mun.) | 789 | Antoine-Labelle | Pontiac-Gatineau-Labelle | Labelle | Claude Comtois, Sec.-Trés., 123, ch du Village, CP 1, St-Aimé-du-Lac-des-Iles J0W 1J0 – 819/597-2047, Fax: 819/597-2554 |
| St-Alban (Mun.) | 1,159 | Portneuf | Portneuf | Portneuf | Myriam Falardeau, Sec.-Trés., 204, rue Principale, St-Alban G0A 3B0 – 418/268-8026, Fax: 418/268-5073 |
| St-Albert-de-Warwick (P) | 1,430 | Arthabaska | Richmond-Arthabaska | Richmond | Suzanne Crête-Corriveau, Sec.-Trés., 25, rue des Loisirs, CP 100, St-Albert J0A 1E0 – 819/353-3300, Fax: 819/353-3313 |
| St-Alexandre (P) | 1,807 | Kamouraska | Kamouraska-Rivière-du-Loup-Témiscouata-Les Basques | Kamouraska-Témiscouata | Lyne Dumont, Sec.-Trés., 723, route 289, CP 10, St-Alexandre G0L 2G0 – 418/495-2440, Fax: 418/495-2659 |
| St-Alexandre (Mun.) | 2,380 | Le Haut-Richelieu | St-Jean | Iberville | Maryse Boucher, Sec.-Trés., 453, rue St-Denis, CP 60, St-Alexandre J0J 1S0 – 514/346-6641, Fax: 514/346-0538 |

Urban Centres (Villes) in CAPITALS; Villages marked (V); Townships/Cantons marked (Canton);United townships/Cantons unis marked (Cantons); Parishes marked (P); Municipalities marked (Mun.).; Northern villages/Villages nordiques marked (NV); Cree Villages/Villages Cris marked (VC); Naskapi Villages/Villages Naskapi marked (VN); In the third column, Urban Community/Communauté Urbaine marked Urb. Com. An in-depth listing for municipalities marked with * appears in Part 2 (check Index for page numbers).

| MUNICIPALITY | 1996 POP. | REGIONAL COUNTY MUN. | FEDERAL ELECTORAL DISTRICT | PROVINCIAL ELECTORAL DISTRICT | CONTACT PERSON WITH ADDRESS, PHONE & FAX |
|---|---|---|---|---|---|
| St-Alexandre-des-Lacs (P) | 350 | La Matapédia | Matapédia-Matane | Matapédia | Rita Angers-Rioux, Sec.-Trés., 17, rue de l'Église, St-Alexandre-des-Lacs G0J 2C0 – 418/778-3532, Fax: 418/778-3532 |
| St-Alexis (P) | 755 | Montcalm | Berthier-Montcalm | Rousseau | Rémy Lanoue, Sec.-Trés., 232, rue Principale, St-Alexis J0K 1T0 – 514/839-7277, Fax: 514/839-6241 |
| St-Alexis (V) | 503 | Montcalm | Berthier-Montcalm | Rousseau | Rémy Lanoue, Sec.-Trés., 232, rue Principale, St-Alexis J0K 1T0 – 514/839-7277, Fax: 514/839-6241 |
| St-Alexis-de-Matapédia (P) | 747 | Avignon | Matapédia-Matane | Bonaventure | Lise Pitre, Sec.-Trés., 121, rue Rustico nord, CP 99, St-Alexis-de-Matapédia G0J 2E0 – 418/299-2030, Fax: 418/299-3011 |
| St-Alexis-des-Monts (P) | 2,741 | Maskinongé | St-Maurice | Maskinongé | Gilles Frappier, Sec.-Trés., 101, rue de l'Hôtel-de-Ville, CP 300, St-Alexis-des-Monts J0K 1V0 – 819/265-2046, Fax: 819/265-2481 |
| St-Alfred (Mun.) | 467 | Robert-Cliche | Beauce | Beauce-Nord | Diane Jacques, Sec.-Trés., 194, rang Ste-Marie, St-Alfred G0M 1L0 – 418/774-2068, Fax: 418/774-2068 |
| St-Alphonse (Mun.) | 866 | Bonaventure | Bonaventure-Gaspé-Îles-de-la-Madeleine-Pabok | Bonaventure | Reina Goulet, Sec.-Trés., 127, rue Principale est, CP 40, St-Alphonse G0C 2V0 – 418/388-5214, Fax: 418/388-2435 |
| St-Alphonse (P) | 2,889 | La Haute-Yamaska | Shefford | Brome-Missisquoi | Danielle Bonneau, Sec.-Trés., 360, rue Principale, St-Alphonse J0E 2A0 – 514/375-4570, Fax: 514/375-4717 |
| St-Alphonse-Rodriguez (Mun.) | 2,461 | Matawinie | Berthier-Montcalm | Berthier | François Legendre, Sec.-Trés., 101, rue de la Plage, St-Alphonse-Rodriguez J0K 1W0 – 514/883-2264, Fax: 514/883-0833 |
| St-Amable (Mun.) | 7,105 | Lajemmerais | Verchères | Verchères | Michel Martel, Sec.-Trés., 616, rue de l'Église, St-Amable J0L 1N0 – 514/649-3555, Fax: 514/922-0728 |
| St-Ambroise (Mun.) | 3,605 | Le Fjord-du-Saguenay | Lac-St-Jean | Dubuc | Jean-Rock Claveau, Sec.-Trés., 330, rue Gagnon, St-Ambroise G0V 1R0 – 418/672-4765, Fax: 418/672-6126 |
| St-Ambroise-de-Kildare (P) | 3,406 | Joliette | Joliette | Joliette | Yvon Ducharme, Sec.-Trés., 740, rue Principale, CP 57, Kildare J0K 1C0 – 514/755-4782, Fax: 514/755-4784 |
| St-Anaclet-de-Lessard (P) | 2,546 | Rimouski-Neigette | Rimouski-Mitis-Mitis | Rimouski | Alain Lapierre, Sec.-Trés., 318, rue Principale ouest, CP 99, St-Anaclet G0K 1H0 – 418/723-2816, Fax: 418/723-0436 |
| St-André (Mun.) | 598 | Kamouraska | Kamouraska-Rivière-du-Loup-Témis-couata-Les Basques | Kamouraska-Témis-couata | Claudine Lévesque, Sec.-Trés., 143, rue Principale, St-André-de-Kamouraska G0L 2H0 – 418/493-2085, Fax: 418/493-2373 |
| St-André-Avellin (P) | 1,588 | Papineau | Argenteuil-Papineau | Papineau | Claire Tremblay, Sec.-Trés., 119, rue Principale, CP 490, St-André-Avellin J0V 1W0 – 819/983-2318, Fax: 819/983-2344 |
| St-André-Avellin (V) | 1,710 | Papineau | Argenteuil-Papineau | Papineau | Claire Tremblay, Sec.-Trés., CP 490, St-André-Avellin J0V 1W0 – 819/983-2318, Fax: 819/983-2344 |
| St-André-d'Acton (P) | 2,487 | Acton | St-Hyacinthe-Bagot | Johnson | Marthe Gauthier, Sec.-Trés., 1053, boul St-André, Acton Vale J0H 1A0 – 514/546-2406, Fax: 514/546-3275 |
| St-André-d'Argenteuil (P) | 1,192 | Argenteuil | Argenteuil-Papineau | Argenteuil | Nancy Le Moignan, Sec.-Trés., 10, rue de la Mairie, CP 179, St-André-Est J0V 1X0 – 514/537-3676, Fax: 514/537-3070 |
| St-André-de-Resti-gouche (Mun.) | 220 | Avignon | Matapédia-Matane | Bonaventure | Blandine Parent, Sec.-Trés., 163, rue Principale, CP 4, St-André-de-Restigouche G0J 2G0 – 418/865-2234 |
| St-André-du-Lac-St-Jean (V) | 580 | Le Domaine-du-Roy | Roberval | Lac-St-Jean | Marcel Lapointe, Sec.-Trés., 11, rue du Collège, St-André-du-Lac-St-Jean G0W 2K0 – 418/349-8167, Fax: 418/349-8167 |
| St-André-Est (V) | 1,471 | Argenteuil | Argenteuil-Papineau | Argenteuil | Linne Roquebrune, Sec.-Trés., 10, rue de la Mairie, CP 149, St-André-Est J0V 1X0 – 514/537-3527, Fax: 514/537-3070 |
| St-Ange-Gardien (P) | 1,312 | Rouville | Shefford | Iberville | André Parent, Sec.-Trés., 249, rue St-Joseph, CP 120, L'Ange-Gardien-de-Rouville J0E 1E0 – 514/293-7575, Fax: 514/293-6635 |
| Ste-Angèle-de-Mérici (Mun.) | 1,162 | La Mitis | Rimouski-Mitis-Mitis | Matapédia | Alain Gravel, Sec.-Trés., 23, rue de la Fabrique, CP 129, Ste-Angèle-de-Mérici G0J 2H0 – 418/775-7733, Fax: 418/775-5722 |
| Ste-Angèle-de-Monnoir (P) | 1,481 | Rouville | Shefford | Iberville | Jacqueline Houle, Sec.-Trés., 7, ch du Vide, CP 30, Ste-Angèle-de-Monnoir J0L 1P0 – 514/460-7838, Fax: 514/460-3853 |
| Ste-Angèle-de-Prémont (Mun.) | 637 | Maskinongé | St-Maurice | Maskinongé | Gilles Gerbeau, Sec.-Trés., 2451, rue Camirand, Ste-Angèle-de-Prémont J0K 1R0 – 819/268-5526, Fax: 819/268-5526 |

Urban Centres (Villes) in CAPITALS; Villages marked (V); Townships/Cantons marked (Canton);United townships/Cantons unis marked (Cantons); Parishes marked (P); Municipalities marked (Mun.).; Northern villages/Villages nordiques marked (NV); Cree Villages/Villages Cris marked (VC); Naskapi Villages/Villages Naskapi marked (VN); In the third column, Urban Community/Communauté Urbaine marked Urb. Com. An in-depth listing for municipalities marked with * appears in Part 2 (check Index for page numbers).

| MUNICIPALITY | 1996 POP. | REGIONAL COUNTY MUN. | FEDERAL ELECTORAL DISTRICT | PROVINCIAL ELECTORAL DISTRICT | CONTACT PERSON WITH ADDRESS, PHONE & FAX |
|---|---|---|---|---|---|
| Ste-Angélique (P) | 634 | Papineau | Argenteuil-Papineau | Papineau | Jacqueline Paul, Sec.-Trés., 266, rue Viger, CP 279, Papineauville J0V 1R0 – 819/427-5221, Fax: 819/427-8318 |
| St-Anicet (P) | 2,549 | Le Haut-St-Laurent | Beauharnois-Salaberry | Beauharnois-Huntingdon | Claudette Génier-Leblanc, Sec.-Trés., 335, av Jules-Léger, St-Anicet J0S 1M0 – 514/264-2555, Fax: 514/264-2395 |
| STE-ANNE-DE-BEAUPRÉ | 3,023 | La Côte-de-Beaupré | Beauport-Montmorency-Orléans | Charlevoix | Roch Lemieux, Sec.-Trés., 9336, av Royale, Ste-Anne-de-Beaupré G0A 3C0 – 418/827-3191, Fax: 418/827-8275 |
| STE-ANNE-DE-BELLEVUE | 4,700 | Montréal (Urb. Com.) | Lac-St-Louis | Nelligan | Jacques Turgeon, Gref., 109, rue Ste-Anne, CP 40, Ste-Anne-de-Bellevue H9X 1M2 – 514/457-5500, Fax: 514/457-6087 |
| Ste-Anne-de-la-Pérade (Mun.) | 2,181 | Francheville | Champlain | Champlain | René Roy, Sec.-Trés., 200, rue Principale, CP 308, Ste-Anne-de-la-Pérade G0X 2J0 – 418/325-2841, Fax: 418/325-3070 |
| Ste-Anne-de-la-Pocatière (P) | 1,862 | Kamouraska | Kamouraska-Rivière-du-Loup-Témiscouata-Les Basques | Kamouraska-Témiscouata | René Pelletier, Sec.-Trés., 175, ch des Sables est, Ste-Anne-de-la-Pocatière G0R 1Z0 – 418/856-3192 |
| Ste-Anne-de-la-Rochelle (Mun.) | 644 | Le Val-St-François | Shefford | Brome-Missisquoi | France Lagrandeur, Sec.-Trés., 142, rue Lagrandeur, Ste-Anne-de-la-Rochelle J0E 2B0 – 514/539-1654, Fax: 514/539-1654 |
| Ste-Anne-de-Portneuf (Mun.) | 990 | La Haute-Côte-Nord | Charlevoix | Saguenay | Gontran Tremblay, Sec.-Trés., 170, rue Principale, CP 98, Ste-Anne-de-Portneuf G0T 1P0 – 418/238-2642, Fax: 418/238-5319 |
| Ste-Anne-de-Sabrevois (P) | 1,910 | Le Haut-Richelieu | St-Jean | Iberville | Michèle Dupuis, Sec.-Trés., 1218, rte 133, Sabrevois J0J 2G0 – 514/347-0066, Fax: 514/347-4040 |
| Ste-Anne-de-Sorel (P) | 2,795 | Le Bas-Richelieu | Richelieu | Richelieu | Luc Papillon, Sec.-Trés., 1685, ch du Chenal-du-Moine, Ste-Anne-de-Sorel J3P 5N3 – 514/742-1616, Fax: 514/742-1118 |
| Ste-Anne-des-Lacs (P) | 2,236 | Les Pays-d'en-Haut | Laurentides | Bertrand | Claude Panneton, Sec.-Trés., 773, ch de Ste-Anne-des-Lacs, Ste-Anne-des-Lacs J0R 1B0 – 514/224-2675, Fax: 514/224-8672 |
| STE-ANNE-DES-MONTS | 5,617 | Denis-Riverin | Matapédia-Matane | Matane | Sylvie Lepage, Sec.-Trés., 6, 1re av ouest, CP 458, Ste-Anne-des-Monts G0E 2G0 – 418/763-5511, Fax: 418/763-3473 |
| STE-ANNE-DES-PLAINES | 12,908 | Thérèse-de-Blainville | Terrebonne-Blainville | Blainville | Serge Lepage, Gref., 139, boul Ste-Anne, Ste-Anne-des-Plaines J0N 1H0 – 514/478-0211, Fax: 514/478-5660 |
| Ste-Anne-du-Lac (Mun.) | 623 | Antoine-Labelle | Pontiac-Gatineau-Labelle | Labelle | Denise Beaudry, Sec.-Trés., 1, rue St-François-Xavier, Ste-Anne-du-Lac J0W 1V0 – 819/586-2110, Fax: 819/586-2110 |
| Ste-Anne-du-Lac (V) | 63 | L'Amiante | Frontenac-Mégantic | Frontenac | Richard Samson, Sec.-Trés., 421, rue des Tulipes, CP 112, Thetford Mines G6G 5R9 – 418/338-0467, Fax: 418/338-6784 |
| Ste-Anne-du-Sault (P) | 1,385 | Arthabaska | Lotbinière | Nicolet-Yamaska | Lyne Bertrand, Sec.-Trés., 634, rue Principale, CP 38, Daveluyville G0Z 1C0 – 819/367-2210, Fax: 819/367-2210 |
| St-Anselme (P) | 1,405 | Bellechasse | Bellechasse | Bellechasse | Louis Felteau, Sec.-Trés., 134, rue Principale, CP 400, St-Anselme G0R 2N0 – 418/885-4977, Fax: 418/885-9834 |
| St-Anselme (V) | 1,912 | Bellechasse | Bellechasse | Bellechasse | Louis Felteau, Sec.-Trés., 134, rue Principale, CP 400, St-Anselme G0R 2N0 – 418/885-4977, Fax: 418/885-9834 |
| ST-ANTOINE | 10,806 | La Rivière-du-Nord | Laurentides | Prévost | Serge Forget, Gref., 854, boul St-Antoine, St-Antoine J7Z 3C5 – 514/436-1762, Fax: 514/436-3057 |
| St-Antoine-de-Lavaltrie (P) | 4,385 | D'Autray | Berthier-Montcalm | Berthier | Yvon Mousseau, Sec.-Trés., 49, ch de Lavaltrie, St-Antoine-de-Lavaltrie J0K 1H0 – 514/586-1331, Fax: 514/586-4060 |
| St-Antoine-de-l'Isle-aux-Grues (P) | 176 | Montmagny | Bellechasse-Etchemins-Montmagny-L'Islet | Montmagny-L'Islet | Adèle Roy-Lavoie, Sec.-Trés., l'Isle-aux-Grues G0R 1P0 – 418/248-8060, Fax: 418/248-8060 |
| St-Antoine-de-Tilly (Mun.) | 1,381 | Lotbinière | Lotbinière | Lotbinière | Mario Léonard, Sec.-Trés., 3837, ch de Tilly, St-Antoine-de-Tilly G0S 2C0 – 418/886-2441, Fax: 418/886-2075 |
| St-Antoine-sur-Richelieu (Mun.) | 1,533 | La Vallée-du-Richelieu | Verchères | Verchères | Gisèle Collette, Sec.-Trés., 1060, rue des Ormes, CP 208, St-Antoine-sur-Richelieu J0L 1R0 – 514/787-3497, Fax: 514/787-2852 |
| St-Antonin (P) | 3,368 | Rivière-du-Loup | Kamouraska-Rivière-du-Loup-Témiscouata-Les Basques | Rivière-du-Loup | Gina Dionne, Sec.-Trés., 261, rue Principale, CP 340, St-Antonin G0L 2J0 – 418/862-1056, Fax: 418/862-3268 |

Urban Centres (Villes) in CAPITALS; Villages marked (V); Townships/Cantons marked (Canton);United townships/Cantons unis marked (Cantons); Parishes marked (P); Municipalities marked (Mun.).; Northern villages/Villages nordiques marked (NV); Cree Villages/Villages Cris marked (VC); Naskapi Villages/Villages Naskapi marked (VN); In the third column, Urban Community/Communauté Urbaine marked Urb. Com. An in-depth listing for municipalities marked with * appears in Part 2 (check Index for page numbers).

| MUNICIPALITY | 1996 POP. | REGIONAL COUNTY MUN. | FEDERAL ELECTORAL DISTRICT | PROVINCIAL ELECTORAL DISTRICT | CONTACT PERSON WITH ADDRESS, PHONE & FAX |
|---|---|---|---|---|---|
| St-Apollinaire (Mun.) | 3,716 | Lotbinière | Lotbinière | Lotbinière | Jean Blais, Sec.-Trés., 94, rue Principale, St-Apollinaire G0S 2E0 – 418/881-3996, Fax: 418/881-4152 |
| Ste-Apolline-de-Patton (P) | 705 | Montmagny | Bellechasse-Etchemins-Montmagny-L'Islet | Montmagny-L'Islet | Raynald Bernard, Sec.-Trés., 497, route Principale, Ste-Apolline de-Patton G0R 2P0 – 418/469-3031, Fax: 418/469-3031 |
| St-Armand (Mun.) | 1,047 | Brome-Missisquoi | Brome-Missisquoi | Brome-Missisquoi | Jacqueline C.-Chisholm, Sec.-Trés., 414, ch Luke, St-Armand J0J 1T0 – 514/248-2344, Fax: 514/248-2344 |
| St-Arsène (P) | 1,198 | Rivière-du-Loup | Kamouraska-Rivière-du-Loup-Témiscouata-Les Basques | Rivière-du-Loup | François Michaud, Sec.-Trés., #201, 49, rue de l'Église, St-Arsène G0L 2K0 – 418/867-2205, Fax: 418/867-2025 |
| St-Athanase (Mun.) | 391 | Témiscouata | Kamouraska-Rivière-du-Loup-Témiscouata-Les Basques | Kamouraska-Témiscouata | Francine Morin-Bélanger, Sec.-Trés., 6081, ch de l'Église, CP 40, St-Athanase G0L 2L0 – 418/859-2575, Fax: 418/859-3415 |
| St-Athanase (P) | 6,546 | Le Haut-Richelieu | St-Jean | Iberville | Carole Bergeron-Laurin, Sec.-Trés., 90, rte 104, Ste-Athanase J2X 1H1 – 514/347-9716, Fax: 514/347-0703 |
| St-Aubert (Mun.) | 1,343 | L'Islet | Bellechasse-Etchemins-Montmagny-L'Islet | Montmagny-L'Islet | Serge Roussel, Sec.-Trés., 14, rue des Loisirs, St-Aubert G0R 2R0 – 418/598-3368, Fax: 418/598-3369 |
| St-Augustin (Mun.) | 683 | Manicouagan | Duplessis | Duplessis | Nicole Driscoll, Sec.-Trés., CP 279, St-Augustin G0G 2R0 – 418/947-2404, Fax: 418/947-2533 |
| St-Augustin (P) | 486 | Maria-Chapdelaine | Roberval | Roberval | Maud Larouche, Sec.-Trés., 686, rue Principale, St-Augustin G0W 1K0 – 418/374-2147, Fax: 418/374-2984 |
| St-Augustin-de-Desmaures (Mun.) | 14,771 | Québec (Urb. Com.) | Portneuf | La Peltrie | Michel Beauchemin, Sec.-Trés., 200, rte Fossambault, St-Augustin-de-Desmaures G3A 2E3 – 418/878-2955, Fax: 418/878-4986 |
| St-Augustin-de-Woburn (P) | 715 | Le Granit | Frontenac-Mégantic | Mégantic-Compton | Gaétane Allard-Lavoie, Sec.-Trés., 590, rue St-Augustin, CP 120, Woburn G0Y 1R0 – 819/544-4211, Fax: 819/544-9236 |
| Ste-Aurélie (Mun.) | 867 | Les Etchemins | Beauce | Beauce-Sud | Sophie Fortin, Sec.-Trés., 6, rue des Saules, Ste-Aurélie G0M 1M0 – 418/593-3021, Fax: 418/593-3961 |
| Ste-Barbe (P) | 1,277 | Le Haut-St-Laurent | Beauharnois-Salaberry | Beauharnois-Huntingdon | Marc Rémillard, Sec.-Trés., 470, ch de l'Église, Ste-Barbe J0S 1P0 – 514/371-2504, Fax: 514/371-2575 |
| St-Barnabé (P) | 1,284 | Maskinongé | Trois-Rivières | Maskinongé | Denis Gélinas, Sec.-Trés., 70, rue Duguay, St-Barnabé G0X 2K0 – 819/264-2085, Fax: 819/264-2079 |
| St-Barnabé-Sud (Mun.) | 902 | Les Maskoutains | St-Hyacinthe-Bagot | St-Hyacinthe | Nicole Bélanger, Sec.-Trés., 251, rang de Michaudville, St-Barnabé-Sud J0H 1G0 – 514/792-3030, Fax: 514/792-3759 |
| St-Barthélemy (P) | 2,075 | D'Autray | Berthier-Montcalm | Berthier | Jean Charland, Sec.-Trés., 1980, rue Bonin, St-Barthélemy J0K 1X0 – 514/885-3511, Fax: 514/885-2165 |
| St-Basile (P) | 840 | Portneuf | Portneuf | Portneuf | Roger Proulx, Sec.-Trés., 39, av Garnier, CP 70, St-Basile G0A 3G0 – 418/329-2969, Fax: 418/329-3743 |
| ST-BASILE-LE-GRAND | 11,771 | La Vallée-du-Richelieu | Chambly | Chambly | Luce Doucet, Gref., 204, rue Principale, St-Basile le-Grand J3N 1M1 – 514/653-4261, Fax: 514/653-8028 |
| St-Basile-Sud (V) | 1,684 | Portneuf | Portneuf | Portneuf | Paulin Leclerc, Sec.-Trés., 40, av Garnier, CP 370, St-Basile G0A 3G0 – 418/329-2204, Fax: 418/329-2788 |
| Ste-Béatrix (Mun.) | 1,617 | Matawinie | Berthier-Montcalm | Berthier | Danielle Lambert, Sec.-Trés., 861, rue de l'Église, Ste-Béatrix J0K 1Y0 – 514/883-2245, Fax: 514/883-1772 |
| St-Benjamin (Mun.) | 917 | Les Etchemins | Beauce | Beauce-Sud | France Veilleux, Sec.-Trés., 440, av du Collège, CP 100, St-Benjamin G0M 1N0 – 418/594-8156, Fax: 418/594-6068 |
| St-Benoît-du-Lac (Mun.) | 53 | | Brome-Missisquoi | Brome-Missisquoi | Jacques Bolduc, Directeur général, Abbaye-St-Benoît, St-Benoît-du-Lac J0B 2M0 – 819/843-4080, Fax: 819/843-3199 |
| St-Benoît-Labre (Mun.) | 1,553 | Beauce-Sartigan | Beauce | Beauce-Sud | Gaétane Vallée, Sec.-Trés., 216, boul des Érables, St-Benoît-Labre G0M 1P0 – 418/228-9250, Fax: 418/228-0518 |
| St-Bernard (Mun.) | 2,023 | La Nouvelle-Beauce | Beauce | Beauce-Nord | Madeleine Nadeau, Sec.-Trés., 551, rue Vaillancourt, CP 70, St-Bernard G0S 2G0 – 418/475-6060, Fax: 418/475-6069 |
| St-Bernard-de-Lacolle (P) | 1,544 | Les Jardins-de-Napierville | Beauharnois-Salaberry | Beauharnois-Huntingdon | Daniel Striletsky, Sec.-Trés., 113, rang Saint-Claude, St-Bernard-de-Lacolle J0J 1V0 – 514/246-3348, Fax: 514/246-4380 |
| St-Bernard-Sud (P) | 607 | Les Maskoutains | St-Hyacinthe-Bagot | Richelieu | Sylvie Chaput, Sec.-Trés., 410, rue Principale, St-Bernard-de-Michaudville J0H 1C0 – 514/792-3190, Fax: 514/792-3591 |
| St-Blaise-sur-Richelieu (Mun.) | 2,067 | Le Haut-Richelieu | St-Jean | St-Jean | Francine Leblanc, Sec.-Trés., 795, rue des Loisirs, St-Blaise-sur-Richelieu J0J 1W0 – 514/291-5944, Fax: 514/291-3832 |

Urban Centres (Villes) in CAPITALS; Villages marked (V); Townships/Cantons marked (Canton);United townships/Cantons unis marked (Cantons); Parishes marked (P); Municipalities marked (Mun.).; Northern villages/Villages nordiques marked (NV); Cree Villages/Villages Cris marked (VC); Naskapi Villages/Villages Naskapi marked (VN); In the third column, Urban Community/Communauté Urbaine marked Urb. Com. An in-depth listing for municipalities marked with * appears in Part 2 (check Index for page numbers).

| MUNICIPALITY | 1996 POP. | REGIONAL COUNTY MUN. | FEDERAL ELECTORAL DISTRICT | PROVINCIAL ELECTORAL DISTRICT | CONTACT PERSON WITH ADDRESS, PHONE & FAX |
|---|---|---|---|---|---|
| Ste-Blandine (P) | 2,114 | Rimouski-Neigette | Rimouski-Mitis-Mitis | Rimouski | Monique Sénéchal, Sec.-Trés., 3, rue du Collège, Ste-Blandine G0K 1J0 – 418/735-2752, Fax: 418/735-2708 |
| St-Bonaventure (Mun.) | 1,071 | Drummond | Drummond | Nicolet-Yamaska | Claire Côté, Sec.-Trés., 720, rue Plante, St-Bonaventure J0C 1C0 – 819/396-2335, Fax: 819/396-2335 |
| St-Boniface-de-Shawinigan (V) | 3,998 | Le Centre-de-la-Mauricie | St-Maurice | St-Maurice | Jacques Caron, Sec.-Trés., 140, rue Guimont, St-Boniface-de-Shawinigan G0X 2L0 – 819/535-3811, Fax: 819/535-1242 |
| Ste-Brigide-d'Iberville (Mun.) | 1,371 | Le Haut-Richelieu | St-Jean | Iberville | Réjeanne Giroux, Sec.-Trés., 480, rue de l'Hôtel-de-Ville, CP 30, Ste-Brigide J0J 1X0 – 514/293-7511, Fax: 514/293-7511 |
| Ste-Brigitte-de-Laval (Mun.) | 3,214 | La Jacques-Cartier | Charlesbourg | Montmorency | Jacques Vallée, Sec.-Trés., 1, rue Auclair, Ste-Brigitte-de-Laval G0A 3K0 – 418/825-2515, Fax: 418/825-3114 |
| Ste-Brigitte-des-Saults (P) | 736 | Drummond | Drummond | Nicolet-Yamaska | Nicole Comtois, Sec.-Trés., 400, rue Principale, CP 1038, Ste-Brigitte-des-Saults J0C 1E0 – 819/336-4460, Fax: 819/336-4410 |
| St-Bruno (Mun.) | 2,422 | Lac-St-Jean-Est | Lac-St-Jean | Lac-St-Jean | Claude Moisan, Sec.-Trés., 541, av St-Alphonse, CP 39, St-Bruno G0W 2L0 – 418/343-2303, Fax: 418/343-2662 |
| St-Bruno-de-Guigues (Mun.) | 1,117 | Témiscamingue | Témiscamingue | Rouyn-Noranda-Témiscamingue | Serge Côte, Sec.-Trés., 21, rue Principale nord, CP 130, St-Bruno-de-Guigues J0Z 2G0 – 819/728-2186, Fax: 819/728-2404 |
| St-Bruno-de-Kamouraska (Mun.) | 529 | Kamouraska | Kamouraska-Rivière-du-Loup-Témiscouata-Les Basques | Kamouraska-Témiscouata | Suzanne Dionne, Sec.-Trés., 4, rue du Couvent, CP 28, St-Bruno-de-Kamouraska G0L 2M0 – 418/492-2612, Fax: 418/492-2612 |
| ST-BRUNO-DE-MONTARVILLE | 23,714 | La Vallée-du-Richelieu | St-Bruno-St-Hubert | Chambly | Chantal Sainte-Marie, Gref., 1585, rue Montarville, St-Bruno-de-Montarville J3V 3T8 – 514/653-2443, Fax: 514/461-3649 |
| St-Calixte (Mun.) | 4,681 | Montcalm | Berthier-Montcalm | Rousseau | Denis Malouin, Sec.-Trés., 6230, rue de l'Hôtel-de-Ville, St-Calixte J0K 1Z0 – 514/222-2782, Fax: 514/222-2789 |
| St-Camille (Canton) | 459 | Asbestos | Richmond-Arthabaska | Richmond | Marie Pigeon, Sec.-Trés., 85, rue Desrivières, St-Camille J0A 1G0 – 819/828-3222, Fax: 819/828-3723 |
| St-Camille-de-Lellis (P) | 963 | Les Etchemins | Bellechasse-Etchemins-Montmagny-L'Islet | Bellechasse | Nicole Mathieu, Sec.-Trés., 7, rue Carrier, CP 70, St-Camille-de-Lellis G0R 2S0 – 418/595-2233, Fax: 418/595-2233 |
| St-Casimir (P) | 436 | Portneuf | Portneuf | Portneuf | Ginette Paquin, Sec.-Trés., 220, boul de la Montagne, 3e étage, CP 250, St-Casimir G0A 3L0 – 418/339-2676, Fax: 418/339-3105 |
| St-Casimir (Mun.) | 1,347 | Portneuf | Portneuf | Portneuf | Carole Germain, Sec.-Trés., 220, boul de la Montagne, CP 220, St-Casimir G0A 3L0 – 418/339-2543, Fax: 418/339-3105 |
| STE-CATHERINE | 13,724 | Roussillon | Châteauguay | La Prairie | Carole Cousineau, Gref., 5465, boul Marie-Victorin, Ste-Catherine J0L 1E0 – 514/632-0590, Fax: 514/632-3298 |
| Ste-Catherine-de-Hatley (Mun.) | 1,859 | Memphrémagog | Compton-Stanstead | Orford | François Bachand, Sec.-Trés., 35, ch de North-Hatley, CP 30, Katevale J0B 1W0 – 819/843-1935, Fax: 819/843-8527 |
| Ste-Catherine-de-la-Jacques-Cartier (Mun.) | 4,428 | La Jacques-Cartier | Portneuf | Portneuf | Marcel Grenier, Sec.-Trés., 1, rue Rouleau, CP 250, Ste-Catherine-de-la-Jacques-Cartier G0A 3M0 – 418/875-2758, Fax: 418/875-2170 |
| Ste-Cécile-de-Lévrard (P) | 420 | Bécancour | Lotbinière | Lotbinière | Réjean Poisson, Sec.-Trés., 235, rue Principale, Ste-Cécile-de-Lévrard G0X 2M0 – 819/263-2104, Fax: 819/263-2104 |
| Ste-Cécile-de-Milton (Canton) | 1,889 | La Haute-Yamaska | Shefford | Shefford | Ronald Sauriol, Sec.-Trés., 136, rue Principale, CP 33, Ste-Cécile-de-Milton J0E 2C0 – 514/378-1942, Fax: 514/378-4621 |
| Ste-Cécile-de-Whitton (Mun.) | 821 | Le Granit | Frontenac-Mégantic | Mégantic-Compton | Linda Deschiever, Sec.-Trés., 4557, rue Principale, Ste-Cécile-de-Whitton G0Y 1J0 – 819/583-0770, Fax: 819/583-0770 |
| St-Célestin (Mun.) | 670 | Nicolet-Yamaska | Richelieu | Nicolet-Yamaska | Gisèle P.-Morin, Sec.-Trés., 990, rang du Pays-Brûlé, St-Célestin J0C 1G0 – 819/229-3745, Fax: 819/229-1386 |
| St-Célestin (V) | 765 | Nicolet-Yamaska | Richelieu | Nicolet-Yamaska | Claude Bouchard, Sec.-Trés., 420, rue Houde, St-Célestin J0C 1G0 – 819/229-3642, Fax: 819/229-1149 |
| St-Césaire (P) | 1,945 | Rouville | Shefford | Iberville | Louise Benoit, Sec.-Trés., 2046, rte 112, St-Césaire J0L 1T0 – 514/469-3700, Fax: 514/469-2398 |
| ST-CÉSAIRE | 2,990 | Rouville | Shefford | Iberville | Pierre Despars, Sec.-Trés., 1111, av St-Paul, St-Césaire J0L 1T0 – 514/469-3108, Fax: 514/469-5275 |

Urban Centres (Villes) in CAPITALS; Villages marked (V); Townships/Cantons marked (Canton);United townships/Cantons unis marked (Cantons); Parishes marked (P); Municipalities marked (Mun.).; Northern villages/Villages nordiques marked (NV); Cree Villages/Villages Cris marked (VC); Naskapi Villages/Villages Naskapi marked (VN); In the third column, Urban Community/Communauté Urbaine marked Urb. Com. An in-depth listing for municipalities marked with * appears in Part 2 (check Index for page numbers).

| MUNICIPALITY | 1996 POP. | REGIONAL COUNTY MUN. | FEDERAL ELECTORAL DISTRICT | PROVINCIAL ELECTORAL DISTRICT | CONTACT PERSON WITH ADDRESS, PHONE & FAX |
|---|---|---|---|---|---|
| St-Charles-Borromée (Mun.) | 10,013 | Joliette | Joliette | Joliette | François Thériault, Sec.-Trés., 525, rue de la Visitation, St-Charles-Borromée J6E 4P2 – 514/759-4415, Fax: 514/759-3393 |
| St-Charles-de-Bellechasse (Mun.) | 2,197 | Bellechasse | Bellechasse-Etchemins-Montmagny-L'Islet | Bellechasse | Denis Labbé, Sec.-Trés., 25, av Commerciale, St-Charles G0R 2T0 – 418/887-6600, Fax: 418/887-6779 |
| St-Charles-de-Bourget (Mun.) | 715 | Le Fjord-du-Saguenay | Lac-St-Jean | Dubuc | Colombe Bergeron, Sec.-Trés., 357, 2e rang, St-Charles-de-Bourget G0V 1G0 – 418/672-2624, Fax: 418/672-4403 |
| St-Charles-de-Drummond (Mun.) | 5,046 | Drummond | Drummond | Drummond | Gilles Proulx, Sec.-Trés., 1250, rue Proulx, St-Charles-de-Drummond J2C 5A2 – 819/477-4530, Fax: 819/477-0697 |
| St-Charles-de-Mandeville (Mun.) | 1,824 | D'Autray | Berthier-Montcalm | Berthier | Francine Bergeron, Sec.-Trés., 162, boul Desjardins, St-Charles-de-Mandeville J0K 1L0 – 514/835-2055, Fax: 514/835-7795 |
| St-Charles-Garnier (P) | 337 | La Mitis | Rimouski-Mitis | Matapédia | Josette Bouillon, Sec.-Trés., CP 39, St-Charles-Garnier G0K 1K0 – 418/798-4305, Fax: 418/798-4305 |
| St-Charles-sur-Richelieu (Mun.) | 1,710 | La Vallée-du-Richelieu | Verchères | Verchères | Francyne Hébert, Sec.-Trés., 12, rue de l'Union, CP 150, St-Charles-sur-Richelieu J0H 2G0 – 514/584-3484, Fax: 514/584-2965 |
| Ste-Christine (P) | 797 | Acton | St-Hyacinthe-Bagot | Johnson | Bernadette Rodier-Chagnon, Sec.-Trés., 629, rue des Loisirs, Ste-Christine J0H 1H0 – 819/858-2828, Fax: 819/858-2828 |
| Ste-Christine-d'Auvergne (Mun.) | 337 | Portneuf | Portneuf | Portneuf | Réjeanne Plamondon, Sec.-Trés., 80, rue Principale, CP 639, Ste-Christine-d'Auvergne G0A 1A0 – 418/329-3304, Fax: 418/329-3356 |
| St-Christophe-d'Arthabaska (P) | 2,264 | Arthabaska | Richmond-Arthabaska | Arthabaska | Francine Moreau, Sec.-Trés., 418, av Pie-X, St-Christophe-d'Arthabaska G6P 6S1 – 819/357-9031, Fax: 819/357-9087 |
| St-Chrysostome (V) | 850 | Le Haut-St-Laurent | Beauharnois-Salaberry | Beauharnois-Huntingdon | Pauline Primeau, Sec.-Trés., #10, 124, rue Notre-Dame, CP 190, St-Chrysostome J0S 1R0 – 514/826-3035, Fax: 514/826-3607 |
| Ste-Claire (Mun.) | 3,160 | Bellechasse | Bellechasse-Etchemins-Montmagny-L'Islet | Bellechasse | Serge Gagnon, Sec.-Trés., 55, rue de la Fabrique, CP 189, Ste-Claire G0R 2V0 – 418/883-3314, Fax: 418/883-3845 |
| St-Claude (Mun.) | 1,004 | Le Val-St-François | Richmond-Arthabaska | Richmond | France Lavertu, Sec.-Trés., 295, rte de l'Église, St-Claude J0B 2N0 – 819/845-7795, Fax: 819/845-2479 |
| St-Clément (P) | 566 | Les Basques | Kamouraska-Rivière-du-Loup-Témiscouata-Les Basques | Rivière-du-Loup | Line Caron, Sec.-Trés., 25A, rue St-Pierre, CP 40, St-Clément G0L 2N0 – 418/963-2258, Fax: 418/963-2619 |
| St-Cléophas (P) | 404 | La Matapédia | Matapédia-Matane | Matapédia | Lise Turbide, Sec.-Trés., 350, rue Principale, St-Cléophas G0J 3N0 – 418/536-3023, Fax: 418/536-3023 |
| St-Cléophas (P) | 283 | D'Autray | Berthier-Montcalm | Berthier | Chantal Piette, Sec.-Trés., 750, rue Principale, St-Cléophas-de-Brandon J0K 2A0 – 514/889-5683, Fax: 514/889-8007 |
| St-Clet (Mun.) | 1,524 | Vaudreuil-Soulanges | Vaudreuil-Soulanges | Salaberry-Soulanges | Nathalie Pharand, Sec.-Trés., 4, rue du Moulin, St-Clet J0P 1S0 – 514/456-3363, Fax: 514/456-3879 |
| Ste-Clothilde-de-Horton (P) | 883 | Arthabaska | Richmond-Arthabaska | Richmond | Marlène Langlois, Sec.-Trés., rue du Parc, CP 29, Ste-Clothilde-de-Horton J0A 1H0 – 819/336-5344, Fax: 819/336-5440 |
| Ste-Clotilde-de-Beauce (Mun.) | 583 | L'Amiante | Frontenac-Mégantic | Beauce-Sud | Marcel Pomerleau, Sec.-Trés., 1045, rue Principale, Ste-Clotilde-de-Beauce G0N 1C0 – 418/427-2637, Fax: 418/427-2637 |
| Ste-Clotilde-de-Châteauguay (P) | 1,595 | Les Jardins-de-Napierville | Beauharnois-Salaberry | Beauharnois-Huntingdon | Nicole Marcil-Lefebvre, Sec.-Trés., 2452, ch de l'Église, Ste-Clotilde-de-Châteauguay J0L 1W0 – 514/826-3129, Fax: 514/826-3217 |
| Ste-Clotilde-de-Horton (V) | 378 | Arthabaska | Richmond-Arthabaska | Richmond | Roger Boissonneault, Sec.-Trés., 11, route 122, CP 189, Ste-Clotilde-de-Horton J0A 1H0 – 819/336-2033 |
| St-Colomban (P) | 5,569 | La Rivière-du-Nord | Argenteuil-Papineau | Argenteuil | Josée Shewchuck, Sec.-Trés., 330, montée de l'Église, St-Colomban J0R 1N0 – 514/436-1453, Fax: 514/436-5955 |
| St-Côme (P) | 1,921 | Matawinie | Berthier-Montcalm | Berthier | Alice Riopel, Sec.-Trés., 1673, 55e rue, St-Côme J0K 2B0 – 514/883-2726, Fax: 514/883-6431 |
| St-Côme-Linière (Mun.) | 3,241 | Beauce-Sartigan | Beauce | Beauce-Sud | Yvan Bélanger, Sec.-Trés., 1375, 18e rue, CP 219, St-Côme-Linière G0M 1J0 – 418/685-3825, Fax: 418/685-2566 |
| ST-CONSTANT | 21,933 | Roussillon | Châteauguay | La Prairie | Vacant, Gref., 147, rue St-Pierre, CP 130, St-Constant J5A 2G2 – 514/638-2010, Fax: 514/638-5919 |

Urban Centres (Villes) in CAPITALS; Villages marked (V); Townships/Cantons marked (Canton);United townships/Cantons unis marked (Cantons); Parishes marked (P); Municipalities marked (Mun.).; Northern villages/Villages nordiques marked (NV); Cree Villages/Villages Cris marked (VC); Naskapi Villages/Villages Naskapi marked (VN); In the third column, Urban Community/Communauté Urbaine marked Urb. Com. An in-depth listing for municipalities marked with * appears in Part 2 (check Index for page numbers).

| MUNICIPALITY | 1996 POP. | REGIONAL COUNTY MUN. | FEDERAL ELECTORAL DISTRICT | PROVINCIAL ELECTORAL DISTRICT | CONTACT PERSON WITH ADDRESS, PHONE & FAX |
|---|---|---|---|---|---|
| Ste-Croix (P) | 825 | Lotbinière | Lotbinière | Lotbinière | Hélène Boucher, Sec.-Trés., 6310, rue Principale, CP 100, Ste-Croix G0S 2H0 – 418/926-2212, Fax: 418/926-2212 |
| Ste-Croix (V) | 1,618 | Lotbinière | Lotbinière | Lotbinière | Bertrand Fréchette, Sec.-Trés., 6310, rue Principale, CP 609, Ste-Croix G0S 2H0 – 418/926-3494, Fax: 418/926-2570 |
| St-Cuthbert (P) | 1,722 | D'Autray | Berthier-Montcalm | Berthier | Richard Lauzon, Sec.-Trés., 1891, rue Principale, CP 100, St-Cuthbert J0K 2C0 – 514/836-4852, Fax: 514/836-4833 |
| St-Cyprien (Mun.) | 1,274 | Rivière-du-Loup | Kamouraska-Rivière-du-Loup-Témiscouata-Les Basques | Rivière-du-Loup | Guy Dubé, Sec.-Trés., 101B, rue Collin, CP 9, St-Cyprien G0L 2P0 – 418/963-2730, Fax: 418/963-3490 |
| St-Cyprien (P) | 617 | Les Etchemins | Bellechasse-Etchemins-Montmagny-L'Islet | Bellechasse | Pauline Fortier, Sec.-Trés., 399, rue Principale, CP 100, St-Cyprien G0R 1B0 – 418/383-5274, Fax: 418/383-5269 |
| St-Cyprien-de-Napierville (P) | 1,307 | Les Jardins-de-Napierville | Beauharnois-Salaberry | Beauharnois-Huntingdon | Pauline Roy, Sec.-Trés., 121, rang Cyr, St-Cyprien-de-Napierville J0J 1L0 – 514/245-3658, Fax: 514/245-3658 |
| St-Cyrille-de-Lessard (P) | 830 | L'Islet | Bellechasse-Etchemins-Montmagny-L'Islet | Montmagny-L'Islet | Raymonde Dubé, Sec.-Trés., 282, rue Principale, CP 87, St-Cyrille-de-L'Islet G0R 2W0 – 418/247-5186, Fax: 418/247-5186 |
| St-Cyrille-de-Wendover (Mun.) | 3,849 | Drummond | Drummond | Richmond | Mario Picotin, Sec.-Trés., 4055, rue Principale, St-Cyrille-de-Wendover J1Z 1C8 – 819/397-4226, Fax: 819/397-5505 |
| St-Damase (P) | 439 | La Matapédia | Matapédia-Matane | Matane | Colette Dastous, Sec.-Trés., 18, av du Centenaire, St-Damase G0J 2J0 – 418/776-2103, Fax: 418/776-5705 |
| St-Damase (V) | 1,362 | Les Maskoutains | St-Hyacinthe-Bagot | St-Hyacinthe | Yvon Tétreault, Sec.-Trés., 223, rue Principale, St-Damase J0H 1J0 – 514/797-3341, Fax: 514/797-3543 |
| St-Damase (P) | 1,362 | Les Maskoutains | St-Hyacinthe-Bagot | St-Hyacinthe | Yvon Tétreault, Sec.-Trés., 223, rue Principale, St-Damase J0H 1J0 – 514/797-3341, Fax: 514/797-3543 |
| St-Damase-de-L'Islet (Mun.) | 630 | L'Islet | Bellechasse-Etchemins-Montmagny-L'Islet | Montmagny-L'Islet | Paulette Lord-Lapointe, Sec.-Trés., 26, rue du Villlage est, CP 10, St-Damase-de-L'Islet G0R 2X0 – 418/598-9370, Fax: 418/598-9370 |
| St-Damien (P) | 1,760 | Matawinie | Berthier-Montcalm | Berthier | Josée Tellier, Sec.-Trés., 6850, rte 347, CP 240, St-Damien J0K 2E0 – 514/835-3419, Fax: 514/835-5538 |
| St-Damien-de-Buckland (P) | 2,216 | Bellechasse | Bellechasse-Etchemins-Montmagny-L'Islet | Bellechasse | Jacques Thibault, Sec.-Trés., 75, rte St-Gérard, St-Damien-de-Buckland G0R 2Y0 – 418/789-2526, Fax: 418/789-2125 |
| St-David (P) | 873 | Le Bas-Richelieu | Richelieu | Nicolet-Yamaska | Sylvie Letendre, Sec.-Trés., 11, rue de la Rivière-David, St-David J0G 1L0 – 514/789-2288, Fax: 514/789-3023 |
| St-David-de-Falardeau (Mun.) | 2,137 | Le Fjord-du-Saguenay | Lac-St-Jean | Dubuc | Daniel Hudon, Sec.-Trés., 140, boul St-David, CP 130, St-David-de-Falardeau G0V 1C0 – 418/673-4647, Fax: 418/673-3266 |
| St-Denis (P) | 488 | Kamouraska | Kamouraska-Rivière-du-Loup-Témiscouata-Les Basques | Kamouraska-Témiscouata | Thérèse Dumais-Charest, Sec.-Trés., 23, route 132 ouest, CP 69, St-Denis-De La Bouteillerie G0L 2R0 – 418/498-2968, Fax: 418/498-2948 |
| St-Denis (P) | 1,147 | La Vallée-du-Richelieu | Verchères | Verchères | André Cabana, Sec.-Trés., #200, 636, ch des Patriotes, St-Denis-sur-Richelieu J0H 1K0 – 514/787-2092, Fax: 514/787-2635 |
| St-Denis (V) | 994 | La Vallée-du-Richelieu | Verchères | Verchères | Pierre Pétrin, Sec.-Trés., 601, ch des Patriotes, St-Denis-sur-Richelieu J0H 1K0 – 514/787-2244, Fax: 514/787-3721 |
| St-Denis-de-Brompton (P) | 2,289 | Le Val-St-François | Richmond-Arthabaska | Johnson | Marc Laflamme, Sec.-Trés., 2050, Ernest-Camiré, CP 120, St-Denis-de-Brompton J0B 2P0 – 819/846-2744, Fax: 819/846-0915 |
| St-Didace (P) | 583 | D'Autray | Berthier-Montcalm | Berthier | André Allard, Sec.-Trés., 380, rue Principale, St-Didace J0K 2G0 – 514/835-4184, Fax: 514/835-4184 |
| St-Dominique (Mun.) | 2,236 | Les Maskoutains | Vaudreuil-Soulanges | St-Hyacinthe | Agnès Archambault, Sec.-Trés., 467, rue Deslandes, St-Dominique J0H 1L0 – 514/774-9939, Fax: 514/774-1595 |
| St-Dominique-du-Rosaire (Mun.) | 457 | Abitibi | Abitibi | Abitibi-Ouest | Lucille Ferron, Sec.-Trés., 235A, rue Principale, St-Dominique-du-Rosaire J0Y 2K0 – 819/727-9544, Fax: 819/727-4344 |
| St-Donat (P) | 812 | La Mitis | Rimouski-Mitis | Matapedia | Gil Bérubé, Sec.-Trés., 194, av du Mont-Comi, CP 70, St-Donat-de-Rimouski G0K 1L0 – 418/739-4634, Fax: 418/739-5003 |
| St-Donat (Mun.) | 3,262 | Matawinie | Berthier-Montcalm | Bertrand | Jean Robidoux, Sec.-Trés., 475, rue Desrochers, CP 460, St-Donat-de-Montcalm J0T 2C0 – 819/424-2383, Fax: 819/424-5020 |

Urban Centres (Villes) in CAPITALS; Villages marked (V); Townships/Cantons marked (Canton);United townships/Cantons unis marked (Cantons); Parishes marked (P); Municipalities marked (Mun.).; Northern villages/Villages nordiques marked (NV); Cree Villages/Villages Cris marked (VC); Naskapi Villages/Villages Naskapi marked (VN); In the third column, Urban Community/Communauté Urbaine marked Urb. Com. An in-depth listing for municipalities marked with * appears in Part 2 (check Index for page numbers).

| MUNICIPALITY | 1996 POP. | REGIONAL COUNTY MUN. | FEDERAL ELECTORAL DISTRICT | PROVINCIAL ELECTORAL DISTRICT | CONTACT PERSON WITH ADDRESS, PHONE & FAX |
|---|---|---|---|---|---|
| St-Edmond (Mun.) | 239 | La Matapédia | Matapédia-Matane | Matapédia | Philippe Lavigne, Sec.-Trés., 880, 4e rang, Lac-au-Saumon G0J 1M0 – 418/778-3478, Fax: 418/778-3478 |
| St-Edmond (Mun.) | 585 | Maria-Chapdelaine | Roberval | Roberval | Danielle Bernard, Sec.-Trés., 561, ch Principale, St-Edmond-les-Plaines G0W 2M0 – 418/274-3069, Fax: 418/274-5629 |
| St-Edmond-de-Grantham (P) | 572 | Drummond | Drummond | Drummond | Hervé Lafleur, Sec.-Trés., 393, Notre-Dame-de-Lourdes, St-Edmond-de-Grantham J0C 1K0 – 819/395-2562, Fax: 819/395-2562 |
| St-Édouard (P) | 1,257 | Les Jardins-de-Napierville | Châteauguay | Beauharnois-Huntingdon | Daniel Théroux, Sec.-Trés., 405C, montée Lussier, CP 120, St-Édouard J0L 1Y0 – 514/454-6333, Fax: 514/454-6333 |
| St-Édouard-de-Fabre (P) | 734 | Témiscamingue | Témiscamingue | Rouyn-Noranda-Témiscamingue | Aline Desjardins, Sec.-Trés., 1323, rue Principale, CP 70, Fabre J0Z 1Z0 – 819/634-4441, Fax: 819/634-2646 |
| St-Édouard-de-Frampton (P) | 1,278 | La Nouvelle-Beauce | Beauce | Beauce-Nord | Josée Audet, Sec.-Trés., 107, rue Ste-Anne, CP 40, St-Édouard-de-Frampton G0R 1M0 – 418/479-5363, Fax: 418/479-5363 |
| St-Édouard-de-Lotbinière (P) | 1,278 | Lotbinière | Lotbinière | Lotbinière | Anna Blondin, Sec.-Trés., 105, route Soucy, CP 188, St-Édouard G0S 1Y0 – 418/796-2971, Fax: 418/796-2228 |
| St-Édouard-de-Maskinongé (Mun.) | 744 | Maskinongé | St-Maurice | Maskinongé | Gilles Gerbeau, Sec.-Trés., 3800, rue St-André, St-Édouard-de-Maskinongé J0K 2H0 – 819/268-2833, Fax: 819/268-2833 |
| Ste-Edwidge-de-Clifton (Canton) | 530 | Coaticook | Compton-Stanstead | Mégantic-Compton | Réjean Fauteux, Sec.-Trés., 203, rue Principale Nord, Ste-Edwidge-de-Clifton J0B 2R0 – 819/849-7740, Fax: 819/849-7740 |
| St-Élie (P) | 1,455 | Le Centre-de-la-Mauricie | St-Maurice | Maskinongé | Micheline Allard, Sec.-Trés., 22, ch des Loisirs, CP 39, St-Élie G0X 2N0 – 819/221-2839, Fax: 819/221-4039 |
| St-Élie-d'Orford (Mun.) | 6,148 | Sherbrooke | Compton-Stanstead | Orford | Pierre Auger, Sec.-Trés., 161, ch St-Roch, St-Élie-d'Orford J0B 2S0 – 819/566-5466, Fax: 819/566-1163 |
| Ste-Élisabeth (P) | 1,559 | D'Autray | Berthier-Montcalm | Berthier | Pauline Ladouceur, Sec.-Trés., 2270, rue Principale, Ste-Élizabeth J0K 2J0 – 514/759-2875, Fax: 514/756-4312 |
| Ste-Élisabeth-de-Warwick (P) | 431 | Arthabaska | Richmond-Arthabaska | Richmond | Lucille Gosselin, Sec.-Trés., 230, 4e rang, CP 75, Ste-Élisabeth-de-Warwick J0A 1M0 – 819/358-5162, Fax: 819/358-5162 |
| St-Éloi (P) | 340 | Les Basques | Kamouraska-Rivière-du-Loup-Témiscouata-Les Basques | Rivière-du-Loup | Annie Roussel, Sec.-Trés., 183, rue Principale, CP 9, St-Éoi G0L 2V0 – 418/898-2734, Fax: 418/898-2734 |
| St-Elphège (P) | 321 | Nicolet-Yamaska | Richelieu | Nicolet-Yamaska | France Dionne, Sec.-Trés., 245, rang St-Antoine, St-Elphège J0G 1J0 – 514/568-0288, Fax: 514/568-0288 |
| St-Elzéar (Mun.) | 565 | Bonaventure | Bonaventure-Gaspé-Îles-de-la-Madeleine-Pabok | Bonaventure | Lucille Ferlatte, Sec.-Trés., 148, ch Principal, CP 40, St-Elzéar G0C 2W0 – 418/534-2611, Fax: 418/534-2611 |
| St-Elzéar (Mun.) | 374 | Témiscouata | Kamouraska-Rivière-du-Loup-Témiscouata-Les Basques | Kamouraska-Témiscouata | Nanny Lévesque, Sec.-Trés., 209, rue de l'Église, St-Elzéar-de-Témiscouata G0L 2W0 – 418/854-7690, Fax: 418/854-7690 |
| St-Elzéar (Mun.) | 1,665 | La Nouvelle-Beauce | Beauce | Beauce-Nord | Solange Marcoux, Sec.-Trés., 672, av Principale, St-Elzéar G0S 2J0 – 418/387-2534, Fax: 418/387-4378 |
| Ste-Émélie-de-l'Énergie (Mun.) | 1,437 | Matawinie | Berthier-Montcalm | Berthier | Guylaine Comtois, Sec.-Trés., 241, rue Coutu, Ste-Émélie-de-L'Énergie J0K 2K0 – 514/886-3823, Fax: 514/886-3824 |
| ST-ÉMILE | 9,889 | Québec (Urb. Com.) | Charlesbourg | Chauveau | Jean Savard, Gref., 6180, rue des Érables, St-Émile G3E 1K6 – 418/842-3000, Fax: 418/842-7081 |
| St-Émile-de-Suffolk (Mun.) | 433 | Papineau | Argenteuil-Papineau | Papineau | Gisèle Éthier, Sec.-Trés., 299, rte des Cantons, Saint-Émile-de-Suffolk J0V 1Y0 – 819/426-2987, Fax: 819/426-2947 |
| Ste-Emmélie (P) | 322 | Lotbinière | Lotbinière | Lotbinière | Francine Demers, Sec.-Trés., 189, rang du Portage, Leclercville G0S 2K0 – 819/292-2331, Fax: 819/292-2639 |
| St-Éphrem-de-Beauce (P) | 1,280 | Beauce-Sartigan | Beauce | Beauce-Sud | Charlotte Longchamps, Sec.-Trés., #1, 34, rue de la Station, CP 369, St-Éphrem-de-Beauce G0M 1R0 – 418/484-5716, Fax: 418/484-5715 |
| St-Éphrem-de-Tring (V) | 1,248 | Beauce-Sartigan | Beauce | Beauce-Sud | Thérèse Bolduc, Sec.-Trés., 34, rue de la Station, CP 87, St-Éphrem-de-Tring G0M 1R0 – 418/484-2114, Fax: 418/484-2305 |
| St-Éphrem-d'Upton (P) | 858 | Acton | St-Hyacinthe-Bagot | Johnson | Robert Leclerc, Sec.-Trés., 863, rue Lanoie, St-Éphrem-d'Upton J0H 2E0 – 514/549-4361, Fax: 514/549-5045 |

Urban Centres (Villes) in CAPITALS; Villages marked (V); Townships/Cantons marked (Canton);United townships/Cantons unis marked (Cantons); Parishes marked (P); Municipalities marked (Mun.).; Northern villages/Villages nordiques marked (NV); Cree Villages/Villages Cris marked (VC); Naskapi Villages/Villages Naskapi marked (VN); In the third column, Urban Community/Communauté Urbaine marked Urb. Com. An in-depth listing for municipalities marked with * appears in Part 2 (check Index for page numbers).

| MUNICIPALITY | 1996 POP. | REGIONAL COUNTY MUN. | FEDERAL ELECTORAL DISTRICT | PROVINCIAL ELECTORAL DISTRICT | CONTACT PERSON WITH ADDRESS, PHONE & FAX |
|---|---|---|---|---|---|
| St-Épiphane (Mun.) | 895 | Rivière-du-Loup | Kamouraska-Rivière-du-Loup-Témis-couata-Les Basques | Rivière-du-Loup | Denis Lagacé, Sec.-Trés., 280, rue Bernier, CP 69, St-Épiphane G0L 2X0 – 418/862-0052, Fax: 418/862-7753 |
| St-Esprit (P) | 1,908 | Montcalm | Berthier-Montcalm | Rousseau | Nathalie Rochon, Sec.-Trés., 21, rue Principale, St-Esprit J0K 2L0 – 514/839-3629, Fax: 514/839-6070 |
| St-Étienne-de-Beau-harnois (Mun.) | 799 | Beauharnois-Salab-erry | Beauharnois-Salaberry | Beauharnois-Hunt-ingdon | Ginette Prud'homme, Sec.-Trés., 489, ch St-Louis, St-Étienne-de-Beauharnois J0S 1S0 – 514/225-1000, Fax: 514/225-1011 |
| St-Étienne-de-Beaumont (P) | 2,067 | Bellechasse | Bellechasse-Etchemins-Montmagny-L'Islet | Bellechasse | Serge Richard, Sec.-Trés., 6, boul Mercier, St-Étienne-de-Beaumont G0R 1C0 – 418/833-3369, Fax: 418/833-4788 |
| St-Étienne-de-Bolton (Mun.) | 400 | Memphrémagog | Brome-Missisquoi | Brome-Missisquoi | Rose-Marie Doucet, Sec.-Trés., 9, rang de la Montagne, St-Étienne-de-Bolton J0E 2E0 – 514/297-3353, Fax: 514/297-0412 |
| St-Étienne-de-Lauzon (Mun.) | 8,207 | Les Chutes-de-la-Chaudière | Lévis | Chutes-de-la-Chaudière | Sébastien Hamel, Sec.-Trés., 1, place Chamberland, CP 339, St-Étienne-de-Lauzon G6J 1M5 – 418/831-4023, Fax: 418/831-7198 |
| St-Étienne-des-Grès (P) | 3,823 | Francheville | St-Maurice | Maskinongé | Hélène Boisvert, Sec.-Trés., 1230, rue Principale, CP 130, St-Étienne-des-Grès G0X 2P0 – 819/535-3113, Fax: 819/535-1246 |
| St-Eugène (P) | 1,158 | L'Islet | Bellechasse-Etchemins-Montmagny-L'Islet | Montmagny-L'Islet | Ginette Gagné, Sec.-Trés., 79, rue Mgr-Bernier, St-Eugène G0R 1X0 – 418/247-5340, Fax: 418/247-5052 |
| St-Eugène (Mun.) | 1,058 | Drummond | Drummond | Drummond | Chantal Herman, Sec.-Trés., 1065, rang de l'Église, CP 30, St-Eugène J0C 1J0 – 819/396-3000, Fax: 819/396-3576 |
| St-Eugène (Mun.) | 651 | Maria-Chapdelaine | Roberval | Roberval | Frédéric Lemieux, Sec.-Trés., 439, rue Principale, CP 70, St-Eugène G0W 1B0 – 418/276-1787, Fax: 418/276-1787 |
| St-Eugène-de-Guigues (Mun.) | 423 | Témiscamingue | Témiscamingue | Rouyn-Noranda-Té-miscamingue | Raynald Julien, Sec.-Trés., 4, rue Notre-Dame ouest, CP 1070, St-Eugène-de-Guigues J0Z 3L0 – 819/785-2301, Fax: 819/785-3512 |
| St-Eugène-de-Ladrière (P) | 479 | Rimouski-Neigette | Rimouski-Mitis | Rimouski | Huguette Proulx, Sec.-Trés., 159, rue Principale, St-Eugène-de-Ladrière G0L 1P0 – 418/869-2582, Fax: 418/869-2582 |
| Ste-Eulalie (Mun.) | 879 | Nicolet-Yamaska | Richelieu | Nicolet-Yamaska | Laurent Champagne, Sec.-Trés., 488, rang des Érables, CP 70, Ste-Eulalie G0Z 1E0 – 819/225-4345, Fax: 819/225-4078 |
| Ste-Euphémie-sur-Rivière-du-Sud (Mun.) | 376 | Montmagny | Bellechasse-Etchemins-Montmagny-L'Islet | Montmagny-L'Islet | Benoît Roth, Sec.-Trés., 220, rue Principal est, Ste-Euphémie-sur-Rivière-du-Sud G0R 2Z0 – 418/469-3427, Fax: 418/469-3427 |
| St-Eusèbe (P) | 662 | Témiscouata | Kamouraska-Rivière-du-Loup-Témis-couata-Les Basques | Kamouraska-Témis-couata | Andréa Deschamps, Sec.-Trés., 222, rue Principale, St-Eusèbe G0L 2Y0 – 418/899-2762, Fax: 418/899-0194 |
| ST-EUSTACHE | 39,848 | Deux-Montagnes | St-Eustache-Ste-Thérèse | Deux-Montagnes | Gilles Gougeon, Gref., 145, rue St-Louis, St-Eustache J7R 1X9 – 514/974-5000, Fax: 514/974-5229 |
| St-Évariste-de-Forsyth (Mun.) | 638 | Beauce-Sartigan | Beause | Beauce-Sud | Claude Poulin, Sec.-Trés., 495, rue Principale, CP 38, St-Évariste-de-Forsyth G0M 1S0 – 418/459-6488, Fax: 418/459-6268 |
| St-Fabien (P) | 1,838 | Rimouski-Neigette | Rimouski-Mitis | Rimouski | Murielle Cloutier, Sec.-Trés., 10, 7e av, CP 9, St-Fabien G0L 2Z0 – 418/869-2950, Fax: 418/869-2950 |
| St-Fabien-de-Panet (P) | 1,061 | Montmagny | Bellechasse-Etchemins-Montmagny-L'Islet | Montmagny-L'Islet | Claude Saint-Pierre, Sec.-Trés., 195, rue Bilodeau, CP 9, St-Fabein-de-Panet G0R 2J0 – 418/249-4471, Fax: 418/249-4471 |
| Ste-Famille (P) | 913 | L'Île-d'Orléans | Beauport-Mont-morency-Orléans | Montmorency | Lise Lapointe, Sec.-Trés., 3894, ch Royal, Ste-Famille G0A 3P0 – 418/829-3572, Fax: 418/829-2513 |
| St-Faustin-Lac Carré (Mun.) [5] | 1,609 | Les Laurentides | Laurentides | Labelle | Sylvain Rolland, Sec.-Trés., 100, Place de la Mairie, St-Faustin-Lac Carré J0T 2G0 – 819/688-2161, Fax: 819/688-6791 |
| ST-FÉLICIEN [6] | 9,599 | Le Domaine-du-Roy | Roberval | Roberval | Luc Bergeron, Gref., 1209, boul Sacré-Coeur, CP 7000, St-Félicien G8K 2R5 – 418/679-0251, Fax: 418/679-1449 |
| Ste-Félicité (Mun.) | 472 | L'Islet | Bellechasse-Etchemins-Montmagny-L'Islet | Montmagny-L'Islet | Julie Bélanger, Sec.-Trés., 5, route de l'Église nord, Ste-Félicité G0R 4P0 – 418/359-2321, Fax: 418/359-2321 |
| Ste-Félicité (Mun.) [7] | 612 | Matane | Matapédia-Matane | Matane | Yves Chassé, Sec.-Trés., 192, rue St-Joseph, CP 9, Ste-Félicité G0J 2K0 – 418/733-4628, Fax: 418/733-8377 |
| St-Félix-de-Dalquier (Mun.) | 978 | Abitibi | Abitibi | Abitibi-Ouest | Richard Michaud, Sec.-Trés., 20, rue Principale sud, St-Félix-de-Dalquier J0Y 1G0 – 819/727-1732, Fax: 819/727-1732 |

Urban Centres (Villes) in CAPITALS; Villages marked (V); Townships/Cantons marked (Canton);United townships/Cantons unis marked (Cantons); Parishes marked (P); Municipalities marked (Mun.).; Northern villages/Villages nordiques marked (NV); Cree Villages/Villages Cris marked (VC); Naskapi Villages/Villages Naskapi marked (VN); In the third column, Urban Community/Communauté Urbaine marked Urb. Com. An in-depth listing for municipalities marked with * appears in Part 2 (check Index for page numbers).

| MUNICIPALITY | 1996 POP. | REGIONAL COUNTY MUN. | FEDERAL ELECTORAL DISTRICT | PROVINCIAL ELECTORAL DISTRICT | CONTACT PERSON WITH ADDRESS, PHONE & FAX |
|---|---|---|---|---|---|
| St-Félix-de-Valois (P) | 3,912 | Matawinie | Berthier-Montcalm | Berthier | Gaston Charette, Sec.-Trés., 600, ch Joliette, CP 220, St-Félix-de-Valois J0K 2M0 – 514/889-5589, Fax: 514/889-5259 |
| St-Félix-de-Valois (V) | 1,530 | Matawinie | Berthier-Montcalm | Berthier | Suzanne Ricard, Sec.-Trés., 4881, rue Principale, CP 69, St-Félix-de-Valois J0K 2M0 – 514/889-5581, Fax: 514/889-5293 |
| St-Félix-d'Otis (Mun.) | 715 | Le Fjord-du-Saguenay | Chicoutimi | Dubuc | Bertrand Boudreault, Sec.-Trés., 455, rue Principale, CP 38, St-Félix-d'Otis G0V 1M0 – 418/544-5543, Fax: 418/544-9122 |
| St-Ferdinand (Mun.) | 771 | L'Érable | Frontenac | Frontenac | Michèle Lacroix, Sec.-Trés., 821, rue Principale, CP 160, St-Ferdinand G0N 1N0 – 418/428-3480, Fax: 418/428-9724 |
| St-Ferréol-les-Neiges (Mun.) | 2,219 | La Côte-de-Beaupré | Beauport-Montmorency-Orléans | Charlevoix | François Drouin, Sec.-Trés., 33, rue de l'Église, St-Ferréol-les-Neiges G0A 3R0 – 418/826-2253, Fax: 418/826-0489 |
| St-Fidèle-de-Mont-Murray (P) | 946 | Charlevoix-Est | Charlevoix | Charlevoix | Raynald Tremblay, Sec.-Trés., 79, rue Principale, CP 40, St-Fidèle G0T 1T0 – 418/434-2447, Fax: 418/434-2315 |
| Ste-Flavie (P) | 920 | La Mitis | Rimouski-Mitis | Matapédia | Suzanne Landreville, Sec.-Trés., 775, rte Jacques-Cartier, Ste-Flavie G0J 2L0 – 418/775-7050, Fax: 418/775-5672 |
| St-Flavien (P) | 657 | Lotbinière | Lotbinière | Lotbinière | Mario Roy, Sec.-Trés., 6, rue Caux, St-Flavien G0S 2M0 – 418/728-4190, Fax: 418/728-4190 |
| St-Flavien (V) | 796 | Lotbinière | Lotbinière | Lotbinière | Mario Roy, Sec.-Trés., 6, rue Caux, St-Flavien G0S 2M0 – 418/728-4190, Fax: 418/728-4190 |
| Ste-Florence (Mun.) | 546 | La Matapédia | Matapédia-Matane | Matapédia | Huguette Gagné, Sec.-Trés., 29, rue des Loisirs, CP 9, Ste-Florence G0J 2M0 – 418/756-3491, Fax: 418/756-3491 |
| St-Fortunat (Mun.) | 275 | L'Amiante | Frontenac-Mégantic | Richmond | Alcide Bédard, Sec.-Trés., 107, rue Principale, St-Fortunat G0P 1G0 – 819/344-5431, Fax: 819/344-5431 |
| *STE-FOY | 72,330 | Québec (Urb. Com.) | Louis-Hébert | Jean-Talon; La Peltrie; Louis-Hébert | René Damphousse, Gref. et Directeur général adjoint, 1130, rte de l'Église, CP 218, Ste-Foy G1V 4E1 – 418/650-7925, Fax: 418/650-7972 |
| St-François (P) | 484 | L'Île-d'Orléans | Beauport-Montmorency-Orléans | Montmorency | Roland Gosselin, Sec.-Trés., 337, rue Lemelin, St-François G0A 3S0 – 418/829-3100, Fax: 418/829-1004 |
| St-François-d'Assise (P) | 897 | Avignon | Matapédia-Matane | Bonaventure | Suzanne Roy, Sec.-Trés., 457, ch Central, CP 39, St-François-d'Assise G0J 2N0 – 418/299-2066, Fax: 418/299-3037 |
| St-François-de-Beauce (Mun.) | 1,357 | Robert-Cliche | Beauce | Beauce-Nord | Dorothy Fortin-Thibodeau, Sec.-Trés., 572, rang St-Charles (La Plée), CP 5, Beauceville-Est G0S 1A0 – 418/774-5259, Fax: 418/774-5259 |
| St-François-de-la-Rivière-du-Sud (Mun.) | 1,609 | Montmagny | Bellechasse-Etchemins-Montmagny-L'Islet | Montmagny-L'Islet | Yves Laflamme, Sec.-Trés., 534, ch St-François ouest, CP 68, St-François-de-la-Rivière-du-Sud G0R 3A0 – 418/259-7228, Fax: 418/259-2056 |
| St-François-de-Pabos (Mun.) | 708 | Pabok | Bonaventure-Gaspé-Îles-de-la-Madeleine-Pabok | Gaspé | Nancy Huard, Sec.-Trés., 168, route St-François, CP 219, St-François-de-Pabos G0C 2H0 – 418/689-6620, Fax: 418/689-7082 |
| St-François-de-Sales (Mun.) | 717 | Le Domaine-du-Roy | Roberval | Roberval | Renaud Blanchette, Sec.-Trés., 541, rue Principale, St-François de Sales G0W 1M0 – 418/348-6736, Fax: 418/348-9439 |
| St-François-du-Lac (P) | 1,095 | Nicolet-Yamaska | Richelieu | Nicolet-Yamaska | Nancy Mercier, Sec.-Trés., 56, route Marie-Victorin, CP 240, St-François-du-Lac J0G 1M0 – 514/568-2124, Fax: 514/568-7465 |
| St-François-du-Lac (V) | 907 | Nicolet-Yamaska | Richelieu | Nicolet-Yamaska | Carmen Forcier, Sec.-Trés., 480, rue Notre Dame, CP 60, St-François-du-Lac J0G 1M0 – 514/568-3728, Fax: 514/568-1130 |
| St-François-Ouest (Mun.) | 1,263 | Robert-Cliche | Beauce | Beauce-Nord | Huguette Rodrigue, Sec.-Trés., 345, rang du Bord-de-l'Eau, St-François-Ouest G0M 1A0 – 418/774-5177, Fax: 418/774-5177 |
| St-François-Xavier-Brompton (P) | 2,008 | Le Val-St-François | Richmond-Arthabaska | Johnson | Mario Chabot, Sec.-Trés., 94, rue Principale, CP 10, St-François-Xavier-de-Brompton J0B 2V0 – 819/845-3954, Fax: 819/845-7711 |
| St-François-Xavier-de-Viger (Mun.) | 305 | Rivière-du-Loup | Kamouraska-Rivière-du-Loup-Témiscouata-Les Basques | Rivière-du-Loup | Yvette Beaulieu, Sec.-Trés., 123, rue Principale, St-François-Xavier-de-Viger G0L 3C0 – 418/497-2302, Fax: 418/497-2302 |
| Ste-Françoise (Mun.) | 505 | Bécancour | Lotbinière | Lotbinière | Isabelle Dubois, Sec.-Trés., 563, 11e rang est, Ste-Françoise-de-Lotbinière G0S 2N0 – 819/287-5755, Fax: 819/287-5838 |

Urban Centres (Villes) in CAPITALS; Villages marked (V); Townships/Cantons marked (Canton);United townships/Cantons unis marked (Cantons); Parishes marked (P); Municipalities marked (Mun.).; Northern villages/Villages nordiques marked (NV); Cree Villages/Villages Cris marked (VC); Naskapi Villages/Villages Naskapi marked (VN); In the third column, Urban Community/Communauté Urbaine marked Urb. Com. An in-depth listing for municipalities marked with * appears in Part 2 (check Index for page numbers).

| MUNICIPALITY | 1996 POP. | REGIONAL COUNTY MUN. | FEDERAL ELECTORAL DISTRICT | PROVINCIAL ELECTORAL DISTRICT | CONTACT PERSON WITH ADDRESS, PHONE & FAX |
|---|---|---|---|---|---|
| Ste-Françoise (P) | 467 | Les Basques | Kamouraska-Rivière-du-Loup-Témis-couata-Les Basques | Rivière-du-Loup | Andrée Rioux, Sec.-Trés., 156, rue Jérémie-Beaulieu, Ste-Françoise G0L 3B0 – 418/851-1502, Fax: 418/851-0926 |
| St-Frédéric (P) | 1,006 | Robert-Cliche | Beauce | Beauce-Nord | Jacqueline Lehoux, Sec.-Trés., 389, rue du Parc, CP 87, St-Frédéric G0N 1P0 – 418/426-3357, Fax: 418/426-3357 |
| St-Fulgence (Mun.) | 2,078 | Le Fjord-du-Saguenay | Lac-St-Jean | Dubuc | Gilles Tremblay, Sec.-Trés., 253, rue Saguenay, CP 70, St-Fulgence G0V 1S0 – 418/674-2588, Fax: 418/674-9213 |
| St-Gabriel (Mun.) | 1,223 | La Mitis | Rimouski-Mitis | Matapédia | Marie-Paule Rioux, Sec.-Trés., 248, rue Principale, CP 10, St-Gabriel G0K 1M0 – 418/798-4938, Fax: 418/798-4108 |
| ST-GABRIEL | 2,862 | D'Autray | Berthier-Montcalm | Berthier | Raymond Gagnon, Sec.-Trés., 45, rue Beausoleil, CP 750, St-Gabriel-de-Brandon J0K 2N0 – 514/835-2212, Fax: 514/835-9852 |
| St-Gabriel-de-Brandon (P) | 2,608 | D'Autray | Berthier-Montcalm | Berthier | André Comtois, Sec.-Trés., 5111, ch du Lac, CP 929, St-Gabriel-de-Brandon J0K 2N0 – 514/835-3494, Fax: 514/835-3495 |
| St-Gabriel-de-Valcartier (Mun.) | 2,204 | La Jacques-Cartier | Charlesbourg | Chauveau | Joan Sheehan, Sec.-Trés., 1743, boul Valcartier, St-Gabriel-de-Valcartier G0A 4S0 – 418/844-1218, Fax: 418/844-3030 |
| St-Gabriel-Lalemant (Mun.) | 883 | Kamouraska | Kamouraska-Rivière-du-Loup-Témis-couata-Les Basques | Kamouraska-Témis-couata | Gina Lévesque, Sec.-Trés., 20, rue Principale, CP 9, Kamouraska G0L 3E0 – 418/852-2801, Fax: 418/852-3390 |
| St-Gédéon (Mun.) | 1,877 | Lac-St-Jean-Est | Lac-St-Jean | Lac-St-Jean | Dany Dallaire, Sec.-Trés., 208, ch De Quen, St-Gédéon G0W 2P0 – 418/345-8001, Fax: 418/345-2306 |
| St-Gédéon (P) | 584 | Beauce-Sartigan | Beauce | Beauce-Sud | Jean-Paul Jolin, Sec.-Trés., 102, 1re av, CP 429, St-Gédéon G0M 1T0 – 418/582-6435, Fax: 418/582-6016 |
| St-Gédéon (V) | 1,770 | Beauce-Sartigan | Beauce | Beauce-Sud | Pierre-Alain Pelchat, Sec.-Trés., 102 - 1re av sud, St-Gédéon G0M 1T0 – 418/582-3341, Fax: 418/582-6016 |
| STE-GENEVIÈVE | 3,339 | Montréal (Urb. Com.) | Pierrefonds-Dollard | Nelligan | Rita Allaire, Gref., 13, rue Chauret, Ste-Geneviève H9H 2X2 – 514/626-2535, Fax: 514/626-0312 |
| Ste-Geneviève-de-Batiscan (P) | 1,044 | Francheville | Champlain | Champlain | Robert Néron, Sec.-Trés., 30, rue St-Charles, CP 70, Ste-Geneviève-de-Batiscan G0X 2R0 – 418/362-2078, Fax: 418/362-2111 |
| Ste-Geneviève-de-Berthier (P) | 2,402 | D'Autray | Berthier-Montcalm | Berthier | Lincoln LeBreton, Sec.-Trés., 400, rang de la Rivière-Bayonne sud, Ste-Geneviève-de-Berthier J0K 1A0 – 514/836-4333, Fax: 514/836-7260 |
| St-Georges (V) | 3,929 | Le Centre-de-la-Mauricie | St-Maurice | Laviolette | Vacant, Sec.-Trés., 505, 105e av, St-Georges G9T 3H3 – 819/538-8631, Fax: 819/538-8634 |
| ST-GEORGES | 20,057 | Beauce-Sartigan | Beauce | Beauce-Sud | Laurent Nadeau, Gref., 11700, boul Lacroix, St-Georges G5Y 1L3 – 418/228-5555, Fax: 418/228-3855 |
| St-Georges-de-Cacouna (P) | 664 | Rivière-du-Loup | Kamouraska-Rivière-du-Loup-Témis-couata-Les Basques | Rivière-du-Loup | Thérèse Dubé, Sec.-Trés., 263, rte 132 est, CP 40, Cacouna G0L 1G0 – 418/862-1937, Fax: 418/862-0136 |
| St-Georges-de-Cacouna (V) | 1,130 | Rivière-du-Loup | Kamouraska-Rivière-du-Loup-Témis-couata-Les Basques | Rivière-du-Loup | Jacques St-Pierre, Sec.-Trés., 415, rue St-Georges, CP 249, Cacouna G0L 1G0 – 418/867-1781, Fax: 418/867-5677 |
| St-Georges-de-Clarenceville (Mun.) | 980 | Le Haut-Richelieu | Brome-Missisquoi | Iberville | Thérese Lacombe, Sec.-Trés., 1350, ch Middle, St-Georges-de-Clarenceville J0J 1B0 – 514/294-2464, Fax: 514/294-2016 |
| St-Georges-de-Windsor (Mun.) | 874 | Asbestos | Richmond-Arthabaska | Richmond | Armande Perreault, Sec.-Trés., 485, rue Principale, St-Georges-de-Windsor J0A 1J0 – 819/828-2716, Fax: 819/828-0213 |
| St-Georges-Est (P) | 3,555 | Beauce-Sartigan | Beauce | Beauce-Sud | Yvon Gilbert, Sec.-Trés., 15480, boul Lacroix, St-Georges G5Y 1R7 – 418/228-2925, Fax: 418/228-2925 |
| St-Gérard (V) | 514 | Le Haut-St-François | Frontenac-Mégantic | Mégantic-Compton | Francine Blanchette, Sec.-Trés., 183, rue Principale, CP 3B C3, St-Gérard G0Y 1K0 – 819/877-2839, Fax: 819/877-2839 |
| St-Gérard-des-Laurentides (P) | 2,113 | Le Centre-de-la-Mauricie | St-Maurice | St-Maurice; La Violette | Denis Brodeur, Sec.-Trés., 431, rue des Frênes, St-Gérard-des-Laurentides G9N 6T6 – 819/539-9121, Fax: 819/539-8622 |
| St-Gérard-Majella (P) | 4,207 | L'Assomption | Joliette | Rousseau | Marius Savoie, Sec.-Trés., 2700, ch du Roy, St-Gérard-Majella J5X 1B1 – 514/588-5536, Fax: 514/588-7161 |

Urban Centres (Villes) in CAPITALS; Villages marked (V); Townships/Cantons marked (Canton);United townships/Cantons unis marked (Cantons); Parishes marked (P); Municipalities marked (Mun.).; Northern villages/Villages nordiques marked (NV); Cree Villages/Villages Cris marked (VC); Naskapi Villages/Villages Naskapi marked (VN); In the third column, Urban Community/Communauté Urbaine marked Urb. Com. An in-depth listing for municipalities marked with * appears in Part 2 (check Index for page numbers).

| MUNICIPALITY | 1996 POP. | REGIONAL COUNTY MUN. | FEDERAL ELECTORAL DISTRICT | PROVINCIAL ELECTORAL DISTRICT | CONTACT PERSON WITH ADDRESS, PHONE & FAX |
|---|---|---|---|---|---|
| St-Gérard-Majella (P) | 258 | Le Bas-Richelieu | Richelieu | Nicolet-Yamaska | Roger Proulx, Sec.-Trés., 370, rang Ste-Catherine, St-Gérard-d'Yamaska J0G 1X0 – 514/789-2630, Fax: 514/789-0336 |
| St-Germain (P) | 300 | Kamouraska | Kamouraska-Rivière-du-Loup-Témis-couata-Les Basques | Kamouraska-Témis-couata | Hélène B.-Bernier, Sec.-Trés., 146, rang des Côtes, St-Germain G0L 3G0 – 418/492-5203 |
| St-Germain-de-Grantham (Mun.) | 3,509 | Drummond | Drummond | Drummond | Jocelyn Légaré, Sec.-Trés., 233, ch Yamaska, CP 190, St-Germain-de-Grantham J0C 1K0 – 819/395-5496, Fax: 819/395-5200 |
| Ste-Germaine-Boulé (Mun.) | 1,076 | Abitibi-Ouest | Témiscamingue | Abitibi-Ouest | Gisèle Bisson-Lapointe, Sec.-Trés., 199, rue Roy, CP 5, Ste-Germaine-Boulé J0Z 1M0 – 819/787-6221, Fax: 819/787-6221 |
| Ste-Germaine-de-l'Anse-aux-Gascons (P) | 1,281 | Pabok | Bonaventure-Gaspé-Îles-de-la-Madeleine-Pabok | Bonaventure | Thérèse Chapados, Sec.-Trés., 63, route 132 ouest, CP 39, Gascons G0C 1P0 – 418/396-5400, Fax: 418/396-2333 |
| Ste-Germaine-du-Lac-Etchemin (P) | 1,565 | Les Etchemins | Bellechasse-Etchemins-Montmagny-L'Islet | Bellechasse | Pierre Dallaire, Sec.-Trés., 208, 2e av, Sainte-Germaine-du-Lac-Etchemin G0R 1S0 – 418/625-2291, Fax: 418/625-2292 |
| Ste-Gertrude-Manneville (Mun.) | 809 | Abitibi | Abitibi | Abitibi-Ouest | Gertrude Bilodeau, Sec.-Trés., 391, rte 395, Ste-Gertrude-de-Villeneuve J0Y 2L0 – 819/727-2244, Fax: 819/727-2244 |
| St-Gervais (Mun.) | 1,875 | Bellechasse | Bellechasse-Etchemins-Montmagny-L'Islet | Bellechasse | Gilles Breton, Sec.-Trés., 36, rue de la Fabrique, CP 69, St-Gervais G0R 3C0 – 418/887-6116, Fax: 418/887-6312 |
| St-Gilbert (P) | 323 | Portneuf | Portneuf | Portneuf | Michelle Robitaille, Sec.-Trés., 3, rue Principale, St-Gilbert G0A 3T0 – 418/268-8194, Fax: 418/268-8194 |
| St-Gilles (P) | 1,806 | Lotbinière | Lotbinière | Lotbinière | Aline Martin, Sec.-Trés., 161, rue O'Hurley, St-Gilles G0S 2P0 – 418/888-3198, Fax: 418/888-5145 |
| St-Godefroi (Canton) | 488 | Bonaventure | Bonaventure-Gaspé-Îles-de-la-Madeleine-Pabok | Bonaventure | Jocelyne Joseph, Sec.-Trés., 109, route 132, CP 157, St-Godefroi G0C 3C0 – 418/752-6316, Fax: 418/752-6316 |
| St-Grégoire-de-Greenlay (V) | 611 | Le Val-St-François | Richmond-Arthabaska | Johnson | Bernice McAdams, Sec.-Trés., #201, 3, rue Greenlay sud, Greenlay J1S 2S1 – 819/845-7667, Fax: 819/845-2644 |
| St-Guillaume (Mun.) | 1,598 | Drummond | Drummond | Nicolet-Yamaska | Hélène Philips, Sec.-Trés., 106, rue St-Jean-Baptiste, St-Guillaume J0C 1L0 – 819/396-2403, Fax: 819/396-0184 |
| St-Guy (Mun.) | 108 | Les Basques | Kamouraska-Rivière-du-Loup-Te@mis-couata | Rimouski | Lisa Caron, Sec.-Trés., 54, rue Principal, St-Guy G0K 1W0 – 418/963-2601, Fax: 418/963-2601 |
| Ste-Hedwidge (Mun.) | 863 | Le Domaine-du-Roy | Roberval | Roberval | Serge Simard, Sec.-Trés., 1090, rue Principale, Ste-Hedwidge G0W 2R0 – 418/275-3020, Fax: 418/275-4163 |
| Ste-Hélène (P) | 933 | Kamouraska | Kamouraska-Rivière-du-Loup-Témis-couata-Les Basques | Kamouraska-Témis-couata | Nathalie Blais, Sec.-Trés., 531, rue de l'Église sud, CP 216, Ste-Hélène G0L 3J0 – 418/492-6830, Fax: 418/492-1854 |
| Ste-Hélène-de-Bagot (Mun.) | 1,495 | Les Maskoutains | St-Hyacinthe-Bagot | Johnson | Denise P.-Arsenault, Sec.-Trés., 379, 7e av, Ste-Hélène-de-Bagot J0H 1M0 – 514/791-2455, Fax: 514/791-2550 |
| Ste-Hélène-de-Breakeyville (P) | 3,423 | Les Chutes-de-la-Chaudière | Lévis | Chutes-de-la-Chaudière | Jean-Guy Brassard, Sec.-Trés., 22, rue Ste-Hélène, Ste-Hélène-de-Breakeyville G0S 1E2 – 418/832-0356, Fax: 418/832-0358 |
| Ste-Hélène-de-Mancebourg (P) | 415 | Abitibi-Ouest | Témiscamingue | Abitibi-Ouest | Sylvie Boutin-Bergeron, Sec.-Trés., 686, 1er rang, Mancebourg J0Z 2T0 – 819/333-5766, Fax: 819/333-5766 |
| Ste-Hénédine (P) | 1,175 | La Nouvelle-Beauce | Beauce | Beauce-Nord | Yvon Marcoux, Sec.-Trés., 111, rue Principale, CP 6, Ste-Hénédine G0S 2R0 – 418/935-7125, Fax: 418/935-7125 |
| St-Henri (Mun.) | 3,886 | Desjardins | Lévis | Lévis | Jacques Risler, Sec.-Trés., 219, rue Commerciale, St-Henri G0R 3E0 – 418/882-2401, Fax: 418/882-0302 |
| St-Henri-de-Taillon (Mun.) | 743 | Lac-St-Jean-Est | Lac-St-Jean | Lac-St-Jean | Léonard Dufour, Sec.-Trés., 401, rue de l'Hôtel-de-Ville, St-Henri-de-Taillon G0W 2X0 – 418/347-3243, Fax: 418/347-3243 |
| St-Herménégilde (Mun.) | 616 | Coaticook | Compton-Stanstead | Mégantic-Compton | Céline Bessette-Dubois, Sec.-Trés., 776, rue Principale, St-Herménégilde J0B 2W0 – 819/849-4443, Fax: 819/849-4443 |
| St-Hilaire-de-Dorset (P) | 121 | Beauce-Sartigan | Beauce | Beauce-Sud | Johanne Jacques, Sec.-Trés., 847, rue Principale, St-Hilaire-de-Dorset G0M 1G0 – 418/459-6872, Fax: 418/459-6872 |
| St-Hilarion (P) | 1,215 | Charlevoix | Charlevoix | Charlevoix | Joseph Rochefort, Sec.-Trés., 215, ch Principale, St-Hilarion G0A 3V0 – 418/457-3463, Fax: 418/457-3805 |

Urban Centres (Villes) in CAPITALS; Villages marked (V); Townships/Cantons marked (Canton);United townships/Cantons unis marked (Cantons); Parishes marked (P); Municipalities marked (Mun.).; Northern villages/Villages nordiques marked (NV); Cree Villages/Villages Cris marked (VC); Naskapi Villages/Villages Naskapi marked (VN); In the third column, Urban Community/Communauté Urbaine marked Urb. Com. An in-depth listing for municipalities marked with * appears in Part 2 (check Index for page numbers).

| MUNICIPALITY | 1996 POP. | REGIONAL COUNTY MUN. | FEDERAL ELECTORAL DISTRICT | PROVINCIAL ELECTORAL DISTRICT | CONTACT PERSON WITH ADDRESS, PHONE & FAX |
|---|---|---|---|---|---|
| St-Hippolyte (P) | 5,672 | La Rivière-du-Nord | Laurentides | Bertrand | Yvon Veillette, Sec.-Trés., 2253, ch des Hauteurs, St-Hippolyte J0R 1P0 – 514/563-2505, Fax: 514/563-2362 |
| St-Honoré (Mun.) | 3,851 | Le Fjord-du-Saguenay | Lac-St-Jean | Dubuc | Hugues Blackburn, Sec.-Trés., 3611, boul Martel, CP 250, St-Honoré G0V 1L0 – 418/673-3405, Fax: 418/673-3871 |
| St-Honoré (Mun.) | 838 | Témiscouata | Kamouraska-Rivière-du-Loup-Témis-couata-Les Basques | Kamouraska-Témis-couata | Lucie April, Sec.-Trés., 99, rue Principale, CP 70, St-Honoré G0L 3K0 – 418/497-2588, Fax: 418/497-1656 |
| St-Honoré (P) | 691 | Beauce-Sartigan | Beauce | Beauce-Sud | Francine Talbot, Sec.-Trés., 289, route de Shenley ouest, CP 249, St-Honoré G0M 1V0 – 418/485-6781, Fax: 418/485-6781 |
| St-Hubert (P) | 1,374 | Rivière-du-Loup | Kamouraska-Rivière-du-Loup-Témis-couata-Les Basques | Rivière-du-Loup | Lisette Claveau, Sec.-Trés., 4, ch Taché est, CP 218, St-Hubert G0L 3L0 – 418/497-3394, Fax: 418/497-1187 |
| *ST-HUBERT | 77,042 | Champlain | St-Bruno-St-Hubert | Laporte; Vachon | Bernard Houle, Directeur, Sécretariat administratif et juridique, 5900, boul Cousineau, St-Hubert J3Y 7K8 – 514/445-7600, Fax: 514/445-7847 |
| St-Hugues (Mun.) | 1,340 | Les Maskoutains | St-Hyacinthe-Bagot | St-Hyacinthe | Raymonde Gauvin, Sec.-Trés., 508, rue Notre-Dame, St-Hugues J0H 1N0 – 514/794-2030, Fax: 514/794-2474 |
| ST-HYACINTHE | 38,981 | Les Maskoutains | St-Hyacinthe-Bagot | St-Hyacinthe | Hélène Beauchesne, Gref., 700, av de l'Hôtel-de-Ville, CP 10, St-Hyacinthe J2S 5B2 – 514/778-8300, Fax: 514/778-8628 |
| St-Hyacinthe-le-Confesseur (P) | 1,126 | Les Maskoutains | St-Hyacinthe-Bagot | St-Hyacinthe | Lise Lemonde, Sec.-Trés., 345, rue Mondor, St-Hyacinthe J2S 5A6 – 514/774-9666, Fax: 514/774-2909 |
| St-Ignace-de-Loyola (P) | 1,883 | D'Autray | Berthier-Montcalm | Berthier | Fabrice Saint-Martin, Sec.-Trés., 25, rue Laforest, St-Ignace-de-Loyola J0K 2P0 – 514/836-3376, Fax: 514/836-1400 |
| St-Ignace-de-Stanbridge (P) | 692 | Brome-Missisquoi | Brome-Missisquoi | Brome-Missisquoi | Monique Aubry-Santerre, Sec.-Trés., 678, rang de l'Église nord, St-Ignace-de-Stanbridge J0J 1Y0 – 514/296-4467, Fax: 514/296-4467 |
| Ste-Irène (P) | 352 | La Matapédia | Matapédia-Matane | Matapédia | Lucie Desjardins, Sec.-Trés., 362, rue de la Fabrique, Ste-Irène G0J 2P0 – 418/629-5705, Fax: 418/629-3220 |
| St-Irénée (P) | 643 | Charlevoix-Est | Charlevoix | Charlevoix | Marie-Claude Lavoie, Sec.-Trés., 122, rue Principale, CP 68, St-Irénée G0T 1V0 – 418/452-3231, Fax: 418/452-8221 |
| St-Isidore (P) | 2,401 | Roussillon | Châteauguay | Châteauguay | Daniel Vinet, Sec.-Trés., 671, rue St-Régis, CP 240, St-Isidore J0L 2A0 – 514/454-3919, Fax: 514/454-7485 |
| St-Isidore (Mun.) | 2,657 | La Nouvelle-Beauce | Beauce | Beauce-Nord | Nancy Labrecque, Sec.-Trés., 128, rte Coulombe, St-Isidore G0S 2S0 – 418/882-5670, Fax: 418/882-5902 |
| St-Isidore-d'Auckland (Mun.) | 604 | Le Haut-St-François | Compton-Stanstead | Mégantic-Compton | Gaétan Perron, Sec.-Trés., 66, ch Auckland, St-Isidore-d'Auckland J0B 2X0 – 819/658-3637, Fax: 819/658-9070 |
| St-Jacques (P) | 1,554 | Montcalm | Berthier-Montcalm | Joliette | Voir St-Jacques (Village), a/s Village de St-Jcques, 16, rue Marechal, St-Jacques J0K 2R0 – 514/839-3671, Fax: 514/839-2387 |
| St-Jacques (V) | 2,261 | Montcalm | Berthier-Montcalm | Joliette | Gilles Sincerny, Sec.-Trés., 16, rue Maréchal, St-Jacques J0K 2R0 – 514/839-3671, Fax: 514/839-2387 |
| St-Jacques-de-Horton (Mun.) | 225 | Arthabaska | Richmond-Arthabaska | Richmond | Jean-Paul Fleurant, Sec.-Trés., 711, rue St-Antoine, Notre-Dame-du-Bon-Conseil J0C 1A0 – 819/336-5402 |
| St-Jacques-de-Leeds (Mun.) | 750 | L'Amiante | Frontenac-Mégantic | Frontenac | Nathalie Laflamme, Sec.-Trés., 430, rue Principale, CP 9, St-Jacques-de-Leeds G0N 1J0 – 418/424-3321, Fax: 418/424-0126 |
| St-Jacques-le-Majeur-de-Causapscal (P) | 731 | La Matapédia | Matapédia-Matane | Matapédia | Jacques Tremblay, Sec.-Trés., 677, route 132 ouest, CP 400, Causapscal G0J 1J0 – 418/756-3996, Fax: 418/756-3996 |
| St-Jacques-le-Majeur-de-Wolfestown (P) | 179 | L'Amiante | Frontenac-Mégantic | Frontenac | Linda Bolduc, Sec.-Trés., 877, route 263, Saint-Jacques-le-Majeur G0N 1E0 – 418/449-1531, Fax: 418/449-1531 |
| St-Jacques-le-Mineur (P) | 1,612 | Les Jardins-de-Napi-erville | Châteauguay | St-Jean | Chantal Guinois, Sec.-Trés., 91, rue Principale, St-Jacques-le-Mineur J0J 1Z0 – 514/347-5446, Fax: 514/347-5754 |
| St-Janvier-de-Joly (Mun.) | 936 | Lotbinière | Lotbinière | Lotbinière | Céline Biron, Sec.-Trés., 729, rue des Loisirs, CP 70, Joly G0S 1M0 – 418/728-2984, Fax: 418/728-2984 |
| St-Jean (P) | 847 | L'Île-d'Orléans | Beauport-Mont-morency-Orléans | Montmorency | Esther Bourdages, Sec.-Trés., 2336, ch Royal, St-Jean G0A 3W0 – 418/829-2206, Fax: 418/829-2206 |

Urban Centres (Villes) in CAPITALS; Villages marked (V); Townships/Cantons marked (Canton);United townships/Cantons unis marked (Cantons); Parishes marked (P); Municipalities marked (Mun.).; Northern villages/Villages nordiques marked (NV); Cree Villages/Villages Cris marked (VC); Naskapi Villages/Villages Naskapi marked (VN); In the third column, Urban Community/Communauté Urbaine marked Urb. Com. An in-depth listing for municipalities marked with * appears in Part 2 (check Index for page numbers).

| MUNICIPALITY | 1996 POP. | REGIONAL COUNTY MUN. | FEDERAL ELECTORAL DISTRICT | PROVINCIAL ELECTORAL DISTRICT | CONTACT PERSON WITH ADDRESS, PHONE & FAX |
|---|---|---|---|---|---|
| St-Jean-Baptiste (Mun.) | 759 | La Mitis | Rimouski-Mitis | Matapédia | Madeleine Roy, Sec.-Trés., 251, ch du Sanatorium, Mont-Joli G5H 1V6 – 418/775-8678, Fax: 418/775-8566 |
| St-Jean-Baptiste (P) | 2,913 | Rouville | Chambly | Borduas | Denis Meunier, Sec.-Trés., 3100, rue Principale, St-Jean-Baptiste J0L 2B0 – 514/467-3456, Fax: 514/467-8813 |
| St-Jean-Baptiste-de-l'Isle-Verte (Mun.) | 596 | Rivière-du-Loup | Kamouraska-Riviére-du-Loup-Témis-couata | Rivière-du-Loup | Léonard Dion, Sec.-Trés., 141, rue St-Jean-Baptiste, CP 248, L'Isle-Verte G0L 1K0 – 418/898-3284, Fax: 418/898-2788 |
| St-Jean-Baptiste-de-Nicolet (P) | 3,076 | Nicolet-Yamaska | Richelieu | Nicolet-Yamaska | Sylvie Provencher, Sec.-Trés., 525, rte du Port, St-Jean-Baptiste-de-Nicolet J3T 1W3 – 819/293-6161, Fax: 819/293-6616 |
| St-Jean-Chrysostome (P) | 1,737 | Le Haut-St-Laurent | Beauharnois-Salaberry | Beauharnois-Huntingdon | Céline Ouimet, Sec.-Trés., 124, rang Notre-Dame, CP 70, St-Jean-Chrysostome J0S 1R0 – 514/826-3911, Fax: 514/826-0568 |
| ST-JEAN-CHRYSOSTOME | 16,161 | Les Chutes-de-la-Chaudière | Lévis | Chutes-de-la-Chaudière | Jacques Leblond, Gref., 959, rue de l'Hôtel-de-Ville, St-Jean-Chrysostome G6Z 2N8 – 418/839-9417, Fax: 418/839-4244 |
| St-Jean-de-Brébeuf (Mun.) | 390 | L'Amiante | Frontenac-Mégantic | Frontenac | Solange Bolduc-Dostie, Sec.-Trés., 344, ch Craig, St-Jean-de-Brébeuf G6G 5R5 – 418/453-7774, Fax: 418/453-2339 |
| St-Jean-de-Cherbourg (P) | 239 | Matane | Matapédia-Matane | Matane | Jacinthe Imbeault, Sec.-Trés., 10, 7e rang ouest, St-Jean-de-Cherbourg G0J 2R0 – 418/733-4710, Fax: 418/733-4710 |
| St-Jean-de-Dieu (Mun.) | 1,828 | Les Basques | Kamouraska-Rivière-du-Loup-Témis-couata-Les Basques | Rivière-du-Loup | Normand Morency, Sec.-Trés., 32, rue Principale sud, St-Jean-de-Dieu G0L 3M0 – 418/963-3529, Fax: 418/963-2903 |
| St-Jean-de-la-Lande (Mun.) | 323 | Témiscouata | Kamouraska-Riviére-du-Loup-Témis-couata | Kamouraska-Témis-couata | Francine Dubé, Sec.-Trés., 810A, rue Principale, St-Jean-de-la-Lande G0L 3N0 – 418/853-3475, Fax: 418/853-3703 |
| St-Jean-de-la-Lande (P) | 763 | Beauce-Sartigan | Beauce | Beauce-Sud | Claudette Deschênes, Sec.-Trés., 600, rue Principale, St-Jean-de-la-Lande G0M 1E0 – 418/227-4363, Fax: 418/227-9266 |
| St-Jean-de-Matha (Mun.) | 3,624 | Matawinie | Berthier-Montcalm | Berthier | D. Nicole Archambault, Sec.-Trés., 170, rue Ste-Louise, CP 60, St-Jean-de-Matha J0K 2S0 – 514/886-3867, Fax: 514/886-3398 |
| St-Jean-des-Piles (P) | 640 | Le Centre-de-la-Mauricie | St-Maurice | Laviolette | Maryse Flageole, Sec.-Trés., 1594, rue Principale, St-Jean des Piles G0X 2V0 – 819/538-3829, Fax: 819/538-3155 |
| St-Jean-Port-Joli (Mun.) | 3,402 | L'Islet | Bellechasse-Etchemins-Montmagny-L'Islet | Montmagny-L'Islet | Denis Gaudreault, Sec.-Trés., 7, Place de l'Église, CP 488, St-Jean-Port-Joli G0R 3G0 – 418/598-3084, Fax: 418/598-3085 |
| ST-JEAN-SUR-RICHELIEU | 36,435 | Le Haut-Richelieu | St-Jean | St-Jean | Jacques Jutras, Gref., 188, rue Jacques-Cartier nord, CP 1025, St-Jean-sur-Richelieu J3B 7B2 – 514/357-2100, Fax: 514/357-2285 |
| Ste-Jeanne-d'Arc (P) | 371 | La Mitis | Rimouski-Mitis | Matapédia | Madeleine Lévesque, Sec.-Trés., 205, rue Principale, CP 40, Ste-Jeanne-d'Arc G0J 2T0 – 418/776-5660, Fax: 418/776-5660 |
| Ste-Jeanne-d'Arc (V) | 1,158 | Maria-Chapdelaine | Roberval | Roberval | Régis Martin, Sec.-Trés., 378, rue François-Bilodeau, CP 39, Ste-Jeanne-d'Arc G0W 1E0 – 418/276-3166, Fax: 418/276-7648 |
| ST-JÉRÔME | 23,916 | La Rivière-du-Nord | Laurentides | Prévost | Louise Pepin, Gref., #301, 10, rue St-Joseph, St-Jérôme J7Z 5L1 – 514/436-1511, Fax: 514/436-6626 |
| St-Jérôme-de-Matane (P) | 1,165 | Matane | Matapédia-Matane | Matane | Cécile Dion, Sec.-Trés., 378, av St-Jérôme, Matane G4W 3B2 – 418/562-2548, Fax: 418/562-2548 |
| St-Joachim (P) | 1,493 | La Côte-de-Beaupré | Beauport-Montmorency-Orléans | Charlevoix | Danielle Paré-Lessard, Sec.-Trés., 172, rue de l'Église, St-Joachim G0A 3X0 – 418/827-3755, Fax: 418/827-8574 |
| St-Joachim-de-Courval (P) | 644 | Drummond | Drummond | Nicolet-Yamaska | Monique-M. Richard, Sec.-Trés., 546, rue Principale, St-Joachim-de-Courval J1Z 2C3 – 819/397-2334, Fax: 819/397-4648 |
| St-Joachim-de-Shefford (P) | 1,142 | La Haute-Yamaska | Shefford | Shefford | Réal Pitt, Sec.-Trés., 567, 1er rang ouest, St-Joachim-de-Shefford J0E 2G0 – 514/539-3201, Fax: 514/539-3145 |
| St-Joseph-de-Beauce (P) | 1,121 | Robert-Cliche | Beauce | Beauce-Nord | Jean-Louis Lessard, Sec.-Trés., 289, rte 276, St-Joseph-de-Beauce G0S 2V0 – 418/397-5858, Fax: 418/397-4390 |
| ST-JOSEPH-DE-BEAUCE | 3,240 | Robert-Cliche | Beauce | Beauce-Nord | Hélène Renaud, Sec.-Trés., 843, av du Palais, CP 850, St-Joseph-de-Beauce G0S 2V0 – 418/397-4358, Fax: 418/397-5715 |

Urban Centres (Villes) in CAPITALS; Villages marked (V); Townships/Cantons marked (Canton);United townships/Cantons unis marked (Cantons); Parishes marked (P); Municipalities marked (Mun.).; Northern villages/Villages nordiques marked (NV); Cree Villages/Villages Cris marked (VC); Naskapi Villages/Villages Naskapi marked (VN); In the third column, Urban Community/Communauté Urbaine marked Urb. Com. An in-depth listing for municipalities marked with * appears in Part 2 (check Index for page numbers).

| MUNICIPALITY | 1996 POP. | REGIONAL COUNTY MUN. | FEDERAL ELECTORAL DISTRICT | PROVINCIAL ELECTORAL DISTRICT | CONTACT PERSON WITH ADDRESS, PHONE & FAX |
|---|---|---|---|---|---|
| St-Joseph-de-Blandford (P) | 446 | Bécancour | Lotbinière | Lotbinière | Mario Geoffroy, Sec.-Trés., 200, rue Roux, CP 200, Manseau G0X 1V0 – 819/356-2450, Fax: 819/356-2721 |
| St-Joseph-de-Cléricy (Mun.) | 538 | Rouyn-Noranda | Témiscamingue | Rouyn-Noranda-Témiscamingue | Charlène Ferron, Sec.-Trés., 931, rue du Souvenir, Clericy J0Z 1P0 – 819/637-2131, Fax: 819/637-2133 |
| St-Joseph-de-Coleraine (Mun.) | 1,735 | L'Amiante | Frontenac-Mégantic | Frontenac | Eloy Gravel, Sec.-Trés., 88, rue St-Patrick, CP 40, Coleraine G0N 1B0 – 418/423-4000, Fax: 418/423-4150 |
| St-Joseph-de-Ham-Sud (P) | 233 | Asbestos | Richmond-Arthabaska | Richmond | Monique Polard, Sec.-Trés., 9, ch Gosford sud, St-Joseph-de-Ham-Sud J0B 3J0 – 819/877-3258, Fax: 819/877-5121 |
| St-Joseph-de-Kamouraska (P) | 412 | Kamouraska | Kamouraska-Rivière-du-Loup-Témiscouata-Les Basques | Kamouraska-Témiscouata | Ginette Castonguay, Sec.-Trés., 161, 5e rang est, St-Joseph-de-Kamouraska G0L 3P0 – 418/493-2214, Fax: 418/493-2214 |
| St-Joseph-de-la-Pointe-de-Lévy (P) | 894 | Desjardins | Lévis | Lévis | Michel Blais, Sec.-Trés., 910, rte Mgr Bourget, St-Joseph-de-la-Pointe-de-Lévy G6V 6N4 – 418/833-3882, Fax: 418/833-7895 |
| St-Joseph-de-la-Rive (V) | 204 | Charlevoix | Charlevoix | Charlevoix | Nicole Girard, Sec.-Trés., 183, rue des Saules, CP 39, St-Joseph-de-la-Rive G0A 3Y0 – 418/635-2742, Fax: 418/635-2742 |
| St-Joseph-de-Lanoraie (P) | 1,855 | D'Autray | Berthier-Montcalm | Berthier | Michel Dufort, Sec.-Trés., 361, rue Notre-Dame, CP 400, Lanoraie J0K 1E0 – 514/887-2381, Fax: 514/887-7593 |
| St-Joseph-de-Lepage (P) | 587 | La Mitis | Rimouski-Mitis | Matapédia | Renée Roy, Sec.-Trés., 70, rue de la Rivière, Mont-Joli G5H 3N8 – 418/775-4171, Fax: 418/775-3004 |
| St-Joseph-de-Maskinongé (P) | 1,151 | Maskinongé | Trois-Rivières | Maskinongé | Gisèle Lemyre, Sec.-Trés., 154, rte 138, St-Joseph-de-Maskinongé J0K 1N0 – 819/227-2243, Fax: 819/227-2097 |
| ST-JOSEPH-DE-SOREL | 1,875 | Le Bas-Richelieu | Richelieu | Richelieu | Martin Valois, Sec.-Trés., 700, rue Montcalm, St-Joseph-de-Sorel J3R 1C9 – 514/742-3744, Fax: 514/742-1315 |
| St-Joseph-des-Érables (Mun.) | 455 | Robert-Cliche | Beauce | Beauce-Nord | Raymonde Tardif, Sec.-Trés., 224, route des Fermes, St-Joseph-de-Beauce G0S 2V0 – 418/397-6617 |
| St-Joseph-du-Lac (P) | 4,930 | Deux-Montagne | Argenteuil-Papineau | Deux-Montagnes | Fernand Larocque, Sec.-Trés., 1110, ch Principal, St-Joseph-du-Lac J0N 1M0 – 514/623-1072, Fax: 514/623-2889 |
| St-Jovite (P) | 1,708 | Les Laurentides | Laurentides | Labelle | François Perreault, Sec.-Trés., 75, ch Napoléon, St-Jovite J0T 2H0 – 819/425-8641, Fax: 819/425-9414 |
| ST-JOVITE | 4,609 | Les Laurentides | Laurentides | Labelle | Lise Julien, Sec.-Trés., 1145, rue Ouimet, CP 159, St-Jovite J0T 2H0 – 819/425-8614, Fax: 819/425-9247 |
| St-Jude (Mun.) | 1,143 | Les Maskoutains | St-Hyacinthe-Bagot | Richelieu | Francine Gilbert, Sec.-Trés., 940, rue du Centre, St-Jude J0H 1P0 – 514/792-3855, Fax: 514/792-3828 |
| St-Jules (Mun.) | 412 | Bonaventure | Bonaventure-Gaspé-Îles-de-la-Madeleine-Pabok | Bonaventure | Susan Legouffe, Sec.-Trés., 55, route Gallagher, Saint-Jules G0C 1T0 – 418/392-4042, Fax: 418/392-4042 |
| St-Jules (P) | 537 | Robert-Cliche | Beauce | Beauce-Nord | Maurice Cloutier, Sec.-Trés., 390, route Principale, St-Jules G0N 1R0 – 418/397-5444, Fax: 418/397-5444 |
| Ste-Julie (Mun.) | 671 | L'Érable | Lotbinière | Lotbinière | Danielle B.-Bilodeau, Sec.-Trés., 140, rue Grenier, Laurierville G0S 1P0 – 819/365-4200, Fax: 819/365-4200 |
| STE-JULIE | 24 | Lajemmerais | Verchères | Marguerite-D'Youville | Brigitte Boisvert, Gref., 1580, ch du Fer-à-Cheval, Ste-Julie J3E 1Y2 – 514/922-7111, Fax: 514/922-7108 |
| St-Julien (P) | 420 | L'Amiante | Frontenac-Mégantic | Frontenac | Raymonde Gouin, Sec.-Trés., 787, ch St-Julien, St-Julien G0N 1B0 – 418/423-4295, Fax: 418/423-2761 |
| Ste-Julienne (P) | 6,778 | Montcalm | Berthier-Montcalm | Rousseau | Claude Arcoragi, Sec.-Trés., 1400, route 125, CP 250, Ste-Julienne J0K 2T0 – 514/831-2688, Fax: 514/831-4433 |
| St-Just-de-Bretenières (Mun.) | 881 | Montmagny | Bellechasse-Etchemins-Montmagny-L'Islet | Montmagny-L'Islet | Isabelle Simard, Sec.-Trés., 250, rue Principale, CP 40, St-Just-de-Bretenières G0R 3H0 – 418/244-3637, Fax: 418/244-3637 |
| St-Juste-du-Lac (Mun.) | 654 | Témiscouata | Kamouraska-Rivière-du-Loup-Témiscouata-Les Basques | Kamouraska-Témiscouata | Nicole Dubé-Chouinard, Sec.-Trés., 28, ch Principale, CP 38, St-Juste-du-Lac G0L 3R0 – 418/899-2855, Fax: 418/899-2938 |
| St-Justin (P) | 1,152 | Maskinongé | St-Maurice | Maskinongé | Raymonde Baril, Sec.-Trés., 1281, rue Gérin, St-Justin J0K 2V0 – 819/227-2838, Fax: 819/227-4876 |
| Ste-Justine (Mun.) | 1,939 | Les Etchemins | Bellechasse-Etchemins-Montmagny-L'Islet | Bellechasse | Gilles Vézina, Sec.-Trés., 167, rte 204, CP 10, Ste-Justine G0R 1Y0 – 418/383-5397, Fax: 418/383-5398 |
| Ste-Justine-de-Newton (P) | 934 | Vaudreuil-Soulanges | Vaudreuil-Soulanges | Vaudreuil | Denis Perrier, Sec.-Trés., 2627, rue Principale, CP 28, Ste-Justine-de-Newton J0P 1T0 – 514/764-3573, Fax: 514/764-3180 |

Urban Centres (Villes) in CAPITALS; Villages marked (V); Townships/Cantons marked (Canton);United townships/Cantons unis marked (Cantons); Parishes marked (P); Municipalities marked (Mun.).; Northern villages/Villages nordiques marked (NV); Cree Villages/Villages Cris marked (VC); Naskapi Villages/Villages Naskapi marked (VN); In the third column, Urban Community/Communauté Urbaine marked Urb. Com. An in-depth listing for municipalities marked with * appears in Part 2 (check Index for page numbers).

| MUNICIPALITY | 1996 POP. | REGIONAL COUNTY MUN. | FEDERAL ELECTORAL DISTRICT | PROVINCIAL ELECTORAL DISTRICT | CONTACT PERSON WITH ADDRESS, PHONE & FAX |
|---|---|---|---|---|---|
| St-Lambert (P) | 268 | Abitibi-Ouest | Témiscamingue | Abitibi-Ouest | Nicole Garant, Sec.-Trés., RR#1, Des Méloizes J0Z 1V0 – 819/788-2491, Fax: 819/788-2491 |
| ST-LAMBERT | 20,971 | Champlain | St-Lambert | Laporte | Louise Grégoire-Marsh, Gref., 55, rue Argyle, St-Lambert J4P 2H3 – 514/672-4444, Fax: 514/672-3732 |
| St-Lambert-de-Lauzon (P) | 4,590 | Les Chutes-de-la-Chaudière | Lotbinière | Chutes-de-la-Chaudière | Magdalen Blanchet, Sec.-Trés., 1200, rue du Pont, St-Lambert-de-Lauzon G0S 2W0 – 418/889-9715, Fax: 418/889-0660 |
| St-Laurent (P) | 1,576 | L'Île-d'Orléans | Beauport-Montmorency-Orléans | Montmorency | Claudette Pouliot, Sec.-Trés., 1430, ch Royale, St-Laurent G0A 3Z0 – 418/828-2322, Fax: 418/828-2170 |
| *SAINT-LAURENT | 74,240 | Montréal (Urb. Com.) | St-Laurent-Cartierville | Acadie; St-Laurent | Édith Baron-Lafrenière, Gref., 777, boul Marcel-Laurin, Saint-Laurent H4M 2M7 – 514/855-6000, Fax: 514/855-5999 |
| St-Lazare (P) | 11,193 | Vaudreuil-Soulanges | Vaudreuil-Soulanges | Vaudreuil | Lucie Gendron, Sec.-Trés., 1960, ch Ste-Angélique, CP 360, St-Lazare J7T 3A3 – 514/424-8000, Fax: 514/455-4712 |
| St-Lazare-de-Bellechasse (Mun.) | 1,249 | Bellechasse | Bellechasse-Etchemins-Montmagny-L'Islet | Bellechasse | Richard Côté, Sec.-Trés., 114, rue Leroux, CP 159, St-Lazare-de-Bellechasse G0R 3J0 – 418/883-3841, Fax: 418/883-2551 |
| St-Léandre (P) | 401 | Matane | Matapédia-Matane | Matane | Carmen Laderoute, Sec.-Trés., 3025, rue Principale, St-Léandre G0J 2V0 – 418/737-4973, Fax: 418/737-4973 |
| St-Léon-de-Standon (P) | 1,237 | Bellechasse | Bellechasse-Etchemins-Montmagny-L'Islet | Bellechasse | Gérald Patry, Sec.-Trés., 100A, rue St-Pierre, CP 130, St-Léon-de-Standon G0R 4L0 – 418/642-5034, Fax: 418/642-2570 |
| St-Léon-le-Grand (P) | 1,145 | La Matapédia | Matapédia-Matane | Matapédia | Suzanne Poirier, Sec.-Trés., 277, rue Plourde, CP 188, St-Léon-le-Grand G0J 2W0 – 418/743-2914, Fax: 418/743-2914 |
| St-Léon-le-Grand (P) | 955 | Maskinongé | Trois-Riviéres | Maskinongé | Gabrielle Lampron, Sec.-Trés., 49, rue de la Fabrique, St-Léon-le-Grand J0K 2W0 – 819/228-3236, Fax: 819/228-8088 |
| *ST-LÉONARD | 71,327 | Montréal (Urb. Com.) | St-Léonard-St-Michel | Jeanne-Mance; Viger | Georges Larivée, Gref., 8400, boul Lacordaire, St-Léonard H1R 3B1 – 514/328-8400, Fax: 514/328-8479 |
| St-Léonard-d'Aston (Mun.) | 2,216 | Nicolet-Yamaska | Richelieu | Nicolet-Yamaska | Ginette L.-Richard, Sec.-Trés., 370, rue Principale, CP 520, St-Léonard-d'Aston J0C 1M0 – 819/399-2596, Fax: 819/399-2333 |
| St-Léonard-de-Portneuf (Mun.) | 988 | Portneuf | Portneuf | Portneuf | Eddy Alain, Sec.-Trés., 260, rue Pettigrew, St-Léonard-de-Portneuf G0A 4A0 – 418/337-6741, Fax: 418/337-6742 |
| St-Liboire (Mun.) | 2,594 | Les Maskoutains | St-Hyacinthe-Bagot | St-Hyacinthe | Denise Breton, Sec.-Trés., 121, rue Paquette, CP 120, St-Liboire J0H 1R0 – 514/793-2811, Fax: 514/793-4428 |
| St-Liguori (P) | 1,730 | Montcalm | Berthier-Montcalm | Joliette | Gilles Fredette, Sec.-Trés., 750, rue Principale, St-Liguori J0K 2X0 – 514/753-3570, Fax: 514/753-4638 |
| St-Lin (Mun.) | 9,336 | Montcalm | Berthier-Montcalm | Rousseau | Jean-Guy Gervais, Sec.-Trés., 250, 12e av, CP 220, Laurentides J0R 1C0 – 514/439-3130, Fax: 514/439-1525 |
| St-Louis (P) | 715 | Les Maskoutains | St-Hyacinthe-Bagot | Richelieu | Jocelyne Brouillard, Sec.-Trés., 765B, rue St-Joseph, St-Louis J0G 1K0 – 514/788-2631, Fax: 514/788-2231 |
| St-Louis-de-Blandford (P) | 806 | Arthabaska | Lotbinière | Lotbinière | Danielle B.-Bédard, Sec.-Trés., 80, rue Principale, CP 140, St-Louis de Blandford G0Z 1B0 – 819/364-7007, Fax: 819/364-2781 |
| ST-LOUIS-DE-FRANCE | 7,327 | Francheville | Champlain | Champlain | Robert Bouchard, Gref., 100, rue de la Mairie, St-Louis-de-France G8W 1S1 – 819/374-6550, Fax: 819/374-0659 |
| St-Louis-de-Gonzague (Mun.) | 455 | Les Etchemins | Bellechasse-Etchemins-Montmagny-L'Islet | Bellechasse | Colombe Bilodeau, Sec.-Trés., 103, rue de l'Église, Ravignan G0R 2L0 – 418/267-5931, Fax: 418/267-5930 |
| St-Louis-de-Gonzague (P) | 1,380 | Beauharnois-Salaberry | Beauharnois-Salaberry | Salaberry-Soulanges | Micheline J.-Carrière, Sec.-Trés., 140, rue Principale, CP 382, St-Louis-de-Gonzague J0S 1T0 – 514/371-0523, Fax: 514/371-6229 |
| St-Louis-de-Gonzague-du-Cap-Tourmente (P) | 4 | La Côte-de-Beaupré | Beauport-Montmorency-Orléans | Charlevoix | Roberge Jacques, Administrateur, 1, rue des Remparts, Québec G1R 5L7 – 418/692-3981, Fax: 418/692-4345 |
| St-Louis-du-Ha!-Ha! (P) | 1,513 | Témiscouata | Kamouraska-Rivière-du-Loup-Témiscouata-Les Basques | Kamouraska-Témiscouata | Gratien Ouellet, Sec.-Trés., 95, rue St-Charles, St-Louis-du-Ha!-Ha! G0L 3S0 – 418/854-2260, Fax: 418/854-0717 |
| St-Louis/Cap-Tourmente (P) | | | Beauport-Montmorency-Orléans | Charlevoix | 1, rue des Remparts, Québec G1R 5L7 – 418/692-3981, Fax: 418/692-4345 |
| Ste-Louise (P) | 823 | L'Islet | Bellechasse-Etchemins-Montmagny-L'Islet | Kamouraska-Témiscouata | Ghislain Lizotte, Sec.-Trés., 80, rte de la Station, Ste-Louise G0R 3K0 – 418/354-2509, Fax: 418/354-7730 |

Urban Centres (Villes) in CAPITALS; Villages marked (V); Townships/Cantons marked (Canton);United townships/Cantons unis marked (Cantons); Parishes marked (P); Municipalities marked (Mun.).; Northern villages/Villages nordiques marked (NV); Cree Villages/Villages Cris marked (VC); Naskapi Villages/Villages Naskapi marked (VN); In the third column, Urban Community/Communauté Urbaine marked Urb. Com. An in-depth listing for municipalities marked with * appears in Part 2 (check Index for page numbers).

| MUNICIPALITY | 1996 POP. | REGIONAL COUNTY MUN. | FEDERAL ELECTORAL DISTRICT | PROVINCIAL ELECTORAL DISTRICT | CONTACT PERSON WITH ADDRESS, PHONE & FAX |
|---|---|---|---|---|---|
| St-Luc (P) | 899 | Matane | Matapédia-Matane | Matane | Guylaine Labrie, Sec.-Trés., 3, rue de l'Église, St-Luc-de-Matane G0J 2X0 – 418/562-2916, Fax: 418/562-8754 |
| St-Luc (P) | 524 | Les Etchemins | Bellechasse-Etchemins-Montmagny-L'Islet | Bellechasse | Lorette S.-Jolin, Sec.-Trés., 230A, rue Principale, St-Luc G0R 1L0 – 418/636-2176, Fax: 418/636-2176 |
| ST-LUC | 18,371 | Le Haut-Richelieu | St-Jean | St-Jean | Lise Bigonesse, Gref., 347, boul Saint-Luc, Saint-Luc J2W 2A2 – 514/359-2400, Fax: 514/359-2407 |
| St-Luc-de-Vincennes (Mun.) | 623 | Francheville | Champlain | Champlain | Rita Massicotte, Sec.-Trés., 600, rue Principale, CP 450, St-Luc-de-Vincennes G0X 3K0 – 819/295-3782, Fax: 819/295-3782 |
| Ste-Luce (P) | 1,419 | La Mitis | Rimouski-Mitis | Matapédia | Gaétan Ross, Sec.-Trés., 1, rue Langlois, CP 40, Ste-Luce G0K 1P0 – 418/739-4317, Fax: 418/739-4823 |
| Ste-Lucie-de-Beauregard (Mun.) | 408 | Montmagny | Bellechasse-Etchemins-Montmagny-L'Islet | Montagny-L'Islet | Yvon Leclerc, Sec.-Trés., 146, rue Principale, Ste-Lucie-de-Beauregard G0R 3L0 – 418/223-3122, Fax: 418/223-3122 |
| Ste-Lucie-des-Laurentides (Mun.) | 999 | Les Laurentides | Laurentides | Bertrand | Monique Paiement, Sec.-Trés., 2057, 10e rue, Ste-Lucie-des-Laurentides J0T 2J0 – 819/326-3198, Fax: 819/326-0592 |
| St-Lucien (P) | 1,220 | Drummond | Drummond | Richmond | Louise Tessier, Sec.-Trés., 5350, 7e rang, St-Lucien J0C 1N0 – 819/397-4679, Fax: 819/397-2732 |
| St-Ludger (V) | 173 | Le Granit | Frontenac-Mégantic | Beauce-Sud | Ghislaine Poulin-Duquette, Sec.-Trés., 158, rue des Fleurs, CP 24, St-Ludger G0M 1W0 – 819/548-5843 |
| St-Ludger-de-Milot (Mun.) | 752 | Lac-St-Jean-Est | Lac St-Jean | Lac-St-Jean | Rita Ouellet, Sec.-Trés., 739, rue Gaudreault, CP 9, St-Ludger-de-Milot G0W 2B0 – 418/373-2266, Fax: 418/373-2554 |
| Ste-Madeleine (V) | 1,993 | Les Maskoutains | St-Hyacinthe-Bagot | Verchères | Sylvie Fréchette, Sec.-Trés., 850, rue St-Simon, CP , Ste-Madeleine J0H 1S0 – 514/795-3822, Fax: 514/795-3736 |
| Ste-Madeleine-de-la-Rivière-Madeleine (Mun.) | 482 | Denis-Riverin | Matapédia-Matane | Gaspé | Martine Fournier, Sec.-Trés., 142, rte Principale, Madeleine-Centre G0E 1P0 – 418/393-2428, Fax: 418/393-2869 |
| St-Magloire-de-Bellechasse (Mun.) | 800 | Les Etchemins | Bellechasse-Etchemins-Montmagny-L'Islet | Bellechasse | Irène Mercier, Sec.-Trés., 130, rue Principale, CP 40, St-Magloire G0R 3M0 – 418/257-4421, Fax: 418/257-4421 |
| St-Majorique-de-Grantham (P) | 871 | Drummond | Drummond | Drummond | Colette Tessier, Sec.-Trés., 1966, boul St-Joseph ouest, RR#5, Saint-Majorique-de-Grantham J2B 8A8 – 819/478-7058, Fax: 819/478-8479 |
| St-Malachie (P) | 1,355 | Bellechasse | Bellechasse-Etchemins-Montmagny-L'Islet | Bellechasse | Hélène Bissonnette, Sec.-Trés., 610, 7e rue, CP 99, St-Malachie G0R 3N0 – 418/642-2102, Fax: 418/642-2231 |
| St-Malachie-d'Ormstown (P) | 2,096 | Le Haut-St-Laurent | Beauharnois-Salaberry | Beauharnois-Huntingdon | Jean-Claude Marcil, Sec.-Trés., 81, rue Lambton, Ormstown J0S 1K0 – 514/829-2625, Fax: 514/829-4162 |
| St-Malo (Mun.) | 375 | Le Haut-St-François | Compton-Stanstead | Mégantic-Compton | Jean-Paul Roy, Sec.-Trés., 116A, rue Principale, St-Malo J0B 2Y0 – 819/658-3556, Fax: 819/658-9010 |
| St-Marc-de-Figuery (P) | 580 | Abitibi | Abitibi | Abitibi-Ouest | Aline Guénette, Sec.-Trés., 10, av Michaud, CP 12, St-Marc-de-Figuery J0Y 1J0 – 819/732-8501, Fax: 819/732-8501 |
| St-Marc-des-Carrières (V) | 2,955 | Portneuf | Portneuf | Portneuf | Maryon Leclerc, Sec.-Trés., 965, av Bona-Dussault, CP 157, St-Marc-des-Carrières G0A 4B0 – 418/268-3862, Fax: 418/268-8776 |
| St-Marc-du-Lac-Long (P) | 486 | Témiscouata | Kamouraska-Rivière-du-Loup-Témiscouata-Les Basques | Kamouraska-Témiscouata | Claudette Beaulieu, Sec.-Trés., 12, rue de l'Église, St-Marc-du-Lac-Long G0L 1T0 – 418/893-2643, Fax: 418/893-7228 |
| St-Marc-sur-Richelieu (Mun.) | 1,999 | Le Vallée-du-Richelieu | Verchères | Verchères | Sylvie Burelle, Sec.-Trés., 102, rue de la Fabrique, St-Marc-sur-Richelieu J0L 2E0 – 514/584-2258, Fax: 514/584-2795 |
| St-Marcel (Mun.) | 548 | L'Islet | Bellechasse-Etchemins-Montmagny-L'Islet | Montmagny-L'Islet | Angèle Bélanger, Sec.-Trés., 48, rue Taché est, CP 10, St-Marcel-de-L'Islet G0R 3R0 – 418/356-2691, Fax: 418/356-2820 |
| St-Marcel-de-Richelieu (Mun.) | 619 | Les Maskoutains | St-Hyacinthe-Bagot | Nicolet-Yamaska | Sylvie Viens, Sec.-Trés., 500, rue de l'École, St-Marcel-de-Richelieu J0H 1T0 – 514/794-2832, Fax: 514/794-1140 |
| St-Marcellin (P) | 313 | Rimouski-Neigette | Rimouski-Mitis | Rimouski | Brigitte Couturier, Sec.-Trés., 337, rte 234, St-Marcellin G0K 1R0 – 418/798-4382, Fax: 418/798-4382 |
| Ste-Marcelline-de-Kildare (Mun.) | 1,221 | Matawinie | Berthier-Montcalm | Joliette | Micheline Miron, Sec.-Trés., 435, 1re rue du Pied-de-la-Montagne, Ste-Marcelline J0K 2Y0 – 514/883-2241, Fax: 514/883-2242 |
| Ste-Marguerite (Mun.) | 235 | La Matapédia | Matapédia-Matane | Matapédia | Odette Corbin, Sec.-Trés., 15, rte de La Vérendrye, Ste-Marguerite-Marie G0J 2Y0 – 418/756-3364, Fax: 418/756-3364 |

Urban Centres (Villes) in CAPITALS; Villages marked (V); Townships/Cantons marked (Canton);United townships/Cantons unis marked (Cantons); Parishes marked (P); Municipalities marked (Mun.).; Northern villages/Villages nordiques marked (NV); Cree Villages/Villages Cris marked (VC); Naskapi Villages/Villages Naskapi marked (VN); In the third column, Urban Community/Communauté Urbaine marked Urb. Com. An in-depth listing for municipalities marked with * appears in Part 2 (check Index for page numbers).

| MUNICIPALITY | 1996 POP. | REGIONAL COUNTY MUN. | FEDERAL ELECTORAL DISTRICT | PROVINCIAL ELECTORAL DISTRICT | CONTACT PERSON WITH ADDRESS, PHONE & FAX |
|---|---|---|---|---|---|
| Ste-Marguerite (P) | 985 | La Nouvelle-Beauce | Beauce | Beauce-Nord | Jacqueline Giroux, Sec.-Trés., 235, rue St-Jacques, Ste-Marguerite G0S 2X0 – 418/935-7103, Fax: 418/935-3709 |
| Ste-Marguerite-du-Lac-Masson (P) | 2,251 | Les Pays-d'en-Haut | Laurentides | Bertrand | Denis Lemay, Sec.-Trés., 414, boul du Baron-Empain, CP 180, Lac-Masson J0T 1L0 – 514/228-2543, Fax: 514/228-4008 |
| STE-MARIE | 10,966 | La Nouvelle-Beauce | Beauce | Beauce-Nord | Benoît Fecteau, Gref., 270, av Marguerite-Bourgeoys, CP 1750, Ste-Marie G6E 3C7 – 418/387-2301, Fax: 418/387-2454 |
| Ste-Marie-de-Blandford (Mun.) | 476 | Bécancour | Lotbinière | Lotbinière | Josée Charest, Sec.-Trés., 473, rue des Bosquets, Ste-Marie-de-Blandford G0X 2W0 – 819/283-2127, Fax: 819/283-2127 |
| Ste-Marie-de-Monnoir (P) | 2,126 | Rouville | Chambly | Iberville | Francine Guertin, Sec.-Trés., 146, ch Ruisseau-Barré, Ste-Marie-de-Monnoir J3M 1P2 – 514/460-2251, Fax: 514/460-4532 |
| Ste-Marie-Madeleine (P) | 2,262 | Les Maskoutains | St-Hyacinthe-Bagot | Verchères | Sylvie McDuff, Sec.-Trés., 3541, boul Laurier, Ste-Marie-Madeleine J0H 1S0 – 514/795-6272, Fax: 514/795-3180 |
| Ste-Marie-Salomé (P) | 1,189 | Montcalm | Berthier-Montcalm | Joliette | Gérard Martin, Sec.-Trés., 690, ch St-Jean, Ste-Marie-Salomé J0K 2Z0 – 514/839-6212, Fax: 514/839-6106 |
| Ste-Marthe (Mun.) | 1,090 | Vaudreuil-Soulanges | Vaudreuil-Soulanges | Vaudreuil | Bernard Charlebois, Sec.-Trés., 776, rue des Loisirs, Ste-Marthe J0P 1W0 – 514/459-4284, Fax: 514/459-4627 |
| Ste-Marthe-du-Cap (Mun.) | 6,150 | Francheville | Champlain | Champlain | Marcel Milot, Sec.-Trés., 1001, rang St-Malo, CP 158, Ste-Marthe-du-Cap G8T 7W2 – 819/378-5949, Fax: 819/378-0561 |
| STE-MARTHE-SUR-LE-LAC | 8,295 | Deux-Montagnes | St-Eustache-St-Thérèse | Deux-Montagnes | Jean-Marc Rivest, Gref., 3000, ch d'Oka, Ste-Marthe-sur-le-Lac J0N 1P0 – 514/472-7310, Fax: 514/472-4283 |
| St-Martin (P) | 2,546 | Beauce-Sartigan | Beauce | Beauce-Sud | Carmelle Veilleux, Sec.-Trés., 131, 1e av est, CP 99, St-Martin G0M 1B0 – 418/382-5035, Fax: 418/382-5035 |
| Ste-Martine (Mun.) | 2,316 | Beauharnois-Salaberry | Beauharnois-Salaberry | Beauharnois-Huntingdon | Claudette Lefebvre-Dubuc, Sec.-Trés., 3, rue des Copains, Ste-Martine J0S 1V0 – 514/427-3050, Fax: 514/427-7331 |
| St-Mathias-sur-Richelieu (Mun.) | 4,014 | Rouville | Chambly | Chambly | Normande Vigeant, Sec.-Trés., 37, ch des Épinettes, St-Mathias-sur-Richelieu J3L 5Z7 – 514/658-2841, Fax: 514/447-1416 |
| St-Mathieu (Mun.) | 1,929 | Roussillon | Châteauguay | La Prairie | Francine Fleurent, Sec.-Trés., 299, ch Saint-Édouard, St-Mathieu J0L 2H0 – 514/632-9528, Fax: 514/632-9544 |
| St-Mathieu (P) | 1,151 | Le Centre-de-la-Mauricie | Kamouraska-Rivière-du-Loup-Témiscouata-Les Basques | St-Maurice | Vacant, Sec.-Trés., 561, ch Déziel, St-Mathieu-du-Parc G0X 1N0 – 819/532-2205, Fax: 819/532-2415 |
| St-Mathieu-de-Beloeil (P) | 2,143 | La Vallée-du-Richelieu | Chambly | Borduas | Monique Beaudry, Sec.-Trés., 5000, rue des Loisirs, St-Mathieu-de-Beloeil J3G 2C9 – 514/467-7490, Fax: 514/467-2999 |
| St-Mathieu-de-Rioux (P) | 565 | Les Basques | Kamouraska-Rivière-du-Loup-Témiscouata-Les Basques | Rimouski | Michelle Lafontaine, Sec.-Trés., 224A, rue de l'Église, CP 40, St-Mathieu-de-Rioux G0L 3T0 – 418/738-2953, Fax: 418/738-2454 |
| St-Mathieu-d'Harricana (Mun.) | 717 | Abitibi | Abitibi | Abitibi-Ouest | Claudine Harvey, Sec.-Trés., 203, ch des 3e-et-4e-rangs, CP 63, Harricana-Ouest J0Y 1M0 – 819/727-9557, Fax: 819/727-9557 |
| St-Maurice (P) | 2,295 | Francheville | Champlain | Champlain | Gisèle Lefèbvre, Sec.-Trés., 2510, rang St-Jean, CP 9, St-Maurice G0X 2X0 – 819/374-4525, Fax: 819/374-9132 |
| St-Maxime-du-Mont-Louis (Mun.) | 1,499 | Denis-Riverin | Matapédia-Matane | Gaspé | Hilaire Lemieux, Sec.-Trés., 1, 1re av ouest, CP 130, Mont-Louis G0E 1T0 – 418/797-2310, Fax: 418/797-2928 |
| St-Médard (Mun.) | 314 | Les Basques | Kamouraska-Rivière-du-Loup-Témiscouata-Les Basques | Rimouski | Nancy Rioux, Sec.-Trés., 64, rue Principale est, CP 9, St-Médard G0L 3V0 – 418/963-6276, Fax: 418/963-6468 |
| Ste-Mélanie (P) | 2,474 | Joliette | Joliette | Berthier | Réjean Marsolais, Sec.-Trés., 10, rue Louis-Charles-Panet, Ste-Mélanie J0K 3A0 – 514/889-5871, Fax: 514/889-4527 |
| St-Méthode-de-Frontenac (Mun.) | 1,613 | L'Amiante | Frontenac-Mégantic | Frontenac | Bernardin Hamann, Sec.-Trés., 24, rue Principale ouest, CP 10, St-Méthode-de-Frontenac G0N 1S0 – 418/422-2135, Fax: 418/422-2135 |
| St-Michel (P) | 2,451 | Les Jardins-de-Napierville | Châteauguay | Beauharnois-Huntingdon | Micheline Lemay, Sec.-Trés., 410, Place St-Michel, CP 60, St-Michel J0L 2J0 – 514/454-4502, Fax: 514/454-4502 |

Urban Centres (Villes) in CAPITALS; Villages marked (V); Townships/Cantons marked (Canton);United townships/Cantons unis marked (Cantons); Parishes marked (P); Municipalities marked (Mun.).; Northern villages/Villages nordiques marked (NV); Cree Villages/Villages Cris marked (VC); Naskapi Villages/Villages Naskapi marked (VN); In the third column, Urban Community/Communauté Urbaine marked Urb. Com. An in-depth listing for municipalities marked with * appears in Part 2 (check Index for page numbers).

| MUNICIPALITY | 1996 POP. | REGIONAL COUNTY MUN. | FEDERAL ELECTORAL DISTRICT | PROVINCIAL ELECTORAL DISTRICT | CONTACT PERSON WITH ADDRESS, PHONE & FAX |
|---|---|---|---|---|---|
| St-Michel-de-Bellechasse (Mun.) | 1,676 | Bellechasse | Bellechasse-Etchemins-Montmagny-L'Islet | Bellechasse | Ronald Gonthier, Sec.-Trés., 129, rte 132 est, St-Michel-de-Bellechasse G0R 3S0 – 418/884-2865, Fax: 418/884-2866 |
| St-Michel-de-Rougemont (P) | 1,463 | Rouville | Shefford | Iberville | Marielle Guertin, Sec.-Trés., 61, ch Marieville, Saint-Michel-de-Rougemont J0L 1M0 – 514/469-3790, Fax: 514/469-0309 |
| St-Michel-des-Saints (Mun.) | 2,339 | Matawinie | Berthier-Montcalm | Berthier | Alain Bellerose, Sec.-Trés., 390, rue Matawin, CP 160, St-Michel-des-Saints J0K 3B0 – 514/833-6941, Fax: 514/833-6081 |
| St-Michel-du-Squatec (P) | 1,380 | Témiscouata | Kamouraska-Rivière-du-Loup-Témiscouata-Les Basques | Kamouraska-Témiscouata | Gilles Morin, Sec.-Trés., 150, rue St-Joseph, CP 280, Squatec G0L 4H0 – 418/855-2185, Fax: 418/855-2935 |
| St-Michel-d'Yamaska (P) | 1,017 | Le Bas-Richelieu | Richelieu | Richelieu | Brigitte Vachon, Sec.-Trés., 137, rue Principale, CP 120, Yamaska J0G 1W0 – 514/789-2489, Fax: 514/789-2970 |
| St-Modeste (P) | 891 | Rivière-du-Loup | Kamouraska-Rivière-du-Loup-Témiscouata-Les Basques | Rivière-du-Loup | Diane Castonguay, Sec.-Trés., 312, rue Principale, St-Modeste G0L 3W0 – 418/867-2352, Fax: 418/867-5359 |
| St-Moïse (P) | 625 | La Matapédia | Matapédia-Matane | Matapédia | Simone Beaulieu, Sec.-Trés., 62, rue Principale, CP 8, St-Moïse G0J 2Z0 – 418/776-2833, Fax: 418/776-2833 |
| Ste-Monique (Mun.) | 954 | Lac-St-Jean-Est | Lac-St-Jean | Lac-St-Jean | Jean-Claude Duchesne, Sec.-Trés., 101, rue Honfleur, CP 9, Ste-Monique G0W 2T0 – 418/347-3592, Fax: 418/347-4368 |
| Ste-Monique (V) [8] | 192 | Nicolet-Yamaska | Richelieu | Nicolet-Yamaska | Lucie Lambert, Sec.-Trés., 310, rue St-Antoine, Ste-Monique J0G 1N0 – 819/289-2051, Fax: 819/289-2051 |
| St-Narcisse (P) | 1,937 | Francheville | Champlain | Champlain | René Pinard, Sec.-Trés., 353, rue Notre-Dame, CP 139, St-Narcisse G0X 2Y0 – 418/328-8645, Fax: 418/328-4348 |
| St-Narcisse-de-Beaurivage (P) | 1,080 | Lotbinière | Lotbiniére | Lotbinière | Solange Boulanger, Sec.-Trés., #1, 508, rue de l'École, St-Narcisse-de-Beaurivage G0S 1W0 – 418/475-6842, Fax: 418/475-6842 |
| St-Narcisse-de-Rimouski (P) | 996 | Rimouski-Neigette | Rimouski-Mitis | Rimouski | Gilles Lepage, Sec.-Trés., 7, rue du Pavillon, CP 1040, St-Narcisse-de-Rimouski G0K 1S0 – 418/735-2638, Fax: 418/735-6021 |
| St-Nazaire (Mun.) | 2,095 | Lac-St-Jean-Est | Lac-St-Jean | Lac-St-Jean | Roger Bouchard, Sec.-Trés., 199, rue Principale, CP 130, St-Nazaire-du Lac-Saint-Jean G0W 2V0 – 418/662-4154, Fax: 418/662-5467 |
| St-Nazaire-d'Acton (P) | 932 | Acton | St-Hyacinthe-Bagot | Johnson | Guylaine Bourgoin, Sec.-Trés., 750, rue des Loisirs, St-Nazaire-d'Acton J0H 1V0 – 819/392-2347, Fax: 819/392-2039 |
| St-Nazaire-de-Dorchester (P) | 406 | Bellechasse | Bellechasse-Etchemins-Montmagny-L'Islet | Bellechasse | Jacques Bruneau, Sec.-Trés., 98, rte Émile-Lachance, St-Nazaire G0R 3T0 – 418/642-2249, Fax: 418/642-2945 |
| St-Nérée (P) | 832 | Bellechasse | Bellechasse-Etchemins-Montmagny-L'Islet | Bellechasse | Jean-Louis Chabot, Sec.-Trés., 1990, rte Principale, St-Nérée G0R 3V0 – 418/243-2735, Fax: 418/243-2136 |
| St-Nicéphore (Mun.) | 9,251 | Drummond | Drummond | Drummond | Stephen-F. Watkins, Sec.-Trés., 4677, av Traversy, St-Nicéphore J2A 2G2 – 819/477-5144, Fax: 819/474-6766 |
| ST-NICOLAS | 15,594 | Les Chutes-de-la-Chaudière | Lévis | Chutes-de-la-Chaudière | Marcel Frigon, Gref., 1240, ch Filteau, St-Nicolas G7A 1A5 – 418/831-2877, Fax: 418/831-8907 |
| St-Noël (V) | 509 | La Matapédia | Matapédia-Matane | Matane | Manon Caron, Sec.-Trés., 51, rue de l'Église, CP 88, St-Noël G0J 3A0 – 418/776-2936, Fax: 418/776-5521 |
| St-Norbert (P) | 1,070 | D'Autray | Berthier-Montcalm | Berthier | Martine Laberge, Sec.-Trés., 2150, rue Principale, St-Norbert J0K 3C0 – 514/836-4700, Fax: 514/836-4700 |
| St-Norbert-d'Arthabaska (Mun.) | 893 | Arthabaska | Richmond-Arthabaska | Arthabaska | René Savoie, Sec.-Trés., 250, route de la Rivière, Norbertville G0P 1B0 – 819/369-9318, Fax: 819/369-9318 |
| St-Norbert-de-Mont-Brun (Mun.) | 537 | Rouyn-Noranda | Témiscamingue | Rouyn-Noranda-Témiscamingue | Marielle Fortier-Migneault, Sec.-Trés., Maison du Partage, 956, rue Principale, Mont-Brun J0Z 2Y0 – 819/637-7045, Fax: 819/637-7045 |
| St-Octave-de-Métis (P) | 575 | La Mitis | Rimouski-Mitis | Matane | Line-Hélène Bérubé, Sec.-Trés., 220, 3e rang ouest, CP 107, St-Octave-de-Métis G0J 3B0 – 418/775-2996, Fax: 418/775-0099 |
| Ste-Odile-sur-Rimouski (P) | 1,412 | Rimouski-Neigette | Rimouski-Mitis | Rimouski | Dolorès Beaulieu, Sec.-Trés., 160, ch des Pointes, Ste-Odile-sur-Rimouski G5L 7B5 – 418/724-4925, Fax: 418/724-7388 |
| St-Odilon-de-Cranbourne (P) | 1,448 | Robert-Cliche | Beauce | Beauce-Nord | André Fecteau, Sec.-Trés., 106, rue de l'Hôtel-de-Ville, CP 100, St-Odilon G0S 3A0 – 418/464-4801, Fax: 418/464-4800 |

Urban Centres (Villes) in CAPITALS; Villages marked (V); Townships/Cantons marked (Canton);United townships/Cantons unis marked (Cantons); Parishes marked (P); Municipalities marked (Mun.).; Northern villages/Villages nordiques marked (NV); Cree Villages/Villages Cris marked (VC); Naskapi Villages/Villages Naskapi marked (VN); In the third column, Urban Community/Communauté Urbaine marked Urb. Com. An in-depth listing for municipalities marked with * appears in Part 2 (check Index for page numbers).

| MUNICIPALITY | 1996 POP. | REGIONAL COUNTY MUN. | FEDERAL ELECTORAL DISTRICT | PROVINCIAL ELECTORAL DISTRICT | CONTACT PERSON WITH ADDRESS, PHONE & FAX |
|---|---|---|---|---|---|
| St-Omer (P) | 1,381 | Avignon | Matapédia-Matane | Bonaventure | Michelyne Leblanc, Sec.-Trés., 303, rte 132 ouest, CP 157, St-Omer G0C 2Z0 – 418/364-3682, Fax: 418/364-6049 |
| St-Omer (Mun.) | 363 | L'Islet | Bellechasse-Etchemins-Montmagny-L'Islet | Montmagny-L'Islet | Lise B. Guillot, Sec.-Trés., 243, ch des Pelletier, CP 1765, Saint-Omer G0R 4R0 – 418/356-5634, Fax: 418/356-5081 |
| St-Onésime-d'Ixworth (P) | 649 | Kamouraska | Kamouraska-Rivière-du-Loup-Témiscouata-Les Basques | Kamouraska-Témiscouata | Isabelle St-Laurent, Sec.-Trés., 12, rte de l'Église, St-Onésime-d'Ixworth G0R 3W0 – 418/856-3018, Fax: 418/856-3018 |
| ST-OURS | 1,619 | Le Bas-Richelieu | Richelieu | Richelieu | France Blain, Sec.-Trés., 2540, rue de l'Immaculée-Conception, CP 129, St-Ours J0G 1P0 – 514/785-2203, Fax: 514/785-2254 |
| St-Pacôme (Mun.) | 1,799 | Kamouraska | Kamouraska-Rivière-du-Loup-Témiscouata-Les Basques | Kamouraska-Témiscouata | Maryse Ouellet, Sec.-Trés., 27, rue St-Louis, CP 370, St-Pacôme G0L 3X0 – 418/852-2356, Fax: 418/852-2977 |
| ST-PAMPHILE | 2,990 | L'Islet | Bellechasse-Etchemins-Montmagny-L'Islet | Montmagny-L'Islet | Richard Pelletier, Sec.-Trés., 3, rte Elgin sud, CP 638, St-Pamphile G0R 3X0 – 418/356-5501, Fax: 418/356-5502 |
| St-Pascal (Mun.) | 1,346 | Kamouraska | Kamouraska-Rivière-du-Loup-Témiscouata-Les Basques | Kamouraska-Témiscouata | Réjean Pelletier, Sec.-Trés., 506, rue Taché, 2e étage, CP 756, St-Pascal G0L 3Y0 – 418/492-3817 |
| ST-PASCAL | 2,504 | Kamouraska | Kamouraska-Rivière-du-Loup-Témiscouata-Les Basques | Kamouraska-Témiscouata | Louise Saint-Pierre, Gref., 405, rue Taché, CP 250, St-Pascal G0L 3Y0 – 418/492-2312, Fax: 418/492-9862 |
| St-Patrice-de-Beaurivage (Mun.) | 1,125 | Lotbinière | Lotbinière | Lotbinière | Lise Demers, Sec.-Trés., 530, rue Principale, St-Patrice-de-Beaurivage G0S 1B0 – 418/596-2362, Fax: 418/596-2362 |
| St-Patrice-de-la-Rivière-du-Loup (P) | 3,080 | Rivière-du-Loup | Kamouraska-Rivière-du-Loup-Témiscouata-Les Basques | Rivière-du-Loup | Adryen Sénéchal, Sec.-Trés., 252, rue Fraser, St-Patrice-de-la-Rivière-du-Loup G5R 3Y4 – 418/862-8722, Fax: 418/862-2287 |
| St-Patrice-de-Sherrington (P) | 1,960 | Les Jardins-de-Napierville | Beauharnois-Salaberry | Beauharnois-Huntingdon | Lucie Riendeau, Sec.-Trés., 300, rue St-Patrice, Sherrington J0L 2N0 – 514/454-4959, Fax: 514/454-5677 |
| St-Paul (Mun.) | 3,644 | Joliette | Joliette | Joliette | Richard B. Morasse, Sec.-Trés., 18, boul Brassard, St-Paul J0K 3E0 – 514/759-4040, Fax: 514/759-6396 |
| St-Paul-d'Abbotsford (P) | 2,789 | Rouville | Shefford | Iberville | Daniel Rainville, Sec.-Trés., 926, rue Principale est, CP 69, St-Paul-d'Abbotsford J0E 1A0 – 514/379-5408, Fax: 514/379-9905 |
| St-Paul-de-Châteauguay (Mun.) | 1,411 | Beauharnois-Salaberry | Beauharnois-Salaberry | Beauharnois-Huntingdon | Léopold Vanier, Sec.-Trés., #1C, 55, rue Saint-Joseph, Ste-Martine J0S 1V0 – 514/427-3703, Fax: 514/427-2548 |
| St-Paul-de-la-Croix (P) | 402 | Rivière-du-Loup | Kamouraska-Rivière-du-Loup-Témiscouata-Les Basques | Rivière-du-Loup | Hélène Malenfant, Sec.-Trés., 3, route de l'Église nord, CP 70, St-Paul-de-la-Croix G0L 3Z0 – 418/898-2031, Fax: 418/898-2322 |
| St-Paul-de-l'Île-aux-Noix (P) | 1,847 | Le Haut-Richelieu | St-Jean | St-Jean | Marie-Lili Lenoir, Sec.-Trés., 959, rue Principale, St-Paul-de-l'Île-aux-Noix J0J 1G0 – 514/291-3166, Fax: 514/291-5930 |
| St-Paul-de-Montminy (Mun.) | 931 | Montmagny | Bellechasse-Etchemins-Montmagny-L'Islet | Montmagny-L'Islet | René Gagné, Sec.-Trés., 309, 4e av, CP 160, St-Paul-de-Montminy G0R 3Y0 – 418/469-3120, Fax: 418/469-3120 |
| St-Paul-du-Nord (Mun.) | 767 | La Haute-Côte-Nord | Charlevoix | Saguenay | Hélène Boulianne, Sec.-Trés., 201, rte 138, CP 39, St-Paul-du-Nord G0T 1W0 – 418/231-2344, Fax: 418/231-2577 |
| Ste-Paule (Mun.) | 228 | Matane | Matapédia-Matane | Matane | Gilles Desjardins, Sec.-Trés., 191, rue de l'Église, Ste-Paule G0J 3C0 – 418/737-4296, Fax: 418/737-9460 |
| St-Paulin (Mun.) | 1,599 | Maskinongé | St-Maurice | Maskinongé | Ghislain Lemay, Sec.-Trés., 3051, rue Bergeron, CP 120, St-Paulin J0K 3G0 – 819/268-2026, Fax: 819/268-2890 |
| Ste-Perpétue (Mun.) | 2,028 | L'Islet | Bellechasse-Etchemins-Montmagny-L'Islet | Montmagny-L'Islet | Marie-Claude Chouinard, Sec.-Trés., 366, av Principale, 2e étage, Ste-Perpétue G0R 3Z0 – 418/359-2966, Fax: 418/359-2707 |
| Ste-Perpétue (P) | 1,024 | Nicolet-Yamaska | Richelieu | Nicolet-Yamaska | Silvie Leclerc, Sec.-Trés., 2480, rang St-Joseph, CP 98, Ste-Perpétue J0C 1R0 – 819/336-6740, Fax: 819/336-6770 |
| Ste-Pétronille (V) | 1,090 | L'Île-d'Orléans | Beauport-Montmorency-Orléans | Montmorency | Gaston Lebel, Sec.-Trés., 3, ch de l'Église, Ste-Pétronille G0A 4C0 – 418/828-2270, Fax: 418/828-1364 |
| St-Philémon (P) | 853 | Bellechasse | Bellechasse-Etchemins-Montmagny-L'Islet | Bellechasse | Diane Labrecque, Sec.-Trés., 1531, rue Principale, CP 10, St-Philémon G0R 4A0 – 418/469-2890, Fax: 418/469-2726 |

Urban Centres (Villes) in CAPITALS; Villages marked (V); Townships/Cantons marked (Canton);United townships/Cantons unis marked (Cantons); Parishes marked (P); Municipalities marked (Mun.).; Northern villages/Villages nordiques marked (NV); Cree Villages/Villages Cris marked (VC); Naskapi Villages/Villages Naskapi marked (VN); In the third column, Urban Community/Communauté Urbaine marked Urb. Com. An in-depth listing for municipalities marked with * appears in Part 2 (check Index for page numbers).

| MUNICIPALITY | 1996 POP. | REGIONAL COUNTY MUN. | FEDERAL ELECTORAL DISTRICT | PROVINCIAL ELECTORAL DISTRICT | CONTACT PERSON WITH ADDRESS, PHONE & FAX |
|---|---|---|---|---|---|
| St-Philibert (Mun.) | 414 | Beauce-Sartigan | Beauce | Beauce-Sud | Marie-Jeanne O.-Rodrigue, Sec.-Trés., 329, rue Principale, CP 9, St-Philibert G0M 1X0 – 418/228-8759, Fax: 418/228-3906 |
| St-Philippe (Mun.) | 3,656 | Roussillon | Argenteuil-Papineau | La Prairie | Anne-Marie Piérard, Sec.-Trés., 2225, rte Édouard-VII, CP 30, St-Philippe J0L 2K0 – 514/659-7701, Fax: 514/659-7702 |
| St-Philippe-de-Néri (P) | 967 | Kamouraska | Kamouraska-Rivière-du-Loup-Témiscouata-Les Basques | Kamouraska-Témiscouata | Pierre Leclerc, Sec.-Trés., 12, côte de l'Église, CP 130, St-Philippe-de-Néri G0L 4A0 – 418/498-2744, Fax: 418/498-2193 |
| Ste-Philomène-de-Fortierville (P) | 286 | Bécancour | Lotbinière | Lotbinière | Claude Martel, Sec.-Trés., 405, route 265, Ste-Philomène-de-Fortierville G0S 1J0 – 819/287-4577, Fax: 819/287-4577 |
| St-Pie (P) | 2,400 | Les Maskoutains | St-Hyacinthe-Bagot | Iberville | Cécile Charron, Sec.-Trés., 70, rue St-François, CP 519, St-Pie J0H 1W0 – 514/772-2481, Fax: 514/772-2482 |
| St-Pie (V) | 2,249 | Les Maskoutains | St-Hyacinthe-Bagot | Iberville | Christiane Côté, Sec.-Trés., 77, rue Saint-Pierre, St-Pie J0H 1W0 – 514/772-2488, Fax: 514/772-2233 |
| St-Pie-de-Guire (P) | 471 | Drummond | Drummond | Nicolet-Yamaska | René Dumont, Sec.-Trés., 100 - 9e rang, St-Pie-de-Guire J0G 1R0 – 514/784-2278, Fax: 514/784-0133 |
| St-Pierre (P) | 1,982 | L'Île-d'Orléans | Beauport-Montmorency-Orléans | Montmorency | Marie-Paule Corriveau, Sec.-Trés., 515, route des Prêtres, CP 100, St-Pierre G0A 4E0 – 418/828-2855, Fax: 418/828-2855 |
| St-Pierre (V) | 357 | Joliette | Joliette | Joliette | Édith Gagné, Sec.-Trés., 485, ch Village de St-Pierre nord, Joliette J6E 3Z1 – 514/756-2592, Fax: 514/756-2735 |
| ST-PIERRE | 4,739 | Montréal (Urb. Com.) | Notre-Dame-de-Grâce-Lachine | Marquette | Pierre Bernardin, Gref., 69, 5e av, St-Pierre H8R 1P1 – 514/368-5700, Fax: 514/368-5717 |
| St-Pierre-Baptiste (P) | 508 | L'Érable | Lotbinière | Lotbinière | Suzanne Savage, Sec.-Trés., 532B, rte de l'Église, St-Pierre-Baptiste G0P 1K0 – 418/453-2286, Fax: 418/453-2286 |
| St-Pierre-de-Broughton (Mun.) | 871 | L'Amiante | Frontenac-Mégantic | Frontenac | Berthe Boulanger, Sec.-Trés., 29, rue de la Fabrique, CP 68, St-Pierre-de-Broughton G0N 1T0 – 418/424-3572, Fax: 418/424-3572 |
| St-Pierre-de-la-Rivière-du-Sud (P) | 889 | Montmagny | Bellechasse-Etchemins-Montmagny-L'Islet | Montmagny-L'Islet | Georges Baillargeon, Sec.-Trés., 645 - 2e av, St-Pierre-de-la-Rivière-du-Sud G0R 4B0 – 418/248-8277, Fax: 418/248-7068 |
| St-Pierre-de-Lamy (Mun.) | 138 | Témiscouata | Kamouraska-Rivière-du-Loup-Témiscouata-Les Basques | Kamouraska-Témiscouata | Odette Caron, Sec.-Trés., 115, rte de l'Église, St-Pierre de Lamy G0L 4B0 – 418/497-2447, Fax: 418/497-2447 |
| St-Pierre-de-Véronne-à-Pike-River (Mun.) | 614 | Brome-Missisquoi | Brome-Missisquoi | Brome-Missisquoi | Lucie Fortin, Sec.-Trés., 548, rte 202, CP 93, St-Pierre-de-Véronne-à-Pike-River J0J 1P0 – 514/248-2120, Fax: 514/248-4772 |
| St-Pierre-les-Becquets (Mun.) | 1,336 | Bécancour | Lotbinière | Lotbinière | Marcelle Lafleur, Sec.-Trés., 110, rue des Loisirs, St-Pierre-les-Becquets G0X 2Z0 – 819/263-2622, Fax: 819/263-2622 |
| St-Placide (Mun.) | 1,479 | Deux-Montagnes | Argenteuil-Papineau | Deux-Montagnes | Françoise Duplessis, Sec.-Trés., 281, rang St-Vincent, CP 60, St-Placide J0V 2B0 – 514/258-2305, Fax: 514/258-3059 |
| St-Polycarpe (Mun.) | 1,676 | Vaudreuil-Soulanges | Vaudreuil-Soulanges | Salaberry-Soulanges | Fleurette Pilon-Sauvé, Sec.-Trés., 1263, ch Élie-Auclair, CP 380, St-Polycarpe J0P 1X0 – 514/265-3777, Fax: 514/265-3010 |
| Ste-Praxède (P) | 354 | L'Amiante | Frontenac-Mégantic | Frontenac | Josée Vachon, Sec.-Trés., 4795, rte 263, Ste-Praxède G0N 1E0 – 418/449-2250, Fax: 418/449-2250 |
| St-Prime (Mun.) | 2,685 | Le Domaine-du-Roy | Roberval | Roberval | Régis Girard, Sec.-Trés., 599, rue Principale, St-Prime G8J 1T2 – 418/251-2116, Fax: 418/251-2823 |
| St-Prosper (Mun.) | 3,772 | Les Etchemins | Beauce | Beauce-Sud | Johanne Nadeau, Sec.-Trés., 2025 - 29e rue, St-Prosper G0M 1Y0 – 418/594-8135, Fax: 418/594-8865 |
| St-Prosper (P) | 548 | Francheville | Champlain | Champlain | Jeannine Mongrain, Sec.-Trés., 375, rue St-Joseph, CP 68, St-Prosper G0X 3A0 – 418/328-8449, Fax: 418/328-4267 |
| St-Raphaël (Mun.) | 2,187 | Bellechasse | Bellechasse-Etchemins-Montmagny-L'Islet | Bellechasse | Armand Picard, Sec.-Trés., 19, av Chanoine-Audet, CP 159, St-Raphaël G0R 4C0 – 418/243-2853, Fax: 418/243-2605 |
| St-Raphaël-d'Albertville (P) | 364 | La Matapédia | Matapédia-Matane | Matapédia | Diane Petrie, Sec.-Trés., 1058, rue Principale, CP 8, Albertville G0J 1A0 – 418/756-3554, Fax: 418/756-3554 |
| St-Raphaël-Sud (P) | 219 | Nicolet-Yamaska | Richelieu | Nicolet-Yamaska | Jacqueline Laplante, Sec.-Trés., 1360 - 3e rang, Aston-Jonction G0Z 1A0 – 819/226-3232, Fax: 819/226-3013 |
| ST-RAYMOND | 8,733 | Portneuf | Portneuf | Portneuf | Réjeanne Julien, Sec.-Trés., 375, rue St-Joseph, CP 880, St-Raymond G0A 4G0 – 418/337-2202, Fax: 418/337-2203 |

Urban Centres (Villes) in CAPITALS; Villages marked (V); Townships/Cantons marked (Canton);United townships/Cantons unis marked (Cantons); Parishes marked (P); Municipalities marked (Mun.).; Northern villages/Villages nordiques marked (NV); Cree Villages/Villages Cris marked (VC); Naskapi Villages/Villages Naskapi marked (VN); In the third column, Urban Community/Communauté Urbaine marked Urb. Com. An in-depth listing for municipalities marked with * appears in Part 2 (check Index for page numbers).

| MUNICIPALITY | 1996 POP. | REGIONAL COUNTY MUN. | FEDERAL ELECTORAL DISTRICT | PROVINCIAL ELECTORAL DISTRICT | CONTACT PERSON WITH ADDRESS, PHONE & FAX |
|---|---|---|---|---|---|
| ST-RÉDEMPTEUR | 6,358 | Les Chutes-de-la-Chaudière | Lévis | Chutes-de-la-Chaudière | Jean Marion, Gref., 95, 19e rue, St-Rédempteur G6K 1E5 – 418/831-4488, Fax: 418/831-7550 |
| ST-RÉMI | 5,707 | Les Jardins-de-Napierville | Châteauguay | Beauharnois-Huntingdon | Serge Brazeau, Gref., 105, rue Perras, CP 578, St-Rémi J0L 2L0 – 514/454-3993, Fax: 514/454-7978 |
| St-Rémi-de-Tingwick (P) | 477 | Arthabaska | Richmond-Arthabaska | Richmond | Élise Gendron, Sec.-Trés., 141A, rue Principale, St-Rémi-de-Tingwick J0A 1K0 – 819/359-2731, Fax: 819/359-2731 |
| St-René (P) | 573 | Beauce-Sartigan | Beauce | Beauce-Sud | Michel Gilbert, Sec.-Trés., 778, rte Principale, St-René G0M 1Z0 – 418/382-5226, Fax: 418/382-3655 |
| St-René-de-Matane (Mun.) | 1,065 | Matane | Matapédia-Matane | Matane | Yvette Boulay, Sec.-Trés., 178, av St-René, CP 58, St-René-de-Matane G0J 3E0 – 418/224-3306, Fax: 418/224-3259 |
| Ste-Rita (Mun.) | 387 | Les Basques | Kamouraska-Rivière-du-Loup-Témiscouata-Les Basques | Rivière-du-Loup | Brigitte Pelletier, Sec.-Trés., #25, 1, rue de l'Église est, CP 39, Ste-Rita G0L 4G0 – 418/963-2967, Fax: 418/963-6539 |
| St-Robert (P) | 1,905 | Le Bas-Richelieu | Richelieu | Richelieu | Éloi Lemoine, Sec.-Trés., 650, ch de Saint-Robert, CP 150, St-Robert J0G 1S0 – 514/782-2844, Fax: 514/782-2844 |
| St-Robert-Bellarmin (Mun.) | 687 | Le Granit | Beauce | Beauce-Sud | Suzanne Lescomb, Sec.-Trés., 10, rue Nadeau, CP 27, St-Robert-Bellarmin G0M 2E0 – 418/582-3420, Fax: 418/582-3420 |
| St-Roch-de-l'Achigan (P) | 4,305 | Montcalm | Berthier-Montcalm | Rousseau | Philippe Riopelle, Sec.-Trés., 30, rue du Dr-Wilfrid-Locat nord, CP 480, St-Roch-de-l'Achigan J0K 3H0 – 514/588-2211, Fax: 514/588-4478 |
| St-Roch-de-Mékinac (P) | 298 | Mékinac | Champlain | Laviolette | Robert Jourdain, Sec.-Trés., 1210, rte Ducharme, St-Roch-de-Mékinac G0X 2E0 – 819/646-5635, Fax: 819/646-5635 |
| St-Roch-de-Richelieu (P) | 1,739 | Le Bas-Richelieu | Richelieu | Verchères | Guylaine Pelletier, Sec.-Trés., 1111, rue du Parc, St-Roch de Richelieu J0L 2M0 – 514/785-2755, Fax: 514/785-3098 |
| St-Roch-des-Aulnaies (P) | 1,008 | L'Islet | Bellechasse-Etchemins-Montmagny-L'Islet | Kamouraska-Témiscouata | Cécile Morin, Sec.-Trés., 379, rte de l'Église, St-Roch-des-Aulnaies G0R 4E0 – 418/354-2892, Fax: 418/354-2059 |
| St-Roch-Ouest (Mun.) | 350 | Montcalm | Berthier-Montcalm | Rousseau | Christiane Archambault, Sec.-Trés., 840, ch du Ruisseau-St-Jean, St-Roch-Ouest J0K 3H0 – 514/588-2146, Fax: 514/588-6060 |
| St-Romain (Mun.) | 682 | Le Granit | Frontenac-Mégantic | Mégantic-Compton | Nicole P. Roy, Sec.-Trés., 355, rue Principale, CP 90, St-Romain G0Y 1L0 – 418/486-7374, Fax: 418/486-7875 |
| ST-ROMUALD | 10,604 | Les Chutes-de-la-Chaudière | Lévis | Chutes-de-la-Chaudière | Danielle Bilodeau, Gref., 2175, ch du Fleuve, CP 43100, St-Romuald G6W 7W9 – 418/839-4141, Fax: 418/839-5548 |
| St-Rosaire (P) | 741 | Arthabaska | Lotbinière | Arthabaska | Jacques Boucher, Sec.-Trés., 9, rue St-Pierre, CP 125, St-Rosaire G0Z 1K0 – 819/752-6178, Fax: 819/752-3959 |
| Ste-Rosalie (P) | 1,571 | Les Maskoutains | St-Hyacinthe-Bagot | St-Hyacinthe | Johanne Beaudoin, Sec.-Trés., 1115, rue du Centre, Ste-Rosalie J0H 1X0 – 514/799-3707, Fax: 514/799-1707 |
| Ste-Rosalie (V) | 4,153 | Les Maskoutains | St-Hyacinthe-Bagot | St-Hyacinthe | Jacques DesOrmeaux, Sec.-Trés., 3205, rue Morissette, Ste-Rosalie J0H 1X0 – 514/799-4141, Fax: 514/799-3835 |
| Ste-Rose-de-Watford (Mun.) | 814 | Les Etchemins | Bellechasse-Etchemins-Montmagny-L'Islet | Bellechasse | Diane Vachon, Sec.-Trés., 695, rue Carrier, CP 39, Ste-Rose-de-Watford G0R 4G0 – 418/267-5811, Fax: 418/267-5330 |
| Ste-Rose-du-Nord (P) | 403 | Le Fjord-du-Saguenay | Lac-St-Jean | Dubuc | Maryse Girard, Sec.-Trés., 126, rue de la Descente-des-Femmes, Ste-Rose-du-Nord G0V 1T0 – 418/675-2250, Fax: 418/675-2250 |
| Ste-Sabine (P) | 455 | Les Etchemins | Bellechasse-Etchemins-Montmagny-L'Islet | Bellechasse | Gaétan Lemieux, Sec.-Trés., 4, rue Saint-Charles, Ste-Sabine G0R 4H0 – 418/383-5488, Fax: 418/383-5488 |
| Ste-Sabine (P) | 1,036 | Brome-Missisquoi | Brome-Missisquoi | Brome-Missisquoi | Francine Surprenant, Sec.-Trés., 185, rue Principale, Ste-Sabine J0J 2B0 – 514/293-7686, Fax: 514/293-7686 |
| St-Samuel (P) | 726 | Arthabaska | Richmond-Arthabaska | Richmond | Lucie Arel-Constant, Sec.-Trés., 141, rue de l'Église, St-Samuel-de-Horton G0Z 1G0 – 819/353-1242, Fax: 819/353-1242 |
| St-Sauveur (P) | 3,970 | Les Pays-d'en-Haut | Laurentides | Bertrand | René Lachance, Sec.-Trés., 125, ch Jean-Adam, Saint-Sauveur J0R 1R2 – 514/227-4633, Fax: 514/227-8564 |
| St-Sauveur-des-Monts (V) | 2,904 | Les Pays-d'en-Haut | Laurentides | Bertrand | Normand Patrice, Sec.-Trés., 30, av Filion, St-Sauveur-des-Monts J0R 1R0 – 514/227-2668, Fax: 514/227-8818 |

Urban Centres (Villes) in CAPITALS; Villages marked (V); Townships/Cantons marked (Canton);United townships/Cantons unis marked (Cantons); Parishes marked (P); Municipalities marked (Mun.).; Northern villages/Villages nordiques marked (NV); Cree Villages/Villages Cris marked (VC); Naskapi Villages/Villages Naskapi marked (VN); In the third column, Urban Community/Communauté Urbaine marked Urb. Com. An in-depth listing for municipalities marked with * appears in Part 2 (check Index for page numbers).

| MUNICIPALITY | 1996 POP. | REGIONAL COUNTY MUN. | FEDERAL ELECTORAL DISTRICT | PROVINCIAL ELECTORAL DISTRICT | CONTACT PERSON WITH ADDRESS, PHONE & FAX |
|---|---|---|---|---|---|
| St-Sébastien (Mun.) | 829 | Le Granit | Frontenac-Mégantic | Mégantic-Compton | Martine Rouleau, Sec.-Trés., 582, rue Principale, St-Sébastien G0Y 1M0 – 819/652-2727, Fax: 819/652-2584 |
| St-Sébastien (P) | 799 | Le Haut-Richelieu | Brome-Missisquoi | Iberville | Micheline Benoit, Sec.-Trés., 176, rue Dussault, CP 126, St-Sébastien J0J 2C0 – 514/244-5237, Fax: 514/244-6264 |
| Ste-Séraphine (P) | 399 | Arthabaska | Richmond-Arthabaska | Richmond | Denise Gaudreau, Sec.-Trés., 2660, rue du Centre-Communautaire, Ste-Séraphine J0A 1E0 – 819/336-3200, Fax: 819/336-3200 |
| St-Sévère (P) | 358 | Maskinongé | Trois-Rivières | Maskinongé | Anne-Marie Sauvageau, Sec.-Trés., 47, rue Principale, St-Sévère G0X 3B0 – 819/264-5656, Fax: 819/264-5656 |
| St-Séverin (P) | 272 | Robert-Cliche | Beauce | Beauce-Nord | Georgette L.-Grégoire, Sec.-Trés., 900, rue des Lacs, St-Séverin G0N 1V0 – 418/426-2423, Fax: 418/426-2423 |
| St-Séverin (P) | 976 | Mékinac | Champlain | Laviolette | Ginette Hamelin, Sec.-Trés., 1986, pl du Centre, CP 120, St-Séverin G0X 2B0 – 418/365-5844, Fax: 418/365-7544 |
| St-Siméon (P) | 1,211 | Bonaventure | Bonaventure-Gaspé-Îles-de-la-Madeleine-Pabok | Bonaventure | Jean-Pierre Gauthier, Sec.-Trés., 107D, av de l'Église, CP 39, St-Siméon G0C 3A0 – 418/534-2155, Fax: 418/534-3830 |
| St-Siméon (P) | 477 | Charlevoix-Est | Charlevoix | Charlevoix | Gérald Bouchard, Sec.-Trés., 500, rue St-Laurent, CP 116, St-Siméon G0T 1X0 – 418/638-2451, Fax: 418/638-5177 |
| St-Siméon (V) | 1,012 | Charlevoix-Est | Charlevoix | Charlevoix | Sylvie Foster, Sec.-Trés., 502, rue St-Laurent, CP 98, St-Siméon G0T 1X0 – 418/638-2691, Fax: 418/638-5145 |
| St-Simon (P) | 504 | Les Basques | Kamouraska-Rivière-du-Loup-Témiscouata-Les Basques | Rimouski | Johanne Bélisle, Sec.-Trés., 36, rue de l'Église, CP 40, St-Simon G0L 4C0 – 418/738-2896, Fax: 418/738-2934 |
| St-Simon (P) | 1,168 | Les Maskoutains | St-Hyacinthe-Bagot | St-Hyacinthe | Sylvain Drolet, Sec.-Trés., 45, rue du Couvent, Saint-Simon J0H 1Y0 – 514/798-2276, Fax: 514/798-2498 |
| St-Simon-les-Mines (Mun.) | 383 | Beauce-Sartigan | Beauce | Beauce-Sud | Francine P.-Thibodeau, Sec.-Trés., 3384, rue Principale, St-Simon-les-Mines G0M 1K0 – 418/774-3317 |
| St-Sixte (Mun.) | 456 | Papineau | Argenteuil-Papineau | Papineau | Alain Hotte, Sec.-Trés., 5, rue Emery, Saint-Sixte J0X 3B0 – 819/983-3155, Fax: 819/983-3409 |
| Ste-Sophie (Mun.) | 317 | L'Érable | Lotbinière | Frontenac | Réjean Gosselin, Sec.-Trés., 505, rue Principale, Ste-Sophie G0P 1L0 – 819/362-3465, Fax: 819/362-3465 |
| Ste-Sophie (Mun.) | 8,534 | La Rivière-du-Nord | Berthier-Montcalm | Rousseau | Daniel Jetté, Sec.-Trés., 2212, rue de l'Hôtel-de-Ville, CP 69, Ste-Sophie J0R 1S0 – 514/438-7784, Fax: 514/438-1080 |
| Ste-Sophie-de-Lévrard (P) | 777 | Bécancour | Lotbinière | Lotbinière | Micheline St-Onge, Sec.-Trés., 184A, Saint-Antoine, Ste-Sophie-de-Lévrard G0X 3C0 – 819/288-5804, Fax: 819/288-5804 |
| St-Stanislas (Mun.) | 1,174 | Francheville | Champlain | Champlain | Raymonde Bordeleau, Sec.-Trés., 33, rue du Port, CP 96, St-Stanislas G0X 3E0 – 418/328-3245, Fax: 418/328-4121 |
| St-Stanislas (Mun.) | 319 | Maria-Chapdelaine | Roberval | Roberval | Majella Gagnon, Sec.-Trés., 953, rue Principale, St-Stanislas G0W 2C0 – 418/276-4476, Fax: 418/276-4476 |
| St-Stanislas-de-Kostka (P) | 1,643 | Beauharnois-Salaberry | Beauharnois-Salaberry | Salaberry-Soulanges | Lucile Benoit, Sec.-Trés., 221, rue Centrale, CP 120, St-Stanislas-de-Kostka J0S 1W0 – 514/373-8944, Fax: 514/373-8949 |
| St-Sulpice (P) | 3,307 | L'Assomption | Joliette | L'Assomption | Huguette Archambault, Sec.-Trés., 1089, rue Notre-Dame, St-Sulpice J5W 1G1 – 514/589-4450, Fax: 514/589-9647 |
| St-Sylvère (Mun.) | 863 | Bécancour | Lotbinière | Nicolet-Yamaska | Ginette Richard, Sec.-Trés., 837, 8e rang, St-Sylvère G0Z 1H0 – 819/285-2075, Fax: 819/285-2075 |
| St-Sylvestre (Mun.) [9] | 605 | Lotbinière | Lotbinière | Lotbinière | Céline Bilodeau, Sec.-Trés., 423B, rue Principale, CP 70, St-Sylvestre G0S 3C0 – 418/596-2384, Fax: 418/596-2384 |
| St-Télésphore (P) | 837 | Vaudreuil-Soulanges | Vaudreuil-Soulanges | Salaberry-Soulanges | Danielle Bourgon, Sec.-Trés., 1425, rte 340, St-Télésphore J0P 1Y0 – 514/269-2999, Fax: 514/269-2257 |
| St-Tharcisius (P) | 557 | La Matapédia | Matapédia-Matane | Matapédia | Sophie Fournier, Sec.-Trés., 55, rue Principale, CP 10, St-Tharcisius G0J 3G0 – 418/629-4727, Fax: 418/629-4727 |
| Ste-Thècle (Mun.) | 2,698 | Mékinac | Champlain | Laviolette | Louise T.-Rompré, Sec.-Trés., 301, rue St-Jacques, Ste-Thècle G0X 3G0 – 418/289-2070, Fax: 418/289-3014 |
| St-Théodore-d'Acton (P) | 1,633 | Acton | St-Hyacinthe-Bagot | Johnson | Florence Gauthier, Sec.-Trés., 1661, rue Principale, CP 150, St-Théodore-d'Acton J0H 1Z0 – 514/546-2634, Fax: 514/546-2526 |

Urban Centres (Villes) in CAPITALS; Villages marked (V); Townships/Cantons marked (Canton);United townships/Cantons unis marked (Cantons); Parishes marked (P); Municipalities marked (Mun.).; Northern villages/Villages nordiques marked (NV); Cree Villages/Villages Cris marked (VC); Naskapi Villages/Villages Naskapi marked (VN); In the third column, Urban Community/Communauté Urbaine marked Urb. Com. An in-depth listing for municipalities marked with * appears in Part 2 (check Index for page numbers).

| MUNICIPALITY | 1996 POP. | REGIONAL COUNTY MUN. | FEDERAL ELECTORAL DISTRICT | PROVINCIAL ELECTORAL DISTRICT | CONTACT PERSON WITH ADDRESS, PHONE & FAX |
|---|---|---|---|---|---|
| St-Théophile (Mun.) | 823 | Beauce-Sartigan | Beauce | Beauce-Sud | Paula Lacoursière, Sec.-Trés., 644, rue du Collège, CP 10, St-Théophile G0M 2A0 – 418/597-3998, Fax: 418/597-3015 |
| STE-THÉRÈSE | 23,477 | Thérèse-de-Blainville | St-Eustache-St-Thérèse | Groulx | Jean-Luc Berthiaume, Gref., 6, rue de l'Église, CP 100, Ste-Thérèse J7E 4H7 – 514/434-1440, Fax: 514/434-1499 |
| Ste-Thérèse-de-Gaspé (Mun.) | 1,262 | Pabok | Bonaventure-Gaspé-Îles-de-la-Madeleine-Pabok | Gaspé | Luc Lambert, Sec.-Trés., 374, route 132, CP 160, Ste-Thérèse-de-Gaspé G0C 3B0 – 418/385-3313, Fax: 418/385-3799 |
| Ste-Thérèse-de-la-Gatineau (Mun.) | 411 | La Vallée-de-la-Gatineau | Pontiac-Gatineau-Labelle | Gatineau | Mariette Rochon, Sec.-Trés., CP 155, Ste-Thérèse-de-la-Gatineau J0X 2X0 – 819/449-4134, Fax: 819/449-2194 |
| St-Thomas (Mun.) | 2,987 | Joliette | Joliette | Joliette | Roger Drainville, Sec.-Trés., 770, rue Principale, CP 390, St-Thomas J0K 3L0 – 514/759-3405, Fax: 514/759-0059 |
| St-Thomas-d'Aquin (P) | 4,196 | Les Maskoutains | St-Hyacinthe-Bagot | St-Hyacinthe | Murielle Archambault, Sec.-Trés., 105, rue Prévert, St-Thomas-d'Aquin J0H 2A0 – 514/796-5885, Fax: 514/796-1851 |
| St-Thomas-de-Pierreville (P) | 705 | Nicolet-Yamaska | Richelieu | Nicolet-Yamaska | Carmelle L. Dupuis, Sec.-Trés., 82, rue Shooner, CP 428, Pierreville J0G 1J0 – 514/568-3366, Fax: 514/568-0021 |
| St-Thomas-Didyme (Mun.) | 855 | Maria-Chapdelaine | Roberval | Roberval | Jean-Marc Paradis, Sec.-Trés., 9, av du Moulin, CP 40, St-Thomas-Didyme G0W 1P0 – 418/274-3638, Fax: 418/274-4176 |
| St-Thuribe (P) | 360 | Portneuf | Portneuf | Portneuf | Lise Labonté, Sec.-Trés., 378, rue Principale, CP 69, St-Thuribe G0A 4H0 – 418/339-2171 |
| ST-TIMOTHÉE | 8,495 | Beauharnois-Salaberry | Beauharnois-Salaberry | Salaberry-Soulanges | Annie Bouchard, Gref., 88, rue St-Laurent, St-Timothée J6S 6J9 – 514/371-4013, Fax: 514/371-4771 |
| St-Tite (P) | 1,445 | Mékinac | Champlain | Laviolette | B. Cadotte, Sec.-Trés., 540, rue Notre Dame, 2e étage, St-Tite G0X 3H0 – 418/365-5093, Fax: 418/365-4296 |
| ST-TITE | 2,555 | Mékinac | Champlain | Laviolette | Pierre Massicotte, Sec.-Trés., 540, rue Notre-Dame, St-Tite G0X 3H0 – 418/365-5143, Fax: 418/365-4020 |
| St-Tite-des-Caps (Mun.) | 1,522 | La Côte-de-Beaupré | Beauport-Montmorency-Orléans | Charlevoix | Gilles Ménard, Sec.-Trés., 1, rue Leclerc, St-Tite-des-Caps G0A 4J0 – 418/823-2239, Fax: 418/823-2527 |
| St-Ubalde (Mun.) | 1,540 | Portneuf | Portneuf | Portneuf | Serge Deraspe, Sec.-Trés., 427B, boul Chabot, St-Ubalde G0A 4L0 – 418/277-2124, Fax: 418/277-2055 |
| St-Ulric (V) | 754 | Matane | Matapédia-Matane | Matane | M. Paquet, Sec.-Trés., 128, av Ulric-Tessier, CP 130, St-Ulric G0J 3H0 – 418/737-4341, Fax: 418/737-4341 |
| St-Ulric-de-Matane (P) | 945 | Matane | Matapédia-Matane | Matane | Louise Coll, Sec.-Trés., 302, route Centrale, St-Ulric-de-Matane G0J 3H0 – 418/737-4051, Fax: 418/737-4051 |
| St-Urbain (P) | 1,528 | Charlevoix | Charlevoix | Charlevoix | Guy Bouchard, Sec.-Trés., 989, rue St-Edouard, CP 100, St-Urbain G0A 4K0 – 418/639-2467, Fax: 418/639-2467 |
| St-Urbain-Premier (P) | 1,179 | Beauharnois-Salaberry | Beauharnois-Salaberry | Beauharnois-Huntingdon | Nicole Sainte-Marie, Sec.-Trés., 204, rue Principale, St-Urbain-Premier J0S 1Y0 – 514/427-3987, Fax: 514/427-3987 |
| Ste-Ursule (P) | 1,431 | Maskinongé | St-Maurice | Maskinongé | Diane Faucher, Sec.-Trés., 215, rue Lessard, CP 60, Ste-Ursule J0K 3M0 – 819/228-4345, Fax: 819/228-8326 |
| St-Valentin (P) | 490 | Le Haut-Richelieu | St-Jean | St-Jean | Diane Richer-Fournier, Sec.-Trés., 790, ch de la Quatrième Ligne, St-Valentin J0J 2E0 – 514/291-5422, Fax: 514/291-5327 |
| St-Valère (Mun.) | 1,337 | Arthabaska | Lotbinière | Arthabaska | Jocelyn Jutras, Sec.-Trés., 1641A, rte 161, St-Valère G0P 1M0 – 819/353-2219, Fax: 819/353-2290 |
| St-Valérien (P) | 830 | Rimouski-Neigette | Rimouski-Mitis | Rimouski | Marie-Paule Cimon, Sec.-Trés., 181, route Centrale, CP 9, St-Valerien G0L 4E0 – 418/736-5047, Fax: 418/736-5922 |
| St-Valérien-de-Milton (Canton) | 1,776 | Les Maskoutains | St-Hyacinthe-Bagot | Johnson | Fernande Bessette, Sec.-Trés., 1384, rue Principale, CP 150, St-Valérien J0H 2B0 – 514/549-2463, Fax: 514/549-2993 |
| St-Vallier (Mun.) | 1,042 | Bellechasse | Bellechasse-Etchemins-Montmagny-L'Islet | Bellechasse | Jean Lemieux, Sec.-Trés., 375, montée de la Station, St-Vallier G0R 4J0 – 418/884-2559, Fax: 418/884-2454 |
| St-Venant-de-Paquette (Mun.) | 111 | Coaticook | Compton-Stanstead | Mégantic-Compton | Robert Plante, Sec.-Trés., 5, ch du Village, St-Venant-de-Paquette J0B 1S0 – 819/658-3660 |
| Ste-Véronique (V) | 1,088 | Antoine-Labelle | Pontiac-Gatineau-Labelle | Labelle | Suzanne Ranger-Dubé, Sec.-Trés., 341, boul F. Lafontaine, CP 150, Ste-Véronique J0W 1X0 – 819/275-3256, Fax: 819/275-2095 |
| St-Vianney (Mun.) | 592 | La Matapédia | Matapédia-Matane | Matapédia | Adrien Beaupré, Sec.-Trés., 140, av Centrale, CP 39, St-Vianney G0J 3J0 – 418/629-4082, Fax: 418/629-4821 |

Urban Centres (Villes) in CAPITALS; Villages marked (V); Townships/Cantons marked (Canton);United townships/Cantons unis marked (Cantons); Parishes marked (P); Municipalities marked (Mun.).; Northern villages/Villages nordiques marked (NV); Cree Villages/Villages Cris marked (VC); Naskapi Villages/Villages Naskapi marked (VN); In the third column, Urban Community/Communauté Urbaine marked Urb. Com. An in-depth listing for municipalities marked with * appears in Part 2 (check Index for page numbers).

| MUNICIPALITY | 1996 POP. | REGIONAL COUNTY MUN. | FEDERAL ELECTORAL DISTRICT | PROVINCIAL ELECTORAL DISTRICT | CONTACT PERSON WITH ADDRESS, PHONE & FAX |
|---|---|---|---|---|---|
| St-Viateur (P) | 201 | D'Autray | Berthier-Montcalm | Berthier | Jean Charland, Sec.-Trés., 1980, rue Bonin, St-Barthélemy J0K 1X0 – 514/885-3511, Fax: 514/885-2165 |
| Ste-Victoire-de-Sorel (P) | 2,318 | Le Bas-Richelieu | Richelieu | Richelieu | Michel Saint-Martin, Sec.-Trés., 517, ch Ste-Victoire, Ste-Victoire-de-Sorel J0G 1T0 – 514/782-3111, Fax: 514/782-2687 |
| St-Victor (Mun.) [10] | 1,253 | Robert-Cliche | Beauce | Beauce-Nord | Marc Bélanger, Sec.-Trés., 287, rue Marchand, CP 40, St-Victor G0M 2B0 – 418/588-6854, Fax: 418/588-6855 |
| St-Wenceslas (Mun.) | 1,170 | Nicolet-Yamaska | Richelieu | Nicolet-Yamaska | Lucie Allard, Sec.-Trés., 1240, rue Principale, CP 68, St-Wenceslas G0Z 1J0 – 819/224-7784, Fax: 819/224-7784 |
| St-Zacharie (Mun.) | 2,180 | Les Etchemins | Beauce | Beauce-Sud | Martin Roy, Sec.-Trés., 735 - 15e rue, CP 249, St-Zacharie G0M 2C0 – 418/593-3185, Fax: 418/593-3085 |
| St-Zénon (P) | 1,146 | Matawinie | Berthier-Montcalm | Berthier | Danielle Rondeau, Sec.-Trés., 6101, rue Principale, St-Zénon J0K 3N0 – 514/884-5987, Fax: 514/884-5285 |
| St-Zénon-du-Lac-Humqui (P) | 464 | La Matapédia | Matapédia-Matane | Matapédia | Claudine Dechamplain, Sec.-Trés., 156, rte 195, Lac-Humqui G0J 1N0 – 418/743-2177, Fax: 418/743-2177 |
| St-Zéphirin-de-Courval (P) | 796 | Nicolet-Yamaska | Richelieu | Nicolet-Yamaska | Christiane Janelle, Sec.-Trés., 1471, rue St-Pierre, CP 40, St-Zéphirin-de-Courval J0G 1V0 – 514/564-2188, Fax: 514/564-2339 |
| St-Zotique (V) | 3,683 | Vaudreuil-Soulanges | Vaudreuil-Soulanges | Salaberry-Soulanges | Pierre Chevrier, Sec.-Trés., 1250, rue Principale, St-Zotique J0P 1Z0 – 514/267-9335, Fax: 514/267-0907 |
| Saints-Anges (P) | 938 | La Nouvelle-Beauce | Beauce | Beauce-Nord | Marie-Paule Marquis, Sec.-Trés., 317, rte des Érables, CP 157, Saints-Anges G0S 3E0 – 418/253-5230, Fax: 418/253-5230 |
| Saints-Martyrs-Canadiens (P) | 206 | Arthabaska | Richmond-Arthabaska | Richmond | Thérèse Lemay, Sec.-Trés., 13, ch du Village, CP 27, Saint-Martyrs G0Y 1B0 – 819/344-5171, Fax: 819/344-5171 |
| SALABERRY-DE-VALLEYFIELD | 26,600 | Beauharnois-Salaberry | Beauharnois-Salaberry | Salaberry-Soulanges | Claude Barrette, Sec.-Trés., 61, rue Ste-Cécile, Salaberry-de-Valleyfield J6T 1L8 – 514/370-4800, Fax: 514/370-4343 |
| Salluit (NV) | 929 | Kativik | Abitibi | Ungava | Donald L. Cameron, Sec.-Trés., Salluit J0M 1S0 – 819/255-8953, Fax: 819/255-8802 |
| Sault-au-Mouton (V) | 643 | La Haute-Côte-Nord | Charlevoix | Saguenay | France Brassard, Sec.-Trés., 70, route 138, CP 99, Sault-au-Mouton G0T 1Z0 – 418/231-2710, Fax: 418/231-2163 |
| Sawyerville (V) | 832 | Le Haut-St-François | Compton-Stanstead | Mégantic-Compton | Lise Houle, Sec.-Trés., 11, ch Clifton, CP 186, Sawyerville J0B 3A0 – 819/889-2252, Fax: 819/889-2252 |
| Sayabec (Mun.) | 2,069 | La Matapédia | Matapédia-Matane | Matapédia | Joël Harrisson, Sec.-Trés., 3, rue Keable, CP 39, Sayabec G0J 3K0 – 418/536-5440, Fax: 418/536-5572 |
| SCHEFFERVILLE | 578 | Caniapiscau | Manicouagan | Duplessis | Nicole Saint-Amand, Sec.-Trés., 505, rue Fleming, CP 1600, Schefferville G0G 2T0 – 418/585-2471, Fax: 418/585-2256 |
| SCOTSTOWN | 680 | Le Haut-St-François | Frontenac-Mégantic | Mégantic-Compton | Claudette Cloutier, Sec.-Trés., 101, ch Victoria ouest, CP 130, Scotstown J0B 3B0 – 819/657-4965, Fax: 819/657-4965 |
| Scott (Mun.) | 1,544 | La Nouvelle-Beauce | Beauce | Beauce-Nord | Lucie Pomerleau, Sec.-Trés., 132, rte du Président-Kennedy, Scott G0S 3G0 – 418/387-2037, Fax: 418/387-1837 |
| Senneterre (P) | 1,169 | Vallée-de-l'Or | Abitibi | Abitibi-Est | Georgette Dumont, Sec.-Trés., 171, rte 113 sud, CP 700, Senneterre J0Y 2M0 – 819/737-2842, Fax: 819/737-2842 |
| SENNETERRE | 3,488 | Vallée-de-l'Or | Abitibi | Abitibi-Est | Hélène Veillette, Gref., 551, 10e av, CP 789, Senneterre J0Y 2M0 – 819/737-2296, Fax: 819/737-4215 |
| Senneville (V) | 906 | Montréal (Urb. Com.) | Lac-St-Louis | Nelligan | Suzanne Lalande, Gref., 35, ch Senneville, Senneville H9X 1B8 – 514/457-6020, Fax: 514/457-0447 |
| SEPT-ÎLES | 25,224 | Sept-Rivières | Manicouagan | Duplessis | Claude Bureau, Gref., 546, av De Quen, Sept-Iles G4R 2R4 – 418/962-2525, Fax: 418/964-3213 |
| Shannon (Mun.) | 3,751 | La Jacques-Cartier | Portneuf | Chauveau | Dale Feeney, Sec.-Trés., 50, ch St-Patrick, Shannon G0A 4N0 – 418/844-3778, Fax: 418/844-2111 |
| SHAWINIGAN | 18,678 | Le Centre-de-la-Mauricie | St-Maurice | St-Maurice | Louise Panneton, Gref., 550, av de l'Hôtel-de-Ville, CP 400, Shawinigan G9N 6V3 – 819/536-7211, Fax: 819/536-7255 |
| SHAWINIGAN-SUD | 11,804 | Le Centre-de-la-Mauricie | St-Maurice | St-Maurice | Yves Vincent, Gref., 1550, 118e rue, Shawinigan-Sud G9P 3G8 – 819/536-5671, Fax: 819/536-5225 |
| Shawville (V) | 1,632 | Pontiac | Pontiac-Gatineau-Labelle | Pontiac | Charles Dale, Sec.-Trés., 350, rue Main, CP 339, Shawville J0X 2Y0 – 819/647-2979, Fax: 819/647-3732 |

Urban Centres (Villes) in CAPITALS; Villages marked (V); Townships/Cantons marked (Canton);United townships/Cantons unis marked (Cantons); Parishes marked (P); Municipalities marked (Mun.).; Northern villages/Villages nordiques marked (NV); Cree Villages/Villages Cris marked (VC); Naskapi Villages/Villages Naskapi marked (VN); In the third column, Urban Community/Communauté Urbaine marked Urb. Com. An in-depth listing for municipalities marked with * appears in Part 2 (check Index for page numbers).

| MUNICIPALITY | 1996 POP. | REGIONAL COUNTY MUN. | FEDERAL ELECTORAL DISTRICT | PROVINCIAL ELECTORAL DISTRICT | CONTACT PERSON WITH ADDRESS, PHONE & FAX |
|---|---|---|---|---|---|
| Sheen-Esher-Aberdeen-et-Malakoff (Cantons) | 127 | Pontiac | Pontiac-Gatineau-Labelle | Pontiac | Donald Marion, Sec.-Trés., Sheenboro J0X 2Z0 – 819/683-2944, Fax: 819/683-3590 |
| Shefford (Canton) | 4,496 | La Haute-Yamaska | Shefford | Shefford | Sylvie Gougeon, Sec.-Trés., 107, rue Lewis ouest, CP 1300, Waterloo J0E 2N0 – 514/539-2258, Fax: 514/539-4951 |
| Shenley (Canton) | 1,009 | Beauce-Sartigan | Beauce | Beauce-Sud | Roger LeBlond, Sec.-Trés., 499, rue Principale, CP 128, St-Honoré G0M 1V0 – 418/485-6738, Fax: 418/485-6738 |
| *SHERBROOKE | 76,786 | Sherbrooke | Sherbrooke | St-François; Sherbrooke | Pierre Huard, Gref. et Directeur, Services juridiques, 191, rue du Palais, CP 610, Sherbrooke J1H 5H9 – 819/821-5500, Fax: 819/822-6064, URL: http://ville.sherbrooke.qc.ca |
| Shigawake (Mun.) | 392 | Bonaventure | Bonaventure-Gaspé-Îles-de-la-Madeleine-Pabok | Bonaventure | Elton Hayes, Sec.-Trés., CP 334, Shigawake G0C 3E0 – 418/752-2474, Fax: 418/752-2474 |
| Shipshaw (Mun.) | 2,858 | Le Fjord-du-Saguenay | Jonquière | Dubuc | Gary James, Sec.-Trés., 3760, route St-Léonard, Shipshaw G7P 1G9 – 418/542-4533, Fax: 418/542-6173 |
| Shipton (Mun.) | 2,753 | Asbestos | Richmond-Arthabaska | Richmond | Michel Lecours, Sec.-Trés., 150, rue Water, CP 209, Danville J0A 1A0 – 819/839-2771, Fax: 819/839-2918 |
| SILLERY | 12,003 | Québec (Urb. Com.) | Louis-Hébert | Jean Talon; Louis-Hébert | Constance Corriveau, Gref., 1445, av Maguire, Sillery G1T 2W9 – 418/684-2100, Fax: 418/684-2199 |
| SOREL | 23,248 | Le Bas-Richelieu | Richelieu | Richelieu | Jean Charbonneau, Gref., 71, rue Charlotte, CP 368, Sorel J3P 7K1 – 514/780-5600, Fax: 514/780-5625 |
| Stanbridge (Canton) | 856 | Brome-Missisquoi | Brome-Missisquoi | Brome-Missisquoi | Vera Gendreau, Sec.-Trés., 12, rue Maple, CP 240, Stanbridge-Est J0J 2H0 – 514/248-3188, Fax: 514/248-3188 |
| Stanbridge-Station (Mun.) | 363 | Brome-Missisquoi | Brome-Missisquoi | Brome-Missisquoi | Serge Therrien, Sec.-Trés., 229, ch Principale, Stanbridge-Station J0J 2J0 – 514/248-2125, Fax: 514/248-1132 |
| STANSTEAD | 3,112 | Memphrémagog | Compton-Stanstead | Orford | Diane Pérusse-Groleau, Sec.-Trés., 96, rue Main, Stanstead J0B 2K0 – 819/876-7181, Fax: 819/876-5560 |
| Stanstead (Canton) | 883 | Memphrémagog | Compton-Stanstead | Orford | Thérèse McCutcheon, Sec.-Trés., 778, ch Sheldon, Magog J1X 3W4 – 819/876-2948, Fax: 819/876-7007 |
| Stanstead-Est (Mun.) | 668 | Coaticook | Compton-Stanstead | Orford | Scott Lothrop, Sec.-Trés., 2310, ch Curtis, Stanstead-Est J0B 3E0 – 819/876-7292, Fax: 819/876-7292 |
| Stoke (Mun.) | 2,409 | Le Val-St-François | Richmond-Arthabaska | Johnson | Diane Roy-Dubois, Sec.-Trés., 403, rue Principale, CP 30, Stoke J0B 3G0 – 819/878-3790, Fax: 819/878-3804 |
| Stoneham-et-Tewkesbury (Cantons) | 4,842 | La Jacques-Cartier | Charlesbourg | Chauveau | Denis Robitaille, Sec.-Trés., 325, ch du Hibou, Stoneham-et-Tewkesbury G0A 4P0 – 418/848-2381, Fax: 418/848-1748 |
| Stornoway (Mun.) | 564 | Le Granit | Frontenac-Mégantic | Mégantic-Compton | Claude Philie, Sec.-Trés., 507, route 108 ouest, CP 98, Stornoway G0Y 1N0 – 819/652-2800, Fax: 819/652-2105 |
| Stratford (Canton) | 786 | Le Granit | Frontenac-Mégantic | Mégantic-Compton | Hélène Lessard, Sec.-Trés., 165, av Centrale nord, Stratford G0Y 1P0 – 418/443-2307, Fax: 418/443-2603 |
| Stukely (Mun.) | 444 | Memphrémagog | Brome-Missisquoi | Brome-Missisquoi | Élise Guertin, Sec.-Trés., 160, ch George-Bonnallie, CP 209, Eastman J0E 1P0 – 514/297-3440, Fax: 514/297-3448 |
| Stukely-Sud (V) | 882 | Memphrémagog | Brome-Missisquoi | Brome-Missisquoi | Lise Côté, Sec.-Trés., 101, pl de la Mairie, CP 30, Stukely-Sud J0E 2J0 – 514/297-3407, Fax: 514/297-3759 |
| Sullivan (Mun.) | 3,312 | Vallée-de-l'Or | Abitibi | Abitibi-Est | Houle Réal, Sec.-Trés., 456, rue de l'Hôtel-de-Ville, CP 40, Sullivan J0Y 2N0 – 819/874-4576, Fax: 819/874-3175 |
| Sutton (Canton) | 1,701 | Brome-Missisquoi | Brome-Missisquoi | Brome-Missisquoi | Suzanne Lessard-Gilbert, Sec.-Trés., 11, rue Principale sud, CP 160, Sutton J0E 2K0 – 514/538-2290, Fax: 514/538-0930 |
| SUTTON | 1,617 | Brome-Missisquoi | Brome-Missisquoi | Brome-Missisquoi | Nicole Bonnal, Gref., 11A, rue Principale sud, CP 959, Sutton J0E 2K0 – 514/538-2230, Fax: 514/538-0955 |
| Tadoussac (V) | 913 | La Haute-Côte-Nord | Charlevoix | Saguenay | Vacant, Sec.-Trés., 162, rue des Jésuites, Tadoussac G0T 2A0 – 418/235-4446, Fax: 418/235-4433 |
| Taschereau (Mun.) | 460 | Abitibi-Ouest | Témiscamingue | Abitibi-Ouest | Linda Chabot, Sec.-Trés., 780A, ch des Pionniers, CP 30, Taschereau J0Z 3N0 – 819/796-2744, Fax: 819/796-2744 |

Urban Centres (Villes) in CAPITALS; Villages marked (V); Townships/Cantons marked (Canton);United townships/Cantons unis marked (Cantons); Parishes marked (P); Municipalities marked (Mun.).; Northern villages/Villages nordiques marked (NV); Cree Villages/Villages Cris marked (VC); Naskapi Villages/Villages Naskapi marked (VN); In the third column, Urban Community/Communauté Urbaine marked Urb. Com. An in-depth listing for municipalities marked with * appears in Part 2 (check Index for page numbers).

| MUNICIPALITY | 1996 POP. | REGIONAL COUNTY MUN. | FEDERAL ELECTORAL DISTRICT | PROVINCIAL ELECTORAL DISTRICT | CONTACT PERSON WITH ADDRESS, PHONE & FAX |
|---|---|---|---|---|---|
| Taschereau (V) | 641 | Abitibi-Ouest | Témiscamingue | Abitibi-Ouest | Yves Aubut, Sec.-Trés., 52, rue Morin, CP 150, Taschereau J0Z 3N0 – 819/796-2219, Fax: 819/796-2219 |
| Tasiujaq (V) | 191 | Kativik | Abitibi | Ungava | Jeannie Cain, Sec.-Trés., Tasiujaq J0M 1T0 – 819/633-9924, Fax: 819/633-5026 |
| TÉMISCAMING | 3,112 | Témiscamingue | Témiscamingue | Rouyn-Noranda-Témiscamingue | Sylvie Bourque, Gref., 451, ch Kipawa, CP 730, Témiscaming J0Z 3R0 – 819/627-3273, Fax: 819/627-3019 |
| Terrasse-Vaudreuil (Mun.) | 1,977 | Vaudreuil-Soulanges | Vaudreuil-Soulanges | Vaudreuil | Gaétan Lemieux, Sec.-Trés., 74 - 7e av, Terrasse-Vaudreuil J7V 3M9 – 514/453-8120, Fax: 514/453-1180 |
| TERREBONNE | 42,214 | Les Moulins | Terrebonne-Blainville | Terrebonne | Denis Bouffard, Gref., 775, rue St-Jean-Baptiste, Terrebonne J6W 1B5 – 514/471-4192, Fax: 514/471-4482 |
| THETFORD MINES | 17,635 | L'Amiante | Frontenac-Mégantic | Frontenac | Denise Veilleux, Gref., 144, rue Notre-Dame sud, CP 489, Thetford Mines G6G 5T3 – 418/335-2981, Fax: 418/335-7089 |
| Thetford-Partie-Sud (Canton) | 3,030 | L'Amiante | Frontenac-Mégantic | Frontenac | Lucie Picard, Sec.-Trés., 2093, rue Notre-Dame nord, Thetford-Partie-Sud G6G 2V9 – 418/338-3533, Fax: 418/338-9443 |
| Thorne (Canton) | 397 | Pontiac | Pontiac-Gatineau-Labelle | Pontiac | Robert Charette, Sec.-Trés., 775, rte 366, Ladysmith J0X 2A0 – 819/647-3206, Fax: 819/647-2086 |
| THURSO | 2,498 | Papineau | Argenteuil-Papineau | Papineau | Vacant, Trés., 161, rue Galipeau, CP 1140, Thurso J0X 3B0 – 819/985-2701, Fax: 819/985-0134 |
| Tingwick (P) | 1,278 | Arthabaska | Richmond-Arthabaska | Richmond | Chantale Ramsay, Sec.-Trés., 48, rue de l'Hôtel-de-Ville, CP 150, Tingwick J0A 1L0 – 819/359-2454, Fax: 819/359-2233 |
| Tourelle (Mun.) | 1,566 | Denis-Riverin | Matapédia-Matane | Matane | Murielle Tanguay, Sec.-Trés., 9, boul Perron est, CP 39, Tourelle G0E 2J0 – 418/763-2629, Fax: 418/763-9004 |
| Tourville (Mun.) | 800 | L'Islet | Bellechasse-Etchemins-Montmagny-L'Islet | Montmagny-L'Islet | Normand Blier, Sec.-Trés., 946, rue Principale, CP 206, Tourville G0R 4M0 – 418/359-2106, Fax: 418/359-2106 |
| TRACY | 12,773 | Le Bas-Richelieu | Richelieu | Richelieu | Laval Tardif, Gref., 3025, boul de la Mairie, Tracy J3R 1C2 – 514/742-5671, Fax: 514/742-5770 |
| Trécesson (Canton) | 1,145 | Abitibi | Abitibi | Abitibi-Ouest | Marlène Fortin, Sec.-Trés., 314, rue Sauvé, Villemontel J0Y 2S0 – 819/732-8524, Fax: 819/732-8322 |
| Tremblay (Canton) | 3,665 | Le Fjord-du-Saguenay | Lac St-Jean | Dubuc | Chantal Girard, Sec.-Trés., 1215, rte Martel, Tremblay G7H 5B2 – 418/543-6875, Fax: 418/543-6803 |
| Très-St-Rédempteur (P) | 622 | Vaudreuil-Soulanges | Vaudreuil-Soulanges | Vaudreuil | Lise Couët, Sec.-Trés., 769, rte Principale, Très-St-Rédempteur J0P 1P0 – 514/451-5203, Fax: 514/451-5203 |
| Très-St-Sacrement (P) | 1,283 | Le Haut-St-Laurent | Beauharnois-Salaberry | Beauharnois-Huntingdon | Suzanne Côté, Sec.-Trés., 63, rue Lambton, CP 192, Howick J0S 1G0 – 514/825-0192, Fax: 514/825-0193 |
| Tring-Jonction (V) | 1,387 | Robert-Cliche | Beauce | Beauce-Nord | Marcel Poulin, Sec.-Trés., 100, av Commerciale, CP 10, Tring-Jonction G0N 1X0 – 418/426-2497, Fax: 418/426-2497 |
| Trois-Lacs (Mun.) | 502 | Asbestos | Richmond-Arthabaska | Richmond | Ghyslaine Leroux, Sec.-Trés., 134, rue Larochelle, Trois-Lacs J1T 3M7 – 819/879-5783, Fax: 819/879-7175 |
| TROIS-PISTOLES | 3,807 | Les Basques | Kamouraska-Rivière-du-Loup-Témiscouata-Les Basques | Rivière-du-Loup | Gabriel Desjardins, Sec.-Trés., 5, rue Notre-Dame est, CP 550, Trois-Pistoles G0L 4K0 – 418/851-1995, Fax: 418/851-3567 |
| TROIS-RIVIÈRES | 48,419 | Francheville | Trois-Rivières | Trois-Rivières | Gilles Poulin, Gref., 1325, Place de l'Hôtel-de-Ville, CP 368, Trois-Rivières G9A 5H3 – 819/374-3521, Fax: 819/372-4631 |
| TROIS-RIVIÈRES-OUEST | 22,886 | Francheville | Trois-Rivières | Maskinongé | Claude Touzin, Gref., 500, côte Richelieu, Trois-Rivières-Ouest G9A 2Z1 – 819/375-7731, Fax: 819/375-2815 |
| Ulverton (Mun.) | 304 | Drummond | Drummond | Johnson | France Turcotte, Sec.-Trés., 151, rte 143, Ulverton J0B 2B0 – 819/826-5049, Fax: 819/826-5181 |
| Umiujaq (NV) | 315 | Kativik | Abitibi | Ungava | Annie Kasudluak, Sec.-Trés., Umiujaq J0M 1Y0 – 819/331-7000, Fax: 819/331-7057 |
| Upton (V) | 1,070 | Acton | St-Hyacinthe-Bagot | Johnson | Louise Quintal, Sec.-Trés., 863, rue Lanoie, Upton J0H 2E0 – 514/549-5611, Fax: 514/549-5045 |
| Val-Alain (Mun.) | 895 | Lotbinière | Lotbinière | Lotbinière | France Bisson, Sec.-Trés., 1245 - 2e rang, CP 10, Val-Alain G0S 3H0 – 819/744-3222, Fax: 819/744-3222 |
| Val-Barrette (V) | 611 | Antoine-Labelle | Pontiac-Gatineau-Labelle | Labelle | Claude Meilleur, Sec.-Trés., 135, rue St-Joseph, CP 60, Val-Barrette J0W 1Y0 – 819/585-3131, Fax: 819/585-4915 |
| VAL-BÉLAIR | 20,176 | Québec (Urb. Com.) | Portneuf | Chauveau | Suzanne Paquet, Sec.-Trés., 1105, av de l'Église nord, Val-Bélair G3K 1X5 – 418/842-7184, Fax: 418/842-1945 |

Urban Centres (Villes) in CAPITALS; Villages marked (V); Townships/Cantons marked (Canton);United townships/Cantons unis marked (Cantons); Parishes marked (P); Municipalities marked (Mun.).; Northern villages/Villages nordiques marked (NV); Cree Villages/Villages Cris marked (VC); Naskapi Villages/Villages Naskapi marked (VN); In the third column, Urban Community/Communauté Urbaine marked Urb. Com. An in-depth listing for municipalities marked with * appears in Part 2 (check Index for page numbers).

| MUNICIPALITY | 1996 POP. | REGIONAL COUNTY MUN. | FEDERAL ELECTORAL DISTRICT | PROVINCIAL ELECTORAL DISTRICT | CONTACT PERSON WITH ADDRESS, PHONE & FAX |
|---|---|---|---|---|---|
| Val-Brillant (Mun.) | 1,040 | La Matapédia | Matapédia-Matane | Matapédia | Louise Bérubé, Sec.-Trés., 11, rue St-Pierre ouest, CP 220, Val-Brillant G0J 3L0 – 418/742-3212, Fax: 418/742-3624 |
| Val-David (V) | 3,473 | Les Laurentides | Laurentides | Bertrand | André Desjardins, Sec.-Trés., 2579, de l'Église, Val-David J0T 2N0 – 819/322-2900, Fax: 819/322-6327 |
| Val-des-Bois (Mun.) | 668 | Papineau | Argenteuil-Papineau | Papineau | Lynda Melanson, Sec.-Trés., 595, route 309, CP 69, Val-des-Bois J0X 3C0 – 819/454-2280, Fax: 819/454-2211 |
| Val-des-Lacs (Mun.) | 627 | Les Laurentides | Laurentides | Bertrand | Réjane Gagnon, Sec.-Trés., 349, ch de Val-des-Lacs, Val-des-Lacs J0T 2P0 – 819/326-5624, Fax: 819/326-7065 |
| Val-des-Monts (Mun.) | 7,231 | Les Collines-de-l'Outaouais | Pontiac-Gatineau-Labelle | Papineau | Patricia Fillet, Sec.-Trés., 1, route du Carrefour, Val-des-Monts J8N 4E9 – 819/457-9400, Fax: 819/457-4141 |
| VAL-D'OR | 24,285 | Vallée-de-l'Or | Abitibi | Abitibi-Est | Normand Gélinas, Gref., 855, 2e av, CP 400, Val-d'Or J9P 4P4 – 819/824-9613, Fax: 819/825-6650 |
| Val-Joli (Mun.) | 1,536 | Le Val-St-François | Richmond-Arthabaska | Johnson | Lucie Camiré, Sec.-Trés., 500, rte 249, Val-Joli J1S 2L5 – 819/845-7663, Fax: 819/845-7663 |
| Val-Morin (Mun.) | 2,043 | Les Laurentides | Laurentides | Bertrand | Manon Bernard, Sec.-Trés., 6120, rue Morin, CP 210, Val-Morin J0T 2R0 – 819/322-3635, Fax: 819/322-3923 |
| Val-Racine (P) | 104 | Le Granit | Frontenac-Mégantic | Mégantic-Compton | Denise Hallé, Sec.-Trés., 2991, ch St-Léon, CP 1, Milan G0Y 1E0 – 819/657-4790, Fax: 819/657-4790 |
| Val-St-Gilles (Mun.) | 187 | Abitibi-Ouest | Témiscamingue | Abitibi-Ouest | Hélène Richer, Sec.-Trés., 801, rue Principale, Val-St-Gilles J0Z 3T0 – 819/333-2158, Fax: 819/333-3116 |
| Val-Senneville (Mun.) | 2,408 | Vallée-de-l'Or | Abitibi | Abitibi-Est | Nicole Guilbert, Sec.-Trés., 656, route des Campagnards, CP 30, Val-Senneville J0Y 2P0 – 819/824-2910, Fax: 819/824-5549 |
| Valcourt (Canton) | 1,030 | Le Val-St-François | Shefford | Johnson | Lucie Beauchemin, Sec.-Trés., 9040B, rue de la Montagne, CP 219, Valcourt J0E 2L0 – 514/532-2688, Fax: 514/532-5570 |
| VALCOURT | 2,442 | Le Val-St-François | Shefford | Johnson | Manon Beauchemin, Gref., 1155, rue St-Joseph, CP 340, Valcourt J0E 2L0 – 514/532-3313, Fax: 514/532-3424 |
| Vallée-Jonction (Mun.) | 1,827 | La Nouvelle-Beauce | Beauce | Beauce-Nord | Gervais Boily, Sec.-Trés., 218, rue Labbé, CP 218, Vallée-Jonction G0S 3J0 – 418/253-5515, Fax: 418/253-6731 |
| VANIER | 11,174 | Québec (Urb. Com.) | Québec-Est | Vanier | Marie-Josée Dumais, Gref., 233, boul Pierre-Bertrand, Vanier G1M 2C7 – 418/687-3530, Fax: 418/681-9433 |
| VARENNES | 18,842 | Lajemmerais | Verchères | Verchères | Yves G. Vincent, Gref., 175, rue Ste-Anne, CP 5000, Varennes J3X 1T5 – 514/652-9888, Fax: 514/652-2655 |
| Vassan (Mun.) | 988 | Vallée-de-l'Or | Abitibi | Abitibi-Est | Brigitte Grandmont, Sec.-Trés., 504, rte 111, CP 610, Vassan J0Y 2R0 – 819/824-8550, Fax: 819/824-5623 |
| VAUDREUIL-DORION | 18,466 | Vaudreuil-Soulanges | Vaudreuil-Soulanges | Vaudreuil | Lise Roy, Gref., 2555, rue Dutrisac, Vaudreuil-Dorion J7V 7E6 – 514/455-3371, Fax: 514/455-0087 |
| Vaudreuil-sur-le-Lac (V) | 928 | Vaudreuil-Soulanges | Vaudreuil-Soulanges | Vaudreuil | Claudia Chebin, Sec.-Trés., 44, rue de l'Église, Vaudreuil-sur-le-Lac J7V 8P3 – 514/455-1133, Fax: 514/455-8614 |
| Venise-en-Québec (Mun.) | 1,108 | Le Haut-Richelieu | Brome-Missisquoi | Iberville | Diane Bégin, Sec.-Trés., 237, 16e av ouest, CP 270, Venise-en-Québec J0J 2K0 – 514/244-5838, Fax: 514/244-5550 |
| Verchères (Mun.) | 4,854 | Lajemmerais | Verchères | Verchères | Luc Forcier, Sec.-Trés., 581, boul Marie-Victorin, Verchères J0L 2R0 – 514/583-3307, Fax: 514/583-3637 |
| *VERDUN | 59,714 | Montréal (Urb. Com.) | Verdun-St-Henri | Verdun | Gérard Cyr, Gref., 4555, rue de Verdun, Verdun H4G 1M4 – 514/765-7000, Fax: 514/765-7048 |
| Vianney (Mun.) | 183 | L'Érable | Lotbinière | Frontenac | Constant Marcoux, Sec.-Trés., 522, rue Principale, CP 12, Vianney G0N 1N0 – 418/428-3461, Fax: 418/428-3016 |
| VICTORIAVILLE | 38,174 | Arthabaska | Richmond-Arthabaska | Arthabaska | Jean Poirier, Gref., 1, rue Notre-Dame ouest, CP 370, Victoriaville G6P 6T2 – 819/758-1571, Fax: 819/758-9292 |
| VILLE-MARIE | 2,855 | Témiscamingue | Témiscamingue | Rouyn-Noranda-Témiscamingue | Pierre Genest, Sec.-Trés., 9, rue Notre-Dame-de-Lourdes, CP 730, Ville-Marie J0Z 3W0 – 819/629-2881, Fax: 819/629-3215 |
| VILLEROY | 493 | L'Érable | Lotbinière | Lotbinière | Angèle Germain, Sec.-Trés., 380, rue Principale, Villeroy G0S 3K0 – 819/385-4605, Fax: 819/385-4605 |
| Waltham-et-Bryson (Cantons) | 496 | Pontiac | Pontiac-Gatineau-Labelle | Pontiac | Fernand Roy, Sec.-Trés., CP 29, Waltham J0X 3H0 – 819/683-3027, Fax: 819/683-2694 |

Urban Centres (Villes) in CAPITALS; Villages marked (V); Townships/Cantons marked (Canton);United townships/Cantons unis marked (Cantons); Parishes marked (P); Municipalities marked (Mun.).; Northern villages/Villages nordiques marked (NV); Cree Villages/Villages Cris marked (VC); Naskapi Villages/Villages Naskapi marked (VN); In the third column, Urban Community/Communauté Urbaine marked Urb. Com. An in-depth listing for municipalities marked with * appears in Part 2 (check Index for page numbers).

| MUNICIPALITY | 1996 POP. | REGIONAL COUNTY MUN. | FEDERAL ELECTORAL DISTRICT | PROVINCIAL ELECTORAL DISTRICT | CONTACT PERSON WITH ADDRESS, PHONE & FAX |
|---|---|---|---|---|---|
| Warden (V) | 330 | La Haute-Yamaska | Shefford | Shefford | Danielle Corriveau-Verhoef, Sec.-Trés., 172, rue Principale, CP 90, Warden J0E 2M0 – 514/539-1349, Fax: 514/539-1349 |
| Warwick (Canton) | 1,972 | Arthabaska | Richmond-Arthabaska | Richmond | Lise Lemieux, Sec.-Trés., 281A, rue St-Louis ouest, CP 160, Warwick J0A 1M0 – 819/358-6197, Fax: 819/358-2164 |
| WARWICK | 2,904 | Arthabaska | Richmond-Arthabaska | Richmond | Jacques Hamel, Sec.-Trés., 8, rue de l'Hôtel-de-Ville, CP 70, Warwick J0A 1M0 – 819/358-4300, Fax: 819/358-4309 |
| Waskaganish (VC) | | | Abitibi | Ungava | CP 60, Waskaganish J0M 1R0 – 819/895-8980, Fax: 819/895-8901 |
| Waswanipi (VC) | | | Abitibi | Ungava | Sam C. Gull, Sec.-Trés., Édifice Diom-Blacksmith, Waswanipi J0Y 3C0 – 819/753-2587, Fax: 819/753-2555 |
| WATERLOO | 4,040 | La Haute-Yamaska | Shefford | Shefford | Denyse Bélanger, Gref., 417, rue de la Cour, CP 50, Waterloo J0E 2N0 – 514/539-2282, Fax: 514/539-3257 |
| WATERVILLE | 1,332 | Sherbrooke | Compton-Stanstead | St-François | Alain Gamache, Sec.-Trés., 170, rue Principale sud, CP 40, Waterville J0B 3H0 – 819/837-2456, Fax: 819/837-2456 |
| Weedon (Canton) [11] | 757 | Le Haut-St-François | Frontenac-Mégantic | Mégantic-Compton | Robert Tardif, Sec.-Trés., 450, 2e av, Weedon J0B 3J0 – 819/877-2727, Fax: 819/877-2255 |
| Wemindji (VC) | | | Abitibi | Mégantic-Compton | Billy Atsynia, Sec.-Trés., 16, rue Beaver, CP 60, Wemindji J0M 1L0 – 819/978-0264, Fax: 819/978-0258 |
| Wentworth (Canton) | 379 | Argenteuil | Argenteuil-Papineau | Argenteuil | Louise Bruneau, Sec.-Trés., 114, ch du Lac-Louisa, Lachute J8H 3W8 – 514/562-0701, Fax: 514/562-0703 |
| Wentworth-Nord (Mun.) | 1,039 | Les Pays-d'en-Haut | Argenteuil-Papineau | Argenteuil | Pauline Legault, Sec.-Trés., 3488, rue Principale, Laurel J0T 1Y0 – 514/226-2416, Fax: 514/226-2109 |
| Westbury (Canton) | 978 | Le Haut-St-François | Compton-Stanstead | Mégantic-Compton | Chantal Bellavance, Sec.-Trés., 140, rue Angus nord, CP 40, East Angus J0B 1R0 – 819/832-3966, Fax: 819/832-3966 |
| WESTMOUNT | 20,420 | Montréal (Urb. Com.) | Westmount-Ville-Marie | Westmount-St-Louis | Marie-France Paquet, Gref., 4333, rue Sherbrooke, Westmount H3Z 1E2 – 514/989-5200, Fax: 514/989-5480 |
| Whapmagoostui (VC) | | | Abitibi | Ungava | Robbie Masty, Sec.-Trés., CP 390, Poste-de-la-Baleine J0M 1G0 – 819/929-3384, Fax: 819/929-3203 |
| Wickham (Mun.) | 2,376 | Drummond | Drummond | Johnson | Réal Dulmaine, Sec.-Trés., 893, rue Moreau, CP 9, Wickham J0C 1S0 – 819/398-6878, Fax: 819/398-7166 |
| WINDSOR | 4,904 | Le Val-St-François | Richmond-Arthabaska | Johnson | Joseph Plante, Gref., 22, rue St-Georges, Windsor J1S 1J3 – 819/845-7888, Fax: 819/845-7606 |
| Wotton (Mun.) | 1,583 | Asbestos | Richmond-Arthabaska | Richmond | Carole Vaillancourt, Sec.-Trés., 400, rue Mgr-L'Heureux, CP 60, Wotton J0A 1N0 – 819/828-2112, Fax: 819/828-3594 |
| Wright (Canton) | 1,202 | La Vallée-de-la-Gatineau | Pontiac-Gatineau-Labelle | Gatineau | Louise Carpentier, Sec.-Trés., 185, route 105, RR#3, Gracefield J0X 1W0 – 819/463-2143, Fax: 819/463-1050 |
| Yamachiche (Mun.) | 2,776 | Maskinongé | Trois-Rivières | Maskinongé | Paul Desaulniers, Sec.-Trés., 366, rue Ste-Anne, CP 430, Yamachiche G0X 3L0 – 819/296-3795, Fax: 819/296-3542 |
| Yamaska (V) | 466 | Le Bas-Richelieu | Richelieu | Richelieu | France Nadeau, Sec.-Trés., 110, rue de Mgr-Parenteau, Yamaska J0G 1W0 – 514/789-2333, Fax: 514/789-2998 |
| Yamaska-Est (V) | 250 | Le Bas-Richelieu | Richelieu | Richelieu | Diane Bibeau-Desmarais, Sec.-Trés., 43, rue Guilbault, Yamaska-Est J0G 1X0 – 514/789-2175, Fax: 514/789-2175 |

1. Effective January 3, 1996 the new city of Baie-St-Paul was created through the amalgamation of the city of Baie-St-Paul, the paroisse of Baie-St-Paul & the muncipality of Rivière-du-Gouffre.
2. Effective August 21, 1996 the new municipality of Chénéville was created through the amalgamation of the village of Chénéville & the municipality of Vinoy.
3. Effective October 23, 1996 the new municipality of Crabtree was created through the amalgamation of the municipalities of Crabtree & Sacré-coeur-de-Crabtree.
4. Effective January 3, 1996 the new city of Pont-Rouge was created through the amalgamation of the village of Pont-Rouge & the municipality of Ste-Jeanne-de-Pont-Rouge.
5. Effective January 3, 1996 the new municipality of St-Faustin-Lac-Carré was created through the amalgamation of the municipality of St-Faustin & the village of Lac-Carré.
6. Effective June 12, 1996 the new municipality of St-Félicien was created through the amalgamation of the city of St-Félicien & the municipality of St-Méthode.
7. Effective January 10, 1996 the new municipality of Ste-Félicité was created through the amalgamation of the village of Ste-Félicité & the paroisse of Ste-Félicité.
8. Effective January 3, 1996 the new municipality of Ste-Monique was created through the amalgamation of the village of Ste-Monique & the paroisse of Ste-Monique.
9. Effective December 4, 1996 the new municipality of St-Sylvestre was created through the amalgamation of the paroisse of St-Sylvestre & the village of St-Sylvestre.
10. Effective December 31, 1996 the new municipality of St-Victor was created through the amalgamation of the municipality of St-Victor-de-Tring & the village of St-Victor.
11. Effective December 11, 1996 the new municipality of Weedon was created through the amalgamation of the village of Weedon Centre & the canton of Weedon.

## REGIONAL COUNTY MUNICIPALITIES/MUNICIPALITÉS DE COMTÉ, QUEBEC

| MUNICIPALITY | 1996 POP. | CONTACT PERSON WITH ADDRESS & PHONE |
|---|---|---|
| Abitibi | 25,280 | Michel Roy, Gref., 571 - 1re rue est, CP 214, Amos J9T 2H3 – 819/732-5356 |
| Abitibi-Ouest | 23,571 | Nicole Breton, Gref., #105, 6 - 8e av est, La Sarre J9Z 1N6 – 819/339-5671 |
| Acton | 15,303 | Yvan Talbot, Gref., 1037, rue Beaugrand, CP 1590, Acton Vale J0H 1A0 – 514/546-3256 |
| Antoine-Labelle | 33,904 | Pierre Borduas, Gref., 400, boul Albiny-Paquette, Mont-Laurier J9L 1J9 – 819/623-3485 |
| Argenteuil | 28,505 | Marc Carrière, Gref., 430, rue Grâce, Lachute J8H 1M6 – 514/562-2474 |
| Arthabaska | 62,917 | Gilles Gagnon, Gref., 40, route de la Grande-Ligne, Victoriaville G6P 6R9 – 819/752-2444, Fax: 819/752-3623 |
| Asbestos | 15,005 | Madeleine Lamoureux, Gref., #303, 185, rue du Roi, Asbestos J1T 1S4 – 819/879-6661 |
| Avignon | 15,898 | Gaétan Bernatchez, Gref., 470, rue Francoeur, CP 128, Nouvelle G0C 2E0 – 418/794-2221 |
| Beauce-Sartigan | 46,318 | Gilles Piché, Gref., 12220 - 2e av, St-Georges G5Y 1X4 – 418/228-8418 |
| Beauharnois-Salaberry | 59,769 | Jean Tétrault, Gref., #300, 600, rue Ellice, Beauharnois J6N 3P7 – 514/225-0870 |
| Bécancour | 19,683 | Laval Dubois, Gref., 3691, Pl le Jardin, Gentilly G0X 1G0 – 819/298-2070 |
| Bellechasse | 29,674 | Clément Fillion, Gref., 100, rue Mgr-Bilodeau, CP 130, St-Lazare G0R 3J0 – 418/883-3347 |
| Bonaventure | 19,550 | Anne-Marie Flowers, Gref., 138, rue Principale, CP 40, New Carlisle G0C 1Z0 – 418/752-6601 |
| Brome-Missisquoi | 45,987 | Robert Desmarais, Gref., 3, rue Principale, CP 150, Bedford J0J 1A0 – 514/248-3326 |
| Caniapiscau | | Gervais Boucher, Gref., 100, place Daviault, CP 1420, Fermont G0G 1J0 – 418/287-5339 |
| Champlain | 314,306 | Sylvie Cossette, Gref., #100, 1000, rue de Sérigny, Longueuil J4K 5B1 – 514/646-6199 |
| Charlevoix | 13,437 | Sylvain Boulianne, Gref., 4, Place de l'Église, CP 549, Baie-St-Paul G0A 1B0 – 418/435-2639 |
| Charlevoix-Est | 16,941 | Pierre Girard, Gref., 172, boul Notre-Dame, CP 610, Clermont G0T 1C0 – 418/439-3947 |
| Coaticook | 15,919 | Guy Charland, Gref., #106, 57, rue Main est, Coaticook J1A 1N1 – 819/849-9166, URL: http://www.multi-medias.ca/mrc_Coaticook/ |
| D'Autray | 37,553 | Claude Joyal, Gref., 180, rue Champlain, CP 1500, Berthierville J0K 1A0 – 514/836-7007 |
| Denis-Riverin | 13,733 | Michel Thibeault, Gref., 122 - 1re av ouest, CP 969, Ste-Anne-des-Monts G0E 2G0 – 418/763-7791 |
| Desjardins | 51,222 | André Roy, Gref., #301 - 13, rue Saint-Louis, Lévis G6V 4E2 – 418/833-1519 |
| Deux-Montagnes | 78,960 | Yvon Bélair, Gref., #201, 400, boul de Deux-Montagnes, Deux-Montagnes J7R 7C2 – 514/491-1818 |
| Drummond | 84,250 | Raymond Malouin, Gref., 436, rue Lindsay, Drummondville J2B 1G6 – 819/477-2230 |
| Francheville | 140,541 | Pierre St-Onge, Gref., 3275, rue Foucher, CP 367, Trois-Rivières G9A 5G4 – 819/378-8088 |
| Joliette | 53,811 | Alain Beaulieu, Gref., 632, rue de Lanaudière, Joliette J6E 3M7 – 514/759-2237 |
| Kamouraska | 23,215 | Guy Lavoie, Gref., 425, av Patry, CP 1120, St-Pascal G0L 3Y0 – 418/492-1660 |
| La Côte-de-Beaupré | 21,632 | Jacques Pichette, Gref., 7007, av Royale, Château-Richer G0A 1N0 – 418/824-3444 |
| La Côte-de-Gaspé | 20,851 | Henri Preston, Gref., 37, rue du Banc, CP 57, Rivière-au-Renard G0E 2A0 – 418/269-7718 |
| La Haute-Côte-Nord | 13,439 | Alain Tremblay, Gref., #1, 9, rue Roussel, CP 790, Les Escoumins G0T 1K0 – 418/233-2102 |
| La Haute-Yamaska | 77,006 | Johanne Gaouette, Gref., 739, rue Dufferin, Granby J2H 2H5 – 514/378-9975, Fax: 514/378-2465 |
| La Jacques-Cartier | 24,819 | Claude Hallé, Gref., 60, St-Patrick, Shannon G0A 4N0 – 418/844-2160 |
| La Matapédia | 20,883 | Jean-Pierre Morneau, Gref., 123, rue Desbiens, CP 2020, Amqui G0J 1B0 – 418/629-2053 |
| La Mitis | 20,160 | Gilles Goulet, Gref., 300, av du Sanatorium, Mont-Joli G5H 1V7 – 418/775-8445 |
| La Nouvelle-Beauce | 25,058 | Ghislain Poulin, Gref., 700, rue Notre-Dame nord, Ste-Marie G6E 2K9 – 418/387-3444 |
| La Rivière-du-Nord | 83,773 | Carole Leduc, Gref., #204, 236, rue du Palais, St-Jérôme J7Z 1X8 – 514/436-9321 |
| La Vallée-de-la-Gatineau | 20,262 | André Beauchemin, Gref., 42, rue Principale, CP 307, Gracefield J0X 1W0 – 819/463-3241 |
| La Vallée-du-Richelieu | 113,832 | Pierre Bélanger, Gref., 630, rue Richelieu, Beloeil J3G 5E8 – 514/464-0339 |
| Lac-St-Jean-Est | 53,066 | Guy Gagnon, Gref., 675, rue Collard ouest, Alma G8B 1N1 – 418/668-3023 |
| Lajemmerais | 95,618 | Maryse Vermette, Gref., 609, rte Marie-Victorin, Verchères J0L 2R0 – 514/583-3301 |
| L'Amiante | 45,020 | Serge Nadeau, Gref., 320, boul Frontenac, Black-Lake G0N 1A0 – 418/423-2757 |
| L'Assomption | 102,188 | Roger Carrier, Gref., 300A, rue Dorval, CP 5057, L'Assomption J0K 1G0 – 514/589-2288 |
| Laval | 330,393 | Ronald Bourcier, Gref., 1, Place du Souvenir, CP 422, Laval H7V 3Z4 – 514/662-4101 |
| Le Bas-Richelieu | 52,288 | Denis Boisvert, Gref., 1275, ch des Patriotes, Sorel J3P 2N4 – 514/743-2703, Fax: 514/743-7313 |
| Le Centre-de-la-Mauricie | 67,103 | Lyne Ricard, Gref., 550, av de l'Hôtel-de-Ville, CP 127, Shawinigan G9N 6T8 – 819/536-4477 |
| Le Domaine-du-Roy | 33,860 | Denis Taillon, Gref., #101, 901, boul St-Joseph, Roberval G8H 2L8 – 418/275-5044 |
| Le Fjord-du-Saguenay | 172,343 | Rénald Gaudreault, Gref., 475, boul Talbot, Chicoutimi G7H 4A3 – 418/696-2521 |
| Le Granit | 21,287 | Serge Bilodeau, Gref., 5090, rue Frontenac, Lac-Mégantic G6B 1H3 – 819/583-0181 |
| Le Haut-Richelieu | 97,539 | Joane Saulnier, Gref., 380, 4e av, CP 90, Iberville J2X 1W9 – 514/346-3636 |
| Le Haut-St-François | 21,946 | Claude Brochu, Gref., 85, rue Principale ouest, CP 250, Cookshire J0B 1M0 – 819/875-3966 |
| Le Haut-St-Laurent | 22,007 | François Landreville, Gref., 23, rue King, Huntingdon J0S 1H0 – 514/264-5411, Fax: 514/264-6885 |
| Le Haut-St-Maurice | 16,293 | Daniel Prince, Gref., 800, rue Réal, La Tuque G9X 2S9 – 819/523-6111 |
| Le Val-St-François | 33,422 | Guy-Lin Beaudoin, Gref., 810, montée du Parc, CP 1869, Richmond J0B 2H0 – 819/826-6505 |
| L'Érable | 24,684 | Victoire Renaud, Gref., 1636, av St-Louis, Plessisville G6L 2M9 – 819/362-6395 |
| Les Basques | 10,204 | François Gosselin, Gref., 122, rue Notre-Dame ouest, CP 399, Trois-Pistoles G0L 4K0 – 418/851-3206 |
| Les Chutes-de-la-Chaudière | 75,598 | Benoît Chevalier, Gref., 8100, rue du Blizzard, Charny G6X 1C9 – 418/832-2496 |
| Les Collines-de-l'Outaouais | 33,662 | Norman Vachon, Gref., 216, ch Old Chelsea, Chelsea J0X 1N0 – 819/827-0516 |
| Les Etchemins | 18,356 | Jean-Claude Morin, Gref., 93, route 277, CP 10, Ste-Germaine-Station G0R 2B0 – 418/625-9000, Fax: 418/625-9005 |
| Les Îles-de-la-Madeleine | 13,802 | Lise Chevrier, Gref., CP 339, Cap-aux-Meules G0B 1B0 – 418/986-4251, Fax: 418/986-4206 |
| Les Jardins-de-Napierville | 22,936 | Nicole Inkel, Gref., 361, rue St-Jacques, CP 1030, Napierville J0J 1L0 – 514/245-7527 |
| Les Laurentides | 36,335 | Denis Savard, Gref., 1111, ch du Lac-Colibri, CP 30, St-Faustin J0T 2G0 – 819/688-3661 |
| Les Maskoutains | 78,754 | Alain Beauregard, Gref., #200, 2200, rue Pratte, St-Hyacinthe J2S 4B6 – 514/774-3141 |
| Les Moulins | 103,213 | Daniel Pilon, Gref., 148, rue St-André, Terrebonne J6W 3C3 – 514/471-9576 |
| Les Pays-d'en-Haut | 28,237 | Yvan Genest, Gref., #200, 1332, boul Ste-Adèle, CP 1380, Ste-Adèle J0R 1L0 – 514/229-6637 |
| L'Île-d'Orléans | 6,892 | Jules Prémont, Gref., 3893, ch Royal, Ste-Famille G0A 3P0 – 418/829-3104 |
| L'Islet | 19,823 | Benoît Lévesque, Gref., 364, rue Verreault, CP 790, St-Jean-Port-Joli G0R 3G0 – 418/598-3076 |
| Lotbinière | 26,921 | Daniel Patry, Gref., CP 430, Ste-Croix G0S 2H0 – 418/926-3407 |
| Manicouagan | 36,271 | André Blais, Gref., 1384, rue Anticosti, Baie-Comeau G5C 3R2 – 418/589-9594 |
| Maria-Chapdelaine | 28,045 | Christian Bouchard, Gref., 209, boul des Pères, Mistassini G8M 3A8 – 418/276-2131, Fax: 418/276-7043 |
| Maskinongé | 23,791 | Janyse L. Pichette, Gref., 651, boul St-Laurent est, Louiseville J5V 1J1 – 819/228-9461, Fax: 819/228-2193 |
| Matane | 23,723 | Michel Barriault, Gref., 572, rue du Phare est, Matane G4W 1B1 – 418/562-6734 |
| Matawinie | 41,322 | Yves Gaillardetz, Gref., 3184 - 1re av, CP 1239, Rawdon J0K 1S0 – 514/834-5441 |
| Mékinac | 13,480 | Claude Beaulieu, Gref., 560, rue Notre-Dame, CP 490, St-Tite G0X 3H0 – 418/365-5151 |
| Memphrémagog | 38,461 | Guy Jauron, Gref., 455, rue Macdonald, Magog J1X 1M2 – 819/843-9292, Fax: 819/843-7295 |

| MUNICIPALITY | 1996 POP. | CONTACT PERSON WITH ADDRESS & PHONE |
|---|---|---|
| Minganie | 12,684 | Martin Larue, Gref., 8788, boul de l'Escale, CP 1146, Havre-St-Pierre G0G 1P0 – 418/538-2732 |
| Mirabel | 22,689 | Suzanne Mireault, Gref., 14111, rue St-Jean, CP 60, Ste-Monique J0N 1R0 – 514/476-0360 |
| Montcalm | 38,053 | Gaétan Hudon, Gref., 1530, rue Albert, CP 308, Ste-Julienne J0K 2T0 – 514/831-2182, Fax: 514/831-4712 |
| Montmagny | 23,794 | Bernard Létourneau, Gref., 159, rue St-Louis, CP 38, Montmagny G5V 1N5 – 418/248-5985 |
| Nicolet-Yamaska | 23,673 | Donald Martel, Gref., 400, rue Notre-Dame, CP 420, St-François-du-Lac J0G 1M0 – 514/568-3144 |
| Pabok | 21,340 | Gaétan Lelièvre, Gref., 46, boul René-Lévesque ouest, CP 128, Chandler G0C 1K0 – 418/689-4313 |
| Papineau | 20,332 | Ghislain Menard, Gref., 266, rue Viger, CP 278, Papineauville J0V 1R0 – 819/427-6243 |
| Pontiac | 15,576 | Luc Séguin, Gref., CP 460, Campbell's Bay J0X 1K0 – 819/648-5689 |
| Portneuf | 46,185 | Yves Laroche, Gref., 185, rte 138, Cap-Santé G0A 1L0 – 418/285-3744 |
| Rimouski-Neigette | 52,677 | Louise Audet, Gref., 220, av de la Cathédrale, CP 1297, Rimouski G5L 5J2 – 418/724-5154 |
| Rivière-du-Loup | 32,120 | André Guay, Gref., 310, rue St-Pierre, CP 938, Rivière-du-Loup G5R 3V3 – 418/867-2485 |
| Robert-Cliche | 18,712 | Gilbert Caron, Gref., 111A, 107e rue de la Station, Beauceville G0S 1A0 – 418/774-9828 |
| Roussillon | 132,167 | Pierre Largy, Gref., 50, rue Ste-Thérèse, Delson J0L 1G0 – 514/638-1221 |
| Rouville | | #100, 500 rue Desjardins, Marieville J3M 1E1 – 514/460-2127 |
| Rouyn-Noranda | 42,638 | Pierre Monfette, Gref., 332, rue Perreault est, Rouyn-Noranda J9X 3C6 – 819/762-6541 |
| Sept-Rivières | 40,905 | Suzanne Cyr, Gref., #200, 106, rue Napoléon, Sept-Îles G4R 3L7 – 418/962-1900, Fax: 418/962-3365 |
| Sherbrooke | 147,384 | Gilles Moreau, Gref., 390, rue King ouest, Sherbrooke J1H 1R4 – 819/821-2446 |
| Témiscamingue | 18,027 | Denis Clermont, Gref., 21, rue Notre-Dame-de-Lourdes, CP 548, Ville-Marie J0Z 3W0 – 819/629-2829 |
| Témiscouata | 23,082 | Jean-Pierre Laplante, Gref., 3, rue Hôtel de Ville, CP 460, Notre-Dame-du-Lac G0L 1X0 – 418/899-6725 |
| Thérèse-de-Blainville | 119,240 | Lucille Vincelli, Gref., 100, rue Charbonneau, Rosemère J7A 3W1 – 514/621-4752 |
| Vallée-de-l'Or | 44,389 | Louis Bourget, Gref., 42, Place Hammond, Val-d'Or J9P 3A9 – 819/825-7733 |
| Vaudreuil-Soulanges | 95,318 | André Boisvert, Gref., #200, 420, av Roche, Vaudreuil-Dorion J7V 2N1 – 514/455-5753 |

## QUÉBEC URBAN COMMUNITIES (REGIONAL GOVERNMENTS)

In-depth listings for the regional districts appear in Part 3 (check Index for page numbers).

| MUNICIPALITY | 1996 POP. | CONTACT PERSON WITH ADDRESS & PHONE |
|---|---|---|
| Montréal | 1,775,846 | Gérard Divay, Gref., 1550, rue Metcalfe, Montréal H3A 3P1 – 514/280-3450, Fax: 514/280-4232, URL: http://www.cum.qc.ca |
| l'Outaouais | 307,441 | Jacques Tremblay, Gref., #500, 25, rue Laurier, CP 2210, Hull J8X 3Z4 – 819/770-1380, Fax: 819/770-8479 |
| Québec | 202,865 | Serge Allen, Gref., 399, rue St-Joseph est, Québec G1K 8E2 – 418/529-8771, Fax: 418/529-2219 |

## SASKATCHEWAN

Acts governing the municipal system in Saskatchewan are The Urban Municipality Act, 1984; The Rural Municipality Act, 1989; and The Northern Municipalities Act. In the province there are the following types of incorporated municipalities: Rural Municipalities, Villages, Resort Villages, Towns, and Cities, as well as Northern Towns, Northern Villages, Northern Hamlets and Northern Settlements. The incorporation of these municipalities is voluntary. Thus a Village that qualifies to be named a Town, can remain a Village if the population so wishes.

Rural Municipalities: are divided into divisions. A Reeve is elected at large every two years. Councillors are also elected every two years but in "staggered" sequence.

Villages: are defined as communities with not less than 100 permanent residents and not less than 50 dwellings and/or business premises. The Village is represented by a Mayor and two to four Councillors. They Mayor and Councillors are elected by the eligible electorate every three years.

Towns: are defined as communities with not less that 500 permanent residents. They are represented by a Mayor and six Councillors elected at large by the eligible electorate every three years.

Cities: are defined as communities with not less than 5,000 residents. They are represented by a Mayor and Councillors (the number varies).

Northern Municipalities: have similar criteria as above.

Elections for all are every three years.

Rural municipal nominations are received until the third Monday in October and elections are held on the third Wednesday after the nomination period. Nominations are held in Urban Municipalities on the second Wednesday in October and elections on the fourth Wednesday in October.

Cities in CAPITALS; Towns marked †; Villages marked (V); Northern Villages marked (NV); Resort Villages not listed. An in-depth listing for municipalities marked with * appears in Part 2 (check Index for page numbers).

| MUNICIPALITY | 1996 POP. | FEDERAL ELECTORAL DISTRICT | PROVINCIAL ELECTORAL DISTRICT | CONTACT PERSON WITH ADDRESS, PHONE & FAX |
|---|---|---|---|---|
| Abbey (V) | 162 | Swift Current-Maple Creek-Assiniboia | Cypress Hills | Richard B. Sylvestre, Adm., PO Box 210, Abbey S0N 0A0 – 306/689-2412, Fax: 306/689-2901 |
| Aberdeen † | 474 | Saskatoon-Humboldt | Humboldt | Angela Banman, Adm., PO Box 130, Aberdeen S0K 0A0 – 306/253-4311, Fax: 306/253-4744 |
| Abernethy (V) | 232 | Qu'Appelle | Melville | Leona Ward, Clerk, PO Box 189, Abernethy S0A 0A0 – 306/333-2271, Fax: 306/333-2271 |
| Adanac (V) | 6 | Battlefords-Lloydminster | Battleford-Cut Knife | Victoria Ralston, Clerk, PO Box 1736, Unity S0K 4L0 – 306/228-2037 |
| Admiral (V) | 34 | Cypress Hills-Grasslands | Wood River | Madeleine Spetz, Clerk, PO Box 44, Admiral S0N 0B0 – 306/297-6356 |
| Air Ronge (NV) | 957 | Churchill River | Cumberland | Joyce L. Forrest, Adm., PO Box 100, Air Ronge S0J 3G0 – 306/425-2107, Fax: 306/425-3108 |
| Alameda † | 304 | Souris-Moose Mountain | Cannington | Ron Burness, Adm., PO Box 36, Alameda S0C 0A0 – 306/489-2077, Fax: 306/489-4602 |
| Albertville (V) | 122 | Prince Albert | Saskatchewan Rivers | Colleen Lavoie, Clerk, General Delivery, Albertville S0J 0A0 – 306/929-2110, Fax: 306/929-2123 |
| Alida (V) | 158 | Souris-Moose Mountain | Cannington | Tammy McCannell, Clerk, PO Box 6, Alida S0C 0B0 – 306/443-2228 |
| Allan † | 702 | Blackstrap | Watrous | Christine Dyck, Adm., PO Box 159, Allan S0K 0C0 – 306/257-3272, Fax: 306/257-3337 |
| Alsask (V) | 237 | Battleford-Lloydminster | Kindersley | Ronald A. Henry, Clerk, PO Box 219, Alsask S0L 0A0 – 306/968-2394, Fax: 306/968-2300 |

Cities in CAPITALS; Towns marked †; Villages marked (V); Northern Villages marked (NV); Resort Villages not listed. An in-depth listing for municipalities marked with * appears in Part 2 (check Index for page numbers).

| MUNICIPALITY | 1996 POP. | FEDERAL ELECTORAL DISTRICT | PROVINCIAL ELECTORAL DISTRICT | CONTACT PERSON WITH ADDRESS, PHONE & FAX |
|---|---|---|---|---|
| Alvena (V) | 79 | Saskatoon-Humboldt | Humboldt | Germaine Muzyka, Clerk, PO Box 8, Alvena S0K 0E0 – 306/943-2101 |
| Aneroid (V) | 81 | Cypress Hills-Grasslands | Wood River | Marcel Gervais, Adm., PO Box 226, Aneroid S0N 0C0 – 306/588-2300 |
| Annaheim (V) | 214 | Saskatoon-Humboldt | Kelvington-Wadena | Brenda Nagy, Adm., PO Box 70, Annaheim S0K 0G0 – 306/598-2122, Fax: 306/598-4526 |
| Antler (V) | 64 | Souris-Moose Mountain | Cannington | Yvonne Bauche, Adm., PO Box 83, Antler S0C 0E0 – 306/452-6155 |
| Arborfield † | 437 | Prince Albert | Carrot River Valley | Allan Frisky, Adm., PO Box 280, Arborfield S0E 0A0 – 306/769-8533, Fax: 306/769-8301 |
| Archerwill (V) | 254 | Saskatoon-Humboldt | Kelvington-Wadena | Paulette Althouse, Clerk, PO Box 130, Archerwill S0E 0B0 – 306/323-2161, Fax: 306/323-2101 |
| Arcola † | 517 | Souris-Moose Mountain | Cannington | Sheila Sim, Adm., PO Box 359, Arcola S0C 0G0 – 306/455-2212, Fax: 306/455-2445 |
| Arelee (V) | 19 | Saskatoon-Rosetown-Biggar | Redberry Lake | Lloyd R. Cross, Adm., PO Box 100, Arelee S0K 0H0 – 306/237-4424, Fax: 306/237-4294 |
| Arran (V) | 53 | Yorkton-Melville | Canora-Pelly | Mike Burtnack, Clerk, PO Box 40, Arran S0A 0B0 – 306/595-4521, Fax: 306/595-4521 |
| Asquith † | 533 | Saskatoon-Rosetown-Biggar | Redberry Lake | Holly Cross, Acting Clerk, PO Box 160, Asquith S0K 0J0 – 306/329-4341, Fax: 306/329-4969 |
| Assiniboia † | 2,653 | Cypress Hills-Grasslands | Wood River | Bruce L. Masur, Adm., PO Box 670, Assiniboia S0H 0B0 – 306/642-3382, Fax: 306/642-5622 |
| Atwater (V) | 35 | Yorkton-Melville | Saltcoats | Doreen D. Rausch, Clerk, PO Box 58, Atwater S0A 0C0 – 306/745-3809 |
| Avonlea (V) | 402 | Palliser | Thunder Creek | Tim Forer, Adm., PO Box 209, Avonlea S0H 0C0 – 306/868-2221, Fax: 306/868-2221 |
| Aylesbury (V) | 59 | Regina-Lumsden-Lake Centre | Arm River | Dorothy M. Wright, Clerk, PO Box 151, Aylesbury S0G 0B0 – 306/734-5125 |
| Aylsham (V) | 91 | Prince Albert | Carrot River Valley | Dorothy E. Blue, Clerk, PO Box 64, Aylsham S0E 0C0 – 306/862-9415 |
| Balcarres † | 661 | Qu'Appelle | Melville | Don A. Warner, Clerk, PO Box 130, Balcarres S0G 0C0 – 306/334-2566, Fax: 306/334-2907 |
| Balgonie † | 1,132 | Qu'Appelle | Regina Wascana Plains | Barbara Marcia, Adm., PO Box 310, Balgonie S0G 0E0 – 306/771-2284, Fax: 306/771-2899 |
| Bangor (V) | 57 | Yorkton-Melville | Saltcoats | Joan C. Bomerak, Clerk, PO Box 35, Bangor S0A 0E0 – 306/728-4084 |
| Battleford † | 3,936 | Battlefords-Lloydminster | Battleford-Cut Knife | Sheryl Ballendine, Adm., PO Box 40, Battleford S0M 0E0 – 306/937-6200, Fax: 306/937-2450 |
| Beatty (V) | 87 | Prince Albert | Melfort-Tisdale | James D. Mason, Clerk, PO Box 51, Beatty S0J 0C0 – 306/752-3980 |
| Beauval (NV) | 785 | Churchill River | Athabasca | Vacant, Clerk, PO Box 19, Beauval S0M 0G0 – 306/288-2110, Fax: 306/288-2348 |
| Beechy (V) | 281 | Cypress Hills-Grasslands | Rosetown-Biggar | Heather Meaden, Clerk, PO Box 153, Beechy S0L 0C0 – 306/859-2205, Fax: 306/859-2270 |
| Belle Plaine (V) | 64 | Palliser | Thunder Creek | Reg E. McKee, Clerk, PO Box 63, Belle Plaine S0G 0G0 – 306/692-3390 |
| Bengough † | 488 | Souris-Moose Mountain | Weyburn-Big Muddy | Wanda McGonigal, Adm., PO Box 188, Bengough S0C 0K0 – 306/268-2927, Fax: 306/268-2988 |
| Benson (V) | 89 | Souris-Moose Mountain | Estevan | Nadine Leclair, Clerk, PO Box 27, Benson S0C 0L0 – 306/634-4904 |
| Bethune (V) | 375 | Regina-Lumsden-Lake Centre | Arm River | Patti Garrett, Clerk, PO Box 209, Bethune S0G 0H0 – 306/638-3188, Fax: 306/638-3188 |
| Bienfait † | 826 | Souris-Moose Mountain | Estevan | Brian Shauf, Adm., PO Box 220, Bienfait S0C 0M0 – 306/388-2969, Fax: 306/388-2960 |
| Big River † | 826 | Churchill River | Shellbrook-Spiritwood | Bernice Swanson, Adm., PO Box 220, Big River S0J 0E0 – 306/469-2112, Fax: 306/469-5755 |
| Biggar † | 2,351 | Saskatoon-Rosetown-Biggar | Rosetown-Biggar | R.G. Tyler, Adm., PO Box 489, Biggar S0K 0M0 – 306/948-3317, Fax: 306/948-5134 |
| Birch Hills † | 945 | Prince Albert | Saskatchewan Rivers | Darlene Cochrane, Adm., PO Box 206, Birch Hills S0J 0G0 – 306/749-2232, Fax: 306/749-2220 |
| Birsay (V) | 58 | Cypress Hills-Grasslands | Rosetown-Biggar | Murray Cook, Clerk, PO Box 115, Birsay S0L 0G0 – 306/573-2047, Fax: 306/573-2111 |
| Bjorkdale (V) | 262 | Yorkton-Melville | Carrot River Valley | Joanne Kehrig, Clerk, PO Box 27, Bjorkdale S0E 0E0 – 306/886-2167, Fax: 306/886-4446 |
| Bladworth (V) | 76 | Blackstrap | Arm River | Marion Bessey, Clerk, PO Box 90, Bladworth S0G 0J0 – 306/567-4364 |
| Blaine Lake † | 516 | Wanuskewin | Redberry Lake | Eleanora Boyko, Adm., PO Box 10, Blaine Lake S0J 0J0 – 306/497-2531, Fax: 306/497-2511 |
| Borden (V) | 217 | Wanuskewin | Redberry Lake | Sandra Long, Adm., PO Box 210, Borden S0K 0N0 – 306/997-2134 |
| Bounty (V) | 18 | Saskatoon-Rosetown-Biggar | Rosetown-Biggar | Vacant, Clerk, RR#1, PO Box 160, Bounty S0L 0L0 – 306/856-2114 |

Cities in CAPITALS; Towns marked †; Villages marked (V); Northern Villages marked (NV); Resort Villages not listed. An in-depth listing for municipalities marked with * appears in Part 2 (check Index for page numbers).

| MUNICIPALITY | 1996 POP. | FEDERAL ELECTORAL DISTRICT | PROVINCIAL ELECTORAL DISTRICT | CONTACT PERSON WITH ADDRESS, PHONE & FAX |
|---|---|---|---|---|
| Bracken (V) | 56 | Cypress Hills-Grasslands | Wood River | Donna Peakman, Clerk, PO Box 41, Bracken S0N 0G0 – 306/293-2945 |
| Bradwell (V) | 145 | Blackstrap | Watrous | Robert Thurmeier, Adm., PO Box 100, Bradwell S0K 0P0 – 306/257-4141, Fax: 306/257-3303 |
| Bredenbury † | 368 | Yorkton-Melville | Saltcoats | Olga Mosiman, Clerk, PO Box 87, Bredenbury S0A 0H0 – 306/898-2055, Fax: 306/898-2103 |
| Briercrest (V) | 125 | Palliser | Thunder Creek | Eileen Jeffery, Clerk, PO Box 25, Briercrest S0H 0K0 – 306/799-2053 |
| Broadview † | 751 | Souris-Moose Mountain | Moosomin | Phil Boivin, Adm., PO Box 430, Broadview S0G 0K0 – 306/696-2533, Fax: 306/696-3573 |
| Brock (V) | 142 | Battlefords-Lloydminster | Kindersley | Barry Knight, Clerk, PO Box 70, Brock S0L 0H0 – 306/379-2116, Fax: 306/379-2024 |
| Broderick (V) | 86 | Blackstrap | Arm River | Elaine Nadeau, Adm., PO Box 29, Broderick S0H 0L0 – 306/867-8009, Fax: 306/867-9271 |
| Brownlee (V) | 72 | Regina-Lumsden-Lake Centre | Arm River | Denise Smith, Clerk, PO Box 89, Brownlee S0H 0M0 – 306/759-2302 |
| Bruno † | 648 | Saskatoon-Humboldt | Humboldt | Orrin Redden, Adm., PO Box 370, Bruno S0K 0S0 – 306/369-2514, Fax: 306/369-2514 |
| Buchanan (V) | 279 | Yorkton-Melville | Canora-Pelly | Eleanor Hadubiak, Adm., PO Box 479, Buchanan S0A 0J0 – 306/592-2144 |
| Buena Vista (V) | 343 | Regina-Lumsden-Lake Centre | Arm River | Anne Fink, Clerk, PO Box 154, Regina Beach S0G 4C0 – 306/729-4385, Fax: 306/729-4518 |
| Buffalo Narrows (NV) | 1,053 | Churchill River | Athabasca | Laura Durocher, Clerk, PO Box 98, Buffalo Narrows S0M 0J0 – 306/235-4225, Fax: 306/235-4699 |
| Bulyea (V) | 99 | Regina-Lumsden-Lake Centre | Last Mountain-Touchwood | Kelly Hansen, Clerk, PO Box 37, Bulyea S0G 0L0 – 306/725-4936 |
| Burstall † | 426 | Cypress Hills | Cypress Hills | Elaine K. Brodie, Adm., PO Box 250, Burstall S0N 0H0 – 306/679-2000, Fax: 306/679-2275 |
| Cabri † | 529 | Cypress Hills-Grasslands | Cypress Hills | Anne P. Francis, Adm., PO Box 200, Cabri S0N 0J0 – 306/587-2500 |
| Cadillac (V) | 97 | Cypress Hills-Grasslands | Wood River | Twila St. Jacques, Clerk, PO Box 189, Cadillac S0N 0K0 – 306/785-2100 |
| Calder (V) | 106 | Yorkton-Melville | Saltcoats | Helen Tkachuk, Clerk, PO Box 47, Calder S0A 0K0 – 306/742-2158 |
| Cando (V) | 106 | Battlefords-Lloydminster | Battleford-Cut Knife | Dora Beckman, Clerk, PO Box 6, Cando S0K 0V0 – 306/937-3052 |
| Canora † | 2,208 | Yorkton-Melville | Canora-Pelly | Patrick N. Dergousoff, Adm., PO Box 717, Canora S0A 0L0 – 306/563-5773, Fax: 306/563-4336 |
| Canwood (V) | 345 | Churchill River | Shellbrook-Spiritwood | Terry Lofstrom, Adm., PO Box 172, Canwood S0J 0K0 – 306/468-2016, Fax: 306/468-2666 |
| Carievale (V) | 253 | Souris-Moose Mountain | Cannington | Donalene McMillen, Clerk, PO Box 88, Carievale S0C 0P0 – 306/928-2033, Fax: 306/928-2021 |
| Carlyle † | 1,252 | Souris-Moose Mountain | Cannington | Norm Riddell, Adm., PO Box 10, Carlyle S0C 0R0 – 306/453-2363, Fax: 306/453-6380 |
| Carmichael (V) | 23 | Cypress Hills-Grasslands | Cypress Hills | Collette Jones, Clerk, PO Box 420, Gull Lake S0N 1A0 – 306/672-3501, Fax: 306/672-3879 |
| Carnduff † | 1,069 | Souris-Moose Mountain | Cannington | Kevin Stephenson, Adm., PO Box 100, Carnduff S0C 0S0 – 306/482-3300, Fax: 306/482-3422 |
| Caronport (V) | 1,147 | Palliser | Thunder Creek | Debra Frank, Adm., PO Box 550, Caronport S0H 0S0 – 306/756-2225, Fax: 306/756-2225 |
| Carragana (V) | 39 | Yorkton-Melville | Kelvington-Wadena | Olga Smith, Clerk, PO Box 42, Carragana S0E 0K0 – 306/278-3487 |
| Carrot River † | 1,032 | Prince Albert | Carrot River Valley | Duril Touet, Adm., PO Box 147, Carrot River S0E 0L0 – 306/768-2515, Fax: 306/768-2930 |
| Central Butte † | 521 | Cypress Hills-Grasslands | Arm River | Don Wildeman, Adm., PO Box 10, Central Butte S0H 0T0 – 306/796-2288, Fax: 306/796-2223 |
| Ceylon (V) | 148 | Souris-Moose Mountain | Weyburn-Big Muddy | Vaughan B. McClarty, Adm., PO Box 188, Ceylon S0C 0T0 – 306/454-2202, Fax: 306/454-2627 |
| Chamberlain (V) | 114 | Regina-Lumsden-Lake Centre | Arm River | Rhonda Lang, Clerk, PO Box 8, Chamberlain S0G 0R0 – 306/638-4680 |
| Chaplin (V) | 314 | Cypress Hills-Grasslands | Thunder Creek | Carol Andrews, Clerk, PO Box 210, Chaplin S0H 0V0 – 306/395-2221, Fax: 306/395-2555 |
| Choiceland † | 417 | Churchill River | Saskatchewan Rivers | Colleen Digness, Adm., PO Box 279, Choiceland S0J 0M0 – 306/428-2070, Fax: 306/428-2071 |
| Christopher Lake (V) | 200 | Churchill River | Saskatchewan Rivers | Cheryl Heleta, Adm., PO Box 163, Christopher Lake S0J 0N0 – 306/982-4242, Fax: 306/982-4242 |
| Churchbridge † | 815 | Yorkton-Melville | Saltcoats | Dawn Dressler, Adm., PO Box 256, Churchbridge S0A 0M0 – 306/896-2240, Fax: 306/896-2240 |
| Clavet (V) | 339 | Blackstrap | Watrous | Susan Bonokoski, Clerk, PO Box 68, Clavet S0K 0Y0 – 306/933-2425, Fax: 306/933-2425 |
| Climax (V) | 206 | Cypress Hills-Grasslands | Wood River | Ronald James Johnson, Adm., PO Box 30, Climax S0N 0N0 – 306/293-2124, Fax: 306/293-2702 |

Cities in CAPITALS; Towns marked †; Villages marked (V); Northern Villages marked (NV); Resort Villages not listed. An in-depth listing for municipalities marked with * appears in Part 2 (check Index for page numbers).

| MUNICIPALITY | 1996 POP. | FEDERAL ELECTORAL DISTRICT | PROVINCIAL ELECTORAL DISTRICT | CONTACT PERSON WITH ADDRESS, PHONE & FAX |
|---|---|---|---|---|
| Coderre (V) | 64 | Cypress Hills-Grasslands | Thunder Creek | Faye Johnstone, Clerk, PO Box 9, Coderre S0H 0X0 – 306/394-2070, Fax: 306/394-2031 |
| Codette (V) | 278 | Prince Albert | Carrot River Valley | Eunice Rudy, Clerk, PO Box 100, Codette S0E 0P0 – 306/862-9551, Fax: 306/862-9551 |
| Cole Bay (NV) | 153 | Churchill River | Athabasca | Delphine Bouvier, Adm., General Delivery, Cole Bay S0M 0M0 – 306/829-4232, Fax: 306/829-4312 |
| Coleville (V) | 323 | Battlefords-Lloydminster | Kindersley | Gloria Johnson, Adm., PO Box 249, Coleville S0L 0K0 – 306/965-2281, Fax: 306/965-2466 |
| Colgate (V) | 40 | Souris-Moose Mountain | Estevan | Laurie Bell, Clerk, PO Box 5, Colgate S0C 0V0 – 306/456-2472, Fax: 306/456-2512 |
| Colonsay † | 428 | Blackstrap | Watrous | Joanne Binsfeld, Adm., PO Box 190, Colonsay S0K 0Z0 – 306/255-2313, Fax: 306/255-2800 |
| Conquest (V) | 195 | Saskatoon-Rosetown-Biggar | Rosetown-Biggar | Daen Fontaine, Clerk, PO Box 250, Conquest S0L 0L0 – 306/856-2114 |
| Consul (V) | 107 | Cypress Hills-Grasslands | Cypress Hills | Carrie Funk, Adm., PO Box 185, Consul S0N 0P0 – 306/299-2030 |
| Coronach † | 949 | Souris-Moose Mountain | Wood River | Murray H. Setrum, Adm., PO Box 90, Coronach S0H 0Z0 – 306/267-2150, Fax: 306/267-2296 |
| Craik † | 441 | Regina-Lumsden-Lake Centre | Arm River | Nora Bakken, Clerk, PO Box 60, Craik S0G 0V0 – 306/734-2250, Fax: 306/734-2898 |
| Craven (V) | 278 | Regina-Lumsden-Lake Centre | Last Mountain-Touchwood | Linda Stevens, Clerk, PO Box 30, Craven S0G 0W0 – 306/731-3452 |
| Creelman (V) | 128 | Souris-Moose Mountain | Indian Head-Milestone | May Allan, Clerk, PO Box 177, Creelman S0G 0X0 – 306/433-2011 |
| Creighton † | 1,713 | Churchill River | Cumberland | Therese Wheeler, Adm., PO Box 100, Creighton S0P 0A0 – 306/688-8253, Fax: 306/688-4764 |
| Cudworth † | 752 | Saskatoon-Humboldt | Humboldt | Donna Bendig, Clerk, PO Box 69, Cudworth S0K 1B0 – 306/256-3492, Fax: 306/256-3515 |
| Cumberland House (NV) | 836 | Churchill River | Cumberland | Pat McKenzie, Adm., PO Box 190, Cumberland House S0E 0S0 – 306/888-2066, Fax: 306/888-2103 |
| Cupar † | 592 | Qu'Appelle | Last Mountain-Touchwood | Cecile Daradich, Adm., PO Box 397, Cupar S0G 0Y0 – 306/723-4324, Fax: 306/723-4324 |
| Cut Knife † | 585 | Battlefords-Lloydminster | Battleford-Cut Knife | Richard Emanuel, Adm., PO Box 338, Cut Knife S0M 0N0 – 306/398-2363, Fax: 306/398-2568 |
| Dafoe (V) | 23 | Qu'Appelle | Watrous | Lana M. Bolt, Clerk, PO Box 142, Dafoe S0K 1C0 – 306/554-3250 |
| Dalmeny † | 1,470 | Wanuskewin | Rosthern | Shelley Funk, Adm., PO Box 400, Dalmeny S0K 1E0 – 306/254-2133, Fax: 306/254-2142 |
| Davidson † | 1,105 | Regina-Lumsden-Lake Centre | Arm River | Gary Edom, Adm., PO Box 340, Davidson S0G 1A0 – 306/567-2040, Fax: 306/567-4730 |
| Debden (V) | 423 | Churchill River | Shellbrook-Spiritwood | Carmen Jean, Adm., PO Box 400, Debden S0J 0S0 – 306/724-2040, Fax: 306/724-2220 |
| Delisle † | 840 | Saskatoon-Rosetown-Biggar | Redberry Lake | Mark Dubkowski, Adm., PO Box 40, Delisle S0L 0P0 – 306/493-2242, Fax: 306/493-2344 |
| Denare Beach (NV) | 776 | Churchill River | Cumberland | Beverley J. Wheeler, Clerk, PO Box 70, Denare Beach S0P 0B0 – 306/362-2054, Fax: 306/362-2257 |
| Denholm (V) | 63 | Battlefords-Lloydminster | Redberry Lake | Lila Yuhasz, Clerk, PO Box 71, Denholm S0M 0R0 – 306/445-7330 |
| Denzil (V) | 194 | Battlefords-Lloydminster | Kindersley | Janet Vetter, Adm., PO Box 100, Denzil S0L 0S0 – 306/358-2118, Fax: 306/358-4828 |
| Deschambault Lake (NV) | 695 | Churchill River | Cumberland | Laura Clarke, Clerk, General Delivery, Deschambault Lake S0P 0C0 – 306/632-4522, Fax: 306/632-4507 |
| Dilke (V) | 85 | Regina-Lumsden-Lake Centre | Arm River | Colleen R. Duesing, Clerk, PO Box 58, Dilke S0G 1C0 – 306/488-4866, Fax: 306/488-4866 |
| Dinsmore (V) | 328 | Saskatoon-Rosetown-Biggar | Rosetown-Biggar | Jim Main, Clerk, PO Box 278, Dinsmore S0L 0T0 – 306/846-2220, Fax: 306/846-2999 |
| Disley (V) | 51 | Regina-Lumsden-Lake Centre | Arm River | Rhonda Keith, Clerk, PO Box 18, Lumsden S0G 3C0 – 306/731-2918 |
| Dodsland (V) | 241 | Battlefords-Lloydminster | Kindersley | Wendy L. Davis, Clerk, PO Box 400, Dodsland S0L 0V0 – 306/356-2106, Fax: 306/356-2055 |
| Dollard (V) | 43 | Cypress Hills-Grasslands | Cypress Hills | Richard E. Goulet, Adm., PO Box 1115, Shaunavon S0N 2M0 – 306/297-2108, Fax: 306/297-2108 |
| Domremy (V) | 156 | Saskatoon-Humboldt | Humboldt | Lil Georget, Clerk, PO Box 208, Domremy S0K 1G0 – 306/423-5244, Fax: 306/423-5244 |
| Dore Lake (NV) | 40 | Churchill River | Athabasca | Eugenie Aubichon, Clerk, PO Box 608, Big River S0J 0E0 – 306/832-4528, Fax: 306/832-4525 |
| Dorintosh (V) | 133 | Churchill River | Meadow Lake | Barbara Galger, Clerk, PO Box 40, Dorintosh S0M 0T0 – 306/236-5166 |
| Drake (V) | 247 | Blackstrap | Watrous | Elsie Schroeder, Clerk, PO Box 18, Drake S0K 1H0 – 306/363-2109 |
| Drinkwater (V) | 87 | Palliser | Thunder Creek | Tracey Morrissette, Clerk, PO Box 66, Drinkwater S0H 1G0 – 306/693-5093 |

Cities in CAPITALS; Towns marked †; Villages marked (V); Northern Villages marked (NV); Resort Villages not listed. An in-depth listing for municipalities marked with * appears in Part 2 (check Index for page numbers).

| MUNICIPALITY | 1996 POP. | FEDERAL ELECTORAL DISTRICT | PROVINCIAL ELECTORAL DISTRICT | CONTACT PERSON WITH ADDRESS, PHONE & FAX |
|---|---|---|---|---|
| Dubuc (V) | 95 | Yorkton-Melville | Melville | Leona Kaczur, Clerk, PO Box 126, Dubuc S0A 0R0 – 306/877-2172 |
| Duck Lake † | 667 | Wanuskewin | Shellbrook-Spiritwood | Betty Fiolleau, Adm., PO Box 430, Duck Lake S0K 1J0 – 306/467-2277, Fax: 306/467-4434 |
| Duff (V) | 43 | Yorkton-Melville | Melville | Reta M. Schick, Clerk, PO Box 57, Duff S0A 0S0 – 306/728-3592 |
| Dundurn † | 476 | Blackstrap | Arm River | Marion D. Beaucage, Adm., PO Box 185, Dundurn S0K 1K0 – 306/492-2202, Fax: 306/492-2202 |
| Duval (V) | 98 | Regina-Lumsden-Lake Centre | Last Mountain-Touchwood | Leonard Wm. Jones, Clerk, PO Box 70, Duval S0G 1G0 – 306/725-3767 |
| Dysart (V) | 240 | Qu'Appelle | Last Mountain-Touchwood | Bernadette Rothecker, Clerk, PO Box 70, Dysart S0G 1H0 – 306/432-2100, Fax: 306/432-2255 |
| Earl Grey (V) | 268 | Regina-Lumsden-Lake Centre | Last Mountain-Touchwood | Shelley Mohr, Adm., PO Box 100, Earl Grey S0G 1J0 – 306/939-2062, Fax: 306/939-2144 |
| Eastend † | 616 | Cypress Hills-Grasslands | Cypress Hills | Debbra Lewis, Adm., PO Box 520, Eastend S0N 0T0 – 306/295-3322, Fax: 306/295-3571 |
| Eatonia † | 469 | Cypress Hills-Grasslands | Kindersley | Darlene L. Olson, Adm., PO Box 237, Eatonia S0L 0Y0 – 306/967-2251, Fax: 306/967-2267 |
| Ebenezer (V) | 166 | Yorkton-Melville | Yorkton | Norman Zayshley, Clerk, PO Box 97, Ebenezer S0A 0T0 – 306/782-5758 |
| Edam (V) | 398 | Battlefords-Lloydminster | Lloydminster | Trudy McMurphy, Adm., PO Box 203, Edam S0M 0V0 – 306/397-2223, Fax: 306/397-2626 |
| Edenwold (V) | 198 | Qu'Appelle | Indian Head-Milestone | Liz Kletzel, Clerk, PO Box 130, Edenwold S0G 1K0 – 306/771-4121 |
| Elbow (V) | 295 | Blackstrap | Arm River | Valerie C. Hundeby, Adm., PO Box 8, Elbow S0H 1J0 – 306/854-2277, Fax: 306/854-2229 |
| Elfros (V) | 167 | Qu'Appelle | Last Mountain-Touchwood | Mary Corby, Clerk, PO Box 40, Elfros S0A 0V0 – 306/328-2123, Fax: 306/328-4490 |
| Elrose † | 557 | Cypress Hills-Grasslands | Rosetown-Biggar | Barb Trayhorne, Adm., PO Box 458, Elrose S0L 0Z0 – 306/378-2202, Fax: 306/378-2966 |
| Elstow (V) | 93 | Blackstrap | Watrous | Elva Greschuk, Clerk, PO Box 29, Elstow S0K 1M0 – 306/257-3889 |
| Endeavour (V) | 173 | Yorkton-Melville | Kelvington-Wadena | Cindy Greba, Adm., PO Box 307, Endeavour S0A 0W0 – 306/547-3484 |
| Englefeld (V) | 223 | Saskatoon-Humboldt | Kelvington-Wadena | Roman Zimmerman, Clerk, PO Box 44, Englefeld S0K 1N0 – 306/287-3151, Fax: 306/287-3139 |
| Ernfold (V) | 51 | Cypress Hills-Grasslands | Thunder Creek | Diane Marie McLaren, Clerk, PO Box 100, Ernfold S0H 1K0 – 306/629-3866 |
| Esterhazy † | 2,602 | Yorkton-Melville | Saltcoats | Brian Sych, Adm., PO Box 490, Esterhazy S0A 0X0 – 306/745-3942, Fax: 306/745-6797 |
| ESTEVAN | 10,752 | Souris-Moose Mountain | Estevan | Zella Reed, Assessor, 1102 - 4 St., Estevan S4A 0W7 – 306/634-1800, Fax: 306/634-9790 |
| Eston † | 1,119 | Cypress Hills-Grasslands | Kindersley | Helen M. Cowan, Adm., PO Box 757, Eston S0L 1A0 – 306/962-4444, Fax: 306/962-4224 |
| Evesham (V) | 40 | Battlefords-Lloydminster | Battleford-Cut Knife | Melody Stephens, Clerk, PO Box 29, Evesham S0L 1B0 – 306/753-2459 |
| Eyebrow (V) | 175 | Regina-Lumsden-Lake Centre | Arm River | Joy Harms, Clerk, PO Box 159, Eyebrow S0H 1L0 – 306/759-2167 |
| Fairlight (V) | 56 | Souris-Moose Mountain | Moosomin | Diana Sauter, Clerk, PO Box 55, Fairlight S0G 1M0 – 306/646-5709 |
| Fenwood (V) | 58 | Yorkton-Melville | Melville | Doreen Dohms, Clerk, PO Box 66, Fenwood S0A 0Y0 – 306/728-4069 |
| Fife Lake (V) | 50 | Cypress Hills-Grasslands | Wood River | Cecil L. Keast, Clerk, PO Box 688, Coronach S0H 0Z0 – 306/267-3234, Fax: 306/267-3234 |
| Fillmore (V) | 286 | Souris-Moose Mountain | Indian Head-Milestone | Brian Beare, Adm., PO Box 185, Fillmore S0G 1N0 – 306/722-3330, Fax: 306/722-3370 |
| Findlater (V) | 57 | Regina-Lumsden-Lake Centre | Arm River | Penny Fishley, Clerk, PO Box 10, Findlater S0G 1P0 – 306/638-4630 |
| Flaxcombe (V) | 126 | Battlefords-Lloydminster | Kindersley | Charlotte Helfrich, Clerk, PO Box 136, Flaxcombe S0L 1E0 – 306/463-6397 |
| Fleming † | 89 | Souris-Moose Mountain | Moosomin | Barb Cuthill, Clerk, PO Box 62, Fleming S0G 1R0 – 306/435-4244 |
| Flin Flon (V) | 289 | Churchill River | Cumberland | |
| Foam Lake † | 1,303 | Yorkton-Melville | Canora-Pelly | G. Emily Kreuger, Adm., PO Box 57, Foam Lake S0A 1A0 – 306/272-3359, Fax: 306/272-3738 |
| Forget (V) | 62 | Souris-Moose Mountain | Cannington | Carrie Johnston, Clerk, PO Box 100, Forget S0C 0X0 – 306/455-2486 |
| Fort Qu'Appelle † | 1,997 | Qu'Appelle | Indian Head-Milestone | Sandra Schlamp, Adm., PO Box 309, Fort Qu'Appelle S0G 1S0 – 306/332-5266, Fax: 306/332-5087 |
| Fosston (V) | 85 | Saskatoon-Humboldt | Kelvington-Wadena | John Reschny, Clerk, PO Box 160, Fosston S0E 0V0 – 306/322-4521 |
| Fox Valley (V) | 359 | Cypress Hills-Grasslands | Cypress Hills | Michelle Sehn, Clerk, PO Box 207, Fox Valley S0N 0V0 – 306/666-3020 |

Cities in CAPITALS; Towns marked †; Villages marked (V); Northern Villages marked (NV); Resort Villages not listed. An in-depth listing for municipalities marked with * appears in Part 2 (check Index for page numbers).

| MUNICIPALITY | 1996 POP. | FEDERAL ELECTORAL DISTRICT | PROVINCIAL ELECTORAL DISTRICT | CONTACT PERSON WITH ADDRESS, PHONE & FAX |
|---|---|---|---|---|
| Francis † | 190 | Wascana | Indian Head-Milestone | Joyce A. Carroll, Clerk, PO Box 128, Francis S0G 1V0 – 306/245-3624 |
| Frobisher (V) | 165 | Souris-Moose Mountain | Estevan | Diane Truscott, Clerk, PO Box 235, Frobisher S0C 0Y0 – 306/486-2140, Fax: 306/486-4504 |
| Frontier (V) | 309 | Cypress Hills-Grasslands | Cypress Hills | Raymond J. Dubé, Adm., PO Box 30, Frontier S0N 0W0 – 306/296-2030, Fax: 306/296-2175 |
| Gainsborough (V) | 296 | Souris-Moose Mountain | Cannington | Valerie A. Olney, Adm., PO Box 120, Gainsborough S0C 0Z0 – 306/685-2010, Fax: 306/685-2161 |
| Gerald (V) | 164 | Yorkton-Melville | Saltcoats | Karen Assailly, Clerk, PO Box 155, Gerald S0A 1B0 – 306/745-6786 |
| Girvin (V) | 33 | Regina-Lumsden-Lake Centre | Arm River | Marcia Palmer, Clerk, PO Box 70, Girvin S0G 1X0 – 306/567-4236 |
| Gladmar (V) | 49 | Souris-Moose Mountain | Weyburn-Big Muddy | Darlene Petterson, Clerk, PO Box 92, Gladmar S0C 1A0 – 306/969-4837 |
| Glaslyn (V) | 374 | Battlefords-Lloydminster | Shellbrook-Spiritwood | Linda Sandwick, Adm., PO Box 279, Glaslyn S0M 0Y0 – 306/342-2144, Fax: 306/342-2144 |
| Glen Ewen (V) | 148 | Souris-Moose Mountain | Cannington | Darlene Carefoot, Clerk, PO Box 99, Glen Ewen S0C 1C0 – 306/925-2211, Fax: 306/925-2211 |
| Glenavon (V) | 230 | Souris-Moose Mountain | Moosomin | James Hoff, Adm., PO Box 327, Glenavon S0G 1Y0 – 306/429-2011, Fax: 306/429-2260 |
| Glenside (V) | 69 | Blackstrap | Arm River | Ethel Rooke, Clerk, General Delivery, PO Box 99, Glenside S0H 1T0 – 306/867-8932 |
| Glentworth (V) | 88 | Cypress Hills-Grasslands | Wood River | E.P. Gasper, Adm., PO Box 70, Glentworth S0H 1V0 – 306/266-4920, Fax: 306/266-2077 |
| Glidden (V) | 48 | Cypress Hills-Grasslands | Kindersley | Lois Haug, Clerk, PO Box 40, Glidden S0L 1H0 – 306/463-3338, Fax: 306/463-4748 |
| Golden Prairie (V) | 78 | Cypress Hills-Grasslands | Cypress Hills | Quinton Jacksteiit, Adm., PO Box 9, Golden Prairie S0N 0Y0 – 306/662-2883, Fax: 306/662-2883 |
| Goodeve (V) | 71 | Yorkton-Melville | Melville | Louise Rathgeber, Clerk, PO Box 160, Goodeve S0A 1C0 – 306/876-4633 |
| Goodsoil (V) | 278 | Churchill River | Meadow Lake | Donna Weinkauf, Clerk, PO Box 176, Goodsoil S0M 1A0 – 306/238-2094, Fax: 306/238-2094 |
| Goodwater (V) | 29 | Souris-Moose Mountain | Estevan | Kevin Melle, Adm., PO Box 280, Weyburn S4H 2K1 – 306/456-2566, Fax: 306/456-2566 |
| Govan † | 316 | Regina-Lumsden-Lake Centre | Last Mountain-Touchwood | Michelle Cruise, Adm., PO Box 160, Govan S0G 1Z0 – 306/484-2011, Fax: 306/484-2113 |
| Grand Coulee (V) | 336 | Regina-Lumsden-Lake Centre | Regina Qu'Appelle Valley | Patrick Seeley, Clerk, RR#2, Site 1, Box 72, Regina S4P 2Z2 – 306/352-8694 |
| Gravelbourg † | 1,211 | Cypress Hills-Grasslands | Thunder Creek | Aline Kirk, Adm., PO Box 359, Gravelbourg S0H 1X0 – 306/648-3301, Fax: 306/648-3400 |
| Grayson (V) | 223 | Yorkton-Melville | Melville | Eileen Parker, Clerk, PO Box 69, Grayson S0A 1E0 – 306/794-2044, Fax: 306/794-4655 |
| Green Lake (NV) | 536 | Churchill River | Athabasca | Brad Weiss, Adm., PO Box 128, Green Lake S0M 1B0 – 306/832-2131, Fax: 306/832-2124 |
| Grenfell † | 1,106 | Souris-Moose Mountain | Moosomin | Leslie McGhie, Adm., PO Box 1120, Grenfell S0G 2B0 – 306/697-2815, Fax: 306/697-2484 |
| Guernsey (V) | 129 | Blackstrap | Watrous | Eleanor Uchacz, Clerk, PO Box 93, Guernsey S0K 1W0 – 306/365-4376, Fax: 306/365-3386 |
| Gull Lake † | 1,078 | Cypress Hills-Grasslands | Cypress Hills | Abe Funk, Adm., PO Box 150, Gull Lake S0N 1A0 – 306/672-3361, Fax: 306/672-3777 |
| Hafford † | 424 | Wanuskewin | Redberry Lake | Charles W. Linnell, Adm., PO Box 220, Hafford S0J 1A0 – 306/549-2331, Fax: 306/549-2331 |
| Hague † | 688 | Wanuskewin | Rosthern | Ivan M. Gabrysh, Adm., PO Box 180, Hague S0K 1X0 – 306/225-2155, Fax: 306/225-4410 |
| Halbrite (V) | 111 | Souris-Moose Mountain | Estevan | Gail Silver, Clerk, PO Box 10, Halbrite S0C 1H0 – 306/458-2252 |
| Handel (V) | 42 | Battlefords-Lloydminster | Rosetown-Biggar | Dean Evanisky, Clerk, PO Box 19, Handel S0K 1Y0 – 306/658-4244 |
| Hanley † | 491 | Blackstrap | Arm River | Tony Obrigewitch, Adm., PO Box 270, Hanley S0G 2E0 – 306/544-2223, Fax: 306/544-2223 |
| Hardy (V) | 15 | Souris-Moose Mountain | Weyburn-Big Muddy | Marie Fettes, Clerk, General Delivery, Hardy S0C 1J0 – 306/869-2800 |
| Harris (V) | 245 | Saskatoon-Rosetown-Biggar | Rosetown-Biggar | Peggy Garner, Clerk, PO Box 124, Harris S0L 1K0 – 306/656-2122, Fax: 306/656-2151 |
| Hawarden (V) | 81 | Blackstrap | Arm River | Darice Carlson, Clerk, PO Box 7, Hawarden S0H 1Y0 – 306/855-2020 |
| Hazenmore (V) | 73 | Cypress Hills-Grasslands | Wood River | D. Koenig, Clerk, PO Box 2, Hazenmore S0N 1C0 – 306/264-3218 |
| Hazlet (V) | 120 | Cypress Hills-Grasslands | Cypress Hills | Terry Erdelyan, Adm., PO Box 150, Hazlet S0N 1E0 – 306/678-2131, Fax: 306/678-2132 |
| Hepburn (V) | 442 | Wanuskewin | Rosthern | Gerald Lepage, Adm., PO Box 217, Hepburn S0K 1Z0 – 306/947-2170, Fax: 306/947-4202 |

Cities in CAPITALS; Towns marked †; Villages marked (V); Northern Villages marked (NV); Resort Villages not listed. An in-depth listing for municipalities marked with * appears in Part 2 (check Index for page numbers).

| MUNICIPALITY | 1996 POP. | FEDERAL ELECTORAL DISTRICT | PROVINCIAL ELECTORAL DISTRICT | CONTACT PERSON WITH ADDRESS, PHONE & FAX |
|---|---|---|---|---|
| Herbert † | 855 | Cypress Hills-Grasslands | Thunder Creek | Sandra MacArthur, Adm., PO Box 370, Herbert S0H 2A0 – 306/784-2400, Fax: 306/784-2402 |
| Herschel (V) | 44 | Saskatoon-Rosetown-Biggar | Rosetown-Biggar | Deborah C. Rea, Clerk, PO Box 88, Herschel S0L 1L0 – 306/377-2014, Fax: 306/377-2014 |
| Heward (V) | 26 | Souris-Moose Mountain | Cannington | Dolores Mitchall, Clerk, PO Box 10, Heward S0G 2G0 – 306/457-2852 |
| Hodgeville (V) | 207 | Cypress Hills-Grasslands | Thunder Creek | Sheila Cooper, Clerk, PO Box 307, Hodgeville S0H 2B0 – 306/677-2223, Fax: 306/677-2466 |
| Holdfast (V) | 216 | Regina-Lumsden-Lake Centre | Arm River | Harvey Hemingway, Clerk, PO Box 160, Holdfast S0G 1H0 – 306/488-2000 |
| Hubbard (V) | 53 | Qu'Appelle | Melville | Diane M. Olech, Adm., PO Box 190, Ituna S0A 1N0 – 306/795-2202, Fax: 306/795-2202 |
| Hudson Bay † | 1,883 | Yorkton-Melville | Carrot River Valley | Richard Dolezsar, Adm., PO Box 730, Hudson Bay S0E 0Y0 – 306/865-2261, Fax: 306/865-2800 |
| Humboldt † | 5,074 | Saskatoon-Humboldt | Humboldt | Robert G. Smith, Adm., PO Box 640, Humboldt S0K 2A0 – 306/682-2525, Fax: 306/682-3144 |
| Hyas (V) | 119 | Yorkton-Melville | Canora-Pelly | Robert Newman, Clerk, PO Box 40, Hyas S0A 1K0 – 306/594-2817, Fax: 306/594-2817 |
| Île à la Crosse (NV) | 1,403 | Churchill River | Athabasca | Rose Daigneault, Adm., PO Box 280, Ile à la Crosse S0M 1C0 – 306/833-2122, Fax: 306/833-2132 |
| Imperial † | 382 | Regina-Lumsden-Lake Centre | Arm River | Sheila Newlove, Adm., PO Box 90, Imperial S0G 2J0 – 306/963-2220, Fax: 306/963-2445 |
| Indian Head † | 1,833 | Qu'Appelle | Indian Head-Milestone | Lawrence Natyshak, Adm., PO Box 460, Indian Head S0G 2K0 – 306/695-3344, Fax: 306/695-2398 |
| Insinger (V) | 17 | Yorkton-Melville | Canora-Pelly | Bettie Thompson, Adm., PO Box 179, Insinger S0A 1L0 – 306/647-2422, Fax: 306/647-2422 |
| Invermay (V) | 295 | Yorkton-Melville | Kelvington-Wadena | Veronica L. Wolski, Clerk, PO Box 234, Invermay S0A 1M0 – 306/593-2242, Fax: 306/593-2242 |
| Ituna † | 743 | Qu'Appelle | Melville | Lawrence Skoretz, Adm., PO Box 580, Ituna S0A 1N0 – 306/795-2272, Fax: 306/795-2272 |
| Jans Bay (V) | 199 | Churchill River | Athabasca | Rose Morin, Clerk, General Delivery, Canoe Narrows S0M 0K0 – 306/829-4320, Fax: 306/829-4424 |
| Jansen (V) | 167 | Blackstrap | Watrous | Elaine Kral, Clerk, PO Box 116, Jansen S0K 2B0 – 306/364-2148 |
| Jedburgh (V) | 13 | Yorkton-Melville | Melville | Jerry T. Kuziak, Adm., PO Box 10, Jedburgh S0A 1R0 – 306/647-2450, Fax: 306/647-2450 |
| Kamsack † | 2,264 | Yorkton-Melville | Saltcoats | Bruno Kossman, Adm., PO Box 729, Kamsack S0A 1S0 – 306/542-2155, Fax: 306/542-2975 |
| Keeler (V) | 21 | Regina-Lumsden-Lake Centre | Arm River | Reg E. McKee, Clerk, PO Box 33, Keeler S0H 2E0 – 306/692-3390 |
| Kelfield (V) | 5 | Battlesfords-Lloydmin-ster | Rosetown-Biggar | Patti Turk, Adm., PO Box 8, Kelfield S0K 2C0 – 306/932-4931, Fax: 306/932-4931 |
| Kelliher (V) | 338 | Qu'Appelle | Last Mountain-Touchwood | Elizabeth A. Clark, Clerk, PO Box 190, Kelliher S0A 1V0 – 306/675-2226, Fax: 306/675-2226 |
| Kelvington † | 1,046 | Yorkton-Melville | Kelvington-Wadena | Beverly Anne Link, Adm., PO Box 10, Kelvington S0A 1W0 – 306/327-4482, Fax: 306/327-4946 |
| Kenaston (V) | 323 | Blackstrap | Arm River | Mark J. Zdunich, Adm., PO Box 129, Kenaston S0G 2N0 – 306/252-2211, Fax: 306/252-2240 |
| Kendal (V) | 98 | Wascana | Indian Head-Milestone | Nadine Jensen, Clerk, PO Box 97, Kendal S0G 2P0 – 306/424-2722 |
| Kennedy (V) | 231 | Souris-Moose Mountain | Cannington | Amaret Smyth, Clerk, PO Box 93, Kennedy S0G 2R0 – 306/538-2194 |
| Kenosee Lake (V) | 202 | Souris-Moose Mountain | Cannington | Helen Gurski, Adm., PO Box 30, Kenosee Lake S0C 2S0 – 306/577-2139, Fax: 306/577-2261 |
| Kerrobert † | 1,109 | Battlefords-Lloydminster | Kindersley | Sharon Pope, Adm., PO Box 558, Kerrobert S0L 1R0 – 306/834-2361, Fax: 306/834-2633 |
| Khedive (V) | 29 | Souris-Moose Mountain | Weyburn-Big Muddy | Wayne Lozinsky, Adm., PO Box 189, Pangman S0C 2C0 – 306/442-2131, Fax: 306/442-2144 |
| Killaly (V) | 88 | Yorkton-Melville | Melville | Vern Huber, Clerk, PO Box 69, Killaly S0A 1X0 – 306/748-2311 |
| Kincaid (V) | 177 | Cypress Hills-Grasslands | Wood River | Diana Lott, Clerk, PO Box 177, Kincaid S0H 2J0 – 306/264-3910 |
| Kindersley † | 4,679 | Battlefords-Lloydminster | Kindersley | James V. Toye, Adm., PO Box 1269, Kindersley S0L 1S0 – 306/463-2675, Fax: 306/463-4577 |
| Kinistino † | 691 | Prince Albert | Melfort-Tisdale | Shirley Jackson, Adm., PO Box 10, Kinistino S0J 1H0 – 306/864-2461, Fax: 306/864-2880 |
| Kinley (V) | 31 | Saskatoon-Rosetown-Biggar | Redberry Lake | Pam McMahon, Adm., PO Box 51, Kinley S0K 2E0 – 306/237-4359, Fax: 306/237-4202 |
| Kipling † | 1,004 | Souris-Moose Mountain | Moosomin | Dave Petz, Adm., PO Box 299, Kipling S0G 2S0 – 306/736-2515, Fax: 306/736-8448 |
| Kisbey (V) | 209 | Souris-Moose Mountain | Cannington | Verna Reed, Clerk, PO Box 249, Kisbey S0C 1L0 – 306/462-2212 |
| Krydor (V) | 29 | Wanuskewin | Redberry Lake | W. Grewa, Clerk, PO Box 195, Krydor S0J 1K0 – 306/931-2393 |
| Kyle † | 479 | Cypress Hills-Grasslands | Rosetown-Biggar | Marlene Pederson, Adm., PO Box 520, Kyle S0L 1T0 – 306/375-2525, Fax: 306/375-2525 |

Cities in CAPITALS; Towns marked †; Villages marked (V); Northern Villages marked (NV); Resort Villages not listed. An in-depth listing for municipalities marked with * appears in Part 2 (check Index for page numbers).

| MUNICIPALITY | 1996 POP. | FEDERAL ELECTORAL DISTRICT | PROVINCIAL ELECTORAL DISTRICT | CONTACT PERSON WITH ADDRESS, PHONE & FAX |
|---|---|---|---|---|
| La Loche (NV) | 1,966 | Churchill River | Athabasca | Doug Gailey, Clerk, PO Box 310, La Loche S0M 1G0 – 306/822-2032, Fax: 306/822-2078 |
| La Ronge † | 2,964 | Churchill River | Cumberland | John Wade, Adm., PO Box 5680, La Ronge S0J 1L0 – 306/425-2066, Fax: 306/425-3883 |
| Lafleche † | 476 | Cypress Hills-Grasslands | Wood River | Lorraine McIvor, Adm., PO Box 250, Lafleche S0H 2K0 – 306/472-5292, Fax: 306/472-3076 |
| Laird (V) | 235 | Wanuskewin | Rosthern | Grant Peters, Clerk, PO Box 189, Laird S0K 2H0 – 306/223-4343, Fax: 306/223-4220 |
| Lake Alma (V) | 40 | Souris-Moose Mountain | Estevan | Myrna Lohse, Clerk, PO Box 163, Lake Alma S0C 1M0 – 306/447-2002 |
| Lake Lenore (V) | 290 | Saskatoon-Humboldt | Humboldt | Barb Politeski, Clerk, PO Box 148, Lake Lenore S0K 2J0 – 306/368-2344, Fax: 306/368-2226 |
| Lampman † | 648 | Souris-Moose Mountain | Cannington | Rodney Audette, Adm., PO Box 70, Lampman S0C 1N0 – 306/487-2462, Fax: 306/487-2285 |
| Lancer (V) | 99 | Cypress Hills-Grasslands | Cypress Hills | Bertha E. Hopfauf, Clerk, PO Box 3, Lancer S0N 1G0 – 306/689-2925, Fax: 306/689-2890 |
| Landis (V) | 189 | Battlefords-Lloydminster | Battleford-Cut Knife | Beryl Hart, Clerk, PO Box 153, Landis S0K 2K0 – 306/658-2155, Fax: 306/658-2117 |
| Lang (V) | 189 | Souris-Moose Mountain | Indian Head-Milestone | Colleen Christopherson, Clerk, PO Box 97, Lang S0G 2W0 – 306/464-2024, Fax: 306/464-2024 |
| Langenburg † | 1,119 | Yorkton-Melville | Saltcoats | Howard McCullough, Adm., PO Box 400, Langenburg S0A 2A0 – 306/743-2432, Fax: 306/743-2723 |
| Langham † | 1,104 | Wanuskewin | Redberry Lake | Randy J. Sherstobitoff, Adm., PO Box 289, Langham S0K 2L0 – 306/283-4842, Fax: 306/283-4842 |
| Lanigan † | 1,368 | Blackstrap | Watrous | Jack R. Dvernichuk, Adm., PO Box 280, Lanigan S0K 2M0 – 306/365-2809, Fax: 306/365-2960 |
| Lashburn † | 674 | Battlefords-Lloydminster | Lloydminster | Vicki Seabrook, Adm., PO Box 328, Lashburn S0M 1H0 – 306/285-3533, Fax: 306/285-3358 |
| Leader † | 983 | Cypress Hills-Grasslands | Cypress Hills | R. Kim Hauta, Adm., PO Box 39, Leader S0N 1H0 – 306/628-3868, Fax: 306/628-4337 |
| Leask (V) | 435 | Wanuskewin | Redberry Lake | Rick Poole, Adm., PO Box 190, Leask S0J 1M0 – 306/466-2229, Fax: 306/466-2000 |
| Lebret (V) | 226 | Qu'Appelle | Melville | Bernadette Huber, Clerk, PO Box 40, Lebret S0G 2Y0 – 306/332-6545, Fax: 306/332-5338 |
| Lemberg † | 353 | Yorkton-Melville | Melville | Joyce Hauck, Clerk, PO Box 399, Lemberg S0A 2B0 – 306/335-2244, Fax: 306/335-2911 |
| Leoville (V) | 359 | Churchill River | Shellbrook-Spiritwood | Mona Chalifour, Clerk, PO Box 280, Leoville S0J 1N0 – 306/984-2140, Fax: 306/984-2337 |
| Leross (V) | 82 | Qu'Appelle | Last Mountain-Touchwood | Elaine Klyne, Clerk, PO Box 68, Leross S0A 2C0 – 306/675-4429 |
| Leroy † | 420 | Saskatoon-Humboldt | Watrous | Mark Fedak, Adm., PO Box 40, Leroy S0K 2P0 – 306/286-3288, Fax: 306/286-3400 |
| Leslie (V) | 34 | Qu'Appelle; Yorkton-Melville | Last Mountain-Touchwood | Norman Casement, Clerk, PO Box 97, Leslie S0A 2E0 – 306/272-3959 |
| Lestock (V) | 301 | Qu'Appelle | Last Mountain-Touchwood | Luelle Frisko, Clerk, PO Box 209, Lestock S0A 2G0 – 306/274-2277 |
| Liberty (V) | 101 | Regina-Lumsden-Lake Centre | Arm River | Michele Cruise, Clerk, PO Box 59, Liberty S0G 3A0 – 306/847-2033 |
| Limerick (V) | 165 | Cypress Hills-Grasslands | Wood River | Mary Jean Alligham, Adm., PO Box 129, Limerick S0H 2P0 – 306/263-2020, Fax: 306/263-2013 |
| Lintlaw (V) | 208 | Yorkton-Melville | Kelvington-Wadena | Sandy Siddons, Clerk, PO Box 10, Lintlaw S0A 2H0 – 306/325-2006, Fax: 306/325-2006 |
| Lipton (V) | 345 | Qu'Appelle | Last Mountain-Touchwood | Marlene L. Bausmer, Clerk, PO Box 219, Lipton S0G 3B0 – 306/336-2505, Fax: 306/336-2505 |
| LLOYDMINSTER | 7,636 [1] | Battlefords-Lloydminster | Lloydminster | Tom Lysyk, Clerk, 5011 - 49 Ave., Lloydminster S9V 0T8 – 306/825-6184, Fax: 306/825-7170 |
| Lockwood (V) | 24 | Blackstrap | Watrous | Irene Hurley, Clerk, PO Box 55, Lockwood S0K 2R0 |
| Loon Lake (V) | 390 | Churchill River | Meadow Lake | Michael Williamson, Clerk, PO Box 220, Loon Lake S0M 1L0 – 306/837-2090, Fax: 306/837-4735 |
| Loreburn (V) | 150 | Blackstrap | Arm River | Muriel Stronski, Clerk, PO Box 177, Loreburn S0H 2S0 – 306/644-2097, Fax: 306/644-2099 |
| Love (V) | 83 | Churchill River | Saskatchewan Rivers | Una J. Fee, Clerk, PO Box 94, Love S0J 1P0 – 306/276-2525, Fax: 306/276-2320 |
| Loverna (V) | 12 | Battlefords-Lloydminster | Kindersley | Beverly A. Dahl, Adm., PO Box 70, Marengo S0L 2K0 – 306/968-2922, Fax: 306/968-2278 |
| Lucky Lake (V) | 353 | Cypress Hills-Grasslands | Rosetown-Biggar | Edna A. Laturnus, Adm., PO Box 99, Lucky Lake S0L 1Z0 – 306/858-2234, Fax: 306/858-2234 |
| Lumsden † | 1,530 | Regina-Lumsden-Lake Centre | Regina Qu'Appelle Valley | Wayne Zerff, Adm., PO Box 160, Lumsden S0G 3C0 – 306/731-2404, Fax: 306/731-3572 |
| Luseland † | 622 | Battlefords-Lloydminster | Kindersley | Harold Trew, Adm., PO Box 130, Luseland S0L 2A0 – 306/372-4218, Fax: 306/347-4700 |
| Macklin † | 1,281 | Battlefords-Lloydminster | Battleford-Cut Knife | Kim G. Gartner, Adm., PO Box 69, Macklin S0L 2C0 – 306/753-2256, Fax: 306/753-3234 |

Cities in CAPITALS; Towns marked †; Villages marked (V); Northern Villages marked (NV); Resort Villages not listed. An in-depth listing for municipalities marked with * appears in Part 2 (check Index for page numbers).

| MUNICIPALITY | 1996 POP. | FEDERAL ELECTORAL DISTRICT | PROVINCIAL ELECTORAL DISTRICT | CONTACT PERSON WITH ADDRESS, PHONE & FAX |
|---|---|---|---|---|
| MacNutt (V) | 95 | Yorkton-Melville | Saltcoats | Cheryl Peppler, Clerk, PO Box 10, MacNutt S0A 2K0 – 306/742-4391 |
| Macoun (V) | 148 | Souris-Moose Mountain | Estevan | Bernice Mohns, Clerk, PO Box 58, Macoun S0C 1P0 – 306/634-2289 |
| Macrorie (V) | 110 | Saskatoon-Rosetown-Biggar | Rosetown-Biggar | Noreen Andrew, Clerk, PO Box 37, Macrorie S0L 2E0 – 306/243-2010, Fax: 306/243-2131 |
| Madison (V) | 11 | Cypress Hills-Grasslands | Kindersley | Judy E. Douglas, Clerk, PO Box 70, Madison S0L 2G0 – 306/967-2594 |
| Maidstone † | 962 | Battlefords-Lloydminster | Lloydminster | Bernice Swanson, Adm., PO Box 208, Maidstone S0M 1M0 – 306/893-2373, Fax: 306/893-2373 |
| Major (V) | 72 | Battlefords-Lloydminster | Kindersley | Louise Kollman, Clerk, PO Box 94, Major S0L 2H0 – 306/834-5390, Fax: 306/834-1010 |
| Makwa (V) | 104 | Churchill River | Meadow Lake | Penny L. Barker, Clerk, PO Box 67, Makwa S0M 1N0 – 306/236-3919 |
| Mankota (V) | 326 | Cypress Hills-Grasslands | Wood River | Jody Penna, Adm., PO Box 336, Mankota S0H 2W0 – 306/478-2331, Fax: 306/478-2525 |
| Manor (V) | 347 | Souris-Moose Mountain | Cannington | Joan Mills, Adm., PO Box 295, Manor S0C 1R0 – 306/448-2273 |
| Mantario (V) | 17 | Cypress Hills-Grasslands | Kindersley | Beverly A. Dahl, Adm., PO Box 47, Mantario S0L 2J0 – 306/968-2922, Fax: 306/968-2278 |
| Maple Creek † | 2,307 | Cypress Hills-Grasslands | Cypress Hills | Tim Leson, Adm., PO Box 428, Maple Creek S0N 1N0 – 306/662-2244, Fax: 306/662-4131 |
| Marcelin (V) | 182 | Wanuskewin | Redberry Lake | Brenda Desjardins, Clerk, PO Box 39, Marcelin S0J 1R0 – 306/226-2168, Fax: 306/226-2168 |
| Marengo (V) | 61 | Battlefords-Lloydminster | Kindersley | Beverly A. Dahl, Adm., PO Box 70, Marengo S0L 2K0 – 306/968-2922, Fax: 306/968-2278 |
| Margo (V) | 127 | Yorkton-Melville | Kelvington-Wadena | Vivian G. Rothlander, Clerk, PO Box 28, Margo S0A 2M0 – 306/324-2134 |
| Markinch (V) | 72 | Qu'Appelle | Last Mountain-Touchwood | Rita T. Orb, Adm., PO Box 29, Markinch S0G 3J0 – 306/726-4355 |
| Marquis (V) | 98 | Regina-Lumsden-Lake Centre | Arm River | Ronald J. Gasper, Adm., PO Box 40, Marquis S0H 2X0 – 306/788-2022, Fax: 306/788-2168 |
| Marsden (V) | 263 | Battlefords-Lloydminster | Battleford-Cut Knife | Jason Boyle, Adm., PO Box 69, Marsden S0M 1P0 – 306/826-5215, Fax: 306/826-5512 |
| Marshall (V) | 605 | Battlefords-Lloydminster | Lloydminster | Lorne Kachur, Adm., PO Box 125, Marshall S0M 1R0 – 306/387-6340, Fax: 306/387-6161 |
| Martensville † | 3,477 | Wanuskewan | Rosthern | Phillip W. Ratzlaff, Adm., PO Box 970, Martensville S0K 2T0 – 306/931-2166, Fax: 306/933-2468 |
| Maryfield (V) | 363 | Souris-Moose Mountain | Moosomin | Ward Fraser, Adm., PO Box 58, Maryfield S0G 3K0 – 306/646-2143 |
| Maymont (V) | 156 | Wanuskewin | Redberry Lake | E. Lynne Tolley, Adm., PO Box 160, Maymont S0M 1T0 – 306/389-2051, Fax: 306/389-2051 |
| Mazenod (V) | 33 | Cypress Hills-Grasslands | Thunder Creek | Mary-Ellen McKechnie, Clerk, PO Box 427, Mossbank S0H 3G0 – 306/354-2878 |
| McLean (V) | 262 | Qu'Appelle | Indian Head-Milestone | Lyla Grad, Clerk, PO Box 56, McLean S0G 3E0 – 306/699-7279, Fax: 306/699-2347 |
| McTaggart (V) | 124 | Souris-Moose Mountain | Weyburn-Big Muddy | Nichol Lynch, Adm., PO Box 134, McTaggart S0G 3G0 – 306/842-5911 |
| Meacham (V) | 79 | Blackstrap | Watrous | Elizabeth Saretzky, Clerk, PO Box 9, Meacham S0K 2V0 – 306/376-2003 |
| Meadow Lake † | 4,813 | Churchill River | Meadow Lake | Richard Levesque, Adm., 120 - 1st St. East, Meadow Lake S9X 1P8 – 306/236-3622, Fax: 306/236-4299 |
| Meath Park (V) | 210 | Prince Albert | Saskatchewan Rivers | Elaine Esopenko, Adm., PO Box 255, Meath Park S0J 1T0 – 306/929-2112, Fax: 306/929-2281 |
| Medstead (V) | 162 | Battlefords-Lloydminster | Shellbrook-Spiritwood | Darrin Beaudoin, Adm., PO Box 148, Medstead S0M 1W0 – 306/342-4609, Fax: 306/342-4609 |
| MELFORT | 5,759 | Prince Albert | Melfort-Tisdale | Joanne Forer, Clerk, PO Box 2230, Melfort S0E 1A0 – 306/752-5911, Fax: 306/752-5556 |
| MELVILLE | 4,646 | Yorkton-Melville | Melville | Ron J. Walton, City Clerk, PO Box 1240, Melville S0A 2P0 – 306/728-6840, Fax: 306/728-5911 |
| Mendham (V) | 53 | Cypress Hills-Grasslands | Cypress Hills | Sandra Ehnisz, Clerk, PO Box 55, Mendham S0N 1P0 – 306/628-3567 |
| Meota (V) | 274 | Battlefords-Lloydminster | North Battleford | Allie R. Raycraft, Adm., PO Box 80, Meota S0M 1X0 – 306/892-2061, Fax: 306/892-2061 |
| Mervin (V) | 161 | Battlefords-Lloydminster | Lloydminster | V. Dawn Simkins, Clerk, PO Box 35, Mervin S0M 1Y0 – 306/845-2784 |
| Meyronne (V) | 40 | Cypress Hills-Grasslands | Wood River | Hazel Diebel, Clerk, PO Box 119, Meyronne S0H 3A0 – 306/264-3773 |
| Michel Village (NV) | 75 | Churchill River | Athabasca | Rita Maurice, Clerk, General Delivery, Michel Village via Dillon S0M 0S0 – 306/282-4401, 4402, Fax: 306/282-2155 |
| Midale † | 522 | Souris-Moose Mountain | Estevan | Bonnie Bjorndalen, Adm., PO Box 128, Midale S0C 1S0 – 306/458-2400, Fax: 306/458-2588 |

Cities in CAPITALS; Towns marked †; Villages marked (V); Northern Villages marked (NV); Resort Villages not listed. An in-depth listing for municipalities marked with * appears in Part 2 (check Index for page numbers).

| MUNICIPALITY | 1996 POP. | FEDERAL ELECTORAL DISTRICT | PROVINCIAL ELECTORAL DISTRICT | CONTACT PERSON WITH ADDRESS, PHONE & FAX |
|---|---|---|---|---|
| Middle Lake (V) | 268 | Saskatoon-Humboldt | Humboldt | Carol Winkel, Clerk, PO Box 119, Middle Lake S0K 2X0 – 306/367-2149 |
| Milden (V) | 208 | Saskatoon-Rosetown-Biggar | Rosetown-Biggar | Barb Barteski, Clerk, PO Box 70, Milden S0L 2L0 – 306/935-2131, Fax: 306/935-2020 |
| Milestone † | 540 | Souris-Moose Mountain | Indian Head-Milestone | Ernest P. Audette, Adm., PO Box 74, Milestone S0G 3L0 – 306/436-2130, Fax: 306/436-2051 |
| Minton (V) | 101 | Souris-Moose Mountain | Weyburn-Big Muddy | Joyce Axten, Clerk, PO Box 52, Minton S0C 1T0 – 306/969-2144, Fax: 306/969-2244 |
| Missinipe (NV) | 40 | Churchill River | Cumberland | Shirley Glass, Clerk, PO Box 1617, La Ronge S0J 1L0 – 306/635-4540, Fax: 306/635-4434 |
| Mistatim (V) | 114 | Yorkton-Melville | Carrot River Valley | Elsie Leblanc, Clerk, PO Box 145, Mistatim S0E 1B0 – 306/889-2114 |
| Montmartre (V) | 485 | Wascana | Indian Head-Milestone | Dale Brenner, Clerk, PO Box 146, Montmartre S0G 3M0 – 306/424-2040, Fax: 306/424-2040 |
| MOOSE JAW | 32,973 | Palliser | Moose Jaw North; Moose Jaw Wakamow | Brian Hamblin, City Clerk & Solicitor, 228 Main St. North, Moose Jaw S6H 3J8 – 306/694-4400, Fax: 306/692-4518 |
| Moosomin † | 2,420 | Souris-Moose Mountain | Moosomin | Paul Listrom, Adm., PO Box 730, Moosomin S0G 3N0 – 306/435-2988, Fax: 306/435-3343 |
| Morse † | 284 | Cypress Hills-Grasslands | Thunder Creek | Darlene Klassen, Adm., PO Box 270, Morse S0H 3C0 – 306/629-3300 |
| Mortlach (V) | 276 | Cypress Hills-Grasslands | Thunder Creek | Maureen Grajczyk, Clerk, PO Box 10, Mortlach S0H 3E0 – 306/355-2239 |
| Mossbank † | 410 | Palliser | Thunder Creek | Judy L. Bolton, Adm., PO Box 370, Mossbank S0H 3G0 – 306/354-2294, Fax: 306/354-7725 |
| Muenster (V) | 381 | Saskatoon-Humboldt | Kelvington-Wadena | Cheryl Chapman, Clerk, PO Box 98, Muenster S0K 2Y0 – 306/682-2794 |
| Naicam † | 789 | Saskatoon-Humboldt | Kelvington-Wadena | Ruby J. Lindsay, Adm., PO Box 238, Naicam S0K 2Z0 – 306/874-2280, Fax: 306/874-5444 |
| Neilburg (V) | 345 | Battlefords-Lloydminster | Battleford-Cut Knife | Dale Bryden, Adm., PO Box 280, Neilburg S0M 2C0 – 306/823-4321, Fax: 306/823-4477 |
| Netherhill (V) | 39 | Battlefords-Lloydminster | Kindersley | Judy Shaver, Clerk, PO Box 70, Netherhill S0L 2M0 – 306/463-3562 |
| Neudorf (V) | 331 | Yorkton-Melville | Melville | Donna Litzenberger, Clerk, PO Box 187, Neudorf S0A 2T0 – 306/748-2551 |
| Neville (V) | 88 | Cypress Hills-Grasslands | Thunder Creek | Susan Fehr, Clerk, PO Box 88, Neville S0N 1T0 – 306/627-3255 |
| Nipawin † | 4,318 | Prince Albert | Carrot River Valley | Peter M. Cannon, Adm., PO Box 2134, Nipawin S0E 1E0 – 306/862-9866, Fax: 306/862-3076 |
| Nokomis † | 469 | Regina-Lumsden-Lake Centre | Watrous | Wilma Staff, Adm., PO Box 189, Nokomis S0G 3R0 – 306/528-2010, Fax: 306/528-2010 |
| Norquay † | 505 | Yorkton-Melville | Cabora-Pelly | Rodney C. Johnson, Adm., PO Box 327, Norquay S0A 2V0 – 306/594-2101, Fax: 306/594-2347 |
| NORTH BATTLEFORD | 14,051 | The Battlefords-Lloyd-minster | North Battleford | Doug McEwen, City Clerk, PO Box 460, North Battleford S9A 2Y6 – 306/445-1700, Fax: 306/445-0411 |
| North Portal (V) | 148 | Souris-Moose Mountain | Estevan | Barry Carlberg, Clerk, PO Box 15, North Portal S0C 1W0 – 306/927-5050 |
| Odessa (V) | 268 | Wascana | Indian Head-Milestone | Sheila Leurer, Clerk, PO Box 91, Odessa S0G 3S0 – 306/957-2020, Fax: 306/957-2075 |
| Ogema † | 349 | Souris-Moose Mountain | Weyburn-Big Muddy | Peggy Tumback, Adm., PO Box 159, Ogema S0C 1Y0 – 306/459-2230, Fax: 306/459-2762 |
| Osage (V) | 23 | Souris-Moose Mountain | Indian Head-Milestone | Linda Kreutzer, Clerk, PO Box 96, Osage S0G 3T0 – 306/722-3747 |
| Osler † | 618 | Wanuskewin | Rosthern | Sarah Peters, Adm., PO Box 190, Osler S0K 3A0 – 306/239-2155, Fax: 306/239-2155 |
| Outlook † | 2,116 | Blackstrap; Saskatoon-Rosetown-Biggar | Arm River | Lawrence W. Zarubiak, Adm., PO Box 518, Outlook S0L 2N0 – 306/867-8663, Fax: 306/867-9898 |
| Oxbow † | 1,163 | Souris-Moose Mountain | Cannington | Geraldine Gervais, Adm., PO Box 149, Oxbow S0C 2B0 – 306/483-2300, Fax: 306/483-5277 |
| Paddockwood (V) | 187 | Prince Albert | Saskatchewan Rivers | Lillian Sauer, Clerk, PO Box 188, Paddockwood S0J 1Z0 – 306/989-2033 |
| Palmer (V) | 29 | Cypress Hills-Grasslands | Thunder Creek | Mary-Ellen McKechnie, Clerk, PO Box 368, Palmer S0H 3G0 – 306/354-2878 |
| Pangman (V) | 251 | Souris-Moose Mountain | Weyburn-Bug Muddy | Wayne Lozinsky, Clerk, PO Box 189, Pangman S0C 2C0 – 306/442-2131, Fax: 306/442-2131 |
| Paradise Hill (V) | 466 | Battlefords-Lloydminster | Meadow Lake | Marion Hougham, Clerk, PO Box 270, Paradise Hill S0M 2G0 – 306/344-2206, Fax: 306/344-4941 |
| Parkside (V) | 119 | Wanuskewin | Shellbrook-Spiritwood | Gwen Olson, Clerk, PO Box 48, Parkside S0J 2A0 – 306/747-2235, Fax: 306/747-3395 |
| Patuanak (NV) | 89 | Churchill River | Athabasca | Vacant, Clerk, General Delivery, Patuanak S0M 2H0 – 306/396-2020, Fax: 306/396-2092 |
| Paynton (V) | 161 | Battlefords-Lloydminster | Lloydminster | Gina Bernier, Clerk-Adm., PO Box 10, Paynton S0M 2J0 – 306/895-2023, Fax: 306/895-2020 |

Cities in CAPITALS; Towns marked †; Villages marked (V); Northern Villages marked (NV); Resort Villages not listed. An in-depth listing for municipalities marked with * appears in Part 2 (check Index for page numbers).

| MUNICIPALITY | 1996 POP. | FEDERAL ELECTORAL DISTRICT | PROVINCIAL ELECTORAL DISTRICT | CONTACT PERSON WITH ADDRESS, PHONE & FAX |
|---|---|---|---|---|
| Pelican Narrows (NV) | 445 | Churchill River | Cumberland | Doreen Linklater, Clerk, PO Box 10, Pelican Narrows S0P 0E0 – 306/632-2225, Fax: 306/632-2006 |
| Pelly (V) | 331 | Yorkton-Melville | Canora-Pelly | Ella Klimm, Clerk, PO Box 160, Pelly S0A 2Z0 – 306/595-2124, Fax: 306/595-2162 |
| Pennant (V) | 135 | Cypress Hills-Grasslands | Cypress Hills | Kim Valentine, Clerk, PO Box 57, Pennant S0N 1X0 – 306/626-3316 |
| Pense (V) | 534 | Palliser | Thunder Creek | Carol Bellefeuille, Adm., PO Box 125, Pense S0G 3W0 – 306/345-2332, Fax: 306/345-2332 |
| Penzance (V) | 46 | Regina-Lumsden-Lake Centre | Arm River | Brenda Olson, Clerk, PO Box 86, Penzance S0G 3X0 – 306/488-4683 |
| Perdue (V) | 403 | Saskatoon-Rosetown-Biggar | Redberry Lake | Pam McMahon, Clerk, PO Box 190, Perdue S0K 3C0 – 306/237-4337, Fax: 306/237-4202 |
| Piapot (V) | 55 | Swift Current-Maple Creek-Assiniboia | Cypress Hills | Nicole Drinkwater, Clerk, PO Box 129, Piapot S0N 1Y0 – 306/558-2007 |
| Pierceland (V) | 488 | Churchill River | Meadow Lake | Jane Eistetter, Clerk, PO Box 39, Pierceland S0M 2K0 – 306/839-2015, Fax: 306/839-2057 |
| Pilger (V) | 106 | Saskatoon-Humboldt | Humboldt | Luella Bregenser, Clerk, PO Box 70, Pilger S0K 3G0 – 306/367-4927 |
| Pilot Butte † | 1,469 | Qu'Appelle | Regina Wascana Plains | Ed Sigmeth, Adm., PO Box 253, Pilot Butte S0G 3Z0 – 306/781-4547, Fax: 306/781-4477 |
| Pinehouse (NV) | 922 | Churchill River | Athabasca | Marie Lavallee, Clerk, PO Box 298, Pinehouse Lake S0J 2B0 – 306/884-2030, Fax: 306/884-2021 |
| Plato (V) | (') | Cypress Hills-Grasslands | Rosetown-Biggar | Judy Mathers, Acting Clerk, PO Box 57, Plato S0L 2P0 – 306/574-2110 |
| Pleasantdale (V) | 113 | Saskatoon-Humboldt | Kelvington-Wadena | Dianne M. Dodd, Adm., PO Box 147, Pleasantdale S0K 3H0 – 306/874-5743 |
| Plenty (V) | 138 | Battlefords-Lloydminster | Kindersley | Maxine Woods, Clerk, PO Box 177, Plenty S0L 2R0 – 306/932-2045, Fax: 306/932-2045 |
| Plunkett (V) | 85 | Blackstrap | Watrous | Helen Miller, Clerk, PO Box 149, Plunkett S0K 3J0 – 306/944-4514 |
| Ponteix † | 544 | Cypress Hills-Grasslands | Wood River | Daniel Gervais, Adm., PO Box 330, Ponteix S0N 1Z0 – 306/625-3222, Fax: 306/625-3204 |
| Porcupine Plain † | 866 | Yorkton-Melville | Kelvington-Wadena | Barry Warsylewicz, Clerk, PO Box 310, Porcupine Plain S0E 1H0 – 306/278-2262, Fax: 306/278-3378 |
| Preeceville † | 1,148 | Yorkton-Melville | Canora-Pelly | Connie Hryciuk, Adm., PO Box 560, Preeceville S0A 3B0 – 306/547-2810, Fax: 306/547-3116 |
| Prelate (V) | 189 | Cypress Hills-Grasslands | Cypress Hills | Darlene Wagner, Clerk, PO Box 40, Prelate S0N 2B0 – 306/673-2340, Fax: 306/673-2340 |
| Primate (V) | 69 | Battlefords-Lloydminster | Kindersley | Dianne Latendresse, Clerk, PO Box 6, Primate S0L 2S0 – 306/753-2897 |
| PRINCE ALBERT | 34,777 | Prince Albert | Prince Albert Carlton; Prince Albert Northcote | Charmaine Code, Director & City Clerk, Legislative Services, City Hall, 1084 Central Ave., Prince Albert S6V 7P3 – 306/953-4305, Fax: 306/953-4353 |
| Prud'homme (V) | 224 | Saskatoon-Humboldt | Humboldt | Kim Sopotyk, Clerk, PO Box 38, Prud'homme S0K 3K0 – 306/654-2001, Fax: 306/654-2001 |
| Punnichy (V) | 338 | Qu'Appelle | Last Mountain-Touchwood | Nancy L. Benko, Clerk, PO Box 250, Punnichy S0A 3C0 – 306/835-2135, Fax: 306/835-2100 |
| Qu'Appelle † | 632 | Qu'Appelle | Indian Head-Milestone | Carol Wickenheiser, Adm., PO Box 60, Qu'Appelle S0G 4A0 – 306/699-2279, Fax: 306/699-2306 |
| Quill Lake (V) | 463 | Saskatoon-Humboldt | Watrous | Judy L. Kanak, Adm., PO Box 9, Quill Lake S0A 3E0 – 306/383-2592 |
| Quinton (V) | 138 | Qu'Appelle | Last Mountain-Touchwood | Ralph Brockman, Clerk, PO Box 128, Quinton S0A 3G0 – 306/835-2515 |
| Rabbit Lake (V) | 117 | Battlefords-Lloydminster | Redberry Lake | Ian McLennan, Adm., PO Box 9, Rabbit Lake S0M 2L0 – 306/824-2044, Fax: 306/824-2044 |
| Radisson † | 403 | Wanuskewin | Redberry Lake | Kimberly Waterhouse, Clerk, PO Box 69, Radisson S0K 3L0 – 306/827-2218, Fax: 306/827-2218 |
| Radville † | 823 | Souris-Moose Mountain | Weyburn-Big Muddy | Lyle R. Fisher, Clerk, PO Box 339, Radville S0C 2G0 – 306/869-2477, Fax: 306/869-3100 |
| Rama (V) | 99 | Yorkton-Melville | Canora-Pelly | Lorraine Kaminski, Clerk, PO Box 205, Rama S0A 3H0 – 306/593-6065, Fax: 306/593-2273 |
| Raymore † | 667 | Qu'Appelle | Last Mountain-Touchwood | Elaine Perry, Adm., PO Box 10, Raymore S0A 3J0 – 306/746-2100, Fax: 306/746-4314 |
| Redvers † | 965 | Souris-Moose Mountain | Cannington | Janice Burnett, Adm., PO Box 249, Redvers S0C 2H0 – 306/452-3533, Fax: 306/452-3701 |

Cities in CAPITALS; Towns marked †; Villages marked (V); Northern Villages marked (NV); Resort Villages not listed. An in-depth listing for municipalities marked with * appears in Part 2 (check Index for page numbers).

| MUNICIPALITY | 1996 POP. | FEDERAL ELECTORAL DISTRICT | PROVINCIAL ELECTORAL DISTRICT | CONTACT PERSON WITH ADDRESS, PHONE & FAX |
|---|---|---|---|---|
| *REGINA | 180,400 | Palliser; Qu'Appelle; Regina-Lumsden-Lake Centre; Wascana | Regina Centre; Regina Coronation Park; Regina Dewdney; Regina Elphinstone; Regina Lakeview; Regina Northeast; Regina Qu'Appelle Valley; Regina Sherwood; Regina South; Regina Victoria; Regina Wascana Plains | Randy Markewich, City Clerk, PO Box 1790, Regina S4P 3C8 – 306/777-7262, Fax: 306/777-6809, URL: http://www.cityregina.com |
| Regina Beach † | 984 | Regina-Lumsden-Lake Centre | Arm River | Pearl Peters, Adm., PO Box 10, Regina Beach S0G 4C0 – 306/729-2202, Fax: 306/729-3411 |
| Rhein (V) | 197 | Yorkton-Melville | Saltcoats | Linda Napady, Clerk, PO Box 233, Rhein S0A 3K0 – 306/273-2155, Fax: 306/273-2155 |
| Richard (V) | 17 | Wanuskewin | Redberry Lake | Ed A. Sargent, Clerk, 1541 - 94 St., North Battleford S9A 0E6 – 306/446-4475, Fax: 306/446-4475 |
| Richmound (V) | 203 | Cypress Hills-Grasslands | Cypress Hills | Shelly Dirk, Adm., PO Box 29, Richmound S0N 2E0 – 306/669-2166 |
| Ridgedale (V) | 104 | Prince Albert | Melfort-Tisdale | Bev Sochaski, Clerk, PO Box 27, Ridgedale S0E 1L0 – 306/277-2002 |
| Riverhurst (V) | 158 | Cypress Hills-Grasslands | Arm River | Jo-ann Shooter, Clerk, PO Box 116, Riverhurst S0H 3P0 – 306/353-2220 |
| Robsart (V) | 19 | Cypress Hills-Grasslands | Cypress Hills | W.D. Olmsted, Clerk, PO Box 119, Robsart S0N 2G0 |
| Rocanville † | 875 | Souris-Moose Mountain | Moosomin | Mel Strong, Adm., PO Box 265, Rocanville S0A 3L0 – 306/645-2022, Fax: 306/645-4492 |
| Roche Percée (V) | 149 | Souris-Moose Mountain | Estevan | Charlotte Wrigley, Clerk, PO Box 237, Bienfait S0C 0M0 – 306/634-4661 |
| Rockglen † | 481 | Cypress Hills-Grasslands | Wood River | Diane Griffin, Adm., PO Box 267, Rockglen S0H 3R0 – 306/476-2144, Fax: 306/476-2339 |
| Rockhaven (V) | 33 | Battlefords-Lloydminster | Battleford-Cut Knife | Louise Denton, Clerk, PO Box 9, Rockhaven S0M 2R0 – 306/398-2734, Fax: 306/398-2868 |
| Rose Valley † | 406 | Saskatoon-Humboldt | Kelvington-Wadena | Marvin H. Holm, Adm., PO Box 460, Rose Valley S0E 1M0 – 306/322-2232, Fax: 306/322-4461 |
| Rosetown † | 2,496 | Saskatoon-Rosetown-Biggar | Rosetown-Biggar | Gary W. Crowder, Adm., PO Box 398, Rosetown S0L 2V0 – 306/882-2214, Fax: 306/882-3166 |
| Rosthern † | 1,564 | Wanuskewin | Rosthern | Brenda Kereluke, Adm., PO Box 416, Rosthern S0K 3R0 – 306/232-4826, Fax: 306/232-5638 |
| Rouleau † | 449 | Palliser | Thunder Creek | Elizabeth Busby, Adm., PO Box 250, Rouleau S0G 4H0 – 306/776-2270, Fax: 306/776-2482 |
| Ruddell (V) | 24 | Wanuskewin | Redberry Lake | E. Lynne Tolley, Adm., PO Box 7, Ruddell S0M 2S0 – 306/389-2051, Fax: 306/389-2051 |
| Rush Lake (V) | 71 | Cypress Hills-Grasslands | Thunder Creek | Adeline Steinley, Clerk, PO Box 126, Rush Lake S0H 3S0 – 306/784-3504 |
| Ruthilda (V) | 14 | Battlefords-Lloydminster | Rosetown-Biggar | Anita Gilles, Clerk, PO Box 90, Ruthilda S0K 3S0 – 306/932-4426 |
| St. Benedict (V) | 119 | Saskatoon-Humboldt | Humboldt | Joan Martin, Clerk, PO Box 99, St. Benedict S0K 3T0 – 306/289-2072, Fax: 306/289-2022 |
| St. Brieux (V) | 507 | Saskatoon-Humboldt | Humboldt | Gailene Gallais, Adm., PO Box 280, St. Brieux S0K 3V0 – 306/275-2257, Fax: 306/275-4949 |
| St. George's Hill (NV) | 85 | Churchill River | Athabasca | Edward Lalonde, Clerk, General Delivery, Dillon S0M 0S0 – 306/282-4408, Fax: 306/282-2002 |
| St. Gregor (V) | 128 | Saskatoon-Humboldt | Kelvington-Wadena | Ann-Marie Block, Clerk, PO Box 19, St. Gregor S0K 3X0 – 306/366-2141, Fax: 306/366-2032 |
| St. Louis (V) | 437 | Saskatoon-Humboldt | Humboldt | Rita Ferland, Adm., PO Box 99, St. Louis S0J 2C0 – 306/422-8471 |
| St. Victor (V) | 47 | Cypress Hills-Grasslands | Wood River | Evelyn Ducharme, Clerk, PO Box 25, St. Victor S0H 3T0 – 306/642-3257 |
| St. Walburg † | 685 | Battlefords-Lloydminster | Meadow Lake | Muriel G. Rosser-Swift, Adm., PO Box 368, St. Walburg S0M 2T0 – 306/248-3232, Fax: 306/248-3484 |
| Saltcoats † | 531 | Yorkton-Melville | Saltcoats | Joyce Morgan, Clerk, PO Box 120, Saltcoats S0A 3R0 – 306/744-2212, Fax: 306/744-2212 |
| Salvador (V) | 42 | Battlefords-Lloydminster | kindersley | Leona Sieben, Clerk, PO Box 10, Salvador S0L 2W0 – 306/372-4757 |
| Sandy Bay (NV) | 959 | Churchill River | Cumberland | Elwood H. Hennings, Adm., PO Box 130, Sandy Bay S0P 0G0 – 306/754-2165, 2181, Fax: 306/754-2157 |

Cities in CAPITALS; Towns marked †; Villages marked (V); Northern Villages marked (NV); Resort Villages not listed. An in-depth listing for municipalities marked with * appears in Part 2 (check Index for page numbers).

| MUNICIPALITY | 1996 POP. | FEDERAL ELECTORAL DISTRICT | PROVINCIAL ELECTORAL DISTRICT | CONTACT PERSON WITH ADDRESS, PHONE & FAX |
|---|---|---|---|---|
| *SASKATOON | 193,647 | Blackstrap; Saskatoon-Humboldt; Saskatoon-Rosetown-Biggar; Wanuskewin | Saskatoon Eastview; Saskatoon Fairview; Saskatoon Greystone; Saskatoon Idylwyld; Saskatoon Meewasin; Saskatoon Mount Royal; Saskatoon Northwest; Saskatoon Nutana; Saskatoon Riversdale; Saskatoon Southest; Saskatoon Sutherland | Janice Mann, City Clerk, City Hall, 222 - 3 Ave. North, Saskatoon S7K 0J5 – 306/975-3240, Fax: 306/975-2782 |
| Sceptre (V) | 154 | Cypress Hills-Grasslands | Cypress Hills | Sherry Egeland, Clerk, PO Box 128, Sceptre S0N 2H0 – 306/623-4244, Fax: 306/623-4229 |
| Scott † | 118 | Battlefords-Lloydminster | Kindersley | Linda F. Nielsen, Clerk, PO Box 96, Scott S0K 4A0 – 306/247-2100 |
| Sedley (V) | 305 | Wascana | Indian Head-Milestone | Helen Weinberger, Clerk, PO Box 130, Sedley S0G 4K0 – 306/885-2133, Fax: 306/885-2133 |
| Semans (V) | 315 | Regina-Lumsden-Lake Centre | Watrous | Sharon Church, Adm., PO Box 113, Semans S0A 3S0 – 306/524-2144, Fax: 306/524-2145 |
| Senlac (V) | 78 | Battlefords-Lloydminster | Wilkie | Thomas J. Forbes, Adm., PO Box 93, Senlac S0L 2Y0 – 306/228-4330 |
| Shackleton (V) | 10 | Cypress Hills-Grasslands | Cypress Hills | Marjorie A. Cator, Clerk, PO Box 7, Shackleton S0N 2L0 – 306/587-2910 |
| Shamrock (V) | 30 | Cypress Hills-Grasslands | Thunder Creek | Cathy Marchessault, Clerk, PO Box 119, Shamrock S0H 3W0 – 306/648-2736 |
| Shaunavon † | 1,857 | Cypress Hills-Grasslands | Wood River | Charmaine Bernath, Adm., PO Box 820, Shaunavon S0N 2M0 – 306/297-2605, Fax: 306/297-2608 |
| Sheho (V) | 181 | Yorkton-Melville | Canora-Pelly | Pamela Hawreluik, Clerk, PO Box 130, Sheho S0A 3T0 – 306/849-2044 |
| Shell Lake (V) | 172 | Churchill River | Shellbrook-Spiritwood | Brian C. Fisher, Clerk, PO Box 280, Shell Lake S0J 2G0 – 306/427-2272, Fax: 306/427-2272 |
| Shellbrook † | 1,234 | Prince Albert | Shellbrook-Spiritwood | Kenneth G. Danger, Adm., PO Box 40, Shellbrook S0J 2E0 – 306/747-2177, Fax: 306/747-3111 |
| Silton (V) | 86 | Regina-Lumsden-Lake Centre | Last Mountain-Touchwood | Maxine Flotre, Clerk, PO Box 1, Silton S0G 4L0 – 306/731-3222 |
| Simpson (V) | 208 | Regina-Lumsden-Lake Centre | Watrous | Donn Bergsveinson, Adm., PO Box 10, Simpson S0G 4M0 – 306/836-2020, Fax: 306/836-4460 |
| Sintaluta † | 189 | Qu'Appelle | Indian Head-Milestone | Ann B. Dolter, Clerk, PO Box 150, Sintaluta S0G 4N0 – 306/727-2100 (YD |
| Smeaton (V) | 192 | Churchill River | Saskatchewan Rivers | Diana M. Jensen, Clerk, PO Box 70, Smeaton S0J 2J0 – 306/426-2044, Fax: 306/426-2291 |
| Smiley (V) | 68 | Battlefords-Lloydminster | Kindersley | Don M. Fizell, Clerk, PO Box 90, Smiley S0L 2Z0 – 306/838-2020, Fax: 306/838-4343 |
| Southend Reindeer (NV) | 168 | Churchill River | Cumberland | Bella Cook, Clerk, General Delivery, Southend S0J 2L0 – 306/758-2044, Fax: 306/758-2044 |
| Southey † | 679 | Qu'Appelle | Last Mountain-Touchwood | Connie C. Hall, Adm., PO Box 248, Southey S0G 4P0 – 306/726-2202, Fax: 306/726-2202 |
| Sovereign (V) | 58 | Saskatoon-Rosetown-Biggar | Rosetown-Biggar | Lenora Anton, Clerk, PO Box 2, Sovereign S0L 3A0 – 306/882-3704 |
| Spalding (V) | 281 | Saskatoon-Humboldt | Kelvington-Wadena | Olinda Elsasser, Adm., PO Box 280, Spalding S0K 4C0 – 306/872-2276, Fax: 306/872-2100 |
| Speers (V) | 84 | Wanuskewin | Redberry Lake | Ronald Tanchak, Adm., PO Box 974, Speers S0M 2V0 – 306/246-2114, Fax: 306/246-2171 |
| Spiritwood † | 924 | Churchill River | Shellbrook-Spiritwood | Jack Klamot, Adm., PO Box 460, Spiritwood S0J 2M0 – 306/883-2161, Fax: 306/883-3212 |
| Springside † | 542 | Yorkton-Melville | Melville | Joan M. Popoff, Adm., PO Box 414, Springside S0A 3V0 – 306/792-2022 |
| Springwater (V) | 20 | Saskatoon-Rosetown-Biggar | Rosetwon-Biggar | Debbie Peterson, Clerk, PO Box 39, Springwater S0K 0M0 – 306/948-2958, Fax: 306/948-2335 |
| Spruce Lake (V) | 73 | Battlefords-Lloydminster | Meadow Lake | Debbie Behnke, Clerk, PO Box 13, Spruce Lake S0M 2W0 – 306/845-2291 |
| Spy Hill (V) | 264 | Yorkton-Melville | Saltcoats | Audrey Clark, Clerk, PO Box 69, Spy Hill S0A 3W0 – 306/534-2255 |
| Stanley Mission (NV) | 190 | Churchill River | Cumberland | Cliff Friesen, Clerk, General Delivery, Stanley Mission S0J 2P0 – 306/635-2222, Fax: 306/635-2145 |
| Star City † | 492 | Prince Albert | Melfort-Tisdale | Cathy Coleman, Clerk, PO Box 250, Star City S0E 1P0 – 306/863-2282, Fax: 306/863-2277 |
| Stenen (V) | 100 | Yorkton-Melville | Canora-Pelly | Donna Lee Olson, Clerk, PO Box 160, Stenen S0A 3X0 – 306/548-4334, Fax: 306/548-4334 |
| Stewart Valley (V) | 101 | Cypress Hills-Grasslands | Swift Current | Valerie L. Ferguson, Clerk, PO Box 10, Stewart Valley S0N 2P0 – 306/778-3611 |
| Stockholm (V) | 356 | Yorkton-Melville | Saltcoats | Mona M. Jacob, Adm., PO Box 265, Stockholm S0A 3Y0 – 306/793-2151 |

Cities in CAPITALS; Towns marked †; Villages marked (V); Northern Villages marked (NV); Resort Villages not listed. An in-depth listing for municipalities marked with * appears in Part 2 (check Index for page numbers).

| MUNICIPALITY | 1996 POP. | FEDERAL ELECTORAL DISTRICT | PROVINCIAL ELECTORAL DISTRICT | CONTACT PERSON WITH ADDRESS, PHONE & FAX |
|---|---|---|---|---|
| Stony Rapids (NV) | 233 | Churchill River | Athabasca | Joyce Roy, Clerk, General Delivery, Stony Rapids S0J 2R0 – 306/439-2173, Fax: 306/439-2098 |
| Stornoway (V) | 8 | Yorkton-Melville | Saltcoats | Peter Mandzuik, Clerk, PO Box 100, Stornoway S0A 3Z0 – 306/273-4718 |
| Storthoaks (V) | 119 | Souris-Moose Mountain | Cannington | Agnes Smith, Adm., PO Box 40, Storthoaks S0C 2K0 – 306/449-2210, Fax: 306/449-2210 |
| Stoughton † | 726 | Souris-Moose Mountain | Cannington | Gerald W. Figler, Adm., PO Box 397, Stoughton S0G 4T0 – 306/457-2413, Fax: 306/457-3162 |
| Strasbourg † | 760 | Regina-Lumsden-Lake Centre | Last Mountain-Touchwood | W. Doug Hunter, Adm., PO Box 369, Strasbourg S0G 4V0 – 306/725-3707, Fax: 306/725-3613 |
| Strongfield (V) | 49 | Blackstrap | Arm River | Yvonne Jess, Clerk, PO Box 87, Strongfield S0H 3Z0 – 306/857-4403 |
| Sturgis † | 684 | Yorkton-Melville | Canora-Pelly | Louise Baht, Adm., PO Box 520, Sturgis S0A 4A0 – 306/548-2108, Fax: 306/548-2948 |
| Success (V) | 49 | Cypress Hills-Grasslands | Cypress Hills | Rhonda Day, Clerk, PO Box 40, Success S0N 2R0 – 306/773-7909 |
| SWIFT CURRENT | 14,890 | Cypress Hills-Grasslands | Swift Current | Delores Cox, Clerk, PO Box 340, Swift Current S9H 3W1 – 306/778-2723, Fax: 306/773-6239 |
| Tantallon (V) | 137 | Yorkton-Melville;Souris-Moose Mountain | Saltcoats | Heather Godwin, Clerk, PO Box 70, Tantallon S0A 4B0 – 306/643-2112 |
| Tessier (V) | 29 | Saskatoon-Rosetown-Biggar | Rosetown-Biggar | Paula Richmond, Clerk, PO Box 34, Tessier S0L 3G0 – 306/656-4580 |
| Theodore (V) | 434 | Yorkton-Melville | Canora-Pelly | Ron Sebulsky, Clerk, PO Box 417, Theodore S0A 4C0 – 306/647-2315, Fax: 306/647-2476 |
| Timber Bay (NV) | 101 | Churchill River | Cumberland | Trudy McDowell, Clerk, General Delivery, Timber Bay S0J 2T0 – 306/663-5885, Fax: 306/663-5052 |
| Tisdale † | 2,966 | Prince Albert | Melfort-Tisdale | Merv T. Vey, Adm., PO Box 1090, Tisdale S0E 1T0 – 306/873-2681, Fax: 306/873-5700 |
| Togo (V) | 138 | Yorkton-Melville | Saltcoats | Rosemarie G. Hamell, Clerk, PO Box 100, Togo S0A 4E0 – 306/597-2114 |
| Tompkins (V) | 201 | Cypress Hills-Grasslands | Cypress Hills | Denise Willows, Clerk, PO Box 247, Tompkins S0N 2S0 – 306/622-2020, Fax: 306/622-2139 |
| Torquay (V) | 285 | Souris-Moose Mountain | Estevan | Linda M. Dugan, Clerk, PO Box 6, Torquay S0C 2L0 – 306/923-2172, Fax: 306/923-2172 |
| Tramping Lake (V) | 118 | Battlefords-Lloydminster | Kindersley | Rose Simon, Clerk, PO Box 157, Tramping Lake S0K 4H0 – 306/755-2002 |
| Tribune (V) | 49 | Souris-Moose Mountain | Estevan | Dallas Locken, Clerk, PO Box 61, Tribune S0C 2M0 – 306/456-2213, Fax: 306/456-2213 |
| Tugaske (V) | 132 | Regina-Lumsden-Lake Centre | Arm River | Daryl Dean, Adm., PO Box 159, Tugaske S0H 4B0 – 306/759-2211, Fax: 306/759-2249 |
| Turnor Lake (NV) | 198 | Churchill River | Athabasca | Victorina Montgrand, Clerk, General Delivery, Turnor Lake S0M 3E0 – 306/894-2080, 2023, Fax: 306/894-2138 |
| Turtleford † | 467 | Battlefords-Lloydminster | Lloydminster | Deanna Kahl-Lundberg, Adm., PO Box 38, Turtleford S0M 2Y0 – 306/845-2156, Fax: 306/845-3320 |
| Tuxford (V) | 102 | Regina-Lumsden-Lake Centre | Arm River | Reg E. McKee, Clerk, PO Box 28, Tuxford S0H 4C0 – 306/692-3390 |
| Unity † | 2,200 | Battlefords-Lloydminster | Battleford-Cut Knife | Jim Weninger, Adm., PO Box 1030, Unity S0K 4L0 – 306/228-2621, Fax: 306/228-4221 |
| Val Marie (V) | 157 | Cypress Hills-Grasslands | Wood River | Andre Parenteau, Clerk, PO Box 178, Val Marie S0N 2T0 – 306/298-2022, Fax: 306/298-2062 |
| Valparaiso (V) | 18 | Prince Albert | Melfort-Tisdale | Ann Campbell, Clerk, PO Box 473, Star City S0E 1P0 – 306/863-2522, Fax: 306/863-2255 |
| Vanguard (V) | 207 | Cypress Hills-Grasslands | Thunder Creek | Ronald W. Kehoe, Adm., PO Box 187, Vanguard S0N 2V0 – 306/582-2010, Fax: 306/582-4811 |
| Vanscoy (V) | 316 | Saskatoon-Rosetown-Biggar | Redberry Lake | Beatrice V. Thomas, Adm., PO Box 223, Vanscoy S0L 3J0 – 306/668-2008 |
| Vawn (V) | 49 | Battlefords-Lloydminster | Lloydminster | Sylvia Duhaime, Clerk, PO Box 22, Vawn S0M 2Z0 – 306/397-2885, Fax: 306/397-2213 |
| Veregin (V) | 90 | Yorkton-Melville | Canora-Pelly | Eva D. Moskal, Clerk, PO Box 160, Veregin S0A 4H0 – 306/542-4338 |
| Vibank (V) | 363 | Wascana | Indian Head-Milestone | Jeanette Schaeffer, Adm., PO Box 204, Vibank S0G 4Y0 – 306/762-2130, Fax: 306/762-4722 |
| Viceroy (V) | 64 | Souris-Moose Mountain | Weyburn-Big Muddy | Mervin A. Guillemin, Adm., PO Box 95, Viceroy S0H 4H0 – 306/268-4555, Fax: 306/268-4547 |
| Viscount (V) | 295 | Blackstrap | Watrous | Lloyd Wilkie, Clerk, PO Box 99, Viscount S0K 4M0 – 306/944-2199, Fax: 306/944-2199 |
| Vonda † | 289 | Saskatoon-Humboldt | Humboldt | Lionel Diederichs, Adm., PO Box 190, Vonda S0K 4N0 – 306/258-2035, Fax: 306/258-2035 |
| Wadena † | 1,477 | Saskatoon-Humboldt | Kelvington-Wadena | Michael Hotsko, Adm., PO Box 730, Wadena S0A 4J0 – 306/338-2145, Fax: 306/338-3804 |
| Wakaw † | 869 | Saskatoon-Humboldt | Humboldt | Sheri Schitka, Adm., PO Box 669, Wakaw S0K 4P0 – 306/233-4223, Fax: 306/233-5234 |

Cities in CAPITALS; Towns marked †; Villages marked (V); Northern Villages marked (NV); Resort Villages not listed. An in-depth listing for municipalities marked with * appears in Part 2 (check Index for page numbers).

| MUNICIPALITY | 1996 POP. | FEDERAL ELECTORAL DISTRICT | PROVINCIAL ELECTORAL DISTRICT | CONTACT PERSON WITH ADDRESS, PHONE & FAX |
|---|---|---|---|---|
| Waldeck (V) | 335 | Cypress Hills-Grasslands | Thunder Creek | Kathy Lang, Clerk, PO Box 97, Waldeck S0H 4J0 – 306/773-6275 |
| Waldheim † | 841 | Wanuskewin | Rosthern | D. Chris Adams, Adm., PO Box 460, Waldheim S0K 4R0 – 306/945-2161, Fax: 306/945-2360 |
| Waldron (V) | 24 | Yorkton-Melville | Melville | Karen Handke, Clerk, PO Box 87, Waldron S0A 4K0 – 306/728-5366 |
| Wapella † | 387 | Souris-Moose Mountain | Moosomin | Nancy Campbell, Clerk, PO Box 189, Wapella S0G 4Z0 – 306/532-4343, Fax: 306/532-4884 |
| Warman † | 2,839 | Wanuskewin | Rosthern | John Janeson, Adm., PO Box 340, Warman S0K 4S0 – 306/933-2133, Fax: 306/933-1987 |
| Waseca (V) | 153 | Battlefords-Lloydminster | Lloydminster | Rachael Gustafson, Clerk, PO Box 128, Waseca S0M 3A0 – 306/893-2211 |
| Watrous † | 1,860 | Blackstrap | Watrous | Willard Struck, Clerk, PO Box 730, Watrous S0K 4T0 – 306/946-3369, Fax: 306/946-2974 |
| Watson † | 837 | Saskatoon-Humboldt | Watrous | Jacqueline Lamarre, Adm., PO Box 276, Watson S0K 4V0 – 306/287-3224, Fax: 306/287-3442 |
| Wawota † | 620 | Souris-Moose Mountain | Cannington | Lynne Swanson, Adm., PO Box 58, Wawota S0G 5A0 – 306/739-2216, Fax: 306/739-2222 |
| Webb (V) | 42 | Cypress Hills-Grasslands | Cypress Hills | Don Haley, Adm., PO Box 100, Webb S0N 2X0 – 306/674-2230, Fax: 306/674-2324 |
| Weekes (V) | 84 | Yorkton-Melville | Kelvington-Wadena | Brenda Kipling, Clerk, PO Box 159, Weekes S0E 1V0 – 306/278-2800 |
| Weirdale (V) | 63 | Prince Albert | Saskatchewan Rivers | Elaine Krawec, Clerk, General Delivery, Weirdale S0J 2Z0 – 306/929-2329, Fax: 306/929-3104 |
| Weldon (V) | 225 | Prince Albert | Saskatchewan Rivers | Fanuel Lima, Adm., PO Box 190, Weldon S0J 3A0 – 306/887-2070 |
| Welwyn (V) | 146 | Souris-Moose Mountain | Moosomin | Elaine Olsen, Adm., PO Box 118, Welwyn S0A 4L0 – 306/733-2077, Fax: 306/435-4313 |
| West Bend (V) | 7 | Yorkton-Melville | Canora-Pelly | Valerie Dlugan, Clerk, PO Box 11, West Bend S0A 4M0 – 306/675-4554 |
| Weyakwin (NV) | 171 | Churchill River | Cumberland | Jemima Nelson, Clerk, PO Box 295, Weyakwin S0J 1W0 – 306/663-5820, Fax: 306/663-5112 |
| WEYBURN | 9,723 | Souris-Moose Mountain | Weyburn-Big Muddy | Fred C. Martyn, City Clerk, PO Box 370, Weyburn S4H 2K6 – 306/848-3209, Fax: 306/842-2001 |
| White City (V) | 905 | Qu'Appelle | Regina Wascana Plains | Darlene Woloshyn, Clerk, PO Box 220, White City S0G 5B0 – 306/781-2355, Fax: 306/781-2194 |
| White Fox (V) | 402 | Churchill River | Carrot River Valley | Wendy Nycholat, Adm., PO Box 38, White Fox S0J 3B0 – 306/276-2106, Fax: 306/276-2131 |
| Whitewood † | 985 | Souris-Moose Mountain | Moosomin | John Billington, Adm., PO Box 129, Whitewood S0G 5C0 – 306/735-2210, Fax: 306/735-2262 |
| Wilcox (V) | 311 | Palliser | Indian Head-Milestone | K.S. Ritchie, Adm., PO Box 130, Wilcox S0G 5E0 – 306/732-2030, Fax: 306/732-4495 |
| Wilkie † | 1,364 | Battlefords-Lloydminster | Battleford-Cut Knife | Julie Brooks, Adm., PO Box 580, Wilkie S0K 4W0 – 306/843-2692, Fax: 306/843-3151 |
| Willow Bunch † | 431 | Cypress Hills-Grasslands | Wood River | Collette Walter, Clerk, PO Box 189, Willow Bunch S0H 4K0 – 306/473-2450, Fax: 306/473-2450 |
| Willowbrook (V) | 41 | Yorkton-Melville | Melville | Christine Kellar, Adm., PO Box 60, Willowbrook S0A 4P0 – 306/783-6751 |
| Windthorst (V) | 239 | Souris-Moose Mountain | Moosomin | Martha J. Hassler, Clerk, PO Box 98, Windthorst S0G 5G0 – 306/224-2033 |
| Wiseton (V) | 125 | Saskatoon-Rosetown-Biggar | Rosetown-Biggar | Sandra E. Elliott, Clerk, PO Box 160, Wiseton S0L 3M0 – 306/357-2022 |
| Wishart (V) | 153 | Qu'Appelle | Last Mountain-Touchwood | Jim Turanich, Adm., PO Box 160, Wishart S0A 4R0 – 306/576-2252, Fax: 306/576-2132 |
| Wollaston Lake (NV) | 229 | Churchill River | Cumberland | Vacant, Clerk, General Delivery, Wollaston Lake S0J 3C0 – 306/633-2193, Fax: 306/633-2020 |
| Wolseley † | 821 | Qu'Appelle | Moosomin | Norman R. Hicks, Clerk, PO Box 310, Wolseley S0G 5H0 – 306/698-2477, Fax: 306/698-2953 |
| Wood Mountain (V) | 31 | Cypress Hills-Grasslands | Wood River | Jocelyn Beauregard, Clerk, PO Box 89, Wood Mountain S0H 4L0 – 306/266-2002, Fax: 306/266-2020 |
| Woodrow (V) | 17 | Cypress Hills-Grasslands | Wood River | Pauline Crone, Clerk, PO Box 68, Woodrow S0H 4M0 |
| Wroxton (V) | 49 | Yorkton-Melville | Saltcoats | Linda Napady, Clerk, PO Box 160, Wroxton S0A 4S0 – 306/742-4557 |
| Wynyard † | 1,954 | Qu'Appelle | Last Mountain-Touchwood | Sheila Hitchings, Adm., PO Box 220, Wynyard S0A 4T0 – 306/554-2123, Fax: 306/554-3224 |
| Yarbo (V) | 127 | Yorkton-Melville | Saltcoats | Joan Kerr, Clerk, PO Box 96, Yarbo S0A 0X0 – 306/745-3532 |
| Yellow Creek (V) | 73 | Saskatoon-Humboldt | Melfort-Tisdale | Sally Wojcichowsky, Adm., PO Box 219, Yellow Creek S0K 4X0 – 306/279-2191 |
| Yellow Grass † | 488 | Souris-Moose Mountain | Indian Head-Milestone | Gail Blaney, Adm., PO Box 270, Yellow Grass S0G 5J0 – 306/465-2400, Fax: 306/465-2802 |
| YORKTON | 15,154 | Yorkton-Melville | Yorkton | Laurie-Anne Rusnak, Clerk, PO Box 400, Yorkton S3N 2W3 – 306/786-1700, Fax: 306/786-6880 |
| Young (V) | 320 | Blackstrap | Watrous | Jean Jack, Clerk, PO Box 359, Young S0K 4Y0 – 306/259-2242 |

Cities in CAPITALS; Towns marked †; Villages marked (V); Northern Villages marked (NV); Resort Villages not listed. An in-depth listing for municipalities marked with * appears in Part 2 (check Index for page numbers).

| MUNICIPALITY | 1996 POP. | FEDERAL ELECTORAL DISTRICT | PROVINCIAL ELECTORAL DISTRICT | CONTACT PERSON WITH ADDRESS, PHONE & FAX |
|---|---|---|---|---|
| Zealandia † | 117 | Saskatoon-Rosetown-Biggar | Rosetown-Biggar | Nora Hoffman, Clerk, PO Box 52, Zealandia S0L 3N0 – 306/882-3825 |
| Zelma (V) | 43 | Blackstrap | Watrous | Maxine Fischer, Clerk, Zelma GMB #14, Allan S0K 0C0 – 306/257-3927, Fax: 306/257-4155 |
| Zenon Park (V) | 259 | Prince Albert | Melfort-Tisdale | Lisa LeBlanc, Clerk, PO Box 278, Zenon Park S0E 1W0 – 306/767-2233, Fax: 306/767-2226 |

1. The population figure reflects total population for Alberta & Saskatchewan populations combined.

## RURAL MUNICIPALITIES IN SASKATCHEWAN

| MUNICIPALITY | 1996 POP. | CONTACT PERSON WITH ADDRESS & PHONE |
|---|---|---|
| Aberdeen No. 373 | 758 | Mary Glenister, Adm., PO Box 40, Aberdeen S0K 0A0 – 306/253-4312, Fax: 306/253-4445 |
| Abernethy No. 186 | 497 | Evan G. Behrns, Adm., PO Box 183, Abernethy S0A 0A0 – 306/333-2044, Fax: 306/333-2285 |
| Antelope Park No. 322 | 179 | Beverly A. Dahl, Adm., PO Box 70, Marengo S0L 2K0 – 306/968-2922, Fax: 306/968-2278 |
| Antler No. 61 | 664 | John H.J. Eberl, Adm., PO Box 70, Redvers S0C 2H0 – 306/452-3263, Fax: 306/452-3518 |
| Arborfield No. 456 | 498 | Allan Frisky, Adm., PO Box 280, Arborfield S0E 0A0 – 306/769-8533, Fax: 306/769-8301 |
| Argyle No. 1 | 301 | Valerie A. Olney, Adm., PO Box 120, Gainsborough S0C 0Z0 – 306/685-2010, Fax: 306/685-2161 |
| Arlington No. 79 | 335 | Richard E. Goulet, Adm., PO Box 1115, Shaunavon S0N 2M0 – 306/297-2108, Fax: 306/297-2108 |
| Arm River No. 252 | 304 | Norman Sagen, Adm., PO Box 250, Davidson S0G 1A0 – 306/567-3103, Fax: 306/567-3266 |
| Auvergne No. 76 | 430 | Linda J. Linnen, Adm., PO Box 60, Ponteix S0N 1Z0 – 306/625-3210, Fax: 306/625-3681 |
| Baildon No. 131 | 694 | Debra A. Matlou, Adm., PO Box 1902, Moose Jaw S6H 7N6 – 306/693-2166, Fax: 306/693-2166 |
| Barrier Valley No. 397 | 615 | Fern Lucas, Adm., PO Box 246, Archerwill S0E 0B0 – 306/323-2101, Fax: 306/323-2101 |
| Battle River No. 438 | 854 | Betty Johnson, Adm., PO Box 148, Battleford S0M 0E0 – 306/937-2235, Fax: 306/937-2235 |
| Bayne No. 371 | 615 | Lonnie Sowa, Adm., PO Box 130, Bruno S0K 0S0 – 306/369-2511, Fax: 306/369-2511 |
| Beaver River No. 622 | 1,090 | Debra Johnson, Adm., PO Box 129, Pierceland S0M 2K0 – 306/839-2060, Fax: 306/839-2178 |
| Bengough No. 40 | 405 | Holly Dahl, Adm., PO Box 429, Bengough S0C 0K0 – 306/268-2055, Fax: 306/268-2055 |
| Benson No. 35 | 435 | Laureen Keating, Adm., PO Box 69, Benson S0C 0L0 – 306/634-9410, Fax: 306/634-9410 |
| Big Arm No. 251 | 299 | Walter Krawchuk, Adm., PO Box 10, Stalwart S0G 4R0 – 306/963-2402 |
| Big Quill No. 308 | 748 | Glenn Thompson, Adm., PO Box 898, Wynyard S0A 4T0 – 306/554-2335, Fax: 306/554-3935 |
| Big River No. 555 | 872 | Wendy Gowda Drummond, Adm., PO Box 219, Big River S0J 0E0 – 306/469-2323, Fax: 306/469-2323 |
| Big Stick No. 141 | 215 | Quinton Jacksteit, Adm., PO Box 9, Golden Prairie S0N 0Y0 – 306/662-2883, Fax: 306/662-2883 |
| Biggar No. 347 | 1,022 | Adele McLeod, Adm., PO Box 280, Biggar S0K 0M0 – 306/948-2422, Fax: 306/948-2250 |
| Birch Hills No. 460 | 775 | Sandra Barber, Adm., PO Box 369, Birch Hills S0J 0G0 – 306/749-2233, Fax: 306/749-2220 |
| Bjorkdale No. 426 | 1,111 | Spencer H. Abbs, Adm., PO Box 10, Crooked River S0E 0R0 – 306/873-2470, Fax: 306/873-2470 |
| Blaine Lake No. 434 | 374 | James V. Burak, Adm., PO Box 38, Blaine Lake S0J 0J0 – 306/497-2282, Fax: 306/497-2511 |
| Blucher No. 343 | 1,155 | Robert Thurmeier, Adm., PO Box 100, Bradwell S0K 0P0 – 306/257-3344, Fax: 306/257-3303 |
| Bone Creek No. 108 | 458 | Rhonda Bellefeuille, Adm., PO Box 459, Shaunavon S0N 2M0 – 306/297-2570, Fax: 306/297-2570 |
| Bratt's Lake No. 129 | 371 | Kevin S. Ritchie, Adm., PO Box 130, Wilcox S0G 5E0 – 306/732-2030, Fax: 306/732-4495 |
| Britannia No. 502 | 1,358 | B. Bonnie Mills-Midgley, Adm., PO Box 661, Lloydminster S9V 0Y7 – 306/825-2610, Fax: 306/825-2610 |
| Brock No. 64 | 356 | Bruce F. Waddell, Adm., PO Box 247, Kisbey S0C 1L0 – 306/462-2010, Fax: 306/462-2016 |
| Brokenshell No. 68 | 340 | Lorelei Zdunich, Adm., PO Box 10, Trossachs S0C 2N0 – 306/842-5820, Fax: 306/842-7530 |
| Browning No. 34 | 552 | Greg Wallin, Adm., PO Box 40, Lampman S0C 1N0 – 306/487-2444, Fax: 306/487-2496 |
| Buchanan No. 304 | 546 | Karren Statchuk, Adm., PO Box 10, Buchanan S0A 0J0 – 306/592-2055 |
| Buckland No. 491 | 3,444 | C. Lorne Marshall, Adm., 99 River St. E., Prince Albert S6V 0A1 – 306/763-2585, Fax: 306/763-6369 |
| Buffalo No. 409 | 473 | Jeanette Nicholson, Adm., PO Box 100, Wilkie S0K 4W0 – 306/843-2301, Fax: 306/843-2455 |
| Calder No. 241 | 542 | Rona Seidle, Adm., PO Box 10, Wroxton S0A 4S0 – 306/742-4233, Fax: 306/742-4559 |
| Caledonia No. 99 | 409 | Ernest P. Audette, Adm., PO Box 328, Milestone S0G 3L0 – 306/436-2050, Fax: 306/436-2051 |
| Cambria No. 6 | 344 | Dale Shauf, Adm., PO Box 210, Torquay S0C 2L0 – 306/923-2000 |
| Cana No. 214 | 1,014 | John B. Chesney, Adm., PO Box 550, Melville S0A 2P0 – 306/728-5645, Fax: 306/728-3807 |
| Canaan No. 225 | 171 | Edna A. Laturnus, Adm., PO Box 99, Lucky Lake S0L 1Z0 – 306/858-2234, Fax: 306/858-2234 |
| Canwood No. 494 | 1,718 | Hugh Otterson, Adm., PO Box 10, Canwood S0J 0K0 – 306/468-2014, Fax: 306/468-2666 |
| Carmichael No. 109 | 462 | Collette Jones, Adm., PO Box 420, Gull Lake S0N 1A0 – 306/672-3501, Fax: 306/672-3879 |
| Caron No. 162 | 534 | Sandra Sparkes, Adm., PO Box 85, Caron S0H 0R0 – 306/756-2353, Fax: 306/756-2250 |
| Chaplin No. 164 | 198 | Doris Bauck, Adm., PO Box 60, Chaplin S0H 0V0 – 306/395-2244, Fax: 306/395-2767 |
| Chester No. 125 | 521 | James R. Hoff, Adm., PO Box 180, Glenavon S0G 1Y0 – 306/429-2110, Fax: 306/429-2260 |
| Chesterfield No. 261 | 598 | Garry Ritsco, Adm., PO Box 70, Eatonia S0L 0Y0 – 306/967-2222, Fax: 306/967-2424 |
| Churchbridge No. 211 | 876 | Casmer P. Chyz, Adm., PO Box 211, Churchbridge S0A 0M0 – 306/896-2522, Fax: 306/896-2743 |
| Clayton No. 333 | 886 | Douglas W. Ferder, Adm., PO Box 220, Hyas S0A 1K0 – 306/594-2832, Fax: 306/594-2832 |
| Clinworth No. 230 | 331 | Naida Dillman, Adm., PO Box 120, Sceptre S0N 2H0 – 306/623-4229, Fax: 306/623-4229 |
| Coalfields No. 4 | 419 | Vera Abrams, Adm., PO Box 190, Bienfait S0C 0M0 – 306/388-2323, Fax: 306/388-2330 |
| Colonsay No. 342 | 322 | Katherine Templeman, Adm., PO Box 130, Colonsay S0K 0Z0 – 306/255-2233, Fax: 306/255-2291 |
| Connaught No. 457 | 815 | Keith Hummel, Adm., PO Box 25, Tisdale S0E 1T0 – 306/873-2657, Fax: 306/873-4442 |
| Corman Park No. 344 | 7,152 | Fred J. Sutter, Adm., 111 Pinehouse Dr., Saskatoon S7K 5W1 – 306/242-9303, Fax: 306/242-6965 |
| Cote No. 271 | 687 | Kim McIvor, Adm., PO Box 669, Kamsack S0A 1S0 – 306/542-2121, Fax: 306/542-2121 |
| Coteau No. 255 | 475 | Murray Cook, Adm., PO Box 30, Birsay S0L 0G0 – 306/573-2047, Fax: 306/573-2111 |
| Coulee No. 136 | 584 | Connie Sorenson, Adm., 1680 Chaplin St. East, Swift Current S9H 1K8 – 306/773-5420, Fax: 306/773-1859 |
| Craik No. 222 | 351 | Tim Fox, Adm., PO Box 420, Craik S0G 0V0 – 306/734-2242, Fax: 306/734-2688 |
| Cupar No. 218 | 576 | Loretta Young, Adm., PO Box 400, Cupar S0G 0Y0 – 306/723-4726, Fax: 306/723-4726 |
| Cut Knife No. 439 | 486 | Donald McCallum, Adm., PO Box 70, Cut Knife S0M 0N0 – 306/398-2353, Fax: 306/398-2839 |
| Cymri No. 36 | 517 | Curtis. Herzberg, Adm., PO Box 238, Midale S0C 1S0 – 306/458-2244, Fax: 306/458-2699 |
| Deer Forks No. 232 | 242 | Rodney J. Quinton, Adm., PO Box 250, Burstall S0N 0H0 – 306/679-2000, Fax: 306/679-2275 |
| Douglas No. 436 | 478 | Ronald A. Tanchak, Adm., PO Box 964, Speers S0M 2V0 – 306/246-2171, Fax: 306/246-2171 |

| MUNICIPALITY | 1996 POP. | CONTACT PERSON WITH ADDRESS & PHONE |
|---|---|---|
| Duck Lake No. 463 | 953 | Lois McCormick, Adm., PO Box 250, Duck Lake S0K 1J0 – 306/467-2011, Fax: 306/476-4423 |
| Dufferin No. 190 | 582 | Rick Hicks, Adm., PO Box 67, Bethune S0G 0H0 – 306/638-3112, Fax: 306/638-3112 |
| Dundurn No. 314 | 555 | Violet P. Barna, Adm., PO Box 159, Dundurn S0K 1K0 – 306/492-2132, Fax: 306/492-2132 |
| Eagle Creek No. 376 | 601 | Lloyd Cross, Adm., PO Box 100, Arelee S0K 0H0 – 306/237-4424, Fax: 306/237-4294 |
| Edenwold No. 158 | 2,738 | Donna L. Strudwick, Adm., PO Box 10, Balgonie S0G 0E0 – 306/771-2522, Fax: 306/771-2631 |
| Elcapo No. 154 | 663 | Mervin J. Schmidt, Adm., PO Box 668, Broadview S0G 0K0 – 306/696-2703, Fax: 306/696-2474 |
| Eldon No. 471 | 838 | Ken E. Reiter, Adm., PO Box 130, Maidstone S0M 1M0 – 306/893-2391, Fax: 306/893-4644 |
| Elfros No. 307 | 615 | Mary Corby, Adm., PO Box 40, Elfros S0A 0V0 – 306/328-2011, Fax: 306/328-4490 |
| Elmsthorpe No. 100 | 328 | Lawrence Harty, Adm., PO Box 240, Avonlea S0H 0C0 – 306/868-2011, Fax: 306/868-2011 |
| Emerald No. 277 | 644 | Jim Turanich, Adm., PO Box 160, Wishart S0A 4R0 – 306/576-2002, Fax: 306/576-2132 |
| Enfield No. 194 | 414 | Joe Van Leuken, Adm., PO Box 70, Central Butte S0H 0T0 – 306/796-2025, Fax: 306/796-2025 |
| Enniskillen No. 3 | 523 | Bill J. Ringguth, Adm., PO Box 179, Oxbow S0C 2B0 – 306/483-2277, Fax: 306/483-2277 |
| Enterprise No. 142 | 265 | Darryl Altman, Adm., PO Box 150, Richmound S0N 2E0 – 306/669-2000, Fax: 306/669-2052 |
| Estevan No. 5 | 1,078 | Dale Malmgren, Adm., 721 Henry St., Estevan S4A 2B7 – 306/634-2222, Fax: 306/634-2223 |
| Excel No. 71 | 563 | Mervin Guillemin, Adm., PO Box 100, Viceroy S0H 4H0 – 306/268-4555, Fax: 306/268-4547 |
| Excelsior No. 166 | 892 | Christina Patoine, Adm., PO Box 180, Rush Lake S0H 3S0 – 306/784-3121, Fax: 306/784-3121 |
| Eye Hill No. 382 | 691 | Calvin Giggs, Adm., PO Box 69, Macklin S0L 2C0 – 306/753-2075, Fax: 306/753-3234 |
| Eyebrow No. 193 | 318 | Herbert A. White, Adm., PO Box 99, Eyebrow S0H 1L0 – 306/759-2101 |
| Fertile Belt No. 183 | 962 | B. Darlene Maier, Adm., PO Box 190, Stockholm S0A 3Y0 – 306/793-2061, Fax: 306/793-2063 |
| Fertile Valley No. 285 | 610 | Donna G. Haug, Adm., PO Box 70, Conquest S0L 0L0 – 306/856-2037, Fax: 306/856-2211 |
| Fillmore No. 96 | 344 | Allan Dionne, Adm., PO Box 130, Fillmore S0G 1N0 – 306/722-3251, Fax: 306/722-3775 |
| Fish Creek No. 402 | 380 | Richard W. Kindrachuk, Adm., PO Box 160, Wakaw S0K 4P0 – 306/233-4412, Fax: 306/233-4412 |
| Flett's Springs No. 429 | 822 | Clinton W. Tetarenko, Adm., PO Box 160, Melfort S0E 1A0 – 306/752-3606, Fax: 306/752-3882 |
| Foam Lake No. 276 | 838 | Ron Kostiuk, Adm., PO Box 490, Foam Lake S0A 1A0 – 306/272-3334, Fax: 306/272-4722 |
| Fox Valley No. 171 | 387 | Daniel S. Buye, Adm., PO Box 190, Fox Valley S0N 0V0 – 306/666-2055, Fax: 306/666-2074 |
| Francis No. 127 | 805 | Claude A. Caron, Adm., PO Box 36, Francis S0G 1V0 – 306/245-3256, Fax: 306/245-3203 |
| Frenchman Butte No. 501 | 1,331 | Isabelle Jasper, Adm., PO Box 180, Paradise Hill S0M 2G0 – 306/344-2034, Fax: 306/344-4434 |
| Frontier No. 19 | 333 | Raymond Dubé, Adm., PO Box 30, Frontier S0N 0W0 – 306/296-2030, Fax: 306/296-2175 |
| Garden River No. 490 | 709 | Francine Kenzle, Adm., PO Box 70, Meath Park S0J 1T0 – 306/929-2020, Fax: 306/929-2281 |
| Garry No. 245 | 565 | Jerry T. Kuziak, Adm., PO Box 10, Jedburgh S0A 1R0 – 306/647-2450, Fax: 306/647-2450 |
| Glen Bain No. 105 | 388 | Dianne Debert, Adm., PO Box 39, Glen Bain S0N 0X0 – 306/264-3607, Fax: 306/264-3607 |
| Glen McPherson No. 46 | 172 | Michael E. Sherven, Adm., PO Box 277, Mankota S0H 2W0 – 306/478-2323, Fax: 306/478-2606 |
| Glenside No. 377 | 394 | Pamela Fareniak, Adm., PO Box 1084, Biggar S0K 0M0 – 306/948-3681, Fax: 306/948-3684 |
| Golden West No. 95 | 547 | Edward A. Mish, Adm., PO Box 70, Corning S0G 0T0 – 306/224-4456, Fax: 306/224-4456 |
| Good Lake No. 274 | 722 | David W. Popowich, Adm., PO Box 896, Canora S0A 0L0 – 306/563-5244, Fax: 306/563-5244 |
| Grandview No. 349 | 480 | Patti Turk, Adm., PO Box 39, Kelfield S0K 2C0 – 306/932-4911, Fax: 306/932-4911 |
| Grant No. 372 | 490 | Lionel J. Diederichs, Adm., PO Box 190, Vonda S0K 4N0 – 306/258-2022, Fax: 306/258-2035 |
| Grass Lake No. 381 | 553 | Brenda M. Kasas, Adm., PO Box 40, Reward S0K 3N0 – 306/228-2988, Fax: 306/228-4188 |
| Grassy Creek No. 78 | 416 | Grace Potter, Adm., PO Box 400, Shaunavon S0N 2M0 – 306/297-2520 |
| Gravelbourg No. 104 | 491 | Shirley M. Parker, Adm., PO Box 510, Gravelbourg S0H 1X0 – 306/648-2412, Fax: 306/648-2603 |
| Grayson No. 184 | 653 | Eileen M. Parker, Adm., PO Box 69, Grayson S0A 1E0 – 306/794-2044, Fax: 306/794-4655 |
| Great Bend No. 405 | 542 | Ken Tanchak, Adm., PO Box 150, Borden S0K 0N0 – 306/997-2101, Fax: 306/997-2101 |
| Griffin No. 66 | 421 | Audrey L. Trombley, Adm., PO Box 70, Griffin S0C 1G0 – 306/842-6298, Fax: 306/842-6400 |
| Gull Lake No. 139 | 282 | Ida-Mae Leek, Adm., PO Box 180, Gull Lake S0N 1A0 – 306/672-4430, Fax: 306/672-3879 |
| Happy Valley No. 10 | 217 | Vernon R. Palmer, Adm., PO Box 39, Big Beaver S0H 0G0 – 306/267-4540, Fax: 306/267-2391 |
| Happyland No. 231 | 432 | Joseph C. Ries, Adm., PO Box 339, Leader S0N 1H0 – 306/628-3800, Fax: 306/628-4228 |
| Harris No. 316 | 276 | Jim Angus, Adm., PO Box 146, Harris S0L 1K0 – 306/656-2072, Fax: 306/656-2151 |
| Hart Butte No. 11 | 340 | Vernon Palmer, Adm., PO Box 210, Coronach S0H 0Z0 – 306/267-2005, Fax: 306/267-2391 |
| Hazel Dell No. 335 | 796 | Kathy L. Ritchie, Adm., PO Box 87, Okla S0A 2X0 – 306/325-4315, Fax: 306/352-4589 |
| Hazelwood No. 94 | 398 | Gary Vargo, Adm., PO Box 270, Kipling S0G 2S0 – 306/736-8121, Fax: 306/736-2496 |
| Heart's Hill No. 352 | 359 | Vern Gintaut, Adm., PO Box 458, Luseland S0L 2A0 – 306/372-4224, Fax: 306/372-4224 |
| Hillsborough No. 132 | 154 | James W. Nichols, Adm., #3, 54 Stadacona St. West, Moose Jaw S6H 1Z1 – 306/693-1329, Fax: 306/693-2810 |
| Hillsdale No. 440 | 615 | Dale M. Bryden, Adm., PO Box 280, Neilburg S0M 2C0 – 306/823-4321, Fax: 306/823-4477 |
| Hoodoo No. 401 | 676 | Lloyd Wedewer, Adm., PO Box 250, Cudworth S0K 1B0 – 306/256-3281, Fax: 306/256-7147 |
| Hudson Bay No. 394 | 1,577 | Linda Purves, Adm., PO Box 520, Hudson Bay S0E 0Y0 – 306/865-2691, Fax: 306/865-2857 |
| Humboldt No. 370 | 960 | Fred W. Saliken, Adm., PO Box 420, Humboldt S0K 2A0 – 306/682-2242, Fax: 306/682-3239 |
| Huron No. 223 | 263 | Daryl Dean, Adm., PO Box 159, Tugaske S0H 4B0 – 306/759-2211, Fax: 306/759-2249 |
| Indian Head No. 156 | 449 | Jody Crossman, Adm., PO Box 39, Indian Head S0G 2K0 – 306/695-3464, Fax: 306/695-3462 |
| Insinger No. 275 | 567 | Bettie Thompson, Adm., PO Box 179, Insinger S0A 1L0 – 306/647-2422, Fax: 306/647-2422 |
| Invergordon No. 430 | 724 | Barry Kuzyk, Adm., PO Box 40, Crystal Springs S0K 1A0 – 306/749-2852, Fax: 306/749-2499 |
| Invermay No. 305 | 514 | Greg Wolkowski, Adm., PO Box 130, Invermay S0A 1M0 – 306/593-2152, Fax: 306/593-2152 |
| Ituna Bon Accord No. 246 | 559 | Diane M. Olech, Adm., PO Box 190, Ituna S0A 1N0 – 306/795-2202, Fax: 306/795-2202 |
| Kellross No. 247 | 541 | Robert Jorgensen, Adm., PO Box 10, Leross S0A 2C0 – 306/675-4423, Fax: 306/675-4423 |
| Kelvington No. 366 | 668 | Tim G. Leurer, Adm., PO Box 519, Kelvington S0A 1W0 – 306/327-4222, Fax: 306/327-4222 |
| Key West No. 70 | 470 | Peggy Tumback, Adm., PO Box 159, Ogema S0C 1Y0 – 306/459-2262, Fax: 306/459-2762 |
| Keys No. 303 | 448 | Sharon Ciesielski, Adm., PO Box 899, Canora S0A 0L0 – 306/563-5331, Fax: 306/563-6759 |
| Kindersley No. 290 | 1,188 | Audrey Hebert, Adm., PO Box 1210, Kindersley S0L 1S0 – 306/463-2524, Fax: 306/463-4197 |
| King George No. 256 | 271 | Jamie McIntosh, Adm., PO Box 100, Dinsmore S0L 0T0 – 306/846-2022, Fax: 306/846-2022 |
| Kingsley No. 124 | 524 | Tim C. Lozinsky, Adm., PO Box 239, Kipling S0G 2S0 – 306/736-2272, Fax: 306/736-2272 |
| Kinistino No. 459 | 866 | Larry W. Edeen, Adm., PO Box 310, Kinistino S0J 1H0 – 306/864-2474, Fax: 306/864-2880 |
| Kutawa No. 278 | 352 | Marlene I. Benko, Adm., PO Box 40, Punnichy S0A 3C0 – 306/835-2110, Fax: 306/835-2100 |
| Lac Pelletier No. 107 | 498 | Rose Lawrence, Adm., PO Box 70, Neville S0N 1T0 – 306/627-3226, Fax: 306/627-3641 |
| Lacadena No. 228 | 786 | Johann F.H. Penner, Adm., PO Box 39, Lacadena S0L 1V0 – 306/574-4753, Fax: 306/574-4753 |
| Laird No. 404 | 1,070 | Brenda Strembicki, Adm., PO Box 160, Waldheim S0K 4R0 – 306/945-2133 |
| Lajord No. 128 | 1,034 | Rod J. Heise, Adm., PO Box 36, Lajord S0G 2V0 – 306/781-2744, Fax: 306/781-2744 |
| Lake Alma No. 8 | 335 | Darlene Lund, Adm., PO Box 100, Lake Alma S0C 1M0 – 306/447-2022, Fax: 306/447-2022 |

| MUNICIPALITY | 1996 POP. | CONTACT PERSON WITH ADDRESS & PHONE |
|---|---|---|
| Lake Johnston No. 102 | 195 | H. Sam Edgerton, Adm., PO Box 160, Mossbank S0H 3G0 – 306/354-2414, Fax: 306/354-7725 |
| Lake Lenore No. 399 | 555 | Gailene Gallais, Adm., PO Box 280, St. Brieux S0K 3V0 – 306/275-2066, Fax: 306/275-4949 |
| Lake of the Rivers No. 72 | 423 | F.A. Kornfeld, Adm., PO Box 610, Assiniboia S0H 0B0 – 306/642-3533, Fax: 306/642-4382 |
| Lakeland No. 521 | 581 | Howard Paterson, Adm., PO Box 27, Christopher Lake S0J 0N0 – 306/982-2010, Fax: 306/982-2589 |
| Lakeside No. 338 | 523 | Judy Kanak, Adm., PO Box 9, Quill Lake S0A 3E0 – 306/383-2261, Fax: 306/383-2255 |
| Lakeview No. 337 | 585 | J. Ann Sanderson, Adm., PO Box 220, Wadena S0A 4J0 – 306/338-2341, Fax: 306/338-2595 |
| Langenburg No. 181 | 768 | Mary L. Angus-Yanke, Adm., PO Box 489, Langenburg S0A 2A0 – 306/743-2341, Fax: 306/743-5282 |
| Last Mountain Valley No. 250 | 395 | Michelle Cruise, Adm., PO Box 160, Govan S0G 1Z0 – 306/484-2011, Fax: 306/484-2113 |
| Laurier No. 38 | 434 | Darlene J. Paquin, Adm., PO Box 219, Radville S0C 2G0 – 306/869-2255, Fax: 306/869-2524 |
| Lawtonia No. 135 | 461 | Art Thompson, Adm., PO Box 10, Hodgeville S0H 2B0 – 306/677-2266, Fax: 306/677-2446 |
| Leask No. 464 | 846 | Rick Poole, Adm., PO Box 190, Leask S0J 1M0 – 306/466-2000, Fax: 306/466-2000 |
| Leroy No. 339 | 667 | Joan Fedak, Adm., PO Box 100, Leroy S0K 2P0 – 306/286-3261, Fax: 306/286-3400 |
| Lipton No. 217 | 533 | Melony K. Materi, Adm., PO Box 40, Lipton S0G 3B0 – 306/336-2244, Fax: 306/336-2244 |
| Livingston No. 331 | 497 | Mike Burtnack, Adm., PO Box 40, Arran S0A 0B0 – 306/595-4521, Fax: 306/595-4521 |
| Lomond No. 37 | 381 | Kevin Melle, Adm., PO Box 280, Weyburn S4H 2K1 – 306/456-2566, Fax: 306/456-2566 |
| Lone Tree No. 18 | 203 | Ronald J. Johnson, Adm., PO Box 30, Climax S0N 0N0 – 306/293-2124, Fax: 306/293-2702 |
| Longlaketon No. 219 | 973 | Shelly Mohr, Adm., PO Box 100, Earl Grey S0G 1J0 – 306/939-2144 |
| Loon Lake No. 561 | 881 | Darren D. Elder, Adm., PO Box 40, Loon Lake S0M 1L0 – 306/837-2076, Fax: 306/837-2282 |
| Loreburn No. 254 | 422 | Nona Stronski, Adm., PO Box 40, Loreburn S0H 2S0 – 306/644-2022, Fax: 306/644-2064 |
| Lost River No. 313 | 230 | Christine Dyck, Adm., PO Box 159, Allan S0K 0C0 – 306/257-3272, Fax: 306/257-3337 |
| Lumsden No. 189 | 1,376 | John E. Spicer, Adm., PO Box 160, Lumsden S0G 3C0 – 306/731-2231, Fax: 306/731-3572 |
| Manitou Lake No. 442 | 618 | Jason Boyle, Adm., PO Box 69, Marsden S0M 1P0 – 306/826-5215, Fax: 306/826-5512 |
| Mankota No. 45 | 506 | Michael E. Sherven, Adm., PO Box 148, Mankota S0H 2W0 – 306/478-2323, Fax: 306/478-2606 |
| Maple Bush No. 224 | 221 | Garry L. Gross, Adm., PO Box 160, Riverhurst S0H 3P0 – 306/353-2292, Fax: 306/353-2292 |
| Maple Creek No. 111 | 1,193 | Debbie Kusler, Adm., PO Box 188, Maple Creek S0N 1N0 – 306/662-2300, Fax: 306/662-3566 |
| Mariposa No. 350 | 291 | Joe Fruhstuk, Adm., PO Box 228, Kerrobert S0L 1R0 – 306/834-5037, Fax: 306/834-5037 |
| Marquis No. 191 | 445 | Ronald J. Gasper, Adm., PO Box 40, Marquis S0H 2X0 – 306/788-2022, Fax: 306/788-2168 |
| Marriott No. 317 | 493 | Jim P. Reiter, Adm., PO Box 366, Rosetown S0L 2V0 – 306/882-4030, Fax: 306/882-4401 |
| Martin No. 122 | 370 | Holly J. McFarlane, Adm., PO Box 99, Wapella S0G 4Z0 – 306/532-4332, Fax: 306/435-4313 |
| Maryfield No. 91 | 479 | Doreen Jurkovic, Adm., PO Box 70, Maryfield S0G 3K0 – 306/646-2033, Fax: 306/646-2033 |
| Mayfield No. 406 | 484 | Laurie DuBois, Adm., PO Box 100, Maymont S0M 1T0 – 306/389-2112, Fax: 306/389-2112 |
| McCraney No. 282 | 478 | Gregory M. Brkich, Adm., PO Box 129, Kenaston S0G 2N0 – 306/252-2240, Fax: 306/252-2248 |
| McKillop No. 220 | 545 | W. Doug Hunter, Adm., PO Box 369, Strasbourg S0G 4V0 – 306/725-3230, Fax: 306/725-3613 |
| McLeod No. 185 | 677 | Murray J. Hanowski, Adm., PO Box 130, Neudorf S0A 2T0 – 306/748-2233, Fax: 306/748-2647 |
| Meadow Lake No. 588 | 2,612 | Darryl J. Wilkinson, Adm., #1, 225 Centre St., Meadow Lake S9X 1L5 – 306/236-5651, Fax: 306/236-3115 |
| Medstead No. 497 | 651 | Darrin Beaudoin, Adm., PO Box 148, Medstead S0M 1W0 – 306/342-4609, Fax: 306/342-4609 |
| Meeting Lake No. 466 | 508 | Debbie L. Wohlberg, Adm., PO Box 26, Mayfair S0M 1S0 – 306/246-4228, Fax: 306/246-4228 |
| Meota No. 468 | 800 | Allie R. Raycraft, Adm., PO Box 80, Meota S0M 1X0 – 306/892-2061, Fax: 306/892-2061 |
| Mervin No. 499 | 1,169 | L. Ryan. Domotor, Adm., PO Box 130, Turtleford S0M 2Y0 – 306/845-2045, Fax: 306/845-2950 |
| Milden No. 286 | 326 | Melody Nieman, Adm., PO Box 160, Milden S0L 2L0 – 306/935-2181, Fax: 306/935-2181 |
| Milton No. 292 | 227 | Beverly A. Dahl, Adm., PO Box 70, Marengo S0L 2K0 – 306/968-2922, Fax: 306/968-2278 |
| Miry Creek No. 229 | 600 | Richard B. Sylvestre, Adm., PO Box 210, Abbey S0N 0A0 – 306/689-2281, Fax: 306/689-2901 |
| Monet No. 257 | 613 | Lori A. McDonald, Adm., PO Box 370, Elrose S0L 0Z0 – 306/378-2212, Fax: 306/378-2212 |
| Montmartre No. 126 | 574 | Dale Brenner, Adm., PO Box 120, Montmartre S0G 3M0 – 306/424-2040, Fax: 306/424-2040 |
| Montrose No. 315 | 693 | Raymond N. French, Adm., PO Box 755, Delisle S0L 0P0 – 306/493-2694, Fax: 306/493-2694 |
| Moose Creek No. 33 | 416 | Betty Ann Rattray, Adm., PO Box 10, Alameda S0C 0A0 – 306/489-2044, Fax: 306/489-2112 |
| Moose Jaw No. 161 | 1,856 | James W. Nichols, Adm., 170 Fairford St. West, Moose Jaw S6H 1V3 – 306/692-3446, Fax: 306/691-0015 |
| Moose Mountain No. 63 | 565 | Ron Matsalla, Adm., PO Box 445, Carlyle S0C 0R0 – 306/453-6175, Fax: 306/453-2430 |
| Moose Range No. 486 | 1,300 | Richard C. Colborn, Adm., PO Box 699, Carrot River S0E 0L0 – 306/768-2212, Fax: 306/768-2211 |
| Moosomin No. 121 | 530 | Holly J. McFarlane, Adm., PO Box 1109, Moosomin S0G 3N0 – 306/435-3113, Fax: 306/435-4313 |
| Morris No. 312 | 448 | Rolande Davis, Adm., PO Box 130, Young S0K 4Y0 – 306/259-2211, Fax: 306/259-2225 |
| Morse No. 165 | 528 | Mark Wilson, Adm., PO Box 340, Morse S0H 3C0 – 306/629-3282, Fax: 306/629-3212 |
| Mount Hope No. 279 | 644 | Jim Down, Adm., PO Box 190, Semans S0A 3S0 – 306/524-2055, Fax: 306/524-2055 |
| Mount Pleasant No. 2 | 477 | Brian R. Miller, Adm., PO Box 278, Carnduff S0C 0S0 – 306/482-3313, Fax: 306/482-5278 |
| Mountain View No. 318 | 371 | Glenda Giles, Adm., PO Box 130, Herschel S0L 1L0 – 306/377-2144, Fax: 306/377-2144 |
| Newcombe No. 260 | 349 | Lois L. Haug, Adm., PO Box 40, Glidden S0L 1H0 – 306/463-3338, Fax: 306/463-4748 |
| Nipawin No. 487 | 1,269 | Eunice Rudy, Adm., PO Box 250, Codette S0E 0P0 – 306/862-9551, Fax: 306/862-9551 |
| North Battleford No. 437 | 984 | Bruce W. Kosolofski, Adm., 1101 - 101 St., North Battleford S9A 0Z5 – 306/445-3604, Fax: 306/445-3604 |
| North Qu'Appelle No. 187 | 828 | Beverly van der Breggen, Adm., PO Box 99, Fort Qu'Appelle S0G 1S0 – 306/332-5202, Fax: 306/332-6028 |
| Norton No. 69 | 296 | Wayne Lozinsky, Adm., PO Box 189, Pangman S0C 2C0 – 306/442-2131, Fax: 306/442-2144 |
| Oakdale No. 320 | 354 | Gloria Johnson, Adm., PO Box 249, Coleville S0L 0K0 – 306/965-2281, Fax: 306/965-2466 |
| Old Post No. 43 | 531 | Doreen Koester, Adm., PO Box 70, Wood Mountain S0H 4L0 – 306/266-2002, Fax: 306/266-2020 |
| Orkney No. 244 | 1,810 | Grant Doupe, Adm., 26 - 5 Ave. North, Yorkton S3N 0Y8 – 306/782-2333, Fax: 306/782-5177 |
| Paddockwood No. 520 | 1,062 | Carole Moritz, Adm., PO Box 187, Paddockwood S0J 1Z0 – 306/989-2124, Fax: 306/989-2124 |
| Parkdale No. 498 | 691 | Tannys Mannix, Adm., PO Box 310, Glaslyn S0M 0Y0 – 306/342-2015, Fax: 306/342-2015 |
| Paynton No. 470 | 301 | Gina Bernier, Adm., PO Box 10, Paynton S0M 2J0 – 306/895-2020, Fax: 306/895-2020 |
| Pense No. 160 | 536 | Carolynn Meadows, Adm., PO Box 190, Pense S0G 3W0 – 306/345-2303, Fax: 306/345-2583 |
| Perdue No. 346 | 439 | John de Gooijer, Adm., PO Box 208, Perdue S0K 3C0 – 306/237-4202, Fax: 306/237-4202 |
| Piapot No. 110 | 380 | Sidney C. McGillivray, Adm., PO Box 100, Piapot S0N 1Y0 – 306/558-2011, Fax: 306/558-2125 |
| Pinto Creek No. 75 | 271 | Henrietta J. Lott, Adm., PO Box 239, Kincaid S0H 2J0 – 306/264-3277, Fax: 306/264-3277 |
| Pittville No. 169 | 291 | Terry Erdelyan, Adm., PO Box 150, Hazlet S0N 1E0 – 306/678-2131, Fax: 306/678-2132 |
| Pleasant Valley No. 288 | 418 | Jim P. Reiter, Adm., PO Box 2080, Rosetown S0L 2V0 – 306/882-4030, Fax: 306/882-4401 |
| Pleasantdale No. 398 | 709 | Lowell Prefontaine, Adm., PO Box 70, Naicam S0K 2Z0 – 306/874-5732, Fax: 306/874-2225 |
| Ponass Lake No. 367 | 767 | Bonnie W. Lengyel, Adm., PO Box 98, Rose Valley S0E 1M0 – 306/322-2162, Fax: 306/322-2162 |
| Poplar Valley No. 12 | 307 | Evan Strelioff, Adm., PO Box 11, Rockglen S0H 3R0 – 306/476-2062, Fax: 306/476-2062 |
| Porcupine No. 395 | 1,150 | Ed F. Poniatowski, Adm., PO Box 190, Porcupine Plain S0E 1H0 – 306/278-2368, Fax: 306/278-3473 |

| MUNICIPALITY | 1996 POP. | CONTACT PERSON WITH ADDRESS & PHONE |
|---|---|---|
| Prairie No. 408 | 559 | Raymond W. Toews, Adm., PO Box 159, Battleford S0M 0E0 – 306/937-2321 |
| Prairie Rose No. 309 | 364 | Dennis C. McBurney, Adm., PO Box 89, Jansen S0K 2B0 – 306/364-2013, Fax: 306/364-4643 |
| Prairiedale No. 321 | 263 | Donald M. Fizell, Adm., PO Box 90, Smiley S0L 2Z0 – 306/838-2020, Fax: 306/838-4343 |
| Preeceville No. 334 | 1,202 | Lynn Larsen, Adm., PO Box 439, Preeceville S0A 3B0 – 306/547-2029, Fax: 306/547-2081 |
| Prince Albert No. 461 | 3,322 | Terry-Lynn Zahara, Adm., 99 River St. East, Prince Albert S6V 0A1 – 306/763-2469, Fax: 306/763-6369 |
| Progress No. 351 | 377 | Harold Trew, Adm., PO Box 130, Luseland S0L 2A0 – 306/372-4322, Fax: 306/372-4700 |
| Reciprocity No. 32 | 475 | Lyle McDonald, Adm., PO Box 70, Alida S0C 0B0 – 306/443-2212, Fax: 306/443-2287 |
| Redberry No. 435 | 464 | Alan Tanchak, Adm., PO Box 160, Hafford S0J 1A0 – 306/549-2333, Fax: 306/549-2333 |
| Redburn No. 130 | 313 | Elizabeth Busby, Adm., PO Box 250, Rouleau S0G 4H0 – 306/776-2270, Fax: 306/776-2482 |
| Reford No. 379 | 367 | Jeanette Nicholson, Adm., PO Box 689, Wilkie S0K 4W0 – 306/843-2342, Fax: 306/843-2455 |
| Reno No. 51 | 539 | Jan Stern, Adm., PO Box 90, Consul S0N 0P0 – 306/299-2133, Fax: 306/299-4433 |
| Riverside No. 168 | 552 | Sharlene Higginson, Adm., PO Box 129, Pennant S0N 1X0 – 306/626-3255, Fax: 306/626-3661 |
| Rocanville No. 151 | 627 | G. Dennis Giegle, Adm., PO Box 298, Rocanville S0A 3L0 – 306/645-2055, Fax: 306/645-2697 |
| Rodgers No. 133 | 157 | Linda K. Coates, Adm., PO Box 70, Courval S0H 1A0 – 306/394-4305, Fax: 306/394-4305 |
| Rosedale No. 283 | 520 | Darlene Walker, Adm., PO Box 150, Hanley S0G 2E0 – 306/544-2202, Fax: 306/544-2202 |
| Rosemount No. 378 | 208 | Gary A. Dziadyk, Adm., PO Box 184, Landis S0K 2K0 – 306/658-2034, Fax: 306/658-2034 |
| Rosthern No. 403 | 1,816 | James F. Spriggs, Adm., PO Box 126, Rosthern S0K 3R0 – 306/232-4393, Fax: 306/232-5321 |
| Round Hill No. 467 | 458 | Ian McLennan, Adm., PO Box 9, Rabbit Lake S0M 2L0 – 306/824-2044, Fax: 306/824-2044 |
| Round Valley No. 410 | 474 | Mervin Bosch, Adm., PO Box 538, Unity S0K 4L0 – 306/228-2248, Fax: 306/228-3483 |
| Rudy No. 284 | 428 | Larry W. Hubbard, Adm., PO Box 1010, Outlook S0L 2N0 – 306/867-9349, Fax: 306/867-8038 |
| St. Andrews No. 287 | 620 | Darcy Olson, Adm., PO Box 488, Rosetown S0L 2V0 – 306/882-2314, Fax: 306/882-3166 |
| St. Louis No. 431 | 1,227 | Leo G. Gareau, Adm., PO Box 28, Hoey S0J 1E0 – 306/422-6170, Fax: 306/422-8520 |
| St. Peter No. 369 | 949 | Brenda Nagy, Adm., PO Box 70, Annaheim S0K 0G0 – 306/598-2122, Fax: 306/598-4526 |
| St. Philips No. 301 | 331 | Victoria Makohoniuk, Adm., PO Box 220, Pelly S0A 2Z0 – 306/595-2050, Fax: 306/595-2050 |
| Saltcoats No. 213 | 886 | Ronald R.. Risling, Adm., PO Box 150, Saltcoats S0A 3R0 – 306/744-2202, Fax: 306/744-2455 |
| Sarnia No. 221 | 327 | Harvey Hemingway, Adm., PO Box 160, Holdfast S0G 2H0 – 306/488-2033 |
| Saskatchewan Landing No. 167 | 529 | Caroll Wallace, Adm., PO Box 40, Stewart Valley S0N 2P0 – 306/778-2105, Fax: 306/778-2105 |
| Sasman No. 336 | 1,031 | Jim Little, Adm., PO Box 130, Kuroki S0A 1Y0 – 306/338-2263, Fax: 306/338-2043 |
| Scott No. 98 | 299 | Paul P. Thiele, Adm., PO Box 210, Yellow Grass S0G 5J0 – 306/465-2512, Fax: 306/465-2512 |
| Senlac No. 411 | 296 | Janet Leibel, Adm., PO Box 130, Senlac S0L 2Y0 – 306/228-3339, Fax: 306/228-2264 |
| Shamrock No. 134 | 312 | Edwin A. Henry, Adm., PO Box 40, Shamrock S0H 3W0 – 306/648-3594, Fax: 306/648-3687 |
| Shellbrook No. 493 | 1,793 | Kenneth G. Danger, Adm., PO Box 40, Shellbrook S0J 2E0 – 306/747-2177, Fax: 306/747-3111 |
| Sherwood No. 159 | 1,056 | Donna Rollie, Adm., 1840 Cornwall St., Regina S4P 2K2 – 306/525-5237, Fax: 306/352-1760 |
| Silverwood No. 123 | 608 | Eileen Grassl, Adm., PO Box 700, Whitewood S0G 5C0 – 306/735-2500, Fax: 306/735-2524 |
| Sliding Hills No. 273 | 650 | Todd Steele, Adm., PO Box 70, Mikado S0A 2R0 – 306/563-5285, Fax: 306/563-5285 |
| Snipe Lake No. 259 | 598 | Carol D. Dale, Adm., PO Box 786, Eston S0L 1A0 – 306/962-3214, Fax: 306/962-4330 |
| Souris Valley No. 7 | 422 | Jo Ann Larsen, Adm., PO Box 40, Oungre S0C 1Z0 – 306/456-2676, Fax: 306/456-2480 |
| South Qu'Appelle No. 157 | 1,135 | Sandra Drinnan, Adm., PO Box 66, Qu'Appelle S0G 4A0 – 306/699-2257, Fax: 306/699-2856 |
| Spalding No. 368 | 681 | Robert J. McPherson, Adm., PO Box 10, Spalding S0K 4C0 – 306/872-2166, Fax: 306/872-2166 |
| Spiritwood No. 496 | 1,504 | Gloria Teer, Adm., PO Box 340, Spiritwood S0J 2M0 – 306/883-2034, Fax: 306/883-2557 |
| Spy Hill No. 152 | 496 | Tracy L. Smith, Adm., PO Box 129, Spy Hill S0A 3W0 – 306/534-2022, Fax: 306/534-2022 |
| Stanley No. 215 | 696 | Marie Steiner, Adm., PO Box 70, Melville S0A 2P0 – 306/728-2818, Fax: 306/728-2818 |
| Star City No. 428 | 1,052 | Ann T. Campbell, Adm., PO Box 370, Star City S0E 1P0 – 306/863-2522, Fax: 306/863-2255 |
| Stonehenge No. 73 | 592 | Mary Jean Allingham, Adm., PO Box 129, Limerick S0H 2P0 – 306/263-2020, Fax: 306/263-2013 |
| Storthoaks No. 31 | 462 | Elaine R. Morgan, Adm., PO Box 40, Storthoaks S0C 2K0 – 306/449-2262, Fax: 306/449-2210 |
| Surprise Valley No. 9 | 231 | Joyce Axten, Adm., PO Box 52, Minton S0C 1T0 – 306/969-2144, Fax: 306/969-2244 |
| Sutton No. 103 | 344 | H. Sam Edgerton, Adm., PO Box 100, Mossbank S0H 3G0 – 306/354-2414, Fax: 306/354-7725 |
| Swift Current No. 137 | 1,547 | Dave Dmytruk, Adm., PO Box 1210, Swift Current S9H 3X4 – 306/773-7314, Fax: 306/773-9538 |
| Tecumseh No. 65 | 359 | Zandra Slater, Adm., PO Box 300, Stoughton S0G 4T0 – 306/457-2277 |
| Terrell No. 101 | 343 | Ernest P. Karlson, Adm., PO Box 60, Spring Valley S0H 3X0 – 306/475-2803, Fax: 306/475-2803 |
| Three Lakes No. 400 | 682 | Tim Schmidt, Adm., PO Box 100, Middle Lake S0K 2X0 – 306/367-2172, Fax: 306/367-2011 |
| Tisdale No. 427 | 1,137 | Terry Hvidston, Adm., PO Box 128, Tisdale S0E 1T0 – 306/873-2334, Fax: 306/873-4442 |
| Torch River No. 488 | 1,827 | Jacques A. Bertrand, Adm., PO Box 40, White Fox S0J 3B0 – 306/276-2066, Fax: 306/276-2099 |
| Touchwood No. 248 | 413 | Marlene I. Benko, Adm., PO Box 160, Punnichy S0A 3C0 – 306/835-2110, Fax: 306/835-2100 |
| Tramping Lake No. 380 | 408 | Karen Wiley, Adm., PO Box 129, Scott S0K 4A0 – 306/247-2033, Fax: 306/247-2055 |
| Tullymet No. 216 | 331 | Darwin Chatterson, Adm., PO Box 190, Balcarres S0G 0C0 – 306/334-2366, Fax: 306/334-2930 |
| Turtle River No. 469 | 374 | Joseph McMurphy, Adm., PO Box 128, Edam S0M 0V0 – 306/397-2311, Fax: 306/397-2311 |
| Usborne No. 310 | 598 | Keith Schulze, Adm., PO Box 310, Lanigan S0K 2M0 – 306/365-2924, Fax: 306/365-2808 |
| Val Marie No. 17 | 523 | Barry W. Dixon, Adm., PO Box 59, Val Marie S0N 2T0 – 306/298-2009, Fax: 306/298-2224 |
| Vanscoy No. 345 | 2,423 | Shawn Antosh, Adm., PO Box 187, Vanscoy S0L 3J0 – 306/668-2060, Fax: 306/668-1338 |
| Victory No. 226 | 494 | Rita Fraser, Adm., PO Box 100, Beechy S0L 0C0 – 306/859-2270, Fax: 306/859-2270 |
| Viscount No. 341 | 494 | Patrick T. Clavelle, Adm., PO Box 100, Viscount S0K 4M0 – 306/944-2044, Fax: 306/944-2044 |
| Wallace No. 243 | 1,044 | Grant Doupe, Adm., 26 - 5 Ave. North, Yorkton S3N 0Y8 – 306/782-2333, Fax: 306/782-5177 |
| Walpole No. 92 | 454 | Rhonda M. Hall, Adm., PO Box 117, Wawota S0G 5A0 – 306/739-2545, Fax: 306/739-2777 |
| Waverley No. 44 | 428 | Ed P. Gasper, Adm., PO Box 70, Glentworth S0H 1V0 – 306/266-4920, Fax: 306/266-2077 |
| Wawken No. 93 | 708 | Jane Laich, Adm., PO Box 90, Wawota S0G 5A0 – 306/739-2332, Fax: 306/739-2222 |
| Webb No. 138 | 465 | Don Haley, Adm., PO Box 100, Webb S0N 2X0 – 306/674-2230, Fax: 306/674-2324 |
| Wellington No. 97 | 403 | Janice E. Mus, Adm., PO Box 1390, Weyburn S4H 3J9 – 306/842-5606 |
| Weyburn No. 67 | 867 | Lloyd E. Muma, Adm., 23 - 6 St. NE, Weyburn S4H 1A7 – 306/842-2314, Fax: 306/842-1002 |
| Wheatlands No. 163 | 226 | Gary Wapple, Adm., PO Box 129, Mortlach S0H 3E0 – 306/355-2233, Fax: 306/355-2233 |
| Whiska Creek No. 106 | 505 | Kathy Countryman, Adm., PO Box 10, Vanguard S0N 2V0 – 306/582-2133, Fax: 306/582-4950 |
| White Valley No. 49 | 615 | Yvonne Wilton, Adm., PO Box 520, Eastend S0N 0T0 – 306/295-3553, Fax: 306/295-3571 |
| Willner No. 253 | 316 | Norman Sagen, Adm., PO Box 250, Davidson S0G 1A0 – 306/567-3103, Fax: 306/567-3266 |
| Willow Bunch No. 42 | 514 | Margaret L. Brown, Adm., PO Box 220, Willow Bunch S0H 4K0 – 306/473-2302, Fax: 306/473-2302 |
| Willow Creek No. 458 | 918 | Bert Ross, Adm., PO Box 5, Brooksby S0E 0H0 – 306/863-4143, Fax: 306/863-2366 |
| Willowdale No. 153 | 408 | Patricia Henry, Acting Adm., PO Box 58, Whitewood S0G 5C0 – 306/735-2344, Fax: 306/735-4495 |

| MUNICIPALITY | 1996 POP. | CONTACT PERSON WITH ADDRESS & PHONE |
|---|---|---|
| Wilton No. 472 | 1,564 | Trent Michelman, Adm., PO Box 40, Marshall S0M 1R0 – 306/387-6244, Fax: 306/387-6598 |
| Winslow No. 319 | 390 | Wendy Davis, Adm., PO Box 310, Dodsland S0L 0V0 – 306/356-2106, Fax: 306/356-2085 |
| Wise Creek No. 77 | 297 | Grace Potter, Adm., PO Box 400, Shaunavon S0N 2M0 – 306/297-2520 |
| Wolseley No. 155 | 549 | Dale A. Harvey, Adm., PO Box 370, Wolseley S0G 5H0 – 306/698-2522, Fax: 306/698-2664 |
| Wolverine No. 340 | 641 | Coleen Bowman, Adm., PO Box 28, Burr S0K 0T0 – 306/682-3640, Fax: 306/682-3640 |
| Wood Creek No. 281 | 351 | Donn Bergsveinson, Adm., PO Box 10, Simpson S0G 4M0 – 306/836-2020, Fax: 306/836-4460 |
| Wood River No. 74 | 437 | Derek Thiele, Adm., PO Box 250, Lafleche S0H 2K0 – 306/472-5235 |
| Wreford No. 280 | 232 | Lois M. Friend, Adm., PO Box 99, Nokomis S0G 3R0 – 306/528-2202, Fax: 306/528-4411 |
| The Gap No. 39 | 278 | Vaughan B. McClarty, Adm., PO Box 188, Ceylon S0C 0T0 – 306/454-2202, Fax: 306/454-2627 |

## YUKON TERRITORY

LEGISLATION: Municipal Act, Municipal Finance & Community Grants Act, Assessment and Taxation Act.

Requirements for incorporation in the Yukon are based on population: village 300-1,000, town 500-3,000, city over 2,500. Any community may become a hamlet, an advisory body to the minister, as a first step towards becoming a municipality.

Municipal elections are held every three years and polling day is the third Thursday of October in each election year. Mayors and councillors are elected for a three-year period.

Cities in CAPITALS; Towns marked †; Villages marked (V); Hamlets marked (H). An in-depth listing for municipalities marked with * appears in Part 2 (check Index for page numbers).

| MUNICIPALITY | 1996 POP. | FEDERAL ELECTORAL DISTRICT | TERRITORIAL ELECTORAL DISTRICT | CONTACT PERSON WITH ADDRESS, PHONE & FAX |
|---|---|---|---|---|
| Beaver Creek (H) | 131 | Yukon | Kluane | Gary Knickle, President, Community Club, Beaver Creek Y0B 1A0 – 867/862-7211 |
| Burwash Landing (H) | 58 | Yukon | Kluane | Liz Johnson, Mgr., Kluane First Nation, Mile 1093, General Delivery, Burwash Landing Y1A 3V4 – 867/841-4274, Fax: 867/841-5900 |
| Carcross (H) | 196 | Yukon | Ross River-Southern Lakes | Rhonda Passmore, President, Community & Curling Club, PO Box 48, Carcross Y0B 1B0 – 867/821-3101 |
| Carmacks (V) | 466 | Yukon | Mayo-Tatchun | Mike Richards, CAO, Village of Carmacks Y0B 1C0 – 867/863-6271, Fax: 867/863-6606 |
| Dawson City † | 1,287 | Yukon | Klondike | Jim Kincaid, CAO, PO Box 308, Dawson City Y0B 1G0 – 867/993-7400, Fax: 867/993-7434 |
| Destruction Bay (H) | 34 | Yukon | Kluane | Jim Flumerfelt, President, Kluane Lake Athletic Assn., Destruction Bay Y0B 1C0 – 867/841-4211 |
| Faro † | 1,261 | Yukon | Faro | Colin Dean, CAO, PO Box 580, Faro Y0B 1K0 – 867/994-2728, Fax: 867/994-3154 |
| Haines Junction (V) | 574 | Yukon | Kluane | Sheila O'Hanlon, Clerk-Treas., PO Box 5339, Haines Junction Y0B 1L0 – 867/634-2291, Fax: 867/634-2008 |
| Ibex Valley (H) | 322 | Yukon | Kluane | Bob Atkinson, Chairperson, RR#2, Site 3, Comp 24, Whitehorse Y1A 5W2 – 867/633-6131, Fax: 867/633-5213 |
| Mayo (V) | 324 | Yukon | Mayo-Tatchun | Margarit Wozniak, CAO, PO Box 160, Mayo Y0B 1M0 – 867/996-2317, Fax: 867/996-2907 |
| Mount Lorne (H) | | Yukon | Mount Lorne | Brent Walden, Chairperson, RR#1, Site 20, Comp 9, Whitehorse Y1A 4Z6 – 867/668-6310, Fax: 867/633-5884 |
| Old Crow (H) | 278 | Yukon | Vuntut Gwichin | Randall Tetlichi, Chief, Vuntut Gwichin First Nation, Old Crow Y0B 1N0 – 867/966-3261, Fax: 867/966-3800 |
| Pelly Crossing (H) | 238 | Yukon | Mayo-Tatchun | Pat Van Bibber, Chief, Selkirk First Nation, Pelly Crossing Y0B 1P0 – 867/537-3331, Fax: 867/537-3902 |
| Ross River (H) | 352 | Yukon | Ross River-Southern Lakes | Norma McLeod, Sec., Ross River Community Club, Ross River Y0B 1S0 – 867/969-2536, Fax: 867/969-2903 |
| Stewart Crossing (H) | 42 | Yukon | Mayo-Tatchun | Dan McDiarmid, President, Stewart Crossing Community Club, Stewart Crossing Y1A 4N1 – 867/996-2514 |
| Tagish (H) | 69 | Yukon | Ross River-Southern Lakes | Art Smith, President, Tagish Community Association, Tagish Y0B 1T0 – 867/399-3407 |
| Teslin (V) | 189 | Yukon | Ross River-Southern Lakes | Jerry Bruce, CAO, Village of Teslin Y0A 1B0 – 867/390-2530, Fax: 867/390-2104 |
| Upper Liard (H) | 111 | Yukon | Watson Lake | Fran Byers, Mgr., Liard First Nation, PO Box 328, Watson Lake Y0A 1C0 – 867/536-2131, Fax: 867/536-2332 |
| Watson Lake † | 993 | Yukon | Watson Lake | Steve Conway, CAO, PO Box 590, Watson Lake Y0A 1C0 – 867/536-2246, Fax: 867/536-2498 |
| *WHITEHORSE | 19,157 | Yukon | Lake Laberge Whitehorse C; McIntyre-Takhini; Porter Creek N; Porter Creek S; Riverdale N; Riverdale S; Riverside; Whitehorse W | 2121 - 2 Ave., Whitehorse Y1A 1C2 – 867/667-6401, Fax: 867/668-8384, URL: http://www.city.whitehorse.yk.ca |

# MAJOR MUNICIPALITIES

## Part 2 (Alphabetical list of major cities, including Council & senior administrative officials)

The population figures shown are 1996 StatsCan census figures. Each local municipality listing includes a main address & general phone & fax number. Some listings include Email and websites (URLs). Use these addresses & numbers if no other phone or fax follows the name of listed persons. Election results from autumn 1997 are includedin these pages, with a few exceptions; refer to the Addenda at the back of the book for any election results not included here.

## City of ABBOTSFORD

32315 South Fraser Way, Abbotsford BC V2T 1W7
604/853-2281, Fax: 604/853-1934
Email: city.abby.bc.ca, URL: http://www.city.abby.bc.ca.abby
Incorporated: January 1, 1995
Area: 35,851 ha
Population: 105,403 (1996)

#### COUNCIL

Mayor, George F. Ferguson
Councillors: Edward Fast; Simon Gibson; Moe Gill; Wendy Lee; George Peary; Patricia Ross; A. Mark Warawa; C.D. Wiebe
*Next Election:* November 1999 (3 year terms)

#### ADMINISTRATION

City Clerk, Toiressa O. Strong, 604/864-5506
Treasurer, Dan Bottrill, 604/864-5524; Fax: 604/853-7968
City Manager, Hedda Cochran, 604/864-5506
Airport Manager, Mike Colmant, 604/855-1001; Fax: 604/855-1066
Chief Constable, Barry Daniel, 604/859-5225; Fax: 604/859-2527
Director, Development Services, Richard Danziger, Fax: 604/853-4981
Director, Engineering, Ed Regts, P.Eng., 604/864-5514; Fax: 604/853-2219
Director, Finance, Dan Bottrill, 604/864-5524; Fax: 604/853-7968
Director, Parks & Recreation, Ken Yates, 604/859-3134; Fax: 604/854-5077
Economic Development Officer, Malcolm Harvey, 604/864-5505
Fire Chief, Lex Haagen, 604/853-3566; Fax: 604/853-7941

## Town of AJAX

65 Harwood Ave. South, Ajax ON L1S 2H9
905/683-4550, Fax: 905/683-1061
Incorporated: 1950
Area: 65.3 sq. km
Population: 64,430 (1996)

#### COUNCIL

Mayor, Steve Parish
Councillors & Wards: 1) Danielle Holmes; 2) S.A. Crawford; 3) Colleen Jordan; 4) P.A. Brown
Regional Councillors: 1&2) Scott Crawford; 3&4) Jim McMaster
*Next Election:* November 2000 (3 year terms)

#### ADMINISTRATION

Clerk, Martin J. de Rond
Director, G.D. Kirkbride
Chief Administrative Officer, Richard Parisotto, Fax: 905/686-8352
Director, Human Resources, Vacant, Fax: 905/686-8352
Director, Operations, F.J. Hull, Fax: 905/686-0360
Director, Parks & Recreation, T.W. Flood, 905/427-8811; Fax: 905/427-3821
Director, Planning & Development, Leo DeLoyde, Fax: 905/686-0360
Director, Transit, T. Barnett, 905/427-5710; Fax: 905/427-3473
Fire Chief (Emergency Response), Randall J. Wilson, 905/683-3050
General Manager, Commercial Planning & Research, Peter Tollefsen, M.C.I.P., Fax: 905/686-0360
General Manager, Development Approval, G. Whittington, Fax: 905/686-0360

## City of BARRIE

70 Collier St., PO Box 400, Barrie ON L4M 4T5
705/726-4242, Fax: 705/739-4243
URL: http://www.city.barrie.on.ca/citymin.htm
Incorporated: 1853
Area: 27 sq. mi (7,265 ha)
Population: 79,191 (1996)

#### COUNCIL

Mayor, Janice Laking
Aldermen & Wards: Anne Black; 1) Bonnie Ainsworth; 3) Rob Warman; 4) Dave Morrison; 5) Alison Eadie; 6) Steve Trotter; 7) Patricia Copeland; 8) Andy Gibson; 9) Jean Sweezie; 10) Mike Ramsay
*Next Election:* November 2000 (3 year terms)

#### ADMINISTRATION

City Clerk, John E. Craig
Treasurer, Lorne Knowles, Fax: 705/739-4237
City Administrator, Peter Lee, Fax: 705/739-4244
Administrator, Social Services, Gary Calvert, Fax: 705/739-4245
Director, Municipal Works, Kerry Columbus, Fax: 705/739-4247
Director, Parks & Recreation, Sid Armatage, Fax: 705/739-4238
Director, Planning & Development, Jim Taylor, Fax: 705/739-4240
Fire Chief, Jim Lemieux, 705/728-1277; Fax: 705/728-4439
Manager, Public Utilities, George Todd, 705/722-6168; Fax: 722-6159
Manager, Traffic, Transit & Parking, George Kaveckas, Fax: 705/739-4247
Police Chief, Jack Delcourt, Fax: 705/728-2971
Purchasing Agent, Noel Banavage, Fax: 705/739-4237
Economic Development Officer, Nancy Tuckett, Fax: 705/739-4246

## Ville de BEAUPORT

10, rue de l'Hôtel-de-Ville, CP 5187, Beauport QC G1E 6P4
418/666-2121, Fax: 418/666-6124
Incorporée: 1855
Superficie: 90.4 sq. km
Population: 72,920 (1996)

#### CONSEIL

Maire, Jacques Langlois
Conseillers et Districts: 1. Petit-Village) Raymond Cantin; 2. St-Ignace) Lise Paradis; 3. Vieux-Moulin) Yolande B. Filion; 4. Cascades) Jean-Luc Duclos; 5. Fargy) Claude Boulet; 6. Orléans) Fernand Trudel; 7. Nordique) Lisette Lepage; 8. Ruisseau) Francine Therien; 9. Cap St-Michel) Stephen Mathieu; 10. Laurentides) Jean Blanchet; 11. Lisieux) Raymond Vézina; 12. Rivière) Sylvie Boutet; 13. Vachon) Mariette Cabana; 14. Montmorency) Carol St-Pierre
*Prochaine election:* novembre 2000 (mandat de 4 ans)

#### ADMINISTRATION

Greffière, Josette Tessier
Trésorier, Jean Grenier, c.g.a.
Directeur général, André Letendre
Directeur, Approvisionnements, Pierre Tessier
Directeur, Communications, Yves Marchand
Directeur, Développement économique, Bernard Auger
Directeur, Loisirs et Parcs, Paul-André Lavigne
Directeur, Personnel, Louis-Philippe Hébert
Directeur, Police, Richard Renaud
Directeur, Services environnementaux, Jean Vézina
Directeur, Services techniques/Génie, Roger Robert, ing.
Asst. Directeur, Incendies, Henri Labadie
Asst. Directeur, Travaux publics, Clement Villeneuve, ing.
Procureur, Jean-Charles Lord
Urbaniste, Jacques Dompierre

## City of BRAMPTON

2 Wellington St. West, Brampton ON L6Y 4R2
905/874-2000, Fax: 905/874-2119
URL: http://www.city.brampton.on.ca/
Incorporated: January 1, 1974
Area: 103.5 sq. mi
Population: 268,251 (1996)

#### COUNCIL

Mayor, Peter Robertson
City Councillors & Wards: 1) Bob Hunter; 2) Linda Jeffrey; 3) Bob Callahan; 4) Susan DiMarco; 5) Grant Gibson; 6) John Hutton; 7) Bill Cowie; 8) Peter Richards; 9) Dick Metzak; 10) John Sprovieri; 11) Sandra Hames
*Next Election:* November 2000 (3 year terms)

#### ADMINISTRATION

City Clerk & Director, Administration, Leonard Mikulich
Treasurer, Paul Caine
City Manager, Al Solski
Commissioner, Community Services, M.J. Neeb
Commissioner, Legal Services, J.G. Metras, Q.C.
Commissioner, Planning & Building, J. Marshall, 905/874-2055
Commissioner, Public Works & Transportation, Larry T. Koehle
Chief Building Official, Building, Percy Hornblow
Chief Economic Development Officer, Dennis Cutjar, 905/874-2662
Director, Human Resources, Mariann Love
Director, Information Technology, J. Wright
Director, Parks Development, K. Walsh
Director, Planning & Development Services, J. Corbett
Director, Recreation Facilities & Programs, H. Newlove
Director, Transit, G. Marshall
Director, Urban Design & Zoning, W. Lee
Fire Chief & EMO, V. Clark
Manager, Supply & Services, Martin Lingard, 905/874-2271

## City of BRANDON

410 - 9 St., Brandon MB R7A 6A2
204/729-2186, Fax: 204/729-8244
Incorporated: May 30, 1882
Area: 25.88 sq. miles
Population: 39,175 (1996)

#### COUNCIL

Mayor, Reg Atkinson
Councillors & Wards: 1. Assiniboine) Joe Kay; 2. Rosser) Drew Caldwell; 3. Victoria) Don Kille; 4. University) Rick Chrest; 5. Meadows) Laurie MacKenzie; 6. South Centre) Jim Reid; 7. Linden Lanes) Scott Smith; 8. Richmond) Margo Campbell;

9. Riverview) Ross Martin; 10. Green Acres) Don Jessiman
*Next Election:* October 1998 (3 year terms)

**ADMINISTRATION**

Clerk, W. Ian Ford, 204/729-2210
Treasurer, Rod Burkard, 204/729-2209
City Manager, Vacant, 204/729-2204; Fax: 204/729-0975
City Engineer, Environmental Services, Ted Snure, 204/729-2214
City Solicitor, Robyn Singleton, 204/729-2246
Coordinator, Safety & EMO, Brian Kayes, 204/729-2239
Director, Human Resources, Rick J. Boyd, 204/729-2242; Fax: 204/729-1904
Director, Parks & Recreation, Brian LePoudre, 204/729-2268
Director, Social Services, Edna Thomassen, 204/729-2293
Fire Chief, Garry Winters, 204/729-2401
Manager, Economic Development, Don Allan, 204/728-3287
Manager, Public Works, Vacant, 204/729-2277; Fax: 204/726-8546
Manager, Transportation Services, Robert C. MacDonald, 204/729-2195; Fax: 204/726-8546
Officer, Planning & Development, Dave Wallace, 204/729-2295
Police Chief, Richard B. Scott, 204/729-2305; Fax: 204/726-1323
Supervisor, Purchasing, Scotty McIntosh, 204/729-2251; Fax: 204/726-8546

## City of BRANTFORD

City Hall, 100 Wellington Sq., Brantford ON N3T 2M3
519/759-4150, Fax: 519/759-7840
URL: http://207.61.52.13:80/brantford/
Incorporated: May 31, 1877
Area: 17,957 acres
Population: 84,764 (1996)

**COUNCIL**

Mayor, Chris Friel
Councillors & Wards: 1) Larry Kings, Paul Urbanowicz; 2) Vince Bucci, John Sless; 3) Mike Hancock, Bob Taylor; 4) Richard Carpenter, Pat Franklin; 5) Marguerite Ceschi-Smith, Wally Lucente
*Next Election:* November 2000 (3 year terms)

**ADMINISTRATION**

City Clerk, Vacant
Treasurer, Calvin Hawke
Chief Administrative Officer, Geoff Wilson
Administrator, Parks & Recreation, Hans Loewig
Chief Building Official, D. Ferguson, Fax: 519/752-1874
City Engineer, A. Gretzinger, P.Eng., 519/759-1350
Director, Economic Development, D. Amos, Fax: 519/752-6775
Director, Environmental Services, Terry Spiers, P.Eng., 519/759-1350
Director, Golf & Aquatics, C. Beachey
Director, Human Resources, David Clarke
Director, Parks & Properties, V. Hergott, 519/756-1500
Director, Planning, P. Atcheson, Fax: 519/752-6977
Director, Tourism, Marketing & Administrative Services, Eric Finkelstein
Purchasing Officer, G. Sturgeon
Superintendent, Works, W. Garabedian, 519/752-4832

## Ville de BROSSARD

2001, boul de Rome, Brossard QC J4W 3K5
514/923-7000, Fax: 514/923-7016
URL: http://www.ville.brossard.qc.ca
Incorporée: 14 fevrier, 1958
Superficie: 44.77 sq. km
Population: 65,927 (1996)

**CONSEIL**

Maire, Paul Leduc
Conseillers et Districts: 1) Nicole Carrier; 2) Claude Moses; 3) Claude Dufresne; 4) Pierre Fortier; 5) Louis-Philippe Blain; 6) Louis-Carol Duchesne; 7) Breda Nadon; 8) Joseph Vassallo; 9) Yves Lampron; 10) Noé Leclerc
*Prochaine election:* novembre 1998 (mandat de 4 ans)

**ADMINISTRATION**

Greffier, Daniel Carrier
Trésorier, André Paquette
Directeur général, Mark Laroche
Directeur, Incendie, Robert Imbeault
Directeur, Loisirs, Aubert Gallant
Directeur, Mesures d'urgence, Mark B. Laroche
Directeur, Police, Gilles Frigon
Directeur, Travaux publics, Alain Cousson
Directeur, Urbanisme, Michel Boyer

## City of BURLINGTON

City Hall, 426 Brant St., PO Box 5013, Burlington ON L7R 3Z6
905/335-7777, Fax: 905/335-7881
Email: cob@worldchat.com, URL: http://worldchat.com/cob
Incorporated: January 1, 1974
Area: 72.65 sq. miles
Population: 136,976 (1996)

**COUNCIL**

Mayor, Robert MacIsaac
City Councillors & Wards: 1) Lynda Schreiber; 2) Joan Lougheed; 3) John Taylor; 4) Jack Dennison; 5) Mike Wallace; 6) Carol D'Amelio
*Next Election:* November 2000 (3 year terms)

**ADMINISTRATION**

City Clerk, Ronald C. Lathan, 905/335-7705
Director, Finance, Robert Carrington, 905/335-7654; Fax: 905/335-7877
City Manager, Tim Dobbie, 905/335-7609
General Manager, Business Affairs, Douglas Brown, 905/335-7614; Fax: 905/335-7842
General Manager, Community Services, Gary Goodman, 905/335-7642; Fax: 905/335-7880
General Manager, Development & Infrastructure, Edward Sajecki, 905/335-7883; Fax: 905/335-7842
Director, Building, Dan Mousseau, 905/335-7731; Fax: 905/335-7876
Director, Engineering, Tom Eichenbaum, 905/335-7795
Director, Environmental & Maintenance Services, Bob Young, 905/335-7873
Director, Management Information Services, Rick Kawai, 905/335-7743
Director, Parks & Recreation, James E. Olmstead, 905/335-7736; Fax: 905/335-7782
Director, Planning, Michael Hall
Director, Transit & Traffic, Vince Mauceri, 905/335-7797; Fax: 905/335-7878
Economic Development Officer, Office of Business Development, Gary Ridgway, 905/335-7712
Fire Chief, Glen Peace, 905/335-1867; Fax: 905/333-1570
Supervisor, Buying, Ken Charles, 905/335-7710

## City of BURNABY

4949 Canada Way, Burnaby BC V5G 1M2
604/294-7944, Fax: 604/294-7537
Incorporated: September 22, 1892
Population: 179,209 (1996)

**COUNCIL**

Mayor, Doug Drummond
Councillors: Derek Corrigan; Doug Evans; Dan Johnston; Doreen Lawson; Lee Rankin; Celeste Redman; Nick Volkow; Jim Young
*Next Election:* November 1999 (3 year terms)

**ADMINISTRATION**

City Clerk, Chad Turpin, 604/294-7283; Fax: 604/294-7537
Treasurer, Rick Earle, 604/294-7360; Fax: 604/294-7544
City Manager, R.H. Moncur, 604/294-7103; Fax: 604/294-7733
Deputy City Manager, Corporate Labour Relations, George Harvie, 604/294-7684; Fax: 604/294-7733
Deputy City Manager, Corporate Services, Chad Turpin, 604/294-7285; Fax: 604/294-7733
Chief Building Inspector, G.R. Humphrey, 604/294-7158; Fax: 604/294-7220
City Solicitor, P.W. Flieger, 604/294-7380; Fax: 604/294-7985
Coordinator, Emergency Program, John Plesha, 604/294-7105; Fax: 604/294-7733
Director, Engineering, W.Craig Sinclair, 604/294-7468; Fax: 604/294-7425
Director, Planning & Building Inspection, D.G. Stenson, 604/294-7413; Fax: 604/294-7220
Director, Recreation & Cultural Services, Dennis Gaunt, 604/294-7102; Fax: 604/294-7710
Fire Chief, W. Brassington, 604/294-7195; Fax: 604/294-0490
Medical Health Officer, Dr. Nadine Loewen, 604/294-7280; Fax: 604/660-7050
Purchasing Agent, John Vissers, 604/294-7377; Fax: 604/294-7529

## City of CALGARY

PO Box 2100, Stn M, Calgary AB T2P 2M5
403/268-2111, Fax: 403/268-2633
URL: http//www.gov.calgary.ab.ca/
Incorporated: January 1, 1894
Area: 721.36 sq. km
Population: 768,082 (1996)

**COUNCIL**

Mayor, Al Duerr, 403/268-5622; Fax: 403/268-8130
Aldermen & Wards: 1) Dale Hodges; 2) Joanne Kerr; 3) John Schmal; 4) Bob Hawkesworth; 5) Ray Jones; 6) David Bronconnier; 7) Bev Longstaff; 8) Jon Lord; 9) Joe Ceci; 10) Ray Clark; 11) Barry Erskine; 12) Sue Higgins; 13) Patti Grier; 14) Linda Fox-Mellway
*Next Election:* October 1998 (3 year terms)

**ADMINISTRATION**

Clerk, D. L. Garner, 403/268-5861; Fax: 403/268-2362; Email: dgarner@gov.calgary.ab.ca
Commissioner, Finance & Administration, A.J. Habstritt, 403/268-5631; Fax: 403/268-1581; Email: ahabstritt@gov.calgary.ab.ca
Chief Commissioner, Paul Dawson, 403/268-5631; Fax: 403/268-1581; Email: pdawson@gov.calgary.ab.ca
Commissioner, Operations & Utilities, R.L. Ward, 403/268-5631; Fax: 403/268-1581; Email: lward@gov.calgary.ab.ca
Commissioner, Planning, Transportation & Community Services, R.J. Holmes, 403/268-5631; Fax: 403/268-1581; Email: rjholmes@gov.calgary.ab.ca
Chief of Police, C. Silverberg, 403/265-5900; Fax: 403/268-4552; Email: csilverberg@gov.calgary.ab.ca
City Assessor & Director, Assessment, I.W. McClung, 403/268-4609; Fax: 403/268-8278; Email: imcclung@gov.calgary.ab.ca
City Solicitor, Law Dept., A. Abougoush, Q.C., 403/268-2441; Fax: 403/268-4634; Email: aaabougoush@gov.calgary.ab.ca

Director, Data Processing Services, J. Umbach, 403/268-4811; Fax: 403/268-2456; Email: jumbach@gov.calgary.ab.ca
Director, Emergency Medical Services, S.W. Cartwright, 403/268-2785; Fax: 403/268-4696; Email: scartwright@gov.calgary.ab.ca
Director, Finance, B. Loach, 403/268-2601; Fax: 403/268-2578; Email: bloach@gov.calgary.ab.ca
Director, Fleet Services, M. Bamford, 403/268-1122; Fax: 403/266-2496; Email: mbamford@gov.calgary.ab.ca
Director, Human Resources, S. Mallon, 403/268-8110; Fax: 403/268-4680; Email: smallon@gov.calgary.ab.ca
Director, Management Audit, R.D. MacLean, 403/268-5670; Fax: 403/268-5411; Email: rmaclean@gov.calgary.ab.ca
Director, Parks & Recreation, K. Knights, 403/268-5200; Fax: 403/268-5265; Email: kknights@gov.calgary.ab.ca
Director, Planning & Building, R. Parker, 403/268-5311; Fax: 403/268-1528; Email: rparker@gov.calgary.ab.ca
Acting Director, Public Information, H. Lauridsen, 403/268-8844; Fax: 403/268-8105; Email: hlauridsen@gov.calgary.ab.ca
Director, Social Services, J. Bader, 403/268-5111; Fax: 403/268-8275; Email: jbader@gov.calgary.ab.ca
Director, Supply Management Services, J.B. Trahan, 403/268-5540; Fax: 403/268-5523; Email: btrahan@gov.calgary.ab.ca
Director, Transportation, Oliver Bowen, 403/268-1574; Fax: 403/268-1633; Email: obowen@gov.calgary.ab.ca
Fire Chief, J.C. Ross, 403/287-4299; Fax: 403/243-9947; Email: jross@gov.calgary.ab.ca
General Manager, Electric System, K. Bosma, 403/268-2820; Fax: 403/265-8419; Email: kbosma@gov.calgary.ab.ca
Leader, Corporate Properties Group, R.J. Shaw, 403/268-2700; Fax: 403/268-1948; Email: bshaw@gov.calgary.ab.ca
President, Calgary Economic Development Authority, J. Jong, 403/221-7831; Fax: 403/221-7837
City Engineer, Engineering & Environmental Services, Terry Montgomery, P.Eng., 403/268-5700; Fax: 403/268-8291

## City of CAMBRIDGE

73 Water St. North, PO Box 669, Cambridge ON N1R 5W8
519/623-1340, Fax: 519/740-3011
Email: calderd@city.cambridge.on.ca
Incorporated: January, 1973
Area: 44.5 sq. mi
Population: 101,429 (1996)

#### COUNCIL

Mayor, Jane Brewer
Councillors & Wards: 1) Rick Cowsill; 2) Greg Durocher; 3) Karl Kiefer; 4) Ben Tucci; 5) Victoria Clark; 6) Gary Price
*Next Election:* November 2000 (3 year terms)

#### ADMINISTRATION

Commissioner (City Clerk), James Anderson, 519/740-4680 ext.4584
Commissioner (Treasurer), Frank Gowman, 519/740-4685 ext.4588
Chief Administrative Officer, Don Smith, 519/740-4683 ext.4518; Fax: 519/740-4512
Commissioner, Community Services, Jim King, 519/740-4681 ext.4559
Commissioner, Engineering & Public Works, Garth James, 519/740-4682 ext.4546; Fax: 519/622-6184
Commissioner, Planning, Wendy Wright, 519/740-4650 ext.4576; Fax: 519/622-6184
Director, Economic Development, Bozena Densmore, 519/740-4536 ext.4511; Fax: 519/740-4512
Director, Public Works, Brian Jones, 519/740-4684 ext.4547; Fax: 519/622-8032
Director, Purchasing & Inventory, David Farrar, 519/740-4637 ext.4293; Fax: 519/740-0834
Fire Chief, Fire Department, Terry Allen, 519/621-6001 ext.7444; Fax: 519/621-4521

## Regional Municipality of CAPE BRETON

320 Esplanade, Sydney NS B1P 1A7
902/563-5005, Fax: 902/564-0481
Incorporated: August 1, 1995

#### COUNCIL

Mayor, David N. Muise
Councillors & Districts: 1) Victor Hanham; 2) Troy Jenkins; 3) Gerard Burke; 4) Ron Burrows; 5) Darren Bruckschwaiger; 6) Ray Kavanaugh; 7) Frank Morrison; 8) Vince Hall; 9) Lorne Green; 10) Douglas MacDonald; 11) Ray Paruch; 12) Jim MacEachern; 13) Arnie Mombourquette; 14) Ivan Doncaster; 15) Claire Dethridge; 16) Rod MacArthur; 17) Mike White; 18) Murray Johnson; 19) Walter Russell; 20) Brian Boudreau; 21) Ross MacKeigan

#### ADMINISTRATION

Clerk, Bernie White
Director, Finances, Rick Farmer
Chief Administrative Officer, Jerry Ryan, 902/563-5006
Internal Audit, Bob MacNeil
Administrator, Corporate Services, Jim MacCormack
Administrator, Public Services, Gordon MacInnis
Chief of Police, Edgar MacLeod
Director, Engineering, Frank Potter
Director, Fire, Rescue & Building Services, Bernie MacKinnon
Director, Human Resources, Rhona Green
Director, Planning, Doug Foster
Director, Public Works, Kevin MacDonald
Director, Recreation, Culture & Facilities, John Fraser
Director, Technology & Communications, Debbie Rudderham

## Ville de CHARLESBOURG

160, 76e rue est, Charlesbourg QC G1H 7H5
418/624-7500, Fax: 418/624-7525
Incorporée: 1 janvier, 1855
Superficie: 67.31 sq. km
Population: 70,942 (1996)

#### CONSEIL

Maire, Ralph Mercier
Conseillers et Districts: 1) Clément Coulombe; 2) Jacques Mitchell; 3) Charles Leduc; 4) Lise Perron-Simard; 5) Louisette Lachance; 6) André Gignac; 7) Claude Gosselin; 8) Guy Poirier; 9) Jean-Marie Laliberté; 10) Régent Légaré; 11) Charles-Henri Verret
*Prochaine election:* novembre 2000 (mandat de 4 ans)

#### ADMINISTRATION

Greffier, Jacques Dorais, 418/624-7537
Directeur, Finances, Clément Guay, 418/624-7550; Fax: 418/624-7655
Directeur général, Michel Lavoie, 418/624-7804
Directeur, Communications, Richard Sévigny, 418/624-7520
Directeur, Loisirs, Serge Paquin, 418/624-7760
Directeur, Travaux publics, Serge Côté, 418/624-7700; Fax: 418/624-7707
Directeur, Urbanisme, Jean-Laval Gagné, 418/624-7512

## City of CHARLOTTETOWN

PO Box 98, Charlottetown PE C1A 7K2
902/566-5548, Fax: 902/566-4701
Email: chtownpe@bud.peinet.pe.ca, URL: http://www.munisource.org/charlottetown/welcome.html
Incorporated: 1855
Area: 42.18 sq. km
Population: 32,531 (1996)

#### COUNCIL

Mayor, George MacDonald
Councillors: 1.) Clifford Lee; 2.) Richard Brown; 3.) Mike Duffy; 4.) Mitchell Tweel; 5.) Frank Zakem; 6.) Roger Birt; 7.) Kathleen Casey; 8.) Brendon McCloskey; 9.) Jim McQuaid; 10.) Allan Poulton
*Next Election:* November 2000 (3 year terms)

#### ADMINISTRATION

CAO, Harry Gaudet
Treasurer, Doug Morton
Chief of Police, Paul Smith
Director, Corporate Services, Donna Waddell
Director, Public Services, Joe Coady
Manager, Fire Services, Bill Hogan
Manager, Human Resources, Phil Handrahan
Manager, Parks & Recreation, Sue Hendricken
Manager, Public Works, Paul Johnston
Utility Manager, Reagh Clark

## Ville de CHICOUTIMI

201, rue Racine est, CP 129, Chicoutimi QC G7H 5B8
418/698-3000, Fax: 418/698-3019
Incorporée: 1 janvier, 1976
Population: 63,061 (1996)

#### CONSEIL

Maire, Jean Tremblay
Conseillers et Districts: 1) Jean-Guy Villeneuve; 2) Carl Savard; 3) Marina Larouche; 4) Jacques Bouchard; 5) Florian Pilote; 6) Jacques Fortin; 7) Jean-Guy Girard; 8) Jacques Cleary; 9) Marcel Jean; 10) Rémi Hamel
*Prochaine election:* novembre 2001(mandat de 4 ans)

#### ADMINISTRATION

Greffière, Services juridiques, Hélène Savard
Trésorière et Directrice, Services financiers, Rina Zampieri
Directeur général, Coordonnateur Mesures d'urgence, Marcel Demers, Fax: 418/698-3019
Directeur général adjoint, Robert Bouchard
Directeur général adjoint, Louison Lepage
Directeur, Ressources humaines, Roger Gonthier
Directeur, Sûreté municipale, Christian Harvey
Directeur, Service technique, Daniel Richard, 150, boul du Saguenay Est, CP 129, Chicoutimi QC G7H 5B8, 418/698-3131
Directeur, Service des incendies, Denis Simard, 2587, rue Roussel, CP 129, Chicoutimi QC G7H 5B8, 418/698-3382; Fax: 418/698-3389
Directeur, Service d'urbanisme, François Hains, 150, boul du Saguenay est, CP 129, Chicoutimi QC G7H 5B8, 418/698-3116
Directeur, Service des travaux publics, Guy St-Gelais, 504, boul Saguenay ouest, CP 129, Chicoutimi QC G7H 5B8, 418/698-3183; Fax: 418/698-3189

## Municipality of CLARINGTON

40 Temperance St., Bowmanville ON L1C 3A6
905/623-3379, Fax: 905/623-4169

Email: jennifer.cookel@sympatico.ca, URL: http://www.municipality.clarington.on.ca
Population: 60,615 (1996)

#### COUNCIL

Mayor, Diane Hamre
Councillors: Charlie Trim; 1) Jane Rowe; 2) Jim Schell; 3) Troy Young
*Next Election:* November 2000 (3 year terms)

#### ADMINISTRATION

Clerk, Patti Barrie
Treasurer, Marie Marano
Chief Administrative Officer, W. H. (Bill) Stockwell
Chief Building Officer, Stephen Vokes, Fax: 905/623-0830
Director, Community Services, Joe Caruana
Director, Planning & Development, Frank Wu
Director, Public Works, Stephen Vokes
Fire Chief, Mike Creighton
Officer, Tourism & Marketing, Jennifer Cooke
Purchasing Agent, Lou-Ann Birkett
Senior Planner, Community Planning Branch, Janice Auger Szwarz, ext.319; Fax: 905/623-0830

## City of COQUITLAM

1111 Brunette Ave., Coquitlam BC V3K 1E9
604/664-1400, Fax: 604/664-1650
URL: http://www.gov.coquitlam.bc.ca/
Incorporated: December 1, 1992
Area: 69 sq. mi
Population: 101,820 (1996)

#### COUNCIL

Mayor, Louis Sekora
Councillor: Kent Becker; Louella Hollington; Jon Kingsbury; Bill Melville; Jim Stangier; Diane Thorne
*Next Election:* November 1999 (3 year terms)

#### ADMINISTRATION

Clerk, Warren Jones
Treasurer, Robin D. Hicks
City Manager, Dr. N. Cook
City Engineer, Neil Nyberg, 604/664-1531; Fax: 604/664-1654
City Planner, Deb Day, 604/664-1481; Fax: 604/664-1652
City Solicitor, Deborah Brown
Director, Corporate Services, Don Buchanan
Director, Leisure & Parks Services, Barry Elliott, 604/933-6019; Fax: 604/933-6099
Director, Permits & Licences, K. Wright
Director, Personnel, Vacant
Fire Chief, K.D. Johnson
Purchasing Agent, Richard Baller

## Corporation of DELTA

4500 Clarence Taylor Cres., Delta BC V4K 3E2
604/946-4141, Fax: 604/946-3390
Incorporated: November 10, 1879
Population: 95,930 (1996)

#### COUNCIL

Mayor, Beth Johnson
Councillors: Krista Engelland; George Hawksworth; Vicki Huntington; Lois Jackson; Wendy Jeske; R. Bruce McDonald
*Next Election:* November 1999 (3 year terms)

#### ADMINISTRATION

Clerk, Tanalee Hesse
Chief Administrative Officer, Tom Fletcher
Director, Corporate Services, Rick Elligott
Director, Engineering, Peter Steblin
Director, Human Resources, J.C. Lambie
Director, Parks & Recreation, David Kalinovich
Acting Director, Permits & Licences, Ron Everett
Director, Planning, Wayne Dickinson
Fire Chief, Randy Wolsey
Police Chief, Jim Cessford

## Borough of EAST YORK

850 Coxwell Ave., East York ON M4C 5R1
416/778-2000, Fax: 416/778-9134
Incorporated: January 1, 1967
Area: 8.3 sq. miles
Population: 107,822 (1996)
**Editor's Note:** The Borough of East York, along with the other five member municipalities that make up Metropolitan Toronto, will amalgamate into a single City of Toronto effective January 1998. The present City of Toronto & Metropolitan Toronto will cease to exist & the new City of Toronto will assume responsibility for providing all municipal services. The amalgamation was in effect for municipal elections, November 1997, and a new council for the amalgamated City of Toronto was elected; *see* City of Toronto listing for the new mayor and council.

#### ADMINISTRATION

Borough Clerk, William Alexander, Jr., 416/778-2001
Treasurer & Director, Finance, Glenn Kippen, 416/778-2063
Chief Administrative Officer, Virginia West, 416/778-2160
Commissioner, Development Services, Richard Tomaszewicz, 416/778-2041
Commissioner, Parks, Recreation & Operations, Clair Tucker-Reid, 416/778-2180
Director, Human Resources, Vacant
Director, Parks & Operations, Don Boyle
Director, Transportation & Engineering Services, John W. Thomas
Environmental Engineer, Victor A. Chao-Ying, 416/778-2218; Fax: 416/466-9877
Fire Chief, John Miller, 416/396-3750
Manager, Planning, David Oikawa
Solicitor, Charles Loopstra, 416/778-2065

## City of EDMONTON

City Hall, 1 Sir Winston Churchill Sq., Edmonton AB T5J 2R7
403/496-8222, Fax: 403/496-8220
URL: http://www.gov.edmonton.ab.ca/
Incorporated: 1904
Area: 700.64 sq. km
Population: 616,306 (1996)

#### COUNCIL

Mayor, Bill Smith
Aldermen & Wards: 1) Leroy Chahley, Wendy Kinsella; 2) Allan Bolstad, Rose Rosenberger; 3) Brian Mason, Robert Noce; 4) Michael Phair, Jim Taylor; 5) Larry Langley, Brent Maitson; 6) Terry Cavanagh
*Next Election:* October 1998 (3 year terms)

#### ADMINISTRATION

City Clerk, David Edey, 403/496-8178
City Manager, Bruce E. Thom
Auditor General, Office of the Auditor General, André Bolduc, Chancery Hall, 3 Sir Winston Churchill Sq., 9th Fl., Edmonton AB T5J 2C3, 403/496-8303; Fax: 403/496-8062
Chief of Police, Police Services, John Lindsay, 9620 - 103A Ave., Edmonton AB T5H 0H7, 403/421-3460; Fax: 403/421-2211
City Solicitor, Law Branch, Anne Massing, Chancery Hall, 3 Sir Winston Churchill Sq., 9th Fl., Edmonton AB T5J 2C3, 403/496-7203; Fax: 403/496-7267
Fire Chief, Emergency Response, Jim Sales, 10351 - 96 St., Edmonton AB T5H 2H5, 403/496-3801; Fax: 403/496-1518
General Manager & City Engineer, Asset Management & Public Works Dept., Al B. Maurer, Century Place, 9803 - 102A Ave., 3rd Fl., Edmonton AB T5J 3A3, 403/496-5656; Fax: 403/496-5636
General Manager, Planning & Development Dept., Bruce Duncan, Exchange Building, 10250 - 101 St., 8th Fl., Edmonton AB T5J 2X6, 403/496-6050; Fax: 403/496-6104
General Manager, Community & Family Services, Joyce Tustian, Century Place, 9803 - 102A Ave., 4th Fl., Edmonton AB T5J 3A3, 403/496-5656; Fax: 403/496-5996
General Manager, Transportation Dept., R. Millican, Century Place, 9803 - 102A Ave., 15th Fl., Edmonton AB T5J 3A3, 403/496-2808; Fax: 403/496-2803
General Manager, Corporate Services Dept., Ronald J. Liteplo, Chancery Hall, 3 Sir Winston Churchill Sq., 4th Fl., Edmonton AB T5J 2C3, 403/496-7201; Fax: 403/496-5109
General Manager, Human Resources, W. Wetterberg, Century Place, 9803-102A Ave., 10th Fl., Edmonton AB T5J 3A3, 403/496-7800; Fax: 403/496-8063

## City of ETOBICOKE

City Hall, 399 The West Mall, Etobicoke ON M9C 2Y2
416/394-8000, Fax: 416/394-8895
Incorporated: June 29, 1983
Area: 48.3 sq. miles
Population: 328,718 (1996)
URL: http://www.busdev.city.etobicoke.on.ca
**Editor's Note:** The City of Etobicoke, along with the other five member municipalities that make up Metropolitan Toronto, will amalgamate into a single City of Toronto effective January 1998. The present City of Toronto & Metropolitan Toronto will cease to exist & the new City of Toronto will assume responsibility for providing all municipal services. The amalgamation was in effect for municipal elections, November 1997, and a new council for the amalgamated City of Toronto was elected; *see* City of Toronto listing for the new mayor and council.

#### ADMINISTRATION

Clerk-Treas. & Commissioner, Administrative Services, Brenda Glover, 416/394-8070
Acting City Manager, Tom Denes, 416/394-8921; Fax: 416/394-6067
Commissioner, Parks & Recreation Services, J.T. Riley, 416/394-8501
Commissioner, Urban Development, Karen Bricker, 416/394-8211; Fax: 416/394-6063
Commissioner, Works, Tom G. Denes, 416/394-8341; Fax: 416/394-8942
Director, Business Development & Corporate Affairs, Rick A. Field, 416/394-8949
Director, Purchasing Services, Tim Collet, 416/394-8155; Fax: 416/394-6065
Medical Officer of Health, A. Egbert, 416/394-8263; Fax: 416/394-8893
Sec.-Treas., Committee of Adjustment, D. Mungovan, 416/394-8063; Fax: 416/394-6042

## City of FREDERICTON

PO Box 130, Fredericton NB E3B 4Y7
506/460-2020, Fax: 506/460-2042
URL: http://www.city.fredericton.nb.ca
Incorporated: 1848
Area: 53 sq. miles
Population: 46,507 (1996)

#### COUNCIL

Mayor, Brad Woodside
Councillors & Wards: 1) G. Skead; 2) R.W. Turnbull; 3) M.J. Smith; 4) P.R. Bird; 5) W. Brown; 6) T. Cam-

eron; 7) D.I. Bentley; 8) R.W. Jackson; 9) T.J. Jellinek; 10) B. Sansom; 11) J. Burns; 12) D.E. Kelly
*Next Election:* May 1998 (3 year terms)

**ADMINISTRATION**

City Clerk, Donna Lavigne
City Treasurer, M. Marven Grant
City Administrator, Paul R. Stapleton
Assistant City Administrator & Director, Development Services, Jake Rudolph
City Engineer, E. John Bliss
City Solicitor, Bruce A. Noble
Director, Community Services, Robert A. Mabie, 506/460-2232
Director, Economic Development, Jacques Dubé
Director, Human Resources, J. David King
Director, Transit, Ronald Steeves, 506/460-2204
Fire Chief, Bert Fusk, 506/460-2511
Manager, Janice Legace, 506/460-2155
Manager, Purchasing, Robert Cormier
Manager, Tourism, Nancy Lockerbie
Manager, Development Division, Alex Forbes
Police Chief, Gordon M. Carlisle, 506/460-2343

## Ville de GATINEAU

144, boul de l'Hôpital, Gatineau QC J8T 7S7
819/243-2345, Fax: 819/243-2338
URL: http://gamma.omnimage.ca/clients/gatineau/
Incorporée: 1975
Superficie: 141 sq. km (54.4 sq. miles)
Population: 100,702 (1996)

**CONSEIL**

Maire, Guy Lacroix
Conseillers et Districts: 5) Jean Deschênes; 6) Jacques Forget; 8) Richard Migneault; 9) Jean René Monette; 12) Yvon Boucher; Bellevue) Richard Côté; De Touraine) Thérèse Cyr; Des Belles-Rives) Jean-Pierre Charette; Du Ruisseau) Marcel Schryer; La Baie) Berthe Miron; Le Baron) Richard Canuel; Limbour) Simon Racine
*Prochaine election:* novembre 1999 (mandat de 4 ans)

**ADMINISTRATION**

Greffier, J.C. Laurin, 819/243-2350
Directeur général adjoint & trésorier, Robert Bélair, 819/243-2313
Directeur général, Claude Doucet, 819/243-2310
Directeur, Communications, Jean Boileau, 819/243-2330
Directeur, Cour municipale, Jacques Dionne, 819/669-2541
Directrice, Loisirs et Culture, Hélène Grand'Maître, 819/243-4343
Directeur, Ressources humaines, Marc Pageau, 819/243-2490
Directeur, Securité publique, Joël Chéruet, 819/246-6125; Fax: 819/246-6051
Directeur, Services techniques, Marcel Roy, 819/669-2500; Fax: 819/669-2399
Directeur, Urbanisme, Jacques Perrier, 819/243-2450
Directeur adjoint, Incendies, Pierre Bertrand, 819/246-6065
Responsable des approvisionnements, Services financiers, Lynda Gariépy, 819/243-2025

## City of GLOUCESTER

1595 Telesat Court, PO Box 8333, Gloucester ON K1G 3V5
613/748-4100, Fax: 613/748-0235
Email: corp@city.gloucester.on.ca, URL: http://www.city.gloucester.on.ca/
Incorporated: January 1, 1981
Area: 29,526 ha
Population: 104,022 (1996)

**COUNCIL**

Mayor, Claudette Cain
Councillors in Wards: 1) Michael Denny; 2) Patricia Clark; 3) Rainer Bloess; 4) René Danis; 5) Ken Vowles; 6) George Barrett
*Next Election:* November 2000 (3 year terms)

**ADMINISTRATION**

Clerk, Michèle Giroux, 613/748-4104
Treasurer, Karen Tippett, 613/748-4158
City Manager, Pierre Tessier, 613/748-4125
Deputy City Manager, Community Development, D.J. Darch, P.Eng., 613/748-4191
Deputy City Manager, Corporate Services, Jo-Anne Poirier, 613/748-4293
Deputy City Manager, Operations & Fire, Brian Futterer, 613/748-4235
Director, Information Systems, Brenda Esson, 613/748-4196
Director, Recreation & Culture, Clem Pelot, 613/748-4138
Director, Human Resources, Gail Horsman, 613/748-4108
Fire Chief, Hubert Labelle, 613/748-4204
General Manager, Economic Adjustment, Don Loguisto, 613/748-4300
Manager, Corporate Communications, Liz Fauteux, 613/748-4259
Manager, Purchasing & Risk, Ted Allan, 613/748-4201

## City of GUELPH

59 Carden St., Guelph ON N1H 3A1
519/822-1260, Fax: 519/763-1269
Incorporated: 1879
Area: 26.53 sq. miles
Population: 95,821 (1996)

**COUNCIL**

Mayor, Joe Young
Councillors & Wards: 1. St Patrick's) Karen Farbridge, Rocco J. Furfaro; 2. St George's) Sean Farrelly, Garry Walton; 3. St John's) Norm Jary, Dan Schnurr; 4. St David's) Phil Cumming, Gloria Kovach; 5. St Andrew's) Cathy Downer, Bill McAdams; 6. St James) Christine Billings, Linda Prior
*Next Election:* November 2000 (3 year terms)

**ADMINISTRATION**

Clerk & Director, Information Services, Lois A. Giles, 519/837-5603; Fax: 519/763-1269
Director, Finance, David Kennedy, 519/837-5610; Fax: 519/837-5631
City Administrator, D.R. Creech, 519/837-5602; Fax: 519/822-8277
City Solicitor, Lois Payne, 519/837-5637; Fax: 519/822-8217
Director, Community Services, Gus Stahlmann, 519/837-5618; Fax: 519/763-9240
Director, Electric-Guelph Hydro, J.A. MacKenzie, 519/822-3017
Director, Personnel, J.D. Kentner, 519/837-5601; Fax: 519/763-2685
Director, Planning & Business Development, Tom Slomke, 519/837-5600; Fax: 519/837-5636
Director, Works, R.D. Funnell, P.Eng., 519/837-5604; Fax: 519/837-5635
Fire Chief, Art Cutten, 519/824-6590
Medical Officer of Health, Dr. D. Kittle, 519/837-5611
Police Chief, Lenna Bradburn, 519/824-1212
Purchasing Agent, Mark Bolzon, 519/837-5611; Fax: 519/837-5631
Transportation, Vacant , 50 Municipal St., Guelph ON N1G 1G9

## Regional Municipality of HALIFAX

1841 Argyle St., PO Box 1749, Halifax NS B3J 3A5
902/490-4000, Fax: 902/490-4208
URL: http://www.region.halifax.ns.ca/
Population: 332,518 (1996)

**COUNCIL**

Mayor, Walter R. Fitzgerald, 902/490-4010; Fax: 902/490-4012
Councillors: Stephen Adams; Barry Barnet; Jerry Blumenthal; Ron Cooper; John Cunningham; Bill Dooks; Graham L. Downey; Howard Epstein; Jack Greenough; Ron Hanson; Bob Harvey; David Hendsbee; Bruce Hetherington; Peter J. Kelly; Harry McInroy; Jack Mitchell; Reg Rankin; Condo Sarto; Clint Schofield; Gordon Snow; Bill Stone; Larry Uteck; Russell Walker
*Next Election:* 2000

**ADMINISTRATION**

Chief Administrative Officer, Kenneth R. Meech, 902/490-4026; Fax: 902/490-4044
Chief, Police, Vincent J. MacDonald
Commissioner, Community Services, Dan English
Commissioner, Corporate Services, Lawrence Corrigan
Commissioner, Fire Services, Gary Greene
Commissioner, Priority & Policy, Valerie Spencer
Commissioner, Regional Operations, George McLellan
Director, Administrative Services, Wayne Anstey
Director, Bus Operations, Brian Smith
Director, Engineering Services, Kulvinder Dhillon, P.Eng.
Director, Finance, Ron Singer
Director, Information Services, Chuck Keith
Director, Works & Natural Services, Doug Quinn
General Manager, Business Parks, Tom Rath
Manager, Human Resources, Kim Hominchuk
Manager, Tourism, Lewis M. Rogers

## City of HAMILTON

City Hall, 71 Main St. West, Hamilton ON L8P 4Y5
905/546-2700, Fax: 905/546-2095
Incorporated: 1846
Area: 54.38 sq. miles
Population: 322,352 (1996)

**COUNCIL**

Mayor, Bob Morrow, 905/546-4537
Aldermen & Wards: 1) Marvin Caplan, Mary Kiss; 2) V.J. Agro, W.M. McCulloch; 3) Don Drury, Bernie Morelli; 4) Geraldine Copps, Dave Wilson; 5) Chad Collins, Fred Eisenberger; 6) Bob Charters, Tom Jackson; 7) Terry Anderson, Henry Merling; 8) Frank D'Amico, Don Ross
*Next Election:* November 2000 (3 year terms)

**ADMINISTRATION**

City Clerk, Joseph J. Schatz, 905/546-4605
Treasurer, Allan Ross, 905/546-4524; Fax: 905/546-2449
Chief Administrative Officer, Joseph Pavelka, 905/546-4535; Fax: 905/546-3915
Commissioner, Building, Len King, 905/546-2775; Fax: 905/546-2764
Commissioner, Human Resources, John Johnston, 905/546-4330; Fax: 905/546-2650
Chief Executive Officer, Ken Roberts, 905-546-3200 ext.3214; Fax: 905/546-3202
City Solicitor, P. Noë-Johnson, 905/546-4635; Fax: 905/546-2142
Commissioner, Public Works & Traffic, Doug Lobo, 905/546-4623; Fax: 905/546-3972
Director, Culture & Recreation, Ross Fair, 905/546-4616; Fax: 905/546-2338

Director, Information Systems, Jim Hindson, 905/546-4563
Director, Planning, Victor Abraham, 905/546-4134; Fax: 905/546-9202
Fire Chief, Wesley H. Shoemaker, 905/546-3345; Fax: 905/546-3344
General Manager, Peter Baker, 905/540-6000; Fax: 905/540-6001
Managing Director & CEO, Gabe Macaluso, 905/546-4047; Fax: 905/521-0924

## Ville de HULL

25, rue Laurier, CP 1970, Succ B, Hull QC J8X 3Y9
819/595-7180, Fax: 819/595-7192
Incorporée: 1875
Superficie: 37.32 sq. km
Population: 62,339 (1996)

### CONSEIL

Maire, Yves Ducharme
Conseillers et Districts: Georges-Vanier) Denise Gagné; Hautes-Plaines) Roch Cholette; Lafontaine) Pierre Chénier; Laurier) Pierre Leduc; Madeleine-de-Verchères) Claude Bonhomme; Montcalm) Roland Michaud; Parc-de-la-Montagne) Lynus Godin; Saint-Raymond) Pierre Philion; Wright) Ghislaine Boucher; de l'Université) Claude Millette
*Prochaine election:* novembre 1999 (mandat de 4 ans)

### ADMINISTRATION

Directeur général adjoint, Jean-Pierre Chabot, 819/595-7147; Fax: 819/595-7138
Directeur, Finances, Michel Tremblay, 819/595-7210; Fax: 819/595-7215
Directeur général, Paul Préseault, o.m.a, 819/595-7131; Fax: 819/595-7138
Directeur général adjoint, Jacques Filiatrault, o.m.a., c.g.a., 819/595-7141; Fax: 819/595-7138
Directeur général adjoint, François Trottier, 819/595-7145; Fax: 819/595-7138
Directeur, Approvisionnements, François Bellemare, 819/595-7501; Fax: 819/595-7519
Directrice, Arts et Culture, Jacqueline Tardif, 819/595-7429; Fax: 819/595-7425
Directeur, Bibliothèque, Denis Boyer, 819/595-7461; Fax: 819/595-7487
Directeur, Développement économique, Rock Lapointe, 819/595-8001; Fax: 819/595-7784
Directeur, Développement organisationnel, Serge Brousseau, 819/595-7151; Fax: 819/595-7849
Directeur, Incendie, Jean-Maurice Roy, 819/595-7521; Fax: 819/595-7546
Directeur, Loisirs, Louis-Paul Guindon, 819/595-7401; Fax: 819/595-7425
Directeur, Operations immobilières, André Croteau, 819/595-7291; Fax: 819/595-7888
Directeur, Police, Claude Papineau, 819/595-7601; Fax: 819/595-7824
Directeur, Travaux publics et Ingénierie, Yves Patry, 819/595-7321; Fax: 819/595-7321
Directeur, Urbanisme, Pierre Tanguay, 819/595-7331; Fax: 819/595-7326
Greffière, Cour municipale, Lucie Poulin, 819/595-7270; Fax: 819/595-7280
Relationniste-conseil, Communications, David Coulombe, 819/595-7179; Fax: 819/595-7178
Responsable, Congrès et Tourisme, Pierre Normandin, 819/595-8013; Fax: 819/595-9755

## Ville de JONQUIÈRE

Hôtel de Ville, 2890, Place Davis, CP 2000, Jonquière QC G7X 7W7
418/546-2222, Fax: 418/699-6018
Email: courrier@ville.jonquiere.qc.ca , URL: http://ville.jonquiere.qc.ca
Incorporée: January 1, 1975
Superficie: 208.28 sq. km
Population: 56,503 (1996)

### CONSEIL

Maire, Marcel Martel
Conseillers et Districts: Lucie Gagnon; Sylvie Gaudreault; Réginald Gervais; Daniel Giguère; Jean-Eudes Girard; Gaston Laforest; Réjean Laforest; Robert Lavoie; Huguette Poirier; Claude Tremblay
*Prochaine election:* novembre 1999 (mandat de 4 ans)

### ADMINISTRATION

Greffier, Pierre Brassard, 418/699-6005; Fax: 418/699-6119
Trésorier, Serges Chamberland, 418/546-2040; Fax: 418/546-2043
Chef du cabinet du Maire, Marcel Fortin, 418/699-6053; Fax: 418/699-6057
Directeur général, Jean-Marc Gagnon, 418/699-6012
Directeur général adjoint, Gérard Leroux, 418/699-6013
Commissaire Industriel, Développement économique, Daniel Larouche
Directeur, Personnel, André Barrette, 418/699-6019
Directeur, Service de la protection publique, Gaston Tardif, 418/546-2007; Fax: 418/546-2038
Directeur, Services des loisirs, Laval Boucher, 418/699-6078; Fax: 418/699-6095
Directeur, Services techniques, Daniel Gaudreault, 418/699-6033; Fax: 418/699-6097
Directeur, Travaux publics, Roger Lavoie, 418/546-2122; Fax: 418/546-2118
Directrice du Contentieux, Jocelyne Trépanier, 418/699-6052; Fax: 418/699-6057
Chef de division, Atelier mécanique, Lionel Débigaré, 418/546-2230; Fax: 418/546-2229
Chef de division, Budget et Rémunération, Edouard Tremblay, 418/546-2056; Fax: 418/546-2043
Chef de division, Comptabilité, Trésorerie, André Cyr, 418/546-2044; Fax: 418/546-2043
Chef de division, Inspection et Permis, Alain Jean, 418/546-2149; Fax: 418/546-2161
Coordonnateur, Communications, Jeannot Allard, 418/699-6017; Fax: 418/699-6018
Directeur, Service des incendies, Normand Laplante, 418/546-2102; Fax: 418/546-2043

## City of KAMLOOPS

7 Victoria St. West, Kamloops BC V2C 1A2
250/828-3311, Fax: 250/828-3578
Incorporated: 1893
Area: 31,142.2 ha
Population: 76,394 (1996)

### COUNCIL

Mayor, Clifford G. Branchflower
Councillors: Shirley O. Culver; Sharon E. Frissell; Russell S. Gerard; Patricia K. Kaatz; Joe N. Leong; Grant R. Robertson; Patricia A. Wallace; William H. Walton
*Next Election:* November 1999 (three year terms)

### ADMINISTRATION

City Clerk/Asst. Administrator, Wayne Vollrath, 250/828-3446
Treasurer & Director, Finance, Wayne Ridgway, 250/828-3413; Fax: 250/828-0845; Email: wridgway@city.kamloops.bc.ca
City Administrator, J.E. Martignago, 250/828-3498; Email: jmartigna@city.kamloops.bc.ca
Asst. Administrator, City Engineer, E.G. Kurtz, 250/828-3452; Fax: 250/828-0952
Director, Development Services, R.H. Diehl, 250/828-3566; Fax: 250/828-7848
Director, Human Resources, K.D. Stinson, 250/828-3439; Fax: 250/372-1351
Director, Parks & Recreation Services, D.E. Kujat, 250/828-3489; Fax: 250/372-1673
Fire Chief & EMO, Doug Norman, 250/828-3490; Fax: 250/372-1447
Collector, R.O. Gowing, 250/828-3432
Manager, Engineering, M. Gravelle, 250/828-3464; Fax: 250/828-0952
Manager, Tourism, Karen McLaughlin, 250/828-3488; Fax: 250/828-7848
Purchasing Agent, E. Wild, 250/828-3503; Fax: 250/828-1766

## City of KELOWNA

City Hall, 1435 Water St., Kelowna BC V1Y 1J4
250/763-6011, Fax: 250/862-3399
Incorporated: May 4, 1905
Area: 87.7 sq. miles
Population: 89,442 (1996)

### COUNCIL

Mayor, Walter Gray
Councillors: Andre F. Blanleil; Marion Irene Bremner; Ron Cannan; Colin B. Day; Robert Douglas Hobson; Joe D. Leask; Smiley Nelson; Sharon Shepherd
*Next Election:* November 1999 (3 year terms)

### ADMINISTRATION

Clerk, David L. Shipclark, 250/862-3308
Treasurer, Tun Wong, Fax: 250/470-0690
City Administrator, R.A. Born
Collector, Lynn Walter, Fax: 250/862-3391
Director, Corporate Services, Linda Kerr
Director, Finance, Cliff Kraft, Fax: 250/470-0690
Director, Human Resources, R.W. Baker, 250/862-3376; Fax: 250/862-3318
Director, Leisure Services, David Graham, 250/862-3381; Fax: 250/470-0699
Director, Planning & Development Services, Ron Mattiussi, 250/862-3304; Fax: 250/862-3320
Director, Works & Utilities, Rod McRae, 250/862-3341; Fax: 250/862-3349
Fire Chief, Gerry Zimmermann, 250/860-6419; Fax: 250/862-3571
Manager, Information Services, D. Rasmussen
Medical Health Officer, Dr. B. Moorehead, 250/868-7700; Fax: 250/868-7760
Supervisor, Purchasing & Stores, R. Reiter, 250/862-3346
City Assessor, Assessment Department, J. Farkas, #201, 1665 Ellis St., Kelowna BC, 250/763-8300; Fax: 250/861-6136
Police Chief, RCMP City Detachment, Supt. Gary Forbes, 350 Doyle Ave., Kelowna BC V1Y 6V7, 250/762-3300; Fax: 250/762-3751

## City of KINGSTON

City Hall, 216 Ontario St., Kingston ON K7L 2Z3
613/546-4291, Fax: 613/546-5232
URL: http://www.city.kingston.on.ca
Incorporated: 1846
Area: 11.69 sq. miles
Population: 55,947 (1996)

### COUNCIL

Mayor, Gary Bennett
Councillors & Wards: 1) George Sutherland; 2) Randy Reid; 3) Bill Campbell; 4) George Beavis; 5) Peter Jardine; 6) George Stoparczyk; 7) Dave Meers; 8) Ken Matthews; 9) John Clements; 10) Don B. Rogers; 11) Rick Downes; 12) Leonore Foster
*Next Election:* November 2000 (3 year terms)

### ADMINISTRATION

City Clerk, Sheila Birrell, ext.247
City Treasurer, Richard Fiebig, ext.246

Chief Administrative Officer, Richard Fiebig
Commissioner, Kingston Municipal Operations, B. Sheridan, ext.239
Administrator, Social Services, B. Mason, 613/546-2695 ext.2071
Chief Building Official, T. Beltrami
City Solicitor, Norm Jackson, ext.208
Director, Human Resources, B. Bishop, ext.269
Director, Planning & Urban Renewal, Rupert Dobbin, ext.278
Director, Purchasing, R. Plumley, ext.236
Fire Chief, R. Thurlby, 613/542-9727
Manager, Public Utilities Commission, R. J. Reynolds, 613/546-1181 ext.203
Officer, Home Improvement Program, D. Werden, ext.214
Police Chief, W. Closs, 613/549-4660; Fax: 613/549-3111

## City of KITCHENER

City Hall, 200 King St. West, PO Box 1118, Kitchener ON N2G 4G7
519/741-2286, Fax: 519/741-2705
Email: kcouncil@hookup.net, URL: http://www.oceta.on.ca/city.kitchener
Incorporated: June 10, 1912
Area: 13,382 ha
Population: 178,420 (1996)

#### COUNCIL

Mayor, Carl Zehr
Councillors & Wards: 1. Centre) Karen Taylor-Harrison; 2. Rockway-Victoria) Mark Yantzi; 3. Bridgeport-North) John D. Smola; 4. Grand River) Jake Smola; 5. Chicopee) Berry Vrbanovic; 6. Doon-Pioneer) Jean Haalboom; 7. Fairview) James Ziegler; 8. South) Tom Galloway; 9. Forest) Geoff L.J. Lorentz; 10. West) Christina Weylie
*Next Election:* November 2000 (3 year terms)

#### ADMINISTRATION

City Clerk & Commissioner, General Services, Robert W. Pritchard, 519/741-2280; Email: bop.pritchard@city.kitchener.on.ca
Commissioner, Finance, John A. Gazzola, 519/741-2350; Fax: 519/741-2750; Email: jgazzola@city.kitchener.on.ca
Interim Chief Administrative Officer, John A. Gazzola, 519/741-2350; Email: jgazzola@city.kitchener.on.ca
General Manager, Parks & Recreation, Tom Clancy, 519/741-2394; Fax: 519/741-2723; Email: parks@city.kitchener.on.ca
General Manager, Planning & Development, Tim McCabe, 519/741-2320; Fax: 519/741-2624; Email: plan@city.kitchener.on.ca
General Manager, Public Works, Ed Kovacs, 519/741-2420; Fax: 519/741-2633
Asst. General Manager, Planning & Development, T. Brock Stanley, 519/741-2302; Fax: 519/741-2775
Asst. General Manager, Public Works, Steve J. Gyorffy, 519/741-2410
City Solicitor, James Shivas, 519/741-2263; Fax: 519/741-2702; Email: legal@city.kitchener.on.ca
Director, Economic Development, V. Gibaut, 519/741-2291; Fax: 519/741-2722; Email: ecodev@city.kitchener.on.ca
Director, Human Resources, Doug Paterson, 519/741-2252; Fax: 519/741-2400; Email: humres@city.kitchener.on.ca
Director, Transit, Vacant, 519/741-2560; Fax: 519/741-2640; Email: transit@city.kitchener.on.ca
Environmental Engineer, Chris Ford, 519/741-2215; Fax: 519/741-2222; Email: chris.ford@city.kitchener.on.ca
Fire Chief, James Hancock, 519/741-2500; Fax: 519/741-2697; Email: jim.hancock@city.kitchener.on.ca

## Corporation of the Township of LANGLEY

4914 - 221 St., Langley BC V3A 3Z8
604/534-3211, Fax: 604/533-6098
Incorporated: 1873
Area: 303.05 sq. km
Population: 80,179 (1996)

#### COUNCIL

Mayor, John Scholtens
Councillors: Muriel Arnason; May Barnard; Dean Drysdale; Karen Kersey; Mel Kositsky; Heather McMullan
*Next Election:* November 1999 (3 year terms)

#### ADMINISTRATION

Municipal Clerk, Rodney T. Edwards, 604/533-6003
Director, Finance & Corporate Services, Phil Revees
Administrator, Mark Bakken
Director, Engineering, Jamie Umpleby
Director, Human Resources, Mike Zora, 604/533-6121
Director, Parks & Recreation, David Steele
Director, Planning & Development, Terry Lyster
Fire Chief, W. Markel, 604/888-7755; Fax: 604/888-7088

## Ville de LASALLE

55, av Dupras, LaSalle QC H8R 4A8
514/367-1000, Fax: 514/367-6600
Incorporée: 1912
Superficie: 4,789 arpents
Population: 72,029 (1996)

#### CONSEIL

Maire, Michel Leduc, m.d.
Conseillers et Districts: 1) Gilbert Vachon; 2) Pierre Lussier; 3) François Dupuis; 4) Ross Blackhurst; 5) Manon Barbe; 6) Antonio Massana; 7) Monique Vallée; 8) Daniel Zizian; 9) Vincenzo Cesari; 10) Alvaro Farinacci; 11) Frank Talarico; 12) Alain Chénier
*Prochaine election:* novembre 1999 (mandat de 4 ans)

#### ADMINISTRATION

Greffière, Nicole Herby, 514/367-6392; Fax: 514/367-6607
Trésorier, Service des finances, Maurice Martel, 514/367-6230; Fax: 514/367-3520
Directeur général, Gervais Lemay, 514/367-6200
Chef de Cabinet du Maire, Pierre Guérin, 514/367-6209
Chef, Génie, Yvon Rousseau, 514/367-6770; Fax: 514/367-6602
Chef, Service des achats, Robert Martineau, 514/367-6720; Fax: 514/367-6602
Commissaire, Corporation de développement économique de LaSalle, Chantal Malo, 514/367-6380
Directrice, Service de la culture, Rachel Laperrière, 514/367-6370; Fax: 514/367-5840
Directeur, Service de protection contre l'incendie, Pierre Damico, 514/367-6320; Fax: 514/368-1436
Directeur, Service des communications, loisirs et dév. communautaire, Gérald Lawrence, 514/367-6490; Fax: 514/367-6607
Directeur, Service des ressources humaines, Michel Beaudoin, 514/367-6400; Fax: 514/367-5840
Directeur, Services techniques, Mario Vachon, 514/367-6700; Fax: 514/367-6602

## Ville de LAVAL

Hôtel de Ville, 1, Place du Souvenir, CP 422, Succ St-Martin, Laval QC H7V 1W7
514/978-8000, Fax: 514/978-5943
URL: http://www.ville.laval.qc.ca/
Incorporée: 6 aout, 1965
Superficie: 242.41 sq. km (93.6 sq. miles)
Population: 330,393 (1996)

#### CONSEIL

Maire, Gilles Vaillancourt
Conseillers: 1) Jacques St-Jean; 2) Maurice Clermont; 3) Michel Poirier; 4) Georges Gauthier; 5) Georges Gagné; 6) Jean-Jacques Lapierre; 7) Benoit Fradet; 8) Norman Girard; 9) Yvon Doré; 10) Philippe Garceau; 11) Michelle Major; 12) Jocelyn Guertin; 13) Ginette Legault-Bernier; 14) Basile Angelopoulos; 15) Richard Goyer; 16) Pierre Cléroux; 17) Jean-Jacques Beldié; 18) Robert Plante; 19) Yvon Bromley; 20) André Boileau; 21) Pierre D'Amico
*Prochaine election:* novembre 2001 (mandat de 4 ans)

#### ADMINISTRATION

Greffier, Guy Collard, 514/978-3950; Fax: 514/978-3966
Budget, Achats et Informatique, Richard Beaudry, 514/978-3900; Fax: 514/978-3915
Pierre Bélanger, 514/978-5959; Fax: 514/978-5970
Directeur général, Claude Asselin, 514/978-3676; Fax: 514/978-3692
Communications, Pierre René de Cotret, 514/978-8000; Fax: 514/978-5943
Contentieux, Jean Allaire, 514/978-5866; Fax: 514/978-5871
Culture, Loisirs et Vie communautaire, Paul Lemay, 514/662-4343; Fax: 514/669-4729
Évaluation, Claude Globensky, 514/978-8777; Fax: 514/978-8710
Finances, André Bourgeois, 514/978-5704; Fax: 514/978-5789
Ingénierie, Claude de Guise, 514/662-4550; Fax: 514/662-5091
Protection des citoyens (Police), Jean Marc-Aurèle, 514/662-4242; Fax: 514/662-7282
Ressources humaines, Pierre Comeau, 514/978-6560; Fax: 514/978-6561
Travaux publics et Environnement urbain, André Perrault, 514/662-4600; Fax: 514/662-7279
Urbanisme, Normand Gariépy, 514/662-4333; Fax: 514/662-7250

## City of LETHBRIDGE

City Hall, 910 - 4 Ave. South, Lethbridge AB T1J 0P6
403/320-3900, Fax: 403/320-9369
URL: http://www.city.lethbridge.ab.ca
Incorporated: 1906
Area: 48 sq. miles (12,413 ha)
Population: 63,053 (1996)

#### COUNCIL

Mayor, David B. Carpenter, Fax: 403/320-7575; Email: mayor@city.lethbridge.ab.ca
Aldermen: Jeffrey Coffman; Barbara Lacey; Don M. Lebaron; Ed J. Martin; Joe Mauro; Frank Peta; Shaun Ward; Greg Weadick
*Next Election:* October 1998 (3 year terms)

#### ADMINISTRATION

City Clerk, Dianne Nemeth, 403/320-3821; Fax: 403/320-7575; Email: dnemeth@city.lethbridge.ab.ca
Director, Finance & Utilities, Garth Sherwin, 403/320-3985; Fax: 403/327-6571
City Manager, Bryan Horrocks, 403/320-3900; Fax: 403/320-9369
Director, Community Services, Tom Hudson, 403/320-3002; Fax: 403/380-2512
Chief Librarian, Duncan Rand, 403/380-7340; Fax: 403/329-1478
Chief of Police, John LaFlamme, 403/327-2210; Fax: 403/328-6999; Email: laflamm@city.lethbridge.ab.ca
City Solicitor, Douglas Hudson, 403/320-3903; Fax: 403/320-9369; Email: dhudson@city.lethbridge.ab.ca
Comptroller, Barry Sawada, 403/320-3981; Fax: 403/327-4195; Email: bsawada@city.lethbridge.ab.ca

Deputy Fire Chief, Disaster Services, Ted Bochan, 403/320-3802; Fax: 403/327-3503; Email: fire@city.lethbridge.ab.ca
Development & Forestry Supervisor, Parks, Dave Mitchell, 403/320-3019; Fax: 403/320-2823; Email: dmitchell@city.lethbridge.ab.ca
Director, Enterprise Development, Brian Bourassa, 403/320-3010; Fax: 403/320-9369
Director, Enterprise Development, Kathy Hopkins, 403/320-3015; Fax: 403/320-9369; Email: khopkins@city.lethbridge.ab.ca
Fire Chief, Tom Wickersham, 403/320-3803; Fax: 403/327-3503; Email: fire@city.lethbridge.ab.ca
General Manager, Development Services, Felix Michna, 403/320-3921; Fax: 403/320-6571; Email: fmichna@city.lethbridge.ab.ca
Infrastructure Steward, Bud Hogeweide, 403/320-3094; Fax: 403/329-4657; Email: hogeweid@city.lethbridge.ab.ca
Interim Leader, Human Resources, Casey Hellawell, 403/320-3913; Fax: 403/320-9361; Email: hellawel@city.lethbridge.ab.ca
Manager, Assessment & Taxation, Barrie Hosack, 403/320-3951; Fax: 403/320-4956
Manager, Computer Services, Joe Feller, 403/320-3971; Fax: 403/327-6571; Email: jfeller@city.lethbridge.ab.ca
Manager, Economic Development, Darrel McKenzie, 1-800-332-1801; Fax: 403/320-4259; Email: ecodev@city.lethbridge.ab.ca
Manager, Fleet Services, Doug Brandvold, 403/329-7368; Fax: 403/328-4467
Manager, Human Resources, Paul Petry, 403/320-3912; Fax: 403/320-9369; Email: ppetry@city.lethbridge.ab.ca
Manager, Leisure Facilities, Tom Hopkins, 403/320-3012; Fax: 403/380-2512; Email: thopkins@city.lethbridge.ab.ca
Manager, Lethbridge Power, Juergen Renter, 403/320-3933; Fax: 403/380-2541; Email: powerline@city.lethbridge.ab.ca
Manager, Purchasing, Al Burghardt, 403/320-3961; Fax: 403/328-0501
Manager, Risk & Insurance, Leo VandenHeuvel, 403/320-3902; Fax: 403/329-4657; Email: vandenhe@city.lethbridge.ab.ca
Manager, Solid Waste & Recycling, Walter Brodowski, 403/320-3090; Fax: 403/329-4657; Email: walterb@city.lethbridge.ab.ca
Manager, Sportsplex, Ashley Matthews, 403/320-4040; Fax: 403/327-3620
Manager, Traffic Operations, Brian Johnson, 403/320-3092; Fax: 403/329-4657; Email: bjohnson@city.lethbridge.ab.ca
Acting Manager, Transit, Tom Hopkins, 403/320-3884; Fax: 403/380-3876; Email: thopkins@city.lethbridge.ab.ca
Medical Health Officer, Community & Wellness, Dr. Paul Hasselback, 403/382-6014; Fax: 403/382-6011; Email: phassel@crha.sas.ab.ca
Urban Designer, Gary Weikum, 403/320-4269; Fax: 403/329-4657; Email: gweikum@city.lethbridge.ab.ca

## City of LONDON

City Hall, 300 Dufferin Ave., PO Box 5035, London ON N6A 4L9
519/661-4500, Fax: 519/661-4892
URL: http://www.city.london.on.ca
Incorporated: 1855
Area: 43,667 ha
Population: 325,646 (1996)

### COUNCIL

Mayor, Dianne Haskett
Councillors & Wards: 1) John Irvine, Sandy Levin; 2) Rob Alder, Robert Beccarea; 3) Bernard R. MacDonald, Fred Tranquilli; 4) William Armstrong, W.J. Polhill; 5) Cheryl Miller, Gary E. Williams; 6) Ben Veel, Megan Walker; 7) Gordon Hume, Martha E. Joyce
*Next Election:* November 2000 (3 year terms)

### ADMINISTRATION

City Clerk, Jeffrey A. Malpass
City Treasurer & Commissioner, Linda H. Reed
Acting City Adminstrator, Linda H. Reed
Commissioner, Planning & Development, Victor A. Coté
Chief of Police, J. Fantino
Commissioner & City Engineer, John W. Jardine
Director, Economic Development, Vacant
Director, Human Resources, H. Ross Rowe
Director & Medical Officer of Health, Dr. G.L. Pollett
Fire Chief, Gary W. Weese
Manager, Parks & Community Programs, Bob Graham

## Ville de LONGUEUIL

350, rue Saint-Charles, CP 5000, Longueuil QC J4K 4Y7
514/646-8218, Fax: 514/646-8080
Incorporée: 1874
Superficie: 45 sq. km
Population: 127,977 (1996)

### CONSEIL

Maire, Claude Gladu, 514/646-8215; Fax: 514/646-8203
Conseillers et Districts: 1. Charles-Lemoyne) Joël Gamache; 2. Pierre d'Iberville) Cécile Langevin; 3. Fernand-Bouffard) Henri Dubois; 4. St.Pierre-Apôtre) Sylvie Robidas; 5. Coteau-Rouge) Nicole Béliveau-Zeitter; 6. Octavien-Vincent) Normand Caisse; 7. Hubert-Perron) Alain St-Pierre; 8. St-Vincent-de-Paul) Johane Fontaine Deshais; 9. Adrien-Laflamme) Nicole Lafontaine; 10. Christ-Roi) Manon Hénault; 11. Emérillon) Serge Sévigny; 12. Sieur-de-Roberval) Lise Sauvé; 13. Lionel-Groulx) Bertrand Girard; 14. Adrien-Gamache) Michel Timpiero; 15. Saint-Pie-X) Florent Charest; 16. Saint-Antoine) Pierre Beaudry; 17. Fatima) Pierre Racicot; 18. Bellerive) Jacques Milette; 19. Gentilly) Claudette Tessier; 20. Du Tremblay) Simon Crochetière
*Prochaine election:* novembre 1998 (mandat de 4 ans)

### ADMINISTRATION

Greffier, Claude Comtois, 514/646-8225
Directeur général, Massimo Iezzoni, Fax: 514/646-8255
Directeur général adjoint et Directeur des services financiers, Pierre Pouliot, 514/646-8710
Chef de division, Hygiène du milieu, Pierre Lemoyne, 514/646-8404
Directeur, Communications, Jean Racicot, 514/646-8669
Directeur, Contentieux, Me Claude Séguin, 514/646-8235
Directeur, Loisirs et Culture, Martin Lelievre, 514/646-8647
Directeur, Police, Marc Quimper, 514/646-8510; Fax: 514/646-8497
Directeur, Prévention des incendies, Gilles Lamadeleine, 514/646-8270
Directeur, Ressources humaines, Raymond Patry, 514/646-8790
Directeur, Urbanisme et Permis, Claude Doyon, 514/646-8420

## Town of MARKHAM

101 Town Centre Blvd., Markham ON L3R 9W3
905/477-7000, Fax: 905/479-7771
URL: http://www.city.markham.on.ca
Incorporated: January 1, 1971
Area: 52,890 acres
Population: 173,383 (1996)

### COUNCIL

Mayor, Don Cousens, 905/470-6622; Fax: 905/479-7775
Regional Councillors: Ralph Aselin; Bill Fisch; Gordon Landon; Frank Scarpitti
Ward Councillors: 1) Bill O'Donnell; 2) Randy Barber; 3) Joe Virgilio; 4) George McKelvey; 5) Jack Heath; 6) David Allison; 7) Tony Wong; 8) Alex Chiu
*Next Election:* November 2000 (3 year terms)

### ADMINISTRATION

Clerk, Bob Panizza
Treasurer & Director, Finance, Joann Chechalk
Chief Administrative Officer, Lorne V. McCool, ext.263; Fax: 905/479-7764
Commissioner, Community Services, Dalo Keliar, ext.265; Fax: 905/479-7766
Commissioner, Corporate Services, Robert Swayze, Fax: 905/479-7764
Commissioner, Development Services, Mary-Francis Turner
Director, Economic Development, Stephen Chait
Director, Human Resources, Jim Hamill
Director, Recreation, Barbara Roth
Director, Roads, Ted Mortson
Fire Chief, Anthony Mintoff
Manager, Administrative Services, Andrew Vickery

## City of MISSISSAUGA

300 City Centre Dr., Mississauga ON L5B 3C1
905/896-5000, Fax: 905/896-5220
URL: http://www.city.mississauga.on.ca
Incorporated: January 1, 1974
Area: 111 sq. miles
Population: 544,382 (1996)

### COUNCIL

Mayor, Hazel McCallion
Councillors & Wards: 1) Carmen Corbasson; 2) Patricia Mullin; 3) Maja Prentice; 4) Frank Dale; 5) Frank McKechnie; 6) David Culham; 7) Nando Iannicca; 8) Katie Mahoney; 9) Pat Saito
*Next Election:* November 2000 (3 year terms)

### ADMINISTRATION

Deputy City Clerk, Arthur Grannum, 905/896-5419
Commissioner & Clerk/Treasurer, Corporate Services, William H. Munden, 905/896-5262; Fax: 905/615-4181
City Manager, David S. O'Brien, 905/896-5550; Fax: 905/615-3376
Commissioner, Community Services, Paul Mitcham, 905/615-3100
Commissioner, Human Resources, David Bray, 905/896-5023
Commissioner, Planning & Building, Thomas Mokrzycki, 905/896-5561; Fax: 905/896-5553
Commissioner, Transportation & Works, Angus McDonald, 905/896-5112; Fax: 905/896-5504
City Solicitor, Shelley Pohjola, 905/896-5393; Fax: 905/896-5106
Director, Communications, Susan Amring, 905/896-5047; Fax: 905/615-3078
Director, Economic Development, Karen Campbell, 905/896-5012; Fax: 905/615-3376
Director, Finance, Jeffrey Jackson, 905/896-5477; Fax: 905/896-5133
Director, Material Management, Brenda Breault, 905/896-5395; Fax: 905/615-4181
Director, Recreation & Parks, John Lohuis, 905/615-3700; Fax: 905/615-3469
Director, Works, Martin Powell, 905/896-5086; Fax: 905/896-5583

Fire Chief, Cyril Hare, 905/615-3750; Fax: 905/615-3773
General Manager, Mississauga Transit, Ed Dowling, 905/615-3840; Fax: 905/615-3833

## City of MONCTON

655 Main St., Moncton NB E1C 1E8
506/853-3333, Fax: 506/859-4225
Incorporated: 1890
Area: 58.06 sq. miles
Population: 59,313 (1996)

**COUNCIL**

Mayor, Léopold F. Belliveau
Councillors & Wards: 1) Norman H. Crossman, Brian Murphy; 2) S. Boyd Anderson, Joan MacAlpine; 3) John W. Betts, George H. LeBlanc; 4) Charles J. Gillespie, Q.C., Yvon Goguen
Councillors at Large: Judith E. Jacobson; Stan McGrath
*Next Election:* May 1998 (3 year terms)

**ADMINISTRATION**

Clerk, Elizabeth Reade, 506/853-3550; Email: elizabeth.reade@moncton.org
Commissioner, Finance & Administration, H.T. Eno, Fax: 506/859-2676; Email: tom.eno@moncton.org
City Manager, L.E. Strang, 506/853-3550; Email: al.strang@moncton.org
Commissioner, Engineering & Public Works, J.G. Greenough, Fax: 506/853-3543; Email: geoff.greenough@moncton.org
Commissioner, Policy & Corporate Resources, M.B. Sullivan; Email: mike.sullivan@moncton.org
Chief of Police, G.D.J. Cohoon, 506/857-2400; Fax: 506/857-2414; Email: greg.cohoon@moncton.org
City Solicitor, William E. Cooper, Fax: 506/859-2610; Email: bill.cooper@moncton.org
Director, Community Services, Community Development & Partnership, Ian Fowler, Fax: 506/859-2629; Email: ian.fowler@moncton.org
Director, Community Services/Operations, Rod Higgins, Fax: 506/859-2679; Email: rod.higgins@moncton.org
Director, Greater Moncton District Planning Commission, Kenneth D. Stevens
Director, Purchasing, R. Melanson, Fax: 506/859-2675
Director, Special Projects, Ron LeBlanc, Fax: 506/853-3543; Email: ron.leblanc@moncton.org
Fire Chief, Bruce Morrison, 506/857-8800; Fax: 506/856-4353; Email: bruce.morrison@moncton.org
President, Greater Moncton Economic Commission, Ron Gaudet
Chair, EMO, & Manager, Codiac Transit Commission, John Allain, 280 Pacific Ave., Moncton NB E1E 2G8, 506/857-2008; Fax: 506/859-2680
General Manager, Moncton Industrial Development, Peter Belliveau, #102, 910 Main St., Moncton NB E1C 1G6, 506/857-0700; Fax: 506/859-7206

## Ville de MONTRÉAL

Hôtel de Ville, 275, rue Notre-Dame est, Montréal QC H2Y 1C6
514/872-1111, Fax: 514/872-5655
URL: http://www.ville.montreal.qc.ca/
Incorporée: 1832
Superficie: 192.47 sq. km (74.2 sq. mi)
Population: 1,016,376 (1996)

**CONSEIL**

Maire, Pierre Bourque
Conseillers et Districts: 1. Cartierville) Pierre Gagnier; 2. L'Acadie) Noushig Eloyan; 3. Ahuntsic) Hasmig Belleli; 4. Saint-Sulpice) Maurice Beauchamp; 5. Fleury) Colette St-Martin; 6. Sault-au-Récollet) Serge-Éric Bélanger; 7. Saint-Michel) Paolo Tamburello; 8. Jean-Rivard) Daniel Boucher; 9. François-Perreault) Vittorio Capparelli; 10. Villeray) Sylvain Lachance; 11. Octave-Crémazie) Anie Samson; 12. Jarry) Achille Polcaro; 13. Parc-Extension) Konstantinos Georgoulis; 14. Saint-Édouard) Pierre Goyer; 15. Père-Marquette) Robert Laramée; 16. Louis-Hébert) Hubert Deraspe; 17. Étienne-Desmarteau) Michelle Daines; 18. Marie-Victorin) Kettly Beauregard; 19. Bourbonnière) Andrée Lavallée; 20. Rosemont) Robert Côté; 21. Lorimier) Richard Théorêt; 22. Plateau Mont-Royal) Thérèse Daviau; 23. Laurier) Louise Roy; 24. Mile-End) Helen Fotopulos; 25. Jeanne-Mance) Michel Prescott; 26. Peter McGill) Georgine Coutu; 27. Cote-des-Neiges) Pierre-Yves Melançon; 28. Darlington) Jack Chadirdjian; 29. Victoria) Saulie Zajdel; 30. Snowdon) Marvin Rotrand; 31. Notre-Dame-de-Grâce) Michael Applebaum; 32. Loyola) Jeremy Searle; 33. Décarie) Sam Boskey; 34. Émard) Robert Gagnon; 35. Saint-Paul) Philippe Bissonnette; 36. Saint-Henri) Germain Prégent; 37. Pointe-Saint-Charles) Marcel Sévigny; 38. Saint-Jacques) Sammy Forcillo; 39. Sainte-Marie) Martin Lemay; 40. Hochelaga) Luc Larivée; 41. Maisonneuve) Nathalie Malépart; 42. Pierre-de-Coubertin) Benoît Parent; 43. Louis-Riel) Jacques Charbonneau; 44. Longue-Pointe) Claire St-Arnaud; 45. Honoré-Beaugrand) Ivon Le Duc; 46. Tétreaultville) Jean-Guy Deschamps; 47. Marc-Aurèle-Fortin) Giovanni De Michele; 48. Rivière-des-Prairies) Aimé Charron; 49. Pointe-aux-Trembles) Marie Lebeau; 50. La Rousselière) Colette Paul; 51. Bout-de-l'Île) Johanne Lorrain
*Prochaine election:* novembre 1998 (mandat de 4 ans)

**ADMINISTRATION**

Directeur, Léon Laberge, 514/872-3142
Secrétariat administratif, Danielle Rondeau, 872-8155; Fax: 872-8433
Avocate en Chef & Directrice, Service du contentieux, Suzanne Jalbert, 514/872-2919; Fax: 514/872-2828
Directeur, Service de la prévention des incendies, Alain Michaud, 4040, av du Parc, Montréal QC H1M 2S6, 514/872-3761; Fax: 514/868-3180
Directeur, Service des immeubles, André Blain, 385, rue Sherbrooke est, Montréal QC H2X 1E3, 514/872-5380; Fax: 514/872-4049
Directeur, Service de l'habitation, Fabien Cournoyer, #4.100, 303, rue Notre-Dame est, Montréal QC H2Y 3Y8, 514/872-3882; Fax: 514/872-3883
Directeur, Service du personnel, Jean Des Trois Maisons, 413, rue St-Jacques, 4e étage, Montréal QC H2Y 1N9, 514/872-5809; Fax: 514/872-8430
Directeur, Service du développement économique, Jean-Marc Lajoie, 500, Place d'Armes, 13e étage, Montréal QC H2Y 1N9, 514/872-6404; Fax: 514/872-9812
Directeur, Service de l'urbanisme, Pierre Ouellet, 303, rue Notre-Dame est, 5e étage, Montréal QC H2Y 3Y8, 514/872-4523; Fax: 514/872-0024
Directeur, Service de la sécurité du revenu, Robert Guay, 1125, rue Ontario est, 2e étage, Montréal QC H2L 1R2, 514/872-4940; Fax: 514/872-6020
Directeur, Service des finances et du contrôle budgétaire, Roger Galipeau, #207, 155, rue Notre-Dame est, Montréal QC H2Y 1B5, 514/872-6630; Fax: 514/872-3145
Directeur, Service de la circulation & du transport, Yann Davies, #1.220, 700, rue St-Antoine est, Montréal QC H2Y 1A6, 514/872-3130; Fax: 514/872-1727
Directeur, Service de l'approvisionnement et du soutien technique, Yves Provost, 9515, rue St-Hubert, Montréal QC H2M 1Z4, 514/872-7014; Fax: 514/872-7510
Direction, Service de la culture, Vacant, 5650, rue d'Iberville, 5e étage, Montréal QC H2G 3E4, 514/872-1149; Fax: 514/872-0425
Direction, Service de la propreté, Vacant, #1.100, 700, rue St-Antoine est, Montréal QC H2Y 1A6, 514/872-1266; Fax: 514/872-3505
Directrice, Service des permis & inspections, Céline Topp, #2.100, 303, rue Notre-Dame est, Montréal QC H2Y 2Y8, 514/872-3111; Fax: 514/872-3587
Directrice, Service des travaux publics, Johanne Falcon, #R-230, 700, rue St-Antoine est, Montréal QC H2Y 1A6, 514/872-9278; Fax: 514/872-8990
Directrice, Service des parcs, jardins et espaces verts, Lise Cormier, #200, 4590, rue d'Orléans, Montréal QC H1X 2K4, 514/872-1457; Fax: 514/872-1458
Directrice, Service des sports, des loisirs et du développement social, Stella Guy, #201, 7400, boul St-Michel, Montréal QC H2A 2Z8, 514/872-2465; Fax: 514/872-4561
Directrice, Service de la gestion financière des caisses de retraite, Thieu Quan Hoang, 413, rue St-Jacques, 7e étage, Montréal QC H2Y 1N9
Vérificateur, Bureau du Vérificateur, Guy Lefebvre, c.a., #605, 276, rue St-Jacques, Montréal QC H2Y 1N3, 514/872-2208; Fax: 514/872-6950

## Ville de MONTRÉAL-NORD

4242, Place de l'Hôtel-de-Ville, Montréal-Nord QC H1H 1S5
514/328-4000, Fax: 514/328-4299
Incorporée: 15 mars, 1915
Superficie: 427.6 ha
Population: 81,581 (1996)

**CONSEIL**

Maire, Yves Ryan
Conseillers et Districts: 1) Antonin Dupont; 2) Michelle Allaire; 3) Pierre Blain; 4) Georgette Morin; 5) Maurice Bélanger; 6) Jean-Marc Gibeau; 7) Jean-Paul Lessard; 8) Normand Fortin; 9) James V. Infantino; 10) André Coulombe; 11) Raymond Paquin; 12) Robert Guerriero
*Prochaine election:* novembre 1998 (mandat de 4 ans)

**ADMINISTRATION**

Greffe, Hélène Simoneau
Directeur, Finances, Michel Labrecque
Directeur général, Michel Archambault
Chef, Approvisionnement, Yvon Ménard, 514/328-4051; Fax: 514/328-4055
Chef, Informatique, Jean-Claude Bérubé
Chef, Personnel, Jean-Pierre Masse
Directeur, Génie, Yvon Paquette, ing., 514/328-4007; Fax: 514/328-4055
Directeur, Protection incendie, André Morin
Directeur, Services des loisirs et de la vie communautaire, François Boucher, 514/328-4166; Fax: 514/328-4064
Directeur, Travaux publics, Environnement et Mesures d'urgence, Roland de Grandpré, ing., 514/328-4104; Fax: 514/328-4065
Directice, Centres biblio-culturels, Céline Dénommée

## City of NANAIMO

455 Wallace St., Nanaimo BC V9R 5J6
250/754-4251, Fax: 250/755-4436
URL: http://www.city.nanaimo.bc.ca/
Incorporated: December 24, 1874
Area: 88,190 sq. km
Population: 70,130 (1996)

**COUNCIL**

Mayor, Gary Richard Korpan, 250/755-4400; Email: gkorpan@city.nanaimo.bc.ca
Councillors: Bill King; Jack Little; Paulette McCarthy; Blake McGuffie; Larry McNabb; Doug Rispin; Lloyd Sherry; David Thompson
*Next Election:* November 1999 (3 year terms)

#### ADMINISTRATION
City Clerk, Jim Bowden, 250/755-4404; Fax: 250/755-4435; Email: jbowden@city.nanaimo.bc.ca
Director, Finance, Connie Davis, Fax: 250/755-4440; Email: cdavis@city.nanaimo.bc.ca
City Administrator, Gerald D. Berry, 250/755-4401; Email: gberry@city.nanaimo.bc.ca
Economic Development, Melinda Entwistle, 250/755-4465; Fax: 250/754-8263; Email: mentwist@city.nanaimo.bc.ca
Director, Development Services, Brian Mehaffey, 250/755-4423; Fax: 250/755-4437; Email: bmehaffe@city.nanaimo.bc.ca
Director, Human Resources, Judy Constable, 250/754-4406; Fax: 250/755-4449; Email: jconstab@city.nanaimo.bc.ca
Director, Parks, Recreation & Culture, Andy Laidlaw, 250/755-7500; Fax: 250/753-7277; Email: alaidlaw@city.nanaimo.bc.ca
Director, Strategic Planning & Engineering, D.L. (Les) King, 250/755-4428; Email: lking@city.nanaimo.bc.ca
Fire Chief, Ray Digby, 250/753-7311; Fax: 250/753-5480; Email: rdigby@city.nanaimo.bc.ca
General Manager, Corporate Services, Al Kenning, 250/755-4410; Email: akenning@city.nanaimo.bc.ca
General Manager, Operations, Ken. Davis, 250/758-5222; Fax: 250/756-5326; Email: kdavis@city.nanaimo.bc.ca
Managing Director, Public Works, Mac Mackenzie, 250/756-5301; Fax: 250/756-5326; Email: mmackenz@city.nanaimo.bc.ca

### City of NEPEAN
Nepean Civic Square, 101 Centrepointe Dr., Nepean ON K2G 5K7
613/727-6600, Fax: 613/727-6701
Email: webmaster@city.nepean.on.ca, URL: http://www.city.nepean.on.ca
Incorporated: 1850
Area: 78.84 sq. miles (50,400 acres)
Population: 115,100 (1996)

#### COUNCIL
Mayor, Mary Pitt
Councillors & Wards: 1. Lakeshore) Mervyn Sullivan; 2. Nepean Centre) Rick Chiarelli; 3. Evergreen) Wayne Phillips; 4. Knoxdale) Margaret Rywak; 5. Merivale) Lee Farnworth; 6. Barrhaven) Jan Harder
*Next Election:* November 2000 (3 year terms)

#### ADMINISTRATION
Commissioner & City Clerk, John LeMaistre, 613/727-6612
Commissioner, Finance, Lloyd Russell, 613/727-6615
Chief Administrative Officer, Robert R. Letourneau, 613/727-6607
Commissioner, Human Resources, Grant Armstrong, 613/727-6624
Commissioner, Parks & Recreation, R.J. (Bob) Sulpher, 613/727-6640
Commissioner, Planning & Development, Jack D. Stirling, 613/727-6626
Commissioner, Public Works, A. Clarke Bellinger, 613/727-6630
Director, Information Services, Andrea McCormick, 613/727-6634
Fire Chief & Commissioner, Emergency Services, Chris Powers, 613/825-2020

### City of NIAGARA FALLS
City Hall, 4310 Queen St., PO Box 1023, Niagara Falls ON L2E 6X5
905/356-7521, Fax: 905/356-9083
URL: http://www.niagara.com/city.niagara-falls
Incorporated: January 1, 1904
Area: 80.92 sq. miles
Population: 76,917 (1996)

#### COUNCIL
Editor's Note: Results of the November 1997 election were not available at press time; up to date results may appear in the Addenda at the back of this book.
*Next Election:* November 2000 (3 year terms)

#### ADMINISTRATION
City Clerk, Elwood Wagg
Director, Finance, Ken Burden
Chief Administrative Officer, Edward P. Lustig
City Solicitor, R. Kallio
Director, Community Services, John MacDonald
Director, Municipal Works, Larry A. Oates
Director, Planning & Development, Doug Darbyson
Manager, Business Development, Serge Felicetti
Manager, Corporate Services, Tony Ravenda
Manager, Parks, Recreation & Culture, Adele Kon
Fire Chief, Fire Dept., Pete Corfield, 5815 Morrison St., Niagara Falls ON L2E 2E8, 905/356-1324

### City of NORTH BAY
City Hall, 200 McIntyre St. East, PO Box 360, North Bay ON P1B 8H8
705/474-0400, Fax: 705/495-4353
URL: http://www.city.north-bay.on.ca/northbay.htm
Incorporated: 1925
Area: 128.9 sq. miles
Population: 54,332 (1996)

#### COUNCIL
Editor's Note: Results of the November 1997 election were not available at press time; up to date results may appear in the Addenda at the back of this book.
*Next Election:* November 2000 (3 year terms)

#### ADMINISTRATION
City Clerk, Bonny Harrison
Director, Financial Services, Brian Rogers
Chief Administrative Officer, C.M. Timothy Sheffield
Chief Building Inspector, Brian Horsman
Chief of Police, Ron Nagel
City Solicitor, M.B. Burke
Director, Human Resources, R.A. Young
Director, Planning & Economic Development, Steve M. Sajatovic
Director, Transportation & Works, Brian Baker
Fire Chief, E. (Ted) McCullough
Manager, Economic Development, Rick Evans
Manager, Environmental Services, Peter Bullock
Manager, Transit, Terry Brent
Medical Officer of Health, Dr. Catherine Whiting

### District Municipality of NORTH VANCOUVER
PO Box 86218, North Vancouver BC V7L 4K1
604/987-7131, Fax: 604/984-9637
URL: http://www.district.north-van.bc.ca/
Incorporated: 1891
Area: 40,121 acres
Population: 80,418 (1996)

#### COUNCIL
Mayor, Don Bell
Councillors: Trevor Carolan; Ernest F. Crist; Glenys Deering-Robb; Janice Harris; Pat Munroe; Lisa Muri
*Next Election:* November 1999 (3 year terms)

#### ADMINISTRATION
Municipal Clerk, Dennis Back
Director, Financial Services, M.S. Hoskin
Municipal Manager, G.M. Howie
Chief, Fire Services, R.A. Grant
Director, Corporate Services, D.C. Stuart
Director, Parks & Engineering Services, R. West-Sells
Director, Planning & Development Services, R.E. Plunkett
Director, Recreation, Gary Young, 604/984-4181; Fax: 604/984-4294
Manager, Parks, Cameron Cairncross, 604/986-9141; Fax: 604/986-7968
Manager, Permits & Licenses, D.E. Pawson
Manager, Purchasing, Mike Chapman, 604/990-2261; Fax: 604/987-7185
Coordinator, North & West Vancouver Emergency Program, G.R. Peterson, 165 East 13th St., North Vancouver BC V7L 2L3, 604/985-3713; Fax: 604/985-3733
Medical Health Officer, Health Department, Dr. Brian O'Connor, 132 West Esplanade, North Vancouver BC V7M 1A2, 604/983-6701; Fax: 604/983-6839

### City of NORTH YORK
5100 Yonge St., North York ON M2N 5V7
416/395-6910, Fax: 416/395-6920
Incorporated: Februrary 14, 1979
Area: 69.5 sq. miles
Population: 589,653 (1996)
**Editor's Note:** The City of North York, along with the other five member municipalities that make up Metropolitan Toronto, will amalgamate into a single City of Toronto effective January 1998. The present City of Toronto & Metropolitan Toronto will cease to exist & the new City of Toronto will assume responsibility for providing all municipal services. The amalgamation was in effect for municipal elections, November 1997, and a new council for the amalgamated City of Toronto was elected; *see* City of Toronto listing for the new mayor and council.

#### ADMINISTRATION
City Clerk, Denis G. Kelly, 416/395-7372; Fax: 416/395-7337
Commissioner, Building, E. Yarman Uzumeri, P.Eng, 416/395-7513; Fax: 416/395-7589
Commissioner, City Hall Building Services, Bob West, 416/395-6903
Commissioner, Human Resources, Ron Yarwood, 416/395-6970; Fax: 416/395-6985
Commissioner, Parks & Recreation, Joe Halstead, 416/395-6188
Commissioner, Planning, Paula Dill, 416/395-7150; Fax: 416/395-7155
Commissioner, Public Works, Alan Wolfe, P.Eng., 416/395-6242; Fax: 416/395-6200
Commissioner, Transportation, Jim Kinrade, 416/395-7474; Fax: 416/395-7482
City Solicitor, George M. Dixon, 416/395-7055; Fax: 416/395-7056
Medical Officer of Health, Public Health, Dr. Barbara Yaffe, 416/395-7611; Fax: 416/395-7691
Senior Officer, Economic Development, John Tracogna, 416/395-7407; Fax: 416/395-7431

### Town of OAKVILLE
1225 Trafalgar Rd., PO Box 310, Oakville ON L6J 5A6
905/845-6601, Fax: 905/815-2025
Incorporated: May 27, 1857
Area: 55 sq. miles
Population: 128,405 (1996)

#### COUNCIL
Mayor, Ann Mulvale
Councillors & Wards: 1) Kevin Flynn; 2) Kathy Graham; 3) F. Keith Bird; 4) Stephen Sparling; 5) Liz Behrens, Janice Caster; 6) Mark Farrow, Kurt Franklin
*Next Election:* November 2000 (3 year terms)

#### ADMINISTRATION
Town Clerk, Judith Muncaster, 905/338-4178
Treasurer & Director, Finance, Michelle A. Séguin, ext.3062
Town Manager, Harry E. Henderson, 905/338-4176
Deputy Town Manager, Administrative Services, M.K. Wood, ext.3166
Deputy Town Manager, Community Services, P.F. Wagland, ext.3165
Director, Building Services, R.H.B. Foy, ext.3091
Commissioner, By-law Enforcement & Licensing, P.J. Bouillon, ext.3252; Fax: 905/338-4230
Director, Human Resources, John Snelgrove, ext.3244
Director, Parks & Recreation, R.G. Perkins, ext.3112
Director, Planning Services, E.C. (Ted) Salisbury, 905/338-4185
Director, Public Works, Ray Green, ext.3300
Director, Purchasing & Office Services, R.J. Cournoyer, ext.3087
Fire Chief, D. Wayne Gould, 905/338-4426
General Manager, Economic Development Office, John Meyerstein, ext.3030
Town Solicitor, D.L. Gates, Fax: 905/338-4184

## City of OSHAWA
City Hall, 50 Centre St. South, Oshawa ON L1H 3Z7
905/725-7351, Fax: 905/436-5697
Incorporated: March 8, 1924
Area: 14,245 ha (143 sq. km)
Population: 134,364 (1996)

#### COUNCIL
Mayor, Nancy Diamond, Fax: 905/436-5691
City Councillors & Wards: 1&2) Mike Nicholson; 2&4) Joe Kolodzie; 5&6) Dina Dykstra
Regional & City Councillors & Wards: 1) Brian Nicholson; 2) John Gray; 3) Nester Pidwerbecki; 4) Bob Boychyn; 5) Cathy Clarke; 6) Clare Aker; 7) Irv Harrell
*Next Election:* November 2000 (3 year terms)

#### ADMINISTRATION
City Clerk, Brian Suter, Fax: 905/436-5697
City Treasurer, N. Tellis, Fax: 905/436-5618
City Manager, J. Brown, 905/436-5622; Fax: 905/436-5623
Commissioner, Community Services, S. Bedford, Fax: 905/436-5692
Commissioner, Development & Planning Services, T. Goodchild, Fax: 905/436-5699
Commissioner, Corporate Services, J. Baker, Fax: 905/436-5689
Commissioner, Public Works Services, A. Myklebost, Fax: 905/436-5694
Director, Budget Services, R. Stockman
Director, Economic Development, Don O'Leary
Director, Engineering, J. Simmonds
Director, Information Management Services, D. Powell
Director, Legal Services, R. Evans, Fax: 905/436-5689
Director, Byron Simmons, Fax: 905/436-5694
Director, Parks & Facilities, N. Hutchinson
Director, Personnel, B.D. Gough, Fax: 905/436-5698
Director, Program & Operational Support Services, M. Sims
Director, Treasury & Fiscal Services, A.P. Geboers
Fire Chief (Emergency Response), M. Wilson, Fax: 905/433-0276
Manager, Buildings, G.N. Bilous
Manager, Planning, B. Hunt
Tax Collector, T. Dwyre
Manager, Oshawa Transit, N. Tweedle, 710 Raleigh Ave., Oshawa ON L1H 3T2, 905/579-2471; Fax: 905/579-1050

## City of OTTAWA
City Hall, 111 Sussex Dr., Ottawa ON K1N 5A1
613/244-5300, Fax: 613/244-5396
Email: info@city.ottawa.on.ca, URL: http://city.ottawa.on.ca
Incorporated: December 18, 1854
Area: 110.15 sq. km
Population: 323,340 (1996)

#### COUNCIL
Mayor, Jim Watson
Councillors & Wards: 1. Britannia-Richmond) Ron Kolbus; 2. Carleton) Brian Mackey; 3. Southgate) Diane Deans; 4. Rideau) Richard Cannings; 5. Bruyère-Strathcona) Stéphane Émard-Chabot; 6. Somerset) Elisabeth Arnold; 7. Kitchissippi) Shawn Little; 8. Mooney's Bay) Karin Howard; 9. Capital) Inez Berg; 10. Alta Vista-Canterbury) Allan Higdon
*Next Election:* November 2000 (3 year terms)

#### ADMINISTRATION
City Clerk, Pierre Pagé, ext.3625; Fax: 613/244-5417
Treasurer & Director, Corporate Finance, Mona Monkman, ext.3889; Fax: 613/244-5457
Chief Administrative Officer, John Burke, ext.5381; Fax: 613/244-5395
Commissioner, Corporate Services, Rosemarie Leclair, ext.3033; Fax: 613/244-5465
Acting Commissioner, Planning, Economic Development & Housing, Ted Robinson, ext.5388; Fax: 613/244-5480
City Auditor, Peter O'Callaghan, ext.3050; Fax: 613/244-5395
City Solicitor & Director, Corporate Law, Jerald Bellomo, ext.3309; Fax: 613/244-5461
Acting Commissioner, Community Services, Janette Foo, ext.4088; Fax: 613/244-5443
Director, Human Resources, Pierre Charette, ext.3419; Fax: 613/244-5467
Chief, Fire Department, Gary Richardson, 1445 Carling Ave., Ottawa ON K1Z 7L9, 613/798-8827; Fax: 613/798-8994

## City of PETERBOROUGH
500 George St. North, Peterborough ON K9H 3R9
705/742-7771, Fax: 705/743-7825
Incorporated: 1850
Area: 51.82 sq. km
Population: 69,535 (1996)

#### COUNCIL
Mayor, Sylvia Sutherland
Aldermen & Wards: 1) Nancy Branscombe, Jeffrey Leal; 2) Henry Clarke, Michael McIntyre; 3) James Bradburn, M. Edwards; 4) John E. Duncan; 4.) D. Paul Ayotte; 5) Bob Ball, Paul Crough
*Next Election:* November 2000 (3 year terms)

#### ADMINISTRATION
City Clerk, Steven F. Brickell, 705/748-8816
City Treasurer, B. Horton, 705/748-8863
City Administrator, R. Chittick, 705/748-8810
Chief of Police, K. McAlpine, 705/876-1122
City Engineer, Barry Poulton, 705/748-8885; Fax: 705/876-4610
City Solicitor, J. Hart, 705/748-8896; Fax: 705/742-3947
Director, Community Services, R. Browne, 705/748-8822
Director, Planning & Development, Malcolm Hunt, 705/748-8881; Fax: 705/742-5218
Emergency Planning Officer, R. Manley, 705/748-8820
Fire Chief, L. Grant, 705/745-2460
Manager, Public Works, P. Southall, 705/745-1386; Fax: 705/743-3223
Manager, Transportation, J. Kimble, 705/748-8895

## Town of PICKERING
Pickering Civic Complex, One The Esplanade, Pickering ON L1V 6K7
905/420-2222, Fax: 905/420-0515
URL: http://www.town.pickering.on.ca
Incorporated: early 1800s
Area: 55,974 acres (22,652 ha)
Population: 78,989 (1996)

#### COUNCIL
Mayor, Wayne Arthurs
Local Councillors & Wards: 1) Dave Ryan; 2) Mark Holland; 3) David Pickles
Regional Councillors & Wards: 1) Maurice Brenner; 2) Doug Dickerson; 3) Rick Johnson
*Next Election:* November 2000 (3 year terms)

#### ADMINISTRATION
Town Clerk, Bruce J. Taylor, 905/420-4611; Fax: 905/420-9685; Email: btaylor@town.pickering.on.ca
Director, Gilles Patterson, 905/420-4634; Fax: 905/420-2596; Email: gpatterson@town.pickering.on.ca
Town Manager, Thomas J. Quinn, 905/420-4648; Fax: 905/420-6064; Email: tquinn@town.pickering.on.ca
Director, Culture & Recreation, Stephen Reynolds, 905/420-4620
Director, Human Resources, Baba Gajadharsingh, 905/420-4627; Fax: 905/420-6064
Director, Legal Services, Penny Wyger, 905/420-4626; Fax: 905/420-7648; Email: pwyger@town.pickering.on.ca
Director, Parks & Facilities, Everett Buntsma, 905/420-4624; Fax: 905/420-7648
Director, Planning, Neil Carroll, 905/420-4617; Fax: 905/420-7648; Email: ncarroll@town.pickering.on.ca
Director, Public Works, Richard Holborn, 905/420-4360; Fax: 905/420-4650; Email: rholborn@town.pickering.on.ca
Fire Chief, Rick Pearsall, 905/839-8095; Fax: 905/839-6327; Email: rpearsall@town.pickering.on.ca
Manager, Transportation, Neil Killens, 905/683-1179; Fax: 905/683-5314; Email: nkillens@town.pickering.on.ca

## City of PRINCE GEORGE
City Hall, 1100 Patricia Blvd., Prince George BC V2L 3V9
250/561-7600, Fax: 250/561-0183
Incorporated: 1915
Area: 123 sq. miles
Population: 75,150 (1996)

#### COUNCIL
Mayor, Colin Kinsley
Councillors: Cliff Dezell; Denise Goodkey; Don Grantham; Shirley Gratton; Murray Krause; Anne Martin; Dan Rogers; Ronald Thiel
*Next Election:* November 1999 (3 year terms)

#### ADMINISTRATION
City Clerk, Allan Chabot, 250/561-7602
Treasurer & Director, Bill Kennedy, 250/561-7602
City Engineer, Dwayne Halldorson, P.Eng., 250/561-7500; Fax: 250/561-7502
City Manager, George Paul, 250/561-7602
Director, Development Services, Peter Monteith, 250/561-7679; Fax: 250/561-7721
Director, Fire Services, Mike Dornbierier, 250/561-7667; Fax: 250/561-7703
Director, Human Resources, Kathleen Soltis, 250/561-7626; Fax: 250/561-7719
Director, Leisure Services, Tom Madden, 250/561-7633; Fax: 250/561-7718
Director, Public Works, Gary Champagne, 250/561-7500; Fax: 250/561-7502

Manager, Bylaw Services, Norm Hudon, 250/561-7622; Fax: 250/561-7745
Manager, Police Services, Carol Wells, 250/561-3300; Fax: 250/562-8331
Purchasing Agent, Scott Bone, 250/561-7510; Fax: 250/563-8420

## Ville de QUÉBEC

Hôtel de ville, 2, rue des Jardins, CP 700, Succ Haute-Ville, Québec QC G1R 4S9
418/691-4636, Fax: 418/691-2346
URL: http://www.megatoon.com/web-quebec
Incorporée: 25 avril, 1883
Superficie: 88.9 sq. km
Population: 167,264 (1996)

#### CONSEIL

Maire, Jean-Paul L'Allier
Conseillers et Districts: 1) France Dupont; 2) Claude Larose; 3) Martin Forgues; 4) R. Chamberland; 5) Caroline Dion; 6) Odile Roy; 7) R.B. Gauvin; 8) Réjean Gignac; 9) Yvon Gignac; 10) André Marier; 11) Lynda Cloutier; 12) Lyse Poirier; 13) Charles R. Amyot; 14) Yvon Bussières; 15) Guylaine Noël; 16) Gérald Poirier; 17) Yvon Patry; 18) François Picard; 19) Claude Cantin; 20) Jacques Jobin
*Prochaine election:* novembre 2001 (mandat de 4 ans)

#### ADMINISTRATION

Greffier, Me. Antoine Carrier, LL.B., 418/691-6076
Trésorier et Directeur, Finances et Administration, Guy Martineau, c.a., 418/691-6024; Fax: 418/691-6088
Directeur général, Serge Viau, ing., Fax: 418/691-6313
Directeur général adjoint, Hervé Brosseau, LL.B., Fax: 418/691-6313
Avocat, Contentieux, Me Denis Boutin, Fax: 418/691-7622
Directeur, Approvisionnement, Jean Chabot, Fax: 418/691-7025
Directeur, Centre de développement économique et urbain (CDÉU), Réal Charest, 418/691-6201; Fax: 418/691-7916
Directeur, Commission de l'exposition provinciale, René Proulx, Fax: 418/691-7249
Directeur, Communications et Relations extérieures, Gilbert Athot, 418/691-7672; Fax: 418/691-7219
Directeur, Entretien des équipements, Michel Hallé, ing., Fax: 418/691-7421
Directrice, Environnement, Madeleine Paulin, 418/691-6899; Fax: 418/691-7642
Directeur, Gestion de l'information, André Boucher, Fax: 418/691-7681
Directeur, Ingénierie, Claude Goulet, ing., 418/691-6702; Fax: 418/691-4684
Directeur, Loisir, Culture et Vie communautaire, Michel Choquette, Fax: 418/691-4683
Directeur, Office municipal d'habitation de Québec & de Champlain, Jocely Bigras, Fax: 418/691-7358
Directeur, Planification, Pierre-Paul Gingras, 418/691-6204; Fax: 418/691-6161
Directeur, Police, Richard Renaud, 418/691-6263; Fax: 418/691-4747
Directeur, Protection contre l'incendie, Henri Labadie, 418/691-6720; Fax: 418/691-6989
Directeur, Ressources humaines, François Jutras, Fax: 418/691-7635
Directeur, SOM-HADEC, Michel Beaumont, Fax: 418/691-7508
Directeur, Travaux publics, Jean Lavoie, ing., 418/691-6392; Fax: 418/691-6707
Vérificateur, Lambert Legaré, c.a.

## Regional Municipality of Queens

PO Box 1264, Liverpool NS B0T 1K0
902/354-3453, Fax: 902/354-7473

#### COUNCIL

Mayor, Chris Clarke
*Next Election:* 2000

#### ADMINISTRATION

Clerk, Vacant
CAO, David Clattenburg

## City of RED DEER

City Hall, PO Box 5008, Red Deer AB T4N 3T4
403/342-8111, 8132, Fax: 403/346-6195
URL: http://www.city.red-deer.ab.ca/
Incorporated: March 25, 1913
Area: 59.5 sq. km
Population: 60,075 (1996)

#### COUNCIL

Mayor, Gail Surkan
Councillors: Jeffrey Dawson; Morris Flewwelling; Bev Hughes; Bill Hull; Dennis Moffat; Robert E. Schnell; Jason Volk; Lorna Watkinson-Zimmer
*Next Election:* October 1998 (3 year terms)

#### ADMINISTRATION

Clerk, Kelly Kloss, 403/342-8132
Manager, Treasury Services, Doug Norris, 403/342-8203
City Manager, Mike Day, 403/342-8154
City Assessor, Al Knight, 403/342-8119
Director, Community Services, Lowell Hodgson, 403/342-8308
Director, Corporate Services, Alan Wilcock, 403/342-8203
Director, Development Services, Bryon Jeffers, 403/342-8158
Fire Chief, Gord Stewart, 403/346-5511; Fax: 403/343-1866
Inspector, RCMP City Detachment, Scott Sutton, 403/341-2000
Manager, Engineering Development, Ken Haslop, 403/342-8158
Manager, Information Technology Services, Dale Smith, 403/342-8392
Manager, Inspections & Licensing, Ryan Strader, 403/342-8195; Fax: 403/347-1138
Manager, Land & Economic Development, Alan Scott, 403/342-8106
Manager, Personnel, Grant Howell, 403/342-8148
Manager, Public Works, Paul Goranson, 403/342-8238; Fax: 403/343-7074
Manager, Recreation, Parks & Culture, Don Batchelor, 403/342-8159
Manager, Transit, Kevin Joll, 403/342-8225
Purchasing Agent, Shirley McKenzie, 403/342-8293

## City of REGINA

PO Box 1790, Regina SK S4P 3C8
306/777-7262, Fax: 306/777-6809
URL: http://www.cityregina.com
Incorporated: June 19, 1903
Area: 114.06 sq. km
Population: 180,400 (1996)

#### COUNCIL

Mayor, Doug Archer
Councillors: 1) Mike Badham; 2) Bill Hutchison; 3) Fred Clipsham; 4) Michael Fougere; 5) Bill Gray; 6) Rob Deglau; 7) Ray Hamilton; 8) Vic McDougall; 9) Darlene Hincks; 10) Bill Wells
*Next Election:* October 2000 (3 year terms)

#### ADMINISTRATION

City Clerk, Randy Markewich, 306/777-7264; Fax: 306/777-6809
Director, Finance, Doug Fisher, 306/777-7317; Fax: 306/777-6810
City Manager, Bob Linner, 306/777-7314; Fax: 306/777-6810
Director, Support Services, Randy Garvey, 306/777-7222; Fax: 306/777-6723
City Auditor General, Wolfgang Langenbacher, 306/777-7619
City Solicitor, Leslie Shaw, 306/777-7472; Fax: 306/777-6818
Director, Community Services, Bland Brown, 306/777-7318; Fax: 306/777-6828
Director, Fire Services, Hugh Gordon, 306/777-7833; Fax: 306/777-6807
Director, Human Resources, Cal Barks, 306/777-7703; Fax: 306/777-6825
Director, Municipal Engineering, David Calam, 306/777-7411; Fax: 306/777-6806
Director, Property Development, L. Boyko, 306/777-7491
Director, Public Affairs, M. Gregory, 306/777-7499; Fax: 306/777-6803
Director, Public Works, Bill Aldcorn, 306/777-7650; Fax: 306/777-6801
Director, Transit, Don Hnetka, 306/777-7775; Fax: 306/777-6811
General Manager, Information Systems, Dale Ward, 306/777-7258

## Ville de RÉPENTIGNY

435, boul Iberville, Répentigny QC J6A 2B6
514/654-2323, Fax: 514/654-2421
Population: 53,824 (1996)

#### CONSEIL

Editor's Note: Results of the November 1997 election were not available at press time; up to date results may appear in the Addenda at the back of this book.
*Prochaine election:* 2001

#### ADMINISTRATION

Gref., Jean Fafard
Directeur, Services urbains, Rejean Durocher, ing.

## City of RICHMOND

6911 - No. 3 Rd., Richmond BC V6Y 2C1
604/276-4000, Fax: 604/278-5139
Email: cityofrichmond@city.richmond.bc.ca, URL: http://www.city.richmond.bc.ca
Incorporated: 1879
Area: 16,818 ha (41,529 acres)
Population: 148,867 (1996)

#### COUNCIL

Mayor, Greg Halsey-Brandt
Councillors: Malcolm Brodie; Derek Dang; Lyn Greenhill; Ken Johnston; Kiichi Kumagai; Bill McNulty; Corisande Percival-Smith; Harold Steves
*Next Election:* November 1999 (3 year terms)

#### ADMINISTRATION

City Clerk, Richard McKenna, 604/276-4007
Finance Administrator, Jim Bruce, 604/276-4095
City Administrator, George Duncan, 604/276-4338
Administrator, Community Services, Mike Brow, 604/276-4127
Administrator, Public Works, Vacant
Administrator, Urban Development, David McLellan, 604/276-4083
City Solicitor, Paul Kendrick, 604/276-4104
Director, Information Services, Brian Sameshima, 604/276-4080
Fire Chief, John Lysholm, 604/278-5131
Manager, Human Resources, Anne Smith, 604/276-4105
Manager, Land Use, Terry Crowe, 604/276-4139
Manager, Roads, Dykes & Field Services, Eric Gilfillan, 604/244-1206

Medical Health Officer, Dr. John Garry, 604/276-4050
RCMP Officer-in-Charge, Supt. Ernie MacAulay, 604/278-1212

## Town of RICHMOND HILL

225 East Beaver Creek Rd., PO Box 300, Richmond Hill ON L4C 4Y5
905/771-8800, Fax: 905/771-2502
Incorporated: 1957
Area: 25,167 acres
Population: 101,725 (1996)

#### COUNCIL

Mayor, William Bell, Fax: 905/771-2500
Councillors & Wards: 1) Vito Spadafora; 2) Brenda Hogg; 3) David L. Cohen; 4) David Bishop; 5) Nick Papa; 6) Joe Di Paola
Regional & Local Councillors: David Barrow; Janet Mabley
*Next Election:* November 2000 (3 year terms)

#### ADMINISTRATION

Town Clerk, Robert Douglas
Treasurer & Commissioner, Finance, S. Zorbas, Fax: 905/771-2501
Chief Administrative Officer, C.D. Weldon, Fax: 905/771-2406
Commissioner, Parks & Recreation, Lynton Friedberg, 905/771-8870; Fax: 905/771-2481
Commissioner, Planning & Development, J.E. Babcock, 905/771-8910; Fax: 905/771-2404
Commissioner, Transportation & Works, M.A. McCauley, 905/771-8830; Fax: 905/771-2405
Fire Chief, R.G. Kennedy, 905/883-5444; Fax: 905/883-0866
Manager, Corporate Communications, C. Moore, Fax: 905/771-2520
Manager, Transit, W.J. Newton, Fax: 905/771-5438
Town Solicitor, A.T. Kowalishin, Fax: 905/771-2408

## Corporation of the District of SAANICH

770 Vernon Ave., Victoria BC V8X 2W7
250/475-1775, Fax: 250/475-5400
Incorporated: March 1, 1906
Area: 41.42 sq. miles
Population: 101,388 (1996)

#### COUNCIL

Mayor, Frank Leonard, 250/479-6710
Councillors: Judy Brownoff; David Cubberley; John Garrison; Robert Gillespie; Sheila Orr; Carol Pickup; Leif Wergeland; Raymond Williams
*Next Election:* November 1999 (3 year terms)

#### ADMINISTRATION

Municipal Clerk, Terry R. Kirk, ext.3500; Fax: 250/475-5440
Controller-Treasurer, Ronald Porter
Fire Chief, Murray Bryden, 250/475-5500, ext.3612; Fax: 250/475-5505
Administrator, R.M. Sharp
Chief of Police, D. Egan
City Solicitor, C.G. Nation
Director, Parks & Recreation, D.W. Hunter, ext.5422; Fax: 250/475-5450
Director, Personnel, L. Teal
Manager, Engineering Services, Hugh McKay, ext.3450; Fax: 250/475-5450
Manager, Public Works, Chris Pease, 250/744-5300, ext.3322; Fax: 250/744-5333
Manager, Purchasing, Neil Duckworth, ext.3480
Municipal Planner, Alan Hopper, ext.3400; Fax: 250/475-5450

## City of ST CATHARINES

City Hall, 50 Church St., PO Box 3012, St. Catharines ON L2R 7C2
905/688-5600, Fax: 905/641-4450
Incorporated: 1876
Area: 38.38 sq. miles
Population: 130,926 (1996)

#### COUNCIL

Mayor, Tim Rigby
Councillors & Wards: 1. Merriton) Wendy Patriquin; 1. Merritton) James Almas; 2. St Andrew) Judy Casselman; 2. St. Andrew) Joseph Kushner; 3. St. George) Alex Christie, Greg Washuta; 4. St. Patrick) Carol Disher, Ronna Katzman; 5. Grantham) Mark T. Brickell, Brian Heit; 6. Port Dalhousie) Norm St. George, Bruce Williamson
*Next Election:* November 2000 (3 year terms)

#### ADMINISTRATION

City Clerk & Director, Corporate Support Services, Kenneth R. Todd, C.M.O.
City Treasurer & Director, Financial Management Services, Colin E. Briggs
Chief Administrative Officer, B. Robert Puhach
Director, Planning & Development, George Borivilous
Director, Recreation & Community Services, William Fenwick
Director, Transportation & Environmental Services, Paul Mustard
Manager, Operations, David Shantz
Building Inspector, John Fisher
Solicitor, A. Poulin
General Manager, St. Catharines Transit Commission, Eric Gillespie, 2012 First St. South, RR#3, St. Catharines ON L2S 3V9, 905/685-4228; Fax: 905/685-4050

## Ville de STE-FOY

1130, rte de l'Église, CP 218, Ste-Foy QC G1V 4E1
418/650-7925, Fax: 418/650-7972
Incorporée: 1949
Superficie: 83.32 sq. km
Population: 72,330 (1996)

#### CONSEIL

Editor's Note: Results of the November 1997 election were not available at press time; up to date results may appear in the Addenda at the back of this book.
*Prochaine election:* 3 novembre 2001 (mandat de 4 ans)

#### ADMINISTRATION

Greffier et Directeur général adjoint, René Damphousse, 418/650-7925
Directeur, Trésorerie, Rémi Beaudoin, 418/650-7949
Directeur général, Alain Marcoux, 418/650-7958
Chef, Incendies, Pierre Leclair
Coordonnateur, Communications, Gilles Noël, 418/650-7906
Coordonnateur, Contentieux, Me Serge Giasson, 418/650-7927
Directeur, Contrôle du développement et de la cartographie, Roch Laliberté, 418/650-7902
Directrice, Loisirs, Pascale Guimont, 418/650-7935
Directeur, Personnel, Pierre-André Thomas, 418/650-7936
Directeur, Protection publique, Pierre Leclair, 418/654-4261
Directeur, Service du génie, Clément Bérubé, 418/650-7922
Directeur, Systèmes, Claude Hudon, 418/650-7907
Directeur, Travaux publics, Jacques Tessier, 418/650-7955

## Ville de ST-HUBERT

5900, boul Cousineau, St-Hubert QC J3Y 7K8
514/445-7600, Fax: 514/445-7847
Incorporée: 1860
Superficie: 68 sq. km
Population: 77,042 (1996)

#### CONSEIL

Maire, Michel Latendresse, 514/445-7663, 656-9516
Conseillers et Districts: 1) Jacques Thibault; 2) Carole Martin Chartré; 3) Suzanne Charbonneau; 4) Mario Boutin; 5) Jacques E. Poitras; 6) Monique Messier; 7) Yvan Laurin; 8) Jacques Lemire; 9) Roger Roy; 10) Jean-Guy Fortin; 11) Brian Taupier; 12) Lise Dutil; 13) Ronald Smith; 14) Marguerite Pearson Richard
*Prochaine election:* novembre 2000 (mandat de 4 ans)

#### ADMINISTRATION

Directeur, Sécretariat administratif et juridique, Bernard Houle
Directeur général, Guy Benedetti
Chef de division, Permis, Jean Larose
Conseiller, Développement et projets spéciaux, Roger Inkel
Directeur, Loisir et de la vie communautaire, Donald Courcy
Directeur, Permis et évaluation, Gilles Rodrigue
Directrice, Planification et développement, Huguette Béland
Directeur, Police, incendies et mesures d'urgence, Pierre Trudeau
Directeur, Services administratifs, Pierre Archambault
Directeur, Services techniques, Denis Gélinas, ing.
Directeur, Travaux publics, Michel Sarrazin, ing.F.
Directeur adjoint, Informatique, Daniel Doiron

## City of SAINT JOHN

City Hall, Market Sq., PO Box 1971, Saint John NB E2L 4L1
506/658-2800, Fax: 506/658-2802
URL: http://www.city.saint-john.nb.ca
Incorporated: May 18, 1785
Area: 121.69 sq. miles
Population: 72,494 (1996)

#### COUNCIL

Mayor, Shirley McAlary
Councillors: Shirley Arthurs; Walter Ball; Sterling Brown; Derek Chase; Stephen Fitzpatrick; Arthur L. Gould; Dennis R. Knibb; Peter Trites; M.A. Vincent; Christopher Waldschutz
*Next Election:* May 1998 (3 year terms)

#### ADMINISTRATION

Common Clerk, Mary L. Munford, 506/658-2862
Commissioner, Finance, Daryl Wilson, 506/658-2951
City Manager, Terrence Totten, 506/658-2913
Commissioner, Municipal Operations, Charles Robichaud, P.Eng., 506/658-2818; Fax: 506/658-2852
Commissioner, Community Services, William Butler, P.Eng., Fax: 506/658-2879
Commissioner, Environment & Development Services, Claude MacKinnon, P.Eng., 506/658-2876; Fax: 506/658-2837
Commissioner, Human Resources, Paul Groody, 506/658-2866
Building Inspector, Bill Edwards, P.Eng., 506/658-2911; Fax: 506/658-2879
City Solicitor, John Nugent, 506/658-2860
Director, Engineering, Stuart Armstrong, P.Eng., 506/658-2818; Fax: 506/658-2852
Director, Municipal Works, Shayne Galbraith, P.Eng., 506/658-2826; Fax: 506/658-4740
Director, Parks, Bernard Morrison, 506/658-2841; Fax: 506/658-2902
Director, Recreation, J. Brownell, 506/658-2908
Director, Tourism & Communications, Yvonne Huntington, 506/658-2990; Fax: 506/632-6118

Fire Chief, Glen Tait, 506/658-2910; Fax: 506/658-2916
General Manager, Economic Development, Steve Carson
Manager, Planning, Jim Baird
Police Chief, D. Sherwood, Fax: 506/648-3304
Purchasing Agent, David Logan, Fax: 506/658-4742
General Manager, Transit, Frank McCarey, PO Box 3860, Saint John NB E2M 5C2, 506/658-4700; Fax: 506/658-4704

## City of ST. JOHN'S

City Hall, PO Box 908, St. John's NF A1C 5M2
709/576-8600, Fax: 709/576-8474
Incorporated: 1888
Area: 493 sq. km
Population: 101,936 (1996)

#### COUNCIL

Mayor, Andrew Wells
Councillors: Shannie Duff; Peter Miller; Dennis O'Keefe; Dorothy Wyatt; 1) Sean Hanrahan; 2) Frank Galgay; 3) Keith Coombs; 4) Gerry Colbert; 5) John Dinn
Deputy Mayor: Marie White
*Next Election:* November 2001 (4 year terms)

#### ADMINISTRATION

City Clerk & Director, Administrative Services, Damien Ryan
Treasurer & Director, Finance, Robert Bishop, C.A., 709/576-8696; Fax: 709/576-8564
Chief Commisssioner & City Solicitor, Ron Penney, 709/576-8557; Fax: 709/576-8561
Assoc. Commissioner & Director, Building & Property Management, Wayne Purchase, 709/576-8701; Fax: 709/576-8160
Assoc. Commissioner & Director, Engineering & Planning, Art Cheeseman, 709/576-8658; Fax: 709/576-8625
Director, Human Resources, Guy Annable, 709/576-8213; Fax: 709/576-8575
Director, Public Works & Parks, Paul Mackey, 709/576-8303; Fax: 709/576-8026
Manager, Economic Development, Elizabeth Lawrence, 709/576-8203; Fax: 709/576-8246
Manager, Environmental Initiatives, Geraldine King, 709/576-8613; Fax: 709/576-8625
Manager, Parks Service, Jim Clark, 709/576-8541; Fax: 709/576-8026
Manager, Tourism Division, Kevin Gushue, 709/567-8545; Fax: 709/576-8246
Purchasing Agent, Melvin Rowe, 709/576-8152; Fax: 709/576-8470
Real Estate Officer, Garth Griffiths, C.E.T., 709/576-8440; Fax: 709/576-8561
Staff Engineer, Transportation, Robin King, 709/576-8232; Fax: 709/576-8625
St. John's Transportation Commission, 245 Freshwater Rd., St. John's NF A1B 1B3, 709/722-3929; Fax: 709/722-0018

## Ville de SAINT-LAURENT

777, boul Marcel-Laurin, Saint-Laurent QC H4M 2M7
514/855-6000, Fax: 514/855-5999
Incorporée: 27 février, 1893
Superficie: 43 sq. km (16.6 sq. mi)
Population: 74,240 (1996)

#### CONSEIL

Maire, Dr. Bernard Paquet
Conseillers et Districts: 1) Ivette Biondi; 2) Michèle D. Biron; 3) Pierre Lambert; 4) René Dussault; 5) Micheline Roy; 6) Roland Bouchard; 7) Charles. Benchimol; 8) Jean-René Taschereau; 9) Alan De-Sousa; 10) Ronald Moreau; 11) Irving Grundman; 12) Maurice Cohen; 13) Alfred Giannetti; 14) François Ghali
*Prochaine election:* novembre 1998 (mandat de 4 ans)

#### ADMINISTRATION

Greffière, Édith Baron-Lafrenière
Trésorier, Jean Kahalé, c.g.a.
Directeur général, Pierre Lebeau, c.g.a.
Directeur, Communications, Jacques Viens, 514/855-5701; Fax: 514/855-5709
Directeur, Ingénierie et Environnement, Robert P. Fortin, ing., 514/855-5960; Fax: 514/855-5959
Directeur, Loisirs, Guy Bourgon
Directeur, Prévention de l'incendie, Charles St-Onge, 514/956-2504; Fax: 514/855-5838
Directeur, Travaux publics, Jacques Brassard
Directeur, Urbanisme, Claude Charette, ing., urb.
Directeur adjoint, Inspection et permis, Mario Duchesne, arch., 514/855-5975

## Ville de ST-LÉONARD

8400, boul Lacordaire, St-Léonard QC H1R 3B1
514/328-8400, Fax: 514/328-8479
Incorporée: 1886
Superficie: 13.63 sq. km
Population: 71,327 (1996)

#### CONSEIL

Maire, Frank Zampino
Conseillers et Districts: 1) John Valentini; 2) Tommaso Nanci; 3) Mario Battista; 4) Italo Barone; 5) Alexandre Pacetti; 6) Dominic Perri; 7) Yvette Bissonnet; 8) Vincenzo Arciresi; 9) André Chrétien; 10) Domenico Moschella; 11) Jean-Jacques Goyette; 12) Robert L. Zambito
*Prochaine election:* novembre 1998 (mandat de 4 ans)

#### ADMINISTRATION

Greffier, Georges Larivée, o.m.a.
Finances, Sylvie A. Brunet
Directeur général, Pierre Santamaria, ing.
Directeur général adjoint, Gérard Soulard
Génie, Pierre Egesborg, ing.
Loisirs communautaires, Claude Martineau
Personnel, Jean-Claude Durand
Prévention des incendies, André Medzalabanleth
Services techniques, Vilis Preiss, ing., 514/328-8345
Urbaniste, M.F. Frigon

## City of SARNIA

City Hall, 255 North Christina St., PO Box 3018, Sarnia ON N7T 7N2
519/332-0330, Fax: 519/332-3995
Incorporated: May 7, 1914
Area: 43,762 acres
Population: 72,738 (1996)

#### COUNCIL

Mayor, Mike Bradley
City & County Aldermen & Wards: 1) Jim Foubister; 2) Anne Khan; 3) Rod Brown; 4) Al Brogden
City Aldermen & Wards: 1) Caroline DiCocco; 2) Mike Kelch; 3) Pat O'Brien; 4) Andy Bruziewicz
*Next Election:* November 2000 (3 year terms)

#### ADMINISTRATION

City Clerk, Ann Tuplin
City Treasurer, Dean A. Anderson
City Manager, Ronald E. Brooks
Administrator, Legal Services, Valerie M'Garry
Co-Manager, Transit, Pauline Chenier
Co-Manager, Jim Stevens
Director, Building Services, Jacques Skutt
Director, Community Services, Terry McCallum, ext.200
Director, Development Planning, Michael Shnare
Director, Economic Renewal & Coporate Planning, Peter Hungerford
Director, Engineering, Reg McMichael, ext.284
Director, Human Resources, Lloyd Fennell
Director, Information Services, Ronald Marshall
Director, Operations, A.J. Morrison
EMO Officer, Bruce Middleton
Fire Chief, Vacant
Police Chief, Bill O'Brien
Purchasing Agent, M. José

## City of SASKATOON

City Hall, 222 - 3 Ave. North, Saskatoon SK S7K 0J5
306/975-3240, Fax: 306/975-2782
Incorporated: May 26, 1906
Area: 14,574.04 ha
Population: 193,647 (1996)

#### COUNCIL

Mayor, Henry Dayday, 306/975-3202
Councillors: 1) James Maddin; 2) Anita Langford; 3) Rik Steernberg; 4) Myles Heidt; 5) Peter McCann; 6) Kate Waygood; 7) Patricia Roe; 8) Howard Harding; 9) Donna Birkmaier; 10) Don Atchinson
*Next Election:* October 2000 (3 year terms)

#### ADMINISTRATION

City Clerk, Janice Mann, 306/975-3240; Fax: 306/975-2784
General Manager, Asset Management, Larry Ollenberger, 306/975-2990; Fax: 306/975-3034
Auditor General, Bob Prosser, 306/975-3274; Fax: 306/975-2784
City Solicitor, Theresa Dust, 306/975-3270; Fax: 306/975-7828
General Manager, Environmental Services, Randy Munch, P.Eng., 306/975-2562; Fax: 306/975-2553
General Manager, Finance, Phil Richards, 306/975-3206; Fax: 306/975-7975
General Manager, Fire & Protective Services, William Hewitt, 306/975-2575; Fax: 306/975-2589
General Manager, Human Resources, Shelley Chirpilo, 306/975-3265; Fax: 306/975-3073
General Manager, Leisure Services, Paul Gauthier, 306/975-3337; Fax: 306/975-3185
General Manager, Planning & Building, Lee Ann Coveyduck, 306/975-2654; Fax: 306/975-7712
General Manager, Public Works, Stewart Uzelman, P. Eng., 306/975-2450; Fax: 306/975-2971
General Manager, Transportation, Tom Mercer, P. Eng., 306/975-2630; Fax: 306/975-7672
Police Chief, Dave Scott, 306/975-8286; Fax: 306/975-8319

## City of SAULT STE. MARIE

Civic Centre, 99 Foster Dr., PO Box 580, Sault Ste Marie ON P6A 5N1
705/759-2500, Fax: 705/759-2310
Email: ssmdpil@soonet.ca, URL: http://www.sault-canada.com
Incorporated: 1912
Area: 92 sq. miles
Population: 80,054 (1996)

#### COUNCIL

Mayor, Stephen E. Butland
Councillors & Wards: 1) David Orazietti, Charles Swift; 2) Jody Curran, Brady Irwin; 3) Mary Borowicz, Derek Brandt; 4) Sam Lepore, Rick Niro; 5) Debbie Amaroso, Duane Jones; 6) Mary Pascuzzi, Peter Vaudry
*Next Election:* November 2000 (3 year terms)

#### ADMINISTRATION

City Clerk, Donna P. Irving, 705/759-5388

Treasurer & Commissioner, Finance, William Freiburger, 705/759-5350
Chief Administrative Officer, Joseph M. Fratesi, 705/759-5347
Commissioner, Community Services, Walter Lamming, 705/759-5310
Commissioner, Engineering & Planning, Mel Brechin, 705/759-5378
Commissioner, Human Resources, John Luszka, 705/759-5361
Commissioner, Public Works & Transportation, Reginald. Avery, 705/541-7000; Fax: 705/541-7010
Executive Director, Economic Development Corporation, Bruce Strapp, 705/759-5432; Fax: 705/759-2185
Chief Building Official, Maurice Kukoraitis, 705/759-5410
Chief of Police, Robert Davies, 705/949-6300; Fax: 705-759-7820
City Solicitor, Lorie A. Bottos, 705/759-5400
City Tax Collector, Garry B. Mason, 705/759-5290
Director, Environmental Engineering, Jim Elliott, 705/759-5381
Director, Planning, John M. Bain, 705/759-5368
Fire Chief, Lynn McCoy, 705/949-3335; Fax: 705/949-2341
Manager, Purchasing, Iain Little, 705/759-5299
Manager, Transit, Terry Ireland, 705/759-5438; Fax: 705/759-4534

## City of SCARBOROUGH

Civic Centre, 150 Borough Dr., Scarborough ON M1P 4N7
416/396-7111, Fax: 416/396-6920, Hazardous Waste: 416/392-4330; Recycling: 416/396-7372
URL: http://www.city.scarborough.on.ca/
Incorporated: June 29, 1983
Area: 72.5 sq. miles
Population: 558,960 (1996)

**Editor's Note:** The City of Scarborough, along with the other five member municipalities that make up Metropolitan Toronto, will amalgamate into a single City of Toronto effective January 1998. The present City of Toronto & Metropolitan Toronto will cease to exist & the new City of Toronto will assume responsibility for providing all municipal services. The amalgamation was in effect for municipal elections, November 1997, and a new council for the amalgamated City of Toronto was elected; *see* City of Toronto listing for the new mayor and council.

#### ADMINISTRATION

City Clerk, W. Drew Westwater, 416/396-7279; Fax: 416/396-4301
Treasurer & Commissioner, Finance & Corporate Services, Estelle Lo, 416/396-7248; Fax: 416/396-5677
Acting City Manager, Michael A. Price, 416/396-7344; Fax: 416/396-5681
Commissioner, Planning & Building, Lorne Ross, 416/396-7343; Fax: 416/396-4265
Commissioner, Recreation, Parks & Culture, Bruce F. Fleury, 416/396-7404; Fax: 416/396-5399
Commissioner, Works & Environment, Michael A. Price, 416/396-7344; Fax: 416/396-5681
City Solicitor, John R. Ratchford, 416/396-7124; Fax: 416/396-4262
Director, Central Services (Purchasing), Bill Adams, 416/396-7228; Fax: 416/396-5677
Director, Parks & Urban Forestry, Tom Tusek, 416/396-7377
Executive Director, Economic Development, Brenda Librecz, 416/396-7744; Fax: 416/396-4241
Fire Chief, Thomas Powell, 416/396-7786; Fax: 416/396-7665
Medical Officer of Health, Dr. Colin D'Cunha, 416/396-7445; Fax: 416/396-5150
Senior Director, Human Resource Services, Alan Deans, 416/396-7759; Fax: 416/396-7217

## Ville de SHERBROOKE

191, rue du Palais, CP 610, Sherbrooke QC J1H 5H9
819/821-5500, Fax: 819/822-6064
URL: http://ville.sherbrooke.qc.ca
Superficie: 22 sq. miles
Population: 76,786 (1996)

#### CONSEIL

Maire, Jean Perrault
Conseillers et Districts: 1. Le Triolet) Jean François Rouleau; 2. Mont-Bellevue) Laurier Custeau; 3. Immaculée-Conception) Lise Drouin-Paquette; 4. Centre-Ville) Serge Paquin; 5. Vieux-Nord) Alain Leclerc; 6. St-Jean-Baptiste) Michel Carrier; 7. Marie-Reine) Sylvie Lapointe; 8. Jardins-Fleuris) Bernard F. Tanguay; 9. Parc-Victoria) Serge Cardin; 10. St-Alphonse) Camille Fortier; 11. Montcalm) Jean-Luc Lavoie; 12. Carrefour) Jacques Jubinville
*Prochaine election:* novembre 1998 (mandat de 4 ans)

#### ADMINISTRATION

Greffier et Directeur, Services juridiques, Me Pierre Huard, 819/821-5425; Fax: 819/822-6064
Trésorier, François Poulette, 819/821-5490; Fax: 819/822-6091
Directeur général, Jacques Lacroix, 819/821-5618; Fax: 819/823-5121
Directeur général adjoint-population, Gilles Veilleux, 819/821-5910; Fax: 819/823-5121
Chef de Cabinet - Mairie, Jean-Yves LaFlamme, 819/821-5969; Fax: 819/822-6131
Chef de division, Communications, Charlotte Gosselin, 819/821-5572; Fax: 819/823-5153
Chef de division, Évaluation, Richard Gagné, 819/821-5708; Fax: 819/821-5777
Chef de division, Informatique, Denis Dore, 819/821-5623; Fax: 819/821-5470
Chef de division, Ingénierie, vacant, 819/821-5925
Chef de division, Protection contre les incendies, Jacques Denault, 819/821-5514; Fax: 819/821-5516
Directeur, Hydro-Sherbrooke, Roger Vachon, 819/821-5718; Fax: 819/822-6085
Directeur, Planification et Travaux publics, Guy Labbé, 819/821-5798; Fax: 819/822-6070
Directeur, Ressources financières, Denys Maurice, 819/821-5490; Fax: 819/821-6091
Directeur, Ressources humaines, Claude Lessard, 819/821-5689; Fax: 819/821-6086
Directeur, Ressources matérielles, Marc Latendresse, 819/821-5666; Fax: 819/821-5426
Directeur, Services de protection de la communauté, Michel Carpentier, 819/821-1985
Directeur, Services récréatifs & communautaires, Alvin Doucet, 819/821-5772; Fax: 819/823-5168
Président, SDRS - Industrie, Jean Perrault, 819/821-5969; Fax: 819/822-6131

## City of STONEY CREEK

777 Hwy. 8, PO Box 9940, Stoney Creek ON L8G 4N9
905/643-1261, Fax: 905/643-6161
Email: snelling@binatech.on.ca
Population: 54,318 (1996)

#### COUNCIL

Mayor, Anne Bain
Councillors & Wards: 1) Doug Conley; 2) Frank Cefaloni; 3) Maria Pearson; 4) R. Menegazzo; 5) Larry Di Ianni; 6) Peter Janack; 7) Paul Miller
*Next Election:* November 2000 (3 year terms)

#### ADMINISTRATION

City Clerk, Rose Caterini
Treasurer, Frank Carrocci
Chief Administrative Officer, William F. Allcock
Chief Building Official, Henry Dekker
Chief Municipal Law Enforcement Officer, Susan McGrath
Director, Engineering, Ian Neville
Director, Human Resources, Mary A. Adamson
Director, Planning, Ronald Marini
Director, Recreation & Parks, Philip J. Bruckler
Fire Chief, Richard Playfair
Manager, Operations, Murray Dinning

## City of SUDBURY

City Hall, Civic Square, 200 Brady St., PO Box 5000, Stn A, Sudbury ON P3A 5P3
705/674-3141, Fax: 705/673-3096
Email: bjmangi@city.sudbury.on.ca, URL: http://www.city.sudbury.on.ca
Incorporated: 1972
Area: 26,723 ha
Population: 92,059 (1996)

#### COUNCIL

*Next Election:* November 2000 (3 year terms)
Editor's Note: Results of the November 1997 election were not available at press time; up to date results may appear in the Addenda at the back of this book.

#### ADMINISTRATION

Clerk, Thom M. Mowry, Fax: 705/671-8118; Email: cctyclrk@city.sudbury.on.ca
Director & City Treasurer, Finance, Larry Laplante
City Manager & Asst. City Manager, Corporate Services, Gary Polano, Fax: 705/671-9327
Asst. City Manager, Community Services, Brian Cottam
Asst. City Manager, Physical Services, Richard Hinton
City Solicitor, W. Fred Dean
Director, Administrative Services, Lise Poratto-Mason
Director, Engineering & Construction, Angelo D'Agostino
Director, Human Resources, Wayne Baker
Director, Information Services, Bruno Mangiardi
Director, Leisure Services, Don Waddell
Director, Maintenance, Greg Clausen
Fire Chief, Don McLean
Chief Executive Officer, Sudbury Public Library, Marian Ridge
Executive Director, Sudbury Metro Centre, Maureen M. Luoma

## City of SURREY

14245 - 56 Ave., Surrey BC V3X 3A2
604/591-4011, Fax: 604/591-4357
URL: http://www.city.surrey.bc.ca/
Incorporated: November 10, 1879
Area: 132 sq. miles
Population: 304,477 (1996)

#### COUNCIL

Mayor, Doug McCallum
Councillors: Edmund P. Caissie; Jeanne Eddington; J.E. (Judy) Higginbotham; J. Marvin Hunt; Pam Lewin; Gary T. Robinson; Judy Villeneuve; Dianne Watts
*Next Election:* November 1999 (3 year terms)

#### ADMINISTRATION

City Clerk & General Manager, Legislative Services, Donna Kenny, 604/591-4113; Fax: 604/591-8731
General Manager, Finance, Gary Guthrie, 604/591-4817; Fax: 604/591-3654
City Manager, D. Lychak, 604/591-4122; Fax: 604/591-4357
General Manager, Engineering, U. Mital, 604/591-4219; Fax: 604/591-8693
General Manager, Human Resources, Len Posyniak, 604/591-4114; Fax: 604/591-4517
Acting General Manager, Parks & Recreation, Owen Croy, 604/591-4418; Fax: 604/591-9566

General Manager, Planning & Development, L. Walker, 604/591-4474; Fax: 604/591-2507
Director & Medical Health Officer, Dr. Roland Guasparini, 604/572-2600; Fax: 604/594-0949
Fire Chief, James Bale, 604/543-6701; Fax: 604/543-6715
Manager, Business Development, Bruce Siudut, 604/591-4549
Manager, Engineering Planning, Paul Ham, 604/591-4243
Manager, Operations, Jamie Umploby, 604/590-7211

## City of THUNDER BAY

City Hall, 500 Donald St. East, Thunder Bay ON P7E 5V3
807/625-2230, Fax: 807/623-5468
Incorporated: January 1, 1970
Area: 156 sq. miles
Population: 113,662 (1996)

#### COUNCIL

Editor's Note: Results of the November 1997 election were not available at press time; up to date results may appear in the Addenda in the back of this book.
*Next Election:* November 2000 (3 year terms)

#### ADMINISTRATION

City Clerk, M. Elaine Bahlieda, 807/625-2480
General Manager, Finance, P. Milligan, 807/625-2242; Fax: 807/622-7963
City Manager, Brian D. MacRae, 807/622-2224; Fax: 807/622-6669
Chief of Police, Protective Services, B. Chambers, 807/625-1304; Fax: 807/623-9242
General Manager, Community Services, G. Davies, 807/625-3320; Fax: 807/625-3292
General Manager, Corporate Services, G. Alexander, 807/625-3525; Fax: 807/625-0181
General Manager, Planning & Building Services, J. Favron, 807/625-2544; Fax: 807/623-2206
General Manager, Telephone & Information Services, S. Hacio, 807/625-2121; Fax: 807/623-0518
General Manager, Transportation & Works, R.H. Wright, 807/625-2137; Fax: 807/625-3588
Manager, Transit, A. Grant, 570 Fort William Rd., Thunder Bay ON P7B 2Z8, 807/625-2187; Fax: 807/345-5744

## City of TORONTO

City Hall, 100 Queen St. West, Toronto ON M5H 2N2
416/392-9111, Fax: 416/392-6990, TDD: 416/392-7354; Telex: 06-219570
Email: info@city.toronto.on.ca, URL: http://www.city.toronto.on.ca/
Incorporated: March 6, 1834
Area: Land 101 sq. km
Population: 2,385,421 (1996)
**Editor's Note:** The City of Toronto, along with the other five member municipalities that make up Metropolitan Toronto, will amalgamate into a single City of Toronto effective January 1998. The present City of Toronto & Metropolitan Toronto will cease to exist & the new City of Toronto will assume responsibility for providing all municipal services. The amalgamation was in effect for municipal elections, November 1997, and a new council for the amalgamated City of Toronto was elected; see below. The population figure above reflects the population of the new city of Toronto.

#### COUNCIL

Mayor, Mel Lastman
Councillors & Wards: 1. East York) Case Ootes, Michael Prue; 2. Lakeshore Queensway) Irene Jones, Blake Kinahan; 3. Kingsway Humber) Mario Giansante, Gloria Luby; 4. Markland) Doug Holyday, Dick O'Brien; 5. Rexdale Thistletown) Elizabeth Brown, Bruce Sinclair; 6. North York Humber) George Mammoliti, Judy Sgro; 7. Black Creek) Maria Augimeri, Peter LiPreti; 8. North York Spadina) Mike Feldman, Howard Moscoe; 9. North York Centre South) Milton Berger, Joanne Flint; 10. North York Centre) John Filion, Norman Gardner; 11. Don Parkway) Gordon Chong, Denzil Minnan-Wong; 12. Seneca Heights) Joan King, David Shiner; 13. Scarborough Bluffs) Gerry Altobello, Brian Ashton; 14. Scarborough Wexford) Norm Kelly, Mike Tzekas; 15. Scarborough City Centre) Lorenzo Berardinetti, Brad Duguid; 16. Scarborough Highland Creek) Frank Faubert, Ron Moeser; 17. Scarborough Agincourt) Doug Mahood, Sherene Shaw; 18. Scarborough Malvern) Raymond Cho, Edith Montgomery; 19. High Park) Chris Korwin-Kuczynski, David Miller; 20. Trinity-Niagara) Joe Pantalone, Mario Silva; 21. Davenport) Betty Disero, Tony Letra; 22. North Toronto) Anne Johnston, Michael Walker; 23. Midtown) John Adams, Ila Bossons; 24. Downtown) Olivia Chow, Kyle Rae; 25. Don River) Jack Layton, Peter Tabuns; 26. East Toronto) Sandra Bussin, Tom Jakobek; 27. York Humber) Frances Nunziata, Bill Saundercook; 28. York Eglinton) Robert Davis, Joe Mihevc
*Next Election:* November 2000 (3 year terms)

#### ADMINISTRATION

City Clerk, Novina Wong
Treasurer, Wanda Liczyk
Chief Adminstrative Offier, Michael Garrett
City Auditor, John S. Woods, 416/392-7171; Fax: 416/392-7959
Fire Chief, Alan Speed
Commissioner, City Works Services, Barry Gutteridge, 416/392-1819; Fax: 416/392-1827
Commissioner, Corporate Services, Margaret Rogrigues
Commissioner, Urban Development Services, John Morand, 416/392-1819; Fax: 416/392-1827
City Solicitor, Sylvia Watson, Q.C., 416/392-7221; Fax: 416/392-1199
Commissioner, Community Services, Tom Greer

## City of VANCOUVER

453 West 12 Ave., Vancouver BC V5Y 1V4
604/873-7011, Fax: 604/873-7419
URL: http://www.city.vancouver.bc.ca/
Incorporated: 1886
Area: 44 sq. miles
Population: 514,008 (1996)

#### COUNCIL

Mayor, Philip W. Owen, 604/873-7621; Fax: 604/873-7750
Councillors: Don Bellamy; Nancy A. Chiavario; Jennifer Clarke; Alan Herbert; Lynne Kennedy; Daniel Lee; Don Lee; Gordon Price; George Puil; Sam Sullivan
*Next Election:* November 1999 (3 year terms)

#### ADMINISTRATION

Clerk, Maria Kinsella, 604/873-7266
General Manager, Corporate Services, Ken. Stoke, 604/873-7220; Fax: 604/873-7107
City Manager, Ken Dobell, 604/873-7627; Fax: 604/873-7641
General Manager, Engineering Services, Dave Rudberg, 604/873-7300; Fax: 604/871-6119
General Manager, Fire & Rescue Services, Glen Maddess, 604/665-6051; Fax: 604/665-6016
General Manager, Parks, Vic Kondrosky, 604/257-8448; Fax: 604/257-8427
Chief Constable, Bruce Chambers, 604/665-3444; Fax: 604/665-3417
Communications Advisor, Scott MacRae, 604/874-7270
Corporation Counsel, Terrance R. Bland, 604/873-7505; Fax: 604/873-7445
Director, Civic Theatres, Rae Ackerman, 604/665-3020; Fax: 604/665-3001
Director, Emergency Management, Vacant, 604/873-7756; Fax: 604/871-6116
Director, Equal Opportunity Employment Program, Lorna McCreath, 604/873-7799; Fax: 604/871-6251
Director, Legal Services, Francie Connell, 604/873-7508; Fax: 604/873-7445
General Manager, Community Services, Ted Droettboom, 604/873-6254; Fax: 604/873-7898
General Manager, Human Resource Services, Marilyn Clark, 604/873-7655; Fax: 604/873-7696

## City of VAUGHAN

2141 Major Mackenzie Dr., Vaughan ON L6A 1T1
905/832-2281, Fax: 905/832-8535
Email: ecdev@city.vaughan.on.ca, URL: http://www.city.vaughan.on.ca
Incorporated: January 1, 1971
Area: 101 sq. miles
Population: 132,549 (1996)

#### COUNCIL

Mayor, Lorna Jackson, 905/832-2281 ext.8345
Local & Regional Councillors: Michael Di Biase; Joyce Frustaglio
Local Councillors & Wards: 1) Mario Ferri; 2) Gino Rosati; 3) Bernard Di Vona; 4) Mario G. Racco; 5) Susan Kadis
*Next Election:* November 2000 (3 year terms)

#### ADMINISTRATION

City Clerk, J.D. Leach
Treasurer & Commissioner, Finance, Clayton D. Harris
Chief Administrative Officer, S.C. Somerville
Commissioner, Community Services, G.D. Haas
Commissioner, Economic Development, Frank Miele, 905/832-8521, ext.8244; Fax: 905/832-6248
Commissioner, Legal & Corporate Services, T.A. Caron
Commissioner, Planning, John Stevens, 905/832-8565, ext.8208; Fax: 905/832-6080
Director, Building Services, M.M. Navabi
Director, Engineering, Bill Robinson, 905/832-8525, ext.8247; Fax: 905/832-6145
Director, Human Resources, R.G. Nagel
Director, Operations, David Moy, 905/832-8562, ext.6116; Fax: 905/303-2005
Director, Parks, Domenic Lunardo, 905/832-8577, ext.8795; Fax: 905/852-8550
Director, Recreation, J.S. Epstein
Fire Chief, J.B. Sutton, ext.8205; Fax: 905/832-8572
Manager, Purchasing, G.A. Wilson, 905/832-8555, ext.8269; Fax: 905/832-8522

## Ville de VERDUN

4555, rue de Verdun, Verdun QC H4G 1M4
514/765-7000, Fax: 514/765-7048
Incorporée: 1907
Superficie: 9.96 sq. km
Population: 59,714 (1996)

#### CONSEIL

Maire, Georges Bossé
Conseillers et Quartiers: 1) Catherine Chauvin; 2) Robert Isabelle; 3) Ernie Chiasson; 4) Robert Filiatrault; 5) Danielle Mimeault; 6) Laurent Dugas; 7) Nicole Santerre; 8) France Lecocq; 9) Claude Ravary; 10) John Gallagher
*Prochaine election:* novembre 2001 (mandat de 4 ans)

**ADMINISTRATION**

Greffier, Gérard Cyr
Finances, Gilles Champagne
Directeur général, Gaétan Laberge
Méthodes & Procédures, Jean Roy
Prévention des incendies et Sécurité publique, Raymond Therrien, 514/765-7118
Ressources humaines, Johanne Jolicoeur
Service développement de la communauté, Daniel L'Écuyer
Services techniques, Raymond Fréchette, 514/765-7075
Travaux publics, Pierre Boutin, 514/765-7181
Urbanisme et environnement, Dany Tremblay, 514/765-7080

## City of VICTORIA

One Centennial Sq., Victoria BC V8W 1P6
250/385-5711, Fax: 250/361-0348
URL: http://www.city.victoria.bc.ca/
Incorporated: August 2, 1862
Area: 4,641 acres
Population: 73,504 (1996)

**COUNCIL**

Mayor, Bob Cross
Councillors: Chris. Coleman; Bob Friedland; Bea Holland; Helen Hughes; Jane Lunt; Pamela Madoff; David McLean; Geoff Young
*Next Election:* November 1999 (3 year terms)

**ADMINISTRATION**

Clerk & Director, Corporate Services, Mark Johnston
Director, Finance, David Gawley
City Manager, Don Roughley
Chief Constable, Doug Richardson
City Solicitor, John Basey, 250/361-0212; Fax: 250/385-3592
Director, Engineering, Parks & Public Works, Steve Yoshino
Acting Director, Human Resources, Bonnie Donnelly
Director, Planning & Community Services, Len Vopnfjord, 250/361-0382; Fax: 250/361-0386
Fire Chief, Victoria Emergency Program, Frank Thoresen, 250/920-3350; Fax: 920-3370

## City of WATERLOO

City Hall, 100 Regina St. South, PO Box 337, Waterloo ON N2J 4A8
519/886-1550, Fax: 519/747-8760
URL: http://www.city.waterloo.on.ca
Incorporated: January 1, 1948
Area: 6.646 ha (25.7 sq. miles)
Population: 77,949 (1996)

**COUNCIL**

Editor's Note: Results of the November 1997 election were not available at press time; up to date results may appear in the Addenda at the back of this book.
*Next Election:* November 2000 (3 year terms)

**ADMINISTRATION**

City Clerk, Lew Ayers, 519/747-8704; Fax: 519/747-8510; Email: layers@gateway.city.waterloo.on.ca
City Treasurer, Bob Mavin; Email: bmavin@gateway.city.waterloo.on.ca
Director, Garry Bezruki; Email: gbezruki@gateway.city.waterloo.on.ca
Director, Bob McFarland; Email: bmcfarla@gateway.city.waterloo.on.ca
Chief Administrative Officer, Tom Stockie, 519/747-8702; Fax: 519/747-8500; Email: tstockie@gateway.city.waterloo.on.ca
Asst. CAO & Director, Human Resources, Kathy Durst, 519/747-8735; Fax: 519/747-8754; Email: kdurst@gateway.city.waterloo.on.ca
Director, Economic Development, Marketing & Promotions, Doug McKenzie; Email: dmckenzi@gateway.city.waterloo.on.ca
Director, Purchasing, Jim Walsh, 519/747-8725; Fax: 519/886-5788
Director & City Engineer, Engineering, Gordon Lemon, 519/747-8741; Fax: 519/747-8775; Email: glemon@gateway.city.waterloo.on.ca
Fire Chief, Max Hussey, 519/884-2121; Fax: 519/884-0242
Landscape Architect, Development Services, Barb Magee-Turner, 519/747-8757; Fax: 519/747-8792

## Town of WHITBY

575 Rossland Rd. East, Whitby ON L1N 2M8
905/668-5803, Fax: 905/686-7005
Email: clerk@town.whitby.on.ca, URL: http://town.whitby.on.ca
Incorporated: 1968
Area: 56.87 sq. miles (36,400 acres)
Population: 73,794 (1996)

**COUNCIL**

Mayor, Marcel Brunelle
Councillors & Wards: 1. North) Don Mitchell; 2. West) Mark McKinnon; 3. Centre) Shirley Scott; 4. East) Dennis Fox
Regional Councillors: Joe Drumm; Gerry Emm; Pat Perkins
*Next Election:* November 2000 (3 year terms)

**ADMINISTRATION**

Town Clerk, Donald G. McKay
Treasurer, R.A. Claringbold
Administrator, Wm. H. Wallace
Director, Marketing & Economic Development, P.G. Lebel
Director, Parks & Recreation, L.J. Morrow
Director, Planning, R.B. Short
Director, Public Works, W.J. Hancock
Fire Chief, A.J. VanDoleweerd

## City of WHITEHORSE

2121 - 2 Ave., Whitehorse YT Y1A 1C2
867/667-6401, Fax: 867/668-8384
Email: cityclerk@city.whitehorse.yk.ca, URL: http://www.city.whitehorse.yk.ca
Incorporated: 1950
Area: 162 sq. miles
Population: 19,157 (1996)

**COUNCIL**

Mayor, Kathy Watson
Councillors: Dan Boyd; Duke Connelly; Barb Harris; Allan Jacobs; Bernie Phillips; Dave Stockdale
*Next Election:* October 2000 (3 year terms)

**ADMINISTRATION**

Director, Corporate Services, Patricia Burke, 403/668-8611
City Manager, Bill Newell, 403/668-8638; Fax: 403/668-8639
City Engineer, Mitchell Moroziuk, 403/668-8307; Fax: 403/668-8386
Director, Community Development, Rob Roycroft, 403/668-8624
Director, Municipal Services, vacant, 403/668-8300; Fax: 403/668-8386
Fire Chief, Brian Monahan, 403/668-8383; Fax: 403/668-8389
Chief Building Inspector, Marvin Brooks, 403/668-8340; Fax: 403/668-8395
Manager, By-law, Russ Juby, 403/668-8318; Fax: 403/668-8386
Manager, Common Services, George White, 403/668-8302
Manager, Information Services, Glen Jolly, 403/668-8670
Manager, Parks & Recreation, Cathy Carlile, 403/668-8326; Fax: 403/668-8324
Manager, Planning Services, Dennis Shewfelt, 403/668-8338; Fax: 403/668-8395
Manager, Public Works, George Mair, 403/668-8350; Fax: 403/668-8386

## City of WINDSOR

City Hall, 350 City Hall Sq., PO Box 1607, Windsor ON N9A 6S1
519/255-6500, Fax: 519/255-6868
URL: http://www.city.windsor.on.ca/
Incorporated: 1854
Area: 49.6 sq. miles
Population: 197,694 (1996)

**COUNCIL**

Mayor, Mike Hurst
Councillors & Wards: 1) Mike Roach, Margaret Williams; 2) Peter Carlesimo, Brian Masse; 3) Donna Gamble, Alan Halberstadt; 4) Dave Cassivi, Bill Marra; 5) Rick Limoges, Tom Wilson
*Next Election:* November 2000 (3 year terms)

**ADMINISTRATION**

City Clerk, Thomas W. Lynd, 519/255-6222; Email: clerks@city.windsor.on.ca
Acting Commissioner, Finance, Gerry Pinsonneault, 519/255-6253; Fax: 519/255-7310; Email: financedept@city.windsor.on.ca
Chief Administrative Officer, Chuck Wills, 519/255-6311; Fax: 519/255-1861; Email: caodept@city.windsor.on.ca
Commissioner, Building, E. Link, 519/255-6267; Fax: 519/255-7170; Email: buildingdept@city.windsor.on.ca
Commissioner, Human Resources, Archie Glajch, 519/255-6206; Fax: 519/255-6874; Email: hrdept@city.windsor.on.ca
Commissioner, Planning, John Atkins, 519/255-6281; Fax: 519/255-6680; Email: planningdept@city.windsor.on.ca
Commissioner, Public Works, Gord Harding, 519/255-6257; Fax: 519/255-9847; Email: pubworks@city.windsor.on.ca
Acting City Solicitor, B. Halliwill, 519/255-6468; Fax: 519/255-6933
Manager, Environmental Services, Ron McConnell, 519/974-1010 ext.223
Acting Commissioner, Property Dept., Bill Salzer, 68 Chatham St. East, Windsor ON N9A 2W1, 519/255-6400; Fax: 519/255-7910, Email: prophouse@city.windsor.on.ca
Chief of Police, Police Dept., John Kousik, 445 City Hall Sq., Windsor ON N9A 1K5, 519/255-6630; Fax: 519/255-6191
Commissioner, Social Services, D. Howe, 755 Louis Ave., Windsor ON N9A 1X3, 519/255-5200; Fax: 519/255-7619, Email: socserv@city.windsor.on.ca
Commissioner, Traffic Engineering, J. Tofflemire, 1269 Mercer St., Windsor ON N8X 3P4, 519/255-6248; Fax: 519/255-7371, Email: trafficdept@city.windsor.on.ca
Commissioner, Parks & Recreation Dept., Lloyd Burridge, 2450 McDougall St., Windsor ON N8X 3N6, 519/253-2300; Fax: 519/255-7990, Email: parkrec@city.windsor.on.ca
Commissioner, Windsor-Essex County Development Commission, Paul Bondy, #215, 333 Riverside Dr. West, Windsor ON N9A 7C5, 519/255-9200; Fax: 519/255-9987
Fire Chief, Fire Dept., David Fields, 815 Goyeau St., Windsor ON N9A 1H7, 519/253-6573; Fax: 519/255-6832

General Manager, Windsor Utilities Commission, K.L. Edwards, 787 Ouellette Ave., Windsor ON N9A 4J4, 519/255-2727; Fax: 519/255-2767
Manager, Purchasing, Don Mills, 185 City Hall Sq., Windsor ON N9A 6W5, 519/255-6272; Fax: 519/255-9891
Medical Officer of Health, Metro Windsor-Essex County Health Unit, Dr. Allen Heimann, 1005 Ouellette Ave., Windsor ON N9A 4J8, 519/258-2146; Fax: 519/258-6003

## City of WINNIPEG

Council Building, Civic Centre, 510 Main St., Winnipeg MB R3B 1B9
204/986-2196, Fax: 204/949-0566
URL: http://www.city.winnipeg.mb.ca/city
Incorporated: November 8, 1873
Area: 570 sq. km (57.053 ha)
Population: 618,477 (1996)

#### COUNCIL

Mayor, Susan A. Thompson
Councillors & Wards: Charleswood/Fort Garry) Bill Clement; Daniel McIntyre) Amaro Silva; Elmwood) Lillian Thomas; Fort Rouge) Glen Murray; Mynarski) Harry Lazarenko; North Kildonan) Mark Lubosch; Old Kildonan) Mike O'Shaughnessy; Point Douglas) John Prystanski; River Heights) Garth Steek; St. Boniface) Daniel Vandal; St. Charles) Pat Phillips; St. James) Jae Eadie; St. Norbert) John Angus; St. Vital) Allan Golden; Transcona) Shirley Timm-Rudolph
*Next Election:* October 1998 (3 year terms)

#### ADMINISTRATION

City Clerk, Dorothy E. Browton, 204/986-2436; Fax: 204/947-3452
Director, Corporate Finance, K. Dowdall, 204/986-2510; Fax: 204/949-9301
Chief Commissioner, Finance & Administration, R. L. Frost, 204/986-2375; Fax: 204/949-1174
Commissioner, Planning & Community Services, T. Yauk, 204/986-2376; Fax: 204/949-1174
Commissioner, Protection, Parks & Culture, L.H. Reynolds, 204/986-2379; Fax: 204/949-1174
Commissioner, Works & Operations, W.D. Carroll, 204/986-2377; Fax: 204/949-1174
Chief Financial Officer, Robert Gannon, 204/986-2378; Fax: 204/949-1174
Coordinator, Emergency Program, M. Bennett, 204/986-4691; Fax: 204/942-5082
Director, Business Liaison & Intergovernmental Affairs, D. Kalcsics, 204/986-5160; Fax: 204/986-7196
Manager, Financial Planning & Budgets, J. Ferrier, 204/986-2186; Fax: 204/986-2237
Chief, Police Dept., David Cassels, Public Safety Bldg., 151 Princess St., Winnipeg MB R3B 1L1, 204/986-6037; Fax: 204/986-6077
City Assessor, Assessment, Brian Moore, 65 Garry St., Winnipeg MB R3C 4K4, 204/986-2951; Fax: 204/986-6105
City Solicitor & Manager, Legal Services, U. Goeres, 185 King St., 3rd Fl., Winnipeg MB R3B 1J1, 204/986-2408; Fax: 204/947-9155
Director, Materials Management Division, Corporate Finance, E. Van Mierlo, 185 King St., 1st Fl., Winnipeg MB R3B 1J1, 204/986-2451; Fax: 204/949-1178
Director, Parks & Recreation Dept., J. Hreno, 2799 Roblin Blvd., Winnipeg MB R3B 0B8, 204/986-3800; Fax: 204/832-7134
Director, Streets & Transportation Dept., J. Thomson, 100 Main St., Winnipeg MB R3C 1A4, 204/986-5285; Fax: 204/942-4811
Director, Social Services Dept., L. King, 705 Broadway, Winnipeg MB R3G 0X2, 204/986-5600; Fax: 204/944-8451
Director, Land & Development Services, P.A. Hamilton, 65 Garry St., 2nd Fl., Winnipeg MB R3C 4K4, 204/986-5235; Fax: 204/944-8476
Director, Winnipeg Hydro, R.J. Linton, 1315 Notre Dame Ave., Winnipeg MB R3E 3G2, 204/986-2320; Fax: 204/772-3872
Director, Transit Dept., R.L. Borland, 421 Osborne St., Winnipeg MB R3L 2A2, 204/986-5724; Fax: 204/986-6863
Fire Chief, Fire Dept., B.J. Lough, Public Safety Bldg., 151 Princess St., Winnipeg MB R3B 1L1, 204/986-6330; Fax: 204/947-0164
Medical Health Officer, Community Services, Dr. M. Fast, 280 William Ave., Winnipeg MB R3B 0R1, 204/986-3400; Fax: 204/986-3706

## City of YELLOWKNIFE

PO Box 580, Yellowknife NT X1A 2N4
867/920-5600, Fax: 867/920-5649
Email: city@internorth.com, URL: http://www.city.yellowknife.nt.ca
Incorporated: January 1, 1970
Area: 13,857 ha
Population: 17,275 (1996)

#### COUNCIL

Mayor, Dave Lovell
Aldermen: Cheryl Best; Bob Brooks; Blake Lyons; Ben McDonald; Peggy Near; Kevin O'Reilly; Dave Ramsay; Robert Slaven
*Next Election:* October 2000 (3 year terms)

#### ADMINISTRATION

Sr. Administration Officer, Douglas Lagore, 403/920-5685
Director, Finance, Robert Charpentier, 403/920-5666
City Administrator, Douglas B. Lagore, 403/920-5624
Director, Community Services, Max Hall, 403/920-5634
Director, Human Resources, Sheila Dunn, 403/920-5677
Director, Planning & Lands, Bob McKinnon, 403/920-5672
Director, Public Safety, Dave Nicklen, 403/920-5653
Director, Public Works & Engineering, Neil Jamieson, 403/920-5653
Executive Director, Economic Development, Archie Gillies, 403/873-5772
Manager, Public Works & Engineering, Adrian Bader, 403/920-5639

## City of YORK

2700 Eglinton Ave. West, Toronto ON M6M 1V1
416/394-2507, Fax: 416/394-2681
Email: info@city.york.on.ca, URL: http://www.city.york.on.ca
Incorporated: July 1, 1973
Area: 2,335 ha
Population: 146,534 (1996)
**Editor's Note:** The City of York, along with the other five member municipalities that make up Metropolitan Toronto, will amalgamate into a single City of Toronto effective January 1998. The present City of Toronto & Metropolitan Toronto will cease to exist & the new City of Toronto will assume responsibility for providing all municipal services. The amalgamation was in effect for municipal elections, November 1997, and a new council for the amalgamated City of Toronto was elected; *see* City of Toronto listing for the new mayor and council.

#### ADMINISTRATION

City Clerk, Ron W. Maurice
Treasurer & Director, Financial Services, John Ford
City Manager, Barry Coopersmith
Commissioner, Buildings, P. Hansen
Commissioner, Community Services, Ken Dickin
Commissioner, Kenneth Whitwell
Commissioner, Operation Services, Bill Dunford
Commissioner, Planning, E. Sajecki
Senior Director, Human Resources, Patrick Kelly
City Solicitor, George Bartlett
Director, Economic Development, Bill Steiss
Fire Chief, Steven Stewart
Manager of Purchasing Services, Financial Services, Jim Price
Acting Medical Officer of Health, Dr. Zofia Davison

# REGIONAL GOVERNMENT

### Part 3 (Alphabetical list of regional municipalities in major population areas of British Columbia, Ontario & Québec)

## BRITISH COLUMBIA REGIONAL GOVERNMENTS

For a complete list of Regional Governments in BC see part 1 of this Section.

## CAPITAL Regional District

524 Yates St., PO Box 1000, Victoria BC V8W 2S6
250/360-3000, Fax: 250/360-3130, Email for general enquiries only: rkirstein@wpo.gov.bc.ca
URL: http://vvv.com/crd/
Incorporated: February 1, 1966
Area: 934 mi$^2$
Population: 317,989 (1996)
Member Areas include: District Municipality of Central Saanich; City of Colwood; Town of Esquimalt; District Municipality of Highlands; District of Langford; District Municipality of Metchosin; District Municipality of North Saanich; District Municipality of Oak Bay; Corporation of Saanich; Town of Sidney; City of Victoria; Town of View Royal
Chairperson, Geoff Young
Executive Director, William Jordan, 250/360-3124
Director, Finance (Purchasing), Diana Lokken, 250/360-3010; Fax: 250/360-3023
General Municipal Services, Yoon Chee, 250/642-1620; Fax: 250/642-5274
Health Planning, Jeremy Tate, 250/360-3145; Fax: 250/360-3120
Administrator, Regional Parks, Lloyd Rushton, 250/478-3344; Fax: 250/478-5416
Chief Engineer, Michael Williams, 250/360-3092; Fax: 250/360-3079
Community Relations Officer, Ron Kirstein, 250/360-3133; Fax: 250/360-3226
Director, Human Resources, Bill Eccleston, 250/360-3073; Fax: 250/360-3076
Manager, Regional Planning Services, Jane Seright, 250/360-3162; Fax: 250/360-3159

## GREATER VANCOUVER Regional District

4330 Kingsway, Burnaby BC V5H 4G8
604/432-6200, Fax: 604/432-6248
URL: http://www.gvrd.bc.ca/index.html
Incorporated: June 29, 1967
Area: 2,931.4 sq. km
Population: 1,831,665 (1996)
Member Areas include: Village of Anmore; Village of Belcarra; City of Burnaby; City of Coquitlam; Corporation of Delta; City of Langley; Township of Langley; Village of Lions Bay; District Municipality of Maple Ridge; City of New Westminster; District Municipality of North Vancouver; City of North Vancouver; District Municipality of Pitt Meadows; City of Port Coquitlam; City of Port Moody; City of Richmond; City of Surrey; City of Vancouver; District Municipality of West Vancouver; City of White Rock

Chair, George Puil
Secretary, Paulette Vetleson
Manager, Finance, Administration & Properties, Ian Jarvis
Chief Administrative Officer, Johnny Carline
Manager, Air Quality, Barrie Mills, P.Eng.
Manager, Communications & Education, Robert Paddon
Manager, Personnel & Labour Relations, Mark Leffler
Manager, Regional Parks, R.A. Hankin
Manager, Sewerage & Drainage, Hew McConnell, P.Eng.
Manager, Solid Waste, Len Hayton, P.Eng.
Manager, Strategic Planning, Kenneth D. Cameron
Manager, Water Engineering & Construction, John Morse, P.Eng.
Senior Project Engineer, Andrew Marr, P.Eng., 604/436-6800; Fax: 604/436-6811; Email: AMarr@gvrd.bc.ca
Administrator, Hospital Planning, Greg Stump
Manager, Regional Housing, Garry Charles

## ONTARIO REGIONAL GOVERNMENTS

### Regional Municipality of DURHAM

605 Rossland Rd. East, PO Box 623, Whitby ON L1N 6A3
905/668-7711, Fax: 905/668-9963
Incorporated: January 1, 1974
Area: 954 mi$^2$ (2,471 sq. km)
Population: 458,616 (1996)
Member Areas include: Town of Ajax; Township of Brock; Municipality of Clarington; City of Oshawa; Town of Pickering; Township of Scugog; Township of Uxbridge; Town of Whitby
Chair, James Y. Witty, Fax: 905/668-1567
Councillors: Ajax) Roger Anderson, Jim McMaster; Brock) Terry Clayton; Clarington) Ann Dreslinski, Carson Elliott, Larry Hannah; Oshawa) John Aker, Pauiline Beal, Bob Boychyn, Cathy Clarke, John Gray, Irv Harrell, Robert Lutczyk, Brian Nicholson, Nester Pidwerbecki, Jim Potticary; Pickering) Wayne Arthurs, Maurice Brenner, Doug Dickerson, Rick Johnson; Scugog) Marilyn Pearce; Uxbridge) Susan Para; Whitby) Marcel Brunelle, Joseph Drumm, Gerry Emm
Clerk, Patricia M. Madill, ext. 4243
Commissioner, Economic Development Department, P.W. Olive, 1615 Dundas St. East, Whitby ON L1N 2L1,905/723-0023; Fax: 905/436-5359, Toll free: 1-800-706-9857
Commissioner, Finance Department, R.J. Clapp, 60 Bond St. West, PO Box 618, Oshawa ON L1H 8B6,905/571-3311; Fax: 905/571-7460
Medical Officer of Health, Health Department, Dr. R.J. Kyle, 1615 Dundas St. East, Whitby ON L1N 2L1,905/723-8521; Fax: 905/723-6026
Director, Information Systems, J. Hermes, 60 Bond St. West, PO Box 618, Oshawa ON L1H 8B6,905/571-3311; Fax: 905/571-7307
Commissioner, Planning Department, A.L. Georgieff, 1615 Dundas St. East, Whitby ON L1N 2L1,905/728-7731; Fax: 905/436-6612
Chief, Police Department, K. McAlpine, 77 Centre St. N., Oshawa ON L1G 4B7,905/579-1520; Fax: 905/433-5053, URL: http://www.police.durham.on.ca
Commissioner, Social Services, Vacant, 850 King St. W., Oshawa ON L1J 8N5,905/721-6150; Fax: 905/721-6135
Commissioner, Works Department, V.A. Silgailis, 105 Consumers Dr., Whitby ON L1N 1C4,905/668-7721; Fax: 905/668-2051

### Regional Municipality of HALDIMAND-NORFOLK

70 Town Centre Dr., Townsend ON N0A 1S0
519/587-4911, Fax: 519/587-5554
Incorporated: April 1, 1974
Area: 1,103 mi$^2$
Population: 102,575 (1996)
Member Areas include: Township of Delhi; Town of Dunnville; Town of Haldimand; City of Nanticoke; Township of Norfolk; Town of Simcoe
Regional Clerk, Gerald van der Wolf
Treasurer & Commissioner, Finance, Robert Johnstone
Chief Administrative Officer, Gerry Taylor
Regional Chair, John Harrison
Commissioner, Engineering, Eric D'Hondt
Commissioner, Human Resources, Richard Beaumont
Commissioner, Planning & Economic Development, Lee Kennaley
Medical Officer of Health, Dr. Megan Ward
Regional Solicitor, Thomas A. Cline

### Regional Municipality of HALTON

1151 Bronte Rd., Oakville ON L6M 3L1
905/825-6000, Fax: 905/825-8838
URL: http://www.region.halton.on.ca
Incorporated: January 1, 1974
Area: 987 sq. km
Population: 339,875 (1996)
Member Areas include: City of Burlington; Town of Halton Hills; Town of Milton; Town of Oakville
Chair, Joyce Savoline
Councillors: Liz Behrens; Colin Best; Keith Bird; Bob Brechin; Don Carter; Al Cook; John Day; Jack Dennison; Anne Fairfield; Kevin Flynn; Kathy Gastle; Kathy Graham; Gordon Krantz; Barry Lee; Denis Lee; Robert MacIsaac; Walter Mulkewich; Ann Mulvale; Barry Quinn; Ralph Scholtens; Marilyn Serjeantson; Stephen Sparling; Bob Wood
Regional Clerk, Joan A. Eaglesham, ext.7237; Email: regionalclerk@region.halton.on.ca
Commissioner, Corporate Services, Joseph Rinaldo, Fax: 905/825-8820
Chief Administrative Officer, Barry Malmsten, ext. 7236; Fax: 905/825-8839
Acting Commissioner, Planning & Public Works, Brent Marshall, 905/825-6030; Fax: 905/825-0267
Commissioner, Social & Community Services, Bonnie Ewart, Fax: 905/825-8836
Commissioner & Medical Officer of Health, Dr. Bob Nosal, 905/825-6060; Fax: 905/825-8588
Chief of Police, Peter Campbell, 905/825-4777
Director, Human Resources, Vacant, Fax: 905/825-4032
Manager, Purchasing, Andrea Mindenhall, Fax: 905/825-8820
Regional Fire Coordinator, Bill Cunningham, 905/877-1133
Regional Solicitor, Mark Meneray, ext.6010

### Regional Municipality of HAMILTON-WENTWORTH

119 King St. West, PO Box 910, Hamilton ON L8N 3V9
905/546-4111, Fax: 905/546-2546
Incorporated: January 1, 1974
Area: 1113 sq. km
Population: 467,799 (1996)
Member Areas include: Town of Ancaster; Town of Dundas; Town of Flamborough; Township of Glanbrook; City of Hamilton; City of Stoney Creek
Regional Chair, Terry Cooke
Councillors: John Addison; Vince Agro; Terry Anderson; Anne Bain; Dave Braden; Marvin Caplan; Bob Charters; Chad Collins; Geraldine Copps; Frank D'Amico; Don Drury; Fred Eisenberger; Glen Etherington; Tom Jackson; Mary Kiss; Frank MacIntyre; William McCulloch; Ted McMeekin; Henry Merling; Bernie Morelli; Robert Morrow; Russ Powers; Don Ross; Grant Shaw; Ann Sloat; Robert Wade; Dave Wilson
Regional Clerk, Robert C. Prowse, 905/546-4140; Fax: 905/546-2546
Acting Treasurer & Commissioner, Finance, Jim Bruzzese, 905/546-4106; Fax: 905/546-2584
Chief Administrative Officer, Michael Fenn, 905/546-4263; Fax: 905/546-2340
Chief, Hamilton-Wentworth Regional Police Dept., R. Middaugh, 905/546-4700; Fax: 905/546-4752
Commissioner, Human Resource Services, John Johnston, 905/546-2361; Fax: 905/546-2650
Commissioner, Regional Community Services, Mike Schuster, 905/546-4839; Fax: 905/546-2454
Commissioner, Regional Environment, J.D. Thoms, 905/546-4339; Fax: 905/546-4473
Commissioner, Regional Transportation, Dale Turvey, 905/528-4200; Fax: 905/546-6050
Commissioner & Corporate Counsel, Regional Legal Services, Rand Roszell, 905/546-4232; Fax: 905/546-4370
Director, Economic Development, Nick Catalano, 905/546-4234; Fax: 905/546-4107
Director, Information Systems, Jim Hindson, 905/546-4562; Fax: 905/546-4276
Medical Officer of Health, Regional Public Health, Dr. Marilyn James, 905/546-3501; Fax: 905/546-4075

### MUSKOKA District Municipality

70 Pine St., Bracebridge ON P1L 1N3
705/645-2231, Fax: 705/645-5319
Email: info@dom.muskoka.com
Incorporated: January 1, 1971
Area: 4,035.29 sq. km
Population: 50,463 (1996)
Member Areas include: Town of Bracebridge; Township of Georgian Bay; Town of Gravenhurst; Town of Huntsville; Township of Lake of Bays; Township of Muskoka Lakes
Clerk & Chief Administrative Officer, William C. (Bill) Calvert
Treasurer & Commissioner, Finance & Administration, John McRae
Solicitor, D. Royston
Commissioner, Engineering & Public Works, Tony White, Fax: 705/645-7599
Commissioner, Human Services, I. Turnbull
Commissioner, Planning & Economic Development, James Green, Fax: 705/646-2207
Secretary, Land Division Committee, M. Wylie

### Regional Municipality of NIAGARA

2201 St. David's Rd., PO Box 1042, Thorold ON L2V 4T7
905/685-1571, Fax: 905/687-4977, Toll Free: 1-800-263-7215
Email: regional.niagara.on.ca, URL: http://www.regional.niagara.on.ca
Incorporated: January 1, 1970
Area: 1,850 sq. km
Population: 403,504 (1996)
Member Areas include: Town of Fort Erie; Town of Grimsby; Town of Lincoln; City of Niagara Falls; Town of Niagara on the Lake; Town of Pelham; City of Port Colborne; City of St Catharines; City of Thorold; Township of Wainfleet; City of Welland; Township of West Lincoln
Chair: Brian Merrett
Councillors: Roy Adams; Nick Andrechuk; Ralph Beamer; Stan Brickell; Harold Clement; John Dawson; Mike Dietsch; Larry Dykstra; Jill Hildreth; Jane Hughes; Tim Kenny; Ray Konkle; George Marshall; Lorne Nelson; Peter Partington; Stan Pettitt; Neal Schoen; Winston Sims; William Smeaton;

Peter Sobol; Wayne Thomson; D. Bruce Timms; Alan Unwin; James White; Mal Woodhouse
Regional Clerk, Thomas R. Hollick; Email: rhollick@regional.niagara.on.ca
Director, Finance, Michael T. Trojan
Chief Administrative Officer, Michael H. Boggs; Email: mboggs@regional.niagara.on.ca
Director, Human Resources, John Nicol
Director, Planning, Alan Veale
Director, Public Works, John Kernahan
Director, Social Services & Senior Citizens, Susan R. Reid, 905/984-6900; Fax: 905/984-8760
Medical Officer of Health, Dr. Robin C. Williams, 905/688-3762; Fax: 905/682-3901; Email: williams@regional.niagara.on.ca
Purchasing, Pat Crow
Solicitor, Bruce Banting
Police Chief, Niagara Regional Police Dept., Grant Waddell, 68 Church St., St. Catharines ON L2R 3C6

## Regional Municipality of OTTAWA-CARLETON

Cartier Sq., 111 Lisgar St., Ottawa ON K2P 2L7
613/560-1337, Fax: 613/560-6017
URL: http://www.rmoc.on.ca (English) http://www.rmoc.on.ca/Bienvenue.html (French)
Incorporated: January 1, 1969
Area: 2,766 sq. km
Population: 721,136 (1996)
Member Areas include: Township of Cumberland; City of Gloucester; Township of Goulbourn; City of Kanata; City of Nepean; Township of Osgoode; City of Ottawa; Township of Rideau; Village of Rockcliffe Park; City of Vanier; Township of West Carleton
Chair: Peter D. Clark, 613/560-2068; Fax: 613/560-6010
Councillors: Dan Beamish, 613/560-1216; Email: beamishda@rmoc.on.ca; Michel Bellemare, 613/560-1217; Email: bellemarmi@rmoc.on.ca; Richard Cantin, 613/560-1205; Email: cantinri@rmoc.on.ca; Alex Cullen, 613/560-1211; Email: aa111@freenet.carleton.ca; Linda Davis, 613/560-1222; Email: davisli@rmoc.on.ca; Betty Hill, 613/560-1209; Email: hillbe@rmoc.on.ca; Diane Holmes, 613/560-1220; Email: holmesdi@rmoc.on.ca; Peter Hume, 613/560-1227; Email: humepe@rmoc.on.ca; Gord Hunter, 613/560-1215; Email: huntergo@rmoc.on.ca; Herb Kreling, 613/560-1204; Email: krelinghe@rmoc.on.ca; Jacques Legendre, 613/560-1219; Email: legendreja@rmoc.on.ca; Al Loney, 613/560-1212; Email: loneyal@rmoc.on.ca; Brian McGarry, 613/560-1224; Email: mcgarrybr@rmoc.on.ca; Madeleine Meilleur, 613/560-1218; Email: by262@freenet.carleton.ca; Alex Munter, 613/560-1207; Email: munteral@rmoc.on.ca; Wendy Stewart, 613/560-1223; Email: stewartwe@rmoc.on.ca; Vina Waddell, 613/560-1206; Email: waddellvi@rmoc.on.ca; Robert van den Harn, 613/560-1210; Email: vandenharo@rmoc.on.ca
Regional Clerk, Mary Jo Woollam, 613/560-1246; Fax: 613/560-1380
Commissioner, Finance, Jack C. LeBelle, 613/560-2069; Fax: 613/560-6004
Chief Administrative Officer, C. Mervyn Beckstead, 613/560-1335 ext.534; Fax: 613/560-6047
Commissioner, Environment & Transportation, Michael Sheflin, 613/560-1335, ext.1285; Fax: 613/560-6068
Commissioner, Homes for the Aged, Garry Armstrong, 613/560-2081; Fax: 613/560-6008
Commissioner, Human Resources, Joyce Potter, 613/560-2060; Fax: 560-1392
Commissioner, Planning & Development Approvals, Nick Tunnacliffe, 613/560-6065, ext. 1539; Email: tunnacni@rmoc.on.ca
Director, Information & Public Affairs, Rob Dolan, 613/560-1337, ext.1566; Fax: 613/560-6017; Email: dolanro@rmoc.on.ca
Regional Internal Auditor, Internal Audit, Richard Palmer, 613/560-1335; Fax: 613/560-6047
Regional Solicitor, Douglas Cameron, 613/560-2056; Fax: 613-560-1383
Medical Officer of Health, Health Department, Dr. Rob Cushman, 495 Richmond Rd., Ottawa ON K2A 4A4,613/724-4122, ext.3684; Fax: 613/724-4152, Email: cushmaro@rmoc.on.ca
Commissioner, Social Services Department, Dick Stewart, 495 Richmond Rd., Ottawa ON K2A 4A4,613/728-3913; Fax: 613/724-4150

## Regional Municipality of PEEL

10 Peel Centre Dr., Brampton ON L6T 4B9
905/791-7800, Fax: 905/791-4792, 905/791-7800 (for automated attendant)
URL: http://www.region.peel.on.ca
Incorporated: October 15, 1973
Area: 1,257.2 sq. km
Population: 852,526 (1996)
Member Areas include: City of Brampton; Town of Caledon; City of Mississauga
Chair: Emil Kolb
Councillors: Rhoda Begley; Lorna Bissell; Carmen Corbasson; David Culham; Frank Dale; Susan Fennell; David Hughes; Nando Iannicca; Pierre Klein; Katie Mahoney; Hazel McCallion; Frank McKechnie; Gael Miles; Marolyn Morrison; Patricia Mullin; Paul Palleschi; Maja Prentice; Peter Robertson; Pat Saito; Carol Seglins; Richard Whitehead
Regional Clerk, Bonnie J. Zeran, ext.4325
Treasurer, Joseph Pennachetti, ext.4528; Fax: 905/791-4195
Chief Administrative Officer, M. Garrett, ext. 4312; Fax: 905/791-2567
Commissioner, Corporate Services & Regional Solicitor, R.K. Gillespie, ext.4315; Fax: 905/791-2567
Commissioner, Planning, Peter E. Allen, ext.4349; Fax: 905/791-7920
Commissioner, Public Works, Mitch Zamojc, ext.4395; Fax: 905/791-0728
Commissioner, Social Services, P. Vezina, ext.4931; Fax: 905/791-0946
Commissioner & Medical Officer of Health, Dr. P. Cole, ext.2215; Fax: 905/796-0970
Commissioner, Housing & General Manager, Peel Living, R. Maloney, ext.2246; Fax: 905/796-0972
Director, Engineering Services, Cope Otten, 905/791-7800, ext 4404; Fax: 905/791-0728
Director, Human Resources, Paul Vivian, ext.4201; Fax: 905/791-6118
Director, Operations, John Savage, ext.4578; Fax: 905/791-0728
Manager, Emergency Program, J. Moore, ext.4730
Sec.-Treas., Land Division Committee, D.B. Cowtan, ext. 4328; Fax: 905/791-3990
Chief of Police, Peel Regional Police, R. Lunney, 7755 Hurontario St., Brampton ON,905/453-3311

## Regional Municipality of SUDBURY

200 Brady St., PO Box 3700, Stn A, Sudbury ON P3A 5W5
705/673-2171, Fax: 705/673-2960
URL: http://www.region.sudbury.on.ca
Incorporated: January 1, 1973
Area: 1,079.8 mi$^2$ (2,796 km$^2$)
Population: 164,049 (1996)
Member Areas include: Town of Capreol; Town of Nickel Centre; Town of Onaping Falls; Town of Rayside-Balfour; City of Sudbury; Town of Valley East; Town of Walden
Chair: Tom Davies
Councillors: Ronald Bradley; Ted Callaghan; Doug Craig; J. Austin Davey; Peter Dow; John Fera; Eldon Gainer; Jim Gordon; Jim Griffin; Stan Hayduk; Jim Ilnitski; Terry Kett; Lionel Lalonde; Ron MacDonald; Frank Mazzuca; Gerry McIntaggart; Ted Nicholson; Robert Parker; John Robert; Ricardo de la Riva
Regional Clerk, Angie Haché
Regional Treasurer & Director, Financial Services, Sandra Jonasson
Chief Administrative Officer, Jim R. Rule
Commissioner, Corporate Services, Doug Wuksinic
Commissioner, Health & Social Services, M. Mieto
Commissioner, Planning & Development, Bill Lautenbach
Commissioner, Public Works, Patrick J. Morrow
Chief Building Official, Guido Mazza
Chief of Police, Regional Police Services, Alex McCauley
Communications & Public Relations Officer, Paul Philion, ext.4507
Coordinator, Environmental Services, David Caverson, 705/674-4455 ext.4327
Director, Human Resources, Patrick Thomson
Director, Legal Services, R. Swiddle
Director, Operations, Brian Bilodeau, 705/560-2022; Fax: 705/560-9641
General Manager, Sudbury Regional Development Corp., Frank Hess, ext.4308; Fax: 705/671-6767

## Municipality of METROPOLITAN TORONTO

Metro Hall, Station 1071, 55 John St., 7th Fl., Toronto ON M5V 3C6
416/392-8000, Fax: 416/392-2980, Commercial Waste Reduction Hotline: 416/392-4200; Hazardous Waste Hotline: 416/392-4330; Water & Wastewater Info Hotline: 416/392-4546
URL: http://www.metrotor.on.ca/
Incorporated: April 15, 1953
Area: 240 mi$^2$
Member Areas include: Borough of East York; City of Etobicoke; City of North York; City of Scarborough; City of Toronto; City of York
**Editor's Note:** The Municipality of Metropolitan Toronto, along with its six member municipalities, will amalgamate into a single City of Toronto effective January 1998. The present City of Toronto & Metropolitan Toronto will cease to exist & the new City of Toronto will assume responsibility for providing all municipal services. The amalgamation was in effect for municipal elections, November 1997, and a new council for the amalgamated City of Toronto was elected; *see* City of Toronto listing for the new mayor and council.
Metropolitan Chairman, Alan Tonks, 416/392-8001; Fax: 416/392-3799; Email: chairman tonks@metrodesk.metrotor.on.ca
Treasurer & Commissioner, Finance, Louise Eason, 416/392-8065; Fax: 416/392-3649
Acting Chief Administrative Officer, Shirley Hoy, 416/392-8683; Fax: 416/392-3751
Commissioner, Ambulance Services, John Dean, 416/392-2200; Fax: 416/392-2115
Commissioner, Community Services, Shirley Hoy, 416/397-8302; Fax: 416/392-8492
Commissioner, Corporate & Human Resource Services, Earl Rowe, 416/397-0820; Fax: 416/392-3966
Commissioner, Parks & Culture, Ray Biggart, 416/392-8147; Fax: 416/392-3355
Commissioner, Planning, David Gurin, 416/392-8771; Fax: 416/392-3821
Commissioner, Transportation, Douglas P. Floyd, 416/392-8300; Fax: 416/392-4426
Commissioner, Works, Michael Thorne, 416/392-8200; Fax: 416/392-4540
Chair, Board of Management, The Guild Inn, Bernard Rasch, 416/266-4449; Fax: 416/266-4375

Chair, Metropolitan Toronto Police Services Board, Maureen Prinsloo, 416/808-8080; Fax: 416/808-8082
Chief Admin. Officer/Sec.-Treas., Metropolitan Toronto & Region Conservation Authority, Craig Mather, 416/661-6600; Fax: 416/661-6898
Chief General Manager, Toronto Transit Commission, David Gunn, 416/393-4000; Fax: 416/488-6198
Chief of Police, Metropolitan Toronto Police, David Boothby, 416/808-8000; Fax: 416/808-8202
Director, Catholic Children's Aid Society of Metropolitan Toronto, Dr. C.J. Maloney, 416/395-1500; Fax: 416/395-1581
Director, Metropolitan Library Board, Frances Schwenger, 416/393-7000; Fax: 416/392-3102
Executive Director, Children's Aid Society of Metropolitan Toronto, Bruce Rivers, 416/924-4646; Fax: 416/324-2485
Executive Director, Community Information Centre of Metro Toronto, Allison Hewitt, 416/392-0505; Fax: 416/392-4404
Acting Executive Director, Economic Development, Philip Fontaine, 416/392-3378; Fax: 416/397-0906
General Manager, Hummingbird Centre for the Performing Arts, Elizabeth Bradley, 416/393-7474; Fax: 416/393-7454
General Manager, Metropolitan Licensing Commission, Carol Ruddell-Foster, 416/392-3000; Fax: 416/392-3102
General Manager, Metropolitan Toronto Housing Co. Ltd., Joanne Campbell, 416/392-6000; Fax: 416/392-3974
General Manager, Metropolitan Toronto Zoo, Calvin White, 416/392-5900; Fax: 416/392-5934
Interim General Manager, Exhibition Place, Brian Tisdale, 416/393-6000; Fax: 416/393-6372
Metropolitan Auditor, Vacant, 416/392-8030; Fax: 416/392-3754
Metropolitan Solicitor, H.W. Osmond Doyle, 416/392-8047; Fax: 416/392-5624
President, Metropolitan Toronto Convention & Visitors Association, Kirk Shearer, 416/203-2600; Fax: 416/203-7943

## Regional Municipality of WATERLOO

Regional Administration Bldg., 150 Frederick St., Kitchener ON N2G 4J3
519/575-4400, Fax: 519/575-4481
URL: http://www.oceta.on.ca/region.waterloo/
Incorporated: January 1, 1973
Area: 1,345 sq. km
Population: 405,435 (1996)
Member Areas include: City of Cambridge; City of Kitchener; Township of North Dumfries; City of Waterloo; Township of Wellesley; Township of Wilmot; Township of Woolwich
Regional Chair, Ken Seiling
Councillors: Murray Aberle; Jane Brewer; Richard Christy; Mike Connolly; Doug Craig; Ted Fairless; Frank Friedmann; Tom Galloway; Fred Kent; David Leis; Geoff Lorentz; Joe Martens; Bruce McKenty; Joan McKinnon; Lynn Myers; Karen Redman; John Smola; William Struck; Grace Sudden; Brian Turnbull; Mike Wagner; William Weichel; Christina Weylie; Mark Yantsi; Jim Ziegler
Regional Clerk, Evelyn L. Stettner, 519/575-4410; Fax: 519/575-4481
Chief Financial Officer, Larry Ryan, 519/575-4542; Fax: 519/575-4448
Chief Administrative Officer, Gerry A. Thompson, 519/575-4425; Fax: 519/575-4440
Asst. Chief Administrative Officer, Human Resources, Cheryl Lowe, 519/575-4485; Fax: 519/575-4454
Co-Director, Human Resources Services, P. Mellor, 519/575-4701; Fax: 519/575-4454
Co-Director, Human Resources Services, C. VanAndel, 519/575-4701; Fax: 519/575-4454
Commissioner, Corporate Resources & Regional Solicitor, C.P. Giller, 519/575-4460; Fax: 519/575-4466
Commissioner, Engineering, William R. Pyatt, 519/575-4540; Fax: 519/575-4453 Medical Officer of Health & Commissioner, Community Health, Dr. R. Sax, 99 Regina St. South, Waterloo ON N2J 4V3,519/883-2000; Fax: 519/883-2241
Commissioner, Social Services, P. Johnston, 99 Regina St. South, PO Box 1612, Waterloo ON N2J 4G6,519/883-2170; Fax: 519/519/883-2234
Acting Commissioner, Planning & Culture, Paul Mason, 519/575-4512; Fax: 519/575-4449
Director, Child Care, M. Parker, 519/883-2177; Fax: 519/883-2234
Director, Communicable Disease & Sexuality Resources, J. Daley, 519/883-2250; Fax: 519/883-2248
Director, Community Health Administration, A. Schlorff, 519/883-2242; Fax: 519/883-2241
Director, Design & Construction, W. Brodribb, 519/575-4457; Fax: 519/575-4430
Director, Employment & Income Support, F. Pizzuto, 519/883-2179; Fax: 519/883-2234
Director, Environmental Health & Lifestyle Resources, B. Hatton, 519/883-2270; Fax: 519/883-2241
Director, Facilities Management & Fleet Services, K. Noonan, 519/575-4711; Fax: 519/575-4430
Director, Family & Community Resources, T. Schumilas, 519/883-2554; Fax: 519/883-2241
Director, Financial Services, L. Ryan, 519/575-4542; Fax: 519/575-4547
Director, Information Systems, W. Gasparini, 519/575-4570, ext.3077
Director, Legal Services, D. Fisher, 519/575-4518; Fax: 519/575-4466
Director, Library Services, K. Manley, 519/575-4589; Fax: 519/634-5371
Director, Transportation, J. Hammer, 519/575-4401; Fax: 519/575-4453
Director, Waste Management, J. Archibald, 519/575-4774; Fax: 519/575-4452
Director, Water Services, M. Murray, 519/575-4403; Fax: 519/575-4452
Coordinator, Community Safety & Crime Prevention, C. Sadeler, 519/575-4794; Fax: 519/575-4440
Coordinator, Emergency Planning, M. Verbeek, 519/575-4740; Fax: 519/575-4440
Coordinator, Social Planning & Administration, B. Blowes, 519/883-2190; Fax: 519/883-2234

## Regional Municipality of YORK

17250 Yonge St., PO Box 147, Newmarket ON L3Y 6Z1
905/731-0201, Fax: 905/895-3031
URL: http://www.region.york.on.ca
Incorporated: January 1, 1971
Area: 663 mi$^2$
Population: 592,445 (1996)
Member Areas include: Town of Aurora; Town of East Gwillimbury; Town of Georgina; Township of King; Town of Markham; Town of Newmarket; Town of Richmond Hill; City of Vaughan; Town of Whitchurch-Stouffville
Regional Chair, Eldred King, 905/640-2876
Councillors: Carole Bell; William Bell; Margaret Black; Gail Blackburn; John Cole; Donald Cousens; Fred Cox; Michael DiBiase; Wayne Emmerson; Bill Fisch; Joyce Frustaglio; Robert Grossi; Lorna Jackson; Tim Jones; Gordon Landon; Janet Mabley; James Mortson; Tom Taylor; Danny Wheeler
Regional Clerk, Dennis Hearse
Treasurer & Commissioner, Finance, S. Cartwright
Chief Administrative Officer, Alan Wells
Commissioner, Planning & Development Services, J. Livey
Commissioner, Transportation & Works, K. Schipper
Medical Officer of Health & Commissioner, Health Services, Dr. H. Jaczek
Regional Solicitor & Commissioner, Corporate & Legal Services, P. Carlyle
Administrator, Social Services, J. Simmons
Chief of Police, Bryan Cousineau
Director, Human Resources, Sheila Tyndall
Fire Coordinator, Ken Beckett

# QUÉBEC REGIONAL GOVERNMENTS

## Communauté urbaine de MONTRÉAL

1550, rue Metcalfe, Montréal QC H3A 3P1
514/280-3450, Fax: 514/280-4232
URL: http://www.cum.qc.ca
Incorporée: December 23, 1969
Superficie: 1,190.88 mi$^2$
Population: 1,775,846 (1996)
Member Areas include: Ville d'Anjou; Ville de Baie-d'Urfé; Ville de Beaconsfield; Cité de Côte-St-Luc; Ville de Dollard-des-Ormeaux; Ville de Dorval; Ville de Hampstead; Ville de Kirkland; Ville de Lachine; Ville de LaSalle; Village de L'Île-Bizard; Ville de L'Île-Dorval; Ville de Mont-Royal; Ville de Montréal; Ville de Montréal-Est; Ville de Montréal-Nord; Ville de Montréal-Ouest; Ville d'Outremont; Ville de Pierrefonds; Ville de Pointe-Claire; Ville de Roxboro; Ville de Ste-Anne-de-Bellevue; Ville de Ste-Geneviève; Ville de Saint-Laurent; Ville de St-Léonard; Ville de St-Pierre; Village de Senneville; Ville de Verdun; Ville de Westmount
Director General, Gérard Divay, 514/280-3535; Fax: 514/280-4232; Email: gerard_divay@smtpgwy.cum.qc.ca
Treasurer, Michel Bélanger, 514/280-3600; Fax: 514/280-3693; Email: michel_belanger@smtpgwy.cum.qc.ca
Secretary, Nicole Lafond, 514/280-3445; Fax: 514/280-3594; Email: nicole_lafond@smtpgwy.cum.qc.ca
Director, 911 Emergency Centre / Taxi Bureau, Richard Boyer, 514/280-6600; Fax: 514/280-6596; Email: richard_boyer@smtpgwy.cum.qc.ca
Director, Air & Water Purification / Food Inspection, Dr. Jean Troalen, 514/280-4283; Fax: 514/280-4318; Email: jean_troalen@smtpgwy.cum.qc.ca
Director, Planning and Urban Affairs, Amara Ouerghi, 514/280-6722; Fax: 514/280-6744; Email: amara_ouerghi@smtpgwy.cum.qc.ca
Director, Police, Jacques Duchesneau, 514/280-2000; Fax: 514/280-2008; Email: francine.chometon@spcum.qc.ca
Director, Regional Parks, Jacques-Errol Guérin, 514/280-6704; Fax: 514/280-6787; Email: jacques-errol_guerin@smtpgwy.cum.qc.ca
Director, Technical Services, Serge Allie, 514/280-3530; Fax: 514/280-3597; Email: serge_allie@smtpgwy.cum.qc.ca
Director, Valuation, Jean Bélanger, 514/280-3800; Fax: 514/280-3899; Email: jean_belanger@smtpgwy.cum.qc.ca
Director, Wastewater Treatment Plant, Réjean Levesque, 514/280-4355; Fax: 514/280-4346; Email: rejean_levesque@smtpgwy.cum.qc.ca
Director General & Secretary, Arts Council, Jacques Cleary, 514/280-3582; Fax: 514/280-3789
Internal Auditor, Gaétan Foisy, 514/280-3540; Fax: 514/280-4090; Email: gaetan_foisy@smtpgwy.cum.qc.ca
Administrator, Corporate Affairs & Information, Stéphane Venne, 514/280-3592; Fax: 514/280-4243; Email: stephane_venne@smtpgwy.cum.qc.ca
Director, Civil Security Centre, Jean-Bernard Guindon, 514/280-4040; Fax: 514/280-4044; Email: jean-bernard_guindon@smtpgwy.cum.qc.ca
Director, Human Resources, Jacques Robillard, 514/280-3702; Fax: 514/280-6673; Email: jacques_robillard@smtpgwy.cum.qc.ca

Director, Economic Development Office, Sylvie Mercier, Tour Scotia, 1002, rue Sherbrooke ouest, Suite 2400, Montréal QC H3A 3L6,514/280-4251; Fax: 514/280-4266
Directeur, Service de l'environnement, Assainissement de l'air et de l'eau, Dr. Jean Troalen, m.v., #301, 827, boul Crémazie est, Montréal QC H2M 2T8,514/280-4283; Fax: 514/280-4318

## Communauté urbaine de l'OUTAOUAIS

#500, 25, rue Laurier, CP 2210, Succ B, Hull QC J8X 3Z4
819/770-1380, Fax: 819/770-8479
Population: 307,441 (1996)
Member Areas include: Ville d'Aylmer; Ville de Buckingham; Ville de Gatineau; Ville de Hull; Ville de Masson-Angers
Directeur général, Jacques Tremblay
Trésorière, Gladys Guérin
Président du conseil, Marc Croteau
Vice-président du conseil, Luc Montreuil
Directeur, Évaluation & Ressources humaines, Michel Hervieux
Directeur, Environnement (Génie), Claude Robert
Directeur, Environnement (Opérations), Lawrence Gangur
Directeur, Planification, Nelson Tochon

## Communauté urbaine de QUÉBEC

399, rue St-Joseph est, Québec QC G1K 8E2
418/529-8771, Fax: 418/529-2219
Incorporée: December 23, 1969
Superficie: 575 sq. km
Population: 202,865 (1996)
Member Areas include: Ville de Beauport; Municipality of Boischatel; Ville de Cap-Rouge; Ville de Charlesbourg; Ville de Lac-St-Charles; Ville de L'Ancienne-Lorette; Ville de Loretteville; Ville de Québec; Paroisse de St-Augustin; Ville de St-Émile; Ville de Ste-Foy; Ville de Sillery; Ville de Val-Bélair; Ville de Vanier
Chair, Executive Committee, Jean-Paul L'Allier, Fax: 418/529-4655
General Manager, Serge Allen, Fax: 418/529-4655
Treasurer, Raynald Bédard
Secretary., Pierre Rousseau
Chair, Transport Commission, Claude Larose
Directeur, Aménagement du territoire, Jean Guyard
Director, Assessment, Jean-Guy Kirouac
Director, Communications, Benoit Jobidon, Fax: 418/529-8727
Director, Environmental Services, René Gélinas, Fax: 418/529-4299
Director, Human Resources, Pierre Lemay
Director, Information Management, Gilles Bélanger
Director, Legal, Estelle Alain
Director, Tourism & Convention Office, Pierre Labrie

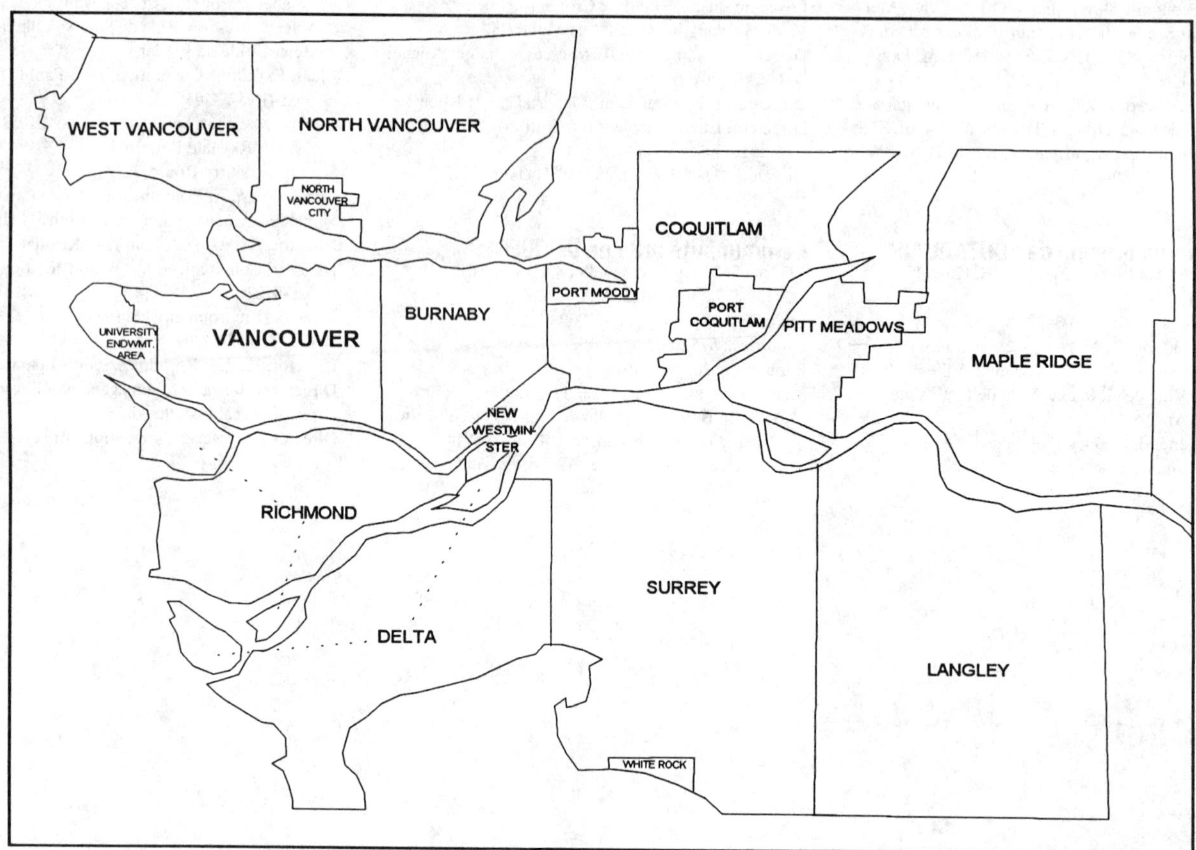
WEST VANCOUVER
NORTH VANCOUVER
NORTH VANCOUVER CITY
COQUITLAM
PORT MOODY
BURNABY
VANCOUVER
UNIVERSITY ENDOWMT. AREA
PORT COQUITLAM
PITT MEADOWS
MAPLE RIDGE
NEW WESTMINSTER
RICHMOND
SURREY
DELTA
LANGLEY
WHITE ROCK



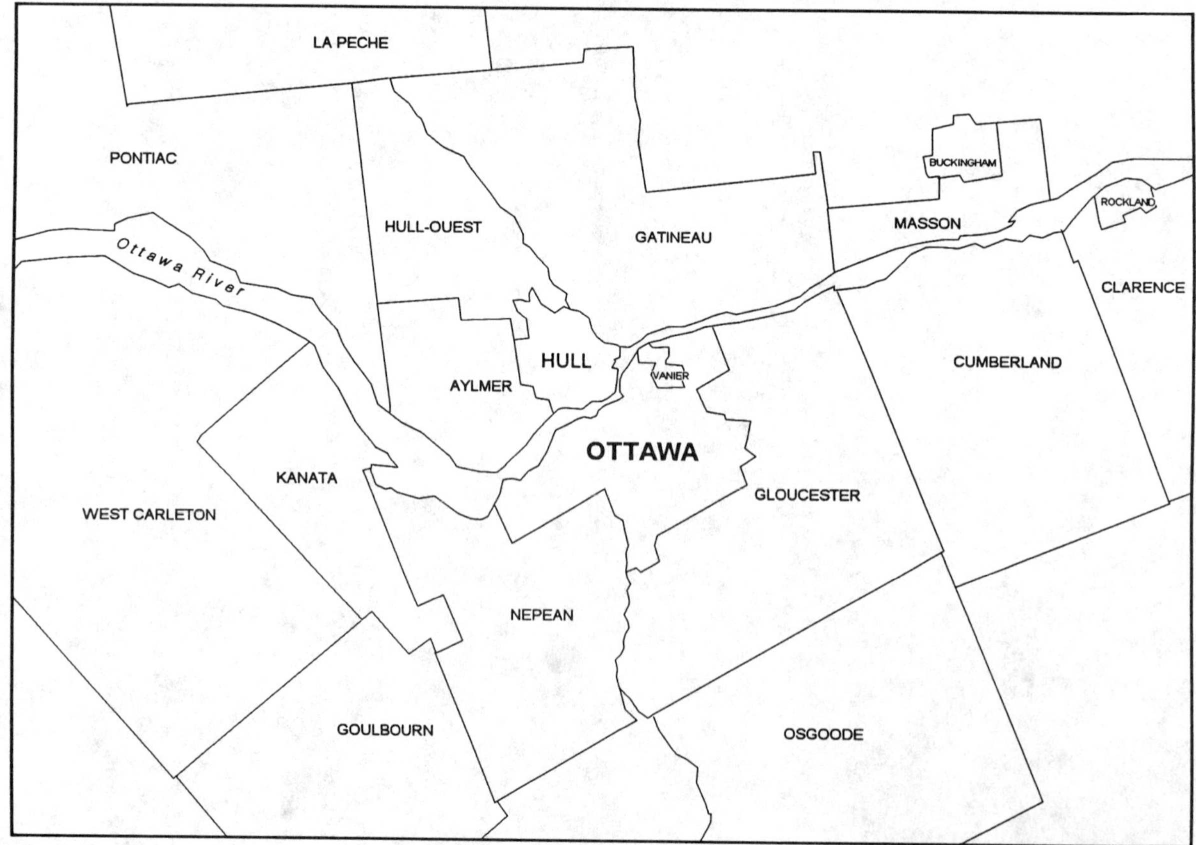
LA PECHE
PONTIAC
BUCKINGHAM
ROCKLAND
MASSON
HULL-OUEST
GATINEAU
Ottawa River
CLARENCE
HULL
VANIER
AYLMER
CUMBERLAND
OTTAWA
KANATA
GLOUCESTER
WEST CARLETON
NEPEAN
GOULBOURN
OSGOODE

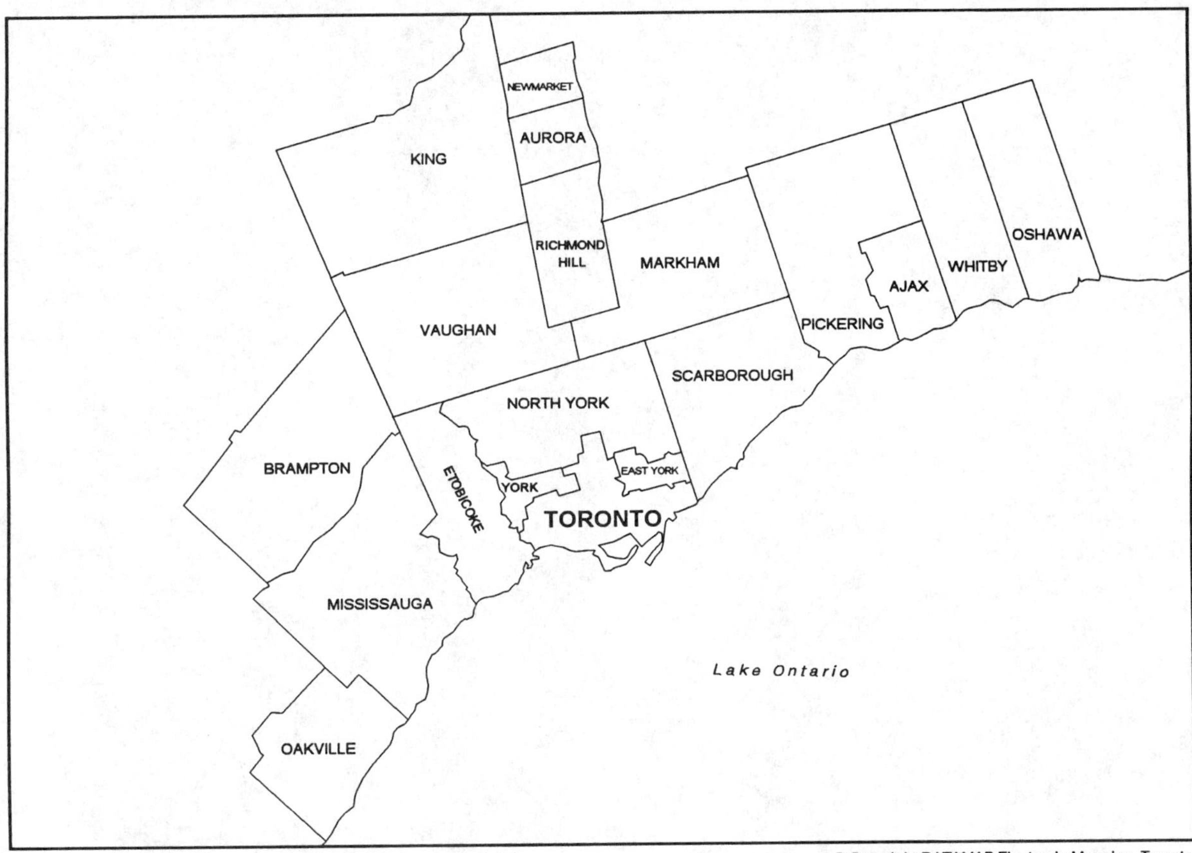




NOTE: Effective January 1, 1998 the constituent municipalities of Metropolitan Toronto were amalgamated into a single new City of Toronto. Metropolitan Toronto & the former cities of Toronto, Etobicoke, North York, Scarborough & York, & the Borough of East York have ceased to exist.

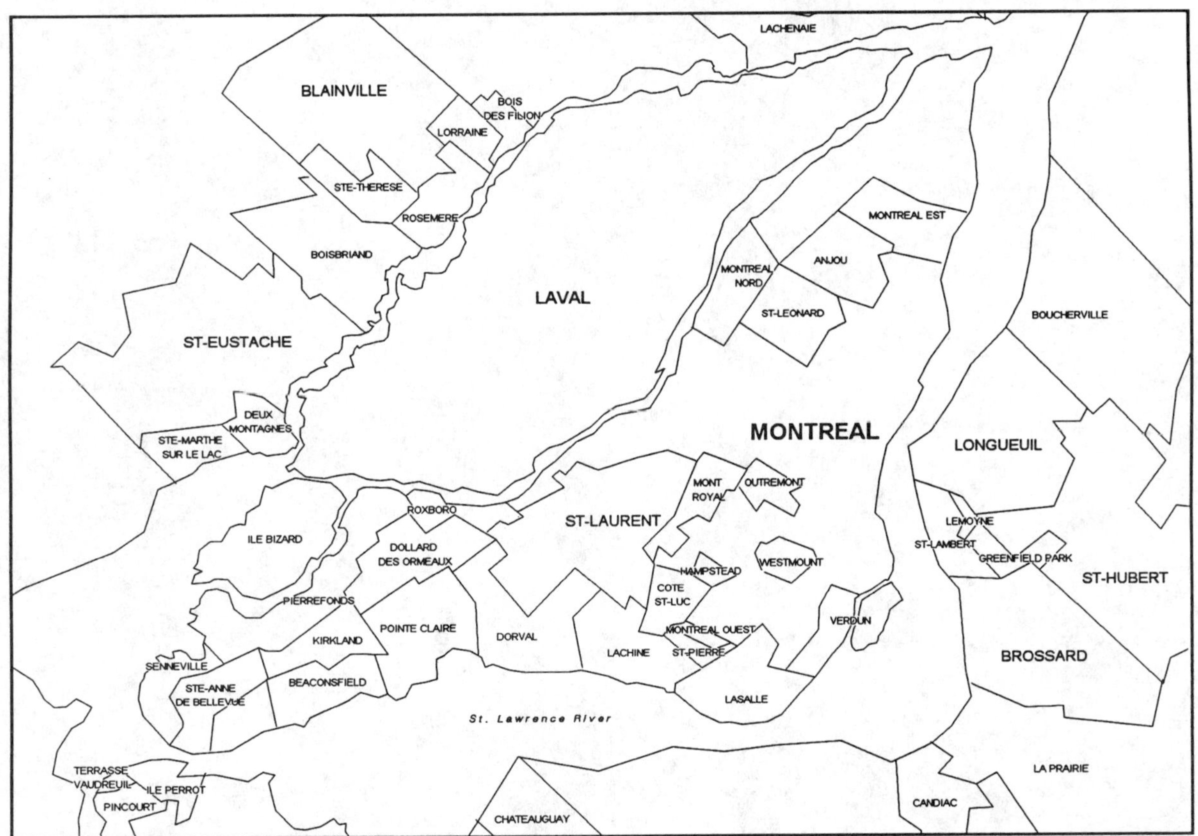

# SECTION 5

## COMMUNICATIONS & INFORMATION MANAGEMENT DIRECTORY



**See ADDENDA at the back of this book for late changes & additional information.**

## LIBRARIES

### The National Library of Canada/Bibliothèque nationale du Canada

395 Wellington St., Ottawa ON K1A 0N4 – 613/995-9481; TTY 613/992-6969; Fax: 613/943-1112; Email: reference@nlc-bnc.ca; URL: http://www.nlc-bnc.ca/; Symbol: OONL

The National Library is governed by the National Library Act, 1969; primary functions are: to promote knowledge & use of the published heritage of Canada; to ensure its acquisition & preservation & to support Canadian studies; to foster library development throughout Canada; to facilitate Canadian library & information resource-sharing. Offers interlibrary loan, reference, info. & advisory services; administers the legal deposit regulations which require that two copies of current Canadian publications be deposited with the Library; publishes national bibliography, Canadiana, (lists new publications relating to Canada); maintains online union catalogues of Canadian libraries; enters into agreements with libraries & coordinates the development of Canadian bibliographic & communications networking to facilitate the sharing of library resources. Collections of Canadian materials include monographs, microforms, newspapers, periodicals, government publications, educational kits, sound recordings, videos & CD-ROMs.

National Librarian, Marianne Scott, 613/996-1623, Email: marianne.scott@nlc-bnc.ca

Acquisitions & Bibliographic Services, Director General, Ingrid Parent, 819/994-6887, Email: ingrid.parent@nlc-bnc.ca

Corporate Policy & Communications, Director General, Tom Delsey, 613/943-1939, Email: tom.delsey@nlc-bnc.ca

Information Technology Services, Director General, Louis Forget, 819/997-7223, Email: louis.forget@nlc-bnc.ca

Information Resource Management, Director General, Paul McCormick, 613/996-2892, Email: paul.mccormick@nlc-bnc.ca

National & International Program, Director General, Gwynneth Evans, 613/995-3904, Email: gwynneth.evans@nlc.bnc.ca

Research & Information Services, Director General, Mary Jane Starr, 613/996-0680, Email: mary-jane.starr@nlc-bnc.ca

Access AMICUS, 819/997-7227, Fax: 819/994-6835, Email: ENVOY 100: its.cic; cic@nlc-bnc.ca

Canadian Book Exchange Centre, 613/952-8902, Fax: 613/954-9891, Email: cbecccel@nlc-bnc.ca

Canadian Children's Literature Service, 613/996-7774, Fax: 613/995-1969, Email: ENVOY 100: OONL.CLS; clsslj@nlc-bnc.ca

Canadian Literature Research Service, 613/947-0827, Fax: 613/995-1969, Email: clrssrlc@nlc-bnc.ca

Canadian Thesis Service, 819/953-6221, Fax: 819/997-7517, Email: theses@nlc-bnc.ca

Canadiana (The National Bibliography), 819/994-6918, Fax: 819/953-0291, Email: canadiana@nlc-bnc.ca

Cataloguing Standards - CAN/MARC Office, 819/994-6936, Fax: 819/994-6835, Email: canmarc@nlc-bnc.ca

Cataloguing Standards - Standards & Support, 819/994-6934, Fax: 819/953-0291, Email: cataloguing.standards@nlc-bnc.ca

Cataloguing in Publication (CIP), 819/994-6881, Fax: 819/997-7517, Email: cip@nlc-bnc.ca

Gifts & Exchanges, 819/994-6955, Fax: 819/997-2395, Email: exchanges@nlc-bnc.ca; gifts@nlc-bnc.ca

Interlibrary Loan (ILL), 613/996-3566, Fax: 613/996-4424, Email: ENVOY 100: OONL.ILL.PEB

International Standard Numbers - Canadian ISBN & ISMN, 819/953-8508, Fax: 819/997-7519, Email: isbn@nlc-bnc.ca

International Standard Numbers - ISSN Canada, 819/994-6895, Fax: 819/953-0291, Email: issn@nlc-bnc.ca

Jacob M. Lowy Collection, 613/995-7960, Fax: 613/995-1969, Email: lowy@ncl-bnc.ca

Legal Deposit, 819/997-9565, Fax: 819/953-8508, Email: legal.deposit@nlc-bnc.ca

Library Information Service, 613/995-8717, Fax: 613/943-2946, Email: ENVOY 100: OONL.LDC; lissib@nlc-bnc.ca

Literary Manuscript Collection, 613/947-0827, Fax: 613/995-1969, Email: litmss@nlc-bnc.ca

MARC Records Distribution Service (MRDS), 819/994-6913, Fax: 819/953-0291, Email: mrds@nlc-bnc.ca

Marketing & Publishing, 613/995-7969, Fax: 613/991-9871, Email: publications@nlc-bnc.ca

Music Division, 613/996-2300, Fax: 613/952-2895, Email: ENVOY 100: OONL.MUS; music@nlc-bnc.ca

Preservation, 613/996-3945, Fax: 613/996-7941

Public Programs, 613/992-9988, Fax: 613/943-2343, Email: public.programs@nlc-bnc.ca

Rare Book Collection, 613/947-0828, Fax: 613/995-1969, Email: rare.books.livres.rares@nlc-bnc.ca

Reading Room (2nd Fl.), 613/996-7428, Fax: 613/943-1112, Email: reference@nlc-bnc.ca

Reference & Information Services, 613/995-9481; TTY: 613/992-6969, Fax: 613/943-1112, Email: reference@nlc-bnc.ca

Union Catalogue, 819/997-7990; 819/953-0291, Fax: 819/947-2706, Email: union.catalogue@nlc-bnc.ca

### Government Departments in Charge of Libraries

ALBERTA: Alberta Community Development-Arts & Libraries Branch, Standard Life Centre, #901, 10405 Jasper Ave., Edmonton AB T5J 4R7 – 403/427-6315; Fax: 403/422-9132; Email: pjackson@mcd.gov.ab.ca – Manager, Punch Jackson; Library Development Officer, Christine E. Nelson

BRITISH COLUMBIA: BC Ministry of Municipal Affairs-Library Services Branch, Administration, PO Box 9490, Victoria BC V8W 9N7 – 250/356-1791; Fax: 250/953-3225; Toll Free: 1-800-663-7051 – Director, Barbara Greeniaus, Email: bgreeniaus@hq.marh.gov.bc.ca; Policy & Legislation, Manager, Chris Peppler, 250/387-4133, Email: cpeppler@hq.marh.gov.bc.ca; Technology & Information Services, Manager, Jim Looney, 250/660-7346, Email: jlooney@hq.marh.gov.bc.ca; Library Consultant, Laurel Prysiazny, 250/387-5277, Email: lprysiazny@hq.marh.gov.bc.ca; Library Consultant, Barbara Chouinard, 250/356-0413, Email: bchouinard@hq.marh.gov.bc.ca; Library

Consultant, Dawn Stoppard, 250/356-1790, Email: dstoppard@hq.marh.gov.bc.ca

MANITOBA: Manitoba Culture, Heritage & Citizenship-Public Library Services, #200, 1525 - 1 St., Brandon MB R7A 7A1 – 204/726-6590; Fax: 204/726-6868 – Director, Sylvia Nicholson

NEW BRUNSWICK: New Brunswick Library Services, PO Box 6000, Fredericton NB E3B 5H1 – 506/453-2354; Fax: 506/453-2416 – Director, Jocelyne LeBel

NEWFOUNDLAND: Newfoundland Provincial Public Libraries Board, Arts & Culture Centre, 125 Allendale Rd., St. John's NF A1B 3A3 – 709/737-3964; Fax: 709/737-3009; Email: dagale@calvin.stemnet.nf.ca – Director, David Gale

NORTHWEST TERRITORIES: Northwest Territories Library Services, Rm# 207 & 209, Wright Centre, 62 Woodland Dr., Hay River NT X0E 1G1 – 867/874-6531; Fax: 867/874-3321; Email: ENVOY: NWT.Library.Services – A/Territorial Librarian, Suliang Feng; Technical Services, Head, Brian Dawson; Administrative Secretary, Heather Beck; Order Clerk, Theresa Lafferty; Technical Services Clerk, Shannon Coady; Shipping Clerk, Alison Kilgour

NORTHWEST TERRITORIES: Northwest Territories Library Services-Baffin Region, Bag 189A, Iqaluit NT X0A 0H0 – 867/979-5401; Fax: 867/979-1373

NORTHWEST TERRITORIES: Northwest Territories Library Services-Keewatin Region, Bag 002, Rankin Inlet NT X0C 0G0 – 867/645-5035; Fax: 867/645-2889

NOVA SCOTIA: Nova Scotia Provincial Library, 3770 Kempt Rd., Halifax NS B3K 4X8 – 902/424-2400; Fax: 902/424-0633; Email: admin@nshpl.library.ns.ca; Symbol: NSHPL – Provincial Librarian, Marion L. Pape; User Services, Andrea John; Administration & Systems, Elizabeth Armstrong; Technical Services, Bridget Turner

ONTARIO: Ministry of Citizenship, Culture & Recreation-Cultural Partnerships Branch, 77 Bloor St. West, 3rd Fl., Toronto ON M7A 2R9 – 416/314-7611; Fax: 416/314-7635 – Director, Michael Langford

PRINCE EDWARD ISLAND: Prince Edward Island Provincial Library, Red Head Rd., PO Box 7500, Morell PE C0A 1S0 – 902/961-7320; Fax: 902/961-7322; TLX: 014-44154; – Director of Archives & Libraries, Harry Holman

QUÉBEC: Ministère de la Culture et des Communications-Direction des politiques et de la coordination des programmes, Bloc C, 225, Grande Allée est, 2e étage, Québec QC G1R 5G5 – 418/644-0485; Téléc: 418/643-4080 – Directeur, Denis Delangie

SASKATCHEWAN: Saskatchewan Provincial Library, 1352 Winnipeg St., Regina SK S4P 3V7 – 306/787-2976; Fax: 306/787-2029; Email: srp.admin@provlib.lib.sk.ca; URL: http://www.lib.sk.ca/provlib/; http://www.lib.sk.ca/pleis/; Symbol: SRP – Provincial Librarian, Maureen Woods; Public Library & Client Services, Director, Joylene Campbell; Client Projects & Assessment, Head, Marie Sakon; Client Services, Reference & Interlibrary Loans, Head, Ved Arora; Multitype Coordinator Services, Coordinator, Marilyn Jenkins; Technical & Internal Services, Director, Gloria Materi

YUKON TERRITORY: Government of Yukon, Dept. of Education, Libraries & Archives Division, PO Box 2703, Whitehorse YT Y1A 2C6 – 867/667-5309; Fax: 867/393-6253; Email: jourom@gov.yk.ca – Director, Linda R. Johnson, Email: Ljohnson@gov.yk.ca; Public Library Services, Manager, Julianne Ourom, 403/667-5447, Fax: 403/393-6333

## ALBERTA

### Regional Library Systems with Member Libraries

#### CHINOOK ARCH REGIONAL LIBRARY SYSTEM

2902 - 7th Ave. North, Lethbridge AB T1H 5C6 – 403/380-1500; Fax: 403/380-3550; Email: mmacdonald@chinookarch.ab.ca; Symbol: ALCA

CEO, Maggie Macdonald

Arrowwood Public Library, PO Box 88, Arrowwood AB T0L 0B0 – 403/534-3932; Fax: 403/534-3932 – Librarian, Dorothy Way

Cardston & District Public Library, PO Box 1560, Cardston AB T0K 0K0 – 403/653-4775 – Head Librarian, Lei Shimbashi

Carmangay & District Municipal Library, PO Box 67, Carmangay AB T0L 0N0 – 403/643-3777 – Head Librarian, Marion Schibbelhute

Vulcan County Municipal Library Board, PO Box 84, Carmangay AB T0L 0N0 – Secretary, Margaret Shaw

Champion Municipal Library, PO Box 177, Champion AB T0L 0R0 – 403/897-3099 – Head Librarian, Grete Christiansen

Claresholm Municipal Library, PO Box 548, Claresholm AB T0L 0T0 – 403/625-4168 – Head Librarian, Kathy Bantle

Coaldale Public Library, PO Box 1207, Coaldale AB T1M 1N1 – 403/345-1340; Fax: 403/345-1342 – Head Librarian, Jane Franz

Fort MacLeod RCMP Centennial Library, PO Box 1479, Fort Macleod AB T0L 0Z0 – 403/553-3880; Fax: 403/553-2643 – Librarian, Sharon Edwards

Glenwood Municipal Library, PO Box 1156, Glenwood AB T0K 2R0 – 403/626-3660 – Librarian, Twylla Oviatt

Granum Municipal Library, PO Box 300, Granum AB T0L 1A0 – 403/687-3912 – Head Librarian, Linda DeMaere

Lethbridge Public Library, 810 - 5 Ave. South, Lethbridge AB T1J 4C4 – 403/380-7341; Fax: 403/329-1478; Email: drand@chinookarch.ab.ca – Head Librarian, Duncan Rand

Lomond Public Library, PO Box 290, Lomond AB T0L 1G0 – 403/792-3934 – Head Librarian, Donna Dietrich

Magrath Public Library, PO Box 295, Magrath AB T0K 1J0 – 403/758-6498; Fax: 403/758-6333 – Head Librarian, Cyd Cunningham

Milo Municipal Library, PO Box 30, Milo AB T0L 1L0 – 403/599-3850 – Head Librarian, Barbara Godkin

Thelma Fanning Memorial Library, PO Box 310, Nanton AB T0L 1R0 – 403/646-5535; Email: nantrlibr@telusplanet.net – Contact, Marie-Jeanne Zetchus

Picture Butte Municipal Library, PO Box 1130, Picture Butte AB T0K 1V0 – 403/732-4141 – Head Librarian, Bonnie Lewis; Circulation Librarian, Anne Withage

Raymond Public Library, PO Box 258, Raymond AB T0K 2S0 – 403/752-4785 – Head Librarian, Linda Sheen

Stavely Municipal Library, PO Box 100, Stavely AB T0L 1Z0 – 403/549-2190 – Head Librarian, Jean Cochlan

Theodore Bradley Library, PO Box 100, Stirling AB T0K 2E0 – 403/756-3665 – Head Librarian, Donna Clawson

Taber Public Library, PO Box 2019, Taber AB T0K 2G0 – 403/223-4343 – Head Librarian, Kim Price

Vauxhall Public Library, PO Box 265, Vauxhall AB T0K 2K0 – 403/654-2370 – Head Librarian, Vera Lowen

Vulcan Municipal Library, PO Box 1120, Vulcan AB T0L 2B0 – 403/485-2571 – Head Librarian, Patricia Crosby

#### MARIGOLD LIBRARY SYSTEM

710 - 2 St., Strathmore AB T1P 1K4 – 403/934-5334; Fax: 403/934-5331; Toll Free: 1-800-332-1077; Email: rlunn@freenet.calgary.ab.ca; Symbol: ASMLS

Director, Rowena Lunn

Assistant Director, Karen Labuik

Consultant/Library Services, Laurie Harrison

Consultant/Computer Manager, Arlene Hammer

Acme Municipal Library, PO Box 326, Acme AB T0M 0A0 – 403/546-3845; Fax: 403/546-2248 – Librarian, Connie Rieger

Banff Public Library, PO Box 996, Banff AB T0L 0C0 – 403/762-2661; Fax: 403/762-3805; Email: jfish@banff.net – Librarian, Jeannette Fish

Beiseker Municipal Library, PO Box 8, Beiseker AB T0M 0G0 – 403/947-3230; Fax: 403/947-2146 – Librarian, Cherry Greer

Sheep River Municipal Library, PO Box 90, Black Diamond AB T0L 0H0 – 403/933-3278; Fax: 403/933-7373; Email: srcl@cadvision.com – Librarian, Tracey Walshaw

Berry Creek Community Library, RR#2, Cessford, Brooks AB T1R 1E2 – 403/566-3743; Fax: 403/566-3736 – Librarian, Gina Lundquist

Canmore Public Library, 950 - 8 Ave., Canmore AB T1W 2T1 – 403/678-2468; Fax: 403/678-2165; Email: jluthy@banff.net – Librarian, Jean Luthy

Carbon Municipal Library, PO Box 70, Carbon AB T0M 0L0 – 403/572-3440; Email: library@supernet.ab.ca – Librarian, Elaine Murphy

Cereal & District Municipal Library, PO Box 218, Cereal AB T0J 0N0 – 403/326-3853; Fax: 403/326-2003 – Librarian, Joanne Barrack

Consort Municipal Library, Bag Service #2, Consort AB T0C 1B0 – 403/577-3654; Fax: 403/577-2112 – Librarian, Shelley Beier

Delia Municipal Library, PO Box 302, Delia AB T0J 0W0 – 403/364-3777; Fax: 403/364-3805; Email: delia@schnet.edc.gov.ab.ca – Librarian, Leah Hunter

Drumheller Public Library, PO Box 1599, Drumheller AB T0J 0Y0 – 403/823-5382; Fax: 403/823-3651; Email: drumli@dns.magtech.ab.ca – Librarian, Linde Turner

East Coulee Community Library, PO Box 600, East Coulee AB T0J 1B0 – 403/822-2149 – Librarian, Beatrice Foose

Empress Municipal Library, PO Box 188, Empress AB T0J 1E0 – 403/565-3938 – Librarian, Wilma Schafer

Exshaw Community Library, PO Box 157, Exshaw AB T0L 2C0 – 403/673-3571 – Librarian, Rose Reid

Gleichen Municipal Library, PO Box 160, Gleichen AB T0J 1N0 – 403/734-2390 – Librarian, Dorien Jackson

Hanna Municipal Library, PO Box 878, Hanna AB T0J 1P0 – 403/854-3865; Fax: 403/854-2772; Email: hml@supernet.ab.ca – Librarian, Mary McKay

High River Centennial Library, 909 - 1st St. West, High River AB T1V 1A5 – 403/652-2917; Fax: 403/652-7203; Email: hrcl@cadvision.com – Librarian, Deborah Gardiner

Hussar Municipal Library, General Delivery, Hussar AB T0J 1S0 – 403/787-3766; Fax: 403/787-3922 – Librarian, Myrtle Pentelchuk

Irricana & District Municipal Library, PO Box 299, Irricana AB T0M 1B0 – 403/935-4818 – Librarian, Kathleen Beagle

Linden Community Library, PO Box 120, Linden AB T0M 1J0 – 403/546-3757; Fax: 403/546-4220 – Librarian, Debbie Martin

Longview Municipal Library, PO Box 189, Longview AB T0L 1H0 – 403/558-3922 – Librarian, Lise Robert

Millarville Community Library, PO Box 59, Millarville AB T0L 1K0 – 403/931-3919; Fax: 403/931-2475 – Librarian, Norma Dawson

Morrin Municipal Library, PO Box 284, Morrin AB T0J 2B0 – 403/772-3922 – Librarian, Josey DeMille

Okotoks Public Library, PO Box 310, Okotoks AB T0L 1T0 – 403/938-2220; Fax: 403/938-4317; Email: okolibry@cadvision.com – Librarian, Marg Proctor

Oyen Municipal Library, PO Box 328, Oyen AB T0J 2J0 – 403/664-3580; Fax: 403/664-2520; Email: omlibry@supernet.ab.ca – Librarian, Charlotte Lester

Rockyford Municipal & District Library, PO Box 277, Rockyford AB T0J 2R0 – 403/533-9904 – Librarian, Frances Garriott

Rumsey Community Library, PO Box 113, Rumsey AB T0J 2Y0 – 403/368-3939 – Librarian, Isabella Taylor

Standard Municipal Library, PO Box 305, Standard AB T0J 3G0 – 403/644-3995 – Librarian, Betty Christensen

Strathmore Municipal Library, 85 Lakeside Blvd., Strathmore AB T1P 1A0 – 403/934-5440; Email: stmunlib@cal.cybersurf.net – Librarian, Margie Lavoie

Three Hills Municipal Library, PO Box 207, Three Hills AB T0M 2A0 – 403/443-2360; Fax: 403/443-2360 – Librarian, Sharon Wood

Trochu Municipal Library, PO Box 396, Trochu AB T0M 2C0 – 403/442-2458 – Librarian, Brenda Cunningham

Youngstown Municipal Library, PO Box 39, Youngstown AB T0J 3P0 – 403/779-3864; Fax: 403/779-2279 – Librarian, Wendy Mainhood

### NORTHERN LIGHTS LIBRARY SYSTEM

PO Bag 8, Elk Point AB T0A 1A0 – 403/724-2596; Fax: 403/724-2597; Email: nlls@ccinet.ab.ca; Symbol: AEPNL

Chair, Iris English

Public Services Librarian, Linda MacCallum

Finance & Administrative Officer, Loretta Swedgan

Bonnyville Municipal District Municipal Library Board, PO Box 1010, Bonnyville AB T9N 2J7 – 403/826-3710; Fax: 403/826-4524; Symbol: ABM – Chair, Polly Kopala

Cold Lake Public Library, #1301 - 8th Ave., Cold Lake AB T0A 0V2 – 403/639-3967; Fax: 403/639-3963 – Librarian, Hansa Thaleshvar

Elk Point Public Library, PO Box 750, Elk Point AB T0A 1A0 – 403/724-3737; Fax: 403/724-3737 – Librarian, Michele Duczek

Grand Centre & District Public Library, PO Box 1049, Grand Centre AB T0A 1T0 – 403/594-5101; Fax: 403/594-0007 – Librarian, Mary Anne Penner

Kitscoty Municipal Library, PO Box 300, Kitscoty AB T0B 2P0 – 403/846-2121; Fax: 403/846-2930 – Librarian, Wanda Berg

Lloydminster Public Library, 5010 - 49 Ave., Lloydminster AB T9V 0K2 – 403/875-0850; 306/825-2618 (Sask.); Fax: 403/875-6523; Email: Lloydlib@supernet.ab.ca – Chief Librarian, Ron Gillies

Marwayne Public Library, PO Box 174, Marwayne AB T0B 2X0 – 403/847-3930; Fax: 403/847-3796 – Clerk Librarian, Carol Killam

Medley Public Library, PO Box 1400, Medley AB T0A 2M0 – 403/594-4254 – Librarian, Dale Gratton

County of Two Hills #21 Municipal Library Board, PO Box 204, Myrnam AB T0B 3K9 – 403/366-3302 – Secretary, Beverly Myroniuk

Myrnam Community Library, General Delivery, Myrnam AB T0B 3K0 – 403/366-3801; Fax: 403/366-2332 – Librarian, Anne Godziuk

Three Cities Public Library, PO Box 60, Paradise Valley AB T0B 3R0 – 403/745-2277 (school); Fax: 403/745-2641 – Librarian, Sandra Babcock

St. Paul Municipal Library, PO Box 1328, St. Paul AB T0A 3A0 – 403/645-4904; Fax: 403/645-5198; Email: astp@telusplanet.net – Librarian, Rachel Holman

Smoky Lake Municipal Library, PO Box 460, Smoky Lake AB T0A 3C0 – 403/656-4212; Fax: 403/656-4212 – Chair, Carole Carpenter; Librarian, Doris Muraca

Alice Melnyk Public Library, PO Box 460, Two Hills AB T0B 4K0 – 403/657-3553; Fax: 403/657-3553 – Chair, Esther Zayak; Librarian, Liz Wells

Vermilion Public Library, 5001 - 49 Ave., Vermilion AB T9X 1B8 – 403/853-4288; Fax: 403/853-1783 – Librarian, Karla Palichuk

Anne Chorney Public Library, PO Box 130, Waskatenau AB T0A 3P0 – 403/358-2777; Fax: 403/358-2332 – Librarian, Cathy Zon

### PARKLAND REGIONAL LIBRARY SYSTEM

5404 - 56 Ave., Lacombe AB T4L 1G1 – 403/782-3850; Fax: 403/782-4650; URL: http://www.rtt.ab.ca/rtt/prl; Symbol: ALAP

Director, Margaret Law

Assistant Director, Clive Maishment

Reference Librarian, Patricia Silver

Alix Public Library, PO Box 69, Alix AB T0C 0B0 – 403/747-3233 – Librarian, Debra Cowan

Alliance Municipal Library, PO Box 185, Alliance AB T0B 0A0 – 403/879-3733 – Librarian, Mandy Fuller

Bashaw Municipal Library, PO Box 669, Bashaw AB T0B 0H0 – 403/372-4055 – Librarian, Beth Richardson

Bawlf Public Library, PO Box 33, Bawlf AB T0B 0J0 – 403/373-3882 – Librarian, Linda Nikiforuk

Bentley Municipal Library, PO Box 361, Bentley AB T0C 0J0 – 403/748-4626 – Librarian, Valerie Anderson

Blackfalds Public Library, PO Box 70, Blackfalds AB T0M 0J0 – 403/885-2343 – Librarian, Darlene Stone

Bowden Public Library, PO Box 218, Bowden AB T0M 0K0 – 403/224-3688 – Librarian, Doreen Lee

Camrose Public Library, 4710 - 50 Ave., Camrose AB T4V 0R8 – 403/672-4214; Fax: 403/672-9165 – Librarian, Robin Brown

Caroline Municipal Library, PO Box 339, Caroline AB T0M 0M0 – 403/722-4060; Fax: 403/722-4050 – Librarian, Viola Larsen

Bob Clarke Municipal Library, PO Box 941, Carstairs AB T0M 0N0 – 403/337-3943 – Librarian, Anne Strilchuk

Clive Public Library, PO Box 82, Clive AB T0C 0Y0 – 403/784-3131 – Librarian, Donna Hunter

Cremona Municipal Library, General Delivery, Cremona AB T0M 0R0 – 403/637-3763; Fax: 403/637-2101 – Librarian, Sandra Herbert

Daysland Public Library, PO Box 700, Daysland AB T0B 1A0 – 403/374-3730 – Librarian, Carol Pennycook

Delburne Municipal Library, PO Box 405, Delburne AB T0M 0V0 – 403/749-3848; Fax: 403/749-2800 – Librarian, Sheila Reczseidler

Didsbury Municipal Library, PO Box 305, Didsbury AB T0M 0W0 – 403/335-3142; Fax: 403/335-3142 – Librarian, Mark Fischer

Lone Pine Public Library, RR#2, Didsbury AB T0M 0W0 – 403/337-2888 – Librarian, Ruth Good

Eckville Municipal Library, PO Box 492, Eckville AB T0M 0X0 – 403/746-3240 – Librarian, Cathy Rolfsen

Edberg Public Library, General Delivery, Edberg AB T0B 1J0 – 403/877-2538; Fax: 403/877-2562 – Librarian, Amanda McCrea

Elnora Public Library, General Delivery, Elnora AB T0M 0Y0 – 403/773-3922 – Librarian, Christine Hunter

Forestburg Public Library, PO Box 579, Forestburg AB T0B 1N0 – 403/582-4110 – Librarian, Judy Oberg

Galahad Public Library, PO Box 58, Galahad AB T0B 1R0 – 403/583-3917 – Librarian, Lori Wegenast

Hardisty & District Public Library, General Delivery, Hardisty AB T0B 1V0 – 403/888-3947 – Librarian, Trudy Vickerman

Hay Lakes Municipal Library, PO Box 69, Hay Lakes AB T0B 1W0 – 403/878-3366 – Librarian, Nora Klappstein

Heisler Municipal Library, PO Box 111, Heisler AB T0B 2A0 – Fax: 403/889-2280 – Librarian, Linda Calon

Innisfail Public Library, 4949 - 49 St., PO Box 220, Innisfail AB T4G 1A5 – 403/227-4407; Fax: 403/227-3122 – Librarian, Virginia Robblee

Killam & District Municipal Library, PO Box 329, Killam AB T0B 2L0 – 403/385-3032 – Librarian, Karen Auburn

Lacombe Public Library, #6, 5033 - 52 St., Lacombe AB T4L 2A6 – 403/782-7572 – Librarian, Christina Landry

Lougheed & District Public Library, PO Box 179, Lougheed AB T0B 2V0 – 403/386-3730 – Librarian, Debra Smith

Mirror Municipal Library, PO Box 254, Mirror AB T0B 3C0 – 403/788-3044 – Librarian, Jeanne Kingston

Nordegg Public Library, General Delivery, Nordegg AB T0M 2H0 – 403/721-3949; Fax: 403/721-2057 – Librarian, Heather Clement

Olds Municipal Library, 5217 - 52 St., Olds AB T4H 1S8 – 403/556-6460; Fax: 403/556-6692 – Librarian, Donna Phillips

Penhold & District Public Library, PO Box 10, Penhold AB T0M 1R0 – 403/886-2636 – Librarian, Gertrude Hingley

Ponoka Jubilee Library, PO Box 4160, Ponoka AB T4J 1R6 – 403/783-3843; Fax: 403/783-6745 – Librarian, Norma-Jean Colquhoun

Rimbey Municipal Library, PO Box 1130, Rimbey AB T0C 2J0 – 403/843-2841 – Librarian, Susan Grieshaber-Otto

Rocky Mountain House Memorial Library, PO Box 1497, Rocky Mountain House AB T0M 1T0 – 403/845-2042; Fax: 403/845-5633 – Librarian, Myrna G. Speers

Sedgewick & District Municipal Library, PO Box 569, Sedgewick AB T0B 4C0 – 403/384-3003 – Librarian, Judy Ferrier

Sundre Municipal Library, PO Box 539, Sundre AB T0M 1X0 – 403/638-4000; Fax: 403/638-4000 – Librarian, Charlene Siegfried

Sylvan Lake Municipal Library, PO Box 46, Sylvan Lake AB T0M 1Z0 – 403/887-2130; Fax: 403/887-3660; Email: sylvan-lake-library@ccinet.ab.ca – Librarian, Alice Swabey

Water Valley Public Library, General Delivery, Water Valley AB T0M 2E0 – 403/637-3899 – Librarian, Harriet Green

### PEACE LIBRARY SYSTEM

8301 - 110 St., Grande Prairie AB T8W 6T2 – 403/538-4656; Fax: 403/539-5285; Email: pls@terranet.ab.ca

Acting Director, Sharon Siga

Public Services Librarian, Linda Duplessis

Technical Services Coordinator, Sharon Nuttycombe

Materials Purchasing Supervisor, Padmini Ramaswamy

Bear Point Community Library, PO Box 5, Bear Canyon AB T0H 0B0 – 403/595-3771; Fax: 403/595-3777; Email: bearcan@schnet.edc.gov.ab.ca – Librarian, Shirley Fredrickson

Alberta RCMP Century Public Library, PO Box 119, Beaverlodge AB T0H 0C0 – 403/354-2569; Fax: 403/

354-3612; Email: beaverlb@terranet.ab.ca – Librarian, Linda Senenko

Berwyn Women's Institute Municipal Library, PO Box 89, Berwyn AB T0H 0E0 – 403/338-3616 – Librarian, Leanne Bowness

Menno-Simons Community School Library, PO Bag 100, Cleardale AB T0H 3Y0 – 403/585-3623; Fax: 403/685-3665; Email: menno@schnet.edc.gov.ab.ca – Librarian, Marie Zacharias

Fairview Public Library, PO Box 248, Fairview AB T0H 1L0 – 403/835-2613; Fax: 403/835-2613 – Librarian, Chris Burkholder

Bibliothèque Dentinger, CP 60, Falher AB T0H 1M0 – 403/837-2776 – Bibliothécaire, Rita Brodeur

Grande Prairie County Library Board, 8611 - 108 St., Grande Prairie AB T8V 4C5 – 403/532-9722 – Secretary, Jean Rycroft

Grande Prairie Municipal Library, 9910 - 99 Ave., Grande Prairie AB T8V 0R5 – 403/532-3580; Fax: 403/538-4983; Email: gppl@terranet.ab.ca – Librarian, Rick Leech

Grimshaw Municipal Library, PO Box 588, Grimshaw AB T0H 1W0 – 403/332-4553 – Librarian, Linda Chmilar

High Level Municipal Library, PO Box 1380, High Level AB T0H 1Z0 – 403/926-2097; Fax: 403/926-2899; Email: hlplsys@ccinet.ab.ca – Librarian, Sheryl Pelletier

High Prairie Municipal Library, PO Box 890, High Prairie AB T0G 1E0 – 403/523-3838; Email: hplibrary@inetnorth.ab.ca – Librarian, Janet G. Lemay

Hines Creek Municipal Library, PO Box 750, Hines Creek AB T0H 2A0 – 403/494-3879; Fax: 403/494-3605 – Librarian, Betty Ann Tachit

Hythe Municipal Library, PO Box 601, Hythe AB T0H 2C0 – 403/356-3014 – Librarian, Karen Bass

Kinuso Municipal Library, PO Box 60, Kinuso AB T0G 1K0 – 403/775-3694; Fax: 403/775-3650 – Librarian, Susan Moody

La Glace Community Library, PO Box 209, La Glace AB T0H 2J0 – 403/568-4696 – Librarian, Doris Fast

Manning Municipal Library, PO Bag 1400, Manning AB T0H 2M0 – 403/836-3054; Fax: 403/836-3570 – Librarian, Barbara Mulcahy

McLennan Municipal Library, PO Box 298, McLennan AB T0H 2L0 – 403/324-3767; Fax: 403/324-2288 – Librarian, Mariette Limoges

Nampa Municipal Library, PO Box 509, Nampa AB T0H 2R0 – 403/322-3805; Fax: 403/322-2100 – Librarian, Cathy Rasmussen

Peace River Municipal Library, 9807 - 97 Ave., Peace River AB T8S 1H6 – 403/624-4076; Fax: 403/624-4664 – Librarian, Sharon Keene

Rainbow Lake Municipal Library, PO Box 266, Rainbow Lake AB T0H 2Y0 – 403/956-3656; Fax: 403/956-3794; Email: rl_lib@agt.net – Librarian, Donna Misner

Sexsmith Shannon Municipal Library, PO Box 266, Sexsmith AB T0H 3C0 – 403/568-4333; Fax: 403/568-2200 – Librarian, Sherrill Robinson

Spirit River Municipal Library, PO Box 490, Spirit River AB T0H 3G0 – 403/864-4038 – Librarian, Carol Bergstrom

Valhalla Centre Community Library, PO Box 68, Valhalla Centre AB T0H 3M0 – 403/356-3834; Fax: 403/356-3834 – Librarian, Gail Perry

Valleyview Municipal Library, PO Box 897, Valleyview AB T0H 3N0 – 403/524-3033; Fax: 403/524-2727; Email: vlibrary@vvw-teg.net – Librarian, Sophie Major

Worsley & District Library, PO Box 210, Worsley AB T0H 3W0 – 403/685-3842; Fax: 403/685-3766 – Librarian, Colleen Rook

### SHORTGRASS LIBRARY SYSTEM

2375 - 10 Ave. SW, Medicine Hat AB T1A 8E2 – 403/529-0550; Fax: 403/528-2473; Email: ENVOY: SHORTGRASS

Director, Raymond Lusty

Bow Island Municipal Library, PO Box 608, Bow Island AB T0K 0G0 – 403/545-2828; Fax: 403/545-6642 – Librarian, Susan Andersen

Brooks Municipal Library, PO Box 1149, Brooks AB T0J 0J0 – 403/362-2947; Fax: 403/362-8111 – Librarian, Karen Armbruster

Foremost Municipal Library, PO Box 397, Foremost AB T0K 0X0 – 403/867-3855 – Librarian, Betty Van Staalduine

Manyberries Library, c/o Manyberries School, General Delivery, Manyberries AB T0K 1L0 – 403/868-3762 (School) – School Secretary, Karen Jakubowsky

Medicine Hat Public Library, 414 First St. SE, Medicine Hat AB T1A 0A8 – 403/527-5528; Fax: 403/527-4595 – Librarian, Bruce Evans

Redcliff Municipal Library, PO Box 280, Redcliff AB T0J 2P0 – 403/548-3335 – Librarian, Reita Wilson

### YELLOWHEAD REGIONAL LIBRARY SYSTEM

433 King St., PO Box 400, Spruce Grove AB T7X 2Y1 – 403/962-2003; Fax: 403/962-2770; Email: yellowhd@freenet.edmonton.ab.ca; URL: http://www.ccinet.ab.ca/yrl/; Symbol: ASGY

Director, Clive Maishment

Assistant Director, Louise Frolek

Alberta Beach Public Library, PO Box 186, Alberta Beach AB T0E 0A0 – 403/924-3491 – Librarian, Anne Allen

Alder Flats Public Library, PO Box 148, Alder Flats AB T0C 0A0 – 403/388-3898; Fax: 403/388-3887 – Librarian, Ivy Seely

Barrhead Public Library, 5103 - 53 Ave., Barrhead AB T7N 1N9 – 403/674-8519; Fax: 403/674-8520; Email: yslemko@ls.barrhead.ab.ca – Coordinator of Libraries, Yvonne Slemko; Library Technician, Darlene Bush

Bibliothèque de Beaumont Library, 5202 - 50 St., Beaumont AB T4X 1K7 – 403/929-2665; Fax: 403/929-8729 – Librarian, Valerie McGillivray

Breton Public Library, PO Box 447, Breton AB T0C 0P0 – 403/696-3740; Fax: 403/696-3590 – Librarian, Diane Shave

Calmar Public Library, PO Box 328, Calmar AB T0C 0V0 – 403/985-3472; Fax: 403/985-3039 – Librarian, Carol Nystrom

Clyde Public Library, PO Box 190, Clyde AB T0G 0P0 – 403/348-5356 – Librarian, Wanda Tollenaar

Darwell Public Library, PO Box 206, Darwell AB T0E 0L0 – 403/892-3199 – Librarian, Heather Hamel

Drayton Valley Public Library, 5120 - 52 St., PO Box 6240, Drayton Valley AB T0E 0M0 – 403/542-2228; Fax: 403/542-5753; Email: nnaidoo@ccinet.ab.ca – Librarian, Nesen Naidoo

Duffield Public Library, PO Box 479, Duffield AB T0E 0N0 – 403/892-2644; Fax: 403/892-3344 – Librarian, Jutta Kube

Keephills Community Library, RR#1, Duffield AB T0E 0N0 – 403/731-3973; Fax: 403/731-2433 – Librarian, Catherine Wagner

Sunwapta Shores Public Library, Box 4, Site 4, RR#1, Duffield AB T0E 0N0 – 403/797-2424 – Librarian, Vicki Richardson

Entwistle Public Library, PO Box 323, Entwistle AB T0E 0S0 – 403/727-4332 – Librarian, Judy Spring

M. Alice Frose Library, PO Box 150, Fawcett AB T0G 0Y0 – 403/954-3827; Fax: 403/954-2570 – Library Clerk, Marie Meyn

Flatbush Public Library, PO Box 82, Flatbush AB T0G 0Z0 – 403/681-3773 – Librarian, Rose Pichota

Fort Assiniboine Library, General Delivery, Fort Assiniboine AB T0G 1A0 – 403/584-2227; Fax: 403/584-2227 – Librarian, Louise Davison

Grande Cache Municipal Library, PO Box 809, Grande Cache AB T0E 0Y0 – 403/827-2081 – Library Coordinator, Gabriela Fleissner

Rich Valley Public Library, RR#1, Gunn AB T0E 1A0 – 403/967-3525 – Librarian, Sylvia Fitzgerald

Jarvie Community Library, PO Box 119, Jarvie AB T0G 1H0 – 403/954-3935; Fax: 403/954-3885 – Librarian, Kim Klein

Leduc Public Library, #2, Alexandra Park, Leduc AB T9E 4C4 – 403/986-2637; Fax: 403/986-3462; Email: bat@freenet.edmonton.ab.ca – Librarian, Beth Anne Thomas

Mayerthorpe Public Library, PO Box 810, Mayerthorpe AB T0E 1N0 – 403/786-2404; Fax: 403/786-4590 – Librarian, Karen Watson

Millet Public Library, PO Box 30, Millet AB T0C 1Z0 – 403/387-5222 – Librarian, Claudia Wagner

Neerlandia Public & School Library, PO Box 10, Neerlandia AB T0G 1R0 – 403/674-5384; Fax: 403/674-2927 – Librarian, Sandra Olthuis

New Sarepta Municipal Library, PO Box 10, New Sarepta AB T0B 3M0 – 403/941-3924; Fax: 403/941-2224 – Librarian, Karen Hipkin

Onoway Public Library, PO Box 484, Onoway AB T0E 1V0 – 403/967-2445; Fax: 403/967-3226; Email: onowaypl@freenet.edmonton.ab.ca – Librarian, Barb McIntyre

Sangudo Public & High School Library, PO Box 524, Sangudo AB T0E 2A0 – 403/785-2365 – Librarian, Helga Jossy

Seba Beach Public Library, PO Box 159, Seba Beach AB T0E 2B0 – 403/797-3940; Fax: 403/797-3800 – Librarian, Chris Newson

Spruce Grove Public Library, #15, 420 King St., Spruce Grove AB T7X 2C6 – 403/962-4423; Fax: 403/962-4826; Email: amwatson@freenet.edmonton.ab.ca – Librarian, Joy Huebert

Stony Plain Public Library, #103, 4613 - 52 Ave., Stony Plain AB T7Z 1E7 – 403/963-5440; Fax: 403/963-5439; Email: sppublic@freenet.edmonton.ab.ca – Librarian, Sandy Sylvestre

Thorsby Municipal Library, PO Box 319, Thorsby AB T0C 2P0 – 403/789-3808 – Librarian, Carolyn Hoffman

Tomahawk Community School Library, PO Box 69, Tomahawk AB T0E 2H0 – 403/339-3935 – Librarian, Chris Goerz

Vimy Public Library, PO Box 29, Vimy AB T0G 2J0 – 403/961-3014 – Librarian, Pauline Despins

Wabamun Municipal Library, PO Box 89, Wabamun AB T0E 2K0 – 403/892-2713 – Librarian, Donna Holoiday

Warburg Public Library, PO Box 299, Warburg AB T0C 2T0 – 403/848-2391; Fax: 403/848-2296 – Librarian, Meta Siemens

Lakedell Area Community Library, RR#1, Westerose AB T0C 2V0 – 403/586-2415; Email: lakedell@ccinet.ab.ca – Librarian, Yvonne M. Adair

Linaria Public Library, RR#1, Westlock AB T7P 2N9 – 403/349-2531 – Librarian, Olga Hadley

Westlock Municipal Library, #1, 10007 - 100 Ave., Westlock AB T7P 2H5 – 403/349-3060; Fax: 403/349-3060 – Librarian, Carolyne Musterer

Wetaskiwin Municipal Library, 5002 - 51 Ave., Wetaskiwin AB T9A 0V1 – 403/352-4055; Fax: 403/352-3266 – Librarian, Leah Tymko

Whitecourt & District Public Library, PO Box 150, Whitecourt AB T7S 1N3 – 403/778-2900; Fax: 403/778-4166 – Librarian, Thyra Ferguson

Winfield Community Library, PO Box 360, Winfield AB T0C 2X0 – 403/682-2498 – Librarian, Ileane Cox

## Municipal, Public & Community Libraries

Airdrie Municipal Library, PO Box 3310, Airdrie AB T4B 2B6 – 403/948-0600; Fax: 403/948-6567 – Head

Librarian, Mary Westcott; Public Services Librarian, Vivyan Oneil; Technical Services Librarian, Debbie Hobberfield

Amisk Public Library, PO Box 71, Amisk AB T0B 0B0 – 403/856-3980 – Librarian, Donna Holte

Andrew Municipal Library, PO Box 449, Andrew AB T0B 0C0 – 403/365-3501; Fax: 403/365-3734 – Librarian, Denise Dorland

Ashmont Public Library, PO Box 330, Ashmont AB T0A 0C0 – 403/726-3877; Fax: 403/726-3777 – Librarian, Donna Karpyshyn – Branch of St. Paul County Municipal Library Board (*see* Heinsburg)

Athabasca County Municipal Library Board, PO Box 540, Athabasca AB T0G 0B0 – 403/675-2285; Fax: 403/675-3544 – Secretary, Robert Tannas – See also following branches: Grassland Community Library, Rochester Community Library

Athabasca: Alice B. Donahue Library & Archives, PO Box 2099, Athabasca AB T0G 0B0 – 403/675-2735; Fax: 403/675-5933 – Librarian, Judy Flax

Barnwell Public Library, 490 Cottonwood St., PO Box 261, Barnwell AB T0K 0B0 – 403/223-3626 – Librarian, Karenne Stuckart

Bassano Municipal Memorial Library, PO Box 658, Bassano AB T0J 0B0 – 403/641-4065 – Librarian, Anne MacPhail

Bellevue Public Library, PO Box 489, Bellevue AB T0K 0C0 – 403/564-5201 – Librarian, Doreen Glavin – Branch of Crowsnest Pass Municipal Library Board (*see* Blairmore)

Big Valley Municipal Library, PO Box 205, Big Valley AB T0J 0G0 – 403/876-2642 – Librarian, Cheryl Wildman

Blairmore: Crowsnest Pass Municipal Library Board, PO Box 1177, Blairmore AB T0K 0E0 – 403/562-8393 – Secretary, Wendy Rossi – See also following branches: Bellevue Public Library, Blairmore Public Library

Blairmore Public Library, PO Box 1177, Blairmore AB T0K 0E0 – 403/562-8393 – Librarian, Judy Bradley – Branch of Crowsnest Pass Municipal Library Board

Bodo Community Library, PO Box 93, Bodo AB T0B 0M0 – 403/753-6647 – Librarian, Kelly Paulgaard – Branch of Provost Municipal District Library Board

Bon Accord Public Library, PO Box 749, Bon Accord AB T0A 0K0 – 403/921-2540; Fax: 403/921-3585 – Librarian, Julie Saunders

Bonnyville Municipal Library, PO Box 8058, Bonnyville AB T9N 2J3 – 403/826-3071; Fax: 403/826-2058 – Librarian, Gil Heney

Boyle Public Library, PO Box 450, Boyle AB T0A 0M0 – 403/689-4161 – Head Librarian, Katherine Bulmer

Brocket: Oldman River Cultural Centre Library, PO Box 70, Brocket AB T0J 0H0 – 403/965-3939 – Librarian, Jo-Ann YellowHorn

Brownfield Community Library, PO Box 54, Brownfield AB T0C 0R0 – 403/578-2487 – Librarian, Annette Barnes

Brownvale: Municipal District of Peace #135 Municipal Library Board, PO Box 57, Brownvale AB T0H 0L0 – 403/597-2250 – Sec.-Treas., Maureen Osowetski – See also following branches: Brownvale Public Library

Brownvale Public Library, General Delivery, Brownvale AB T0H 0L0 – 403/597-3781 – Librarian, Faye McEachnie – Branch of Municipal District of Peace #135 Municipal Library Board

Bruderheim Municipal Library, PO Box 250, Bruderheim AB T0B 0S0 – 403/796-3032 – Librarian, Annette Bjorkquist

Cadogan Public Library, General Delivery, Cadogan AB T0B 0T0 – 403/753-2434 – Librarian, Avis Jickling – Branch of Provost Municipal District Library Board

Calgary Public Library, 616 Macleod Trail SE, Calgary AB T2G 2M2 – 403/260-2600; Fax: 403/237-5393; Email: ENVOY: ILL.AC; Symbol: AC – Director, Gerry Meek; Collection & Electronic Resources, Manager, Beth Barlow, 403/260-2607; Support Services, Manager, Anne Sawa, 403/260-2668; Planning, Manager, Barbara Killick, 403/260-2634; Human Resources, Manager, Ellen Humphrey, 403/260-2627; Youth Services, Manager, J. Hardman, 403/260-2679 – See also following branches: Alexander Calhoun Branch Library, Bowness Branch Library, Chinook Branch Library, Fish Creek Area Library, Forest Lawn Branch Library, Georgina Thomson Branch Library, Louise Riley Branch Library, Memorial Park Branch Library, Millican-Ogden Branch Library, Nose Hill Area Library, Shaganappi Branch Library, Southwood Branch Library, Thorn-Hill Branch Library, Village Square Area Library, W.R. Castell Central Library

Calgary: Alexander Calhoun Branch Library, 3223 - 14 St. SW, Calgary AB T2T 3V8 – 403/221-2010 – Manager, Barbara Lake – Branch of Calgary Public Library

Calgary: Bowness Branch Library, 7930 Bowness Rd. NW, Calgary AB T3B 0H3 – 403/221-2022 – Jean Ludlam – Branch of Calgary Public Library

Calgary: Chinook Branch Library, Chinook Centre, Bowladrome Level, 6455 MacLeod Trail South, Calgary AB T2H 0K8 – 403/221-2072 – Manager, Janet MacKinnon – Branch of Calgary Public Library

Calgary: Fish Creek Area Library, 11161 Bonaventure Dr. SE, Calgary AB T2J 6S1 – 403/221-2090; Fax: 403/225-2526 – Manager, Susan Beatty – Branch of Calgary Public Library

Calgary: Forest Lawn Branch Library, 4807 - 8 Ave. SE, Calgary AB T2A 4M1 – 403/221-2070 – Manager, Janet MacKinnon – Branch of Calgary Public Library

Calgary: Georgina Thomson Branch Library, 51 Cornell Rd. NW, Calgary AB T2L 0L4 – 403/221-2040 – Jean Ludlam – Branch of Calgary Public Library

Calgary: Louise Riley Branch Library, 1904 - 14 Ave. NW, Calgary AB T2N 1M5 – 403/221-2046 – Manager, Marilyn Wallace – Branch of Calgary Public Library

Calgary: Memorial Park Branch Library, 1221 - 2 St. SW, Calgary AB T2R 0W5 – 403/221-2006 – Manager, Aruna Marthe – Branch of Calgary Public Library

Calgary: Millican-Ogden Branch Library, 7005 - 18 St. SE, Calgary AB T2C 1Y1 – 403/221-2080 – Manager, Aruna Marathe – Branch of Calgary Public Library

Calgary: Nose Hill Area Library, 1530 Northmount Dr. NW, Calgary AB T2G 0G6 – 403/221-2030 – Manager, Jane Haney – Branch of Calgary Public Library

Calgary: Shaganappi Branch Library, Shaganappi Multi-Service Centre, 3415 - 8 Ave. SW, Calgary AB T3C 0E8 – 403/221-2020 – Manager, Carolyn Murray – Branch of Calgary Public Library

Calgary: Southwood Branch Library, 924 Southland Dr. SW, Calgary AB T2W 0J9 – 403/221-2082 – Manager, Mary Enright – Branch of Calgary Public Library

Calgary: Thorn-Hill Branch Library, Thorn-Hill Community Centre, 6617 Centre St. North, Calgary AB T2K 4Y5 – 403/221-2050 – Manager, Ann Austin – Branch of Calgary Public Library

Calgary: Village Square Area Library, Village Square Leisure Centre, 2623 - 56 St. NE, Calgary AB T1Y 6E7 – 403/221-2060; Fax: 403/280-8965 – Manager, Carole McCloy – Branch of Calgary Public Library

Calgary: W.R. Castell Central Library, 616 McLeod Trail SE, Calgary AB T2G 2M2 – 403/260-2600; Fax: 403/237-5393 – Manager, Central & Area Libraries, Peg Hofmann – Branch of Calgary Public Library

Castor Municipal Library, PO Box 699, Castor AB T0C 0X0 – 403/882-3999 – Librarian, Wendy Bozek

Chauvin Municipal Library, PO Box 129, Chauvin AB T0B 0V0 – 403/858-3744; Fax: 403/858-2392; Email: folkin@schnt.gov.ab.ca – Librarian, Linda Granigan

Chestermere Municipal Library, 156 East Chestermere Dr., Chestermere AB T1X 1C1 – 403/272-9744; Fax: 403/569-0512 – Municipal Administrator, Kathy Nikkel

Clyde Municipal Library, PO Box 190, Clyde AB T0G 0P0 – 403/348-5356 (Village Office) – Librarian, Wanda Tollenaar

Cochrane: Nan Boothby Memorial Library, PO Box 996, Cochrane AB T0L 0W0 – 403/932-4353; Fax: 403/932-4353 – Librarian, Brenda J. Hughes

Coronation Memorial Library, PO Box 453, Coronation AB T0C 1C0 – 403/578-3445 – Librarian, Eileen Merchant

Coutts Municipal Library, PO Box 216, Coutts AB T0K 0N0 – 403/344-3804; Fax: 403/344-3815 – Librarian, Sharon Wollersheim

Crossfield Municipal Library, PO Box 355, Crossfield AB T0M 0S0 – 403/946-4232 – Librarian, Sylvia Ramage

Czar Municipal Library, PO Box 127, Czar AB T0B 0Z0 – 403/857-3870 – Librarian, Robyn Long

Debolt Public Library, PO Box 480, Debolt AB T0H 1B0 – 403/957-3770 – Librarian, Karen Downey

Derwent Public Library, General Delivery, Derwent AB T0B 1C0 – 403/741-3792 – Librarian, Leona Bielech

Devon Public Library, 105 Athabasca Ave., Devon AB T9G 1A4 – 403/987-3720 (School) – Librarian, Audrey Benjamin

Donalda Municipal Library, PO Box 40, Donalda AB T0B 1H0 – 403/883-2345; Fax: 403/883-2022 – Librarian, Leigh-Ann Ensign

Duchess Public Library, PO Box 88, Duchess AB T0J 0Z0 – 403/378-4369 – Librarian, Cathy Neufeld

Eaglesham Public Library, PO Box 206, Eaglesham AB T0H 1H0 – 403/359-3792; Fax: 403/359-3745 – Library Clerk, Norma Bolster

Edgerton Public Library, General Delivery, Edgerton AB T0B 1K0 – 403/755-3820 (res.) – Sec.-Treas., Brenda Redhead

Edmonton Public Library, 7 Sir Winston Churchill Sq., Edmonton AB T5J 2V4 – 403/496-7000; Fax: 403/496-1885; Email: penny@freenet.edmonton.ab.ca – Director, Penelope McKee; Reference Librarian, Louise Reimer; Circulation Librarian, Michael Dell; Children's Librarian, Joanne Griener; Deputy Director, Public Services, Keith Turnbull; Deputy Director, Support Services, Al Davis; Acquisitions Librarian, Mary Flannagan – See also following branches: Calder Branch Library, Capilano Branch Library, Castledowns Branch Library, Highlands Branch Library, Idylwylde Branch Library, Jasper Place Branch Library, Londonderry Branch Library, Millwoods Branch Library, Southgate Branch Library, Sprucewood Branch Library, Strathcona Branch Library, Woodcroft Branch Library

Edmonton: Calder Branch Library, 12522 - 132 Ave., Edmonton AB T5L 3P9 – 403/496-7090; Fax: 403/496-1453 – Branch Manager, Jack de Graaf – Branch of Edmonton Public Library

Edmonton: Capilano Branch Library, 201 Capilano Mall, Edmonton AB T6A 0A1 – 403/496-1803; Fax: 403/496-7009 – Branch Manager, Barbara Bulat – Branch of Edmonton Public Library

Edmonton: Castledowns Branch Library, 15333 Castledowns Rd. #9, Edmonton AB T5X 3Y7 – 403/496-1805; Fax: 403/496-7005 – Branch Manager, Jack de Graaf – Branch of Edmonton Public Library

Edmonton: Highlands Branch Library, 6710 - 118 Ave., Edmonton AB T5B 0P3 – 403/496-1806; Fax: 403/496-7012 – Branch Manager, Howard Saunders – Branch of Edmonton Public Library

Edmonton: Idylwylde Branch Library, 8310 - 88 Ave., Edmonton AB T6C 1L1 – 403/496-1809; Fax: 403/496-7092 – Branch Manager, Barbara Bulat – Branch of Edmonton Public Library

Edmonton: Jasper Place Branch Library, 9010 - 156 St., Edmonton AB T5R 5X7 – 403/496-1810; Fax: 403/496-7004 – Branch Manager, Skip Wilson – Branch of Edmonton Public Library

Edmonton: Londonderry Branch Library, L10A Londonderry Mall, Edmonton AB T5C 3C8 – 403/496-1816; Fax: 403/496-1452; Symbol: LON – Branch Manager, Andrea Smith – Branch of Edmonton Public Library

Edmonton: Millwoods Branch Library, 601 Millwoods Town Centre, 2331 - 66 St., Edmonton AB T6K 4B5 – 403/496-1820; Fax: 403/496-1450 – Branch Manager, Hazel Spratt – Branch of Edmonton Public Library

Edmonton: Southgate Branch Library, 48 Southgate Mall, Edmonton AB T6H 4M6 – 403/496-1825; Fax: 403/496-7007 – Branch Manager, Joanne Griener – Branch of Edmonton Public Library

Edmonton: Sprucewood Branch Library, 11555 - 95 St., Edmonton AB T5G 1L5 – 403/496-7098; Fax: 403/496-7010 – Branch Manager, Howard Saunders – Branch of Edmonton Public Library

Edmonton: Strathcona Branch Library, 8331 - 104 St., Edmonton AB T6E 4E9 – 403/496-1828; Fax: 403/496-1451 – Branch Manager, Pat Arnold – Branch of Edmonton Public Library

Edmonton: Woodcroft Branch Library, 13420 - 114 Ave., Edmonton AB T5M 2Y5 – 403/496-1831; Fax: 403/496-7089 – Branch Manager, Pat Arnold – Branch of Edmonton Public Library

Edson & District Public Library, 4726 - 8 Ave., Edson AB T7E 1S8 – 403/723-6691; Fax: 403/723-3508; Email: boothlj@mgltd.ab.ca; Symbol: AED – Head Librarian, Lisbeth J. Booth

Enchant Public Library, PO Box 3000, Enchant AB T0K 0V0 – 403/739-3835 – Librarian, Sandy Severtson – Branch of Taber Municipal District Library Board

Evansburg & District Municipal Library, PO Box 339, Evansburg AB T0E 0T0 – 403/727-3872; Fax: 403/727-2437 – Librarian, E. Lauer

Falher: Municipal District of Smoky River No. 130 Municipal Library Board, PO Box 210, Falher AB T0H 1M0 – 403/837-2221 – Secretary, Roger Laflamme

Fort McMurray Public Library, Jubilee Centre, 9907 Franklin Ave., Fort McMurray AB T9H 2K4 – 403/743-7800; Fax: 403/743-7037; Email: ENVOY: ILL.FOR – Director, Carol Cooley; Public Services Librarian, Paula Benson

Fort Saskatchewan Public Library, 10011 - 102 St., Fort Saskatchewan AB T8L 2C5 – 403/998-4275; Fax: 403/992-3255; Email: fsasklib@freenet.edmonton.ab.ca – Library Director, J. Robin Brown

Fort Vermilion Community Library, PO Box 4, Fort Vermilion AB T0H 1N0 – 403/927-4279; Symbol: AFVC – Librarian, Anne Martens

Fox Creek Municipal Library, PO Box 1078, Fox Creek AB T0H 1P0 – 403/622-2343; Fax: 403/622-3482 – Librarian, Carol Downing

Gem: County of Newell Library Board, PO Box 35, Gem AB T0J 1M0 – 403/641-2155 – Sec.-Treas., Betty Neufeld – See also following branches: Alcoma Public Library, Gem Jubilee Library, Rolling Hills Public Library

Gem: Gem Jubilee Library, PO Box 37, Gem AB T0J 1M0 – 403/641-2261 – Librarian, Shelly Heryford – Branch of County of Newell Library Board

Gibbons Public Library, PO Box 510, Gibbons AB T0A 1N0 – 403/923-2004; Fax: 403/923-3691 – Librarian, Julie Saunders

Grassland Community Library, PO Box 57, Grassland AB T0A 1V0 – 403/525-3733; Fax: 403/525-3750 – Librarian, Lori Zachkewich – Branch of Athabasca County Municipal Library Board

Grassy Lake Community Library, PO Box 690, Grassy Lake AB T0K 0Z0 – 403/655-2232; Fax: 403/655-2259 – Librarian, Cindy Orr

Hairy Hill Municipal Library, PO Box 126, Hairy Hill AB T0B 1S0 – 403/768-3840; Email: dlaing@agt.net – Librarian, Don Laing

Hays: Taber Municipal District Library Board, PO Box 63, Hays AB T0K 1B0 – 403/725-3750 – Sec.-Treas., Diane Wickenheiser – See also following branches: Enchant Public Library, Hays Public Library

Hays Public Library, PO Box 36, Hays AB T0K 1B0 – 403/725-3744 – Librarian, Diane Wickenheiser – Branch of Taber Municipal District Library Board

Heinsburg: St. Paul County Municipal Library Board, General Delivery, Heinsburg AB T0A 1X0 – Chair, Bob Smith – See also following branches: Ashmont Public Library, Bibliothèque Mallaig Community Library, Heinsburg Public Library, Lafond Public Library

Heinsburg Public Library, General Delivery, Heinsburg AB T0A 1X0 – 403/943-3913; Fax: 403/943-3773 – Librarian, Cathy Botting – Branch of St. Paul County Municipal Library Board

Hinton Municipal Library, 803 Switzer Dr., Hinton AB T7V 1V1 – 403/865-2363; Fax: 403/865-4292; Email: hettwild@gyrd.ab.ca – Librarian, Hetty Wilderdijk

Holden Municipal Library, PO Box 26, Holden AB T0B 2C0 – 403/688-3838; Fax: 403/688-2091 – Librarian, Sandy Kluczny

Hughenden Public Library, PO Box 36, Hughenden AB T0B 2E0 – 403/856-3830 – Librarian, Leslie McDevitt

Irma Municipal Library, PO Box 340, Irma AB T0B 2H0 – 403/754-3752; Fax: 403/754-3802 – Librarian, Marj Guiltner

Irvine Municipal Library, PO Box 67, Irvine AB T0J 1V0 – Chairperson, Brenda Reigel

Jasper Municipal Library, PO Box 1170, Jasper AB T0E 1E0 – 403/852-3652; Fax: 403/852-5841; Email: jlibrary@incentre.net – Librarian, Judy Krefting

Keg River Community Library, PO Box 3, Keg River AB T0H 2G0 – 403/981-2128 – Librarian, Janice Freeman

La Crete Community Library, PO Box 609, La Crete AB T0H 2H0 – 403/928-3166; Fax: 403/928-3000 – Librarian, Helen Wiebe

Lac La Biche & District Public Library, PO Box 2039, Lac La Biche AB T0A 2C0 – 403/623-7467; Fax: 403/623-3510 – Librarian, Ron Weir

Lafond Public Library, PO Box 20, Lafond AB T0A 2G0 – 403/645-2432 – Librarian, Joanne Ternovoy – Branch of St. Paul County Municipal Library Board (*see* Heinsburg)

Lamont Public Library, PO Box 180, Lamont AB T0B 2R0 – 403/895-2228; Fax: 403/895-2600 – Librarian, Rosemarie Konsorada

Lethbridge: County of Lethbridge Municipal Library, 905 - 4 Ave. South, Lethbridge AB T1J 4E4 – 403/328-5525 – Sec.-Treas., S. Steinke

Mallaig: Bibliothèque Mallaig Community Library, CP 90, Mallaig AB T0A 2K0 – 403/635-3858; Téléc: 403/635-3938 – Librarian, Anne-Marie Amyotte – Branch of St. Paul County Municipal Library Board (*see* Heinsburg)

Mannville Municipal Library, PO Box 186, Mannville AB T0B 2W0 – 403/763-3611 – Librarian, Theresa Myroniuk

Milk River: Warner County Municipal Library Board, PO Box 8, Milk River AB T0K 1M0 – 403/344-2128 – Treasurer, Joy Nett – See also following branch: Wrentham Public Library

Milk River Municipal Library, PO Box 579, Milk River AB T0K 1M0 – 403/647-3793 – Librarian, Velora Kundert

Morinville Public Library, 10119 - 100 Ave., Morinville AB T8R 1S1 – 403/939-3292; Email: mvillep@freenet.edmonton.ab.ca – Librarian, Mark Oberg

Nanton: Municipal District of Willow Creek Library Board, PO Box 751, Nanton AB T0L 1R0 – 403/646-5467 – Secretary, Colleen Kindt

Nanton: Thelma Fanning Memorial Library, PO Box 310, Nanton AB T0L 1R0 – 403/646-5535; Fax: 403/646-2653; Email: nantlibr@telusplanet.net – Librarian, Marie-Jeanne Zetchus

Newbrook Community Public Library, PO Box 208, Newbrook AB T0A 2P0 – 403/576-3771; Fax: 403/576-2115 – Librarian, Jan Rosenthal – Branch of Thorhild County Municipal Library Board

Niton Junction: Green Grove Community Library, PO Box 219, Niton Junction AB T0E 1S0 – 403/795-3782; Fax: 403/795-3933 – Librarian, Wendy Langard

Pincher Creek Municipal Library, PO Box 2020, Pincher Creek AB T0K 1W0 – 403/627-3813 – Librarian, Gwendy Donegani

Plamondon Municipal Library, PO Box 90, Plamondon AB T0A 2T0 – 403/798-3852; Fax: 403/798-3850; Email: plamonee@schnet.edc.gov.ab.ca – Librarian, Emilie Chevigny

Provost Municipal District Library Board, PO Box 300, Provost AB T0B 3S0 – 403/753-2774 – Secretary, Kelly Paulgaard – See also following branches: Bodo Community Library, Cadogan Public Library

Provost Municipal Library, PO Box 449, Provost AB T0B 3S0 – 403/753-2801 – Librarian, Colleen Vaughan

Radway & District Municipal Library, PO Box 220, Radway AB T0A 2V0 – 403/736-3548 (Rec. Centre) – Librarian, Fern Mulyk

Rainier: Alcoma Public Library, General Delivery, Rainier AB T0J 2M0 – 403/362-3741; Fax: 403/362-3741 – Librarian, Joyce Aasen – Branch of County of Newell Library Board (*see* Ge,)

Ralston: Graham Community Library, PO Box 40, Ralston AB T0J 2N0 – 403/544-3670 – Librarian, Barbara Janecke

Red Deer Public Library, 4818 - 49 St., Red Deer AB T4N 1T9 – 403/346-4576; Fax: 403/341-3110; Email: info@rdpl.red-deer.ab.ca; URL: http://www.rdpl.red-deer.ab.ca – Director, Dean Frey; Children's Librarian, Donna Alberts, 403/346-7470; Adult Services Librarian, Cynthia Belanger, 403/346-2100; Information Technology, Scott Stanley – See also following branches: Dawe Public Library

Red Deer: Dawe Public Library, 56 Holt St., Red Deer AB T4N 6A6 – 403/341-3822; Fax: 403/343-2120 – Jill Griffith – Branch of Red Deer Public Library

Redwater Public Library, PO Box 384, Redwater AB T0A 2W0 – 403/942-3464 – Librarian, Anne Schmidt

Rochester Community Library, PO Box 309, Rochester AB T0G 1Z0 – 403/698-3970; Fax: 403/698-2290 – Librarian, Doris Briggs – Branch of Athabasca County Municipal Library Board

Rolling Hills Public Library, PO Box 40, Rolling Hills AB T0J 2S0 – 403/964-3640; Fax: 403/964-3659 – Librarian, Johnene Amulung – Branch of County of Newell Library Board (*see* Gem)

Rosemary Municipal Library, PO Box 210, Rosemary AB T0J 2W0 – 403/378-4493 – Librarian, Donna Janzen

Rycroft Municipal Library, PO Box 248, Rycroft AB T0H 3A0 – 403/765-3973; Fax: 403/765-2002 – Librarian, Valerie Twelvetree

Ryley: Beaver County No. 9 Municipal Library Board, PO Box 140, Ryley AB T0B 4A0 – 403/663-3730 – Sec.-Treas., Margaret Jones

Ryley: McPherson Municipal Library, PO Box 139, Ryley AB T0B 4A0 – 403/663-3999 – Librarian, Lori Yachimec

St. Albert Public Library, 5 St. Anne St., St. Albert AB T8N 3Z9 – 403/459-1530; Fax: 403/458-5772; Email: sapl@freenet.edmonton.ab.ca – Library Director, Pamela Forsyth, 403/459-1681; Adult Services/Reference Librarian, Jill Armitage, 403/459-1682; Circulation Librarian, Rosanne Delaney, 403/459-1537; Children's Librarian, Arlene Kissau, 403/459-1536; Systems/Technical Services Librarian, David Rushton, 403/459-1684

St. Isidore Community Library, PO Box 1168, St Isidore AB T0H 3B0 – 403/624-8182 – Librarian, Marie Lavoie

Sherwood Park: Strathcona County Municipal Library, 104 Sherwood Park Mall, 2020 Sherwood Dr., Sherwood Park AB T8A 5P7 – 403/449-5800; Fax: 403/467-6861; Email: scml@freenet.edmonton.ab.ca; Symbol: SPS – Library Director, Marilyn Corbett; Children's Librarian, Mary Card, 403/449-5809; Public Relations & Adult Services Librarian, Joan Urshel, 403/449-5807

Silver Valley: Savanna Community Library, PO Box 49, Silver Valley AB T0H 3E0 – 403/351-3808

Slave Lake Municipal Library, PO Box 540, Slave Lake AB T0G 2A0 – 403/849-5250; Fax: 403/849-2633 – Librarian, Anne McMeekin

Spirit River: Municipal District of Spirit River No. 133 Municipal Library, PO Box 389, Spirit River AB T0H 3G0 – 403/864-2463 – Secretary, Giselle Lewchuk

Stettler Public Library, 6202 - 44 Ave., 2nd Fl., Stettler AB T0C 2L1 – 403/742-2292; Fax: 403/742-3480; Email: spl@heartland.ab.ca – Head Librarian, Eileen Scheerschmidt

Swan Hills Public Library, PO Box 386, Swan Hills AB T0G 2C0 – 403/333-4505 – Head Librarian, Cheryl Oulton; Children's Librarian, Sandra Berg

Tangent Community Library, PO Box 63, Tangent AB T0H 3J0 – 403/359-2388 – Librarian, Lina M. Boily

Thorhild County Municipal Library Board, PO Box 615, Thorhild AB T0A 3J0 – 403/576-2180 – Chairperson, Barb Koistinen – See also following branches: Newbrook Community Public Library

Thorhild & District Municipal Library, PO Box 658, Thorhild AB T0A 3J0 – 403/398-3502; Fax: 403/398-2100; Email: thorlib@telusplanet.net; Symbol: ATHOM – Librarian, Rose Alexander

Tilley & District Public Library, PO Box 225, Tilley AB T0J 3K0 – 403/377-2233; Fax: 403/377-2703 – Librarian, Brenda Arnold

Tofield Municipal Library, 5407 - 50 St., PO Box 479, Tofield AB T0B 4J0 – 403/662-3838; Fax: 403/662-3929; Email: tml@supernet.ab.ca – Librarian, Elizabeth Hubbard, Email: ehubbard@supernet.ab.ca

Vegreville Public Library, PO Box 129, Vegreville AB T9C 1R1 – 403/632-3491; Fax: 403/632-3423; Email: library@vegnet.afternet.com – Librarian, Janet Kolisniak

Veteran Municipal Library, PO Box 527, Veteran AB T0C 2S0 – 403/575-3915 – Librarian, Shirley Kary

Viking Municipal Library, PO Box 300, Viking AB T0B 4N0 – 403/336-4992; Fax: 403/334-2660 – Library Clerk, Kaye Roddick

Vilna & District Municipal Library, PO Box 119, Vilna AB T0A 3L0 – 403/636-3667 – Librarian, Frank D. Barry

Wainwright: Municipal District of Wainwright Municipal Library Board, 717 - 14 Ave., Wainwright AB T9W 1B3 – 403/842-4454; Fax: 403/842-2463 – Secretary, Janice Frost

Wainwright Public Library, 921 - 3rd Ave., Wainwright AB T9W 1C4 – 403/842-2673; Fax: 403/842-2340; Email: wainlib@agt.net – Wendy Sears Ilnicki

Wandering River Women's Institute Community Library, General Delivery, Wandering River AB T0A 3M0 – 403/771-3928

Wanham Community Library, General Delivery, Wanham AB T0H 3P0 – 403/694-3828 – Librarian, Alice Hillaby

Warner Memorial Library, PO Box 270, Warner AB T0K 2L0 – 403/642-3988 – Librarian, Colleen Irwin

Waskatenau: Anne Chorney Public Library, PO Box 130, Waskatenau AB T0A 3P0 – 403/358-2777 – Librarian, Cathy Zon

Wildwood Community Public Library, PO Box 243, Wildwood AB T0E 2M0 – 403/325-2108; Fax: 403/325-3783 – Librarian, Ann Myrholm

Willingdon & District Public Library, PO Box 270, Willingdon AB T0B 4R0 – 403/367-2222 – Librarian, Frances Hols

Wrentham Public Library, PO Box 111, Wrentham AB T0K 2P0 – 403/222-2485 – Librarian, Brenda Jurgens – Branch of Warner County Municipal Library Board (*see* Milk River)

## Special & College Libraries & Resource Centres

### AIRDRIE

Kids First Parent Association of Canada – Library, POBox 5256, Airdrie AB T4B 2B3 – 403/289-1440 – National Secretary, Cathy Buchanan

### ATHABASCA

Athabasca University - Library, 1 University Dr., POBox 10000, Athabasca AB T9S 1A1 – 403/675-6254; Fax: 403/675-6477; Toll Free: 1-800-788-9041; Email: library@admin.athabascau.ca; URL: http://www.athabasca.ca; Symbol: AEAU

- Library Services, Director, Steve Schafer, 403/675-6259
- Technical Services & Systems, Head, Doug Kariel, 403/675-6261
- Reference Services Librarian, Lorna Young, 403/675-6232
- Circulation Supervisor, Eileen Hendy, 404/675-6271
- Interlibrary Loans Supervisor, Judy Stady, 403/675-6251

### BANFF

The Banff Centre for the Arts - Library, POBox 1020, Banff AB T0L 0CO – 403/762-6265; Fax: 403/762-6236; Email: Envoy: LIBRARY.BNFFCNTR; URL: http://www.banffcentre.ab.ca/Library/Index.html; Symbol: ABSFA

- Head Librarian, Bob Foley
- Music Librarian, P. Lawless

Banff Mineral Springs Hospital – Health Records, POBox 1050, Banff AB T0L 0C0 – 403/762-2222; Fax: 403/762-4193 – Director, Health Records, Eldene Heikkila

Whyte Museum of the Canadian Rockies - Archives Library, 111 Bear St., POBox 160, Banff AB T0L 0C0 – 403/762-2291; Fax: 403/762-8919; Symbol: ABA – Librarian, Mary Andrews

### BARRHEAD

Alberta Distance Learning Centre - Library, POBox 4000, Barrhead AB T7N 1P4 – 403/674-5333; Fax: 403/674-6561; Email: Dhagan@edc.gov.ab.ca – Librarian, Dawn I. Hagan

### BEAVERLODGE

Beaverlodge Research Centre - Library, POBox 29, Beaverlodge AB T0H 0C0 – 403/354-2212; Fax: 403/354-8171; Symbol: ABEAG – Librarian, Shelley M. Pirnak, Email: pirnaks@em.agr.ca

### BIG VALLEY

Canadian Northern Society – Library, POBox 142, Big Valley AB T0J 0G0 – 403/672-3099; Fax: 403/742-1477 – Lori Pratt

### BLAIRMORE

Crowsnest Pass Symphony – Library, POBox 567, Blairmore AB T0K 0E0 – 403/562-2127 – Librarian, C. Kovach

### CALGARY

Aboriginal Tourism Authority Inc., POBox 1240, Calgary AB T2P 2L2 – 403/261-3022; Fax: 403/261-5676; Toll Free: 1-800-821-5703 – Communications Coordinator, Ryan Horner

Acres International Limited - Library, 10201 Southport Rd. SW, 5th Fl., Calgary AB T2W 4X9 – 403/253-9161, ext.300; Fax: 403/255-2444 – Librarian, Evelyn Ross

AIDS Calgary Awareness Association – Library, #300, 1021 - 10 Ave. SW, Calgary AB T2R 0B7 – 403/228-0198; Fax: 403/229-2077 – Education Coordinator, Pia Anderson

Alberta Association of Rehabilitation Centres – Library, Box 105, 2725 - 12 St. NE, Calgary AB T2E 7J2 – 403/250-9495; Fax: 403/291-9864

Alberta College of Art & Design - Luke Lindoe Library, 1407- 14 Ave. NW, Calgary AB T2N 4R3 – 403/284-7631; Fax: 403/289-6682; Toll Free: 1-800-251-8290; URL: http://www.acad.ab.ca/CALENDAR/LINDOE/lindoe.htm; Symbol: ACAA – Director, Christine E. Sammon, Email: christine.sammon@acad.ab.ca

Alberta Energy & Utilities Board - Library, 640 - 5 Ave. SW, Calgary AB T2P 3G4 – 403/297-8242; Fax: 403/297-3517; Email: librae@mail.eub.gov.ab.ca; Symbol: ACER – Librarian, Liz Johnson

Alberta Energy Co. Ltd. - Library, #3900, 421 - 7 Ave SW, Calgary AB T5K 2P6 – 403/422-1306; Fax: 403/266-8185

- Library Acquisitions, Catherine Vrielink, Email: cvrielink@aec.ca
- Supervisor, Information Centre, June Crichton

Alberta Justice - Law Society of Alberta Library, Courthouse, 611 - 4 St. SW, Calgary AB T2P 1T5 – 403/297-6148; Fax: 403/297-5171; Email: lawseare@cia.com – Regional Librarian, Robert Leigh

- Office of the Chief Medical Examiner, Southern Region - Library, 4070 Bowness Rd. NW, Calgary AB T3B 3R7 – 403/297-8123; Fax: 403/297-3429; Email: mcmanus@just.gov.ab.ca; Symbol: ACCME – Librarian, Karen McManus
- Southern Alberta Region, Provincial Court Library, 323 - 6 Ave. SE, 5th Fl., Calgary AB T2G 4V1 – 403/297-3126; Fax: 403/297-2981; Email: powels@agt.net – Librarian, Susan Powelson

Alberta Natural Gas Co. Ltd. - Information Centre, Amoco Centre, #2900, 240 - 4 Ave. SW, 27th Fl., Calgary AB T2P 4L7 – 403/691-7760; Fax: 403/691-7888; Email: ENVOY: ACAS.ILL – Administrator, Paul Mankelow

Alberta Playwrights' Network – Script Library/Reading Room, 1134 - 8 Ave. SW, 2nd Fl., Calgary AB T2P 1J5 – 403/269-8564; Fax: 403/269-8564; Toll Free: 1-800-268-8564

Alberta Speleological Society – Library, POBox 22324, Calgary AB T2P 4J1 – 403/245-8823 – Librarian, John Chaychuk

Alberta Sulphur Research Ltd. – Library, Chemistry Department, University of Calgary, 2500 University Dr. NW, Calgary AB T2N 1N4 – 403/220-5372; Fax: 403/284-2054; Email: asrinfo@chem.ucalgary.ca

Alberta Wheat Pool – Library, 505 - 2 St. SW, POBox 2700, Calgary AB T2P 2P5 – 403/290-5581; Fax: 403/290-5550 – Librarian, Jane Fournier

Alberta Wilderness Association – Library, 455 - 12 St. NW, POBox 6398, Calgary AB T2P 2E1 – 403/492-2311; Fax: 403/492-2364

Arusha Centre Society – Resource Centre, 233 - 10 St. NW, Calgary AB T2N 1V5 – 403/270-3200; Fax: 403/270-8832 – Paddy Campbell

Baptist Leadership Training School - Library, 4330 - 16 St. SW, Calgary AB T2T 4H9 – 403/243-3770; Fax: 403/287-1930; Toll Free: 1-800-549-4675 – Principal, Marcel Leffelaar

Bennett Jones Verchere - Law Library, Bankers Hall East, #4500, 855 - 2 St. SW, Calgary AB T2P 4K7 – 403/298-3165; Fax: 403/265-7219
- Chief Librarian, Shelagh Mikulak, Email: mikulaks@bjv.ca
- Reference Librarian, Bernadette Gunn, 403/298-3691
- Reference Services Librarian, Kathy Kurceba, 403/298-3691
- Librarian, Kathleen Hogan, 403/298-3692
- Senior Library Technician, Bonnie Buchanan, 403/298-3143
- Library Technician, Yolanda Jung, 403/298-3006
- Library Clerk, Lorie Larry, 403/298-3226

Blake, Cassels & Graydon Law Office - Library, Bankers Hall East, #3500, 855 - 2 St. SW, Calgary AB T2P 4J8 – 403/260-9600; Fax: 403/263-9895 – Librarian, Jane Hillard

Burnet, Duckworth & Palmer, Barristers & Solicitors - Information & Research Services, First Canadian Centre, #1400, 350 - 7 Ave. SW, Calgary AB T2P 3N9 – 403/260-0187; Fax: 403/260-0332; Email: pfh@bdplaw.mhs.compuserve.com
- Information & Research, Research Lawyer/Director, Penelope F. Hamilton
- Assistant Librarian, Brenda Nixon
- Library Assistant, Susan Russell

Calgary Board of Education - Educational Resources & Services, 3610 - 9 St. SE, Calgary AB T2G 3C5 – 403/294-8542; Fax: 403/287-9739
- Acquisitions, Head, Frankie Steele, 403/294-8539
- Biblio Systems & Services, Head, Yasmin Peerani, 403/294-8589
- Circulation (Film & Video), Head, Doreen Johnson, 403/294-8733
- Processing, Head, Maureen Akins, 403/294-8590
- Media Production, Head, Penny Dowswill, 403/294-8576
- School Library Technology, Frank Karas, 403/294-8559

The Calgary Herald - Library, 215 - 16 St. SE, POBox 2400, Calgary AB T2P 0W8 – 403/235-7361; Fax: 403/235-7379 – Library Team Manager, Karen Crosby

Calgary Horticultural Society – Library, 208 - 50 Ave. SW, Calgary AB T2S 2S1 – 403/287-3469; Fax: 403/287-6986 – Director, Library/Books, Barbara Nobert

Calgary Humane Society – Resource Centre, 1323 - 36 Ave. NE, Calgary AB T2E 6T6 – 403/250-7722, ext.345; Fax: 403/291-9818 – Education Coordinator, Judy Weisbrot

Calgary Learning Centre - Library, 3930 - 20 St. SW, Calgary AB T2T 4Z9 – 403/686-9300; Fax: 403/686-0627; Email: calearnc@cadvision.com
- Librarian, Carolyn Patterson, 403/686-9300, Email: cpatters@acs.ucalgary.ca
- Library Technician, Janice Caskey

Calgary Philharmonic Society – Library, 205 - 8 Ave. SE, Calgary AB T2G 0K9 – 403/571-0270; Fax: 403/294-7424 – Librarian, Rob Grewcock

Calgary Regional Health Authority - Peter Lougheed Centre - Hospital Library, 3500 - 26 Ave. NE, Calgary AB T1Y 6J4 – 403/291-8736; Fax: 403/291-8888; Email: ENVOY: ILL.ACPLC; Symbol: ACPLC – Medical Library Technician, Kathie Gaudes

Calgary Society for Students with Learning Difficulties – Learning Centre Library, 3930 - 20 St. SW, Calgary AB T2T 4Z9 – 403/686-9322; Fax: 403/686-0627 – Librarian, Carolyn Patterson

Calgary Sun - Library, 2615 - 12 St. NE, Calgary AB T2E 7W9 – 403/250-4200; Fax: 403/250-4180; URL: http://www.canoe.ca/CalgarySun/home.html – Chief Librarian, Kathryn Dilts, 403/250-4159

Canadian Association for Suicide Prevention – Library, #201, 1615 - 10th Ave. SW, Calgary AB T3C 0J7 – 403/245-3900 – Karen Kiddey

Canadian Association of Oilwell Drilling Contractors – Library, #800, 540 - 5 Ave. SW, Calgary AB T2P 0M2 – 403/264-4311; Fax: 403/263-3796 – Coordinator, Economic Analysis, Alan Laws

Canadian Energy Research Institute – I.N. McKinnon Memorial Library, #150, 3512 - 33 St. NW, Calgary AB T2L 2A6 – 403/220-2394; Fax: 403/284-4181; Email: ENVOY: ILL.ACINM; Symbol: ACERR – Library Technician, Lynne Buist

Canadian Heritage - Parks Canada, Western Region - Library, #551, 220 - 4 Ave. SE, Calgary AB T2P 3H8 – 403/292-4455; Fax: 403/292-6679; Email: bitzl@pkswro.dots.doe.ca; Symbol: ACIA – Librarian, Leonard Bitz, Email: Len_Bitz@pch.gc.ca

Canadian Hunter Exploration Ltd. - Library, #2000, 605 - 5 Ave. SW, Calgary AB T2P 3H5 – 403/260-1772; Fax: 403/260-1899; Symbol: ACHE – Library Coordinator, Wendy Mayer

Canadian Institute of Resources Law – Library, PF-B 3330, University of Calgary, 2500 University Dr. NW, Calgary AB T2N 1N4 – 403/220-3200; Fax: 403/282-6182 – Secretary, Sue Parsons

Canadian Music Centre - Prairie Region – Branch Library, Library Tower, #911, 2500 University Dr. NW, Calgary AB T2N 1N4 – 403/220-7403; Fax: 403/289-4877

Canadian Nazarene College - Thomson Library, #610, 833 - 4th Ave. SW, Calgary AB T2P 3T5 – 403/571-2550; Fax: 403/571-2556; Toll Free: 1-800-363-6896
- Head Librarian, Carolyn J. Alho
- Administrative Assistant, Heather J. Liebenberg

Canadian Occidental Petroleum Ltd. - Library, #1500, 635 - 8 Ave. SW, Calgary AB T2P 3Z1 – 403/234-6437; Fax: 403/263-8673; Symbol: ACCO – Librarian, Marlene Robertson

Canadian Pacific Railway - Business Information Services, #2000, 401 - 9 Ave SW, Calgary AB T2P 4Z4 – 403/218-6191; Fax: 403/218-6257; Email: cprbis@agt.net; URL: http://www.cprailway.com/; Symbol: QMCP – Manager, Carole Lacourte, 403/218-6193

City of Calgary - Engineering & Environmental Library, #8026, 800 Macleod Trail SE, POBox 2100, Calgary AB T2P 2M5 – 403/268-2793; Fax: 403/268-8260; Email: astubbs@gov.calgary.ab.ca; Symbol: ACE – Library Specialist, Allisen Stubbs

City of Calgary Electric System - Resource Centre, POBox 2100, Calgary AB T2P 2M5 – 403/268-1100; Fax: 403/269-1833 – Supervisor, Shannon-Dean Christoffersen, 403/268-1268

City of Calgary Planning & Building Department - Information Centre, POBox 2100, Calgary AB T2P 2M5 – 403/268-5438; Fax: 403/268-1528; Email: plngbldg@gov.calgary.ab.ca; Symbol: ACPL – Linda D. Read

City of Calgary Social Services Dept. - Library, POBox 8116, Calgary AB T2P 2M5 – 403/268-5115; Fax: 403/268-5765; Email: rempelj@gov.calgary.ab.ca; URL: http://www.gov.calgary.ab.ca/81/ – Research Social Planner, Judith Rempel

Clean Calgary Association – Clean Calgary Environmental Resource Library, #100, 3811 Edmonton Trail NE, Calgary AB T2E 3P5 – 403/230-1443; Fax: 403/230-1458

The Coal Association of Canada – Library, #502, 205 - 9 Ave. SE, Calgary AB T2G 0R3 – 403/262-1544, ext.4; Fax: 403/265-7604; Toll Free: 1-800-910-2625 – Administrative Assistant, Communication & Library Services, Susan Howes

Code Hunter Wittmann - Library, #1200, 700 - 2nd Ave. SW, Calgary AB T2P 4V5 – 403/298-1000; Fax: 403/263-9193; Symbol: CODH – Librarian, Susan Hammer, 403/298-1088

Commonwealth Microfilm - Library, 901 - 10 Ave. SW, Calgary AB T2R 0B5 – 403/245-2555; Fax: 403/244-6426 – Regional General Manager, Irene Price

Corporate-Higher Education Forum – Library, #440, 1010 - 8 Ave. SW, Calgary AB T2P 1J2 – 514/543-1171; Fax: 514/543-1175

Cottonwood Consultants Ltd. – Library, 615 Deercroft Way SE, Calgary AB T2J 5V4 – 403/271-1408 – Environmental Researcher, Cliff Wallis

Deloitte & Touche - Library, Scotia Centre, #2400, 700 - 2 St. SW, Calgary AB T2P 0S7 – 403/267-1783; Fax: 403/264-2871; Email: deloitte@cadvision.com; Symbol: ACTR – Library Technician, Heather Gellner

Developmental Disabilities Resource Centre of Calgary – Resource Centre, 4631 Richardson Way SW, Calgary AB T3E 7B7 – 403/240-3111, ext.335; Fax: 403/240-3230 – Coordinator, Education & Counselling, Adette Dantzer-Skoglunt

DeVry Institute of Technology - Library, 803 Manning Rd. NE, Calgary AB T2E 7M8 – 403/235-3450; Fax: 403/273-3554; Toll Free: 1-800-363-5558 – LRC Coordinator, Darlene Hittel, 403/235-3450, ext. 145, Email: dhittel@acs.ucalgary.ca

Education on Media & Pornography – EMAP Resource Library, #312, 223 - 12 Ave. SW, Calgary AB T2R 0G9 – 403/264-6778

Ernst & Young - Business Information Services, #1300, 707 - 7 Ave. SW, Calgary AB T2P 3H6 – 403/290-4183, 4216; Fax: 403/290-4265; Email: joan.faulk@ca.eyi.com; Symbol: ACCG
- Manager, Joan Faulk
- Library Technician, Liz Henry

Fluor Daniel Canada Inc. - Technical Information Centre, 10101 Southport Rd. SW, Calgary AB T2W 3N2 – 403/259-1110; Fax: 403/259-1222; Email: ENVOY: FLUOR.LIB – Supervisor, Nancy Topper

Foothills Pipe Lines Ltd. - Library, #3100, 707 - 8 Ave. SW, Calgary AB T2P 3W8 – 403/294-4471; Fax: 403/294-4171; Symbol: ACF – Library Technician, Susan Jones, Email: susan.jones@foothillspipe.com

Geological Survey of Canada (Calgary) - Library, 3303 - 33 St. NW, Calgary AB T2L 2A7 – 403/292-7165; Fax: 403/292-5377; Email: gscill@NRCan.gc.ca; URL: http://www.NRCan.gc.ca/ess/esic/esic_e.html; Symbol: ACSP – Head Librarian, John McIsaac, 403/292-7169

Glenbow Museum - Library, 130 - 9 Ave. SE, Calgary AB T2G 0P3 – 403/268-4197; Fax: 403/232-6569; Email: glenbow@glenbow.org; URL: http://www.glenbow.org/library.htm; Symbol: ACG
- Senior Librarian, Lindsay Moir
- Reference Librarian, Catherine Myhr

Grace Women's Health Centre – Dr. Alfred Rothwell Library, 1441 - 29 St. NW, Calgary AB T2N 4JB – 403/670-2200; Fax: 403/284-0228 – Shirley A. Thistlewood

Gulf Canada Resources - Library, POBox 130, Calgary AB T2P 2H7 – 403/233-3905; Fax: 403/233-3070; Symbol: ACGO
- Team Leader - Library/Record Management, Susan Lowe
- Reference Librarian, Guy Trott
- Library Technician, Sherri Querengesser

Heart & Stroke Foundation of Alberta – Library, 1825 Park Rd. SE, Calgary AB T2G 3Y6 – 403/264-5549; Fax: 403/237-0803 – Tracey Ginn

Howard, Mackie Law Office - Library, Canterra Tower, #1000, 400 - 3 Ave. SW, Calgary AB T2P 4H2

– 403/232-9500; Fax: 403/266-1395, 1397 – Joan Scilley

Husky Oil Limited - Library, POBox 6525, Calgary AB T2P 3G7 – 403/298-7057; Fax: 403/298-7464 – Librarian, Wanda Oleszkiwicz

Immigration & Refugee Board - Documentation Centre, 205 - 9th Ave. SE, Calgary AB T2G 0R3 – 403/292-6130; Fax: 403/292-6116 – Chief, Michael Embaie

Imperial Oil Limited - Information Resources, 237 - 4 Ave. SW, 12th Fl., Calgary AB T2P 0H6 – 403/237-4520; Fax: 403/237-3728; Email: ENVOY: ILL.ESSO.MAIN; Symbol: ACI – Information Collections Management, Barbara Landes

Research Library, 3535 Research Rd. NW, Calgary AB T2L 2K8 – 403/284-7417; Fax: 403/284-7589; Email: ENVOY: ILL.ESSO.RESEARCH; Symbol: ACIPRD – Information Specialist, Abe Cohen

Insurance Institute of Southern Alberta – Library, #801, 1015 - 4 St. SW, Calgary AB T2R 1J4 – 403/266-3427; Fax: 403/269-3199

International Association of Hydrogeologists - Canadian National Chapter – Library, c/o Dept. of Geology & Geophysics, University of Calgary, 2500 University Dr. NW, Calgary AB T2N 1N4 – 403/220-4512; Fax: 403/284-0074 – Librarian, Beverley Foss

MacKimmie Matthews Law Office - Library, Gulf Canada Sq., #700, 401 - 9 Ave. SW, POBox 2010, Calgary AB T2P 2M2 – 403/232-0765; Fax: 403/232-0888 – Manager of Library Services, Judy Harvie

Macleod, Dixon - Law Library, Canterra Tower, #3700, 400 - 3 Ave. SW, Calgary AB T2P 4H2 – 403/267-8141; Fax: 403/264-5973; Email: barretl@macleoddixon.com; Symbol: ACMD – Librarian, Lana Barrett, 403/267-8141

Manalta Coal Ltd. - Resource Centre, 700 - 9 Ave. SW, Calgary AB T2P 3V4 – 403/231-7102; Fax: 403/269-8075 – Administrative Clerk, Debra Nault

McCarthy Tétrault - Library, #3200, 421 - 7 Ave. SW, Calgary AB T2P 4K9 – 403/260-3500; Fax: 403/260-3501 – Librarian, Colleen A. Maier

McManus Anderson Miles Law Office - Library, Bow Valley Square, #2200, 250 - 6 Ave. SW, Calgary AB T2P 3H7 – 403/263-2190; Fax: 403/263-6840 – Librarian, Leila Lukowski

Milner Fenerty Law Office - Library, Fifth Avenue Place, 237 - 4th Ave. SW, 30th Fl., Calgary AB T2P 4X7 – 403/268-7055; Fax: 403/268-3100 – Head Librarian, Anil Tiwari

Mobil Oil Canada - Library, POBox 800, Calgary AB T2P 2J7 – 403/260-7857; Fax: 403/260-7600; Email: ENVOY: ILL.ACM; Symbol: ACM – Senior Legal Secretary & Law Librarian, June A. Lux

Monenco AGRA Inc. - Information Resource Centre, Monenco Place, #900, 801 - 6 Ave. SW, Calgary AB T2P 3W3 – 403/298-4673; Fax: 403/298-4125; Email: ENVOY: MONENCO.LIBRARY – Manager, Lyn McCluskey

Mount Royal College - Learning Resources Centre, 4825 Richard Rd. SW, Calgary AB T3E 6K6 – 403/240-6124; Fax: 403/240-6698; Email: ENVOY: ADMIN/ILL.ACMR – Director of Library Services, Madeleine Bailey

National Energy Board - Library, 311 - 6 Ave. SW, Calgary AB T2P 3H2 – 403/299-3561; Fax: 403/292-5576; Email: library@neb.gc.ca; Symbol: ACNEB – Manager, Library Services, Shawn Aitkin

Norcen Energy Resources Ltd. - Library, 425 - 1 St. SW, Calgary AB T2P 4V4 – 403/231-0245; Fax: 403/231-0383; Email: rmclauch@norcen.com; Symbol: ACNER – Librarian, Robert McLauchlin

Nova Gas Transmission - Business Information Centre, 801 - 7 Ave. SW, POBox 2535, Calgary AB T2P 2N6 – 403/290-7505; Fax: 403/290-8940 – Acquisitions Librarian, Jody Barrett

NOVA Knowledge Resource Network, 2928 - 16 St. NE, Calgary AB T2E 7K7 – 403/250-4794; Fax: 403/291-3208; Email: library@novachem.com; Symbol: ACNH – Team Leader, John McIntyre

PanCanadian Petroleum Ltd. - Corporate Library, 150 - 9th Ave. SW, POBox 2850, Calgary AB T2P 2S5 – 403/268-7645; Fax: 403/268-7649; Email: Pat_Bolander@pcp.ca; Symbol: ACPP – Library Technician, Pat Bolander

Parlee McLaws, Barristers & Solicitors - Library, Western Canadian Place, #3400, 707 - 8 Ave. SW, Calgary AB T2P 1H5 – 403/294-7000; Fax: 403/265-8263; Symbol: ACPML – Reference Technician, Phyllis L. Thornton, 403/294-7059

Petro-Canada - Library, POBox 2844, Calgary AB T2P 3E3 – 403/296-8955; Fax: 403/296-3805; Email: reference@peomega.pccw.petro-canada.ca; Symbol: ACPC – ILL/PEB, Rose Taylor

Petroleum Communication Foundation – Library, #214, 311 - 6th Ave. SW, Calgary AB T2P 3H2 – 403/264-6064; Fax: 403/237-6286 – Information Coordinator, Tony Laramée

Petroleum Industry Training Service – Library, #13, 2115 - 27 Ave. NE, Calgary AB T2E 7E4 – 403/250-0883; Fax: 403/291-9408; Toll Free: 1-800-667-5557 – Library Technician, Brad Tickell

Petroleum Recovery Institute – Library, #100, 3512 - 33 St. NW, Calgary AB T2L 2A6 – 403/282-1211; Fax: 403/289-1988; Email: darwent@pri.ab.ca – Darryl Darwent

Planned Parenthood Alberta – Reproductive Health Resource Centre, #304, 301 - 14 St. NW, Calgary AB T2N 2A1 – 403/283-8591; Fax: 403/270-3209 – Executive Director, Melanie Anderson

Price Waterhouse - Calgary Library, #1200, 425 - 1 St. SW, Calgary AB T2P 3V7 – 403/267-1200; Fax: 403/233-0883 – Library Technician, Laureen Matthews

Ranson, Smith, Neef & Barnes - Library, #2120, 520 - 5 Ave. SW, Calgary AB T2P 3R7 – 403/269-5400; Fax: 403/265-8118; Email: rsnb@cadvision.com – Partner, Clarke D. Barnes

Reid Crowther & Partners Ltd. – Library, #210, 340 Midpark Way SE, Calgary AB T2X 1P1 – 403/254-3301, ext.653; Fax: 403/254-3366 – Technical Librarian, Doreen Munsie

Revenue Canada - Research & Library Services, #732, 220 - 4 Ave. SE, Calgary AB T2G 0L1 – 403/691-8711; Fax: 403/691-8793; Symbol: ACRCT

Rigel Oil & Gas Ltd. - Library, Bow Valley Square 3, #1900, 255 - 5 Ave. SW, Calgary AB T2P 3G6 – 403/267-3057; Fax: 403/267-3087; Email: cjmorrisey@rigelenergy.com; Symbol: ACTP – Librarian, Cheryl Morrisey

Rocky Mountain College - Library, 4039 Brentwood Rd. NW, Calgary AB T2L 1L1 – 403/284-5100; Fax: 403/220-9567 – Head Librarian, Ronald A. Fox

Rockyview General Hospital – Library Services, 7007 - 14th St. SW, Calgary AB T2V 1P9 – 403/541-3143; Fax: 403/541-3486; Email: Tuyet.Lam@crha-health.ab.ca; Symbol: ACRVH – Librarian, Kim Polvi

Singleton Urquhart Scott Law Office - Library, #203, 200 Barclay Parade SW, Calgary AB T2P 4R5 – 403/261-9043; Fax: 403/265-4632 – Office Services, Cris Salazar

Society for Technology & Rehabilitation – Technical Resource Centre, #200, 1201 - 5 St. SW, Calgary AB T2R 0Y6 – 403/262-9445; Fax: 403/262-4539

Southern Alberta Institute of Technology - Educational Resources Centre, 1301 - 16 Ave. NW, Calgary AB T2M 0L4 – 403/284-8616, 8860; Fax: 403/284-8619; Email: library@sait.ab.ca; Symbol: ACSA

Educational Resources, Director, R. Thornborough

Library Operations, T. Skinner, 403/284-8701

Media Production, M. Sinotte, 403/284-8381

Sproule Associates Ltd. Library, North Tower, Sun Life Plaza, 140 - 4 Ave. SW, 9th Fl., Calgary AB T2P 3N3 – 403/294-5514; Fax: 403/294-5590 – Supervisor, Marilyn Marsden

Statistics Canada - Prairie Regional Reference Centre - Southern Alberta, Discovery Place, #201, 3553 - 31 St. NW, Calgary AB T2L 2K7 – 403/292-6717; Fax: 403/292-4958; Toll Free: 1-800-563-7828

Stikeman, Elliott Law Office - Library, Bankers Hall, #1500, 855 - 2nd St. SW, Calgary AB T2P 4J7 – 403/266-9000; Fax: 403/266-9034 – Librarian, Lynne Gibson

Suicide Information & Education Centre – Resource Centre, #201, 1615 - 10 Ave. SW, Calgary AB T3C 0J7 – 403/245-3900; Fax: 403/245-0299; Symbol: ACSIEC – Library Coordinator, Karen Kiddey

Suncor Inc. - Library, 112 - 4th Ave. SW, Calgary AB T2P 2V5 – 403/269-8128; Fax: 403/269-6200; Email: info@suncor.com; URL: http://www.suncor.com – Information Specialist, Dave Yadav, Email: dyadav@suncor.com

Talisman Energy Inc. - Information Resources Centre, #2400, 855 - 2 St. SW, Calgary AB T2P 4J9 – 403/237-1040; Fax: 403/237-1902 – Coordinator, Cathy Ross

Toronto-Dominion Bank - Corporate & Investment Banking Group Library, #800, Home Oil Tower, Toronto-Dominion Sq., 324 - 8 Ave. SW, Calgary AB T2P 2Z2 – 403/292-1296; Fax: 403/292-2772 – Librarian, V. Swanson

Towers Perrin - Information Centre, #3700, 150 - 8 Ave. SW, Calgary AB T2P 3Y7 – 403/261-1400; Fax: 403/237-6733 – Librarian, Mary Davey

TransAlta Utilities Corporation - Information Resource Centre, POBox 1900, Calgary AB T2P 2M1 – 403/267-7388; Fax: 403/267-3727; Symbol: ACTU

Information Resource Specialist, Shamin Kassam

Information Resource Specialist, Cheryl McNeil

Information Resource Specialist, Carol Thiessen

TransCanada Pipelines - Library, POBox 1000, Calgary AB T2P 4K5 – 403/267-6498; Fax: 403/267-6266; Symbol: ACTRPL – Librarian, Tracy Angel

University of Calgary - Library, 2500 University Dr. NW, Calgary AB T2N 1N4 – 403/220-5953; Fax: 403/282-6837, 1218; URL: http://www.ucalgary.ca/UofC/departments/INFO/library/

Acting Library Director, Yvonne Hinks, 403/220-3767, Email: 471011@ucdasvm1.admin.ucalgary.ca

Collections & Technical Services, Coordinator, Ada-Marie Atkins Nechka, 403/220-3755, Email: 4710143@ucdasvm1.admin.ucalgary.ca

Acquisitions, Manager, Sandra Telfer, 403/220-7215, Email: 471017@ucdasvm1.admin.ucalgary.ca

Bibliographic Services, Manager, Ross Thrasher, 403/220-3479, Email: rthrashe@acs.ucalgary.ca

Collection Services, Manager, Jan Roseneder, 403/220-3606, Email: rosenede@acs.ucalgary.ca

Access Services, Manager, Darlene Warren, 403/220-6043, Email: dcwarren@acs.ucalgary.ca

Library Research Services, Manager, William Sgrazzutti, Email: sgrazzut@acs.ucalgary.ca

Information Technology Services, Coordinator, Mary Westell, 403/220-3764, Email: westell@acs.ucalgary.ca

Gallagher Library of Geology & Geophysics, Head, Rhys Williams, 403/220-6043, Email: rgwillia@acs.ucalgary.ca

Law Library, Acting Head, Don Sanders, 403/220-6702, Email: sanders@acs.ucalgary.ca

Management Resource Centre, Head, Arden Matheson, 403/220-7577, Email: amatheso@mgmt.ucalgary.ca
Medical Library, Head, John Cole, 403/220-6858, Email: jhcole@acs.ucalgary.ca
Environmental Science Librarian, Marilyn Nasserden, 403/220-3447, Email: nasserde@acs.ucalgary.ca

Vocational & Rehabilitation Research Institute – Dr. Randy Tighe Resource Centre, 3304 - 33 St. NW, Calgary AB T2L 2A6 – 403/284-1121,ext.431; Fax: 403/289-6427 – Librarian, Bob McGowan

Walsh Wilkins, Barristers & Solicitors - Library, #2800, 801 - 6 Ave. SW, Calgary AB T2P 4A3 – 403/267-8400; Fax: 403/264-9400 – Librarian, Frankie Wilson

Zenith Hookenson Boyle Law Office - Library, #1050, 10201 Southport Rd. SW, Calgary AB T2W 3X6 – 403/259-5041; Fax: 403/258-0719 – Receptionist, Carole Sabados

**CAMROSE**

Augustana University College - Library, 4901 - 46 Ave., Camrose AB T4V 2R3 – 403/679-1189; Fax: 403/679-1594; Email: goebn@augustana.ab.ca; URL: http://www.augustana.ab.ca; Symbol: ACAL
Head Librarian, Nancy Goebel
Reference Librarian, Paul Neff

**CANMORE**

Alpine Club of Canada – Library, POBox 8040, Canmore AB T1W 2T8 – 403/678-5940; Fax: 403/678-3224; Email: bbendell@banff.net – Librarian, Bev Bendell

**CLARESHOLM**

Appaloosa Horse Club of Canada – APHCC Museum & Archives, POBox 940, Claresholm AB T0L 0T0 – 403/625-3326; Fax: 403/625-2274

**COLLEGE HEIGHTS**

Canadian Union College - Library, 50 Ramona Dr., College Heights AB T4L 2B7 – 403/782-3381; Fax: 403/782-3977; Email: cuclibrary@ccinet.ab.ca
Librarian, Joyce Van Scheik
Assistant Librarian, Carol Nicks

**DIDSBURY**

Didsbury & District Historical Society – Library, POBox 1175, Didsbury AB T0M 0W0 – 403/335-9295; Fax: 403/335-8931 – Office Coordinator, Denise Stevens

**DRAYTON VALLEY**

The Pembina Institute for Appropriate Development – Library, POBox 7558, Drayton Valley AB T7A 1S7 – 403/542-6272; Fax: 403/542-6464

**DRUMHELLER**

Royal Tyrrell Museum of Palaeontology - Library, POBox 7500, Drumheller AB T0J 0Y0 – 403/823-7707; Fax: 403/823-7131; Email: rtmp@dns.magtech.ab.ca; Symbol: ADTMP
Library Technician, Deborah Lister, 403/823-7707, ext.333
Special Collections, Corinne Pugh

Solicitor General Canada - Drumheller Institution - Library, POBox 3000, Drumheller AB T0J 0Y0 – 403/823-5101, ext.166; Symbol: AADI – Librarian, Sharen Nadasdi

**EDMONTON**

Alberta Research Council – Library, 250 Karl Clark Rd., POBox 8330, Edmonton AB T6H 5X2 – 403/450-5260; Fax: 403/450-8996; Email: STORMS@arc.ab.ca – Library Contact, Barb Storms

ACCESS - Media Resource Centre, 3720 - 76 Ave, Edmonton AB T6B 2N9 – 403/440-7777; Fax: 403/440-8899; Toll Free: 1-800-352-8293; Email: access@incentre.net; URL: http://www.accesstv.ab.ca – Librarian, Darnell Waldner

AIDS Network of Edmonton Society – Tom Edge Memorial Resource Centre, Ross Armstrong Office, #201, 11456 Jasper Ave., Edmonton AB T5K 0M1 – 403/488-5742; Fax: 403/488-3735 – Resource Coordinator, Heather Syren

Alberta Advanced Education & Career Development - Labour Market Information Centre, 10030 - 107 St., South Tower, Edmonton AB T5J 4X7 – 403/427-3722; Fax: 403/427-4778
Coordinator, Dorothy Humphrey
Administrative Support, Lorelei Pritchard

Alberta Agriculture, Food & Rural Development & Alberta Public Works, Supply & Services - Neil Crawford Provincial Centre Library, 7000 - 113 St., Edmonton AB T6H 5T6 – 403/427-2104; Fax: 403/422-2484; Email: library@agric.gov.ab.ca; Symbol: AEAG
Head Librarian, Robert Bateman, Email: bateman@agric.gov.ab.ca
Reference Librarian, Connie Hruday
Reference Librarian, Jennifer Fullen
Technical Services Librarian, Jane Starr
Interlibrary Loan Technician, Fran Harris

Alberta Arbitration & Mediation Society – Library, University of Alberta, 110 Law Centre, Edmonton AB TG6 2H5 – 403/433-4881; Fax: 403/433-9024; Toll Free: 1-800-232-7214 – Librarian, Kay Forsyth

Alberta Association for Community Living – Reg Peters Resource Centre, 11724 Kingsway Ave., Edmonton AB T5G 0X5 – 403/451-3055; Fax: 403/453-5779; Toll Free: 1-800-252-7556 – Information Resource Coordinator, Marta Carmona

Alberta Association of Architects – Library, Duggan House, 10515 Saskatchewan Dr., Edmonton AB T6E 4S1 – 403/432-0224; Fax: 403/439-1431 – Assistant Registrar, Nurjehan Jamal

Alberta Associations for Bright Children – Bright Site, The Bright Site, #1280, 6240 - 113 St., Edmonton AB T6H 3L2 – 403/422-0362; Fax: 403/413-1631

Alberta Band Association – R. Bruce Marsh Memorial Library, #808, 10136 - 100 St., Edmonton AB T5J 0P1 – 403/429-0482; Fax: 403/429-0559

Alberta Choral Federation – Choral Lending Library, #209, 14218 Stony Plain Rd., Edmonton AB T5N 3R3 – 403/488-7464; Fax: 403/488-4132 – Patricia Cook

Alberta Community Development - Citizenship Services Branch - Library, Standard Life Centre, #802, 10405 Jasper Ave., Edmonton AB T5J 4R7 – 403/427-2927; Fax: 403/422-6348; Symbol: AEAC – Research Assistant, Mary Louise Mitchell, Email: mlmitchell@mcd.gov.ab.ca

Alberta Craft Council – Alberta Craft Resource Centre, 10106 - 124 St., Edmonton AB T5N 1P6 – 403/488-6611; Fax: 403/488-8855; Toll Free: 1-800-362-7238 – Nancy St. Hilaire

Alberta Dance Alliance – Resource Centre/Library, 11759 Groat Rd., 2nd Fl., Edmonton AB T5M 3K6 – 403/422-8107; Fax: 403/422-8161; Toll Free: 1-888-422-8107

Alberta Economic Development & Tourism - Library, 10155 - 102 St., 5th Fl., Edmonton AB T5J 4L6 – 403/427-4957; Fax: 403/422-1262; URL: http://gate.library.ualberta.ca; Symbol: AEED – Librarian, Donna M. Gordon, Email: gordodon@censsw.gov.ab.ca

Alberta Education - Library, Devonian Building, West Tower, 11160 Jasper Ave., 4th Fl., Edmonton AB T5K 0L2 – 403/427-2985; Fax: 403/427-5927; Email: librarian@edc.gov.ab.ca; Symbol: AEE – Manager, Library Services, Christina Andrews
Materials Resource Centre for the Visually Impaired, 12360 - 142 St., Edmonton AB T5L 4X9 – 403/427-4681; Fax: 403/427-6683; Email: materialsresourcecentre@edc.gov.ab.ca; Symbol: AEEM – Manager, Kathryn Ribeiro, 403/427-5212

Alberta Energy - Oil Sands Information Services, North Petroleum Plaza, 9945 - 108 St., Edmonton AB T5K 2G6 – 403/427-8382; Fax: 403/427-3198; Symbol: AOSIS
Manager, Helga Petri
Technical Information Officer, Dagmar Losert
Technical Information Officer, James Li
Administrative Assistant, Valerie Pinkoski
Information Clerk, May Fallis
Calgary Branch, Technical Information Officer, Gary Whitehead, 403/297-3380
Calgary Branch, Library Assistant, Brenda Belland, 403/297-3380

Alberta Environmental Protection - Library, 9920 - 108 St., 6th Fl., Edmonton AB T5K 2M4 – 403/427-5870; Fax: 403/422-0170; Email: library@env.gov.ab.ca; Symbol: AEEN – Head Librarian, Lucy Chang

Alberta Health - Library Services Branch, 10025 Jasper Ave., 9th Fl., Edmonton AB T5J 2P4 – 403/427-8720; Fax: 403/427-1643; Email: ahlib2@mail.health.gov.ab.ca; Symbol: AEHE
Health Librarian, Peggy Yeh
Librarian, Linda Bumstead
ILL, Anna Duerr

Alberta Health Record Association – Library, POBox 1752, Edmonton AB T5J 2P1 – 403/413-7239

Alberta Justice - Library, Bowker Bldg., #403, 9833 - 109 St., Edmonton AB T5K 2E8 – 403/498-3413; Fax: 403/427-6821; Symbol: AEATG – Justice Law Librarian, Andrew Balázs
Office of the Chief Medical Examiner, Northern Region - Library, 7007 - 116 St., Edmonton AB T6H 5R8 – 403/427-4987; Fax: 403/422-1265; Email: woodside@mgate.just.gov.ab.ca; Symbol: AEOCME – Librarian, Cathy Woodside

Alberta Labour - Library, #302, 10808 - 99 Ave., Edmonton AB T5K 0G5 – 403/427-8533; Fax: 403/422-0084; Email: labour-library@lab.gov.ab.ca; URL: http://www.gov.ab.ca/~lab/library/library.html; Symbol: AEML – Librarian, Debbie Hunter

Alberta Legislative Assembly - Library, #216, Legislature Bldg., 10800 - 97 Ave. NW, Edmonton AB T5K 2B6 – 403/427-2473; Fax: 403/427-6016; Email: lbuhr@assembly.ab.ca; URL: http://www.assembly.ab.ca; Symbol: AEP – Librarian, Lorne Buhr

Alberta Museums Association – Library, Rossdale House, 9829 - 103 St., Edmonton AB T5K 0X9 – 403/424-2626; Fax: 403/425-1679 – Administrative Assistant, Wendy Griswold

Alberta Pensions Administration Board - Library, Park Plaza Bldg., 10611 - 98 Ave., 4th Fl., Edmonton AB T5K 2P7 – 403/427-3354; Fax: 403/421-1652 – Librarian, Theresa Frauenfeld

Alberta Public Works, Supply & Services - Standards & Specifications Library, 12360 - 142 St., 2nd Fl, Edmonton AB T5L 2H1 – 403/427-3222, ext.274; Fax: 403/427-0834 – Administrator, Wendy Proch

Alberta Rehabilitation Council for the Disabled – Resource Centre, #400, 10909 Jasper Ave., Edmonton AB T5J 3L9 – 403/429-0137; Fax: 403/429-1937 – Library Technician, Gwen Sanderson

Alberta Safety Council – Library, #201, 10526 Jasper Ave., Edmonton AB T5J 1Z7 – 403/428-7555; Fax: 403/428-7557 – Office Manager, Carol Reimer

Alberta School for the Deaf - Library, 6240 - 113 St., Edmonton AB T6H 3L2 – 403/422-0244; Fax: 403/422-2036

Alberta Securities Commission - Library, 10025 Jasper Ave., 19th Fl., Edmonton AB T5J 3Z5 – 403/422-3036; Fax: 403/422-0777; Email: Richard.Farrelly@gov.ab.ca – Librarian, Richard Farrelly

Alberta Teachers' Association – Library, Barnett House, 11010 - 142 St., Edmonton AB T5N 2R1 –

403/453-2411; Fax: 403/455-6481; Email: eatwood@teachers.ab.ca – Librarian, Elaine Atwood
Alberta Treasury - Tax Resource Library, Sir Frederick Haltain Bldg., 9811 - 109 St., 2nd Fl. NE, Edmonton AB T5K 2L5 – 403/427-9425; Fax: 403/427-0348 – Librarian, M. Davies
Association canadienne-française de l'Alberta – Bibliothèque, #303, 8527, rue Marie-Anne-Gaboury, Edmonton AB T6C 3N1 – 403/466-1680; Téléc: 403/465-6773 – Louise Lavallée
Baptist General Conference of Canada – BGC Canada Archives, 4306 - 97 St., Edmonton AB T6E 5R9 – 403/438-9127; Fax: 403/435-2478
Bishop & McKenzie Law Office - Library, #2500, 10104 - 103 Ave., Edmonton AB T5J 1V3 – 403/426-5550; Fax: 403/426-1305 – Librarian, Catherine Mackenzie
Brownlee Fryett Law Office - Library, Commerce Place, #2200, 10155 - 102 St., Edmonton AB T5J 4G8 – 403/497-4800; Fax: 403/424-3254 – Librarian, Tara Veylan
Bryan & Company Law Office - Library, Manulife Place, #2600, 10180 - 101 St., Edmonton AB T5J 3Y2 – 403/423-5730; Fax: 403/428-6324 – Janet Anderson
Canadian Broadcasting Corporation - Record Library, POBox 555, Edmonton AB T5J 2P4 – 403/468-7465; Fax: 403/468-7471 – Music Librarian, Shirley Thorvaldson
Canadian Institute of Ukrainian Studies – Library, #352 Athabasca Hall, University of Alberta, 26 University Campus NW, Edmonton AB T6G 2E8 – 403/492-2972; Fax: 403/492-4967; TLX: 037-2979
Canadian Libraries in Occupational Safety & Health – Library, c/o Alberta Labour Library, 10808 - 99 Ave, 3rd Fl., Edmonton AB T5K 0G5 – 403/427-8533; Fax: 403/422-0084; Email: labour-library@lab.gov.ab.ca; Symbol: AEML – Debbie Hunter
Canadian Organization of Small Business Inc. – Library, POBox 11246, Edmonton AB T5H 3J5 – 403/423-2672; Fax: 403/423-2751 – Administrative Coordinator, Linda Stevens
CANSPEC Group - Library, 7450 - 18 St., Edmonton AB T6P 1N8 – 403/440-2131; Fax: 403/440-1167; Toll Free: 1-800-663-9729; Symbol: AEHM – Head of Library Services, Connie Vogler
Communitas Group Ltd. - Resource Centre, #200, 12120 - 106 Ave., Edmonton AB T5N 0Z2 – 403/482-5467; Fax: 403/488-5102 – Librarian, Lesley Connley
Cross Cancer Institute - Abdul Khaliq Library, 11560 University Ave., 3rd Fl., Edmonton AB T6G 1Z2 – 403/432-8593; Fax: 403/432-8411; Email: ILL.ZJU; Symbol: AECCI – Medical Librarian, Linda Harris
Cruickshank Karvellas Law Office - Library, Manulife Pl., #3400, 10180 - 101 St., Edmonton AB T5J 4W9 – 403/970-5279; Fax: 403/424-1311 – Librarian, Lyla Reid
Deloitte & Touche - Information Centre, #2000, 10180 - 101 St., Edmonton AB T5J 4E4 – 403/421-3790; Fax: 403/421-3782; Email: cengbers@planet.eon.net – Manager, Cea Engbers
Earthkeeping: Food & Agriculture in Christian Perspective – Earthkeeping Resource Centre, #205, 10711 - 107 Ave., Edmonton AB T5H 0W6 – 403/428-6981; Fax: 403/428-1581
Edmonton Archives - Library, 10440 - 108 Ave., Edmonton AB T5H 3Z9 – 403/496-8710; Fax: 403/496-8732; Email: bibsen@gov.edmonton.ab.ca; URL: http://www.gov.edmonton.ab.ca/parkrec/archives – City Archivist, Bruce Ibsen
Edmonton Social Planning Council – Roger Soderstrom Resource Library, #41, 9912 - 106 St., Edmonton AB T5K 1C5 – 403/423-2031; Fax: 403/425-6244 – Publications Editor, Sheila Hallett-Kushniruk
Edmonton Stamp Club – Library, POBox 399, Edmonton AB T5J 2J6 – 403/479-6067; Fax: 403/492-7196 – Librarian, Maurice Hampson
Edmonton Symphony Orchestra – Library, 10160 - 103 St., Edmonton AB T5J 0X6 – 403/428-1108; Fax: 403/425-0167 – Librarian, Sheila Jones
Emery Jamieson Law Office - Library, Oxford Tower, Edmonton Centre, #1700, 10235 - 101 St., Edmonton AB T5J 3G1 – 403/426-5220; Fax: 403/420-6277 – Librarian, Ana San Miguel
Enviro-Test Laboratories - Division of ETL Chemspec Analytical Ltd. – Library, 9936 - 67 Ave., Edmonton AB T6E 0P5 – 403/413-5227; Fax: 403/437-2311; Toll Free: 1-800-668-9878 – Inside Sales, Sylvia Ouellette
Environment Canada - Atmospheric Environment Service, Prairie & Northern Region - Library, #200, 4999 - 98 Ave., Edmonton AB T6B 2X3 – 403/951-8817, 8818; Fax: 403/951-8819; Symbol: AEEPS; AEEAE – Chief Librarian, Terri Fraser
The Environmental Law Centre (Alberta) Society – Library, #204, 10709 Jasper Ave., Edmonton AB T5J 3N3 – 403/424-5099; Fax: 403/424-5133; Toll Free: 1-800-661-4238; Symbol: AEELC – Librarian, Dolores Noga
Fédération des parents francophones de l'Alberta – Centre de ressources prescolaires Guy-Lacombe, #205, 8925 - 82 Ave., Edmonton AB T6C 0Z2 – 403/468-6934; Téléc: 403/469-4799 – Coordonnateur, Richard Vaillancourt
Field Atkinson Perraton Law Office - Library, Oxford Tower, Edmonton Centre, #2000, 10235 - 101 St., Edmonton AB T5J 3G1 – 403/423-3003; Fax: 403/428-9329; 424-7116 – Librarian, Linda Statt, 403/423-3003, ext.249
Glenrose Rehabilitation Hospital – Library Services, 10230 - 111 Ave., Edmonton AB T5G 0B7 – 403/471-2262; Fax: 403/474-8863; Email: pschoenberg@cha.ab.ca; Symbol: AEG – Librarian, Peter Schoenberg
Grant MacEwan Community College - Resource Centre for Voluntary Organizations, #5-132, 10700 - 104 Ave., Edmonton AB T5J 4S2 – 403/497-5616; Fax: 403/497-5209; Email: robertsonl@admin.gmcc.ab.ca; Symbol: RCVO
  Coordinator, Lynda Robertson, 403/497-5617
  Coordinator, Karen Spiess
Grey Nuns Community Health Centre – Library, 1100 Youville Dr. West, Edmonton AB T6L 5X8 – 403/450-7301; Fax: 403/450-7202 – Librarian, Sheila Fynn
Industry Canada - The Business Link, #100, 10237 - 104 St., Edmonton AB T5J 1B1 – 403/422-7722; Fax: 403/422-0055; Toll Free: 1-800-272-9675; Email: buslink@cbsc.ic.gc.ca; URL: http://www.cbsc.org/alberta/
Institute for Peace & Global Education – Library, Department of Secondary Education, University of Alberta, 57 University Campus, Edmonton AB T6G 2G5 – 403/492-5504; Fax: 403/492-9402 – Vimbi Nhundu
Judo Alberta – Video Library, Percy Page Centre, 11759 Groat Rd., Edmonton AB T5M 3K6 – 403/453-8679 – Joyce Syrenne
Justice Canada - Prairies & Northwest Territories Region, Edmonton Regional Office - Law Library, #211, 10199 - 101 St., Edmonton AB T5J 3Y4 – 403/495-2973; Fax: 403/495-2964; Email: lawlib.cajedmonton@justice.x400.gc.ca; Symbol: AEJ
  Law Librarian, Suzan A. Hebditch, Email: suzan.hebditch@justice.x400.gc.ca
  Library Technician, Eve Poirier
Natural Resources Canada-Canadian Forest Service: Northwest Region – Library, 5320 - 122 St., Edmonton AB T6H 3S5 – 403/435-7323, 7324; Fax: 403/435-7356; Email: ill@nofc.forestry.ca; Symbol: AEF – Head, Library Services, Edith M. Hopp
North American Baptist Conference - Canadian Headquarters – Schalm Memorial Library, 11525 - 23 Ave., Edmonton AB T6J 4T3 – 403/437-1960; Fax: 403/434-9170; Email: library@nabcebs.ab.ca – Librarian, Aileen Wright
Northern Alberta Institute of Technology - McNally Library, Learning Resources Centre, #3000, 11762 - 106 St., Edmonton AB T5G 2R1 – 403/471-8844; Fax: 403/471-8813; Email: suec@nait.ab.ca; URL: http://www.nait.ab.ca; Symbol: AENA
Planned Parenthood Association of Edmonton – Phyllis Harris Library, #50, 9912 - 106 St., Edmonton AB T5K 1C5 – 403/423-3737; Fax: 403/425-1782 – Counselling Coordinator, Jeni Adler
Society for the Retired & Semi-Retired – Heritage Library, 15 Sir Winston Churchill Sq., Edmonton AB T5J 2E5 – 403/423-5510; Fax: 403/426-5175 – Resource Librarian, A. Webster
Solicitor General Canada - Edmonton Institution - Library, POBox 2290, Edmonton AB T5J 3H7 – 403/472-6052, ext.265; Fax: 403/495-6036; Symbol: AEEIS – Librarian, Sikhumbuzo Maqubela
Stanley Technology Group Inc. – Library, 10160 - 112 St., Edmonton AB T5K 2L6 – 403/917-7066; Fax: 403/421-7149; Email: dmeen@stantech.com; Symbol: AESAE – Librarian, Donna Meen
Statistics Canada - Prairie Regional Reference Centre - North of Alberta & NWT, Park Sq., 10001 Bellamy Hill, 9th Fl., Edmonton AB T5J 3B6 – 403/495-3027; Fax: 403/495-5318; Toll Free: 1-800-263-1136; Email: ewieall@statcan.ca
  Assistant Director, Advisory Services, Connie Leclair
  Data Dissemination, Officer, Carmel Forbes
  Data Dissemination, Officer, Nadia Danyliuk
Tarrabain & Company - Law Library, #2150, Tower One, Scotia Place, Edmonton AB T5J 3R8 – 403/429-1010; Fax: 403/429-0101 – Barrister, M. Deborah Stewart
Theatre Alberta Society – Theatre Alberta Library, 11759 Groat Rd., 3rd Fl., Edmonton AB T5M 3K6 – 403/422-8162; Fax: 403/422-2663 – Librarian, Natalie Chute
Toxics Watch Society of Alberta – Resource Centre, 10511 Saskatchewan Dr., Edmonton AB T6E 4S1 – 403/433-4808; Fax: 403/439-5081
Transport Canada - Airworthiness Technical Reference Centre, Canada Place, #1100, 9700 Jasper Ave., Edmonton AB T5J 4E6 – 403/495-5223; Fax: 403/495-6659 – Librarian, David J.S. Robinson
  Regional Library Edmonton, #1100, 9700 Jasper Ave., 11th Fl., Edmonton AB T5J 4E6 – 403/495-3801; Fax: 403/495-6460; Symbol: AETR – Regional Librarian, Patricia Nelson, Email: nel-sopj@tc.gc.ca
United Nurses of Alberta – Library, Park Plaza, 10611 - 98 Ave., 9th Fl., Edmonton AB T5K 2P7 – 403/425-1025; Fax: 403/426-2093 – Melanie Chapman
University of Alberta - Libraries, 28 University Campus NW, Edmonton AB T6G 2J8 – 403/492-3790; Fax: 403/492-8302; URL: http://www.library.ualberta.ca/library.html; Symbol: AEU
  Learning Support Systems, Associate Vice-President, Ernie Ingles, 403/492-5569
  Associate Director, K. DeLong, 403/492-0073
  Operational Support Services, Associate Director, S. Rooney, 403/492-3793
  Library Development & Public Relations, Assistant Director, M. Distad, 403/492-1429
  Herbert T. Coutts (Education) Library, Education Librarian, Deborah Dancik, 403/492-5759, Fax: 403/492-8367, Email: educref@library.ualberta.ca
  Humanities & Social Sciences Library, Librarian, Deborah Dancik, 403/492-1405, Fax: 403/492-5083
  John Alexander Weir Memorial Law Library, Acting Law Librarian, Deborah Dancik, 403/492-1569, Fax: 403/492-7546

John W. Scott Health Sciences Library, Acting Health Sciences Librarian, Robin Minion, 403/492-7936, Fax: 403/492-6960

Science & Technology Library, Acting Librarian, Robin Minion, 403/492-7324, Fax: 403/492-2721

Canadian Circumpolar Library, Head Librarian, Robin Minion, 403/492-4409

Mathematics Library, Supervisor, J. Lin, 403/492-3529

William C. Wonders Map Collection, 403/492-7912

Winspear Business Reference Room, Head, Kathy West, 403/492-7931

Dept. of Biochemistry, C.J. Smith Reading Room, Librarian, Susan Smith, 403/492-3358

Data Library, Data Library Coordinator, Chuck Humphrey, 403/492-5212

Music Resources Centre, Librarian, James Whittle, 403/492-5708

Rural Economy Library, Librarian, Barbara Johnson, 403/492-4225

Information Technology Services, Head, D. Poff, 403/492-4770, Fax: 403/492-9243

Interlibrary Loans & Document Delivery, Head, A. Gibb, 403/492-7882, Fax: 403/492-4327

Bibliothèque Saint-Jean, Bibliothécaire, Juliette Henley, 403/465-8710, Fax: 403/468-2550

Bruce Peel Special Collections Library, Head, John Charles, 403/492-7928

Dept. of Extension, Legal Resource Centre Library, Administrative Librarian, Elaine Hutchinson, 403/492-5732

Development Disabilities Centre Library, Librarian, H. de Groot, 403/492-4439

Faculty of Extension, Educational Media Services, Head, James Shaw, 403/492-5047 (Adult Studies); 5039 (Film & Video)

MacLeod Memorial Library, Librarian, Theresa Burwell, 403/492-8337

St. Joseph's College Library, Librarian, Paula Sheedy, 403/492-7681

Book & Record Depository, V. Munro, 403/466-5270

Willson & Associates Law Office - Library, 10316 - 121 St., Edmonton AB T5N 1K8 – 403/482-6670; Fax: 403/482-2518

World Trade Center Edmonton – Resource Center, POBox 1480, Edmonton AB T5J 2N5 – 403/471-7283; Fax: 403/477-0128 – Secretary, Kathy Jansen

Writers Guild of Alberta – Library, Percy Page Centre, 11759 Groat Rd., 3rd Fl., Edmonton AB T5M 3K6 – 403/422-8174; Fax: 403/422-2663; Toll Free: 1-800-665-5354

#### HINTON

Johnson & McClelland Law Office - Library, 221 Pembina Ave., POBox 6060, Hinton AB T7V 1X4 – 403/865-2222; Fax: 403/865-8857

#### INNISFAIL

Solicitor General Canada - Bowden Institution - Library, POBox 6000, Innisfail AB T0M 1A0 – 403/227-3391, ext.361; Fax: 403/227-6022; Symbol: AIBI – Librarian, Frank Turner

#### LETHBRIDGE

Agriculture & Agri-Food Canada-Lethbridge Research Centre – Library, Hwy. 3 East, POBox 3000, Lethbridge AB T1J 4B1 – 403/327-4561; Fax: 403/382-3156; Email: library@ABRSLE.gov.ca; Symbol: ALAG – Librarian, Cheryl M. Ronning-Mains

Native Counselling Services of Alberta – Library, #208, 324 - 7 St. South, Lethbridge AB T1J 2G2 – 403/423-2141; Fax: 403/380-2562 – Librarian, Alexandra Nowacka

University of Lethbridge - Library, 4401 University Dr., Lethbridge AB T1K 3M4 – 403/327-2263 – Library Contact, Business, Andrea Glover

#### MEDICINE HAT

National Defence (Canada)-Defence Research Establishment Suffield – Library, POBox 4000, Medicine Hat AB T1A 8K6 – 403/544-4011; Fax: 403/544-3388 – Librarian, Jerry Fitzgerald

Unisphere Global Resource Centre – Library, 101 - 6 St. SE, Medicine Hat AB T1A 1G7 – 403/529-2656; Fax: 403/529-0540

#### MEDLEY

National Defence - Aerospace Engineering Test Establishment - Technical Reference Library, CFB Cold Lake, POBox 1000-3450, Medley AB T0A 2M0 – 403/840-8000, ext.8062; Fax: 403/840-7381; Email: reflib@aete.coldlake.dnd.ca; Symbol: AMECFA – Librarian, John MacIntyre

#### RED DEER

Red Deer College - Library, POBox 5005, Red Deer AB T4N 5H5 – 403/342-3300; Fax: 403/346-8500; Email: reference@rdc.ab.ca; URL: http://www.rdc.ab.ca/rdc/library/; Symbol: ARDC – Alice McNair

#### STETTLER

Buffalo Lake Naturalists Club – Library, Box 1802, Stettler AB T0C 2L0 – 403/742-1837 – Librarian, Lloyd Lohr

## BRITISH COLUMBIA

### Municipal Public Libraries

Burnaby Public Library, 6100 Willingdon Ave., Burnaby BC V5H 4N5 – 604/436-5427; Fax: 604/436-2961 – Chief Librarian, Paul Whitney; Assistant Chief Librarian, Jon O'Grady, 604/436-5432; Circulation Supervisor, Brenda Lincoln; Children's Services, Coordinator, Joyce Pinsker; Technical Services Librarian, Carolyn Hoffman, 604/436-5424; Acquisitions Librarian, John Davenport, 604/436-5435 – See also following branches: Bob Prittie Metrotown Branch Library, Cameron Branch Library, Kingsway Branch Library, McGill Branch Library

Burnaby: Bob Prittie Metrotown Branch Library, 6100 Willingdon Ave., Burnaby BC V5H 4N5 – 604/436-5410; Fax: 604/436-2961; Email: ENVOY: F.BPL; Symbol: BB – Branch Librarian, Jon O'Grady – Branch of Burnaby Public Library

Burnaby: Cameron Branch Library, 9523 Cameron St., Burnaby BC V3J 1L6 – 604/421-5454; Fax: 604/436-2961 – Branch Librarian, Linda Shineton – Branch of Burnaby Public Library

Burnaby: Kingsway Branch Library, 7252 Kingsway, Burnaby BC V5E 1G3 – 604/522-3971; Fax: 604/436-2961 – Branch Librarian, Caroline Christie – Branch of Burnaby Public Library

Burnaby: McGill Branch Library, 4595 Albert St., Burnaby BC V5C 2G6 – 604/299-8955; Fax: 604/299-5167 – Branch Librarian, Linnea Gibbs – Branch of Burnaby Public Library

Coquitlam Public Library, 575 Poirier St., Coquitlam BC V3J 6A9 – 604/931-2416; Fax: 604/931-6739 – Director, Stan Pukesh – See also following branches: Lincoln Branch Library, Poirier St. Main Library

Coquitlam: Lincoln Branch Library, 3020 Lincoln Ave., Coquitlam BC V3J 6B4 – 604/464-1112; Fax: 604/464-3380 – Branch Supervisor, Marlene Winters – Branch of Coquitlam Public Library

Coquitlam: Poirier St. Main Library, 575 Poirier St., Coquitlam BC V3J 6A9 – 604/931-1293; Fax: 604/931-1460 – Branch Head, Elspeth Richmond, 604/931-1293; Reference Librarian, Gillian Campbell, 604/931-1444; Children's Librarian, Deborah Duncan, 604/931-1292; Public Services Librarian, Leslie Utsunomiya, 604/937-0455 – Branch of Coquitlam Public Library

Dawson Creek Public Library, 1001 McKellar Ave., Dawson Creek BC V1G 4W7 – 250/782-4662; Fax: 250/782-4667; Email: bdc.ill@pris.bc.ca – Librarian, Mary Toma, Email: mtoma@pris.bc.ca; Assistant Librarian, Jenny Snyder

Mackenzie Public Library, 400 Skeena Dr., Bag Service 750, Mackenzie BC V0J 2C0 – 250/997-6343; Fax: 250/997-5792; Symbol: BMK – Librarian, Patricia Dauphinee

Nelson Municipal Library, 602 Stanley St., Nelson BC V1L 1N4 – 250/352-6333; Fax: 250/354-1799; Email: dthomas@netidea.com; URL: http://www.netidea.com/~nellib; Symbol: BNE – Chief Librarian, Deborah Thomas; Reference Librarian, Martha Scott; Circulation & Acquisitions Librarian, Deb Thomas; Children's Librarian, Nancy Radonich

New Westminster Public Library, 716 - 6 Ave., New Westminster BC V3M 2B3 – 604/521-8874; Fax: 604/521-6647; URL: http://www.nwpl.new-westminster.bc.ca; Symbol: BNW – City Librarian, Ron Clancy, Email: rclancy@nwpl.new-westminster.bc.ca; Reference Librarian, Joan G. Halverson; Circulation Librarian, Maureen Allen; Children's Librarian, Ellen Heaney; Public Services Librarian, Debra Nelson; Technical Services Librarian, Jean Simpson

North Vancouver District Public Library, 1280 East 27 St., North Vancouver BC V7J 1S1 – 604/984-0286; Fax: 604/984-7600; URL: http://www.nvdpl.north-van.bc.ca – Chief Librarian, Noreen A. Ballantyne; Reference Coordinator, Vicki Ringe; Adult Coordinator, Blair G. Thompson; Children's & Young Adult Coordinator, Allison Haupt; Manager, Collections & Services, Barbara Jo May; Manager, Technical Services, Alison J. Hill; Manager, Systems & Technology, Jacqueline Van Dyk; Audiovisual Coordinator, Jean McCarran – See also following branches: Capilano Branch Library, Lynn Valley Branch Library, Parkgate Branch Library

North Vancouver: Capilano Branch Library, 3045 Highland Blvd., North Vancouver BC V7R 2X4 – 604/987-4471; Fax: 604/987-0956 – Branch Manager, Teresa James, Email: tjames@nvdpl.north-van.bc.ca – Branch of North Vancouver District Public Library

North Vancouver: Lynn Valley Branch Library, 1280 East 27 St., North Vancouver BC V7J 1S1 – 604/984-0286; Fax: 604/984-7600; Email: pforsyth-manchester@nvdpl.north-van.bc.ca – Branch Manager, Penny Forsyth-Manchester – Branch of North Vancouver District Public Library

North Vancouver City Library, 121 - 14th St. West, North Vancouver BC V7M 1P2 – 604/980-0581; Fax: 604/983-3624; Email: ENVOY: F.NVC – Chief Librarian, Joe Lavery

North Vancouver: Parkgate Branch Library, 3675 Banff Ct., North Vancouver BC V7H 2Y7 – 604/929-3727; Fax: 604/929-0758 – Branch Manager, Helen Kaiser, Email: hgk@nvdpl.north-van.bc.ca – Branch of North Vancouver District Public Library

Penticton Public Library, 785 Main St., Penticton BC V2A 5E3 – 250/492-0024; Fax: 250/492-0440 – Director, R.M. McIvor; Children's Librarian, K. Kellerman; Systems Librarian, S. Murphy; Assistant Director, L. Little

Port Moody Public Library, 240 Ioco Rd., PO Box 37, Port Moody BC V3H 2E1 – 604/469-4580; Fax: 604/469-4576 – Chief Librarian, Lynne Russell;

Children's Librarian, Vicki Donaghue; Public Services Librarian, Eva Lederer

Pouce Coupe Public Library, PO Box 75, Pouce Coupe BC V0C 2C0 – 250/786-5765; Fax: 250/786-5257; Symbol: BPOC – Librarian, Laraine Guidry

Prince George Public Library, 887 Dominion St., Prince George BC V2L 5L1 – 250/563-9251; Fax: 250/563-0892; Symbol: BPG – Director, Edel Toner-Rogala, 250/563-9251, ext.129; Adult Services Manager, Joan Jarman, 250/563-9251, ext.128; Children's Services Manager, Barb Dean, 250/563-9251, ext.105; Support Services Manager, Joseph Stibrany, 250/563-9251, ext.130; Finance & Administrative Services Manager, Noreen Redman, 250/563-9251, ext.134; Community Relations Manager, Joan Jarman, 250/563-9251, ext.128 – See also following branches: Nechako Branch Library

Prince George: Nechako Branch Library, 6547 Hart Hwy., Prince George BC V2K 3A4 – 250/962-9710 – Branch of Prince George Public Library

Prince Rupert Library, 101 - 6 Ave. West., Prince Rupert BC V8J 1Y9 – 250/627-1345; Fax: 250/627-7743; Email: library@citytel.net; Symbol: BPR – Librarian, Michele Cook; Deputy Librarian, Michael Purcell

Richmond Public Library, #100, 7700 Minoru Gate, Richmond BC V6Y 1R9 – 604/231-6422; Fax: 604/273-0459; URL: http://www.rpl.richmond.bc.ca; Symbol: BRI – Chief Librarian, Greg Buss; Deputy Chief Librarian, Cate McNeely – See also following branches: Steveston Branch Library

Richmond: Steveston Branch Library, 4111 Moncton St., Richmond BC V7E 3A8 – 604/274-2012 – Branch Head, Andrée Duval – Branch of Richmond Public Library

Surrey Public Library, 13742 - 72 Ave., Surrey BC V3W 2P4 – 604/572-8269; Fax: 604/596-8523 – Chief Librarian, Stan Smith – See also following branches: Cloverdale Branch, Guildford Branch, Newton Branch Library, Ocean Park Branch Library, Port Kells Branch Library, Whalley Branch Library

Surrey: Cloverdale Branch, 5642 - 176A St., Surrey BC V3S 4G9 – 604/576-1384; Fax: 604/576-0120 – Branch Manager, Jennifer Herfst – Branch of Surrey Public Library

Surrey: Guildford Branch, 15105 - 105 Ave., Surrey BC V3R 7G8 – 604/588-5015; Fax: 604/588-5627 – Branch Manager, Jane Knight – Branch of Surrey Public Library

Surrey: Newton Branch Library, 13795 - 70 Ave., Surrey BC V3W 0E1 – 604/596-7401; Fax: 604/597-3792 – Branch Manager, Melanie Houlden – Branch of Surrey Public Library

Surrey: Ocean Park Branch Library, 12854 - 17th Ave., Surrey BC V4A 1T5 – 604/531-5044; Fax: 604/531-3951 – Community Librarian, Jane Gifford – Branch of Surrey Public Library

Surrey: Port Kells Branch Library, 18885 - 88th Ave., Surrey BC V4N 3G5 – 604/882-0733; Fax: 604/882-0733 – Community Librarian, Sharon Ward – Branch of Surrey Public Library

Surrey: Whalley Branch Library, 10347 - 135th St., Surrey BC V3T 4C3 – 604/588-5951; Fax: 604/588-0457 – Branch Manager, Patricia Miller – Branch of Surrey Public Library

Trail & District Public Library, 1051 Victoria St., Trail BC V1R 3T3 – 250/364-1731; Fax: 250/364-2176; Email: trailib@knet.kootenay.net – Director, Julie Spurrell

Vancouver Public Library, 350 West Georgia St., Vancouver BC V6B 6B1 – 604/331-4001; Fax: 604/331-4080; Email: ENVOY: VPL.ILL; Symbol: VPL – Director, Madeleine Aalto; Circulation Librarian, Susan Everall; Technical Services Librarian, Pat Haffenden – See also following branches: Britannia Community Branch Library, Carnegie Branch Library, Champlain Heights Branch Library, Collingwood Branch Library, Dunbar Branch Library, Firehall Branch Library, Fraserview Branch Library, Hastings Branch Library, Joe Fortes Branch Library, Kensington Community Library, Kerrisdale Branch Library, Kitsilano Branch Library, Marpole Branch Library, Mount Pleasant Branch Library, Oakridge Branch Library, Renfrew Branch, Riley Park Branch Library, South Hill Branch Library, Strathcona Branch Library, West Point Grey Branch Library

Vancouver: Britannia Community Branch Library, 1661 Napier St., Vancouver BC V5L 4X4 – 604/665-2222 – Branch Head, Catherine Connell – Branch of Vancouver Public Library

Vancouver: Carnegie Branch Library, 401 Main St., Vancouver BC V6A 2T7 – 604/665-3010 – Branch Head, Eleanor Kelly – Branch of Vancouver Public Library

Vancouver: Champlain Heights Branch Library, #101, 3200 East 54th Ave., Vancouver BC V5S 3T8 – 604/665-3955 – Branch Head, Susan Watson – Branch of Vancouver Public Library

Vancouver: Collingwood Branch Library, 2985 Kingsway, Vancouver BC V5R 5J4 – 604/665-3953 – Branch Head, Janet Wynne-Edwards – Branch of Vancouver Public Library

Vancouver: Dunbar Branch Library, 4515 Dunbar St., Vancouver BC V6S 2G7 – 604/665-3968 – Branch Head, Andrew Kevlahan – Branch of Vancouver Public Library

Vancouver: Firehall Branch Library, 1455 West 10th Ave., Vancouver BC V6H 1J8 – 604/665-3970 – Branch Head, Judi Walker – Branch of Vancouver Public Library

Vancouver: Fraserview Branch Library, 1950 Argyle Dr., Vancouver BC V5P 2A8 – 604/665-3957 – Branch Head, Marsha Robinson – Branch of Vancouver Public Library

Vancouver: Hastings Branch Library, 2674 Hastings St. East, Vancouver BC V5K 1Z6 – 604/665-3959 – Branch Head, Donna Meadwell – Branch of Vancouver Public Library

Vancouver: Joe Fortes Branch Library, 870 Denman St., Vancouver BC V6G 2L8 – 604/665-3972 – Branch Head, Thomas Quigley – Branch of Vancouver Public Library

Vancouver: Kensington Community Library, 3927 Knight St., Vancouver BC V5N 3L8 – 604/665-3961 – Branch Head, Anne Kyler – Branch of Vancouver Public Library

Vancouver: Kerrisdale Branch Library, 2112 West 42nd Ave., Vancouver BC V6M 2B6 – 604/665-3974 – Branch Head, Jane White – Branch of Vancouver Public Library

Vancouver: Kitsilano Branch Library, 2425 MacDonald St., Vancouver BC V6K 3Y9 – 604/665-3976; Fax: 604/731-6931 – Branch Head, Linda Kalman – Branch of Vancouver Public Library

Vancouver: Marpole Branch Library, 8386 Granville St., Vancouver BC V6P 4Z7 – 604/665-3978 – Branch Head, Chris Middlemass – Branch of Vancouver Public Library

Vancouver: Mount Pleasant Branch Library, 370 East Broadway, Vancouver BC V5T 4G5 – 604/665-3962 – Branch Head, Del Tait – Branch of Vancouver Public Library

Vancouver: Oakridge Branch Library, Oakridge Shopping Centre, #191, 650 West 41 Ave., Vancouver BC V5Z 2M9 – 604/665-3980 – Branch Head, Peter Archibald – Branch of Vancouver Public Library

Vancouver: Renfrew Branch, 2969 East 22nd Ave., Vancouver BC V5M 2Y3 – 604/257-8705 – Branch Head, Stephanie Bohlin – Branch of Vancouver Public Library

Vancouver: Riley Park Branch Library, Little Mountain Neighbourhood House, 3981 Main St., Vancouver BC V5V 3P3 – 604/665-3964 – Branch Head, Anne Kyler – Branch of Vancouver Public Library

Vancouver: South Hill Branch Library, 6076 Fraser St., Vancouver BC V5W 2Z7 – 604/665-3965 – Branch Head, Tish McMurtry – Branch of Vancouver Public Library

Vancouver: Strathcona Branch Library, 592 East Pender St., Vancouver BC V6A 1V5 – 604/665-3967 – Branch Head, Heather Scoular – Branch of Vancouver Public Library

Vancouver: West Point Grey Branch Library, 4480 West 10th Ave., Vancouver BC V6R 2H9 – 604/665-3982 – Head Librarian, Susan Bridgman – Branch of Vancouver Public Library

Victoria: Greater Victoria Public Library, 735 Broughton St., Victoria BC V8W 3H2 – 250/382-7241; Fax: 250/382-7125 – Chief Librarian, Sandra Anderson; Children's Librarian, Colleen Stewart; Technical Services Librarian, Barbara Irwin; Acquistions Librarian, Glenda Payzant – See also following branches: Bruce Hutchison Branch Library, Esquimalt Branch Library, Juan de Fuca Branch at Royal Roads University, Nellie McClung Branch Library, Oak Bay Branch Library, Saanich-Victoria Branch Library

Victoria: Bruce Hutchison Branch Library, 4636 Elk Lake Dr., Victoria BC V8Z 7K2 – 250/727-0104 – Branch Head, Ruth Scott, Email: rscott@gvpl.victoria.bc.ca – Branch of Greater Victoria Public Library

Victoria: Esquimalt Branch Library, 1149 Esquimalt Rd., Victoria BC V9A 3N6 – 250/385-1021 – Branch Head, Cheryl Osborn, Email: cosborn@gvpl.victoria.bc.ca – Branch of Greater Victoria Public Library

Victoria: Juan de Fuca Branch at Royal Roads University, 2005 Sooke Rd., Victoria BC V9B 5Y2 – 250/391-0653; Fax: 250/391-0879 – Branch Head, Gillian Pearson, Email: gpearson@gvpl.victoria.bc.ca – Branch of Greater Victoria Public Library

Victoria: Nellie McClung Branch Library, 3950 Cedar Hill Rd., Victoria BC V8P 3Z9 – 250/477-7111 – Branch Head, Barbara Hutcheson, Email: bhutches@gvpl.victoria.bc.ca – Branch of Greater Victoria Public Library

Victoria: Oak Bay Branch Library, 1442 Monterey Ave., Victoria BC V8S 4W1 – 250/592-2489 – Branch Head, H. Wetselaar, Email: hwetsela@gvpl.victoria.bc.ca – Branch of Greater Victoria Public Library

Victoria: Saanich-Victoria Branch Library, 3500 Blanshard St., Victoria BC V8X 1W3 – 250/475-6100 – Branch Head, Penny Watson – Branch of Greater Victoria Public Library

West Vancouver Memorial Library, 1950 Marine Dr., West Vancouver BC V7V 1J8 – 604/925-7400; Fax: 604/925-5933; URL: http://www.wvml.jeslacs.bc.ca; Symbol: BWV – Chief Librarian, Ann Goodheart; Reference Services, Head, Ted Benson; Adult Services, Head, Cheryl McGregor; Youth Services, Head, Julia Hedley; Support Services, Head, Lauren Henderson; Technical Services/Systems, Head, Roy Hunter; Acquisitions Clerk, Andrea Tartaglio

## Regional Library Districts with Member Libraries

### FRASER VALLEY REGIONAL LIBRARY

34589 Delair Rd., Abbotsford BC V2S 5Y1 – 604/859-7141; Fax: 604/852-5701; Email: jean.dirksen@fvrl.bc.ca

Chief Administrative Officer, Jean Dirksen
Public Services, Director, Bill Mitchell
Systems & Technical Services, Director, Diana Guinn
Collection Development Coordinator, Sybil Harrison

Abbotsford MSA Centennial Branch Library, 33660 South Fraser Way, Abbotsford BC V2S 2B9 – 604/853-1753; Fax: 604/853-7861 – Community Librarian, Judy Casey

Clearbrook Branch Library, 32320 Dahlstrom Ave., Abbotsford BC V2T 6N4 – 604/859-7814; Fax: 604/859-7329 – Area Coordinator, Barbara Emerson

Agassiz Branch Library, #1805 Hwy. 9, Agassiz BC V0M 1A0 – 604/796-9510; Fax: 604/796-9517 – Community Librarian, Earla Legault

Aldergrove Branch Library, 26770 - 29 Ave., Aldergrove BC V4W 3B8 – 604/856-6415; Fax: 604/856-6415 – Community Librarian, Yvonne Holden

Boston Bar Branch Library, 47643 Old Boston Bar Rd., PO Box 400, Boston Bar BC V0K 1C0 – 604/867-8847 – Community Librarian, Cora Dunlop

Chilliwack Branch Library, 45860 - 1 Ave., Chilliwack BC V2P 7K1 – 604/792-1941; Fax: 604/792-7483 – Area Coordinator, Kathy Brown

George Mackie Branch Library, 8440 - 112 St., Delta BC V4C 4W9 – 604/594-8155; Fax: 604/594-9364 – Area Coordinator, Barbara Hynek

Ladner (Delta Pioneer) Branch Library, 4683 - 51 St., Delta BC V4K 2V8 – 604/946-6215; Fax: 604/946-7821 – Community Librarian, Cecilia Duncan

South Delta Branch Library, 1321A - 56 St., Delta BC V4L 2A6 – 604/943-2271 – Community Librarian, Jean Minch

Fort Langley Branch Library, 9167 Glover Rd., PO Box 312, Fort Langley BC V1M 2R6 – 604/888-0722; Fax: 604/882-0729 – Community Librarian, Mary Marquette

Hope Branch Library, 1005 - 6th Ave., Hope BC V0X 1L0 – 604/869-2313; Fax: 604/869-2472 – Community Librarian, Sydney Mason

Brookswood Branch Library, 20045 - 40 Ave., Langley BC V3A 2W2 – 604/534-7055; Fax: 604/532-7432 – Community Librarian, Marina Kristjanson

Langley Centennial Branch Library, 20355 Douglas Cres., Langley BC V3A 4B3 – 604/534-3284; Fax: 604/534-2985 – Area Coordinator, Mary Kierans

Walnut Grove Branch Library, 8889 Walnut Grove Dr., Langley BC V1M 2N7 – 604/882-0410; Fax: 604/882-3754 – Community Librarian, Bea Rawlings

Maple Ridge Branch Library, 22420 Dewdney Trunk Rd., Maple Ridge BC V2X 3J5 – 604/466-2601; Fax: 604/467-7596 – Branch Librarian, Kathryn Feeney

Mission Branch Library, 33247 - 2 Ave., Mission BC V2V 1J7 – 604/826-6610; Fax: 604/826-6614 – Branch Librarian, Rhian Piprell

Mount Lehman Branch Library, 5875 Mt. Lehman Rd., Mount Lehman BC V0X 1V0 – 604/856-4988; Fax: 604/856-4908 – Community Librarian, Taylor Jorgenson-Shaw

Pitt Meadows Branch Library, 12047 Harris Rd., Pitt Meadows BC V3Y 1Z2 – 604/465-4113; Fax: 604/465-9732 – Community Librarian, Sandra Richardson

Terry Fox Branch Library, 2470 Mary Hill Rd., Port Coquitlam BC V3C 3B1 – 604/927-7999; Fax: 604/941-8365 – Area Coordinator, Ada Con

White Rock Branch Library, 15342 Buena Vista Ave., White Rock BC V4B 1Y6 – 604/541-2201; Fax: 604/541-2209 – Community Librarian, Mary Anne Johnson

Yale Branch Library, c/o Yale Elementary School, 65050 Albert St., Yale BC V0K 2S0 – 604/863-2279; Fax: 604/863-2279 – Community Librarian, Karen Rushlow

Yarrow Public Library, 4670 Community St., PO Box 370, Yarrow BC V2R 5H8 – 604/823-4664; Fax: 604/823-4686 – Community Librarian, Gail Berger

**OKANAGAN REGIONAL LIBRARY**

1430 KLO Rd., Kelowna BC V1W 3P6 – 250/860-4033; Fax: 250/861-8696; Symbol: BKO

Executive Director, Lesley Dieno

Public Services Manager, Lorraine Hladik

Technical Services Librarian, Paula Neumann

Children's Services Coordinator, Judy Arter

Media Librarian, Georgia McKay

Armstrong Branch Library, PO Box 189, Armstrong BC V0E 1B0 – 250/546-8311 – Community Librarian, Charlene Woodbury

Celista Branch, PO Box 233, Celista BC V0E 1L0 – 250/955-8198 – Community Librarian, Angela Stevenson

Cherryville Branch, RR#1-6E, Lumby BC V0E 2G0 – 250/547-9776 – Librarian, Colleen Primley

Enderby Branch, City Hall Complex, Hwy. 97, PO Box 226, Enderby BC V0E 1V0 – 250/838-6488 – Community Librarian, Kathleen Moerman

Falkland Branch, PO Box 33, Falkland BC V0E 1W0 – 250/379-2705 – Community Librarian, Julie Schoenberger

Golden Branch, PO Box 750, Golden BC V0A 1H0 – 250/344-6516 – Community Librarian, Lynda Whitwell

Hedley Branch, PO Box 155, Hedley BC V0X 1K0 – 250/292-8209 – Community Librarian, Martha Chambers

Kaleden Branch, PO Box 370, Kaleden BC V0H 1K0 – 250/497-8066 – Community Librarian, Louise Gardiner

Kelowna Resource Centre, 1626 Richter St., Kelowna BC V1Y 2M3 – 250/762-2800 – Kelowna Area Librarian, Beth McKee

Mission Branch, #5, 3818 Gordon Dr., Kelowna BC V1W 3G8 – 250/868-3391 – Community Librarian, Sharron Cooper

Keremeos Branch, PO Box 330, Keremeos BC V0X 1N0 – 250/499-2313 – Community Librarian, Isabel Chatfield

Lumby Branch, Lumby Community Centre, 2250 Shields Ave., PO Box 116, Lumby BC V0E 2G0 – 250/547-9528 – Community Librarian, Darlene Gudeit

Naramata Branch, PO Box 190, Naramata BC V0H 1N0 – 250/496-5679 – Community Librarian, Carol A. McGibney

Okanagan Falls Branch, PO Box 299, Okanagan Falls BC V0H 1R0 – 250/497-5886 – Community Librarian, Ruell Smith

Oliver Branch, PO Box 758, Oliver BC V0H 1T0 – 250/498-2242 – Community Librarian, Kaye-Marie Yuckin

Osoyoos Branch, PO Box 1038, Osoyoos BC V0H 1V0 – 250/495-7637 – Community Librarian, Kathy Burton

Oyama Branch, PO Box 55, Oyama BC V0H 1W0 – 250/548-3377 – Community Librarian, Helen Edgar

Peachland Branch, PO Box 21, Peachland BC V0H 1X0 – 250/767-9111 – Community Librarian, Pat Fowler

Princeton Branch, PO Box 958, Princeton BC V0X 1W0 – 250/295-6495 – Community Librarian, Joan Muir

Revelstoke Branch, PO Box 1289, Revelstoke BC V0E 2S0 – 250/837-5095 – Community Librarian, Joan Holzer

Rutland Branch, PO Box 2104, Rutland BC V1X 3B2 – 250/765-8165 – Community Librarian, Sheila Mitchell

Salmon Arm Branch, PO Box 1630, Salmon Arm BC V1E 4P7 – 250/832-6161 – Librarian, Leslie Stafford

Silver Creek Branch, RR#1, Site 9, Comp. 60, Salmon Arm BC V1E 4M1 – 250/832-4719 – Community Librarian, Marlene Campbell

Seymour Arm Branch, RR#2, Sicamous BC V0E 2V0 – 250/832-8775 – Community Librarian, Holly MacKenzie

Sicamous Branch, PO Box 15, Sicamous BC V0E 2V0 – 250/836-4845 – Community Librarian, Sharon Dyck

Sorrento Branch, PO Box 54, Sorrento BC V0E 2W0 – 250/675-4818 – Community Librarian, Glenna Hines

Summerland Branch, PO Box 1198, Summerland BC V0H 1Z0 – 250/494-5591 – Community Librarian, Jan Carlson

Trout Lake Branch, PO Box 46, Trout Lake BC V0G 1R0 – Community Librarian, Nancy Savage

Vernon Branch, 3001 - 32 Ave., Vernon BC V1T 2L8 – 250/542-7610 – Vernon Area Librarian, Wendy Stevens

Westbank Branch, PO Box 46, Westbank BC V4T 1Z1 – 250/768-4369 – Community Librarian, Marnie Keath

Winfield Branch, PO Box 477, Winfield BC V0H 2C0 – 250/766-3141 – Community Librarian, Angela MacPherson

**VANCOUVER ISLAND REGIONAL LIBRARY**

6250 Hammond Bay Rd., PO Box 3333, Nanaimo BC V9R 5N3 – 250/758-4697; Fax: 250/758-2482; Email: ENVOY: ILL.VIRL; DF.MEADOWS; Symbol: ORCA

Director, Donald F. Meadows

Public Services, Assistant Director, Penny Grant

Support Services, Assistant Director, Mary Maquega

Personnel, Head, Ann Lowrie

Personnel Officer, Ann Lowrie

Reference Services, Coordinator, Marion Wildin

Catalogue & Computer Services, Coordinator, Gloria Novak

Collections, Coordinator, Shev O'Hara

Bella Coola Branch Library, PO Box 68, Bella Coola BC V0T 1C0 – 250/799-5330; Fax: 250/799-5330 – Branch Head, Linda Chapman

Brentwood/Central Saanich Branch Library, 1209 Clarke Rd., Brentwood Bay BC V8M 1P8 – 250/652-2013; Fax: 250/652-6224 – Branch Head, Katherine Day

Campbell River Branch Library, 1240 Shopper's Row, Campbell River BC V9W 2C8 – 250/287-3655; Fax: 250/287-2119 – Branch Head, Julia Clausen

Chemainus Branch Library, 2592 Legion St., PO Box 72, Chemainus BC V0R 1K0 – 250/246-9471; Fax: 250/246-9411 – Branch Head, Heather Aikenhead

Comox Branch Library, 1729 Comox Ave., Comox BC V9M 3M2 – 250/339-2971; Fax: 250/339-2940 – Branch Head, Judy Van Sickle

Courtenay Branch Library, 410 Cliffe Ave., Courtenay BC V9N 2J2 – 250/334-3369; Fax: 250/334-0910 – Branch Head, Diane Taggart

Cumberland Branch Library, Dunsmuir Ave., PO Box 378, Cumberland BC V0R 1S0 – 250/336-8121; Fax: 250/336-8121 – Branch Head, Ellen Wise

Cowichan Branch Library, 2687 James St., Duncan BC V9L 2X5 – 250/746-7661; Fax: 250/746-5595 – Branch Head, Rhonda Nott

Gold River Branch Library, 396 Nimpkish Dr., PO Box 309, Gold River BC V0P 1G0 – 250/283-2502; Fax: 250/283-2502 – Branch Head, Ann Henkelman

Hornby Island Branch Library, 1765 Sollans Rd., PO Box 37, Hornby Island BC V0R 1Z0 – 250/335-0044; Fax: 250/335-0044 – Branch Head, Denyse Wallace

Ladysmith Branch Library, #3, 740 - 1st Ave., PO Box 389, Ladysmith BC V0R 2E0 – 250/245-2322; Fax: 250/245-2393 – Branch Head, Florence Edgar

Lake Cowichan Branch Library, #1, 38 King George, PO Box 918, Lake Cowichan BC V0R 2G0 – 250/749-3431; Fax: 250/749-3401 – Branch Head, Deborah Maher

Masset Branch Library, 2123 Collison, PO Box 710, Masset BC V0T 1M0 – 250/626-3663; Fax: 250/626-3663 – Branch Head, Andrea Gee

South Cowichan Branch Library, #33, 2720 Mill Bay Rd., PO Box 2000, Mill Bay BC V0R 2P0 – 250/743-5436; Fax: 250/743-5506 – Branch Head, Pat Fiddis

Nanaimo Branch Library, 90 Commercial St., Nanaimo BC V9R 5G2 – 250/753-1154; Fax: 250/754-1483 – Branch Head, Leif Rosvold

Wellington Branch Library, 3032 Barons Rd., Nanaimo BC V9T 4B5 – 250/758-5544; Fax: 250/758-7513 – Branch Head, Laurene Miller

Parksville Branch Library, 162 Morrison Ave., PO Box 508, Parksville BC V9P 2G6 – 250/248-3841; Fax: 250/248-0170 – Branch Head, Vivienne Wilson

Port Alberni Branch Library, 4245 Wallace St., Port Alberni BC V9Y 3Y6 – 250/723-9511; Fax: 250/723-5366 – Branch Head, Mary Howarth

Port Alice Branch Library, Marine Dr., PO Box 190, Port Alice BC V0N 2N0 – 250/284-3554; Fax: 250/284-3554 – Branch Head, Cheryl Reaume

Port Clements Branch Library, 35 Cedar Ave. West, PO Box 283, Port Clements BC V0T 1R0 – 250/557-4402; Fax: 250/557-4402 – Branch Head, Sheila Heit

Port Hardy Branch Library, 7110 Market St., PO Box 251, Port Hardy BC V0N 2P0 – 250/949-6661; Fax: 250/949-6600 – Branch Head, Barbara Bruner

Port McNeill Branch Library, #4, Broughton Plaza, PO Box 786, Port McNeill BC V0N 2R0 – 250/956-3669; Fax: 250/956-3669 – Branch Head, Bonnie Vandervalk

Port Renfrew Branch Library, General Delivery, Elementary School, Port Renfrew BC V0S 1K0 – 250/647-5423; Fax: 250/647-5534 – Branch Head, Joan Levy

Quadra Island Branch Library, Heriot Bay, 712 Cramer Rd., PO Box 310, Quadra Island BC V0P 1H0 – 250/285-2216; Fax: 250/285-2216 – Branch Head, Barbara Van Orden

Qualicum Beach Branch Library, #101, 660 Primrose St., PO Box 397, Qualicum Beach BC V9K 1S9 – 250/752-6121; Fax: 250/752-6630 – Branch Head, Diana Wilson

Queen Charlotte Branch Library, 138 Bay St., PO Box 339, Queen Charlotte City BC V0T 1S0 – 250/559-4518; Fax: 250/559-4518 – Branch Head, Marnie Andrews

Sandspit Branch Library, Seabreeze Plaza, PO Box 228, Sandspit BC V0T 1T0 – 250/637-2247; Fax: 250/637-2247 – Branch Head, Adriana Spighi

Sayward Branch Library, Sayward Centre Mall, 641C Kelsey Way, PO Box 310, Sayward BC V0P 1R0 – 250/282-5551; Fax: 250/282-5551 – Branch Head, Heather Sprout

Sidney/North Saanich Branch Library, 10091 Resthaven Dr., Sidney BC V8L 3G3 – 250/656-0944; Fax: 250/656-6400 – Branch Head, Wendy Gibbs

Sointula Branch Library, PO Box 187, Sointula BC V0N 3E0 – 250/973-6493; Fax: 250/973-6493 – Branch Head, Denise Aleksich

Sooke Branch Library, 2065 Anna Marie Rd., PO Box 468, Sooke BC V0S 1N0 – 250/642-3022; Fax: 250/642-3994 – Branch Head, Marilyn Boes

Tahsis Branch Library, 977 South Maquinna Rd., PO Box 458, Tahsis BC V0P 1X0 – 250/934-6621; Fax: 250/943-6621 – Branch Head, Penelope Leach

Tofino Branch Library, 121 - 3rd St., PO Box 97, Tofino BC V0R 2Z0 – 250/725-3713; Fax: 250/725-3713 – Branch Head, Linda White

Ucluelet Branch Library, 1768 Peninsula, PO Box 247, Ucluelet BC V0R 3A0 – 250/726-4642; Fax: 250/726-4642 – Branch Head, Ann Novak

Union Bay Branch Library, 5527 Island Hwy., PO Box 81, Union Bay BC V0R 3B0 – 250/335-2433; Fax: 250/335-2433 – Branch Head, Bryanna Grogan

Woss Public Branch Library, PO Box 5280, Woss BC V0N 3P0 – 250/281-2263; Fax: 250/281-2263 – Branch Head, Lori Kaube

## Integrated Public Library System with Member Libraries

### CARIBOO LIBRARY NETWORK

Network Office, #2, 487 Borland St., Williams Lake BC V2G 1R9 – 250/392-3637; Fax: 250/392-7399; Email: admin@cln.bc.ca; Symbol: BWLCR

Director of Libraries, Colleen Swift

100 Mile House Library, PO Box 278, 100 Mile House BC V0K 2E0 – Wendy Hamblin

Alexis Creek Branch, General Delivery, Alexis BC V0L 1A0 – 250/394-4346

Alkali Lake Branch, General Delivery, Alkali Lake BC V0L 1B0 – 250/440-5618

Anahim Lake Branch, General Delivery, Anahim Lake BC V0L 1C0 – 250/742-3235 – Librarian, Sue Glenn

Big Lake Branch, General Delivery, Big Lake BC V0L 1G0

Bridge Lake Branch, General Delivery, Bridge Lake BC V0K 1E0 – 250/593-4545

Forest Grove Branch, PO Box 8, Forest Grove BC V0K 1M0 – 250/397-2927 – Librarian, Mary Bourne

Horsefly Branch, PO Box 48, Horsefly BC V0L 1L0 – 250/620-3345

Lac La Hache Branch, PO Box 246, Lac La Hache BC V0K 1T0 – 250/396-7642 – Librarian, Elva Ogden

Likely Branch, PO Box 86, Likely BC V0L 1N0 – 250/790-2234 – Librarian, Janis Ulrich

McLeese Lake Branch, PO Box 100, McLeese Lake BC V0L 1P0 – 250/297-6533 – Librarian, Evelyn Suski

Nazko Branch, RR#5, Quesnel BC V2J 3H9 – Librarian, Marlene Cline, 604/992-8626

Quesnel Library, 593 Barlow Ave., Quesnel BC V2J 2C5 – 250/992-7912; Fax: 250/992-9882 – Librarian, Barbara McKenzie

Tatla Lake Branch, General Delivery, Tatla Lake BC V0L 1V0 – 250/476-1242 – Librarian, Jean Fell

Wells Branch, PO Box 35, Wells BC V0K 2R0 – 250/994-3424

Williams Lake Branch, 110 Oliver St., Williams Lake BC V2G 1L8 – 250/392-3630; Fax: 250/392-3518; Email: wlake@cln.bc.ca – Librarian, Lillian Mack

### THOMPSON-NICOLA REGIONAL DISTRICT LIBRARY SYSTEM

Administration Centre, 906 Laval Cres., Kamloops BC V2C 5P5 – 250/374-8866; Fax: 250/374-8355; Email: postmaster@tnrdlib.bc.ca; URL: http://www.tnrdlib.bc.ca

Director of Libraries, Alice Dalton

Reference Librarian, Alex MacDonald

Manager of Library & Support Services, Kevin Kierans

Ashcroft Library, 201 Brink St., PO Box 789, Ashcroft BC V0K 1A0 – 250/453-9042; Fax: 250/453-9042 – Branch Head, Margaret Vallance

Barrière Library, 643 Barriere Town Rd., PO Box 100, Barriere BC V0E 1E0 – 250/672-5811; Fax: 250/672-5811 – Branch Head, Linda Kelley

Blue River Library, PO Box 2, Blue River BC V0E 1J0 – 250/673-8235; Fax: 250/673-8235 – Branch Head, Judith Mitchell

Cache Creek Library, 1390 Quartz Rd., PO Box 429, Cache Creek BC V0K 1H0 – 250/457-9953; Fax: 250/457-9953 – Branch Head, Fran White

Chase Library, 614 Shuswap Ave., PO Box 590, Chase BC V0E 1M0 – 250/679-3331; Fax: 250/679-3331 – Branch Head, Jill Bewza

Clearwater Library, RR#1, PO Box 1913, Clearwater BC V0E 1N0 – 250/674-2543; Fax: 250/674-2543 – Branch Head, Darlene Cowie

Clinton Library, 1506 Tingley St., PO Box 550, Clinton BC V0K 1K0 – 250/459-7752; Fax: 250/459-7752 – Branch Head, Catheryn Munro

Kamloops Library, #101, 63 Victoria St. West, Kamloops BC V2C 6L4 – 250/372-5145; Fax: 250/372-5614 – Branch Head, Alex MacDonald

Logan Lake Library, #70, 150 Opal Dr., PO Box 310, Logan Lake BC V0K 1W0 – 250/523-6745; Fax: 250/523-6745 – Branch Head, Sophie Douglas

Lytton Library, PO Box 220, Lytton BC V0K 1Z0 – 250/455-2521; Fax: 250/455-2521 – Branch Head, Shirley Mountford

Merritt Library, 2058 Granite Ave., PO Box 1510, Merritt BC V1K 2B0 – 250/378-4737; Fax: 250/378-3706 – Branch Head, Deborha Merrick

North Kamloops Library, 795 Tranquille Rd., North Kamloops BC V2B 3J3 – 250/554-1124; Fax: 250/376-3825 – Branch Head, Michael Killick

Savona Library, 640 Tingley St., PO Box 169, Savona BC V0K 2J0 – 250/373-2666; Fax: 250/373-2666 – Branch Head, Sandra Rawson

## Federated Public Library System

Burnaby: InterLINK Federated Public Library System, #110, 6545 Bonsor Ave., Burnaby BC V5H 1H3 – 604/437-8441; Fax: 604/430-8595 – Acting Director, Stan Pukesh

## Public Library Associations

Alert Bay Public Library, PO Box 208, Alert Bay BC V0N 1A0 – 250/974-5721; Fax: 250/974-5470 – Librarian, Joyce M. Wilby

Bowen Island Public Library, 6 Cates Hill, 495 Mt. Gardner Rd., PO Box 10, Bowen Island BC V0N 1G0 – 604/947-9788; Fax: 604/947-0148 – Librarian, Tina Nielsen

Burns Lake Public Library, 613 Government St., PO Box 449, Burns Lake BC V0J 1E0 – 250/692-3192; Fax: 250/692-7488; Symbol: BBUL – Chief Librarian, Gwynne Nelson; Children's Librarian, Linda Palmer

Castlegar & District Public Library, 1005 - 3 St., Castlegar BC V1N 2A2 – 250/365-7765; Email: ENVOY: ILL.BCD – Librarian, Judy Wearmouth; Assistant Librarian, Kay Ross; Assistant Librarian, Julie Kalesnikoff

Chetwynd Public Library, 5012 - 46 St., PO Box 1420, Chetwynd BC V0C 1J0 – 250/788-2559; Fax: 250/788-2186 – Librarian, Fay Asleson

Cranbrook Public Library, 20 - 17 Ave. North, Cranbrook BC V1C 3W8 – 250/426-4063; Fax: 250/426-2098; Symbol: BCR – Director, Patricia Adams

Creston Public Library, 205 - 7 Ave. North, PO Box 1639, Creston BC V0B 1G0 – 250/428-4141; Fax: 250/428-4703 – Chief Librarian, Michelle Southam

Elkford Public Library, 816 Michel Rd., PO Box 280, Elkford BC V0B 1H0 – 250/865-2912; Fax: 250/865-2460 – Librarian, Sharon Gumowsky

Fernie Public Library, 592 - 3 Ave., PO Box 448, Fernie BC V0B 1M0 – 250/423-4458; Fax: 250/423-3050; Symbol: BF – Librarian, Diane Sharp

Fort Nelson Public Library, PO Box 330, Fort Nelson BC V0C 1R0 – 250/774-6777; Fax: 250/774-6777; Symbol: BFN – Librarian, Nola Newman

Fort St. James Public Library, 389 Stuart Dr., PO Box 729, Fort St. James BC V0J 1P0 – 250/996-7431; Fax: 250/996-2248; Email: fortlib@glynx.com – Librarian, Kay Biron

Fort St. John Public Library, 10015 - 100 Ave., Fort St. John BC V1J 1Y7 – 250/785-3731; Fax: 250/785-1510; Symbol: BFSJ – Director, Angela Mehmel

Fraser Lake Public Library, PO Box 520, Fraser Lake BC V0J 1S0 – 250/699-8888; Fax: 250/699-8899 – Head Librarian, Judith Loza

Fruitvale: Beaver Valley Public Library, PO Box 429, Fruitvale BC V0G 1L0 – 250/367-7114; Fax: 250/367-7130; Symbol: BFBV – Acting Chief Librarian, Dianne Kniss

Gibsons & District Public Library, 470 South Fletcher Rd., PO Box 109, Gibsons BC V0N 1V0 – 604/886-

2130; Fax: 604/886-2689; Email: gibsons_library@sunshine.net – Chief Librarian, Dace Beggs
Goldbridge Public Library, General Delivery, Goldbridge BC V0K 1P0 – 250/238-2437 – Contact, Sheena Aitken – Branch of Lillooet Area Public Library
Grand Forks & District Public Library, PO Box 1539, Grand Forks BC V0H 1H0 – 250/442-3944; Fax: 250/442-2645 – Librarian, Lorraine Kelley
Granisle Public Library, PO Box 550, Granisle BC V0J 1W0 – 250/697-2713; Fax: 250/697-2306; Symbol: BGR – Community Librarian, Sherry Smith
Greenwood Public Library, 346 South Copper St., PO Box 279, Greenwood BC V0H 1J0 – 250/445-6111; Email: bgreill@awinc.com; Symbol: BGRE – Librarian, Judy Foucher
Hazelton District Public Library, PO Box 323, Hazelton BC V0J 1Y0 – 250/842-5961; Fax: 250/842-2176; Symbol: BHA – Librarian, Janet Willson
Houston Public Library, PO Box 840, Houston BC V0J 1Z0 – 250/845-2256; Fax: 250/845-2088; Email: library2@netshop.net; Symbol: BH – Librarian, Janet Marren
Hudson's Hope Library, PO Box 269, Hudson's Hope BC V0C 1V0 – 250/783-9414; Fax: 250/783-5788; Symbol: BHH – Librarian, Wendy McIver
Invermere Public Library, PO Box 989, Invermere BC V0A 1K0 – 250/342-6416; Fax: 250/342-6416; Symbol: BIN – Librarian, Elizabeth Burke
Kaslo & District Public Library, PO Box 760, Kaslo BC V0G 1M0 – 250/353-2942; Fax: 250/353-7559; Symbol: BKASL – Community Librarian, Denise Fournier
Kemano Public Library, PO Box 90, Kemano BC V0T 1K0 – 250/634-5495; Fax: 250/634-5255; Symbol: BKE – Librarian, Judith Halland
Kimberley Public Library, 115 Spokane St., Kimberley BC V1A 2E5 – 250/427-3112; Fax: 250/427-7157; Symbol: BKI – Librarian, Beverley J. Varty
Kitimat Public Library, 940 Wakashan Ave., Kitimat BC V8C 2G3 – 250/632-2665; Fax: 250/632-2630; Symbol: BKIT – Chief Librarian, Mike Burris
Lillooet Area Public Library, PO Box 939, Lillooet BC V0K 1V0 – 250/256-7944; Fax: 250/256-4037 – Librarian, Sheila Pfeiffer – See also following branches: Bridge River Public Library, Goldbridge Public Library
McBride & District Public Library, 241 Dominion St., PO Box 489, McBride BC V0J 2E0 – 250/569-2411; Fax: 250/569-2411; Email: ENVOY: ILL.BMB – Librarian, Margaret Griffiths
Midway Public Library, PO Box 268, Midway BC V0H 1M0 – 250/449-2620; Fax: 250/449-2616; Symbol: BM – Librarian, Rosemary Santopinto
Nakusp Public Library, 92 - 6 Ave. NW, PO Box 297, Nakusp BC V0G 1R0 – 250/265-3363; Fax: 250/265-3788; Email: ENVOY: ILL.BNA – Librarian, Evelyn Goodell
Pemberton & District Public Library, PO Box 430, Pemberton BC V0N 2L0 – 604/894-6916; Fax: 604/894-6916; Symbol: BPE – Librarian, Janet Naylor
Pender Island Public Library, RR#1, PO Box 12, Pender Island BC V0N 2M0 – 250/629-3722; Fax: 250/629-3788; Symbol: BPI – Librarian, Susan St. John
Powell River District Public Library, 4411 Michigan Ave., Powell River BC V8A 2S3 – 604/485-4796; Fax: 604/485-2913; Symbol: BPRDP – Chief Librarian, Elaine Julian
Rossland Public Library, PO Box 190, Rossland BC V0G 1Y0 – 250/362-7611; Fax: 250/362-5399; Symbol: BR – Library Director, Myra Skaronski
Salmo Public Library, 120 - 4th St., PO Box 458, Salmo BC V0G 1Z0 – 250/357-2312; Fax: 250/357-2596 – Librarian, June Stockdale
Salt Spring Island Public Library, 129 McPhillips Ave., Salt Spring Island BC V8K 2T6 – 250/537-4666; Fax: 250/537-4666; Symbol: BGSI – Chair, Lois Slotten; Chief Librarian, Norma Keech; Reference Librarian, Anthony Burridge, 250/537-5029; Children's Librarian, Merle Sheffield, 250/537-9520
Sechelt Public Library Association, 5520 Trail Ave., PO Box 2104, Sechelt BC V0N 3A0 – 604/885-3260; Fax: 604/885-5183; Symbol: BSE – Librarian, Rose Toenders
Shalalth: Bridge River Public Library, PO Box 19, Shalalth BC V0N 3C0 – 250/259-8242 – Contact, Edith Lovey – Branch of Lillooet Area Public Library
Smithers Public Library, PO Box 55, Smithers BC V0J 2N0 – 250/847-3043
Sparwood Public Library, 110 Pine Ave., PO Box 1060, Sparwood BC V0B 2G0 – 250/425-2299; Fax: 250/425-0229; Symbol: BSPA – Librarian, James Bertoia
Squamish Public Library, PO Box 1039, Squamish BC V0N 3G0 – 604/892-3110; Fax: 604/892-1083; Symbol: BSQ – Librarian, Maureen Painter
Stewart Public Library, PO Box 546, Stewart BC V0T 1W0 – 250/636-2380; Fax: 250/636-9247 – Librarian, Joanne Hoffman
Terrace Public Library, 4610 Park Ave., Terrace BC V8G 1V6 – 250/638-8177; Fax: 250/635-6207; Symbol: BTE – Librarian, Ed Curell
Tumbler Ridge Library, 340 Front St., PO Box 70, Tumbler Ridge BC V0C 2W0 – 250/242-4778; Fax: 250/242-4707; Email: tr-lib2@pris.bc.ca; URL: http://sun.pris.bc.ca/tr-library/ – Librarian, Peggy Holden
Valemount Public Library, 1070 Main St., PO Box 368, Valemount BC V0E 2Z0 – 250/566-4367; Fax: 250/566-4278; Email: bvale@cancom.net; Symbol: BVALE – Librarian, Linda Hedberg
Vanderhoof Public Library, PO Bag 6000, Vanderhoof BC V0J 3A0 – 250/567-4060; Fax: 250/567-4060; Email: ENVOY: ILL.BVDH – Librarian, Jane Gray
Victoria: View Royal Public Library, 279 Island Hwy., Victoria BC V9B 1G4 – 250/479-2723; Fax: 250/479-6246; Symbol: BVIVR – Librarian, Maxeen Brookhart
Whistler Public Library, 4329 Main St., PO Box 95, Whistler BC V0N 1B0 – 604/932-5564; Fax: 604/932-0664; Email: bw.ill@whistler.net – Head Librarian, Joan Richoz

## Reading Centres

Atlin Public Library, PO Box 208, Atlin BC V0W 1A0 – 250/651-7572 – Librarian, Carol Boyko
Brisco Reading Centre, PO Box 50, Brisco BC V0A 1B0 – 250/346-3229 – Librarian, Ruth Wingert
Burton Community Reading Centre, PO Box 142, Burton BC V0G 1E0 – 250/265-4509 – Librarian, Twyla Davies
Crawford Bay: Eastshore Community Reading Centre, PO Box 85, Crawford Bay BC V0B 1E0 – 250/227-9457 – Librarian, Cathy Poch
Dease Lake Reading Centre, PO Box 237, Dease Lake BC V0C 1L0 – 250/771-3636 – Librarian, Carolyn Moore
Edgewater Reading Centre, PO Box 129, Edgewater BC V0A 1E0 – 250/347-9558 – Librarian, Linda Prudden
Edgewood: Inonoaklin Valley Reading Centre, PO Box 129, Edgewood BC V0G 1J0 – 250/269-7212 – Librarian, Susan Bampton
Fauquier Community Reading Centre, PO Box 99, Fauquier BC V0G 1K0 – 250/269-7348 – Librarian, Anna Siebold
Grasmere Reading Centre, PO Box 75, Grasmere BC V0B 1R0 – 250/887-3487 – Librarian, Bonnie Crosson
Lions Bay Reading Centre, 400 Centre Rd., PO Box 326, Lions Bay BC V0N 2E0 – 604/921-6944 – Librarian, Mansje More
Madeira Park: Pender Harbour Reading Centre, PO Box 278, Madeira Park BC V0N 2H0 – 604/883-2983 – Librarian, Anne Wutzke
Mayne Island Reading Centre, Comp. 38, Miner's Bay Rd., Mayne Island BC V0N 2J0 – Librarian, Terry Harvey
Moyie Reading Centre, General Delivery, PO Box 124, Moyie BC V0B 2A0 – 250/829-0508 – Librarian, Arlene Pervin
New Denver Reading Centre, PO Box 38, New Denver BC V0G 1S0 – 250/358-2221 – Chairperson, Agnes Emary
Riondel Community Reading Centre, PO Box 29, Riondel BC V0B 2B0 – 250/225-3494 – Librarian, Edith Nelson
Roberts Creek Reading Centre, General Delivery, Roberts Creek BC V0N 2W0 – 604/885-9401; Fax: 604/886-7973 – Librarian, Allan Case
Saturna Island Reading Centre, PO Box 131, Saturna Island BC V0N 2Y0 – 250/539-5908 – Librarian, Marjorie Nelson
Telkwa Reading Centre, PO Box 313, Telkwa BC V0J 2X0 – 250/846-9286 – Librarian, Christine Tessier
Wardner: Steeples' View Reading Centre, PO Box 79, Wardner BC V0B 2J0 – 250/429-3625 – Librarian, Tamara Ekman

## Special & College Libraries & Resource Centres

### 100 MILE HOUSE

BC Courthouse Library Society, Courthouse, POBox 1628, 100 Mile House BC V0K 2E0

### ABBOTSFORD

Solicitor General Canada - Matsqui Institution - Library, POBox 2500, Abbotsford BC V2S 4P3 – 604/859-4841, ext.313; Fax: 604/850-8375; Symbol: BAMIS – Librarian, Jill Hummerstone
  Regional Psychiatric Centre (Pacific) - Library, POBox 3000, Abbotsford BC V2S 4P4 – 604/853-7464, ext.259; Fax: 604/853-6992; Symbol: BARP – Contract Librarian, Jennifer Joslin
University College of the Fraser Valley - Library, 33844 King Rd., Abbotsford BC V2S 7M9 – 604/854-4510; Fax: 604/853-8055; Email: harris@ucfv.bc.ca; URL: http://www.ucfv.bc.ca/library/; Symbol: BCLF
  Director of Libraries, W.E. Harris
  Technical Services, Judy Inouye
  Public Services, Anne Knowlan
Western Pentecostal Bible College - Lorne Philip Hudson Memorial Library, POBox 1700, Abbotsford BC V2S 7E7 – 604/853-7491, local 30; Fax: 604/853-8951
  Librarian, Laurence M. Van Kleek
  Library Work Supervisor, Darlene H. Van Kleek
  Library Technologist, Leona Krause

### AGASSIZ

Pacific Agri-Food Research Centre (Agassiz) - Library, 6947 Hwy. 7, POBox 1000, Agassiz BC V0M 1A0 – 604/796-2221, ext.250; Fax: 604/796-0359; Email: boydl@em.agr.ca; Symbol: BAGAG – Librarian, Lynne Stack Boyd
Solicitor General Canada - Kent Institution - Library, POBox 1500, Agassiz BC V0M 1A0 – 604/796-2121, ext.467; Fax: 604/796-9563; Symbol: BAKI – Librarian, Catherine Ings
  Mountain Institution - Library, POBox 1600, Agassiz BC V0M 1A0 – 604/796-2231, ext.484; Fax: 604/796-1450; Symbol: BAMI – Librarian, Joanne Bean

### ALERT BAY

U'mista Cultural Society – Library, POBox 253, Alert Bay BC V0N 1A0 – 250/974-5403; Fax: 250/974-5499 – Collections Manager, Juanita Pascos

**BURNABY**

Association of British Columbia Teachers of English as an Additional Language – Mel Henderson Collection, #177, 4664 Lougheed Hwy., Burnaby BC V5C 5T5 – 604/294-8325; Fax: 604/294-8355 – Librarian, Diane Jones

BC Hydro - Information Centre, #B02, 6911 Southpoint Dr., Burnaby BC V3N 4X8 – 604/528-3065; Fax: 604/528-3137; Symbol: BCH – Information Services, Manager, H. Elizabeth McLaren

BC Tel Information - Resource Centre, #5, 3777 Kingsway, Burnaby BC V5H 3Z7 – 604/432-2671; Fax: 604/435-0510; Email: shelley_tegart@bctel.com; Symbol: BVABT – Manager, IRC, Shelley Tegart

British Columbia Institute of Technology - Library Services, 3700 Willingdon Ave., Burnaby BC V5G 3H2 – 604/432-8371; Fax: 604/430-5443; Email: ENVOY: BCIT; Symbol: BBIT
- Chief Librarian, Brigitte Peter-Cherneff, 604/432-8360
- Acquisitions/Serials, Coordinator, Robert Roy, 604/432-8364
- Cataloguer, Yu Mei Choi, 604/432-8922
- Systems Librarian, Merilee MacKinnon, 604/432-8647
- Pacific Marine Training Institute, Librarian, Linda Matsuba, 604/985-0622, ext.330
- Electronics Librarian, Linda Matsuba
- Public Services, Coordinator, Tony O'Kelly
- Academic Studies Librarian, Merilee Mackinnon
- Business, Gerry Weeks, 604/432-8856
- Engineering, Margot Allingham, 604/432-8793
- Health, Ana Ferrinho, 604/432-8546
- Trades, Tony O'Kelly, 604/432-8764

Burnaby Hospital – H.H.W. Brooke Memorial Library, 3935 Kincaid St., Burnaby BC V5G 2X6 – 604/431-4734; Fax: 604/431-4734; Email: hlim@a.teleserve.ca – Librarian, Houng Lim

Columbia College - Library, 6037 Marlborough Ave., Burnaby BC V5H 3L6 – 604/430-6422; Fax: 604/430-6761 – Head Librarian, Yvonne de Souza

Golder Associates Ltd. - Library, #500, 4260 Still Creek Dr., Burnaby BC V5C 6C6 – 604/298-6623; Fax: 604/298-5253; Email: lwills@golder.com; Symbol: GA – Librarian, Lisa Wills

Greater Vancouver Regional District - Library, 4330 Kingsway, Burnaby BC V5H 4G8 – 604/432-6335; Fax: 604/432-6445; Email: fchristo@gvrd.bc.ca; URL: http://www.gvrd.bc.ca; Symbol: BBGV – Chief Librarian, Frances Christopherson, Email: fchristo@gvrd.bc.ca

Health Canada - Health Protection Branch - Regional Library, 3155 Willingdon Green, Burnaby BC V5G 4P2 – 604/666-3147; Fax: 604/666-3149 – Librarian, Elizabeth Hardacre

Kerfoot, Cameron & Company Law Office - Library, #314, 9600 Cameron St., Burnaby BC V3J 7N3 – 604/421-7144; Fax: 604/421-2912 – Berry Kerfoot

MacMillan Bloedel Research (MB Research) - Technical Library, 4225 Kincaid St., Burnaby BC V5G 4P5 – 604/439-8602; Fax: 604/439-8627; Symbol: MACB
- Research Librarian, Marjory Jardine, Email: me.jardine@mbltd.com
- Library Technician, Lana Sloan

Mechanical Contractors Association of British Columbia – Library, 3210 Lake City Way, Burnaby BC V5A 3A4 – 604/420-9714; Fax: 604/420-0127

MPR Teltech Ltd. - Information Resources Centre, 8999 Nelson Way, Burnaby BC V5A 4B5 – 604/293-5381; Fax: 604/293-5787; Email: ENVOY: MPR.LIB Patrice Hall; Symbol: BBMT – Reference Librarian, Patrice Hall

Simon Fraser University - W.A.C. Bennett Library, 8888 Barnet Hwy., Burnaby BC V5A 1S6 – 604/291-3265; Fax: 604/291-4908; Email: libloan@sfu.ca; URL: http://www.lib.sfu.ca/; Symbol: BVAS
- University Librarian, Ted C. Dobb
- Collections Management, Division Head, Sharon Thomas, 604/291-3263
- Loans/Circulation, Head, Giselle Pomerleau, 604/291-3274
- Processing Division, Head, Mary Harris, 604/291-3184
- Reference, Head, Perce Groves, 604/291-3252
- Research Data Library, Librarian, Walter Piovesan, 604/291-1313
- Systems & Monographs, Head, Vacant, 604/291-3184
- Belzberg Branch, Head Librarian, Karen Marotz, 604/291-5054
- Business, Librarian, Elaine Fairey, 604/291-3044
- Business, Librarian, Sylvia Bell, 604/291-3044
- Inter-Library Loans, Head, Todd Mundle, 604/291-5596

**BURNS LAKE**

BC Courthouse Library Society - Library, 508 Yellowhead Hwy., POBox 244, Burns Lake BC V0J 1E0

**CAMPBELL RIVER**

BC Courthouse Library Society – Library, Courthouse, 500 - 13 Ave., Campbell River BC V9W 6P1

North Island College - Campbell River Campus Library, 1480 Elm St., Campbell River BC V9W 3A6 – 250/286-8957; Fax: 250/287-4537; Symbol: BCOMN – Library Clerk, Marion Summerer, Email: summerer@nic.bc.ca

Strathcona Park Lodge & Outdoor Education Centre – Library, POBox 2160, Campbell River BC V9W 5C9 – 250/286-3122; Fax: 250/286-6010 – COLT Director, Chris Lawrence

**CASTLEGAR**

BC Courthouse Library Society - Library, 555 Columbia Ave., Castlegar BC V1N 1G8

Selkirk College - Library, 301 Frank Beinder Way, POBox 1200, Castlegar BC V1N 3J1 – 250/365-1229; Fax: 250/365-7259; URL: http://www.selkirk.bc.ca; Symbol: BCS
- Library Director, John Mansbridge, 250/365-7292, ext.263
- Reference Librarian, Ron Welwood
- Technical Services Librarian, Judy Deon

West Kootenay/Boundry AIDS Network, Outreach & Support Society – Library, 903 - 4th St., Castlegar BC V1N 3P3 – 250/365-2437; Fax: 250/304-2437; Toll Free: 1-800-421-2437 – Claire Davison

**CHASE**

BC Courthouse Library Society - Library, POBox 581, Chase BC V0E 1M0

**CHETWYND**

Northern Lights College - Chetwynd Campus Library, POBox 1180, Chetwynd BC V0C 1J0 – 250/788-2248; Fax: 250/788-9706 – Library Contact, Kathy Hecker

**CHILLIWACK**

BC Courthouse Library Society - Library, Courthouse, 9391 College St., Chilliwack BC V2P 4L7

University College of the Fraser Valley - Library, 45635 Yale Rd., Chilliwack BC V2P 6T4 – 604/795-2824; Fax: 604/792-2388; URL: http://www.ucfv.bc.ca/library/; Symbol: BCLF
- Director, W.E. Harris, Email: Harris@ucfv.bc.ca
- Public Services Librarian, Anne Knowlan

**CLEARBROOK**

Columbia Bible College - Library, 2940 Clearbrook Rd., Clearbrook BC V2T 2Z8 – 604/853-3358; Fax: 604/853-3063 – Librarian, David Giesbrecht, 604/853-3567

**COQUITLAM**

Pacific Institute for Advanced Study – Library, 936 Thermal Dr., Coquitlam BC V3J 6R8 – 604/469-7946; Fax: 604/469-3552

Registered Psychiatric Nurses Association of British Columbia – Library, #251, 3041 Anson Ave., Coquitlam BC V3B 2H6 – 604/294-6539; Fax: 604/944-4945

Warnock Hersey Professional Services Ltd. - Library, 211 Schoolhouse St., Coquitlam BC V3K 4X9 – 604/520-3321; Fax: 604/524-9186 – Librarian, Regina Frackowiak

**COURTENAY**

BC Courthouse Library Society - Library, Courthouse, 420 Cumberland, Courtenay BC V9N 5M6

North Island College - Comox Valley Campus Library, 2300 Ryan Rd., Courtenay BC V9N 8N6 – 250/334-5001; Fax: 250/334-5291; Email: thomas@nic.bc.ca; Symbol: BCOMN
- Librarian, Shiloa Thomas
- Library Assistant, Helen Wickins
- Library Clerk, Debby Scott

**CRANBROOK**

BC Courthouse Library Society - Library, Courthouse, 102 - 11 Ave. South, Cranbrook BC V1C 2P2

College of the Rockies - Library, POBox 8500, Cranbrook BC V1C 5L7 – 250/489-2751; Fax: 250/489-8256; Email: reference@cotr.bc.ca; URL: http://www.cotr.bc.ca; Symbol: BCRK
- Director, Learning Resources Centre, Heather Schneider
- Public Services Librarian, Barbara Janzen
- Coordinator LRC-Teleconferencing, Jim Duncan

**CRESTON**

BC Courthouse Library Society - Library, 224 - 10th Ave. North, POBox 1790, Creston BC V0B 1G0

**DAWSON CREEK**

BC Courthouse Library Society - Library, Courthouse, 1201 - 103 Ave., Dawson Creek BC V1G 4J2

Northern Lights College - Dawson Creek Campus Library, 11401 - 8 St., Dawson Creek BC V1G 4G2 – 250/784-7533; Fax: 250/782-6069; Email: jbeavers@nlc.bc.ca; URL: http://www.nlc.bc.ca/; Symbol: BDCNL – Regional Librarian, Janet H. Beavers

**DELTA**

BC Courthouse Library Society - Library, 4450 Clarence Taylor Cres., Delta BC V4K 3W3

British Columbia Waterfowl Society – Library, 5191 Robertson Rd., RR#1, Delta BC V4K 3N2 – 604/946-6980; Fax: 604/946-6980

Souch Severide Law Office - Library, #220, 4977 Trennant St., Delta BC V4K 2K5 – 604/946-1249

**DEWDNEY**

The Canadian Orthodox Church – Library, 37323 Hawkins Pickle Rd., Dewdney BC V0M 1H0 – 604/826-9336; Fax: 604/820-9758 – Librarian, Father Moses Armstrong

**DUNCAN**

BC Courthouse Library Society - Library, Courthouse, 238 Government St., Duncan BC V9L 1A5

BC School District 65 - District Resource Centre, 2557 Beverly St., Duncan BC V9L 2X3 – 250/748-0321, ext.243; Fax: 250/748-3497 – Coordinator, John Caldwell

**FERNIE**

BC Courthouse Library Society - Library, Courthouse, PO Bag 1000, Fernie BC V0B 1M0

**FORT NELSON**

Northern Lights College - Fort Nelson Campus Library, POBox 860, Fort Nelson BC V0C 1R0 – 250/774-2741; Fax: 250/774-2750 – Library Contact, Alison Starr

**FORT ST. JOHN**

BC Courthouse Library Society - Library, Courthouse, 10600 - 100 St., Fort St. John BC V1J 4L6

Northern Lights College - Fort St. John Campus Library, POBox 1000, Fort St. John BC V1J 6K1 – 250/785-6213; Fax: 250/785-1294; Email: knoble@nlc.bc.ca; Symbol: BDCNL – Library Contact, Kathy Noble

**FORT STEELE**

Fort Steele Heritage Town - Research Library & Archives, General Delivery, Fort Steele BC V0B 1N0 – 250/489-3351; Fax: 250/489-2624; Symbol: OTHSC – Archivist/Librarian, Derryll White

**GOLDEN**

BC Courthouse Library Society - Library, 837 Park Dr., Golden BC V0A 1H0

**GRAND FORKS**

BC Courthouse Library Society - Library, 524 Central Ave., POBox 1059, Grand Forks BC V0H 1H0

**HOPE**

BC Courthouse Library Society - Library, 999 Water Ave., POBox 610, Hope BC V0X 1L0

**INVERMERE**

BC Courthouse Library Society - Library, Courthouse, 645 - 7th Ave., POBox 128, Invermere BC V0A 1K0

**KAMLOOPS**

BC Courthouse Library Society - Library, Courthouse, 455 Columbia St., Kamloops BC V2C 6K4 – 250/828-4385; Fax: 250/828-4734 – Denise Caldwell

BC School District 24 - Henry Grube Education Centre, 245 Kitcherner Cres., Kamloops BC V2B 1B9 – 250/376-2260; Fax: 250/376-7966 – Teacher/Librarian, Corinne Paravantes

Morelli, Chertkow Law Office - Library, #300, 180 Seymour St., Kamloops BC V2C 2E3 – 250/374-3344; Fax: 250/374-1144 – Library Assistant, Mary Buchanan

Royal Inland Hospital – Library, 311 Columbia St., Kamloops BC V2C 2T1 – 250/314-2234; Fax: 250/314-2333 – Manager, Library Services, Teresa Prior

University College of the Cariboo - Library, POBox 3010, Kamloops BC V2C 5N3 – 250/828-5300; Fax: 250/828-5313; Symbol: CR
- Director, Nancy Levesque, 250/828-5305
- Reference Librarian, Peter Peller, 250/828-5304
- Technical Services Librarian, Penny Haggarty, 250/828-5303

**KASLO**

Kaslo Arts Council – Langham Arts Instruction Library, POBox 1000, Kaslo BC V0G 1M0 – 250/353-2661; Fax: 250/353-7559

**KELOWNA**

BC Courthouse Library Society - Library, Courthouse, 1355 Water St., Kelowna BC V1Y 9R3 – 250/470-6980; Fax: 250/470-6995

Okanagan Symphony Society – Library, POBox 1120, Kelowna BC V1Y 7P8 – 250/763-7018; Fax: 250/763-3553 – Librarian, David Benda

Okanagan University College - KLO Road Campus Library, 1000 KLO Rd., Kelowna BC V1Y 4X8 – 250/762-5445; Fax: 250/762-9743; URL: http://www.okanagan.bc.ca; Symbol: BKOC – University College Library, Dean, G. Zilm
- North Kelowna Campus Library, 3333 College Way, Kelowna BC V1V 1V7 – 250/762-5445; Fax: 250/470-6003

Salloum Doak Law Office - Library, #200, 537 Leon Ave., Kelowna BC V1Y 2A9 – 250/763-4323; Fax: 250/763-4780; Email: salloum.doak@awinc.com
- Librarian, Pat Flett
- Library Assistant, Ab Estephan

Weddell, Horn & Company Law Office - Library, #1, 1737 Pandosy St., Kelowna BC V1Y 1R2 – 250/762-2011; Fax: 250/861-3980 – Librarian, Jennifer Finlay

**KITIMAT**

BC Courthouse Library Society - Library, 603 City Centre, Kitimat BC V8C 2N1

Wozney & Donaldson Law Office - Library, #366, City Centre, Kitimat BC V8C 1T6 – 250/632-7151; Fax: 250/632-7100; Email: rwozney@kitimat.sno.net – Manager, R.W. Wozney

**LAKE COWICHAN**

School District 66 (Lake Cowichan) - District Resource Center, POBox 980, Lake Cowichan BC V0R 2G0 – 250/749-3822; Fax: 250/749-3543 – Coordinator, Linda Nelson

**LANGLEY**

Eagles Nest Resource Centre, #13, 5965 - 205A St., Langley BC V3A 8C4 – 604/532-3107; Fax: 604/532-3109 – Ann Mebs

Fleming, Olson & Taneda - Library, 4038 - 200B St., Langley BC V3A 1N9 – 604/533-3411; Fax: 604/533-8749

Northwest Baptist Theological College - ACTS Library, POBox 790, Langley BC V3A 8B8 – 604/888-7511,ext.3906; Fax: 604/888-3354; Email: badke@charity.twu.ca – Librarian, W.B. Badke, Email: badke@charity.twu.ca

Recreation Vehicle Dealers Association of British Columbia – Library, #209, 20353 - 64 Ave., Langley BC V2Y 1N5 – 604/533-4200; Fax: 604/533-0795

Roofing Contractors Association of British Columbia – Library, 9734 - 201st St., Langley BC V1M 3E8 – 604/882-9734; Fax: 604/882-1744

Society of Christian Schools in BC – Library, 7600 Glover Rd., Langley BC V3A 6H4 – 604/888-6366; Fax: 604/888-2791 – Education Coordinator, J. Vanderhoek

Trinity Western University - Norma Marion Alloway Library, 7600 Glover Rd., Langley BC V2Y 1Y1 – 604/888-7511; Fax: 604/888-3786; Email: twiest@twu.ca; URL: http://www.twu.ca/Library.htm; Symbol: TWV
- Chief Librarian, David Twiest
- Reference Librarian, Ron Braid
- Media Librarian, Ted Goshulak
- Systems Librarian, Stan Olson
- Cataloguing Librarian, Rick Wiebe

**MAPLE RIDGE**

Dewdney-Alouette Railway Society – Library, 22520 - 116 Ave., Maple Ridge BC V2X 0S4 – 604/463-5311 – Archivist, John R. Maughan

**MASSET**

BC Courthouse Library Society - Library, 1666 Orr St., POBox 230, Masset BC V0T 1M0

**MERRITT**

BC Courthouse Library Society - Library, 1840 Nicola Ave., POBox 4400, Merritt BC V1K 1B8

**MISSION**

Solicitor General Canada - Mission Institution - Library, POBox 60, Mission BC V2V 4L8 – 604/826-1231, ext.325; Symbol: BMMI – Librarian, J. Joslin

University College of the Fraser Valley - Mission Campus Library, 33700 Prentis Ave., POBox 1000, Mission BC V2V 7B1 – 604/820-4587; Fax: 604/826-0681; URL: http://www.ucfv.bc.ca/library/; Symbol: BCLF – Director ol Libraries, W.E.C. Harris

Westminster Abbey - Seminary of Christ the King Library, POBox 30, Mission BC V2V 4L8 – 604/826-8975 – Librarian, Boniface Aicher

**NANAIMO**

BC Courthouse Library Society - Library, Courthouse, 35 Front St., Nanaimo BC V9R 5J1

Fisheries & Oceans Canada-Pacific Biological Station – Library, Hammond Bay Rd., POBox 3190, Nanaimo BC V9R 5K6 – 250/756-7071; Fax: 250/756-7053; Email: library@pbs.dfo.ca; Envoy: DFO.LIB.NANAIMO; Symbol: BNP – Head, Library Services, Gordon Miller

**NELSON**

BC Courthouse Library Society - Library, Courthouse, 320 Ward St., Nelson BC V1L 1S6

Chamber of Mines of Eastern British Columbia – Library of Government Geological Reports, 215 Hall St., Nelson BC V1L 5X4 – 250/352-5242; Fax: 250/352-7227

The Daily News Library, 266 Baker St., Nelson BC V1L 4H3 – 250/352-3552

Selkirk College - Nelson Campus Library, 2001 Silver King Rd., Nelson BC V1L 1C8 – 250/352-6601, ext.254 – Campus Librarian, Barb Cavalier

**NEW WESTMINSTER**

BC Courthouse Library Society - Library, The Law Courts, Begbie Sq., New Westminster BC V3M 1C9 – 604/660-8577; Fax: 604/660-1715 – Josephine Lord

Douglas College - Library, POBox 2503, New Westminster BC V3L 5B2 – 604/527-5568; Fax: 604/527-5193; Email: lib_media@douglas.bc.ca; URL: http://www.douglas.bc.ca/library.html; Symbol: CABNWD
- Director, Virginia Chisholm, 604/527-5182, Email: chisholmv@douglas.bc.ca
- Reference Librarian, Jean Cockburn, 604/527-5184
- Audio Visual Librarian, Susan Ashcroft, 604/527-5189
- Technical Services Librarian, Penny Swanson, 604/527-5259
- Collections Librarian, Joan Wenman, 604/527-5181
- Circulation Librarian, Patti Romanko, 604/527-5183
- Serials Librarian, Len McIver, 604/527-5190
- Extension Librarian, Mary Matthews, 604/527-5190
- Orientation Librarian, Sandra Hochstein, 604/527-5181
- Public Service Librarian, Diane Hewitt, 604/527-5184

Econotech Services Ltd. – Library, 852 Derwent Way, New Westminster BC V3M 5R1 – 604/526-4221; Fax: 604/526-1898; Toll Free: 1-800-463-5700; Symbol: ECON – Librarian, Norma Becker

HOPE International Development Agency – Hope Global Resource Centre, 214 - 6 St., New Westminster BC V3L 3A2 – 604/525-5481; Fax: 604/525-3471 – Coordinator/Resource Centre, Leah Libsekal

Justice Institute of British Columbia – Library, 715 McBride Blvd., New Westminster BC V3L 5T4 – 604/528-5594; Fax: 604/660-9637;

Email: april_haddad@sfu.ca; Symbol: BVAJI – Librarian, April Haddad

Royal Columbian Hospital – Library, 330 Columbia St. East, New Westminster BC V3L 3W7 – 604/520-4281; Fax: 604/520-4804 – Manager, S. Abzinger

**NORTH VANCOUVER**

Capilano College - Library, 2055 Purcell Way, North Vancouver BC V7J 3H5 – 604/984-4944; Fax: 604/984-1728; URL: http://www.capcollege.bc.ca; Symbol: BVAC
- College Librarian, Frieda Wiebe, 604/984-4943
- Reference Coordinator, George Modenesi, 604/986-1911, ext.2111
- Circulation Librarian, David Lambert, 604/986-1911, ext.2108
- Collections Librarian, Maureen Witney, 604/986-1911, ext.2141
- Technical Services Librarian, Sidney Myers, 604/986-1911, ext.1770
- Systems Librarian, Annette Lorek, 604/986-1911, ext.2143
- Media Production Supervisor, Edna Sakata, 604-986-1911, ext.2117

Environment Canada - Pacific & Yukon Region, 224 West Esplanade, North Vancouver BC V7M 3H7 – 604/666-5914; Fax: 604/666-1788; Email: nvan.library@ec.gc.ca; Symbol: BVAEP – Librarian, Andrew Fabro

EVS Consultants Ltd. – Library, 195 Pemberton Ave., North Vancouver BC V7P 2R4 – 604/986-4331; Fax: 604/662-8548 – Librarian, Rhona Karbusicky

Healing Our Spirit – Library, 319 Seymour Blvd. North, North Vancouver BC V7M 1A6 – 604/983-8774; Fax: 604/983-2667; Email: hoscdev@intergate.bc.ca – Community Development Officer, Barb Cowan

Insurance Corporation of BC - Information Resource Center, #249, 151 West Esplanade, North Vancouver BC V7M 3H9 – 604/661-6322; Fax: 604/443-7304; Email: ENVOY: ICBC.LIB; Symbol: ICBC
- Librarian/Manager, Grace Makarewicz
- Information Technician, Ida Bradd

Lions Gate Hospital – Carson Memorial Library, 231 East 15 St., North Vancouver BC V7L 2L7 – 604/988-3131; Fax: 604/984-5838 – Director, Sharon Lyons

**OLIVER**

BC Courthouse Library Society - Library, PO Bag 5000, Oliver BC V0H 1T0

**PENTICTON**

BC Courthouse Library Society - Library, Courthouse, 100 Main St., Penticton BC V2A 5A5

Okanagan University College - Penticton Campus Library, 583 Duncan Ave., Penticton BC V2A 8E1 – 250/492-4305; Fax: 250/490-3954

**PORT ALBERNI**

BC Courthouse Library Society - Library, Courthouse, 2999 - 4 Ave., Port Alberni BC V9Y 8A5

North Island College - Port Alberni Campus Library, 3699 Roger St., Port Alberni BC V9Y 8E3 – 250/724-8733; Fax: 250/724-8780; Email: krupninski@nicad3.nic.bc.ca; URL: http://www.nic.bc.ca; Symbol: BCOMN
- Library Assistant, Sherry Kropninski
- Library Technician, Monica Mooney

**PORT COQUITLAM**

BC Courthouse Library Society - Library, 2620 Mary Hill Rd., Port Coquitlam BC V3C 3B2

Riverview Hospital - Library Services, 500 Lougheed Hwy., Port Coquitlam BC V3C 4J2 – 604/524-7576; Fax: 604/524-7021; Email: library@bcmhs.bc.ca – Manager, Library Services, Patricia Fortin, 604/524-7018

**PORT HARDY**

BC Courthouse Library Society - Library, Mailbag 11,000, Port Hardy BC V0N 2P0

North Island College - Port Hardy Campus Library, POBox 901, Port Hardy BC V0N 2P0 – 250/949-2863; Fax: 250/949-2617; Email: newman@nic.bc.ca – Diane Newman

**POWELL RIVER**

BC Courthouse Library Society - Library, Courthouse, 6953 Alberni St., Powell River BC V8A 2B8

**PRINCE GEORGE**

BC Courthouse Library Society, Law Courts, JO Wilson Sq., 250 George St., Prince George BC V2L 5S2 – 250/614-2763; Fax: 250/614-2788 – Library Assistant, Julie Loerke

The Citizen Newspaper - Library, POBox 5700, Prince George BC V2L 5K9 – 250/562-2441; Fax: 250/562-7453 – Librarian, Leslie Barclay

College of New Caledonia - Library, 3330 - 22 Ave., Prince George BC V2N 1P8 – 250/562-2131; Fax: 250/561-5845; Email: cnclibrary@cnc.bc.ca; Symbol: BPGC
- Associate Director, Resource Centres, Katherine Plett
- Reference Librarian, Kathryn Ruffle
- Technical Services Librarian, Brenda Yee
- Orientation/Instruction Librarian, Sandra Chulka

Hope Heinrich Law Office - Library, 1598 - 6 Ave., Prince George BC V2L 5G7 – 250/563-0681; Fax: 250/562-3761 – Administrator, Ruth Langner

Prince George Regional Hospital – Medical Library, 2000 - 15 Ave., Prince George BC V2M 1S2 – 250/565-2219; Fax: 604/563-6850 – Librarian, Anne M. Allgaier

**PRINCE RUPERT**

BC Courthouse Library Society - Library, Courthouse, 100 Market Pl., Prince Rupert BC V8J 1B8

**QUESNEL**

BC Courthouse Library Society - Library, Courthouse, 350 Barlow Ave., Quesnel BC V2J 2C1

**REVELSTOKE**

BC Courthouse Library Society - Library, Courthouse, 1123 - 2nd St. West, POBox 2820, Revelstoke BC V0E 2S0

Canadian Avalanche Association – Library, POBox 2759, Revelstoke BC V0E 2S0 – 250/837-2435; Fax: 250/837-4624

**RICHMOND**

British Columbia Genealogical Society – BCGS Resource Centre, PO Box 88054, Lansdowne Mall, Richmond BC V6X 3T6 – 604/502-9119; Fax: 604/263-4952

Canadian Holistic Nurses Association – Archives, #209, 6051 Gilbert Rd., Richmond BC V7C 3V3 – 403/451-0043; Fax: 403/452-3276

Klohn-Crippen Consultants Ltd. – Library, 10200 Shellbridge Way, Richmond BC V6X 2W7 – 604/279-4315; Fax: 604/279-4300; Email: dawsone@rmd.klohn.com; Symbol: KLL – Library/Records Coordinator, Elaine Dawson

MacDonald Dettwiler and Associates Ltd. – Library, 13800 Commerce Pkwy., Richmond BC V6V 2Y3 – 604/278-3411; Fax: 604/278-2117; Symbol: MD – Librarian, Darlene Cripps

Triton Environmental Consultants Ltd. – Library, #120, 13511 Commerce Pkwy., Richmond BC V6V 2L1 – 604/279-2093; Fax: 604/279-2047; Email: LArchibald@Triton-Env.com; Symbol: BVAEN – Librarian, Louise Archibald

Union of BC Municipalities – Library, #15, 10551 Shellbridge Way, Richmond BC V6X 2W9 – 604/270-8226; Fax: 604/660-2271 – Technical Services Librarian, Frank Storey

Workers' Compensation Board - Library, 6951 Westminster Hwy., Richmond BC V7C 1C6 – 604/231-8450; Fax: 604/279-7608; Email: library@wcb.bc.ca; URL: http://www.wcb.bc.ca; Symbol: BVAWC – Librarian, Lance Nordstrom

**ROSSLAND**

BC Courthouse Library Society - Library, POBox 1448, Rossland BC V0G 1Y0

**SAANICHTON**

BC School District 63 - District Resource Centre, 2125 Keating Cross Rd., Saanichton BC V8M 2A5 – 250/652-7320; Fax: 250/544-1254; Email: Linda_Coupal@sd63.bc.ca; URL: http://www.sd63.bc.ca – Teacher-Librarian, Linda Coupal

**SALMON ARM**

BC Courthouse Library Society - Library, c/o Court Registry, POBox 100, Salmon Arm BC V1E 4S4

Okanagan University College - Salmon Arm Campus Library, 2552 Trans Canada Hwy. NE, Salmon Arm BC V1E 4N3 – 250/804-8851; Fax: 250/804-8852

**SECHELT**

BC Courthouse Library Society - Library, POBox 1488, Sechelt BC V0N 3A0

Capilano College - Sechelt Campus Library, 5627 Inlet Ave., Sechelt BC V0N 3A0 – 604/885-9310 – Becky Wayte

**SIDNEY**

Esperanto Association of Canada – Libraro Ludovika, POBox 2159, Sidney BC V8L 3S6 – 902/477-5251; Fax: 250/656-7012 – Librarian, Stevens T. Norvell Jr.

Fisheries & Oceans Canada-Institute of Ocean Sciences – Library, 9860 West Saanich Rd., POBox 6000, Sidney BC V8L 4B2 – 250/363-6392; Fax: 250/363-6749; Symbol: BVIEM – Librarian, Sharon Thomson

**SMITHERS**

BC Courthouse Library Society - Library, POBox 5000, Smithers BC V0J 2N0

**SQUAMISH**

BC Courthouse Library Society - Library, 38073 - 2nd Ave., POBox 1580, Squamish BC V0N 3G0

Capilano College - Squamish Campus Library, 1150 Carson Pl., Squamish BC V0N 3G0 – 604/892-5322 – Regional Assistant, Susan Herity

**SUMMERLAND**

Agriculture & Agri-Food Canada-Pacific Agri-Food Research Centre – Canadian Agriculture Library, Hwy. 97, Summerland BC V0H 1Z0 – 250/494-7711; Fax: 250/494-0755; Email: lbbsuag@ncccot.agr.ca; Symbol: BSUAG – Librarian, Margaret A. Watson

**SURREY**

BC Hydro - Powertech Labs Inc. – Library, 12388 - 88 Ave., Surrey BC V3W 7R7 – 604/590-7456; Fax: 604/590-5347; Symbol: BCH – Librarian, Janet Kibblewhite

BC Courthouse Library Society - Library, Courthouse, 14340 - 57 Ave., Surrey BC V3X 1B2

British Columbia Forestry Association – Library, 9800A - 140 St., Surrey BC V3T 4M5 – 604/582-0100; Fax: 604/582-0101 – Cheryl Zida

Forest Education BC – Green Timbers Forest Education Centre, 9800A - 140th St., Surrey BC V3T 4M5 – 604/582-7170; Fax: 604/582-0101 – Environmental Education Assistant, Michelle Kwok

Learning Disabilities Association of British Columbia – Resource Centre, #203, 15463 - 104 St., Surrey BC V3R 1N9 – 604/588-6322; Fax: 604/588-6344

Surrey Memorial Hospital – Library, 13750 - 96th Ave., Surrey BC V3V 1Z2 – 604/585-5666, ext.2467; Fax: 604/585-5540; Email: lhoward@smhpo1.hosp.gov.bc.ca; Symbol: SMH – Librarian, Linda Howard

### TERRACE

BC Courthouse Library Society - Library, Courthouse, 3408 Kalum St., Terrace BC V8G 2N6

Northwest Community College - Learning Resource Centre, 5331 McConnell Ave., Terrace BC V8G 4C2 – 250/638-5407; Fax: 250/635-3511; Email: barnes@noradm.nwcc.bc.ca; Symbol: BTENW
Coordinator, Patricia Barnes
Technical Services Librarian, Liz Ball

### TRAIL

Cominco Ltd. - Central Technical Library, Cominco Research, POBox 2000, Trail BC V1R 4S4 – 250/364-4408; Fax: 250/364-4456; Symbol: BTC
Licensing & Information Specialist, Stan Greenwood
Library Assistant, Randi Walsh

### TUMBLER RIDGE

Northern Lights College - Tumbler Ridge Campus Library, POBox 180, Tumbler Ridge BC V0C 2W0 – 250/242-5591; Fax: 250/242-3109 – Library Contact, Heidi Bevington

### VANCOUVER

Affiliation of Multicultural Societies & Service Agencies of BC – Resource Centre, 385 South Boundary Rd., Vancouver BC V5K 4S1 – 604/718-2777; Fax: 604/298-0747 – Research Coordinator, Bernard Bouska

AIDS Vancouver – Pacific AIDS Resource Centre Library, c/o Pacific AIDS Resource Centre, 1107 Seymour St., Vancouver BC V6B 5S8 – 604/681-2122; Fax: 604/893-2211 – Librarian, Janice Linton

Alexander, Holburn, Beaudin & Lang Law Office - Library, #2700, 700 West Georgia St., POBox 10057, Vancouver BC V7Y 1B8 – 604/688-1351; Fax: 604/669-7642; Email: ahblinfo@direct.ca – Librarian, Susan Daly

Asia Pacific Foundation of Canada – Library, #666, 999 Canada Pl., Vancouver BC V6C 3E1 – 604/684-5986; Fax: 604/681-1370 – Rachel Charron

Association for Educators of Gifted, Talented & Creative Children – Library, c/o British Columbia Teachers' Federation, #100, 550 - 6th Ave. West, Vancouver BC V5Z 4P2 – 604/871-1848; Fax: 604/871-2291

Association of Book Publishers of British Columbia – Library, #107, 100 West Pender St., Vancouver BC V6B 1R8 – 604/684-0228; Fax: 604/684-5788 – Executive Director, Margaret Reynolds

Autism Society of British Columbia – Library, 1584 Rand Ave., Vancouver BC V6P 3G2 – 604/261-8888; Fax: 604/261-7898 – Librarian, Dwain Weese

BC Courthouse Library Society – Vancouver Courthouse Library, 800 Smithe St., Vancouver BC V6Z 2E1 – 604/660-2841; Fax: 604/660-2821; Toll Free: 1-800-665-2570

BC Lung Association – Film Library, 2675 Oak St., Vancouver BC V6H 2K2 – 604/731-5864; Fax: 604/731-5810

BC Rail - Library, POBox 8770, Vancouver BC V6B 4X6 – 604/984-5090; Fax: 604/984-5090; Symbol: BCRL – Librarian, Kathryn Boegel

BC Research Inc. – Library, 3650 Westbrook Mall, Vancouver BC V6S 2L2 – 604/224-4331; Fax: 604/224-0540; Email: nglass@bcr.bc.ca; Symbol: BVAR – Research Librarian, Nancy Glass

BC Securities Commission - Library, 865 Hornby St., 10th Fl., Vancouver BC V6Z 2H4 – 604/660-9692; Fax: 604/660-5473; Email: carol_s_williams@email.bcse.gov.bc.ca; URL: http://www.bcsc.bc.ca; Symbol: BVASEC – Librarian, Carol Williams

The Bible Holiness Movement – Library, POBox 223, Vancouver BC V6C 2M3 – 250/498-3895

Blake, Cassels & Graydon Law Office - Library, #1700, 1030 West Georgia St., Vancouver BC V6E 2Y3 – 604/631-3300; Fax: 604/631-3309, 3305 – Librarian, Maureen Hall

British Columbia Epilepsy Society – Dr. Norman Auckland Library, #120, 535 - 10th Ave. West, Vancouver BC V5Z 1K9 – 604/875-6704; Fax: 604/875-0617; Toll Free: 1-800-223-3366 – Executive Assistant, Suzanne Drahotsky

British Columbia Health Association – Library, #600, 1333 Broadway West, Vancouver BC V6H 4C7 – 604/734-2423; Fax: 604/734-7202; TLX: 04-54300 – Librarian, Carolyn Hall

British Columbia Real Estate Association – Library, #309, 1155 Pender St. West, Vancouver BC V6E 2P4 – 604/683-7702; Fax: 604/683-8601; Symbol: BCREA – Director of Research, Theresa Murphy

British Columbia Teachers' Federation – Information Centre, #100, 550 - 6th Ave. West, Vancouver BC V5Z 4P2 – 604/871-2283; Fax: 604/871-2294; Email: dbroome@bctf.bc.ca; Symbol: BVATF – Librarian, Diana Broom

British Columbia Trade & Investment Office - Trade Resource Centre, #730, 999 Canada Place, Vancouver BC V6C 3E1 – 604/844-1900; Fax: 604/660-2457; Email: rwilliam@van.ei.gov.bc.ca
Client Service Coordinator, Renate Williams
Client Service Coordinator, J. Boecky

Bull, Housser & Tupper Law Office - Library, Royal Centre, 1055 Georgia St. West, POBox 11130, Vancouver BC V6E 3R3 – 604/687-6575; Fax: 604/641-4949; Symbol: BHT – Chief Librarian, Catherine Ryan

Campney & Murphy, Barristers & Solicitors - Library, #2100, 1111 Georgia St. West, POBox 48800, Vancouver BC V7X 1K9 – 604/688-8022; Fax: 604/688-0829; Email: cmlaw@campneymurphy; Symbol: CM – Law Librarian, Anna Holeton

Canada/British Columbia Business Service Centre - Small Business Library, 601 West Cordova St., Vancouver BC V6B 1G2 – 604/775-5601; Fax: 604/775-5515

Canadian Broadcasting Corporation - TV News Library, 700 Hamilton St., POBox 4600, Vancouver BC V6B 4A2 – 604/662-6855; Fax: 604/662-6878; Symbol: BVACBV – Librarian, Colin Preston

Canadian HIV Trials Network – Library, #620, 1081 Burrard St., Vancouver BC V6Z 1Y6 – 604/631-5327; Fax: 604/631-5210; Toll Free: 1-800-661-4664; Email: heath@hivnet.ubc.ca – Information Officer, Heather Fowlie

Canadian Music Centre - British Columbia Region – Branch Library, #200, 2021 - 4 Ave West, Vancouver BC V6J 1N3 – 604/734-4622; Fax: 604/734-4627

Canadian Pelvic Inflammatory Disease Society – Library, POBox 33804, Vancouver BC V6J 4L6 – 604/684-5704

Le Centre culturel francophone de Vancouver – Bibliothèque, 1551 - 7 Ave. West, Vancouver BC V6J 1S1 – 604/736-9806; Téléc: 604/736-4661 – Marie-Christine Wilson

Centre for Human Settlements - Disaster Preparedness Resource Centre, 2206, The East Mall, Vancouver BC V6T 1Z3 – 604/822-5518; Fax: 604/822-6164; Symbol: DPRC

Chemetics International Company – Library, 1818 Cornwall Ave., Vancouver BC V6J 1C7 – 604/734-1200; Fax: 604/734-0304 – Librarian, Claudia Chandler

Clark, Wilson Law Office - Library, #800, 885 West Georgia St., Vancouver BC V6C 3H1 – 604/687-5700; Fax: 604/687-6314; Email: central@cwilson.com – Library Assistant, Diane Snyder

College Institute Educators' Association of BC – Library, #301, 555 - 8 Ave. West, Vancouver BC V5Z 1C6 – 604/873-8988; Fax: 604/873-8865 – Administrative Assistant, Nancy Yip

College of Physicians & Surgeons of British Columbia – Medical Library Service, 1807 West 10th Ave., Vancouver BC V6J 2A9 – 604/733-6671; Fax: 604/737-8582; Toll Free: 1-800-461-3008; Email: ENVOY: BCMLS; Symbol: BCMLS – Director, Jim Henderson

Cominco Ltd. - Corporate/Legal Library, 200 Burrard St., Vancouver BC V6C 3L7 – 604/685-3055; Fax: 604/844-2509; Email: Keith.Low@Cominco.com; Symbol: BVACOM – Librarian, Keith Low

The Commonwealth of Learning – Information Resource Centre, #600, 1285 West Broadway, Vancouver BC V6H 3X8 – 604/775-8234; Fax: 604/775-8210; Symbol: VACL – Library Technician, Sue Parker

Connell Lightbody - Library, Box 11161, Royal Centre, #1900, 1055 Georgia St. West, Vancouver BC V6E 4J2 – 604/684-1181; Fax: 604/641-3916; Email: conlight@connelllightbody.com – Librarian, Carole F. Burley

Continuing Legal Education Society of BC – Library, #300, 845 Cambie St., Vancouver BC V6B 5T2 – 604/669-3544; Fax: 604/669-9260; Toll Free: 1-800-663-0437; Email: kimeson@cle.bc.ca – Karen Imeson

Coopers & Lybrand - Library, 1111 Hastings St. West, Vancouver BC V6E 3R2 – 604/661-5700; Fax: 604/661-5709; Symbol: CLY – Librarian, Jane Moxon

Deloitte & Touche - Library, 4 Bentall Centre, Bental IV, #2000, 1055 Dunsmuir St., POBox 49279, Vancouver BC V7X 1P4 – 604/640-3040; Fax: 604/685-0458; Symbol: DT
Librarian, Iona Douglas
Assistant Librarian, Nada Djurovic

Early Childhood Multicultural Services – Westcoast Child Care Resource Centre, #201, 1675 - 4th Ave. West, Vancouver BC V6J 1L8 – 604/739-9456; Fax: 604/739-3289 – Coordinator, Lesley Richardson

EcoDesign Resource Society – Resource Centre, #201, 225 Smithe St., POBox 3981, Vancouver BC V6B 3Z4 – 604/689-7622; Fax: 604/689-7016

Edwards, Kenny & Bray Law Office - Library, 1040 Georgia St. West, 19th Fl., Vancouver BC V6E 4H3 – 604/689-1811; Fax: 604/689-5177 – Librarian, Stephanie Taggart

Emily Carr Institute of Art & Design - Library, Granville Island, 1399 Johnston St., Vancouver BC V6H 3R9 – 604/844-3840; Fax: 604/844-3801; Email: sheilaw@eciad.bc.ca; URL: http://www.eciad.bc.ca/ – Library Director, Sheila Wallace

Ernst & Young, Pacific Centre, 700 Georgia St. West, POBox 10101, Vancouver BC V7Y 1C7 – 604/683-7133; Fax: 604/643-5422; Symbol: EY – Librarian, Ellen Roth

The Family History Association of Canada – Library, #404, 4620 West 10th Ave., Vancouver BC V6R 2H2 – 250/222-2112

Farris, Vaughan, Wills & Murphy Law Office - Library, Pacific Centre South, 700 West Georgia St., POBox 10026, Vancouver BC V7Y 1B3 – 604/684-9151; Fax: 604/661-9349; Email: tgleave@farris.com – Librarian, Teresa Gleave

Federation of British Columbia Writers – Reference Library, #600, 890 West Pender St., POBox 2206, Vancouver BC V6B 3W2 – 604/683-2057; Fax: 604/683-8269

Feller Drysdale Law Office - Library, #1550, 400 Burrard St., POBox 58, Vancouver BC V6C 3A6 –

604/689-2626; Fax: 604/681-5354 – Receptionist, Carol White

Fisheries & Oceans Canada - Fisheries Management Regional Library, 555 West Hastings St., Vancouver BC V6E 5G3 – 604/666-3851; Fax: 604/666-3450; Email: ENVOY: DFO.LIB.VANCOUVER; Symbol: BVAFI – Coordinator, Library & Information Services, Marcia Croy Vanwely, Email: vanwelym@mailhost.pac.dfo.ca

Fluor Daniel – Technical Information Centre, #500, 1075 West Georgia St., Vancouver BC V6E 4M7 – 604/488-2289; Fax: 604/488-0582 – Librarian, Leonie Page

Forest Alliance of British Columbia – Library, 1055 Dunsmuir St., POBox 49312, Vancouver BC V7X 1L3 – 604/685-7507; Fax: 604/685-5373; Toll Free: 1-800-567-8733; Email: tam@mail.fabc.bc.ca – Information Services Manager, Kit Tam

Forintek Canada Corp. – Western Laboratory Library, 2665 East Mall, Vancouver BC V6T 1W5 – 604/222-5668; Fax: 604/222-5690; Email: holder@van.forintek.ca; Symbol: BVAFP – Librarian, Barbara Holder

Fraser & Beatty Law Office - Library, Grosvenor Bldg., 1040 West Georgia St., 15th Fl., Vancouver BC V6E 4H8 – 604/687-4460; Fax: 604/683-5214 – Library Assistant, Lynda Mitchell

The Fraser Institute – Library, 626 Bute St., 2nd Fl., Vancouver BC V6E 3M1 – 604/688-0221; Fax: 604/688-8539; Toll Free: 1-800-665-3558 – Marie Morris

Geological Survey of Canada - Geoscience Research Library, Natural Resources Canada, 605 Robson St., 15th Fl., Vancouver BC V6B 5J3 – 604/666-3812; Fax: 604/666-7186; Email: libvan@gsc.nrcan.gc.ca; Symbol: BVAG
- Library Services, Manager, Mary Akehurst, 604/666-1147, Email: makehurst@gsc.emr.ca
- Library Technician, Fontaine Hwang, 604/666-3812

Goethe-Institut/German Cultural Centre (Vancouver) – Library, 944 - 8th Ave. West, Vancouver BC V5Z 1E5 – 604/732-4339; Fax: 604/732-5062; Email: libr@goethe-van.org – Librarian, Ingrid Cuk

H.A. Simons Ltd. – Library, #400, 111 Dunsmuir St., Vancouver BC V6B 5W3 – 604/664-4311; Fax: 604/664-3368; Email: jwallace@hasimons.com; Symbol: HAS – Corporate Librarian, Jan Wallace

Harper Grey Easton Law Office - Library, #3100, Vancouver Centre, 650 West Georgia St., POBox 11504, Vancouver BC V6B 4P7 – 604/687-0411; Fax: 604/669-9385; Email: hge@hgelaw.com – Librarian, Liisa Tella

Hospital Employees Union (CLC) – Library, 2006 - 10 Ave. West, Vancouver BC V6J 4P5 – 604/734-3431; Fax: 604/734-3163 – Librarian, Elaine Samwald

Human Resources Development Canada - Regional Economic Services Branch - Library, 1055 West Georgia St., 11th Fl., PO Box 11145, Stn Royal Centre, Vancouver BC V6E 2P8 – 604/666-2611; Symbol: BVAMI – Statistical Officer, Tom Caspersen

Immigration & Refugee Board - Documentation Centre, #1510, 1600 - 800 Burrard St., Vancouver BC V6Z 2J9 – 604/666-5945; Fax: 604/666-7370 – Chief, Alta Haggarty

Industry Canada - Business Service Centre, 601 West Cordova St., Vancouver BC V6B 1G1 – 604/775-5525; Fax: 604/775-5520; Toll Free: 1-800-667-2272; Email: yee.judy@cbsc.ic.gc.ca; URL: http://www.cbsc.org/bc/

Institute of Asian Research – Asian Library, C.K. Choi Bldg., 1855 West Mall, Vancouver BC V6T 1Z2 – 604/822-5905; Fax: 604/822-5207; Email: ljoe@unixg.ubc.ca – Head, Asian Library, Linda Joe

Institute of Certified Management Consultants of British Columbia – Library, #1501, 650 Georgia St. West, POBox 11606, Vancouver BC V6B 4N9 – 604/681-1419; Fax: 604/687-6688

International Development Education Resource Association – Library, #200, 2678 Broadway Ave. West, Vancouver BC V6K 2G3 – 604/732-1496; Film Line: 604/739-8815; Fax: 604/738-8400

Jewish Historical Society of BC – Nemetz Jewish Community Archives, #206, 950 - 41 Ave. West, Vancouver BC V5Z 2N7 – 604/257-5199; Fax: 604/257-5199 – Archivist, Diane M. Rodgers

Justice Canada - Vancouver Regional Office - Library, #900, 840 Howe St., Vancouver BC V6Z 2S9 – 604/666-0549; Fax: 604/666-2760; Symbol: BVAJ – Librarian, Judy Deavy, Email: judy.deavy@justice.x400.gc.ca

Killam, Whitelaw & Twining - Law Library, #100, 200 Granville St., POBox 25, Vancouver BC V6C 1S4 – 604/682-5466; Fax: 604/682-5217 – Phyllis Gordon

KPMG Peat Marwick Thorne - Library, Pacific Centre, 777 Dunsmuir St., POBox 10426, Vancouver BC V7Y 1K3 – 604/691-3292; Fax: 604/691-3031; Email: dlee@kpmg.ca – Librarian, Diane Lee, 604/691-3292

Labour Relations Board of BC - Library, #900, 360 West Georgia St., Vancouver BC V6B 6B2 – 604/660-1300; Fax: 604/660-7321; Email: Astrid.Kenning@lrb02.lrb.gov.bc.ca; Symbol: IRC
- Librarian, Astrid Kenning
- Technician, Krystyna Kwiatkowska
- Assistant, Carole Choquette
- Assistant, Heather Shkuratoff

Ladner Downs Barristers & Solicitors - Library, #1200, 200 Burrard St., POBox 48600, Vancouver BC V7X 1T2 – 604/640-4012; Fax: 604/687-1415 – Librarian, Anne Beresford

Lang Michener Lawrence & Shaw - Library, #1500, 1055 West Georgia St., POBox 11117, Vancouver BC V6E 4N7 – 604/689-9111; Fax: 604/685-7084; Email: library@lmls.com – Library Manager, Anne Ikeda

Langara College - Library, 100 - 49 Ave. West, Vancouver BC V5Y 2Z6 – 604/323-5384; Fax: 604/323-5512; URL: http://www.langara.bc.ca; Symbol: BVaVCL
- Library, Media & Bookstore Services, Director, David Pepper, 604/323-5460, Fax: 604/323-5512
- Public Services Librarian, John Burgess, 604/323-5465, Fax: 604/323-5512
- Technical Services Librarian, Jo Toon, 604/323-5457, Fax: 604/323-5649
- Acquisitions, Charlotte Wynne, 604/323-5385, Fax: 604/323-5649
- Media Services, Linda Prince, 604/323-5459, Fax: 604/323-5577
- Systems, Halina Mitton, 604/323-5243, Fax: 604/323-5649

The Laurier Institution – Library, #608, 1030 West Georgia St., Vancouver BC V6E 2Y3 – 604/669-3638 – A. Roberts

Lawson, Lundell, Lawson & McIntosh Law Office - Library, #1600, 925 Georgia St. West, Vancouver BC V6C 3L2 – 604/685-3456; Fax: 604/669-1620; Email: ghoar@lawsonlundell.com
- Librarian, Gwendoline Hoar, 604/631-9167
- Library Technician, Cecilia Hui

Lindsay Kenney Law Office - Library, 700 West Pender St., 17th Fl., Vancouver BC V6C 1G8 – 604/687-1323; Fax: 604/687-2347; Email: info@lindsaykenney.bc.ca; URL: http://www.lindsaykenney.bc.ca – Library Manager, Lynn Smith

McCarthy Tétrault - Library, Pacific Centre, #1300, 777 Dunsmuir St., POBox 10424, Vancouver BC V7Y 1K2 – 604/643-7100; Fax: 604/643-7900; URL: http://www.mccarthy.ca
- Head Librarian, Susan Crysler, 604/643-7931, Email: smc@mccarthy.ca
- Reference Librarian, Debbie Benson, 604/643-7178
- Technician, Natasha Lyndon, 604/643-7199

Muslim Education & Welfare Foundation of Canada – Jannat Bibi Library, Aljameeatul Islaameeyah Lit-Tarbeeya War-Riaayah (Canada), 2580 McGill St., Vancouver BC V5K 1H1 – 604/255-9941; Fax: 604/255-9941 – Dr. Nazih Kamal Hammad

Myasthenia Gravis Association of British Columbia – Library, 2805 Kingsway Ave., Vancouver BC V5R 5H9 – 604/451-5511; Fax: 604/451-5651 – Brenda Kelsey

Native Investment & Trade Association – NITA Resource Library, #410, 890 West Pender St., Vancouver BC V6C 1J9 – 604/684-0880; Fax: 604/684-0881; Toll Free: 1-888-684-0881 – Myrna Kane

Norecol, Dames & Moore Inc. - Vancouver – Library, #1900, 650 West Georgia St., POBox 11507, Vancouver BC V6B 4NT – 604/681-1672; Fax: 604/687-3446; Symbol: NORE – Manager, Business Admin., Starlet Lum

Northwest Wildlife Preservation Society – NWPS Wildlife Library, POBox 34129, Vancouver BC V6J 4M1 – 604/736-8750; Fax: 604/736-9615

Owen, Bird Law Office - Library, Three Bentall Centre, #2900, 595 Burrard St., POBox 49130, Vancouver BC V7X 1J5 – 604/688-0401; Fax: 604/688-2827 – Library Technician, Nancy Connor

Pacific Cinémathèque Pacifique – Film Reference Library, #200, 1131 Howe St., Vancouver BC V6Z 2L7 – 604/688-8202; Fax: 604/688-8204

Pacific Salmon Commission - Library, #600, 1155 Robson St., Vancouver BC V6E 1B5 – 604/684-8081; Fax: 604/666-8707; Email: PACSALM.LIB; tarita@psc.org; Symbol: PSAL – Librarian, Teri Tarita

Persons with AIDS Society of British Columbia – Pacific AIDS Resource Centre Library, c/o Pacific AIDS Resource Centre, 1107 Seymour St., Vancouver BC V6B 5S8 – 604/681-2122, ext.294; Fax: 604/893-2211; Email: library@parc.org – Librarian, Janice Linton

Planned Parenthood Association of British Columbia – Library, #201, 1001 West Broadway, Vancouver BC V6K 2G8 – 604/731-4252; Fax: 604/731-4698; Toll Free: 1-800-739-7367 – Education Director, Faye Bebb

Price Waterhouse - Vancouver Library, #1400, 601 Hastings St. West, Vancouver BC V6B 5A5 – 604/443-2631; Fax: 604/443-2635; Symbol: PW – Librarian, Janet Parkinson

Pulp & Paper Research Institute of Canada - UBC Pulp & Paper Centre, 2385 East Mall, Vancouver BC V6T 1Z4 – 604/822-8568; Fax: 604/822-8563; Email: library@ppc.ubc.ca; Symbol: BVAPPC – Librarian, Rita M. Penco
- Vancouver Laboratory Library, 3800 Wesbrook Mall, Vancouver BC V6S 2L9 – 604/222-3200; Fax: 604/222-3262; Email: library@vanlab.paprican.ca; Symbol: BVAPPR – Librarian, Linda Everett

Recycling Council of British Columbia – Waste Reduction Library, #201, 225 Smithe St., Vancouver BC V6B 4X7 – 604/683-6009; Fax: 604/683-7255; Toll Free: 1-800-667-4321 – Library Coordinator, Jo Bergstrand

Registered Nurses Association of British Columbia – Library, 2855 Arbutus St., Vancouver BC V6J 3Y8 – 604/736-7331; Fax: 604/738-2272; Toll Free: 1-800-565-6505 – Library Manager, Joan Andrews

Revenue Canada - Research & Library Services, 1166 West Pender St., Vancouver BC V6E 3H8 – 604/691-4782; Fax: 604/689-7536; Email: ENVOY: TAYLOR.EV; Symbol: BVATC – Team Coordinator, Library Services, Evelyn Taylor

Russell & DuMoulin Law Office - Library, #2100, 1075 Georgia St. West, Vancouver BC V6E 3G2 – 604/631-3131; Fax: 604/631-3232;

Email: ref@rdcounsel.com; Symbol: BVARD – Manager, Library Services, Joan D. Bilsland

Sandwell Inc. – Library, #700, 1190 Hornby St., Vancouver BC V6Z 2H6 – 604/684-9311; Fax: 604/688-5913; Email: kgreen@vancouver.western.sandwell; Symbol: VASA – Librarian, Kim Green

Sierra Legal Defence Fund – Library, #214, 131 Water St., Vancouver BC V6B 1H6 – 604/685-5618; Fax: 604/685-7813 – Office Administrator, Joy Fai

Singleton Urquhart Scott Law Office - Library, #1200, 1125 Howe St., Vancouver BC V6Z 2K8 – 604/682-7474; Fax: 604/682-1283; URL: http://www.singleton.com

SNC-Lavalin Inc. - Vancouver Library, 1075 Georgia St. West, 12th Fl., Vancouver BC V6E 3C9 – 604/662-3555; Fax: 604/683-1672 – Librarian, Brenda Oscar

Society of Kabalarians of Canada – Resource Centre, 5912 Oak St., Vancouver BC V6M 2W2 – 604/263-9551; Fax: 604/263-5514

Society Promoting Environmental Conservation – Library, 2150 Maple St., Vancouver BC V6J 3T3 – 604/737-7732; Fax: 604/736-7115

Statistics Canada - Pacific Regional Reference Centre, Sinclair Centre, #600, 300 West Georgia St., Vancouver BC V6B 6C7 – 604/666-3691; Fax: 604/666-4863; Toll Free: 1-800-263-1136; Email: stcvan@statcan.ca; URL: http://www.statcan.ca – Manager, Data Dissemination, D.G. Meakins

Teck Corporation Library, #600, 200 Burrard St., Vancouver BC V6C 3L9 – 604/687-1117; Fax: 604/687-6100 – Librarian, Mary-Anne Pomphrey

Teck Mining Group Ltd., #600, 200 Burrard St., Vancouver BC V6C 3L9 – 604/687-1117; Fax: 604/687-6100 – Librarian, Mary-Anne Pamphrey

Thorsteinssons Law Office - Library, Three Bentall Centre, 595 Burrard St., 27th Fl., POBox 49123, Vancouver BC V7X 1J2 – 604/689-1261; Fax: 604/688-4711; Email: 73742.3144@compuserve.com – Librarian, Yoko Beriault

Towers Perrin - Information Centre, #1600, 1100 Melville St., Vancouver BC V6E 4A6 – 604/691-1034; Fax: 604/691-1062; Email: lepagec@towers.com – Senior Information Specialist, Carey LePage

Trans Mountain Pipe Line Company Ltd. Library, #900, 1333 Broadway West, Vancouver BC V6H 4C2 – 604/739-5286; Fax: 604/739-5008; Email: janetg@vcr.tmpl.ca; Symbol: TMPL – Library/Records Coordinator, Janet Graham

Transport Canada - Library, Pacific Region, #620, 800 Burrard St., Vancouver BC V6Z 2J8 – 604/666-5868; Fax: 604/666-2320; Email: rowland@unixg.ubc.ca; Symbol: BVATCA – Regional Librarian, J. Jill Rowland

Union of British Columbia Indian Chiefs – Library, 342 Water St., 5th Fl., Vancouver BC V6B 1B6 – 604/602-9555; Fax: 604/684-5726; Symbol: BVAUBCI – Librarian, Wendy Ancell

University of British Columbia - Libraries, 1956 Main Mall, Vancouver BC V6T 1Z1 – 604/822-3871; Fax: 604/822-3893; Email: ENVOY: R.PATRICK@UNIXG.UBC.CA

- University Librarian, Dr. Ruth Patrick, 604/822-2298
- Public Services, Associate Librarian, Heather Keate, 604/822-2396
- Human Resources, Assistant Librarian, Erik de Bruijn, 604/822-4555
- Technical Services, Assistant Librarian, Nadine Baldwin, 604/822-2740
- Catalogue Division, Head, N.E. Omelusik, 604/822-9103
- Government Publications/Humanities & Social Sciences, Head, Jocelyn Godolphin, 604/822-2160
- Resource Sharing, Head, Patrick Dunn, 604/822-4430
- Order Division, Head, Nadine Baldwin, 604/822-5038
- Asian Library, Head, Linda Joe, 604/822-2427
- Biomedical Branch, Librarian, Nancy Forbes, 604/875-4505
- Data Library, Head, Hilde Colenbrander, 604/822-6742
- Education Library, Head, Howard Hurt, 604/822-8680
- Eric Hamber Memorial Branch, Librarian, Pat Lysyk, 604/875-2153
- Fine Arts/Music/Special Collections, Head, Brenda Peterson, 604/228-2720
- Law Library, Head, Thomas Shorthouse, 604/822-2275
- MacMillan Forestry/Agriculture Library, Head, Lee Ann Bryout, 604/822-6333
- Map Library, Map Librarian, Tim Ross, 604/822-2231
- School of Library, Archival & Information Studies, Director, Dr. Ken Haycock, 604/822-2404
- Science & Engineering Division Library, Head, Bonita Stableford, 604/228-3295
- St. Paul's Hospital Branch, Librarian, Barbara Saint, 604/631-5425
- Woodward Biomedical Library, Head, Margaret Price, 604/822-2762
- David Lam Library Management Research Library, Head, Elizabeth Caskey, 604/822-9399

Urban Development Institute of Canada – Library, 717 Pender St. West, 3rd Fl., Vancouver BC V6C 1G9 – 604/669-9585; Fax: 604/689-8691; Symbol: UDI – Librarian, David Helem

Urban Native Indian Education Society – NEC Library, Native Education Centre, 285 - 5 Ave. East, Vancouver BC V5T 1H2 – 604/873-3761; Fax: 604/873-9152 – Library Coordinator, Donna Chester

Vancouver Aquarium - Robin Best Library, POBox 3232, Vancouver BC V6B 3X8 – 604/685-3364; Fax: 604/631-2529; Symbol: VAQ – Librarian, Treva Ricou

Vancouver Board of Trade – Library, #400, 999 Canada Place, Vancouver BC V6C 3C1 – 604/681-2111; Fax: 604/681-0437 – Librarian, Lucia Park

Vancouver Community College - Libraries, 1155 East Broadway, POBox 24620, Vancouver BC V5N 5T9 – 604/871-7318; Fax: 604/871-7100; Email: bappleton@vcc.bc.ca; URL: http://www.vcc.bc.ca; Symbol: BVAVCC

- College Librarian, Brenda Appleton
- Acquisitions, Coordinator, Virginia Adams, 604/871-7385, Fax: 604/871-7446
- Technical Services, Department Chair, J. Toon, 604/324-5457, Fax: 604/324-5512
- Circulation Services, Campus Librarian, Eva Sharel, 604/443-8349, Fax: 604/443-8329
- Information Services, Campus Librarian, Aphrodite Harris, 604/871-7319, Fax: 604/871-7446

Vancouver Holocaust Centre Society - A Museum for Education & Remembrance – Resource Centre, #50, 950 West 41st Ave., Vancouver BC V5Z 2N7 – 604/264-0499; Fax: 604/264-0497

The Vancouver Maritime Museum Society, 1905 Ogden Ave., Vancouver BC V6J 1A3 – 604/257-8300; Fax: 604/737-2621 – Curator of Collections, J. Thornley

Vancouver Symphony Society – VSO Library, 601 Smithe St., Vancouver BC V6B 5G1 – 604/684-9100; Fax: 604/684-9264 – Librarian, Minella Lacson

Vancouver Youth Symphony Orchestra – Library, 3214 - 10th Ave. West, Vancouver BC V6K 2L2 – 604/737-0714; Fax: 604/731-4133 – C. Epp

VanDusen Botanical Gardens Association – VanDusen Library, 5251 Oak St., Vancouver BC V6M 4H1 – 604/257-8668; Fax: 604/263-1777 – Librarian, Barbara J. Fox

Victory Square Law Office - Library, #300, 198 West Hastings St., Vancouver BC V6B 1H2 – 604/684-8421; Fax: 604/684-8427; Email: vslo@vslo.bc.ca – Greg Wurzer

Watson Goepel Maledy Law Office - Library, #3023, 595 Burrard St., POBox 49096, Vancouver BC V7X 1G4 – 604/688-1301; Fax: 604/688-8193 – Administrator, Deborah A. Welch

West Coast Environmental Law Research Foundation – Library, #1001, 207 Hastings St. West, Vancouver BC V6B 1H7 – 604/684-7378; Fax: 604/684-1312; Toll Free: 1-800-330-9235 – Research Coordinator, Catherine Ludgate

West Coast Women & Words Society – Library, #219, 1675 - 8th Ave. West, Vancouver BC V6J 1V2 – 604/730-1034

Westcoast Energy Inc. - Library, 1333 Georgia St. West, 14th Fl., Vancouver BC V6E 3K9 – 604/691-5517; Fax: 604/691-5994; Symbol: WEI – Librarian, Beatrice Yakimchuk

Western Canada Wilderness Committee – Library, 20 Water St., Vancouver BC V6B 1A4 – 604/683-8220; Fax: 604/683-8229; Toll Free: 1-800-661-9453 – Sue Fox

### VANDERHOOF

BC Courthouse Library Society - Library, 2440 Bute Ave., POBox 1220, Vanderhoof BC V0J 3A0

Yinka Dene Language Institute – Library, PO Bag Service 7000, Vanderhoof BC V0J 3A0 – 250/567-9236; Fax: 250/567-3851 – Ruby Ephrom

### VERNON

BC Courthouse Library Society – Library, Courthouse, 3001 - 27th St., Vernon BC V1T 4W5

Edward F. Kenny Barrister & Solicitor - Library, 3009 - 28 St., Vernon BC V1T 4Z7 – 250/545-0587; Fax: 250/545-8660 – Office Manager, Joyce Hodgson

Okanagan University College - Vernon Campus Library, 7000 College Way, Vernon BC V1B 2N5 – 250/545-7291; Fax: 250/558-4963

### VICTORIA

BC Ministry of Forests - Research Branch – Library, 1450 Government St., Victoria BC V8W 3E7 – 250/387-3628; Fax: 604/953-3079; Symbol: BVIFO – Manager, Susanne Barker

AIDS Vancouver Island – Library, #304, 733 Johnston St., Victoria BC V8W 3C7 – 250/384-2366; Fax: 250/380-9411; Toll Free: 1-800-665-2437 – Aaron Severs

BC Courthouse Library Society - Library, POBox 9246, Victoria BC V8W 9J2 – 250/387-3239; Fax: 250/387-0698 – Library Assistant, Sheila Folka

BC Employment & Investment - Library Services, 1810 Blanshard St., POBox 9321, Victoria BC V8W 9N3 – 250/952-0658; Fax: 250/952-0581

- Librarian, Margaret Palmer, Email: mpalmer@eivic.ei.gov.bc.ca
- Kathy Gower, Email: kgower@eivic.ei.gov.bc.ca
- Jennifer Siemens, Email: jsiemens@eivic.ei.gov.bc.ca

BC Legislative Library, #214, Parliament Bldgs., Victoria BC V8V 1X4 – 250/387-6510; Fax: 250/356-1373

- Director, Joan A. Barton, 250/387-6500
- Manager, Reference Services, Maureen Lawson

BC Ministry Labour - Library, POBox 9566, Victoria BC V8W 9K1 – 250/953-3378; Fax: 250/356-8322; Email: vbruce@galaxy.bc.ca; Symbol: BVIML – Librarian, Vivienne Bruce

BC Ministry of Energy, Mines & Petroleum Resources - Library, 1810 Blanshard St., 8th Fl., Victoria BC

V8V 1X4 – 250/952-0582; Fax: 250/952-0581; Email: mpalmer@eivic.ei.gov.bc.ca
Head Librarian, Margaret Palmer
Librarian, Sharon Ferris

BC Ministry of Environment, Lands & Parks - Library, Public Affairs & Communications Branch, 810 Blanshard St., 1st Fl., Victoria BC V8V 1X4 – 250/387-9747; Fax: 250/387-9741; Email: ENVOY: ENVLIB.BC; Symbol: BVILFW
Reference Librarian, Kathy Neer, Email: kneer@pubaffair.env.gov.bc.ca
ILL Technician, Bonnie Brugger
Acquisitions Clerk, Carol Smith

Parks Library, Parks Division Services, 800 Johnson St., 2nd Fl., Victoria BC V8V 1X4 – 250/389-3974; Fax: 250/387-5757; Email: ENVOY: PARKSLIB; Symbol: VIPB
Librarian, Shirley Desrosiers
ILL Library Assistant, John Pinn
Circulation, A/V Library Assistant, Louise Noble

BC Ministry of Health & Ministry Responsible for Seniors - Library/Audio Visual Resource Centre, 1515 Blanshard St., Main Fl., Victoria BC V8W 3C8 – 250/952-2196; Fax: 250/952-2180; Email: hlthlibr@bcsc02.gov.bc.ca; URL: http://www.hlth.gov.bc.ca/library/index.html
Head Librarian, Elizabeth Woodworth
Head Librarian, Peter Rose

BC School District 61 - Greater Victoria School District Learning Resource Centre, 923 Topaz Ave., Victoria BC V8T 2M2 – 250/360-4300; Fax: 250/360-4308 – District Resource Centre Coordinator, Shannon Glover, 250/360-4302

BC School District 62 - District Resource Centre, 3143 Jacklin Rd., Victoria BC V9B 5R1 – 250/474-9800; Fax: 250/474-9825

British Columbia Heritage Trust - Library, 800 Johnson St., 5th Fl., Victoria BC V8V 1X4 – 250/356-1440; Fax: 250/356-7796 – Librarian, Romi Casber

British Columbia Museums Association – Library, 514 Government St., Victoria BC V8V 4X4 – 250/387-3315; Fax: 250/387-1251

Camosun College - Library, 3100 Foul Bay Rd., Victoria BC V8P 5J2 – 250/370-3604; Fax: 250/370-3624; URL: http://www.camosun.bc.ca/~library; Symbol: BVIC – Coordinator, Catherine Winter, Email: winter@camosun.bc.ca

Defence Research Establishment - Pacific - Information Services Library, Forces Mail Office, Victoria BC V0S 1B0 – 250/380-2854; Fax: 250/363-2856; Symbol: BEPN – Head, Antony Cheung

Greater Victoria Chamber of Commerce – Library, 525 Fort St., Victoria BC V8W 1E8 – 250/383-7191; Fax: 250/385-3552 – Business Information Officer, Lynda Boyd

Island Deaf & Hard of Hearing Centre – Library, #300, 1627 Fort St., Victoria BC V8R 1H8 – 250/592-8144; Fax: 250/592-8199; Toll Free: 1-800-667-5448 – Susan Low

Natural Resources Canada-Canadian Forest Service: Pacific Forestry Centre – Library, 506 West Burnside Rd., Victoria BC V8Z 1M5 – 250/363-0600; Fax: 604/363-6035; Email: asolyma@a1.pfc.forestry.ca; Symbol: BVIF – Head, Library Services, Alice Solyma

The Right to Die Society of Canada – Library, POBox 39018, Victoria BC V8V 4X8 – 250/380-1112; Fax: 250/386-3800 – Head Librarian, Evelyn Martens

Royal Roads University - Library & Learning Resources Centre, 2005 Sooke Rd., Victoria BC V9B 5Y2 – 250/391-2575; Fax: 250/391-2594; URL: http://www.royalroads.ca/docs/library/home.html; Symbol: BRC
Manager, Barry Jensen, MLS, 250/391-2596, Email: bjensen@royalroads.ca
Assistant, Aquisitions, Rachanee Tannas, 250/391-2595, Email: rtannas@royalroads.ca
Assistant, Circulation & Interlibrary Loan, Melanie Martens, 250/391-2575, Email: mmartens@royalroads.ca

Royal United Services Institute of Vancouver Island – CFB Esquimalt Library, Bay Street Armoury, 715 Bay St., Victoria BC V8T 1R1 – 250/384-1331

Smith, Hutchison Law Office - Library, 823 Broughton St., Victoria BC V8W 1E5 – 250/388-6666; Fax: 250/389-0400; Email: mhutchqc@sprynet.com – J. Michael Hutchison, QC

Solicitor General Canada - William Head Institution - Library, POBox 4000, Victoria BC V8X 3Y8 – 250/363-4642, ext.245; Fax: 250/363-5983; Symbol: BVIW – Librarian, Kim Rempel

South Pacific Peoples Foundation of Canada – Resource Centre, 1921 Fernwood Rd., Victoria BC V8T 2Y6 – 250/381-4131; Fax: 250/388-5258

Thurber Environmental Consultants Ltd. – Library, #210, 4475 Viewmont Ave., Victoria BC V8Z 6L8 – 250/727-7332; Fax: 250/727-3710; Symbol: BVIT – Librarian, Rose Mary Ormerod

United World Colleges – Library, Lester B. Pearson College of the Pacific, 650 Pearson College Dr., Victoria BC V9C 4H7 – 250/391-2421; Fax: 250/391-2412; Email: Library@pearson-college.uwc.ca – Bette Kirchner

University of Victoria - McPherson Library, POBox 1800, Victoria BC V8W 3H5 – 250/721-8211; Fax: 250/721-8215; URL: http://gateway.uvic.ca; Symbol: CABVIV
University Librarian, Marnie Swanson
Access Services, Head, Jessie Kurtz
Bibliographic & Authorities Records Unit, Coordinator, Hugh Irving
Business Librarian, Hazel Cameron
Cataloguing Database Management Unit, Coordinator, John Dell
Cataloguing Librarian, Sam Acquila
Collection Management Services, Head, Donna Signori
Communications Librarian/Reference Librarian, Betty Gibb
Continuing Studies Library Services, Program Director, Sandy Slade
External Services Librarian, Kathryn Paul
Humanities Librarian, Ken Cooley
Library Staff Relations, Manager, Wendie McHenry
Library Systems & Budget, Manager, L. Declerck
Public Services, Director, Joan Sandllands
Reference, Head, Don White
Science Librarian, Katy Nelson
Serials Management Unit, Coordinator, Elena Romaniuk
Systems Librarian, Kathleen Matthews
Technical Services, Director, Hana Komorous
University Archivist & Head, Special Collections, Chris Petter
Reference/ILL Librarian, Cheryl Lumley

Victoria Persons with AIDS Society – AIDS Treatment Information Library, 613 Superior St., Victoria BC V8V 1V1 – 250/383-7494; Fax: 250/383-1617; Toll Free: 1-800-434-2959 – David Hillman

#### WEST VANCOUVER

Fisheries & Oceans Canada - West Vancouver Laboratory Library, 4160 Marine Dr., West Vancouver BC V7V 1N6 – 604/666-4813; Fax: 604/666-3497; Email: DFO.LIB.WESTVAN; Symbol: BVAPE – Librarian, Mei-Shuen Fok

#### WILLIAMS LAKE

BC Courthouse Library Society – Library, Courthouse, 540 Borland St., Williams Lake BC V2G 1R8

Council of Forest Industries – Library, #203, 197 Second Ave. North, Williams Lake BC V2G 1Z5 – 250/392-7770; Fax: 250/392-5188; Symbol: COFI – Administrative Assistant, Norma Poole

University College of the Cariboo - Williams Lake Campus, 351 Hodgson Rd., Williams Lake BC V2G 3P7 – 250/392-8030; Fax: 250/392-8032; Email: mcoyne@cariboo.bc.ca; Symbol: BWLCC – Librarian, Michael Coyne

## MANITOBA

### Regional Library Systems with Member Libraries

#### BORDER REGIONAL LIBRARY

312 Seventh Ave. South, PO Box 970, Virden MB R0M 2C0 – 204/748-3862; Email: vwcap#2@techplus.com; Symbol: MVE
Regional Library Coordinator, Gaylene Oliver
Librarian, Linda Grant-Braybrook

Elkhorn Branch Library, 110 Richhill Ave. East, PO Box 370, Elkhorn MB R0M 0N0 – 204/845-2292 – Librarian, Ellen Rae Overand

Mc Auley Branch Library, PO Box 234, Mc Auley MB R0M 1H0 – 204/722-2221 – Library Personnel, Mary Ellen Warkentin

#### EVERGREEN REGIONAL LIBRARY

63 - 1 Ave., PO Box 1140, Gimli MB R0C 1B0 – 204/642-7912; Fax: 204/642-8056; Symbol: MGE
Head Librarian, Valerie Eyolfson

Arborg Branch Library, PO Box 4053, Arborg MB R0C 0A0 – 204/376-5388; Fax: 204/642-8056 – Branch Head, Linda Hegg

Riverton Branch Library, Riverton MB R0C 2R0 – 204/378-2988; Fax: 204/642-8056 – Branch Head, Sigrid Palsson

#### JOLYS REGIONAL LIBRARY

PO Box 118, St-Pierre-Jolys MB R0A 1V0 – 204/433-7729; Email: stplibrary@pli.mb.ca; Symbol: MSTP
Head Librarian, Claudette Desharnais

St. Malo Library, Chalet Malouin, St. Malo MB R0A 1T0 – 204/347-5606; Email: stmlibrary@pli.mb.ca – Librarian, Carole Arpin

#### LAKELAND REGIONAL LIBRARY

318 Williams Ave., PO Box 970, Killarney MB R0K 1G0 – 204/523-4949; Fax: 204/523-7460; Email: lrl@mail.techplus.com; Symbol: MKL
Librarian, Carol Ross

Cartwright Branch Library, Railway Ave., Cartwright MB R0K 0L0 – 204/529-2261; Symbol: MCCB – Branch Head, Cherie Melvin

Pilot Mound Branch Library, PO Box 126, Pilot Mound MB R0G 1P0 – 204/825-2035; Symbol: MPM – Branch Head, Allison MacAulay

#### NORTH-WEST REGIONAL LIBRARY

PO Box 999, Swan River MB R0L 1Z0 – 204/734-3880; Email: nwrl@swanvalley.freenet.mb.ca; Symbol: MSRNW
Head Librarian, Bonnie Ray

Benito Branch Library, General Delivery, Benito MB R0L 0C0 – 204/539-2446; Email: benlib@swanvalley.freenet.mb.ca; Symbol: MBB – Branch Head, Mabel Cooke

**PARKLAND REGIONAL LIBRARY**

504 Main St. North, Dauphin MB R7N 1C9 – 204/638-6410; Fax: 204/638-9483; Email: parklibr@mts.net; Symbol: MDP

Director, Glenn Butchart

Siglunes District Library, PO Box 368, Ashren MB R0C 0E0 – 204/768-2048; Email: ashlib@mb.sympatico.ca – Librarian, Kathi Budge

Birch River & District Branch Library, 3rd St., PO Box 245, Birch River MB R0L 0E0 – 204/236-4419; Email: birchlib@mb.sympatico.ca – Attendant, Gwenda Wotton

Birtle Branch Library, PO Box 207, Birtle MB R0M 0C0 – 204/842-3418; Email: birtlelib@mb.sympatico.ca – Librarian, Susan Barteaux

Bowsman Branch Library, PO Box 209, Bowsman MB R0L 0H0 – 204/238-4615; Email: bowslib@mb.sympatico.ca – Librarian, Fern De Groot

Dauphin Branch Library, 504 Main St. North, Dauphin MB R7N 1C9 – 204/638-3055; Email: daulibr@mts.net – Librarian, Lynn Innerst

Erickson District Library, PO Box 385, Erickson MB R0J 0P0 – 204/636-2325; Email: ericklib@mail.techplus.com – Librarian, Imeke Kerr

Foxwarren Branch Library, PO Box 204, Foxwarren MB R0J 0R0 – 204/847-2030 – Librarian, Pearl Clunie

Gilbert Plains Branch Library, Gilbert Plains MB R0L 0X0 – 204/548-2733; Email: gilblib@mb.sympatico.ca – Librarian, Sudesh Malik

Gladstone District Library, PO Box 720, Gladstone MB R0J 0T0 – 204/385-2641; Email: gladlib@mb.sympatico.ca – Librarian, Margaret Broadfoot

Grandview Branch Library, General Delivery, Grandview MB R0L 0Y0 – 204/546-2398; Email: grandlib@mb.sympatico.ca – Librarian, Marion Storozinski

Hamiota Centennial Library, PO Box 610, Hamiota MB R0M 0T0 – 204/764-2680; Email: hamlib@mb.sympatico.ca – Librarian, Gladys Mathison

Langruth Library, PO Box 154, Langruth MB R0H 0N0 – 204/445-2030 – Librarian, Karen Dick

McCreary District Library, PO Box 297, McCreary MB R0J 1B0 – 204/835-2629; Email: mccrlib@mb.sympatico.ca – Attendant, Germaine Longtin

Minitonas Branch Library, Minitonas MB R0L 1G0 – 204/525-4840; Email: minitlib@mb.sympatico.ca – Librarian, Betty MacCumber

Ochre River Branch Library, General Delivery, Ochre River MB R0L 1K0 – 204/733-2293; Email: ochrelib@mb.sympatico.ca – Librarian, Orla Berkvens

Roblin & District Library, PO Box 1342, Roblin MB R0L 1P0 – 204/937-2443; Email: roblib@mb.sympatico.ca – Librarian, Marlene Beattie

Shoal Lake Community Library, PO Box 428, Shoal Lake MB R0J 1Z0 – 204/759-2242; Email: shoallib@mb.sympatico.ca – Librarian, Donna Charney

Winnipegosis Branch Library, Winnipegosis MB R0L 2G0 – 204/656-4876; Email: wpglib@mb.sympatico.ca – Librarian, Kim Fehr

**PORTAGE PLAINS REGIONAL LIBRARY**

170 Saskatchewan Ave. West, Portage la Prairie MB R1N 0M1 – 204/857-4271; Fax: 204/239-4387; URL: library@freenet.mb.ca; Symbol: MPLP

Percy Gregoire-Voskamp

Regional Municipality of Victoria Branch Library, Holland MB R0G 0X0 – 204/526-2011; Email: viclib@trehearne.com; Symbol: MHP – Librarian, Linda Clark

**RUSSELL & DISTRICT REGIONAL LIBRARY**

PO Box 340, Russell MB R0J 1W0 – 204/773-3127; Symbol: MRD

Librarian, Florence Pushka

Librarian, Louise Sidoryk

Binscarth Branch Library, General Delivery, Binscarth MB R0J 0G0 – 204/532-2342 – Librarian, Doris Barrett

**SOUTH CENTRAL REGIONAL LIBRARY**

Civic Centre, 185 Main St., Winkler MB R6W 1B4 – 204/325-5864; Fax: 204/325-5915; Email: irisloew@mbnet.mb.ca; Symbol: MMOW

Head Librarian, Iris Loewen

Altona Branch Library, PO Box 650, Altona MB R0G 0B0 – 204/324-1503; Email: scrla@altona.man.net; Symbol: MWOW – Branch Librarian, Liz Forrester

Morden Branch Library, 514 Stephen St., Morden MB R6M 1T7 – 204/822-4092; Email: scrlibm@mbnet.mb.ca – Branch Librarian, Kathy Ginter

Winkler Branch Library, Civic Centre, 185 Main St., Winkler MB R6W 1B4 – 204/325-7174; Fax: 204/325-5915; Email: scrlibw@mbnet.mb.ca; Symbol: MAOW – Branch Librarian, Patricia Hildebrand

**SOUTH INTERLAKE REGIONAL LIBRARY**

385 Main St., Stonewall MB R0C 2Z0 – 204/467-8415; Symbol: MSTOS

Chief Librarian/Administrator, Heather Kowalchuk

Bookmobile Contact, Peggy Armstrong

Teulon Branch Library, 70 Main St., Teulon MB R0C 3B0 – 204/886-3648; Symbol: MTSIR – Branch Librarian, Barb Bowman

**SOUTHWESTERN MANITOBA REGIONAL LIBRARY**

149 Main St. South, PO Box 670, Melita MB R0M 1L0 – 204/522-3923; Fax: 204/522-3421; Email: swmblib@mail.techplus.com; URL: http://www.techplus.com/swlib/index.htm; Symbol: MESM

Head Librarian, Valorie Wray

Napinka Branch Library, Napinka MB R0M 1N0 – 204/665-2282 – Librarian, Deb Green

Pierson Branch Library, PO Box 39, Pierson MB R0M 1S0 – 204/634-2215 – Librarian, Viki Miner

**WESTERN MANITOBA REGIONAL LIBRARY**

638 Princess Ave., Brandon MB R7A 0P3 – 204/727-6648; Fax: 204/727-4447; Email: wmrlibrary@tkm.mb.ca; Symbol: MBW

Chief Librarian, Kathy Thornborough

Children's Librarian, Shelley Mortensen

Brandon Public Library, 638 Princess Ave., Brandon MB R7A 0P3 – 204/727-6648; Fax: 204/727-4447; Email: wmrlibrary@tkm.mb.ca – Chief Librarian, Kathy Thornborough

Carberry/North Cypress Branch Library, PO Box 382, Carberry MB R0K 0H0 – 204/834-3043; Fax: 204/834-2736 – Branch Supervisor, Isabel Cathcart

Glenboro/South Cypress Branch Library, PO Box 429, Glenboro MB R0K 0X0 – 204/827-2874; Fax: 204/827-2127 – Branch Supervisor, Jackie Steele

Neepawa Branch Library, PO Box 759, Neepawa MB R0J 1H0 – 204/476-5648; Fax: 204/476-5939; Email: neepawalib@mail.techplus.com – Branch Supervisor, Jean Forsman

## Public Libraries

Baldur: Regional Municipality of Argyle Public Library, PO Box 358, Baldur MB R0K 0B0 – 204/535-2314; Fax: 204/535-2242; Symbol: MBA – Librarian, Cheri McLaren

Beausejour: Brokenhead River Regional Library, PO Box 1087, Beausejour MB R0E 0C0 – 204/268-3588; Symbol: MBBR – Librarian, Karen Berry

Boissevain & Morton Regional Library, PO Box 340, Boissevain MB R0K 0E0 – 204/534-6478; Email: mbom@mail.techplus.com; Symbol: MBOM – Librarian, Phyllis Hallett

Carman: Boyne Regional Library, 15 - 1st Ave. SW, PO Box 788, Carman MB R0G 0J0 – 204/745-3504; Symbol: MCB – Head Librarian, Helen Stewart

Churchill Public Library, PO Box 730, Churchill MB R0B 0E0 – 204/675-2731; Symbol: MCH – Librarian, Juliette Lee; Archivist, Anne Gould; Part-time Librarian, Beverley Mulhern

Deloraine: Bren Del Win Centennial Library, PO Box 584, Deloraine MB R0M 0M0 – 204/747-2415; Symbol: MDB – Librarian, Lorraine Stovin

Eriksdale Public Library, PO Box 219, Eriksdale MB R0C 0W0 – 204/739-2668; Symbol: MEL – Librarian, Jean Heroux

Flin Flon Public Library, 58 Main St., Flin Flon MB R8A 1J8 – 204/687-3397; Fax: 204/687-4233; Symbol: MFF – Library Administrator, Gretta Redahl

Gillam Public Library, PO Box 400, Gillam MB R0B 0L0 – 204/652-2617; Symbol: MGI – Head Librarian, Gerry Belbas

Headingley Municipal Library, 121 Alboro St., Unit 3, Box 2, Headingley MB R4J 1A3 – 204/888-5410; Symbol: MHH – Librarian, Audrey Teichroeb

La Broquerie: Bibliothèque Saint-Joachim, PO Box 10, La Broquerie MB R0A 0W0 – 204/424-5287; Fax: 204/424-5610 – Librarian, Diane Boily

Lac du Bonnet Regional Library, 84 - Third St., PO Box 216, Lac du Bonnet MB R0E 1A0 – 204/345-2653; Email: mldb@granite.mb.ca; Symbol: MLDB – Head Librarian, Rosalind M. Burt

Leaf Rapids Public Library, PO Box 190, Leaf Rapids MB R0B 1W0 – 204/473-2742; Symbol: MLR – Head Librarian, Traci Dunn

Lundar: Pauline Johnson Library, PO Box 698, Lundar MB R0C 1Y0 – 204/762-5367; Symbol: MLPJ – A/Librarian, Jane Nikkel

Lynn Lake Centennial Library, PO Box 1127, Lynn Lake MB R0B 0W0 – 204/356-8222 – Librarian, Margaret Thomson

MacGregor: North Norfolk MacGregor Regional Library, PO Box 622, MacGregor MB R0H 0R0 – 204/685-2796; Symbol: MMNN – Librarian, Lorraine Burt

Manitou Public Library, PO Box 432, Manitou MB R0G 1G0 – 204/242-3134; Email: manitlib@cici.mb.ca; Symbol: MMA – Librarian, Beverley Boote

Minnedosa Regional Library, PO Box 1226, Minnedosa MB R0J 1E0 – 204/867-2585; Fax: 204/867-5204; Symbol: MMR – Librarian, Georgina Johnson

Morris: Valley Regional Library, PO Box 397, Morris MB R0G 1K0 – 204/746-2136; Symbol: MMVR – Librarian, Diane DeKezel

Notre Dame de Lourdes: Bibliothèque Père Champagne, Centre Dom Benoit, 55, rue Rodgers, CP 399, Notre Dame de Lourdes MB R0G 1M0 – 204/248-2386; Symbol: MNDP – Président, Denis Bibault; Bibliothécaire, Colette Compté

Pinawa Public Library, Pinawa MB R0E 1L0 – 204/753-2496; Email: plibrary@eastman.freenet.mb.ca; Symbol: MP – Librarian, Brenda Johnson

Rapid City Regional Library, PO Box 8, Rapid City MB R0K 1W0 – 204/826-2732; Symbol: MRA – Librarian, Jocelyn Aimoe

Reston District Library, PO Box 340, Reston MB R0M 1X0 – 204/877-3673; Symbol: MRP – Librarian, Onagh Williamson

Rivers: Prairie Crocus Regional Library, PO Box 609, Rivers MB R0K 1X0 – 204/328-7613; Symbol: MRIP – Librarian, Beth Schafer

Rossburn Regional Library, PO Box 87, Rossburn MB R0J 1V0 – 204/859-2687; Symbol: MRO – Librarian, Ann Hrycak

St Adolphe: Bibliothèque Ritchot Library, CP 123, St Adolphe MB R5A 1AY – 204/388-4016; Symbol: MIBR – Bibliothécaire, Lousie Durand

Ste Anne: Bibliothèque Ste. Anne Library, CP 220, Ste Anne MB R5H 1H8 – 204/422-9958; Symbol: MSA – Librarian, Monica Ball

St-Claude: Bibliothèque Saint-Claude Library, 50 - 1 St., CP 203, St-Claude MB R0G 1Z0 – 204/379-2524; Téléc: 204/379-2014; Symbol: MSCL – Librarian, Lynn Gobin

St-Georges: Bibliothèque Allard Library, St-Georges Community Club, PO Box 157, St-Georges MB R0E 1V0 – 204/367-8443; Email: allard@granite.mb.ca; Symbol: MSTG – Head Librarian, Janet Robert

St-Jean-Baptiste: Bibliothèque Montcalm Library, CP 345, St-Jean-Baptiste MB R0G 2B0 – 204/758-3137; Courrier électronique: biblio@mb.sympatico.ca; Symbol: MSJB – Head Librarian, Diane Bérard

Ste. Rose Regional Library, Ste. Rose du Lac MB R0L 1S0 – 204/447-2527; Fax: 204/447-3474; Symbol: MSTR – Librarian, Sonja Saquet

Selkirk Community Library, 303 Main St., Selkirk MB R1A 1S7 – 204/482-3522; Fax: 204/482-6166; Symbol: MSEL – Librarian, Linda Pleskach

Snow Lake Community Library, PO Box 760, Snow Lake MB R0B 1M0 – 204/358-2322; Symbol: MSL – Librarian, Dorothy Salahub

Somerset: Bibliothèque Somerset Library, 289 Carlton Ave., Somerset MB R0G 2L0 – 204/744-2170; Symbol: MS – Bibliothécaire, Lucille Labossière

Souris: Glenwood & Souris Regional Library, PO Box 760, Souris MB R0K 2C0 – 204/483-2757; Symbol: MSOG – Librarian, Margaret Greaves

Steinbach Public Library, 255 Elmdale St., PO Box 2050, Steinbach MB R0A 2A0 – 204/326-6841; Fax: 204/326-6859; Email: steinlib@rocketmail.com; Symbol: MSTE – Librarian, Valerie Kasper

The Pas Public Library, 53 Edwards St., PO Box 4100, The Pas MB R9A 1R2 – 204/623-2023; Fax: 204/623-4594; Email: the_pas_library@mbnet.mb.ca; Symbol: MTP – Library Administrator, Roberta Day

Thompson Public Library, 81 Thompson Dr. North, Thompson MB R8N 0C3 – 204/677-3717; Fax: 204/778-5844; Email: ThompsonPublib@NorCom.mb.ca; Symbol: MTH – Administrator, Edward Reece

Winnipeg Public Library, 251 Donald St., Winnipeg MB R3C 3P5 – 204/986-6472; Fax: 204/942-5671; URL: http://www.mbnet.mb.ca/~wwwlib/libindex.htm; Symbol: MW – Director of Libraries, David Weismiller, Email: dweismil@city.winnipeg.mb.ca; Branch Services, Manager, Carol Mahe, 204/986-6473, Email: cmahe@city.winnipeg.mb.ca; Community Relations, Coordinator, Heather Graham, 204/986-5579, Email: hgraham@city.winnipeg.mb.ca; Systems Services, Manager, Al Pritchard, 204/986-6416, Email: apritcha@city.winnipeg.mb.ca; Support Services-Materials, Manager, Betty Parry, 204/986-5002, Email: bparry@city.winnipeg.mb.ca – See also following branches: Bibliothèque de St-Boniface, Centennial Library, Charleswood Branch Library, Cornish Branch Library, Fort Garry Branch Library, Henderson Branch Library, Louis Riel Branch Library, Munroe Branch Library, Osborne Branch Library, Pembina Trail Branch Library, River Heights Branch Library, Sir William Stephenson Branch Library, St. James-Assiniboia Branch Library, St. John's Branch Library, St. Vital Branch Library, Transcona Branch Library, West End Branch Library, West Kildonan Branch Library, Westwood Branch Library, Windsor Park Branch Library

Winnipeg: Bibliothèque de St-Boniface, #100, 131, boul Provencher, Winnipeg MB R2H 0G2 – 204/986-4330; Téléc: 204/986-6827 – Coordinator of French Language Services, Danielle Chagnon; Reference Librarian, Liv Thorseth, 204/986-4331, Email: lthorset@city.winnipeg.mb.ca; Children's Librarian, Édith Boulet, 204/986-4332, Email: eboulet@city.winnipeg.mb.ca – Branch of Winnipeg Public Library

Winnipeg: Centennial Library, 251 Donald St., Winnipeg MB R3C 3P5 – 204/986-6450; Fax: 204/986-4072; Email: vandrysi@city.winnipeg.mb.ca; Symbol: MW – Manager, Vera Andrysiak, 204/986-6458 – Branch of Winnipeg Public Library

Winnipeg: Charleswood Branch Library, 5014 Roblin Blvd., Winnipeg MB R3R 0G7 – 204/986-3069; Fax: 204/986-3545; Email: tfurmani@city.winnipeg.mb.ca – Branch Head, Terry Furmaniuk, 204/986-3074 – Branch of Winnipeg Public Library

Winnipeg: Cornish Branch Library, 20 West Gate, Winnipeg MB R3C 2B1 – 204/986-4679; Fax: 204/986-7126; Email: rwatkins@city.winnipeg.mb.ca – Branch Head, Rick Watkins, 204/986-4680 – Branch of Winnipeg Public Library

Winnipeg: Fort Garry Branch Library, 1360 Pembina Hwy., Winnipeg MB R3T 2B4 – 204/986-4910; Fax: 204/986-3399; Email: kborland@city.winnipeg.mb.ca – Acting Branch Head, Karin Borland, 204/986-4917 – Branch of Winnipeg Public Library

Winnipeg: Henderson Branch Library, #1, 1050 Henderson Hwy., Winnipeg MB R2K 2M5 – 204/986-4314; Fax: 204/986-3065; Email: rwalker@city.winnipeg.mb.ca – Area Head, Rick Walker, 204/986-4318 – Branch of Winnipeg Public Library

Winnipeg: Louis Riel Branch Library, 1168 Dakota St., Winnipeg MB R2N 3T9 – 204/986-4568; Fax: 204/986-3274; Email: epiush@city.winnipeg.mb.ca – Branch Head, Evelyn Piush, 204/986-4571 – Branch of Winnipeg Public Library

Winnipeg: Munroe Branch Library, 489 London St., Winnipeg MB R2K 2Z4 – 204/986-3736; Fax: 204/986-7125; Email: ggrainge@city.winnipeg.mb.ca – Branch Head, Gale Grainger, 204/986-3738 – Branch of Winnipeg Public Library

Winnipeg: Osborne Branch Library, 625 Osborne St. South, Winnipeg MB R3L 2B3 – 204/986-4775; Fax: 204/986-7124; Email: spopowic@city.winnipeg.mb.ca – Branch Head, Sharon Popowich – Branch of Winnipeg Public Library

Winnipeg: Pembina Trail Branch Library, 2724 Pembina Hwy., Winnipeg MB R3T 2H7 – 204/986-4370; Fax: 204/986-3290; Email: kmadansi@city.winnipeg.mb.ca – Branch Head, Kamini Madansingh, 204/986-4378 – Branch of Winnipeg Public Library

Winnipeg: River Heights Branch Library, 1520 Corydon Ave., Winnipeg MB R3N 0J6 – 204/986-4934; Fax: 204/986-3544; Email: jjohnsto@city.winnipeg.mb.ca – Branch Head, C. Jill Johnston, 204/986-4937 – Branch of Winnipeg Public Library

Winnipeg: St. James-Assiniboia Branch Library, 1910 Portage Ave., Winnipeg MB R3J 0J2 – 204/986-5583; Fax: 204/986-3798; Email: bnorquay@city.winnipeg.mb.ca – Acting Branch Head, Brenda Norquay, 204/986-3426 – Branch of Winnipeg Public Library

Winnipeg: St. John's Branch Library, 500 Salter St., Winnipeg MB R2W 4M5 – 204/986-4689; Fax: 204/986-7123; Email: lcarmich@city.winnipeg.mb.ca – Branch Head, Lynn Carmichael, 204/986-4690 – Branch of Winnipeg Public Library

Winnipeg: St. Vital Branch Library, 6 Fermor Ave., Winnipeg MB R2M 0Y2 – 204/986-5625; Fax: 204/986-3173 – Branch Head, Vacant – Branch of Winnipeg Public Library

Winnipeg: Sir William Stephenson Branch Library, 765 Keewatin, Winnipeg MB R2X 3B9 – 204/986-7070; Fax: 204/986-7201 – Branch Head, Theresa Yauk, 204/986-7156, Email: tyauk@city.winnipeg.mb.ca – Branch of Winnipeg Public Library

Winnipeg: Transcona Branch Library, 111 Victoria Ave. West, Winnipeg MB R2C 1S6 – 204/986-3950; Fax: 204/986-3172; Email: dfillion@city.winnipeg.mb.ca – Branch Head, Doris Fillion, 204/986-3953 – Branch of Winnipeg Public Library

Winnipeg: West End Branch Library, 823 Ellice Ave., Winnipeg MB R3G 0C3 – 204/987-4677; Fax: 204/986-7129; Email: jturnbul@city.winnipeg.mb.ca – Branch Head, Joan Turnbull, 204/986-4678 – Branch of Winnipeg Public Library

Winnipeg: West Kildonan Branch Library, 365 Jefferson Ave., Winnipeg MB R2V 0N3 – 204/986-4384; Fax: 204/986-3373; Email: tgretzin@city.winnipeg.mb.ca – Acting Branch Head, Tannis Gretzinger, 204/986-4387 – Branch of Winnipeg Public Library

Winnipeg: Westwood Branch Library, 66 Allard Ave., Winnipeg MB R3K 0T3 – 204/986-4742; Fax: 204/986-3799; Email: dbates@city.winnipeg.mb.ca – Branch Head, Diane Bates, 204/986-4745 – Branch of Winnipeg Public Library

Winnipeg: Windsor Park Branch Library, 955 Cottonwood Rd., Winnipeg MB R2J 1G3 – 204/986-4945; Fax: 204/986-7122; Email: dsouchan@city.winnipeg.mb.ca – Branch Head, Diane Souchan, 204/986-4948 – Branch of Winnipeg Public Library

## Special & College Libraries & Resource Centres

### BRANDON

Agriculture & Agri-Food Canada-Brandon Research Centre – Library & Information Centre, RR#3, POBox 1000A, Brandon MB R7A 5Y3 – 204/726-7650; Fax: 204/728-3858; Email: cenns@em.agr.ca – Aquisition Librarian, Carol Enns

Assiniboine Community College - Library, 1430 Victoria Ave. East, Brandon MB R7A 2A9 – 204/726-6635; Fax: 204/726-7014; Email: armstrong@accnet.assiniboinec.mb.ca; URL: http://www.assiniboinec.mb.ca

Librarian, Sandra Armstrong
Library Technician, Anni de Cangas
Library Technician, Ann Marie Melvie
Library Clerk, Dory Yorobe

Brandon General Hospital – Library Services, 150 McTavish Ave. East, Brandon MB R7A 2B3 – 204/727-2257; Fax: 204/727-0317; Email: Envoy: ILL.MBGH; Symbol: MBGH – Director of Library Services, Dianna Derouin

Brandon University - John E. Robbins Library, 270 - 18th St., Brandon MB R7A 6A9 – 204/727-9645; Fax: 204/726-1072; Email: interloan@brandonu.ca; URL: http://www.brandonu.ca/Library/; Symbol: MBC

Public Services, Head, Linda Burridge
Extension Librarian, Carmen Kazakoff

Child & Family Services of Western Manitoba – Library, #100, 340 - 9 St., Brandon MB R7A 6C2 – 204/726-6030; Fax: 204/726-6775; Toll Free: 1-800-483-8980 – Executive Assistant, Joan Kennedy

Hunt, Miller & Combs Law Office - Library, 148 - 8 St., Brandon MB R7A 3X1 – 204/727-8491; Fax: 204/727-4350 – Partner, J.D. Cram

The Marquis Project, Inc. – Laura Delamater Resource Centre, #200, 107 - 7 St., Brandon MB R7A 3S5 – 204/727-5675; Fax: 204/727-5683 – Resource Coord./Educator, Debra Jennings

**CHURCHILL**

Churchill Health Centre – Library, Churchill Town Centre, General Delivery, Churchill MB R0B 0E0 – 204/675-8381; Fax: 204/675-2243 – Wanda O'Brien

Churchill Northern Studies Centre - Library, POBox 610, Churchill MB R0B 0E0 – 204/675-2307; Fax: 204/675-2139 – Executive Director, Michael Carter

**DAUPHIN**

Canadian Coalition for Ecology, Ethics & Religion – Library, 1021 Jackson St., Lot 75, Dauphin MB R7N 2N5 – 204/638-4319; Fax: 204/638-5733

Manitoba Heritage Federation Inc. – MHF Heritage Library, 21 - 2nd Ave. NW, 2nd Fl., Dauphin MB R7N 1H1 – 204/638-9154; Fax: 204/638-0683 – Administrative Assistant, Sheila Goraluk

Western Christian College - Library, POBox 5000, Dauphin MB R7N 2V5 – 204/638-8801; Fax: 204/638-7054; Email: lhusband@mbnet.mb.ca – Teacher Librarian, Loreen Husband

**HAMIOTA**

Hamiota District Health Centre – Library, 177 Birch Ave., Hamiota MB R0M 0T0 – 204/764-2412; Fax: 204/764-2049 – Health Educator, Jody Allan

**MORDEN**

Agriculture & Agri-Food Canada - Canadian Agriculture Library, #100-101, Route 100, Morden MB R6M 1Y5 – 204/822-4471; Fax: 204/822-6841; Email: cscharf@em.agr.ca – Secretary/Librarian, Cheryl Sharf

**OAK HAMMOCK MARSH**

Ducks Unlimited Canada – Library, Oak Hammock Marsh Conservation Centre, 1 Mallard Bay at Hwy. 220, POBox 1160, Oak Hammock Marsh MB R0C 2Z0 – 204/467-3276; Fax: 204/467-9028; Toll Free: 1-800-665-3825; Email: iwwr@ducks.ca – Hal Loewen

**OTTERBURNE**

Providence College & Seminary - Library, POBox 1-138, Otterburne MB R0A 1G0 – 204/433-7488; Fax: 204/433-7158; Email: lwild@providence.mb.ca; URL: http://www.providence.mb.ca; Symbol: BCW
- Head Librarian, Larry Wild
- Circulation Librarian, Murray Harrison
- Technical Services Librarian, Martha Loeppky, Email: mloeppky@providence.mb.ca

**PINAWA**

Atomic Energy of Canada Limited-Whiteshell Laboratories – WL Information Centre, General Delivery, Pinawa MB R0E 1L0 – 204/753-2311; Fax: 204/753-8490; Email: ENVOY: WNRE.LIBRARY; REFdesk2@aecl.ca; Symbol: MPW – Library Supervisor, Sharon Taylor

**PORTAGE LA PRAIRIE**

Manitoba Rural Development - Food Development Centre – Library, 810 Phillips St., POBox 1240, Portage La Prairie MB R1N 3J9 – 204/239-3162; Fax: 204/239-3180; Toll Free: 1-800-870-1044; Email: lpetriuk@fdc.mb.ca; Symbol: MPCFP – Librarian, Linda Petriuk

The Daily Graphic & Herald Leader Press - Library, 1941 Saskatchewan Ave. West, POBox 130, Portage La Prairie MB R1N 3B4 – 204/857-3427; Fax: 204/239-1270; Email: pdg@cpnet.net
- Office Manager, M. Barter
- Chief Librarian, Tom Tenszen
- Reference Librarian, Ian White

David Winton Bell Memorial Library - Delta Waterfowl & Wetlands Research Station, RR#1, Box 1, Portage La Prairie MB R1N 3A1 – 204/239-1900; Fax: 204/239-5950; Email: dw4ducks@portage.net; URL: http://deltawaterfowl.com; Symbol: MDW – Library Technician, Heidi den Haan

Manitoba Developmental Centre - Memorial Library, POBox 1190, Portage La Prairie MB R1N 3C6 – 204/856-4205; Fax: 204/856-4258; Symbol: MPLPM – Library Technician, Jo-Anne Doan

**SELKIRK**

Selkirk Mental Health Centre – Library, 825 Manitoba Ave. West, POBox 9600, Selkirk MB R1A 2B5 – 204/482-3810, ext.411; Fax: 204/785-8936 – Library Technician, Lorna Weiss

**STEINBACH**

Evangelical Mennonite Conference – EMC Archives, POBox 1268, Steinbach MB R0A 2A0 – 204/326-6401; Fax: 204/326-1613 – Secretary, Martha Kroeker

Red River Apiarists' Association – Library, POBox 1448, Steinbach MB R0A 2A0 – 204/326-3763; Fax: 204/326-3763 – Librarian, Ron Rudiak

Steinbach Bible College - Library, POBox 1420, Steinbach MB R0A 2A0 – 204/326-6451; Fax: 204/326-6908; Email: sbcpr@sbcollege.mb.ca – Technical Services Librarian, Lois Loeppky

**THE PAS**

Keewatin Community College - Library, POBox 3000, The Pas MB R9A 1M7 – 204/623-3416, ext.261; Fax: 204/623-7316
- Librarian, Elena Ruivivar
- Library Technician, Sharyl Latta
- Library Technician, John Schoen

The Sam Waller Museum - Library, 306 Fischer Ave., POBox 185, The Pas MB R9A 1K4 – 204/623-3802; Fax: 204/623-5506 – Director, Laura MacLean

**THOMPSON**

Keewatin Community College - Thompson Campus Library, 504 Princeton Dr., Thompson MB R8N 0A5 – 204/677-6408; Fax: 204/677-6439 – Librarian, Shelly Doman, Email: sdoman@kccnet.keewatincc.mb.ca

**WINNIPEG**

Economic Innovation & Technology Council - Environmental Sciences Centre – Library, Environmental Research, 745 Logan Ave., Winnipeg MB R3E 3L5 – 204/945-3804; Fax: 204/945-0763 – Librarian, Helen Woo

Aboriginal Women's Network Inc. – Aboriginal Women's Resource Centre, 181 Higgins Ave., 3rd Fl., Winnipeg MB R3A 3G1 – 204/942-2711; Fax: 204/942-3445

Addictions Foundation of Manitoba – William Potoroka Memorial Library, 1031 Portage Ave., Winnipeg MB R3G 0R8 – 204/944-6277; Fax: 204/786-7768; Email: library@afm.mb.ca; Symbol: MWAF – Library Technician, Pat Klimack

Agriculture & Agri-Food Canada-Cereal Research Centre – Canadian Agriculture Library, 195 Dafoe Rd., Winnipeg MB R3T 2M9 – 204/983-0721; Fax: 204/983-4604; Email: lbmwag@em.agr.ca – Librarian, Mike Malyk

Aikins, MacAulay & Thorvaldson Law Office - Library, Commodity Exchange Tower, 360 Main St., 30th Fl., Winnipeg MB R3C 4G1 – 204/957-4785; Fax: 204/957-0840 – Librarian, Shu Huang

Arcor Resource Library, 265 Notre Dame Ave., Winnipeg MB R3B 1N9 – 204/943-9400; Fax: 204/943-4088 – Librarian, Arthur Short

Associated Manitoba Arts Festivals, Inc. – Music & Resource Library, #424, 100 Arthur St., Winnipeg MB R3B 1H3 – 204/945-4578; Fax: 204/948-2073

Benedictine Sisters of Manitoba – St. Benedict's Monastery Library, 225 Masters Ave., Winnipeg MB R4A 2A1 – 204/338-4601; Fax: 204/339-8775

Bethania Mennonite Personal Care Home Inc. – Library, 1045 Concordia Ave., Winnipeg MB R2K 3S7 – 204/667-0795; Fax: 204/667-7078 – Staff Education Coordinator, Esther Fransen

Buchwald Asper Gallagher Henteleff Barristers & Attorneys-at-Law - Library, Commodity Exchange Tower, 360 Main St., 25th Fl., Winnipeg MB R3C 4H6 – 204/956-0560, ext.373; Fax: 204/957-0227; Email: bagh@escape.ca; Symbol: MWBAH – Librarian, Edie Biberdorf

Canadian Artists' Representation Manitoba – Library, #221, 100 Arthur St., Winnipeg MB R3B 1H3 – 204/943-7211; Fax: 204/942-1555; Symbol: VARC – Program Coordinator, Helma Rogge

Canadian Brain Injury Coalition – Library, 29 Pearce Ave., Winnipeg MB R2V 2K3 – 204/334-0471; Fax: 204/339-1034

Canadian Broadcasting Corporation - Music & Record Library, 541 Portage Ave., POBox 160, Winnipeg MB R3C 2H1 – 204/788-3222; Fax: 204/788-3685; Symbol: MWC – Senior Librarian, Mary Worobec

Canadian Grain Commission - Library, #300, 303 Main St., Winnipeg MB R3C 3G8 – 204/983-0878; Fax: 204/983-6098; Email: Library@cgc.ca; URL: http://www.cgc.ca; Symbol: MWGR
- Chief Librarian, Elva Simundsson
- Technical Services & Loans, C. Wallman

Canadian Home Economics Association Foundation – Gwenyth Bailey Simpson Video Resource Library, 303 Ashland Ave., Winnipeg MB R3L 1L6 – 204/475-1508

Canadian Mennonite Bible College - Library, 600 Shaftesbury Blvd., Winnipeg MB R3P 0M4 – 204/888-6781; Fax: 204/831-5675; Email: cmbclib@mbnet.mb.ca – Librarian, Paul Friesen

Canadian Wheat Board - Library, 423 Main St., POBox 816, Winnipeg MB R3C 2P5 – 204/983-3437; Fax: 204/983-4031; Email: library@cwb.ca; Symbol: MWCWB – Librarian, Ruth Reedman, Email: ruth_reedman@cwb.ca

Catherine Booth Bible College - Library, 447 Webb Place, Winnipeg MB R3B 2P2 – 204/947-6701; Fax: 204/942-3856; Symbol: CBBA – Director of Library Services, Adrian Dalwood

Centre for Mennonite Brethren Studies – Library, 169 Riverton Ave., Winnipeg MB R2L 2E5 – 204/669-6575; Fax: 204/654-1865; Email: adueck@cdnmbconf.ca; URL: http://www.cdnmbconf.ca/mb/cmbs.htm
- Director, Abe Dueck
- Archivist, Alf Redekop

City of Winnipeg - Waterworks, Waste & Disposal Dept. - Resource Centre, 1500 Plessis Rd., Winnipeg MB R2C 2Z9 – 204/986-3250, 4481; Fax: 204/224-0032; Email: JdaSilva@City.Winnipeg.MB.CA.; Symbol: MWWW – Library Technician, Joann de Silva

Collège universitaire de Saint-Boniface - Bibliothèque Alfred-Monnin, 200, av de la Cathedrale, Winnipeg MB R2H 0H7 – 204/235-4403; Téléc: 204/233-9472; Symbol: MSC
- Bibliothécaire en chef, Marcel Boulet, 204/235-4402
- Bibliothécaire, Madeleine Samuda

Community Therapy Services Inc. - Library, 35 King St., 5th Fl., Winnipeg MB R3B 1H4 – 204/949-0533; Fax: 204/942-1428 – Education Coordinator, Monica Brechka

Concord College - Library, 169 Riverton Ave., Winnipeg MB R2L 2E5 – 204/669-6583; Fax: 204/663-2468; Email: thiessen@uwpg02.uwinnipeg.ca; Symbol: MWMBC – Librarian, Richard Thiessen

Concordia Hospital – Library, 1095 Concordia Ave., Winnipeg MB R2K 3S8 – 204/661-7163; Fax: 204/663-7301 – Library Technician, Peggy Prins

Council on Homosexuality & Religion – Library, POBox 1912, Winnipeg MB R3C 3R2 – 204/474-

0212; Fax: 204/478-1160 – Resource Officer, Jeremy Buchner
Crafts Guild of Manitoba Inc. – Library, 183 Kennedy St., Winnipeg MB R3C 1S6 – 204/943-1190; Fax: 204/989-2254 – Librarian, M. Wilson
Deer Lodge Centre - J.W. Crane Memorial Library, 2109 Portage Ave., Winnipeg MB R3J 0L3 – 204/831-2152; Fax: 204/888-1805; Email: jwclib@pangea.ca; URL: http://www.deerlodge.mb.ca/deerlod2.html; Symbol: MWDL
  Director, Judy Inglis
  Technical Services/Systems Librarian, Laurie Blanchard
  Library Technician, Janice Saunders
  Library Technician, Christine Shaw-Daigle
Duboff Edwards Haight & Schachter Law Office - Library, 175 Carlton St., 2nd Fl., Winnipeg MB R3C 3H9 – 204/942-3361; Fax: 204/943-4498; Email: duboff@mbnet.mb.ca – Neil Duboff
Environment Canada - Atmospheric Environment Service, Central Region - Library, #1000, 266 Graham Ave., Winnipeg MB R3C 3V4 – 204/983-2024; Fax: 204/983-4884 – Secretary, Scientific Services, Patti Graham
Epilepsy Manitoba – Resource Centre, 825 Sherbrook St., Winnipeg MB R3A 1M5 – 204/783-0466; Fax: 204/786-0860
Fédération provinciale des comités de parents du Manitoba – Centre de ressources éducatives à l'enfance (CRÉE), 531 Marion St., Winnipeg MB R2J 0J9 – 204/237-9666; Téléc: 204/231-1436 – Directrice, Suzanne Lagassé
Fillmore & Riley - Law Library, #1700, 360 Main St., Winnipeg MB R3C 3Z3 – 204/956-2970; Fax: 204/957-0516 – Librarian, Christine Stewart
Fire Fighters Historical Society of Winnipeg, Inc. – Library, Winnipeg Fire Department, 151 Princess St., 5th Fl., Winnipeg MB R3B 1L1 – 204/888-8021 – Director, Barb Kuryluk
Fisheries & Oceans Canada-Freshwater Institute – Eric Marshall Aquatic Research Library, 501 University Cr., Winnipeg MB R3T 2N6 – 204/983-5170; Fax: 204/983-6285; Email: library@fwi.dfo.ca; Symbol: MWFW – Acting Manager, Mary Layton
Folk Arts Council of Winnipeg – Library, #300, 180 King St., Winnipeg MB R3B 3J8 – 204/982-6210; Fax: 204/943-1956 – Resources Officer, Eslyn Glasgow
Gays for Equality – Gay/Lesbian Resource Centre, #1, 222 Osborne St., POBox 1661, Winnipeg MB R3C 2Z6 – 204/474-0212; Fax: 204/478-1160
German Society of Winnipeg – Library, 121 Charles St., Winnipeg MB R2W 4A6 – 204/589-7724; Fax: 204/589-0030 – Secretary, K. Turner
Gould Goszer Law Office - Library, 175 Carlton St., 2 Fl., Winnipeg MB R3C 3H9 – 204/943-0571; Fax: 204/943-4498
Grand Lodge of Manitoba, Ancient, Free & Accepted Masons – Grand Lodge of Manitoba Library, Masonic Memorial Temple, 420 Corydon Ave., Winnipeg MB R3L 0N8 – 204/453-7410; Fax: 204/284-3527 – Grand Librarian, Charles A. Merrick
The Great-West Life Assurance Company - Great-West Compagnie d'Assurance Vie – Library, 100 Osborne St. North, POBox 6000, Winnipeg MB R3C 3A5 – 204/946-8906; Fax: 204/946-7838; Email: ENVOY: D.NELSON; Symbol: MWGW – Corporate Librarian, Dale Nelson
Heritage Winnipeg – Library, #509, 63 Albert St., Winnipeg MB R3B 1G4 – 204/942-2663; Fax: 204/942-2094
Human Resources Development Canada - Manitoba Region Resource Centre, #500, 259 Portage Ave., Winnipeg MB R3B 3L4 – 204/983-7229; Fax: 204/983-2117 – Technical Services Assistant, Donna Martin, 204/983-7229
Industrial Technology Centre - Library, 1329 Niakwa Rd. East, Winnipeg MB R2J 3T4 – 204/945-1413; Fax: 204/945-1784; Email: bedearth@itc.mb.ca; URL: http://www.itc.mb.ca; Symbol: MWMRC – Librarian, Betty J. Dearth
Industry Canada - Business Service Centre, 330 Portage Ave., 8th Fl., POBox 2609, Winnipeg MB R3C 4B3 – 204/984-2272; Fax: 204/983-3852; Toll Free: 1-800-665-2019; Email: manitoba@cbsc.ic.gc.ca; URL: http://www.cbsc.org/manitoba/
Institute of Urban Studies – Library, University of Winnipeg, 346 Portage Ave., Winnipeg MB R3C 0C3 – 204/982-1145; Fax: 204/943-4695 – Librarian, Nancy Klos
International Institute for Sustainable Development – Library, 161 Portage Ave. East, 6th Fl., Winnipeg MB R3B 0Y4 – 204/958-7724; Fax: 204/958-7710; Email: mroy@iisd.ca – Programme Officer, Marlene Roy
Jewish Historical Society of Western Canada – Archives, #404, 365 Hargrave St., Winnipeg MB R3B 2K3 – 204/942-4822; Fax: 204/942-9299 – Archivist, Bonnie Tregobon
Jewish Public Library, 1725 Main St., Winnipeg MB R2V 1Z4 – 204/338-8408 – Librarian, Nina Thompson
The John Howard Society of Manitoba – Justice Resource Centre, 583 Ellice Ave., Winnipeg MB R3B 1Z7 – 204/775-1514; Fax: 204/775-1670 – Volunteer Coordinator, Mike Collins
Justice Canada - Winnipeg Regional Office - Library, #301, 310 Broadway, Winnipeg MB R3C 0S6 – 204/983-2391; Fax: 204/983-3636 – Barbara Shields
Law Society of Manitoba – Library, 219 Kennedy St., Winnipeg MB R3C 1S8 – 204/942-5571; Fax: 204/956-0624
League for Life in Manitoba – Library, 579 Des Meurons St., Winnipeg MB R2H 2P6 – 204/233-8047, 7283; Fax: 204/233-0523; Toll Free: 1-800-665-0570 – Barbara Gommerman
Learning Disabilities Association of Manitoba – Resource Centre, 60 Maryland St., 2nd Fl., Winnipeg MB R3G 1K7 – 204/774-1821; Fax: 204/788-4090
Legal Aid Manitoba - Library, #402, 294 Portage Ave., Winnipeg MB R3C 0B9 – 204/985-8500; Fax: 204/944-8582
Manitoba Archaeological Society Inc. – Library, POBox 1171, Winnipeg MB R3C 2Y4 – 204/942-7243; Fax: 204/942-3749 – Office Manager, Leo Pettipas
Manitoba Association for the Promotion of Ancestral Languages – Resource Centre, 1574 Main St., Winnipeg MB R2W 5J8 – 204/338-7951; Fax: 204/334-8277 – Secretary, Leanna Burgess
Manitoba Association of Playwrights – Library, #503, 100 Arthur St., Winnipeg MB R3B 1H3 – 204/942-8941; Fax: 204/942-1555
Manitoba Blind Sport Association – Library, 200 Main St., Winnipeg MB R3C 4M2 – 204/925-5694; Fax: 204/925-5703
Manitoba Cancer Treatment & Research Foundation – Library, 100 Olivia St., Winnipeg MB R3E 0V9 – 204/787-2136; Fax: 204/783-6875; Symbol: MWCT
Manitoba Child Care Association – Resource Library, 364 McGregor St., Winnipeg MB R2W 4X3 – 204/586-8587; Fax: 204/589-5613 – Resource/Research Dev. Officer, Katalin Nagy
Manitoba Crafts Council – Library, #003, 100 Arthur St., Winnipeg MB R3B 1H3 – 204/942-1816; Fax: 204/989-2254
Manitoba Culture, Heritage & Citizenship - Legislative Library, 200 Vaughan St., Winnipeg MB R3C 1T5 – 204/945-4330; Fax: 204/948-2008; Email: refserv@che.gov.mb.ca; URL: http://www.gov.mb.ca/manitoba/leg-lib/contents.html; Symbol: MWP
  Legislative Librarian, Susan Bishop, 204/945-3968
  Reference Services, Head, Rick MacLowick
  Collection Development, Head, Doreen Schafer
Manitoba Eco-Network Inc. – Library, #2, 70 Albert St., Winnipeg MB R3B 1E7 – 204/947-6511; Fax: 204/946-6514
Manitoba Education & Training - Direction des Resources éducatives françaises, #S208, 200 Cathedral Ave., Winnipeg MB R2H 0H7 – 204/945-8594; Téléc: 204/945-0092; Symbol: MWDRE
  Acting Director, Doris Lemoine, 204/945-8554
  Librarian, Gemma Boily, 204/945-2010
  Reference Librarian, Norma Rocan, 204/945-4782
  Acquisitions Librarian, Nicole Baudry, 204/945-2743
  Library Coordinator, Huguette Dandeneau, 204/945-6859
 Instructional Resources, 1181 Portage Ave., Winnipeg MB R3G 0T3 – 204/945-7833; Fax: 204/945-8756; Email: irb@minet.gov.mb.ca; Symbol: MWE
  Coordinator, John Tooth
  Resource Sharing, Phyllis Barich, 204/945-5764
  Collection Management, Lorrie Andersen, 204/945-7823
  Circulation, Debbie Somerville, 204/945-5371
  Technical Services, Atarrha Wallace, 204/945-7834
  Information Services, Diane Dwarka, 204/945-4015
  Assistant Coordinator/Marketing, Elaine Seepish, 204/945-7830
 Special Materials Services, #215, 1181 Portage Ave., Winnipeg MB R3G 0T3 – 204/945-7842; Fax: 204/945-7914; Toll Free: 1-800-282-8069 – Circulation Supervisor, Denise Speliers
Manitoba Energy & Mines - Library, #360, 1395 Ellice Ave., Winnipeg MB R3G 3P2 – 204/945-6569; Fax: 204/945-8427; Email: library@em.gov.mb.ca; URL: http://www.gov.mb.ca/em/library/index.html; Symbol: MWEMM
  Library Technician, Monique Lavergne
  Library Technician, Debbie Rind
Manitoba Environment - Environment Library/Bibliothèque de l'Environnement, #160, 123 Main St., Winnipeg MB R3C 1A5 – 204/945-7125; Fax: 204/948-2357; URL: http://www.gov.mb.ca/environ/pages/library.html; Symbol: MEW
  Librarian, Shelley Penziwol, Email: shelleyp@mb.sympatico.ca
  Library Technician, Wendy Barber, Email: barber@mbnet.mb.ca
Manitoba Federation of Labour – Occupational Health Centre, #101, 275 Broadway, Winnipeg MB R3C 4M6 – 204/949-0811; Fax: 204/943-4276 – Library Technician, Pat Hebert
Manitoba Finance - Federal-Provincial Relations & Research Library, #910, 386 Broadway, Winnipeg MB R3C 0S9 – 204/945-3757; Fax: 204/945-5051 – Librarian, Beatrice Miller
Manitoba Genealogical Society Inc. – Resource Centre, 885 Notre Dame Ave., Winnipeg MB R3E 0M4 – 204/944-1153; Fax: 204/783-0190
Manitoba Health - Library, 599 Empress St., Winnipeg MB R3G 3H2 – 204/786-7124; Fax: 204/945-5063; Email: mbrooke@gov.mb.ca; URL: http://www.gov.mb.ca/health/library/; Symbol: MWHP
  Manager, Marilyn Brooke, 204/786-7192
  Customer Services Supervisor, Doug Carlson, 204/786-7109
  Customer Services Support, Gail Kohut, 204/945-7198
Manitoba Hydro - Library, 820 Taylor Ave., POBox 815, Winnipeg MB R3C 2P4 – 204/474-3614; Fax: 204/453-1838; Email: rmepp@hydro.mb.ca; Symbol: MWH
  Corporate Librarian, Rhona Lapierre
  Reference Librarian, Ruth Epp, 204/474-3212
Manitoba Indian Cultural Education Centre – People's Library, Branch Office, 119 Sutherland Ave.,

Winnipeg MB R2W 3C9 – 204/942-0228; Fax: 204/947-6564 – Librarian, Vi Chalmers

Manitoba Industry, Trade & Tourism - Audio Visual Library, #510, 155 Carlton St., Winnipeg MB R3C 3H8 – 204/945-3998; Fax: 204/945-2302 – Manager, John W.G. Giesbrecht, 204/945-2036

Business Library, 155 Carlton St., 5th Fl., Winnipeg MB R3C 3H8 – 204/945-2036; Fax: 204/945-2804 Manager, Business Library, John W.G. Giesbrecht

Public Services Technician, P. Jane Bullied

Manitoba Justice - Attorney General's Library, 405 Broadway, 6th Fl., Winnipeg MB R3C 3L6 – 204/945-2895 – Librarian, Brian Chesworth

Great Library, Law Courts Bldg., #331, 408 York Ave., Winnipeg MB R3C 0P9 – 204/945-1958; Fax: 204/948-2138 – Chief Librarian, Garth Niven

Legal Library Resources, #235, 405 Broadway, Winnipeg MB R3C 3L6 – 204/945-0968; Fax: 204/948-2150 – Director, Legal Library Resources, Marilyn Hernandez

Manitoba Labour - Research & Planning Library, #409, 401 York Ave., Winnipeg MB R3C 0P8 – 204/945-3412; Fax: 204/948-2085 – Research Analyst, Glenda Segal

Workplace Safety & Health Library, #200, 401 York Ave., Winnipeg MB R3C 0P8 – 204/945-0580; Fax: 204/945-4556; Toll Free: 1-800-282-8069; URL: http://www.gov.mb.ca/manitoba/safety; Symbol: MWLW – Librarian, Jean Van Walleghem, Email: jvan@labour.gov.mb.ca

Manitoba Labour Board - Library, #402, 258 Portage Ave., Winnipeg MB R3C 0B6 – 204/945-3783; Fax: 204/945-1296 – Research Analyst, Jodi Gilmore, 204/945-5046

Manitoba Legislative Assembly - Library, 200 Vaughan St., Winnipeg MB R3C 1T5 – 204/945-4330; Fax: 204/948-2008; Email: legislative_library@chc.gov.mb.ca; URL: http://www.gov.mb.ca/leg-lib/; Symbol: MWP

Legislative Librarian, Susan Bishop

Reference Services, Head, F.B. MacLowick

Manitoba Library Association – Library, #208, 100 Arthur St., Winnipeg MB R3B 1H3 – 204/943-4567; Fax: 204/942-1555

Manitoba Museum of Man & Nature - Library, 190 Rupert Ave., Winnipeg MB R3B 0N2 – 204/988-0692, 0662; Fax: 204/942-3679; Email: steffan@museummannature.mb.ca; Symbol: MWMM

Head Librarian, Cindi Steffan

Library Technician, Judy Carnegie

Manitoba Natural Resources - Land Information Centre - Air Photo Library, 1007 Century St., Winnipeg MB R3H 0W4 – 204/945-6669; Fax: 204/945-1365; Email: mapsales@nr.gov.mb.ca – Manager, Product Distribution, Valerie Borkowsky

Library, 200 Saulteaux Cres., POBox 26, Winnipeg MB R3J 3W3 – 204/945-6610 – Librarian, Michelle Swanson

Manitoba Ombudsman - Library, #750, 500 Portage Ave., Winnipeg MB R3C 3X1 – 204/786-6483; 1-800-665-0531 (Manitoba); Fax: 204/942-7803 – Office Manager, L. Foster

Manitoba Society of Artists – Archives, 504 Daer Blvd., Winnipeg MB R3K 1C5 – 204/837-1754 – Secretary, Barbara K. Endres

Manitoba Society of Pharmacists Inc. – Pharmacy House Library, 187 St. Mary's Rd., Winnipeg MB R2H 1J2 – 204/233-1411; Fax: 204/237-3468 – Director, Continuing Education, Janet McGillivray

Manitoba Telephone System - Corporate Library, 489 Empress St., POBox 6666, Winnipeg MB R3C 3V6 – 204/941-6344; Fax: 204/772-2155; Email: ENVOY: MTS.LIBRARY; Symbol: MWTS – Tanya L. Evancio

Manitoba Trucking Association – Library, 25 Bunting St., Winnipeg MB R2X 2P5 – 204/632-6600; Fax: 204/694-7134 – Research Coordinator, Dianne Milton

Manitoba Writers' Guild – MWG Resource Centre, #206, 100 Arthur St., Winnipeg MB R3B 1H3 – 204/942-6134; Fax: 204/942-5754 – Administrative Assistant, Kathie Axtell

Meadowood Manor – Nursing Resource Centre, 577 St. Anne's Rd., Winnipeg MB R2M 5B2 – 204/257-2394; Fax: 204/254-5402 – Education Coordinator, Elaine Wardrop

Mines Accident Prevention Association of Manitoba – Film & Reference Library, #700, 305 Broadway, Winnipeg MB R3C 3J7 – 204/942-2789; Fax: 204/943-4371

Misericordia General Hospital – Library, 99 Cornish Ave., Winnipeg MB R3C 1A2 – 204/788-8109; Fax: 204/744-7834 – Sharon Allentuck

National Defence - CFB Winnipeg - Base Recreational Library, 3 Jameswood Dr., Winnipeg MB R3J 0T0 – 204/831-7252 – Head Librarian, L. Schaffer

National Energy Conservation Association – Library, #200, 281 McDermot Ave., Winnipeg MB R3B 0S9 – 204/956-5888; Fax: 204/956-5819; Toll Free: 1-800-263-5974

Pitblado & Hoskin Law Office - Library, #1900, 360 Main St., Winnipeg MB R3C 3Z3 – 204/944-2580; Fax: 204/957-1790; Email: lawyers@pitblado.mb.ca – Librarian, Carla Moore

Red River Community College - Library, 2055 Notre Dame Ave., Winnipeg MB R3H 0J9 – 204/632-2322; Fax: 204/697-4791; URL: http://www.rrcc.mb.ca/~library; Symbol: MWRR

Director, Library Services, Patricia Bozyk

Head, Technical Services, Martin Beckwith

Coordinator, Reference Services, Norman Beattie

Coordinator, Access Services, Karen Hunt

Resource Conservation Manitoba Inc. – Resource Centre, #2, 70 Albert St., Winnipeg MB R3B 1E7 – 204/925-3777; Fax: 204/942-4207 – Information Officer, Darrell Keating

Revenue Canada - Research & Library Services, 325 Broadway, 5th Fl., Winnipeg MB R3C 4T4 – 204/983-1013; Fax: 204/983-1015; Symbol: MWRE – Librarian, Don Albright

Royal Canadian Mounted Police Forensic Laboratory - Scientific Information Centre, 621 Academy Rd., Winnipeg MB R3N 0E7 – 204/983-6586; Fax: 204/983-6399 – Librarian, June Poitras

St. Boniface General Hospital – Carolyn Sifton - Helene Fuld Library, 409 Tache Ave., Winnipeg MB R2H 2A6 – 204/237-2807; Fax: 204/235-3339; Email: rabnett@sbrc.umanitoba.ca; Symbol: MWSBM – Head Librarian, Mark Rabnett

The Salvation Army Grace General Hospital – Winnipeg Library, 300 Booth Dr., Winnipeg MB R3J 3M7 – 204/837-0127; Fax: 204/885-7905; Email: jkochan@mbnet.mb.ca; Symbol: MWGH – Library Technician, Janet Kochan

Seven Oaks General Hospital – Library, 2300 McPhillips St., Winnipeg MB R2V 3M3 – 204/632-3107; Fax: 204/694-9469 – Library Technician, Arthur Short

Société historique de Saint-Boniface – Centre de documentation, 200, av de la Cathédrale, Winnipeg MB R2H 0H7 – 204/233-4888; Téléc: 204/233-4888

Society for Manitobans with Disabilities Inc. – Stephen Sparling Library, 825 Sherbrook St., Winnipeg MB R3A 1M5 – 204/786-5601 ext.319; Fax: 204/783-2919; Toll Free: 1-800-282-8041 – Librarian, Edith Konoplenko

Solicitor General Canada - Stony Mountain Institution - Library, POBox 4500, Winnipeg MB R3C 3W8 – 204/453-5541, ext.5673; Fax: 204/453-5541; Symbol: MWSM – Librarian, Peter Kulyk

Spina Bifida & Hydrocephalus Association of Canada – Library, #220, 388 Donald St., Winnipeg MB R3B 2J4 – 204/957-1784; Fax: 204/957-1794; Toll Free: 1-800-565-9488 – Mary Meldrum

Sport Manitoba – Library, 200 Main St., Winnipeg MB R3C 4M2 – 204/925-5619; Fax: 204/925-5916 – Faye Finch

Statistics Canada - Prairie Regional Reference Centre - Manitoba, Via Rail Bldg., #200, 123 Main St., Winnipeg MB R3C 4V9 – 204/983-4020; Fax: 204/983-7543; Toll Free: 1-800-263-1136; Email: statswpg@Solutions.net

Assistant Regional Director, B. Gloyn

Data Dissemination Officer, Ron Wonneck

Taylor McCaffrey Law Office - Library, 400 St. Mary Ave., 9th Fl., Winnipeg MB R3C 4K5 – 204/988-0463; Fax: 204/957-0945; Email: taylorm@mbnet.mb.ca; URL: http://www.mbnet.mb.ca/~taylorm – Librarian, Jane Bridle

Thompson Dorfman Sweatman Law Office - Library, Toronto-Dominion Centre, 2200 - 201 Portage Ave., Winnipeg MB R3B 3L3 – 204/957-1930; Fax: 204/943-6445 – Librarian, P. Betcher

Transport Canada - Central Region Library, Aviation Audio Visual Library, 333 Main St., 16th Fl., POBox 8550, Winnipeg MB R3C 0P6 – 204/983-6853; Fax: 204/984-2255; Symbol: MWTCR – A/Regional Librarian, Lisa Wong

Travel Manitoba – Industry, Trade & Tourism Business Library, Dept. SA7, 155 Carlton St., 7th Fl., Winnipeg MB R3C 3H8 – 204/945-2036; Fax: 204/945-2302; Toll Free: 1-800-665-0040 – Librarian, John Giesbrecht

Ukrainian Cultural & Educational Centre - Library, 184 Alexander Ave. East, Winnipeg MB R3B 0L6 – 204/942-0218; Fax: 204/943-2857; Email: ucec@mb.sympatico.ca – Librarian, Larissa Tolchinsky

Ukrainian Orthodox Church of Canada – Library, 9 St. Johns Ave., Winnipeg MB R2W 1G8 – 204/586-3093, 582-8709; Fax: 204/582-5241 – Archivist/Librarian, Wolodymyr G. Senchuk

UMA Engineering Ltd. - Library, 1479 Buffalo Pl., Winnipeg MB R3T 1L7 – 204/284-0580; Fax: 204/475-3646 – Bernice Kandrac

United Grain Growers Ltd. – Corporate Library, #2800, 201 Portage Ave., POBox 6600, Winnipeg MB R3C 3A7 – 204/944-5754; Fax: 204/944-5415 – Library Technician, Jackie Garrity

University of Manitoba - Libraries, 66 Chancellors Circle, Winnipeg MB R3T 2N2 – 204/474-9881; Fax: 204/261-1515; URL: http://www.cc.umanitoba.ca/academic_support/libraries/

Director of Libraries, Carolynne Presser

Finance & Planning, Executive Assistant, Janice Chaturvedi

Personnel, Executive Assistant, Linda Lassman

Collections Management, Coordinator, Donna Breyfogle

Collections, Associate Director, Michael Angel

Information Services & Systems, Associate Director, Susan Suart

Albert D. Cohen Management Library, Head, Dennis Felbel, 204/474-8440

Architecture & Fine Arts Library, Head, Mary Lochhead, 204/474-9216

D.S. Woods Education Library, Head, David Thirlwall, 204/474-9976

Donald W. Craik Engineering Library, Head, Norma Godavari, 204/474-9445

E.K. Williams Law Library, Head, Neil A. Campbell, 204/474-9995

Eckhardt-Gramatté Music Library, Head, Vladimir Simosko, 204/474-9567

Elizabeth Dafoe Library, Head, Nicole Michaud-Oystryk, 204/474-9211

Neil John Maclean Health Sciences Library, Head, Ada Ducas, 204/789-3821

Science Library, Head, Judy Harper, 204/474-8171

St. Andrew's College Library, Head, Raisa Moroz, 204/474-8901
St. John's College Library, Head, Patrick Wright, 204/474-8542
Fr. Harold Drake Library, Head, Earle Ferguson, 204/474-8585
Neil John Maclean Health Sciences Library, 770 Bannatyne Ave., Winnipeg MB R3E 0W3 – 204/789-3342; Fax: 204/775-0788; Email: infodesk@bldghsc.lan1.umanitoba.ca; URL: http://www.cc.umanitoba.ca/libraries/units/njmhsl/ – Ada M. Ducas
University of Winnipeg - Library, 515 Portage Ave., Winnipeg MB R3B 2E9 – 204/786-9801; Fax: 204/783-8910, 786-1824; URL: http://www.mercury.uwinnipeg.ca; Symbol: MWUC
University Librarian, W.R. Converse, 204/786-9801
Associate University Librarian, Coreen Koz, 204/786-9802
Acquisitions, Head, Kathy Buschhausen, 204/786-9806
Circulation, Head, Pat Russell, 204/786-9807
Computerized Information Systems & Networks, Head, William Pond, 204/786-9812
Interlending & Document Supply Services (IDSS), Heather Mathieson, 204/786-9814
Technical Services, Head, Joan Scanlon, 204/786-9803
Cataloguing Librarian, Kam Wing Lee
Collection Librarian, Linwood DeLong, 204/786-9124
Government Documents/Reference Librarian, Linda Dixon
Special Projects Librarian, Sandra Zuk, 204/786-9813
Reference/Public Services & Systems, Head, William Pond, 204/786-9812
Project Manager, Allison Dixon, 204/786-9031
Victoria General Hospital – Library, 2340 Pembina Hwy., Winnipeg MB R3T 2E8 – 204/477-3307; Fax: 204/261-0223 – Lynne Hardy
Volunteer Centre of Winnipeg, 5 Donald St. South, 3rd Fl., Winnipeg MB R3L 2T4 – 204/477-5180; Fax: 204/284-5200 – Librarian, Jennifer King
Walsh, Micay and Company Law Office - Library, Richardson Bldg., One Lombard Pl., 10th Fl., Winnipeg MB R3B 3H1 – 204/942-0081; Fax: 204/957-1261 – Partner, A. Dalmyn
Western Economic Diversification - Canada Business Service Centre, #800, 330 Portage Ave., Winnipeg MB R3C 2V2 – 204/984-2272; Fax: 204/983-3852; Toll Free: 1-800-665-2019; Email: manitoba@cbsc.ic.gc.ca; URL: http://www.cbsc.org/manitoba/index.html
Chief Librarian, Oliver Bernuetz, 204/983-6182
Manager, Shannon Coughlin
Business & Trade Services Officer, Lee Gregg, 204/983-8036
Business Officer, Daria Gawronsky
William Molloy Memorial Library, 19 Linacre Rd., Winnipeg MB R3T 3G5 – 204/261-9366 – Sandra Konrad
Winnipeg Art Gallery - The Clara Lander Library, 300 Memorial Blvd., Winnipeg MB R3C 1V1 – 204/786-6641; Fax: 204/788-4998; Email: cathwag@mb.sympatico.mb; URL: http://www.wag.mb.ca; Symbol: MWWA – Librarian, Catherine Shields
Winnipeg Clinic - Library, 425 St. Mary Ave., Winnipeg MB R3C 0N2 – 204/957-1900, ext.512; Fax: 204/943-2164 – Librarian, S. Loeppky
Winnipeg Free Press - Library, 1355 Mountain Ave., Winnipeg MB R2X 3B6 – 204/697-7289; Fax: 204/697-7412; Email: library@freepress.mb.ca – Librarian, J. Williamson, 204/697-7290
Winnipeg Gay/Lesbian Resource Centre, #1, 222 Osborne St. South, Winnipeg MB R3C 2Z6 – 204/284-5208; 474-0212; Fax: 204/478-1160 – Services Coordinator, Jeremy Buckner
The Winnipeg Sun - Library, 1700 Church Ave., Winnipeg MB R2X 3A2 – 204/694-2022 – Marcia P. Stephenson
Winnipeg Symphony Orchestra Inc. – Music Library, #101, 555 Main St., Winnipeg MB R3B 1C3 – 204/949-3950; Box Office: 949-3999; Fax: 204/956-4271 – Margo Hodgson
YM-YWCA - Women's Resource Centre, 301 Vaughan St., Winnipeg MB R3B 2N7 – 204/989-4140; Fax: 204/943-6159 – Volunteer Librarian, Babs Friesen

## NEW BRUNSWICK

### Regional Library Systems with Member Libraries

#### ALBERT-WESTMORLAND-KENT REGIONAL LIBRARY

#201, 644 Main St., Moncton NB E1C 1E2 – 506/869-6032; Fax: 506/869-6022; Email: potvin@gov.nb.ca
Regional Librarian, Claude Potvin
Reference Librarian, Thérèse Arsenault
Children's Librarian, Nancy Cohen

Bibliothèque publique de Bouctouche, 84, boul Irving, Bouctouche NB E0A 1G0 – 506/743-7263; Téléc: 506/743-7263 – Bibliothécaire, Carmen Leger
Bibliothèque publique de Dieppe, 333, av Acadie, Dieppe NB E1A 1G9 – 506/877-7945; Téléc: 506/877-7910 – Bibliothécaire, Claudia Losier
Dorchester Public Library, Dorchester NB E0A 1M0 – 506/379-6611 – Librarian, Daphne Holmes
Hillsborough Public Library, PO Box 8, Hillsborough NB E0A 1X0 – 506/734-3722 – Barbara Alcorn
Hopewell Cape Public Library, Hopewell Cape NB E0A 1Y0 – Librarian, Shirley Teahan
Moncton Public Library, #101, 644 Main St., Moncton NB E1C 1E2 – 506/869-6000; Fax: 506/869-6022 – Librarian, Jeanne Maddix
Petitcodiac Public Library, 31 Main St., PO Box 369, Petitcodiac NB E0A 2H0 – 506/756-3144; Fax: 506/756-3142 – Librarian, Janet Coates-Mason
Port Elgin Public Library, PO Box 38, Port Elgin NB E0A 2K0 – 506/538-2120; Fax: 506/538-2263 – Librarian, Betty Davis
Bibliothèque publique de Richibuctou, 81, rue Main, CP 397, Richibuctou NB E0A 2M0 – 506/523-7851; Téléc: 506/523-7851 – Bibliothécaire, Michele-Ann Goguen
Riverview Public Library, 34 Honour House Ct., Riverview NB E1B 3Y9 – 506/387-2108; Fax: 506/387-4970 – Librarian, Lynn Cormier
Sackville Public Library, 33 West Main St., PO Box 1769, Sackville NB E0A 3C0 – 506/536-3184; Fax: 506/364-0427 – Librarian, Allan Alward
Bibliothèque publique de St-Antoine, 11, av Jeanne d'Arc, CP 328, St-Antoine NB E0A 2X0 – 506/525-4028; Téléc: 506/525-4028 – Bibliothécaire, Paulette Leger
Bibliothèque publique de Memramcook, CP 98, St-Joseph NB E0A 2Y0 – 506/758-4029; Téléc: 506/758-4030 – Bibliothécaire, Jocelyne Leblanc
Salisbury Public Library, 205 Main St., PO Box 419, Salisbury NB E0A 3E0 – 506/372-3240 – Librarian, Margaret Crosthwaite
Bibliothèque publique de Shediac, 161, rue Main, CP 1448, Shediac NB E0A 3G0 – 506/532-7014; Téléc: 506/532-6156 – Bibliothécaire, Gabrielle LeBlanc

#### CHALEUR REGIONAL LIBRARY

88 Sister Green Rd., PO Box 607, Campbellton NB E3N 3H1 – 506/789-6599; Fax: 506/789-7318; Email: libcr@gov.nb.ca
Regional Director, James Violette

Bibliothèque publique d'Atholville, 272A, rue Notre-Dame, Atholville NB E3N 3Z9 – 506/789-2914; Fax: 506/789-2914 – Responsable, A.M. Bernard
Bibliothèque publique de Bas-Caraquet, 8185, rue St-Paul, CP 149, Bas-Caraquet NB E0B 1E0 – 506/726-2775; Téléc: 506/726-2770 – Responsable, M. David
Bibliothèque du Centenaire Népisiguit, 360, av Douglas, CP 86, Bathurst NB E2A 3Z1 – 506/548-0706; Téléc: 506/548-0708 – Bibliothécaire, Jacques Filiatrault
Bibliothèque publique Mgr. Robichaud, 855, rue Principale, CP 600, Beresford NB E0B 1H0 – 506/542-2704; Téléc: 506/542-2702 – Responsable, M. Imbeault
Campbellton Centennial Library, 2, rue Aberdeen, PO Box 130, Campbellton NB E3N 3G1 – 506/753-5253; Fax: 506/753-3803 – Librarian, James Katan
Bibliothèque publique Mgr. Paquet, 10A, rue Colisée, Caraquet NB E1W 1A5 – 506/726-2681; Téléc: 506/726-2685 – Responsable, C. Hébert-LeBouthillier
Bibliothèque du centenaire de Dalhousie, 405, rue Adelaide, CP 1980, Dalhousie NB E0K 1B0 – 506/684-7370; Téléc: 506/684-7374 – Bibliothécaire, Myrian Doiron
Bibliothèque publique de Lamèque, 46, rue du Pêcheur nord, CP 922, Lamèque NB E0B 1V0 – 506/344-3262; Téléc: 506/344-3263 – Responsable, J.M. Noël
Bibliothèque publique de Petit-Rocher, 702, rue Principale, CP 490, Petit-Rocher NB E0B 2E0 – 506/542-2744; Téléc: 506/542-2745 – Responsable, Claudette Boudreau
Bibliothèque publique de Shippagan, 244, boul J.D. Gauthier, CP 739, Shippagan NB E0B 2P0 – 506/336-3920; Téléc: 506/336-3921 – Responsable, P. Godin
Bibliothèque publique de Tracadie-Sheila, 3620, rue Principale, CP 3654, Tracadie-Sheila NB E1X 1G5 – 506/393-4005; Téléc: 506/395-4009 – Responsable, I. Aubie

#### BIBLIOTHÈQUE RÉGIONALE DU HAUT-SAINT-JEAN

135A, rue St-François, Edmundston NB E3V 1E8 – 506/739-7331; Téléc: 506/735-2745; Courrier électronique: libhr@gov.nb.ca; Symbol: NBEBR
Bibliothécaire régional, Guy Lefrançois

Bibliothèque publique Mgr. W.J. Conway, 74, rue Canada, Edmundston NB E3V 1V5 – 506/735-4713; Téléc: 506/737-6848 – Bibliothécaire, J. Robert Daigle
Bibliothèque publique de Grand-Sault, 136, rue Church, CP 850, Grand-Sault NB E3Z 1C3 – 506/475-7781; Téléc: 506/475-7783 – Bibliothécaire, Patricia Toner
Bibliothèque publique de Kedgwick, 17, rue Jeanne-Mance, CP 250, Kedgwick NB E0K 1C0 – 506/284-2757; Téléc: 506/284-4557 – Responsable, Mariette St-Pierre
Bibliothèque publique Mgr. Plourde, 15, rue Bellevue, St-François NB E7A 1A4 – 506/992-6052; Téléc: 506/992-6047; Courrier électronique: bibliofr@nbnet.nb.ca – Responsable, Bertin Nadeau
Bibliothèque publique Dr. Lorne J. Violette, 180, rue St-Jean, CP 789, St-Léonard NB E0L 1M0 – 506/423-3025; Téléc: 506/423-3026 – Responsable, Nicole Malenfant
Bibliothèque publique La Moisson de St-Quentin, 206, rue Canada, St-Quentin NB E0K 1J0 – 506/235-1955; Téléc: 506/235-1952 – Responsable, Yvette Quimper

#### SAINT JOHN REGIONAL LIBRARY

1 Market Sq., Saint John NB E2L 4Z6 – 506/643-7220; Fax: 506/643-7225; Email: libsr@gov.nb.ca; Symbol: NBS
Regional Librarian, Pamela Stevens Rosolen

Information Technology/Branch Development, Manager, Barbara A. Malcolm
Public Relations/Development Librarian, Jean Cunningham
Youth Services Librarian, Joann Hamilton-Barry
Information Services Librarian, Diane Buhay

Campobello Public Library, 3 Welshpool St., PO Box 51, Campobello NB E0G 3H0 – 506/752-7082; Fax: 506/752-7083 – Branch Manager, Glenna Cline
Kennebecasis Public Library, 1 Landing Ct., Quispamsis NB E2E 4R2 – 506/849-5314; Fax: 506/849-5318 – Branch Manager, Leslye McVicar
Ross Memorial Library, 110 King St., PO Box 367, St. Andrews NB E0G 2X0 – 506/529-5125; Fax: 506/529-5129 – Branch Supervisor, Lesa Pomeroy
Bibliothèque Le Cormoran, Centre Samuel de Champlain, RR#1, 67 Ragged Point, Saint John NB E2K 5C3 – 506/658-4610; Fax: 506/658-3984 – Branch Supervisor, Mireille Mercure
East Branch Public Library, 545 Westmorland Rd., Saint John NB E2J 2G5 – 506/643-7250 – Branch Manager, Valerie Bauer
Saint John Free Public Library, 1 Market Sq., Saint John NB E2L 4Z6 – 506/643-7220; Fax: 506/643-7225 – City Librarian, Ian A. Wilson
West Branch Public Library, Lancaster Mall, 621 Fairville Blvd., Saint John NB E2M 4X5 – 506/643-7260 – Branch Manager, Barbara MacKay
Saint Croix Public Library, 1 Budd Ave., St. Stephen NB E3L 1E8 – 506/466-7529; Fax: 506/466-7574 – Branch Manager, Elva Hatt
Sussex Public Library, #597, 601 Main St., PO Box 1550, Sussex NB E0E 1P0 – 506/432-4585; Fax: 506/432-4583; Symbol: NBS – Branch Manager, Pauline Giberson

**YORK REGIONAL LIBRARY**

4 Carleton St., Fredericton NB E3B 5P4 – 506/453-5380; Fax: 506/457-4878; Email: libyr@gov.nb.ca; Symbol: NBFYR
Regional Librarian, Laurette Mackey
Reference Librarian, Greg Blake
Children's Librarian, Marilyn Lohnes
Technical Services Librarian, Geraldine Stanaway

Boiestown Community-School Library, PO Box 99, Boiestown NB E0H 1A0 – 506/369-2022; Fax: 506/369-2023 – Branch Manager, Gail Ross
Chipman Public Library, PO Box 40, Chipman NB E0E 1C0 – 506/339-5852; Fax: 506/339-6197 – Branch Manager, Krista Blyth
Doaktown Community-School Library, 430 Main St., PO Box 58, Doaktown NB E0C 1G0 – 506/365-2018; Fax: 506/365-2019 – Branch Manager, Belva Brown
Andrew & Laura McCain Public Library, PO Box 270, Florenceville NB E0J 1K0 – 506/392-5294; Fax: 506/392-6143 – Branch Manager, Lorena Green
Bibliothèque Dr Marguerite Michaud, Centre communautaire Ste-Anne, 715, rue Priestman, Fredericton NB E3B 5W1 – 506/455-1740; Téléc: 506/453-3958 – Bibliothécaire, Françoise Caron
Fredericton Public Library, 12 Carleton St., Fredericton NB E3B 5P4 – 506/460-2800; Fax: 506/460-2801 – City Librarian, William Molesworth
Minto Public Library, 19 Maple St., Minto NB E0E 1J0 – 506/327-3220; Fax: 506/327-3041; Email: minto1@nbtel.nb.ca – Branch Manager, Mary Lambropoulos
Nashwaaksis Public School Library, 324 Fulton Ave., Fredericton NB E3A 2C3 – 506/453-3241; Fax: 506/444-4129 – Branch Manager, Ruth Russell
Dr. Walter Chestnut Public Library, 395 Main St., PO Box 120, Hartland NB E0J 1N0 – 506/375-4876; Fax: 506/375-6816 – Branch Manager, Ann Ellis
Harvey Community Library, PO Box 10, Harvey Station NB E0H 1H0 – 506/366-2206; Fax: 506/366-2210 – Branch Manager, Joanne Cole
McAdam Public Library, 146 Saunders Rd., McAdam NB E0H 1K0 – 506/784-1403; Fax: 506/784-1402 – Branch Manager, Catherine Dougherty
Bibliothèque Père-Louis-Lamontagne, Carrefour-Beausoleil, 300, ch Beaverbrook, Miramichi NB E1V 1A1 – 506/627-4084; Téléc: 506/622-6361 – Bibliothécaire, Sylvan Lavoie
Chatham Public Library, PO Box 446, Miramichi NB E1N 3A8 – 506/773-6274; Fax: 506/773-6963 – Branch Manager, Patricia Clancy
Newcastle Public Library, 100 Fountain Head Lane, Miramichi NB E1V 4A1 – 506/627-2545; Fax: 506/623-2335 – Librarian, Catherine Reid
Nackawic Public & School Library, Landegger Dr., Nackawic NB E0H 1P0 – 506/575-2136; Fax: 506/575-2336 – Branch Manager, Carolyn Munroe
Oromocto Public Library, 54 Miramichi Rd., Oromocto NB E2L 1S2 – 506/357-3320; Fax: 506/357-2266 – Librarian, Muriel Morton
Perth-Andover Public Library, PO Box 128, Perth-Andover NB E0J 1V0 – 506/273-2843; Fax: 506/273-1913 – Branch Manager, Tammie De Merchant
Plaster Rock Public-School Library, Tobique Valley High School, PO Box 249, Plaster Rock NB E0J 1W0 – 506/356-6018; Fax: 506/356-6019 – Branch Manager, Carolyn Knowlton
Stanley Public Library, PO Box 108, Stanley NB E0H 1T0 – 506/367-2492; Fax: 506/367-3166 – Branch Manager, Rhonda Smith
L.P. Fisher Public Library, 679 Main St., PO Box 1540, Woodstock NB E0J 2B0 – 506/328-6880; Fax: 506/325-9527 – Branch Manager, Jonathan Tait

## Special & College Libraries & Resource Centres

**BATHURST**

Chaleur Regional Hospital – Library, 1750 Sunset Dr., Bathurst NB E2A 4L7 – 506/344-2261; Fax: 506/545-1429 – Suzanne Doucet
New Brunswick Community College - Bathurst Campus Library, rue Collège, CP 266, Bathurst NB E2A 3Z2 – 506/547-7495; Fax: 506/547-2174; Symbol: NBBCC – Bibliothécaire, Lucien Chassé

**DORCHESTER**

Solicitor General Canada - Dorchester Penitentiary - Library, POBox A, Dorchester NB E0A 1M0 – 506/857-6363, ext.2508; Symbol: NBDD – Librarian, Bill Geier
Westmorland Institution - Library, POBox 130, Dorchester NB E0A 1M0 – 506/379-2471, ext.3503; Symbol: NBDW – Librarian, Tim Atkinson

**EDMUNDSTON**

Centre international pour le développement de l'inforoute en français – Cyberthèque, 165, boul Hébert, Edmundston NB E3V 2S8 – 506/737-5280; Téléc: 506/737-5281 – Documentaliste et cyberthécaire, Cécile Lointier
Fraser Paper Inc. – Central Technical Research Library, 27 Rice St., Edmundston NB E3V 1S9 – 506/735-5551 – Manager, Jean-Claude Martin
New Brunswick Community College - Edmundston Campus Library, POBox 70, Edmundston NB E3V 3K7 – 506/735-2500; Fax: 506/735-1108; Email: kclarkgorey@brunswickmicro.nb.ca; Symbol: NBECC – Librarian, Kenda Clark-Gorey
Université de Moncton - Campus d'Edmundston, 165, boul Hebert, Edmundston NB E3V 2S8 – 506/737-5058; Téléc: 506/737-5373; Symbol: NBESLM – Bibliotechnicienne, Claire Charest

**FREDERICTON**

New Brunswick Department of Agriculture - Land Resources Branch – Library, POBox 6000, Fredericton NB E3B 5H1 – 506/453-2109; Fax: 506/457-7267
New Brunswick Research & Productivity Council – RPC Info Centre, 921 College Hill Rd., Fredericton NB E3B 6Z9 – 506/452-1381; Fax: 506/452-1395; Email: vjackson@rpc.unb.ca; Symbol: NPFRP – Coordinator, Virginia Jackson
ADI Group Inc. – Library, #300, 1133 Regent St., Fredericton NB E3B 3Z2 – 506/452-9000; Fax: 506/459-3954; Email: dee@adi.ca – Librarian, Debra Edmondson
Agriculture & Agri-Food Canada-Potato Research Centre – Library, 850 Lincoln Rd., POBox 20280, Fredericton NB E3B 4Z7 – 506/452-3260; Fax: 506/452-3316; Email: andersonrm@em.agr.ca; Symbol: NBFAG – Librarian, Richard Anderson
AIDS New Brunswick – Resource Centre/Centre des ressources, 65 Brunswick St., Fredericton NB E3B 1G5 – 506/459-7518, 450-2620; Fax: 506/459-5782 – George Flanders
Association des enseignantes et des enseignants francophones du Nouveau-Brunswick – Bibliothèque, CP 712, Fredericton NB E3B 5B4 – 506/452-8921; Téléc: 506/453-9795 – Germaine Burns
Association Museums New Brunswick – Resource Centre/Centre de documentation, 503 Queen St., POBox 116, Fredericton NB E3B 4Y2 – 506/452-2908; Fax: 506/459-0481
Canada/New Brunswick Service Centre - Resource Centre, 570 Queen St., Fredericton NB E3B 6Z6 – 506/444-6158; Toll Free: 1-800-668-1010; URL: http://www.cbsc.org/nb/index.html – Business Information Officer, Paulianne Howe
Conservation Council of New Brunswick – Library, 180 St. John St., Fredericton NB E3B 4A9 – 506/458-8747; Fax: 506/458-1047
Dr. Everett Chalmers Hospital – Health Sciences Library, POBox 9000, Fredericton NB E3B 5N5 – 506/452-5432; Fax: 506/452-5571; Email: r3pclark@health.nb.ca; Symbol: NBFDEC – Librarian, Paul Clark
Industry Canada - Business Service Centre, 570 Queen St., Fredericton NB E3B 6Z6 – 506/444-6140; Fax: 506/444-6172; Toll Free: 1-800-668-1010; Email: cbscnb@cbsc.ic.gc.ca; URL: http://www.cbsc.org/nb/
Law Society of New Brunswick – Library, Justice Bldg., #206, 1133 Regent St., Fredericton NB E3B 3Z2 – 506/453-2500; Fax: 506/453-9438 – Law Librarian, Diane Hanson
Natural Resources Canada-Canadian Forest Service: Atlantic Forestry Centre – Library, Hugh John Flemming Forestry Centre, College Hill, POBox 4000, Fredericton NB E3B 5P7 – 506/452-3541; Fax: 506/452-3525; Email: mrenner@fcmr.forestry.ca; Symbol: NBFE – Head Librarian, Melinda Renner
New Brunswick Advanced Education & Labour - Library, 470 York St., POBox 6000, Fredericton NB E3B 5H1 – 506/453-8247; Fax: 506/453-3618; Email: mcomeau@gov.nb.ca – Administrative Services Officer, Mary Comeau
New Brunswick Agriculture - Publication Centre, POBox 6000, Fredericton NB E3B 5H1 – 506/453-2333; Fax: 506/453-7978 – Information Officer, Amrik Jaswal
New Brunswick College of Craft & Design - Library, POBox 6000, Fredericton NB E3B 5H1 – 506/453-2305; Fax: 506/457-7352 – Honorary Librarian, Barbara M. Smith
New Brunswick Department of the Environment - Library, 364 Argyle St., 2nd Fl., Fredericton NB E3B 1T9 – 506/453-2566; Fax: 506/453-3843; Symbol: NBFME – Librarian, Gail Darby
New Brunswick Economic Development & Tourism - Records Management/Library, POBox 6000, Fredericton NB E3B 5H1 – 506/453-2187; Fax: 506/444-5299
Records Manager, Sandra Thomas

Departmental Library, Frances Scott

New Brunswick Education - Library, POBox 6000, Fredericton NB E3B 5H1 – 506/453-3229; Fax: 506/453-3325; Symbol: NBFED – Librarian, Judith Colter, M.L.S.

New Brunswick Federation of Agriculture – Library, #206, 1115 Regent St., Fredericton NB E3B 3Z2 – 506/452-8101; Fax: 506/452-1085 – Policy Officer, Bruce Oliver

New Brunswick Finance - Library, #373, Centennial Bldg., POBox 6000, Fredericton NB E3B 5H1 – 506/453-2511 – Chief Librarian, Katherine Brennan

New Brunswick Health & Community Services - Library, Carleton Place, 3rd Fl., POBox 5100, Fredericton NB E3B 5G8 – 506/453-3715; Fax: 506/453-2958; Email: librarydoh@gov.nb.ca; Symbol: NBFH – Chief Librarian, Carole Ford, 506/453-3715

New Brunswick Healthcare Association – Library, 861 Woodstock Rd., Fredericton NB E3B 7R7 – 506/451-0750; Fax: 506/451-0760 – Librarian, Linda-Ann Sturgeon

New Brunswick Legislative Library, Legislative Bldg., POBox 6000, Fredericton NB E3B 5H1 – 506/453-2338; Fax: 506/444-5889; Email: leglibbib@gov.nb.ca; Symbol: NBFL
- Chief Librarian, Eric L. Swanick
- Reference Librarian, Margaret Pacey
- Government Publications Librarian, Janet McNeil
- Technical Services Librarian, Jean-Claude Arcand

New Brunswick Lung Association – Library, Victoria Health Centre, #257, 65 Brunswick St., Fredericton NB E3B 1G5 – 506/455-8961; Fax: 506/462-0939; Toll Free: 1-800-565-5864 – Program Coordinator, Susan Kelso

New Brunswick Natural Resources & Energy - Library, POBox 6000, Fredericton NB E3B 5H1 – 506/453-5478; Fax: 506/444-4367; Symbol: NBFNR – Library Technician, Sheila Robinson

New Brunswick Ombudsman - Library, POBox 6000, Fredericton NB E3B 5H1 – 506/453-2789; Fax: 506/444-4087; Toll Free: 1-800-561-4021 – Secretary, Giséle Girouard

New Brunswick Statistics Agency - Library, Centennial Bldg., #248, 670 King St., Fredericton NB E3B 5H1 – 506/453-2381; Fax: 506/453-7970 – Secretary, Mary Lou Cotter

New Brunswick Supply & Services - Information Services Group Library, #200, Westmorland Pl., POBox 6000, Fredericton NB E3B 5H1 – 506/453-3807; Fax: 506/453-2270; Email: ENVOY: NBFDSS; Symbol: NBFDSS – Librarian, David Campbell

New Brunswick Teachers' Federation – Library, POBox 1535, Fredericton NB E3B 5R6 – 506/452-1726; Fax: 506/453-9795; Email: burnsg@nbnet.nb.ca; Symbol: NBFTF – Germaine Burns

New Brunswick Translation Bureau - Library, Marysville Place, POBox 6000, Fredericton NB E3B 5H1 – 506/453-2920; Fax: 506/459-7911; Email: luciela@gov.nb.ca; Symbol: NBFT
- Chief Librarian, Lucie Laperrière
- Assistant Librarian, Suzanne Pelletier

New Brunswick Transportation - Library, POBox 6000, Fredericton NB E3B 5H1 – 506/453-2535; Fax: 506/444-5790; Email: adm041@gov.nb.ca; Symbol: NBFTR
- Library Manager, Bonnie Ellis
- Library Assistant, Lisette Dionne

Nurses Association of New Brunswick – Library, 165 Regent St., Fredericton NB E3B 3W5 – 506/458-8731; Fax: 506/459-2838 – Librarian, Barbara Thompson

Tourism Industry Association of New Brunswick Inc. – Library, Prospect Place, #206, 191 Prospect St., Fredericton NB E3B 2T7 – 506/458-5646; Fax: 506/459-3634 – Program Director, Karen Richard

University of New Brunswick - Harriet Irving Library, POBox 7500, Fredericton NB E3B 5H5 – 506/453-4572; Fax: 506/453-4595; Symbol: NBFU
- Director of Libraries, John D. Teskey
- Associate Director of Libraries, Dr. Alan Burk
- Technical Services, Head, Judith Aldus
- Collection Development, Head, Judith Colson
- Engineering Library, Head, Doris Rauch, 506/453-4747
- Science & Forestry Library, Head, Eszter Schwenke, 506/453-4601
- Education Resource Centre, Head, Patricia Johnston, 506/453-3516
- Reference Services, Coordinator, Janet Phillips, 506/453-4749

Writers' Federation of New Brunswick – Library, POBox 37, Fredericton NB E3B 4Y2 – 506/459-7228; Fax: 506/459-7228 – Project Coordinator, Anna Mae Snider

### GRAND-SAULT

New Brunswick Community College - Grand-Sault Campus Library, 160, rue Réservoir, POBox 1270, Grand-Sault NB E3Z 1C6 – 506/473-7733; Fax: 506/473-7769 – Librarian, Kenda Clark-Gorey

### MONCTON

Association acadienne des artistes professionnelles du Nouveau-Brunswick inc. – Centre de ressources des arts et de la culture, #17, 140, rue Botsford, Moncton NB E1C 4X4 – 506/852-3313; Téléc: 506/852-3401 – Directrice, Jeanne Farrah

Atlantic Baptist University - George A. Rawlyk Library, POBox 6004, Moncton NB E1C 9L7 – 506/858-8970; Fax: 506/858-9694; Email: ldouthwright@abu.nb.ca; Symbol: NBMAB – Librarian, Ivan W. Douthwright

Atlantic Canada Opportunities Agency - Library, 644 Main St., 3rd Fl., POBox 6051, Moncton NB E1C 9J8 – 506/851-2144; Fax: 506/851-7403 – Librarian, Malcolm MacBeath

Atlantic Lottery Corporation - Information & Research Centre, POBox 5500, Moncton NB E1C 8W6 – 506/867-5846; Fax: 506/867-5738; Email: atloto6@nbnet.nb.ca – Librarian, Wendy Donnahee

Canadian Air Transport Administration - Atlantic Regional Library, Place Heritage Court, 95 Foundry St., 5th Fl., POBox 42, Moncton NB E1C 8K6 – 506/857-7360; Fax: 506/851-3018; Symbol: NBMOTA

Embroiderers' Association of Canada, Inc. – Leonida Leatherdale Library, 1311 Salisbury Rd., RR#1, Moncton NB E1C 8J5 – 604/466-7530; Fax: 506/478-2879 – Librarian, Helen McCrindle

Environment Canada-Environmental Quality Laboratories: Moncton – Library, Environmental Science Centre, POBox 23005, Moncton NB E1A 6S8 – 506/851-6606; Fax: 506/851-6608 – Administrative Assistant, L. Boulter

Fisheries & Oceans Canada - Fisheries Centre Library, 343 Archibald St., POBox 5030, Moncton NB E1C 9B6 – 506/851-6264; Fax: 506/857-7732; Email: paulette.levesque@maritimes.dfo.ca; Symbol: NBMF – Librarian, Paulette Lévesque, 506/857-6226

Fowler & Fowler Law Office - Library, #11, 885 Main St., POBox 721, Moncton NB E1C 8M9 – 506/857-8811; Fax: 506/857-9297 – James E. Fowler

Hôpital Dr. Georges L. Dumont – Bibliothèque des sciences de la santé, 330, rue Archibald, Moncton NB E1C 2Z3 – 506/862-4247; Téléc: 506/862-4246; Courrier électronique: martheb@health.nb.ca; Symbol: NBMHD – Bibliothécaire, Marthe Brideau

Moncton Hospital – Health Sciences Library - South-East Health Care Corp., 135 MacBeath Ave., Moncton NB E1C 6Z8 – 506/857-5447; Fax: 506/857-5785; Symbol: NBMMH – Librarian, S.P. Libby

New Brunswick Community College - Moncton Campus Library, 1234 Mountain Rd., Moncton NB E1C 8H9 – 506/856-2226; Fax: 506/856-3288; Symbol: NBMOCC – Librarian, Bill Hegan

Public Works & Government Services Canada - Superannuation Branch - Reference Library, POBox 5010, Moncton NB E1C 8Z5 – 506/533-5681; Fax: 506/533-5558; Symbol: NBMOS – Documentation Coordinator, Marie-Marthe Sarrazin

Université de Moncton - Bibliothèque Champlain, Centre universitaire de Moncton, Moncton NB E1A 3E9 – 506/858-4012; Téléc: 506/858-4086; URL: http://www.umoncton.ca/champ/index.html; Symbol: NBMOU
- Bibliothécaire en chef, Gilles Chiasson
- Bibliothèque de droit, Directrice, Simoine Clermont, 506/858-4547
- Centre d'études acadiennes, Bibliothécaire, Vacant, 506/858-4085
- Centre de ressources pédagogiques, Directrice, Berthe Boudreau, 506/858-4356
- Centre universitaire de Shippagan, Directrice, Rose-Marie Gauthier
- Centre universitaire St-Louis-Maillet, Directrice, Jeannine Michaud, 506/737-5050

### NEWCASTLE

Newcastle Hospital – Library, 673 King George Hwy., POBox 420, Newcastle NB E1V 3M5 – 506/627-7041; Fax: 506/627-7029; Email: mirhslib@nbnet.nb.ca; Symbol: NBNM – Health Sciences Librarian, Nancy McAllister

### PRINCE WILLIAM

Kings Landing Library, Route 2, Exit 259, Prince William NB E0H 1S0 – 506/363-5090; Fax: 506/363-5757; Email: cnbkl@chin.cycor.ca
- Director, Bob Dallison
- Curator of Collections, Don Lemon

### RENOUS

Solicitor General Canada - Atlantic Institution - Library, POBox 102, Renous NB E9E 2E1 – 506/623-4060; Fax: 506/623-4017; Symbol: NBRA – Librarian, Murray Baillie

### ROTHESAY

Colin Mackay Memorial Library - RCS-Netherwood, General Delivery, Rothesay NB E0G 2W0 – 506/847-8224; Fax: 506/849-9101; Email: rcsnthwd@nbnet.nb.ca – Librarian, Jennifer Leger, M.L.I.S.

### SACKVILLE

Environment Canada - Canadian Wildlife Service, Atlantic Region - Library, POBox 1590, Sackville NB E0A 3C0 – 506/364-5019; Fax: 506/364-5062; Email: sealyj@ns.doe.ca; Symbol: NBSACW – Librarian, Jean Sealy

Mount Allison University - Ralph Pickard Bell Library, POBox 1-2158, Sackville NB E0A 3C0 – 506/364-2562; Fax: 506/364-2617; URL: http://library.mta.ca; Symbol: NBSaM
- University Librarian, Sara Lochhead
- Technical Services, Head, Ruthmary MacPherson

### ST. ANDREWS

Atlantic Salmon Federation – Library, POBox 429, St. Andrews NB E0G 2X0 – 506/529-4581; Fax: 506/529-4438

Fisheries & Oceans Canada-St. Andrews Biological Station – Library, Dept. of Fisheries & Oceans, Brandy Cove Rd., St. Andrews NB E0G 2X0 – 506/529-8854; Fax: 506/529-5862;

Email: library@sta.dfo.ca; Symbol: NBAB – Librarian, Marilynn Rudi

New Brunswick Community College - St. Andrews Campus Library, POBox 427, St. Andrews NB E0G 2X0 – 506/529-5070; Fax: 506/529-5009; Email: md5070@gov.nb.ca; Symbol: NBSTAC – Librarian, Mary Doon, 506/529-5070

**SAINT JOHN**

Atlantic Health Sciences Corporation – Library Services, c/o Saint John Regional Hospital, POBox 2100, Saint John NB E2L 4L2 – 506/648-6763; Fax: 506/648-6764; Email: Library@ Reg2.Health.nb.ca; Symbol: NBSRH – Director, Anne Kilfoil

Centre communautaire Samuel-de-Champlain – Bibliothèque de Cormoran, 67 Ragged Point Rd., Saint John NB E2K 5C3 – 506/658-4600; Téléc: 506/ 658-3984 – Bibliothécaire, Mireille Mercure

New Brunswick Community College - Saint John Campus - L.R. Fulton Library & Audio Visual Centre, POBox 2270, Saint John NB E2L 3V1 – 506/ 658-6727; Fax: 506/658-6792 – Librarian, Dewan Sachdeva

New Brunswick Historical Society – The Loyalist Library, 120 Union St., Saint John NB E2L 1A3 – 506/652-3590 – Librarian, Margaret Earle

New Brunswick Museum - Library, 277 Douglas Ave., Saint John NB E2K 1E5 – 506/643-2322; Fax: 506/ 643-2360; Symbol: NBSM – Coordinator, Gary Hughes, 506/643-2322

New Brunswick Youth Orchestra – Library, 38 Cliff St., Saint John NB E2L 3A7 – 506/657-1498 – Librarian, Charles Estabrooks

Saint John Jewish Historical Museum – Dr. Moses I. Polowin Memorial Library, 29 Wellington Row, Saint John NB E2L 3H4 – 506/633-1833; Fax: 506/ 633-1833 – Assistant to the Curator, Katherine Biggs

Saint John Law Society – Library, 110 Charlotte St., Saint John NB E2L 2J3 – 506/658-2542; Fax: 506/ 634-7556 – Librarian, Marilyn Brown

University of New Brunswick - Ward Chipman Library, POBox 5050, Saint John NB E2L 4L5 – 506/648-5700; Fax: 506/648-5701; URL: http://www.unbsj.ca/ library/home1.htm; Symbol: NBSU
- Reference Librarian, William Kerr, Email: kerr@ unbsj.ca
- Director, Susan Collins

**ST. MARTINS**

Carson Memorial Library, POBox 1-30, St. Martins NB E0G 2Z0 – 506/833-4740 – Librarian, Elizabeth Thibodeau, 506/833-4324

**SUSSEX**

Bethany Bible College - Rogers Memorial Library, POBox 1-2350, Sussex NB E0E 1P0 – 506/432-4400, ext.470; Fax: 506/432-4425
- Library Services, Director, Myrna Griffith
- Library Assistant, Rebecca Louden

**WOODSTOCK**

New Brunswick Community College - Woodstock Library, POBox 1175, Woodstock NB E0J 2B0 – 506/325-4400; Fax: 506/328-8426; Email: NBCCWood@nbnet.nb.ca; Symbol: NBWC – Librarian, Margaret McAllister

## NEWFOUNDLAND

### Regional Library Systems with Member Libraries

**CENTRAL NEWFOUNDLAND LIBRARY DIVISION**

PO Box 3333, Gander NF A1V 1X2 – 709/651-2781; Fax: 709/256-2194; Email: rdale@ calvin.stemnet.nf.ca

Librarian, Patricia Parsons, Email: pmparson@ calvin.stemnet.nf.ca

Manager, Ralph Dale

Baie Verte Public Library, PO Box 178, Baie Verte NF A0K 1B0 – 709/532-8361 – Library Technician, Debbie Yetman

Bishop's Falls Public Library, PO Box 329, Bishop's Falls NF A0H 1C0 – 709/258-6244 – Library Technician, Cora Stanley

Botwood Public Library, PO Box 749, Botwood NF A0H 1E0 – 709/257-2091 – Library Technician, Mariem Gill

Buchans Public Library, PO Box 99, Buchans NF A0H 1G0 – 709/672-3859 – Library Technican, Diane Burton

Carmanville Public Library, Carmanville NF A0G 1N0 – 709/534-2370 – Library Technician, Kay Butt

Centreville Public Library, PO Box 100, Wareham-Centreville NF A0G 4P0 – 709/678-2700 – Library Technician, Gertrude Collins

Change Islands Public Library, PO Box 40, Change Islands NF A0G 1R0 – 709/621-5566 – Library Technician, Christine Hoffe

Dover Public Library, PO Box 250, Dover NF A0G 1X0 – 709/537-5763 – Library Technician, Linda Rogers

Fogo Island Public Library, Fogo Island NF A0G 2B0 – 709/266-2210 – Library Technician, Marion Foley

Gambo Public Library, PO Box 10, Gambo NF A0G 1T0 – 709/674-5052 – Librarian, Sylvia Collins

Gander Public Library, PO Box 4444, Gander NF A1V 1X2 – 709/256-3282 – Library Technician, Glenda Peddle

Gaultois Public Library, PO Box 100, Gaultois NF A0H 1N0 – Library Technican, Phyllis Harris

Glenwood Public Library, PO Box 40, Glenwood NF A0G 2K0 – 709/679-5700 – Library Technician, Michelle Stuckless

Alexander Bay Public Library, PO Box 70, Glovertown NF A0G 2L0 – 709/533-6688 – Library Technician, Audrey Lane

Harmsworth Public Library, Arts & Culture Centre, Cromer Ave., Grand Falls-Windsor NF A2A 1W9 – 709/489-2303 – Library Technician, Elizabeth Waye

Greenspond Public Library, PO Box 70, Greenspond NF A0G 2N0 – 709/269-3434 – Library Technician, Mae Dyke

Harbour Breton Public Library, PO Box 569, Harbour Breton NF A0H 1P0 – 709/885-2165 – Library Technician, Vivian Bennett

Hare Bay Public Library, Hare Bay NF A0G 2P0 – 709/ 537-2391 – Library Technician, Gertrude Collins

Harry's Harbour Public Library, Harry's Harbour NF A0J 1E0 – Library Technician, Ellen King

Hermitage Public Library, PO Box 159, Hermitage NF A0H 1S0 – 709/883-2421 – Library Technician, Bernice Willmott

Tilley Memorial Public Library, PO Box 23, Kings Point NF A0J 1H0 – 709/268-2282 – Library Technician, Greta Noble

La Scie Public Library, La Scie NF A0K 3M0 – 709/675-2004 – Library Technician, Mrs. Jackie Sheppard

Lewisporte Public Library, Lewisporte NF A0G 3A0 – 709/535-2519 – Library Technician, Judy Snow

Lumsden Public Library, Lumsden NF A0G 3E0 – 709/ 530-2617 – Library Technician, Beatrice Stagg

John B. Wheeler Public Library, PO Box 130, Musgrave Harbour NF A0G 3J0 – 709/655-2730 – Library Technician, Donna Noseworthy

Norris Arm Public Library, PO Box 100, Norris Arm NF A0G 3M0 – 709/653-2531 – Library Technician, Leona Rowsell

Point Leamington Public Library, PO Box 76, Point Leamington NF A0H 1Z0 – 709/484-3541 – Library Technician, Emma Rolfe

Roberts Arm Public Library, PO Box 119, Roberts Arm NF A0J 1R0 – 709/652-3100 – Library Technician, Helen Sooley

St Albans Public Library, PO Box 70, St Albans NF A0H 2E0 – 709/538-3034 – Library Technician, Melinda Walsh

Seal Cove Public Library, PO Box 70, Seal Cove NF A0K 5E0 – 709/531-2505 – Library Technician, Madeline Parsons

Naskapi School Public Library, Sops Arm NF A0K 5K0 – 709/482-2422 – Library Technician, Beatrice Pinksen

Springdale Public Library, PO Box 100, Springdale NF A0J 1T0 – 709/673-4169 – Library Technician, Golda Burton

Summerford Public Library, Summerford NF A0G 4E0 – 709/629-3244; Fax: 709/629-3419 – Library Technician, Mavis Boyd

Twillingate Public Library, PO Box 338, Twillingate NF A0G 4M0 – 709/884-2353 – Library Technician, Barbara Hamlyn

Wesleyville Public Library, Wesleyville NF A0G 4R0 – 709/536-5777 – Library Technician, Beverley Hounsell; Library Technician, Marion Hennebury

**EASTERN NEWFOUNDLAND LIBRARY DIVISION**

Arts & Culture Centre, Allendale Rd., St. John's NF A1B 3A3 – 709/737-3505; 3508; Fax: 709/737-2660; Symbol: NFED

Regional Manager, John White, Email: jfwhite@ calvin.stemnet.nf.ca

Librarian, Derek Bussey, Email: dbussey@ calvin.stemnet.nf.ca

Arnold's Cove Public Library, PO Box 239, Arnold's Cove NF A0B 1A0 – 709/463-8707 – Library Technician, Lisa Giles

Bay Roberts Public Library, PO Box 610, Bay Roberts NF A0A 1G0 – 709/786-9629 – Library Technician, Linda Miller; Library Technician, Marilyn Clarke

Bell Island Public Library, PO Box 760, Bell Island NF A0A 4H0 – 709/488-2413 – Library Technician, Lois Clarke

Bonavista Memorial Library, PO Box 400, Bonavista NF A0C 1B0 – 709/468-2185 – Library Technician, Brenda Wilton

Brigus Public Library, Brigus NF A0A 1K0 – 709/528-3156 – Library Technician, Elsie Percy

Burin Memorial Library, PO Box 306, Burin NF A0E 1E0 – 709/891-1924 – Library Technician, Marilyn Beazley

Carbonear Public Library, PO Box 928, Carbonear NF A1Y 1C4 – 709/596-3382 – Library Technician, Brenda Peach

Joseph Clouter Memorial Library, Catalina NF A0C 1J0 – 709/469-3045 – Library Technician, Kimberley Johnson

Clarenville Public Library, PO Box 2550, Clarenville NF A0E 1J0 – 709/466-7634 – Library Technician, Marvin Pitts

Fortune Memorial Library, Fortune NF A0E 1P0 – 709/ 832-0232 – Library Technician, Fay Dominie

Fox Harbour Public Library, PO Box 74, Fox Harbour NF A0B 1V0 – 709/227-2271 – Library Technician, Catherine Murray

G. Hollett Memorial Library, PO Box 190, Garnish NF A0E 1T0 – 709/826-2371 – Library Technician, Anne Riley

Grand Bank Memorial Library, PO Box 1000, Grand Bank NF A0E 1W0 – 709/832-0310 – Library Technician, Mildred Watts

Harbour Grace Public Library, PO Box 40, Harbour Grace NF A0A 2M0 – 709/596-3894 – Library Technician, Doreen Quinn

Holyrood Public Library, PO Box 263, Holyrood NF A0A 2R0 – 709/229-7852 – Library Technician, Diane Mann

Conception Bay South Public Library, PO Box 580, Manuels NF A1W 1N1 – 709/834-4241 – Library Technician, Bertha Rideout
Marystown Memorial Library, PO Box 1270, Marystown NF A0E 2M0 – 709/279-1507 – Library Technician, Patricia Mayo
Mount Pearl Public & Resource Library, PO Box 880, Mount Pearl NF A1N 3C8 – 709/368-3603 – Library Technician, Linda Quinn
Old Perlican Public Library, Old Perlican NF A0A 3G0 – 709/587-2639 – Library Technician, Christina McNeil
Placentia Public Library, Placentia NF A0B 2Y0 – 709/227-3621 – Library Technician, Doris Bowering
Pouch Cove Public Library, PO Box 40, Pouch Cove NF A0A 3L0 – 709/335-2652 – Library Technician, Diane Mulley
Cape Shore Public Library, St. Bride's NF A0B 2Z0 – 709/337-2360 – Library Technician, Mary Coffey
St. Lawrence Public Library, Memorial Dr., PO Box 366, St. Lawrence NF A0E 2V0 – 709/873-2650 – Library Technician, Meta Turpin
Southern Harbour Public Library, Southern Habour NF A0B 3H0 – 709/463-8814 – Library Technician, Bride Whiffen
E. Morey Memorial Public Library, 1288A Torbay Rd., Torbay NF A1K 1B2 – 709/437-6571 – Library Technician, Marie Evans
Trepassey Public Library, Trepassey NF A0A 4B0 – 709/438-2224 – Library Technician, Ted Winter
Victoria Public Library, Victoria NF A0A 4G0 – 709/596-3682 – Library Technician, Mary Sutton
Whitbourne Public Library, Whitbourne NF A0B 3K0 – 709/759-2461 – Library Technician, Gloria Somerton
Winterton Public Library, PO Box 119, Winterton NF A0B 3M0 – 709/583-2810 – Library Technician, Betty Pitcher

#### NEWFOUNDLAND PROVINCIAL RESOURCE LIBRARY

Arts & Culture Centre, Allendale Rd., St. John's NF A1B 3A3 – 709/737-3946; Fax: 709/737-2660; Email: cameron@morgan.ucs.mun.ca; URL: http://www.stemnet.nf.ca/Community/PublicLibrary/; Symbol: NFSG
Manager, Charles Cameron
Reference Librarian, Anne Lawson
Lending Services Librarian, Victoria Murphy
Children's Librarian, Heather Myers
Newfoundland Collection Librarian, Brenda Parmenter
Audio-Visual Librarian, Jewel Cousens

A.C. Hunter Library, Arts & Culture Centre, Allendale Rd., St. John's NF A1B 3A3 – 709/737-2133 (Adults); 737-3953 (Children); Fax: 709/737-3953
Marjorie Mews Library, Highland Plaza, 18 Highland Dr., St. John's NF A1A 3C5 – 709/737-2621 – Library Technician, Glenda Quinn
Michael Donovan Library, 655 Topsail Rd., St. John's NF A1E 2E3 – 709/737-2621 – Library Technician, Rita Roberts

#### WEST NEWFOUNDLAND-LABRADOR LIBRARY DIVISION

5 Union St., Corner Brook NF A2H 5M7 – 709/634-7333; Fax: 709/634-7313; Email: schilcot@calvin.stemnet.nf.ca
Librarian, Elinor Benjamin, Email: elinorb@morgan.ucs.mun.ca
Manager, Sandy Chilcote

Burgeo Public Library, PO Box 370, Burgeo NF A0M 1A0 – 709/886-2730 – Library Technician, Freda MacDonald
Cape St. George Public Library, Cape St. George NF A0N 1E0 – 709/644-2852; Email: cmstuckl@calvin.stemnet.nf.ca – Library Technician, Cynthia Stuckless
Cartwright Public Library, PO Box 166, Cartwright NF A0K 1V0 – 709/938-7219 – Library Technician, Heather Martin
Churchill Falls Public Library, PO Box 160, Churchill Falls NF A0R 1A0 – 709/925-3281 – Library Technician, Loretta Bryant
Cormack Public Library, RR#2, PO Box 524, Cormack NF A0K 2E0 – 709/635-7022 – Library Technician, Marie Morris
Corner Brook Public Library, Sir Richard Squires Bldg., Mt. Bernard Ave., Corner Brook NF A2H 6J8 – 709/634-0013; Fax: 709/634-0330; Email: lwest@calvin.stemnet.nf.ca – Librarian, Lynne West
Cow Head Public Library, Cow Head NF A0K 2A0 – 709/243-2467 – Library Technician, Nora Shears
Daniel's Harbour Public Library, PO Box 39, Daniel's Harbour NF A0K 2C0 – 709/898-2283 – Library Technician, Edith Guinchard
Deer Lake Public Library, PO Bag 2002, Deer Lake NF A0K 2E0 – 709/635-3671; Email: wcramm@calvin.stemnet.nf.ca – Library Technician, Worneta Cramm
Codroy Valley Public/School Library, General Delivery, Doyles NF A0N 1J0 – 709/955-2940; Fax: 709/955-2620 – Library Technician, Judy Gillis
Melville Public Library, Elizabeth Goudie Bldg., Happy Valley NF A0P 1E0 – 709/896-8045 – Library Technician, Hyra Skoglund
Labrador City Public Library, 306 Hudson Dr., Labrador City NF A2V 1L5 – 709/944-2190; Fax: 709/944-3674; Email: efoley@calvin.stemnet.nf.ca – Library Technician, Ethel Foley
Labrador South Public Library, L'Anse au Loup NF A0K 3L0 – 709/927-5542 – Library Technician, Phyllis O'Brien
Blow-Me-Down Public/School Library, Lark Harbour NF A0L 1H0 – 709/681-2620; Email: npickett@calvin.stemnet.nf.ca – Library Technician, Norma Pickett
Lourdes Public/School Library, PO Box 129, Lourdes NF A0N 1R0 – 709/642-5248; Email: esnook@calvin.stemnet.nf.ca – Library Technician, Elizabeth Snook
Norris Point Public Library, Norris Point NF A0K 3V0 – 709/458-2118; Email: jsamms@calvin.stemnet.nf.ca – Library Technician, Judy Samms
Pasadena Public Library, 16 Tenth Ave., Pasadena NF A0L 1K0 – 709/686-2792 – Library Technician, Gloria Campbell
Curran Memorial Library, Port au Port East NF A0N 1T0 – 709/648-9401 – Shirley Crane
Port Au Port West Public/School Library, General Delivery, Port au Port NF A0N 1T0 – Library Technician, Maureen Abbott
Channel-Port-aux-Basques Public Library, PO Box 790, Port-aux-Basques NF A0M 1C0 – 709/695-3471; Email: bingram@calvin.stemnet.nf.ca – Library Technician, Brenda Ingram
Ingornachoix Public Library, PO Box 59, Port Saunders NF A0K 4H0 – 709/861-3690 – Library Technician, Evelyn Biggin
Marie S. Penney Memorial Library, PO Box 59, Ramea NF A0M 1N0 – 709/625-2344 – Library Technician, Frances Lushman
Rocky Harbour Public Library, Rocky Harbour, St. Barbe South NF A0K 4N0 – 709/458-2900 – Library Technician, Margaret Parsons
St. Anthony Public Library, PO Box 129, St. Anthony NF A0K 4S0 – 709/454-3025; Email: besmith@calvin.stemnet.nf.ca – Library Technician, Bernice Smith
Bay St. George South Public/School Library, PO Box 70, St. Fintan's NF A0N 1Y0 – 709/645-2780, ext.35; 645-2052 – Library Technician, Anita MacInnis
St Georges Public Library, PO Box 249, St Georges NF A0N 1Z0 – 709/647-3808 – Library Technician, Joan Downey
St. Lunaire-Griquet Public Library, St. Lunaire NF A0K 2X0 – 709/623-2904 – Library Technician, Mae Bussey
Kindale Public Library, 45 Carolina Ave., Stephenville NF A2N 3P8 – 709/643-4262; Fax: 709/643-5781; Email: ymcisaac@calvin.stemnet.nf.ca – Library Technician, Yvonne McIsaac
Stephenville Crossing Public Library, PO Box 610, Stephenville Crossing NF A0N 2C0 – 709/646-2086 – Library Technician, Joan Downey
Wabush Public Library, PO Box 179, Wabush NF A0R 1B0 – 709/282-3479 – Library Technician, Alfreda Harkins
Edgar L. Roberts Memorial Library, PO Box 179, Woody Point NF A0K 1P0 – 709/453-2556 – Library Technician, Barbara Wheeler

### Special & College Libraries & Resource Centres

#### BONAVISTA

Eastern College of Applied Arts, Technology & Continuing Education - Bonavista Campus Library, POBox 670, Bonavista NF A0C 1B0 – 709/468-2610

#### BURIN

Eastern College of Applied Arts, Technology & Continuing Education - Burin Campus Library, POBox 369, Burin NF A0E 1E0 – 709/891-1253; Fax: 709/891-2256 – Librarian, Gary Peschell

#### CARBONEAR

Eastern College of Applied Arts, Technology & Continuing Education - Carbonear Campus, POBox 60, Carbonear NF A1Y 1B5 – 709/596-6139; Fax: 709/596-2688; Email: agoff@calvin.stemnet.nf.ca
Learning Resources Specialist, Alexandra Goff
Library Technician, Sophie Colbourne

#### CLARENVILLE

Eastern College of Applied Arts, Technology & Continuing Education - Clarenville Campus Library, POBox 308, Clarenville NF A0E 1J0 – 709/466-0328; Fax: 709/466-2771 – Learning Resources Coordinator, Lynn Cuff

#### CORNER BROOK

Newfoundland & Labrador Department of Natural Resources - Newfoundland Forest Service - Library, Herald Bldg., POBox 2006, Corner Brook NF A2H 6J8 – 709/637-2307; Fax: 709/637-2403; Email: bboland@atcon.com; Symbol: NFCBF – Bruce Boland
Sir Wilfred Grenfell College - Ferriss Hodgett Library, Memorial University of Newfoundland, University Dr., Corner Brook NF A2H 3A3 – 709/637-6236; Fax: 709/639-8125; Email: ENVOY: GRENFELL.COLLEGE; URL: http://www.swgc.mun.ca/library; Symbol: NFCBM – Associate University Librarian, Elizabeth Behrens, Email: ebehrens@beothuk.swgc.mun.ca
Western Memorial Regional Hospital – Health Sciences Library, POBox 2005, Corner Brook NF A2H 6J7 – 709/637-5395; Fax: 709/634-2649; Symbol: WMRH – Librarian, Kimberly Hancock
Westviking College - Corner Brook Campus Library, POBox 822, Corner Brook NF A2H 6H6 – 709/637-8528; Fax: 709/634-2126 – Librarian, Marian Burnett

#### GANDER

James Paton Memorial Hospital – Medical Library, 125 TransCanada Hwy., Gander NF A1V 1P7 – 709/256-5760; Fax: 709/256-7800; Email: educ.jpm@nf.sympatico.ca – Library Technician, Marion Brake

**GRAND FALLS-WINDSOR**

Central Newfoundland Regional Health Centre – Medical Library, 50 Union St., Grand Falls-Windsor NF A2A 2E1 – 709/292-2228; Fax: 709/292-2249 – Head Librarian, Ellen C. Fewer

**HAPPY VALLEY-GOOSE BAY**

Melville Hospital – Medical Library, Postal Station A, Happy Valley-Goose Bay NF A0P 1S0 – 709/896-2417; Fax: 709/896-8966 – Secretary, Glenda Simon

Them Days Inc. – Library, 3 Courtemanche, POBox 939, Happy Valley-Goose Bay NF A0P 1E0 – 709/896-8531 – Office Manager/Archivist, Gillian H. Saunders

**LABRADOR CITY**

Captain William Jackman Memorial Hospital – Medical Library, 410 Booth Ave., Labrador City NF A2V 2K1 – 709/944-2632; Fax: 709/944-6045 – Librarian, Margaret Sullivan

**MOUNT PEARL**

Heywood, Kennedy, Belbin Law Office - Library, 184 Park Avenue, POBox 250, Mount Pearl NF A1N 2C3 – 709/747-9613; Fax: 709/747-9723 – Jackie Brazil, LL.B.

**PLACENTIA**

Eastern College of Applied Arts, Technology & Continuing Education - Placentia Campus Library, POBox 190, Placentia NF A0B 1J0 – 709/227-2037

**ST ANTHONY**

Charles S. Curtis Memorial Hospital – Library, West St., POBox 1-628, St Anthony NF A0K 4S0 – 709/454-3333; Fax: 709/454-2052 – Joan Hillier

**ST. JOHN'S**

Newfoundland & Labrador Department of Environment & Labour - Industrial Environmental Engineering – Library, Confederation Bldg., POBox 8700, St. John's NF A1B 4J6 – 709/729-2110; Fax: 709/729-1930

Newfoundland & Labrador Department of Fisheries, Food & Agriculture - Soil, Plant & Feed Laboratory – Library, Brookfield Rd., POBox 8700, St. John's NF A1B 4J6 – 709/729-6587; Fax: 709/729-6046

Action: Environment – Resource Centre, POBox 2549, St. John's NF A1C 6K1 – 709/579-3729; Fax: 709/579-3729

Agriculture & Agri-Food Canada-Atlantic Cool Climate Crop Research Centre – Canadian Agriculture Library, 308 Brookfield Rd., POBox 7098, St. John's NF A1N 2C1 – 709/772-4169; Fax: 709/772-6064; Email: library@nfrssj.agr.ca; Symbol: LBNFSA – Librarian, Hélène Sabourin

Association of Newfoundland & Labrador Archives – Library, Colonial Building, Military Rd., St. John's NF A1C 2C9 – 709/726-2867; Fax: 709/729-0578

Canada-Newfoundland Offshore Petroleum Board - Library, #500, TD Place, 140 Water St., St. John's NF A1C 6H6 – 709/778-1450; Fax: 709/778-1473
- Librarian, J. Ryan
- Library Technician/Clerk, Lisa Clarke

Canadian Broadcasting Corporation - Broadcast Materials Library, POBox 12010, St. John's NF A1B 3T8 – 709/576-5049; Fax: 709/576-5011 – Supervisor, Larry O'Brien

Centre for Nursing Studies - Learning Resources Centre, 250 Waterford Bridge Rd., St. John's NF A1E 1E3 – 709/737-3834; Fax: 709/737-3836; Email: cathy@nurse.nf.ca – Instructional Materials Specialist, Cathy Ryan

College of the North Atlantic - Prince Philip Drive Campus Library, POBox 1693, St. John's NF A1C 5P7 – 709/758-7274; Fax: 709/758-7231; Email: bneable@admin.cabot.nf.ca
- Librarian, Beverley Neable
- Engineering Technology Centre Library, Librarian, Chitra Paranjape, 709/758-7099
- Topsail Road Campus Library, Librarian, Joan Roberts, 709/758-7622

Community Services Council, Newfoundland & Labrador – Library, Virginia Park Plaza, 201 Newfoundland Dr., St. John's NF A1A 3E9 – 709/753-9860; Fax: 709/753-6112

Dr. Leonard A. Miller Centre – Library, 1 - 100 Forest Rd., St. John's NF A1A 1E5 – 709/778-4344; Fax: 709/778-4333; Email: smensink@morgan.ucs.mun.ca – Librarian, Sheila Mensinkai

Enterprise Newfoundland & Labrador - Business Resource Centre, Viking Building, 136 Crosbie Rd., St. John's NF A1B 3K3 – 709/729-7150; Fax: 709/729-7183; Symbol: NFSNLD
- Manager, Business Resource Centre, Corinne Hynes
- Reference Librarian, Darlene Abbott
- Online Librarian, Heather Roberts

Environment Canada-Environmental Quality Laboratories: St. John's – Library, Northwest Atlantic Fisheries Centre, POBox 5037, St. John's NF A1C 5V3 – 709/772-5488; Fax: 709/772-5097

Environmental Design Consultants - Division of BFL Consultants Ltd. – Library, BFL Place, 133 Crosbie Rd., POBox 12070, St. John's NF A1B 1H3 – 709/753-6252; Fax: 709/739-5458 – Documents Clerk, Debbie Dooley

Fisheries & Oceans Canada-Northwest Atlantic Fisheries Centre – Library, POBox 5667, St. John's NF A1C 5X1 – 709/772-2022; Fax: 709/772-2156; Email: conroy@athena.nwafc.nf.ca; Symbol: NFSF – Library Contact, Audrey Conroy

The General Hospital/Health Sciences Centre – Health Sciences Library, 300 Prince Philip Dr., St. John's NF A1B 3V6 – 709/758-1308; Fax: 709/737-6770 – Librarian, Cathy Sheehan

Heritage Foundation of Newfoundland & Labrador – Library, POBox 5171, St. John's NF A1C 5V5 – 709/739-1892; Fax: 709/739-5413

The Hub - Specialized Information Centre, POBox 13788, St. John's NF A1B 4G3 – 709/754-0352; Fax: 709/722-2110 – Coordinator, Donna Underhay

Industry Canada - Business Service Centre, 90 O'Leary Ave., POBox 8687, St. John's NF A1B 3T1 – 709/772-6022; Fax: 709/772-6090; Toll Free: 1-800-668-1010; Email: st.johns@cbsc.ic.gc.ca; URL: http://www.cbsc.org/nfld/

Law Society of Newfoundland – Library, Atlantic Place, 5th Fl., 215 Water St., POBox 1028, St. John's NF A1C 5M3 – 709/753-7770; Fax: 709/753-0054 – Law Librarian, Gail A. Hogan

Learning Disabilities Association of Newfoundland, POBox 26036, St. John's NF A1E 5T9 – 709/754-3665; Fax: 709/754-3665 – Diane White

Memorial University - Libraries, 234 Elizabeth St., St. John's NF A1B 3Y1 – 709/737-7428; Fax: 709/737-3118; Symbol: NFSM
- University Librarian, Richard H. Ellis
- Acquisitions/Periodicals, Head, Victoria Marshall, 709/737-7438
- Cataloguing, Head, Charles Pennell, 709/737-7433
- Collections, Head, Dorothy Milne, 709/737-7421
- Information Services, Head, Joy Tillotson, 709/737-7427
- Lending Services, Head, Louise White, 709/737-4352
- Maps, Head, Alberta Auringer Wood, 709/737-8892
- Systems, Head, Slavko Manojlovich, 709/737-7470
- Centre for Cold Ocean Resources Engineering, Researcher, Judith Whittick, 709/737-8351, Email: ENVOY: C.CORE
- Centre for Newfoundland Studies, Head, Anne Hart, 709/737-7475
- Health Sciences, Librarian, George Beckett, 709/737-6670
- Ocean Engineering Information Centre, K-1000, Bartlett Bldg., 240 Prince Philip Dr., St. John's NF A1B 3X5 – 709/737-8377; Fax: 709/737-4706; Email: ccore@morgan.ucs.mun.ca; URL: http://www.mun.ca/ccore; Symbol: NFSMO
- Information Researcher, Sherry Wall
- Information Researcher, Norma Matthews

Memorial University of Newfoundland - Fisheries & Marine Institute - Library, 155 Ridge Rd., POBox 4920, St. John's NF A1C 5R3 – 709/778-0662; Fax: 709/778-0346; URL: http://www.ifmt.nf.ca; Symbol: NFSCF – Librarian, D.E. Taylor-Harding, Email: dharding@inseine.ifmt.nf.ca

Morris & Pittman Law Office - Library, 139 Water St., POBox 2355, St. John's NF A1C 6E7 – 709/754-8474; Fax: 709/754-8036 – Barbara Hearn

National Research Council-Institute for Marine Dynamics – Library, POBox 12093, St. John's NF A1B 3T5 – 709/772-2468; Fax: 709/772-3670; Email: library@minnie.imd.nrc.ca; Symbol: NFSNM – Librarian, Susan Salo

Natural Resources Canada-Canadian Forest Service: Atlantic Region – Library, Pleasantville Complex, Bldg. 304, POBox 6028, St. John's NF A1C 5X8 – 709/772-4672; Fax: 709/772-2576; Email: ENVOY: ILL.NFRC; Symbol: NFSEC – Librarian, Patricia Tilley

Newfoundland & Labrador Alliance of Technical Industries – NATI Library, Parsons Bldg., 1st Fl., 90 O'Leary Ave., St. John's NF A1B 2C7 – 709/722-8324; Fax: 709/722-3213

Newfoundland & Labrador Department of Development & Rural Renewal - Business Resource Centre, Viking Bldg., 136 Crosbie Rd., St. John's NF A1B 3K3 – 709/729-7150; Fax: 709/729-7183; Email: brc_requests@porthole.entnet.nf.ca – Corinne Hynes

Newfoundland & Labrador Department of Environment & Labour - Environment Library, Confederation Bldg., West Block, 4th Fl., POBox 4750, St. John's NF A1C 5T7 – 709/729-3394; Fax: 709/729-1930

Newfoundland & Labrador Department of Finance - Departmental Library, POBox 8700, St. John's NF A1B 4J6 – 709/729-2341 – Director, Government Accounting, Ron Williams

Newfoundland & Labrador Department of Fisheries, Food & Agriculture - Library, Provincial Fisheries Bldg., 30 Strawberry Marsh Rd., POBox 8700, St. John's NF A1B 4J6 – 709/729-3723; Fax: 709/729-6082 – Library Technician, Sandra Hallett

Newfoundland & Labrador Department of Justice - Law Library, Confederation Bldg., POBox 8700, St. John's NF A1B 4J6 – 709/729-2912; Fax: 709/729-1370; Symbol: NFSJL
- Library Director, Mona B. Pearce
- Library Technician, Brenda Blundon
- Legal Librarian, Sean M. Dawe

Newfoundland & Labrador Department of Mines & Energy - Geological Survey Library, 50 Elizabeth Ave., POBox 8700, St. John's NF A1B 4J6 – 709/729-3159; Fax: 709/729-3493; Email: mcp@zeppo.geosurv.gov.nf.ca; URL: http://www.geosurv.gov.nf.ca; Symbol: NFSMEM – Geologist, Catherine Patey

Newfoundland & Labrador Department of Municipal & Provincial Affairs - Urban & Rural Planning Division Library, Confederation Bldg., West Block, POBox 8700, St. John's NF A1B 4J6 – 709/729-3090; Fax: 709/729-2609

Newfoundland & Labrador Genealogical Society Inc. – Newfoundland & Labrador Genealogical Resource Centre, Colonial Building, Military Rd., St. John's NF A1C 2C9 – 709/754-9525

Newfoundland & Labrador Teachers' Association – Resource Centre, 3 Kenmount Rd., St. John's NF

A1B 1W1 – 709/726-3223; Fax: 709/726-4302; Toll Free: 1-800-563-3599 – Researcher, Susan Cardoulis

Newfoundland Association of Public Employees – Library, POBox 8100, St. John's NF A1B 3M9 – 709/754-0700; Fax: 709/754-0726; Toll Free: 1-800-563-4442 – Research Officer, Trudi Brake

Newfoundland Cancer Treatment & Research Foundation – Elaine Deluney Patient & Family Resource Library, Dr. H. Bliss Murphy Cancer Centre, Health Sciences Centre, 300 Prince Philip Dr., St. John's NF A1B 3V6 – 709/757-4244; Fax: 709/753-0927 – Social Worker, Valarie Barrington

Newfoundland House of Assembly - Legislative Library, Confederation Bldg., POBox 8700, St. John's NF A1B 4J6 – 709/729-3604; Fax: 709/729-0234 – Legislative Librarian, N.J. Richards

Pentecostal Assemblies of Newfoundland – Library, POBox 8248, St. John's NF A1B 3T2 – 709/753-6314; Fax: 709/753-4945 – General Manager, Dept. of Lit., C. Buckle

Provincial Archives of Newfoundland & Labrador - Library, Military Rd., St. John's NF A1C 2C9 – 709/729-3065; Fax: 709/729-0578; Symbol: PANL
- Director, Provincial Archives, David J. Davis, 709/729-0724, Email: ddavis@tourism.gov.nf.ca
- Reference Archivist, R. Calvin Best, 709/729-0475
- Pre-1949, Government Records Archivist, Anthony Murphy, 709/729-0496
- Post-1949, Government Records Archivist, John Mowbray
- Still & Moving Images Archivist, Ann Devlin-Fischer
- Records Manager, Paul Kenny

Queen's College - Library, Prince Philip Dr., St. John's NF A1B 3R6 – 709/753-0116; Fax: 709/753-1214; Symbol: NFSQ – Susan Foley

St. Clare's Mercy Hospital – Library, 154 Lemarchant Rd., St. John's NF A1C 5B8 – 709/778-3414; Fax: 709/738-1216 – Librarian, Catherine Lawton

Salvation Army Grace General Hospital - C.A. Pippy Jr. Medical Library, 241 Le Marchant Rd., St. John's NF A1E 1P9 – 709/778-6796 – Librarian, Elizabeth Duggan

Waterford Hospital – Library & Information Services, 306 Waterford Bridge Rd., St. John's NF A1E 4J8 – 709/758-3368; Fax: 709/758-3988; Email: hcc.keade@hccsj.nf.ca; Symbol: WTFD – Library Technician, Debra Kearsey

Women's Enterprise Bureau – Library, 30 Harvey Rd., St. John's NF A1C 2G1 – 709/754-5555; Fax: 709/754-0079; Email: ACOA/ENTERPRISE.NETWORK – Faye Worthman

#### STEPHENVILLE

Sir Thomas Roddick Hospital – Library, 89 Ohio Dr., Stephenville NF A2N 2V6 – 709/643-7400; Fax: 709/643-2700 – Regional Director, Education Services, Karen Alexander

Westviking College of Applied Arts, Technology & Continuing Education - Library, POBox 5400, Stephenville NF A2N 2Z6 – 709/643-7752; Fax: 709/643-5407; Email: jcarter@westvikingc.nf.ca; Symbol: NFSBS
- Bay St. George Campus, Librarian, Jim Carter
- Library Technician, Tina Foote
- L.A. Bown Campus, Library Technician, Cathy Ash
- Stephenville Crossing Campus, Library Technician, Barb King

#### TWILLINGATE

Notre Dame Bay Memorial Health Centre – Library, POBox 1-748, Twillingate NF A0G 4M0 – 709/884-2131; Fax: 709/884-2586 – Library Technician, Barbara Hamlyn

## NORTHWEST TERRITORIES

### Public Libraries

Arviat: Donald Suluk Library, PO Bag 4000, Arviat NT X0C 0E0 – 867/857-2579; Fax: 867/857-2743 – Local Librarian, Susan Arloo

Baker Lake: Thomas Tapatai Library, PO Box 189, Baker Lake NT X0C 0A0 – 867/793-2909; Fax: 867/793-2509 – Local Librarian, Sarah Segova

Cambridge Bay: May Hakongak Community Library, PO Box 1106, Cambridge Bay NT X0E 0C0 – 867/983-2406; Fax: 867/983-2455 – Local Librarian, Kim Crockatt

Clyde River Community Library, PO Box 150, Clyde River NT X0A 0E0 – 867/924-6266; Fax: 867/924-6247 – Branch of Baffin Regional Library

Fort Norman Community Library, General Delivery, Fort Norman NT X0E 0K0 – 867/588-4361; Fax: 867/588-3912 – Local Librarian, Nancy Norn-Lennie

Fort Simpson: John Tsetso Memorial Library, PO Box 258, Fort Simpson NT X0E 0N0 – 867/695-3276; Fax: 867/695-2722 – Local Librarian, Grace Crisp

Fort Smith: Mary Kaeser Library, PO Box 630, Fort Smith NT X0E 0P0 – 867/872-2296; Fax: 867/872-5303 – Local Librarian, Jeri Miltenberger

Hay River Dene Village Library, c/o Chief Sunrise Education Centre, PO Box 3055, Hay River NT X0E 1G4 – 867/874-2128; Fax: 867/874-3229 – Local Librarian, Kathleen Graham

Hay River: Northwest Territories Centennial Library, 75 Woodland Dr., PO Bag 5003, Hay River NT X0E 1G1 – 867/874-6486; Fax: 867/874-3321 – Local Librarian, Marilyn Barnes

Igloolik: Amitturmiut Library, PO Box 260, Igloolik NT X0A 0L0 – 867/934-8812; Fax: 867/934-8779 – Local Librarian, Sylvia Ivalu – Branch of Baffin Regional Library

Inuvik Centennial Library, PO Box 1640, Inuvik NT X0C 0T0 – 867/979-2749; Fax: 867/979-3221; Email: icl@inuvik.net; URL: http://www.inuvik.net/~icl/ – Librarian, Deb Sullivan

Iqaluit: Baffin Regional Library, PO Bag 189A, Iqaluit NT X0A 0H0 – 867/979-5401; Fax: 867/979-1373 – Library Technician, Carol Rigby – See also following branches: Amitturmiut Library, Clyde River Community Library, Iqaluit Centennial Library, Kugluktuk Community Library, Nanisivik Community Library, Qimiruvik Library

Iqaluit Centennial Library, PO Bag 189A, Iqaluit NT X0A 0H0 – 867/979-5400; Fax: 867/979-1373 – Local Librarian, Marilyn Scott; Local Librarian, Sylvia Wiffin – Branch of Baffin Regional Library

Kugluktuk Community Library, PO Box 190, Kugluktuk NT X0E 0E0 – 867/982-3098; Fax: 867/982-3060 – Local Librarian, Lucy Nivingalok – Branch of Baffin Regional Library

Nanisivik Community Library, PO Box 115, Nanisivik NT X0A 0X0 – 867/436-7445; Fax: 867/436-7588 – Local Librarian, Marissa Gillingham – Branch of Baffin Regional Library

Norman Wells Community Library, PO Box 97, Norman Wells NT X0E 0V0 – 867/587-2956; Fax: 867/587-2956 – Local Librarian, Lori Shapansky; Assistant Librarian, Lori Graca

Pangnirtung: Qimiruvik Library, PO Box 403, Pangnirtung NT X0A 0R0 – 867/473-8678; Fax: 867/473-8685 – Local Librarian, Rita Kisa – Branch of Baffin Regional Library

Pond Inlet: Rebecca Panikpak Idlout Library, PO Bag 212, Pond Inlet NT X0A 0S0 – 867/899-8972; Fax: 867/899-8175

Rankin Inlet: John Ayaruaq Library, PO Bag 002, Rankin Inlet NT X0C 0G0 – 867/645-5034; Fax: 867/645-2889

Tulita Community Library, General Delivery, Tulita NT X0E 0K0 – 867/588-4361; Fax: 867/588-3912 – Local Librarian, Nancy Norn-Lennie

Yellowknife Public Library, PO Box 694, Yellowknife NT X1A 2N5 – 867/920-5642; Fax: 867/920-5671; Symbol: NWY – Library Manager, Eileen Murdoch

### Special & College Libraries & Resource Centres

#### FORT SMITH

Science Institute of the NWT - South Slave Research Centre – Library, POBox 45, Fort Smith NT X0E 0P0 – 867/872-4909; Fax: 867/872-4922

Aurora College - Thebacha Campus Library, PO Bag 2, Fort Smith NT X0E 0P0 – 867/872-7544; Fax: 867/872-4511; Symbol: NWFST
- Librarian, Alexandra Hook
- Library Technician, Janet Lanoville

Canadian Heritage - Wood Buffalo National Park Library, POBox 750, Fort Smith NT X0E 0P0 – 867/872-2349; Fax: 867/872-3910; Symbol: NWFSW – Librarian, Jenny Belyea

#### HAY RIVER

Northwest Territories Court Library - Hay River Branch, POBox 1276, Hay River NT X0E 0R0

#### IGLOOLIK

Nunavut Research Institute - Igloolik Research Centre – Library, POBox 210, Igloolik NT X0A 0L0 – 867/934-8836; Fax: 867/934-8792

#### INUVIK

Aurora Research Institute - Inuvik Research Centre – Library, POBox 1430, Inuvik NT X0E 0T0 – 867/979-3838; Fax: 867/979-3570; Symbol: NWII – Library Manager, Vanessa Bebee

Ingamo Hall Friendship Centre – Resource Centre, POBox 1293, Inuvik NT X0E 0T0 – 867/979-2166 – Coordinator, Bryan Edwards

Inuvik Research Centre - Library, College West, POBox 1430, Inuvik NT X0E 0T0 – 867/979-3838; Fax: 867/979-3570

Northwest Territories Court Library - Inuvik Branch, POBox 1965, Inuvik NT X0E 0T0

#### IQALUIT

Nunavut Research Institute - Iqaluit Research Centre – Library, Aeroplex Bldg., POBox 160, Iqaluit NT X0A 0H0 – 867/979-4114; Fax: 867/979-4119

Northwest Territories Association of Provincial Court Judges – Law Library, Court House, POBox 297, Iqaluit NT X0A 0H0 – 867/979-5450; Fax: 867/979-6384 – Chief Librarian, Sue Baer

Northwest Territories Court Library - Iqaluit Branch, Iqaluit Courthouse, POBox 297, Iqaluit NT X0A 0H0

Nunavut Arctic College - Nunatta Campus Library, POBox 600, Iqaluit NT X0A 0H0 – 867/979-7220; Fax: 867/979-4579; Email: ENVOY: AC.IQ.LIB; Symbol: NWIAC
- Librarian, Gayle Jessop
- Library Technician, Brenda Mowbray

#### YELLOWKNIFE

Ecology North – Recycling Resource Centre, POBox 2888, Yellowknife NT X1A 2N1 – 867/873-6019; Fax: 867/873-3654 – Resource Centre Manager, Paula Webber

Environment Canada - Prairie & Northern Region, Library, POBox 637, Yellowknife NT X1A 2N5 – 867/920-8531; Fax: 867/873-8185; Symbol: NWYECW – In Charge, Kevin McCormick

Fédération franco-ténoise – Bibliothèque, CP 1325, Yellowknife NT X1A 2N9 – 867/920-2919; Téléc: 867/873-2158 – Caroline Millette

Industry Canada - Business Service Centre, Scotia Centre, 8th Fl., POBox 1320, Yellowknife NT X1A 2L9 – 867/873-7958; Fax: 867/873-0575; Toll Free: 1-800-661-0599; Email: yel@cbsc.ic.gc.ca; URL: http://www.cbsc.org/nwt/

National Defence - Northern Region Headquarters - Library, POBox 6666, Yellowknife NT X1A 2R3 – 867/873-4011, ext.817; Fax: 867/873-0856; Email: CSN: 620-1961, ext.540; Symbol: NWYND – Library Clerk, Evans Block

Northwest Territories Aboriginal Affairs - Library, Precambrian Bldg., 7th Fl., POBox 1320, Yellowknife NT X1A 2L9 – 867/873-7143; Fax: 867/873-0233 – Executive Secretary, Kathy Green

Northwest Territories Court Library, Courthouse, 4903 - 49 St., 1st Fl., POBox 1320, Yellowknife NT X1A 2L9 – 867/920-8617; Fax: 867/873-0368; Email: courtlib@ssimicro.com; Symbol: NWYC
Librarian, Susan Baer, 403/920-8617
Library Technician, Kelly Chiu

Northwest Territories Federation of Labour – Library, POBox 2787, Yellowknife NT X1A 2R1 – 867/873-3695; Symbol: NWTFL – Researcher, Peter Atamanenko

Northwest Territories Legislative Branch Library, Centre Square Tower, 2nd Fl., POBox 1320, Yellowknife NT X1A 2L9 – 867/873-7628; Fax: 867/873-0395
Branch Librarian, Bev Speight
Library Technician, Marni McDonald

Northwest Territories Legislative Library, Legislative Assembly Building, POBox 1320, Yellowknife NT X1A 2L9 – 867/669-2202, 2203; Fax: 867/873-0207; Email: NWT.GOVTLIB; Symbol: NWYGI
Legislative Librarian, Vera Raschke
Legislative Branch Library, Branch Librarian, Bev Speight

Northwest Territories Resources, Wildlife & Economic Development - Library, Scotia Centre-5, POBox 1320, Yellowknife NT X1A 2L9 – 867/920-8606; Fax: 867/873-0293; Email: alison_welch@gov.nt.ca; Symbol: NWYRR – Librarian, Alison Welch

Northwest Territories Safety & Public Services - Resource Centre Library, Government of NWT, Box 1320, PA-3, Yellowknife NT X1A 2L9 – 867/873-7470; Fax: 867/873-0262
Library Technician, Rita Denneron
Manager, Occupational Safety & Health Section, Al Schreiner

Prince of Wales Northern Heritage Centre - Culture & Heritage Division, POBox 1320, Yellowknife NT X1A 2L9 – 867/873-7698; Fax: 867/873-0205; Email: nwtarchives@ece.learnet.nt.ca; Symbol: NWYWNH – Territorial Archivist, Richard Valpy

## NOVA SCOTIA

### Regional Library Systems with Member Libraries

#### ANNAPOLIS VALLEY REGIONAL LIBRARY

PO Box 640, Bridgetown NS B0S 1C0 – 902/665-2995; Fax: 902/662-4899; Email: avradmin@nsar.library.ns.ca; Symbol: NSAR
Chief Librarian, David Witherly
Reference Librarian, Corinne Frantel

Annapolis Royal Branch Library, St. George St., PO Box 579, Annapolis Royal NS B0S 1A0 – 902/532-2226 – Branch Librarian, Dorothy Abbott

Berwick Branch Library, 236 Commercial St., Berwick NS B0P 1E0 – 902/538-9517 – Branch Librarian, Marian Prout

Bridgetown Branch Library, Town Hall, 271 Granville St., PO Box 39, Bridgetown NS B0S 1C0 – 902/665-2758 – Branch Librarian, Betty Chazalon

Mobile Branch #1, PO Box 640, Bridgetown NS B0S 1C0 – 902/665-2995; Fax: 902/665-4899

Hantsport Branch Library, Hantsport School, 11 School St., Box 542, Hantsport NS B0P 1P0 – 902/584-3488 – Branch Librarian, Diana Thompson

Kentville Branch Library, 95 Cornwallis St., PO Box 625, Kentville NS B4N 3X7 – 902/679-2544 – Branch Contact, Winnie Stephen-Wills

Mobile Branch #2, PO Box 625, Kentville NS B4N 3X7 – 902/679-6653; Fax: 902/679-6653

Kingston Branch Library, 671 Main St., PO Box 430, Kingston NS B0P 1R0 – 902/765-3631 – Branch Librarian, Andrea Leeson

Lawrencetown Branch Library, 479 Main St., PO Box 88, Lawrencetown NS B0S 1M0 – 902/584-3044 – Branch Librarian, Dene Marshall

Middleton Branch Library, 45 Gates Ave., PO Box 667, Middleton NS B0S 1P0 – 902/825-4835 – Branch Librarian, Susan Aldred

Port Williams Branch Library, Community Centre, 131 Main St., Port Williams NS B0P 1T0 – 902/542-3005; Fax: 902/542-3005 – Branch Librarian, Connie Millett

Windsor Branch Library, 78 Thomas St., Windsor NS B0N 2T0 – 902/798-5424 – Branch Librarian, Peggy Hamilton

Wolfville Branch Library, 21 Elm Ave., PO Box 880, Wolfville NS B0P 1X0 – 902/542-5760; Fax: 902/542-5780 – Branch Librarian, Sharon Wendt

#### CAPE BRETON REGIONAL LIBRARY

50 Falmouth St., Sydney NS B1P 6X9 – 902/562-3279; Fax: 902/564-0765; Email: inssc@nssc.library.ns.ca; URL: http://www.nshpl.library.ns.ca/regionals/cbr/; Symbol: NSSC
Regional Librarian, Ian R. MacIntosh

Baddeck Branch Library, Chebucto St., PO Box 88, Baddeck NS B0E 1B0 – 902/295-2055

Victoria County Bookmobile, 526 Chebucto St., Baddeck NS B0E 1B0 – 902/295-2055

Dominion Branch Library, 78 Commercial St., Dominion NS B0A 1E0 – 902/849-3590

Donkin Branch Library, Donkin Elementary School, 81 Centre Ave., Donkin NS B0A 1G0 – 902/737-1154

Florence Branch Library, 380 Main St., Florence NS B0C 1J0 – 902/736-1988

Glace Bay Library, 121 Union St., Glace Bay NS B1A 2P8 – 902/849-8657

Louisbourg Branch Library, 10 Upper Warren St., Louisbourg NS B0A 1M0 – 902/733-3608

Main-A-Dieu Branch Library, Credit Union Bldg., Main-A-Dieu NS B0A 1N0 – 902/733-5708

New Waterford Branch Library, 3390 Plummer Ave., PO Box 12, New Waterford NS B1H 4K4 – 902/862-2892

Ingonish Branch Library, 35962 Cabot Trail, North Ingonish NS B0C 1K0 – 902/285-2544

Wilfred Oram Centennial Library, 299 Commercial St., North Sydney NS B2A 1B9 – 902/794-3272

Tompkins Memorial Library, 2249 Sydney Rd., Reserve Mines NS B0A 1V0 – 902/849-6685

Martha Hollett Memorial Library, 113 Main St., PO Box 102, Sydney Mines NS B1V 2L4 – 902/736-3219

Cape Breton County Bookmobile, 50 Falmouth St., Sydney NS B1P 6X9 – 902/562-3279

James McConnell Memorial Library, 50 Falmouth St., Sydney NS B1P 6X9 – 902/562-3161; Email: mcconne@nssc.library.ns.ca

#### COLCHESTER-EAST HANTS REGIONAL LIBRARY

754 Prince St., Truro NS B2N 1G9 – 902/895-4183; Fax: 902/895-7149; Email: anstc@nstc.library.ns.ca; Symbol: NSTC
Regional Library Director, Janet D. Pelley
Adult Services, Administrator, Daphne Cragg
Children's Services, Administrator, M. Lynda Marsh
Technical & Automated Services, Administrator, Michelle G. Walters

Elmsdale Branch Library, Elmsdale NS B0N 1M0 – 902/883-9838 – Branch Assistant, Rosalind Morrison

Stewiacke Branch Library, Stewiacke NS B0N 2J0 – 902/639-2481 – Branch Assistant, Evelyn Caldwell

Tatamagouche Branch Library, Tatamagouche NS B0K 1V0 – 902/657-3064 – Branch Assistant, Glenn Hamilton

Truro Branch Library, 754 Prince St., Truro NS B2N 1G9 – 902/895-4183; Fax: 902/895-7149

#### CUMBERLAND REGIONAL LIBRARY

Confederation Memorial Bldg., Ratchford St., PO Box 220, Amherst NS B4H 3Z2 – 902/667-2135; Fax: 902/667-1360; Email: insamc@rs6000.nshpl.library.ns.ca
Chief Librarian, Beverly True
Assistant Librarian, Frances Newman

Advocate Branch Library, Fundy Tides Recreation Centre, Advocate Harbour NS B0M 1A0 – 902/392-2214; Email: advocate@rs6000.nshpl.library.ns.ca – Jeannine Grant

Four Fathers Memorial Library, Acadia St., PO Box 220, Amherst NS B3H 3Z2 – 902/667-2549; Fax: 902/667-1360 – Frances Newman

Oxford Branch Library, Water St., PO Box 309, Oxford NS B0M 1P0 – 902/447-2440; Email: oxford@rs6000.nshpl.library.ns.ca – Debra Millard

Parrsboro Branch Library, Queen St., PO Box 397, Parrsboro NS B0M 1S0 – 902/254-2046; Email: parrsbor@rs6000.nshpl.library.ns.ca – Saundra Spence

Pugwash Branch Library, Durham St., Pugwash NS B0K 1L0 – 902/243-3331; Email: pugwash@rs6000.nshpl.library.ns.ca – Helen Feeley

River Hebert Miners Memorial Branch Library, Tidal View Health Centre, 2730 Barrons Field Rd., River Hebert NS B0L 1G0 – 902/251-2324; Email: riverheb@rs6000.nshpl.library.ns.ca – Maureen Glennie

Springhill Branch Library, Main St., Springhill NS B0M 1X0 – 902/597-2211; Email: springhi@rs6000.nshpl.library.ns.ca – Sharon Simons; Mary Guthro

#### EASTERN COUNTIES REGIONAL LIBRARY

390 Murray St., PO Bag 2500, Mulgrave NS B0E 2G0 – 902/747-2597; Fax: 902/747-2500; Email: info@nsme.library.ns.ca; URL: http://www.library.ns.ca/regionals/ecr/; Symbol: NSME
Automation Library/Bookmobile Coordinator, David Cumby
User Services Librarian, Heather Halliday
Coordinatrice des services en langue française, Lorraine Fennell

Canso Branch Library, 18 School St., PO Box 44, Canso NS B0H 1H0 – 902/366-2955; Fax: 902/366-2955; Email: canso@nsme.library.ns.ca

Cyril Ward Memorial Library, 27 Pleasant St., PO Box 191, Guysborough NS B0H 1N0 – 902/533-3586; Fax: 902/533-3586; Email: guysboro@nsme.library.ns.ca

Drs. Coady & Tompkins Memorial Library, 7972 Cabot Trail, General Delivery, Margaree Forks NS B0E 2A0 – 902/248-2821; Fax: 902/248-2821; Email: margaree@nsme.library.ns.ca

Mulgrave Branch Library, 390 Murray St., PO Box 2500, Mulgrave NS B0E 2G0 – 902/747-2597; Fax: 902/747-2500; Email: mulgrave@nsme.library.ns.ca

Petit de Grat Branch Library, PO Box 151, Petit de Grat NS B0E 2L0 – 902/226-3534; Fax: 902/226-3534; Email: petitdeg@nsme.library.ns.ca

Port Hawkesbury Branch Library, 304 Pitt St., PO Box 996, Port Hawkesbury NS B0E 2V0 – 902/625-2729; Fax: 902/625-2729; Email: porthawk@nsme.library.ns.ca

Sherbrooke Branch, Main St., PO Box 177, Sherbrooke NS B0J 3C0 – 902/522-2180; Fax: 902/522-2180; Email: sherbroo@nsme.library.ns.ca

**HALIFAX REGIONAL LIBRARY**

60 Alderney Dr., Dartmouth NS B2Y 4P8 – 902/490-5744; Fax: 902/490-5762; Email: ansh@nsh.library.ns.ca; Symbol: NSH

Director, Judith Hare
Deputy Director/Public Services Manager, Susan McLean
Planning & Development, Manager, Paula Saulnier
Systems & Technical Services, Manager, Deborah Nicholson
Finance, Manager, Al LeBlanc
Community Services, Manager, Joan Brown Hicks
Collections, Manager, Laura Jantek
Service Delivery, Manager, Linda Hodgins
Information Services Manager, Michael Colborne

Bedford Branch Public Library, Wardour Centre, 15 Dartmouth Rd., Bedford NS B4A 3X6 – 902/490-5740; Fax: 902/490-5752 – Branch Head, Sarah Wenning

Cole Harbour Public Library, Cole Harbour Place, 2 Forest Hills Pkwy., Cole Habour NS B2W 6C6 – 902/434-7228; Fax: 902/434-7448 – Branch Head, Darlene Beck

Alderney Gate Public Library, 60 Alderney Dr., Dartmouth NS B2Y 4P8 – 902/490-5745 – Branch Head, Andrew Poplawski

Dartmouth North Public Library, Highfield Park Drive, 134 Pinecrest Dr., Dartmouth NS B3A 2J9 – 902/490-5840; Fax: 902/490-5842 – Branch Head, Troy Myers

Woodlawn Public Library, Woodlawn Centre, 114 Woodlawn Rd., Dartmouth NS B2W 2S7 – 902/435-8352; Fax: 902/435-8380 – Branch Head, Charby Slemin

Captain William Spry Public Library, Captain William Spry Community Centre, 10 Kidston Rd., Halifax NS B3R 2J7 – 902/490-5734; Fax: 902/490-5741 – Branch Head, Jennifer Evans

Halifax North Memorial Public Library, 2285 Gottingen St., Halifax NS B3K 3B7 – 902/490-5723; Fax: 902/490-5737 – Branch Head, Tracey Jones

Spring Garden Road Library, 5381 Spring Garden Rd., Halifax NS B3J 1E9 – 902/490-5700; Reference Services: 902/490-5710; Fax: 902/490-5746; Symbol: NSH – Branch Head, Ranjani Masih

Thomas Raddall Public Library, 255 Lacewood Dr., Halifax NS B3M 4G2 – 902/490-5738; Fax: 902/490-5739 – Branch Head, Jean Morgan

J.D. Shatford Memorial Library, Hubbards NS B0J 1T0 – 902/857-9176; Fax: 902/857-1397 – Branch Head, Paige Rockwell

Sackville Public Library, Sackville Commercial Centre, 636 Sackville Dr., Lower Sackville NS B4C 2E1 – 902/865-8653; Reference: 902/865-3744; Fax: 902/865-2370 – Branch Head, Kathleen Peverill

Musquodoboit Harbour Public Library, The Strip Mall, Musquodoboit Harbour NS B0J 1T0 – 902/889-2227; Fax: 902/889-3799 – Branch Head, Mary Lorimer

Sheet Harbour Public Library, Blue Water Business Centre, Sheet Harbour NS B0J 3B0 – 902/885-2391; Fax: 902/885-2749 – Branch Head, Mary Lorimer

**PICTOU-ANTIGONISH REGIONAL LIBRARY**

PO Box 276, New Glasgow NS B2H 5E3 – 902/755-6031; Fax: 902/755-6775; Email: requests@nsngp.library.ns.ca; URL: http://www.library.ns.ca/regionals/par/; Symbol: NSNGP

Director, Ann Ripley
Children's Librarian, Linda Arsenault
Technical Services Librarian, Fred Popowich
Systems Librarian, Eric Stackhouse

Antigonish Library, PO Box 1741, Antigonish NS B2G 2M5 – 902/863-4276; Email: antigoni@nsngp.library.ns.ca – Contact, Rhynda Tudor

New Glasgow Library, PO Box 276, New Glasgow NS B2H 5E3 – 902/752-8233; Email: newglaso@nsngp.library.ns.ca – Branch Supervisor, Carol A. MacMillan

Pictou Library, PO Box 622, Pictou NS B0K 1H0 – 902/485-5021; Email: pictou@nsngp.library.ns.ca – Contact, Bonnie Allan

River John Library, PO Box 104, River John NS B0K 1N0 – 902/351-2599; Email: riverjoh@nsngp.library.ns.ca – Contact, Margaret MacLean

Stellarton Library, PO Box 1372, Stellarton NS B0K 1S0 – 902/755-1638; Email: stellart@nsngp.library.ns.ca – Contact, Peggy Vienneau

Trenton Library, Main St., PO Box 612, Trenton NS B0K 1X0 – 902/752-5181; Email: trenton@nsngp.library.ns.ca – Contact, Shelley MacLean

Westville Library, Queen St., PO Box 627, Westville NS B0K 2A0 – 902/396-5022 – Contact, Gina Snell

**SOUTH SHORE REGIONAL LIBRARY**

PO Box 34, Bridgewater NS B4V 2W6 – 902/543-2548; Fax: 902/543-8191; Email: ansbs@rs6000.nshpl.library.ns.ca; URL: http://rs6000.nshpl.library.ns.ca/regionals/ssr/; Symbol: NSBS

Chief Librarian, Janet Clark
Branch/Extension Librarian, Frances Anderson
Mobile Branch/Technical Services Librarian, Cathy MacDonald

Bridgewater Branch Library, 547 King St., Bridgewater NS B4V 1B3 – 902/543-9222

DeWolfe Memorial Library, Gorham St., PO Box 9, Liverpool NS B0T 1K0 – 902/354-5270

Lunenburg Branch Library, 19 Pelham St., Lunenburg NS B0J 2C0 – 902/634-8008

**WESTERN COUNTIES REGIONAL LIBRARY**

405 Main St., Yarmouth NS B5A 1G3 – 902/742-2486; Fax: 902/742-6920; Email: ansy@nsy.library.ns.ca; Symbol: NSY

Regional Library Director, Trudy Amirault
Reference Librarian, Virginia Stoddard
Children's Librarian, Joanne Head
French Services Librarian, Janice Boudreau

Barrington Branch Library, PO Box 310, Barrington Passage NS B0W 1G0 – 902/637-3348; Email: barringt@nsy.library.ns.ca – Contact, Margo Chetwynd

Clarks Harbour Branch Library, PO Box 189, Clarks Harbour NS B0W 1P0 – 902/745-2885; Email: clarksha@nsy.library.ns.ca – Contact, Shelly Smith

Digby Branch Library, Town Hall, Sydney St., PO Box 730, Digby NS B0V 1A0 – 902/245-2163; Email: digby@nsy.library.ns.ca – Contact, Thelma Pulsifer

Lockeport Branch Library, PO Box 265, Lockeport NS B0T 1L0 – 902/656-2817; Email: lockepor@nsy.library.ns.ca – Contact, Mary Anne Turner

Clare Branch Library, PO Box 265, Meteghan NS B0W 2J0 – 902/645-3350; Email: clare@nsy.library.ns.ca – Contact, Aline Deveau

Pubnico Branch Library, PO Box 22, Pubnico NS B0W 2W0 – 902/762-2204; Fax: 902/762-3208; Email: pubnico@nsy.library.ns.ca – Contact, Beatrice Adams

Shelburne Branch Library, PO Box 158, Shelburne NS B0T 1W0 – 902/875-3615; Fax: 902/875-1015; Email: mckaymem@nsy.library.ns.ca – Branch Head, Edith Bower

Westport Branch Library, PO Box 1194, Westport NS B0V 1H0 – 902/839-2955; Email: westport@nsy.library.ns.ca – Branch Head, Charlotte Dixon

Weymouth Branch Library, PO Box 340, Weymouth NS B0W 3T0 – 902/837-4596; Email: weymouth@nsy.library.ns.ca – Contact, Marguerite Thibault

Yarmouth Branch Library, 405 Main St., Yarmouth NS B5A 1G3 – 902/742-5040; Fax: 902/742-6920; Email: yarmouth@nsy.library.ns.ca – Librarian, Joanne Head

## Special & College Libraries & Resource Centres

**AMHERST**

Amherst Township Historical Society – Genealogical Archives, c/o Cumberland County Museum, 150 Church St., Amherst NS B4H 3C3 – 902/667-2561; Fax: 902/667-2561 – Education Officer, Joan Fillmore

Cumberland County Family Planning Association – Library, 16 Church St., Lower Level, POBox 661, Amherst NS B4H 4B8 – 902/667-7500 – Community Director, Ruthie Patriquin

Indian & Northern Affairs Canada - Library, 40 Havelock St., POBox 160, Amherst NS B4H 3Z3 – 902/661-6233; Fax: 902/667-9947; Symbol: NSAIN – Public Inquiries Officer, Debbi Adams

**ANTIGONISH**

Coady International Institute – Marie Michael Library, St. Francis Xavier University, POBox 5000, Antigonish NS B2G 2W5 – 902/867-3964; Fax: 902/867-3907; Email: sadams@juliet.stfx.ca; Symbol: NSASF – Librarian, Sue Adams

St. Francis Xavier University - Angus L. Macdonald Library, POBox 5000, Antigonish NS B2G 2W5 – 902/867-2267; Fax: 902/867-5153; Email: rcampbel@stfx.ca; URL: http://cwaves.stfx.ca/libraries/welcome.html; Symbol: NSAS

Chief Librarian, Rita Campbell
Reference Librarian, Barbara Phillips, 902/867-2242
Circulation Supervisor, Jane Synishin, 902/867-2228
Systems Librarian, Gordon Bertrand, 902/867-2114
Acquisitions Supervisor, Kevin MacNeil, 902/867-2168

**ARMDALE**

Nova Scotia Teachers Union – Library, 3106 Dutch Village Rd., Armdale NS B3L 4L7 – 902/477-5621; Fax: 902/477-3517; Toll Free: 1-800-565-6788; Email: library@nstu.ns.ca; Symbol: NSHTU – Librarian, Maureen Phinney

**BEDFORD**

Environment Canada - Atmospheric Environment Service, Atlantic Region - Library, 1496 Bedford Hwy., Bedford NS B4A 1E5 – 902/426-9278; Fax: 902/426-9158; Email: joan.backer@ec.gc.ca; Symbol: NSHW – Librarian, Joan Backer, 902/426-9187

**BERWICK**

Western Kings Memorial Health Centre – Library, 121 Orchard St., POBox 490, Berwick NS B0P 1E0 – 902/538-3111; Fax: 902/538-9590; Symbol: NSBWK – Administrator, John Dow

**CHETICAMP**

La Société Saint-Pierre – Les Trois Pignons, CP 430, Cheticamp NS B0E 1H0 – 902/224-2612; Téléc: 902/224-1579 – Éditeur, Edmond J. Burns

**CHURCH POINT**

Université Sainte-Anne - Bibliothèque Louis R. Comeau, POBox 1-242, Church Point NS B0W 1M0 – 902/769-2114, ext.161; Fax: 902/769-0137; Email: ENVOY: ILL.NSCS; Symbol: NSCS

University Librarian, Mildred Comeau

Reference Librarian, Cecile Pothier
Circulation, Rejeanne LeBlanc-Comeau
ILL, Corinne Arsenault

**CLEMENTSPORT**

The Lester B. Pearson Canadian International Peacekeeping Training Centre – Library, Cornwallis Park, POBox 100, Clementsport NS B0S 1E0 – 902/638-8611; Fax: 902/638-8888; Email: nauby@ppc.cdnpeacekeeping.ns.ca – Librarian, Lana J. Kamennof-Sine

**DARTMOUTH**

Nova Scotia Innovation Corporation – Library, 101 Research Dr., POBox 790, Dartmouth NS B2Y 3Z7 – 902/424-8670, ext.181; Fax: 902/424-4679; Toll Free: 1-800-565-7051; Email: library@innovacorp.ns.ca; Symbol: NSHR – Information Services Manager, Mary Veling

Black Cultural Centre for Nova Scotia – Library, 1149 Main St., Dartmouth NS B2Z 1A8 – 902/434-6223; Fax: 902/434-2306 – Curator, Henry Bishop

Cole Harbour Rural Heritage Society – Library, 471 Poplar Dr., Dartmouth NS B2W 4L2 – 902/434-0222 – Curator, Terry Eyland

Defence Research Establishment - Atlantic - Reference Library, 9 Grove St., POBox 1012, Dartmouth NS B2Y 3Z7 – 902/426-3100, ext.135; Fax: 902/426-9654; Email: ENVOY: DREA.INFO.SVCS; URL: http://www.drea.dnd.ca; Symbol: NSHN – Information Services, Iris Ouellette, Email: Ouellette@drea.dnd.ca

Environment Canada-Environmental Quality Laboratories: Dartmouth – Library, Bedford Institute of Oceanography, 1 Challenger Dr., POBox 1006, Dartmouth NS B2Y 4A2 – 902/426-3288; Fax: 902/426-8041 – Librarian, Dawn Taylor-Prime

Environment Canada - Atlantic Region Library, Queen Sq., 45 Alderney Dr., 5th Fl., Dartmouth NS B2Y 2N6 – 902/426-7219; Fax: 902/426-6143; Symbol: NSDE
Librarian, Dawn Taylor-Prime, Email: Dawn.Taylor-Prime@ec.gc.ca
ILL Librarian, Angela Ward, 902/426-7232

Fisheries & Oceans Canada-Bedford Institute of Oceanography – Maritimes Regional Library, 1 Challenger Dr., POBox 1006, Dartmouth NS B2Y 4A2 – 902/426-3675; Fax: 902/496-1544; Email: biolib@maritimes.dfo.ca; Symbol: NSDB – Chief, Library Services, Anna Fiander

Health Canada - Health Protection Branch - Library, POBox 1060, Dartmouth NS B2Y 3Z7 – 902/426-6694; Fax: 902/426-6676 – Librarian, Adeline MacDonald

Lupus Society of Nova Scotia – Library, POBox 38038, Dartmouth NS B3B 1X2 – 902/434-4511; Fax: 902/685-3953; Toll Free: 1-800-394-0125 – Librarian, Birdie Fiddes

Nova Scotia Community College - Akerley Campus Library, 21 Woodlawn Rd., Dartmouth NS B2W 2R7 – 902/434-2020, ext.336; Fax: 902/462-4320; Symbol: NSDRV – Librarian, P.T.H. Huang

Nova Scotia Hospital – Health Sciences Library, 300 Pleasant St., POBox 1004, Dartmouth NS B2Y 3Z9 – 902/464-3254; Fax: 902/464-4804; Symbol: NSDNSH – Library Technician, Myrna Lawson

Schizophrenia Society of Nova Scotia – Library, Administration Office, Nova Scotia Hospital, POBox 1004, Dartmouth NS B2Y 3Z9 – 902/465-2601, 464-3456; Fax: 902/465-5479; Toll Free: 1-800-465-2601 – Resource Librarian, Geri Cooper

Transport Canada - Maritimes Regional Library, Queen's Square Bldg., #1215, 45 Alderney Dr., POBox 1013, Dartmouth NS B2Y 4K2 – 902/426-5182; Fax: 902/426-8337; Symbol: NSHMT – Library Technician, Gary Keirstead

**DIGBY**

Digby General Hospital – Health Records Library, Warwick St., POBox 820, Digby NS B0V 1A0 – 902/245-2501; Fax: 902/245-5517; Symbol: NSDG – Shirley Dugas

**HALIFAX**

AIDS Coalition of Nova Scotia – Library, #600, 5675 Spring Garden Rd., Halifax NS B3J 1H1 – 902/425-4882; Fax: 902/422-6200 – Rosanne LeBlanc

Alzheimer Society of Nova Scotia – Alzheimer Resource Centre, 5954 Spring Garden Rd., Halifax NS B3H 1Y7 – 902/422-7961; Fax: 902/422-7971 – Program Coordinator, Johnann MacGillivray

Armbrae Academy - Library, 1400 Oxford St., Halifax NS B3H 3Y8 – 902/423-7920; Fax: 902/423-9731; Email: head@ambrae.ns.ca; URL: http://www.armbrae.ns.ca/isnet/armbrae/ – Headmaster, Eric T. MacKnight

Atlantic School of Theology - Library, 640 Francklyn St., Halifax NS B3H 3B5 – 902/423-7986; Fax: 902/423-7941; Email: ENVOY: nshph.ill; URL: http://novanet.ns.ca/ast/homepage.html; Symbol: NSHPH
Head Librarian, Dr. D. Davis
Cataloguing, Technical Services Librarian, Lloyd J. Melanson
Reference, Librarian, Elaine Murray
Assistant Technical Services Librarian, Michael Bramah

Burchell, MacAdam & Hayman Law Office - Library, 1801 Hollis St., 18th Fl., POBox 36, Halifax NS B3J 2L4 – 902/423-6361; Fax: 902/420-9326 – Michael Wood

Cambridge Military Library, RA Park, 1565 Queen St., Halifax NS B3J 2H9 – 902/427-7193; Email: cml@istar.ca – M.Cpl. Rebecca Hanbigde-Kock

Canadian Broadcasting Corporation - Broadcasting Materials Library, 5600 Sackville St., POBox 3000, Halifax NS B3J 2E9 – 902/420-4186; Fax: 902/420-4281; Email: kirby@halifax.cbc.ca – Senior Broadcast Material Librarian, Doug Kirby, 902/420-4160
Music & Record Library, 5600 Sackville St., POBox 3000, Halifax NS B3J 3E9 – 902/420-4404; Fax: 902/420-4414; Symbol: NSHCB – Senior Record Librarian, Caroline Grant

Canadian Environmental Remediation Services – Library, POBox 2564, Halifax NS B3J 3N5 – 902/422-5949 – Chief Librarian, Nick Wright

Canadian Heritage - Parks Canada, Atlantic Region Library, Historic Properties, Upper Water St., Halifax NS B3J 1S9 – 902/426-8951; Fax: 902/426-7012; Email: ENVOY: PARKSATLANTIC.LB; Symbol: NSHIAP
Chief, Information Holdings Management, David Palmer, 902/426-8951, Email: palmerd@pch.gc.ca
Librarian, Lynn O'Brien, 902/426-4621
Library Clerk, Shirley McNeil, 902/426-7266
Records Management, Coordinator, Gail Collins, 902/426-7327
Records, Clerk, Linda Soulis, 902/426-3426
Records, Clerk, Wayne O'Melia, 902/426-3426
Parks Canada, Halifax Citadel National Historic Site - Library, POBox 9080, Halifax NS B3K 5M7 – 902/426-1992; Fax: 902/426-4228; Symbol: NSHCN – Head, Ron McDonald

The Chronicle-Herald & The Mail Star - Herald Information Services, 1650 Argyle St., POBox 610, Halifax NS B3J 2T2 – 902/426-3080; Fax: 902/426-2810; Email: online@herald.ns.ca; URL: http://www.herald.ns.ca
Librarian, Alberta Dubé
Library Assistant, Debbie Reid

The Clean Nova Scotia Foundation – Library, 1675 Bedford Row, POBox 2528, Halifax NS B3J 3N5 – 902/420-3474; Fax: 902/424-5334; Toll Free: 1-800-665-5377 – Information Officer, Debbie Neilson

Council of Nova Scotia Archives – Library, c/o Public Archives of Nova Scotia, 6016 University Ave., Halifax NS B3H 1W4 – 902/424-7093; Fax: 902/424-0628 – Archivist, Johanna Smith

Cox Downie Law Office - Library, PO Box 2380, RPO Central, Halifax NS B3J 3E5 – 902/421-6262; Fax: 902/421-3130; Email: lawyer@coxdownie.ns.ca; URL: http://coxdowie.ns.ca – Librarian, Linda Matte

Daley, Black & Moreira Law Office - Library, #400, TD Centre, 1791 Barrington St., POBox 355, Halifax NS B3J 2N7 – 902/423-7211; Fax: 902/420-1744 – Librarian, Mary Gibson

Dalhousie University - Kellogg Health Science Library, Tupper Bldg., Main Fl., University Ave. & College St., Halifax NS B3H 4H7 – 902/494-1617; Fax: 902/494-3798; Email: betty.sutherland@dal.ca
Killam Library, 6225 University Ave., Halifax NS B3H 4H8 – 902/494-3601; Fax: 902/494-2062; Symbol: NSHD
University Librarian, Dr. William F. Birdsall, Email: bill.birdsall@dal.ca
Collections Development, Head, Holly Melanson
Technical Services, Head, Elaine Boychuk
Science Services, Head, Patricia Lutley
Pharmacy Library, Information Officer, Elizabeth Foy, 902/494-1671
Law Library, Weldon Law Bldg., University Ave., Halifax NS B3H 4H9 – 902/494-2124; Fax: 902/494-6669 – Law Librarian, Christine Wiktor
School for Resource & Environmental Studies Library, 1312 Robie St., Halifax NS B3H 3E2 – 902/494-3728; Fax: 902/494-1359; Email: SRES@is.dal.ca – Librarian, Judith Reade

Dalhousie University Polytechnic - Library, PO Box 1000, Stn Central RPO, Halifax NS B3J 2X4 – 902/420-7700; Fax: 902/420-7831; Email: library@tuns.ca; URL: http://www.tuns.ca/~library; Symbol: NSHT
University Librarian, Donna Richardson
Public Services Librarian, Helen Powell, 902/420-7595
Reference Librarian, Sharon Murphy, 902/420-2614
Head of Circulation, Bill Slauenwhite, 902/420-2630
Technical Services Librarian, Mark Bartlett, 902/420-7562

Ecology Action Centre – Library, #31, 1568 Argyle St., Halifax NS B3J 2B3 – 902/429-2202; Fax: 902/422-6410 – Librarian, Ellen Redden

Fisheries & Oceans Canada - Scotia-Fundy Regional Library, Halifax Fisheries Library, 1707 Lower Water St., POBox 550, Halifax NS B3J 2S7 – 902/426-7160; Fax: 902/426-1862; Email: Hfx.Library@maritimes.dfo.ca; URL: http://www.maritimes.dfo.ca/corporate/library/halifax.html; Symbol: NSHF
Head Librarian, Lori Collins
ILL, Diane Stewart

Halifax Regional Multicultural Council, #209, 2786 Agricola St., Halifax NS B3K 4E1 – 902/455-1619; Fax: 902/455-1619 – Administrator, I. Illyas

Health Canada - Library, 1557 Hollis St., Halifax NS B3J 3V4 – 902/426-8440 – Library, Anne MacAlpine

Heart & Stroke Foundation of Nova Scotia – Resource Centre, City Centre Atlantic, #204, 5523 Spring Garden Rd., Halifax NS B3J 3T1 – 902/423-7530; Fax: 902/492-1464; Toll Free: 1-800-423-4432

Industry Canada - Business Service Centre, 1575 Brunswick St., Halifax NS B3J 2G1 – 902/426-8604; Fax: 902/426-6530; Toll Free: 1-800-668-1010;

Email: halifax@cbsc.ic.gc.ca; URL: http://www.cbsc.org/ns/

International Education Centre - Saint Mary's University – Resource Centre, Saint Mary's University, 923 Robie St., Halifax NS B3H 3C3 – 902/420-5525; Fax: 902/420-5288 – Ron Houlihan

IWK-Grace Health Centre for Children, Women & Families – Health Sciences Library, 5980 University Ave., Halifax NS B3H 4N1 – 902/420-3058; Fax: 902/422-3009; Email: Library@iwkgrace.ns.ca; Symbol: NSHGH – Manager, Library Services, Darlene Chapman

Justice Canada - Halifax Regional Office - Library, #1400, 5251 Duke St., Halifax NS B3J 1P3 – 902/426-3260; Fax: 902/426-2329 – Administrative Assistant, Samantha Boorman

Lane Environment Limited – Library, 1663 Oxford St., Halifax NS B3H 3Z5 – 902/423-8197; Fax: 902/429-8089 – Administrative Assistant, Suzanne Sleigh

Maritime Conservatory of Music - Library, 6199 Chebucto Rd., Halifax NS B3L 1K7 – 902/423-6995; Fax: 902/423-6029 – Office Manager, Janet Hillier

Maritime Museum of the Atlantic - Library, 1675 Lower Water St., Halifax NS B3J 1S3 – 902/424-7890; Fax: 902/424-0612; Symbol: NSHMM

McInnes Cooper & Robertson - Law Library, 1601 Lower Water St., POBox 730, Halifax NS B3J 2V1 – 902/424-1340; Fax: 902/425-6386, 6350; Email: mcrhfx@mcrlaw.com; URL: http://fox.nstn.ca/~mcrhfx/; Symbol: NSHMCR
- Librarian, Lindy L. Stephens
- Library Technician, L.H. Paris

Mount Saint Vincent University - Library, 166 Bedford Hwy., Halifax NS B3M 2J6 – 902/457-6120; Fax: 902/457-3175; Email: ENVOY: ADMIN/MT.ST.VINCENTUNIV; URL: http://www.msvu.ca/; Symbol: NSHV
- Reference Services/Collections Development, Head, Terrence Paris, 902/457-6526
- User Services Systems Librarian, Meg Raven, 902/457-6403
- Bibliographic Services Librarian, Peter Glenister, 902/457-6402
- Chief Librarian, Lillian Beltaos, 902/457-6121

National Defence - CFB Halifax - Reference & Recreation Library, Forces Mail Office, Halifax NS B3K 2X0 – 902/427-8398; Symbol: NSHN – Base Librarian, Jackie Lombard

Nova Scotia Association of Health Organizations – Library, Bedford Professional Centre, 2 Dartmouth Rd., Halifax NS B4A 2K7 – 902/832-8500; Fax: 902/832-8505 – Pam Shipley

Nova Scotia Barristers' Society – Library, 1815 Upper Water St., Halifax NS B3J 1S7 – 902/425-2665; Fax: 902/422-1697; Email: nsbarlib@atcon.com – Director, Library Services, Barbara Campbell

Nova Scotia College of Art & Design - Library, 5163 Duke St., Halifax NS B3J 3J6 – 902/494-8196; Fax: 902/425-2420; Email: ilga@nscad.ns.ca; URL: http://www.nscad.ns.ca; Symbol: NSHCA – Director of Library Services, Ilga Leja, 902/494-8181

Nova Scotia Community College - Halifax Campus Library, 1825 Bell Rd., Halifax NS B3H 2Z4 – 902/424-7972; Fax: 902/424-0553 – Deborah Costelo

Institute of Technology Library, 5685 Leeds St., POBox 2210, Halifax NS B3J 3C4 – 902/424-4224; Fax: 902/424-0534; Email: brennand@nscc.ns.ca; Symbol: NSHTI
- Librarian, Nola Brennan
- Library Clerk, Veronica Paris

Nova Scotia Community Services - Library, POBox 696, Halifax NS B3J 2T7 – 902/424-7906; Fax: 902/424-0502; Email: coms.phillija@gov.ns.ca; Symbol: NSHSS – Librarian, Jane Phillips

Nova Scotia Department of Health - Library, Joseph Howe Bldg., 1681 Granville St., 10th Fl., Halifax NS B3J 2R8 – 902/424-8694; Fax: 902/424-0663; Email: library@gov.ns.ca; Symbol: NSHH – Librarian, Ruth Vaughan

Nova Scotia Economic Renewal Agency - Library, 1800 Argyle St., POBox 519, Halifax NS B3J 2R7 – 902/424-5807, 6178; Fax: 902/424-0748; Email: econ.library@gov.ns.ca; URL: http://www.gov.ns.ca/ecor/cs/library.htm; Symbol: NSHDD
- Librarian, Donald Purcell
- Library Assistant, Eileen Dunphy

Nova Scotia Education & Culture - Library, #402, 2021 Brunswick St., POBox 587, Halifax NS B3J 2S9 – 902/424-5264; Fax: 902/424-0519; Email: educ_lib@gov.ns.ca; URL: http://www.ednet.ns.ca/educ/policy/library/homepage/library.htm; Symbol: NSHVTT
- Librarian, K. Arbuckle, Email: arbuckkl@gov.ns.ca
- Information Services Librarian, M. Dewar, Email: dewarma@gov.ns.ca
- Technical Services, Jennifer Millman, Email: millmajl@gov.ns.ca

Nova Scotia Environment - Library, 5151 Terminal Rd., 5th Fl., POBox 2107, Halifax NS B3J 3B7 – 902/424-5300; Fax: 902/424-2372; Email: lauferje@gov.ns.ca; Symbol: NSHDE – Research & Statistics Officer, Janice E. Laufer, 902/424-2372

Nova Scotia Finance - Federal-Provincial Taxation & Fiscal Relations Library, POBox 187, Halifax NS B3J 2N3 – 902/424-2595; Fax: 902/424-0590 – Sheila Crummell

Nova Scotia Housing & Municipal Affairs - Library, POBox 216, Halifax NS B3J 2M4 – 902/424-5965; Fax: 902/424-0531; Symbol: NSHMA – Librarian, Audrey Manzer, Email: amanzer@gov.ns.ca

Nova Scotia Human Rights Commission - Library, POBox 2221, Halifax NS B3J 3C4 – 902/424-4111; Fax: 902/424-0596; Email: hlfxlord.hrc.jennifer@gov.ns.ca; Symbol: NSHRC – Central Registry Clerk, Jennifer Downey

Nova Scotia Justice - Library, 5151 Terminal Rd., 3rd Fl., POBox 7, Halifax NS B3J 2L6 – 902/424-7699; Fax: 902/424-4556; Symbol: NSHOL – Library Contact, Marie DeYoung

Nova Scotia Labour - Library, POBox 697, Halifax NS B3J 2T8 – 902/424-8474; Fax: 902/424-3239; Email: ENVOY 100: ILL.NSHDOL; Symbol: NSHDOL – Librarian, JoAnn Richling

Nova Scotia Legislative Library, Province House, POBox 396, Halifax NS B3J 2P8 – 902/424-5932; Fax: 902/424-0574; Email: nsleglib@fox.nstn.ca; URL: http://www.gov.ns.ca/legi; Symbol: NSHL
- Legislative Librarian, Margaret F. Murphy
- Reference Librarian, Sandra Cook, 902/424-5625
- Technical Services Librarian, Jean Sawyer

Nova Scotia Museum - Library, 1747 Summer St., Halifax NS B3H 3A6 – 902/424-7198; Fax: 902/424-0560; Email: burlesdl@gov.ns.ca; Symbol: NSHM – Librarian, Debra Burleson

Nova Scotia Natural Resources - Library, 1701 Hollis St., 3rd Fl., POBox 698, Halifax NS B3J 2T9 – 902/424-8633; Fax: 902/424-7735; Symbol: NSHDOM
- Head, Library Services, Valerie Brisco
- Reference Librarian, Barbara DeLory

Nova Scotia Ombudsman - Library, POBox 2152, Halifax NS B3J 3B7 – 902/424-6780; Fax: 902/424-6675; Toll Free: 1-800-670-1111 – Secretary, Muriel Mappin

Nova Scotia Youth Orchestra – Library, #200, 1541 Barrington St., Halifax NS B3J 1Z5 – 902/423-5984; Fax: 902/423-5984

Nova Scotian Institute of Science – Library, Science Services, University Library, Dalhousie University, 6225 University Ave., Halifax NS B4H 4H8 – 902/494-2384; Fax: 902/494-2062 – Librarian, Sharon Longard

Patterson Palmer Hunt Murphy - Library, #1600, 5151 George St., POBox 247, Halifax NS B3J 2N9 – 902/492-2000; Fax: 902/429-5215 – Librarian, Lynda Feetham

Public Archives of Nova Scotia - Library, 6016 University Ave., Halifax NS B3H 1W4 – 902/424-6060; Fax: 902/424-0628 – Provincial Archivist, Brian Speirs

Public Legal Education Society of Nova Scotia – Reference Library, #911, 6080 Young St., Halifax NS B3K 5L2 – 902/454-2198; Fax: 902/455-3105; Toll Free: 1-800-665-9779

Queen Elizabeth II Health Sciences Centre - Health Sciences Library, 1796 Summer St., Halifax NS B3H 3A7 – 902/473-4287; Fax: 902/473-7168; Email: qelib@istar.ca; Symbol: NSHQ – Director, Anitra Laycock, Email: alaycock@fox.nstn.ca

Queen Elizabeth II Health Sciences Centre (Victoria General Hospital) – Health Sciences Library - Bethune Bldg., 1278 Tower Rd., Halifax NS B3H 2Y9 – 902/428-2429; Fax: 902/428-7456; Email: vghl@fox.nstn.ca; Symbol: NSHVGH – Director, Anitra Laycock

Ringette Nova Scotia – Resource Library, 5516 Spring Garden Rd., POBox 3010, Halifax NS B3J 3G6 – 902/425-5450, ext.350

St. Mary's University - Patrick Power Library, 923 Robie St., Halifax NS B3H 3C3 – 902/420-5544; Fax: 902/420-5561; Email: ill@admin.stmarys.ca; URL: http://www.stmarys.ca/administration/library/; Symbol: NSHS
- Acting University Librarian, Margot E. Schenk, 902/420-5532
- Reference/Research Librarian, Douglas Vaisey, 902/420-5540
- Systems & Training Librarian, Rashid Tayyeb, 902/420-5545

Statistics Canada - Atlantic Regional Information Centre, 1770 Market St., 3rd Fl., Halifax NS B3J 3M3 – 902/426-5331; Fax: 902/426-9538; Toll Free: 1-800-263-1136; Email: atlantic.info@statcan.ca – Bert Losier

Stewart McKelvey Stirling Scales - Library, 1959 Upper Water St., 9th Fl., POBox 997, Halifax NS B3J 2X2 – 902/420-3200; Fax: 902/420-1417; Email: cjm@email.smss.com; Symbol: NSHSMC
- Director, Information Services, Cynthia Murphy, 902/420-3373
- Library Assistant, Christine Johannesen, 902/420-3200, ext.104

Tourism Industry Association of Nova Scotia – Library, The World Trade & Convention Centre, #402, 1800 Argyle St., Halifax NS B3J 3N8 – 902/423-4480; Fax: 902/422-0184; Toll Free: 1-800-948-4267

Union of Nova Scotia Municipalities – Library, #1106, 1809 Barrington St., Halifax NS B3J 3K8 – 902/423-8331; Fax: 902/425-5592 – Ken Simpson

The United Church of Canada - Maritime Conference Archives, 640 Francklyn St., Halifax NS B3H 3B5 – 902/429-4819 – Conference Archivist, Carolyn Earle

University of King's College - Library, 6350 Coburg Rd., Halifax NS B3H 2A1 – 902/422-1271, ext.171; Fax: 902/423-3357; Symbol: NSHK
- Chief Librarian, H. Drake Petersen, 902/422-1271, ext.173
- Circulation, Head, M. Elaine Galey, 902/422-1271, ext.171
- Assistant Librarian, Patricia L. Chalmers, 902/422-1271, ext.174
- Serials/Acquisitions, Head, Paulette C. Drisdelle, 902/422-1271, ext.172
- Assistant Archivist, Janet K. Hathaway, 902/422-1271, ext.175

Visual Arts Nova Scotia – Resource Centre, #901, 1809 Barrington St., Halifax NS B3J 3K8 – 902/423-4694; Fax: 902/422-0881 – Executive Secretary, Dinah Simmons

Writers' Federation of Nova Scotia – Library, #901, 1809 Barrington St., Halifax NS B3J 3K8 – 902/423-8116; Fax: 902/422-0881

**KENTVILLE**

Agriculture & Agri-Food Canada-Atlantic Food & Horticulture Research Centre – Library, 32 Main St., Kentville NS B4N 1J5 – 902/679-5508; Fax: 902/679-2311; Email: melansonpa@em.agr.ca; minerj@em.agr.ca; Symbol: NSKR – Librarian, Jerry R. Miner

Efamol Research Institute, Scotia Pharmaceuticals Canada Ltd. - Library, 15 Chipman Dr., POBox 818, Kentville NS B4N 4H8 – 902/678-5534, ext.165; Fax: 902/678-9440; Email: scotlib@fox.nstn.ca; Symbol: NSKER – Research Library Manager, Barbara J. Stailing

Kemic Bioresearch Laboratories Ltd. – Library, 70 Exhibition St., POBox 878, Kentville NS B4N 4H8 – 902/678-8195; Fax: 902/678-2839 – Librarian, Susan Goodall, B.Sc.

Nova Scotia Community College - Kingstec Campus Library, POBox 487, Kentville NS B4N 3X3 – 902/678-7341; Fax: 902/679-1141; Email: ILL@Kingstec.nscc.ns.ca; URL: http://www.kingstec.nscc.ns.ca; Symbol: NSKKR
- Librarian, Idella Miner, Email: MINERIM@kingstec.nscc.ns.ca
- Library Technician, Paula Coldwell

Valley Regional Hospital – Library, 150 Exhibition St., Kentville NS B4N 5E3 – 902/679-2657, ext.3299; Fax: 902/679-1904; Email: kublin@fox.nstn.ca; Symbol: NSKVH – Librarian, Joyce Kublin

**LAWRENCETOWN**

College of Geographic Sciences - J.B. Hall Memorial Library, 50 Elliott Rd., RR#1, Lawrencetown NS B0S 1M0 – 902/584-2226; Fax: 902/584-7211; Symbol: NSLAL – Librarian, Donna M. Eisner

**LOUISBOURG**

Canadian Heritage - Fortress of Louisbourg - Library, POBox 160, Louisbourg NS B01 1M0 – 902/733-2280; Fax: 902/733-2362; Email: Louisbourg_info@PCH.gc.ca; URL: http://fortress.uccb.ns.ca; Symbol: NSLF – Librarian, Judith Romard

**LUNENBURG**

D.W.T. Brattston Law Office - Library, POBox 1599, Lunenburg NS B0J 2C0 – 902/634-8474; Fax: 902/634-9400

Lunenburg Marine Museum Society – Library, 68 Bluenose Dr., POBox 1363, Lunenburg NS B0J 2C0 – 902/634-4794 – Heather Getson

**MIDDLETON**

Annapolis Valley Historical Society – Library, POBox 925, Middleton NS B0S 1P0 – 902/825-6116 – Library Assistant, Krista Toole

Soldiers' Memorial Hospital – Library, POBox 730, Middleton NS B0S 1P0 – 902/825-3411, ext.357; Fax: 902/825-4811; Email: medical@soldiersmem.ns.ca; Symbol: NSMS – Librarian, Joyce Dagley

**NEW GLASGOW**

Aberdeen Hospital – Dr. G.R. Douglas Memorial Library, 835 East River Rd., New Glasgow NS B2H 3S6 – 902/752-7600,ex.213; Fax: 902/755-2356 – Debbie Kaleva

**PORT HASTINGS**

Port Hastings Historical Society – Genealogy Records, POBox 115, Port Hastings NS B0E 2T0 – 902/625-1295

**PORT HAWKESBURY**

Nova Scotia Community College - Strait Area Campus - Library, 226 Reeves St., POBox 1225, Port Hawkesbury NS B0E 2V0 – 902/625-2380; Fax: 902/625-0193; Email: maclealb@nscc.ns.ca
- Librarian, Lana B. MacLean
- Library Clerk, Glenda Charlton
- Acting Library Clerk, Margaret Eager

**SPRINGHILL**

Correctional Service Canada - Springhill Institution - Library, POBox 2140, Springhill NS B0M 1X0 – 902/597-8651, ext.301; Fax: 902/597-3888; Symbol: NSSS
- Library Supervisor, Donna Morrison
- Library Assistant, Carolyn Mooring

**STELLARTON**

Nova Scotia Community College - Pictou Campus Library, POBox 820, Stellarton NS B0K 1S0 – 902/752-2002; Fax: 902/752-5446; Email: hratch@north.nsis.com – Librarian, Harvey Ratchford

**SYDNEY**

Canadian Coast Guard College - Library, 1990 Westmount Rd., POBox 4500, Sydney NS B1P 6L1 – 902/564-3660; Fax: 902/564-3672; URL: http://www.cgc.ns.ca; Symbol: NSSCG – Librarian, D.N. MacSween, Email: macsween@cgc.ns.ca

Canadian Music Educators' Association – Library, 43 Victoria Hill, Sydney NS B1R 1N9 – 902/567-2398; Fax: 902/564-0123

Cape Breton Health Care Complex – Health Sciences Library, 1482 George St., Sydney NS B1P 1P3 – 902/567-8000, ext.2738; Fax: 902/567-7878; Email: edserv1@atcon.com; Symbol: NSSCBH – Librarian, Patricia Foley

Cape Breton Regional Hospital - Health Sciences Library, 1492 George St., Sydney NS B1P 1P2 – 902/562-2322, ext.137; Fax: 902/562-8593; Symbol: NSSSRH – Librarian, Patricia Colford Keough

Centre for International Studies (Nova Scotia) – Library, #256, Campus Centre, University College of Cape Breton, POBox 5300, Sydney NS B1P 6L2 – 902/563-1286; Fax: 902/562-0119

Community Economic Development Institute – Library, University College of Cape Breton, POBox 5300, Sydney NS B1P 6L2 – 902/564-1366; Fax: 902/564-1366 – Manager, Cecil Cameron

University College of Cape Breton - Library, POBox 5300, Sydney NS B1P 6L2 – 902/563-1388; Fax: 902/563-1177; Symbol: NSSX
- University College Librarian, Penelope Marshall, 902/539-5300, ext.388
- Public Services Librarian, Laura Pervill
- Technical Services Librarian, Mary Dobson

**TATAMAGOUCHE**

Tatamagouche Historical & Cultural Society – Library, Main St., Tatamagouche NS B0K 1V0 – Librarian, Glen Hamilton

**TRURO**

Nova Scotia Department of Agriculture & Marketing - Plant Industry Branch – Library, PO Box 550, Truro NS B2N 5E3 – 902/895-1571; Fax: 902/893-0244

Burchell MacDougall - Law Library, 710 Prince St., POBox 1128, Truro NS B2N 5H1 – 902/895-1561; Fax: 902/895-7709; Email: truro@burmac.ns.ca – Krista McNutt

Colchester Historical Society – Library, POBox 412, Truro NS B2N 5C5 – 902/895-6284; Fax: 902/895-9530 – Archivist, Nan Harvey

Native Council of Nova Scotia – Library, 324 Abenaki Rd., POBox 1320, Truro NS B2N 5N2 – 902/895-1524, 1525; Fax: 902/895-0024; Toll Free: 1-800-565-4372 – Communications, Ramona Greene

Nova Scotia Agricultural College - MacRae Library, POBox 550, Truro NS B2N 5E3 – 902/893-6669; Fax: 902/895-0934; URL: http://www.nsac.ns.ca/nsac/lib/index.html; Symbol: NSTA
- Chief Librarian, Bonnie Waddell, 902/893-6670, Email: bwaddell@ca.nsac.ns.ca
- Systems Librarian, F. Lai, 902/893-6669

Nova Scotia Teachers' College - Learning Resources Centre, POBox 810, Truro NS B2N 5G5 – 902/893-5326; Fax: 902/893-5610; Email: ptiwana@fox.nstn.nsw.ca; Symbol: NSTT
- Acquisitions & Serials, Paul Tiwana
- Circulation & Reference, Sheila Pearl
- Cataloguing, Tom Acker, 902/895-5306, ext.259

**WINDSOR JUNCTION**

Nova Scotia Transportation & Communications - Materials Laboratory Library, Site #37, RR#1, Windsor Junction NS B0N 2V0 – 902/861-1911, ext.56; Fax: 902/861-4828 – Librarian, M. Reid

**WOLFVILLE**

Acadia University - Vaughan Memorial Library, Wolfville NS B0P 1X0 – 902/585-1249; Fax: 902/585-1073; Email: ref-desk@acadiau.ca; URL: http://www.acadiau.ca/vaughan/home.html; Symbol: NSWA
- University Librarian, Lorraine McQueen, Email: lorraine.mcqueen@acadian.ca
- Acquisitions, Roni Fenwick, 902/585-1248
- Information Services, Betty Jeffrey, 902/585-1403
- Electronic Resources, Mary MacLeod, 902/585-1734

Wolfville Historical Society – WHS Library, POBox 38, Wolfville NS B0P 1X0 – 902/542-9775; Fax: 902/542-4319 – Librarian, Shirley Elliott

**YARMOUTH**

Yarmouth County Historical Society – Library, 22 Collins St., Yarmouth NS B5A 3C8 – 902/742-5539; Fax: 902/749-1120 – Librarian/Archivist, Laura Bradley

# ONTARIO

## Public Libraries

Acton Public Library, 17 River St., Acton ON L7J 1C2 – 519/853-0301; Fax: 519/853-3110 – Branch Head, Catherine Yestadt – Branch of Halton Hills Public Library (*see* Georgetown)

Addison: Elizabethtown Twp. Public Library Board, RR#2, Addison ON K0E 1A0 – 613/924-9525 – Librarian, Ruth Blanchard – See also following branches: Lyn Branch Library

Ailsa Craig Branch Library, 160 Main St., Ailsa Craig ON N0M 1A0 – 519/293-3441; Fax: 519/293-3441 – Supervisor, Joan McDonald – Branch of Middlesex County Library (*see* Arva)

Ailsa Craig: Beechwood Library, RR#1, Ailsa Craig ON N0M 1A0 – Supervisor, Elizabeth McLachlan – Branch of Middlesex County Library

Ajax Public Library, 65 Harwood Ave. South, Ajax ON L1S 2H8 – 905/683-4000; Fax: 905/683-6960; URL: http://www.io.org/~bruin/; Symbol: OAJ – CEO/Librarian, Geoffrey P. Nie; Support Services Manager, Dan Gioiosa – See also following branches: Administration & Technical Services, McLean Community Branch Library, Pickering Village Branch Library

Ajax: Administration & Technical Services, 539 Westney Rd. South, Ajax ON L1S 4N7 – 905/683-6632; Fax: 905/683-6944; Email: nieg@gov.on.ca – Branch of Ajax Public Library

Ajax: McLean Community Branch Library, 95 Magill Dr., Ajax ON L1T 3K7 – 905/428-8489; Fax: 905/428-3743 – Branch Head, Cindy Kimber – Branch of Ajax Public Library

Ajax: Pickering Village Branch Library, 58 Church St. North, Ajax ON L1T 2W6 – 905/683-1140; Fax: 905/683-1140 – Branch Head, Cindy Kimber – Branch of Ajax Public Library

Alexandria Branch Library, PO Box 1030, Alexandria ON K0C 1A0 – 613/525-3241 – Area Supervisor, Darlene McRae – Branch of Stormont, Dundas & Glengarry County Library (*see* Finch)

Alliston: New Tecumseth Public Library, PO Box 399, Alliston ON L9R 1V6 – 705/435-0250; Fax: 705/435-0750 – CEO, Pam Kirkpatrick – See also following branches: Alliston Memorial Branch Library, Beeton Branch Library, Tottenham Branch Library

Alliston Memorial Branch Library, 17 Victoria St. East, Alliston ON L9R 1V6 – 705/435-5651; Fax: 705/435-0750 – Brenda Herring – Branch of New Tecumseth Public Library (*see* Alliston)

Almonte Public Library, PO Box 820, Almonte ON K0A 1A0 – 613/256-1037; Fax: 613/256-4423; Email: pnelson@almonte.library.on.ca; Symbol: OA – Head Librarian, Peter Nelson; Children's Librarian, Monica Blackburn

Alton Branch, 15 Station St., Alton ON L0N 1A0 – 519/941-5480; Fax: 519/941-5480; Email: altonlib@headwaters.com – Branch Head, Donna St. Jacques – Branch of Caledon Public Library (*see* Bolton)

Alvinston Library, 3251 River St., PO Box 44, Alvinston ON N0N 1A0 – 519/898-2921 – Librarian, Ruth Leitch – Branch of Lambton County Library (*see* Wyoming)

Ameliasburgh Twp. Library, Site 1-0, RR#1, Ameliasburg ON K0K 1A0 – 613/968-9327, 962-2551; Fax: 613/962-1514; Email: pleavey@ameliasburgh.library.on.ca; Symbol: OAAP – CEO/Chief Librarian, Peggy Leavey – See also following branches: Consecon Branch Library

Amherstburg Library, 232 Sandwich St. South, Amherstburg ON N9V 2A4 – 519/736-4632 – Supervisor, Jean Hunt – Branch of Essex County Library

Ancaster Public Library, 300 Wilson St. East, Ancaster ON L9G 2B9 – 905/648-6911; Fax: 905/648-2961 – Branch Head, Kay McDonald – Branch of Wentworth Libraries (*see* Hamilton)

Angus: Essa Centennial Library, 36 King St., PO Box 280, Angus ON L0M 1B0 – 705/424-6531; Fax: 705/424-6531 – CEO/Administrator, Loretta Metcalfe; Administrative Assistant/ILLO, Angie Wishart

Apsley: Burleigh, Anstruther & Chandos Union Public Library, Main St., PO Box 335, Apsley ON K0K 1A0 – 705/656-4333 – Chief Librarian, Susan Mycroft

Arden Branch Library, General Delivery, Arden ON K0H 1B0 – 613/335-2570 – Sue DesRosiers – Branch of Frontenac County Library (*see* Kingston)

Arkona Library, 16 Smith St., PO Box 12, Arkona ON N0M 1B0 – 519/828-3406 – Librarian, Helen Batten – Branch of Lambton County Library (*see* Wyoming)

Arnprior Public Library, 21 Madawaska St., Arnprior ON K7S 1R6 – 613/623-2279; Fax: 613/623-9882; Email: j.barker@sauron.globalx.net; Symbol: OAR – Chief Librarian, Judy Barker; Children's Librarian, Patricia Bouchard; ILL Librarian, Gail Whalen

Arthur Branch Library, 183 George St., Arthur ON N0G 1A0 – 519/848-3999; Fax: 519/846-2066 – Branch Supervisor, Trudy Gohn – Branch of Wellington County Library (*see* Fergus)

Arva: Middlesex County Library, Centennial Bldg., 11 St. John's Dr., Arva ON N0M 1C0 – 519/660-8368; Fax: 519/660-6511 – County Librarian, Margaret Rule; Reference Librarian, Carol Roberts; Systems Librarian, Beverly Sweezie – See also following branches: Ailsa Craig Branch Library, Avon Library, Beechwood Library, Coldstream Library, Delaware Library, Dorchester Library, Glencoe Library, Harrietsville Library, Komoka Library, London Twp. Library, Lucan Library, Melbourne Library, Mount Brydges Library, Newbury Library, Parkhill Library, Putnam Library, Wardsville Library, West Nissouri Library

Astorville: East Ferris Twp. Public Library Board, East Ferris Public Library, Astorville ON P0H 1B0 – 705/752-2042 – CEO, Claudette Quinn

Athens Public Library, PO Box 309, Athens ON K0E 1B0 – 613/924-2048 – CEO, Freda Schaafsma

Atikokan Public Library, Civic Centre, Atikokan ON P0T 1C0 – 807/597-4406; Fax: 807/597-1514 – Librarian, Doris B. Brown

Auburn Branch Library, Auburn ON N0M 1E0 – Branch Supervisor, Laura May Chamney – Branch of Huron County Library (*see* Goderich)

Aurora Public Library, 56 Victoria St., Aurora ON L4G 1R2 – 905/727-9493; Fax: 905/727-9374 – Librarian, Colleen Abbott

Avonmore Branch Library, PO Box 70, Avonmore ON K0C 1C0 – 613/346-2137 – Area Supervisor, Fiona Fraser – Branch of Stormont, Dundas & Glengarry County Library (*see* Finch)

Avon Library, Avon ON N0L 2J0 – 519/269-3652 – Supervisor, Anita Crandall – Branch of Middlesex County Library (*see* Arva)

Aylmer Old Town Hall Library, 38 John St. South, Aylmer ON N5H 2C2 – 519/773-2439 – Supervisor, Christina Mayhew – Branch of Elgin County Library (*see* St. Thomas)

Ayr: Ayr Branch Library, Stanley St., PO Box 339, Ayr ON N0B 1E0 – 519/632-7298 – Branch Supervisor, Diane Schmidt – Branch of Waterloo Regional Library (*see* Kitchener)

Ayton: Normanby Twp. Public Library, Ayton ON N0G 1C0 – 519/665-7784 – Librarian, Miriam Long

Azilda Branch Library, PO Box 818, Azilda ON P0M 1B0 – 705/983-2650 – Librarian, Solange Jolicoeur – Branch of Rayside-Balfour Library (*see* Chelmsford)

Baden Branch Library, 115 Snyder's Rd. East, PO Box 214, Baden ON N0B 1G0 – 519/634-8933 – Asst. Branch Supervisor, Connie Miller – Branch of Waterloo Regional Library (*see* Kitchener)

Baillieboro Branch Library, 199 Hwy. 28, Baillieboro ON K0L 1B0 – 705/939-6510; Fax: 705/939-1096 – Branch Head, Vilda Nurse – Branch of Cavan, Millbrook, South Monaghan Union Library (*see* Millbrook)

Bala Public Library, Bala Community Centre, PO Box 50, Bala ON P0C 1A0 – 705/762-0576 – Librarian, Mari Carson – Branch of Port Carling Public Library

Bala: Wahta Mohawks Library, PO Box 327, Bala ON P0C 1A0 – 416/762-3343; Fax: 416/762-5744 – CEO, Lila Commandant

Balmertown: Twp. of Golden - Balmertown Public Library, PO Box 280, Balmertown ON P0V 1C0 – 807/735-2110; Fax: 807/735-2110 – CEO/Librarian, Arlene Johnson

Bancroft Public Library, 14 Flint St., PO Box 127, Bancroft ON K0L 1C0 – 613/332-3380 – CEO, Betty Lambeck

Bancroft: United Public Library, c/o Herman Public School, RR#4, Bancroft ON K0L 1C0 – 613/332-2897 – CEO, Ursula O'Connor

Barrie Public Library, 60 Worsley St., Barrie ON L4M 1L6 – 705/728-1010; Fax: 705/728-4322 – Director of Library Services, Adele Kostiak; Circulation Services, Joanne Comper; Information Services, Katherine Wallis; Technical Services Librarian, Dunja Conroy

Barrie: Southern Ontario Library Service - Barrie, 30 Morrow Rd., Barrie ON L4N 3V8 – 705/733-0051; Fax: 705/733-1143

Barry's Bay Public Library, Opeongo Line, PO Box 970, Barry's Bay ON K0J 1B0 – 613/756-2000 – Librarian, A. Lorbetskie – See also following branches: Sherwood Jones & Burns Branch

Barwick Community Library, PO Box 4, Barwick ON P0W 1A0 – 807/487-2354 – Librarian, Doris Dyson

Batawa: Sidney Twp. Public Library, 1 Haig St., PO Box 1057, Batawa ON K0K 1E0 – 613/398-7344 – CEO, Robert Amesse – See also following branches: Bayside Branch Library

Bath Branch Library, PO Box 400, Bath ON K0H 1G0 – 613/352-3361 – Supervisor, Phyllis Strain – Branch of Lennox & Addington County Library (*see* Napanee)

Bath: Sandhurst Branch Library, RR#1, Bath ON K0H 1G0 – 613/352-5007 – Supervisor, Phyllis Strain – Branch of Lennox & Addington County Library (*see* Napanee)

Battersea: Storrington Twp., Sunbury Branch Library, RR#2, Battersea ON K0H 1H0 – 613/353-6333 – Carol Lee Riley – Branch of Frontenac County Library (*see* Kingston)

Bayfield Branch Library, PO Box 2090, Bayfield ON N0M 1G0 – 519/565-2886 – Branch Supervisor, Anny Johnston – Branch of Huron County Library (*see* Goderich)

Baysville: Lake of Bays Public Library, University Ave., Baysville ON P0B 1A0 – 705/767-2361; Fax: 705/767-3933; Email: linla@muskoka.com – CEO, Linda Lacroix – See also following branches: Dwight Public Library

Beachburg Public Library, 202 Main St., PO Box 159, Beachburg ON K0J 1C0 – 613/582-7090 – CEO, Marilyn Labow

Beachville Public Library, Beachville ON N0J 1A0 – 519/423-6533 – Supervisor, Teresa Van Rees – Branch of Oxford County Library (*see* Woodstock)

Beamsville: Lincoln Public Library, 4996 Beam St., PO Box 460, Beamsville ON L0R 1B0 – 905/563-7014; Fax: 905/563-1810; Email: linclib2@vaxxine.com – CEO, A. Lorene Sims; Children's Librarian, Elizabeth Peters – See also following branches: Moses F. Rittenhouse Branch Library

Beardmore Public Library, 185 Main St., PO Box 240, Beardmore ON P0T 1G0 – 807/875-2212; Fax: 807/875-2212 – Head Librarian, Dianne Coté

Bearskin Lake Public Library, Bearskin Lake ON P0V 1E0 – 807/363-2518; Fax: 807/363-1066

Beaverton Branch, 401 Simcoe St., PO Box 310, Beaverton ON L0K 1A0 – 705/426-9283 – Librarian, Brigitta Johnston – Branch of Brock Twp. Public Library (*see* Sunderland)

Beeton Branch Library, 42 Main St. West, PO Box 305, Beeton ON L0G 1A0 – 905/729-3726 – Janice Day – Branch of New Tecumseth Public Library (*see* Alliston)

Belfountain Branch, 17247 Shaw's Creek Rd., Belfountain ON L0N 1B0 – 519/927-5701; Fax: 519/927-5662 – Branch Assistant, Caroline Butson – Branch of Caledon Public Library (*see* Bolton)

Belle River Public Library, 467 Notre Dame St., PO Box 459, Belle River ON N0R 1A0 – 519/728-2324 – CEO, Christina Ouellette

Belleville Public Library, 223 Pinnacle St., Belleville ON K8N 3A7 – 613/968-6731; Fax: 613/968-6841; Symbol: OBE – CEO, Leona Hendry; Reference Librarian, Elizabeth Mitchell; Circulation Supervisor, Fanny Tom; Children's Librarian, Barbara Coulman; Technical Services Librarian, Brian Naulls; Systems Manager, Carlene Martin – See also following branches: East Branch Library

Belleville: Bayside Branch Library, RR#2, Belleville ON K8N 4Z2 – 613/962-5695 – Branch Head, Iris Claveau – Branch of Sidney Twp. Public Library (*see* Batawa)

Belleville: East Branch Library, 495 Victoria Ave., Belleville ON K8N 2G4 – 613/962-1681 – Branch Head, Winnifred Voogt – Branch of Belleville Public Library

Belmont Public Library, PO Box 149, Belmont ON N0L 1B0 – 519/644-1560 – Supervisor, Maria Smit – Branch of Elgin County Library (*see* St. Thomas)

Binbrook Public Library, Hwy. 56, PO Box 89, Binbrook ON L0R 1C0 – 905/692-3323; Fax: 905/

692-3323 – Branch Head, Carolyne Timms – Branch of Wentworth Libraries (*see* Hamilton)

Birch Island: Whitefish River First Nation Public Library, PO Box A, Birch Island ON P0P 1A0 – 705/285-0028; Fax: 705/285-4532 – Librarian, Crystal McGregor

Blenheim Branch Library, George St., Blenheim ON N0P 1A0 – 519/676-3174; Fax: 519/676-2304 – Branch Librarian, Diane Sanford – Branch of Kent County Library (*see* Chatham)

Blind River Public Library, 17 Michigan Ave., PO Box 880, Blind River ON P0R 1B0 – 705/356-7616; Fax: 705/356-7343 – Librarian, Rhea Marcellus

Blind River: Mississauga First Nation Library, PO Box 1299, Blind River ON P0R 1B0 – 705/356-1621; Fax: 705/356-1740 – CEO, Clifford Niganobe

Bloomfield-Hallowell Union Library, 36 Main St., PO Box 9, Bloomfield ON K0K 1G0 – 613/393-3400; Fax: 613/393-1323 – Librarian, Barbara Sweet

Bloomingdale Branch Library, PO Box 16, Bloomingdale ON N0B 1K0 – 519/745-3151 – Asst. Branch Supervisor, Janice Martin – Branch of Waterloo Regional Library (*see* Kitchener)

Bluevale Branch Library, Bluevale ON N0G 1G0 – Branch Supervisor, Bonnie Grieg – Branch of Huron County Library (*see* Goderich)

Blyth Branch Library, PO Box 388, Blyth ON N0M 1H0 – 519/523-4400 – Branch Supervisor, Pat Brigham – Branch of Huron County Library (*see* Goderich)

Bobcaygeon Branch Library, Bobcaygeon ON K0M 1A0 – 705/738-2088; Fax: 705/738-2088; Email: boblib@knet.flemingc.on.ca – Branch Supervisor, Carolyn Warren – Branch of Victoria County Public Library (*see* Lindsay)

Bolton: Caledon Public Library, Albion-Bolton Community Centre, 150 Queen St. South, Bolton ON L7E 1E3 – 905/857-1400; Fax: 905/857-8280; URL: http://www.hookup.net/~caledon/ – Chief Librarian, Rod Hall; Reference/Acquisitions Librarian, Louisa Cooper, 519/927-5662; Children's Librarian, Kelley Potter; Public Services Librarian, Gladys Rennie; Technical Services Librarian, Margaret Fleetwood – See also following branches: Albion-Bolton Branch, Alton Branch, Belfountain Branch, Caledon East Branch, Caledon Village Branch, Inglewood Branch

Bolton: Albion-Bolton Branch, Albion-Bolton Community Centre, 150 Queen St. South, Bolton ON L7E 1E3 – 905/857-1400; Fax: 905/857-8280; Email: caledon@hookup.net – Branch Head, Les Szollosy – Branch of Caledon Public Library (*see* Bolton)

Bond Head Branch, Bond Head Community Centre, PO Box 58, Bond Head ON L0G 1B0 – 905/775-6875 – Lynn Flack – Branch of Bradford West Gwillimbury Public Libraries

Bonfield Public Library, Hwy. 531, Bonfield ON P0H 1E0 – 705/776-2641 – Librarian, Jeanette Shields

Borden: Base Borden Public & Military Library, PO Box 430, Borden ON L0M 1C0 – 705/424-1200; Fax: 705/423-2892; Email: baselib@mail.transdata.ca; Symbol: CFB101 – Head Librarian, Terri Bristow

Bothwell Branch Library, Main St., Bothwell ON N0P 1C0 – 519/695-2844 – Branch Librarian, Marianne Buchanan – Branch of Kent County Library (*see* Chatham)

Bothwell: Caldwell First Nation Library, 215 Main St., PO Box 250, Bothwell ON N0P 1C0 – 519/695-3920; Fax: 519/695-2358 – Librarian, Larry Johnson

Bourget: Bibliothèque publique de Canton de Clarence, CP 143, Bourget ON K0A 1E0 – Librarian, Marthe Boileau – See also following branches: Succursale de Bourget, Succursale de Clarence Creek, Succursale de Hammond, Succursale de St-Pascal-Baylon

Bourget: Succursale de Bourget, 11 Laval St. East, CP 98, Bourget ON K0A 1E0 – Bibliothécaire, Thérèse D. Lalonde – Branch of Bibliothèque publique de Canton de Clarence (*see* Bourget)

Bowmanville: Clarington Public Library, 62 Temperance St., Bowmanville ON L1C 3A8 – 905/623-7322; Fax: 905/623-9905 – Library Director, Cynthia Mearns – See also following branches: Clarke Branch Library, Courtice Branch Library, Newcastle Village Branch Library

Bracebridge Public Library, 94 Manitoba St., PO Box 1537, Bracebridge ON P1L 1S1 – 705/645-4171; Fax: 705/645-1262 – Chief Librarian, Ann-Marie Mathieu

Bradford West Gwillimbury Public Libraries, 100 Holland Crt., PO Box 130, Bradford ON L3Z 2A7 – 905/775-3328; Fax: 905/775-1236 – CEO, Alannah Hegedus; Reference/Children's, Anita Sikma; Circulation, Adrienne Price; Technical Services, Liz Fenwick; ILL, Flora Nydam – See also following branches: Bond Head Branch, Newton Robinson Branch

Bradford: Newton Robinson Branch, Site #5, RR#2, PO Box 27, Bradford ON L3Z 2A7 – 705/458-4515 – Gwen Taylor – Branch of Bradford West Gwillimbury Public Libraries

Brampton Public Library, 65 Queen St. East, Brampton ON L6W 3L6 – 905/453-2444; Fax: 905/453-4602; Email: drynant@gov.on.ca; Symbol: BRAM – CEO, Tom Drynan – See also following branches: Chinguacousy Resource Branch, Cyril Clark Branch Library, Four Corners Branch Library, South Fletcher Branch Library

Brampton: Chinguacousy Resource Branch, 150 Central Park Dr., Bramalea ON L6T 1B4 – 905/793-4636; Fax: 905/793-0506; Symbol: OBRA – Branch Manager, Cynthia Toniolo – Branch of Brampton Public Library

Brampton: Cyril Clark Branch Library, 20 Loafer's Lake Lane, Brampton ON L6Z 1X9 – 905/846-7310; Fax: 905/846-4278 – Branch Supervisor, Catherine Carreiro – Branch of Brampton Public Library

Brampton: Four Corners Branch Library, 65 Queen St. East, Brampton ON L6W 3L6 – 905/453-2444; Fax: 905/453-4602 – Manager, Branch Libraries, Gary Baumbach – Branch of Brampton Public Library

Brampton: South Fletcher Branch Library, City South Plaza, 500 Ray Lawson Blvd., Brampton ON L6Y 5B3 – 905/453-1038; Fax: 905/453-8425 – Branch Supervisor, Arleta Wang – Branch of Brampton Public Library

Brantford Public Library, 173 Colborne St., Brantford ON N3T 2G8 – 519/756-2220; Fax: 519/756-4979; Email: wnewman@brantford.library.on.ca; URL: http://www.worldchat.com/library; Symbol: OBRT – CEO, Wendy Newman; Circulation, Mary Varga; Reference & Branch Services, Christopher Stanley; Technical Services, June Hibbert; Business Administrator, Shirley Allan; Public Services, Lorie Macdonald – See also following branches: St. Paul Avenue Branch Library

Brantford: St. Paul Avenue Branch Library, 441 St. Paul Ave., Brantford ON N3R 4N8 – 519/753-2179; Fax: 519/753-3557 – Reference & Branch Services, Christopher Stanley – Branch of Brantford Public Library

Brechin: Mara Twp. Public Library, Brechin ON L0K 1B0 – 705/484-0476 – Librarian, A. Lambert – See also following branches: Atherley Branch Library

Bridgenorth: Smith Twp. Public Library, Ward St., PO Box 500, Bridgenorth ON K0L 1H0 – 705/292-5065; Fax: 705/292-6695; Email: joanmac@smith.twp.library.on.ca; Symbol: OBRIS – Library Technician, Joan MacDonald

Brigden Library, 1540 Duncan St., PO Box 339, Brigden ON N0N 1B0 – 519/864-1142 – Head Librarian, Janet Eves – Branch of Lambton County Library (*see* Wyoming)

Brighton Public Library, PO Box 129, Brighton ON K0K 1H0 – 613/475-2511 – CEO, Maureen Venton

Brights Grove Library, 2600 Hamilton Rd., PO Box 339, Brights Grove ON N0N 1C0 – 519/869-2351 – Librarian, Mavis Schmid – Branch of Lambton County Library (*see* Wyoming)

Brinston Branch Library, PO Box 40, Brinston ON K0E 1C0 – 613/652-2045 – Area Supervisor, Elizabeth Porter – Branch of Stormont, Dundas & Glengarry County Library (*see* Finch)

Britt Area Public Library, PO Box 2, Britt ON P0G 1A0 – 705/383-2292 – Librarian, Barbara Wohleber

Britt: Magnetawan First Nation Public Library, RR#1, PO Box 15, Britt ON P0G 1A0 – 705/383-0208; Fax: 705/383-2566 – CEO, Kim Charles

Brockville: Augusta Twp. Public Library, RR#2, Brockville ON K6V 5T2 – 613/926-2449; Fax: 613/926-0440; Email: augusta@recorder.ca – Head Librarian, Eleanor Denny; Assistant Librarian, Linda Parrott; Assistant Librarian, Lois Byrnes

Brockville Public Library, 21 George St., PO Box 100, Brockville ON K6V 5T7 – 613/342-3936; Fax: 613/342-9598; Email: bville1@mulberry.com; URL: http://www.mulberry.com/~bville1/ – CEO, Margaret Williams; Reference Librarian, Monica Fazekas; Children's Librarian, Maureen Wharton

Brooklin Branch Library, PO Box 430, Brooklin ON L0B 1C0 – 905/655-3191 – Branch Head, Margaret Edwards – Branch of Whitby Public Library

Brownsville Public Library, Brownsville ON N0L 1C0 – 519/877-2938 – Supervisor, Lois Cole – Branch of Oxford County Library (*see* Woodstock)

Bruce Mines & Plumber Additional Union Library, Desbarats St., PO Box 249, Bruce Mines ON P0R 1C0 – 705/785-3370; Fax: 705/785-3370 – Librarian, Gail Bennett

Brussels Branch Library, PO Box 80, Brussels ON N0G 1H0 – 519/887-6448 – Branch Supervisor, Susan Nichol – Branch of Huron County Library (*see* Goderich)

Brussels: Cranbrook Branch Library, RR#3, Brussels ON N0G 1H0 – Branch Supervisor, Carmie Newman – Branch of Huron County Library (*see* Goderich)

Buckhorn: Harvey Twp. Public Library, General Delivery, Buckhorn ON K0L 1J0 – 705/657-3695; Fax: 705/657-9077; Symbol: OBH – CEO, Maria Bradburn

Burford Twp. Public Library, 120 King St., PO Box 255, Burford ON N0E 1A0 – 519/449-5371; Fax: 519/449-5371; Email: Burfordpl@bfree.on.ca – Librarian, E. Stroud

Burgessville Public Library, Burgessville ON N0L 1C0 – 519/424-2404 – Supervisor, Linda Visser – Branch of Oxford County Library (*see* Woodstock)

Burk's Falls Armour & Ryerson Union Public Library, Yonge & Copeland Sts., PO Box 620, Burk's Falls ON P0A 1C0 – 705/382-3327; Fax: 705/382-2497 – CEO, Margaret Ross, 705/382-2852, Fax: 705/382-5555

Burlington Public Library, 2331 New St., Burlington ON L7R 1J4 – 905/639-3611; Fax: 905/681-7277; Email: schickw@bpl.on.ca; URL: http://199.235.184.2/library/bpl/bpl.html; Symbol: OBU – CEO, Wendy M. Schick; Deputy CEO, Sonia Lewis; Adult Services Librarian, Judy Walker; Children's Librarian, Andrea Gordon; Technical Services Librarian, Gwen Forsyth; Branches, Head, Maureen Barry – See also following branches: Aldershot Branch Library, Kilbride Branch Library, New Appleby Branch Library, Tansley Woods Branch Library, Tyandaga Branch Library

Burlington: Aldershot Branch Library, 335 Plains Rd. East, Burlington ON L7T 2C7 – 905/333-9995; Fax: 905/681-7277; Email: warrickd@bpl.on.ca –

Branch Head, Diane Warrick – Branch of Burlington Public Library

Burlington: New Appleby Branch Library, 676 Appleby Line, Burlington ON L7L 5Y1 – 905/639-6373; Fax: 905/681-7277; Email: williamsl@bpl.on.ca – Branch Head, Laura Williams – Branch of Burlington Public Library

Burlington: Tyandaga Branch Library, 1500 Upper Middle Rd., Burlington ON L7P 3P5 – 905/335-2209; Fax: 905/681-7277; Email: powellm@bpl.on.ca – Branch Head, Marilyn Powell – Branch of Burlington Public Library

Burnt River Branch Library, Burnt River ON K0M 1C0 – 705/454-8045 – Branch Supervisor, June Hunter – Branch of Victoria County Public Library (*see* Lindsay)

Burritt's Rapids: Oxford-on-Rideau Twp. Public Library, PO Box 119, Burritt's Rapids ON K0G 1B0 – 613/269-3636 – Librarian, Olivia Mills – See also following branches: Burritt's Rapids Library, Oxford Mills Library

Burritt's Rapids Library, PO Box 119, Burritt's Rapids ON K0G 1B0 – 613/269-3636 – Librarian, Olivia Mills – Branch of Oxford-on-Rideau Twp. Public Library (*see* Burritt's Rapids)

Cache Bay Public Library, 77 Cache St., Cache Bay ON P0H 1G0 – CEO, Clare Lisk

Calabogie: Bagot & Blythfield Twp. Public Library, Calabogie ON K0J 1H0 – 613/752-2317 – Librarian, Lois Mulvihill

Caledon East Branch, 24 Church St., Caledon East ON L0N 1E0 – 905/584-1456; Fax: 905/584-1456; Email: ceastlib@headwaters.com – Branch Head, Gerry Lawlor – Branch of Caledon Public Library (*see* Bolton)

Caledon Village Branch, 18313 Hurontario St., Caledon Village ON L0N 1C0 – 519/927-5800; Fax: 519/927-5800; Email: caledonlib@headwaters.com – Branch Head, Glenda Dolan – Branch of Caledon Public Library (*see* Bolton)

Caledonia: Haldimand Public Libraries, 28 Cayuga St. North, Caledonia ON N0A 1E0 – 905/772-5467 – Donna Armstrong – See also following branches: Caledonia Public Library, Cayuga Public Library, Hagersville Public Library

Caledonia Public Library, 25 Caithness St. West, Caledonia ON N3W 1B7 – 905/765-2634 – Branch Manager, Mary Edwards – Branch of Haldimand Public Libraries

Callander: North Himsworth Twp. Public Library, 30 Catherine St., PO Box 149, Callander ON P0H 1H0 – 705/752-2544; Fax: 705/752-2819; Email: nhpl@efni.com – CEO, Helen McDonnell

Cambray Branch Library, Cambray ON K0M 1E0 – 705/374-4900 – Branch Supervisor, Isabel Barton – Branch of Victoria County Public Library (*see* Lindsay)

Cambridge Public Library, 20 Grand Ave. North, Cambridge ON N1S 2K6 – 519/621-0460; Fax: 519/621-2080; Email: illsmsg.ogal@sols.on.ca; Symbol: OGAL – Information Services, Head, Cathy Kiedrowski; Circulation & Children's Librarian, Dixie Alkier; Automation Systems Librarian, Christine Wilson – See also following branches: Hespeler Branch, Preston Branch

Cambridge: Hespeler Branch, 5 Tannery St., Cambridge ON N3C 2C1 – 519/658-4412; Fax: 519/621-2080 – Librarian, Liz Krist – Branch of Cambridge Public Library

Cambridge: Preston Branch, 435 King St. East, Cambridge ON N3H 3N1 – 519/653-3632; Fax: 519/621-2080 – Librarian, Angela Caretta – Branch of Cambridge Public Library

Camden East Branch, PO Box 10, Camden East ON K0K 1J0 – 613/378-2101 – Supervisor, Mary Lou Fraser – Branch of Lennox & Addington County Library (*see* Napanee)

Camlachie Library, 6707 Camlachie Sideroad, PO Box 130, Camlachie ON N0N 1E0 – 519/899-2202 – Librarian, Anne Ross – Branch of Lambton County Library (*see* Wyoming)

Campbellcroft: Garden Hill Branch Library, RR#1, Campbellcroft ON L0A 1B0 – 905/797-2473 – Branch Head, Merrylin Caldwell – Branch of Northumberland County Public Library (*see* Hastings)

Campbellford/Seymour Branch Library, Bridge St., Campbellford ON K0L 1L0 – 705/653-3611 – Branch Head, Mae Bailey – Branch of Northumberland County Public Library (*see* Hastings)

Canfield: Caistorville Branch Library, RR#2, Canfield ON N0A 1C0 – 905/692-4290 – Branch Head, Barb Stolys – Branch of West Lincoln Public Library (*see* Smithville)

Cannington Branch, Ann St. North, Cannington ON L0E 1E0 – 705/432-2867 – Branch Head, Susan Ross – Branch of Brock Twp. Public Library (*see* Sunderland)

Capreol Public Library, Morin St., PO Box 520, Capreol ON P0M 1H0 – 705/858-1622 – Librarian, Barbara Finnson

Cardiff: Bicroft Branch Library, Cardiff ON K0L 1M0 – 613/339-2804 – Supervisor, Cathy Passaretti – Branch of Haliburton County Public Library

Cardinal Public Library, Lewis St., PO Box 490, Cardinal ON K0E 1E0 – 613/657-3822 – Librarian, Betty Donaldson

Cargill Branch Library, King St., Cargill ON N0G 1J0 – 519/366-2259 – Branch Supervisor, Cheryl Parker – Branch of Bruce County Public Library (*see* Port Elgin)

Carleton Place Public Library, 101 Beckwith St., Carleton Place ON K7C 2T3 – 613/257-2702 – Librarian, Janet French-Baril

Carlisle Library, PO Box 320, Carlisle ON L0R 1H0 – 905/689-8769 – Branch Head, Elizabeth Vervaeke – Branch of Wentworth Libraries (*see* Hamilton)

Carp: West Carleton Twp. Public Library, 3911 Carp Rd., Carp ON K0A 1L0 – 613/839-5412; Fax: 613/839-0179; Email: wmckay@westcarleton.twp.library.on.ca – CEO, Wendy McKay; Main Branch Supervisor, Barbara Enright – See also following branches: Constance & Buckham's Bay Branch, Fitzroy Harbour Branch

Carp: Constance & Buckham's Bay Branch, c/o Constance & Buckham's Bay Community Centre, 262 Len Purcell Dr., Constance Bay ON K0A 1L0 – 613/839-5412; Fax: 613/839-0179 – Supervisor, Mary Porritt – Branch of West Carleton Twp. Public Library

Carp: Fitzroy Harbour Branch, Fitzroy Harbour Community Centre, 100 Victoria St., PO Box 220, Carp ON K0A 1L0 – 613/839-5412; Fax: 613/839-0179 – Supervisor, Mary Porritt – Branch of West Carleton Twp. Public Library

Cartier Public Library, Cartier ON P0M 1J0 – 705/965-2001; Fax: 705/965-2500 – Librarian, Simonne McGowan

Casselman Public Library, PO Box 340, Casselman ON K0A 1M0 – 613/764-5505 – Librarian, Thérèse Chenier

Castleton: Cramahe Twp. Public Library, Town Hall, PO Box 82, Castleton ON K0K 1M0 – 905/344-7320; Fax: 905/344-5040 – Chief Librarian, Suzanne LaBerge

Cavan: Mount Pleasant Branch Library, RR#2, Cavan ON L0A 1C0 – 705/799-7841 – Librarian, Bonnie Bullock – Branch of Cavan, Millbrook, South Monaghan Union Library (*see* Millbrook)

Cayuga Public Library, 28 Cayuga St., PO Box 550, Cayuga ON N0A 1E0 – 905/772-5726; Symbol: EBHA – Branch Manager, Donna Armstrong – Branch of Haldimand Public Libraries (*see* Caledonia)

Chalk River Public Library, PO Box 160, Chalk River ON K0J 1J0 – 613/589-2966 – Librarian, Judy Field

Chapleau Public Library, PO Box 910, Chapleau ON P0M 1K0 – 705/864-0852 – Chief Librarian, Diane Collings

Chatham: Kent County Library, 455 Grand Ave. West, Chatham ON N7L 1C5 – 519/351-1010, ext.301 (voice mail); Fax: 519/351-7570; Email: mscott@kent.county.on.ca – Director, Margaret Scott – See also following branches: Blenheim Branch Library, Bothwell Branch Library, Dresden Branch Library, Highgate Branch Library, Merlin Branch Library, North Maple Mall Branch Library, Ridgetown Branch Library, Thamesville Branch Library, Tilbury Branch Library, Wallaceburg Branch Library, Wheatley Branch Library

Chatham Public Library, 120 Queen St., Chatham ON N7M 2G6 – 519/354-2940; Fax: 519/354-7352; Symbol: OCHA – Director, Library Services, Sally Scherer; Children's Librarian, Dianne Thompson; Public Services Coordinator, Sheila Gibbs; Technical Services Coordinator, Pam Sojczynski; Acquisitions Coordinator, Lynne Brown

Chatham: North Maple Mall Branch Library, 801 St. Clair St., Chatham ON N7M 5J7 – 519/354-7922; Fax: 519/354-9373 – Branch Librarian, Karen Charbonneau – Branch of Kent County Library (*see* Chatham)

Chelmsford: Rayside-Balfour Library, PO Box 1720, Chelmsford ON P0M 1L0 – 705/855-9333; Fax: 705/855-4629; Email: raybalpl@cyberbeach.net – Librarian, Jacqueline Vaillancourt – See also following branches: Azilda Branch Library

Chesley Branch Library, 102 - 1 Ave. Southibrary, PO Box 220, Chesley ON N0G 1L0 – 519/363-2239 – Branch Supervisor, Mary Witzke – Branch of Bruce County Public Library (*see* Port Elgin)

Chesterville Branch Library, PO Box 120, Chesterville ON K0C 1H0 – 613/448-2616 – Area Supervisor, Renate True – Branch of Stormont, Dundas & Glengarry County Library (*see* Finch)

Christian Island: Beausoleil First Nation Library, Cedar Point PO, Christian Island ON L0K 1C0 – 705/247-2011; Fax: 705/247-2239 – Librarian, Carlene Montague

Churchill Branch Library, RR#1, Churchill ON L0L 1K0 – 705/456-2671; Fax: 705/456-4467 – Branch Head, Paula Wright – Branch of Innisfil Public Library (*see* Stroud)

Clarence Creek: Succursale de Clarence Creek, Clarence Creek ON K0A 1N0 – Bibliothécaire, Raymond Lafleur – Branch of Bibliothèque publique de Canton de Clarence (*see* Bourget)

Clarence Creek: Succursale de Hammond, CP 102, Hammond ON K0A 2A0 – Bibliothécaire, Pierrette Hillier – Branch of Bibliothèque publique de Canton de Clarence (*see* Bourget)

Clarksburg: L.E. Shore Memorial Library, 175 Bruce St. South, PO Box 357, Thornbury ON N0H 2P0 – 519/599-3681; Fax: 519/599-7951; Email: leonard@georgian.net – CEO, Ken Haigh

Clifford Branch Library, Clifford ON N0G 1M0 – 519/327-8328; Fax: 519/846-2066 – Branch Supervisor, Henny Derbecker – Branch of Wellington County Library (*see* Fergus)

Clinton Branch Library, 27 Albert St., PO Box 370, Clinton ON N0M 1L0 – 519/482-3673 – Branch Supervisor, Ingrid Bos – Branch of Huron County Library (*see* Goderich)

Cloyne: Barrie Twp., Cloyne Branch Library, PO Box 190, Cloyne ON K0H 1K0 – 613/336-8744 – Janet Black – Branch of Frontenac County Library (*see* Kingston)

Cobalt Public Library, PO Box 170, Cobalt ON P0J 1C0 – 705/679-8120 – CEO, B. Eno

Cobden Public Library, 44 Main St., PO Box 40, Cobden ON K0J 1K0 – 613/646-7592 – Librarian, Shirley A. Sutherland

Coboconk Branch Library, PO Box 73, Coboconk ON K0M 1K0 – 705/454-1777; Fax: 705/454-1777 – Branch of Victoria County Public Library (*see* Lindsay)

Cobourg Public Library, 200 Ontario St. South, Cobourg ON K9A 5P4 – 905/372-9271; Fax: 905/372-4538 – Chief Librarian, Valerie Scott

Cochrane Public Library, 143 - 3rd St., PO Box 700, Cochrane ON P0L 1C0 – 705/272-4178; Fax: 705/272-4165 – CEO, Audrey Andrews; Children's Librarian, Beatrice Fortin; Head, Interlibrary Loans, Carole Bernard

Codrington: Brighton Twp. Branch Library, RR#2, Codrington ON K0K 1R0 – Branch Head, Grace McLean – Branch of Northumberland County Public Library (*see* Hastings)

Coe Hill: Wollaston & Limerick Union Public Library, Coe Hill Public School, PO Box 100, Coe Hill ON K0L 1P0 – 613/337-5711 – Librarian, Catherine Giroux

Colborne Public Library, 1 Toronto St., PO Box 190, Colborne ON K0K 1S0 – 905/355-3722; Fax: 905/355-3430; Email: ocolb@eagle.ca; Symbol: OCOLB – Librarian, Pat Johnson

Coldwater Memorial Public Library, 31 Coldwater Rd., PO Box 278, Coldwater ON L0K 1E0 – 705/686-3601 – CEO, Shirley Jennett

Collingwood Public Library, 100 Second St., Collingwood ON L9Y 1E5 – 705/445-1571; Fax: 705/445-3704; Email: clib@georgian.net – Chief Librarian/CEO/Pubic Relations, Kerri Robinson; Reference Coordinator, Debra Kuehl; Children's Coordinator, Lynda Reid; Technical Services Coordinator, Judith Koenig; Audio Visual Coordinator, Ruth Branget; Systems Administrator, Karen Berry

Comber Branch Library, 6400 Main St., PO Box 250, Comber ON N0P 1J0 – 519/687-2832 – Supervisor, Gisèle Lévesque – Branch of Essex County Library

Coniston Branch Library, 30 Second Ave., Coniston ON P0M 1M0 – 705/694-5511; Fax: 705/694-0992 – Head Librarian, Jane Shannon – Branch of Nickel Centre Public Library (*see* Garson)

Consecon Branch Library, PO Box 130, Consecon ON K0K 1T0 – 613/392-1106; Fax: 613/962-1514 – Branch of Ameliasburgh Twp. Library

Cookstown Branch Library, 19 Queen St., PO Box 261, Cookstown ON L0L 1L0 – 705/458-1273; Fax: 705/458-1294; Email: sbaues@innisfil.library.on.ca – Branch Head, Susan Baues – Branch of Innisfil Public Library (*see* Stroud)

Copper Cliff Centennial Library, 11 Balsam St., PO Box 790, Copper Cliff ON P0M 1N0 – 705/673-1155, ext.280; Fax: 705/682-4520 – Branch Supervisor, Heini Heinonen-Kari; Branch Assistant, Joanne Charbonneau – Branch of Sudbury Public Library

Cornwall: Akwesasne Library, PO Box 579, Cornwall ON K6H 5T3 – 518/358-2240; Fax: 518/358-2649 – Director/Circulation Librarian, Carol C. White, 518/358-2240; Acquisitions Librarian, Corinne White, 518/358-2240

Cornwall Public Library, 45 Second St. East, PO Box 939, Cornwall ON K6H 5V1 – 613/932-4796; Fax: 613/932-2715; Symbol: OC – CEO/Chief Librarian, Robert Hubsher; Deputy Chief Librarian, Magdalene Albert; Information Services Librarian, Dawn Kiddel; Office Manager, Abigail MacLean; Young Adult & Children's Librarian, Susan Bloos

Corunna Library, 417 Lyndock St., PO Box 460, Corunna ON N0N 1G0 – 519/862-1132 – Librarian, Elizabeth Cusden – Branch of Lambton County Library (*see* Wyoming)

Cottam Branch Library, 122 Fox St., PO Box 159, Cottam ON N0R 1B0 – 519/839-5040 – Supervisor, Emily Somerville – Branch of Essex County Library

Courtice Branch Library, 2950 Courtice Rd., Courtice ON L1E 2H8 – 905/404-0707 – Branch Supervisor, Christine Evans – Branch of Clarington Public Library

Courtright Library, 1534 - 4th St., PO Box 182, Courtright ON N0N 1H0 – 519/867-2712 – Librarian, Diane Leizert – Branch of Lambton County Library (*see* Wyoming)

Creemore Branch, 165 Jane St., PO Box 279, Creemore ON L0M 1G0 – 705/466-3011; Fax: 705/466-3011 – Branch Head, Joyce Smith – Branch of Clearview Public Library (*see* Staynor)

Crysler Branch Library, PO Box 190, Crysler ON K0A 1R0 – 613/987-2090 – Area Supervisor, Darlene McRae – Branch of Stormont, Dundas & Glengarry County Library (*see* Finch)

Curve Lake Band Library, Curve Lake PO, Curve Lake ON K0L 1R0 – 705/657-3217; Fax: 705/657-8707 – CEO, Kathleen Taylor

Cutler: Serpent River First Nation Public Library, Village Rd., Cutler ON P0P 1B0 – 705/844-2131; Fax: 705/844-2757 – Librarian, Virginia McLeod

Dalkeith Branch Library, PO Box 70, Dalkeith ON K0B 1E0 – 613/874-2337 – Area Supervisor, Darlene McRae – Branch of Stormont, Dundas & Glengarry County Library (*see* Finch)

Deep River: Rolph, Buchanan, Wylie & McKay Twp. Public Library, Municipal Hall, RR#1, Deep River ON K0J 1P0 – 613/584-2714; Fax: 613/584-3285; Symbol: OROLP – Librarian, Maureen L. Bakewell

Deep River: W.B. Lewis Public Library, 55 Ridge Rd., PO Box 278, Deep River ON K0J 1P0 – 613/584-4244; Fax: 613/584-1405; Email: jfoster@deepriver.library.on.ca; Symbol: RYDR – CEO, Jill Foster; Children's Librarian, Kelly Thompson

Delaware Library, Lion's Park, Young St., Delaware ON N0L 1E0 – 519/652-9978; Fax: 519/652-0166 – Supervisor, Linda Verberne – Branch of Middlesex County Library (*see* Arva)

Delhi Twp. Public Library, 192 Main St., Delhi ON N4B 2M2 – 519/582-1791; Fax: 519/582-8376; Email: delpub@simcom.on.ca; URL: http://www.simcom.on.ca/~delpub/index.html; Symbol: DE – CEO, Gwen Wood; Circulation Librarian, Kim Handsaeme; Technical Services Librarian, Jennifer Grohs

Delta Branch Library, Delta ON K0E 1G0 – 613/928-2991 – Librarian, Lois Braidwood – Branch of Rideau Lakes Union Library (*see* Elgin)

Deseronto Public Library, Main St. West, PO Box 302, Deseronto ON K0K 1X0 – 613/396-2744 – Librarian, R. Glendon Brant

Deseronto: Ka:nhiote Tyendinaga Territory Public Library, Tyendinaga Mohawk Territory, RR#1, Deseronto ON K0K 1X0 – 613/967-6264; Fax: 613/396-3627 – CEO, Karen Lewis

Devlin: Naicatchewenin Band Library, Rainy Lake Indian Reserve 17A, RR#1, PO Box 15, Devlin ON P0W 1C0 – 807/486-3407; Fax: 807/486-3704 – Librarian, Darlene Smith

Dobie: Gauthier Public Library, PO Box 11, Dobie ON P0K 1B0 – 705/567-1189 – Librarian, Jim Malherbe

Dorchester Library, 54 Dorchester Rd., Dorchester ON N0L 1G0 – 519/268-3451; Fax: 519/268-3451 – Supervisor, Margaret Trevitt – Branch of Middlesex County Library (*see* Arva)

Dorion Public Library, RR#1, Dorion ON P0T 1K0 – 807/857-2318 – Librarian, Betty Chambers, 807/857-2265; Librarian's Assistant, Janet Harris; Librarian's Assistant, Claudia Hubbard

Dorset: Sherborne Branch Library, PO Box 195, Dorset ON P0A 1E0 – 705/766-9969 – Branch Head, Carol Anger – Branch of Haliburton County Public Library

Douglas: Bromley-St. Michael Community Library, Hwy. 60, PO Box 130, Douglas ON K0J 1S0 – 613/649-2576 – Librarian, Anne English

Douro Twp. Public Library, General Delivery, Douro ON K0L 1S0 – 705/745-6803 – Librarian, Pauline Beyer

Dowling: Lionel Rheaume Public Library, 31 Sturgeon St., PO Box 520, Dowling ON P0M 1R0 – 705/855-9028; Fax: 705/855-7702 – Librarian, Bonnie Rhude – See also following branches: Earle Jarvis Public Library, Levack Branch Library

Drayton Branch Library, PO Box 130, Drayton ON N0G 1P0 – 519/638-3788; Fax: 519/846-2066 – Branch Supervisor, B. Van Soest – Branch of Wellington County Library (*see* Fergus)

Dresden Branch Library, 187 Brown St., Dresden ON N0P 1M0 – 519/683-4922; Fax: 519/683-1857 – Branch Librarian, Carol Richmond – Branch of Kent County Library (*see* Chatham)

Drumbo Public Library, PO Box 69, Drumbo ON N0J 1G0 – 519/463-5321 – Supervisor, Barbara Blake – Branch of Oxford County Library (*see* Woodstock)

Dryden Public Library, 36 Van Horne Ave., Dryden ON P8N 2A7 – 807/223-1475; Fax: 807/223-4312 – CEO, Bryan C. Buffett

Dubreuilville (Bibliothèque publique), 23, rue des Pins, Dubreuilville ON P0S 1B0 – 705/884-2284 – Bibliothécaire, Denise B. Gagné

Dunchurch: Hagerman Twp. Public Library, General Delivery, Dunchurch ON P0A 1G0 – 705/389-3311 – Librarian, Marlane Andersen

Dundalk Public Library, Main St., PO Box 190, Dundalk ON N0C 1B0 – 519/923-3248; Fax: 519/923-2685; Symbol: DD – CEO/Librarian, Dianne Walker

Dundas Public Library, 18 Ogilvie St., Dundas ON L9H 2S2 – 905/627-3507; Fax: 905/627-4391 – Interim CEO, D. Varley

Dunnville Public Library, 317 Chestnut St., Dunnville ON N1A 2H4 – 905/774-4240; Fax: 905/774-4294; Email: djackson@netinc.ca – Librarian, Debra Jackson

Dunsford Branch Library, Dunsford Community Centre, PO Box 82, Dunsford ON K0M 1L0 – 705/793-3037; Fax: 705/793-3037 – Branch Librarian, Shelley Ferguson – Branch of Victoria County Public Library (*see* Lindsay)

Durham Public Library, PO Box 706, Durham ON N0G 1R0 – 519/369-2107; Fax: 519/369-5962; Email: melridge@durham.library.on.ca; Symbol: DU – Chief Librarian, Marlaine Elvidge

Dutton Public Library, PO Box 69, Dutton ON N0L 1J0 – 519/762-2780 – Supervisor, Mary Lou McMillan – Branch of Elgin County Library (*see* St. Thomas)

Dwight Public Library, PO Box 172, Dwight ON P0A 1H0 – 705/635-3319; Fax: 705/635-3319; Email: lakebay@muskoka.com – Librarian, Peggy Hurley – Branch of Lake of Bays Public Library (*see* Baysville)

Ear Falls Twp. Public Library, 1 Balsalm St., PO Box 369, Ear Falls ON P0V 1T0 – 807/222-3209 – Librarian, Krishna Singh

Earlton: Bibliothèque publique du canton d'Armstrong, 35 - 10th St., CP 39, Earlton ON P0J 1E0 – 705/563-2717; Téléc: 705/563-2093 – Directrice générale, Aline Lefebvre

East York Public Library, #34, 2 Thorncliffe Park Dr., East York ON M4H 1H2 – 416/396-3800; Fax: 416/396-3812; URL: http://www.eypl-eastyork.com – CEO, Alice R. Lorriman; Technology & Support Services, Manager, Carol Ufford; User Services, Nancy Chavner – See also following branches: Dawes Rd. Library, Leaside Library, S. Walter Stewart Library, Thorncliffe Library, Todmorden Library

East York: Dawes Rd. Library, 416 Dawes Rd., East York ON M4B 2E8 – 416/396-3820; Fax: 416/396-3825 – Branch Librarian, Caroline Ingvaldsen – Branch of East York Public Library

East York: Leaside Library, 165 McRae Dr., East York ON M4G 1S8 – 416/396-3835; Fax: 416/396-3840 –

Branch Manager, Mary Ann San Juan – Branch of East York Public Library

East York: S. Walter Stewart Library, 170 Memorial Park Ave., East York ON M4J 2K5 – 416/396-3975; Fax: 416/396-3842 – Branch Manager, Nancy Chavner – Branch of East York Public Library

East York: Thorncliffe Library, 48 Thorncliffe Park Dr., East York ON M4H 1J7 – 416/396-3865; Fax: 416/396-3866 – Branch Librarian, Margaret Adair – Branch of East York Public Library

East York: Todmorden Library, Pape Community Centre, 1081-1/2 Pape Ave., East York ON M4K 3W6 – 416/396-3875 – Branch Manager, Nancy Chavner – Branch of East York Public Library

Eganville: Bonnechere Union Public Library, 75 Wallace St., PO Box 39, Eganville ON K0J 1T0 – 613/628-2400 – Librarian, T. Smith

Elgin: Rideau Lakes Union Library, Halladay St., PO Box 189, Elgin ON K0G 1E0 – 613/359-5315 – Coordinator, Susan Warren – See also following branches: Delta Branch Library, Elgin Branch Library, Lyndhurst Branch Library, Portland Branch Library, Seeley's Bay Branch

Elgin Branch Library, Elgin ON K0G 1E0 – 613/359-5315 – Librarian, Marjorie Keates – Branch of Rideau Lakes Union Library

Elk Lake Public Library, PO Box 218, Elk Lake ON P0J 1G0 – 705/678-2340 – Librarian, Dorothy Tessier

Elliot Lake Public Library, Algo Centre Mall, 151 Ontario Ave., Elliot Lake ON P5A 2T2 – 705/461-7204; Fax: 705/461-7244 – Librarian, Barbara Fazekas

Elmira Branch Library, 65 Arthur St. South, Elmira ON N3B 2M6 – 519/669-5477 – Branch Supervisor, Mary Anne Kirkness – Branch of Waterloo Regional Library (*see* Kitchener)

Elmvale: Flos-Elmvale Public Library, 64 Queen St. West, PO Box 430, Elmvale ON L0L 1P0 – 705/322-1482 – Branch Head, Lynn Patkau – Branch of Springwater Public Library (*see* Midhurst)

Elora Branch Library, Elora ON N0B 1S0 – 519/846-0190; Fax: 519/846-2066 – Branch Supervisor, Bonnie Moebus – Branch of Wellington County Library (*see* Fergus)

Embro Public Library, Huron St., Embro ON N0J 1G0 – 519/475-4172 – Supervisor, Sue Butt – Branch of Oxford County Library (*see* Woodstock)

Embrun: Russell Twp. Public Library, #2, 717 Notre Dame St., Embrun ON K0A 1W1 – 613/443-3636; Fax: 613/443-0668; Symbol: OERT – Directrice générale, Lucille Legault – See also following branches: Marionville Branch Library, Russell Branch Library

Emeryville Library, 104 Emery Dr., PO Box 160, Emeryville ON N0R 1C0 – 519/727-6464 – Supervisor, Angela Rice – Branch of Essex County Library

Emo: Emo Public Library, Mill St., PO Box 490, Emo ON P0W 1E0 – 807/482-2575; Fax: 807/482-2575 – CEO/Librarian, Shirley D. Sheppard

Emo: Manitou Library, PO Box 450, Emo ON P0W 1E0 – 807/482-2479

Emsdale: Perry Twp. Public Library, PO Box 39, Emsdale ON P0A 1J0 – 705/636-5454 – Librarian, Pat Aitchison

Englehart Public Library, 71 Fourth Ave., Englehart ON P0J 1H0 – 705/544-2100; Fax: 705/544-2238; Email: englib@nt.net; Symbol: OENG – Librarian/CEO, Pam Milton

Ennismore Twp. Public Library, Ennismore PO, Ennismore ON K0L 1T0 – 705/292-8022; Fax: 705/292-8022 – Librarian, Carol Crough

Enterprise Branch Library, PO Box 163, Enterprise ON K0K 1Z0 – 613/358-2058 – Supervisor, Joan Larkin – Branch of Lennox & Addington County Library (*see* Napanee)

Erin Village Branch Library, #4, 140 Main St., Erin ON N0B 1T0 – 519/833-2216; Fax: 519/846-2066 – Branch Supervisor, Virginia Hogan – Branch of Wellington County Library (*see* Fergus)

Espanola Public Library, 245 Avery Dr., Espanola ON P5E 1S4 – 705/869-2940; Fax: 705/869-6463; Email: library@etown.net – Chief Librarian, Mark Gagnon, Email: markg@engrg.uwo.ca

Essex County Library, 360 Fairview Ave. West, Essex ON N8M 1Y3 – 519/776-5241; Fax: 519/776-4455; URL: http://www.essex.county.library.on.ca – Chief Librarian, Edward R. George; Technical Services, Manager, Patricia Knight; Branches, Manager, Marilyn Thompson – See also following branches: Amherstburg Library, Comber Branch Library, Cottam Branch Library, Emeryville Library, Essex Library, Harrow Branch Library, Kingsville Library, LaSalle Library, Malden Road Library, McGregor Library, Ruthven Library, St. Clair Beach Library, Stoney Point Library, Tecumseh Branch Library, Woodslee Library

Essex Library, 18 Gordon Ave., Essex ON N8M 2M4 – 519/776-8962 – Supervisor, Judy Ward – Branch of Essex County Library

Etobicoke Public Libraries, 65 Hartsdale Dr., Etobicoke ON M9R 2S8 – 416/394-5000; Fax: 416/394-5050; Email: jmilne@library.epl.etobicoke.on.ca; URL: http://www.library.epl.etobicoke.on.ca – CEO, Jennifer Milne; Public Services, Director, Anne Bailey; Collection Development, Director, Judy Paisley – See also following branches: Albion Library, Alderwood Library, Brentwood Public Library, Eatonville Library, Elmbrook Park Library, Humber Bay Library, Humberwood Library, Long Branch Library, Mimico Centennial Library, New Toronto Library, Northern Elms Library, Rexdale Library, Richview Central Library

Etobicoke: Albion Library, 1515 Albion Rd., Etobicoke ON M9V 1B2 – 416/394-5170; Fax: 416/394-5185; Email: lnorth@library.epl.etobicoke.on.ca – Branch Manager, Lesley North – Branch of Etobicoke Public Libraries

Etobicoke: Alderwood Library, 525 Horner Ave., Etobicoke ON M8W 2B9 – 416/394-5310; Email: crichardson@library.epl.etobicoke.on.ca – Branch Manager, Cathy Richardson – Branch of Etobicoke Public Libraries

Etobicoke: Brentwood Public Library, 36 Brentwood Rd. North, Etobicoke ON M8X 2B5 – 416/394-5240; Fax: 416/394-5257; Email: vvanvliet@library.epl.etobicoke.on.ca – Branch Manager, Virginia Van Vliet – Branch of Etobicoke Public Libraries

Etobicoke: Eatonville Library, 430 Burnhamthorpe Rd., Etobicoke ON M9B 2B1 – 416/394-5270; Email: pmoffet@library.epl.etobicoke.on.ca – Branch Manager, Peter Moffet – Branch of Etobicoke Public Libraries

Etobicoke: Elmbrook Park Library, 2 Elmbrook Cres., Etobicoke ON M9C 5B4 – 416/394-5290; URL: spatrick@library.epl.etobicoke.on.ca – Branch Manager, Sue Patrick – Branch of Etobicoke Public Libraries

Etobicoke: Humber Bay Library, 200 Parklawn Rd., Etobicoke ON M8Y 3J1 – 416/394-5300; Email: mjgaudet@library.epl.etobicoke.on.ca – Branch Manager, Mark Gaudet – Branch of Etobicoke Public Libraries

Etobicoke: Humberwood Library, 850 Humberwood Blvd., Etobicoke ON M9W 7A6 – 416/394-5210; Fax: 416/394-5215; Email: acampbell@library.epl.etobicoke.on.ca – Branch Manager, Anne Campbell – Branch of Etobicoke Public Libraries

Etobicoke: Long Branch Library, 3500 Lake Shore Blvd. West, Etobicoke ON M8W 1N6 – 416/394-5320; Email: bcrandall@library.epl.etobicoke.on.ca – Branch Manager, Bert Crandall – Branch of Etobicoke Public Libraries

Etobicoke: Mimico Centennial Library, 47 Station Rd., Etobicoke ON M8V 2R1 – 416/394-5330; Fax: 416/394-5338; Email: mrice@library.epl.etobicoke.on.ca – Branch Manager, Margaret Rice – Branch of Etobicoke Public Libraries

Etobicoke: New Toronto Library, 110 - 11 St., Etobicoke ON M8V 3G5 – 416/394-5350; Fax: 416/394-5358; Email: shumphries@library.epl.etobicoke.on.ca – Branch Manager, Susan Humphries – Branch of Etobicoke Public Libraries

Etobicoke: Northern Elms Library, Rexdale Plaza, 2267 Islington Ave., Etobicoke ON M9W 3W7 – 416/394-5230; Email: mpatrick@library.epl.etobicoke.on.ca – Branch Manager, Marliese Patrick – Branch of Etobicoke Public Libraries

Etobicoke: Rexdale Library, 2243 Kipling Ave., Etobicoke ON M9W 4L5 – 416/394-5200; Email: plabbe@library.epl.etobicoke.on.ca – Branch Manager, Pat Llabbe – Branch of Etobicoke Public Libraries

Etobicoke: Richview Central Library, 1806 Islington Ave., Etobicoke ON M9C 5H8 – 416/394-5120; Fax: 416/394-5158; Email: iabbott@library.epl.etobicoke.on.ca – Branch Manager, Ilka Abbott – Branch of Etobicoke Public Libraries

Exeter Branch Library, PO Box 610, Exeter ON N0M 1S6 – 519/235-1890 – Branch Supervisor, Helen Hodgins – Branch of Huron County Library (*see* Goderich)

Falconbridge Branch Library, Edison St. Community Centre, PO Box 460, Falconbridge ON P0M 1S0 – 705/693-2423 – Branch Head, Marlene Bilsborough – Branch of Nickel Centre Public Library (*see* Garson)

Fauquier-Strickland Public Library, PO Box 100, Fauquier ON P0L 1G0 – 705/339-2521; Fax: 705/339-2421 – Librarian, Odile Tremblay

Fenelon Falls Branch Library, 21 Market St., PO Box 867, Fenelon Falls ON K0M 1N0 – 705/887-6300; Fax: 705/887-6300; Email: fenlib@knet.flemingc.on.ca – Branch Head, Valerie Garland – Branch of Victoria County Public Library (*see* Lindsay)

Fenwick: Maple Acre Branch Library, 782 Canboro Rd., General Delivery, Fenwick ON L0S 1C0 – 905/892-5226 – Librarian, Peggy Grady – Branch of Pelham Public Library (*see* Fonthill)

Fergus: Wellington County Library, Wellington Place, RR#1, Fergus ON N1M 2W3 – 519/846-0918; Fax: 519/846-2066; Email: path@county.wellington.on.ca; Symbol: OFERW – CEO, Patrick Harvie – See also following branches: Arthur Branch Library, Centre Wellington Branch Library, Clifford Branch Library, Drayton Branch Library, Elora Branch Library, Erin Village Branch Library, Harriston Branch Library, Mount Forest Branch Library, Palmerston Branch Library, Puslinch Branch Library

Fergus: Centre Wellington Branch Library, RR#1, Fergus ON N1M 2W3 – 519/846-0918; Fax: 519/846-2066 – Branch of Wellington County Library

Fergus Public Library, 190 St. Andrew St. West, Fergus ON N1M 1N5 – 519/843-1180; Fax: 519/843-5743 – Librarian, G. Kozak Selby

Field Public Library, 59 Ecole St., Field ON P0H 1M0 – 705/758-6610; Fax: 705/758-9529 – CEO, Lucienne Desjardins

Finch: Stormont, Dundas & Glengarry County Library, PO Box 217, Finch ON K0C 1K0 – 613/346-2501; Fax: 613/246-2461 – CEO, Leanne Clendening – See also following branches: Alexandria Branch Library, Avonmore Branch Library, Brinston Branch Library, Chesterville Branch Library, Crysler Branch Library, Dalkeith Branch Library,

Finch Branch Library, Glen Robertson Branch, Ingleside Branch Library, Lancaster Branch Library, Lancaster Twp. Branch Library, Long Sault Branch Library, Maxville Branch Library, Moose Creek Branch Library, Morewood Branch Library, Morrisburg Branch Library, South Mountain Branch Library, St. Andrews West Branch, Williamsburg Branch Library, Williamstown Branch Library, Winchester Branch Library

Finch Branch Library, PO Box 250, Finch ON K0C 1K0 – 613/984-2807 – Area Supervisor, Fiona Fraser – Branch of Stormont, Dundas & Glengarry County Library (*see* Finch)

Flesherton Public Library, 10 Elizabeth St., Flesherton ON N0C 1E0 – 519/924-2241 – Librarian, Wilda Allen

Flinton: Kaladar, Anglesea & Effingham Twps. Public Library, Main St., Flinton ON K0H 1P0 – Librarian, Yvonne Brushey

Florence Library, 531 Florence Rd., PO Box 102, Florence ON N0P 1R0 – 519/692-3213 – Librarian, Mary Emerick – Branch of Lambton County Library (*see* Wyoming)

Florence: Shetland Library, 1279 Shetland Rd., Florence ON N0P 1R0 – 519/695-3330 – Librarian, Barbara Beckett – Branch of Lambton County Library (*see* Wyoming)

Foleyet Public Library, PO Box 147, Foleyet ON P0M 1T0 – 705/899-2280 – Librarian, William J. Kilgour

Fonthill: Pelham Public Library, PO Box 830, Fonthill ON L0S 1E0 – 905/892-6443; Fax: 905/892-3392; Symbol: OFP – CEO, Hugh D. Molson – See also following branches: Maple Acre Branch Library

Fordwich Branch Library, RR#1, Fordwich ON N0G 1V0 – Branch Supervisor, Marion Feldskov – Branch of Huron County Library (*see* Goderich)

Forester's Falls: Ross Twp. Public Library, Forester's Falls ON K0J 1V0 – 613/646-2543 – Librarian, Debbie Byce, 613/646-2496

Forest: Chippewas of Kettle & Stony Point Library, RR#2, 53 Indian Lane, Forest ON N0N 1J0 – 519/786-6903; Fax: 519/786-6904; Email: lhenry@xcelco.on.ca – CEO, Linda Henry

Forest Library, 61 King St. West, PO Box 370, Forest ON N0N 1J0 – 519/786-5152 – Librarian, M. Wallace – Branch of Lambton County Library (*see* Wyoming)

Fort Erie Public Library, 136 Gilmore Rd., Fort Erie ON L2A 2M1 – 905/871-2546; Fax: 905/871-9884 – CEO, Elizabeth Rossnagel; Reference Librarian, Lorne Featherston; Children's Librarian, Hazel Reinhart; Adult Services Librarian, Lynda Goodridge; Technical Services Librarian, Dee Thompson – See also following branches: Crystal Ridge Branch Library, Stevensville Branch Library

Fort Erie: Crystal Ridge Branch Library, c/o 136 Gilmore Ave., Fort Erie ON L2A 2M1 – 905/894-1281 – Branch of Fort Erie Public Library

Fort Erie: Stevensville Branch Library, c/o 136 Gilmore Ave., Fort Erie ON L2A 2M1 – 905/382-2051 – Branch of Fort Erie Public Library

Fort Frances Public Library, 363 Church St., Fort Frances ON P9A 1C9 – 807/274-9879; Fax: 807/274-4496; Email: libff@fort-frances.lakeheadu.ca – Librarian, Margaret Sedgwick

Frankford Public Library, 22 Trent St. North, PO Box 550, Frankford ON K0K 2C0 – 613/398-7572; Fax: 613/398-8826 – Librarian, L. Wallington

Frankville: Kitley Twp. Public Library, Frankville ON K0E 1H0 – 613/275-2093 – CEO, Judi Osler

Freelton Library, PO Box 15, Freelton ON L0R 1K0 – 905/659-7639 – Branch Head, Valerie Lawson – Branch of Wentworth Libraries (*see* Hamilton)

Gananoque Public Library, 100 Park St., Gananoque ON K7G 2Y5 – 613/382-2436 – Librarian, J. Love

Gananoque: Howe Island Branch Library, Gananoque ON K7G 2V6 – 613/549-7972 – Yvonne Kane – Branch of Frontenac County Library (*see* Kingston)

Garson: Nickel Centre Public Library, 214 Orell St., Garson ON P3L 1V2 – 705/693-2729; Fax: 705/693-5540 – CEO, Lillian Bergeron – See also following branches: Coniston Branch Library, Falconbridge Branch Library, Garson Branch Library, Skead Branch Library

Garson Branch Library, 214 Orell St., Garson ON P3L 1V2 – 705/693-2729; Fax: 705/693-5540 – Head Librarian, Verna Thompson – Branch of Nickel Centre Public Library

Georgetown: Halton Hills Public Library, 9 Church St., Georgetown ON L7G 2A3 – 905/873-2681; Fax: 905/873-6118; Email: cornwelb@hhpl.on.ca; URL: http://www.hhpl.on.ca/library/hhpl/hhpl.htm; Symbol: CAOGTN – CEO, Betsy Cornwell; Deputy Chief/Systems Administrator, Walter Lewis; Children's/Public Services Librarian, Cindy Cooper; Information Services Librarian, Geoffrey Cannon – See also following branches: Acton Public Library, Georgetown Branch Library

Georgetown Branch Library, 9 Church St., Georgetown ON L7G 2A3 – 905/873-2681; Fax: 905/873-6118 – Public Services Librarian, Cindy Cooper – Branch of Halton Hills Public Library

Geraldton Centennial Public Library, PO Box 40, Geraldton ON P0T 1M0 – 807/854-1490; Fax: 807/854-2351 – Librarian, Donna Mae Mikkonen

Gilmour: Tudor & Cashel Public Library, RR#2, PO Box 430, Gilmour ON K0L 1W0 – 613/474-2583 – Librarian/CEO, Cynthia Wannamaker

Glanworth Library, 2950 Glanworth Dr., Glanworth ON N0L 1L0 – 519/681-6797; Fax: 519/663-5396 – Branch Head, Judy Shaw – Branch of London Public Library

Glen Morris Branch Library, Glen Morris ON N0B 1W0 – 519/740-2122; Fax: 519/740-2122; Symbol: OGMS – Branch Head, Kelly Dinsmore – Branch of South Dumfries Twp. Public Library

Glen Robertson Branch, PO Box 92, Glen Robertson ON K0B 1H0 – 613/874-2250 – Area Supervisor, Darlene McRae – Branch of Stormont, Dundas & Glengarry County Library (*see* Finch)

Glencoe Library, 178 McKellar St., PO Box 490, Glencoe ON N0L 1M0 – 519/287-2735; Fax: 519/287-2735 – Supervisor, Karen J. Kendrick-Diamond – Branch of Middlesex County Library (*see* Arva)

Gloucester: Bibliothèque publique de Gloucester, 1400 Blair Place, 5th Fl., CP 8333, Gloucester ON K1J 3V5 – 613/748-4226; Téléc: 613/748-4114; Courrier électronique: ao682@freenet.carleton.ca; Symbol: BPG – Director, Arch Campbell; Deputy Director, Elaine Condos – See also following branches: Services Techniques, Succursale Blackburn Hamlet, Succursale Blossom Park, Succursale Hôtel de Ville, Succursale Orléans

Gloucester: Services Techniques, #7, 2950 Bank St., Gloucester ON K1T 1N8 – 613/523-2957; Téléc: 613/523-9378 – Chef des services techniques, Marie Desaulniers; Chef de cataloguage, Céline Lefebvre-Turcotte – Branch of Bibliothèque publique de Gloucester

Gloucester: Succursale Blackburn Hamlet, 199 Glen Park Dr., Gloucester ON K1B 5B8 – 613/824-6926; Téléc: 613/824-8848; Symbol: OGBH – Branch Head, Marcia Aronson – Branch of Bibliothèque publique de Gloucester

Gloucester: Succursale Blossom Park, #7, 2950 Bank St., Gloucester ON K1T 1N8 – 613/731-9907; Fax: 613/731-0744 – Branch Head, Sonia Chippendale – Branch of Bibliothèque publique de Gloucester

Gloucester: Succursale Hôtel de Ville, 1400 Blair Pl., CP 8333, Gloucester ON K1G 3V5 – 613/748-4208; Téléc: 613/748-4314; Symbol: OGO – Branch Head, Dave Thomas – Branch of Bibliothèque publique de Gloucester

Gloucester: Succursale Orléans, 1705 Orléans Blvd., Gloucester ON K1C 4W2 – 613/824-1962; Téléc: 613/748-4114; Symbol: OGB – Branch Head, Abe Schwartz – Branch of Bibliothèque publique de Gloucester

Goderich: Huron County Library, RR#5, Clinton ON N0M 1L0 – 519/482-5457; Fax: 519/482-7820; Symbol: OGOH – County Librarian, Beth Ross; Deputy County Librarian, Sharon Cox – See also following branches: Auburn Branch Library, Bayfield Branch Library, Bluevale Branch Library, Blyth Branch Library, Brussels Branch Library, Centralia Branch Library, Clinton Branch Library, Cranbrook Branch Library, Exeter Branch Library, Fordwich Branch Library, Goderich Branch Library, Gorrie Branch Library, Hensall Branch Library, Kirkton Branch Library, Seaforth Branch Library, Wingham Branch Library, Zurich Branch Library

Goderich Branch Library, 52 Montreal St., Goderich ON N7A 2G4 – 519/524-9261 – Branch Supervisor, Marg Bushell – Branch of Huron County Library

Gogama Public Library, PO Box 238, Gogama ON P0M 1W0 – 705/894-2448 – Volunteer Head Librarian/CEO, Sue Primeau

Gogama: Mattagami Indian Band Library, PO Box 250, Gogama ON P0M 1W0 – 705/894-2003

Golden Lake First Nation Library, PO Box 100, Golden Lake ON K0J 1X0 – 613/625-2402; Fax: 613/625-2332 – Librarian, Linda Sarazin

Gooderham: Glamorgan Branch Library, Gooderham ON K0M 1R0 – 705/447-3163 – Branch Head, Marilyn Billings – Branch of Haliburton County Public Library

Gore Bay Union Public Library, 15 Water St., PO Box 225, Gore Bay ON P0P 1H0 – 705/282-2221; Fax: 705/282-3076 – CEO/Librarian, Johanna Allison

Gorrie Branch Library, Gorrie ON N0G 1X0 – Branch Supervisor, Marion Feldskov – Branch of Huron County Library (*see* Goderich)

Grafton: Centreton Branch Library, RR#1, Grafton ON K0K 2G0 – 905/349-2976 – Branch Head, Heather Viscount – Branch of Northumberland County Public Library (*see* Hastings)

Grafton Branch Library, PO Box 12, Grafton ON K0K 2G0 – 905/349-2424 – Branch Head, Bette LeBarr – Branch of Northumberland County Public Library (*see* Hastings)

Grand Bend Library, 22-81 Gill Rd., PO Box 117, Grand Bend ON N0M 1T0 – 519/238-2067 – Librarian, Cathy Smith – Branch of Lambton County Library (*see* Wyoming)

Grand Valley Public Library, 4 Amaranth St., PO Box 129, Grand Valley ON L0N 1G0 – 519/928-5622; Email: gvpl@flexnet.com – Librarian, S. Leighton

Gravenhurst Public Library, 275 Muskoka Rd. South, Gravenhurst ON P1P 1J1 – 705/687-3382; Email: gplib@muskoka.com – CEO/Librarian, Robena Kirton – See also following branches: Morrison Library Outpost, Ryde Library Outpost

Gravenhurst: Ryde Library Outpost, RR#3, Gravenhurst ON P1P 1R3 – 705/687-2633 – Branch Head, Barb Holden – Branch of Gravenhurst Public Library

Gravenhurst: Walker's Point Public Library, Walker's Point Community Centre, RR#2, Gravenhurst ON P0C 1G0 – 705/687-9965 – Librarian, Susan Pitts – Branch of Port Carling Public Library

Greely Branch Library, 7008 Parkway Rd., PO Box 159, Greely ON K0A 1Z0 – 613/821-3609 – Librarian, Alison Surinskis – Branch of Osgoode Twp. Public Library Board (*see* Metcalfe)

Greensville Library, #5, 59 Kirby St., Greensville ON L9H 4H6 – 905/627-4951 – Branch Head, Terri

Shewfelt – Branch of Wentworth Libraries (*see* Hamilton)

Grimsby Public Library, 25 Adelaide St., Grimsby ON L3M 1X2 – 905/945-5142 – Librarian, Barry Church

Guelph Public Library, 100 Norfolk St., Guelph ON N1H 4J6 – 519/824-6220; Fax: 519/824-8342 – Chief Librarian, Norman McLeod; Reference Librarian, Steven Kraft; Circulation Librarian, Barbara Baxter; Children's Librarian, Kerry Hannah; Technical Services Librarian, Cathy McInnis; Systems Librarian, Linda J. Kearns – See also following branches: Bullfrog Mall Library, Scottsdale Centre Branch Library

Guelph: Bullfrog Mall Library, #36, 380 Eramosa Rd., Guelph ON N1E 6R2 – 519/824-6220; Fax: 519/824-8342 – Librarian, Kate Gilchrist – Branch of Guelph Public Library

Guelph: Puslinch Branch Library, RR#3, Guelph ON N1H 6H9 – 519/763-8026; Fax: 519/846-2066 – Branch Supervisor, F.E. Shaw – Branch of Wellington County Library (*see* Fergus)

Guelph: Scottsdale Centre Branch Library, #1, 650 Scottsdale Dr., Guelph ON N1G 2M3 – 519/824-6220; Fax: 519/824-8342 – Librarian, Robin Tunney – Branch of Guelph Public Library

Hagersville Public Library, 13 Alma St. North, PO Box 219, Hagersville ON N0A 1H0 – 905/768-5941 – Branch Manager, L. Diane Schweyer – Branch of Haldimand Public Libraries (*see* Caledonia)

Hagersville: Mississaugas of New Credit Band Library, RR#6, Hagersville ON N0A 1H0 – 905/768-5686; Fax: 905/768-1225 – CEO, Carolyn King

Haileybury Public Library, 545 Lakeshore, PO Bag O, Haileybury ON P0J 1K0 – 705/672-3707; Fax: 705/672-5966; Symbol: JHAB – CEO, Elizabeth A. Bishop

Haliburton County Public Library, 2001 Mountain St., PO Box 119, Haliburton ON K0M 1S0 – 705/457-2241; Email: joel-levis@canrem.com; Symbol: OHAL – Director, Joel Levis; Technical Services Librarian, Carol Madill; ILL, Arlene Robinson – See also following branches: Bicroft Branch Library, Cardiff Branch Library, Dysart Branch Library, Glamorgan Branch Library, Minden Branch Library, Monmouth Branch Library, Sherborne Branch Library, Snowdon Twp., Lochlin Library, Stanhope Branch Library

Haliburton: Dysart Branch Library, PO Box 119, Haliburton ON K0M 1S0 – 705/457-1791 – Branch Head, Victoria Ross – Branch of Haliburton County Public Library

Haliburton: Stanhope Branch Library, RR#1, Haliburton ON K0M 2K0 – 705/489-2402 – Branch Head, Marjorie Cowen – Branch of Haliburton County Public Library

Hamilton Public Library, 55 York Blvd., PO Box 2700, Stn LCDI, Hamilton ON L8N 4E4 – 905/546-3200; Fax: 905/546-3202; URL: http://www.hpl.hamilton.on.ca – Chief Librarian, Ken Roberts; Deputy Chief Librarian, Don Kilpatrick; Youth Services Librarian, Helen Benoit; Acquisitions Librarian, Pamela Haley – See also following branches: Barton Library, Concession Library, Kenilworth Library, Locke Library, Picton Branch Library, Red Hill Library, Sherwood Library, Terryberry Library, Westdale Library

Hamilton: Wentworth Libraries, #1, 70 Frid St., Hamilton ON L8P 4M4 – 905/546-4126; Fax: 905/522-9083; Symbol: CAOHWL – Chief Librarian, Barbara Baker; Reference Librarian, Jane Skeates; Acquisitions/Technical Services Librarian, Frances Rukavina; Public Services/Circulation Librarian, Leslie Muirhead – See also following branches: Ancaster Public Library, Binbrook Public Library, Carlisle Library, Freelton Library, Greensville Library, Lynden Public Library, Millgrove Public Library, Mount Hope Public Library, Rockton Public Library, Saltfleet Public Library, Sheffield Public Library, Stoney Creek Public Library, Valley Park Library, Waterdown Public Library, Winona Public Library

Hamilton: Barton Library, 571 Barton St. East, Hamilton ON L8L 2Z4 – 905/546-3450; Fax: 905/546-3453 – Librarian, Debbie Rudderham – Branch of Hamilton Public Library

Hamilton: Concession Library, 565 Concession St., Hamilton ON L8V 1A8 – 905/546-3415; Fax: 905/546-3491 – Librarian, Jean Lyall – Branch of Hamilton Public Library

Hamilton: Kenilworth Library, 103 Kenilworth Ave. North, Hamilton ON L8H 4R6 – 905/546-3960; Fax: 905/546-4010 – Librarian, Rita Bozz – Branch of Hamilton Public Library

Hamilton: Locke Library, 285 Locke St. South, Hamilton ON L8P 4C2 – 905/546-3492; Fax: 905/546-3447 – Librarian, Karen Peter – Branch of Hamilton Public Library

Hamilton: Picton Branch Library, 502 James St. North, Hamilton ON L8L 1J4 – 905/546-3494; Fax: 905/546-3496 – Librarian, Debbie Rudderham – Branch of Hamilton Public Library

Hamilton: Red Hill Library, 695 Queenston Rd., Hamilton ON L8G 1A1 – 905/546-2069; Fax: 905/546-3973 – Librarian, Yvonne Patch – Branch of Hamilton Public Library

Hamilton: Sherwood Library, 467 Upper Ottawa, Hamilton ON L8T 3T4 – 905/546-3267; Fax: 905/546-3268 – Librarian, Sheila Gamble – Branch of Hamilton Public Library

Hamilton: Terryberry Library, 100 Mohawk Rd. West, Hamilton ON L9C 1W1 – 905/546-3921; Fax: 905/546-3953 – Librarian, Karen Cooper – Branch of Hamilton Public Library

Hamilton: Valley Park Library, 970 Paramount Dr., Hamilton ON L8J 1Y2 – 905/573-3141 – Branch Head, Jane Henderson – Branch of Wentworth Libraries

Hamilton: Westdale Library, 955 King St. West, Hamilton ON L8S 1K9 – 905/546-3456; Fax: 905/546-3458 – Librarian, Karen Peter – Branch of Hamilton Public Library

Hanmer: Valley East Public Library, 4100 Elmview Dr., Hanmer ON P3P 1J7 – 705/969-5565; Fax: 705/969-7787; Email: vallylib@cyberbeach.net; Symbol: OVC – CEO, Charles Grayson; Public Services Librarian, Lynn Imbeau; Technical Services Librarian, L. Roberts

Hanover Public Library, 451 - 10 Ave., Hanover ON N4N 2P1 – 519/364-1420; Fax: 519/364-1747; Email: library@log.on.ca – Librarian, Linda Manchester

Harrietsville Library, 201 Main St., Harrietsville ON N0L 1N0 – 519/269-3089 – Supervisor, Sharon Churchill – Branch of Middlesex County Library (*see* Arva)

Harriston Branch Library, Elora St., PO Box 130, Harriston ON N0G 1Z0 – 519/338-2396; Fax: 519/846-2066 – Branch Supervisor, Dorothy Pike – Branch of Wellington County Library (*see* Fergus)

Harrow Branch Library, 140 King St. West, PO Box 550, Harrow ON N0R 1G0 – 519/738-6362 – Supervisor, Hilda Enns – Branch of Essex County Library

Hartington: Portland Twp., Hartington Branch Library, Hartington ON K0H 1W0 – 613/372-2524 – Joan Leonard – Branch of Frontenac County Library (*see* Kingston)

Hastings: Northumberland County Public Library, General Delivery, Hastings ON K0L 1Y0 – 705/696-3630; Fax: 705/696-1806 – CEO, Judy Howard; Reference Librarian, Catherine McLeod; Technical Services Librarian, Lily Griffiths – See also following branches: Brighton Twp. Branch Library, Campbellford/Seymour Branch Library, Centreton Branch Library, Garden Hill Branch Library, Grafton Branch Library, Hastings Branch Library, Murray Twp. (Wooler) Branch Library, Roseneath Branch Library, Warkworth (Percy Twp.) Branch Library

Hastings Branch Library, 6 Albert St., PO Box 130, Hastings ON K0L 1Y0 – 705/696-2111 – Branch Head, Ann Sullivan – Branch of Northumberland County Public Library

Havelock Public Library, 13 Quebec St., PO Box 464, Havelock ON K0L 1Z0 – 705/778-2621 – Librarian, Beth LaBarre

Hawkesbury: Bibliothèque publique de Hawkesbury, 550, rue Higginson, Hawkesbury ON K6A 1H1 – 613/632-6656; Téléc: 613/632-8314; Courrier électronique: hawbib@hawk.igs.net – Directeur général, Yvon Léonard; Référence, Frances Pâlin; Prêt entre bibliothèques, Lynn Belle-Isle Guindon; Services techniques, Sophie Legault

Hearst Public Library, PO Bag 5000, Hearst ON P0L 1N0 – 705/362-4700; Fax: 705/362-5902 – Chief Library Technician, Nathalie Proulx

Hensall Branch Library, 198 King St., PO Box 249, Hensall ON N0M 1X0 – 519/262-2445 – Branch Supervisor, Susan Hartman – Branch of Huron County Library (*see* Goderich)

Hepworth Branch Library, 465 Bruce St., PO Box 83, Hepworth ON N0H 1P0 – 519/935-2030 – Branch Supervisor, Barbara Wong – Branch of Bruce County Public Library (*see* Port Elgin)

Hepworth: Sauble Beach Branch Library, RR#1, Sauble Beach ON N0H 2G0 – 519/422-1283; Fax: 519/422-1283 – Branch Supervisor, Bonnie Phair – Branch of Bruce County Public Library (*see* Port Elgin)

Heron Bay: Pic River First Nation Public Library, Pic Day School, Heron Bay ON P0T 1R0 – 807/229-0630; Fax: 807/229-1944 – CEO, Glenda Nabigon

Hickson Public Library, Hickson ON N0J 1L0 – 519/462-2927 – Supervisor, Louise Ross – Branch of Oxford County Library (*see* Woodstock)

Highgate Branch Library, King St., Highgate ON N0P 1T0 – 519/678-3313 – Branch Librarian, Vera Leverton – Branch of Kent County Library (*see* Chatham)

Highland Grove: Cardiff Branch Library, Highland Grove ON K0L 2A0 – 705/448-2652 – Branch Head, Joanne Burroughs – Branch of Haliburton County Public Library

Hillsburgh: Erin Twp. Public Library, 98B Main St., PO Box 490, Hillsburgh ON N0B 1Z0 – 519/855-4010; Fax: 519/855-4873 – Librarian, Barb Thompson

Hilton Union Library, PO Box 117, Hilton Beach ON P0R 1G0 – 705/246-2557 – CEO, Diane Gerhart

Hogansburg: Akwesasne Library & Cultural Centre, St. Regis Mohawk Reservation, Rte. 37, RR#1, PO Box 14C, Hogansburg NY 13655-9705 USA – 518/358-2240; Fax: 518/358-2649 – CEO, Carol White

Holland Landing: East Gwillimbury Public Library, 19513 Yonge St., PO Box 1609, Holland Landing ON L9N 1P2 – 905/836-6492; Fax: 905/836-6499; Email: kmclean@interhop.net – CEO, Karen McLean; Reference Librarian, Alexandra Gutelius; Children's Librarian, Linne Thompson – See also following branch: Mount Albert Branch Library

Holstein: Egremont Twp. Public Library, General Delivery, Holstein ON N0G 2A0 – 519/334-3480; Fax: 519/334-3388 – Librarian, Sandra Bossie

Honey Harbour Branch Library, Honey Harbour ON P0E 1E0 – 705/756-8851; Fax: 705/756-8851 – Librarian, Billie Hewitt – Branch of Georgian Bay Twp. Public Library

Hornepayne Public Library, 200 Front St., PO Box 539, Hornepayne ON P0M 1Z0 – 807/868-2332 – Librarian, L. Kahara

Huntsville Public Library, 7 Minerva St. East, Huntsville ON P1H 1W4 – 705/789-5232; Symbol: OHU – Chief Librarian/CEO, Marguerite Urban

Huron Park: Centralia Branch Library, 117 Wellington Cres., Huron Park ON N0M 1Y0 – Branch Supervisor, Maxine Hyde – Branch of Huron County Library (*see* Goderich)

Ignace Public Library, 36 Main St., PO Box 480, Ignace ON P0T 1T0 – 807/934-2280; Fax: 807/934-6452; Symbol: NZIG – Librarian, Catherine Penney

Ilderton: Coldstream Library, RR#2, Ilderton ON N0M 2A0 – 519/666-1201 – Supervisor, Mary Higgs – Branch of Middlesex County Library (*see* Arva)

Ilderton: London Twp. Library, 40 Heritage Dr., Ilderton ON N0M 2A0 – 519/666-1599; Fax: 519/666-1599 – Supervisor, Carolyne Walden – Branch of Middlesex County Library (*see* Arva)

Ingersoll Library, 130 Oxford St., Ingersoll ON N5C 2V5 – 519/485-2505; Fax: 519/485-4028 – Supervisor, Rosemary Lewis – Branch of Oxford County Library (*see* Woodstock)

Ingleside Branch Library, PO Box 704, Ingleside ON K0C 1M0 – 613/537-2592 – Area Supervisor, Fiona Fraser – Branch of Stormont, Dundas & Glengarry County Library (*see* Finch)

Inglewood Branch, 15825 McLaughlin Rd., Inglewood ON L0N 1K0 – 905/838-3324; Fax: 905/838-3324; Email: inglelib@headwaters.com – Branch Head, Judy Nelson – Branch of Caledon Public Library (*see* Bolton)

Innerkip Public Library, PO Box 104, Innerkip ON N0J 1M0 – 519/469-3824 – Branch Supervisor, Irene Priest – Branch of Oxford County Library (*see* Woodstock)

Inwood Library, 6504 James St., PO Box 41, Inwood ON N0N 1K0 – 519/844-2491 – Librarian, Nola Tait – Branch of Lambton County Library (*see* Wyoming)

Iron Bridge Public Library, PO Box 339, Iron Bridge ON P0R 1H0 – 705/843-2192 – CEO, Bette C. Size

Iroquois Falls Public Library, 725 Synagogue St., PO Box 860, Iroquois Falls ON P0K 1G0 – 705/232-5722; Fax: 705/232-7166 – CEO, Denise Giroux; Circulation Librarian/ILL, Jeannine Beaudoin

Iroquois Public Library, PO Box 39, Iroquois ON K0E 1K0 – 613/652-4377 – Senior Librarian, Eleanor Pietersma

Jarvis: Nanticoke Public Library Board, 17 Talbot St. East, PO Box 399, Jarvis ON N0A 1J0 – 519/587-4293; Fax: 519/519/587-5569; Email: ERNA; Symbol: NAN – CEO, Katherine Bristol; Reference Librarian, Rosemary Hilton; Children's Librarian, Betty Lee; Technical Services Librarian, Heidi Goodale; Acquisitions Librarian, Patricia Reidy – See also following branches: Jarvis Branch Library, Port Dover Branch Library, Selkirk Branch Library, Waterford Branch Library

Jarvis Branch Library, 37 Main St. North, PO Box 636, Jarvis ON N0A 1J0 – 519/587-4746 – Branch Librarian, Rosemary Hilton – Branch of Nanticoke Public Library Board

Kagawong: Billings Twp. Public Library, Kagawong ON P0P 1J0 – 705/282-2944 – CEO, Lillian Boyd

Kakabeka Falls: Conmee Public Library, Conmee Community Centre, RR#1, Kakabeka Falls ON P0T 1W0 – 807/475-5229 – CEO, Selly Pajamaki

Kanata Public Library, 2500 Campeau Dr., Kanata ON K2K 2W3 – 613/592-1321; Fax: 613/592-0891; Email: lslowden@kanata.library.on.ca; Symbol: OKAN – CEO, Linda Sherlow Lowdon; Reference Librarian, Pat Skarzinski; Technical Services Librarian, Laura St. Denis – See also following branches: Beaverbrook Branch Library, Hazeldean Branch Library

Kanata: Beaverbrook Branch Library, 2500 Campeau Dr., Kanata ON K2K 2W3 – 613/592-2712; Fax: 613/592-4592; Email: bw301@freenet.carleton.ca – Branch Manager, Joan Darby – Branch of Kanata Public Library

Kanata: Hazeldean Branch Library, 50 Castlefrank Rd., Kanata ON K2L 2N5 – 613/836-1900; Fax: 613/836-5326; Email: ac578@freenet.carleton.ca – Branch Manager, Anne Robison – Branch of Kanata Public Library

Kapuskasing Public Library, 24 Mundy Ave., Kapuskasing ON P5N 1P9 – 705/335-3363; Fax: 705/335-2464 – CEO, Louise Boucher

Kashechewan First Nation Public Library, c/o St. Andrews School, General Delivery, Kashechewan ON P0L 1S0 – 705/275-4405; Fax: 705/275-4515 – CEO, Lucy Wesley

Kearney & Area Public Library, PO Box 220, Kearney ON P0A 1M0 – 705/636-5849 – CEO/Librarian, Brandi Nolan

Keene: Otonabee Twp. Public Library, PO Box 9, Keene ON K0L 2G0 – 705/295-6814; Fax: 705/295-6814; Symbol: OTO – CEO, Jane Tully – See also following branches: Stewart Hall Branch Library

Keene: Stewart Hall Branch Library, PO Box 9, Keene ON K0L 2G0 – 705/749-5642; Fax: 705/295-6814 – Branch Head, Gail McIntyre – Branch of Otonabee Twp. Public Library

Keewatin Public Library, 812 Ottawa St., PO Box 602, Keewatin ON P0X 1C0 – 807/547-2145; Fax: 807/547-3145; Symbol: OKEE – CEO, Marceline Chagnon; Children's Librarian, Carolyn Heyens; Technical Services Librarian, Shirley Alcock

Kejick: Iskutewisakaygun #39 Independant First Nation Public Library, Kejick PO, Kejick ON P0X 1E0 – 807/733-3772; Fax: 807/733-3773 – CEO, Vernon Fair

Kejick: Shoal Lake #40 First Nation Public Library, Kejick PO, Kejick ON P0X 1E0 – 807/733-3341; Fax: 807/733-3115 – CEO, Ashley Green

Kemptville Public Library, 207 Prescott St., PO Box 538, Kemptville ON K0G 1J0 – 613/258-5577; Email: suehig@kempville.library.on.ca; Symbol: OKEM – CEO/Librarian, Susan Higgins

Kemptville: South Gower Public Library, PO Box 1734, Kemptville ON K0G 1J0 – 613/258-4711 – Librarian, Michelle Stein

Kenora Public Library, 24 Main St. South, Kenora ON P9N 1S7 – 807/467-2081; Fax: 807/467-2085 – CEO, Erin Roussin

Keswick: Georgina Public Libraries, 130 Gwendolyn Blvd., Keswick ON L4P 3W8 – 905/476-7233; Fax: 905/476-8724; Symbol: OKES – Leisure Services, Director, John McLean – See also following branches: Keswick Branch Library, Pefferlaw Library, Sutton Centennial Library

Keswick Branch Library, 130 Gwendolyn Blvd., Keswick ON L4P 3W8 – 905/476-5762; Fax: 905/476-8724 – Head Librarian, Janice Green – Branch of Georgina Public Libraries

Kilbride Branch Library, 68 Paton Rd., Kilbride ON L0P 1G0 – 905/335-4011; Fax: 905/681-7277 – Branch Head, Sandra Ferris – Branch of Burlington Public Library

Killaloe Public Library, Killaloe ON K0J 2A0 – 613/757-2211; Fax: 613/757-3634; Email: kilpublib@mv.igs.net – Librarian, Marnie MacKay

Killarney: Rutherford & George Island Twp. Public Library, 32 Commissioner St., Killarney ON P0M 2A0 – 705/287-2229 – CEO, Susan Tyson

Kimberley: Euphrasia Twp. Public Library, Main St., Kimberley ON N0C 1G0 – 519/599-2589 – Librarian, E. Brooks

Kincardine Branch Library, 727 Queen St., Kincardine ON N2Z 1Z9 – 519/396-3289; Fax: 519/396-3289 – Branch Supervisor, Ann Munn – Branch of Bruce County Public Library (*see* Port Elgin)

King Twp. Public Library, King Side Rd., PO Box 399, King City ON L7B 1A6 – 905/833-5101; Fax: 905/833-0824; Email: saintej@king.twp.library.on.ca – Chief Librarian, Justin Sainte – See also following branches: Ansnorveldt Branch Library, King City Library, Nobleton Branch Library, Schomberg Library

King City: Ansnorveldt Branch Library, PO Box 399, King City ON L7B 1A6 – 905/775-8717; Fax: 905/775-8717 – Branch Head, Sharon Bentley – Branch of King Twp. Public Library

King City Library, King Side Rd., PO Box 339, King City ON L7B 1A6 – 905/833-5101; Fax: 905/833-0824 – Librarian, Sharon Bentley – Branch of King Twp. Public Library

Kingston: Frontenac County Library, County Court House, Court St., Kingston ON K7L 2N4 – 613/548-8657; Fax: 613/548-8193; Email: mwatkins@frontenac.county.library.on.ca – County Librarian, Marion Watkins; Children's Librarian, Nancy Mohan; Technical Services Librarian, Mary McPhee – See also following branches: Arden Branch Library, Barrie Twp., Cloyne Branch Library, Clarendon Miller Twp., Plevna Branch Library, Howe Island Branch Library, Kingston Twp., Days Rd. Branch Library, Loughborough Twp., Sydenham Branch, Olden Twp., Mountain Grove Branch Library, Oso Twp., Sharbot Lake Branch Library, Palmerston North & South Canonto Twp., Ompah Branch Library, Parham Deposit, Pittsburgh Twp., Barriefield Branch Library, Portland Twp., Hartington Branch Library, Storrington Twp., Sunbury Branch Library, Wolfe Island Twp. - Library

Kingston Public Library, 130 Johnson St., Kingston ON K7L 1X8 – 613/549-8888; Fax: 613/549-8476; Email: jordonl@kingston.library.on.ca – Chief Librarian, Lynne Jordon; Children's Librarian, Mary Beaty; Outreach Contact, Stella Carney; Adult Services Librarian, Deborah Defoe; Technical Services Librarian, Jerome McHenry; Branch Services Librarian, Gail Scala, 613/546-0698; 2582; Systems Contact, Lester Webb – See also following branches: Calvin Park Library, Kingscourt Branch

Kingston: Amherstview Branch Library, 108 Amherst Dr., Kingston ON K7N 1H9 – 613/389-6006; Fax: 613/389-6006 – Branch Head, Anne Taylor – Branch of Lennox & Addington County Library (*see* Napanee)

Kingston: Calvin Park Library, 88 Wright Cres., Kingston ON K7L 4T9 – 613/546-2582 – Chief Librarian, Lynne Jordon – Branch of Kingston Public Library

Kingscourt Branch, 115 Kirkpatrick St., Kingston ON K7K 2P4 – 613/546-0698 – Chief Librarian, Lynne Jordon – Branch of Kingston Public Library

Kingston Twp., Days Rd. Branch Library, 130 Days Rd., Kingston ON K7M 3P8 – 613/389-2616; Fax: 613/389-4372 – Librarian, A. Black – Branch of Frontenac County Library

Kingston: Pittsburgh Twp., Barriefield Branch Library, 414 Regent St., Kingston ON K7K 5R1 – 613/542-8222 – Lorna Grice – Branch of Frontenac County Library

Kingsville Library, 28 Division St. South, Kingsville ON N9Y 1P3 – 519/733-5620 – Supervisor, Maxene Guerrieri – Branch of Essex County Library

Kinmount Branch Library, Kinmount ON K0M 2A0 – 705/488-3199 – Branch Supervisor, Bonnie Wilkins – Branch of Victoria County Public Library (*see* Lindsay)

Kintore Public Library, A.J. Baker School, Kintore ON N0M 2C0 – 519/283-6339 – Supervisor, Gail Kavelman – Branch of Oxford County Library (*see* Woodstock)

Kirkfield: Eldon Twp. Branch Library, Kirkfield ON K0M 2B0 – 705/438-3331 – Branch Supervisor, Jane Davis – Branch of Victoria County Public Library (*see* Lindsay)

Kirkland Lake Office, 11 Station Rd. South, Kirkland Lake ON P2N 3H2 – 705/567-3341; Fax: 705/567-9410; Toll Free: 1-800-461-6348 – Branch of Ontario Library Service North

Kirkland Lake Public Library, 10 Kirkland St. East, Kirkland Lake ON P2N 1P1 – 705/567-7966; Fax: 705/568-6303; Email: teck@nt.net – CEO, Barry Holmes

Kirkland Lake: Teck Centennial Library, 10 Kirkland St. East, Kirkland Lake ON P2N 1P1 – 705/567-7966; Fax: 705/568-6303; Email: teck@nt.net – Chief Librarian, B. Holmes

Kirkton Branch Library, RR#1, Kirkton ON N0K 1K0 – 519/229-8854 – Branch Supervisor, Joan Francis – Branch of Huron County Library (*see* Goderich)

Kitchener Public Library, 85 Queen St. North, Kitchener ON N2H 2H1 – 519/743-0271; Fax: 519/743-1261 – CEO, Margaret Y. Walshe; Reference Librarian, Pam Pembroke Leonard; Circulation Librarian, Ann Wood; Children's Librarian, Maureen Sawa; Public Services Manager, Cathy Matyas; Technology Coordinator, Bryan Dunham; Acquisitions Librarian, Cheryl Kaar; Marketing & Community Relations Manager, Harry Froklage – See also following branches: Forest Heights Community Library, Pioneer Park Community Library, Stanley Park Community Library

Kitchener: Waterloo Regional Library, 150 Frederick St., 2nd Fl., Kitchener ON N2G 4J3 – 519/575-4590; Fax: 519/634-5371; Email: kmanley@wrl.library.on.ca – Director of Library Services, Karin Manley; Public Services Librarian, Katherine Seredynska – See also following branches: Ayr Branch Library, Baden Branch Library, Bloomingdale Branch Library, Elmira Branch Library, Linwood Branch Library, New Dundee Branch Library, New Hamburg Branch Library, St. Clements Branch Library, St. Jacobs Branch Library, Wellesley Branch Library

Kitchener: Forest Heights Community Library, 251 Fischer-Hallman Rd., Kitchener ON N2H 2H1 – 519/743-0271; Fax: 519/743-0644 – Branch Head, Sharron Smith – Branch of Kitchener Public Library

Kitchener: Pioneer Park Community Library, 150 Pioneer Dr., Kitchener ON – 519/748-2740; Fax: 519/748-2740 – Branch Head, Maureen Plomske – Branch of Kitchener Public Library

Kitchener: Stanley Park Community Library, 146 Trafalgar Ave., Kitchener ON N2A 1Z7 – 519/896-1736; Fax: 519/896-1736 – Branch Head, Penny Lynn Fielding – Branch of Kitchener Public Library

Kleinburg Library, 10341 Islington Ave. North, Kleinburg ON L0J 1C0 – 905/893-1248; Fax: 905/893-2736 – Manager, Beryl Hall – Branch of Vaughan Public Libraries (*see* Maple)

Komoka Library, 133 Queen St., Komoka ON N0L 1R0 – 519/657-1461; Fax: 519/657-1461 – Supervisor, June Davis – Branch of Middlesex County Library (*see* Arva)

Lake Temagami: Temagami First Nation Public Library, Bear Island PO, Lake Temagami ON P0H 1C0 – 705/237-8943; Fax: 705/237-8959 – Librarian, Tammy Birtch

Lakefield Public Library, 1 Bridge St., PO Box 2200, Lakefield ON K0L 2H0 – 705/652-8623 – Librarian, J.C. Warren

Lambeth Library, 7112 Beattie St., Lambeth ON N0L 1A0 – 519/652-2951; Fax: 519/663-6396 – Branch Head, Bonnie Symons – Branch of London Public Library

Lanark Village, Lavant, Dalhousie & North Sherbrooke Twp., & Lanark Twp. Union Public Library, 75 George St., Lanark ON K0G 1K0 – 613/259-3068; Symbol: OLAU – Librarian/CEO, Mary Arnoldi; Librarian, Wanda Proulx

Lancaster Branch Library, PO Box 129, Lancaster ON K0C 1N0 – 613/347-2311 – Area Supervisor, Donna Parker – Branch of Stormont, Dundas & Glengarry County Library (*see* Finch)

Lancaster Twp. Branch Library, PO Box 571, Lancaster ON K0C 1N0 – 613/347-1748 – Area Supervisor, Donna Parker – Branch of Stormont, Dundas & Glengarry County Library (*see* Finch)

Lansdowne: Front of Leeds & Lansdowne Public Library, 1B Jessie St., PO Box 210, Lansdowne ON K0E 1L0 – 613/659-3885; Fax: 613/659-4192; Email: ylapoint@lansdowne.library.ca; URL: http://www.mulberry.com/~leedslan/; Symbol: OLAN – CEO, Yolande LaPointe

Larder Lake Public Library, 29 Godfrey St., PO Box 189, Larder Lake ON P0K 1L0 – 705/643-2222; Fax: 705/643-2311; Email: llpublib@ntl.sympatico.ca – Librarian, Virginia Kitty

LaSalle Library, 1301 Front Rd., LaSalle ON N9J 2A9 – 519/734-8111 – Supervisor, Donna Spickett – Branch of Essex County Library

Latchford Public Library, 66 Main St., Latchford ON P0J 1N0 – 705/676-2030 – CEO, Beth Inglis

Leamington Public Library, 1 John St., Leamington ON N8H 1H1 – 519/326-3441; Fax: 519/322-1585; Email: lpl@lccia.net; URL: http://www.lpl.leamington.on.ca; Symbol: OLE – Chief Librarian, Jill Nicholson

Lefaivre: Bibliothèque publique du Canton d'Alfred et Plantagenet, CP 10, Lefaivre ON K0B 1J0 – 613/679-4928 – Directrice générale, Hélène Lavoie

Levack Branch Library, 32 School St., PO Box 560, Levack ON P0M 2C0 – 705/966-2140; Fax: 705/966-0710 – Librarian, Anne Matte – Branch of Lionel Rheaume Public Library (*see* Dowling)

Limoges: Bibliothèque publique de Canton de Cambridge, rue Main, CP 70, Limoges ON K0A 2M0 – 613/443-2310 – Bibliothécaire, Yvette Leduc

Lindsay: Victoria County Public Library, PO Box 9000, Lindsay ON K9V 5R8 – 705/324-9411; Fax: 705/878-1859; Email: vcounty@lindsaycomp.on.ca – County Librarian, Moti Tahiliani – See also following branches: Bobcaygeon Branch Library, Burnt River Branch Library, Cambray Branch Library, Carden Twp. Branch Library, Coboconk Branch Library, Dalton Twp. Branch Library, Downeyville Branch Library, Dunsford Branch Library, Eldon Twp. Branch Library, Fenelon Falls Branch Library, Kinmount Branch Library, Little Britain Branch Library, Manilla Branch Library, Norland Branch Library, Oakwood Branch Library, Omemee Branch Library, Woodville Branch Library

Lindsay: Downeyville Branch Library, RR#5, Lindsay ON K9V 4R5 – 705/799-5265 – Branch Supervisor, Shelley Ferguson – Branch of Victoria County Public Library

Lindsay Public Library, 190 Kent St. West, Lindsay ON K9V 2Y6 – 705/324-5632; Fax: 705/324-7140; Email: MTahilia@FlemingC.on.ca – Librarian, M. Tahiliani

Linwood Branch Library, 38 Adelaide St., Linwood ON N0B 2A0 – 519/698-2700 – Asst. Branch Supervisor, Helen Sagle – Branch of Waterloo Regional Library (*see* Kitchener)

Lion's Head & District Branch Library, PO Box 24, Lions Head ON N0H 1W0 – 519/793-3844 – Branch Supervisor, Jacqui Gardiner – Branch of Bruce County Public Library (*see* Port Elgin)

Listowel Public Library, 260 Main St. West, Listowel ON N4W 1A1 – 519/291-4621; Fax: 519/291-2235 – Chief Librarian, Tom Bentley; Children's Librarian, Gail Clarkson; ILL Librarian, Lorna Wherry

Little Britain Branch Library, Little Britain ON K0M 2C0 – 705/786-2088 – Branch of Victoria County Public Library (*see* Lindsay)

Little Current Public Library, 50 Meredith St., PO Box 790, Little Current ON P0P 1K0 – 705/368-2444 – Librarian, Judith Kift

Little Current: Sucker Creek First Nations Public Library, RR#1, PO Box 21, Little Current ON P0P 1K0 – 705/368-3696; Fax: 705/368-3563 – CEO, Beverly Nahwegahbo

Lively: Walden Public Library, 615 Main St., PO Box 189, Lively ON P3Y 1M3 – 705/692-4749; Fax: 705/692-4261; Email: maggi@cyberbeach.net – CEO/Administrator, Margaret LaFramboise; Children's Librarian, Mary Woboditsch, 705/692-4238; Technical Services Librarian, Lea Ann Hicks – See also following branches: Beaver Lake Branch Library, Naughton Branch Library, Whitefish Branch Library

Lively: Beaver Lake Branch Library, c/o Walden Public Library, PO Box 189, Lively ON P3Y 1M3 – 705/866-2958 – Branch of Walden Public Library

Lochlin: Snowdon Twp., Lochlin Library, Lochlin ON K0M 2G0 – Branch Head, Diane Peacock – Branch of Haliburton County Public Library

Lombardy: South Elmsley Twp. Public Library, Lombardy Public School, RR#1, Lombardy ON K0G 1L0 – 613/283-0860; Fax: 613/284-1523 – CEO, Larry Winters

London Public Library, 305 Queens Ave., London ON N6B 3L7 – 519/661-5100; Fax: 519/663-5396; URL: http://discover.lpl.london.on.ca – CEO, Reed Osborne; Public Services, Director, Margaret Mitchell; Technical Support Services, Director, Beth Cada; Community Relations, Director, Carmen Sprovieri; Lending Services, Coordinator, Nancy Ward; Children's Library, Head, Delilah Deane Cummings – See also following branches: Beacock Branch Library, Byron Memorial Branch Library, Eastwood Centre Branch Library, Fred Landon Branch Library, Glanworth Library, Jalna Branch Library, Lambeth Library, Masonville Branch Library, Northridge Branch Library, Pond Mills Branch Library, Richard E. Crouch Branch Library, Sherwood Forest Branch Library, W.O. Carson Branch Library, Westmount Branch Library, Westown Branch Library

London: Beacock Branch Library, 1280 Huron St., London ON N5Y 1A8 – 519/451-8140; Fax: 519/663-5396 – Branch Head, Frances Huber – Branch of London Public Library

London: Byron Memorial Branch Library, 1295 Commissioners Rd. West, London ON N6K 1C9 – 519/471-4000; Fax: 519/663-5396 – Branch Head, Bonnie Symons – Branch of London Public Library

London: Eastwood Centre Branch Library, Eastwood Centre Plaza, 1920 Dundas St. East, London ON N5V 3P1 – 519/451-7600; Fax: 519/663-5396 – Branch Head, Cheryl Fround – Branch of London Public Library

London: Fred Landon Branch Library, 167 Wortley Rd., London ON N6C 3P6 – 519/439-6240; Fax: 519/663-5396 – Branch Head, Gordon Price – Branch of London Public Library

London: Jalna Branch Library, 1119 Jalna Blvd., London ON N6E 3B3 – 519/685-6465; Fax: 519/663-5396 – Branch Head, Arlene Thompson – Branch of London Public Library

London: Masonville Branch Library, 30 North Centre Rd., London ON N5X 3W1 – 519/660-4646 – Branch Head, Beth Whitney – Branch of London Public Library

London: Northridge Branch Library, 1444 Glenora Dr., London ON N5K 1V2 – 519/439-4331; Fax: 519/663-5396 – Branch Head, Frances Huber – Branch of London Public Library

London: Pond Mills Branch Library, 1166 Commissioners Rd. East, London ON N5Z 4W8 – 519/685-1333; Fax: 519/663-5396 – Branch Head, Judy Shaw – Branch of London Public Library

London: Richard E. Crouch Branch Library, 550 Hamilton Rd., London ON N5Z 1S4 – 519/673-0111; Fax: 519/663-5396 – Branch Head, Regina Patterson – Branch of London Public Library

London: Sherwood Forest Branch Library, Sherwood Forest Mall, 1225 Wonderland Rd. North, London ON N6G 2V9 – 519/473-9965; Fax: 519/663-5396 –

Branch Head, Dianne Knoppert – Branch of London Public Library

London: Westmount Branch Library, 507 Village Green Ave., London ON N6J 4G4 – 519/473-4708; Fax: 519/663-5396 – Acting Branch Head, Judy Shaw – Branch of London Public Library

London: Westown Branch Library, Westown Plaza Mall, 301 Oxford St. West, London ON N6H 1S6 – 519/439-6456; Fax: 519/663-5396 – Branch Head, Sandra Lang – Branch of London Public Library

London: W.O. Carson Branch Library, 465 Quebec St., London ON N5W 3Y4 – 519/438-4287; Fax: 519/663-5396 – Branch Head, Regina Patterson – Branch of London Public Library

Long Sault Branch Library, PO Box 550, Long Sault ON K0C 1P0 – 613/534-2605 – Area Supervisor, Fiona Fraser – Branch of Stormont, Dundas & Glengarry County Library (*see* Finch)

Longlac Public Library, 168 Kenogami St., PO Box 760, Longlac ON P0T 2A0 – 807/876-4515; Fax: 807/876-4886 – Librarian, Carole McLean

Lucan Library, 183 Main St., PO Box 400, Lucan ON N0M 1J0 – 519/227-4682; Fax: 519/227-4682 – Supervisor, Donna Atkinson – Branch of Middlesex County Library (*see* Arva)

Lucknow Library, 526 Campbell St., PO Box 130, Lucknow ON N0G 2H0 – 519/528-3011 – Branch Supervisor, Claudia Baskerville – Branch of Bruce County Public Library (*see* Port Elgin)

Lynden Public Library, Main St., PO Box 9, Lynden ON L0R 1T0 – 519/647-2571; Fax: 519/647-2571 – Branch Head, Cathy Bryden – Branch of Wentworth Libraries (*see* Hamilton)

Lyndhurst Branch Library, Lyndhurst ON K0E 1N0 – 613/928-2277 – Librarian, Viola McMachen – Branch of Rideau Lakes Union Library (*see* Elgin)

Lyn: Lyn Branch Library, PO Box 158, Lyn ON K0E 1M0 – 613/345-0033 – Librarian, Beverley LaBrash – Branch of Elizabethtown Twp. Public Library Board

MacDiarmid: Rocky Bay First Nation Public Library, MacDiarmid ON P0T 2B0 – 807/885-3401; Fax: 807/885-3231 – CEO, Roxanne Kowtiash

Mactier: Georgian Bay Twp. Public Library, High St., Mactier ON P0C 1H0 – 705/375-5430; Fax: 705/375-5430 – Librarian, Marilyn Keall – See also following branches: Honey Harbour Branch Library

Mactier: Moose Deer Point Library, PO Box 136, Mactier ON P0C 1H0 – 705/375-5209; Fax: 705/375-2258 – CEO, Gail Russell

Madawaska Local Services Board Public Library, PO Box 59, Madawaska ON K0J 2C0 – 613/637-5533 – CEO, Pamela Aleck

Madoc Public Library, 20 Davidson St., PO Box 6, Madoc ON K0K 2K0 – 613/473-4456; Email: ssmith@madoc.library.on.ca; Symbol: OMAD – CEO, Susan Smith

Magnetawan Chapman Public Library, PO Box 130, Magnetawan ON P0A 1P0 – 705/387-4411; Fax: 705/387-0102 – CEO, Lisa Gillette-Haig

Mallorytown: Front of Escott Twp. Public Library, 1348 County Rd. 2, RR#2, Mallorytown ON K0E 1R0 – 613/659-3800; Fax: 613/659-3521 – Librarian, Linda Mallory

Mallorytown: Front of Yonge Twp. Public Library, PO Box 250, Mallorytown ON K0E 1R0 – 613/923-2442 – Librarian, Jack Tennant

Malton Branch Library, 3540 Morningstar Dr., Malton ON L4T 1Y2 – 905/677-5878; Fax: 905/677-0547 – Manager, Ingrid Masterson – Branch of Mississauga Library System

Manilla Branch Library, Manilla ON K0M 2J0 – 705/357-2768 – Branch Supervisor, Cathy Hamill – Branch of Victoria County Public Library (*see* Lindsay)

Manitoulin Island: Wikwemikong First Nation Public Library, Wikwemikong Reserve, PO Box 112, Manitoulin Island ON P0P 2J0 – 705/859-2692; Fax: 705/859-3851 – CEO, Sheri Mishibinijima

Manitouwadge Public Library, Community Centre, Manitou Rd., Manitouwadge ON P0T 2C0 – 807/826-3913; Fax: 807/826-4640; Email: library@manitouwadge.ca – Librarian, Sheila Durand, 807/826-4789

Manitowaning: Assiginack Public Library, PO Box 280, Manitowaning ON P0P 1N0 – 705/859-2110; Fax: 705/859-3010 Attn:Library – CEO/Librarian, Debbie Robinson

Manotick: Rideau Twp. Public Library Board, PO Box 430, Manotick ON K4M 1A4 – 613/692-3854; Fax: 613/489-2880 – CEO, Verna Preston – See also following branches: Manotick Branch Library, North Gower Branch Library

Manotick Branch Library, PO Box 430, Manotick ON K4M 1A4 – 613/692-3854; Fax: 613/489-2880 – Branch Librarian, Denise Pedersen – Branch of Rideau Twp. Public Library Board

Maple: Vaughan Public Libraries, 8 Merino Rd., Maple ON L6A 1S9 – 905/832-8515; Fax: 905/832-5207 – CEO, Rosemary Bonanno – See also following branches: Ansley Grove Library, Bathurst Clark Library, Dufferin Clark Library, Kleinburg Library, Maple Library, Woodbridge Library

Maple Library, 10190 Keele St., Maple ON L6A 1S9 – 905/832-2959; Fax: 905/832-4971 – Manager, June Orrell – Branch of Vaughan Public Libraries

Marathon Public Library, PO Box 400, Marathon ON P0T 2E0 – 807/229-0740; Fax: 807/229-3336; Symbol: OMAR – Librarian, Lynn Banks

Marionville Branch Library, 4629, rue Grégoire, PO Box 1141, Marionville ON K4R 1E5 – 613/445-0289 – Branch Head, Francine Dagenais – Branch of Russell Twp. Public Library

Markdale Public Library, 21 Main St. East, PO Box 499, Markdale ON N0C 1H0 – 519/986-3436; Fax: 519/986-4799; Email: bdrum@markdale.library.on.ca – CEO/Acquisitions Librarian, Betty Drummond; ILL Officer, Beth Kennedy

Markham Public Libraries, #100, 445 Apple Creek Blvd., Markham ON L3R 9X7 – 905/513-7977; Fax: 905/513-7984 – CEO, Gina La Force; Deputy CEO, Catherine Biss; Acquisitions Supervisor, Suraj Sharma; Chief Financial Officer, Bert Rajaram; Technical Services Manager, Bob Henderson; Computer Services Manager, Karina Boenders – See also following branches: Markham Community Library, Milliken Mills Community Library, Thornhill Community Centre Library, Thornhill Village Library, Unionville Branch Library

Markham Community Library, 6031 Hwy. 7, Markham ON L3P 3A7 – 905/294-2782; Fax: 905/294-7586 – Branch Manager, Suzanne White – Branch of Markham Public Libraries

Markham: Unionville Branch Library, 15 Library Lane, Markham ON L3R 5C4 – 905/477-2641; Fax: 905/477-8608; Symbol: UB – Branch Manager, Bob Henderson – Branch of Markham Public Libraries

Markstay: Hagar Twp. Public Library, 21 Main St., PO Box 39, Markstay ON P0M 2G0 – 705/853-4536 – Librarian, John Grosshauer

Marmora: Deloro Public Library, RR#2, PO Box 63, Marmora ON K0K 2M0 – 613/472-2172 – Librarian, Bernice Young

Marmora Public Library, 37 Forsythe St., PO Box 340, Marmora ON K0K 2M0 – 613/472-3122; Email: marlib@connect.reach.net; URL: http://www.reach.net/~marlib/; Symbol: MO – Librarian, Sheryl Price; Assistant Librarian, Judy Martin

Massey & Twp. Public Library, 185 Grove St., PO Box 40, Massey ON P0P 1P0 – 705/865-2641; Fax: 705/865-2641; Email: massey@etown.net; Symbol: OMAST – CEO, Lilliane Richer

Massey: Sagamok Anishnawbek Public Library, PO Box 610, Massey ON P0P 1P0 – 705/865-2970; Fax: 705/865-3307 – CEO, Colleen Eshkakogan

Matheson: Black River-Matheson Public Library, 352 - 2 St., PO Box 450, Matheson ON P0K 1N0 – 705/273-2760; Fax: 705/273-2760 – CEO, Linda Lougheed – See also following branches: Ramore Branch

Mattawa Public Library, 362 Main St., PO Box 920, Mattawa ON P0H 1V0 – 705/744-5550; Fax: 705/744-1714 – Contact, Lise Moore Asselin

Mattice-Val Côté Public Library, Hwy. 11, PO Box 129, Mattice ON P0L 1T0 – 705/364-5301; Fax: 705/364-6431; Email: biblimat@nt.net – Librarian, Michelle Salonen

Maxville Branch Library, PO Box 58, Maxville ON K0C 1T0 – 613/527-2235 – Area Supervisor, Darlene McRae – Branch of Stormont, Dundas & Glengarry County Library (*see* Finch)

Maynooth: Bangor Wicklow & McClure & Monteagle Union Public Library, Municipal Bldg., Maynooth ON K0L 2S0 – 613/338-2262 – Librarian, C. Browne

McGregor Library, 9532 Walker Rd., McGregor ON N0R 1J0 – 519/726-6311 – Supervisor, Nancy Brown – Branch of Essex County Library

McKellar Twp. Public Library, PO Box 10, McKellar ON P0G 1C0 – 705/389-2611; Fax: 705/389-2611 – Librarian, Joan Ward

Meaford Public Library, 15 Trowbridge St. West, Meaford ON N4L 1V4 – 519/538-3500; Fax: 519/538-1808 – CEO, Donna Binsted; Children's Librarian, Marion Mower

Melbourne Library, 7 Queen St., Melbourne ON N0L 1T0 – 519/289-2405 – Supervisor, Donna Wolfe – Branch of Middlesex County Library (*see* Arva)

Merlin Branch Library, 13 Aberdeen St., Merlin ON N0P 1W0 – 519/689-4944 – Branch Librarian, Dorian Toll – Branch of Kent County Library (*see* Chatham)

Merrickville Public Library, 111 Main St. East, PO Box 460, Merrickville ON K0G 1N0 – 613/269-3326; Symbol: OMER – Librarian, Mary Kate Laphen

Metcalfe: Osgoode Twp. Public Library Board, PO Box 60, Metcalfe ON K0A 2P0 – 613/821-1330 – See also following branches: Greely Branch Library, Metcalfe Branch Library, Osgoode Branch Library, Vernon Branch Library

Metcalfe Branch Library, 2782 Albert St., PO Box 340, Metcalfe ON K0A 2P0 – 613/821-1330 – Librarian, Shirley Mills – Branch of Osgoode Twp. Public Library Board

Midhurst: Springwater Public Library, 12 Finlay Mill Rd., PO Box 129, Midhurst ON L0L 1X0 – 705/737-5650 – CEO, Lynn Patkau; Technical Services Librarian, Dee-anne Byers – See also following branches: Flos-Elmvale Public Library, Minesing Branch Library

Midhurst: County of Simcoe Library Co-operative, Simcoe County Administration Centre, 1110 Hwy. 26, Midhurst ON L0L 1X0 – 705/726-9300, ext.258; Fax: 705/726-3991; Email: daugust@simcoe.county.library.on.ca; URL: http://www.geocities.com/Athens/Forum/9021/; Symbol: OBAS – CEO, Dianne E. Augustson; Reference Librarian, Gayle Hall

Midland Public Library, 320 King St., Midland ON L4R 3M6 – 705/526-4216; Fax: 705/526-1474 – CEO, Michael V. Saddy; Reference Librarian, Marion Locke; Circulation Librarian, Gail Griffith; Children's Librarian, Bonnie Reynolds; Public Services Librarian, Tina Brophy

Mildmay-Carrick Branch Library, Peter St., PO Box 87, Mildmay ON N0G 2J0 – 519/367-2814 – Branch Supervisor, Pat Markle – Branch of Bruce County Public Library (*see* Port Elgin)

Milford Bay Public Library, Milford Bay Community Centre, General Delivery, Milford Bay ON

P0B 1E0 – 705/764-8912 – Librarian, Nancy Kirkpatrick – Branch of Port Carling Public Library

Milford: South Marysburgh Twp. - Ann Farwell Public Library, King St., Milford ON K0K 2P0 – 613/476-4130 – Librarian, Doris Dance, 613/476-3897

Millbrook: Cavan, Millbrook, South Monaghan Union Library, King St., Millbrook ON L0A 1G0 – 705/932-2919; Fax: 705/932-2595 – See also following branches: Baillieboro Branch Library, Millbrook Public Library, Mount Pleasant Branch Library

Millbrook Public Library, 34 King St. East, Millbrook ON L0G 1G0 – 705/932-2919 – Librarian, Margot Loucks – Branch of Cavan, Millbrook, South Monaghan Union Library

Millgrove Public Library, PO Box 220, Millgrove ON L0R 1V0 – 905/689-6582 – Branch Head, Bev Onufer – Branch of Wentworth Libraries (*see* Hamilton)

Milton Public Library, 45 Bruce St., Milton ON L9T 2L5 – 905/875-2665; Fax: 905/875-4324; Email: fitchl@mpl.on.ca; URL: http://www.hhpl.on.ca/library/mpl/mpl.htm – CEO/Chief Librarian, Leslie Fitch; Information Services, Coordinator, Jane MacDonald; Circulation, Coordinator, Lee Wood; Children's Services Librarian, Janis Marshall; Technical Services Coordinator/Systems Manager, Marjorie Bethune

Milverton Public Library, 27 Main St. South, Milverton ON N0K 1M0 – 519/595-8395; Email: library@perth.net – Librarian, S. Riddell

Mindemoya: Carnarvon Twp. Public Library, King St., PO Box 210, Mindemoya ON P0P 1S0 – 705/377-5334; Fax: 705/377-5585 – Chief Librarian, Claire Taylor Witt – See also following branches: Providence Bay Branch Library

Minden Branch Library, PO Box 157, Minden ON K0M 2K0 – 705/286-2491 – Branch Head, Bev Wood – Branch of Haliburton County Public Library

Mine Centre: Seine River First Nation Public Library, PO Box 129, Mine Centre ON P0W 1H0 – 807/599-2870; Fax: 807/599-2871

Minesing Branch Library, PO Box 131, Minesing ON L0L 1Y0 – 705/722-6440 – Branch Head, Carol Grenier – Branch of Springwater Public Library (*see* Midhurst)

Mississauga Library System, 301 Burnhamthorpe Rd. West, Mississauga ON L5B 3Y3 – 905/615-3500; Fax: 905/615-3625; URL: http://www.city.mississauga.on.ca/library – CEO, Don Mills, 905/615-3601; Public Services, Director, Barbara Quinlan, 905/615-3607; Technical Services, Director, Jenny Lorentowicz, 905/615-3646; Automated Services, Director, Bob Eastman, 905/615-3633 – See also following branches: Burnhamthorpe Branch Library, Clarkson-Lorne Park Branch Library, Erin Mills Branch Library, Lakeview Branch Library, Malton Branch Library, Meadowvale West Branch Library, Mississauga Valley Branch Library, Park Royal Branch Library, Port Credit Branch Library, Sheridan Branch Library, Streetsville Branch Library, Woodlands Branch Library

Mississauga: Burnhamthorpe Branch Library, 1350 Burnhamthorpe Rd. East, Mississauga ON L4Y 3V9 – 905/602-6625; Fax: 905/602-6409 – Manager, Kathy Oakleaf – Branch of Mississauga Library System

Mississauga: Clarkson-Lorne Park Branch Library, 1474 Truscott Dr., Mississauga ON L5J 1Z2 – 905/822-1241; Fax: 905/822-1917 – Manager, Kathy Angus – Branch of Mississauga Library System

Mississauga: Erin Mills Branch Library, 2227 South Millway, Mississauga ON L5L 3R6 – 905/820-5442; Fax: 905/820-6396 – Manager, Ann Jacob – Branch of Mississauga Library System

Mississauga: Lakeview Branch Library, 1110 Atwater Ave., Mississauga ON L5E 1M9 – 905/274-5027; Fax: 905/274-2209 – Manager, Larysa Koshil – Branch of Mississauga Library System

Mississauga: Meadowvale West Branch Library, 6855 Meadowvale Town Centre Circle, Mississauga ON L5N 2Y1 – 905/821-7570; Fax: 905/821-3547 – Manager, Hanne von Bulow – Branch of Mississauga Library System

Mississauga Valley Branch Library, 1275 Mississauga Valley Blvd., Mississauga ON L5A 3R8 – 905/276-6890; Fax: 905/615-3452 – Manager, Patricia Kluge, 905/615-3452 – Branch of Mississauga Library System

Mississauga: Park Royal Branch Library, Park Royal Shopping Plaza, 2425 Truscott Dr., Mississauga ON L5J 2B4 – 905/822-3476; Fax: 905/822-8581 – Manager, Kathy Angus – Branch of Mississauga Library System

Mississauga: Port Credit Branch Library, 20 Lakeshore Rd. East, Mississauga ON L5G 1C8 – 905/278-3437; Fax: 905/278-5099 – Manager, Larysa Koshil – Branch of Mississauga Library System

Mississauga: Sheridan Branch Library, 2225 Erin Mills Pkwy., Mississauga ON L5K 1T9 – 905/823-4106; Fax: 905/823-3499 – Manager, Ann Jacob – Branch of Mississauga Library System

Mississauga: Streetsville Branch Library, 112 Queen St. South, Mississauga ON L5M 1K8 – 905/826-3001; Fax: 905/826-0049 – Manager, Al Stray – Branch of Mississauga Library System

Mississauga: Woodlands Branch Library, 1030 McBride Ave., Mississauga ON L5C 1L6 – 905/275-7087; Fax: 905/615-3453 – Manager, Jo Anne Storen – Branch of Mississauga Library System

Mitchell Public Library, 105 St. Andrew St., Mitchell ON N0K 1N0 – 519/348-9234 – Librarian, C. Shewburg

Mobert: Pic Mobert First Nation Public Library, Mobert ON P0M 2J0 – 807/822-2011; Fax: 807/822-2710 – CEO, Cora-Lee Desmoulin

Monetville: Dokis First Nation Library, Monetville PO, Monetville ON P0M 2K0 – 705/763-2211; Fax: 705/763-2087 – Executive Officer, Wanita Dokis; Librarian, Angeline Dokis

Monkton: Elma Twp. Public Library - Atwood Branch, 218A Main St., Atwood ON N0G 1B0 – 519/356-2455 – Librarian, Martha Bosch

Monkton: Elma Twp. Public Library - Monkton Branch, Winstanley St., Monkton ON N0K 1P0 – 519/347-2703 – Librarian, Ellen Illman

Moonbeam: Bibliothèque publique de Moonbeam, 53 St-Aubin St., CP 370, Moonbeam ON P0L 1V0 – 705/367-2462; Téléc: 705/367-2610; Courrier électronique: bibliomo@ntl.sympatico.ca – Bibliothécaire, Gisèle Belisle

Mooretown Library, General Delivery, Mooretown ON N0N 1M0 – 519/867-2823 – Librarian, Pauline Sheriff – Branch of Lambton County Library (*see* Wyoming)

Moose Creek Branch Library, PO Box 40, Moose Creek ON K0C 1W0 – 613/538-2214 – Area Supervisor, Darlene McRae – Branch of Stormont, Dundas & Glengarry County Library (*see* Finch)

Moosonee Public Library, PO Box 130, Moosonee ON P0L 1Y0 – 705/336-2913; Fax: 705/336-2393 – Librarian, Diana Doxtdator

Morewood Branch Library, PO Box 210, Morewood ON K0A 2R0 – 613/448-3822 – Area Supervisor, Renate True – Branch of Stormont, Dundas & Glengarry County Library (*see* Finch)

Morrisburg Branch Library, PO Box 853, Morrisburg ON K0C 1X0 – 613/543-3384 – Area Supervisor, Elizabeth Porter – Branch of Stormont, Dundas & Glengarry County Library (*see* Finch)

Mount Albert Branch Library, 74 Main St., Mount Albert ON L0G 1M0 – 905/473-2472 – Branch Head, Nina Raponi – Branch of East Gwillimbury Public Library (*see* Holland Landing)

Mount Brydges Library, 23 Bowen St. East, Mount Brydges ON N0L 1W0 – 519/264-1061; Fax: 519/264-1061 – Supervisor, Glenna Smith – Branch of Middlesex County Library (*see* Arva)

Mount Elgin Public Library, Mount Elgin ON N0J 1N0 – 519/485-0134 – Supervisor, Lois Kocsis – Branch of Oxford County Library (*see* Woodstock)

Mount Forest Branch Library, Mount Forest ON N0G 2L0 – 519/323-4541; Fax: 519/846-2066 – Branch Supervisor, Gwynne Smith – Branch of Wellington County Library (*see* Fergus)

Mount Hope Public Library, Mount Hope ON L0R 1W0 – 905/679-6445 – Branch Head, Doris Popper – Branch of Wentworth Libraries (*see* Hamilton)

Mountain Grove: Olden Twp., Mountain Grove Branch Library, Mountain Grove ON K0H 2E0 – 613/335-5360 – Cindy Cox – Branch of Frontenac County Library (*see* Kingston)

Muncey: Chippewas of the Thames Library & Resource Centre, RR#1, Muncey ON N0L 1Y0 – 519/797-2781; Fax: 519/264-2203

Muncey: Munsee Deleware Nation Library Services, RR#1, Muncey ON N0L 1Y0 – 519/289-5396; Fax: 519/289-5156 – Library Coordinator, Candy Thomas

Munster Branch Library, 7749 Bleeks Rd., PO Box 470, Munster ON K0A 3P0 – 613/838-2888 – Librarian, Gail Waters – Branch of Goulbourn Twp. Public Library (*see* Stittsville)

Murillo: Oliver Twp. Public Library, PO Box 26, Murillo ON P0T 2G0 – 807/935-2729; Fax: 807/935-2161 – Librarian, Maxine McCulloch

Nakina Public Library, North St., PO Box 300, Nakina ON P0T 2H0 – 807/329-5906 – Chairman, Jean McHarg; Librarian, Marlene Dowhaniuk

Napanee: Lennox & Addington County Library, 37 Dundas St. West, Napanee ON K7R 1Z5 – 613/354-2585; Fax: 613/354-7527 – Manager, Mary Anne Evans – See also following branches: Amherstview Branch Library, Bath Branch Library, Camden East Branch, Enterprise Branch Library, Napanee Public Library, Newburgh Branch Library, Odessa Branch Library, Sandhurst Branch Library, Stella Branch Library, Tamworth Branch Library, Yarker Branch Library

Napanee Public Library, 37 Dundas St. West, Napanee ON K7R 1Z5 – 613/354-2525 – Branch Head, Jane Vanderzande – Branch of Lennox & Addington County Library

Naughton Branch Library, PO Box 121, Naughton ON P0M 2M0 – 705/692-3177 – Branch Head, Petrina Lawrie – Branch of Walden Public Library (*see* Lively)

Naughton: Whitefish Lake First Nation Public Library, PO Box 39, Naughton ON P0M 2M0 – 705/692-9618; Fax: 705/692-5010 – CEO, Connie Brideau

Navan: Cumberland Public Library, 1246 Colonial Rd., PO Box 239, Navan ON K4B 1J4 – 613/835-2665; Fax: 613/835-3677; Email: lindacap@cumberland.canton.library.on.ca – CEO, L. Caporicci; Public Services Librarian, Inta Douglas – See also following branch: Sir Wilfrid Laurier Branch Library

Nepean Public Library, Nepean Civic Square, 101 Centrepointe Dr., Nepean ON K2G 5K7 – 613/727-6637; Fax: 613/727-6677; Email: at058@freenet.carleton.ca; URL: http://www.library.nepean.on.ca – Executive Director, George Skarzynski; Reference Librarian, Peter Loades, 613/727-6659; Circulation Librarian, Ann Marie Madhosingh, 613/727-6660; Children's Librarian, Frank Dimech, 613/727-6649; Coordinator, Community Library Services, Sylvia Teasdale, 613/727-6646; Technical Services Librarian, Catherine Barrette, 613/825-7704; Acquisitions Librarian, Fay Foster, 613/727-6647; Coordinator, Automated & Technical Services, Doris Rankin, 613/727-6647 –

See also following branches: Centennial Branch Library, Emerald Plaza Branch Library, Nepean Central Library, Ruth E. Dickinson Branch Library

Nepean: Centennial Branch Library, 3870 Richmond Rd., Nepean ON K2H 5C4 – 613/828-5142; Fax: 613/828-0515; Symbol: ONCB – Branch Library Manager, Linda Daly – Branch of Nepean Public Library

Nepean: Emerald Plaza Branch Library, 1547 Merivale Rd., Nepean ON K2G 4V3 – 613/224-7874; Fax: 613/224-7876 – Branch Library Manager, Josephine Norton – Branch of Nepean Public Library

Nepean Central Library, 101 Centrepointe Dr., Nepean ON K2G 5K7 – 613/727-6646; Fax: 613/727-6677 – Coordinator, Linda Ward – Branch of Nepean Public Library

Nepean: Ruth E. Dickinson Branch Library, Walter Baker Sports Centre, 100 Malvern Dr., Nepean ON K2J 2G5 – 613/825-3508; Fax: 613/825-3500 – Branch Library Manager, Deborah Dearham – Branch of Nepean Public Library

Nephton: Belmont & Methuen Twp. Public Library, PO Box 10, Havelock ON K0L 1Z0 – 705/778-2721; Fax: 705/778-5248 – CEO, Sandra Harris

Neustadt Public Library, 411 Mill St., Neustadt ON N0G 2M0 – 519/799-5830 – Librarian, Merelda Lantz

New Dundee Branch Library, 136 Main St., New Dundee ON N0B 2E0 – 519/696-3041 – Asst. Branch Supervisor, Lynn Weiss – Branch of Waterloo Regional Library (*see* Kitchener)

New Hamburg Branch Library, 145 Huron St. South, PO Box 179, New Hamburg ON N0B 2G0 – 519/662-1112 – Branch Supervisor, Yvonne Zyma-Stark – Branch of Waterloo Regional Library (*see* Kitchener)

New Liskeard Public Library, Whitewood Ave., PO Box 668, New Liskeard ON P0J 1P0 – 705/647-4215; Fax: 705/647-3199 – CEO, Carla Drury

New Lowell: Sunnidale Branch, General Delivery, New Lowell ON L0M 1N0 – 705/424-6288; Fax: 705/424-6288; Symbol: SU – Branch Head, M. Joyce Smith – Branch of Clearview Public Library (*see* Staynor)

Newburgh Branch Library, PO Box 40, Newburgh ON K0K 2S0 – 613/378-2556 – Supervisor, Rika Blakslee – Branch of Lennox & Addington County Library (*see* Napanee)

Newbury Library, Newbury ON N0L 1Z0 – 519/693-4275 – Supervisor, Sandra Carnegie – Branch of Middlesex County Library (*see* Arva)

Newcastle Village Branch Library, 50 Mill St. North, Newcastle ON L0A 1H0 – 905/987-4844 – Branch Supervisor, Andrea MacDonald – Branch of Clarington Public Library

Newmarket Public Library, 438 Park Ave., Newmarket ON L3Y 1W1 – 905/895-5196; Fax: 905/895-7798; Email: lol@god.on.ca; Symbol: ONE – CEO, Pat Wilson; Adult Services Librarian, Marcia Watt; Circulation, Head, Linda Peppiatt; Children's Services, Head, Marilyn Read-Stark, 905/895-9056; Adult Services, Head, Judith Bealkowski; Library Systems Librarian, Stephen Whelan; Children's Services Librarian, Wendy Zwaal, 905/895-9056; Audio-Visual Services, Head, Karen Mark, 905/895-5728; Administrative Assistant, Anne Dixon

Niagara Falls Public Library, 4848 Victoria Ave., Niagara Falls ON L2E 4C5 – 905/356-8080; Fax: 905/356-7004; Email: nfpl@freenet.niagara.com – Chief Librarian, Joe Longo; Head of Reference & Information Services, Andrew Porteus; Head of Circulation, Connie Dick; Children's Librarian, Colleen Lambert; Public Services Librarian, Claire Beckermann – See also following branches: Chippawa Branch Library, Stamford Centre Branch Library

Niagara Falls: Chippawa Branch Library, 3763 Main St., Niagara Falls ON L2G 6B3 – 905/295-4391 – Branch Head, Mary Joselin – Branch of Niagara Falls Public Library

Niagara Falls: Stamford Centre Branch Library, Town & Country Plaza, 3643 Portage Rd. North, Niagara Falls ON L2J 2K8 – 905/357-0410 – Branch Head, Margaret Ramsay – Branch of Niagara Falls Public Library

Niagara on the Lake Public Library, PO Box 430, Niagara on the Lake ON L0S 1J0 – 905/468-2023; Fax: 905/468-3334; Email: gmolsonl@freenet.niagara.com; Symbol: NL – CEO, Gerda Molson; Children's Librarian, Gerrie Barnim; Technical Services Librarian, Linda Potter

Nipigon Public Library, 25 Third St., PO Box 728, Nipigon ON P0T 2J0 – 807/887-3142; Fax: 807/887-3142; Email: niplib@nipigon.lakeheadu.ca; URL: http://nipigon.lakeheadu.ca/~niplib/nnpl.html – Librarian/CEO, Karrie Matheson

Nobel: Shawanaga First Nation Public Library, RR#1, Nobel ON P0G 1G0 – 705/366-2526; Fax: 705/366-2740 – CEO, Karen Pawis

Nobleton Branch Library, Sheardown Dr., PO Box 670, Nobleton ON L0G 1N0 – 905/859-4188; Fax: 905/859-4188 – Librarian, Mary Oram – Branch of King Twp. Public Library

Noelville: Cosby, Mason & Martland Twp. Public Library, PO Box 130, Noelville ON P0M 2N0 – 705/898-2965; Fax: 705/898-3481; Email: biblicmm@isys.ca – CEO, Colette Prévost

Norland Branch Library, Norland ON K0M 2L0 – 705/454-8552; Email: norlib@knet.flemingc.on.ca – Branch Supervisor, Grace Graham – Branch of Victoria County Public Library (*see* Lindsay)

North Bay Public Library, 271 Worthington St. East, North Bay ON P1B 1H1 – 705/474-4830; Fax: 705/495-4010; Email: library@onlink.net; URL: http://www.city.north-bay.on.ca/library/nbplinfo.htm; Symbol: VGNX – CEO, Paul Walker; Systems, Reference & AV Librarian, Donna Bourne-Tyson, 705/474-3332; Children's Librarian, Nora Elliott; Adult Services Librarian, Judith Bouman; French Services, Robert Boisvert

North Gower Branch Library, Main St., PO Box 280, North Gower ON K0A 2T0 – 613/489-3909; Fax: 613/489-2880 – Branch Librarian, Karen Craig – Branch of Rideau Twp. Public Library Board (*see* Manotick)

North York Public Library, 5120 Yonge St., North York ON M2N 5N9 – 416/395-5500; Fax: 416/395-5542; Email: khuntley@nypl.north-york.on.ca; URL: http://www.nypl.north-york.on.ca – CEO, Josephine Bryant, Email: jbryant@nypl.toronto.on.ca; Deputy CEO, Linda Mackenzie, Email: lmackenz@nypl.toronto.on.ca; Information Technology, Director, Jane Pyper, Email: gthomson@nypl.toronto.on.ca; Administrative Services, Director, Sid Mowder, Email: smowder@nypl.toronto.on.ca; Public Relations & Planning, Manager, Kim Huntley, 416/395-5511; Public Services, Director, Vickery Bowles, Email: vbowles@nypl.toronto.on.ca – See also following branches: Amesbury Park Community Branch, Armour Heights Community Branch, Barbara Frum Library, Bayview Community Branch, Black Creek Community Branch, Brookbanks Community Branch, Centennial Community Branch, Central Library, Don Mills Regional Branch, Downsview Regional Branch, Fairview Regional Branch, Flemingdon Park Community Branch, Hillcrest Community Branch, Humber Summit Community Branch, Jane/Sheppard Community Branch, Pleasant View Community Branch, Victoria Village Community Branch, Woodview Park Community Branch, York Woods Regional Branch Library

North York: Amesbury Park Community Branch, 1565 Lawrence Ave. West, North York ON M6L 1A8 – 416/395-5420; Fax: 416/395-5432 – Branch of North York Public Library

North York: Armour Heights Community Branch, 2140 Avenue Rd., North York ON M5M 4M7 – 416/395-5430; Fax: 416/395-5433 – Branch of North York Public Library

North York: Barbara Frum Library, 20 Covington Rd., North York ON M6A 3C1 – 416/395-5440; Fax: 416/395-5447 – Branch of North York Public Library

North York: Bayview Community Branch, Bayview Village Shopping Centre, 2901 Bayview Ave., North York ON M2K 1E6 – 416/395-5460; Fax: 416/395-5434 – Branch of North York Public Library

North York: Black Creek Community Branch, 2141 Jane St., North York ON M3M 1A2 – 416/395-5470; Fax: 416/395-5435 – Branch of North York Public Library

North York: Brookbanks Community Branch, 210 Brookbanks Dr., North York ON M3A 2T8 – 416/395-5480; Fax: 416/395-5436 – Branch of North York Public Library

North York: Centennial Community Branch, 578 Finch Ave. West, North York ON M2R 1N7 – 416/395-5490; Fax: 416/395-5437 – Branch of North York Public Library

North York: Central Library, 5120 Yonge St., North York ON M2N 5N9 – 416/395-5700; Fax: 416/395-5668 – Branch of North York Public Library

North York: Don Mills Regional Branch, 888 Lawrence Ave. East, North York ON M3C 1P6 – 416/395-5710; Fax: 416/395-5715 – Branch of North York Public Library

North York: Downsview Regional Branch, 2793 Keele St., North York ON M3M 2G3 – 416/395-5720; Fax: 416/395-5727 – Branch of North York Public Library

North York: Fairview Regional Branch, 35 Fairview Mall Dr., North York ON M2J 4S4 – 416/395-5750; Fax: 416/395-5756 – Branch of North York Public Library

North York: Flemingdon Park Community Branch, 29 St. Dennis Dr., North York ON M3C 3J3 – 416/395-5820; Fax: 416/395-5438 – Branch of North York Public Library

North York: Hillcrest Community Branch, 5801 Leslie St., North York ON M2H 1J8 – 416/395-5830; Fax: 416/395-5439 – Branch of North York Public Library

North York: Humber Summit Community Branch, 2990 Islington Ave., North York ON M9L 2K6 – 416/395-5840; Fax: 416/395-5426 – Branch of North York Public Library

North York: Jane/Sheppard Community Branch, Jane Sheppard Mall, #11, 2721 Jane St., North York ON M3L 1S3 – 416/395-5966; Fax: 416/395-5427 – Branch of North York Public Library

North York: Pleasant View Community Branch, 575 Van Horne Ave., North York ON M2J 4S8 – 416/395-5940; Fax: 416/395-5419 – Branch of North York Public Library

North York: Victoria Village Community Branch, 184 Sloane Ave., North York ON M4A 2C4 – 416/395-5950; Fax: 416/395-5418 – Branch of North York Public Library

North York: Woodview Park Community Branch, 16-18 Bradstock Rd., North York ON M9M 1M8 – 416/395-5960; Fax: 416/395-5417 – Branch of North York Public Library

North York: York Woods Regional Branch Library, 1785 Finch Ave. West, North York ON M3N 1M6 – 416/395-5980; Fax: 416/395-5991 – Branch of North York Public Library

Norwich Public Library, 21 Stover St. North, Norwich ON N0J 1P0 – 519/863-3307 – Supervisor, Maureen Baker-Wilkinson – Branch of Oxford County Library (*see* Woodstock)

Norwood Public Library, 60 Colborne St., PO Box 100, Norwood ON K0L 2V0 – 705/639-2228 – CEO, Mabel Dornan

Oakville Public Library, 120 Navy St., Oakville ON L6J 2Z4 – 905/815-2042; Fax: 905/815-2024; Email: jamese@haltonbc.on.ca; URL: http://www.hhpl.on.ca/library/opl/opl.htm – Director, Eleanor James; Deputy Director, Edith Hopkins; Reference Librarian, Florence de Dominicis; Circulation Librarian, Jane Diamanti; Children's Librarian, Daria Sharanewych; Technical Services Manager, Brian Bell; Acquisitions Supervisor, Janet Whaley; Marketing & Development, Pam Sadler – See also following branches: Glen Abbey Branch Library, White Oaks Branch Library, Woodside Branch Library

Oakville: Glen Abbey Branch Library, 1415 Third Line, Oakville ON L6M 3G2 – 905/815-2039; Fax: 905/815-5978; Email: cravens@haltonbc.on.ca – Branch Head, Suzanne Craven – Branch of Oakville Public Library

Oakville: White Oaks Branch Library, 1070 McCraney St. East, Oakville ON L6H 2R6 – 905/815-2038; Fax: 905/815-2024; Email: kullasj@haltonbc.on.ca – Branch Head, Janice Kullas – Branch of Oakville Public Library

Oakville: Woodside Branch Library, 1274 Rebecca St., Oakville ON L6L 1Z2 – 905/815-2036; Fax: 905/815-5954; Email: mazzak@haltonbc.on.ca – Branch Head, Kathryn Mazza – Branch of Oakville Public Library

Oakwood Branch Library, Oakwood ON K0M 2M0 – 705/953-9060; Email: oaklib@knet.flemingc.on.ca – Branch Supervisor, Ruth Teel – Branch of Victoria County Public Library (*see* Lindsay)

Odessa Branch Library, PO Box 250, Odessa ON K0H 2H0 – 613/386-3981 – Supervisor, Mary Lou Fraser – Branch of Lennox & Addington County Library (*see* Napanee)

Ohsweken: Six Nations Public Library, PO Box 149, Ohsweken ON N0A 1M0 – 519/445-2954 – Librarian, Diana Doxtdator

Oil Springs Library, 4596 Oil Springs Line, PO Box 126, Oil Springs ON N0N 1P0 – 519/834-2670 – Librarian, Nancy Byers – Branch of Lambton County Library (*see* Wyoming)

Omemee Branch Library, Coronation Hall, Omemee ON K0L 2W0 – 705/799-5711 – Branch Supervisor, Bev McQuade – Branch of Victoria County Public Library (*see* Lindsay)

Ompah: Palmerston North & South Canonto Twp., Ompah Branch Library, Ompah ON K0H 2J0 – 613/479-2281 – Heather White – Branch of Frontenac County Library (*see* Kingston)

Onaping: Earle Jarvis Public Library, PO Box 160, Onaping ON P0M 2R0 – 705/966-2740; Fax: 705/966-0711 – Librarian, Marilyn Knoll – Branch of Lionel Rheaume Public Library (*see* Dowling)

Orangeville Public Library, One Mill St., Orangeville ON L9W 2M2 – 519/941-0610; Fax: 519/941-4698 – CEO, Janice Hindley; Children's Librarian, Lesley McGill; Public Services Librarian, Olive Vousden; Technical Services Librarian, Janet Scheibler

Orillia: Atherley Branch Library, RR#7, Orillia ON L3V 6H7 – 705/325-5776 – Librarian, Louise Duncan – Branch of Mara Twp. Public Library

Orillia Public Library, 36 Mississaga St. West, Orillia ON L3V 3A6 – 705/325-2338; Fax: 705/327-1744; Email: gward@orillia.library.on.ca; Symbol: OORI – Children's & AV Services, Director, Suzanne Campbell; Technical Services, Director, David Rowe; Information Services, Director, Lynne Gibbon

Orleans: Sir Wilfrid Laurier Branch Library, 1515 Tenth Line, Orleans ON K1E 3E8 – 613/830-5422; Fax: 613/834-4511 – Public Services Librarian, I. Douglas – Branch of Cumberland Public Library (*see* Navan)

Orono: Clarke Branch Library, 127 Church St., Orono ON L0B 1M0 – 905/983-5507 – Branch Supervisor, Andrea MacDonald – Branch of Clarington Public Library

Osgoode Branch Library, 5630 Main St., PO Box 459, Osgoode ON K0A 2W0 – 613/826-2227 – Librarian, Brenda Porteous – Branch of Osgoode Twp. Public Library Board (*see* Metcalfe)

Oshawa Public Library, McLaughlin Bldg., 65 Bagot St., Oshawa ON L1H 1N2 – 905/579-6111; Fax: 905/433-8107 – CEO, Jana S. Schuelke; Children's Services, Head, Dinah E.W. Gough; Adult Services, Head, Richard Ficek; Technical Services, Head, Anne Donnellan; Automated Systems, Manager, Ian J. Heckford – See also following branches: Jess Hann Library, McLaughlin Library, Northview Branch Library

Oshawa: Jess Hann Library, Lake Vista Sq., 199 Wentworth St. West, Oshawa ON L1J 6P4 – 905/728-2441 – Branch Head, Leslie Winston – Branch of Oshawa Public Library

Oshawa: McLaughlin Library, 65 Bagot St., Oshawa ON L1H 1N2 – 905/579-6111; Fax: 905/433-8107; Email: jschuelk@idirect.com – Librarian, Jana S. Schuelke – Branch of Oshawa Public Library

Oshawa: Northview Branch Library, 250 Beatrice St. East, Oshawa ON L1G 7T6 – 905/576-6040 – Branch Head, Kim Pircher – Branch of Oshawa Public Library

Ottawa Public Library, 120 Metcalfe St., Ottawa ON K1P 5M2 – 613/236-0301; Fax: 613/567-4013; URL: http://www.opl.ottawa.on.ca; Symbol: OOC – Chief Librarian, Barbara Clubb; Acting Reference Librarian, Lesley Hoermann; Circulation, Valerie Dodge; Children's Librarian, Barbara Herd; Adult Services Librarian, Fernande Arcand; Technical Services Librarian, Karen Smith; Acquisitions, Anna Dooley; Automated Services Librarian, Linnie Kalloo; Financial Services, Jean Martel – See also following branches: Alta Vista Library, Carlingwood Branch Library, Elmvale Acres Library, Rideau Branch Library, South Branch Library & Mobile Service, St. Laurent Library, West Branch Library

Ottawa: Alta Vista Library, 2516 Alta Vista Dr., Ottawa ON K1V 7T1 – 613/598-4012; Fax: 613/737-4355; Email: lavoiem@opl.ottawa.on.ca – Librarian, Monique Lavoie – Branch of Ottawa Public Library

Ottawa: Carlingwood Branch Library, 281 Woodroffe Ave., Ottawa ON K2A 3W4 – 613/598-4013; Fax: 613/725-2677; Email: claenera@opl.ottawa.on.ca – Acting Head, Anne Claener – Branch of Ottawa Public Library

Ottawa: Elmvale Acres Library, 1910 St. Laurent Blvd., Ottawa ON K1G 1A4 – 613/598-4014; Fax: 613/738-7534; Email: murphyg@opl.ottawa.on.ca – Librarian, Gale Hamilton-Murphy – Branch of Ottawa Public Library

Ottawa: Rideau Branch Library, 377 Rideau St., Ottawa ON K1N 5Y6 – 613/598-4015; Fax: 613/241-0358; Email: moniqued@opl.ottawa.on.ca – Librarian, Monique E. Désormeaux – Branch of Ottawa Public Library

Ottawa: Rockcliffe Park Public Library, 350 Springfield Rd., Ottawa ON K1M 0K7 – 613/745-2562; Fax: 613/749-0127 – Librarian, Barbara Mirsky

Ottawa: St. Laurent Library, 515 Côté St., Ottawa ON K1K 3A7 – 613/598-4016; Fax: 613/748-3546; Email: mattes@opl.ottawa.on.ca – Librarian, Suzanne Matte – Branch of Ottawa Public Library

Ottawa: South Branch Library & Mobile Service, 1049 Bank St., Ottawa ON K1S 3W9 – 613/598-4017; Fax: 613/521-4323; Email: hillmanm@opl.ottawa.on.ca – Head, Missy Hillman – Branch of Ottawa Public Library

Ottawa: Southern Ontario Library Service - Ottawa, #310, 1900 City Park Dr., Ottawa ON K1J 1A3 – 613/742-0707; Français: 613/742-5640; Fax: 613/742-0712; URL: http://www.sols.on.ca; Symbol: OOEO

Ottawa: West Branch Library, 18 Rosemount Ave., Ottawa ON K1Y 1P4 – 613/598-4018; Fax: 613/729-7945; Email: wellerj@opl.ottawa.on.ca – Librarian, Joan Weller – Branch of Ottawa Public Library

Otterville Public Library, North St., Otterville ON N0J 1R0 – 519/879-6984 – Supervisor, Lurene McMullen – Branch of Oxford County Library (*see* Woodstock)

Owen Sound & North Grey Union Public Library, 824 - 1 Ave. West., Owen Sound ON N4K 4K4 – 519/376-6623; Fax: 519/376-7170; Email: aarmitag@owensound.library.on.ca – Library Director, Andrew D. Armitage; Assistant Library Director, Judy Beth Armstrong

Oxford Mills Library, Oxford Mills ON K0G 1S0 – 613/258-5040 – Librarian, Elaine Landry – Branch of Oxford-on-Rideau Twp. Public Library (*see* Burritt's Rapids)

Paisley Branch Library, 274 Queen St., PO Box 219, Paisley ON N0G 2N0 – 519/353-7225 – Branch Supervisor, Cheryl Parker – Branch of Bruce County Public Library (*see* Port Elgin)

Pakenham Public Library, PO Box 250, Pakenham ON K0A 2X0 – 613/624-5306; Fax: 613/624-5646; Email: pakenham@ott.igs.net – CEO, Mary Ellen Jack

Palmerston Branch Library, 265 Bell St., PO Box 340, Palmerston ON N0G 2P0 – 519/343-2142; Fax: 519/846-2066 – Branch Supervisor, Barbara Burrows – Branch of Wellington County Library (*see* Fergus)

Parham Deposit, Long Lake Rd., RR#1, Parham ON K0H 2K0 – Glenda Young – Branch of Frontenac County Library (*see* Kingston)

Paris Public Library, 12 William St., Paris ON N3L 1K7 – 519/442-2433; Fax: 519/442-7582 – Librarian, Werner Mueller

Parkhill Library, 233 Main St., Parkhill ON N0M 2K0 – 519/294-6583; Fax: 519/294-6583 – Supervisor, Karen Woods – Branch of Middlesex County Library (*see* Arva)

Parry Sound: Christie Twp. Public Library, RR#3, Parry Sound ON P2A 2W9 – 705/732-2850; Fax: 705/732-1467 – CEO/Librarian, Liana Bradley

Parry Sound: Humphrey Twp. Public Library, RR#2, Parry Sound ON P2A 2W8 – 705/732-4526 – Librarian, Patricia Coles

Parry Sound Public Library, 29 Mary St., Parry Sound ON P2A 1E3 – 705/746-9601; Fax: 705/746-9601; Email: pslib@zeuter.com – Librarian, Laurine Tremaine

Parry Sound: Wasauksing First Nation Public Library, PO Box 253, Parry Sound ON P2A 2X3 – 705/746-2531; Fax: 705/746-5984 – CEO, Carol M. Pegahmagabow

Pawitik: Whitefish Bay First Nation Public Library, c/o BaiBomBeh Anishinabe School, Pawitik ON P0X 1L0 – 807/226-5698; Fax: 807/226-1089 – CEO, Helen Wesley

Pefferlaw Library, PO Box 220, Pefferlaw ON L0E 1N0 – 705/437-1514 – Branch Head, Mary Reddings – Branch of Georgina Public Libraries (*see* Keswick)

Pelee Island Public Library, West Shore Rd., Pelee Island ON N0R 1M0 – 519/724-2028 – Librarian, Debbie Crawford

Pembroke Public Library, 237 Victoria St., Pembroke ON K8A 4K5 – 613/732-8844; Fax: 613/732-1116; Email: pemlib@fox.nstn.ca; URL: http://www.valleynet.on.ca/Education/Libraries/pemlib.html; Symbol: OPEM – CEO/Chief Librarian, Subhash Mehta; Children's Librarian, Anne Irvine

Penetanguishene Public Library, 24 Simcoe St., Penetanguishene ON L9M 1R6 – 705/549-7164; Fax: 705/549-3932; Email: marchand@barint.on.ca – CEO, Rosemary Marchand

Perth & District Union Public Library, 30 Herriott St., Perth ON K7H 1T2 – 613/267-1224; Fax: 613/267-7899 – Librarian, Faye Cunningham; Children's Librarian, Susan Snyder

Petawawa Village & Twp. Union Public Library, 16 Civic Centre Rd., Petawawa ON K8H 3H5 – 613/687-2227; Fax: 613/687-2527 – Chief Librarian, Jean Risto; Children's Librarian, Carol Goldsmith; Audio-Visual Librarian, Janet Coulas; Languages & Special Collections, Barbara Collmorgen; Memberships & Statistics, Brenda Meighan; Displays & Special Programs, Judy O'Reilly

Peterborough Public Library, 345 Aylmer St. North, Peterborough ON K9H 3V7 – 705/745-5382; Fax: 705/743-8958 – Culture & Heritage Division, Community Services, Manager, Ken Doherty; Head Librarian/Systems Administrator, Becky Rogers; Reference Librarian, Jim Pendergest; Circulation Supervisor, Glenda Underwood; Acquisitions Librarian, Cara Peterman; Children's Librarian, Laurie Woollard; Technical Services Librarian, Ruth Whelham-Umphrey – See also following branches: De La Fosse Library

Peterborough: De La Fosse Library, 729 Park St. South, Peterborough ON K9J 3T3 – 705/745-8653 – Jan Ball – Branch of Peterborough Public Library

Petrolia Library, 4200 Petrolia St., PO Box 70, Petrolia ON N0N 1R0 – 519/882-0771 – Librarian, Shirley Banks – Branch of Lambton County Library

Pickerel: Henvey Inlet First Nation Public Library, Pickerel ON P0G 1J0 – 705/857-2331 – CEO, Fern Panamick

Pickering Public Library, One, The Esplanade, PO Box 368, Pickering ON L1V 2R6 – 905/831-6265; Fax: 905/831-8795; Email: lindal@picnet.org – CEO, Alexander Cameron; Deputy CEO, Valerie Ridgeway; Systems & Technical Services, Head, Elaine Bird; Adult Services Coordinator, Linda Linton; Children's Coordinator, Kathy Williams – See also following branches: Bay Ridges Branch Library, Central Library, Claremont Branch Library, Greenwood Branch Library, Rouge Hill Branch Library, Whitevale Branch Library

Pickering: Bay Ridges Branch Library, PO Box 368, Pickering ON L1V 2R6 – 905/839-3083 – Branch of Pickering Public Library

Pickering: Central Library, One The Esplanade South, Pickering ON L1V 6K7 – 905/831-6265; Fax: 905/831-8795 – Branch of Pickering Public Library

Pickering: Claremont Branch Library, PO Box 368, Pickering ON L1V 2R6 – 905/649-3341 – Branch of Pickering Public Library

Pickering: Greenwood Branch Library, PO Box 368, Pickering ON L1V 2R6 – 905/683-8844 – Branch of Pickering Public Library

Pickering: Rouge Hill Branch Library, PO Box 368, Pickering ON L1V 2R6 – 905/509-2579 – Branch of Pickering Public Library

Pickering: Whitevale Branch Library, PO Box 368, Pickering ON L1V 2R6 – 905/294-0967 – Branch of Pickering Public Library

Pickle Lake: Fort Hope First Nation Public Library, John C. Yesno Education Centre, Eabemet Lake, Pickle Lake ON P0T 1L0 – 807/242-8421; Fax: 807/242-1592 – Librarian, Lucy Slipperjack

Picton Public Library, Main St., PO Box 260, Picton ON K0K 2T0 – 613/476-5962; Fax: 613/476-3325 – Librarian, Valerie Creasy; Children's Librarian, Marie Dawson

Plattsville Public Library, PO Box 40, Plattsville ON N0J 1S0 – 519/684-7390 – Supervisor, Kathy Hofstetter – Branch of Oxford County Library (*see* Woodstock)

Plevna: Clarendon Miller Twp., Plevna Branch Library, Plevna ON K0H 2M0 – 613/479-2542 – Heather White – Branch of Frontenac County Library (*see* Kingston)

Point Edward Library, 220 Michigan Ave., Point Edward ON N7V 1E8 – 519/336-3291 – Librarian, Margaret Scott – Branch of Lambton County Library

Port Burwell Library, PO Box 189, Port Burwell ON N0J 1T0 – 519/874-4754; Symbol: PR – Supervisor, Doris Van Den Eeckhout – Branch of Elgin County Library (*see* St. Thomas)

Port Carling Public Library, Port Community Centre, PO Box 189, Port Carling ON P0B 1J0 – 705/765-5650 – Librarian, Elizabeth H. Glen, 705/765-5392 – See also following branches: Bala Public Library, Milford Bay Public Library, Muskoka Lakes Twp. Public Library Board, Ullswater Public Library, Walker's Point Public Library

Port Carling: Muskoka Lakes Twp. Public Library Board, PO Box 189, Port Carling ON P0B 1J0 – 705/765-5650 – CEO, Elizabeth H. Glen – Branch of Port Carling Public Library

Port Colborne Public Library, 310 King St., Port Colborne ON L3K 4H1 – 905/834-6512; Fax: 905/835-5775 – CEO, Cecil Vincent; Director of Library Services, Jennifer Parry

Port Dover Branch Library, 413 Main St., Port Dover ON N0A 1N0 – 519/583-0622 – Branch Librarian, Betty Lee – Branch of Nanticoke Public Library Board (*see* Jarvis)

Port Elgin: Bruce County Public Library, 1243 Mackenzie Rd., Port Elgin ON N0H 2C2 – 519/832-6935; Fax: 519/832-9000 – Director, Marzio Apolloni; Reference Librarian, Shirley Morningstar – See also following branches: Cargill Branch Library, Chesley Branch Library, Hepworth Branch Library, Kincardine Branch Library, Lion's Head & District Branch Library, Lucknow Library, Mildmay-Carrick Branch Library, Paisley Branch Library, Port Elgin Branch Library, Ripley Branch Library, Sauble Beach Branch Library, Southampton Branch Public Library, Tara Branch Library, Teeswater Branch Library, Tiverton Branch Library, Tobermory Branch Library, Walkerton Branch Library, Wiarton Branch Library

Port Elgin Branch Library, Goderich St., PO Box 609, Port Elgin ON N0H 2C0 – 519/832-2201 – Branch Supervisor, Elizabeth Carter – Branch of Bruce County Public Library

Port Franks Library, 7545 Riverside Dr., PO Box 49, Port Franks ON N0M 2L0 – 519/243-2820 – Librarian, Pat Wells – Branch of Lambton County Library

Port Hope Public Library, 31 Queen St., Port Hope ON L1A 2Y8 – 905/885-4712; Fax: 905/885-4181 – Chief Librarian, Patricia Enright; Children's Librarian, Alison Brown

Port Lambton Library, 507 Stoddard St., PO Box 126, Port Lambton ON N0P 2B0 – 519/677-5217 – Librarian, Theresa Lecky – Branch of Lambton County Library

Port McNicoll Public Library, 701 Fourth St., PO Box 490, Port McNicoll ON L0K 1R0 – 705/534-3511; Fax: 705/534-3511 – Branch Librarian, Lana Wells-Garrett – Branch of Tay Twp. Public Library (*see* Waubaushene)

Port Perry: Mississaugas of Scugog Island First Nation Library, RR#5, Port Perry ON L9L 1B6 – 905/935-3337; Fax: 905/985-8828 – CEO, Kelly Ewing

Port Perry: Scugog Memorial Public Library, 231 Water St., PO Box 1049, Port Perry ON L9L 1A8 – 905/985-7686; Fax: 905/985-7210 – CEO, Tom Bonanno

Port Robinson Branch Library, 46 Cross St., Port Robinson ON L0S 1K0 – 905/384-9513 – Branch Head, L. Wronski – Branch of Thorold Public Library

Port Rowan: Norfolk Twp. Public Library Board, 34 Main St., PO Box 130, Port Rowan ON N0E 1M0 – 519/586-3201; Email: prpl@kwic.com – Librarian, Marsha Johnston – See also following branches: Valley Heights Public Library

Port Rowan: Valley Heights Public Library, PO Box 130, Port Rowan ON N0E 1M0 – 519/586-3532 – Librarian, Donna Graham – Branch of Norfolk Twp. Public Library Board

Port Stanley Public Library, 302 Bridge St., PO Box 280, Port Stanley ON N0L 2A0 – 519/782-4241 – Supervisor, Sue Nemett – Branch of Elgin County Library (*see* St. Thomas)

Portland Branch Library, Portland ON K0G 1V0 – 613/272-2832 – Librarian, Lois Braidwood – Branch of Rideau Lakes Union Library (*see* Elgin)

Powassan & District Union Library, 324 Clark St., PO Box 160, Powassan ON P0H 1Z0 – 705/724-3618 – Chief Librarian & CEO, Mary Hall

Prescott Public Library, 360 Dibble St. West, PO Box 430, Prescott ON K0E 1T0 – 613/925-4340; Fax: 613/925-0100; Email: jmcguire@prescott.on.ca; Symbol: OPRE – Chief Librarian, Jane McGuire

Princeton Library, PO Box 99, Princeton ON N0J 1V0 – 519/475-4172 – Supervisor, Margaret Kipp – Branch of Oxford County Library (*see* Woodstock)

Providence Bay Branch Library, General Delivery, Providence Bay ON P0P 1T0 – 705/377-4503 – Branch of Carnarvon Twp. Public Library (*see* Mindemoya)

Putnam Library, RR#1, Putnam ON N0L 2B0 – 519/485-4946 – Supervisor, Evelyn Rath – Branch of Middlesex County Library (*see* Arva)

Rainy River Public Library, 202 - 4 St., PO Box 308, Rainy River ON P0W 1L0 – 807/852-3375; Email: library@rainyriver.lakeheadu.ca – Librarian/CEO, Shannon Haner

Rama: Chippewas of Rama First Nation Public Library, Rama Rd., PO Box 35, Rama ON L0K 1T0 – 705/326-7323; Fax: 705/325-0879 – CEO, Gail Anderson

Ramore Branch, PO Box 250, Ramore ON P0K 1R0 – 705/236-4225 – Branch Head, Lucille Robillard – Branch of Black River-Matheson Public Library

Red Lake Public Library, PO Box 348, Red Lake ON P0V 2M0 – 807/727-2230; Fax: 807/727-3980; Email: rllib@red-lake.lakeheadu.ca – Librarian/CEO, Darlene Wilson; Reference Librarian, Sherry Boland; Children's Librarian, Tara Brown; Public Services Librarian, Darlene Wilson

Red Rock Public Library, Salls St., PO Box 285, Red Rock ON P0T 2P0 – 807/886-2558; Fax: 807/886-2793 – Chief Librarian, Luella Sumner

Redbridge: Phelps Public Library, RR#1, Redbridge ON P0H 2A0 – 705/663-2720 – CEO, Beverly Reynolds

Renfrew Public Library, 13 Railway Ave., Renfrew ON K7V 3A9 – 613/432-8151 – Chief Librarian, Patricia Eady; Children's Librarian, Susan Klinck

Richards Landing: St. Joseph Twp. Public Library, Richards Landing ON P0R 1J0 – 705/246-2353; Fax: 705/246-2353 – Librarian/CEO, Karen VanSickle

Richmond Hill Public Library, 1 Atkinson St., Richmond Hill ON L4C 0H5 – 905/770-0310; Fax: 905/770-0312 – CEO, Jane Horrocks – See also following branches: Central Library, Oak Ridges Moraine Library, Richvale Library

Richmond Hill: Central Library, 1 Atkinson St., Richmond Hill ON L4C 0H5 – 905/884-9288 – Director of Public Service, Barbara Ransom – Branch of Richmond Hill Public Library

Richmond Hill: Oak Ridges Moraine Library, #12, 13085 Yonge St., Richmond Hill ON L4E 3L2 – 905/773-5533; Fax: 905/773-8107 – Manager of Branch Services, Mary Deciantis – Branch of Richmond Hill Public Library

Richmond Hill: Southern Ontario Library Service, Head Office, #601, 151 Bloor St. West, Toronto ON M5S 1T4 – 416/961-1669; Fax: 416/961-5122 – CEO, Laurey Irvine

Richmond Branch Library, 6240 Perth St., PO Box 1029, Richmond ON K0A 2Z0 – 613/838-2026 – Branch Head, Sharon McMullen – Branch of Goulbourn Twp. Public Library (*see* Stittsville)

Ridgetown Branch Library, Main St. West, Ridgetown ON N0P 2C0 – 519/674-3121; Fax: 519/674-0566 – Branch Librarian, Mary Lou Wootton – Branch of Kent County Library (*see* Chatham)

Ripley Branch Library, Jessie St., PO Box 207, Ripley ON N0G 2R0 – 519/395-5919 – Branch Supervisor, Judy Hawrylyshyn – Branch of Bruce County Public Library (*see* Port Elgin)

Rockland (Bibliothèque publique), 2085, rue Laurier, CP 819, Rockland ON K4K 1L5 – 613/446-5680; Téléc: 613/446-7907 – CEO, Lyne Lapalme

Rockton Public Library, 795 Old Hwy. 8, Rockton PO, Rockton ON L0R 1X0 – 519/647-2272 – Branch Head, Jan Maas – Branch of Wentworth Libraries (*see* Hamilton)

Rockwood: Eramosa Community Library, PO Box 520, Rockwood ON N0B 2K0 – 519/856-4851; Fax: 519/856-2240 – CEO, Linda Hornick; Children's Librarian, Leanne Clark; Assistant Librarian, Susan Marcoux

Rodney Branch Library, 207 Furnival Rd., PO Box 398, Rodney ON N0L 2C0 – 519/785-2100 – Supervisor, Shelley Fleming – Branch of Elgin County Library (*see* St. Thomas)

Roseneath: Alderville Library & Resource Centre, PO Box 46, Roseneath ON K0K 2X0 – 905/352-2488; Fax: 905/352-1080; Email: esimpson@alderville.library.on.ca – CEO, Eileen Simpson

Roseneath Branch Library, PO Box 90, Roseneath ON K0K 2X0 – 905/352-1079 – Branch Head, Bronwyn Cochrane – Branch of Northumberland County Public Library (*see* Hastings)

Rosseau Public Library, PO Box 8, Rosseau ON P0C 1J0 – 705/732-4231 – Librarian, Margaret R. Crawford

Russell Branch Library, 92 Mill St., PO Box 280, Russell ON K4R 1E1 – 613/445-5331 – Branch Head, Hélène Quesnel – Branch of Russell Twp. Public Library

Ruthven Library, 1695 Elgin St., PO Box 279, Ruthven ON N0P 2G0 – 519/326-8758 – Supervisor, Hilda MacDonald – Branch of Essex County Library

St. Albert: Bibliothèque publique de Cambridge-St-Albert, 201, rue Principale, CP 99, St Albert ON K0A 3C0 – 613/987-2143; Téléc: 613/987-2143 – Directrice générale, Thérèse Piché

St. Andrews West Branch, PO Box 90, St Andrews West ON K0C 2A0 – 613/932-6012 – Area Supervisor, Fiona Fraser – Branch of Stormont, Dundas & Glengarry County Library (*see* Finch)

St Catharines Public Library, 54 Church St., St Catharines ON L2R 7K2 – 905/688-6103; Fax: 905/688-6292; Email: scpublib@stcatharines.library.on.ca; URL: http://www.stcatharines.library.on.ca – Interim CEO, Barbara Gledhill; Circulation, Head, A. Penfold; Children's Services, Head, B. Rempel; Acquisitions & Technical Services, Manager, Barbara Gledhill; Fiction & Community Services, Head, D. Andrusko; Audio-Visual Services, Head, P. Errington – See also following branches: Grantham Branch Library, Port Dalhousie Library, William Hamilton Merritt Branch Library

St Catharines: Grantham Branch Library, Scott & Vine Sts., St Catharines ON L2M 3W4 – 905/934-7511; Fax: 905/688-6292 – Head, Branch Library Services, B. Gledhill – Branch of St Catharines Public Library

St Catharines: Port Dalhousie Library, 23 Brock St., St Catharines ON L2N 5E1 – 905/646-0220; Fax: 905/688-6292 – Head, Fiction & Community Services, D. Andrusko – Branch of St Catharines Public Library

St Catharines: William Hamilton Merritt Branch Library, 149 Hartzel Rd., St Catharines ON L2P 1N6 – 905/682-3568; Fax: 905/688-6292 – Head, Branch Library Services, B. Gledhill – Branch of St Catharines Public Library

St Charles: Casimir Jennings & Appleby Twp. Public Library, PO Box 40, St Charles ON P0M 2W0 – 705/867-5332; Fax: 705/867-2511 – CEO, Claudette Pothier

St. Clair Beach Library, 13675 St. Gregory's Rd., St. Clair Beach ON N9N 3E4 – 519/735-3670 – Supervisor, Sheila Eagen – Branch of Essex County Library

St. Clements Branch Library, Main St. North, PO Box 80, St. Clements ON N0B 2M0 – 519/699-4341 – Asst. Branch Supervisor, Annette Gray – Branch of Waterloo Regional Library (*see* Kitchener)

St. George: South Dumfries Twp. Public Library, 36 Main St. South, PO Box 310, St. George ON N0E 1N0 – 519/448-1300; Fax: 519/448-4608; Email: clarkef@southdumfries.twp.library.on.ca – CEO, Fiona Clarke – See also following branches: Glen Morris Branch Library, St. George Branch Library

St. George Branch Library, 36 Main St. South, PO Box 310, St. George ON N0E 1N0 – 519/448-1300; Fax: 519/448-4608; Symbol: OSTG – Branch Head, Betty Ames – Branch of South Dumfries Twp. Public Library

St. Isidore & South Plantagenet Union Public Library, Centre Paroissial Joseph Roy, St Isidore de Prescott ON K0C 2B0 – 613/524-2252; Fax: 613/524-2545 – Director, Huguette Bourdon

St. Jacobs Branch Library, 29 Queen St. South, PO Box 507, St Jacobs ON N0B 2N0 – 519/664-3443 – Asst. Branch Supervisor, Helen Biggar – Branch of Waterloo Regional Library (*see* Kitchener)

St. Marys Public Library, 15 Church St. North, PO Box 700, St. Mary's ON N4X 1B4 – 519/284-3346; Fax: 519/284-2630; Symbol: OSTMY – CEO, Barbara Taylor; Children's Librarian, Vera Symons; Technical Services Librarian, Marlene Weston; Acquisitions Librarian, Barbara Taylor

St-Pascal-Baylon: Succursale de St-Pascal-Baylon, CP 43, St-Pascal-Baylon ON K0A 3N0 – 613/488-2494 – Bibliothécaire, Jocelyne Marton – Branch of Bibliothèque publique de Canton de Clarence (*see* Bourget)

St. Thomas: Elgin County Library, 450 Sunset Dr., St. Thomas ON N5R 5V1 – 519/631-1460, ext.109; Fax: 519/633-7661 – Manager of Library Services, Cathy Bishop; Public Services Librarian, Frank Clarke; Technical Services Librarian, Dianne Palmer; Collection Development, Dorothy Streets – See also following branches: Aylmer Old Town Hall Library, Bayham Twp. Public Library, Belmont Public Library, Dutton Public Library, Port Burwell Library, Port Stanley Public Library, Rodney Branch Library, Shedden Library, Springfield Branch Library, Vienna Branch Library, West Lorne Library

St. Thomas Public Library, 153 Curtis St., St. Thomas ON N5P 3Z7 – 519/631-6050; Fax: 519/631-1987; Email: kneeshaw@elgin.net; Symbol: OSTT – CEO, Carolyn Kneeshaw; Public Services, Head, Peter Bailey; Circulation, Head, Maxine Beleutz; Children's Librarian, Julie Siegel; Technical Services, Head, Geri Claridge; Support Services, Stephen Cummings

Sarnia: Chippewas of Sarnia Library, Chippewa Band Community Centre, Marlborough Lane, Sarnia ON N7T 7Y8 – 519/337-7836 – Librarian, Stephanie Williams – Branch of Lambton County Library

Sarnia: Mallroad Library, 1652 Lambton Mall Rd., Sarnia ON N7S 5A1 – 519/542-2580 – Librarian, Wendy Washington – Branch of Lambton County Library

Sarnia Library, 124 Christina St. South, Sarnia ON N7T 2M6 – 519/337-3291; Fax: 519/337-3041 – Branch Manager, April James – Branch of Lambton County Library

Sarnia Reserve Chippewa Library, 1972 Virgil Ave., Sarnia ON N7T 7Y9 – 519/337-7836; Fax: 519/336-0382 – CEO, Stephanie Williams

Sault Ste. Marie Public Library, 50 East St., Sault Ste Marie ON P6A 3C3 – 705/759-5230; Fax: 705/759-8752 – Director, Wilhelm Eisenbichler; Asst. Director & Head of Children's & Audio-Visual Services, Valerie Dawson, 705/759-5244; Technical Services, Head, Robert McWilliam, 705/759-5234; Adult Services, Head, Stephanie Stowe, 705/759-5243; Systems & Circulation, Head, Irma Sauvola – See also following branches: Churchill Branch Library, Korah Library

Sault Ste. Marie: Batchewana First Nation Public Library, 236 Frontenac St., Sault Ste. Marie ON P6A 5K9 – 705/759-0914; Fax: 705/759-9171 – Librarian, Darlene Syrette

Sault Ste. Marie: Churchill Branch Library, 150 Churchill Blvd., Sault Ste. Marie ON P6A 3Z9 – 705/759-5248; Fax: 705/759-8752 – Branch Head, Stephanie Stowe – Branch of Sault Ste. Marie Public Library

Sault Ste. Marie: Garden River First Nation Public Library, RR#4, Site 5, PO Box 7, Sault Ste. Marie ON P6A 5K9 – 705/946-6300; Fax: 705/945-1415 – Librarian, Lisa Cress

Sault Ste. Marie: Korah Library, 496 Second Line West, Sault Ste. Marie ON P6C 2K4 – 705/759-5249; Fax: 705/759-8752 – Branch Head, Stephanie Stowe – Branch of Sault Ste. Marie Public Library

Sault Ste. Marie: Prince Twp. Public Library, 3042 Second Line West, Sault Ste. Marie ON P6A 6K4 – 705/779-3653; Fax: 705/779-2725 – CEO, Elizabeth Papineau

Savant Lake Community Library, General Delivery, Savant Lake ON P0V 2S0 – 807/584-2242; Fax: 807/584-2272

Scarborough Public Library Board, 1076 Ellesmere Rd., Scarborough ON M1P 4P4 – 416/396-8800; Fax: 416/396-8808; Email: aeddie@splb.scarborough.on.ca – CEO, Ann Eddie; Deputy CEO, David Reddin; Director, Service Development & Promotion, Michele Topa; Coordinator of Children & Young Adult Services, Ken Setterington; Coordinator of Multicultural Services, Chryss Mylopoulos; Coordinator of Communications, Marcus Wiseman; Bibliographic & Information Systems, Director, Stan Algoo; Adult Collection, Coordinator, Laurie Saunders; Bibliographic Support Services, Head, Ellen Jaaku; Northern Division, Director, Donald McKenzie; Southern Division, Director, Anna Kwan – See also following branches: Agincourt District Library, Albert Campbell District Library, Bendale Neighbourhood Branch Library, Bridlewood Neighbourhood Branch Library, Cedarbrae District Library, Cliffcrest Neighbourhood Branch Library, Eglinton Square Neighbourhood Branch Library, Goldhawk Park Neighbourhood Branch Library, Guildwood Neighbourhood Branch Library, Highland Creek Neighbourhood Branch Library, Kennedy/Eglinton Neighbourhood Branch Library, Malvern Community Library, Maryvale Neighbourhood Branch Library, McGregor Park Neighbourhood Branch Library, Morningside Neighbourhood Branch Library, Port Union Neighbourhood Branch Library, Steeles Neighbourhood Branch Library, Taylor Memorial Neighbourhood Branch Library, Woodside Square Neighbourhood Branch Library

Scarborough: Agincourt District Library, 155 Bonis Ave., c/o 1076 Ellesmere Rd., Scarborough ON M1P 4P4 – 416/396-8943 – Branch Head, Charna Kofsky; Adult Services Librarian, Bill Hamade; Children's Services Librarian, Mee-Shan Lau – Branch of Scarborough Public Library Board

Scarborough: Albert Campbell District Library, 496 Birchmount Rd., c/o 1076 Ellesmere Rd.,

Scarborough ON M1P 4P4 – 416/396-8890 – Branch Head, Rodger McLennan; Adult Services Librarian, Susan Zadek; Children's Services Librarian, Mary Allen – Branch of Scarborough Public Library Board

Scarborough: Bendale Neighbourhood Branch Library, 1515 Danforth Rd., c/o 1076 Ellesmere Rd., Scarborough ON M1P 4P4 – 416/369-8910 – Branch Supervisor, Carol Ives – Branch of Scarborough Public Library Board

Scarborough: Bridlewood Neighbourhood Branch Library, Bridlewood Mall, c/o 1076 Ellesmere Rd., Scarborough ON M1P 4P4 – 416/396-8960 – Branch Supervisor, Usha Reddy – Branch of Scarborough Public Library Board

Scarborough: Cedarbrae District Library, 545 Markham Rd., c/o 1076 Ellesmere Rd., Scarborough ON M1P 4P4 – 416/396-8850; Fax: 416/396-8864 – Branch Head, Sylvia King; Adult Services Librarian, Visjna Brcic; Children's Services Librarian, Joanne Hawthorne – Branch of Scarborough Public Library Board

Scarborough: Cliffcrest Neighbourhood Branch Library, Cliffcrest Plaza, c/o 1076 Ellesmere Rd., Scarborough ON M1P 4P4 – 416/396-8916 – Branch Supervisor, Donna Clifton – Branch of Scarborough Public Library Board

Scarborough: Eglinton Square Neighbourhood Branch Library, Eglinton Square Mall, c/o 1076 Ellesmere Rd., Scarborough ON M1P 4P4 – 416/396-8920 – Branch Supervisor, Roz Mida – Branch of Scarborough Public Library Board

Scarborough: Goldhawk Park Neighbourhood Branch Library, 295 Alton Towers Circle, c/o 1076 Ellesmere Rd., Scarborough ON M1P 4P4 – 416/ 396-8964 – Branch Head, Paula Smith – Branch of Scarborough Public Library Board

Scarborough: Guildwood Neighbourhood Branch Library, Guildwood Plaza, c/o 1076 Ellesmere Rd., Scarborough ON M1P 4P4 – 416/396-8872 – Branch Supervisor, Barbara More – Branch of Scarborough Public Library Board

Scarborough: Highland Creek Neighbourhood Branch Library, c/o 1076 Ellesmere Rd., Scarborough ON M1P 4P4 – 416/396-8876 – Branch Supervisor, Patricia Green – Branch of Scarborough Public Library Board

Scarborough: Kennedy/Eglinton Neighbourhood Branch Library, Liberty Square Shopping Plaza, c/ o 1076 Ellesmere Rd., Scarborough ON M1P 4P4 – 416/396-8924 – Branch Supervisor, Marilyn Sansome – Branch of Scarborough Public Library Board

Scarborough: Malvern Community Library, 30 Sewells Rd., c/o 1076 Ellesmere Rd., Scarborough ON M1P 4P4 – 416/396-8969 – Branch Head, Russell Hanley – Branch of Scarborough Public Library Board

Scarborough: Maryvale Neighbourhood Branch Library, Parkway Plaza, c/o 1076 Ellesmere Rd., Scarborough ON M1P 4P4 – 416/396-8931 – Branch Supervisor, Sheryl Hyland – Branch of Scarborough Public Library Board

Scarborough: McGregor Park Neighbourhood Branch Library, 2219 Lawrence Ave. East, c/o 1076 Ellesmere Rd., Scarborough ON M1P 4P4 – 416/ 396-8935 – Branch Supervisor, Thea Adams – Branch of Scarborough Public Library Board

Scarborough: Morningside Neighbourhood Branch Library, Morningside Mall, c/o 1076 Ellesmere Rd., Scarborough ON M1P 4P4 – 416/396-8881 – Branch Head, Linda Martin – Branch of Scarborough Public Library Board

Scarborough: Port Union Neighbourhood Branch Library, 5450 Lawrence Ave. East, c/o 1076 Ellesmere Rd., Scarborough ON M1P 4P4 – 416/ 396-8885 – Branch Supervisor, Bonnie McAteer – Branch of Scarborough Public Library Board

Scarborough: Steeles Neighbourhood Branch Library, Bamburgh Gardens Shopping Centre, c/o 1076 Ellesmere Rd., Scarborough ON M1P 4P4 – 416/ 396-8975 – Branch Supervisor, Carol Silverberg – Branch of Scarborough Public Library Board

Scarborough: Taylor Memorial Neighbourhood Branch Library, 1440 Kingston Rd., c/o 1076 Ellesmere Rd., Scarborough ON M1P 4P4 – 416/ 396-8939 – Branch Supervisor, Linda Flavell – Branch of Scarborough Public Library Board

Scarborough: Woodside Square Neighbourhood Branch Library, Woodside Square Mall, c/o 1076 Ellesmere Rd., Scarborough ON M1P 4P4 – 416/ 396-8979 – Branch Supervisor, Vincent Bowes – Branch of Scarborough Public Library Board

Schomberg Library, PO Box 9, Schomberg ON L0G 1T0 – 905/939-2102; Fax: 905/939-2102 – Librarian, Linda Chadwick – Branch of King Twp. Public Library

Schreiber Twp. Public Library, PO Box 39, Schreiber ON P0T 2S0 – 807/824-2477; Fax: 807/824-3241; Email: schlib@schreiber.lakeheadu.ca – Librarian, Howard Alexander

Scotland: Oakland Twp. Public Library, 281 Oakland Rd., PO Box 40, Scotland ON N0E 1R0 – 519/446-0181 – CEO, Linda Zylstra

Seaforth Branch Library, PO Box 490, Seaforth ON N0K 1W0 – 519/527-1430 – Branch Supervisor, Trudy Broome – Branch of Huron County Library (*see* Goderich)

Sebright: Carden Twp. Branch Library, RR#1, Sebright ON L0K 1W0 – 705/833-2845; Fax: 705/833-2845 – Branch Supervisor, Joyce Townes – Branch of Victoria County Public Library (*see* Lindsay)

Sebright: Dalton Twp. Branch Library, RR#1, Sebright ON L0K 1W0 – 705/833-2858 – Branch Supervisor, June Hill – Branch of Victoria County Public Library (*see* Lindsay)

Seeley's Bay Branch, Main St., Seeley's Bay ON K0H 2N0 – 613/387-3909 – Librarian, Hilda Simpson – Branch of Rideau Lakes Union Library (*see* Elgin)

Selkirk Branch Library, 34 Main St., PO Box 130, Selkirk ON N0A 1P0 – 905/776-2127 – Branch Librarian, Pat Reidy – Branch of Nanticoke Public Library Board (*see* Jarvis)

Severn Bridge: Morrison Library Outpost, RR#1, Severn Bridge ON P0E 1N0 – Branch Head, Leanne De Vries – Branch of Gravenhurst Public Library

Shannonville: Tyendinaga Twp. Public Library, Queen St., Shannonville ON K0K 3A0 – 613/967-0606 – CEO, Frances Smith

Sharbot Lake: Oso Twp., Sharbot Lake Branch Library, PO Box 251, Sharbot Lake ON K0H 2P0 – 613/279-2583 – Sue Hunter – Branch of Frontenac County Library (*see* Kingston)

Shedden Library, PO Box 10, Shedden ON N0L 2E0 – 519/764-2081 – Supervisor, Cathy Bishop – Branch of Elgin County Library (*see* St. Thomas)

Sheffield Public Library, 1256 Sheffield Rd., Sheffield ON L0R 1Z0 – 519/623-2681 – Branch Head, Jan Maas – Branch of Wentworth Libraries (*see* Hamilton)

Shelburne Public Library, Owen Sound St., PO Box 127, Shelburne ON L0N 1S0 – 519/925-2168; Symbol: SPL – CEO, Mary Lynne Armstrong; Children's Librarian, Jeanne Cruikshank

Simcoe Public Library, 46 Colborne St. South, Simcoe ON N3Y 4H3 – 519/426-3506; Fax: 519/426-0657; Email: spl@kwic.com; URL: http:// www.spl.kwic.com; Symbol: SIM – CEO, Autar Ganju; Reference Librarian, Carole Henderson; Circulation Librarian, Deborah Verhoeven; Children's Librarian, Wendy Gedy; Technical Services/Acquisitions Librarian, Maryann Armstrong

Sioux Lookout Public Library, PO Box 1028, Sioux Lookout ON P8T 1B3 – 807/737-3660; Fax: 807/737-4046; Email: mwilli@sl.lakeheadu.ca; Symbol: OSI – Chief Librarian, Marianne Williamson

Sioux Narrows Public Library, PO Box 417, Sioux Narrows ON P0X 1N0 – 807/226-5204; Fax: 807/226-5712 – Librarian, J. Reid

Skead Branch Library, D2-7, Skead ON P0M 2Y0 – 705/969-2416 – Librarian, Rose Rice – Branch of Nickel Centre Public Library (*see* Garson)

Smiths Falls Public Library, 81 Beckwith St. North, Smiths Falls ON K7A 2B9 – 613/283-2911; Fax: 613/ 283-9834; Email: sflibrary@falls.igs.net – Librarian, K. Schecter

Smithville: West Lincoln Public Library, PO Box 28, Smithville ON L0R 2A0 – 905/957-3756; Fax: 905/ 957-3219 – Chief Librarian, Catharine Vaughan – See also following branches: Caistorville Branch Library, Wellandport Branch Library

Smooth Rock Falls Public Library, 120 Ross St., PO Box 670, Smooth Rock Falls ON P0L 2B0 – 705/338-2318; Fax: 705/338-2330 – Librarian, Suzanne Petit

Sombra Library, 3464 St. Clair Parkway, PO Box 39, Sombra ON N0P 2H0 – 519/892-3711 – Librarian, Elizabeth MacDonell – Branch of Lambton County Library

South Gillies Community Library, Municipal Bldg., South Gillies ON P0T 2U0 – 807/475-3185; Fax: 807/ 473-0767 – CEO, Shelbie Brown

South Mountain Branch Library, PO Box 230, South Mountain ON K0E 1W0 – 613/989-2199 – Area Supervisor, Renate True – Branch of Stormont, Dundas & Glengarry County Library (*see* Finch)

South Porcupine: C.M. Shields Centennial Library, 99 Bloor St., PO Box 400, South Porcupine ON P0N 1H0 – 705/235-4974; Email: tpl_1@ city.timmins.on.ca – Branch Head, Kathi Martin – Branch of Timmins Public Library

South River-Machar Union Public Library, 22 Marie St., South River ON P0A 1X0 – 705/386-0222; Fax: 705/386-0702 – Librarian, Jan Heinonen; Assistant Librarian, Jeananne Brooks

South Woodslee: Woodslee Library, 118 Malden Rd., PO Box 158, South Woodslee ON N0R 1V0 – 519/ 975-2433 – Supervisor, Susan Tuck – Branch of Essex County Library

Southampton: Saugeen First Nation Library, RR#1, PO Box 1534, Southampton ON N0H 2L0 – 519/ 797-5986; Fax: 519/797-5987 – Band Librarian, Dorothy Ladd

Southampton Branch Public Library, 215 High St., PO Box 130, Southampton ON N0H 2L0 – 519/797-3586; Fax: 519/797-1221 – Branch Supervisor, Linda Mewhinney – Branch of Bruce County Public Library (*see* Port Elgin)

Southwold: Onyota'a:ka Language & Cultural Centre, RR#2, Southwold ON N0L 2G0 – 519/652-6227; Fax: 519/652-9287 – Band Librarian, Corey Nicholas; Librarian's Assistant, Judith Cornelius

Spanish Public Library, PO Box 329, Spanish ON P0P 2A0 – 705/844-2555; Fax: 705/844-2550 – Chief/ Reference Librarian, Hanne Sauve; Children's Librarian, Christine Grose

Spencerville: Edwardsburg Twp. Public Library, PO Box 130, Spencerville ON K0E 1X0 – 613/658-5575 – Librarian, Marva Sothmann

Springfield Branch Library, 106 Main St., PO Box 9, Springfield ON N0L 2J0 – 519/765-4515 – Supervisor, Maria Smit – Branch of Elgin County Library (*see* St. Thomas)

Stayner: Clearview Public Library, 201 Huron St., PO Box 160, Stayner ON L0M 1S0 – 705/428-3595; Fax: 705/428-3595; Symbol: OSTA – CEO, Jennifer La Chapelle; Children's Librarian, Amy Bray; Technical Services Librarian, Sandra Squire – See also following branches: Creemore Branch, Sunnidale Branch

Stella Branch Library, Stella ON K0H 2S0 – 613/389-3393 – Supervisor, Karen Fleming – Branch of

Lennox & Addington County Library (*see* Napanee)

Stirling Public Library, 43 Front St., PO Box 730, Stirling ON K0K 3E0 – 613/395-2837; Fax: 613/395-2837 – CEO, Christopher Faiers

Stittsville: Goulbourn Twp. Public Library, 1637 Main St., PO Box 760, Stittsville ON K2S 1A9 – 613/836-4600; Fax: 613/836-7790; Email: dmcginn@sols.on.ca; Symbol: OSGS – Chief Librarian, Dorothy McGinn – See also following branches: Munster Branch Library, Richmond Branch Library, Stittsville Branch Library

Stittsville Branch Library, 1637 Main St., PO Box 760, Stittsville ON K2S 1A9 – 613/836-3381 – Branch Head, Sharon Ashton – Branch of Goulbourn Twp. Public Library

Stonecliffe: Head, Clara & Maria Twp. Public Library, Stonecliffe ON K0J 2K0 – 613/586-2526; Fax: 613/586-2596 – Sec.-Treas., Diane Beauchamp; Circulation Librarian, Clarence Leach

Stoney Creek: Saltfleet Public Library, 377 Hwy. 8 & Worsley Rd., Stoney Creek ON L8G 1E7 – 905/662-8611; Fax: 905/662-5196 – Branch Head, Nancy Evans – Branch of Wentworth Libraries (*see* Hamilton)

Stoney Creek Public Library, 10 Second St. North, Stoney Creek ON L8G 1Y6 – 905/662-2211; Fax: 905/662-1340 – Branch Head, Stella Clark – Branch of Wentworth Libraries (*see* Hamilton)

Stoney Point Library, 6720 Tecumseh Rd., PO Box 14, Stoney Point ON N0R 1N0 – 519/798-3373 – Supervisor, Mary Pardy – Branch of Essex County Library

Stouffville: Whitchurch-Stouffville Public Library, 6240 Main St., Stouffville ON L4A 1E2 – 905/640-2395; Fax: 905/640-1384; Email: ferguson.gov.on.ca – Librarian, M. Ferguson

Straffordville: Bayham Twp. Public Library, PO Box 209, Straffordville ON N0J 1Y0 – 519/866-3584 – Supervisor, Doris Van Den Eeckhout – Branch of Elgin County Library (*see* St. Thomas)

Stratford Public Library, 19 St. Andrew St., Stratford ON N5A 1A2 – 519/271-0220; Fax: 519/271-3843; Email: slibrary@cims.net; URL: http://www.cims.net/presence/stratfordpublic/ – Library Director/CEO, Jane E. Kirkpatrick; Deputy Director, N. MacPherson

Strathroy Public Library, 34 Frank St., Strathroy ON N7G 2R4 – 519/245-1290; Fax: 519/245-0647; Email: jcummer@strathroy.library.on.ca – Librarian, J. Cummer

Stratton Community Library, PO Box 40, Stratton ON P0W 1N0 – 807/483-5455 – CEO, Anna Boily

Stroud: Innisfil Public Library, PO Box 310, Stroud ON L0L 2M0 – 705/436-1681; Fax: 705/436-7547; Email: sdowns@innisfil.library.on.ca; URL: http://www.sols.on.ca/~innisfil – Chief Librarian/CEO, Susan Downs – See also following branches: Churchill Branch Library, Cookstown Branch Library

Sturgeon Falls: Nipissing First Nation Public Library, 36 Semo Rd., Sturgeon Falls ON P0H 2G0 – 705/753-2050; Fax: 705/753-0207 – CEO, Karen Commanda

Sturgeon Falls Public Library, 225 Holditch St., PO Box 180, Sturgeon Falls ON P0H 2G0 – 705/753-2620; Fax: 705/753-3950 – CEO, Carole Marion

Sudbury: Ontario Library Service North, Administration Office, 334 Regent St., Sudbury ON P3C 4E2 – 705/675-6467; Fax: 705/675-6108; Toll Free: 1-800-461-6348 – CEO, Alan G. Pepper, Email: alan@olsn.on.ca – See also following branches: Kirkland Lake Office, Thunder Bay Office

Sudbury Public Library, 74 MacKenzie St., Sudbury ON P3C 4X8 – 705/673-1155; Fax: 705/673-6145 – CEO, Marian F. Ridge; Reference Librarian, Michaele Mueller; Information Services & Systems Librarian, Anne Fabbro; Community Services Librarian, Marg Hardie; Children's Services, Normand Vermette; Public Services Librarian, Claire Zuliani – See also following branches: Copper Cliff Centennial Library, South Branch Library, W. Clarence Sinclair Library

Sudbury: South Branch Library, 1991 Regent St. South, Sudbury ON P3E 5V3 – 705/673-1155, ext. 250; Fax: 705/522-7788 – Branch Supervisor, Heini Heinonen-Kari – Branch of Sudbury Public Library

Sudbury: W. Clarence Sinclair Library, New Sudbury Shopping Centre, 1346 LaSalle Blvd., Sudbury ON P3A 1Z6 – 705/673-1155, ext.260; Fax: 705/524-2868 – Branch Supervisor, Connie Lee – Branch of Sudbury Public Library

Sunderland: Brock Twp. Public Library, Church St., PO Box 208, Sunderland ON L0C 1H0 – 705/357-3109 – Librarian, Carole Wetheral – See also following branches: Beaverton Branch, Cannington Branch, Sunderland Branch

Sunderland Branch, Church St., PO Box 208, Sunderland ON L0H 1H0 – 705/357-3109; Fax: 705/357-2541 – Branch Head, Carole Wetheral – Branch of Brock Twp. Public Library

Sundridge-Strong Union Public Library, 110 Main St., PO Box 429, Sundridge ON P0A 1Z0 – 705/384-7311; Fax: 705/384-7311 – CEO, Frances Therrien

Sutton West: Georgina Island First Nation Library, RR#2, Sutton West ON L0E 1R0 – 705/437-4328; Fax: 705/437-4597 – Librarian, Georgina Charles

Sutton Centennial Library, 5279 Black River Rd., PO Box 338, Sutton West ON L0E 1R0 – 905/722-5702; Fax: 905/722-6309 – Branch Head, Mary Flint – Branch of Georgina Public Libraries (*see* Keswick)

Sydenham: Loughborough Twp., Sydenham Branch, PO Box 88, Sydenham ON K0H 2T0 – 613/376-3437 – Joanne Stewart-Normans – Branch of Frontenac County Library (*see* Kingston)

Tamworth Branch Library, PO Box 10, Tamworth ON K0K 3G0 – 613/379-2511 – Supervisor, Joan Larkin – Branch of Lennox & Addington County Library (*see* Napanee)

Tara Branch Library, Whites Ave., PO Box 59, Tara ON N0H 2N0 – 519/934-2626 – Branch Supervisor, Doreen Hills – Branch of Bruce County Public Library (*see* Port Elgin)

Tavistock Public Library, PO Box 190, Tavistock ON N0B 2R0 – 519/655-3013 – Supervisor, Deb Schurink – Branch of Oxford County Library (*see* Woodstock)

Tecumseh Branch Library, 949 Lesperance Rd., Tecumseh ON N8N 1W9 – 519/735-9385 – Supervisor, Kathleen Jullien – Branch of Essex County Library

Teeswater Branch Library, Clinton St., PO Box 260, Teeswater ON N0G 2S0 – 519/367-2835 – Branch Supervisor, Lynda Benninger – Branch of Bruce County Public Library (*see* Port Elgin)

Tehkummah Twp. Public Library, RR#1, Tehkummah ON P0P 2C0 – 705/859-3301; Fax: 705/859-2605 – CEO, Judy McDermid

Temagami First Nations Public Library, Bear Island PO, Temagami ON P0H 1C0 – 705/237-8943; Fax: 705/237-8954 – CEO, Bonnie Turner

Temagami Public Library, PO Box 220, Temagami ON P0H 2H0 – 705/569-2945; Fax: 705/569-2834 – CEO, Paulette Turgeon

Terrace Bay Public Library, PO Box 369, Terrace Bay ON P0T 2W0 – 807/825-3819; Email: library2@schreiber.lakeheadu.ca – CEO, Jeanne Marcella

Thamesford Public Library, PO Box 220, Thamesford ON N0M 2M0 – 519/285-3219 – Supervisor, Nancy Van Geel – Branch of Oxford County Library (*see* Woodstock)

Thamesville: Deleware Nation Library, RR#3, Thamesville ON N0P 2K0 – 519/692-3936; Fax: 519/692-5522 – CEO, Darryl Stonefish

Thamesville Branch Library, Town Hall, Thamesville ON N0P 2K0 – 519/692-4251 – Branch Librarian, Debby Kennedy – Branch of Kent County Library (*see* Chatham)

Thedford Library, #2, 115 Main St., PO Box 204, Thedford ON N0M 2N0 – 519/296-4459 – Librarian, Mary Ellen Anderson – Branch of Lambton County Library

Thessalon Union Public Library, PO Box 549, Thessalon ON P0R 1L0 – 705/842-2306; Fax: 705/842-2605 – CEO, Mary Bockman

Thornbury: Leonard E. Shore Memorial Library, 175 Bruce St. South, PO Box 357, Thornbury ON N0H 2P0 – 519/599-3681; Fax: 519/599-7951; Email: leonard@georgian.net – CEO, Ken Haigh

Thorndale: West Nissouri Library, RR#3, PO Box 88, Thorndale ON N0M 2P0 – 519/461-0219; Fax: 519/461-0219 – Supervisor, Reta Young – Branch of Middlesex County Library (*see* Arva)

Thornhill: Bathurst Clark Library, 900 Clark Ave. West, Thornhill ON L4J 8C1 – 905/709-1103; Fax: 905/709-1099 – Manager, Lilita Stripnieks – Branch of Vaughan Public Libraries (*see* Maple)

Thornhill: Dufferin Clark Library, 1441 Clark Ave. West, Thornhill ON L4J 7R4 – 905/660-0374; Fax: 905/660-7202 – Manager, Pat Stegenga – Branch of Vaughan Public Libraries (*see* Maple)

Thornhill: Richvale Library, 40 Pearson Ave., Richmond Hill ON L4C 6T7 – 905/889-2847; Fax: 905/889-2435 – Manager of Branch Services, Mary Deciantis – Branch of Richmond Hill Public Library

Thornhill Community Centre Library, 7755 Bayview Ave., Thornhill ON L3T 4P1 – 905/881-5668; Fax: 905/881-2935 – Branch Manager, Cynthia Teitelman – Branch of Markham Public Libraries

Thornhill Village Library, 10 Colborne St., Thornhill ON L3T 1Z6 – 905/881-8299; Fax: 905/881-0149 – Branch Manager, Mary Lou Allen – Branch of Markham Public Libraries

Thorold Public Library, 14 Ormond St. North, Thorold ON L2V 1Y8 – 905/227-2581; Fax: 905/227-2311 – Chief Librarian, Patricia Bronson; Reference Librarian, C. Bowman; Children's Services, Lou Anne Wronski – See also following branches: Port Robinson Branch Library

Thunder Bay Public Library, 285 Red River Rd., Thunder Bay ON P7B 1A9 – 807/344-3585; Fax: 807/345-8727; Email: ILL.OTB – CEO, Karen Harrison; Head, Adult Services, Barbara Philp; Head, Children's Services, Angela Meady; Public Services Coordinator, Carole Aitken, 807/623-0925; Head, Automated Services, Larry Joseph – See also following branches: Brodie Resource Library, Mary J.L. Black Branch Library, Victoriaville Branch Library, Waverley Resource Library

Thunder Bay: Brodie Resource Library, 216 South Brodie St., Thunder Bay ON P7E 1C2 – 807/623-0925; Fax: 807/623-0875 – Branch Head, Carole Aitken – Branch of Thunder Bay Public Library

Thunder Bay: Mary J.L. Black Branch Library, 151 West Brock St., Thunder Bay ON P7E 4H9 – 807/475-5906 – Branch Head, Carole Aitken – Branch of Thunder Bay Public Library

Thunder Bay Office, 910 Victoria Ave. East, Thunder Bay ON P7C 1B4 – 807/626-1670; Fax: 807/623-4623; Toll Free: 1-800-461-7763 – Branch of Ontario Library Service North

Thunder Bay: Victoriaville Branch Library, 700 Victoria Ave. East, Thunder Bay ON P7C 5P7 – 807/623-4472 – Branch Head, Carole Aitken – Branch of Thunder Bay Public Library

Thunder Bay: Waverley Resource Library, 285 Red River Rd., Thunder Bay ON P7B 1A9 – 807/344-3585; Fax: 807/345-8727 – Branch Head, Carole Aitken – Branch of Thunder Bay Public Library

Tilbury Branch Library, 2 Queen St., PO Box 999, Tilbury ON N0P 2L0 – 519/682-0100; Fax: 519/682-

2392 – Branch Librarian, Maxine Gardiner – Branch of Kent County Library (*see* Chatham)

Tillsonburg Public Library, 2 Library Lane, Tillsonburg ON N4G 4S7 – 519/842-5571; Fax: 519/842-2941; Email: matt@oxford.net – CEO, Matthew Scholtz; Children's Librarian, Dianne Moore

Timmins Public Library, 236 Algonquin Blvd. East, Timmins ON P4N 1B2 – 705/267-8451; Fax: 705/268-9185; Email: tpl_2@city.timmins.on.ca; URL: http://timmins.vianet.on.ca/community/tpl/ – CEO, Brian Nimeroski; Adult Librarian, Colleen Mares; Children's Librarian, Susan Hoffman; Head, French Services, Colette Proulx; Head, Technical Services, Teresa Woodrow; Systems Administrator, Lucy Gowers – See also following branches: C.M. Shields Centennial Library

Tiverton Branch Library, King St., PO Box 140, Tiverton ON N0G 2T0 – 519/368-5655 – Branch Supervisor, Mary MacKay – Branch of Bruce County Public Library (*see* Port Elgin)

Tobermory Branch Library, Bay St., PO Box 159, Tobermory ON N0H 2R0 – 519/596-2446 – Branch Supervisor, Kathryn MacLeod – Branch of Bruce County Public Library (*see* Port Elgin)

Toronto: Metropolitan Toronto Reference Library, 789 Yonge St., Toronto ON M4W 2G8 – 416/393-7000; Fax: 416/393-7229 – CEO, Frances Schwenger; Business & Government Information Centre, Greg Kelner – See also following branches: Metro Urban Affairs Library

Toronto Public Library, 281 Front St. East, Toronto ON M5A 4L2 – 416/393-7500; Fax: 416/393-7782; URL: http://www.tpl.toronto.on.ca – CEO, Gabriele Lundeen; Collections Coordinator, Susan Caron; Children's Services Specialist, Katherine Palmer; Public Services, Director, Stephanie Hutcheson; Access & Information Services Coordinator, George Levin; Multicultural Services Specialist, Janice Lavery; Literacy Services Specialist, Brenda Livingston – See also following branches: Annette Library, Beaches Library, Bloor & Gladstone Library, Charles R. Sanderson Library, City Hall Public Library, College/Shaw Library, Danforth/Coxwell Library, Davenport Library, Deer Park Library, Dufferin-St.Clair Library, Forest Hill Library, George H. Locke Branch, Gerrard-Ashdale Library, High Park Library, Jones Ave. Library, Lillian H. Smith Library, Main Street Library, Mount Pleasant Branch, Northern District Library, Palmerston Library, Pape-Danforth Library, Parkdale Library, Parliament Street Library, Perth-Dupont Library, Queen-Saulter Library, Riverdale Library, Runnymede Library, Spadina Rd. Library, St. Clair-Silverthorn Library, St. Lawrence Library/Library on Wheels Branch, Swansea Memorial Branch, Wychwood Library, Yorkville Library

Toronto: Annette Library, 145 Annette St., Toronto ON M6P 1P3 – 416/393-7692 – Branch Head, Marlene Archambeau – Branch of Toronto Public Library

Toronto: Beaches Library, 2161 Queen St. East, Toronto ON M4L 1J1 – 416/393-7703 – Branch Head, Pat Bull – Branch of Toronto Public Library

Toronto: Bloor & Gladstone Library, 1101 Bloor St. West, Toronto ON M6H 1M7 – 416/393-7674; Fax: 416/393-7502 – Branch Head, Brigitte Richter – Branch of Toronto Public Library

Toronto: Charles R. Sanderson Library, 327 Bathurst St., Toronto ON M5T 1J1 – 416/393-7653 – Branch Head, Jim Montgomery – Branch of Toronto Public Library

Toronto: City Hall Public Library, Nathan Phillips Sq., Toronto ON M5H 2N3 – 416/393-7650; Fax: 416/393-7665 – Branch Supervisor, Nancy Jessop – Branch of Toronto Public Library

Toronto: College/Shaw Library, 766 College St. West, Toronto ON M6G 1C4 – 416/393-7668 – Branch Head, Pat O'Sullivan – Branch of Toronto Public Library

Toronto: Danforth/Coxwell Library, 1675 Danforth Ave., Toronto ON M4C 5P2 – 416/393-7783; Symbol: DA – Branch Head, Maggie Gosselin – Branch of Toronto Public Library

Toronto: Davenport Library, 1246 Shaw St., Toronto ON M6G 3P1 – 416/393-7732 – Branch Supervisor, Jean Lee – Branch of Toronto Public Library

Toronto: Deer Park Library, 40 St. Clair Ave. East, Toronto ON M4T 1M9 – 416/393-7657; Fax: 416/393-7696; Symbol: DP – Branch Head, Linda Steinberg – Branch of Toronto Public Library

Toronto: Dufferin-St.Clair Library, 1625 Dufferin St., Toronto ON M6H 3L9 – 416/393-7712 – Branch Head, Ewa Piatkowski – Branch of Toronto Public Library

Toronto: Evelyn Gregory Branch Library, 120 Trowell Ave., Toronto ON M6M 1L7 – 416/394-1006 – Branch Head, B. Warzocha – Branch of City of York Public Library

Toronto: Forest Hill Library, 700 Eglinton Ave. West, Toronto ON M5N 1B9 – 416/393-7706 – Branch Head, Phyllis Malette – Branch of Toronto Public Library

Toronto: George H. Locke Branch, 3083 Yonge St., Toronto ON M4N 2K7 – 416/393-7730; Symbol: LO – Branch Head, Tiiu Kubjas – Branch of Toronto Public Library

Toronto: Gerrard-Ashdale Library, 1432 Gerrard St. East, Toronto ON M4L 1Z6 – 416/393-7717 – Branch Head, Pam Hancock – Branch of Toronto Public Library

Toronto: High Park Library, 228 Roncesvalles Ave., Toronto ON M6R 2L7 – 416/393-7671 – Branch Head, Barrie Gray – Branch of Toronto Public Library

Toronto: Jane-Dundas Branch Library, 620 Jane St., Toronto ON M6S 4A6 – 416/394-1014 – Branch Head, George N. Shirinian – Branch of City of York Public Library

Toronto: Jones Ave. Library, 118 Jones Ave., Toronto ON M4M 2Z9 – 416/393-7715; Symbol: JO – Branch Head, Beverley Howatson – Branch of Toronto Public Library

Toronto: Lillian H. Smith Library, 239 College St., Toronto ON M5T 1R5 – 416/393-7746 – Branch Head, Mary Anne Cree – Branch of Toronto Public Library

Toronto: Main Street Library, 137 Main St., Toronto ON M4E 2V9 – 416/393-7700 – Branch Head, Nancy Harbour – Branch of Toronto Public Library

Toronto: Metro Urban Affairs Library, 55 John St., Toronto ON M5V 3C6 – 416/393-7131; Fax: 416/397-7245; Email: ENVOY: OTMSM – Manager, Berenice Campagne, 416/392-7230 – Branch of Metropolitan Toronto Reference Library

Toronto: Mount Dennis Branch Library, 1123 Weston Rd., Toronto ON M6N 3S3 – 416/394-1008 – Branch Head, B. Warzocha – Branch of City of York Public Library

Toronto: Mount Pleasant Branch, 599 Mount Pleasant Rd., Toronto ON M4S 2M5 – 416/393-7737 – Branch Supervisor, Barbara Forsythe – Branch of Toronto Public Library

Toronto: Northern District Library, 40 Orchard View Blvd., Toronto ON M4R 1B9 – 416/393-7610; Fax: 416/393-7740 – Branch Head, Cheryl Skovronek – Branch of Toronto Public Library

Toronto: Palmerston Library, 560 Palmerston Ave., Toronto ON M6G 2P7 – 416/393-7680; Fax: 416/393-7740 – Branch Head, Rose Marie Spearpoint – Branch of Toronto Public Library

Toronto: Pape-Danforth Library, 701 Pape Ave., Toronto ON M4K 3S6 – 416/393-7727; Fax: 416/393-7503 – Branch Head, Ann Thoburn – Branch of Toronto Public Library

Toronto: Parkdale Library, 1303 Queen St. West, Toronto ON M6K 1L6 – 416/393-7686 – Branch Head, Linda Karlinsky – Branch of Toronto Public Library

Toronto: Parliament Street Library, 269 Gerrard St. East, Toronto ON M5A 2G3 – 416/393-7663 – Branch Head, Nancy Wade-Stadler – Branch of Toronto Public Library

Toronto: Perth-Dupont Library, 1589 Dupont St., Toronto ON M6P 3S3 – 416/393-7677 – Branch Supervisor, Carmen Martino – Branch of Toronto Public Library

Toronto: Queen-Saulter Library, 765 Queen St. East, Toronto ON M4M 1H3 – 416/393-7723 – Branch Supervisor, Miguelita Costes – Branch of Toronto Public Library

Toronto: Riverdale Library, 370 Broadview Ave., Toronto ON M4P 1X4 – 416/393-7720 – Branch Head, Fidelia Lau – Branch of Toronto Public Library

Toronto: Runnymede Library, 2178 Bloor St. West, Toronto ON M6S 1M8 – 416/393-7697 – Branch Head, Holly Benson – Branch of Toronto Public Library

Toronto: St. Clair-Silverthorn Library, 1748 St. Clair Ave. West, Toronto ON M6N 1J4 – 416/393-7709 – Branch Supervisor, Pat Coulter – Branch of Toronto Public Library

Toronto: St. Lawrence Library/Library on Wheels Branch, 171 Front St. East, Toronto ON M4M 1H3 – 416/393-7655 – Branch Supervisor, Linda Goldman – Branch of Toronto Public Library

Toronto: Spadina Rd. Library, 10 Spadina Rd., Toronto ON M5R 2S7 – 416/393-7666 – Branch Head, Vivienne James – Branch of Toronto Public Library

Toronto: Swansea Memorial Branch, 95 Lavinia Ave., Toronto ON M6S 3H9 – 416/393-7695 – Branch Head, Holly Benson – Branch of Toronto Public Library

Toronto: Weston Branch Library, 2 King St., Toronto ON M9N 1K9 – 416/394-1016; Fax: 416/394-2781 – Branch Head, Linda Davis – Branch of City of York Public Library

Toronto: Wychwood Library, 1431 Bathurst St., Toronto ON M5R 3J2 – 416/393-7683 – Branch Head, Diana Arris – Branch of Toronto Public Library

Toronto: Yorkville Library, 22 Yorkville Ave., Toronto ON M4W 1J4 – 416/393-7660 – Branch Head, Janice Long – Branch of Toronto Public Library

Tottenham Branch Library, 18 Queen St. North, PO Box 339, Tottenham ON L0G 1W0 – 905/936-2291 – Janine Grady – Branch of New Tecumseth Public Library (*see* Alliston)

Trenton: Murray Twp. (Wooler) Branch Library, RR#1, Trenton ON K8V 5P4 – 613/392-4435 – Branch Head, Esther Maples – Branch of Northumberland County Public Library (*see* Hastings)

Trenton Memorial Public Library, 18 Albert St., Trenton ON K8V 4S3 – 613/394-3381; Symbol: OTRE – Acting CEO, Rosemary Kirby

Trout Creek Public Library, McCarthy St., PO Box 310, Trout Creek ON P0H 2L0 – 705/723-5351 – CEO, Jeannette Schmelefske

Tweed Public Library, 320 Colborne St., PO Box 628, Tweed ON K0K 3J0 – 613/478-1066 – CEO/Librarian, Jane Ferguson

Unionville: Milliken Mills Community Library, 7600 Kennedy Rd., Unit 1, Unionville ON L3R 9S5 – 905/940-8323; Fax: 905/940-8326 – Branch Manager, Larry Pogue – Branch of Markham Public Libraries

Utterson: Ullswater Public Library, Ullswater Community Hall, RR#1, Utterson ON P0B 1M0 – 705/769-3792 – Librarian, Phyllis Olsen – Branch of Port Carling Public Library

Uxbridge Twp. Public Library, 9 Toronto St. South, PO Box 279, Uxbridge ON L9P 1P7 – 905/852-9747; Fax: 905/852-9748 – Chief Librarian, Cathy Thomson; Children's Librarian, Pam Noble – See also following branches: Scott Branch Library

Val Rita-Harty Public Library, Government St., PO Box 69, Val Rita ON P0L 2G0 – 705/335-8700 – CEO, Cecile Lamontagne

Vanier Public Library, 310 Pères Blancs Ave., Vanier ON K1L 7L5 – 613/745-0861; Téléc: 613/747-8795 – Directrice générale, Liliane Pinard

Vankleek Hill Public Library, PO Box 520, Vankleek Hill ON K0B 1R0 – 613/678-2216 – Head Librarian, Margaret Higginson

Verner: Caldwell Twp. Public Library, PO Box 59, Verner ON P0H 2M0 – 705/594-2800; Fax: 705/594-9153 – Librarian, Diane Tellier

Vernon Branch Library, 4082 Dominion St., PO Box 59, Vernon ON K0A 3J0 – 613/821-3389 – Librarian, Kay Porteous – Branch of Osgoode Twp. Public Library Board (*see* Metcalfe)

Victoria Harbour Public Library, Albert St., Victoria Harbour ON L0K 2A0 – 705/534-3581; Fax: 705/534-3581 – Branch Librarian, Carol Vanderhart – Branch of Tay Twp. Public Library (*see* Waubaushene)

Vienna Branch Library, PO Box 5, Vienna ON N0J 1Z0 – 519/874-4118 – Librarian, Doris Van Den Eeckhout – Branch of Elgin County Library (*see* St. Thomas)

Vineland: Moses F. Rittenhouse Branch Library, 4080 John Charles Blvd., Vineland ON L0R 2C0 – 905/562-5711; Fax: 905/562-3454; Email: linclib1@vaxxine.com – Technical Services, Mona McMaster – Branch of Lincoln Public Library (*see* Beamsville)

Virginiatown: McGarry Public Library, PO Box 250, Virginiatown ON P0K 1X0 – 705/634-2312; Fax: 705/634-9312; Email: mcgarry@ntl.sympatico.ca – Librarian/CEO, Anne-Marie Boucher

Wainfleet Twp. Public Library, 19M9 Park St., Wainfleet ON L0S 1V0 – 905/899-1277; Fax: 905/899-2495; Email: mpodolya@freenet.npiec.on.ca; URL: http://ont.net/wainfleet/lib.html; Symbol: WA – CEO/Head Librarian, Mary Podolyak; Reference Librarian/Circulation Librarian, Lorrie Atkinson; Children's Librarian/ Public Services Librarian/Acquisitions Librarian, Mary Podolyak; Technical Services Librarian, Lorrie Atkinson

Walkerton Branch Library, 253 Durham St., PO Box 250, Walkerton ON N0G 2V0 – 519/881-3240; Fax: 519/881-3240 – Branch Supervisor, Tracey Knapp – Branch of Bruce County Public Library (*see* Port Elgin)

Wallaceburg: Bkejwanong First Nations Community Library, RR#3, Wallaceburg ON N8A 4R9 – 519/627-7034; Fax: 519/627-7035 – CEO, Jean Wrightman

Wallaceburg Branch Library, 209 James St., Wallaceburg ON N8A 2N4 – 519/627-5292; Fax: 519/627-3039 – Branch Librarian, Alla Steen – Branch of Kent County Library (*see* Chatham)

Wardsville Library, Main St., Wardsville ON N0L 2N0 – 519/693-4208 – Supervisor, Janice Moniz – Branch of Middlesex County Library (*see* Arva)

Warkworth (Percy Twp.) Branch Library, Main & Church Sts., Warkworth ON K0K 3K0 – 705/924-3116 – Branch Head, Claire Jenney – Branch of Northumberland County Public Library (*see* Hastings)

Warren: Ratter & Dunnet Twp. Public Library, 8 Dyke St., PO Box 250, Warren ON P0H 2N0 – 705/967-2702 – Librarian, Janis Lamothe

Wasaga Beach Public Library, 120 Glenwood Dr., PO Box 530, Wasaga Beach ON L0L 2P0 – 705/429-5481; Fax: 705/429-5481 – CEO/Librarian, Jackie Marshall-Beaudin

Waterdown Public Library, 25 Mill St. North, Waterdown ON L0R 2H0 – 905/689-6269; Fax: 905/689-4684 – Branch Head, Elizabeth Wright – Branch of Wentworth Libraries (*see* Hamilton)

Waterford Branch Library, 15 Main St., Waterford ON N0E 1Y0 – 519/443-7682 – Branch Librarian, Heidi E. Goodale – Branch of Nanticoke Public Library Board (*see* Jarvis)

Waterloo Public Library, 35 Albert St., Waterloo ON N2L 5E2 – 519/886-1310; Fax: 519/886-7936; Email: wpl@hookup.net – Chief Librarian, Joanne Tate – See also following branches: McCormick Branch Library

Waterloo: McCormick Branch Library, 500 Parkside Dr., Waterloo ON N2L 5J4 – 519/885-1920 – Branch Supervisor, Doreen Disney – Branch of Waterloo Public Library

Watford: Warwick Library, 6199 First School Rd., RR#5, Watford ON N0M 2S0 – 519/849-5533 – Librarian, Jean O'Neil – Branch of Lambton County Library

Watford Library, 5317 Nauvoo Rd., PO Box 9, Watford ON N0M 2S0 – 519/876-2204 – Librarian, Sheryl Mendritzki – Branch of Lambton County Library

Waubaushene: Tay Twp. Public Library, Waubaushene Public Library, 9 Maple St., PO Box 280, Waubaushene ON L0K 2C0 – 705/538-1122; Fax: 705/538-1122 – Chief Librarian/CEO, Sheila Hamilton – See also following branches: Port McNicoll Public Library, Victoria Harbour Public Library

Wawa: Michipicoten Twp. Public Library, PO Box 1730, Wawa ON P0S 1K0 – 705/856-2062; Fax: 705/856-2120 – CEO, Sandra Weitzel

Webbwood Public Library, Webbwood ON P0P 2G0 – 705/869-4147; Fax: 705/869-1394 – CEO, Benva Lea Bentley, 705/869-2806

Welland Public Library, 140 King St., Welland ON L3B 3J3 – 905/734-6210; Fax: 905/734-8955; Symbol: WPL – CEO/Chief Librarian, Janet C. Booth; Reference Librarian, Douglas Abbott; Children's Librarian, Janet Hodgkins; Public Services Librarian, Stephen Hanns; Support Services Librarian, Laura Kmety; Audio-Visual Librarian, William Wallis – See also following branches: Northwest Branch Library

Wellandport Branch Library, Wellandport ON L0R 2J0 – 905/386-6792 – Branch Head, Colleen Keizer – Branch of West Lincoln Public Library (*see* Smithville)

Welland: Northwest Branch Library, 650 South Pelham Rd., Welland ON L3C 3C8 – 905/735-4231 – Branch Head, Shelley Beckett – Branch of Welland Public Library

Wellesley Branch Library, 10 Henry St., PO Box 190, Wellesley ON N0B 2T0 – 519/656-2001 – Asst. Branch Supervisor, Elizabeth Earle – Branch of Waterloo Regional Library (*see* Kitchener)

Wellington Public Library, 261 Main St., PO Box 370, Wellington ON K0K 3L0 – 613/399-2023 – Chief Librarian, Dianne Cranshaw

Wendover: Bibliothèques publiques du Canton de Plantagenet-Nord, Succ. Wendover, Wendover ON K0A 3K0 – 613/673-2923 – Directrice générale, Catherine Bélisle – See also following branches: Succursale Curran, Succursale Wendover

Wendover: Succursale Wendover, Wendover ON K0A 3K0 – 613/673-2923 – Branch of Bibliothèques publiques du Canton de Plantagenet-Nord

West Bay First Nations Public Library, PO Box 331, West Bay ON P0P 1G0 – 705/377-5540; Fax: 705/377-5080; Email: 3sanda@kanservu – Librarian, Sandra Bayer

West Lorne Library, 160 Main St., PO Box 10, West Lorne ON N0L 2P0 – 519/768-1150 – Supervisor, Shelley Fleming – Branch of Elgin County Library (*see* St. Thomas)

Westport-North Crosby Union Public Library, 3 Spring St., PO Box 28, Westport ON K0G 1X0 – 613/273-3223 – Librarian, P. Stuffles

Westwood: Asphodel Public Library, PO Box 2, Westwood ON K0L 3B0 – 705/696-2744 – CEO, Nelda Beavis

Wheatley Branch Library, 35 Talbot St. West, Wheatley ON N0P 2P0 – 519/825-7131 – Branch Librarian, Merle Richmond – Branch of Kent County Library (*see* Chatham)

Whitby Public Library, 405 Dundas St. West, Whitby ON L1N 6A1 – 905/668-6531; Fax: 905/668-7445; Email: nharsanyi@whitby.library.on.ca; URL: http://www.sols.on.ca/~whitby/ – Chief Librarian, Nancy Harsanyi; Reference Librarian, L. Evans; Circulation Supervisor, Pauline Baxter; Children's Librarian, R. Jessup; Public Services Librarian, T. Driesschen; Technical Services Supervisor, Elaine Yatulis – See also following branches: Brooklin Branch Library, Rossland Branch Library

Whitby: Rossland Branch Library, 701 Rossland Rd. East, Whitby ON L1N 8Y9 – 905/668-1886 – Branch Head, Judy McIntosh – Branch of Whitby Public Library

White River Public Library, PO Box 458, White River ON P0M 3G0 – 807/822-2406 – CEO, Mary Lue Constantineau

Whitedog: Islington First Nation Public Library, General Delivery, Whitedog PO, Whitedog ON P0X 1P0 – 807/927-2286 – CEO, Darlene Bunting

Whitefish Branch Library, c/o R.H. Murray Public School, 3 Henry St., Whitefish ON P0M 3E0 – 705/866-2651 – Branch Head, Gabrielle Makela – Branch of Walden Public Library (*see* Lively)

Whitney: Airy Twp. Public Library, PO Box 208, Whitney ON K0J 2M0 – 613/637-5471 – CEO, Carol A. Watson

Wiarton: Chippewas of Nawash Public Library, RR#5, Wiarton ON N0H 2T0 – 519/534-1508; Fax: 519/534-2130 – Librarian, Mary Lynne Pedoniquotte

Wiarton Branch Library, 542 Bedford St., PO Box 250, Wiarton ON N0H 2T0 – 519/534-2602; Fax: 519/534-2602 – Branch Supervisor, Clare Drury – Branch of Bruce County Public Library (*see* Port Elgin)

Wilberforce: Monmouth Branch Library, Wilberforce ON K0L 3C0 – 705/448-2510 – Branch Head, Bessie Croft – Branch of Haliburton County Public Library

Wilkesport Library, 1349 Main St., General Delivery, Wilkesport ON N0P 2R0 – 519/846-4000 – Librarian, Shelley Lucier – Branch of Lambton County Library

Williamsburg Branch Library, PO Box 69, Williamsburg ON K0C 2H0 – 613/535-2185 – Area Supervisor, Elizabeth Porter – Branch of Stormont, Dundas & Glengarry County Library (*see* Finch)

Williamstown Branch Library, PO Box 68, Williamstown ON K0C 2J0 – 613/347-3397 – Area Supervisor, Donna Parker – Branch of Stormont, Dundas & Glengarry County Library (*see* Finch)

Wilno: Sherwood Jones & Burns Branch, Wilno ON K0J 2N0 – Branch Head, Angela E. Lorbetskie – Branch of Barry's Bay Public Library

Winchester Branch Library, PO Box 444, Winchester ON K0C 2K0 – 613/774-2612 – Area Supervisor, Renate True – Branch of Stormont, Dundas & Glengarry County Library (*see* Finch)

Windsor Public Library, 850 Ouellette Ave., Windsor ON N9A 4M9 – 519/255-6770; Fax: 519/255-7207; Email: wpl@city.windsor.on.ca; URL: http://www.city.windsor.on.ca/wpl – CEO, Steve Salmons, 519/255-6750; Deputy CEO, Gail Juris; Technical Services Coordinator, Aziz Chowdhury – See also following branches: Ambassador Library, Forest Glade-Optimist Library, Main Library, Nikola Budimir Library, Remington Park Library, Riverside Library, Seminole Library, South Walkerville Library

Windsor: Ambassador Library, 1564 Huron Church Rd., Windsor ON N9C 2L1 – 519/253-7340; Fax: 519/253-7340 – Librarian, Elizabeth Watson – Branch of Windsor Public Library

Windsor: Forest Glade-Optimist Library, 3211 Forest Glade Dr., Windsor ON N8R 1W7 – 519/735-6803; Fax: 519/735-6803 – Librarian, David Eady – Branch of Windsor Public Library

Windsor: Main Library, 850 Ouellette Ave., Windsor ON N9A 4M9 – 519/255-6770; Fax: 519/973-1213 – Manager, Blodwen Reitz – Branch of Windsor Public Library

Windsor: Malden Road Library, 5860 Malden Rd., Windsor ON N9H 1S4 – 519/969-0771 – Supervisor, Annette Isaac – Branch of Essex County Library

Windsor: Nikola Budimir Library, 1310 Grand Marais Rd. West, Windsor ON N9E 1E4 – 519/969-5880; Fax: 519/969-5880 – Manager, Elizabeth Watson – Branch of Windsor Public Library

Windsor: Remington Park Library, 2710 Lillian St., Windsor ON N8X 4B5 – 519/966-3441; Fax: 519/966-3441 – Manager, Elizabeth Watson – Branch of Windsor Public Library

Windsor: Riverside Library, 6275 Wyandotte St. East, Windsor ON N8S 1N5 – 519/945-7568; Fax: 519/945-7568 – Manager, David Eady – Branch of Windsor Public Library

Windsor: Seminole Library, 4285 Seminole St., Windsor ON N8Y 1Z5 – 519/945-6467; Fax: 519/945-6467 – Manager, David Eady – Branch of Windsor Public Library

Windsor: South Walkerville Library, 1425 Tecumseh Rd. East, Windsor ON N8W 1C2 – 519/253-3600; Fax: 519/253-3600 – Manager, Elizabeth Watson – Branch of Windsor Public Library

Wingham Branch Library, 281 Edward St., PO Box 208, Wingham ON N0G 2W0 – 519/357-3312 – Branch Supervisor, Paula Mackie – Branch of Huron County Library (*see* Goderich)

Winona Public Library, 1304 Hwy. 8, Winona ON L8E 5R1 – 905/643-2912 – Branch Head, Marg Lee – Branch of Wentworth Libraries

Wolfe Island Twp. - Library, Wolfe Island ON K0H 2Y0 – 613/385-2112 – Brenda MacDonald – Branch of Frontenac County Library (*see* Kingston)

Woodbridge: Ansley Grove Library, 350 Ansley Grove Rd., Woodbridge ON L4L 5C9 – 905/856-6551; Fax: 905/856-6151 – Manager, Jane Salmon – Branch of Vaughan Public Libraries (*see* Maple)

Woodbridge Library, 150 Woodbridge Ave., Woodbridge ON L4L 2S7 – 905/851-1296; Fax: 905/851-2322 – Branch Manager, Beryl Hall – Branch of Vaughan Public Libraries (*see* Maple)

Woodstock: Oxford County Library, The Town Centre, 130 Oxford St., Ingersoll ON N5C 2V5 – Fax: 519/485-4028; Email: jmoore@ocl.net; URL: http://www.ocl.net/oxlib/index.html; Symbol: OWOO – Chief Librarian, Sam Coghlan – See also following branches: Beachville Public Library, Brownsville Public Library, Burgessville Public Library, Drumbo Public Library, East Oxford Public Library, Embro Public Library, Hickson Public Library, Ingersoll Library, Innerkip Public Library, Kintore Public Library, Mount Elgin Public Library, Norwich Public Library, Otterville Public Library, Plattsville Public Library, Princeton Library, Tavistock Public Library, Thamesford Public Library

Woodstock: East Oxford Public Library, RR#4, Woodstock ON N4S 7V8 – 519/424-9378 – Supervisor, Heather Taylor – Branch of Oxford County Library (*see* Woodstock)

Woodstock Public Library, 445 Hunter St., Woodstock ON N4S 4G7 – 519/539-4801; Fax: 519/539-5246; Email: snelson@ocl.net; URL: http://www.ocl.net/oxlib/woodstkpl.html; Symbol: OWO – Chief Librarian, Stephen Nelson; Reference Librarian, Penny Quinn; Children's Librarian, Ursula Benoit; Head of Information Services, Susan Start

Woodville Branch Library, General Delivery, Woodville ON K0M 2T0 – 705/439-2160 – Branch of Victoria County Public Library (*see* Lindsay)

Wroxeter: Belmore Community Library, RR#1, Wroxeter ON N0G 2X0 – 519/392-6634 – Supervisor, Jane McQuarrie

Wyoming: Lambton County Library, 787 Broadway St., PO Box 3100, Wyoming ON N0N 1T0 – 519/845-3324; Fax: 519/845-0700; Symbol: LA – Director of Libraries, Museums & Cultural Services, Robert Krieg; Reference Librarian, Darlene LaBelle; Adult Services Librarian, Carol Leckie; Children's Librarian, Paulette Thompson; Public Services Manager, Maureen McKay; Technical Services Manager, Krystyna Stalmach; Manager, Branch Services, Carol Gardiner – See also following branches: Alvinston Library, Arkona Library, Brigden Library, Brights Grove Library, Camlachie Library, Chippewas of Sarnia Library, Corunna Library, Courtright Library, Florence Library, Forest Library, Grand Bend Library, Inwood Library, Mallroad Library, Mandaumin Library, Mooretown Library, Oil Springs Library, Petrolia Library, Point Edward Library, Port Franks Library, Port Lambton Library, Sarnia Library, Shetland Library, Sombra Library, Thedford Library, Warwick Library, Watford Library, Wilkesport Library, Wyoming Library

Wyoming: Mandaumin Library, 3019 Confederation Line, RR#1, Wyoming ON N0N 1T0 – 519/383-8085 – Librarian, Shirley Deelstra – Branch of Lambton County Library

Wyoming Library, 617 Broadway St., Wyoming ON N0N 1T0 – 519/845-0181 – Librarian, Phyllis Brooks – Branch of Lambton County Library

Yarker Branch Library, PO Box 160, Yarker ON K0K 3N0 – 613/377-6698 – Supervisor, Rika Blakslee – Branch of Lennox & Addington County Library (*see* Napanee)

York: City of York Public Library, 1745 Eglinton Ave. West, Toronto ON M6E 2H4 – 416/394-1000; Fax: 416/394-2781 – CEO, Bohus Derer; Branch Head, Maria Shchuka – See also following branches: Evelyn Gregory Branch Library, Jane-Dundas Branch Library, Mount Dennis Branch Library, Weston Branch Library

Zephyr: Scott Branch Library, Zephyr ON L0E 1T0 – 905/473-2375 – Branch Head, Judy Harrison – Branch of Uxbridge Twp. Public Library

Zurich Branch Library, PO Box 201, Zurich ON N0M 2T0 – 519/236-4965 – Branch Supervisor, Helene Ducharme – Branch of Huron County Library (*see* Goderich)

Burlington: Tansley Woods Branch Library, 1996 Itabashi Way, Burlington ON L7M 4J8 – 905/336-5583; Fax: 905/336-4266; Email: susanfb@haltonbe.on.ca – Branch Head, Susan Fitzgerald-Bell – Branch of Burlington Public Library

Curran: Succursale Curran, Curran ON K0B 1C0 – 613/673-5490 – Carole Mainville – Branch of Bibliothèques publiques du Canton de Plantagenet-Nord (*see* Wendover)

## Special & College Libraries & Resource Centres

### ALFRED

Alfred College of Agriculture & Food Technology - Library, POBox 580, Alfred ON K0B 1A0 – 613/679-2443; Fax: 613/679-2430

Chief Librarian, Robert St-Amant

Library Technician, Lyne Gagné-Lalonde

Loyalist College - Resource Centre, POBox 4200, Belleville ON K8N 5B9 – 613/969-1913; Fax: 613/962-1376; Email: LO@LoyalistC.on.ca – Educational Resources, Director, Beatrice Lo

Wright & Wright Law Office - Library, 329 Front St., Belleville ON K8N 2Z9 – 613/966-9711; Fax: 613/962-6833 – Richard Wright

### BRAMPTON

Against Drunk Driving – Library, POBox 397, Brampton ON L6V 2L3 – 905/793-4233; Fax: 905/793-4233 – Office Manager, Kathleen Close

Canadian Air Line Pilots Association (Ind.) – Library, 1300 Steeles Ave. East, Brampton ON L6T 1A2 – 905/453-8210; Fax: 905/453-8757 – Manager, Information Services, Roger Burgess Webb

Ontario Ministry of the Solicitor General & Correctional Services - Ontario Correctional Institute Library, 109 McLaughlin Rd. South, POBox 1888, Brampton ON L6V 2P1 – 905/457-7050; Fax: 905/452-8606 – Library Technician, Jeanette Fletcher

Vanier Centre for Women Library, 205 McLaughlin Rd. South, POBox 1150, Brampton ON L6V 2M5 – 905/459-9100, ext.158; Fax: 905/459-5735 – Library Technician, Angie Zanotti

Ontario Provincial Police Academy - Library, POBox 266, Brampton ON L6V 2L1 – 905/874-3154; Fax: 905/874-4032 – Librarian, Catherine Dowd

Ontario Provinicial Police Academy - Library, POBox 266, Brampton ON L6V 2L1 – 905/459-4193; Fax: 905/324-3688

Peel Law Association – Library, 7755 Hurontario St., Brampton ON L6V 2M7 – 905/451-2924; Fax: 905/451-3137 – Librarian, Marilyn Elkin

Peel Memorial Hospital – Health Sciences Library, 20 Lynch St., Brampton ON L6W 2Z8 – 905/796-4015; Fax: 905/451-5552 – Coordinator, Clare Pirie

Sheridan College - Brampton Campus Library, McLaughlin Rd., POBox 7500, Brampton ON L6V 1G6 – 905/459-7533; Fax: 905/459-7054; Symbol: OBRASC – Peggy Bram

Spar Aerospace Limited - Spar Space Systems Library/Information Resource Centre, 9445 Airport Rd., Brampton ON L6S 4J3 – 905/790-2800, ext.4108; Fax: 905/790-4423; Email: ENVOY: RMSD.LIB; ttrip@spar.ca; Symbol: OWSA – Library Supervisor, Tim Tripp

### BRANTFORD

Brant Historical Society – Library, 57 Charlotte St., Brantford ON N3T 2W6 – 519/752-2483

Canadian Foresters Life Insurance Society – Library, POBox 850, Brantford ON N3T 5S3 – 905/525-9559 – Personnel Administrator, Gail Newman

Insulating Glass Manufacturers Association of Canada – Library, POBox 25013, Brantford ON N3T 6K5 – 519/449-2487; Fax: 519/449-2887

Mohawk College - Brantford Campus Library, 411 Elgin St., Brantford ON N3T 5V2 – 519/758-6019; Fax: 519/758-6043 – Supervisor, Gail Sekine

Ontario Ministry of the Solicitor General & Correctional Services - Burtch Correctional Centre Library, POBox 940, Brantford ON N3T 5S6 – 519/484-2461; Fax: 519/484-2587 – Library Technician, Laurie D'Eon

Woodland Cultural Centre – Library, 184 Mohawk St., POBox 1506, Brantford ON N3T 5V6 – 519/759-2650 ext.224; Fax: 519/759-8912 – Library Technician, Winnie Jacobs

### BROCKVILLE

Leeds & Grenville Law Association - County Courthouse Library, 10 Wall St., Brockville ON K6V 7A8 – 613/342-1832; Fax: 613/342-2462 – Librarian, Florence Atkinson

St. Lawrence College - Learning Resource Centre, 2288 Parkedale Ave., Brockville ON K6V 5X3 – 613/345-0660, ext.3104; Fax: 613/345-2231; Email: staf1277@slcsl.stlawrencec.on.ca; Symbol: OBSL – Group Leader, Sara Manoll

**BURLINGTON**

The Bible League of Canada – Library, POBox 5037, Burlington ON L7R 3Y8 – 905/319-9500; Fax: 905/319-0484; Toll Free: 1-800-363-9673

Canadian Society of Mayflower Descendants – Library, 2071 Wellington Ave., Burlington ON L7R 1P4 – Arthur Harris

Christian Reformed World Relief Committee of Canada – CRWRC Development Education Library, 3475 Mainway, POBox 5070, Burlington ON L7R 3Y8 – 905/336-2920; Fax: 905/336-8344; Toll Free: 1-800-730-3490

City of Burlington - Clerk's Department Library, 426 Brant St., Burlington ON L7R 3Z6 – 905/335-7701; Fax: 905/335-7881; Email: cob@worldchat.com; URL: http://wchat.on.ca/cob – Records Coordinator, Annie Budz, Email: budza@city.burlington.on.ca

CUMIS General Insurance Co. - Library, 151 North Service Rd., POBox 5065, Burlington ON L7R 4C2 – 905/632-1221; Fax: 905/632-9412; Toll Free: 1-800-263-9120 – Librarian, Ann Higgins

Environment Canada - Canada Centre for Inland Waters - Library, 867 Lakeshore Rd., Burlington ON L7R 4A6 – 905/336-4530; Fax: 905/336-4428; Email: library@cciw.ca; Symbol: OBUC – Head, Library Services, Eve Dowie

Halton Board of Education - J.W. Singleton Education Library, 2050 Guelph Line, POBox 5005, Burlington ON L7R 3Z2 – 905/335-3665, ext.3312; Fax: 905/335-9802; Email: susan_mickalow@halton.tor.hookup.net
- Supervisor, Media & Libraries, Susan Mickalow
- Technical Services, Library Technician, Bonnie Starr

Joseph Brant Memorial Hospital – Organizational Development, 1230 North Shore Blvd., Burlington ON L7R 4C4 – 905/632-3730; Fax: 905/336-6480; Email: jbmh@fhs.mcmaster.ca – Librarian, Marnie E. Lynn

**CAMBRIDGE**

Heritage Baptist College & Heritage Theological Seminary - Library, 175 Holiday Inn Dr., Cambridge ON N3C 3T2 – 519/651-2869; Fax: 519/651-2870; Toll Free: 1-800-465-1961; Symbol: OTCBS – Librarian, Marion E. Meadows

**CAMPBELLFORD**

Solicitor General Canada - Warkworth Institution - Library, POBox 760, Campbellford ON K0L 1L0 – 705/924-2210, ext.2730; Fax: 705/924-3351; Symbol: OCWI – Librarian, Thomas Johnston

**CARLETON PLACE**

Postal History Society of Canada – Library, 216 Mailey Dr., Carleton Place ON K7C 3X9 – 613/257-5453

**CHALK RIVER**

Chalk River Laboratories - Information Centre, GPO, Chalk River ON K0J 1J0 – 613/584-8811, ext.3900; Fax: 613/584-1745; Email: refdesk@crl.aecl.ca; Symbol: OCKA
- Technical Leader, Monica Lim, Email: limm@crl.aecl.ca
- Acquistions Librarian, Linda Crawford

**CHATHAM**

Chatham-Kent Health Alliance - St. Joseph's Campus – Library of the Healing Arts, 519 King St. West, Chatham ON N7M 1G8 – 519/352-2500; Fax: 519/352-5261 – Librarian, Mary Gillies

St. Clair College - Thames Campus Resource Centre, 1001 Grand Ave. West, POBox 2017, Chatham ON N7M 5W4 – 519/354-9100, ext.3232, 3273; Fax: 519/354-5496; Email: mtales@sccoll.stclairc.on.ca
- Manager, Barry Van Biesbrouck
- Library Technician, Linda Grineage
- Library Specialist, Matt Tales

Union Gas Ltd. - Library Services, 50 Keil Dr. North, Chatham ON N7M 5M1 – 519/352-3100, ext.2495 – Assistant Librarian, Maureen Mason

**COBOURG**

Cobourg & District Historical Society – The Cobourg & District Historical Society Archives, POBox 911, Cobourg ON K9A 4W4 – 905/377-0413

Ontario Ministry of the Solicitor General & Correctional Services - Brookside Youth Centre Library, 390 King St. East, POBox 159, Cobourg ON K9A 4K6 – 905/372-5451; Fax: 905/372-7788 – Library Assistant, Gail Cunningham

**CONCORD**

CMS Group Inc. – Library, #3, 140 Snow Blvd., Concord ON L4K 4C1 – 905/660-7580; Fax: 905/660-0243 – Administrator, Lynda Bennare

**CORNWALL**

Canadian Heritage - Parks Canada - Information Resource Centre, 111 Water St. East, Cornwall ON K6H 6S3 – 613/938-5787; Fax: 613/938-5766; Email: ENVOY: PARKS.ILL.OCN; Symbol: OCN – Librarian, Joan Lipscombe

Cornwall & Seaway Valley Tourism – Library, 231 Augustus St., Cornwall ON K6J 3W2 – 613/938-4748; Fax: 613/938-4751; Toll Free: 1-800-937-4748 – Candy Pollard

North American Indian Travelling College – Library, RR#3, Cornwall ON K6H 5R7 – 613/932-9452; Fax: 613/932-0092

Stormont, Dundas & Glengarry Law Association – Courthouse Library, POBox 35, Cornwall ON K6H 5R9 – 613/932-5411

Transport Canada Training Institute - Library, 1950 Montreal Rd., Cornwall ON K6H 6L2 – 613/936-5018; Fax: 613/936-5044; Symbol: OOTI – Supervisor, Judith Daoust

**DEEP RIVER**

Deep River Symphony Orchestra – Library, POBox 1496, Deep River ON K0J 1P0 – 613/584-3311, x.3743 – Librarian, George Doubt

**DELHI**

Agriculture & Agri-Food Canada - Canadian Agriculture Library, Pest Management Research Centre, Delhi Farm, Schafer Rd., POBox 186, Delhi ON N4B 2W9 – 519/582-1950; Fax: 519/582-4223; Symbol: ODEAG – Librarian, Robert Duff

**DORSET**

Ontario Ministry of Environment & Energy - Dorset Environmental Science Centre – Library, Bellwood Acres Rd., Dorset ON P0A 1E0 – 705/766-2418; Fax: 705/766-2254; Email: dillonpe@epo.gov.on.ca – Manager, Peter Dillon

Leslie M. Frost Natural Resources Centre - Library, General Delivery, Dorset ON P0A 1E0 – 705/766-2451; Fax: 705/766-9677 – Education Specialist, David Gibson

**DUNDAS**

Peace Research Institute - Dundas – Peace Research Library, 25 Dundana Ave., Dundas ON L9H 4E5 – 905/628-2356; Fax: 905/628-1830 – Documentation Specialist, Linda Carroll

**ELMIRA**

Woolwich Community Services – Kids & I Resource Centre, 73 Arthur St. South, Elmira ON N3B 2M8 – 519/669-5139; Fax: 519/669-4210 – Coordinator, Elizabeth deBoer

**EMBRUN**

James D. Campbell Law Office - Library, #1, 165 Bay St., Embrun ON K0A 1W1 – 613/443-5683; Fax: 613/443-3285

**EXETER**

Shared Library Services – Library, South Huron Hospital, 24 Huron St. West, Exeter ON N0M 1S2 – 519/235-2700, ext.249; Fax: 519/235-3405; Email: lwilcox@julian.uwo.ca; Symbol: OESH
- Director, Linda Wilcox
- Library Assistant, Susan Oke

**FERGUS**

Wilson, Jack & Grant Law Office - Library, POBox 128, Fergus ON N1M 2W7 – 519/843-1960; Fax: 519/843-6888 – Partner, Douglas C. Jack

**FORT ERIE**

Adult Literacy Council of Greater Fort Erie – Library, #14, 427 Garrison Rd., Fort Erie ON L2A 6E6 – 905/871-6626; Fax: 905/871-7719

**FORT FRANCES**

United Native Friendship Centre – Library, 516 Portage Ave., POBox 752, Fort Frances ON P9A 3N1 – 807/274-3207; Fax: 807/274-4110 – Literacy Coordinator, Mike Anderson

**GEORGETOWN**

Esquesing Historical Society – Halton Hills Public Library, Georgetown Branch, POBox 51, Georgetown ON L7G 4T1 – 905/873-2681; Fax: 905/873-6118 – Information Services Librarian, Geoffrey Cannon

North Halton Association for the Developmentally Handicapped – Library, 62 Park Ave., Georgetown ON L7G 4Z1 – 905/873-8181; Fax: 905/873-8184 – Executive Assistant, Etta Mills

**GLOUCESTER**

Federation of Canadian Archers Inc. – Sport Information Resource Centre, #211, 1600 James Naismith Dr., Gloucester ON K1B 5N4 – 613/748-5658; Fax: 613/748-5785; Toll Free: 1-800-511-9999; TLX: 053-3660 – Reference Librarian, Ann Romeril

Ottawa-Carleton Children's Aid Society – Library, 1602 Telesat Court, Gloucester ON K1B 1B1 – 613/747-7800, ext.2750; Fax: 613/742-1607

Sport Information Resource Centre, Place R. Tait McKenzie, 1600 James Naismith Dr., Gloucester ON K1B 5N4 – 613/748-5658; Fax: 613/748-5701; Toll Free: 1-800-665-6413; Email: moreinfor@sirc.ca; URL: http://www.sirc.ca/; Symbol: OOFS
- President, Gilles Chiasson
- Marketing, Coordinator, Linda Wheeler
- Customer Services, Head, Christine Lalande
- Indexing, Head, Marion Fournier

Telesat Canada - Information Resource Centre, 1601 Telesat Ct., Gloucester ON K1B 5P4 – 613/748-0123; Fax: 613/748-8712; Email: ENVOY: TELESAT.LIBRARY; Symbol: OOTEL
- Information Services Coordinator, Steven Roby
- Library Technician, Suzanne Dion

Transport Canada - Aircraft Services Directorate - Technical Library, 58 Service Rd., Gloucester ON K1V 9B2 – 613/998-8299; Fax: 613/998-8326; Symbol: OOTFS
- Head, Technical Library, Jeff White
- Acquisitions, Sherry Stewart
- Distribution, Jennifer Maguire

Transportation Safety Board - Engineering Branch - Library, 1901 Research Rd., Gloucester ON K1A 1K8 – 613/998-8230, ext.172; Fax: 613/998-5572; Symbol: OOTSE – Library Technician, Janet Thomas

**GUELPH**

Agriculture & Agri-Food Canada-Greenhouse & Processing Crops Research Centre: Guelph – Library, 70 Fountain St. East, Guelph ON N1H 3N6 – 519/826-2086; Fax: 519/826-2090

Canadian Botanical Association – Library, Dept. of Botany, University of Guelph, #158, 50 Stone Rd. East, Guelph ON N1G 2W1 – 613/990-6452; Fax: 519/767-1991 – Archivist, Dr. J.F. Gerrath

Conestoga College - Guelph Campus Library, 460 Speedvale Ave. West, Guelph ON N1H 6N6 – 519/824-9390, ext.126 – Florence Dumas

Farm Safety Association Inc. – Film Service, #22, 340 Woodlawn Rd. West, Guelph ON N1H 1G8 – 519/823-5600; Fax: 519/823-8880

Fellowship of Evangelical Baptist Churches in Canada – Archives, 679 Southgate Dr., Guelph ON N1G 4S2 – 519/821-4830; Fax: 519/821-9829 – Isabel Freeman

Guelph Correctional Centre - Library, POBox 3600, Guelph ON N1H 6P3 – 519/822-0020, ext.2232; Fax: 519/822-4926 – Library Technician, Vanessa Jabelmann

Homewood Health Centre – Library, 150 Delhi St., Guelph ON N1E 4J8 – 519/824-1010, ext.148; Fax: 519/824-1827 – Library Technician, Joyce Pharoah

Jubilee Centre for Agricultural Research – Family Farm Stewardship Library, 115 Woolwich St., Guelph ON N1H 3V1 – 519/837-1620; Fax: 519/824-1835 – Librarian, Nellie van Donkersgoed

Moon, Heath Law Office - Library, 164 Norfolk St., POBox 180, Guelph ON N1H 6K1 – 519/824-2540; Fax: 519/763-6785; Email: moonlaw@sentex.net – Librarian, Pat Breese

Ontario Ministry of Agriculture, Food & Rural Affairs - Audio Visual Library, Visual Communication Services, 1 Stone Rd. West, Guelph ON N1G 4Y2 – 519/826-3680, 3681; Fax: 519/826-3358

Ontario Ministry of the Solicitor General & Correctional Services - Guelph Correctional Centre Library, 785 York Rd., POBox 3600, Guelph ON N1H 6P3 – 519/822-0020, ext.2313/2232; Fax: 519/822-0591 – Library Technician, Vanessa Jabelmann

Rowan Williams Davies & Irwin Inc. – Library, 650 Woodlawn Rd. West, Guelph ON N1K 1B8 – 519/823-1311; Fax: 519/823-1316 – Project Manager, M. Vanderheyden

Uniroyal Chemical Ltd. - Research Labs Library, 120 Huron St., Guelph ON N1H 6N3 – 519/822-3790, ext.455/458; Fax: 519/837-0523; Symbol: OGDR – Manager of Information Services & Legal Liaison, Lorna Cole

The United Brethren Church in Canada – Library, 501 Whitelaw Rd., Guelph ON N1K 1E7 – 519/836-0180; Fax: 519/837-2219

University of Guelph - Library, #158, 50 Stone Rd. East, Guelph ON N1G 2W1 – 519/824-4120, ext.2181; Fax: 519/824-6931; Email: libloan@uoguelph.ca; URL: http://www.lib.uoguelph.ca; Symbol: OGU
- Chief Librarian, Michael Ridley
- Administrative & Facilities Support Services, Head, Pat Hock
- Collections Services, Head, Tim Sauer
- Public Services, Head, Ron MacKinnon
- Special Collections & Library Development, Head, Bernard Katz
- Systems Services, Manager, George Loney
- Technical Services, Head, Ellen Tom

Wellington County Board of Education - Terry James Resource Library, 500 Victoria Rd. North, Guelph ON N1E 6K2 – 519/822-4420, ext.226; Fax: 519/763-6870; Email: library@board.wcbc.on.ca; Symbol: OGWE – Supervisor, Central Library Services, Paola Rowe, 519/822-4420, ext.270, Email: prowe@board.wcbc.on.ca

Wellington County Law Association – Law Library, 74 Woolwich St., Guelph ON N1H 3T9 – 519/763-6365; Fax: 519/763-6847; Symbol: WELN – Librarian, Betty Thiessen

**HAGERSVILLE**

Grand River Polytechnical Institute - Library Resource Centre, Grand River Territory, Six Nations, POBox 728, Hagersville ON N0A 1H0 – 905/768-0448; Fax: 905/768-0424 – Diana Doxdator

**HAILEYBURY**

Northern College - Haileybury School of Mines - Library, PO Bag A, Haileybury ON P0J 1K0 – 705/672-3376, ext.806; Fax: 705/672-2014; Toll Free: 1-800-461-5745; Email: libraryh@kirk.northernc.on.ca – Library Technician, Brenda Morissette

**HAMILTON**

Canadian Academic Accounting Association – Library, Faculty of Management, University of Toronto, #850, 120 King St. West, POBox 176, Hamilton ON L8N 3C3 – 905/525-1884; Fax: 905/525-3046

Canadian Baptist Archives, McMaster Divinity College, 1280 Main St. West, Hamilton ON L8S 4K1 – 905/525-9140, ext.23511; Fax: 905/577-4782; Email: colwellj@mcmail.cis.mcmaster.ca – Archivist, Judith Colwell

Canadian Centre for Occupational Health & Safety – Documentation Resources, 250 Main St. East, Hamilton ON L8N 1H6 – 905/572-4400, 1-800-263-8466; Fax: 905/572-2206; Toll Free: 1-800-668-4284; Email: library@kate.ccohs.ca; Symbol: OHOHS – Manager, Documentation Resources & Records Management, Peter Lukas

Canadian Society of Laboratory Technologists – Library, POBox 2830, Hamilton ON L8N 3N8 – 905/528-8642; Fax: 905/528-4968

Centre for Canadian Historical Horticultural Studies, POBox 399, Hamilton ON L8N 3H8 – 905/527-1158, ext. 246; Fax: 905/577-0375; Symbol: OHRB – Librarian, Linda Brownlee

Chedoke-McMaster Hospital – Chedoke Hospital Library, 1200 Main St. West, POBox 2000, Hamilton ON L8N 3Z5 – 905/521-2100, ext.7741; Fax: 905/521-5090; Email: wyndham@fhs.csu.mcmaster.ca – Librarian, Lois Wyndham

Community Information Service Hamilton-Wentworth – Library, 55 York Blvd., POBox 2700, Hamilton ON L8N 4E4 – 905/528-0104; Fax: 905/528-7764

Dofasco Inc. - Library Resource Centre, POBox 2460, Hamilton ON L8N 3J5 – 905/548-7200, ext.2794; Fax: 905/548-4630 – Coordinator, Linda Pauloski

Greater Hamilton Symphony Association – Library, 991 King St. West, POBox 89007, Hamilton ON L8S 4R5 – 905/526-6690; Fax: 905/526-1050 – Librarian, Enid Pottinger

Greater Hamilton Technology Enterprise Centre – BAC Library, #100, 7 Innovation Dr., Hamilton ON L9J 1K3 – 905/689-2400; Fax: 905/689-2200; Email: kzavitz@bac.net – Manager, Help Services, Kara Zavitz

Hamilton & District Chamber of Commerce – Business Reference Library, 555 Bay St. North, Hamilton ON L8L 1H1 – 905/522-1151; Fax: 905/522-1154

Hamilton Board of Education - Dr. Harry Paikin Library, 100 Main St. West, Hamilton ON L8N 3L1 – 905/521-2518; Fax: 905/521-2541; Symbol: OHEC
- Chief Librarian, Ingrid Scott, 905/521-2518, ext.2335
- Research Librarian, Karyn Hogan, 905/527-5092, ext.2308
- Library Technician, Leslie Ferguson, 905/521-2518
- Library Secretary, Sue McCormick, 905/527-5092, ext.2309
- Library Technician, Cherilyn Waterfield, 905/527-5092, ext.2283
- Library Technician, Jane Holbrook, 905/527-5092, ext.2332

Hamilton Law Association – Anthony Pepe Memorial Law Library, 50 Main St. East, Hamilton ON L8N 1E9 – 905/522-1563; Fax: 905/572-1188 – Librarian, Wendy Hearder-Moan

Hamilton Psychiatric Hospital – Library Resource Centre, 100 - 5th St. West, POBox 585, Hamilton ON L8L 2B3 – 905/388-2511; Fax: 905/575-6035; Email: devries@fhs.csu.mcmaster.ca – Librarian, Anne Devries

Hamilton Regional Indian Centre – Resource Library, 712 Main St. East, Hamilton ON L8M 1K8 – 905/548-9593; Fax: 905/545-4077 – Laura Williams

Hamilton Spectator - Library, 44 Frid St., Hamilton ON L8N 3G3 – 905/526-3315; Fax: 905/526-3399; Email: tdanciu@ham.southam.ca
- Senior Information Technician, Tammie Danciu, 905/526-3209
- Information Technician, Marilyn McGrory, 905/526-3379

Inch, Easterbrook & Shaker Law Office - Library, 1 King St. West, 15th Fl., Hamilton ON L8P 4X8 – 905/525-4481, ext.31; Fax: 905/525-0031; Email: ies@inchlaw.com; URL: http://www.inchlaw.com – Library Technician, Margery Bylsma

McMaster University - Libraries, 1280 Main St. West, Hamilton ON L8S 4L6 – 905/525-9140; Fax: 905/546-0625, 522-1277; Email: ILL.OHM; URL: http://www.mcmaster.ca; Symbol: OHM
- University Librarian, Graham R. Hill
- Administrative Services, Head, Mary Ruth Linkert
- Archives & Research Collections, Director, Charlotte Stewart
- Collection Management & Development, Assistant University Librarian, Victor Nunn
- Processing Services, Director, Carol Racheter
- Readers Services, Assistant University Librarian, Sheila Pepper
- Systems Development, Associate University Librarian, Marju Drynan
- Health Sciences Library, Director, Dorothy Fitzgerald
- Innis Library, Business Librarian, Kathryn Ball
- Lloyd Reeds Map Library/Urban Documentation Centre, Documentalist, Cathy Moulder
- Science & Engineering, Librarian, Peggy Findlay

Mohawk College - Health Sciences Education Centre Library, 630 Sanitorium Rd., Hamilton ON L8N 3Z5 – 905/575-2509 – Maureen Price
- Library Resource Centre, 135 Fennell Ave. West, POBox 2034, Hamilton ON L8N 3T2 – 905/575-2077; Fax: 905/575-2011; Email: hykl@oper-atns.mohawkc.on.ca; Symbol: OHMC
- Director of Learning Resources, Sandra Black
- Media & Technology Services, Head, Valerie Parke
- Circulation/Reference, Head, Marilyn McDermott

Native Indian/Inuit Photographer's Association – Resource Centre, 134 James St. South, Hamilton ON L8P 2Z4 – 905/529-7477 – Communictions Specialist, Steve Loft

NDE Institute of Canada – Library, 135 Fennell Ave. West, Hamilton ON L8N 3T2 – 905/387-1655; Fax: 905/574-6080

New Hamilton Orchestra – Library, Hamilton Place, #705, 25 Main St. West, Hamilton ON L8P 1H1 – 905/526-1677; Fax: 905/526-1606 – Librarian, Nancy Elbeck

Ontario Cancer Treatment & Research Foundation - Library, 699 Concession St., Hamilton ON L8V 5C2 – 905/387-9711, ext.5100; Fax: 905/575-6317;

Email: fraumeni@fhs.csu.mcmaster.ca – Library Manager, Michael Fraumeni

Ross & McBride Law Office - Library, 1 King St. West, 10 - 11th Fl., POBox 907, Hamilton ON L8N 3P6 – 905/526-9800; Fax: 905/526-0732 – Librarian, K. Kennett

Royal Botanical Gardens – Library, POBox 399, Hamilton ON L8N 3H8 – 905/527-1158, ext.246; Fax: 905/577-0375; Symbol: OHRB – Linda Brownlee

St. Joseph's Hospital – Library Services, 50 Charlton Ave. East, Hamilton ON L8N 4A6 – 905/522-1155, x.3410; Fax: 905/521-6111; Email: marag@fhs.mcmaster.ca – Director, Library Services, Jean Maragno

SHAIR International Resource Centre – Library, 255 West Ave. North, Hamilton ON L8L 5C8 – 905/528-9055; Fax: 905/522-9374

Simpson, Wigle - Law Library, #1030, 120 King St. West, POBox 990, Hamilton ON L8N 3R1 – 905/528-8411 – Library Technician, M. Bylsma

Society of Canadian Cine Amateurs – Library, 45 Highcliffe Ave., Hamilton ON L9C 2Y4 – 905/575-1063 – Librarian, Neil Upshall

Society of Management Accountants of Canada – CMA Library, #850, 120 King St. West, POBox 176, Hamilton ON L8N 3C3 – 905/525-4100; 416/847-0373 (Toronto line); Fax: 905/525-4533; Toll Free: 1-800-263-7622

Stelco Inc. - Research & Development Dept. - Corporate Information Centre, POBox 2030, Hamilton ON L8N 3T1 – 905/528-2511, ext.2076; Fax: 905/308-7012; Email: strblib@netaccess.on.ca; Symbol: OHSCC – Research Library Technician, Carol Cernile

### HARROW

Agriculture & Agri-Food Canada-Greenhouse & Processing Crops Research Centre: Harrow – Library, Hwy. 18 East, Harrow ON N0R 1G0 – 519/738-2251; Fax: 519/738-2929; Email: lboharag@ncccot.agr.ca; Symbol: OHARAG – Research Librarian, Eric Champagne

Harrow Early Immigrant Research Society – Library, POBox 53, Harrow ON N0R 1G0 – 519/738-4368; Fax: 519/738-9315 – Librarian, J. Ferguson

### HEARST

Collège universitaire de Hearst - Bibliothéque Maurice-Saulnier, CP 580, Hearst ON P0L 1N0 – 705/372-1781; Téléc: 705/362-7518 – Johanne Morin-Corbeil

### HULL

Industry Canada - Canadian Intellectual Property Office Library, Place du Portage, Phase 1, 50, rue Victoria, 11e étage, Hull ON K1A 0C9 – 819/997-2964; Fax: 819/997-5585; URL: http://info.ic.gc.ca/opengov/cipo/; Symbol: OOSP
- Librarian, Rita Bolar
- Library Technician, Thérèse Renaud

### KANATA

Canadian Marconi Co. - Library, 415 Legget Dr., Kanata ON K2K 2B2 – 613/592-6500; Fax: 613/592-7427; URL: http://www.marconi.ca; Symbol: OKCM – Chief Librarian, Lois Brimacombe

Fleet Technology Limited – Library, 311 Legget Dr., Kanata ON K2K 1Z8 – 613/592-2830; Fax: 613/592-4950 – Librarian, Faye Bennett

Mitel Corporation - Library, 350 Legget Dr., Kanata ON K2K 1X3 – 613/592-2122; Fax: 613/592-4784 – Librarian, Marie P. Paul, 613/592-2122, ext.4188

### KAPUSKASING

Northern College of Applied Arts & Technology - Kapuskasing Campus Library, 3 Aurora Ave., Kapuskasing ON P5N 1J6 – 705/335-8504; Fax: 705/335-8343; Toll Free: 1-800-461-2167; Email: mehta@kirk.northernc.ca – Academic Coordinator, Kishor Mehta

### KEMPTVILLE

Kemptville College - Purvis Library, PO Bag 2003, Kemptville ON K0G 1J0 – 613/258-8634; Fax: 613/258-8384; Email: purvis3@igs.net; URL: http://home.istar.ca/~kcat/purvis.htm; Symbol: OKEMC – Librarian, D. Simpson

Professional Photographers of Ontario Inc. – PPO Library, 2833 Donnelly Dr., RR#4, Kemptville ON K0G 1J0 – 613/258-5432; Fax: 613/258-5432; Toll Free: 1-800-368-6776 – Library Chair, Mark Robinson

### KING CITY

Seneca College - King Campus Library Resource Centre, 13990 Dufferin St., King City ON L7B 1B3 – 905/833-3333, ext.5105; Fax: 905/833-1106 – Campus Librarian, Marjorie Hale, 905/833-3333, ext.5106

### KINGSTON

Alcan International Ltd. - Kingston Research & Development Centre Technical Library, POBox 8400, Kingston ON K7L 5L9 – 613/541-2065, 2071; Fax: 613/547-2134; Email: brian_chenoweth@alcan.com
- Coordinator, Brian Chenoweth
- Specialist, Cindy Cain-Lough

Canadian Land Force Command & Staff College - Fort Frontenac Library, Fort Frontenac, POBox 1700, Kingston ON K7K 7B4 – 613/541-5010, ext.5815; Fax: 613/546-0589; Symbol: OKF
- Chief Librarian, Serge Campion, 613/541-5010, ext.5829
- Technical Services Librarian, D. Willis

Cunningham, Swan, Carty, Little & Bonham Law Office - Library, Empire Life Bldg., #500, 259 King St. East, POBox 460, Kingston ON K7L 4W6 – 613/544-0211; Fax: 613/542-9814 – Librarian, Elizabeth A. Marshall

Frontenac Law Association – Frontenac County Courthouse Library, County Courthouse, Court St., Kingston ON K7L 2N4 – 613/542-0034; Fax: 613/531-9764 – Librarian, Jackie Hawkins

Hôtel-Dieu Hospital – Staff Library, 166 Brock St., Kingston ON K7L 5G2 – 613/544-3310; Fax: 613/544-7175 – Director, Lynda Silver

International Centre – Education Abroad Resource Library, Queen's University, John Deutsch University Centre, 99 University Ave., Kingston ON K7L 3N6 – 613/545-2604; Fax: 613/545-6190 – Senior Secretary, Asha Joneja

Kingston Area Economic Development Commission – Small Business Centre, #200, 181 Wellington St., Kingston ON K7L 3E3 – 613/544-2725; Fax: 613/546-2882 – Administrative Assistant, Sharon Fitch

Kingston District Community Information Centre – Library, 130A Johnson St., Kingston ON K7L 1X8 – 613/542-1001; Fax: 613/547-6521 – Database Manager, Jane McDonald

Kingston General Hospital – Library, 76 Stuart St., Kingston ON K7L 2V7 – 613/549-6666, ext.4076; Fax: 613/548-6042; Email: KGHLIB@qucdn.queensu.ca; Symbol: OKGH – Manager, Library Services, Margaret Darling

Kingston Penitentiary - Library, 555 King St., POBox 22, Kingston ON K7L 4V7 – 613/545-8460, ext.1505; Fax: 613/545-0826; Symbol: OKK – Librarian, N. Rudolph Meier

Kingston Psychiatric Hospital – Staff Library, 752 King St. West, POBox 603, Kingston ON K7L 4X3 – 613/546-1101, ext.5745; Fax: 613/548-5577; Email: gagnon@qucdn.queensu.ca; Symbol: OKPH – Hospital Librarian, Karen Gagnon

Marine Museum of the Great Lakes at Kingston - Audrey Rushbrook Memorial Library & Archives, 55 Ontario St., Kingston ON K7L 2Y2 – 613/542-2261; Fax: 613/542-0043; URL: http://www.marmus.ca – Archivist, Librarian, Earl Moorhead

Queen's University - Libraries, Joseph S. Stauffer Library, Union St., Kingston ON K7L 5C4 – 613/545-2519; Fax: 613/545-6362; Email: web@stauffer.queensu.ca; URL: http://stauffer.queensu.ca; Symbol: OKQ
- Chief Librarian, Paul Wiens, Email: wiensp@qucdn.queensu.ca
- Collection Development, Coordinator, Dianne Cook, Email: cookdc@stauffer.queensu.ca
- Access Services, Head, Melody Burton, Email: burtonm@stauffer.queensu.ca
- Acquisitions, Head, Sam Kalb, Email: kalbs@post.queensu.ca
- Information & Reference, Head, Constance Adamson, Email: adamsonc@stauffer.queensu.ca
- ILL Coordinator, Nancy Lemon, Email: lemonn@stauffer.queensu.ca
- Documents Unit, Head, Jeff Moon, Email: moonj@stauffer.queensu.ca
- Special Collections, Head, Barbara Teatero, Email: teaterob@qucdn.queensu.ca
- Special Readers' Services, Coordinator, Michele Chittenden, Email: chittend@stauffer.queensu.ca
- Systems & Development, Assistant Librarian, Gene Clevenger, Email: cleveng@stauffer.queensu.ca
- Art Library, Art Librarian, Jane Law, Email: lawj@qucdn.queensu.ca
- Bracken (Health Sciences) Library, Head, Vivien Ludwin, Email: ludwinv@stauffer.queensu.ca
- Education Library, Librarian, Sandra Casey, Email: caseys@qucdn.queensu.ca
- Engineering & Science Libraries, Head, Jane Philipps, 613/545-6846, Email: philipps@stauffer.queensu.c
- May Ball Library, School of Industrial Relations, Head, Carol Williams, 613/545-6623, ext.7077, Email: williamc@post.queensu.ca
- Music Librarian, Vivien Taylor, Email: taylorv@stauffer.queensu.ca
- William R. Lederman Law Library, Chief Law Librarian, Denis Marshall, Email: marshald@qsilver.queensu.ca
- Map & Air Photos, Curator, Shirley Harmer, Email: harmers@stauffer.queensu.ca

Royal Military College of Canada - Library, General Delivery, Kingston ON K7K 5L0 – 613/541-6000, ext.6004; Fax: 613/542-5055; Symbol: OKR
- Chief Librarian, Samuel O. Alexander, 613/541-6229
- Technical Services & Systems, Head, S.J. Toomey, 613/541-6000, ext.6260
- Massey Library, Head, B. Cameron, 613/541-6000, ext.6674
- Science/Engineering Library, Head, N. Turkington, 613/541-6000, ext.6079

Solicitor General Canada - Collins Bay Institution - Library, 455 Bath Rd., POBox 190, Kingston ON K7L 4V9 – 613/545-8598, ext.341; Symbol: OKCB
- Joyceville Institution - Library, POBox 880, Kingston ON K7L 4X9 – 613/542-4554, ext.2491; Symbol: OKJ – Librarian, Lise Maillet

### KIRKLAND LAKE

Northern College of Applied Arts & Technology - Northern College Libraries in South Porcupine & Haileybury, PO Bag 2400, Kirkland Lake ON P2N 3P4 – 705/567-9291, ext.700; Fax: 705/568-8186; Toll

Free: 1-800-461-4991; Email: libraryk@ kirk.northernc.on.ca; Symbol: OKLNC
Library Technician, E. Rose
Library Technician, D. Conway

**KITCHENER**

AIDS Committee of Cambridge, Kitchener/Waterloo & Area – Library, 123 Duke St. East, Kitchener ON N2A 1A4 – 519/570-3687; Fax: 519/570-4034 – Education Coordinator, Rob Gascho

Community Information Centre of Waterloo Region – Library, 25 Frederick St., Lower Level, Kitchener ON N2H 6M8 – 519/579-3800; Fax: 519/578-9185

Conestoga College - Learning Resource Centre, 299 Doon Valley Dr., Kitchener ON N2G 4M4 – 519/748-5220, ext.361; Fax: 519/748-5971
Manager, Grant McGregor, 519/748-5220, ext.355
Coordinator, Jill Douglas, 519/748-5220, ext.240
Coordinator, Cathy Potvin, 519/748-5220, ext.458

Grand River Hospital – Health Sciences Library, Kitchener-Waterloo Health Centre, POBox 9056, Kitchener ON N2G 1G3 – 519/749-4300, ext.2235; Fax: 519/749-4208 – Coordinator, Library Services, Dee Sprung

Grand River Hospital Corp. - Freeport Health Centre, 3570 King St. East, Kitchener ON N2A 2W1 – 519/894-8360, ext.7174; Fax: 519/893-2625 – Librarian, Dawn Bombay

Kitchener-Waterloo Record - Library, 225 Fairway Rd. South, Kitchener ON N2G 4E5 – 519/894-2231; Fax: 519/894-3829; Email: newsroom@ therecord.com
Librarian, Chris Masterman, 519/894-2231, ext.695
Library Assistant, Ken Cenerelli

Kitchener-Waterloo Symphony Orchestra Association Inc. – Library, 101 Queen St. North, Kitchener ON N2H 6P7 – 519/745-4711; Fax: 519/745-4474 – Marianne Leach-Hoffer

St. Mary's General Hospital – Library, 911 Queens Blvd., Kitchener ON N2M 1B2 – 519/749-6549; Fax: 519/749-6484; Email: ebaldwin@ stmaryhosp.on.ca – Medical Librarian, Elaine Baldwin

Waterloo Historical Society – Library, c/o Kitchener Public Library, 85 Queen St. North, Kitchener ON N2H 2H1 – 519/743-0271, ext.252; Fax: 519/570-1360 – Local History Librarian, Susan Hoffman

Waterloo Law Association – Law Library, Court House, 20 Weber St. East, Kitchener ON N2H 1C3 – 519/742-0872; Fax: 519/742-4102 – Librarian, Catherine Whiteman

Waterloo Region Roman Catholic Separate School Board - Resource Centre, 91 Moore Ave., POBox 1116, Kitchener ON N2G 4G2 – 519/578-3660; Fax: 519/884-0158 – Resource Librarian, Elaine Zink

Waterloo Regional Arts Council Inc. – Resource Centre, 25 Frederick St., Kitchener ON N2H 6M8 – 519/744-4552; Fax: 519/744-9342

**KLEINBURG**

Canadian Compensation Association – Library, 10435 Islington Ave., POBox 294, Kleinburg ON L0J 1C0 – 905/893-1689; Fax: 905/893-2392

The McMichael Canadian Art Collection - Library, 10365 Islington Ave., Kleinburg ON L0J 1C0 – 905/893-1121; Fax: 905/893-2588; Email: linda.morita@ mcmichael.on.ca; URL: http://www.mcmichael.com – Librarian, Linda Morita

**LAKEFIELD**

Lakefied College - School Library, Hwy. 28, Lakefield ON K0L 2H0 – 705/652-3324; Fax: 705/652-6320; URL: http://www.lakefieldcs.on.ca/
Head, Manal Stamboulie, Email: MStamboulie@ Lakefieldcs.on.ca
Library Technician, Friedel Hatje

**LEAMINGTON**

Point Pelee National Park - Library, RR#1, Leamington ON N8H 3V4 – 519/322-2365; Fax: 519/322-1277 – Chief, Lily J. Meleg

South Essex Community Centre – Resource Centre, #301, 33 Princess St., Leamington ON N8H 5C5 – 519/326-8629; Fax: 519/326-1529 – Director, Community Education, Christine Tiessen

**LINDSAY**

Sir Sandford Fleming College of Applied Arts & Technology - School of Natural Resources, Frost Campus Educational Resource Centre, POBox 8000, Lindsay ON K9V 5E6 – 705/324-9144; Fax: 705/878-9318; Symbol: OLISF
Library Supervisor, Gale Butterill, Email: GButteri@flemingc.on.ca
LRC Director, Karen Sjolin
Periodicals, Maggie Fry

Victoria/Haliburton Law Association – Library, 440 Kent St. West, Lindsay ON K9V 4T7 – 705/324-7114; Fax: 705/878-1071 – Law Librarian, Ann Neale

**LION'S HEAD**

Bruce Peninsula Environment Group – Library, 30 Main St., POBox 1119, Lion's Head ON N0H 1W0 – 519/793-4123; Toll Free: 1-800-416-2734 – Librarian, Edith Tompkins

**LONDON**

3M Canada Inc. - Technical Information Centre, POBox 5610, London ON N6A 4L6 – 519/451-2500, ext.2486; Fax: 519/452-4714; Email: ENVOY: MMM.TECHINFO; Symbol: OLTMC – Librarian, Cheryl E. Stephenson, Email: cstephenson@ mmm.com

Agriculture & Agri-Food Canada-Pest Management Research Centre – Canadian Agriculture Library, 1391 Sandford St., London ON N5V 4T3 – 905/457-1470, ext.263; Fax: 519/457-3997; Email: DrewD@ em.agr.ca; Symbol: OLAG – Librarian, Dorothy Drew

Board of Education for the City of London - Education Centre Professional Library, 1250 Dundas St., London ON N5W 5P2 – 519/452-2124; Fax: 519/455-7648; Email: greigpa@epo.gov.on.ca – Librarian, Patricia Grieg

Brescia College - Library, 1285 Western Rd., London ON N6G 1H2 – 519/432-8353; Fax: 519/679-6489; Symbol: OLBR – Librarian, Christine Suokaite

Child & Parent Resource Institute – Dr. Joseph Pozsonyi Memorial Library, 600 Sanitorium Rd., London ON N6H 3W7 – 519/471-2540; Fax: 519/641-1922; Email: mmaguire@julian.uwo.ca – Library Supervisor, Maureen Maguire

College of Family Physicians of Canada - Canadian Library of Family Medicine, #170C, Natural Sciences Centre, University of Western Ontario, 1151 Richmond St. North, London ON N6A 5B7 – 519/661-3170; Fax: 519/661-3880; Email: clfm@julian.uwo.ca; URL: http:// www.uwo.ca/fammed/clfm/index.html; Symbol: OLUCL – Director, Library Services, Lynn Dunikowski

The Commonwealth Association for Education in Journalism & Communication – Commonwealth Media Resource Centre, Faculty of Law, University of Western Ontario, 1151 Richmond St., London ON N6A 3K7 – 519/433-9787; Fax: 519/661-3790; TLX: 064-7134; Email: caejc@julian.uwo.ca – Bill Cecil-Smith

Cross Cultural Learner Centre – Resource Library, #225, 17 Dundas St. East, London ON N5W 2Z5 – 519/432-1133; Fax: 519/660-6168 – Global Educator, Suha Velamoor

Fanshawe College - Library, POBox 4005, London ON N5W 5H1 – 519/452-4240; Fax: 519/452-4473; URL: http://www.franshawec.on.ca; Symbol: OLFC
Manager, Library Services, A.K. Frost
Acquisitions/Cataloguing, Technical Services & Systems Librarian, Vicky Mok
Circulation/Reference, Public Services Librarian, Suzanne O'Neill, Email: oneills@ admin.fanshawec.on.ca
Media Services, Librarian, Elaine Vitali

Faxon Canada Ltd. - Reference Library, POBox 2382, London ON N6A 5A7 – 519/472-1005; Fax: 519/472-1072; Email: stuart@faxon.ca – S. Silcox

Fenco MacLaren Inc. - Library, 320 Adelaide St. South, London ON N5Z 3L2 – 519/686-5711; Fax: 519/686-5770 – Library Manager, Jennifer McNenly

Huron College - Silcox Memorial Library, 1349 Western Rd., London ON N6G 1H3 – 519/438-7224, ext.213; Fax: 519/438-3938; Email: pmackay@ julian.uwo.ca; URL: http://www.uwo.ca/huron/ libweb.html – Chief Librarian, Pamela MacKay

King's College - Cardinal Carter Library, 266 Epworth Ave., London ON N6A 2M3 – 519/433-3491, ext.504; Fax: 519/433-0070; Toll Free: 1-800-265-4406; Email: clouston@julian.uwo.ca
Chief Librarian, Dr. John S. Clouston
Assistant Librarian/Systems Manager, Linda Whidden, 519/433-3491, ext.506
Circulation, Head, Toni Barrette, 519/433-3491, ext.505
Public Services Librarian, Susan Evans, 519/433-3491, ext.327

London Chamber of Commerce – Library, 244 Pall Mall St., POBox 3295, London ON N6A 5P6 – 519/432-7551; Fax: 519/432-8063; Email: info@ chamber.london.on.ca – Information Services, Wendy Mills

The London Free Press - Editorial Library, 369 York St., POBox 2280, London ON N6A 4G1 – 519/667-4559 (Reference Library); Fax: 519/667-4528; Email: library@lfpress.com; URL: http://www.lfpress.com – Librarian, Anita McCallum, 519/667-5451, ext.2097, Email: amccallu@lfpress.com

London Health Sciences Centre - University Campus – Library Services, 339 Windermere Rd., London ON N6A 5A5 – 519/663-3300, ext.5865; Fax: 519/663-3198 – Chief Librarian, Jan Figurski
Victoria Campus - Westminister Site, 800 Commissioners Rd. East, POBox 5375, London ON N6A 4G5 – 519/685-8300, ext.2042; Fax: 519/685-8147 – Manager, Learning Services, Mary Gillett

London Psychiatric Hospital – George E. Jenkins Library, 850 Highbury Ave., POBox 2532, London ON N6A 4H1 – 519/455-5110, ext.2167; Fax: 519/455-9986; Symbol: OLPH – Librarian, Mai Why

Middlesex Law Association – Library, 80 Dundas St., Unit N, 6th Fl., London ON N6A 6A1 – 519/679-7046; Fax: 519/672-5917 – Law Librarian, Cynthia Simpson

Ontario Petroleum Institute Inc. – Library, #104, 555 Southdale Rd. East, London ON N6E 1A2 – 519/680-1620 – Librarian, Fran McCallum

Orthodox Missionary Church of Canada – Bishop Matthaios Library, Sts. Cyril & Methodius Parish, #514, 186 King St., London ON N6A 1C7 – 519/438-0734

St. Joseph's Health Centre of London - Library Services, 268 Grosvenor St., London ON N6A 4V2 – 519/646-6000, ext.4439; Fax: 519/646-6006; Symbol: OLSJ – Manager, Library Services, Louise Lin

St. Peter's Seminary - A.P. Mahoney Library, 1040 Waterloo St. North, London ON N6A 3Y1 – 519/

432-1824, 439-3963; Fax: 519/439-5172; Email: lcote@julian.uwa.ca; Symbol: OLSP
Chief Librarian, Lois Côté
Reference Librarian, Frances Theilade
Secretary/Library Assistant, Rita Ulrich

University of Western Ontario - Library System, The D.B. Weldon Library, London ON N6A 3K7 – 519/679-2111; Fax: 519/661-3911; URL: http://www.uwo.ca/libinfo/
Director of Libraries, Catherine Quinlan
Allyn & Betty Taylor Library & Engineering Library, Head, Eeva Munoz
Business Library & Information Centre, Head, Jerry Mulcahy
Cataloguing & Acquisitions, Head, Wendy Kennedy
Collections Management & Coordinator of Document Delivery, Head, Linda Lutz
Collections Management, Coordinator, Jane Pearce Baldwin
Education Library, Head, Claire Callaghan
John & Dotsa Bitove Family Law Library, Head, Lorraine Busby
Music Library, Head, William Guthrie
Public Services, Head, Mary Ann Mavrinac
The J.J. Talman Regional Collection & Special Collections, Head, John Lutman

University of Western Ontario Symphony Orchestra – UWO Music Library, Faculty of Music, University of Western Ontario, 1151 Richmond St. North, London ON N6A 3K7 – 519/661-2043; Fax: 519/661-3531 – Traci Betteridge

Westminster Institute for Ethics & Human Values – Library, 361 Windermere Rd., London ON N6G 2K3 – 519/673-0046; Fax: 519/673-5016 – Librarian, Ms. D. Smith

### MAPLE

Ahmadiyya Movement in Islam (Canada) – Reference Library, 10610 Jane St., Maple ON L6A 1S1 – 905/832-2669; Fax: 905/832-3220 – Aslam Chaudhary

Anco Chemicals Inc. – Library, 85 Malmo Ct., Box 2, Comp. 13, Maple ON L6A 1R4 – 905/832-2276; Fax: 905/832-3701; Toll Free: 1-888-268-2626 – Technical Manager, John Humphrey

Ontario Ministry of Natural Resources - Research Library, 10401 Dufferin St., POBox 5000, Maple ON L6A 1S9 – 905/832-7145; Fax: 905/832-7149; Email: ENVOY: ILL.OMAPFW; Symbol: OMAPFW
Research Library, Head, Helle Arro
Reference, Technician, Ann Chalk, 905/832-7101
Technical Services, Librarian, Ginnie Galloway, 905/832-7248
Acquisitions, Technician, Judy Kucopy, 905/832-7100

### MARKHAM

Evangelical Fellowship of Canada – Library, POBox 3745, Markham ON L3S 0Y4 – 905/479-5885; Fax: 905/479-4742 – Bruce Clemenger

FinSec Services Inc. - Library, 2820 - 14 St., Markham ON L3R 0S9 – 905/477-4420; Fax: 905/477-4426 – Reference Librarian, Jonathan Corbett

Gartner Lee Limited – Library, #102, 140 Renfrew Dr., Markham ON L3R 6B3 – 905/477-8400; Fax: 905/477-1456 – Librarian, Bev Foss

International Reference & Serials Library, #21, 90 Nolan Ct., Markham ON L3R 4L9 – 905/946-9588; Fax: 905/946-9590; Symbol: IPP – Librarian, B. Sethi

Vehicle Information Centre of Canada – Library, #220, 175 Commerce Valley Dr. West, Markham ON L3T 7P6 – 905/764-5560; Fax: 905/764-6846

### MERRICKVILLE

Canadian Recreational Canoeing Association – Library, 446 Main St. West, POBox 398, Merrickville ON K0G 1N0 – 613/269-2910; Fax: 613/269-2908 – Nancy Gough

Ontario Ministry of the Solicitor General & Correctional Services - Rideau Correctional/Treatment Centre Library, RR#3, Merrickville ON K0G 1N0 – 613/269-4771, ext.267; Fax: 613/269-3583 – Library Technician, Elizabeth Smith

### MIDLAND

Huronia Historical Parks - Resource Centre, POBox 160, Midland ON L4R 4K8 – 705/526-7838; Fax: 705/526-9193; Symbol: OMIH – Pierre Lefaive

Industrial Research & Development Institute – Library, 649 Prospect Blvd., POBox 518, Midland ON L4R 4L3 – 705/526-2163; Fax: 705/526-2701; Email: j.tilson@irdi.on.ca – Technical Librarian, Jeannie Tilson

### MILLBROOK

Ontario Ministry of the Solicitor General & Correctional Services - Millbrook Correctional Centre Library, POBox 300, Millbrook ON L0A 1G0 – 705/932-2624; Fax: 705/932-2962 – Library Technician, Margaret Monis

### MILTON

Halton County Law Association – Courthouse Library, 491 Steeles Ave. East, Milton ON L9T 1Y7 – 905/878-1272; Fax: 905/878-8298 – Librarian, Betty Dykstra

Information Milton – Library, 311 Commerical St., Milton ON L9T 3Z9 – 905/876-4365; Fax: 905/876-0430 – Coordinator, Sue McCormack

Ontario Electric Railway Historical Association – Archives, POBox 578, Milton ON L9T 5A2 – 519/856-9802 – Archivist, A. Paterson

Ontario Ministry of the Solicitor General & Correctional Services - Maplehurst Correctional Centre Library, 661 Martin St., POBox 10, Milton ON L9T 2Y3 – 905/878-8141, ext.273; Fax: 905/878-1572 – Library Technician, Jutta Legler

### MISSISSAUGA

ORTECH Corporation – Business Resource Centre, Sheridan Science & Technology Park, 2395 Speakman Dr., Mississauga ON L5K 1B3 – 905/822-4111; Fax: 905/823-1446; Email: brc@ortech.on.ca – Christine McCutcheon

Abitibi-Price Inc. - Technology Centre Library, Sheridan Park, 2240 Speakman Dr., Mississauga ON L5K 1A9 – 905/822-4770, ext.212; Fax: 905/823-9651; Symbol: OMABP – Librarian, Gina Grassi

Allelix Biopharmaceuticals Inc. - Information Centre, 6850 Goreway Dr., Mississauga ON L4V 1V7 – 905/677-0831; Fax: 905/677-9595; Symbol: OMAI
Library Information Specialist, Daphne Bruce, Email: dbruce@ftn.net
Library Technician, Sureena Dhillon

Allergy Asthma Information Association – Library, 30 Eglinton Ave. West, Mississauga ON L5R 3E7 – 905/712-2242; Fax: 905/712-2245

Atomic Energy of Canada Limited-AECL-CANDU - Mississauga Laboratory – Information Resources Centre, 2251 Speakman Dr., Mississauga ON L5K 1B2 – 905/823-9060, ext.5002; Fax: 905/823-8229; Email: matulewiczi@aecl.ca; Symbol: OTAE – Senior Information Resources Technician, Iwona Matulewicz

Canadian Islamic Organization Inc. – Library, 2069 Kempton Park Dr., Mississauga ON L5M 2Z4 – 905/820-4655; Fax: 905/820-0382 – Public Services Librarian, Rayed Abou-Hawtash

Canadian Marfan Association – Resource Centre, 4216 Pheasant Run, Mississauga ON L5L 2B9 – 416/393-7056 – Sharon Gaylor

Canadian Plastics Industry Association – Technical Information Resource Centre, #500, 5925 Airport Rd., Mississauga ON L4V 1W1 – 905/678-7748; Fax: 905/678-0774; Email: spress@cpia.ca – Librarian, Sally Press

Canadian Society for Nondestructive Testing, Inc. – Library, #7, 966 Pantera Dr., Mississauga ON L4W 2S1 – 905/238-4846; Fax: 905/238-0689 – Office Administrator, Angie Giglio

Canadian Trotting Association – Standardbred Canada Library, 2150 Meadowvale Blvd., Mississauga ON L5N 6R6 – 905/858-3060; Fax: 905/858-3111 – Librarian, Elynne Lewis

Canadian Welding Bureau – Gooderham Centre Library, 7250 West Credit Ave., Mississauga ON L5N 5N1 – 905/542-1312; Fax: 905/542-1318 – Manager, Andrew McCartney

CanTox Inc. – Library, #308, 2233 Argentia Rd., Mississauga ON L5N 2X7 – 905/542-2900; Fax: 905/542-1011 – Librarian, Sandra Stewart

Cominco Ltd. Product Technology Centre - Gerald P. Lewis Library, 2380 Speakman Dr., Mississauga ON L5K 1B4 – 905/822-2022; Fax: 905/822-2882; Symbol: OMCS
Technical Information Specialist, Pat Doyle
Library Technician, Vera Rodic

Credit Institute of Canada – Library, #501, 5090 Explorer Dr., Mississauga ON L4W 3T9 – 905/629-9805; Fax: 905/629-9809

The Credit Valley Hospital – Dr. Keith G. MacDonald Health Sciences Library, 2200 Eglinton Ave. West, Mississauga ON L5M 2N1 – 905/820-2411; Fax: 905/820-4101 – Librarian, Alexander Lyubechansky

DeVry Institute of Technology - Mississauga Campus Library, 5860 Chedworth Way, Mississauga ON L5R 3W3 – 905/501-1210 – Library Technician, Kasia Skorupska

DuPont Canada Inc. - Central Library, POBox 2300, Mississauga ON L5M 2J4 – 905/821-5782; Fax: 905/821-5519; Symbol: OMDC – Caren Larner, Email: caren.larner@conoco.dupont.com

General Electric Canada Inc. - Legal Library, 2300 Meadowvale Blvd., Mail Drop T30, Mississauga ON L5N 5P9 – 905/858-5227; Fax: 905/858-5234 – Lori Lyle

Glaxo Wellcome Inc. - Information Centre, 7333 Mississauga Rd. North, Mississauga ON L5N 6L4 – 905/819-3403; Fax: 905/819-3096; Symbol: OTGX
Manager, Marion Greer
Information Analyst, Maria-Jésus Senas
Library Specialist, Susan Sequeira
Library Assistant, Donna Walsh

Golder Associates Ltd. – Library, 2180 Meadowvale Blvd., Mississauga ON L5N 5S3 – 905/567-4444; Fax: 905/567-6561; Email: mwrezel@golder.com; Symbol: OMGA – Librarian, Mira Wrezel

Goodfellow Consultants Inc., #160, 7070 Mississauga Rd., Mississauga ON L5N 7G2 – 905/858-4424; Fax: 905/858-4426; Toll Free: 1-800-649-4424 – Ana Liberatori

Hoffmann-La Roche Ltd. - Corporate Library, 2455 Meadowpine Blvd., Mississauga ON L5N 6L7 – 905/542-5542; Fax: 905/542-7130; Symbol: OMHL
Manager, Corporate Information, Colin Hoare
Circulation Librarian, Nancy Millwood

ICI Forest Products – Research Library, Sheridan Park Research Centre, 2101 Hadwen Rd., Mississauga ON L5K 2L3 – 905/403-2726; Fax: 905/823-0044; Email: morgant@hookup.net; Symbol: OMCILCR – Library Services Coordinator, Tracy Morgan

Inco Limited - J. Roy Gordon Research Laboratory, 2060 Flavelle Blvd., Mississauga ON L5K 1Z9 – 905/403-2487; Fax: 905/403-2401; URL: http://www.incoltd.com; Symbol: OMIN
Research Librarian, Janet MacLachlan
Library Technologist, Diane Baksa

Mississauga Heritage Foundation Inc. – Library, #1055, 300 City Centre Dr., Mississauga ON L5B 3C9 – 905/272-1432; Fax: 905/615-4171

Northern Telecom Limited - Information Resource Centre, 3 Robert Speck Parkway, Mississauga ON

L4Z 3C8 – 905/897-9000; Fax: 905/566-3332 – Jo-Anne Wong

OMF International - Canada – OMF Archives, 5759 Coopers Ave., Mississauga ON L4Z 1R9 – 416/489-4660; Fax: 905/568-9974; Email: dmichell@cproject.com – OMF Ontario Director, Dr. David Michell

Peel Board of Education - J.A. Turner Professional Library, 5650 Hurontario St., Mississauga ON L5R 1C6 – 905/890-1010, ext.2583; Fax: 905/890-4780; Toll Free: 1-800-668-1146
 Librarian, Dr. Catherine Wilkins
 Information Resources Technician, Marsha Hunt

Petro-Canada - Products/Lubricants Research & Development Library, 2489 North Sheridan Way, Mississauga ON L5K 1A8 – 905/896-6726; Fax: 905/896-6740 – Library Administrator, Jane McAndless

Revenue Canada - Research & Library Services, 77 City Centre Dr., POBox 6000, Mississauga ON L5A 4E9 – 905/803-7400; Fax: 905/566-6018; Symbol: OMRCT – Librarian, Maureen Reeves

World Vision Canada – DevEd Library, 6630 Turner Valley Rd., Mississauga ON L5N 2S4 – 905/821-3033, ext.375; Fax: 905/821-1354; Toll Free: 1-800-268-5863; Email: doug_blackburn@worldvision.ca – Resource Coordinator, Doug Blackburn

Xerox Research Centre of Canada - Technical Information Centre, 2660 Speakman Dr., Mississauga ON L5K 2L1 – 905/823-7091; Fax: 905/822-7022; Email: xrcc_tic@xn.xerox.com; Symbol: OMX
 Manager, Technical Information Centre, Carolyne Sidey
 Senior Technical Information Assistant, Gisela Smithson

### MORRISBURG

Upper Canada Village - Reference Library, RR#1, Morrisburg ON K0C 1X0 – 613/543-3704; Fax: 613/543-7847; Symbol: OMUC – Librarian/Archivist, Jack Schecter

### MOUNT HOPE

Canadian Warplane Heritage – Library, #300, 9300 Airport Rd., Mount Hope ON L0R 1W0 – 905/679-4183; Fax: 905/679-4186 – Library Volunteer, Tervor Melorum

### NAPANEE

Lennox & Addington Law Association - Courthouse Library, 167 Adelphi St., Napanee ON K7R 1T6 – Librarian, Carol Sirman, 613/354-5469

### NEPEAN

Algonquin College - Woodroffe Campus Resource Centre, 1385 Woodroffe Ave., Nepean ON K2G 1V8 – 613/727-4723, ext.7713; Fax: 613/727-7684 – Jocelyne Chaperon-Beck

Canadian Federation of Humane Societies – Library, #102, 30 Concourse Gate, Nepean ON K2E 7V7 – 613/224-8072; Fax: 613/723-0252 – Gail Dellaire

Carleton Board of Education - Resource Centre, 133 Greenbank Rd., Nepean ON K2H 6L3 – 613/721-1820, ext.432; Fax: 613/820-6968; URL: http://www.ocebe.edu.on.ca; Symbol: OOCBE – Library Supervisor, Joanne Larocque

Gandalf Canada - Library, 130 Colonnade Rd., Nepean ON K2E 7M4 – 613/274-6500; Fax: 613/274-6501; URL: http://www.gandalf.ca; Symbol: OOGDC – Corporate Librarian, Dawna Kluver, 613/274-6500, ext.8783, Email: dkluver@gandalf.ca

The Naval Officers Association of Canada – Library, 72 Robertson Rd., POBox 26083, Nepean ON K2H 9R6 – 613/224-7577; Fax: 613/832-3917; Email: laurief@magi.com – National Archivist, Laurie Farrington

Organization of Military Museums of Canada, Inc. – Canadian War Museum Library, 72 Robertson Rd., POBox 26106, Nepean ON K2H 9R6 – 819/776-8654; Fax: 613/829-0280 – Librarian, Jean Langdon-Ford

Professional Institute of The Public Service of Canada – Library, 53 Auriga Dr., Nepean ON K2E 8C3 – 613/228-6310; Fax: 613/228-9048; Toll Free: 1-800-267-0446 – Head, Research, Kathryn Brookfield

R.A. Vanier Law Office - Library, 90 Centrepointe Dr., Nepean ON K2G 6B1 – 613/226-3336; Fax: 613/226-8767 – Assistant, Jodi Dean

Shooting Federation of Canada – Library, 45 Shirley Blvd., Nepean ON K2K 2W6 – 613/828-7338; Fax: 613/828-7333

### NEW LISKEARD

École St-Michel - Bibliothèque, CP 1-3040, New Liskeard ON P0J 1P0 – 705/647-6614 – Bibliotechnicienne, Thérèse Benoit

### NEWCASTLE

Newcastle Village & District Historical Society – Massey Memorial Library, #3, 20 King St. West, POBox 15, Newcastle ON L1B 1L9 – 905/987-5411 – Collection Chairperson, Pat Mcdonnell

### NEWMARKET

Toronto Society of Model Engineers – TSME Library, 166 Millard Ave., Newmarket ON L3Y 1Y9 – 416/534-0550 – Librarian, Steve Estok

### NIAGARA FALLS

Acres International Limited - Library, 4342 Queen St., POBox 1001, Niagara Falls ON L2E 6W1 – 905/374-5200, ext.5247; Fax: 905/374-1157; Email: mdamboise@niagarafalls.acres.com; Symbol: ONFA – Librarian, Marion D'Amboise, Email: mdamboise@nf.acres.com

Arcturus Environmental - Division of Conor Pacific Environmental Technologies Inc. – Library, 7900 Canadian Dr., Niagara Falls ON L2E 6S5 – 905/357-6424; Fax: 905/357-6447

Greater Niagara General Hospital – Health Sciences Library, 5546 Portage Rd., POBox 1018, Niagara Falls ON L2E 6X2 – 905/358-4937, ext.3470; Fax: 905/358-8437; Email: jdunn@freenet.npiec.on.ca – Library Technician, John Dunn

Martin, Sheppard, Fraser Law Office - Library, 4607 Huron St., POBox 900, Niagara Falls ON L2E 6V7 – 905/354-1611; Fax: 905/354-5540; Toll Free: 1-800-263-2502 – Janet McQuay

Niagara College - Maid of the Mist Centre, 5881 Dunn St., Niagara Falls ON L2J 2N9 – 905/374-7454, ext.3605; Fax: 905/374-1116; Email: BDupuis@niagarac.on.ca; Symbol: LRC – Library Technician, Beth Dupuis

Niagara Parks Botanical Gardens - School of Horticulture - C.H. Henning Library, POBox 150, Niagara Falls ON L2E 6T2 – 905/356-7670, ext.226; Fax: 905/356-5488 – Library Technician, Ruth Stoner

### NIAGARA ON THE LAKE

Niagara Historical Research Centre, c/o Niagara on the Lake Public Library, 26 Queen St., Rear, POBox 430, Niagara on the Lake ON L0S 1J0 – 905/468-2023; Fax: 905/468-3334; Symbol: EBNL
 Chief Librarian, Gerda Molson
 Local History Librarian, Linda Gula
 Reference Librarian, Linda Potter
 Circulation Librarian, Gerrie Barnim

Shaw Festival – Stelco Library, POBox 774, Niagara on the Lake ON L0S 1J0 – 905/468-2153; Fax: 905/468-5438; Toll Free: 1-800-511-7429 – Librarian, Nancy Butler

### NORTH BAY

AIDS Committee of North Bay & Area – Library, #202, 240 Algonquin Ave., North Bay ON P1B 4V9 – 705/497-3560; Fax: 705/497-7850 – Secretary-Receptionist, Kerry Powers

Education Centre - Library, POBox 5002, North Bay ON P1B 8L7 – 705/474-3450, ext.4220; Fax: 705/497-1455; Email: ENVOY: ONBNU or ONBCC
 Director, Library Services, Brian Nettlefold
 Associate Director, Barbara Lee

Nipissing District Law Association – The Court House Library, 360 Plouffe St., North Bay ON P1B 9L5 – 705/495-3271(am only); Fax: 705/495-3487; Symbol: NIPI

North Bay Literacy Council – Library, 1000 High St., North Bay ON P1B 6S6 – 705/494-9416; Fax: 705/494-9856

North Bay Psychiatric Hospital – Library, POBox 3010, North Bay ON P1B 8L1 – 705/474-1200; Fax: 705/472-1694

North Bay Symphony Orchestra – Library, #106, 269 Main St. West, North Bay ON P1B 2T8 – 705/494-7744; Fax: 705/494-7663 – Librarian, Judy Statham

The Nugget Newspaper - Library, POBox 570, North Bay ON P1B 8J6 – 705/472-3200; Fax: 705/472-5128 – Librarian, Allison Barrett

Ontario Natural Resources Safety Association – ONRSA Resource Library, 690 McKeown Ave., POBox 2050, North Bay ON P1B 9P1 – 705/474-7233; Fax: 705/472-5800; Toll Free: 1-800-850-5519 – Customer Service Representative, Jocelyne Leroux

### OAKVILLE

Appleby College - Library, 540 Lakeshore Rd. West, Oakville ON L6K 3P1 – 905/845-4681, ext.217; Fax: 905/845-9828; URL: http://www.appleby.on.ca – Librarian, Isabel Hodge

Monarchist League of Canada – King George III Memorial Library, POBox 1057, Oakville ON L6J 5E9 – 905/482-4157; Fax: 905/972-9179; Toll Free: 1-800-465-6925 – Dominion Librarian, Claudia Willetts

O'Connor MacLeod Law Office - Library, 700 Kerr St., Oakville ON L6K 3W5 – 905/842-8030; Fax: 905/842-2460 – Librarian, Ken Watts

### ORILLIA

Crawford, Worling, McKenzie & Donnelly Law Office - Library, 40 Coldwater St. E., POBox 520, Orillia ON L3V 6K4 – 705/325-2753; Fax: 705/325-4913 – Karen L. Wilford

Georgian College - Orillia Campus Learning Resources Centre, 825 Memorial Ave., POBox 2316, Orillia ON L3V 6S2 – 705/325-2705, ext.3050; Fax: 705/325-3690; Email: ENVOY: ILL.GEO.OR; Symbol: OORIGC – Campus/Systems Librarian, Jennifer Varcoe

Ontario Ministry of Community & Social Services - Huronia Regional Centre Library, POBox 1000, Orillia ON L3V 6L2 – 705/326-7361, ext. 2441; Fax: 705/326-3445; Symbol: OOHUR – Maureen Maguire

Ontario Provincial Police - General Headquarters Library, 777 Memorial Ave., Orillia ON L3V 7V3 – 705/329-6886; Fax: 705/329-6887; Symbol: OOP – Librarian, Catherine Dowd, Email: dowdsa@epo.gov.on.ca

Orillia Soldiers' Memorial Hospital – Library, 170 Colborne St. West, Orillia ON L3V 2Z3 – 705/325-2201; Fax: 705/325-7953 – Dir., Devel. & Library Service, Christie Whitman

### ORLEANS

Advocacy Group for the Environmentally Sensitive – Library, 1887 Chaine Ct., Orleans ON K1C 2W6 – 613/830-5722 – Librarian, Claudette Guibord

## OSHAWA

Alzheimer Society of Durham Region – Charles McGibbon Resource Centre, #205, 419 King St. West, Oshawa ON L1J 2K5 – 905/576-2567; Fax: 905/576-2033 – Program Services Coordinator, Kim Fernandes

Christian Record Services Inc. – Lending Library for the Blind, #119, 1300 King St. East, Oshawa ON L1H 8N9 – 905/436-6938; Fax: 905/436-7102

Creighton, Victor, Alexander, Hayward & Morison Law Office - Library, 235 King St. East, POBox 26010, Oshawa ON L1H 8R4 – 905/723-3446; Fax: 905/432-2323

Durham College - Main Library, 2000 Simcoe St. North, POBox 385, Oshawa ON L1H 7L7 – 905/721-3082 – Director, Learning Resources, Susan Barclay-Pereira

Information Oshawa – Resource Centre, #204A, 419 King St. West, Oshawa ON L1J 2KS – 905/434-4636; Fax: 905/434-6007

Kingsway College & High School - Library, 1200 Leland Rd., Oshawa ON L1K 2H4 – 905/433-1144, ext.267; Fax: 905/433-1156; Email: kingsway@globalserve.net – Librarian, Carroll Ryan

Ontario Ministry of Finance - Library Services - Oshawa, 33 King St. West, POBox 627, Oshawa ON L1H 8H5 – 905/433-6136; Fax: 905/433-6037; Symbol: OTREV
- Group Leader, Wendy Craig, 905/433-6135, Email: craigw@gov.on.ca
- Senior Library Technician, Penni Lee

Oshawa-Durham Symphony Orchestra – Library, POBox 444, Oshawa ON L1H 7L5 – 905/683-2680 – Librarian, Mr. Leslie Siklos

Oshawa General Hospital – Library, 24 Alma St., Oshawa ON L1G 2B9 – 905/576-8711, ext.3334/3567; Fax: 905/433-4338; Email: library@hospital.oshawa.on.ca – Director of Library Services, Susan E. Hendricks

Oshawa Historical Society – Oshawa Commuity Archives at the Sydenham Museum, 1450 Simcoe St. South, Oshawa ON L1H 8S8 – 905/436-7624; Fax: 905/436-7625 – Interim Director, Cathy Molloy

## OTTAWA

Aboriginal Nurses Association of Canada – Library, 192 Bank St., Ottawa ON K2P 1W8 – 613/236-3373; Fax: 613/236-3599 – Anna White

Academy of Medicine, Ottawa – Library, #1, 1867 Alta Vista Dr., POBox 8223, Ottawa ON K1G 3H7 – 613/733-2604; Fax: 613/731-1779

Agriculture & Agri-Food Canada - Canadian Agriculture Library, Sir John Carling Bldg., 930 Carling Ave., Ottawa ON K1A 0C5 – 613/759-7068; Fax: 613/759-6627; Email: CALREF@em.agr.ca; Symbol: OOAG
- Director, Victor Desroches, Email: desrochesv@em.agr.ca
- Systems & Network Services, Librarian, Marie-Josée Boisvenue
- Marketing & New Services, Chief, Janet Stitt
- Technical Services, Chief, Julia Goodman
- Public Services, Chief, Emil Daniel
- Acquisitions & Technical Services, Assistant Director, Mae Cutler, Email: cutlerm@em.agr.ca

Canadian Agriculture Library, Animal Diseases Research Institute, 3851 Fallowfield Rd., Ottawa ON K2H 8P9 – 613/998-9320; Fax: 613/952-2285; Email: lbooaga@ncccot.agr.ca; Symbol: OOAGA – Librarian, Linda Hopson

Eastern Cereal Oilseed & Research Library, K.W. Neatby Bldg., Rm. 4061, Ottawa ON K1A 0C6 – 613/759-1806; Fax: 613/759-1924; Email: ecore@em.agr.ca; Symbol: OOAGE – Librarian, Dena Rabow

Plant Research Library, #219, W.M. Saunders Bldg., Ottawa ON K1A 0C6 – 613/759-1368; Fax: 613/759-1599; Symbol: OOAGB – Lise Robillard

Agudath Israel Congregation - Malca Pass Library, 1400 Coldrey Ave., Ottawa ON K1Z 7P9 – 613/728-3501; Fax: 613/728-4468 – Librarian, Donna Guttman

Algonquin College - Rideau Campus Learning Resource Centre, 200 Lees Ave., Ottawa ON K1S 0C5 – 613/727-4723, ext. 3332; Fax: 613/598-3346; URL: http://www.algonquinc.on.ca/algweb/planning/lrc/lrc.html; Symbol: OOACR – Maureen Sheppard

Alliance canadienne des responsables et enseignants en français (Langue maternelle) – Bibliothèque, Faculté d'éducation, Université d'Ottawa, 145, rue Jean-Jacques Lussier, CP 415, Ottawa ON K1N 6N5 – 613/562-5800, ext.4144; Téléc: 613/562-5146

American Information Resource Center, United States Embassy, 150 Wellington St., 3rd Fl., Ottawa ON K1P 5A4 – 613/238-4470, ext.391; Fax: 613/563-7701; Email: refott@usia.gov; URL: http://www.usis-canada.usia.gov; Symbol: OOUSI
- Centre Director, Kyle Malone Ward, 613/238-4470, ext.321
- Reference Librarian, Allison Abraszko, 613/238-4470, ext.311
- Reference Librarian, Gail McKeating, 613/238-4470, ext.391

Assembly of First Nations – Resource Centre, One Nicholas St., 10th Fl., Ottawa ON K1N 7B7 – 613/241-6789; Fax: 613/241-5808; Email: keesh@afn.ca – Coordinator, Kelly Whiteduck

Association des enseignantes et des enseignants franco-ontariens – Bibliothèque, 681 Belfast Rd., Ottawa ON K1G 0Z4 – 613/244-2336; Téléc: 613/563-7718

Association for Baha'i Studies – Library, 34 Copernicus St., Ottawa ON K1N 7K4 – 613/233-1903; Fax: 613/233-3644 – Librarian, Betty Butterill

Association for the Export of Canadian Books – Library, #504, One Nicholas St., Ottawa ON K1N 7B7 – 613/562-2324; Fax: 613/562-2329 – Information Officer, Catherine Montgomery

Association of Canadian Community Colleges – Information Resource Centre, #200, 1223 Michael St. North, Ottawa ON K1J 7T2 – 613/746-2222; Fax: 613/746-6721 – Contact, Ginette Bourdon

Association of Canadian Distillers – Library, #1100, 90 Sparks St., Ottawa ON K1P 5T8 – 613/238-8444, ext.214; Fax: 613/238-3411; TLX: 0533783 – Researcher & Information Specialist, Sandi Bokij

Association of Consulting Engineers of Canada – Library, #616, 130 Albert St., Ottawa ON K1P 5G4 – 613/236-0569; Fax: 613/236-6193 – F. Stone

Association of Public Service Financial Administrators (Ind.) – Library, #302, 666 Kirkwood Ave., Ottawa ON K1Z 5X9 – 613/728-0695; Fax: 613/761-9568 – Peter Seguin

Association of Universities & Colleges of Canada – Library, #600, 350 Albert St., Ottawa ON K1R 1B1 – 613/563-1236; Fax: 613/563-9745; Symbol: OOCU – Reference Librarian, Jane Szepesi

Atomic Energy Control Board - Library, 280 Slater St., POBox 1046, Ottawa ON K1P 5S9 – 613/995-7120; Fax: 613/995-5086; Symbol: OOAECB
- Librarian, Jane Naisbitt
- Circulation Technician, Carole Blais, 613/995-1359
- Acquisitions Librarian, Frank Rauterkranz, 613/995-2060
- Proprietary Library, Mary Didyk, 613/992-8292

Atomic Energy of Canada Limited - Library, 344 Slater St., Ottawa ON K1A 0S4 – 613/237-3270, ext.5138; Fax: 613/782-2065; Symbol: OOAECL

Bank of Canada - Library, 234 Wellington St., Ottawa ON K1A 0G9 – 613/782-8466; Fax: 613/782-7387; URL: http://www.bank-banque-canada.ca/library; Symbol: OOB – Chief Librarian, Carly Hunt

Brewers Association of Canada – Library, Heritage Place, #1200, 155 Queen St., Ottawa ON K1P 6L1 – 613/232-9601; Fax: 613/232-2283; Email: egregory@brewers.ca; Symbol: OOBA – Librarian & Information Specialist, Ed Gregory

Buchan, Lawton, Parent Ltd. – Library, 5370 Canotek Rd., Ottawa ON K1J 9E6 – 613/748-3762 – Researcher, Carol Ann Hinde

Bytown Railway Society – Library, POBox 141, Ottawa ON K1N 8V1 – 613/745-1201 – Archivist, Richard Bonnycastle

CAL Corporation - Information Resource Centre, 1050 Morrison Dr., Ottawa ON K2H 8K7 – 613/820-8280; Fax: 613/820-8314; Email: ENVOY: CAL.IRC; Symbol: 125-OOCAA – Library Administrative Assistant, Sandra Spence, 613/820-8280, ext.1149

The Canada Council - Library, 99 Metcalfe St., POBox 1047, Ottawa ON K1P 5V8 – 613/598-4308; Fax: 613/566-4390; Symbol: OOCAC – Librarian, Carol Barton

Canada Labour Relations Board - Research & Reference Centre, C.D. Howe Bldg., 240 Sparks St., 4th Fl. West, Ottawa ON K1A 0X8 – 613/947-5404; Fax: 613/947-5407; Email: oolrb@istar.ca; URL: http://home.iSTAR.ca/~clrbccrt/; Symbol: OOLRB
- Director, Gloria Anderson
- Deputy Director, Joy Patel

Canada Mortgage & Housing Corporation - Canadian Housing Information Centre, 700 Montreal Rd., Ottawa ON K1A 0P7 – 613/748-2367; Fax: 613/748-4069; URL: http://www.cmhc-schl.gc.ca; Symbol: OOCM
- Manager, Leslie Jones, 613/748-2362
- Acting Chief Reference Librarian, Tony Westenbrock, 613/748-2567
- Technical Services Librarian, Edward Savic, 613/748-2371

Canada Ports Corporation - Business Information Centre & Library, 99 Metcalfe St., Ottawa ON K1A 0N6 – 613/957-6778; Fax: 613/995-3501; Symbol: OOPOR – Librarian, Sylvia Hodel

Canada Post Corporation - Corporate Library, #N0080, 2701 Riverside Dr., Ottawa ON K1A 0B1 – 613/734-7928; Fax: 613/734-7558; Symbol: OOPO – Corporate Librarian, Bruce Moreland

Canadian Association of Chiefs of Police – Library, #1710, 130 Albert St., Ottawa ON K1P 5G4 – 613/233-1106; Fax: 613/233-6960 – Administration, Alexia Roure

The Canadian Association of Family Resource Programs – Library, #101, 30 Rosemount Ave., Ottawa ON K1Y 1P4 – 613/728-3307; Fax: 613/729-5421; Email: kellerma@frp.ca – Project Manager, Maureen Kellerman

Canadian Association of Independent Living Centres – Library, #1004, 350 Sparks St., Ottawa ON K1R 7S8 – 613/563-2581; Fax: 613/235-4497 – Services & Development Consultant, Michael Herne

Canadian Association of Occupational Therapists – Library, Carleton Technology & Training Centre, #3400, 1125 Colonel By Dr., Ottawa ON K1S 5R1 – 613/523-2268; Fax: 613/523-2552; Toll Free: 1-800-434-2268 – Executive Director, Anne Strickland

Canadian Association of the Deaf – Library, #205, 2435 Holly Lane, Ottawa ON K1V 7P2 – 613/526-4785; Fax: 613/526-4718

Canadian Association of University Teachers – Library, 2675 Queensview Dr., Ottawa ON K2B 8K2 – 613/820-2270; Fax: 613/820-7244

Canadian Automobile Association – Library, #200, 1145 Hunt Club Rd., Ottawa ON K1V 0Y3 – 613/247-0117; Fax: 613/247-0118 – Rosalinda Weisbrod

Canadian Broadcasting Corporation - Documentation Centre/Centre de documentation, POBox 3220,

Ottawa ON K1Y 1E4 – 613/724-5075; Fax: 613/724-5074 – Responsable, Louise Petitclerc

Canadian Bureau for International Education – Library, #1100, 220 Laurier Ave. West, Ottawa ON K1P 5Z9 – 613/237-4820; Fax: 613/237-1073; TLX: 053-3255; Email: mkane@cbie.ca – Editor/Program Manager, Mary Kane

Canadian Centre for Management Development - Management Resource Centre, POBox 420, Ottawa ON K1N 8V4 – 819/995-6165; Fax: 819/995-0331; Symbol: OOCCM – Director, Lorraine McQueen

Canadian Centre on Substance Abuse – Library, #300, 75 Albert St., Ottawa ON K1P 5E7 – 613/235-4048, ext.222; Fax: 613/235-8101; Toll Free: 1-800-559-4514; Email: breimer@ccsa.ca – Information Specialist, Bette Reimer

Canadian Chapter of the International Council of Community Churches – Archives, 30 Briermoor Cres., Ottawa ON K1T 3G7 – 613/738-2942; Fax: 613/738-7835 – Bishop, S.A. Thériault

Canadian Child Care Federation – Library, #306, 120 Holland Ave., Ottawa ON K1Y 0X6 – 613/729-5289; Fax: 613/729-3159 – Information Officer, Jennifer Murphy-Hupé

Canadian Co-operative Association – CCA Information Centre, #400, 275 Bank St., Ottawa ON K2P 2L6 – 613/238-6711; Fax: 613/567-0658; Email: carol@coopcca.com – Carol Hunter

Canadian Coalition for High Blood Pressure Prevention & Control – Library, #200, 160 George St., Ottawa ON K1N 9M2 – 613/241-4361, ext.317; Fax: 613/241-3278

Canadian Coast Guard - Fleet Systems Library, Canada Bldg., #737, 344 Slater St., Ottawa ON K1A 0N7 – 613/998-1801; Fax: 613/993-8659; Symbol: OOTTD – Senior Information Officer, Ginette Dion

Canadian Commercial Corp. - Reference Section, 50 O'Connor St., Ottawa ON K1A 0S6 – 613/996-2655; Fax: 613/947-3903; Email: info@ccc.ca; URL: http://www.ccc.ca – Reference Section, Terry Scott

Canadian Conference of Catholic Bishops – Resource Centre, 90 Parent Ave., Ottawa ON K1N 7B1 – 613/241-9461; Fax: 613/241-8117; Toll Free: 1-800-769-1147 – Archivist, Anita Bissonnette

Canadian Conference of the Arts – Library, 189 Laurier Ave. East, Ottawa ON K1N 6P1 – 613/238-3561; Fax: 613/238-4849; Toll Free: 1-800-463-3561 – Sharon Griffiths

Canadian Conservation Institute – CCI Library, 1030 Innes Rd., Ottawa ON K1A 0M5 – 613/998-3721; Fax: 613/998-4721; Email: alicia.prata@banyan.dgim.doc.c; Symbol: OONMCC – Chief, Library Services, Alicia Prata

Canadian Coordinating Office for Health Technology Assessment – Library, #110, 955 Green Valley Cres., Ottawa ON K2C 3V4 – 613/226-2553; Fax: 613/226-5392 – Librarian, Leigh Ann Topfer

Canadian Council for Multicultural & Intercultural Education – Library, #200, 144 O'Connor St., Ottawa ON K1P 5M9 – 613/233-4916; Fax: 613/233-4735

Canadian Council for Tobacco Control – National Clearinghouse on Tobacco & Health, #1000, 170 Laurier Ave. West, Ottawa ON K1P 5V5 – 613/567-3050; Fax: 613/567-2730 – Librarian, Jennifer Soutter

Canadian Council on Animal Care – Library, Constitution Square, Tower II, #315, 350 Albert St., Ottawa ON K1R 1B1 – 613/238-4031; Fax: 613/238-2837; Email: lmatthews@bart.ccac.ca – Receptionist, L. Matthews

Canadian Council on International Law – Library, #215, 236 Metcalfe St., Ottawa ON K2P 1R3 – 613/235-0442; Fax: 613/230-5978

Canadian Criminal Justice Association – Library, #304, 383 Parkdale Ave., Ottawa ON K1Y 4R4 – 613/725-3715; Fax: 613/725-3720

Canadian Dental Association – Library, 1815 Alta Vista Dr., Ottawa ON K1G 3Y6 – 613/523-1770; Fax: 613/523-7736; Email: library@cda-adc.ca

Canadian Federation of Labour – Library, #300, 107 Sparks St., Ottawa ON K1P 5B5 – 613/234-4141; Fax: 613/234-5188

Canadian Film Institute – Library, 2 Daly Ave., Ottawa ON K1N 6E2 – 613/232-8769; Fax: 613/232-6727 – Film Librarian, Chris Robinson

Canadian General Standards Board – Library, #1402, 222 Queen St., Ottawa ON K1A 1G6 – 613/941-8709, 8703 (Sales Centre); Fax: 613/941-8706; Toll Free: 1-800-665-2472

Canadian Hard of Hearing Association – Clearinghouse, #205, 2435 Holly Lane, Ottawa ON K1V 7P2 – 613/526-1584; Fax: 613/526-4718; Toll Free: 1-800-263-8068 – Special Projects Clerk, Karla Johnston

Canadian Home Care Association – Library, #401, 17 York St., Ottawa ON K1R 7F8 – 613/569-1585; Fax: 613/569-1604 – Odile Girard

Canadian Horticultural Council – Library, #310, 1101 Prince of Wales Dr., Ottawa ON K2C 3W7 – 613/226-4187; Fax: 613/226-2984

Canadian Human Rights Commission - Library, Place de Ville, Tower A, #1413, 320 Queen St., Ottawa ON K1A 1E1 – 613/943-9109; Fax: 613/996-9661; Email: ENVOY: LIBRARY.CHRC; Symbol: OOCHR – Head Librarian, Suzanne Tourigny

Canadian Institute of Financial Accountants – Library, 2380 Holly Lane, 2nd Fl., Ottawa ON K1V 7P2 – 613/521-0620; Fax: 613/521-1185 – Susan Singh

Canadian Institute of Geomatics – Library, #120, 162 Cleopatra Dr., Ottawa ON K2G 5X2 – 613/224-9851; Fax: 613/224-9577 – Susan Pugh

Canadian Intergovernmental Conference Secretariat - Intergovernmental Document Centre, 110 O'Connor St., 10th Fl., POBox 488, Ottawa ON K1N 8V5 – 613/995-4310; Fax: 613/996-6091; Email: joan.murphy@scics.x400.gc.ca; Symbol: OOCIC – Manager, Joan Murphy

Canadian International Trade Tribunal - Library, 333 Laurier Ave. West, Ottawa ON K1A 0G7 – 613/990-2418; Fax: 613/990-2439; Email: uschultz@citt.qc.ca; URL: http://www.citt.qc.ca; Symbol: OOCITT
- Chief Librarian, Ursula Schultz
- Library Technician, Marthe Seguin-Muntz

Canadian Labour Congress – Library, 2841 Riverside Dr., Ottawa ON K1V 8X7 – 613/521-3400; Fax: 613/521-4655; TLX: 053-4750; Symbol: OOCLC – Librarian, Nora Lezada Côté

Canadian Livestock Records Corporation – Library, 2417 Holly Lane, Ottawa ON K1V 0M7 – 613/731-7110; Fax: 613/731-0704 – Bruce Hunt

Canadian Meat Council – Library, Dow's Lake Court, #410, 875 Carling Ave., Ottawa ON K1S 5P1 – 613/729-3911; Fax: 613/729-4997

Canadian Medical Association – Library, 1867 Alta Vista Dr., Ottawa ON K1G 3Y6 – 613/731-9331; Fax: 613/731-9013; Toll Free: 1-800-267-9703

Canadian Museum of Nature - Library & Archives, POBox 3443, Ottawa ON K1P 6P4 – 613/364-4042; Fax: 613/364-4026; Email: cmnlib@mus-nature.ca; URL: http://www.nature.ca; Symbol: OONMNS
- Chief, Library & Archives, Arch Stewart, 613/364-4040
- Reference Librarian, Mireille Boudreau, 613/364-4044
- Cataloguer, Patrice Stevenson, 613/364-4045
- Archivist, Chantal Dussault, 613/364-4047

Canadian Musical Heritage Society – Library, 50 Rideau St., POBox 53161, Ottawa ON K1N 1C5 – 613/520-2600, ext.8265; Fax: 613/520-6677 – G. Leclerc

Canadian Nature Federation – Library, #606, One Nicholas St., Ottawa ON K1N 7B7 – 613/562-3447; Fax: 613/562-3371; Toll Free: 1-800-267-4088 – Jodi Joy

Canadian Nurses Association – Helen K. Mussallem Library, 50 Driveway, Ottawa ON K2P 1E2 – 613/237-2133; Fax: 613/237-3520 – Library Manager, Elizabeth Hawkins-Brady

Canadian Organic Growers Inc. - Mail-Lending Library, POBox 6408, Ottawa ON K2A 3Y6 – 613/256-1848; Fax: 613/256-4453 – Librarian, Leeanne McCormick

Canadian Paediatric Society – Library, #100, 2204 Walkley Rd., Ottawa ON K1G 4G8 – 613/526-9397, ext.231; Fax: 613/526-3332

Canadian Payments Association – Library, #1212, 50 O'Connor St., Ottawa ON K1P 6L2 – 613/238-4173; Fax: 613/233-3385 – Senior Legal Administrator, Debra Dunkerley

Canadian Petroleum Products Institute – Library, #1000, 275 Slater St., Ottawa ON K1P 5H9 – 613/232-3709, ext.217; Fax: 613/232-4345 – Betty Jean Mark

Canadian Pork Council – Library, 75 Albert St., Ottawa ON K1P 5E7 – 613/236-9239; Fax: 613/236-6658 – Executive Secretary, Martin Rice

Canadian Printing Industries Association – Library, #906, 75 Albert St., Ottawa ON K1P 5E7 – 613/236-7208; Fax: 613/236-8169

The Canadian Public Relations Society, Inc. – Library, #720, 220 Laurier Ave. West, Ottawa ON K1P 5Z9 – 613/232-1222; Fax: 613/232-0565 – Pam Bannister

Canadian Radio-Television & Telecommunications Commission - Library, #202, 1, Promenade du Portage, Ottawa ON K1A 0N2 – 819/997-4484; Fax: 819/994-6337; Email: library@crtc.x400.gc.ca; Symbol: CORT
- Manager, Library Services, Karla Weys
- Acquisitions Librarian, Sheila Roussel, 819/997-4226
- Technical Services Librarian, Lorraine Pigeon

The Canadian Red Cross Society – National Office Library, 1800 Alta Vista Dr., Ottawa ON K1G 4J5 – 613/739-2573; Fax: 613/731-1411; TLX: 05-33784; Symbol: OOCRC – Librarian, Ann M. Butryn

Canadian Research Institute for the Advancement of Women – Library, #408, 151 Slater St., Ottawa ON K1P 5H3 – 613/563-0681; Fax: 613/563-0682 – Secretary/Receptionist, Céline Bessette

Canadian Security Intelligence Service - General Information Centre, Ottawa Terminal, POBox 9732, Ottawa ON K1G 4G4 – 613/782-0021; Fax: 613/782-0705 – Deputy Director General, Mary Joan Dunn

Canadian Society for International Health – Library, #902, 170 Laurier Ave. West, Ottawa ON K1P 5V5 – 613/230-2654, ext.305; Fax: 613/230-8401 – Communications Officer, Mary Bridgeo

Canadian Teachers' Federation – George A. Croskery Memorial Library, 110 Argyle Ave., Ottawa ON K2P 1B4 – 613/232-1505; Fax: 613/232-1886 – Program Assistant, Marita Moll

Canadian Tobacco Manufacturers' Council – Information Centre, #701, 99 Bank St., Ottawa ON K1P 6B9 – 613/238-2799; Fax: 613/238-4463; Email: CANTOB.INFO; Symbol: OOCTM – Manager, Information, Philip Gordon

Canadian Tourism Commission - Tourism Reference & Documentation Centre, 235 Queen St., Ottawa ON K1A 0H6 – 613/954-3943; Fax: 613/954-3945; Email: trdc.ctc@ic.gc.ca; URL: http://www.info.ic.gc.ca/Tourism; Symbol: OOTB – Chief Librarian, Judith M. Cameron, Email: cameron.judith@ic.gc.ca

Canadian War Museum - Library, 330 Sussex Dr., Ottawa ON K1A 0M8 – 819/776-8654; Fax: 819/776-8657; Symbol: OONMC – Librarian, Jean Langdon-Ford

Canadian Wildlife Federation – Library, 2740 Queensview Dr., Ottawa ON K2B 1A2 – 613/721-

2286; Fax: 613/721-2902; Toll Free: 1-800-563-9453 – Education Programs Director, Luba Mycio-Mommers

Canadian Wood Council – Library, #350, 1730 St. Laurent Blvd., Ottawa ON K1G 5L1 – 613/247-7077; Fax: 613/247-7856 – Librarian, Audrey Mattila

Capital Region Centre for the Hearing Impaired – Library, 310 Elmgrove Ave., Ottawa ON K1Z 6V1 – 613/729-1467 (Voice); Fax: 613/729-5167 – Administrative Assistant, Camilla Strickland

Carleton County Law Association – Ottawa Courthouse Library, Ottawa Courthouse, #2004, 161 Elgin St., Ottawa ON K2P 2K1 – 613/233-7386; Fax: 613/238-3788; Symbol: OOCCL

Carleton University - Library, 1125 Colonel By Dr., Ottawa ON K1S 5B6 – 613/520-2735; Fax: 613/520-2750; Email: library_ill@carleton.ca; URL: http://www.library.carleton.ca; Symbol: OOCC
- University Librarian, Martin Foss, 613/788-2600, ext.2725
- Access Services, Head, Bozena Clarke
- Acquisitions, Head, Gail Catley
- Cataloguing, Head, Alison Hall
- Collections Librarian, Anita Hui
- Gifts Librarian, Dorothy Rogers
- Interlibrary Loans, Head, Callista Kelly
- Maps, Data & Government Information Centre, Head, Susan Jackson
- Reference Services, Head, Elizabeth Knight
- Systems & Technical Services, Associate Librarian, Terry Clark
- Information Services, Associate Librarian, Linda Rossman
- Library Administrative Services, Manager, Suzanne Doraty

Catholic Health Association of Canada – Library, 1247 Kilborn Pl., Ottawa ON K1H 6K9 – 613/731-7148; Fax: 613/731-7797 – Technical Services Librarian, Annette Foucault

Child Welfare League of Canada – Canadian Resource Centre on Children & Youth, #312, 180 Argyle Ave., Ottawa ON K2P 1B7 – 613/788-5102; Fax: 613/788-5075 – Elizabeth Bourgue

Children's Hospital of Eastern Ontario – Library Services, 401 Smyth Rd., Ottawa ON K1H 8L1 – 613/737-2206; Fax: 613/738-4806; Email: johnston@cheo.on.ca; Symbol: OOCHEO – Library Director, Patricia Johnston

City of Ottawa - Planning & Development Library, 111 Sussex Dr., Ottawa ON K1N 5A1 – 613/564-3095; Fax: 613/564-8077; Symbol: OOCPB
- Chief Librarian, Evelina Leal
- Associate Librarian, Peter McNaughton

Commissioner of Official Languages - Library, 110 O'Connor St., Ottawa ON K1A 0T8 – 613/995-0403; Fax: 613/993-5082; Email: mimi_benoit@ocol-clo.gc.ca; URL: http://ocol-clo.gc.ca; Symbol: OOCOL – Librarian, Rosemarie Benoit

Commonwealth War Graves Commission - Canadian Agency – Library, #1707, 66 Slater St., Ottawa ON K1A 0P4 – 613/992-3224; Fax: 613/995-0431 – Office Supervisor, Johanne Neville

Communications, Energy & Paperworkers Union of Canada (CLC) – Library, 350 Sparks St., 19th Fl., Ottawa ON K1R 1A4 – 613/230-5200, ext.222; Fax: 613/230-5801; Email: martin@cep.ca – Librarian/Researcher, Martin McGreal

Community Foundation of Ottawa-Carleton – Library, #301, 75 Albert St., Ottawa ON K1P 5E7 – 613/236-1616; Fax: 613/236-1621

Competition Tribunal - Library, 90 Sparks St., 6th Fl., Ottawa ON K1P 5B4 – 613/954-0449; Fax: 613/957-3170; Symbol: OOCOT – Library Manager, Lydia Austin, 613/954-0449

Computing Devices Canada - Technical Library, POBox 8508, Ottawa ON K1G 3M9 – 613/596-7273; Fax: 613/820-5081; Symbol: OOCDC – Librarian, Elaine Tigges, Email: elaine.tigges@gpo.canada.cdev.com

The Conference Board of Canada – Information Centre, 255 Smyth Rd., Ottawa ON K1H 8M7 – 613/526-3280; Fax: 613/526-4857; TLX: 053-3343 – Manager, Information Services, Laurie McCarthy

Consulting & Audit Canada - Information Centre, Place de Ville, Tower B, Rm.# 1009, 112 Kent St., Ottawa ON K1A 0S5 – 613/996-3348; Fax: 613/947-2381; URL: http://w3.pwgsc.gc.ca/cac/; Symbol: OOBMC – Agency Information Centre Officer, Marie-Claire Girouard

Cree Naskapi Commission – Library, Capital Square Bldg., #305, 222 Queen St., Ottawa ON K1P 5V9 – 613/234-4288; Fax: 613/234-8102 – Librarian, Nicole Cheechoo

Defence Research Establishment - Ottawa - Information Services Library, 3701 Carling Ave., Ottawa ON K1A 0Z4 – 613/998-2657; Fax: 613/991-2964; Email: ENVOY: DREO.INFO.SVCS; Symbol: OODRC – Head, Susan G. McIntyre

Dendron Resource Surveys Inc. – Library, #206, 880 Lady Ellen Place, Ottawa ON K1Z 5L9 – 613/725-2971; Fax: 613/725-1716 – Office Manager, Catherine Smyth

E.B. Eddy Forest Products Ltd. - Library, Central Laboratory, 6 Booth St., Ottawa ON K1R 6K8 – 613/782-2645; Fax: 613/782-2515 – Librarian/Secretary, Margaret Jean-Louis

Elections Canada - Library, 1595 Telesat Court, Ottawa ON K1A 0M6 – Fax: 613/954-5880; Toll Free: 1-800-46368683; Email: tony.coulson@electc.x400.gc.ca; Symbol: OOELC
- Supervisor, Library, Alain Pelletier
- Assistant to the Supervisor, Library, Tony Coulson

Federal Court of Canada - Library, 90 Sparks St., 12th Fl., Ottawa ON K1A 0H9 – 613/995-1382; Fax: 613/954-7714; Email: rosalie.fox@fct-cf.x400.gc.ca; Symbol: OOFC
- Head Librarian, Rosalie Fox
- Reference Librarian, Wendy Reynolds, 613/943-0839
- Cataloguing, Systems Librarian, Louise Houston, 613/996-8735
- Collection Development Librarian, Fiona McPherson, 613/947-3906

Fédération des communautés francophones et acadienne du Canada – Bibliothèque, #1404, One Nicholas St., Ottawa ON K1N 7B7 – 613/563-0311; Téléc: 613/241-6046 – Documentaliste, Micheline Gleixner

Fédération nationale des femmes canadiennes-françaises – Bibliothèque, #302, 450 Rideau St., Ottawa ON K1N 5Z4 – 613/241-3500; Téléc: 613/241-6679

Finance & Treasury Board Canada - Library, 140 O'Connor St., 11th Fl. East, Ottawa ON K1A 0G5 – 613/996-5491; Fax: 613/992-6411; Symbol: OOF – Chief Librarian, Trent Reid

Fisheries & Oceans Canada - Library, 200 Kent St., 10th Fl., Ottawa ON K1A 0E6 – 613/993-2950; Fax: 613/990-4901; Email: ENVOY: DFO.LIB.OTTAWA; Symbol: OOFI – Head, Library Policy & Services, Heather Cameron

Foreign Affairs & International Trade Canada - Legal Library, 125 Sussex Dr., Ottawa ON K1A 0G2 – 613/992-4383; Fax: 613/992-2467; Symbol: OOELB – In Charge, Marilyn McLennan
- Library, Lester B. Pearson Bldg., 125 Sussex Dr., Ottawa ON K1A 0G2 – 613/992-6150; Fax: 613/944-0222; Email: refdesk@magi.com; Symbol: OOE – Client Services, Head, Marjorie Bull

Friends of the Earth – Library, #306, 47 Clarence St., Ottawa ON K1N 9K1 – 613/241-0085; Fax: 613/241-7998 – Information Officer, Marian Lenczewski

Fur Institute of Canada – Library, #804, 255 Albert St., Ottawa ON K1P 6A9 – 613/231-7099; Fax: 613/231-7940

Government House - Library, 1 Sussex Dr., Ottawa ON K1A 0A1 – 613/993-5278; Fax: 613/990-7636; Symbol: OOGH – Archivist/Librarian, Sandy Allen

Gowlings - Library, 160 Elgin St., Ottawa ON K1P 1C3 – 613/233-1781; Fax: 613/563-9869, 563-7938 – Librarian, Linda Marchand, 613/233-1781, ext.7335

Health Canada-Environmental Health Directorate – Library, Bldg. 8, Environmental Health Centre, Tunney's Pasture, 120 Parkdale Ave., Ottawa ON K1A 0L2 – 613/957-1725; Fax: 613/952-2206; Symbol: OONHH – Manager, Lorna Adcock

Health Canada - Health Protection Branch Library Network, Sir Frederick G. Banting Research Centre, Ross Ave., Postal Locator 2202B, Ottawa ON K1A 0L2 – 613/957-1026; Fax: 613/941-6958; Symbol: OONHBR – Chief, Scientific Information & Document Services, Merle McConnell

Heart & Stroke Foundation of Canada – Library, #200, 160 George St., Ottawa ON K1N 9M2 – 237-4361 ext. 225; Fax: 613/241-3278 – Paula Coutts

Heraldry Society of Canada – Library, POBox 8128, Ottawa ON K1G 3H9 – 613/737-4587; Fax: 613/737-4150 – Librarian, Howard Keck

Hôpital Montfort – Bibliothèque médicale Annie Powers, 713, ch Montréal, Ottawa ON K1K 0T2 – 613/746-4621; Fax: 613/748-4947

Human Rights Institute of Canada – Library, #303, 246 Queen St., Ottawa ON K1P 5E4 – 613/232-2920; Fax: 613/232-3735 – Assistant to the President, Mary Neufeld

Immigration & Refugee Board - Resource Centre, 222 Nepean Rd., Ottawa ON K1A 0K1 – 613/996-0741; Reference: 613/996-0703; Fax: 613/954-1228; URL: http://www.irb.gc.ca/; Symbol: OOIRB – Coordinator, Dianne Parsonage

Indian & Northern Affairs Canada - Library, 10 Wellington St., Ottawa ON K1A 0H4 – 613/997-8204; Fax: 613/953-5491; Email: ENVOY: INA.ILL; Symbol: OORD – Departmental Librarian, Sue Hanley

Indian Claims Commission - Library, Enterprise Bldg., #400, 427 Laurier Ave. West, POBox 1750, Ottawa ON K1P 1A2 – 613/947-0750; Fax: 613/943-0157; Symbol: OOICC – Librarian, Joanne Debassige, Email: JDebassige@IndianClaims.ca

Industry Canada - Communications Research Centre Library, 3701 Carling Ave., POBox 11490, Ottawa ON K2H 8S2 – 613/998-2202; Fax: 613/998-1216; URL: http://www.crc.doc.ca/library/library.html; Symbol: OORPL
- Manager, Carole Laplante, 613/998-2705
- Circulation & ILL, Jean-Marc Lapointe, 613/998-2202
- Acquisitions Clerk, Miriam Poole, 613/998-2255
- Cataloguer, Brenda Creighton, 613/998-2679

Journal Towers Library, #1420, 300 Slater St., Ottawa ON K1A 0C8 – 613/941-4943; Fax: 613/990-7016; Symbol: OOCO – Senior Reference Librarian, Monique Perrier

Library Services, 235 Queen St., Ottawa ON K1A 0H5 – 613/954-2791; Reference: 613/954-2728; Fax: 613/954-0135; Email: ISTC.LIBRARY; Symbol: OOTC
- Director, Claire Renaud-Frigon
- Senior Reference Librarian, Nicole Ménard

Portage Library, Place du Portage, 14th Fl., 50 Victoria St., Ottawa ON K1A 0C9 – 819/997-1632; Fax: 819/997-2378; Email: ENVOY: ILL.OOCI; Symbol: OCI – Senior Reference Librarian, John Marosi

Infertility Awareness Association of Canada – Library, #201, 396 Cooper St., Ottawa ON K2P 2H7 – 613/730-1322; Fax: 613/730-1323; Toll Free: 1-800-263-2929 – Pamela Lee

Information & Privacy Commissioners of Canada - Library, Place de Ville, Tower B, 112 Kent St., Ottawa ON K1A 1H3 – 613/995-1009; Fax: 613/995-1501; Toll Free: 1-800-267-0441; Symbol: OOIPC
- Head, Library Services, Diane Melski
- Library Technician, Francine Ryan

Institut canadien-français d'Ottawa – Bibliothèque, 316, rue Dalhousie, Ottawa ON K1N 7E7 – 613/241-3522 – Directeur culturel & bibliothécaire, Camille Cheff

Institute of Speculative Philosophy – Library, POBox 913, Ottawa ON K1P 5P9 – 613/594-5881; Fax: 613/594-3952

Institute on Governance – Information Resource Centre, 122 Clarence St., Ottawa ON K1N 5P6 – 613/562-0092, ext.229; Fax: 613/562-0097 – Program Officer, Ioanna Sahas Martin

International Association of Fire Fighters (AFL-CIO/CLC) - Canadian Office – Library, #403, 350 Sparks St., Ottawa ON K1R 7S8 – 613/567-8988; Fax: 613/567-8986 – Research Assistant, Donald Mallon

International Council for Canadian Studies – Library, #800, 325 Dalhousie St., Ottawa ON K1N 7G2 – 613/789-7834; Fax: 613/789-7830; Symbol: OOICCS – Librarian, Linda Jones

International Development Research Centre – IDRC Library, 250 Albert St., 10th Fl., POBox 8500, Ottawa ON K1G 3H9 – 613/236-6163; Fax: 613/563-0815; Email: reference@idrc.ca; pub@idrc.ca; Symbol: OOID – Director, Carole Joling

International Joint Commission - Library, 100 Metcalfe St., 18th Fl., Ottawa ON K1P 5M1 – 613/995-2984; Fax: 613/993-5583

Islamic Information & Education of Canada – Library, 393 Cooper St., Ottawa ON K2P 0G8 – 613/232-0210 – Hilmi El-Sharief

Jewish Community Council of Ottawa – Library, 151 Chapel St., Ottawa ON K1N 7Y2 – 613/789-1818; Fax: 613/789-4593 – Librarian, Estelle Backman

Jewish Youth Library of Ottawa, 185 Switzer Ave., Ottawa ON K1Z 7H8 – 613/729-7712; Fax: 613/724-3855 – Devora Caytak

Justice Canada - Library Services, Justice Bldg, 239 Wellington St., 8th Fl., Ottawa ON K1A 0H8 – 613/957-4607; Fax: 613/952-5792; Symbol: OOJ – Director, Mireille McCullough

Lapp-Hancock Associates Limited – Library, #904, 280 Albert St., Ottawa ON K1P 5G8 – 613/238-2483; Fax: 613/238-1734 – Library Assistant, Heather McLeod

Learning Disabilities Association of Canada – Library, #200, 323 Chapel St., Ottawa ON K1N 7Z2 – 613/238-5721; Fax: 613/235-5391

Library of Parliament, 111 Wellington St., Ottawa ON K1A 0A9 – 613/992-3122; Fax: 613/992-1269; Email: CN/CP COMO444; Symbol: LP/BP
- Parliamentary Librarian, Richard Paré, 613/992-3122
- Director General, Research Branch, Hugh Finsten, 613/992-1132
- Director General, Information & Technical Services Branch, F. LeMay, 613/996-4934
- Director General, Administration & Personnel, Jean-Jacques Cardinal, 613/996-4477

M.E. Association of Canada – Library, #400, 246 Queen St., Ottawa ON K1P 5E4 – 613/563-1771; Fax: 613/567-0614; Email: tharvey@mecan.ca – Tina Harvey

Medical Research Council of Canada - Library, Tower B, 1600 Scott St., 5th Fl., Ottawa ON K1A 0W9 – 613/954-1809; Fax: 613/954-1800; Email: mrcinfocrm@hpb.hwc.ca – Special Projects Assistant, Suzane Faltacas

National Archives of Canada - Library, 395 Wellington St., Ottawa ON K1A 0N3 – 613/992-6534; Fax: 613/943-8491; Email: library@archives.ca; Symbol: OOA – Acting Director, Alex Delvaux, 613/996-7685

National Association of Friendship Centres – Library, #204, 396 Cooper St., Ottawa ON K2P 2H7 – 613/563-4844; Fax: 613/594-3428 – Monique Godin-Beers

National Aviation Museum - Library, Ottawa Terminal, POBox 9724, Ottawa ON K1G 5A3 – 613/993-2303; Fax: 613/990-3655; Email: aviation@istar.ca; URL: http://www.nmstc.aviation.ca; Symbol: OONMA
- Librarian, Fiona Hale
- Library Assistant, Ian A. Leslie

National Capital Commission - Library, 40 Elgin St., Ottawa ON K1P 1C7 – 613/239-5123; Fax: 613/239-5274; Symbol: OONCC
- Head, Library Services, Gwyneth Hughes
- Library Assistant, Lauretta Bédard

National Clearinghouse on Tobacco & Health – Library, #1000, 170 Laurier Ave. West, Ottawa ON K1P 5V5 – 613/567-3050; Fax: 613/567-2730 – Information/Systems Specialist, Suzanna Gardner

National Defence (Canada)-Emergency Preparedness Canada, Jackson Bldg., 122 Bank St., 2nd Fl., Ottawa ON K1A 0W6 – 613/991-7725; Fax: 613/996-0995; Symbol: OOEPC

National Defence Headquarters - National Defence Records & Library Services, Major-General George R. Pearkes Bldg., 101 Colonel By Dr., Ottawa ON K1A 0K2 – 613/996-0831; Reference: 613/996-0832; Fax: 613/995-8176; Email: ENVOY: ILL.OOND; Symbol: OOND
- Departmental Librarian, Peter Greig
- Head/NDRLS, Jacques N. Goulet

National Defence Medical Centre – Medical Library, 1745 Alta Vista Dr., Ottawa ON K1A 0K6 – 613/945-6517; Fax: 613/998-8093; Symbol: OONDM – Chief Librarian, Philip B. Allan

National Educational Association of Disabled Students – Library, Carleton University, 4th Level Unicentre, 1125 Colonel By Dr., Ottawa ON K1S 5B6 – 613/526-8008; Fax: 613/520-3704

National Federation of Pakistani Canadians Inc. – Library, #1100, 251 Laurier Ave. West, Ottawa ON K1P 5J6 – 613/232-5346; Fax: 613/232-6607

National Gallery of Canada - Library, 380 Sussex Dr., POBox 427, Ottawa ON K1N 9N4 – 613/998-8949; Fax: 613/990-9818; Email: ngcref@ngc.chin.gc.ca; URL: http://national.gallery.ca; Symbol: CAOONG
- Chief Librarian, Murray Waddington
- Reader Services, Head, Peter Trepanier
- Technical Services Librarian, Roy Engfield
- Archivist, Cyndie Campbell
- ILL, Bonnie Bates

National Museum of Science & Technology - Library & Information Services, 2380 Lancaster Rd., POBox 9724, Ottawa ON K1G 5A3 – 613/990-7874, Resource Centre: 613/993-0306; Fax: 613/990-3636; URL: http://www.science-tech.nmstc.ca/research/library/elibinfo.htm; Symbol: OONMST – Manager, Catherine Campbell

National Research Council Canada - Canada Institute for Scientific & Technical Information, Bldg. M-55, Montréal Rd., Ottawa ON K1A 0S2 – 613/993-1600 (general), 2013 (reference & referral); Fax: 613/952-9112; Toll Free: 1-800-668-1222; Email: cisti.reference@nrc.ca; URL: http://www.cisti.nrc.ca/cisti/cisti.html; Symbol: OON
- Director General, Margot J. Montgomery
- Information Resource Management, Director, Brenda Hurst
- Communications, Head, Elizabeth Katz
- Biodiagnostics Research Branch, Head, David Colborne
- Biotechnology (Montréal), Head, Sylvie Belzile, 514/496-6119
- Construction Research Branch, Head, Scott Mellon, 613/993-2466
- Document Delivery, Manager, Kathryn Mikoski
- Dominion Astrophysical Observatory Branch (Victoria), Head, Eric LeBlanc, 604/388-0020
- Dominion Radio Astrophysical Observatory Branch (Penticton), Contact, B. Jones, 604/497-5321
- Electronic Products & Services, Manager, Leo Grigaitis
- Industrial Materials/Matériaux industriels (Boucherville), Head, Patrice Dupont, 514/641-2280
- Information Services & Product Development, Director, Ferrers Clark
- Information Services, Head, Morna Paterson
- Institute for Biodiagnostics (Winnipeg), Head, Dianne Pammett
- J.H. Parkin Branch, Head, Kathy Wallace
- Marine Biosciences Branch (Halifax), Head, Vacant, 902/426-8250
- Marine Dynamics Branch (St. John's), Head, Vacant, 709/772-2468
- National Measurements Standards Branch, Head, Carol Fairbrother, 613/993-6400
- Operations, Director, Bernard Dumouchel
- Plant Biotechnology Branch (Saskatoon), Head, Vacant, 306/975-5256
- Sussex Branch CISTI, Head, Bonnie Bullock, 613/990-6027, Fax: 613/947-2064, Email: library@biologysx.lan.nrc.ca

Institute for Research in Construction - Information Service, Bldg. M-20, 1500 Montréal Rd., Ottawa ON K1A 0R6 – 613/993-2466; Fax: 613/952-7671; Email: irc.library@nrc.ca; URL: http://www.nrc.ca/irc; Symbol: OONBR – Head, Information Services, Scott Mellon

Natural Resources Canada-Canada Centre for Remote Sensing – Client Services, 588 Booth St., Ottawa ON K1A 0Y7 – 613/947-1216; Fax: 613/947-1385; Email: jill.marriner@ccrs.nrcan.gc.ca – Jill Marriner

Natural Resources Canada - Canadian Forest Service - Library, Place Vincent Massey, 351 St. Joseph Blvd., 17th Fl., Ottawa ON K1A 1G5 – 613/997-1107, ext.1741; Fax: 613/997-8697; Email: ENVOY: ILL.OOFR; Symbol: OOFR – Chief, Library Services, Vicki Ritchie

CANMET Information Centre, 555 Booth St., Ottawa ON K1A 0G1 – 613/995-4132; Fax: 613/995-8730; URL: http://www.es.nrcan.gc.ca/msd/cic/cicintro.htm; Symbol: OOM
- Chief, Leslie Hamel
- Circulation, Lucille Tremblay
- Reference, Margaret Ahearn
- Collection Development, Lidia Taylor, 613/943-8770
- ILL, Technician, Heather Lindsay, 613/995-4147
- Cataloguing, Technician, José Gelinas, 613/943-8766
- Bells Corners Library, Jean Macaulay, 613/996-1112
- Energy Diversification Research Laboratory Library, Robin Majumdar, 514/652-3210

Earth Sciences Information Centre - Geology Collection, #350, 601 Booth St., Ottawa ON K1A 0E8 – 613/996-3919; Fax: 613/943-8742; Email: library@gsc.nrcan.gc.ca; URL: http://www.nrcan.gc.ca/ess/esic/esic_e.html; Symbol: OOG – Acting Head, Beverly Chen

Earth Sciences Information Centre - Geomatics Collection, #121, 601 Booth St., Ottawa ON K1A 0E8 – 613/992-9550; Fax: 613/943-8742; Email: Library@gsc.nrcan.gc.ca; URL: http://www.nrcan.gc.ca/ess/esic/esic_e.html; Symbol: OOG – Acting Head, Beverly Chen

Headquarters Library, 580 Booth St., Ottawa ON K1A 0E4 – 613/996-8282; Fax: 613/992-7211; URL: http://www.NRCan.gc.ca/css/imb/hqlib; Symbol: OOMR – Chief Librarian, Sharon Henry, 613/996-0144

National Air Photo Library, 615 Booth St., Room 180, Ottawa ON K1A 0E9 – 613/996-9369; Fax: 613/995-4568; Symbol: OOMNA – Acting Chief, Marjorie Elwood

Nortel Technology - Information Resource Network - Ottawa, POBox 3511, Ottawa ON K1Y 4H7 – 613/763-5728; Fax: 613/763-4282; Email: jkealy@bnr.com; Symbol: OONORE – Manager, Bibi Patel

Office of the Auditor General - Information & Library Services, West Tower, C.D. Howe Bldg., 240 Sparks St., 11th Fl., Ottawa ON K1A 0G6 – 613/995-3708; Fax: 613/952-5131; Email: oooag@oag.bvg.gc.ca; Symbol: OOOAG
- Manager, Shayla Mindell
- Client Services, Head, Judy Chamberland
- Reference Assistant, Jim Trigg
- Reference/Cataloguing Librarian, Cathy Ray
- Technical Services, Head, Gail Rawlings
- Acquisitions Clerk, Carol Skippen
- Serials Clerk, Susan Ames

Office of the Superintendent of Financial Institutions – Library, 255 Albert St., Ottawa ON K1A 0H2 – 613/990-7729; Fax: 613/952-8219; Toll Free: 1-800-385-8647; Symbol: OOIN – Library Technician, Luanne Larose

Ontario Public Interest Research Group - Ottawa – Resource Centre, University of Ottawa, 631 King Edward, 3rd Fl., Ottawa ON K1N 7N8 – 613/230-3076; Fax: 613/230-4830 – Librarian, Leszek Nowosielski

Osler, Hoskin & Harcourt - Library, #1500, 50 O'Connor St., Ottawa ON K1P 6L2 – 613/787-1100; Fax: 613/235-2867; Email: mstenson@osler.com; URL: http://www.osler.com; Symbol: OOOH – Library Technician, Monique Stenson

Ottawa Citizen Library, 1101 Baxter Rd., Ottawa ON K2C 3M4 – 613/596-3742; Fax: 613/726-1198; Email: a1715@freenet.carleton.ca; URL: http://www.ottawacitizen.com
- Chief Librarian, Ron Tysick, 613/596-3744
- Graphics Librarian, Charlene Ruberry, 613/596-3742
- Photo Librarian, Lois Kirkup, 613/596-3744
- Special Projects, Liisa Tuomenin, 613/596-3744

Ottawa Civic Hospital – Dr. George S. Williamson Health Sciences Library, 1053 Carling Ave., Ottawa ON K1Y 4E9 – 613/761-4459; Fax: 613/761-5292; Email: ifrogley@civich.ottawa.on.ca; Symbol: OOOCH – Manager, Kyungja Shin

Ottawa General Hospital – Library, 501 Smyth Rd., Ottawa ON K1H 8L6 – 613/737-8530; Fax: 613/737-8521; Email: ENVOY: ILL.OGH – Manager, Jessie McGowan

Ottawa Tourism & Convention Authority, #1800, 130 Albert St., Ottawa ON K1P 5G4 – 613/237-5150, ext.118; Fax: 613/237-7339; Toll Free: 1-800-363-4465 – Researcher, Martin Winges

The Parliamentary Centre – Library, 250 Albert St., 4th Fl., Ottawa ON K1P 6M1 – 613/237-0143; Fax: 613/235-8237 – Librarian, Theresa Bruneau

Pauktuutit Inuit Women's Association – Library, 192 Bank St., Ottawa ON K2P 1W8 – 613/238-3977; Fax: 613/238-1787

People, Words & Change – Library, 211 Bronson Ave., Ottawa ON K1R 6H5 – 613/234-2494; Fax: 613/234-4223 – Win Burrows

Perley-Robertson, Panet, Hill & McDougall Law Office - Library, 99 Bank St., Ottawa ON K1P 6C1 – 613/238-2022; Fax: 613/238-8775 – Chief Librarian, Emer Cronin

Potvin Law Office - Library, #1000, 141 Laurier Ave. West, Ottawa ON K1P 5J3 – 613/236-6628; Fax: 613/234-7529; Email: iplaw@synapse.com

Privy Council Office - Information & Research Centre, #1000, 85 Sparks St., Ottawa ON K1A 0A3 – 613/957-5125; Fax: 613/957-5043; Email: library@pco.gc.ca; Symbol: OOPC – Manager, Jean Weerasinghe

Public Service Alliance of Canada (CLC) – PSAC Library, 233 Gilmour St., Ottawa ON K2P 0P1 – 613/560-4211; Fax: 613/567-0385 – Library Supervisor, Louise Laplante

Public Service Commission of Canada - Library, #B1123 West Tower, 300 Laurier Ave. West, Ottawa ON K1A 0M7 – 613/992-4068; Fax: 613/992-4329; Email: ENVOY: ILL.OOCS; Symbol: OOCS – Head, Library Services, Gregory Renaud

Public Service Staff Relations Board - Library, POBox 1525, Ottawa ON K1P 5V2 – 613/990-1813; Fax: 613/990-1849 – Chief Librarian, Richard Harkin

Public Works & Government Services Canada - Departmental Library, #1E, Phase 3, 11 Laurier St., Ottawa ON K1A 1B2 – 819/956-3460; Fax: 819/997-8909; Symbol: OODP
- Chief Librarian, Henne Kahwa, 819/956-3461
- Acquisitions Librarian, Sylvette Forget-Séguin, 819/956-3462
- Cataloguing Technician, Lois Marcil, 819/956-3441
- Circulation Clerk, Cathy Talbot, 819/956-3460
- Reference Librarian, Elizabeth Kirby, 819/956-3465

Translation Bureau - Military Terminology Documentation Centre, 390 Laurier St. West, 5th Fl., Ottawa ON K1A 0S5 – 613/990-7964; Fax: 613/990-9020 – Head, M. Drolet

Translation Bureau - Military Translation Documentation Centre, North Tower, Rm. 168, 101 Colonel By Dr., 18th Fl., Ottawa ON K1A 0M5 – 613/947-7151; Fax: 613/992-8808 – Head, J. Tomlinson

Translation Bureau - Parliamentary & Interpretation Services Documentation Centre, 171 Slater St., 3rd Fl., Ottawa ON K1A 0S5 – 613/996-7438; Fax: 613/996-8794 – Head, N. Vilandré

Tupper Library, #B321, Sir Charles Tupper Bldg., 2323 Riverside Dr., Ottawa ON K1A 0M2 – 613/736-2396; Fax: 613/736-2401; Symbol: OOPW – Branch Librarian, Marilyn Dyck

Queen's University of Ottawa - Economic Projects Library, POBox 1503, Ottawa ON K1P 5R5 – 613/567-7489; Fax: 613/567-7640; Symbol: OOQEP – Librarian, Deborah Scott-Douglas

Regional Municipality of Ottawa-Carleton - Corporate Resource Centre, 111 Lisgar St., Ottawa ON K2P 2L7 – 613/560-2058; Fax: 613/560-1380; Symbol: OORM
- Corporate Librarian, V. El-Zorkany
- Library Technician, M. O'Donnell

Legal Department Library, 111 Lisgar St., 3rd Fl., Ottawa ON K2P 2L7 – 613/560-2056; Fax: 613/590-1383 – Library Technician, Alice Rabb

The Rehabilitation Centre – Reading Room, 505 Smyth Rd., Ottawa ON K1H 8M2 – 613/737-7350; Fax: 613/737-7056; Email: illooro@rohcg.on.ca – Cathy Cuzner

RESORS Canada Centre for Remote Sensing - Library, #121, 615 Booth St., Ottawa ON K1A 0Y7 – 613/943-8833; Fax: 613/947-0574; Symbol: OOCCR – Database Manager, Louis Marcotte

Revenue Canada - Departmental Library, Albion Tower, #1100, 25 Nicholas St., Ottawa ON K1A 0L5 – 613/957-2278; Fax: 613/957-9514; Symbol: OONR – Library Services, Assistant Director, Lorraine Wilkinson, 613/957-2275

Scientific & Technical Information Centre, 79 Bentley Ave., Ottawa ON K1A 0L5 – 613/954-9944; Fax: 613/952-7825; Symbol: OOSTI – Head, Ted Racine

Riverside Hospital of Ottawa – Scobie Health Sciences Library, 1967 Riverside Dr., Ottawa ON K1H 7W9 – 613/738-8230; Fax: 613/738-8532; Symbol: OORH – Coordinator, Paula M. Coutts

Royal Canadian Mint - Library, 320 Sussex Dr., Ottawa ON K1A 0G8 – 613/993-3614; Fax: 613/991-2294; Symbol: OOCRM – Manager, Information Systems, Monic Bourgon, 613/991-2028

Royal Canadian Mounted Police - Canadian Police College Library, St. Laurent Blvd. & Sandridge Rd., POBox 8900, Ottawa ON K1G 3J2 – 613/993-3225; Fax: 613/993-2220; Email: library@cpc.gc.ca; URL: http://www.cpc.gc.ca; Symbol: OOR
- Manager, Nancy Park, 613/998-0774
- Head of Client Services, Emmett Will
- Head of Technical Services, Margaret Brignell

Scientific Information Centre, Ident Tower, CPS Bldg., #502, 1200 Vanier Pkwy., POBox 8885, Ottawa ON K1G 3M8 – 613/998-6282; Fax: 613/956-0152; Email: ENVOY: RCMPCPS.LIB; Symbol: OORS

Royal Ottawa Health Care Group – Rhodes Chalke Library, 1145 Carling Ave., Ottawa ON K1Z 7K4 – 613/722-6521, ext.6268; Fax: 613/722-5048; Email: illooro@rohcg.on.ca; Symbol: OORO – Cathy Cuzner

The Royal Society of Canada – Library, #308, 225 Metcalfe St., Ottawa ON K2P 1P9 – 613/991-5760; Fax: 613/991-6996 – Kathy Riikonen

Saint Paul University - Library, 223 Main St., Ottawa ON K1S 1C4 – 613/236-1393; Fax: 613/782-3005; Symbol: OOSU
- Chief Librarian, Larry Eshelman, 613/236-1393, ext.2314, Email: larrye@spu.stpaul.uottawa.ca
- Principal Cataloguer, Edwin Galipeau
- Acquisitions Librarian, André Paris

Scott & Aylen Law Office - Legal Library, 60 Queen St., Ottawa ON K1P 5Y7 – 613/237-5160; Fax: 613/230-8842; Email: snixon@scottaylen.com
- Library Services, Director, Sherril Nixon
- Library Assistant, Katharine Heney

Scouts Canada – Library, 1345 Baseline Rd., PO Box 5151, LCD Merivale, Ottawa ON K2C 3G7 – 613/224-5131; Fax: 613/224-3571 – Librarian, Valerie Charron

Smart & Biggar Law Office - Library, #900, 55 Metcalfe St., Ottawa ON K1P 6L5 – 613/232-2486; Fax: 613/232-8440; Symbol: OOSB – Chief Librarian, Andrea Billingham

Social Sciences & Humanities Research Council - Library, 255 Albert St., POBox 1610, Ottawa ON K1P 6G4 – 613/992-0638 (morning only); Fax: 613/992-1787; Symbol: OOSSHR – Library Assistant, Diane Séguin

Solar Energy Society of Canada Inc. – Library, #702, 116 Lisgar St., Ottawa ON K1A 0K1 – 613/234-4151; Fax: 613/234-2988

Solicitor General Canada - Library, 340 Laurier Ave. West, Ottawa ON K1A 0P8 – 613/991-2787; Fax: 613/941-6171; Email: library@sgc.gc.ca; Symbol: OOSG
- Chief Librarian, Heather Moore, 613/991-2779
- Head, Client Services, Leonard Bonavero, 613/991-2780
- ILL/Reference Officer, Noëlla Morvan, 613/991-2787
- Technical Services Librarian, France Grenier, 613/991-2784

Soloway, Wright - Library, #900, 427 Laurier Ave. West, Ottawa ON K1R 7Y2 – 613/236-0111; Fax: 613/238-8507 – Librarian, Norma Vincent

South Asia Partnership Canada – Resource Centre, #200, One Nicholas St., Ottawa ON K1N 7B7 – 613/241-1333; Fax: 613/241-1129 – Canadian Program Manager, Faruq Faisel

Standards Council of Canada - Document Centre, #1200, 45 O'Connor St., Ottawa ON K1P 6N7 – 613/238-3222; Fax: 613/995-4564; Email: info@scc.ca; URL: http://www.scc.ca; Symbol: OOST – Customer Services, Manager, Kathy Millar

Statistics Canada - Library, R.H. Coats Bldg., 2nd Fl., 120 Parkdale Ave., Ottawa ON K1A 0T6 – 613/951-8219; Fax: 613/951-0939; Symbol: OOS

Director, Library Services, Susan Feeney
Director, Advisory Services, Gail Graser, 613/951-9285

Status of Women Canada - Documentation Centre, #700, 360 Albert St., Ottawa ON K1A 1C3 – 613/995-4008; Fax: 613/957-3359; Symbol: OOSW – Chief, Records & Library Services, Céline Champagne

Supreme Court of Canada - Library, Kent & Wellington Streets, Ottawa ON K1A 0J1 – 613/996-8120; Fax: 613/952-2832; Email: library@scc-csc.gc.ca; Symbol: OOSC
Director, F. Diane Teeple, 613/996-8026
Chief, Reader Services, Judith Rubin, 613/996-8579
Reference Librarian, Daphne Phillips, 613/943-8879
Reference Librarian, Alicia Loo, 613/996-7996
Chief, Technical Services, Ken Lane, 613/996-8183
Manager, Collection Development, Adela Romero, 613/996-0166
Chief, Systems & Database Administration, Tara Naraynsingh, 613/947-1636

Tax Court of Canada - Library, 200 Kent St., Ottawa ON K1A 0M1 – 613/992-1704; Fax: 613/943-8449; Symbol: OOTR
Manager, Library Services, Denis Roussel
Library Technician, Chantal Beauregard

Traffic Injury Research Foundation of Canada – Resource Centre, #200, 171 Nepean St., Ottawa ON K2P 0B4 – 613/238-5235; Fax: 613/238-5292 – Steve Brown

Transport Canada - Library & Information Services, Place de Ville, Tower C, 15th Fl., 330 Sparks St., Ottawa ON K1A 0N5 – 613/998-5128; Fax: 613/954-4731; Email: ENVOY: ILL.OOT; Symbol: OOT – Director, Gary Brenton
Road Safety Library, Canada Bldg., Minto Place, #1305, 344 Slater St., Ottawa ON K1A 0N5 – 613/998-1980; Fax: 613/998-4831; Symbol: OOTRS – Librarian, Suzan Zimmerman

Transportation Association of Canada – Technical Information Centre, 2323 St. Laurent Blvd., Ottawa ON K1G 4K6 – 613/736-1350; Fax: 613/736-1395; Email: tis@tac-atc.ca – Librarian, Jocelyne Blanchard

United Nations Association in Canada – Resource Centre, #900, 130 Slater St., Ottawa ON K1P 6E2 – 613/232-5751; Fax: 613/563-2455 – Research & Information Officer, Rory O'Connor

United Steelworkers of America (AFL-CIO/CLC) - Canadian Office – Library, #201, 885 Meadowlands Dr. East, Ottawa ON K2C 3N2 – 416/487-1571, ext.214; Fax: 613/727-1825 – Librarian/Researcher, Lesley Stodart

University of Ottawa - Library Network, 65 University Cres., Ottawa ON K1N 9A5 – 613/562-5888; Fax: 613/562-5195; Email: ill.oou@uottawa.ca; URL: http://www.uottawa.ca/library/; Symbol: OOU
University Chief Librarian, Richard Greene
Morisset Library, Director, Jean LeBlanc, 613/562-5800, ext.3645
Law Library, Director, Jules Larivière, 613/562-5845
Health Sciences Library, Director, Dianne Kharouba, 613/562-5418
Collections & Public Services, Librarian, Jean LeBlanc, 613/564-5921
Music Library, Head, Debra Begg, 613/562-5800, ext.3638
Map Library, Head, Grace Welch, 613/562-5800, ext.3634
Media Resources, Head, Guillaume Blais, 613/562-5800, ext.3581
Systems, Leslie Weir, 613/562-5228
Technical Services Librarian, Pierre Daoust, 613/562-5800, ext.3581
Archives & Special Collections, Librarian, Andrea Trudel, 613/562-5910

Vietnamese Canadian Federation – Library, 249 Rochester St., Ottawa ON K1R 7M9 – 613/230-8282; Fax: 613/230-8282 – Librarian, Quy Do

World University Service of Canada – Library, POBox 3000, Ottawa ON K1Y 4M8 – 613/798-7477; Fax: 613/798-0990 – Information Officer, Daun Kennedy

#### OWEN SOUND

Georgian College - Learning Resource Centre, 1150 - 8 St. East, POBox 700, Owen Sound ON N4K 5R4 – 519/376-0682, ext.2037; Fax: 519/376-5395; Email: ENVOY: ILL.GEO.OS; Symbol: OOWGC – Supervisor, Karen L. McPhatter

Grey-Bruce Regional Health Centre - Health Sciences Library, 1400 - 8 St. East, POBox 1400, Owen Sound ON N4K 6M9 – 519/376-2121 ext.2043; Fax: 519/376-1846; Email: ENVOY: GBRHC; Symbol: OOWGM – Health Sciences Librarian, Peggy Binkle

Grey County Law Association – Courthouse Library, 595 - 9 Ave. East, Owen Sound ON N4K 3E3 – 519/371-5495; Fax: 519/371-4606 – Librarian, Teresa Cullen

#### PEMBROKE

Algonquin College - Pembroke Campus Resource Centre, 315 Pembroke St. East, Pembroke ON K8A 3K2 – 613/735-4707; Fax: 613/735-8801; Symbol: OPEMAC – Library Technician, Jean Lopushanski

#### PENETANGUISHENE

Deacon Taws Friend - Library, 90 Main St., POBox 869, Penetanguishene ON L0K 1P0 – 705/549-3131; Fax: 705/549-4682 – Midland, Administrator, Phil Marley, CMA, 705/526-3791, Fax: 705/526-2688

Penetanguishene Mental Health Centre - Library, 500 Church St., Penetanguishene ON L9M 1G3 – 705/549-3181, ext.2342; Fax: 705/549-6467; Email: patreid@mhcp.on.ca; Symbol: OPENM – Librarian, Patricia Reid

#### PERTH

Algonquin College - Lanark County Resource Centre, 7 Craig St., Perth ON K7H 1X7 – 613/267-2859, ext.5607; Fax: 613/267-3950; Symbol: OPAC – Head, Ann L. MacPhail, Email: macphaa@algonquinc.on.ca

#### PETERBOROUGH

City of Peterborough - Planning Division Library, City Hall, 500 George St. North, Peterborough ON K9H 3R9 – 705/748-8881; Fax: 705/742-5218 – Secretary, Planning & Economic Development, Judy Reader

Greater Peterborough Chamber of Commerce – Library, 175 George St. North, Peterborough ON K9J 3G6 – 705/748-9771; Fax: 705/743-2331 – Don Frise

H. Girvin Devitt Law Office - Library, 858 Chemong Rd., POBox 1449, Peterborough ON K9H 7H6 – 705/742-5471 – Bookkeeper, Michelle Towns

Kawartha World Issues Centre – Library, #10, 180 Barnardo Ave., Peterborough ON K9H 5V3 – 705/745-1380; Fax: 705/745-9720 – Resource Coordinator, Marisa Kaczmarczyk

Ontario Federation of Anglers & Hunters – Eaton Conservation Resource Library, POBox 2800, Peterborough ON K9J 8L5 – 705/748-6324; Fax: 705/748-9577 – Freya Long

Ontario Ministry of Natural Resources - Library, 300 Water St., POBox 7000, Peterborough ON K9J 8M5 – 705/755-1888; Fax: 705/755-1882; Email: mnr-library@gov.on.ca; Symbol: OTLF – Group Leader, Wendy Craig

Ontario Public Interest Research Group - Peterborough – Library, Peter Robinson College, Trent University, Peterborough ON K9J 7B8 – 705/748-1767; Fax: 705/748-1795

Ontario Trails Council – Library, Trail Studies Unit, Environmental Sciences Bldg., Trent University, POBox 4800, Peterborough ON K9J 7B8 – 709/748-1419; Fax: 709/748-1205

Peterborough Civic Hospital – Hospital Library, 1 Hospital Dr., Peterborough ON K9J 7C6 – 705/876-5005; Fax: 705/743-0188; Email: jmacinto@pch.sjhhc.org; Symbol: OPETCH – Librarian, Judy MacIntosh

St. Joseph's General Hospital – Library, 384 Rogers St., Peterborough ON K9H 7B6 – 705/743-4251; Fax: 705/740-8345; Email: mconchel@sjhhc.org; Symbol: OPETSJ – Librarian, Mary Conchelos

Sir Sandford Fleming College of Applied Arts & Technology - Sutherland Campus, Educational Resources Centre, Brealey Dr., Peterborough ON K9J 7B1 – 705/743-5610; Fax: 705/749-5556; Symbol: OPETSF
Learning Resource Centre, Director, Karen Sjolin
Periodicals, Library Technician, D. Sloan
Reference & Acquisition, Library Technician, R. O'Grady
Reference & Acquisition, Library Technician, S. Coones
Interlibrary Loans, Library Technician, P. Moher
Circulation Services, Circulation Clerk, B. McGee
Audiovisual Services, AV Technician, G. Richards
Media Resources, Media Resources Technician, A. Callan

Survivors of Suicide Support Program – Resource Centre, #301, 349A George St. North, Peterborough ON K9H 3P9 – 705/748-6711; Fax: 705/748-2577 – Health Promotion Coordinator, Anne Cole

Trent University - Thomas J. Bata Library, POBox 4800, Peterborough ON K9J 7B8 – 705/748-1324; Fax: 705/748-1315; Email: ENVOY 100: ILL.OPET or MW.GENOE; Symbol: OPET
University Librarian, Murray W. Genoe
Information Services, Head, J. Luyben
Monographs (Cat. & Acq.), Head, M.A. Scigliano
Government Publications & Maps, Head, B. Znamirowski
Serials, Microforms & Photoreproduction Services, Head, J. Millard
Collection Development, A. McCalla

#### PICKERING

Purdue Frederick - Library, 575 Granite Ct., Pickering ON L1W 3W8 – 905/420-4991; Fax: 905/420-4193; Email: karens@inforamp.net – Librarian, Karen Smith

#### POINT EDWARD

Owens Corning Canada - Technical Information Centre, 704 Mara St., Point Edward ON N7V 1X4 – 519/336-5670; Fax: 519/336-5906 – Information Clerk, Carol Scott

#### RICHMOND HILL

Canadian Bottled Water Federation – Library, #203-1, 70 East Beaver Creek Rd., Richmond Hill ON L4B 3B2 – 905/886-6928; Fax: 905/886-9531

Environmental Auditors Ltd., York Corporate Centre, #240, 100 York Blvd., Richmond Hill ON L4B 1J8 – 905/886-7965; Fax: 905/886-7967

Helpmate Community Information & Volunteer Bureau – Library, 10100 Yonge St., Richmond Hill ON L4C 1T8 – 905/884-3839; Toll Free: 1-800-363-2412 – Anne Rout

SENES Consultants Limited – Information Centre, #12, 121 Granton Dr., Richmond Hill ON L4B 3N4 – 905/764-9380; Fax: 905/764-9386; Email: hguttman@senes.on.ca; Symbol: OWSCL – Supervisor, Library Services, Henny Guttman

York Central Hospital – Douglas Storms Memorial Library, 10 Trench St., Richmond Hill ON L4C 4Z3 – 905/883-2018; Fax: 905/883-2293

**RIDGETOWN**

Ridgetown College - Library, Main St. East, Ridgetown ON N0P 2C0 – 519/674-1540; Fax: 519/674-1530; Email: iroadhou@ridgetownc.on.ca; URL: http://www.ridgetownc.on.ca/library.htm; Symbol: ORCAT – Librarian, Iona Roadhouse

**ST CATHARINES**

AIDS Niagara – Library, #200, 50 William St., St Catharines ON L2R 5J2 – 905/984-8684; Fax: 905/988-1921 – Joan Blanchard

Alzheimer Society of Niagara Region – Library, 203 Ontario St., St Catharines ON L2R 5L2 – 905/687-3914; Fax: 905/687-9952 – Executive Asst., Cynthia Smith

Association of Self Employment Developers of Ontario – Library, 59 Welland Vale Rd., St Catharines ON L2R 6V6 – 905/685-3418; Fax: 905/684-1282 – Coordinator, Douglas Crawford

Brock University - James A. Gibson Library, 500 Glenridge Ave., St Catharines ON L2S 3A1 – 905/688-5550, ext.3226; Fax: 905/988-5490; Email: jhogan@spartan.ac.brocku.ca; URL: http://www.brocku.ca/library/; Symbol: OSTCB
- University Librarian, James W. Hogan, 905/688-5550, ext.3226
- Circulation Librarian, Robert Rossini, 905/688-5550, ext.3727
- Information & Resource Management, Associate Librarian, Margaret Grove, 905/688-5550, ext.3198
- Acquisitions Supervisor, Catherine Foreman, 905/688-5550, ext.3265
- Serials Librarian, Esther Sleep, 905/688-5550, ext.3266
- University Map Library, Map Librarian, Colleen Beard, 905/688-5550, ext.3468
- Business Librarian, Douglas Suarez, 905/688-5550, ext.4083
- Reference Information Services Librarian, Phyllis Wright, 905/688-5550, ext.3961
- Cataloguing Librarian, Brigitte Schimek, 905/688-5550, ext.4468

Canadian Canal Society – Canadian Canal Society Library/Archives, PO Box 23016, RPO Midtown, St Catharines ON L2R 7P6 – 905/688-5550, ext.3264; Fax: 905/988-5490 – John Burtniak

Family & Children's Services Niagara – Library, 311 Geneva St., POBox 24028, St Catharines ON L2R 7P7 – 905/937-7731; Fax: 905/646-7085; Toll Free: 1-888-937-7731

Lincoln County Board of Education - Educational Resource Library, 191 Carlton St., St Catharines ON L2R 7P4 – 905/641-1550, ext.2305; Fax: 905/685-8511; Email: lin100@niagara.com
- Library Technician, Corrine McKernan
- Library Technician, Nicole Kitchen

Niagara College - St Catharines Campus Learning Resource Centre, 59 Welland Vale Rd., POBox 340, St Catharines ON L2R 6V6 – 905/684-4315, ext.2402; Fax: 905/684-3167 – Campus Librarian, Maria Edelman

Niagara Youth Orchestra Association – Library, Ridley Sq., #148, 111 Fourth Ave., St Catharines ON L2S 3P5 – 905/945-4160; Fax: 905/704-0558 – Librarian, Barbara Bewlay

Ontario Ministry of Transportation - MTO Library, 301 St. Paul St., 2nd Fl. North, St Catharines ON L2R 7R4 – 905/704-2065; Fax: 905/704-2004; Email: zvejniek@mto.gov.on.ca; Symbol: OTDT
- Public Services Librarian, Judy Martin
- Technical Services Librarian, Laila Zvejnieks

Ontario Public Buyers Association, Inc. – OPBA Internal Databank, Ridley Square, #361, 111 Fourth Ave., St Catharines ON L2S 3P5 – 905/356-7521, ext.4300; Fax: 905/682-3788; Email: miller@city.niagara-falls.on.ca – Executive Vice-President of Technology, Ray Miller

Ontario Public Interest Research Group - Brock – Library, Brock University, #306, Student Centre, St Catharines ON L2S 3A1 – 905/688-5550, ext.3499; Fax: 905/641-7581 – Karin Perry

Rodman Hall Arts Centre - Library, 109 St. Paul Cres., St Catharines ON L2S 1M3 – 519/684-2925 – Curator of Education & Extensions, Debra Attenborough

Worldwise International Resource Centre – Worldwise Library, 125 Welland Ave., St Catharines ON L2R 2N5 – 905/641-2525; Fax: 905/682-4314

**ST MARYS**

St Marys & District Association for Community Living – Library, POBox 1618, St Marys ON N4X 1B9 – 519/284-1455; Fax: 519/284-3120 – Manager, Community Involvement, Charlotte Dingwall

**ST THOMAS**

Elgin County Courthouse - Library, 8 Wellington St., St Thomas ON N5R 2P2 – 519/631-7650; Fax: 519/633-9837

**SARNIA**

Bayer Inc. - Rubber Division - Information Centre, POBox 3001, Sarnia ON N7T 7M2 – 519/337-8251, ext.5711; Fax: 519/339-7748; Email: rosemary.odonnell.bi@bayer.com; Symbol: OPS
- Information Services Supervisor, Rosemary O'Donnell
- Reference Librarian, Tina Demars, 519/337-8251, ext. 5106
- Reference Librarian, Sharon Freeman, 519/337-8251, ext.5388

Canadian Centre for Pollution Prevention – Pollution Prevention Library, #112, 265 North Front St., Sarnia ON N7T 7X1 – 519/337-3423; Fax: 519/337-3486; Toll Free: 1-800-667-9790

Imperial Oil - Research Technical Information Centre, 453 Christina St. South, POBox 3022, Sarnia ON N7T 7M1 – 519/339-2902; Fax: 519/339-4436; Symbol: OSI
- Information Specialist, Nancy Bourque, 519/339-2617
- Library Assistant, Jackie Baley, 519/339-2626

Lambton College - Resource Centre, 1457 London Rd., Sarnia ON N7S 6K4 – 519/542-7751, ext.489; Fax: 519/542-1103; Email: leeann@lambton.on.ca; URL: http://www.lambton.on.ca; Symbol: OSLC – Learning Technology & Information Systems, Director, Jim Elliot

Lambton County Board of Education - Professional Library, 200 Wellington St., POBox 2019, Sarnia ON N7T 7L2 – 519/336-1500, ext.2422; Fax: 519/383-8937; Email: mccaffd@lambto.lcbe.edu.on.ca – Librarian, Denise McCaffrey

Lambton Industrial Society: An Environmental Co-operative – Library, #111, 265 Front St. North, Sarnia ON N7T 7X1 – 519/332-2010; Fax: 519/332-2015

**SAULT STE MARIE**

Algoma University College - Arthur A. Wishart Library, 1520 Queen St. East, Sault Ste Marie ON P6A 2G4 – 705/949-2101; Fax: 705/949-6583; Email: ENVOY: ILL.OSTMA; URL: http://www.auc.on.ca
- Library Director, Patricia V. Burt, 705/949-2301, ext.351
- Technical Services Librarian, Warrick Chin
- Information Services Librarian, John D. Blackwell, 705/949-2301, ext.352, Email: blackwel@thunderbird.auc.laurentian.ca

Clean North – Environmental Resource Room, POBox 1204, Sault Ste Marie ON P6A 6N1 – 705/945-1573; Fax: 705/945-0595

Fisheries & Oceans Canada - Sea Lamprey Control Centre Library, 1 Canal Dr., Sault Ste Marie ON P6A 6W4 – 705/941-3000; Fax: 705/941-3025 – Administrative Officer, Jackie Bassett, 705/941-3002

Natural Resources Canada-Canadian Forest Service: Great Lakes Forestry Centre – Library, 1219 Queen St. East, POBox 490, Sault Ste Marie ON P6A 5M7 – 705/949-9461, ext.2000; Fax: 705/759-5700; Email: ENVOY: OTMF.ILL; Symbol: OSTMF – N.J. Dukes

Ontario Ministry of the Solicitor General & Correctional Services - Northern Treatment Centre Library, 800 Great Northern Rd., Sault Ste Marie ON P6A 5K7 – 705/946-0995, ext.242; Fax: 705/946-2925; Symbol: OSTMNT – Library Technician, Mary Campbell

Sault Area Hospitals – Health Sciences Library, 969 Queen St. East, Sault Ste Marie ON P6A 2C4 – 705/759-3434, ext.4368; Fax: 705/759-3847; Email: youkathy@soonet.ca; Symbol: OSTMPH – Librarian, Kathy You

Sault College - Library, 443 Northern Ave., POBox 60, Sault Ste Marie ON P6A 5L3 – 705/759-2554, ext.711; Fax: 705/759-1319; Email: ENVOY: SAULT.CAATLIB

Sault Community Information & Career Centre – Resource Centre, 8 Albert St. East, Sault Ste Marie ON P6A 2H6 – 705/949-6565; Toll Free: 1-800-461-2259

Sault Symphony Association – Music Library, #2, 121 Brock St., Sault Ste Marie ON P6A 3B6 – 705/945-5337; Fax: 705/945-5337 – Music Librarian, Guy Traficante

**SIMCOE**

Ontario Ministry of the Solicitor General & Correctional Services - Sprucedale Youth Centre - Library, 660 Ireland Rd., POBox 606, Simcoe ON N3Y 4L8 – 519/426-3561, ext.248; Fax: 519/428-1407 – Library Technician, Ruth Ann Misener

**SOUTH PORCUPINE**

Northern College of Applied Arts & Technology - Porcupine Campus Learning Resources Centre, Hwy. 101 East, POBox 3211, South Porcupine ON P4N 8R6 – 705/235-3211, ext.150; Fax: 705/235-7279; Toll Free: 1-800-461-2167; Email: libraryp@kirk.northernc.on.ca; Symbol: OSPNC
- Library Technician, Maire Leigh Sheppard
- Library Technician, Eileen Pope
- Library Technician, Christine Dorval

**STONEY CREEK**

Contemporary Information Analysis Ltd., 2 Lakeview Dr., Stoney Creek ON L8E 5A5 – 905/643-1094; Fax: 416/927-0427

Mohawk College - Stoney Creek Campus Library, 481 Barton St. East, Stoney Creek ON L8E 2L7 – 905/662-3700, ext.5001; Fax: 905/664-0253 – Library Supervisor, Carol Farr

**STRATFORD**

County of Perth Law Association – Law Library, County Court House, 1 Huron St., Stratford ON N5A 5S4 – 519/271-1871; Fax: 519/271-3522

**SUDBURY**

Cambrian College - Library Services, 1400 Barrydowne Rd., Sudbury ON P3A 3V8 – 705/566-8101, ext.7333; Fax: 705/671-7329; Email: ENVOY: CAM.COLL.LIBRARY; Symbol: OSUC – Manager, Library Services, Caroline Hallsworth, MLIS, 705/566-8101, ext.7406, Email: cmhallsworth@venus.cambrianc.on.ca

Centre franco-ontarien de ressources en alphabétisation – Centre FORA, 533, rue Notre-Dame, Sudbury ON P3C 5L1 – 705/673-7033; Téléc: 705/673-5520 – Responsable à la clientèle, Roxanne Lépine

Laurentian Hospital – Medical Library, 41 Ramsey Lake Rd., Sudbury ON P3E 5J1 – 705/522-2200; Fax: 705/523-7017; Symbol: OSULH – Director, Library Services, Rannah Brosseau

Laurentian University - J.N. Desmarais Library, 935 Ramsey Lake Rd., Sudbury ON P3E 2C6 – 705/675-1151, ext.4803; Fax: 705/673-6524; Email: ENVOY: ILL.OSUL; URL: http://www.laurentian.ca; Symbol: OSUL
- Director of Library, Joyce C. Garnett
- Access Services, Chair, TBA
- Public Information, Chair, Ashley Thomson

Miller, Maki Law Office - Library, 176 Elm St., Sudbury ON P3C 1T7 – 705/675-7503; Fax: 705/675-8669

Oldtime Radio-Show Collector's Association – Library, 45 Barry St., Sudbury ON P3B 3H6 – 705/560-3095, 2957 – Librarian, Reg Hubert

Ontario Ministry of Northern Development & Mines - Willet Green Miller Centre, Mines Library, 933 Ramsey Lake Rd., Level A3, Sudbury ON P3E 6B5 – 705/670-5615; Fax: 705/670-5622; Email: davisl@gov.on.ca; Symbol: CAOTDM
- Linda Davis
- Janice Brissor

Ontario Ministry of the Solicitor General & Correctional Services - Cecil Facer Youth Centre Library, 2500 South Lane Rd., POBox 850, Sudbury ON P3E 4S3 – 705/522-1250; Fax: 705/522-6017 – Library Technician, Lydia Katulka

Service familial de la région de Sudbury inc. – Bibliothèque, #402, 51 Elm St., Sudbury ON P3C 1S3 – 705/674-5456 – Suzanne Paquin

Sudbury General Hospital – Library, 700 Paris St., Sudbury ON P3B 3B5 – 705/674-3181; Fax: 705/675-4781; Symbol: OSUGH – Librarian, Donald M. Hawryliuk

**THORNHILL**

The Baha'i Faith in Canada – Library, Baha'i National Centre, 7200 Leslie St., Thornhill ON L3T 6L8 – 905/889-8168; Fax: 905/889-8184; TLX: 06 96413 – Regan Brit

Epilepsy Ontario – Resource Centre, #308, 1 Promenade Circle, Thornhill ON L4J 4P8 – 905/764-5099; Fax: 905/764-1231; Toll Free: 1-800-463-1119 – Communication Officer, John Phair

**THOROLD**

Donohue Inc. - Library, Allanburg Rd., Thorold ON L2V 3Z5 – 905/227-1121, ext.3306; Fax: 905/227-2353; Email: iridgway@niagara.com; Symbol: OTHOP – Librarian, Isabelle Ridgway

**THUNDER BAY**

Ontario Hydro - Thunder Bay G.S. Laboratory – Library, Mission Island, POBox 816, Thunder Bay ON P7C 4X7 – 807/625-6455; Fax: 807/623-3619 – Librarian, Impi Sawchuk

Buset & Partners Law Office - Library, 1121 Barton St., Thunder Bay ON P7B 5N3 – 807/623-2500; Fax: 807/622-7808 – Librarian, Carolyn Enns

Confederation College - Challis Resource Centre, POBox 398, Thunder Bay ON P7C 4W1 – 807/475-6241; Fax: 807/622-3258; Email: tapak@confed.confederationc.on.ca; URL: http://www.confederationc.on.ca; Symbol: OTBCC – Director, Laraine Tapak

Lakehead Psychiatric Hospital – Northwestern Regional Mental Health Library, 580 Algoma St. North, POBox 2930, Thunder Bay ON P7B 5G4 – 807/343-4351; Fax: 807/343-4387; Email: hhyvarin@microage-tb.com; Symbol: OTBLP – Library Technician, Helen Hyvarinen

Lakehead University - Library, 855 Oliver Rd., Thunder Bay ON P7B 5E1 – 807/343-8205; Fax: 807/343-8007; URL: http://www.lakeheadu.ca; Symbol: OPAL
- Chief Librarian, Fred McIntosh
- Reference Librarian, Shirley Boneca, 807/343-8165
- Circulation Supervisor, Frank Sebesta, 807/343-8212
- Technical Services Librarian, Ian Dew, 807/343-8315
- Acquisitions Librarian, Anne Deighton, 807/343-8211
- Education Librarian, Jim Arnot, 807/343-8719

Northwestern Ontario Sports Hall of Fame & Museum – Library, 2203 Moodie St. East, Thunder Bay ON P7E 4Z5 – 807/622-2852; Fax: 807/622-2736

Ontario Ministry of the Solicitor General & Correctional Services - Thunder Bay Correctional Centre Library, POBox 1900, Thunder Bay ON P7B 5G3 – 807/475-8401; Fax: 807/475-9240 – Library Technician, Marjorie Brumwell

Thunder Bay Law Association – District Courthouse Library, 277 Camelot St., Thunder Bay ON P7A 4B3 – 807/344-3481; Fax: 807/345-9091; Email: lmoody@flash.lakeheadu.ca – LaRea Moody

Thunder Bay Symphony Orchestra Association – Music Library, POBox 24036, Thunder Bay ON P7A 7A9 – 807/345-4331; Fax: 807/345-8915 – Librarian, Valerie Patton

**TILBURY**

Tilbury & District Chamber of Commerce – Tilbury Odette Memorial Library, POBox 1355, Tilbury ON N0P 2L0 – 519/682-1766; Fax: 519/682-1766 – Librarian, Maxine Gardiner

**TIMMINS**

Ojibway & Cree Cultural Centre – Resource Centre, #304, 210 Spruce St. South, Timmins ON P4N 1C6 – 705/267-7911; Fax: 705/267-4988 – Supervisor, Christopher Duval

Rape Crisis Centre Timmins – Library, 355 Wilson Ave., Timmins ON P4N 2T7 – 705/268-8381; Fax: 705/268-3332 – Public Education Coordinator, Kathy Dionne

**TOBERMORY**

Ontario Marine Heritage Committee – Library, POBox 221, Tobermory ON N0H 2R0 – 519/596-2947; Fax: 519/596-2947 – Joy Buckingham

**TORONTO**

Ontario Hydro - Ontario Hydro Technologies – InfoPlace, 800 Kipling Ave., Toronto ON M8Z 5S4 – 416/207-6706; Fax: 416/231-6738; Email: infoplace@oht.hydro.on.ca – Senior Librarian, Donna Gardner

Ontario Ministry of Environment & Energy - Laboratory Services Branch – Laboratory Library, 125 Resources Rd., Etobicoke ON M9P 3V6 – 416/235-5751; Fax: 416/235-0189; Email: crawfotr@ene.gov.on.ca; Symbol: OTMENL – Interlibrary Loans, Traceyann Crawford

Academy of Medicine, Toronto - William Boyd Library, c/o The Toronto Hospital Library, 200 Elizabeth St., BW 9th Fl., Toronto ON M5G 2C4 – 416/340-3259; Fax: 416/340-4384; Symbol: OTA

Acres International Limited - Library, 480 University Ave., 13th Fl., Toronto ON M5G 1V2 – 416/595-2000, ext.5247; Fax: 416/595-2004; Symbol: OTAC – Librarian, Marion D'Amboise

Addiction Research Foundation – Library, 33 Russell St., Toronto ON M5S 2S1 – 416/595-6144; Fax: 416/595-6036; Toll Free: 1-800-463-6273; Email: arf@vax.library.utoro – Library Manager, Louise Hamel

Advocacy Resource Centre for the Handicapped – Library, #255, 40 Orchard View Blvd., Toronto ON M4R 1B9 – 416/482-8255; Fax: 416/482-2981

AIDS Committee of Toronto – Library, 399 Church St., 4th Fl., POBox 55, Toronto ON M4Y 2L4 – 416/340-2437, ext.223; Fax: 416/340-8224 – Mark Robertson

Aird & Berlis - Law Library, BCE Place, #1800, North Tower, 181 Bay St., POBox 754, Toronto ON M5J 2T9 – 416/863-1500; Fax: 416/863-1515; Email: durquhart@airdberlis.com – Librarian, Dawn Urquhart, 416/865-7756

Al-Anon Family Groups – Library, 1771 Avenue Rd., POBox 54533, North York ON M5M 4N5 – 416/366-4072; Toll Free: 1-800-443-4525

Albert & Temmy Latner Jewish Public Library, 4600 Bathurst St., North York ON M2R 3V3 – 416/635-2996 – Executive Director, Rabbi Zigmund Wolkenstein

Alexander Consulting Group - Resource Centre, #1900, 20 Bay St., Toronto ON M5J 2N9 – 416/868-5501; Fax: 416/868-5786 – Research Librarian, S. Shapero

Alfa Romeo Club of Canada – Library, POBox 62, Toronto ON M4T 2L7 – 416/498-6553; Fax: 416/499-7129

Alliance for Canadian New Music Projects – Library, Canadian Music Centre, 20 St. Joseph St., 3rd Fl., Toronto ON M4Y 1J9 – 416/963-5937; Fax: 416/961-7198

ALPHA Ontario - The Literacy & Language Training Resource Centre, 21 Park Rd., Toronto ON M4W 2N1 – 416/397-5900 (English), 397-5902 (Français); Fax: 416/397-5915; Toll Free: 1-800-363-0007; Email: alphaont@gwmail.mtrl.toronto.on.ca; URL: http://www.mtrl.toronto.on.ca/centres/alpha/ – Collections, Services & Outreach, Manager, Lucie Goulet

Alzheimer Society for Metropolitan Toronto – Alzheimer Resource Centre, #500, 2323 Yonge St., Toronto ON M4P 2C9 – 416/322-6560; Fax: 416/322-6656 – Librarian, Emmie Leung

Amyotrophic Lateral Sclerosis Society of Canada – ALS Resource Centre, #220, 6 Adelaide St. East, Toronto ON M5C 1H6 – 416/362-0269; Fax: 416/362-0414; Toll Free: 1-800-267-4257 – Manager of National Services, Helene Vassos

The Anglican Church of Canada – Library, Anglican Church House, 600 Jarvis St., Toronto ON M4Y 2J6 – 416/924-9192; Book Centre: 924-1332; Fax: 416/968-7983 – Karen Evans

Angus Environmental Ltd. – Library, 1127 Leslie St., North York ON M3C 2J6 – 416/443-8360; Fax: 416/443-8380

Animal Alliance of Canada – Animal Alliance Resource Centre, #101, 221 Broadview Ave., Toronto ON M4M 2G3 – 416/462-9541; Fax: 416/462-9647

Archives of Ontario - Library, #300, 77 Grenville St., Toronto ON M5S 1B3 – 416/327-1553; Fax: 416/327-1999; Toll Free: 1-800-668-9933; Email: vankalf@gov.on.ca; Symbol: OTAR
- Librarian, Frank van Kalmthout
- Library Technician, Susan Watt

Armstrong, Dunne Law Office - Library, #1400, 141 Adelaide St. West, Toronto ON M5H 3L5 – 416/868-0180; Fax: 416/863-1814; Email: adsclaw@inforamp.net – Librarian, Cynthia McKeich

Art Gallery of Ontario - Edward P. Taylor Research Library & Archives, 317 Dundas St. West, Toronto ON M5T 1G4 – 416/979-6642; Fax: 416/979-6602; Email: library@ago.net; URL: http://

www.AGO.net/library.html; Symbol: OTAG – Chief Librarian, Karen McKenzie

Arthur Andersen & Co. - Information Centre, Toronto-Dominion Centre, PO Box 29, Stn Toronto-Dominion, Toronto ON M5K 1B9 – 416/947-7898; Fax: 416/947-7878 – Head, Information Centre, Sean Forbes

Association canadienne-française de l'Ontario – Bibliothèque, #1711, 2, rue Carlton, Toronto ON M5B 1J3 – 416/595-5585; Téléc: 416/595-0202

Association of Canadian Orchestras – Resource Centre, #311, 56 The Esplanade, Toronto ON M5E 1A7 – 416/366-8834; Fax: 416/366-1780

Association of Canadian Publishers – Library, #301, 2 Gloucester St., Toronto ON M4Y 1L5 – 416/413-4929; Fax: 416/413-4920

Association of Municipalities of Ontario – Resource Centre, #1701, 393 University Ave., Toronto ON M5G 1E6 – 416/971-9856; Fax: 416/971-6191; Email: svukelic@amo.municom.com – Resources Manager, Snezana Vukelic

Association of Ontario Health Centres – Resource Centre, #102, 5233 Dundas St. West, Etobicoke ON M9B 1A6 – 416/236-2539; Fax: 416/236-0431

AT&T Canada Long Distance Services - Regulatory Information Centre, 200 Wellington St. West, Toronto ON M5V 3C7 – 416/345-2336; Fax: 416/345-2878 – Regulatory Research, Senior Manager, Tracy Tennant

AT&T Global Information Solutions - Marketing Information Retrieval Library, 320 Front St. West, Toronto ON M5V 3C4 – 416/351-2105; Fax: 416/351-2287
- Administration Manager, Mary Quattromini
- Esther Balevi

Audit Bureau of Circulations – Library of Print Media Circulation Statistics, Canadian Member Service Office, #850, 151 Bloor St. West, Toronto ON M5S 1S4 – 416/962-5840; Fax: 416/962-5844 – Supvr., Cdn. Member Services, Marian C. Robertson

B'nai Brith Canada – Library, 15 Hove St., North York ON M3H 4Y8 – 416/633-6224; Fax: 416/630-2159 – Sharon Anisman

Baker & McKenzie - Library, #2100, 181 Bay St., POBox 874, Toronto ON M5J 2T3 – 416/863-1221; Fax: 416/863-6275 – Librarian, Irene Batna

Bank of Montreal - Business Information Centre, 100 King St. West, Level B2, Toronto ON M5X 1A1 – 416/867-5833; Fax: 416/867-6951 – Manager, Diane F. James

Bank of Nova Scotia - Business Research Library, POBox 7007, Toronto ON M5C 2K7 – 416/866-6257; Fax: 416/866-4036 – Chief Librarian, Marion Miwa, 416/866-4403
- Technical Resource Centre, 2201 Eglinton Ave. East, Scarborough ON M1L 4S2 – 416/288-3571; Fax: 416/288-4445 – Manager, Lynda Cavanagh

Bell Canada - Information Resource Centre, F-1N Bell Trinity Square, Toronto ON M5G 2E1 – 416/581-4256; Fax: 416/340-0324; Symbol: OTBCIR – Rhona Glazer

Bereaved Families of Ontario – Resource Centre, #204, 214 Merton St., Toronto ON M4S 1A6 – Toll Free: 1-800-236-6364

Bereavement Services & Community Education – Library, 1403 Bayview Ave, Toronto ON M4G 3A8 – 416/485-6415; Fax: 416/487-4395 – Program Co-ordinator, Patricia Corrigall

Beth Tzedec Congregation - Max & Beatrice Wolfe Library, 1700 Bathurst St., Toronto ON M5P 3K3 – 416/781-3511, ext.25; Fax: 416/781-0150; URL: http://www.uscj.org/ontario/torontobt/
- Chief Librarian, Zina Glassman
- Children's Librarian, Fagie Goldfarb

Big Sisters Association of Ontario – Resource Centre, 2750 Dufferin St., Toronto ON M6B 3R4 – 416/789-7859; Fax: 416/789-7850 – Serivice Coordinator, Neil Burke

Blake, Cassels & Graydon Law Office - Library, Commerce Court West, POBox 25, Toronto ON M5L 1A9 – 416/863-2650; Fax: 416/863-4261
- Library Manager, Sandra M. Morris
- Research Librarian, Wray Roulston, 416/863-3851
- Research & Technology Librarian, Martin Tomlinson, 416/863-5827

Bloorview Macmillan Centre - Bloorview Site – Health Sciences Library, 25 Buchan Court, Willowdale ON M2J 4S9 – 416/425-6220, ext.6040; Fax: 416/494-9985; Email: wongpy@library.utoronto.ca – Pui-ying Wong

Bloorview MacMillan Centre - Macmillan Site - Health Sciences Library, 350 Rumsey Rd., Toronto ON M4G 1R8 – 416/425-6220, ext.3517; Fax: 416/425-6591; Email: wongpy@library.utoronto.ca – Librarian, Pui-ying Wong

Board of Trade of Metropolitan Toronto – Resource Centre, World Trade Centre, One First Canadian Place, POBox 60, Toronto ON M5X 1C1 – 416/366-6811; Fax: 416/366-4906 – Director, Information Services, Mary de Reus

Bob Rumball Centre for the Deaf – Library Resource Centre, 2395 Bayview Ave., North York ON M2L 1A2 – 416/449-9651 (Voice & TDD); Fax: 416/449-8881; Toll Free: 1-800-841-9663

Borden & Elliot Law Office - Library, Scotia Plaza, #4400, 40 King St. West, Toronto ON M5H 3Y4 – 416/367-6370; Fax: 416/361-2752 – Manager, Information Services, Vivienne Denton, 416/367-6369

British Consulate-General - Library, #2800, 777 Bay St., Toronto ON M5G 2G2 – 416/593-1290; Fax: 416/593-1229 – Valerie Strand

British Methodist Episcopal Church Conference of Canada – Norval Johnson Heritage Library, 460 Shaw St., Toronto ON M6G 3L3 – 416/534-3831; Fax: 416/383-6856 – Librarian, Wilma Morrison

Business Development Centre (Toronto) – Library, 1801 Eglinton Ave. West, Toronto ON M6E 2H8 – 416/789-2485; Fax: 416/789-0365

Cadillac Fairview - Records Centre, 20 Queen St. West, 4th Fl., Toronto ON M5H 3R4 – 416/598-8440; Fax: 416/598-8607
- Records Librarian, Simonne Nord
- Records Clerk, Esther Kim

Calmeadow – Calmeadow Resource Centre, #600, 365 Bay St., Toronto ON M5H 2V1 – 416/362-9670, ext.241; Fax: 416/362-0769 – Librarian, Audrey Malloch

Canada Academy & Association of Chinese Acupuncture/Medicine – Library, #407, 3852 Finch Ave. East, Scarborough ON M1T 3T6 – 416/222-1428 – Dr. Ding

Canada-Latin America Resource Centre – Library, 603 1/2 Parliament St., Toronto ON M4X 1P9 – 416/921-4424; Fax: 416/921-0071

The Canada Life Assurance Company – Corporate Library Services, 330 University Ave., Toronto ON M5G 1R8 – 416/597-1456, ext.5266; Fax: 416/597-8537 – Nathalie Richard

Canadian Abortion Rights Action League – Video Library, #306, 344 Bloor St. West, Toronto ON M5S 3A7 – 416/961-1507; Fax: 416/961-5771

Canadian Alliance in Solidarity with the Native Peoples – Library, 39 Spadina Rd., POBox 574, Toronto ON M5R 2S9 – 416/972-1573; Fax: 416/972-6232 – Maogostia Pyjor

The Canadian Art Foundation – Library, 70 The Esplanade, 2nd Fl., Toronto ON M5E 1R2 – 416/368-8854; Fax: 416/368-6135 – Production Manager, Lisa Ghione

Canadian Association for Co-operative Education – Library, #310, 55 Eglinton Ave. East, Toronto ON M4P 1G8 – 416/535-6993; Fax: 416/483-3365

Canadian Association for Community Living – Information Services, Kinsmen Building, York University Campus, 4700 Keele St., North York ON M3J 1P3 – 416/661-9611; Fax: 416/661-5701 – Director, Information Services & Technology, Miriam Ticoll

Canadian Association of Food Banks – Library, 530 Lakeshore Blvd. West, Toronto ON M5V 1A5 – 416/203-9241; Fax: 416/203-9244 – Membership Coordinator, Aynsley Morris

Canadian Association of Photographers & Illustrators in Communications – Library, #322, 100 Broadview Ave., Toronto ON M4M 2E8 – 416/462-3700; Fax: 416/462-3678 – John Martin

Canadian Aviation Historical Society – Library, POBox 224, North York ON M2N 5S8 – 416/488-2247; Fax: 416/488-2247 – Bill Turner

Canadian Bankers Association – Banking Information Centre, Commerce Court West, 30th Fl., PO Box 348, Stn Commerce Court, Toronto ON M5L 1G2 – 416/362-6092; Fax: 416/362-7705; Toll Free: 1-800-263-0231

Canadian Bible Society – Library, 10 Carnforth Rd., Toronto ON M4A 2S4 – 416/757-4171; Fax: 416/757-3376; Toll Free: 1-800-465-2425 – Archives/Editor, Connie Stamp

Canadian Bookbinders & Book Artists Guild – Craft Resource Centre, #309, 176 John St., Toronto ON M5T 1X5 – 416/581-1071 – Chairperson, Ann Douglas

Canadian Broadcasting Corporation - Reference Library, POBox 500, Toronto ON M5W 1E6 – 416/205-3244; Fax: 416/205-3733; Symbol: OTBC – Head Librarian, Leone Earls, Email: learls@toronto.cbc.ca

Canadian Camping Association – Bookstore, #303, 1810 Avenue Rd., Toronto ON M5M 3Z2 – 416/781-4717; Fax: 416/781-7875 – Administrator, Dawn Hunter

Canadian Centre for Victims of Torture – Resource Centre, 194 Jarvis St., Toronto ON M5B 2B7 – 416/363-1066; Fax: 416/363-2122 – Mulugeta Abai

The Canadian Centre/International P.E.N. – Library, 24 Ryerson Ave., Toronto ON M5T 2P3 – 416/703-8448; Fax: 416/703-3870

The Canadian Children's Book Centre – Library, 35 Spadina Rd., Toronto ON M5R 2S9 – 416/975-0010; Fax: 416/975-1839

Canadian Civil Liberties Association – Library, #403, 229 Yonge St., Toronto ON M5B 1N9 – 416/363-0321; Fax: 416/861-1291 – Stephen McCammon

Canadian Congress for Learning Opportunities for Women – Library, 47 Main St., Toronto ON M4E 2V6 – 416/699-1909; Fax: 416/699-2145

Canadian Copper & Brass Development Association – Library, #375, 10 Gateway Blvd., North York ON M3C 3A1 – 416/421-0788; Fax: 416/421-8092 – Librarian, Sandra J. Knapp

Canadian Copyright Institute – Library, 35 Spadina Rd., Toronto ON M5R 2S9 – 416/975-1756; Fax: 416/975-1839 – Nancy Fleming

Canadian Council for Public-Private Partnerships – Library, #4700, Toronto Dominion Bank Tower, PO Box 48, Stn Toronto Dominion, Toronto ON M5K 1E6 – 416/601-8333; Fax: 416/868-0673

Canadian Council on Rehabilitation & Work – Library, 20 King St. West, 9th Fl., Toronto ON M5H 1C4 – 416/974-2461; Fax: 416/974-5577 – Project Planner, Amy Pike

Canadian Direct Marketing Association – Library, #607, One Concorde Gate, North York ON M3C 3N6 – 416/391-2362; Fax: 416/441-4062 – Communications Manager, Irene Payne

Canadian Drug Manufacturers Association – Library, #409, 4120 Yonge St., Toronto ON M2P 2B8 – 416/223-2333; Fax: 416/223-2425 – Director, Professional & Scientific Affairs, Julie Tam

Canadian Education Association – Library, #8-200, 252 Bloor St. West, Toronto ON M5S 1V5 – 416/924-7721; Fax: 416/924-3188 – Librarian, Diane Sibbett

Canadian Environmental Law Association – Resource Library for the Environment & the Law, #401, 517 College St., Toronto ON M6G 4A2 – 416/960-2284; Fax: 416/960-9392 – Chief Librarian, Mary Vise

Canadian Federation of Independent Business – Library, #401, 4141 Yonge St., North York ON M2P 2A6 – 416/222-8022; Fax: 416/222-4337 – Katalin Coorsh

Canadian Feed the Children – Library, 174 Bartley Dr., Toronto ON M4A 1E1 – 416/757-1220; Fax: 416/757-3318; Toll Free: 1-800-387-1221

Canadian Film & Television Production Association – Library, #806, 175 Bloor St. East, Toronto ON M4W 3R8 – 416/927-8942; Fax: 416/922-4038 – Cindy Lewis

Canadian Filmmakers Distribution Centre – Library, #220, 37 Hanna Ave., Toronto ON M6K 1W8 – 416/588-0725; Fax: 416/588-7956

Canadian Flag Association – Library, 50 Heathfield Dr., Scarborough ON M1M 3B1 – 416/267-9618; Fax: 416/267-9618

Canadian Forces College - Information Resource Centre, 215 Yonge Blvd., Toronto ON M5M 3H9 – 416/482-6846; Fax: 416/482-6908; Email: ENVOY: CFC.LIBRARY; Symbol: OTRC – Chief Librarian, Cathy Murphy

Canadian Foundation for Children, Youth & the Law – Resource Centre, #405, 720 Spadina Ave., Toronto ON M5S 2T9 – 416/920-1633; Fax: 416/920-5855

Canadian Foundation for Economic Education – Library, #501, 2 St. Clair Ave. West, Toronto ON M4V 1L5 – 416/968-2236; Fax: 416/968-0488 – Resource Centre Director, Judith Jackson

Canadian Friends Historical Association – Arthur Garratt Dorland Friends Historical Collection, 60 Lowther Ave., Toronto ON M5R 1C7 – 905/895-1700 – Archivist/Librarian, Jane Zavitz Bond

Canadian Friends of Soviet People – Library, 280 Queen St. West, Toronto ON M5V 2A1 – 416/977-5819; Fax: 416/593-0781 – Secretary, Helen Lucas

Canadian Friends Service Committee – Friends House Library, 60 Lowther Ave., Toronto ON M5R 1C7 – 416/921-0368 – Library Coordinator, Jane Sweet

Canadian Gas Association – Library & Information Services, #1200, 243 Consumers Rd., North York ON M2J 5E3 – 416/498-1994; Fax: 416/498-7465 – Librarian, Barbara Cayley

Canadian German Chamber of Industry & Commerce Inc. – Library, #1410, 480 University Ave., Toronto ON M5G 1V2 – 416/598-3355; Fax: 416/598-1840 – Elisabeth Feil

Canadian Hearing Society – Library, 271 Spadina Rd., Toronto ON M5R 2V3 – 416/964-9595; TTY: 416/964-0023; Fax: 416/928-2506; Toll Free: 1-800-465-4327 – Education Resource Officer, Angela Palmer

Canadian Imperial Bank of Commerce – Business Information, Commerce Court, PO Box 1, Stn Commerce Court, Toronto ON M5L 1A2 – 416/980-3053; Fax: 416/861-3666 – Manager, Cynthea C. Penman

Canadian Institute for Radiation Safety – Resource Centre, #607, 1120 Finch Ave. West, Toronto ON M3J 3H7 – 416/650-9090; Fax: 416/650-9920; Toll Free: 1-800-263-5803 – Information Officer, Tina de Geus

Canadian Institute of Chartered Accountants – Studies & Standards Dept. Library, 277 Wellington St. West, Toronto ON M5V 3H2 – 416/204-3307; Fax: 416/977-8585; Symbol: OTCI – Library Contact, Gerald B. Gerard

Canadian Institute of Chartered Life Underwriters & Chartered Financial Consultants – Library, 41 Lesmill Rd., North York ON M3B 2T3 – 416/444-5251; Fax: 416/444-8031 – Manager/Library Services, Ilse Selwyn

Canadian Institute of Cultural Affairs – Library, 579 Kingston Rd., Toronto ON M4E 1R3 – 416/691-2316; Fax: 416/691-2491 – Jeannette Stanfield

Canadian Institute of International Affairs – The John Holmes Library, 5 Devonshire Pl., Toronto ON M5S 2C8 – 416/979-1851; Fax: 416/979-8575; Toll Free: 1-800-668-2442; Email: jen.mcnenly@utoronto.ca – Librarian, Jennifer McNenly

Canadian Institute of Strategic Studies – Library, Box 2321, #402, 2300 Yonge St., Toronto ON M4P 1E4 – 416/322-8128; Fax: 416/322-8129; Toll Free: 1-800-831-5695 – Susan McNisha

Canadian Lesbian & Gay Archives – James Fraser Library, #201, 56 Temperance St., POBox 639, Toronto ON M5W 1G2 – 416/777-2755

Canadian Life & Health Insurance Association Inc. – Research & Information Library, #1700, One Queen St. East, Toronto ON M5C 2X9 – 416/777-2221; Fax: 416/603-9019; Toll Free: 1-800-268-8099 – Records & Information Manager, Lillian Premovic

Canadian Magazine Publishers Association – CMPA Resource Centre, #202, 130 Spadina Ave., Toronto ON M5V 2L4 – 416/504-0274, ext.24; Fax: 416/504-0437 – Research Assistant, Heather MacKay

Canadian Management Centre of AMA (American Management Association) International – Library, 150 York St., 5th Fl., Toronto ON M5H 3S5 – 416/214-5678; Fax: 416/214-1453

Canadian Memorial Chiropractic College – CC Clemmer Health Sciences Library, 1900 Bayview Ave., Toronto ON M4G 3E6 – 416/482-2340; Fax: 416/482-9745 – Director, Marina Englesakis

Canadian Music Centre – Ettore Mazzolini Library, Chalmers House, 20 St. Joseph St., Toronto ON M4Y 1J9 – 416/961-6601; Fax: 416/961-7198 – National Librarian, Glenn Ford

The Canadian National Institute for the Blind – CNIB Library for the Blind, 1929 Bayview Ave., Toronto ON M4G 3E8 – 416/480-7520; Fax: 416/480-7677 – Executive Director, Rosemary Kavanagh

Canadian Natural Health Association – Library, #5, 439 Wellington St. West, Toronto ON M5V 1E7 – 416/977-2642; Fax: 416/977-1536 – Book Dept. Coordinator, Michelle Doucette

Canadian Newspaper Association – Library, #200, 890 Yonge St., Toronto ON M4W 3P4 – 416/923-3567; Fax: 416/923-7206 – Bryan Cantley

Canadian Nuclear Society – Library, #475, 144 Front St. West, Toronto ON M5J 2L7 – 416/977-6152; Fax: 416/979-8356; Toll Free: 1-800-387-4477 – A. Laughlin

Canadian Opera Company – Library, 227 Front St. East, Toronto ON M5A 1E8 – 416/363-6671, ext.328; Fax: 416/363-5584; Toll Free: 1-800-250-4653 – Archivist, Birthe Joergensen

Canadian Paraplegic Association (Ontario) – Library, 520 Sutherland Dr., Toronto ON M4G 3V9 – 416/422-5644; Fax: 416/422-5943 – Information & Resources Coordinator, Jane Lundgren

Canadian Physicians for Aid & Relief – Library, #202, 111 Queen St. East, Toronto ON M5C 1S2 – 416/369-0865; Fax: 416/369-0294; Toll Free: 1-800-263-2727; Email: CPAR@WEB 2:254/70 – Administrative Assistant, Sylvia Opena

Canadian Physiotherapy Association – Library, #410, 2345 Yonge St., Toronto ON M4P 2E5 – 416/932-1888; Fax: 416/932-9708; Toll Free: 1-800-387-8679 – Customer Relations Coordinator, Christine McQuade

Canadian Poetry Association – Small Press Reference Library, PO Box 22571, RPO St. George, Toronto ON M5S 1V0 – 905/874-1414, 416/944-3985; Fax: 905/874-1414; Email: lurc.lspc@onlinesys.com – Librarian, Wayne Ray

The Canadian Press – Library, 36 King St. East, Toronto ON M5C 2L9 – 416/364-0321; Broadcast News: 364-3172; Fax: 416/364-0207; TLX: 06-217715; 06-2 – Asma Khan

Canadian Professional Sales Association – Library, #310, 145 Wellington St. West, Toronto ON M5J 1H8 – 416/408-2685; Fax: 416/408-2684; Toll Free: 1-800-267-2772 – Librarian, Anna Fredericks

Canadian Publishers' Council – Library, #203, 250 Merton St., Toronto ON M4S 1B1 – 416/322-7011; Fax: 416/322-6999

Canadian Restaurant & Foodservices Association – CRFA Resource Centre, 316 Bloor St. West, Toronto ON M5S 1W5 – 416/923-8416; Fax: 416/923-1450; Toll Free: 1-800-387-5649 – Information Specialist, Erica Dennis

Canadian Sanitation Supply Association – Library, #G10, 300 Mill Rd., Etobicoke ON M9C 4W7 – 416/620-9320; Fax: 416/620-7199

Canadian Schizophrenia Foundation – Library, 16 Florence Ave., North York ON M2N 1E9 – 416/733-2117; Fax: 416/733-2352 – Administrative Assistant, Claire D'Intino

The Canadian Society for Mesopotamian Studies – Library, 4 Bancroft Ave., 4th Fl., Toronto ON M5S 1A1 – 416/978-4531; Fax: 416/978-3305 – Archivist, Grant Frame

Canadian Standards Association – Information Centre, 178 Rexdale Blvd., Etobicoke ON M9W 1R3 – 416/747-4007; Fax: 416/747-2475; Toll Free: 1-800-463-6727; TLX: 06-989344; Symbol: OTCSA – Coordinator, Susan Morley

Canadian Sugar Institute – Library, Water Park Place, #620, 10 Bay St., Toronto ON M5J 2R8 – 416/368-8091; Fax: 416/368-6426 – Luana Simpkins

Canadian Training Institute – Resource Centre, Kinsmen Bldg., 4700 Keele St., North York ON M3J 1P3 – 416/665-3889; Toll Free: 1-800-336-4908; Email: fsipek@inforamp.net – Frances Sipek

Canadian University Press – CUP Resource Centre, #404, 73 Richmond St., Toronto ON M5H 1Z4 – 416/364-0258; Fax: 416/364-6512

Canadian Urban Transit Association – Library, #901, 55 York St., Toronto ON M5J 1R7 – 416/365-9800; Fax: 416/365-1295 – Manager of Research, Brendon Hemily

Canadian Water Quality Association – Library, #330, 295 The West Mall, Etobicoke ON M9C 4Z4 – 416/695-3068; Fax: 416/695-2945 – Ralph Suppa

Candlelighters Childhood Cancer Foundation Canada – Childhood Cancer Library, #401, 55 Eglinton Ave. East, Toronto ON M4P 1G8 – 416/489-6440; Fax: 416/489-9812; Toll Free: 1-800-363-1062 – Executive Assistant, Janet Evans

Cassels, Brock & Blackwell Law Office - Library, Scotia Plaza, #2100, 40 King St. West, Toronto ON M5H 3C2 – 416/869-5436; Fax: 416/360-8877; URL: http://www.nstn.ca/cbb/index.html; Symbol: OTCBB
- Library Manager, Clare Lyons, Email: clyons@casselsbrock.com
- Reference Librarian, Elizabeth Baranecki, Email: ebaranecki@casselsbrock.com
- Library Technician, Karen Hunter, Email: khunter@casselsbrock.com
- Library Assistant, Lourdes Bourgouin

Catholic Biblical Association of Canada – Resource Centre, 3275 St. Clair Ave. East, Scarborough ON M1L 1W2 – 416/285-9552; Fax: 416/285-9174 – Librarian, Christopher Hay

C.C. Clemmer Health Sciences - Library, 1900 Bayview Ave., Toronto ON M4G 3E6 – 416/482-2340; Fax: 416/482-9745; Email: reference@cmcc.ca; Symbol: OTCMC
- Director of Library Services, Marina Englesakis, 416/482-2340, ext.159
- Media Services, Head, Margaret Butkovic
- Public Services, Reference Librarian, Valda Svede
- Technical Services, Head, Claire M. Bowman

C.D. Howe Institute – Library, 125 Adelaide St. East, Toronto ON M5C 1L7 – 416/865-1904; Fax: 416/865-1866 – Librarian, Susan Knapp

Centenary Health Centre – Health Sciences Library, 2867 Ellesmere Rd., Scarborough ON M1E 4B9 – 416/281-7101; Fax: 416/281-7360; Email: poplak@library.utoronto.ca – Librarian, Valda Poplak

Centennial College - Learning & Resource Centres, POBox 631, Scarborough ON M1K 5E9 – 416/289-5000, ext.2601; Fax: 416/289-5228 – Executive Director, Learning & Resource Centres, Janice Hayes, Email: jhayes@cencol.on.ca

Centre for Christian Studies - Library, 77 Charles St. West, Toronto ON M5S 1K5 – 416/923-1168; Fax: 416/923-5496 – Librarian, Shelagh Telford

Centre for Refugee Studies - Andrew Forbes Refugee Resource Centre, York Lanes, York University, #314, 4700 Keele St., North York ON M3J 1P3 – 416/736-5663; Fax: 416/736-5837; Email: lwong@yorku.ca; URL: http://www.yorku.ca/research/crs – Documentalist, Len Wong

Centre for Research on Latin America & The Caribbean – Documentation Centre, 240 York Lanes, York University, 4700 Keele St., North York ON M3J 1P3 – 416/736-5237; Fax: 416/736-5737 – Administrative Assistant, Liddy Gomes

Centre for Spanish Speaking Peoples – Spanish Language Library, 1004 Bathurst St., Toronto ON M5R 3G7 – 416/533-8545; Fax: 416/533-5731

Centre of Forensic Sciences - H. Ward Smith Library, 25 Grosvenor St., 2nd Fl., Toronto ON M7A 2G8 – 416/314-3218; Fax: 416/314-3225; Symbol: OTCF – Library Technician, Carolyn Regan

C.G. Jung Foundation of the Ontario Association of Jungian Analysts – C.G. Jung Library, 223 St. Clair Ave. West, 3rd Fl., Toronto ON M4V 1R3 – 416/961-9767 – Administrator, Edith Leslie

CH2M Gore & Storrie Limited – Library, #401, 255 Consumers Rd., North York ON M2J 5B6 – 416/499-0090, ext.305; Fax: 416/499-4687; Symbol: OTGS – Librarian, Dianne Sawh

Childbirth By Choice Trust – Library, #306, 344 Bloor St. West, Toronto ON M5S 3A7 – 416/961-1507; Fax: 416/961-5771 – Jane Koster

Children's Aid Society of Metropolitan Toronto – Library, 33 Charles St. East, Toronto ON M4Y 1R9 – 416/924-4646; Fax: 416/324-2485 – Librarian, Andrea Sutton

The Christian & Missionary Alliance in Canada – Library, POBox 7900, North York ON M2K 2R6 – 416/492-8775; Fax: 416/492-7708 – Director, Communications, Irene J. Alexander

The Church Army in Canada – Cowan Memorial Library, Headquarters & College of Evangelism, 397 Brunswick Ave., Toronto ON M5R 2Z2 – 416/924-9279; Fax: 416/924-2931 – Sister, Ruth Wylie

CIBC Wood Gundy Securities Inc. - Library & Information Services, BCE Place, POBox 500, Toronto ON M5J 2S8 – 416/594-7716, 7717; Fax: 416/594-7713
  Cheif Librarian, Cheryl Dhillon
  Acquisitions Librarian, S. Parker

Citizens for Public Justice – Library, #311, 229 College St., Toronto ON M5T 1R4 – 416/979-2443; Fax: 416/979-2458

City of Scarborough - Health Resource Centre, #500, 55 Town Centre Ct., Scarborough ON M1P 4X4 – 416/396-7453; Fax: 416/396-5299 – Resource Librarian, Dianne Beal

City of Toronto - Dept. of Buildings & Inspections Library, City Hall, East Tower, 100 Queen St. West, 17th Fl., Toronto ON M5H 2N2 – 416/392-7608; Fax: 416/392-0677 – Coordinator, Library Services, Irene Moore
  Urban Development Services - Library, City Hall, East Tower, 100 Queen St. West, 11th Fl., Toronto ON M5H 2N2 – 416/392-1526; Fax: 416/392-0071 – Head Librarian, Deborah Fowler

Civic Garden Centre - Library, 777 Lawrence Ave. East, North York ON M3C 1P2 – 416/397-1340; Fax: 416/397-1354 – Librarian, Roslyn Theodore, 416/397-1353

Clarke Institute of Psychiatry – Farrar Library, 250 College St., Toronto ON M5T 1R8 – 416/979-6824; Fax: 416/979-6817; Email: library@clarke-inst.on.ca; Symbol: OTUDP – Head, Library Services, Diane Thomas

Communications Information Technology Ontario – Library, D.L. Pratt Building, #286, 6 King's College Rd., Toronto ON M5S 3H5 – 416/978-7203; Fax: 416/978-7207 – Administrative Assistant, Roseanne Reid

Community AIDS Treatment Information Exchange – CATIE Resources, #420, 517 College St., Toronto ON M6G 4A2 – 416/944-1916; Fax: 416/928-2185; Toll Free: 1-800-263-1638 – Information Manager, Robert MacKay-Melrose

Community Legal Education Ontario – Library, #600, 119 Spadina Ave., Toronto ON M5V 2L1 – 416/408-4420; Fax: 416/408-4424 – Librarian, Susan Moses

Congregation of St-Basil (Basilian Fathers) – Library, c/o John Kelly Library, 113 St. Joseph St., Toronto ON M5S 1J4 – 416/926-7279; Fax: 416/926-7262 – Archivist, Rev. Kevin Kirley, CSB

Connaught Laboratories Ltd. - Balmer Neilly Library, 1755 Steeles Ave. West, North York ON M2R 3T4 – 416/667-2662; Fax: 416/667-2850; Email: library@ca.pmc-vacc.com; Symbol: OTCL – Library Services Manager, Hugh W. McNaught

Connexions Information Sharing Services – Library, POBox 158, Toronto ON M6P 3J8 – 416/537-3949 – Ulli Diemer

Conseil des écoles françaises de la communauté urbaine de Toronto – Bibliothèque, #207, One Concorde Gate, North York ON M3C 3N6 – 416/391-1264; Téléc: 416/391-3892 – Hélène Amyot

Conseil des organismes francophones du Toronto Métropolitain – Bibliothèque, 20 Lower Spadina Ave., Toronto ON M5V 2Z1 – 416/203-1220; Téléc: 416/203-1165

Conservation Council of Ontario – Library, #506, 489 College St., Toronto ON M6G 1A5 – 416/969-9637; Fax: 416/960-8053

Consumers Gas - Information Resource Centre, 500 Consumers Rd., North York ON M2J 1P8 – 416/495-5490; Fax: 416/495-5402 – Manager, Mirren Hinchley, 416/495-5814

COSTI – Library, 1710 Dufferin St., Toronto ON M6E 3P2 – 416/658-1600; Fax: 416/658-8537 – Executive Assistant, Mary Cellucci

Council of Ontario Universities – Library, #203, 444 Yonge St., Toronto ON M5B 2H4 – 416/979-2165, ext.201; Fax: 416/979-8635; Email: alevine@coupo.cou.on.ca – Research Analyst & Librarian, Arlene Levine

Cross Cultural Communication Centre – Library, 2909 Dundas St. West, Toronto ON M6P 1Z1 – 416/760-7855; Fax: 416/767-4352 – Resource Librarian, Carmen Alcalde

Cryonics Society of Canada – Library, POBox 788, Toronto ON M5W 1G3 – 416/534-0967 – Douglas Quinn

Czech & Slovak Association of Canada – Library, 740 Spadina Ave., Toronto ON M5S 2J2 – 416/925-2241; Fax: 416/925-1940

Dale & Lessmann - Library, #2000, Commercial Union Tower, Box 73, Toronto Dominion Centre, Toronto ON M5K 1E7 – 416/863-1010; Fax: 416/863-1009 – Librarian, Bettina Hakala

de Havilland Inc. - Library Services, Mail Stop N17-09, Garratt Blvd., Downsview ON M3K 1Y5 – 416/375-3365; Fax: 416/375-4533 – Librarian, Cathy Parsons

Delcan Corporation - Division of Delcan Group – Library, 133 Wynford Dr., North York ON M3C 1K1 – 416/441-4111; Fax: 416/441-4131 – Librarian, Gillian Henderson

Deloitte & Touche – National Research Centre, #1300, 95 Wellington St. West, Toronto ON M5J 2P4 – 416/601-5933; Fax: 416/601-5975 – Manager, Suzanne Levasseur
  National Tax Resource Centre, BCE Place, #1400, 181 Bay St., Toronto ON M5J 2V1 – 416/601-6286; Fax: 416/601-6151; Email: trc@ftn.net
  Manager, Mina Woodruff
  Information Specialist, Laurie A. Smith
  Administrative Assistant, Michelle Martin

Design Exchange – Resource Centre, Toronto Dominion Centre, 234 Bay St., POBox 18, Toronto ON M5K 1B2 – 416/216-2125; Fax: 416/368-0684 – Curator, Rachel Gotlieb

Designers Walk - Resource Centre, 168 Bedford Rd., Toronto ON M5R 2K9 – 416/961-1211; Fax: 416/928-9683; Email: dwincres@istar.ca; URL: http://www.designerswalk.com – Coordinator, Shauna Levy

Developing Countries Farm Radio Network – Library, Box 12, #227B, 40 Dundas St. West, Toronto ON M5G 2C2 – 416/593-3751; Fax: 416/593-3752 – Librarian, Joan Beckley

DeVry Institute of Technology - North York Campus Library, 2201 Finch Ave. West, North York ON M9M 2Z4 – 416/741-9220; Fax: 416/741-3633
  Director, Susan Heinrich
  Library Technician, Sherry Taylor
  Scarborough Campus Library, 670 Progress Ave., Scarborough ON M1H 3A4 – 416/289-3642 – Library Technician, Gosha Trzaski

Dianne Saxe, Barrister & Solicitor, D.Jur. - Library, 66 Russell Hill Rd., Toronto ON M4V 2T2 – 416/962-5882; Fax: 416/962-8817; Email: dsaxe@envirolaw.com; URL: http://www.magic.ca/saxe/

Dillon Consulting Ltd. – Library, #300, 100 Sheppard Ave. East, Toronto ON M2N 6N5 – 416/229-4646; Fax: 416/229-4692

Dingwall, McLauchlin, #2100, Commercial Union Tower, Box 69, Toronto Dominion Centre, Toronto ON M5K 1E7 – 416/863-1000; Fax: 416/863-1007 – Librarian, Bettina Hakala

Doctors Hospital - Health Sciences Library, 340 College St., 6th Fl., Toronto ON M5T 3A9 – 416/963-7677, ext.7464; Email: dh@library.utoronto.ca; Symbol: OTDHS
  Health Sciences Librarian, Sharon Virtue
  Assistant Librarian, Keith Denny

The Donwood Institute – The Donwood Library, 175 Brentcliffe Rd., Toronto ON M4G 3Z1 – 416/425-3930; Fax: 416/425-7896 – Chris Kirby

Dystonia Medical Research Foundation – Library, #116, 230 Heath St. West, Toronto ON M5P 1N8 – 416/487-8326; Fax: 416/488-6974; Toll Free: 1-800-361-8061

East End Literacy - Library, 265 Gerrard St. East, Toronto ON M5A 2G3 – 416/968-6989; Fax: 416/968-0597

The Easter Seal Society (Ontario) – Easter Seal Resource Centre, #200, 250 Ferrand Dr., North York ON M3C 3P2 – 416/421-8377, ext.364; Fax: 416/696-1035; Toll Free: 1-800-668-6252; Email: dgordon@easterseals.org – Resource Centre Assistant, Debbie Gordon

Education Wife Assault – Library, 427 Bloor St. West, Toronto ON M5S 1X7 – 416/968-3422; Fax: 416/968-2026 – Librarian, Tiffany Veinot

Employment & Immigration Canada - Ontario Region Library, #700, 4900 Yonge St., North York ON M2N 6A8 – 416/954-7682; Fax: 416/954-7537; Symbol: OTMIO – Chief Librarian, F.R. Hersom

Energy Probe Research Foundation – Library, 225 Brunswick Ave., Toronto ON M5S 2M6 – 416/964-9223; Fax: 416/964-8239; Toll Free: 1-800-263-2784 – Frank Cianflone

Environment Canada-Climate & Atmospheric Research Directorate – Library, c/o Atmospheric Environment Service, 4905 Dufferin St., Toronto ON M3H 5T4 – 416/739-4995; Fax: 416/739-4265 – Head Librarian, Maria Latyszewskyj

Environment Canada - Library - Downsview, 4905 Dufferin St., Downsview ON M3H 5T4 – 416/739-4828; Fax: 416/739-4212;
Email: maria.latyszewskyj@ec.gc.ca; Symbol: OTM
Head, Maria A. Latyszewskyj
Reference Librarian, Roberta McCarthy, 416/739-5702
Technical Services, Supervisor, Sheila Osborne, 416/739-4831
Circulation/Interlibrary Loans, Clerk, Mary Bozickovic, 416/739-4225

Environmental Commissioner of Ontario - Library, #605, 1075 Bay St., Toronto ON M5S 2B1 – 416/325-0559; Fax: 416/325-3370; Email: ellensch@web.net – Librarian, Ellen Schwartzel

Ernst & Young - National Tax Library, Toronto-Dominion Centre, 31st Fl., PO Box 251, Stn Toronto Dominion, Toronto ON M5K 1J7 – 416/943-3152; Fax: 416/943-3120
Supervisor, Diane Conwath
Assistant, Anna Difelice

Estonian Central Council in Canada – Library, #308, 958 Broadview Ave., Toronto ON M4K 2R6 – 416/465-2219; Fax: 416/461-0488 – Contact, Maimu Palumäe

Etobicoke Education Centre - Resource Library, One Civic Centre Ct., Etobicoke ON M9C 2B3 – 416/394-7309; Fax: 416/394-7308 – Coordinator of Media Studies, Alice Churchman

The Etobicoke General Hospital – Library, 101 Humber College Blvd., Etobicoke ON M9V 1R8 – 416/747-3466; Fax: 416/747-8608 – Executive Director, Valery Close

Etobicoke Philharmonic Orchestra, 19 Hilldowntree Rd., Etobicoke ON M9A 2Z4 – 416/233-5665 – Librarian, Mary-Grace Knox

Family Service Association of Metropolitan Toronto – Library, 355 Church St., Toronto ON M5B 1Z8 – 416/595-9230; Fax: 416/595-0242 – Theresa Sit

Fasken Campbell Godfrey - Law Library, Toronto-Dominion Centre, PO Box 20, Stn Toronto-Dominion, Toronto ON M5K 1N6 – 416/865-5143; Fax: 416/364-7813; Email: Michele_Miles@fasken.com – Head Librarian, Michele L. Miles

Federation of Ontario Naturalists – Library, 355 Lesmill Rd., North York ON M3B 2W8 – 416/444-8419; Fax: 416/444-9866; Toll Free: 1-800-440-2366 – Receptionist, Dianne Slyford

The Financial Post - Library, 333 King St. East, Toronto ON M5A 4N2 – 416/350-6690; Fax: 416/350-6301 – Library Manager, Theresa M. Butcher, 416/350-6693

Foodshare Metro Toronto – Library, 238 Queen St. West., Lower Level, Toronto ON M5V 1Z7 – 416/392-1669; Fax: 416/392-6650

Foster Parents Plan – Library, #1001, 95 St. Clair Ave. West, Toronto ON M4V 3B5 – 416/920-1654; Fax: 416/920-9942; Toll Free: 1-800-387-1418

Frank Anrep & Associates Ltd. – Library, #402, 505 Consumers Rd., Willowdale ON M2J 4V8 – 416/502-0540; Fax: 416/502-3284 – Marketing Coordinator, Helen Anrep

Fraser & Beatty Law Office - Library, One First Canadian Place, PO Box 100, Stn First Canadian Place, Toronto ON M5X 1B2 – 416/863-4581; Fax: 416/863-4592; Email: Jan_Barrett@FraserBeatty.ca; URL: http://www.FraserBeatty.ca
Chief Librarian, Jan Barrett, 416/863-4581
Chief Librarian, Linda Boss, 416/863-4581
Reference Librarian, Ian Colvin, 416/862-3489
ILL Technician, Trish Richardson, 416/862-3472
Filing Technician, Marg Goger

George Brown College - Resource Centre, POBox 1015, Toronto ON M5T 2T9 – 416/415-2676; Email: jhardy@gbrownc.on.ca – Education Resources, Director, John L. Hardy

Giffels Associates Limited – Library, 30 International Blvd., Etobicoke ON M9W 5P3 – 416/675-5950; Fax: 416/675-4620; Toll Free: 1-800-567-8918 – Information Centre Giffels, Desiree Singh

Girl Guides of Canada – Resource Centre, 50 Merton St., Toronto ON M4S 1A3 – 416/487-5281; Fax: 416/487-5570 – Resource Centre Administrator, Lynn Austin

The Globe and Mail Ltd. - Library, 444 Front St. West, Toronto ON M5V 2S9 – 416/585-5076; Fax: 416/585-5085 – Head Librarian, Amanda Valpy

Goethe-Institut Toronto – Library, 163 King St. West, Toronto ON M5H 4C6 – 416/593-5257; Fax: 416/593-5145 – Head Librarian, Ulla Habekost

Goodman & Carr Law Office - Library, #2300, 200 King St. West, Toronto ON M5H 3W5 – 416/595-2300; Fax: 416/595-0567; Email: jsimpson@goodmancarr.com
Librarian, Jane Simpson
Assistant Librarian, Gaye Lefebvre

Goodwill Toronto – Library, 234 Adelaide St. East, Toronto ON M5A 1M9 – 416/362-4711; Fax: 416/362-0720 – Life Skills Coordinator, Renée Rowe

Gowlings - Library, #4900, Commerce Court West, PO Box 149, Stn Commerce Court, Toronto ON M5L 1J3 – 416/862-5735; Fax: 416/862-7661; Email: rataiclj@gowlings.com
Chief Librarian, Joan Rataic-Lang, 416/862-5735
Assistant Librarian, Joanne Berent, 416/862-4382
Library Technician, Elisabeth Adams-Quan, 416/862-3505
Library Clerk, Ewa Zarska, 862-4383

The Green Brick Road – Library, 8 Dumas Ct., Don Mills ON M3A 2N2 – 905/465-1597; Toll Free: 1-800-473-3638

Hay Management Consultants - Information Resource Centre, #700, 121 King St. West, Toronto ON M5H 3X7 – 416/868-1371; Fax: 416/868-6871; Email: haytor@hookup.net; URL: http://www.haygroup.com – Staff Librarian, Merle Johnson

Health Canada - Health Protection Branch - Regional Library, 2301 Midland Ave., Scarborough ON M1P 4R7 – 416/973-1556; Fax: 416/973-1559; Symbol: OTNHH – Librarian, Sandra Brockhurst

Hemophilia Ontario – Library, #308, 60 St. Clair Ave. East, Toronto ON M4T 1N5 – 416/972-0641; Fax: 416/972-0307 – Administrative Assistant, Marc Laprise

Heritage Toronto – Library, Administrative Offices, 205 Yonge St., Toronto ON M5B 1N2 – 416/392-6827; Fax: 416/392-6834 – Assistant Curator, John Summers

Hewitt Associates - Research Practice, #800, 25 Sheppard Ave. West, Toronto ON M2N 6T1 – 416/225-5001; Fax: 416/225-9790; URL: http://www.hewitt.com

Hicks Morley Hamilton Stewart Storie Law Office - Library, Toronto Dominion Bank Tower, Toronto-Dominion Centre, 30th Fl., POBox 371, Toronto ON M5K 1K8 – 416/362-1011; Fax: 416/362-9680; Email: library@hicks.com – Library Technician, Lorenza G. Thompson, 416/362-1011, ext.119

The Hincks Centre for Children's Mental Health - Jackman Library, Silverman Bldg., 114 Maitland St., Toronto ON M4Y 1E1 – 416/972-1935, ext.3308; Fax: 416/924-9808; Symbol: HTC – Librarian, Rita M. Bondi

Holden Day Wilson Law Office - Library, #2400, T-D Bank Tower, T-D Centre, POBox 52, Toronto ON M5K 1E7 – 416/361-1444; Fax: 416/361-1258
Chief Librarian, James Allan, 416/863-5686
Technician, John Brennan
Technical Services, Diane Rooke

Holocaust Education & Memorial Centre of Toronto – Holocaust Resource Centre, 4600 Bathurst St., North York ON M2R 3V2 – 416/631-5689; Fax: 416/635-0925

Hong Fook Mental Health Association – Library, #408, 260 Spadina Ave., Toronto ON M5T 2L5 – 416/595-1103; Fax: 416/595-6332 – Office Manager, Theresa Chung

Hospice Association of Ontario – Lending Resource Centre, #313, 40 Wynford Dr., North York ON M3C 1J5 – 416/510-3880; Fax: 416/510-3882 – Manager, Membership Services, Jeanette Browne

The Hospital for Sick Children – Library, 555 University Ave., Toronto ON M5G 1X8 – 416/813-6693; Fax: 416/813-7523 – Director, Elizabeth Uleryk

Houser, Henry & Syron Law Office - Library, #2000, 145 King St. West, Toronto ON M5H 2B6 – 416/362-3411; Fax: 416/362-3757 – Librarian, Sandra Findlay

Hughes, Amys Law Office - Library, Box 401, #5050, One First Canadian Place, Toronto ON M5X 1E3 – 416/367-1608; Fax: 416/367-8821; Email: pas@h_amys.mhs.compuserve.com – Librarian, Penny Sheehan

Huguenot Society of Canada – Library, #105, 4936 Yonge St., North York ON M2N 6S3 – Fax: 416/226-0043 – Archivist, Paul Litt

Human Resources Development Canada - Ontario Regional Library, #700, 4900 Yonge St., North York ON M2N 6A8 – 416/224-4858; Fax: 416/224-4860; Symbol: OTMIO – Acting Librarian, Flaka Hersom

Humber College of Applied Arts & Technology - Lakeshore Campus Library, 3199 Lakeshore Blvd. West, Toronto ON M8V 1K8 – 416/675-6622, ext.3247; Fax: 416/252-0918; URL: http://admin.humberc.on.ca/~library/
North Campus Library, 205 Humber College Blvd., Etobicoke ON M9W 5L7 – 416/675-5079; Fax: 416/675-7439; URL: http://admin.humberc.on.ca/~library/

IBI Group – Library, 230 Richmond St. West, 5th Fl., Toronto ON M5V 1V6 – 416/596-1930, ext.107; Fax: 416/596-0644; Email: josther@pathcom.com – Librarian, Jennifer Osther

IBM Canada Limited - Information Resource Centre, 844 Don Mills Rd., North York ON M3C 1V7 – 416/448-3555; Fax: 416/448-3545
Librarian, Barbara Wallace, 416/448-3418
Library Assistant, Desiree Lloyd

Immigration & Refugee Board - Documentation Centre, 1 Front St. West, Ground Fl., Toronto ON M5J 1A5 – 416/973-8568; Fax: 416/973-7149; Symbol: OTIR – Chief, Theresa Smith
Documentation Centre, 70 University Ave., 8th Fl., Toronto ON M5J 2M5 – 416/954-1179; Fax: 416/954-1191; Symbol: OTIRB – Chief, Elizabeth Bennett

Imperial Oil Limited - Engineering & Petroleum Information Centre, #4104, 90 Wynford Dr., North York ON M3C 1K5 – 416/441-7858; Fax: 416/441-7926 – Information Specialist, Kathy Wallace

Inco Limited - Records & Information Management, #1500, 145 King St. West, Toronto ON M5H 4B7 – 416/361-7763; Fax: 416/361-7781, 7782; URL: http://www.incoltd.com
Manager, Records & Information Management, Jennifer Myrie
Librarian, Christina Wu, 416/361-7518

Industrial Accident Prevention Association Ontario – Information Centre, Eaton Tower, 250 Yonge St., 28th Fl., Toronto ON M5B 2N4 – 416/506-8888; Fax: 416/506-8880; Toll Free: 1-800-669-4939 – Supervisor, Zuzka Hora

Industrial Accident Victims Group of Ontario – Library, #203, 489 College St., Toronto ON M6G 1A5 – 416/924-6477; Fax: 416/924-2472

Institute for Aerospace Studies – Library, University of Toronto, 4925 Dufferin St., North York ON M3H 5T6 – 416/667-7712; Fax: 416/667-7799 – Librarian, Judy Mills

Institute for Policy Analysis – Library, University of Toronto, #707, 140 Saint George St., Toronto ON

M5S 1A1 – 416/978-4854; Fax: 416/978-5519 – Ursula Gutenburg

Institute of Canadian Advertising – Library, #500, 2300 Yonge St., POBox 2350, Toronto ON M4P 1E4 – 416/482-1396; Fax: 416/481-1856; Toll Free: 1-800-567-7422

Institute of Municipal Assessors of Ontario – Library, #303, 109 Railside Rd., North York ON M3A 1B2 – 416/447-7213; Fax: 416/447-3452 – Executive Director, W.J. Lettner

Insurance Bureau of Canada – Library, #1800, 151 Yonge St., Toronto ON M5C 2W7 – 416/362-2031, x350; Fax: 416/361-5952; Toll Free: 1-800-387-2880; Email: ibclib@ibc.ca – Librarian, Sandra Rakovac

Insurance Institute of Canada – Library, 18 King St. East, 6th Fl., Toronto ON M5C 1C4 – 416/362-8586; Fax: 416/362-4239 – Librarian, Nancy MacGillivray

Insurers' Advisory Organization (1989) Inc. – Library, #700, 18 King St. East, Toronto ON M5C 1C4 – 416/368-1801; Fax: 416/368-0333; Toll Free: 1-800-268-8080

Intergovernmental Committee on Urban & Regional Research – Library, #301, 150 Eglinton Ave. East, Toronto ON M4P 1E8 – 416/973-1339; Fax: 416/973-1375; Email: vgregor@icurr.org – Senior Information Officer, Vicky Gregor

International Commission for the Co-ordination of Solidarity Among Sugar Workers – Sugar Workers & Industry Education Resource Library, #3, 2084 Danforth Ave., Toronto ON M4C 1J9 – 416/467-8621; Fax: 416/467-9143; Symbol: SWIERL

International Council for Adult Education – Resource Centre, #500, 720 Bathurst St., Toronto ON M5S 2R4 – 416/588-1211; Fax: 416/588-5725 – Resource Centre/Outreach Coordinator, Eva Kupidura

International Relief Agency Inc. – Library, 95 Wood St., Toronto ON M4Y 2Z3 – 416/922-7120; Fax: 416/928-0901 – Office Manager, Eileen Brown

Investor Learning Centre of Canada – ILC Investment Library, 121 King St. West, 15th Fl., Toronto ON M5H 3T9 – 416/364-6666; Fax: 416/364-9315

ISM (Information Systems Management) - Corporation Library, 251 Consumers Rd., 10th Fl., North York ON M2J 4R3 – 416/351-6741; Fax: 416/351-6294 – Systems Librarian, Wai Lai

Italian Cultural Institute – Library, Istituto Italiano di Cultura, 496 Huron St., Toronto ON M5R 2R3 – 416/921-3802; Fax: 416/962-2503 – Administrative Coordinator, Mariolina Franceschetti

Janssen-Ortho Inc. - Information Resource Centre, 19 Green Belt Dr., North York ON M3C 1L9 – 416/442-2500; Fax: 416/449-2520
- Manager, Information Resources, Teresa Helik, 416/382-5106, Email: thelik@joica.jnj.com
- Information Specialist, Karen Gaggi

Japanese External Trade Organization – Japan Trade Centre, #1600, 181 University Ave., Toronto ON M5H 3M7 – 416/861-0000; Fax: 416/861-9666

The Jesuit Centre for Social Faith & Justice – Library, 947 Queen St. East, Toronto ON M4M 1J9 – 416/469-1123; Fax: 416/469-3579 – JRS/Canada Coordinator, Ezat Mossallanejad

Jewish Genealogical Society of Canada – North York Central Library, Canadiana Room, POBox 446, North York ON M2N 2T1 – 416/395-5623 – Debora Pekilis

Jewish Student Federation – Library, #442, Student Centre, York University, 4700 Keele St., North York ON M3J 1P3 – 416/736-5178; Fax: 416/736-5102

The John Howard Society of Ontario – Library, 6 Jackson Pl., Toronto ON M6P 1T6 – 416/604-8412; Fax: 416/604-8948

John Milton Society for the Blind in Canada – Library, #202, 40 St. Clair Ave. East, Toronto ON M4T 1M9 – 416/960-3953 – Librarian, Rena Riley

Justice Canada - Toronto Regional Office - Library, #3400, 2 First Canadian Place, PO Box 36, Stn First Canadian Place, Toronto ON M5X 1K6 – 416/973-2334; Fax: 416/973-3586; Symbol: OTJ – Librarian, Alison Colvin

Kelly, White & Smith Law Office - Library, #1020, 130 Adelaide St. West, Toronto ON M5H 3P5 – 416/366-5900; Fax: 416/366-1799 – Lori Sangiuliano

Kids Help Phone – Library, 439 University Ave., Toronto ON M5G 1Y8 – 416/586-0100; Fax: 416/586-1880; Toll Free: 1-800-668-6868 – Manager, Information/Grants, Wendy Josberg

Knox College - Caven Library, 59 St. George St., Toronto ON M5S 2E6 – 416/978-4504; Fax: 416/971-2133; Email: tucker@vax.library.utoronto.ca; URL: http://www.utoronto.ca/knox; Symbol: OTK
- Readers Services Librarian, Kathleen Gibson
- Technical Services Librarian, Chris Tucker

KPMG - John Walker Library, POBox 31, Toronto ON M5L 1B2 – 416/777-8515; Fax: 416/777-8586; Email: cgareau@kpmg.ca
- Manager/Librarian, Cathy Gareau, 416/777-8512
- Reference Specialist, M. Ulehla, 416/777-8513
- Library Clerk, B. Gravelle, 416/777-8093
- Tax Library, Reference, L. Boyko, 416/777-3307
- Technical Services Information Specialist, J. Andersen, 416/777-8092

Lang Michener - Library, BCE Pl., #2500, 181 Bay St., POBox 747, Toronto ON M5J 2T7 – 416/360-8600; Fax: 416/365-1719
- Manager, Library Services, Nancy L. Clarke, 416/307-4158
- Senior Library Technician, Margaret Harrop, 416/307-4140
- Library Technician, Jacquie Gray, 416/360-8611, ext.2083
- Library Clerk, Suzanna La Rose, 416/360-8611, ext.2226

Law Society of Upper Canada – Great Library, Osgoode Hall, 130 Queen St. West, Toronto ON M5H 2N6 – 416/947-3300; Fax: 416/947-5967; Toll Free: 1-800-668-7380 – Glen W. Howell

League for Human Rights of B'nai Brith Canada – Education & Training Centre, 15 Hove St., Downsview ON M3H 4Y8 – 416/633-6227; Fax: 416/630-2159; Email: tklein@bnaibrith.ca – Executive Assistant, Talia Klein

The League of Canadian Poets – Poetry Library, 54 Wolseley St., 3rd Fl., Toronto ON M5T 1A5 – 416/504-1657; Fax: 416/703-0059 – Program Manager, Sandie Drzewiecki

Learning Disabilities Association of Ontario – LDAO Resource Library, Box 39, #1004, 365 Bloor St. East, Toronto ON M4W 3L4 – 416/929-4311; Fax: 416/929-3905 – Resource Counsellor, Diane Wagner

Leprosy Mission Canada – Library, #1410, 75 The Donway West, North York ON M3C 2E9 – 416/441-3618; Fax: 416/441-0203 – Director, Communications, Nicholas Hunter

Life Underwriters Association of Canada, 41 Lesmill Rd., North York ON M3B 2T3 – 416/444-5251; Fax: 416/444-8031 – Librarian, Ilse Selwyn

Lilly Anderson Morgan - Library, #900, 330 Bay St., Toronto ON M5H 2S8 – 416/365-6300; Fax: 416/365-7429 – Librarian, Micky Wylie

Litton Systems Canada Ltd. - Library, 25 City View Dr., Etobicoke ON M9W 5A7 – 416/249-1231; Fax: 416/246-2016 – Librarian, Jackie Brown

Lyndhurst Hospital – Health Sciences Library, 520 Sutherland Dr., Toronto ON M4G 3V9 – 416/422-5551; Fax: 416/422-5216 – Ann Marie Chin

Maclean's Magazine - Library, 777 Bay St., 7th Fl., Toronto ON M5W 1A7 – 416/596-5340; Fax: 416/596-7730 – Chief Librarian, Basil Guinane

The Manufacturers Life Insurance Company – Business Library, 200 Bloor St. East, Toronto ON M4W 1E5 – 416/926-5221; Fax: 416/926-5540; Email: frances_mcmanus@manulife.com; Symbol: MLF – Head Librarian, Frances McManus

Marsh & McLennan Ltd. - Information Centre, Canada Trust Tower, BCE Place, 161 Bay St., POBox 502, Toronto ON M5J 2S4 – 416/868-2697; Fax: 416/868-2870 – M. Cavers

Massey College - Robertson Davies Library, 4 Devonshire Place, Toronto ON M5S 2E1 – 416/978-2893; Fax: 416/978-1759; Symbol: CoOTMC – Librarian, Marie Korey

McCarthy Tétrault - John J. Robinette Library, #4700, T-D Bank Tower, T-D Centre, POBox 48, Toronto ON M5K 1E6 – 416/601-8200; Fax: 416/868-0673; Email: library@mccarthy.ca – Head Librarian, Mary Percival, 416/601-7843

McLean & Kerr Law Office - Library, #2800, 130 Adelaide St. West, Toronto ON M5H 3P5 – 416/364-5371; Fax: 416/366-8571 – Librarian, Audrey Jessup

McMillan Binch Law Library, Royal Bank Plaza, South Tower, POBox 38, Toronto ON M5J 2J7 – 416/865-7031; Fax: 416/865-7048; Email: randersen@mcbinch.com; URL: http://www.mcbinch.com
- Manager, Library Services, Ricki Anne Andersen, 416/865-7031
- Reference Librarian, Lenie Ott, 416/865-7269
- Technical Services Technician, Lynn Alvernaz, 416/865-7870
- Acquisitions Clerk, Suzan Walzak, 416/865-7867

MediaWatch – Reference Library, #204, 517 Wellington St. West, Toronto ON M5V 1G1 – 416/408-2065; Fax: 416/408-2069 – Outreach Coordinator, Josie Marchese

Meighen Demers Law Office - Library, Merrill Lynch Canada Tower, Box 11, #1100, 200 King St. West, Toronto ON M5H 3T4 – 416/977-8400; Fax: 416/977-5239 – Librarian, Janine Miller

Merrill Lynch Canada Inc. - Corporate Library, 200 King St. West, 5th Fl., Toronto ON M5H 3W3 – 416/586-6016; Fax: 416/586-6419 – Manager, Corporate Library, Susan Bryant

Metropolitan Separate School Board - Catholic Education Centre Library, 80 Sheppard Ave. East, North York ON M2N 6E8 – 416/222-8282, ext.5324; Fax: 416/229-5345 – Program Coordinator, Judy Smith

Metropolitan Toronto Association for Community Living – AV/Reference Services, 20 Spadina Rd., Toronto ON M5R 2S7 – 416/968-0650; Fax: 416/968-6463 – Library Technician, Susan Rawle

Metropolitan Toronto Convention & Visitors Association – Information Centre, Queen's Quay Terminal at Harbourfront, #590, 207 Queen's Quay West, POBox 126, Toronto ON M5J 1A7 – 416/203-2600; Fax: 416/203-6753; Toll Free: 1-800/363-1990 – Advertising Manager, Ken Gruber

Metropolitan Toronto Lawyers Association – Library, 361 University Ave., Toronto ON M5G 1T3 – 416/327-5700; Fax: 416/947-9148 – Library Manager, Anne Matthewman

Metropolitan Toronto Zoo - Resource Centre, 361A Old Finch Ave., Scarborough ON M1B 5K7 – 416/392-5961; Fax: 416/392-4979; URL: http://www.torontozoo.com – Administration, Linda Ervine

The Michener Institute for Applied Health Sciences – Library, 222 St. Patrick St., Toronto ON M5T 1V4 – 416/596-3101, ext.3123; Fax: 416/596-3123 – Supervisor, Susan Reynolds

Midland Walwyn Capital Inc. - Library, 40 King St. West, 34th Fl., Toronto ON M5H 1B5 – 416/369-7547; Fax: 416/369-2803 – Librarian, Sonia Solomon

The Migraine Association of Canada – Library, #1912, 365 Bloor St. East, Toronto ON M4W 3L4 – 416/920-4916; Fax: 416/920-3677; Toll Free: 1-800-663-3557 – Communications Manager, Shaaron McDonald

Miller Thomson Law Office - Library, #2700, 20 Queen St. West, Toronto ON M5H 3S1 – 416/595-8537; Fax: 416/595-8695 – Librarian, Ines Freeman

Mizrachi-Hapoel Hamizrachi Organization of Canada – Library, 296 Wilson Ave., North York ON M3H

1S8 – 416/630-9266; Fax: 416/630-2305 – Rochelle Shulman

Molson Breweries - Technical Services Centre, 33 Carlingview Dr., Etobicoke ON M9W 5E4 – 416/798-1786; Fax: 416/798-8390 – TSC Administrator, Sophia A. (Sandi) Lloyd

Morgan Stanley Canada Ltd. - Library, #3700, 181 Bay St., Toronto ON M5J 2T3 – 416/943-8413; Fax: 416/368-0796 – Librarian, Frances Main

Morris, Rose, Ledgett Law Office - Library, Canada Trust Tower, BCE Place, 161 Bay St., Toronto ON M5J 2S1 – 416/981-9400; Fax: 416/863-9500; Email: mrl@mrl.on.ca – Librarian, Helen Hochberg

Morrison Hershfield Ltd. – Library, 4 Lansing Sq., North York ON M2J 1T1 – 416/499-3110; Fax: 416/499-9658

Moss Lawson & Co. Ltd. - Library, #410, 1 Toronto St., Toronto ON M5C 2W3 – 416/864-2700; Fax: 416/864-2756 – Librarian, Anne Frelich

Mount Sinai Hospital – Sidney Liswood Library, 600 University Ave., Toronto ON M5G 1X5 – 416/586-4614; Fax: 416/586-4998; Email: msh@library.utoronto.ca – Director, Library Services, Linda Devore

Multicultural History Society of Ontario – Resource Centre, 43 Queen's Park Cres. East, Toronto ON M5S 2C3 – 416/979-2973; Fax: 416/979-7947 – Library Technician, Ljubomir Medjesi

Multiple Sclerosis Society of Canada – Information Resource Centre, #1000, 250 Bloor St. East, Toronto ON M4W 3P9 – 416/922-6065; Fax: 416/922-7538; Toll Free: 1-800-268-7582 – Librarian, Nancy Crozier

National Action Committee on the Status of Women – Library, #203, 234 Eglinton Ave. East, Toronto ON M4P 1K5 – 416/932-1718; Fax: 416/932-0646; Toll Free: 1-800-665-5124 – Laura Cabarrocas

National Automobile, Aerospace, Transportation & General Workers Union of Canada (CLC) – Library, 205 Placer Ct., North York ON M2H 3H9 – 416/497-4110; Fax: 416/495-6559; Symbol: OWCA – Librarian, Kathy Bennett

National Defence (Canada)-Defence & Civil Institute of Environmental Medicine – Library, 1133 Sheppard Ave. West, POBox 2000, North York ON M3M 3B9 – 416/635-2070; Fax: 416/635-2104; Email: sic@dciem.dnd.ca; Symbol: OTDR – Head, Scientific Information Centre, Stewart Harrison

National Eating Disorder Information Centre – Library, College Wing 1-211, 200 Elizabeth St., Toronto ON M5G 2C4 – 416/340-4156; Fax: 416/340-4736

National Trust Mutual Funds – Reference Library, One Financial Place, One Adelaide St. East, Toronto ON M5C 2W8 – 416/361-3863; Fax: 416/361-5563; Toll Free: 1-800-563-4683 – Patricia Greenwell

Native Womens Resource Centre of Toronto – Library, 191 Gerrard St. East, Toronto ON M5A 2E5 – 416/963-9963; Fax: 416/963-9573 – Literacy Coordinator, Jody MacDonald

Nesbitt Burns - Library, One First Canadian Place, PO Box 150, Stn 1st Cdn Place, Toronto ON M5X 1H3 – 416/359-4587; Fax: 416/365-5394 – Manager of Information Services, Dani Breen

Nickel Development Institute – Library, #510, 214 King St. West, Toronto ON M5H 3S6 – 416/591-7999; Fax: 416/591-7987; TLX: 06-218565 – Publications Manager, Barbara Fell

Noranda Mining & Exploration Inc. - Information Centre, #2700, One Adelaide St. East, Toronto ON M5C 2Z6 – 416/982-7238; Fax: 416/982-7021

North York Board of Education - The F.W. Minkler Library, 3 Tippett Rd., North York ON M3H 2V1 – 416/395-8289; Fax: 416/395-8292; Email: fwm@hookup.net; Symbol: OTNYE
- Librarian/Cataloguer, J. Ameline
- Librarian/Archivist, J. Creelman

North York General Hospital – W. Keith Welsh Library, 4001 Leslie St., Willowdale ON M2K 1E1 – 416/756-6142; Fax: 416/756-6605 – Director, Library Services, Marjory Morphy

North York Symphony Association – Music Library, #109, 1210 Sheppard Ave. East, North York ON M2K 1E3 – 416/499-2204; Fax: 416/490-9739 – Librarian, Linda Perkins

Northern Miner - Library, 1450 Don Mills Rd., North York ON M3B 2X7 – 416/442-2164; Fax: 416/442-2181; Email: tnm@southam.ca; URL: http://www.northernminer.ca – Administrative Assistant, Mariann Semkiw

Office of the Fire Marshall - Fire Sciences Library, 5775 Yonge St., North York ON M2M 4J1 – 416/325-3235; Email: kendalb@epo.gov.on.ca – Librarian, Barry Kendall

Ombudsman Ontario - Communications Team, 125 Queen's Park Cres., Toronto ON M5S 2C7 – 416/586-3300; Fax: 416/586-3485; Toll Free: 1-800-263-1830 – Administrative Assistant, Dean Morra, 416/586-3353

The Ontario Archaeological Society Inc. – Library, 126 Willowdale Ave., North York ON M2N 4Y2 – 416/730-0797; Fax: 416/730-0797 – Librarian, Charles Garrad

Ontario Association of Art Galleries – Library, #306, 489 King St. West, Toronto ON M5V 1K4 – 416/598-0714; Fax: 416/598-4128

Ontario Association of Distress Centres – Library, #418, 99 Atlantic Ave., Toronto ON M6K 3J8 – 416/537-7373; Fax: 416/537-6739 – Office Manager, Kate Hunter

Ontario Association of Volunteer Bureaux/Centres – Library, #203, 2 Dunbloor Rd., Etobicoke ON M9A 2E4 – 416/236-0588; Fax: 416/236-0590 – Iga Jakubowska

Ontario Bible College & Theological Seminary - J. Wm. Horsey Library, 25 Ballyconnor Ct., North York ON M2M 4B3 – 416/226-6380; Fax: 416/226-6746; Email: library@obcots.on.ca; URL: http://www.obcots.on.ca; Symbol: OWOBC
- Library Director, Sandy Finlayson
- Reference Librarian, Hugh Rendle

Ontario Black History Society – Library, Ontario Heritage Centre, #202, 10 Adelaide St. East, Toronto ON M5C 1J3 – 416/867-9420; Fax: 416/867-8691 – Everette Moore

Ontario Cancer Institute – Library, Princess Margaret Hospital, 610 University Ave., Toronto ON M5G 2M9 – 416/946-4482; Fax: 416/946-2084

Ontario Centre for Environmental Technology Advancement – Library, 63 Polson St., 2nd Fl., Toronto ON M5A 1A4 – 416/778-5275; Fax: 416/778-5624 – Information Manager, Nancy Shepherd

Ontario College of Art - Dorothy H. Hoover Library, 100 McCaul St., Toronto ON M5T 1W1 – 416/977-6000; Fax: 416/977-0235; Symbol: OTCA
- Director, Jill Patrick, Email: jpatrick@oca.on.ca
- Head, A/V Services, Angelo Rao
- Head, Technical Support, Jim Forrester
- Media Librarian, Tom Ready
- Circulation Technician, Lee Henderson

Ontario Crafts Council – Library, Chalmer's Building, 35 McCaul St., Toronto ON M5T 1V7 – 416/977-3551; Fax: 416/977-3552 – Information Officer, Jane Moore

Ontario Energy Board - Library, 2300 Yonge St., 26th Fl., POBox 2319, Toronto ON M4P 1E4 – 416/440-7655; Fax: 416/440-7656 – Librarian, Lina Buccilli

Ontario Environmental Assessment Advisory Committee - Library, 65 St. Clair Ave. East, 7th Fl., Toronto ON M4T 2Y3 – 416/323-2666 – Administrative Assistant, Trish Shayne

Ontario Federation of Agriculture – Library, 40 Eglinton Ave. West, 5th Fl., Toronto ON M4P 3A2 – 416/485-3333; Fax: 416/485-9027 – Cecil Bradley

Ontario Federation of Labour – Library, #202, 15 Gervais Dr., North York ON M3C 1Y8 – 416/441-2731; Fax: 416/441-0722 – Secretary-Librarian, Judy Robins

Ontario Genealogical Society – Library, #102, 40 Orchard View Blvd., Toronto ON M4R 1B9 – 416/395-5623; Fax: 416/489-9803 – Coordinator, Library Division, Jean Bircham

Ontario Hydro - Library Services, 700 University Ave., Toronto ON M5G 1X6 – 416/592-2716; Fax: 416/592-7532; Email: cic@hydro.on.ca; Symbol: OTH – Information Resources Supervisor, Kim Cornell

Ontario Institute for Studies in Education of the University of Toronto - Library, 252 Bloor St. West, Toronto ON M5S 1V6 – 416/923-6641, Fax: 416/926-4745
- Co-Director, Information Resources & Services, Judith Snow, Email: judysnow@oise.utoronto.ca
- Collection Management, Valerie Downs
- Acquisitions Control, Helen Fitzpatrick
- Cataloguing, Special Collections, Stephanie Swift
- Reference, Technology, Marian Press
- Resource Sharing, Distance Education, Patricia Serafini
- Circulation, Instruction, & Media, Carol Calder

Ontario Insurance Commission - Library, 5160 Yonge St., POBox 85, North York ON M2N 6L9 – 416/590-7135; Fax: 416/590-7070; Email: shanfij@gov.on.ca; Symbol: OTOI – Librarian, Joy Shanfield

Ontario Labour Relations Board - Library, 400 University Ave., 4th Fl., Toronto ON M7A 1V4 – 416/326-7468; Fax: 416/326-7531; Symbol: OTOLR – Manager, Kevin Jenkins, 416/326-7468

Ontario Legislative Library, Legislative Bldg., Queen's Park, Toronto ON M7A 1A9 – 416/325-3900; Fax: 416/325-3925; Email: ONT.LEG.LIB; Symbol: OTL
- Executive Director, Mary Dickerson
- Information & Reference Services, Donna Burton, 416/325-3945
- Collections Development, Brian Tobin, 416/325-3910
- Press Clipping Service, Karen Wierucki, 416/314-8534
- Technical Services & Systems, Pamela Stoksik, 416/314-8520
- Acquisitions Librarian, Deirdre Grimes, 416/314-8525
- Legislative Research Service, Cynthia Smith, 416/325-3637

Ontario Lung Association – Environmental Information Centre, #201, 573 King St. East, Toronto ON M5A 4L3 – 416/864-9911; Fax: 416/864-9916; Toll Free: 1-800-668-7682 – Environmental Program Manager, Ian Morton

Ontario Lupus Association – Resource Centre, #1700, 393 University Ave., Toronto ON M5G 1E6 – 416/979-7228; Fax: 416/979-8366; Toll Free: 1-800-321-1433 – Staff Liaison, Violet Turalba

Ontario Management Board Secretariat - Library & Resource Centre, Ferguson Block, 77 Wellesley St. West, 4th Fl., Toronto ON M7A 1N3 – 416/327-2533; Fax: 416/327-2530; Email: Mackelm@gov.on.ca; Symbol: OTOM
- Coordinator, Marilyn MacKellar
- Library Assistant, Fabiola Colavizza, 416/327-2534, 0996

Ontario March of Dimes – Resource Centre, 10 Overlea Blvd., Toronto ON M4H 1A4 – 416/425-3463; Fax: 416/425-1920; Toll Free: 1-800-263-3463

Ontario Medical Association – Corporate Information, #300, 525 University Ave., Toronto ON M5G 2K7 – 416/340-2914; Fax: 416/599-9309 – Manager, Vivian Hung

Ontario Ministry of Community & Social Services - Library & Learning Resources, 880 Bay St., 4th Fl.,

Toronto ON M7A 1E9 – 416/326-6442; Fax: 416/326-6453; Email: ENVOY: ILL.OTPW
Library Manager, Dolly Lyn, 416/326-6446
Reference Librarian, Elizabeth Sharp, 416/326-6448
Technical Services, Sallie Thayer, 416/326-6450
Circulation, Anna DiFelice, 416/326-6442
Acquisitions, Perry Tom, 416/326-6443
Ontario Ministry of Economic Development, Trade & Tourism - InfoSource, Hearst Block, 900 Bay St., 3rd Fl., Toronto ON M7A 2E1 – 416/325-6626; Fax: 416/325-6635
Information Retrieval Specialist, Lynda Bond, Email: bondl@gov.on.ca
Information Retrieval Specialist, Lindsay Wood Coolidge, Email: coolidl@gov.on.ca
Ontario Ministry of Education & Training - Online Research Library, Mowat Block, 900 Bay St., 13th Fl., Toronto ON M7A 1L2 – 416/325-2665; Fax: 416/325-4235 – Librarian, Simon Loban
Ontario Ministry of Environment & Energy - Approvals Branch Library, 250 Davisville Ave., 3rd Fl., Toronto ON M4S 1H2 – 416/440-6985; Fax: 416/440-6973; Email: camerope@ene.gov.on.ca; Symbol: OTMEAB – Library Technician, Peggy Cameron
Energy Board Library, 2300 Yonge St., 26th Fl., Toronto ON M4P 1E4 – 416/440-7666 – Lina Buccilli
Energy Library, 40 St. Clair Ave. West, 5th Fl., Toronto ON M4V 1M2 – 416/327-1247 – Heather Ara
Environmental Assessment Library, 250 Davisville Ave., 5th Fl., Toronto ON M4S 1H2 – 416/440-6985 – Library Technician, Peggy Cameron
Legal Services Library, 135 St Clair Ave. West, 10th Fl., Toronto ON M4V 1P5 – 416/323-4309 – Jane Thompson
Program Development Branch Library, 40 St Clair Ave. West, 14th Fl., Toronto ON M4V 1M2 – 416/314-7959; Fax: 416/314-4128; Symbol: OTMEP – Maria Nicolescu, Email: Nicolem@gov.on.ca
Public Information Centre, 135 St. Clair Ave. West, Toronto ON M4V 1P5 – 416/323-4321; Fax: 416/323-4564; Toll Free: 1-800-565-4923 – Researcher/Group Leader, Fania Urbina
Regional Operations Division - Library, 250 Davisville Ave., 3rd Fl., Toronto ON M4S 1H2 – 416/440-6985; Fax: 416/440-6973 – Library Technician, Peggy Cameron
Science & Technology Library, 2 St Clair Ave. West, 14th Fl., Toronto ON M4V 1L5 – 416/323-5131; Fax: 416/323-5031; Symbol: OTMEW – Emilita Lacson
Standards Development Branch Library, 2 St Clair Ave. West, 12th Fl., Toronto ON M4V 1L5 – 416/323-5009 – Iraj Rahmani
Ontario Ministry of Finance - Library Services, Frost Bldg. North, 1st Fl., 95 Grosvenor St., Toronto ON M7A 1Y8 – 416/325-1200; Fax: 416/325-1212; Symbol: OTDRE – Coordinator, Library Services, Helen Katz
Ontario Ministry of Health - Laboratory Services Branch, POBox 9000, Toronto ON M5W 1R5 – 416/235-5935; Symbol: OTDHL – Librarian, Doris Standing
Ontario Ministry of Labour - Library Services, 400 University Ave., 10th Fl., Toronto ON M7A 1T7 – 416/326-7840; Fax: 416/326-7844; Symbol: OTDL – Head, Library Services, Sandra Gold
Ontario Ministry of Municipal Affairs & Housing - Library, 777 Bay St., 2nd Fl., Toronto ON M5G 2E5 – 416/585-6527; Fax: 416/585-7300; Symbol: OTOH
Chief Librarian, Annette Dignan
Information Specialist, Michele Fleet
Ontario Ministry of the Attorney General - Law Library, 720 Bay St., 9th Fl., Toronto ON M5G 1K1 – 416/326-4566; Fax: 416/326-4562; Symbol: OTMAG – Manager, Gina Cullen, 416/326-4563
Ontario Ministry of the Solicitor General & Correctional Services - Mimico Correctional Complex Library, 130 Horner Ave., POBox 75, Toronto ON M8V 3S9 – 416/314-9684; Fax: 416/314-9698 – Library Technician, Laurie Fenton
Office of the Fire Marshal, Audio-Visual Resource Centre, Place Nouveau, 5775 Yonge St., 7th Fl., North York ON M2M 3T7 – 416/325-3121; Fax: 416/325-3213; Symbol: OTFM – Audio-Visual Clerk, Sophie Greco
Office of the Fire Marshal, Fire Sciences Library, Place Nouveau Bldg., 5775 Yonge St., 7th Fl., North York ON M2M 3T7 – 416/325-3235, 3236; Fax: 416/325-3213; Email: kendalb@epo.gov.on.ca; Symbol: OTFM
Librarian, Barry Kendall
Library Technician, Gabrielle Gaedecke
Ontario Museum Association – Library, George Brown House, 50 Baldwin St., Toronto ON M5T 1L4 – 416/348-8672; Fax: 416/348-0438 – Publications Coordinator, Sandra Black
Ontario Nurses' Association – Library, #600, 85 Grenville St., Toronto ON M5S 3A2 – 416/964-8833; Fax: 416/964-8864; Toll Free: 1-800-387-5580 – Library Technician, Vicky White
Ontario Physical & Health Education Association – Library, #501, 1185 Eglinton Ave. East, North York ON M3C 3C6 – 416/426-7120; Fax: 416/426-7373
Ontario Public Interest Research Group – Library, #201, 455 Spadina Ave., Toronto ON M5S 2G8 – 416/978-7770 – Toronto Coordinator, Andrea Calver
Ontario Public School Boards Association – Library, Phoenix House, 439 University Ave., 18th Fl., Toronto ON M5G 1Y8 – 416/340-2540; Fax: 416/340-7571 – Carol Cohen
Ontario Public Service Employees Union – Library, 100 Lesmill Rd., North York ON M3B 3P8 – 416/443-8888; Fax: 416/448-7454; Toll Free: 1-800-268-7376; Email: akeung@opseu.org – Librarian, Annie Keung
Ontario Recreational Canoeing Association – Library, #104, 1185 Eglinton Ave. East, North York ON M3C 3C6 – 416/426-7170; Fax: 416/426-7363 – Communications Director, Chris Beckett
Ontario Safety League – OSL Film & Video Library, #100, 21 Four Seasons Pl., Etobicoke ON M9B 6J8 – 416/620-1720, ext.21; Fax: 416/620-5977 – Film & Video Librarian, Adele Ross
Ontario Science Centre - Library, 770 Don Mills Rd., North York ON M3C 1T3 – 416/696-3149; Fax: 416/696-3157; Email: Valerie_Hatten@fcgate1.osc.on.ca; URL: http://www.osc.on.ca; Symbol: OTST – Librarian, Valerie Hatten
Ontario Securities Commission - Library, 20 Queen St. West, 8th Fl., Toronto ON M5H 3S8 – 416/593-8268; Fax: 416/593-8240; Email: dsinclair@osc.gov.on.ca – Librarian, Donna Sinclair
Ontario Sports & Recreation Centre Inc. – Sports & Recreation Resource Centre, 1185 Eglinton Ave. East, North York ON M3C 3C6 – 416/426-7060; Fax: 416/426-7353; Email: hstewart@osrc.com – Coordinator, Heather Stewart
Ontario Teachers' Federation – Library, #700, 1260 Bay St., Toronto ON M5R 2B5 – 416/966-3424; Fax: 416/966-5450 – Elfrieda Young
Ontor Ltd. – Library, 12 Leswyn Rd., Toronto ON M6A 1K3 – 416/781-5286; Fax: 416/781-7680 – Marketing Coordinator, Mary Borg
Orchestras Ontario – Resource Centre, #311, 56 The Esplanade, Toronto ON M5E 1A7 – 416/366-8834; Fax: 416/366-1780
Orthopaedic & Arthritic Hospital – Health Sciences Library, 43 Wellesley St. East, Toronto ON M4Y 1H1 – 416/967-8545; Fax: 416/967-8593 – Susan Baillie
Osteoporosis Society of Canada – Lindy Fraser Resource Library, 33 Laird Dr., Toronto ON M4G 3S9 – 416/696-2663; Fax: 416/696-2673; Toll Free: 1-800-463-6842
Outerbridge, Miller, Sefton, Willms & Shier - Library, #900, 4 King St. West, Toronto ON M5H 1B6 – 416/863-0711; Fax: 416/863-1938 – Librarian, Lesley Rhodes
Pay Equity Commission - Library, 150 Eglinton Ave. East, 5th Fl., Toronto ON M4P 1E8 – 416/481-4464; Fax: 416/314-8741; Email: walkerc@gov.on.ca; Symbol: OTPE – Librarian, Catherine A. Walker, 416/481-4464, ext.667
Periodical Writers Association of Canada – Library, #203, 54 Wolseley St., Toronto ON M5T 1A5 – 416/504-1645; Fax: 416/703-0059
Photographic Historical Society of Canada – Library, 1712 Avenue Rd., POBox 5420, Toronto ON M5M 4N5 – 416/691-1555; Fax: 416/693-0018 – Gerry Loban
Playwrights Union of Canada – Drama Reading Room, 54 Wolseley St., 2nd Fl., Toronto ON M5T 1A5 – 416/703-0201; Fax: 416/703-0059; Toll Free: 1-800-561-3318 – Customer Service, James Wilkinson
Polten & Hodder Law Office - Library, Guardian of Canada Tower, #2200, 181 University Ave., Toronto ON M5H 3M7 – 416/601-6766; Fax: 416/947-0909; Email: info@poltenhodder.com; URL: http://www.poltenhodder.com/~ph – Acquisitions Librarian, Lise Kunzelmann
Price Waterhouse - National/Toronto Office Library, #3300, One First Canadian Place, PO Box 190, Stn First Canadian Place, Toronto ON M5X 1H7 – 416/863-1133; Fax: 416/947-8921
Manager, Nancy Wells
Head of Reference/Public Services, Margaret Ashton
Manager, National Tax Library, H. Kerr, 365-8151
Probe International – Library, 225 Brunswick Ave., Toronto ON M5S 2M6 – 416/964-9223; Fax: 416/964-8239; Email: adavis@nextcity.com – Information Officer, Andrea Davis
Prospectors & Developers Association of Canada – Library, 34 King St. East, 9th Fl., Toronto ON M5C 2X8 – 416/362-1969; Fax: 416/362-0101 – Saley Lawton
The Prudential Insurance Company of America – Library, 200 Consilium Pl., Scarborough ON M1H 3E6 – 416/296-0777; Fax: 416/296-3180 – Elinor Major
Public Works & Government Services Canada - Translation Bureau - Ontario Regional Library, #814, 55 St Clair Ave. East, Toronto ON M4T 1M2 – 416/973-1154; Fax: 416/973-3325; Email: pwgsctb@inforamp.net; Symbol: OTGSC-C – Head, S. Castaneda
The Queen Elizabeth Hospital – Library Services, 550 University Ave., Toronto ON M5G 2A2 – 416/597-3050; Fax: 416/597-6625; Email: qeh@library.utoronto.ca – Manager, Helen Michael
Queen Street Mental Health Centre – Library, 1001 Queen St. West, Toronto ON M6J 1H4 – 416/535-8501; Fax: 416/583-4307 – Mary-Ann Georges
Quetico Foundation – John B. Ridley Research Library, #610, 48 Yonge St., Toronto ON M5E 1G6 – 807/929-2571; Fax: 416/941-9236 – Librarian, Andrea Allison
Real Estate Institute of Canada – Library, #208, 5407 Eglinton Ave. West, Toronto ON M9C 5K6 – 416/695-9000; Fax: 416/695-7230; Toll Free: 1-800-542-7342
Recycling Council of Ontario – Library, #504, 489 College St., Toronto ON M6G 1A5 – 416/960-1025, ext.21; Fax: 416/960-8053; Toll Free: 1-800-263-2849 – Library Coordinator, Ebun Arimah
Reed Stenhouse Ltd. - National Resource Centre, 20 Bay St., Toronto ON M5J 2N9 – 416/868-5520;

Fax: 416/868-5580; Symbol: OTRS – Research Manager, O. Gil

Retail Council of Canada – Library, #1210, 121 Bloor St. West, Toronto ON M4W 3M5 – 416/922-6678; Fax: 416/922-8011; Toll Free: 1-888-373-8245 – Researcher, Irene Fedyushina

Revenue Canada - Research & Library Services, #1000, 5001 Yonge St., North York ON M2N 6R9 – 416/218-4597; Fax: 416/512-2558; Symbol: OTNYR – Librarian, Harinder Guraya

Research & Library Services, 36 Adelaide St. East, Toronto ON M5C 1J7 – 416/973-9359; Fax: 416/954-6015; Symbol: OTRCT – Librarian, Paul Sawa

Richardson Greenshields of Canada Ltd. - Library, #1400, 130 Adelaide St. West, Toronto ON M5H 1T8 – 416/860-3432; Fax: 416/368-2481 – Librarian, Alison Crawley

Right to Life Association of Toronto – Resource Centre, #700, 120 Eglinton Ave. East, Toronto ON M4P 1E2 – 416/483-7869; Fax: 416/483-7052 – June Scandiffio

Rio Algom Ltd. - Information Centre, 120 Adelaide St. West, Toronto ON M5H 1W5 – 416/365-6800; Fax: 416/365-6870; Symbol: OTRAL – Manager, Information Services, Penny Lipman, Email: plipman@rioalgom.com

The Riverdale Hospital – Staff Library, 14 St. Matthews Rd., Toronto ON M4M 2B5 – 416/461-8251; Fax: 416/461-1670 – Librarian, Richard Kopak

The Roeher Institute – Library, Kinsmen Building, York University, 4700 Keele St., North York ON M3J 1P3 – 416/661-9611; Fax: 416/661-5701; Toll Free: 1-800-856-2207; Symbol: OTNIIR – Director, Information Services, Miriam Ticoll

Rose Technology Group Ltd. – Library, 255 Consumers Rd., North York ON M2J 1R4 – 416/756-4170; Fax: 416/756-1825 – Librarian, Gillian Henderson

Rothmans, Benson & Hedges Inc. - Library, 1500 Don Mills Rd., North York ON M3B 3L1 – 416/449-5525; Fax: 416/449-6142 – Jacqui Clarke

Royal Astronomical Society of Canada – Library, 136 Dupont St., Toronto ON M5R 1V2 – 416/924-7973; Fax: 416/924-2911

Royal Bank of Canada - Technical Resource Centre, 315 Front St. West, 2nd Fl., Toronto ON M5V 3A4 – 416/348-5821; Fax: 416/348-5880 – Manager, Susan Reid

Toronto Office, Royal Bank Plaza, Lower Concourse, POBox 1, Toronto ON M5J 2J5 – 416/974-2780; Fax: 416/974-0135; Toll Free: 1-800-263-9191; Symbol: OTRBI – Manager, Sandra Walsh

Royal Canadian Academy of Arts – Library, Office of the Secretary, 163 Queen St. East, POBox 2, Toronto ON M5A 1S1 – 416/363-9612; Fax: 416/363-9612

Royal Canadian College of Organists – Library, #302, 112 St. Clair Ave. West, Toronto ON M4V 2Y3 – 416/929-6400; Fax: 416/929-6400 – Sharon Beckstead

Royal Canadian Military Institute – Library, 426 University Ave., Toronto ON M5G 1S9 – 416/597-0286; Fax: 416/597-6919 – Librarian, Anne Melvin

Royal Ontario Museum - Library, 100 Queen's Park, Toronto ON M5S 2C6 – 416/586-5595; Fax: 416/586-5863; Email: matthewsj@vax.library.utoronto.ca – Head, Julia Matthews

The Royal Philatelic Society of Canada – Library, POBox 929, Toronto ON M4T 2P1 – 416/979-7474; Fax: 416/979-1144

RP Research Foundation - Fighting Blindness – Library, #910, 36 Toronto St., Toronto ON M5C 2C5 – 416/360-4200; Fax: 416/360-0060; Toll Free: 1-800-461-3331

R.V. Anderson Associates Limited – Library, #400, 2001 Sheppard Ave. East, North York ON M2J 4Z8 – 416/497-8600; Fax: 416/497-0342; Email: lindad@rvanderson.com – Librarian, Linda Diener

Ryerson Polytechnic University - Library, 350 Victoria St., Toronto ON M5B 2K3 – 416/979-5144; Fax: 416/979-5215; Email: interlib@acs.ryerson.ca; URL: http://hugo.lib.ryerson.ca; Symbol: CaOTR

Chief Librarian, R. Malinski

Access Services, Head, D. Phelan, 416/979-5000, ext.7160

Information Services, Head, O. Cheung, 416/979-5025

Public Services, Associate Librarian, E. Bishop, 416/979-5000, ext.6909

Systems & Technical Support, Associate Librarian, B. Jackson, 416/979-5147

Technical Services, Head, E. Friesen, 416/979-5146

St. Augustine's Seminary - Library, 2661 Kingston Rd., Scarborough ON M1M 1M3 – 416/261-7207, ext.236 – Librarian, Sr. Jean Harris

St. John's Rehabilitation Hospital – Beeston Staff Library, 285 Cummer Ave., North York ON M2M 2G1 – 416/226-6790, ext.7350; Fax: 416/226-6265 – Librarian, Sister Margaret Ann

St. Joseph's Health Centre – George Pennal Library, 30 The Queensway, Toronto ON M6R 1B5 – 416/530-6726; Fax: 416/530-6034 – Librarian, Barbara Iwasiuk

St. Michael's Hospital – Health Sciences Library, 30 Bond St., Toronto ON M5B 1W8 – 416/864-5059; Fax: 416/864-5296; Email: OTS.MH; Symbol: OTSM – Director, Anita Wong

St. Vladimir Institute - Resource Centre for Ukrainian Studies, 620 Spadina Ave., Toronto ON M5S 2H4 – 416/923-3318 – Ihor Krut

The Salvation Army - College for Officer Training - Library, 2130 Bayview Ave., Toronto ON M4N 3K6 – 416/481-6131, ext.306; Fax: 416/481-5389; Email: whporter@cfot.sallenet.org – Librarian, Bill Porter

The Salvation Army in Canada - George Scott Railton Heritage Centre & Library, 2031 Bayview Ave., North York ON M4N 3K6 – 416/481-4441; Fax: 416/481-6096 – Librarian, Paul Murray

The Salvation Army Scarborough Grace General Hospital – Glenn Gould Memorial Library, 3030 Birchmount Rd., Scarborough ON M1W 3W3 – 416/495-2437; Fax: 416/495-2432; Email: lambert@library.utoronto.ca – Coordinator, Deborah Lambert

Scarborough Board of Education - A.B. Patterson Professional Library, 140 Borough Dr., Level 1, Scarborough ON M1P 4N6 – 416/396-7515; Fax: 416/396-5418; Email: Professional_Library@sbe.scarborough.on.ca – Supervisor, Rowan Amott

Scarborough General Hospital – Health Sciences Library, 3050 Lawrence Ave. East, Scarborough ON M1P 2V5 – 416/431-8114; Fax: 416/431-8204; Email: sgh@library.utoronto.ca – Library Coordinator, Bonnie Brownstein

Scarborough Historical Society – Library & Archives, POBox 593, Scarborough ON M1K 5C4 – 416/396-6930; Fax: 416/282-9482; Email: rick_schofield@sbe.scarborough.on.ca – Archivist, R. Schofield

Schizophrenia Society of Canada – Library, #814, 75 The Donway West, North York ON M3C 2E9 – 416/445-8204; Fax: 416/445-2270 – Jessie Barretto

Scotia Capital Markets - Information Centre, Scotia Plaza, 40 King St. West, POBox 4085, Toronto ON M5W 2X6 – 416/863-7737; Fax: 416/863-7839; URL: http://wealth.passport.ca/wealth

Associate Director, Angela Devlin

Reference Librarian, Ann Struthers

Technical Services Librarian, Yvonne Rollins

Technical Services Librarian, Jane Crowder

Reference Librarian, Mari Wilson

Sculptor's Society of Canada – Library, Exchange Tower, First Canadian Place, 130 King St. West, POBox 40, Toronto ON M5X 1B5 – 416/883-3075 – Archivist, Karen Stoskopf Harding

Sears Canada Inc. - Corporate & Marketing Research/Library Resource Centre, 222 Jarvis St., 3rd Fl., Toronto ON M5B 2B8 – 416/941-2544; Fax: 416/941-4514 – Research Assistant, Doris Hamilton

Sedgwick Limited – Library, Commercial Union Tower, Toronto-Dominion Centre, POBox 439, Toronto ON M5K 1M3 – 416/361-6976; Fax: 416/361-6763 – Barbara Wilson

Self-Help Resource Centre of Greater Toronto – Library, #219, 40 Orchard View Blvd., Toronto ON M4R 1B9 – 416/487-4355; Fax: 416/487-0344 – Office Manager, Ruth Richardson

Seneca College - Leslie Campus Library, 1255 Sheppard Ave. East, North York ON M2K 1E2 – 416/491-5050, ext.6261; Fax: 416/494-9323 – Campus Librarian, Vinh Le

Newnham Campus Library, 1750 Finch Ave. East, North York ON M2J 2X5 – 416/491-5050, ext.2100; Fax: 416/491-3349; Symbol: OTSC

Director, Library Resource Centres, Tanis Fink, 416/491-5050, ext.2096

Associate Director, Library Resource Centres, Doreen London, 416/491-5050, ext.2097

Satellite Campus Libraries, Campus Librarian & Manager, Carolyn Lam, 905/833-3333, ext.5105

Newnham Campus, Campus Librarian, Rhonda Roth

Public Services, Librarian, Rosalie Walker

Technical Services, Campus Librarian, Linda Oldham

Sheppard Campus Library, 43 Sheppard Ave. East, North York ON M2N 2Z8 – 416/491-5050, ext.6444; Fax: 416/733-3855 – Campus Librarian, Joy Muller

Sex Information & Education Council of Canada – Library, 850 Coxwell Ave., East York ON M4C 5R1 – 416/466-5304; Fax: 416/778-0785 – Librarian, Mary Bissell

Shibley Righton Law Office - Library, #1900, 401 Bay St., POBox 32, Toronto ON M5H 2Z1 – 416/214-5294; Fax: 416/214-5438 – Librarian, Karen Cohen

Sky Works Charitable Foundation – Film Library, 566 Palmerston Ave., Toronto ON M6G 2P7 – 416/536-6581; Fax: 416/536-7728

Smith & Andersen Consulting Engineering – Library, 505 Eglinton Ave. West, Toronto ON M5N 1B1 – 416/487-8151; Fax: 416/487-9104 – Associate, David Vickery

SNC-Lavalin Inc. - Ontario Branch Library, Atria North, Phase II, 2235 Sheppard Ave. East, North York ON M2J 5A6 – 416/756-2300, ext.4601; Fax: 416/756-2266; Symbol: OWSNC – Librarian, Tze-Ling Kong, Email: kongl@snc-lavalin.com

Social Investment Organization – Library, #443, 366 Adelaide St. East, Toronto ON M5A 3X9 – 416/360-6047; Fax: 416/360-6380

Society for the Study of Egyptian Antiquities – Library, POBox 578, Toronto ON M5S 2T1 – 416/586-5632; Fax: 416/978-5294

Spina Bifida & Hydrocephalus Association of Ontario – Resource Lending Library, #310, 35 McCaul St., Toronto ON M5T 1V7 – 416/979-5514; Fax: 416/979-0849; Toll Free: 1-800-387-1575 – Information & Services Director, Joan Booth

Statistics Canada - Ontario Regional Reference Centre, Arthur Meighen Bldg., 25 St. Clair Ave. East, 10th Fl., Toronto ON M4T 1M4 – 416/973-6586; Fax: 416/973-7475; Toll Free: 1-800-263-1136 – Communications Officer, Sandra Lee McIntyre

Sterling Pulp Chemicals Ltd. - Central Library, 2 Gibbs Rd., Toronto ON M9B 1R1 – 416/239-7111, ext.213; Fax: 416/234-7441; Symbol: OIE – Corporate Librarian, Nancy Logan

Stikeman, Elliott - Library, Commerce Court West, POBox 85, Toronto ON M5L 1B9 – 416/869-5575;

Fax: 416/947-0866, 862-8518; Email: duber@tor.stikeman.com – Library Manager, Richard Dubé

Stone & Webster Canada Limited – Library, 2300 Yonge St., Toronto ON M4P 2W6 – 416/932-4400; Fax: 416/482-2865 – Librarian, Jennifer Webster

Sun Life Assurance Co. of Canada - Research Library, 225 King St. West, Toronto ON M5V 3C5 – 416/408-8840; Fax: 416/359-0346; Email: TMLIB@interlog.com

Manager, Research Library, Elizabeth Gibson, 416/408-8841

Reference Librarian, Faye Mitchell

Sunnybrook Health Science Centre – Health Sciences Library, 2075 Bayview Ave., North York ON M4N 3M5 – 416/480-6100,ex.4562; Fax: 416/480-6848; Email: ENVOY OTSMC – Chief Librarian, Linda McFarlane

Sus-Ward Editorial Library, 382 Balliol St., Toronto ON M4S 1E2 – Librarian, Emma Ward

Tandem International Inc. - Information Centre, #300, 3625 Dufferin St., Downsview ON M3K 1Z2 – 416/630-8971; Fax: 416/630-9211 – Library Technician, Rita D'Onorio

Ten Days for Global Justice – Resource Centre, #401, 77 Charles St. West, Toronto ON M5S 1K5 – 416/922-0591; Fax: 416/922-1419 – Resource Coordinator, Julie Graham

Thistletown Regional Centre Library, 51 Panorama Ct., Etobicoke ON M9V 4L8 – 416/326-0717; Fax: 416/326-9078; Symbol: TRC – Acting Supervisor of Libraries, Mary Beth Arrigo

Times Change Women's Employment Service – Access Centre, #1704, 365 Bloor St. East, Toronto ON M4W 3L4 – 416/927-1900; Fax: 416/927-7212

Toronto Artscape Inc. – Toronto Artscape, #111, 60 Atlantic Ave., Toronto ON M6K 1X9 – 416/392-1038; Fax: 416/392-1059 – Office/Library Manager, Jelica Vrana

Toronto Board of Education - Education Centre Reference Library, 155 College St., Toronto ON M5T 1P6 – 416/397-3011; Fax: 416/397-3044; Symbol: OTEC – Supervisor, Reference Services, Joan Culley

The Toronto-Dominion Bank – Dept. of Economic Research Library, TD Centre, PO Box 1, Stn Toronto-Dominion, Toronto ON M5K 1A2 – 416/982-8068; Fax: 416/982-6884; Toll Free: 1-800-387-2092 – Patricia Domine

Toronto East General & Orthopaedic Hospital – Health Sciences Library, 825 Coxwell Ave., Toronto ON M4C 3E7 – 416/469-6010; Fax: 416/469-6106 – Librarian, Jennifer Reiswig

Toronto Family History Library, 95 Melbert Rd., POBox 1, Etobicoke ON M9C 4V2 – 416/621-4607 – Director, E.G. Lansitie

The Toronto Hospital, Toronto General Division - Fudger Health Sciences Library, 585 University Ave., Toronto ON M5G 2C4 – 416/340-3429; Fax: 416/340-4384 – Library & Information Services, Director, J. Bayne, Email: jbayne@torhosp.toronto.on.ca

The Toronto Hospital, Toronto Western Division - R.C. Laird Health Science Library, 399 Bathurst St., Toronto ON M5T 2S8 – 416/603-5750; Fax: 416/603-5326; Email: ENVOY: OTTWH.LIB; Symbol: OTTWH – Library & Information Services, Director, J. Bayne, Email: jbayne@torhosp.toronto.on.ca

Toronto International Film Festival – Film Reference Library, 2 Carlton St., 16th Fl., Toronto ON M5B 1J3 – 416/967-1517; Fax: 416/967-0628 – Director, Sylvia Frank

Toronto Jewish Media Centre – Library, #252, 4600 Bathurst St., North York ON M2R 3V3 – 416/633-7770; Fax: 416/633-7535

The Toronto Mendelssohn Choir – Library, 60 Simcoe St., Toronto ON M5J 2H5 – 416/598-0422; Fax: 416/598-2992 – Librarian, Roger Hobbs

Toronto PWA Foundation – Treatment Resource Centre, 399 Church St., 2nd Fl., Toronto ON M5B 2J6 – 416/506-1400; Fax: 416/506-1404; Toll Free: 1-800-558-7923 – Treatment Resources Coordinator, Derek Thaczuk

Toronto Real Estate Board – Resource Centre, 1400 Don Mills Rd., North York ON M3B 3N1 – 416/443-8152; Fax: 416/443-0028, 1495 – Resource Library Administrator, Michael Murphy

Toronto Star Newspapers Ltd. - Library, One Yonge St., Toronto ON M5E 1E6 – 416/869-4490; Fax: 416/865-3994; Email: snoble@thestar.ca – Chief Librarian, Sonja Noble

Toronto Stock Exchange - Information Resource Centre, Exchange Tower, 2 First Canadian Place, PO Box 450, Stn 1st Can Place, Toronto ON M5X 1J2 – 416/947-4653; Fax: 416/947-4662; Email: sfroebel@tse.com – Senior Information Specialist, Shonna Froebel

Toronto Sun - News Research Centre, 333 King St. East, Toronto ON M5A 3X5 – 416/947-2257; Fax: 416/947-2043; Email: research@sunpub.com; URL: http://www.canoe.ca/Sunlib – Manager, News Research, Julie Kirsh, Email: jkirsh@sunpub.com

The Toronto Symphony Orchestra – Resource Centre, 212 King St. West, 5th Fl., Toronto ON M5H 1K5 – 416/593-7769, ext.315; Fax: 416/977-2912 – Principal Librarian, Gary Corrin

Toronto Transportation Society – Library, POBox 5187, Toronto ON M5W 1N5 – 416/883-3322 – Adam Zhelka

Tory Tory DesLauriers & Binnington - Law Library, #3000, Aetna Tower, Toronto-Dominion Centre, PO Box 270, Stn Toronto-Dominion, Toronto ON M5K 1N2 – 416/865-8158; Fax: 416/865-7380

Library Services, Director, Louis Mirando

Reference Librarian, Mary Almey

Tourette Syndrome Foundation of Canada – Resource Centre, #203, 3675 Keele St., North York ON M3J 1M6 – 416/636-2800; Fax: 416/636-1688; Toll Free: 1-800-361-3120 – Administrative Assistant, Bonnie Strachan-Oman

Towers Perrin - Information Centre, #1501, 175 Bloor St. East, Toronto ON M4W 3T6 – 416/960-2600; Fax: 416/960-2819; Email: torinfo@inforamp.net – Information Services Specialist, Lorraine Flanigan

Transport Canada - Ontario Region Library, #300, 4900 Yonge St., North York ON M2N 6A5 – 416/952-0441; Fax: 416/952-0440; Email: chinge@tc.gc.ca; URL: http://www.tc.gc.ca; Symbol: OTTOA – Librarian, Eng K. Ching

Treasury Management Association of Canada – National Resource Centre, #1010, 8 King St. East, Toronto ON M5C 1B5 – 416/367-8501; Fax: 416/367-3242

TVOntario - Library, 2180 Yonge St., Toronto ON M4S 2C1 – 416/484-2651; Fax: 416/484-7771; Toll Free: 1-800-613-0513; Email: rcchildc_volpatti@tvo.org; URL: http://www.tvo.org; Symbol: OTET – Supervisor, Rechilde Volpatti

Ukrainian Canadian Research & Documentation Centre – Research & Documentation Centre, #200, 620 Spadina Ave., Toronto ON M5S 2H4 – 416/966-1819; Fax: 416/966-1820

Ukrainian National Federation - Library, 297 College St., Toronto ON M5T 1S2 – 416/922-1617; Fax: 416/485-9387 – Director, Nell A. Nakoneczny

United Empire Loyalists' Association of Canada – Reference Library, Dominion Office, The George Brown House, 50 Baldwin St., Toronto ON M5T 1L4 – 416/591-1783; Fax: 416/591-1783

University of Toronto Libraries, John P. Robarts Research Library, 130 Saint George St., Toronto ON M5S 1A5 – Email: askus@library.utoronto.ca; URL: http://www.library.utoronto.ca; Symbol: CAOTU

Robarts Reference Department, Head, Sharon Brown, 416/978-6215

A. E. MacDonald Ophthalmic Library, Librarian, Judy Cardwell, 416/978-2635, Email: j.cardwell@utoronto.ca

Architecture Library, Librarian, Pamela Manson-Smith, 416/978-2649

Astronomy Library, Librarian, Marlene Cummins, 416/978-4268

Audiovisual Library, Acting Head, Shauna Dorskind, 416/978-6520, Email: avlib@library.utoronto.ca

Bora Laskin Law Library, Chief Librarian, Ann Rae, 416/978-0944

Business Information Centre, Manager, Vicki Whitmell, 416/978-1924

Canadian Institute of International Affairs Library, Head Librarian, Jennifer McNenly, MA, MLS, 416/979-1851

Centre for Computing in the Humanties Library, Information Officer, Claire Smith, 416/978-2535, Email: csmith@epas.utoronto.ca

Charles H. Best Institute Library, Colin Savage, 416/978-2588

Chemistry Library, Librarian, Judy Mills, 416/978-3587

Cheng Yu Tung East Asian Library, Head, Anna U, 416/978-3300, Email: u@library.utoronto.ca

Computer Science Library, Librarian, Stephanie Johnston, 416/978-2987, Email: steph@cs.toronto.edu

Connaught Laboratories Ltd. (Balmer Neilly Library), Librarian, Hugh McNaught, 416/667-2662, Email: library@toronto.connaught.com

Criminology Library, Head Librarian, Catherine J. Matthews, 416/978-7068, Email: criminology.library@utoronto.ca

Dentistry Library, Librarian, Susan Goddard, 416/979-4916, ext.4560

Emmanuel College Library, Theology Librarian, Rev. Douglas Fox, 416/585-4550

Engineering Library, Librarian, Elaine Granatstein, 416/978-6494

Erindale College Library, College Librarian, Catherine Matthews, 905/828-5235, Email: matthews@credit.erin.utoronto.ca

Faculty of Information Studies Library, Co-Manager, Marte Misiek, 416/978-7060

Fine Art Library, Librarian, Andrea Retfalvi, 416/978-5006

First Nations Library, Chanze Gamble, 416/978-8227, Email: littlewillie@utoronto.ca

Gerstein Science Information Centre, Joan Leishman, 416/978-2280

Information Technology Services, Director, Marshall (Peter) Clinton, 416/978-7639, Email: its@library.utoronto.ca

Innis College Library, Library Technician, Leonard Ferstman, 416/978-4497

Institute for Aerospace Studies, Librarian, Judy Mills, 416/667-7712

Institute for Policy Analysis Library, Ursula Gutenburg, 416/978-8623

Jean and Dorothy Newman Industrial Relations Library, Head Librarian, Elizabeth Perry, 416/978-2928

Knox College Library, Readers Services, Kathleen Gibson, 416/978-6719

Language Teaching Resource Library, Alice Weinrib, 416/923-6641, ext.2646

Mathematics Library, Librarian, Chibeck Graham, 416/978-8624

Media Centre, Director, Michael T. Edmunds, 416/978-6049

Music Library, Librarian, Kathleen McMorrow, 416/978-3734

New College Library, Librarian, Jeanne Guillaume, 416/978-2493

Noranda Earth Sciences Library, Librarian, Jenny Mendelsohn, 416/978-3024
Petro Jacyk Central and East European Resource Centre, Librarian, Sofija Skoric, 416/978-0588, Email: pjrc@vax.library.utoronto.ca
Physics Library, Librarian, Barbara Chu, 416/978-5188
Pontifical Institute of Mediaeval Studies Library, Chief Librarian, James K. Farge, CSB, 416/926-7146
R.O. Hurst Pharmacy Library, Librarian, S.P. Newman, 416/978-2872
Regis College, Librarian, Barbara Geiger, 416/922-0536
Robertson Davies (Massey College) Library, Librarian, Marie Korey, 416/978-2893
St. Michael's College Library, Chief Librarian, Louise Girard, 416/926-7114
Thomas Fisher Rare Book Library, Director, Richard Landon, 416/978-5285
Trinity College Library, College Librarian, Linda W. Corman, 416/978-2653
University College Library, Librarian, Carolyn Murray, 416/978-8107
Victoria University Libraries, Chief Librarian, Dr. Robert C. Brandeis, 416/585-4470
Women's Educational Resources Centre, Coordinator, Frieda Forman, 416/926-4706
Wycliffe College Library, Librarian, Cindy Derrenbacker, 416/979-2870, ext.37
Zoology Library, Kim Gallant, 416/978-3515

University of Toronto at Scarborough - V.W. Bladen Library, 1265 Military Trail, Scarborough ON M1C 1A4 – 416/287-7508; Fax: 416/287-7507; Email: miller@macpost.scar.utoronto.ca; URL: http://library.scar.utoronto.ca/; Symbol: OTSCC – Chief Librarian, M. Miller, 416/287-7497

Urban Alliance on Race Relations – Library, #202, 675 King St. West, Toronto ON M5V 1M9 – 416/703-6607; Fax: 416/703-4415

VideoFACT, A Foundation to Assist Canadian Talent – Resource Centre, #508, 151 John St., Toronto ON M5V 2T2 – 416/596-8696; Fax: 416/596-6861

Vision Institute of Canada – Bobier-Fisher-Lyle Vision Science Library, York Mills Centre, #110, 16 York Mills Rd., North York ON M2P 2E5 – 416/224-2273; Fax: 416/224-9234 – Dr. C. Chiarelli

Visual Arts Ontario – Resource Library, 439 Wellington St. West, 3rd Fl., Toronto ON M5V 1E7 – 416/591-8883; Fax: 416/591-2432

Voice for Hearing Impaired Children – Library, #420, 124 Eglinton Ave. West, Toronto ON M4R 2G8 – 416/487-7719; Fax: 416/487-7423 – Executive Assistant, Kathy Antaya

Volunteer Centre of Metro Toronto – Resource Centre on Volunteerism, #207, 344 Bloor St. West, Toronto ON M5S 3A7 – 416/961-6888 – Administrative Assistant, Shani Doucet

Warner-Lambert Canada Inc. - Scientific Information Centre, 2200 Eglinton Ave. East, Scarborough ON M1L 2N3 – 416/288-2200; Fax: 416/288-2174 – Philloza Suleman

Waterfront Regeneration Trust - Library, Box 129, #580, 207 Queens Quay West, Toronto ON M5J 1A7 – 416/314-4660; Fax: 416/314-9497; Email: info@wrtrust.com – Librarian, Janet Hollingsworth

Watts, Griffis & McOuat Ltd. - Library, #400, 8 King St. East, Toronto ON M5C 1B5 – 416/364-6244; Fax: 416/864-1675; Email: wgmtor@ican.net – Librarian, A. Street-Bishop

Weir & Foulds Law Office - Library, Exchange Tower, 2 First Canadian Pl., POBox 480, Toronto ON M5X 1J5 – 416/947-5057; Fax: 416/365-1876; Symbol: OTWF
Librarian, Jim Spence, Email: spencej@weirfoulds.com
Assistant Librarian, Theresa Kennedy, Email: kennedyt@weirfoulds.com

The Wellesley Central Hospital - Wellesley Site – Library, 160 Wellesley St. East, Toronto ON M4Y 1J3 – 416/926-7071; Fax: 416/926-4908; Email: WELLESLEY.LIBRARY – Manager, Library Services, Verla Empey

William M. Mercer Limited - Information/Research Centre, BCE Place, Box 501, 161 Bay St., Toronto ON M5J 2S5 – 416/868-2005; Fax: 416/868-7002
Manager, Merle J. Ramdial, 416/868-7697
Reference Librarian, Jo-Anne Weiler
Technical Services Librarian, Lise McLeod

The Women & Environments Education & Development Foundation – WEED Resource Centre, 736 Bathurst St., Toronto ON M5S 2R4 – 416/516-2600; Fax: 416/531-6214 – Office Manager, Jennifer Jackson

Women's Art Resource Centre – Library, #389, 401 Richmond St. West, Toronto ON M5V 3A8 – 416/977-0097; Fax: 416/977-7425

Women's College Hospital – Library, 76 Grenville St., Toronto ON M5S 1B2 – 416/323-6078; Fax: 416/323-7311 – Librarian, Shahida Rashid

Women's Inter-Church Council of Canada, #402, 815 Danforth Ave., Toronto ON M4J 1L2 – 416/462-2528; Fax: 416/462-3915

Women's Legal Education & Action Fund – Library, #403, 489 College St., Toronto ON M6G 1A5 – 416/963-9654; Fax: 416/963-8455

Workers' Compensation Appeals Tribunal - Library, 505 University Ave., 7th Fl., Toronto ON M5G 1X4 – 416/598-4638, ext.203; Fax: 416/326-3558; URL: http://www.wcat.on.ca; Symbol: OTWCA
Reference Librarian, Felicity Fowke
Reference Librarian, Trevor Hennig

Workers' Compensation Board - Reference Library, 200 Front St. West, Toronto ON M5V 3J1 – 416/927-4972, 3667; Fax: 416/927-4995 – Coordinator, Angela Osterreiche

World Trade Centre Toronto – International Trade Library, First Canadian Place, POBox 375, Toronto ON M5X 1E2 – 416/366-6811; Fax: 416/366-4906

Wyatt Company - Canadian Research & Information Centre, #1210, 1 Queen St. East, Toronto ON M5C 2Y1 – 416/594-5811; Fax: 416/862-2193 – Librarian, Janice Sipus

Wyeth-Ayerst Canada - Medical Library, POBox 370, North York ON M3M 3A8 – 416/225-7500; Fax: 416/225-6111; Toll Free: 1-800-268-1946 – Drug Information & Surveillance, Manager, Shamim Jamal-Rajan

York Board of Education - Professional Library, 2 Trethewey Dr., Toronto ON M6M 4A8 – 416/394-2168; Fax: 416/394-3397
Head Librarian, Sheila Moll
Head Librarian, Pat Steenbergen

York-Finch General Hospital – Thomas J. Malcho Memorial Library, 2111 Finch Ave. West, Downsview ON M3N 1N1 – 416/744-2500; Fax: 416/747-3872; Symbol: OTYF – Coordinator, Hospital Library, Mona Frantzke

York Pioneer & Historical Society – Library, 2482 Yonge St., POBox 45026, Toronto ON M4P 3E3 – 416/489-4188 – Archivist, Paul Litt

York University - Libraries, 4700 Keele St., North York ON M3J 1P3 – 416/736-5601; Fax: 416/736-5451; URL: http://www.library.yorku.ca
University Librarian, Ellen Hoffmann, 416/736-5601
Acquisitions, Head, Karen Cassel
Bibliographic Services, Head, Dale Irwin
Business & Government Publications Library, Head, Elizabeth Watson, 416/736-5139
Circulation, Head, Linda Hansen
Library Computing Services, Director, Robert Thompson, 416/736-5601
Library Computing, Manager, Doug Fenwick
Library Facilities, Head, John Thompson
Public Services, Associate University Librarian, Toni Olshen
Technical Services, Associate University Librarian, Vale Irwin
Law Library, Librarian, Balfour J. Halévy, 416/736-5587
Leslie Frost Library, Glendon Campus, Head, Julianna Drexler, 416/487-6729
Steacie Science Library, Brian Wilks, 416/736-5639

York University Staff Association – Library, Suite F, East Office Bldg., 4700 Keele St., North York ON M3J 1P3 – 416/736-5109; Fax: 416/736-5519

Youth Assisting Youth – Resource Library, #4080, 3080 Yonge St., Toronto ON M4N 3N1 – 416/932-1919 – Program Director, Robert Mout

## UXBRIDGE

Nuclear Awareness Project – Library, POBox 104, Uxbridge ON L9P 1M6 – 905/852-0571; Fax: 905/852-0571 – Irene Kock

## VANIER

Fédération des caisses populaires de l'Ontario – Bibliothèque, 214, ch Montreal, Vanier ON K1L 8L8 – 613/789-7777, poste 622; Téléc: 613/746-3063 – Ginette Gagnon

Fédération canadienne pour l'alphabétisation en français – Bibliothèque, #205, 235, ch Montréal, Vanier ON K1L 6C7 – 613/749-5333; Téléc: 613/749-2252 – Luce Lapierre

## VERNON

Osgoode Twp. Historical Society – Museum Archives, POBox 74, Vernon ON K0A 3J0 – 613/821-4062 – Archivist, Donna Bowen

## VINELAND STATION

Horticultural Research Institute of Ontario – Library, POBox 7000, Vineland Station ON L0R 2E0 – 905/562-4141, ext.131; Fax: 905/562-3413; Email: wannerj@gov.on.ca – Librarian, Judith Wanner

## WALKERTON

Bruce Law Association – Courthouse Library, 215 Cayley St., POBox 818, Walkerton ON N0G 2V0 – 519/881-2384; Fax: 519/881-2384 – Librarian, Laurie McDonald

## WATERLOO

Canadian Association for Music Therapy – CAMT Library, Wilfrid Laurier University, 75 University Ave. West, Waterloo ON N2L 3C5 – 519/884-1970, ext.6828; Fax: 519/884-8853; Toll Free: 1-800-996-2268 – Administrative Coordinator, Lynda Tracy

Canadian Industrial Innovation Centre – Library, 156 Columbia St. West, Waterloo ON N2L 3L3 – 519/885-5870; Fax: 519/885-5729; Toll Free: 1-800-265-4559

Conrad Grebel College - Library, 84 Waterloo University Campus, Waterloo ON N2L 3G6 – 519/885-0220, ext.239; Fax: 519/885-0014 – Librarian, Sam Steiner, Email: steiner@library.uwaterloo.ca

Ecologistics Ltd. – Library, #A1, 490 Dutton Dr., Waterloo ON N2L 6H7 – 519/886-0522; Fax: 519/888-7864 – Library Manager, Brenda Fansher

Global Community Centre – Library, #89, 91 King St. North, Waterloo ON N2J 2X3 – 519/746-4090; Fax: 519/746-4096 – Resources Coordinator, Lucy Harrison

Kitchener-Waterloo Vegetarian Association – Library, 103 Marshall St., Waterloo ON N2J 2T5 – 519/747-0870 – Librarian, Dianne Meloun

Manulife Securities International Ltd. – Law Library, 500 King St. North, Waterloo ON N2J 4C6 – 519/

747-7000, ext.6240; Fax: 519/747-6325; Toll Free: 1-800-265-7401 – Law Librarian, Diana Robertson

Mutual Life of Canada - Business Information Service, 227 King St. South, Waterloo ON N2J 4C5 – 519/888-2262; Fax: 519/888-3899
- Corporate Archivist/Librarian, Nancy Maitland, 519/888-2769, Email: 102232.2046@compuserve.com
- Library Coordinator, Marianna Martisek, 519/888-2262, Email: 102232.2047@compuserve.com

The Network: Interaction for Conflict Resolution – Library, Conrad Grebel College, 84 Waterloo University Campus, Waterloo ON N2L 3G6 – 519/885-0880; Fax: 519/885-0806 – Coordinator, Jennifer Newcombe

Ontario Numismatic Association – Library, PO Box 40033, Stn Waterloo Square, Waterloo ON N2J 4V1 – 519/745-3104 – Librarian, T. Masters

Ontario Public Interest Research Group - Waterloo – Library, University of Waterloo, 200 University Ave. West, Waterloo ON N2L 3G1 – 519/888-4882; Fax: 519/746-6530

Project Ploughshares – Library, Institute of Peace & Conflict Studies, Conrad Grebel College, 84 Waterloo University Campus, Waterloo ON N2L 3G6 – 519/888-6541; Fax: 519/885-0806 – Program Associate, Bill Robinson

Renison College - Library, Westmount Rd. North, Waterloo ON N2L 3G4 – 519/884-4404, ext.646; Email: JEGMITCHELL@RENISON.watstar.uwaterloo.ca – Librarian, Jane Mitchell

St. Jerome's College - Library, 81 Waterloo University Campus, Waterloo ON N2L 3G3 – 519/884-8110, ext.285; Fax: 519/884-5759; Email: dgdraper@library.uwaterloo.ca – Librarian, Dr. Gary Draper

University of Waterloo - Library, 200 University Ave. West, Waterloo ON N2L 3G1 – 519/888-4567, ext.2282; Fax: 519/747-4606; Email: liboff09@watserv1.uwaterloo.ca; URL: http://www.lib.uwaterloo.ca; Symbol: OWTU
- University Librarian, Murray C. Shepherd, 519/888-4567, ext.2281, Email: mcshephe@library.uwaterloo.ca
- Information Services & Systems, Associate Librarian, Mark Haslett, 519/888-4567, ext.3568, Email: mhaslett@library.uwaterloo.ca
- Library Resources Management, Coordinator, Lorraine Beattie, 519/888-4567, ext.2618, Email: lbeattie@library.uwaterloo.ca
- Special Collections, Head, Susan Bellingham, 519/888-4567, ext.3122, Email: sbelling@library.uwaterloo.ca
- Dana Porter Reference & Collections Development Dept., Head, Margaret Hendley, 519/888-4567, ext.3992, Email: mlhendle@library.uwaterloo.ca
- Davis Reference Centre, Head, Joan Macdonald, 519/888-4567, ext.3319, Email: jmacdona@library.uwaterloo.ca
- University Map & Design Library, Head, Richard Pinnell, 519/888-4567, ext.3412, Email: rhpinnel@library.uwaterloo.ca
- ILL/Document Delivery, Head, Faye Abrams, 519/888-4567, ext.3520, Email: fabrams@library.uwaterloo.ca
- Environment & Resource Studies, Liaison Librarian, Margaret Aquan-Yuen, 519/888-4567, ext.3783, Email: maquanyu@library.uwaterloo.ca
- Conrad Grebel College Library, Librarian & Archivist, Sam Steiner, 519/885-0220, Email: steiner@library.uwaterloo.ca
- Renison College Library, Librarian, Jane Mitchell, 519/884-4404, ext.646, Email: jegmitchell@renison.watstar.uwaterloo.ca
- St. Jerome's College Library, Dr. Gary Draper, 519/884-8110

Wilfrid Laurier University - Central Library, 75 University Ave., Waterloo ON N2L 3C5 – 519/884-0710, ext.3380; Fax: 519/884-8023; Email: 22ill@mach1.wlu.ca; URL: http://www.wlu.ca/~wwwlib; Symbol: OWTL
- University Librarian, Virginia Gillham
- Acquisitions/Bibliographic Searching, Head, John Arndt
- Cataloguing, Head, Brooke Skelton
- Access Services, Head, Vera Fesnak
- Documents & Serials, Head, Linda Cracknell
- Systems, Head, Herbert Schwartz
- Reference Department, Head, Diane Wilkins, 519/884-0710, ext.3417

#### WELLAND

Niagara College - Welland Campus Learning Resource Centre, POBox 1005, Welland ON L3B 5S2 – 416/735-2211; Fax: 416/735-5365

#### WHITBY

Durham Region Law Association – Durham District Courthouse Library, 605 Rossland Rd. East, Whitby ON L1N 5S4 – 905/668-2177; Fax: 905/668-0692 – Libarian, Monica Schjott

Whitby Mental Health Centre – Library, 700 Gordon St., POBox 613, Whitby ON L1N 5S9 – 905/430-4015; Fax: 905/430-4032; Email: wardc@wmhc1.moh.gov.on.ca – Librarian, Cathy Ward

#### WINDSOR

Canadian Association of Moldmakers – Library, 424 Tecumseh Rd. East, Windsor ON N8X 2R6 – 519/255-7863; Fax: 519/255-9446; Toll Free: 1-800-567-2266 – Executive Secretary, Patricia Papp

Essex Law Association – County Courthouse Library, 245 Windsor Ave., Windsor ON N9A 1J2 – 519/252-8418; Fax: 519/252-9686 – Doug Hewitt

Glos Engineering Ltd – Library, 3155 Huron Church Rd., Windsor ON N9E 4H6 – 519/966-6750; Fax: 519/966-6753 – Librarian, Jean-Guy Dupuis

Great Lakes United – Library, POBox 548, Windsor ON N9A 6M6 – 519/255-7141 – Associate Director, Mary Ginnebaugh

Hôtel Dieu Grace Hospital – Library, 1030 Ouellette Ave., Windsor ON N9A 1E1 – 519/255-2245; Fax: 519/255-2458 – Librarian, A. Henshaw

International Joint Commission - Reference Resource Centre, 100 Ouellette Ave., 8th Fl., Windsor ON N9A 6T3 – 519/257-6700; Fax: 519/257-6740; Symbol: OWIJC – Reference Resource Clerk, Mae Carter, 519/257-6702

John XXIII Centre - Library, 2275 Wellesley Ave., Windsor ON N8W 2G1 – 519/254-2090; Fax: 519/254-0330 – Librarian, J.A. Rocheleau

Paroian, Raphael, Courey, Cohen & Houston Law Office - Library, 875 Ouellette Ave., POBox 970, Windsor ON N9A 6S7 – 519/258-1166; Fax: 519/258-8361 – Clerk, Doye DeLauw

St. Clair College - Library Resource Centre, 2000 Talbot Rd., Windsor ON N9A 6S4 – 519/972-2739; Fax: 519/966-2737

University of Windsor - Leddy Library, 401 Sunset Ave., Windsor ON N9B 3P4 – 519/973-7023; Fax: 519/973-7076, 971-3638; URL: http://www.uwindsor.ca/library/leddy/; Symbol: OWA
- University Librarian, Gwendolyn Ebbett
- Associate University Librarian, Cynthia Archer
- University Archivist, Brian Owens
- Access Services, Head, Cathy Maskell
- Collections Services, Head, Martha Wolfe
- Reference Dept., Head, Joan Dalton
- Systems Dept., Head, Art Rhyno
- Paul Martin Law Library, Law Librarian, Prof. Paul Murphy

Windsor & District Chamber of Commerce – Library, 2575 Ouellette Place, Windsor ON N8X 1L9 – 519/966-3696; Fax: 519/966-0603

The Windsor Regional Hospital – Health Sciences Library - Metropolitan Campus, 1995 Lens Ave., Windsor ON N8W 1L9 – 519/254-5577, ext.2329; Fax: 519/254-3150 – Coordinator, Loretta Joyce Jewer
- Western Campus, 1453 Prince Rd., Windsor ON N9C 3Z4 – 519/257-5232, 257-2037; Fax: 519/257-5244; Email: jjewer@mnsi.net – Loretta Joyce Jewer

The Windsor Star - Library, 167 Ferry St., Windsor ON N9A 4M5 – 519/255-5711; Fax: 519/255-5515 – Metro Editor, Bill Hickey, 519/255-5714

#### WOODSTOCK

Oxford Law Association – Library, POBox 1029, Woodstock ON N4S 8A4 – 519/539-7711; Fax: 519/539-7962; Email: dlewis-lib@sympatico.ca – Librarian, Doreen Lewis

## PRINCE EDWARD ISLAND

### PEI Provincial Library System

#### PRINCE EDWARD ISLAND PROVINCIAL LIBRARY SERVICE

Red Head Rd., PO Box 7500, Morell PE C0A 1S0 – 902/961-7320; Fax: 902/961-7322; Email: plshq@gov.pe.ca; Symbol: PC

Director of Archives & Libraries, Harry Holman

Alberton Public Library, PO Box 449, Alberton PE C0B 1B0 – 902/853-3049 – Helen Wallace

Borden Public Library, Borden PE C0B 1X0 – 902/437-2225 – Sharon Leard

Breadalbane Public Library, Breadalbane PE C0A 1E0 – 902/964-2520 – Joan Sutton

Carrefour de l'Isle Saint-Jean, 5, rue Acadien, Charlottetown PE C1C 1M2 – 902/368-6092 – Linda Allain

Confederation Centre Public Library, PO Box 7000, Charlottetown PE C1A 8G8 – 902/368-4642; Fax: 902/368-4652; Email: ccpl@gov.pe.ca – Chief Librarian, Don Scott; Reference Librarian, Gary Ramsay; Children's Librarian, Barbara Kissick

Government Services Library, Basement, Shaw Bldg., PO Box 2000, Charlottetown PE C1A 7N8 – 902/368-4653 – Librarian, Nichola Cleaveland

Cornwall Public Library, Cornwall PE C0A 1H0 – 902/629-8415 – Elmer Power

Crapaud Public Library, PO Box 96, Crapaud PE C0A 1J0 – 902/658-2722 – Luann Molyneaux

Georgetown Public Library, Georgetown PE C0A 1L0 – 902/652-2832 – Brenda Batchilder

Hunter River Public Library, Hunter River PE C0A 1N0 – 902/964-2800 – Pam Wheatley

Kensington Public Library, PO Box 394, Kensington PE C0B 1M0 – 902/836-3721 – Mary McInnis

Kinkora Public Library, Kinkora PE C0B 1N0 – 902/887-2868 – Catherine Arsenault

Montague Public Library, PO Box 129, Montague PE C0A 1R0 – 902/838-2528 – Jane Harris

Morell Public Library, PO Box 7500, Morell PE C0A 1S0 – 902/961-7321 – Carol McGrath

Mount Stewart Public Library, Mount Stewart PE C0A 1T0 – Bertha Dennis

Murray Harbour Public Library, Murray Harbour PE C0A 1V0 – 902/962-3875 – Kaye MacLean

Murray River Public Library, Murray River PE C0A 1W0 – 902/962-2667 – Ruth Moore

O'Leary Public Library, O'Leary PE C0B 1V0 – 902/859-8788 – Verna Smallman

St. Peter's Public Library, St. Peter's Bay PE C0A 2A0 – 902/961-2268 – Ann MacInnis

Souris Public Library, PO Box 603, Souris PE C0A 2B0 – 902/687-2157 – Tina Davis

Rotary Regional Library, 192 Water St., Summerside PE C1N 1B1 – 902/436-7323; Fax: 902/888-8055 – Librarian, Johanne Jacob

Tignish Public Library, Tignish PE C0B 2B0 – 902/882-2681 – Dianne McCue

Tyne Valley Public Library, Tyne Valley PE C0B 2C0 – 902/831-2928 – Carolyn Millar

Abram Village Bibliothèque publique, c/o École Evangeline, RR#3, Wellington PE C0B 2E0 – 902/854-3077; Téléc: 902/854-3077 – Judith Arsenault; French Services Librarian, Johanne Jacob

### Special & College Libraries & Resource Centres

#### CHARLOTTETOWN

Agriculture & Agri-Food Canada-Charlottetown Research Centre – Agriculture & Agri-Food Canada Library, 440 University Ave., POBox 1210, Charlottetown PE C1A 7M8 – 902/566-6861; Fax: 902/566-6821; Email: stanfieldb@em.agr.ca; Symbol: PCAG – Librarian, Barrie Stanfield

Canadian Pension Commission - Policy Reference Library, POBox 9900, Charlottetown PE C1A 8V6 – 902/566-8870; Fax: 902/566-8879; Symbol: PCCP – Custodian, Kathy Stewart

Community Legal Information Association of Prince Edward Island – Library, Sullivan Building, #158, 20 Fitzroy, POBox 1207, Charlottetown PE C1A 7M8 – 902/892-0853; Fax: 902/368-4096

Confederation Centre Art Gallery & Museum - Resource Centre, 145 Richmond St., Charlottetown PE C1A 1J1 – 902/628-6111; Fax: 902/566-4648 – Director/Curator, Terry Graff, 902/628-6121

Farmer & MacLeod, Barristers, Solicitors, Notaries - Library, National Bank Tower, #605, 134 Kent St., POBox 2500, Charlottetown PE C1A 8C2 – 902/368-3733; Fax: 902/566-4265

Heart & Stroke Foundation of Prince Edward Island – Library, 40 Queen St., POBox 279, Charlottetown PE C1A 7K4 – 902/892-7441; Fax: 902/368-7068 – Education Director, Donalda Clow

Holland College - Library, Charlottetown Centre, 140 Weymouth St., Charlottetown PE C1A 4Z1 – 902/566-9558; Fax: 902/566-9505; Email: brady@vega.cc.hollandc.pe.ca; Symbol: PCHC – College Librarian, Brenda Brady
- Technology Centre Library, 40 Enman Cres., Charlottetown PE C1E 1E6 – 902/566-9358; Fax: 902/566-9355; Email: astewart@hollande.pe.ca – Manager, Andrea Stewart

Industry Canada - Business Service Centre, 75 Fitzroy St., POBox 40, Charlottetown PE C1A 7K2 – 902/368-0771; Fax: 902/566-7377; Toll Free: 1-800-668-1010; Email: pei@cbsc.ic.gc.ca; URL: http://www.cbsc.org/pei/

Institute for Bioregional Studies – Library, #126, 449 University Ave., Charlottetown PE C1A 8K3 – 902/892-9578

Law Society of Prince Edward Island – Law Library, 49 Water St., POBox 128, Charlottetown PE C1A 7K2 – 902/368-6099; Fax: 902/368-7557 – Librarian, Pamela Borden

Medical Society of Prince Edward Island – Library, 559 North River Rd., Charlottetown PE C1E 1J7 – 902/368-7303; Fax: 902/566-3934

PEI Council of the Arts – Library, 115 Richmond St., Charlottetown PE C1A 1H7 – 902/368-4410; Fax: 902/368-4418 – Administrative Assistant, Ferne Taylor

PEI Food Technology Centre - Library, POBox 2000, Charlottetown PE C1A 7N8 – 902/566-1725; Fax: 902/566-5627; Email: peiftc@peinet.pe.ca; URL: http://www.gov.pe.ca/info/ftc/; Symbol: PCFT
- Chief Librarian, Mary Jane Grant
- Acquisitions Librarian, Kathy MacEwen

PEI Government - Media Centre, Richmond St., Charlottetown PE C1A 1J1 – 902/368-4641, 4644; Fax: 902/368-4621 – Secretary, Rita Sahajpal

PEI Multicultural Council – Resource Centre, 115 Richmond St., 3rd Fl., POBox 1994, Charlottetown PE C1A 7N7 – 902/368-8393; Fax: 902/628-8717

Prince Edward Island Museum & Heritage Foundation – Library, 2 Kent St., Charlottetown PE C1A 1M6 – 902/368-6604; Fax: 902/368-6608 – Curator of History, Edward MacDonald

Prince Edward Island Teachers' Federation – Library, POBox 6000, Charlottetown PE C1A 8B4 – 902/569-4157; Fax: 902/569-3682

Queen Elizabeth Hospital – Frank J. MacDonald Library, POBox 6600, Charlottetown PE C1A 8T5 – 902/894-2371; Fax: 902/894-2385; Symbol: PCQEH – Librarian, Marion K. MacArthur

University of Prince Edward Island - Robertson Library, 550 University Ave., Charlottetown PE C1A 4P3 – 902/566-0696; Fax: 902/628-4305; Email: ENVOY: ILL.PCU; Symbol: PCU
- University Librarian, Daniel A. Savage
- Reference, Head, Cathy Callaghan, 902/566-0681
- Circulation Librarian, Sharon Neill, 902/566-0581
- Special Collection Librarian, Frank Pigot, 902/566-0536
- Systems Librarian, Suzanne Jones, 902/566-0393
- Collections Librarian, Corine Hanns, 902/566-0479
- Cataloguing Librarian, Janet Arsenault, 902/566-0741
- Reference Librarian, Jennifer Taylor, 902/566-0453
- Periodicals Librarian, Cathy Dillon, 902/566-0556

Veterans Affairs Canada - Library, POBox 7700, Charlottetown PE C1A 8M9 – 902/566-8988; Fax: 902/566-8508; Email: jgaudet@peinet.pe.ca; Symbol: PCV – Librarian, Joyce Gaudet

#### SHERWOOD

Prince Edward Island Humane Society – Library, POBox 20022, Sherwood PE C1A 9E3 – 902/892-1190; Fax: 902/892-1190; Toll Free: 1-800-892-1191

#### SUMMERSIDE

Holland College - Harbourside Centre Library, 298 Water St., Summerside PE C1N 1B8 – 902/888-6452; Fax: 902/888-6401; Email: lykow@harbour.hc.hollandc.pe.ca – Manager, Jean Lykow

Prince County Hospital – Medical Library, 259 Beattie Ave., Summerside PE C1A 2A9 – 902/436-9131; Fax: 902/436-1501 – Health Records Administrator, Joy Jenkins

## QUÉBEC

### Centres régionaux de services aux bibliothèques publiques (CRSBP)

Abitibi-Témiscamingue: CRSBP de l'Abitibi-Témiscamingue, 20, boul Québec, Rouyn-Noranda QC J9X 2E6 – 819/762-4305; Téléc: 819/797-1161; URL: http://www.crsbpat.qc.ca – Directeur général, Norman Fink, Email: norman.fink@crsbpat.qc.ca; Responsable des services administratifs, Lydia Turgeon, Email: lydia.turgeon@crsbpat.qc.ca; Responsable des services techniques, Monic Frigon, Email: monic.frigon@crsbpat.qc.ca; Responsable du soutien professionel, Chantal Baril, Email: chantal.baril@crsbpat.qc.ca

Alma: CRSBP de Saguenay-Lac-St-Jean, 100, rue Price ouest, Alma QC G8B 4S1 – 418/662-6425; Téléc: 418/662-7593; URL: http://www.crsbpslsj.biblio.qc.ca – Directrice générale, Johanne Belley, Email: johanne@crsbpslsj.biblio.qc.ca

Charny: CRSBP Régions de Québec-Chaudière-Appalaches, 3189, av Albert-Demers, Charny QC G6X 3A1 – 418/832-6166; Téléc: 418/832-6168; Courrier électronique: info@crsbp-qca.qc.ca; Symbol: CRSBP-RQCA – Directeur général, Réal Messier; Public Services Librarian, Denis Gravel; Acquisitions Librarian, Lucie Gobeil

Côte-Nord: CRSBP de la Côte-Nord, 59, rue Napoléon, Sept-Îles QC G4R 5C5 – 418/962-1020; Téléc: 418/962-5124; Courrier électronique: crsbpcn@quebectel.com; URL: http://www.quebectel.com/crsbpcn/ – Directeur général, Jean-Roch Gagnon; Secrétaire administrative, Sylvie Landry

Estrie: CRSBP Estrie, 4155, rue Brodeur, Sherbrooke QC J1L 1K4 – 819/565-9744 – Administrateur délégué, Normand Bernier

Gaspésie: CRSBP de Gaspésie-Îles-de-la-Madeleine, 31, rue des Écoliers, CP 340, Cap-Chat QC G0J 1E0 – 418/786-5597; Téléc: 418/786-2024; Courrier électronique: grochett@quebectel.com; URL: http://www.quebectel.com/crsbp/ – Directeur général, Gilles Rochette

Laurentides: CRSBP des Laurentides, 29, rue Brissette, CP 239, Ste-Agathe-des-Monts QC J8C 3A3 – 819/326-6440; Téléc: 819/326-0885; URL: http://www.crsbpl.qc.ca – Directeur général, Marcel Bouchard

Mauricie: CRSBP de Mauricie, 3125, rue Girard, Trois-Rivières QC G8Z 2M4 – 819/375-9623; Téléc: 819/375-0132 – Administrateur délégué, Pierre L'Hérault; Public Services Librarian, Judith Dansereau; Technical Services/Acquisitions Librarian, Sonia Loubier

Montérégie: CRSBP de la Montérégie, 275, rue Conrad-Pelletier, La Prairie QC J5R 4V1 – 514/444-5433; Téléc: 514/659-3364; Courrier électronique: info.biblio@monteregie.crsbp.qc.ca; URL: http://www.iti.qc.ca/iti/users/crsbp-mont/index.html – Administrateur délégué, Richard Boivin; Responsable du développement des bibliothèques affiliées, Claire Dionne; Responsable de la gestion des systèmes d'information, Jacqueline Labelle

Outaouais: CRSBP de l'Outaouais, 736, av Principale, Gatineau QC J8T 5L8 – 819/561-6008; Téléc: 819/561-6767; Courrier électronique: biblio@crspbo.qc.ca; URL: http://www.crsbpo.qc.ca; Symbol: CRSBPO – Directrice générale, Hélène Arseneau; Technical Services & Acquisitions Librarian, Danielle Sauvé

Portages: CRSBP du Bas-Saint-Laurent, 465, rue St-Pierre, Rivière-du-Loup QC G5R 4T6 – 418/867-1682; Téléc: 418/867-3434 – Directeur général, Yves Savard

### Bibliothèques publiques

Alma: Bibliothèque municipale d'Alma, 500, rue Collard ouest, Alma QC G8B 1N2 – 418/669-5139; Téléc: 418/669-5089; URL: http://www.alma.biblio.qc.ca; Symbol: QA – Responsable, Martin Bouchard

Amos: Bibliothèque municipale d'Amos, 222 - 1e avenue est, Amos QC J9T 1H3 – 819/732-6070; Téléc: 819/732-3242; Courrier électronique: bibliotheque@ville.amos.qc.ca – Bibliothécaire, Jean Chabot

Amqui: Bibliothèque municipale d'Amqui, 24, promenade de l'Hôtel de Ville, CP 1628, Amqui QC G0J 1B0 – 418/629-4216; Téléc: 418/629-4090; Courrier électronique: biblio@quebectel.com – Responsable, Marie Côté

Anjou: Bibliothèque municipale d'Anjou, 7500, av Goncourt, Anjou QC H1K 3X9 – 514/493-8270; Téléc: 514/493-8273; Symbol: QAN – Chef de division/Bibliothèque, Marie-Thérèse Stephen, M. Bibl.; Public Services Librarian, Ivan Filion;

Technical Services Librarian, Sylvaine Tétreault – See also following branches: Succursale de la Bibliothèque d'Anjou

Anjou: Succursale de la Bibliothèque d'Anjou, 7070, rue Jarry est, Anjou QC H1J 1G2 – 514/493-8271 – Branch of Bibliothèque municipale d'Anjou

Arthabaska: Succursale Alcide-Fleury, 841, boul Bois-Francs Sud, Arthabaska QC G6P 5W3 – 819/357-8240; Téléc: 819/357-2099 – Branch of Bibliothèque Charles-Édouard-Mailhot

Asbestos: Bibliothèque municipale d'Asbestos, 187, rue du Roi, CP 117, Asbestos QC J1T 1S4 – 819/879-4363; Téléc: 819/879-2343; Courrier électronique: bibliasb@interlinx.qc.ca – Responsable, Julie Fontaine

Aylmer: Bibliothèque municipale d'Aylmer, 120, rue Principale, Aylmer QC J9H 3M3 – 819/685-5005, poste 4700; Téléc: 819/685-5038; URL: http://WWW.OUTAOUAIS.NET/biblioaylmer/; Symbol: QAY – Bibliothécaire, Guy Dubois

Baie-Comeau: Bibliothèque municipale de Baie-Comeau, 6, av Radisson, Baie-Comeau QC G42 1W4 – 418/296-8305; Téléc: 418/296-3759; Symbol: QBCM – Responsable, Joan Sirois

Baie-d'Urfé: Bibliothèque Baie-d'Urfé Library, 20551, ch Bord du Lac, Baie-d'Urfé QC H9X 1R3 – 514/457-3274 – President, Ray Tunmer; Children's Librarian, G. Berard; Technical Services Librarian, D. Stanmers; Acquisitions Librarian, E. Wells

Beaconsfield: Bibliothèque municipale de Beaconsfield, 303, boul Beaconsfield, Beaconsfield QC H9W 4A7 – 514/428-4466; Téléc: 514/428-4477 – Responsable, Linda Burdayron

Beauharnois: Bibliothèque municipale de Beauharnois, 600, rue Ellice, Beauharnois QC J6N 3P7 – 514/429-3546; Téléc: 514/429-6663 – Responsable, Marielle Groulx

Beauport: Bibliothèque municipale de Beauport, 3095, ch Royal, CP 5187, Beauport QC G1E 6P4 – 418/666-2188; Téléc: 418/666-6173 – Denis Couture – See also following branches: Bibliothèque Étienne-Parent, Bibliothèque Succursale

Beauport: Bibliothèque Étienne-Parent, 3515, Clémenceau, CP 5187, Beauport QC G1E 6P4 – Branch of Bibliothèque municipale de Beauport

Beauport: Bibliothèque Succursale, 3095, ch Royal, CP 5187, Beauport QC G1E 6P4 – Branch of Bibliothèque municipale de Beauport

Bécancour: Bibliothèque municipale de Bécancour, 1295, av Nicolas-Perrot, Bécancour QC G0X 1B0 – 819/294-6500; Téléc: 819/294-6535; Symbol: QBEC – Bibliothécaire, Johane Aubry – See also following branches: Bibliothèque municipale de Gentilly, Bibliothèque municipale de Précieux-Sang, Bibliothèque municipale de St-Grégoire, Bibliothèque municipale de Ste-Angèle-de-Laval, Bibliothèque municipale de Ste-Gertrude

Bellefeuille: Bibliothèque publique de Bellefeuille, 450, boul La Salette, Bellefeuille QC J0R 1A0 – 514/432-1226; Téléc: 514/565-2920; Courrier électronique: belfbibl@citenet.net – Responsable, Claudine Richer

Beloeil: Bibliothèque municipale de Beloeil, 620, rue Richelieu, Beloeil QC J3G 5E8 – 514/467-7872; Téléc: 514/467-3257 – Directrice du Service de la bibliothèque, Johanne Guevremont

Black Lake: Bibliothèque publique de Black Lake, 302, rue St-Désiré, Black Lake QC G0N 1A0 – 418/423-4291; Téléc: 418/423-4909 – Responsable, Claude Matte

Blainville: Bibliothèque municipale de Blainville, 980, ch du Plan-Bouchard, Blainville QC J7C 3S9 – 514/434-5370; Téléc: 514/434-5378 – Directrice, Maud Lefebvre

Bois-des-Filion: Bibliothèque publique de Bois-des-Filion, 60, 36e av sud, Bois-des-Filion QC J6Z 3S8 – 514/621-2041; Téléc: 514/621-8483 – Responsable, Marc Bineault

Boisbriand: Bibliothèque de Boisbriand, 901, boul de la Grande Allée, Boisbriand QC J7G 1W6 – 514/435-7466; Téléc: 514/435-0627 – Bibliothécaire, Ghislaine Lauzon

Boucherville: Bibliothèque Montarville-Boucher-De la Bruère, 501, ch du Lac, Boucherville QC J4B 6V6 – 514/449-8353; Téléc: 514/449-6865 – Directeur, Sylvie Provost

Brossard: Bibliothèque municipale Brossard, 3200, boul Lapinière, Brossard QC J4Z 2L4 – 514/923-7045; Téléc: 514/926-7908; Symbol: QB – Directrice, Danielle Champagne; Reference Librarian, Brigitte Gagnon; Technical Services Librarian, Sylvie Morin; Acquisitions Librarian, Patricia Lemieux

Buckingham: Bibliothèque municipale de Buckingham, 181, rue Joseph, Buckingham QC J8L IG6 – 819/986-4211; Téléc: 819/986-4206 – Responsable, Lise Robitaille

Candiac: Bibliothèque municipale Candiac, #100, 4, boul Montcalm nord, Candiac QC J5R 3M2 – 514/444-6030; Téléc: 514/444-6039; Courrier électronique: biblio.candiac@sympatico.ca – Responsable, Maryse St-Onge-Hansen

Cap-de-la-Madeleine: Bibliothèque municipale de Cap-de-la-Madeleine, 70, rue Saint-Pierre, CP 368, Cap-de-la-Madeleine QC G8T 6V8 – 819/378-8826; Téléc: 819/378-5539 – Bibliothécaire, Francine Marcouiller

Cap-Rouge: Bibliothèque municipale de Cap-Rouge, 4705, rue de la Promenade-des-Soeurs, Cap-Rouge QC G1Y 2W2 – 418/650-7501; Téléc: 418/650-7795 – Responsable, Lucie Dion

Chambly: Bibliothéque municipale Chambly, 1691, rue Bourgogne, Chambly QC J3L 1Y8 – 514/658-2711; Téléc: 514/447-4525 – Bibliotechnicienne, Carole Mainville-Beriault

Charlesbourg: Bibliothèque municipale de Charlesbourg, 7950, 1e av, Charlesbourg QC G1H 2Y4 – 418/624-7742; Téléc: 418/624-7886; Courrier électronique: biblio2@total.net – Activités culturelles, Chef de division, Constance Grégoire; Services publiques, Chef de section, Lina Rousseau; Services techniques, Technicienne principale, Sylvie Brown

Charny: Bibliothèque Marguerite-Yourcenar, 2504, av du Viaduc, Charny QC G6X 2V3 – 418/832-7620; Téléc: 418/832-9286 – Responsable, Jacques Rochette

Châteauguay: Bibliothèque municipale de Châteauguay, 15, boul Maple, Châteauguay QC J6J 3P7 – 514/698-3095; Téléc: 514/698-3109 – Responsable, Céline Lussier

Chibougamau: Bibliothèque municipale de Chibougamau, 601, 3e rue, Chibougamau QC G8P 3A2 – 418/748-2497; Téléc: 418/748-6562 – Responsable, Lise Matte

Chicoutimi: Bibliothèque publique de Chicoutimi, 155, rue Racine est, Chicoutimi QC G7H 5B8 – 418/698-5350; Téléc: 418/698-5359; Courrier électronique: martine@chicoutimi.biblio.qc.ca; URL: http://www.chicoutimi.biblio.qc.ca – Régisseur, Andre Y. Duchesne

Coaticook: Bibliothèque publique de Coaticook, 34, rue Main est, Coaticook QC J1A 1N2 – 819/849-4013; Téléc: 819/849-7918; Courrier électronique: ggrenier@cscoaticook.qc.ca; URL: http://www.cscoaticook.qc.ca/biblcoat/index.html – Directrice, Ginette Grenier

Contrecoeur: Bibliothèque municipale de Contrecoeur, 4970, rue Marie-Victorin, Contrecoeur QC J0L 1C0 – 514/587-8145; Téléc: 514/587-5855 – Responsable, Martine Tremblay

Côte-St-Luc: Bibliothèque municipale de Côte-Saint-Luc, 5851, boul Cavendish, Côte-St-Luc QC H4W 2X8 – 514/485-6900; Téléc: 514/485-6966; Symbol: QMCSL – Director, Eleanor London

Cowansville: Bibliothèque municipale de Cowansville, 175, rue Principale, Cowansville QC J2K 1T4 – 514/263-4071; Téléc: 514/263-9357 – Responsable, Anne-Marie Landry

Deux-Montagnes: Bibliothèque municipale de Deux-Montagnes, 200, rue Henri-Dunant, Deux-Montagnes QC J7R 4W6 – 514/473-2702; Téléc: 514/473-2816; Courrier électronique: bibdm@videotron.net – Director, Johanne Chaput

Dolbeau: Bibliothèque municipale de Dolbeau, 175, 4ieme av, Dolbeau QC G8L 2W6 – 418/276-5169; Téléc: 418/276-8188; Courrier électronique: lapointe@dolbeau.biblio.qc.ca – Directrice, Pauline Lapointe

Dollard-des-Ormeaux: Bibliothèque intermunicipale de Dollard-des-Ormeaux, 12001, boul de Salaberry, Dollard-des-Ormeaux QC H9B 2A7 – 514/684-1496; Téléc: 514/684-9184 – Bibliothécaire, Michèle Dupuy

Dorval: Bibliothèque municipale de Dorval, 1401, ch Bord-du-Lac, Dorval QC H9S 2E5 – 514/633-4170; Téléc: 514/633-4177; Courrier électronique: dorval@total.net; Symbol: QD – Manager, Jill Roberts; Reference Librarian, Cathy Maxwell; Public Services Librarian, Gail Warren; Technical Services Librarian, Roland Guerin; Technical Services Librarian, Roland Guerin – See also following branches: Surrey Branch

Dorval: Surrey Branch, 1945 Parkfield Ave., Dorval QC H9P 1X5 – 514/633-4072; Fax: 514/633-4165 – Manager, Jill Roberts – Branch of Bibliothèque municipale de Dorval

Drummondville: Centre d'information documentaire Côme-Saint-Germain, 545, rue des Écoles, Drummondville QC J2B 1J6 – 819/474-8881; Téléc: 819/478-0399; Symbol: CID – Responsable, Pierre Meunier

Farnham: Bibliothèque publique de Farnham, 479, rue Hôtel-de-Ville nord, Farnham QC J2N 2H3 – 514/293-3375; Téléc: 514/293-2989 – Responsable, Lise Gagnon

Fermont: Bibliothèque publique de Fermont, CP 10, Fermont QC G0G 1J0 – 418/287-3227; Téléc: 418/287-3274 – Responsable, Rose Vaillancourt

Gatineau: Bibliothèque municipale de Gatineau, 855, boul de la Gappe, Gatineau QC J8T 8H9 – 819/243-2506; Téléc: 819/243-2569; Courrier électronique: biblio@ville.gatineau.qc.ca; URL: http://www.ville.gatineau.qc.ca/biblio – Chef de la division, Paule Brochu; Responsable des services techniques, François Gagnon; Responsable des services au public, Nicole Proulx – See also following branches: Succursale de la Riviera, Succursale Docteur-Jean-Lorrain

Gatineau: Succursale de la Riviera, Centre communautaire de la Riviera, 12, rue de Picardie, Gatineau QC J8T 1N9 – 819/243-2543 – Branch of Bibliothèque municipale de Gatineau

Gatineau: Succursale Docteur-Jean-Lorrain, 20, boul Lorrain, Gatineau QC J8T 2C8 – 819/669-5201 – Branch of Bibliothèque municipale de Gatineau

Gentilly: Bibliothèque municipale de Gentilly, 1920, boul Bécancour, Gentilly QC G0X 1G0 – 819/298-3948 – Bénévole responsable, Lise Emond – Branch of Bibliothèque municipale de Bécancour

Granby: Bibliothèque municipale de Granby, 11, rue Dufferin, Granby QC J2G 4W5 – 514/776-8310; Téléc: 514/776-8211 – Service technique et informatique, Coordonnatrice, Réjeanne Rheault

Grand'Mère: Bibliothèque Hélène-B.-Beauséjour, 650 - 8e rue, Grand'Mère QC G9T 6K1 – 819/538-5555 – Librarian, Janine Vaugeois-Patry

Greenfield Park: Bibliothèque municipale de Greenfield Park, 225, av Empire, Greenfield Park QC J4V 1T9 – 514/672-7500; Téléc: 514/671-0517 – Librarian, Linda Travis

Hull: Bibliothèque municipale de Hull, 25, rue Laurier, CP 1970, Succ. B, Hull QC J8X 3Y9 – 819/595-7460;

Téléc: 819/595-7487; Courrier électronique: BMH; Symbol: QH – Librarian, Denis Boyer; Public Services Librarian, Pierre Tessier; Acquisitions, Francine Chevrier – See also following branches: Succursale Aurélien-Doucet, Succursale Lucien-Lalonde

Hull: Succursale Aurélien-Doucet, 207, boul du Mont-Bleu, Hull QC J8Z 3G3 – 819/595-7490; Téléc: 819/595-7376 – Responsable, Denis Boyer – Branch of Bibliothèque municipale de Hull

Hull: Succursale Lucien-Lalonde, 225, rue Berri, Hull QC J8Y 4K1 – 819/595-7480; Téléc: 819/595-7479 – Responsable, Denis Boyer – Branch of Bibliothèque municipale de Hull

Île-Bizard: Bibliothèque municipale de St-Raphaël-de-l'Île-Bizard, 500, rue de l'Église, Île-Bizard QC H9C 1G9 – 514/620-6331; Téléc: 514/620-4153 – Responsable, Louise-Hélène Lefebvre

Joliette: Bibliothèque de la Maison de la culture Bonsecours, 585, rue Archambault, Joliette QC J6E 2W7 – 514/755-6400; Téléc: 514/755-6426; Courrier électronique: bibliojoliette.qc.ca; URL: http://www.bibliojoliette.qc.ca – Responsable, Chantal Émard

Jonquière: Bibliothèque municipale de Jonquière, 2850, Place Davis, CP 2000, Jonquière QC G7X 7W7 – 418/699-6068; Téléc: 418/699-6046; Courrier électronique: boudreau@jonquiere.biblio.qc.ca; URL: http://www.jonquiere.biblio.qc.ca – Chef de division bibliothèques, Mireille Boudreault – See also following branches: Succursale Kenogami, Succursale St-Michel

Jonquière: Succursale Kenogami, 3750, boul du Royaume, CP 2000, Jonquière QC G7X 7W7 – 418/546-2175 – Responsable, Pierre Côté – Branch of Bibliothèque municipale de Jonquière

Jonquière: Succursale St-Michel, 3885, boul Harvey, CP 2000, Jonquière QC G7X 7W7 – 418/546-2173 – Responsable, Suzanne Potvin – Branch of Bibliothèque municipale de Jonquière

Kirkland: Bibliothèque municipale de Kirkland, 17100, boul Hymus, Kirkland QC H9J 2W2 – 514/630-2726; Téléc: 514/630-2716; Courrier électronique: kirkev@cam.org; Symbol: QK – Bibliothécaire, Claire Clément; Reference Librarian, Beverley Gilbertson; Technical Services Librarian, Gisele Laforce

La Baie: Bibliothèque publique de La Baie, 1911, 6e av, La Baie QC G7B 1S1 – 418/697-5085; Téléc: 418/697-5087 – Directeur, Anne Lebel

La Malbaie: Bibliothèque publique de La Malbaie, 395, rue St-Etienne, CP 232, La Malbaie QC G5A 1J7 – 418/665-6027 – Responsable, Thomas Claude Tremblay

La Plaine: Bibliothèque publique de La Plaine, 6900, rue Guérin, La Plaine QC J0N 1B0 – 514/968-2626; Téléc: 514/968-3130 – Directrice, Francine Piché

La Prairie: Bibliothèque municipale de La Prairie, 500, rue Saint-Laurent, La Prairie QC J5R 5X2 – 514/659-9135; Téléc: 514/444-9133 – Bibliothécaire, Marie-Josée Benoit

La Salle: Bibliothèque L'Octogone, 1080, av Dollard, La Salle QC H8N 2T9 – 514/367-6488; Téléc: 514/367-6604 – Chef de division, Marie-Andrée Marcoux, 514/367-6488; Reference Librarian, Nicole Cromp, 514/367-6385; Circulation Librarian, France Lecours, 514/367-6372; Children's Librarian, Louise Gagné, 514/367-6379; Technical Services Librarian, Lise Filiatrault, 514/367-6382

La Sarre: Bibliothèque Richelieu de La Sarre, 195, rue Principale sud, La Sarre QC J9Z 1Y3 – 819/333-2294; Téléc: 819/333-3090; Courrier électronique: droy@lino.com – Responsable, Denise Roy

La Tuque: Bibliothèque municipale de La Tuque, 575, rue St-Eugène, La Tuque QC G9X 2T5 – 819/523-3100; Téléc: 819/523-5419 – Bibliothécaire, Alain Michaud

Lac Brome: Bibliothèque Commemorative Pettes, 276, rue Knowlton, CP 177, Lac Brome QC J0E 1V0 – 514/243-6128 – Head Librarian, Susan Bailey-Godin

Lac-Etchemin: Bibliothèque municipale de Lac-Etchemin, 208 - 2e av, Lac-Etchemin QC G0R 1S0 – 418/625-8741; Téléc: 418/625-3175 – Responsable, Louise Poulin

Lac-Mégantic: Bibliothèque municipale de Lac-Mégantic, 5086, rue Frontenac, Lac-Mégantic QC G6B 1H3 – 819/583-0876; Téléc: 819/583-0878 – Directeur, Yves Tanguay

Lachenaie: Bibliothèque municipale de Lachenaie, 3060, ch Saint-Charles, Lachenaie QC J6V 1A1 – 514/471-9267; Téléc: 514/471-9872 – Directrice, Céline Paquette

Lachine: Bibliothèque municipale Saul-Bellow, 3100, rue St-Antoine, Lachine QC H8S 4B8 – 514/634-3471; Téléc: 514/634-8194 – Directrice, JoAnne Turnbull; Adult Services, Andrée Allard; Children's Librarian, Francine Dupuis

Lachute: Bibliothèque municipale de Lachute, 378, rue Principale, Lachute QC J8H 1Y2 – 514/562-3781; Téléc: 514/562-1431; Courrier électronique: biblachb@citenet.net – Bibliothécaire, Louise Beaulieu-Couture; Bibliotechnicienne, Chantal Belisle

L'Ancienne-Lorette: Bibliothèque Marie-Victorin, 1635, rue Notre-Dame, L'Ancienne-Lorette QC G2E 3B4 – 418/877-9703; Téléc: 418/877-4336 – Responsable, Camille Deschênes

Laval: Bibliothèque municipale de Laval, 1535, boul Chomedey, Laval QC H7V 3Z4 – 514/978-5848; Téléc: 514/978-5833 – Directrice, Monique Normandin; Public Services Librarian, Ghislaine Bélanger – See also following branches: Bibliothèque Alain-Grandbois, Bibliothèque Émile-Nelligan, Bibliothèque Gabrielle-Roy, Bibliothèque Germaine-Guèvrement, Bibliothèque Laure-Conan, Bibliothèque Marius-Barbeau, Bibliothèque Multiculturelle, Bibliothèque Philippe-Panneton, Bibliothèque Sylvain-Garneau, Bibliothèque Yves-Thériault

Laval: Bibliothèque Alain-Grandbois, 4300, boul Samson, Laval QC H7W 2G9 – 514/978-3671; Téléc: 514/686-8270 – Branch of Bibliothèque municipale de Laval

Laval: Bibliothèque Émile-Nelligan, 325, boul Cartier, Laval QC H7N 2J5 – 514/662-4973; Téléc: 514/668-9374 – Branch of Bibliothèque municipale de Laval

Laval: Bibliothèque Gabrielle-Roy, 3505, boul Dagenais, Laval QC H7P 4V9 – 514/978-8909; Téléc: 514/628-5992 – Branch of Bibliothèque municipale de Laval

Laval: Bibliothèque Germaine-Guèvrement, 2900, boul de la Concorde, Laval QC H7E 2B6 – 514/662-4001; Téléc: 514/661-0215 – Branch of Bibliothèque municipale de Laval

Laval: Bibliothèque Laure-Conan, 4660, boul des Laurentides, Laval QC H7M 2M8 – 514/662-4975; Téléc: 514/628-4674 – Branch of Bibliothèque municipale de Laval

Laval: Bibliothèque Marius-Barbeau, 455, Montée du Moulin, Laval QC H7A 1Z2 – 514/662-4004; Téléc: 514/665-9889 – Branch of Bibliothèque municipale de Laval

Laval: Bibliothèque Multiculturelle, 1535, boul Chomedey, Laval QC H7V 3Z4 – 514/978-5995; Téléc: 514/978-5833 – Branch of Bibliothèque municipale de Laval

Laval: Bibliothèque Philippe-Panneton, 4747, boul Arthur-Sauvé, Laval QC H7N 5P5 – 514/978-8919; Téléc: 514/627-5928 – Branch of Bibliothèque municipale de Laval

Laval: Bibliothèque Sylvain-Garneau, 216, boul Ste-Rose, Laval QC H7L 1L6 – 514/978-3940; Téléc: 514/963-6002 – Branch of Bibliothèque municipale de Laval

Laval: Bibliothèque Yves-Thériault, 670, Place Publique, Laval QC H7X 1G1 – 514/978-6599; Téléc: 514/969-3285 – Branch of Bibliothèque municipale de Laval

Le Gardeur: Bibliothèque municipale de Le Gardeur, 1, Montée des Arsenaux, Le Gardeur QC J5Z 2C1 – 514/582-8288; Téléc: 514/585-5221 – Directrice, Ginette Martin

Lévis: Bibliothèque municipale de Lévis, 7, rue Monseigneur-Gosselin, Lévis QC G6V 5J9 – 418/838-4126; Téléc: 418/838-4124 – Régisseur, Suzanne Rochefort – See also following branches: Bibliothèque Lauzon, Bibliothèque St-David

Lévis: Bibliothèque Lauzon, 10, rue Giguère, Lévis QC G6V 1N6 – 418/838-4143; Téléc: 418/838-4948 – Branch of Bibliothèque municipale de Lévis

Lévis: Bibliothèque St-David, 4, rue Olympique, Lévis QC G6W 6N3 – 418/838-4127; Téléc: 418/838-4955 – Branch of Bibliothèque municipale de Lévis

L'Île-Bizard: Bibliothèque municipale de L'Île-Bizard, 500, rue de l'Église, L'Île-Bizard QC H9C 1G9 – 514/626-8505; Téléc: 514/620-4153; Symbol: OSTR – Responsable, Hélène Rouette

L'Île-Perrot: Bibliothèque municipale de L'Île-Perrot, 150, boul Perrot, L'Île-Perrot QC J7V 3G1 – 514/453-1751; Téléc: 514/453-0999 – Bibliothécaire, Chantal Lepage

Longueuil: Bibliothèque municipale de Longueuil, 100, rue St-Laurent ouest, Longueuil QC J4K 4Y7 – 514/646-8615; Téléc: 514/646-8874; Symbol: PLO – Bibliothécaire en chef, Yves Ouimet

Loretteville: Bibliothèque municipale de Loretteville, 307, rue Racine, Loretteville QC G2B 1E7 – 418/842-1924; Téléc: 418/842-2585 – Directeur, France Lemay

Lorraine: Bibliothèque municipale de Lorraine, 33, boul de Gaulle, Lorraine QC J6Z 3W9 – 514/621-1071; Téléc: 514/621-6585 – Director, Juanita Sales

Magog: Bibliothèque Memphrémagog, 61, rue Merry nord, Magog QC J1X 2E7 – 819/843-1330; Téléc: 819/843-1594; Symbol: QMAGB – Bibliothécaire, Diane Boulé

Malartic: Bibliothèque municipale de Malartic, 870, rue Royale, CP 4170, Malartic QC J0Y 1Z0 – 819/757-4449 – Responsable, Lucille Mikolajczak

Maniwaki: Bibliothèque municipale de Maniwaki, 8, rue Comeau, Maniwaki QC J9E 2R8 – 819/449-2738 – Directrice, Jocelyne Leclair

Marieville: Bibliothèque commémorative Desautels, 1801, rue du Pont, Marieville QC J3M 1J7 – 514/460-4988 – Directeur, Daniel Lalonde, M.Bibl.

Mascouche: Bibliothèque publique de Mascouche, 2685, ch Sainte-Marie, Local P, Mascouche QC J7K 1M8 – 514/474-4159; Téléc: 514/474-3410 – Directrice, Diane Allard

Matane: Bibliothèque municipale de Matane, 230, av Saint-Jérôme, Matane QC G4W 3A2 – 418/562-9233; Téléc: 418/562-4869 – Responsable, Lise Whittom Grenier

Mercier: Bibliothèque municipale de Mercier, 16, rue du Parc, Mercier QC J6R 1E5 – 514/692-6780; Téléc: 514/691-6529 – Directeur, Daniel Morin

Mirabel: Bibliothèque municipale de Mirabel, 13908, boul du Curé Labelle, CP 1170, Mirabel QC J7J 1A1 – 514/430-4563; Téléc: 514/430-2868 – Directrice, Claudette Poulin

Mistassini: Bibliothèque municipale de Mistassini, 173, boul St-Michel, Mistassini QC G8M 1E9 – 418/276-3685; Téléc: 418/276-8164 – Responsable, Carold Sasseville

Mont-Joli: Bibliothèque Jean-Louis-Desrosiers, 1477, boul Jacques-Cartier, CP 576, Mont-Joli QC G5H 3L3 – 418/775-4106; Téléc: 418/775-6320 – Responsable, Julie Bélanger

Mont-Laurier: Bibliothèque municipale de Mont-Laurier, 485, rue Mercier, Mont-Laurier QC

J9L 3N8 – 819/623-1833; Téléc: 819/623-4840 – Responsable, Edith Whear

Mont-Royal: Bibliothèque Reginald J.P. Dawson, 1967, boul Graham, Mont-Royal QC H3R 1G9 – 514/734-2967; Téléc: 514/734-3089; Symbol: QMRRD – Head Librarian, Sharon Huffman; Librarian, English Adult Services, Lisa Rasmussen, 514/734-2970; Librarian, French Adult Services, Denis Chouinard, 514/734-2969; Children's Librarian, Julie-Anne Cardella; Children's Librarian, Leanne Bowler; Technical Services Supervisor, Angèle Mailloux; Acquisitions Technician, Elaine Charness; ILL, Chantal Galarneau, 514/734-2971

Mont-Saint-Hilaire: Bibliothèque municipale de Mont-Saint-Hilaire, #101, 150, rue du Centre Civique, Mont-Saint-Hilaire QC J3H 5Z5 – 514/467-2854; Téléc: 514/446-5879 – Responsable de la bibliothèque, Francine Ledoux-Nadeau

Montréal: Bibliothèque de Montréal, #400, 5650, rue d'Iberville, Montréal QC H2G 3E4 – 514/872-5923, 2900; Téléc: 514/872-4911; URL: http://www.ville.montreal.qc.ca/biblio/pageacc.htm; Symbol: QMBM – Bibliothécaire en chef, Jacques Panneton; Division du traitement documentaire, chef de division, Jacques Aird; Division des systèmes et des nouvelles technologies, Isabel Assunçao; Division de la Bibliothèque centrale, chef de division, Michèle Régnier; Division du développement des ressources et services, Hélène Roussel; Section de la préparation matérielle, chef de section, Claire Lahaie; Section des services annexes, chef de section (Div. B. Centrale), Brigitte Raymond – See also following branches: Bibliobus, Bibliothèque Acadie, Bibliothèque Ahuntsic, Bibliothèque Benny, Bibliothèque Centrale, Bibliothèque Centrale-Annexe, Bibliothèque Côte-des-Neiges, Bibliothèque de Rosemont, Bibliothèque Frontenac, Bibliothèque Georges-Vanier, Bibliothèque Hochelaga, Bibliothèque la Petite Patrie, Bibliothèque Langelier, Bibliothèque le Prevost, Bibliothèque Maisonneuve, Bibliothèque Marie-Uguay, Bibliothèque Métro McGill, Bibliothèque Mercier, Bibliothèque Mile-End, Bibliothèque Notre-Dame, Bibliothèque Notre-Dame-de-Grace, Bibliothèque Plateau-Mont-Royal, Bibliothèque Pointe-aux-Trembles, Bibliothèque Rivière-des-Prairies, Bibliothèque Saint-Charles, Bibliothèque Saint-Michel, Bibliothèque Salaberry, Phonothèque

Montréal: Bibliobus, #400, 5650, rue d'Iberville, Montréal QC H2G 3E4 – 514/872-5690; Téléc: 514/872-4911 – Rachel Boisjoly – Branch of Bibliothèque de Montréal

Montréal: Bibliothèque Acadie, 11833, boul de l'Acadie, Montréal QC H3M 2T5 – 514/872-6989; Téléc: 514/872-0510 – Responsable, Édith Saucier – Branch of Bibliothèque de Montréal

Montréal: Bibliothèque Ahuntsic, 770, boul Henri-Bourassa est, Montréal QC H2C 1E6 – 514/872-6992 (adultes), 872-6994 (jeunes); Téléc: 514/872-0518 – Responsable, Marie Pilon – Branch of Bibliothèque de Montréal

Montréal: Bibliothèque Benny, 3465, av Benny, Montréal QC H4B 2R9 – 514/872-4147 (adultes), 872-4636 (jeunes); Téléc: 514/872-0515 – Responsable, Lorraine Guay – Branch of Bibliothèque de Montréal

Montréal: Bibliothèque Centrale, 1210, rue Sherbrooke est, Montréal QC H2L 1L9 – 514/872-5923 (adultes), 872-1633 (jeunes); Téléc: 514/872-1626 – Responsable, Michèle Régnier – Branch of Bibliothèque de Montréal

Montréal: Bibliothèque Centrale-Annexe, 1160, rue Sherbrooke est, Montréal QC H2L 1L7 – 514/872-2198; Téléc: 514/872-1626 – Evelyne Caron – Branch of Bibliothèque de Montréal

Montréal: Bibliothèque Côte-des-Neiges, 5290, ch de la Côte-des-Neiges, Montréal QC H3T 1Y4 – 514/872-6603 (adultes), 872-5118 (jeunes); Téléc: 514/872-0516 – Responsable, Chantal Trottier – Branch of Bibliothèque de Montréal

Montréal: Bibliothèque de Rosemont, 3131, boul Rosemont, Montréal QC H1Y 1M4 – 514/872-4701 (adultes), 872-6139 (jeunes); Téléc: 514/872-0527 – Responsable, Sylvie Burelle – Branch of Bibliothèque de Montréal

Montréal: Bibliothèque Frontenac, 2550, rue Ontario est, Montréal QC H2K 1W7 – 514/872-7888; Téléc: 514/872-0520 – Responsable, Johanne Prud'Homme – Branch of Bibliothèque de Montréal

Montréal: Bibliothèque Georges-Vanier, 530, rue Vinet, Montréal QC H3J 2E6 – 514/872-2001 (adultes), 872-2002 (jeunes); Téléc: 514/872-0511 – Responsable, Hélène Desmeules – Branch of Bibliothèque de Montréal

Montréal: Bibliothèque Hochelaga, 1870, rue Davidson, Montréal QC H1W 2Y6 – 514/872-3666 – Responsable, Johanne Petel – Branch of Bibliothèque de Montréal

Montréal: Bibliothèque la Petite Patrie, 6707, av de Lorimier, Montréal QC H2G 2P8 – 514/872-1733 (adultes), 872-1732 (jeunes); Téléc: 514/872-0526 – Responsable, Suzanne Élie – Branch of Bibliothèque de Montréal

Montréal: Bibliothèque Langelier, 6473, rue Sherbrooke est, Montréal QC H1N 1C5 – 514/872-2640 (adultes), 872-4227 (jeunes); Téléc: 514/872-0523 – Responsable, Josée Valiquette – Branch of Bibliothèque de Montréal

Montréal: Bibliothèque le Prevost, 7355, av Christophe-Colomb, Montréal QC H2R 2S5 – 514/872-1523 (adultes), 872-1526 (jeunes); Téléc: 514/872-0529 – Responsable, Louise Robichaud – Branch of Bibliothèque de Montréal

Montréal: Bibliothèque Maisonneuve, 4120, rue Ontario est, Montréal QC H1V 1J9 – 514/872-4213 (adultes), 872-4214 (jeunes); Téléc: 514/872-0522 – Responsable, François Séguin – Branch of Bibliothèque de Montréal

Montréal: Bibliothèque Marie-Uguay, 6052, boul Monk, Montréal QC H4A 1H2 – 514/872-4097 (adultes), 872-4414 (jeunes); Téléc: 514/872-0513 – Responsable, Jean-Pierre Leduc – Branch of Bibliothèque de Montréal

Montréal: Bibliothèque Mercier, 8105, rue Hochelaga, Montréal QC H1L 2K9 – 514/872-8738 (adultes), 872-8739 (enfants); Téléc: 514/872-0524 – Responsable, Diane Tremblay – Branch of Bibliothèque de Montréal

Montréal: Bibliothèque Métro McGill, #310, 2001, rue University, Montréal QC H3A 2A6 – 514/872-4154; Téléc: 514/872-0530 – Luce Forest-Doyon – Branch of Bibliothèque de Montréal

Montréal: Bibliothèque Mile-End, 5434, av du Parc, Montréal QC H2V 4G7 – 514/872-2141 (adultes), 872-2142 (jeunes); Téléc: 514/872-0531 – Responsable, Van Be Lam – Branch of Bibliothèque de Montréal

Montréal: Bibliothèque municipale de St-Pierre, 183, rue des Érables, St-Pierre QC H8R 1B1 – 514/368-5740; Téléc: 514/368-5747 – Responsable, Monique Charette

Montréal: Bibliothèque Notre-Dame, 4700, rue Notre-Dame ouest, Montréal QC H4C 1S8 – 514/872-2879 (adultes), 872-4698 (jeunes); Téléc: 514/872-0512 – Responsable, Jacques Charbonneau – Branch of Bibliothèque de Montréal

Montréal: Bibliothèque Notre-Dame-de-Grace, 3755, rue Botrel, Montréal QC H4A 3G8 – 514/872-2398 (adultes), 872-2377 (jeunes); Téléc: 514/872-0517 – Responsable, Michèle Lavigne – Branch of Bibliothèque de Montréal

Montréal: Bibliothèque Plateau-Mont-Royal, 465, av du Mont-Royal est, Montréal QC H2J 1W3 – 514/872-2270 (adultes); 872-2271 (jeunes); Téléc: 514/872-0532 – Responsable, Daniel Legault – Branch of Bibliothèque de Montréal

Montréal: Bibliothèque Pointe-aux-Trembles, 1515, boul du Tricentennaire, Montréal QC H1B 3A9 – 514/872-6987; Téléc: 514/872-0525 – Responsable, Nicole St-Vincent – Branch of Bibliothèque de Montréal

Montréal: Bibliothèque Rivière-des-Prairies, 9001, boul Perras, Montréal QC H1E 3J7 – 514/872-9425 (adultes), 872-9494 (jeunes) – Responsable, Gloria Maïstrelli – Branch of Bibliothèque de Montréal

Montréal: Bibliothèque Saint-Charles, 2333, rue Mullins, Montréal QC H3K 3E3 – 514/872-3092 (adultes), 872-3035 (jeunes); Téléc: 514/872-0514 – Responsable, France Machet – Branch of Bibliothèque de Montréal

Montréal: Bibliothèque Saint-Michel, 7601, rue François-Perrault, Montréal QC H2A 3L6 – 514/872-3899 (adultes), 872-4250 (jeunes); Téléc: 514/872-0528 – Responsable, Suzanne Thibault – Branch of Bibliothèque de Montréal

Montréal: Bibliothèque Salaberry, 4170, rue Salaberry, Montréal QC H4J 1H1 – 514/872-1521; Téléc: 514/872-0519 – Responable, Danièle Bouffard – Branch of Bibliothèque de Montréal

Montréal: La Magnétothèque, #304, 1030, rue Cherrier, Montréal QC H2L 1H9 – 514/524-6831; Téléc: 514/524-5828 – Responsable, André Hamel

Montréal: Phonothèque, 880, rue Roy est, Montréal QC H2L 1E6 – 514/872-2860; Téléc: 514/872-7735 – Responsable, Gérald Forget – Branch of Bibliothèque de Montréal

Montréal: Westmount Public Library, 4574, rue Sherbrooke ouest, Westmount QC H3Z 1G1 – 514/989-5300; Fax: 514/989-5485; Email: wpl@westlib.org; URL: http://www.westlib.org; Symbol: QWSMM – Director of Library & Cultural Services, Caroline Thibodeau; Reference Librarian, Ann Moffat; Circulation Librarian, Craig Wright; Children's Librarian, Joanne Stanbridge; Technical Services Librarian, Isabelle Seguin; Adult Services, Brenda Smith; French Services, Lysanne Ferron-Godin

Montréal : Bibliothèque municipale de Montréal-Est, 11370, rue Notre-Dame est, Montréal-Est QC H1B 2W6 – 514/645-7431; Téléc: 514/645-0107; Courrier électronique: qmem@ville.montreal-est.qc.ca; URL: http://www.ville.montreal-est.qc.ca; Symbol: QMEM – Directeur, Jean Ko; Public Services Librarian, Nathalie Joly; Technical Services Librarian, Anne Marie Dufort

Montréal : Centres Biblio-culturels de Montréal-Nord, 5400, boul Henri-Bourassa est, Montréal-Nord QC H1G 2S9 – 514/328-4128; Téléc: 514/328-4298 – Responsable, Céline Dénommée

Normandin: Bibliothèque municipale de Normandin, 1156, Valois, Normandin QC G8M 3Z8 – 418/274-2241; Téléc: 418/274-7171; Courrier électronique: dmorin@normandin.biblio.qc.ca; URL: http://www.normandin.biblio.qc.ca – Responsable, Denise Morin-Larouche

Notre-Dame-de-l'Île-Perrot: Bibliothèque municipale Nôtre-Dame-de-l'Île-Perrot, 2254, boul Perrot, Notre-Dame-de-l'Île-Perrot QC J7V 8P4 – 514/453-0013; Téléc: 514/453-8961 – Responsable, Guylaine Lauzon

Outremont: Bibliothèque municipale d'Outremont, 544, av Davaar, Outremont QC H2V 2B9 – 514/495-6209; Téléc: 514/495-6287 – Bibliothécaire, Guy Laverdière

Pierrefonds: Bibliothèque intermunicipale de Pierrefonds, 13555, boul Pierrefonds, Pierrefonds QC H9A 1A6 – 514/620-4181; Téléc: 514/620-5503; Symbol: QPD – Head Librarian, Michèle Dupuis; Reference/Acquisitions Librarian, Daniel Proulx;

Reference Librarian, Louise Zampini; Circulation Librarian, Lise Bertrand; Circulation Librarian, Jennifer Reeves; Children's Librarian, Serrolyn Campbell; Children's Librarian, Micheline Patton; Public Services Librarian, Lise Brosseau, 514/684-1496; Technical Services Librarian, Maurice Houle

Pincourt: Bibliothèque municipale de Pincourt, 375, boul. Cardinal Léger, Pincourt QC J7V 9H6 – 514/453-3788; Téléc: 514/453-1839 – Régisseure, Rose-Marie Desjardins

Plessisville: Bibliothèque intermunicipale de Plessisville, 1699, rue St-Calixte, Plessisville QC G6L 1R2 – 819/362-6628; Téléc: 819/362-6421 – Bibliothécaire, Suzanne Bédard

Pointe-Claire: Bibliothèque publique de Pointe-Claire, 100, av Douglas Shand, Pointe-Claire QC H9R 4V1 – 514/630-1218; Téléc: 514/630-1261; Symbol: QPOC – Directrice de la bibliothèque et des activités culturelles, Claire Coté; Reference Librarian, Suzanne Lauzier; Children's Librarian, Carole Lanthier-Boiteau; Technical Services Librarian, Céline Laperrière; Programming Librarian, Cristina Segura – See also following branches: Bibliothèque publique de Stewart Hall, Bibliothèque publique de Valois

Pointe-Claire: Bibliothèque publique de Stewart Hall, 176, Bord du Lac, Pointe-Claire QC H9S 4J7 – 514/630-1221 – Responsable, Gwen Murray – Branch of Bibliothèque publique de Pointe-Claire

Pointe-Claire: Bibliothèque publique de Valois, 68, av Prince Edward, Pointe-Claire QC H9R 4C7 – 514/630-1219; Téléc: 514/695-9924 – Responsable, Mary Pupil – Branch of Bibliothèque publique de Pointe-Claire

Pointe-du-Lac: Bibliothèque Simone-L.-Roy, 101, Grande Allée, Pointe-du-Lac QC G0X 1Z0 – 819/377-4289; Téléc: 819/377-2415 – Responsable, Louise Houle

Port-Cartier: Bibliothèque municipale de Port-Cartier, 40, av Parent, Port-Cartier QC G5B 2G5 – 418/766-2345; Téléc: 418/766-3561 – Bibliothécaire, Stéphane Harvey; Technical Services Librarian, Chantal Maltais

Précieux-Sang: Bibliothèque municipale de Précieux-Sang, 10995, St-Laurent, Précieux-Sang QC G0X 2A0 – 819/294-1173 – Bénévole responsable, Louise Labarre – Branch of Bibliothèque municipale de Bécancour

Québec: Bibliothèque de Québec, 350, rue St-Joseph est, Québec QC G1K 3B2 – 418/529-0924; Téléc: 418/529-1588; Courrier électronique: courrier@icqbdq.qc.ca; URL: http://www.icqbdq.qc.ca – Directeur général, Jean Payeur; Reference Librarian, Sylvie Fournier; Animation culturelle, Directrice, Marie Goyette; Directeur des services techniques, Hughes Bélanger; Acquisitions Librarian, Jean-Pierre Germain; Directeur des services administratifs, Jean Debonville – See also following branches: Bibliothèque Canardière, Bibliothèque Collège-des-Jésuites, Bibliothèque Duberger, Bibliothèque Les Saules, Bibliothèque Neufchâtel, Bibliothèque Saint-Albert, Bibliothèque Saint-André, Bibliothèque Saint-Charles, Bibliothèque Saint-Jean-Baptiste, Bibliothèque Vieux-Québec, Comptoir Lebourgneuf

Québec: Bibliothèque Canardière, 1601, ch de la Canardière, Québec QC G1J 2E1 – 418/666-8791; Téléc: 418/529-1588; Courrier électronique: courrier@icqbdq.qc.ca – Responsable, Nadia Pizzamiglio – Branch of Bibliothèque de Québec

Québec: Bibliothèque Collège-des-Jésuites, 1120, boul René-Lévesque oust, Québec QC G1S 4W4 – 418/691-6378; Téléc: 418/529-1588; Courrier électronique: courrier@icqbdq.qc.ca – Responsable, Lise Beaudoin – Branch of Bibliothèque de Québec

Québec: Bibliothèque Duberger, 2475, boul Central, Québec QC G1P 4S1 – 418/529-0924; Téléc: 418/529-1588; Courrier électronique: jgrantham@icqbdq.qc.ca – Responsable, Jean Grantham – Branch of Bibliothèque de Québec

Québec: Bibliothèque Les Saules, 2035, boul Masson, Québec QC G1P 1J3 – 418/872-5086; Téléc: 418/529-1588; Courrier électronique: jgrantham@icqbdq.qc.ca – Responsable, Jean Grantham – Branch of Bibliothèque de Québec

Québec: Bibliothèque Neufchâtel, 4060, rue Blain, Québec QC G2B 4P3 – 418/843-1395; Téléc: 418/529-1588; Courrier électronique: courrier@icqbdq.qc.ca – Nancy Duscheneau – Branch of Bibliothèque de Québec

Québec: Bibliothèque Saint-Albert, 5, rue des Ormes, Québec QC G1L 1M5 – 418/623-7996; Téléc: 418/529-1588; Courrier électronique: courrier@icqbdq.qc.ca – Responsable, Nadia Pizzamiglio – Branch of Bibliothèque de Québec

Québec: Bibliothèque Saint-André, 2155, boul Bastien, Québec QC G2B 1B8 – 418/843-3263; Téléc: 418/529-1588; Courrier électronique: courrier@icqbdq.qc.ca – Responsable, Fabienne Labadie – Branch of Bibliothèque de Québec

Québec: Bibliothèque Saint-Charles, 400, 4e av, Québec QC G1J 2Z9 – 418/691-6358; Téléc: 418/529-1588; Courrier électronique: courrier@icqbdq.qc.ca – Responsable, Hélène Dufour – Branch of Bibliothèque de Québec

Québec: Bibliothèque Saint-Jean-Baptiste, 755, rue Saint-Jean, Québec QC G1R 1G1 – 418/691-6492; Téléc: 418/529-1588; Courrier électronique: courrier@icqbdq.qc.ca – Responsable, Isabelle Picard – Branch of Bibliothèque de Québec

Québec: Bibliothèque Vieux-Québec, 37, rue Sainte-Angèle, Québec QC G1R 4G5 – 418/691-6357; Téléc: 418/529-1588; Courrier électronique: courrier@icqbdq.qc.ca – Responsable, Monique Lemieux – Branch of Bibliothèque de Québec

Québec: Comptoir Lebourgneuf, 1650, boul La Morille, Québec QC G2K 2L2 – 418/623-5058; Téléc: 418/529-1588; Courrier électronique: courrier@icqbdq.qc.ca – Responsable, Fabienne Labadie – Branch of Bibliothèque de Québec

Repentigny: Bibliothèque municipale de Repentigny, 1, place D'Évry, Repentigny QC J6A 8H7 – 514/654-2346; Téléc: 514/654-2409 – Régisseure, Célyne Ross; Reference Librarian, Maryse Trudeau

Rimouski: Bibliothèque Lisette-Morin, 110, rue de l'Éveché est, CP 710, Rimouski QC G5L 7C7 – 418/724-3164; Téléc: 418/724-3180 – Bibiothécaire responsable, Nicole Gagnon

Rivière-du-Loup: Bibliothèque Françoise-Bédard, Maison de la culture, 67, rue du Rocher, Rivière-du-Loup QC G5R 1J8 – 418/862-4252; Téléc: 418/862-3478; Symbol: QRL – Head Librarian, Marlène Létourneau; Head, Technical Services, Aline Bourgoin

Roberval: Bibliothèque municipale de Roberval, 829, boul St-Joseph, Roberval QC G8H 2L6 – 418/275-2333; Téléc: 418/275-1699; Courrier électronique: laflamme@roberval.biblio.qc.ca – Responsable, Francine Laflamme-Lachance

Rock Forest: Bibliothèque municipale de Rock Forest, 6630, rue Fontaine, Rock Forest QC J1N 2T3 – 819/864-6288; Téléc: 819/864-0809 – Responsable, Johanne Lavoie

Rosemère: Bibliothèque municipale de Rosemère, 339, ch de la Grande-Côte, Rosemère QC J7A 1K2 – 514/621-6132; Téléc: 514/621-6131; Courrier électronique: bibliros@cam.org – Directrice, Carole Trépanier

Rouyn-Noranda: Bibliothèque municipale de Rouyn-Noranda, 201, av Dallaire, Rouyn-Noranda QC J9X 4T5 – 819/762-0944; Téléc: 819/797-7136 – Responsable, Luc Sigouin

Roxboro: Bibliothèque de Roxboro, 110, rue Cartier, Roxboro QC H8Y 1G8 – 514/684-8247; Téléc: 514/684-8563 – Directrice, Lesley DesAutels; Reference Librarian, Claudette Fournier; ILL, Jeannine Reinart

Ste-Adèle: Bibliothèque municipale de Ste-Adèle, 170, rue Morin, CP 1046, Ste-Adèle QC J0R 1L0 – 514/229-2921; Téléc: 514/229-4179 – Responsable, Monique Auger

Ste-Agathe-des-Monts: Bibliothèque municipale de Ste-Agathe-des-Monts, 10, rue St-Donat, Ste-Agathe-des-Monts QC J8C 1P5 – 819/326-2848; Téléc: 819/326-5784 – Responsable, France Bélanger

Ste-Angèle-de-Laval: Bibliothèque municipale de Ste-Angèle-de-Laval, 14700, boul Bécancour, Ste-Angèle-de-Laval QC G0X 2H0 – 819/222-5735 – Bénévole responsable, Pauline Pratt – Branch of Bibliothèque municipale de Bécancour

Ste-Anne-des-Monts: Bibliothèque Blanche-Lamontagne, 120, 7e rue ouest, CP 670, Ste-Anne-des-Monts QC G0E 2G0 – 418/763-9167; Téléc: 418/763-3473 – Responsable, Jacques Lavoie

Ste-Anne-des-Plaines: Bibliothèque publique de Ste-Anne-des-Plaines, 155, rue des Cèdres, Ste-Anne-des-Plaines QC J0N 1H0 – 514/478-4337; Téléc: 514/478-6733; Courrier électronique: steanne@citenet.net; URL: http://ville.ste-anne-des-plaines.qc.ca/biblio/ – Directrice, Danielle Labelle

St-Antoine: Bibliothèque municipale de St-Antoine, 500, boul des Laurentides, St-Antoine QC J7Z 4M2 – 514/431-1388; Téléc: 514/431-3684 – Directrice de la bibliothèque, Chantal Paquin

St-Augustin-de-Desmaures: Bibliothèque Alain-Grandbois, 160, rue Jean-Juneau, St-Augustin-de-Desmaures QC G3A 2P1 – 418/878-4423; Téléc: 418/878-5473; Courrier électronique: biblio@st-augustin.org – Bibliothécaire, Claire Sénéclauze

St-Basile-le-Grand: Bibliothèque municipale de St-Basile-le-Grand, 40, rue Savaria, CP 1010, St-Basile-le-Grand QC J3N 1M5 – 514/653-0287; Téléc: 514/653-8028 – Directrice, France Goyette

St-Bruno-de-Montarville: Bibliothèque municipale de St-Bruno-de-Montarville, 82, rue Seigneuriale ouest, St-Bruno-de-Montarville QC J3V 5N7 – 514/653-2443; Téléc: 514/441-0431; Symbol: QSTB – Bibliothécaire en chef, Guylaine Pellerin

Ste-Catherine: Bibliothèque municipale de Ste-Catherine, 5465, boul Marie-Victorin, Ste-Catherine QC J0L 1E0 – 514/632-9951; Téléc: 514/632-9908 – Responsable, Lise Forcier

St-Constant: Bibliothèque publique de St-Constant, 80, rue Brodeur, St-Constant QC J5A 1X8 – 514/632-8732; Téléc: 514/635-8414 – Responsable, Nadine Géroli

St-Eustache: Bibliothèque Guy-Bélisle, 80, boul Arthur-Sauvé, St-Eustache QC J7R 2H7 – 514/974-5035; Téléc: 514/974-5054 – Directrice, Nicole Grimard; Reference Technician, Danielle Touchette

St-Félicien: Bibliothèque municipale de St-Félicien, 1209, boul Sacré-Coeur, St-Félicien QC G8K 2R5 – 418/679-5334; Téléc: 418/679-1449 – Responable, Johanne Laprise

Ste-Foy: Bibliothèque Monique-Corriveau, 999, av Roland-Beaudin, Ste-Foy QC G1V 4E1 – 418/654-4676; Téléc: 418/654-4172; Courrier électronique: bibliomc@ville.sainte-foy.qc.ca; URL: http://www.bibliotheques.qc.ca/bmc/index.htm; Symbol: QSF – Responsable, Claudette Auger – See also following branches: Succursale Champigny

Ste-Foy: Succursale Champigny, 1465, rue Félix-Antoine-Savard, Ste-Foy QC – 418/654-4676; Téléc: 418/654-4172 – Responsable, Claudette

Auger – Branch of Bibliothèque Monique-Corriveau

Ste-Geneviève: Bibliothèque municipale de Ste-Geneviève, 35, rue Sainte-Anne, Ste-Geneviève QC H9H 2Z2 – 514/626-2537; Téléc: 514/626-0312 – Responsable, Cécile Picard

Saint-Georges: Bibliothèque municipale de Saint-Georges, 250, 18e Rue, Saint-Georges QC G5Y 4S9 – 418/226-2271; Téléc: 418/228-1321; Courrier électronique: sgbliol@quebectel.com; URL: http://www.bibliotheques.qc.ca – Bibliothécaire, Julie Michaud

Ste-Gertrude: Bibliothèque municipale de Ste-Gertrude, 6095, av des Pins, Ste-Gertrude QC G0X 2S0 – 819/297-2555 – Bénévole responsable, Lise Montambault – Branch of Bibliothèque municipale de Bécancour

St-Grégoire: Bibliothèque municipale de St-Grégoire, 4000, Port-Royal, St-Grégoire QC G0X 2T0 – 819/233-4177 – Bénévole responsable, Michelle Nepton – Branch of Bibliothèque municipale de Bécancour

St-Hubert: Bibliothèque municipale de St-Hubert, 5900, boul Cousineau, St-Hubert QC J3Y 7K8 – 514/445-7761; Téléc: 514/445-7836 – Bibliothécaire, Linda Moisan – See also following branches: Bibliothèque J.-W.-Gendron

Saint-Hubert: Bibliothèque J.-W.-Gendron, 3875, Grande-Allée, Saint-Hubert QC J4T 2V8 – 514/445-7790; Téléc: 514/445-6741 – Branch of Bibliothèque municipale de St-Hubert

St-Hyacinthe: Bibliothèque T.A. St-Germain, 2720, rue Dessaulles, St-Hyacinthe QC J2S 2V7 – 514/773-4865; Téléc: 514/773-3398 – Directeur, Denis Boisvert

St-Jacques-de-Montcalm: Bibliothèque municipale de St-Jacques-de-Montcalm, 16, rue Maréchal, CP 370, St-Jacques-de-Montcalm QC J0K 2R0 – 514/839-3926; Téléc: 514/839-2387; Courrier électronique: bibliostjacques@pandore.qc.ca – Responsable, Francine Roy

St-Jean-Chrysostome: Bibliothèque Francine-McKenzie, 100, Place Centre-Ville, St-Jean-Chrysostome QC G6Z 3B9 – 418/839-0012; Téléc: 418/839-8818 – Bibliothécaire, Suzanne Fortin

St-Jean-sur-Richelieu: Bibliothèque Adélard-Berger, 180, rue Laurier, CP 1025, St-Jean-sur-Richelieu QC J3B 7B2 – 514/357-2113; Téléc: 514/357-2055; Courrier électronique: bricault@access-cible.net – Directrice, Camille Bricault; Public Services Librarian, Lise Gosselin

St-Jérôme: Bibliothèque municipale de Saint-Jérôme, 185, rue du Palais, St-Jérôme QC J7Z 1X6 – 514/432-0571; Téléc: 514/436-1211; Courrier électronique: CTSJ1376@citenet.net – Directrice, Renée Masse

St-Jovite: Bibliothèque municipale de St-Jovite, 901, rue Ouimet, CP 200, St-Jovite QC J0T 2H0 – 819/425-2337; Téléc: 819/425-9247 – Responsable, Christiane Langlois

Ste-Julie: Bibliothèque municipale de Ste-Julie, 1580, ch du Fer-à-Cheval, Sainte-Julie QC J3E 1Y2 – 514/922-7070; Téléc: 514/922-7077 – Responsable, Nicole Perras

St-Lambert: Bibliothèque municipale de St-Lambert, 490, av Mercille, St-Lambert QC J4P 2L5 – 514/465-4508; Téléc: 514/465-0681; Symbol: QSTLB – Bibliothécaire en chef, Micheline Perreault – See also following branches: Bibliothèque de Préville

Saint-Lambert: Bibliothèque de Préville, 120, rue de Poitou, Saint-Lambert QC J4S 1E1 – 514/671-2152 – Micheline Perreault – Branch of Bibliothèque municipale de St-Lambert

St-Laurent: Bibliothèque municipale de St-Laurent, 1380, rue de l'Église, St-Laurent QC H4L 2H2 – 514/855-6130; Téléc: 514/855-6129; Symbol: QSTL – Chef de division, Florian Dubois; Public Services & Reference, Sonia Djevalikian; Technical Services, Head, Josiane Querghi; Special Services, Head, Elaine Sauvé

St-Lazare: Bibliothèque municipale de St-Lazare, 1811, ch Sainte-Angélique, CP 690, St-Lazare QC J0P 1V0 – 514/424-6472; Téléc: 514/424-8822 – Responsable, Michel Piché

St-Léonard: Bibliothèque municipale de St-Léonard, 8420, boul Lacordaire, St-Léonard QC H1R 3G5 – 514/328-8585; Téléc: 514/328-7002 – Chef de division, France Huvelin; Reference Librarian, Murielle Alary, 514/328-8589; Circulation/Public Services Librarian, Reine Harvey, 514/328-8517; Technical Services/Acquisitions Librarian, Huguette Desmarais, 514/328-8520; Reading Activities Librarian, Claire Séguin

Saint-Louis-de-France: Bibliothèque de la Franciade, 100, av de la Mairie, Saint-Louis-de-France QC G8W 1S1 – 819/374-6419; Téléc: 819/374-0659 – Directrice, Lise Thériault

St-Luc: Bibliothèque municipale de St-Luc, 347, boul St-Luc, St-Luc QC J2W 2A2 – 514/348-4128; Téléc: 514/348-5889 – Directrice, Sylvette Toutant

Ste-Marie: Bibliothèque Honorius-Provost, 80, rue St-Antoine, CP 1750, Ste-Marie QC G6E 3C7 – 418/387-2240; Téléc: 418/387-2454 – Responsable, Caroline Dion

Ste-Marthe-sur-le-Lac: Bibliothèque municipale de Ste-Marthe-sur-le-Lac, 3075, ch Oka, local 110, Ste-Marthe-sur-le-Lac QC J0N 1P0 – 514/974-7111; Téléc: 514/472-4283 – Responsable, Brigitte Boiteau, BA, MBSI

St-Nicolas: Bibliotheque publique de Bernières-Saint-Nicolas, 220, route du Pont, St-Nicolas QC G0S 2Z0 – 418/831-7090; Téléc: 418/831-8395 – Responsable, Nathalie Ouellet

Saint-Pierre: Bibliothèque municipale de Saint-Pierre, 183, rue des Érables, Saint-Pierre QC H8R 1B1 – 514/368-368-5740; Téléc: 514/368-5717 – Responsable, Monique Charette

St-Rémi: Bibliothèque municipale de Saint-Rémi, 25, rue Saint-Sauveur, CP 578, St-Rémi QC J0L 2L0 – 514/454-2418; Téléc: 514/454-4083; Courrier électronique: biblir_mi@cedep.net – Responsable, Nathalie Groulx

St-Romuald: Bibliothèque municipale de St-Romuald, 2161, ch du Fleuve, CP 43100, St-Romuald QC G6W 5P8 – 418/839-5242; Téléc: 418/839-5323 – Responsable, Martine Boulay

Ste-Thérèse: Bibliothèque municipale de Ste-Thérèse, 150, boul du Séminaire, Ste-Thérèse QC J7E 1Z2 – 514/434-1442; Téléc: 514/434-6070; Courrier électronique: nadeaul@ville.sainte-therese.qc.ca; Symbol: QMBST – Directeur, Léonard Nadeau; Reference Librarian, Nicole Bouchard

Saint-Timothée: Bibliothèque publique de Saint-Timothée, #400, 5100, boul Hébert, Saint-Timothée QC J0S 1X0 – 514/371-6854; Téléc: 514/371-7205 – Responsable, Andrée Julien

Salaberry-de-Valleyfield: Bibliothèque municipale de Salaberry-de-Valleyfield, 75, rue St-Jean-Baptiste, Salaberry-de-Valleyfield QC J6T 1Z6 – 514/370-4860; Téléc: 514/370-4888 – Responsable, Manon Allen

Sept-Îles: Bibliothèque municipale de Sept-Îles, 500, av Jolliet, Sept-Îles QC G4R 2B4 – 418/964-3355; Téléc: 418/964-3353 – Bibliothécaire en chef, Jocelyne Boudreau

Shawinigan: Bibliothèque municipale de Shawinigan, 550, av de l'Hôtel-de-Ville, CP 400, Shawinigan QC G9N 6V3 – 819/536-7219; Téléc: 819/536-0808 – Bibliothécaire, Charlotte Lecours-Picard

Sherbrooke: Bibliothèque Eva-Senécal, 450, rue Marquette, Sherbrooke QC J1H 1M4 – 819/821-5860; Téléc: 819/822-6110; Courrier électronique: bibliotheque@ville.sherbrooke.qc.ca; URL: http://ville.sherbrooke.qc.ca:9006/~secbib/ – Directrice, Diane Verville-Caron; Adultes, Bibliothécaire, Jocelyne Valence; Enfants, Bibliothécaire, Jeanne Desautels; Services techniques, André Bruneau

Sillery: Bibliothèque Charles-H.-Blais, 1245, av du Chanoine-Morel, Sillery QC G1S 4B1 – 418/684-2140; Téléc: 418/684-2169 – Responsable, Madeleine Dumais

Sorel: Bibliothèque municipale de Sorel, 145, rue George, Sorel QC J3P 1C7 – 514/780-5750; Téléc: 514/780-5758; Symbol: QSO – Directeur, Guy Desjardins

Terrebonne: Bibliothèque municipale de l'Île-des-Moulins, 855, Place Île-des-Moulins, Terrebonne QC J6W 4N7 – 514/471-4192; Téléc: 514/471-2872 – Directrice, Françoise Martin – See also following branches: Bibliothèque André-Guérard

Terrebonne: Bibliothèque André-Guérard, 3425, av Camus, RR#40, Terrebonne QC J6Y 1L2 – 514/471-4192; Téléc: 514/471-2872 – Directrice, Françoise Martin – Branch of Bibliothèque municipale de l'Île-des-Moulins

Thetford Mines: Bibliothèque publique de Thetford Mines, 5, rue de la Fabrique, CP 489, Thetford Mines QC G6G 5T3 – 418/335-6111; Téléc: 418/335-0919 – Directeur, Maryse Pomerleau

Tracy: Bibliothèque municipale de Tracy, 3025, boul de la Mairie, Tracy QC J3R 1C2 – 514/742-8321; Téléc: 514/746-8894 – Responsable, Alain Larouche

Trois-Rivières-Ouest: Bibliothèque municipale de Trois-Rivières-Ouest, 5575, boul Jean-XXIII, Trois-Rivières-Ouest QC G8Z 4A8 – 819/374-6525; Téléc: 819/374-5126; Courrier électronique: bibliotheque.tro-2@cgocable.ca; URL: http://www.bibliombf.qc.ca/tro.htm – Bibliothécaire, France René

Trois-Rivières: Bibliothèque Gatien-Lapointe, 1225, Place de l'Hôtel-de-Ville, CP 1713, Trois-Rivières QC G9A 5L9 – 819/374-3521; Téléc: 819/693-1892 – Chef de service, Michel Lacoursière; Technical Services Librarian, Odette Pelletier; Acquisitions Librarian, Madeleine Bessette

Val-Bélair: Bibliothèque Félix-Leclerc, 1130, boul Pie XI nord, CP 8310, Val-Bélair QC G3K 1Y9 – 418/843-6197; Téléc: 418/843-9970; Symbol: QVBFL – Directeur, Patrice Robitaille, Ph.D.

Val-d'Or: Bibliothèque municipale de Val-d'Or, 600, 7e rue, Val-d'Or QC J9P 3P3 – 819/824-2666; Téléc: 819/825-3062; Courrier électronique: biblvd@uqat.uquebec.ca; URL: http://pyrite.uqat.uquebec.ca/~biblvd – Bibliothécaire, Alain Cloutier

Vanier: Bibliothèque de Vanier, 320, rue Chabot, Vanier QC G1M 3J5 – 418/683-2908; Téléc: 418/681-9433; Courrier électronique: bibliol@oricom.ca; URL: http://www.bibliotheques.qc.ca/bv/index.htm – Technicienne en documentation, Martine Caouette

Varennes: Bibliothèque Jacques-Le Moyne-de-Ste-Marie, 2221, boul René-Gaultier, Varennes QC J3X 1E3 – 514/652-3949; Téléc: 514/652-2349 – Bibliothécaire, Michèle Lamoureux

Vaudreuil-Dorion: Bibliothèque municipale de Vaudreuil-Dorion, 51, rue Jeannotte, Vaudreuil-Dorion QC J7V 6E6 – 514/455-5588; Téléc: 514/455-5653 – Directrice-adjointe de la bibliothèque et culture, Michelle Dupuy

Verdun: Bibliothèque de Verdun, 5955, av Bannantyne, Verdun QC H4H 1H6 – 514/765-7170; Téléc: 514/765-7167; Symbol: QVEC – Bibliothécaire en chef, Loïs Ann Clouthier

Victoriaville: Bibliothèque Charles-Édouard-Mailhot, 2, rue de l'Ermitage, CP 370, Victoriaville QC G6P 6T2 – 819/758-8441; Téléc: 819/357-2099 – Directrice, Sylvie Filiatrault – See also following branches: Succursale Alcide-Fleury

Warwick: Bibliothèque municipale de Warwick, 104, rue St-Louis, CP 577, Warwick QC J0A 1M0 – 819/358-4325; Téléc: 819/358-4309; Courrier électronique: bibliow@ivic.qc.ca – Responsable, Pauline L. Picard

Waterloo: Bibliothèque publique de Waterloo, 650, rue de la Cour, CP 883, Waterloo QC J0E 2N0 – 514/539-2268 – Bibliothécaire, Gisèle Dupuis

Windsor: Bibliothèque municipale de Windsor, 54, rue St-Georges, Windsor QC J1S 1J5 – 819/845-7115; Téléc: 819/845-5516 – Responsable, Marie-Pascale Morin

## Special & College Libraries & Resource Centres

### ACTON VALE

Société d'histoire des Six Cantons – Bibliothèque, CP 236, Acton Vale QC J0H 1A0 – 514/546-2093

### ALMA

CEGEP d'Alma - Bibliothèque, 675, boul Auger ouest, Alma QC G8B 2B7 – 418/668-2387; Fax: 418/668-3806; Email: jtrepanier@calma.qc.ca;
Symbol: QALC – Bibliothécaire, Janic Trépanier

Centre locale de services communautaires Le Norois - Centre de documentation, Édifice du complexe J. Gagnon, 100, rue St-Joseph sud, Alma QC G8B 7A6 – 418/668-4563; Téléc: 418/668-5403 – Isabelle Dufour

Conseil de la culture de la région Saguenay/Lac-St-Jean/Chibougamau/Chapais – Bibliothèque, #101, 414, rue Collard ouest, Alma QC G8B 1N2 – 418/662-6623; Téléc: 418/662-1071 – Secrétaire-comptable, Suzette Villeneuve

Morency, Duchesne & Associé Law Office - Bibliothèque, 521, rue Sacré-Coeur ouest, Alma QC G8B 1M4 – 418/668-3011; Téléc: 418/668-0209 – Technicienne, Marlene Hudon

Société d'histoire du Lac-St-Jean – Centre d'archives de la MRC Lac-Saint-Jean Est, 54, rue St. Joseph, CP 787, Alma QC G8B 3E4 – 418/668-2606; Téléc: 418/668-5851 – Archiviste, Gaston Martel

### BAIE-COMEAU

CEGEP de Baie-Comeau - Centre de ressources éducatives: documentation, 537, boul Blanche, Baie-Comeau QC G5C 2B2 – 418/589-5707;
Fax: 418/589-9842; Symbol: QHAC – Bibliothécaire en chef, Richard Lachance

Centre hospitalier régional - Pavillon Le Royer – Bibliothèque médicale, 635, boul Joliet, Baie Comeau QC G5C 1P1 – 418/589-0693; Téléc: 418/589-7101 – Technicienne en documentation, Marcelle Vallée

Centre local de services communautaires de l'Aquilon - Centre de documentation, 600, rue Jalbert, Baie-Comeau QC G5C 1Z9 – 418/589-2191; Téléc: 418/589-7784; Symbol: QBCCL – Technicienne, Anne Côté

Services Myriam Beth-léhem – Bibliothèque Myriam, 105, boul Lasalle, Baie-Comeau QC G4Z 1R7 – 418/296-6223; Téléc: 418/294-2257 – Bibliothécaire, Sylvie Grenier

### BAIE-SAINT-PAUL

Centre hospitalier de Charlevoix – Bibliothèque, 74, rue Ambroise-Fafard, CP 5000, Baie-Saint-Paul QC G0A 1B0 – 418/435-5150; Téléc: 418/435-3315 – Louise Leblanc

### BEAUPORT

Centre hospitalier Robert Giffard – Bibliothèque professionnelle, 2601, rue de la Canardière, Beauport QC G1J 2G3 – 418/663-5300; Téléc: 418/666-9416; Courrier électronique: bibichrg@qbc.clic.net; Symbol: QBRG – Technicienne Documentation, Nicole Drolet

### BOUCHERVILLE

Canadian Society for Education through Art – Library, 675, Samuel de Champlain, Boucherville QC J4B 6C4 – 514/655-2435; Fax: 514/655-4379

National Research Council-Industrial Materials Institute – Centre d'information du CNRC, 75, boul de Montagne, Boucherville QC J4B 6Y4 – 514/641-5131; Fax: 514/641-5133; Email: patrice.dupont@nrc.ca – Spécialiste en information, Patrice Dupont

### BRIGHAM

Les Centres Butters-Savoy et Horizon – Centre de documentation, 278, av des Érables, Brigham QC J0E 1J0 – 514/263-3545; Téléc: 514/263-1145 – Technicien, Jean-Yves Dufort

### CAP-DE-LA-MADELEINE

Hôpital Cloutier – Bibliothèque, 155, rue Toupin, CP 218, Cap-de-la-Madeleine QC G8T 7W3 – 819/370-2100; Téléc: 819/379-6511 – Lise Caron

René Gervais Inc., Consultants – Library, 303, rue Dessureault, Cap-de-la-Madeleine QC G8T 2L8 – 819/371-3313; Téléc: 819/371-2288 – Technical Director, Réjean Blais

### CHARLESBOURG

Jardin zoologique du Québec – Bibliothèque, 9141, av du Zoo, Charlesbourg QC G1G 4G4 – 418/622-0313; Téléc: 418/644-9004 – Personne ressource, Danielle Martel

Ministère des ressources naturelles - Centre de documentation - Énergie, Mines, 5700 - 4e av ouest, #B-208, Charlesbourg QC G1H 6R1 – 418/643-4624; Téléc: 418/643-5928; TLX: 051-2274;
Symbol: QQER – Responsable, Marie-Ève Varin, 418/528-1752, 643-4624

### CHÂTEAUGUAY

Centre hospitalier Anna-Laberge – Centre de documentation, 200, boul Brisebois, Châteauguay QC J6K 4W8 – 514/699-2451; Téléc: 514/699-2525 – B. Gagnon

### CHELSEA

Historical Society of the Gatineau – Archives, POBox 485, Chelsea QC J0X 1N0 – 819/827-4432; Fax: 819/827-5380 – Archivist, Jay Atherton

### CHIBOUGAMAU

Hôpital Chibougamau Ltée – Centre de documentation, 51, 3e rue, Chibougamau QC G8P 1N1 – 418/748-7741; Téléc: 418/748-6391 – Carol Meilleur

### CHICOUTIMI

CEGEP de Chicoutimi - Centre de médias, 534, rue Jacques Cartier est, Chicoutimi QC G7H 1Z6 – 418/549-9520, poste 330; Téléc: 418/549-1315; Courrier électronique: lgaudrea@cegep-chicoutimi.qc.ca;
URL: http://www.cegep-chicoutimi.qc.ca;
Symbol: QCCEC – Référence/Services publiques, Responsable, Louis Gaudreau, 418/549-9520, poste 345

Complexe hospitalier de la Sagamie – Bibliothèque, 305, av Saint-Vallier, CP 5006, Chicoutimi QC G7H 5H6 – 418/549-2195; Téléc: 418/549-0607 – Marcelle Frigon

Institut Roland-Saucier – Bibliothèque médicale, 150, rue Pinel, CP 2250, Chicoutimi QC G7G 3W4 – 418/549-5474; Téléc: 418/549-8143 – Chef de service, Lorraine Berube

Séminaire de Chicoutimi - Bibliothèque, 679, rue Chabanel, Chicoutimi QC G7H 1Z7 – 418/549-0190, poste 320 – Technicien en documentation, Lucien Fortin

Société généalogique du Saguenay, inc. – Archives, #102, 121, rue Racine est, CP 814, Chicoutimi QC G7H 5E8 – 418/674-2487 – Archiviste, Annie Lavoie

Société historique du Saguenay – Bibliothèque, CP 456, Chicoutimi QC G7H 5C8 – 418/549-2805 – Archiviste, Roland Bélanger

Université du Québec à Chicoutimi - Bibliothèque Paul-Emile-Boulet, 555, boul de l'Université, Chicoutimi QC G7H 2B1 – 418/545-5031;
Téléc: 418/693-5896; Courrier électronique: QCU
Head, Information Services, Gilles Caron
Reference Librarian, Serge Harvey
Circulation Librarian, Réginald Gamache

### COATICOOK

Centre hospitalier de Coaticook – Centre de documentation, 138, rue Jeanne-Mance, Coaticook QC J1A 1W3 – 819/849-2115; Téléc: 819/849-6735 – Robert Simard

### CONTRECOEUR

Sidbec-Dosco Inc. - Centre de documentation, 3900, route des Aciéries, Contrecoeur QC J0L 1C0 – 514/392-3200; Téléc: 514/392-3222 – Library Coordinator, Therese Levesque, 514/392-3258

### COWANSVILLE

Hôpital Brôme-Missisquoi-Perkins – Centre de documentation, 950, rue Principale, Cowansville QC J2K 1K3 – 514/266-4342; Téléc: 514/263-8669 – André Marcoux

Solicitor General Canada - Cowansville Establishment - Library, 400 Fordyce St., POBox 5000, Cowansville QC J2K 3N7 – 514/263-3073, ext.271;
Symbol: QCCE – Librarian, Rose Sybille

### DONNACONNA

Solicitor General Canada - Donnaconna Institution - Library, 1538 Hwy. 138, Donnaconna QC G0A 1T0 – 418/285-2455, ext.2501; Symbol: QDSG – Librarian, Hélène Pellerin

### DRUMMONDVILLE

Hôpital Ste-Croix – Bibliothèque, 570, rue Heriot, Drummondville QC J2B 1C1 – 819/478-6464; Téléc: 819/478-6461; Symbol: QDHSC – Technicienne, Thérèse Henault

Société d'histoire de Drummondville – Archives, 545, rue des Écoles, Drummondville QC J2B 1J6 – 819/474-2318; Téléc: 819/478-2582 – Archiviste, Jean-Pierre Bélanger

Solicitor General Canada - Drummond Establishment - Library, 2025, rue Jean-de-Brébeuf, Drummondville QC J2B 7Z6 – 819/477-5112, ext.285; Fax: 819/477-5664; Symbol: QDD – Librarian, Mohammed Ben Abdallah

### GASPÉ

Ministère de l'agriculture, des pêcheries et de l'alimentation - Centre de documentation, 96, Montée Sandy Beach, CP 1070, Gaspé QC G0C 1R0 – 418/368-7618; Téléc: 418/368-8400;
Symbol: QGAP
Documentalist, Paul Carrier, 418/368-7615
Chef, Acquisitions et services techniques, Jocelyne Anglehart, 418/368-7616
Prêt - PIB - Circulation, Brenda Lapierre, 418/368-7618

### GATINEAU

Centre hospitalier de Gatineau – Bibliothèque médicale, 909, boul de la Verendrye ouest, CP 2000, Gatineau QC J8P 7H2 – 819/561-8106; Téléc: 819/561-8306; Symbol: QGCH – Michel Turpin

### GRANBY

Centre hospitalier de Granby – Bibliothèque médicale, 205, boul Leclerc, Granby QC J2G 1T7 – 514/372-5495, poste 2147; Téléc: 514/372-7197;
Symbol: QGCHG – Technicienne en documentation, Lise Trudel

Centre local de services communautaires de la Haute Yamaska - Centre de documentation, 294, rue Déragon, Granby QC J2G 5J5 – 514/375-1442; Téléc: 514/375-5655 – Brigitte Dionne

**GREENFIELD PARK**

Hôpital Charles Lemoyne – Bibliothèque, 121, boul Taschereau, Greenfield Park QC J4V 2H1 – 514/466-5410; Téléc: 514/466-5779 – Bibliothécaire, Daniel Lamagnère

**HULL**

Canadian Environmental Assessment Agency - Reference Centre, Édifice Fontaine, 200, boul Sacré-Coeur, Hull QC K1A 0H3 – 819/994-2578; Fax: 819/953-2891; Email: parents@fox.nstn.ca; URL: http://www.ceaa.qc.ca; Symbol: OOFE – Reference Clerk, Stéphane Parent

Canadian Heritage - Departmental Library, Les Terrasses de la Chaudière, 15, rue Eddy, Hull QC K1A 0M5 – 819/994-5478; Fax: 819/953-7988; Email: ENVOY:OOSS; Symbol: OOSS
- Chief Librarian, Réjean Héroux, 819/997-3981, Email: rejean_heroux_at_TC3@ccmail.chin.doc.ca
- Public Services Librarian, Louis Belanger, 819/994-2229
- Acquisitions, Denis Parizeau, 819/997-2345
- Wellington Library, Mezzanine Level, 10 Wellington St., Hull QC K1A 0M5 – 819/997-6679; Fax: 819/953-9312; Symbol: OOPAC

Canadian International Development Agency - Development Information Centre, Place du Centre, 200 Promenade du Portage, 8e étage, Hull QC K1A 0G4 – 819/953-8168; Fax: 819/953-8132; Symbol: OOCD – Chief, Nicole Sansfaçon

Canadian Museum of Civilization - Information Management Services (IMSD), 100, rue Laurier, POBox 3100, Hull QC J8X 4H2 – 819/776-7173 (Ref.Desk); Fax: 819/776-8491; Email: library@cmcc.muse.digital.ca; URL: http://www.cmcc.muse.digital.ca; Symbol: OONMM
- Director, Manon Guilbert, 819/776-7179, Email: manon.guilbert@cmcc.muse.digital.ca
- Reference Librarian, Brigitte Lafond, 819/776-7151
- Documentation & Technical Services, Head, Margaret McGarry, 819/776-8498
- Acquisitions Assistant, Sam Morgulis, 819/776-8307
- ILL, Sylvie Laflamme, 819/776-7174
- Information Access Services, Head, Geneviève Eustache, 819/776-8183
- Copyright Licensing, Nicole Chamberland, 819/776-8499

Centre hospitalier Pierre Janet – Centre de documentation, 20, rue Pharand, Hull QC J9A 1K7 – 819/771-7761; Téléc: 819/771-2908 – Nguyen Lam

Centre hospitalier régional de l'Outaouais – Bibliothèque, 116, boul Lionel Emond, Hull QC J8Y 1W7 – 819/595-6050; Téléc: 819/595-6327; Symbol: QHSC – Bibliotechnicienne, Dianne Couture

Collège de l'Outaouais - Bibliothèque Gabrielle Roy, 333, boul Cité des Jeunes, Hull QC J8Y 6M5 – 819/770-4012; Téléc: 819/770-3855; Courrier électronique: MFRA@fedecegeps.qc.ca; URL: http://www.coll-outao.qc.ca – Directeur, Marthe Marthe Francoeur

Environment Canada-Technology Development Directorate – Library, Environmental Protection Service, Place Cartier, 425, boul St-Joseph, 4e étage, Hull QC K1A 0H3 – 819/997-1768; Fax: 819/953-9029 – Librarian, Diana Dale

Environment Canada - Departmental Library, 351, St Joseph Blvd., Hull QC K1A 0H3 – 819/997-1767; Fax: 819/997-5349; Email: librarypvm@ncrsv2.am.doe.ca; URL: http://www.doe.ca/library/libhome.html; Symbol: OOFF

Heritage College - Library, 325, boul Cité des Jeunes, Hull QC J8Y 6T3 – 819/778-2270; Fax: 819/778-7364; Symbol: QHCH
- Librarian, Kate Hughes
- Library Technician, Rachel Patry

Human Resources Development Canada - Canadian Clearinghouse on Disability Issues, Status of Disabled Persons Secretariat, #100, 25, rue Eddy, Hull QC K1A 0M5 – 819/994-7514; Fax: 819/953-4797; Toll Free: 1-800-665-9017; Symbol: OOCCD – Manager, Terri Tomchyshyn
- Main Library, Place du Portage, Phase IV, 1st Fl., 140, Promenade du Portage, Hull QC K1A 0J9 – 819/994-2603; Fax: 819/953-5482; Symbol: OOMI
- Acting Departmental Librarian, Joanne Cournoyer, 819/994-1683
- Acting Chief, Information Access, Sara Sprague, 819/953-9021
- Phase II Library, Place du Portage, Phase II, 7th Fl., 165, rue Hôtel-de-Ville, Hull QC K1A 0J9 – 819/997-3541; Fax: 819/953-2098; Symbol: OOL – Chief, Client Information Services, Phase II, Michèle Auger, 819/953-0032

National Transportation Agency of Canada - Library, 15, rue Eddy, 17e étage, Hull QC K1A 0N9 – 819/997-7160; Fax: 819/953-9815; Email: NTA.LIBRARY; natlib@magi.com; Symbol: OOTT – R. Pareanen

Pavillon Jellinek – Bibliothèque, 25, rue Saint-François, Hull QC J9A 1B1 – 819/776-5584; Téléc: 819/776-0255 – Technicien, Pierre Hamelin

Public Service Commission of Canada - Asticou Centre, 241, boul Cité des Jeunes, Hull QC J8Y 6L2 – 819/953-7879; Fax: 819/953-2392; Symbol: QHCFP

Public Works & Government Services Canada - Translation Bureau - Documentation Services Division, Place du Portage, Phase II, 165, rue Hôtel-de-Ville, 23e étage, Hull QC K1A 0S5 – 819/997-4840; Fax: 819/994-3735
- Chief, Lise Sabourin
- Cataloguing, Brigitte Lepage
- Acquisitions, Johanne Bertrand
- Translation Bureau - Multilingual Documentation Centre, Place du Portage II, West Tower, 165, rue Hotel-de-Ville, 5e étage, Hull QC K1A 0S5 – 819/997-0258; Fax: 819/994-5900; Symbol: OOSSTM – Head, Martin Tremblay
- Translation Bureau - Terminology Documentation Centre, Place du Portage, Phase II, 165, rue Ho^tel-de-Ville, 3e étage, Hull QC K1A 0S5 – 819/994-5904; Fax: 819/953-9691; Symbol: OOSSTE-195 – Librarian, Yves Ranger
- Translation Bureau - Translation Services Documentation Centre, Place du Portage, Phase II, 165, rue Hôtel-de-Ville, 23e étage, Hull QC K1A 0S5 – 819/994-0859; Fax: 819/994-3735 – Head, J. Lachapelle

Régie régionale de la santé et des services sociaux de l'Outaouais – Centre de documentation, 104, rue Lois, Hull QC J8Y 3R7 – 819/770-7747; Téléc: 819/771-8632; Symbol: QHCRS – Bibliotechnicienne, Christiane Boyer

Société de généalogie de l'Outaouais – Bibliothèque, CP 2025, Hull QC J8X 3Z2 – 819/682-5576; Téléc: 819/682-3252

Transportation Safety Board - Library, Place du Centre, 4th Fl., 200 Promenade du Portage, Hull QC K1A 1K8 – 819/994-8020; Fax: 819/997-2239; Symbol: OOTAI – Librarian, Louis Morin

Université du Québec à Hull - Bibliothèque, CP 1250, Hull QC J8X 3X7 – 819/773-1790; Téléc: 819/773-1699; Courrier électronique: ENVOY: PEB.QHU; URL: http://www.uqah.uquebec.ca
- Chief Librarian, Monique Légère
- Public Services Librarian, Danielle Boisvert, 819/595-2374
- Public Services Librarian, Gilles Bergeron, 819/773-1789
- Public Services Librarian, Daniel Pouloit, 819/773-1799
- Indexing Librarian, Monique Picard, 819/595-3809

**JOLIETTE**

CEGEP de Lanaudière - Bibliothèque, 20, rue St-Charles sud, Joliette QC J6E 4T1 – 514/759-1661; Téléc: 514/759-4468; URL: http://www.collanaud.qc.ca
- Bibliothécaire en chef, Robert Corriveau, 514/759-1661, ext.134
- Bibliotechnicienne, Martine Gagnon, 514/759-1661, ext.288
- Bibliotechnicienne, Francine Grosleau, 514/759-1661, ext.261
- Bibliotechnicienne, Danielle Gagnon, 514/759-1661, ext.160

Département de santé communautaire de Lanaudière - Centre de documentation, Centre hospitalier régional de Lanaudière, 1000, boul Ste-Anne, Joliette QC J6E 6J2 – 514/759-9900; Téléc: 514/759-5149; Symbol: QJCH – Suzie Desilets

**JONQUIÈRE**

Alcan International Ltd. - Bibliothèque, CP 1250, Jonquière QC G7S 4K8 – 418/699-2844; Téléc: 418/699-3996 – Bibliothécaire, P. Leclerc

CEGEP de Jonquière - Centre de ressources éducatives, 2505, rue St-Hubert, Jonquière QC G7X 7W2 – 418/547-2191; Téléc: 418/547-3359; URL: http://college.cjonquiere.qc.ca
- Conseiller pédagogique, Jean-Pierre Dufour, 418/547-2191, ext.266
- Reference Librarian, Armande Déry-Allard, 418/547-2191, ext.302
- Circulation Librarian, Rémi Savard, 418/547-2191, ext.268
- Public Services Librarian, Yvon Tremblay, 418/547-2191, ext.302
- Technical Services Librarian, Monique Laforte, 418/547-2191, ext.379
- Acquisitions Librarian, Jacques Fortin, 418/547-2191, ext.269

Centre hospitalier Jonquière – Centre de ressources éducatives, 2230, rue de l'Hôpital, CP 1200, Jonquière QC G7X 7X2 – 418/695-7700; Téléc: 418/695-4437

Fédération des syndicats du secteur de l'aluminium inc. (ind.) – Bibliothèque, 1924, boul Mellon, Jonquière QC G7S 3H3 – 418/548-7075; Téléc: 418/548-7992

**KNOWLTON**

Brome County Historical Society – Library, 130 Lakeside Rd., POBox 690, Knowlton QC J0E 1V0 – 514/243-6782 – Archivist, Marion L. Phelps

**L'ASSOMPTION**

Collège de l'Assomption - Centre de documentation, 270, boul l'Ange-Gardien, L'Assomption QC J0K 1G0 – 819/589-5621 – Bibliothécaire, Réjean Oliver

**LA MACAZA**

Solicitor General Canada - La Macaza Establishment - Library, 321 Airport Rd., La Macaza QC J0T 1R0 – 819/275-2315, ext.7046; Téléc: 819/275-3079; Symbol: QLML – Librarian, Daniel Lapointe

**LA POCATIÈRE**

CEGEP de La Pocatière - Bibliothèque François-Hertel, 140, 4e av, La Pocatière QC G0R 1Z0 – 418/856-1525; Téléc: 418/856-4589; Courrier électronique: jldemers@cglapocatiere.qc.ca;

URL: http://cegep.cglapocatiere.qc.ca – Bibliothécaire en chef, Jean-Louis Demers

Collège de Ste-Anne-de-la-Pocatière - Bibliothèque, 100, 4e av, La Pocatière QC G0R 1Z0 – 418/856-3012; Téléc: 418/856-5611 – Responsable, Marcel Mignault

Institut de technologie agro-alimentaire de La Pocatière - Centre de documentation, 401, rue Poiré, La Pocatière QC G0R 1Z0 – 418/856-1110, poste 258; Téléc: 418/856-1719; Ligne sans frais: 1-800-463-1351; Symbol: QPES
- Bibliothécaire, Denis Dumont
- Bibliotechnicienne, Ginette Lévesque
- Agente de bureau, Agathe Plante

Société historique de la Côte-du-Sud – Centre de documentation, CP 937, La Pocatière QC G0R 1Z0 – 418/856-2104; Téléc: 418/856-2104

### LA SARRE

Centre local de services communautaires des aurores boréales - Centre de documentation, 285, 1re rue est, La Sarre QC J9Z 3K1 – 819/333-2354; Téléc: 819/333-3111 – Lorraine Carbonneau

### LA TÛQUE

Centre hospitalier Saint-Joseph de La Tuque – Centre de documentation, 885, boul Ducharme, La Tûque QC G9X 3C1 – 819/523-4581; Téléc: 819/523-7992 – Bibliothécaire, Nicole Saint-Pierre

### LENNOXVILLE

Agriculture & Agri-Food Canada-Dairy & Swine Research & Development Centre: Lennoxville – Bibliothèque canadienne de l'agriculture, 2000, rte 108 est, CP 90, Lennoxville QC J1M 1Z3 – 819/565-9171; Téléc: 819/564-5507; Courrier électronique: gagnegigueres@em.agr.ca; Symbol: QLAG – Bibliothécaire, Suzanne Gagné-Giguère

Bishop's University - John Bassett Memorial Library, PO Box 5000, Stn Lennoxville, Lennoxville QC J1M 1Z7 – 819/822-9600, ext.2605; Fax: 819/822-9644; URL: http://www.ubishops.ca; Symbol: QLB
- University Librarian, William M. Curran, 819/822-9600, ext.2606, Email: wcurran@ubishops.ca
- Public Services, Head, Wendy L. Durrant, 819/822-9600, ext.2708
- Technical Services & Systems, Head, Pierre Lafrance, 819/822-9600, ext.2707
- Acquisitions Librarian, Terry Skeats, 819/822-9600, ext.2604
- Reference Librarian, Gary McCormick, 819/822-9600, ext.2608

### LÉVIS

Assurance vie Desjardins-Laurentienne Inc. – Centre de documentation, 200, av des Commandeurs, Lévis QC G6V 6R2 – 418/838-7390, 7626; Fax: 418/833-3271; Toll Free: 1-800-463-7870 – Technicienne en documentation, Louise Bédard

Cégep de Lévis-Lauzon - Bibliothéque, 205, Mgr Ignace Bourget, Lévis QC G6V 6Z9 – 418/833-5110; Téléc: 418/833-7323; URL: http://www.clevislauzon.qc.ca/
- Responsable des services publics, Alain Gendron, Email: alain.gendron@clevislauzon.qc.ca
- Responsable des services techniques, Jean-Claude Gosselin

Collège de Lévis - Bibliothéque, 9, av Mgr. Gosselin, Lévis QC G6V 5K1 – 418/833-1249, poste 140; Téléc: 418/833-1974; Symbol: QCL – Responsable, Josée Audet

Confédération des caisses populaires et d'économie desjardins du Québec - Division des ressources informationnelles et documentaires, 100, av des Commandeurs, Lévis QC G6V 7N5 – 418/835-4593; Téléc: 418/833-5873; Ligne sans frais: 1-800-463-4810; Courrier électronique: GESDOC; Symbol: QLCCP
- Documentaliste, Benjamin Fortin
- Technicienne, Lise Petel
- Technicienne, Jacqueline Dubé

Conseil de la coopération du Québec – Bibliothèque, #304, 4950, boul de la Rive Sud, Lévis QC G6V 4Z6 – 418/835-3710; Téléc: 418/835-6322

Fédération des associations coopérative d'économie familiale du Québec - ACEF Rive-Sud de Québec – Bibliothèque, #2, 11, av Bégin, Lévis QC G6V 4B6 – 418/835-6633

Hôtel-Dieu de Lévis – Bibliothèque, 143, rue Wolfe, Lévis QC G6V 3Z1 – 418/835-7121, ext.3274; Téléc: 418/835-7133; Symbol: QLHD – Secretaire, J. Dufour

### LONGUEUIL

Association béton Québec – Bibliothèque, #107, 85, rue St-Charles ouest, Longueuil QC J4H 1C5 – 514/463-3569; Téléc: 514/463-1704 – Diane Morin

Centre hospitalier Pierre-Boucher – Centre de documentation, 1333, boul Jacques-Cartier est, Longueuil QC J4M 2A5 – 514/468-8111; Téléc: 514/468-8029; Courrier électronique: cdochpb@cam.org; Symbol: QLOPB – Dominique Lefrançois

Les Centres jeunesse de la Montérégie – Centre de documentation, 25, boul Lafayette, Longueuil QC J4K 5C8 – 514/679-0140; Téléc: 514/679-3731; Symbol: QLOCSS – Line Marquis

Collège Edouard-Montpetit - Centre des ressources documentaires, 945, ch de Chambly, Longueuil QC J4H 3M6 – 514/679-2630, poste 609; Téléc: 514/677-2945
- Coordonnatrice, Gisèle Laramée
- Responsable de la référence et des services publiques, Francine Paquin
- Responsable des services techniques, Janine Boucher

Conseil culturel de la Montérégie inc. – Bibliothèque, 305, boul Saint-Jean, Longueuil QC J4H 2X4 – 514/651-0694; Téléc: 514/651-6020 – Rita Harvie

Health Canada - Direction générale de la protection de la santé - Bibliothèque régionale, 1001, boul Saint-Laurent ouest, Longueuil QC J4K 1C7 – 514/646-1353, poste 312; Téléc: 514/928-4102; Courrier électronique: france_lachapelle@inet.hwc.ca; Symbol: QMNHH – Library Technician, France Lachapelle

Institut Nazareth et Louis-Braille - Bibliothèque braille, 1111, rue Saint-Charles ouest, Longueuil QC J4K 5G4 – 514/463-1710; Téléc: 514/463-0243; Ligne sans frais: 1-800-361-7063 – Bibliothécaire, Linda Laberge

Institut Nazareth et Louis Braille - Centre d'information typhlophilique, 1111, rue Saint-Charles ouest, Longueuil QC J4K 5G4 – 514/463-1710; Téléc: 514/463-0243; Ligne sans frais: 1-800-361-7063; Symbol: QLNLB
- Bibliothécaire, Linda Laberge
- Directeur, André Vincent

Pratt & Whitney Canada Inc. - Library, 1000, rue Marie-Victorin, Longueuil QC J4G 1A1 – 514/647-7341; Fax: 514/647-7797; TLX: 05-267509; Symbol: QLOU
- Librarian Supervisor, Elizabeth Reader, 514/647-7341, Email: elizabeth.reader@pwc.utc.com
- Reference Librarian, L. St. Amour, 514/647-2607
- Circulation, M. Andrews, 514/647-7342
- Public Services Librarian, B. Pawlowsky, 514/647-7342
- Technical Services, E. Lacombe, 514/647-4694
- Acquisitions, K. Portanier, 514/647-7343
- Circulation, M. Chaput, 514/647-7342

Société d'histoire de Longueuil – Maison André-Lamarre, 255, rue Saint-Charles est, Longueuil QC J4H 1B3 – 514/674-0349

Société historique du Marigot inc. – Centre de documentation, 440, ch de Chambly, Longueuil QC J4H 3L7 – 514/677-4573; 670-7399

### MATANE

Collège de Matane - Bibliothèque, 616, rue St-Rédempteur, Matane QC G4W 1L1 – 418/562-1240, poste 2128; Fax: 418/566-2115 – Bibliothécaire, Colette Côté

Société d'histoire et de généalogie de Matane – Bibliothèque, CP 608, Matane QC G4W 3P6 – 418/562-9766, 2808 – Secrétaire, J. Bernier

### MIRABEL

Bell Helicopter Textron - Library, 12800, rue de l'Avenir, Mirabel QC J7J 1R4 – 514/437-6041; Fax: 514/437-6382; Email: engineer@bhtc.com; URL: http://www.bellhelicopter.textron.com; Symbol: QSTTB – Supervisor, Engineering Support, Gerda-Marie Gritzka

### MONT-JOLI

Fisheries & Oceans Canada-Institut Maurice-Lamontagne – Bibliothèque, 850, rte de la Mer, CP 1000, Mont-Joli QC G5H 3Z4 – 418/775-0551; Téléc: 418/775-0542; Courrier électronique: ENVOY: DFO.LIB.QUEBEC; biblio@dfo-mpo.gc.ca; Symbol: QQPSM – Bibliothécaire, Guy Michaud

Hôpital de Mont-Joli Inc. – Bibliothèque médicale, 800, ch du Sanatorium, Mont-Joli QC G5H 3L6 – 418/775-7261, ext.4323; Téléc: 418/775-8607; Symbol: QMJH – Bibliotechnicienne, Hélène Jean

### MONTRÉAL

Québec Ministère des Transports - Service de l'environnement – Bibliothèque, 35, rue de Port-Royal est, 4e étage, Montréal QC H3L 3T1 – 514/864-1668; Fax: 514/873-7630; Email: vnguyen@mtg.gouv.qc.ca; Symbol: QMTRA – Bibliothécaire, Vy-Khanh Nguyen

Transportation Development Centre – Judith Nogrady Library, 800, boul René-Lévesque ouest, 6e étage, Montréal QC H3B 1X9 – 514/283-0007; Fax: 514/283-7158; Email: ludgatg@tc.gc.ca; Symbol: QMTD – Head Librarian, George Ludgate

A. Foster Higgins & Cie - Employee Benefit Documentation Centre, #2624, 800 Victoria Sq., Montréal QC H4Z 1C3 – 514/878-4035; Fax: 514/878-4708 – Coordinator, Documentation Centre, Claire Gendreau

Agence francophone pour l'enseignement supérieur et la recherche – Bibliothèque, Direction générale-Rectorat, CP 400, Succ Côte des Neiges, Montréal QC H3C 2S7 – 514/343-6630; Téléc: 514/343-2107; TLX: 055-60955 – Documentaliste, Céline Brunel

Agriculture & Agri-Food Canada - Bibliothèque canadienne de l'agriculture, #746, 2001, rue University, Montréal QC H3A 3N2 – 514/283-8888; Téléc: 514/283-3143; Courrier électronique: lbqmtlag@nccot.agr.ca; Symbol: QMPCA – Bibliothécaire, Pierre DiCampo, 514/283-8888, ext.201

Alcan Aluminum Ltd. - Information Centre, 1188, rue Sherbrooke ouest, POBox 6090, Montréal QC H3C 3A7 – 514/848-8187; Fax: 514/848-1469; Symbol: QMA – Manager, Information Centre, Lucie Dion, 514/848-8319

Allan Memorial Institute of Psychiatry - Eric D. Wittkower Library, 1025, av des Pins ouest, Montréal QC H3A 1A1 – 514/842-1231, poste 4528; Fax: 514/843-1644; Symbol: QMAM – Medical Librarian, Beverley Bailey, Email: bbailey@rvhmed.lan.mcgill.ca

Alliance des professeures et professeurs de Montréal – Bibliothèque, 8225, boul Saint-Laurent, Montréal QC H2P 2M1 – 514/383-4880; Téléc: 514/384-5756 – Documentaliste-archiviste, Régent Séguin

Amnistie internationale, Section canadienne (Francophone) – Bibliothèque, 6250, boul Monk, Montréal QC H4E 3H7 – 514/766-9766; Téléc: 514/766-2088 – Responsable archives, Marguerite Hug

The Asbestos Institute – Library, #1750, 1002, rue Sherbrooke ouest, Montréal QC H3A 3L6 – 514/844-3956; Fax: 514/844-1381 – John Di Gironimo

Association des auxiliaires bénévoles des établissements de santé du Québec – Bibliothèque, #400, 505, boul de Maisonneuve ouest, Montréal QC H3A 3C2 – 514/282-4264; Téléc: 514/282-4289 – Bibliothécaire, Viera Grmela

Association des conseils des médecins, dentistes et pharmaciens du Québec, 308, boul St-Joseph est, Montréal QC H2T 1J2 – 514/842-5059; Téléc: 514/842-5356 – Documentaliste, Marc Guévin

Association coopérative d'économie familiale - Montréal (Nord) – Centre de documentation, 7500, av Chateaubriand, Montréal QC H2R 2M1 – 514/277-7959; Téléc: 514/277-7730 – Hélène Talbot

Association féminine d'éducation et d'action sociale – Bibliothèque, 5999, rue de Marseille, Montréal QC H1N 1K6 – 514/251-1636; Téléc: 514/251-9023 – Documentaliste, Huguette Dalpé

Association for Canadian Studies – Documentation Centre, c/o UQAM, V-5130, CP 8888, Succ Centre-Ville, Montréal QC H3C 3P8 – 514/987-7784; Fax: 514/987-8210 – Publications Officer, Danielle Comeau

Association des hôpitaux du Québec – Centre de documentation, #400, 505, boul de Maisonneuve ouest, Montréal QC H3A 3C2 – 514/842-4861; Téléc: 514/282-4271; Symbol: QMAHQ – Virginie Jamet

Association des ingénieurs-conseils du Québec – Bibliothèque, #1200, 2050, rue Mansfield, Montréal QC H3A 1Y9 – 514/288-2032; Téléc: 514/288-2306 – Adjointe administrative, Joanne Cook

Association des libraires du Québec – Bibliothèque, 1306, rue Logan, Montréal QC H2L 1X1 – 514/526-3349; Téléc: 514/526-3340 – Adjointe et responsable du Service de recherche, Francine Déry

Association de manutention du Québec – Bibliothèque, 62A, Labelle, Laval QC H7N 2S3 – 514/662-3717; Téléc: 514/662-6096 – Bibliothécaire, Stephanie Born

Association de Montréal pour la déficience intellectuelle – Centre de documentation multi-média, #100, 633, boul Crémazie est, Montréal QC H2M 1L9 – 514/381-2307; Téléc: 514/381-0454 – Documentaliste, Michelle Jacques

Association nationale des éditeurs de livres – Bibliothèque, 2514, boul Rosemont, Montréal QC H1Y 1K4 – 514/273-8130; Téléc: 514/273-9657 – Lise Oligny

Association paritaire pour la santé et la sécurité du travail - Affaires municipales – Bibliothèque, #710, 715, carré Victoria, Montréal QC H2Y 2H7 – 514/849-8373; Téléc: 514/849-8873; Toll Free: 1-800-465-1754 – Personne ressource, Jeanne Taussig

Association paritaire pour la santé et la sécurité du travail - Construction – Bibliothèque, #301, 7905, boul Louis-H.-Lafontaine, Anjou QC H1K 4E4 – 514/355-6190; Téléc: 514/355-7861; Toll Free: 1-800-361-2061 – Bibliothécaire, Lucie Brunet

Association pour l'éducation interculturelle du Québec – Bibliothèque, #530, 7400, boul Saint-Laurent, Montréal QC H2R 2Y1 – 514/276-8883; Téléc: 514/948-1231

Association professionnelle des technologistes médicaux du Québec (ind.) – Bibliothèque, 1595, rue St-Hubert, 3e étage, Montréal QC H2L 3Z2 – 514/524-3734; Téléc: 514/524-7863; Toll Free: 1-800-361-4306 – Commis-relation de travail, Robert Francine

Association du Québec pour l'intégration sociale – Centre de documentation, 3958, rue Dandurand, Montréal QC H1X 1P7 – 514/725-7245; Téléc: 514/725-2976; Courrier électronique: cdocigdi@total.net; Symbol: QMIQDI – Claude F. Leclair

Association québécoise de loisir pour personnes handicapées – Bibliothèque, 4545, av Pierre de Coubertin, CP 1000, Montréal QC H1V 3R2 – 514/252-3144; Téléc: 514/252-3164 – Marie-Josée Duchesne

Association québécoise des marionnettistes – Centre de documentation, Centre UNIMA au Québec, CP 7, Succ De Lorimier, Montréal QC H2H 2N6 – 514/499-0875

Association québécoise pour les troubles d'apprentissage – Centre de ressources, #300, 284, rue Notre-Dame ouest, Montréal QC H2Y 1T7 – 514/847-1324; Téléc: 514/281-5187 – Agente d'information, Jeannette Côté

Association québécoise de l'épilepsie - Epilepsie Montréal – Bibliothèque, #115, 3800, rue Radisson, Montréal QC H1M 1X6 – 514/252-0859; Téléc: 514/252-0598

Association québécoise de l'industrie du disque, du spectacle et de la vidéo – Bibliothèque, #706, 3575, boul St-Laurent, Montréal QC H2X 2T7 – 514/842-5147; Téléc: 514/842-7762 – Documentaliste, Marie-Berthe Lefebvre

Association des services de réhabilitation sociale du Québec inc. – Bibliothèque, 2000, boul St-Joseph est, 2e étage, Montréal QC H2H 1E4 – 514/521-3733; Téléc: 514/521-3753 – Chantal Traversy

Association des sexologues du Québec – Bibliothèque, #300, 6915, rue St-Denis, Montréal QC H2S 2S3 – 514/270-9289; Téléc: 514/270-9289 – Sylviane Larose

L'Association de spina-bifida et d'hydrocéphalie du Québec – Bibliothèque, #425, 5757, rue Decelles, Montréal QC H3S 2C3 – 514/340-9019; Téléc: 514/340-9109; Toll Free: 1-800-567-1788 – Adjointe à la direction, Ginette Bélisle

Atelier d'histoire Hochelaga-Maisonneuve – Centre de documentation, 1691, boul Pie IX, Montréal QC H1V 2C3 – 514/523-5930 – Documentaliste, Mario Laverge

Atomic Energy of Canada Limited-AECL-CANDU - Montréal Laboratory – Information Resources, 1155 Metcalfe St., Montréal QC H3B 2V6 – 514/871-1116; Fax: 514/934-1322

Bank of Montreal – Business Information Centre, 129, rue St-Jacques ouest, Montréal QC H2Y 1L6 – 514/877-9383; Fax: 514/877-8189; Toll Free: 1-800-555-3000 – Manager, Sylvia Piggott

Barreau de Montréal – Bibliothèque, Palais de Justice, #980, 1, rue Notre Dame est, Montréal QC H2Y 1B6 – 514/393-2057; Téléc: 514/879-8592 – Directrice, Celine Amnotte

Batshaw Youth & Family Centre – Centre de documentation, #1010, 2155, rue Guy, Montréal QC H3H 2R9 – 514/989-1885, poste 274; Fax: 514/939-3609; Symbol: QMVM – Janet Sand

Bell Canada - Bibliothèque du service juridique, #1830, 1800, av McGill College, Montréal QC H3A 3J6 – 514/870-2683; Fax: 514/288-0717 – Research Assistant, Carolyne Bourgon

Information Resource Centre, #C29, 700, de la Gauchetière ouest, Montréal QC H3B 4L1 – 514/870-8500; Fax: 514/876-8826; Email: ENVOY100: IRC.MTL.GENERAL; Symbol: QMB – Associate Director, S. Boyd, 514/870-8922

Bendix Avelex Inc. - Engineering Library, POBox 2140, Saint-Laurent QC H4L 4X8 – 514/744-2811, ext.7141; Fax: 514/748-4420 – Rafik Rabbat

Berkowitz Strauber Goldman Law Office - Library, #300, 4141, Sherbrooke ouest, Montréal QC H3Z 1B8 – 514/931-1788; Téléc: 514/931-3061

Bibliothèque générale C.N.D., Maison-mère, 4873, av Westmount, Westmount QC H3Y 1X9 – 514/487-2420, poste 251; Courrier électronique: ENVOY: IDEM – Bibliothécaire-responsable, Carmen Brabant

Bibliothèque nationale du Québec, Édifice Marie-Claire-Daveluy, 125, rue Sherbrooke ouest, Montréal QC H2X 1X4 – 514/873-1100; Téléc: 514/873-4310; Ligne sans frais: 1-800-363-9028; Courrier électronique: web@biblinat.gouv.qc.ca; URL: http://www.biblinat.gouv.qc.ca/

Président/Directeur général, Philippe Sauvageau, 514/873-1100, poste 402

Directeur de la référence, Yvon-André Lacroix, 514/873-1100, poste 441

Directrice des acquisitions, Carole Urbain, 514/873-1100, poste 431

Directeur de l'analyse documentaire, Van Khoa Nguyen, 514/873-1100, poste 447

Directeur de la conservation, Richard Thouin, 514/873-1100, poste 111

Salle de consultation des livres et ouvrages de référence, Édifice Saint-Sulpice, 1700, rue Saint-Denis, Montréal QC H2X 3K6 – 514/873-1100, poste 441; Téléc: 514/873-9932; Ligne sans frais: 1-800-363-9028; Courrier électronique: reference@biblinat.gouv.ac.ca; URL: http://www.biblinat.gouv.qc.ca – Directeur de la référence, Yvon-André Lacroix, Email: ya_lacroix@biblinat.gouv.qc.ca

Salle de consultation des revues, journaux et publications gouvernementales, Édifice Aegidius-Fauteux, 4499, av de l'Esplanade, Montréal QC H2W 1T2 – 514/873-1100, poste 244; Téléc: 514/873-9933; Ligne sans frais: 1-800-363-9028; Courrier électronique: reference@biblinat.gouv.qc.ca; URL: http://www.biblinat.gouv.qc.ca; Symbol: QMBN – Chef de Division, Louise Tessier

Biothermica International Inc. – Library, #440, 3333, boul Cavendish, Montréal QC H4B 2M5 – 514/488-3881; Téléc: 514/488-3125; Toll Free: 1-800-837-6422 – Marketing, Marie-Josée Leroux

Bombardier Inc. - Canadair Division, Technical Information Centre, CP 6087, Succ Centre-Ville, Montréal QC H3C 3G9 – 514/855-5000, ext.6185; Fax: 514/855-7203; Symbol: QMCA – Supervisor, Technical Information & Recordkeeping, Judith Costello

Bristol-Myers Squibb Canada - Medical Library, 2365, côte de Liesse, Montréal QC H4N 2M7 – 514/333-2057; Fax: 514/331-6387; Email: gibson_D@BMS.can; URL: http://www.bms.com; Symbol: QMSQC

Medical Librarian, Donna Gibson

Library Assistant, Hayley Fitzsimmons

Business Development Bank of Canada - Corporate Research Centre, #400, 5, Place Ville Marie, Montréal QC H4Z 1L4 – 514/283-7632; Fax: 514/283-4039; Symbol: QMFBD

Librarian, Jane Patterson, 514/283-3639

Library Technician, Maria Szulhan

Byers Casgrain - Library, #3900, 1, Place Ville Marie, Montréal QC H3B 4M7 – 514/878-8800; Fax: 514/866-2241; Symbol: QMBC – Librarian, Sonya Eder

CAE Electronics Ltd. - Reference Library, 8585, Côte de Liesse, Montréal QC H4T 1D6 – 514/341-6780, ext.2113; Fax: 514/734-5616 – Reference Librarian, Barbara Clement, Email: barbara@cae.ca

Caisse de dépôt et placement du Québec - Bibliothèque, 1981, av McGill College, Montréal QC H3A 3C7 – 514/842-3261; Fax: 514/842-4833 – Responsable, Pauline Corbeil

Canada Human Resources Development - Québec Regional Library, 1441, rue St-Urbain, Montréal QC H2X 2M6 – 514/283-4695; Fax: 514/283-3874; Symbol: QMMIQ

Chief Librarian, Jacinthe Castonguay, 514/283-7586

Reference & Technical Services, Angèle Viau, 514/283-4707

Reference & Acquisitions Clerk, Lise Chamberland, 514/283-4695

Canadian Centre for Architecture – Bibliothèque, 1920, rue Baile, Montréal QC H3H 2S6 – 514/939-7000; Fax: 514/939-7020; Symbol: QMCA – Head, Reader Services, Renata Guttman

Canadian Centre for Ecumenism – Library, 2065, rue Sherbrooke ouest, Montréal QC H3H 1G6 – 514/937-9176; Fax: 514/937-2684 – Coordinator, Bernice Baranowski

Canadian Crossroads International - Group Program Office – Library, 912, rue Sherbrooke est, Montréal QC H2L 1L2 – 514/528-5363; Téléc: 514/528-5367

Canadian HIV/AIDS Legal Network – Library/ Resource Centre, 4007, rue de Mentana, Montréal QC H2L 3R9 – 514/526-1796; Fax: 514/526-5543 – Research Associate, Louise Shap

Canadian Institute for Jewish Research – Library, #550, 5250, boul Decarie, Montréal QC H3X 2H9 – 514/486-5544; Fax: 514/488 3064 – Guy Mizrachi

Canadian Institute of Hypnotism – Library, 110, rue Greystone, Montréal QC H9R 5T6 – 514/426-1010; Fax: 514/426-4680 – Maxine Kershaw

Canadian Institute of Mining, Metallurgy & Petroleum – Library, #1210, 3400, boul de Maisonneuve ouest, Montréal QC H3Z 3B8 – 514/939-2710; Fax: 514/939-2714

Canadian Jewish Congress – Library, 1590, av Docteur Penfield, Montréal QC H3G 1C5 – 514/931-7531; Fax: 514/931-0548 – Archivist, Janice Rosen

Canadian Music Centre - Région du Québec – Bibliothèque, #300, 430, rue St-Pierre, Montréal QC H2Y 2M5 – 514/849-9176; Téléc: 514/849-9177

Canadian National Railway - Dechief Information & Documentation Centre, 1060, rue University, Montréal QC H3B 3A2 – 514/399-3781; Téléc: 514/399-8258; Courrier électronique: library@cn.ca – D. Bélanger

Canadian Psychoanalytic Society – Library, 7000, ch Côte-des-Neiges, Montréal QC H3S 2C1 – 514/738-6105; Fax: 514/738-6393

Canadian Pulp & Paper Association – Library, Sun Life Building, 1155, rue Metcalfe, 19e étage, Montréal QC H3B 4T6 – 514/866-6621; Fax: 514/866-3035 – Librarian, Karen Fountain

Caron, Bélanger, Ernst & Young - Library, #2400, 1 Place Ville Marie, Montréal QC H3B 3M9 – 514/875-6060; Fax: 514/871-8713; Symbol: QMCGLI – Librarian, Margaret Cameron

Carrefour des cèdres – Library, 2376, rue Quesnel, Montréal QC H3J 1G5 – 514/932-3961 – G. Baraghid

CEGEP André Laurendeau - Bibliothèque, 1111 Lapierre, La Salle QC H8N 2J4 – 514/364-3320; Téléc: 514/364-2627; Courrier électronique: lstp@fedecegeps.qc.ca – Spécialiste en moyens et techniques d'enseignement, Louise St-Pierre

CEGEP Marie-Victorin - Bibliothèque, 7000, rue Marie-Victorin, Montréal QC H1G 2J6 – 514/325-0150; Téléc: 514/328-3830 – Bibliothécaire, Réjean Charette

Centraide du Grand Montréal – Bibliothèque, 493, rue Sherbrooke ouest, Montréal QC H3A 1B6 – 514/288-1261; Téléc: 514/844-9900 – Monique Berthiaume

Centrale des syndicats démocratiques – Bibliothèque, 5100, rue Sherbrooke est, 8e étage, Montréal QC H1V 3R9 – 514/899-1070; Téléc: 514/899-1216 – Personne ressource, Catherine Escojido

Centrale de l'enseignement du Québec – Centre de documentation, 9405, rue Sherbrooke est, Montréal QC H1L 6P3 – 514/356-8888; Téléc: 514/356-9999; Symbol: QSTFCE – Louise Grondines

Centre d'action bénévole de Montréal – Centre de documentation, 235, rue St-Jacques, Montréal QC H2Y 1M6 – 514/842-3351; Téléc: 514/842-8977 – Marisa Gelfusa

Centre d'animation de développement et de recherche en éducation – Bibliothèque, 1940, boul Henri-Bourassa est, Montréal QC H2B 1S2 – 514/381-8891; Téléc: 514/381-4086; Toll Free: 1-888-381-8891 – Documentaliste, Roland Desrosiers

Centre des auteurs dramatiques – Centre de documentation, 3450, rue St. Urbain, Montréal QC H2X 2N5 – 514/288-3384; Téléc: 514/288-7043 – Daniel Gauthier

Centre d'auto-perfectionnement des enseignants de français langue seconde – Centre de documentation, 7105, rue Saint-Hubert, Montréal QC H2S 2N1 – 514/273-5329; Téléc: 514/273-0710

Centre canadien d'étude et de coopération internationale – Centre de documentation, 180, rue Sainte-Catherine est, Montréal QC H2X 1K9 – 514/875-9911; Téléc: 514/875-6469; Courrier électronique: carmenh@ceci.ca – Directeur, Robert Hazel

Centre de caractérisation microscopique des matériaux – École Polytechnique Bibliothèque, CP 6079, Montréal QC H3C 3A7 – 514/340-4847; Téléc: 514/340-4468

Centre de documentation sur l'éducation des adultes et la condition féminine – Bibliothèque, #340, 1265, rue Berri, Montréal QC H2L 4X4 – 514/844-3674; Téléc: 514/844-1598; Symbol: QMICE

Centre Dollard-Cormier - Centre québécoise de documentation en toxicomanie, 950, rue Louvain, Montréal QC H2M 2E8 – 514/385-0046; Téléc: 514/385-5728; Symbol: QMCADM – Monique Gauthier

Centre d'éducation interculturelle et de compréhension internationale – Centre de documentation, 3925, rue Villeray, Montréal QC H2A 1H1 – 514/721-8122; Téléc: 514/721-8613 – Bibliothécaire, Michel Craig

Centre d'études et de documentation d'amérique latine – Nouvelles Solidarités, #460, 3680, rue Jeanne-Mance, Montréal QC H2X 2K5 – 514/982-6664; Téléc: 514/982-6122 – Documentaliste, Louise Lavallée

Centre hospitalier de l'Université de Montréal - Pavillon Saint-Luc – Bibliothèque, 1058, rue St-Denis, Montréal QC H2X 3J4 – 514/281-2121, poste 5867; Téléc: 514/281-2501; Courrier électronique: ENVOY: QMHSL; Symbol: QMHSL – Chef du service de soutien à l'enseignement, Pierre Duchesneau

Centre hospitalier Angrignon – Bibliothèque médicale, 4000, boul Lasalle, Verdun QC H4G 2A3 – 514/765-8121; Téléc: 514/765-7306; Symbol: QMHGC – Marc Lamarre

Pavillon LaSalle, 8585, Terrasse Champlain, Lasalle QC H8P 1C1 – 514/365-1510, poste 1435; Téléc: 514/595-2227 – Technicienne, Manon Rivest

Centre hospitalier Catherine Booth – Bibliothèque du personnel, 4375, av Montclair, Montréal QC H4B 2J5 – 514/481-0431; Téléc: 514/481-0029 – Karen Honegger

Centre hospitalier Côte-des-Neiges – Centre de documentation, 4565, ch de la Reine Marie, Montréal QC H3W 1W5 – 514/340-1424; Téléc: 514/340-2815; Courrier électronique: bourbonl@ere.umontreal.ca; Symbol: QMQ – Bibliothécaire en chef, Louise Bourbonnais

Centre hospitalier Fleury – Centre de documentation, 2180, rue Fleury est, Montréal QC H2B 1K3 – 514/381-9311; Téléc: 514/383-5086; Symbol: QMHGF – Bibliotechnicienne, Lise Paradis

Centre hospitalier gériatrique Maimonides – Health Information Centre, 5795, av Caldwell, Cote-Saint-Luc QC H4W 1W3 – 514/483-2121, ext.217; Téléc: 514/483-1086; Symbol: QMMHH – Health Information Officer, D. Scipio

Centre hospitalier Jacques Viger – Centre de documentation, 1051, rue St-Hubert, Montréal QC H2L 3Y5 – 514/842-7181; Téléc: 514/842-1212; Symbol: QMHM – Technicienne en documentation, Danielle Cayer

Centre Hospitalier Richardson – Bibliothèque médicale, 5425, av Bessborough, Montréal QC H4V 2S7 – 514/483-2694; Téléc: 514/483-4596; Courrier électronique: qmhjr@mail.accent.net; Symbol: QMHJR – Christine J. Bolduc

Centre hospitalier de St. Mary – Bibliothèque des sciences de la santé, 3830, av Lacombe, Montréal QC H3T 1M5 – 514/345-3317; Téléc: 514/345-3695; Symbol: QMSMA – Jeannine Lawlor

Centre hospitalier de l'Univeristé de Montréal - Pavillon Hôtel-Dieu – Centre de documentation, 3840, rue St-Urbain, Montréal QC H2W 1T8 – 514/843-2611, poste 5355; Téléc: 514/843-2730; Courrier électronique: boyerg@ere.umontreal.ca; Symbol: QMHD – Chef du centre de documentation, Ginette Boyer

Centre hospitalier de l'Université de Montréal - Pavillon Notre-Dame – Bibliothèque, 1560, rue Sherbrooke est, Montréal QC H2L 4M1 – 514/876-7217; Téléc: 514/876-6748; Symbol: QMHND – Bibliothécaire en chef, André Allard

Centre international de criminologie comparée – Centre de documentation, CP 6128, Montréal QC H3C 3J7 – 514/343-7065; Téléc: 514/343-2269

Centre Justice et Foi - Bibliothèque Édmond Desrochers, 25, rue Jarry ouest, Montréal QC H2P 1S6 – 514/387-2541; Fax: 514/387-4244 – Directeur, Luc Trépanier, 514/387-2541

Centre québécois du droit de l'environnement – Bibliothèque, #307, 2360, rue Notre-Dame ouest, Montréal QC H3G 1N4 – 514/931-9190; Téléc: 514/931-1926 – Bibliothécaire, Dora Knez

Centre de réadaptation Constance-Lethbridge – Bibliothèque médicale, 7005, boul de Maisonneuve ouest, Montréal QC H4B 1T3 – 514/487-1891, poste 220; Téléc: 514/487-5494; Symbol: QMLR – Personne ressource, Jane Petrov

Centre de recherche et développement en économique – Centre de documentation, Pavillon Lionel-Groulx, Université de Montréal, CP 6128, Succ Centre-Ville, Montréal QC H3C 3J7 – 514/343-6111; Téléc: 514/343-5831 – Fethy Mili

Centre de recherche industrielle du Québec - Centre de documentation, 8475, rue Christophe-Colomb, Montréal QC H2P 2X1 – 514/383-1550; Téléc: 514/383-3238; TLX: 05-827887; Courrier électronique: ENVOY: QMCRI.PEB; Symbol: QMCRI – Carole Lamoureux

Centre de recherche Lionel-Groulx – Bibliothèque, 261, av Bloomfield, Outremont QC H2V 3R6 – 514/271-4759; Téléc: 514/271-6369 – Bibliothécaire, Jean-Pierre Chalifoux

Centre des services sociaux de Montréal Métropolitain – Centre de documentation, 4675, rue Bélanger est, Montréal QC H2T 1C2 – 514/593-3979; Téléc: 514/593-3982; Symbol: QMCSS – Hélène Neilson

Les Centres jeunesse de Montréal – Centre de documentation, 840, Côte Vertu, Saint-Laurent QC H4L 1Y4 – 514/855-5055; Téléc: 514/855-5071; Symbol: QMCJH – Bibliothécaire, Jeanne Bazinet

Chait Amyot - Law Library, #1900, 1, Place Ville Marie, Montréal QC H3B 2C3 – 514/879-1353; Fax: 514/879-1460; Email: biblio@chait-amyot.ca; URL: http://www.chait-amyot.ca – Librarian, Pauline Housden

Chambre de commerce du Montréal métropolitain – Info Entrepreneurs, Niveau plaza, #12500, 5, Place Ville-Marie, Montréal QC H3B 4Y2 – 514/496-4636; Téléc: 514/871-1255 – Directeur général, Yvan Deslauriers

Chambre des notaires du Québec – Bibliothèque, Tour de la Bourse, #700, 800, Place Victoria, CP 162, Montréal QC H4Z 1L8 – 514/879-2903; Téléc: 514/879-1923

Chinese Nationalist League of Canada – Chung Shan Library, Montréal Branch, 1101, rue Clark, Montréal QC H2Z 1K3 – 514/861-5382, 926-1377; Fax: 514/861-5382 – Principal, Yi-Hsiung Shih

La Cinémathèque québécoise – Médiathèque Guy-L.-Coté, 335, boul de Maisonneuve est, Montréal QC H2X 1K1 – 514/842-9763; Téléc: 514/842-1816; Courrier électronique: rbeauclair@cinematheque.qc.ca – Directeur, René Beauclair

Cité de la santé de Laval – Centre de documentation, 1755, boul René-Laennec, CP 440, Laval QC H7M 3L9 – 514/975-5493; Téléc: 514/975-5572; Courrier électronique: labellel@ere.umontreal.ca; Symbol: QLACS – Bibliothécaire, France Pontbriand

Coalition des organismes communautaires québécois de lutte contre le sida – Bibliothèque, #320, 4205, rue St-Denis, Montréal QC H2J 2K9 – 514/844-2477; Téléc: 514/844-2498 – André Roy

Collège d'Ahuntsic - Bibliothèque, 9155, rue St-Hubert, Montréal QC H2M 1Y8 – 514/389-5921; Téléc: 514/389-4554; Courrier électronique: jean.lortie@collegeahuntsic.qc.ca
- Jean Lortie
- Louise Grenier

Collège de Bois-de-Boulogne - Centre des ressources didactiques et pédagogiques, 10555, av de Bois-de-Boulogne, Montréal QC H4N 1L4 – 514/332-3000; Téléc: 514/332-0083; Symbol: CRDP
- Bibliothécaire en chef, Eduardo Brito
- Bibliothécaire, Anne Marie Lachance, 514/332-3000, poste 220

Collège Français - Bibliothèque, 185, av Fairmount ouest, Montréal QC H2T 2M6 – 514/495-2581, poste 141; Téléc: 514/271-2823 – Responsable de la bibliothèque, Suzanne Howison

Collège Jean-de-Brebeuf - Bibliothèque, 5625, rue Decelles, Montréal QC H3T 1W4 – 514/342-1320, poste 261; Téléc: 514/342-0130 – Bibliothécaire, Alain Roberge

Collège LaSalle - Centre de documentation, 2000, rue Ste-Catherine ouest, Montréal QC H3H 2T2 – 514/939-2006; Téléc: 514/939-2015
- Bibliothécaire en chef, Madeleine Lambert
- Bibliotechnicienne, Josée Berthelette
- Bibliotechnicienne, Sylvie Auger

Collège de Maisonneuve - Centre des médias (Bibliothèque), 3800, rue Sherbrooke est, Montréal QC H1X 2A2 – 514/254-7131; Téléc: 514/254-2517; Courrier électronique: mdevost@cmaisonneuve.qc.ca; URL: http://www.cmaisonneuve.qc.ca
- Adjointe administrative, Monique Devost-Rivard
- Bibliothécaire, Nathalie Ouellet
- Acquisitions, Regine Millaire

Collège des médecins du Québec – Centre de documentation, 2170, boul René-Lévesque ouest, Montréal QC H3H 2T8 – 514/933-4441, poste 254; Téléc: 514/933-3112; Toll Free: 1-800-633-3246; Symbol: QMCPM – Bibliotechnicienne, Hélène Landry

Collège Montmorency - Centre des ressources didactiques, 475, boul de l'Avenir, Laval QC H7N 5H9 – 514/975-6100; Téléc: 514/975-6153
- Directeur, France Bordeleau
- Responsable de la référence et des services publics, Gilbert Baillargeon, 514/975-6272

Collège de Montréal - Bibliothèque, 1931, rue Sherbrooke ouest, Montréal QC H3H 1E3 – 514/933-7397; Téléc: 514/933-3225 – Responsable, Sylvie Caron

College O'Sullivan - Library, 1191, rue de la Montagne, Montréal QC H3G 1Z2 – 514/866-3124; Fax: 514/866-0668 – Librarian, Krishna Pal, 514-866-4622

Collège de Rosemont - Bibliothèque, 6400, 16e av, Montréal QC H1X 2S9 – 514/376-1620, poste 261; Téléc: 514/376-8279; Courrier électronique: rbeaudry.biblio@crosemont.qc.ca – Bibliothécaire, Raymonde Beaudry

Comité canadien des éléctrotechnologies – Bibliothèque, 1010, Ste-Catherine ouest, 9e étage, Montréal QC H3C 4S7 – 514/392-8446; Téléc: 514/392-8416 – Jacques Constantineau

Comité des personnes atteintes du VIH du Québec – Library, #1415, 1301, rue Sherbrooke est, CP 958, Montréal QC H2L 4V2 – 514/521-8720; Téléc: 514/521-9630 – Gilles Picard

Commission d'appel en matière de lésions professionnelles - Centre de documentation, #350, 1200, av McGill College, Montréal QC H4A 2K9 – 514/873-1654; Téléc: 514/873-7529; Symbol: QMCAML – Chief Librarian, Monique Desrochers

Commission des droits de la personne et des droits de la jeunesse - Bibliothèque, 360, rue Saint-Jacques, 2e étage, Montréal QC H2Y 1P5 – 514/873-5146; Téléc: 514/873-6032; Courrier électronique: cdpdjbiblio@drpers.gouv.qc.ca; Symbol: QMQDP
- Bibliothécaire, Madeleine Beaudoin
- Technicienne, Diane Dupont

Commission de la construction du Québec - Ressources documentaires, 3530, rue Jean-Talon ouest, Montréal QC H3R 2G3 – 514/341-7740; Téléc: 514/341-6354; Courrier électronique: ENVOY: PEB.QMOC – Chef, section ressources documentaires, Nicole Côté

Commission de la santé et de la sécurité du travail du Québec - Audiovidéothèque, 1199, rue de Bleury, 4e étage, Montréal QC H3B 3J1 – 514/873-2494; Téléc: 514/873-6593; Symbol: QQCAT

Centre de documentation, 1199, rue de Bleury, 4e étage, CP 6067, Montréal QC H3C 4E2 – 514/873-3160; Téléc: 514/864-2617; Courrier électronique: Envoy: PEB.QMCSST; URL: http://www.csst.qc.ca; Symbol: QMCSST
- Chef de service, Marc Fournier
- Responsable, Sylvie Lacerte, 514/873-6883
- Bibliothécaire, Carole Bergeron, 514/873-6225

Commission des services juridiques - Bibliothèque, #1404, 2, Complexe Desjardins, Montréal QC H5B 1B3 – 514/873-3562; Téléc: 514/873-9263; Symbol: QMJSJ – Documentaliste, Francine Godin

Commission des valeurs mobilières - Bibliothèque, 800 Place Victoria, 17e étage, CP 246, Montréal QC H4Z 1G3 – 514/873-5326; Téléc: 514/873-3090; Symbol: QMCVM
- Chef de service, Jean-François Doutrelepont
- Référence & services publics, Librarian, Lucie Lafrance
- Référence, Gilles Lachance

Communauté Sépharade du Québec – Bibliothèque, 4735, Côte Ste-Catherine, Montréal QC H3W 1M1 – 514/733-4998; Téléc: 514/733-3158 – Elie Benchetrit

Concordia University - Libraries, 1455, boul de Maisonneuve ouest, Montréal QC H3G 1M8 – 514/848-7695; Fax: 514/848-2882; URL: http://juno.concordia.ca; Symbol: CAQMG
- Chief Librarian, Dr. Roy Bonin, 514/848-7695
- Information Services, Head, Judy Appleby, 514/848-7769
- Access Services, Head, TBA, 514/848-7702
- Planning & Priorities, Assistant Director, Robert Wrightson, 514/848-7691
- Library Personnel, Assistant Director, Charlotte MacLaurin, 514/848-7693
- User Services, Assistant Director, Irene Sendek, 514/848-7699
- Vanier Library, Head, Helena Bairos, 514/848-7721
- Guidance Library, Head, Marlis Hubbard, 514/848-3556
- Periodicals & Media, Head, Judy Appleby, 514/848-7769
- Government Publications & Special Collections, Head, Louise Carpentier, 514/848-7709
- Collection Services, Assistant Director, Mia Massicotte, 514/848-7782

Confédération québécoise des centres d'hébergement et de réadaptation – Bibliothèque, #1100, 1001, boul de Maisonneuve est, Montréal QC H2L 4P9 – 514/597-1007; Téléc: 514/873-5411 – Responsable, Nicole Tardif

Confédération des syndicats nationaux – Bibliothèque, 1601, av de Lorimier, Montréal QC H2K 4M5 – 514/598-2121; Téléc: 514/598-2089

Conférence des recteurs et des principaux des universités du Québec – Bibliothèque, #1200, 300, Léo Pariseau, CP 952, Succ Place du Parc, Montréal QC H2W 2N1 – 514/288-8524; Téléc: 514/288-0554 – Personne ressource, Roger Charland

Conseil des arts textiles du Québec – Centre de Documentation, 811A, rue Ontario est, Montréal QC H2L 1P1 – 514/524-6645; Téléc: 514/525-2621

Conseil du patronat du Québec – Bibliothèque, #606, 2075, rue Université, Montréal QC H3A 2L1 – 514/288-5161; Téléc: 514/288-5165 – Ginette Bourbonnais

Conservatoire d'art dramatique de Montréal - Bibliothèque, 100, rue Notre Dame est, Montréal QC H2Y 1C1 – 514/873-3002; Téléc: 514/873-7943; Symbol: QMCADQ – Responsable, Daniel Laflamme

Conservatoire de musique de Montréal - Bibliothèque, 100, rue Notre-Dame est, Montréal QC H2Y 1C1 – 514/873-7482; Téléc: 514/873-4601; Courrier électronique: CMM.Bibliotheque@mccq.gouv.qc.ca; Symbol: QMCOM – Directrice, Annette Bolduc

Coopers & Lybrand - Information Centre, 1170 Peel St., Montréal QC H3B 4T2 – 514/876-1500; Fax: 514/876-1502, 1527; Symbol: QMCCL – Librarian, Danielle Martin, Email: dmartin@login.net

Corporation des bibliothécaires professionnels du Québec – Bibliothèque, #320, 307, rue Ste-Catherine ouest, Montréal QC H2X 2A3 – 514/845-3327; Téléc: 514/845-1618

Corporation d'Urgences-santé de la région de Montréal métropolitain - Centre de documentation, 3232, rue Bélanger est, Montréal QC H1Y 3H5 – 514/723-5754; Téléc: 514/723-5790; Courrier électronique: ussdoc@consulan.com; Symbol: QMCUS – Diane Pelletier

David M. Stewart Museum at the Fort, Île Sainte-Hélène - Library, POBox 1200, Montréal QC H3C 2Y9 – 514/861-6701; Fax: 514/284-0123; Email: mdms@quebectel.com; URL: http://www.mlink.net/~stewart/; Symbol: QMDS – Librarian, Eileen Meillon

Dawson College - Library, 3040 Sherbrooke St. West, Westmount QC H3Z 1A4 – 514/931-8731; Fax: 514/931-3567; Email: cgilmore@dawsoncollege.qc.ca
- Public Services, Coordinator, Carolyn Gilmore
- Reference Librarian, Beryl Moser
- Reference Librarian, David Jones
- Technical Services, Coordinator, Anne Scott

De Grandpré, Godin Law Office - Bibliothèque, #2900, 1000 rue de la Gauchetière ouest, Montréal QC H3B 4W5 – 514/878-4311; Téléc: 514/878-4333
- Technicienne en droit, Manon Savoie
- Directeur général, Hélène Schampaert

DES Action Canada – Library, #203, 5890 Monkland Ave., POBox 233, Montréal QC H3X 3T4 – 514/482-3204; Fax: 514/482-1445; Toll Free: 1-800-482-1337 – Librarian, Vasi Mathioudakis

Le Devoir - Centre de documentation, 2050, rue de Bleury, 9e étage, Montréal QC H3A 3M9 – 514/985-3423; Téléc: 514/985-3360 – Head Librarian, Gilles Paré

Direction de santé publique - Centre de documentation, 4835, av Christophe-Colomb, Montréal QC H2J 3G8 – 514/528-2400, poste 3960; Téléc: 514/528-2598; Symbol: QMSPM
- Bibliothécaire, Francine Fiore
- Technicienne en documentation, Raymonde Champagne

Domtar Inc. – Library, 22025, route Transcanada ouest, Senneville QC H9X 3L7 – 514/457-8208; Fax: 514/457-2983 – Library Assistant, Marilyn Hussey

École des Hautes Études Commerciales - Bibliothèque, 5255, av Decelles, Montréal QC H3T 1V6 – 514/340-6220; Fax: 514/340-6230 – Directeur, Reference, Gerald Boudreau

École Peter Hall inc. - Centre de documentation, 1455, rue Rochon, Saint-Laurent QC H4L 1W1 – 514/748-6727, local 229; Téléc: 514/748-5122; URL: http://www.peterhall.qc.ca – Secretary, Louise Leblanc

École polytechnique de Montréal - Bibliothèque, Campus de l'Université de Montréal, CP 6079, Succ Centre-ville, Montréal QC H3C 3A7 – 514/340-4666; Téléc: 514/340-4026; Courrier électronique: biblio@mailsrv.polymtl.ca; Symbol: QMEP

- Directeur de la Bibliothèque, Olivier Paradis, 514/340-4847
- Information Access Services, Richard Dumont, 514/340-4652
- Technical Services & Acquisitions Librarian, Claire Pelletier, 514/340-4641
- Systems Librarian, Minh-Thu Nguyen, 514/340-4993
- Fee-based Services, Marie-Hélène Dupuis, 514/340-4213
- Circulation, Marlène Aubin, 514/340-4659

Ecological Agriculture Projects – Library, Centennial Centre, 21111 Lakeshore Rd., Ste-Anne-de-Bellevue QC H9X 3V9 – 514/398-7771; Fax: 514/398-7621

Environment Canada - Canadian Meteorological Centre - Library, #508, 2121 Trans-Canada Hwy., Dorval QC H9P 1J3 – 514/421-4754; Fax: 514/421-2106; Symbol: QMEA – Head, Maryse Ferland

ERS Youth Development Corporation – Library, #520, 5250 Ferrier St., Montréal QC H4P 1L4 – 514/731-3419; Fax: 514/731-4999

Facultés de la Compagnie de Jésus - Bibliothèque de théologie, 5605, av Decelles, Montréal QC H3T 1W4 – 514/737-1465; Téléc: 514/739-2896; Symbol: QMFCJ – Directeur, Claude-Roger Nadeau

Fédération acadienne du Québec – Centre de documentation, #102, 2201, rue Sherbrooke est, Montréal QC H2K 1E2 – 514/527-2127; Téléc: 514/527-2679 – Ernest Thériault

Fédération des affaires sociales inc. (CSN) – Bibliothèque, 1601, av de Lorimier, Montréal QC H2K 4M5 – 514/598-2210; Téléc: 514/598-2223 – Personne ressource, Lucie Courtemanche

Fédération des associations coopérative d'économie familiale du Québec – Bibliothèque, #305, 5225, rue Berri, Montréal QC H2J 2S4 – 514/271-7004 – Johanne Groulx

Fédération des cégeps – Bibliothèque, 500, boul Crémazie est, Montréal QC H2P 1E7 – 514/381-8631; Téléc: 514/381-2263 – Lucie Varin

Fédération de gymnastique du Québec – Bibliothèque, 4545, av Pierre-de-Coubertin, CP 1000, Montréal QC H1V 3R2 – 514/252-3043; Téléc: 514/252-3169

Fédération des infirmières et infirmiers du Québec – Bibliothèque, 2050, rue de Bleury, 4e étage, Montréal QC H3A 2J5 – 514/861-8328, poste 243; Téléc: 514/987-7273 – Archiviste, Martine Dubé

Fédération des médecins omnipraticiens du Québec – Centre de documentation, #1000, 1440, rue Ste-Catherine ouest, Montréal QC H3G 1R8 – 514/878-1911; Téléc: 514/878-4455; Toll Free: 1-800-361-8499; Symbol: QMFMO – Technicienne, Ghislaine Lincourt

Fédération nationale des associations de consommateurs du Québec – Bibliothèque, #103, 1215, rue de la Visitation, Montréal QC H2L 3B5 – 514/521-6820; Téléc: 514/521-0736

Fédération du plongeon amateur du Québec – Bibliothèque, 4545, av Pierre-de-Coubertin, CP 1000, Montréal QC H1V 3R2 – 514/252-3096; Téléc: 514/252-3094 – Donald Normond

Fédération du Québec pour le planning des naissances – Bibliothèque, #302, 4428, boul St-Laurent, Montréal QC H2W 1Z5 – 514/844-3721; Téléc: 514/844-8736 – Coordonnatrice à l'information, France Tardif

Fédération des sociétés d'histoire du Québec – Centre de documentation, 4545, av Pierre-De-Coubertin, CP 1000, Montréal QC H1V 3R2 – 514/252-3031; Téléc: 514/251-8038

Fédération des travailleurs et travailleuses du Québec – Centre de documentation de la FTQ, 545, boul Crémazie est, 17e étage, Montréal QC H2M 2V1 – 514/383-8025; Téléc: 514/383-8001; Symbol: QMFTQ – Documentaliste, Isabelle Reny

Fonds de la recherche en santé du Québec - Centre de documentation, #1950, 550, rue Sherbrooke ouest, Montréal QC H3A 1B9 – 514/873-2114; Téléc: 514/873-8768 – Rédactrice scientifique, Michelle Dubuc

Forest Engineering Research Institute of Canada – Information Resources, 580, boul Saint-Jean, Pointe Claire QC H9R 3J9 – 514/694-1140; Fax: 514/694-4351 – Head, Information Resources, Christel Mukhopadhyay

Frank W. Horner Inc. - Research Library, 5485, rue Ferrier, POBox 959, Montréal QC H3C 2W6 – 514/731-3931, ext.259; Fax: 514/738-5509 – Librarian, Yvon Dugas

The Fraser-Hickson Institute - Free Library, 4855 Kensington, Montréal QC H3X 3S6 – 514/489-5301; Fax: 514/489-5302; Email: fratrick@cam.org – Chief Librarian, Frances W. Ackerman

Fraternité nationale des charpentiers-menuisiers, forestiers et travailleurs d'usine (CTC) – Bibliothèque, #205, 3730, boul Crémazie est, Montréal QC H2A 1B4 – 514/374-5871; Téléc: 514/374-8800; Toll Free: 1-800-465-9791 – Directeur du personnel, G. Marois

Grand Séminaire de Montréal - Bibliothèque, 2065, rue Sherbrooke ouest, Montréal QC H3H 1G6 – 514/935-1169; Téléc: 514/935-5497 – Jean-Pierre Lussier

Groupe d'action pour la prévention du sida – Bibliothèque, #101, 2577A, rue Jean Talon est, Montréal QC H2A 1T8 – 514/722-5655; Téléc: 514/722-0063 – Responsable, Suzon F. Jean-Pierre

Groupe interuniversitaire de recherche en informatique cognitive des organisations – Bibliothèque, #912, 276, rue St-Jacques, Montréal QC H2Y 1N3 – 514/985-5459; Téléc: 514/985-2720 – Jocelyne Gonthier

Groupe de recherche en écologie sociale – Bibliothèque, Dépt. de Soc., Université de Montréal, CP 6128, Montréal QC H3C 3J7 – 514/343-5959; Téléc: 514/343-5722

Groupement des assureurs automobiles – Centre de documentation, #600, 500, rue Sherbrooke ouest, Montréal QC H3A 3C6 – 514/288-1537; Téléc: 514/288-0753 – Documentaliste, Claude Garceau

Guy & Gilbert Law Office - Bibliothèque, #2300, 770, rue Sherbrooke ouest, Montréal QC H3A 1G1 – 514/281-1766; Téléc: 514/281-1059, 9948, 5799 – Technical Services & Acquisitions, Librarian, Lise Zaucher

Hébert Denault Law Office - Bibliothèque, 359, Place Royale, Montréal QC H2Y 2V3 – 514/288-4424; Téléc: 514/288-7859 – Responsable, Colette Bastien

Heenan Blaikie Law Office - Bibliothèque, #2500, 1250, boul René-Lévesque ouest, Montréal QC H3B 4W8 – 514/281-1212; Téléc: 514/281-1776 – Bibliotecnicienne, Dianne Bellemare

Héritage Montréal – Bibliothèque, 1181, rue de la Montagne, Montréal QC H3G 1Z2 – 514/875-2985; Téléc: 514/875-0935 – Documentaliste, Robert Klein

Historic Theatres' Trust – Library, POBox 387, Montréal QC H3Z 2V8 – 514/933-8077; Fax: 514/933-8012

L'Hôpital Chinois de Montréal – Bibliothèque, 7500, rue St-Denis, Montréal QC H2R 2E6 – 514/273-9154; Téléc: 514/273-2446; Symbol: QMHCM – Technicienne, Cécile Desjardins

Hôpital Douglas – Staff Library, 6875, boul Lasalle, Verdun QC H4H 1R3 – 514/762-3029; Téléc: 514/762-3039; Courrier électronique: biblio@douglas.mcgill.ca; Symbol: QMDH – Chief Librarian, Elaine Mancina

Hôpital général Juif Sir Mortimer B. Davis – Library, 3755, ch Côte Ste-Catherine, Montréal QC H3T 1E2 – 514/340-8222,ext5390; Téléc: 514/340-7530 – Arlene Greenberg

Hôpital général de Montréal/The Montréal General Hospital – Nurses' Library, Rm. E6-181, 1650, av Cedar, Montréal QC H3G 1A4 – 514/937-6011, x4189; Fax: 514/934-8250; Email: bcovingt@is.muhc.mcgill.ca; Symbol: QMGHN – Nurses' Librarian, Barbara Covington

Hôpital Jean-Talon – Bibliothèque médicale, 1385, rue Jean-Talon est, Montréal QC H2E 1S6 – 514/495-6767; Téléc: 514/495-6772; Symbol: QMHJT – Pierrette Galarneau

Hôpital Louis-H. Lafontaine – Bibliothèque du personnel, 7401, rue Hochelaga, Montréal QC H1N 3M5 – 514.251-4000, ext. 2964; Téléc: 514/251-0270; Symbol: QMLHL – Bibliothécaire en chef, Camil Lemire

Hôpital Maisonneuve-Rosemont – Bibliothèque médicale, 5415, boul de l'Assomption, Montréal QC H1T 2M4 – 514/252-3462; Téléc: 514/252-3574; Courrier électronique: lachaped@ere.umontreal.ca; Symbol: QMHMR – Chef-bibliothécaire, Hélène Lauzon

- Direction de la santé publique - Centre de documentation, #240, 75, rue de Port-Royal Est, Montréal QC H3L 3T1 – 514/858-7510, poste 267; Téléc: 514/858-5993; Courrier électronique: ddiamond@santepub-mtl.qc.ca; URL: http://www.santepub-mtl.qc.ca; Symbol: QMSPS – Bibliothécaire, Denise Diamond

Hôpital Marie Enfant – Centre de documentation, 5200, rue Belanger est, Montréal QC H1T 1C9 – 514/374-1710, poste 2033; Téléc: 514/374-6803; Symbol: QMHME – Bibliothécaire, Anca Cojocaru

Hôpital de Montréal pour enfants – Bibliothèque médicale, 2300, rue Tupper, Montréal QC H3H 1P3 – 514/934-4400; Téléc: 514/934-4345 – Joanne Baird

Hôpital Nôtre-Dame de la Merci – Centre de documentation, 555, boul Gouin ouest, Montréal QC H3L 1K5 – 514/331-3020, ext.367; Téléc: 514/331-3358; Symbol: QMNDM – Bibliothécaire, Mario Tessier

Hôpital Rivière-des-Prairies – Bibliothèque du personnel, 7070, boul Perras, Montréal QC H1E 1A4 – 514/323-7260; Téléc: 514/323-8622; Courrier électronique: fortinsy@ere.umontreal.ca; Symbol: QMHRP – Head, Robert Aubin

Hôpital Royal Victoria – Bibliothèque du pavillon des femmes, 687, av des Pins ouest, Montréal QC H3A 1A1 – 514/842-1231; Téléc: 514/843-1678; Symbol: QMRVW – Bibliothécaire, Lynda Dickson

Hôpital du Sacré-Coeur de Montréal – Bibliothèque Norman-Bethune, 5400, boul Gouin ouest, Montréal QC H4J 1C5 – 514/338-2222, poste 2577; Téléc: 514/338-3154; Courrier électronique: morisset@ere.umontreal.ca; Symbol: QMHSC – Chef de service - documentation, Jean-Pierre Morissette

- Bibliothèque Albert-Prévost, 6555, boul Gouin ouest, Montréal QC H4K 4M1 – 514/338-2160; Symbol: QMIAP – Bibliothécaire, Jean-Pierre Morissette

Hôpital Saint-Luc - Département de santé communautaire - Centre de documentation, 1001, rue Saint-Denis, Montréal QC H2X 3H9 – 514/281-4076; Téléc: 514/281-4099 – Colette Bérubé

Hôpital Sainte-Anne – Centre de documentation, 305, rue Saint-Pierre, Sainte-Anne-de-Bellevuew QC H9X 1Y9 – 514/457-2761; Téléc: 514/457-5741 – Technicien, Pierre Turcotte

Hôpital Sainte-Jeanne d'Arc de Montréal – Bibliothèque médicale, 3570, rue St-Urbain, Montréal QC H2X 2N8 – 514/282-6951; Téléc: 514/282-9206

Hôpital Sainte-Justine – Centre d'information sur la santé de l'enfant, 3175, ch de la Côte Ste-Catherine, Montréal QC H3T 1C5 – 514/345-4680; Téléc: 514/345-4806; Courrier électronique: Envoy: QMSTJ; lecomptl@ere.umo; Symbol: QMSTJ – Chef de service, Louis-Luc Lecompte

Hôpital Santa Cabrini – Centre de documentation, 5655, rue St-Zotique est, Montréal QC H1T 1P7 – 514/252-6488; Téléc: 514/252-6535; Courrier électronique: gmhsca@cam.org;
Symbol: QMHSCA – Bibliotechnicienne, Diane Séguin

Human Resources Development Canada - Regional Library, 1441, rue St-Urbain, CP 7500, Montréal QC H3C 3L4 – 514/283-7586; Reference: 514/283-4695; Téléc: 514/283-1386; Symbol: QMMIQ – Regional Chief, Jacinthe Castonguay

Hydro-Québec - Bibliothèque, 75, boul René-Lévesque ouest, Montréal QC H2Z 1A4 – 514/289-2145; Téléc: 514/289-3750; Courrier électronique: se1024@mailgtway.vpi.hydro.qc.ca; Symbol: QMH – Chef de service, Line McMurray

Hydrogen Industry Council – Hydrogen Library, #2610, 1800, av McGill College, Montréal QC H3A 3J6 – 514/288-5139; Fax: 514/843-6079

Immigration & Refugee Board - Documentation Centre, #102, 200, boul René-Lévesque ouest, Montréal QC H2Z 1X4 – 514/496-6530; Reference: 514/496-6529; Fax: 514/496-1709; Symbol: QMCIS – Chief, Serge Vallée

Imperial Tobacco Ltd. - Corporate Library, 3810, rue Saint-Antoine ouest, POBox 6500, Montréal QC H3C 3L6 – 514/932-6161; Fax: 514/932-0383; Symbol: QMIT – Corporate Librarian, Yolande Mukherjee

Industry Canada - Centre for Information Technologies Innovation, 1575, boul Chomedey, Laval QC H7V 2X2 – 514/973-5740; Fax: 514/973-5757; Email: siri@citi.doc.ca
Manager, Marcel Simoneau
Reference Librarian, Marie-Cecile Domeco, 514/973-5748
Library Technician, Chantal Gasse
Indexation Librarian, Anne Simard

Info Entrepreneurs - Documentation Centre, #12500, 5, Place Ville Marie, Niveau Plaza, Montréal QC H3B 4Y2 – 514/496-4636; Téléc: 514/496-5934; Ligne sans frais: 1-800-322-4636; URL: http://www.cbsc.org/quebec/;
Symbol: QMBFD
Chief, Documentation Centre, Nicole Beaudry
Reference Librarian, Sylvie Paquette
Circulation Librarian, Carole Tousignant
Technical Services Librarian, Claire Lavoie
Acquisitions Librarian, Chantal Jetté

Institut du cancer de Montréal – Centre de documentation, 1560, rue Sherbrooke est, Montréal QC H2L 4M1 – 514/281-6055; Téléc: 514/896-4689; Symbol: QMINC – Technicienne, Chantal Corriveau

Institut de cardiologie de Montréal – Bibliothèque, 5000, rue Bélanger est, Montréal QC H1T 1C8 – 514/376-3330; Téléc: 514/593-2540; Symbol: QMICM

Institut d'études médiévales – Bibliothèque, 2715, ch Côte Ste-Catherine, Montréal QC H3T 1B6 – 514/739-9868

Institut d'histoire de l'Amérique française – Centre de recherches Lionel-Groulx, 261, av Bloomfield, Montréal QC H2V 3R6 – 514/278-2232; Téléc: 514/271-6369

Institut interculturel de Montréal – Centre de documentation, 4917, rue St-Urbain, Montréal QC H2T 2W1 – 514/288-7229; Téléc: 514/844-6800 – Documentaliste, Réal Bathalon

Institut national de la recherche scientifique - Division de santé – Bibliothèque, 245, boul Hymus, Pointe-Claire QC H9R 1G6 – 514/630-8812; Fax: 514/630-8850; Email: gilbert_leblanc@inrs-sante.uquebec.ca; Symbol: QMUQIS – Bibliothécaire, Gilbert Leblanc

Institut Philippe Pinel de Montréal – Centre de documentation, 10905, boul Henri-Bourassa est, Montréal QC H1C 1H1 – 514/648-8461; Téléc: 514/494-4406; Courrier électronique: beaudetn@ere.umontreal.ca – Normand Beaudet

Institut Raymond-Dewar - Centre de documentation spécialisé en déficience auditive, 3600, rue Berri, Montréal QC H2L 4G9 – 514/284-2214, poste 3610; Téléc: 514/284-5086; Symbol: QMISM – Responsable, Louise Comtois

Institut de réadaptation de Montréal - Centre de documentation, 6300, av Darlington, Montréal QC H3S 2J4 – 514/340-2085, poste 2270; Téléc: 514/340-2176; Symbol: QMRI – Head of Library Services, Maryse Boyer

Institut de recherche en santé et en sécurité de travail - Québec – Bibliothèque, 505, boul de Maisonneuve ouest, Montréal QC H3A 3C2 – 514/288-1551; Téléc: 514/288-0998; TLX: 055 61348 – Bibliothécaire, Jacques Blain

Institut de recherches cliniques - Centre de documentation, 110, av des Pins ouest, Montréal QC H2W 1R7 – 514/987-5599; Téléc: 514/987-5675; Courrier électronique: ENVOY: QMIRC; Symbol: QMIRC – Bibliothécaire en chef, L.D. Bielmann

Institut Teccart inc. - Bibliothèque, 3155, rue Hochelaga, Montréal QC H1W 1G4 – 514/526-2501; Téléc: 514/526-9192 – Technicienne, Monique Thérien

Institut de tourisme et d'hôtellerie du Québec – Médiathèque, 401, rue de Rigaud, Montréal QC H2L 4P3 – 514/282-5114; Téléc: 514/282-5163; Toll Free: 1-800-361-5111; Symbol: QMTH – Services techniques, Céline Beauchemin

Institute of Community & Family Psychiatry - Library, Sir Mortimer B. Davis Jewish General Hospital, 4333, ch Côte Ste-Catherine, Montréal QC H3T 1E4 – 514/340-8210, ext.5243; Fax: 514/340-7507; Email: adll@musica.mcgill.ca; Symbol: QMJGI – Librarian, Ruth Stilman

International Centre for Human Rights & Democratic Development – Documentation Centre, #100, 63, rue de Bresoles, Montréal QC H2Y 1V7 – 514/283-6073; Fax: 514/283-3792 – Head, Documentation, Lucie Lamoureux

International Civil Aviation Organization - Library, 999, rue Université, Montréal QC H3C 5H7 – 514/285-8207; Fax: 514/954-6077; TLX: 05-24513; Symbol: QMIC

International Day Committee for the Eradication of Poverty – Library, 6747, rue Drolet, Montréal QC H2S 2T1 – 514/279-0468; Fax: 514/279-7759 – Claude Dimitroff

Italian Chamber of Commerce in Canada – Library, #680, 550, rue Sherbrooke ouest, Montréal QC H3A 1B9 – 514/844-4249; Fax: 514/844-4875; Toll Free: 1-800-263-4372

Jardin botanique de Montréal - Bibliothèque, 4101, rue Sherbrooke est, Montréal QC H1X 2B2 – 514/872-1824; Téléc: 514/872-3765; Courrier électronique: celine_arseneault@ville.montreal.qc.ca; Symbol: QMJB – Botanist/Responsable, Céline Arseneault

Jewish Information Service Montréal – Library, 5151, Côte Ste-Catherine, Montréal QC H3W 1M6 – 514/737-2221; Toll Free: 1-888-252-5477

Jewish Public Library, 5151, ch Côte Ste-Catherine, Montréal QC H3W 1M6 – 514/345-2627; Fax: 514/342-6477
Executive Director, Zipporah Shnay
Reference Librarian, Ron Finegold
Circulation Librarian, Eleanor Steinberg
Public Services Librarian, Clare Stern
Technical Services Librarian, Helen Bassal
Archivist, Carol Katz
Children's Librarian, Eva Raby

Jewish Rehabilitation Hospital – Health Sciences Information Centre, 3205, Place Alton-Goldbloom, Laval QC H7V 1R2 – 514/688-9550, ext.226; Téléc: 514/688-3673; Courrier électronique: axis@musica.mcgill.ca; Symbol: OCHJC – Librarian, Irene Shanefield

John Abbott College - Library, POBox 2000, Ste-Anne-de-Bellevue QC H9X 3L9 – 514/457-6610, ext.331; Fax: 514/457-4730
Chief Librarian, Janette Wygergangs
Public Services Librarian, Douglas Armstrong
Technical Services Librarian, Dale Biteen
Collections Development Librarian, Sue Evans

Justice Canada - Montréal Regional Office - Library, Guy Favreau Complex, 200, boul René-Lévesque ouest, Montréal QC H2Z 1X4 – 514/283-6674; Fax: 514/283-9690; Symbol: QMJM – Bibliothécaire en chef, André Archambault, 514/283-8739

Laboratoire de santé publique du Québec - Centre de documentation, 20045, ch Sainte-Marie, Ste-Anne-de-Bellevue QC H9X 3R5 – 514/457-2070; Téléc: 514/457-6346; Courrier électronique: lspq@InterLink.NET; Symbol: QSABS – Technicien, Marc-André Jobin

Laboratoire de sciences judiciaires et de médecine légale - Centre de documentation, CP 1500, Montréal QC H2L 4K6 – 514/873-2704; Téléc: 514/873-4847; Symbol: QMJLP – Technicienne, Françoise Pothier

Lafarge Canada Inc. - Corporate Technical Services Library, 6150 Royalmount Ave., Montréal QC H4P 2R3 – 514/738-1202; Fax: 514/738-1124; Symbol: QMLC – Head Librarian, Iréne M. Paulmier, 514/738-1202, ext.2274

Langlois Gaudreau Law Office - Bibliothèque, Tour Scotia, 1002, rue Sherbrooke ouest, 28e étage, Montréal QC H3A 3L6 – 514/842-9512; Téléc: 514/845-6573; Symbol: QMLR – Chief Librarian, Jacqueline Chan Seng

Ligue de sécurité du Québec – Bibliothèque spécialisée en prévention des accidents, 2536, rue Lapierre, Lasalle QC H8N 2W9 – 514/595-9110; Téléc: 514/595-3398

Loisir littéraire du Québec – Bibliothèque, 4545, av Pierre-de-Coubertin, CP 1000, Montréal QC H1V 3R2 – 514/252-3033; Téléc: 514/251-8038

Lower Canada College - Library, 4090 Royal Ave., Montréal QC H4A 2M5 – 514/482-9916; Fax: 514/482-0195 – Head Librarian, Maria Varvarikos

Loyola Peace Institute – Library, 2480 West Broadway, Montréal QC H4B 2A5 – 514/848-7799; Fax: 514/848-7799

Mackenzie Gervais Law Office - Library, #1300, 770 Sherbrooke St. West, Montréal QC H3A 1G1 – 514/842-9831; Téléc: 514/288-7389 – Librarian, Georges R. Thibaudeau

La Maison Jean Lapointe - Centre de documentation, 111, rue Normand, Montréal QC H2Y 2K6 – 514/288-2611; Téléc: 514/288-2919; Ligne sans frais: 1-800-567-9543 – Responsable des communications, Christine Maltais

Marchand, Magnan, Melançon, Forget Law Office - Bibliothèque, #1640, 600, rue De La Gauchetière ouest, Montréal QC H3B 4L8 – 514/393-1155; Téléc: 514/861-0727 – Technicienne, Nadine Lemieux

Marius Barbeau - Centre de documentation en arts et traditions populaires, 6560, rue Chambord,

Montréal QC H2G 3B9 – 514/274-5656; Téléc: 514/274-7418

Martineau, Walker - Law Library, #3400, Tour de la Bourse, Carré Victoria, POBox 242, Montréal QC H4Z 1E9 – 514/397-4307; Fax: 514/397-7600, 7601; Email: biblio@martineau-walker.com – Librarian, Linda Patry

McCarthy Tétrault - Bibliothèque, 1170, rue Peel, Montréal QC H3B 4S8 – 514/397-4214; Téléc: 514/875-6246; Courrier électronique: abujold@mccarthy.ca; URL: http://www.mccarthy.ca – Directrice de la bibliothèque, Agathe Bujold

McDougall, Caron - Bibliothèque/Library, #2600, 1000, rue de la Gauchetière ouest, Montréal QC H3B 4W5 – 514/399-1000; Fax: 514/399-1026 – Stephanie Alyanakian

McGill Institute for the Study of Canada – Library, 3463, rue Peel, Montréal QC H3A 1W7 – 514/398-8346; Fax: 514/398-7336; Email: saubin@heps.lan.mcgill.ca – Receptionist, Suzanne Aubin

McGill University - Blacker-Wood Biology Library, Redpath Library Bldg, 3459, rue McTavish, Montréal QC H3A 1Y1 – 514/398-4744; Fax: 514/398-8231; Email: maclean@lib1.lan.mcgill.ca; Symbol: QMMBZ – Biology Librarian, Eleanor MacLean

Edward Rosenthall Mathematics & Statistics Library, Burnside Hall, #1105, 805, rue Sherbrooke ouest, Montréal QC H3A 2K6 – 514/398-4676; Fax: 514/398-3899; URL: http://www.library.mcgill.ca/math.htm;
Symbol: QMMER
Librarian, Hanna Waluzyniec
Library Administrative Secretary, Monique Lemire

Health Sciences Library, McIntyre Medical Sciences Bldg, 3655, rue Drummond, Montréal QC H3G 1Y6 – 514/398-4475; Fax: 514/398-3890;
Email: Refdesk@healthlib.lan.mcgill.ca;
URL: http://www.health.library.mcgill.ca;
Symbol: QMMM – Life Sciences Area Librarian, David Crawford

Libraries, 3459, rue McTavish, Montréal QC H3A 1Y1 – 514/398-4677; Fax: 514/398-3561;
URL: http://www.library.mcgill.ca;
Symbol: QMM
Director of Libraries, Frances Groen, Email: groen@lib1.lan.mcgill.ca
Associate Director, John Hobbins, 514/398-7486
Life Sciences, Librarian, David Crawford, 514/398-4475, Fax: 514/398-3890
McLennan Library of Humanities & Social Sciences, Acting Librarian, John Hobbins, 514/398-4698
Law Library, Librarian, Robert Clarke, 514/398-4715, Fax: 514/398-3585
Branch Services, Librarian, Michael Renshawe, 514/398-7112, Email: renshawe@lib1.lan.mcgill.ca
Blackader-Lauterman Library of Architecture & Art, Head Librarian, Marilyn Berger, 514/398-4742, Fax: 514/398-6695
Education Library, Head Librarian, Marilyn Cohen, 514/398-4687, Fax: 514/398-2165
Howard Ross Library of Management, Head Librarian, Michael Renshawe, 514/398-4691, Fax: 514/398-5046
Islamic Studies Library, Head Librarian, Adam Gacek, 514/398-4688, Fax: 514/398-8189
Marvin Duchow Music Library, Head Librarian, Cynthia Leive, 514/398-4694, Fax: 514/398-8276

Macdonald Campus Library, Barton Bldg, 21111, rue Lakeshore, Ste-Anne-de-Bellevue QC H9X 3V9 – 514/398-7879; Fax: 514/398-7960;
Email: Envoy: PEB.QMAC; Symbol: QMAC
Head Librarian, Janet Finlayson, 514/398-7876, Fax: 514/398-7960
Public Services Librarian, Bruce Grainger

Osler Library (History of Medicine), McIntyre Medical Sciences Bldg, 3655, rue Drummond, 3e étage, Montréal QC H3G 1Y6 – 514/398-4475, ext.094163; Fax: 514/398-5747; Email: lily@healthlib.lan.mcgill.ca; URL: http://www.health.library.mcgill.ca/osler/welcome.html; Symbol: QMMO – History of Medicine Librarian, June Schachter, 514/398-4475, ext.094168

Physical Sciences & Engineering Library, Macdonald Stewart Library Bldg, 809, rue Sherbrooke ouest, Montréal QC H3A 2K6 – 514/398-4769; Fax: 514/398-3903; Email: pseref@lib1.lan.mcgill.ca; URL: http://www.library.mcgill.ca/psel/physci.htm; Symbol: QMME – Librarian, Hanna Waluzyniec, 514/398-4763

Walter Hitschfeld Environmental Earth Sciences Library, Burnside Hall, 805, rue Sherbrooke ouest, 5e étage, Montréal QC H3A 2K6 – 514/398-8095; Symbol: QMM – Librarian, Carol Marley, 514/398-7453, Fax: 514/398-3903

McMaster Meighen Law Office - Library, 630, boul René-Lévesque ouest, Montréal QC H3B 4H7 – 514/954-3159; Fax: 514/878-0605, 4428 – Librarian, Ronald Charest

Mendelsohn Rosentzveig Shacter Law Office - Bibliothèque, 1000, rue Sherbrooke ouest, 27e étage, Montréal QC H3A 3G4 – 514/987-5043; Téléc: 514/987-1213; Courrier électronique: mrs@mrslaw.com – Bibliothécaire, Marina Bélanger

Merck Frosst Canada Inc. - Research Library & Information Centre, POBox 1005, Pointe-Claire QC H9R 4P8 – 514/428-3323; Fax: 514/428-8535; Email: claire.kelly@merck.com; Symbol: QMCF – Manager, Claire B. Kelly

Ministère des Affaires internationales - Centre de documentation, 380, rue Saint-Antoine ouest, 4e étage, Montréal QC H2Y 3X7 – 514/499-2170; Téléc: 514/873-7825; Symbol: QMCED – Library Technician, Marielle Bernard

Ministère de la santé et des services sociaux - Service de la documentation, 201, rue Crémazie est, R.C. 04, Montréal QC H2M 1L2 – 514/873-3685; Téléc: 514/873-2125; Symbol: QMSA – Bibliothécaire, Gérard Darlington

Ministère de la Sécurité publique - Laboratoire de sciences judiciaires et de médecine légale - Centre de documentation, 1701, rue Parthenais, CP 1500, Montréal QC H2L 4K6 – 514/873-2704; Téléc: 514/873-4847; Symbol: QMJLP – Bibliotechnicienne, Françoise Pothier

Ministère du loisir, de la chasse et de la pêche - Bibliothèque, 6255, 13e av, Montréal QC H1X 3E6 – 514/374-5840; Téléc: 514/873-2100;
Symbol: QMMLCP – Bibliothécaire, Richard Mathien, 514/374-5840, poste 271

Ministère des relations avec les citoyens et de l'immigration - Centre de documentation, 360, rue McGill, Montréal QC H2Y 2E9 – 514/873-3255; Téléc: 514/864-2468; Symbol: QMIMM – Bibliothécaire, Denis Robichaud, 514/873-8379

Ministère des Relations avec les citoyens et de l'Immigration - Centre de documentation, #14, 360, rue McGill, Montréal QC H2Y 2E9 – 514/873-2594; Téléc: 514/864-2468

Ministère des transports - Centre de documentation, 35, rue de Port-Royal est, 3e étage, Montréal QC H3L 3T1 – 514/864-1666; Téléc: 514/873-7389; Symbol: QMTRA – Librarian, Vy-Khanh Nguyen

Montréal Gazette - Library, 250, rue St-Antoine ouest, Montréal QC H2Y 3R7 – 514/987-2583; Fax: 514/987-2433; Email: library@thegazette.southam.ca; URL: http://www.montrealgazette.com;
Symbol: QMGA – Reference Librarian, Donna MacHutchin

The Montréal Holocaust Memorial Centre – Library, 5151, ch Côte-Ste-Catherine, Montréal QC H3W 1M6 – 514/345-2605; Fax: 514/344-2651 – Archivist, Carole Katz

Montréal International – Library, #3200, 380, rue Saint-Antoine ouest, Montréal QC H2Y 3X7 – 514/849-1999; Téléc: 514/987-1948 – Osvaldo Nunez

Montréal Neurological Institute - Library, 3801 University St., Montréal QC H3A 2B4 – 514/398-1980; Fax: 514/398-5077; Email: ENVOY: ILL.QMNIH
Head Librarian, Carol Wiens
Reference Librarian, Avis Antel
Circulation Librarian, Claudia Ugolik

Mouvement ATD Quart Monde – Centre de documentation Pauvreté et Droits Humains, 6747, rue Drolet, Montréal QC H2S 2T1 – 514/279-0468; Téléc: 514/279-7759 – Responsable, Elisa Hamel

Mouvement québécois de la qualité – Centre de documentation, #404, 455, rue Saint-Antoine ouest, Montréal QC H2Z 1J1 – 514/874-9933; Téléc: 514/866-4600 – Agent d'information, Denise Cote

Musée d'art contemporain de Montréal - Médiathèque, 185, rue Ste-Catherine ouest, Montréal QC H2X 1Z8 – 514/847-6254; Téléc: 514/847-6916; Courrier électronique: adepoca@cam.org; URL: http://Media.MACM.qc.ca; Symbol: QMMAC
Bibliothécaire responsable, Michelle Gauthier
Bibliothécaire de référence, Élaine Bégin, 514/847-6257
Technicienne en documentation, Jacqueline Bélanger, 514/847-6260
Technicienne en documentation, Ginette Bujold, 514/847-6259
Technicienne en documentation, Régine Francoeur, 514/847-6256
Technicienne en documentation, Johanne Lefebvre, 514/847-6255
Agente de bureau, Nicole St-Pierre, 514/847-6261
Agente de bureau auxiliaire, Dominique Chicoine, 514/847-6923

Musée des beaux-arts de Montréal - Bibliothèque, CP 3000, Montréal QC H3G 2T9 – 514/285-1600; Téléc: 514/285-5655; Symbol: QMFA
Bibliothécaire en chef, Joanne Dery
Bibliotechnicienne, Danielle Blanchette
Librarian, Thérèse Bourgault

Le Musée Marc-Aurèle Fortin – Bibliothèque, 118, rue St-Pierre, Montréal QC H2Y 2L7 – 514/845-6108; Téléc: 514/845-6100 – Adjointe au directeur, Marcelle Trudeau

Musicaction – Bibliothèque, #209, 455, rue Saint-Antoine ouest, Montréal QC H2Z 1J1 – 514/861-8444; Téléc: 514/861-4423 – Secrétaire, Suzie Champagne

National Bank of Canada – Centre de documentation, 600, rue de La Gauchetière ouest, Montréal QC H3B 4L2 – 514/394-5000, poste 5470; Fax: 514/394-4167; Symbol: QMBAN – Bibliothécaire, Agathe Sabourin

National Film Board of Canada - Communications - Reference Library, POBox 6100, Montréal QC H3C 3H5 – 514/283-9045; Fax: 514/283-5729; Toll Free: 1-800-267-7710; URL: http://www.nfb.ca;
Symbol: QMNF – Head, Reference Library, Rose-Aimée Todd, Email: r.a.todd@nfb.ca

National Research Council-Biotechnology Research Institute – Library, 6100, av Royalmount, Montréal QC H4P 2R2 – 514/496-6117; Fax: 514/496-7885; Email: eveline@landa.nrc.ca; Symbol: QMNB – Librarian, Eveline Landa

National Theatre School - Library, 5030 St-Denis, Montréal QC H2J 2L8 – 514/842-7954; Fax: 514/842-5661
Head Librarian, Wolfgang Noethlichs
Assistant to the Librarian, Monique Forest

Native Friendship Centre of Montréal Inc. – Library, 2001, boul St-Laurent, Montréal QC H2X 2T3 – 514/499-1854; Fax: 514/499-9436 – Socio-Cultural Coordinator, Skawennati Tricia Fragnito

Nesbitt Burns - Library, #300, 1501, av McGill College, Montréal QC H3A 3M8 – 514/286-7200; Fax: 514/282-8104 – Librarian, Nicole Piggott

Noranda Technology Centre - Library, 240, boul Hymus, Pointe Claire QC H9R 1G5 – 514/630-9524; Fax: 514/630-9379; Symbol: QMNR

Chief Librarian, N. De Brouwer

Reference Librarian, Jean Barrette, 514/630-9300, ext.213

Circulation Librarian, E. Eaton, 514/630-9404

Office des congrès et du tourisme du Grand Montréal – Bibliothèque, #600, 1555, rue Peel, Montréal QC H3A 3L8 – 514/844-5400; Téléc: 514/844-5757 – Personne ressource, Louise Lessard

Office franco-québécois pour la jeunesse - Centre de références, #301, 1441, boul René Lévesque ouest, Montréal QC H3G 1T7 – 514/873-4255, 1-800-465-4255 (Québec); Téléc: 514/873-0067 – Responsable, Michel Lagacé

Office de la langue française - Service des bibliothèques, 800, place Victoria, 15e étage, CP 316, Montréal QC H4Z 1G8 – 514/873-2997; Téléc: 514/873-2884; Courrier électronique: OLF.BIBLMTL; Symbol: QMOLF – Bibliothécaire, Chantal Robinson, 514/873-2996

Office des personnes handicapées du Québec - Centre de documentation, 600, rue Fullum, bureau 5.08, Montréal QC H2K 3L6 – 514/873-3574; Téléc: 514/873-9706; Symbol: QDOPH – Responsable, Sophie Janik

Office des services de garde à l'enfance - Centre de documentation, 100, rue Sherbrooke est, Montréal QC H2X 1C3 – 514/873-2323; Téléc: 514/873-4250; Ligne sans frais: 1-800-363-0310; Symbol: QMSGE – Responsable, Claire Bergeron

Ogilvy Renault Law Office - Library, #1100, 1981, av McGill College, Montréal QC H3A 3C1 – 514/847-4747; Téléc: 514/286-5474 – Chief Librarian, Carole Méhul, 514/847-4701

Oratoire St-Joseph - Bibliothèque Sainte-Croix, 3800, ch Reine-Marie, Montréal QC H3V 1H6 – 514/733-8211, poste 2341; Fax: 514/733-9735; Symbol: BSC – Directeur, Pierre Germain

Orchestre symphonique de Montréal – Bibliothèque, 260, boul de Maisonneuve, Montréal QC H2X 1Y9 – 842-3402, poste 213; Téléc: 514/842-0728 – Archiviste, Jean Prévost

Ordre des infirmières et infirmiers auxiliaires du Québec – Bibliothèque, 531, rue Sherbrooke est, Montréal QC H2L 1K2 – 514/282-9511; Téléc: 514/282-0631; Toll Free: 1-800-283-9511 – JoAnne Beaulieu

Ordre des infirmières et infirmiers du Québec – Centre de documentation, 4200, boul Dorchester ouest, Westmount QC H3Z 1V4 – 514/935-2501; Téléc: 514/935-1799; Toll Free: 1-800-363-6048; Courrier électronique: cdoc@oiiq.org – Chef du service, Maryse Dumas

Ordre des ingénieurs du Québec – Bibliothèque, 2020, rue University, 18e étage, Montréal QC H3A 2A5 – 514/845-6141; Téléc: 514/845-1833; Toll Free: 1-800-461-6141 – Documentaliste, Hélène Larouche

Ordre des orthophonistes et audiologistes du Québec – Bibliothèque, #730, 1265, rue Berri, Montréal QC H2L 4X4 – 514/282-9123; Téléc: 514/282-9541

Ordre des pharmaciens du Québec – Bibliothèque, #301, 266, rue Notre Dame ouest, Montréal QC H2Y 1T6 – 514/284-9588; Téléc: 514/284-3420; Toll Free: 1-800-363-0324 – Directrice communications, Elaine Lacaille

Ordre des technologues en radiologie du Québec – Bibliothèque, #420, 7400, boul les Galeries d'Anjou, Anjou QC H1M 3M2 – 514/351-0052; Téléc: 514/355-2396; Toll Free: 1-800-361-8759 – Sec. de direction, Josée Turcotte

Pfizer Canada Inc. - Medical Library, POBox 800, Pointe-Claire QC H9R 4V2 – 514/426-7060; Fax: 514/426-6997; Email: goodwin1@pfizer.com; Symbol: QKPC

Librarian, Maureen Goodwin

Assistant Librarian, Jocelyne Leclerc

Phillips, Friedman, Kotler - Law Library, #900, Place du Canada, Montréal QC H3B 2P8 – 514/878-3371; Fax: 514/878-3691, 4676 – Librarian, Barbara Shapiro

Polish Institute of Arts & Sciences - Library, 3479, rue Peel, Montréal QC H3A 1W7 – 514/398-6978; Fax: 514/398-8184; Email: cxsw@musica.mcgill.ca

Director, Prof. Hanna M. Pappius

Cataloguing Librarian, Sophie Boganski

Librarian, Stefan Wladysiuk

Pouliot, Mercure Law Office - Bibliothèque, 1155, boul René-Lévesque ouest, 31e étage, Montréal QC H3B 3S6 – 514/875-5210; Courrier électronique: poumer@cedep.com – Bibliothécaire, François Trudeau

Presbyterian College - Library, 3495 University St., Montréal QC H3A 2A8 – 514/288-5256 – Librarian, Daniel Shute

Protestant School Board of Greater Montréal - Professional Library, 6000 Fielding Ave., Montréal QC H3X 1T4 – 514/483-7269 – Librarian, J. Wrench

Provincial Association of Protestant Teachers of Québec – Library, #1, 17035 Brunswick Blvd., Kirkland QC H9H 5G6 – 514/694-9777; Fax: 514/694-0189

Public Works & Government Services Canada - Translation Bureau - Montréal Documentation Centre, #307, 200, boul René-Lévesque ouest, Montréal QC H2Z 1X4 – 514/283-7519; Fax: 514/283-3877 – Head, L. Rebelo

Pulp & Paper Research Institute of Canada – Library, 570, boul St-Jean, Pointe Claire QC H9R 3J9 – 514/630-4100; Fax: 514/630-4105; Symbol: QMPP – Marilyn McNamee

Québec Community Newspaper Association – Library, Glenaladale House, MacDonald College, 21111, rue Lakeshore, Ste-Anne-de-Bellevue QC H9X 3V9 – 514/398-7706; Fax: 514/398-7972 – Member Services Coordinator, Michelle Faladreau

Québec Family History Society – Library, POBox 1026, Pointe Claire QC H9S 4H9 – 514/695-1502 – Librarian, Penelope Redmile

Québec Federation of Home & School Associations – Library, #562, 3285, boul Cavendish, Montréal QC H4B 2L9 – 514/481-5619; Fax: 514/481-5619 – Donna Sauriol

Radio-Québec - Centre des ressources documentaires, 800, rue Fullum, Montréal QC H2K 3L7 – 514/521-2424, poste 2094; Téléc: 514/873-7464; Symbol: QMRQ – Chef de service, Nicole Charest

Raymond, Chabot, Martin Paré et associés - Bibliothèque, Tour de la Banque nationale, #1900, 600, rue de la Gauchetière ouest, Montréal QC H3B 4L8 – 514/878-2691; Téléc: 514/878-2127 – Bibliothécaire, Michele Bernard

Reader's Digest Magazines Ltd. - Editorial Library, 215 Redfern, Westmount QC H3Z 2V9 – 514/934-0751; Fax: 514/934-2357; Symbol: QMRD – Librarian, Pierre Charlebois, 514/934-0751, poste 4125

Régie du cinéma du Québec - Centre de documentation, 455, rue Sainte-Hélène, Montréal QC H2Y 2L3 – 514/873-2371; Téléc: 514/864-3229 – Directrice du classement des films, Carmen Watson

Régie du logement - Centre de documentation, Loc. 23.60, 5199, rue Sherbrooke est, Montréal QC H1T 3X1 – 514/873-6575; Téléc: 514/873-6805; Symbol: QMRL – Responsable, Ginette Belair

Regroupement loisir Québec – Bibliothèque, 4545, av Pierre-de-Coubertin, CP 1000, Montréal QC H1V 3R2 – 514/252-3126; Téléc: 514/253-7156 – Directeur, Communications, Daniel Caron

Revenue Canada - Research & Library Services, 3131, boul St-Martin ouest, Laval QC H7T 2A7 – 514/956-7052; Fax: 514/956-6915 – Library Technician, Claire Rozon

Research & Library Services, 305, boul René-Lévesque ouest, Montréal QC H2Z 1A6 – 514/283-7725; Téléc: 514/283-6944; Courrier électronique: ENVOY: QMRE.PEB; Symbol: QMRE – Coordonnatrice, Gestion de l'information, Lucie Rebelo, Email: rebellu@cam.org

Robinson Sheppard Shapiro Law Office - Library, Stock Exchange Tower, #4700, 800, Place Victoria, POBox 322, Montréal QC H4Z 1H6 – 514/878-2631; Fax: 514/878-1865 – Librarian, Angela Tietolman, 514/393-4009

Rolls-Royce Canada Ltd. - Library, 9500 Côte de Liesse Rd., Lachine QC H8T 1A2 – 514/631-3541; Fax: 514/636-9969 – Technical Librarian, Juliette Martin

Royal Bank of Canada – Information Resources, Place Ville Marie, CP 6001, Montréal QC H3C 3A9 – 514/874-2343; Téléc: 514/874-2445 – Librarian, John O'Shaughnessy

Samson Bélair/Deloitte & Touche - Centre de documentation, #3000, 1, Place Ville Marie, Montréal QC H3B 4T9 – 514/393-5066; Téléc: 514/393-7140; Courrier électronique: linda.patry@sympatico.ca – Librarian, Linda Patry

Sandoz Canada Inc. - Bibliothèque, 385, boul Bouchard, Dorval QC H9S 1A9 – 514/631-6775; Fax: 514/631-1867; Email: ENVOY: QMSAC; Symbol: QMSAC – Bibliothécaire, Sharon Pipon

Sir Mortimer B. Davis Jewish General Hospital - Health Sciences Library, East Wing, Pavilion A, Room 200, 3755, côte Ste-Catherine, Montréal QC H3T 1E2 – 514/340-8222, ext.5927

Chief Medical Librarian, Arlene Greenberg, Email: cyag@musica.mcgill.ca

Circulation & Acquisitions, Paula Calestagne, Email: ad70@musica.mcgill.ca

Serials, Liz Breier, Email: axlz@musica.mcgill.ca

ILL & Reference, Blanka Glowacki, Email: axbl@musica.mcgill.ca

Lady Davis Institute for Medical Research Library, Contact, Beverly Caplan, 514/340-8260, ext.3795, Email: axbc@musica.mcgill.ca

Institute of Community and Family Psychiatry Library, Contact, Judy Grossman, 514/340-8210, ext.5243, Email: ad11@musica.mcgill.ca

SNC-Lavalin Environment Inc. – Library, 455, boul René-Lévesque ouest, Montréal QC H2Z 1Z3 – 514/393-1000; Téléc: 514/866-6709; Symbol: QMSNC – Manager, Library & Records Management Services, Linda Thivierge

Social Justice Committee of Montréal – Library, 1857, rue de Maisonneuve ouest, Montréal QC H3H 1J9 – 514/933-6797; Fax: 514/933-9517 – Coordinator, Derek McCuish

Société catholique de la Bible – Bibliothèque, #519, 7400, boul St-Laurent, Montréal QC H2R 2Y1 – 514/274-4381; Téléc: 514/274-5184

Société de criminologie du Québec – Bibliothèque, #210, 2000, boul Saint-Joseph est, Montréal QC H2H 1E4 – 514/529-4391; Téléc: 514/521-3753 – Denise Trottier

Société de développement des entreprises culturelles – Centre de documentation, #200, 1755, boul René-Lévesque est, Montréal QC H2K 4P6 – 514/873-7768; Téléc: 514/873-4388; Symbol: SODEC – Responsable, Micheline Gougeon

Société d'habitation du Québec - Direction générale de la planification et de la recherche - Centre de documentation, Tour Nord, 25e étage, 3, Place Desjardins, Montréal QC H5B 1B3 – 514/873-9611; Téléc: 514/873-2849; Courrier électronique: Centredoc@SHQ.gouv.qc.ca; Symbol: QMSHQ – Bibliothécaire, Barbara Maass

Société historique de Montréal – Centre de documentation, 460, Place Jacques-Cartier, 2e étage, Montréal QC H2Y 3B3 – 514/878-9008; Téléc: 514/878-0085

La Société des musées québécois – Bibliothèque, CP 8888, Succ Centre-Ville, Montréal QC H3C 3P8 – 514/987-3264; Téléc: 514/987-3379

Société québécoise de développement de la main-d'oeuvre - Région de Montréal - Centre de documentation, 5350, rue Lafond, Montréal QC H1X 2X2 – 514/725-5221, poste 310; Téléc: 514/725-4311; Symbol: QMCFP – Nicole Dumoulin

Société québécoise d'espéranto – Bibliothèque, 6358A, rue de Bordeaux, Montréal QC H2G 2R8 – 514/272-0151; Téléc: 514/495-8442 – Responsable, Normand Fleury

Société québécoise de spéléologie – Centre de documentation, 4545, av Pierre-de-Coubertin, CP 1000, Montréal QC H1V 3R2 – 514/252-3006; Téléc: 514/252-3201; Toll Free: 1-800-338-6636

Société Radio-Canada - Bibliothèque, C74, 1400, boul René-Lévesque est, Montréal QC H2L 2M2 – 514/597-4776; Téléc: 514/597-6236; Symbol: QMCB – Directeur, Cyr Devost

Bibliothèque de l'ingénierie, 7925, ch Côte St-Luc, Montréal QC H4W 1R5 – 514/485-5546; Téléc: 514/485-5885; Courrier électronique: stlauren@srcing.login.qc.ca; Symbol: QMCBE – Technicienne, Lysane St-Laurent

Music Library, 1400, boul René-Lévesque est, CP 6000, Montréal QC H3C 3A8 – 514/597-6420; Téléc: 514/597-6241; Symbol: QMCBM – Acting Chief, Guy Peloquin

Société de télédiffusion du Québec - Info-Centre, 655, rue Parthenais, Montréal QC H2K 3R7 – 514/521-2424, poste 2091; Téléc: 514/873-5729; Symbol: QMRQ – Bibliothécaire, Danielle Marion

Société de transport de la communauté urbaine de Montréal - Bibliothèque, 800, la Gauchetiere ouest, Montréal QC H5A 1J6 – 514/280-5219; Téléc: 514/280-5631; Courrier électronique: stcumoc@mlink.net

Bibliothécaire, Michelle Chartier

Technicienne en documentation, Dominique Constantin

Sodarcan - Centre de documentation, #804, 1140, boul de Maisonneuve ouest, Montréal QC H3A 1M8 – 514/288-0100, poste 3704; Fax: 514/282-9405; Symbol: QMGP – Odette Lavoie

Solicitor General Canada - Federal Training Centre - Library, 6099, boul Lévesque est, Laval QC H7C 1P1 – 514/661-7786, ext.4505; Fax: 514/661-9485; Symbol: QLASGP – Librarian, Claire Jutras

Leclerc Establishment - Library, 400, Montée St-François, Laval QC H7C 1S7 – 514/664-1320, ext.5505; Fax: 514/664-6719; Symbol: QLL – Librarian, Isabelle Lapointe

The Spiritual Science Fellowship of Canada – Library, POBox 1387, Montréal QC H3G 2N3 – 514/937-8539; Fax: 514/937-5380 – B. Lyman

Statistics Canada - Québec Regional Reference Centre, Complexe Guy-Favreau, Tour Est, 4e étage, 200, boul René-Lévesque ouest, Montréal QC H2Z 1X4 – 514/283-5725; Téléc: 514/283-9350; Ligne sans frais: 1-800-263-1136

Sureté du Québec - Centre de documentation, 1701, rue Parthenais, Montréal QC H2K 3S7 – 514/598-4330; Téléc: 514/596-3682; Symbol: QMSU

Bibliothécaire, Maureen Clapperton

Bibliothécaire de référence, France Blackburn

Technicienne, Francine Cusson

Tecsult Inc. – Bibliothèque, 85, rue Ste-Catherine ouest, Montréal QC H2X 3P4 – 514/287-8546; Téléc: 514/287-8643; Courrier électronique: biblitec@tecsult.com; Symbol: QMABB – Librarian, Louise Pichet

Teleglobe Canada Inc. - Bibliothèque centrale, 680, rue Sherbrooke ouest, Montréal QC H3A 2S4 – 514/868-7272; Fax: 514/868-7234 – Lise Gill

Towers Perrin - Information Centre, 1800, av McGill College, 22e étage, Montréal QC H3A 3J6 – 514/982-9411; Fax: 514/982-9269; Email: tpinfo@lanter.net – Information Specialist, Josée Plamondon

Union Carbide/Pétromont - Documentation Centre, PO Box 700, Succ. Pointe-aux-Trembles, Montréal QC H1B 5K8 – 514/640-6400, ext.1312; Fax: 514/645-8149 – M.C. de Jesus

Union des municipalités du Québec – Bibliothèque, #680, 680, rue Sherbrooke ouest, Montréal QC H3A 2M7 – 514/282-7700; Téléc: 514/282-7711

Union of the Vietnamese Buddhist Churches in Canada – Bibliothèque Tam Bao Som, 4450, av Van Horne, Montréal QC H3S 1S1 – 819/687-2183; Fax: 514/733-5860 – Secretary & Principal, Rév. Pho Tinh

Université de Montréal - Services des bibliothèques, 2910, boul Édouard-Montpetit, CP 6128, Succ Centre-Ville, Montréal QC H3C 3J7 – 514/343-6905, 7643; Téléc: 514/343-2252; Courrier électronique: joffe@brise.ere.umontreal.ca; URL: http://brise.ere.umontreal.ca/~bullj/servbib/; Symbol: QMU

Directrice générale, Arlette Joffe-Nicodème, 514/343-6905

Services aux usagers, Directeur, Gilles Picard, 514/343-7643

Services techniques, Directrice, Ginette Darbon, 514/343-7687

Bureau des systèmes, Directeur, Paul-Emil Provost, 514/343-2080

Adjoint général, Jacques Boyer, 514/343-7646

Banques de donnés, Adjointe, Christiane Robert-Guertin, 514/343-6070

Développement des collections, Adjointe, Mireille Janeau, 514/343-7653

Gestion du personnel, Adjoint, Michel Goulet, 514/343-7757

Service de l'Audiovidéothèque, Chef, Ginette Gagnier, 514/343-7344

Service de catalogage, Chef, Ginette Grégoire, 514/343-6899

Service des acquisitions, Chef, Suzanne Simoneau, 514/343-7197

Services des collections spéciales, Chef, Geneviève Bazin, 514/343-7753

Service du prêt entre bibliothèques, Chef, Sylvie April, 514/343-6903

Bibliothèque d'aménagement, Chef, Marc Joanis, 514/343-6009

Bibliothèque de bibliothéconomie, Chef, Georges Clonda, 514/343-6047

Bibliothèque de biologie, Chef, Ginette Gagnier, 514/343-7073

Bibliothèque de chimie, Directrice, Josée Schepper, 514/343-6459

Bibliothèque d'éducation physique, Chef, Johanne Hopper, 514/343-6765

Bibliothèque de droit, Directeur, Clément Tremblay, 514/343-7095

Bibliothèque EPC (Éducation, psychologie, communication), Chef, Robert Gauthier, 514/343-7242

Bibliothèque de géographie, Directrice, Pâquerette Ranger, 514/343-8063

Bibliothèque des lettres et des sciences humaines, Directrice, Pâquerette Ranger, 514/343-7430

Bibliothèque d'optométrie, Chef, Danielle Tardif, 514/343-7674

Bibliothèque de mathématiques et d'informatique, Chef, Jules Giroux, 514/343-6703

Bibliothèque de médecine vétérinaire, Chef, Bernard Bédard, 514/773-8521

Bibliothèque de musique, Chef, Marc Joanis, 514/343-6432

Bibliothèque para-médicale, Chef, Johanne Hopper, 514/343-6180

Bibliothèque de physique, Chef, Jules Giroux, 514/343-6613

Bibliothèque de psycho-éducation, Chef, Tamara Rosenthal, 514/385-2556

Bibliothèque de la santé, Directrice, Diane Raymond-Clerk, 514/343-6826

Bibliothèque des sciences de la santé, Directrice, Diane Raymond-Clerk, 514/343-7810

Bibliothèques scientifiques, Directrice, Josée Schepper, 514/343-5665

Université du Québec - Bibliothèque de l'Institut nationale de la recherche scientifique - Santé, 245, boul Hymus, Pointe-Claire QC H9R 1G6 – 514/630-8812; Téléc: 514/630-8850; Symbol: QMUQIS – Documentalist, Gilbert Leblanc

Université du Québec à Montréal - Direction des bibliothèques, 455, boul René-Lévesque est, CP 8889, Montréal QC H3C 3P8 – 514/987-6124; Téléc: 514/987-7787; Symbol: QMUQ

Directeur général, Jean-Pierre Côté

Adjointe au Directeur général, Diane Polrucky

Bibliothèques spécialisées, Directrice, Lisette Dupont

Bibliothèque des arts, Directrice, Daphné Dufresne

Bibliothèque centrale, Directeur, Rénald Beaumier

Bibliothèque des sciences, Directeur, Conrad Corriveau

Bibliothèque des sciences de l'éducation, Responsable, Lucie Verreault

Bibliothèque des sciences juridiques, Directrice, Micheline Drapeau

Services informatisés, Directeur, André Champagne

Services techniques, Directrice adjointe, Claire Boisvert

Vanier College - Library, 821 Ste-Croix Ave., Saint-Laurent QC H4L 3X9 – 514/744-7540; Fax: 514/744-7545; Email: ENVOY: VANIER.COLL.LIBRARY; Symbol: QMVC

Chief Librarian, Beverly Chandler, 514/744-7543

Collections Librarian, Carol Anne Inglis, 514/744-7538

Reference Specialist, Michel Starenky, 514/744-7541

Data Base Manager, Wendy Loucks, 514/744-7551

Automation Coordinator & Systems Manager, Cheryl Holmes, 514/744-7550

Vidéographe – Centre de documentation, 4550, rue Garnier, Montréal QC H2J 3S7 – 514/866-4720; Téléc: 514/866-4725 – Vidéothécaire, Chantal Molleur

Villa Maria - Bibliothèque, 4245, boul Décarie, Montréal QC H4A 3K4 – 514/484-4950; Téléc: 514/484-4492 – Irene Wagner

Ville de Montréal - Service de l'urbanisme, Centre de documentation, #5.100, 303, rue Notre-Dame est, Montréal QC H2Y 3Y8 – 514/872-4119; Téléc: 514/872-0350 – Danielle Fortin, 514/872-4119

William M. Mercer Ltée - Information Centre, #1100, 600, boul de Maisonneuve ouest, Montréal QC H3A 3J4 – 514/285-1802; Fax: 514/285-8831; Email: monique_delorme@mercer.ca; Symbol: QMWMM

Manager, Information Centre, Monique Delorme

Library Technician, Sylvie Bourgoin

Wyeth-Ayerst Research. - Département de l'information scientifique, 1025, boul Marcel Laurin, Montréal QC H4R 1J6 – 514/748-3734; Téléc: 514/744-0550; Courrier électronique: pilonn@war.wyeth.com; Symbol: QMAY
Nicole B. Pilon
René Pageau
Carole Brouillette

**NICOLET**

Institut de police du Québec - Centre de documentation, 350, rue Marguerite-d'Youville, Nicolet QC J3T 1X4 – 819/293-8631; Téléc: 819/293-4018; Courrier électronique: ipq@itr.qc.ca; Symbol: QNIP – Technicienne en documentation, Nathalie Rheault

Séminaire de Nicolet - Bibliothèque, #110, 900, boul Louis-Fréchette, Nicolet QC J3T 1V5 – 819/293-4838; Téléc: 819/293-4161; Symbol: QNICS – Archiviste, Marie Pelletier

**NOTRE-DAME-DU-LAC**

Hôpital Notre-Dame-du-Lac – Bibliothèque médicale, 58, rue de l'Eglise, CP 310, Notre-Dame-du-Lac QC G0L 1X0 – 418/899-6751; Téléc: 418/899-2809 – Christine David

**PASPÉBIAC**

Centre local de services communautaires Chaleurs - Centre de documentation, CP 7000, Paspébiac QC G0C 2K0 – 418/752-6611; Téléc: 418/752-6734 – Pierre Provost

**PORT-CARTIER**

Solicitor General Canada - Port-Cartier Establishment - Library, Airport Rd., POBox 7070, Port-Cartier QC G5B 2W2 – 418/766-7070; Fax: 418/766-6258; Symbol: QPCP – Librarian, Mick Boucher

**QUÉBEC**

Assemblée nationale du Québec - Bibliothèque, Édifice Pamphile-Lemay, 1035, rue des Parlementaires, Québec QC G1A 1A5 – 418/643-4408; Téléc: 418/646-3207; Courrier électronique: ENVOY: PEB.QQL; Symbol: QQL
Directeur, Gaston Bernier, 418/643-4032, Fax: 418/646-4873
Reference, Circulation & Public Services, Head, Jean-Luc Fortin, 418/643-2708
Catalogue, Technical Services & Acquisitions, Head, Clément Lebel, 418/643-1204
Archives, Head, J.G. Pelletier, 418/646-0695
Research, Head, Gaston Deschênes, 418/643-4567
Clipping, Head, Jean-Claude Duval, 418/643-7596

Barreau de Québec - Bibliothèque, Palais de Justice, #5.03, 300, boul Jean-Lesage, Québec QC G1K 8K6 – 418/649-3536; Téléc: 418/522-4560 – Directrice, Anne Demers, 418/529-0301

Bureau de la statistique du Québec - Centre d'information et de documentation, 200, ch Sainte-Foy, 3e étage, Québec QC G1R 5T4 – 418/691-2401; Téléc: 418/643-4129; Ligne sans frais: 1-800-463-4090; Courrier électronique: cid@bsq.gouv.qc.ca; URL: http://www.bsq.gouv.qc.ca/bsq/bsq.html; Symbol: QQBS – Technicienne en documentation, Lorraine Carrier

Carrefour Tiers-Monde – Centre de documentation, 454, rue Caron, Québec QC G1K 8K8 – 418/647-5853; Téléc: 418/647-5719 – Agente d'éducation, Lyse Nadeau

Centre d'arbitrage commercial national et international du Québec – Bibliothèque, Édifice la Fabrique, #090, 295, boul Charest est, Québec QC G1K 3G8 – 418/649-1374; Montréal: 519/393-3774; Téléc: 418/649-0845 – Céline Vallières

Centre hospitalier universitaire de Québec - Pavillon St-François-d'Assise – Bibliothèque médico-administrative, 10, rue de l'Espinay, Québec QC G1L 3L5 – 418/525-4408; Téléc: 418/525-4426 – Coordonnateur administratif, Ulric Lefebvre

Centre local de services communautaire de la Basse-Ville-Limoilou - Centre de documentation, 50, rue St-Joseph est, Québec QC G1K 3A5 – 418/529-6592, poste 483; Téléc: 418/529-1376; Symbol: QQCBV – Responsable, Ginette Rouleau

Collège François-Xavier Garneau - Centre des Médias, 1660, boul de l'Entente, Québec QC G1S 4S3 – 418/688-8310; Téléc: 418/681-9384, 688-0087; Courrier électronique: sfortin@cegep-fxg.qc.ca
Gestion, Sylvie Fortin
Service du Prêt, Bibliotechnicienne, Christiane Lavoie
Bibliotechnicienne aux acquisitions, Christine Lavoie

Collège Jésus-Marie de Sillery - Bibliothèque, 2047, Chemin Saint-Louis, Québec QC G1T 1P3 – 418/687-9250; Téléc: 418/687-9847 – Bibliothécaire, Jacqueline Lamontagne

Collège Limoilou - Bibliothèque, CP 1400, Québec QC G1K 7H3 – 418/647-6600, poste 733; Téléc: 418/647-6793; Courrier électronique: mgod@fedecegeps.qc.ca; URL: http://www.climoilou.qc.ca/bibli/accueil/cadre.html
Bibliothécaire, Danielle Fleury
Responsable du développement des collections, M. Godin
Campus de Charlesbourg, Responsable, Centre des médias, Ann Murchison, 418/624-3612

Collège Mérici - Bibliothèque, 755, ch St-Louis, Québec QC G1S 1C1 – 418/683-1591; Téléc: 418/682-8938; Courrier électronique: mmessely@college-merici.qc.ca; Symbol: QQCM – Bibliothécaire, Maryse Messely, 418/683-1591, poste 2213

Commission d'acces à l'information - Centre de documentation, #315, 900, boul René-Lévesque est, Québec QC G1R 2B5 – 418/528-7741; Téléc: 418/529-3102; Courrier électronique: cai.communications@cai.gouv.gc.ca; Symbol: QCAI – Responsable, Suzanne Plante

Commission d'appel en matière de lésions professionnelles - Centre de documentation, 900, Place d'Youville, 7e étage, Québec QC G1R 3P7 – 418/644-4618; Téléc: 418/644-8237; Symbol: QQCAML – Techniciennne, Monique Boies

Commission de la fonction publique du Québec - Centre de documentation, 8, rue Cook, 4e étage, Québec QC G1R 5J8 – 418/643-1425; Téléc: 418/643-7264; Symbol: QQCFP – Bibliotechnicienne, Louise Guy

Commission des normes du travail - Centre de documentation, 400, boul Jean-Lesage, 7e étage, CP 18500, Québec QC G1K 8W1 – 418/646-8713; Téléc: 418/643-5132; URL: http://www.cnt.gouv.qc.ca; Symbol: QQCDT – Responsable, Mireille Barrière

Commission de toponymie du Québec - Bibliothèque, 1060, rue Louis-Alexandre-Taschereau, 4e étage, Québec QC G1R 5V8 – 418/643-8922; Téléc: 418/644-9466; Courrier électronique: toponymie@toponymie.gouv.qc.ca; URL: http://www.toponymie.gouv.qc.ca; Symbol: QQCT – Responsable de la documentation, Yolande Morency

Commission des transports du Québec - Bibliothèque, 200, ch Ste-Foy, 7e étage, Québec QC G1R 5V5 – 418/643-2078; Téléc: 418/643-8368; Courrier électronique: courrier@ctq.gouv.qc.ca; URL: http://www.ctq.gouv.qc.ca – Bibliothécaire en chef, Yvon Déry

Conseil des colleges du Québec - Centre de documentation, 905, Autoroute Dufferin-Montmorency, 3e étage, Québec QC G1R 5M6 – 418/644-2928; Téléc: 418/643-9019; Symbol: QQCC – Responsable, Micheline Poulin

Conseil de la famille - Centre de documentation, #1.66, 875, Grande Allée est, Québec QC G1R 4Y8 – 418/646-5865; Téléc: 418/643-9832; Symbol: QQASF – Responsable, Suzanne Lamy

Conseil de la langue française - Centre de documentation, 800, Place d'Youville, 13e étage, Québec QC G1R 3P4 – 418/646-1127; Téléc: 418/644-7654; Courrier électronique: dbelley@clf.gouv.qc.ca; Symbol: QQCLF – Responsable, Donald Belley

Conseil de presse du Québec – Centre de documentation, 55 1/2, rue Saint-Louis, Québec QC G1R 3Z2 – 418/692-3008; Téléc: 418/692-5148 – Documentaliste, recherchiste, Lisette Lapointe

Conseil du Statut de la Femme - Centre de documentation, #300, 8, rue Cook, 3e étage, Québec QC G1R 5J7 – 418/643-4326; Téléc: 418/643-8926; Ligne sans frais: 1-800-463-2851; Courrier électronique: centre.doc@csf.gouv.qc.ca; URL: http://www.csf.gouv.qc.ca; Symbol: QQCSF – Responsable, Gabrielle Poirier

Conseil du trésor - Centre de documentation, a/s Direction des communications, 875, Grande Allée est, Section 1-F, Québec QC G1R 5R8 – 418/644-9447 – Technicienne en documentation, Nancy Roy

Conservatoire d'art dramatique de Québec - Bibliothèque, 31, Mont-Carmel, Québec QC G1R 4A6 – 418/643-9184; Téléc: 418/646-9255; Symbol: QQCADQ – Responsable de la bibliothèque, Denise Gagné

Conservatoire de musique de Québec - Bibliothèque, 270, rue St-Amable, Québec QC G1R 5G1 – 418/643-2068; Téléc: 418/644-9658; Courrier électronique: cmq-b@mccq.gouv.qc.ca; Symbol: QQCMQ – Bibliothécaire, Denise Prince

Fondation québécoise du cancer - Centre de documentation, 1675, ch Ste-Foy, Québec QC G1S 2P7 – 418/681-9989; Téléc: 418/681-9947; Ligne sans frais: 1-800-363-0063; Courrier électronique: fqc.oool@ibm.net; URL: http://cancer.multiservices.com
Directrice, Claire Voyer Gosselin
Documentaliste, France Bélanger

Hôpital de l'Enfant-Jesus – Bibliothèque scientifique Charles-Auguste-Gauthier, 1401, 18e rue, Québec QC G1J 1Z4 – 418/649-5686; Téléc: 418/649-5627; Symbol: QQHEJ – Responsable, Madeleine Dumais

Hôtel-Dieu de Québec - Bibliothèque, 11, côte du Palais, Québec QC G1R 2J6 – 418/667-9577; Symbol: QQHD – Lizette Germain

Hôtel-Dieu du Sacré-Coeur de Jésus de Québec - Bibliothèque médicale, 1, av du Sacré-Coeur, Québec QC G1N 2W1 – 418/529-6851, poste 278; Téléc: 418/529-2971; Symbol: QQHDS – Christian Martel

L'Inspecteur général des institutions financières - Bibliothèque, 800, Place d'Youville, Québec QC G1R 4Y5 – 418/694-5008; Téléc: 418/643-3336; Symbol: QQIF
Bibliotechnicienne, Sylvie Nadeau
Ghislaine Gagnon

Institut de réadaptation en déficience physique en Québec – Centre de documentation, 525, boul Wilfrid Hamel, Québec QC G1M 2S8 – 418/529-9141; Téléc: 418/529-3723; Symbol: QQCF – Bibliothécaire, Anne Potvin

Institut de l'Énergie des pays ayant en commun l'usage du français – Bibliothèque, 56, rue St-Pierre, 3e étage, Québec QC G1K 4A1 – 418/692-5727; Téléc: 418/692-5644 – Chef, Service Documentation, Henriette Dumont

Literary & Historical Society of Québec – Library, 44 St-Stanislas, Québec QC G1R 4H3 – 418/694-9147 – Sylviane Dubois

MFQ Vie, Corporation d'Assurance - Centre de documentation, CP 16040, Québec QC G1K 7X8 – 418/644-4269; Téléc: 418/646-0370; Ligne sans frais: 1-800-463-5549 – Technicienne en documentation, F. Labrecque

Ministère des Affaires municipales - Centre de documentation, 20, av Chauveau, Québec QC G1R 4J3 – 418/691-2018; Téléc: 418/646-9266; Symbol: QQAM – Responsable, Ernest-B. Roy

Ministère des Communications - Centre de documentation, #320, 580, Grand Allée est, Québec QC G1R 2K2 – 418/643-8537; Téléc: 418/643-7853; Symbol: QQCOM – Documentaliste, Michel Gagné

Ministère des finances - Bibliothèque, #2.12, 12, rue St-Louis, Québec QC G1R 5L3 – 418/691-2256; Téléc: 418/646-1631; Symbol: QQMDF – Responsable, Michèle Lavoie

Ministère de la Culture et des Communications - Bibliothèque de l'édifice Guy-Frégault, 225, Grande Allée est, Québec QC G1R 5G5 – 418/643-3078; Téléc: 418/528-1060; Courrier électronique: Helene_Larouche@mcc.gouv.qc.ca; Symbol: QQAC – Bibliothécaire, Hélène Larouche

Ministère de la santé et des services sociaux - Service de la documentation, 845, av Joffre, R.C., Québec QC G1S 3L8 – 418/643-5572; Téléc: 418/646-2134; Symbol: QQIAS – Chef de service, Yvon Papillion, 418/643-5572

Ministère des Relations avec les citoyens et de l'Immigration - Bibliothèque - Édifices G & H, 1056, rue Louis-Alexandre-Taschereau, Québec QC G1R 5E6 – 418/643-1515 (G), 643-2377 (H); Téléc: 418/646-8132; Courrier électronique: Telereference@riq.qc.ca; Symbol: QQMC, QQMCH
- Directeur, Jean-Pierre Gagnon, 418/646-0976
- Responsable de la référence et des services publiques (G), Gilbert Plaisance
- Responsable des services techniques, Marcel Plourde
- Responsable de la référence et des services publiques (H), Lise Villeneuve

Ministère des ressources naturelles - Centre de documentation - Forêts, Édifice Bois-Fontaine, 880, ch Sainte-Foy, Québec QC G1S 4X4 – 418/643-2570; Téléc: 418/646-0802; Symbol: QQFO
- Responsable, Marie-Ève Varin
- Référence, PEB, Jacques Hébert
- Acquisitions, Pierrette Labbé
- Traitement, Francine Vachon

Ministère du tourisme - Centre de documentation, #344, 900, boul René-Lévesque est, Québec QC G1R 2B5 – 418/643-5090; Téléc: 418/644-7514; Courrier électronique: centre_doc@tourisme.gouv.qc.ca; URL: http://www.tourisme.gouv.qc.ca; Symbol: QQTO – Responsable, François Cantin

Ministère des transports - Centre de documentation, 700, boul René-Lévesque est, 21e étage, Québec QC G1R 5H1 – 418/643-3578; Téléc: 418/646-2343; Symbol: QQTR – Responsable, Donald Blais
- Centre de documentation, 930, ch Ste-Foy, 6e étage, Québec QC G1S 4X9 – 418/643-2256; Téléc: 418/646-6195; Courrier électronique: doc-qtrd@mtg.gouv.qc.ca; Symbol: QQTRD – Bibliothécaire, Nicole Brind Amour

Ministère de l'agriculture, des pêcheries et de l'alimentation - Bibliothèque, 200A, ch Ste-Foy, Québec QC G1R 4X6 – 418/643-2428; Téléc: 418/646-0829; Symbol: QQAG – Bibliothécaire, Chef de service, Hélène Babineau, 418/644-6244

Ministère de l'Éducation - Centre de documentation, Direction générale des affaires universitaires et scientifiques, 1035, rue de la Chevrotière, 19e étage, Québec QC G1R 5A5 – 418/643-1572; Symbol: QQESE – Responsable, Claudine Tremblay
- Centre d'information multimédia, 1035, rue de la Chevrotière, 11e étage, Québec QC G1R 5A5 – 418/643-6363; Téléc: 418/646-6561; Courrier électronique: dir_com@meq.gouv.qc.ca; Symbol: QQED – Responsable, Solange Cyr

Ministère de l'industrie, du commerce, de la science et de la technologie - Bibliothèque et gestion documentaire, #203, 710, Place d'Youville, Québec QC G1R 4Y4 – 418/691-5972; Téléc: 418/643-9719; Symbol: QQIC – Directeur, Jacques Fournier

Mouvement d'information et d'entraide dans la lutte contre le sida à Québec – Bibliothèque, #200, 175, rue St-Jean, Québec QC G1R 1N4 – 418/649-1720; Téléc: 418/649-1256

Musée de la civilisation - Centre de documentation, 85, rue Dalhousie, CP 155, Québec QC G1K 7A6 – 418/643-2158; Téléc: 418/646-8779; Symbol: QQMUC – Responsable, Danielle Aubin

Musée du Québec - Bibliothèque, Parc des Champs-de-Bataille, Québec QC G1R 5H3 – 418/643-7134; Téléc: 418/646-3330
- Bibliothécaire en chef, Louise Allard, 418/644-9908
- Reference, Bibliothécaire, Lucienne Gariepy, 418/643-7134
- Bibliothécaire, Richard St-Gelais, 418/646-4412
- Bibliotechnicienne, Nicole Gastonguay
- Bibliotechnicienne, Lina Doyon

Musée de l'Amérique française - Bibliothèque du Séminaire - Fonds ancien, 9, rue de l'Université, Québec QC G1R 4R7 – 418/643-2158; Courrier électronique: mcqarch@mcq.org; URL: http://www.mcq.org; Symbol: QQS – Directrice, Danielle Aubin

Office de la langue française - Bibliothèque, 200, ch Sainte-Foy, 4e étage, Québec QC G1R 5S4 – 418/643-4575; Téléc: 418/643-3210; Courrier électronique: qqolf@olf.gouv.qc.ca; Symbol: QQOLF – Responsable, Micheline Gagnon

Office des professions du Québec - Direction de la recherche/Centre de documentation, 320, rue St-Joseph est, Québec QC G1K 8G5 – 418/643-6912; Téléc: 418/643-0973; Courrier électronique: dmartineau@opq.gouv.qc.ca; Symbol: QQEDOP
- Documentaliste, André Contant
- Bibliotechnicienne, Denise Martineau

Patrimoine Canadien - Parcs Canada, Région du Québec, Bibliothèque, 3, rue Buade, CP 6060, Succ Haute-Ville, Québec QC G1R 4V7 – 418/648-7380; Téléc: 418/648-4234; Courrier électronique: PARCS. QQPCQ.PEB; Symbol: QQPCQ
- Bibliothécaire, Hélène Tardif, 418/649-8259
- Technicienne, Hélène D'Amours

Pavillon Saint-Sacrement – Bibliothèque Delâge-Couture, 1050, ch Ste-Foy, Québec QC G1S 4L8 – 418/682-7730; Téléc: 418/682-7972; Symbol: QQHSS – Bibliotechnicienne, Diane St-Pierre

Le Petit Séminaire de Québec - Bibliothèque, 3, de l'Université, Québec QC G1R 5X8 – 418/694-1020; Téléc: 418/694-3363
- Directeur, Louis-J. Lépine
- Services techniques, Georges-Henri De Champlain

Régie des rentes du Québec - Centre de documentation, Carrefour de la Capitale, 670, rue Bouvier, Québec QC G2J 1A7 – 418/644-3003; Téléc: 418/646-7181; Symbol: QQRRQ – Responsable, Nicole Paquin

Revenu Canada - Services Fiscaux, Québec - Bibliothèque, 165, rue de la Pointe-aux-Lièvres sud, Québec QC G1K 7L3 – 418/649-4999, poste 3115; Téléc: 418/649-6765; Courrier électronique: Christine.Roy@riq.qc.ca; Symbol: QQRT – Bibliothécaire, Christine Roy

Société d'habitation du Québec - Centre de documentation, Succursale de Québec, 1054, rue L.-A.-Taschereau, 3e étage, Québec QC G1R 5E7 – 418/646-7915; Téléc: 418/643-4059; Courrier électronique: Centredoc@SHQ.gouv.qc.ca; Symbol: QQSHQ – Technicienne en documentation, Jeanne-Mance Caron

Société historique de Québec – Bibliothèque, 72, Côte de la Montagne, Québec QC G1K 4E3 – 418/692-0556; Téléc: 418/692-0614 – Bibliothécaire, Rev. Honorius Provost

Société de l'assurance automobile du Québec – Bibliothèque, 333, boul Jean-Lesage, CP 19 600, Québec QC G1K 8J6 – 418/528-4291; Téléc: 418/644-0339; Symbol: QQRAA – Bibliothécaire en chef, Michel Dupuis

Le Soleil ltée - Bibliothèque, 925, ch St-Louis, CP 1547, Québec QC G1K 7J6 – 418/686-3394, poste 2510; Téléc: 418/686-3374; Courrier électronique: documentation@lesoleil.com; URL: http://www.lesoleil.com – Responsable de la documentation, Claudine Gagnon

Syndicat de la fonction publique du Québec inc. (ind.) – Centre de documentation, 5100, boul des Gradins, Québec QC G2J 1N4 – 418/623-2424; Téléc: 418/623-6109 – Bibliotechnicienne, Denise Joncas

Tourisme Québec - Centre de documentation, #344, 900, boul René-Lévesque est, Québec QC G1R 2B5 – 418/643-5090; Téléc: 418/644-7514; Courrier électronique: centre_doc@tourisme.gouv.qc.ca; URL: http://www.tourisme.gouv.qc.ca; Symbol: QMTQ – Bibliothécaire, François Cantin

Union québécoise pour la conservation de la nature – Bibliothèque, 690, Grande Allée est, 4e étage, Québec QC G1R 2K5 – 418/648-2104; Téléc: 418/648-0991 – Diane Neron

Université Laval - Bibliothèque, Pavillon Jean-Charles-Bonenfant, Cité Universitaire, CP 2208, Québec QC G1K 7P4 – 418/656-2131; Téléc: 418/656-7897; URL: http://www.bibl.ulaval.ca; Symbol: QQLA, QQLAS
- Directeur, Claude Bonnelly
- Acquisitions, Jo-Anne Belair, 418/656-2131, ext.5991
- Adj. Systems, Daniel Prémont, 418/656-2131, ext.3448
- Cataloguing, Claude Ochietti, 418/656-2131, ext.6313
- Circulation, Françoise Sorieul, 418/656-2131, ext.3224
- Collections sciences humaines et sociales, Alain Bourque, 418/656-2131, ext.5196
- Collections scientifiques, Lorraine Vallières, 418/656-2131, ext.2948
- Services de support et de développement, Claude Busque, 418/656-2131, ext.3918, Email: claude.busque@bibl.ulaval.ca
- Michel Fournier, 418/656-2131, ext.2871
- Charles H. Pelletier, 418/656-2131, ext.2888

### REPENTIGNY

Centre hospitalier Le Gardeur – Centre de documentation, 135, boul Claude David, Repentigny QC J6A 1N6 – 514/654-9600; Téléc: 514/585-5939 – Michèle Paquette

### RICHELAIN

National Defence - CFB Saint-Jean, POBox 1-119, Richelain QC J0J 1R0 – 514/358-7509; Fax: 514/358-7800; Symbol: QSTJCF – Library Technician, Réjean Messier

### RICHMOND

Centre local de services communautaires du Val Saint-François - Centre de documentation, 110, rue Barlow, CP 890, Richmond QC J0B 2H0 – 819/826-3781; Symbol: QRVSF – Martha Lemieux

**RIMOUSKI**

Centre hospitalier Régional de Rimouski – Centre de documentation, 150, av Rouleau, Rimouski QC G5L 5T1 – 418/724-8394; Téléc: 418/724-8615; Courrier électronique: chrr.doc@sie.qc.ca; Symbol: QRCH – Bibliotechnicienne, Nicole Bélanger

Institut maritime du Québec - Centre de documentation, 53, rue St-Germain ouest, Rimouski QC G5L 4B4 – 418/724-2822; Téléc: 418/724-0606
- Bibliothécaire, Bruno Lavoie
- Technicienne en documentation, Lise Gagné
- Responsable, Janine Lepage

Société généalogique de l'est du Québec – Bibliothèque, CP 253, Rimouski QC G5L 7C1 – 418/722-3500 – Archiviste, Donald O'Farrell

Université du Québec à Rimouski - Bibliothèque, 300, Allée des Ursulines, Rimouski QC G5L 3A1 – 418/724-1476; Téléc: 418/724-1621; Courrier électronique: ENVOY: PEB.QRU **Directeur; Symbol: QRU
- Directeur, Gaston Dumont, 418/723-1986, poste 1470
- Reference Librarian, Christian Bielle, 418/723-1986, poste 1479
- Circulation Librarian, Claude Durocher, 418/723-1986, poste 1474
- Archives Dept., Pierre Collins, 418/723-1986, poste 1669
- Acquisitions Librarian, Gérard Mercure, 418/723-1986, poste 1237

**RIVIÈRE-DU-LOUP**

Centre hospitalier régional du Grand-Portage – Bibliothèque médicale, 75, rue St-Henri, Rivière-du-Loup QC G5R 2A4 – 418/868-1000; Téléc: 418/862-5778 – Hadrien Thériault

Collège de Rivière-du-Loup - Bibliothèque, 80, rue Frontenac, Rivière-du-Loup QC G5R 1R1 – 418/862-6903, poste 238; Téléc: 418/862-4959 – Bibliothécaire, responsable du Centre des ressources didactiques, Marielle Tétreault

**ROBERVAL**

Hôtel-Dieu de Roberval – Bibliothèque médicale, 450, rue Brassard, Roberval QC G8H 1B9 – 418/275-0110; Téléc: 418/275-2322; Symbol: QRHD – Bibliotechnicienne, Lise Laflame

**ROUYN-NORANDA**

CEGEP de l'Abitibi-Témiscamingue - Bibliothèque, 425 - boul du Collège, CP 8000, Rouyn-Noranda QC J9X 5M5 – 819/762-0931, poste 1339; Téléc: 819/762-3815; Symbol: QRCN
- Directeur, André Béland
- Secrétaire, Lucie Laprise

Conseil de la culture de L'Abitibi-Témiscamingue – Bibliothèque, 51, Mgr Tessier ouest, Rouyn-Noranda QC J9X 2S5 – 819/764-9511; Téléc: 819/764-6375 – Agente d'information/Recherche, Camille Gauthier

**STE-ANNE-DES-MONTS**

Société d'histoire et d'archéologie des Monts – Bibliothèque SHAM, 675, ch du Roy, CP 1192, Ste-Anne-des-Monts QC G0E 2G0 – 418/763-7871 – Directeur, Père Roland Provost

**STE-ANNE-DES-PLAINES**

Solicitor General Canada - Archambault Institution - Library, 242, Montée Gagnon, Ste-Anne-des-Plaines QC J0H 1H0 – 514/478-5960, ext.4505; Symbol: QSAA – Librarian, Lise Roy
- Regional Reception Centre - Library, 246, Montée Gagnon, Ste-Anne-des-Plaines QC J0N 1H0 – 514/478-5977, ext.7555; Fax: 514/478-7661; Symbol: QSAS – Bibliotechnicienne, Madeleine Montpetit

**ST-AUGUSTIN-DE-DESMAURES**

Campus Notre-Dame-de-Foy - Bibliothèque, 5000, rue Clément-Lockquell, St-Augustin-de-Desmaures QC G3A 1B3 – 418/872-8041; Téléc: 418/872-3448 – Bibliothécaire, Albert Pruneau

Collège St-Augustin - Bibliothèque, 4950, rue Lionel-Groulx, St-Augustin-de-Desmaures QC G3A 1V2 – 418/872-0954, poste 47; Téléc: 418/872-8249 – Directeur, Yvon Germain

**ST-BENOÎT-DU-LAC**

Abbaye Saint-Benoît-du-Lac - Bibliothèque, General Delivery, St-Benoît-du-Lac QC J0B 2M0 – 819/843-4080 – Bibliothécaire, Père Martin Chamberlain

**ST-CHARLES-BORROMEE**

Centre hospitalier régional de Lanaudière - Bibliothèque, 1000, boul Ste-Anne, St-Charles-Borromee QC J6E 6J2 – 514/759-8222; Téléc: 514/759-7463; Courrier électronique: ENVOY: ILL.QMJG; Symbol: QJH – Bibliothécaire, Francine Garneau

**ST-CHARLES-SUR-RICHELIEU**

Urgel Delisle & Associés inc. – Library, 426, ch des Patriotes, CP 60, St-Charles-sur-Richelieu QC J0H 2G0 – 514/584-2207; Téléc: 514/584-2523 – Engineer, François Granger

**ST-EUSTACHE**

Saulnier, Leroux & associés - Bibliothèque, #5070, 430, boul Arthur Sauve, St-Eustache QC J7R 6V6 – 514/472-0031; Téléc: 514/472-7910 – Mylene Turcotte

**ST-FÉLICIEN**

CEGEP de St-Félicien - Centre de documentation, CP 7300, St-Félicien QC G8K 2R8 – 418/679-5412; Téléc: 418/679-8357 – Responsable, Serge Bérubé

**STE-FOY**

Centre de recherche industrielle du Québec – Centre de documentation, 333, rue Franquet, Ste-Foy QC G1P 4C7 – 418/652-2210; Fax: 418/652-2225; Email: hbeaumon@criq.qc.ca; Symbol: QSFCR – Chef de groupe, Madeleine Savard

Agriculture & Agri-Food Canada-Soils & Crops Research & Development Centre – Bibliothèque canadienne de l'agriculture, 2560, boul Hochelaga, Ste-Foy QC G1V 2J3 – 418/657-7980; Téléc: 418/648-2402; Courrier électronique: cotes@em.agr.ca; lbqsfag@nccco; Symbol: QSFAG – Spécialiste en information, Suzanne Côté

Archives nationales du Québec - Bibliothèque, 1210, av du Séminaire, CP 10450, Ste-Foy QC G1V 4N1 – 418/644-4787; Téléc: 418/646-0868; URL: http://www.anq.gouv.qc.ca; Symbol: QQA – Chef des services au public, Jean-Pierre Therrien

Association professionnelle des meuniers du Québec – Bibliothèque, #115, 2323, boul Versant nord, Ste-Foy QC G1N 4P4 – 418/688-9227; Téléc: 418/688-3575

Association de santé et sécurité des pâtes et papiers du Québec inc. – Bibliothèque, #102, 1200, av Germain-des-Prés, Ste-Foy QC G1V 3M7 – 418/657-2267; Téléc: 418/651-4622 – Secrétaire, Elisabeth Boily

Centre for Entrepreneurship & Small Business – Library, Maison Eugène-Roberge, Cité Universitaire, Université Laval, POBox 2208, Ste-Foy QC G1K 7P4 – 418/656-2490; Fax: 418/656-3337

Centre hospitalier de l'Université de Québec – Bibliothèque des sciences de la santé/Centre de recherche, 2705, boul Laurier, Ste-Foy QC G1V 4G2 – 418/687-1090; Téléc: 418/654-2247, 2714; Courrier électronique: ENVOY 100:BIBLIO.CHUL – Technicienne, Sylvie Bélanger

Centre international de recherche en aménagement linguistique – Bibliothèque, Pav. Charles-de-Koninck, Cité Universitaire, Université Laval, CP 2208, Ste-Foy QC G1K 7P4 – 418/656-3232; Téléc: 418/656-7144 – Claude Rocheleau

Centre de toxicologie du Québec – Section Information-documentation, Centre hospitalier de l'Université Laval, 2705, boul Laurier, Ste-Foy QC G1V 4G2 – 418/654-2254; Téléc: 418/654-2148; Courrier électronique: ENVOY: PEB.QQCTO; Symbol: QQCTQ
- Director, Albert J. Nantel
- Deputy Director, Jean-Philippe Weber

Complexe scientifique - Centre de documentation, 2700, rue Einstein, F2, Ste-Foy QC G1P 3W8 – 418/643-9730; Téléc: 418/643-3361; Courrier électronique: Michel.Levesque@agr.gouv.qc.ca; Symbol: QQAGCS – Michel Lévesque

Conseil de la science et de la téchnologie du Québec - Centre de documentation, 2050, boul René-Lévesque ouest, 5e étage, Ste-Foy QC G1V 2K8 – 418/644-4187; Téléc: 418/646-0920; Symbol: QQST – Bibliothécaire, Edith Dubois

Conseil supérieur de l'éducation - Centre de documentation, #320, 1200, Route de l'Église, Ste-Foy QC G1V 4Z4 – 418/643-2845; Téléc: 418/644-2530; Courrier électronique: prehel@cse.gouv.qc.ca; Symbol: QSFCSE
- Bibliotechnicienne, Patricia Réhel
- Bibliotechnicienne, Francine Vallée

Directeur général des élections du Québec - Centre de documentation, 3460, rue de la Pérade, Ste-Foy QC G1X 3Y5 – 418/644-9948; Téléc: 418/643-7291; Courrier électronique: dgeq@dgeq.qc.ca; URL: http://www.dgeq.qc.ca; Symbol: QSFE – Responsable, Jacques Gilbert

Environment Canada - Région du Québec, Bibliothèque, 1141, Rte de l'Église, CP 10100, Ste-Foy QC G1V 4H5 – 418/649-6545; Téléc: 418/649-6861; Symbol: QQE
- Head, Library & Records Management, Cécile Morin, 418/648-4768
- Library Technician, Carmen Joseph
- Reference, Librarian, Julia Innes, 418/649-6545

Fédération des commissions scolaires du Québec – Bibliothèque, 1001, av Bégon, CP 490, Ste-Foy QC G1V 4C7 – 418/651-3220; Téléc: 418/651-2574 – Clermont Provencher

Fédération québécoise des sociétés de généalogie – Bibliothèque, CP 9454, Ste-Foy QC G1V 4B8 – 418/653-3940

Forintek Canada Corp. - Eastern Laboratory Library, 319, rue Franquet, Ste-Foy QC G1P 4R4 – 418/659-2647; Fax: 418/659-2922; Email: doreen.liberty@qc.forintek.ca; URL: http://www.forintek.ca; Symbol: QSFF
- Librarian, Doreen Liberty
- Assistant Librarian, Odile Fleury, Email: odile.fleury@qc.forintek.ca

Geological Survey of Canada (Québec) - Bibliothèque, 2535, boul Laurier, CP 7500, Ste-Foy QC G1V 4C7 – 418/654-2677; Téléc: 418/654-2615

Hôpital Laval – Bibliothèque des sciences de la santé, 2725, ch Ste-Foy, Ste-Foy QC G1V 4G5 – 418/656-4563; Téléc: 418/656-4720; Courrier électronique: jocelyne.bellemare@crhl.ulaval.ca; Symbol: QSFHL – Bibliothécaire, Jocelyne Bellemare

Institut de la technologie du magnésium – Bibliothèque, 357, rue Franquet, Ste-Foy QC G1P 4N7 – 418/650-3167; Téléc: 418/650-3190

Institut national de la recherche scientifique – Bibliothèque INRS-Géoressources, #640, 2600, boul Laurier, CP 7500, Ste-Foy QC G1V 4C7 – 418/654-2677; Téléc: 418/654-2525 – Sonia Dupuis
- Division de l'eau, #040, 2800, rue Einstein, CP 7500, Ste-Foy QC G1V 4C7 – 418/654-2649; Téléc: 418/654-2600; Courrier électronique: renaudso@inrs-eau.uquebec.ca; Symbol: QQUIE – Sophie Renaud

Institut de réadaptation physique de Québec – Centre de documentation René-Paquet, Cité Centre Cardinal-Villeneuve, 2975, ch Saint-Louis, Ste-Foy QC G1W 1P9 – 418/653-8766; Téléc: 418/653-9263

Ministère de la justice - Bibliothèque, 1200, Route de l'Église, 4e étage, Ste-Foy QC G1V 4M1 – 418/643-8409; Téléc: 418/643-9749; Courrier électronique: mricard@riq.qc.ca; Symbol: QQJ
- Responsable, Michel Ricard
- Martine Boivin
- Paulette Landry
- Solange Tardif

Ministère de la sécurité publique - Centre de documentation, 2525, boul Laurier, 5e étage, Ste-Foy QC G1V 2L2 – 418/646-6620; Téléc: 418/643-3194; Symbol: QSFCP – Responsable, Cécile Goudreault

Ministère du revenu - Bibliothèque, 3800, rue Marly, Ste-Foy QC G1X 4A5 – 418/652-5765; Téléc: 418/643-4962; Symbol: QQRE – Responsable, Venise L. Roy

Ministère de l'Environnement et de la Faune - Centre de documentation, #57, 3900, rue Marly, 3e étage, Ste-Foy QC G1X 4E4 – 418/643-5363; Téléc: 418/528-0406; Courrier électronique: ENVOY 100: PEB.QQEN; Symbol: QQEN
- Responsable, Gérard Nobréga
- Bibliothécaire de référence, Véronique Paré
- Technicienne en documentation, Alain Aubin
- Technicienne en documentation, Carole Robitaille
- Secteur Faune, Louise Buisson, 418/643-7522, Fax: 418/643-3330, Email: ENVOY 100: PEB.QQLCP

National Optics Institute – Library, 369, rue Franquet, Ste-Foy QC G1P 4N8 – 418/657-7006; Fax: 418/657-7009; Email: cbeau@ino.qc.ca – Librarian, Chantal Beauregard

Natural Resources Canada-Canadian Forest Service: Laurentian Forestry Centre – Bibliothèque, 1055, rue du P.E.P.S., CP 3800, Ste-Foy QC G1V 4C7 – 418/649-6956; Téléc: 418/648-5849; Courrier électronique: ENVOY:QQMF.BIB; bizier@am.cfl.forestry.ca; Symbol: QQMF – Librarian, Gilles Bizier

Le Protecteur du citoyen - Centre de documentation, 2875, boul Laurier, Ste-Foy QC G1V 2M2 – 418/643-2688; Téléc: 418/643-8759; Courrier électronique: patrick.robarde@ombuds.gouv.qc.ca; URL: http://www.ombuds.gouv.qc.ca; Symbol: QSTFP – Documentaliste, France Prévost, 418/644-6565

Public Works & Government Services Canada - Translation Bureau - Québec Documentation Centre, 1141, rte de l'Église, 3e étage, Ste-Foy QC G1V 3W5 – 418/648-3906; Fax: 418/648-5700 – Head, M. Guilbault

Québec Geoscience Centre Library - INRS - Georessources, 2535, boul Laurier, POBox 7500, Ste-Foy QC G1V 4C7 – 418/654-2677; Fax: 418/654-2615; Email: ENVOY 100: CGQ.BIB; Symbol: QSFIG
- Library Coordinator, Sonia Dupuis
- Library Technician, Anne Robitaille

REXFOR - Centre de documentation, 1195, rue Lavigerie, Ste-Foy QC G1V 4N3 – 418/659-4530; Téléc: 418/643-4037; Symbol: QSTFR
- Directrice des communications, Danielle Dussault
- Technicienne en documentation, Réjeanne Fournier

Société de généalogie de Québec – Bibliothèque, CP 9066, Ste-Foy QC G1V 4A8 – 418/651-9127; Téléc: 418/651-2643 – Bibliothécaire, René Doucet

Société québécoise d'exploration minière - Centre de documentation, Tour Belle Cour, 2600, boul Laurier, 5e étage, Ste-Foy QC G1V 4M6 – 418/658-5400; Téléc: 418/658-5459; Symbol: QSFS – Technicien, Daniel Sauser

### ST-GEORGES

CEGEP Beauce-Appalaches - Bibliothèque, 1055, rue 116e, St-Georges QC G5Y 3G1 – 418/228-8896; Fax: 418/228-0562 – Georges-Henri Goulet

### SAINT-HUBERT

Association des collaboratrices et partenaires en affaires – Bibliothèque, 2099, boul Edouard, Saint-Hubert QC J4T 2A2 – 514/465-4565; Téléc: 514/923-0810 – Yvonne Boucher

Centre local de services communautaires St-Hubert - Centre de documentation, 6800, boul Cousineau, St-Hubert QC J3Y 8Z4 – 514/443-7413; Téléc: 514/676-4645 – Technicienne, Hélène Goggin

### SAINT-HYACINTHE

Agriculture & Agri-Food Canada-Food Research & Development Centre – Bibliothèque du CRDA, 3600, boul Casavant ouest, Saint-Hyacinthe QC J2S 8E3 – 514/773-1105; Téléc: 514/773-8461, 2888; Courrier électronique: bernarf@em.agr.ca; Symbol: QSHAG – Librarian, Francine Bernard

Fondation du conseil des gouverneurs du centre de recherche et de développement sur les aliments inc. – CRDA, 3600, boul Casavant ouest, Saint-Hyacinthe QC J2S 8E3 – 514/773-1105; Téléc: 514/773-8461 – Bibliothécaire, Francine Bernard

Réseau Santé Richelieu-Yamaska - Pavillon Hôtel-Dieu – Centre de documentation, 1800, rue Dessaulles, Saint-Hyacinthe QC J2S 2T2 – 514/774-6495; Téléc: 514/774-0947 – Paul-Albert Dufour

Séminaire de St-Hyacinthe - Bibliothèque, 650, rue Girouard est, CP 370, Saint-Hyacinthe QC J2S 7B7 – 514/774-8977; Téléc: 514/774-7101 – Bibliothécaire, Bernard Auger

### ST-JEAN-SUR-RICHELIEU

Agriculture & Agri-Food Canada-Horticulture Research & Development Centre – Bibliothèque canadienne de l'agriculture, 430, boul Gouin, St-Jean-sur-Richelieu QC J3B 3E6 – 514/346-4494; Téléc: 514/346-7740; Courrier électronique: lbqstjag@ncccot.agr.ca; Symbol: QSTJAG – Library Assistant, Lise Lavallée

CEGEP St-Jean-sur-Richelieu - Bibliothèque, 30, boul du Séminaire, CP 1018, St-Jean-sur-Richelieu QC J3B 7B1 – 514/347-5301; Téléc: 514/347-3329
- Bibliothécaire en chef, Michel Robert
- Bibliothécaire, Robert Dufort
- Chef, Services techniques, Johanne Lorion

Corporation du Fort Saint-Jean - Bibliothèque, Pavillon Lahaie, Campus du Fort Saint-Jean, 15, rue Jacques-Cartier nord, St-Jean-sur-Richelieu QC J3B 8R8 – 514/358-6602; Téléc: 514/358-6799; Symbol: QSTJ
- Directrice, Gretchen Cheung, 514/358-6602
- Bibliothécaire, Paul Tremblay, 514/358-6608
- Librarian, Léandre Racicot, 514/358-6506
- Acquisitions Librarian, Lise Laflèche, 514/358-6607

Hôpital du Haut-Richelieu – Bibliothèque médicale, 920, boul du Séminaire, St-Jean-sur-Richelieu QC J3A 1B7 – 514/359-5055; Téléc: 514/359-5064; Symbol: QSTJH – Technicienne, Hélène Héroux-Bouchard
- Santé Publique, 485, rue Saint-Jacques, St-Jean-sur-Richelieu QC J3B 2M1 – 514/346-3220; Téléc: 514/346-8787; Symbol: QSTJC – Technicienne, Hélène Bouchard

Oerlikon Aerospace Inc. - Bibliothèque, 225, boul du Seminaire, St-Jean-sur-Richelieu QC J3B 8E9 – 514/358-2000; Téléc: 514/358-1744

### ST-JÉRÔME

Association monnaies des Laurentides – Bibliothèque, CP 252, St-Jérôme QC J7Z 5T9 – 819/322-7224 – Directeur, Claude Proulx

CEGEP St-Jérôme - Bibliothèque, 455, rue Fournier, St-Jérôme QC J7Z 4V2 – 514/436-1580; Téléc: 514/436-1756
- Coordinateur, Claude Riendeau
- Bibliothécaire, Daniele Montreuil

Hôtel-Dieu de St-Jérôme – Bibliothèque, 290, rue Montigny, St-Jérôme QC J7Z 5T3 – 514/431-8200, poste 2157; Téléc: 514/431-8280; Symbol: QSJHD – Bibliotechnicienne, Francine Henri

Le Pavillon André Boudreau - Centre de documentation, 910, rue Labelle, St-Jérôme QC J7Z 5M5 – 514/432-1395; Téléc: 514/432-8654 – Réal Daoust

Société de Jésus - Bibliothèque, 175, boul des Hauteurs, CP 130, St-Jérôme QC J7Z 5T8 – 514/438-3993, ext.258; Téléc: 514/438-6617
- Chief Librarian, Joseph Cossette, 514/438-3593, ext.258
- Reference Librarian, Martine Proulx, 514/438-3593, ext.258

### ST-LAMBERT

Champlain Regional College - Resource Centre, 900 Riverside Dr., St-Lambert QC J4P 3P2 – 514/672-7360, ext.221; Fax: 514/672-9299
- Coordinator, Resource Centre, Peggy Herlinger, 514/672-7360, ext.220, Email: herling@ChamplainCollege.qc.ca
- Reference Librarian, Dale Huston, 514/672-7360, ext.345, Email: huston@ChamplainCollege.qc.ca

### STE-THÉRÈSE-DE-BLAINVILLE

Collège Lionel-Groulx - Bibliothèque, 100, rue Duquet, Ste-Thérèse-de-Blainville QC J7E 3G6 – 514/430-3120; Téléc: 514/430-2783 – Responsable de la bibliothèque, Marcel Paquin

### SALABERRY-DE-VALLEYFIELD

Centre hospitalier régional du Suroît – Centre de documentation, 150, rue St-Thomas, Salaberry-de-Valleyfield QC J6T 6C1 – 514/371-9925, poste 2121; Téléc: 514/371-7454 – Chef Service Archives, Lise Clovel

### SEPT-ILES

Centre hospitalier régional de Sept-Iles – Bibliothèque, 45, rue Père Divet, Sept-Iles QC G4R 3N7 – 418/962-9761; Téléc: 418/968-9723 – Bibliothécaire, Brigitte Chiasson

### SHAWINIGAN

Centre hospitalier Sainte-Thérèse – Centre de documentation, 1705, av Georges, Shawinigan QC G9N 2N1 – 819/537-9351, poste 343; Téléc: 819/537-4737; Symbol: OSHST – Responsable du Centre de documentation, Lise Gélinas

Collège de Shawinigan - Bibliothèque, 2263, av du Collège, Shawinigan QC G9N 6V8 – 819/539-6401; Téléc: 819/539-8819; Courrier électronique: Information@CollegeShawinigan.qc.ca; URL: http://www.CollegeShawinigan.qc.ca – Colette Caron

### SHAWINIGAN-SUD

Centre hospitalier régional de la Mauricie – Bibliothèque médicale, 50, 118e rue, Shawinigan-Sud QC G9P 4E7 – 819/536-7665; Téléc: 819/537-7687; Symbol: QSHCH – Responsable de la bibliothèque, Guylaine Vaugeois

### SHERBROOKE

Centre universitaire de santé de l'Estrie - site Bowen – Bibliothèque, 580, rue Bowen sud, Sherbrooke QC

J1G 2E8 – 819/569-2551; Téléc: 819/822-6767; Symbol: QSHERHD – Technicienne, Gilberte Poirier

College du Sacré-Coeur - Bibliothèque, 155, rue Belvédère nord, Sherbrooke QC J1H 4A7 – 819/569-9457; Fax: 819/820-0636 – Christiane St Martin

Collège de Sherbrooke - Centre des médias, 475, rue Parc, Sherbrooke QC J1H 5M7 – 819/564-6233; Téléc: 819/564-4025; Courrier électronique: cmedias@collegesherbrooke.qc.ca; URL: http://www.CollegeSherbrooke.qc.ca – Gaétan Roy

Le Groupe Teknika – Bibliothèque, 150, rue de Vimy, Sherbrooke QC J1J 3M7 – 819/562-3871; Téléc: 819/563-3663 – Raymond Demers

Hôpital de St-Vincent de Paul de Sherbrooke – Bibliothèque médicale, 300, rue King est, Sherbrooke QC J1G 1B1 – 819/563-2366; Téléc: 819/563-5201; Courrier électronique: g.poirier@login.net; Symbol: QSHERSV – Responsable, Gilberte Poirier

Institut universitaire de gériatrie de Sherbrooke – Centre de documentation et d'audio-visuel, 1036, rue Belvédère sud, Sherbrooke QC J1H 4C4 – 819/821-5100, ext.2237; Téléc: 819/821-2065; Symbol: QSHERY – Technicienne, Louise Routhier

Intervention régionale et information sur le sida en Estrie – Centre de documentation, 20, rue Robidoux, Sherbrooke QC J1J 2W1 – 819/823-6704; Téléc: 819/823-5537 – Daniel Gladu

Séminaire de Sherbrooke - Bibliothèque, 195, rue Marquette, Sherbrooke QC J1H 1L6 – 819/563-2050, ext.46; Téléc: 819/562-8261; Courrier électronique: semsherb@login.net; URL: http://www.login.net/semsherb – Directrice, Ghislaine Pinard

Société de généalogie des Cantons de l'Est – Bibliothèque, CP 635, Sherbrooke QC J1H 5K5 – 819/821-5414 – Ginette Arguin

Société d'histoire de Sherbrooke – Bibliothèque, 275, rue Dufferin, Sherbrooke QC J1H 4M5 – 819/821-5406; Téléc: 819/821-5417

Syndicat des professeures et professeurs de l'Université de Sherbrooke – Bibliothèque, 2500, boul Université, Sherbrooke QC J1K 2R1 – 819/821-7656; Téléc: 819/821-7995

Université de Sherbrooke - Services des bibliothèques, 2500, boul Université, Sherbrooke QC J1K 2R1 – 819/821-7550; Téléc: 819/821-7935; Courrier électronique: vitrine@biblio.usherb.ca; URL: http://www.biblio.usherb.ca; Symbol: QSHERU

Chief Librarian, Michel Beaudoin
Public Services Librarian, Michel Beaudoin
Acquisitions Librarian, Alain Keroack
Assistant Director, Pierre Gaudette
Bibliothèque des sciences de la santé, Germain Chouinard, 819/564-5297, Fax: 819/564-5378
General Library, Diane Quirion, 819/821-7553
Music Library, Sylvie Bareil, 819/821-8201
Law Library, Guy Tanguay, 819/821-7519
Science Library, Roger B. Bernier, 819/821-7099
Business Librarian, Daniel Beaulyeu

#### SILLERY

Régie de l'assurance-maladie du Québec - Bibliothèque, 1125, ch Saint-Louis, 7e étage, CP 6600, Sillery QC G1K 7T3 – 418/682-5118; Téléc: 418/646-1167; Courrier électronique: bibliotheque@ramq.gouv.qc.ca; Symbol: QQRAMQ – Technicienne de la documentation, Angèle Pouliot

#### SOREL

Hôtel-Dieu de Sorel – Centre de documentation, 400, av Hôtel-Dieu, Sorel QC J3P 1N5 – 514/746-6068; Téléc: 514/746-2782 – Claudette Laverdiere

#### STANSTEAD

Stanstead College - Bibliothèque, POBox 1-540, Stanstead QC J0B 3E0 – 819/876-7891, ext.278; Fax: 819/876-5891; URL: http://www.stansteadc.qc.ca – Bibliothécaire, J. Philip

#### THETFORD MINES

Centre hospitalier de la région de l'Amiante – Bibliothèque, 1717, rue Notre-Dame nord, Thetford Mines QC G6G 2V4 – 418/338-0976; Téléc: 418/338-7786; Symbol: QTMH – Bibliotechnicienne, Jacinthe Ouellet

Thetford Mines (Succursale Collège de la Région de l'Amiante) - Centre des ressources éducatives, 671, boul Smith sud, Thetford Mines QC G6G 1N1 – 418/338-8591; Téléc: 418/338-0380 – Responsable, André Gamache

#### TRACY

CEGEP de Sorel-Tracy - Centre de documentation, 3000, boul de la Mairie, Tracy QC J3R 5B9 – 514/742-6651; Courrier électronique: biblio@cegep-sorel-tracy.qc.ca; URL: http://www.cegep-sorel-tracy.qc.ca – Bibliothécaire, Jean-Marie Riopel

#### TROIS-RIVIÈRES

CEGEP de Trois-Rivières - Bibliothèque, 3500, rue de Courval, CP 97, Trois-Rivières QC G9A 5E6 – 819/376-1721; Téléc: 819/693-9409; Courrier électronique: Pierre.Gagnon@cegeptr.qc.ca

Coordonnateur, Pierre Gagnon
Bibliothécaire, Daniéle Baillargeon
Bibliothécaire, Monique Paradis
Bibliothécaire, Quy LeDuy

Centre hospitalier St-Joseph – Bibliothèque médicale, 731, rue Ste-Julie, Trois-Rivières QC G9A 1Y1 – 819/379-8112; Téléc: 819/372-3581 – Solange De Rouyn

Centre hospitalier Sainte-Marie – Bibliothèque médicale, 1991, boul du Carmel, Trois-Rivières QC G8Z 3R9 – 819/378-9878; Téléc: 819/378-9850 – Lucie Grondin

Centre de santé publique à Trois-Rivières - Département de santé communautaire - Centre de documentation, 3350, boul Royal, Trois-Rivières QC G9A 5Z4 – 819/378-9813; Téléc: 819/378-6600; Symbol: OTCRS – Technicienne, Jocelyne Drolet

Comité de solidarité tiers-monde/Trois-Rivières – Bibliothèque, 942, rue Ste-Genevieve, Trois-Rivières QC G9A 3X6 – 819/373-2598; Téléc: 819/373-7892 – Animatrice, Violette Tousignant

Conseil de la culture du Coeur-du-Québec – Bibliothèque, 956, rue St-Paul, Trois-Rivières QC G9A 1J3 – 819/374-3242; Téléc: 819/374-2649

Fédération des caisses populaires Desjardins - Centre du Québec – Bibliothèque, 2000, boul des Récollets, CP 1000, Trois-Rivières QC G9A 5K3 – 819/374-3594, poste 258; Téléc: 819/374-2486 – Chef de gestion documentaire, Nicole Garneau

Régie de la sécurité dans les sports du Québec – Bibliothèque, #302, 100, rue Laviolette, Trois-Rivières QC G9A 5S9 – 819/371-6033; Téléc: 819/371-6992 – Responsable, Micheline Denis

Séminaire St-Joseph - Bibliothèque, 858, rue Laviolette, Trois-Rivières QC G9A 5S3 – 819/376-4459; Téléc: 819/378-0607 – Bibliothécaire, Danielle Cossette

Université du Québec à Trois-Rivières - Service de la bibliothèque, 3351, boul des Forges, Trois-Rivières QC G9A 5H7 – 819/376-5005; Téléc: 819/376-5144; Courrier électronique: Michel_Jacob@uqtr.uquebec.ca; URL: http://www.uqtr.uquebec.ca/biblio/; Symbol: QTU – Directeur, Michel Jacob

#### VAL-BÉLAIR

Defence Research Establishment - Valcartier - Library, 2459, boul Pie XI nord, Val-Bélair QC G3J 1X5 – 418/844-4262; Téléc: 418/844-4624; Symbol: QQC

#### VAL-D'OR

Centre hospitalier de Val d'Or – Bibliothèque médicale, 725, 6e rue, Val-d'Or QC J9P 3Y1 – 819/825-6711; Téléc: 819/825-4615 – Janine Desjardins

#### VARENNES

Institut de recherche d'Hydro-Québec – IREQ Library, 1800, boul Lionel-Boulet, Varennes QC J3X 1S1 – 514/652-8413; Téléc: 514/652-8161 – Librarian, Régis Côté

Natural Resources Canada - Energy Diversification Research Laboratory - Library Services, 1615, boul Lionel-Boulet, POBox 4800, Varennes QC J3X 1S6 – 514/652-3210; Fax: 514/652-5177

Library Services, Robin Majumdar, Email: robin.majumdar@ccsmtp.nrcan.gc.ca
Communications Coordinator, Jean-Claude Cloutier

#### VICTORIAVILLE

Association québécoise du théâtre amateur inc. – Bibliothèque, 6, rue de l'Exposition, CP 977, Victoriaville QC G6P 8Y1 – 819/752-2501; Téléc: 819/758-4466 – Joceline Levis

Bureau local d'intervention traitant du sida – Bibliothèque, #110, 59, rue Monfette, Victoriaville QC G6P 1J8 – 819/758-2662; Téléc: 819/758-8270

CEGEP de Victoriaville - Centre de documentation, 475, rue Notre-Dame est, POBox 68, Victoriaville QC G6P 4B3 – 819/758-6401; Fax: 819/758-0333; Symbol: QVC – Documentaliste, Hélène Lupien

#### VILLAGE-DES-HURONS

Institut culturel et éducatif montagnais – Bibliothèque, #7, 40, rue Chef François Gros-Louis, Village-des-Hurons QC G0A 4V0 – 418/843-0258 – Coordonnatrice de la culture, Marlène Rock

## SASKATCHEWAN

### Regional Library Systems with Member Libraries

#### CHINOOK REGIONAL LIBRARY

1240 Chaplin St. West, Swift Current SK S9H 0G8 – 306/773-3186; Fax: 306/773-0434; Symbol: SCR

Director, Michael Keaschuk
Branch Supervisor, Myra Leyshon

Abbey Branch Library, PO Box 185, Abbey SK S0N 0A0 – 306/689-2202 – Librarian, Marilyn Turgeon

Admiral Branch Library, PO Box 152, Admiral SK S0N 0B0 – 306/297-6354 – Librarian, C. Duclos

Burstall Branch Library, PO Box 309, Burstall SK S0N 0H0 – 306/679-2177 – Librarian, Judith Winter

Cabri Branch Library, PO Box 18, Cabri SK S0N 0J0 – 306/587-2500 – Librarian, Ruby Franke

Central Butte Branch Library, PO Box 276, Central Butte SK S0H 0T0 – 306/796-2222 – Librarian, Virginia Hemsworth

Chaplin Branch Library, PO Box 225, Chaplin SK S0H 0V0 – 306/395-2597 – Librarian, Carolyn Walls

Climax Branch Library, PO Box 322, Climax SK S0N 0N0 – 306/293-2006 – Librarian, Sue Smith

Consul Branch Library, PO Box 121, Consul SK S0N 0P0 – 306/299-2118 – Librarian, Linda Brown

Eastend Branch Library, PO Box 91, Eastend SK S0N 0T0 – 306/295-3788 – Librarian, Betty Ann Huhn

Fox Valley Branch Library, PO Box 42, Fox Valley SK S0N 0V0 – 306/666-2045 – Librarian, Valerie Reinboldt
Frontier Branch Library, 1 St. West, Frontier SK S0N 0W0 – 306/296-2147 – Librarian, Cindy Puszkar
Glentworth Branch Library, Main St., Glentworth SK S0H 1V0 – 306/266-2185 – Librarian, Meryle Iwanicki
Gravelbourg Library, PO Box 568, Gravelbourg SK S0H 1X0 – 306/648-3177 – Librarian, Bargara Douglas
Gull Lake Branch Library, Cultural Complex, Conrad St., PO Box 653, Gull Lake SK S0N 1A0 – 306/672-3277 – Librarian, Carol Springer
Hazlet Branch Library, PO Box 73, Hazlet SK S0N 1E0 – 306/678-2155 – Librarian, Linda Kulferst
Herbert Branch Library, PO Box 176, Herbert SK S0H 2A0 – 306/784-2484 – Librarian, Jane Epp
Hodgeville Branch Library, Main St., PO Box 68, Hodgeville SK S0H 2B0 – 306/677-2223 – Librarian, Edna Sauder
Kincaid Branch Library, PO Box 146, Kincaid SK S0H 2J0 – 306/264-3910 – Librarian, Trudy Turgeon
Lafleche Library, 157 Main St., PO Box 132, Lafleche SK S0H 2K0 – 306/472-5466 – Librarian, Diane Clermont
Leader Branch Library, 151 - 1 St. West, Leader SK S0N 1H0 – 306/628-3830 – Librarian, Delores Hudec
Mankota Branch Library, 1st Ave., Mankota SK S0H 2W0 – 306/478-2331 – Librarian, Doreen McCallum
Maple Creek Branch Library, 205 Jasper St., PO Box 760, Maple Creek SK S0N 1N0 – 306/662-3522 – Librarian, Violet Bethel
Morse Branch Library, Main St., Morse SK S0H 3C0 – 306/629-3335 – Librarian, Margaret Ferguson
Pennant Public Library, Standard St., PO Box 219, Pennant SK S0N 1X0 – 306/626-3316 – Librarian, Joanne Heeg-Williams
Piapot Branch Library, McDonald St., Piapot SK S0N 1Y0 – Librarian, Marlene Meacock
Ponteix Library, PO Box 700, Ponteix SK S0N 1Z0 – 306/625-3353 – Librarian, Marie Kouri
Prelate Branch Library, Main St., Drawer 40, Prelate SK S0N 2B0 – 306/673-2340 – Librarian, Darlene Wagner
Sceptre Branch Library, PO Box 128, Sceptre SK S0N 2H0 – 306/623-4244 – Librarian, Sherry Egeland
Shaunavon Branch Library, PO Box 1116, Shaunavon SK S0N 2M0 – 306/297-3844 – Librarian, Pauline James
Simmie Branch Library, PO Box 51, Simmie SK S0N 2N0 – 306/297-6217 – Librarian, Lorna Irish
Stewart Valley Branch Library, Stewart Valley SK S0N 2P0 – Librarian, Kathy King
Swift Current Branch Library, 411 Herbert St. East, Swift Current SK S9H 1M5 – 306/778-2752 – Librarian, Myra Leyshon
Tompkins Library, Main St., Tompkins SK S0N 2S0 – 306/622-2255 – Librarian, Carol Mitchell
Val Marie Branch Library, PO Box 205, Val Marie SK S0N 2T0 – 306/298-2133 – Librarian, Mildred Harbor
Vanguard Branch Library, Main St., Vanguard SK S0N 2V0 – 306/582-2244 – Librarian, Doris Burns

#### LAKELAND LIBRARY REGION

10023 Thatcher Ave., PO Box 813, North Battleford SK S9A 2Z3 – 306/445-6108; Fax: 306/445-5717; Symbol: SNB
A/Regional Director, Marie Sakon

Battleford Branch Library, PO Box 220, Battleford SK S0M 0E0 – 306/937-2646 – Librarian, Helen MacKay
Borden Branch Library, Borden SK S0K 0N0 – 306/997-2220 – Librarian, Helen Sutherland
Red Pheasant Branch Library, PO Box 155, Cando SK S0K 0V0 – 306/937-7761 – Librarian, Alvena Baptiste
Cut Knife Branch Library, Cut Knife SK S0M 0N0 – 306/398-2342 – Librarian, Shirley Bertoria
Denzil Branch Library, Denzil SK S0L 0S0 – 306/358-2118 – Librarian, Rose Reiniger
Edam Library, PO Box 203, Edam SK S0M 0V0 – 306/397-2223 – Librarian, Trudy McMurphy
Sweet Grass Branch Library, PO Box 80, Gallivan SK S0M 0X0 – 306/937-2974 – Librarian, Johanna Whitecalf
Glaslyn Library, Glaslyn SK S0M 0Y0 – 306/342-4748 – Librarian, Karen Smith
Goodsoil Branch Library, Goodsoil SK S0M 1A0 – 306/238-2155 – Librarian, Collette Himmelsbach
Hafford Branch Library, Hafford SK S0J 1A0 – 306/549-2373 – Librarian, Shelly Hrabia
Lashburn Branch Library, Lashburn SK S0M 1H0 – 306/285-4144 – Librarian, Theresa Coolidge
Lloydminster Public Library, 5010 - 49th St., Lloydminster SK T9V 0K2 – 403/875-0850; Fax: 403/875-6523; Email: ENVOY: ILL.LAL – Librarian, Ronald J. Gillies
Island Lake Library, PO Box 460, Loon Lake SK S0M 1L0 – 306/837-2188; Fax: 306/837-2266 – Librarian, Dorothy Waugh
Loon Lake Branch Library, PO Box 216, Loon Lake SK S0M 1L0 – 306/837-2186 – Librarian, Dorothy Waugh
Macklin Branch Library, Macklin SK S0L 2C0 – 306/753-2933 – Librarian, Hilda Gartner
Maidstone Branch Library, Maidstone SK S0M 1M0 – 306/893-4153 – Librarian, Joyce Weston
Makwa Branch Library, Makwa SK S0M 1N0 – 306/236-3995 – Librarian, Lynda Bertrand
Marsden Branch Library, Marsden SK S0M 1P0 – 306/826-5666 – Librarian, Denise Polkinghorne
Marshall Branch Library, Marshall SK S0M 1R0 – 306/387-6555 – Librarian, Donna Ferguson
Maymont Library, Maymont SK S0M 1T0 – 306/389-2006 – Librarian, Mary Scott
Meadow Lake Branch Library, PO Box 1237, Meadow Lake SK S0M 1V0 – 306/236-5396 – Librarian, Gwyn Breland
Medstead Branch Library, Medstead SK S0M 1W0 – 306/342-4609 – Librarian, Pauline Bovair
Meota Library, Meota SK S0M 1X0 – 306/892-2113 – Librarian, Doreen Griffith
Mervin Branch Library, PO Box 130, Mervin SK S0M 1Y0 – 306/845-2784 – Librarian, Mildred Cormack
Neilburg Branch Library, Neilburg SK S0M 2C0 – 306/823-4234 – Librarian, Sharon Schempp
Mosquito Branch Library, PO Box 368, North Battleford SK S9A 2Z3 – 306/937-2093 – Librarian, Audrey Wahobin
North Battleford Public Library, 1392 - 101st St., North Battleford SK S9A 1A2 – 306/445-3206 – Librarian, Anne Marie Hillson
Saskatchewan Hospital Branch Library, c/o Saskatchewan Hospital, PO Box 39, North Battleford SK S9A 2X8 – 306/446-7913 – Librarian, Dianne Philippon
Paradise Hill Branch Library, Paradise Hill SK S0M 2G0 – 306/344-2206 – Librarian, Dianne Palsich
Little Pine Branch Library, PO Box 327, Paynton SK S0M 2J0 – 306/398-2925 – Librarian, Eileen Frank
Paynton Branch Library, Paynton SK S0M 2J0 – 306/895-2175 – Librarian, Bev Webb
Poundmaker Branch Library, PO Box 329, Paynton SK S0M 0N0 – 306/398-4966 – Librarian, Arlene Chickosis
Joseph Bighead Branch Library, c/o Chief Napayo School, Pierceland SK S0M 2K0 – 306/839-2297 – Librarian, Donna Weinkauf
Pierceland Library, Pierceland SK S0M 2K0 – 306/839-2166 – Librarian, Anita Murphy
Rabbit Lake Branch Library, Rabbit Lake SK S0M 2L0 – 306/824-2089 – Librarian, Laura Ricketts
Radisson Branch Library, Radisson SK S0K 3L0 – 306/827-2118 – Librarian, Linda Brookman
St. Walburg Branch Library, St Walburg SK S0M 2T0 – 306/248-3250 – Librarian, Gen Etcheverry
Speers Branch Library, Speers SK S0M 2V0 – 306/246-4866 – Librarian, Maureen Kachmarski
Thunderchild Branch Library, PO Box 34, Turtleford SK S0M 2Y0 – 306/845-2071 – Librarian, Elaine Standingwater
Turtleford Branch Library, Turtleford SK S0M 2Y0 – 306/845-2074 – Librarian, June Heath
Waterhen Lake Branch Library, Waterhen Lake SK S0M 3B0 – 306/236-4723; Fax: 306/236-6523 – Librarian, Delphine Vincent

#### PAHKISIMON NUYEAH LIBRARY SYSTEM

PO Box 6600, La Ronge SK S0J 1L0 – 306/425-4525; Fax: 306/425-4572; Email: pnlshq@pnls.lib.sk.ca; Symbol: SLPN
Director, Audrey Mark
Teacher/Librarian, Harriet Roy, 306/425-4598

Beauval Public Library, Bag Service 9000, Beauval SK S0M 0G0 – 306/288-2022; Fax: 306/288-2202 – Carol Edquist
Wisewood Public Library, PO Box 309, Buffalo Narrows SK S0M 0J0 – 306/235-4240; Fax: 306/235-4452 – Darlene Petit
Deschambault Lake Library, General Delivery, Deschambault Lake SK S0P 0C0 – 306/632-4446; Fax: 306/632-4700
Ile a la Crosse Public Library, PO Box 70, Ile a la Crosse SK S0M 1C0 – 306/833-2010; Fax: 306/833-2322 – Myra Gardiner
La Loche Public Library, PO Box 4, La Loche SK S0M 1G0 – 306/822-2151; Fax: 306/822-2280 – Chris Cardinal
La Ronge Public Library, PO Box 5680, La Ronge SK S0J 1L0 – 306/425-2160; Fax: 306/425-3883 – Arlene Kolosky
Senator Miles Venne School Public Library, PO Box 328, La Ronge SK S0J 1L0 – 306/425-2478; Fax: 306/425-2815 – Edna Mirasty
Montreal Lake Community Library, General Delivery, Montreal Lake SK S0J 1Y0 – 306/663-5602; Fax: 306/663-5652 – Deidre MacGregor
Tawowikamik Public Library, PO Box 100, Pelican Narrows SK S0P 0E0 – 306/632-2161; Fax: 306/632-2110 – Marilyn Ballantyne
Sandy Bay Public Library, PO Box 150, Sandy Bay SK S0P 0G0 – 306/754-2139; Fax: 306/754-2130 – Geraldine Merasty
Keethanow Public Library, General Delivery, Stanley Mission SK S0J 2P0 – 306/635-2104; Fax: 306/635-2050 – Lucy Ratt

#### PALLISER REGIONAL LIBRARY

366 Coteau St. West, PO Box 2500, Moose Jaw SK S6H 6Y2 – 306/693-3669; Fax: 306/692-5657; Email: smjp.ill@palliser.lib.sk.ca
Director, Cora Greer

Assiniboia Library, 110 - 4 Ave. West, PO Box 940, Assiniboia SK S0H 0B0 – 306/642-3631; Email: as.pall.lib@sk.sympatico.ca – Librarian, Cindy Susut
Avonlea Library, Main St. West, PO Box 351, Avonlea SK S0H 0C0 – 306/868-2076 – Librarian, Gina Sudom
Bethune Branch Library, Community Hall, Bethune SK S0G 0H0 – 306/638-3046 – Librarian, Mildred Kistner
Briercrest Library, Main St., Briercrest SK S0H 0K0 – 306/799-2137 – Librarian, Eleanor Anderson

Bushell Park Library, Bushell Park SK S0H 0N0 – 306/694-2367 – Librarian, Gayle Kitchen
Caronport Branch Library, Health Care Centre, Caronport SK S0H 0S0 – 306/756-3343 – Librarian, Lorraine Tanner
Coronach Library, Main St., Coronach SK S0H 0Z0 – 306/267-3260 – Librarian, Maxine Thurlow
Craik Library, PO Box 339, Craik SK S0G 0V0 – 306/734-2388; Email: library@dig.craik.sk.ca – Librarian, Linda McMillan
Davidson Library, Garfield St., PO Box 754, Davidson SK S0G 1A0 – 306/567-2022 – Librarian, Janice Johnson
Elbow Branch Library, Main St., Elbow SK S0H 1J0 – 306/845-2277 – Librarian, Wendy Cafferata
Holdfast Branch Library, PO Box 205, Holdfast SK S0G 2H0 – 306/488-2140 – Librarian, Shelley Harms
Imperial Branch Library, Town Office, Main St., Imperial SK S0G 2J0 – 306/963-2272 – Librarian, Donalda MacLellan
Loreburn Branch Library, Village Office, Loreburn SK S0H 2S0 – 306/644-2097 – Librarian, Barbara Kelman
Moose Jaw Public Library, 461 Langdon Cres., Moose Jaw SK S6H 0X6 – 306/692-2787; Fax: 306/692-3368 – Head Librarian, Anne Warriner
Mortlach Branch Library, Main St., Mortlach SK S0H 3E0 – 306/355-2202 – Librarian, Phyllis Wolf
Mossbank Public Library, PO Bag Service, 3 St. West, Mossbank SK S0H 3G0 – 306/354-2474 – Librarian, Debbie Sullivan
Riverhurst Library, Main St., Riverhurst SK S0H 3P0 – 306/353-2130 – Librarian, Della Bartzen
Rockglen Library, Main St., Rockglen SK S0H 3R0 – 306/476-2350 – Librarian, Claudette Schnell
Rouleau Library, Main St., Rouleau SK S0G 4H0 – 306/776-2322 – Librarian, Hazel Anaka
Tugaske Branch Library, Main St., Tugaske SK S0H 4B0 – 306/759-2215; Fax: 306/759-2253; Email: tug.lib@sk.sympatico.ca – Librarian, Kathy Russell
Willow Bunch Branch Library, PO Box 280, Willow Bunch SK S0H 4K0 – 306/473-2405 – Librarian, Christine Lemieux
Wood Mountain Library, 2nd Ave., Wood Mountain SK S0H 4L0 – 306/266-2110 – Librarian, Edith Klein

**PARKLAND REGIONAL LIBRARY**

95A Broadway West, Yorkton SK S3N 0L9 – 306/782-2876; Fax: 306/782-2844; Email: ENVOY: ILL.SYP
Acting Regional Librarian, Gladys Stasiuk

Annaheim Branch Library, Annaheim SK S0K 0G0 – 306/598-2155 – Librarian, Joyce Kimmen
Balcarres Branch Library, PO Box 640, Balcarres SK S0G 0C0 – 306/334-2966 – Librarian, Elaine Chatterson
Bredenbury Branch Library, Bredenbury SK S0A 0H0 – 306/898-2299 – Librarian, Lois Smandych
Buchanan Library, Buchanan SK S0A 0J0 – 306/592-2137 – Librarian, Marie Kupchinski
Calder Branch Library, General Delivery, Calder SK S0A 0K0 – Librarian, Margie Mankish
Canora Branch Library, PO Box 694, Canora SK S0A 0L0 – 306/563-6877 – Librarian, Joan Chernoff
Churchbridge Branch Library, PO Box 530, Churchbridge SK S0A 0M0 – 306/896-2322 – Librarian, Jocelyn Mehrer
Cupar Branch Library, Cupar SK S0G 0Y0 – 306/723-4600 – Librarian, Marie Reed
Earl Grey Library, General Delivery, Earl Grey SK S0G 1J0 – 306/939-2212 – Librarian, Lynda Bailey
Elfros Branch Library, PO Box 70, Elfros SK S0A 0V0 – 306/328-2175 – Librarian, Stella Stephanson
Englefeld Branch Library, PO Box 22, Englefeld SK S0K 1N0 – 306/287-3497 – Librarian, Gladys Freriks
Esterhazy Branch Library, Esterhazy SK S0A 0X0 – 306/745-6406 – Librarian, Pamela Knourek
Foam Lake Branch Library, PO Box 181, Foam Lake SK S0A 1A0 – 306/272-3660 – Librarian, Olive Beattie
Govan Branch Library, PO Box 40, Govan SK S0G 1Z0 – 306/484-2122 – Librarian, Gloria Davis
Invermay Branch Library, Invermay SK S0A 1M0 – 306/593-4990 – Librarian, Doreen Johnson
Ituna Library, Ituna SK S0A 1N0 – 306/795-2672 – Librarian, Staffa Renkas
Jansen Branch Library, PO Box 113, Jansen SK S0K 2B0 – 306/364-2122
Kamsack Branch Library, PO Box 1870, Kamsack SK S0A 1S0 – 306/542-3787 – Librarian, Nancy Brunt
Kelliher Library, PO Box 161, Kelliher SK S0A 1V0 – 306/675-2110 – Librarian, Laurel Rugland
Kelvington Branch Library, PO Box 429, Kelvington SK S0A 1W0 – 306/327-4322 – Librarian, Kim Kizlyk
Lake Lenore Branch Library, Lake Lenore SK S0K 2J0 – 306/368-2344 – Librarian, Lucille Eberle
Langenburg Library, PO Box 549, Langenburg SK S0A 2A0 – 306/743-5394 – Librarian, Marlies Nerbas
Lemberg Branch Library, PO Box 339, Lemberg SK S0A 2B0 – 306/335-2267 – Librarian, Barbara Kanciruk
Leroy Branch Library, PO Box 310, Leroy SK S0K 2P0 – 306/286-3356 – Librarian, Tracy Muller
Lintlaw Branch Library, Lintlaw SK S0A 2H0 – 306/325-2166 – Librarian, Georgie Little
Lipton Branch Library, Lipton SK S0G 3B0 – 306/336-2288 – Librarian, Marlene Huber
MacNutt Branch Library, PO Box 150, MacNutt SK S0A 2K0 – Librarian, Cheryl Peppler
Melville Library, PO Box 489, Melville SK S0A 2P0 – 306/728-2171 – Librarian, Evelyn Trost
Muenster Library, Muenster SK S0K 2Y0 – 306/682-5252 – Librarian, Sally Muench
Neudorf Branch Library, Neudorf SK S0A 2T0 – 306/748-2553 – Librarian, Linda Hanowski
Norquay Library, PO Box 460, Norquay SK S0A 2V0 – 306/594-2347; Fax: 306/594-2076 – Librarian, Lori Hudye
Pelly Branch Library, PO Box 40, Pelly SK S0A 2Z0 – 306/595-2243
Punnichy Branch Library, Punnichy SK S0A 3C0 – 306/835-2176 – Librarian, Audrey Brown
Quill Lake Branch Library, PO Box 271, Quill Lake SK S0A 3E0 – 306/383-2242 – Librarian, Kelly Berlinic
Raymore Branch Library, PO Box 244, Raymore SK P0M 1L0 – 306/746-2166
Rose Valley Library, PO Box 384, Rose Valley SK S0E 1M0 – 306/332-2001 – Librarian, Cheryl Holt
Saltcoats Library, Saltcoats SK S0A 3R0 – 306/744-2911 – Librarian, Barbara Straker
Semans Library, PO Box 220, Semans SK S0A 3S0 – 306/524-2224 – Librarian, Donna Oblander
Southey Library, Southey SK S0G 4P0 – 306/726-2907 – Librarian, Sharon Hakl
Spalding Branch Library, Spalding SK S0K 4C0 – 306/872-2184 – Librarian, Olwen Hoffman
Springside Branch Library, Springside SK S0A 3V0 – 306/792-2255 – Librarian, Marion Ockochinski
Spy Hill Branch Library, PO Box 160, Spy Hill SK S0A 3W0 – 306/534-2122 – Librarian, Jeanette Blakley
Stockholm Branch Library, Stockholm SK S0A 3Y0 – 306/793-2102 – Librarian, Carol Closson
Strasbourg Branch Library, PO Box 331, Strasbourg SK S0G 4V0 – 306/725-3239 – Librarian, Patricia Kelln
Sturgis Branch Library, Sturgis SK S0A 4A0 – 306/548-2824 – Librarian, Kathereen Brodu
Theodore Branch Library, Theodore SK S0A 4C0 – 306/647-2369 – Librarian, Darlene Fleming
Wadena Library, PO Box 297, Wadena SK S0A 4J0 – 306/338-2293 – Librarian, Francis Ekstrom
Watson Branch Library, PO Box 489, Watson SK S0K 4V0 – 306/287-3642 – Librarian, Linda Ceaser
Wishart Branch Library, PO Box 58, Wishart SK S0A 4R0 – 306/576-2150 – Librarian, Donna McDougall
Wynyard Library, PO Box 477, Wynyard SK S0A 4T0 – 306/554-3321 – Librarian, Wendy Howie
Yorkton Public Library, 93 Broadway West, Yorkton SK S3N 0L9 – 306/783-3523, 782-2877; Fax: 306/782-2844; Email: ENVOY: ILLSYP – Chief Librarian, Dan Calef

**SOUTHEAST REGIONAL LIBRARY**

PO Box 550, Weyburn SK S4H 2K7 – 306/842-3432; Fax: 306/842-2665; Email: ENVOY: ILL.SRL
Regional Director, Allan Johnson

Alameda Branch Library, PO Box 144, Alameda SK S0C 0A0 – 306/489-2066 – Librarian, Diane Miller
Arcola Branch Library, 100 Main St., Arcola SK S0C 0G0 – 306/455-2321 – Librarian, Ivy Chandler
Balgonie Branch Library, PO Box 389, Balgonie SK S0G 0E0 – 306/637-2332 – Librarian, Carolyn Selinger
Bengough Branch Library, PO Box 71, Bengough SK S0C 0K0 – 306/268-2022 – Librarian, Maureen Schmaltz
Bienfait Branch Library, PO Box 433, Bienfait SK S0C 0M0 – 306/388-2223 – Librarian, S. Tuchscherer
Broadview Branch Library, 515 Main St., General Delivery, Broadview SK S0G 0K0 – 306/696-2414 – Librarian, Catherine Adams
Carievale Branch Library, Carievale SK S0C 0P0 – 306/928-4619 – Librarian, Diana Cook
Carnduff Branch Library, PO Box 9, Carnduff SK S0C 0S0 – 306/482-3255 – Librarian, Judy Thompson
Estevan Public Library, 701 Souris Ave., Estevan SK S4A 2T1 – 306/634-3933; Fax: 306/634-2151; Email: greg@southeast.lib.sk.ca – Librarian, Greg Salmers
Fillmore Branch Library, Main St., PO Box 68, Fillmore SK S0G 1N0 – 306/722-3369 – Librarian, Wendy Dionne
Fort Qu'Appelle Branch Library, 148 Company Ave., PO Box 218, Fort Qu'Appelle SK S0G 1S0 – 306/332-6411 – Librarian, Shirley Dryden
Standing Buffalo Branch Library, PO Box 1771, Fort Qu'Appelle SK S0G 1S0 – 306/332-4414 – Librarian, Natalie Yuzicappi
Gainsborough Branch Library, PO Box 57, Gainsborough SK S0C 0Z0 – 306/685-2229 – Library, Marjorie Johnson
Glenavon Branch Library, PO Box 162, Glenavon SK S0G 1Y0 – 306/429-2180 – Librarian, Carol Nyiri
Grenfell Branch Library, Civic Building, Wolseley Ave., Grenfell SK S0G 2B0 – 306/697-2455 – Librarian, Ann Neuls
Indian Head Branch Library, PO Box 986, Indian Head SK S0G 2K0 – 306/695-3922 – Librarian, K. Baydak
Kennedy Branch Library, PO Box 217, Kennedy SK S0G 2R0 – 306/438-2020 – Librarian, Wendy Cancade
Kipling Branch Library, PO Box 608, Kipling SK S0G 2S0 – 306/736-2911 – Librarian, Debbie Toppings
Lake Alma Branch Library, Lake Alma SK S0C 1M0 – 306/447-2061 – Librarian, Bernice Bloor
Lampman Branch Library, Main St., PO Box 9, Lampman SK S0C 1N0 – 306/487-2202 – Librarian, Lee Ann Hutt
Lumsden Branch Library, Centennial Hall, 3rd Ave., Lumsden SK S0G 3C0 – 306/731-2247 – Librarian, Mary Ellen Hengen
Manor Branch Library, Main St., PO Box 115, Manor SK S0C 1R0 – 306/448-2266 – Librarian, Rita Kyle
Maryfield Branch Library, Maryfield SK S0G 3K0 – 306/646-2143 – Librarian, Judy Moore

Midale Branch Library, PO Box 206, Midale SK S0C 1S0 – 306/458-2263 – Librarian, Corrine Sjodin
Milestone Library, 112 Main St., Milestone SK S0G 3L0 – 306/436-2112 – Librarian, Connie Kinvig
Montmartre Regional Library, 133 - 1 Ave. West, Montmartre SK S0G 3M0 – 306/424-2029 – Librarian, Val Perras
Moosomin Branch Library, PO Box 1470, Moosomin SK S0G 3N0 – 306/435-2107 – Librarian, Paulette Green
Odessa Branch Library, Odessa SK S0G 3S0 – 306/957-2020 – Librarian, Sheila Leurer
Ogema Branch Library, Main St., PO Box 185, Ogema SK S0C 1Y0 – 306/459-2985 – Librarian, Valerie Dunn
Oungre Branch Library, PO Box 88, Oungre SK S0C 1Z0 – 306/456-2662 – Librarian, R. Graefer
Oxbow Branch Library, 516 Prospect Ave., Oxbow SK S0C 2B0 – 306/483-5175 – Librarian, Marty James
Pangman Library, Pangman SK S0C 2C0 – 306/442-2119 – Librarian, Carol Colbow
Pilot Butte Branch Library, PO Box 568, Pilot Butte SK S0G 3Z0 – 306/781-4494 – Librarian, Anne Wolfe
Qu'Appelle Branch Library, Walsh & 9 St., PO Box 450, Qu'Appelle SK S0G 4A0 – 306/699-2279 – Librarian, Cindy Duesterbeck
Radville Branch Library, PO Box 791, Radville SK S0C 2G0 – 306/869-2742 – Librarian, Bridget Harder
Redvers Library, 12 Broadway, PO Box 392, Redvers SK S0C 2H0 – 306/452-3255 – Librarian, Janet Dauvin
Regina Beach Branch Library, Main St., PO Box 596, Regina Beach SK S0G 4C0 – 306/729-2062 – Librarian, Karin Bjerke-Lisle
Rocanville Branch Library, PO Box 263, Rocanville SK S0A 3L0 – 306/645-2088 – Librarian, Marcia Birkenshaw
Stoughton Branch Library, PO Box 595, Stoughton SK S0G 4T0 – 306/457-2484 – Librarian, Marjorie Brown
Tribune Branch Library, Rienze St., PO Box 159, Tribune SK S0C 2M0 – 306/456-2200 – Librarian, Amy Pattyson
Vibank Branch Library, 2nd Ave., PO Box 241, Vibank SK S0G 3Y0 – 306/762-2270 – Librarian, S. Fahlman
Wapella Branch Library, 519 Main St., PO Box 130, Wapella SK S0G 4Z0 – 306/532-4419 – Librarian, Sharon Matheson
Wawota Branch Library, 308 Railway, PO Box 65, Wawota SK S0G 5A0 – 306/739-2375 – Librarian, Cheryl Weatherald
Weyburn Public Library, 45 Bison Ave., Weyburn SK S4H 0H9 – 306/842-4352 – Librarian, Marlene Yurkowski
White City Branch Library, PO Box 308, White City SK S0G 5B0 – 306/781-2118 – Librarian, Debi Bruer
Whitewood Library, 731 Lalonde St., PO Box 488, Whitewood SK S0G 5C0 – 306/735-4233 – Librarian, Wendy Paquin
Yellow Grass Branch Library, Main St., PO Box 31, Yellow Grass SK S0G 5J0 – 306/465-2574 – Librarian, Cheryl Watson

**WAPITI REGIONAL LIBRARY**

145 - 12 St. East, Prince Albert SK S6V 1B7 – 306/764-0712; Fax: 306/922-1516; Email: ILL.SPANC
Regional Director, Kitty Pope
Business Administrator, Anne McLeod

Alvena Public Library, Alvena SK S0K 0E0 – 306/943-2031 – Librarian, Sharon Jungwirth
Arborfield Public Library, Arborfield SK S0E 0A0 – 306/769-8729 – Librarian, Ida Miezianko
Archerwill Public Library, Archerwill SK S0E 0B0 – 306/323-2128 – Librarian, Gwen Wiles
Big River Public Library, PO Box 154, Big River SK S0J 0E0 – 306/469-2152 – Librarian, Joyce Ahearn
Birch Hills Public Library, Civic Centre, PO Box 396, Birch Hills SK S0J 0G0 – 306/749-3281 – Librarian, Bettye Bouchard
Bjorkdale Public Library, Bjorkdale SK S0E 0E0 – 306/886-2135 – Librarian, Trudy Mahussier
Blaine Lake Public Library, Blaine Lake SK S0J 0J0 – 306/497-3130 – Librarian, Lucy Cheveldayoff
Canwood Public Library, Main St., Canwood SK S0J 0K0 – 306/468-2016 – Librarian, H. Butz
Carrot River Public Library, PO Box 10001, Carrot River SK S0E 0L0 – 306/768-2501 – Librarian, Joanne Rempel
Choiceland Public Library, Choiceland SK S0J 0M0 – 306/428-2216 – Librarian, Janice Bakker
Christopher Lake Public Library, RM Building, PO Box 27, Christopher Lake SK S0J 0N0 – 306/982-2010 – Librarian, Gail Anderson
Crystal Springs Public Library, Crystal Springs SK S0K 1A0 – 306/749-2809 – Librarian, Ethel LaRoche
Cudworth Public Library, PO Box 401, Cudworth SK S0K 1B0 – 306/256-3492 – Librarian, Luella Frie
Debden Public Library, PO Box 143, Debden SK S0J 0S0 – 306/724-2240 – Librarian, Priscilla Charpentier
Duck Lake Public Library, Duck Lake SK S0K 1J0 – 306/467-2016 – Librarian, Diane Perrin
Gronid Public Library, PO Box 10, Gronid SK S0E 0W0 – 306/277-4633 – Librarian, Olga Dobrowolsky
Hudson Bay Public Library, PO Box 109, Hudson Bay SK S0E 0Y0 – 204/865-3110 – Librarian, Elly Ferguson
Humboldt Public Library, PO Box 1330, Humboldt SK S0K 2A0 – 306/682-2034 – Librarian, Tina Colistro
Kinistino Public Library, PO Box 774, Kinistino SK S0J 1H0 – 306/864-2537 – Librarian, Evelyn Sjolin
Leask Public Library, PO Box 117, Leask SK S0J 1M0 – 306/466-2000 – Librarian, Irene Bold
Leoville Public Library, Leoville SK S0J 1N0 – 306/984-2057 – Librarian, Anne Marie Laventure
Marcelin Public Library, Marcelin SK S0J 1R0 – 306/226-2110 – Librarian, Julie Bonin
Meath Park Public Library, PO Box 122, Meath SK S0J 1T0 – 306/929-2555 – Librarian, Michele Sachkowski
Melfort Public Library, PO Box 429, Melfort SK S0E 1A0 – 306/752-2022 – Librarian, Bonnie Rogers
Mistatim Public Library, Mistatim SK S0E 1B0 – 306/889-2144 – Librarian, Bethol Kennedy
Naicam Public Library, PO Box 587, Naicam SK S0K 2Z0 – 306/874-2156 – Librarian, Darla Christianson
Nipawin Public Library, PO Box 1720, Nipawin SK S0E 1E0 – 306/862-4867 – Librarian, Nancy Budd
Paddockwood Public Library, Paddockwood SK S0J 1Z0 – 306/989-2033 – Librarian, Rhonda Alland
Pilger Public Library, Pilger SK S0K 3G0 – 306/367-4809 – Librarian, Betty Bregenser
Porcupine Plain Public Library, PO Box 162, Porcupine Plain SK S0E 1H0 – 306/278-2488 – Librarian, Joanne Yacyshyn
Prairie River Public Library, Prairie River SK S0E 1J0 – 306/889-4521 – Librarian, Lorraine Waskouic
John M. Cuelenaere Library, 125 - 12 St. East, Prince Albert SK S6V 1B7 – 306/763-8496; Fax: 306/922-1516 – Library Director, Eleanor Acorn
Ridgedale Public Library, Ridgedale SK S0E 1L0 – 306/277-2061 – Librarian, Diane Rorke
St. Benedict Public Library, St. Benedict SK S0K 3T0 – 306/289-2072 – Librarian, Rose Mary Reynaud
St. Brieux Public Library, RM Building, St. Brieux SK S0K 3V0 – 306/275-2314 – Librarian, Muriel Lafreniere
St. Louis Public Library, St. Louis SK S0J 2C0 – 306/422-8630 – Librarian, Monique Tremblay
Shell Lake Public Library, PO Box 310, Shell Lake SK S0J 2G0 – 306/427-2272 – Librarian, Joan Ens
Shellbrook Public Library, Shellbrook SK S0J 2E0 – 306/747-3419 – Librarian, Linda Mazurkewich
Sturgeon Lake Public Library, Sturgeon Lake Central School, RR#1, Site 12, Comp. 5, Shellbrook SK S0J 0E0 – 306/764-5506 – Librarian, Sharon Daniels
Smeaton Public Library, Smeaton SK S0J 2J0 – 306/426-2202 – Librarian, Levina Pearson
Spiritwood Public Library, Spiritwood SK S0J 2M0 – 306/883-2337 – Librarian, Joyce Carriere
Star City Public Library, Centennial Recreational Centre, Star City SK S0E 1P0 – 306/863-2545 – Librarian, Pauline Stenzel
Tisdale Public Library, Civic Centre, PO Box 2499, Tisdale SK S0E 1T0 – 306/873-4767 – Librarian, Joan Burroughs
Wakaw Public Library, PO Box 464, Wakaw SK S0K 4P0 – 306/233-5552 – Librarian, Lucille Reynaud
Waskesiu Public Library, Montreal Dr., PO Box 157, Waskesiu SK S0J 2Y0 – 306/663-5999 – Librarian, Deidre MacGregor
Weldon Public Library, Weldon SK S0J 3A0 – Librarian, Myrna Peterson
White Fox Public Library, White Fox SK S0J 3B0 – Librarian, Violet Johnson
Yellow Creek Public Library, Yellow Creek SK S0K 4X0 – 306/279-2191 – Librarian, Sally Wojcicjowsky
Zenon Park Public Library, PO Box 175, Zenon Park SK S0E 1W0 – 306/777-6091 – Librarian, Bev Favreau

**WHEATLAND REGIONAL LIBRARY**

806 Duchess St., Saskatoon SK S7K 0R3 – 306/652-5077; Fax: 306/931-7611; Email: bcameron@wheatland.lib.sk.ca; URL: http://www.wheatland.lib.sk.ca; Symbol: WRL
Executive Director, Bruce Cameron
Reference Librarian, Paul Hand
Public Services Librarian, Betty Miller
Acquisitions Librarian, Bruce Cameron

Aberdeen Library, PO Box 130, Aberdeen SK S0K 0A0 – 306/253-4311 – Librarian, Ron Minielly
Allan Library, PO Box 40, Allan SK S0K 0C0 – 306/257-4222 – Librarian, Sandra Wilson
Beechy Library, PO Box 154, Beechy SK S0L 0C0 – 306/859-2032 – Librarian, Lois Meaden
Biggar Library, PO Box 157, Biggar SK S0K 0M0 – 306/948-3911; Email: biggar.library@sk.sympatico.ca – Librarian, Darlene Stainbrook
Bruno Library, PO Box 2, Bruno SK S0K 0S0 – 306/369-2353; Email: bruno.library@sk.sympatico.ca – Librarian, Donna Olchawsk
Coleville Library, PO Box 45, Coleville SK S0L 0K0 – 306/965-2551 – Librarian, Wendy Bahm
Colonsay Library, PO Box 172, Colonsay SK S0K 0Z0 – 306/255-2232; Email: colonsay.library@sk.sympatico.ca – Librarian, Mrs. Val Pidlisney
Conquest Library, PO Box 130, Conquest SK S0L 0L0 – 306/856-4555 – Librarian, Jean Jones
Delisle Library, PO Box 340, Delisle SK S0L 0P0 – 306/493-8288 – Librarian, Carole Merkosky
Dinsmore Library, PO Box 369, Dinsmore SK S0L 0T0 – 306/846-2011 – Librarian, Mary McBain
Dodsland Library, PO Box 100, Dodsland SK S0L 0V0 – 306/356-2180 – Librarian, Tracey Johnson
Dundurn Library, PO Box 185, Dundurn SK S0K 1K0 – 306/492-2366 – Librarian, Ruth McDonald
Eatonia Public Library, PO Box 100, Eatonia SK S0L 0Y0 – 306/967-2224 – Librarian, Gisela Steinke
Elrose Library, General Delivery, PO Box 185, Elrose SK S0L 0Z0 – 306/378-2808 – Librarian, Catherine McDonald
Eston Library, PO Box 387, Eston SK S0L 1A0 – 306/962-3513 – Librarian, Nancy Stevenson
Hanley Library, PO Box 263, Hanley SK S0G 2E0 – 306/544-2546 – Librarian, Sonja English

Kenaston Library, PO Box 309, Kenaston SK S0G 2N0 – 306/252-2130 – Librarian, Ina-Mae Collins
Kerrobert Library, PO Box 618, Kerrobert SK S0L 1R0 – 306/834-5211 – Librarian, Heather Wack
Kindersley Plains Library, 104 Princess St., Kindersley SK S0L 1S2 – 306/463-4141; Email: kindersley.library@sk.sympatico.ca – Librarian, Marilyn Shea
Kyle Public Library, Main St., PO Box 370, Kyle SK S0L 1T0 – 306/375-2566 – Librarian, Elva Akister
Landis Library, General Delivery, Landis SK S0K 2K0 – 306/658-2177; Email: landis.library@sk.sympatico.ca – Librarian, Vera Halter
Langham Library, PO Box 697, Langham SK S0K 2L0 – 306/283-4362 – Librarian, Brenda Tallmadge
Lanigan Library, Town Office, PO Box 70, Lanigan SK S0K 2M0 – 306/365-2472 – Librarian, Linda Gibney
Lucky Lake Library, PO Box 340, Lucky Lake SK S0L 1Z0 – 306/858-2246 – Librarian, Linda Peters
Luseland Library, PO Box 550, Luseland SK S0L 2A0 – 306/372-4808 – Librarian, Diane Hurford
Martensville Library, PO Box 1180, Martensville SK S0K 2T0 – 306/956-7311 – Librarian, Christel Epp
Milden Library, PO Box 7, Milden SK S0L 2L0 – 306/935-4600 – Librarian, Lorraine Fennell
Nokomis Library, PO Box 38, Nokomis SK S0G 3R0 – 306/528-2251; Email: nokomis.library@sk.sympatico.ca – Librarian, Irene Proseilo
Osler Library, PO Box 190, Osler SK S0K 3A0 – 306/239-4774 – Librarian, Colleen Rempel
Outlook Library, PO Box 547, Outlook SK S0L 2N0 – 306/867-8823 – Librarian, Susan Jebson
Perdue Library, PO Box 253, Perdue SK S0K 3C0 – 306/237-4227 – Librarian, Marge Featherstone
Plenty Library, PO Box 70, Plenty SK S0L 2R0 – 306/932-2045 – Librarian, Susan McCleod
Rosetown Library, PO Box 1208, Rosetown SK S0L 2V0 – 306/882-3566 – Librarian, Janey Johnson
Rosthern Library, PO Box 27, Rosthern SK S0K 3R0 – 306/232-5377 – Librarian, Andy Lehmann
Sonningdale Library, PO Box 40, Sonningdale SK S0K 4B0 – 306/237-9533 – Librarian, Sharon Farnell
Stranraer Book Deposit, PO Box 34, Stranraer SK SOL 3B0 – 306/377-4845 – Librarian, Linda Ek
Unity Library, General Delivery, Unity SK S0K 4L0 – 306/228-2802; Email: unity.library@sk.sympatico.ca
Viscount Library, 5 Donald St., 3rd Fl., PO Box 117, Viscount SK S0K 4M0 – 306/944-2155 – Librarian, Carol Brown
Waldheim Library, PO Box 265, Waldheim SK S0K 4R0 – 306/945-2221 – Librarian, Irene Balman
Warman Library, PO Box 788, Warman SK S0K 4S0 – 306/933-4387 – Librarian, Kim Cadrain
Watrous Library, PO Box 460, Watrous SK S0K 4T0 – 306/946-2244; Email: watrous.library@sk.sympatico.ca – Librarian, Kathleen Kimmie
Wilkie Library, PO Box 189, Wilkie SK S0K 4W0 – 306/843-2616 – Librarian, Terri Dueck
Young Branch, PO Box 288, Young SK S0K 4Y0 – 306/259-2227 – Librarian, Helen Weber

## Municipal Resource Library Systems

### REGINA PUBLIC LIBRARY

2311 - 12 Ave., PO Box 2311, Regina SK S4P 3Z5 – 306/777-6099; Fax: 306/352-5550; Email: kjensen@rpl.regina.sk.ca
Library Director, Ken Jensen
Central Public Services, Head, André Gagnon
Technical Support Services, Head, Vivien Cartmell
Branch Services, Head, Lubbert van der Laan
Finance & Administration, Head, Colleen Schommer
Public Relations, Head, Anne Campbell
Dunlop Art Gallery, Director/Curator, Helen Marzolf

Albert Branch, 1401 Robinson St., Regina SK S4T 2N7 – 306/777-6076; Fax: 306/777-6223 – Branch Head, Wendy Sinclair
Connaught Branch, 3435 - 13 Ave., Regina SK S4T 1P8 – 306/777-6079; Fax: 306/352-5550 – Branch Head, Ann Stuart
George Bothwell Branch, 2965 Gordon Rd., Regina SK S4S 6H7 – 306/777-6091; Fax: 306/777-6213 – Branch Head, Anne James
Glen Elm Branch, 1601 Dewdney Ave. East, Regina SK S4N 4N6 – 306/777-6080; Fax: 306/352-5550 – Branch Head, Charles Ottosen
Interlibrary Loans, 2311 - 12th Ave., PO Box 2311, Regina SK S4P 3Z5 – 306/777-6024; Fax: 306/777-6105; Email: illstaff@rpl.regina.sk.ca – ILLO Supervisor, Janet Craig
Prince of Wales Branch, 2188 Broder St., Regina SK S4N 3S4 – 306/777-6085; Fax: 306/352-5550 – Branch Head, Anna Mann
Regent Place Branch, 107 Albert St., Regina SK S4R 2N3 – 306/777-6086; Fax: 306/777-6215 – Branch Head, Warren James
Sherwood Village Branch, 6121 Rochdale Blvd., Regina SK S4X 2R1 – 306/777-6088; Fax: 306/777-6214 – Branch Head, Bernard Vander Ziel
Sunrise Branch, 3131 East Woodhams Dr., Regina SK S4V 2P9 – 306/777-6095; Fax: 306/777-6212 – Branch Head, Janet Hilderman

### SASKATOON PUBLIC LIBRARY SYSTEM

311 - 23 St. East., Saskatoon SK S7K 0J6 – 306/975-7574; Fax: 306/975-7542; Email: ENVOY: ILL.SS
Director, Zenon Zuzak
Reference Librarian, Anne Craggs
Children's Librarian, Judy Buckle
Public Services Librarian, Muriel Dickson
Technical Services Librarian, Diane Vinish

Carlyle King Branch, 3130 Laurier Dr., Saskatoon SK S7L 5J7 – 306/975-7592 – Branch Head, Donna Wells
Cliff Wright Branch, 1635 McKercher Dr., Saskatoon SK S7H 5J9 – 306/975-7550 – Branch Head, Wenda McArthur
J.S. Wood Branch, 1801 Landsdowne Ave., Saskatoon SK S7H 2C4 – 306/975-7590 – Branch Head, Josephine Bischoff
Mayfair Branch, 602 - 33 St. West, Saskatoon SK S7L 0W1 – 306/975-7591 – Branch Supervisor, Trudy Harder
Rusty Macdonald Branch, 225 Primrose Dr., Saskatoon SK S7K 5E4 – 306/975-7600; Fax: 306/975-7603 – Branch Head, Bryan Foran
Sutherland Branch, 449 Central Ave., Saskatoon SK S7N 2E9 – 306/975-7593 – Branch Supervisor, Laura Sauffert

## Special & College Libraries & Resource Centres

### AIR RONGE

Northlands College - Library, POBox 1000, Air Ronge SK S0J 3G0 – 306/425-4480

### CARONPORT

Briercrest Bible College - Archibald Library, 510 College Dr., Caronport SK S0H 0S0 – 306/756-3252; Fax: 306/756-3366; URL: http://www.briercrest.ca; Symbol: SCA – Head Librarian, Laura Klassen, 306/756-3262

### CREIGHTON

Northlands College - Eastern Region Library, POBox 400, Creighton SK S0P 0A0 – 306/688-3474; Fax: 306/688-7710

### FORT QU'APPELLE

Niel Halford Law Office - Library, POBox 817, Fort Qu'appelle SK S0G 1S0 – 306/332-5661

### HAFFORD

Redberry Pelican Project Inc. – Library, POBox 221, Hafford SK S0J 1A0 – 306/549-2400; Fax: 306/549-2199 – Eileen Laviolette

### HUMBOLDT

Prairie Agricultural Machinery Institute – Library, Hwy. 5 West, POBox 1900, Humboldt SK S0K 2A0 – 306/682-2555; Fax: 306/682-5080; Toll Free: 1-800-567-7264; Symbol: SHPA – Head Librarian, Sharon Deopker

### INDIAN HEAD

Agriculture & Agri-Food Canada-Shelterbelt Centre – Resource Centre, POBox 940, Indian Head SK S0G 2K0 – 306/695-2284; Fax: 306/695-2568 – Head, Administration, Murray Hurford
Indian Head Research Farm - Library, POBox 760, Indian Head SK S0G 2K0 – 306/695-2274; Fax: 306/695-3445 – Office Manager, B.A. Robb

### MOOSE JAW

Moose Jaw Union Hospital – Medical Library, 455 Fairford St. East, Moose Jaw SK S6H 1H3 – 306/694-1515; Fax: 306/692-5596 – Director, Health Records, I. Alraum
Providence Place for Holistic Health – Staff Library, 100 Second Ave. NE, Moose Jaw SK S6H 1B8 – 306/694-8081; Fax: 306/694-8804 – Director, Resident Information, Eileen Blandford
Saskatchewan Institute of Applied Science & Technology - Palliser Institute Library, POBox 1420, Moose Jaw SK S6H 4R4 – 306/694-3256; Fax: 306/694-3427; Email: Palliser-library@www.siast.sk.ca; URL: http://www.siast.sk.ca/~pallstu/library.htm; Symbol: SMJT
Program Head/Library, Beverley Brooks, 306/694-3255
Library Technician, Shawna North
Acquisitions Clerk, Brenda Fallis
Saskatchewan Water Corporation - Library, 111 Fairford St. East, Moose Jaw SK S6H 7X9 – 306/694-3980; Fax: 306/694-3944 – Executive Secretary, Doreen Jerred
Valley View Centre - Harrison Memorial Library, POBox 1300, Moose Jaw SK S6H 4R2 – 306/694-3096; Fax: 306/694-3003 – Records/Librarian, Diane Gray

### MOOSOMIN

Osman, Gardner, Gordon Law Office - Library, Box 280, 626 Carleton St., Moosomin SK S0G 3N0 – 306/435-3851; Fax: 306/435-3962 – Partner, Don Osman

### MUENSTER

St. Peter's Abbey & College - Library, POBox 10, Muenster SK S0K 2Y0 – 306/682-1760; Fax: 306/682-4402; URL: stpetes@orion.sk.sympatico.ca; Symbol: SMSP – Managing Librarian, Brenda McNabb

### NIPAWIN

Cumberland Regional College - Information Centre, POBox 2225, Nipawin SK S0E 1E0 – 306/862-9833; Fax: 306/862-4940

### NORTH BATTLEFORD

Battlefords Union Hospital – Memorial Library, 1092 - 107 St., North Battleford SK S9A 1Z1 – 306/446-7350; Fax: 306/446-7301
Lojek, Jones & Hudec Law Office - Library, 10211 - 12 Ave., POBox 1179, North Battleford SK S9A 3X5 – 306/446-2211; Fax: 306/446-3022 – Manager, James G. Burkinshaw
North West Regional College - Career & Educational Information Centre, 1381 - 101 St., North Battleford SK S9A 0Z9 – 306/937-5100; Fax: 306/445-1575 – Coordinator, Michael Brokop

**OUTLOOK**

Saskatchewan Irrigation Development Centre - Library, POBox 700, Outlook SK S0L 2N0 – 306/867-5400; Fax: 306/867-9656 – Administrator, Library, Marlene Martinson

**PRINCE ALBERT**

Gabriel Dumont Institute of Native Studies & Applied Research – SIAST Library, Kelsey Campus, 48 - 12 St. East, Prince Albert SK S6V 1B2 – 306/922-6466; Fax: 306/764-3995

Prince Albert Model Forest Association Inc. – PAMF Reference Library, POBox 2406, Prince Albert SK S6V 7G3 – 306/922-1944; Fax: 306/763-6456 – Communications Director, Ian Monteith

Saskatchewan Environment & Resource Management - Forestry Branch Library, McIntosh Mall, POBox 3003, Prince Albert SK S6V 6G1 – 306/953-2448; Fax: 306/953-2360; Email: battiste@derm.gov.sk.ca; Symbol: SPAE – Library Contact, Angela Battiste

Saskatchewan Forestry Association – Library, POBox 400, Prince Albert SK S6V 5R7 – 306/763-2189; Fax: 306/764-7463 – Carol Adams

Saskatchewan Institute of Applied Science & Technology - Woodland Campus Library Services/ Technical Centre, 1100 - 15 St. East, POBox 3003, Prince Albert SK S6V 6G1 – 306/953-7098, 7108; Fax: 306/953-7099 – Librarian, Martine Morency

Solicitor General Canada - Saskatchewan Penitentiary, POBox 160, Prince Albert SK S6E 5R6 – 306/953-8500, ext.386; Symbol: SPASP – Librarian, Erin McCrumb

Victoria Union Hospital – Medical Library, 1200 - 24th St. West, Prince Albert SK S6V 5T4 – 306/953-0521; Fax: 306/763-2871 – Coordinator, Health Records, Heather Painchaud

**REGINA**

Saskatchewan Highways & Transportation - Planning & Coordination – Library & Geotechnical Branch Library, 1855 Victoria Ave., 8th Fl., Regina SK S4P 3V5 – 306/787-2099; Fax: 306/787-1007; Email: basle@explorer.sasknet.sk.ca; Symbol: SRHP – Librarian, Ellen Basler

Agriculture & Agri-Food Canada - Prairie Farm Rehabilitation Administration Information Centre, #603, 1800 Hamilton, Regina SK S4P 0R5 – 306/780-5100; Fax: 306/780-5018; Email: pfrainfo@em.agr.ca; URL: http://www.agr.ca/pfra; Symbol: SRRE – Manager, Information Centre, Charlene Dusyk

Allan Blair Cancer Centre - Gerald H. Ewing Library, 4101 Dewdney Ave., Regina SK S4T 7T1 – 306/766-2203; Fax: 306/766-2322; Symbol: SRAB – Medical Secretary/Librarian, Barbara Karchewski

Alzheimer Association of Saskatchewan Inc. – Library, #301, 2550 - 12th Ave., Regina SK S4P 3X1 – 306/949-4141; Fax: 306/949-3069; Toll Free: 1-800-263-3367

Association des juristes d'expression française de la Saskatchewan – Bibliothèque, 2132 Broad St., Regina SK S4P 1Y5 – 306/565-2507; Téléc: 306/781-7916

Baha'i Local Spiritual Assembly of Regina - Library, 2900 - 15 Ave., Regina SK S4T 1S7 – 306/584-2771 – Librarian, Joan Prentice-Naqvi

Basketball Saskatchewan Inc. – Library, 2205 Victoria Ave., Regina SK S4P 0S4 – 306/791-3660; Fax: 306/525-4009 – Roger Bakes

Bertram, Scrivens, Prior & Stradecki Law Office - Library, #1730, 2002 Victoria Ave., Regina SK S4P 0R7 – 306/525-2737; Fax: 306/565-3244 – Robert H. Bertram

Canadian Bible College - Archibald Foundation Library, 4400 - 4 Ave., Regina SK S4T 0H8 – 306/545-1515; Fax: 306/545-0210; Symbol: SRCB – Director of Library Services, H.D. Sandy Ayer, Email: hdayer@cbccts.sk.ca

Court of Appeal - Library, Courthouse, 2425 Victoria Ave., Regina SK S4P 3V7 – 306/787-7399; Fax: 306/787-0505 – Librarian, Shirley A. Hurnard

Crown Life Insurance Co. - Crown Life Library, 1901 Scarth St., Regina SK S4P 4L4 – 306/751-6078; Fax: 306/751-7070; Email: sprid@sasknet.sk.ca – Librarian, Darlene Springer

Law Library, 1901 Scarth St., 8th Fl., Regina SK S4P 3B1 – 306/751-6108; Fax: 306/751-6100; Email: lcook@crownlife.ca – Reference Librarian, Cheryl Charron

Early Childhood Intervention Program - Regina Region – Toy & Reference Libraries, 2180 - 23 Ave., Regina SK S4S 0A5 – 306/766-5300; Fax: 306/766-5519 – Toy Library Coordinator, Joan Anderson

Environment Canada - Atmospheric & Hydrobiological Sciences Division - Library, POBox 4800, Regina SK S4P 3Y4 – 306/780-5739; Fax: 306/780-7588; Symbol: SREAE – Officer-in-Charge, Ronald F. Hopkinson

Prairie & Northern Region - Library, #300, 2365 Albert St., Regina SK S4P 4K1 – 306/780-5306; Fax: 306/780-5311; Symbol: SREIW – In Charge, Priya Montgomery

Indian & Northern Affairs Canada - Resource Centre, 2110 Hamilton St., Regina SK S4P 4K4 – 306/780-5945; Fax: 306/780-5733; Symbol: SRIN – Information Assistant, Marilyn Hill

Law Society of Saskatchewan - Library, Courthouse, 2425 Victoria Ave., POBox 5032, Regina SK S4P 3M3 – 306/569-8020; Fax: 306/569-0155 – Reference Librarian, M. Seeley

Leader-Post Ltd. - Library, 1964 Park St., POBox 2020, Regina SK S4P 3G4 – 306/565-8234

Luther College - Library, University of Regina, #108, 3737 Wascana Pkwy., Regina SK S4S 0A2 – 306/585-5030; Fax: 306/585-5267; Email: judy.halliday@uregina.ca – Library Coordinator, Judith L. Halliday

Museums Association of Saskatchewan – Library, 1808 Smith St., Regina SK S4P 2N4 – 306/780-9279; Fax: 306/359-6758 – Museums Advisor, Wendy Fitch

Pasqua Hospital – Health Sciences Library, 4101 Dewdney Ave., Regina SK S4T 1A5 – 306/359-2370; Fax: 306/766-2751 – Director, Leona Lang

Plains Health Centre – Health Sciences Library, Regina Health District, 4500 Wascana Pkwy., Regina SK S4S 5W9 – 306/766-6426; Fax: 306/766-6722; Email: ENVOY 100: SRHS; esilzer@cableregina.com; Symbol: SRHS – Director, Beth Silzer

Provincial Auditor Saskatchewan - Library, #1500, 1920 Broad St., Regina SK S4P 3V7 – 306/787-6398; Fax: 306/787-6383; Symbol: SRPA – Librarian, Rita Schiller

Randall Wellsch & Simaluk - Library, #200, 2425 - 13 Ave., Regina SK S4P 0W1 – 306/569-1530; Fax: 306/569-0121 – Harvey Randall

Regina General Hospital – Health Sciences Library, 1440 - 14 Ave., Regina SK S4P 0W5 – 306/359-4314; Fax: 306/359-4723; Email: envoy: ill.srg. – Coordinator, T. Bouchard

Regina Humane Society Inc. – Library, POBox 3143, Regina SK S4P 3G7 – 306/543-6363; Fax: 306/545-7661 – Lisa Koch

Regina Police Service - Resource Centre, 1717 Osler St., POBox 196, Regina SK S4P 2Z8 – 306/777-8614; Fax: 306/757-5461 – Planning & Research Analyst, Lois Wallace

Regina School Division #4 - Alex Robb Resource Centre, 1600 - 4 Ave., Regina SK S4R 8C8 – 306/791-8261, 8272; Fax: 306/352-2898

Learning Resources Consultant, Dianna Dushinski

Resource Centre Assistant, Yvette Ast

Regina Symphony – Library, 200 Lakeshore Dr., Regina SK S4P 3V7 – 306/586-9555; Fax: 306/586-2133 – James Fitzpatrick

Resource Centre for Sport, Culture & Recreation, #210, 3303 Hillsdale St., Regina SK S4S 6W9 – 306/780-9411; Fax: 306/780-9442; Email: rbakes@ucomnet.unibase.com; URL: http://www.cableregina.com/nonprofits/spra/rc_page.htm; Symbol: SRCR – Roger Bakes

Royal Canadian Mounted Police - Training Academy Resource Centre, POBox 6500, Regina SK S4P 3J7 – 306/780-5824; Fax: 306/780-7599; Email: depot.res@sk.sympatico.ca; Symbol: IS – Manager, Resource Centre, Ruth Hoffart

Saskatchewan Agriculture & Food - Library, Walter Scott Bldg., #B5, 3085 Albert St., Regina SK S4S 0B1 – 306/787-5151; Fax: 306/787-0216; Email: library@agr.gov.sk.ca; Symbol: SRAG – Librarian, Hélène Stewart

Saskatchewan Archives Board - Resource Centre, University of Regina, 3303 Hillsdale St., Regina SK S4S 0A2 – 306/787-4066; Fax: 306/787-1975 – Provincial Archivist, Trevor J.D. Powell

Saskatchewan Association for Multicultural Education – Resource Centre, #201, 2205 Victoria Ave., Regina SK S4P 0S4 – 306/780-9428; Fax: 306/525-4009

Saskatchewan Association of Licensed Practical Nurses – Library, 2310 Smith St., Regina SK S4P 2P6 – 306/525-1436; Fax: 306/347-7784 – Ede Leeson

Saskatchewan Association of Rural Municipalities – Library, 2075 Hamilton St., Regina SK S4P 2E1 – 306/757-3577; Fax: 306/565-2141; Toll Free: 1-800-667-3604

Saskatchewan Bureau of Statistics - Library, 2350 Albert St., 5th Fl., Regina SK S4P 4A6 – 306/787-6333; Fax: 306/787-6311 – Statistical Clerk, Yvonne Small

Saskatchewan Choral Federation – Library, 1860 Lorne St., Regina SK S4P 2L7 – 306/780-9230; Fax: 306/781-6021; Email: ylozow@unibase.unibase.com – Librarian, Merle Bintner

Saskatchewan Council for International Co-operation – Library, 2138 McIntyre St., Regina SK S4P 2R7 – 306/757-4669; Fax: 306/757-3226

Saskatchewan Department of Education & Department of Post-Secondary Education & Skills Training - Resource Centre, 2220 College Ave., Regina SK S4P 3V7 – 306/787-2262; Fax: 306/787-2223; Email: ENVOY: ILL.SRED; URL: http://www.sasked.gov.sk.ca/resources/lib4_hom.html; Symbol: SRED – Head Librarian, Charlene Kramer, 306/787-2262

Saskatchewan Drama Association – Library, #203, 2135 Albert St., Regina SK S4P 2V1 – 306/525-0151; Fax: 306/525-6277

Saskatchewan Education - Library, 2220 College Ave., Regina SK S4P 3V7 – 306/787-2262 – Librarian, Charlene Kramer

Saskatchewan Energy & Mines - Marketing & Publications, 1914 Hamilton St., Regina SK S4P 4V4 – 306/787-2528; Fax: 306/787-2527 – Terry Theiss, 306/787-7643

Saskatchewan Environment & Resource Management - Resource Library, #238, 3211 Albert St., Regina SK S4S 5W6 – 306/787-6114, 0902; Fax: 306/787-3941; Email: ENVOY: SPRC; Symbol: SRE – Librarian, Janice Szuch

Saskatchewan Genealogical Society – Library, #201, 1870 Lorne St., POBox 1894, Regina SK S4P 3E1 – 306/780-9207; Fax: 306/781-6021 – Librarian, Laura M. Hanowski

Saskatchewan Government Insurance - Library, 2260 - 11 Ave., 10th Fl., Regina SK S4P 0J9 – 306/751-1830; Fax: 306/359-7333

Saskatchewan Health - Resource Centre, 3475 Albert St., Regina SK S4S 6X6 – 306/787-3090; Fax: 306/787-3823; Email: library@health.gov.sk.ca; Symbol: SRPH – Manager, Lynn Kozun

Saskatchewan History & Folklore Society Inc. – Library, 1860 Lorne St., Regina SK S4P 2L7 – 306/

780-9204; Fax: 306/781-6021; Toll Free: 1-800-919-9437

Saskatchewan Indian Federated College - Library, Rm. 118, College West Bldg., University of Regina, Regina SK S4S 0A2 – 306/779-6299; Fax: 306/584-0955; URL: http://www.sifc.edu
- Head Librarian, Phyllis G. Lerat, Email: plerat@tansi.sifc.edu
- Assistant Librarian, Rob Nestor, Email: rnestor@tanis.sifc.edu
- Administration Assistant, Suzanne Pelletier

Saskatchewan Institute of Applied Science & Technology - Wascana Insitute, Library Services, Parkway Centre, 4635 Wascana Pkwy., POBox 556, Regina SK S4P 3A3 – 306/787-4323; Fax: 306/787-0560; Email: waslib@siast.sk.ca; URL: http://www.siast.sk.ca/~wascana/waslib.htm; Symbol: SRRI
- Learning Centre, Program Head, Colleen Warren, 306/787-4321
- Technical Services, Duane Meyers, 306/787-4277
- Parkway Centre Library, Library Technician, Ruth Prentice, 306/787-4323, 0564
- St. John Centre Library, Library Technician, Chris Ast, 306/787-4344
- Albert South Library, Public Services Librarian, TBA, 306/787-4005
- 8 Ave. North Library, Library Technician, Charlotte Ewert, 306/787-6036
- Maxwell Cres. Library, Library Technician, Anand Vaid, 306/787-4713
- Winnipeg North Library, Public Services Library, Heather West, 306/787-0728
- Interlibrary Loans, Laureen Marchuk, 306/787-4323

Saskatchewan Justice - Civil Law Library, 1874 Scarth St., 9th Fl., Regina SK S4P 3V7 – 306/787-7281; Fax: 306/787-0581; Email: AStirling@Justice.gov.sk.ca; Symbol: SRJC – Librarian, Andrew Stirling

Saskatchewan Labour - Resource Centre, 1870 Albert St., Regina SK S4P 3V7 – 306/787-2429; Fax: 306/787-7229; Symbol: SRDL

Saskatchewan Legislative Library, #234, Legislative Bldg., Regina SK S4S 0B3 – 306/787-2276; Fax: 306/787-1772; Email: Reference@legassembly.sk.ca; URL: http://www.legassembly.sk.ca; Symbol: SRL
- Legislative Librarian, Marian Powell, 306/787-2277
- Secretary to the Legislative Librarian, Sandra M. Gardner, 306/787-1824
- Reference Librarian, Michele Howland, 306/787-2276

Saskatchewan Municipal Government - Housing Division, Library, 1855 Victoria Ave., 7th Fl., Regina SK S4P 3V7 – 306/787-4198; Fax: 306/787-5166 – Librarian, Kathy Reece

Saskatchewan Music Festival Association Inc. – Library & Archives, #201, 1819 Cornwall St., Regina SK S4P 2K4 – 306/757-1722; Fax: 306/347-7789

Saskatchewan Palliative Care Association Inc. – Resource Library, #332, 845 Broad St., Regina SK S4R 8G9 – 306/359-7484; Fax: 306/757-8161

Saskatchewan Parks & Recreation Association – Library, #210, 3303 Hillsdale St., Regina SK S4S 6W9 – 306/791-3666; Fax: 306/780-9257 – Roger Bakes

Saskatchewan Securities Commission Library, 1914 Hamilton St., 8th Fl., Regina SK S4P 3V7 – 306/787-5645; Fax: 306/787-5899 – Deputy Director, Legal, Dean Murrison

Saskatchewan Social Services - Resource Centre, 1920 Broad St., Regina SK S4P 3V6 – 306/787-3680; Fax: 306/787-3441; Symbol: SRSS – Library Technician, Muriel Griffiths

Saskatchewan Society for the Autistic Inc. – Library, 3510 - 25 Ave., Regina SK S4S 1L8 – 306/569-0858; Fax: 306/586-4615

Saskatchewan Wheat Pool - Corporate Library, 2625 Victoria Ave., Regina SK S4T 7T9 – 306/569-4480; Fax: 306/569-4885; Email: dbehrns@swp.com; URL: http://www.swp.com; Symbol: SRW
- Corporate Librarian, Diana Behrns, Email: dbehrns@swp.com
- Public Serives Librarian, Shannon Ponsford, 306/569-4753

Saskatchewan Writers Guild Inc. – Library, POBox 3986, Regina SK S4P 3R9 – 306/757-6310; Fax: 306/565-8554 – Communications Officer, April Davies

SaskPower - Technical Services & Research Library, 2025 Victoria Ave., Regina SK S4P 0S1 – 306/566-3333; Fax: 306/566-3348; Symbol: SRPCRD – Librarian/Private Secretary, D.A. Tsakires

SaskTel - Corporate Library, 2121 Saskatchewan Dr., 7th Fl., Regina SK S4P 3Y2 – 306/347-2249; Fax: 306/359-9022; Symbol: SRST – Manager, Information Resources, Basil Pogue, 306/777-2004

Statistics Canada - Prairie Regional Reference Centre - Saskatchewan, Avord Tower, 2002 Victoria Ave., 9th Fl., Regina SK S4P 0R7 – 306/780-5405; Fax: 306/780-5403; Toll Free: 1-800-263-1136; Email: statcan@sk.sympatico.ca

Tourism Saskatchewan - Photo Library, 1900 Albert St., Regina SK S4P 4L9 – 306/787-6298; Fax: 306/787-0715; Email: alan.mills@sasktourism.com
- Director, Neil Sawatsky
- Image Library, Coordinator, Alan Mills, 306/787-6298

University of Regina - Library, #100, 3737 Wascana Pkwy., Regina SK S4S 0A2 – 306/585-4134; Fax: 306/585-4878, 586-9862; Toll Free: 1-800-667-6014; Email: wmaes@max.cc.uregina.ca; Symbol: SRU
- Director of Libraries & Information Services, William R. Maes, 306/585-4132
- Acquisitions, Manager, E. Magee, 306/585-4398
- Cataloguing, Head, Bibliographic Services, B. Browne, 306/585-5101
- Circulation/Reference, Associate Librarian/Client Services, C.L. Adams, 306/585-4289
- Resources, Associate Librarian/Resources, Margaret A. Hammond, 306/585-4283
- Campion College Library, Librarian, Myfanwy Truscott, 306/359-1234
- Education Branch Library, Education Librarian, Del Affleck, 306/585-4642
- Fine Arts Branch Library, Library Supervisor, Margaret Steffensen, 306/779-4826
- Luther College Library, Librarian, Judith Halliday, 306/585-5030
- Language Institute Library, Librarian, Richard Lapointe, 306/585-5241

Wascana Rehabilitation Centre – Health Sciences Library, 2180 - 23 Ave., Regina SK S4S 0A5 – 306/359-5441; Fax: 306/359-5554; Email: SRSH.WASCANA; Symbol: SRSH – Library Technician, Lily Walter-Smith

Woloshyn Mattison Law Office - Library, Saskatchewan Pl., #200, 1870 Albert St., Regina SK S4P 4B7 – 306/352-9676; Fax: 306/569-8411 – Dirk Silversides

Workers' Compensation Board - Resource Centre, #200, 1881 Scarth St., Regina SK S4P 4L1 – 306/787-2112; Fax: 306/787-3915; Toll Free: 1-800-667-7590; Email: wcbrc@unibase.unibase.com; Symbol: SRWCB – Library Technician, Nick Langshaw

## SASKATOON

Ag-West Biotech Inc. – Library, #230, 111 Research Dr., Saskatoon SK S7N 3R2 – 306/975-1939; Fax: 306/975-1966 – Chief Librarian, Toni Clendening

Agriculture & Agri-Food Canada-Saskatoon Research Centre – Canadian Agriculture Library, 107 Science Place, Saskatoon SK S7N 0X2 – 306/956-7222; Fax: 306/956-7247; Email: KeaneV@em.agr.ca; Symbol: SSAGR – Librarian, Van Keane

Canadian Institute for Radiation Safety - National Laboratory & Centre for Public Education – Library, #102, 110 Research Dr., Saskatoon SK S7N 3R3 – 306/975-0566; Fax: 306/975-0494 – Administrative Assistant, Colette LePoudre

Catholic Health Association of Saskatchewan – Library, 1702 - 20 St. West, Saskatoon SK S7M 0Z9 – 306/655-5330; Fax: 306/655-5333 – Secretary, Marilyn Ellis

Certified General Accountants Association of Saskatchewan – Library, #4, 2345 Ave. C North, Saskatoon SK S7L 5Z5 – 306/955-4622; Fax: 306/373-9219; Toll Free: 1-800-667-5745

Cogema Resources Inc. - Library, #817, 825 - 45 St. West, POBox 9204, Saskatoon SK S7K 3X5 – 306/343-4530; Fax: 306/343-4632 – Professional Librarian, Cathy Padfield, 306/343-4530

College of Emmanuel & St. Chad - Library, 1337 College Dr., Saskatoon SK S7N 0W6 – 306/975-1554; Fax: 306/934-2683 – Librarian, Judith Postle

Dance Saskatchewan – Library, 152 - 2nd Ave. North, POBox 8789, Saskatoon SK S7K 6S6 – 306/931-8480; Fax: 306/244-1520; Toll Free: 1-800-667-8480 – Librarian, Maria Teresa Colambani

Entomological Society of Saskatchewan – Library, Agriculture Canada Research Stn., 107 Science Pl., Saskatoon SK S7N 0X2 – 306/975-7014

Environment Canada - Canadian Wildlife Service, Prairie & Northern Wildlife Research Centre - Library, 115 Perimeter Rd., Saskatoon SK S7N 0X4 – 306/975-4096; Fax: 306/975-4089; Email: cwslibrary@ec.gc.ca; Symbol: SSECW – Library Technician, Patricia Yeudall, Email: pat.yeudall@ec.gc.ca
- National Hydrology Research Centre Library, 11 Innovation Blvd., Saskatoon SK S7N 3H5 – 306/975-5559; Fax: 306/975-5143; URL: http://www.ednet.ns.ca/educ/policy/library/homepage/library.htm; Symbol: SSEH – Library Technician, Heather Popoff

Industry Canada - Business Service Centre - Resource Library, 122 - 3 Ave. North, Saskatoon SK S7K 2H6 – 306/956-2323; Fax: 306/956-2328; Toll Free: 1-800-667-4374; Email: saskatooncsbsc@cbsc.ic.gc.ca; URL: http://www.cbsc.org/sask/ – Information Officer, Carol Tanner

Law Society of Saskatchewan - Library, Courthouse, 520 Spadina Cres. East, Saskatoon SK S7K 3G7 – 306/933-5141; Fax: 306/933-5166; Email: lawlib@link.ca – Librarian, Peta J. Bates

Learning Disabilities Association of Saskatchewan – Kinsmen Resource Centre, Albert Community Centre, #26, 610 Clarence Ave. South, Saskatoon SK S7H 2E2 – 306/652-4114; Fax: 306/652-3220 – Administrative Assistant, Sheri Gavin

Mendel Art Gallery - Library, 950 Spadina Cres. East, POBox 569, Saskatoon SK S7K 3L6 – 306/975-7611; Fax: 306/975-7670; Email: maglib@eagle.wmb.ca; URL: http://www.mendel.saskatoon.sk.ca – Librarian, Frances Daw Bergles, 306/975-8058

National Research Council-Plant Biotechnology Institute – Library, 110 Gymnasium Pl., Saskatoon SK S7N 0W9 – 306/975-5256; Fax: 306/975-6144; Email: dpammett@pbi.nrc.ca – Head, NRC Information Centre, Saskatoon, Dianne Pammett

Nutana Collegiate Institute - Memorial Library & Art Gallery, 411 - 11 St. East, Saskatoon SK S7N 0E9 – 306/683-7593; Fax: 306/683-7587 – Librarian, Ron Berntson, Email: berntson@duke.usask.ca

One Sky, The Saskatchewan Cross Cultural Centre Inc. – Resource Centre, 120 - 33 St. East, Saskatoon SK S7K 0S2 – 306/244-1146; Fax: 306/665-6520 – Librarian, Jim Bruce

Persons Living with AIDS Network of Saskatchewan Inc. – Library, POBox 7123, Saskatoon SK S7K 4J1 – 306/373-7766; Fax: 306/374-7743 – Tracie Wood

Photographers Gallery Society Inc. – Library, 12 - 23 St. East, 2nd Fl., Saskatoon SK S7K 0H5 – 306/244-8018; Fax: 306/665-6568

POS Information Services – Library, 118 Veterinary Rd., Saskatoon SK S7N 2R4 – 306/975-7066; Fax: 306/975-3766; Symbol: SSPP – Manager, Information Services, Betty Vankoughnett

Potash Corporation of Saskatchewan Inc. - Library, #500, 122 - 1 Ave. South, Saskatoon SK S7K 7G3 – 306/933-8501; Fax: 306/652-2699; Toll Free: 1-800-667-0403; Email: pcsinc@sk.sympatico.ca; URL: http://www.potash.corp.com; Symbol: SSPCT – Library Coordinator, Marybelle White

Public Health Services - Resource Centre, 101 - 310 Idylwyld Dr. North, Saskatoon SK S7L 0Z2 – 306/655-4600; Fax: 306/655-4718; Symbol: SSCHE – Resource Coordinator, Helen Beaven

Public Legal Education Association of Saskatchewan, Inc. – Library, #115, 701 Cynthia St., Saskatoon SK S7L 6B7 – 306/653-1868; Fax: 306/653-1869

Robertson Stromberg Law Office - Library, #600, 105 - 21 St. East, Saskatoon SK S7K 0B3 – 306/652-7575; Fax: 306/652-2445; Email: robertson.stromberg@sasknet.sk.ca – Library Technician, Ann Marie Melvie

St. Andrew's College - Library, 1121 College Dr., Saskatoon SK S7N 0W3 – 306/966-8983; Fax: 306/966-8981; Email: bergerman@sklib.usask.ca; Symbol: SSLL – Librarian, Joe Bergerman

St. Paul's Hospital – Library, 1702 - 20 St. West, Saskatoon SK S7M 0Z9 – 306/655-5224; Fax: 306/655-5716; Symbol: SSS – Library Technician, Colleen Haichert

St. Thomas More College - Shannon Library, 1437 College Dr., Saskatoon SK S7N 0W6 – 306/966-8962; Fax: 306/966-8904; Symbol: SSM – Librarian, Jane Morris

Saskatchewan Abilities Council – Library, 2310 Louise Ave., Saskatoon SK S7J 2C7 – 306/374-4448; Fax: 306/373-2665 – Library Clerk, Anne Cox

Saskatchewan Archaeological Society – Resource Centre, #5, 816 - 1 Ave. North, Saskatoon SK S7K 1Y3 – 306/664-4124; Fax: 306/665-1928

Saskatchewan Archives Board - Resource Centre, University of Saskatchewan, 3 Campus Dr., Saskatoon SK S7N 5A4 – 306/933-5832; Fax: 306/933-7305; Symbol: SSA – Director, D'Arcy Hande

Saskatchewan Association for Community Living – John Dolan Resource Centre, 3031 Louise St., Saskatoon SK S7J 3L1 – 306/955-3344; Fax: 306/373-3070; Email: jdolanlibrary@quadrant.net – Librarian, Lalita Martfeld

Saskatchewan Environmental Society – Library, #203, 115 - 2nd Ave. North, POBox 1372, Saskatoon SK S7K 3N9 – 306/665-1915; Fax: 306/665-2128

Saskatchewan Indian Cultural Centre – Library & Information Services, 120 - 33rd St. East, Saskatoon SK S7K 0S2 – 306/244-1146; Fax: 306/665-6520

Saskatchewan Indian Federated College - Saskatoon Campus Library, 310 - 20 St. East, Saskatoon SK S7K 0A7 – 306/931-1825; Fax: 306/665-0175
- Library Technician, April Chiefcalf
- Assistant, Yvonne Littlecrow

Saskatchewan Institute of Applied Science & Technology - Kelsey Institute Learning Resources Centre, POBox 1520, Saskatoon SK S7K 3R5 – 306/933-6417; Fax: 306/933-6490; Email: ENVOY: ILL.SSSI; Symbol: SSSI
- Librarian, T.K. Harrison
- A/V Librarian, Ethel Crosthwaite

Saskatchewan Research Council - Information Services, 15 Innovation Blvd., Saskatoon SK S7N 2X8 – 306/933-5454; Fax: 306/933-7446; Email: macleod@src.sk.ca; URL: http://www.src.sk.ca/; Symbol: SSR – Coordinator, Colleen MacLeod

Saskatchewan Teachers' Federation – Stewart Resource Centre, 2317 Arlington Ave., Saskatoon SK S7K 2H8 – 306/373-1660; Fax: 306/374-1122 – Teacher Librarian, Joan Elliott

Saskatchewan Women's Institutes – Library, #137, Kirk Hall, University of Saskatchewan, 117 Science Pl., Saskatoon SK S7N 0W0 – 306/966-5566; Fax: 306/966-8717

Saskatoon City Hospital – Medical Library, 701 Queen St., Saskatoon SK S7K 0M7 – 306/655-8228; Fax: 306/655-8727 – Library Technician, Shirley Blanchette

SED Systems Inc. - Library, 18 Innovation Blvd., POBox 1464, Saskatoon SK S7K 3P7 – 306/933-1672; Fax: 306/933-1486; Symbol: SSSED – DM Coordinator, Lynn Kennedy

Solicitor General Canada - Regional Psychiatric Centre (Prairies) - Library, POBox 9243, Saskatoon SK S7K 3X5 – 306/975-5442; Fax: 306/975-6024; Symbol: SSRP – Library Technician, Rose Brandt

Star-Phoenix Newspaper - Library, 204 - 5 Ave. North, Saskatoon SK S7K 2P1 – 306/664-8242; Fax: 306/664-0437 – Librarian, Miriam Clemence

University of Saskatchewan - Libraries, Murray Bldg., Room 103 Main Library, 3 Campus Dr., Saskatoon SK S7N 5A4 – 306/966-5927; Fax: 306/966-6040; URL: http://library.usask.ca; Symbol: CASSU
- Director of Libraries, Frank Winter
- Education Library, Education Librarian, Debbie McGugan, 306/966-5975
- Engineering Library, Head, David Salt, 306/966-5976
- Geology/Physics Library, Science Librarian, Vacant, 306/966-6049
- Health Sciences Library, Librarian, Wilma Sweaney, 306/966-5991
- Law Library, Law Librarian, Edward Stanek, 306/966-5999
- Thorvaldson Library, Librarian, Vacant, 306/966-6038
- Veterinary Medicine Library, Librarian, Ken Ladd, 306/966-7205
- Reference Librarian, Linda Fritz, 306/966-6003
- Public Services Librarian, Margaret Baldock, 306/966-5927
- Technical Services Librarian, Marian Dworaczek, 306/966-5049
- Acquisitions Librarian, Diana Kichuk

Western Development Museum - George Shepherd Library, 2935 Melville St., Saskatoon SK S7J 5A6 – 306/934-1400; Fax: 306/934-4467 – Exhibits Curator, Warren Clubb, 306/934-1400

#### SWIFT CURRENT

Agriculture & Agri-Food Canada-Semiarid Prairie Agricultural Research Centre – Canadian Agriculture Library, Airport Rd., POBox 1030, Swift Current SK S9H 3X2 – 306/778-7260; Fax: 306/773-9123; Email: wiltonk@em.agr.ca; Symbol: SSCAG – Librarian, Karen Wilton

Canadian Feed Information Centre – Library, POBox 1251, Swift Current SK S9H 3X4 – 306/773-5401; Fax: 306/773-3955 – Librarian, K. Wilton

Douglas J. Heinricks Law Office - Library, 327 Central Ave. North, POBox 1327, Swift Current SK S9H 3X4 – 306/773-7226; Fax: 306/773-5696

MacBean Tessem Law Office - Library, Box 550, 151 First Ave. NE., Swift Current SK S9H 3W4 – 306/773-9343; Fax: 306/773-3828 – Librarian, Robert J. Hale

#### WEYBURN

Souris Valley Extended Care Centre - Health Sciences Library, POBox 2003, Weyburn SK S4H 2Z9 – 306/842-8706; Fax: 306/842-7710; Symbol: SWSVC – Librarian, Melva Cooke

Weyburn & Area Early Childhood Intervention Program Inc. – Library, 415 Souris Ave., Weyburn SK S4H 0C9 – 306/842-2686; Fax: 306/842-2686 – Peggy Borshowa

Weyburn Mental Health Centre - Library, POBox 1056, Weyburn SK S4H 2L4 – 306/848-2800; Fax: 306/848-2835 – Shirley Biliak

#### WILCOX

Athol Murray College of Notre Dame - Lane Hall Memorial Library, POBox 220, Wilcox SK S0G 5E0 – 306/732-2080, ext.137 – Chief Librarian, James Williams

#### YORKTON

East Central Health District – Information Resource Centre, 270 Bradbrooke Dr., Yorkton SK S3N 2K6 – 306/786-3170; Fax: 306/782-3359; Symbol: SYU – Information Technician, Callie Pickering

Parkland Regional College - University Program & Resource Centre, 72 Melrose Ave., Yorkton SK S3N 1Z2 – 306/783-6566; Fax: 306/786-7866 – University Coordinator, Christine Hudy

## YUKON TERRITORY

### Public Libraries

Carcross: Isabelle Pringle Library, PO Box 93, Carcross YT Y0B 1B0 – 867/821-3801; Symbol: YCL

Carmacks Community Library, PO Box 131, Carmacks YT Y0B 1C0 – 867/863-5901

Dawson City Community Library, PO Box 1410, Dawson City YT Y0B 1G0 – 867/993-5571; Fax: 867/993-6112; Email: dcoffice@yknet.yk.ca; URL: http://users.yknet.yk.ca/dcpages/

Faro Community Library, PO Box 279, Faro YT Y0B 1K0 – 867/994-2684; Email: farolibrary@hotmail.com

Haines Junction Community Library, PO Box 5350, Haines Junction YT Y0B 1L0 – 867/634-2215; Email: hjpublib@hotmail.com

Mayo Community Library, PO Box 158, Mayo YT Y0B 1M0 – 867/995-2541

Pelly Crossing Community Library, Pelly Crossing YT Y0B 1P0 – 403/537-3615

Ross River Library, General Delivery, Ross River YT Y0B 1S0 – 867/969-2909

Teslin Community Library, PO Box 161, Teslin YT Y0A 1B0 – 867/390-2802; Fax: 867/390-2104; Email: tcapsite@yknet.yk.ca

Watson Lake Community Library, PO Box 390, Watson Lake YT Y0A 1C0 – 867/536-7517; Fax: 867/536-7515; Email: wlklib@hotmail.com

Whitehorse Public Library, PO Box 2703, Whitehorse YT Y1A 2C6 – 867/667-5239; Email: whselib@gov.yk.ca

### Special & College Libraries & Resource Centres

#### WHITEHORSE

Anton, Campion, Macdonald & Phillips Law Office - Library, #200, 204 Lambert St., Whitehorse YT Y1A 3T2 – 867/667-7885; Fax: 867/667-7600 – Librarian, Karen St. Pierre

Canadian Heritage - Parks Canada, Yukon National Historic Sites Library, #205, 300 Main St., Whitehorse YT Y1A 2B5 – 867/667-3910; Fax: 867/668-3780 – Manager, Program Services, Ernest Depatie, 403/667-3912

Environment Canada - Pacific & Yukon Region - Library, Mile 917.6 Alaska Hwy., Whitehorse YT Y1A 5X7 – 867/667-3407; Fax: 867/667-7962; Email: library@ywc.yk.doe.ca; Symbol: YWEEP – Librarian, Mary Martin

Indian & Northern Affairs Canada - Yukon Region Library, #345, 300 Main St., Whitehorse YT Y1A

2B5 – 867/667-3111; Fax: 867/667-3196; Email: dyrlib@yknet.yk.ca; Symbol: YWIN
Manager, Library Services, Brenda Oziewicz
Reference Librarian, Donna McBee
Industry Canada - Business Service Centre, #201, 208 Main St., Whitehorse YT Y1A 2A9 – 403/633-6257; Fax: 403/633-2533; Toll Free: 1-800-661-0543; Email: perry.debbie@cbsc.ic.gc.ca; URL: http://www.cbsc.org/yukon/
Law Society of Yukon – Library, #201, 302 Steele St., Whitehorse YT Y1A 2C5 – 403/667-3086; Fax: 867/667-7556 – Librarian, Jenny Nesbitt-Dufort
Learning Disabilities Association of Yukon Territory – Resource Centre, #205, 4133 - 4 Ave., POBox 4853, Whitehorse YT Y1A 4N6 – 867/668-5167; Fax: 867/668-6504
Public Service Alliance of Canada (CLC) - Yukon Employees Union/Syndicat des employés du Yukon – Library, 208 Strickland St., Whitehorse YT Y1A 2J8 – 867/667-2332; Fax: 867/667-6521 – Administrations Assistant, Carolyn Booker
Yukon Archives - Library, POBox 2703, Whitehorse YT Y1A 2C6 – 867/667-5321; Fax: 867/393-6253; Email: yarchive@gov.yk.ca; Symbol: YWA – Archives Librarian, Peggy D'Orsay, 403/667-5625
Yukon Chamber of Commerce – Business Service Centre, #201, 208 Main St., Whitehorse YT Y1A 2A9 – 867/667-2000; Fax: 867/667-4507; Toll Free: 1-800-661-0500 – Business Information Officer, Debby Parry
Yukon Chamber of Mines – Library, POBox 4427, Whitehorse YT Y1A 3T5 – 867/667-2090; Fax: 867/668-7127 – Office Manager, Patty O'Brien
Yukon College - Library, POBox 2799, Whitehorse YT Y1A 5K4 – 867/668-8870; Fax: 867/668-8808; Symbol: YCLIB
Manager, Rob Sutherland, Email: rsuther@yukoncollege.yk.ca
Reference Librarian, Sally Bremner
Circulation Librarian, Bente Sorenson
Public Services Librarian, Maureen Long
Technical Services Librarian, Eileen Edmunds
AV/Computers, Richard Klassen
Yukon Conservation Society – Library, 302 Hawkins St., POBox 4163, Whitehorse YT Y1A 3T3 – 867/668-5678; Fax: 867/668-6637
Yukon Economic Development - Library, POBox 2703, Whitehorse YT Y1A 2C6 – 867/667-5818; Fax: 867/667-8601; Email: margaret.donnelly@gov.yk.ca; Symbol: YWED
Librarian, Margaret Donnelly
Oil & Gas Library, Monica Woelfel, 403/667-3427
Geoscience Library, Diane Carruthers, 403/667-8808
Yukon Family Services Association – Library, 4071 - 4th Ave., Whitehorse YT Y1A 1H3 – 867/667-2970; Fax: 867/633-3557 – Office Supervisor, Haley Argen
Yukon Health & Social Services - Library, POBox 2703, Whitehorse YT Y1A 2C6 – 867/667-5919; Fax: 867/667-3096; Toll Free: 1-800-661-0408; Email: jpelchat@gov.yk.ca; Symbol: ywhhr
Librarian, Judy Pelchat
Alchohol & Drug Services Collection, J. Gauthier, 403/667-5777
Biblio-Santé, J. Wackett, 403/667-8949
Child Care Services Collection, M. Caley, 403/667-3447
Yukon Law Library, POBox 2703, Whitehorse YT Y1A 2C6 – 867/667-3086; Fax: 867/393-6301; Email: ywl@yknet.yk.ca; Symbol: YWL
Librarian, Tanya Astika
Librarian, Jenny Nesbitt-Dufort
Yukon Public Legal Education Association – Library, Yukon College, POBox 2799, Whitehorse YT Y1A 5K4 – 867/668-5297; Fax: 867/668-5541; Toll Free: 1-800-668-5297
Yukon Renewable Resources - Library, POBox 2703, Whitehorse YT Y1A 2C6 – 867/667-3029 – Contact, Kate Moylan-Smith, Email: moylan@yknet.yk.ca
Yukon Workers' Compensation Health & Safety Board - Library, 401 Strickland St., Whitehorse YT Y1A 5N8 – 867/667-8983; Fax: 867/393-6279 – Bonnie King

# BOOK PUBLISHERS

**Includes Book Publishers, Distributors, Publishers' Representatives, with ISBN (International Standard Book Number) & SAN (Standard Address Number) where available.**

49th Avenue Press
100 West 49th Ave., Vancouver BC V5Y 2Z6
604/323-5374; Fax: 604/323-5597
ISBN: 0-921218

Aardvark Enterprises (Div. of Speers Investments Ltd.)
204 Millbank Dr. SW, Calgary AB T2Y 2H9
403/256-4639
ISBN: 0-921057; ISSN: 0831-1919

Abbeyfield Publishers
33 Springbank Ave., Scarborough ON M1N 1G3
416/698-8687; Fax: 416/698-8687
Email: caamlb@inforamp.net
ISBN: 0-9680045, 0-9682274

Academic Printing & Publishing
PO Box 4218, Edmonton AB T6E 4T2
403/435-5898; Fax: 403/435-5852
Email: app@freenet.edmonton.ab.ca
ISBN: 0-920980

Acadiensis Press
Campus House, University of New Brunswick, PO Box 4400, Stn A, Fredericton NB E3B 5A3
506/453-4978; Fax: 506/453-4599
Email: acadnsis@unb.ca
ISBN: 0-919107; SAN: 115-2386

Acorn Press
PO Box 22024, Charlottetown PE C1A 9J2
902/892-8151; Fax: 902/566-0758
Email: brinklow@upei.ca
ISBN: 0-9698606

Actualisation
#705, 300, av Léo-Parizeau, CP 1142, Succ Place du Parc, Montréal QC H2W 2P4
514/284-2622; Fax: 514/284-2625
Email: formatio@actualisation.com; URL: http://www.actualisation.com
ISBN: 2-920007, 2-921547

Actuel Inc. Livres Français
492 Hurontario St., Collingwood ON L9Y 2N1
705/444-2424; Fax: 705/445-8600; Toll Free: 1-800-461-9177

Ad Astra Books
PO Box 53081, Stn Dorval, Dorval QC H9S 5W4
514/636-6080
Email: adastra@hexonx.com; URL: http://www.aero.com/adastra/
ISBN: 0-9691416

Addiction Research Foundation
33 Russell St., Toronto ON M5S 2S1
416/595-6059; Fax: 416/593-4694; Toll Free: 1-800-661-1111
Email: mktg@arf.org; URL: http://www.arf.org
ISBN: 0-88868; SAN 115-0081

Addison-Wesley Publishers Ltd.
26 Prince Andrew Pl., PO Box 580, North York ON M3C 2T8
416/447-5101, 6489 (customer service); Fax: 416/443-0948
URL: http://www.aw.com/canada
ISBN: 0-201; SAN 115-0022

Ages Publications
#153, 1054-2 Centre St., Thornhill ON L4J 8E5
905/709-3929; Fax: 905/731-1778
ISBN: 1-896280, 1-886508; SAN: 117-3103

Aggie Blinkhorn Organization Inc.
#101, 13753 - 72nd Ave., PO Box 88549, Surrey BC V3W 0X1
604/594-7607; Fax: 604/594-7289
ISBN: 0-9696248; SAN: 118-5039

Alcuin Society
PO Box 3216, Vancouver BC V6B 3X8
604/872-2376; Fax: 604/888-9052
ISBN: 0-919026

Alexis Press
PO Box 755, Guelph ON N1H 6L8
519/821-7653; Fax: 519/836-3369
Email: rlcent@sentex.net
ISBN: 0-9694159

Alive Books
Canadian Health Reform Products Ltd., 7436 Fraser Park Dr., Burnaby BC V5J 5B9
604/438-1919; Fax: 604/435-4888; Toll Free: 1-800-663-6513
Email: editorial@ultranet.ca
ISBN: 0-920470; SAN: 115-7078

Alliage éditeur
30, rue Palmerston, Mont Royal QC H3P 1V2
514/277-5456; Fax: 514/277-2934
ISBN: 2-9800671, 2-921327

Almark & Co. - Booksellers
PO Box 7, Thornhill ON L3T 3N1
905/764-2665; Fax: 905/764-2665
Email: almarkco@aol.com; URL: http://www.75711.2144@compuserve.com

Alpel Publishing
PO Box 203, Chambly QC J3L 4B3
514/658-6205; Fax: 514/658-3514
Email: alpelie@accent.net; URL: http://www.accent_net/alpelie/
ISBN: 0-9691932, 0-921993

Alter Ego Editions
3447, av Hôtel-de-Ville, Montréal QC H2X 3B5
514/849-9886; Fax: 514/849-9886
Email: alterego@rocler.qc.ca; URL: http://www.alterego.montreal.qc.ca
ISBN: 1-896743

The Alternate Press
272 Hwy. 5, RR#1, St. George ON N0E 1N0
519/448-4001; Fax: 519/448-4411
Email: natural@life.ca; URL: http://www.life.ca
ISBN: 0-920118

Althouse Press
University of Western Ontario, 1137 Western Rd., London ON N6G 1G7
519/661-2096; Fax: 519/661-3833
Email: press@edu.uwo.ca; URL: http://www.uwo.ca/edu/press
ISBN: 0-920354; SAN: 115-2440

Altitude Publishing Ltd.
1500 Railway Ave., Canmore AB T1W 1P6
403/678-6888; Fax: 403/678-6951; Toll Free: 1-800-957-6888
Email: altitude@telusplanet.net
ISBN: 1-55153

Angel Publications
#123, 3691 Albion Rd. South, Gloucester ON K1T 1P2
URL: http://www.magi.com/~angelpub/
ISBN: 1-896700

Anglican Book Centre
600 Jarvis St., Toronto ON M4Y 2J6
416/924-9192; Fax: 416/924-2760; Toll Free: 1-800-268-1168
Email: dbenson@national.anglican.ca
ISBN: 0-919030, 0-919891, 0-921846, 1-55126

Annick Press Ltd.
15 Patricia Ave., North York ON M2M 1H9
416/221-4802; Fax: 416/221-8400
Email: annickpress@powerwindows.ca
ISBN: 0-920236, 920303, 1-55037; SAN: 115-0065

Annron Sales Ltd.
#4, 5155 Spectrum Way, Mississauga ON L4W 5A1
905/624-1009; Fax: 905/624-5499; Toll Free: 1-800-668-0492

Anson-Cartwright Editions
229 College St., Toronto ON M5T 1R4
416/979-2441; Fax: 416/979-2441
Email: hac@interlog.com; URL: http://www.interlog.com/~hac
ISBN: 0-919974

Anthem Marketing & Distribution *see* Commonwealth Publications Inc.

Anvil Press
#204A, 175 East Broadway, Vancouver BC V5T 1W2
604/876-8710; Fax: 604/879-2667
Email: suber@pinc.com
ISBN: 1-895636

Apple Press Publishing
#9, 57 Glen Cameron Rd., Thornhill ON L3T 1P3
905/882-0988; Fax: 905/881-8770
ISBN: 0-919972

Aquila Communications Ltd.
2646 Diab St., St. Laurent QC H4S 1E8
514/338-1065; Fax: 514/338-1948; Toll Free: 1-800-667-7071
Email: aquila@generation.net; URL: http://www.generation.net/~aquila
ISBN: 0-88510, 2-89054; SAN: 115-2483, 115-8295

Arbor Studio Press Ltd.
PO Box 81091, Stn Lake Bonavista, Calgary AB T2J 7C9
403/271-1731; Fax: 403/278-4327
ISBN: 1-896160

Argenta Friends Press
Argenta BC V0G 1B0
250/366-4314
ISBN: 0-920367

Ariane Editions Inc.
#110, 1209, av Bernard ouest, Outremont QC H2V 1V7
514/276-2949; Fax: 514/276-2141
URL: http://www.mlink.net/~ariane
ISBN: 2-920987

Arion
10570, rue Elisabeth-II, Québec QC G2A 1Y3
418/842-4622; Fax: 418/842-4622
ISBN: 2-921493

Arnold Publishing Ltd.
11016 - 127 St., Edmonton AB T5M 0T2
403/454-7477; Fax: 403/454-7463; Toll Free: 1-800-563-2665
Email: info@arnold.ca; URL: http://www.arnold.ca
ISBN: 0-919913, 1-896081

Arsenal Pulp Press Ltd.
#103, 1014 Homer St., Vancouver BC V6B 2W9
604/687-4233; Fax: 604/669-8250
Email: arsenal@pinc.com
ISBN: 0-88978, 1-55152; SAN: 115-0847

Art Global
384, av Laurier ouest, Montréal QC H2V 2K7
514/272-6111; Fax: 514/272-8609
ISBN: 2-920718

Art Metropole
788 King St. West, Toronto ON M5V 1N6
416/703-4400; Fax: 416/703-4404
Email: art_metropole@inagg.web.net
ISBN: 0-920956; SAN: 156-9902

Artel Educational Resources Ltd.
5528 Kingsway, Burnaby BC V5H 2G2
604/435-4949; Fax: 604/435-1955; Toll Free: 1-800-665-9255
SAN: 116-029X

Artemis Enterprises
578 Ofield Rd. North, RR#2, PO Box 54, Dundas ON L9H 5E2
905/628-0596; Fax: 905/628-0596
Email: artemis@icom.ca
ISBN: 1-895247

Artery Enterprises Ltd.
#102, 1037 West Broadway, Vancouver BC V6H 1E3
604/730-2520; Fax: 604/730-7959
ISBN: 0-920431; SAN: 117-0198

Artexte Information Centre/Centre d'information Artexte
#508, 460, rue Sainte-Catherine ouest, Montréal QC H3B 1A7
514/874-0049; Fax: 514/874-0316
Email: xxartexte@canelle.telcom.uqam.ca; URL: http://www.unites.uqam.ca/bib/artexte/
ISBN: 2-98006

Ascension Books
3 Iolanta Ct., Etobicoke ON M9W 6H2
416/798-1731; Fax: 416/798-1731
ISBN: 0-929431; SAN: 117-0198

Asian Educational Services (Canada) Ltd.
1975 Fairbanks Ave., Ottawa ON K1H 5Y5
613/738-2163; Fax: 613/247-0256
Email: educa@travel-net.com; URL: http://www.travel-net.com/~educa/aesmain.htm
ISBN: 1-89675

Asquith House Limited/Michael Preston Associates
94 Asquith Ave., Toronto ON M4W 1J8
416/925-3577; Fax: 416/925-8823
Email: m.preston@sympatico.ca

Athabasca University
PO Box 10,000, Athabasca AB T9S 1A1
403/675-5864

Athena Publisher's Agency
2146 - 17 Ave. SW, Calgary AB T2T 0G3
403/245-2087; Fax: 403/245-2098

Atlantic Book Ltd.
35 Cobequid Dr., PO Box 1910, Truro NS B2N 5R1
902/895-6666; Fax: 902/893-1464
SAN: 111-0608

Augsburg Fortress Canada
#1, 216 - 40 Ave. NE, Calgary AB T2E 8C6
403/276-7000; Fax: 403/230-1165; Toll Free: 1-800-661-8379

Aviation Publishers Co. Ltd.
PO Box 1361, Stn B, Ottawa ON K1P 5R4
613/745-2943; Fax: 613/745-9851
Email: aviationpub@igs.net; URL: http://www.aviationpublishers.com
ISBN: 0-9690054

Avon Books *see* The Hearst Book Group of Canada

Aya Press *see* The Mercury Press

B. Broughton Co. Ltd.
2105 Danforth Ave., Toronto ON M4C 1K1
416/690-4777; Fax: 416/690-5357; Toll Free: 1-800-268-4449
SAN: 168-4213

Bacon & Hughes
13 Deerlane Ave., Nepean ON K2E 6W7
613/226-8136; Fax: 613/226-8121

Ballantine-Fawcett Books *see* Random House of Canada Ltd.

Balmuir Book Publishing Ltd.
128 Manning Ave., Toronto ON M6J 2K5
416/861-9129; Fax: 416/861-8702
ISBN: 0-919511; SAN: 115-6551

Banff Centre Press
The Banff Centre, PO Box 1020-50, Banff AB T0L 0C0
403/762-7532; Fax: 403/762-6699
Email: press@banffcentre.ab.ca; URL: http://www.banffcentre.ab.ca
ISBN: 0-920159

Bantam Books Canada Inc.
105 Bond St., 4th Fl., Toronto ON M5B 1Y3
416/340-0777; Fax: 416/340-1069; Toll Free: 1-800-387-5621
ISBN: 0-553; SAN: 115-1479

Bare Bones Publishing
#305, 4625 Varsity Dr. NW, Box 355, Calgary AB T3A 0Z9
403/239-7555; Fax: 403/239-0563
Email: barebones@cadvision.com
ISBN: 0-9696095, 1-896865

Barron's Educational Series Inc.
34 Armstrong Ave., Georgetown ON L7G 4R9
905/458-5506; Fax: 905/877-5575; Toll Free: 1-800-247-7160
ISBN: 0-8120; SAN: 115-2033

The Battered Silicon Dispatch Box
PO Box 204, Shelburne ON L0N 1S0
519/925-3022; Fax: 519/925-3482
Email: gav@gbd.com
ISBN: 1-896648

Battle Street Books
175 Battle St., Kamloops BC V2C 2L1
250/372-1119; Fax: 250/372-1830
URL: http://www.llnetpage.bc.ca/battlestreetbooks
ISBN: 1-896452

Beach Holme Publishers Limited
#226, 2040 West 12th Ave., Vancouver BC V6J 2G2
604/733-4868; Fax: 604/733-4860; Toll Free: 1-800-551-6655
Email: bhp@beachholme.bc.ca; URL: http://www.swifty.com
ISBN: 0-88878; SAN: 115-0812

Beacon Distributing/Cook Communications
55 Woodslee Ave., PO Box 98, Paris ON N3L 3E5
519/442-7853; Fax: 519/442-1303; Toll Free: 1-800-263-2664
Email: pape@cook.ca; URL: http://www.cook.ca
ISBN: 0-89693; SAN: 170-0197

BeJo Sales Ltd.
#52, 7050B Bramalea Rd., Mississauga ON L5S 1S9
905/677-0730; Fax: 905/677-0905; Toll Free: 1-800-668-7932
SAN: 115-2602

Bella Flor Enterprises
#3, 2250 Leckie Rd., Kelowna BC V1X 7K1
250/860-3377; Fax: 250/860-0833; Toll Free: 1-800-667-1902
Email: bellaflor@okanagan.net

Ben-Simon Publications
PO Box 318, Brentwood Bay BC V0S 1A0
250/652-6332; Fax: 250/652-6332
Email: bensimon@simon-sez.com; URL: http://www.simon-sez.com
ISBN: 0-920808; SAN: 115-2637

Benben Publications
1483 Carmen Dr., Mississauga ON L5G 3Z2
905/274-4380
ISBN: 0-920808

Bendall Books
PO Box 115, Mill Ray BC V0R 2P0
250/743-2946; Fax: 250/743-2910
Email: bendallbooks@islandnet.com; URL: http://www.islandnet.com/bendallbooks
ISBN: 0-9696985

Bergman & Associates Inc.
731 South Dr., Winnipeg MB R3T 0C2
204/475-0652; Fax: 204/475-6515
Email: ephb@compuserve.com

The Best of Bridge Publishing Ltd.
6037 - 6 St. SE, Calgary AB T2H 1L8
403/252-0119; Fax: 403/252-0206
ISBN: 0-9690425

Betelgeuse Books
#193, 55 McCaul St., Toronto ON M5T 2W7
ISBN: 0-9690783

Between the Lines
#404, 720 Bathurst St., Toronto ON M5S 2R4
416/535-9914; Fax: 416/535-1484
Email: mamorris@web.apc.org; URL: http://www.btl.on.ca
ISBN: 0-919946, 0-921284; SAN: 115-0189

Bilkin Enterprises Ltd.
4853 Brentlawn Dr., Burnaby BC V5C 3V4
604/291-2459; Fax: 604/291-1855
Email: wanatoos@direct.ca
ISBN: 0-9680199
Black Moss Press
2450 Byng Rd., PO Box 143, Stn A, Windsor ON N9A 6K1
519/252-2551; Fax: 519/253-7809
ISBN: 0-88753; SAN: 115-2645
Black Rose Books
PO Box 1258, Stn Place du Parc, Montréal QC H2W 2R3
514/844-4076; Fax: 514/849-1956
Email: blackrose@web.apc.org; URL: http://www.webnet/blackrosebooks
Blizzard Publishing Ltd.
73 Furby St., Winnipeg MB R3B 2C2
204/775-2923; Fax: 204/775-2947; Toll Free: 1-800-694-9256
Email: atwood@blizzard.mb.ca; URL: http://www.blizzard.mb.ca/catalog
ISBN: 0-921368
Blue Nun Press
3226 Midland Pl., Duncan BC V9L 4H7
250/748-4545
Blue Ribbon Bookhouse
PO Box 158, Shakespeare ON N0B 2P0
519/655-3360; Fax: 519/655-3167
ISBN: 0-895; SAN: 115-1878
Book Express
8680 Cambie St., Vancouver BC V6P 6M9
604/323-7106; Fax: 604/323-7109; Toll Free: 1-800-663-5714
Email: info@raincoast.com
SAN: 115-0871
The Book Room
1546 Barrington St., PO Box 272, Halifax NS B3J 2N7
902/423-8271; Fax: 902/423-0398; Toll Free: 1-800-387-2665
ISBN: 0-9690177, 0-9682065; SAN: 168-020X
Bookfellows
3404 Connorton Lane, Victoria BC V8P 3K1
250/380-2665; Fax: 250/380-2664
Bookworm Literary Productions
PO Box 2095, Kingston ON K7L 5J8
613/544-6946
Borealis/Tecumseh Presses Ltd.
9 Ashburn Dr., Ottawa ON K2E 6N4
613/224-6837; Fax: 613/829-7783
ISBN: 0-919594, 0-88887
Boston Mills Press
132 Main St., Erin ON N0B 1T0
519/833-2407; Fax: 519/833-2195
URL: http://www.boston-mills.on.ca
ISBN: 0-919822, 0-919783, 1-55046; SAN: 115-0138
Bow-Dell Publishing Ltd.
PO Box 40620, Stn UpperBrant, Burlington ON L7P 4W1
905/333-9049; Fax: 905/333-6780
SAN: 115-270X
Bradley Publications
2352 Smith St., Regina SK S4P 2P6
306/525-3305; Fax: 306/757-1810
Braun & Braun Educational Enterprise Ltd.
PO Box 84129, Stn Market Mall, Calgary AB T2A 5C4
403/282-1584; Fax: 403/282-1584
ISBN: 0-9690605
Breakwater Books Ltd.
(Breakwater Educational Consortium)
100 Water St., PO Box 2188, St. John's NF A1C 6E6
709/722-6680; Fax: 709/753-0708; Toll Free: 1-800-563-3333
Email: breakwater@nfld.com; URL: http://www.nfld.com/~krose/breakw.htm
ISBN: 0-919519, 0-920911, 1-55081; SAN 115-0154
Brendan Kelly Publishing Inc.
2122 Highview Dr., Burlington ON L7R 3X4
905/335-5954; Fax: 905/335-5104
Email: bkelly@hookup.net
ISBN: 1-895997
Breton Books
RR#1, Wreck Cove, Victoria County, Englishtown NS B0C 1H0
902/539-5140, 929-2372; Fax: 902/539-9117
Email: speclink@atcom.com
ISBN: 1-895415
Brick Books
431 Boler Rd., PO Box 20081, London ON N6K 4G6
519/657-8579; Fax: 519/657-8579
Email: brick.books@sympatico.ca
ISBN: 0-919626; SAN: 115-0162
Broadview Press
PO Box 1243, Peterborough ON K9J 7H5
705/743-8990; Fax: 705/743-8353
Email: 75322.44@compuserve.com; URL: http://www.broadviewpress.com
Western Office: #627, 604 - 1st St. SW, Calgary AB T2P 1M7
403/232-6863; Fax: 403/233-0001
ISBN: 0-921149, 1-55111; SAN: 115-6772
Broken Jaw Press *see* Maritimes Arts Projects Productions
Broquet inc./Broquet Publishing Company Inc.
418, ch des Frênes, L'Acadie QC J2Y 1J1
514/357-9626; Fax: 514/357-9625
Email: broquet@stjeannet.ca; URL: http://www.stjeannet.ca/broquet
ISBN: 2-89000
Brucedale Press
PO Box 2259, Port Elgin ON N0H 2C0
519/832-6025; Fax: 519/389-4962
ISBN: 0-9698716, 1-896922
BRYCEFINLEY
501 Dupee Rd., Christina Lake BC V0H 1E3
604/442-7107
Email: bfinley@awinc.com
ISBN: 1-896245
Bungalo Books
#100, 17 Elk Ct., Kingston ON K7M 7A4
613/389-2494; Fax: 613/389-2351
Email: bungalo@cgocable.net; URL: http://www.bungalobooks.com
ISBN: 0-921285
Bunker to Bunker Books
34 Blue Spruce Cres., Winnipeg MB R2M 4C2
204/255-5843; Fax: 204/255-8537
ISBN: 0-9699039
Burgher Books
#504, 555 Richmond St. West, Toronto ON M5V 3B1
416/504-3471; Fax: 416/504-6604
Email: info@burgher.com
Butterfly Books Ltd.
PO Box 294, Maple Creek SK S0N 1N0
Butterworths Canada Ltd.
75 Clegg Rd., Markham ON L6G 1A1
905/479-2665; Fax: 905/479-2826; Toll Free: 1-800-668-6481
Email: info@butterworths.ca; URL: http://www.butterworths.ca
Western Office: #1721, 808 Nelson St., Vancouver BC V6Z 2H2
604/684-4116; Fax: 604/682-5779
ISBN: 0-409, 0-433; SAN: 115-2750
C. Kirkness Press
93B Woodbridge Ave., PO Box 56510, Woodbridge ON L4L 8V3
905/851-4660; Fax: 905/851-5507
ISBN: 0-86596, 0-04150
Caboodle & Co.
217 Pickering St., Toronto ON M4E 3J9
416/699-0669; Fax: 416/699-2651
ISBN: 0-9694654
Cacanadadada Press *see* Ronsdale Press
The Caitlin Press
PO Box 2387, Stn B, Prince George BC V2N 2S6
250/964-4953; Fax: 250/964-4953
Email: caitlin_press@bc.sympatico.ca
ISBN: 0-920576; SAN: 115-2793
Callawind Publications Inc./Publications Callawind inc.
#205, 3383, boul Sources, Dollard-des-Ormeaux QC H9B 1Z8
514/685-9109; Fax: 514/685-7055
Email: info@callawind.com; URL: http://www.callawind.com
ISBN: 1-896511
Camden House Publishing
Harrowsmith Country Life, #100, 25 Sheppard Ave. West, Toronto ON M2N 6S7
416/733-7600; Fax: 416/733-7981; Toll Free: 1-800-267-7833
ISBN: 0-920656, 0-921820; SAN: 115-7086
Campbell Communications Inc.
#1, 1218 Langley St., Victoria BC V8W 1W2
250/388-7231; Fax: 250/383-1140
Email: frocus@octonet.com
ISBN: 1-895297
Can-Ed Media Ltd.
43 Moccasin Trail, North York ON M3C 1Y5
416/445-3900; Fax: 416/445-9976
ISBN: 0-920102
Canada Communications Group Publishing/Groupe Communication Canada - Édition
Dept. of Public Works & Government Services Canada, #D2200, 45, boul Sacre-Coeur, Hull QC K1A 0S9
819/956-4800; Fax: 819/994-1498
Email: publishing@ccg.gcc.ca; URL: http://www.ccg.gcc.ca
ISBN: 0-662, 0-660; SAN: 115-2882
Canada Law Book Inc.
240 Edward St., Aurora ON L4G 3S9
905/841-6472; Fax: 905/841-5085; Toll Free: 1-800-263-2037
URL: http://www.canadalawbook.ca
ISBN: 0-88804
Canada Publishing Corporation
164 Commander Blvd., Agincourt ON M1S 3C7
416/293-8141; Fax: 416/293-9009
ISBN: 0-7715, 7705
Canadian Almanac & Directory Publishing Company
200 Adelaide St. West, 3rd Fl., Toronto ON M5H 1W7
416/597-1616; Fax: 416/597-1617, 8941; Toll Free: 1-800-815-9417
Email: info@mail.canadainfo.com; orders@mail.canadainfo.com; URL: http://www.canadainfo.com
ISBN: 1-895021
Canadian Book Review Annual
#3205, 44 Charles St. West, Toronto ON M4Y 1R8
416/961-8537; Fax: 416/961-1855
Email: cbra@interlog.com; URL: http://www.interlog.com/~cbra
ISBN: 0-9697390
Canadian Caboose Press
(Good Medicine Books)
PO Box 844, Skookumchuck BC V0B 2E0
ISBN: 0-920698
Canadian Educators' Press
1230 White Clover Way, Mississauga ON L5V 1K7
905/826-0578; Fax: 905/826-0578
ISBN: 1-896191
Canadian Manda Group
#105, One Atlantic Ave., Toronto ON M6K 3E7
416/516-0911; Fax: 416/516-0917
Email: manda@sympatico.ca

Canadian News
1530 Erin St., Winnipeg MB R3E 3K5
204/786-3465; Fax: 204/772-1316

Canadian Paperbacks Publishing Ltd.
17 Gwynne Ave., Ottawa ON K1Y 1X1
613/722-1171
ISBN: 0-919554

Canadian Professional Information Centre Ltd.
#108, 6200 Dixie Rd., Mississauga ON L5T 2E1
905/670-1250; Fax: 905/670-1252
Email: web@idirect.com

Canadian Scholars' Press Inc.
#402, 180 Bloor St. West, Toronto ON M5S 2V6
416/929-2774; Fax: 416/929-1926
Email: info@cspi.org
ISBN: 0-921627, 1-55130

Canadian Stage and Arts Publications Limited
104 Glenrose Ave., Toronto ON M4T 1K8
416/484-4534; Fax: 416/484-6214
Email: kbell@interlog.ca
ISBN: 0-919952

CANAV Books
51 Balsam Ave., Toronto ON M4E 3B6
416/698-7559; Fax: 416/693-4344
ISBN: 0-9690703

Canbook Distribution Services
1220 Nicholson Rd., Newmarket ON L3Y 7B1
905/713-3852; Fax: 1-800-363-2665; Toll Free: 1-800-399-6858

Captus Press
York University Campus, 4700 Keele St., North York ON M3J 1P3
416/736-5537; Fax: 416/736-5793
Email: info@captus.com; URL: http://www.captus.com
ISBN: 0-921801, 1-895712

Caravan Books Co. Ltd.
121 Lee Ave., Toronto ON M4E 2P2
416/298-9540, 9541; Fax: 416/298-9541
Warehouse & Showroom: #1, 70 Weybright Ct., Scarborough ON M1S 4E4
416/298-9540, 9541; Fax: 416/298-9541
SAN: 115-3048

Cariad Ltd.
#1103, 89 Isabella St., Toronto ON M4Y 1N8
416/924-1918; Fax: 416/962-9966

Carib-Can Communications Inc.
555 Bloor St. W., 2nd Fl., Toronto ON M5S 1Y6
416/531-3414; Fax: 416/531-3197
Email: ccrc@ccrc.org
ISBN: 0-920997

Carleton University Press Inc.
Carleton University, #1400, 1125 Colonel By Dr., Ottawa ON K1S 5B6
613/788-3740; Fax: 613/788-2893
Email: cu_press@carleton.ca
ISBN: 0-88629; SAN: 115-3056

Carraig Books/Livres Carraig
PO Box 8733, Ste. Foy QC G1V 4N6
418/651-5918
ISBN: 0-9690805

Carswell
One Corporate Plaza, 2075 Kennedy Rd., Scarborough ON M1T 3V4
416/609-8000; Fax: 416/298-5094; Toll Free: 1-800-387-5351
URL: http://www.carswell.com/carswell.home
Distribution Centre: 245 Bartley Dr., Toronto ON M4A 2V8
416/759-4411; Fax: 416/759-5415; Toll Free: 1-800-387-5164
ISBN: 0-459, 0-88820; SAN: 115-0316

Castlefield Press
892 Castlefield Ave., Toronto ON M6B 1C8
416/782-3116; Fax: 416/782-3116
Email: 75533.3202@compuserve.com
ISBN: 0-9632554; SAN: 119-6251

Cavendish Books Inc.
#5, 801 West 1st St., North Vancouver BC V7P 1A4
604/985-2969; Fax: 604/985-2955; Toll Free: 1-800-665-3166
Email: sales@cavendishbooks.com; URL: http://www.gardenbooks.com
ISBN: 0-929050; SAN: 115-0944

CCH Canadian Limited
#300, 90 Sheppard Ave. East, North York ON M2N 6X1
416/224-2224; Fax: 416/224-2243; Toll Free: 1-800-461-4131
URL: http://www.ca.cch.com/
ISBN: 0-88796, 1-55141; SAN: 115-2785

C.D. Howe Institute
125 Adelaide St. East, Toronto ON M5C 1L7
416/865-1904; Fax: 416/865-1866
Email: cdhowe@cdhowe.org; URL: http://www.cdhowe.org
ISBN: 0-88806; SAN: 115-0502

Cedar Cave Publishing
PO Box 867, Stn F, Toronto ON M4Y 2N7
416/657-8621; Fax: 416/658-0327
Email: iw@io.org
ISBN: 0-929403

Centax Books & Distribution
1150 - 8th Ave., Regina SK S4R 1C9
306/525-2304; Fax: 306/757-2439; Toll Free: 1-800-236-6438
Email: centax@printwest.com; URL: http://www.printwest.com/centax
ISBN: 0-919845, 1-895292, 1-894022; SAN: 115-1630

Chapters Inc.
90 Ronson Dr., Etobicoke ON M9W 1C1
416/243-3138; Fax: 416/243-8964
ISBN: 0-7740; SAN: 115-3102

Charlemagne Press
1384 Hope Rd., North Vancouver BC V7P 1W7
604/988-7724; Fax: 604/984-7718
Email: coadpuppet@aol.com
ISBN: 0-921845

The Charlton Press
2010 Yonge St., Toronto ON M4S 1Z9
416/488-1418; Fax: 416/488-4656; Toll Free: 1-800-442-6042
Email: charltonpress@charltonpress.com; URL: http://www.charltonpress.com
ISBN: 0-88968: SAN: 115-0235

Chenelière/McGraw Hill
215, rue Jean-Talon est, Montréal QC H2R 1S9
514/273-1066; Fax: 514/276-0324
Email: chene@dlcmcgrawhill.ca
ISBN: 2-89310, 2-89461

Cherev Canada Inc.
RR#3, PO Box 698, Markdale ON N0C 1H0
519/986-4353; Fax: 519/986-3103; Toll Free: 1-800-263-2408
Email: cherevca@headwaters.com

The Chessnut Press/Éditions Fou des Échecs
7306, rue Sherbrooke ouest, Montréal QC H4B 1R7
514/489-6733; Fax: 514/485-3828
Email: drknight@odyssee.net; URL: http://www.odyssee.net/~drknight
ISBN: 0-919848

Child's Play
c/o Vanwell Publishing, 1 Northrup Cres., PO Box 2131, St Catharines ON L2R 7S2
905/937-3100; Fax: 905/937-1760
ISBN: 0-85953

Childe Thursday
29 Sussex Ave., Toronto ON M5S 1J6
416/979-2544
ISBN: 0-920459

The Children's Book Store
2532 Yonge St., Toronto ON M4P 2H7
416/480-0233; Fax: 416/480-9345; Toll Free: 1-800-265-5622
Email: cbs@imforamp.net

Christie & Christie Associates
261 Alice St., Kincardine ON N2Z 2P9
519/396-9553; Fax: 519/396-9554; Toll Free: 1-800-263-1991

Christie Communications
#1002, 10611 - 98 Ave., Edmonton AB T5K 2P7
403/424-4433; Fax: 403/424-4888
Email: christie@mrg.sas.ab.ca
ISBN: 0-929099

Claude M. Diffusion Ltd.
1544, rue Villeray, Montréal QC H2E 1H1
514/376-9723; Fax: 514/727-0899

CMC Distribution
590 York Rd., Niagara-on-the-Lake ON L0S 1J0
905/641-0631; Fax: 905/641-8824; Toll Free: 1-800-387-6950

Coach House Books
401 Huron St., Toronto ON M5S 2G5
416/979-2217; Fax: 416/977-1158
Email: chp@chbooks.com; URL: http://www.chbooks.com

Coïncidence/Jeunesse
60, rue Lorrain, CP 143, Iberville QC J2X 4J5
514/346-6958; Fax: 514/347-6727
ISBN: 2-89397

Coles Publishing *see* Chapters Inc.

Colombo & Company
42 Dell Park Ave., Toronto ON M6B 2T6
416/782-6853; Fax: 416/782-0285
Email: jrc@inforamp.net; URL: http://www.inforamp.net/~JRC
ISBN: 1-896308

Commoners' Publishing Society Inc.
73 Eccles St., Ottawa ON K1R 6S5
613/238-3699; Fax: 613/238-3491
ISBN: 0-88970; SAN: 115-0243

Commonwealth Publications Inc.
9764 - 45th Ave., Edmonton AB T6E 5C5
403/465-7316; Fax: 403/432-9409
Email: cpub@worldgate.com; URL: http://www.commonwealthpub.com

The Communications Project
9 Lobraico Lane, Whitchurch-Stouffville ON L4A 7X5
905/640-8914; Fax: 905/640-2922
ISBN: 1-896232

Company's Coming Publishing Limited
PO Box 8037, Stn F, Edmonton AB T6H 4N9
403/450-6223; Fax: 403/450-1857
URL: http://www.companyscoming.com
ISBN: 0-9690695, 1-895444; SAN: 115-3129

Computofacts
209 Sheppard Ave. East, North York ON M2N 5W2
416/222-4361
ISBN: 0-919640; SAN: 115-3137

Continental Records Co. Ltd.
PO Box 2604, Brampton ON L6T 5M6
905/450-6660; Fax: 905/457-9417; Toll Free: 1-800-494-6129
Email: conrecs@gocontinental.com; URL: http://www.gocontinental.com
ISBN: 0-920325

Copp Clark Ltd. *see* Addison-Wesley Publishers Ltd.

Copp Clark Professional
200 Adelaide St. West, 3rd Fl., Toronto ON M5H 1W7
416/597-1616; Fax: 416/597-1617; Toll Free: 1-800-815-9417
Email: info@mail.canadainfo.com; URL: http://www.coppclark.com

Cordillera Publishing Co.
8415 Granville St., PO Box 46, Vancouver BC V6P 4Z9
604/261-1695; Fax: 604/266-4469
ISBN: 1-895590

Cormorant Books Inc.
RR#1, Dunvegan ON K0C 1J0
613/527-3348; Fax: 613/527-2262

Email: cormoran@glen-net.ca
ISBN: 0-920953, 1-896951; SAN: 115-4176
Coteau Books/Thunder Creek Publishing Cooperative
#401, 2206 Dewdney Ave., Regina SK S4R 1H3
306/777-0170; Fax: 306/522-5152; Toll Free: 1-800-440-4471
Email: coteau@coteau.unibase.com; URL: http://www.coteau.unibase.com
ISBN: 0-919926, 0-55050; SAN: 115-0391
Cottage Life Books
#408, 111 Queen St. East, Toronto ON M5C 1S2
416/360-6880; Fax: 416/360-6814
Email: zikovitz@cotagelife.com
ISBN: 0-9696922
La Courte Échelle
5243, boul Saint-Laurent, Montréal QC H2T 1S4
514/274-2004; Fax: 514/270-4160
ISBN: 2-89021, 2-7625; SAN: 116-0249
Crabtree Publishing Co. Ltd.
360 York St., RR#4, Niagara on the Lake ON L0S 1J0
905/682-5221; Fax: 905/682-7166
Email: marketng@crabtree-pub.com; URL: http://www.crabtree-pub.com
ISBN: 0-86505; SAN: 115-1436
Crane Editions
PO Box 460, Dundurn SK S0K 1K0
306/492-2128; Fax: 306/492-2202
ISBN: 1-895285
Creative Book Publishing Ltd.
PO Box 8660, St. John's NF A1B 3T7
709/722-8500; Fax: 709/722-2228
ISBN: 0-920021, 1-895387
Creative Bound Inc.
151 Tansley Dr., PO Box 424, Carp ON K0A 1L0
613/831-3641; Fax: 613/831-3643
Email: baird@igs.net
ISBN: 0-921165; SAN: 116-7413
Cross Canada Books
354 Wellesley St. East, PO Box 550, Stn P, Toronto ON M5S 2T1
416/925-7807; Fax: 416/925-7807
Crown Publications Inc.
521 Fort St., Victoria BC V8W 1E7
250/386-4636; Fax: 250/386-0221
Email: crown@pinc.com; URL: http://www.com/crownpub/
ISBN: 0-9696417
Culture Concepts Inc.
69 Ashmount Cres., Toronto ON M9R 1C9
416/245-8119; Fax: 416/245-3383
Email: cultureconcepts@sympatico.ca; URL: http://www3.sympatico.ca/cultureconcepts
ISBN: 0-921472
Daillac éditeur
99, rue Beaumont ouest, Saint-Bruno QC J3V 2P3
514/653-7226
ISBN: 2-9801025
Dance Collection Danse Press/es
145 George St., Toronto ON M5A 2M6
416/365-3233; Fax: 416/365-3169; Toll Free: 1-800-665-5320
Email: dancecol@web.net; URL: http://www.dancecollection.danse.on.ca/dancecol
ISBN: 0-929003
David C. Cook Publishing (Canada) Ltd. *see* Beacon Distributing/Cook Communications
Davis Press
6060 Doulton Ave., Richmond BC V7C 4Y4
604/277-6003; Fax: 604/277-6003
ISBN: 0-895209; SAN: 115-7588
D.C. Books/Livres DC
950, rue Decarie, PO Box 662, Montréal QC H4L 4V9
514/843-8130
ISBN: 0-919688; SAN: 115-8988
D.C. Heath Canada Ltd. *see* ITP Nelson

Décarie éditeur inc.
233, av Dunbar, Mont-Royal QC H3P 2H4
514/343-8500; Fax: 514/342-3982
ISBN: 2-89137
Dempsey - Your Distributor Inc.
#200, 1396 Richards St., Vancouver BC V6B 3G6
604/683-5541; Fax: 604/683-5521; Toll Free: 1-800-667-3399
Detselig Enterprises Ltd.
#210, 1220 Kensington Rd. NW, Calgary AB T2N 3P5
403/283-0900; Fax: 403/283-6947
Email: temeron@telusplanet.net
ISBN: 0-920490, 1-55059; SAN: 115-0324
Deutsche Buch-Gesellschaft
475 Dominion St., Winnipeg MB R3G 2N1
204/774-7157; Fax: 204/783-4100
SAN: 115-3250
Development Press
5096 Catalina Terrace, Victoria BC V8Y 2A5
250/658-1323; Fax: 250/658-8110
Email: connor@connor.bc.ca; URL: http://www.cibbir,bc,ca/~connor
ISBN: 0-929136
Didacta Inc.
1228, rue St-Mathieu, Montréal QC H3H 2H7
514/931-0707; Fax: 514/931-0708
ISBN: 2-89199; SAN: 115-3269
Diffulivre Inc.
817, rue McCaffrey, St-Laurent QC H4T 1N3
514/738-2911; Fax: 514/738-8512
Email: diffulivre@interlink.net
Diffusion Dimedia Inc.
539, boul Lebeau, Montréal QC H4N 1S2
514/336-3941; Fax: 514/331-3916
Email: dimedia@infopuq.uquebec.ca
Diffusion Inter-livres enr.
1703, av Belleville, Lemoyne QC J4P 3M2
514/465-0037; Fax: 514/923-8966
Diffusion du Livre Mirabel
5757, rue Cypihot, St-Laurent QC H4S 1R3
514/334-2690; Fax: 514/334-4720; Toll Free: 1-800-263-3678
Email: erpidlm@odyssee.net
ISBN: 0-88527
Diffusion Prologue
1650, boul Lionel-Bertrand, Boisbriand QC G7E 4H4
514/434-0306; Fax: 514/434-2627; Toll Free: 1-800-363-2864
Diffusion et Promotion du Livre Universitaire Inc. (DPLU)
#112, 5165, rue Sherbrooke ouest, Montréal QC H4A 1T6
514/484-3940; Fax: 514/484-9325
Diffusion Raffin, inc.
7870, rue Fleuricourt, St-Léonard QC H1R 2L3
514/325-5553; Fax: 514/325-7329; Toll Free: 1-800-361-4293
Diffusion Rive-nord
1977, boul Industriel, Laval QC H7S 1P6
514/662-1975; Fax: 514/662-2125
Diffusion Soussan Edilivre Inc.
5740, rue Ferrier, Ville Mont-Royal QC H4P 1H7
514/738-0202; Fax: 514/738-5102
ISBN: 2-89393
Distican Inc.
35 Fulton Way, Richmond Hill ON L4B 2N4
905/764-0073; Fax: 905/764-0086; Toll Free: 1-800-268-3216
Email: order_desk@distican.com
DMH Limited Editions
PO Box 181, Noelville ON P0M 2N0
705/898-2055
ISBN: 1-896620
DMR Distribution Inc.
3700A, boul St-Laurent, Montréal QC
514/499-0072; Fax: 514/499-0851

Doubleday Canada Ltd.
105 Bond St., Toronto ON M5B 1Y3
416/340-0777; Fax: 416/340-1069; Toll Free: 1-800-387-5621
URL: http://www.bold.com
ISBN: 0-385; SAN: 115-0340
Douglas & McIntyre Ltd.
Adult Trade Division, 1615 Venables St., Vancouver BC V5L 2H1
604/254-7191; Fax: 604/254-9099; Toll Free: 1-800-667-6902
Email: dm@douglas-mcintyre.com
ISBN: 0-88894, 1-55054; SAN: 115-1886, 115-2270
Doutre et Vandal, editeurs *see* Groupe Beauchemin, éditeur ltée
Dovehouse Editions Inc.
1890 Fairmeadow Cres., Ottawa ON K1H 7B9
613/731-7601
ISBN: 0-919473, 1-895537
Dragon Hill Publishing
5541 - 39th Ave., Edmonton AB T6L 1B7
403/465-5279; Fax: 403/466-3999
Email: dragon@superiway.net
ISBN: 1-896124
Dundurn Press Ltd.
#200, 8 Market St., Toronto ON M5E 1M6
416/214-5544; Fax: 416/214-5556; Toll Free: 1-800-565-9523
Email: orders@dundurn.com
ISBN: 0-919670, 1-55002, 0-88924, 1-895681, 0-88882, 0-969054
Durkin Hayes Publishing Ltd.
3375 North Service Rd., #B7, Burlington ON L7N 3G2
905/335-0393; Fax: 905/332-3008; Toll Free: 1-800-263-5224
ISBN: 0-88625, 0-88646, 1-55204; SAN: 115-3765
Earthscan Canada
225 Brunswick Ave., Toronto ON M5S 2M6
416/978-5602; Fax: 416/978-3824
Email: earthscan@nextcity.com; URL: http://www.nextcity.com/earthscan/pubearth.htm
ISBN: 185383; SAN: 116-838X
Ecrits des Forges
PO Box 335, Trois-Rivières QC G9A 5G4
819/379-9813; Fax: 819/376-0774
ISBN: 2-89046
ECW Press
(Essays on Canadian Writing)
#200, 2120 Queen St. East, Toronto ON M4E IE2
416/694-3348; Fax: 416/698-9906
Email: ecw@sympatico.ca; URL: http://www.ecw.ca/press
ISBN: 1-55022; SAN: 115-1274
Éd-Archambault-Inc.
500, rue Sainte-Catherine est, Montréal QC H2L 2C6
514/849-6201; Fax: 514/849-0764
EDIMAG inc.
CP 325, Succ Rosemont, Montréal QC H1X 3B8
514/522-2244; Fax: 514/522-6301
Email: pnadeau@edimag.com; URL: http://www.edimag.com
ISBN: 2-921207
Edipress inc.
945, av Beaumont, Montréal QC H3N 1W3
514/272-6141; Fax: 514/273-7021
Edisem Inc.
2475, av Sylva-Clapin, CP 295, Saint-Hyacinthe QC J2S 7B6
514/774-8118; Fax: 514/774-3017
ISBN: 2-89130
Les Éditions d'Acadie ltée
236, rue St-Georges, PO Box 885, Moncton NB E1C 8N8
506/857-8490; Fax: 506/855-3130
Email: edacadie@nbnet.nb.ca
ISBN: 2-7600

Éditions Adage
12306, boul O'Brien, Montréal QC H4J 1Z4
514/336-2938; Fax: 514/336-0614
ISBN: 2-9801053
Éditions Agence d'Arc *see* Groupe Éducalivres inc. - Éditions Études Vivantes
Éditions Anne Sigier inc.
1073, boul René-Lévesque ouest, Sillery QC G1S 4R5
418/687-6086; Fax: 418/687-3565; Toll Free: 1-800-463-6846
Email: sigier@megatoon.com
ISBN: 2-89129
Éditions Arts, Lettres et Techniques Inc.
901, boul Ste-Croix, Montréal QC H4L 3Y5
514/747-4784, 747-4785; Fax: 514/747-5366
Éditions Behaviora
151, ch Bellevue, CP 91, Eastman QC J0E 1P0
514/297-0515; Fax: 514/297-0516
Email: rotis@interlinx.qc.ca
ISBN: 2-7629
Éditions Bellarmin
165, rue Deslauriers, Saint-Laurent QC H4N 2S4
514/745-4290; Fax: 514/745-4299
ISBN: 0-88502, 2-89007
Éditions Bibi et Geneviève
3409, rue Saint-Antoine, Westmount QC H3Z 1X1
514/931-6190; Fax: 514/939-2034
ISBN: 2-921577
Les Éditions du Blé
CP 31, Saint-Boniface MB R3H 3B4
204/237-8200; Fax: 204/233-2373
Email: alexis@magic.mb.ca; URL: http://www.magic.mb.ca/~alexis
ISBN: 0-920640, 2-921347
Editions du Bois-de-Coulonge
1140, av de Montigny, Sillery QC G1S 3T7
418/683-6332; Fax: 418/683-6332
Email: acces@ebc.qc.ca; URL: http://www.ebc.qc.ca
ISBN: 2-9801397
Éditions du Boréal
4447, rue St-Denis, Montréal QC H2J 2L2
514/287-7401; Fax: 514/287-7664
Email: boreal@mlink.net
ISBN: 2-89052
Les Éditions Brault et Bouthillier
(B & B Publishing)
#275, 4823, rue Sherbrooke ouest, Westmount QC H3Z 1G7
514/932-9466; Fax: 514/932-5929
ISBN: 0-88537, 2-7615
Éditions Brimar Inc.
338, rue Saint-Antoine est, Montréal QC H2Y 1A3
514/954-1441; Fax: 514/954-1443
ISBN: 2-920845
Éditions Centre FORA
(Centre franco-ontarien de ressources en alphabétisation)
533, rue Notre-Dame, Sudbury ON P3C 5L1
705/673-7033; Fax: 705/673-5520
Email: yclement@centrefora.on.ca; URL: http://www.centrefora.on.ca
ISBN 2-921706
Éditions Ceres
CP 1386, Succ Place Bonaventure, Montréal QC H5A 1H3
514/937-7138; Fax: 514/937-7138
ISBN: 0-919089
Éditions de la Chenelière inc. *see* Chenelière/McGraw Hill
Les Éditions Compton
#110, 55, rue Belvédère nord, Sherbrooke QC J1H 6B2
819/562-9082
ISBN: 2-920482
Éditions Doberman inc.
CP 2021, Saint-Nicholas est QC G7A 4X5
418/831-1304; Fax: 418/836-3645
Email: pgerrits@qui.qc.ca; URL: http://www.qui.qc.ca/clients/doberman
ISBN: 2-921204; music publishers
Éditions École Active
2244, rue de Rouen, Montréal QC H2K 1L5
514/527-3425; Fax: 514/527-6713
ISBN: 2-89069
Éditions Fides
165, rue Deslauriers, Saint-Laurent QC H4N 2S4
514/745-4290; Fax: 514/745-4299
Email: editions@fides.qc.ca
ISBN: 2-7621, 2-89007
Les Éditions Flammarion Ltée
375, av Laurier ouest, Montréal QC H2V 2K3
514/277-8807; Fax: 514/278-2085
Email: flammarion@sympatico.ca; URL: http://www.flammarion.qc.ca
ISBN: 2-89077
Éditions FM
3281, av Jean-Béraud, Laval QC H7T 2L2
514/334-5912; Fax: 514/688-6269; Toll Free: 1-800-361-4504
URL: http://www.beauchemin.qc.ca
ISBN: 2-89047, 0-88519
Les Éditions Françaises inc.
1411, rue Ampère, Boucherville QC J4B 5Z5
514/641-0514; Fax: 514/641-4893; Toll Free: 1-800-361-9635
ISBN: 0-7756; SAN: 115-7756
Éditions La Frégate inc.
CP 157, Succ H, Montréal QC H3G 2K7
514/481-6368; Fax: 514/683-5014
ISBN: 2-920047
Les Éditions Ganesha inc.
CP 484, Succ Youville, Montréal QC H2P 2W1
514/641-2395; Fax: 514/641-2989
ISBN: 2-89145
Les Éditions le Griffon d'argile
7649, boul Wilfrid-Hamel, Ste-Foy QC G2G 1C3
418/871-6898; Fax: 418/871-6818
URL: http://www.griffondargile.com
ISBN: 2-920210, 2-920922, 2-89443
Éditions les Herbes rouges
#304, 3575, boul St-Laurent, Montréal QC H2X 2T7
514/845-4039; Fax: 514/845-3629
ISBN: 2-89419
Les Éditions Heritage
300, rue Arran, Saint-Lambert QC J4R 1K5
514/875-0327; Fax: 514/672-5448
ISBN: 2-7625, 0-7773
Les Éditions de l'Hexagone
1010, rue de la Gauchetière est, Montréal QC H2L 2N5
514/523-1182; Fax: 514/282-7530
ISBN: 2-89006, 2-89295
Éditions de l'Homme *see* Sogides Ltée
Éditions Hurtubise HMH Ltée
1815, av De Lorimier, Montréal QC H2K 3W6
514/523-1523; Fax: 514/523-5955; Toll Free: 1-800-361-1664
ISBN: 2-89045, 2-89428
Les Éditions l'Image de l'art
3281, av Jean-Béraud, Montréal QC H7T 2L2
514/334-5912; Toll Free: 1-800-361-2598
URL: http://www.beauchemin.qc.ca
ISBN: 2-920822, 2-9211370, 2-921580
Éditions de l'Instant même
865, av Moncton, Québec QC G1S 2Y4
418/527-8690; Fax: 418/681-6780
ISBN: 2-921197
Les Éditions internationales Alain Stanké ltée
1212, rue St-Mathieu, Montréal QC H3H 2H7
514/935-7452; Fax: 514/931-1627
ISBN: 2-7604, 0-88566
Les Éditions JCL inc.
930, rue Jacques-Cartier est, Chicoutimi QC G7H 2A9
418/696-0536; Fax: 418/696-3132
Email: jlc@saglac.qc.ca
ISBN: 2-89431, 2-920176
Les Éditions la Liberté inc.
3020, ch Ste-Foy, Ste-Foy QC G1X 3V6
418/658-3763; Fax: 418/658-3763; Toll Free: 1-800-567-5449
Email: liberte@mediom.qc.ca
ISBN: 2-89084
Les Éditions Libre expression ltée
2016, rue St-Hubert, Montréal QC H2L 3Z5
514/849-5259; Fax: 514/849-1388
ISBN: 2-89111
Éditions Logiques
1225, rue de Condé, Montréal QC H3K 2E4
514/933-2225; Fax: 514/933-2182
Email: logique@com.org; URL: http://www.logique.com
ISBN: 2-89381
Éditions Marie-France ltée
3651, rue Fleury est, Montréal QC H1H 2S5
514/329-3700, 3701; Fax: 514/329-0630; Toll Free: 1-800-563-6644
ISBN: 2-89168
Éditions Médiaspaul
3965, boul Henri-Bourassa est, Montréal QC H1H 1L1
514/322-7341; Fax: 514/322-4281
ISBN: 0-88840, 2-89039, 2-89420
Éditions du Meridien
#870, 550, rue Sherbrooke ouest, Montréal QC H3A 1B9
514/845-5445; Fax: 514/843-9491
ISBN: 2-920417
Les Éditions Modus vivendi inc.
(Presses Aventure)
CP 213, Succ Ste-Dorothée, Laval QC H7X 2T4
514/627-7093; Fax: 514/962-6577
ISBN: 2-92155, 2-922148 (Presses Aventure)
Éditions du Mortagne
CP 116, Boucherville QC J4B 5E6
514/641-2387; Fax: 514/655-6092
ISBN: 2-89074
Éditions Multimondes
930, rue Pouliot, Ste-Foy QC G1V 3N9
418/651-3885; Fax: 418/651-6822; Toll Free: 1-800-840-3029
Email: multimondes@multim.com; URL: http://multim.com
ISBN: 2-921146
Éditions du Nordir
17, rue Berville, CP 580, Hearst ON P0L 1N0
705/362-8964; Fax: 705/362-8964
ISBN: 2-921365
Les Éditions du Noroît
CP 156, Succ de Lorimier, Montréal QC H2H 2N6
514/563-1644; Fax: 514/563-1644
ISBN: 2-89018
Les Éditions de la nouvelle plume, coopérative ltée
PO Box 3663, Regina SK S4P 3N8
306/352-7435; Fax: 306/585-1657
URL: http://www.dicwest.com/~acfc/Associations/Nouvelleplume/nouvelleplume.html
ISBN: 2-921385
Les Éditions d'Orphée
2770, rue Darling, Montréal QC H1W 2X5
514/523-5307
ISBN: 2-89418
Éditions de la paix
125, rue Lussier, Saint-Alphonse-de-Granby QC J0E 2A0
514/375-4765; Fax: 514/375-4765
Email: editpaix@total.net; URL: http://www.net-graphe.qc.ca/editpaix
ISBN: 2-921255
Éditions Papyrus
745, av Eymard, Québec QC G1S 3Z9

418/688-9694
ISBN: 2-9800941
Éditions la Pensée inc.
#1, 4243, rue Beaubien est, Montréal QC H1T 1S5
514/593-1144; Fax: 514/593-6380; Toll Free: 1-800-667-5422
URL: http://www.lidec.qc.ca
ISBN: 2-921187
Éditions Phidal inc.
5740, rue Ferrier, Mount-Royal QC H4P 1M7
514/738-0202; Fax: 514/738-5102; Toll Free: 1-800-738-7349
ISBN: 2-89393
Editions Pierre Tisseyre *see* Éditions du Renouveau Pédagogique inc.
Les Éditions des Plaines
202, boul Provencher, CP 123, Saint-Boniface MB R2H 3B4
204/235-0078; Fax: 204/233-7741
ISBN: 0-920944, 1-895173
Les Éditions de la Pleine Lune
#223, 34e av, Lachine QC H8T 1Z4
514/637-6366; Fax: 514/637-6366
ISBN: 2-89024
Éditions Québec-Amérique
329, rue de la Commune ouest, 3e étage, Montréal QC H2Y 2E1
514/499-3000; Fax: 514/499-3010
Email: montreal@editionsqa.qc.ca
ISBN: 0-88552, 2-89037
Éditions Quebecor
7, ch Bates, Outremont QC H2V 1A6
514/270-1746; Fax: 514/270-5313
ISBN: 2-89089, 2-7640
Editions Quinze *see* VLB Éditeur
Les Éditions du Remue-Ménage inc.
#404, 4428, boul St-Laurent, Montréal QC H2W 1Z5
514/982-0730; Fax: 514/982-9831
ISBN: 2-89091
Les Éditions le Renouveau Charlesbourg inc.
870, Carré de Tracy est, CP 7605, Charlesbourg QC G1G 5W6
418/628-3445; Fax: 418/624-2277
ISBN: 2-89254
Éditions du Renouveau Pédagogique inc.
5757, rue Cypihot, Saint-Laurent QC H4S 1R3
514/334-2690; Fax: 514/334-4720; Toll Free: 1-800-263-3678
Email: erpidlm@odyssee.net
ISBN: 2-7613, 2-89041
Éditions Reynald Goulet
40, rue Mireault, Repentigny QC J6A 1M1
514/654-2626; Fax: 514/654-5433; Toll Free: 1-800-663-3021
Email: infro@goulet.ca; URL: http://www.goulet.ca
ISBN: 2-89377
Éditions du Roseau
6521, rue Louis Hémon, Montréal QC H2G 2L1
514/725-7772; Fax: 514/725-5889
ISBN: 2-920083, 2-894660
Éditions Saint-Martin
#3203, 5000, rue Iberville, Montréal QC H2H 2S6
514/529-0920; Fax: 514/529-8384
ISBN: 2-89035
Éditions Saint-Yves
CP 9638, Ste-Foy QC G1V 4C2
418/657-4399; Fax: 418/657-2096
ISBN: 2-89034
Éditions Sciences et culture inc.
5090, rue de Bellechasse, Montréal QC H1T 2A2
514/253-0403; Fax: 514/256-5078
ISBN: 2-89092, 2-920052
Les Éditions Sedes
755, rue Robitaille, Saint-Lambert QC J4P 1C5
514/465-1077; Fax: 514/465-0328
ISBN: 2-921140
Éditions du Septentrion
1300, av Maguire, Sillery QC G1T 1Z3
418/688-3556; Fax: 418/527-4978
Email: sept@zone.ca
ISBN: 2-921114, 2-89448
Les Éditions du Sphinx
CP 8742, Ste-Foy QC G1V 4N6
418/666-0548; Fax: 418/666-6336
ISBN: 2-920123
Les Éditions Thémis
Faculté de droit, Université de Montréal, CP 6128, Succ A, Montréal QC H3C 3J7
514/739-9945; Fax: 514/343-2199
ISBN 2-920376
Éditions Tormont
#300, 338, rue Saint-Antoine est, Montréal QC H2Y 1A3
514/954-1441; Fax: 514/954-1443
ISBN: 2-89429
Les Éditions Transcontinental inc.
1253, rue de Condé, Montréal QC H3K 2E4
514/925-4996; Fax: 514/933-8823; Toll Free: 1-888-933-9884
Email: bedard@mail.transc.com; URL: http://www.logique.com
ISBN: 2-921030, 2-89472
Éditions du Trécarré
817, rue McCaffrey, St Laurent QC H4T 1N3
514/738-2911; Fax: 514/738-8512
Email: diffulivre@interlink.net
ISBN: 2-89249
Éditions Trois
2033, av Jessop, Laval QC H7S 1X3
514/663-4028; Fax: 514/663-1639
Email: ed3ama@contact.net
ISBN: 2-920887
Les Éditions un Monde différent ltée
3925, boul Grand-Allée, Saint-Hubert QC J4T 2V8
514/656-2660; Fax: 514/445-9098; Toll Free: 1-800-443-CLUB
ISBN: 2-92000, 2-89225
Éditions Vents d'ouest
99, rue Montcalm, Hull QC J8X 2L9
819/770-6377; Fax: 819/770-0559
ISBN: 2-921603
Les Éditions Villes Nouvelles - Villes Anciennes
CP 192, Succ Côte-des-Neiges, Montréal QC H3S 2S5
514/733-6689
ISBN: 2-9801943
Les Éditions Yvon Blais inc.
CP 180, Cowansville QC J2K 3H6
514/266-1086; Fax: 514/263-9256; Toll Free: 1-800-363-3047
Email: cowansvillw@editionsyvonblais.qc.ca
ISBN: 0-89073, 0-89451
Ekstasis Editions
PO Box 8474, Stn Main, Victoria BC V8W 3S1
250/385-3378; Fax: 250/385-3378
Email: ekstasis@ampsc.com
ISBN: 0-921215, 1-896860
Elan Publishing Inc.
PO Box 21009, Stn Dominion SW, Calgary AB T2P 4H5
403/293-1030; Fax: 403/280-1400
ISBN: 0-9694626
Ellis Ivison & Lindsay Music Productions
PO Box 1809, Kingston ON K7L 5J6
613/542-6987; Fax: 613/542-6987
ISBN: 1-8952411
Emond Montgomery Publications Ltd.
58 Shaftesbury Ave., Toronto ON M4T 1A3
416/975-3925; Fax: 416/975-3924
Email: info@emp.on.ca; orders@emp.on.ca; URL: http://www.emp.on.ca
ISBN: 0-920722
Empyreal Press
PO Box 1746, Stn Place du Parc, Montréal QC H2W 2R7
ISBN: 0-921852
Encyclopaedia Britannica Publications Ltd.
186 Shoemaker St., PO Box 9055, Kitchener ON N2G 4X1
519/893-0499; Fax: 519/893-7106; Toll Free: 1-800-465-9439
ISBN: 0-7738; SAN: 115-1363
English Literary Studies
Dept. of English, University of Victoria, PO Box 3045, Victoria BC V8W 3P4
250/721-7237; Fax: 250/721-6498
ISBN: 0-920604; SAN: 115-3366
Ergo Productions
PO Box 4460, London ON N5W 5J2
519/432-4357
ISBN: 0-920516; SAN: 115-3374
Erin Publications
82 Edenstone View NW, Calgary AB T3A 4T5
403/239-4318; Fax: 403/239-6044
ISBN: 0-9690609
Escart Press *see* Upney Editions
L'Etincelle editeur inc. *see* Robert Davies Multimedia Publishing
Evangelical Tract Distributors
PO Box 146, Edmonton AB T5J 2G9
403/477-1538
Everyday Publications Inc.
#2, 421 Nugget Ave., Scarborough ON M1S 4L8
416/291-9411; Fax: 416/291-9411
Email: 102604.1530compuserve.com
ISBN: 0-88873, 0-919586; SAN: 115-3398
Exile Editions Ltd.
20 Dale Ave., Toronto ON M4W 1K4
416/969-8877; Fax: 416/969-9556
ISBN: 1-55096, 0-920428; SAN: 115-3404
Exportlivre
289, boul Desaulniers, Saint-Lambert QC J4P 1M8
514/671-3888; Fax: 514/671-2121
URL: http://www.cyberglake.net/users/exportlivre
Fairmount Books Ltd.
120 Duffield Dr., Markham ON L6G 1B5
905/475-0988; Fax: 905/475-1072
ISBN: 0-921372; SAN: 106-7886
Falcon's Roost
PO Box 610, Nackawic NB E3B 2T7
506/575-2460
ISBN: 0-919859
Fernwood Publishing Co. Ltd.
PO Box 9409, Stn A, Halifax NS B3K 5S3
902/422-3302; Fax: 902/422-3179
Email: esharpe@bbs.mmcs.com
ISBN: 1-895686
Fiddlehead Poetry Books *see* Goose Lane Editions
Fifth House Publishers
#201, 165 - 3rd Ave. South, Saskatoon SK S7K 1L8
306/242-4936; Fax: 306/242-7667
ISBN: 0-920079, 1-895618; SAN: 115-141X
Firefly Books Ltd.
3680 Victoria Park Ave., North York ON M2H 3K1
416/499-8412; Fax: 416/499-8313; Toll Free: 1-800-387-6192
ISBN: 0-920668; SAN: 115-3439
First Avenue Publications
1328 Avenue Rd., Toronto ON M5N 2G9
416/483-1564; Fax: 416/481-4721
ISBN: 0-9695315
Fisher House Publishing
10907 - 34A Ave., Edmonton AB T6J 2T9
403/988-0321; Fax: 403/468-2058
Email: fisher@ocii.com; URL: http://www.ocii.com/~fisher/shp.htm
ISBN: 1-896255
Fitzhenry & Whiteside Limited
195 Allstate Pkwy., Markham ON L3R 4T8

905/477-9700; Fax: 905/477-9179; Toll Free: 1-800-387-9776
Email: godwit@fitzhenry.ca; URL: http://www.fitzhenry.ca
ISBN: 0-55041, 0-88902; SAN: 115-1444
Fleurbec
198, ch de la Grande-Grillade, St-Henri-de-Lévis QC G0R 3E0
418/882-0843; Fax: 418/882-6133
Email: floraqca@versicolores.ca
ISBN: 2-920174
Formac Publishing Ltd.
5502 Atlantic St., Halifax NS B3H 1G4
902/421-7022; Fax: 902/425-0166; Toll Free: 1-800-565-1975
ISBN: 0-88780; SAN: 115-1371
Fortress Publications
221 Barton St. East, Unit B, Stoney Creek ON L8E 2K3
905/662-3505; Fax: 905/662-3855
ISBN: 0-9690486, 0-9191945; SAN: 115-3455
F.P. Hendricks Publishing Ltd.
10301 - 104 St., PO Box 756, Edmonton AB T5J 1B9
403/742-6483
Email: fphendriks_pub@wildrose.net
ISBN: 0-9699619
The Fraser Institute
626 Bute St., 2nd Fl., Vancouver BC V6E 3M1
604/688-0221; Fax: 604/688-8539
Email: infro@fraserinstitute.ca; URL: http://www.fraserinstitute.ca
ISBN: 0-88975; SAN: 115-3498
Frederick Harris Music Co. Ltd.
#1, 5865 McLaughlin Rd., Mississauga ON L5R 1B8
905/501-1595; Fax: 905/501-0929; Toll Free: 1-800-387-4013
Future Directions
7 Pittypat Ct., Aurora ON L4G 6J6
905/841-5689; Fax: 905/841-3616
ISBN: 1-896504
Gaétan Morin editeur Ltée
171, boul de Mortagne, Boucherville QC J4B 6G4
514/449-2369; Fax: 514/449-1096
ISBN: 2-89105
Gage Educational Publishing
Division of Canada Publishing Corporation
164 Commander Blvd., Scarborough ON M1S 3C7
416/293-8141; Fax: 416/293-9009; Toll Free: 1-800-667-1115
ISBN: 0-7715, 7705; SAN: 115-0375
Gale Canada
#100, 1120 Birchmount Rd., Scarborough ON M1K 5G4
416/752-7338; Fax: 416/752-9646; Toll Free: 1-800-701-9130
Garamond Press
#403, 77 Mowat Ave., Toronto ON M6K 3E3
416/516-2709; Fax: 416/533-5652
Email: garamond@web.apc.org; URL: http://www.garamond.ca/garamond
ISBN: 0-920059; SAN: 115-1339
Gaspereau Press
PO Box 143, Wolfville NS B0P 1X0
GB Publishing
PO Box 6292, Stn D, Calgary AB T2P 2C9
403/228-6897
General Publishing Co. Limited
30 Lesmill Rd., North York ON M3B 2T6
416/445-3333; Fax: 416/445-5967
ISBN: 0-7736, 0-7737; SAN: 115-0391
General Store Publishing House Inc.
One Main St., Burnstown ON K0J 1G0
613/432-7697; Fax: 613/432-7184; Toll Free: 1-800-465-6072
ISBN: 0-919431; SAN: 115-6853
Get a Life Publishing
#127, 2255B Queen St. East, Toronto ON M4E 1G3
416/699-6070; Fax: 416/536-9101
ISBN 0-9697755
Gilpin Publishing
PO Box 597, Alliston ON L9R 1V7
705/424-6507; Fax: 705/424-6507
ISBN: 0-921046
Ginn Publishing Canada Inc. *see* Prentice-Hall Canada Inc.
Global Geneological Books
158 Laurier Ave., Milton ON L9T 4S2
905/875-2176; Fax: 905/875-1887
Global Press *see* Macmillan Canada
Globe Information Services
444 Front St. West, Toronto ON M5V 2S9
416/585-5250; Fax: 416/585-5249; Toll Free: 1-800-268-9128
ISBN: 0-921925
Goddard-Zaxis Inc.
#200, 510 Front St. West, Toronto ON M5V 3H3
416/599-8975; Fax: 416/408-4704
Email: zaxis@interlog.com
Godwin Books
PO Box 4781, Vancouver BC V6B 4A4
604/988-2407; Fax: 604/984-9821
Email: thomsonr@direct.ca
ISBN: 0-9696774
Golden Books Publishing
200 Sheldon Dr., Cambridge ON N1R 5X2
519/623-3590; Fax: 519/623-3598
Email: manager@goldenbooks.com; URL: http://www.senetex.net~goldenbk
ISBN: 0-307; SAN: 115-5598
The Golden Dog Press
409 Oxford St. East, PO Box 393, Kemptville ON KOG 1J0
613/258-3882; Fax: 613/258-3882
ISBN: 0-919614
Good Medicine Books *see* Canadian Caboose Press
Goodread Biographies
5502 Atlantic St., Halifax NS B3H 1G4
902/421-7022; Fax: 902/425-0166
ISBN: 0-88780; SAN: 115-1371
Goose Lane Editions
469 King St., Fredericton NB E3B 1E5
506/450-4251; Fax: 506/459-4991
Email: gooselan@sympatico.nb.ca; URL: http://www.cygnus.nb.ca/bookstr/glane/glogo.html
ISBN: 0-919197, 0-86492, 0-920110; SAN: 115-3420
Gordon Soules Book Publishers Ltd.
1354B Marine Dr., West Vancouver BC V7T 1B5
604/922-6588; Fax: 604/688-5442
Email: books@gordonsoules.com; URL: http://www.gordonsoules.com
ISBN: 0-919574; SAN: 115-0987
Gordon V. Thompson Music
85 Scarsdale Rd., Toronto ON M3B 2R2
416/445-3131; Fax: 416/445-2473; Toll Free: 1-800-268-7736
ISBN: 1-55122; SAN: 115-7159
Gospel Publishing House
6745 Century Ave., Mississauga ON L5N 6P7
905/542-8340; Fax: 905/542-1624; Toll Free: 1-800-567-2420
SAN: 115-3528
Great Pacific News
2500 Vauxhall Pl., Richmond BC V6V 1Y8
604/278-4841; Fax: 604/278-5642
Email: gpn@direct.ca
Great Plains Publications Ltd.
#3, 161 Stafford St., Winnipeg MB R3M 2X9
204/475-6799; Fax: 204/475-6799
Email: greatplains@prodigy.com
ISBN: 0-9697804
Greey de Pencier Books *see* Owl Books
Grolier Limited
12 Banigan Dr., Toronto ON M4H 1A6
416/425-1924; Fax: 416/425-8858; Toll Free: 1-800-563-3231
Grolier limitée: 45, rue Montpellier, Saint-Laurent QC H4N 3H6
514/747-5000; Fax: 514/747-0444; Toll Free: 1-800-361-5873
Email: grolltee@infobannos.com
ISBN: 0-7172; SAN 115-3668
Grosvenor Books Canada *see* MRA Books
Grosvenor House Press Inc./Éditions Grosvenor inc.
1456, rue Sherbrooke ouest, Montréal QC H3G 1K4
514/284-1138; Fax: 514/284-0415
Email: info-ntl@pegasus.ca
Toronto office: #203, 2 Pardee Ave., Toronto ON M6K 3H5
416/532-3211; Fax: 416/532-9277
ISBN: 0-919959; SAN: 115-3684
Groundwood Books
Division of Douglas & McIntyre Ltd.
Juvenile Trade Division, 585 Bloor St. West, 2nd Fl., Toronto ON M6G 1K5
250/537-2501
ISBN: 0-88899; SAN 115-2270
Groupe Beauchemin, éditeur ltée
3281, av Jean-Béraud, Laval QC H7T 2L2
514/334-5912; Toll Free: 1-800-361-2598
Email: manon.bergeron@beauchemin.qc.ca; URL: http://www.beauchemin.qc.ca
ISBN: 2-7616, 2-89410
Groupe Communication Canada - Edition *see* Canada Communications Group Publishing
Groupe Éducalivres inc. - Éditions Études Vivantes
955, rue Bergar, Laval QC H7L 4Z7
514/334-8466; Fax: 514/334-8387
ISBN: 2-7607, 0-88586, 0-289022
Guérin éditeur ltée
4501, rue Drolet, Montréal QC H2T 2G2
514/842-3481; Fax: 514/842-4923
Email: francel@guerin-editeur.qc.ca
ISBN: 2-7601, 0-7764
Guernica Editions Inc.
PO Box 117, Stn P, Toronto ON M5S 2S6
416/658-9888; Fax: 416/657-8885
Email: 102026.1331@compuserve.com; URL: http://ourworld.compuserve.com/hompages/guernica
ISBN: 0-919349, 2-89135, 0-920717; SAN: 115-0421
Guidance Centre
712 Gordon Baker Rd., Toronto ON M2H 3R7
416/502-1262; Fax: 416/502-1101; Toll Free: 1-800-668-6247
Email: dhughes@oise.utoronto.ca; URL: http://www.utor.ca/guidance
ISBN: 0-7713; SAN: 110-2818
Gutter Press
PO Box 600, Stn Q, Toronto ON M4T 2N4
416/822-8708; Fax: 416/822-8709
Email: gutter@salzmann.com; URL: http://www.salzmann.com/gutter
ISBN: 0-9696520
Guy Saint-Jean éditeur
#200B, 674, Place Publique, Laval QC H7X 1G1
514/689-6402; Fax: 514/689-9393
Email: jacques@mlink.net
ISBN: 2-920340, 2-89455
gynergy books *see* Ragweed Press Inc./gynergy books
Hancock House Publishers Ltd.
19313 Zero Ave., Surrey BC V4P 1M7
604/538-1114; Fax: 604/538-2262; Toll Free: 1-800-938-1114
Email: hancock@uniserve.com
ISBN: 0-88839, 0-919654; SAN: 115-3730
Hans Schaffler & Co. Ltd.
#2, 1252 Speers Rd., Oakville ON L6L 5N9
905/825-2185; Fax: 905/825-2130
Email: cp507@freenet.toronto.on.ca
Harbour Publishing Co. Ltd.
PO Box 219, Madeira Park BC V0N 2H0
604/883-2730; Fax: 604/883-9451; Toll Free: 1-800-667-2988

Email: harbour@sunshine.net
ISBN: 0-920080, 1-55017
Harcourt Brace & Company Canada, Ltd.
55 Horner Ave., Toronto ON M8Z 4X6
416/255-4491; Fax: 416/255-4046; Toll Free: 1-800-387-7278
Email: hbc_can@harcourtbrace.com; URL: http://www.harcourtbrace-canada.com
ISBN: 0-7747, 0-7216; SAN: 115-1754
Hargreaves, Fuller & Company
#13, 4335 West 10th Ave., Vancouver BC V6R 2H6
604/222-2955; Fax: 604/222-2965
Harlequin Enterprises Ltd.
225 Duncan Mill Rd., Toronto ON M3B 3K9
416/445-5860; Fax: 416/445-8655, 8736; Toll Free: 1-800-387-0112
URL: http://www.romance.net
ISBN: 0-373; SAN: 115-3749
Harry Cuff Publications Ltd.
94 LeMarchant Rd., St. John's NF A1C 2H2
709/726-6590; Fax: 709/726-0902
Email: hcp@public.comusult.nf.ca
ISBN: 0-919095, 0-921191
Hartley & Marks Publishers
3661 Broadway West, Vancouver BC V6R 2B8
604/739-1771; Fax: 604/738-1913
Email: hartmark@direct.ca
ISBN: 0-88179; SAN: 115-3757
Harvest House Ltd.
#1, 1200, av Atwater, Montréal QC H3Z 1X4
514/932-0666; Fax: 514/489-4287
ISBN: 0-88772; SAN: 115-0456
H.B. Fenn and Company Ltd.
34 Nixon Rd., Bolton ON L7E 1W2
905/951-6600; Fax: 905/951-6601; Toll Free: 1-800-267-3366
ISBN: 0-919768, 1-55168; SAN: 115-1746
The Hearst Book Group of Canada
#603, 130 Spadina Ave., Toronto ON M5V 2L4
416/504-0106; Fax: 416/504-6394; Toll Free: 1-800-268-3531
ISBN: 0-380, 0-688; SAN: 115-1460
Heartbeat Productions
PO Box 633, Abbotsford BC V2S 7
604/852-3761; Fax: 604/852-3761
Email: winw@direct.ca
ISBN: 1-895112
Heirloom Publishing Inc.
6509B Mississauaga Rd., Mississauga ON L5N 1A6
905/821-1152; Fax: 905/821-1158
ISBN: 0-9692182, 0-9694247
Hemlock Press
#201, 89 Colborne St. East, Orillia ON L3V 1T8
705/484-1096
ISBN: 0-829066; SAN: 116-0931
Herald Press
490 Dutton Dr., Waterloo ON N2L 6H7
519/747-5722; Fax: 519/747-5721; Toll Free: 1-800-245-7894
Email: mpcan%5904477@mcimail.com
ISBN: 0-8361; SAN: 116-0931
Heritage House Publishing Co. Ltd.
Outrigger Rd., RR#2, PO Box 115, Nanoose Bay BC V0R 2R0
250/468-5328; Fax: 250/468-5318; Toll Free: 1-800-665-3302
Email: herhouse@island.net; URL: http://www.island.net/~herhouse
ISBN: 0-919214, 1-895811; SAN: 115-8287
H.H. Marshall News Group
3731 Mackintosh St., PO Box 9301, Stn A, Halifax NS B3K 5N5
902/454-8381; Fax: 902/455-3652; Toll Free: 1-800-456-7881
Highway Book Shop
Hwy. 11, Cobalt ON P0J 1C0
705/679-8375; Fax: 705/679-8511; Toll Free: 1-800-461-2062
Email: bookshop@onlink.net; URL: http://www.onlink.net/cybermail/bookshop/index.htm
ISBN 0-88954; SAN 115-0464
Hinterland Publshers
PO Box 198, Sandy Hook MB R0C 2W0
204/389-3842
Email: hinterland@gatewest.net; URL: http://www.hinterland.mb.ca
Historical Trails West/Historical Research Centre
1115 - 8th Ave. South, Lethbridge AB T1J 1P7
403/328-9011; Fax: 403/328-9011
Email: haig@upanet.uleth.ca
ISBN: 0-921624
HMS Press
PO Box 340, Stn B, London ON N6A 4W1
519/438-8677; Fax: 519/432-6299
Email: hmspress@mirror.org; URL: http://www.mirror.org/commerce/hmspress
ISBN: 0-919957, 1-895700, 1-57105; SAN: 115-0480
Hogrefe & Huber Publishers
12 Bruce Park Ave., Toronto ON M4P 2S3
416/482-6339; Fax: 416/482-5127; Toll Free: 1-800-228-3749
URL: http://www/hhpub.com
ISBN: 0-88937, 0-920887; SAN: 115-379X
Holt, Rinehart & Winston of Canada Ltd. *see* Harcourt Brace & Company Canada, Ltd.
Hornblower Books Ltd.
#201, 4001 Berri St., Montréal QC H2L 4H2
514/843-7410; Fax: 514/843-7798
Email: hbgen@axess.com
Horsdal & Schubart Publishers Ltd.
#623, 425 Simcoe St., Victoria BC V8V 4T3
250/360-2031; Fax: 250/360-0829
ISBN: 0-920663; SAN: 115-7094
Hounslow Press *see* Dundurn Press Ltd.
House of Anansi Press
1800 Steeles Ave. West, Concord ON L4K 2P3
905/660-0611; Fax: 905/660-0676
Email: anansi@irwin-pub.com; URL: http://www.irwin-pub.com/irwin/anansi/
ISBN: 0-88784; SAN: 115-0391
Humanica Press
#110, 186 Sutton Place, Beaconsfield QC H9W 5S3
514/695-0834; Fax: 514/694-2059
ISBN: 0-9693115
Humanitas
990, rue Picard, Montréal QC J4W 1S5
514/466-9737; Fax: 514/466-9737
Email: humanitas@cyberglobe.net
ISBN: 2-89396, 2-9800950
Hushion House Publishing Ltd.
36 Northline Rd., Toronto ON M4B 3E2
416/285-6100; Fax: 416/285-1777
Email: jbeau@hushion.com; URL: http://www.hushion.com
Hyperion Press Ltd.
300 Wales Ave., Winnipeg MB R2M 2S9
204/256-9204; Fax: 204/255-7845
ISBN: 0-920534; SAN: 115-124X
D'Ici et d'ailleurs
343, 4e av, CP 314, Val-d'Or QC J9P 4P4
819/824-4248; Fax: 819/825-8953
ISBN: 2-921055
ICURR Press/Les Presses du CIRUR
#301, 150 Eglinton Ave. East, Toronto ON M4P 1E8
416/973-5629; Fax: 416/973-1375
Email: awexler@icurr.org; URL: http://www.icurr.org/icurr/
ISBN: 1-895469
IDRC Books/Les Éditions du CRDI
PO Box 8500, Ottawa ON K1G 3H9
613/236-6163; Fax: 613/238-7230
Email: order@idrc.ca; URL: http://www.idrc.ca/
ISBN: 0-88936
Impressions Publishers
124 Peter St., Kitchener ON N2G 3K2
519/744-8953
ISBN: 0-920553
Inclusion Press International
24 Thome Cres., Toronto ON M6H 2S5
416/658-5363; Fax: 416/658-5067
Email: 74640.1124@compuserve; URL: http://www.inclusion.com
ISBN: 1-895418
Inner City Books
PO Box 1271, Stn Q, Toronto ON M4T 2P4
416/927-0355; Fax: 416/924-1814
Email: icb@inforamp.net; URL: http://www.inforamp.net/~icb
ISBN: 0-919123; SAN: 115-3870
Insomniac Press
378 Delaware Ave., Toronto ON M6H 2T8
416/536-4308; Fax: 416/588-4198
Email: insomna@pathcom.com; URL: http://www.insomniacpress.com
ISBN: 1-895837
The Institute for Research on Public Policy/L'Institut de recherche en politiques publiques
#200, 1470, rue Peel, Montréal QC H3A 1T1
514/985-2461; Fax: 514/985-2559
Email: irpp@irpp.org; URL: http://www.irpp.org
ISBN: 0-920380, 0-88645; SAN: 115-3889, 115-0537
International Press Publications Inc.
#21, 90 Nolan Ct., Markham ON L3R 4L9
905/946-9588; Fax: 905/946-9590; Toll Free: 1-800-679-2514
Email: ipp@interlog.com; URL: http://www.interlog.com/~ipp
ISBN: 1-896128; SAN: 170-0049
I.P.I. Publishing Ltd.
#708, 50 Prince Arthur Ave., Toronto ON M5R 1B5
416/944-1141; Fax: 416/944-1153
ISBN: 0-920702; SAN: 115-3854
Iris Diffusion *see* Éditions Sciences et culture inc.
Iroqrafts
RR#2, Ohsweken ON N0A 1M0
519/445-0414; Fax: 519/445-0580
Email: iroqraft@worldchat.com
ISBN: 0-919645; SAN: 159-236X
Irwin Publishing
Division of General Publishing Co. Limited
1800 Steeles Ave. West, Concord ON L4K 2P3
905/660-0611; Fax: 905/660-0676; Toll Free: 1-800-263-7824
Email: irwin@irwin-pub.com; URL: http://www.irwin-pub.com/irwin/
ISBN: 0-7725; SAN: 115-0391
Is Five Press
#4, 400 Mount Pleasant Rd., Toronto ON M4S 2L6
416/480-2408; Fax: 416/480-2546
ISBN: 0-920934; SAN: 115-3943
ISER Books (Institute of Social & Economic Research)
Memorial University of Newfoundland, PO Box 4200, Stn C, St. John's NF A1C 5S7
709/737-7450; Fax: 709/737-7560
Email: jgleeson@morgan.ucs.mun.ca
ISBN: 0-919666; SAN: 115-3897
Israel's The Judaica Centre
897 Eglinton Ave. West, Toronto ON M6C 2C1
416/256-2858; Fax: 416/256-2750
SAN: 115-396X
ITMB Publishing Ltd.
345 West Broadway, Vancouver BC V5Y 1P8
604/879-3621; Fax: 604/879-4521
URL: http:/www.nas.com/travelmaps
ISBN: 0-921463, 1-895907
ITP Nelson
1120 Birchmount Rd., Scarborough ON M1K 5G4
416/752-9100; Fax: 416/752-9646; Toll Free: 1-800-268-2222
Email: inquire@nelson.com; URL: http://www.nelson.com/nelson.html
ISBN: 0-17; SAN: 115-0669

J. Gordon Shillingford Publishing Inc.
905 Corydon Ave., PO Box 86, Winnipeg MB R3M 3S3
204/779-6967; Fax: 204/779-6970
Email: shillingfo@vir.com
ISBN: 1-896239, 0-919754, 0-969761, 0-920486

J & L Macpherson Educational Services Ltd.
3030 Collens Hill Rd., Kelowna BC V1Z 1P5
250/769-4321; Fax: 250/769-3297
Email: envirocan@fichther.com; URL: http://www.fichther.com/envirocan

Jack The Bookman Ltd.
#16, 10 Newkirk Rd. South, Richmond Hill ON L4C 5S3
905/884-6177; Fax: 905/884-2411; Toll Free: 1-800-563-5168

Jam Ink Publishing
261 Alice St., Kincardine ON N2Z 2P9
519/396-9553; Fax: 519/396-9554; Toll Free: 1-800-263-1991
ISBN: 1-895268

James Lorimer & Co. Publishers
35 Britain St., Toronto ON M5A 1R7
416/362-4762; Fax: 416/362-3939; Toll Free: 1-800-565-1975
Email: formac@ns.sympatico.ca
Sales & Marketing Offices: 5502 Atlantic St., Halifax NS B3H 1G4
902/421-7022 (customer service); Fax: 902/425-0166; Toll Free: 1-800-565-1975
ISBN: 0-88862, 1-55028; SAN: 115-1134

J.E.S.L. Educational Products
58 Glen Park Ave., Toronto ON M6B 2C2
416/785-7941; Fax: 416/785-7941
Email: 75567.3155@compuserve.com
ISBN: 0-9691264

Jesperson Press
39 James Lane, St. John's NF A1E 3H3
709/753-0633; Fax: 709/753-5507
ISBN: 0-920502, 0-921692; SAN: 115-1320

Jeux de mots /Wordplay
711, av Hartland, Outremont QC H2V 2X5
514/272-5389; Fax: 514/279-4768
Email: sales@wordplay1.com; URL: http://www.jeuxdemots.qc.ca
2-9209867

J.L.H. Law Books Ltd.
(The Law Bookstore)
#8, 166 Bullock Dr., Markham ON L3P 1W2
905/472-0219; Fax: 905/472-5578; Toll Free: 1-800-637-5947
Email: lawbook@io.org; URL: http://www.lawbookstores.com

J.M. LeBel Enterprises Ltd.
10335 - 61 Ave., Edmonton AB T6H 1K9
403/436-8205; Fax: 403/437-5256; Toll Free: 1-800-882-0667
ISBN: 0-920008; SAN: 115-1282

JMC Press Ltd./Les Presses JMC Ltée
34, rue Fleury ouest, Montréal QC H3L 1S9
514/382-3000; Fax: 514/382-3007; Toll Free: 1-800-363-7800

John Coutts Library Services Ltd.
6900 Kinsmen Ct., PO Box 1000, Niagara Falls ON L2E 7E7
905/356-6382; Fax: 905/356-5064; Toll Free: 1-800-263-1686
Email: coutts@wizbang.countts.on.ca; URL: http://wizbang.coutts.on.ca
SAN: 169-5401

John Markham & Associates
11210 Elderberry Way, Sidney BC V8L 5J6
250/655-1823; Fax: 250/655-1826
ISBN: 0-903001

John Wiley & Sons Canada Ltd.
22 Worcester Rd., Etobicoke ON M9W 1L1
416/236-4433; Fax: 416/236-4448; Toll Free: 1-800-567-4797
Email: canada@wiley.com; URL: http://www/wiley.com
Sales & Marketing (courier address only): 5353 Dundas St. West, 4th Fl., Etobicoke ON M9B 6H8
416/236-4433; Fax: 416/236-4448; Toll Free: 1-800-567-4797
Email: canada@wiley.com
ISBN: 0-471

Johnson Gorman Publishers
3669 - 41 Ave., Red Deer AB T4N 2X7
403/342-0917; Fax: 403/342-0917
ISBN 0-921835

J.P. Delf Companies
13020 Delf Pl., Richmond BC V6V 2A2
604/278-4600; Fax: 604/278-6540
Email: delf@helix.net
ISBN: 1-55056

Juno Press
PO Box 502, Port Hope ON L1A 3Z4
905/885-9653; Fax: 905/372-5847
ISBN: 0-921516

Karver Distributors
85 Linden Ave., Winnipeg MB R2K 0M7
800/563-3290; Fax: 800/567-2908

The Kashtan Press
22 Gretna Green, Kingston ON K7M 3J2
613/546-8364
ISBN: 1-896354

Kate Walker & Co. Ltd.
8660 Cambie St., Vancouver BC V6P 6M9
604/323-7111; Fax: 604/323-7118
SAN: 115-7213

Kellington & Associates
#901, 88 Mutual St., Toronto ON M5B 2N3
416/368-3737; Fax: 416/368-3380

Keng Seng Enterprises
#227, 4030, rue St-Ambroise, Montréal QC H4C 2C7
514/939-3971; Fax: 514/989-1922
Email: canada@kengseng.com; URL: http://www.kengseng.com
ISBN: 1-895494

Key Porter Books Limited
70 The Esplanade, Toronto ON M5E 1R2
416/862-7777; Fax: 416/862-2304
Email: keyporter.com@onramp; URL: http://www/keyporter.com
ISBN: 0-919493, 1-55013; SAN: 115-0561

Kids Can Press Ltd.
29 Birch Ave., Toronto ON M4V 1E2
416/925-5437; Fax: 416/960-5437
ISBN: 0-919964, 0-921103, 1-55074; SAN: 115-4001

Kinbridge Publications
PO Box 89065, RPO Westdale, Hamilton ON L8S 4R5
ISBN 0-9693233

Kindred Productions
#4, 169 Riverton Ave., Winnipeg MB R2L 2E5
204/669-6575; Fax: 204/654-1865; Toll Free: 1-800-545-7322
Email: kindred@cdnmbconf.ca; URL: http://www.mbconf.org/mbc/kp/kindred.htm
ISBN: 0-919797, 0-921788

Kirkton Press Ltd.
396 Grills Rd., RR#2, Baltimore ON K0K 1C0
905/349-3443; Fax: 905/349-3420
ISBN: 0-9693768

Kitchener News Company Ltd.
455 Dutton Dr., PO Box 274, Stn Waterloo, Waterloo ON N2J 4A4
519/884-3710; Fax: 519/885-4640; Toll Free: 1-800-265-8839
Email: cosgrove@nic.wat.hookup,net; URL: http://www.kitnews.com
ISBN 0-394

Knopf Canada
#210, 33 Yonge St., Toronto ON M5E 1G4
416/777-9477; Fax: 416/777-9470
Orders & Customer Service: 1265 Aerowood Dr., Mississauga ON L4W 1B9
905/624-0672; Fax: 905/624-6217; Toll Free: 1-800-668-4247
ISBN: 0-394

Knowbuddy Resources
PO Box 37, Collingwood ON L9Y 3Z7
Fax: 705/444-0274; Toll Free: 1-800-667-1121
Email: info@knoebuddyresources.com; URL: http://www.knowbuddyresources.com

Koala Books of Canada Ltd.
14327 - 95A Ave., Edmonton AB T5N 0B6
403/452-5149; Fax: 403/452-5149
SAN: 169-9385

Kosoy Travel Guides
112 Fairholme Ave., Toronto ON M6B 2W9
416/256-0974; Fax: 416/256-1216
ISBN: 0-919632; SAN: 115-8724

Kugh Enterprises
PO Box 5573, Whitehorse YK Y1A 3T3
403/633-2118; Fax: 403/633-3307
Email: mbraver@yknet.yk.ca; URL: http://www.yukon.web.com/tourism/kugh
ISBN: 1-896

Kylix Media Inc.
#414, 5165, rue Sherbrooke ouest, Montréal QC H4A 1T6
514/481-6606; Fax: 514/481-9699
ISBN: 0-919571

Lambrecht Publications
1763 Maple Bay Rd., Duncan BC V9L 5N6
250/748-8722; Fax: 250/748-8722
Email: helgal@cowichan.com
ISBN: 0-919383; SAN: 115-057X

Lancelot Press Ltd.
PO Box 425, Hantsport NS B0P 1P0
902/684-9129; Fax: 902/684-3685
Email: lancelot@atcon.com; URL: http://www.atcon.com/lancelot
ISBN: 0-88999; SAN: 115-4052

Laurier Books Ltd.
PO Box 2694, Stn D, Ottawa ON K1P 5W6
613/738-2163; Fax: 613/247-0256
Email: laurierbooks@intertel.net
ISBN: 1-895959; SAN: 168-2806

Lawson-Falle Ltd.
1245 Franklin Blvd., PO Box 940, Cambridge ON N1R 5X9
519/622-1941; Fax: 519/622-2755
SAN: 115-4052

Lazara Press
PO Box 2269, Stn Main, Vancouver BC V6B 3W2
604/872-1134; Fax: 604/874-6661
ISBN 0-920999

Learnxs Press
155 College St., Toronto ON M5T 1P6
416/397-3911; Fax: 416/393-9969
ISBN: 0-920020; SAN: 115-4060

Leméac éditeur Inc.
1124, rue Marie-Anne est, Montréal QC H2J 2B7
514/524-5558; Fax: 514/524-3145
ISBN: 2-7609, 0-7761

Lester Publishing *see* Key Porter Books Limited

Lexa Publishers' Representatives
215 Ashworth Ave., Toronto ON M6G 2A6
416/535-6494; Fax: 416/535-6599
Email: lmcclory@interlog.com

Librairie Champlain
468 Queen St. East, Toronto ON M5A 1T7
416/364-4345; Fax: 416/364-8843
ISBN: 0-9209

Librairie Raffin, inc.
7870, rue Fleuricourt, St-Léonard QC H1R 2L3
514/325-5553, 5555; Fax: 514/325-7329; Toll Free: 1-800-361-4293

Librairie Wilson & Lafleur Ltée
40, rue Notre-Dame est, Montréal QC H2Y 1B9

514/875-6326; Fax: 514/875-8356; Toll Free: 1-800-363-2327
ISBN: 2-89127
Librarie du Soleil
434, boul St-Joseph, Hull QC J8Y 3Y7
819/595-2414; Fax: 819/595-3672
Library Bound
200C Frobisher Dr., Waterloo ON N2V 2A2
519/885-3233; Fax: 519/885-2662; Toll Free: 1-800-363-4728
Email: lbi@librarybound.com; URL: http://www.librarybound.com
SAN: 116-9203
The Library Services Centre
141 Dearborn Pl., Waterloo ON N2J 4N5
519/746-4420; Fax: 519/746-4425; Toll Free: 1-800-265-3360
Email: mckim@lsc.on.ca
ISBN: 0-921830; SAN: 319-2024
Lidec Inc.
4350, av de l'Hôtel-de-Ville, Montréal QC H2W 2H5
514/843-5991; Fax: 514/843-5252
ISBN: 2-7608
Life Cycle Books Ltd.
2205 Danforth Ave., Toronto ON M4C 1K4
416/690-5860; Fax: 416/690-8532
ISBN: 0-919225; SAN: 115-8417
Lifestyle Books
6 Dawe Cres., Grand Falls NF A2A 2T2
709/489-6796; Fax: 709/489-6796
ISBN: 0-9691126, 0-9699031
Lilmur Publishing
147 Brooke Ave., Toronto ON M5M 2K3
416/486-0145; Fax: 416/486-5380
ISBN: 0-9692729; SAN: 115-7035
Literary Press Group of Canada
#301, 2 Gloucester St., Toronto ON M4Y 1L5
416/413-1887; Fax: 416/413-9443; Toll Free: 1-800-717-7702
Email: claudrum@lpg.ca; URL: http://www.lpg.ca
Little Brick Schoolhouse Inc.
1235 Trafalgar Rd., PO Box 84001, Oakville ON L6H 3J0
905/844-4669; Fax: 905/844-4669
Email: littlebrick@globalserve.net; URL: http://www.littlebrick.com
ISBN: 0-919788
Little Brown & Co.
148 Yorkville Ave., Toronto ON M5R 1C2
416/967-3888; Fax: 416/967-4591; Toll Free: 1-800-387-6922
ISBN: 0-316; SAN: 115-4109
Livres Mercier ltée
RR#2, Tara ON N0H 2N0
519/934-0262; Fax: 519/934-0262
Log House Publishing Co. Ltd.
RR#1, Pender Island BC V0N 2M0
250/629-6521; Fax: 250/629-2010
ISBN: 0-920270; SAN: 115-0588
Logidisque inc. *see* Éditions Logiques
Login Brothers Canada
324 Saulteaux Cres., Winnipeg MB R3J 3T2
204/837-2987; Fax: 204/837-3116; Toll Free: 1-800-665-0103
SAN: 119-6049
Lone Pine Publishing
#206, 10426 - 81 Ave., Edmonton AB T6E 1X5
403/433-9333; Fax: 403/433-9646; Toll Free: 1-800-661-9017
Email: editors@lonepinepublishing.com; URL: http://www.lonepinepublishing.com
ISBN: 0-919433, 1-55105; SAN: 115-4125
Lorraine Greey Publications Limited
#303, 56 The Esplanade, Toronto ON M5E 1A7
416/422-3995; Fax: 416/422-3995
Lost Moose, The Yukon Publishers
58 Kluane Cres., Whitehorse YT Y1A 3G7
867/688-5076; Fax: 867/668-6223
Email: lmoose@yknet.yk.ca; URL: http://www.yukonweb.com/business/lost_moose
ISBN: 0-9694612, 1-896758
Louise Courteau, éditrice inc.
1, Lac St-Louis est, CP 481, Saint-Zénon QC J0K 3N0
514/884-5958; Fax: 514/884-5913
URL: http://club-culture.com/club/
ISBN: 2-89239
Le Loup de Gouttière
347, rue Saint-Paul, Québec QC G1K 3X1
418/694-2224; Fax: 418/694-2225
ISBN: 2-921310
Loyal Colonies Press
304 Olympus Ave., Kingston ON K7M 4T9
613/389-0866
ISBN: 0-929832
Lugus Publications Ltd.
(Lugus Libros Latinamerica Inc.)
48 Falcon St., Toronto ON M4S 2P5
416/322-5113; Fax: 416/484-9512
Email: lugust@tvo.org; URL: http://www.travel-net.com/blochfd/lugus.html
ISBN: 0-921633
Lyalta Publishing
1403 - 2nd St. SW, Calgary AB T2R 0W7
403/233-2558
ISBN: 0-9699
Macfarlane Walter & Ross
37A Hazelton Ave., Toronto ON M5R 2E3
416/924-7595; Fax: 416/924-4254
Email: mwandr@interlog.com
ISBN: 0-921912
Macmillan Canada
Division of Canada Publishing Corporation
29 Birch Ave., Toronto ON M4V 1E2
416/963-8830, 293-8464 (customer service); Fax: 416/923-4821; Toll Free: 1-800-667-1115
ISBN: 0-7715, 0-7705; SAN: 115-0375
MacNeill Library Service
1701 West 3rd Ave., Vancouver BC V6J 1K7
604/732-1335; Fax: 604/732-3765; Toll Free: 1-800-663-1174
Email: macneill@literascape.com
Madison Press Books
40 Madison Ave., Toronto ON M5R 2S1
416/923-5027; Fax: 416/923-9708
Madonna House Publications
Madonna House, Combermere ON K0S 1L0
613/756-3728
ISBN: 0-921440
Magra Publishing
44 Tally-Ho Dr., Hamilton ON L9H 3M6
905/628-4388; Fax: 905/628-4388
ISBN: 0-9693817
La Maison de l'Education inc.
10485, boul Saint-Laurent, Montréal QC H3L 2P1
514/384-4401; Fax: 514/384-4844
Email: maiseduc@prisco.net
Malin Head Press
PO Box 72172, Stn Kanata North, Kanata ON K2K 2P4
613/592-4453; Fax: 613/592-7078
Email: shearonj@magi.com; URL: http://www.magi.com/~shearonj
ISBN: 0-9698039
Mandragore
127A Castlerock Dr., Richmond Hill ON L4C 6A1
905/770-0183; Fax: 905/881-6710
Marcus Books
PO Box 327, Queensville ON L0G 1R0
905/478-2201; Fax: 905/478-8338
ISBN: 0-919951; SAN: 115-4249
Marginal Distribution
#102, 277 George St. North, Peterborough ON K9J 3G9
705/745-2326; Fax: 705/745-2326
Email: marginal@ptbo.igs.net; URL: http://www.ptbo.igs.net/~marginal
SAN: 115-4257
Marine Press of Canada Ltd.
295, rue de la Montagne, Montréal QC H3C 4K4
514/932-8342; Fax: 514/931-3711
Maritimes Arts Projects Productions
(Broken Jaw Press)
PO Box 596, Stn A, Fredericton NB E3B 5A6
506/454-5127; Fax: 506/454-5127
Email: jblades@nbnet.nb.ca
ISBN: 0-921411; SAN: 117-1437
Marshall Cavendish
93B Woodbridge Ave., PO Box 56510, Woodbridge ON L4L 8V3
905/851-4660; Fax: 905/851-5507
ISBN: 1-85435
Martin & Ziegler Ltd.
6958 Laburnum St., Vancouver BC V6P 5M9
604/261-4615; Fax: 604/266-6472
Marvin Melnyk Associates Ltd
PO Box 220, Queenston ON L0S 1L0
905/262-4964; Fax: 905/262-4974; Toll Free: 1-800-682-0029
Email: meljack@niagara.com
ISBN: 0-919803; SAN: 115-4281
MasterAthlete Book Publishing
#8, 100 West Beaver Creek, Richmond Hill ON L4B 1H4
905/707-8464; Fax: 905/707-8464; Toll Free: 1-800-363-9709
Email: sports@passport.ca
ISBN: 0-921016; SAN: 118-3613
MAXAM inc.
3436, rue Archambault, Longueuil QC J4M 2W8
514/448-5049; Fax: 514/448-9898
ISBN: 2-9801115
McBeth of Canada
#2, 110 Morton Ave. East, Brantford ON N3S 7J7
519/753-1903; Fax: 519/753-4811
SAN: 169-9717
McClelland & Stewart Inc.
#900, 481 University Ave., Toronto ON M5G 2E9
416/598-1114; Fax: 416/598-7764; Toll Free: 1-800-788-1074
ISBN: 0-7710; SAN: 115-4192
McGill-Queen's University Press
3430 McTavish St., Montréal QC H3A 1X9
514/398-3750; Fax: 514/398-4333; Toll Free: 1-800-565-9523
Email: mqup@printing.lan.mcgill.ca; URL: http://www.mcgill.ca/mqupress
Queen's University: 184 Union St., Kingston ON K7L 2P6
613/545-2155; Fax: 613/545-6822
ISBN: 0-7735
McGilligan Books
859 Dundas St. West, PO Box 16024, Toronto ON M6J 1W0
416/538-0945; Fax: 416/538-0547
ISBN: 0-9698064
McGraw-Hill Ryerson Limited
300 Water St., Whitby ON L1N 9B6
905/430-5000; Fax: 905/430-5020
Email: johnd@mcgrawhill.ca; URL: http://www.mcgrawhill.ca
ISBN: 0-07; SAN: 115-060X
McMaster University Press
c/o Title Bookstore, 1280 Main St. West, Hamilton ON L8S 4L8
905/525-9140, ext.23355; Fax: 905/572-7160
Email: mup@mcmaster.ca
Meakin and Associates
#17, 81 Auriga Dr., Nepean ON K2E 7Y5
613/226-4381; Fax: 613/226-1687
ISBN: 1-895195; SAN: 115-7183
The Mercury Press
2569 Dundas St. West, Toronto ON M6P 1X7

416/767-4352; Fax: 416/767-4631
ISBN: 0-920544, 1-55128; SAN: 115-009X
Messageries A.D.P. inc.
955, rue Amherst, Montréal QC H2C 3K4
514/523-1182; Fax: 514/521-4434; Toll Free: 1-800-603-0433
Michael Reynolds & Associates
#202, 1224 Hamilton St., Vancouver BC V6B 2S8
604/688-6918; Fax: 604/687-4624
Email: mra@mindlink.net
Michelin North America (Canada) Inc.
Maps & Guides Division, 2450, boul Daniel Johnson, Laval QC H7T 2T9
514/856-8855; Fax: 514/856-0551; Toll Free: 1-800-361-8236
URL: http://www.michelin-travel.com
ISBN: 2-06; SAN: 115-0618
Michi-Mook Enterprises
664 Queen St. East, Sault Ste Marie ON P6A 2A4
705/946-5746, 253-8543
Micromedia Limited
20 Victoria St., Toronto ON M5C 2N8
416/362-5211; Fax: 416/362-6161; Toll Free: 1-800-387-2689
Email: info@mmltd.com; URL: http://www.mmltd.com
ISBN: 0-88892; SAN: 115-4303
Midwestern News Agency
344 Portage Ave., Saskatoon SK S7J 4C6
306/934-4414; Fax: 306/934-3515
Mile Oak Publishing
#81, 20 Mineola Rd. East, Mississauga ON L5G 4N9
905/274-4356
Email: 102535.312@compuserve.com
ISBN: 1-896819
Milestone Publications Inc.
3284 Heather St., Vancouver BC V5Z 3K5
604/875-0611; Fax: 604/738-5135
URL: http://www.milestonepub.com
SAN: 115-169X
Mind Resources Inc.
PO Box 126, Kitchener ON N2G 3W9
519/895-0330; Fax: 519/895-0331
SAN: 115-3986
Mini Mocho Press
PO Box 57424, Stn Jackson, Hamilton ON L8P 4X2
905/523-1518
Minnow Books Inc.
1251 Northside Rd., Burlington ON L7M 1H7
905/336-4003; Fax: 905/336-3766; Toll Free: 1-800-262-5210
Misthorn Press
RR#6, Site 660 C-11, Courtenay BC V9N 8H9
250/335-2237; Fax: 250/338-8469
ISBN: 0-9680159
MLR Editions Canada
Dept. of English, Wilfrid Laurier University, Waterloo ON N2L 3C5
519/884-1970
Email: ptiessen@machi1.wlu.ca
ISBN: 0-9692539
Modulo Publisher Inc./Modulo Editeur Inc.
#300, 233, av Dunbar, Montréal QC H3P 2H4
514/738-9818; Fax: 514/738-5838
ISBN: 2-89113
Monarch Books of Canada
5000 Dufferin St., Downsview ON M3H 5T5
416/663-8231; Fax: 416/736-1702; Toll Free: 1-800-404-7404
SAN: 111-171X
Mondia éditeurs inc.
105, de Martigny ouest, Saint-Jérôme QC J7Y 2G2
514/438-8479; Fax: 514/432-3892; Toll Free: 1-800-561-2371
ISBN: 0-88556, 2-89114
Moneyjar Publishing
#1711, 642 Sheppard Ave. East, North York ON M2K 1B9
416/223-7312; Fax: 416/223-7312
Email: millyard@tvo.org
ISBN: 0-9695889
moonprint
PO Box 293, Winnipeg MB R3C 2G9
204/237-5504
URL: http://www/escape/ca/~elle
Moonstone Press
167 Delaware St., London ON N5Z 2N6
519/659-5784
ISBN: 0-920259; SAN: 115-4354
Mosaic Press
1252 Speers Rd., Unit 1, Oakville ON L6L 5N9
905/825-2130; Fax: 905/825-2130
ISBN: 0-88962
Mosby Yearbook *see* Times Mirror Professional Publishing
Mostly Books
736 Pritchard Farm Rd., East St. Paul MB R2E 0B4
204/663-8166; Fax: 204/663-8228
Email: mjudge@mb.sympatico.ca
Moulin Publishing Ltd.
PO Box 560, Norval ON L0P 1K0
905/877-3555; Fax: 905/877-3555
URL: http://www.moulinpub.com
ISBN: 0-9697079
Moving Publications Ltd.
#100, 44 Upjohn Rd., North York ON M2B 2W1
416/441-1168; Fax: 416/441-1641
Email: movingto@idirect.com
ISBN: 1-895020
MRA Books
#500, 251 Bank St., Ottawa ON K2P 1X3
613/230-7197; Fax: 613/230-4233
Email: mra@web.net
ISBN: 0-85239, 0-901269; SAN: 115-7515
Multicultural Books
2384 Yonge St., PO Box 1279, Stn K, Toronto ON M4P 3E5
416/488-9997; Fax: 416/488-4831
Email: mul@io.org
ISBN: 0-9694933
Munsey Music
PO Box 511, Richmond Hill ON L4C 4Y8
905/737-0208; Fax: 905/737-0208
Email: terrence_munsey@tvo.org; URL: http://www.digiserve.com/stoneman/
ISBN: 0-9697066; SAN: 116-967X
The Muses' Company *see* J. Gordon Shillingford Publishing Inc.
Musson Publishing *see* General Publishing Co. Limited
Napoleon Publishing Inc.
#1005, 3266 Yonge St., Toronto ON M4N 3P6
416/730-9052; Fax: 416/226-9975; Toll Free: 1-800-387-8028
Email: transmedia@sympatico.ca
ISBN: 0-929141; SAN: 115-0022
National Book Network
39 Glenaden Ave. East, Toronto ON M8Y 2L4
416/239-5232; Fax: 416/232-1934
Email: lpetriw@nbnbooks.com
National Book Service
25 Kodiak Cres., North York ON M3J 3E5
416/630-2950; Fax: 416/630-0274; Toll Free: 1-800-387-3178
Email: nbs@nbs.com; URL: http://www.nbs.com
SAN: 108-0830
National News Co. Ltd.
2655 Lancaster Rd., Ottawa ON K1B 4L5
613/731-2840; Fax: 613/731-2320
Natural Heritage/Natural History Inc.
PO Box 95, Stn O, Toronto ON M4A 2M8
416/694-7907; Fax: 416/690-0819; Toll Free: 1-800-725-9982
ISBN: 0-920474, 1-896219; SAN: 115-4559
NC Press Limited
#400, 345 Adelaide St. West, Toronto ON M5V 1R5
416/593-6284; Fax: 416/593-6204
Email: ncpress@fox.nstn.ca
ISBN: 0-919, 0-920, 1-55021; SAN: 115-0650
Negev Importing Co. Ltd. House of Judaica
3509 Bathurst St., Toronto ON M6A 2C5
416/781-9356; Fax: 416/781-0071
SAN: 170-0154
Netherlandic Press
3 Pearson Rd., Brampton ON L6Y 2M9
905/451-8916; Fax: 905/451-1956
ISBN: 0-919417
New Magazine Publishing Co. Ltd.
PO Box 390, Stn A, Ottawa ON K1N 8V4
613/236-0982; Fax: 613/236-1408
ISBN: 0-921032
New Orphic Publishers
1095 Victoria Dr., Vancouver BC V5L 4G3
604/255-9074
ISBN: 0-9699162
New Society Publishers
PO Box 189, Gabriola Island BC V0R 1X0
250/247-9737; Fax: 250/247-7471; Toll Free: 1-800-567-6772
Email: nsp@island.net; URL: http://www.newsociety.com
ISBN: 1-55092, 0-86571
New Star Books Ltd.
2504 York Ave., Vancouver BC V6K 1E3
604/738-9429; Fax: 604/738-9332
Email: newstar@pinc.com
ISBN: 0-919888, 0-919573, 0-921586; SAN: 115-1908
NeWest Publishers Ltd.
(NeWest Press)
#201, 8540 - 109 St., Edmonton AB T6G 1E6
403/432-9427; Fax: 403/433-3179
Email: newest@planet.eon.net
ISBN: 0-920316, 0-920897, 1-896300
Newport Bay Publishing
356 Cyril Owen Place, RR#3, Victoria BC V8X 3X1
250/479-4616; Fax: 250/479-3836
Email: newport.bay@islanbnet.com
ISBN: 0-921513
The News Group - Edmonton Distribution Centre
16504 - 121A Ave., Edmonton AB T5V 1J9
403/454-0306; Fax: 403/453-3687
The News Group - Vancouver Distribution Centre
2500 Vauxhall Pl., Richmond BC V6V 1Y8
604/278-4841; Fax: 604/231-6195
Email: gnp@direct.ca
News West
5716 Burbank Rd. SE, Calgary AB T2H 1Z4
403/253-8856; Fax: 403/252-9743
Email: general@newswest.ca
NewsWest Corp.
5716 Burbank Rd. SE, Calgary AB T2H 1Z4
403/253-8856; Fax: 403/252-9743; Toll Free: 1-888-639-7868
Email: info@newswest.ca
Nicholas Hoare Ltd.
2165, av Madison, Montréal QC H4B 2T2
514/489-9341; Fax: 514/489-1784
SAN: 170-0332
Nightwood Editions
#13, RR#2, Site 26, Gibson BC V0N 1V0
604/885-0212; Fax: 604/885-0212
ISBN: 0-88971; SAN: 115-2661
Nimbus Publishing Ltd.
PO Box 9301, Stn A, Halifax NS B3K 5N5
902/454-4286; Fax: 902/455-3652; Toll Free: 1-800-646-2879
ISBN: 0-920852, 0-921054, 1-55109; SAN: 115-0685
Nine Pines Publishing
1128 Church St., Manotick ON K4M 1A5
613/692-1601; Fax: 613/692-1602; Toll Free: 1-800-465-3287
Email: unity_arts/nine_pines@bcon.com
ISBN: 1-895456
Non-Entity Press Ltd./New Ireland Press
217 Aberdeen St., Fredericton NB E3B 1R6

506/454-1153
ISBN: 0-9690215, 0-920483-88-7
Norbry Publishing
15838 Shaws Creek Rd., Terra Cotta ON L0P 1N0
Fax: 905/838-0214; Toll Free: 1-800-667-2791
Email: mikep@norbry.com
ISBN: 0-921282
Norris-Whitney Communications Inc.
#7, 23 Hannover St., St. Catharines ON L2W 1A3
905/641-3471641-1648; Toll Free: 1-800-265-8481
Email: order@nor.com
ISBN: 0-9691272
North 49 Books
35 Prince Andrew Pl., Toronto ON M3C 2H2
416/449-4000; Fax: 416/449-9924; Toll Free: 1-800-490-4049
Email: north49@idirect.com
SAN: 117-2689
Northstone Publishing
#330, 1980 Cooper Rd., Kelowna BC V1Y 9G8
250/766-2926; Fax: 250/766-1201; Toll Free: 1-800-299-2926
Email: info@northstone.doc
ISNB: 1-55145, 1-896836; SAN: 117-7436
Les Nouvelles Éditions de l'Arc
5844, rue Duquesne, Montréal QC H1M 2K4
514/251-7625
ISBN: 2-89016
Novalis
6255, rue Hutchison, Montréal QC H2V 4C7
514/278-3020; Fax: 514/278-3030; Toll Free: 1-800-668-2547
Email: novalis@odyssee.net
Toronto Office: 49 Front St. East, 2nd Fl., Toronto ON M5E 1B3
416/363-3303; Fax: 416/363-9409; Toll Free: 1-800-387-7164
Email: novalis@interlog.com
ISBN: 2-89088
Nuage Éditions
PO Box 8, Stn E, Montréal QC H2T 3A5
514/272-5226; Fax: 514/271-5722
ISBN: 0-921833
Oasis Press
38 Nina St., Toronto ON M5R 1Z4
416/537-8421
ISBN: 1-895092
Oberon Press
#400, 350 Sparks St., Ottawa ON K1R 7S8
613/238-3275; Fax: 613/238-3275
ISBN: 0-88750, 0-7780; SAN: 115-0723
Ocapt Publications
27 Donna Marie Dr., Welland ON L3C 2X7
905/735-2967; Fax: 905/788-0839; Toll Free: 1-888-579-3013
Email: ocapt@iaw.com
OISE Press
(Ontario Institute for Studies in Education Press)
252 Bloor St. West, Toronto ON M5S 1V5
416/926-4707; Fax: 416/926-4725
ISBN: 0-7744; SAN: 115-2818
Ontario Outdoor Publications
1431 Stavebank Rd., Mississauga ON L5G 2V5
905/891-1714; Fax: 905/891-2352
ISBN: 0-9690474; SAN: 115-4672
Oolichan Books
PO Box 10, Lantzville BC V0R 2H0
250/390-4839; Fax: 250/390-4839
ISBN: 0-88982; SAN: 115-4680
Optimum Publishing International Inc.
PO Box 237, Stn Victoria, Westmount QC H3Z 2V5
514/483-0901; Fax: 514/483-0641
ISBN: 0-88890
Orca Book Publishers Ltd.
PO Box 5626, Stn B, Victoria BC V8R 6S4
250/380-1229; Fax: 250/380-1892; Toll Free: 1-800-210-5277
Email: orca@pinc.com; URL: http://www.swifty.com/orca/index.htm
ISBN: 0-920501, 1-55143; SAN: 115-7485
Orchard Press Inc.
55 Lismer, PO Box 72144, Stn Kanata North, Kanata ON K2K 2P4
613/592-6226; Fax: 613/592-9315
ISBN: 0-919741
Otter Press
81 Albert St., Waterloo ON N2L 3S6
519/885-4130
ISBN: 0-9690963
Our Schools/Our Selves
107 Earl Grey Rd., Toronto ON M4J 3L6
416/463-6978; Fax: 416/463-6978; Toll Free: 1-800-565-1975
ISBN: 0-921908
Outcrop, The Northern Publishers
PO Box 1350, Yellowknife NT X1A 2N9
867/920-4652; Fax: 867/873-2844
ISBN: 0-919315; SAN: 115-4710
Outport Publishing
PO Box 1072, Lewisporte NF A0G 3A0
709/535-8464; Fax: 709/535-0382
ISBN: 0-9696544
Owl Books
#500, 179 John St., Toronto ON M5T 3G5
416/971-5275; Fax: 416/971-5294
Email: owlbooks@owl.on.ca; URL: http://www.owl.on.ca
ISBN: 0-919872, 0-920775, 1-895688; SAN: 115-4044
Owl's Head Press
PO Box 57, Alma NB E0A 1B0
506/887-2073; Fax: 506/887-2074
ISBN: 0-929635
Oxford University Press
70 Wynford Drive, North York ON M3C 1J9
416/441-2941; Fax: 416/444-0427; Toll Free: 1-800-387-8020
Email: custserv@oupcan.com; URL: http://www.oupcan.com
ISBN: 0-19; SAN: 115-731
OZ New Media
10050 - 117 St., Edmonton AB T5K 1X2
403/414-1148; Fax: 403/488-5834; Toll Free: 1-800-436-2414
Email: oznet@onewmedia.com; URL: http://www.newmedia.com
ISBN: 1-896295
Pacesetter Press
236 Sunset Cres., PO Box 326, Stroud ON L0L 2M0
705/431-6898; Fax: 705/431-6898; Toll Free: 1-800-813-7223
ISBN: 0-9697317
Pacific Edge Publishing
Comp. 50, Site 21, Gabriola BC V0R 1X0
250/247-8806; Fax: 250/247-8299; Toll Free: 1-800-668-8806
Email: pacedge@island.net; URL: http://www.schoolnet.ca/vp/cdncont/
ISBN: 1-895110
Pacific Educational Press
Faculty of Education, U.B.C., 6365 Bioilogical Sciences Rd., Vancouver BC V6T 1Z4
604/822-5385; Fax: 604/822-6603
Email: cedwards@interchange.ubc.ca
ISBN 0-88865; SAN 115-1266
Pacific-Rim Publishers
Comp. 7, Site 28, RR#1, Gabriola BC V0R 1X0
250/247-0014; Fax: 250/247-0015
Email: prp@island.net
ISBN: 0-921358
Paideia Press Ltd.
PO Box 1000, Jordan Station ON L0R 1S0
905/562-5719; Fax: 905/562-7828
ISBN: 0-88815; SAN: 115-4761
Palmerston Press
822 Manning Ave., Toronto ON M6G 2W8
416/516-9056; Fax: 416/5160282
Pannonia Books - The Hungarian Bookstore
PO Box 716, Stn P, Toronto ON M5S 2Y4
416/966-5156; Fax: 416/966-5156
Email: pannonia@interlog.com; URL: http://www.panbooks.com
ISBN: 0-919368; SAN: 168-5104
paperplates books
19 Kenwood Ave., Toronto ON M6C 2RB
416/651-2551, 656-4559
Parchment Press
90 Charlton Blvd., North York ON M2M 1B9
416/221-2088
ISBN: 0-9695504
Pathway Publishers
RR#4, Aylmer ON N5H 2R3
ISBN: 0-919374
Pauline Books & Media
3022 Dufferin St., Toronto ON M6B 3T5
416/781-9131; Fax: 416/783-1615; Toll Free: 1-800-668-2078
Email: pauline@netrover.com; URL: http://www.netrover.com/~pauline
ISBN: 0-8198
P.D. Meany Publishers
PO Box 118, Streetsville ON L5M 2B7
905/567-5803; Fax: 905/567-1687
ISBN: 0-88835; SAN: 115-4273
Pegasus Publishing
Causeway Rd., Site 19, PO Box 26, Seaforth NS B0J 1N0
902/827-3204
Email: aj401@ccn.cs.dal.ca
ISBN 0-9692552
Peguis Publishers Limited
#100, 318 McDermot Ave., Winnipeg MB R3A 0A2
204/987-3500; Fax: 204/947-0080; Toll Free: 1-800-667-9673
Email: peguis@peguis.mb.ca
ISBN: 0-920541, 1-895411; SAN: 115-480X
Pembroke Publishers Limited
538 Hood Rd., Markham ON L3R 3K9
905/477-0650; Fax: 905/477-3691; Toll Free: 1-800-997-9807
Email: pembroke@istar.ca
ISBN: 0-921217, 1-55138
Pemmican Publications
#2, 1635 Burrows Ave., Winnipeg MB R2X 0T1
204/589-6346; Fax: 204/589-2063
Email: pemmican@fox.nstn.ca; URL: http://fox.nstn.ca/~pemmican
ISBN: 0-921827; SAN: 115-1657
Pendas Press
32 Hammersmith Ave., Toronto ON M4E 2W4
416/699-5338
ISBN: 0-920820
Pendragon House Ltd.
PO Box 338, Stn Port Credit, Mississauga ON L5G 4L8
905/823-0222; Fax: 905/823-9931; Toll Free: 1-800-727-2751
ISBN: 0-88761; SAN: 156-7764
Penguin Books Canada Ltd.
#300, 10 Alcorn Ave., Toronto ON M4V 3B2
416/925-2249; Fax: 416/925-0068
URL: http://www.penguin.ca
ISBN: 0-14; SAN: 115-4826, 115-074X
Penumbra Press
PO Box 40062, Ottawa ON K1V 0W8
613/526-3232; Fax: 613/526-3244; Toll Free: 1-800-567-6591
ISBN: 0-921254, 0-929806; SAN: 115-0774
Peterborough Publishing
RR#2, 621 Lily Lake Rd., Peterborough ON K9J 6X3
705/742-0298; Fax: 705/743-9878
ISBN: 0-9693497
Petheric Press Ltd. *see* Nimbus Publishing Ltd.

Phoenix Publishing Inc.
821 - 254 St., Langley BC V4W 2R8
604/878-0248; Toll Free: 1-800-563-6050
ISBN: 0-91345
Playwrights Canada Press
54 Wolseley St., 2nd Fl., Toronto ON M5T 1A5
416/947-0201; Fax: 416/947-0159; Toll Free: 1-800-561-3318
Email: cdplays@interlog.com; URL: http://www.puc.ca
ISBN: 0-88754, 0-919834; SAN: 115-0766
Point-to-Point
PO Box 133, Stn B, Ottawa ON K1P 6C3
613/237-4658
Email: cz173@freenet.carleton.ca
ISBN: 0-9695731
Polar Bear Press *see* North 49 Books
Polestar Press Ltd.
1011 Commercial Dr., 2nd Fl., Vancouver BC V5L 3X1
604/251-9718; Fax: 604/251-9718
ISBN: 0-919591; SAN 115-4931
Polyscience Publications Inc.
44 Seize Arpents, PO Box 148, Morin Heights QC J0R 1H0
514/226-5870; Fax: 514/226-5866; Toll Free: 1-800-840-5870
Email: polysci@ietc.com; URL: http://www.ietc.ca/polysci/
ISBN: 0-921317; SAN: 115-4419
Porcepic Books *see* Beach Holme Publishers Limited
Porcupine's Quill Inc.
68 Main St., Erin ON N0B 1T0
519/833-9158; Fax: 519/833-9158
ISBN: 0-88984; SAN: 115-0820
Porphry Press
148 McComber Cres., Thunder Bay ON P7A 7E8
807/767-2705
ISBN: 0-9693138, 0-9680686
Portage & Main Press *see* Peguis Publishers Limited
Porthole Press Ltd.
2082 Neptune Rd., RR#3, Sidney BC V8L 3X9
250/656-7902; Fax: 250/652-1521
ISBN: 0-919931
Potentials Within
161 Franklin Ave., North York ON M2N 1C6
416/512-1168; Fax: 416/512-1168
ISBN: 0-9695781; SAN: 118-413X
Potlatch Publications Limited
30 Berry Hill, Waterdown ON L0R 2H4
905/689-1632
ISBN: 0-919676; SAN: 115-1355
Pottersfield Press
RR#2, Porters Lake NS B0J 2S0
902/827-4517; Fax: 902/455-3652 (orders)
ISBN: 0-919001; SAN: 115-0790
Power Engineering Books Ltd.
7 Perron St., St Albert AB T8N 1E3
403/458-3155, 459-2525; Fax: 403/460-2530; Toll Free: 1-800-667-3155
Email: power@nucleus.com; URL: http://powerengbooks.com
SAN: 115-4850
Prairie House Books
PO Box 84007, Stn Market Mall, Calgary AB T3A 5C4
403/229-2040; Fax: 403/247-3675
ISBN: 1-895012
Prairie Lily Books
PO Box 1673, Saskatoon SK S7K 3R8
306/955-4238
The Prairie Publishing Co.
PO Box 2997, Winnipeg MB R3C 4B5
204/885-6496; Fax: 204/775-3277
ISBN: 0-919576; SAN: 115-4869
Prentice-Hall Canada Inc.
1870 Birchmount Rd., Scarborough ON M1P 2J7
416/293-3621; Fax: 416/299-2540; Telex: 065-25184
URL: http://prenhall.com/
ISBN: 0-13; SAN; 115-0839
Press Gang Publishers Feminist Co-operative
#101, 225 - 17th Ave. East, Vancouver BC V5V 1A6
604/876-7787; Fax: 604/876-7892
Email: pgangpub@portal.ca; URL: http://www.pressgang.bc.ca
ISBN: 0-88974; SAN: 115-4893
Presses d'Amérique
#100, 50, rue Saint-Paul ouest, Montréal QC H2Y 1Y8
514/847-1953; Fax: 514/847-1647
ISBN: 2-921378
Presses d'Or
#105, 7875, boul Louis-H-Lafontaine, Anjou QC H1K 4E4
514/355-7703; Fax: 514/354-3144
ISBN: 2-920903
Les Presses de l'Université Laval
Cité universitaire, #3103, Pavillon Maurice-Pollack, Ste-Foy QC G1K 7P4
418/656-7381; Fax: 418/656-3305
Email: presses@pul.ulaval.ca
ISBN 2-7637
Les Presses de l'Université de Montréal
CP 6128, Succ A, Montréal QC H3C 3J7
514/343-6929; Fax: 514/343-2232
Email: pumedit@ere.umontreal.ca; URL: http://www.pum.umontreal.ca/pum/
ISBN: 2-7606
Presses de l'Université du Québec
2875, boul Laurier, Sainte-Foy QC G1V 2M3
418/657-3551; Fax: 418/657-2096
Email: marketing@puq.uquebec.ca
ISBN 0-7770, 2-7605, 2-920073
Primary Press
PO Box 372, Peterborough ON K9J 6Z3
705/749-9276; Fax: 705/742-7651
ISBN: 0-919895; SAN: 118-4113
Prime Books Inc.
166 Bayview Fairways Dr., Thornhill ON L3T 2Y8
905/881-2853; Fax: 905/881-4334
ISBN: 0-920814, 0-921573, 2-89423
Prise de Parole Inc.
#205, 109 Elm St., PO Box 550, Stn B, Sudbury ON P3E 4R2
705/675-6491; Fax: 705/673-1817
Email: pdp@vianet.on.ca
ISBN: 0-920814, 0-921573, 2-89423
Productions Boule de neige
1175, rue Notre-Dame ouest, Victoriaville QC G6P 7L1
819/758-5073; Fax: 819/758-4787; Toll Free: 1-800-567-2531
ISBN: 2-921380
Productive Publications
PO Box 7200, Stn A, Toronto ON M5W 1X8
416/483-0634; Fax: 416/322-7434
ISBN: 0-920847, 1-896210
Prologue Inc.
1650, boul Lionel-Bertrand, Boisbriand QC J7H 1N7
514/434-0306; Fax: 514/434-2627; Toll Free: 1-800-363-2864
Promotional Book Company
36 Northline Rd., Toronto ON M4B 3E2
416/759-2226; Fax: 416/759-2150
Email: 75030.1713@compuserve.com
Prosveta Inc.
3950 Albert Mines, North Hatley QC J0B 2C0
819/564-8212; Fax: 819/564-1823; Toll Free: 1-800-854-8212
Email: prosveta@abacom.com; URL: http://www.prosveta.com
Vancouver Office: #202, 141 West 7th Ave., Vancouver BC V5Y 1L8
604/872-7292; Fax: 604/872-7292
ISBN: 1-895978, 2-920344, 2-85566; SAN 115-6896
Provincial News Co.
16504 - 121A Ave., Edmonton AB T5V 1J9
403/454-0306; Fax: 403/453-3687
Ptarmigan Press
(Kask Graphics Ltd.)
1372 - 16th Ave., Campbell River BC V9W 2E1
250/286-0878; Fax: 250/286-9749; Toll Free: 1-800-215-5275
ISBN: 0-919537; SAN: 116-0281
Publications Chant de mon pays
860, ch de la Montagne, CP 28, Beloeil QC J3S 4S8
514/464-1837; Fax: 514/464-2146
ISBN: 2-921124
Les Publications Graficor
175, boul de Mortagne, Boucherville QC J4B 6G4
514/449-2369; Fax: 514/449-7808
ISBN: 2-89242
Publications Ontario
50 Grosvenor St., Toronto ON M7A 1N8
416/326-5300; Fax: 416/326-5317; Toll Free: 1-800-668-9938
ISBN: 0-7743, 0-7729, 0-7778
Les Publications du Québec
1500D, boul Charest ouest, 1er étage, Ste-Foy QC G1N 2E5
418/643-5150; Fax: 418/643-6177; Toll Free: 1-800-463-2100
ISBN: 2-551
Publishers Group West
#223, 543 Richmond St. West, PO Box 106, Toronto ON M5V 1Y6
416/504-3900; Fax: 416/504-3902; Toll Free: 1-800-747-8147
Email: alan.zweig@pgw.com
SAN: 117-0171
Purich Publishing
PO Box 23032, Stn Market Mall, Saskatoon SK S7J 5H3
306/373-5311; Fax: 306/373-5315
Email: purich@sk.sympatico.ca
ISBN: 1-895830
Purpleville Publishing
#5, 3405 American Dr., Mississauga ON L4V 1T6
905/678-2855; Fax: 905/678-6036
ISBN: 0-9695306
Quarry Press
PO Box 1061, Kingston ON K7L 4Y5
613/548-8429; Fax: 613/548-1556
ISBN: 0-919627; SAN: 115-4958
Québec dans le Monde
#302, 1001, rte de l'Eglise, CP 8503, Ste-Foy QC G1V 4N5
418/659-5540; Fax: 418/659-4143
Email: quebecmonde@total.net; URL: http://www.total.net/~quebecmonde
ISBN: 2-921309
Québec Livres
2185, autoroute des Laurentide, Laval QC H7S 1Z6
514/687-1210; Fax: 514/687-1331
ISBN: 2-920596
Québec Science Éditeur
425, rue de la Gauchetière est, Montréal QC H2L 2M7
514/843-6888; Fax: 514/843-4897
Email: courier@QuebecScience.qc.ca
ISBN: 2-920073
Quintin Publishers/Éditions Michel Quintin
PO Box 340, Waterloo QC J0E 2N0
514/539-3774; Fax: 514/539-4905
ISBN: 2-920438, 2-89435; SAN: 116-5356
Quon Editions
10103 - 97A Ave., Edmonton AB T5K 2T3
403/428-3333; Fax: 403/428-3966; Toll Free: 1-800-565-9398
Email: quon@quoned.com; URL: http://www.quoned.com
ISBN: 0-9694432, 0-9695539, 0-9696831

Ragweed Press Inc./gynergy books
PO Box 2023, Charlottetown PE C1A 7N7
902/566-5750; Fax: 902/566-4473
Email: gb@gynergy.com
ISBN: 0-920304, 0-921556, 0-921881; SAN: 115-0863

Rainbird Press
3456 Dunbar St., PO Box 206, Vancouver BC V6S 2C2
604/224-4756; Fax: 604/731-3511
ISBN: 0-9690504

Rainbow House Distributors
#10, 160 Frobisher Dr., Waterloo ON N2V 2B1
519/746-8921; Fax: 519/746-5244; Toll Free: 1-800-265-8887

Raincoast Books Distribution Ltd. (Raincoast Books)
8680 Cambie St., Vancouver BC V6P 6M9
604/323-7100; Fax: 604/323-2600; Toll Free: 1-800-663-5714
Email: info@raincoast.com
ISBN: 0-920417, 1-895714; SAN 115-087

Random House of Canada Ltd.
1265 Aerowood Dr., Mississauga ON L4W 1B9
905/624-0672; Fax: 905/624-6217; Toll Free: 1-800-668-2427
URL: http://www.randomhouse.com
Editorial & Publicity Offices: #210, 33 Yonge St., Toronto ON M5E 1G4
416/777-9477; Fax: 416/777-9470
ISBN: 0-394, 0-679; SAN: 115-088X

Reader's Digest Association (Canada) Ltd.
215, av Redfern, Montréal QC H3Z 2V9
514/934-0751; Fax: 514/934-6177
Warehouse & Customer Service: 300 Orenda Rd. East, Brampton ON L6T 1G2
905/793-8221; Fax: 905/793-0846; Toll Free: 1-800-363-6259
ISBN: 0-88850; SAN 115-0898, 115-4974

Rebel Publishing
PO Box 2294, Peterborough ON K9J 7Y8
705/742-4831; Fax: 705/749-9226
URL: http://www.oncomdis.on.ca/bounty.htm
ISBN: 0-9680197

Red Deer College Press
PO Box 5005, Red Deer AB T4N 5H5
403/342-3321; Fax: 403/357-3639
Email: vmix@admin.rdc.ab.ca
ISBN 0-88995; SAN 115-1819

Reference Press
PO Box 70, Teeswater ON N0G 2S0
519/392-6634; Fax: 519/392-8043
Email: refpress@wcl.on.ca; URL: http://www.wcl.on.ca/~refpress
ISBN: 0-919981; SAN: 115-687X

Reference West
2450 Central Ave., Victoria BC V8S 2S8
250/598-0096
ISBN: 1-895362, 1-89410

Reflections
PO Box 178, Gabriola BC V0R 1X0
250/247-8685; Fax: 250/247-8116
ISBN: 0-9692570

Regina News Ltd.
1201 Lorne St., Regina SK S4R 2J9
306/525-3757; Fax: 306/569-9899; Toll Free: 1-800-665-8135

Reid Publishing Ltd.
109 Thomas St., PO Box 69559, Oakville ON L6J 7R4
905/842-4428; Fax: 905/842-9327; Toll Free: 1-800-4464797
ISBN: 0-921601; SAN: 116-0478

Reidmore Books
#1200, 10109 - 106 St., Edmonton AB T5J 3L7
403/424-4420; Fax: 403/441-9919; Toll Free: 1-800-661-2859
Email: reidmore@compusmart.ab.ca; URL: http://www.reidmore.com
ISBN: 0-919091, 1-895073

Renewable Energy in Canada
15010 Yonge St., Aurora ON L4G 1M6
905/841-5551; Fax: 905/841-6744
ISBN: 0-920456; SAN: 115-4990

Renouf Publishing Co. Ltd./Editions Renouf limitee
5369 Canotek Rd., Ottawa ON K1J 9J3
613/745-2665; Fax: 613/745-7660
Email: order.dept@renoufbooks.com; URL: http://www.renoufbooks.com
ISBN: 0-88852; SAN: 170-8066

Repository Press
137 South Lyon St., Prince George BC V2M 3K7
250/562-7074; Fax: 250/561-7094
Email: harris@cnc.bc.ca
ISBN: 0-920104; SAN: 115-5016

Research Press
60 Rankin St., Waterloo ON N2V 1V9
519/747-2477; Fax: 519/747-0062; Toll Free: 1-800-265-3375
ISBN: 0-87822; SAN: 115-5024

The Resource Centre Inc.
PO Box 190, Waterloo ON N2J 3Z9
519/885-0826; Fax: 519/747-5629
ISBN: 0-920701; SAN: 115-5032

Revue Cap-aux-Diamants (Editions Cap-aux-Diamants)
1, Côte de la Fabrique, CP 609, Succ HauteVille, Québec QC G1R 4S2
418/656-5040; Fax: 418/656-7282
ISBN: 2-920069

R.G. Mitchell Family Books Inc.
565 Gordon Baker Rd., Willowdale ON M2H 2W2
416/499-4615; Fax: 416/499-6340; Toll Free: 1-800-268-3445
Email: messages@rgm.ca; URL: http://www.rgm.ca
ISBN: 0-9293201; SAN: 115-8511

The Riverbank Press
10 Wolfrey Ave., Toronto ON M4K 1K8
416/462-1295

Riverwood Publishers Ltd.
6 Donlands Ave., PO Box 70, Sharon ON L0G 1V0
905/478-8396; Fax: 905/478-8380
Email: rwpub@interlog.com
ISBN: 1-895121; SAN: 116-1288

Robert Davies Multimedia Publishing/Editions multimedia Robert Davies inc.
#330, 4999, rue Ste-Catherine ouest, Westmount QC H3Z 1T3
514/481-2440; Fax: 514/481-9973; Toll Free: 1-800-481-2440
Email: rdppub@vir.com; URL: http://www.rdppub.com
ISBN: 1-895854, 1-55207, 2-89019, 2-89462

Robert Rose Inc.
#12, 156 Duncan Mill Rd., Don Mills ON M3B 3N2
416/449-3535; Fax: 416/449-9887
ISBN: 1-896503

Robert S. Ing Publishers
#102, 1170 Bay St., Toronto ON M5S 2B4
416/580-7508; Fax: 416/928-0243
ISBN: 0-9692707, 1-895377; SAN: 115-6934

Rockland Press
c/o Ken Haycock & Associates Inc., #343, 101-1001 West Broadway, Vancouver BC V6H 4E4
604/925-0266; Fax: 604/925-0566
Email: eml@rockland.com
ISBN: 0-920175

Rocky Mountain Books
4 Spruce Centre SW, Calgary AB T3C 3B3
403/249-9490; Fax: 403/249-2968; Toll Free: 1-800-566-3336
Email: tonyd@rmbooks.com; URL: http://www.rmbooks.com
ISBN: 0-9690038, 0-921102; SAN: 115-5040

Ron Belanger & Associates Inc.
217 Fairview Ave., Toronto ON M6P 3A6
416/763-0101; Fax: 416/763-0508
Email: rbelan@netcom.ca

Ronald P. Frye & Company (Publisher)
55 Lismer, Kanata ON K2K 1A5
613/592-6226; Fax: 613/592-9315
ISBN: 0-919741; SAN: 115-351X

Ronsdale Press
3350 West 21st. Ave., Vancouver BC V6S 1G7
604/738-1195; Fax: 604/731-4548
Email: ronhatch@pinc.com; URL: http://www.ronsdalepress.com
ISBN: 0-921870; SAN: 116-2454

A Room of One's Own Press
PO Box 5215, Stn B, Victoria BC V8R 6N4
250/598-8458; Fax: 250/598-8458
ISBN: 0-919998

Roseway Publishing Co.
RR#1, Lockeport NS B0T 1L0
902/656-2223; Fax: 902/656-2223
Email: ktudor@atcon.com
ISBN: 0-9694180, 1-896496

Roussan Publishers Inc./Roussan éditeur inc.
#100, 2110, boul Decarie, Montréal QC H4A 3J3
514/487-2895; Fax: 514/487-2899
URL: http://www.magnet.ca/roussan
ISBN: 1-896184, 2-921212

Rowland & Jacob Inc.
PO Box 545, Stn P, Toronto ON M5S 2T1
416/921-9557; Fax: 416/921-0408
ISBN: 0-921430

Rubicon Publishing Inc.
#1, 116 Thomas St., Oakville ON L6J 3A8
905/849-8777; Fax: 905/849-7579
Email: rubicon@pathway1.pathcom.com
ISBN: 0-921156; SAN 115-432X49-7579

S & B Books Ltd.
3043 Universal Dr., Mississauga ON L4X 2E2
905/629-5055; Fax: 905/629-5054; Toll Free: 1-800-997-7299
SAN: 119-6014

S & B Large Print & Special Lines Ltd.
4132 Dundas St. West, Toronto ON M8X 1X3
416/234-5015; Fax: 416/234-8781
SAN: 170-7736

S. Rosoph Publishers & Representatives
631, av Smart, Montréal QC H4X 1T2
514/488-3395
ISBN: 0-920341; SAN: 115-0936

Sage Books Canada
209 Bell St. North, Ottawa ON K1R 7E1
613/233-7243; Fax: 613/233-8626; Toll Free: 1-800-363-2845

Salem Press
93B Woodbridge Ave., PO Box 56510, Woodbridge ON L4L 8V3
905/851-4660; Fax: 905/851-5507

Sandhill Book Marketing
#99, 1270 Ellis St., Kelowna BC V1Y 1Z4
250/763-1406; Fax: 250/763-5211
Email: sandhill@awinc.com
ISBN: 0-920923; SAN: 115-2181

Saturn Distributing Inc.
25 Bodrington Ct., Markham ON L6G 1B6
905/470-2666; Fax: 905/470-2672

Saunders Book Co.
199 Campbell St., PO Box 308, Collingwood ON L9Y 3Z7
705/445-4777; Fax: 705/445-9569; Toll Free: 1-800-461-9120
Email: info@saundersbook.ca; URL: http://www.saundersbook.ca
ISBN: 1-89505; SAN: 169-9768

Saxon House Canada
PO Box 6947, Stn A, Toronto ON M5W 1X6
416/488-7171
ISBN: 0-9693934

SBF Media Limited
2201 Dunwin Dr., Mississauga ON L5L 1X2
905/828-6620; Fax: 905/828-2761; Toll Free: 1-800-268-4557
Email: sbfmedia@idirect.com; URL: http://www.sbfmedia.com
ISBN: 0-921932; SAN 115-5083

Scholar's Choice
2323 Trafalgar St., PO Box 4214, London ON N5W 5W3
519/453-7470; Fax: 519/455-2214; Toll Free: 1-800-265-1095
Email: scholars@wwdc.com
ISBN: 0-88809; SAN: 170-0014

Scholarly Book Services Inc.
#405, 77 Mowat Ave., Toronto ON M6K 3E3
416/533-5490; Fax: 416/533-5652; Toll Free: 1-800-847-9736
Email: sbookscan@globalserve.net; URL: http://www.globalserve.net/~sbookscan
SAN: 115-1339

Scholars' Books International Ltd.
(The Hathorne Bookshop)
PO Box 5218, Stn B, Victoria BC V8R 6W4
250/383-3215; Fax: 250/382-5512
SAN: 115-5148

Scholastic Canada Ltd.
123 Newkirk Rd., Richmond Hill ON L4C 3G5
905/883-5300; Fax: 905/883-4113
URL: http://www.scholastic.ca
ISBN: 0-590; SAN: 115-5164

School Book Fairs Limited *see* SBF Media Limited

Script Publishing Inc.
#200, 839 - 5 Ave. SW, Calgary AB T2P 3C8
403/290-0800; Fax: 403/241-8575; Toll Free: 1-800-661-1096
URL: http://www.ioe-design.com/script/
ISBN: 0-9694287, 1-896015

Seal Books
105 Bond St., Toronto ON M5B 1Y3
416/340-0777; Fax: 416/340-1069
ISBN: 0-7704; SAN 115-5210

Second Story Press
#301, 720 Bathurst St., Toronto ON M5S 1R4
416/537-7850; Fax: 416/537-7850
Email: secstory@fox.nstn.ca
ISBN: 0-929005

SeeMore Information Systems *see* Reidmore Books

Self-Counsel Press Ltd.
1481 Charlotte Rd., North Vancouver BC V7J 1H1
604/986-3366; Fax: 604/986-3947; Toll Free: 1-800-663-3007
Email: sales@self-counsel.com; URL: http://www.self-counsel.com
Toronto Office: 4 Bram Ct., Brampton ON L6W 3R6
905/450-0336; Fax: 905/450-7626; Toll Free: 1-800-387-3362
Email: scpress@total.net
ISBN: 0-88908, 1-55180; SAN: 115-0545

September Dreams Publishing
9419 Fairmount Dr. SE, Calgary AB T2J 0R1
403/253-0284; Fax: 403/253-3441
Email: septdrms@cal.cybersurf.net
ISBN: 0-9695763

Services Documentaires Multimedia Inc.
#300, 75, Port-Royal est, Montréal QC H3L 3T1
514/382-0895; Fax: 514/384-9139
Email: info@sdm.qc.ca; URL: http://www.sdm.qc.ca

Servidec
50 Main St., Ottawa ON K1S 1B2
613/237-5577; Fax: 613/230-1762; Toll Free: 1-800-265-0375

Shard Press
4 Garview Ct., Etobicoke ON M9K 4B9
416/249-5522; Fax: 416/249-5522
Email: kyril@shard.com
ISBN: 0-9696455

Sheltus & Picard Inc.
CP 1321, Bedford QC J0J 1A0
514/248-7319; Fax: 514/248-2057
Email: sandp@acbm.qc.cq
ISBN: 0-9696296

Shirley Lewis Information Services *see* National Book Service

Shoreline/Littoral
23, rue Sainte-Anne, Sainte-Anne-de-Bellevue QC H9X 1L1
514/457-5733; Fax: 514/457-5733
Email: bookline@total.net; URL: http://www.total.net/~bookline
ISBN: 0-9695180, 0-9698752, 1-896754; SAN 116-9564

Siddall & Associates
#101, 873 Beatty St., Vancouver BC V6B 2M6
604/662-3511; Fax: 604/683-7540
Email: general@siddall-assoc.com

Sinai Books
7356 Ontario St., Vancouver BC V5X 3B8
604/327-6694
Email: sinai@sportsx.com
ISBN: 1-8962771

Sister Vision Press
PO Box 217, Stn E, Toronto ON M6H 4E2
416/533-9353; Fax: 416/533-9676
Email: sisvis@web.net
ISBN: 0-920813, 1-896705

Slabtown Press
141 Bradley St., St. Catharines ON L2T 1R8
905/227-2699
Email: kphutchin@freenet.npiec.on.ca

Slavuta Publishers
72 Westbrook Dr., Edmonton AB T6J 2E1
403/434-2449
ISBN: 0-919452

Snowapple Press
PO Box 66024, Stn Heritage, Edmonton AB T6J 6T4
403/437-0191
ISBN: 1-895592

Socadis Inc.
350, boul Lebeau, Ville St-Laurent QC H4N 1W6
514/331-3300; Fax: 514/745-3282; Toll Free: 1-800-361-2847

Sogides Ltée
955, rue Amherst, Montréal QC H2L 3K4
514/523-1182; Fax: 514/521-4434; Toll Free: 1-800-361-4806
ISBN: 2-7619

Somabec Ltée
2475, av Sylva-Clapin, Saint-Hyacinthe QC J2S 7B6
514/774-8118; Fax: 514/774-3017

Somerset Books Ltd.
RR#2, PO Box 1500, Stayner ON L0M 1S0
705/428-0378; Fax: 705/428-0310
SAN: 115-8260

Somerville House Books Limited
#5000, 3080 Yonge St., Toronto ON M4N 3N1
416/488-5938; Fax: 416/488-5506
Email: sombooks@goodmedia.com; URL: http://www.goodmedia.com/somervillehouse
ISBN: 0-921051

Sono Nis Press
1725 Blanshard St., Victoria BC V8W 2J8
250/382-1024; Fax: 250/382-0775
URL: http://www.islandnet.com/~sononis/
ISBN: 0-919462, 0-919203, 1-55039; SAN: 115-1398

Sound And Vision Publishing Ltd.
359 Riverdale Ave., Toronto ON M4J 1A4
416/465-2828; Fax: 416/465-0755
URL: http://www.soundandvision.com
ISBN: 0-920151; SAN: 115-0979

Southam Magazine & Information Group
1450 Don Mills Rd., North York ON M3B 2X7
416/445-6641; Fax: 416/442-2077; Toll Free: 1-800-268-7742
Email: irhind@southam.ca; URL: hhtp://www.southam.com
SAN: 115-5253

Southwest Québec Publishing
(Dialogue)
2311 Rockburn Rd., Franklin Centre QC J0S 1E0
514/264-6618; Fax: 514/264-5387; Toll Free: 1-800-706-1819
Email: dialogue@rocler.qc.ca
ISBN: 1-895656

Spectrum Educational Supplies Ltd.
125 Mary St., Aurora ON L4G 1G3
905/841-0600; Fax: 905/727-6265; Toll Free: 1-800-668-0600
SAN: 116-0311

Spindrift Publishing
PO Box 50, Barrington NS B0W 1E0
902/637-2569
ISBN: 0-9691458

Springbank Publishing
5425 Elbow Dr. SW, Calgary AB T2V 1H7
403/640-9137; Fax: 403/640-9138
ISBN: 1-895653

Squeegee Press
1727 Adanac St., Victoria BC V8R 2C4
ISBN: 0-9680715

Stanton & MacDougall *see* Kate Walker & Co. Ltd.

Statistics Canada
c/o Circulation Management, 120 Parkdale Ave., Ottawa ON K1A 9Z9
613/951-7277; Fax: 613/951-1584; Toll Free: 1-800-700-1033
Email: order@statcan.ca; URL: http://www.statcan.ca
ISBN: 0-660, 0-662

Stewart House
c/o Canbook Distribution Services, 1220 Nicholson Rd., Newmarket ON L3Y 7B1
800/399-6858; Fax: 800/363-2665
ISBN: 1-895246; SAN: 115-4192

Stoddart Publishing Co. Limited
34 Lesmill Rd., Toronto ON M3B 2T6
416/445-3333; Fax: 416/445-5967
Email: stoddart@gen.pub.com; URL: http://www.genpub.com/stoddart/index.html
ISBN: 0-7737; SAN: 115-0391

Stoneycroft Publishing
RR#1, PO Box 1710, Yarmouth NS B5A 4A5
902/742-2667
ISBN: 1-896269

Subway Books Ltd.
247 Albany Ave., Toronto ON M5R 3C7
416/535-5572; Fax: 416/538-3317
ISBN: 0-9681660

Summerhill Books *see* Breakwater Books Ltd.

Summerthought Ltd.
PO Box 1420, Banff AB T0L 0C0
403/762-3919; Fax: 403/762-4126
ISBN: 0-919934; SAN: 115-2149

Summit Educational Services
PO Box 149, Richmond Hill ON L4C 4X9
905/883-9427; Fax: 905/770-8576; Toll Free: 1-800-741-5956
ISBN: 1-895187

Sun-Scape Enterprises Ltd.
PO Box 793, Stn F, Toronto ON M4Y 2N7
905/470-8634; Toll Free: 1-800-437-1454
Email: 74601.2021@compuserve.com; URL: http://www.sun-scape.com
ISBN: 0-919842

Synaxis Press
37323 Hawkins Rd., Dewdney BC VOM 1HO
604/826-9336; Fax: 604/820-9758
ISBN: 0-919672; SAN: 115-532

Talmage Book Centre
1260 Lakeshore Rd. East, Mississauga ON L5E 3B8

905/271-7173; Fax: 905/274-1843
Email: tbc@terraport.net; URL: http://www.terraport.net/tbc/tbc.htm
SAN: 118-1327

Talon Books Ltd.
#104, 3100 Production Way, Burnaby BC V5A 4R4
604/444-4889; Fax: 604/444-4119
Email: talon@pinc.com; URL: http://www.swifty.com/talon
ISBN: 0-88922; SAN: 115-5334; Telebook: S1150391

Tanager Press
(Groupe Tanager)
145 Troy St., Mississauga ON L5G 1S8
905/891-2502; Fax: 905/891-6884
ISBN: 1-895410

Tantalas Books
PO Box 255, Gander NF A1V 1W6
709/651-3136; Fax: 709/651-3849
ISBN: 0-9695519

Temeron Books Inc.
#210, 1220 Kensington Rd. NW, Calgary AB T2N 3P5
403/283-0900; Fax: 403/283-6947
Email: temeron@telusplanet.net
ISBN: 1-895510

Terrific Titles for Young Readers
PO Box 545, Stn P, Toronto ON M5S 2T1
416/921-9557; Fax: 416/921-0408

Theytus Books
PO Box 20040, Penticton BC V2A 6K3
250/493-7181; Fax: 250/493-5302
ISBN: 0-919441; SAN: 115-1517

Thistledown Press Ltd.
633 Main St., Saskatoon SK S7H 0J8
306/244-1722; Fax: 306/244-1762
Email: thistle@sk.sympatico.ca; URL: http://www.thistledown.sk.ca
ISBN: 0-920066, 0-920633, 1-895449; SAN: 115-1061

Thomas Allen & Son Ltd./Saunders of Toronto
390 Steelcase Rd. East, Markham ON L3R 1G2
905/475-9126; Fax: 905/475-6747; Toll Free: 1-800-458-5504
ISBN: 0-919028; SAN: 115-1762

Thompson Educational Publishing, Inc.
#105, 14 Ripley Ave., Toronto ON M6S 3N9
416/766-2763; Fax: 416/766-0398
Email: thompson@canadabooks.ingenia.com
ISBN: 1-55077, 1-921332

Tikka Books
PO Box 242, Chambly QC J3L 4B3
514/658-6205; Fax: 514/658-3514
Email: alpelie@accent.net; URL: http://www.accent.net/alpelie/
ISBN: 1-896106

Times Mirror Professional Publishing
130 Flaska Dr., Markham ON L6G 1B8
905/470-6739; Fax: 905/470-6780; Toll Free: 1-800-268-4178
ISBN: 0-8016; SAN: 115-4389

Tralco Educational Services Inc.
297 Brucedale Ave. East, Hamilton ON L9A 1R2
905/575-5717; Fax: 905/575-1783; Toll Free: 1-800-487-2524
Email: tralco@binatech.on.ca
ISBN: 0-921376

Trans-Canada Press *see* Who's Who Publications

Tree Frog Press Ltd.
10144 - 89 St., Edmonton AB T5H 1P7
403/429-1947; Fax: 403/425-8760
ISBN: 0-88967; SAN: 115-1053

Tree House Press Inc.
85 Lansing Dr., Unit O, Hamilton ON L8W 2Z9
905/574-3399; Fax: 905/574-0228; Toll Free: 1-800-776-8733
ISBN 1-895165

Tri-Fold Books (Distributor)
55 Wyndham St. North, PO Box 29078, Guelph ON N1H 8J4
519/821-9901; Fax: 519/821-5333
SAN: 106-4320

Trifolium Books Inc.
#28, 238 Davenport Rd., Toronto ON M5R 1J6
416/925-0765; Fax: 416/485-5563
Email: trifolio@ican.net; URL: http://www.pubcouncil.ca/trifolium
ISBN: 1-895579

Trilobyte Press
1486 Willowdown Rd., Oakville ON L6L 1X3
905/847-7366; Fax: 905/847-3258
Email: admin@successatschool.com; URL: http://www.successatschool.com
ISBN: 1-895482

True Remainders Ltd. *see* Paideia Press Ltd.

TSAR Publications
PO Box 6996, Stn A, Toronto ON M5W 1X7
416/483-7191; Fax: 416/486-0706
ISBN: 0-929661

Tumbleweed Press
#11, 401 Magnetic Dr., Downsview ON M3J 3H9
416/964-1771; Fax: 416/667-0460

Tundra Books Inc. *see* McClelland & Stewart Inc.

TUNS Press
Faculty of Architecture, Dalhousie University, PO Box 1000, Halifax NS B3J 2X4
902/420-7641; Fax: 902/423-6672
Email: press@tuns.ca; URL: http://www.tuns.ca/press
ISBN: 0-929112

Turner-Warwick Publications Inc.
PO Box 1029, North Battleford SK S9A 3E6
306/445-7261; Fax: 306/445-3223
ISBN: 0-919899

Turnstone Press
#607, 100 Arthur St., Winnipeg MB R3B 1H3
204/947-1555, 1556; Fax: 204/942-1555
Email: Editor@TurnstonePress.mb.ca; Marketing@TurnstonePress.mb.ca
ISBN: 0-88801; SAN: 115-1096

Tyro Publishing
194 Carlbert S., Sault Ste. Marie ON P6A 5E1
705/253-6402; Fax: 705/942-3625
ISBN: 0-921249

Ulverscroft Large Print (Canada) Ltd.
PO Box 80038, Burlington ON L7L 6B1
905/637-8734; Fax: 905/333-6788; Toll Free: 1-888-860-3365
Email: ulpbcan@worldchat.com; URL: http://dspace.dial.pipex.com/town/plaza/hfss/
ISBN: 0-7089

Ulysses Books & Maps Distribution/Éditions Ulysse
4176, rue Saint-Denis, Montréal QC H2W 2M5
514/843-9882; Fax: 514/843-9448
URL: http://www.ulysse.ca
ISBN: 2-921444; SAN: 115-7167

Umbrella Press
56 Rivercourt Blvd., Toronto ON M4J 3A4
416/696-6665; Fax: 416/696-9189
Email: umbpress@interlog.com; URL: http://www.interlog.com/~umbpress
ISBN: 1-895642

United Church Publishing House
3250 Bloor St. West, 4th Fl., Etobicoke ON M8X 2Y4
416/231-7680, ext.4113; Fax: 416/232-6004
Email: bparker@uccan.org; URL: http://www.@uccan.org
ISBN: 0-919000, 1-55134; SAN: 115-3013

United Library Services
7140 Fairmount Dr. SE, Calgary AB T2H 0X4
403/252-4426; Fax: 403/258-3426; Toll Free: 1-800-342-5857
Email: service@uls.com
SAN: 169-9342

The Unitrade Press
(Unitrade Associates)
95 Floral Pkwy., Toronto ON M6L 2C4
416/242-5900; Fax: 416/242-6115
ISBN: 0-919801, 0-895909; SAN: 115-544X

University of Alberta Press
141 Athabasca Hall, University of Alberta, Edmonton AB T6G 2E8
403/492-3662; Fax: 403/492-0719; Toll Free: 1-800-668-0821
Email: uap@gpu.srv.ualberta.ca; URL: http://www.ualberta.ca/~uap
ISBN: 0-88864; SAN: 115-110X

University of British Columbia Press
(UBC Press)
UBC, 6344 Memorial Rd., Vancouver BC V6T 1Z2
604/822-3259; Fax: 604/822-6083; Toll Free: 1-800-668-0821
Email: orders@ubcpress.ubc.ca; URL: http://www.ubcpress.ubc.ca
ISBN: 0-7748; SAN: 115-1118

University of Calgary Press
2500 University Dr. NW, Calgary AB T2N 1N4
403/220-7578; Fax: 403/282-0085; Toll Free: 1-800-668-0821
Email: 75001@aoss.ucalgary.ca; URL: http://www.ucalgary.ca/UCPress
ISBN: 0-919813, 1-895176, 1-55238

University College of Cape Breton Press
PO Box 5300, Stn A, Sydney NS B1P 6L2
902/503-1604; Fax: 902/563-1177
Email: pmarshall@caper2.uccb.ns.ca
ISBN 0-920336; SAN 115-5458

University Extension Press
Rm. 118, Kirk Hall, University of Saskatchewan, 117 Science Pl., Saskatoon SK S7N 5C8
306/966-5558; Fax: 306/966-5567
Email: bert.wolfe@usask.ca; URL: http://www.extension.usask.ca/

University of Manitoba Press
#244, 15 Gilson St., Winnipeg MB R3T 5V6
204/474-9495; Fax: 204/474-7511
URL: http://www.umanitoba.ca/publications.uofmpress
ISBN: 0-88755; SAN: 115-5474

University of Ottawa Press/Presses de l'Université d'Ottawa
542 King Edward St., Ottawa ON K1N 6N5
613/562-5246; Fax: 613/562-5247
Email: press@uottawa.ca; URL: http://www.uopress.uottawa.ca
ISBN: 0-7766, 2-7603; SAN: 115-5482

University of Toronto Press
#700, 10 St. Mary St., Toronto ON M4Y 2W8
416/978-2239; Fax: 416/978-4738
Email: utpbooks@gpu.utcc.utoronto.ca; URL: http://www.library.utoronto.ca/www/utpress/depthome.htm
Order Department & Distribution: 5201 Dufferin St., North York ON M3H 5T8
416/667-7791; Fax: 416/667-7832; Toll Free: 1-800-565-9523
ISBN: 0-8020; SAN: 115-1134

Upney Editions
19 Appalachian Cres., Kitchener ON N2E 1A3
ISBN: 0-9681403

Uris Analytica Publishing Inc.
PO Box 47036, Stn Edmonton Ctr., Edmonton AB T5J 4N1
403/432-9458; Fax: 403/413-8207
ISBN: 0-9698958

Vancouver Community College Press *see* 49th Avenue Press

Vanwell Publishing Limited
1 Northrup Cres., PO Box 2131, St. Catharines ON L2M 6P5
905/937-3100; Fax: 905/937-1760; Toll Free: 1-800-661-6136
ISBN: 0-92027, 1-55068

Véhicule Press
PO Box 125, Stn Place du Parc, Montréal QC H2W 2M9
514/844-6073; Fax: 514/844-7543
Email: vpress@cam.org; URL: http://www.cam.org/~vpress
ISBN: 0-919890, 1-55065; SAN: 115-1150

Vesta Publications Ltd.
PO Box 1641, Cornwall ON K6H 5V6
613/932-2135; Fax: 613/932-7735
Email: sgill@glen-net.ca
ISBN: 0-919806, 1-55065; SAN: 115-5520

VLB Éditeur
1010, rue de la Gauchetière est, Montréal QC H2L 2N5
514/523-1182; Fax: 514/282-7530
ISBN: 2-89295

Voyageur Publishing
3 Richmond St., Maitland ON K0E 1P0
613/348-3166; Fax: 613/348-3065
ISBN: 0-921842

Wall & Emerson, Inc.
(Wall & Thompson)
6 O'Connor Dr., Toronto ON M4K 2K1
416/467-8685; Fax: 416/696-2460
Email: wall@maple.net
ISBN: 1-895131, 0-921332; SAN: 116-0486

Warwick Publishing
#111, 388 King St. West, Toronto ON M5V 1K2
416/596-1555; Fax: 416/596-1520
ISBN: 1-895629

Waterloo Music Co. Ltd.
3 Regina St. North, Waterloo ON N2J 4A5
519/886-4990; Fax: 519/886-4999
ISBN: 0-88909; SAN: 157-9363

Weigl Educational Publishers
1900 - 11th St. SE, Calgary AB T2G 3G2
403/233-7747; Fax: 403/233-7769; Toll Free: 1-800-668-0766
ISBN: 0-9690637, 0-919879; SAN: 115-1312, 115-5536

West Coast Paradise Publishing
#5, 9060 Tronson Rd., Vernon BC V1T 6L7
250/545-4186; Fax: 250/545-4194
ISBN: 0-9697494, 1-896779

West Wind Press
#304, 5805 - 112 St., Edmonton AB T6H 3J4
403/434-4362
ISBN: 0-9692942

Western Extension College Publishers
PO Box 110, Saskatoon SK S7K 3K1
306/373-6399; Fax: 306/892-2046

Western Publishing (Canada) Inc. *see* Golden Books Publishing

White Wolf Publishers
Bay R, 7004 - 5th St. SE, Calgary AB T2H 2G3
403/252-2006; Fax: 403/894-0332
Email: sales@tdimports.com; URL: http://www.tdimports.com
ISBN: 1-56504

Whitecap Books Ltd.
351 Lynn Ave., North Vancouver BC V7J 2C4
604/980-9852; Fax: 604/980-8197
Email: whitecap@pinc.com; URL: http://www.whitecap.ca
Toronto Office: 602 Richmond St. West, Toronto ON M5Y 1Y9
416/777-0929
ISBN: 1-895099; SAN: 115-1290

Whitehots Inc.
#2, 2 Vata Ct., Aurora ON L4G 4B6
905/727-9188; Fax: 905/727-8756; Toll Free: 1-800-567-9188
Email: whitehot@idirect.com

Who's Who Publications
777 Bay St., 5th Fl., Toronto ON M5W 1A7
416/595-5100; Fax: 416/596-5155
ISBN: 0-920966; SAN: 115-1045

Wilfrid Laurier University Press
75 University Ave. West, Waterloo ON N2L 3C5
519/884-0710, ext.6124; Fax: 519/725-1399
Email: press@mach1.wlu.ca; URL: http://www.wlu.ca/~wwwpress/
ISBN: 0-88920; SAN: 115-1525

William Street Press
PO Box 21114, Stratford ON N5A 7X4
519/263-5973; Fax: 519/263-5973
ISBN: 0-9691075, 0-9695097

Williams Books
3007 Granville St., Vancouver BC V6H 3J9
604/733-1326; Fax: 604/733-1326

Wilson et Lafleur
40, rue Notre-Dame, Montréal QC H2Y 1B9
514/875-6326; Fax: 514/875-8356
Email: cwilson@quebecor.com; URL: http://www.wilsonlafleur.com
ISBN: 2-89127

Windflower Communications
844K McLeod Ave., Winnipeg MB R2G 2T7
204/668-7475; Fax: 204/661-8530; Toll Free: 1-800-465-6564
Email: windflower@brandtfamily.com; URL: http://www.infobahn.mb.ca/brandtfamily
ISBN: 1-895308

Windsor News Educational Division
3350 North Talbot Rd., Oldcastle ON N0R 1L0
519/737-6923; Fax: 519/737-1612; Toll Free: 1-800-265-2892

Wolsak & Wynn Publishers Ltd.
PO Box 316, Stn Don Mills, Don Mills ON M3C 2S7
416/222-4690; Fax: 416/237-0291
ISBN: 0-919897; SAN: 115-749

Women's Press
(Women's Educational Press)
#302, 517 College St., Toronto ON M6G 4A2
416/921-2425; Fax: 416/921-4428
Email: wompress@web.apc.org
ISBN: 0-88961; SAN: 115-5628

Wood Lake Books, Inc.
10162 Newene Rd., Winfield BC V4V 1R2
250/766-2778; Fax: 250/766-2736; Toll Free: 1-800-663-2775
Email: info@woodlane.com
ISBN: 0-919599, 0-929032; SAN: 115-5636

Word Alive
60 Cedar St., Niverville MB R0A 1E0
Fax: 204/388-9999; Toll Free: 1-800-665-1468

World Book Childcraft of Canada Ltd.
#240, 4411 East Hastings St., Burnaby BC V5C 2K1
604/298-3915; Fax: 604/298-8273
ISBN: 0-7166; SAN: 115-5644, 115-5662

Wuerz Publishing Ltd.
895 McMillan Ave., Winnipeg MB R3M 0T2
204/453-7429; Fax: 204/453-6598
Email: swuerz@wuerzpuble.mb.ca; URL: http://www.mbnet.mb.ca/~swuerz
ISBN: 0-929963

Wyman & Son Publishers
866 Campbell Ave., Ottawa ON K2A 2C5
613/729-8495; Fax: 613/729-9230; Toll Free: 1-800-668-3283

XYZ Éditeur
1781, rue Saint-Hubert, Montréal QC H2L 3Z1
514/525-2170; Fax: 514/525-7537
ISBN: 2-89261

York Press Ltd.
#305, 77 Carlton St., Toronto ON M5B 2J7
416/599-6652; Fax: 416/599-2657
ISBN: 0-919966, 1-896761; SAN: 115-5687

Young Readers Ltd.
11 Banington Cres., Brampton ON L7A 1G4
905/840-1765; Fax: 905/840-0463

# NEWSPAPERS

## Alberta Daily Newspapers

### CALGARY:

Calgary Herald, Southam Inc., 215 - 16 St. SE, PO Box 2400, Stn M, Calgary AB T2P 0W8 – 403/235-7100; Fax: 403/235-7113; Email: theherald.southam.ca; Telex: 038-22793 – Circ.: 140,000; Morning – Publisher, Ken King; Editor, Crosbie Cotton

The Calgary Sun, 2615 - 12 St. NE, Calgary AB T2E 7W9 – 403/250-4200; Fax: 403/491-4116; URL: http://www.canoe.ca/CalgarySun/home.html – Circ.: 67,526, Mon.-Sat.; 98,480, Sun.; Morning – Publisher, Lester Pyette

### EDMONTON:

The Edmonton Journal, Southam Inc., 10006 - 101 St., PO Box 2421, Edmonton AB T5J 2S6 – 403/429-5100; Fax: 403/429-5500; URL: http://www.southam.com/edmontonjournal/ – Circ.: 150,500; Morning – President & Publisher, Linda Hughes; Editor-in-chief, Murdoch Davis; Reader Sales & Service, Dave Reidie

The Edmonton Sun, #250, 4990 - 92 Ave., Edmonton AB T6B 3A1 – 403/468-0100; Fax: 403/468-0139; Email: sun.letters@ccinet.ab.ca; URL: http://www.canoe.ca – Circ.: 73,036, Mon.-Sat.; 113,297, Sun.; Morning – Publisher, Craig Martin; Editor-in-chief, Paul Stanway

### FORT MCMURRAY:

Fort McMurray Today, Bowes Publishers Ltd., 8550 Franklin Ave., Fort McMurray AB T9H 3G1 – 403/743-8186; Fax: 403/790-1006; Email: today@ccinet.ab.ca – Circ.: 4,909, Mon.-Thur.; 7,248, Fri.; Afternoon/evening, Mon.-Fri. – Publisher, Tim O'Rouke; Managing Editor, Darrell Skidnuk

### GRANDE PRAIRIE:

Daily Herald-Tribune, Bowes Publishers Ltd., 10604 - 100 St., PO Box 3000, Grande Prairie AB T8V 6V4 – 403/532-1110; Fax: 403/532-2120 – Circ.: 8,500, Mon.-Thur.; 12,130, Fri.; Afternoon – Publisher, Peter J. Woolsey; Managing Editor, David Lassner

### LETHBRIDGE:

The Lethbridge Herald, Thomson Newspapers Co. Ltd., 504 - 7th St. South, Lethbridge AB T1J 3Z7 – 403/328-4411; Fax: 403/328-4536; URL: http://www.lis.ab.ca/lhearld/ – Circ.: 22,370, Mon.-Sat.; 20,416, Sun.; Morning – Publisher, Greg Lutes; Managing Editor, Bill Whitelaw; Circulation Manager, Garth Leddy

### MEDICINE HAT:

Medicine Hat News, Southam Inc., 3257 Dunmore Rd. SE, PO Box 10, Medicine Hat AB T1A 7E6 – 403/527-1101; Fax: 403/527-6029 – Circ.: 14,500; Evening – Publisher, Mike Hertz

### RED DEER:

Red Deer Advocate, 2950 Bremner Ave., PO Box 5200, Red Deer AB T4N 5G3 – 403/343-2400; Fax: 403/342-4051 – Circ.: 20,800; Afternoon – Publisher, Howard D. Janzen; Editor, Joe McLaughlin; Circulation Manager, Allan Melbourne

## Other Newspapers in Alberta

Airdrie & District Echo, PO Box 3820, Airdrie AB T4B 2B9 – 403/948-7280 – Wed.

Athabasca: The Advocate, 4917B - 49 St., Athabasca AB T9S 1C5 – 403/675-9222; Fax: 403/675-3143 –

Circ.: 5,000; Tue. – Publisher & Editor, Donny Rajoo

Banff: The Banff Crag & Canyon, 201 Bear St., 2nd Fl., PO Box 129, Banff AB T0L 0C0 – 403/762-2453; Fax: 403/762-5274; Email: banffweb@telusplanet.net – Circ.: 3,993; Wed. – Publisher, Sandra Santa Lucia; Editor, Sherri Bickifoose; Circulation Manager, Anne Bosma

Barrhead Leader, PO Box 4520, Barrhead AB T7N 1A4 – 403/674-3823; Fax: 403/674-6337; Email: leader@west-teq.net – Circ.: 3,959; Tue. – Publisher, Carol Farnalls; Editor, John Ollerenshaw

Bashaw Star, PO Box 188, Bashaw AB T0B 0H0 – 403/372-3608; Fax: 403/372-4445 – Tue. – Manager, Ross Hunter

Bassano Times, PO Box 780, Bassano AB T0J 0B0 – 403/641-3636; Fax: 403/641-3952 – Circ.: 749; Mon. – Publisher & Editor-in-chief, Mary Lou Brooks

Beaumont La Nouvelle, 5021B - 52nd Ave., Beaumont AB T4X 1E5 – 403/929-5552; Fax: 403/929-5553 – Circ.: 1,800; Mon.; English & French – Publisher, Hugh Johnston; Editor, Kimberly Carr

Beaverlodge & District Advertiser, PO Box 300, Beaverlodge AB T0H 0C0 – 403/354-2460 – Wed.

Bentley: Bentley Bugle, PO Box 380, Rimbey AB T0C 2J0 – 403/843-2231; Fax: 403/843-2990 – Circ.: 1,850; Monthly – Publisher, Ed Moller; Editor, John Roberts; Circulation Manager, E. Archer

Blairmore: The Crowsnest Pass Promoter, PO Box 1019, Blairmore AB T0K 0E0 – 403/562-8884; Fax: 403/562-2242 – Circ.: 2,500; Tue. – Publisher, Jim Prentice; Editor, Ross Purnell

Blairmore: The Pass Herald, PO Box 960, Blairmore AB T0K 0E0 – 403/562-2248; Fax: 403/562-2242 – Tue.

Bonnyville Nouvelle, PO Box 8174, Bonnyville AB T9N 2J5 – 403/826-3876 – Tue.; English & French

Bow Island: The 40-Mile County Commentator, PO Box 580, Bow Island AB T0K 0G0 – 403/545-2258; Fax: 403/545-6886 – Tue.

Bowden: The Voice of Bowden, PO Box 209, Bowden AB T0M 0K0 – 403/224-2288; Fax: 403/224-3010 – Circ.: 1,000; Tues. – Publisher & Editor, Wray Hutchison

Brooks Bulletin, Nesbitt Publishing Co., 124 - 3rd St. West, PO Box 1450, Brooks AB T1R 1C3 – 403/362-5571; Fax: 403/362-5080; Email: nesbittj@cadvision.com – Wed. – Publisher, J.L. Nesbitt Sr.; Editor, Jamie Nesbitt Jr.

Calgary Community Digest, #453, 3545 - 32nd Ave. NE, Calgary AB T1Y 6M6 – 403/275-8275 – Circ.: 25,000; Fri.

Calgary Herald Neighbors, PO Box 2400, Stn M, Calgary AB T2P 0W8 – 403/235-8680; Fax: 403/235-7379 – Thur.; 6 city area editions

Calgary Mirror, 2615 - 12 St. NE, Calgary AB T2E 7W9 – 403/250-4329; Fax: 403/250-4176 – Circ.: 156,000; Wed.; 2 city area editions

Calgary: Calgary Rural Times, 315 First St. East, Cochrane AB T0L 0W1 – 403/932-3000; Fax: 403/932-3935; Email: ctw@nucleus.com – Circ.: 12,063; Tue. – Publisher, Kelvin Thera; Editor, David Forbes

Calgary: Le Chinook, 4 Hunterhorn Rd. NE, Calgary AB T2K 6E8 – 403/274-7320; Email: chinook@nucleus.com – Tirage: 10 000; Mensuel; français – Rédacteur, Richard Belanger

Calmar Community Voice, A.F. Keller & Associates Ltd., PO Box 6000, Spruce Grove AB T7X 2Z5 – 403/962-9228; Fax: 403/962-1021 – Circ.: 4,600; Every other Tue. – Editor, Al Keller

Camrose Booster, 4925 - 48 St., Camrose AB T4V 1L7 – 403/672-3142; Fax: 403/672-2518; Email: booster@cable-lynx.net; URL: http://www.ifpa.com – Circ.: 12,357; Tue. – Publisher, Blain Fowler; Editor, Berdie Fowler; Circulation Manager, Doug Schwartz

Camrose Canadian, 4903 - 49 Ave., Camrose AB T4V 0M9 – 403/672-4421; Fax: 403/672-5323; Email: canadian@telusplanet.net – Circ.: 3,875; Wed.; also Camrose Canadian Extra (Mon.) – Publisher, Lynne Chernin; Editor, Tim Chamberlin; Circulation Manager, Karen Olsen

Canmore: The Canmore Leader, #201, 802 - 8th St., Canmore AB T1W 2B7 – 403/678-2365; Fax: 403/678-2996; Email: canmore1@telusplanet.net – Tue.; also Rockies: the magazine (2 times a year) – Publisher, Shari Bishop

Cardston Chronicle, PO Box 1800, Cardston AB T0K 0K0 – 403/653-2222; Fax: 403/653-1935 – Tue.

Carstairs Courier, PO Box 40, Irricana AB T0M 1B0 – 403/935-4688; Fax: 403/337-3160 – Circ.: 3,100; Tue. – Publisher, Fred Denishuk; Editor, Leanne Rekiel

Castor Advance, PO Box 120, Castor AB T0C 0X0 – 403/882-4044; Fax: 403/882-2010 – Thur.

Claresholm Local Press, PO Box 520, Claresholm AB T0L 0T0 – 403/625-4474; Fax: 403/625-2828 – Wed.

Coaldale: Sunny South News, PO Box 30, Coaldale AB T1M 1M2 – 403/345-3081; Fax: 403/345-5408 – Circ.: 4,025; Tue. – Publisher, Coleen Campbell, 403/223-9659; Editor, Harley Richards; Circulation Manager, Valerie Wiebe

Cochrane This Week, 315 First St. East, Cochrane AB T0L 0W1 – 403/932-3000; Fax: 403/932-3935; Email: ctw@nucleus.com – Circ.: 2,284; Tue. – Publisher, Kevin Thera; Editor, David Forbes

Cold Lake Courier, CFB Cold Lake, PO Box 6190, Cold Lake AB T9M 2R7 – 403/594-5206; Fax: 403/594-2139 – Wed.

Consort Enterprise, PO Box 129, Consort AB T0C 1B0 – 403/577-3611; Fax: 403/577-3611; Email: consort_entrprise@awnet.net – Circ.: 1,201; Tue. – Publisher, Wm. J. Readman; Editor, Mary K. Readman; Circulation Manager, Carol Readman

Coronation Review, PO Box 70, Coronation AB T0C 1C0 – 403/578-4111; Fax: 403/578-2088; Email: coronation_review@awnet.net – Tue.

Didsbury Review, PO Box 760, Didsbury AB T0M 0W0 – 403/335-3301; Fax: 403/335-8143 – Circ.: 1,782; Tue. – Publisher, Gene Hartmann; Editor-in-chief, Janice Harrington

Drayton Valley Western Review, PO Box 6960, Drayton Valley AB T7A 1SE – 403/542-5380; Fax: 403/542-9200 – Tue. – Editor, Mark Mellott

Drumheller Mail, PO Box 1629, Drumheller AB T0J 0Y0 – 403/823-2580 – Wed.

Eckville Examiner, PO Box 380, Rimbey AB T0C 2J0 – 403/843-2231; Fax: 403/843-2990; Email: eckville_examiner@awnet.net – Circ.: 1,000; Tue. – Publisher, Ed Moller; Editor, John Roberts; Circulation Manager, E. Archer

Edmonton City News, Alberta Business Research Ltd, #800, 10179 - 105 St., Edmonton AB T5J 3N1 – 403/424-0190; Fax: 403/421-7677 – Circ.: 40,000; Monthly; also Edmonton Senior Newspaper – Publisher, Lorne Silverstein; Editor, Colin Smith

Edmonton Examiner, 17533 - 106 Ave., Edmonton AB T5S 1E7 – 403/483-6000; Fax: 403/483-2000, 487-9691 – Circ.: 153,000; Fri.; 7 city area editions – Publisher, Don Sinclair; Editor-in-chief, Maurice Tougas; Circulation Manager, Kent Verlick

Edmonton Jewish Life, #107, 10342 - 107 St., Edmonton AB T5J 1K2 – 403/488-7276 – Monthly

Edmonton: Le Franco Albertain, #201, 8527 - 91 St., Edmonton AB T6C 03N1 – 403/465-6581; Fax: 403/465-3647; Email: lefranco@compusmart.ab.ca – Circ.: 3,000; Vendredi; français – Rédacteur, François V. Pageau

Edmonton: The Garrison Times, Edmonton Garrison, PO Box 10500, Edmonton AB T5J 4J5 – 403/473-7764; Fax: 403/973-1881 – Every other Thur. – Producer, George Hodgson; Editor, Capt. Rob Patterson-Burton

Edmonton: Windspeaker, 15001 - 112 Ave., Edmonton AB T5M 2V6 – 403/455-2700; Fax: 403/455-7639 – Circ.: 15,000; Monthly – Publisher, Bert Crowfoot; Managing Editor, Linda Caldwell

Edson Leader, PO Box 6330, Edson AB T7E 1T8 – 403/723-3301 – Mon.

Edson: The Weekly Anchor, PO Box 6870, Edson AB T7E 1V2 – 403/723-5787; Fax: 403/723-5725; Email: anchor@yellowhead.com – Circ.: 5,500; Every other Mon. – Publisher, Craig McArthur

Elk Point Review, PO Box 309, Elk Point AB T0A 1A0 – 403/724-4087; Fax: 403/724-4211 – Tue.

Fairview Post, PO Box 1900, Fairview AB T0H 1L0 – 403/835-4925; Fax: 403/835-4227; Email: Fairview_Post@telusplanet.net; URL: http://www.Bowesnet.com/Fairview – Circ.: 3,800; Tue. – Publisher, Bob Doornenbal; Editor-in-chief, Darcy Cheek

Falher: Smoky River Express, PO Box 644, Falher AB T0H 1M0 – 403/837-2585; Fax: 403/837-2102; Email: spn@inetnorth.net – Circ.: 2,500; Wed., English with some French – Publisher, Jeff Burgar; Advertising Manager, Leona Jorgenson

Fort Macleod: Macleod Gazette, PO Box 720, Fort Macleod AB T0L 0Z0 – 403/553-3391; Fax: 403/553-2961 – Circ.: 1,591; Wed. – Publisher & Editor, Jack Murphy

Fort Saskatchewan Record, #155, 10420 - 98 Ave., Fort Saskatchewan AB T8L 2N6 – 403/998-7070; Fax: 403/998-5515 – Tue.

Fort Saskatchewan This Week, 10109 - 99 Ave., Fort Saskatchewan AB T8L 1X7 – 403/998-1638; Fax: 403/998-3258 – Fri.

Gibbons: The Free Press, PO Box 330, Gibbons AB T0A 1N0 – 403/421-9715; Fax: 403/942-2515 – Circ.: 4,668; Mon.

Grande Cache Mountaineer, PO Box 660, Grande Cache AB T0E 0Y0 – 403/827-3539; Fax: 403/827-3530; Email: grande.cache.mountaineer@awnet.net – Circ.: 1,462; Tue. – Publisher, Noel Edey; Editor, Arthur Veitch

Grande Centre: Cold Lake Sun, 5517 - 55 St., Grande Centre AB T0A 1T0 – 403/594-5881; Fax: 403/594-2120 – Tue.

Grande Prairie: Peace Country Extra, 10604 - 100 St., PO Box 3000, Grande Prairie AB T8V 2M5 – 403/532-1110 – Circ.: 12,123; bi-weekly; also Peace Country Farmer (circ. 29,190)

Grimshaw: The Mile Zero News, PO Box 1010, Grimshaw AB T0H 1W0 – 403/332-2215; Fax: 403/332-4380 – Wed.

Hanna Herald, PO Box 790, Hanna AB T0J 1P0 – 403/854-3366; Fax: 403/854-3256 – Wed.

High Level Echo, PO Box 240, High Level AB T0H 1Z0 – 403/926-2000; Fax: 403/926-2001 – Wed.

High Prairie: The Mirror, 4732 - 53 Ave., PO Box 269, High Prairie AB T0G 1E0 – 403/523-3706 – Circ.: 2,061; Monthly

High Prairie: South Peace News, PO Box 1000, High Prairie AB T0G 1E0 – 403/523-4484 – Wed.

High River Times, 618 Centre St. South, High River AB T1V 1E9 – 403/652-2034; Fax: 403/652-3962 – Tue.

Hinton Parklander, 104 McLeod Ave., Hinton AB T7V 2A9 – 403/865-3115; Fax: 403/865-1252 – Circ.: 3,061; Mon. – Publisher, Neil Sutcliffe; Editor, Rod Kelley; Circulation Manager, Merna Strawson

Hythe Headliner, Hythe Family & Community Support Services, 10011A - 100 St., PO Box 622, Hythe AB T0H 2C0 – 403/356-2000; Fax: 403/356-2009 – Circ.: 1,000; Bi-weekly – Editor, Bonnie Joyes

Innisfail Booster, 4932 - 49th St., Innisfail AB T4G 1N2 – 403/227-3477; Fax: 403/227-3330 – Circ.: 7,500; Tue. – Publisher & Editor, Ray Brinson

Innisfail Province, PO Box 9, Innisfail AB T0M 1A0 – 403/227-3612; Fax: 403/222-1570 – Mon.

Irricana/Rocky View/Five Village Weekly, PO Box 40, Irricana AB T0M 1B0 – 403/935-4688; Fax: 403/935-4221 – Circ.: 9,992; Mon. – Publisher, Susan Denischuk

Jasper Booster, PO Box 940, Jasper AB T0E 1E0 – 403/852-3620; Fax: 403/852-3384; Email: jasboo@telusplanet.net – Circ.: 1,980; Wed.; also Jasper This Week – Publisher, Cathy Burwood; Editor, Peter Glenn; Circulation Manager, Karen Young

Lac La Biche Post, PO Box 508, Lac La Biche AB T0A 2C0 – 403/623-4221; Fax: 403/623-4230; Email: Lac_La_Biche_Post@awnet.net – Circ.: 2,600; Tue. – Fisal Asiff

Lamont: Lifestyle Regional News, 5028 - 50 Ave., PO Box 182, Lamont AB T0B 2R0 – 403/895-2063; Fax: 403/895-2063 – Circ.: 4,000; Thur.

Leduc & County This Week, 4712 - 50 Ave., Leduc AB T9E 6Y6 – 403/986-0860; Fax: 403/986-8870; Email: thisweek@compusmart.ab.ca; URL: http://www.compusmart.ab.ca/thisweek – Circ.: 15,336; Fri. – Publisher, Maureen Klatt; Editor, Kimberly Carr

Leduc Representative, 4504 - 61 Ave., Leduc AB T9E 3Z1 – 403/986-2271; Fax: 403/986-6397; Email: leducrep@ccinet.ab.ca; URL: http://www.bowesnet.com/leduc – Circ.: 10,800; Sun. – Publisher, Neil Sutcliffe; Managing Editor, Jerold Leblanc

Leslieville: The Western Star, PO Box 100, Leslieville AB T0M 1H0 – 403/729-3000 – Wed.

Lethbridge Shopper, 234 - 12B St. North, Lethbridge AB T1H 2K7 – 403/329-8225; Fax: 403/329-8211 – Circ.: 32,500; Sat., supplement to West Lethbridge Sun – Publisher & Editor, Ted Ominski; Circulation Manager, John Sheer

Manning Banner Post, PO Box 686, Manning AB T0H 2M0 – 403/836-3588 – Wed.

Mayerthorpe: The Freelancer, PO Box 599, Mayerthorpe AB T0E 1N0 – 403/786-2602; Fax: 403/786-2663; Email: may-free@telusplanet.net; URL: http://www.bowesnet.com/mayerthorpe – Circ.: 1,738; Wed. – Publisher, Jim Gray; Editor, Kevin Laliberte

Medicine Hat Shopper, 922 Allowance Ave. SE, Medicine Hat AB T1A 3G7 – 403/527-5777; Fax: 403/526-7352 – Circ.: 23,500; Sat. – Publisher, Ted Ominski

Morinville Gazette, PO Box 263, St. Albert AB T8N 1N3 – 403/459-2240; Fax: 403/460-8220 – Tue.; supplement, Homestyle

Morinville Mirror, 10205 - 100 Ave., Morinville AB T8R 1P9 – 403/939-2133; Fax: 403/939-2425 – Circ.: 5,355; Tue.

Nanton News, PO Box 429, Nanton AB T0L 1R0 – 403/646-2023; Fax: 403/646-2848 – Wed.

Okotoks: The Western Wheel, PO Bag 9, Okotoks AB T0L 1T0 – 403/938-6397 – Wed.

Olds: Mountain View County News, PO Box 3870, Olds AB T4H 1P6 – 403/556-3351; Fax: 403/556-3464 – Every other Fri. – Editor, M.J. Harper

The Olds Albertan, 5018 - 57th Ave., Olds AB T4H 1J1 – 403/556-7510 – Circ.: 8,200; Wed.

Olds Gazette, PO Box 3870, Olds AB T4H 1P6 – 403/556-3351; Fax: 403/556-3464 – Wed. – Editor, M.J. Harper

Onoway Community Voice, A.F. Keller & Associates Ltd., PO Box 6000, Spruce Grove AB T7X 2Z5 – 403/962-9228; Fax: 403/962-1021 – Circ.: 4,600; Every other Tue. – Editor, Al Keller

Oyen Echo, PO Box 420, Oyen AB T0J 2J0 – 403/664-3622; Fax: 403/664-3622; Email: oyenecho@agt.net; URL: http://www.inter.ab.ca/oyen – Circ.: 1,411; Wed. – Publisher, Ronald Holmes; Editor, Diana Walker; Co-Editor, H.E. Ball

Peace River Record-Gazette, PO Box 6870, Peace River AB T8S 1S6 – 403/624-2591; Fax: 403/624-8600; Email: rgazette@agt.net – Circ.: 4,097; Wed. – Publisher, Shaun Jessome; Editor, Irene Chomokovski; Circulation Manager, Penny Ashdown

Pincher Creek Echo, PO Box 1000, Pincher Creek AB T0K 1W0 – 403/627-3252; Fax: 403/627-3949 – Tue.

Ponoka Herald, PO Box 4308, Ponoka AB T0C 2H0 – 403/783-3074; Fax: 403/783-5350; Email: ponoka_herald@awnet.net – Circ.: 6,300; Mon. – Publisher, Frank Ryan; Editor, John Roberts

Ponoka News & Advertiser, PO Box 4217, Ponoka AB T0C 2H0 – 403/783-3311; Fax: 403/783-3311 – Mon.

Provost News, PO Box 180, Provost AB T0B 3S0 – 403/753-2564; Fax: 403/753-6117 – Wed.

Raymond: The County Review, PO Box 315, Raymond AB T0K 2S0 – 403/752-3635 – Tue.

Red Deer Express, PO Bag 5012, Red Deer AB T4N 6R4 – 403/346-3356; Fax: 403/347-6620; Email: rdpub@ccinet.ab.ca – Circ.: 24,277; Wed. – Publisher, Cal Dallas; Editor, Glen Werkman; Circulation Manager, Murray Wieting

Redwater Tribune, PO Box 1180, Redwater AB T0A 2W0 – 403/942-4535; Fax: 403/939-2425 – Tue.

Redwater: The Review, PO Box 850, Redwater AB T0A 2W0 – 403/942-2023; Fax: 403/942-2515 – Circ.: 4,772; Mon. – Publisher, Wanda Cowley; Editor, Edwin Cowley

Rimbey Record, PO Box 380, Rimbey AB T0C 2J0 – 403/843-2231; Fax: 403/843-2990; Email: rimbey_record@awnet.net – Circ.: 2,060; Tue. – Publisher, Ed Moller; Editor, John Roberts; Circulation Manager, E. Archer

Rocky Mountain House: The Mountaineer, 4814 - 49 St., Rocky Mountain House AB T0M 1T1 – 403/845-3334; Fax: 403/845-5570; Email: publish@/editor@/advert@rmh-mountaineer.com; URL: http://www.rmhnet.com/mountaineer/index – Tue. – Publisher, Glen Mazza; Editor, Brian Mazza

Rycroft: The Central Peace Signal, PO Box 250, Rycroft AB T0H 3A0 – 403/765-3604; Fax: 403/765-2188 – Tue.

St. Albert Gazette, PO Box 263, St. Albert AB T8N 1N3 – 403/460-5500; Fax: 403/460-8220; URL: http://www.greatwest.ca – Wed. & Sat.; supplement Homestyle (Wed.)

St. Albert This Week, #150, 44 Riel Dr., St. Albert AB T8N 5C4 – 403/459-5446; Fax: 403/460-2437 – Circ.: 17,620; Fri.; also Edmonton Suburban This Week (Fri., circ. 75,000)

St. Michael: Elk Island Triangle, PO Box 170, St. Michael AB T0B 4B0 – 403/896-2223; Fax: 403/896-2281 – Circ.: 1,600; Every other week – Publisher, Joanne Paltzat

St. Paul Journal, PO Box 159, St. Paul AB T0A 3A0 – 403/645-3342; Fax: 403/645-2346 – Tue.

Sedgewick: The Community Press, PO Box 99, Sedgewick AB T0B 4C0 – 403/384-3641; Fax: 403/384-2244 – Tue.

Sherwood Park: The News, 168 Kaska Rd., Sherwood Park AB T8A 4G7 – 403/464-0033; Fax: 403/464-2117; Email: parknews@telusplanet.net; URL: http://www.bowesnet.com/spnews/ – Circ.: 17,000; Wed. – Publisher, Brian Bentt

Sherwood Park This Week, #112A, 101 Granada Blvd., Sherwood Park AB T8A 4W2 – 403/464-5176; Fax: 403/467-4125; Email: thisweek@compusmart.ab.ca; URL: http://www.compusmart.ab.ca/thisweek – Circ.: 20,600; Fri. – Publisher, John Putters; Editor, Jackie Bibby; Circulation Manager, Paul Percival

Slave Lake: Lakeside Leader, PO Box 849, Slave Lake AB T0G 2A0 – 403/849-4380; Fax: 403/849-3903 – Wed.

Slave Lake Scope, PO Box 1130, Slave Lake AB T0G 2A0 – 403/849-4350; Fax: 403/849-2433; Email: scope@connect.ab.ca – Circ.: 2,000; Sat. – Bruce D. Thomas

Smoky Lake Signal, PO Box 328, Smoky Lake AB T0A 2A0 – 403/656-4114 – Wed.

Spruce Grove: The Examiner, PO Box 4206, Spruce Grove AB T7X 3B4 – 403/962-4257; Fax: 403/962-0658; Email: spruce_grove_examiner@awnet.net – Circ.: 5,120; Sun. – Publisher, Inez Scheideman; Editor, Rich Gossen; Circulation Manager, Lyle Martin

Spruce Grove/Stony Plain This Week, 322 McLeod Ave., PO Box 3006, Spruce Grove AB T7X 3A4 – 403/962-8457; Fax: 403/962-2902; Email: thisweek@compusmart.ab.ca – Circ.: 13,450; Fri. – Editor, Joe Langford; Sales Coordinator, Dan Holman

Stettler Independent, 5006 - 50th Ave., PO Box 310, Stettler AB T0C 2L0 – 403/742-2395; Fax: 403/742-8050; Email: stetnews@telusplanet.net – Circ.: 4,200; Wed. – Publisher, Alan Willis

Stony Plain Reporter, PO Box 780, Stony Plain AB T0E 2G0 – 403/963-2291; Fax: 403/963-9716 – Tue.

Strathmore Standard, 136 - 2nd Ave., PO Box 2250, Strathmore AB T1P 1K2 – 403/934-3021; Fax: 403/934-5011; Email: strathmore_standard@awnet.net – Circ.: 3,671; Tue. – Publisher, John Snelgrove; Editor, George Brown

Sundre Round-Up, PO Box 599, Sundre AB T0M 1X0 – 403/638-3577; Fax: 403/638-3077 – Circ.: 2,245; Wed. – Publisher, Monica Leatherdale; Editor, Dan Singleton

Swan Hills Grizzly Gazette, PO Box 1000, Swan Hills AB T0G 2C0 – 403/333-2100; Fax: 403/333-2111 – Circ.: 637; Tue. – Publisher, Carol Webster

Sylvan Lake News, #103, 5020 - 50A St., Sylvan Lake AB T4S 1R2 – 403/887-2331; Fax: 403/887-2081; Email: elnews@telusplanet.net – Circ.: 4,200; Wed. – Barry Hibbert

Taber Times, 6304 - 52nd St., Taber AB T1G 1J7 – 403/223-2266; Fax: 403/223-1408 – Circ.: 3,365; Wed. – Publisher, Coleen Campbell; Editor, Jason Lothian

Three Hills Capital, PO Box 158, Three Hills AB T0M 2A0 – 403/443-5133; Fax: 403/443-7331 – Circ.: 3,900; Wed. – Publisher & Editor, Timothy J. Sherlaw; Circulation Manager, Denean Denis

Tofield Mercury, PO Box 150, Tofield AB T0B 4J0 – 403/662-4046; Fax: 403/662-3735; Email: newsdesk@tofieldmercury.com; URL: http://www@tofieldmercury.com – Tue. – Anne Francoeur

Trochu: Highway 21 News, PO Box 665, Trochu AB T0M 2C0 – 403/442-2711; Fax: 403/442-2633; Email: trochu_highway_21_news@awest.net – Circ.: 6,100; Tue. – Publisher, Ed Moller; Editor, Frank Ryan

Two Hills Times, PO Box 430, Two Hills AB T0B 4K0 – 403/657-2530; Fax: 403/657-2721 – Tue.

Valley Views, Valley Views Publishing Ltd., PO Box 787, Valleyview AB T0H 3N0 – 403/524-3490; Fax: 403/524-4545; Email: valley_views@awnet.net – Circ.: 1,538; Wed. – Co-Publisher, Wayne Plaxton; Co-Publisher & Editor, Joan Plaxton; Circulation Manager, Betty Kobe

Vauxhall Advance, PO Box 302, Vauxhall AB T0K 2K0 – 403/654-2122 – Thur.

Vegreville News Advertiser, PO Box 810, Vegreville AB T9C 1R9 – 403/632-2861; Fax: 403/632-7981; Email: VNAprod@digitalweb.net – Circ.: 10,700; Mon. – Publisher, Dan Beaudrette; General Manager, Arthur Beaudrette

Vegreville Times Observer, 4910 - 50th St., PO Box 160, Vegreville AB T9C 1R2 – 403/632-2353 – Circ.: 5,200; Tue.

Vermilion News Advertiser, PO Box 810, Vegreville AB T9C 1R9 – 403/853-6397; Fax: 403/853-6526 – Circ.: 6,800; Mon. – Editor, Dan Beaudrette

Vermilion Standard, 4917 - 50 Ave., Vermilion AB T9X 1A6 – 403/853-5344; Fax: 403/853-5203; Email: stand1@telusplanet.net; URL: http://www/bowesnet.com/Vermilion – Circ.: 3,400; Tue.

Veteran Eagle, PO Box 462, Veteran AB T0C 2S0 – 403/575-3892; Fax: 403/575-3938; Email: veagle@agt.net; URL: http://www.geocities.com/Eureka/8053 – Circ.: 550 – Publisher, Les Hainer

Viking: The Weekly Review, PO Box 240, Viking AB T0B 4N0 – 403/336-3422; Fax: 403/336-2550 – Tue.

Vulcan Advocate, PO Box 389, Vulcan AB T0L 2B0 – 403/485-2036; Fax: 403/485-2911 – Wed.

Wabamun Community Voice, A.F. Keller & Associates Ltd., PO Box 6000, Spruce Grove AB T7X 2Z5 – 403/962-9228; Fax: 403/962-1021 – Circ.: 4,600; Every other Tue. – Editor, Al Keller

Wainwright Star-Chronicle, 414 - 10 St., Wainwright AB T9W 1P5 – 403/842-4465; Fax: 403/842-2760 – Circ.: 1,920; Wed.; also Wainwright Star Regional

Westlock News, PO Box 40, Westlock AB T0G 2L0 – 403/349-3033; Fax: 403/349-3677 – Mon. – Editor, Town & Country Section, Les Dunford

Wetaskiwin Times Advertiser, PO Box 6900, Wetaskiwin AB T9A 2G5 – 403/352-2231; Fax: 403/352-4333; Email: wtimes@ccinet.ab.ca; URL: http://www.bowesnet/wtimes – Circ.: 12,625; Mon. – Publisher, Kent Keebaugh; Editor, Barbara Stewart

Whitecourt Star, PO Box 630, Whitecourt AB T7S 1N7 – 403/778-3977; Fax: 403/778-6459 – Wed.

## British Columbia Daily Newspapers

**CRANBROOK:**

Daily Townsman, E. Kootenay Newspapers Ltd., 822 Cranbrook St. North, Cranbrook BC V1C 3R9 – 250/426-5201; Fax: 250/426-5003 – Circ.: 4,300 – Publisher, Nigel Lark; Editor, David Sands

**DAWSON CREEK:**

Peace River Block News, Sterling Newspapers Ltd., 901 - 100th Ave., PO Box 180, Dawson Creek BC V1G 4G6 – 250/782-4888; Fax: 250/782-6770; Email: PRBNEWS@PRIS.BC.CA; URL: http://www.sterlingnews.com/peace – Circ.: 2,572; Mon.-Fri; also Peace River Block News Regional Weekly (Sun., circ. 10,788) – Publisher, Margaret Forbes; Circulation Manager, Tiffany Lewis

**FORT ST. JOHN:**

Alaska Highway News, Sterling Newspapers Ltd., 9916 - 98th St., Fort St. John BC V1J 3T8 – 250/785-5631; Fax: 250/785-3522; Email: ahnews@awinc.com; URL: http://www.sterlingnews.com/Alaska – Circ.: 3,100; Mon.-Fri. – Publisher, Bruce Lantz; Circulation Manager, Sarah Brown

**KAMLOOPS:**

The Kamloops Daily News, Southam Inc., 393 Seymour St., Kamloops BC V2C 6P6 – 250/372-2331; Fax: 250/374-3884 – Circ.: 16,900; Morning – Publisher, Dale Brin; Editor, Mel Rothenburger

**KELOWNA:**

Daily Courier, Thomson Newspapers Co. Ltd., 550 Doyle Ave., Kelowna BC V1Y 7V1 – 250/762-4445; Fax: 250/762-3866 – Circ.: 17,002, Mon.-Sat.; 16,205, Sun.; Morning – Publisher & General Manager, Peter Kapyrka; Managing Editor, Gord Smiley

**KIMBERLEY:**

The Daily Bulletin, E. Kootenay Newspapers Ltd., 335 Spokane St., Kimberley BC V1A 1Y9 – 250/427-5333; Fax: 250/427-5336; Email: Bulletin@cyberlink.bc.ca – Circ.: 8,200; Afternoon – Publisher, Michelle Jaques; Circulation Manager, Laura Butler

**NANAIMO:**

Nanaimo Daily News, Thomson Newspapers Co. Ltd., #B1, 2577 McCullough Rd., Nanaimo BC V9S 5W5 – 250/758-4917; Fax: 250/758-7304 – Circ.: 12,700; Morning, Mon.-Sat. – Publisher & General Manager, Ron Mitchell; Managing Editor, Doyle Mackinnon

**NELSON:**

Daily News, News Publishing Co., 266 Baker St., Nelson BC V1L 4H3 – 250/352-3552; Fax: 250/352-2418 – Circ.: 4,345; Afternoon – Publisher, John A. Smith

**PENTICTON:**

Herald, Thomson Newspapers Co. Ltd., 186 Nanaimo Ave. West, Penticton BC V2A 1N4 – 250/492-4002; Fax: 250/492-2403 – Circ.: 8,600; Morning, Mon.-Sat. – Publisher, Jane Howard; Circulation Manager, Dave Hamilton

**PORT ALBERNI:**

Alberni Valley Times, Sterling Newspapers Ltd., 4918 Napier St., PO Box 400, Port Alberni BC V9Y 7N1 – 250/723-8171; Fax: 250/723-0586; Email: avtimes@cedar.alberni.net; URL: http://www.alberni.net/~avtimes/index.html – Circ.: 6,500; Evening – Publisher, N.E. Hannaford; Circulation Manager, John Richardson

**PRINCE GEORGE:**

The Citizen, Southam Inc., 150 Brunswick St., PO Box 5700, Prince George BC V2L 5K9 – 250/562-2441; Fax: 250/562-7453 – Circ.: 17,679, Mon.-Thur., Sat.; 20,273, Fri.; Morning – Publisher, Bob McKenzie; Editor, Peter Godfrey

**PRINCE RUPERT:**

Daily News, Sterling Newspapers Ltd., 801 - 2nd Ave. West, Prince Rupert BC V8J 1H6 – 250/624-6781; Fax: 250/624-2851; Email: prdnews@kaien.awinc.com; URL: http://www.sterlingnews.com – Circ.: 3,612; Evening, Mon.-Fri. – Publisher, Robert Ritchie; Circulation Manager, Margaret Bob

**TRAIL:**

Times, 1163 Cedar Ave., Trail BC V1R 4B8 – 250/364-1416; Fax: 250/368-8550; Email: trailtimes@awinc.com; URL: http://haven.uniserve.com/~swise – Circ.: 6,200; Afternoon; also West Kootenay Weekender (29,000), Fri. – Publisher, Raymon D. Picco; Editor, Tracy Konschuk; Circulation Manager, Terry Finlay

**VANCOUVER:**

The Province, Pacific Press Ltd., 2250 Granville St., Vancouver BC V6H 3G2 – 604/732-2478; Fax: 604/732-2704 – Circ.: 158,490, 192,271 Sun.; Morning, Sun.-Fri. – Managing Editor, Neil Graham

The Vancouver Sun, Pacific Press Ltd., 2250 Granville St., Vancouver BC V6H 3G2 – 604/732-2111; Fax: 604/732-2323 – Circ.: 192,300 Mon.-Thur., 252,000 Fri., 253,900 Sat.; Morning – Editor-in-chief, John Cruickshank

**VICTORIA:**

Times Colonist, Thomson Newspapers Co. Ltd., 2621 Douglas St., PO Box 300, Victoria BC V8T 4M2 – 250/380-5211; Fax: 250/380-5353; Email: times@interlink.bc.ca – Circ.: 79,000; Morning – Publisher, Peter Baillie; Editor-in-chief, Bob Poole; Reader Sales & Service Director, Stephen Hastings

## Other Newspapers in British Columbia

Abbotsford News, 34375 Cyril St., Abbotsford BC V2S 2H5 – 604/856-9543; Fax: 604/853-9808 – Circ.: 15,000, 40,000 Sat.; Tue., Thur., Sat.; also Sumas & Matsqui Times

Abbotsford Times, #1, 30887 Peardonville Rd., Abbotsford BC V2T 6K2 – 604/854-5244; Fax: 604/854-1140; Email: abby@direct.ca – Circ.: 37,000; Tue., Fri. – Publisher, Rod Thomson; Editor, Phil Melnychuk

Agassiz-Harrison Advance, 1892 Park St., PO Box 410, Agassiz BC V0M 1A0 – 604/796-3633; Fax: 604/796-3182 – Wed. – Publisher, Steve Dills

Agassiz-Harrison Observer, PO Box 129, Agassiz BC V0M 1A0 – 604/796-2022 – Wed.

Aldergrove Star, CFV Star Publishing Ltd., 3089 - 272 St., Aldergrove BC V4W 3R9 – 604/856-8303; Fax: 604/856-5212; Email: online@aldstar.com; URL: http://www.aldstar.com – Wed. – Publisher, Rudy Langmann; Editor, Kurt Langmann; Advertising Manager, Inge B. Langmann

Armstrong Advertiser, PO Box 610, Armstrong BC V0E 1B0 – 250/546-3121 – Wed.

Ashcroft Journal, PO Box 190, Ashcroft BC V0K 1A0 – 250/453-2261, 2655; Fax: 250/453-9625 – Tue. – Publisher, Judy Van Allen; Editor, Barry Tait; Circulation Manager, Dawn Lanyon

Barriere: North Thompson Star/Journal, PO Box 1020, Barriere BC V0E 1E0 – 250/672-5611; Fax: 250/672-9900 – Mon.

Burnaby News Leader, 6569 Kingsway, Burnaby BC V5E 1E1 – 604/526-9696 – Circ.: 46,300; Wed., Sun.

Burnaby Now, #205A - 3430 Brighton Ave., Burnaby BC V5A 3H4 – 604/444-3451; Fax: 604/444-3460 – Sun., Wed.

Burns Lake: Lakes District News, PO Box 309, Burns Lake BC V0J 1E0 – 250/692-7526 – Wed.

Campbell River Courier-Islander, PO Box 310, Campbell River BC V9W 5B5 – 250/287-7464 – Circ.: 7,500; Wed., Fri.

Campbell River Mirror, #104 - 250 Dogwood St., Campbell River BC V9W 2X9 – 250/287-9227; Fax: 250/287-3238 – Circ.: 7,980; Wed.; also North Island Weekender (Sat., circ. 21,000)

Campbell River: The Wrap, 1040 Cedar St., Campbell River BC V9W 5B5 – 250/287-7464 – Circ.: 21,000; Sat.

Castlegar Sun, 233 Columbia Ave., Castlegar BC V1N 1G3 – 250/365-2278; Fax: 250/365-7762 – Circ.: 3,600; Wed. – Publisher, Marilyn Strong; Editor, Sharlene Imhoff, 250/365-5266

Chetwynd Echo, #215, 5021 - 49th Ave., PO Box 750, Chetwynd BC V0C 1J0 – 250/788-2246; Fax: 250/788-9988; Email: chetecho@pris.bc.ca – Circ.: 1,900; Tues. – Publisher, Margaret Mould; Editor, Rick Davison

Chilliwack Progress, 45860 Spadina Ave., Chilliwack BC V2P 6H9 – 604/792-1931; Fax: 604/792-4936 – Wed., Fri. – Publisher, Julian Galbecka; Editor, Paul Bucci; Circulation Manager, Kellee Taylor

Chilliwack Times, #102 - 45951 Tretheway Ave., Chilliwack BC V2P 1K4 – 604/792-9117; Fax: 604/792-9300 – Circ.: 25,400; Tue., Fri.

Clearwater: North Thompson Times, RR#1, PO Box 1102, Clearwater BC V0E 1N0 – 250/674-3343; Fax: 250/674-3777; Email: mail.netshop.net – Circ.: 3,822; Tue. – Publisher, Bruce Chappell; Editor, Nancy Chappell

Coquitlam: Now, #1, 2700 Barnet Hwy., Coquitlam BC V3B 1B8 – 604/942-4192 – Circ.: 47,784; Wed., Sun.

Coquitlam: The Tri-City News, 1405 Broadway, Port Coquitlam BC V3C 5W9 – 604/526-9696 – Sun., Wed.

Courtenay: Comox Valley Echo, 407D Fifth St., Courtenay BC V9N 1J7 – 250/334-4722; Fax: 250/334-3172; Email: echo@mars.ark.com – Circ.: 19,000; Tue., Fri. – Dave MacDonald

Courtenay: Comox Valley Record, PO Box 3729, Courtenay BC V9N 7P1 – 250/338-5811; Fax: 250/338-5568 – Circ.: 18,200; Wed., Fri. – Publisher, Grant Lawrence; Editor, Bruce Winfield; Circulation Manager, Vicky Butters

Cranbrook: East Kootenay Weekly, 822 Cranbrook St. North, Cranbrook BC V1C 3R9 – 250/426-5201; Fax: 250/426-5003 – Circ.: 15,000; Wed. – Publisher, Carol Murray; Editor, David Sands

Cranbrook: The Kootenay Advertiser, Koocanusa Publications Inc., 1510 - 2nd St. North, Cranbrook BC V1C 3L2 – 250/489-3455; Fax: 250/489-3743; Email: advertiser@cyberlink.bc.ca – Circ.: 31,260; Mon.; TV listing supplement, 7 Days Magazine (Mon.) – Publisher & Editor, Daryl D. Shellborn

Cranbrook: The Rocky Mountain Weekender, 19 Ninth Ave. South, Cranbrook BC V1C 2L9 – 250/

426-6119; Fax: 250/426-6070 – Circ.: 25,500; Sat. – Publisher, Melba Hanson; Editor, Deb Saffin

Creston Valley Advance, 115 - 10th Ave., PO Box 1279, Creston Valley BC V0B 1G0 – 250/428-2266; Fax: 250/428-3320; Email: advance@kootenay.awinc.com – Circ.: 4,086; Mon., Thur. – Publisher, Helena E. White; Editor, Brian Bell; Circulation Manager, Dianne Audette

Dawson Creek Mirror, 10224 - 10th St., Dawson Creek BC V1G 3T4 – 250/782-9424; Fax: 250/782-9454; Email: mirror@neonet.bc.ca – Circ.: 10,000; Weekly

Delta Optimist, 5485 - 48 Ave., Delta BC V4K 1X2 – 604/946-4451; Fax: 604/946-5680 – Circ.: 15,700; Wed., Sat.

Delta: North Delta Sentinel, 10680 - 84 Ave., Delta BC V4C 2L2 – 604/589-2233; Fax: 604/581-1519 – Circ.: 10,000; Monthly

Duncan: The Citizen, 469 Whistler St., Duncan BC V9L 4X5 – 250/748-2666; Fax: 250/748-1552; Email: citizen@mail.duncan.island.net – Circ.: 20,200; Sun., Wed.

Duncan: Cowichan News Leader, 2742 James St., PO Box 910, Duncan BC V9L 2X9 – 250/746-4471; Fax: 250/746-8529 – Circ.: 19,000; Wed., also Cowichan Pictorial (Sun.)

Enderby Commoner, PO Box 190, Enderby BC V0E 1V0 – 250/838-7229 – Wed.

Esquimalt: Esquimalt News, 538 Fraser St., Victoria BC V9A 6H7 – 250/381-5664; Fax: 250/361-9283; Email: esquimaltn@sonati.com – Circ.: 7,500; Wed. – Publisher, Marilyn Cowie; Editor, Alanna Jorde

Esquimalt: Lookout, c/o CFB Esquimalt, PO Box 17000, Stn Forces, Victoria BC V9A 7N2 – 250/385-0313; Fax: 250/361-3512; Email: lookout@horizon.bc.ca – Circ.: 5,000; Wed.; English & French – Managing Editor, Corina DeGuire

Fernie: Elk Valley Extra, Sterling Newspapers, 342 - 2nd Ave., PO Box 500, Fernie BC V0B 1M0 – 250/423-4666; Fax: 250/423-3110; Email: ferniefp@elkvalley.net – Circ.: 6,400; Fri.

Fernie Free Press, PO Bag 5000, Fernie BC V0B 1M0 – 250/423-4666; Fax: 250/423-3110 – Tue.

Fort Nelson News, #3, Sikanni Bldg., 5004 - 52nd Ave. West, PO Box 600, Fort Nelson BC V0C 1R0 – 250/774-2357; Fax: 250/774-3612; Email: jkenyon@cancom.net – Wed.

Fort St. James Caledonia Courier, PO Box 1007, Vanderhoof BC V0J 3A0 – 250/567-9258; Fax: 250/567-2070 – Circ.: 1,100; Wed. – Publisher, Mark Warner; Editor, Roger Knox

Fort St. John: The Northerner, 9908 - 101 Ave., Fort St. John BC V1J 1B2 – 250/785-2890; Fax: 250/785-1638 – Circ.: 4,000; Tues. – General Manager, Brian Amesbury

Fort St. John: North Peace Express, Sterling Newspapers Ltd., 9916 - 98 St., Fort St. John BC V1J 3T8 – 250/785-5631; Fax: 250/785-3522; Email: ahnews@awinc.com; URL: http://www.sterlingnews.com/Alaska – Circ.: 10,800; Sun. – Publisher, Bruce Lantz; Editor, Karen Marshall

Gabriola Sounder, Box 56, Site 17, RR#1, Gabriola BC V0R 1X0 – 250/247-9337; Fax: 250/247-8147; Email: sounder@island.net – Circ.: 3,500; Every other Fri. – Publisher, Bill de Carteret; Editor, Sue de Carteret; Circulation Manager, Terri Hawkins

Gibsons: Coast Independent, PO Box 125, Gibsons BC V0N 1V0 – 604/886-4003; Fax: 604/886-4993; Email: independent@sunshine.net – Circ.: 12,990; Mon.

Gold River: The Record, PO Box 279, Gold River BC V0P 1G0 – 250/283-2324; Fax: 250/283-2527; Email: record@goldrvr.island.net – Circ.: 1,500; Twice monthly – Publisher, Jerry West

Golden News, PO Box 4114, Golden BC V0A 1H0 – 250/344-6333 – Wed.

Golden Star, PO Box 149, Golden BC V0A 1H0 – 250/344-5251; Fax: 250/344-7344 – Circ.: 2,302; Wed.; also Columbia Valley This Week (Wed.) – Publisher, Holly Magoon; Editor, Bill Costello; Circulation Manager, Patti Roberts

Golden: Windermere Valley Shoppers Guide, PO Box 4114, Golden BC V0A 1H0 – 250/344-6333 – Mon.

Grand Forks: Boundary Bulletin, PO Box 700, Grand Forks BC V0H 1H0 – 250/442-2191; Fax: 250/442-3336; Email: gfgazedt@sunshinecable.com – Circ.: 5,195; Mon. – Publisher, Sandra Watts; Editor, Richard Finnigan; Circulation Manager, Shirley Larsen

Grand Forks Gazette, 7330 - 2nd St., PO Box 700, Grand Forks BC V0H 1H0 – 250/442-2191; Fax: 250/442-3336; Email: gfgazedt@sunshinecable.com – Circ.: 3,076; Wed. – Publisher, Sandra Watts; Editor, Richard Finnigan; Circulation Manager, Shirley Larsen

Greenwood: Boundary Creek Times, PO Box 99, Greenwood BC V0H 1J0 – 250/445-2233; Fax: 250/445-2240 – Wed. – Richard Furness; Joyce Furness

Hagensborg: Coast Mountain News, PO Box 250, Hagensborg BC V0T 1H0 – 250/982-2696; Fax: 250/982-2512 – Circ.: 3,500; Every other Thur. – Publisher & Editor, Angela Hall

Hope Standard, 895 - 3rd Ave., Unit 3, PO Box 1090, Hope BC V0X 1L0 – 604/869-2421; Fax: 604/869-7351 – Circ.: 2,372; Thur.

Houston Today, PO Box 899, Houston BC V0J 1Z0 – 250/845-2890; Fax: 250/845-7893 – Wed.

Invermere: The Valley Echo, PO Box 70, Invermere BC V0A 1K0 – 250/342-9216; Fax: 250/342-3930; Email: echonews@rockies.net – Circ.: 3,500; Wed. – Publisher, Sheila Tutty; Editor, Ian Cobb, 250/342-3223

Kamloops This Week, 1365B Dalhousie Dr., Kamloops BC V2C 5P6 – 250/374-7467; Fax: 250/374-1033 – Sun., Wed., Fri. – Publisher, Linda Hooton; Editor, Gene Laverty

Kaslo-Kootenay Lake Pennywise, PO Box 430, Kaslo BC V0G 1M0 – 250/353-2602 – Wed.; also Nelson Pennywise, New Denver/Winlaw/Slocan Valley Pennywise, Salmo-Fruitvale Pennywise

Kelowna: Capital News, 2495 Enterprise Way, Kelowna BC V1X 7K2 – 250/763-3212; Fax: 250/763-8469 – Sun., Wed., Fri; supplement TV Week (Fri.)

Keremeos: Gazette of the Similkameen, PO Box 299, Keremeos BC V0X 1N0 – 250/499-2920 – Wed.

Kitimat: Northern Sentinel, 626 Enterprise Ave., Kitimat BC V8C 2E4 – 250/632-6144; Fax: 250/639-9373; Email: sentinel@sno.net – Circ.: 2,600; Wed; supplement, TV & Video Scanner (Wed); also Weekend Advertiser (Sat., circ. 15,800) – Publisher, Sandra Dugdale; Editor, Malcolm Baxter

Ladysmith-Chemainus Chronicle, PO Box 400, Ladysmith BC V0R 2E0 – 250/245-2277; Fax: 250/245-2260 – Circ.: 3,000; Tue. – Publisher, Bobby Cloke; Editor, John McKinley

Lake Cowichan Gazette, PO Box 2500, Lake Cowichan BC V0R 2G0 – 250/749-4383 – Circ.: 2,500; Wed.

Lake Cowichan: The Lake News, PO Box 962, Lake Cowichan BC V0R 2G0 – 250/749-3143; Fax: 250/749-3153; Email: lakenews@island.net – Circ.: 2,552; Wed.

Langley Advance News, #111, 20353 - 6th Ave., Langley BC V2Y 1N5 – 604/534-8641; Fax: 604/534-3383; Email: lan@direct.ca – Circ.: 37,900; Tues., Fri. – Marilyn Boswyk; R. Fowler

Langley Times, PO Box 3097, Langley BC V3A 4R3 – 604/533-4157; Fax: 604/533-0219 – Wed., Sat.

The Lantzville Log, Lantzville Log Society, PO Box 268, Lantzville BC V0R 2H0 – 250/390-2847 – Circ.: 3,075; Monthly – Editor, Lynn Reeve

Lazo: Comox Totem Times, CFB Comox, Lazo BC V0R 2K0 – 250/339-2541; Fax: 250/339-8673 – Circ.: 2,300; Monthly – Editor, Joel Clarkson

Lillooet: Bridge River-Lillooet News, 979 Main St., PO Box 709, Lillooet BC V0K 1V0 – 250/256-4219; Fax: 250/256-4210 – Wed.

Lumby Valley Times, #3, 1879 Vernon St., PO Box 408, Lumby BC V0E 2G0 – 604/547-6990 – Wed.

Mackenzie: The Times, PO Box 609, Mackenzie BC V0J 2C0 – 250/997-6675 – Tue.

Maple Ridge-Pitt Meadows Times, 22334 Selkirk Ave., Maple Ridge BC V2X 2X5 – 604/463-2281; Fax: 604/463-9943 – Circ.: 23,000; Wed. & Sun. – Publisher, Lois Lee; Editor, Chris Campbell

Merritt Herald, PO Box 9, Merritt BC V0N 2B0 – 250/378-4241 – Wed.

Merritt: The Merritt News, PO Box 939, Merritt BC V1K 1B8 – 250/378-8876; Fax: 250/378-8853; Email: news@merritt-news.bc.ca; URL: http://www.merritt-news.bc.ca – Wed.

Merritt: Nicola-Thompson Today, PO Box 9, Merritt BC V0K 2B0 – 250/378-4241 – Mon.

Mission: Record, 33047 First Ave., Mission BC V2V 1G2 – 604/826-6221; Fax: 604/826-8266 – Circ.: 4,986; Thur.

Nakusp: Arrow Lakes News, PO Box 189, Nakusp BC V0G 1R0 – 250/265-3823; Fax: 250/265-3841 – Circ.: 2,200; Wed. – Publisher, Paul Deleske; Circulation Manager, Linda McInnis

Nanaimo: The Bulletin - Nanaimo News Bulletin, 777B Poplar St., Nanaimo BC V9S 2H7 – 250/753-3707; Fax: 250/753-0788; Email: bulletin@island.net – Circ.: 28,900; Mon., Thur. – Publisher, Roy Linder; Editor, Kevin Laird

Nelson: Kootenay Weekly Express, 554 Ward St., Nelson BC V1L 1S9 – 250/354-3910; Fax: 250/352-5075; Email: express@netidea.com – Circ.: 12,814; Wed. – Publisher & Editor, Nelson Becker

Nelson: West Kootenay Weekender & TV Today, 266 Baker St., Nelson BC V1L 4H3 – 250/352-3552; Fax: 250/352-2418 – Circ.: 29,230; Fri; supplement to Nelson Daily News, Trail Daily Times, & Castlegar Sun

New Westminster Now/Royal City Record, 418 - 6th St., New Westminster BC V3L 3B2 – 604/525-6306 – Circ.: 16,219; Sat., Wed.

North Shore News, 1139 Lonsdale Ave., North Vancouver BC V7M 2H4 – 604/985-2131; Fax: 604/985-2104; Email: trenshaw@direct.ca; URL: http://www.nsnews.com – Circ.: 58,000; Wed., Fri., Sun. – Publisher, Peter Speck; Managing Editor, Timothy Renshaw

Oliver Chronicle, PO Box 880, Oliver BC V0H 1T0 – 250/498-3711; Fax: 250/498-3966; Email: chronicle@img.net; URL: http://www.img.net/oliver – Circ.: 3,380; Wed. – Publisher, Michael Newman; Editor, Kathleen Connolly

One Hundred Mile House Free Press, PO Box 459, One Hundred Mile House BC V0K 2E0 – 250/395-2219; Fax: 250/395-3939 – Wed.

Osoyoos Times, PO Box 359, Osoyoos BC V0H 1V0 – 250/495-7225; Fax: 250/495-6616; Email: pturner@ftcnet.com – Circ.: 2,637; Wed. – Co-Publisher, C. Stodola; Editor & Co-Publisher, Patrick Turner

Parksville: The Morning Sun, 114 East Hirst Ave., PO Box 45, Parksville BC V9P 2G3 – 250/954-0600 – Circ.: 15,000; Wed.

Parksville-Qualicum News, PO Box 1180, Parksville BC V9P 2H2 – 250/248-4341; Fax: 250/248-4655; Email: kpqnews@island.net – Circ.: 16,117; Tue., Fri. – Publisher, Judi Thompson; Editor, Jeff H. Vircoe; Circulation Manager, Lenore Gibson

Pender Island: Gulf Islands, Island Tides, Island Tides Publishing Ltd., PO Box 55, Pender Island BC V0N 2M0 – 250/629-3660; Fax: 250/629-3838; Email: islandtides@gulfislands.com – Circ.: 8,500; Every other Thur. – President & Editor, Christa Grace-Warrick

Penticton: Western News Advertiser, 2250 Camrose St., Penticton BC V2A 8R1 – 250/492-0444; Fax: 250/492-9843 – Circ.: 21,260; Wed., Fri.

Port Alberni: Pennyworth, 3017 - 3rd Ave., Port Alberni BC V9Y 2A5 – 250/723-3709 – Wed.

Port Hardy: North Island Gazette, PO Box 458, Port Hardy BC V0N 2P0 – 250/949-6225; Fax: 250/949-7655 – Circ.: 3,382; Wed. – Publisher, Chuck Bennett; Editor, Rob Giblak; Circulation Manager, Sandy Haydamack

Port Hardy: The View, PO Box 458, Port Hardy BC V0N 2P0 – 250/949-6225 – Wed.

Powell River News, 7030 Alberni St., Powell River BC V8A 2C3 – 604/485-4255; Fax: 604/485-5832; Email: prnews@thecentre.com – Circ.: 5,600; Wed. – Publisher, Pam Krompocker; Editor, Terry Kruger

Powell River Peak, 4312A Franklin Ave., Powell River BC V8A 5L7 – 604/485-5313; Email: peak@prcn.org; URL: http://www.windspirit.com/peak/ – Circ.: 8,700; Thur. – Joyce Carlsdon

Powell River Town Crier, 7030 Alberni St., Powell River BC V8A 2C3 – 604/485-4255; Fax: 604/485-5832; Email: prnews@thecentre.com – Circ.: 5,600; Mon. – Publisher, Pam Krompocker; Editor, Terry Kruger

Prince George Free Press, #200, 1515 - 2nd Ave., Prince George BC V2L 3B8 – 250/564-0005 – Circ.: 29,500; Thur.

Prince George This Week, 145 Brunswick St., Prince George BC V2L 2B2 – 250/563-9988; Fax: 250/562-5012 – Sun.; also Central Interior Buy & Sell (Thurs.), Central Interior Business Magazine (4 times a year) – General Manager, Toni Drake

Prince Rupert This Week, 413 - 3rd Ave. East, Prince Rupert BC V8J 1K7 – 250/627-8482 – Sun.

Princeton: Similkameen Spotlight, PO Box 340, Princeton BC V0X 1W0 – 250/295-3535 – Wed.

Queen Charlotte Islands Observer, PO Box 205, Queen Charlotte BC V0T 1S0 – 250/559-4680; Fax: 250/559-8433 – Circ.: 1,800; Thur. – Jeff King

Quesnel: Cariboo Observer, 188 Carson Ave., Quesnel BC V2J 2A8 – 250/992-2121; Fax: 250/992-5229 – Wed., Sun.

Revelstoke Times Review, 402 Third St. West, PO Box 20, Revelstoke BC V0E 2S0 – 250/837-4667; Fax: 250/837-3070 – Wed.

Richmond News, 5731 No. 3 Rd., Richmond BC V6X 2C9 – 604/270-8031; Fax: 604/270-2248 – Wed. & Sun.

Richmond Review, #120, 5851 No. 3 Rd., Richmond BC V6X 2C9 – 604/526-9696 – Sat.

Saanich News, 1824 Store St., Victoria BC V8T 4R4 – 250/920-2090; Fax: 250/920-7352 – Circ.: 32,800; Wed. – Publisher, Trevor Flatman; Editor, Jennifer Blyth; Circulation Manager, Susan Glover

Salmon Arm Observer, PO Box 550, Salmon Arm BC V1E 4N7 – 250/832-2131; Fax: 250/832-5140 – Circ.: 5,200; Wed. – Publisher, Ron Lovestone; Editor, Gordon Priestman; Circulation Manager, Liz Smith

Salmon Arm Shoppers' Guide, PO Box 1270, Salmon Arm BC V1E 4P4 – 250/832-9461; Fax: 250/832-5246 – Circ.: 15,000; Mon. – Publisher, Sally Scales; Editor, G. Paul Skelhorne

Salmon Arm: The Shuswap Market News, PO Box 550, Salmon Arm BC V1E 4N7 – 250/832-2131; Fax: 250/832-5140 – Circ.: 17,000; Sat. – Publisher, Ron Lovestone; Editor, Lorne Reimer

Salmon Arm: The Shuswap Sun, PO Box 729, Salmon Arm BC V1E 4N8 – 250/832-6364; Fax: 250/832-2206; Email: writeon@jetstream.com – Circ.: 15,800; Thur. – Publisher, Robin Campbell; Editor, Chris Ladd

Salt Spring Island: Gulf Islands Driftwood, Driftwood Publishing Ltd., 328 Lower Ganges Rd., Salt Spring Island BC V8K 2V3 – 250/537-9933; Fax: 250/537-2613; Email: trichards@gulfislands.net; URL: http://www.driftwood.bc.ca – Circ.: 4,700; Wed. – Publisher & Editor, Tony Richards; Circulation, Linda Pickell

Sechelt Express, PO Box 920, Sechelt BC V0N 3A0 – 604/885-6228; Fax: 604/885-6199 – Circ.: 12,990; Thur.

Sicamous: Eagle Valley News, 1133 Parksville St., PO Box 113, Sicamous BC V0E 2V0 – 250/836-2570; Fax: 250/836-2661 – Circ.: 1,300; Wed. – Publisher, Ron Lovestone

Sidney: Peninsula News Review, PO Box 2070, Sidney BC V8L 3S5 – 250/656-1151; Fax: 250/656-5526 – Circ.: 13,830; Wed.

Smithers: Interior News, PO Box 2560, Smithers BC V0J 2N0 – 250/847-3266; Fax: 250/847-2995; Email: swan@stargazer.netshop.net – Circ.: 4,398; Wed. – Publisher, Vic Swan; Editor, John Young

Sooke News Mirror, PO Box 339, Sooke BC V0S 1N0 – 250/642-5752; Fax: 250/642-4767 – Wed.

Sparwood: The Elk Valley Miner, PO Box 820, Sparwood BC V0B 2G0 – 250/425-6411; Fax: 250/425-6201; Email: evminer@titanlink.com – Circ.: 2,803; Tue. – Publisher, Fritz Brockel; Editor, Richard Collicutt; Circulation Manager, Wendy Fitzmaurice

Squamish Chief, PO Box 3500, Squamish BC V0N 3G0 – 604/892-9161 – Tue.

Summerland/Peachland Bulletin, PO Box 309, Summerland BC V0H 1Z0 – 250/494-5406; Fax: 250/494-5453; Email: slandreview@img.net – Circ.: 5,500; Mon.; also Summerland Review (Thur., circ. 2,850) – Publisher, Juanita Gibney; Editor, Bill Hodgson; Circulation Manager, Sonja Waller

Surrey: The Leader, PO Box 276, Surrey BC V3T 4W8 – 604/588-4313; Fax: 604/588-1863 – Wed., Sun.

Surrey-North Delta Now, #201, 7889 - 132nd St., Surrey BC V3W 4N2 – 604/572-0064; Fax: 604/572-6438 – Circ.: 105,000; Wed., Sat. – Publisher, Frank Teskey; Editor, Jeff Beamish

Terrace: Skeena Messenger, 4663 Lazelle Ave., Terrace BC V8G 1S4 – 250/638-1681; Fax: 250/638-1606 – Monthly – Publisher/Editor, Mike Kelly

Terrace: The Terrace Standard, 3210 Clinton Ave., Terrace BC V8G 5R2 – 250/638-7283; Fax: 250/638-8432 – Circ.: 8,200; Wed.; also The Skeena Marketplace (Sat., circ. 14,100) – Publisher & Editor, Rod Link

Terrace Times, #4, 3240 Kalum St., Terrace BC V8G 2N4 – Wed.

Tumber Ridge: Tumbler Ridge Observer, 901 - 100 Ave., Dawson Creek BC V1G 1W2 – 250/782-4888; Fax: 250/782-6770 – Circ.: 1,808; Tue. – Publisher, Margaret Forbes; Editor, Kathleen Couturier

Ucluelet: The Westerly News, PO Box 317, Ucluelet BC V0R 3A0 – 250/726-7029 – Wed.

Valemount: The Valley Sentinel, PO Box 688, Valemount BC V0E 2Z0 – 250/566-4425; Fax: 250/566-4528 – Circ.: 1,324; Wed.

Vancouver: East Side Revue, 1736 - 33rd Ave. East, Vancouver BC V5N 3E2 – 604/327-0221 – Circ.: 5,600; Every other Thur.; also West Side Revue (every other Sun.) – Publisher & Editor, Rod Raglin

Vancouver: Jewish Western Bulletin, #203, 873 Beatty St., Vancouver BC V6B 2M6 – 604/689-1520 – Circ.: 5,000; Weekly – Associate Publisher, Rick Wolk

Vancouver: The Link, #201, 225 - 17th Ave. East, Vancouver BC V5V 1A6 – 604/876-9300; Email: Indolink@mindlink.bc.ca – Circ.: 10,000; Wed., Sat. – Publisher & Editor, Promod Puri

Vancouver: Le Soleil de Colombie, #2405, 1177 West Hastings, Vancouver BC V6E 2K3 – 604/730-9575; Fax: 604/730-9576 – Tirage: 3,000; Vendredi; français – Editeur, Jacques Baillout; Rédactrice, Hélène Péronny

Vancouver/False Creek News, 661A Market Hill, Leg-in-Boot Sq., False Creek South, Vancouver BC V5Z 4B5 – 604/876-6770 – Fri.

The Vancouver Courier, 1574 - West Sixth Ave., Vancouver BC V6J 1R2 – 604/738-1411; Fax: 604/731-1474 – Circ.: 61,500, Wed.; 124,500, Sun.; Wed., Sun. – Co-Publisher, Phil Hager; Co-Publisher, Peter Ballard; Editor, Mick Maloney; General Manager, Jack Lynburner

Vancouver Echo, 3355 Grandview Hwy., Vancouver BC V5M 1Z5 – 604/439-2671; Email: rshore@vanecho.com; URL: http://www.vannet.com/vanecho – Circ.: 47,000; Wed. – Publisher, R. Mark Walker; Editor, Randy Shore; Circulation Manager, Linda Caravatta

Vancouver: Westender, #103, 2145 West Broadway, Vancouver BC V6K 4L3 – 604/733-6397; Fax: 604/733-6398; Email: westender@Jumppoint.com – Circ.: 60,000; Thur., Westender (Thur.,); also Bowen Island Undercurrent (Fri.) – Regional Publisher, Dave McCullough; Editor, Ted Townsend

Vancouver: West End Times, #501, 68 Water St., Vancouver BC V6B 1A4 – 604/682-1424; Fax: 604/682-1425 – Circ.: 25,000; Fri. – Bruce Coney

Vanderhoof: Omineca Express Bugle, PO Box 1007, Vanderhoof BC V0J 3A0 – 250/567-9258; Fax: 250/567-2070 – Circ.: 2,300; Wed. – Publisher, Mark Warner; Editor, Mark Nielsen

Vernon: The Morning Star, 4407 - 25th St., Vernon BC V1T 1P5 – 250/545-3322; Fax: 250/542-1510 – Circ.: 29,475; Sun., Wed., Fri. – Publisher, Don Kendall

Victoria: Goldstream News Gazette, 77 Goldstream Ave., Stn D, Victoria BC V9B 2X5 – 250/478-9552; Fax: 250/478-6545 – Circ.: 13,360; Wed. – Publisher, Jane Norman; Editor, Keith Norbury; Circulation, Ev Melanson

Victoria: Oak Bay News, #219, 2187 Oak Bay Ave., Victoria BC V8R 1G1 – 250/598-4123; Fax: 250/598-1896 – Circ.: 9,400; Wed., Fri. – Publisher, Carol Bailey; Editor, David Lennam; Circulation Manager, Sharon Tiffin

Victoria News, 1824 Store St., Victoria BC V8T 4R4 – 250/381-3484; Fax: 250/386-2624 – Circ.: 25,127; Wed.

Westside Weekly, #140, 2300 Carrington Rd., Westbank BC V4T 2E6 – 604/768-5030 – Circ.: 11,604; Wed., Fri.

Whistler: The Whistler Question, #238, 4370 Lorimer Rd., Whistler BC VON 1B4 – 604/932-5131; Fax: 604/932-2862; Email: question@#whistler.net; URL: http://www.whistlerquestion.com – Mon. (circ. 3,457), Thur. (circ. 4,611) – Publisher, Bruce McGregor; Editor, John Wells; Circulation Manager, Henry Lacroix

White Rock: The Peace Arch News, #101, 1440 George St., White Rock BC V4B 4A3 – 604/531-1711; Fax: 604/531-7977; Email: pa_news@deepcove.com – Circ.: 28,000; Wed., Sun. – Publisher, Fred Gorman; Editor, Diane Strandberg

Williams Lake: The Tribune, 188 - 1st Ave. North, Williams Lake BC V2G 1Y8 – 250/392-2331; Fax: 250/392-7253; Email: bphillip@awinc.com – Circ.: 6,600; Tue., Thur; also the Weekender (circ. 10,300) – Publisher, Gary Crosina; Editor, Bill Phillips; Circulation Manager, Ramona Strombom

Winfield: The Calendar, PO Box 54, Winfield BC V0H 2C0 – 250/766-4688 – Wed.

## Manitoba Daily Newspapers

**BRANDON:**

Brandon Sun, Thomson Newspapers Co. Ltd., 501 Rosser Ave., Brandon MB R7A 5Z6 – 204/727-2451; Fax: 204/725-0976, editorial 727-0385 – Circ.: 18,980; Evening; supplement - CoverSTORY (Sun., circ. 23,000) – Publisher, Rob Forbes; Managing Editor, Brian D. Marshall

**FLIN FLON:**

The Reminder, Eagles Printers, 10 North Ave., Flin Flon MB R8A 0T2 – 204/687-3454; Fax: 204/687-4473 – Circ.: 3,800; Evening – Publisher, Randy Daneliuk

**PORTAGE LA PRAIRIE:**

The Daily Graphic, Bowes Publishers Ltd., 1941 Saskatchewan Ave. West, PO Box 130, Portage La Prairie MB R1N 3B4 – 204/857-3427; Fax: 204/239-1270 – Circ.: 4,148; Evening – Publisher, Tom Tenszen; Editor, Simon Blake; Circulation Manager, Carolyn Miller

**WINNIPEG:**

Winnipeg Free Press, Thomson Newspapers Co. Ltd., 1355 Mountain Ave., Winnipeg MB R2X 3B6 – 204/697-7000; Fax: 204/697-7412 – Circ.: 133,530 Mon.-Fri., 207,720 Sat., 141,131 Sun.; Morning – Publisher, H.R. Redekop; Editor, Duncan McMonagle

The Winnipeg Sun, 1700 Church Ave., Winnipeg MB R2X 3A2 – 204/694-2022; Fax: 204/697-0759 – Circ.: 47,214 Mon.-Sat., 62,822 Sun.; Morning – Publisher, Richard Boyer; Managing Editor, Glen Cheater

## Other Newspapers in Manitoba

Altona Red River Valley Echo, Interlake Publishing, PO Box 700, Altona, MB R0G 0B0 – 204/324-5001; Fax: 204/324-1402 – Circ.: 2,400; Mon. – Editor & Business Manager, Liz Wieler

Baldur Gazette, PO Box 280, Baldur MB R0K 0B0 – 204/535-2127; Fax: 204/535-2350 – Tue.

Birtle Eye-Witness, PO Box 160, Shoal Lake MB R0J 1Z0 – 204/759-2644; Fax: 204/759-2521; Email: gnesbitt@lpm.net – Circ.: 1,100; Mon.; supplement Crossroads (circ. 4,400) – Publisher & Editor, Greg Nesbitt

Boissevain Recorder, PO Box 220, Boissevain MB R0K 0E0 – 204/534-6479; Fax: 204/534-2977; Email: brecorder@mail.techplus.com; URL: http://www.techplus.com/recorder.recorderhome.htm – Circ.: 1,624; Wed. – Publisher & Editor, Miles G. Phillips

Brandon: Westman Review, 501 Rosser Ave., Brandon MB R7A 0K4 – 204/727-2451 – Circ.: 20,000; Tue.

Carberry News-Express, PO Box 220, Carberry MB R0K 0H0 – 204/834-2153; Fax: 204/834-2714; Email: newsexpress@mail.techplus.com – Circ.: 1,377; Wed. – Editor & Publisher, John W.H. Lupton; Circulation Manager, Diana Fisher

Carman: The Valley Leader, 70 Main St. South, PO Box 70, Carman MB R0G 0J0 – 204/745-2051; Fax: 204/745-3976 – Circ.: 7,300; Mon.

Cartwright: Southern Manitoba Review, PO Box 249, Cartwright MB R0K 0L0 – 204/529-2342 – Tue.

Dauphin Herald, PO Box 548, Dauphin MB R7N 2V4 – 204/638-4420; Fax: 204/638-8760 – Tue.

Deloraine Times & Star, PO Box 407, Deloraine MB R0M 0M0 – 204/747-2249 – Wed.

Gimli: The Interlake Spectator, 70 - 2nd Ave., PO Box 450, Gimli MB R0C 1B0 – 204/467-2421 – Circ.: 13,316; Mon.

Glenboro Gazette, PO Box 10, Glenboro MB R0K 0X0 – 204/827-2343; Fax: 204/827-2207 – Tue. – Co-Publisher, Travis Johnson; Co-Publisher & Editor, Michael Johnson; Circulation Manager, Agnes Witherspoon

Grandview Exponent, PO Box 39, Grandview MB R0L 0Y0 – 204/546-2555; Fax: 204/546-3081 – Circ.: 1,506; Wed. – Publisher & Editor, Clayton Chaloner

Hamiota Echo, PO Box 160, Shoal Lake MB R0J 1Z0 – 204/759-2644; Fax: 204/759-2521; Email: gnesbitt@lpm.net – Circ.: 1,250; Mon.; supplement Crossroads – Publisher, Greg Nesbitt

Killarney Guide, PO Box 670, Killarney MB R0K 1G0 – 204/523-4611 – Tue.

Lac du Bonnet Leader, PO Box 910, Lac du Bonnet MB R0E 1A0 – 204/345-8611; Fax: 204/345-6344 – Tue.

Manitou Western Canadian, PO Box 190, Manitou MB R0G 1G0 – 204/242-2555; Fax: 204/242-3137 – Circ.: 1,850; Tue. – Publisher & Editor, Bryan Klippenstein

Melita New Era, 149 Main St., PO Box 820, Melita MB R0M 1L0 – 204/522-3491 – Tue.

Minnedosa Tribune, PO Box 930, Minnedosa MB R0J 1E0 – 204/867-3816; Fax: 204/867-5171; Email: tribune@mail.techplus.com; URL: http://www.techplus.com/trib/index.htm – Tues. – Publisher & Editor, R.M. Mummery

The Morden Times, PO Box 1356, Winkler MB R6W 4B3 – 204/325-4771 – Mon.

Neepawa Banner, PO Box 699, Neepawa MB R0J 1H0 – 204/476-3401; Fax: 204/476-5073; Email: banner@mail.techplus.com; URL: http://www.techplus.com/banner – Mon.; also Farmers' Advocate (11,500) – Publisher, Ken Waddell; Editor, Rod Nickel; Circulation Manager, Chris Waddell

Neepawa Press, Sundance Publications Ltd., PO Box 939, Neepawa MB R0J 1H0 – 204/476-2309; Fax: 204/476-5802; Email: neepress@mts.net – Circ.: 3,000; Tue. – Publisher, Ewan Pow; Editor, Jack Gibson

Pilot Mound: The Sentinel Courier, PO Box 179, Pilot Mound MB R0G 1P0 – 204/825-2772; Fax: 204/825-2772 – Circ.: 1,400; Tue. – Publisher, Jeff Howell; Editor, Sheila Howell

Portage La Prairie: Herald Leader Press, 1941 Saskatchewan Ave. West, Portage La Prairie MB R1N 2B4 – 204/857-3427; Fax: 204/239-1270 – Circ.: 6,500; Tue. – Publisher, Tom Tenszen; Editor, Simon Blake; Circulation Manager, Carolyn Miller

Reston Recorder, PO Box 10, Reston MB R0M 1X0 – 204/877-3321; Fax: 204/877-3331 – Mon.

The Rivers Banner, PO Box 70, Rivers MB R0K 1X0 – 204/328-7494; Fax: 204/328-5212 – Circ.: 650; Mon. – Publisher, Ken Waddell; Managing Editor, Sheila Runions; Circulation Manager, Chris Waddell

Roblin Review, PO Box 938, Roblin MB R0L 1P0 – 204/937-8377; Fax: 204/937-8212 – Tue.

Rossburn: Rossburn Review, PO Box 160, Shoal Lake MB R0J 1Z0 – 204/759-2644; Fax: 204/759-2521; Email: gnesbitt@lpm.net – Circ.: 1,100; Mon.; supplement Crossroads – Publisher & Editor, Greg Nesbitt

Russell Banner, PO Box 100, Russell MB R0J 1W0 – 204/773-2069; Fax: 204/773-2645 – Tue. – Publisher & Editor, Clayton G. Chaloner

St. Boniface: La Liberté, CP 190, St. Boniface MB R2H 3B4 – 204/237-4823; Fax: 204/231-1998; Email: la_liberte@presse-ouest.mb.ca; URL: http://www.presse.ouest.mb.ca – Tirage: 4,000; Vendredi; français – Editrice & Rédactrice, Sylviane Lanthier

Selkirk Journal, 217 Clandeboye Ave., Selkirk MB R1A 0X2 – 204/482-7402 – Mon.

Shilo Stag, CFB Shilo, Shilo MB R0K 2A0 – 204/765-3013 – Every other Tue.

Shoal Lake Star, PO Box 160, Shoal Lake MB R0Z 1Z0 – 204/759-2644; Fax: 204/759-2521; Email: gnesbitt@lpm.net – Circ.: 1,100; Mon.; supplement Crossroads – Publisher & Editor, Greg Nesbitt

Souris Plaindealer, PO Box 488, Souris MB R0K 2C0 – 204/483-2070; Fax: 204/483-3866 – Circ.: 1,400; Mon.

Steinbach: The Carillon, 377 Main St., Steinbach MB R0A 2A0 – 204/326-3421; Fax: 204/326-4860; Email: theqarillon@derksenprinters.com; URL: http://www/derksenprinters.com – Circ.: 12,000; Mon. – Publisher, Rick Derksen; Editor, Peter Dyck; Ad Manager, John Wiebe

Stonewall Argus & Teulon Times, Interlake Publishing, 410 Main St., PO Box 190, Stonewall MB R0C 2Z0 – 204/467-2421; Fax: 204/467-5967 – Circ.: 4,627; Mon.

Swan River Star & Times, PO Box 670, Swan River MB R0L 1Z0 – 204/734-3858; Fax: 204/734-4935 – Wed. – Manager/Owner, Bob Gilroy

The Pas: Opasquia Times, PO Box 750, The Pas MB R9A 1K8 – 204/623-3435; Fax: 204/623-5601 – Wed., Fri.

Thompson: The Citizen, PO Box 887, Thompson MB R8N 1N8 – 204/677-4534; Fax: 204/677-3681 – Mon., Wed., Fri. – Grant Wright

Thompson Nickel Belt News, PO Box 887, Thompson MB R8N 1N8 – 204/677-4534; Fax: 204/677-3681 – Circ.: 6,921; Mon. – Publisher, Joan Wright

Treherne: The Times, PO Box 50, Treherne MB R0G 2V0 – 204/723-2542 – Mon.

Virden Empire Advance, 300 Nelson St. West, PO Box 250, Virden MB R0M 2C0 – 204/748-3931; Fax: 204/748-1816; Email: empire@mail.techplus.com; URL: http://www.techplus.com/empire/homepage.htm – Circ.: 2,128; Tues. – Publisher, J.H. McLachlan; Editor, B. Griffith

Westwin: Winnipeg Voxair, CFB Winnipeg, Westwin MB R3J 0T0 – 204/889-3963; Fax: 204/885-4176; Email: voxair@vulcanachq.dnd.ca – Circ.: 4,000; Every other Wed.; English & French – Editor-in-chief, Lt.-Col. S. Marcott; Managing Editor, Maj. C.M. Walton-Simm; Circulation Manager, Maureen Walls

The Winkler Times, PO Box 1356, Winkler MB R6W 4B3 – 204/325-4771; Fax: 204/325-5059 – Mon.

Winnipeg: The Herald, Canadian Publishers, 1465 James St., Winnipeg MB R3H 0W9 – 204/949-6100; Fax: 204/949-6122 – Circ.: 38,000; Tue.

Winnipeg: The Jewish Post & News, 117 Hutchings St., Winnipeg MB R2X 2V4 – 204/694-3332; Fax: 204/694-3916; Email: jewishpost@pangee.ca; URL: http://www.jewishpost.mb.ca – Circ.: 5,500; Wed.; supplement, Lifestyles (6 times a year; circ. 30,000) – Co-Publisher, Bernie Bellan; Editor, Matt Bellan

Winnipeg: The Lance, Canadian Publishers, 1465 James St., Winnipeg MB R3H 0W9 – 204/949-6100; Fax: 204/949-6122 – Circ.: 48,500; Tue.

Winnipeg: The Metro, Canadian Publishers, 1465 James St., Winnipeg MB R3H 0W9 – 204/949-6100; Fax: 204/949-6122 – Circ.: 50,300; Tue.

Winnipeg: The Times, Canadian Publishers, 1465 James St., Winnipeg MB R3H 0W9 – 204/949-6100; Fax: 204/949-6122 – Circ.: 33,000; Tue.

## New Brunswick Daily Newspapers

**CARAQUET:**

L'Acadie Nouvelle, 476, boul St-Pierre ouest, Caraquet NB E0B 1K0 – 506/727-4444; Fax: 506/727-4277 – Tirage: 17,761; Matin; français – Rédacteur, Hermel Vienneau

**FREDERICTON:**

Daily Gleaner, PO Box 3370, Fredericton NB E3B 5A2 – 506/452-6671; Fax: 506/452-7405; Email: dgnews@nbnet.nb.ca; URL: http://www.DailyGleaner.com – Circ.: 29,828; Evening, Mon.-Sat. – Publisher, Brian Butters; Circulation Manager, Kevin Chase

**MONCTON:**

The Times-Transcript, 939 Main St., PO Box 1001, Moncton NB E1C 8P3 – 506/859-4900; Fax: 506/859-4904 – Circ.: 42,234 Mon.-Fri., 55,946 Sat.; Evening – Publisher & General Manager, Johnathan Franklin

**SAINT JOHN:**

Telegraph-Journal/Times-Globe, 210 Crown St., PO Box 2350, Saint John NB E2L 3V8 – 506/632-8888; Fax: 506/648-2652; Email: tjetg@nbnet.nb.ca; URL: http://www.nbpub.nb.ca – Circ.: 28,000 morning, 28,000 evening; Telegraph-Journal morning; Times-Globe evening – President & Publisher, Jamie Milne; Editor-in-chief, Scott Honeyman; Director of Reader Sales & Service, Terry Willows

## Other Newspapers in New Brunswick

Bathurst: Northern Light, Southam Inc., PO Box 416, Bathurst NB E2A 3Z3 – 506/546-4491; Fax: 506/546-1491 – Wed., includes Marketplace (Sun.)

Campbellton: L'Aviron, CP 637, Campbellton NB E3N 3H1 – 506/753-7637; Fax: 506/759-7738; Email: laviron@nbnet.nb.ca – Mercredi; français – Directeur de production, Marc Pitre

Campbellton: The Tribune, PO Box 486, Campbellton NB E3N 3G9 – 506/753-4413; Fax: 506/759-9595; Email: trib@nbnet.nb.ca – Circ.: 8,000; Wed.; English & French – Publisher & Editor, Terrence Raymond; Circulation Manager, Nancy Cook

Edmundston: Le Madawaska, 20 St. François, Edmundston NB E3V 1E3 – 506/735-5575; Fax: 506/735-8086; Email: pag@nbnet.nb.ca; URL: http://www.terra-tech.nb.ca/madawaska – Tirage: 7,600; Mercredi; français – Editeur, J.P. Boucher

Grand Falls: Cataract, PO Box 2756, Grand Falls NB E0J 1M0 – 506/473-3083; Fax: 506/473-3083 – Circ.: 3,084; Wed., English & French

Hartland Observer, 65 Jane St., PO Box 330, Hartland NB E0J 1N0 – 506/375-4458 – Wed.

Miramichi Leader, 65 Jane St., PO Box 500, Miramichi NB E1V 3M6 – 506/622-1600; Fax: 506/622-7422; Email: mleader@auracom.com – Circ.: 7,734; Tue. – Publisher, David Cadogan; Editor, Joanne Cadogan; Sales Director, Bill MacIntosh

Miramichi Weekend, 371 Water St., PO Box 250, Miramichi NB E1N 3A6 – 506/622-2600, 773-5853; Fax: 506/622-6506; Email: mleader@auracom.com; URL: http://www.mibe.nb – Circ.: 7,989; Fri. – Publisher, David Cadogan; Editor, Joanne Cadogan

Oromocto Post-Gazette, 291 Restigouche Rd., Oromocto NB E2V 2H5 – 506/357-9813; Fax: 506/357-6440; Email: oropost@nbnet.nb.ca – Circ.: 4,200; Wed. – Editor, James Haley

Perth-Andover: Victoria County Record, PO Box 990, Perth-Andover NB E0J 1V0 – 506/273-2285; Fax: 506/273-4441; Email: vcrecord@nbnet.nb.ca – Circ.: 4,700; Wed.

Richibucto: Pro-Kent, PO Box 280, Richibucto NB E0A 2M0 – 506/523-9148; Fax: 506/523-7556 – Circ.: 11,000; Wed. English & French – Editeur, Raymond Beaudouin; Rédacteur, Mario Tardif

Sackville Tribune-Post, PO Box 1530, Sackville NB E0A 3C0 – 506/536-2500; Fax: 506/536-4024; Email: tribune@nbnet.nb.ca; URL: http://www.media.medianet.ca/trib/ – Circ.: 3,800; Wed. – Publisher, Vince Arbing; Editor, Lourdes Ann Richard; Circulation Manager, Mary Estabrooks

St. Croix Courier, Courier Newspapers Ltd., PO Box 250, St. Stephen NB E3L 2X2 – 506/466-3220; Fax: 506/466-9950; Email: courier@nbnet.nb.ca – Circ.: 5,700; Tue; also: Courier Weekend, Atlantic Coast Guide – Editor, Chuck Brown

Shediac: Le Moniteur Acadien, C.P. 1807, Shediac NB E0A 3G0 – 506/532-6680; Fax: 506/532-6681; Email: moniteur@nbnet.nb.ca – Jeudi; français – Rédactrice en chef, Carole Friolet

Sussex: Kings County Record, Cadogan Publishing Ltd., PO Box 40, Sussex NB E0E 1P0 – 506/433-1070; Fax: 506/432-3532 – Circ.: 5,500; Tue. – Editor, Jamie Roach; Circulation Manager, Teresa Perry

Woodstock: The Bugle, PO Box 130, Woodstock NB E0J 2B0 – 506/328-8863; Fax: 506/328-3208 – Wed.

## Newfoundland Daily Newspapers

### CORNER BROOK:

The Western Star, Southam Inc., PO Box 460, Corner Brook NF A2H 6E7 – 709/634-4348; Fax: 709/634-9824 – Circ.: 11,590; Evening, Mon.-Sat. – Publisher, Ian Baird; Editor, Richard Williams

### ST JOHN'S:

The Evening Telegram, Southam Inc., Columbus Dr., PO Box 5970, St John's NF A1C 5X7 – 709/364-6300; Fax: 709/364-9333; Email: telegram@eveningtelegram.com; URL: http://www.eveningtelegram.com – Circ.: 40,649 Mon.-Fri., 62,807 Sat., 40,211 Sun.; Evening – Publisher, Miller H. Ayre; Managing Editor, Paul Sparkes

## Other Newspapers in Newfoundland

Bay Roberts: The Compass, PO Box 530, Bay Roberts NF A0A 1G0 – 709/786-7014; Fax: 709/786-0666 – Circ.: 8,778; Tues. – Editor, Heather May

Channel-Port aux Basques: The Gulf News, PO Box 129, Grand Falls NF A2A 2J4 – 709/722-8500 – Circ.: 3,342; Mon.

Clarenville: The Packet, PO Box 129, Grand Falls NF A2A 2J4 – 709/722-8500 – Circ.: 6,347; Mon.

Corner Brook: Humber Log, PO Box 129, Grand Falls NF A2A 2J4 – 709/722-8500 – Circ.: 3,422; Wed.

Gander: Beacon, PO Box 129, Gander NF A2A 2J4 – 709/256-4371; Fax: 709/256-3826; Email: beacon@rb.nf.ca; URL: http://www.rb.nf.ca/beacon – Circ.: 6,072; Wed. – Business Manager, Iris Warren; Editor, Rob Antle

Grand Falls: Advertiser, PO Box 129, Grand Falls NF A2A 2J4 – 709/489-2162; Fax: 709/489-4817 – Circ.: 4,309; Wed.

Happy Valley/Goose Bay: The Labradorian, PO Box 39, Stn B, Happy Valley/Goose Bay NF A0P 1E0 – 709/896-3341; Fax: 709/896-8781 – Circ.: 3,500; Mon. – Publisher, Robinson Blackmore; Editor, Bert Pomeroy

Harbour-Breton-Bay d'Espoir: The Coaster, PO Box 129, Grand Falls NF A2A 2J4 – 709/722-8500 – Circ.: 1,822; Thur.

Labrador City: The Aurora, Labrador Mall, 500 Vanier Ave., PO Box 423, Labrador City NF A2V 2K7 – 709/944-2957; Fax: 709/944-2958 – Circ.: 3,600; Mon. – Publisher, Robinson Blackmore; Editor, Gordon Parsons; Circulation Manager, Wilson Hiscock

Lewisporte: The Pilot, PO Box 129, Grand Falls NF A2A 2J4 – 709/722-8500 – Circ.: 4,759; Wed.

Marystowns: Southern Gazette, PO Box 1116, Marystowns NF A0G 2M0 – 709/279-3188 – Tue.

Paradise: The Shoreline News, PO Box 850, Paradise NF A1L 1E2 – 709/834-2169; Fax: 709/834-4364 – Tue.

St. Anthony: The Northern Pen, PO Box 520, St. Anthony NF A0K 4S0 – 709/454-2191; Fax: 709/454-3718 – Wed. – Publisher, Bernard Bromley; Editor, Allan Bock; Circulation, Frances Reardon

St. John's: The Express, PO Box 8660, St. John's NF A1B 3T7 – 709/579-1312 – Wed.

Springdale: The Nor-Wester, PO Box 129, Grand Falls NF A2A 2J4 – 709/722-8500 – Circ.: 933; Wed.

Stephenville: Le Gaboteur, 41, rue Main, Stephenville NF A2N 1H5 – 709/643-9585; Fax: 709/643-9586; Email: gaboteur@nf.sympatico.ca – Tirage: 1,000; Bi-mensuel; français – Printer, Robinson Blackmore; Rédactrice en chef, Angélique Gridel

Stephenville: The Georgian, PO Box 283, Stephenville NF A2N 2Z4 – 709/643-4531; Fax: 709/643-5041; Email: georgian@rb.nf.ca – Circ.: 3,016; Tue. – Business Manager, Steve Dunne; Editor, Chisholm Pothier

## Newspapers in Northwest Territories

Fort Smith: Slave River Journal, PO Box 990, Fort Smith NT X0E 0P0 – 867/872-2734; Fax: 867/872-2754; Email: slaveriver@aol.com; URL: http://www.auroranet.nt.casrj – Circ.: 2,193; Tues. – Publisher, Don Jaque; Editor-in-chief, James Carroll; Circulation Manager, Dinesh Deonarian

Hay River: The Hub, @105, 3 Capital Dr., Hay River NT X0E 1G2 – 867/874-6577; Fax: 867/874-2679 – Tue. – Publisher & Editor, Chris Brodeur

Inuvik: The Drum, PO Box 2820, Yellowknife NT X1A 2R1 – 867/873-4031; Fax: 867/873-8507; Email: nnsl@nnsl.com; URL: http://www.nnsl.com – Circ.: 1,636; Thur. – Publisher, J.W. Sigvaldson; General Manager, Michael Scott

Iqaluit: Nunatsiaq News, PO Box 8, Iqaluit NT X0A 0H0 – 867/979-5357; Fax: 867/979-4763; Email: nunat@nunanet.com; URL: http://www.nunanet.com/~nunat – Circ.: 6,500; Fri.; English & Inukitut – Publisher, Steven Roberts; Editor, Todd Phillips; Circulation Manager, Doug Hawey

Yellowknife: L'Aquilon, CP 1325, Yellowknife NT X1A 2N9 – 867/873-6603; Fax: 867/873-2158; Email: aquilon@internorth.com – Vendredi; français

Yellowknife: News/North, PO Box 2820, Yellowknife NT X1A 2R1 – 867/873-8109; Fax: 867/873-8507; Email: nnsl@nnsl.com; URL: http://www.nnsl.com – Circ.: 12,333; Mon. – Publisher, Jack W. Sigvaldson; General Manager, Michael Scott

Yellowknifer, 5108 - 50th St., PO Box 2820, Yellowknife NT X1A 2R1 – 867/873-4031 – Circ.: 5,375; Wed., Fri.

## Nova Scotia Daily Newspapers

### AMHERST:

Daily News, Cumberland Publishing Ltd., PO Box 280, Amherst NS B4H 3Z2 – 902/667-5102; Fax: 902/667-0419 – Circ.: 4,071 Mon.-Fri., 6,225 Sat.; Morning, Mon.-Sat. – President & Publisher, Earl J. Gouchie

### HALIFAX:

The Chronicle-Herald and The Mail-Star, 1650 Argyle St., Halifax NS B3J 2T2 – 902/426-2811; Fax: 902/426-3014; Email: sarahd@herald.ns.ca; URL: http://www.herald.ns.ca – Circ.: 96,744 morning, 45,817 evening; The Chronicle-Herald morning, The Mail-Star evening – Publisher, G.W. Dennis; Managing Editor, Jane Purves; Circulation Manager, Scott Boyle

The Daily News, PO Box 8330, Stn A, Halifax NS B3K 5M1 – 902/465-1222; Fax: 902/468-2645 news, 468-3609 adv.; Email: citydesk@nfxnews.com; URL: http://www.hfxnews.com – Circ.: 26,400 Mon.-Sat., 43,200 Sun.; Morning; also Sunday Daily News (Circ. 45,408) – Publisher, Mark Richardson; Editor-in-chief, Douglas MacKay

### NEW GLASGOW:

The Evening News, Southam Inc., 352 East River Rd., New Glasgow NS B2H 5E2 – 902/752-3000; Fax: 902/752-1945 – Circ.: 10,695; Evening – Publisher & General Manager, Richard Russell; Managing Editor, Doug MacNeil

### SYDNEY:

Cape Breton Post, Southam Inc., 255 George St., PO Box 1500, Sydney NS B1P 6K6 – 902/564-5451; Fax: 902/562-7077 – Circ.: 31,398; Morning – Publisher & General Manager, Milton Ellis; Managing Editor, Fred Jackson

### TRURO:

The Daily News, Southam Inc., 6 Louise St., PO Box 220, Truro NS B2N 5C3 – 902/893-9405; Fax: 902/893-0518 – Circ.: 8,809 Mon.-Fri., 10,498 Sat.; Evening, Sat. morning – Publisher, Leith Orr; Managing Editor, Bill McGuire

## Other Newspapers in Nova Scotia

Amherst: The Citizen, PO Box 280, Amherst NS B4H 3Z2 – 902/667-5116; Fax: 902/667-0419 – Sat.

Annapolis: The Royal Spectator, PO Box 250, Bridgetown NS B0S 1C0 – 902/665-4441; Fax: 902/665-4014 – Tue.

Antigonish: The Casket, PO Box 1300, Antigonish NS B2G 2L6 – 902/863-4370; Fax: 902/863-5808 – Tue.

Berwick Register, PO Box 640, Berwick NS B0P 1E0 – 902/538-3189; Fax: 902/538-8583 – Wed.

Bible Hill: The Light, 228 Main St., Bible Hill NS B2N 4H2 – 902/895-7946; Fax: 902/893-1427 – Monthly; also TV This Week (Wed.)

Bridgetown Monitor, PO Box 250, Bridgetown NS B0S 1C0 – 902/665-4441; Fax: 902/665-4014 – Circ.: 1,445; Tue.; also Mirror-Examiner (Wed.)

Bridgewater Bulletin, Lighthouse Publishing Ltd., 353 York St., Bridgewater NS B4V 3K2 – 902/543-2457; Fax: 902/543-2228; Email: lightse@fox.nstn.ca; URL: http://fox.nstn.ca/~lighthse/ – Circ.: 8,600; Wed; also South Shore Living (Wed.) & Lighthouse Log (Mon.)

Bridgewater: Progress Enterprise, 353 York St., Bridgewater NS B4V 3K2 – 902/543-2457; Fax: 902/543-2228; Email: lighthse@fox.nstn.ca – Circ.: 4,500; Wed.; also South Shore Living (Wed.) & Lighthouse Log (Mon.)

Digby Courier, PO Box 670, Digby NS B0V 1A0 – 902/245-4715; Fax: 902/245-4715 – Wed. – Editor, John DeMings

Enfield: The Weekly Press, 287 Hwy. 2, Enfield NS B2T 1C9 – 902/883-3181; Fax: 902/420-0524 – Circ.: 2,620; Wed.

Glace Bay: Cape Breton Regional Gazette, 17 Commercial St., PO Box 113, Glace Bay NS B1A 5V1 – 902/849-1830 – Circ.: 5,000; Wed. – Publisher, Ken Cotter

Greenwood: The Aurora, CFB Greenwood, PO Box 99, Greenwood NS B0P 1N0 – 902/765-1494, ext.5440; Fax: 902/765-1717; Email: aurora@auracom.com; URL: http://www.14wing.qrwd.dnd.ca – Circ.: 5,900; Mon.; English & French

Halifax: Maritime Command Trident, Trident Military Newspaper, PO Box 3308, Halifax NS B3J 3J1 – 902/427-4235; Fax: 902/427-4234 – Circ.: 10,000; Every other Thur; English & French – Publisher, Sheila Fournier; Editor, Len Canfield; Circulation Manager, Kim Cameron

Inverness: The Oran, PO Box 100, Inverness NS B0E 1N0 – 902/258-2253 – Wed.

Kentville: The Advertiser, PO Box 430, Kentville NS B4N 3X4 – 902/681-2121; Fax: 902/681-0830 – Tue., Fri; also Kentville Teleguide (Wed.)

Liverpool Advance, PO Box 10, Liverpool NS B0T 1K0 – 902/354-3441; Fax: 902/354-2455 – Wed.

Oxford Journal, PO Box 10, Oxford NS B0M 1P0 – 902/447-2051; Fax: 902/447-2055 – Circ.: 3,008; Wed.

Pictou Advocate, PO Box 1000, Pictou NS B0K 1H0 – 902/485-8014; Fax: 902/752-4816 – Circ.: 6,000; Wed. – Publisher, George Bellefontaine; Editor, Gordon Stiles; General Manager, Andrew Robertson

Port Hawkesbury: The Reporter, PO Box 3300, Port Hawkesbury NS B0E 2V0 – 902/625-3300; Fax: 902/625-2369 – Circ.: 4,525; Tue.

Port Hawkesbury: The Scotia Sun, PO Box 599, Port Hawkesbury NS B0E 2V0 – 902/625-1900 – Thur.

Shearwater: The Warrior, PO Box 190, Shearwater NS B0J 3A0 – 902/460-1013; Fax: 902/460-1796 – Circ.: 6,500; Bi-weekly; English & French – Managing Editor, Jon Houston

Sheet Harbour: The Eastern Shore Sandpiper, PO Box 136, Sheet Harbour NS B0J 3B0 – 902/885-2146; Fax: 902/885-3424 – Circ.: 13,500; Monthly – Co-Publisher, Heather Robinson; Co-Publisher, James Robinson

Shelburne: The Coast Guard, PO Box 100, Shelburne NS B0T 1W0 – 902/875-3244; Fax: 902/875-3545; Email: coastg@auracom.com; URL: http://www.klis.com/fundy/coastguard – Circ.: 5,000; Tue.

Springhill & Parrsboro Record, PO Box 670, Springhill NS B0M 1X0 – 902/597-3731; Fax: 902/667-1402 – Wed.

Truro: The Weekly Record, 615 Prince St., Truro NS B2N 1G2 – 902/895-7946 – Circ.: 4,978; Wed.

Waverley: The Laker, 287 Hwy. 2, Enfield NS B2T 1C9 – 902/883-3181 – Monthly

Windsor: Hants Journal, PO Box 550, Windsor NS B0N 2T0 – 902/798-8371; Fax: 902/798-5451 – Wed.

Yarmouth: Le Courrier de la Nouvelle-Ecosse, 236B Water St., PO Box 4, Yarmouth NS B5A 4P8 – 902/742-9119; Fax: 902/742-9110; Email: courrier@fox.nstn.ca – Vendredi; français

Yarmouth: The Vanguard, PO Box 128, Yarmouth NS B5A 4B1 – 902/742-7111; Fax: 902/742-2311 – Tue., Fri; also Telecaster (Tue.)

## Ontario Daily Newspapers

### BARRIE:

Barrie Examiner, Hollinger Inc., 16 Bayfield St., Barrie ON L4M 4T6 – 705/726-6537; Fax: 705/726-7706; Email: examiner@sympatico.com – Circ.: 44,353; Evening, Mon.-Sat. – Publisher, Ron Laurin

### BELLEVILLE:

The Intelligencer, Hollinger Inc., 45 Bridge St. East, PO Box 5600, Belleville ON K8N 5C7 – 613/962-9171; Fax: 613/962-9652; Email: intel@intranet.ca.on – Circ.: 18,670 Mon.-Sat., 16,998 Sun.; Afternoon – Publisher & General Manager, Peter E. Leichnitz; Circulation Manager, Ron Prins

### BRANTFORD:

The Expositor, Southam Inc., 53 Dalhousie St., Brantford ON N3T 5S8 – 519/756-2020; Fax: 519/756-9470 – Circ.: 26,593; Morning – Publisher, William R. Findlay; Reader Sales Manager, Susan Azzopardi

### BROCKVILLE:

Recorder and Times, 23 King St. West, PO Box 10, Brockville ON K6V 5T8 – 613/342-4441; Fax: 613/342-4456; URL: http://www.recorder.ca – Circ.: 17,001, 18,300 Fri.; Evening, Mon.-Sat. – Co-Publisher, Hunter S. Grant; Co-Publisher & Editor, Perry S. Beverley, 613/342-4443

### CAMBRIDGE:

Cambridge Reporter, Hollinger Inc., 26 Ainslie St. South, Cambridge ON N1R 3K1 – 519/621-3810; Fax: 519/621-8239 – Circ.: 10,070; Evening – Publisher, Verne Shaull; Circulation Manager, Sue Wood

### CHATHAM:

Chatham Daily News, Southam Inc., 45 Fourth St., PO Box 2007, Chatham ON N7M 2G4 – 519/354-2000; Fax: 519/436-0949 – Circ.: 16,273; Evening – Publisher & General Manager, John Cheek; Managing Editor, Jim Blake

### COBOURG:

Cobourg Daily Star, Northumberland Publishers Ltd., 415 King St. West, PO Box 400, Cobourg ON K9A 4L1 – 905/372-0131; Fax: 905/372-2391; Email: letters@eagle.ca – Circ.: 5,632; Evening – Publisher, Earl Bateman

### CORNWALL:

Standard-Freeholder, Southam Inc., 44 Pitt St., Cornwall ON K6J 3P3 – 613/933-3160; Fax: 613/933-7521 – Circ.: 18,497; Morning – Publisher, John A. Farrington; Circulation Manager, Dale David

### ETOBICOKE:

Daily Racing Form, 47 Voyageur Ct. North, Etobicoke ON M9W 4Y6 – 416/798-1911; Fax: 416/798-1921 – Circ.: 3,570 Mon., 5,529 Tue.-Fri., 9,558 Sat., 8,465 Sun.; Morning – Editor, Bill Tallon

### FORT FRANCES:

Daily Bulletin, PO Box 339, Fort Frances ON P9A 3M7 – 807/274-5373; Fax: 807/274-7286; Email: fftimes@ff.lakeheadu.ca – Circ.: 2,778; Afternoon – Publisher, J.R. Cumming; Editor, Mike Behan

### GUELPH:

The Guelph Mercury, Hollinger Inc., #8, 14 Macdonell St., PO Box 3604, Guelph ON N1H 6P7 – 519/822-4310; Fax: 519/767-1681; Email: mercury@in.on.ca – Circ.: 16,655 Mon.-Sat., 15,521 Sun.; Evening – Publisher & General Manager, Stephen Rhodes; Managing Editor, Ed Cassavoy

### HAMILTON:

The Hamilton Spectator, Southam Inc., 44 Frid St., Hamilton ON L8N 3G3 – 905/526-3333; Fax: 905/522-1696; Toronto line: 416/825-0111; Telex: 06-18390; URL: http://www.southam.com/hamilton-spector – Circ.: 110,611, 132,091 Sat.; Evening – Publisher, Patrick J. Collins; Reader Sales & Serv. Dir., Terry Willows

### KENORA:

Daily Miner & News, Bowes Publishers Ltd., 33 Main St. South, PO Box 1620, Kenora ON P9N 3X7 – 807/468-5555; Fax: 807/468-4318; Email: kendmn@akenora.com – Circ.: 4,792; Evening – Publisher, Mitch Wolfe; Circulation Manager, Bob Stewart

### KINGSTON:

The Kingston Whig-Standard, 306 King St. East, Kingston ON K7L 4Z7 – 613/544-5000; Fax: 613/544-6994 – Circ.: 28,127 Mon.-Fri., 36,176 Sat.; Morning & evening – Publisher, Fred Laflamme; Editor, Lynn Messerschmidt

### KIRKLAND LAKE:

Northern Daily News, Southam Inc., 8 Duncan Ave., Kirkland Lake ON P2N 3L4 – 705/567-5321; Fax: 705/567-6162 – Circ.: 5,319; Evening – Publisher & Manager, Syl Belisle; Editor, Tom Perry

### KITCHENER:

Kitchener-Waterloo Record, Southam Inc., 225 Fairway Rd. South, Kitchener ON N2G 4E5 – 519/894-2231; Fax: 519/894-3912; Toronto line: 416/826-9182 – Circ.: 74,000; Afternoon, 6 days a week – Publisher, Wayne MacDonald; Editor, Carolyne Rittinger

### LINDSAY:

The Lindsay Daily Post, Hollinger Inc., 15 William St. North, Lindsay ON K9V 3Z8 – 705/324-2114; Fax: 705/324-0174 – Circ.: 8,066; Morning – Publisher, Jim Ambrose

### LONDON:

The London Free Press, Sun Media Corp., 369 York St., PO Box 2280, London ON N6A 4G1 – 519/667-5451; Fax: 519/667-4523; Email: letters@lfpress.com; URL: http://www.lfpress.com – Circ.: 108,501 Mon.-Fri., 137,725 Sat.; Morning – Publisher & CEO, John Paton; Editor-in-chief, Phil McLeod; Director of Reader Sales & Marketing, John Muszak

### NIAGARA FALLS:

Review, Hollinger Inc., 4801 Valley Way, PO Box 270, Niagara Falls ON L2E 6T6 – 905/358-5711; Fax: 905/356-0785 – Circ.: 46,500; Evening – Publisher, David A. Beattie; Editor, Michael Brown

**NORTH BAY:**

North Bay Nugget, Southam Inc., 259 Worthington St. West, PO Box 570, North Bay ON P1B 8J6 – 705/472-3200; Fax: 705/472-5128 – Circ.: 22,500; Evening, Mon.-Fri.; morning, Sat. – Publisher, Robert Hull; Managing Editor, Bruce Cowan; Circulation Manager, Ron Bean

**ORILLIA:**

Packet and Times, Hollinger Inc., 31 Colborne St. East, Orillia ON L3V 1T4 – 705/325-1355; Fax: 705/325-7691 – Circ.: 9,628; Evening – General Manager, Bruce MacIntyre; Managing Editor, Jeff Day

**OTTAWA:**

Le Droit, #222, 47 Clarence St., CP 8860, Succ T, Ottawa ON K1G 3J9 – 613/560-2747; Fax: 613/560-2572 – Tirage: 35,020 lun.-ven., 42,490 sam.; Matin; français – Editeur, Pierre Bergeron; Rédacteur, Claude Beauregard

The Ottawa Citizen, Southam Inc., 1101 Baxter Rd., PO Box 5020, Ottawa ON K2C 3M4 – 613/829-9100; Fax: 613/829-5032 – Circ.: 152,751 Mon.-Fri., 210,256 Sat., 139,745 Sun.; All day – Publisher, Russ Mills; Executive News Editor, Don Butler; Circulation Manager, Harold Lundy

Ottawa Sun and Sunday Sun, 380 Hunt Club Rd., PO Box 9729, Stn T, Ottawa ON K1G 5H7 – 613/739-7000; Fax: 613/739-8043 – Circ.: 51,035 Mon.-Fri., 60,063 Sun.; Morning – Interim Publisher, John Paton; Managing Editor, Mike Therien

**OWEN SOUND:**

Sun Times, Southam Inc., 290 - 9th St. East, PO Box 200, Owen Sound ON N4K 5P2 – 519/376-2250; Fax: 519/376-7190; Email: owstimes@southam.ca; URL: http://www.southam.com/owensoundsuntimes/ – Circ.: 22,000; Evening – Publisher, Clyde Wicks; Editor, Jim Merriam; Circulation Manager, Dan Patterson

**PEMBROKE:**

The Daily Observer, Hollinger Inc., 186 Alexander St., Pembroke ON K8A 4L9 – 613/732-3691; Fax: 613/732-2645 – Circ.: 8,000; Evening – Publisher, Steve Gloster; Editor, Peter Lapinskie; Circulation Manager, David Bell

Pembroke Daily News, Runge Newspapers, Inc., 86 Pembroke St. West, PO Box 10, Pembroke ON K8A 6X1 – 613/735-3141; Fax: 613/732-7214 – Morning – General Manager, Jim Badgley

**PETERBOROUGH:**

Examiner, Hollinger Inc., 400 Water St., PO Box 3890, Peterborough ON K9J 8L4 – 705/745-4641; Fax: 705/743-4581 – Circ.: 25,453 Mon.-Sat., 23,367 Sun.; Morning – Publisher, Jim Ambrose; Managing Editor, Ed Arnold

**ST. CATHARINES:**

The St. Catharines Standard, 17 Queen St., St. Catharines ON L2R 5G5 – 905/684-7251; Fax: 905/684-8011 – Circ.: 38,720 Mon.-Fri., 47,047 Sat.; Afternoon – Publisher, D. Gaynor; Managing Editor, Doug Firby; News Editor, Paul Harvey

**ST. THOMAS:**

Times-Journal, Bowes Publishers Ltd., 16 Hincks St., St. Thomas ON N5R 5Z2 – 519/631-2790; Fax: 519/631-5653 – Circ.: 9,154; Evening – Publisher, Terry Carroll; Managing Editor, Ross Porter

**SARNIA:**

Observer, Southam Inc., 140 South Front St., PO Box 3009, Sarnia ON N7T 7M8 – 519/344-3641; Fax: 519/332-2951 – Circ.: 24,000; Evening – Publisher, Daryl Smith; News Editor, Frank Rupnik; Circulation Manager, Terry Pimlatt

**SAULT STE. MARIE:**

Star, Southam Inc., 145 Old Garden Rd., PO Box 460, Sault Ste. Marie ON P6A 5M5 – 705/759-3030; Fax: 705/942-8690, 759-0102; Email: ssmstar@southam.ca; URL: http://www.saultstar.com – Circ.: 24,500, Mon. - Sat.; Evening (morning Sat.) – Publisher, Robert Richardson; Editor, John Halucha; Manager, Lou Maulucci

**SIMCOE:**

Reformer, Southwestern Ontario Publishing Ltd., 105 Donly Dr. South, PO Box 370, Simcoe ON N3Y 4L2 – 519/426-5710; Fax: 519/426-9255; Email: refedit@swopp.com; URL: http://www.swopp.com/reformer – Circ.: 9,584; Evening – Publisher, Michael Fredericks; Managing Editor, Kim Novak

**STRATFORD:**

The Beacon-Herald, 108 Ontario St., PO Box 430, Stratford ON N5A 6T6 – 519/271-2220; Fax: 519/271-1026 – Circ.: 13,283; Evening – Publisher & Editor, Charles W. Dingman; Managing Editor, Don Carson

**SUDBURY:**

The Sudbury Star, Southam Inc., 33 MacKenzie St., Sudbury ON P3C 4Y1 – 705/674-5271; Fax: 705/674-0624; Email: ss-publisher@cwconnect.ca; URL: http://sudbury.siteseet.ca – Circ.: 26,333 Mon.-Sat., 23,960 Sun.; Morning – Publisher, Ken Sequin; Managing Editor, Roger Cazabon; Circulation Manager, Dave Paquette

**THUNDER BAY:**

The Chronicle-Journal, Thomson Newspapers Co. Ltd., 75 South Cumberland St., Thunder Bay ON P7B 1A3 – 807/343-6200; Fax: 807/345-5991; Email: cj-editorial@cwconnect.ca; URL: http://netreader.com/tbay/index2.html – Circ.: 7,058 morning, 28,306 evening, 40,918 Sat., 33,843 Sun. – Publisher & General Manager, Colin Bruce; Circulation Manager, Shannon Simpson

**TIMMINS:**

Daily Press, Southam Inc., 187 Cedar St. South, Timmins ON P4N 2G9 – 705/268-5050; Fax: 705/268-7373; Email: tdp@nt.net; URL: http://www.timminspress.com – Circ.: 12,000; Morning – Publisher, Syl Belisle; Editor, David McGee

**TORONTO:**

The Financial Post, 333 King St. East, Toronto ON M5A 4N2 – 416/350-6300; Fax: 416/350-6301; Email: letters@finpost.com; Advertising Email: advertising@fpadv.finpost.com; URL: http://www.canoe.ca/FP – Circ.: 78,463 Tue.-Fri., 170,380 Sat.; Morning, Tue.-Sat. – Publisher & CEO, Bill Neill; Editor, Diane Francis, 416/350-6350

The Globe and Mail, 444 Front St. West, Toronto ON M5V 2S9 – 416/585-5000; Fax: 416/585-5085; URL: http://www.globeandmail.com – Circ.: 313,747; Morning, Mon. to Sat.; also Report on Business, Broadcast Week, & Gusto – Publisher & CEO, Roger P. Parkinson; Editor-in-chief, William Thorsell

The Toronto Star, One Yonge St., Toronto ON M5E 1E6 – 416/367-2000; Fax: 416/869-4328 editorial, 869-4215 advtg.; Email: newsroom@inforamp.net; URL: http://www.thestar.com – Circ.: 463,218 Mon.-Fri., 712,873 Sat., 469,738 Sun.; Morning, 2 editions – Publisher, John Honderich; VP, Marketing, Jeff Shearer

The Toronto Sun, Sun Media Corp., 333 King St. East, Toronto ON M5A 3X5 – 416/947-2222; Fax: 416/947-1664; Email: sun@inforamp.net; URL: http://www.canoe.ca – Circ.: 247,187, daily; 430,140, Sunday; Morning – Publisher, Hartley Steward; Executive Editor, Peter O'Sullivan; Manager, News Research, Julie Kirsh, 416/947-2257

**WELLAND:**

Welland-Port Colborne Tribune, Hollinger Inc., 228 East Main St., Welland ON L3B 5P5 – 905/732-2411; Fax: 905/732-4883; Email: tribune@iaw.on.ca – Circ.: 18,000; Morning, Mon. to Sat. – Publisher, David A. Beattie; Managing Editor, Gary W. Manning; Circulation Manager, Karin Vanderzee

**WINDSOR:**

The Windsor Star, Southam Inc., 167 Ferry St., Windsor ON N9A 4M5 – 519/255-5711; Fax: 519/255-5778; Email: letters@win.smoutham.ca; URL: http://www/southam.com/windsorstar/ – Circ.: 82,077 Mon.-Fri., 94,849 Sat.; Evening – Publisher, Jim McCormack; Editor, Gerry Nott

**WOODSTOCK:**

Sentinel-Review, Southwestern Ontario Publishing Ltd., #16, 18 Brock St., PO Box 1000, Woodstock ON N4S 8A5 – 519/537-2341; Fax: 519/537-3049 – Circ.: 10,049; Evening; supplement - CoverStory (weekly, circ. 15,200) – Publisher, Pat Logan; Circulation Manager, Andy Clifford

## Other Newspapers in Ontario

Ajax/Pickering News Advertiser, Metroland Printing Publishing & Distribution, 130 Commercial Ave., Ajax ON L1S 2H5 – 905/683-5110; Fax: 905/683-7363 – Circ.: 39,555; Wed., Fri., Sun. – Tim Whittaker

Alexandria: Glengarry News, PO Box 10, Alexandria ON K0C 1A0 – 613/525-2020; Fax: 613/525-3824 – Wed.

Alliston Herald, Metroland Printing Publishing & Distribution, 169 Dufferin St. South, Unit 22, Alliston ON L9R 1E6 – 705/435-6228; Fax: 705/435-3342 – Circ.: 4,709; Wed; also The Herald Courier (Sat., circ. 18,791) – Publisher, Joe Anderson

Almonte Gazette, PO Box 130, Almonte ON K0A 1A0 – 613/256-1311; Fax: 613/256-5168 – Wed.

Amherstburg: The Amherstburg Echo Community News, 238 Dalhousie St., Amherstburg ON N9V 1W4 – 519/736-2147; Fax: 519/736-8384; Email: aecho@wincom.net; URL: http://www.bowesnet.com/amherstburgecho – Circ.: 7,500; Tue. – Publisher, Jack Kindred

Ancaster News, 311 Wilson St. East, Ancaster ON L9G 2B8 – 905/628-6313; Fax: 905/648-7458 – Circ.: 8,172; Wed.

Angus Star, Star Group Community Newspapers Inc., 3 Caroline St. West, PO Box 70, Creemore ON L0M 1G0 – 705/466-2002; Fax: 705/466-3433 – Circ.: 3,200; Wed.; also publishes: Clearview Star (Wed.), Elmvale Lance (Wed.), & Wasaga Star Times (Wed.)

Arnprior Chronicle Guide, 116 John St. North, Arnprior ON K7S 2N6 – 613/623-6571; Fax: 613/623-7518 – Circ.: 4,783; Wed.; also The Arnprior Weekend Chronicle (circ. 13,000) – Publisher, Marjory McBride; News Editor, Rita Racicot; Circulation Manager, Beverly Quattrocchi

Arnprior News, 98 John St. North, Arnprior ON K7S 2N3 – 613/623-5064; Fax: 613/623-0110 – Circ.: 10,705; Sun.

Arthur Enterprise-News, 106 Charles St. East, PO Box 310, Arthur ON N0G 1A0 – 519/848-2410; Fax: 519/848-3665 – Circ.: 1,443; Wed. – Publisher, Clive Williams; Editor, Mike Robinson

Astra: Contact, 8 Wing, PO Box 1000, Stn 40, Astra ON K0K 3W0 – 613/965-7248; Fax: 613/965-7490 – Circ.: 3,500; Wed.; English & French – Editor-in-chief, Capt. Peter Thorp-Levitt; Managing Editor, M.J. Thistle; Circulation Manager, Keith Cleaton

Atikokan Progress, PO Box 220, Atikokan ON P0T 1C0 – 807/597-2731; Fax: 807/597-6103; Email: aprogress@atikokan.lakeheadu.ca – Circ.: 1,769; Mon. – Publisher, Eve Shine; Editor, Michael P. McKinnon; Circulation Manager, Marie Cornell

Aurora Weekly, 237 Romina Dr., Unit 2, Concord ON L4K 4V3 – 905/660-9556 – Wed.

Aurora: Newmarket/Aurora Era Banner, Metroland Printing Publishing & Distribution, 580 Steven Ct., Bldg. B, PO Box 236, Aurora ON L3Y 4X1 – 905/493-1300; Fax: 905/853-4629 – Wed., Fri., Sun. – Publisher, Bruce Annan

Aylmer Express, 390 Talbot St. East, PO Box 160, Aylmer ON N5H 2R9 – 519/773-3126; Fax: 519/773-3147 – Wed.

Ayr News, 40 Piper St., Ayr ON N0B 1E0 – 519/632-7432; Fax: 519/632-7743 – Circ.: 4,350; Wed. – Publisher, James W. Schmidt; Editor, John P. Schmidt

Bancroft Times, 93 Hastings St. North, Bancroft ON K0L 1C0 – 613/332-2300 – Wed.

Barrie Advance, Metroland Printing Publishing & Distribution, 21 Patterson Rd., Barrie ON L4N 7W6 – 705/726-0573; Fax: 705/726-9350 – Circ.: 28,000 Fri., 45,500 Sat,; Wed., Fri., Sun. – Publisher, Joe Anderson

Barrie: Super Shopper, Buy, Trade & Sell, 124 Brock St., Barrie ON L4N 2M2 – 705/726-6015; Fax: 705/726-6015; Email: tyler@bconnex.net – Circ.: 15,000; Thur.

Barry's Bay This Week, PO Box 220, Barry's Bay ON K0J 1B0 – 613/756-2944; Fax: 613/756-2994 – Circ.: 5,500; Tue. – Publisher, Phil Conway; Editor, Helen Conway

Beamsville: Lincoln Post Express, 4309 Central Ave., PO Box 400, Beamsville ON L0R 1B0 – 905/563-5393; Fax: 905/563-7977 – Wed.

Beaverton: Brock Citizen, 390 Simcoe St., PO Box 10, Beaverton ON L0K 1A0 – 705/426-7443; Fax: 705/426-5953 – Circ.: 2,800; Wed. – Publisher, Angie McCabe; Editor, Jeff Bower

Beeton Record Sentinel, PO Box 310, Beeton, ON L0G 1A0 – 905/729-2287; Email: york@simcoe.igs.net – Circ.: 1,325; Wed. – John Archibald; Bruce Haire

Belle River: North Essex News, c/o Phoenix Media Group Inc., PO Box 429, Belle River ON N0R 1A0 – 519/728-1082; Fax: 519/728-4551 – Circ.: 2,500; Wed. – Editor, Karen Fallon

Belleville Shopper's Market, Bowes Publishers, 366 North Front St., PO Box 446, Belleville ON K8N 5A5 – 613/962-3422; Fax: 613/962-1353 – Circ.: 42,800; Sat. – General Manager, Charles Parker

Blenheim News-Tribune, 62 Talbot St. West, PO Box 160, Blenheim ON N0P 1A0 – 519/676-3321; Fax: 519/676-5454 – Wed.

Blind River Sentinel, PO Box 640, Thessalon ON P0R 1L0 – Fax: 705/356-3485 – Thur. – Publisher, Randy Rankin; Editor, Kelly James

Blyth: The Citizen, North Huron Publishing Co. Inc., 136 Queen St. South, PO Box 429, Blyth ON N0M 1H0 – 519/523-4792; Fax: 519/523-9140; Email: norhuronm@huropn.net – Circ.: 2,191; Wed. – Publishers, Keith Roulston; Editor, Bonnie Grupp; Circulation Manager, Jill Roulston

Bobcaygeon Independent, 49 Main St., PO Box 220, Bobcaygeon ON K0M 1A0 – 705/738-2212; Fax: 705/738-4332 – Wed.

Bolton Enterprise, 2 Marconi Ct., Unit 13, Bolton ON L7E 1E5 – 905/857-3433; Fax: 905/857-5002 – Circ.: 10,000; Sun. – Publisher, Bill Anderson; Editor, Bill Whitbread

The Borden Citizen, CFB Borden, Borden ON L0M 1C0 – 705/423-2567; Fax: 705/423-3452 – Circ.: 4,000; Wed., English & French – L.Col. Hardiman

Bothwell Times, PO Box 40, Bothwell ON N0P 1C0 – 519/692-3105 – Wed.

Bracebridge Examiner, 16 Manitoba St., PO Box 1049, Bracebridge ON P0B 1C0 – 705/645-1718 – Wed.

Bracebridge: The Muskokan, 16 Manitoba St., PO Box 1049, Bracebridge ON P1L 1S1 – 705/645-8771 – Thur. – Editor, Susan Pryle

Bracebridge: Muskoka Advance, #203, 175 Manitoba St., PO Box 1600, Bracebridge ON P1L 1V6 – 705/645-4463; Fax: 705/645-3928 – Circ.: 23,000; Sun.

Bracebridge: Muskoka Sun, #203, 175 Manitoba St., PO Box 1600, Bracebridge ON P1L 1V6 – 705/645-4463; Fax: 705/645-3928; Email: sun@muskoka.com – Circ.: 22,000; Thur.; also Muskoka Life (annually)

Bradford West Gwillimbury Times, 32 Holland St. East, PO Box 1570, Bradford ON L3Z 2B8 – 905/775-4471; Fax: 905/775-4489; Email: rfonger@times.net – Circ.: 7,800; Wed. – Publisher, Richard Fonger; Editor, Miriam King

Brampton Guardian, Metroland Printing Publishing & Distribution, 685 Queen St. West, RR# 2, Brampton ON L6V 1A1 – 905/454-4344; Fax: 905/454-4385 – Circ.: 60,000; Wed., Fri., Sun. – Publisher, Ken Nugent; Editor-in-chief, Lorne Drury

Brampton Pennysaver, 56 Bramsteele Rd., Unit 1, Brampton ON L6W 3M7 – 905/454-0854 – Sun.; also publish: Caledon Pennysaver, Malton Pennysaver, Mississauga Pennysaver, & Rexdale Pennysaver

Brantford/Tekawennake-6 Nations-New Credit Reporter, PO Box 130, Ohsweken ON N0A 1M0 – 519/753-0077; Fax: 519/753-0011 – Wed.

Brantford Pennysaver, 61 Dalkeith Dr., Unit 5, Brantford ON N3P 1M1 – 519/756-0076 – Sat.

Brant News, #301, 446 Grey St., Brantford ON N3S 7L6 – 519/759-5550; Fax: 519/759-8425; Email: brntnews@bis.on.ca – Circ.: 35,000; Tue. – Publisher, Fred Huxley; Editor, Peter Muir

Brighton Independent, 1 Young St., PO Box 1030, Brighton ON K0K 1H0 – 613/475-0255; Fax: 613/475-4546; Email: brighton_independent@ocna.org – Tue., also Brighton Independent East Northumberland (Tue.) – Publisher, Stasha Conolly

Burford Times, 115 King St., Burford ON N0E 1A0 – 519/449-5478; Fax: 519/449-5478 – Circ.: 2,000; Wed. – Publisher & Editor, Bill Johnston

Burks Falls: Almaguin News, PO Box 518, Burks Falls ON P0A 1C0 – 705/382-3843; Fax: 705/382-3440; Email: aldennis@onlink.com – Circ.: 7,200; Wed. – Publisher, Peter Barr; Editor, Allan Dennis

Burks Falls Marketplace, 183 Ontario St., PO Box 518, Burks Falls ON P0A 1C0 – 705/382-3843; Fax: 705/382-3440 – Circ.: 12,600; Almaguin News 6,200; Mon., Wed. – Publisher, Peter Barr; Editor, Allan Dennis

Burlington Post, 2317 Fairview St., Burlington ON L7R 2E3 – 905/632-4444; Fax: 905/632-6604 – Wed., Fri., Sun. – Publisher, Ian Oliver

Caledon Citizen, 25 Queen St. North, Bolton ON L7E 1C1 – 905/857-6626; Fax: 905/857-6363 – Circ.: 7,800; Wed. – Publisher, Bruce Haire; Editor, Mark Pavilons

Caledonia: Grand River Sachem, PO Box 160, Caledonia ON N0A 1A0 – 905/765-4441; Fax: 905/765-3651; Email: grand.river.sachem@ocna.org – Circ.: 2,400; Thur. – Publisher, Neil Dring; Editor, Kim Huson; Circulation Manager, Lynda Dunn

Cambridge Times, 240 Holiday Inn Dr., Units B & C, Cambridge ON N3C 3X4 – 519/651-2390 – Circ.: 31,567; Wed., Sat.

The Campbellford Courier, Cembal Publications Ltd., PO Box 250, Marmora ON K0K 2M0 – 613/472-2431; Fax: 613/472-5026 – Circ.: 4,435; Wed. – Editor, Rolly Ethier

Campbellville: Nassagaweya News & Rockwood Area, PO Box 478, Campbellville ON L0P 1B0 – Monthly

Cardiff Courier, PO Box 99, Cardiff ON K0L 1M0 – 613/332-3889 – Circ.: 1,000; Every other Thur. – Stewart Smith; Ann Smith

Carleton Place: The Canadian, PO Box 430, Carleton Place ON K7C 3P5 – 613/257-1303; Fax: 613/257-7373 – Wed.

Cayuga: The Haldimand Press, PO Box 100, Cayuga ON N0A 1E0 – 905/772-3852; Fax: 905/772-5465 – Circ.: 4,313; Wed.

Chapleau Sentinel, PO Box 158, Chapleau ON P0M 1K0 – 705/864-0640; Fax: 705/864-2317 – Circ.: 1,400; Weds.; French & English – Editor, Rene C. Decosse

Chatham Pennysaver, 930 Richmond St., Unit 7, Chatham ON N7M 5L1 – 519/351-4362 – Sun.

Chatham Shopper, 55 St. Clair St., PO Box 758, Chatham ON N7M 5L1 – 519/351-8360 – Circ.: 24,000; Wed.

Chatham This Week, 930 Richmond St., Unit 7, Chatham ON N7M 5J5 – 519/351-7331 – Wed.

Chesley Enterprise, PO Box 250, Chesley ON N0G 1L0 – 519/363-2414; Fax: 519/363-2726 – Wed. – Editor & General Manager, Mary Golem

Chesterville Record, PO Box 368, Chesterville ON K0C 1H0 – 613/448-2321; Fax: 613/448-3260 – Wed.

Clarington/Courtice Independent, PO Box 190, Bowmanville ON L1C 3K9 – 905/623-3303; Fax: 905/623-6161; Email: statesman@ocna.org – Circ.: 18,865; Wed.; also Canadian Statesman (Wed., circ. 6,256) – Publisher, John M. James; Editor, Peter Parrott; Circulation Manager, Angela Luscher

Clinton News-Record, 53 Albert St., PO Box 39, Clinton ON N0M 1L0 – 519/482-3443; Fax: 519/482-7341; Email: clinton.news@odyssey.on.ca; URL: http://www.bowesnet.com/newsrecord – Wed.

Cobden Sun, 36 Crawford St., PO Box 100, Cobden ON K0J 1K0 – 613/646-2380; Fax: 613/628-3291 – Wed.

Cochrane Northland Post, PO Box 10, Cochrane ON P0L 1C0 – 705/272-4363; Fax: 705/272-2935 – Wed.

Colborne Chronicle, 11 King St. East, PO Box 208, Colborne ON K0K 1S0 – 905/355-2843; Fax: 905/355-1639 – Circ.: 1,760; Wed. – Publisher, Cheryl McMenemy; Editor, Eileen Argyris

Collingwood Connection, Metroland Printing, Publishing & Distributing Ltd., 25 Second St., Collingwood ON L9Y 1E4 – 705/444-1875 – Wed., Sun. – Joe Anderson

Collingwood Enterprise-Bulletin, 77 Marie St., PO Box 98, Collingwood ON L9Y 3Z4 – 705/445-4611; Fax: 705/444-6477; Email: mwalsh@eb.georgian.net; URL: http://www.eb.georgian.net – Circ.: 5,600; Wed.; also Enterprise-Bulletin This Week (Sat., circ. 13,500) – Publisher, Michael Walsh; Editor, Ian Chadwick; Circulation Manager, Rick Matty

Cornwall: Le Journal, 113 Montréal Rd., Cornwall ON K6H 1B2 – 613/938-1433; Fax: 613/938-2798; Email: rlduplan@glen-net.ca – Tirage: 2,300; Jeudi; français – President, Roger Duplantie

Cornwall: Seaway News, 329 - 2nd St. West, Cornwall ON K6J 1G8 – 613/933-0014; Fax: 613/933-0024; Email: snews@glen-net.ca – Circ.: 31,499; Mon. – Publisher & Editor, R.N. Aubry

Courtice/Bowmanville News, 211 Waterloo St., Oshawa ON L1H 3W9 – 905/433-1629, 5546; Fax: 905/433-7050 – Circ.: 30,000; Wed. – Publisher, Sandra McDowell; Editor, Greg McDowell; Circulation Manager, Dave Cole

Deep River: North Renfrew Times, 25A Champlain St., PO Box 310, Deep River ON K0J 1P0 – 613/584-4161 – Wed.

Delhi News-Record, 222 Argyle St., Delhi ON N4B 2Y1 – 519/582-2510; Fax: 519/582-4040; Email: deleditorial@swopp.com; URL: http:www.swopp.com/delhi-records – Circ.: 3,500; Tues. – Publisher, Cam McKnight; Editor, Jeff Helsdon

Dorchester Signpost, 15 Brydge St., Dorchester ON N0L 1G02 – 519/268-7337; Fax: 519/268-3260 – Circ.: 2,128; Wed.

Drayton: The Community News, PO Box 189, Drayton ON N0G 1P0 – 519/638-3066 – Wed.

Dresden: North Kent Leader, PO Box 490, Dresden ON N0P 1M0 – 519/683-4485 – Wed.

Dryden Observer, Coldstream Ltd., PO Box 3009, Dryden ON P8N 2Y9 – 807/223-2390; Fax: 807/223-2907; Email: editor.observer@awcoldstream.on.ca; URL: http://www.awc/on.ca.observer – Circ.: 6,200; Wed. – Publisher, Alex Wilson; Editor, Sylvia Veal

Dundalk Herald, Herald Publishing Co., PO Box 280, Dundalk ON N0C 1B0 – 519/923-2203; Fax: 519/923-2747 – Circ.: 3,400; Wed. – Publisher, Matthew Walls; Editor, Melodee Lovering; Circulation Manager, Cathy Walls

Dundas-Ancaster Recorder, 264 East 22nd St., PO Box 68041, Stn Blakely PO, Hamilton ON L8M 3M7 – 905/385-7192 – Tue.

Dundas Star, 47 Cootes Dr., Dundas ON L9H 1B5 – 905/628-6313; Fax: 905/628-5485 – Circ.: 10,477; Wed.

Dunnville Chronicle, 131 Lock St. East, PO Box 216, Dunnville ON N1A 2X5 – 905/774-5855 – Circ.: 4,275; Wed.; also CoverStory (Sat.)

Durham Chronicle, PO Box 230, Durham ON N0G 1R0 – 519/369-2504; Fax: 519/369-3560 – Circ.: 1,700; Wed. – Marie David

Dutton Advance, PO Box 220, Dutton ON N0L 1J0 – 519/762-2310 – Circ.: 1,700; Wed. – Publisher, D.W. Moore; Editor, Marlene Moore

Eganville Leader, 154 John St., PO Box 310, Eganville ON K0J 1T0 – 613/628-2332 – Circ.: 6,500; Wed. – Co-Publisher, Ron Tracey; Editor & Co-Publisher, Gerald Tracey

Elgin: The Rideau Review, PO Box 220, Elgin ON K0G 1E0 – 613/359-5544 – Wed. – Publisher, David Morris; Circulation Manager, Penny Griffin

Elliot Lake Standard, 14 Hillsdale Dr. South, Elliot Lake ON P5A 1M6 – 705/848-7195 – Wed.; also North Shore Market Place (Sat.)

Elmira Independent, 15 King St., Elmira ON N3B 2R1 – 519/669-5155; Fax: 519/669-5928; Email: enews@bond.net – Circ.: 8,611; Mon. – Editor, J. Robert Verdun

Embrun: Le Reflet, #3, 793 Notre-Dame St., Embrun ON K0A 1W0 – 613/443-2741; Fax: 613/443-1865 – Tirage.: 15 600; Mercredi; français

Erin Advocate, #5, 8 Thompson Cres., Erin ON N0B 1T0 – 519/833-9603 – Wed.

Espanola: Mid-North Monitor, #15, 417 Second Ave., Espanola ON P5E 1L1 – 705/869-0588; Fax: 705/869-0587 – Wed., English & French

Essex Free Press, 16 Centre St., Essex ON N8M 1N9 – 519/776-4268; Fax: 519/776-4014 – Circ.: 4,300; Wed. – Editor, W.R. Brett

Etobicoke Guardian, Metroland Printing, Publishing & Distributing Ltd., 260 Galaxy Blvd., Etobicoke ON M9W 5R8 – 416/675-4390; Fax: 416/675-9296 – Circ.: 64,998 Wed., 6,011 Sun.; also Monthly Business – Publisher, Betty Carr

Etobicoke Life, 3874 Bloor St. West, Etobicoke ON M9B 1L3 – 416/231-6809; Fax: 416/231-2035; Email: etobicoke_life@ocna.org – Circ.: 30,000; Wed. – Publisher, W. Domanski; Editor, Patrick McConnell; Circulation Manager, Karyn Haystead

Exeter Times-Advocate, PO Box 850, Exeter ON N0M 1S6 – 519/235-1331; Fax: 519/235-0766 – Wed.

Fenelon Falls Gazette, PO Box 340, Fenelon Falls ON K0M 1N0 – 705/887-2940 – Wed.

Fergus-Elora News-Express, 390 Tower St. South, PO Box 130, Fergus, ON N1M 2W7 – 519/843-1310; Fax: 519/843-1334; Email: express@ionline.net – Circ.: 3,971; Wed.

Fergus: The Wellington Advertiser, 180 St. Andrews St. East, PO Box 252, Fergus ON N1M 2W8 – 519/843-5410 – Mon.

Flesherton: Flesherton Advance, Herald Publishing Co. Ltd., PO Box 280, Dundalk ON N0C 1B0 – 519/923-2203; Fax: 519/923-2747; Email: herald@headwaters.com – Matt Walls; Cathy Walls

Forest Standard, PO Box 220, Forest ON N0N 1J0 – 519/786-5242; Fax: 519/786-4884 – Wed.

Fort Erie: The Times, 450 Garrison Rd., Unit 5, PO Box 1219, Fort Erie ON L2A 5Y2 – 905/871-3100; Fax: 905/871-5243; Email: mrobinson@rannie.com; URL: http://www.rannie.com – Tue. (circ. 10,900), Sat. (circ. 11,500) – Publisher, Tim Dundas; Editor, Mike Robinson; Circulation Manager, Petrina Richardson

Fort Frances Times, PO Box 339, Fort Frances ON P9A 3M7 – 807/274-5373; Fax: 807/274-7286; Email: fftimes@ff.lakeheadu.ca; URL: http://www.fftimes.com – Wed. – Publisher, Jim Cumming; Editor, Mike Behan

Gananoque Reporter, 79 King St. East, Gananoque ON K7G 1E8 – 613/382-2156 – Wed.

Georgetown Independent/Acton Free Press, Metroland Printing, Publishing & Distributing Ltd., 211 Armstrong Ave., Georgetown ON L7G 4X5 – 905/873-0301; Fax: 905/877-0442 – Wed., Sun; also Acton Free Press – Publisher, Ken Nugent

Geraldton: Times Star, 401 Main St., PO Box 490, Geraldton ON P0T 1M0 – 807/854-1919; Fax: 807/854-1682 – Wed.

Gladstone Enterprise, Sundance Publications Ltd., PO Box 939, Neepawa ON R0J 1H0 – 204/476-2309; Fax: 204/476-5802; Email: neepress@mts.net – Circ.: 2,200; Tue. – Publisher, Ewan Pow; Editor, Jack Gibson

Glencoe: Transcript & Free Press, 243 Main St., PO Box 400, Glencoe ON N0L 1M0 – 519/287-2615 – Circ.: 2,720; Wed. – Publisher & Editor, Walter Vanderkwaak

Goderich Signal-Star, Industrial Park, PO Box 220, Goderich ON N7A 4B6 – 519/524-2614; Fax: 519/524-5145 – Circ.: 5,600; Wed; also Focus (every other Tues.) – Publisher, John Buchanan; Editor, Dave Sykes; Circulation Manager, Irene Ott

Gore Bay: Manitoulin Recorder, PO Box 235, Gore Bay ON P0P 1H0 – 705/282-2003; Fax: 705/282-2432 – Circ.: 4,178; Wed. – Publisher & Editor, Margaret E. Robinson; Circulation Manager, Nancy Noland

Grand Valley Star & Vidette, PO Box 119, Grand Valley ON L0N 1G0 – 519/928-2822 – Wed.

Gravenhurst Banner, 140 Muskoka Rd. South, PO Box 849, Gravenhurst ON P0C 1G0 – 705/687-6674 – Wed.

Grimsby Independent, 19 Adelaide St., PO Box 310, Grimsby ON L3M 4G5 – 905/945-9264; Fax: 905/945-0540 – Wed.

Guelph Pennysaver, Netmar Inc., 86 Dawson Rd., Guelph ON N1H 1A8 – 519/823-5070; Fax: 519/823-2161 – Sat.

The Guelph Tribune, 650 Woodlawn Rd. W., Unit 11 & 12, Guelph ON N1K 1B8 – 519/763-3333; Fax: 519/763-4814 – Wed.

Haliburton County Echo, PO Box 360, Haliburton ON K0M 1S0 – 705/457-1037; Fax: 705/457-3275 – Circ.: 5,000; Tue. – Publisher, Len Pizzey; Editor, Martha Perkins

Hamilton News, Mountain Edition, 333 Arvin Ave., Stoney Creek ON L8E 2M6 – 905/523-5800 – Circ.: 44,369; Wed.

Hamilton Recorder, PO Box 68041, Stn Blakely, Hamilton ON L8M 3M7 – 905/561-1090 – Wed.

Hanover Post & Grey Bruce This Week, 413 - 18th Ave., Hanover ON N4N 3S5 – 519/364-2001; Fax: 519/364-6950 – Tue; also The Hanover Post (Tue.), Grey Bruce This Week (Wed.) & Grey Bruce This Weekend (Sat.) – Publisher, Marie David

Hanover: The Saugeen City News, 414 - 10th St., Hanover ON N4N 1P6 – 519/364-4597; Fax: 519/364-6869; Email: scn@bmts.com – Circ.: 12,400; Tue.

Harriston Review, PO Box 370, Harriston ON N0G 1Z0 – 519/338-2341 – Circ.: 1,068; Tue. – Publisher, Clive Williams, 519/848-2410

Harrow & Colchester South This Week, 72 King St. East, Harrow, ON N0R 1G0 – 519/738-2000 – Wed.

Harrow News, PO Box 310, Harrow ON N0R 1G0 – 519/738-2542; Fax: 519/738-3874 – Wed.

Hastings Star, Cembal Publications Ltd., PO Box 250, Marmora ON K0K 2M0 – 613/472-2431; Fax: 613/472-5026 – Circ.: 1,400; Wed. – Editor, Bill Freeman

Havelock Citizen, Cembal Publications Ltd., PO Box 250, Stn , Marmora ON K0K 2M0 – 613/472-2431; Fax: 613/472-5026 – Circ.: 2,280; Wed. – Editor, Nancy Powers

Hawkesbury: Le Carillon, CP 1000, Hawkesbury ON K6A 3H1 – 613/632-4155; Fax: 613/632-6122 – Tirage: 10,000; Mercredi; français

Hawkesbury Tribune/Express, 299, rue Principale est, Hawkesbury ON K6A 3H1 – 613/632-4605 – Circ.: 23,000; Sat., English & French

Hawkesbury: Le/The Regional, 124, rue Principale est, Hawkesbury ON K6A 1A8 – 613/632-0112 – Circ.: 30,000; Fri.; English & French

Hearst: Le Nord, 905, rue Georges, CP 2320, Hearst ON P0L 1N0 – 705/372-1233; Fax: 705/362-5954; Email: lenord@nt.net – Tirage: 3,500; Mercredi; français et anglais – Editeur & Rédacteur, Omer Cantin

Hornepayne: The Bear News, 79 Front St., PO Box 660, Hornepayne ON P0M 1Z0 – 807/868-2701; Fax: 807/868-3337 – Wed.

Huntsville Forester, #1, 72 Main St. East, Huntsville ON P1H 2C7 – 705/789-5541; Fax: 705/789-9381 – Wed.

Ignace Driftwood, PO Box 989, Ignace ON P0T 1T0 – 807/934-6482 – Wed.

Ingersoll Times, 19 King St. West, Ingersoll ON N5C 2J2 – 519/485-3631; Fax: 519/485-6652 – Circ.: 3,600; Wed. – Publisher, Pat Logan; Editor, Geoff Dale; Circulation Manager, Mary Pinney

Innisfil Scope, PO Box 310, Beeton ON L0G 1A0 – 905/458-4434; Email: york@simcoe.igs.net – Circ.: 1.800; Wed. – John Archibald; Bruce Haire

Iroquois: The Chieftain, PO Box 529, Iroquois ON K0E 1K0 – 613/652-4395; Fax: 613/652-2508; Email: comnews@magmacom.com – Circ.: 2,000; Wed. – Publisher, Brian Crawford; Editor, Michael Bailey; Circulation Manager, Karen Cooke

Iroquois Falls A: The Enterprise, PO Box 834, Iroquois Falls A ON P0K 1G0 – 705/232-4081 – Wed.; English & French

Kanata Kourier-Standard, 3 Beaverbrook Rd., Kanata ON K2K 1L2 – 613/591-3060; Fax: 613/591-8503 – Circ.: 16,781; Fri. – Publisher, Angie Shepherd; Editor, Sally Gunther

Kapuskasing Northern Times, 51 Riverside Dr., Kapuskasing ON P5N 1A7 – 705/335-2283; Fax: 705/337-1222; Email: ntimes@sumpatico.ca – Circ.: 5,300; Wed.; English & French – Publisher, Rene Piché; Editor & General Manager, Wayne Major; Director of Finance & Marketing, Linda Leblanc

Kemptville Weekly Advance, PO Box 669, Kemptville ON K0G 1J0 – 613/258-3451; Fax: 613/258-7734; Email: comnews@magmacom.com – Wed; also Kemptville Accent Magazine (monthly) – Publisher, Brian Crawford

Keswick: Georgina Advocate, 204 Simcoe Ave., Keswick ON L4P 3S6 – 905/476-7753; Fax: 905/476-5785 – Circ.: 14,000; Mon. – Publisher, Mark Skelton; Editor, John Slyknuis

Kincardine: The Independent, PO Box 1240, Kincardine ON N2Z 2Z4 – 519/396-3111; Fax: 519/396-3899 – Circ.: 3,100; Wed. – Editor, Eric Howard

Kincardine News, 708 Queen St., Kincardine ON N2Z 2A3 – 519/396-2963; Fax: 519/396-3790 – Wed.

King Weekly, 237 Romina Dr., Unit 2, Concord ON L4K 4V3 – 905/660-9556; Fax: 905/660-9558 – Wed.

Kingston: The Heritage Newspaper, 784 Bath Rd., Kingston ON K7M 4Y2 – 613/389-8884; Fax: 613/389-1870 – Circ.: 29,600; Tue.

Kingston This Week, Metroland Printing, Publishing & Distributing Ltd., 677 Gardiners Rd., Kingston ON K7M 3Y4 – 613/389-7400; Fax: 613/389-7507 – Circ.: 46,200; Wed., Sat. – Publisher, Cam Inglis; Editor, Dan Donohue; Circulation Manager, Margaret Amsun

Kingsville Reporter, 17 Chestnut St., Kingsville ON N9Y 1J9 – 519/733-2211; Fax: 519/733-6464 – Tue.

Kitchener This Week, 677 Gardiners Rd., Kitchener ON K7M 3Y4 – 519/576-5300 – Circ.: 58,000; Wed., Sat.

Kitchener: K.W. Real Estate News, 540 Riverbend Dr., Kitchener ON N2K 3S0 – 519/749-1400; Fax: 519/749-0488 – Circ.: 9,000; Fri. – Publisher & Editor, Bob Verdun

Kitchener: Pennysaver, 685 Wabanaki Dr., Kitchener ON N2C 2G3 – 519/894-1400 – Sat.

Lakefield: Katchewanooka Herald, 112 Queen St., PO Box 1000, Lakefield ON K0L 2H0 – 705/652-6594; Fax: 705/652-6912; Email: The_Herald@ocna.org – Circ.: 2,200; Mon. – Publisher, June K. Helwig; Editor, Neil Boughen; Circulation Manager, Eva Smith

Lambeth News-Star, PO Box 490, Lambeth ON N0L 1S0 – 519/652-3421 – Thur.

Leamington Pennysaver, NETMAR, 60 Oak St. East, Leamington ON N8H 2C2 – 519/322-0400; Fax: 519/322-0405 – Circ.: 18,500; Sun. – Publications Manager, Kanita Thiessen; Editor, Shelley Fellows

Leamington Post & News, Bowes Publishers Ltd., 27 Princess St., Leamington ON N8H 2X8 – 519/326-4434; Fax: 519/326-2171; Email: lempost@wincom.net; URL: http://www.bowenet.com – Circ.: 5,400; Wed.; also Leamington Shopper (Tues., circ. 16,491) – Publisher, Don Gage; Editor, Mike Thibodeau, 519/326-4434; Circulation Manager, John Patterson

Lindsay Performer, 15 William St. North, Lindsay ON K9V 3Z8 – 705/324-2114 – Fri. – Publisher, F.M. Dundas

Lindsay This Week, Metroland Printing, Publishing & Distributing Ltd., 96 Albert St. South, Lindsay ON K9V 3H7 – 705/324-8600; Fax: 705/324-5694 – Circ.: 27,500; Wed., Sat. – Hugh Nicholson

Listowel Banner, 185 Wallace Ave. North, Listowel ON N4W 1K8 – 519/291-1660; Fax: 519/291-3771 – Circ.: 5,000; Wed.; also Independent & Independent Plus (Mon.) – Publisher, Paul Teahen; Editor, Marion Duke

Little Current: The Manitoulin Expositor, PO Box 369, Little Current ON P0P 1K0 – 705/368-2744; Fax: 705/368-3822; Email: manitoulin_expositor@ocna.org – Circ.: 5,800; Wed. – Publisher, R.L. McCutcheon; Editor, Ross Muir

London Pennysaver, 244 Adelaide St. South, London ON N5Z 3L1 – 519/685-2020; Fax: 519/649-0908 – Circ.: 144,000; Sun. – General Manager, Marj Bastow

Lucknow Sentinel, Bowes Publishers, PO Box 400, Lucknow ON N0G 2H0 – 519/528-2822; Fax: 519/528-3529 – Circ.: 2,000; Wed. – Editor, Pat Livingstone; Circulation Manager, Phyllis Matthews Helm

Madoc Review, Cembal Publications Ltd., PO Box 250, Marmora ON K0K 2M0 – 613/472-2431; Fax: 613/472-5026 – Circ.: 2,680; Wed. – Editor, Jeff Wilson

Manitouwadge: The Echo, PO Box 550, Manitouwadge ON P0T 2C0 – 807/826-3788; Fax: 807/826-3910 – Circ.: 1,750; Wed. – Publisher & Editor, B.J. Schermann

Marathon Mercury, PO Box 369, Marathon ON P0T 2E0 – 807/229-1520; Fax: 807/229-1595 – Wed.

Markdale Standard, PO Box 465, Markdale ON N0C 1H0 – 519/986-3151 – Wed.

Markham Economist & Sun, 9 Heritage Rd., Markham ON L3P 1M3 – 905/294-2200; Fax: 905/294-1538; Toronto line: 416/798-7624 – Circ.: 45,000; Wed. & Sat. – Publisher, Patricia Pappas; Editor-in-chief, Jo Ann Stevenson; Editor, Alan Shackleton

Marmora: Land O'Lakes Sun, Cembal Publications Ltd., PO Box 250, Marmora ON K0K 2M0 – 613/472-2431; Fax: 613/472-5026 – Circ.: 6,740; Sat.

Marmora Herald, Cembal Publications Ltd., PO Box 250, Marmora ON K0K 2M0 – 613/472-2431; Fax: 613/472-5026 – Circ.: 1,880; Tue. – Editor, Nancy Powers

Mattawa Recorder, 341 McConnell St., PO Box 67, Mattawa ON P0H 1V0 – 705/744-5361; Fax: 705/744-5361 – Circ.: 1,050; Wed. – Publisher, Carole Edwards

Meaford: The Courier Herald, 68 Sykes St. North, Meaford ON N4L 1R2 – 519/599-3760; Fax: 519/599-3214 – Wed.; also Meaford Express (Wed., circ. 2,521)

Midland/Penetanguishene Mirror, Metroland Printing, Publishing & Distributing Ltd., 99 Woodland Dr., Unit 2, Midland ON L4R 4V3 – 705/527-5500 – Circ.: 18,500; Thur., Sun. – Publisher, Joe Anderson

Midland: Penetanguishene Free Press, 248 First St., Midland ON L4R 4K6 – 705/526-5431; Fax: 705/526-1771 – Wed., Fri.

Mildmay Town & Country Crier, PO Box 190, Mildmay ON N0G 2J0 – 519/367-2681; Fax: 519/367-5417 – Every other Tue.

Millbrook Times, 28 King St. East, Millbrook ON L0A 1G0 – 705/932-3001; Fax: 705/932-3377 – Circ.: 2,000; Mon. – Publisher & Editor, Lynda Todd

Milton Canadian Champion, Metroland Printing, Publishing & Distributing Ltd., 191 Main St, Milton ON L9T 1N7 – 905/878-2341; Fax: 905/878-4943 – Wed., Fri. – Publisher, Ian Oliver

Minden: The Times, PO Box 97, Minden ON K0M 2K0 – 705/286-1288; Fax: 705/286-4768; Email: mindentimes@halhinet.on.ca; URL: http://www.mindentimes.on.ca – Mon. – Editor, Jack B. Brezina

Mississauga Booster, 24 Falconer Dr., Mississauga ON L5N 1B1 – 905/826-3672; Fax: 905/567-7299 – Every other Wed.

Mississauga News, Metroland Printing, Publishing & Distributing Ltd., 3145 Wolfedale Rd., Mississauga ON L5C 3A9 – 905/273-8118 – Tue., Thur., Sun; supplement, Community News (Wed.) – Publisher, Ron Lenyk

Mitchell Advocate, PO Box 669, Mitchell ON N0K 1N0 – 519/348-8431; Fax: 519/348-8836 – Wed.

Morrisburg Leader, PO Box 891, Morrisburg ON K0C 1X0 – 613/543-2987 – Circ.: 2,500; Wed. – Publisher & Editor, Sam Laurin

Mount Forest Confederate, PO Box 130, Mount Forest ON N0G 2L0 – 519/323-1550; Fax: 519/323-4548 – Wed.

Napanee Beaver, 72 Dundas St. East, Napanee ON K7R 1H9 – 613/354-6641; Fax: 613/354-2622 – Wed.

Napanee Weekly Guide, 12 Dundas St. East, Napanee ON K7R 1H5 – 613/354-6648; Fax: 613/354-6708 – Tue.

Nepean Clarion, 25 Greenbank Rd., Nepean ON K2H 8S1 – 613/820-3126; Fax: 613/820-6147 – Sun.

New Hamburg Independent, 91 Peel St., PO Box 670, New Hamburg ON N0B 2G0 – 519/662-1240; Fax: 519/662-3521 – Wed.

New Liskeard/Temiskaming Speaker, PO Box 580, New Liskeard ON P0J 1P0 – 705/647-6791 – Wed.

Newmarket: Aurora/Newmarket Town Crier, 17817 Leslie St., Unit 19, Newmarket ON L3Y 8C8 – 416/853-5056 – Wed.

Niagara on Lake Review Weekly, 4801 Valley Way, Niagara Falls ON L2E 6T6 – 905/358-5711 – Circ.: 5,600; Wed.; also Fort Erie Review Weekly (Tue., circ. 11,000)

Niagara Shopping News, 4949 Victoria Ave., Niagara Falls ON L2E 4C7 – 905/357-2440 – Wed., Sat.

Nipigon-Red Rock Gazette, PO Box 1057, Nipigon ON P0T 2J0 – 807/887-3583 – Tue.

North Bay Shield, CFB North Bay, Hornell Heights ON P0H 1P0 – 705/494-6011; Fax: 705/494-2108; Email: shield@onlink.net – Circ.: 1,000; Monthly; English & French – Dan Noble

North York: Hi-Rise, 95 Leewad Glenway, Unit 121, North York ON M3C 2Z6 – 416/424-1393 – Monthly

Norwich Gazette, 46 Main St. West, PO Box 459, Norwich ON N0J 1P0 – 519/863-2262; Fax: 519/863-3229 – Circ.: 2,000; Wed. – Publisher, Pat Logan; Editor, John Tapley; Circulation Manager, Deb Clifford

Norwood Register, Cembal Publications Ltd., PO Box 250, Marmora ON K0K 2M0 – 613/472-2431; Fax: 613/472-5026 – Circ.: 2,210; Wed. – Editor, Bill Freeman

Oakville: Abbey Oaks News, PO Box 306, Oakville ON L6J 5A2 – 905/825-2229 – Circ.: 15,000; Thur.

Oakville: Milton Shopping News, 1158 South Service Rd. West, Oakville ON L6L 5T7 – 905/827-2244; Fax: 905/827-2308 – Circ.: 16,865; Tue. – Bill Whitaker Sr.

Oakville Beaver, Metroland Printing, Publishing & Distributing Ltd., 467 Speers Rd., Oakville ON L6K 3S4 – 905/845-3824; Fax: 905/845-3085 – Circ.: 21,000; Wed., Fri., Sun.; also North News (Fri.), & Oakville Marketplace (Tue.) – Publisher, Ian Oliver; Editor, Norm Alexander; Circulation Manager, Martin Doherty

Oakville Free Press Journal, 1158 South Service Rd. West, Oakville ON L6L 5T7 – 905/827-2596; Fax: 905/827-2308; Email: oakville.free.press.journal@ocna.org – Circ.: 37,000; Tue. – Publisher, Arnold L. Huffman; Editor, Don Redmond

Oakville North News, 467 Speers Rd., Oakville ON L6K 3S4 – 905/845-3824 – Circ.: 17,500; Fri.; also Oakville Marketplace (Tue., circ. 39,000)

Oakville Shopping News, 1158 South Service Rd. West, Oakville ON L6L 5T7 – 905/827-2244; Fax: 905/827-2308 – Circ.: 37,000; Tue., Fri. – Bill Whitaker Sr.

Orangeville Banner, 37 Mill St., Orangeville ON L9W 2M4 – 519/941-1350; Fax: 519/941-9600 – Circ.: 6,305; Wed., Fri; supplement, Orangeville & District Shopping News (Fri.) – Publisher, David J. Mitchell; Editor, Steve Harron; Circulation Manager, Patricia Mahrle

Orangeville Citizen, 14 Mill St., Orangeville ON L9W 2M3 – 519/941-2230; Fax: 519/941-9361; Email: editor@headwaters.com; URL: http://www.headwaters.com/citizen/citizen.html – Circ.: 10,700; Wed. – Publisher, Pamela Claridge; Editor, Sheila Duncan; Circulation Manager, Sandi Jovic

Orillia Today, Metroland Printing, Publishing & Distributing Ltd., #7, 12 Centre St., Orillia ON L3V 6H1 – 705/329-2058 – Sun., Wed. – Publisher, Joe Anderson

Orleans Community Weekly Journal, #205, 815 Taylor Creek Dr., Orleans ON K1C 1T1 – 613/830-3005; Fax: 613/830-2284; Email: ocwj@cyberplus.ca; URL: http://www.ocwj.on.ca – Circ.: 28,000; Sat. – Caroline Andrews; Mike Curran

Orleans Express, #209, 1455 Youville Dr., Orleans ON K1C 4R1 – 613/830-2000; Fax: 613/830-9338 – Tirage: 36,500; Mardi; français

Orleans: The Star, #209, 1455 Youville Dr., Orleans ON K1C 4R1 – 613/830-7827; Fax: 613/830-1116 – Circ.: 44,000; Wed. – Publisher, Derek Walter; Editor, Michael Curran

Orono Weekly Times, PO Box 209, Orono ON L0B 1M0 – 905/983-5301; Fax: 905/983-5301 – Wed. – Publisher & Editor, Troy Young; Circulation Manager, Christine Faulkner

Oshawa/Whitby This Week, 865 Farewell Ave., PO Box 481, Oshawa ON L1H 7L5 – 905/579-4400; Fax: 905/579-2238; Toronto line: 416-798-7672 – Wed., Fri., Sun. – Publisher, Tim Whittaker

Oshawa News, 211 Waterloo St., Oshawa ON L1H 3W9 – 905/433-1629, 5546; Fax: 905/433-7050 –

Circ.: 17,000; Wed. – Publisher, Sandra McDowell; Editor, Greg McDowell
Ottawa: The Alta Vista News, Ottawa News Publishing, #3B, 15 Antares Dr., Nepean ON K2E 7Y9 – 613/723-5970; Fax: 613/723-1862 – Circ.: 12,000; Every other Wed. – Publisher, Michael Wollock; Editor, Patrick Uguccioni
Ottawa: Greenboro Hunt Club Park News, Ottawa News Publishing, #3B, 15 Antares Dr., Nepean ON K2E 7Y9 – 613/723-5970; Fax: 613/723-1862 – Circ.: 12,000; Every other Wed.
Ottawa: The Hill Times, 69 Sparks St., Ottawa ON K1P 5A5 – 613/232-5952; Fax: 613/232-9055; Email: hilltimes@achilles.net; URL: http://www.thehilltimes.ca – Circ.: 15,000; Mon. – Publisher, Ross Dickson; Co-Publisher & Editor, Jim Creskey
Ottawa: Hunt Club Riverside News, Ottawa News Publishing, #3b, 15 Antares Dr., Nepean ON K2E 7Y9 – 613/723-5970; Fax: 613/723-1862 – Circ.: 10,000; Every other Wed.
Ottawa: The Ottawa-Carleton This Month, #202, 1142 Tigne St., PO Box 102, Manotick ON K4M 1A2 – 613/692-3211; Fax: 613/692-2456; Email: comnews@magmacom.com – Circ.: 13,500; Monthly; also Ottawa-Carleton This Month – Brian Crawford, 613/258-3451
Ottawa/Centretown News, c/o Carleton University School of Journalism, Colonel By Dr., Ottawa ON K1S 5B6 – 613/564-6388 – Every other Fri.
Ottawa: Ottawa Pennysaver, 48 Colonnade Rd., Nepean ON K2E 7J6 – 613/723-1707 – Sat.
Palmerston Observer, PO Box 757, Palmerston ON N0G 2P0 – 519/343-2440; Fax: 519/343-2267; Email: palmerston_observer@ocha.org – Wed. – Laverne Long
Paris Star, 59 Grand River St. North, Paris ON N3L 2M3 – 519/442-7866; Fax: 519/442-3100 – Wed.
Parkhill Gazette, PO Box 400, Parkhill ON N0M 2K0 – 519/294-6264; Fax: 519/294-6391 – Wed.
Parry Sound Beacon/Star, 67 James St., Parry Sound ON P2A 1T6 – 705/746-4228; Fax: 705/746-8369 – Sun.
Parry Sound North Star, PO Box 370, Parry Sound ON P2A 2X4 – 705/746-2104; Fax: 705/746-8369 – Wed.
Penetanguishene: Le Goût de Vivre, 351, rue Principale, RR#3, Lafontaine, Penetanguishene ON L9M 1R3 – 705/533-3349; Fax: 705/533-3422; Email: goutvivr@bconnex.net; URL: http://www.bconnex.net/~legout – Tirage: 500; Tous les deux jeudi; français
Perth Courier, PO Box 156, Perth ON K7H 3E3 – 613/267-1100; Fax: 613/267-3986 – Wed.
Petawawa Messenger, 35A Highway St., Petawawa ON K8H 1Z3 – 613/687-1440 – Circ.: 7,600; Thur.
Petawawa Post, Bldg. P-106, Petawawa ON K8H 2X3 – 613/687-5511, ext.5386; Fax: 613/588-6996; Email: ppost@renc.igs.net – Circ.: 6,000; Wed. – Editor, Carol Bullied
Peterborough This Week, 884 Ford St., Peterborough ON K9J 5V3 – 705/749-3383; Fax: 705/749-0074 – Circ.: 42,500; Wed., Sat. – Publisher, Hugh Nicholson
The Petrolia Topic, 4182 Petrolia Line, PO Box 40, Petrolia ON N0N 1R0 – 519/882-1770; Fax: 519/882-3212 – Circ.: 3,300; Wed. – Publisher, Denise Thibeault; Editor, David Pattenaude
Picton: The County Guide, 281 Main St., Picton ON K0K 2T0 – 613/476-5838 – Circ.: 9,825; Sun.
Picton Gazette, PO Box 80, Picton ON K0K 2T0 – 613/476-3201; Fax: 613/476-3464; Email: gazette@connect.reach.net – Circ.: 4,400; Wed., Sat.; also Picton Gazette Regional (Sat., circ. 12,000) – Publisher, Jean M. Morrison; Editor, Kevin Wood; Circulation Manager, David Fabius
Port Dover Maple Leaf, 351 Main St., Port Dover ON N0A 1N0 – 519/583-0112 – Wed.
Port Elgin: The Beacon Times, PO Box 580, Port Elgin ON N0H 2C0 – 519/832-9001; Fax: 519/389-4793 – Wed.
Port Elgin: Shoreline News, 685 Goderich St., Port Elgin ON N0H 2C0 – 519/389-4733 – Wed.
Port Hope Evening Guide, 415 King St. West, Cobourg ON K9A 4L1 – 905/372-0131; Fax: 905/372-4966 – Afternoon, Mon.-Fri.
Port Perry Star, 188 Mary St., PO Box 90, Port Perry ON L9L 1B7 – 905/985-7383; Fax: 905/985-3708 – Circ.: 5,000; Tue; supplement, Port Perry Weekend Star (Fri., circ. 18,500) – Publisher, Peter Huidsten; Editor, Jeff Mitchell; General Manager, Don MacLeod
Prescott Journal, PO Box 549, Prescott ON K0E 1T0 – 613/925-4265; Fax: 613/925-3472 – Wed.
Rainy River Record, PO Box 280, Rainy River ON P0W 1L0 – 807/852-3366; Fax: 807/852-4434; Email: Rainy_River_Record@ocna.org – Circ.: 1,500; Wed. – Publisher, J.R. Cumming; Editor, Ken Johnston
Rainy River: The Westend Weekly, PO Box 188, Rainy River ON P0W 1L0 – 807/852-3815 – Circ.: 8,050; Fri.
Red Lake District News, PO Box 425, Red Lake ON P0V 2M0 – 807/727-2618; Fax: 807/727-3717 – Circ.: 2,800; Wed. – Publisher, Rick Smit; Circulation Manager, Wendy Beidler
Renfrew Mercury, PO Box 400, Renfrew ON K7V 4A8 – 613/432-3655 – Circ.: 7,000; Wed.; also Weekender (Sat., circ. 14,000) – Publisher, Fred Runge; Editor, Elaine Dick
Renfrew News, 250 Raglan St. South, Renfrew ON K7V 1R4 – 613/432-7544; Fax: 613/432-9798 – Circ.: 13,186; Sun. – General Manager, Jim Kwiatkowski
Richmond Hill: The Liberal, Metroland Printing, Publishing & Distributing Ltd., 9350 Yonge St., PO Box 390, Richmond Hill ON L4C 4Y6 – 905/881-3373; Fax: 905/881-9924; Email: news.room@rhliberal.net; Toronto line: 416/661-0047 – Circ.: 68,000; Tues.. Thur., Sun – Publisher, Ian Proudfoot; Editor, Debora Kelly
Richmond Hill Weekly, 237 Romina Dr., Unit 2, Concord ON L4K 4V3 – 905/660-9556 – Wed.
Rodney: The Chronicle, 246 Furnival Rd., PO Box 400, Rodney ON N0L 2C0 – 519/785-2455; Fax: 519/785-2455 – Circ.: 4,800; Weekly
Russell Villager, PO Box 550, Russell ON K4R 1E1 – 613/445-3805 – Circ.: 1,265; Thur.
St. Catharines Shopping News, 140 Welland Ave., Unit 1, St. Catharines ON L2R 2N6 – 905/688-4332; Fax: 905/688-6313 – Circ.: 46,500; Wed.
St. Marys Journal-Argus, PO Box 1030, St. Marys ON N4X 1B7 – 519/284-2440; Fax: 519/284-3650 – Wed.
Sarnia: Lambton-Sarnia Shopping News, 1383 Confederation St., Sarnia ON N7S 5P1 – 519/336-1100 – Sat. – Publisher, Peter Wilpstra
Sarnia: This Week, 1383 Confederation St., PO Box 99, Sarnia ON N7S 5P1 – 519/336-1100; Fax: 519/336-1833 – Circ.: 21,500; Wed. – Editor, Jim Connelly
Sault Ste. Marie This Week, PO Box 188, Sault Ste. Marie ON P6A 2T9 – 705/949-6111 – Wed.
Scarborough: Bluffs Monitor, 14 Lynn Rd., Scarborough ON M1N 2A3 – 416/691-4085 – Circ.: 23,000; Monthly – Publisher, L. Graves
Scarborough: Toronto East End Express, 80 Nashdene Rd., Unit 15, Scarborough ON M1V 5E4 – 416/463-4634 – Wed.
Schomberg: Schomberg Record Sentinel, PO Box 310, Beeton ON L0G 1A0 – 905/939-5008; Fax: 905/729-2541; Email: york@simcoe.igs.net – Circ.: 925; Wed. – John Archibald; Bruce Haire
Seaforth Huron Expositor, 100 Main St., PO Box 69, Seaforth ON N0K 1W0 – 519/527-0240; Fax: 519/527-2858; Email: hronexp@odyssey.on.ca; URL: http://www.bowesnet.com/expositor – Circ.: 2,782; Wed. – Publisher, Bill Dempsey; Editor, David Scott
Shelburne Free Press & Economist, PO Box 100, Shelburne ON L0N 1S0 – 519/925-2832; Fax: 519/925-5500 – Wed.
Simcoe: Tuesday Times-Reformer, 105 Donly Dr. South, PO Box 370, Simcoe ON N3Y 4L2 – 519/426-5710; Fax: 519/426-9504; Email: refedit@swopp.com; URL: http://www.swopp.com/reformer – Circ.: 17,200; Tue. – Publisher, Michael Fredericks; Editor, Kimberley Novak; Circulation Manager, Steve Smithson
Sioux Lookout Bulletin, 40 Front St., PO Box 1389, Sioux Lookout ON P8T 1B7 – 807/737-3209, advtg. 737-4207; Fax: 807/737-3084 – Circ.: 4,717; Wed. – Editor, Jason van Rassel
Sioux Lookout: Wawatay News, Wawatay Native Communications Society, PO Box 1180, Sioux Lookout ON P8T 1B7 – 807/737-2951; Fax: 807/737-3224 – Circ.: 8,000; Every other Thur.; English & Ojibwe – Editor-in-chief, Bryan Phelan
Smiths Falls Record News, PO Box 158, Smith Falls ON K7A 4T1 – 613/283-3182; Fax: 613/283-7480 – Circ.: 4,402; Wed; supplement, Record News EMC (Sun., circ. 35,727) – Publisher, Chuck Hudson; Editor, Michael Hayes
Stayner Sun, PO Box 80, Stayner ON L0M 1S0 – 705/428-2638; Fax: 705/428-6909 – Circ.: 1,056; Wed.; also Wasaga Sun (Wed., circ. 3,900)
Stirling: The Community Press, PO Box 88, Stirling ON K0K 3E0 – 613/395-3015; Fax: 613/395-2992 – Circ.: 54,937; Sat. – Publisher, John Seckar; Editor, Alan Coxwell; Circulation Manager, Dan Kennedy
Stirling News-Argus, Cembal Publications Ltd., PO Box 250, Marmora ON K0K 2M0 – 613/472-2431; Fax: 613/472-5026 – Circ.: 4.960; Tue. – Editor, Jeff Wilson
Stittsville News, PO Box 610, Stittsville ON K2S 1A7 – 613/836-1357; Fax: 613/836-5621 – Circ.: 4,400; Wed. – Publisher & Editor, John Curry
Stoney Creek News, 333 Arvin Ave., Stoney Creek ON L8E 2M6 – 905/561-1090; Fax: 905/664-3102 – Circ.: 25,000; Wed.; also The Real Estate News & Buyer's Guide (Wed.) – Publisher, Dave O'Reilly, 905/523-5800; Editor, Stephen Beecroft, 905/523-5800; Circulation Manager, Dave Settle
Stouffville Sun, 6306 Main St., PO Box 154, Stouffville ON L4A 7Z5 – 905/640-2612; Fax: 905/640-8778 – Wed.
Stouffville Tribune, Metroland Printing, Publishing & Distributing Ltd., 6244 Main St., Stouffville ON L4A 1E2 – 905/640-2100; Toronto line: 416/798-7625 – Wed. – Publisher, Patricia Pappas
Stratford This Week, 108 Ontario St., PO Box 430, Stratford ON N5A 6T6 – 519/271-2220; Fax: 519/271-1026 – Circ.: 14,604; Wed. – Publisher, Charles W. Dingman
Strathroy Age-Dispatch, 8 Front St. East, Strathroy ON N7G 1Y4 – 519/245-2370 – Wed.
Sturgeon Falls Tribune, PO Box 900, Sturgeon Falls ON P0H 2G0 – 705/753-2930 – Tue.; English & French
Sudbury: Northern Life, 158 Elgin St., Sudbury ON P3E 3N5 – 705/673-5667; Fax: 705/673-4652 – Wed.
Sudbury: South Side Story, #204, 469 Bouchard St., Sudbury ON P3E 2K8 – 705/523-2339
Sudbury: Le Voyageur, 20 St. Anne St., Sudbury ON P3A 5N4 – 705/673-3377; Fax: 705/673-5854; Email: voyageur@vianet.on.ca – Tirage: 3,900; Mercredi; français – Editeur, Guy Lemieux; Rédacteur, Jacques des Bacquets
Tavistock Gazette, PO Box 70, Tavistock ON N0B 2R0 – 519/655-2341 – Wed.
Tecumseh: Le Rempart, 7515 Forest Glade, Tecumseh ON N8N 2M1 – 519/234-6735; Email: publicat@netcare.ca – Mercredi; français
Tecumseh: Shoreline Week, 1614 Lesperance Rd., Tecumseh ON N8N 1Y3 – 519/735-2080; Fax: 519/

735-2082 – Circ.: 12,500; Wed. – Publisher, Gary Baxter

Teeswater: The Midwest Weekly News, 13 Clinton St., PO Box 250, Teeswater ON N0G 2S0 – 519/327-8668, 392-6175; Fax: 519/392-8345; Email: midwest.news@ocna.org – Wed.

Terrace Bay: Terrace Bay Schreiber News, PO Box 730, Schreiber ON P0T 2S0 – 807/824-2021 – Tue.

Thamesville Herald, 65 London Rd., Thamesville ON N0P 2K0 – 519/692-3825 – Wed.

Thessalon: The North Shore Sentinel, PO Box 640, Thessalon ON P0R 1L0 – 705/842-2504; Fax: 705/842-2679 – Circ.: 3,500; Wed. – Publisher, Randy Rankin; Editor, D. Brent Rankin; Circulation Manager, Jackie Dauphin

Thorold News, 13 Front St., Thorold ON L2V 1X3 – 905/227-1141; Fax: 905/227-0222 – Tue.

Thunder Bay Post, 1126 Roland St., Thunder Bay ON P7B 5M4 – 807/622-8588; Fax: 807/622-2779; Email: tbpost@air.on.ca; URL: http://www.tb-source.com – Circ.: 48,000; Tues.

Tilbury Times, PO Box 490, Tilbury ON N0P 2L0 – 519/682-0411; Fax: 519/682-3633 – Wed.

Tillsonburg Independent, 25 Townline Rd., Tillsonburg ON N4G 2R5 – 519/688-6892 – Circ.: 9,909; Mon., also Lakeshore Shopper (Sat., circ. 35,977)

Tillsonburg News, PO Box 190, Tillsonburg ON K4G 4H6 – 519/688-6397; Fax: 519/842-3511 – Circ.: 5,746; Wed., Fri.

Timmins: The Freighter, 550 Lamminen, Timmins ON P4N 4R3 – 705/268-4282 – Wed.

Timmins: Les Nouvelles, 187, rue Cedar sud, Timmins ON P4N 2G9 – 705/268-2955; Fax: 705/268-3614 – Lundi; français – Editeur, Sylvid Belisle

Timmins Times, The 101 Mall, 38 Pine St. North, PO Box 1006, Timmins ON P4N 6K6 – 705/628-6252; Fax: 705/268-2255; Email: timmins.times@ocna.org – Circ.: 19,157; Sat.; English & French – Publisher & Editor, Kevin Vincent

Tobermory: The Bruce Peninsula Press, PO Box 89, Tobermory ON N0H 2R0 – 519/596-2658; Fax: 519/596-8030; Email: tobpress@kanservu.ca – Circ.: 3,000; 16 times a year – Publisher, John Francis; Editor, Paddy Donovan

Toronto: Beach Metro Community News, Ward Nine Community News Inc., 2196 Gerrard St. East, Toronto ON M4E 2G7 – 416/698-1164; Fax: 416/698-1253 – Circ.: 30,000; Every other Tue. except 1 issue only in Aug. – Editor, Carole Stimmell; Circulation Manager, Sheila Blinoff

Toronto: East Toronto Advocate, WenDay Publishing Ltd., #301, 146 Laird Dr., Toronto ON M4G 3V7 – 416/467-7037; Fax: 416/467-6700 – Thur. – Co-Publisher, Patrick Daley; Co-Publisher, Wendy Daley

Toronto: East York Times, WenDay Publishing Ltd., #301, 146 Laird Dr., Toronto ON M4G 3V7 – 416/467-7037; Fax: 416/467-7000 – Thur.

Toronto: L'Express, 17 Carlaw Ave., Toronto ON M4M 2R6 – 416/465-2107 – Mardi; français; et: L'Observateur, London; L'Information, Hamilton/Burlington, & Le Courrier d'Oshawa

Toronto: Forest Hill Journal, WenDay Publishing Ltd., #301, 146 Laird Dr., Toronto ON M4G 3V7 – 416/467-7037; Fax: 416/467-6700 – Every other Thur.

Toronto: North Toronto Post, Post Newspapers Inc., 340 Sheppard Ave. East, Toronto ON M2N 3B4 – 416/250-7979; Fax: 416/250-1737; Email: postnews@idirect.com – Circ.: 35,000; Monthly; also publishes: Bayview Post, Thornhill Post, The Village Post, Richmond Hill Post

Toronto: Nouveau Canada, #500, 120 Eglinton Ave. East, Toronto ON M4P 1E2 – 416/481-7793 – Tirage: 10,000; Vendredi; français – Hasanat Ahmad Syed

Toronto etc...News, 201 Leslie St., Toronto ON M4M 3C6 – 416/465-7554; Fax: 416/465-8190 – Circ.: 25,000; Monthly – Publisher, Bruce Brackett; Editor, Terry Brackett

Toronto: Toronto Jewish Press, PO Box 142, Downsview ON M3M 3A3 – 416/633-0202 – Fri.; English & Hebrew

Toronto: The Toronto Voice, 249 Sherbourne St., Toronto ON M5A 2R9 – 416/927-0150 – Circ.: 32,500; Monthly – Publisher & Editor-in-chief, Barbara Neyedly

Toronto: Town Crier, #327, 2510 Yonge St., Toronto ON M4P 2H8 – 416/488-4779; Fax: 416/488-4918; Email: tcrier@idirect.com – Monthly; seven separate newspapers: Leaside-Rosedale Town Crier (circ. 25,000); North Toronto Town Crier (circ. 30,000); Forest Hill Town Crier (circ. 26,000); Bayview Mills Town Crier (circ. 25,000); – Publisher, Julie Wang Morris; Acting Editor, Andrew Gordham

Toronto: Villager, 2259 Bloor St. West, Toronto ON M6S 1N8 – 416/767-3644; Fax: 416/767-4880 – Circ.: 42,000; Monthly – Publisher, George Longo; Editor, Ian McMillan

Tottenham: Tottenham Times, PO Box 310, Beeton ON L0G 1A0 – 905/729-2287; Fax: 905/729-2541; Email: york@simcoe.igs.net – Circ.: 2,100; Wed. – John Archibald; Bruce Haire

Trenton Trentonian, PO Box 130, Trenton ON K8V 5R3 – 613/392-6501 – Circ.: 7,677; Mon., Wed., Fri.; also CoverStory (Fri.)

Tweed News, PO Box 550, Tweed ON K0K 3J0 – 613/478-2017; Fax: 613/478-2749 – Circ.: 2,100; Wed. – Publisher & Editor, Ivy Hanna; Circulation Manager, Roseann Turcotte

Uxbridge Times Journal, 8 Church St., PO Box 459, Uxbridge ON L9P 1M9 – 905/852-9141; Fax: 905/852-9341 – Circ.: 5,000; Wed. – Publisher, Don MacLeod; Managing Editor, Jim Belyea

Vankleek Hill Review, PO Box 160, Vankleek Hill ON K0B 1R0 – 613/678-3327; Fax: 613/678-2700; Email: review@hawk.IGS.net – Circ.: 4,500; Wed.; English & French – Publisher, Louise Sproule; Editor, Richard Mahoney

Virgil: Niagara Advance, PO Box 430, Virgil ON L0S 1T0 – 905/468-3283; Fax: 905/468-3137 – Circ.: 5,750; Tue. – Publisher, Tim Dundas; Editor, Doug Morton

Walkerton Herald-Times, 10 Victoria St., PO Box 190, Walkerton ON N0G 2V0 – 519/881-1600; Fax: 519/881-0276 – Wed.

Wallaceburg Courier-Press, 820 Dufferin Ave., Wallaceburg ON N8A 4X1 – 519/627-1488 – Circ.: 11,350; Wed.

Wallaceburg News, 222 Wellington St., Wallaceburg ON N8A 2X9 – 519/627-2243 – Wed.

Waterdown Flamborough Review, 30 Main St. North, PO Box 20, Waterdown ON L0R 2H0 – 905/689-4841 – Wed.

Waterloo Chronicle, 75 King St. South, 2nd Fl., Waterloo ON N2J 1P2 – 519/886-2830; Fax: 519/886-9383; Email: Editor@waterloo-chronicle.com – Circ.: 25,000; Wed. – Publisher, Cheryl McMenemy; Editor, Deborah Crandall; Circulation Manager, Carolyn Anstey

Watford Guide-Advocate, 5292 Nauvoo Rd., Watford ON N0M 2S0 – 519/876-2809; Fax: 519/876-2322 – Circ.: 1,408; Wed.

Wawa/Algoma News Review, PO Box 528, Wawa ON P0S 1K0 – 705/856-2267; Fax: 705/856-4952 – Circ.: 1,850; Wed. – Publisher & Editor, W. Robert Avis; Circulation Manager, Nancy Pavlic

Welland Regional Shopping News, 440 Niagara St., Unit 7, Welland ON L3C 1L5 – 905/735-9222 – Wed.

West Lincoln: West Lincoln Review, PO Box 40, Smithville ON L0R 2A0 – 905/957-3315 – Wed.

Westport & Rideau Valley Mirror, PO Box 130, Westport ON K0G 1X0 – Circ.: 2,511; Wed.

Wheatley Journal, PO Box 10, Wheatley ON N0P 2P0 – 519/825-4541 – Wed.

Wiarton Echo, PO Box 220, Wiarton ON N0H 2T0 – 519/534-1560; Fax: 519/534-4616 – Wed. – Publisher, Clyde Wicks

Willowdale: Scarborough/North York Mirror, Metroland Printing, Publishing & Distributing Ltd., 10 Tempo Ave., Willowdale ON M2H 2N8 – 416/493-4400; Fax: 416/493-4703 – Circ.: 106,000; Wed., Sun. – Publisher, Betty Carr; Editor, Tracy Kibble

Winchester Press, 2woMor Publications Inc., PO Box 399, Winchester ON K0C 2K0 – 613/774-2524; Fax: 613/774-3967 – Circ.: 4,300; Wed. – Publisher, John Morris; Editor, Liz Edwards; Circulation Manager, Connie Hart

Windsor Pennysaver, 2610 Pillette Rd., Windsor ON N8T 1R1 – 519/944-7070 – Sun.

Wingham Advance-Times, PO Box 390, Wingham ON N0G 2W0 – 519/357-2320; Fax: 519/357-2900; Email: advance@wcl.on.ca; URL: http://www.eedy.com/advancetimes/ – Circ.: 2,010; Wed. – Publisher, Jim Beckett

Woodbridge Advertiser, RR#1, Palgrave ON L0N 1P0 – 905/729-4501; Fax: 905/729-3961; Email: auctions@bconnex.net – Tue.

Woodstock: Oxford Shopping News, 809 Dundas St., Woodstock ON N4S 1G2 – 519/537-6657 – Circ.: 27,800; Tue., Fri.

Zurich: The Lakeshore Advance, PO Box 190, Zurich ON N0M 2T0 – 519/236-4312; Fax: 519/236-7558; Email: ladvance@hay.net; URL: http://www.bowesnet.com/ladvance/ – Wed. – General Manager, Gail Lawson; Editor, C. Cowan

## Prince Edward Island Daily Newspapers

### CHARLOTTETOWN:

The Guardian, Southam Inc., 165 Prince St., Charlottetown PE C1A 4R7 – 902/629-6000; Fax: 902/566-3808 – Circ.: 23,225 morning; Morning – Publisher & General Manager, Don Brander; Circulation Manager, Julie Murtha

### SUMMERSIDE:

Journal Pioneer, 4 Queen St., PO Box 2480, Summerside PE C1N 4K5 – 902/436-2121; Fax: 902/436-3027 – Circ.: 10,891; Evening – Publisher, Steen O. Jorgensen

## Other Newspapers in Prince Edward Island

Alberton: West Prince Graphic, PO Box 790, Montague PE C0A 1R0 – 902/838-2515; Fax: 902/838-4392; Email: wgraphic@cycor.ca – Circ.: 2,149; Wed. – Publisher & Editor, Jim MacNeill; Circulation Manager, Hazel Easter

Montague: The Eastern Graphic, PO Box 790, Montague PE C0A 1R0 – 902/838-2515; Fax: 902/838-4392 – Circ.: 5,789; Wed.

Summerside: La Voix Acadienne, 340, rue Court, CP 1420, Summerside PE C1N 4K2 – 902/436-6005; Fax: 902/888-3976; Email: lavoix@auracom.com – Mercredi; français – Marcia Enman

## Québec Daily Newspapers

### CHICOUTIMI:

Le Quotidien, 1051, boul Talbot, Chicoutimi QC G7H 5C1 – 418/545-4474; Fax: 418/690-8824 – Tirage: 30,562; Matin; français – Directeur de tirage, Jean-Louis Lavoie

### GRANBY:

La Voix de L'Est, 76, rue Dufferin, Granby QC J2G 9L4 – 514/375-4555; Fax: 514/777-7221 – Tirage: 15,324 lun.-ven., 19,151 sam.; Matin; français – Rédacteur en chef, Dany Doucet

**MONTRÉAL:**

Le Devoir, 2050, rue de Bleury, Montréal QC H3A 3M9 – 514/985-3399; Fax: 514/985-3390; Email: devoir@cam.org; URL: http://www.ledevoir.com – Tirage: 29,534 lun.-ven., 34,948 sam.; Matin; français – Editrice, Lise Bissonnette

The Gazette, 250, rue St-Antoine ouest, Montréal QC H2Y 3R7 – 514/987-2222; Fax: 514/987-2323; URL: http://www.montrealgazette.com – Circ.: 148,092 Mon.-Fri., 217,456 Sat., 138,204 Sun.; Morning; also South Shore Edition (Thur., circ. 21,747), West End Edition (Thur., circ. 35,512), West Island Edition (Thur., circ. 40,000) – Publisher, Michael Goldbloom; Editor-in-chief, Alan Allnutt; Reader Sales & Service VP, Cathy Hamilton Lambie

Le Journal de Montréal, Groupe Québécor Inc., 4545, rue Frontenac, Montréal QC H2H 2R7 – 514/521-4545; Fax: 514/521-5442 – Tirage: 277,383 lun.-ven., 336,294 sam., 292,691 dim.; Matin; français – Editeur, Pierre Francoeur

La Presse, 7, rue St-Jacques, Montréal QC H2Y 1K9 – 514/285-7306; Fax: 514/845-8129 – Tirage: 190,623 lun.-ven., 331,082 sam., 192,552 dim.; Matin; français – Editeur, Roger D. Landry

**QUÉBEC:**

Le Soleil, 925, chemin Saint-Louis, CP 1547, Succ Terminus, Québec QC G1K 7J6 – 418/686-3233; Fax: 418/686-3374 & 686-3260; URL: http://www.lesoleil.com – Matin; français – Rédacteur en chef, Gilbert Lavoie

**SHERBROOKE:**

Record, Groupe Québécor Inc., 2850, rue Delorme, Sherbrooke QC J1K 1A1 – 819/569-9525; Fax: 819/569-3945 – Circ.: 5,500; Morning, five days a week – Publisher, Randy Kinnear

La Tribune, 1950, rue Roy, Sherbrooke QC J1K 2X8 – 819/564-5450; Fax: 819/564-5455 – Tirage: 32,246 lun.-ven., 43,557 sam.; Matin; français – Editeur, Raymond Tardif; Rédacteur en chef, Jacques Pronovost

**TROIS-RIVIÈRES:**

Le Nouvelliste, 1920, rue Bellefeuille, Trois-Rivières QC G9A 3Y2 – 819/376-2501; Fax: 819/376-0946 – Tirage: 49,347; Matin; français – Rédacteur en chef, Bernard Champoux

**VANIER:**

Le Journal de Québec, Groupe Québécor Inc., 450, rue Bechard, Vanier QC G1M 2E9 – 418/683-1573; Fax: 418/683-1027 – Tirage: 102,701 lun.-ven., 122,079 sam., 99,905 dim.; Matin; français – Editeur, Jean-Claude L'Abbée; Rédacteur, Serge Côté; Directeur de tirage, Marc Couture

## Other Newspapers in Québec

Alma: L'Echo de La Tuque, 525, av du Pont sud, CP 520, Alma QC G8B 5W1 – 819/523-6141; Fax: 819/523-6143 – Tirage: 7 166

Alma: Le Lac Saint-Jean, 525, av du Pont, CP 520, Alma QC G8B 5W1 – 418/668-4545; Fax: 418/668-8522 – Tirage: 19 716; Dimanche

Amqui: L'Avant-Poste Gaspesien, CP 410, Rimouski QC G5L 7C4 – 418/723-4800; Fax: 418/722-4078 – Dimanche

Arthabaska: L'Union, 43, rue Notre-Dame est, CP 130, Arthabaska QC G6P 3Z4 – 514/357-8232; Fax: 514/357-3623 – Tirage: 25,150; Mercredi

Asbestos: Les Actualités, 78, rue St-Jean, Asbestos QC J1T 3R3 – 819/879-6681; Fax: 819/879-2355 – Samedi

Aylmer Bulletin d'Aylmer, 9, rue Principale, Aylmer QC J9H 3K9 – 819/684-4755; Fax: 819/684-6428 – Mon.; English & French – Owner, Fred Ryan; Editor, David DuCharme

Baie-Comeau Objectif-Plein-Jour, Rive-nord medias inc., 896, rue de Puyjalon, Baie-Comeau QC G5C 1N1 – 418/589-5900; Fax: 418/589-5263; Email: objectif@qubectel.com – Samedi; aussi Plein jour sur la Manicouagan (mercredi, tirage 15 687) – Directeur-général régional, Claude Mercier

Baie-Comeau: Le Plein-Jour en Haute Côte-Nord, Rive-nord medias inc., 896, rue de Puyjalon, Baie-Comeau QC G5C 1N1 – 418/589-5900; Fax: 418/589-5263; Email: objectif@qubectel.com – Lundi – Directeur-général régional, Claude Mercier

Beauport Express, Groupe Quebecor inc., 597 av Royale, Beauport QC G1E 1Y6 – 418/663-6131; Fax: 418/663-3469 – Tirage: 40,000; Hebdomadaire – Directeur général, Paul Lessard

Bedford: Journal des Rivières, CP 960, Bedford QC J0J 1A0 – 514/248-3303; Fax: 514/248-7540 – Tirage: 6,562; Samedi – Rédacteur, Richard Hamel

Beloeil: L'Oeil Régional, 393, boul Laurier, Beloeil QC J3G 4H6 – 514/467-1821; Fax: 514/467-3087 – Tirage: 27,000; Samedi – Editeur, Guy Gilbert

Boucherville: Journal La Relève, 528, rue St-Charles, Boucherville QC J4B 3M5 – 514/641-4844; Fax: 514/641-4849 – Tirage: 24 500; Samedi – Directeur-général, Charles Desmarteau

Boucherville: La Seigneurie, 391, boul de Montagne, Boucherville QC J4B 1B7 – 514/641-3360; Fax: 514/655-9752 – Tirage: 30 000; Samedi – Rédacteur, S. Landry

Bromont: Ici maintenant Bromont, a/s Imprimerie Désourdy, 30, rue Pacifique est, Bromont QC J0E 1L0 – 514/534-2823 – Marianik Gagnon

Brossard-Eclair Extra, #A105, 7900, boul Taschereau, Brossard QC J4X 1C2 – 514/466-3344; Fax: 514/466-9019 – Circ.: 23 800; Sun.; French & English

Buckingham: Le Bulletin, 435, rue Principale, Buckingham QC J8L 2G8 – 819/986-5089; Fax: 819/986-2073 – Tirage: 10 200; Mercredi

Buckingham: La Vie à Buckingham Life, #203, 585 James St., PO Box 180, Buckingham QC J8L 2R7 – 819/986-8557; Fax: 819/986-8167 – Circ.: 7,000; Wed.

Cabano: Le Touladi, CP 430, Cabano QC G0L 1E0 – 418/854-2766; Fax: 418/854-2830 – Tirage: 9 800; Dimanche

Cacouna: Journal Epik de Cacouna, 245, rue Principale, Cacouna QC G0L 1G0 – Circ.: 770

Cap-aux-Meules/Iles-de-la-Madeleine: Le Radar, L'Hebos des Iles-de-la-Madeleine, CP 580, Cap-aux-Meules/Iles-de-la-Madeleine QC G0B 1B0 – 418/986-2345; Fax: 418/986-6358; Email: radar@cancom.net – Tirage: 3,000; Vendredi; français – Editeur, Achille Hubert; Rédacteur, Yves Marcotte; Directrice de tirage, Nancy Gallant

Cap-de-la-Madeleine: L'Hebdo-Journal, 44, rue de la Fonderie, Cap-de-la-Madeleine QC G8T 2E8 – 819/379-1490; Fax: 819/379-0705 – Tirage: 44 500; Dimanche

Chambly: Le Journal de Chambly, 1685 Bourgogne, CP 175, Chambly QC J3L 1Y8 – 514/658-6516; Fax: 514/658-3785 – Tirage: 20,725; Mardi – Rédacteur, Daniel Noiseux

Chandler: Le Havre, CP 410, Rimouski QC G5L 7C4 – 418/723-4800; Fax: 418/722-4078 – Tirage: 8 035; Dimanche

Châteauguay: L'Information Regional, #202, 243, boul d'Anjou, Châteauguay QC J6J 2R3 – 514/691-3863; Fax: 514/691-3883 – Tirage: 27 105; Mercredi – Rédacteur, André Gendron

Châteauguay: Le Soleil du St-Laurent, Hebdos Montérégiens, 82, boul Salaberry sud, Châteauguay QC J6J 4J6 – 514/692-8555; Fax: 514/692-3460 – Tirage: 25 250; Samedi – Manager, Jeanne D'Arc Germain, 514/692-8552; Rédacteur en chef, Michel Thibault

Chelsea: The Low Down to Hull & Back News, PO Box 99, Wakefield QC J0X 3G0 – 819/459-2222; Email: wakefield_news@ocna.org – Circ.: 2,500; Mon. – Publisher, K.J. Mantell; Editor, Arthur Mantell

Chibougamau: La Sentinelle, CP 250, Chibougamau QC G8P 2K7 – 819/748-6406 – Tirage: 3 200; Mardi; aussi Le Radissonien (mensuel)

Chicoutimi: Le Progrès Dimanche, 1051, boul Talbot, Chicoutimi QC G7H 5C1 – 418/545-4474; Fax: 418/690-8824 – Tirage: 47 703; Dimanche

Chicoutimi: Le Réveil à Chicoutimi, 3388, boul St-François, Jonquière QC G7X 2W9 – 418/695-2601 – Tirage: 30 610; Dimanche

Coaticook: Le Progrès, CP 150, Coaticook QC J1A 2S9 – 819/849-3616 – Tirage: 7 585; Samedi

Cookshire: Le Haut St-François, 80, rue Principale est, CP 292, Cookshire QC J0B 1M0 – 819/875-5501; Fax: 819/875-3135 – Tirage: 9 500; Mensuel – Pierre Hébert

Côte-Saint-Luc: The Suburban, 8170, ch Wavell, Côte-Saint-Luc QC H4W 1M3 – 514/484-1107; Fax: 514/484-7284 – Wed., 8 area editions: Cote-des-Neiges/Snowdon, Côte-Saint-Luc, Hampstead, Chomedy/St-Laurent, Montréal-ouest, Town of Mount Royal, Westmount, The West Island

Cowansville: Le Citoyen, 352, rue Principale, St-Alphonse-de-Granby QC J0E 2A0 – 514/777-1636 – Lundi

Cowansville: Le Guide, 245, rue Principale, Cowansville QC J2K 1J4 – 514/263-5288; Fax: 514/263-9435 – Tirage: 16 000; Samedi

Delson: Le Reflet, 54, boul Marie-Victorin, Delson QC J0L 1E0 – Tirage: 26 500; Samedi

Donnacona: Le Courrier de Portneuf, 274, rue Notre-Dame, CP 1030, Donnacona QC G0A 1T0 – 418/285-0211; Fax: 418/285-2441 – Tirage: 29,700; Samedi – Rédacteur, Maurice Marcotte

Drummondville: L'Express, 1050, rue Cormier, Drummondville QC J2C 2N6 – 819/477-3773; Email: unimedia@9bit.qc.ca – Tirage: 40 600; Dimanche – Rédacteur, Real Brodeur

Drummondville: La Parole, 1050, rue Cormier, Drummondville QC J2C 2N6 – 819/478-8171; Fax: 819/478-4306; Email: unimedia@9bit.qc.ca – Tirage: 35 835; Mercredi – Rédacteur, Real Brodeur

Farnham: L'Avenir, 322A, rue Principale est, Farnham QC J2N 1L7 – 514/293-3138; Fax: 514/293-2093 – Tirage: 41 398; Samedi

Fermont: Le Trait d'Union du Nord, Ctr. L.J. Patterson, CP 561, Fermont QC G0G 1J0 – 418/287-5432; Fax: 418/287-3874; Email: sprecour@cancom.net – Tirage: 1 800

Fort Coulonge/Pontiac Journal, 289, rue Principale, PO Box 893, Fort Coulonge QC J0X 1V0 – 819/683-3582; Fax: 819/683-2977 – Circ.: 9,855; Every other Tue.; English & French – Publisher & Editor, Fred Ryan; Circulation Manager, Peter L. Smith

Gaspé Peninsula Spec, 128 Main St., PO Box 99, New Carlisle QC G0C 1Z0 – 418/752-5400, 5070; Fax: 418/752-6932; Email: specs@quebectel.com – Circ.: 3,200; Sun. – Publisher, Sharon Farrell; Editor, Cynthia Dow

Gaspé: Le Pharillon, CP 410, Rimouski QC G5L 7C4 – 418/723-4800; Fax: 418/722-4078 – Tirage: 8 470; Dimanche

Gatineau: La Revue de Gatineau, #106, 430, boul de l'Hôpital, Gatineau QC J8V 1T7 – 819/568-7736; Fax: 819/568-7038 – Tirage: 36,947; Mercredi – Editeur, Yves Blondin; Rédacteur, Sylvain Dupras

Gatineau: Week-end Outaouais, 430, boul de L'Hôpital, Gatineau QC J8V 1T7 – 819/568-7736 – Tirage: 64 700; Dimanche

Granby: Samedi Express, 21, St-Charles sud, Granby QC J2G 9M2 – 514/777-4515; Fax: 514/777-4516 – Circ.: 44 000; Hebdomadaire – Ben Gaudreau

Granby: La Voix de l'est plus, 76, rue Dufferin, Granby QC J2G 9L4 – 514/375-6993 – Tirage: 40 142; Dimanche

Grosse Île, Magdalen Islands: First Informer, PO Box 148, Grosse Île, Magdalen Islands QC G0B 1M0 –

418/985-2100; Fax: 418/985-2274 – Fri. – Publisher & Editor, Norma Jean Clarke

Hudson: Lake of Two Mountains Gazette, PO Box 70, Hudson QC J0P 1H0 – 514/458-5482; Fax: 514/458-3337 – Circ.: 8,000; Wed. – Publisher & Editor, G. Jones

Hull: Bonjour Dimanche, 825, boul de la Carrière, Hull QC J8Y 6T7 – 819/770-2205 – Tirage: 77 000; Dimanche

Hull: Le Régional combiné Outaouais, 141, rue Jean-Proulx, Hull QC J8Z 1T4 – 514/844-3131 – Tirage: 10 650; Mercredi

Hull: Le Regional Hull, 141, rue Jean-Proulx, Hull QC J8Z 1T4 – 819/776-1063; Fax: 819/776-1668 – Tirage: 26 352; Mercredi

Huntingdon: The Gleaner/La Source, PO Box 130, Huntingdon QC J0S 1H0 – 514/264-5364; Fax: 514/264-9521 – Circ.: 4,230; Wed.; English & French – Publisher, Jocelyn Ranger; Editor, Judith Taylor

Joliette: L'Expression de Lanaudière, 342, Beaudry nord, Joliette QC J6E 6A6 – 514/752-0447; Fax: 514/759-2988; Email: expression@pandore.qc.ca – Tirage: 45 500; Hebdomadaire – Jean-Pierre Malo

Joliette: Le Régional de Lanaudière, 262, boul l'Industrie, Joliette QC J6E 3Z1 – 514/759-3664 – Tirage: 20 965; Mercredi

Joliettte: L'Action, 262, boul l'Industrie, Joliettte QC J8E 3Z1 – 514/759-3664; Fax: 514/759-9828 – Tirage: 44 000; Dimanche

Jonquière: Le Réveil à Jonquière, 3388, boul St-François, Jonquière QC G7X 2W9 – 418/695-2601 – Tirage: 26 992; Dimanche; aussi Le Point (dimanche), Le Réveil à la Baie (dimanche)

Knowlton: Brome County News, 88 Lakeside, Knowlton QC J0E 1V0 – Wed.

La Malbaie: L'Hebdo Charlevoisien, 203, rue Nairn, La Malbaie QC G5A 1M4 – 418/665-1299 – Tirage: 13 033; Samedi

La Malbaie: Le Plein Jour Charlevoix, #110, 249, rue Nairn, La Malbaie QC G5A 1M4 – 418/665-6121; Flax: 418/665-3105 – Tirage: 12 118; Samedi

La Plaine: Journal le Plainois, 5333, boul Laurier, La Plaine QC J7M 1W1 – 514/964-4444 – Tirage: 19 000; Mercredi

Lac Etchemin: La Voix du Sud, CP 789, Lac Etchemin QC G0R 1S0 – 418/625-7471; Fax: 418/625-5200 – Tirage: 19 400; Dimanche

Lac-Mégantic: L'Echo de Frontenac, 5040, boul des Vétérans, Lac-Mégantic QC G6B 2G5 – 819/583-1630; Fax: 819/583-1124 – Tirage: 9 050; Dimanche; français – Editeur, Gaétan Poulin; Rédacteur en chef, Rémi Tremblay; Directrice de tirage, Suzanne Poulin

Lachine: Le Messager de Lachine, 9216, rue Boivin, LaSalle QC H8R 2E7 – 514/637-2381; Fax: 514/637-8273 – Tirage: 18 100; Wed.; English & French

Lachute: L'Argenteuil, 52, rue Principale, Lachute QC J8H 3A8 – 514/562-2494; Fax: 514/562-1434 – Tirage: 12,900; Mercredi; français – Editeur, André Paquette; Rédacteur, François Legault; Directeur de tirage, Alain Morris

Lachute: Tribune/Express, 52, rue Principale, Lachute QC J8H 3A8 – 514/562-8593; Fax: 514/562-1434; Email: watchman@ocna.org – Circ.: 12.900; Sat.; English & French – Publisher, André Paquette; Editor, François Legault; Circulation Manager, Alain Morris

LaSalle: Le Messenger de LaSalle, 9216, rue Boivin, LaSalle QC H8R 2E7 – 514/363-5656; Fax: 514/363-3151 – Circ.: 26,600; Sun.; English & French

Laurier Station: Le Peuple de Lotbinière, 1000, ch St-Joseph, CP 130, Laurier Station QC G0S 1N0 – 418/728-2131; Fax: 418/728-4819 – Tirage: 10 971; Dimanche; français – Denys Simoneau

Lennoxville: The Townships Sun, 7 Conley St., PO Box 28, Lennoxville QC J1M 1Z3 – 819/566-7424; Fax: 819/566-7424 – Circ.: 1,000; Monthly – Editor, Patricia Ball

Levis-Lauzon: Le Peuple-Tribune, 45, rue Desjardins, Levis-Lauzon QC G6V 5V3 – 418/833-9398; Fax: 418/833-8177 – Tirage: 27 705; Samedi

Longueuil: Le Courrier du Sud, 267, rue St-Charles ouest, Longueuil QC J4H 1E3 – 514/646-3333; Email: courrier-du-sud.comm – Tirage: 118 000; Dimanche; aussi Longueuil Extra (dimanche, tirage 53 000)

Louiseville: L'Echo de Louiseville/Berthier, 50, rue St-Aimé, Louiseville QC J5V 2Y7 – 819/228-2766 – Tirage: 8 745; Mercredi; aussi Salut Dimanche (dimanche, tirage 17 599)

Magog: Le Progres de Magog, 355, rue Principale ouest, Magog QC J1X 2B1 – 819/843-2000; Fax: 819/843-2608 – Samedi

Magog: Le Reflect du Lac, 106, Place du Commerce, Magog QC J1X 5G6 – 819/843-3500; Fax: 819/843-3085 – Dimanche

Malartic: Le Courrier de Malartic, CP 4020, Malartic QC J0Y 1Z0 – 819/757-4712; Fax: 819/757-4712 – Tirage: 1 200; Mardi; français – Editrice, Denyse Roberge

Maniwaki: La Gatineau, 114, rue de la Ferme, Maniwaki QC J9E 3J9 – 819/449-1725; Fax: 819/449-5108 – Vendredi; français – Superviseur, Denise Lacourcière

Maniwaki: La Gazette de Maniwaki, 93, rue Notre-Dame, Maniwaki QC J9E 2H5 – 819/449-2233; Fax: 819/449-7067 – Tirage: 10,200; Dimanche; français – Editrice, Denise Carrière

Matane: La Voix Gaspesienne, #107, 305, rue de la Gare, Matane QC G4W 3M5 – 418/562-4040; Fax: 418/562-4607 – Tirage: 4 938; Mercredi; aussi La Voix du dimanche (dimanche)

Mont Joli: L'Information, 135, rue Doucet, Mont Joli QC G5H 1R6 – 418/775-4381 – Tirage: 12 000; Dimanche

Mont-Laurier: Le Choix, 501, boul Paquette, Mont-Laurier QC J9L 1K8 – Tirage: 14 624; Vendredi

Mont-Laurier: L'Echo de la Lievre, 506, rue Carillon, Mont-Laurier QC J9L 1P9 – 819/623-5250 – Tirage: 11 610; Dimanche

Montmagny: L'Oie Blanche, #401, 1, Place de l'Eglise, Montmagny QC G5V 2L9 – Tirage: 19 672; Samedi

Montmagny: Le Peuple de la Côte-du-Sud, CP 430, Montmagny QC G5V 3S7 – 418/248-0415 – Tirage: 19 200; Vendredi

Montréal: Canadian Jewish News, #341, 6900, boul Decarie, Montréal QC H3X 2T8 – 514/735-2612; Fax: 514/735-9090; Email: torCJN1@aol.com – Circ.: 20,000; Thur.; English with some French – Editor, Mordechai Ben-Dat; Advertising Manager, Louise Wolman

Montréal: Le Citoyen de Saint-Lambert, #902, 1550, rue Metcalfe, Montréal QC H3A 1X6 – 514/845-8724 – Tue.; English & French

Montréal: Contact Laval, 189, rue Laval, Laval-des-Rapides QC H7N 3V8 – 514/667-4360; Fax: 514/667-9498 – Tirage: 98 158; Mercredi; aussi Courrier Laval (dimanche; tirage 90 200) – Editeur & Rédacteur, Jacques Dion; Directrice de tirage, Lynn Fortin

Montréal: Échos du Vieux-Montréal, 230, rue St-Paul ouest, Montréal QC H2Y 1Z9 – 514/844-2133 – Vincent Di Candido

Montréal: L'Express d'Outremont, 230, av Laurier ouest, Montréal QC H2T 2N8 – 514/276-9615; Fax: 514/274-5564 – Tirage: 16 000; Vendredi, tous les deux semaines; français – Editeur, Jean Lessard; Editeur & Rédacteur, Alain Tittley

Montréal: Les Hebdos Metropolitains de Montréal, #202, 6424, rue Jean Talon est, Montréal QC H1S 1M8 – 514/899-5888; Fax: 514/899-5001 – Mardi; publie: Le Flambeau de l'Est, Anjou (tirage 45 908), Nouvelles de l'Est (tirage 27 031), Le Guide Mont-Royal (tirage 16 900), La Petite Patrie (tirage 18 097), Le Journal de Rosemont (tirage 35 125)

Montréal: Messager de Verdun Messenger, 1735, av de l'Eglise, Montréal QC H4E 1G6 – 514/768-1920; Fax: 514/768-3306 – Circ.: 24,500; Tue.; English & French – Diane Bissonnette; Louis Mercier

Montréal: Le Monde, CP 7, Succ St-Michel, Montréal QC H2A 7L8 – 514/722-7708 – Vendredi – Editeur, Normand Lalonde; Rédacteur, Guy Jolicoeur

Montréal: The Monitor, #12, 5890, av Monkland, Montréal QC H4A 1G2 – 514/481-7510; Fax: 514/481-3492 – Circ.: 30,000; Wed.; English & French – Publisher, Peter Yakimchuk; Editor, Leonard J. Gervais; Circulation Manager, Kim Gribeauval

Montréal: Nouvelles Parc-Extension News, #340, 400, boul Curé-Labelle, Montréal QC H7V 2S7 – 514/272-0252 – Sat.; English & French

Montréal: La Voix Populaire, 1735, rue de l'Église, Montréal QC H4E 1G6 – 514/768-1920; Fax: 514/768-3306 – Tirage: 23 500; Mercredi – Diane Bissonnette; Louis Mercier

Montréal/Ahuntsic: Courrier Ahuntsic, 189, rue Laval, Laval-des-Rapides QC H7N 3V8 – 514/667-4360; Fax: 514/667-9498 – Tirage: 33 366; Dimanche – Rédacteur, Jacques Dion

Mount-Royal: Le Journal de Ville Mont-Royal, CP 697, Succ Mont-Royal, Mount-Royal QC H3P 3G4 – 514/739-5839 – Mensuel; aussi Town of Mount Royal Journal (English)

Mount-Royal: Weekly Post/L'Hebdo de Ville Mount-Royal, #280, 1255, boul Laird, Mount-Royal QC H3P 2T1 – 514/739-3302; Fax: 514/739-3304 – Thur.; English & French

Napierville: Coup D'Oeil, 350, rue St-Jacques, Napierville QC J0J 1L0 – 514/245-3344; Fax: 514/245-7419 – Tirage: 12,270; Samedi

New Richmond: L'Echo de la Baie, 140, boul Perron ouest, CP 129, New Richmond QC G0C 2B0 – 418/392-5083; Fax: 418/392-6605 – Mardi

Nicolet Courrier-Sud, Les Publications J.T.C. inc., 3255, rue Marie Victorin, Nicolet QC J3T 1X5 – 819/293-4551; Fax: 819/293-8758 – Tirage: 21,544; Dimanche – Rédacteur, Jean Blanchette

Nun's Island Magazine, #200, 5, Place du Commerce, Nun's Island QC H3E 1M8 – 514/767-7154; Fax: 514/767-1978; Email: magazine@axess.com – Circ.: 8,000; Wed.; English & French

Outremont: Le Journal d'Outremont, 812, av Davaar, CP 727, Succ Outremont, Outremont QC H2V 3B5 – 514/276-6671; Fax: 514/276-1011 – Tirage: 16 000; Mensuel; français – Editeur, Patrice Dauzet; Editrice, Louise Perron

Plessisville: La Feuille d'Erable, CP 160, Plessisville QC G6L 2Y7 – 819/362-7049; Fax: 819/362-2216 – Tirage: 5 000; Mardi

Pointe-aux-Trembles: Journal PAT/ME, 1004, rue Notre-Dame, Repentigny QC J5Y 1S9 – Tirage: 19 653; Mardi

Pointe-Claire: The Chronicle, 15 Cartier Ave., Pointe-Claire QC H9S 4R7 – 514/630-6688; Fax: 514/630-7340 – Tirage: 19,049; Wed.

Québec: Droit de parole, 301, rue Carillon, Québec QC G1K 5B3 – 418/648-8043 – Tirage: 150 000 – President, Michele Dionne

Québec: Journal le Carrefour, Editions du Joyeux Drille, 155, boul Charest est, Québec QC G1K 3G6 – 418/649-0775; Fax: 418/649-7531; Email: carrefour@webnet.qc.ca – Tirage: 70 000; Dimanche

Repentigny: L'Artisan, 1004, rue Notre-Dame, Repentigny QC J5Y 1S9 – 514/581-5120; Fax: 514/581 6509 – Tirage: 43 680; Mardi – Helenè Ouellette

Repentigny: Hebdo Rive-Nord, 1004, rue Notre-Dame, Repentigny QC J5Y 1S9 – 514/581-5120; Fax: 514/581-6509 – Tirage: 40 240; Dimanche – Helenè Ouellette

Richelain: Journal Servir, Base des Forces canadiennes de Montréal, PO Box 100, Stn Bureau Chef, Richelain QC J0J 1R0 – 514/358-7099, ext.7426; Fax: 514/358-7423; Email: servir@aei.ca – Circ.: 4,000; Engish & French – Rédacteur, Alain Gauthier

Rimouski: Le Progrès Echo Dimanche, CP 410, Rimouski QC G5L 7C4 – 418/723-4800; Fax: 418/722-4078 – Tirage: 28 244; Jeudi

Rimouski: Le Rimouskois, 156, Lepage, Rimouski QC G5L 3H2 – 418/723-2571; Fax: 418/722-4078 – Tirage: 23 317; Mardi

Rivière-du-Loup: Info Dimanche, 72, rue Fraser, Rivière-du-Loup QC G5R 1C6 – 418/862-1911; Fax: 418/862-6165 – Tirage: 20,350; Dimanche – Editeur & Rédacteur, Michel Chalifour

Rivière-du-Loup: Le Portage, 16, rue du Domaine, Rivière-du-Loup QC G5R 2R2 – 418/862-1774; Fax: 418/862-4387 – Dimanche

Rouyn-Noranda: Le Citoyen, CP 490, Rouyn-Noranda QC J9X 5C4 – 819/797-2450; Fax: 819/762-4361 – Tirage: 57,000; Dimanche; supplement, Journal du Nord-Ouest – Directeur, Andre Renaud, 819/762-4361

Rouyn-Noranda: La Frontière, 25, rue Gamble est, CP 490, Rouyn-Noranda QC J9X 4F9 – 819/762-4361 – Tirage: 13 681; Mercredi

Ste-Adèle: Le Journal des Pays D'en Haut, c/o Quebecor, CP 1890, Ste-Adèle QC J0R 1L0 – 514/229-6664; Fax: 514/229-6063 – Tirage: 17,000; Mercredi – Directeur-General, Michel Gareau

St-Andre-Avelin: La Revue de la Petite Nation, Publications Dumont inc., 70, Principale, CP 440, St-Andre-Avelin QC J0V 1W0 – 819/983-2725; Fax: 819/983-6844 – Tirage: 8 150; Lundi – Rédacteur, Michel Blais

Saint-Bruno: L'Écho de Saint-Bruno, 1688, Place Seigneuriale, Saint-Bruno QC J3V 4E4 – 514/653-5295 – Tirage: 10 000; Mensuel – Faouzi Majeri

Saint-Bruno: Le Journal de Saint-Bruno, 1507, rue Roberval, Saint-Bruno QC J3V 3P8 – Tirage: 14 900; Samedi

St-Donat: Journal Altitude, CP 1350, St-Donat QC J0T 2C0 – 819/424-2610; Fax: 819/424-3615 – Tirage: 4,000; Vendredi; français – Directrice de tirage, Marthe Lafortune; Rédacteur, Jean Lafortune

St-Eustache: La Concorde, 53, rue St-Eustache, St-Eustache QC J7R 2L2 – 514/473-1700 – Tirage: 37 500; Mercredi; aussi L'Eveil (dimanche; tirage 37 400)

St-Eustache: Courrier Deux-Montagnes, 189, rue Laval, Laval-des-Rapides QC H7N 1X1 – 514/667-4360; Fax: 514/667-9498 – Tirage: 33 366; Dimanche – Editeur & Rédacteur, Jacques Dion; Directrice de tirage, Lynn Fortin

Sainte-Foy: Québec Chronicle-Telegraph, 3484, ch Ste-Foy, Sainte-Foy QC G1X 1S8 – 418/650-1764; Fax: 418/650-1764; Email: QUEBEC_Chron-Telegraph@ocna.org – Circ.: 2,000; Wed. – Publisher & Editor, Karen Macdonald

Sainte-Geneviève: Cités Nouvelles, 15716, boul Gouin ouest, Sainte-Geneviève QC H9H 1C4 – Circ.: 55 000; Sun.; English & French

Saint-Georges: L'Impact, 225, rue 125, Saint-Georges QC G5Y 2Y3 – 418/227-7700; Fax: 418/227-7711; URL: http://www.belin.qc.ca/impact – Tirage: 24,700; Vendredi – Rédacteur, Paul-André Parent

St-Georges-Est: L'Eclaireur Progrès-Nouvelle, 12625, av 1e, St-Georges-Est QC G5Y 2E8 – 418/228-8858 – Tirage: 26 850; Mercredi, samedi

Saint-Hubert: Le Journal de St-Hubert, 5863, boul Cousineau, Saint-Hubert QC J3Y 7P5 – 514/445-2812; Fax: 514/445-6347 – Tirage: 27 800; Mardi

Saint-Hyacinthe: Le Clairon Regional, 655, av Ste-Anne, Saint-Hyacinthe QC J2S 5G4 – 514/774-5375; Fax: 514/773-0344 – Tirage: 22 107; Samedi

Saint-Hyacinthe: Le Courrier de Saint-Hyacinthe, 655, rue Ste-Anne, CP 340, Saint-Hyacinthe QC J2S 7B6 – 514/773-6028; Fax: 514/773-3115 – Tirage: 14 500; Mardi; français – Directeur-général, Benoit Chartier; Rédacteur en chef, Jean Vigneault

Saint-Hyacinthe: Le Regional Maskoutain, 592, av Ste-Marie, Saint-Hyacinthe QC J2S 4R5 – 514/778-1045; Fax: 514/773-3115 – Tirage: 30 900; Dimanche

St-Jean-sur-Richelieu: Le Canada Français, 84, rue Richelieu, St-Jean-sur-Richelieu QC J3B 6X3 – 514/347-0323; Fax: 514/347-4539 – Tirage: 18 000; Mercredi; aussi Le Richelieu Dimanche (dimanche)

St-Jérôme: Journal Le Mirabel, 179, rue St-Georges, St-Jérôme QC J7Z 4Z8 – 514/436-8200; Fax: 514/436-8912 – Tirage: 7 999; Dimanche

St-Jérôme: Journal Le Nord, #1, 287, rue Labelle, St-Jérôme QC J7Z 5L2 – 514/438-8383; Fax: 514/438-4174 – Tirage: 34 288; Mercredi – President, François Laferrière

St-Jovite: L'Information du Nord, 1107, rue Ouimet, CP 1480, St-Jovite QC J0T 2H0 – 819/425-8658; Fax: 819/425-7713 – Tirage: 7 999; Samedi

Sainte-Julie: L'Information, #2, 566, rue Jules-Choquet, Sainte-Julie QC J3E 1W6 – Samedi

Saint-Lambert Journal, 574, rue Victoria, Saint-Lambert QC J4P 2J5 – 514/671-0014 – Circ.: 10,800; Wed.; English & French

Saint-Lambert: South Shore/Greenfield Park Journal, 574 Victoria St., Saint-Lambert QC J4P 2J5 – 514/932-1454 – Wed.

Saint-Laurent: Nouvelles Saint-Laurent, #101, 685, boul Décarie, Saint-Laurent QC H4L 5G4 – Circ.: 25 650; Tue.; English & French

Sainte-Marie: Beauce Media, CP 400, Sainte-Marie QC G0S 2Y0 – 418/387-8000; Fax: 418/387-4495 – Tirage: 16 807; Lundi

Sainte-Marie: Beauce Week-End, 450, 2e av, Sainte-Marie QC G6E 1B6 – 418/387-6969 – Tirage: 15 200; Lundi

Sainte-Martine: Le Regional, 290, rue St. Joseph, Sainte-Martine QC J0S 1V0 – 514/427-2306; Fax: 514/427-0120 – Circ.: 13,500; Wed.; English & French – Directeur, Pierre Doré

St-Pascal: Le Placoteux, 491, rue d'Anjou, CP 1199, St-Pascal QC G0L 3Y0 – 418/492-2706; Fax: 418/492-9706 – Tirage: 16,623; Dimanche – Directeur-général, Raymond Freve

St-Sauveur-des-Monts: Le Journal de la Vallée, 43, rue Filion, CP 2100, St-Sauveur-des-Monts QC J0R 1R0 – Tirage: 27 500; Jeudi

St-Siméon: Le Goéland, 127, boul Perron ouest, CP 250, St-Siméon QC G0C 3A0 – 418/534-2026 – Micheline Babin

Ste-Thérèse/Blainville: Courrier de Groulx, 189, rue Laval, Laval-des-Rapides QC H7N 3V8 – 514/667-4360; Fax: 514/667-9498 – Tirage: 34 816; Dimanche – Editeur & Rédacteur, Jacques Dion; Directrice de tirage, Lynn Fortin

Ste-Thérèse/Blainville: Le Nord Info, 53, rue St-Eustache, St-Eustache QC J7R 2L3 – 514/473-1700 – Tirage: 47 100; Dimanche

Sept-Îles: Le Nord-Est, 365, boul Laure, Sept-Îles QC G4R 1X2 – 418/962-4100; Fax: 418/962-0439 – Tirage: 12 305; Dimanche; aussi Le Nord-Est Plus (mercredi)

Sept-Îles: Le Port-Cartois, 8, boul des Iles, Sept-Îles QC G5B 2N1 – 418/766-5322; Fax: 418/766-5329 – Tirage: 3 600; Dimanche

Shawinigan: Hebdo du St-Maurice, CP 10, Shawinigan QC G9N 6T8 – 819/537-5111; Fax: 819/537-5471 – Dimanche; français – Rédacteur, Michel Matteau

Shawville: The Equity, PO Box 430, Shawville QC J0X 2Y0 – 819/647-2204; Fax: 819/647-2206 – Circ.: 4,523; Wed.; English & French – Publisher, Heather Dickson; Editor, Richard Wills

Sherbrooke: Entrée Libre, #317, 187, rue Laurier, Sherbrooke QC J1H 4Z4 – 819/821-2270 – Normand Gilbert

Sherbrooke: La Nouvelle de Sherbrooke, 716, rue Short, Sherbrooke QC J1H 2E8 – 819/566-8022; Fax: 819/563-1977 – Tirage: 43,500; Dimanche – Editrice, Cèline Maheu; Rédacteur, Richard Gendron

Sorel: Les 2 Rives, 77, rue George, Sorel QC J3P 1B9 – 514/742-9409 – Tirage: 28 000; Mardi

Sorel: Journal La Voix, 38, rue Augusta, Sorel QC J3P 1A3 – 514/743-8466; Fax: 514/742-8567 – Tirage: 27 850; Hebdomadaire, samedi – Editrice & directrice-générale, Johanne Berthiaume; Rédacteur, Marc Laprise

Stanstead Journal, 25A Dufferin St., CP 30, Stanstead QC J0B 3E0 – 819/876-7514; Fax: 819/876-7515; Email: journal@together.net; URL: http://www.tomifobia.com – Wed. – Greg Duncan; Ross Murray

Terrebonne: La Revue de Terrebonne, 231, rue Ste-Marie, Terrebonne QC J6W 3E4 – 514/964-4444; Fax: 514/471-1023 – Tirage: 39 850; Mardi – Editeur, Marie-France Despatis; Rédacteur, Gilles Bordonado

Thetford Mines: Le Courrier Frontenac, 541, boul Smith nord, CP 789, Thetford Mines QC G6G 5V3 – 418/338-5181; Fax: 418/338-5482 – Tirage: 19,530; Dimanche; aussi Le Flect du Lac Aylmer (mensuel) – Rédacteur, Carol Isabel

Trois-Pistoles: Le Courrier de Trois-Pistoles, CP 759, Trois-Pistoles QC G0L 4K0 – 418/851-3644 – Tirage: 8 901; Dimanche

Trois-Rivières: La Gazette Populaire, 952, rue Ste-Geneviève, Trois-Rivières QC G9A 3X6 – 819/375-4012 – Tirage: 51 000; Mensuel – Rédacteur, Martine Lévesque

Val-David: Ski-se-dit, 1280, rue Dion, CP 1080, Val-David QC J0T 2N0 – Mensuel

Val d'Or: Les Echos Abitibiens, CP 100, Val d'Or QC J9P 4P2 – 819/825-3755; Fax: 819/825-0361 – Tirage: 17 700; Mercredi; (Amos, Lasarre, Malartic, Matagami)

Valleyfield: Le St-François Journal, 55, rue Jacques-Cartier, Valleyfield QC J6T 4R4 – 514/371-6222; Fax: 514/371-7254 – Tirage: 30,000; Mardi – Rédacteur, Andre Pomerleau

Vaudreuil: 1ere Edition du Sud-Ouest, 123, rue Dumont, Vaudreuil QC J7V 1W9 – 514/455-7955; Fax: 514/455-1050 – Circ.: 34 982; Sat.; English & French

Vaudreuil-Dorion: L'Etoile de l'Outaouais St-Laurent, 123, rue Dumont, Vaudreuil-Dorion QC J7V 1W9 – 514/455-6111; Fax: 514/455-0596 – Tirage: 34 243; Mercredi

Victoriaville: La Nouvelle, CP 130, Victoriaville QC G6P 3Z4 – 819/752-6718; Fax: 819/758-2759 – Tirage: 38 000; Dimanche

Ville-Marie: Le Journal Témiscamien, CP 219, Ville-Marie QC J0Z 3W0 – 819/629-2618 – Tirage: 8 500; Mercredi

Ville-Marie: Le Reflet, Le Reflet Témiscamein inc., CP 877, Ville-Marie QC J0Z 3W0 – 819/622-1313; Fax: 819/622-1333 – Tirage: 8,500; Mardi – Rédacteur en chef, Monic Ray

Westmount Examiner, 210 Victoria Ave., Westmount QC H3Z 2M4 – 514/932-3157; Fax: 514/932-5700 – Thur.

Windsor: L'Etincelle, 193, rue St-Georges, Windsor QC J1S 1J7 – 819/845-2705; Fax: 819/845-5520 – Mardi

## Saskatchewan Daily Newspapers

### LLOYDMINSTER:

Lloydminster Daily Times, 4828 - 44th St., Lloydminster SK S9V 0G8 – 306/825-5522; Fax: 306/825-3207; Email: times@bordercity.com – Editor, Timm D. Schaffer

### MOOSE JAW:

Times-Herald, Hollinger Inc., 44 Fairford St. West, Moose Jaw SK S6H 6E4 – 306/692-6441; Fax: 306/692-2101; Email: moose.jaw.times@sasknet.sk.ca – Circ.: 10,261; Evening – Publisher, A.B. Calvert; Editor, Carl DeGurse; Circulation Manager, Kathy Sterzuk

**PRINCE ALBERT:**

Daily Herald, Hollinger Inc., 30 - 10th St. East, Prince Albert SK S6V 5R9 – 306/764-4276; Fax: 306/763-3331; Email: pa.dailyherald@sk.sympatico.ca – Circ.: 10,036; Evening – Publisher & General Manager, Robert W. Gibb

**REGINA:**

The Leader-Post, 1964 Park St., Regina SK S4P 3G4 – 306/565-8211; Fax: 306/565-8350 – Circ.: 67,958; Afternoon – Publisher, Robert Hughes; Editor, Bob Hughes

**SASKATOON:**

Star-Phoenix, 204 - 5th Ave. North, Saskatoon SK S7K 2P1 – 306/664-8340; Fax: 306/664-8208 – Circ.: 58,866 Mon.-Thur., 76,154 Fri., 65,594 Sat.; Morning – Publisher, Lyle Sinkewicz; Editor, Steve K. Gibb

## Other Newspapers in Saskatchewan

Assiniboia Times, PO Box 910, Assiniboia SK S0H 0B0 – 306/642-5901; Fax: 306/642-4519; Email: assiniboia.times@sk.sympatico.ca – Mon.; also Assiniboia Today – Glen Hall; Linda Hall

Biggar Independent, PO Box 40, Biggar SK S0K 0M0 – 306/948-3344 – Mon.

Broadview: Broadview Express, PO Box 189, Grenfell SK S0G 2B0 – 306/697-2722; Fax: 306/697-2689 – Tue.

Canora Courier, PO Box 746, Canora SK S0A 0L0 – 306/563-5131; Fax: 306/563-6144 – Circ.: 2,240; Wed.

Carlyle Observer, PO Box 160, Carlyle SK S0C 0R0 – 306/453-2525; Fax: 306/453-2938; also The Prairie Progress(Wed.) – Tue.

Carnduff Gazette-Post News, PO Box 220, Carnduff SK S0C 0S0 – 306/482-3252; Fax: 306/482-3373 – Wed.

Coronach: Triangle News, PO Box 689, Coronach SK S0H 0Z0 – 306/267-3381 – Wed.

Craik Weekly News, PO Box 360, Craik SK S0G 0V0 – 306/734-2313 – Wed.

Creighton: The Gold Belt Gazette, PO Box 900, Creighton SK S0P 0A0 – 306/688-3999; Fax: 306/688-3919 – Wed.

Cut Knife: Highway 40 Courier, PO Box 400, Cut Knife SK S0M 0N0 – 306/398-4901; Fax: 306/398-4909 – Circ.: 700; Wed. – Carla Schwindt; Todd Schwindt

Davidson Leader, PO Box 786, Davidson SK S0G 1A0 – 306/567-2047; Fax: 306/567-2900; Email: lmt@sk.sympatico.ca – Circ.: 1,750; Mon. – Publisher, Lyle Emmons

Esterhazy Potashville Miner-Journal, PO Box 1000, Esterhazy SK S0A 0X0 – 306/745-6669; Fax: 306/745-2699 – Circ.: 1,700; Wed. – Publisher & Editor, Robert Koskie

Estevan Mercury, PO Box 730, Estevan SK S4A 2A6 – 306/634-2654; Fax: 306/634-3934; Email: mercury@sk.sympatico.ca – Wed.

Estevan This Week, 1330 - 4th St., Estevan SK S4A 0T6 – 306/634-6088; Fax: 306/634-4964 – Sat. – Publisher, Andrea Heath; Editor, P. Glenn Froh

Estevan: The Southeast Trader Express, 814 - 4th St., PO Box 730, Estevan SK S4A 2A6 – 306/634-2654; Fax: 306/634-3934; Email: mercury@sk.sympatico.ca – Circ.: 11,484; Mon. – Publisher, Peter Ng; Editor, Jonas Weinraueh

Eston: The Press Review, PO Box 787, Eston SK S0L 1A0 – 306/962-3221; Fax: 306/962-4445 – Tue. – Publisher, Verna Thompson

Foam Lake Review, PO Box 550, Foam Lake SK S0A 1A0 – 306/272-3262; Fax: 306/272-4521 – Mon. – Publisher, Bob Johnson

Fort Qu'Appelle Times, PO Box 940, Fort Qu'Appelle SK S0G 1S0 – 306/332-5526 – Tue.

Gravelbourg: Tribune, PO Box 1017, Gravelbourg SK S0H 1X0 – 306/648-3479; Fax: 306/648-2520; Email: Gravelbourgtribune@awnet.net – Circ.: 1,552; Mon.; English & French – Publisher, Paul Boisvert; Editor, Lindsay Mitchell

Grenfell Sun, PO Box 189, Grenfell SK S0G 2B0 – 306/697-2722; Fax: 306/697-2689 – Tue.

Gull Lake Advance, PO Box 628, Gull Lake SK S0N 1A0 – 306/672-3373 – Tue.

Hafford: The Riverbend Review, PO Box 1029, North Battleford SK S9A 3E6 – 306/445-7261; Fax: 306/445-3223; Email: battlefords.publishing@sk.sympatico.ca – Wed.

Herbert Herald, PO Box 399, Herbert SK S0H 2A0 – 306/784-2422; Fax: 306/784-3246 – Circ.: 1,700; Tue. – Publisher & Editor, Rhonda Ens

Hudson Bay Post-Review, PO Box 10, Hudson Bay SK S0E 0Y0 – 306/865-2771; Fax: 306/865-2340 – Circ.: 1,800; Tue. – Publisher, Bob Gilroy; Editor, Bruce Paproske

Humboldt Journal, PO Box 970, Humboldt SK S0K 2A0 – 306/682-2561; Fax: 306/682-3322 – Circ.: 3,865; Mon. & Wed; also, Humboldt Trader Regional (Mon.) – Publisher, Chad Charbonneau; Editor, Sharon Domotor

Indian Head-Wolseley News, PO Box 70, Indian Head SK S0G 2K0 – 306/695-3565 – Tue.

The Ituna News, PO Box 413, Ituna SK S0A 1N0 – 306/795-2412; Fax: 306/795-3621 – Circ.: 1,033; Mon. – Editor, Susan Antonishyn

Kamsack Times, PO Box 746, Canora SK S0A 0L0 – 306/563-5131; Fax: 306/563-6144 – Circ.: 1,700; Thur.

Kelvington Radio, PO Box 100, Wadena SK S0A 4J0 – 306/338-2231 – Circ.: 1,395; Weds. – Publisher & Editor, James R. Headington

Kerrobert Citizen, PO Box 1150, Kindersley SK S0L 1S0 – 306/463-4611; Fax: 306/463-6505 – Wed.

Kindersley Clarion, PO Box 1150, Kindersley SK S0L 1S0 – 306/463-4611; Fax: 306/463-6505 – Wed.

Kindersley: West Central Crossroads, PO Box 1150, Kindersley SK S0L 1S0 – 306/463-4611; Fax: 306/463-6505 – Circ.: 17,058; Wed.

Kinistino: Birch Hills Post Gazette, PO Box 340, Kinistino SK S0J 1H0 – 306/864-2266; Fax: 306/752-5358 – Wed.

Kipling Citizen, PO Box 329, Kipling SK S0J 2S0 – 306/736-2535; Fax: 306/736-8445 – Sun.

La Ronge: The Northerner, PO Box 1350, La Ronge SK S0J 1L0 – 306/425-3344; Fax: 306/425-2827; Email: northerner@rongenet.sk.ca – Weekly – Publishers & Editor, Scott Boyes

Langenburg: The Four-Town Journal, PO Box 68, Langenburg SK S0A 2A0 – 306/743-2617; Fax: 306/743-2299 – Circ.: 1,966; Wed. – Publisher & Editor, Bill Johnston

Lanigan Advisor, PO Box 1029, Lanigan SK S0K 2M0 – 306/365-2010; Fax: 306/365-3388 – Mon.

Lloydminster: CCA Rodeo News, Canadian Cowboys Association, PO Box 1877, Lloydminster SK S9V 1N4 – 306/825-7116; Fax: 306/825-7762; Email: rodeo@sk.sympatico.ca – Circ.: 2,000; 10 times a year – Editor, Rhonda Phipps

Lumsden: Waterfront Press, PO Box 507, Lumsden SK S0G 3C0 – 306/731-3143; Fax: 306/731-2277; Email: watpress@eagle.wbm.ca – Circ.: 1,602; Thur. – Co-Publisher, Lucien Chouinard; Co-Publisher, Jacqueline Chouinard

Macklin Mirror, PO Box 100, Macklin SK S0L 2C0 – 306/753-2424; Fax: 306/753-2424 – Wed.

Maidstone Mirror, PO Box 308, Maidstone SK S0M 1M0 – 306/893-2251; Fax: 306/893-4707; Email: battlefords.publishing@sk.sympatico.ca – Thur.

Maple Creek News, PO Box 1360, Maple Creek SK S0N 1N0 – 306/662-2133; Fax: 306/662-3092 – Tue.

Meadow Lake Progress, 311 Centre St., Meadow Lake SK S9X 1L7 – 306/236-5265; Fax: 306/236-3130; Email: meadow.lake.progress@sk.sympatico.ca – Circ.: 4,500; Tue. – Publisher, Al Guthro; Editor, Dan McPherson

Meadow Lake: Northern Pride, 205A - 3rd Ave. East, Meadow Lake SK S9X 1L7 – 306/236-5353; Fax: 306/236-5962 – Mon. – Publisher, Terry Villeneuve

Melfort Journal, Phillips Publishers Ltd., PO Box 1300, Melfort SK S0E 1A0 – 306/752-5737; Fax: 306/752-5358; supplement – Circ.: 4,215; Tue. – Editor, Ron Phillips

Melville Advance, PO Box 1420, Melville SK S0A 2P0 – 306/728-5448; Fax: 306/728-4004 – Circ.: 4,000; Wed. – Publisher, Mark Orosz; Editor, Lin Orosz

Moose Jaw This Week, 44 Fairford St. West, Moose Jaw SK S6H 6E4 – 306/692-2325; Fax: 306/674-1216 – Tue. – Publisher, A.B. Calvert

Moosomin World-Spectator, PO Box 250, Moosomin SK S0G 3N0 – 306/435-2445; Fax: 306/435-3969; Email: talk2us@world-spectator.com; URL: http://www.world-spectator.com – Circ.: 3,350; Mon. – Co-Publisher, Bruce Penton; Co-Publisher, Barb Penton; Editor, Kevin Weedmark

The Naicam News, PO Box 507, Watson SK S0K 4V0 – 306/287-4388; Fax: 306/287-3308 – Circ.: 540; Mon. – Publisher, Debbie Schueller; Editor, Linda Griffith

Nipawin Journal, PO Box 2014, Nipawin SK S0E 1E0 – 306/862-4618; Fax: 306/862-4566 – Circ.: 4,700; Wed. – Publisher, Donna Bohnen; Editor, Dennis Hegland

Nipawin N.E. Region Community Booster, PO Box 2014, Nipawin SK S0E 1E0 – 306/862-4618; Fax: 306/862-4566 – Circ.: 18,750; Every other Mon. – Publisher & Editor, Ken Nelson

Nokomis: Last Mountain Times, PO Box 340, Nokomis SK S0G 3R0 – 306/528-2020; Fax: 306/528-2090; Email: lmt@sk.sympatico.ca – Circ.: 1,800; Tue.; also The Market Connection (6,410) – Publisher, Lyle Emmons

Norquay North Star, PO Box 746, Canora SK S0A 0L0 – 306/563-5131; Fax: 306/563-6144 – Circ.: 841; Thur.

North Battleford News-Optimist, Battleford Publishing Ltd., PO Box 1029, North Battleford SK S9A 3E6 – 306/445-7261; Fax: 306/445-3223 – Circ.: 3,500; Wed. – Publisher, Steven Dills; Editor, Lorne Cooper

North Battleford: Regional Optimist/Advertiser-Post, PO Box 1029, North Battleford SK S9A 3E6 – 306/445-7261; Fax: 306/445-3223 – Circ.: 20,000; Mon.; also: The Telegraph (Fri., circ. 3,444); Northwest Neighbours, Turtleford (Wed., circ. 693) – Publisher, Steven Dills; Editor, Lorne Cooper

North Battleford: The Telegraph, Battleford Publishing Ltd., PO Box 1029, North Battleford SK S9A 3E6 – 306/445-7261; Fax: 306/445-3223 – Circ.: 3,500; Fri. – Publisher, Steven Dills; Editor, Lorne Cooper

Outlook: The Outlook, PO Box 399, Outlook SK S0L 2N0 – 306/867-8262; Fax: 306/867-9556; Email: the_outlook@awnet.net – Circ.: 2,431; Mon. – Publisher, Roland Jenson; Editor, Debra Murphy; Circulation Manager, Denise Jenson

Oxbow Herald, PO Box 420, Oxbow SK S0C 2B0 – 306/483-2323; Fax: 306/483-5258 – Circ.: 1,402; Tue. – Publisher & Editor, J.K. Pedlar

Pierceland: The Beaver River Banner, General Delivery, Pierceland SK S0M 2K0 – 306/839-4496; Fax: 306/839-2306; Email: beav@sk.sympatico.ca – Circ.: 1,820; Mon. – Publisher, Lillian Mein

Preeceville Progress, PO Box 746, Canora SK S0A 0L0 – 306/563-5131; Fax: 306/563-6144 – Circ.: 1,636; Thur.

Radville Star, PO Box 370, Radville SK S0C 2G0 – 306/869-2202 – Thur.

Redvers: The Optimist, PO Box 490, Redvers SK S0C 2H0 – 306/452-3363 – Tue.

Regina: Journal L'eau vive, 2604, rue Central, Regina SK S4N 2N9 – 306/347-0481; Fax: 306/565-3450; Email: leauvive@dlcwest.com – Jeudi; français – Directeur-général, Francis Potié

Regina Sun, 1964 Park St., PO Box 2020, Regina SK S4P 3G4 – 306/565-8250; Fax: 306/565-8350 – Circ.: 67,318 Wed.; 68,212 Sun., city, 20,528 Sun., rural; Wed., Sun.

Rosetown Eagle, PO Box 130, Rosetown SK S0L 2V0 – 306/882-4202; Fax: 306/882-4204 – Circ.: 2,638; Mon. – Publisher & Editor, Dan Page

Rosthern: Saskatchewan Valley News, PO Box 10, Rosthern SK S0K 3R0 – 306/232-4865 – Thur.

Saskatoon Free Press, 2270 Northridge Dr., Saskatoon SK S7; 1B9 – 306/978-3733 – Thur., Sun.

Saskatoon Sun, 204 - 5th Ave., North, Saskatoon SK S7K 2P1 – 306/664-8340 – Sun.

Shaunavon Standard, PO Box 729, Shaunavon SK S0N 2M0 – 306/297-4144; Fax: 306/297-3357; Email: standard@sk.sympatico.ca – Tue.

Shellbrook Chronicle, PO Box 10, Shellbrook SK S0J 2E0 – 306/747-2442; Fax: 306/747-3000 – Mon.; also Cross Country Connection

Shellbrook: Spiritwood Herald, PO Box 10, Shellbrook SK S0J 2E0 – 306/747-2442; Fax: 306/747-3000 – Mon.

Swift Current: The City Sun, PO Box 1330, Swift Current SK S9H 3Y4 – 306/773-9321; Fax: 306/773-9136; Email: swbooster@sk.sympatico.ca – Circ.: 19,685; Wed. – Publisher, Bill Mann; Editor, Scott Anderson

Swift Current: The Southwest Booster, PO Box 1330, Swift Current SK S9H 3X4 – 306/773-9321; Fax: 306/773-9136; Email: swbooster@sk.sympatico.ca – Circ.: 19,000; Sat. – Publisher, Bill Mann; Editor, Scott Anderson

Tisdale Recorder, PO Box 1660, Tisdale SK S0E 1T0 – 306/873-4515; Fax: 306/873-4712 – Circ.: 2,200; Mon. – Publisher, Larry Mitchell; Editor, Peggy Todd

Unity: The Northwest Herald, 304 Main St., PO Box 309, Unity SK S0K 4L0 – 306/228-2267; Fax: 306/228-2767 – Mon.

Wadena News, PO Box 100, Wadena SK S0A 4J0 – 306/338-2231 – Circ.: 3,500; Wed. – Publisher & Editor, James R. Headington

Wakaw Recorder, PO Box 9, Wakaw SK S0K 4P0 – 306/233-4325; Fax: 306/233-4386 – Circ.: 1,900; Wed. – Editor, D. Biccum

Watrous Manitou, PO Box 100, Watrous SK S0K 4T0 – 306/946-3343 – Mon.

Watson Witness, PO Box 746, Canora SK S0A 0L0 – 306/287-3245; Fax: 306/287-4333 – Circ.: 600; Wed.

Weyburn Review, PO Box 400, Weyburn SK S4H 2K4 – 306/842-7487; Fax: 306/842-0282 – Circ.: 5,800; Wed.; also Weyburn Booster (Mon.) – Publisher, Darryl Ward; Editor-in-chief, Patricia Ward

Weyburn This Week, 19 - 11th St., Weyburn SK S4H 1J1 – 306/842-3900; Fax: 306/842-2515 – Circ.: 9,819; Sat. & Tue. – Publisher, Andrea L. Heath; Editor, P. Glenn Froh; Circulation Manager, Margaret Medwed

Whitewood Herald, 3rd St., PO Box 160, Whitewood SK S0G 5C0 – 306/735-2230 – Mon.

Wilkie Press, PO Box 309, Unity SK S0K 4L0 – 306/228-2267; Fax: 306/228-2767 – Mon.

The Wolseley Bulletin, PO Box 89, Wolseley SK S0G 5H0 – 306/698-2271; Fax: 306/698-2808 – Circ.: 800; Fri. (50 times a year) – Publisher, Rick Dahlman; Editor, Eleanor Dahlman

Wynyard Advance/Gazette, PO Box 10, Wynyard SK S0A 4T0 – 306/554-2224; Fax: 306/554-3226 – Mon. – Ray Lachambre

Yorkton: The News, 29 - 2nd Ave. North, Yorkton SK S3N 1G1 – 306/783-7355; Fax: 306/783-9138; Email: the.news@sk.sympatico.ca – Circ.: 31,188; Mon. – Ken Chyz

Yorkton This Week & Enterprise, Hollinger Inc., PO Box 1300, Yorkton SK S3N 2X3 – 306/782-2465; Fax: 306/786-1898 – Circ.: 7,941; Wed. & Sat; also Marketplace (Fri., circ. 39,900) – Editor, Girard Hengen

## Yukon Daily Newspapers

**WHITEHORSE:**

The Whitehorse Star, 2149 - 2nd Ave., Whitehorse YT Y1A 1C5 – 867/668-2063; Fax: 867/668-7130 – Circ.: 5,000; Daily, weekdays – Publisher, Bob Erlam

## Other Newspapers in Yukon

Whitehorse: L'Aurore Boréale, PO Box 5205, Whitehorse YT Y1A 4Z1 – 867/667-2931; Fax: 867/668-3511; Email: aureb@yknet.yk.ca – Tirage: 1,000; Mensuel; français

Whitehorse: Yukon News, 211 Wood St., Whitehorse YT Y1A 2E4 – 867/667-6285; Fax: 867/668-3755; Email: steverob@yknet.yk.ca; URL: http://www.yukonweb.com/community/yukon-news – Circ.: 7,447 Wed., 8,893 Fri. – Publisher, Doug Bell

# MAGAZINE INDEX

# MAGAZINES

## BUSINESS PUBLICATIONS

### ADVERTISING, MARKETING, SALES

Adnews, #212, 80 Park Lawn Rd., Etobicoke ON M8Y 3H8 – 416/252-9400; Fax: 416/252-8002; Email: adnews@io.org; URL: http://www.adnews.com – Weekly – Publisher, Rob Bale; Managing Editor, Mike Deibert

Canadian Advertising Rates & Data (Published by Maclean Hunter Publishing), 777 Bay St., Toronto ON M5W 1A7 – 416/596-2790; Fax: 416/596-5158; Email: bmason@inforamp.net; URL: http://www.cardmedia.com – Circ.: 2,197; Monthly – Publisher, Gloria Gallagher; Editor, Beth Mason; Circulation Manager, Bruce Murray

Canadian Direct Marketing News, c/o Lloydmedia Inc., #301, 1200 Markham Rd., Scarborough ON M1H 3C3 – 416/439-4083; Fax: 416/439-4086; Email: lloydmedia@compuserve.com; URL: http://www.dmlinks.com – Circ.: 7,000; Monthly, plus annual directory of suppliers – Publisher, Stephen P. Lloyd

The Chronicle of Healthcare Marketing (Published by Chronicle Information Resources Ltd.), 1270 The Queensway, Toronto ON M8Z 1S3 – 416/503-3957; Fax: 416/503-4118; Email: health@chronicle.org – Circ.: 1,884; 6 times a year – Publisher, Mitchell Shannon; Editorial Director, R. Allan Ryan

Contact, Canadian Professional Sales Assn., #310, 145 Wellington St. West, Toronto ON M5J 1H8 – 416/408-2685; Fax: 416/408-2684; URL: http://www.cpsa.com – Circ.: 35,000; 6 times a year – Director, Sharon Armstrong; Consulting Editor, David Napier

Ethnic Media & Markets (Published by Maclean Hunter Publishing), 777 Bay St., Toronto ON M5W 1A7 – 416/596-5893; Fax: 416/596-5158; Email: bmason@mhpublishing.com – 2 times a year – Group Publisher, Gloria Gallagher, 416/596-5913

Info Presse Communications (Published by Editions Info Presse inc.), 4316, boul St-Laurent, Montréal QC H2W 1Z3 – 514/842-5873; Fax: 514/842-2422; Email: pubipc@infopresse.com; redaipc@

infopresse.com; URL: http://www.infopresse.com – 10 fois par an – Editeur, Bruno Gautier; Rédacteur, Romain Bédard

Marketing (Published by Maclean Hunter Publishing), 777 Bay St., Toronto ON M5W 1A7 – 416/596-5835; Fax: 416/593-3170; Email: marketmh@aol.com; Telex: 06-219547; URL: http://www.marketingmag.ca – Circ.: 14,200; Weekly – Publisher, Cameron Gardner; Editor, Stan Sutter; Circulation Manager, Victoria Newland

The Media Book, #1511, 2 Carlton St., Toronto ON M5B 1J3 – 416/599-3737; Fax: 416/599-5730; Email: staff@mediastop.net; URL: http://www.mediastop.com – Circ.: 27,000; 2 times a year – Publisher, Tom Monson, Email: tjm@meadiastop.net; Editor, Janet Forbes, Email: jkforbes@meadiastop.net

The National List of Advertisers (Published by Maclean Hunter Publishing), 777 Bay St., Toronto ON M5W 1A7 – 416/596-2790; Fax: 416/596-5158 – Circ.: 3,000; Annually, Dec. – Publisher, Gloria Gallagher; Editor, Beth Mason; Circulation Manager, Bruce Murray

Publication Profiles (Published by Maclean Hunter Publishing), 777 Bay St., Toronto ON M5W 1A7 – 416/596-2790; Fax: 416/596-5158; Email: bmason@inforamp.net – Circ.: 4,400; Annually, Sept. – Publisher, Gloria Gallagher; Publisher, Beth Mason; Circulation Manager, Bruce Murray

Sales Promotion (Published by Clifford Elliott & Associates Ltd.), 3228 South Service Rd., 2nd Fl., Burlington ON L7N 3H8 – 905/634-2100; Fax: 905/634-2338; Email: mb@industrialsourcebook.com; URL: http://www.industrialsourcebook.com – Circ.: 20,600; 6 times a year – Publisher, Mark Barber; Editorial Director, Jackie Roth

Signals, Northworthy Communications, 39 Bedford Park Ave., Richmond Hill ON L4C 2N9 – 905/508-7374; Fax: 905/508-7376 – Circ.: 7,200; 11 times a year – Publisher, Steve Brown; Editor, Kevin Press

Signs Canada (Published by Kenilworth Publishing), #201, 27 West Beaver Creek, Richmond Hill ON L4B 1M8 – 905/771-7333; Fax: 905/771-7336; Email: sales@kenilworth.com – Publisher, Jim Davidson

Strategy (Published by Brunico Communications), #500, 366 Adelaide St. West, Toronto ON M5V 1R9 – 416/408-2300; Fax: 416/408-0870; URL: http://www.bulldog.ca/burnico/ – Circ.: 16,000; 25 times a year – President & Executive Publisher, James Shenkman; Editor, Mark Smyka

**ARCHITECTURE**

ARQ/La Revue d'Architecture, 1463, rue Préfontaine, Montréal QC H1W 2N6 – 514/523-6832, 4900 – Circ.: 5,000; 6 times a year; English & French

Award Magazine (Published by Canada Wide Magazines & Communications Ltd.), 4180 Lougheed Hwy., 4th Fl., Burnaby BC V5C 6A7 – 604/299-7311; Fax: 604/299-9188 – Circ.: 7,500; 6 times a year – Publisher, Peter Legge; Editor, Janet Collins; Circulation Manager, Mark Weeks

Buildcore Product Source, Construction Market Data Canada Inc., 280 Yorkdale Blvd., North York ON M2J 4Z6 – 416/494-4990; Fax: 416/756-2767; Email: info@buildcore.com; URL: http://www.buildcore.com – Circ.: 8,738; Annually – Publisher, Susan Steele; Editor, Nigel Heseltine

Canadian Architect (Published by Southam Magazine Group), 1450 Don Mills Rd., Don Mills ON M3B 2X7 – 416/445-6641; Fax: 416/442-2077 – Circ.: 10,000; Monthly – Publisher, Gord Carley; Managing Editor, Bronwen Ledger

Construction Canada, 316 Adelaide St. West, Toronto ON M5V 1R1 – 416/977-8104; Fax: 416/598-0658 – Circ.: 6,671; 6 times a year – Publisher & Editor, Jim Tobros

Perspectives (Published by Omnicom Publications Inc.), #300, 512 King St. East, Toronto ON M5A 1M1 – 416/955-1550; Fax: 416/955-1391 – Circ.: 6,000; 4 times a year; also Profiles (annually) – Publisher, Richard Soren; Editor, Gordon Grice

Sweet's Canadian Construction Catalogue File, McGraw-Hill Information Systems Company of Canada Limited, 270 Yorkland Blvd., North York ON M2J 1R8 – 416/496-3100; Fax: 416/496-3123 – Circ.: 6,660; Annually – Director, Finance & Admin., Eve L. Brown

**ARTS, ART & ANTIQUES**

Canadian Gift and Collectibles Retailer (Published by Trajan Publishing Corp.), #202, 103 Lakeshore Rd., St Catharines ON L2N 2T6 – 905/646-7744; Fax: 905/646-0995; Email: newsroom@trajan.com; URL: http://www.trajan.com/trajan – Circ.: 8,000; 6 times a year – Publisher, Paul Fiocca; Editor, Bret Evans; Circulation Manager, Tammy Kruck

**AUTOMOBILE, CYCLE, & AUTOMOTIVE ACCESSORIES**

Aftermarket Canada, 2050 Speers Rd., Unit 1, Oakville ON L6L 2X8 – 905/847-0277; Fax: 905/847-7752 – Circ.: 11,000; Monthly – President/Publisher, Shirley G. Brown; Editor, Steve Manning

L'Automobile, Southam Business Communications, #410, 3300, Place Côte Vertu, Saint-Laurent QC H4R 2B7 – 514/339-1399; Fax: 514/339-1396; URL: http://www.southam.com/b1-1-1.html – Tirage: 11,804; 6 fois par an; français – Rédacteur, Marc Beauchamp

Automotive Parts & Technology, Cardiff Communications Ltd., 130 Belfield Rd., Etobicoke ON M9W 1G1 – 416/614-0955; Fax: 416/614-2781; Email: apt@onramp.ca – Circ.: 30,490; 9 times a year – Publisher, Bill James; Editor, Allan Janssen

Automotive Retailer, #1, 8980 Fraserwood Ct., Burnaby BC V5J 5H7 – 604/432-7987; Fax: 604/432-1756; Email: rromero@axionet.com – Circ.: 10,000; 6 times a year – Publisher & Editor, Reg Romero; Circulation Manager, Angela Cook

Automotive Service Data Book (Published by Southam Magazine Group), 1450 Don Mills Rd., Don Mills ON M3B 2X7 – 416/445-6641; Fax: 416/442-2261 – Annually, Dec. – Editor, David Booth

Bodyshop (Published by Southam Magazine Group), 1450 Don Mills Rd., Don Mills ON M3B 2X7 – 416/445-6641; Fax: 416/442-2213; Email: bharper@southam.ca; URL: http://www.southam.com/b1-1-2.html – Circ.: 12,863; 6 times a year – Group Publisher, Paul Wilson; Editor, Brian Harper

Canadian Automotive Fleet, Bobit Publishing, #207, 95 Barber Greene Rd., Don Mills ON M3C 3E9 – 416/383-0302; Fax: 416/383-0313 – Circ.: 12,350; 6 times a year – Publisher, Jake McLaughlin; Managing Editor, Kevin Sheehy

Canadian Auto World (Published by Helpard Publishing Inc.), #300, 1200 Markham Rd., Scarborough ON M1H 3C3 – 416/438-7777; Fax: 416/438-5333 – Circ.: 5,700; 12 times a year – Publisher, Lynn R. Helpard; Executive Editor, Joe Knycha; Circulation Manager, Susan Brown

Corporate Fleet Management (Published by Maclean Hunter Publishing), 777 Bay St., Toronto ON M5W 1A7 – 416/596-5086, 595-5704; Fax: 416/593-3201 – 4 times a year – Publisher, Tim Dimopoulos

Jobber News (Published by Southam Magazine Group), 1450 Don Mills Rd., Don Mills ON M3B 2X7 – 416/445-6641; Fax: 416/442-2077; URL: http://www.southam.com/b1-1-3.html – Circ.: 11,000; Monthly – Group Publisher, Paul D. Wilson

Motor Fleet Management (Published by Toro Communications), #209B, 1450 Midland Ave., Scarborough ON M1P 4Z8 – 416/757-6080; Fax: 416/757-6288 – Circ.: 12,300 – Publisher & Editor, Dan Radulescu

Octane (Published by Maclean Hunter Publishing Ltd.), #2450, 101 - 6th Ave. SW, Calgary AB T2P 3P4 – 403/266-8700; Fax: 403/266-6634; Email: oilweek@cadvision.com – Circ.: 6,863; 6 times a year – Publisher, Phil Boyd; Editor, Gordon Jaremko

Pickup 4X4 & SUV Review (Published by Baum Publications Ltd.), #201, 2323 Boundary Rd., Vancouver BC V5M 4V8 – 604/291-9900; Fax: 604/291-1906 – Circ.: 83,200; 4 times a year – Publisher, Engelbert Baum; Editor, Stan Sauerwein

La Revue le garagiste, Les Editions du Cerf inc., #270, 1555, boul Jean-Paul Vincent, Longueuil QC J4N 1L6 – 514/448-2220; Fax: 514/448-1041; Email: gargist@microtec.net – Tirage: 17,100; 10 fois par an – Editeur, Rémy L. Rousseau

Service Station & Garage Management (Published by Southam Magazine Group), 1450 Don Mills Rd., Don Mills ON M3B 2X7 – 416/445-6641; Fax: 416/442-2077; Email: hostmaster@southam.com; URL: http://www.southam.com/b1-1-4.html – Circ.: 25,000; Monthly – Publisher, Rob Wilkins; Editor, Gary Kenez

Speciality & Performance Magazine (Published by Southam Magazine Group), 1450 Don Mills Rd., Don Mills ON M3B 2X7 – 416/445-6641; Fax: 416/442-2213 – Circ.: 10,000; 4 times a year – Publisher, Robert Lauder; Editor, Andrew Ross

Taxi News, 38 Fairmount Cres., Toronto ON M4L 2H4 – 416/466-2328; Fax: 416/466-4220 – Circ.: 10,200; Monthly – Publisher, John Duffy; Editor, William McOuat; Circulation Manager, Barb Whitehurst

Thunder Bay Car & Truck News (Published by North Superior Publishing Inc.), 1145 Barton St., Thunder Bay ON P7B 5N3 – 807/623-2348; Fax: 807/623-7515; Email: nsuperior@norlink.net – Circ.: 30,000; 24 times a year – Publisher/Editor, Scott Sumner

Western Automotive Repair (Published by New Horizons West Ltd.), PO Box 64011, Winnipeg MB R2K 4K6 – 204/654-3573; Fax: 204/667-8922 – Circ.: 10,757; 6 times a year – Publisher, Ilan Moyle; Editor, Dan Proudley

Western Collision Repair (Published by New Horizons West Ltd.), PO Box 64011, Winnipeg MB R2K 4K6 – 204/654-3573; Fax: 204/667-8922 – Circ.: 5,781; 5 times a year – Publisher, Ilan Moyle; Editor, Dan Proudley

**AVIATION & AEROSPACE**

Airforce, c/o Airforce Productions Ltd., 100 Metcalfe St., PO Box 2460, Stn D, Ottawa ON K1P 5W6 – 613/992-2355; Fax: 613/995-2196; Email: vjohnson@airforce.ca; URL: http://www.airforce.ca – Circ.: 20,200; 4 times a year – Publisher, Bob Tracy; Editor, Vic Johnson

Airports Americas (Published by Baum Publications Ltd.), #201, 2323 Boundary Rd., Vancouver BC V5M 4V8 – 604/298-3004; Fax: 604/291-3966 – Circ.: 15,000; 4 times a year – Publisher, Heri R. Baum; Editor, Toni Dabbs

Atlantic Region Aviation Business Directory (Published by OP Publishing), #300, 780 Beatty St., Vancouver BC V6B 2N1 – 604/687-1581 – Annually – Publisher, Rex Armstead

Calgary & Area Airport Business Directory (Published by OP Publishing), #300, 780 Beatty St., Vancouver BC V6B 2N1 – 604/606-4644; Fax: 604/687-1925 – Annually – Publisher, Rex Armstead

Canadian Aviation & Aircraft for Sale, PO Box 4755, Hamilton ON L8H 7S7 – 800/567-5966 – 6 times a year – Publisher, Gerry Boyar

Canadian Flight, #1001, 75 Albert St., Ottawa ON K1P 5E7 – 613/565-0881; Email: editorial@copanational.org; URL: http://www.copanational.org – Circ.: 20,000; Monthly; includes: Canadian Homebuilt Aircraft News, Canadian Ultalight News, Executive Flight News, Seaplane News, Aircraft Maintenance Engineers News, Canadian

Plane Trade, Aviation Museum News – Publisher, Garth Wallace; Editor, Doris Ohlmann

Edmonton & Area Airport Business Directory (Published by OP Publishing), #300, 780 Beatty St., Vancouver BC V6B 2N1 – 604/606-4644; Fax: 604/687-1925 – Annually – Publisher, Rex Armstead

Helicopters (Published by Corvus Publishing Group), #320, 3115 - 12 St. NE, Calgary AB T2E 7J2 – 403/735-5000; Fax: 403/735-0537 – Circ.: 5,750; 4 times a year – Publisher/Editor, Paul J. Skinner

ICAO Journal, International Civil Aviation Organization, 999, rue University, Montréal QC H3C 5H7 – 514/954-8222; Fax: 514/954-6376; Telex: 05-24513 ICAO – Circ.: 66,758; 10 issues a year; English, French & Spanish Editions – Editor-in-chief, Eric MacBurnie

Mid-Canada & Area Airport Business Directory (Published by OP Publishing), #300, 780 Beatty St., Vancouver BC V6B 2N1 – 604/606-4644; Fax: 604/687-1925 – Annually – Publisher, Rex Armstead

Montréal & Area Aviation Business Directory (Published by OP Publishing), #300, 780 Beatty St., Vancouver BC V6B 2N1 – 604/606-4644; Fax: 604/687-1925 – Annually

Toronto & Area Aviation Business Directory (Published by OP Publishing), #300, 780 Beatty St., Vancouver BC V6B 2N1 – 604/606-4644; Fax: 604/687-1925 – Annually

Vancouver & Area Aviation Business Directory (Published by OP Publishing), #300, 780 Beatty St., Vancouver BC V6B 2N1 – 604/606-4644; Fax: 604/687-1925 – Annually

West Coast Aviator Magazine, PO Box 2065, Sidney BC V8L 3S3 – 604/656-7598; Fax: 604/655-4090 – Circ.: 20,000; 6 times a year – Publisher, Colleen Sinclair

Wings (Published by Corvus Publishing Group), #320, 3115 - 12 St. NE, Calgary AB T2E 7J2 – 403/735-5000; Fax: 403/735-0537 – Circ.: 11,000; 6 times a year – Publisher/Editor, Paul J. Skinner

#### BAKING & BAKERS' SUPPLIES

Bakers Journal (Published by Annex Publishing & Printing Inc.), 222 Argyle Ave., Delhi ON N4B 2Y2 – 905/271-1366; Fax: 905/271-6373; Email: bakersj@kjsgroup.com – Circ.: 7,021; 10 times a year – Publisher, David Douglas; Editor, Blair Adams; Circulation Manager, Florence Jacques

La Fournée (Published by Les Éditions du Monde alimentaire inc.), #102, 200, rue MacDonald, Saint-Jacques-sur-Richelieu QC J3B 8J6 – 514/349-0107; Fax: 514/349-6923; Email: ampaqce@cam.org – Tirage: 4 718; 4 fois par an; français – Directrice, Johanne Latour

#### BARBERS & BEAUTICIANS

Salon Beauté (Published by Salon Communications Inc.), #300, 411 Richmond St. East, Toronto ON M5A 3S5 – 416/869-3131; Fax: 416/869-3008; Email: salon@beautynet.com; URL: http://www.salonline.com – Tirage: 14,000; 8 fois par an – Rédactrice, Christine Daviault

Salon Magazine (Published by Salon Communications Inc.), #300, 411 Richmond St. East, Toronto ON M5A 3S5 – 416/869-3131; Fax: 416/869-3008; Email: salon@beautynet.com; URL: http://www.beautynet.com – Circ.: 28,000; 8 times a year; English & French editions – Publisher, Gregory Robins; Editor, Alison Wood; Circulation Manager, Keith Fulford

#### BOATING & YACHTING

Boating Business (Published by Formula Publications Ltd.), #4, 446 Speers Rd., Oakville ON L6K 3S7 – 905/842-6591; Fax: 905/842-6843 – 6 times a year – Publisher, Scott Robinson; Editor, Lizanne Madigan; Circulation Manager, Deadra Worth

Marina News, #211, 4 Cataraqui St., Kingston ON K7K 1Z7 – 613/547-6662; Fax: 613/547-6813 – Circ.: 700; 8 times a year – Editor, Michael Shaw

The Westcoast Mariner (Published by Westcoast Publishing Ltd), 1496 - 72nd Ave. West, Vancouver BC V6P 3C8 – 604/266-7433; Fax: 604/263-8620; Email: wcoast@wimsey.com – Circ.: 10,500; Monthly – Publisher, David Rahn; Editor, Rob Morris

#### BOOKS

Access, c/o Ontario Library Association, #303, 100 Lombard St., Toronto ON M5C 1M3 – 416/363-3388; Fax: 416/941-9581; Email: jgilbert@interlog.com; URL: http://www.OLA.ca.dyna.com – Circ.: 4,000; 3 times a year – Publisher, Jefferson Gilbert; Editor, Lawrence Moore

Canadian Author, Canadian Authors Association, Box 419, Campbellford ON K0L 1L0 – 705/653-0323; Fax: 705/653-0593; URL: http://www.islandnet.com/~caa/national – Circ.: 2,914; 4 times a year – Managing Editor, Welwyn Wilton Katz, 519/641-6768

Canadian Bookseller, Canadian Booksellers Association, 301 Donlands Ave., Toronto ON M4J 3R8 – 416/467-7883; Fax: 416/467-7886; Email: enquiries@cbabook.org; URL: http://www.cbabook.org – Circ.: 2,000; 10 times a year – Editor, Kim Laudrum

CM Magazine, Manitoba Library Association, #208, 100 Arthur St., Winnipeg MB R3B 1H3 – 204/943-4567; Fax: 204/942-1555; Email: camera@mbnet.mb.ca; URL: http://www.mbnet.mb.ca/cm/index.html – Circ.: 1,000; Weekly

Emergency Librarian, #101, 1001 West Broadway, Vancouver BC V6H 4E4 – 604/925-0266; Fax: 604/925-0566; Email: eml@rockland.com – Circ.: 10,000; 5 times a year – Editor, Ken Haycock; Editor, Karin Paul; Circulation Manager, Morganne Mohr

Feliciter, c/o Canadian Library Association, #602, 200 Elgin St., Ottawa ON K2P 1L5 – 613/232-9625, ext.321; Fax: 613/563-9895; Email: az057@freenet.carleton.ca; URL: http://www.cla.amlibs.ca – Circ.: 3,700; 10 times a year – Editor, Mary J. Moore

Quill & Quire, #210, 70 The Esplanade, Toronto ON M5E 1R2 – 416/360-0044; Fax: 416/955-0794; Email: quill@hookup.net – Circ.: 7,200; Monthly; supplement, Canadian Publishers' Directory (June & Dec.); ISSN: 0033-6491 – Publisher, Sharon McAuley; Editor, Scott Anderson

#### BROADCASTING

Broadcaster (Published by Southam Magazine Group), 1450 Don Mills Rd., Don Mills ON M3B 2X7 – 416/510-6835; Fax: 416/442-2213; Email: jbugailiskis@southam.ca; URL: http://www.southam.com/b1-2-1.html – Circ.: 8,000; 10 times a year – Publisher, James A. Cook; Editor, John Bugailiskis; Circulation Manager, Hasina Ahmed

Broadcast Technology & Media Production, 264 Queens Quay West, PO Box 803, Toronto ON M5J 1B5 – 416/260-9364; Fax: 416/260-9372; Email: btmp@goodmedia.com – Circ.: 7,000; 10 times a year, plus July/August Annual Buyers' Guide – Publisher, Doug Loney; Editor, Lee Rickwood

Cablecaster (Published by Southam Magazine Group), 1450 Don Mills Rd., Don Mills ON M3B 2X7 – 416/445-6641; Fax: 416/442-2213 – Circ.: 6,075; 8 times a year – Publisher, James A. Cook; Editor, Steve Pawlett

Cable Communications Magazine, 57 Peachwood Ct., Kitchener ON N2B 1S7 – 519/744-4111; Fax: 519/744-1261 – Circ.: 6,900; 6 times a year – Publisher/Editor, Udo Salwsky

Canada on Location (Published by Brunico Communications), #500, 366 Adelaide St. West, Toronto ON M5V 1R9 – 416/408-2300; Fax: 416/408-0870 – Circ.: 3,523; 2 times a year – Publisher, James Shenkman; Editor, Mary Maddever

Playback (Published by Brunico Communications), #500, 366 Adelaide St. West, Toronto ON M5V 1R9 – 416/408-2300; Fax: 416/408-0870 – Circ.: 10,000; 25 times a year; also Playback International (2 times a year; circ. 2,162) – Publisher, James Shenkman

#### BUILDING & CONSTRUCTION

Alberta Construction, Naylor Communications, 100 Sutherland Ave., Winnipeg MB R2W 3C7 – 204/947-0222; Fax: 204/947-2047; Email: jconnoll@axionet.com – 4 times a year; also Alberta Constuction Association Membership Roster & Buyers' Guide (annual, May) – Editor, Janis Connolly

Atlantic Construction Journal (Published by NCC Specialty Publications), #107, 900 Windmill Rd., Dartmouth NS B3B 1P7 – 902/468-8027; Fax: 902/468-2425 – 4 times a year – Publisher, Reg Priest; Editor, Ken Partridge

B.S.D.A. Newsmagazine, Building Supply Dealers Assn. of BC, #2, 19299 - 94th Ave., Surrey BC V4N 4E6 – 604/513-2205; Fax: 604/513-2206 – 4 times a year – Managing Editor, George R. Tracy

Building & Construction Trades Today, c/o 29 Bernard Ave., Toronto ON M5R 1R3 – 416/944-1217; Fax: 416/944-0133; Email: hize@compuserve.com – Circ.: 4,000; 8 times a year – Publisher, Alan Heisey; Editor, Laura Kosterski; Circulation Manager, Alexandra Irving

Building Magazine (Published by Crailer Communications), 360 Dupont St., Toronto ON M5R 1V9 – 416/966-9944; Fax: 416/966-9946; Email: crailer@interlog.com – Circ.: 14,500; 6 times a year – Publisher, Sheri Craig; Editor, John Fennell; Circulation Manager, Beata Olechnowicz

Canadian Construction Service & Supply Directory - Alberta (Published by June Warren Publishing Ltd.), 9915 - 56 Ave., Edmonton AB T6E 5L7 – 403/944-9333; Fax: 403/944-9500 – Circ.: 16,112; Annually – Publisher, Colin Eicher

Canadian Homebuilder & Renovation Contractor, #403, 1230 Quayside Dr., New Westminster BC V3M 6H1 – 604/522-6033 – General Manager, Mark Bowen

Canadian Masonry Contractor (Published by Perks Publications Ltd.), #7A, 1735 Bayly St., Pickering ON L1W 3G7 – 905/831-4711 – 3 times a year – E. Brian Perks; Editor, Tanja Nowotny

Canadian Property Management (Published by Media Edge Communications), #1000, 5255 Yonge St., North York ON M2N 6P4 – 416/512-8186; Fax: 416/512-8344; Email: janel@mediaedge.ca; URL: http://www.mediaedge.ca – Circ.: 14,500; 8 times a year – Editor, Jane Leckey, 416/512-8186, ext.225

Canadian Roofing Contractor (Published by Perks Publications Ltd.), #7A, 1735 Bayly St., Pickering ON L1W 3G7 – 905/831-4711 – 4 times a year – Publisher, E.B. Perks; Editor, Tanja Nowotny

Canadian Window & Door Manufacturer (Published by Bryarhouse Publishing Ltd.), 10893 Old River Rd., Komoka ON N0L 1R0 – 519/657-2088; Fax: 519/657-2796 – Circ.: 2,077; 2 times a year – Editor, Bruce Munro

Condominium Magazine (Published by Media Edge Communications), #1000, 5255 Yonge St., North York ON M2N 6P4 – 416/512-8186; Fax: 416/512-8344; URL: http://www.mediaedge/ca – Circ.: 2,500; 12 times a year – Editor, Angela Altass

Construction Comment (Published by Naylor Communications Ltd.), 920 Yonge St., 6th Fl., Toronto ON M4W 3C7 – 416/961-1028; Fax: 416/924-4408 – 2 times a year – Publisher, Robert Thompson

Construire, Assn de la construction du Québec, #205, 7400, boul des Galeries-d'Anjou, Anjou QC H1M 3M2 – 514/354-0609; Fax: 514/354-8292 – Tirage:

20,000; 6 fois par an; français - Rédactrice, Christiane Rioux

Daily Commercial News & Construction Record, 280 Yorkland Blvd., Willowdale ON M2J 4Z6 - 416/494-4990; Fax: 416/756-2767 - Circ.: 4,758; Daily - Publisher, Ian Hardy; Editor, Scott Button

Heavy Construction News (Published by Maclean Hunter Publishing), 777 Bay St., Toronto ON M5W 1A7 - 416/596-5848; Fax: 416/593-3193; URL: http://www.io.org/~hcn - Circ.: 21,700; Monthly - Publisher, David J. Fidler

Home Builder Magazine, 4819 St. Charles Blvd., Pierrefonds QC H9H 3C7 - 514/620-2200; Fax: 514/620-6300; Email: work4@total.net - Circ.: 17,400; 6 times a year - Associate Publisher, Ady Artzy; Circulation Manager, Joyce Crandall

Journal Constructo, #200, 1500, boul Jules-Poitras, St-Laurent QC H4N 1X7 - 514/745-5720; Fax: 514/339-2267; Email: groupeconstructo@mail.transc.com - 2 fois par an; français - Editeur, Johanne Rouleau; Rédacteur en chef, Rénald Fortier

Journal of Commerce (Published by Construction Marketing Data Canada Inc.), 4285 Canada Way, Burnaby BC V5G 1H2 - 604/433-8164; Fax: 604/433-9549; Email: jofc@lynx.bc.ca - Circ.: 5,300; 2 times a week - President/Publisher, Brian Martin; Editor, Frank Lillquist

LBMAO Reporter (Published by Perks Publications Ltd.), #7A, 1735 Bayly St., Pickering ON L1W 3G7 - 905/831-4711; Fax: 905/831-4725 - 6 times a year - Managing Editor, Lumber & Bldg. Materials Assn. of Ont., Steve Johns, 416/298-1731, 1-800-465-5270; Fax: 416/298-4865

London & District Construction Association Magazine (Published by Naylor Communications Ltd.), 920 Yonge St., 6th Fl., Toronto ON M4W 3C7 - 416/961-1028; Fax: 416/924-4408 - Annually - Publisher, Robert Thompson

Ontario Home Builder, 1455 Lakeshore Rd., Burlington ON L7S 2J1 - 905/634-5770; Fax: 905/634-8335 - Circ.: 8,000; 5 times a year

Property Management News, K-Rey Publishing Inc., #720, 789 West Pender St., Vancouver BC V6C 1H2 - 604/669-7671; Fax: 604/681-9535 - Circ.: 5,000; 6 times a year - Publisher, Steve Munday; Editor, Margaret Munday; Circulation Manager, Andria Preiss

Provincial Building Trades Yearbook (Published by Naylor Communications Ltd.), 920 Yonge St., 6th Fl., Toronto ON M4W 3C7 - 416/961-1028; Fax: 416/924-4408 - Annually, Oct. - Publisher, Robert Thompson

Québec Construction, #200, 1500, boul Jules-Poitras, St-Laurent QC H4N 1X7 - 514/745-5720, 1-800-363-0910; Fax: 514/339-2267; Email: groupeconstructo@mail.transc.com - 7 fois par an; français - Publisher, Johanne Rouleau; Rédacteur en chef, Rénald Fortier

Québec Habitation, 5930, boul Louis-H.-Lafontaine, Anjou QC H1M 1S7 - 514/353-9960; Fax: 514/353-4825; Email: quebec-hab@apchq.com; URL: http://www.apchq.com - Tirage: 15,000; 6 fois par an; français - Rédactrice, Brigitte Gauvreau; Directrice de tirage, Nathalie Renauld

Sanitation Canada (Published by Perks Publications Ltd.), #7A, 1735 Bayly St., Pickering ON L1W 3G7 - 905/831-4711; Fax: 905/831-4725 - Circ.: 4,500; 7 times a year - Editor, Tanja Nowotny

Siding Windows & Remodelling (Published by Bryarhouse Publishing Ltd.), 10893 Old River Rd., Komoka ON N0L 1R0 - 519/657-2088; Fax: 519/657-2796 - 5 times a year - Publisher/Editor, R.B. Munro

Toronto Construction News, 280 Yorkland Blvd., Willowdale ON M2J 4Z6 - 416/494-4990; Fax: 416/756-2767 - Circ.: 3,900; 4 times a year - Managing Editor, Randy Threndyle

Western Homebuilder & Renovation Contractor (Published by Bowen Communications), #403, 1230 Quayside Dr., New Westminster BC V3M 6H1 - 604/522-6033 - 4 times a year - General Manager, Mark Bowen

**BUSINESS & FINANCE**

Advantage for Partners in Trade, #220, 466 Speers Rd., Oakville ON L6K 3W9 - 905/845-8300; Fax: 905/845-9086; Email: wendyp@interlog.com; URL: http://www.infostream.ab.ca/advant - President & Publisher, Thomas Peters; Vice-President, Doreen W. Ruso

Les Affaires (Published by Transcontinental Publications Inc.), 1100, boul René-Levesque ouest, 24e étage, Montréal QC H3B 4X9 - 514/392-9000; Fax: 514/392-1586 - Tirage: 86 500; 51 fois par an; français; aussi Les Affaires 500, Les Affaires plus (10 fois par an, 93 288) - Rédacteur en chef, Jean-Paul Gagné

AfriCan Access Magazine, #201, 1290 Broad St., Vancouver BC V8W 2A5 - 604/598-4940; Fax: 604/598-4977; Email: editor@AfriCanAccess.com; URL: http://www.africanaccess.com - Circ.: 6,000; 4 times a year - Publisher, Chris Roberts

Alberta Venture, 17225 - 109 Ave., Edmonton AB T5S 1H7 - 403/486-4424; Fax: 403/483-1327; Email: venture@compusmart.ab.ca - Circ.: 40,000; 10 times a year - Publisher & Editor, Ruth Kelly

Atlantic Chamber Journal, EastCan Publications Inc., 275 Amirault St., Dieppe NB E1A 1G1 - 506/858-8710; Fax: 506/858-1707; Email: eastpub@nbnet.nb.ca - 6 times a year - Publisher, Elie J. Richard

Atlantic Progress, #603, 1660 Hollis St., Halifax NS B3J 1V7 - 902/494-0999; Fax: 902/494-0997; Email: progress@istar.ca - Circ.: 25,000; 8 times a year; ISSN: 0046-6735 - Publisher, Neville Gilfoy; Editor, David Holt; Circulation Manager, Pamela Scott-Crace

Avantages (Published by Maclean Hunter Publishing), 777 Bay St., Toronto ON M5W 1A7 - 416/596-5070; Fax: 416/596-5071; Email: 74227.2473@compuserve.com - Tirage: 5,000; 6 fois par an; français - Editeur, Paul Williams; Rédacteur, Antoine Di-Lillo; Directrice de tirage, Donna Singh

Le Banquier, Canadian Bankers Assn., Tour Scotia, 1002, rue Sherbrooke ouest, Montréal QC H3A 3M5 - 514/840-8732; Fax: 514/282-7551 - Tirage: 8,500; 6 fois par an; français - Rédacteur, Jacques Hébert

BC Business Magazine (Published by Canada Wide Magazines & Communications Ltd.), 4180 Lougheed Hwy., 4th Fl., Burnaby BC V5C 6A7 - 604/299-7311; Fax: 604/299-9188 - Circ.: 21,572; Monthly; ISSN: 0849-481X - Publisher, Peter Legge; Editor, Bonnie Irving; Circulation Manager, Mark Weeks

Benefits Canada (Published by Maclean Hunter Publishing), 777 Bay St., Toronto ON M5W 1A7 - 416/596-5959; Fax: 416/596-5071; Email: 74227.2743@compuserve.com; URL: http://www.benefitscanada.com - Circ.: 15,400; 11 times a year; English & French - Publisher, Paul Williams; Editor, Lori Bak; Circulation Manager, Donna Singh

Benefits & Pensions Monitor, c/o Powershift Communications Inc., #308, 245 Fairview Mall Dr., North York ON M2J 4T1 - 416/494-1066; Fax: 416/494-2536; Email: pwrshift@idirect.com - Circ.: 15,670; 6 times a year - Publisher, John L. McLaine; Managing Editor, Patricia McCullagh; Circulation Manager, D. Brian McKerchar

Bilan, c/o Ordre des compatables agréés du Québec, 680 Sherbrooke St. West, 7th Fl., Montréal QC H3A 2S3 - 514/982-4620; Fax: 514/843-8375; Email: m.parant@ocaq.qc.ca; URL: http://www.ocaq.qc.ca - Circ.: 19,000; 6 times a year; English & French - Editor, Richard Roch; Circulation Manager, Paul-Marcel Adam

Biz-Hamilton/Halton Business Report (Published by Town Publishing Inc), 875 Main St., Hamilton ON L8S 4R1 - 905/522-6117; Fax: 905/529-2242 - Circ.: 20,000; 4 times a year - Publisher & Editor, Wayne Narciso

The Bottom Line (Published by Butterworths Canada Ltd.), 75 Clegg Rd., Markham ON L6G 1A7 - 905/479-2665; Fax: 905/474-9803; Email: tbl@butterworths.ca; URL: http://www.butterworths.ca/tbl.htm - Circ.: 30,000; Monthly - Publisher, Don Brillinger, 905-415-5801; Editor, Michael Lewis; Circulation Controller, Kim Rattray

The Bruce County Marketplace, 910 Queen St., Kincardine ON N2Z 2Y9 - 519/396-9142; Fax: 519/396-3555 - Circ.: 13,000; 12 times a year - Publisher, James Pannell; Editor, Charles Whipp

Business Bulletin, Mississauga Board of Trade, 100-3 Robert Speck Pkwy., Mississauga ON L4Z 2G5 - 905/273-6151; Fax: 905/273-4937; Email: info@mbot.com; URL: http://www.mbot.com - Circ.: 22,000; 11 times a year - Coordinator, Bill Dzugan

Business Examiner - Mid/North Island Edition, Island Publishers, 777 Poplar St., Nanaimo BC V9S 2H7 - 250/754-8344; Fax: 250/753-0788 - Circ.: 10,400; Monthly - Publisher, Mark A. MacDonald

Business Examiner - South Island Edition, Island Publishers, 1824 Store St., Victoria BC V8T 4R4 - 250/381-3926; Fax: 250/381-5606; Email: be@busex.bc.ca; URL: http://www.busex.bc.ca - Circ.: 14,000; 24 times a year - Publisher, Woodrow Turnquist

The Business Executive, #220, 466 Speers Rd., Oakville ON L6K 3W9 - 905/845-8300; Fax: 905/845-9086; Email: wendyp@interlog.com; URL: http://www.busexec.com - Circ.: 21,000; 17 times a year - Publisher, Thomas Peters; Editor, Wendy Peters; Office Manager, Maria Raposo

Business in Calgary (Published by OT Communications), #600, 237 - 8th Ave. SE, Calgary AB T2G 5C3 - 403/264-3270; Fax: 403/264-3276 - Circ.: 33,500; Monthly - Publisher, Pat Ottmann; Editor, Richard Bronstein

Business in Vancouver, #500, 1155 West Pender St., Vancouver BC V6E 2P4 - 604/688-2398; Fax: 604/688-1963; Email: news@biv.com.bc.ca; URL: http://www.biv.com - Circ.: 9,447; Weekly, Mon. - Editor & Publisher, Peter Ladner

Business People Magazine (Published by McCaine-Davis Communications Ltd.), 232 Henderson Hwy., Winnipeg MB R2L 1L9 - 204/982-4002; Fax: 204/982-4001 - Circ.: 11,000; 4 times a year - Publisher & Editor, Heather McCaine-Davies

The Business & Professional Woman, Val Publications Ltd., 95 Leeward Glenway, Unit 121, Don Mills ON M3C 2Z6 - 416/467-1393; Fax: 416/467-8262 - Circ.: 5,000; 4 times a year - Editor, Valerie Dunn

The Business Times, Netmar Magazine Group, #203, 231 Dundas St., London ON N6A 1H1 - 519/679-4901; Fax: 519/434-7842 - Monthly - General Manager, Katherine Wigget

Business Today, Saskatoon Today Inc., 266 Assiniboine Dr., Stn Main, Saskatoon SK S7K 3K1 - 306/242-3641 - Circ.: 10,000; Monthly - General Manager, Gerald Rekue

Businest, Le Groupe Bellavance inc., 156, rue le Page, Rimouski QC G5L 3H2 - 418/724-6311; Fax: 418/725-4711 - Mensuel; français - Editeur, Claude Bellavance

CA Magazine, 277 Wellington St. West, Toronto ON M5V 3H2 - 416/977-3222; Fax: 416/204-3409; Email: christian.bellavance@cica.ca; URL: http://www.cica.ca - Circ.: 67,000; 10 times a year; English & French - Editor-in-chief, Christian Bellavance; Circulation Manager, Coleen Schoonhoven

Canada Japan Journal, Van Network Ltd., #370, 220 Cambie St., Vancouver BC V6B 2M9 - 604/688-2486; Fax: 604/688-1487; Email: janpan@helix.net - Monthly - Editor, Taka Aoki

Canada Journal (Published by Ruland Communications), 12 Lawton Blvd., Toronto ON M4V 1Z4 – 416/927-9129; Fax: 416/927-9118; Email: ruland@istar.ca – Circ.: 14,250; 6 times a year; German – Publisher/Editor, Joseph F. Ruland; Publisher/Editor, Ulli Nadine Ruland

The Canadian Banker, Canadian Bankers Assn., #3000, Commerce Ct. West, 199 Bay St., PO Box 348, Toronto ON M5L 1G2 – 416/362-6092; Fax: 416/362-8465; URL: http://www.cba.ca – Circ.: 33,400; 6 times a year – President & CEO, Raymond J. Protti; Editor, Simon Hally; Circulation Manager, Karen Bentley

Canadian Business (Published by Maclean Hunter Publishing), 777 Bay St., Toronto ON M5W 1A7 – 416/596-5151, 5100; Fax: 416/596-5152; Email: letters@cbmedia.ca; URL: http://www.canbus.com – Circ.: 82,000; Monthly with quarterly technology supplements; ISSN: 0008-3100 – Publisher, Paul Jones; Editor, Arthur Johnson; Circulation Manager, Allan Landsman

Canadian German Trade (Published by Ruland Communications), 12 Lawton Blvd., Toronto ON M4V 1Z4 – 416/927-9129; Fax: 416/929-9118; Email: ruland@istar.ca – Circ.: 1,500; 8 times a year – Publisher, Ulli N. Ruland

Canadian Investment Review (Published by Maclean Hunter Publishing), 777 Bay St., Toronto ON M5W 1A7 – 416/596-5959; Fax: 416/596-5071; Email: 74227.2743@compuserve.com; URL: http://www.benefitscanada.com/Content/cir/cirhome.html – Circ.: 8,000 – Publisher, Paul Williams; Editor, Jim Helik; Circulation Manager, Donna Singh

The Canadian Manager, Canadian Institute of Management, #310, 2175 Sheppard Ave. East, Willowdale ON M2J 1W8 – 416/493-0155; Fax: 416/491-1670 – 4 times a year – Editor, Ruth Max

Canadian Stock Market Reporter (online), 4252 Commerce Ct., Victoria BC V8Z 4M4 – 250/744-2887; Fax: 250/744-2831; Email: ianm@canstock.com – President, Kit Spence

Canadian Treasurer, c/o Treasury Management Association of Canada, #1010, 8 King St. East, Toronto ON M5C 1B5 – 416/367-8500; Fax: 416/367-3240; Email: info@tmac.ca; URL: http://www.tmac.ca – Circ.: 4,500; 6 times a year – Editor, Bruce McDougall

Central Nova Business News, Advocate Print & Publishing Ltd., 228 Main St., Bible Hill NS B2N 4H2 – 902/895-7948; Fax: 902/893-1427 – Monthly – Publisher, Tom Maclean

CGA Magazine, #700, 1188 Georgia St. West, Vancouver BC V6E 4E2 – 604/669-3555, 1-800-663-1529; Fax: 604/689-5845; Email: editcga@cga-canada.org; URL: http://www.cga-canada.org – Circ.: 47,000; Monthly; English & French – Publisher & Editor, Lesley A. Wood

The Chamber Advocate, 244 Pall Mall St., PO Box 3295, London ON N6A 5P6 – 519/432-7551; Fax: 519/432-8063; Email: info@chamber.london.on.ca; URL: http://www.chamber.london.on.ca – Monthly – Publisher, Gerry Macartney; Editor & Co-Publisher, John Redmond

CMA Magazine, c/o Society of Management Accountants, #850, 120 King St. West, PO Box 1, Hamilton ON L8N 3C3 – 905/525-4100; Fax: 905/525-4533; Email: cma@binatech.on.ca; URL: http://www.cma-canada.org – Circ.: 75,000; 10 times a year; English & French – Publisher, Dan R. Hicks; Circulation Manager, Claire Keane

Commerce and Industry (Published by Mercury Publications Ltd.), 1839 Inkster Blvd., Winnipeg MB R2X 1R3 – 204/697-0835; Fax: 204/633-7784; Email: mp@mercury.mb.ca – Circ.: 13,000; 4 times a year – Publisher, Gren R. Yeo

Commerce News, Edmonton Chamber of Commerce, #600, 10123 - 99 St., Edmonton AB T5J 3G9 – 403/426-4620; Fax: 403/424-7946; Email: ecc@tns.com – Circ.: 15,000; 11 times a year – Publisher, Martin Sabhoum

Durham Business News, PO Box 206, Whitby ON L1N 5S1 – 905/668-6111; Fax: 905/668-0594 – Circ.: 12,500; Monthly – Publisher, Doug Anderson; Editor, Glenn Hendry; Sales Manager, Peter Irvine

L'Économique, 12606, av Rivoli, Montréal QC H4J 2L9 – 514/856-2214; Fax: 514/856-0850 – Circ.: 45,040; 6 times a year – Publisher, Ian Dobson

L'Edition Commerciale, 6885, rue Jarry est, 2e étage, St-Léonard QC – 514/321-7000; Fax: 514/321-7792 – Tirage: 59 500; Mensuel

Edmonton Commerce & Industry, Homersham Advertising Agency, #215, 11802 - 124 St., Edmonton AB T5L 0M3 – 403/454-5540; Fax: 403/453-2553 – Monthly – Publisher, D. Homersham

Entreprendre, Editions Qualité performante inc., #630, 1600, boul St-Martin est, Laval QC H7G 4S7 – 514/669-8373; Fax: 514/669-9078 – Tirage: 50,000; 10 fois par an; français – Rédacteur en chef, Edmond Bourque

The Financial Post 500 (Published by Financial Post Co. Ltd.), 333 King St. East, Toronto ON M5A 4N2 – 416/350-6000; Fax: 416/350-6301 – Circ.: 100,000; Annually, May – Publisher, Bill Neill; Editor, Diane Francis

The Financial Post Magazine Canada (Published by Financial Post Co. Ltd.), 333 King St. East, Toronto ON M5A 4N2 – 416/350-6170; Fax: 416/350-6171; Email: fpmag@nstn.fox.ca; URL: http://www.canoe.ca – 11 times a year – Publisher, David Bailey, 416/350-6198; Editor, Wayne Gooding

The Financial Post Survey of Industrials (Published by Financial Post Co. Ltd.), 333 King St. East, Toronto ON M5A 4N2 – 416/350-6500; Fax: 416/350-6501 – Circ.: 3,870; Annually, Aug. – Director, Data Services, Joanne Bryant

Futur présent, Publi-Relais, 119, boul St-Joseph ouest, Montréal QC H2T 2P7 – 514/278-3344; Fax: 514/278-1543 – Tirage: 10 000; 6 fois par an; français – Rédactrice en chef, Pierrette Gagné

German American Trade (Published by Ruland Communications), 12 Lawton Blvd., Toronto ON M4V 1Z4 – 416/927-9129; Fax: 416/927-9118; Email: ruland@istar.ca – Circ.: 2,600; 10 times a year – Publisher, Ulli N. Ruland

Gestion, 3000, ch de la Côte-Sainte-Catherine, Montréal QC H3T 2A7 – 514/340-6677; Fax: 514/340-6382; Email: Revue-gestion@heg.ca – 4 fois par an; français – Rédacteur, Alain Gosselin

GTA Business Journal, Canadian Business Publications, #111, 388 King St. West, Toronto ON M5V 1K2 – 416/593-5911; Fax: 416/591-8955; Email: 76001.1413@compuserve.com – Circ.: 80,000; Monthly – Publisher, Nick Pitt; Editor-in-chief, Frank Condrun

Head Office at Home, Abaco Communications Ltd., 44 Carlton Rd., Unionville ON L3R 1Z5 – 905/477-4349; Fax: 905/477-0412 – Circ.: 40,000; 5 times a year – Publisher/Editor, Elizabeth Harris

Home Business Report, HB Communications Group Inc., 2949 Ash St., Abbotsford BC V2S 4G5 – 604/854-5530; Fax: 604/854-3087 – 4 times a year – Publisher, Barbara Mowat

Huronia Business Times, 24 Dunlop St. East, 2nd Fl., Barrie ON L4M 1A3 – 705/721-1450; Fax: 705/721-1449 – Circ.: 7,500; 10 times a year – Publisher, Alexander Donald; Editor, Eric Skelton

IE: Money (Published by Investment Executive Inc.), #202, 90 Richmond St. East, Toronto ON M5C 1P1 – 416/366-4200; Fax: 416/366-7846; Email: editorial@iemoney.com; adsales@iemoney.com; URL: http://www.iemoney.com – Circ.: 133,200; 5 times a year – Publisher, Barbara Hyland; Editor, Tessa Wilmott

Info-affaires, Bell Productions inc., CP 399, Richibucto NB E0A 2M0 – 506/523-1123; Fax: 506/523-1122; Email: bellprod@nbnet.nb.ca – Mensuel; français – Editeur, Gilles Belleau

Info Systems Executive (Published by Plesman Publications Ltd.), 2005 Sheppard Ave. East, 4th Fl., Willowdale ON M2J 5B1 – 416/497-9562; Fax: 416/497-5022 – Circ.: 18,000; 6 times a year – Publisher, George Soltys

Interface, 425, rue de la Gauchetière est, Montréal QC H2L 2M7 – 514/849-0045; Fax: 514/849-5558; Email: interface@acfas.ca; URL: http://www.acfas.ca/ – Tirage: 9 000; 6 fois par an; français – Editrice & Rédactrice, Sophie Malavoy

Investment Executive (Published by Investment Executive Inc.), #202, 90 Richmond St. East, Toronto ON M5C 1P1 – 416/366-4200; Fax: 416/366-7844 – Circ.: 23,950; 12 times a year – Editor, Tessa Wilmott

Investor's Digest of Canada, #700, 133 Richmond St. West, Toronto ON M5H 3M8 – 416/869-1177; Fax: 416/869-0616 – Circ.: 20,500; 24 times a year – Editor, Rick Morrison

Italcommerce, Italian Chamber of Commerce in Canada, #680, 550 Sherbrooke St. West, Montréal QC H3A 1B9 – 514/844-4249; Fax: 514/844-4875; Email: info.montreal@italchambers.net – 4 times a year; French, English & Italian – Editor-in-chief, Marianna Simeone

Italy Canada Trade, Italian Chamber of Commerce of Toronto, #306, 901 Lawrence Ave. West, Toronto ON M6A 1C3 – 416/789-7169; Fax: 416/789-7160 – 4 times a year – Editor-in-Chief, Arturo Pelliccione

Ivey Business Quarterly, c/o Richard Ivey School of Business, University of Western Ontario, 1151 Richmond St. North, London ON N6A 3K7 – 519/661-3309; Fax: 519/661-3838; Email: bq@uwo.ca; URL: http://www.ivey.uwo.ca/publications/bq/index.html – Circ.: 10,000; 4 times a year; ISSN: 007-6996 – Publisher & Editor, Angela Smith; Managing Editor, Linda Verde

Le Journal Économique de Québec, 605, boul René Lévesque ouest, Québec QC G1S 1S7 – 418/681-9999; Fax: 418/681-7077; Email: jecono@total.net; URL: http://www.journaleconomique.com – Tirage: 13,023; Mensuel; français – Editeur, Pierre Cassivi

Kootenay Business Magazine (Published by Koocanusa Publications Inc.), 1510 - 2nd St. North, Cranbrook BC V1C 3L2 – 250/426-7253; Fax: 250/426-4125; Email: advertiser@cyberlink.bc.ca – Circ.: 8,000; Monthly – Publisher, Daryl D. Shellborn; Editor, Stacey Curry

London Business Monthly Magazine (Published by Bowes Publishers Ltd.), PO Box 7400, London ON N5Y 4X3 – 519/472-7601; Fax: 519/473-2256 – Circ.: 12,176; Monthly – Publisher, Robert Way; Managing Editor, Janine Foster

Magazine Affaires Plus (Published by Transcontinental Publications Inc.), 1100, boul René-Levesque ouest, 24e étage, Montréal QC H3B 4X9 – 514/392-9000; Fax: 514/392-4726; Email: akplus@mail.transc.com; URL: http://www.transc.com – Tirage: 93,000; 10 fois par an; français – Editeur, André Préfontaine; Rédacteur, Pierre Duhamel; Directeur de tirage, François Blondin

Le Magazine Québec-Franchise, #1002, 350 Prince Arthur St. West, Montréal QC H2X 3R4 – 514/287-9827; Fax: 514/287-9684 – Circ.: 12,500; 4 times a year; English & French – Editor, Jacques Desfurges

Main Streets Business Magazine, 80 - 9th St. East, 2nd Fl., Owen Sound ON N4K 1N4 – 519/376-1177; Fax: 519/376-8666 – Circ.: 7,000; Monthly – Publisher, Paul E. Farrow; Editor, Claudia Stains

Manitoba Business, #502, 310 Broadway, Winnipeg MB R3C 0S6 – 204/943-2931; Fax: 204/943-2942 – Circ.: 7,000; 10 times a year – Editor, Ritchie Gage

Mississauga Business Times (Published by North Island Sound Ltd.), #8, 1606 Sedlescomb Dr.,

Mississauga ON L4X 1M6 – 905/625-7070; Fax: 905/625-4856 – Circ.: 19,000; 10 times a year – Publisher, Alexander Donald; Managing Editor, Rosalind Stefanac

Montréal Business Magazine, #43, 275, rue St-Jacques, Montréal QC H2Y 1M9 – 514/286-8038; Fax: 514/287-7346 – Circ.: 17,700; 6 times a year – Publisher, Mark Weller; Editor, Michael Carin; Sales Manager, Scott Pritchard

Montréal Plus, Board of Trade of Metropolitan Montréal, #12500, 5, Place Ville Marie, Plaza Level, Montréal QC H3B 4Y2 – 514/871-4000; Fax: 514/871-1255 – Circ.: 10,000; 7 times a year; English & French – Editor, Joélle Ganguillet

Niagara Business Report, Southam Community Newspapers Inc., 4309 Central Ave., PO Box 400, Beamsville ON L0R 1B0 – 905/563-1629; Fax: 905/563-7977 – Circ.: 15,000; 4 times a year – Publisher, Tom Haire; Circulation Manager, Pattie Corsini

Northern Ontario Business, Laurentian Publishing Co., 158 Elgin St., Sudbury ON P3E 3N5 – 705/673-5705; Fax: 705/673-9542 – Monthly – Publisher/Editor, Mark Sandford

Northwest Business, Dakota Design & Advertising Ltd., #201, 2915 - 19th St.NE, Calgary AB T2E 7A2 – 403/250-1128; Fax: 403/250-1194 – Circ.: 25,000; 6 times a year – Editor, Donald C. Sylvester

Nova Scotia Business Journal (Published by NCC Specialty Publications), #107, 900 Windmill Rd., Dartmouth NS B3B 1P7 – 902/468-8027; Fax: 902/468-2425 – Circ.: 13,600; Monthly – Publisher, Peter Steele; Editor, Ken Partridge

Okanagan Business Magazine (Published by Byrne Publishing Group Inc), PO Box 1479, Stn A, Kelowna BC V1Y 7V8 – 250/861-5399; Fax: 250/868-3040; Email: oklife@awinc.com – Circ.: 11,000; 8 times a year – Editor, Mike Haines; Circulation Manager, Tammy Tomiye

Ontario, Canada's Business Centre (Published by Kenilworth Publishing), #201, 27 West Beaver Creek, Richmond Hill ON L4B 1M8 – 905/771-7333; Fax: 905/771-7336; Email: sales@kenilworth.com – Publisher, James Davidson

Opportunities Canada, The Type People Inc., 1293 Matheson Blvd. East, Mississauga ON L4W 1R1 – 905/238-3320; Fax: 905/238-3301 – Circ.: 15,000; 3 times a year – Publisher, Robert Sinclair

Ottawa Business Journal, The Business Press Group Inc., #319, 126 York St., Ottawa ON K1N 5T5 – 613/789-0403; Fax: 613/789-0227 – Circ.: 40,000; 52 times a year – Editor, Mark Sutcliffe

Parlons Affaires Beauce/Etchemin, 12625, av 1e est, St-Georges QC G5Y 2E4 – 418/228-8858; Fax: 418/228-0268 – Tirage: 4 300; Mensuel; français

Parlons Affaires Laurentides, Communications Quebecor, 801, rue Sherbrook est, 4e étage, Montréal QC H2L 4X9 – 514/523-5800; Fax: 514/523-5944 – Tirage: 15 000; Mensuel; français – Directrice, Diane Bougie

PME (Le Magazine PME) (Published by Transcontinental Publications Inc.), 1100, boul René-Levesque ouest, 24e étage, Montréal QC H3B 4X9 – 514/392-9000; Fax: 514/392-4726; Email: pme@mail.transc.com; URL: http://www.transc.com – Tirage: 35,000; 10 fois par an; français – Editeur, André Préfontaine; Rédacteur en chef, François Barbes; Directeur de tirage, François Blondin

Profiles, York University, #280, York Lanes, 4700 Keele St., North York ON M3J 1P3 – 416/736-2100, ext.33160; Fax: 416/736-5681 – Circ.: 98,807; 4 times a year – Publisher, Jessie-May Rowntree

Profit: The Magazine for Canadian Entrepreneurs (Published by Maclean Hunter Publishing), 777 Bay St., Toronto ON M5W 1A7 – 416/596-5100; Fax: 416/596-5152; Email: profit@cbmedia.ca; URL: http://www.profit100.com – Circ.: 100,000; 6 times a year – Publisher, Paul Jones; Editor, Rick Spence; Circulation Manager, Allan Landsman

Québec Enterprise, #600, 417, rue St-Pierre, Montréal QC H2Y 2M4 – 514/842-5492; Fax: 514/842-5375 – Tirage: 25 000; 6 fois par an; français – Rédacteur, Daniel Boisvert

Report on Business Magazine, c/o The Globe and Mail, 444 Front St. West, Toronto ON M5V 2S9 – 416/585-5411; Fax: 416/585-5275; Email: robmag@globeandmail.ca; URL: http://www.robmagazine.com – Circ.: 300,000; 12 times a year – Publisher, Stephen Petherbridge; Editor, Patricia Best

Revue Commerce (Published by Transcontinental Publications Inc.), 1100, boul René-Levesque ouest, 24e étage, Montréal QC H3B 4X9 – 514/392-9000; Fax: 514/392-4726; Email: commerce@mail.trtansc.com; URL: http://www.transc.com – Tirage: 39,800; Mensuel; français – Editeur, André Préfontaine; Rédacteur, Pierre Sormany; Directeur du tirage, François Blondin

La Revue Occasions d'Affaires, #145, 425, rue St-Amable, Québec QC G1R 5E4 – 418/640-1686, 1-800-361-1686; Fax: 418/640-1687; Email: roa@qbc.clic.net; URL: http://www.roa.qc.ca – Tirage: 150,000; 6 fois par an; français – Editeur, Pierre Bhérer; Rédacteur, Régis Pelletier; Directrice de tirage, Isabelle Comeau

Saskatchewan Business (Published by Sunrise Publishing), 2213C Hanselman Ct., Saskatoon SK S7L 6A8 – 306/244-5668; Fax: 306/244-5679 – Circ.: 9,000; 6 times a year – Publisher, Twila Reddekopp; Editor, Keith Moon

Silicon Valley North, Silvan Communications Inc., #605, 45 Rideau St., Ottawa ON K1N 5W8 – 613/562-3648; Fax: 613/562-2649; Email: mailroom@silvan.com – Circ.: 30,000; Monthly – Publisher & Editor, Tony Patterson

Sounding Board, The Vancouver Board of Trade, #400, 999 Canada Place, Vancouver BC V6C 3C1 – 604/681-2111; Fax: 604/681-0437; Email: contactus@vancouver.boardoftrade.com – Circ.: 12,000; 10 times a year – Editor, Darcy Rezac

Thunder Bay Business (Published by North Superior Publishing Inc.), 1145 Barton St., Thunder Bay ON P7B 5N3 – 807/623-2348; Fax: 807/623-7515; Email: nsuperior@norlink.net – Circ.: 6,000; Monthly – Publisher/Editor, Scott Sumner

Today's Corporate Investor (Published by Toro Communications), #209B, 1450 Midland Ave., Scarborough ON M1P 4Z8 – 416/757-6080; Fax: 416/757-6288 – Circ.: 15,278; 6 times a year – Publisher, Dan Radulescu

Today's Woman in Business, 113 Old Black River Rd., PO Box 1291, Saint John NB E2L 4H8 – 506/658-0754; Fax: 506/633-0868 – 4 times a year – Publisher/Editor, Carol Maber

The Toronto Stock Exchange Review, 2 First Canadian Place, Exchange Tower, 9th Fl., Toronto ON M5X 1J2 – 416/947-4681; Fax: 416/814-8811; Email: ptraynor@tse.com – Circ.: 2,500; 12 times a year – Publisher, Peter Traynor, 416/947-4602; Editor, G. Daniel Strong

Trade & Commerce, 1700 Church Ave., PO Box 6900, Winnipeg MB R3C 3B1 – 204/632-2606; Fax: 204/694-3040 – 5 times a year – Managing Director, George Mitchell; Editor, Laura Jean Stewart

Upwardly Mobile, 345 Bloor St. East, PO Box 72611, Toronto ON M4W 3S9 – 416/920-0533; Fax: 416/920-0702 – Circ.: 20,000; 4 times a year – Editor, Linda Darmanie

Your Office (Published by Canadian Office Products Association), #911, 1243 Islington Ave., Toronto ON M8X 1X9 – 416/239-2737; Fax: 416/239-1553; Email: darrell.townson@sympatico.ca; URL: http://www.copa.ca – Circ.: 70,000; 4 times a year – Publisher, James Preece

### CERAMICS

Canadian Ceramics Quarterly, #310, 2175 Sheppard Ave. East, Willowdale ON M2J 1W8 – 416/491-2886; Fax: 416/491-1670; Email: taylor@interlog.com – 4 times a year – Editor, Dr. M. Sayer; Circulation Manager, B. Howell

### CHEMICALS & CHEMICAL PROCESS INDUSTRIES

Canadian Chemical News, c/o Chemical Inst. of Canada, #550, 130 Slater St., Ottawa ON K1P 6E2 – 613/232-6252; Fax: 613/232-5862; Email: cic_publ@fox.nstn.ca; URL: http://www.chem-inst-can.org – Circ.: 6,500; 10 times a year – Editor, Nola Haddadian; Circulation Manager, Allison McLean

Canadian Process Equipment & Control News, 343 Eglinton Ave. East, Toronto ON M4P 1L7 – 416/481-6483; Fax: 416/481-6436 – Circ.: 25,000; 6 times a year – Publisher, J.P. Birchard; Editor, V.J. Sharp; Circulation Manager, L. Bargh

Industrial Process Products & Technology (Published by Swan Erickson Publishing Inc.), #1235, 1011 Upper Middle Rd. East, Oakville ON L6H 5Z9 – 905/475-4231; Fax: 905/475-3512 – Circ.: 23,500; 6 times a year – Publisher, M.H. Swan; Editor-in-Chief, Bob Erickson, 905/845-1347

### CHURCH ADMINISTRATION

Church Business Magazine (Published by Sawmill Creek Communications), #11, 4040 Creditview Rd., PO Box 1800, Mississauga ON L5C 3Y8 – 905/569-1800; Fax: 905/813-7117 – 6 times a year – Publisher & Editor, Hugh Parkinson

### CLOTHING & ACCESSORIES

Canadian Apparel Magazine, #801, 555, rue Chabanel, Montréal QC H2N 2H8 – 514/382-4243; Fax: 514/382-4612; Email: ApparelMag@aol.com – Circ.: 5,000; 6 times a year – Editor-in-chief, Gillian Crosby; Circulation Manager, S. Vallée

Fashion femme (Published by McLeish Communications Inc.), 1, rue Pacifique, Ste-Anne-de-Bellevue QC H9X 1C5 – 514/457-2423; Fax: 514/457-2577 – Circ.: 7,584; 6 times a year; English & French – Editor, Barbara McLeish

Kids Creations, c/o Children's Apparel Manufacturers' Association, #3110, 6900 Decarie Blvd., Montréal QC H3X 2T8 – 514/731-7774; Fax: 514/731-7459 – Circ.: 6,000; 4 times a year; English & French – Business Manager & Executive Director, Murray W. Schwartz; Editor, Lisa Peters; Advertising Manager, Della Druick

Luggage, Leathergoods & Accessories (Published by Laurentian Media Inc.), 501 Oakdale Rd., North York ON M3N 1W7 – 416/746-7360; Fax: 416/746-1421; Email: tammy-mang@lti.on.ca – Circ.: 5,100; 4 times a year – Tammy Mang

Style, #302, 1448 Lawrence Ave. East, Toronto ON M4A 2V6 – 416/755-5199; Fax: 416/755-9123 – 12 times a year – Publisher, Patricia MacLean; Editor, Doris Montinara

### COMPUTING & TECHNOLOGY

AutoCAD User (Published by Swan Erickson Publishing Inc.), #1235, 1011 Upper Middle Rd. East, Oakville ON L6H 5Z9 – 905/475-4231; Fax: 905/475-3512 – Circ.: 15,000; 4 times a year – Publisher, R.A. Erickson, 905/845-1347; Editor-in-Chief, K. Pashuk

CAD Systems (Published by Kerrwil Publications Ltd.), 395 Matheson Blvd. East, Mississauga ON L4Z 2H2 – 905/890-1846; Fax: 905/890-5769; Email: kdalton@cadsystems.com; URL: http://www.cadsystems.com – Circ.: 16,200; 6 times a year – Publisher & Editor, Karen Dalton; Circulation Manager, Jean Bilkey

Canadian Computer Reseller (Published by Maclean Hunter Publishing), 777 Bay St., Toronto ON M5W 1A7 – 416/596-2668; Fax: 416/593-3166; Email:

ccrcinforamp.net; URL: http://www.mhbizlink.com/coreseller – Circ.: 15,000; 24 times a year – Publisher, Kathryn Swan; Editor, Alison Eastwood; Circulation Manager, Donna Singh

Canadian Computer Wholesaler, #503, 425 Carrall St., Vancouver BC V6B 6E3 – 604/608-2688; Fax: 604/688-4270 – Circ.: 11,900; Monthly – Publisher, Douglas Alder

CIO Canada (Published by Laurentian Media Inc.), 501 Oakdale Rd., North York ON M3N 1W7 – 416/746-7360; Fax: 416/746-1421 – Circ.: 7,500; 10 times a year – Publisher, Andrew White; Managing Editor, David Charey; Circulation Director, Pauline White

Computer Dealer News (Published by Plesman Publications Ltd.), 2005 Sheppard Ave. East, 4th Fl., Willowdale ON M2J 5B1 – 416/497-9562; Fax: 416/497-9427; Email: cdnedit@plesman.com; URL: http://www.plesman.com/cdn – Circ.: 14,883; 26 times a year – Publisher, George Soltys; Editor, James Bouchok

Computer & Entertainment Retailing (Published by Plesman Publications Ltd.), 2005 Sheppard Ave. East, 4th Fl., Willowdale ON M2J 5B1 – 416/497-9562; Fax: 416/497-9427; Email: ceredit@plesman.com; URL: http://www.plesman.com – Circ.: 6,133 – Publisher, George Soltys; Editor, Pamela Addo

Computer Freelancer, 1800 Sheppard Ave. East, North York ON M2J 5B9 – 416/493-6752; Fax: 416/493-7093 – Circ.: 11,839; 8 times a year – Publisher, Jayanti Parmar

The Computer Paper, #503, 425 Carrall St., Vancouver BC V6B 6E3 – 604/688-2120; Fax: 604/688-4270; Email: editorial@tcp.ca; URL: http://tcp.ca/ – Circ.: 355,000; Monthly – Publisher, Douglas Alder; Editor, David Tanaka

The Computer Post, #660, 125 Garry St., Winnipeg MB R3C 3P2 – 204/947-9766; Fax: 204/947-9767; Email: jstrauss@cpost.mb.ca; URL: http://www.cpost.mb.ca – Circ.: 12,000; Monthly – Publisher, Jonathan Strauss

Computer Reseller News, The Publishing House Inc., #1100, 235 Yorkland Blvd., North York ON M2J 4Y8 – 416/756-9736; Fax: 416/756-1612 – Circ.: 16,200; 26 times a year – General Manager, Harley Broder; Editor, Steve Wexler

Computer World (Published by Laurentian Media Inc.), 501 Oakdale Rd., North York ON M3N 1W7 – 416/746-7360; Fax: 416/746-1421 – Circ.: 40,000; 25 times a year – Publisher, Andrew White; Editor, Ron Glen

Computing Canada (Published by Plesman Publications Ltd.), 2005 Sheppard Ave. East, 4th Fl., Willowdale ON M2J 5B1 – 416/497-9562; Fax: 416/497-9427; Email: ccedit@plesman.com; URL: http://www.plesman.com/cc – Circ.: 35,465; 26 times a year – Publisher, George Soltys; Editor, Martin Slofstra

Direction Informatique (Published by Plesman Publications Ltd.), 2005 Sheppard Ave. East, 4th Fl., Willowdale ON M2J 5B1 – 416/497-9562; Fax: 416/497-9427; URL: http://www.direction-informatique.qc.ca – Tirage: 18,837; Mensuel; français – Éditeur, George Soltys; Rédacteur, Guy Martin

Electronic Composition & Imaging (Published by Youngblood Publishing), #1204, 2240 Midland Ave., Scarborough ON M1R 4R8 – 416/299-6007; Fax: 416/299-6674 – Circ.: 9,000; 6 times a year – Publisher, Sara Young

Government Computer Magazine, #303, 260 St. Patrick St., Ottawa ON K1N 5K5 – 613/789-6431; Fax: 613/789-6433; Email: lee.hunter@hum.com; URL: http://www.hum.com – Circ.: 14,000; 11 times a year – Associate Publisher, E. Murchison; Editor, Lee Hunter; Circulation Manager, Loriel Langille

Government Computing Digest (Published by Synergistic Publications), 132 Adrian Cres., Markham ON L3P 7B3 – 905/472-2801; Fax: 905/472-3091 – Circ.: 9,329; 6 times a year – Publisher, Peter Kitchens; Editor, Gabriel Oak; Circulation Manager, Dianne Osadchuk

Info-tech magazine (Published by Les Editions du Feu vert), 5148, boul St-Laurent, Montréal QC H2T 1R8 – 514/392-9000; Fax: 514/392-2088 – Tirage: 19 600; 11 fois par an; français – Editrice, Francine Tremblay

InfoWorld Canada (Published by Laurentian Media Inc.), 501 Oakdale Rd., North York ON M3N 1W7 – 416/746-7360; Fax: 416/746-1421; Email: infocanada@cis.compuserve.com – Circ.: 30,000; Monthly – Publisher, Andrew White; Editor, Dan McLean; Circulation Manager, Pauline White

Network World Canada (Published by Laurentian Media Inc.), 501 Oakdale Rd., North York ON M3N 1W7 – 416/746-7360; Fax: 416/746-1421; Email: networldcan@cis.compuserve.com – Circ.: 12,000; 24 times a year – Publisher, Andrew White; Editor, Dan McLean; Circulation Manager, Pauline White

Technology in Government (Published by Plesman Publications Ltd.), 2005 Sheppard Ave. East, 4th Fl., Willowdale ON M2J 5B1 – 416/497-9562; Fax: 416/497-9427; Email: tigedit@plesman.com; URL: http://www.plesman.com – Circ.: 24,202; Monthly – Publisher, George Soltys; Editor, Alison Eastwood

Toronto Computes , #408, 99 Atlantic Ave., Toronto ON M6K 3J8 – 416/588-6818; Fax: 416/588-4110; URL: http://www.canadacomputes.com – Circ.: 100,000; Monthly; also publish: Canada Computes BC (60,000 circ.), Canada Computes Alberta (30,000 circ.) & Québec Micro (85,000 circ.) – Publisher, Douglas Alder; Editor, Mara Gulens

Web World (Published by Laurentian Media Inc.), 501 Oakdale Rd., North York ON M3N 1W7 – 416/746-7360; Fax: 416/746-1421 – 4 times a year – Publisher, Andrew White; Editor-in-Chief, John Pickett; Circulation Manager, Pauline White

**CONVENTIONS & MEETINGS**

Association (Published by August Communications Ltd.), #200, 388 Donald St., Winnipeg MB R3B 2J4 – 204/957-0265; Fax: 204/957-0217; Email: august@escape.ca; URL: http://www/august.ca – Circ.: 3,000; 6 times a year; English & French – Publisher, Gladwyn Nickel; Editor, Andrea Kuch

Congrès Mensuel (Published by Publicom inc.), #400, 1055, côte du Beaver Hall, CP 365, Montréal QC H2Y 3H1 – 514/274-0004; Fax: 514/274-5884 – Tirage: 5,500; 10 fois par an; français – Rédacteur en chef, Guy Jonkman

Conventions & Meetings Canada (Published by Maclean Hunter Publishing), 777 Bay St., Toronto ON M5W 1A7 – 416/596-5165; Fax: 416/593-3193; Email: jcharles@mhpublishing.com; URL: http://www.mhbizlink.com/mnit – Annually – Editor, Julie Charles

Meetings & Incentive Travel (Published by Maclean Hunter Publishing), 777 Bay St., Toronto ON M5W 1A7 – 416/596-5165, 2697; Fax: 416/593-3193; Email: jcharles@mhpublishing.com; URL: http://www.mhbizlink.com/mnit – Circ.: 10,000; 8 times a year – Editor, Julie Charles, 416/596-2697

Meetings Monthly (Published by Publicom inc.), #400, 1055, côte du Beaver Hall, CP 365, Montréal QC H2Y 3H1 – 514/274-0004; Fax: 514/274-5884 – Circ.: 12,600; 10 times a year – Editor-in-Chief, Guy J. Jonkman

**COSMETICS**

Cosmetics (Published by Maclean Hunter Publishing), 777 Bay St., Toronto ON M5W 1A7 – 416/596-5817; Fax: 416/596-5179 – Circ.: 13,000; 6 times a year; supplement - Men'sline, for consumer market; also Cosmetiques (2 fois par an; français) – Publisher, Jim Hicks, 416/596-5246; Editor, Ronald A. Wood

Spa Management Journal (Published by Publicom inc.), #400, 1055, côte du Beaver Hall, CP 365, Montréal QC H2Y 3H1 – 514/274-0004; Fax: 514/274-5884; URL: http://www.spamanagement.com – Circ.: 13,200; 8 times a year – Publisher, Guy J. Jonkman

**CREDIT**

The Atlantic Co-operator, Atlantic Co-operative Publishers, PO Box 1386, Antigonish NS B2G 2L7 – 902/863-2776; Fax: 902/863-8077; Email: atlcoop@atcon.com.ca – Circ.: 60,000; Bi-monthly – Editor, Brenda MacKinnon; Circulation Manager, Jerome D'Eon

**DAIRY PRODUCTS**

Canadian Dairy, #205, 3269 Bloor St. West, Toronto ON M8X 1E2 – 416/239-8423; Fax: 416/239-7202; URL: http://www.inforamp.net/~dbattler – Circ.: 2,027; 5 times a year – Publisher & Editor, Iain Macnab

**DENTISTRY**

Dental Practice Management (Published by Southam Magazine Group), 1450 Don Mills Rd., Don Mills ON M3B 2X7 – 416/442-2046; Fax: 416/442-2214; Email: ekay@southam.ca – Circ.: 16,500; 4 times a year – Publisher & Editor, Erla Kay; Managing Editor, Cynthia Keeshan, 416/442-2193

Journal Dentaire du Québec, Ordre des dentistes du Québec, 625, boul René Lévesque ouest, 15e étage, Montréal QC H3B 1R2 – 514/875-8511; Fax: 514/875-9412 – Circ.: 4,800; 10 times a year; English & French – Editor, Dr. Denis Forest

Journal of the Canadian Dental Association, 1815 Alta Vista Dr., Ottawa ON K1G 3Y6 – 613/523-1770; Fax: 613/523-7736 – Circ.: 18,600; Monthly; English & French – Publisher, Jardine Neilson; Editor, Dr. P. Ralph Crawford

Ontario Dentist, 4 New St., Toronto ON M5R 1P6 – 416/922-3900; Fax: 416/922-9005 – Circ.: 6,000; 10 times a year – Publisher, Peter James; Editor-in-Chief, James Shosenberg; Managing Editor, Nadine Hubert

Oral Health (Published by Southam Magazine Group), 1450 Don Mills Rd., Don Mills ON M3B 2X7 – 416/442-2046; Fax: 416/442-2214; Email: ekay@southam.ca; URL: http://www.southam.com/b1-3-1.html – Circ.: 16,500; Monthly – Publisher & Editor, Erla Kay; Managing Editor, Cynthia Keeshan, 416/442-2193

Probe, c/o Canadian Dental Hygienists' Assn., 96 Centrepointe Dr., Nepean ON K2G 6B1 – 613/224-5515; Fax: 613/224-7283 – Circ.: 6,800; 6 times a year – Editorial Director, Ellen Brownstone

**DIRECTORIES & ALMANACS**

Sources, #109, 4 Phipps St., Toronto ON M4Y 1J5 – 416/964-7799; Fax: 416/964-8763; Email: sources@sources.com; URL: http://www.sources.com – Circ.: 14,000; 2 times a year – Publisher, Barrie Zwicker; Editor, Kate MacDougall

**DRUGS**

L'Actualité Pharmaceutique (Published by Maclean Hunter Publishing), 1001, boul de Maisonneuve ouest, Montréal QC H3A 3E1 – 514/843-2542; Fax: 514/845-2063 – Mensuel; français – Editeur, Manon Richer; Rédacteur, Danièle Rudel-Tessier

The Canadian Journal of Hospital Pharmacy, The Cdn. Society of Hospital Pharmacists, #350, 1145 Hunt Club Rd., Ottawa ON K1V 0Y3 – 613/736-9733; Fax: 613/736-5660 – Circ.: 3,600; 6 times a year; English & French – Editor, Scott Walker; Circulation Manager, Sue Dokuchie

Canadian Pharmaceutical Journal, Clifford K. Goodman Inc., 1382 Hurontario St., Mississauga ON L5G 3H4 – 905/278-6700; Fax: 905/278-4850; Email: khc@sympatico.ca; cpj@cyberus.ca –

Circ.: 19,500; 10 times a year – Editor, Andrew Reinboldt

Hospital Pharmacy Practice (Published by Maclean Hunter Publishing), 777 Bay St., Toronto ON M5W 1A7 – 416/596-5000; Fax: 416/596-3499; Email: pharmacy@med-news.com – 6 times a year – Editor, Ruth Hanley

Le Pharmactuel, #900, 1470, rue Peel, Montréal QC H3A 1T1 – 514/286-0776; Fax: 514/286-1081; Email: apes@microtec.net – Tirage: 1,300; 6 fois par an – Rédacteur, Denis Lebel

Pharmacy Post (Published by Maclean Hunter Publishing), 777 Bay St., Toronto ON M5W 1A7 – 416/596-5000; Fax: 416/596-3499; Email: pharmacypost@mhpublishing.com; URL: http://www.mhbizlink.compharmacy – Circ.: 17,000; 12 times a year; OTC Report (March) – Associate Publisher, Janet Smith; Editor, Karen Welds

Pharmacy Practice (Published by Maclean Hunter Publishing), 777 Bay St., Toronto ON M5W 1A7 – 416/596-5000; Fax: 416/596-3499 – Circ.: 20,000; 12 times a year – Editor, Anne Bokma

Québec Pharmacie, 4375, av Pierre-de-Coubertin, Montréal QC H1V 1A6 – 514/254-0346; Fax: 514/254-5010; Email: qpharm@codex.qc.ca – Tirage: 6,700; 10 fois par an; français – Editrice, Jacqueline Racicot; Rédactrice, Monique Richer

**EDUCATION**

The ATA Magazine, The Alberta Teachers' Association, 11010 - 142 St., Edmonton AB T5N 2R1 – 403/447-9400; Fax: 403/455-6481; Email: tjohnston@teachers.ab.ca; URL: http://www.teachers.ab.ca – Circ.: 39,500; 4 times a year – Managing Editor, Raymond Gariépy; Editor, Timothy Johnston

The Canadian School Executive, Bentall Centre, PO Box 48265, Vancouver BC V7X 1A1 – 604/739-8600; Fax: 604/739-8200 – 10 times a year – Publisher & Editor-in-Chief, Dr. James Balderson

Canadian Vocational Journal, Association Canadienne de la formation professionnelle, PO Box 3435, Stn D, Ottawa ON K1P 6L4 – 613/722-7696; Fax: 613/722-7696 – Circ.: 1,000; 4 times a year; English & French – Editor, B. Louks

CAUT Bulletin ACPPU, 2675 Queensview Dr., Ottawa ON K2B 8K2 – 613/820-2270; Fax: 613/820-2417; Email: acppu@caut.ca; URL: http://www.caut.ca – Circ.: 34,000; 10 times a year; English & French; supplements - Income Tax Guide (Feb.), Status of Women in Academe (April), Status of Librarians in Academe (June) – Publications Officer, Liza R. Duhaime

Educational Digest (Published by Zanny Ltd.), 11966 Woodbine Ave., Gormley ON L0H 1G0 – 905/887-5048; Fax: 905/887-0764 – Circ.: 17,000; 4 times a year – Publisher, Janet Gardiner

Education Forum, c/o Ontario Secondary School Teachers' Federation, 60 Mobile Dr., Toronto ON M4A 2P3 – 416/751-8300; Fax: 416/751-3394; Email: walkern@osstfon.ca; URL: http://www.osstf.on.ca – Circ.: 46,000; 4 times a year – Editor, Neil Walker; Circulation Manager, June Pariaug

Education Today, Ontario Public School Board's Assn., 439 University Ave. 18th Fl., Toronto ON M5G 1Y8 – 416/340-2540; Fax: 416/340-7571; Email: admin@opsba.org; URL: http://www.opsba.org – Circ.: 4,000; 3 times a year – Editor, Heather Ropseveare Dion; Circulation Manager, Elsa Moura

Green Teacher: Education for Planet Earth, 95 Robert St., Toronto ON M5S 2K5 – 416/960-1244; Fax: 416/925-3474; Email: greentea@web.ca; URL: http://www.web.ca/~greentea – Circ.: 5,700; 4 times a year – Co-Publisher, Tim Grant; Co-Publisher, Gail Littlejohn

Journal les Enseignants, 1316 Domaine du Moulin, L'Ancienne-Lorette QC G2E 4N1 – 418/872-6966 – Tirage: 5 000; 10 fois par an; français; ISSN: 1196-7838 – Éditeur & Rédacteur, Jean-Louis Jobin, Ph.D.

The Manitoba Teacher, The Manitoba Teachers' Society, 191 Harcourt St., Winnipeg MB R3J 3H2 – 204/888-7961; Fax: 204/831-0877 – Circ.: 17,000; 9 times a year – Managing Editor, Raman Job

OPHEA Journal (Published by Kenilworth Publishing), #201, 27 West Beaver Creek, Richmond Hill ON L4B 1M8 – 905/771-7333; Fax: 905/771-7336; Email: sales@kenilworth.cpm – Circ.: 1,600; 3 times a year – Publisher, Jim Davidson; Editor, Phil Parker

Quebec Home & School News, Québec Federation of Home & School Associations, #562, 3285 Cavendish Blvd., Montréal QC H4B 2L9 – 514/481-5619; Fax: 514/481-5610; Email: qfhsa@total.net – Circ.: 7,450; 4 times a year – Editor, Dorothy Nixon

The Reporter, c/o Ontario English Catholic Teachers' Association, 65 St. Clair Ave. East, Toronto ON M4T 2Y8 – 416/925-2493; Fax: 416/925-7764; Email: a.oconnor@oecta.on.ca; URL: http://www/pecta/pm/cary@sympatico.ca – Circ.: 40,000; 3 times a year – Editor-in-Chief, Aleda O'Connor

School Business Magazine (Published by Sawmill Creek Communications), #11, 4040 Creditview Rd., PO Box 1800, Mississauga ON L5C 3Y8 – 905/569-1800; Fax: 905/813-7117 – 6 times a year – Publisher, Hugh Parkinson

Short Courses & Seminars, Development Publications, 152 Carlton St., PO Box 92530, Toronto ON M5A 2K0 – 416/972-1027; Fax: 416/972-1027 – Circ.: 3,000; 2 times a year – Circulation Manager, Detchena Bowler

The Teacher, c/o Nova Scotia Teachers Union, 3106 Dutch Village Rd., Halifax NS B3L 4L7 – 902/477-5621; Fax: 902/477-3517; Email: theteacher@nstu.ns.ca; URL: http://fox.nstn.ca/~nstu/pub-info/ – Circ.: 15,000; Monthly, Oct. to June (9 times a year) – Editor, Paul R. McCormick; Circulation & Advertising Manager, Sonya Morgan

Teach Magazine, Quadrant Educational Media Services Inc., #206, 258 Wallace Ave., Toronto ON M6P 3M9 – 416/537-2103; Fax: 416/537-3491; Email: teachmag@istar.ca; URL: http://www.teachmag.com – Circ.: 22,000; 5 times a year – Publisher & Editor, Wili Liberman

University Affairs, c/o Assn. of Universities & Colleges of Canada, #600, 350 Albert St., Ottawa ON K1R 1B1 – 613/563-1236; Fax: 613/563-9745; Email: ctausig@aucc.ca; URL: http://www.aucc.ca – Circ.: 31,000; 10 times a year; English & French; ISSN: 0041-9257 – Publisher & Editor, Christine Tausig Ford; Coordinator, Campus Advertising & Circulation, Colleen LaPlante

University Manager (Published by August Communications Ltd.), #200, 388 Donald St., Winnipeg MB R3B 2J4 – 204/957-0265; Fax: 204/957-0217; Email: august@escape.ca; URL: http://www.august.ca – Circ.: 3,000; 4 times a year; English & French – Publisher, Gladwyn Nickel; Editor, Andrea Kuch

**ELECTRICAL EQUIPMENT & ELECTRONICS**

Canadian Electronics (Published by Action Communications Inc.), 135 Spy Ct., Markham ON L3R 5H6 – 905/447-3222; Fax: 905/477-4320; Email: ce@actioncom.com; URL: http://www.industrycan.com – Circ.: 22,000; 6 times a year; also annual directory of supplies – Publisher, Tony Chisholm

EIC (Electronique, industrielle et commerciale), Serpro Communications inc., 8403, rue Oscar-Roland, Montréal QC H2M 2T4 – 514/383-7700; Fax: 514/383-7691 – Tirage: 9,019; 5 fois par an; français – Editeur, J.J. Pierre Tremblay; Rédacteur, Ernest Bourgault

Electrical Bluebook (Published by Kerrwil Publications Ltd.), 395 Matheson Blvd. East, Mississauga ON L4Z 2H2 – 905/890-1846; Fax: 905/890-5769; Email: rbm@inforamp.net – Circ.: 18,000; Annually, Jan. – Publisher, Janet Small; Editor, Roger Burford Mason; Circulation Manager, Jean Bilkey

Electrical Business (Published by Kerrwil Publications Ltd.), 395 Matheson Blvd. East, Mississauga ON L4Z 2H2 – 905/890-1846; Fax: 905/890-5769; Email: ibm@inforamp.net – Circ.: 19,500; Monthly – Publisher, Janet Small; Editor, Roger Burford Mason; Circulation Manager, Jean Bilkey

Electrical Equipment News - The Industrial Buyer (Published by Southam Magazine Group), 1450 Don Mills Rd., Don Mills ON M3B 2X7 – 416/445-6641; Fax: 416/442-2214 – Circ.: 23,516; 2 times a year – Publisher, Alex Papanov; Editor, Olga Markovich; Circulation Manager, Dianne Rakoff

Electrical Line, 3105 Benbow Rd., West Vancouver BC V7V 3E1 – 604/922-5516; Fax: 604/922-5312; Email: kevinb@electricalline.com; URL: http://www.electricalline.com – Circ.: 7,200; 6 times a year – Publisher, Kevin Buhr; Editor, Ken Buhr; Circulation Manager, Sheila Wilson

Electrical Supply & Distribution Annual (Published by Kerrwil Publications Ltd.), 395 Matheson Blvd. East, Mississauga ON L4Z 2H2 – 905/890-1846; Fax: 905/890-5769; Email: rbm@inforamp.net – Circ.: 12,500; Annually, May – Publisher, Janet Small; Editor, Roger Burford Mason; Circulation Manager, Jean Bilkey

Électricité Québec, 5925, boul Decarie, Montréal QC H3W 3C9 – 514/738-2184; Fax: 514/738-2192; URL: http://www.cmeq.org – Tirage: 9 301; 10 fois par an; framçais – Editrice & Rédactrice, Suzanne Desrosiers; Directrice de tirage, Louisette Brousseau

Electricity Today, Hurst Communications, #101, 345 Kingston Rd., Pickering ON L1V 1A1 – 905/509-4448; Fax: 905/509-4451; Email: hq@electricityform.com; URL: http://www.electricityforum.com – Circ.: 12,000; 10 times a year – Publisher, Randolph Hurst; Editor, Richard Douglas; Circulaton Manager, Colleen Hurst

The Electronics Communicator (Published by Evert Communications Ltd.), 1296 Carling Ave., 2nd Fl., Ottawa ON K1Z 7K8 – 613/728-4621; Fax: 613/728-0385; Email: newsdesk@evert.com; URL: http://www.evert.com – 40 times a year – Publisher/Editor, Gordon D. Hutchison; Assistant Editor, Alex Anderson; Circulation Manager, Carole Jeffrey

EP&T, Lakeview Publications, 1200 Aerowood Dr., Unit 27, Mississauga ON L4W 2S7 – 905/624-8100; Fax: 905/624-1760; Email: info@ept.ca; URL: http://www/ept.ca – Circ.: 23,786; 8 times a year; also EP&T's Electrosource Product Reference Guide & Telephone Directory (annually, Jan.) – Publisher, Robert C. Luton; Editor, David Kerfoot

Le Monde de l'electricité (Published by Groupe Constructo), #200, 1500, boul Jules-Poitras, Saint-Laurent QC H4N 1X7 – 514/745-5720; Fax: 514/339-2267 – Tirage: 7 649; 10 fois par an; français – Editeur, Johanne Rouleau

Report on Wireless (Published by Evert Communications Ltd.), 1296 Carling Ave., 2nd Fl., Ottawa ON K1Z 7K8 – 613/728-4621; Fax: 613/728-0385; Email: newsdesk@evert.com; URL: http://www.evert.com – Weekly; by fax, email & www only – Publisher, Gordon D. Hutchison; Editor, Trevor Marshall; Circulation Manager, Carole Jeffrey

**EMERGENCY SERVICES**

Canadian Emergency News, Pendragon Publishing, 7750 Ranchview Dr. NW, PO Box 68010, Calgary AB T3G 3N8 – 403/547-5748, 1-800-567-0911;

Fax: 403/547-5749 – Circ.: 5,000; 6 times a year – Publisher/Editor, Lyle Blumhagen

Emergency Prepardness Direct (Published by Canada Communications Group), #A-2411, 45, boul Sacre-Coeur, Hull QC K1A 0S9 – 819/956-7864; Fax: 819/956-5134; Email: cominfo@x400.gc.ca – Circ.: 3,300; 4 times a year; English & French – Editor, André Lamalice

**ENGINEERING**

Aggregates & Roadbuilding Contractor, Franmore Communications Inc., #215, 4999 Ste-Catherine St. West, Westmount QC H3Z 1T3 – 514/487-9868; Fax: 514/487-9276 – Circ.: 7,627; 8 times a year – Publisher & Editor, Robert L. Consedine

Annuaire Téléphonique de la Construction du Québec, 22, rue St-Charles, CP 590, Ste-Thérèse QC J7E 2A4 – 514/437-1600; Fax: 514/437-0723; Email: optilog@optilog.com; URL: http://www.optilog.com – Annuellement; français – Editeur & Rédacteur, Michel Vaudrin

Canadian Consulting Engineer (Published by Southam Magazine Group), 1450 Don Mills Rd., Don Mills ON M3B 2X7 – 416/445-6641; Fax: 416/442-2214 – Circ.: 8,900; 7 times a year – Publisher, Jack Meli; Editor, Sophie Kneisel

Canadian Heavy Equipment Guide (Published by Baum Publications Ltd.), #201, 2323 Boundary Rd., Vancouver BC V5M 4V8 – 604/291-9900; Fax: 604/291-1906 – Circ.: 30,000; 10 times a year – Publisher, Englebert Baum; Editor, Len Webster

CCLS Focus, The Canadian Council of Land Surveyors, 1043 McNicoll Ave., Scarborough ON M1W 3W6 – 416/491-4009; Fax: 416/491-2576; Email: ccls@interlog.com – 2 times a year – Editor, Brian Munday

Construction Alberta News, 10536 - 106 St., Edmonton AB T5H 2X6 – 403/424-1146; Fax: 403/425-5886 – Circ.: 4,000; 2 times a year – Editor, D. Coates

Energy Manager (Published by Kerrwil Publications Ltd.), 395 Matheson Blvd. East, Mississauga ON L4Z 2H2 – 905/890-1846; Fax: 905/890-5769 – Circ.: 11,000; 6 times a year – Publisher, Gary A. Dugan; Editor, Bryan S. Rogers; Circulation Manager, Jean Bilkey

Engineering Dimensions, #1000, 25 Sheppard Ave. West, North York ON M2N 6S9 – 416/224-1100; Fax: 416/224-8168; Email: spawlett@peo.on.ca; URL: http://www.peo.on.ca – Circ.: 60,000; 6 times a year – Publisher, David Fletcher; Managing Editor, Steve Pawlett

Equipment Journal, Pace Publishing Limited, 5160 Explorer Dr., Unit 6, Mississauga ON L5H 3R2 – 905/274-4883; Fax: 905/274-8686; Email: equipmentjournal@globalserve.net – Circ.: 19,500; 17 issues a year, every 3 weeks – Publisher & Editor, E.E. Abel; Managing Editor, Michael Anderson; Associate Publisher, John Baker

Geomatica, c/o Canadian Institute of Geomatics, PO Box 5378, Stn F, Ottawa ON K2C 3J1 – 613/224-9851; Fax: 613/224-9577; Email: editgeo@magi.com; URL: http://www.cig-acsq.ca – Circ.: 1,600; 4 times a year; English & French – Editor, M. Pinch

Innovation, c/o Assn. of Professional Engineers & Geoscientists of BC, #200, 4010 Regent St., Burnaby BC V5C 6NZ – 604/929-6733; Fax: 604/929-6753; Email: apegomfp@apeg.bc.ca; URL: http://www.apeg.bc.ca – Circ.: 17,080; 10 times a year – Editor, Wayne Gibson, P.Eng.; Advertising Manager, Gillian Cobban

Northpoint (Published by Ontario Association of Certified Engineering Technicians & Technologists), #404, 10 Four Seasons Pl., Etobicoke ON M6B 6H7 – 416/621-9621; Fax: 416/621-8694 – Circ.: 1,300; 4 times a year – Director, Publications & Communications, R.M. Klein; Editor, Robert Fowler

The Ontario Land Surveyor Quarterly, 1043 McNicoll Ave., Scarborough ON M1W 3W6 – 416/491-9020; Fax: 416/491-2576; Email: aols@interlog.com; URL: http://www/interlog.com/~aols – Circ.: 1,600; 4 times a year – Editor, Brian Munday

Ontario Technologist (Published by Ontario Association of Certified Engineering Technicians & Technologists), #404, 10 Four Seasons Pl., Etobicoke ON M6B 6H7 – 416/621-9621; Fax: 416/621-8694; Email: mellor@interlog.com; URL: http://www.oacett.org – Circ.: 21,000; 6 times a year – Editor, Colleen Mellor

The PEGG, APEGGA, Tower One, 15th Fl., 10060 Jasper Ave., Edmonton AB T5J 4A2 – 403/426-3990; Fax: 403/425-1722; Email: email@appega.com; URL: http://www.appega.com – Circ.: 33,000; 10 times a year – Editor, Nordahl Flakstad; Managing Editor, Trevor Maine, P.Eng.; Publications Secretary, Jackie Hessels

Plan, #1800, 2020 University St., Montréal QC H3A 2A5 – 514/845-6141; Fax: 514/845-1833 – Tirage: 40,000; 9 fois par an; français – Rédacteur, Jean-Marc Papineau

Plan Canada, Canadian Institute of Planners, #801, 116 Albert St., Ottawa ON K1P 5G3 – 613/237-7526; Fax: 613/237-7045; Email: hlrplan@limestone.kosone.com; URL: http://www.cip-icu.ca – Circ.: 4,900; 6 times a year – Editor-in-chief, Pamela Robinson

Publiquip/Roucam, 10595, boul Louis-H-Lafontaine, Anjou QC H1J 2E8 – 514/351-1110; Fax: 514/351-1066 – Tirage: 45 300; Mensuel; français – Président, Gilles Chevigny

Supply Post, #108, 19329 Enterprise Way, Surrey BC V3S 6J8 – 604/533-5577; Fax: 604/533-9533 – Circ.: 14,900; 11 times a year – Managing Editor, D. Kenward

**FIRE PROTECTION**

Atlantic Firefighter, Hilden Publishing Ltd., 34 Spring St., PO Box 919, Amherst NS B4H 4E1 – 902/667-3009; Fax: 902/667-2868 – Circ.: 9,073; 11 times a year – Publisher, Earl Gouchie; Editor, Doug Harkness

The Canadian Firefighter, PO Box 95, Stn D, Etobicoke ON M9A 4X1 – 416/233-2516; Fax: 416/233-2051; Email: cdnff@interhop.net; URL: http://www.interhop.net/cdnff/cdnff.html – Circ.: 11,607; 6 times a year – Publisher & Editor, Lorne Campbell; Circulation Manager, R.V. Mullen

Fire Fighting in Canada (Published by Annex Publishing & Printing Inc.), 222 Argyle Ave., Delhi ON N4B 2Y2 – 519/582-2513; Fax: 519/582-4040; Email: firefcan@nornet.on.ca – Circ.: 7,500; 10 times a year – Publisher, David Douglas; Editor, Jim Knisley

**FISHERIES**

Atlantic Fisherman, Graphic Advocate Co. Ltd., #30, 3695 Barrington St. North, Halifax NS B3K 2Y3 – 902/422-4990; Fax: 902/422-4278 – Circ.: 4,486; Monthly – Editor, Karen Futton

Atlantic Fish Farming, PO Box 790, Montague PE C0A 1R0 – 902/838-2515; Fax: 902/838-4392 – 12 times a year – Publisher, Jim MacNeill

The Fisherman, #160, 111 Victoria Dr., Vancouver BC V5L 4C4 – 604/255-1366; Fax: 604/255-3162 – Circ.: 7,700; Monthly – Editor, Sean Griffin

Northern Aquaculture, RR#4, Site 465, C-37, Courtenay BC V9N 7J3 – 250/338-2455, 1-800-661-0368; Fax: 250/338-2466; Email: naqua@mars.ark.com; URL: http://www.naqua.com/ – Circ.: 4,200; 12 times a year – Editor (West Coast), Peter Chettleburgh, Email: chet@islandnet.com; Business Manager, Catherine Egan; Editor (East Coast), John Gracey, Email: jgracey@cycor.ca

The Sou'Wester, Cameron Publishing, PO Box 128, Yarmouth NS B5A 4B1 – 902/742-7111; Fax: 902/742-2311 – Circ.: 10,500; 24 times a year – Editor, Alain Meuse

The Westcoast Fisherman (Published by Westcoast Publishing Ltd), 1496 - 72nd Ave. West, Vancouver BC V6P 3C8 – 604/266-7433; Fax: 604/263-8620; Email: fish@west_coast.com – Circ.: 10,000; Monthly – Publisher, David Rahn

**FLOOR COVERINGS**

Coverings: Floors, Windows & Walls, Mayville Publishing (Canada) Ltd., RR#1, Picton ON K0K 2T0 – 613/476-4244; Fax: 613/476-5233 – Circ.: 8,229; 7 times a year – Publisher, Peter Spragg

Floor Coverings, PO Box 113, Bloomfield ON K0K 1G0 – 613/476-4244; Fax: 613/476-5233 – 7 times a year

Surface, 1475 Maisonneuve, Val-David QC J0T 2N0 – 819/322-7940; Fax: 819/322-1789 – Tirage: 6,325; 8 fois par an; français – Rédacteur, Richard Boiduc

**FLORISTS**

Canadian Florist, Greenhouse & Nursery, Horticulture Publications Ltd., 1090 Aerowood Dr., Unit #1, Mississauga ON L4W 1Y5 – 905/625-2730; Fax: 905/625-1355 – Monthly – Publisher/Editor, Peter Heywood

Cut & Dried, 2 Highview Dr., Simcoe ON N3Y 2K2 – 519/428-8020; Fax: 519/428-1122 – 6 times a year – Publisher, Sue Fredericks

Fleur Design (Published by Editions Versicolores inc.), 1320, boul St-Joseph, Québec QC G2K 1G2 – 418/628-8690; Fax: 418/628-0524 – 6 fois par an; français – Editeur, François Bernatchez; Rédacteur en chef, Caty Bérubé

**FOOD & BEVERAGE**

Canadian Pizza Magazine (Published by Annex Publishing & Printing Inc.), 222 Argyle Ave., Delhi ON N4B 2Y2 – 519/582-2513; Fax: 519/582-4040 – Circ.: 12,250; 4 times a year – Publisher, David W. Douglas

Enoteca Wine & Food Magazine, PO Box 37, Concord ON L4K 1B2 – 905/850-9463; Fax: 905/850-8099 – Circ.: 10,000; 4 times a year – Editor, W. Cavalière

Food in Canada (Published by Maclean Hunter Publishing), 777 Bay St., Toronto ON M5W 1A7 – 416/596-5192; Fax: 416/593-3189; Email: catfood@mhpublishing.com; URL: http://www.mhbizlink.com/food/ – Circ.: 8,384; 9 times a year – Associate Publisher, Ingrid Eilbracht

**FOOTWEAR**

Canadian Footwear Journal (Published by McLeish Communications Inc.), 1, rue Pacifique, Ste-Anne-de-Bellevue QC H9X 1C5 – 514/457-2423; Fax: 514/457-2577; Email: footwear@total.net – Circ.: 7,000; 8 times a year; plus Retail Buyers' Guide (annual), Shoemaking Buyers' Guide (annual) – Publisher, George McLeish; Editor, Peter Matz; Circulation Manager, Ruth Gardiner

**FOREST & LUMBER INDUSTRIES**

Business Farmer (Published by Westcoast Publishing Ltd), 1496 - 72nd Ave. West, Vancouver BC V6P 3C8 – 604/266-7433; Fax: 604/263-8620 – Circ.: 9,000; Monthly – Publisher, David Rahn

The Business Logger (Published by Westcoast Publishing Ltd), 1496 - 72nd Ave. West, Vancouver BC V6P 3C8 – 604/266-7433; Fax: 604/263-8620; Email: wcoast@wimsey.com – Circ.: 9,000; Monthly – Publisher, David Rahn

Canadian Forest Industries (Published by JCFT Forest Communications Inc.), 1, rue Pacifique, Ste-Anne-de-Bellevue QC H9X 1C5 – 514/457-2211; Fax: 514/457-2558; URL: http://www.forestind.com – Circ.: 13,000; 8 times a year – Publisher, Tim Tolton; Editor, Scott Jamieson; Circulation Manager, Carol Nixon

Canadian Wood Products (Published by JCFT Forest Communications Inc.), 1, rue Pacifique, Ste-Anne-de-Bellevue QC H9X 1C5 – 514/457-2211; Fax: 514/457-2558 – Circ.: 7,500; 6 times a year – Publisher, Tim Tolton; Editor, Scott Jamieson; Circulation Manager, Carol Nixon

Le Coopérateur forestier (Published by Les Editions forestières), 520, rue des Méandres, Québec QC G2E 5N4 – 418/877-4583; Fax: 418/877-6449 – Tirage: 5,500; 10 fois par an; français – Rédacteur en chef, Alain Castonguay; Directrice de tirage, Sylvie Julien

Directory of Ontario Lumber & Building Materials Retailers, Buyers' Guide & Product Directory (Published by Naylor Communications Ltd.), 920 Yonge St., 6th Fl., Toronto ON M4W 3C7 – 416/961-1028; Fax: 416/924-4408 – Annually, Oct. – Editor, Lori Knowles

The Forestry Chronicle, Canadian Institute of Forestry, #606, 151 Slater St., Ottawa ON K1P 5H3 – 613/234-2242; Fax: 613/234-6181; Email: cif@cif-ifc.org; URL: http://www.cif-ifc.org – Circ.: 2,822; 6 times a year – Editor, D. Burgess; Editor, V.J. Nordin

Hiballer Forest Magazine, HB Publishers, #11, 106 - 14th St. East, North Vancouver BC V7L 2N3 – 604/984-2002; Fax: 604/984-2820 – 6 times a year – Publisher/Managing Editor, Paul Young

Logging & Sawmilling Journal, PO Box 86670, North Vancouver BC V7L 4L2 – 604/990-9970; Fax: 604/990-9971; Email: stanhope@forestnet.com; URL: http://www.forestnet.com – Circ.: 15,900; 10 times a year – Publisher, Robert Stanhope; Editor, Norm Poole, 604/944-6146

Madison's Canadian Lumber Directory, PO Box 2486, Vancouver BC V6B 3W7 – 604/681-6838; Fax: 604/681-6585; Email: madisons@dowco.com; URL: http://www.dowco.com/cmd/madisons – Circ.: 1,200; Annually, Spring – Publisher, Laurence Cater; Editor, Leah McNutt

Opérations forestières et de scierie (Published by JCFT Forest Communications Inc.), 1, rue Pacifique, Ste-Anne-de-Bellevue QC H9X 1C5 – 514/457-2211; Fax: 514/457-2558 – Tirage: 5,500; 4 fois par an; français – Editeur/Rédacteur, Guy Fortin

Le Resam forestier (Published by Les Editions forestières), 520, rue des Méandres, Québec QC G2E 5N4 – 418/877-4583; Fax: 418/877-6449 – Tirage: 11,700; 10 fois par an; français – Rédacteur, Alain Castonguay; Directrice de tirage, Sylvie Julien

Truck Logger Magazine, #725, 815 West Hastings St., Vancouver BC V6C 1B4 – 604/682-4080; Fax: 604/682-3775; Email: truck_loggers@bc.sympatico.ca; URL: http://www.forestind.com/tla – 6 times a year – Publisher/Editor, David Webster; Sales, Lucy Butler

Yardstick, Craig Kelman & Assoc., #3C, 2020 Portage Ave., Winnipeg MB R3J 0K4 – 204/885-7798; Fax: 204/889-3576 – Circ.: 1,600; 6 times a year; also WRLA Directory & Buyers' Guide (annually, Jan.) – Editor, Jim E. Watson

## FUNERAL SERVICE

Canadian Funeral Director, Halket Publishing Ltd., #206, 174 Harwood Ave. South, Ajax ON L1S 2H7 – 905/427-6121; Fax: 905/427-1660 – Monthly – Publisher, Ray Halket; Editor, Scott Hillier

Canadian Funeral News (Published by OT Communications), #600, 237 - 8th Ave. SE, Calgary AB T2G 5C3 – 403/264-3270; Fax: 403/264-3276 – Monthly – Publisher, Patrick Ottmann; Editor, Natika Sunstrum

Network (Published by OT Communications), #600, 237 - 8th Ave. SE, Calgary AB T2G 5C3 – 403/569-9520; Fax: 403/569-9590 – 6 times a year – Editor, Richard Bronstein

## FUR TRADE

The Canadian Trapper, Coyote Communications Inc., 9748 - 71 Ave., Grand Prairie AB T8V 6P9 – 403/538-9716; Fax: 403/539-9742; Email: wildfur@agt.net – Circ.: 5,700; 6 times a year; also BC Trapper Magazine, 4 times a year (circ. 1,200) – Publisher, Becky McIntosh McDonald

## GARDENING & GARDEN EQUIPMENT

Greenhouse Canada (Published by Annex Publishing & Printing Inc.), 222 Argyle Ave., Delhi ON N4B 2Y2 – 519/582-2513; Fax: 519/582-4040; Email: greenhse@nornet.on.ca – Circ.: 4,500; Monthly – Publisher, Michael V. Fredericks

## GIFTS

Canadian Gifts & Collectibles Retailer (Published by Trajan Publishing Corp.), #202, 103 Lakeshore Rd., St Catharines ON L2N 2T6 – 905/646-7744; Fax: 905/646-0995; Email: fiocca@trajan.com – 6 times a year – Publishers, Paul Fiocca; Editor, Bret Evans

CGTA Retail News, Canadian Gift & Tableware Association, #301, 265 Yorkland Blvd., North York ON M2J 1S5 – 416/497-5771; Fax: 416/497-3448 – Circ.: 33,380; 4 times a year – Editor, Diana Daniels

Gifts & Tablewares (Published by Southam Magazine Group), 1450 Don Mills Rd., Don Mills ON M3B 2X7 – 416/445-6641; Fax: 416/442-2213; Email: lsmith@southam.ca; URL: http://www.southam.com/b1-9-1/html – Circ.: 14,000; 7 times a year – Editor/Publisher, Dawn Dickinson, 416/442-2996

## GLASS

Glass Canada (Published by AIS Communications Ltd.), 145 Thames Rd. West, Exeter ON N0M 1S3 – 519/235-2400; Fax: 519/235-0798 – Circ.: 5,144; 6 times a year – Publisher, Peter Phillips; Editor, Peter Darbishire; Circulation Manager, Jan Jeffery

## GOVERNMENT

BC Municipal Redbook (Published by Construction Marketing Data Canada Inc.), 4285 Canada Way, Burnaby BC V5G 1H2 – 604/433-8164; Fax: 604/433-9549; Email: jofc@lynx.bc.ca – Circ.: 2,000; Annual – Publisher, Judy Sirett; Editor, Anne Crittenden

FCM Forum, Federation of Canadian Municipalities, 24 Clarence St., Ottawa ON K1N 5P3 – 613/241-5221; Fax: 613/241-7440; Email: federation@fcm.ca; URL: http://www.fcm.ca – Circ.: 7,000; 8 times a year; English & French – Director, Bruce Hollands

Focus, The Government Source, 1025 Richmond Rd., Unit 107, Ottawa ON K2B 8G8 – 613/820-3272; Fax: 613/820-3646 – Circ.: 12,700; 8 times a year; English & French – Publisher, Ken Lagasse; Editor, Richard Newport

Government Business (Published by Sawmill Creek Communications), #11, 4040 Creditview Rd., PO Box 1800, Mississauga ON L5C 3Y8 – 905/813-7100; Fax: 905/813-7117 – Circ.: 20,000; 6 times a year – Publisher, Hugh Parkinson; Editor, Jay Barwell

Government Business Opportunities, Sebra Inc., 55 Bloor St. West, 8th Fl., Toronto ON M4W 3N5 – 416/927-5881; Fax: 416/927-5664 – Circ.: 2,000; 3 issues per week; English & French – Editor, Carole Kennedy

Government Purchasing Guide (Published by Moorshead Magazines Ltd.), #490, 10 Gateway Blvd., Toronto ON M3C 3T4 – 416/696-5488; Fax: 416/696-7395; Email: gpg@moorshead.com; URL: http://www.moorshead.com/~magazine.gps/ – Circ.: 17,000; Monthly – Publisher, Halvor Moorshead; Editor, John Dujay; Circulation Manager, Rick Cree

Municipal World, PO Box 399, Stn Main, St. Thomas ON N5P 3V3 – 519/633-0031; Fax: 519/633-1001; Email: mwadmin@municipalworld.com; URL: http://www.municipalworld.com – Circ.: 7,400; Monthly – Publisher & Editor, Michael J. Smither; Circulation Manager, Wanda Tully

Optimum: The Journal of Public Sector Management, Prospectus Inc., #900, 180 Elgin St., Ottawa ON K2P 2Z9 – 613/580-2207; Fax: 613/237-7666; Email: aphillips@prospectus.com; URL: http://www.optimum.prspectus.com – Publisher, Anne Phillips

La Revue Municipale, Publigam, #202, 339, rue Fleury ouest, Montréal QC H3L 1V5 – 514/383-0883; Fax: 514/383-5590; Email: lrm@point-net.com; URL: http://www.revuemunicipale.com – Tirage: 7,332; Mensuel; français – Editeur, Gilles P. Verronneau; Rédacteur, Phillipe Gauthier

Urba, L'Union des municipalitiés de Québec, #680, 680, rue Sherbrooke ouest, Montréal QC H3A 2M7 – 514/282-7700; Fax: 514/282-7711 – Tirage: 8,000; 10 fois par an; français – Rédacteur, Martin Lasalle

## GRAPHIC ARTS

Applied Arts, #324, 885 Don Mills Rd., Don Mills ON M3C 1V9 – 416/510-0909; Fax: 416/510-0913; Email: app-edit@interlog.com; URL: http://www.interlog.com/~app-arts – Circ.: 11,000; 7 times a year – Publisher, George Haroutiun; Editor, Sara Curtis

The Graphic Exchange, Brill Communications Inc., #65090, 358 Danforth Ave., Toronto ON M4K 3Z2 – 416/961-1325; Fax: 416/961-0941 – 6 times a year – Publisher & Editor, Dan Brill

## GROCERY TRADE

L'Alimentation, Les Editions du marchand québécois, 1298, rue St-Zotique est, Montréal QC H2S 1N7 – 514/271-6922; Fax: 514/283-3170 – Tirage: 14 500; 10 fois par an; français – Rédactrice, Françoise Pitt

Canadian Grocer (Published by Maclean Hunter Publishing), 777 Bay St., Toronto ON M5W 1A7 – 416/596-5191; Fax: 416/593-3162; Email: emasters@cycor.ca; URL: http://www.mhbizlink.com/grocer – Circ.: 18,000; Monthly; supplements - The Excecutive Report, Food Brokers Issue, Directory of Non-Food Suppliers, & Who's Who of Grocery Retailing – Publisher, Karen James; Editor, George H. Condon, 416/596-5772; Circulation Manager, Celia Ramwarine

Grocer Today (Published by Canada Wide Magazines & Communications Ltd.), 4180 Lougheed Hwy., 4th Fl., Burnaby BC V5C 6A7 – 604/299-7311; Fax: 604/299-9188 – Circ.: 11,500; 10 times a year – Publisher, Peter Legge; Editor, Janet Collins; Circulation Manager, Mark Weeks

Western Grocer (Published by Mercury Publications Ltd.), 1839 Inkster Blvd., Winnipeg MB R2X 1R3 – 204/697-0835; Fax: 204/633-7784; Email: mp@mercury.mb.ca – Circ.: 11,986; 6 times a year – Publisher, Gren R. Yeo

## HARDWARE TRADE

Centre Magazine (Published by Southam Magazine Group), 1450 Don Mills Rd., Don Mills ON M3B 2X7 – 416/445-6641; Fax: 416/442-2077; URL: http://www.southam.com/b1-9-2.html – Circ.: 14,960; 8 times a year – Editor, Elena Opasini

Le Guide des fournisseurs des centres de rénovation et des quincailleries du Québec (Published by Publiédition inc.), 620, boul Industriel, St-Jean-sur-Richelieu QC J3B 7X4 – 514/856-7821; Fax: 514/359-0836 – Annuellement – Éditeur, Yves Bégnoche

Hardware Merchandising (Published by Maclean Hunter Publishing), 777 Bay St., Toronto ON M5W 1A7 – 416/596-5284, 5259; Fax: 416/593-2642; URL: http://www.hardware-merchandising.com – Circ.: 14,943; 9 times a year – Publisher, Stephen Payne

Home Improvement Retailing, Powershift Communications Inc., #308, 245 Fairview Mall Dr., North York ON M2J 4T1 – 416/494-1066; Fax: 416/

494-2536 – Circ.: 15,600; 6 times a year – Publisher, Dante Piccinin

Quart de rond, Assn des détaillants de matériaux de construction du Québec, 474, Place Trans-Canada, Longueuil QC J4G 1N8 – 514/646-5842; Fax: 514/646-6171; Email: admacq@accent.net – Tirage: 4,400; 8 fois par an; français – Rédacteur, Gabriel Pollender; Directrice de tirage, Lisette Leduc

Quincaillerie-Matériaux (Published by Maclean Hunter Publishing), 777 Bay St., Toronto ON M5W 1A7 – 416/596-5259; Fax: 416/596-5553; URL: http://www.cyberplex.com/quincaillerie – Tirage: 4,900; 6 fois par an; français – Rédacteur, Benoit Bisson

**HEALTH & MEDICAL**

L'Actualité Médicale (Published by Maclean Hunter Publishing), 1001, boul de Maisonneuve ouest, Montréal QC H3A 3E1 – 514/843-2542; Fax: 514/845-2063 – 44 fois par an; français – Editeur, Jacques Lafontaine; Rédactrice en chef, Danièle Rudel-Tessier

The Alberta Doctors' Digest, Alberta Medical Association, 12230 - 106 Ave. NW, Edmonton AB T5N 3Z1 – 403/482-2626; Fax: 403/482-5445; URL: http://www.amda.ab.ca – Circ.: 5,600; 10 times a year – Editor, Dr. Gerald L. Higgins

Annals of the Royal College of Physicians & Surgeons of Canada, Royal College of Physicians & Surgeons of Canada, 774 Promenade Echo Dr., Ottawa ON K1S 5N8 – 613/730-6200; Fax: 613/730-8830; Email:: lynne.quon-mak@rcpsc.edu – Circ.: 29,000; 8 times a year; English & French – Associate Editor, Lynne Quon-Mak

Artère, c/o Les Éditions 2000 Neuf, #330, 606, rue Cathcart, Montréal QC H3B 1K9 – 514/868-0383; Fax: 514/868-0608; Email: 2009@sympatico.ca; URL: http://www.2009.com – Tirage: 6,661; 11 fois par an; français – Rédacteur, Michel Bissonnette, 514/868-2009; Staff Writer, Françoix Marcil, 514/868-0383

British Columbia Medical Journal, c/o BC Medical Association, #115, 1665 West Broadway, Vancouver BC V6J 5A4 – 604/736-5551; Fax: 604/733-7317; Email: cupton@bcma.bc.ca – Circ.: 8,000; Monthly – Editor, James A. Wilson, M.D.

CAEP/ACMU Communiqué (Published by Canadian Medical Association), 1867 Alta Vista Dr., Ottawa ON K1G 3Y6 – 613/731-9331; Fax: 613/523-0937; Email: pubs@cma.ca – Circ.: 1,800; 4 times a year – Editor, Robert Street, M.D.

Canadian Association of Radiologists Journal (Published by Canadian Medical Association), 1867 Alta Vista Dr., Ottawa ON K1G 3Y6 – 613/731-9331; Fax: 613/523-0937; Email: pubs@cma.ca; URL: http://www.cma.ca – Circ.: 1,800; Bi-monthly; English & French – Editor, Dr. A. Dale Vellet

Canadian Family Physician, College of Family Physicians of Canada, 2630 Skymark Ave., Mississauga ON L4W 5A4 – 905/629-0900; Fax: 905/629-0893; Email: national postoffice pek@cfpc.attmail.com – Circ.: 30,000; Monthly – Editorial Director, Dr. Calvin Gutkin

Canadian Healthcare Manager (Published by Maclean Hunter Publishing), 777 Bay St., Toronto ON M5W 1A7 – 416/596-5794; Fax: 416/596-5071 – Circ.: 20,000; 4 times a year 6 – Publisher, John Milne; Editor, Celia Milne; Circulation Manager, Donna Singh

Canadian Journal of Allergy & Immunology (Published by Medicopea International Inc.), #300, 3333, boul Cote-Vertu, Saint-Laurent QC H4R 2N1 – 514/331-4561; Fax: 514/336-1129; Email: Medicopea@nextaxis.qc.ca – Circ.: 3,600; 6 times a year – Publisher, Lawrence Goldstein; Circulation Manager, Mary Di Lemme

Canadian Journal of Anaesthesia, c/o Canadian Anaesthetists' Society, #208, 1 Eglinton Ave. East, Toronto ON M4P 3A1 – 416/480-0602; Fax: 416/480-0320; Email: cas@multinet.net; URL: http://www.cas.ca – Circ.: 5,000; Monthly – Editor, Dr. David R. Bevan; Circulation Manager, Angela Fritsch

Canadian Journal of Cardiology (Published by Pulsus Group Inc.), 2902 South Sheridan Way, Oakville ON L6J 7L6 – 905/829-4770; Fax: 905/829-4799; Email: pulsus@pulsus.com; URL: http://www.pulsus.com.home.htm – Circ.: 16,000; Monthly – Publisher, Robert B. Kalina; Editor, Dr. E.R. Smith

The Canadian Journal of Clinical Pharmacology (Published by Pulsus Group Inc.), 2902 South Sheridan Way, Oakville ON L6J 7L6 – 905/829-4770; Fax: 905/829-4799; Email: pulsus@pulsus.com; URL: http://www.pulsus.com/home.htm – Circ.: 20,000; 4 times a year; English with French abstracts – Publisher, Robert J. Kalina; Editor, Dr. Neil Shear

Canadian Journal of Continuing Medical Education (Published by STA Communications Inc.), #306, 955, boul Saint-Jean, Pointe-Claire QC H9R 5K3 – 514/695-7623; Fax: 514/695-8554 – Circ.: 35,065; Monthly – Publisher, Robert E. Passaretti; Editor, Monica Matys; Circulation Manager, Gail Gafka

Canadian Journal of Dermatology (Published by Rodar International Inc.), 84 Hymus Blvd., Pointe-Claire QC H9R 1E4 – 514/697-7738; Fax: 514/697-4114; Email: cjd@canadianjournals.com – Circ.: 9,300; 4 times a year – Publisher, Bob Fauteux; Managing Editor, Terry O'Shaughnessy

The Canadian Journal of Diagnosis (Published by STA Communications Inc.), #306, 955, boul Saint-Jean, Pointe-Claire QC H9R 5K3 – 514/695-7623; Fax: 514/695-8554 – Circ.: 34,270; Monthly – Publisher, Robert Passaretti; Editor, Tracy Schuppli; Circulation Manager, Gail Gafka

Canadian Journal of Gastroenterology (Published by Pulsus Group Inc.), 2902 South Sheridan Way, Oakville ON L6J 7L6 – 905/829-4770; Fax: 905/829-4799; Email: pulsus@pulsus.com; URL: http://www.pulsus.com/home.htm – Circ.: 17,000; 8 times a year – Publisher, Robert B. Kalina; Co-Editor, Dr. A.B.R. Thomson; Co-Editor, Dr. C.N. Williams

Canadian Journal of Infectious Diseases (Published by Pulsus Group Inc.), 2902 South Sheridan Way, Oakville ON L6J 7L6 – 905/829-4770; Fax: 905/829-4799; Email: pulsus@pulsus.com; URL: http://www.pulsus.com/home.htm – Circ.: 7,500; 6 times a year – Publisher, Robert B. Kalina; Editor, Dr. L.E. Nicolle

Canadian Journal of Medical Laboratory Science, Cdn. Society of Laboratory Technologists, PO Box 2830, Stn LCD 1, Hamilton ON L8N 3N8 – 905/528-8642; Fax: 905/528-4968; Email: cjmls@cslt.com; URL: http://www.sclt.com – Circ.: 18,500; 6 times a year; English & French editions – Publisher, Kurt H. Davis

Canadian Journal of Medical Radiation Technology, Canadian Assn. of Medical Radiation Technologists, #601, 294 Albert St., Ottawa ON K1P 6E6 – 613/234-0012; Fax: 613/234-1097; Email: sbrasier@istar.ca – Circ.: 10,000; 4 times a year; English & French – Director of Communications, Steven Brasier; Registrar, Norma Saunders

Canadian Journal of Neurological Sciences, #810, 906 - 12 Ave. SW, Calgary AB T2R 1K7 – 403/229-9575; Fax: 403/229-1661; Email: cjns@canjneurolsci.org; URL: http://www.canjneurolsci.org – Circ.: 1,600; 4 times a year; English & French – Publisher, Sally Gregg; Editor, James A. Sharpe, M.D.; Circulation Manager, Margaret Peterson

The Canadian Journal of Occupational Therapy, Carleton Technology & Training Ctr., Carleton University Campus, #3400, 1125 Colonel By Dr., Ottawa ON K1S 5R1 – 613/523-2268; Fax: 613/523-2552 – Circ.: 6,000; 5 times a year plus Feb. conference supplement; English & French – Editor, Geraldine Moore

Canadian Journal of Ophthalmology, Canadian Ophthalmological Society, #610, 1525 Carling Ave., Ottawa ON K1Z 8R9 – 613/729-6779; Fax: 613/729-7209; Email: cos@eyesite.ca; URL: http://www.eyesite.ca – 7 times a year – Editor, Dr. B.J. MacInnis

Canadian Journal of Optometry, #301, 1785 Alta Vista Dr., Ottawa ON K1G 3Y6 – 613/738-4412; Fax: 613/738-7161 – 4 times a year – Medical Editor, Dr. Mitch Samek

Canadian Journal of Pediatrics (Published by Rodar International Inc.), 84 Hymus Blvd., Pointe-Claire QC H9R 1E4 – 514/697-7738; Fax: 514/697-4114; Email: cjp@canadinajournals.com – 4 times a year – Publisher, Bob Fauteux; Managing Editor, Jefferey Price

The Canadian Journal of Plastic Surgery (Published by Pulsus Group Inc.), 2902 South Sheridan Way, Oakville ON L6J 7L6 – 905/829-4770; Fax: 905/829-4799; Email: pulsus@pulsus.com; URL: hjttp://www.pulsus.com/home.htm – Circ.: 5,000; 4 times a year; English with French abstracts – Publisher, Robert B. Kalina; Editor, Dr. P. Wyshynski

Canadian Journal of Psychiatry, Cdn. Psychiatric Assn., #260, 441 MacLaren St., Ottawa ON K2P 2H3 – 613/234-2815; Fax: 613/234-9857; Email: statuscjp@medical.org; URL: http://cpa.medical.org – Circ.: 3,300; 10 times a year – Editor, Dr. Q. Rae-Grant; Circulation Manager, Christy Bradnock Paddick

Canadian Journal of Public Health, Canadian Public Health Association, #400, 1565 Carling Ave., Ottawa ON K1Z 8R1 – 613/725-3769; Fax: 613/725-9826; Email: cjph.cpha.ca; URL: http://www.cpha.ca – Circ.: 3,000; Bi-monthly; English & French – Hon. Scientific Editor, Dr. Richard Mathias; Executive Managing Editor, Gerald H. Dafoe; Circulation Manager, Ellan McWeeny

Canadian Journal of Rehabilitation, University of Alberta, Faculty of Rehabilitation Medicine, Edmonton AB T6G 2G4 – 403/492-1734; Fax: 403/492-1626; Email: cjrehab@gpu.srv.ualberta.ca – Circ.: 350; 4 times a year; English & French; ISSN 0828-0827 – Editor, Dr. Hy Day

Canadian Journal of Respiratory Therapy (Published by Canadian Medical Association), 1867 Alta Vista Dr., Ottawa ON K1G 3Y6 – 613/731-9331; Fax: 613/523-0937; Email: pubs@cma.ca; URL: http://www.cma.ca – Circ.: 2,800; 4 times a year – Editor, Dr. Norman Tiffin

Canadian Journal of Surgery (Published by Canadian Medical Association), 1867 Alta Vista Dr., Ottawa ON K1G 3Y6 – 613/731-9331; Fax: 613/523-0937; Email: pubs@cma.ca; URL: http://www.cma.ca – Circ.: 3,100; 6 times a year; English & French – Co-Editor, J.L. Meakins; Co-Editor, J.P. Waddell

Canadian Journal of Women's Health Care (Published by Rodar International Inc.), 84 Hymus Blvd., Pointe-Claire QC H9R 1E4 – 514/697-7738; Fax: 514/697-4114; Email: whc@canadianjournals.com – Circ.: 17,000; 4 times a year – Publisher, Bob Fauteux; Managing Editor, Terry O'Shaughnessy

Canadian Medical Association Journal (Published by Canadian Medical Association), 1867 Alta Vista Dr., Ottawa ON K1G 3Y6 – 613/731-9331; Fax: 613/523-0937; Email: pubs@cma.ca; URL: http://www.cma.ca – Circ.: 58,500; 24 times a year; English & French – Editor, John Hoey, M.D.

Canadian Nursing Home, c/o Health Media, 14453 - 29A Ave., White Rock BC V4P 1P7 – 604/535-7933; Fax: 604/535-9000 – Circ.: 2,800; 4 times a year – Publisher & Adv. Manager, Ron Forster; Editor, Frank Fagan

Canadian Respiratory Journal (Published by Pulsus Group Inc.), 2902 South Sheridan Way, Oakville ON L6J 7L6 – 905/829-4770; Fax: 905/829-4799; Email: pulsus@pulsus.com; URL: http://www.plusus.com/home.htm – Circ.: 15,000; 6 times a year

– Publisher, Robert B. Kalina; Editor, Dr. N.L. Jones

CHAC Review, c/o Catholic Health Association of Canada, 1247 Kilborn Ave., Ottawa ON K1H 6K9 – 613/731-7148; Fax: 613/731-7797; Email: chac@neb.net – Circ.: 2,000; 3 times a year – Editor, Maryse Blouin

The Chronicle of Cardiovascular & Internal Medicine (Published by Chronicle Information Resources Ltd.), 1270 The Queensway, Toronto ON M8Z 1S3 – 416/503-3957; Fax: 416/503-4118; Email: health@chronicle.org – Publisher, Mitchell Shannon; Editorial Director, R. Allan Ryan

The Chronicle of Neurology & Psychiatry (Published by Chronicle Information Resources Ltd.), 1270 The Queensway, Toronto ON M8Z 1S3 – 416/503 3957; Fax: 416/503-4118; Email: health@chronicle.org – Circ.: 6,180; 6 times a year – Publisher, Mitchell Shannon; Editorial Director, R. Allan Ryan

The Chronicle of Skin & Allergy (Published by Chronicle Information Resources Ltd.), 1270 The Queensway, Toronto ON M8Z 1S3 – 416/503-3957; Fax: 416/503-4118 – Circ.: 6,119; 9 times a year – Publisher, Mitchell Shannon; Editorial Director, R. Allan Ryan

The Chronicle of Urology & Sexual Medicine (Published by Chronicle Information Resources Ltd.), 1270 The Queensway, Toronto ON M8Z 1S3 – 416/503-3957; Fax: 416/503-4118 – Circ.: 3,860; 6 times a year – Publisher, Mitchell Shannon; Editorial Director, R. Allan Ryan

Clinical and Investigative Medicine (Published by Canadian Medical Association), 1867 Alta Vista Dr., Ottawa ON K1G 3Y6 – 613/731-9331; Fax: 613/523-0937; Email: pubs@cma.ca; URL: http://www.cma.ca – Circ.: 1,000; 6 times a year – Editor, George D. Sweeney

Le Clinicien (Published by STA Communications Inc.), #306, 955, boul Saint-Jean, Pointe-Claire QC H9R 5K3 – 514/695-7623; Fax: 514/695-8554 – Tirage: 12,984; Mensuel; français – Editeur, Robert Passaretti; Rédactrice, Anne Jamez; Directrice de tirage, Gail Gafka

CMA News (Published by Canadian Medical Association), 1867 Alta Vista Dr., Ottawa ON K1G 3Y6 – 613/731-9331; Fax: 613/523-0937; Email: wharrs@cma.ca; URL: http://www.cma.ca – Circ.: 46,000; Monthly; English & French – Editor, Patrick Sullivan; Editor, Steven Wharry

Coup d'oeil (Published by Martine Breton Communications), #206, 6955, boul Taschereau, Brossard QC J4Z 1A7 – 514/462-2112; Fax: 514/462-3352; Email: breton.inc@videotron.ca – Tirage: 2,737; 6 fois par an – President, Martine Breton

Dermatology Times of Canada (Published by CTC Communications Corp.), #203, 121 Lakeshore Rd. East, Mississauga ON L5G 1E5 – 905/274-3414; Fax: 905/274-2954; Email: dermuroobg@aol.com; URL: http://www.derm.ubc.ca/cme/dermupdat – Circ.: 5,313; 9 times a year – Publisher & CEO, M.E. Farley; Marketing Director, Joseph Duz

Diététique en Action, #703, 1425, boul René-Lévesque ouest, Montréal QC H3G 1T7 – 514/393-3733; Fax: 514/393-3582; Email: opdq@opdq.org; URL: http://www.opdq.org – Circ.: 2,500; 3 times a year; English & French – President, Micheline Seguin Bernier

Doctor's Review (Published by C.M.E. Publishing), 400 McGill St., 3rd Fl., Montréal QC H2Y 2G1 – 514/397-8833; Fax: 514/397-0228; Email: parkhurst@vir.com; URL: http://www.bestmdsite.com – Circ.: 37,370; Monthly – Publisher, David Elkins; Editor, Madeleine Partous; Circulation Manager, Yvonne MacKinder

Family Practice (Published by Maclean Hunter Publishing), 777 Bay St., Toronto ON M5W 1A7 – 416/596-5000; Fax: 416/596-3177 – Circ.: 24,800; 32 times a year – Publisher, Peter Craig; Editor, John Shaughnessy

FMWC Newsletter (Published by Canadian Medical Association), 1867 Alta Vista Dr., Ottawa ON K1G 3Y6 – 613/731-9331; Fax: 613/523-0937; Email: pubs@cma.ca – Circ.: 750; 4 times a year – Editor, Gail Beck, M.D.

Germs & Ideas (Published by Pulsus Group Inc.), 2902 South Sheridan Way, Oakville ON L6J 7L6 – 905/829-4770; Fax: 905/829-4700; URL: http://www.pulsus.com/home.htm – Circ.: 3,200; 4 times a year – Publisher, Robert Kalina

Guide to Canadian Healthcare Facilities, c/o Canadian Healthcare Association, 17 York St., Ottawa ON K1N 9J6 – 613/241-8005; Fax: 613/241-5055; Email: chapress@canadian-healthcare.org; URL: http://www.canadian-healthcare.org – Director, Publishing, Eleanor Sawyer; Editor, Indra Seegobin

Healthcare Management FORUM, Canadian College of Health Service Executives, #402, 350 Sparks St., Ottawa ON K1R 7S8 – 613/235-7218; Fax: 613/235-5451; Email: cchse@canlinks.com; URL: http://www.canlinks.com/cchse/ – Circ.: 3,560; 4 times a year – President, Gaston Levac; Managing Editor, Randall R. Steffan

Hospital Business (Published by Sawmill Creek Communications), #11, 4040 Creditview Rd., PO Box 1800, Mississauga ON L5C 3Y8 – 905/813-7000; Fax: 905/813-7117 – Circ.: 10,000; 6 times a year – Publisher, Hugh Parkinson; Editor, Jay Barwell

Hospital News, Auto Mart Magazines Ltd., 23 Apex Rd., Toronto ON M6A 2V6 – 416/781-5516; Fax: 416/781-5499 – Circ.: 46,000; Monthly – Editor, Cindy Woods

The Journal, Addiction Research Foundation, 33 Russell St., Toronto ON M5S 2S1 – 416/595-6714; Fax: 416/595-6892; Email: adubey@arf.org; URL: http://www.intropage.html – Circ.: 11,000; 6 times a year; English & French – Editor, Anita Dubey

Journal of the Canadian Chiropractic Association, 1396 Eglinton Ave. West, Toronto ON M6C 2E4 – 416/781-5656; Fax: 416/781-7344 – Circ.: 4,500; 4 times a year – Editor, Dr. Allan Gotlib

Journal of the Canadian Dietetic Association, #604, 480 University Ave., Toronto ON M5G 1V2 – 416/596-0857; Fax: 416/596-0603; Email: centralinfo@dietitians.ca; URL: http://www.dietitians.ca – Circ.: 5,000; 4 times a year; French & English – Editor, Eunice Chao

Journal of Cutaneous Medicine & Surgery (Published by Decker Periodicals), 4 Hughson Ct. South, 4th Fl., Hamilton ON L8N 3J1 – 905/522-7017; Fax: 905/522-7839; Email: info@bcdecker.com – Circ.: 2,700; 4 times a year – Publisher, Brian C. Decker; Editor-in-chief, Daniel Sauder, M.D.

Journal of Otolaryngology (Published by Decker Periodicals), 4 Hughson Ct. South, 4th Fl., Hamilton ON L8N 3J1 – 905/522-7017; Fax: 905/522-7839; Email: info@bcdecker.com – Circ.: 1,191; 6 times a year – Publisher, Brian Decker; Editor, Dr. Peter Alberti

Journal of Psychiatry & Neuroscience, Canadian Medical Association, 1867 Alta Vista Dr., Ottawa ON K1G 3Y6 – 613/731-9331; Fax: 613/523-0937; Email: pubs@cma.ca; URL: http://www.cma.ca – Circ.: 2,439; 5 times a year – Editor, Y.D. Lapierre

Journal of Rheumatology, Journal of Rheumatology Publishing Co. Ltd., #115, 920 Yonge St., Toronto ON M4W 3C7 – 416/967-5155; Fax: 416/967-7556; Email: jrheum@jrheum.com; URL: http://www.jrheum.com – Circ.: 3,500; Monthly – Editor-in-Chief, Duncan A. Gordon

Journal SOGC, Ribsome Communications, 50A Hillholm Rd., Toronto ON M5P 1N5 – 416/322-5510; Fax: 416/322-5263; Email: ribosome@inforamp.net – Circ.: 14,000; 14 times a year; English with French abstracts – Publisher, Adrian Stein; Editor, Dr. Patrick J. Taylor; Production/Circulation Manager, Kismet Goodbaum

Linacre's: The Chronicle of Medical Progress & Culture (Published by Chronicle Information Resources Ltd.), 1270 The Queensway, Toronto ON M8Z 1S3 – 416/503-3957; Fax: 416/503-4118; Email: health@chronicle.org – Editorial Director, R. Allan Ryan; National Sales Director, James A. Bentley

Long Term Care, Ontario Nursing Home Association, #202, 345 Renfrew Dr., Markham ON L3R 9S9 – 905/470-8995; Fax: 905/470-9595 – Circ.: 4,200; 4 times a year – Editor, Heather Lang-Runtz

Le Médecin du Québec, Quebec Federation of General Practitioners, #1000, 1440, rue St-Catherine ouest, Montréal QC H3G 1R8 – 514/878-1911; Fax: 514/878-4455; Email: med.que@fmog.org – Tirage: 17,800; Mensuel; français – Rédacteur, Jean-Maurice Turgeon, M.D.; Directrice de tirage, Marie-Hélène Wolford

Médecine/sciences, #203, 3414, av du Parc, Montréal QC H2X 2H5 – 514/288-2247; Fax: 514/288-0520; Email: medecine.sciences@sympatico.ca – Tirage: 1 953; 10 fois par an – Rédacteur, Michel Bergeron

The Medical Post (Published by Maclean Hunter Publishing), 777 Bay St., Toronto ON M5W 1A7 – 416/596-5748; Fax: 416/593-3177; Email: jmcallister@mhpublishing.com; URL: http://www.io.org/~cjaimet/outlook/outlook.html – 44 times a year – Editor-in-Chief, Pat Rich

Medical Scope Monthly Journal, 1015 Hooke Rd., Edmonton AB T5A 4K5 – 403/456-9547; Fax: 403/476-1363; Email: medial@planet.eon.net – 12 times a year – Editor, Patrick McLaughlin

Medical Society of Nova Scotia News, Medical Society of Nova Scotia, 5 Spectacle Lake Dr., Dartmouth NS B3B 1X7 – 902/468-1866; Fax: 902/468-6578 – Circ.: 2,400; 6 times a year – Editor, Donna Christopher

Medicine North America (Published by C.M.E. Publishing), 400 McGill St., 3rd Fl., Montréal QC H2Y 2G1 – 514/397-9393; Fax: 514/397-0228; Email: parkhurst@vir.com; URL: http://bestmdsite.com – Circ.: 30,000; Monthly – Publisher, David Elkins; Editor, Katherine Addleman; Circulation Manager, Yvonne MacKinder

Mediscan (Published by Canadian Medical Association), 1867 Alta Vista Dr., Ottawa ON K1G 3Y6 – 613/731-9331; Fax: 613/523-0937; Email: pubs@cma.ca; URL: http://www.cma.ca – Circ.: 5,500; 3 times a year – President, CFMS, Kevin D. Buscle; Editor, Flora Kwan; Editor, Suparna Madan

The Nutrition Post (Published by Maclean Hunter Publishing), 777 Bay St., Toronto ON M5W 1A7 – 416/596-5726; Fax: 416/593-3177 – Circ.: 40,000; 4 times a year – Publisher, John Milne; Editor, Diana Swift

Obstetrics & Gynaecology 2000 (Published by CTC Communications Corp.), #203, 121 Lakeshore Rd. East, Mississauga ON L5G 1E5 – 905/274-3414; Fax: 905/274-2954 – Circ.: 9,688; 8 times a year – Publisher, Michael E. Farley; Marketing Director, Joseph Duz

L'Omnipraticien (Published by Maclean Hunter Publishing), 1001, boul de Maisonneuve ouest, Montréal QC H3A 3E1 – 514/878-2595; Fax: 514/878-8270 – Tirage: 11 000; 24 fois par an – Rédactrice, Lyse Savard

Ontario Medical Review, Ontario Medical Assn., #300, 525 University Ave., Toronto ON M5G 2K7 – 416/599-2580; Fax: 416/599-9309; Email: kim_secord@oma.org; URL: http://www.oma.org – Circ.: 22,000; 11 times a year – Managing Editor, Elizabeth Petruccelli; Editor, Jeff Henry; Circulation Manager, Kim Secord

Ophthalmic Practice (Published by Medicopea International Inc.), #300, 3333, boul Cote-Vertu, Saint-Laurent QC H4R 2N1 – 514/331-4561; Fax: 514/336-1129; Email: Medicopea@netaxis.

qc.ca – Circ.: 1,200; 6 times a year – Publisher, Lawrence Goldstein; Editor, Dr. Leon Solomon; Circulation Manager, Mary Di Lemme

Opti-Guide (Published by Martine Breton Communications), #206, 6955, boul Taschereau, Brossard QC J4Z 1A7 – 514/462-2112; Fax: 514/462-3352; Email: breton.inc@videotron.ca – Circ.: 5,118; Annual – President, Martine Breton

Optical Prism, Vezcom Inc., 31 Hastings Dr., Unionville ON L3R 4Y5 – 905/475-9343; Fax: 905/477-2821; Email: prism@istar.ca – Circ.: 7,500; 9 times a year – Editor, Allan K. Vezina

L'Optométriste, #740, 1265, rue Berri, Montréal QC H2L 4X4 – 514/288-6272; Fax: 514/288-7071; Email: jplagace@login.net; URL: http://www.login.net/assocopto/index – 6 fois par an; français – Jean-Pierre Lagacé

Paediatrics & Child Health (Published by Pulsus Group Inc.), 2902 South Sheridan Way, Oakville ON L6J 7L6 – 905/829-4770; Fax: 905/829-4799; Email: pulsus@pulsus.com; URL: http://www.pulsus.com/home.htm – Circ.: 16,500; 6 times a year – Publisher, Robert Kalina; Editor, Dr. N. MacDonald

Pain Research Management (Published by Pulsus Group Inc.), 2902 South Sheridan Way, Oakville ON L6J 7L6 – 905/829-4770; Fax: 905/829-4799; Email: pulsus@pulsus.com; URL: http://www.pulsus.com/home.htm – Circ.: 20,000; 4 times a year – Publisher, Robert Kalina; Editor, Dr. H. Merskey

The Parkhurst Exchange (Published by C.M.E. Publishing), 400 McGill St., 3rd Fl., Montréal QC H2Y 2G1 – 514/397-8833; Fax: 514/397-0228 – Circ.: 37,000 – Publisher, David Elkins; Editor, Catherine Addleman; Circulation Manager, Yvonne MacKinder

Patient Care (Published by Maclean Hunter Publishing), 777 Bay St., Toronto ON M5W 1A7 – 416/596-5000; Fax: 416/596-3177 – Circ.: 27,000; 12 times a year – Publisher, Peter Craig; Editor, Vil Meere; Circulation Manager, Denise Brearley

Perspectives in Cardiology (Published by STA Communications Inc.), #306, 955, boul Saint-Jean, Pointe-Claire QC H9R 5K3 – 514/695-7623; Fax: 514/695-8554 – Circ.: 15,269; 9 times a year – Publisher, Robert Passaretti

Physicians' Computing Chronicle (Published by Chronicle Information Resources Ltd.), 1270 The Queensway, Toronto ON M8Z 1S3 – 416/503-3957; Fax: 416/503-4118; Email: health@chronicle.org – Circ.: 36,957; 6 times a year – Publisher, Mitchell Shannon; Editorial Director, R. Allan Ryan

Physiotherapy Canada, The Canadian Physiotherapy Assn., 2345 Yonge St., Toronto ON M4P 2E5 – 416/932-1888; Fax: 416/932-9708 – 4 times a year – Editor, Diane Charter

Practical Optometry (Published by Medicopea International Inc.), #300, 3333, boul Cote-Vertu, Saint-Laurent QC H4R 2N1 – 514/331-4561; Fax: 514/336-1129; Email: Medicopea@NETAXIS.qc.ca – Circ.: 2,700; 6 times a year – Publisher, Lawrence Goldstein; Editor, Dr. John Jantzi; Circulation Manager, Mary Di Lemme

Psychology Canada, #221, 730 Yonge St., Toronto ON M4Y 2B7 – 416/961-5552; Fax: 416/961-5516; Email: ont@hookup.net – Circ.: 1,500; 4 times a year – Editor, Dr. Donald Rudzinski; Publication Manager, Sandra Traub

Rehab & Community Care Management, BCS Communications Ltd., 101 Thorncliffe Park Dr., Toronto ON M4H 1M2 – 416/421-7944; Fax: 416/421-0966 – Circ.: 20,000; 4 times a year – Publisher, Caroline Tapp-McDougall

Stitches: The Journal of Medical Humour (Published by Stitches Publishing Inc.), 16787 Warden Ave., Newmarket ON L3Y 4W1 – 905/853-1884; Fax: 905/853-6565; Email: jcocker@medhumor.com – Circ.: 43,000; 11 times a year – Publisher, Dr. John Cocker; Editor/Associate Publisher, Simon Hally

Strategy (Published by Canadian Medical Association), 1867 Alta Vista Dr., Ottawa ON K1G 3Y6 – 613/731-9331; Fax: 613/523-0937; Email: pubs@cma.ca – Circ.: 46,000; Monthly – Managing Editor, Don Bisch

Urology Times of Canada, CTC Communications Corp., 1382 Hurontario St., Mississauga ON L5G 3H4 – 905/278-6700; Fax: 905/278-4850; Email: derm.urol@sympatico.ca – Circ.: 4,800; 6 times a year – Associate Publisher, Marg Churchill; Editor, Ian Moore; Circulation Manager, Olga Murphy

Vision Magazine (Published by August Communications Ltd.), #200, 388 Donald St., Winnipeg MB R3B 2J4 – 204/957-0265; Fax: 204/957-0217; Email: august@inforamp.net – Circ.: 3,000; 6 times a year; English & French – Publisher, Gladwyn Nickel

**HEATING, PLUMBING, AIR CONDITIONING**

Heating-Plumbing-Air Conditioning, Cowgate Communications, #300, 1370 Don Mills Rd., Don Mills ON M3B 3N7 – 416/759-2500; Fax: 416/759-6979 – Circ.: 16,300; 7 times a year; also Buyers Guide (annually, Aug.) – Publisher, W. Bruce Meacock; Editor, Lynne Erskine-Chelo

Inter-mécanique du bâtiment, 8175, boul St-Laurent, Montréal QC H2P 2M1 – 514/382-2668; Fax: 514/382-1566 – Tirage: 5,500; 10 fois par an; français – Rédacteur, André Dupuis, 1-800-465-2668; Directrice de tirage, Sonia Audet

Mechanical Buyer & Specifier: HVAC/Refrigeration Magazine (Published by Nytek Publishing Inc), 130 Belfield Rd., Etobicoke ON M9W 1G1 – 416/242-8088; Fax: 416/242-8085; Email: rshuker@mechspec.com; URL: http://www.mechspec.com – Circ.: 8,100; 7 times a year – President, R.H. Shuker

Mechanical Buyer & Specifier: Plumbing, Piping & Heating Magazine (Published by Nytek Publishing Inc), 130 Belfield Rd., Etobicoke ON M9W 1G1 – 416/242-8088; Fax: 416/242-8085; Email: rshuker@mechspec.com; URL: http://www.mechspec.com – Circ.: 13,100; 6 times a year – President, R.H. Shuker

**HOTELS & RESTAURANTS**

La Barrique (Published by Kylix Media Inc), #414, 5165 Sherbrooke St. West, Montréal QC H4A 1T6 – 514/481-5892; Fax: 514/481-9699; Email: ryann@odyssee.net; URL: http://www.magnet.ca/wine – Tirage: 8,332; 6 fois par an; français – Editrice, Judy Rochester; Rédactrice, Nicole Barrette-Ryan; Directrice de tirage, Veronica Gumilar

Le Chef du service alimentaire, 252, rte 171, CP 1010, St-Etienne-de-Lauzon QC G6J 1S2 – 418/831-5317; Fax: 418/831-5172 – Tirage: 18,500; 6 fois par an; français – Editeur, Maurice LeBlanc; Rédactrice, Ann Labrecque

Foodservice and Hospitality (Published by Kostuch Publications Ltd.), #101, 23 Lesmill Rd., Don Mills ON M3B 3P6 – 416/447-0888; Fax: 416/447-5333; Email: mkostuch@foodservice.ca; URL: http://www.foodserviceworld.com – Circ.: 24,475; 12 times a year – President/Publisher, Mitch Kostuch; Editor, Rosanna Caira; Business Manager, Jim Kostuch

Hotelier (Published by Kostuch Publications Ltd.), #101, 23 Lesmill Rd., Don Mills ON M3B 3P6 – 416/447-0888; Fax: 416/447-5333; Email: rcaira@foodservice.ca; URL: http://www.foodserviceworld.com – Circ.: 8,000; 6 times a year – Publisher, Mitch Kostuch; Editor, Rosanna Caira; Business Manager, Jim Kostuch

Inn Business Magazine, Perf-Link Publications Inc., 65 St. John Side Rd. East, Aurora ON L4G 3G8 – 905/841-8753; Fax: 905/841-7416; Email: innbusiness@msn.com – Circ.: 13,000; 4 times a year – Publisher, Barbara Baker Howson; Editor, Reginald Baker

The Network (Published by Naylor Communications Ltd.), 920 Yonge St., 6th Fl., Toronto ON M4W 3C7 – 416/961-1028; Fax: 416/924-4408 – Annually – Publisher, Robert Thompson

Ontario Restaurant Association Membership Directory & Buyers' Guide (Published by Naylor Communications Ltd.), 920 Yonge St., 6th Fl., Toronto ON M4W 3C7 – 416/961-1028; Fax: 416/924-4408 – Annually – Publisher, Robert Thompson

Ontario Restaurant News (Published by Ishcom Publications Ltd.), #101, 2065 Dundas St. East, Mississauga ON L4X 2W1 – 905/206-0150; Fax: 905/206-9972 – 12 times a year – Publisher, Steven Isherwood; Editor, Michael Deibart

Western Hospitality News (Published by Ishcom Publications Ltd.), #101, 2065 Dundas St. East, Mississauga ON L4X 2W1 – 905/206-0150; Fax: 905/206-9972 – Circ.: 13,500; 4 times a year – Publisher, Steven Isherwood; Managing Editor, Colleen Isherwood

Western Restaurant News (Published by Mercury Publications Ltd.), 1839 Inkster Blvd., Winnipeg MB R2X 1R3 – 204/697-0835; Fax: 204/633-7784; Email: wrn@mercury.mb.ca – Circ.: 12,366; 4 times a year – Publisher, Gren R. Yeo

**HOUSEWARES**

Canadian Home Style Magazine, Lorell Communications, 598 Stillwater Ct., Burlington ON L7T 4G7 – 905/681-7932; Fax: 905/681-2141 – Circ.: 6,800; 7 times a year – Publisher & Editor, Laurie O'Halloran

**HUMAN RESOURCES**

Canadian HR Reporter, MPL Communications, #700, 133 Richmond St. West, Toronto ON M5H 3M8 – 416/869-1177; Fax: 416/869-3288; Email: chrr@cycor.ca – Circ.: 7,700; 22 times a year – Publisher & Editor, George Pearson

Human Resources Professional, Human Resources Professionals Assn. of Ontario (HRPAO), #1902, 2 Bloor St. West, Toronto ON M4W 3E2 – 416/923-2324; Fax: 416/923-7264 – Circ.: 8,100; 6 times a year – Editor, K. Came; Circulation Manager, Farah Allen-Goldson

**INDUSTRIAL & INDUSTRIAL AUTOMATION**

Canadian Industrial Equipment News (Published by Southam Magazine Group), 1450 Don Mills Rd., Don Mills ON M3B 2X7 – 416/445-6641; Fax: 416/442-2214; URL: http://www.southam.com/b1-5-1.html – Circ.: 23,516; Monthly – Publisher, Alex Papanov; Editor, Olga Markovich; Circulation Manager, Dianne Rakoff

Circuit Industriel, P.A.P. Communications Inc., 1627, boul St-Joseph, Québec QC G2K 1H1 – 418/623-3383; Fax: 418/623-5033; Email: info@promoapageau.qc.ca; URL: http://www.promoapageau.qc.ca – Tirage: 13 878; 6 fois par an; français – Rédacteur, Andre Pageau

Le Journal Industriel du Québec, Info-industriel inc., 2370, boul Henri-Bourassa est, Montréal QC H2B 1T6 – 514/388-8801; Fax: 514/388-7871 – Tirage: 20,900; 10 fois par an; français – Rédacteur, Yvan Gauthier

Manufacturing & Process Automation (Published by Kerrwil Publications Ltd.), 395 Matheson Blvd. East, Mississauga ON L4Z 2H2 – 905/890-1846; Fax: 905/890-5769; Email: mpa@kerrwil.com; URL: http://www.automationmag.com – Circ.: 15,400; 7 times a year – Publisher, Klaus Pirker; Editor, Heather Angus; Circulation Manager, Jean Bilkey

National Industrial, Brymell Publications Inc., #201, 801 York Mills Rd., Don Mills ON M3B 1X7 – 416/446-1404; Fax: 416/446-0502 – Circ.: 25,500; Monthly – Publisher/Editor, W.R. Bryson

New Equipment News, c/o Canadian Engineering Publications Ltd., #1511, 2 Carlton St., Toronto ON M5B 1J3 – 416/599-3737; Fax: 416/599-3730 –

Circ.: 22,500; 10 times a year – Publisher, Tom Monson; Editor, D. Barrie Lehman; Sales Manager, Maureen Wheeler

PEM: Plant Engineering & Maintenance (Published by Clifford Elliott & Associates Ltd.), 3228 South Service Rd., 2nd Fl., Burlington ON L7N 3H8 – 905/634-2100; Fax: 905/634-2238; URL: http://www.industrialsourcebook.com – Circ.: 21,300 – Publisher, George Clifford; Editor, Todd Philips; Circulation Manager, Janice Armbrust

PEM Industrial Sourcebook (Published by Clifford Elliott & Associates Ltd.), 3228 South Service Rd., 2nd Fl., Burlington ON L7N 3H8 – 905/634-2100; Fax: 905/634-2238; Email: cliffell@inforamp.net; URL: http://www.industrialsourcebook.com – Circ.: 20,100; 2 times a year – Publisher, Rae Robb

Plant (Published by Maclean Hunter Publishing), 777 Bay St., Toronto ON M5W 1A7 – 416/596-5777; Fax: 416/596-5552 – Circ.: 34,000; 18 times a year – Publisher, Dan Bordun; Editor, Wayne Karl, 416/596-5761

Produits pour l'industrie québécoise, Action communications inc., CP 357, Pointe Claire QC H9R 4P4 – 514/590-5934; Fax: 514/457-7914 – Tirage: 15,000; 6 fois par an; français – Editeur, Michael L. Doody; Rédacteur, David Terhune

L'Usine (Published by Maclean Hunter Publishing), 1001, boul de Maisonneuve ouest, Montréal QC H3A 3E1 – 514/845-5141; Fax: 514/845-4393 – Tirage: 15,400; 4 fois par an – Editeur, Dan Bordun; Rédacteur, Pierre Deschamps

**INDUSTRIAL SAFETY**

Accident Prevention, Accident Prevention Assn., 250 Yonge St., 28th Fl., Toronto ON M5B 2N4 – 416/506-8888, 1-800-669-4939 – Circ.: 16,388; 6 times a year – Editor, Susan Stanton

Canadian Occupational Safety (Published by Clifford Elliott & Associates Ltd.), 3228 South Service Rd., 2nd Fl., Burlington ON L7N 3H8 – 905/634-2100; Fax: 905/634-2238; Email: re@industrialsourcebook.com; URL: http://www.industrialsourcebook.com – Circ.: 12,100; 6 times a year – Publisher, Ralph Elliot; Editor, Jackie Roth; Circulation Manager, Janice Armbrust

OHS Canada Magazine (Published by Southam Magazine Group), 1450 Don Mills Rd., Don Mills ON M3B 2X7 – 416/445-6641; Fax: 416/442-2200; Email: ddehaas@southam.ca – Circ.: 10,000; 7 times a year – Publisher, Gregory Peek; Editor, David Dehaas

Travail et santé, CP 1089, Napierville QC J0J 1L0 – 514/245-7285; Fax: 514/245-0593 – Tirage: 2,400; 4 fois par an; français – Rédacteur, Robert Richards

**INSURANCE**

Alberta Insurance Directory (Published by Arbutus Publications Ltd.), PO Box 3311, Stn MPO, Vancouver BC V6B 3Y3 – 604/874-1001; Fax: 604/874-3922 – Circ.: 1,050; Annually, Jan. – Publisher & Editor, Bill Earle

The BC Broker (Published by Arbutus Publications Ltd.), PO Box 3311, Stn MPO, Vancouver BC V6B 3Y3 – 604/874-1001; Fax: 604/874-3922 – Circ.: 2,500; 6 times a year – Publisher & Managing Editor, Bill Earle

British Columbia Insurance Directory (Published by Arbutus Publications Ltd.), PO Box 3311, Stn MPO, Vancouver BC V6B 3Y3 – 604/874-1001; Fax: 604/874-3922 – Circ.: 2,095; Annually, April – Editor & Publisher, Bill Earle

Canadian Insurance (Published by Stone & Cox Ltd.), #202, 111 Peter St., Toronto ON M5V 2H1 – 416/599-0772; Fax: 416/599-0867; Email: canadian_insurance@stonecox.com – Monthly – Publisher, J. Kent Chisholm; Editor, Craig Harris

Canadian Insurance Claims Directory, University of Toronto Press, #700, 10 St. Mary St., Toronto ON M4Y 2W8 – 416/978-2239, ext.245; Fax: 416/978-4738 – Circ.: 2,000; Annually, July – Editor, Gwen Peroni

Canadian Underwriter (Published by Southam Magazine Group), 1450 Don Mills Rd., Don Mills ON M3B 2X7 – 416/445-6641; Fax: 416/442-2213; Email: ndunlop@southam.ca; URL: http://www.cdnunderwriter.com – Circ.: 6,250; Monthly; also Rehabilitation Services Guide, Guide to Legal Firms, Insurance Marketer & annual statistical issue – Publisher, Steve Wilson; Managing Editor, Larry Welsh

General Insurance Register (Published by Stone & Cox Ltd.), #202, 111 Peter St., Toronto ON M5V 2H1 – 416/599-0772; Fax: 416/599-0867; Email: gir@stonecox.com – Annually, Jan. – Editor, J. Wyndham

The Insurance Journal (Published by Les Editions du Journal de l'Assurance), #102, 353, rue St-Nicholas, Montréal QC H2Y 2P1 – 514/289-9595; Fax: 514/289-9527; Email: journass@interlink.net – Circ.: 7,500; ISSN: 1205-6189 – Publisher & Editor-in-chief, Serge Therrien

Insurance West (Published by Arbutus Publications Ltd.), PO Box 3311, Stn MPO, Vancouver BC V6B 3Y3 – 604/874-1001; Fax: 604/874-3922 – 4 times a year – Publisher, Bill Earle; Associate Publisher, Jim Bensley

Le Journal de l'Assurance (Published by Les Editions du Journal de l'Assurance), #102, 353, rue St-Nicholas, Montréal QC H2Y 2P1 – 514/289-9595; Fax: 514/289-9527; Email: journass@interlink.net – Tirage: 18 000; 10 fois par an; français; ISSN: 1198-4678 – Editeur/Rédacteur, Serge Therrien; Directeur de tirage, Daniel Campeau

Liaison, #139, 955, rue d'Assigny, Longueuil QC J4K 5C3 – 514/674-6258; Fax: 514/674-3609 – Tirage: 3,000; 6 fois par an – Directrice-génèrale, Claudette Carrier

LUAC Forum, c/o Life Underwriters Association, 41 Lesmill Rd., Don Mills ON M3B 2T3 – 416/444-5251, 1-800-563-5822; Fax: 416/444-8031; URL: http://www.luac.com – Circ.: 18,100; 10 times a year – Director, Val Osborne

Ontario Insurance Directory (Published by Southam Magazine Group), 1450 Don Mills Rd., Don Mills ON M3B 2X7 – 416/445-6641; Fax: 416/442-2213; Email: s.wilson@netcom.ca; URL: http://cdnunderwriter.com – Circ.: 5,500; Annually, Jan. – Publisher, Steve Wilson; Editor, Nancy V. Campbell, 416/510-6840

Le Portefeuille d'assurances, L. Chaput, files et cie ltée, #114, 3328, av Troie, Montréal QC H3V 1B1 – 514/739-2230; Fax: 514/739-1422 – Mensuel – Editeur, Pierre M Chaput

Prospective, Life Underwriters Association of Québec, #500, 1 Westmount Sq., Montréal QC H3Z 2P9 – 514/932-4277; Fax: 514/932-6400; Email: aiapq@eureka.qc.ca – Circ.: 13,000; 9 times a year; English & French – Editor-in-Chief, Louis Garneau

**INTERIOR DESIGN & DECOR**

Azure, 2 Silver Ave., Toronto ON M6R 3A2 – 416/588-2588; Fax: 416/588-2357 – Circ.: 14,000; 6 times a year – Publisher, Sergio Sgaramella; Editor, Nelda Rodger

Canadian Facility Management & Design, 62 Olsen Dr., Don Mills ON M3A 3J3 – 416/447-3417; Fax: 416/447-4410 – Circ.: 6,156; 6 times a year – Publisher, Arvid B. Stonkus; Editor, Victor von Buchstab

Canadian Interiors (Published by Crailer Communications), 360 Dupont St., Toronto ON M5R 1V9 – 416/966-9944; Fax: 416/966-9946; Email: crailer@interlog.com – Circ.: 12,000; 6 times a year – Publisher & Editor, Sheri Craig; Circulation Manager, Beata Olechnowicz

L'Envers du décor, Groupe Inter data inc., #102, 491, boul Lebeau, Ville St-Laurent QC H4N 1S2 – 514/745-0080; Fax: 514/745-0993 – Tirage: 6,000; 6 fois par an

Ontario Design (Published by Homes Publishing Group), 178 Main St., Unionville ON L3R 2G9 – 905/479-4663; Fax: 905/479-4482; URL: http://www.homes.mag.com – Circ.: 12,000; Annually – Publisher, Michael Rosset

**JEWELLERY & GIFTWARE**

Canadian Jeweller, Style Communications, #302, 1448 Lawrence Ave. East, Toronto ON M4A 2V6 – 416/755-5199; Fax: 416/755-9123; Email: canjewel@style.on.ca; URL: http://www/canjewel.polygon.net – Circ.: 6,000; 7 times a year – Publisher, John Peters; Editor, Carol Besler

**JOURNALISM**

Actualité Canada (Published by News Canada Inc.), #606, 366 Adelaide St. West, Toronto ON M5V 1R9 – 416/599-9900; Fax: 416/599-9700 – Mensuel; français – Editeur, Rodney N. Morris; Rédactrice, Linda Kroboth

Media, Carleton University, St. Patrick's Bldg., Rm. 316B, 1125 Colonel By Drive, Ottawa ON K1S 5B6 – 613/233-2801; Fax: 613/233-3904; Email: cf408@freenet.carleton.ca – 4 times a year – Editor, David McKie

News Canada (Published by News Canada Inc.), #606, 366 Adelaide St. West, Toronto ON M5V 1R9 – 416/599-9900; Fax: 416/599-9700 – Monthly – Publisher, Rodney Morris; Editor, Linda Kroboth

Press Review, PO Box 368, Stn A, Toronto ON M5W 1C2 – 416/368-0512; Fax: 416/366-0104 – Circ.: 15,000; 4 times a year – Publisher & Editor, B.M. Cassidy

Ryerson Review of Journalism, School of Journalism, Ryerson Polytechnic University, 350 Victoria St., Toronto ON M5B 2K3 – 416/979-5000, ext.7434; Fax: 416/979-5216; URL: http://www.ryerson.ca/rrj/ – Circ.: 4,000; 2 times a year – Editor, Lynn Cunningham

**LANDSCAPING**

GreenMaster (Published by Kenilworth Publishing), #201, 27 West Beaver Creek, Richmond Hill ON L4B 1M8 – 905/771-7333; Fax: 905/771-7336; Email: sales@kenilworth.com – 6 times a year – Publisher, Jim Davidson

Horticulture Review: The Voice of Landscape Ontario (Published by Landscape Ontario Horticultural Trades Association), 7856 Fifth Line South, RR#4, Stn Main, Milton ON L9T 2X8 – 905/875-1805; Fax: 905/875-0183 – Monthly – Publisher, Rita Weedenburg; Editor, Linda Erskine; Circulation Manager, Crispin Co

Hortwest, c/o British Columbia Nursery Trades Association, #101, 5830 - 176A St., Surrey BC V3S 4E3 – 604/574-7772; Fax: 604/574-7773; Email: bhardy@direct.ca – Circ.: 1,250; 6 times a year – Managing Editor, Jane Stock

Landmark (Published by Charlton Communications), #1000, 1777 Victoria Ave., Regina SK S4P 4K5 – 306/584-1000; Fax: 306/584-2824 – Circ.: 15,680; 6 times a year – Publisher, Mary-Lynn Charlton; Editor, Tom Steve

Landscape Trades (Published by Landscape Ontario Horticultural Trades Association), 7856 Fifth Line South, RR#4, Stn Main, Milton ON L9T 2X8 – 905/875-1805; Fax: 905/875-0183; Email: 10@mail.westonia.com; URL: http://www.hort-trades.com – Circ.: 7,890; 9 times a year – Publisher, Rita Weedenburg; Editor, Linda Erskine; Circulation Manager, Crispin Co

Prairie Landscape Magazine (Published by OT Communications), #600, 237 - 8th Ave. SE, Calgary AB T2G 5C3 – 403/264-3270; Fax: 403/264-3276; Email: bic@lions.com – Circ.: 1,100; 6 times a year – Editor, Nigel Bowles

Québec Vert (Published by Editions Versicolores inc.), 1320, boul St-Joseph, Québec QC G2K 1G2 – 418/628-8690; Fax: 418/628-0524 – 8 fois par an; français – Editeur, François Bernatchez

Turf & Recreation, 123B King St., Delhi ON N4B 1X9 – 519/582-8873; Fax: 519/582-8877 – Circ.: 14,000; 7 times a year – Publisher, Bart Crandon; Editor, Michael Jiggens

**LAUNDRY & DRY CLEANING**

Fabricare Canada, Todd's Your Answer Ltd., PO Box 968, Oakville ON L6J 5E8 – 905/337-0516; Fax: 905/337-0525; Email: martodd@compuserve.com – 6 times a year – Publisher & Editor, Marcia Todd

**LEGAL**

The Advocate, Vancouver Bar Association, 4765 Pilot House Rd., West Vancouver BC V7W 1J2 – 604/925-2122; Fax: 604/925-2065 – Circ.: 9,900; 6 times a year – Editor, Thomas S. Woods; Circulation Manager, Gillian Roberts

Canadian Bar Review, c/o Canadian Bar Association, #902, 50 O'Connor St., Ottawa ON K1P 6L2 – 613/237-2925; Fax: 613/237-0185; Email: info@cba.org, editor.cba@anb.ca – Circ.: 35,525; 2 times a year; English & French – Editor-in-Chief, Prof. Edward Veitch; Circulation Manager, Monique Cassidy

Canadian Lawyer, 240 Edward St., Aurora ON L4G 3S9 – 905/841-6480; Fax: 905/841-5078 – Circ.: 28,300; 10 times a year – Publisher, Stuart Morrison; Executive Editor, D. Michael Fitz-James

Digest Business & Law Journal, 826 Erin St., Winnipeg MB R3G 2W4 – 204/775-8918; Fax: 204/788-4322 – Circ.: 1,600; Weekly – Publisher, Walter Bowden; Editor, Frank Chalmers

Le Journal du Barreau, 445, boul St-Laurent, Montréal QC H2Y 3T8 – 514/954-3439; Fax: 514/954-3477; Email: journal@barreau.qc.ca; URL: http://www/barreau.qc.ca – 20 fois par an; français – Editeur, Léon Bébard; Rédacteur, Marius Marin

Law Now, 11019 - 90 Ave., Edmonton AB T6G 1A6 – 403/492-1751; Fax: 403/492-6180; Email: Pauline.Jacob@ualberta.ca; URL: http://www.extension.ualberta.ca/lawnow/ – Circ.: 3,000; 6 times a year; ISSN: 0841-2626 – Publisher, Lois Gander; Editor, Marsha Mildon

Law Times, 240 Edward St., Aurora ON L4G 3S9 – 905/841-6481; Fax: 905/841-5078; Email: lawtimes@canadalawbook.ca – Circ.: 14,000; 43 times a year – Publisher, Stuart Morrison; Managing Editor, Beth Marlin

The Lawyers Weekly (Published by Butterworths Canada Ltd.), 75 Clegg Rd., Markham ON L6G 1A7 – 905/479-2665, 1-800-668-6481; Fax: 905/479-3758; Email: tlw@butterworths.ca; URL: http://www.butterworths.ca/tlw.htm – Circ.: 7,000; 48 times a year – Publisher, Don Brillinger; Managing Editor, Jordan Furlong; Circulation Controller, Kim Rattray

McGill Law Journal, McGill Law Journal Inc., c/o Faculty of Law, McGill University, 3644 Peel St., Montréal QC H3A 1W9 – 514/874-9038; Fax: 514/874-0679; Email: mlj@lsa.lan.mcgill.ca; URL: http://www.law.library.mcgill.ca/journal – Circ.: 1,320; 4 times a year; English & French – Editor-in-Chief, Sébastien Beaulieu; Managing Editor, Charles J. Prober

Le Monde Juridique, 7423, av de Fougeray, Anjou QC H1K 3K2 – 514/353-3549; Fax: 514/353-4159 – 12 fois par an; français – Editeur/Rédacteur, André Gagnon

National, c/o Canadian Bar Association, #902, 50 O'Connor St., Ottawa ON K1P 6L2 – 613/237-2925; Fax: 613/237-0185; Email: info@cba.org; URL: http://cba.org/abc – Circ.: 35,500; 8 times a year; English & French – Publisher, Jim Farley, 416/596-2538; Editor, J. Stuart Langford; Circulation Manager, Monique Cassidy

Ontario Legal Directory, University of Toronto Press, #700, 10 St. Mary St., Toronto ON M4Y 2W8 – 416/978-2239, ext.245; Fax: 416/978-4738 – Circ.: 6,500; Annually, Feb. – Editor, Elizabeth Lumley

The Ontario Reports (Published by Butterworths Canada Ltd.), 75 Clegg Rd., Markham ON L6G 1A7 – 905/479-2665; Fax: 905/479-3758 – Circ.: 27,000; Weekly – Editor, Anne Eichenberg

Osgoode Hall Law Journal, c/o York University, 4700 Keele St., North York ON M3J 1P3 – 416/736-5354; Fax: 416/736-5736; Email: journal@yorku.ca; URL: http://www.yorku.ca/faculty/osgoode/ohlj – Circ.: 1,500; 4 times a year, plus index; English or French – Editor, Bruce Ryder

**LIGHTING**

Eclairage Plus (Published by Groupe Constructo), #200, 1500, boul Jules-Poitras, Saint-Laurent QC H4N 1X7 – 514/745-5720; Fax: 514/339-2267 – 4 fois par an; français – Editeur, Guy Choinière; Rédacteur, Johanne Rouleau

Lighting Magazine (Published by Kerrwil Publications Ltd.), 395 Matheson Blvd. East, Mississauga ON L4Z 2H2 – 905/890-1846; Fax: 905/890-5769 – Circ.: 7,488; 6 times a year – Publisher, Gary A. Dugan; Editor, Bryan S. Rogers

**MACHINERY MAINTENANCE**

Machinery & Equipment MRO (Published by Southam Magazine Group), 1450 Don Mills Rd., Don Mills ON M3B 2X7 – 416/445-6641; Fax: 416/442-2214; Email: broebuck@southam.ca; URL: http://www.southam.com/b1-5-4.html – Circ.: 22,000; 6 times a year – Publisher, Peter Helston; Editor, William Roebuck; Circulation Manager, Diane Rakoff

**MATERIALS HANDLING & DISTRIBUTION**

Materials Management & Distribution (Published by Maclean Hunter Publishing), 777 Bay St., Toronto ON M5W 1A7 – 416/596-5000; Fax: 416/596-5554; URL: http://www.mhbizlink.com/mm&d – Circ.: 19,000; Monthly; also Bar Code Quarterly (4 times a year) – Publisher, Warren Patterson; Editor, Robert Robertson

**METALWORKING**

Canadian Machinery & Metalworking (Published by Maclean Hunter Publishing), 777 Bay St., Toronto ON M5W 1A7 – 416/596-2667, 5714; Fax: 416/596-5881 – Circ.: 16,600; 7 times a year – Publisher, Glen Alton; Editor, Mike Overment

Metalworking Production & Purchasing (Published by Action Communications Inc.), 135 Spy Ct., Markham ON L3R 5H6 – 905/477-3222; Fax: 905/477-4320; Email: MPP@ACTIONCOM.COM; URL: http://www.actioncom.com – Circ.: 18,200; 6 times a year; also The Dealer – Publisher, Nigel Bishop

**MILITARY**

Canadian Defence Quarterly (Published by Baxter Publishing Co), 310 Dupont St., Toronto ON M5R 1V9 – 416/968-7252; Fax: 416/968-2377; Email: cdq@baxter.net; URL: http://www/baxter.net/cdq/ – Circ.: 5,958; 4 times a year; English & French – Publisher, David McClung; Editor, Martin Shadwick

Canadian Defence Review (Published by Synergistic Publications), 132 Adrian Cres., Markham ON L3P 7B3 – 905/472-2801; Fax: 905/472-3091 – Circ.: 11,000; 4 times a year – Publisher, Peter A. Kitchen; Editor, Nick Stephens; Circulation Manager, Dianne Osadchuk

Garrison, HQ LFCA, 5775 Yonge St., PO Box 17, North York ON M2M 4J7 – 416/733-4681; Fax: 416/363-3944 – Circ.: 11,000; 8 times a year – Editor-in-Chief, Col. G.B. Mitchell; Editor, Capt. R.N. Kennedy, 416/733-4681, ext.5501

**MINING**

Canadian Mines Handbook (Published by Southam Magazine Group), 1450 Don Mills Rd., Don Mills ON M3B 2X7 – 416/510-6779; Fax: 416/442-2272; Email: kcallins@southam.ca – Annually, July – Publisher, Doug Donnelly; Editor, Diane Giancola; Circulation Manager, Sandra Burke

Canadian Mining Journal (Published by Southam Magazine Group), 1450 Don Mills Rd., Don Mills ON M3B 2X7 – 416/442-2094; Fax: 416/442-2175; URL: http://www.southam.com.b1-6-1.html – Circ.: 8,513; 6 times a year – Publisher, Ray Perks; Circulation Manager, Cindi Holder

CIM Bulletin (Published by Canadian Inst. of Mining, Metallurgy & Petroleum), #1210, 3400, boul de Maisonneuve ouest, Montréal QC H3Z 3B8 – 514/939-2710; Fax: 514/939-2714; Email: publications@cim.org; URL: http://www.cim.org – Circ.: 11,000; 10 times a year – Publisher, Yvan Jacques; Editor, Perla Gantz; Circulation Manager, Lynda Battista

CIM Directory (Published by Canadian Inst. of Mining, Metallurgy & Petroleum), #1210, 3400, boul de Maisonneuve ouest, Montréal QC H3Z 3B8 – 514/939-2710; Fax: 514/939-2714; Email: Publications@cm.org – Circ.: 10,531 – Publisher, Yvan Jacques; Editor, Perla Gantz; Circulation Manager, Lynda Battista

CIM Reporter (Published by Canadian Inst. of Mining, Metallurgy & Petroleum), #1210, 3400, boul de Maisonneuve ouest, Montréal QC H3Z 3B8 – 514/939-2710; Fax: 514/939-2714 – Circ.: 6,583 – Publisher, Yvan Jacques; Editor, Perla Gantz; Circulation Manager, Lynda Battista

The Financial Post Survey of Mines & Energy Resources (Published by Financial Post Co. Ltd.), 333 King St. East, Toronto ON M5A 4N2 – 416/350-6500, 1-800-661-7678; Fax: 416/350-6501; Email: fpdg@fpdata.finpost.com – Circ.: 4,300; Annually, Aug. – Editor, Robert Pearson

Mining Review, Naylor Communications, 100 Sutherland Ave., Winnipeg MB R2W 3C7 – 204/947-0222; Fax: 204/204-947-2047 – 4 times a year – Editor, Janis Connolly

Mining Sourcebook (Published by Southam Magazine Group), 1450 Don Mills Rd., Don Mills ON M3B 2X7 – 416/442-2094; Fax: 416/442-2175 – Annually, Nov. – Group Publisher, Doug Donnelly; Publisher, Ray Perks

The Northern Miner (Published by Southam Magazine Group), 1450 Don Mills Rd., Don Mills ON M3B 2X7 – 416/442-2164; Fax: 416/442-2175; Email: tnm@southam.ca; URL: http://www.northernminer.com – Circ.: 25,000; Weekly – Publisher, Doug Donnelly; Executive Publisher, John Cooke; Circulation Manager, Sandra Burke

The Prospector Exploration & Investment Bulletin, K.W. Publishing Ltd., #101, 211 East Georgia St., Vancouver BC V6A 1Z6 – 604/688-2271; Fax: 604/688-2038; Email: prospector@info-mine.com; URL: http://www.info-mine.com/daily.news/ – Circ.: 25,000; 6 times a year – Publisher, Darlene Liboiron; Editor, Blake Desaulniers

**MOTOR TRUCKS & BUSES**

Atlantic Trucking (Published by Naylor Communications Ltd.), 920 Yonge St., 6th Fl., Toronto ON M4W 3C7 – 416/961-1028; Fax: 416/924-4408 – 3 times a year – Publisher, Robert Thompson

Camionneurs, Publications media plus inc., #114, 4058, rue Mouselet, Montréal-Nord QC H1H 2C5 – 514/328-3485; Fax: 514/328-3131; Email: ccqi@camionquevec.com – Tirage: 12,186; 8 fois par an; français

L'Echo du Transport (Published by Les Editions Bomart ltée), #103, 7493 Trans Canada Hwy., St-Laurent QC H4T 1T3 – 514/337-9043; Fax: 514/337-1862; Email: bomart@infobahnos.com; URL: http://www.bomartgroup.com – Tirage: 19,517; 10 fois par an; français – Rédacteur, Steve Bouchard; Directrice de tirage, Ginette Marsolais

Manitoba Ship-by-Truck Directory (Published by Craig Kelman & Associates Ltd.), #3C, 2020 Portage Ave., Winnipeg MB R3J 0K4 – 204/885-7798; Fax: 204/889-3576 – Circ.: 1,000; Annually

Motor Truck (Published by Southam Magazine Group), 1450 Don Mills Rd., Don Mills ON M3B 2X7 – 416/445-6641; Fax: 416/442-2213; URL: http://www.southam.com/b1-10-1.html – Circ.: 29,000; 6 times a year

Today's Trucking, New Communications Group Inc., 130 Belfield Rd., Etobicoke ON M9W 1G1 – 416/614-2200; Fax: 416/614-8861 – Circ.: 29,400; 10 times a year – Publisher, James B. Glionna; Editor, Rolf Lockwood

Truck News (Published by Southam Magazine Group), 1450 Don Mills Rd., Don Mills ON M3B 2X7 – 416/442-2062; Fax: 416/442-2092; Email: jsmith@southam.ca; URL: http://www.southam.com/b1-10-2.html – Circ.: 39,872; Monthly – Publisher, Ted Light; Editor, John G. Smith; Circulation Manager, Keith Fulford

Truck West (Published by Southam Magazine Group), 1450 Don Mills Rd., Don Mills ON M3B 2X7 – 416/442-2268; Email: pcancilla@southam.ca; URL: http://www.southam.com/b1-10-3/html – Circ.: 20,300; Monthly – Publisher, Ted Light

Truck World, HB Publishers Ltd., #11, 106 - 14th St. East, North Vancouver BC V7L 2N3 – 604/984-2002; Fax: 604/984-2820 – Circ.: 14,600; 6 times a year – Publisher/Editor, Paul Young; Managing Editor, Ken Barnsohn

La Voix du vrac, #235, 670, rue Bouvier, Québec QC G2J 1A7 – 418/623-7923; Fax: 418/623-0448 – Tirage: 9 000; 6 fois par an; français – Editeur, André Lavoie

Western Canada Highway News (Published by Craig Kelman & Associates Ltd.), #3C, 2020 Portage Ave., Winnipeg MB R3J 0K4 – 204/985-1780; Fax: 204/985-9795; Email: kelman@escape.ca – Circ.: 4,000; 4 times a year – Publisher, Craig Kelman; Editor, T. Ross

### MUSIC

The Canadian Music Educator, Canadian Music Educators' Assn., 43 Victoria Hill, Sydney NS B1R 1N9 – 902/567-2398; Fax: 902/564-0123; Email: efavaro@fox.nstn.ca; URL: http://www.stemnet.nf.ca/~barobert/.cmea/cmea.html – Circ.: 2,000; 5-7 times a year; includes the CMEA Newsletter – Editor, Dr. Brian Roberts

Canadian Music Trade (Published by Norris-Whitney Communications Inc.), #7, 23 Hannover Dr., St Catharines ON L2W 1A3 – 905/641-3471; Fax: 905/641-1648; Email: info@nor.com; URL: http://nor.com.cmt – Circ.: 3,516; 6 times a year – Publisher, Jim Norris; Consumer Services Director, Maureen Jack

Professional Sound (Published by Norris-Whitney Communications Inc.), #7, 23 Hannover Dr., St Catharines ON L2W 1A3 – 905/641-1512; Fax: 905/641-1648; Email: info@nor.com; URL: http://www.nor.com/ps – Circ.: 12,700; 6 times a year – Publisher, Jim Norris; Consumer Services Director, Maureen Jack

RPM Weekly, 6 Brentcliffe Rd., Toronto ON M4G 3Y2 – 416/425-0257; Fax: 416/425-8629 – Weekly – Publisher, Walt Grealis

### NURSING

A.A.R.N Newsletter, Alberta Association of Registered Nurses, 11620 - 168 St., Edmonton AB T5M 4A6 – 403/451-0043; Fax: 403/452-3276; Email: nurses.ab.ca – Circ.: 26,000; 11 times a year – Editor/Information Officer, Micky Elabdi

Canadian Journal of Cardiovascular Nursing, c/o Canadian Council of Cardiovascular Nurses, #200, 160 George St., Ottawa ON K1N 9M2 – 613/241-4361; Fax: 613/241-3278 – Annually

The Canadian Nurse, Canadian Nurses' Assn., 50 Driveway, Ottawa ON K2P 1E2 – 613/237-2133; Fax: 613/237-3520 – Circ.: 110,000; 10 times a year; English & French

Canadian Oncology Nursing Journal, Pappin Communications, 84 Isabella St., Pembroke ON K8A 5S5 – 613/735-0952; Fax: 613/735-7983; Email: Bever;eu_Page@cancercare.on.ca – Circ.: 1,000; 4 times a year; English & French – Editor, Beverley Page

Canadian Operating Room Nursing Journal, c/o Health Media, 14453 - 29A Ave., Surrey BC V4A 9K8 – 604/535-7933; Fax: 604/535-9000 – Circ.: 2,800; 4 times a year – Publisher, Ronald Forster; Executive Editor, Agnes Forster

The Care Connection, Bldg. 4, #200, 5025 Orbitor Dr., Mississauga ON L4W 4Y5 – 905/602-4664; Fax: 905/602-4666; Email: rpnao@istar.ca – Circ.: 5,500; 4 times a year – Executive Director, Barbara Thornber

Concern, 2066 Retallack St., Regina SK S4T 7X5 – 306/757-4643; Fax: 306/525-0849 – Circ.: 10,000; 6 times a year – Editor, J. Johnson

L'Infirmière du Québec, 4200, boul Dorchester ouest, Montréal QC H3Z 1V4 – 514/935-2501; Fax: 514/935-2055; Email: inf@oiiq.org – Tirage: 67,186; 6 fois par an; français – Rédactrice, Diane Iezzi

Nursing B.C., 2855 Arbutus St., Vancouver BC V6J 3Y8 – 604/736-7331; Fax: 604/738-2272 – Circ.: 36,000; 5 times a year – Editor, Bruce Wells

Pre & Post Natal News (Published by Professional Publishing), 269 Richmond St. West, Toronto ON M5V 1X1 – 416/596-8680; Fax: 416/596-1991 – 3 times a year – Editor, Beverly Topping

Santé Québec, Ordre des infirmières & infirmiers auxiliaires du Québec, 531, rue Sherbrooke est, Montréal QC H2L 1K2 – 514/282-9511; Fax: 514/282-0631 – Tirage: 23,000; 3 fois par an; français – Rédactrice, Madeleine Pelletier

### OFFICE EQUIPMENT

COPA Conversation (Published by Canadian Office Products Association), #911, 1243 Islington Ave., Toronto ON M8X 1X9 – 416/239-2737; Fax: 416/239-1553 – 4 times a year – Publisher, James H. Preece; Editor, Darrell O. Townson

### PACKAGING

Canadian Packaging (Published by Maclean Hunter Publishing), 777 Bay St., Toronto ON M5W 1A7 – 416/596-5744; Fax: 416/596-5810 – Circ.: 12,200; 11 times a year – Publisher, Stephen Dean; Editor, Douglas W. Faulkner, 416/596-5746

### PAINT, FINISHES, COATINGS

Coatings (Published by Kay Publishing), #1, 406 North Service Rd. East, Oakville ON L6H 5R2 – 905/844-9773; Fax: 905/844-5672 – Circ.: 7,200; 6 times a year – Publisher & Editor, G. Barry Kay

### PETROLEUM, OIL & GAS

Alberta Oil & Gas Directory (Published by Armadale Publications Inc.), PO Box 1193, Stn Main PO, Edmonton AB T5J 2M4 – 403/429-1073; Fax: 403/425-5844 – Annually – Editor, Cal Kelly

Canada-Z Oil Gas Mining Directory (Published by Armadale Publications Inc.), PO Box 1193, Stn Main PO, Edmonton AB T5J 2M4 – 403/429-1073; Fax: 403/425-5844 – Annually – Editor, Cal Kelly

Canadian Oilfield Gas Plant Atlas (Published by June Warren Publishing Ltd.), 9915 - 56 Ave., Edmonton AB T6E 5L7 – 403/944-9333; Fax: 403/944-9500 – Circ.: 1,547; Annually – Publisher, Colin Eicher

Canadian Oilfield Service & Supply Directory (Published by June Warren Publishing Ltd.), 9915 - 56 Ave., Edmonton AB T6E 5L7 – 403/944-9333; Fax: 403/944-9500 – Annually – Publisher, Colin Eicher

Canadian Oil Register, Southam, #300, 999 - 8 St. SW, Calgary AB T2R 1N7 – 403/244-6111; Fax: 403/245-8666 – Annually, Sept. – Manager, Doreen McArthur

Energy Processing/Canada (Published by Northern Star Communications Ltd.), 900 - 6 Ave. SW, 5th Fl., Calgary AB T2P 3K2 – 403/263-6881; Fax: 403/263-6886; Email: nstar@cadvision.com – Circ.: 6,420; 6 times a year – Publisher, Scott Jeffrey; Editor, Alister Thomas; Circulation Manager, Kim Glonnie

The Journal of Canadian Petroleum Technology, The Petroleum Society, #320, 101 - 6th Ave. SW, Calgary AB T2P 3P4 – 403/237-5112; Fax: 403/262-4792; Email: petsoc@canpic.ca; URL: http://www.canpic.ca/PETSOC – Circ.: 5,600; 12 times a year – Editor, Catherine Buchanan

Oil & Gas Inquirer (Published by June Warren Publishing Ltd.), 9915 - 56 Ave., Edmonton AB T6E 5L7 – 403/944-9333; Fax: 403/944-9500 – Monthly – Publisher, Colin Eicher

Oil & Gas Product News (Published by Baum Publications Ltd.), #201, 2323 Boundary Rd., Vancouver BC V5M 4V8 – 604/291-9900; Fax: 604/291-1906; Email: ebaum@baumpub.com; URL: http://www.baumpub.com – Circ.: 15,500; 6 times a year – Publisher, Engelbert J. Baum; Editor, Stan Sauerwein

Oil Patch Magazine, Master Publications, 17560 - 107 Ave., 2nd Fl., Edmonton AB T5S 1E9 – 403/486-1295; Fax: 403/484-0884 – 6 times a year – Publisher/Senior Editor, L.M. Hyman

Oilweek (Published by Maclean Hunter Publishing Ltd.), #2450, 101 - 6th Ave. SW, Calgary AB T2P 3P4 – 403/266-8700; Fax: 403/266-6634; Email: oilweek@cadvision.com – Circ.: 7,500; Weekly – Publisher, Philip J. Boyd; Editor, Gordon Jaremko

Propane-Canada (Published by Northern Star Communications Ltd.), 900 - 6 Ave. SW, 5th Fl., Calgary AB T2P 3K2 – 403/263-6881; Fax: 403/263-6886; Email: nstar@cadvision.com – Circ.: 5,500; 6 times a year – Publisher, Scott Jeffrey; Editor, Alister Thomas; Circulation Manager, Eric Anderson

The Roughneck (Published by Northern Star Communications Ltd.), 900 - 6 Ave. SW, 5th Fl., Calgary AB T2P 3K2 – 403/263-6881; Fax: 403/263-6886 – Circ.: 5,700; Monthly – Publisher, Scott Jeffrey; Editor, Alister Thomas; Circulation Manager, Eric Anderson

### PHOTOGRAPHY

Photonews & Electronic Imaging, BCS Communications Ltd., 101 Thorncliffe Park Dr., Toronto ON M4H 1M2 – 416/421-7944; Fax: 416/421-0966; Email: gunter.ott@canrem.com – Circ.: 30,500; 3 times a year – Editor, Gunter Ott

Photo Retailer (Published by Les Publications Apex inc.), 185, rue St-Paul, Québec QC G1K 3W2 – 418/692-2110; Fax: 418/692-3392 – Circ.: 5,000; 3 times a year – Publisher, Curtis J. Sommerville; Editor, Don Long; Circulation Manager, Jeffery A. Sommerville

Professional Photographers of Canada (Published by Craig Kelman & Associates Ltd.), #3C, 2020 Portage

Ave., Winnipeg MB R3J 0K4 – 204/885-7798; Fax: 204/889-3576 – Circ.: 1,600; 6 times a year; English & French; also Professional Photographers of Canada Directory (annually, April) – Editor, Jim E. Watson

**PLASTICS**

Canadian Plastics (Published by Southam Magazine Group), 1450 Don Mills Rd., Don Mills ON M3B 2X7 – 416/445-6641; Fax: 416/442-2213; Email: cmacdonald@southam.ca; URL: http://www.southam.com/magazines/plastics.html – Circ.: 10,100; 8 times a year – Publisher, Judith Nancekivell, 416/442-2067; Editor, Michael LeGault

Canadian Plastics Directory & Buyer's Guide (Published by Southam Magazine Group), 1450 Don Mills Rd., Don Mills ON M3B 2X7 – 416/445-6641; Fax: 416/442-2213; Email: cmacdonald@southam.ca; URL: http://www.magazines.Southam.com/CanPlastics/directorydisk.html – Circ.: 10,100 – Publisher, Judith Nancekivell; Editor, Cindy Macdonald; Circulation Manager, Diane Rakoff

Canadian Plastics Technology Showcase (Published by Southam Magazine Group), 1450 Don Mills Rd., Don Mills ON M3B 2X7 – 416/445-6641; Fax: 416/442-2213; Email: cmacdonald@southam.ca; URL: http://www.southam.com/magazines/plastics.html – Circ.: 10,900; 4 times a year – Publisher, Judith Nancekivell; Editor, Michael LeGault; Circulation Manager, Diane Rakoff

Plastics in Canada Magazine (Published by Kay Publishing), #1, 406 North Service Rd. East, Oakville ON L6H 5R2 – 905/844-9773; Fax: 905/844-5672 – Circ.: 10,145; 6 times a year – Publisher, Larry Bonikowsky

Plastics Industry Reference Guide & Sourcebook (Published by Kenilworth Publishing), #201, 27 West Beaver Creek, Richmond Hill ON L4B 1M8 – 905/771-7333; Fax: 905/771-7336; Email: sales@kenilworth.com – Circ.: 1,020; Annually, May – Publisher, James Davidson

**POLICE**

Blue Line Magazine, #254, Unit 12A, Hwy. 7 East, Markham ON L3R 1N1 – 905/640-3048; Fax: 905/640-7547 – Circ.: 10,000; 10 times a year – Publisher, Morley S. Lymburner

News & Views, Metropolitan Toronto Police Assn., 180 Yorkland Blvd., North York ON M2J 1R5 – 416/491-4301; Fax: 416/494-4948 – Circ.: 9,245; Monthly – Editor, Elizabeth Alexander

Scarlet & Gold, 1215 Alder Bay Walk, Vancouver BC V6H 3T6 – 604/738-4423; Fax: 604/681-5230 – Circ.: 2,000; Annually – Editor & Publisher, J. Murphy

**POWER & POWER PLANTS**

Nuclear Canada Yearbook, #475, 144 Front St., Toronto ON M5J 2L7 – 416/977-6152; Fax: 416/979-8356 – Circ.: 3,000; Annually, May – Publications Editor, Colin Hunt

**PRINTING & PUBLISHING**

Canadian Printer (Published by Maclean Hunter Publishing), 777 Bay St., Toronto ON M5W 1A7 – 416/596-5781; Fax: 416/596-5965; Email: cdaprint@cycor.ca – Circ.: 13,000; 10 times a year – Publisher, Susan Leggat; Editor, Stephen Forbes

Estimators' & Buyers' Guide (Published by North Island Sound Ltd.), #8, 1606 Sedlescomb Dr., Mississauga ON L4X 1M6 – 905/625-7070; Fax: 905/625-4856 – Annually, Feb. – Publisher/Owner, Sandy Alexander Donald

Graphic Monthly (Published by North Island Sound Ltd.), #8, 1606 Sedlescomb Dr., Mississauga ON L4X 1M6 – 905/625-7070; Fax: 905/625-4856 – Circ.: 10,088; 6 times a year – Publisher/Owner, Sandy Alexander Donald; Managing Editor, Nancy Clark

Le Maître Imprimeur, #13, 255, Montée Seraphin, Ste-Adèle QC J0R 1L0 – 514/227-7300; Fax: 514/229-4710 – Tirage: 4,100; Mensuel; français – Editeur, Jules Côte; Rédacteur, Gerard Thérien

Masthead (Published by North Island Sound Ltd.), #8, 1606 Sedlescomb Dr., Mississauga ON L4X 1M6 – 905/625-7070; Fax: 905/625-4856; Email: the-editor@biginc.on.ca; URL: http://www.the-wire.com/bishop/biginc.html – Circ.: 4,300; 10 times a year; ISSN 0832-512X – Publisher, Alexander Donald; Editor, Patrick Walsh

PrintAction (Published by Youngblood Publishing), #1204, 2240 Midland Ave., Scarborough ON M1R 4R8 – 416/299-6007; Fax: 416/299-6674 – Circ.: 11,500; Monthly – Publisher, John Galbraith; Editor, Julian Mills

Production Imprimée (Published by Editions Info Presse inc.), 4316, boul St-Laurent, Montréal QC H2W 1Z3 – 514/842-5873; Fax: 514/842-2422; Email: pubpim@infopresse.com; redapim@infopresse.com – 10 fois par an – Editeur, Bruno Gautier

The Publisher, #206, 90 Eglinton Ave. East, Toronto ON M4P 2Y3 – 416/482-1090; Fax: 416/482-1908; Email: ccna@sentex.net; URL: http://www.ccna.ca – Circ.: 2,100; 10 times a year – Publisher, Michael Anderson; Editor, Robert MacKenzie

Second Impressions, 35 Mill Dr., St. Albert AB T8N 1J5 – 403/458-9889; Fax: 403/458-9839; Email: simttm@supernet.ab.ca – Circ.: 6,650; 6 times a year – Publisher, Loretta Puckrin

**PRODUCT ENGINEERING & DESIGN**

Design Engineering (Published by Maclean Hunter Publishing), 777 Bay St., Toronto ON M5W 1A7 – 416/596-5819; Fax: 416/593-3193 – Circ.: 19,000; 8 times a year – Publisher, Frank Ragan; Editor, James Barnes

Design Product News (Published by Action Communications Inc.), 135 Spy Ct., Markham ON L3R 5H6 – 905/477-3222; Fax: 905/477-4320; Email: DPN@ACTIONCOM.COM – Circ.: 19,158; 6 times a year – Publisher, Michael Doody; Editor, Mike Edwards; Circulation Manager, Carole Halse

**PULP & PAPER**

Forêt Conservation, 175, rue St-Jean, 4 étage, Québec QC G1R 1N4 – 418/529-2542; Fax: 418/529-3021 – Tirage: 6,500; 6 fois par an; français – Rédacteur, Pierre Dubois

Mill Product News (Published by Baum Publications Ltd.), #201, 2323 Boundary Rd., Vancouver BC V5M 4V8 – 604/298-3004; Fax: 604/298-3966 – Circ.: 18,000; 6 times a year – Publisher, Heri R. Baum; Editor, Toni Dabbs

Les Papetières du Québec (Published by Southam Magazine Group), #410, 3300, boul Côte Vertu, Saint-Laurent QC H4R 2B7 – 514/339-1399, 1-800-363-1327; Fax: 514/339-1396; URL: http://www.southam.com/b1-7-1.html – Tirage: 3,733; 4 fois par an; français – Président, W. Mann; Rédacteur, Jaclin Ouellet

Pulp & Paper Canada (Published by Southam Magazine Group), #410, 3300, boul Côte Vertu, Saint-Laurent QC H4R 2B7 – 514/339-1399; Fax: 514/339-1396; URL: http://www.southam.com/b1-7-2.html – Circ.: 9,600; Monthly; aslo Annual Directory (Nov.) – Publisher, Mark Yerbury; Editor, Graeme Rodden

**PURCHASING**

Canadian Purchaser (Published by Canadian Office Products Association), #911, 1243 Islington Ave., Toronto ON M8X 1X9 – 416/239-2737; Fax: 416/239-1553; Email: darrell.townson@sympatico.ca; URL: http://www.copa.ca – Circ.: 20,000; 4 times a year – Publisher, James H. Preece

Canadian Trade Index, c/o Alliance of Manufacturers & Exporters Canada, 75 International Blvd., 4th Fl.., Etobicoke ON M9W 6L9 – 416/798-8000; Fax: 416/798-1627; Email: orders@allianceonline.com; URL: http://www.ctidirectory.com – Annually, March – Editor, Hugh Owen

Fraser's Canadian Trade Directory (Published by Maclean Hunter Publishing), 777 Bay St., Toronto ON M5W 1A7 – 416/596-5086; Fax: 416/593-3201 – Circ.: 8,000; Annually, May – Publisher, Bert Bauer

Modern Purchasing (Published by Maclean Hunter Publishing), 777 Bay St., Toronto ON M5W 1A7 – 416/596-5792, 5704; Fax: 416/596-5866 – Circ.: 20,000; 10 times a year – Publisher, Tim Dimopoulos; Editor, Joe Terrett

**REAL ESTATE**

Canadian Industrial Property Guide, Royal LePage Commercial Inc., #200, 5770 Hurontario S., Mississauga ON L5R 3G5 – 905/568-9500; Fax: 905/568-9444; Email: mailbox@royallepage.com; URL: http://www.royallepage.com – Circ.: 37,000; Annual – Publisher & Editor, Alex Strachan

Canadian Realtor News, Canadian Real Estate Association, #1600, 344 Slater St., Ottawa ON K1R 7Y3 – 613/237-7111; Fax: 613/234-2567; Email: info@crea.ca; URL: http://www.crea.ca – Circ.: 72,000; Monthly; separate English & French editions – Editor, Jim McCarthy

ProAct (Published by Kenilworth Publishing), #201, 27 West Beaver Creek, Richmond Hill ON L4B 1M8 – 905/771-7333; Fax: 905/771-7336; Email: sales@kenilworth.com – Circ.: 8,300; 4 times a year – Publisher, Jim Davidson; Editor, Nicholas Stephens

REM: Canada's Magazine for Real Estate Professionals, House Magazine Inc., 115 Thorncliffe Park Dr., Toronto ON M4H 1M1 – 416/425-3504; Fax: 416/425-0040; Email: jclc@pathcom.com – Circ.: 33,000; 12 times a year – Publisher, Heino Molls; Editor, Jim Adair

The Western Investor, Westward Publications, #501, 1155 West Pender St., Vancouver BC V6E 2P4 – 604/669-8500, 1-800-661-6988; Fax: 604/669-2154 – Circ.: 12,000; Monthly – Publisher, Tracy Chysik; Editor, Anna Lilly

**RENTAL & LEASING EQUIPMENT**

Canadian Rental Service (Published by AIS Communications Ltd.), 145 Thames Rd. West, Exeter ON NOM 1S3 – 519/235-2400; Fax: 519/235-0798 – Circ.: 3,830; 8 times a year – Publisher, Peter Phillips; Editor, Peter Darbishire; Circulation Manager, Jan Jeffery

**RETAILING**

Canadian Retailer, Retail Council of Canada, 121 Bloor St. East, 12th Fl., Toronto ON M4W 3M5 – 416/922-6678; Fax: 416/922-8011; URL: http://www.retailcouncil.org – Circ.: 9,500; 6 times a year – Publisher, Diane J. Brisebois

**SCIENCE, RESEARCH & DEVELOPMENT**

Biochemistry & Cell Biology (Published by National Research Council of Canada - NRC Research Press), Montréal Rd., Ottawa ON K1A 0R6 – 613/993-9085; Fax: 613/952-7656; Email: Hoda.Jabbour@NRC.CA; URL: http://www.cisti.nrc.ca/cisti/journals.rj.html – Circ.: 1.085; Bi-monthly; English & French – Editor, D.L. Brown; Editor, M. Tenniswood

Canadian Geotechnical Journal (Published by National Research Council of Canada - NRC Research Press), Montréal Rd., Ottawa ON K1A 0R6 – 613/993-9085; Fax: 613/952-7656; Email: judy.heyman@nrc.ca; URL: http://

www.nrc.ca/cisti/journals/ – Circ.: 2,553; 6 times a year; English & French – Editor, Dennis Becker

Canadian Journal of Analytical Sciences & Spectroscopy (Published by Polyscience Publications Inc.), 44 Seize Arpents, PO Box 148, Morin-Heights QC J0R 1H0 – 514/226-5870; Fax: 514/226-5866; URL: http://www.ietc.ca/polysci/ – Circ.: 1,000; 6 times a year; English & French – Editor, Dr. Ian Butler

Canadian Journal of Botany (Published by National Research Council of Canada - NRC Research Press), Montréal Rd., Ottawa ON K1A 0R6 – 613/993-0151; Fax: 613/952-7656; Email: heyman.judy@nrc.ca; URL: http://www.nrc.ca/cisti/journals – Circ.: 1,460; Monthly; English & French – Editor, Dr. B.P. Dancik

Canadian Journal of Chemistry (Published by National Research Council of Canada - NRC Research Press), Montréal Rd., Ottawa ON K1A 0R6 – 613/993-9085; Fax: 613/953-7656; Email: Hoda.Jabbour@NRC.CA – Monthly; English & French – Editor, T. Chivers

Canadian Journal of Civil Engineering (Published by National Research Council of Canada - NRC Research Press), Montréal Rd., Ottawa ON K1A 0R6 – 613/993-9085; Fax: 613/953-7656; Email: Hoda.Jabbour@NRC.CA – 6 times a year; English & French – Editor, Dr. M. Isaacson

Canadian Journal of Earth Sciences (Published by National Research Council of Canada - NRC Research Press), Montréal Rd., Ottawa ON K1A 0R6 – 613/993-9085; Fax: 613/953-7656; Email: judy.heyman@nrc.ca; URL: http://www.cisti.nrc.ca/journals/ – Circ.: 1,830; Monthly; English & French – Editor, Dr. B.P. Dancik

Canadian Journal of Forest Research (Published by National Research Council of Canada - NRC Research Press), Montréal Rd., Ottawa ON K1A 0R6 – 613/993-9085; Fax: 613/953-7656; Email: Hoda.Jabbour@NRC.CA – Monthly; English & French – Editor, Dr. W.M. Cheliak

Canadian Journal of Microbiology (Published by National Research Council of Canada - NRC Research Press), Montréal Rd., Ottawa ON K1A 0R6 – 613/993-9085; Fax: 613/953-7656; Email: judy.heyman@nrc.ca; URL: http://www.cisti.nrc.ca/journals/ – Monthly; English & French – Co-Editor, L.M. Nelson

Canadian Journal of Physics (Published by National Research Council of Canada - NRC Research Press), Montréal Rd., Ottawa ON K1A 0R6 – 613/993-9085; Fax: 613/953-7656 – Monthly; English & French – Editor, Dr. Donald Betts

Canadian Journal of Physiology & Pharmacology (Published by National Research Council of Canada - NRC Research Press), Montréal Rd., Ottawa ON K1A 0R6 – 613/993-9085; Fax: 613/953-7656; Email: Hoda.Jabbour@NRC.CA; URL: http://www.cisti.nrc.ca/cisti/journals/rj.html – Circ.: 980; Monthly; English & French – Editor, J.F. Brien; Editor, Dr. J.D. Davison

Canadian Journal of Zoology (Published by National Research Council of Canada - NRC Research Press), Montréal Rd., Ottawa ON K1A 0R6 – 613/993-9085; Fax: 613/953-7656; Email: judy.heyman@nrc.ca; URL: http://www.cisti.nrc.ca/journals/ – Monthly; English & French – Editor, Dr. K.G. Davey; Editor, Dr. A.S.M. Saleuddin

Genome (Published by National Research Council of Canada - NRC Research Press), Montréal Rd., Ottawa ON K1A 0R6 – 613/993-9085; Fax: 613/953-7656; Email: Hoda.Jabbour@NRC.CA; URL: http://www.cisti.nrc.ca/cisti/journals.rj.html – Circ.: 1,270; 6 times a year; English & French – Editor, Dr. Peter Moens

LAB Business, #202, 30 East Beaver Creek Rd., Richmond Hill ON L4B 1J2 – 905/886-5040; Fax: 905/886-6615; Email: chris@jesmar.com; URL: http://www.jesmar.com – Circ.: 43,303; 4 times a year – Publisher, Christopher Forbes

Laboratory Buyers Guide (Published by Southam Magazine Group), 1450 Don Mills Rd., Don Mills ON M3B 2X7 – 416/445-6641; Fax: 416/442-2201 – Annually – Publisher/Editor, Rita Tate, 416/442-2052

Laboratory Product News (Published by Southam Magazine Group), 1450 Don Mills Rd., Don Mills ON M3B 2X7 – 416/445-6641; Fax: 416/442-2201; URL: http://www.southam.com/b1-5-3.html – Circ.: 18,000; 6 times a year – Publisher/Editor, Rita Tate, 416/442-2052

The Microscopical Society of Canada Bulletin, Microscopical Society of Canada, Dept. of Pathology, McMaster Univ., 1200 Main St., Hamilton ON L8N 3Z5 – 905/525-9140, ext.22496; Fax: 905/528-8860; Email: cemerson@kean.ucs.mun.ca; URL: http://www.ualberta.cal~mmid/msc – Circ.: 650; 4 times a year; ISSN 0383-1825 – Editor, Carolyn J. Emerson, 709/737-7515

OSMT Advocate, #600, 234 Eglinton Ave. East, Toronto ON M4P 1K5 – 416/485-6768; Fax: 416/672-0244 – Circ.: 4,000; 4 times a year – Executive Editor, Sam Laldin

Physics in Canada, #112, McDonald Bldg., 150 Louis Pasteur Ave., Ottawa ON K1N 6N5 – 613/562-5614; Fax: 613/562-5615; Email: cap@physics.uottawa.ca; URL: http://www.cap.ca – Circ.: 2,000; 6 times a year; French & English – Publisher, F.M. Ford; Editor, J.S.C. McKee

Research Money (Published by Evert Communications Ltd.), 1296 Carling Ave., 2nd Fl., Ottawa ON K1Z 7K8 – 613/728-4621; Fax: 613/728-0385; Email: services@evert.com; URL: http://www.evert.com – 20 times a year – Publisher, Gordon D. Hutchison; Editor, Mark Henderson; Circulation Manager, Carole Jeffrey

### SECURITY

Canadian Security, c/o Security Publishing, 46 Crockford Blvd., Scarborough ON M1R 3C3 – 416/755-4343; Fax: 416/755-7487 – Circ.: 11,900; 7 times a year – Publisher, Maureen Percival; Editor, Richard Skinulis; Circulation Manager, Lisa Drummond

Security Products & Technology News, Essential Publications Inc., #206, 1085 Bellamy Rd. North, Scarborough ON M1H 3C7 – 416/289-1510; Fax: 416/289-7460; Email: info@sptnews.com – Circ.: 18,437; 6 times a year – Publisher, Bob Rodkin, Email: rodkin@sptnews.com

### SHIPPING & MARINE

British Columbia Commercial Marine Directory & Buyers Guide (Published by Westcoast Publishing Ltd), 1496 - 72nd Ave. West, Vancouver BC V6P 3C8 – 602/266-7433; Fax: 602/263-8620; Email: marinedir@west-coast.com; URL: http://www.west-coast.com – Circ.: 6,000; Annually (Nov.)

Canadian Sailings, 4634 St. Catherine St. West, Montréal QC H3Z 1S3 – 514/934-0373; Fax: 514/934-4708 – Circ.: 10,000; Weekly – Publisher, Brian O'N. Gallery; Editor, Leo Ryan; Circulation Manager, Diane Lazar; Associate Publisher, Bob Sutherland

Captain Lillie's Coast Guide & Radiotelephone Directory (Published by Progress Publishing Co Ltd.), #200, 1865 Marine Dr., West Vancouver BC V7V 1J7 – 604/922-6717; Fax: 604/922-1739 – Biennially – Publisher, M.D. McLellan

Great Lakes Navigation (Published by Canadian Marine Publications), #512, 1434, rue Ste-Catherine ouest, Montréal QC H3G 1R4 – 514/861-6715; Fax: 514/861-0966 – Annually, March – Publisher, John W. McManus; Editor, Megan D. Perkins; Circulation Manager, Marilyn Bélanger

Harbour & Shipping (Published by Progress Publishing Co Ltd.), #200, 1865 Marine Dr., West Vancouver BC V7V 1J7 – 604/922-6717; Fax: 604/922-1739 – Monthly – President/Publisher, M.D. McLellan; Editor, Liz Bennett

Ports Annual (Published by Canadian Marine Publications), #512, 1434, rue Ste-Catherine ouest, Montréal QC H3G 1R4 – 514/861-6715; Fax: 514/861-0966 – Annually, Aug. – Editor, Megan D. Perkins

Westcoast Shipping (Published by Westcoast Publishing Ltd), 1496 - 72nd Ave. West, Vancouver BC V6P 3C8 – 604/266-7433; Fax: 604/263-8620 – Circ.: 2,500; Monthly – Publisher, David Rahn; Editor, Alison Bate

### SHOWS & EXHIBITIONS

Shows & Exhibitions (Published by Maclean Hunter Publishing), 777 Bay St., Toronto ON M5W 1A7 – 416/596-2790; Fax: 416/596-5158 – Circ.: 6,000; 2 times a year – Publisher, Gloria Gallagher; Associate Publisher, Bruce D. Richards

### SPORTING GOODS & RECREATIONAL EQUIPMENT

Eté Contact (Published by Editions Versicolores inc.), 1320, boul St-Joseph, Québec QC G2K 1G2 – 418/628-8690; Fax: 418/628-0524 – 4 fois par an – Editeur, François Bernatchez; Rédacteur, Caty Bérubé

Motorsport Dealer & Trade (Published by Turbopress Inc.), #301, 411 Richmond St. East, Toronto ON M5A 3S5 – 416/362-7966; Fax: 416/362-3950; Email: cyclecan@aol.com – Circ.: 3,500; 6 times a year – Publisher, Jean-Pierre Belmonte; Editor, David Martin

Pool & Spa Marketing, Hubbard Marketing & Publishing Ltd., 270 Esna Park Dr., Unit 12, Markham ON L3R 1H3 – 905/513-0090; Fax: 905/513-1377 – Circ.: 9,000; 7 times a year – Publisher, Richard Hubbard; Editor, David Barnsley

RV Lifestyle Dealer News (Published by Camping Canada), #306, 2585 Skymark Ave., Mississauga ON L4W 4L5 – 905/624-8218; Fax: 905/624-6764 – 4 times a year – Publisher, William E. Taylor; Editor, Peter Tasler

Sports Business, #214, 3883 Hwy. 7, Woodbridge ON L4L 6C1 – 905/856-2600; Fax: 905/856-2667; Email: triscomm@istar.ca – Circ.: 9,100; 5 times a year – Publisher, Tony Muccilli

### SPORTS & RECREATION

Golf Business Canada, Capital Publishers, 400 Cumberland St., Ottawa ON K1N 8X3 – 613/241-7888; Fax: 613/241-3112; Email: cappub@istar.ca – Circ.: 3,000; 4 times a year – Publisher, Stephen Ball

### TELECOMMUNICATIONS

Canadian Communications Network Letter (Published by Evert Communications Ltd.), 1296 Carling Ave., 2nd Fl., Ottawa ON K1Z 7K8 – 613/728-4621; Fax: 613/728-0385; Email: services@evert.com; URL: http://www.evert.com – 40 times a year – Publisher, Gordon D. Hutchison; Editor, Brant Scott; Circulation Manager, Carole Jeffrey

Canadian Communications Reports (Published by Evert Communications Ltd.), 1296 Carling Ave., 2nd Fl., Ottawa ON K1Z 7K8 – 613/728-4621; Fax: 613/728-0385; Email: newsdesk@evert.com; URL: http://www.evert.com – 20 times a year – Publisher, Gordon D. Hutchison; Editor, Debbie Lawes; Circulation Manager, Carole Jeffrey

Canadian Telecom, The ABY Group, #1160, 36 Toronto St., Toronto ON M5C 2C5 – 416/359-2911; Fax: 416/359-9909 – Circ.: 5,520; 6 times a year

Wireless Telecom, #2004, 275 Slater St., Ottawa ON K1P 5H9 – 613/233-4888; Fax: 613/233-2032; Email: mchoma@cwta.ca; URL: http://www.cwta.ca – Circ.: 5,000 – Managing Editor, Marc Choma

### TELEVISION, RADIO, VIDEO & HOME APPLIANCES

Marketnews, Bomar Publishing Inc., 364 Supertest Rd., 2nd Fl., North York ON M3J 2M2 – 416/667-9945; Fax: 416/667-0609; Email: rfranner@ican.net – Circ.: 9,800; Monthly – Publisher, Bob Grierson; Editor, Robert Franner; Circulation Manager, Elizabeth Stolarz

Première: Video Magazine, 1314 Britannia Rd. East, Mississauga ON L4W 1C8 – 905/564-1033; Fax: 905/564-3398 – Circ.: 7,900; 12 times a year – Editor, Salah Bachir

### TEXTILES

Canadian Textile Journal (Published by CTJ-Inc.), 1, rue Pacifique, Ste-Anne-de-Bellevue QC H9X 1C5 – 514/457-2347; Fax: 514/457-2147 – 7 times a year – Publisher, Gillian Crosby

### TOYS

Toys & Games, Toys & Games Publishing Inc., #203, 364 Supertest Rd., North York ON M3J 2M2 – 416/665-4666; Fax: 416/665-2775 – Circ.: 6,300; 6 times a year – Publisher, Graham Kennedy; Editor, Lynn Winston

### TRANSPORTATION, SHIPPING & DISTRIBUTION

Atlantic Transportation Journal (Published by NCC Specialty Publications), #107, 900 Windmill Rd., Dartmouth NS B3B 1P7 – 902/468-8027; Fax: 902/468-2425 – 4 times a year – Managing Editor, Ken Partridge

Canadian Customs Guide, Les Editions adequate inc, #717, 1117, rue Ste-Catherine ouest, Montréal QC H3B 1H9 – 514/843-7660; Fax: 514/843-7174; Email: cacustomsguide@colba.net – Circ.: 14,369; 6 times a year; English & French – Editor, Djamel Lazreg

Canadian Shipper (Published by Maclean Hunter Publishing), 777 Bay St., Toronto ON M5W 1A7 – 416/586-5000; Fax: 416/596-5158 – Circ.: 4,890; 6 times a year – Publisher, Warren Patterson, 416/596-5708; Editor, Robert Robertson

Canadian Transportation Logistics (Published by Southam Magazine Group), 1450 Don Mills Rd., Don Mills ON M3B 2X7 – 416/445-6641; Fax: 416/442-2214; URL: http://www.southam.com/b1-5-2.html – Circ.: 15,280; Monthly – Editor, Bonnie Toews, 416/442-2228

L'Expéditeur (Published by Les Editions Bomart ltée), H4T 1T3#103, 7493 Trans Canada Hwy., St-Laurent QC H4T 1T3 – 514/337-9043; Fax: 514/337-1862; Email: bomart@infobahnos.com; URL: http://www.bomart.com – Tirage: 10,828; 10 fois par an; français – Rédacteur, Alexandre Daudelin; Rédacteur, Steve Bouchard; Directrice de tirage, Ginette Marsolais

Guide du Transport par Camion (Published by Les Editions Bomart ltée), #103, 7493 Trans Canada Hwy., St-Laurent QC H4T 1T3 – 514/337-9043; Fax: 514/337-1862; Email: bomart@infobahnos.com; URL: http://www.bomartgroup.com – Annually, Nov.; French & English – Directrice de tirage, Ginette Marsolais

Maritime Magazine (Published by Productions Maritimes), 175, rue Saint-Paul, Québec QC G1K 3W2 – 418/692-3779; Fax: 418/692-5198 – Tirage: 5,700; 4 fois par an; français et anglais – Rédacteur, Pierre Terrien

Routes et Transports, A.Q.T.R., #100, 1595, rue Saint-Hubert, Montréal QC H2L 3Z2 – 514/523-6444; Fax: 514/523-2666 – Tirage: 1,500; 4 fois par an; français

### TRAVEL

Bulletin Voyages, Distribution ACRA ltée, 78, boul St-Joseph ouest, Montréal QC H2T 2P4 – 514/287-9773; Fax: 514/842-6180; Email: bulletinvoyages@acra.com – Tirage: 8,095; Hebdomadaire; français – Editeur, Etienne Ozan-Groulx

Campground & Cottage Resort Management, Target Publications, RR#1, Elgin ON K0G 1E0 – 613/359-5225; Fax: 613/359-5491; Email: target@adan.kingston.net – Circ.: 5,431; 4 times a year – Publisher & Editor, James Barton

Canadian Traveller (Published by OP Publishing), #300, 780 Beatty St., Vancouver BC V6B 2N1 – 604/606-4644; Fax: 604/606-4612; Email: op@mindlink.bc.ca – Circ.: 15,000; Monthly – Publisher, Susan Youle; Co-Editor, Ursula Retief

Canadian Travel Press (Published by Baxter Publishing Co), 310 Dupont St., Toronto ON M5R 1V9 – 416/968-7252; Fax: 416/968-2377, 7569; Email: ctp@baxter.net; URL: http://www.baxter.net – Circ.: 13,097; 46 times a year – Publisher, David McClung; Editor, Edith Baxter; Circulation Manager, Susan Bedder

Connections Inflight (Published by GSA Publishing Group), #209, 1015 Burrard St., Vancouver BC V6Z 1Y5 – 604/689-2909; Fax: 604/689-2989 – Circ.: 14,000; 4 times a year – Publisher, Frank Cumming; Editor, Richard Williams

Excursions en Autocar (Published by Publicom inc.), #400, 1055, côte du Beaver Hall, CP 365, Montréal QC H2Y 3H1 – 514/274-0004; Fax: 514/274-5884 – Tirage: 5,500; 10 fois par an; français – Editeur, Guy J. Jonkman

Group Travel/Voyage en Groupe, 590, ch St-Jean, La Prairie QC J5R 2L1 – 514/444-5870 – Tirage: 11 336; 6 fois par an; français – Editrice, Monique Papineau

GSA: The Travel Magazine for Western Canada (Published by GSA Publishing Group), #209, 1015 Burrard St., Vancouver BC V6Z 1Y5 – 604/689-2909; Fax: 604/689-2989 – Circ.: 4,500; 24 times a year – Publisher, Frank Cumming; Editor, Lynda Cumming

Le Magazine l'agent de voyages inc., CP 38, Ville d'Anjou QC H1K 4G5 – 514/881-9637; Fax: 514/881-2578; Email: ebit@planisphere.qc.ca – Tirage: 7,000; 26 fois par an; français – Rédacteur en chef, Michel Villeneuve; Directrice ventes, Chantal Lapointe

Personnel Guide to Canada's Travel Industry (Published by Baxter Publishing Co), 310 Dupont St., Toronto ON M5R 1V9 – 416/968-7252; Fax: 416/968-2377, 7569; Email: pg@baxter.net – Circ.: 4,500; 2 times a year – Director of National Sales, Patrick Doherty

Rendez-Vous (Published by Baxter Publishing Co), 310 Dupont St., Toronto ON M5R 1V9 – 416/968-7252; Fax: 416/968-2377 – Annually, May – President, David McClung; Sales Manager, Marlene Schwengers

The Road Explorer (Published by Naylor Communications Ltd.), 920 Yonge St., 6th Fl., Toronto ON M4W 3C7 – 416/961-1028; Fax: 416/924-4408 – 2 times a year – Publisher, Robert Thompson

Spa Destinations (Published by Publicom inc.), #400, 1055, côte du Beaver Hall, CP 365, Montréal QC H2Y 3H1 – 514/274-0004; Fax: 514/274-5884 – Circ.: 20,500; Annually – Publisher, Guy J. Jonkman

Tourisme Plus (Published by Groupe Constructo), #200, 1500, boul Jules-Poitras, Saint-Laurent QC H4N 1X7 – 514/745-5720; Fax: 514/339-9794 – Tirage: 6 882; 44 fois par an; français

Tours on Motorcoach (Published by Publicom inc.), #400, 1055, côte du Beaver Hall, CP 365, Montréal QC H2Y 3H1 – 514/274-0004; Fax: 514/274-5884 – Circ.: 12,000; 10 times a year – Publisher, Guy J. Jonkman

Travel Courier (Published by Baxter Publishing Co), 310 Dupont St., Toronto ON M5R 1V9 – 416/968-7252; Fax: 416/968-2377; Email: tc@baxter.net; URL: http://www.baxter.net/ – Circ.: 7,100; Weekly – Editor-in-chief, Edith Baxter

Travelweek, Concepts Travel Media Ltd., 282 Richmond St. East, Toronto ON M5A 1P4 – 416/365-1500; Fax: 416/365-1504; Email: travelwk@astral.magic.ca – Circ.: 10,000; Weekly – Publisher, Gerald Kinasz; Editor, Patrick Dineen

### VENDING & VENDING EQUIPMENT

Canadian Coin Box Magazine (Published by Annex Publishing & Printing Inc.), 222 Argyle Ave., Delhi ON N4B 2Y2 – 519/582-2513; Fax: 519/582-4040 – Circ.: 1,921; 6 times a year – Publisher, Michael Fredericks; Editor, Sandra L. Anderson-Lloy; Circulation Manager, Flo Jacques

Canadian Vending (Published by Annex Publishing & Printing Inc.), 222 Argyle Ave., Delhi ON N4B 2Y2 – 519/582-1513; Fax: 519/582-4040; URL: http://www.vendnet.com – Circ.: 2,108; 7 times a year – Publisher, David Douglas; Editor, Sandra L. Anderson-Lloy; Circulation Manager, Flo Jacques

### VETERINARY

The Canadian Veterinary Journal, c/o Canadian Veterinary Medical Association, 339 Booth St., Ottawa ON K1R 7K1 – 613/236-1162; Fax: 613/236-9681; Email: jnlscvma@magi.com; URL: http://www.upei.ca/~cvma/ – Circ.: 5,000; Monthly; English & French – Editor, Dr. W.C.D. Hare; Manager, Journals, Kimberley Allen-McGill

Le Médecin Vétérinaire du Québec, Ordre des médecins vétérinaires du Québec, #200, 795, av du Palais, St-Hyacinthe QC J2S 5C6 – 514/774-1427; Fax: 514/774-7635 – Tirage: 2,500; 4 fois par an; français – Rédacteur, Guy-Pierre Martineau, d.m.v.

Le Vétérinarius, #200, 795, av du Palais, St-Hyacinthe QC J2S 5C6 – 514/774-1427; Fax: 514/774-7635 – 6 fois par an; français – Dr. Marcel Bouvier

### WATER & WASTES TREATMENT

Canadian Environmental Protection (Published by Baum Publications Ltd.), #201, 2323 Boundary Rd., Vancouver BC V5M 4V8 – 604/291-9900; Fax: 604/291-1906; Email: ebaum@baumpub.com; URL: http://www.baumpub.com – Circ.: 22,097; 9 times a year – Publisher, Engelbert Baum; Editor, Morena Zanotto

Environmental Science & Engineering, Environmental Science & Engineering Publications Inc., 220 Industrial Pkwy. South, Unit 30, Aurora ON L4G 3V6 – 905/727-4666; Fax: 905/841-7271; Email: esemag@istar.ca; URL: http://www.esemag.com – Circ.: 19,062; 6 times a year; ISSN 0835-605X – Publisher & Editor, Tom Davey

Envirotech, #200, 640, rue St-Paul ouest, Montréal QC H3C 1L9 – 514/393-8862; Fax: 514/393-3568; Email: envirtec@citenet.net; URL: http://www.citenet.net/envirotech/ – Tirage: 9,000; 6 fois par an; français; supplement - Québec Environmental Industry Source Book – Editeur & Rédacteur, Perry Nino

Ground Water Canada (Published by AIS Communications Ltd.), 145 Thames Rd. West, Exeter ON NOM 1S3 – 519/235-2400; Fax: 519/235-0798 – Circ.: 4,040; 4 times a year – Publisher, Peter Phillips; Editor, Peter Darbishire

Hazardous Materials Management Magazine (Published by CHMM Inc.), #4, 951 Denison St., Markham ON L3R 3W9 – 905/305-6155; Fax: 905/305-6255; URL: http://www.hazmatmag.com – Circ.: 20,000; Bi-monthly - also annual Québec regional supplement in French; ISSN 0843-9303 – Publisher, Todd Latham; Editor, Guy Crittenden; Sales Manager, Arnie Gess

Maritime Provinces Water & Wastewater Report (Published by NCC Specialty Publications), #107, 900 Windmill Rd., Dartmouth NS B3B 1P7 – 902/468-8027; Fax: 902/468-2425 – 4 times a year – Editor, Ken Partridge

Recycling Product News (Published by Baum Publications Ltd.), #201, 2323 Boundary Rd., Vancouver BC V5M 4V8 – 604/291-9900; Fax: 604/291-1906; Email: ebaum@baumpub.com; URL: http://www.baumpub.com – Circ.: 14,700; 9 times a year – Publisher, Engelbert J. Baum; Editor, Dan Kennedy

Solid Waste & Recycling Magazine (Published by CHMM Inc.), #4, 951 Denison St., Markham ON L3R 3W9 – 905/305-6155; Fax: 905/305-6255; Email: salesinfo@solidwastemag.com; URL: http://www.solidwastemag.com – Circ.: 10,000; 6 times a year; ISSN: 1206-0879 – Publisher, Todd Latham; Editor, Guy Crittenden; Sales, Manager, Arnie Gess

Vecteur envrionnement, #220, 911, rue Jean-Talon est, Montréal QC H2R 1V5 – 514/270-7110; Fax: 514/270-7154; Email: assqenv@login.net – 6 fois par an; français – Editeur, Christian Scott; Rédacteur en chef, Guy Giasson

Water & Pollution Control (Published by Zanny Ltd.), 11966 Woodbine Ave., Gormley ON L0H 1G0 – 905/887-5048; Fax: 905/887-0764 – 4 times a year

#### WELDING

Welding Canada (Published by Maclean Hunter Publishing), 777 Bay St., Toronto ON M5W 1A7 – 416/596-5713; Fax: 416/596-5881 – 6 times a year – Publisher, Glen Alton, 416/596-5000

#### WOODWORKING

2 x 4, Editions C.R. Inc., PO Box 1010, Victoriaville QC G6P 8Y1 – 819/752-4243; Fax: 819/758-8812 – Circ.: 8,000; 5 times a year; English & French – Editor & Publisher, Claude Roy

Woodworking (Published by Action Communications Inc.), 135 Spy Ct., Markham ON L3R 5H6 – 905/477-3222; Fax: 905/477-4320; Email: woodactioncom.com – Circ.: 11,000; 6 times a year; also Woodworking Sourcer (annually) – Publisher, R. Blair Tullis; Editor, Maurice Holtham; Circulation Manager, Connie Warren

## CONSUMER MAGAZINES

#### AIRLINE INFLIGHT

Above & Beyond, PO Box 2348, Yellowknife NT X1A 2P7 – 867/873-2299, 613/599-4190; Fax: 867/873-2295, 613/599-4191; Email: abeyond@achilles.net; abeyond@internorth.com – Circ.: 30,000; 4 times a year – Publisher & General Manager, Tom Koelbel; Editor, Annelies Pool

Atmosphere Magazine, Melaine Communications Group Inc., #3120, 3300 Bloor St. West, Etobicoke ON M8X 2X3 – 416/233-4348; Fax: 416/233-9367; Email: melaine@inforamp.net – Circ.: 87,750; 2 times a year; English & French – Editor, Susan Melnyk

Canadian Inflight Magazine, Transcontinental Publications Inc., #2700, 777 Bay St., PO Box 148, Toronto ON M5G 2N1 – 416/340-8000; Fax: 416/977-0566 – Circ.: 75,000; Monthly – Publisher, Tim Goodman; Editor, Marianne Tefft

Connections Northwest, #209, 1015 Burrard St., Vancouver BC V6Z 1Y5 – 604/689-2909; Fax: 604/689-2989 – Circ.: 4,500; 4 times a year – Publisher, Frank Cumming; Editor, Richard Williams

enRoute (Published by Publicor), 7, ch Bates, Outremont QC H2V 1A6 – 514/270-1100, ext.260; Fax: 514/270-4050; Email: info@enroute.quebecor.com – Circ.: 113,409; 12 times a year; English & French – Editor, Lise Ravary

#### ANIMALS

Canine Review, SS2, Site 4, Comp. 22, Beaton Rd., Kamloops BC V2C 6C3 – 250/828-1978; Fax: 250/828-0052; Email: caninrv@netshop.net; URL: http://kamloops.netshop.net/canerev/ – Circ.: 1,500; 10 times a year – Publisher/Editor, Helen W. Lee

Dogs, Dogs, Dogs , Kodiak Cycle Ltd., 92 King William St., Unit 2, Huntsville ON P1H 1E4 – 705/788-3647; Fax: 705/787-0722; Email: jenny@netcom.ca; URL: http://www.interlog.com/~dogs – Circ.: 12,000; 6 times a year – Publisher & Editor, Jackie Lindsay

Dogs in Canada, Apex Publishers, #200, 89 Skyway Ave., Etobicoke ON M9W 6R4 – 416/798-9778; Fax: 416/798-9671; Email: info@dogs-in-canada.com; URL: http://www.dogs-in-canada.com – Monthly (13 issues a year, including Dogs in Canada Annual) – Publisher, David Bell; Editor, Allan Rezanik

Pets Magazine (Published by Moorshead Magazines Ltd.), #490, 10 Gateway Blvd., Toronto ON M3C 3T4 – 416/696-5488; Fax: 416/696-7395; Email: pets@moorshead.com; URL: http://www.moorshead.com/magazine/pets – Circ.: 48,500; 6 times a year; also Dog Care Guide, Cat Care Guide, Puppies & Kittens & other things too Care Guide, & First Aid for Dogs & Cats – Publisher, Halvor Moorshead; Editor, Ed Zapletal; Circulation Manager, Rick Cree

Pets Quarterly Magazine (Published by Omnicom Publications Inc.), #300, 512 King St. East, Toronto ON M5A 1M1 – 416/955-1550; Fax: 416/955-1391 – Circ.: 70,000; 4 times a year – Publisher, Jim Eaton; Editor, Richard Soren

#### ARTS, ART & ANTIQUES

Antiques, #702, 27 Queen St. East, PO Box 1860, Toronto ON M5C 2M6 – 416/944-3880; Email: marnia@msn.com – Circ.: 5,000; 6 times a year; ISSN: 1198-8258 – Publisher & Editor, Marni Andrews

Antique Showcase (Published by Trajan Publishing Corp.), #202, 103 Lakeshore Rd., St Catharines ON L2N 2T6 – 905/646-7744; Fax: 905/646-0995; Email: fiocca@trajan.com; URL: http://www.trajan.com/trajan – 9 times a year – Publisher, Paul Fiocca; Editor, Barbara Sutton-Smith; Circulation Manager, Tammy Kruck

Artfocus, PO Box 1063, Stn F, Toronto ON M4Y 2T7 – 416/925-5564; Fax: 416/925-2972; Email: pfleisher@artfocus.com; URL: http://www.artfocus.com – Circ.: 8,000; 4 times a year – Publisher/Editor, Pat Fleisher

Artichoke: Writings about the Visual Arts, #208, 901 Jervis St., Vancouver BC V6E 2B6 – 604/683-1941; Fax: 604/683-1941 – Circ.: 1,000; 3 times a year – Editor, Paula Gustafson

ArtsAtlantic, 145 Richmond St., Charlottetown PE C1A 1J1 – 902/628-6138; Fax: 902/566-4648; Email: artsatlantic@isn.net; URL: http://www.isn.net/artsatlantic – Circ.: 2,500; 3 times a year – Editor, Joseph Sherman; Circulation Manager, Ellen MacPhail

Border Crossings, #500, 70 Arthur St., Winnipeg MB R3B 1G7 – 204/942-5778; Fax: 204/949-0793; Email: bordercr@escape.ca – 4 times a year – Editor, Meeka Walsh; Editor at Large, Robert Enright

Canadian Art, 70 The Esplanade, 2nd Fl., Toronto ON M5E 1R2 – 416/368-8854; Fax: 416/368-6135; Email: canart@istar.ca – Circ.: 20,000; 4 times a year – Publisher, Wendy Ingram; Editor, Richard Rhodes

C Magazine, PO Box 5, Stn B, Toronto ON M5T 2T2 – 416/539-9495; Fax: 416/539-9903 – Circ.: 4,500; 4 times a year – Publisher & Editor, Joyce Mason

Collectibles Canada (Published by Trajan Publishing Corp.), #202, 103 Lakeshore Rd., St Catharines ON L2N 2T6 – 905/646-7744; Fax: 905/646-0095; Email: bret@trajan.com; URL: http://www.trajan.com/collectibles/default.ehtml – Circ.: 12,102; 6 times a year – Publisher, Paul Fiocca; Editor, Joanne Keogh

Contact, Ceramic Contacts Inc., 429 - 12th St. NW, Calgary AB T2N 1Y9 – 403/270-3252 editorial, 905/477-9416 business; Fax: 403/270-3252; Email: btipton.cadvision; URL: http://web.idirect.com/~contact – Circ.: 1,250; 4 times a year; ISSN: 1194-6377 – Editor, Barbara Tipton

Dance International, The Vancouver Ballet Society, 1415 Barclay St., Vancouver BC V6G 1J6 – 604/681-1525; Fax: 604/681-7732 – Circ.: 3,800; 4 times a year – Editor, Maureen Riches

Fusion: The Ontario Clay & Glass Association, The Gardener's Cottage, 225 Conferation Dr., Scarborough ON M1G 1B2 – 416/438-8946; Fax: 416/438-0192; Email: fusion@aracnet.net – Circ.: 700; 3 times a year; also Fusion News Magazine (3 times a year) – President, Robert Têtu; Publications, Brian Truscott

Inter, Les Éditions intervention, CP 227, Haute-Ville QC G1R 4P8 – 418/529-9680; Fax: 418/529-6933; Email: edinter@total.net; URL: http://www.surscene.qc.ca/ielieu-inter – Tirage: 1,200; 3 fois par an – Directrice de tirage, Lise Bourassa

Inuit Art Quarterly, Inuit Art Foundation, 2081 Merivale Rd., Nepean ON K2G 1G9 – 613/224-8189; Fax: 613/224-2907; Email: iaq@inuitart.org; URL: http://www.inuitart.org – Circ.: 3,500; 4 times a year – Editor, Marybelle Mitchell; Circulation Manager, Matthew Fox

Muse, Canadian Museums Assn., #400, 280 Metcalfe St., Ottawa ON K2P 1R7 – 613/567-0099; Fax: 613/233-5438; Email: info@museums.ca; URL: http://www.museums.ca – 4 times a year; English & French – Editor, Catherine Cole

Ontario Craft, Ontario Crafts Council, 35 McCaul St., Toronto ON M5T 1V7 – 416/977-3551; Fax: 416/977-3552 – Circ.: 4,000; 4 times a year – Editor, Wendy Jacob

Parachute, #501, 4060, boul St-Laurent, Montréal QC H2W 1Y9 – 514/842-9805; Fax: 514/287-7146 – 4 times a year; ISSN: 0318-7020 – Rédacteur, C. Pontbriand

Rotunda, c/o Royal Ontario Museum, 100 Queen's Park, Toronto ON M5S 2C6 – 416/586-5590; Fax: 416/586-5887; Email: sandras@rom.on.ca; URL: http://www.rom.on.ca – Circ.: 25,000; 3 times a year – Editor-in-chief, Sandra Shaul

Slate, 155 King St. East, Kingston ON K7L 2Z9 – 613/542-3717; Fax: 613/542-1447; Email: admin@slateartguide.com; URL: http://www.slateartguide.com – 8 times a year – Editor, Sonya Dodich

Vie des Arts, #600, 200, rue Saint-Jacques, Montréal QC H2Y 1M1 – 514/282-0205; Fax: 514/282-0235 – Tirage: 6,600; 4 fois par an; français – Rédacteur en chef, Bernard Lévy

#### AUTOMOBILE, CYCLE, & AUTOMOTIVE ACCESSORIES

Autopinion Annual, Canadian Automobile Association, #200, 1145 Hunt Club Rd., Ottawa ON K1V 0Y3 – 613/247-0117; Fax: 613/247-0018; Email: dsteventon@caa.ca; URL: http://www.caa.ca – Circ.: 56,414; Annually – Editor, David Steventon

Canadian Biker, PO Box 4122, Victoria BC V8X 3X4 – 250/384-0333; Fax: 250/384-1832; Email: canbike@islandnet.com; URL: http://canadianbiker.com – Circ.: 25,000; 8 times a year – Editor & Publisher, Len Creed; Circulation Manager, Chris Creed

Carguide/Le Magazine Carguide (Published by Formula Publications Ltd.), #4, 446 Speers Rd., Oakville ON L6K 3S7 – 905/842-6591; Fax: 905/842-6843; Email: formula@carguideca.com – 6 times a year, English & French editions – Publisher, J. Scott Robinson; Editor, Graham Fletcher; Circulation Manager, Deadra Worth

Cycle Canada (Published by Turbopress Inc.), #301, 411 Richmond St. East, Toronto ON M5A 3S5 – 416/362-7966; Fax: 416/362-3950 – Circ.: 20,000; 10 issues a year – Publisher, Jean-Pierre Belmonte; Editor, Bruce Reeve

DRIVE, #217, 716 Gordon Baker Rd., Toronto ON M2H 3B4 – 416/492-9539; Fax: 416/492-1596 – Circ.: 30,000; 4 times a year – Publisher, C.J. Millar; Executive Editor, Joe Duarte

Lemon-Aid Magazine, c/o Automobile Protection Association, 292, boul St-Joseph ouest, Montréal QC H2V 2N7 – 514/272-5555; Fax: 514/273-0797 – Circ.: 12,000; 4 times a year – Co-Editor, Antoinette Greco, 514/273-1662; Co-Editor, George Iny

Le Monde de l'Auto, Helpard Publishing Inc., #401, 7575 Trans Canada Hwy., St-Laurent QC H4T 1V6 – 514/958-1361; Fax: 514/956-1461 – 6 fois par an; français – Rédacteur, Luc Gagné

Moto Journal (Published by Turbopress Inc.), #301, 411 Richmond St. East, Toronto ON M5A 3S5 – 416/362-7966; Fax: 416/362-3950; Email: motojourna@aol.com – Tirage: 7,000; 10 fois par an – Editeur, Jean-Pierre Belmonte; Rédacteur, Claude Leonard

Old Autos, 348 Main St., PO Box 419, Bothwell ON N0P 1C0 – 519/695-2303; Fax: 519/695-3716 – Circ.: 14,000; 24 times a year – Publisher/Editor, Murray McEwan

Pedal Magazine, #204, 2 Pardee Ave., Toronto ON M6K 3H5 – 416/530-1350; Fax: 416/530-4155 – Circ.: 18,000; 8 times a year – Publisher & Editor, Benjamin Sadavoy

Performance Racing News, Buy & Sell Newspaper Ltd., 593 Yonge St., PO Box 5, Toronto ON M4Y 1Z4 – 416/922-7223; Fax: 416/922-8001; Email: greggo@io.org – Circ.: 10,060; 16 times a year

The Professional's Guide to Luxury Cars, 3 Ainsley Gardens, Etobicoke ON M9A 1M5 – 416/233-2171; Fax: 416/233-2171 – 2 times a year – Publisher, John D. Duncan; Editor, Bob English, 519/833-2089

Vélo Mag (Published by Les Éditions Tricycle inc.), 1251, rue Rachel est, Montréal QC H2J 2J9 – 514/521-8356; Fax: 514/521-5711; Email: velo_mag@velo.qc.ca – Tirage: 20,000; 6 fois par an; français – Editeur & Rédacteur, Pierre Hamel

World of Wheels (Published by Helpard Publishing Inc.), #300, 1200 Markham Rd., Scarborough ON M1H 3C3 – 416/438-7777; Fax: 416/438-5333 – Circ.: 60,000; 6 times a year – Publisher, Lynn R. Helpard; Executive Editor, Joe Knycha; Circulation Manager, Susan Brown

### AVIATION & AEROSPACE

Canadian Aviation Historical Society Journal, PO Box 224, Stn A, Willowdale ON M2N 5S8 – 416/488-2247; Fax: 416/488-2247 – Circ.: 1,300; 4 times a year – Editor, W. Wheeler

### BABIES & MOTHERS

The Baby & Child Care Encyclopaedia (Published by Family Communications Inc.), #1, 37 Hanna Ave., Toronto ON M6K 1W9 – 416/537-2604; Fax: 416/538-1794 – Circ.: 100,000; 2 times a year (May & Nov.). – Publisher, Donald Swinburne; Editor-in-chief, Bettie Bradley

Baby Name Magazine (Published by Family Communications Inc.), #1, 37 Hanna Ave., Toronto ON M6K 1W9 – 416/537-2604; Fax: 416/538-1794 – Circ.: 147,713; Annually – President, Don Swinburne; Editor, Manon Le Moyne

Best Wishes (Published by Family Communications Inc.), #1, 37 Hanna Ave., Toronto ON M6K 1W9 – 416/537-2604; Fax: 416/538-1794 – Circ.: 150,917; 2 times a year (May & Nov.) – Publisher, Donald Swinburne; Editor-in-chief, Bettie Bradley

C'est Pour Quand? Revue prénatale (Published by Family Communications Inc./Communications Famille inc.), 2260, rue des Patriotes, Sainte-Rose QC H7L 3K8 – 514/622-0091; Fax: 514/622-0099 – Tirage: 51 228; 2 fois par an; français – Editeur, Manon Le Moyne

The Compleat Mother, RR#3, Clifford ON N0G 1M0 – 519/327-8785; Email: zyoung@wcl.on.ca – Circ.: 15,000; 4 times a year – Editor, Catherine Young

Expecting (Published by Family Communications Inc.), #1, 37 Hanna Ave., Toronto ON M6K 1W9 – 416/537-2604; Fax: 416/538-1794 – Circ.: 147,713; 3 times a year – President, Donald G. Swinburne

Great Expectations (Published by Professional Publishing), 269 Richmond St. West, Toronto ON M5V 1X1 – 416/596-8680; Fax: 416/596-1991 – Circ.: 200,000; 3 times a year

Mère Nouvelle (Published by Professional Publishing), 269 Richmond St. West, Toronto ON M5V 1X1 – 416/596-8680; Fax: 416/596-1991 – 2 fois par an – Editrice, Beverly Topping; Rédactrice, Fran Fearnley

Mon Bébé Revue Postnatale (Published by Family Communications Inc./Communications Famille inc.), 2260, rue des Patriotes, Sainte-Rose QC H7L 3K8 – 514/622-0091; Fax: 514/622-0099 – Tirage: 51,770; 2 fois par an; français – Editeur, Manon Le Moyne

Mon Enfant (Published by Professional Publishing), 269 Richmond St. West, Toronto ON M5V 1X1 – 416/596-8680; Fax: 416/596-1991 – Tirage: 62,500; 3 fois par an; français – Editrice, Beverly Topping; Rédactrice, Fran Fearnley

New Mother (Published by Professional Publishing), 269 Richmond St. West, Toronto ON M5V 1X1 – 416/596-8680; Fax: 416/596-1991 – Circ.: 165,000; 2 times a year; English & French editions – Publisher, Beverly Topping; Editor-in-chief, Fran Fearnley

Pouponnière (Published by Professional Publishing), 269 Richmond St. West, Toronto ON M5V 1X1 – 416/596-8680; Fax: 416/596-1991 – Tirage: 90,000; Annuellement; français – Editrice, Beverly Topping; Rédactrice, Fran Fearnley

Your Baby (Published by Professional Publishing), 269 Richmond St. West, Toronto ON M5V 1X1 – 416/596-8680; Fax: 416/596-1991 – Circ.: 187,500; 3 times a year – Publisher, Beverly Topping; Editor-in-chief, Fran Fearnley

### BOATING & YACHTING

Boat Guide (Published by Formula Publications Ltd.), #4, 446 Speers Rd., Oakville ON L6K 3S7 – 905/842-6591; Fax: 905/842-6843; Email: formula@carguideca.com – 2 times a year – Publisher, Scott Robinson; Editor, Lizanne Madigan; Circulation Manager, Deadra Worth

Boating East Ports & Cruising Guide, Marble Rock Rd, RR#2, Gananoque ON K7G 2V4 – 613/382-5735; Fax: 613/382-1118 – Circ.: 23,000; Annually, May

Canadian Yachting (Published by Kerrwil Publications Ltd.), 395 Matheson Blvd. East, Mississauga ON L4Z 2H2 – 905/890-1846; Fax: 905/890-5769; Email: canyatch@kerrwil.com; URL: http://www/canyacht.com/canyacht – 6 times a year (April to Oct.) – Editor, Heather Ormerod

DIY Boat Owner, JM Publishing, #515, 2511 Lakeshore Rd. West, Oakville ON L6L 6L9 – 905/847-3009; Fax: 905/847-3590; Email: diy@diy-boat.com; URL: http://www.diy-boat.com – Circ.: 15,000; 4 times a year – Publisher & Editor, Jan Mundy

L'Escale Nautique (Published by Productions Maritimes), 175, rue Saint-Paul, Québec QC G1K 3W2 – 418/692-3779; Fax: 418/692-5198 – Tirage: 6,700; 5 fois par an; français – Redacteur en chef, Michel Sacco

Gam on Yachting, #202, 250 The Esplanade, Toronto ON M5A 1J2 – 416/368-1559; Fax: 416/368-2831 – 8 times a year – Editor, Karin Larson

Pacific Yachting (Published by OP Publishing), #300, 780 Beatty St., Vancouver BC V6B 2N1 – 604/687-1581; Fax: 604/687-1925; Email: op@mindlink.bc.ca – Circ.: 19,126; Monthly – Publisher, Rex Armstead; Editor, Duart Snow

Les Plaisanciers, #310, 970, Montee de Liesse, St-Laurent QC H4T 1W7 – 514/856-0788; Fax: 514/856-0790 – Tirage: 20,000; 5 fois par an; français – Editeur, William E. Taylor; Rédacteur, Claude Leonard; Directrice de tirage, Marlene Jolicover

Port Hole, c/o Canadian Power & Sail Squadrons, 26 Golden Gate Ct., Scarborough ON M1P 3A5 – 416/293-2438; Fax: 416/293-2445; Email: hqg@cps-eckp.ca; URL: http://www.cps-ecp.ca – Circ.: 28,000; 4 times a year; English & French – Editor-in-chief, Alex MacInnis; Managing Editor, D. Zonnenberg

Power Boating Canada, #306, 2585 Skymark Ave., Mississauga ON L4W 4L5 – 905/624-8218; Fax: 905/624-6764 – Circ.: 50,000; 6 times a year – Publisher, William Taylor

Québec Yachting Voile & Moteur (Published by Transcontinental Publications Inc.), 1100, boul René-Levesque ouest, 24e étage, Montréal QC H3B 4X9 – 514/392-9000; Fax: 514/392-4726 – Tirage: 8,000; 6 fois par an; français

Today's Boating, Ranmor Publishing Inc., #606A, 366 Adelaide St. West, Toronto ON M5V 1R9 – 416/595-6439; Fax: 416/599-9700 – Circ.: 25,500; 5 times a year in English, 4 times a year in French – Editor, Mike Milne; Co-Publisher, Rod Morris; Co-Publisher, Ted Rankin

Windsport, True Wind Corp. Ltd., #3266, 2255B Queen St. East, Toronto ON M4E 1G3 – 416/698-0138; Fax: 416/698-8080; Email: infro@windsport.com; URL: http://www.windsport.com – 3 times a year – Editor, Steve Jarrett; Circulation Manager, Duncan O'Brien

### BOOKS

BC BookWorld, A.R.T. BookWorld Productions, 3516 West 13th Ave., Vancouver BC V6R 2S3 – 604/736-4011; Fax: 604/736-4011; Email: bcbook@portal.ca – 4 times a year; ISSN 0847-7728 – Publisher, Alan Twigg; Editor, Katja Pantzar

### BRIDES, BRIDAL

Mariage Québec, #1301, 1155, rue Unviersity, Montréal QC H3B 3A7 – 514/392-9030; Fax: 514/392-0328; Email: mariagequeqc@accent.net; URL: http://www.mariagequebec.com – Tirage: 22,500; 2 fois par an; français – Editrice, Suzanne Hurst; Rédactrice, Juliette Ruer

Sposa Magazine, Imagistix Inc., #407, 77 Mowat Ave., Toronto ON M6K 3E3 – 416/534-1851; Fax: 416/534-0262; Email: sposa@sposa.com; URL: http://www.sposa.com – Circ.: 32,000; 2 times a year – Publisher & Editor, Gulshan Sippy; Assistant Editor, Adriana Suppa

Today's Bride (Published by Family Communications Inc.), #1, 37 Hanna Ave., Toronto ON M6K 1W9 – 416/537-2604; Fax: 416/538-1794 – Circ.: 101,000; 2 times a year – President & Publisher, Don Swinburne; Corporate Editor, Bettie Bradley

WeddingBells, 50 Wellington St. East, 2nd Fl., Toronto ON M5E 1C8 – 416/862-8479; Fax: 416/862-2184; Email: editor@weddingbells.com; URL: http://www.weddingbells.com – 2 times a year – Publisher, Diane Hall; Editor-in-chief, Crys Stewart; Circulation Manager, Marlene Semple

The Wedding Pages, 30 Relroy Ct., Scarborough ON M1W 2Y7 – 416/498-4996; Fax: 416/498-5997 – Circ.: 23,400; 2 times a year – Publisher, Brandon Jones; Publisher, Chris Jones

Weddings & Honeymoons, 65 Helena Ave., Toronto ON M6G 2H3 – 416/653-4986; Fax: 416/653-2291; Email: wedhon@to.org – Circ.: 50,000; 2 times a year; ISSN: 1192-764X – Publisher & Editor, Joyce Barshow; Circulation Manager, Beverley Colbourne

**BUSINESS & FINANCE**

Canadian Business Economics, PO Box 828, Stn B, Ottawa ON K1P 5P9 – 613/238-4831; Fax: 613/238-7698 – 4 times a year; ISSN 0705-8330

Canadian MoneySaver, PO Box 370, Bath ON K0H 1G0 – 613/352-7448; Fax: 613/352-7700 – Circ.: 34,500; 11 times a year – President & Publisher, Dale Ennis

Canadian Shareowner, #1317, 2 Carlton St., Toronto ON M5B 1J3 – 416/595-9557; Fax: 416/595-0400; Email: Questions@shareowner.ca; URL: http://www.shareowner.ca – Circ.: 12,000; 6 times a year – Publisher & Editor, John T. Bart

Pensez-y bien , Editions EJS & Edibec, #110, 455, rue Marais, Vanier QC G1M 3A2 – 418/686-1940; Fax: 418/686-1942 – Circ.: 123,000; 4 fois par an – Editeur, France Begin

Personal Finance Journal, KCO Publishing Inc., #130, 1489 Marine Dr., West Vancouver BC V7T 1B8 – 604/664-1094; Fax: 604/926-7757; Email: rketchen@mindlink.bc.ca – Circ.: 30,000; 9 times a year – Publisher & Editor, Richard Ketchen

**CAMPING & OUTDOOR RECREATION**

Camping Caravaning, Communication Camping Caravaning, 4545, av Pierre de Coubertin, CP 1000, Succ M, Montréal QC H1V 3R2 – 514/252-3003; Fax: 514/254-0694 – Tirage: 13,482; 8 fois par an – Rédacteur en chef, Robert Aubin

Camping in Ontario, Ontario Private Campground Assn., RR#5, Owen Sound ON N4K 5N7 – 519/371-3393; Fax: 519/371-0080; URL: http://www.campgrounds.org – Circ.: 125,000; Annually, Jan. – Managing Director, Marcel Gobeil

Explore, Thompson & Gordon Publishing Co. Ltd., #420, 301 - 14 St. NW, Calgary AB T2N 2A1 – 403/270-8890; Fax: 403/270-7922; Email: explore@cadvision.com; URL: http://www.explore-mag.com – Circ.: 35,000; 7 times a year – Publisher, Peter Thompson; Editor, Marion Harrison, 403/270-8911

Kanawa: Canada's Canoeing & Kayaking Magazine, PO Box 398, Merrickville ON K0G 1N0 – 613/269-2910; Fax: 613/269-2908; Email: staff@crca.ca; URL: http://www.crca.ca/ – Circ.: 20,000; 4 times a year – Publisher & Editor, Joseph Agnew; Circulation Manager, Nancy Gough

RV Lifestyle (Published by Camping Canada), #306, 2585 Skymark Ave., Mississauga ON L4W 4L5 – 905/624-8218; Fax: 905/624-6764 – 7 times a year – Publisher, William E. Taylor; Editor, Peter Tasler

Vie en Plein Air, #310, 970 Montée de Liesse, Ville St-Laurent QC H4T 1W7 – 514/856-0787; Fax: 514/856-0790 – Tirage: 30,000; 1 fois par an; français – Editeur, William E. Taylor; Rédacteur, Claude Leonard

**CHILDREN'S**

ChickaDEE, #300, 370 King St. West, PO Box 53, Toronto ON M5V 1J9 – 416/971-5275; Fax: 416/971-5294; Email: chicka@owl.on.ca; URL: http://www.owlkids.com – Circ.: 100,000; 9 times a year – Publisher, Diane Davy; Editor, Nyla Ahmad; Circulation Manager, Paula Harding

Coulicou (Published by Les Éditions Héritage), 300, rue Arran, Saint-Laurent QC J4R 1K5 – 514/875-0327; Fax: 514/672-5448 – 10 fois par an; français – Editeur, Sylvie Payette

Les Débrouillards, 3995, rue Ste-Catherine est, Montréal QC H1W 2G7 – 514/522-1304; Fax: 514/522-1761; Email: scientifix@lesdebrouillards.qc.ca; URL: http://www.lesdebrouillards.qc.ca – Tirage: 31,000; 10 fois par an; français – Editeur, Felix Maltais; Rédactrice, Sarah Perreault

En Primeur Jeunesse (Published by Tribute Publishing Inc.), 71 Barber Greene Rd., Don Mills ON M3C 2A2 – 416/4445-0544; Fax: 416/445-2894 – Tirage: 50,000; 4 fois par an; français – Rédactrice en chef, Sandra Stewart; Directeur de tirage, Guy Murnaghan

Hibou (Published by Les Éditions Héritage), 300, rue Arran, Saint-Laurent QC J4R 1K5 – 514/875-0327; Fax: 514/672-1481 – 10 fois par an; français – Editeur, Luc Payette

J'Aime Lire (Published by Bayard Presse Canada Inc.), 3995, rue Ste-Catherine est, Montréal QC H1W 2G7 – 514/522-3936; Fax: 514/522-1761 – Tirage: 16,000 – Editrice & Rédactrice, Suzanne Spino

Kids Tribute (Published by Tribute Publishing Inc.), 71 Barber Greene Rd., Don Mills ON M3C 2A2 – 416/445-0544; Fax: 416/445-2894 – Circ.: 300,000; 4 times a year – Publisher & Editor, Sandra Stewart; Circulation Manager, Guy Murnaghan

Kids World Magazine, #108, 93 Lombard Ave., Winnipeg MB R3B 3B1 – 204/985-8160; Fax: 204/943-8991; Email: kidsworld@kidsworld-online.com; URL: http://www.kidsworld-online.com – Circ.: 225,000; 6 times a year – Publisher, Nancy Moore; Editor, Stuart Slayen; Circulation Manager, Sherry Jones

OWL Magazine, #300, 370 King St. West, PO Box 53, Toronto ON M5V 1J9 – 416/971-5275; Fax: 416/971-5294; Email: wiredowl@owl.on.ca; URL: http://www.owlkids.com – Circ.: 110,000; 9 times a year – Publisher, Diane Davy; Editor, Nyla Ahmad; Circulation Manager, Paula Harding

**CITY MAGAZINE**

Alderlea Magazine, 105 Kenneth St., Duncan BC V9L 1N5 – 250/746-6463; Fax: 250/746-7745 – Circ.: 12,700; 12 times a year – Publisher, George E. Spong; Editor, Frank Hird-Rutter

The Coast, 5171 George St., 2nd Fl., Halifax NS B3J 1M6 – 902/422-6278; Fax: 902/425-0013; Email: coast@ra.isisnet.com – Circ.: 17,000; Weekly – Publisher, Catherine Salisbury; Editor, Kyle Shaw; Associate Publisher, Christine Oreskovich

Events Planner, Pearl Publishing, 99 Kimbark Blvd., Toronto ON M5N 2Y3 – 416/782-3322; Fax: 416/787-9299 – Circ.: 2,000; 2 times a year – Publisher, Sybil Levine; Editor, R.S. Diamond

Eye, #207, 57 Spadina Ave., Toronto ON M5V 2J2 – 416/971-8421; Fax: 416/971-9697; URL: http://www.interlog.com:80/eye/ – Circ.: 100,000; Weekly – Managing Editor, Bill Reynolds

Fast Forward Weekly, Great West Publishing, #220, 932 - 17 Ave. SW, Calgary AB T2T 0A4 – 403/244-2235; Fax: 403/244-1431; Email: ffwd@greatwest.ca; URL: http://www.greatwest.ca/ffwd – Circ.: 18,000; Weekly – Managing Editor, Ian Chiclo

The Georgia Straight, 1770 Burrard St., 2nd Fl., Vancouver BC V6J 3G7 – 604/730-7000; Fax: 604/730-7010; Email: info@straight.com; URL: http://www.straight.com – Circ.: 99,253; Weekly – Publisher, Dan McLeod, 604/730-7088; Editor-in-chief, Charles Campbell; Circulation Manager, Nick Collier

Le Guide Prestige Montréal, #1401, 115, rue Sherbrooke ouest, Montréal QC H3A 1H3 – 514/982-9823; Fax: 514/289-9160 – 4 times a year; English & French – Publisher, Peter Weiss; Editor, André Ducharme

Hamilton This Month (Published by Town Publishing Inc), 875 Main St., Hamilton ON L8S 4R1 – 905/522-6117; Fax: 905/529-2242 – Circ.: 40,000; 7 times a year – Publisher, Wayne Narciso; Editor, Elizabeth Kelly; Circulation Manager, Laurie Ann Raynor

Hi-Rise, #121, 95 Leeward Glenway, Don Mills ON M3C 2Z6 – 416/424-1393; Fax: 416/467-8262 – Circ.: 30,000; 11 times a year – Editor & Publisher, Valerie Dunn

Hour, Communications Voir Inc., #302, 4126, rue St-Denis, Montréal QC H2W 2M5 – 514/848-0777; Fax: 514/848-0360; Email: hour@eureka.qc.ca – Circ.: 46,000; 52 times a year – Publisher, Pierre Paquet

L'Important (Published by Groupe Magazines S.A. Inc.), #300, 275, boul des Braves, Terrebonne QC J6W 3H6 – 514/964-7590; Fax: 514/964-2327; Email: magazine@magazinesa.com – 4 fois par an; français – Editeur, Denis Clermont; Rédacteur, Louise Bourbonnais

In Montréal, 5151, ch Côte St-Catherine, Montréal QC H3W 1M6 – 514/345-2624; Fax: 514/345-2643; Email: inmtl@total.net; URL: http://inmtl.total.net – Circ.: 30,000; 9 times a year – Editor-in-chief, Ross Paperman; Editor, Mitch Joel Cohen

International Guide (Published by I.G. Publications Ltd.), #222, 999 - 8 St. SW, Calgary AB T2R 1J5 – 403/244-7343 – Circ.: 16,000; Annually, June – Publisher, Wayne R. Kehoe; Editor, Sharon Komori

Key to Kingston, c/o Kingston Publications, 11 Princess St., PO Box 1352, Kingston ON K7L 5C6 – 613/549-8442; Fax: 613/549-4333 – Circ.: 17,000; 8 times a year – Publisher, Dan Bedford; Editor, Mary Owens

Kootenay Visitor's Magazine (Published by Koocanusa Publications Inc.), 1510 - 2nd St. North, Cranbrook BC V1C 3L2 – 250/426-7253; Fax: 250/489-3743; Email: advertiser@cyberlink.bc.ca – Circ.: 40,000; Annually, June – Publisher, Daryl D. Shellborn; Editor, Stacey Curry

Lethbridge Living, PO Box 22005, Stn Henderson Lake, Lethbridge AB T1K 6X5 – 403/329-1008; Fax: 403/329-0264 – Circ.: 17,200; 4 times a year

London, 244 Adelaide St. South, London ON N5Z 3L1 – 519/685-1624; Fax: 519/649-0908 – Circ.: 35,000; 8 times a year

Monday Magazine, Island Publisher Ltd., 1609 Blanshard St., Victoria BC V8W 5J5 – 250/382-6188; Fax: 250/381-2662 – Circ.: 40,000; Weekly – Publisher, Michael Turnpenny; Editor, James MacKinnon

Montréal Mirror, Communications Gratte-Ciel ltée, 400 McGill St. 1st Fl., Montréal QC H2Y 2G1 – 514/393-1010; Fax: 514/393-3173, 3756; Email: mirror@babylon.montreal.qc.ca – Circ.: 75,000; Weekly, Thur – Production Manager, Catherine Leconte

Montréal Scope, #232, 1253 McGill College, Montréal QC H3B 2Y5 – 514/933-3333; Fax: 514/931-9581 – Circ.: 40,800; 11 times a year – Editor/Publisher, N. Evreinow

Moving to & Around... (Published by Moving Publications Ltd.), 40 Upjohn Rd., Don Mills ON M3B 2W1 – 416/441-1168; Fax: 416/441-1641 – Circ.: 220,000; Annually, or bi-annual issues cover all major Canadian cities & areas; 2 bilingual issues, Montréal, Ottawa/Hull – Publisher, Anita Wood; Editor, Lorraine Hunter; Circulation Manager, Paula Muzzin

New City Magazine, PO Box 26083, Winnipeg MB R3C 4K9 – 204/775-9327; Fax: 204/788-0109 – Circ.: 1,000; 4 times a year; ISSN: 0315-7911 – Publisher, Ross Dobson

Niagara Magazine, #B2, 11 Bond St., St. Catharines ON L2R 4Z4 – 905/641-3505; Fax: 905/687-6911 – Circ.: 30,000; 6 times a year – Publisher, Ted Szymanski; Editor, Wendy Luce

Now, 150 Danforth Ave., Toronto ON M4K 1N1 – 416/461-0871; Fax: 416/461-2886; Email: letters@now.com; URL: http://www.now.com – Circ.: 100,000; Weekly – Editor/Publisher, Michael Hollett; Executive Editor/CEO, Alice Klein

Okanagan Life Magazine (Published by Byrne Publishing Group Inc), PO Box 1479, Stn A, Kelowna BC V1Y 7V8 – 250/861-5399; Fax: 250/868-3040 – Circ.: 18,000; 6 times a year – Publisher, Paul Byrne; Circulation Manager, Tammy Tomiye

Ottawa Magazine, Pegasus Publishing Inc., 1312 Bank St., Ottawa ON K1S 3Y4 – 613/731-9194; Fax: 613/731-9884 – Circ.: 37,999; 6 times a year – Publisher, Peter Ginsberg; Editor, Mark Sutcliffe

The Ottawa X Press, 69 Sparks St., Ottawa ON K1P 5A5 – 613/237-8226; Fax: 613/232-9055; Email: xpress@achilles.net; URL: http://

www.theottawaxpress.ca – Thurs. – Publisher, Ross Dickson; Co-publishers & Executive Editor, Jim Creskey; Associate Editor, Allan Wigney

Pique Newsmagazine, Pique Publishing Inc., #5, 1050 Millar Creek Rd., Whistler BC V0N 1B1 – 604/938-0202; Fax: 604/938-0201; Email: pique@whistler.net – Circ.: 6,840; Weekly, Fri. – Publisher, Kathy Barnett; Editor, Bob Barnett

the prairie dog, 2201 Hamilton St., Regina SK S4D 2E7 – 306/757-8522; Fax: 306/352-9686 – Circ.: 13,000; Monthly – General Manager, Mitch Diamantopoulos

Profile Kingston, PO Box 91, Kingston ON K7L 4V6 – 613/546-6723; Fax: 613/546-0707 – Circ.: 12,000; 6 times a year – Publisher, Bonnie Golomb

Pulse, Dynasty Communciations Inc., 44 Queenston St., Unit #7, St. Catharines ON L2P 2Y9 – 905/682-5999; Fax: 905/682-1414 – Circ.: 11,500; Weekly – Publisher, Sean Rosen; Editor, Walter Sendzic

Richmond Hill Month (Published by Thornhill Publications Ltd.), 7780 Woodbine Ave., Unit 16, Markham ON L3R 2N7 – 905/475-1743 – Monthly – Publisher, P.G. Grosskurth; Editor, Deborah Smith

SEE Magazine, 10310 - 102 Ave., Edmonton AB T5J 2X6 – 403/428-9354; Fax: 403/428-9349; Email: see@greatwest.ca; URL: http://www.greatwest.ca/see – Weekly, Thur. – Editor, Stew Slater

Thornhill Month (Published by Thornhill Publications Ltd.), 7780 Woodbine Ave., Unit 16, Markham ON L3R 2N7 – 905/475-1743 – Monthly – Publisher, P.G. Grosskurth; Editor, Ron Preston

Thunder Bay Guest, 1126 Roland St., Thunder Bay ON P7B 5M4 – 807/623-4424; Fax: 807/622-3140; Email: tbpost4@air.on.ca; URL: http://www.tbsource.com – Circ.: 14,000; Monthly – Publisher, E. Dougall; Editor, Lorraine Deck

Thunder Bay Life (Published by North Superior Publishing Inc.), 1145 Barton St., Thunder Bay ON P7B 5N3 – 807/623-2348; Fax: 807/623-7515; Email: nsuperior@norlink.net – Circ.: 30,000; Bi-monthly – Publisher & Editor, Scott A. Sumnor

Toronto Events Planner, 99 Kimbark Blvd., Toronto ON M5N 2Y3 – 416/782-3322; Fax: 416/787-9299; Email: sybilp@ican.net – 3 times a year, Jan., May, Sept. – Publisher, Sybil Levine; Editor, R.S. Diamond

Toronto Life (Published by Key Publishers), 59 Front St. East, 2nd Fl., Toronto 0N M5E 1B3 – 416/364-3333; Fax: 416/861-1169; URL: http://www.tor-lifeline.com/tl – Circ.: 93,500; Monthly; also monthly Chinese edition co-published with Ming Pao Daily – Publisher, William M. Duron; Editor, John MacFarlane

Uptown Magazine (Published by Canadian Publishers), 1465 St. James St., Winnipeg MB R3H 0W9 – 204/949-8680; Fax: 204/957-0795; Email: uptown@copcomm.mb.ca; URL: http://www.pangea.ca/~uptown – Circ.: 25,000; Weekly – Publisher, Gerald L. Dorge; Editor, Elizabeth Bridge

Vancouver Magazine, Telemedia Publishing Inc., #300, 555 - 12th Ave. West, Vancouver BC V5Z 4L4 – 604/877-7732; Fax: 604/877-4848 – Circ.: 61,000; 8 times a year – Publisher, Greg Hryhorchuk; Editor, Jim Sutherland

View, Dynasty Communications Inc., #300, 149 Main St., Hamilton ON L8N 1G4 – 905/527-3343; Fax: 905/527-3721; Email: view@worldchat.com; URL: http://www.viewmag.com – Circ.: 18,500; Weekly – Publisher, Sean Rosen; Editor, Walter Sendzik

Visitor's Choice (Published by I.G. Publications Ltd.), #222, 999 - 8 St. SW, Calgary AB T2R 1J5 – 403/244-7343 – Annually; also editions for: Banff & Lake Louise, Vancouver, & Victoria – Publisher, Wayne Kehoe; Editor, Sharon Komori

Voilà Québec, 185, rue St-Paul, Québec QC G1K 3W2 – 418/694-1272; Fax: 418/692-3392 – Circ.: 260,000; 4 times a year; English & French – Publisher, Curtis J. Sommerville; Editor, Lynn Magee

Voir, 4130, rue St-Denis, Montréal QC H2W 2M5 – 514/848-0805; Fax: 514/848-9004 – Tirage: 84,600; Hebdomadaire; français, aussi Voir Québec City – Editeur, Pierre Paquet

Vue Weekly, 307 - 10080 Jasper Ave., Edmonton AB T5J 1V9 – 403/426-1996; Fax: 403/426-2889; Email: office@vue.ab.ca; URL: http://vue.ab.ca – Circ.: 30,000; Weekly – Publisher & Editor, Ron Garth

What's Happening Magazine, 135-137 Main St., PO Box 171, Foxboro ON K0K 2B0 – 613/989-8896; Fax: 613/969-1836 – Circ.: 15,000; 4 times a year – Publisher, Susan Kell

Where Calgary, Keywest Publishers, #250, 125 - 9 Ave. SE, Calgary AB T2G 0P6 – 403/299-1888; Fax: 403/299-1899; Email: wherecgy@aol.com; URL: http://www.wheremags.com – Circ.: 25,000; Monthly – Publisher, Thomas Tait; Editor, Jill Sawyer

Where Edmonton, Tanner Publishing Ltd., #4, 9343 - 50 St., Edmonton AB T6B 2L5 – 403/465-3362; Fax: 403/448-0424 – Circ.: 48,000; 4 times a year – Publisher, Rob Tanner

Where Halifax, Metro Guide Publishers, #500, 5475 Spring Garden Rd., PO Box 14, Halifax NS B3J 3T2 – 902/420-9943; Fax: 902/429-9058; Email: mpublis@106.aol – Circ.: 25,000 – Publisher, Sheila Pottie; Editor, Karen Janik; Circulation Manager, Patricia Baxter

Where Ottawa-Hull, 400 Cumberland St., Ottawa ON K1N 8X3 – 613/241-7888; Fax: 613/241-3112 – Circ.: 32,000; Monthly; English with one section in French – Publisher, Stephen Ball; Editor, Marc Choma

Where Rocky Mountains, #250, 125 - 9 Ave. SE, Calgary AB T2G 0P6 – 403/299-1888; Fax: 403/299-1899; URL: http://www.wheremags.com/world – Circ.: 125,000 summer, 150,000 winter; 2 times a year; English with some Japanese – Publisher, Jack Newton, 403/299-1885

Where Toronto, 6 Church St., 2nd Fl., Toronto ON M5E 1M1 – 416/364-3333; Fax: 416/594-3375; Email: 102216.1067@compuserve.com; URL: http://www.wheremags.com – Circ.: 80,000; Monthly; supplements - Where Toronto West, Heart of the City – Publisher, Giorgina Bigioni; Editor-in-chief, Jacquelyn Waller-Vintar; Communications Manager, Marilou Cruz

Where Vancouver, 2208 Spruce St., Vancouver BC V6H 2P3 – 604/736-5586; Fax: 604/736-3465 – Circ.: 32,000; Monthly – Publisher, Peggie Terry; Editor, Louise Whitney

Where Vancouver Island (Published by Pacific Island Publishers Co. Ltd.), 1001 Wharf St., 3rd Fl., Victoria BC V8W 1T6 – 250/388-4324; Fax: 250/388-6166 – Circ.: 60,000; Annually, May – Publisher, Lise Gyorkos

Where Victoria (Published by Pacific Island Publishers Co. Ltd.), 1001 Wharf St., 3rd Fl., Victoria BC V8W 1T6 – 250/388-4324; Fax: 250/388-6166 – Circ.: 22,000; Monthly – Publisher, Anna Scolnick; Editor & Associate Publisher, Caroyln Camilleri

Where Winnipeg, #300, 128 James Ave., Winnipeg MB R3B 0N8 – 204/943-4439; Fax: 204/947-5463 – Monthly – Editor, Alison Kirkland

Word: Toronto's Black Culture Magazine, Working Word Cooperative Ltd., #370, 6-295 Queen St. East, Brampton ON L6W 4S6 – 905/799-1630; Fax: 905/799-2788; Email: word@wordmag.com – Monthly – Publisher & Editor, Phillip Vassell

Zone Outaouais, 35, rue Gamelin, Hull QC J8Y 1V4 – 819/777-5538; Fax: 819/777-8525; Email: zone@journalzone.qc.ca; URL: http://www.journalzone.qc.ca – Tirage: 17 000; Mensuel; français – Editeur, Nicolas Cazelais; Rédactrice en chef, Lara Mainville

### COMPUTING & TECHNOLOGY

Content London, Information London, 325 Queens Ave., London ON N6B 1X2 – 519/432-1105; Fax: 519/432-1106; Email: editor@info.london.on.ca; URL: http://www.info.london.on.ca/content/london/ – Circ.: 6,000; 6 times a year – Publisher & Editor, Joe Swan

Guide Internet (Published by Trustar Ltd.), #2000, 2020, rue University, Montréal QC H5A 2A5 – 514/848-7000; Fax: 514/848-9854 – Circ.: 17,700; 10 times a year – Publisher, Michel Trudeau

INFORMATION highways: The Magazine about Online Information, c/o TCE Information Group Ltd., #102, 1999 Avenue Rd., Toronto ON M5M 4A5 – 416/488-7372; Fax: 416/488-7078; Email: info@tce.on.ca; URL: http://www.flexnet/com/~infohiwy/ – Circ.: 5,000; 6 times a year – Publisher, David Shinwell; Executive Editor, Beverley Watters; Circulation Manager, Mary-Anne Messinger

Sympatico NetLife (Published by Telemedia Publishing), #100, 25 Sheppard Ave. West, North York ON M2N 6S7 – 416/733-7600; Fax: 416/733-8272; Email: giffen@sympatico.ca; URL: http://www.sympatico.ca/mags/netlife/ – Circ.: 80,000; 6 times a year – Associate Publisher, Barbara Warren; Editor, Peter Giffen

We Compute, Read/Write Media Inc., #302A, 1560 Bayview Ave., Toronto ON M4G 3B8 – 416/481-1955; Fax: 416/481-2819 – Circ.: 80,000; 10 times a year – Editor, Eric McMillan

### CULTURE, CURRENT EVENTS

Border/Lines, PO Box 459, Stn P, Toronto ON M5S 5Z9 – 416/921-6446; Fax: 416/921-3984 – 4 times a year

Edges: New Planetary Patterns, 579 Kingston Rd., Toronto ON M4E 1R3 – 416/691-2316; Fax: 416/691-2491; Email: icacan@web.net; URL: http://www.web.net/~icacan – 4 times a year – Editor, Brian Stanfield

Fuse, #454, 401 Richmond St. West, Toronto ON M5V 3A8 – 416/340-8026; Fax: 416/340-0494; Email: fuse@interlog.com – Circ.: 3,300; 4 times a year – Administrator, Petra Chevrier

id magazine, 123 Woolwich St., Guelph ON N1H 3V1 – 519/766-9853, 9336 editorial; Fax: 519/766-9891; Email: jpetrie@idmagazine.com; URL: http://www.idmagazine.com – Circ.: 40,000; Weekly – Publisher, Michael McLarnon

MIX, Parallélogramme Artist-Run Culture & Publishing, #446, 401 Richmond St. West, Toronto ON M5V 3A8 – 416/506-1012; Fax: 416/340-8458; Email: mix@web.net; URL: http://www.mix.web.net/mix/ – 4 times a year; English & French; ISSN: 1204-5349 – Editor, Margaret Christakos; Circulation Manager, Lorne Fromer

The Nation: The News & Cultural Magazine of the James Bay Cree, 5678 Park Ave., PO Box 48036, Montréal QC H2V 4S8 – 514/272-3077; Fax: 514/278-9914; Email: beesum@odyssee.com; URL: http://nisk.creenet.com/~nation/ – 26 times a year; English & James Bay Cree – President, Ernest Webb; Editor, Alex Ruslin

NeWest Review, Sub PO 6, PO Box 394, Saskatoon SK S7N 0W0 – 306/934-1444; Fax: 306/242-5004 – 6 times a year; ISSN: 0380-2917

Outlook, #3, 6184 Ash St., Vancouver BC V5Z 3G9 – 604/324-5101; Fax: 604/325-2470 – 8 times a year – Editor, Henry Rosenthal; Assistant Editor, Carl Rosenberg

This Magazine, Red Maple Foundation, #396, 401 Richmond St. West, Toronto ON M5V 3A8 – 416/979-9429; Fax: 416/979-1143; Email: this_magazine@intacc.web.net – Circ.: 8,000; 6 times a year; ISSN: 9381-3746 – Editor, Clive Thompson

**DIRECTORIES & ALMANACS**

Almanach du Peuple (Published by Le Groupe Polygone éditeurs inc.), 11450, boul Albert-Hudon, Montréal-Nord QC H1G 3J9 – 514/327-4464; Fax: 514/327-0602 – Tirage: 150,000; Annuellement; français – Editeur, Luc Lemay; Directeur de tirage, Robert Ferland

Canadian Forces Base Kingston Official Directory (Published by Kingston Publications), PO Box 1352, Kingston ON K7L 5C6 – 613/549-8442; Fax: 613/549-4333 – Circ.: 3,600; Annually, March; English & French – Publisher & Editor, Mary Laflamme

Locator, #302, 989 Derry Rd. East, Mississauga ON L5T 2J8 – Fax: 905/669-6810 – Annually, 35 editions – Publisher, Paul Moroney

**ENTERTAINMENT**

Bingo News & Gaming Hi-Lites, 10171 Saskatchewan Dr., PO Box 106, Edmonton AB T6E 4R5 – 403/433-9740; Fax: 403/433-9842 – Circ.: 25,000; 11 times a year – Editor & Publisher, Lorraine B. Kramer Kalmbach

Canadian Theatre Review (Published by University of Toronto Press), Journals Division, 5201 Dufferin St., North York ON M3H 5T8 – 416/667-7810; Fax: 416/667-7881; Email: journals@gpu.utcc.utoronto.ca – Circ.: 1,000; 4 times a year; ISSN: 0315 0836 – Co-Editor, Alan Filewod; Co-Editor, Natalie Rewa

Cineaction: Radical Film Criticism & Theory, #705, 40 Alexander St., Toronto ON M4Y 1B5 – 416/323-9083 – 3 times a year; ISSN: 0826-9866

Image de la Mauricie, 564, boul des Prairies, Cap-de-la-Madeleine QC G8T 1K9 – 819/378-2176; Fax: 819/374-2263 – Mensuel; français – Rédacteur, Gilles Mercier

Magazine Le Clap, 2360, ch Ste-Foy, Ste-Foy QC G1V 4H2 – 418/653-2470; Fax: 418/653-6018 – Tirage: 98,000; 8 fois par an; français – Editeur, Michel Aubé

Marquee, #621, 77 Mowat Ave., Toronto ON M6K 3E3 – 416/538-1000; Fax: 416/538-0201 – Circ.: 633,296; 9 times a year – Publisher, David Haslam

Network, 287 MacPherson Ave., Toronto ON M4V 1A4 – 416/928-2909; Fax: 416/928-1357 – Circ.: 146,000; 6 times a year – Managing Editor, Stephen Hubbard

Performing Arts & Entertainment in Canada, 104 Glenrose Ave., Toronto ON M4T 1K8 – 416/484-4534; Fax: 416/484-6214; Email: kbell@interlog.ca – Circ.: 44,000; 4 times a year – Publisher, George Hencz; Editor, Karen Bell; Circulation Manager, Margaret Kennedy

Playboard, Arch-Way Publishers Ltd., 7560 Lawrence Dr., Burnaby BC V5A 1T6 – 604/420-6115; Fax: 604/420-6115 – Circ.: 44,360; Monthly – Publisher, Harold Schiel; Editor, Chuck Davis

Scene Magazine, PO Box 2302, London ON N6A 4E3 – 519/642-4780; Fax: 519/642-0737 – Circ.: 20,000; 26 times a year – Publisher, Bret Downe; News Editor, Barry Wells; Sales Manager, Michael Lavery

Shift Magazine, Behaviour Publishing Inc., #202, 119 Spadina Ave., Toronto ON M5V 2L1 – 416/977-7982; Fax: 416/977-7983; URL: http://www.shift.com/shift.home – Circ.: 30,000; 5 times a year – Publisher, Andrew Heintzman; Editor, Evan Solomon

Tribute Magazine (Published by Tribute Publishing Inc.), 71 Barber Greene Rd., Don Mills ON M3C 2A2 – 416/445-0544; Fax: 416/445-2894 – Circ.: 656,000; 7 times a year – Publisher, Geoffrey Dawe; Editor, Sandra Stewart

Vox, #127 MacEwan Hall, University of Calgary, 2500 University Dr. NW, Calgary AB T2N 1N4 – 403/220-5165; Fax: 403/289-8212; URL: http://www.ucalgary.ca/uofc/students/vox – Monthly

The Wild Life, #8, 103 Jay St., PO Box 665, Banff AB T0L 0C0 – 403/762-8574; Fax: 403/762-8226 – Circ.: 11,500; Monthly – Publisher, Kate Sellers-Tooke; Managing Editor, Lana Riva

**ENVIRONMENT & NATURE**

Alternatives Journal: Environmental Thought, Policy & Action, c/o Faculty of Environmental Studies, University of Waterloo, 200 University Ave. West, Waterloo ON N2L 3G1 – 519/885-1211, ext.6783; Fax: 519/746-0292; Email: alternat@fes.uwaterloo.ca; URL: http://www.fes.uwaterloo.ca/Research/Alternatives/ – 4 times a year – Editor, Bob Gibson

Canadian Wildlife, Canadian Wildlife Federation, 2740 Queensview Dr., Ottawa ON K2B 1A2 – 613/721-2286, 1-800-563-9453; Fax: 613/721-2902; Email: infor@cwf-fcf.org; URL: http://www.toucan.net/cwf-fcf/cwfhome.html – Circ.: 50,000; 5 times a year – Editor, Martin Silverstone; Circulation Manager, Paola Cernicchi

Ecodecision, #924, 276, rue St-Jacques ouest, Montréal QC H2Y 1N3 – 514/284-3043; Fax: 514/284-3045; URL: http://www.ecodec.org – 4 times a year; ISSN: 1183-2355

encompass, Pembina Institute, PO Box 75588, Drayton Valley AB T7A 1S7 – 403/542-6272; Fax: 403/542-6464; Email: encompass@piad.ab.ca – 5 times a year – Editor, Margaret Chandler

Franc-Vert, c/o Union Québecoise pour la conservation de la nature, 690, Grande-Allée est, 4e étage, Québec QC G1R 2K5 – 418/648-2014; Fax: 418/648-0991; Email: evert@uqcn.qc.ca – Tirage: 8,000; 6 fois par an; français – Rédactrice, Louise Desautels

Global Biodiversity, c/o Canadian Museum of Nature, PO Box 3443, Stn D, Ottawa ON K1P 6P4 – 613/990-6671; Fax: 613/990-0318; Email: sswan@mus-nature.ca; URL: http://www.nature.ca/english/gbzine.htm – Circ.: 1,200; 4 times a year; separate English & French editions (La biodiversité mondiale); ISSN: 1195-3101 – Business Manager, Dory Cameron, 613/364-4122; Email: dcameron@mus-nature.ca; Editor, Catherine Ripley, 613/566-4267; Email: cripley@mus-nature.ca; Circulation Manager, Susan Swan, Email: sswan@mus-nature.ca

Heritage Canada, PO Box 1358, Stn B, Ottawa ON K1P 5R4 – 613/237-1066; Fax: 613/237-5987; Email: hercanot@sympatico.ca – 5 times a year; ISSN 1195-5899 – Executive Director, Brian Anthony

Natural Life Magazine, The Alternate Press, 272 Highway 5, RR#1, St. George ON N0E 1N0 – 519/448-4001; Fax: 519/448-4411; Email: natural@life.ca; URL: http://www.life.ca – Circ.: 25,000; 6 times a year; includes "Earthkeeper" & "Growth Spurts" sections; ISSN 0701-8002 – Publisher & Editor, Wendy Priesnitz

Nature Canada, c/o Canadian Nature Federation, #606, 1 Nicholas St., Ottawa ON K1N 7B7 – 613/562-3447; Fax: 613/562-3371; Email: cnf@web.net; URL: http://www.web.net/~cnf – Circ.: 22,000; 4 times a year – Editor, Barbara Stevenson

Seasons, Federation of Ontario Naturalists, 355 Lesmill Rd., Don Mills ON M3B 2W8 – 416/444-8419; Fax: 416/444-9866; Email: fon@web.net; URL: http://www.web.net/fon – Circ.: 15,775; 4 times a year – Editor, Margaret Webb

Watershed Sentinel, PO Box 39, Whaletown BC V0P 1Z0 – 250/935-6992; Email: dbroten@oberon.ark.com – Circ.: 3,000; 6 times a year – Publisher & Editor, Delores Broten

WE International, 736 Bathurst St., Toronto ON M5S 2R4 – 416/516-2600; Fax: 416/531-6214; Email: weed@web.apc.org.; URL: http://www.web.net/~weed – Circ.: 1,200; 4 times a year; ISSN: 0229-0480X – Magazine Manager, Lisa Dale

Wildflower, c/o Canadian Wildflower Society, PO Box 336, Stn F, Toronto ON M4Y 2L7 – 905/294-9075; Fax: 905/294-9075; Email: ann.melvin@sympatico.ca; URL: http://www.acorn-online.com/hedge/cws.html – Circ.: 2,000; 4 times a year; ISSN: 0842-5132

**FAMILIES**

Calgary's Child Magazine, #723, 105-150 Crowfoot Cres. NW, Calgary AB T3G 3T2 – 403/520-1003; Fax: 403/286-9731; Email: calchild@cadvision.com; URL: http://www.calgaryschild.com – Circ.: 41,000; 6 times a year – Publisher & Editor, Ellen Percival; Publisher & Editor, Sherry Kerr

Canadian Family (Published by Multi-Vision Publishing), #1000, 655 Bay St., Toronto ON M5G 2K4 – 416/595-9944; Fax: 416/595-7217 – Circ.: 162,900; 6 times a year – Editor, Kristin Jenkins

City Parent, Metroland Printing, Publishing & Distributing Ltd., 467 Speers Rd., Oakville ON L6K 3S4 – 905/815-0017; Fax: 905/815-0511 – Circ.: 274,500; 12 times a year – Publisher, Ian Oliver; Editor-in-chief, Jane Muller; Circulation, Geoff Hill

Island Parent Magazine, 941 Kings Rd., Victoria BC V8T 1W7 – 250/388-6905; Fax: 250/388-4391 – Circ.: 25,000; Monthly – Publisher/Editor, Selinde Krayehoff

Junior, c/o Les Éditions Multi-concept inc., #425, 1600, boul Henri Bourassa ouest, Montréal QC H3M 3E2 – 514/331-0661; Fax: 514/331-8821 – Tirage: 40 000; 4 fois par an; français – Editeur, Ronald Lapierre; Directrice, Ginette Desjarlais

Le Magazine Enfants Québec (Published by Les Éditions Héritage), 300, rue Arran, Saint-Laurent QC J4R 1K5 – 514/672-7027; Fax: 514/672-5448 – Tirage: 43 755; 6 fois par an; français – Editrice, Sylvie Payette; Rédactrice, Claire Chabot

Owl Canadian Family (Published by Multi-Vision Publishing), #1000, 655 Bay St., Toronto ON M5G 2K4 – 416/595-9944; Fax: 416/595-7217; Email: owlfamily@m-v-p.com – Circ.: 210,000; 6 times a year – Publisher, Lilia Lozinski; Editor, Kristin Jenkins; Circulation Manager, Terri De Rose

Parent-To-Parent, PO Box 85324, Burlington ON L7R 2G6 – 905/335-3549; Fax: 905/336-0761 – Circ.: 60,000; 6 times a year – Publisher, B. Burrows; Editor, A. Greenway

Pomme d'Api Québec (Published by Bayard Presse Canada Inc.), 3995, rue Ste-Catherine est, Montréal QC H1W 2G7 – 514/522-3936; Fax: 514/522-1761 – Tirage: 9,000 – Editeur, Suzanne Spino; Rédacteur, Paule Brière

Today's Parent (Published by Professional Publishing), 269 Richmond St. West, Toronto ON M5V 1X1 – 416/596-8680; Fax: 416/596-1991 – Circ.: 160,000; 10 times a year; also Prenatal Class Guide (annual) – Publisher, Mitchell B. Dent; Editor-in-chief, Fran Fearnley

**FASHION**

Flare (Published by Maclean Hunter Publishing), 777 Bay St., Toronto ON M5W 1A7 – 416/596-5462, 5453; Fax: 416/596-5799; Email: editors@flare.com; URL: http://www.flare.com – Circ.: 182,000; Monthly – Publisher, David Hamilton; Editor-in-chief, Suzanne Boyd

Luxe, Style Communications Inc., #302, 1448 Lawrence Ave. West, Toronto ON M4A 2V6 – 416/755-5199; Fax: 416/755-9123; Email: stylcom@cycor.ca – Circ.: 100,000 – Publisher, John Peters; Editor, Pat MacLean; Circulation Manager, Don Trimm

Toronto Life Fashion Magazine (Published by Key Publishers), 59 Front St. East, 2nd Fl., Toronto 0N M5E 1B3 – 416/364-3334; Fax: 416/594-3374; Email: fasion@istar.ca – Circ.: 129,000; 6 times a year – Publisher, Shelagh Tarleton; Editor, Joan

Harting Barham; Circulation Director, Scott Bullock

Vision Mode (Published by Groupe Magazines S.A. Inc.), #300, 275, boul des Braves, Terrebonne QC J6W 3H6 – 514/964-7590; Fax: 514/964-2327; Email: magazine@magazinesa.com – 3 fois par an; français – Editeur, Denis Clermont; Rédactrice, Sophie Bertrand

**FISHING & HUNTING**

Alberta Fishing Guide, #6C, 5571 - 45 St., Red Deer AB T4N 1L2 – 403/347-5079; Fax: 403/341-5454 – Circ.: 24,269; Annually, March – Publisher, Barry Mitchell; Editor, Ann Mitchell

The Atlantic Salmon Journal, Atlantic Salmon Federation, PO Box 429, St. Andrews NB E0G 2X0 – 506/529-1030; Fax: 506/529-4985; Email: asfpub@nbnet.nb.ca; URL: http://www.flyfishing.comasf – 4 times a year – Editor, Philip Lee

BC Fishing Directory & Atlas (Published by OP Publishing), #300, 780 Beatty St., Vancouver BC V6B 2N1 – 604/606-4644; Fax: 604/687-1925; Email: OP@mindlink – Annually, Saltwater (March, circ. 14,000); Freshwater (Jan., circ. 17,000) – Publisher, Rex Armstead; Editor, Karl Brahn; Circulation Director, Janet Genders

B.C. Outdoors (Published by OP Publishing), #300, 780 Beatty St., Vancouver BC V6B 2N1 – 604/606-4644; Fax: 604/687-1925; Email: op@mindlink.bc.ca – Circ.: 34,868; 8 times a year – Editor, Karl Bruhn

B.C. Sport Fishing Magazine, 909 Jackson Cres., New Westminster BC V3L 4S1 – 604/683-4871 – Circ.: 21,000; 6 times a year – Publisher & Editor, Rikk Taylor

Canadian Sportfishing, #2020, 937 Centre Rd., Waterdown ON L0R 2H0 – 905/689-1112; Fax: 905/689-2065 – 6 times a year – Publisher, Henry Waszczuk; Editor, Kerry Knudsen

Eastern Woods & Waters, Land & Sea Events Ltd., 44 Wildwood Blvd., Dartmouth NS B2W 2L8 – 902/435-4576; Fax: 902/435-4576 – Circ.: 15,600; 6 times a year – Publisher & Editor, Jim Gourlay; Circulation Manager, Faith Drinnan

Newfoundland Sportsman, 803 Water St. West, PO Box 13754, Stn A, St. John's NF A1B 4G5 – 709/754-3515; Fax: 709/754-2490; URL: http://silverweb.nf.ca/nf-sportsman – 6 times a year – Publisher, Dwight J. Blackwood; Editor, Gordon Follet

Ontario Out of Doors (Published by Maclean Hunter Publishing), 777 Bay St., Toronto ON M5W 1A7 – 416/596-5908; Fax: 416/596-2517; Email: 102677.1125@compuserve.com; URL: http://www.cyberplex.com/fishontario – Circ.: 89,000; 10 times a year – Publisher, Ron Goodman; Editor, Burton J. Myers; Circulation Manager, Linda Chick

Outdoor Canada, #202, 703 Evans Ave., Toronto ON M9C 5E9 – 416/695-0311; Fax: 416/695-0382 – Circ.: 93,000; 8 times a year – Publisher, Ildiko Marshall; Editor, James Little; Circulation Manager, Terry Gray

The Outdoor Edge, Keywest Marketing Ltd., 5829 - 97 St., Edmonton AB T6E 3J2 – 403/448-0381; Fax: 403/438-3244 – Circ.: 55,000; 6 times a year – Publisher, Kevin Rolfe

Saskatchewan Fishing & Hunting, Tourism Saskatchewan, #500, 1900 Albert St., Regina SK S4P 4L9 – 306/787-9685; Fax: 306/787-0715 – Circ.: 100,000; Annual

Sentier Chasse-Pêche (Published by Le Groupe Polygone éditeurs inc.), 11450, boul Albert-Hudon, Montréal-Nord QC H1G 3J9 – 514/327-4464; Fax: 514/327-0602 – Tirage: 90,000; 11 fois par an; français – Editeur, Luc Lemay; Rédacteur, Jeannot Ruel; Directeur de tirage, Robert Ferland

Western Sportsman, Canadian Outdoor Publications Inc., 140 Ave. F North, Saskatoon SK S7L 1V8 – 306/665-6302; Fax: 306/244-8859; Email: copi@sk.sympatico.ca; URL: http://www.globalnet.ca/copi – Circ.: 22,000; 6 times a year – Editor, George Gruenefeld

**FOOD & BEVERAGE**

Appeal (Published by Canada Wide Magazines & Communications Ltd.), 4180 Lougheed Hwy., 4th Fl., Burnaby BC V5C 6A7 – 604/299-7311; Fax: 604/299-9188 – Circ.: 415,000; 4 times a year – Publisher, Peter Legge

BCL Guide to Products & Services, B.C. Liquor Distribution Branch, 2625 Rupert St., Vancouver BC V5M 3T5 – 604/252-3034; Fax: 604/252-3044; Email: llmyers@bcsc02.gov.bc.ca – 4 times a year

B.C. Wine Trails, PO Box 1077, Summerland BC V0H 1Z0 – 250/494-7733; Fax: 250/494-7737; URL: http://www/bcwonme/cp,/trails/ – Circ.: 17,500; 4 times a year – Publisher/Editor, Dave Gamble

Coup de Pouce Extra Cuisine (Published by Les Éditions Télémedia), #900, 2001, rue University, Montréal QC H3A 2A6 – 514/499-0561; Fax: 514/499-1844 – 5 fois par an; français – Editrice, Michèle Cyr

Food & Drink, Liquor Control Board of Ontario, 55 Lakeshore Blvd. East, Toronto ON M5E 1A4 – 416/864-6630; Fax: 416/365-5935 – 4 times a year; English & French – Publisher, Debbie Costa; Editor, Michelle Oosterman

Le Guide Cuisine, Communication Duocom Inc., #203, 90, rue Sainte-Anne, Sainte-Anne-de-Bellevue QC H9X 1L8 – 514/457-0144; Fax: 514/457-0226 – Tirage: 19,200; 5 fois par an – Editeur, Nicolas Vallée

Toronto's Fifty Best Restaurants, Twenty First Century Publishing Ltd., 465 Rosewell Ave., Unit 1, Toronto ON M4R 2B6 – 416/482-6400; Fax: 416/482-6729; Email: dhlaikie@tor.ajilon.com – Circ.: 52,000; 2 times a year – Publisher & Editor, Ron Fonte; Associate Publisher, Scott O'Donoghue

WineTidings (Published by Kylix Media Inc), #414, 5165 Sherbrooke St. West, Montréal QC H4A 1T6 – 514/481-5892; Fax: 514/481-9699; Email: winetidings@opim.ca; URL: http://www.cmpa.ca/ – Circ.: 13,391; 8 times a year – Publisher, Judy Rochester; Executive Editor, Tony Aspler; Circulation, Veronica Gumilar

**FRATERNAL, SERVICE CLUBS, ASSOCIATIONS**

KIN Magazine, c/o Kinsmen & Kinette Clubs of Canada, Cambridge ON N3H 5C6 – 519/653-1920; Fax: 519/650-1091 – Circ.: 16,000; 4 times a year – Editor, Joseph Distel

Legion, Canvet Publications, #407, 359 Kent St., Ottawa ON K2P 0R6 – 613/235-8741; Fax: 613/233-7159 – Circ.: 436,675; 5 times a year – Editor, Mac Johnston; Advertising Coordinator, Jan Buchanan-Redden

Mensa Canada Communications, Mensa Canada Society, #232, 329 March Rd., PO Box 11, Kanata ON K2K 2E1 – 613/599-5897; Email: bn628@freenet.toronto.on.ca; URL: http://www.rohcg.onca/mensa/mensa.html – Circ.: 2,100; 10 times a year

Papyrus, c/o Rameses Temple, A.A.O.N.M.S., 3100 Keele St., Downsview ON M3M 2H4 – 416/633-6317; Fax: 416/633-6345 – Circ.: 7,200; 6 times a year – Editor, Otto Yoworski

The Sentinel, c/o Loyal Orange Association, 94 Sheppard Ave. West, Willowdale ON M2N 1M5 – 416/223-1690; Fax: 416/223-1324; URL: http://www.organge.ca – Circ.: 2,229; 6 times a year – Editor, Norman R. Ritchie

**GARDENING & GARDEN EQUIPMENT**

Canadian Gardening (Published by Camar Publications), 130 Spy Ct., Markham ON L3R 5H6 – 905/475-8440; Fax: 905/475-9246, 9560; Email: letters@canadiangardening.com – Circ.: 135,000; 7 times a year – Publisher, Phil Whalen; Editor, Liz Primeau

Chatelaine Gardens (Published by Maclean Hunter Publishing), 777 Bay St., Toronto ON M5W 1A7 – 416/596-5936; Fax: 416/593-3197; Email: editors@chatelaine.com – Circ.: 115,000; Annually, Feb. – Publisher, Lee Simpson; Editor-in-chief, Anita Draycott; Editorial & Administrative Manager, Holly Lee

The Coastal Grower Magazine, c/o Greenheart Publications Ltd., 1075 Alston St., Victoria BC V9A 3S8 – 250/360-0709; Fax: 250/360-1709; Email: grower@islandnet.com; URL: http://www.islandnet.com/~grower/homepage.html – Circ.: 10,000; 9 times a year – Publisher/Editor, Mary Mills; Circulation Manager, John Brant

COGNITION, Canadian Organic Growers, PO Box 116, Collingwood ON L9Y 3Z4 – 705/444-0923; Fax: 705/444-0380; Email: prgamox@georgian.net – 4 times a year – Tomas L. Nimmo

Fleurs, plantes et jardins (Published by Editions Versicolores inc.), 1320, boul St-Joseph, Québec QC G2K 1G2 – 418/628-8690; Fax: 418/628-0524 – Tirage: 53,131; 8 fois par an; français – Editeur, François Bernatchez; Rédacteur, Bertrand Dumont

Gardening Life (Published by Canadian Home Publishers), #120, 511 King St. West, Toronto ON M5V 2Z4 – 416/593-0204; Fax: 416/591-1630; Email: mail@canhomepub.com; URL: http://www.canadianhousenadhome.com – Circ.: 100,000; 4 times a year; ISSN: 1203-858X – Publisher, Donna Murphy; Editior-in-chief, Marjorie Harris; Editor, Nancy Jane Hastings

Gardens West, Cornwall Publishing Co. Ltd., PO Box 2680, Vancouver BC V6B 3W8 – 604/879-4991; Fax: 604/879-5110; Email: grow@gradenswest.com; URL: http://www.gardenswest.com – 9 times a year – Publisher/Editor, Dorothy Horton; Public Relations, Tamy Yates

Plant & Garden (Published by Helpard Publishing Inc.), #300, 1200 Markham Rd., Scarborough ON M1H 3C3 – 416/438-7777; Fax: 416/438-5333 – 5 times a year – Publisher, Lynn R. Helpard; Editor, Lorraine Hunter

Toronto Gardens, Bayview Media Inc., #302A, 1560 Bayview Ave., Toronto ON M4G 3B8 – 416/481-1955; Fax: 416/481-2819 – Circ.: 50,000; 6 times a year; ISSN 1198-8649 – Publisher/Editor, Eric McMillan

**GENERAL INTEREST**

Actif, Édibec inc., 2251, boul Shervchenko, Lasalle QC H8N 2Y8 – 514/366-4436; Fax: 514/366-4495 – 5 fois par an; français – Editeur, Stéphane Leroy

Active Living, Disability Today Publishing Group Inc., #203, 627 Lyons Lane, Oakville ON L6J 5Z7 – 905/338-6894; Fax: 905/338-1836 – Circ.: 45,000; 4 times a year, plus Active Living's Buyers' Guide Product & Service Directory (annual) – Publisher, Jeffrey Tiessen; Editor, Hilda Hoch

Angles, Lavender Publishing Society of BC, 1170 Bute St., Vancouver BC V6E 1Z2 – 604/688-0265; Fax: 604/688-5405 – Circ.: 17,800; Monthly

Beautiful British Columbia Magazine, 929 Ellery St., Victoria BC V9A 7B4 – 250/384-5456; Fax: 250/384-2812; Email: ed@bbcmag.bc.ca – Circ.: 255,000; 4 times a year; also Traveller – Publisher, John Thomson; Editor-in-chief, Bryan McGill

The Beaver Magazine: Exploring Canada's History, Canada's National History Society, #478, 167 Lombard Ave., Winnipeg MB R3B 0T6 – 204/988-9300; Fax: 204/988-9309; Email: beaver@cyberspc.mb.ca; URL: http://www.cyberspc.mb.ca/~otmw/cnhs/cnhs.html – Circ.: 44,560; 6 times a year – Publisher, Laird Rankin; Editor, Christopher Dafoe

The Canadian Forum, #804, 251 Laurier Ave. West, Ottawa ON K1P 5J6 – 613/230-3078; Fax: 613/233-

1458 – Circ.: 10,000; 10 times a year; ISSN: 0008-3631 – Publisher, James Lorimer; Editor, Duncan Cameron

Canadian Geographic, c/o Royal Canadian Geographical Society, 39 McArthur Ave., Vanier ON K1L 8L7 – 613/745-4629; Fax: 613/744-0947; Email: editorial@cangeo.ca; URL: http://www.cangeo.ca – Circ.: 245,000; 6 times a year – Publisher, Edwin O'Dacre; Editor, Rick Boychuk; Circulation Director, Maureen Ogilvie

Cape Breton's Magazine, Wreck Cove NS B0C 1H0 – 902/539-3817; Fax: 902/539-9117; Email: speclink@atcon.com – Circ.: 7,500; 3 times a year – Publisher & Editor, Ronald Caplan

Club News, 393 Main St., Hamilton ON L8N 3T7 – 905/525-1210; Fax: 905/525-1654 – 6 times a year

Common Ground Magazine, #201, 3091 West Broadway, Stn D, Vancouver BC V6K 2G9 – 604/733-2215; Fax: 604/733-4415; Email: cgbc@web.net – Circ.: 80,000; 10 times a year; also annual directory – Publisher, Joseph Roberts

Contact, Cité Universitaire, Université Laval, 3577, Pavillon Alphonse-Desjardins, Québec QC G1K 7P4 – 418/656-2571; Fax: 418/656-2809; Email: contact@scom.ulaval.ca – Tirage: 115,000; 3 fois par an; français – Rédactrice en chef, Diane Dontigny

Continuité, 82, Grande-Allée ouest, Québec QC G1R 2G6 – 418/647-4525; Fax: 418/647-6483 – Tirage: 5 000; 4 fois par an; français – Rédactrice, Micheline Piché

Cottage Life, #408, 111 Queen St. East, Toronto ON M5C 1S2 – 416/360-6880; Fax: 416/360-6814; Email: cottage_life@magic.ca – Circ.: 70,000; 6 times a year – Publisher, Al Zikovitz; Editor, Dave Zimmer

Cottage News, Hwy. 11 North, Gravenhurst ON P1P 1R1 – 705/687-7788; Fax: 705/687-7789 – Circ.: 30,000; 7 times a year – Publisher, Bruce Clark; Editor, Margaret Bellamy

The Country Connection, PO Box 100, Boulter ON K0L 1G0 – 613/332-3651; Fax: 613/332-5183; URL: http://www.cyberus.ca/~queenswood/pinecone/ – Circ.: 15,000; 2 times a year – Editor & Publisher, Gus Zylstra; Circulation Manager, Nancy Zylstra

Dernière heure (Published by Trustar Ltd.), #2000, 2020, rue University, Montréal QC H5A 2A5 – 514/848-7000; Fax: 514/848-9854 – Circ.: 51 000; Hebdomadaire; français – Editeur, Claude J. Charron

Dialogue: A Forum for the Exchange of Ideas, Gabriel Communications, 19383 Kenyon Rd., Apple Hill ON K0C 1B0 – Fax: 613/525-3548; Email: dialogue@dialogue.ca; URL: http://www.dialogue.ca/home.htm – Circ.: 5,000; Monthly – Publisher, Maurice J. King; Editor, Janet Hicks

Equinox (Published by Malcolm Publishing), 11450, boul Albert-Hudon, Montréal-Nord QC H1G 3J9 – 514/327-4464; Fax: 514/327-7592; URL: http://www.equinox.ca – Circ.: 140,296; 6 times a year – Publisher, Michel Paradis; Alan Morantz

The Flag & Banner, International Flag & Banner Inc., 1755 - 4th Ave. West, Vancouver BC V6J 1M2 – 604/736-8161; Fax: 604/736-6439; Email: doreen@flagshop.ca; URL: http://www.flagshop.com – Circ.: 18,000; 2 times a year – Editor, Doreen Braveman; Production Assistant, Dennis Dong

Georgian Bay Today, c/o 29 Bernard Ave., Toronto ON M5R 1R3 – 416/944-1217; Fax: 416/944-0133; Email: hize@compuserve.com – Circ.: 3,500; 4 times a year – Publisher, Alan Heisey; Editor, Sue Russell; Circulation Manager, Alexandra Irving

Globe Magazine, #110, 455, rue Narais, Vanier QC G1M 3A2 – 418/686-1940; Fax: 418/686-1942 – Tirage: 25,000; 5 fois par an; français – Editeur, France Begin

Going Natural, Federation of Canadian Naturists, PO Box 186, Islington ON M9A 4X2 – 416/410-6833; Fax: 416/723-5531 – Circ.: 630; 4 times a year – Editor, Doug Beckett

Going Places Manitoba (Published by Canada Wide Magazines & Communications Ltd.), 4180 Lougheed Hwy., 4th Fl., Burnaby BC V5C 6A7 – 604/299-7311; Fax: 604/299-9188 – Circ.: 102,000; 6 times a year – Publisher, Peter Legge; Editor, Pat Price

Harrowsmith Country Life (Published by Malcolm Publishing), 11450, boul Albert-Hudon, Montréal-Nord QC H1G 3J9 – 514/327-4464; Fax: 514/327-0514 – Circ.: 140,146; 6 times a year; ISSN: 1190-8416 – VP & Group Publisher, Michel Paradis; Editor, Tom Cruikshank; Circulation Manager, Paola Cernicchi

Home Digest, 28 Hearne Cres., Ajax ON L1T 3P5 – 905/686-3093; Fax: 905/686-8680 – Circ.: 513,700; 5 times a year – Publisher, Barry Holmes; Editor, William Roebuck

Humanist in Canada, Canadian Humanist Publications, PO Box 3769, Stn C, Ottawa ON K1Y 4J8 – 613/749-8929; Fax: 613/749-8929 (phone first); Email: jepiercy@cyberus.ca – Circ.: 1,500; 4 times a year – Editor, Joe Piercy; Circulation Manager, Ernie Schreiber

Kindred Spirits of PEI, PO Box 491, Kensington PE C0B 1M0 – 902/436-7329; Fax: 902/436-1787 – Circ.: 5,000; 4 times a year; English & Japanese – Publisher & Editor, George Campbell

Leisureways (Published by Canada Wide Magazines & Communications Ltd.), 4180 Lougheed Hwy., 4th Fl., Burnaby BC V5C 6A7 – 604/299-7311; Fax: 604/299-9188 – Circ.: 665,000; 6 times a year – Publisher, Peter Legge; Editor, Deborah Milton

Leisure World, 1253 Ouellette Ave., Windsor ON N8X 1J3 – 519/971-3207; Fax: 519/977-1197 – Circ.: 338,400; 6 times a year – Editor, Douglas O'Neil

Lifestyles 5758, A.T.E. Publishing Co. Ltd., 155 East Beaver Creek Rd., Unit 25, PO Box 1000, Richmond Hill ON L4B 2N1 – 905/881-3070; Fax: 905/731-6000 – 6 times a year – Publisher, Gabriel Erem; Editor, Jeannette Friedman

Living Safety, c/o Canada Safety Council, 1020 Thomas Spratt Place, Ottawa ON K1G 5L5 – 613/739-1535; Fax: 613/739-1566; Email: csc@safety-council.org; URL: http://www.safety-council.org – 4 times a year – General Manager, Jack A. Smith

Le Lundi (Published by Trustar Ltd.), #2000, 2020, rue University, Montréal QC H5A 2A5 – 514/848-7000; Fax: 514/848-9854 – Tirage: 82,000; Hebdomadaire; français – Rédactrice, Michèle Lemieux

Menz, #610, 4150, rue St-Catharine ouest, Montréal QC H3Z 2X7 – 514/937-3131; Fax: 514/937-3515 – Circ.: 85,000; 6 times a year – Publisher, Bhaskar Patel; Editor-in-chief, Vanessa Berkling

Monarchy Canada, PO Box 1057, Oakville ON L5J 5E9 – 905/975-2608; Fax: 905/975-2608 – 4 times a year

The Next City, PEMA, 225 Brunswick Ave., Toronto ON M5S 2M6 – 416/964-9223, ext.236; Fax: 416/964-8239; Email: letters@nextcity.com; URL: http://www.nextcity.com – Circ.: 10,000; 4 times a year – Publisher & Editor, Lawrence Solomon, Email: LawrenceSolomon@nextcity.com

Nouvelles CEQ, Centrale de l'enseignement du Québec, 9405, rue Sherbrooke est, Montréal QC H1L 6P3 – 514/356-8888; Fax: 514/356-9999 – Tirage: 99,000; 5 fois par an; français – Directeur, Guy Brouillette

OHS Bulletin (Published by Ontario Historical Society), 34 Parkview Ave., Willowdale ON M2N 3Y2 – 416/226-9011; Fax: 416/226-2740 – Circ.: 2,500; 6 times a year – Circulation Manager, Barbara Truax; Editor, Meribeth Clow

Peninsula Magazine, The Peace Arch News, #101, 1440 George St., PO Box 75149, White Rock BC V4B 4A3 – 604/531-1711; Fax: 604/531-7977 – Monthly – Publisher, Fred Gorman; Editor, Diane Strandberg

Reader's Digest, 215 Redfern Ave., Montréal QC H3Z 2V9 – 514/934-0751; Fax: 514/932-3637 – Circ.: 1,537,200; Monthly; English & French editions – Editor, R. Aubin

Safarir, 1342, rue Saint-Pierre, Québec QC G1K 4A7 – 418/692-4499; Fax: 418/692-0942 – Tirage: 39 000; 12 fois par an; français – Editeur, Sylvain Bolduc

Saturday Night, Saturday Night Magazine Ltd., #400, 184 Front St. East, Toronto ON M5A 4N3 – 416/368-7237; Fax: 416/368-5112; Email: coastes@istar.ca – Circ.: 330,000; 10 times a year – Publisher/COO, Maureen M. Cavan; Editor, Ken Whyte

Sky News, National Museum of Science & Technology Corp., 2421 Lancaster Rd., PO Box 9724, Stn T, Ottawa ON K1G 5A3 – 613/377-6364; Fax: 613/990-3635 – Publisher, Wendy McPeake; Editor, Terence Dickinson

Touring: The Car & Travel Magazine, c/o Consultants CGEI inc., 3281, av Jean-Béraud, Chomedey, Laval QC H7T 2L2 – 514/334-5912; Fax: 514/688-6269 – Circ.: 488,000; 4 times a year; English & French – Delegate Publisher, Ginette St-Pierre; Editor, André Ducharme

University of Toronto Magazine, University of Toronto, Dept. of Public Affairs, 21 King's College Circle, Toronto ON M5S 1A1 – 416/978-2106; Fax: 416/978-7430; Email: k.dahlin@utoronto.ca; karen.handley@utoronto.ca – Circ.: 196,400; 4 times a year – Co-Editor, Karina Dahlin; Co-Editor, Karen Hanley

Up Here: Life in Canada's North, Outcrop Ltd., PO Box 1350, Yellowknife NT X1A 2N9 – 867/920-4652; Fax: 867/873-2844; Email: outrcrop@internorth.com – Circ.: 35,000; Bi-monthly – Publisher, Marion LaVigne; Editor, Rosemary Allerston

Urban MO-ZA-IK, Studio Q International Inc., 382 Queen St. East, Toronto ON M5A 1T1 – 416/364-7690; Fax: 416/364-7925; Email: studioq@haven.ios.com; URL: http://www.urbanmozaik.com/studioq/ – Circ.: 15,000; 4 times a year – Editor, Carolyn Quan

Vice Versa, #403, 3575, boul. St-Laurent, Montréal QC H2X 2T7 – 514/847-7558; Fax: 514/847-1593 – 6 times a year; English, French, Spanish & Italian; ISSN: 0821-6827

Western Living, Telemedia, #300, South East Tower, 555 - 12th Ave. West, Vancouver BC V5Z 4L4 – 604/877-7732; Fax: 604/877-4848 – Monthly – Editor, Carolann Rule

Westworld British Columbia (Published by Canada Wide Magazines & Communications Ltd.), 4180 Lougheed Hwy., 4th Fl., Burnaby BC V5C 6A7 – 604/299-7311; Fax: 604/299-9188 – Circ.: 485,000; 4 times a year; also Westworld Sastchewan (circ. 108,000, 4 times a year), Westworld Alberta (circ. 330,000, 6 times a year) – Publisher, Peter Legge; Editor, Pat Price

Why: A Magazine About Life, RAZ Communications, #217, 312 Dolomite Dr., Downsview ON M3J 2N2 – 416/667-9609; Fax: 416/667-9715; Email: whymag@interlog.com – Circ.: 55,000; 4 times a year – Publisher, Orly Sibilia; Editor, Diane Spivak; Circulation Manager, Esther Abbou

**HEALTH & MEDICAL**

Ability Network, 19 Mount Pleasant Ave., Dartmouth NS B3A 3T3 – 902/461-9009; Fax: 902/461-9484 – Circ.: 24,000; 4 times a year – Spencer Bevan-John

alive magazine - The Canadian Journal of Health & Nutrition, Canadian Health Reform Products Ltd., 7436 Fraser Park Dr., Burnaby BC V5J 5B9 – 604/435-1919; Fax: 604/435-4888 – Circ.: 173,000; 12 times a year – Publisher, Siegfried Gursche; Managing Editor, Rhody Lake

Arthritis News, The Arthritis Society, #1700, 393 University Ave., Toronto ON M5G 1E6 – 416/979-

7228; Fax: 416/979-1149 – Circ.: 15,000; 4 times a year; ISSN: 0820-9006 – Editor, Rod Jamer

Arthroexpress, c/o The Arthritis Society, #1700, 393 University Ave., Toronto ON M5G 1W6 – 416/979-7228; Fax: 416/979-1149 – Tirage: 5,000; 4 fois par an; français; ISSN: 1198-7669 – Rédacteur, Rod Jamer

Better Health Magazine, The Harvard Publishing Co., #406, 220 Duncan Mill Rd., North York ON M3B 3J5 – 416/443-0875; Fax: 416/447-0059 – Circ.: 498,000; 2 times a year; English & French – Editor, Frances Litwin; Circulation Manager, Chaya Glezerman

Diabetes Dialogue, #800, 15 Toronto St., Toronto ON M5C 2E3 – 416/363-3373; Fax: 416/363-3393; Email: campbell@cda-nat.org – 4 times a year – Managing Editor, Cindy Campbell

Family Health, PO Box 2421, Edmonton AB T5J 2S6 – 403/429-5189; Fax: 403/498-5661 – 4 times a year; ISSN 0830-0305 – Publisher, Robert Clarke

Future Health, c/o Canadians for Health Research, PO Box 126, Westmount QC H3Z 2T1 – 514/398-7478; Fax: 514/398-8361; Email: chrpat@total.net – Circ.: 2,000; 4 times a year; English & French – Editor, Heather Pengelley; Assistant Editor, Linda Bazinet

Guide Ressources, SWAA Communication Inc., #305, 4388, rue St-Denis, Montréal QC H2J 2L1 – 514/847-0060; Fax: 514/847-0062; Email: swaa@vir.com – Tirage: 15,000; 10 fois par an; français – Editeur, Christian Lamontagne; Rédactrice, Lucie Dumoulin

The Health Journal: Canada's Authorative Health Forum, Gemini Communications, 113 Mildenhall Rd., North York ON M4N 3H4 – 416/488-1513; Fax: 416/484-9377 – Circ.: 200,000; 6 times a year – Co-Publisher, Chantal Goudreau; Co-Publisher, Donnalyn Manitni

Health Naturally, PO Box 580, Parry Sound ON P2A 2X5 – 705/746-7839; Fax: 705/746-7893 – Circ.: 43,000; 6 times a year – Co-Publisher, David Rowland; Editor, Lorrie Imbert; Office Manager, Gloria Marshall

HealthWatch Canada (Published by Multi-Vision Publishing), #1000, 655 Bay St., Toronto ON M5G 2K4 – 416/595-9944; Fax: 416/595-7217; Email: hwatch@m-v-p.com – Circ.: 520,000; 4 times a year – Publisher, Lilia Lozinski; Editor, Kristin Jenkins

Ontario's Common Ground Magazine (Published by New Age Times Ink.), 356 Dupont St., Toronto ON M5R 1V9 – 416/964-0528 – Circ.: 52,000; 4 times a year – Editor, Julia Woodford

Santé (Published by Les Editions du Feu vert), 5148, boul St-Laurent, Montréal QC H2T 1R8 – 514/273-9773; Fax: 514/273-9034; Email: transc.com/abob – Tirage: 65,000; 10 fois par an; français – Editeur, Francine Tremblay; Rédactrice, Hélène Matteau; Directrice de tirage, Sylvie Hamel

Second Wind, The Alberta Lung Assn., 11402 University Ave., 3rd Fl., PO Box 4500, Edmonton AB T6E 6K2 – 403/492-0354; Fax: 403/492-0362; Email: rtelasky@lung.ab.ca – Circ.: 17,000; 4 times a year – Editor, Robin Telasky

Vitalité Québec Mag, 99, rue Laurel, Baie d'Urfé QC H9X 3M6 – 514/990-6040; Fax: 514/457-0385 – Tirage: 38 640; 6 fois par an' français – Président, Pierre Martineau; Rédacteur, Daniel Crisafi

Vitality Magazine (Published by New Age Times Ink.), 356 Dupont St., Toronto ON M5R 1V9 – 416/964-0528 – Circ.: 38,000; 10 times a year – Editor & Publisher, Julia Woodford

### HISTORY & GENEALOGY

The Loyalist Gazette, 50 Baldwin St., Toronto ON M5T 1L4 – 416/591-1783; Fax: 416/591-7506; Email: escott@freenet.npiec.on.ca – Circ.: 3,000; 2 times a year – Editor, Edward Scott

### HOBBIES

Canadian Amateur, C.A.R.F. Publications, #114, 535 Canteval Terrace, Orleans ON K4A 2E4 – 613/837-4477; Fax: 613/837-5723; Email: RDL2@igs.net; URL: http://www.cac.ca – Circ.: 8,500; 11 times a year – Editor, Robin Ludlow; Circulation Manager, Deborah Norman

Canadian Coin News (Published by Trajan Publishing Corp.), #202, 103 Lakeshore Rd., St Catharines ON L2N 2T6 – 905/646-7744; Fax: 905/646-0995; Email: bret@trajan.com; URL: http://www.trajan.com/trajan – 26 times a year – Publisher, Paul Fiocca; Editor, Bret Evans; Circulation Manager, Tammy Kruck

Canadian Railway Modeller, c/o North Kildonan Publications, 1453 Henderson Hwy, PO Box 28006, Winnipeg MB R2G 4E9 – 204/668-0168; Fax: 204/669-9821; Email: morgant@cdnrwymod.com; URL: http://www/cdnrwymod.com – Circ.: 24,000; 6 times a year – Editor, Morgan B. Turney; Editor, John Longhurst; Circulation Manager, Dianne Williams

Canadian Sportscard Collector (Published by Trajan Publishing Corp.), #202, 103 Lakeshore Rd., St Catharines ON L2N 2T6 – 905/646-7744; Fax: 905/646-0995; Email: newsroom@trajan.com; URL: http://www.trajan.com/trajan – Circ.: 25,000; Monthly – Editor, Baron Bedesky

Canadian Stamp News (Published by Trajan Publishing Corp.), #202, 103 Lakeshore Rd., St Catharines ON L2N 2T6 – 905/646-7744; Fax: 905/646-0995; Email: newsroom@trajan.com; URL: http://www.trajan.com/trajan – 26 times a year – Publisher, Paul Fiocca; Editor, Ellen Rodger; Circulation Manager, Tammy Kruck

Canadian Workshop (Published by Camar Publications), 130 Spy Ct., Markham ON L3R 5H6 – 905/475-8440; Fax: 905/475-9246; Email: letters@canadianworkshop.ca; URL: http://www.canadianworkshop.ca – Circ.: 113,000; 11 times a year – Publisher, Phil Whalen; Editor, Tom Hopkins

ÉCHEC+, c/o La Fédération Québécoise des Échecs, CP 640, Succ C, Montréal QC H2L 4L5 – 514/252-3034; Fax: 514/251-8038; Email: fqechec@cam.org; URL: http://www.cam.org/~iqechec/index.html – Tirage: 1,800; 6 fois par an; français – Rédacteur, Jean Hébert; Directeur de tirage, Richard Bérubé

Model Aviation Canada, 5100 South Service Rd., Unit 9, Burlington ON L7L 6A5 – 905/632-9808; Fax: 905/632-3304; URL: http://www.maac.ca – Circ.: 12,600; 6 times a year – Editor, Henry Zwolak, 905/688-1887

Philatélie Québec, Les Editions Phibec inc., CP 1000, Succ M, Montréal QC H1V 3R2 – 514/252-3035; Fax: 514/251-8038 – Tirage: 1,500; 6 fois par an; français – Rédacteur, Jean-Pierre Durard

### HOMES

Build & Green, #D, 2922 West 6th Ave., Vancouver BC V6K 1X3 – 604/730-1940; Fax: 604/730-7860; Email: buildgrn@dowco.com – Circ.: 30,000; 9 times a year – Publisher & Editor, Leonard Wexler

The Canadian Home Planner (Published by Family Communications Inc.), #1, 37 Hanna Ave., Toronto ON M6K 1W9 – 416/537-2604; Fax: 416/538-1794; Email: family@interlog.com; sales@todaysbride.ca; URL: http://www/todaysbride.ca – Circ.: 100,000; 2 times a year – Publisher, Donald Swinburne

Canadian House & Home (Published by Canadian Home Publishers), #120, 511 King St. West, Toronto ON M5V 2Z4 – 416/593-0204; Fax: 416/591-1630; Email: mail@canadianhouseandhome.com; URL: http://www.canadianhouseandhome.com – Circ.: 140,000; 8 times a year – Publisher, Jennifer McLean; Editor, Cobi Ladner; President, Lynda Reeves

Canadian Living (Published by Telemedia Publishing), #100, 25 Sheppard Ave. West, North York ON M2N 6S7 – 416/733-7600; Fax: 416/733-3398; Email: canadianliving@telemedia.org; URL: http://www.canadianliving.com – Circ.: 563,000; 12 times a year – Publisher, Caren King; Editor-in-chief, Bonnie Baker Cowan; Circulation Manager, Darlene Storey

Century Home, Bluestone House Inc., 12 Mill St. South, Port Hope ON L1A 2S5 – 905/885-2449; Fax: 905/885-5355; Email: chome@eagle.ca – Circ.: 35,000; 7 times a year – Publisher & Editor, J. Rumgay

Classic Home (Published by Giroux Publishing), 102 Ellis St., Penticton BC V2A 4L5 – 250/493-0942; Fax: 250/493-7526; Email: cgiroux@awinc.com – Circ.: 10,000; Annually – Publisher, G.T. Giroux; Editor, Michael A. Giroux

Condos de Rêves (Published by Groupe Magazines S.A. Inc.), #300, 275, boul des Braves, Terrebonne QC J6W 3H6 – 514/964-7590; Fax: 514/964-2327; Email: magazine@magazinesa.com – Annuellement; français – Editeur, Denis Clermont

Décoration Chez-Soi (Published by Publicor), 7, ch Bates, Outremont QC H2V 1A6 – 514/270-1100; Fax: 514/270-9618 – Tirage: 63,000; 10 fois par an; français – Directeur, Pierre Deschènes

Décormag (Published by Les Editions du Feu vert), 5148, boul St-Laurent, Montréal QC H2T 1R8 – 514/273-9773; Fax: 514/273-9034 – Tirage: 60,000; 10 fois par an; français – Editrice, Michèle Dubreuil; Rédactrice, Michèle Deraîche; Directrice de tirage, Sylvie Hamel

Del Condominium Life, 4800 Dufferin St., Downsview ON M3H 5S9 – 416/661-3151; Fax: 416/661-8653 – Circ.: 25,000; 3 times a year – Editor-in-chief, Andre Pilish

Designers' Best Home Plans (Published by Giroux Publishing), 102 Ellis St., Penticton BC V2A 4L5 – 250/493-0942; Fax: 250/493-7526; Email: cgiroux@awinc.com – Circ.: 10,000; Annually – Publisher, G.T. Giroux; Editor-in-chief, Michael A. Giroux

First Home Buyer's Guide (Published by Homes for Sale Magazine Ltd.), 178 Main St., Unionville ON L3R 2G9 – 905/479-4663; Fax: 905/479-4482 – Circ.: 300,000; 2 times a year – Publisher, Michael Rosset; Editor, Risë Levy; Circulation Manager, Natalie Armstrong

Habitabec Plus, 8620, rue Berri, Montréal QC H2P 2G4 – 514/389-5943; Fax: 514/385-5982 – 48 times a year; English & French – President & Executive Editor, Jacques Dery

Homes & Cottages, The In-Home Show, #D, 6557 Mississauga Rd., Mississauga ON L5N 1A6 – 905/567-1440; Fax: 905/567-1442; Email: janhre@pathcom.com; URL: http://www.homesandcottages.com – Circ.: 55,000; 8 times a year – Publisher, Steven Griffin; Editor, Janice Naisbly; Circulation, Margaret Good

Homes Magazine (Published by Homes for Sale Magazine Ltd.), 178 Main St., Unionville ON L3R 2G9 – 905/479-4663; Fax: 905/479-4482 – Circ.: 100,000; 8 times a year – Publisher, Michael Rosset; Editor, Risë Levy; Circulation Manager, Natalie Armstrong

Les Idées de ma maison (Published by Publicor), 7, ch Bates, Outremont QC H2V 1A6 – 514/270-1100; Fax: 514/270-6900 – Tirage: 68,000; 10 fois par an; français – Rédactrice, Béatrix Marik

Kitchens & Baths (Published by Maclean Hunter Publishing), 777 Bay St., Toronto ON M5W 1A7 – 416/596-5425; Fax: 416/593-3197; Email: adraycott@chatelaine.com – Annual – Publisher, Lee Simpson; Editor, Anita Draycott

Maison d'aujourd'hui, 3390, boul Métropolitain est, Montréal QC H2A 1A4 – 514/729-0000; Fax: 514/729-2552; Email: courrier@maisondirect.com; URL: http://www.maisondirect.com – Circ.: 22,500; Annual – President, Phillippe Massé

Maître d'Oeuvre (Published by Groupe Ro-na Dismat), 1250, rue Nob, Boucherville QC J4B 5K1 – 514/599-5106; Fax: 514/599-5161 – 2 fois par an; français – Rédacteur en chef, Marcel Soucy

Master Builder (Published by Groupe Ro-na Dismat), 1250, rue Nob, Boucherville QC J4B 5K1 – 514/599-5106; Fax: 514/599-5157 – 2 times a year – Publisher, Daniel Therrien

Muskoka Sun Real Estate Guide, Muskoka Publications Group Inc., PO Box 1600, Bracebridge ON P1L 1V6 – 705/645-4463; Fax: 705/645-3928 – Circ.: 8,713, winter; 22,274, summer; Weekly – Publisher, Donald F. Smith

Plaisirs de vivre/Living in Style, Marekting U.S.P. Inc., 554 Grosvenor Ave., Westmount QC H3Y 2S4 – 514/935-1171; Fax: 514/935-4504 – Circ.: 66,390; 5 times a year – Publisher, Danièle Adam; Editor, Monic Robillard

Plans de Maisons du Québec (Published by Publicor), 7, ch Bates, Outremont QC H2V 1A6 – 514/270-1100; Fax: 514/270-6900 – Tirage: 27,000; 4 fois par an; français – Rédacteur, Claude Leclerc

Practical Homes Home Plans (Published by Giroux Publishing), 102 Ellis St., Penticton BC V2A 4L5 – 250/493-0942; Fax: 250/493-7526; Email: cgiroux@awinc.com – Circ.: 10,000; Annually – Publisher, G.T. Giroux; Editor-in-chief, Michael A. Giroux

Proven & Popular Home Plans (Published by Giroux Publishing), 102 Ellis St., Penticton BC V2A 4L5 – 250/493-0942; Fax: 250/493-7526; Email: cgiroux@awinc.com – Circ.: 10,000; Annually – Publisher, G.T. Giroux; Editor-in-chief, Michael A. Giroux

Real Estate News, 159 Kern Rd., North York ON M3B 1S9 – 416/443-8113; Fax: 416/443-9185 – Circ.: 74,000; Weekly – Vice President & General Manager, Mark Shaprio; Editorial Coordinator, Robert Jones

Real Estate Victoria, Monday Publications, 1609 Blanshard St., Victoria BC V8W 2J5 – 250/382-9171; Fax: 250/382-9172 – Circ.: 25,000; Weekly – Publisher, Andrew Lynch; Editor, Glenda Turner

Rénovation Bricolage (Published by Publicor), 7, ch Bates, Outremont QC H2V 1A6 – 514/270-1100; Fax: 514/270-6900 – Tirage: 34 886; 9 fois par an; français – Rédacteur, Claude LeClerc

Renovation Magazine (Published by Homes for Sale Magazine Ltd.), 178 Main St., Unionville ON L3R 2G9 – 905/479-4663; Fax: 905/479-4482; Email: house@homesmag.com – Circ.: 50,000; 2 times a year – Publisher, Michael Rosset; Editor, Risë Levy; Circulation Manager, Natalie Armstrong

Select Home Designs, #301, 611 Alexander St., Vancouver BC V6A 1E1 – 604/879-4144; Fax: 604/251-3212; Email: selecthomedesigns@msn.com; URL: http://www.selectaplan.com – Circ.: 150,000; 2 times a year – Publisher, Brian Thorn; Editor, Brant Furdyk

Style at Home: Canada's Decorating Magazine (Published by Telemedia Publishing), #100, 25 Sheppard Ave. West, North York ON M2N 6S7 – 416/733-7600; Fax: 416/218-3632; Email: letters@styleathome.com – Circ.: 145,000; 8 times a year – Publisher, Kerry Mitchell; Editor, Gail Johnston Habs

Thunder Bay Real Estate News (Published by North Superior Publishing Inc.), 1145 Barton St., Thunder Bay ON P7B 5N3 – 807/623-2348; Fax: 807/623-7515; Email: nsuperior@norlink.net – Circ.: 30,000; Weekly – Scott A. Sumnor

Touchez-Dubois, 1001, Bromont, Longueuil QC J4M 2P9 – 514/674-6668; Fax: 514/674-6658 – Tirage: 30,000; 10 fois par an – Rédacteur, Robert Dubois

Welcome Home (Published by Maclean Hunter Publishing), 777 Bay St., Toronto ON M5W 1A7 – 416/596-5425; Fax: 416/593-3197; Email: adraycott@chatelaine.com – Circ.: 150,000; Annually, April – Publisher, Lee Simpson; Editor, Anita Draycott

Winnipeg Homes & Lifestyles, 444 Brooklyn St., Winnipeg MB M3J 1M7 – 204/885-5577; Fax: 204/889-2015 – 4 times a year – Publisher, Fred H. Glazerman

**HORSES, RIDING & BREEDING**

Atlantic Horse & Pony, PO Box 1509, Liverpool NS B0T 1K0 – 902/354-3321 – 6 times a year – Editor, Dirk van Loon

Canadian Arabian News, Canadian Arabian Horse Registry, #801 Terrace Plaza, 4445 Calgary Trail, Edmonton AB T6H 4R7 – 403/436-4244; Fax: 403/438-2971 – Circ.: 2,200; 6 times a year – Editor, Peggy Arthurs

Canadian Horseman (Published by Corinthian Publishing Co. Ltd.), 225 Industrial Pkwy. South, PO Box 670, Aurora ON L4G 4J9 – 905/727-0107; Fax: 905/841-1530; Email: horsepower@horsenet.com; URL: http://www.horsenet.com – 6 times a year – Publisher, Susan Jane Anstey; Editor, Lee Benson

The Canadian Sportsman, 25 Old Plank Rd., PO Box 129, Straffordville ON N0J 1Y0 – 519/866-5558; Fax: 519/866-5596; Email: cdnsport@nornet.on.ca – 26 times a year – Editor, Gary Foerster

Canadian Thoroughbred (Published by Corinthian Publishing Co. Ltd.), 225 Industrial Pkwy. South, PO Box 670, Aurora ON L4G 4J9 – 905/727-0107; Fax: 905/841-1530; Email: horsepower@horsenet.com; URL: http://www.horsenet.com – 6 times a year – Publisher, Susan Jane Anstey; Editor, Lee Benson

Le Courrier Hippique, Sportam Inc., 4545, av Pierre-de-Coubertin, CP 1000, Succ M, Montréal QC H1V 3R2 – 514/252-3030; Fax: 514/252-3165; Email: feq@sumpatico.ca – 6 fois par an; français – Directeur général, Richard Mongeau; Publicité, Jocelyne Lortie

Horse Action International, Whitehouse Publishing Co., PO Box 1778, Vernon BC V1T 8C3 – 250/545-9896; Fax: 250/545-9896; Email: whitehouse@junction.net – Circ.: 20,000 – Publisher & Editor, Dr. B.J. (Jan) White

The Horse Chronicle, Grace Publishing, RR#1, Orillia ON L3V 6H1 – Fax: 705/325-6639 – 6 times a year – Publisher & Editor, John D. Kennedy

Horse & Country Canada, Equine Communications & Publications, 8B Sweetnam Dr., Stittsville ON K2S 1A2 – 613/831-2928; Fax: 613/831-0240 – Circ.: 9,000; 6 times a year – Publisher & Editor, Judith H. McCartney

Horsepower: Magazine for Young Horse Lovers (Published by Corinthian Publishing Co. Ltd.), 225 Industrial Pkwy. South, PO Box 670, Aurora ON L4G 4J9 – 905/727-0107; Fax: 905/841-1530; Email: horsepower@horsenet.com; URL: http://www.horsenet.com – Circ.: 20,000; 6 times a year – Publisher, Susan Jane Anstey; Editor, Susan Stafford

Horses All, 278 - 19th St. NE, Calgary AB T2E 8P7 – 403/248-9993; Fax: 403/248-1001; Email: nhpubs@netway.ab.ca – Circ.: 10,000; Monthly – Publisher, Steven Mark; Editor, Vanessa Peterelli; Circulation Manager, Michelle Zaparaniuk

Horse Sport (Published by Corinthian Publishing Co. Ltd.), 225 Industrial Pkwy. South, PO Box 670, Aurora ON L4G 4J9 – 905/727-0107; Fax: 905/841-1530 – Circ.: 10,000; 12 times a year – Publisher, Susan Jane Anstey; Editor, Susan Stafford; Circulation Manager, Karin Appel

Pacific Horse Journal, 10148 Bowerbank Rd., Sidney BC V8L 3T9 – 450/655-8883; Fax: 450/655-8883; Email: pachorse_main@bc.sympatico.ca; URL: http://www.ibnd.com/horsejnl – Circ.: 20,000; 11 times a year – Co-Publisher, Marina Sacht; Editor & Co-Publisher, Kathy Smith

The Rider, 491 Book Rd. West, Ancaster ON L9G 3L1 – 905/648-2035; Fax: 905/648-6977 – Circ.: 9,000; 10 times a year – Publisher, Aidan Finn; Editor, Barry Finn

Trot, c/o Canadian Trotting Association, 2150 Meadowvale Blvd., Mississauga ON L5N 6R6 – 905/858-3060; Fax: 905/858-3111; Email: troton@ican.net – Monthly – Editor, Harold Howe

**LABOUR, TRADE UNIONS**

Our Times, #201A, 1209 King St. West, Toronto ON M6K 1G2 – 416/531-6877 – 6 times a year – Editor, Lorraine Endicott

Socialist Worker, PO Box 339, Stn E, Toronto ON M6H 4E3 – 416/972-6391; Fax: 416/972-6319; Email: sworker@web.net – 24 times a year; ISSN 0836-7094 – Editor, Paul Kellogg

**LITERARY**

absinthe, PO Box 61113, Stn Kensington PO, Calgary AB T2N 4S6; URL: http://www.ucalgary.ca/~amathur/absinthe.html – 2 times a year

The Antigonish Review, St. Francis Xavier University, PO Box 5000, Antigonish NS B2G 2W5 – 902/867-3962; Fax: 902/867-5153; Email: tar@stfx.ca – Circ.: 800; 4 times a year – Editor, George Sanderson

ARC: Canada's National Poetry Magazine, PO Box 7368, Ottawa ON K1L 8E4 – Circ.: 800; 2 times a year; ISSN: 0705-6397 – Co-Editor, John Barton; Co-Editor, Rita Donovan

Blood & Aphorisms, PO Box 702, Stn P, Toronto ON M5S 2Y4 – 416/535-1233; Email: blood@io.org; URL: http://www.io.org/~blood – Circ.: 2,500; 4 times a year – Publisher, Tim Paleczny

Books in Canada, 30A Hazelton Ave., Toronto ON M5R 2E2 – 416/924-2777; Email: BinC@istar.ca – Circ.: 8,000; 9 times a year; ISSN: 0045-2564 – Co-Publisher, Adrian Stein; Editor, Norman Doidge; Managing Editor, Gerald Owen

Brick: A Literary Journal, PO Box 537, Stn Q, Toronto ON M4T 2M5 – 3 times a year; ISSN: 0382-8565

Canadian Fiction Magazine, Quarry Press, PO Box 1061, Kingston ON L7L 4Y5 – 613/548-8429; Fax: 613/548-1556 – Circ.: 2,000; 2 times a year; ISSN: 0045-477X – Editor, Geoff Hancock

The Capilano Review, 2055 Purcell Way, North Vancouver BC V7J 3H5 – 604/984-1712; Fax: 604/984-4985; Email: erains@capcollege.bc.ca; URL: http://www.capcollege.bc.ca/departments.tcr/tcr.html – Circ.: 900; 3 times a year; ISSN: 0315-3754 – Editor, Robert Sherrin; Circulation Manager, Elizabeth Rains

Carousel, c/o University of Guelph, #217, University Centre, Guelph ON N1G 2W1 – 519/824-4120, ext.6748; Fax: 519/673-9603; Email: daniel@uoguelph.ca – Circ.: 600; Annually; ISSN: 0835-7994 – Editor, Daniel Evans

The Chesterton Review, c/o STM College, 1437 College Dr., Saskatoon SK S7N 0W6 – 306/966-8917; Fax: 306/966-8917; Email: morrisj@duke.usask.ca – Circ.: 1,700; 4 times a year; ISSN: 0317-0505 – Editor, Rev. J. Ian Boyd, C.S.B.; Circulation Manager, Jane Morris

The Claremont Review, Claremont Review Publishers, 4980 Wesley Rd., Victoria BC V8Y 1Y9 – 250/658-5221; Fax: 250/658-5387; Email: reviewd@claremont.victoria.bc.ca; URL: http://206.12.151.253 – Circ.: 1,500; 2 times a year – Co-Editor, Bill Stenson

The Dalhousie Review, c/o Dalhousie University, 1456 Henry St., Halifax NS B3H 3J5 – 902/494-2541; Fax: 902/494-3561; Email: dalrev@ac.dal.ca – Circ.: 700; 3 times a year – Editor, Ronald Hubert

Dandelion, Dandelion Magazine Society, #303, 223 - 12th Ave. SW, Calgary AB T2R 0G9 – 403/265-0524 – Circ.: 750; 2 times a year; ISSN 0383-9275

Descant, Descant Arts & Letters Foundation, PO Box 314, Stn P, Toronto ON M5S 2S8 – 416/593-2557 –

Circ.: 1,100; 4 times a year – Editor, Karen Mulhallen

Exile, PO Box 67, Stn B, Toronto ON M5T 2C0 – 416/969-9556 – Circ.: 1,200; 4 times a year – Publisher & Editor, Barry Callaghan

The Fiddlehead, Campus House, University of New Brunswick, PO Box 4400, Stn A, Fredericton NB E3B 5A3 – 506/453-3501; Fax: 506/453-4599 – Circ.: 1,000; 4 times a year – Editor, Ross Leckie; Circulation Manager, S. Campbell

Geist, #103, 1014 Homer St., Vancouver BC V6B 2W9 – 604/681-9161; Fax: 604/669-8250; Email: geist@geist.com – Circ.: 5,000; 4 times a year – Publisher, Stephen Osborne; Editor, Kevin Barefoot

Grain, Saskatchewan Writers Guild, PO Box 1154, Regina SK S4P 3B4 – 306/244-2828; Fax: 306/244-0255; Email: grain.mag@sk.sympatico.ca; URL: http://www.sasknet.com/corporate/skwriter – Circ.: 1,500; 4 times a year – Editor, J.Jill Robinson

Interculture, 4917, rue Saint-Urbain, Montréal QC H2T 2W1 – 514/288-7229; Fax: 514/844-6800 – Circ.: 1,000; 2 times a year; English & French editions; ISSN: 0828-797X – Publisher & Editor, Robert Vachon; Circulation Manager, André Giguere

Literary Review of Canada, 3266 Yonge St., PO Box 1830, Toronto ON M4N 3P6 – Fax: 416/322-4852 – Circ.: 2,000; 11 times a year – Publisher & Editor, P.A. Dutil

The Malahat Review, University of Victoria, PO Box 1700, Victoria BC V8W 2Y2 – 250/721-8524; Fax: 250/721-8653; Email: malahat@uvic.ca – Circ.: 1,800; 4 times a year – Editor, Derk Wynand

Matrix, #LB509-7, 1400, boul de Maisonneuve ouest, Montréal QC H3G 1M8 – 514/848-2340; Fax: 514/848-4501 – 2 times a year; ISSN 0318-3610

The Mystery Review, PO Box 233, Colborne ON K0K 1S0 – 613/475-4440; Fax: 613/475-3400; Email: 71554.551@compuserve.com; URL: http://www:inline-online.com/mystery/ – Circ.: 2.500; 4 times a year – Publisher, Christian von Hessert; Editor, Barbara Davey

The New Quarterly, c/o English Language Proficiency Programme, PAS 2082, U of Waterloo, 200 University Ave. West, Waterloo ON N2L 3G1 – 519/885-1211, ext.2837; Email: mmerikle@watarts.uwaterloo.ca – Circ.: 400; 4 times a year – Managing Editor, Mary Merikle

Nuit Blanche, #403, 1026, rue St-Jean, Québec QC G1R 1R7 – 418/692-1354; Fax: 418/692-1355; URL: http://www.qbc.clic.net/~carl/nuit/nuit.html – Tirage: 5,000; 4 fois par an; français – Rédacteur, Alain Lessard

On Spec: The Canadian Magazine of Speculative Writing, The Copper Pig Writers' Society, PO Box 4727, Edmonton AB T6E 5G6 – 403/413-0215; Fax: 403/413-0215; Email: onspec@earthling.net; URL: http://www.greenwoods.com/onspec/ – Circ.: 2,000; 4 times a year – Publisher's Assistant, Katerina Carastathis

paperplates, 19 Kenwood Ave., Toronto ON M6C 2R8 – 416/651-2551; Fax: 416/651-2910; Email: beekelly@perkolator.com; URL: http://www.hookup.net/~beekelly – 2/3 issues a year; ISSN: 1183-3742 – Publisher & Editor, Bernard Kelly; Circulation Manager, Dan Yashinsky

Paragraph: The Canadian Fiction Review, The Mercury Press, 137 Birmingham St., Stratford ON N5A 2T1 – 519/273-7932; Fax: 519/273-7932 – Circ.: 1,200; 3 times a year – Editor, Beverley Daurio

Poetry Canada, PO Box 1061, Kingston ON K7L 4Y5 – 613/548-8429; Fax: 613/548-1556 – Circ.: 1,750; 4 times a year; ISSN: 0709-3373 – Publisher, Bob Hilderley; Editor, Barry Dempster

Pottersfield Portfolio, The Gatsby Press, PO Box 27094, Halifax NS B3H 4M8 – 902/443-9178; Fax: 902/443-9178; Email: saundc@auracom.com; URL: http://www.auracom.com/~saundc/potters.html – Circ.: 500; 3 times a year – Editor, Ian Colford

Prairie Fire, Prairie Fire Press Inc., #423, 100 Arthur St., Winnipeg MB R3B 1H3 – 204/943-9066; Fax: 204/942-1555 – Circ.: 1,400; 4 times a year; ISSN: 0821-1124 – Editor, Andris Taskand; Circulation Manager, Heidi Harms

Prairie Journal, Prairie Journal Press, PO Box 61203, Stn Brentwood, Calgary AB T2L 2K6 – Circ.: 600; 2 times a year – A. Burke

Prism International, #E462, Dept. of Creative Writing, UBC, 1866 Main Mall, Vancouver BC V6T 1Z1 – 604/822-2514; Email: prism@unixg.ubc.ca; URL: http://www.arts.ubc.ca/crwr/prism/prism.html – 4 times a year – Executive Editor, Tim Mitchell

Quarry, PO Box 1061, Kingston ON K7L 4Y5 – 613/548-8429; Fax: 613/548-1556 – Circ.: 1,200; 3 times a year; ISSN: 0033-5266 – Publisher, Bob Hilderley; Editor, Mary Cameron

Raddle Moon, #518, 350 East 2nd Ave., Vancouver BC V5T 4R8 – Circ.: 700; 2 times a year – Editor, Susan Clark

The Readers Showcase (Published by Suggitt Publishing Ltd.), 10608 - 172 St., Edmonton AB T5S 1H8 – 403/486-5802; Fax: 403/481-9276; Email: suggitt@planet.eon.net; URL: http://www.wwr/.com/suggitt – Circ.: 300,000; 6 times a year – Publisher, Thomas J. Suggitt; Editor, Tanis Nessler

sub-TERRAIN Magazine, sub-TERRAIN Literary Collective Society, PO Box 1575, Stn Bentall Ctr., Vancouver BC V6C 2P7 – 604/876-8710; Fax: 604/879-2667; Email: subter@pinc.com – Circ.: 3,000; 4 issues a year – Managing Editor, Brian Kaufman

TickleAce, PO Box 5353, St. John's NF A1C 5W2 – 709/754-6610; Fax: 709/754-5579; Email: tickleace@nfld.com – Circ.: 1,000; 2 times a year – Editor, Bruce Porter

The Toronto Review of Contemporary Writing Abroad, PO Box 6996, Stn A, Toronto ON M5W 1X7 – 416/483-7191; Fax: 416/486-0706; Email: treview@astral.magic.ca; URL: http://www.candesign.com/tsarbooks – 3 times a year – Editor, M.C. Vassanji

West Coast Line, West Coast Review Publishing Society, 2027 East Academic Annex, Simon Fraser University, Burnaby BC V5A 1S6 – 604/291-4287; Fax: 604/291-5737 – Circ.: 600; 3 times a year – Editor, Roy Miki; Managing Editor, Jacqueline Larson

Whetstone, c/o University of Lethbridge, 4401 University Dr., Lethbridge AB T1K 3M4 – 403/329-2367; Fax: 403/329-5130 – Circ.: 1,000; 2 times a year – Editor, TheresaMarie Tougas

White Wall Review, 63 Gould St., Toronto ON M5B 1E9 – 416/977-1045; Fax: 416/977-7709 – Annually; ISSN: 0712-8991

### MUSIC

Access Magazine, Trafalgar Publications, 109 Morse St., Toronto ON M4M 2P7 – 416/465-9718; Fax: 416/465-6876 – Circ.: 88,000; 10 times a year – Publisher/Editor, Keith Sharp

Bluegrass Canada Magazine, #1, 231 Victoria St., Kamloops BC V2C 2A1 – 250/374-3313; Fax: 250/374-0304 – 6 times a year; ISSN 0035-8495

Canadian Musician (Published by Norris-Whitney Communications Inc.), #7, 23 Hannover Dr., St Catharines ON L2W 1A3 – 905/641-3471; Fax: 905/641-1648; Email: info@nor.com; URL: http://nor.com.cm – Circ.: 30,000; 6 times a year – Publisher, Jim Norris; Consumer Services Director, Maureen Jack

CD Plus Compact Disc Catalogue, 766 Gordon Baker Rd., Willowdale ON M2H 3B4 – 416/490-8850; Fax: 416/490-9662; Email: deve@cd-plus.com; URL: http://www.cd-plus.com – Annual – Publisher, David Cubitt

Chart, Chart Communications Inc., #200, 41 Britain St., Toronto ON M5A 1R7 – 416/363-3101; Fax: 416/363-3109; Email: chart@chartnet.com; URL: http://www.chartnet.com – Circ.: 20,000; Monthly – Co-Publisher, Edward Skira; Co-Publisher, Nada Laskovski

Classical Music Magazine, 81 Lakeshore Rd. East, PO Box 45045, Mississauga ON L5G 4S7 – 905/271-0339; Fax: 905/271-9748; Email: music@inforamp.net; URL: http://www.cmpa.ca/pa3.html – 4 times a year; ISSN: 1185-9717 – Publisher, Anthony D. Copperthwaite; Editor, Derek Deroy

Coda Magazine, PO Box 1002, Stn O, Toronto ON M4A 2N4 – 416/593-7230; Fax: 416/593-7230; Email: codawest@mars.ark.com – Circ.: 3,000; 6 times a year – Publisher, John Norris; Editor, William E. Smith

Country, RR#1, Holstein ON N0G 2A0 – 519/334-3246; Fax: 519/334-3366 – Circ.: 25,000; 6 times a year – Editor/Publisher, Jim Baine

Country Music News, PO Box 7323, Stn Vanier Terminal, Ottawa ON K1L 8E4 – 613/745-6006; Fax: 613/745-0576 – Circ.: 12,500; Monthly – Publisher & Editor, Larry Delaney

Crescendo, Toronto Musicians' Assn., 101 Thorncliffe Park Dr., Toronto ON M4H 1M2 – 416/421-1020; Fax: 416/421-7011 – Circ.: 4,000; 4 times a year – Editor, Joe Macerollo; Circulation Manager, Richard Mendonca

Heart of the Country, 56A Brybeck Circle, Kitchener ON N2M 2C6 – 519/624-8682; Fax: 519/624-8933; Email: hotc1@golden.net; URL: http://www.golden.net/~hotc1 – Circ.: 10,000; Monthly – Editor, Warren Murchie

Le Musicien, 439, rue Ste-Hélène, Longueuil QC J4K 3R3 – 514/928-1726; Fax: 514/670-8683 – Tirage: 13 000; 6 fois par an – Editeur et Rédacteur, Ralph Angelillo; Directeur de tirage, Serge Gamache

Music in our Lives, The Royal Conservatory of Music, 273 Bloor St. West, Toronto ON M5S 1W2 – 416/408-2824; Fax: 416/698-7081; Email: good@inforamp.net – Circ.: 40,000; 4 times a year – Publisher, Ann Francis Oakes; Editor, Louise Yearwood; Director of Circulation, Deborah Wood

Musicworks: The Journal of Sound Explorations, 179 Richmond St. West, 3rd Fl., Toronto ON M5V 1V3 – 416/977-3546; Fax: 416/204-1084 – Circ.: 2,000; 3 times a year; English & French; ISSN:0225-686X – Editor, Gayle Young

Opera Canada, Foundation for Coast to Coast Opera Publication, #434, 366 Adelaide St. East, Toronto ON M5A 3X9 – 416/363-0395; Fax: 416/363-0395 – Circ.: 5,000; 4 times a year

Top Forty Focus (Published by Suggitt Publishing Ltd.), 10608 - 172 St., Edmonton AB T5S 1H8 – 403/486-5802; Fax: 403/481-9276; Email: suggitt@planet.eon.net – Circ.: 50,000; 6 times a year – Publisher, Thomas J. Suggitt; Editor, Tanis Nessler

The Valley Circle, c/o Fraser Valley Square & Round Dance Association, 13665 - 88th Ave., Surrey BC V3W 6H1 – 604/594-6415 – Circ.: 2,500; 9 times a year – Editor, Alex Galbraith; Editor, Jean Galbraith

### NEWS

7 Jours (Published by Trustar Ltd.), #2000, 2020, rue University, Montréal QC H5A 2A5 – 514/848-7000; Fax: 514/848-9854 – Tirage: 166,366; Hebdomadaire – Publisher, Claude J. Charron

L'Actualité (Published by Maclean Hunter Publishing), 1001, boul de Maisonneuve ouest, Montréal QC H3A 3E1 – 514/843-2567; Fax: 514/845-3879; Email: actcour@lactualite.com; URL: http://www.lactualite.com – Tirage: 205,514; 20 fois par an; français – Editeur, Jean Paré

Alberta/Western Report, 17327 - 106A Ave., Edmonton AB T5S 1M7 – 403/486-2277; Fax: 403/489-3280 – Circ.: 43,603; Weekly – Publisher & Editor, Link Byfield

British Columbia Report, #600, 535 Thurlow St., Vancouver BC V6E 3L2 – 604/682-8202; Fax: 604/682-0963; Email: bcreport@axionet.com; URL: http://www.axionet.com/bcreport – Circ.: 27,000; Weekly – Publisher, Ted Byfield; Editor-in-chief, Terry O'Neill

The G-7 Report, PO Box 824, Stn Q, Toronto ON M4T 2N7 – 416/699-3530 – Circ.: 18,800; 4 times a year – Publishers & Editor, William B.Z. Vukson

Maclean's (Published by Maclean Hunter Publishing), 777 Bay St., Toronto ON M5W 1A7 – 416/596-5311, 5386; Fax: 416/596-6001; Email: 76702.2251@compuserve.com; URL: http://www.canoe.ca/macleans – Circ.: 510,000; Weekly; also Chinese edition co-published six times a year with Sing Tao Daily; ISSN: 0024-9262 – Publisher, Brian Segal; Editor-in-chief, Robert Lewis; Managing Editor, Geoffrey Stevens

Southern Africa Report, 603 1/2 Parliament St., Toronto ON M4X 1P9 – 416/967-5562; Fax: 416/978-1547; Email: tclsac@web.apg.org; vise@physics.utoronto.ca – 4 times a year; ISSN: 0820-5582

Time, Time Canada Ltd., #602, 175 Bloor St. East, Toronto ON M4W 3R8 – 416/929-1115; Fax: 416/929-0019 – Circ.: 327,000; Weekly – Managing Director, Sandra F. Berry

Ven'd'est, L'Editions coopératives du ven'd'est ltée, 725, rue de Collège, CP 266, Bathurst NB E2A 3Z2 – 506/548-4097; Fax: 506/545-6299 – Tirage: 4,500; 6 fois par an; français – Rédacteur, Michel St-Onge

**PHOTOGRAPHY**

Blackflash, P.G. Press, 12 - 23rd St. East, 2nd Fl., Saskatoon SK S7K 0H5 – 306/244-8018; Fax: 306/665-6568 – Circ.: 1,300; 4 times a year; ISSN: 0826-3922 – Editor, Wallace Polsom

CV Photo, Productions Ciel Variable, #301, 4060, boul Saint-Laurent, Montréal QC H2W 1Y9 – 514/849-0508; Fax: 514/284-6775; Email: vpopuli@cam.org; URL: http://www.cam.org/~vpopuli – Circ.: 900; 4 times a year; English & French – Publisher, Marcel Blouin; Editor, Franck Michel

Photo Life, Apex Publications, Toronto-Dominion Ctr., PO Box 77, Toronto ON M5K 1E7 – Email: apex@photolife.com; Toll Free Fax: 1-800-664-2739; URL: http://www.photolife.com – Circ.: 45,000; 6 times a year – Publisher, Curtis J. Sommerville; Editor, Jacques Thibault; Circulation Manager, Jeffrey A. Sommerville

Photo Sélection (Published by Les Publications Apex inc.), 185, rue St-Paul, Québec QC G1K 3W2 – 418/692-2110; Fax: 418/692-3392 – Tirage: 17,000; 6 fois par an; français, – Editeur, Curtis J. Sommerville; Rédacteur, Jacques Thibault

**POLITICAL**

bout de papier, #412, 47 Clarence St., Ottawa ON K1N 9K1 – 613/241-1391; Fax: 613/241-5911 – 4 times a year; English & French

Briarpatch, 2138 McIntyre St., Regina SK S4P 2R7 – 306/525-2949; Fax: 306/565-3430 – Circ.: 2,000; 10 times a year – Managing Editor, George Manz

Canadian Speeches: Issues of the Day, 194 King St., PO Box 250, Woodville ON K0M 2T0 – 705/439-2580; Fax: 705/439-1208 – 10 times a year – Publisher & Editor, Earle Grey

Kick it Over, PO Box 5811, Stn A, Toronto ON M5W 1P2 – 416/766-0972; Email: kio@web.apc.ord – Circ.: 1,600; 4 times a year; ISSN: 0823-6526 – Editor, Bob Melcombe

Pacific Current, Pacific New Directions Publishing Society, PO Box 34279, Stn D, Vancouver BC V6J 4P2 – 604/873-1739; Fax: 604/875-1403 – Circ.: 2,000; 6 times a year; ISSN: 1198-838X – Editor, Geoff Meggs

Peace Magazine, 736 Bathurst St., Toronto ON M5S 2R4 – 416/533-7581; Fax: 416/531-6214; Email: mspencer@web.net; URL: http://www.peacemagazine.org – Circ.: 3,000; 6 times a year – Publisher & Editor, Metta Spencer; Circulation Manager, Brian Burch

**RELIGIOUS & DENOMINATIONAL**

The Anglican, 135 Adelaide St. East, Toronto ON M5C 1L8 – 416/604-0082; Fax: 416/604-9409 – Monthly – Editor, Stuart Mann

Anglican Journal, c/o Anglican Church of Canada, 600 Jarvis St., Toronto ON M4Y 2J6 – 416/924-9199; Fax: 416/921-4452 (editorial), 925-8811 (circ. & adv.); Email: anglican_journal@ecunet.org – Circ.: 250,000; 10 times a year – Business Manager, Larry Gee; Editor, Rev. David Harris; Circulation Manager, Beverley Murphy

The Atlantic Baptist, PO Box 756, Kentville NS B4N 3X9 – 902/681-6868; Fax: 902/681-0315; Email: gdunfiel@fox.nstn.ca – Circ.: 7,000; Monthly – Editor, Gary Dunfield; Associate Editor, Andrew Steeves

Canada Lutheran, 1512 St. James St., Winnipeg MB R3H 0L2 – 204/786-6707; Fax: 204/783-7548 – Circ.: 20,000; 9 times a year – Editor, Rev. Kenn Ward

The Canadian Baptist, #414, 195 The West Mall, Etobicoke ON M9C 5K1 – 416/622-8600; Fax: 416/622-0780; Email: thecb@baptist.ca – Circ.: 12,000; 10 times a year – Editor, Dr. Larry Matthews; Circulation Manager, Carol Gouveia

Canadian Jewish News, #420, 10 Gateway Blvd., Don Mills ON M3C 3A1 – 416/422-2331; Fax: 416/422-3790 – Circ.: 50,000; Weekly – President, Don Carr, Q.C.; Editor, Mordechai Ben-Dat; General Manager, Gary Laforet

Canadian Mennonite, #3, 312 Marsland Dr., Waterloo ON N2J 3Z1 – 519/884-3810; Fax: 519/884-3331 – Circ.: 9,000; 25 times a year – Editor, Ron Rempel

The Canadian Messenger, c/o Jesuit Fathers, 661 Greenwood Ave., Toronto ON M4J 4B3 – 416/466-1195 – Circ.: 14,000; 11 times a year – Editor, Rev. F.J. Power

Canadian Orthodox Missionary, 37323 Hawkins Rd., Dewdney BC V0M 1H0 – 604/826-9336; Fax: 604/820-9758 – Bi-monthly – Editor, Fr. Moses Armstrong

Catholic Insight, PO Box 625, Stn Adelaide St. PO, Toronto ON M5C 2J8 – 416/368-4558; Fax: 416/368-8575 – 10 times a yar; ISSN: 1192-5671

Catholic New Times, 80 Sackville St., Toronto ON M5A 3E5 – 416/361-0761; Fax: 416/251-8191 – 20 times a year – Editor, Sister Anne O'Brien

The Catholic Register, #401, 1155 Yonge St., Toronto ON M4T 1W2 – 416/934-3410; Fax: 416/934-3409; Email: newsdept@cathreg.on.ca – Circ.: 23,300; 47 times a year – Editor, Joseph Sinesac

Christian Courier, c/o Reformed Faith Witness, #4, 261 Martindale Rd., St. Catharines ON L2W 1A1 – 905/682-8311; Fax: 905/682-8313; Email: cceditor@aol.com – Circ.: 5,000; Weekly; English & Dutch – Publisher, Stan de Jong; Editor, Bert Witvoet

Christian Info News, #200, 20316 - 56th Ave., Langley BC V3A 3Y7 – 604/534-1444; Fax: 604/534-2970 – Circ.: 31,000; Monthly – Publisher, Allan Stanchi; Editor, Flyn Ritchie

ChristianWeek, #300, 228 Notre Dame Ave., Winnipeg MB R3B 1N7 – 204/982-2060; Fax: 204/947-5632; Email: cw@christianweek.org; URL: http://www.christianweek.org – Circ.: 11,000; Every other Tues., except every 3 weeks in July & Aug. – Publisher, Doug McLeod; Editor-in-chief, Doug Koop

Compass: A Jesuit Journal, 50 Charles St. East, PO Box 400, Stn F, Toronto ON M4Y 2L8 – 416/921-0653; Fax: 416/921-1864; Email: 74163.2472@compuserve.com; URL: http://www.io.org/~gvanv/compass/comphome.html – Circ.: 3,700; 6 times a year – Publisher, William Addley; Editor, Robert Chodos; Circulation Manager, Barbara Barrett

Faith Today, c/o The Evangelical Fellowship of Canada, #300, 600 Alden Rd., Markham ON L3R 0Y4 – 905/479-5885; Fax: 905/479-4742; Email: ft@efc-canada.com – Circ.: 22,000; 6 times a year – Editor, Gary Walsh; Managing Editor, Marianne Meed Ward; Circulation Manager, Juanita Sternbergh

Gospel Herald, c/o Gospel Herald Foundation, 4904 King St., Beamsville ON L0R 1B6 – 905/563-7503; Fax: 905/563-7503; Email: eperry@freenet.npiec.on.ca; eperry9953@aol.com – Circ.: 1,400; Monthly – Editor, Wayne Turner; Managing Editor, Eugene C. Perry

Grail: An Ecumenical Journal, c/o Novalis, Saint Paul University, 223 Main St., Ottawa ON K1S 1C4 – 613/236-1393; Fax: 613/782-3004; Email: cgreen@spu.stpaul.uottawa.ca – Circ.: 700; 4 times a year – Editor, Michael Higgins; Managing Editor, Caryl Green

Jewish Free Press, 8411 Elbow Dr. SW, Calgary AB T2V 1K8 – 403/252-9423; Fax: 403/255-5640 – Circ.: 2,000; Semi-monthly – Editor, Judy Shapiro

The Jewish Tribune, 15 Hove St., Downsview ON M3H 4Y8 – 416/633-6224; Fax: 416/630-2159; URL: http://www.canada_ibm.net/bnaibrith/ – Circ.: 65,000; 24 times a year – Publisher, Frank Dimant; Editor, Dan Horowitz

Mennonite Brethren Herald, Canadian Mennonite Brethern Conference, #3, 169 Riverton Ave., Winnipeg MB R2L 2G5 – 204/669-6575; Fax: 204/654-1865; Email: mbherald@cdnmbconf.ca; URL: http://www.cdnmbconf.ca/mb/mbherald.htm – Circ.: 15,100; Bi-weekly – Managing Editor, Susan Brandt; Editor, Jim Coggins

The New Brunswick Anglican, 773 Glengarry Place, Fredericton NB E3B 5Z8 – 506/459-5358; Fax: 506/459-5358; Email: awatts@nbnet.nb.ca – Circ.: 12,000; Monthly exc. July & Aug. – Editor/Production Manager, Ana Watts

The New Freeman, 1 Bayard Dr., Saint John NB E2L 3L5 – 506/632-9226 – Circ.: 6,850; Weekly – Editor, W.L. Donovan

Niagara Anglican, c/o Anglican Diocese of Niagara, Cathedral Place, 252 James St. North, Hamilton ON L8R 2L3 – 905/521-9598; Fax: 905/546-5255; Email: editor@niagara.anglican.ca – Circ.: 18,000; Monthly exc. July & Aug. – Editor, Larry Perks; Advertising Manager, Roddie Gould-Perks

L'Oratoire, 3800, ch Queen Mary, Montréal QC H3V 1H6 – 514/733-8211; Fax: 514/733-9735 – Circ.: 8,500 English; 58,000 French; 6 fois par an; français – Rédacteur en chef, Gilles Leblanc

The Pentecostal Testimony, The Penetecostal Assemblies of Canada, 6745 Century Ave., Mississauga ON L5N 6P7 – 905/542-7400; Fax: 905/542-7313; Email: testimony@paoc.org – Circ.: 23,700; Monthly – Editor, Rick Hiebert

Prairie Messenger, Benedictine Monks of St. Peter's Abbey, PO Box 190, Muenster SK S0K 2Y0 – 306/682-1772; Fax: 306/682-5285; Email: ccnpm@explorer.sasknet.sk.ca – Circ.: 7,600; 46 times a year – Editor-in-chief, Rev. Andrew M. Britz; Circulation Manager, Gail Kleefeld

Presbyterian Record, 50 Wynford Dr., North York ON M3C 1J7 – 416/441-1111; Fax: 416/441-2825; Email: pcrecord@presbyterian.ca; URL: http://www.presbyterian.ca – Circ.: 58,000; Monthly exc. Aug. – Editor, John Congram

Shalom, The Printer, #305, 1515 South Park St., Halifax NS B3J 2L2 – 902/422-7491; Fax: 902/425-3722; Email: ajc.halifax@ns.sympatico.ca; URL: http://www3.ns.sympatico.ca/ajc.halifax/main.html – Circ.: 1,200; 4 times a year – Editor, Jon M. Goldberg

Studies in Religion, c/o Prof. W. Braun, Bishop's University, Lennoxville QC J1M 1Z7 – 819/822-9600; Fax: 819/822-9661; Email: wbaun@ubishops.ca – Circ.: 1,400; 4 times a year – Editor-in-chief, Monique Dumais; Managing Editor, Willi Braun

The United Church Observer, c/o United Church of Canada, 478 Huron St., Toronto ON M5R 2R3 – 416/960-8500; Fax: 416/960-8477; Email: general@ucobserver.org; URL: http://www.ucobserver.org – Circ.: 134,600; Monthly – Editor, Muriel Duncan

La Voix Sépharade, 4735, ch de la Côte Ste-Catherine, Montréal QC H3W 1M1 – 514/733-4998; Fax: 514/733-3158 – Tirage: 5 000; 5 fois par an – Rédactrice, Perla Serfaty-Garzon

Western Catholic Reporter, 8421 - 101 Ave., Edmonton AB T6A 0L1 – 403/465-8030; Fax: 403/465-8031; Email: wer@supernet.ab.ca – Circ.: 38,000; 43 times a year – Managing Editor, Glen Argan; Circulation Manager, Sharon Bly

World of Chabad, c/o Lubavitch, British Columbia, 5750 Oak St., Vancouver BC V6M 2V9 – 604/266-1313; Fax: 604/263-7934 – Circ.: 6,000; 8 times a year – Editor, Yoseph Thomson

## SCIENCE, RESEARCH & DEVELOPMENT

Québec Science, 425, rue de la Gauchetière est, Montréal QC H2L 2M7 – 514/843-6888; Fax: 514/843-4897; Email: courrier@QuebecScience.qc.ca; URL: http://QuebecScience.qc.ca – Tirage: 15,971; 10 fois par an; français – Editeur, Michel Gauquelin; Rédacteur en chef, Raymond Lemieux

## SENIOR CITIZENS

Active Adult (Published by Homes Publishing Group), 178 Main St., Unionville ON L3R 2G9 – 905/479-4663; Fax: 905/479-4482; Email: hope@homesmag.com – Circ.: 100,000; 2 times a year – Publishers, Michael Rosset; Editor, Diane McDougall

Le Bel Age (Published by Les Editions du Feu vert), 5148, boul St-Laurent, Montréal QC H2T 1R8 – 514/273-9773; Fax: 514/273-9034 – Tirage: 145,000; 11 fois par an; français – Editrice, Francine Tremblay; Rédactrice, Lucie Deaulniers

CARP News, #702, 27 Queen St. East, Toronto ON M5C 2M6 – 416/363-5562; Fax: 416/363-7394 – Circ.: 180,000; 6 times a year – Publisher & Editor, David Tafler

Choices After 50, EMC Marketing Associates Ltd., PO Box 1291, Saint John NB E2L 4H8 – 506/658-0754; Fax: 506/633-0868 – Editor, Carol Maber

Community Resource Directory (Published by Egress Enterprises Inc), PO Box 1094, Stn A, Kelowna BC V1Y 7P8 – 250/765-6065; Fax: 250/765-7346 – 3 annual editions covering different BC regions – Publisher, Joel A. Rickard

The Edmonton Senior (Published by Alberta Business Research Ltd), #800, 10179 - 105 St., Edmonton AB T5J 3N1 – 403/425-1185; Fax: 403/421-7677 – Circ.: 45,000; 12 times a year – Publisher, Lorne Silverstein, 403/429-1610; Editor, Colin Smith

Fifty-Five Plus, c/o Valley Publishing, 95 Abbeyhill Dr., Kanata ON K2L 2M8 – 613/592-3578; Fax: 613/592-9033 – Circ.: 40,000; 6 times a year – Publisher, Brian Warren; Editor, Patricia den Boer

Good Times, Senior Publications, 5148, boul St-Laurent, Montréal QC H2T 1R8 – 514/273-9773; Fax: 514/273-3408 – Circ.: 100,000; 11 times a year – Editor, Denise B. Crawford

The Independent Senior, K.W. Publishing Ltd., #101, 211 East Georgia St., Vancouver BC V6A 1Z6 – 604/688-2271; Fax: 604/688-2038 – Circ.: 48,900; 10 times a year – Publisher, Darlene Liboiron; Editor, Adrian Leonard

Le Magazine FADOQ, Editador, 4545, av Pierre-de-Coubertin, CP 1000, Succ M, Montréal QC H1V 3R2 – 514/252-3017; Fax: 514/252-3154 – Tirage: 108,000; 5 fois par an; français – Directeur, Lyne Rémillard

Mainly for Seniors Lambton-Kent, 4182 Petrolia Line, PO Box 40, Petrolia ON N0N 1R0 – 519/882-1770; Fax: 519/882-3212 – Circ.: 10,000; Monthly – Publisher, Denise Thibeault; Editor, David Pattenaude

Mature Lifestyles, RobJay Holdings Ltd., 6 Trumpourt Ct., Markham ON L3R 1Y9 – 905/475-0586; Fax: 905/474-9851; Email: matulife@netrover.com – Circ.: 25,000; 10 times a year – Publisher, Diane Peterson

Maturity, CYN Investments Ltd., PO Box 397, New Westminster BC V3L 4Y7 – 604/540-7911; Fax: 604/540-7912

MSOS Journal, c/o Manitoba Society of Seniors, 697B Carter Ave., Winnipeg MB R3M 2C3 – 204/453-8502; Fax: 204/475-6853 – Monthly – Editor, Irv Kroeker

New Clarion, PO Box 3151, Stn B, Saint John NB E2M 4X8 – 506/674-2439; Fax: 506/672-1537; Email: paulevns@nbnet.nb.ca – Publisher, Karen Wilson

Prime Time, c/o Canterbury Publishing, 298 Prince St., Peterborough ON K9J 2A5 – 705/749-1895; Fax: 705/749-1105; Email: canterbury@onwmdis.on.ca – Circ.: 8,100; Monthly – Editorial Manager, Leanne Lavender; Circulation Manager, Brian Lavender

The Seniors Choice (Published by Egress Enterprises Inc), PO Box 1094, Stn A, Kelowna BC V1Y 7P8 – 250/765-6065; Fax: 250/765-7346 – Monthly – Publisher, Joel A. Rickard

SeniorsPlus Newspaper, PO Box 1112, Barrie ON L4M 4Y6 – 705/725-9269; Fax: 705/725-9684 – Circ.: 17,000; Monthly – Publisher, W. Moran

The Seniors Review, #B2, 11 Bond St., St. Catharines ON L2R 4Z4 – 905/687-9861; Fax: 905/687-6911 – Circ.: 40,000 – Publisher, David Irwin; Editor, Elaine Irwin

Seniors Today (Published by McCaine-Davis Communications Ltd.), 232 Henderson Hwy., Winnipeg MB R2L 1L9 – 204/982-4000; Fax: 204/982-4001 – 24 times a year – President, Heather McCaine-Davis

The Senior Times, 4077 Decarie Blvd., Montréal QC H4A 3J8 – 514/484-5033; Fax: 514/484-8254 – 22 times a year; also Montreal Resource Directory (bi-annual) – Publisher & Editor, Barbara Moser

The Silver Pages, Silver Pages International, #24, 20 Hanlan Rd., Woodbridge ON L4L 3P6 – 905/264-7233; Fax: 905/264-7242 – Circ.: 250,000; 2 times a year – Publisher & Editor, Joanna M. Bickus

The Silver Pages, MY Publishing Inc., RR#1, Beaslau ON N0B 1M0 – 519/648-2615; Fax: 519/648-9427 – Circ.: 20,000; 2 times a year – Publisher, Gordon Young

Today's Choices, 17533 - 106 Ave., Edmonton AB T5S 1E7 – 403/489-5898; Fax: 403/483-2000 – Circ.: 35,000; Monthly – Publisher, Don Sinclair; Associate Publisher/Editor, Elsie Rose

Today's Seniors, Metroland Printing, Publishing & Distributing Ltd., 467 Speers Rd., Oakville ON L6K 3S4 – 905/815-0017, 0045; Fax: 905/815-0026 – Circ.: 567,000; 12 times a year – Publisher, Ian Oliver; Editor-in-chief, Don Wall

Vitality Newsmagazine, Gold Quill Enterprises Ltd., 208 Princess, 2nd Fl., Winnipeg MB R3B 1L4 – 204/949-9355; Fax: 204/956-0030 – Circ.: 21,000; 10 times a year – Editor, Evelyn Seida; Advertising Manager, Gale Whiteside

Westcoast Reflections, 2604 Quadra St., Victoria BC V8T 4E4 – 250/383-1149; Fax: 250/388-4479; Email: magazine@islandnet.com; URL: http://www.islandnet.com/~magazine/ – Circ.: 20,000; Monthly – Publisher, Jim Bisakowski; Editor, Jane Kezar

## SOCIAL WELFARE

Canadian Dimension, #401, 228 Notre Dame Ave., Winnipeg MB R3B 1N7 – 204/957-1519; Fax: 204/943-4617; Email: info@canadiandimension.mb.ca; URL: http://www.canadiandimension.mb.ca/cd/index.htm – Circ.: 3,500; 6 times a year – Office Manager, Michelle Torrres

Community Action: Canada's Community Service Newspaper, 41 Marbury Cres., PO Box 444, Don Mills ON M3C 2T2 – 416/449-6766; Fax: 416/444-5850; Email: comact@interlog.com; URL: http://www.comact@interlog.com – Circ.: 12,000; 22 times a year – Publisher & Editor, Leon Kumove

Our Schools/Our Selves, 107 Earl Grey Rd., Toronto ON M4J 3L6 – 416/463-6978; Fax: 416/463-6978 – Circ.: 1,000; 6 times a year; ISSN 0840-7339 – David Clandfield; George Martell

Perception, Canadian Council on Social Development, 441 MacLaren, 4th Fl., Ottawa ON K2P 2H3 – 613/236-8977; Fax: 613/236-2750; Email: council@ccsd.ca; URL: http://www.ccds.ca – Circ.: 2,000; 4 times a year; English & French – Editor, Ellen Adelberg; Circulation Manager, Louise Clarke

Rehabilitation Digest, Easter Seals/March of Dimes National Council, #511, 90 Eglinton Ave. East, Toronto ON M4P 2Y3 – 416/932-8382; Fax: 416/932-9844 – Circ.: 2,000; 4 times a year – Editor, Wiliam A. Hoch

The Social Worker, Myropen Publications Ltd., #402, 383 Parkdale Ave., Ottawa ON K1Y 4R4 – 613/729-6668; Fax: 613/729-9608; Email: casw@casw-acts.ca; URL: http://www.intranet.ca/~casw-acts/ – Circ.: 14,500; English/French; 4 times a year – Co-ordination, Penny Sipkes

## SPORTS & RECREATION

Athletics: Canada's National Track & Field/Running Magazine, #601, 1185 Eglinton Ave. East, North York ON M3C 3C6 – 416/426-7215; Fax: 416/426-7358; Email: ontrack@io.org; URL: http://www.io.org/~ontrack – Circ.: 6,000; 9 times a year; ISSN 0229-4966 – Publisher & Editor, Cecil Smith; Circulation Manager, Bernie Eckler

Backspin: Manitoba's Golf Newspaper (Published by Canadian Publishers), 1465 St. James St., Winnipeg MB R3H 0W9 – 204/949-6100; Fax: 204/949-6122 – Circ.: 15,000; 6 times a year – Publisher, Gerald L. Dorge

Boudoir Noir, PO Box 5, Stn F, Toronto ON M4Y 2L4 – 416/591-2387; Fax: 416/591-1572; Email: boudoir@boudoir-noir.com; URL: http://www.boudoir-noir.com – Circ.: 10,000; 4 times a year – Co-Publisher, Mary Dante; Co-Publisher, Robert Dante

Canadian Curling News, #100, 75 The East Mall, Etobicoke ON M8Z 5W3 – 416/253-0022; Fax: 416/253-9356 – Monthly from Sept. to April – Publisher, Brian Cooke; Editor, George Karrys

Canadian Rodeo News, #223, 2116 - 27 Ave. NE, Calgary AB T2E 7A6 – 403/250-7292; Fax: 403/250-6926; Email: rodeonews@iul-ccs; URL: http://www.rodeocanada.com – Circ.: 4,000; Monthly – Editor, P. Kirby Meston; Circulation Manager, Vicki Mowat

Coast the outdoor recreation magazine, PO Box 65837, Stn A, Vancouver BC V5N 5L3 – 604/876-1473; Fax: 604/876-1474; Email: coast@istar.ca; URL: http://www.vanmag.com/outside/ – Circ.: 40,000; 11 times a year – Publisher, Allan Main; Editor, Steven Threndyle

Le Coureur des Neiges (Published by Camar Publications), 130 Spy Ct., Markham ON L3R 5H6 – 905/475-8440; Fax: 905/475-9246; Email: jacquelinehowe@sympataico.ca; URL: SnowGoer.comm – Tirage: 39,400; Annuellement; français – Editeur, Jacqueline Howe; Rédacteur, Chris Knowles

Diver Magazine, #230, 11780 Hammersmith Way, Richmond BC V7A 5E3 – 604/274-4333; Fax: 604/

274-4366; Email: divermag@axionet.com; URL: http://medianetcom.com/divermag – 9 times a year – Publisher, Peter Vassilopoulos; Editor, Stephanie Bold

Fittingly Yours, #184, 1857 West 4th Ave., Vancouver BC V6J 1M4 – 604/878-1297; Fax: 604/582-7382 – Circ.: 40,000; 6 times a year – Publisher & Editor, Karen Zaitchik

Flagstick, #102, 201 McLeod St., Ottawa ON K2P 0Z9 – 613/567-5691; Fax: 613/567-5691; Email: publisher@flagstick.com; URL: http://www.flagstick.com – Circ.: 20,000; 6 times a year – Publisher, Jeff Bauder

Golden Triangle Hockey Magazine, 56a Brybeck Circle, Kitchener ON N2M 2C6 – 519/624-8682; Fax: 519/624-8933; Email: hotc1@golden.net; URL: http://www.golden.net/~hotc1 – Circ.: 10,000; Monthly – Editor, Warren Murchie

Golf Canada, Laurel Oak Marketing, #205, 1455 Lakeshore Rd. South, Burlington ON L7S 2J1 – 905/634-5770; Fax: 905/634-8335 – Circ.: 118,720; 4 times a year – Publisher, Wayne Narcisco

Golf Course Ranking Magazine, Longhurst Golf Corp., #14, 85 West Wilmot St., Richmond Hill ON L4B 1K7 – 905/764-5409; Fax: 905/764-5462 – Circ.: 125,000; Annually – Publisher, Bruce Longhurst

Golf Guide, 16410 - 137 Ave., Edmonton AB T5L 4H8 – 403/447-2128; Fax: 403/447-1933 – Annually, April – Publishers & Editor, Paul McCracken

Golf International, 798, boul Arthur Sauvé, CP 91022, St-Eustache QC J7R 6V9 – 514/386-2927; Fax: 514/974-2212 – Tirage: 28 000; 5 fois par an; français – Editeur et Rédacteur, Jacques Landry

Golf the West (Published by Koocanusa Publications Inc.), 1510 - 2nd St. North, Cranbrook BC V1C 3L2 – 250/426-7253; Fax: 250/426-4125; Email: advertuser@cyberlink.bc.ca – Circ.: 35,000; Annually, spring – Publisher, Daryl D. Shellborn; Editor, Stacey Curry

The Hockey News, Transcontinental Publications Inc., #2700, 777 Bay St., Toronto ON M5G 2C8 – 416/340-8000; Fax: 416/340-2786 – Circ.: 112,837; 42 times a year – Publisher, Ed Pearce; Editor, Steve Dryden

Le Journal Québec Quilles, CP 126, Succ Anjou, Montréal QC H1L 4N7 – 514/351-5224; Fax: 514/351-6818 – Tirage: 26,000; 7 fois par an; français – Editeur, Yves Larocque; Rédacteur, Gilles Poulin

Motoneige Québec, 99, rue Brouillard, Vaudreuil QC J7V 6T5 – 514/252-3163; Fax: 514/254-2066 – Tirage: 59,000; 6 fois par an; français – Rédacteur en chef, Pierre Vaillancourt

National Rugby Post, 13228 - 76 St., Edmonton AB T5C 1B6 – 403/476-0268; Fax: 403/473-1066 – Circ.: 6,000; 6 times a year – Publisher, David C. Graham; Editor, Don Whidden

Northwestern Ontario Snowmobile News (Published by North Superior Publishing Inc.), 1145 Barton St., Thunder Bay ON P7B 5N3 – 807/623-2348; Fax: 807/623-7515; Email: nsuperior@norlink.net – Circ.: 5,000; 6 times a year – Publisher & Editor, Scott A. Summer

Oldtimers' Hockey News, 640 Christopher Rd., PO Box 951, Peterborough ON K9J 7A5 – 705/743-2679; Fax: 705/748-3470 – Circ.: 15,000; 8 times a year – Publisher & Editor, David E. Tatham; Circulation Manager, Deborah Tatham

Ontario Golf News, #400, 2 Billingham Rd., Toronto ON M9B 6E1 – 416/232-2380; Fax: 416/232-9291 – Circ.: 30,000; 5 times a year – Publisher, Ken McKenzie; Editor, Charles Halpin

Ontario Snowmobiler, 18540 Centre St., Mount Albert ON L0G 1M0 – 905/473-7009; Fax: 905/473-5217 – Circ.: 80,000; 5 times a year – Publisher, Terrence D. Kehoe; Editor, Kent Lester; Circulation Manager, D.B. Stevens

Ontario Tennis, Ontario Tennis Association, 1185 Eglinton Ave. East, North York ON M3C 3C6 – 416/426-7135; Fax: 416/426-7370 – Circ.: 16,500; 4 times a year

Outside Guide (Published by Solstice Publishing Inc.), 47 Soho Sq., Toronto ON M5T 2Z2 – 416/595-1252; Fax: 416/595-7255; Email: info@skicanadamag.com; URL: http://www.skicanadamag.com – Circ.: 60,000; 2 times a year – Publisher, Paul Green; Editor, Iain MacMillan; Circulation Manager, Jon Spencer

Pacific Golf Magazine (Published by Canada Wide Magazines & Communications Ltd.), 4180 Lougheed Hwy., 4th Fl., Burnaby BC V5C 6A7 – 604/299-7311; Fax: 604/299-9188 – Publisher, Peter Legge; Editor, Bonnie Irving; Circulation Manager, Mark Weeks

Parks and Recreation Canada, Canadian Parks/Recreation Association, #306, 1600 James Naismith Dr., Ottawa ON K1B 5N4 – 613/748-5651; Fax: 613/748-5854; Email: cpra@activeliving.ca; URL: http://www.activeliving.ca/activeliving/cpra.html – Circ.: 1,500; 6 times a year – Editor, Mary Lynn Charlton; Circulation Manager, Kathleen Luten

Physical Education Digest, 111 Kingsmount Blvd., Sudbury ON P3E 1K8 – Fax: 705/675-5539; Email: pedigest@cyberbeach.net; URL: http://www.cyberbeach.net/pedigest – Circ.: 3,600; 4 times a year – Publisher & Editor, Dick Moss

Pocket Pro Golf Magazine, 85 West Wilmont St., Unit 14, Richmond Hill ON L4B 1K7 – 905/764-5409; Fax: 905/764-5462 – Annually – Publisher, Bruce Longhurst

Québec Soccer, 6900, rue Nenner, 3e étage, Montréal QC H2S 2S2 – 514/278-6399 – 8 fois par an; français

SCORE, 287 MacPherson Ave., Toronto ON M4V 1A4 – 416/928-2909; Fax: 416/928-1357; Email: weeksy@idirect.com – Circ.: 115,900; 6 times a year

Le Ski, 8 Winnifred Ave., Toronto ON M4M 2X3 – 416/462-0611; Fax: 416/462-9419 – Tirage: 22,500; 4 fois par an; français – Editeur, Paul Green, 416/595-1252; Rédacteur en chef, Robert Choquette

Ski Canada Magazine (Published by Solstice Publishing Inc.), 47 Soho Sq., Toronto ON M5T 2Z2 – 416/595-1252; Fax: 416/595-7255; Email: infro@skicanadamag.com; URL: http://www.skicanadamag.com – Circ.: 48,500; 6 times a year – Publisher, Paul Green; Editor, Iain MacMillan; Circulation Manager, Jon Spencer

Ski Press/Ski Presse, 850, rue Bernard-Pilon, McMasterville QC J3G 5X7 – 514/464-3121; Fax: 514/464-9210; Email: skipress@sympatico.ca; URL: http://www.skipress.sympatico.ca – Publisher, Jean Marc Blais; English Editor, Jules Olser; French Editor, Maxime Tremblay

SkiTrax Magazine, #204, 2 Pardee Ave., Toronto ON M6K 3H5 – 416/530-1350; Fax: 416/530-4155; Email: medal@passport.ca; URL: http://www.pedal.com – Circ.: 18,000; 4 times a year – Publisher & Editor, Benjamin Sadavoy

Ski The West (Published by Koocanusa Publications Inc.), 1510 - 2nd St. North, Cranbrook BC V1C 3L2 – 250/426-7253; Fax: 250/426-4125; Email: advertiser@cyberlink.bc.ca – Circ.: 40,000; Annually, Oct. – Publisher, Daryl D. Shellborn; Editor, Stacey Curry

Sno Riders West (Published by Koocanusa Publications Inc.), 1510 - 2nd St. North, Cranbrook BC V1C 3L2 – 250/426-7253; Fax: 250/426-4125; Email: advertiser@cyberlink.bc.ca – Circ.: 35,000; 4 times a year – Publisher, Daryl Shellborn; Editor, Stacey Curry

Snow Goer (Published by Camar Publications), 130 Spy Ct., Markham ON L3R 5H6 – 905/475-8440; Fax: 905/475-9246; Email: jacquelinehowe@sympatico.ca; URL: http://www.snowgoer.com – Circ.: 99,000; 4 times a year – Publisher, Jacqueline Howe; Editor, Chris Knowles

Sporting Scene, 22 Maberley Cres., West Hill ON M1C 3K8 – 416/284-0304; Fax: 416/284-1299 – Circ.: 24,000; Monthly Sept. to May – Publisher & Editor, Peter Martens

Squash Life, c/o Squash Ontario, 1185 Eglinton Ave. East, North York ON M3C 3C6 – 416/426-7201; Fax: 416/426-7393; Email: sq.ont.sherry@sympatico.ca; URL: http://www3.sympatico.ca/squash.ontario – 4 times a year; includes Annual Handbook – Executive Director & Managing Editor, Sherry Funston

Supertrax Int'l, 18540 Centre St., Mount Albert ON L0G 1M0 – 905/473-7009; Fax: 905/473-5217; Email: supertrax@aol.com – Circ.: 160,000; 5 times a year; English & French – Publisher, Terrence D. Kehoe; Editor, Kent Lester; Circulation, Richard Kehoe; General Manager, Ray Kehoe

True North Volleyball Magazine, 416 Cranbrook Ave., North York ON M5M 1N5 – 416/780-9686; Email: 4ewg@qlink.queensv.ca – Circ.: 15,000; 6 times a year – Publisher, Ted Graham; Editor, Tony Martins; Circulation Manager, Paul Brownstein

Water Goer (Published by Camar Publications), 130 Spy Ct., Markham ON L3R 5H6 – 905/475-8440; Fax: 905/475-9246 – Annually – Publisher, Jacqueline Howe

WhyNot Magazine, Canadian Foundation for Physically Disabled Persons, 731 Runnymede Ave., Toronto ON M6N 3V7 – 416/760-7351; Fax: 416/760-9405 – 6 times a year – Publisher, Vim Kochlar; Editor, Marsha Stall

**TELEVISION, RADIO, VIDEO & HOME APPLIANCES**

Bow Valley This Week, 201 Bear St., 2nd Fl., PO Box 129, Banff AB T0L 0C0 – 403/762-2453; Fax: 403/762-5274 – Circ.: 12,249; Weekly – Publisher, Sandra Santa Lucia; Editor, David Rodney; Circulation Manager, Anne Bosma

The Brandon Sun TV Book, 501 Rosser Ave., Brandon MB R7A 5Z6 – 204/727-2451; Fax: 204/725-0976, 0385 (ed.) – Circ.: 24,785; Weekly – Publisher, Rob Forbes; Editor, Cathy Arthur

Broadcast Week, The Globe and Mail, 444 Front St. West, Toronto ON M5V 2S9 – 416/585-5608, 5045; Fax: 416/585-5275, 5085; Email: dbarber@globeandmail.ca – Weekly – Publisher, Stephen Petterbridge; Editor, David Barber

Feature (Your Premium Entertainment Magazine) (Published by Les Publications Feature ltée), 2100, rue Ste-Catherine ouest, 9e étage, Montréal QC H3H 2T3 – 514/939-5024; Fax: 514/939-1515 – Circ.: 650,000; Monthly – Publisher, Marvin Boisvert; Editor, David Sherman; Circulation Manager, Nathalie Abitbul

The Inner Ear Report, 85 Moorehouse Dr., Scarborough ON M1V 2E2 – 416/297-7968; Fax: 416/297-7968; Email: tier@terraport.net – Circ.: 16,000 – Editor, Ernie Fisher

The Newfoundland Herald, PO Box 2015, St. John's NF A1C 5R7 – 709/726-7060; Fax: 709/726-8227 – Weekly – Publisher, Geoff W. Stirling

PrimeTime, Riviera Plaza, 5308 Calgary Trail, Edmonton AB T6H 4J8 – 403/434-7424; Fax: 403/437-0123 – Circ.: 298,000; 12 times a year – Publisher, Harold Roozen; Editor, Ruth Kelly

Primeurs (Published by Les Publications Feature ltée), 2100, rue Ste-Catherine ouest, 9e étage, Montréal QC H3H 2T3 – 514/939-5036; Fax: 514/939-1515 – Tirage: 280,000; Mensuel; français – Editeur, Marvin Boisvert; Rédactrice, Marielle Duhamel; Directrice de tirage, Nathalie Abitbul

Satellite Entertainment Guide, #1109 TD Tower, 10205 - 101 St., Edmonton AB T5J 2Z1 – 403/424-6222; Fax: 403/425-8392 – Circ.: 82,600; Monthly – Publisher, Steven R. Vogel

Signal, TV Ontario, 2180 Yonge St., 5th Fl., PO Box 20, Toronto ON M4T 2T1 – 416/484-2898; Fax: 416/484-6285 – Circ.: 55,000; 10 times a year

Son Hi-Fi Video (Published by Les Editions du Feu vert), 5148, boul St-Laurent, Montréal QC H2T 1R8 – 514/273-9773; Fax: 514/273-9034 – 6 fois par an; français – Editrice, Francine Tremblay; Rédacteur, Claude Corbeil; Directrice de tirage, Sylvie Hamel

StarWeek Magazine, c/o Toronto Star, One Yonge St., 5th Fl., Toronto ON M5E 1E6 – 416/869-4244, 4936; Fax: 416/869-4103 – Circ.: 740,000; Weekly – Publisher, John Honderich; Editor, Jim Atkins, 416/869-4870

Sunday Sun Television Magazine, Calgary Sun, 2615 - 12 St. NE, Calgary AB T2E 7W9 – 403/250-4200; Fax: 403/250-4180; Email: callet@sunpub.com; URL: http://www.canoe.caCalgarySun – Circ.: 100,000; Weekly – Publisher, Les Pyette; Editor, Chris Nelson; Circulation Manager, Joe King

Sunday Sun Television Magazine, c/o Edmonton Sun, #250, 4990 - 92 Ave., Edmonton AB T6B 3A1 – 403/468-0100; Fax: 403/468-0128; Email: edmonton.sun@ccinet.ab.ca – Circ.: 121,800; Weekly – Publisher, Craig Martin

Sunday Sun Television Magazine, c/o Ottawa Sun, 380 Hunt Club Rd., Ottawa ON K1G 3N3 – 613/739-7000; Fax: 613/739-8043; Email: ottsun@ottawa.net; URL: http://www.canoe.ca – Circ.: 55,108 Mon.-Fri., 62,025 Sun.; Weekly – Editor-in-chief, Rick Vansickle

Sunday Sun Television Magazine, c/o Toronto Sun, 333 King St. East, Toronto ON M5A 3X5 – 416/947-2333; Fax: 416/947-3139; Telex: 06-217688 – Circ.: 445,600; Weekly – General Manager, Mark Stevens

Télé Horaire, c/o Le Journal, 4545 Frontenac, Montréal QC H2H 2R7 – 514/521-4545 – Tirage: 331 000; Hebdomadaire; français

Télé Horaire (Québec) (Published by Groupe Québécor Inc.), c/o Le Journal de Québec, 450, rue Bechard, Vanier QC G1M 2E9 – 418/683-1573; Fax: 418/683-1027 – Tirage: 122,000; Hebdomadaire; français – Editeur, Jean-Claude L'Abbée; Rédacteur, Serge Côté; Directeur de tirage, Marc Couture

TéléPlus, 7, rue St-Jacques, Montréal QC H2Y 1K9 – 514/285-7306; Fax: 514/845-8129 – Hebdomadaire; français – Editeur, Roger D. Landry

Téléromans (Published by Trustar Ltd.), #2000, 2020, rue University, Montréal QC H5A 2A5 – 514/499-0561; Fax: 514/843-3529 – Tirage: 70,000; 4 fois par an; français – Editeur, Michel Trudeau; Rédacteur, Thérèse Parisien

Télé Soleil, c/o Le Soleil, 925, ch Saint-Louis, CP 1547, Succ Terminus, Québec QC G1K 7J6 – 418/686-3270; Fax: 418/686-3260; URL: http://www.lesoleil.com – Hebdomadaire; français – Président, Gilbert Lacasse; Rédacteur en chef, Gilbert Lavoie

Thunder Bay Guide, 1126 Roland St., Thunder Bay ON P7B 5M4 – 807/623-5788; Fax: 807/622-3140; Email: tbpost3@air.on.ca; URL: http://www/tbsource.com – Circ.: 10,000; Weekly – Editor, Lois Rogala

TV 7 Jours (Published by Trustar Ltd.), #2000, 2020, rue University, Montréal QC H5A 2A5 – 514/848-7000; Fax: 514/848-9854 – Tirage: 170,000; Hebdomadaire; français – Editeur, Claude J. Charron

TV Guide (Published by Telemedia Publishing), #100, 25 Sheppard Ave. West, North York ON M2N 6S7 – 416/733-7600; Fax: 416/733-3568; Email: tvguideletters@telemedia.ca; URL: http://www.tvguide.sympatico.ca – Circ.: 838,000; Weekly – Publisher, Naomi Judith Rose; Editor, Christopher Loudon

TV Hebdo (Published by Trustar Ltd.), #2000, 2020, rue University, Montréal QC H5A 2A5 – 514/499-0561; Fax: 514/499-1844 – Tirage: 234,000; Hebdomadaire – Editeur, François de Gaspé-Beaubien; Rédacteur en chef, Jean-Louis Podlesak

TV Magazine (Central B.C.), Spartan Printing & Advertising Ltd., 101 Marsh Dr., Quesnel BC V2J 3K3 – 250/992-2713; Fax: 250/992-3902 – Circ.: 4,600; Weekly; also TV Guide Style (weekly) – Co-Editor, J.P. Hartnett; Co-Editor, G. Seale

TV Scene, c/o Thunder Bay Times, 75 South Cumberland St., Thunder Bay ON P7B 1A3 – 807/343-6200; Fax: 807/345-5991; Email: cj-editorial@cwconnect.ca; URL: http://www.netreader.com/tbay/index2.html – Circ.: 40,900; Weekly – Publisher, Colin Bruce; Editor, Peter Haggert; Circulation Manager, Mike Keating

TV Scene, c/o Winnipeg Free Press, 1355 Mountain Ave., Winnipeg MB R2X 3B6 – 204/697-7000; Fax: 204/697-7412 – Weekly

TV Scene Around, Northern Enterprises, 1441 - 100 Ave., Dawson Creek BC V1G 1W7 – 250/782-3190 – Weekly – Publisher, Robin Graham

TV Times (Published by Southam Magazine Group), 1450 Don Mills Rd., Don Mills ON M3B 2X7 – 416/442-3444; Fax: 416/442-2088 – Circ.: 1.8 million; Weekly – Editor, Eric Kohanik

TV Week Magazine (Published by Canada Wide Magazines & Communications Ltd.), 4180 Lougheed Hwy., 4th Fl., Burnaby BC V5C 6A7 – 604/299-7311; Fax: 604/299-9188 – Weekly – Publisher, Peter Legge; Editor, Robin Roberts; Circulation Manager, Mark Weeks

TV Week Stratford, c/o The Beacon Herald of Stratford, PO Box 430, Stratford ON N5A 6T6 – 519/271-2220; Fax: 519/271-1026 – Circ.: 13,283; Weekly – Publisher, Charles Dingman; Editor, Ron Carson

The Winnipeg Sun TV Preview, 1700 Church Ave., Winnipeg MB R2X 3A2 – 204/694-2022; Fax: 204/632-8709; Email: wpgsun@escape.ca – Circ.: 52,000; Weekly – Publisher, Richard Boyer; Managing Editor, Glenn Cheater

**TRAVEL**

AutoRoute, #606, 366 Adelaide St. West, Toronto ON M5V 1R9 – 416/599-9900; Fax: 416/599-9700; Email: kenda@passport.ca – Circ.: 285,000; 4 times a year; English & French – Publisher, Rod Morris; Managing Editor, John Terauds; Associate Publisher, Angela McNab

Bienvenue en Nouvelle-Écosse, Mardelli Publishing, PO Box 811, Yarmouth NS B5K 4K4 – 902/742-4653; Fax: 902/742-2460; Email: welcome@ns.sympatico.ca – Circ.: 150,000; Annually; French & German – Publisher, Bill Mardelli

Coup d'oeil, Les Editions M.C.C. ltée, 1048, d'Avangour, Chicoutimi QC G7H 2T1 – 418/696-4805; Fax: 418/696-1476 – Tirage: 30,000; 4 fois par an; français – Editeur, Chantal Tremblay

Geo Plein Air (Published by Les Éditions Tricycle inc.), 1251, rue Rachel est, Montréal QC H2J 2J9 – 514/521-8356; Fax: 514/521-5711; Email: geo_pleinair@velo.qc.ca – Tirage: 25,000; 6 fois par an; français – Editeur, Pierre Hamel; Rédacteur, Simon Kretz

HolidayMaker, Wild Boar Productions, 23260 - 88 Ave., PO Box 10, Fort Langley BC V1M 2R4 – 604/888-4037; Fax: 604/888-6663; Email: holmaker@aol.com – Circ.: 34,000; 4 times a year – Publisher & Editor, Chris Potter

Latitudes, Plan B Strategies Inc., #217, 45 Sheppard Ave. East, Toronto ON M2N 5W9 – 416/226-1700; Fax: 416/226-2566 – Circ.: 200,000; 4 times a year; English & French – Publisher, Eve Howse; Editor-in-chief, Louis Gauthier

The Laurentians Tourist Guide, #14, 142, rue de la Chapelle, St-Jérôme QC J7Z 5T4 – 514/436-8532; Fax: 514/436-5309; Email: infro-tourisme@laurentides.com; URL: http://www.laurentides.com – Circ.: 60,000, English edition; 170,000, French edition; Annually; English & French editions – General Manager, André Goyer

Leisure Canada, Altracs Multimedia Inc., #300, 5025 Oribitor Dr., Bldg. 4, Mississauga ON L4W 4Y5 – 905/625-1796; Fax: 905/625-0640 – 6 times a year – Publisher & Editor, Jerry Tutunjian

The Pacific Hosteller, c/o Canadian Hostelling Association, #402, 134 Abbott St., Vancouver BC V6B 4K4 – 604/684-7101; Fax: 604/684-7181 – 4 times a year – Publisher, Morris Jenkinson

Resort Weekly, South East Press Ltd., 521 Main St., PO Box 329, Kipling SK S0G 2S0 – 306/736-2535; Fax: 306/736-8445 – Circ.: 2,700; 12 times a year, weekly beginning May 24 – Editor, Scott Kearns

Saskatchewan Vacation Guide, Tourism Saskatchewan, #500, 1900 Albert St., Regina SK S4P 4L9 – 306/787-9685; Fax: 306/767-0715 – Circ.: 300,000; Monthly

Travelworld, Gemini International Inc., #490, 10 Gateway Blvd., North York ON M3C 3T4 – 416/221-0288; Fax: 416/221-0287 – Circ.: 165,000 – Editor, James A. Bruce Sr.

Vacances pour Tous, #110, 455, rue Marais, Vanier QC G1M 3A2 – 418/686-1940; Fax: 418/686-1942 – Tirage: 40,000; 6 fois par an; français – Editeur, Eric Sohier; Rédactrice, Marie-Christine Magnan

**WOMEN'S & FEMINIST**

Action Now, National Action Committee on the Status of Women, #203, 234 Eglinton Ave. West, Toronto ON M4P 1K5 – 416/932-1718; Fax: 416/932-0646; Email: nac@web.net – Circ.: 1,400; 8 times a year – Circulation Manager, Michele Havens

L'Actuelle, 1043, rue Tiffin, Longueuil QC J4P 3G7 – 514/442-3983; Fax: 514/442-4363 – 7 fois par an; français – Editeur, Renel Bouchard

BC Woman, 2061 Cape Horn Ave., Coquitlam BC V3K 1J2 – 604/540-8448; Fax: 604/524-0041 – Circ.: 35,000; Monthly – Publisher, Rosemarie Nakamura; Editor, Nikki Groocock

Canadian Guider, c/o Girl Guides of Canada, 50 Merton St., Toronto ON M4S 1A3 – 416/487-5281; Fax: 416/487-5570; URL: http://www.girlguides.ca – Circ.: 45,000; 5 times a year – Editor, Sharon Pruner

Canadian Woman Studies, 212 Founders College, York University, 4700 Keele St., Downsview ON M3J 1P3 – 416/736-5356; Fax: 416/736-5765; Email: cwscf@yorku.ca; URL: http://www.yorku.ca/org/cwscf/home.html – Circ.: 5,000; 4 times a year – Editor, Luciana Ricciutelli; Circulation Manager, Rosemary Moore

Chatelaine (Published by Maclean Hunter Publishing), 777 Bay St., Toronto ON M5W 1A7 – 416/596-5425; Fax: 416/596-5516; Email: editors@chatelaine.com; URL: http://www.canoe.ca/chatelaine – Circ.: 1,100,000; Monthly; also Welcome Home (annually), Chatelaine Renovates (annually); ISSN 0009-1995 – Publisher, Lee Simpson; Editor-in-chief, Rona Maynard

Châtelaine (Published by Maclean Hunter Publishing), 1001, boul de Maisonneuve ouest, Montréal QC H3A 3E1 – 514/845-5141; Fax: 514/845-4302 – Tirage: 188,000; Mensuel; français – Editeur, Jean-François Douville; Rédactrice, Catherine Elie

Clin d'oeil (Published by Publicor), 7, ch Bates, Outremont QC H2V 1A6 – 514/270-1100; Fax: 514/270-7079; URL: http://www.clindoeil@quebecor.com – Tirage: 100,000; Mensuel; français – Directrice de publication, Sandra Cliche

Contemporary Verse 2, PO Box 3062, Winnipeg MB R3C 4E5 – 204/949-1365 – Circ.: 650; 4 times a year – Editor, Janine Tschuncky

Coup de Pouce (Published by Les Éditions Télémedia), #900, 2001, rue University, Montréal QC H3A 2A6 – 514/499-0561; Fax: 514/499-1844 – Tirage: 155,000; 12 times a year – Editrice, Michéle Cyr; Rédactrice, Sandra Cliche

Edmonton Woman (Published by Alberta Business Research Ltd), #800, 10179 - 105 St., Edmonton AB T5J 3N1 – 403/424-1221; Fax: 403/421-7677 –

Circ.: 40,000; 10 times a year – Publisher, Lorne Silverstein, 403/429-1610; Executive Editor, Colin Smith; Editor, Laurie Rowswell

Elle Québec (Published by Les Éditions Télémedia), #900, 2001, rue University, Montréal QC H3A 2A6 – 514/499-0561; Fax: 514/499-1844 – Tirage: 80 000; Mensuel; français – Editeur, Michéle Cyr

Elm Street (Published by Multi-Vision Publishing), #1000, 655 Bay St., Toronto ON M5G 2K4 – 416/595-9944; Fax: 416/595-7217 – Circ.: 700,000; 6 times a year – Editor-in-chief, Stevie Cameron

L'Essentiel (Published by Publicor), 7, ch Bates, Outremont QC H2V 1A6 – 514/270-1100; Fax: 514/270-6900 – Tirage: 94 750; Mensuel; français – Rédacteur, Sylvie Laplante

Femme d'Aujourd'hui (Published by Trustar Ltd.), #2000, 2020, rue University, Montréal QC H5A 2A5 – 514/848-7000; Fax: 514/848-9854 – Mensuel; français – Editeur, Claude J. Charron

Femme Plus (Published by Publicor), 7, ch Bates, Outremont QC H2V 1A6 – 514/270-1100; Fax: 514/270-6900 – Tirage: 57,790; Mensuel; français – Rédacteur, Jean-Louis Maubois

Filles d'aujourd'hui (Published by Publicor), 7, ch Bates, Outremont QC H2V 1A6 – 514/270-1100; Fax: 514/270-6900 – Tirage: 54,211; Mensuel; français – Rédacteur, Francine Trudeau

Fireweed: A Feminist Quarterly of Writing, Politics, Art & Culture, PO Box 279, Stn B, Toronto ON M5T 2W2 – 416/504-1339 – Circ.: 1,500; 4 times a year – Co-ordinating Editor, Mary Myers

Focus on Women, Campbell Communicatons Inc., #1, 1218 Langley St., Victoria BC V8W 1W2 – 250/388-7231; Fax: 250/383-1140; Email: focus@octonet.com – Circ.: 30,000; Monthly – Publisher, Leslie Campbell; Editor, Kerry Slavens

Herizons, Herizons Magazine Inc., PO Box 128, Stn Main, Winnipeg MB R3C 2G1 – 204/774-6225; Fax: 204/786-8038 – 4 times a year; ISSN 0711-7485 – Business Manager, Yvonne Block; Editor, Penni Mitchell

Homemaker's (Published by Telemedia Publishing), #100, 25 Sheppard Ave. West, North York ON M2N 6S7 – 416/733-7600; Fax: 416/733-8683 – Circ.: 1,600,000; 8 times a year – Publisher, Barrie Pykes; Editor, Sally Armstrong; Circulation Manager, Lisa Rivers

Images (Published by Multi-Vision Publishing), #1000, 655 Bay St., Toronto ON M5G 2K4 – 416/595-9944; Fax: 416/595-7217; Email: Images@m-v-p.com – Circ.: 411,000; 4 times a year – Publishers, Lilia Lozinksi; Editor, Kate MacDonald

JourneyWoman Online, #1703, 50 Prince Arthur Ave., Toronto ON M5R 1B5 – 416/929-7654; Fax: 416/929-1433; Email: editor@journeywoman.com; URL: http://www.journeywoman.com – Published on the Internet only; 6 times a year – Publisher, Cine Eve; Editor, Evelyn Hannon; Advertising Manager, L. Hannon

Kinesis, c/o Vancouver Status of Women, #309, 877 East Hastings, Vancouver BC V6A 3Y1 – 604/255-5499; Fax: 604/255-5511; Email: kinesis@web.net – Circ.: 3,000; 10 times a year – Editor, Agnes Huang

Local Women , Bona Dea Words Inc., 6826 - 135A St., Surrey BC V3W 4X3 – 604/591-6557; Fax: 604/591-6557; Email: whiting@intouch.bc.ca; URL: http://www.localwomen.bc.ca – 10 times a year – Editor, Sharon Whiting

LOOKwest Magazine, #314, 602 - 11 Ave. SW, Calgary AB T2R 1J8 – 403/571-5665; Fax: 403/571-5667; Email: lookwest@cadvision.com; URL: http://www.cadvision.com/lookwest – Circ.: 50,000; 6 times a year – Publisher, Jeff Hunter

Magazine Les Ailes de la mode, Les Editions San Francisco inc., 50, de Lauzon, Boucherville QC J4B 1E6 – 514/449-1313; Fax: 514/449-1317 – Tirage: 45 000; 6 fois par an – Rédactrice, Camille Roberge

Modern Woman (Published by Maclean Hunter Publishing), 777 Bay St., Toronto ON M5W 1A7 – 416/596-5425; Fax: 416/593-3197; Email: editors@modernwoman.com – Circ.: 500,000; Monthly – Publisher, Charlotte Empey; Editor, Judy Allen

Ontario Woman, Merrick Enterprises, 20 Edgevalley Dr., Islington ON M9A 4N7 – Circ.: 35,500; 4 times a year – Publisher, John Merrick

Orah Magazine, Canadian Hadassah-WIZO, #900, 1310 Greene Ave., Westmount QC H3Z 2B8 – 514/937-9431; Fax: 514/933-6483 – Circ.: 14,000; 4 times a year – Editor-in-chief, Patricia Joy Alpert; Editor, Ellen Smiley

Point of View, c/o Holt Renfrew, 50 Bloor St. West, Toronto ON M4W 1A1 – 416/960-2917; Fax: 416/922-3240 – Circ.: 132,000; 2 times a year; English & French – Managing Editor, Nancy Moore

Room of One's Own, Growing Room Collective, PO Box 46160, Stn G, Vancouver BC V6R 4G5 – 4 times a year; ISSN: 0316-1609

Women's Education des femmes, Cdn. Congress for Learning Opportunities for Women, 47 Main St., Toronto ON M4E 2V6 – 416/699-1909; Fax: 416/699-2145; Email: cclow@web.apc.org – Circ.: 1,200; 4 times a year; English & French – Editor, Christina Starr; Circulation Manager, Dianne Palachik

**YOUTH**

Adorable, #600, 132, rue Saint-Pierre, Québec QC G1K 4A7 – 418/692-5123; Fax: 418/692-0942; Email: hbarbeau@aol.com – Tirage: 25 000; Mensuel; français – Directrice, Helene Barbeau

The Canadian Leader, PO Box 5112, Stn F, Ottawa ON K2C 3H4 – 613/224-5131; Fax: 613/224-3571; Email: leader@scouts.ca; URL: http://www/scouts.ca – Circ.: 44,000; 10 times a year – Publisher, Andy McLaughlin

Le Magazine Jeunesse, 7383, rue de la Roche, Montréal QC H2R 2T4 – 514/274-6124; Fax: 514/272-5939; Email: grpjeune@total.net – Tirage: 60,000; 4 fois par an; français – Rédacteur, Yves Daigle

The Secondary Press, Just Publishing, #202, 7 Mary St., Hamilton ON L8R 1J6 – 905/546-1139; Fax: 905/546-9538 – Circ.: 7,500; 20 times a year – Publisher, Ross DePalma

Watch Magazine, #245, 401 Richmond St. West, Toronto ON M5V 1X3 – 416/595-1313; Fax: 416/595-1312 – Circ.: 75,000; 12 times a year – Publisher, Doug Stewart; Managing Editor, Paul Anderson

What! A Magazine, #108, 93 Lombard Ave., Winnipeg MB R3B 3B1 – 204/985-8160; Fax: 204/943-8991; Email: what@fox.nstn.ca – Circ.: 200,000; 5 times a year – Publisher, Nancy Moore; Editor, Stuart Slayen; Circulation Manager, Sherry Jones

Youth Culture Incorporated, Watch Magazines Inc., #245, 401 Richmond St. West, Toronto ON M5V 1X3 – 416/595-1313; Fax: 416/595-1312; Email: watchmag@compuserve.com – Circ.: 75,000; 11 times a year – Publisher, Doug Stewart; Editor, Gary Butler

Youth Today, PO Box 390, Stn A, Ottawa ON K1N 8V4 – 819/771-5591; Fax: 819/595-6838 – 12 times a year

## ETHNIC PUBLICATIONS

**ABORIGINAL**

Aboriginal Voices, #201, 116 Spadina Ave., Toronto ON M5V 2K6 – 416/703-4577; Fax: 416/703-4581; Email: abvoices@inforamp.net; URL: http://www.vli.ca/clients/abc/cmall/abvoices – Circ.: 15,000; 4 times a year – Editor-in-Chief, Gary Farmer; Circulation Manager, David Shilling

Alberta Native News, #330, 10036 Jasper Ave., Edmonton AB T5J 2W2 – 403/421-7966; Fax: 403/424-3951 – Circ.: 12,000; 12 times a year – Editor, Dave Moser

Alberta Sweetgrass, 15001 - 112 Ave., Edmonton AB T5M 2V6 – 403/455-2945; Fax: 403/455-7639 – Circ.: 7,000; Monthly – Publisher, Bert Crowfoot

Kahtou News, 5526 Sinku Dr., PO Box 192, Sechelt BC V0N 3A0 – 604/885-7391; Fax: 604/885-7397 – Circ.: 11,000; Monthly – Editor, Stan Dixon

Micmac-Maliseet Nation News, 840 Willow St., PO Box 1590, Truro NS B2N 5V3 – 902/895-6385; Fax: 902/893-1520; Email: nstn2436@fox.nstn.ca – Circ.: 2,000; Monthly – Editor, Tim Bernard

**ARABIC**

Al-Miraat, 2090, ch Côte-Vertu, Saint-Laurent QC H4R 1N7 – 514/337-1100 – Weekly

Arab News International, 602 Millwood Rd., Toronto ON M5A 1K8 – 416/362-0307; Fax: 416/861-0238; Telex: 06-52629 – Bi-weekly

El-Mahroussa, Egyptian Canadian Friendship Association, 879, av St-Charles, Chomedy QC H7V 3T5 – 514/687-0273; Fax: 514/681-0804 – 12 issues a year

**ARMENIAN**

Abaka, 825, rue Manoogian, St-Laurent QC H4N 1Z5 – 514/747-6680; Fax: 514/747-6162; Email: abakaMtl@aol.com – Circ.: 1,500; Weekly; tabloid; Armenian, French & English – Editor, Arsène Mamourian

**BLACK COMMUNITY**

Share, 658 Vaughan Rd., Toronto ON M6E 2Y5 – 416/656-3400; Fax: 416/656-0691 – Circ.: 43,500; Weekly – Publisher, Arnold Auguste; Managing Editor, Jules Elder

**CARIBBEAN**

Caribbean Camera, #212, 55 Nugget Ave., Scarborough ON M1S 3L1 – 416/412-2905; Fax: 416/412-2134 – Weekly

Equality News, #2500, 2500 Eglinton Ave. East, Scarborough ON M1K 2R5 – 416/266-9711; Fax: 416/282-6534 – Circ.: 37,000; Weekly – Publisher & Editor, Bhaskar Sharma

The Jamaican Weekly Gleaner, 1390 Eglinton Ave. West, Toronto ON M6C 2E4 – 416/784-3002, 1-800-565-3961; Fax: 416/784-5719 – Circ.: 120,000; Weekly – Publisher, John Hudson; Editor, Gail Scala

**CELTIC**

Celtic Heritage, PO Box 8805, Stn A, Halifax NS B3K 5M4 – 902/835-6244; Fax: 902/835-0080; Email: celtic@fox.nstn.ns.ca; URL: http://fox.nstn.ca/~celtic – Circ.: 10,000; 6 times a year – Publisher, Angus M. MacQuarrie; Editor, Alexa Thompson; Circulation Manager, Cabrini Macquarrie

**CHINESE**

The Capital Chinese News, 695 Somerset St. West, Ottawa ON K1R 6P5 – 613/837-3564; Fax: 613/834-1193 – Circ.: 4,200; Monthly – Ping J. Chiu; Shane Hsu

Chinese News, #1616, 705 King St. West, Toronto ON M5V 2W8 – 416/504-0761; Fax: 416/504-4928 – Weekly

Ming Pao Daily News, 1355 Huntingwood Dr., Scarborough ON M1S 3J1 – 416/321-0088; Fax: 416/321-6339 – Circ.: 25,803, Mon.-Wed.; 31,353, Thur.-Fri.; 42,653, Sat.; 51,453, Sun.; Daily; Chinese – Editor-in-chief, K.M. Lui; General Manager, Peter Li

Rice Paper, 311 East - 41st Ave., Vancouver BC V5W 1N9 – 604/322-6616; Fax: 604/322-6616; Email: acww@vcn.bc.ca; URL: http://www.asian.ca – President, Jim Wong-Chu

Shing Wah News, 795 Gerrard St. East, Toronto ON M4M 1Y5 – 416/778-1854; Fax: 416/778-8108 – Monthly

Sing Tao Daily, 417 Dundas St. West, Toronto ON M5T 1G6 – 514/596-8140; Fax: 514/599-6688 – Daily

World Journal (Toronto), 415 Eastern Ave., Toronto ON M4M 1B7 – 416/778-0888; Fax: 416/778-1037 – Daily

World Journal (Vancouver), 2288 Clark Dr., Vancouver BC V5N 3G8 – 604/876-1338; Fax: 604/876-3728 – Circ.: 30,000; Daily; Chinese – Publisher, Wang Shaw Lan; Editor, John Hsu

#### CROATIAN

Croatian Voice, PO Box 596, Nanaimo BC V9R 5L5 – 250/754-8282; Fax: 250/753-4303 – Circ.: 2,500; 12 times a year – Publisher, Dr. Mladen G. Zorkin

Glasnik Hrvatske Seljacke Stranke, PO Box 82187, North Burnaby BC V5C 5P2 – 604/524-2813; Fax: 604/521-0030 – Monthly

#### DUTCH

De Hollandse Krant, #201, 20408 Douglas Cres., Langley BC V3A 4B4 – 604/530-9446; Fax: 604/530-9766; Email: holkrant@awinc.com – Circ.: 7,800; Monthly; Dutch – Editor, Gerald Bonekamp

De Nederlandse Courant, 3019 Harvester Rd., Burlington ON L7N 3G4 – 905/333-3615; Fax: 905/333-5958; Email: dutch@inforamp.net – Circ.: 6,000; 26 times a year; Dutch & English – Publisher, Theo Luykenaar; Editor, Rebecca Saager; Circulation Manager, Mark Luykenaar

#### EAST INDIAN

Charhdi Kala, #6, 7743 - 128th St., Surrey BC V3W 4E6 – 604/590-6397; Fax: 604/591-6397 – Weekly; Punjabi & English

Gujarat Vartman, Gujarat Vartman Ltd., 250 Norfinch Dr., North York ON M3N 1Y4 – 416/736-9699; Fax: 416/736-1640 – Circ.: 3,000; Monthly; Gujarti – Editor, J.D. Shah

Indo-Canadian Times, PO Box 2296, Vancouver BC V6B 3W5 – 604/599-5408; Fax: 604/599-5415; Email: indo@direct.ca; URL: http://www.can.can.com/ – Weekly; Punjabi

Indo Canadian Phulwari, Indo Canadian Phulwari Publications Inc., 14891 Spenser Dr., Surrey BC V3S 7K7 – 604/599-6400; Fax: 604/599-6400 – Monthly; English & Punjabi – Editor, Gurjit Singh Sangra

Kerala Express, 1565 Jane St., PO Box 34556, Toronto ON M9N 2R3 – 416/654-0431 – Circ.: 2,000; Weekly; Malayalam – Publisher, J.P. George

Mehfil Magazine, Vig Communications Inc., #109, 3855 Henning Dr., Burnaby BC V5C 6N3 – 604/473-9005; Fax: 604/473-9828 – Circ.: 25,000; 9 times a year; Indo-Canadian – Publisher, Rana Vig

#### ESTONIAN

Meie Elu, 958 Broadview Ave., Toronto ON M4K 2R6 – 416/466-8404; Fax: 416/466-4339 – Weekly

Vaba Eestlane, c/o Free Estonian Publishers, 120A Willowdale Ave., Willowdale ON M2N 4Y2 – 416/733-4551; Fax: 416/733-4550 – Circ.: 2,500; Bi-weekly; Estonian – Editor-in-chief, Arvi E. Tinits

#### FILIPINO

Filipino Journal, 483 Bannatyne Ave., Winnipeg MB R3A 0G2 – 204/943-4512; Fax: 204/943-4512 – 24 times a year

The Philippine Reporter, 807 Queen St. East, Toronto ON M4M 1H8 – 416/461-8694; Fax: 416/461-7399; Email: infro@phil-reproter.com; URL: http://www.phil-reporter.com – Circ.: 8,000; 24 times a year – Editor, Hermie Garcia

#### FINNISH

Canadan Uutiset, Finnews Ltd., 31 North Court St., Thunder Bay ON P7A 4T4 – 807/344-1611; Fax: 807/344-1879; Email: canuutiset@aol.com – Circ.: 1,800; Weekly; English & Finnish – Editor, Sakri A. Viklund

Vapaa Sana, #22, 50 Weybright Ct., Scarborough ON M1S 5A8 – 416/321-0808; Fax: 416/321-0811 – Weekly

#### GERMAN

Deutsche Presse, #303, 455 Spadina Ave., Toronto ON M5S 2G8 – 416/595-9714; Fax: 416/595-9716 – Weekly

Deutsche Presse B.C., #605, 807A Frederick St., Kitchener ON N2B 2B5 – 519/749-0606; Fax: 519/749-8207 – Circ.: 7,500; Weekly; German – Erhard Matthaes

Kanada Kurier, 955 Alexander Ave., Winnipeg MB R3C 2X8 – 204/774-1883; Fax: 204/783-5740 – Weekly

Die Mennonitische Post, PO Box 1120, Steinbach MB R0A 2A0 – 204/326-6790; Fax: 204/326-6302 – 24 times a year

Mennonitische Rundschau, c/o Bd. of Commun. of the Cdn. Conference of the M.B. Churches, #3, 169 Riverton Ave., Winnipeg MB R2L 2E5 – 204/669-6575; Fax: 204/654-1865 – Circ.: 3,000; Monthly; German – Editor, Lorina Marsch; Circulation Manager, Helga Kosdorf

Die Zeit, 29 Coldwater Rd., Toronto ON M3B 1Y8 – 416/391-4196 – Weekly

#### GREEK

Acropolis, 2122 - 47th St. West, Vancouver BC V6M 2M7 – 604/266-6137; Fax: 604/266-3595 – 24 times a year

Courrier Grec, 5700, boul St-Laurent, Montréal QC H2T 1S8 – 514/278-9299; Fax: 514/278-4572 – Weekly

Greek Canadian Action, 4879 Faulkner St., Chomedey QC H7W 1H9 – 514/272-4000; Fax: 514/687-6330; Email: drassis@chomedeynews.ca – Circ.: 44,000; Weekly – Publisher, George Guzmas

Greek Canadian Reportage, #2, 8060, Birnam, Montréal QC H3N 2T7 – 514/279-7772; Fax: 514/279-7772 – Weekly; Greek, English & French

Greek Canadian Tribune, 7835, av Wiseman, Montréal QC H3N 2N8 – 514/272-6873; Fax: 514/272-3157 – Weekly; Greek & English

Hellenic-Canadian Chronicles, Ledra Publishing Ltd., 437 Danforth Ave., Toronto ON M4K 1P1 – 416/465-4628; Fax: 416/465-6592 – Weekly; English & Greek – Editor, Peter Maniatakos

Hellenic Hamilton News, #2, 8 Morris Ave., Hamilton ON L8L 1X7 – 905/549-9208; Fax: 905/549-7935 – Circ.: 2,000; Monthly; Greek – Publisher & Editor, Panos Andronidis

The Hellenic News, Alpha-Omega Communications, 37 Hillsmount Rd., London ON N6K 1W1 – 519/472-4807 – Circ.: 5,000; Monthly – Editor, A. Drossos

#### HUNGARIAN

Kanadai Magyarsag, 74 Advance Rd., Etobicoke ON M8Z 2T7 – 416/233-3131; Fax: 416/233-5964 – Weekly

Menorah-Egyenloseg, #312, 3089 Bathurst S., North York ON M6E 2A4 – 416/780-9168; Fax: 416/780-9167 – Weekly, Fri. – Publisher, Andy Winter; Editor, William Koseras

#### ICELANDIC

Logberg-Heimskringla, 699 Carter Ave., Winnipeg MB R3M 2C3 – 204/284-5686; Fax: 204/284-3870; URL: http://www.helix.net/~rasgeirs/LH – Circ.: 2,000; Weekly (44 issues a year); English & Icelandic – Publisher, Kevin Johnson; Editor, Laureen Narfason; Circulation Manager, Gunnur Isfeld

#### ITALIAN

Alberta Italian Times, 504 Alder Ave., Sherwood Park AB T8A 1S9 – 403/472-6397; Fax: 403/478-5493 – Weekly – Publisher, Josephine Sicoli

Il Cittadino Canadese, #209, 5960, rue Jean Talon est, Montréal QC H1S 3B1 – 514/253-2332; Fax: 514/253-6574 – Weekly; Italian & French

Il Congresso, Cura Enterprises Ltd., 9322 - 109A Ave., Edmonton AB T5H 1E8 – 403/424-3010; Fax: 403/424-3037 – 26 times a year; Italian – Office Manager, Lina Amodio

Corriere Canadese, 890 Caledonia Rd., Toronto ON M6B 3Y1 – 416/785-4300; Fax: 416/785-4329; Email: corriere@hookup.net – Circ.: 28,500; Daily Mon. to Fri. – Founder, Daniel Iannuzzi; Editor, Elena Caprice; Circulation Manager, Vito Mancini

Corriere Italiano, 6900, rue St-Denis, Montréal QC H2S 2S2 – 514/279-4536; Fax: 514/376-4260 – Weekly

L'Eco D'Italia, Zone Publishing, 3849 Hastings St. East, Burnaby BC V5C 2H7 – 604/294-8707; Fax: 604/291-1707 – Circ.: 5,900; Weekly – Editor, Rino Vultaggio

La Gazzetta, 909 Howard Ave., Windsor ON N9A 1S3 – 519/253-8883; Fax: 519/253-3280 – Weekly; Italian & English

Insieme, 4358, rue Charleroi, Montréal QC H1H 1T3 – 514/328-2062; Fax: 514/328-6562; Email: insieme@total.net – Circ.: 38,000; Weekly; Italian – Publisher, P. Giuseppe De Rossi; Editor, Mimmo Forte

Italian Link, #205, 10342 - 107 St., Edmonton AB T5J 1K2 – 403/473-8136; Fax: 403/478-5493 – Monthly

Lo Specchio/Vaughan, #100, 166 Woodbridge Ave., Woodbridge ON L4L 2S7 – 905/856-2823; Fax: 905/856-2825; Email: lospecchio@msn – Circ.: 16,000; Weekly – Editor, Sergio Tagliavini

Il Nuovo Mondo, 8720 - 137 Ave., Edmonton AB T5E 1X4 – 403/472-6397; Fax: 403/478-5493 – 24 times a year; Italian & English

L'Ora Di Ottawa, 203 Louisa St., Ottawa ON K1R 6Y9 – 613/232-5689; Fax: 613/563-2573 – Weekly – Managing Editor, Renata Coppola

Il Rincontro, 6675 Winderton Ave., Montréal QC H3S 2L8 – 514/739-4213; Fax: 514/344-8238 – Circ.: 11,500; Monthly; Italian – Editor, Tony Vellone

Tandem, 890 Caledonia Rd., Toronto ON M6B 3Y1 – 416/785-4300; Fax: 416/785-4329 – Circ.: 35,000; Weekly, Sat. – Editor, Elena Caprice

#### JAPANESE

The New Canadian, 524 Front St. West, Toronto ON M5V 1B8 – 416/593-6118; Fax: 416/593-1871 – Circ.: 4,000; Thur.; English & Japanese – Publisher, Shin Kawai; Editor, Sakura Torizuka

#### KOREAN

The Korea Times Daily, 287 Bridgeland Ave., North York ON M6A 1Z6 – 416/787-1111; Fax: 416/781-7777 – 5 times a week; Korean – Publisher, Lawrence Kim

#### LATVIAN

Latvija-Amerika, 125 Broadview Ave., Toronto ON M4M 2E9 – 416/465-7902; Fax: 416/465-8168 – Weekly

#### LITHUANIAN

Nepriklausoma Lietuva, 7722, rue George, LaSalle QC H8P 1C4 – 514/366-6220 – Bi-weekly

Teviskes Ziburiai, 2185 Stavebank Rd., Mississauga ON L5C 1T3 – 905/275-4672; Fax: 905/275-1336 – Weekly; Lithuanian – Editor-in-Chief, Dr. P. Gaida

#### MACEDONIAN

Macedonia, 364 Old Kingston Rd., PO Box 97589, Scarborough ON M1C 4Z1 – 416/286-7673 –

Monthly; English & Macedonian – Editor, Tanas Jovanovska

**MULTICULTURAL**

Community Digest, #216, 1755 Robson St., Vancouver BC V6G 3B7 – 604/875-8313; Fax: 604/875-0336 – Weekly

New Canada Weekly, #500, 120 Eglinton Ave. East, Toronto ON M4P 1E2 – 416/481-7793; Fax: 416/481-7793 – Circ.: 10,000; Weekly; English & Urdu & French – Publisher & Editor, Hasanat Ahmad Syed

**PAKISTANI**

Eastern News, PO Box 1061, Stn B, Mississauga ON L4Y 2E0 – 905/858-7525, 858-NEWS (newslines); Fax: 905/858-7951 – Circ.: 5,000; 24 times a year – Publisher, Alia Sultana; Editor, Masood Khan

Fortnightly Universal News, PO Box 21051, Stn Bridgeview, Windsor ON N9B 3T4 – 519/253-5851; Fax: 519/253-8658 – Twice monthly; Urdu

Pakeeza International (Published by Directories International Ltd.), 370 Main St. North, PO Box 44007, Brampton ON L6V 4H5 – 905/455-9839; Fax: 905/452-8133; Email: mansoor@emanon.com – Circ.: 4,000; Wed.; Urdu – Publisher & Editor, Sabih Mansoor; Circulation Manager, Umber Mansoor

Shama, PO Box 1304, Stn B, Mississauga ON L4Y 3W4 – 905/826-6397; Fax: 905/858-7951 – Monthly; Urdu

The South Asian Voice (Published by Directories International Ltd.), 370 Main St. North, PO Box 44007, Brampton ON L6V 4H5 – 905/455-9839; Fax: 905/452-8133; Email: mansoor@emanon.com – Circ.: 4,000; Wed.; English & Urdu – Publisher & Managing Editor, Sabih Mansoor; Circulation Manager, Umber Mansoor

**POLISH**

Kulisy Polonii, 10806 - 81 Ave., Edmonton AB T6E 1Y4 – 403/439-0806, 2215; Fax: 403/439-0806 – Circ.: 4,500; 24 times a year – Editor, Mary Carlton

The Polish Canadian Courier, PO Box 161, Stn P, Toronto ON M5S 2S7 – 416/259-4353; Fax: 416/259-4353; 905/274-1470 – Weekly; Polish & English

**PORTUGUESE**

Acontece, 102 Atlantic Ave., PO Box 614, Stn C, Toronto ON M6J 3R9 – 416/533-7799; Fax: 416/533-2410 – 24 times a year

Correio Português, 793 Ossington Ave., Toronto ON M6G 3T8 – 416/532-9894; Fax: 416/532-1475 – 24 times a year

Portugal Ilustrado, 60 Hanson Rd., Unit 138, Mississauga ON L5B 2P6 – 905/279-8368; Fax: 905/279-8368; URL: http://www.webx.ca/portilus – Circ.: 8,000; Weekly – Editor, Manuel Neto

A Voz de Portugal, 4117A, boul St-Laurent, Montréal QC H2W 1Y7 – 514/844-0388; Fax: 514/844-6283 – Circ.: 10,000; Weekly – Editor, Armando Barquairo

**SERBIAN**

Kanadski Srbobran, Serbian League of Canada, 335 Britannia Ave., Hamilton ON L3H 1Y4 – 905/549-4079; Fax: 905/549-8552; Email: dccom@yesic.com – Circ.: 1,000; 3 times a month – President, Cedo Asanin; Editor, Dragan Ciric, Email: dciric@yesic.com; Administrator, Steve Kangrga

Voice of Canadian Serbs, c/o Serbian National Shield Society of Canada, 1900 Sheppard Ave. East,, PO Box 303, Willowdale ON M2J 4T4 – 416/496-7881; Fax: 416/493-0335 – Circ.: 2,000; Monthly; Serbian & English – Editor, Bora Dragasevich

**SLOVAK, CZECH**

Kanadske Listy, 388 Atwater Ave., Mississauga ON L5G 2A3 – 905/278-4116 – Circ.: 2,500; Monthly; Czech – Publisher & Editor, Mirko Janecek

Novy Domov, Masaryk Memorial Institute Inc., 450 Scarborough Golf Club Rd., Scarborough ON M1G 1H1 – 416/439-9557; Fax: 416/439-4646; Email: novydom@interlog.com – Circ.: 3,000; Bi-weekly; Czech, Slovak & English – Editor, Vera M. Roller

**SPANISH**

Correo Latinoamericano, 2413 Dundas St. West, Toronto ON M6P 1X3 – 416/538-0588; Fax: 416/531-7187 – Weekly – Publisher, Eduardo Uruena

El Popular, 2413 Dundas St. West, Toronto ON M6P 1X3 – 416/531-2495; Fax: 416/531-7187 – Daily – Publisher, Eduardo Uruena; Editor, Walter Seminario; Circulation Manager, Mayde Mauianda

La Voz de Montreal, #209, 5960, rue Jean-Talon est, Montréal QC H1S 1M2 – 514/253-2332; Fax: 514/253-6574 – 24 times a year

**SWEDISH**

Swedish Press, 1294 - 7th Ave. West, Vancouver BC V6H 1B6 – 604/731-6381; Fax: 604/731-2292 – Circ.: 6,000; Monthly; English & Swedish; also Scandinavian Press (4 times a year; English) covers all Nordic countries – Publisher & Editor, Anders Neumuller

**UKRAINIAN**

Homin Ukrainy, 140 Bathurst St., Toronto ON M5V 2R3 – 416/504-3443; Fax: 416/703-0687 – Circ.: 15,000; Weekly; Ukrainian & English – Publisher, W. Okipniuk; Editor, O. Romanyshyn

Moloda Ukraina, c/o Walentina Rodak, 12 Minstrel Dr., Toronto ON M8Y 3H4 – 416/255-8604; Fax: 905/238-9821 – Circ.: 1,050; Monthly – Executive Publisher, P. Rodak; Editor, L. Lishchyna

Novy Shliakh, 297 College St., Toronto ON M5T 1S2 – 416/960-3424; Fax: 416/960-1442 – Weekly; also New Pathway Almanac (annual)

Ukrainian News, c/o Edmonton Lasergraphics, #1, 12227 - 107 Ave., Edmonton AB T5M 1Y9 – 403/488-3693; Fax: 403/488-3859; Email: ukrnews@compusmart.ab.ca – Circ.: 6,500; Bi-weekly; English & Ukrainian – Editor, Marco Levytsky; Circulation Manager, Alexandra Cybulsky

Ukrainsky Holos, 842 Main St., Winnipeg MB R2W 3N8 – 204/589-5101; Fax: 204/586-3618 – Weekly; Ukrainian & English

Zhinochy Svit, Ukrainian Women's Organization of Canada, 937 Main St., Winnipeg MB R2W 3P2 – 204/943-8230; Fax: 204/943-8230 – Circ.: 2,500; 10 issues a year; English & Ukrainian – Managing Editor, Anne Wach

## FARM PUBLICATIONS

The Ad-Viser (Published by Robins Southern Printing (1990) Ltd.), 1320 - 36 St. North, Lethbridge AB T1H 5H8 – 403/328-5114; Fax: 403/328-5443 – Circ.: 20,159; Every other Thurs. – Editor, Rick Gillis; Circulation Manager, Leona Milford

Agri-book: Beans in Canada (Published by AIS Communications Ltd.), 145 Thames Rd. West, Exeter ON N0M 1S3 – 519/235-2400; Fax: 519/235-0798 – Circ.: 22,897; Annually – Publisher, Peter Phillips; Editor, Peter Darbishire; Circulation Manager, Jan Jeffery

Agri-book: Corn in Canada (Published by AIS Communications Ltd.), 145 Thames Rd. West, Exeter ON N0M 1S3 – 519/235-2400; Fax: 519/235-0798 – Circ.: 21,360; Annually – Publisher, Peter Phillips; Editor, Peter Darbishire; Circulation Manager, Jan Jeffery

Agri-book: Custom Operator (Published by AIS Communications Ltd.), 145 Thames Rd. West, Exeter ON N0M 1S3 – 519/235-2400; Fax: 519/235-0798 – Circ.: 3,000; Annual – Publisher, Peter Phillips; Editor, Peter Darbishire

Agri-book: Drainage Contractor (Published by AIS Communications Ltd.), 145 Thames Rd. West, Exeter ON N0M 1S3 – 519/235-2400; Fax: 519/235-0798 – Circ.: 8,425; Annually – Publisher, Peter Phillips; Editor, Peter Darbishire; Circulation Manager, Jan Jeffery

Agri-book: Potatoes in Canada (Published by AIS Communications Ltd.), 145 Thames Rd. West, Exeter ON N0M 1S3 – 519/235-2400; Fax: 519/235-0798 – Circ.: 3,363; Annually – Publisher, Peter Phillips; Editor, Peter Darbishire; Circulation Manager, Jan Jeffery

Agri-book: Top Crop Manager (Published by AIS Communications Ltd.), 145 Thames Rd. West, Exeter ON N0M 1S3 – 519/235-2400; Fax: 519/235-0798 – Circ.: 31,397; 4 times a year – Publisher, Peter Phillips; Editor, Peter Darbishire; Circulation Manager, Jan Jeffery

Agricom, 2474 Champlain St., CP 220, Clarence Creek ON K0A 1N0 – 613/488-2651; Fax: 613/488-2541; Email: info.agricom@atreide.net – 22 times a year – Editor, Pierre Glaude

AgWorld news, The StarPhoenix, 204 - 5th Ave. North, Saskatoon SK S7K 2P1 – 306/664-8340; Fax: 306/664-8208 – Circ.: 67,206; 12 times a year

Alberta Beef, #202, 2915 - 19 St. NE, Calgary AB T2E 7A2 – 403/250-1090; Fax: 403/291-9546 – Circ.: 13,400; 12 times a year – Publisher/Editor, Garth McClintock

Alberta FarmLIFE, #200, 4850 - 51 St., Red Deer AB T2N 2A5 – 403/343-2769; Fax: 403/343-2736 – Circ.: 168,000; 24 times a year – Manager, Keith Rideout

Barley Country, c/o Alberta Barley Commission, #237, 2116 - 27 Ave. NE, Calgary AB T2E 7A6 – 403/291-9111; Fax: 403/291-0190; Email: abbarley@cadvision.com – Circ.: 40,936; 4 times a year – Editor, Shannon Park

B.C. Agri Digest, RR#2, Chase BC V0E 1M0 – 250/679-5362; Fax: 250/679-5362; Email: frankay@netshop.net; URL: http://www.shuswap.bc.ca/sunny/fkay-mg.htm – Circ.: 11,862; 12 times a year; Aug. issue - BC Agri Directory (annual) – Publisher & Editor, Fran Kay; Circulation Manager, Delores Barkman

B.C. Dairy Directory, #108, 10721 - 139 St., Surrey BC V3T 4L8 – 604/582-7288; Fax: 604/583-3000 – Circ.: 1,400; Annually, June – Publisher, Lloyd Mackey; Editor, Edna Mackey

B.C. Orchardist, Growers Publishing, PO Box 423, Salmon Arm BC V1E 4N6 – 250/833-0071; Fax: 250/833-0622 – Monthly – Publisher, Jim Hayward; Editor, E.W. Noonan

B.C. Simmental News, 1860 - 232nd Ave., RR#9, Langley BC V3A 6H5 – 604/533-1054; Fax: 604/533-1054 – Circ.: 4,000; 4 times a year – K. Mary Watt

Beef in B.C. Inc., c/o B.C. Cattlemen's Association, #4, 10145 Durango Rd., Kamloops BC V2C 6T4 – 250/573-3611; Fax: 250/573-5155 – Circ.: 3,000; 7 times a year – Editor, A.L. Leach

Le Bulletin des Agriculteurs, 514/843-2100; Fax: 514/845-6261; Email: bulletin@maclean-hunter-quebec.qc.ca; URL: http://www.cyberplex.com/bulletin – Tirage: 30,000; Mensuel; français – Editeur, Simon M. Guertin; Rédacteur, Marc-Alain Soucy

CAAR Communicator, Canadian Association of Agricultural Retailers, #107, 1090 Waverly St., PO Box 13, Winnipeg MB R3T 0P4 – 204/989-9300; Fax: 204/989-9306; Email: robeva@freenet.mb.ca – Circ.: 3,300; 4 times a year – R. Anderson

Canada Poultryman (Published by Farm Papers Ltd.), #105B, 9547 - 152 St., Surrey BC V3R 5Y5 – 604/585-3131; Fax: 604/585-1504; Email: tgreaves@wimsey.com – Circ.: 7,734; Monthly; English & French – Editor, Tony Greaves; Circulation Manager, Irene Trueman

Canada's Who's Who Of The Poultry Industry (Published by Farm Papers Ltd.), #105B, 9547 - 152 St., Surrey BC V3R 5Y5 – 604/585-3131; Fax: 604/585-1504; Email: tgreavers@wimsey.com –

Circ.: 4,993; Annually, June – Editor, Tony Greaves; Circulation Manager, Irene Trueman

Canadian Ayrshire Review, PO Box 188, Ste-Anne-de-Bellevue QC H9X 1C0 – 514/398-7970; Email: info@ayrshire-canada.com; URL: http://www.ayrshire-canada.com – Monthly; English & French – Business Manager, Linda Ness

Canadian Fruitgrower (Published by Annex Publishing & Printing Inc.), 222 Argyle Ave., Delhi ON N4B 2Y2 – 519/582-2513; Fax: 519/582-4040 – Circ.: 3,200; 9 times a year – Publisher, Dave Douglas

Canadian Guernsey Journal, Canadian Guernsey Assn., 368 Woolwich St., Guelph ON N1H 3W6 – 519/836-2141; Fax: 519/824-9250 – 2 times a year – Editor, V.M. Macdonald

Canadian Hereford Digest, 5160 Skyline Way NE, Calgary AB T2E 6V1 – 403/274-1734 – Monthly, except July; English & French – Publisher & Editor, Kurt Gilmore

Canadian Jersey Breeder, 350 Speedvale Ave. West, Unit 9, Guelph ON N1H 7M7 – 519/821-9150; Fax: 519/821-2723 – 10 times a year – Editor, Betty Clements

Canadian Ostrich (Published by Dakota Design & Advertising Ltd.), #201, 2915 - 19th St. NE, Calgary AB T2E 7A2 – 403/250-1128; Fax: 403/250-1194 – Circ.: 2,600; Monthly – Co-Publisher, Ruth Dunbar; Co-Publisher & Editor, Ingrid Schulz

The Canadian Tobacco Grower (Published by Annex Publishing & Printing Inc.), 222 Argyle Ave., Delhi ON N4B 2Y2 – 519/582-2513; Fax: 519/582-4040 – Circ.: 2,800; 7 times a year – Publisher, David Douglas

Canola Country, Saskatchewan Canola Growers Association, #210, 111 Research Dr., Saskatoon SK S7N 3R2 – 306/668-2380; Fax: 306/975-1126 – Circ.: 1,100; 6 times a year – Editor, Holly Rask

Canola Guide (Published by Farm Business Communications), #2500, 201 Portage Ave., PO Box 6600, Winnipeg MB R3C 3A7 – 204/944-2254; Fax: 204/944-5416; Email: bstrautman@fbc.unitedgrain.ca – Circ.: 26,000; 9 times a year – Managing Director, Palmer Anderson; Editor, Bill Strautman; Circulation Manager, Heather Anderson

Cattlemen Magazine (Published by Farm Business Communications), #2500, 201 Portage Ave., PO Box 6600, Winnipeg MB R3C 3A7 – 204/944-5750; Fax: 204/942-8463; Email: gwinslow@fbc.unitedgrain.ca – Circ.: 27,200; Monthly – Editor, Gren Winslow; Circulation Manager, Andy Sirski

Central Alberta Adviser, Red Deer Publications, 5929 - 48th Ave., PO Box 5023, Stn MPO, Red Deer AB T4N 6R4 – 403/346-3356; Fax: 403/347-6620; Email: RDPUB@cnnet.com – Circ.: 27,327; Weekly – Publisher, Cal Dallas; Editor, Glen Werkman

Central Alberta Farmer (Published by Bowes Publishers Ltd.), 4504 - 61 Ave., Leduc AB T9E 3Z1 – 403/986-2271; Fax: 403/986-6397; Email: leduc_rep@awnet.net – Circ.: 26,428; 12 times a year – Publisher, Neil Sutcliffe

Central Alberta Life (Published by Red Deer Advocate), 2950 Bremner Ave., PO Box 5200, Red Deer AB T4N 5G3 – 403/343-2400; Fax: 403/342-4051 – Circ.: 38,500; Weekly – Publisher, Howard Jenzen; Editor, Joe McLaughlin; Circulation Manager, Allan Melbourne

Charolais Banner (Published by Charolais Banner Ltd.), #205, 3016 - 19 St. NE, Calgary AB T2E 6Y9 – 403/291-1420; Fax: 403/291-0081; URL: http://www/charolaisbanner.com – Circ.: 3,000; 10 times a year – Managing Editor, Rob Pek; Circulation Manager, Sharon Degner

Charolais Connection (Published by Charolais Banner Ltd.), #205, 3016 - 19 St. NE, Calgary AB T2E 6Y9 – 403/291-1420; Fax: 403/291-0081 – Circ.: 30,000; 2 times a year – Managing Editor, Rob Pek

Le Coopérateur Agricole, #200, 9001, boul de l'Acadie, CP 500, Montréal QC H4N 3H7 – 514/384-6450; Fax: 514/858-2025 – Tirage: 25,439; 9 fois par an; français – Rédacteur, Patrick Dupuis

Corn-Soy Guide (Published by Farm Business Communications), #2500, 201 Portage Ave., PO Box 6600, Winnipeg MB R3C 3A7 – 204/944-5760; Fax: 204/942-8463; Email: dwreford@fbc.unitedgrain.ca – Circ.: 22,500; 10 times a year – Editor, Dave Wreford; Circulation Manager, Andy Sirski

Country Guide (Published by Farm Business Communications), #2500, 201 Portage Ave., PO Box 6600, Winnipeg MB R3C 3A7 – 204/944-5761; Fax: 204/942-8463; Email: dwreford@fbc.unitedgrain.ca; URL: http://www.agriculture.com – Circ.: 69,000; 11 times a year – Managing Director, Palmer Anderson; Managing Editor, Dave Wreford; Circulation Manager, Heather Anderson

Country Life in B.C., 3308 King George Hwy., Surrey BC V4P 1A8 – 604/536-7622; Fax: 604/536-5677; Email: countrylife@bc.sympatico.ca – Circ.: 8,176; Monthly – Publisher & Editor, Malcolm Young; Circulation Manager, L.A. Noonan

Dairy Contact, PO Box 549, Onoway AB T0E 1V0 – 403/967-2929; Fax: 403/967-2930 – Monthly – Editor, Allen Parr

Dairy Guide (Published by Farm Business Communications), #2500, 201 Portage Ave., PO Box 6600, Winnipeg MB R3C 3A7 – 204/944-5750; Fax: 204/942-8463; Email: gwinslow@fbc.unitedgrain.ca; URL: http://www.mbnet.mb.ca/~wilkins – Circ.: 18,100; 5 times a year – Editor, Gren Winslow; Circulation Manager, Andy Sirski, 204/944-5762

Economic Planning in Free Societies, Academic Publishing Co., PO Box 145, Mount Royal QC H3P 3B9 – 514/738-5255; Fax: 514/738-5255, 305/463-7020, Nov.-May – Circ.: 1,200; 6 times a year – Editor, Dr. Peter Harsany; Circulation Manager, A. Graul

Equi Links Farm & Ranch, #260, 720 - 28th St. NE, Calgary AB T2A 6R3 – 403/569-7422; Fax: 403/569-0771 – Circ.: 69,500; Monthly – Publisher, Dennis McCormack; Editor, Mickey Dumont

Farm & Country (Published by Agricultural Publishing Co Ltd.), #1504, One Yonge St., Toronto ON M5E 1E5 – 416/364-5324; Fax: 416/364-5857 – Circ.: 51,870; 18 times a year; also Farm Power Today (monthly supplement) – Managing Editor, John Muggeridge

Farmers' Choice (Published by Red Deer Advocate), 2950 Bremner Ave., PO Box 5200, Red Deer AB T4N 5G3 – 403/343-2400; Fax: 403/342-4051 – Circ.: 83,600; Monthly – Publisher, Howard Jenzen; Editor, Joe McLaughlin; Circulation Manager, Allan Melbourne

Farm Focus, Cameron Publishing, PO Box 128, Yarmouth NS B5A 4B1 – 902/742-7111; Fax: 902/742-2311 – Circ.: 7,982; 24 times a year

The Farm Gate, North Waterlook Publishing Ltd., 15 King St., Elmira ON N3B 2R1 – 519/669-5155; Fax: 519/669-5928; Email: enews@bond.net – Circ.: 21,000; Monthly

Farm Light & Power, 2352 Smith St., Regina SK S4P 2P6 – 800/668-3300; Fax: 800/213-9999 – Circ.: 70,363; Monthly – Publisher, Tom Bradley

Farm Review, 12 Dundas St. East, Napanee ON K7R 1H5 – 613/354-6648; Fax: 613/354-6708 – Monthly – Publisher, Victor Mlodecki; Editor, Kathleen Clark

Feather Fancier, 4094 Ross St., RR#5, Forest ON N0N 1J0 – 519/899-2364; Fax: 519/899-2364 – Circ.: 2,800; 11 times a year – Co-Publisher, Linda Gryner; Co-Publisher & Editor, James Gryner

Germination, Issues Ink, #203, 897 Corydon Ave., Winnipeg MB R3M 0W7 – 204/453-1965; Fax: 204/475-5247 – Circ.: 4,000; 4 times a year – Editor, Robynnne Anderson Eva

Gestion et Technologie Agricoles, 655, av Sainte-Anne, St-Hyacinthe QC J2S 5G4 – 514/773-6028; Fax: 514/773-3115 – Tirage: 20,000; 8 fois par an; français – Rédacteur, Louis A. Bernard

Grainews (Published by Farm Business Communications), #2500, 201 Portage Ave., PO Box 6600, Winnipeg MB R3C 3A7 – 204/944-5587; Fax: 204/944-5416; Email: jham@fbc/unitedgrain.ca – Circ.: 52,000; 16 times a year – Managing Director, Palmer Anderson; Editor, Andy Sirski; Circulation Manager, Heather Anderson

The Grower, c/o Ontario Fruit & Vegetable Growers Assn., #103, 355 Elmira Rd., Guelph ON N1K 1S5 – 519/763-6160; Fax: 519/763-6604 – Circ.: 8,000; Monthly – Editor, Gayle Anderson, 519/763-8728

Le Guide de l'Agriculture du Québec (Published by Publiédition inc.), 620, boul Industriel, St-Jean-sur-Richelieu QC J3B 7X4 – 514/856-7821; Fax: 514/359-0836 – Tirage: 5,000; Annuellement – Éditeur, Yves Bégnoche

Holstein Journal, 9120 Leslie St., Unit 105, Richmond Hill ON L4B 3J9 – 905/886-4222; Fax: 905/866-0037 – Circ.: 9,577; Monthly; English & French – Publisher, Peter English; Editor, Bonnie Cooper

Huron Soil & Crop News, c/o Exeter Times-Advocate, 424 Main St., Exeter ON N0M 1S0 – 519/235-1331; Fax: 519/235-0766 – Circ.: 7,000; Annually, March – Editor, Ross Haugh

Island Farmer, PO Box 790, Montague PE C0A 1R0 – 902/838-2515; Fax: 902/838-4392 – Circ.: 2,000; 26 times a year – Publisher, J. MacNeill

The Limousin Leader, Bollum Marketing, #253, 1935 - 32 Ave. NE, Calgary AB T2E 7C8 – 403/291-6770; Fax: 403/291-6744 – 11 times a year – Editor, Randy Bollum

The Manitoba Co-Operator, 220 Portage Ave., PO Box 9800, Winnipeg MB R3C 3K7 – 204/934-0401; Fax: 204/934-0480 – Circ.: 23,600; Weekly – Publisher/Editor, John W. Morriss

Manitoba Farm Life, Deversa Group, #1, 217 - 10th St., Brandon MB R7A 4E9 – 204/727-5459; Fax: 204/729-8965 – 24 times a year – Editor, Craig Laursen

Ma Revue de machinerie agricole, Rubricor inc., CP 454, Drummondville QC J2B 6W4 – 819/478-2136; Fax: 819/478-4819 – Tirage: 35,000; 11 fois par an; français – Rédacteur, Jean-Marc Beland

Le Meunier, #115, 2323, boul du Versant Nord, Ste-Foy QC G1N 4P4 – 418/688-9227; Fax: 418/688-3575 – 4 fois par an; français – Directeur, Andre J. Pilon

Niagara Farmers' Monthly, 131 College St., PO Box 52, Smithville ON L0R 2A0 – 905/957-3751; Fax: 905/957-0088 – Circ.: 18,000; 11 times a year – Publisher & Editor, I.G. Carruthers; Circulation Manager, Rob Shepherd

The Northern Horizon, 901 - 100th Ave., Dawson Creek BC V1G 1W2 – 250/782-4888; Fax: 250/782-6770 – Circ.: 28,055; 25 times a year – Publisher, Margaret Forbes; Editor, Reg Minall; Circulation Manager, Tiffany Lewis

Northern Horse Review (Published by Dakota Design & Advertising Ltd.), #201, 2915 - 19th St. NE, Calgary AB T2E 7A2 – 403/250-1128; Fax: 403/250-1194; Email: dakota@supernet.ab.ca – Circ.: 10,000; 10 times a year – Co-Publisher, Ruth Dunbar; Co-Publisher & Editor, Ingrid Schulz

Northwest Farmer/Rancher (Published by Battleford Publishing Ltd.), PO Box 1029, North Battleford SK S9A 3E6 – 306/445-7261; Fax: 306/445-3223 – Circ.: 15,000; 4 times a year – Publisher, Steven Dills; Editor, Lorne Cooper

Ontario Beef, Ontario Cattlemen's Assn., 130 Malcolm Rd., Guelph ON N1K 1B1 – 519/824-0334; Fax: 519/824-9101; Email: ontbeef@cattle.guelph.on.ca; URL: http://www.cattle.guelph.on.ca – Circ.: 21,000; 5 times a year – Editor, Sandra Eby; Circulation Manager, Donna Corbet

Ontario Beef Farmer (Published by Bowes Publishers Ltd.), PO Box 7400, London ON N5Y 4X3 – 519/

471-8520; Fax: 519/473-2256 – Circ.: 12,800; 4 times a year – Publisher, Mervyn J. Hawkins; Editor, Paul Mahon; Circulation Manager, Arland Klein

Ontario Corn Producer, c/o Ontario Corn Producers Assn., 90 Woodlawn Rd. West, Guelph ON N1H 1B2 – 519/837-1660; Fax: 519/837-1674; Email: ontcorn@ontariocorn.org; http://www.ontariocron.org – Circ.: 21,000; 10 times a year – Editor, Terry Boland

Ontario Dairy Farmer (Published by Bowes Publishers Ltd.), PO Box 7400, London ON N5Y 4X3 – 519/473-0010; Fax: 519/473-2256; Email: ontariofarmer@online.sys.com – Circ.: 13,900; 6 times a year – Publisher, Mervyn J. Hawkins; Editor, Paul Mahon

Ontario Farmer (Published by Bowes Publishers Ltd.), PO Box 7400, London ON N5Y 4X3 – 519/473-0010; Fax: 519/473-2256 – Circ.: 33,800; Weekly, Tues. – Publisher, Mervyn J. Hawkins; Editor, Paul Mahon; Circulation Manager, Arland Klein

Ontario Hog Farmer (Published by Bowes Publishers Ltd.), PO Box 7400, London ON N5Y 4X3 – 519/473-0010; Fax: 519/473-2256 – Circ.: 8,500; 6 times a year – Publisher, Mervyn J. Hawkins; Editor, Paul Mahon; Circulation Manager, Arland Klein

Ontario Milk Producer, Dairy Farmers of Ontario, 6780 Campobello Rd., Mississauga ON L5N 2L8 – 905/821-8970; Fax: 905/821-3160; Email: bdimmick@milk.ong – Circ.: 11,500; Monthly – Editor, Bill Dimmick, 905/821-8035

Porc Québec, 555, boul Roland Therrien, Longueuil QC J4H 3Y9 – 514/679-0530, ext.276; Fax: 514/670-4788; Email: publicite@tcn.upa.qc.ca – Tirage: 3,700; 5 times a year – Hélène Perrault

Pork Producer (Published by Agricultural Publishing Co Ltd.), #1504, One Yonge St., Toronto ON M5E 1E5 – 416/364-5324; Fax: 416/364-5857 – Circ.: 7,300; 4 times a year – Managing Editor, Bernard Tobin

The Prairieland Agricultural Newspaper, L & L Communications Inc., PO Box 1623, Rosetown SK S0L 2V0 – 306/882-2221; Fax: 306/882-2217 – Circ.: 65,400; 20 times a year – Editor, Kevin Hursh

Pro-farm, 1836 Victoria Ave., Regina SK S4N 7K3 – 306/586-5866; Fax: 306/586-2707 – Circ.: 9,000; 6 times a year – Publisher, Chris Dodd; Editor, Alanna Koch; Circulation Manager, Glenys Fox

Le Producteur de lait québécois, Fédération des producteurs de lait du Québec, 555, boul Roland Thérrien, Longueuil QC J4H 3Y9 – 514/679-0530; Fax: 514/670-4788; Email: publicite@tcn.upa.qc.ca – Tirage: 14,099; Mensuel; français – Rédacteur en chef, Jean Vigneault

Producteur Plus, 455A, rue St-Hilaire, CP 147, Farnham QC J2N 2R4 – 514/293-8282; Fax: 514/293-8554 – Tirage: 22,000; 10 fois par an; français – Directeur, Bertrand Beaumont; Rédacteur, Leonard Pigeon

Professional Farm Magazine, 41 West 1st Ave. South, Magrath AB T0K 1J0 – 403/758-3661; Fax: 403/758-3818; Email: pfmag@agt.net – Circ.: 11,500; 6 times a year – Pubisher, Duane Thomson

Québec Farmers' Advocate, CP 80, Ste-Anne-de-Bellevue QC H9X 3L4 – 514/457-2010; Fax: 514/398-7972 – Tirage: 4,000; 11 times a year – Publisher, Hugh Maynard; Managing Editor, Susanne Brown

Rural Roots, 30 - 10th Ave. East, PO Box 550, Prince Albert SK S6V 5R9 – 306/764-4276; Fax: 306/763-3331 – Circ.: 35,000; 50 times a year – Publisher, Bob Gibb; Editor, Barb Gustafson

The Rural Voice (Published by North Huron Publishing Ltd.), 136 Queen St., PO Box 429, Blyth ON N0M 1H0 – 519/523-4311; Fax: 519/523-9140 – Circ.: 15,100; Monthly – Publisher & Editor, Keith Roulston; Circulation Manager, Joan Caldwell

Saskatchewan Farm Life, #4, 75 Lenore Dr., Saskatoon SK S7K 7Y1 – 306/242-5723; Fax: 306/244-6656 – 25 times a year

Simmental Country, Pritchett Publications, #13, 4101 - 19 St. NE, Calgary AB T2E 7C4 – 403/250-5255; Fax: 403/250-5279 – Monthly – Publisher/Editor, Ted Pritchett

Southern Farm Guide, The Weyburn Review, 904 East Ave., PO Box 400, Weyburn SK S4H 2K4 – 306/842-7487; Fax: 306/842-0282 – Circ.: 17,675; 12 times a year – Publisher, Darryl Ward; Editor, Patricia Ward

La Terre de chez-nous, Agricultural Producers Union, 555, boul Roland Thérrien, Longueuil QC J4H 3Y9 – 514/679-0530; Fax: 514/670-4788; Email: publicite@tcn.upa.qc.ca – Tirage: 39,500; Hebdomadaire; français – Rédacteur en chef, France Groulx

Union Farmer Quarterly, National Farmers Union, 250C - 2nd Ave. South, Saskatoon SK S7K 2M1 – 306/652-9465; Fax: 306/664-6226 – Circ.: 4,300; 4 times a year – Editor, Carla Roppel

Voice of the Essex Farmer, 254 Main St., PO Box 490, Dresden ON N0P 1M0 – 519/683-4485; Fax: 519/683-4355 – Circ.: 35,000; Bi-weekly; also - Voice of the Huron Farmer, Voice of the Kent Farmer, Voice of the Lambton Farmer, Voice of the Middlesex Farmer, Voice of the Elgin Farmer, Voice of the Perth Farmer, Voice of the Ox – Publisher, Denise Thibeault; Editor, Peter Epp; Circulation Manager, Marilyn Leitch

Western Dairy Farmer Magazine (Published by Bowes Publishers Ltd.), 4504 - 61 Ave., Leduc AB T9E 3Z1 – 403/986-2271; Fax: 403/986-6397; Email: wdfarmer@ccinet.ab.ca – Circ.: 6,400; 5 times a year – Publisher, Neil Sutcliffe; Editor, Ken Nelson; Circulation Manager, Karen Clayton

Western Hog Journal, Alberta Pork Producers Development Corp., 10319 Princess Elizabeth Ave., Edmonton AB T5G 0Y5 – 403/474-8288; Fax: 403/471-8065 – Circ.: 7,723; 4 times a year – Editorial Director, Ward Toma

The Western Producer, PO Box 2500, Saskatoon SK S7K 2C4 – 306/665-3500, 1-800-667-7776; Fax: 306/653-1255; Email: newsroom@producer.com; URL: http://www.producer.com/ – Circ.: 98,000; Weekly – Publisher, Allan Laughland; Editor, Garry Fairbairn, 306/665-3577; Circulation Manager, Glenn Caleval

## SCHOLARLY PUBLICATIONS

18th Century Fiction (Published by University of Toronto Press), Journals Division, 5201 Dufferin St., North York ON M3H 5T8 – 416/667-7810; Fax: 416/667-7881; Email: journals@utpress.utoronto.ca – Circ.: 560; 4 times a year – Editor, David Blewett; Circulation Manager, Wendy Thornton

Acadiensis: Journal of the History of the Atlantic Region, Campus House, University of New Brunswick, PO Box 4400, Stn A, Fredericton NB E3B 5A3 – 506/453-4978; Fax: 506/453-4599; Email: Acadnsis@unb.ca – Circ.: 900; 2 times a year; English & French – Editor, Gail Campbell

Annals of Air & Space Law, Institute & Centre of Air & Space Law, McGill University, 3661 Peel St., Montréal QC H3A 1X1 – 514/398-3544; Fax: 514/398-8197; Email: annals@falaw.lan.mcgill.ca; URL: http://www.iasl.mcgill.ca – Circ.: 1,000; 2 times a year – Editor, Dr. Michael Milde; Circulation Manager, Melissa Knock

Anthropologica, c/o Dr. Andrew Lyons, Dept. of Sociology & Anthropology, Wilfrid Laurier University, Waterloo ON N2L 3C5 – 519/884-1970; Fax: 519/884-8854; Email: alyons@mach1.wlu.ca; 1christi@mach1.wlu.ca – 2 times a year – Andrew Lyongs, Dr.; Dr. Karen Szala-Meneok

Arctic, c/o Arctic Institute of North America, University of Calgary, 2500 University Dr. NW, Calgary AB T2N 1N4 – 403/220-7515; Fax: 403/282-4609; Email: kmccullo@acs.ucalgary.ca; URL: http://www.ucalgary.ca/aina/ – Circ.: 2,200; 4 times a year; ISSN: 0004-0843 – Editor, Dr. Karen McCullough, 403/220-4049

ARIEL -- A Review of International English Literature, Dept. of English, University of Calgary, 2500 University Dr. NW, Calgary AB T2N 1N4 – 403/220-4657; Fax: 403/289-1123; Email: ariel@acs.ucalgary.ca – Circ.: 1,000; 4 times a year – Editor, Victor J. Ramraj

BC Studies: The British Columbian Quarterly, c/o University of British Columbia, #165, 1855 West Mall, Vancouver BC V6T 1Z2 – 604/822-3727; Fax: 604/822-9452; Email: bcstudies@unixg.ubc.ca; URL: http://www.swifty.com/bcamp/directors/humansci/bcs.html – Circ.: 650; 4 times a year – Co-Editor, Jean Barman; Co-Editor, R. Cole Harris

Canadian Children's Literature, c/o Dept. of English, University of Guelph, Guelph ON N1G 2W1 – 519/824-4120, ext.3189; Fax: 519/837-1315; Email: ccl@uoguelph.ca; URL: http://www.uoguelph.ca/englit/ccl/ – Circ.: 900; 4 times a year; English & French; ISSN 0319-0080 – Co-Editor, Mary Rubio; Co-Editor, Daniel Chouinard

Canadian Ethnic Studies, University of Calgary, 2500 University Dr. NW, Calgary AB T2N 1N4 – 403/220-7257; Fax: 403/284-5467 – 3 times a year; ISSN: 0008-3496

Canadian Folk Music Journal (Published by Becker Associates), PO Box 507, Stn Q, Toronto ON M4T 2M5 – 416/483-7282; Fax: 416/489-1713 – Annually; ISSN 0318-2568 – Editor, Prof. Jay Rahn

Canadian Foreign Policy, PO Box 70030, Ottawa ON K2P 2M3 – 613/241-1391; Fax: 613/241-5911; Email: epotter@gsro.carleton.ca – 3 times a year

The Canadian Historical Review (Published by University of Toronto Press), Journals Division, 5201 Dufferin St., North York ON M3H 5T8 – 416/667-7810; Fax: 416/667-7881; Email: chr@utpress.utoronto.ca – Circ.: 2,200; 4 times a year; English & French – co-Editor, Margaret Conrad; Co-Editor, Keith Walden; Circulation Manager, Wendy Thornton

Canadian Home Economics Journal, Canadian Home Economics Association, #307, 151 Slater St., Ottawa ON K1P 5H3 – 613/238-8817; Fax: 613/238-8972 – Circ.: 2,600; 4 times a year; English & French – Editor, J. Estelle Reddin

Canadian Journal of Development Studies, c/o University of Ottawa, 538 King Edward Ave., Ottawa ON K1N 6N5 – 613/562-5800, ext.1561; Fax: 613/562-5100; Email: cjdsrced@aixl. uottawa.ca; URL: http://www.uottawa.ca/publications/cjds – 3 times a year; English & French – Rédactrice, Brigitte Lévy; Editor, Henry Rempel

Canadian Journal of Economics, University of Toronto Press, #700, 10 St. Mary St., Toronto ON M4Y 2W8 – 416/978-6739; Email: journals@gpw.utcc.utoronto.ca – Circ.: 3,200; 4 times a year – Editor, B. Curtis Eaton, 604/291-5825

Canadian Journal of Higher Education, c/o Canadian Society for the Study of Higher Education, Secretariat, 220 Sinnot Bldg., 70 Dysart Rd., Winnipeg MB R3T 2N2 – 204/474-6211; Fax: 204/474-7607; Email: csshe@cc.umanitoba.ca – Circ.: 550; 3 times a year – Executive Secretary, Dr. Alexander D. Gregor

Canadian Journal of History, Dept. of History, University of Saskatchewan, 9 Campus Dr., Saskatoon SK S7N 5A5 – 306/966-5794; Fax: 306/966-5852; Email: cjh@duke.usask.ca; URL: http://www.usask.ca/history/cjh – Circ.: 725; 3 times a year – Editor-in-Chief, C.A. Kent; Managing Editor, Jacqueline Fraser

The Canadian Journal of Information & Library Science (Published by University of Toronto Press), Journals Division, 5201 Dufferin St., North York

ON M3H 5T8 – 416/667-7810; Fax: 416/667-7881; Email: journals@utpress.utoronto.ca – Circ.: 615; 4 times a year – Editor, Lynne Howarth; Circulation Manager, Wendy Thornton

Canadian Journal of Law & Society, Dept des sciences jurigiques, UQAM, PO Box 8888, Stn Centre-Ville, Montréal QC H3C 3P8 – 514/987-3000, ext.4712; Fax: 514/987-6548; Email: benoist@canelle.telecom.uquam.ca; URL: http://www.juris.uquam.ca/rcds/index_en.htm – Circ.: 400; Biennially; English & French – Editor-in-chief, Roderick Macdonald

Canadian Journal of Linguistics (Published by University of Toronto Press), Journals Division, 5201 Dufferin St., North York ON M3H 5T8 – 416/667-7810; Fax: 416/667-7881; Email: journals@utpress.utoronto.ca – Circ.: 900; 4 times a year – Editor, Anne Rochette; Circulation Manager, Wendy Thornton

Canadian Journal of Mathematics (Published by University of Toronto Press), Journals Division, 5201 Dufferin St., North York ON M3H 5T8 – 416/667-7810; Fax: 416/667-7881 – Circ.: 1,225; 6 times a year – Editor, Dr. Graham Wright; Circulation Manager, Wendy Thornton

Canadian Journal of Philosophy (Published by University of Calgary Press), 2500 University Dr. NW, Calgary AB T2N 1N4 – 403/220-7578; Fax: 403/282-0085; Email: 470513@aoss.ucalgary.ca; URL: http://www.ucalgary.ca/ucpress – Circ.: 1,150; 4 times a year – Editorial Board Coordinator, Dr. T. Hurka

Canadian Journal of Program Evaluation (Published by University of Calgary Press), 2500 University Dr. NW, Calgary AB T2N 1N4 – 403/220-7578; Fax: 403/282-0085; Email: 470513@aoss.ucalgary.ca; URL: http://www.ucalgary.ca/ucpress – Circ.: 1,300; Bi-annually; English & French – Editor, Dr. Robert Segsworth

Canadian Journal of Psychoanalysis (Published by Becker Associates), PO Box 507, Stn Q, Toronto ON M4T 2M5 – 416/483-7282; Fax: 416/489-1713 – Annually; ISSN 0829-3929 – Editor, Dr. Eva P. Lester

Canadian Journal of Sociology, 5-21 Tory Bldg., Dept. of Sociology, University of Alberta, Edmonton AB T6G 2H4 – 403/492-5941; Fax: 403/492-5941; Email: cjscopy@gpu.srv.ualberta.ca – Circ.: 750; 4 times a year; English with French abstracts – Editor, Susan A. McDaniel

Canadian Journal of Women & The Law, 575 King Edward, PO Box 450, Ottawa ON K1N 6N5 – 613/562-5800, ext.3473; Fax: 613/562-5129; Email: cjwlrfd@ftn.net – Circ.: 1,000; 2 times a year; English & French – Editor, Martha Jackman; Circulation Manager, Lucille Béland

Canadian Journal on Aging, Rm. 039, MacKinnon Bldg., University of Guelph, Guelph ON N1G 2W1 – 519/824-4120, ext.6925; Fax: 519/837-9953; Email: rvanderk@uoguelph.ca – Circ.: 1,800; 4 times a year; English & French – Editor, Anne Martin-Matthews; Managing Editor, Rosemary Vanderkamp; Circulation Manager, Christa Parson

Canadian Literature, c/o University of British Columbia, #167, 1855 West Mall, Vancouver BC V6T 1Z2 – 604/822-2780; Fax: 604/822-9452; Email: orders@cdn-lit.ubc.ca; URL: http://www.swifty.com/cdn_lit – Circ.: 1,500; 4 times a year – Editor, E.M. Kröller; Managing Editor, Donna Chin

Canadian Mathematical Bulletin (Published by University of Toronto Press), Journals Division, 5201 Dufferin St., North York ON M3H 5T8 – 416/667-7810; Fax: 416/667-7881 – Circ.: 775; 4 times a year – Editor, Dr. Graham Wright; Circulation Manager, Wendy Thornton

Canadian Modern Language Review (Published by University of Toronto Press), Journals Division, 5201 Dufferin St., North York ON M3H 5T8 – 416/667-7810; Fax: 416/667-7881; Email: cmlr@utpress.utoronto.ca; URL: http://www.utpress.utoronto.ca – Circ.: 1,600; 4 times a year; English & French – Co-Editor, Sharon Lapkin; Circulation Manager, Wendy Thornton

Canadian Poetry: Studies, Documents, Reviews, Dept. of English, University of Western Ontario, Richmond St. North, London ON N6A 3K7 – 519/673-1164; Fax: 519/661-3776; Email: therese@bosshog.arts.wwo.ca – Circ.: 400; 2 times a year – Editor, D.M.R. Bentley

Canadian Public Administration, #401, 1075 Bay St., Toronto ON M5S 2B1 – 416/932-3666; Fax: 416/932-3667; Email: ntl@ipaciapc.ca; URL: http://www.ipaciapc.ca – Circ.: 3,300; 4 times a year – Editor, Paul G. Thomas

Canadian Public Policy, Rm.409, School of Policy Studies, Queen's University, Kingston ON K7L 3N6 – 613/545-6644; Fax: 613/545-6960; Email: constant@qed.econ.queensu.ca; URL: http://qsilver.queensu.ca/~cpp/ – Circ.: 1,500; 4 times a year; English & French – Editor, Charles M. Beach

The Canadian Review of American Studies (Published by University of Calgary Press), 2500 University Dr. NW, Calgary AB T2N 1N4 – 403/220-7578; Fax: 403/282-0085; Email: 470513@aoss.ucalgary.ca; URL: http://www.ucalgary.ca/ucpress – Circ.: 500; 3 times a year; English & French – Editor-in-Chief, Dr. S. Randall

Canadian Review of Comparative Literature (Published by University of Toronto Press), Journals Division, 5201 Dufferin St., North York ON M3H 5T8 – 416/667-7810; Fax: 416/667-7881; Email: journals@utpress.utoronto.ca – Circ.: 260; 4 times a year – Editor, M.V. Dimic; Circulation Manager, Wendy Thornton

Canadian Review of Sociology & Anthropology, #LB-615, 1455 de Maisonneuve West, Montréal QC H3G 1M8 – 514/848-8780; Fax: 514/848-4539; Email: csaa@vax2.concordia.ca – Circ.: 1,700; 4 times a year; French & English – Editor, Rosalind Sydie

Canadian University Music Review, PO Box 507, Stn Q, Toronto ON M4T 2M5 – 416/483-7282; Fax: 416/489-1713; Email: jbecker@interlog.com – Circ.: 400; 2 times a year; ISSN 0710-0353; English & French – Editor, Prof. William R. Bowen; Rédacteur, Marc-André Roberge

Cartographica (Published by University of Toronto Press), Journals Division, 5201 Dufferin St., North York ON M3H 5T8 – 416/667-7810; Fax: 416/667-7881 – Circ.: 1,000; 4 times a year – Editor, Michael Coulson; Circulation Manager, Wendy Thornton

Cheng Review, K.C. Cheng Press, 1462 Queen St. West, Stn Parkdale PO, Toronto ON M6K 1L0 – 416/535-2360; Fax: 416/535-9531 – 4 times a year – Chairman, Kuan-Chyun Cheng

Ctheory, c/o Concordia University, 1455, boul de Maisonneuve ouest, Montréal QC H3G 1M8 – 514/848-2119; Fax: 514/848-4-72; Email: ctheory@vax2.concordia.ca; URL: http://www.ctheory.com – Circ.: 2,500; Weekly; published on the internet – Co-Publisher, Arthur Kroker; Co-Publisher & Editor, Marilouise Kroker, 514/282-9298

Echos du Monde Classique (Published by University of Calgary Press), 2500 University Dr. NW, Calgary AB T2N 1N4 – 403/220-7578; Fax: 403/282-0085; Email: 470513@aoss.ucalgary.ca; URL: http://www.ucalgary.ca/ucpress – Circ.: 750; 3 times a year; English & French – Dr. Mark Joyal

Economics Working Papers, Dept. of Economics, McMaster University, Hamilton ON L8S 4M4 – 905/525-9140, ext.23821; Fax: 905/521-8232; Email: hannank@mcmaster.ca – Circ.: 75; 4 times a year – Editor, Lonnie Magee, Email: magee@mcmaster.ca; Working Papers Secretary, Kathleen Hannan

Ellipse, Faculté des Lettres et sciences humaines, Université de Sherbrooke, Sherbrooke QC J1K 2R1 – 819/821-7238; Fax: 819/821-7285 – Circ.: 750; 2 times a year; English & French – Director, Charly Bouchara, 514/821-7000, ext.3268

Energy Studies Review, McMaster University, Hamilton ON L8S 4M4 – 905/525-9140, ext.4527; Fax: 905/521-8232 – 3 times a year; ISSN: 0843-4379

Environments: A Journal of Interdisciplinary Studies, Heritage Resources Ctr., Faculty of Environmental Studies, University of Waterloo, Waterloo ON N2L 3G1 – 519/885-1211, ext.2072; Fax: 519/746-2031; Email: hrc@fes.uwaterloo.ca; URL: http://www.fes.uwaterloo.ca/Research/HRC/environments.html – 3 times a year – Editor, J. Gordon Nelson; Managing Editor, Kenneth Van Osch

Essays on Canadian Writing, #200, 2120 Queen St. East, Toronto ON M4E 1E2 – 416/694-3348; Fax: 416/698-9906; Email: ecw@sympatico.ca; URL: http://www.ecw.ca/press – Circ.: 1,200; 3 times a year – Publisher & Editor, Jack David; Publisher & Editor, Robert Lecker

Event, c/o Douglas College, PO Box 2503, New Westminster BC V3L 5B2 – 604/527-5293; Fax: 604/527-5095; URL: http://www.douglas.ca/Event/homepage.html – 3 times a year – Editor, Calvin Wharton; Assistant Editor, Bonnie Bauder

Exceptionality Education Canada, c/o Vivanne Timmons, Dean of Education, Univ. of PEI, 550 University Avenue, Charlottetown PE C1A 4P3 – Circ.: 250; 4 times a year

Infor (Published by University of Toronto Press), Journals Division, 5201 Dufferin St., North York ON M3H 5T8 – 416/667-7810; Fax: 416/667-7881; Email: journals@utpress.utoronto.ca – Circ.: 1,700; 4 times a year – Editor, David Wright; Circulation Manager, Wendy Thornton

Journal of Baha'i Studies, 34 Copernicus St., Ottawa ON K1N 7K4 – 613/233-1903; Fax: 613/233-3644; Email: as929freenet.carleton.ca; URL: http://www.pagecreator.com/~newsroom – Circ.: 2,000; 4 times a year; English, French & Spanish – Executive Officer & Editor, Christine Zerbinis

Journal of Canadian Art History, c/o VA-432, Concordia University, 1455, boul de Maisonneuve ouest, Montréal QC H3G 1M8 – 514/848-4699; Fax: 514/848-8627; Email: jcah@vax2.concordia.ca; URL: http://www-fofa.concordia.ca/arth/jcah.intro.htm – 2 times a year; English & French – Publisher, Sandra Paikowsky

Journal of Canadian Poetry, Dept. of English, University of Ottawa, Ottawa ON K1N 6N5 – 613/562-5705; Fax: 613/562-5975 – Circ.: 350; Annually – Editor, David Staines

Journal of Canadian Studies, c/o Trent University, PO Box 4800, Peterborough ON K9J 7B8 – 705/748-1279; Fax: 705/748-1655; Email: jcs_rec@trentu.ca – Circ.: 1,300; 4 times a year; English & French – Acting Editor, James Conley; Managing Editor, Kerry Cannon

Journal of Child & Youth Care, Dept. of Human Services, Malaspina University College, 900 Fifth St., Nanaimo BC V9R 5S5 – Circ.: 450; 4 times a year – Co-Editor, Dr. G. Fewster; Co-Editor, Dr. T. Garfat

Journal of Law and Social Policy (Published by Becker Associates), PO Box 507, Stn Q, Toronto ON M4T 2M5 – 416/483-7282; Fax: 416/489-1713 – Annually; ISSN 0829-3929 – Editor, Paul Dusome

Journal of Scholarly Publishing (Published by University of Toronto Press), Journals Division, 5201 Dufferin St., North York ON M3H 5T8 – 416/667-7810; Fax: 416/667-7881 – Circ.: 1,560; 4 times a year – Editor, Sandra Meadow; Circulation Manager, Wendy Thornton

Labour, c/o Dept. of History, Memorial University, St. John's NF A1C 5S7 – 709/737-2144; Fax: 709/737-4342; Email: joanb@plato.ucs.mun.ca; URL: http://www.mun.ca/cclh – Circ.: 1,000; 2 times a year; English & French – Editor-in-chief, Bryan D.

Palmer; Managing Editor, Irene Whitfield, 709/737-3453

Labour, Capital & Society: A Journal on the Third World, Centre for Developing Area Studies, McGill University, 3715 Peel St., Montréal QC H3A 1X1 – 514/398-3508; Fax: 514/398-8432; Email: ed10@musica.mcgill.ca – Circ.: 700; 2 times a year; English & French – Editor, Dr. Rosalind Boyd

Leisurability (Published by Becker Associates), PO Box 507, Stn Q, Toronto ON M4T 2M5 – 416/483-7282; Fax: 416/489-1713 – 4 times a year; ISSN 0711-222X – Editor, Dr. Peggy Hutchison

Material History Review, c/o National Museum of Science & Technology, PO Box 9724, Stn T, Ottawa ON K1G 5A3 – 613/991-3081; Fax: 613/990-3636 – 2 times a year – Managing Editor, Geoffrey Rider

McGill Journal of Education, c/o Faculty of Education, McGill University, 3700 McTavish St., Montréal QC H3A 1Y2 – 514/398-4246; Fax: 514/398-6968; Email: keenana@education.mcgill.ca – Circ.: 500; 3 times a year; English & French – Editor, William M. Talley; Editorial Assistant, Ann Keenan

McMaster Journal of Theology & Ministry, c/o Divinity College, McMaster University, Main St. West, Hamilton ON L8S 4K1 – 905/525-9140, ext.24401; Fax: 905/577-4782; Email: bellousk@mcmaster.ca; URL: http://www.mcmaster.ca/divinity – 2 times a year – Editor, Kenneth W. Bellous

Modern Drama (Published by University of Toronto Press), Journals Division, 5201 Dufferin St., North York ON M3H 5T8 – 416/667-7781; Fax: 416/667-7832; Email: journals@gpu.utcc.utoronto.ca; editorial office email: moddram@epas.utoronto.ca; URL: http://www/utpress/depthome.htm – Circ.: 2,223; 4 times a year – Editor, Dorothy Parker

The Monograph - Journal of the Ont. Assn. for Geographical & Environmental Education (Published by Becker Associates), PO Box 507, Stn Q, Toronto ON M4T 2M5 – 416/483-7282; Fax: 416/489-1713 – 4 times a year; ISSN 0048-1973 – Editor, Gary Birchall

Monographs in Education, Rm 230, Education Bldg., University of Manitoba, Winnipeg MB R3T 2N2 – 204/474-8309; Fax: 204/275-5962 – Annual – Editor, Dr. A.D. Gregor

Mosaic: A Journal for the Interdisciplinary Study of Literature, Room 208, Tier Bldg., University of Manitoba, Winnipeg MB R3T 2N2 – 204/474-9763; Fax: 204/474-7584; Email: ejhinz@bldgarts.lan1.umanitoba.ca; URL: http://www.umanitoba.ca/publications/mosaic – Circ.: 900; 4 times a year – Editor, Evelyn J. Hinz; Circulation Manager, Donna Derenchuk

Newfoundland Studies, c/o English Dept., Memorial University, St. John's NF A1C 5S7 – 709/737-3453; Fax: 709/737-4342; Email: irenew@plato.ucs.mun.ca; URL: http://www.ucs.mun.ca/~nflds – Circ.: 250; 2 times a year; English & French – Editor-in-chief, Richard Buehler; Managing Editor, Irene Whitfield

Ontario History (Published by Ontario Historical Society), 34 Parkview Ave., Willowdale ON M2N 3Y2 – 416/226-9011; Fax: 416/226-2740 – Circ.: 1,200; 4 times a year – Editor, Dr. Terry Crowley; Circulation Manager, Barbara Truax

Open Letter, 499 Dufferin Ave., London ON N6B 2A1 – 519/673-5732; Fax: 519/673-5857; Email: fdavey@uwo.ca – 3 times a year; ISSN: 0048-1939

Pacific Affairs, c/o University of British Columbia, #164, 1855 West Mall, Vancouver BC V6T 1Z2 – 604/822-6508; Fax: 604/822-5207 – 4 times a year – Editor, Dr. Ian Slater

The Philantropist (Published by Becker Associates), PO Box 507, Stn Q, Toronto ON M4T 2M5 – 416/483-7282; Fax: 416/489-1713 – 4 times a year – Editor, John D. Gregory

Philosophia Mathematica (Published by University of Toronto Press), Journals Division, 5201 Dufferin St., North York ON M3H 5T8 – 416/667-7810; Fax: 416/667-7881 – Circ.: 250; 3 times a year – Editor, Robert S.D. Thomas; Circulation Manager, Wendy Thomas

Policy Options, Inst. for Research on Public Policy, #200, 1470, rue Peel, Montréal QC H3A 1T1 – 514/985-2461; Fax: 514/985-2559; Email: policyop@irpp.org; URL: http://www.irpp.org – 10 times a year – Editor, Alfred Leblanc

Prairie Forum: Journal of the Canadian Plains Research Centre, Canadian Plains Research Centre, University of Regina, Regina SK S4S 0A2 – 306/585-4758; Fax: 306/585-4699; Email: canadian.plains@uregina.ca; URL: http://www.cprc.uregina.ca – Circ.: 300; 2 times a year – Editor, Dr. Patrick Douaud; Circulation Manager, Lorraine Nelson

Public Sector Management et Secteur Public, #401, 1075 Bay St., Toronto ON M5S 2B1 – 416/924-8787; Fax: 416/924-4992; Email: ntl@ipaciapc.ca – Circ.: 4,000 – Editor, Joseph Galimberti

Queen's Quarterly, c/o Queen's University, 184 Union St., Kingston ON K7L 3N6 – 613/545-2667; Fax: 613/545-6822; Email: qquartly@post.queensu.ca; URL: http://www.info.queensu.ca/quarterly – Circ.: 3,000; 4 times a year – Editor, Dr. Boris Castel; Business Manager, Penny Roantree

Renaissance & Reformation (Published by Becker Associates), PO Box 507, Stn Q, Toronto ON M4T 2M5 – 416/483-7282; Fax: 416/489-1713 – 4 times a year; ISSN 0034-429X – Editor, Prof. Francois Paré

Resources for Feminist Research, 252 Bloor St. West, Toronto ON M5S 1V6 – 416/923-6641, ext. 2278; Fax: 416/926-4725; Email: rfrdrf@oise.utoronto.ca; URL: http://www/oise.utoronto.ca/rfr – Circ.: 2,000; 4 times a year – Coordinating Editor, Philinda Masters

Russell: The Journal of the Bertrand Russell Archives, c/o The Bookstore, McMaster University, Main St. West, Hamilton ON L8S 4L6 – 905/525-9140, ext.23355; Fax: 905/572-7160; Email: blackwk@mcmaster.ca; URL: http://bookstore.services.mcmaster.ca/nupress/journals/russell/journal.html – Circ.: 500 – Hon. Russell Archivist & Editor, Kenneth Blackwell

Science Fiction Studies, c/o Veronica Hollinger, Cultural Studies Program, Trent University, Peterborough ON K9J 7B8 – ; Email: vhollinger@trentu.ca – 3 times a year

Scientia Canadensis - Journal of the History of Cdn. Science, Technology & Medicine (Published by Becker Associates), PO Box 507, Stn Q, Toronto ON M4T 2M5 – 416/483-7282; Fax: 416/489-1713 – 2 times a year; ISSN 0829-2507 – Editor, Prof. Yves Gingras

Scrivener, c/o McGill University, 853 Sherbrooke St. West, Montréal QC H3A 2T6 – 514/398-6588; Fax: 514/398-8146; Email: bqgc@musich.mcgill.ca – Circ.: 500; Annually – Editor, Michelle LeLievre

Seminar (Published by University of Toronto Press), Journals Division, 5201 Dufferin St., North York ON M3H 5T8 – 416/667-7810; Fax: 416/667-7881; Email: journals@utpress.utoronto.ca – Circ.: 770; 4 times a year – Editor, Rodney Symington; Circulation Manager, Wendy Thornton

Social History (Published by University of Toronto Press), Journals Division, 5201 Dufferin St., North York ON M3H 5T8 – 416/667-7810; Fax: 416/667-7881 – Circ.: 560; 2 times a year – Editor, Chad Gaffield; Circulation Manager, Wendy Thornton

Studies in Canadian Literature, Hut 5, University of New Brunswick, PO Box 4400, Stn A, Fredericton NB E3B 5A3 – 506/453-4598; Fax: 506/453-4995; Email: scl@unb.ca – Circ.: 500; 2 times a year – Editor, J. Ball; Managing Editor, S. Campbell, 506/453-3501

Studies in Political Economy, Carleton University, Rm. SR303, Stn E, Ottawa ON K1S 5B6 – 613/520-2600, ext.6625; Fax: 613/520-3981; Email: ekillean@ccs.carleton.ca – Circ.: 800; 3 times a year

Tessera, c/o 350 Stong College, York University, 4700 Keele St., North York ON M3J 1P3 – 416/736-5412; Email: jennifer@yorku.ca – Circ.: 500; 2 times a year – Co-Editor, Jennifer Henderson

Texte (Published by University of Toronto Press), Journals Division, 5201 Dufferin St., North York ON M3H 5T8 – 416/667-7810; Fax: 416/667-7881 – Circ.: 150; Annually – Editor, Andrew Oliver; Circulation Manager, Wendy Thornton

Theatre Research in Canada, Graduate Ctr. for Study of Drama, Koffler Student Ctr., U of T, 214 College St., Toronto ON M5S 2Z9 – 416/978-7984; Fax: 416/971-1378; Email: trican@chiss.utoronto.ca – Circ.: 350; 2 times a year; English & French – Co-Editor, Deborah Cottreau; Co-Editor, Stephen Johnson; Co-Editor, Rob Nunn

The Tocqueville Review (Published by University of Toronto Press), Journals Division, 5201 Dufferin St., North York ON M3H 5T8 – 416/667-7781 – Circ.: 800; 2 times a year; English & French – Editor, Henri Mendras

Transcultural Psychiatric Research Review, Psychiatry Dept., McGill University, 1033 Pine Ave. West, Montréal QC H3A 1A1 – 514/398-7302; Fax: 514/398-4370; Email: cylk@musica.mcgill.ca; URL: http://www.mcgill.ca/psychiatry – Circ.: 500; 4 times a year – Editor, Laurence J. Kirmayer, M.D.; Circulation Manager, Margie Gabriel

Ultimate Reality & Meaning (Published by University of Toronto Press), Journals Division, 5201 Dufferin St., North York ON M3H 5T8 – 416/667-7810; Fax: 416/667-7881; Email: journals@utpress.utoronto.ca – Circ.: 380; 4 times a year – Editor, John F. Perry; Circulation Manager, Wendy Thornton

University of Toronto Law Journal (Published by University of Toronto Press), Journals Division, 5201 Dufferin St., North York ON M3H 5T8 – 416/667-7810; Fax: 416/667-7881; Email: journals@utpress.utoronto.ca; URL: http://www.utpress.utoronto.ca/journal.depthome.htm – Circ.: 700; 4 times a year – Editor, Bruce Chapman; Circulation Manager, Wendy Thornton

University of Toronto Quarterly (Published by University of Toronto Press), Journals Division, 5201 Dufferin St., North York ON M3H 5T8 – 416/667-7810; Fax: 416/667-7881; Email: journals@utpress.utoronto.ca; URL: http://www.utpress.utoronto.ca/journal/depthome.htm – Circ.: 940; 4 times a year – Editor, Brian Corman; Circulation Manager, Wendy Thornton

Urban History Review (Published by Becker Associates), PO Box 507, Stn Q, Toronto ON M4T 2M5 – 416/483-7282; Fax: 416/489-1713; Email: jbecker@interlog.com – Circ.: 500; 2 times a year; ISSN 0703-0428 – Editor, Prof. Richard Harris

## STUDENT GUIDES

Campus Canada, 287 MacPherson Ave., Toronto ON M4V 1A4 – 416/928-2909; Fax: 416/966-1181 – Circ.: 125,000; 4 times a year – Publisher, Harvey Wolfe; Editor, Sarah Moore

Campus Reel (Published by Tribute Publishing Inc.), 71 Barber Greene Rd., Don Mills ON M3C 2A2 – 416/445-0544; Fax: 416/445-2894 – Circ.: 270,000; 4 times a year – Publisher & Editor, Sandra Stewart

Magazine Tourisme jeunesse, 4545, av Pierre-de-Coubertin, Montréal QC H1V 3R2 – 514/252-3117; Fax: 514/252-3119 – Tirage: 40 000; 2 fois par an

The Student Traveller, The Canadian Federation of Students - Services, 243 College St., 5th Fl., Toronto ON M5T 2Y1 – 416/977-3703; Fax: 416/977-4796; Email: stutrav@travelcuts.com; URL: http://www.travelcuts.com – 2 times a year – Publisher, Michael T. Fuller

Temps Libre, 4545, Pierre-de-Coubertin, CP 1000, Succ M, Montréal QC H1V 3R2 – 514/252-3117; Fax: 514/252-3119

U-Choose: A Student's Guide to Financial Survival (Published by Moving Publications Ltd.), 40 Upjohn Rd., Don Mills ON M3B 2W1 – 416/441-1168; Fax: 416/441-1641 – Circ.: 305,000 – Publisher, Anita Wood; Editor, Lorraine Hunter; Circulation Manager, Paula Muzzin

Welcome Back Student Magazine (Published by Kingston Publications), PO Box 1352, Kingston ON K7L 5C6 – 613/549-8442; Fax: 613/549-4333 – Circ.: 18,000; Annually – Publisher & Editor, Mary Laflamme

## UNIVERSITY & SCHOOL PUBLICATIONS

**Contact the publication, c/o the school, for editorial purposes. Addresses of the schools are given in the Education Section of the Almanac**

L'Action — Université du Québec à Montréal
Algonquin Times — Algonquin College
L'Alinéa — Cégep Joliette-De Lanaudière
Alumni-News/Bulletin des Anciens — University of Ottawa
Alumni Gazette — University of Western Ontario
Alumni Journal — University of Manitoba
Alumni Journal — Simon Fraser University
Alumni Magazine — The University of Calgary
Alumni News — Carleton University
Aquinian — St. Thomas University
Argosy Weekly — Mount Allison University
The Argus — Lakehead University
ARN Messager — Université de Montréal
Arthur — Trent University
The Athenaeum — Acadia University
Atkinsonian — York University
Audaces — Cégep Joliette-De Lanaudière
Bandersnatch — John Abbott College
The Baron — University of New Brunswick
BCIT Link — BC Institute of Technology
Bilan — Université de Sherbrooke
Bricklayer — Red Deer College
La Brise — Cégep de l'Outaouais
Brock Press — Brock University
The Brunswickian — University of New Brunswick
The Bulletin — University of Toronto
Le Caducée — École des Hautes Études Commerciales
Le Calvaire — Cégep de Rimouski
The Campus — Bishop's University
Campus Times — University of British Columbia
Le Canard Déchaine — Université du Québec à Hull
Caper Times — University College of Cape Breton
Capilano Courier — Capilano College
The Carillon — The University of Regina
CAS — Concordia University
Champlain Bugle — Champlain Regional College
The Charlatan — Carleton University
The Chronicle — Durham College
Cité Universitaire — Université de Montréal
Cityside — The University of Regina
The Concordian — Concordia University
Concordia University Magazine — Concordia University
The Cord Weekly — Wilfrid Laurier University
La Criée — Cégep de Matane
La Crise — Cégep François-Xavier-Garneau
Debit Memo — McGill University
D.E.C. express — Cégep de Baie-Comeau
Défi-Sciences — Université Laval
D'Épiderme — Cégep de Sept-Îles
Les Diplômés — Université de Montréal
Discorder - Student Radio Society of U.B.C — University of British Columbia
Eclosion — Cégep de Ste-Foy
L'Ecorché — Cégep Lionel-Groulx
L'Électic — Cégep de St-Hyacinthe
The Emery Weal — The Southern Alberta Institute of Technology
En Tete — Université du Québec à Trois-Rivières
L'Entremetteur — Cégep de l'Outaouais
Etcetera — Humber College
Excalibur — York University
L'Exemplaire — Cégep de Sorel-Tracy
The Eyeopener — Ryerson Polytechnic University
The Faucet — McGill University
Au Fil des Evénements — Université Laval
Le Forcep — Cégep de Lévis-Lauzon
Forum — Université de Montréal
de Fouille-moi — Cégep de Granby-Haute-Yamaska
Le Front — Université de Moncton
The Fulcrum — University of Ottawa
Gargoyle — University College
Gateway — University of Alberta
The Gauntlet — The University of Calgary
Gazette — Dalhousie University
The Gazette — University of Western Ontario
The Georgian Eye — Georgian College
La Gifle — Cégep de Trois-Rivières
The Gleaner — Vancouver Community College
Golden Words — Queen's University
The Graduate — University of British Columbia
Le Grafitti — Collège Jean-de-Brebeuf Inc.
The Green and White — University of Saskatchewan
La Grenouille — Cégep de Chicoutimi
Guelph Peak — University of Guelph
L'Hermes — Cégep St-Jean-sur-Richelieu
Impact Campus — Université Laval
Imprint — University of Waterloo
in Extremis — Cégep de Sherbrooke
L'Infomane — Cégep de Bois-de-Boulogne
L'Interdit — Collège de Limoilou
L'Interêt — École des Hautes Études Commerciales
The Interpreter — Grant MacEwan Community College
Le Jets — École de Technologie Supérieure
The Journal — Saint Mary's University
Journal l'actif — Cégep de Shawinigan
Journal U.Q.A.M — Université du Québec à Montréal
Lambda — Laurentian University of Sudbury
The Lance — University of Windsor
Lexicon — York University
Liaison — Université de Sherbrooke
The Link — Concordia University
The MacEwan Journalist — Grant MacEwan Community College
Le Majeur — Cégep d'Alma
The Manitoban — University of Manitoba
The Martlet — University of Victoria
Le Matulu — École secondaire Marie-Victorin
McGill Daily — McGill University
McGill French — McGill University
The McGill News — McGill University
McGill Reporter — McGill University
McGill Tribune — McGill University
The McMaster Courier — McMaster University
Medium II — Erindale College
The Meliorist — University of Lethbridge
The Mike — St. Michael's College
La Minerve — Cégep de Saint-Laurent
Le Misanthrope — Cégep Ahuntsic
Le Motdit — Cégep Édouard-Montpetit
Mouton Noir — Cégep de Drummondville
The Muse — Memorial University of Newfoundland
Navigator — Malaspina University College
Le Nénu phare — Cégep de Chicoutimi
New Edition — New College
The Newspaper — University of Toronto
New Trail — University of Alberta
Nexus — Camosun College
Niagara News — Niagara College
Nighviews — Ryerson Polytechnic University
Nomad — St. Lawrence College
Le Nordet — Cégep de La Pocatière
The Nugget — The Northern Alberta Institute of Technology
Obiter Dicta (Osgood Hall) — York University
OK Phoenix — Okanagan University College
The Ontarion — University of Guelph
L'Original déchainé — Laurentian University of Sudbury
Other Press — Douglas College
Over the Edge — University of Northern British Columbia
Panther Prints — University of Prince Edward Island
Pars ailleurs — Cégep de Valleyfield
The Peak — Simon Fraser University
La Petite Caisse — Université du Québec à Chicoutimi
Picaro — Mount Saint Vincent University
La Pige — Cégep de Jonquière
Pigeon Dissident — Université de Montréal
Plant — Dawson College
The Point — University of British Columbia
Polar Press — Confederation College
Le Polyscope — École Polytechnique
Le Profane — Cégep de l'Abitibi-Témiscamingue
Project Magazine — McMaster University
The Pro Tem (Glendon College) — York University
Psycause — Université de Montréal
Quartier Libre — Université de Montréal
Queen's Alumni Review — Queen's University
Queen's Journal — Queen's University
Quill — Brandon University
Reflector — Mount Royal College
La Réplique — Cégep de Victoriaville
The Reporter — McGill University
Le Republique — Cégep du Vieux-Montréal
République étudiante — Cégep de Rosemont
Réseau/U.Q. Network — Université du Québec
La Rotonde — University of Ottawa
Ryersonian — Ryerson Polytechnic University
The Ryerson Rambler — Ryerson Polytechnic University
La Sagace — Université de Sherbrooke
The Saint — St. Clair College
The Satellite — Mohawk College
Le Script — Collège de Lévis
Seneca Impact — Seneca College
Le Sentier — Cégep de St-Félicien
The Sheaf — University of Saskatchewan
The Sheridan Sun — Sheridan College
The Shield — Cambrian College of Applied Arts & Technology
The Silhouette — McMaster University
Siren — Centennial College
Sommets — Université de Sherbrooke
Spoke — Conestoga College
Standard — University of Victoria
The Sting — Concordia University
Strand — Victoria College
Suites — Université du Québec à Montréal
The Tablet — McGill University
Talon — Confederation College
Le Temporel — Université du Québec à Montréal
The Three Penny Beaver — Sir Sandford Fleming College
Thunderbird Sports Magazine — University of British Columbia
Thursday Report — Concordia University
Le Trait d'Union — Cégep de Maisonneuve
Transactions — Université du Québec à Montréal
U.B.C. Alumni Chronicle — University of British Columbia
The Ubyssey — University of British Columbia
L'Ulcère — Cégep de Rivière-du-Loup
Underground — Scarborough College
Unité — Université du Québec à Montréal
The Uniter — University of Windsor
University of Toronto Magazine — University of Toronto
U.Q.A.R. Information — Université du Québec à Rimouski

Uquam — Université du Québec à Montréal
Uquarium — Université du Québec à Rimouski
The UVic Torch — University of Victoria
Vanier Phoenix — Vanier College
The Vanier Vandoo — Vanier College
Varsity — University of Toronto
V.C.C. Voice — Vancouver Community College
Le Virus — Université du Québec à Hull
Vox-Populi — Cégep André-Laurendeau
Le Voyeur — Université du Québec à Trois-Rivières
Le Voyeur — Université du Québec en Abitibi-Témiscamingue
Watch — University of King's College
Western Alumni Gazette — University of Western Ontario
Western News — University of Western Ontario
Window — New College
X-Press — University of Prince Edward Island
Xaverian — St. Francis Xavier University
Le Zèle — Cégep Montmorency

# BROADCASTING STATIONS

## BROADCASTING NETWORK HEAD OFFICES

Astral Entertainment Group, Maison Astral, #900, 2100, rue Ste-Catherine ouest, Montréal QC H3N 2T3 – 514/939-5000; Fax: 514/939-1515

Atlantic Television System (ATV), PO Box 1653, Halifax NS B3J 2Z4 – 902/453-4000; Fax: 902/454-3302; Email: atv@atv.ca

Baton Broadcasting Inc., PO Box 9, Stn O, Toronto ON M4A 2M9 – 416/299-2000; Fax: 416/299-2220

The Blackburn Group Inc, 369 York St., PO Box 2280, London ON N6A 4G1 – 519/667-4545; Fax: 519/667-4530

British Columbia Television (BCTV), 7850 Enterprise St., PO Box 4700, Burnaby BC V6B 4A3 – 604/420-2288; Fax: 604/421-9427

Cablecasting Ltd., #900, 1200 Bay St., Toronto ON M5R 2A5 – 416/964-6411; Fax: 416/964-9206

Canadian Broadcasting Corporation (CBC), 250 Lanark Ave., PO Box 3220, Stn C, Ottawa ON K1Y 1E4 – 613/724-1200; TDD: 613/738-6686

Canadian Broadcasting Corporation - English Network (CBC), PO Box 500, Stn A, Toronto ON M5W 1E6 – 416/205-3311; TDD: 416/205-6688

Radio Canada International, 1055, boul René-Lévesque est, CP 6000, Montréal QC H3C 3A8 – 514/597-7555; Fax: 514/284-0891

Société Radio-Canada - French Network, 1400, boul René-Lévesque est, CP 6000, Montréal QC H3C 3A8 – 514/597-5970; TDD: 514/597-6013

Canadian Satellite Communications Inc. (CANCOM), 50 Burnhamthorpe Rd. West, 10th Fl., Mississauga ON L5B 3C2 – 905/272-4960; Fax: 905/272-3399; Email: pdumas@cancom.ca

Canwest Broadcasting Ltd., 603 St. Mary's Rd., Winnipeg MB R2M 3L8 – 204/233-3304; Fax: 204/233-5615

CHUM Limited, 1331 Yonge St., Toronto ON M4T 1Y1 – 416/925-6666; Fax: 416/926-4042

Cogeco Cable inc., #200, 1630 - 6e rue, Trois-Rivières QC G8Y 5B8 – 819/372-9292; Fax: 819/372-3318

Craig Broadcast Systems Inc., 2940 Victoria Ave., Brandon MB R7B 0N2 – 204/728-1150; Fax: 204/728-1838

Fawcett Broadcasting Ltd. (CFOB/CJRL/CKDR), 242 Scott St., Fort Frances ON P9A 1G7 – 807/274-5341; Fax: 807/274-8746

Forvest Broadcasting Corp., 345 - 4 Ave. South, Saskatoon SK S7K 5S5 – 306/244-1975; Fax: 306/665-8484; Email: cjww.radio@sk.sympatico.ca

Fraser Valley Radio Group, 45715 Hocking Ave., PO Box 386, Chilliwack BC V2P 6J7 – 604/795-5711; Fax: 604/795-6643

Global Television Network, 81 Barber Greene Rd., Don Mills ON M3C 2A2 – 416/446-5311; Fax: 416/446-5447

Golden West Broadcasting Ltd., PO Box 950, Altona MB R0G 0B0 – 204/324-6464; Fax: 204/324-8918

Groupe Videotron Ltée, 300, av Viger est, Montréal QC H2X 3W4 – 514/281-1232; Fax: 514/985-8425

Humber Valley Broadcasting Co. Ltd., 345 O'Connell Dr., PO Box 570, Corner Brook NF A2H 6H5 – 709/634-3111; Fax: 709/634-4081

Inuit Broadcasting Corporation (IBC), #703, 251 Laurier Avenue, Ottawa ON K1P 5J6 – 613/235-1892; Fax: 613/230-8824; Email: ibcicsl@sonetis.com

Knowledge Network, Service of the Open Learning Agency (KN), 4355 Mathissi Place, Burnaby BC V5B 4S8 – 604/431-3000; Fax: 604/525-5511; Email: knowline@ola.bc.ca

Learning Skills Television of Alberta (ACCESS - The Education Station), 3720 - 76 Ave., Edmonton AB T6B 2N9 – 403/440-7777; Fax: 403/440-8899; Email: access@incentre.net

MCTV-TV, 699 Frood Rd., Sudbury ON P3C 5A3 – 705/674-8301; Fax: 705/671-2444

Metro Marketing West, 680C, Leg-in-Boot-Sq., Vancouver BC V5Z 4B5 – 604/874-8463; Fax: 604/874-9300

Moffat Communications Ltd., CKY Bldg., Polo Park, PO Box 220, Stn L, Winnipeg MB R3H 0Z5 – 204/788-3440; Fax: 204/956-2710

Monarch Communications, 361 - 1 St. SE, Medicine Hat AB T1A 0A5 – 403/526-4529; Fax: 403/526-4000

Northern Cable Holdings Ltd., #15 - 500 Barrydowne Rd., PO Box 4500, Sudbury ON P3A 5W1 – 705/560-1560; Fax: 705/560-4752

NTV Network, 446 Logy Bay Rd., PO Box 2020, St. John's NF A1C 5S2 – 709/722-5015; Fax: 709/726-5107

Okalakatiget Society, PO Box 160, Nain NF A0P 1L0 – 709/922-2955; Fax: 709/922-2293

Pelmorex Radio Inc., #200, 186 Robert Speck Pkwy., Mississauga ON L4Z 3G1 – 905/566-9511; Fax: 905/566-8004; Email: prn@pelmorex.ca

Pelmorex Infomedia/Weather (PIW), #200, 186 Robert Speck Pkwy., Mississauga ON L4Z 3G1 – 905/566-9511; Fax: 905/566-9696

Pelmorex Radio Network (PRN), #200, 186 Robert Speck Pkwy., Mississauga ON L4Z 3G1 – 905/566-9511; Fax: 905/566-9696

Quatre Saisons (Le réseau de télévision), 405, av Ogilvy, Montréal QC H3N 2Y4 – 514/271-3535; Fax: 514/271-6231

Radio Corp. Inc. (1290 CJBK), 743 Wellington Rd. South, London ON N6C 4R5 – 519/686-2525; Fax: 519/686-9067; Email: 1290.cjbk@odyssey.on.ca

Radio Futura Ltée, 211, av Gordon, Verdun QC H4G 2R2 – 514/766-2311; Fax: 514/761-2122

Radio Nord inc., 380, rue Murdoch, Rouyn-Noranda QC J9P 1G5 – 819/762-0741; Fax: 819/762-2280

Radiomutuel inc., #405, 1717, boul René-Lévesque est, Montréal QC H2L 4E8 – 514/529-3210; Fax: 514/529-3219

RAWLCO Communications Ltd., 2723 - 37 Ave. NE, Calgary AB T1Y 5R8 – 403/291-0000; Fax: 403/291-0037

Réseau des Appalaches, 327, av Labbé, CP 69, Thetford Mines QC G6S 5S3 – 418/335-7533; Fax: 418/335-9009

Rogers Broadcasting Ltd., 25 Adelaide St. East, 10th Fl., Toronto ON M5C 1H3 – 416/864-2000; Fax: 416/864-2002

Satellite Radio Network, 2440 Ash St., Vancouver BC V5Z 4J6 – 604/873-9583; Fax: 604/873-5305

Rogers Cablesystems Ltd., 1 Valleybrook Dr., 5th Fl., North York ON M3B 2S7 – 416/447-5500; Fax: 416/391-7247

Rogers Communications Inc., Scotia Plaza, #6400, 40 King St. West, PO Box 1007, Toronto ON M5H 3Y2 – 416/864-2373; Fax: 416/864-2385

Shaw Communications Inc. (Shaw Cable), #900, 630 - 3rd Ave. SW, Calgary AB T2P 4L4 – 403/750-4500; Fax: 403/750-4506

Skeena Broadcasters, Division of Okanagan Skeena Group Ltd., 4625 Lazelle Ave., Terrace BC V8G 1S4 – 250/635-6316; Fax: 250/638-6320; Email: info@osg.net

Slaight Communications Inc., 2 St. Clair Ave. West, 11th Fl., Toronto ON M4V 1L6 – 416/960-9911; Fax: 416/323-6828

Standard Broadcasting Corp. Ltd., 2 St. Clair Ave. West, 11th Fl., Toronto ON M4V 1L6 – 416/960-9911; Fax: 416/323-6828

Stentor Telecom Policy Inc., #1800, 45 O'Connor St., Ottawa ON K1P 1A4 – 613/567-7000; Fax: 613/567-7001

SupeRadio, #2400 - 250 Yonge St., Toronto ON M5B 2M6 – 416/599-3949; Fax: 416/599-3958

Taqramiut Nipingat Inc. (Voice of the North) (TNI), #501, 185, av Dorval, Dorval QC H9S 5J9 – 514/631-1394; Fax: 514/631-6258

Télé-Québec (Société de télédiffusion du Québec), 1000, rue Fullum, Montréal QC H2K 3L7 – 514/521-2424; Fax: 514/525-5511; Email: morifran@telequebec.qc.ca

Télémédia Communications inc., 1411, rue Peel, 5e étage, Montréal QC H3A 1S5 – 514/845-6291; Fax: 514/845-3628

Telesat Canada, 1601 Telesat Ct., Gloucester ON K1B 5P4 – 613/748-0123; Fax: 613/748-8784; Email: info@telesat.ca

Television Northern Canada (TVNC), PO Box 1630, Iqaluit NT X0A 0H0 – 867/979-1707; Fax: 867/979-1708; Email: tvnc@sonetis.com

TVA inc. (Le réseau de télévision), 1600, boul de Maisonneuve est, Montréal QC H2L 4P2 – 514/526-9251; Fax: 514/598-6085

TVOntario (Ontario Educational Communications Authority) (CICA), PO Box 200, Stn Q, Toronto ON M4T 2T1 – 416/484-2600; Fax: 416/484-6285

Videotron Communications Ltd., 10450 - 178 St., Edmonton AB T5S 1S2 – 403/486-6500; Fax: 403/486-6506

Wawatay Native Communications Society, PO Box 1180, Sioux Lookout ON P8T 1B7 – 807/737-2951; Fax: 807/737-3224

WIC Western International Communications Ltd., #1960, 505 Burrard St., Vancouver BC V7X 1M6 – 604/687-2844; Fax: 604/687-4118

## AM BROADCASTING STATIONS

| LOCATION | CALL | *CBC Stations/Affiliates †French Language Stations | FREQ. |
|---|---|---|---|
| Abbotsford, BC | CKMA | Fraser Valley Broadcasters Ltd., 2722 Allwood St., Abbotsford BC V2T 3R8 – 604/859-5277; Fax: 604/859-9907; Email: alpen@uniserve.com | 850 |
| Alma, QC | †CFGT | 1441, rue Auger sud, Alma QC G8B 6V3 – 418/662-6673; Fax: 418/662-9269 | 1270 |
| Altona, MB | CFAM | Golden West Broadcasting Ltd., PO Box 950, Altona MB R0G 0B0 – 204/324-6464; Fax: 204/324-8918 | 950 |
| Altona, MB | CKMW | Golden West Broadcasting Ltd., PO Box 950, Altona MB R0G 0B0 – 204/324-6464; Fax: 204/324-8918 | 1570 |
| Amherst, NS | CKDH | Maritime Broadcasting System Ltd., 32 Church St., PO Box 670, Amherst NS B4H 4B8 – 902/667-3875; Fax: 902/667-4490; Email: am90@atcon.com; URL: http://www.atcon.com/~am90/ | 900 |
| Amos, QC | †CHAD | Radio Nord Inc., 751, 1re av ouest, Amos QC J9T 1V7 – 819/762-0741; Fax: 819/732-6310 | 1340 |
| Amqui, QC | †CFVM | Power Broadcasting Inc./Diffusion Power Inc., 111, rue de l'Hopital, CP 1840, Amqui QC G0J 1B0 – 418/629-2025; Fax: 418/629-2599 | 1220 |
| Antigonish, NS | CJFX | Atlantic Broadcasters Ltd., PO Box 5800, Antigonish NS B2G 2R9 – 902/863-4580; Fax: 902/863-6300; Email: cjfx@atcom.com | 580 |
| Antigonish, NS | CFXU | St. Francis Xavier University, PO Box 948, Antigonish NS B2G 1C0 – 902/867-2410; Fax: 902/867-5138 | 690 |
| Arnprior, ON | CHVR-2 | Pelmorex Radio, 490 Didak St., Arnprior ON K7S 3R1 – 613/623-7711; Fax: 613/432-8236 | 1490 |
| Asbestos, QC | †CJAN | Radio Plus BMD Inc., 185, rue du Roi, Asbestos QC J1T 1S4 – 819/879-5439; Fax: 819/879-7922 | 1340 |
| Athabasca, AB | CKBA | Nornet Broadcasting Ltd., #1, 4818 - 49 St., Athabasca AB T9S 1C3 – 403/675-5301; Fax: 403/675-4938 | 850 |
| Atikokan, ON | CKDR-6 | *See* Dryden (CKDR) | 1240 |
| Baie Verte, NF | CKIM | VOCM Radio Newfoundland Ltd., PO Box 620, Baie Verte NF A2A 2K2 – 709/489-2192 | 1240 |
| Bancroft, ON | CJNH | Quinte Broadcasting Co. Ltd., PO Box 1240, Bancroft ON K0L 1C0 – 613/332-1423; Fax: 613/332-0841 | 1240 |
| Banff, AB | CFHC-1 | *See* Canmore (CFHC) | 1340 |
| Bathurst, NB | CKBC | Radio Atlantic (1997) Ltd., 176 Main St., Bathurst NB E2A 1A4 – 506/547-1360; Fax: 506/547-1367 | 1360 |
| Bedford, NS | CFDR | NewCap Broadcasting Inc., #800, 1550 Bedford Hwy., Bedford NS B4A 1E6 – 902/835-6100; Fax: 902/835-1511; Email: qcrew@istar.ca | 780 |
| Belleville, ON | CJBQ | Quinte Broadcasting Co. Ltd., 10 Front St. South, PO Box 488, Belleville ON K8N 5B2 – 613/969-5555; Fax: 613/969-0288 | 800 |
| Blairmore, AB | CJPR | Lethbridge Broadcasting, PO Box 840, Blairmore AB T0K 0E0 – 403/562-2200; Fax: 403/562-8114 | 1490 |
| Blind River, ON | CJNR | *See* Elliot Lake (CJNR) | 730 |
| Boissevain, MB | CJRB | Golden West Broadcasting Ltd., PO Box 1220, Boissevain MB R0K 0E0 – 204/324-6464; Fax: 204/324-8918 | 1220 |
| Brampton, ON | CIAO | CKMW Radio Ltd., 50 Kennedy Rd. South, Unit 20, Brampton ON L6W 3R7 – 905/798-4888; Fax: 905/453-4788 | 530 |
| Brandon, MB | CKLQ | Riding Mountain Broadcasting Ltd., 624 - 14 St. East, Brandon MB R7A 7E1 – 204/726-8888; Fax: 204/726-1270; Email: cklq@techplus.com | 880 |
| Brandon, MB | CKX | Craig Broadcasting Systems Inc., 2940 Victoria Ave., Brandon MB R7B 0N2 – 204/728-1150; Fax: 204/727-2505 | 1150 |
| Brantford, ON | CKPC | Telephone City Broadcast Ltd., 571 West St., Brantford ON N3T 5P8 – 519/759-1000; Fax: 519/753-1470 | 1380 |
| Bridgewater, NS | CKBW | Acadia Broadcasting Co. Ltd., 215 Dominion St., Bridgewater NS B4V 2G8 – 902/543-2401; Fax: 902/543-1208; Email: ckbw@ckbw.com; URL: http://www.ckbw.com | 1000 |
| Brockville, ON | CFJR | St. Lawrence Broadcasting Co. Ltd., PO Box 666, Brockville ON K6V 5V9 – 613/345-1666; Fax: 613/342-2438; Email: cfjr@cfjr.brockville.com | 830 |
| Brooks, AB | CIBQ | NorNet Broadcasting, #7, 403 - 2nd Ave. West, PO Box 180, Brooks AB T1R 1B3 – 403/362-3418; Fax: 403/362-8168 | 1340 |
| Burns Lake, BC | CFLD | BV/LD Radio, PO Box 600, Burns Lake BC V0J 1E0 – 250/692-3414 | 760 |
| Cabano, QC | †CJAF | *See* Rivière-du-Loup (CJFP) | 1340 |
| Calgary, AB | CHQR | Westcom Radio Group Ltd., #1900, 125 - 9 Ave. SE, Calgary AB T2G 0P6 – 403/233-0770; Fax: 403/266-4040 | 770 |
| Calgary, AB | CKMX | Standard Broadcasting Inc., PO Box 2750, Stn M, Calgary AB T2P 4P8 – 403/240-5800; Fax: 403/240-5801 | 1060 |
| Calgary, AB | CFAC | Rogers Broadcasting Ltd., 3320 - 17 Ave. SW, Calgary AB T3E 6X6 – 403/246-9696; Fax: 403/246-6660 | 960 |
| Calgary, AB | CFFR | RAWLCO Communications Ltd., #220, 2723 - 37 Ave. NE, Calgary AB T1Y 5R8 – 403/291-0000; Fax: 403/291-5342 | 660 |
| Calgary, AB | *CBR | CBC, PO Box 2640, Calgary AB T2P 2M7 – 403/521-6000; Fax: 403/521-6007 | 1010 |
| Cambridge, ON | CIAM | Power Broadcasting Inc., 46 Main St., Cambridge ON N1R 1V4 – 519/621-7510; Fax: 519/621-0165 | 960 |
| Campbell River, BC | CFWB | CFCP Radio Ltd., 909 Ironwood St., Campbell River BC V9W 3E5 – 250/287-7106; Fax: 250/287-7170 | 1490 |
| Campbellton, NB | CKNB | Maritime Broadcasting System Ltd., 100 Water St., PO Box 340, Campbellton NB E3N 3G7 – 506/753-4415; Fax: 506/789-9505; Email: cknb@nb.sympatico.ca | 950 |
| Camrose, AB | CFCW | *See* Edmonton (CFCW) | |
| Canmore, AB | CFHC | Rogers Broadcasting Ltd., PO Box 1450, Canmore AB T0L 0M0 – 403/678-2222; Fax: 403/678-6844 | 1450 |
| Caraquet, NB | †CJVA | Radio Acadie Ltée, CP 5694, Caraquet NB E0B 1K0 – 506/727-4426; Fax: 506/727-6707 | 810 |
| Carbonear, NF | CHVO | VOCM Radio Newfoundland Ltd., 1 CHVO Dr., Carbonear NF A1Y 1A2 – 709/596-7144; Fax: 709/596-8626; Email: jd.harvey@nf.sympatico.ca; URL: http://www.vocm.com | 560 |
| Castlegar, BC | CKQR | Valley Broadcasters Ltd., 525 - 11 Ave., Castlegar BC V1N 1J6 – 250/365-7600; Fax: 250/365-8480 | 760 |
| Charlottetown, PE | CFCY | Maritime Broadcasting Ltd., 141 Kent St., PO Box 1060, Charlottetown PE CIA 7M7 – 902/892-1066; Fax: 902/566-1338 | 630 |
| Charlottetown, PE | CHTN | NewCap Broadcasting Ltd., 141 Kent St., PO Box 1060, Charlottetown PE CIA 7M7 – 902/892-8591; Fax: 902/566-1338 | 720 |
| Charlottetown, PE | CIMN | University of P.E.I., Student Union Bldg., 550 University Ave., Charlottetown PE CIA 4P3 – 902/566-0417; Fax: 902/566-0979; Email: cimn@upci.ca | 700 |
| Chatham, ON | CFCO | Bea-Ver Communications Inc., 21 Keil Dr., PO Box 630, Chatham ON N7M 5K9 – 519/352-3000; Fax: 519/352-9690; Email: ckyfm@ciaccess.com | 630 |
| Chibougamau, QC | †CJMD | Groupe Radio Antenne 6, 539, 3e rue, Chibougamau QC G8H 2K6 – 418/275-1831; Fax: 418/275-2475 | 1240 |
| Chicoutimi, QC | †CKRS | Radio Saguenay Ltée, 121, rue Racine est, Chicoutimi QC G7H 5G4 – 418/545-2577; Fax: 418/695-2654 | 590 |
| Chicoutimi, QC | †CJMT | 1200, boul du Royaume ouest, Chicoutimi QC G7H 1T1 – 418/696-1420; Fax: 418/696-4164 | 1420 |
| Chicoutimi, QC | *†CBJ | Société Radio-Canada, 500, rue des Sagueneens, CP 790, Chicoutimi QC G7H 5E7 – 418/696-6600; Fax: 418/696-6689 | 1580 |
| Chilliwack, BC | CHWK | Fraser Valley Broadcasters Ltd., PO Box 386, Chilliwack BC V2P 6J7 – 604/795-5711; Fax: 604/795-6643; URL: http://www.fraservalley.com | 1270 |
| Cobourg, ON | CHUC | Pineridge Broadcasting, PO Box 520, Cobourg ON K9A 4L3 – 905/372-5401; Fax: 905/372-6280; Email: chuc@eagle.ca | 1450 |
| Corner Brook, NF | CFCB | Humber Valley Broadcasting Co. Ltd., PO Box 570, Corner Brook NF A2H 6H5 – 709/634-3111; Fax: 709/634-4081 | 570 |
| Corner Brook, NF | CKXX | Newcap Broadcasting Ltd., PO Box 1039, Corner Brook NF A2H 7B2 – 709/634-1340; Fax: 709/637-1039; Email: kixx1340@atcon.com | 1340 |
| Corner Brook, NF | *CBY | CBC, 162 Premier Dr., PO Box 610, Corner Brook NF A2H 6G1 – 709/634-3141; Fax: 709/634-8506 | 990 |
| Cornwall, ON | CJSS | Tri-Co Broadcasting Ltd., 237 Water St. East, PO Box 969, Cornwall ON K6H 5V1 – 613/932-5180; Fax: 613/938-0355; Email: cjssradio@cnwl.igs.net | 1220 |
| Courtenay, BC | CFCP | CFCP Radio Ltd., 1625 McPhee Ave., Courtenay BC V9N 3A6 – 250/334-2421; Fax: 250/334-1977 | 1440 |

| LOCATION | CALL | *CBC Stations/Affiliates †French Language Stations | FREQ. |
|---|---|---|---|
| Cranbrook, BC | CKEK | Columbia Kootenay Broadcasting Co. Ltd., 19 - 9 Ave. South, Cranbrook BC V1C 2L9 – 250/426-2224; Fax: 250/426-5520 | 570 |
| Crowsnest Pass, AB | CJPR | Lethbridge Broadcasting Ltd., 13213 - 20th Ave., PO Box 840, Crowsnest Pass AB T0K 0E0 – 403/562-2806; Fax: 403/562-8114 | 1490 |
| Dauphin, MB | CKDM | Dauphin Broadcasting Co. Ltd., 27 - 3 Ave. NE, Dauphin MB R7N 0Y5 – 204/638-3230; Fax: 204/638-8257 | 730 |
| Dawson Creek, BC | CJDC | MEGA Communications Ltd., 901 - 102 Ave., Dawson Creek BC V1G 2B6 – 250/782-3341; Fax: 250/782-3154; Email: cjdcam@neonet.bc.ca; URL: http://www.cjdcam.com | 890 |
| Dolbeau, QC | *†CHVD | Radio CHVD Inc., 1975, boul Wallberg, Dolbeau QC G8L 1J5 – 418/276-3333; Fax: 418/276-6755 | 1230 |
| Drumheller, AB | CKDQ | Nor-Net Broadcasting Ltd., PO Box 1480, Drumheller AB T0J 0Y0 – 403/823-3384; Fax: 403/823-7241 | 910 |
| Drummondville, QC | †CHRD | *See* Drummondville (CHRD) | 1480 |
| Dryden, ON | CKDR | Fawcett Broadcasting Ltd., PO Box 580, Dryden ON P8N 2Z3 – 807/223-2355; Fax: 807/223-5090 | 800 |
| Duncan, BC | CKAY | CKAY Radio (1979) Inc., #205, 2700 Beverly St., Duncan BC V9L 5C7 – 250/748-1500; Fax: 250/748-1517 | 1500 |
| Ear Falls, ON | CKDR-4 | *See* Dryden (CKDR) | 1450 |
| Edmonton, AB | CFCW | NewCap Broadcasting Inc., 4752 - 99 St., Edmonton AB T6E 5H5 – 403/437-7879; Fax: 403/436-9803 | 790 |
| Edmonton, AB | CFRN | Standard Radio Inc., #100, 18520 Stony Plain Rd., Edmonton AB T5S 2E2 – 403/486-2800; Fax: 403/489-6927; Email: mforbes@worldgate.com | 1260 |
| Edmonton, AB | CHED | Westcom Radio Group Ltd., 5204 - 84 St., Edmonton AB T6E 5N8 – 403/440-6300; Fax: 403/468-5937 | 630 |
| Edmonton, AB | CHQT | Shaw Radio Ltd., 10550 - 105 St., Edmonton AB T5H 2T3 – 403/424-8800; Fax: 403/426-6502; Email: cisn@compusmart.ab.ca | 880 |
| Edmonton, AB | CJCA | Touch Canada Broadcasting Inc., #206, 4207 - 98 St., Edmonton AB T6E 5R7 – 403/466-4930; Fax: 403/469-5335; Email: canadianplus@msn.com | 930 |
| Edmonton, AB | *CBX | CBC, 7909 - 51 Ave., Edmonton AB T6E 5L9 – 403/468-7500; Fax: 403/468-7515 | 740 |
| Edmonton, AB | *†CHFA | Société Radio-Canada, 7909 - 51 Ave., CP 555, Edmonton AB T5J 2P4 – 403/468-7800; Fax: 403/468-7812 | 680 |
| Edmundston, NB | †CJEM | Edmundston Radio Ltd., 174, rue de l'Église, CP 188, Edmundston NB E3V 3K8 – 506/735-3351; Fax: 506/739-5803 | 570 |
| Edson, AB | CJYR | Yellowhead Broadcasting Ltd., PO Box 6600, Edson AB T7E 1T9 – 403/723-4461; Fax: 403/723-3765 | 970 |
| Elliot Lake, ON | CJNR | North Channel Broadcasters Inc., 15 Charles Walk, Elliot Lake ON P5A 2A2 – 705/356-2209 | 730 |
| Elliott Lake, ON | CKNR | *See* Elliot Lake (CKNR) | 1340 |
| Espanola, ON | CKNS | Pelmorex Radio, 46 Mead Blvd., Espanola ON P0P 1C0 – 705/869-4930; Fax: 705/869-3764 | 930 |
| Estevan, SK | CJSL | Golden West Broadcasting Ltd., 1132 - 5 St., PO Box 1280, Estevan SK S4A 2H8 – 306/634-1280; Fax: 306/634-6364 | 1280 |
| Fernie, BC | CFEK | Columbia Kootenay Broadcasting Co. Ltd., 441 - 2nd Ave., PO Box 1170, Fernie BC V0B 1M0 – 250/423-4449; Fax: 250/423-6009 | 1240 |
| Flin Flon, MB | CFAR | Arctic Radio (1982) Ltd., PO Box 430, Flin Flon MB R8A 1N3 – 204/687-3469; Fax: 204/687-6786 | 590 |
| Forestville, QC | †CFRP | Forestville QC | 620 |
| Fort Frances, ON | CFOB | Fawcett Broadcasting Ltd., 242 Scott St., Fort Frances ON P9A 1G7 – 807/274-5341; Fax: 807/274-2033 | 640 |
| Fort McMurray, AB | CJOK | OK Radio Group Ltd., 9912 Franklin Ave., Fort McMurray AB T9H 2K5 – 403/743-2246; Fax: 403/791-7250 | 1230 |
| Fort Nelson, BC | CFNL | Nor-Net Communications Ltd., PO Box 880, Fort Nelson BC V0C 1R0 – 250/774-2525; Fax: 250/774-2577 | 590 |
| Fort St. John, BC | CKNL | Nor-Net Broadcasting Ltd., 10532 Alaska Rd., Fort St. John BC V1J 1B3 – 250/785-6634; Fax: 250/785-4544 | 560 |
| Fredericton, NB | CIHI | Radio One Ltd., 206 Rookwood Ave., Fredericton NB E3B 2M2 – 506/454-2444; Fax: 506/452-2345 | 1260 |
| Fredericton, NB | *CBZ | CBC, 1160 Regent St., PO Box 2200, Fredericton NB E3B 2M2 – 506/452-8974 | 970 |
| Gander, NF | CKXD | NewCap Broadcasting Ltd., 78 Elizabeth Dr., Gander NF A1V 1G8 – 709/651-2787; Fax: 709/651-2780 | 1010 |
| Gander, NF | CKGA | VOCM Radio Newfoundland Ltd., PO Box 650, Gander NF A1V 1X2 – 709/651-3650; Fax: 709/651-2542 | 650 |
| Gander, NF | *CBG | CBC, 98 Sullivan Ave., PO Box 369, Gander NF A1V 1W7 – 709/256-4311; Fax: 709/651-2021 | 1400 |
| Gaspé, QC | †CHGM | *See* New Carlisle (CHNC) | 1150 |
| Gatineau, QC | †CJRC | Radiomutuel inc., 22, rue St-Louis, Gatineau QC J8T 2R9 – 819/561-8801; Fax: 819/561-9439; Email: cjrc@rheodatum.ca | 1150 |
| Golden, BC | CKGR | Copper Island Broadcasting Ltd., PO Box 1403, Golden BC V0A 1H0 – 250/344-7177; Fax: 250/344-7233 | 1400 |
| Grand Centre, AB | CJCM | Nor-Net Communications, 5414 - 44 St., PO Box 443, Grand Centre AB T0A 1T0 – 403/594-2459; Fax: 403/594-3001 | 1340 |
| Grand Falls, NB | †CKMV | *See* Edmundston (CJEM) | 1490 |
| Grand Falls-Windsor, NF | CKCM | VOCM Radio Newfoundland Ltd., PO Box 620, Grand Falls-Windsor NF A2A 2K2 – 709/489-2192; Fax: 709/489-8626; URL: http://www.vocm.com/ | 620 |
| Grand Falls-Windsor, NF | *CBT | CBC, 2 Harris Ave., PO Box 218, Grand Falls-Windsor NF A2A 2J7 – 709/489-2102; Fax: 709/489-1055; Email: grandfallsnews@stjohns.cbc.ca | 540 |
| Grand Forks, BC | CKGF | Boundary Broadcasting Ltd., PO Box 1570, Grand Forks BC V0H 1H0 – 250/442-5844; Fax: 250/442-3340 | 1340 |
| Grande Prairie, AB | CJXX | Monarch Broadcasting Ltd., #202, 9817 - 101 Ave., Grande Prairie AB T8V 0X6 – 403/532-0840; Fax: 403/538-1266 | 840 |
| Guelph, ON | CJOY | Power Broadcasting Inc., 75 Speedvale Ave. East, Guelph ON N1E 6M3 – 519/824-7000; Fax: 519/824-4118; Email: power@in.on.ca | 1460 |
| Halifax, NS | CFSM | Radio Saint Mary's Association, 5th Fl., Student Union Bldg., Halifax NS B3H 3C3 – 902/496-8776; Fax: 902/425-4636; Email: cfsm@squid.stmarys.ca; URL: http://huskyl.stmarys.ca/~cfsm/ | 550 |
| Halifax, NS | CHNS | Maritime Broadcasting System, 1313 Barrington St., PO Box 400, Halifax NS B3J 2R2 – 902/422-1651; Fax: 902/422-5330 | 960 |
| Halifax, NS | CJCH | CHUM Ltd., 2900 Agricola St., PO Box 1653, Halifax NS B3J 2Z4 – 902/453-2524; Fax: 902/453-3132; Email: 920cjch@newedge.net; URL: http://www.920cjch.talkradio.net | 920 |
| Halifax, NS | CFDR | *See* Bedford (CFDR) | 780 |
| Hamilton, ON | CHAM | Golden West Broadcasting Ltd., 151 York Blvd., Hamilton ON L8R 3M2 – 905/526-8200; Fax: 905/525-1416 | 820 |
| Hamilton, ON | CHML | Westcom Radio Group Ltd., #900, 875 Main St. West, Hamilton ON L8S 4R1 – 905/521-9900; Fax: 905/521-2306 | 900 |
| Hamilton, ON | CKOC | Radio Corp. Inc., #401, 883 Upper Wentworth St., PO Box 1150, Hamilton ON L8N 3P5 – 905/574-1150; Fax: 905/575-6429; Email: ckoc@radiocorp.ca; URL: http://www.radiocorp.ca | 1150 |
| High Level, AB | CKYL | *See* Peace River (CKYL) | 530 |
| High Prairie, AB | CKVH | Nor-Net Broadcasting Ltd., PO Box 2219, High Prairie AB T0G 1E0 – 403/523-5111; Fax: 403/523-3360 | 1020 |
| High River, AB | CHRB | Golden West Broadcasting Ltd., 11 - 5th Ave. SE, High River AB T1V 1G2 – 403/652-2472; Fax: 403/652-7861 | 1140 |
| Hinton, AB | CIYR | 118 Athabasca Ave., PO Box 3140, Hinton AB T7V 2A5 – 403/865-8804; Fax: 403/865-7792 | 1230 |
| Hope, BC | CKGO | Fraser Valley Broadcasters Ltd., PO Box 1600, Hope BC V0X 1L0 – 604/869-9313; Fax: 604/869-2454; URL: http://www.fraservalley.com | 1240 |
| Hudson, ON | CKDR-3 | *See* Dryden (CKDR) | 1400 |
| Ignace, ON | CKDR-1 | *See* Dryden (CKDR) | 1340 |
| Inuvik, NT | *CHAK | CBC, 155 MacKenzie Rd., Bag Service No. 8, Inuvik NT X0E 0T0 – 867/979-4411; Fax: 867/979-4458 | 860 |
| Invermere, BC | CKIR | *See* Golden (CKGR) | 870 |

| LOCATION | CALL | *CBC Stations/Affiliates †French Language Stations | FREQ. |
|---|---|---|---|
| Iqaluit, NT | *CFFB | CBC Eastern Arctic, PO Box 490, Iqaluit NT X0A 0H0 – 867/979-6100; Fax: 867/979-6147; Email: patrick_nagle@cbc.ca; URL: http://www.radio.cbc.ca | 1230 |
| Kamloops, BC | CFJC | Jim Pattison Group, JC55 New Country, 460 Pemberton Terrace, Kamloops BC V2C 1T5 – 250/372-3322; Fax: 250/374-0445; Email: info@jc55.com; URL: http://www.jc55.com | 550 |
| Kamloops, BC | CHNL | NL Broadcasting Ltd., 611 Lansdowne St., PO Box 610, Kamloops BC V2C 1Y6 – 250/372-2292; Fax: 250/372-0682 | 610 |
| Kapuskasing, ON | †CHYK | Kapuskasing ON | 1230 |
| Kapuskasing, ON | CKAP | Pelmorex Radio, 52 Riverside Dr., Kapuskasing ON P5N 1A8 – 705/335-2379; Fax: 705/337-6391; Email: am58@nt.net | 580 |
| Kelowna, BC | CKFR | Okanagan Radio Ltd., 2419 Hwy. 97 North, Kelowna BC V1X 4J2 – 250/860-8600; Fax: 250/886-8856 | 1150 |
| Kelowna, BC | CKOV | Seacoast Communications Group Inc., 3805 Lakeshore Rd., Kelowna BC V1W 3K6 – 250/762-3331; Fax: 250/762-2141; Email: ckov@awinc.com | 630 |
| Kenora, ON | CJRL | Fawcett Broadcasting Ltd., 128 Main St. South, Kenora ON P9N 1S9 – 807/468-3181; Fax: 807/468-4188 | 1220 |
| Kentville, NS | CKEN | Annapolis Valley Radio Ltd., 29 Oakdene Ave., PO Box 310, Kentville NS B4N 1H5 – 902/678-2111; Fax: 902/678-9894; Email: avr@glinx.com | 1490 |
| Kingston, ON | CFFX | Power Broadcasting Inc., 479 Counter St., Kingston ON K7M 7J3 – 613/549-1911; Fax: 613/549-7974 | 960 |
| Kingston, ON | CKLC | St. Lawrence Broadcasting Co. Ltd., 99 Brock St., PO Box 1380, Kingston ON K7L 4Y5 – 613/544-1380; Fax: 613/546-9751 | 1380 |
| Kirkland Lake, ON | *CJKL | Connelly Communications Corp., 5 Kirkland St., PO Box 430, Kirkland Lake ON P2N 3J4 – 705/567-3366; Fax: 705/567-6101 | 560 |
| Kitchener, ON | CKGL | Rogers Broadcasting Ltd., 305 King St. West, Kitchener ON N2G 4E4 – 519/743-2611; Fax: 519/743-7510 | 570 |
| Kitchener, ON | CXLR | Conestoga College, 299 Doon Valley Dr., Kitchener ON N2G 4M4 – 519/748-5220, ext.310; Fax: 519/748-3505 | closed circuit |
| Kitchener, ON | CIAM | *See* Cambridge (CIAM) | |
| Kitchener, ON | CKKW | *See* Waterloo (CKKW) | 1090 |
| Kitimat, BC | CKTK | Skeena Broadcasters, Division of Okanagan Skeena Group Ltd., 350 City Centre, Kitimat BC V8C 1T6 – 250/632-2102 | 1230 |
| La Crete, AB | CKLA | *See* Peace River (CKYL) | 92.1 |
| La Sarre, QC | †CKLS | Radio Nord inc., 122, 5e rue est, La Sarre QC J9Z 2Y1 – 819/333-5505; Fax: 819/333-2066 | 1240 |
| La Tûque, QC | *†CFLM | Radio Haute-Mauricie inc., 529, rue St-Louis, CP 850, La Tûque QC G9X 3P6 – 819/523-4575; Fax: 819/676-8000 | 1240 |
| Labrador City, NF | *CBDQ | CBC, PO Box 576, Labrador City NF A2V 2L3 – 709/944-3616 | 1490 |
| Lac-Etchemin, QC | †CIRB | *See* St-Georges-de-Beauce (CKRB) | 1240 |
| Lac-Mégantic, QC | †CKFL | Radio PLUS Lac-Mégantic inc., 5088, rue Frontenac, Lac-Mégantic QC G6B 1H3 – 819/583-0663; Fax: 819/583-0665 | 1400 |
| Lethbridge, AB | CJOC | Rogers Broadcasting Ltd., PO Box 820, Lethbridge AB T1J 3Z9 – 403/320-1220; Fax: 403/327-5879 | 1220 |
| Lethbridge, AB | CLCC | Lethbridge Community College, Student Service Centre, 3000 College Dr. South, Lethbridge AB T1K 1L6 – 403/320-3256; Fax: 403/320-1461 | 730; closed circuit |
| Lindsay, ON | CKLY | Centario Communications Inc., 249 Kent St. West, Lindsay ON K9V 2Z3 – 705/324-9103; Fax: 705/324-4149 | 910 |
| Lloydminster, AB | CKSA | Saskatchewan-Alberta Broadcasters Ltd., 5026 - 50 St., Lloydminster AB T9V 1P3 – 403/875-3321; Fax: 403/875-4704 | 1080 |
| London, ON | CFPL | Blackburn Radio Inc., 369 York St., PO Box 2580, London ON N6A 4H3 – 519/438-8391; Fax: 519/438-2415 | 980 |
| London, ON | CJBK | London Communications Ltd., 743 Wellington Rd. South, London ON N6C 4R5 – 519/686-2525; Fax: 519/686-3658; Email: 1290.cjbk@odyssey.on.ca; URL: http://www.cjbk.com | 1290 |
| London, ON | CKSL | Telemedia Communications Ontario Inc., 380 Wellington St. South, PO Box 1410, London ON N6A 5J2 – 519/667-1410; Fax: 519/667-2175 | 1410 |
| Mackenzie, BC | CKMK | Radio Station CKPG Ltd., PO Box 1210, Mackenzie BC V0J 2C0 – 250/997-3400; Fax: 250/997-4818 | 1240 |
| Mackenzie, NT | *CFYK-1 | *See* Yellowknife (CFYK) | 1340 |
| Marystown, NF | CHCM | VOCM Radio Newfoundland Ltd., PO Box 560, Marystown NF A0E 2M0 – 709/279-2560; Fax: 709/279-3538 | 740 |
| Matane, QC | †CHRM | Les Communications Matane inc., 800, av du Phare ouest, CP 605, Matane QC G4W 1V7 – 418/562-4141; Fax: 418/562-0778; Email: chrm_am@quebectel.com | 1290 |
| Matane, QC | *†CBGA | Société Radio-Canada Gaspésie, 155, rue St-Sacrament, Matane QC G4W 1Y9 – 418/562-0290; Fax: 418/562-5555 | 1250 |
| Meadow Lake, SK | CJNS | Northwestern Radio Partnership Ltd., PO Box 1660, Meadow Lake SK S0M 1V0 – 306/236-6494; Fax: 306/236-6141 | 1240 |
| Medicine Hat, AB | CHAT | Monarch Broadcasting Ltd., PO Box 1270, Medicine Hat AB T1A 7H5 – 403/529-1270; Fax: 403/529-1292; Email: ddietric@mlc.awinc.com | 1270 |
| Medicine Hat, AB | CJCY | Medicine Hat Broadcasting Ltd., 457 - 3 St. SE, 2nd Fl., Medicine Hat AB T1A 0G8 – 403/529-1390; Fax: 403/527-5971 | 1390 |
| Melfort, SK | CJVR | Radio CJVR Ltd., 611 Main St., PO Box 750, Melfort SK S0E 1A0 – 306/752-2587; Fax: 306/752-5932; Email: cjvr@sk.sympatico.ca; URL: http://www.saskar.sk.ca/cjvr/ | 1420 |
| Merritt, BC | CJNL | Merritt Broadcasting, 1970 Quilchena Ave., Merritt BC V1K 1B8 – 250/378-4288; Fax: 250/378-6979 | 1230 |
| Middleton, NS | CKAD | Annapolis Valley Radio Inc., 10 Bridge St., Middleton NS B0S 1P0 – 902/825-3429; Fax: 902/825-6009; Email: avr@glinx.com; URL: Http://www.glinx.com | 1350 |
| Miramichi, NB | CFAN | Maritime Broadcasting Co. Ltd., 245 Pleasant St., PO Box 338, Miramichi NB E1V 3M4 – 506/622-3311; Fax: 506/627-0335; Email: cfan@nb.sympatico.ca; URL: http://www.cfan.com | 790 |
| Moncton, NB | CKCW | Maritime Broadcasting System Ltd., 1000 St. George Blvd., Moncton NB E1E 4M7 – 506/858-1220; Fax: 506/858-1209 | 1220 |
| Moncton, NB | *CBA | CBC, 250 Archibald St., PO Box 950, Moncton NB E1C 8N8 – 506/853-6666; Fax: 506/853-6739 | 1070 |
| Montréal, QC | CFMB | Radio Montréal, 35, rue York, Montréal QC H3Z 2Z5 – 514/483-2362; Fax: 514/483-1362; Email: admin@cfmb.ca; URL: http://www.cfmb.ca | 1410 |
| Montréal, QC | CFLI | Concordia University, 6931, rue Sherbrooke ouest, Montréal QC H4B 1R6 – 514/848-7470; Fax: 514/848-7450 | closed circuit; 650 & cable FM; 88.9 CF cable; 101.9 Videotron |
| Montréal, QC | CJAD | Standard Radio Inc., 1411, rue du Fort, Montréal QC H3H 2R1 – 514/989-2523; Fax: 514/989-3868 | 800 |
| Montréal, QC | †CKAC | Radio Média, #300, 1411, rue Peel, Montréal QC H3A 3L5 – 514/845-5151; Fax: 514/845-2229 | 730 |
| Montréal, QC | CKIS | CHUM Ltd., 1310, av Greene, Montréal QC H3Z 2B5 – 514/931-4487; Fax: 514/931-4057 | 990 |
| Montréal, QC | *†CBF | Société Radio-Canada, CP 6000, Succ A, Montréal QC H3C 3A8 – 514/597-5970; Fax: 514/597-4100 | 690 |
| Montréal, QC | *CBM | CBC, CP 6000, Succ A, Montréal QC H3C 3A8 – 514/597-4444; Fax: 514/597-4511 | 940 |
| Moose Jaw, SK | CHAB | Golden West Broadcasting, 1704 Main St. North, PO Box 800, Moose Jaw SK S6H 4P5 – 306/694-0800; Fax: 306/692-8880 | 800 |
| Moosonee, ON | CHMO | James Bay Broadcasting Corp. Inc., PO Box 400, Moosonee ON P0L 1Y0 – 705/336-2466; Fax: 705/336-2186 | 1450 |
| Mount Pearl, NF | VOAR | VOAR Christian Radio, PO Box 2520, Mount Pearl NF A1N 4M7 – 709/745-8627; Fax: 709/745-1600; URL: http://www.voar.org1210 | |
| Nanaimo, BC | CKEG | Central Island Broadcasting Ltd., 4550 Wellington Rd., Nanaimo BC V9T 2H3 – 250/758-1131; Fax: 250/758-4644 | 1570 |
| New Carlisle, QC | †CHNC | Radio CHNC Ltée, 153, rue Principale, CP 610, New Carlisle QC G0C 1Z0 – 418/752-2215; Fax: 418/752-6939 | 610 |
| New Glasgow, NS | CKEC | Hector Broadcasting Co. Ltd., 84 Provost St., PO Box 519, New Glasgow NS B2H 5E7 – 902/752-4200; Fax: 902/755-2468 | 1320 |

| LOCATION | CALL | *CBC Stations/Affiliates †French Language Stations | FREQ. |
|---|---|---|---|
| New Liskeard, ON | *CJTT | Connelly Communications Corp., 55 Whitewood Ave., PO Box 1058, New Liskeard ON P0J 1P0 – 705/647-7334; Fax: 705/647-8660; Email: cjtt@nt.net; URL: http://www.nt.net/1230_cjtt/radio.htm | 1230 |
| New Westminster, BC | CKNW | Div. of WIC Radio Ltd., #2000, 700 West Georgia St., New Westminster BC V7Y 1K9 – 604/331-2711; Fax: 604/331-2722; Email: cknw@wic.ca; URL: http://www.cknw.com | 980 |
| Niagara Falls, ON | CJRN | CJRN 710 Inc., PO Box 710, Niagara Falls ON L2E 6X7 – 905/356-6710; Fax: 905/356-6397; Email: rock@theplanet.com | 710 |
| North Battleford, SK | CJNB | Northwestern Radio Partnership, PO Box 1460, North Battleford SK S9A 2Z5 – 306/445-2477; Fax: 306/445-4599 | 1050 |
| North Bay, ON | CHUR | Pelmorex Broadcasting Inc., 215 Oak St. East, North Bay ON P1B 8P8 – 705/472-1110; Fax: 705/476-8400 | 840 |
| North York, ON | CRSC | Seneca College, 1750 Finch Ave. East, North York ON M2J 2X5 – 416/491-5050, ext.2994; Fax: 416/756-2765 | closed circuit |
| Norway House, MB | CJNC | Norway House Communications Inc., PO Box 250, Norway House MB R0B 1B0 – 204/359-4683; Fax: 204/359-6191 | 1340 |
| Oakville, ON | CJMR | CJMR 1320 Radio Ltd., 284 Church St., Oakville ON L6J 7N2 – 905/271-1320; Fax: 905/842-1250 | 1320 |
| Oakville, ON | CHWO | CHWO Radio Ltd., 284 Church St., Oakville ON L6J 7N2 – 905/845-2821; Fax: 905/842-1250 | 1250 |
| 100 Mile House, BC | CKBX | Cariboo Broadcasters Ltd., 260 - 3rd St., PO Box 939, 100 Mile House BC V0K 2E0 – 250/395-3848; Fax: 250/395-4147 | 840 |
| Oshawa, ON | CKDO | Power Broadcasting Inc., 360 King St. West, Oshawa ON L1J 2K2 – 905/571-1350; Fax: 905/571-1150 | 1350 |
| Osoyoos, BC | CJOR | Okanagan Radio Ltd., PO Box 539, Osoyoos BC V0H 1V0 – 250/495-7226; Fax: 250/495-7228 | 1240 |
| Ottawa, ON | CFGO | RAWLCO Communications Ltd., 1575 Carling Ave., Ottawa ON K1Z 7M3 – 613/729-1200; Fax: 613/729-9829 | 1200 |
| Ottawa, ON | CFRA | CHUM Ltd., 1900 Walkley Rd., Ottawa ON K1H 8P4 – 613/738-2372; Fax: 613/523-6423; Email: mailbox@koolcfra.com; http://www.cfra.com | 580 |
| Ottawa, ON | CIWW | Rogers Broadcasting Ltd., #1900, Tower B, Place de Ville, 112 Kent St., Ottawa ON K1P 6J1 – 613/238-7482; Fax: 613/236-5382; Email: oldies-1310@ottawa.net; URL: http://www.ottawa.net/~oldies-1310/ | 1310 |
| Owen Sound, ON | CFOS | Bayshore Broadcasting Corp., 270 - 9 St. East, PO Box 280, Owen Sound ON N4K 5P5 – 519/376-2030; Fax: 519/371-4242; Email: bayshore@radioowensound.com; URL: http://www.radioowensound.com | 560 |
| Parksville, BC | CKCI | Central Island Broadcasting Ltd., #204, 182 Harrison Ave., PO Box 1370, Parksville BC V6P 2H3 – 250/248-4211; Fax: 250/248-4210 | 1350 |
| Peace River, AB | CKYL | Peace River Broadcasting Corp., Bag 300, Peace River AB T8S 1T5 – 403/624-2535; Fax: 403/624-5424 | 610 |
| Penticton, BC | CKOR | Okanagan Radio Ltd., 33 Carmi Ave., Penticton BC V2A 3G4 – 250/492-2800; Fax: 250/493-0370 | 800 |
| Peterborough, ON | CKPT | CHUM Ltd., PO Box 177, Peterborough ON K9J 6Y8 – 705/742-8844; Fax: 705/742-1417; Email: radio@ckpt.com; URL: http://www.ckpt.com | 1420 |
| Peterborough, ON | CKRU | Power Broadcasting Inc., 1925 Television Rd., PO Box 4150, Peterborough ON K9J 6Z9 – 705/742-7708; Fax: 705/742-7274; Email: misinclair@accel.net | 980 |
| Plessisville, QC | †CKTL | Radio Média ltée, CP 142, Plessisville QC G6L 2Y6 – 819/362-3737; Fax: 819/362-3414 | 1420 |
| Pohenegamook, QC | †CHRT | *See* Rivière-du-Loup (CJFP) | 1450 |
| Port Alberni, BC | CJAV | CJAV Ltd., 2970 - 3 Ave. South, Port Alberni BC V9Y 7N4 – 250/723-2455; Fax: 250/723-0797; Email: cjav@cedar.alberni.net; URL: http://www.alberni.net/~cjav/cjav.htm | 1240 |
| Port au Choix, NF | CFNW | *See* Corner Brook (CFCB) | 790 |
| Port aux Basques, NF | CFGN | Humber Valley Broadcasting Co. Ltd., PO Box 1230, Port aux Basques NF A0M 1C0 – 709/695-2183; Fax: 709/695-9614 | 1230 |
| Port Elgin, ON | CFPS | *See* Owen Sound (CFOS) | 1490 |
| Port Hardy, BC | CFNI | CFCP Radio Ltd., PO Box 1240, Port Hardy BC V0N 2P0 – 250/949-6500; Fax: 250/949-6580 | 1240 |
| Port Hawkesbury, NS | CIGO | MacEachern Broadcasting Ltd., Business Park, PO Box 1410, Port Hawkesbury NS B0E 2V0 – 902/625-1220; Fax: 902/625-2664; Email: bob@cigo.com; URL: http://www.cigo.com | 1410 |
| Portage La Prairie, MB | CFRY | Portage-Delta Broadcasting Co. Ltd., 1500 Saskatchewan Ave. West, Portage La Prairie MB R1N 0N6 – 204/239-5111; Fax: 204/857-3456 | 920 |
| Powell River, BC | CHQB | Sunshine Coast Broadcasting Co. Ltd., 6816 Courtenay St., Powell River BC V8A 1X1 – 604/485-4207; Fax: 604/485-4210 | 1280 |
| Prince Albert, SK | CKBI | Central Broadcasting Co. Ltd., PO Box 900, Prince Albert SK S6V 7R4 – 306/763-7421; Fax: 306/764-1850 | 900 |
| Prince George, BC | CJCI | Cariboo Central Interior Radio Inc., 1940 - 3 Ave., Prince George BC V2M 1G7 – 250/564-2524; Fax: 250/562-6611; Email: cjci@solutions-4u.com; URL: http://www.cjci.com | 620 |
| Prince George, BC | *CKPG | Monarch Broadcasting Ltd., 1220 - 6 Ave., Prince George BC V2L 3M8 – 250/564-8861; Fax: 250/562-8768; Email: ckpgmail@ckpg.bc.ca; URL: http://www.ckpg.ca | 550 |
| Prince Rupert, BC | CHTK | Skeena Broadcasting Group Ltd., Division of Okanagan Skeena Group Ltd., 346 Stiles Pl., Prince Rupert BC V8J 3S5 – 250/624-9111; Fax: 250/624-3100 | 560 |
| Prince Rupert, BC | *CFPR | CBC, #1, 222 - 3 Ave. West, Prince Rupert BC V8J 1L1 – 250/624-2161; Fax: 250/627-8594; Email: daybreak@citytel.net | 860 |
| Princeton, BC | CIOR | Princeton Broadcasting Ltd., PO Box 1400, Princeton BC V0X 1W0 – 250/295-6991; Fax: 250/295-6628 | 1400 |
| Québec, QC | *†CBV | Société Radio-Canada, 2505, boul Laurier, CP 10400, Québec QC G1V 2X2 – 418/654-1341; Fax: 418/656-8225 | 980 |
| Québec, QC | *†CHRC | Les Entreprises de Radiodiffusion de la Capitale inc., CP 8080, Québec QC G1V 1R8 – 418/688-8080; Fax: 418/682-8429 | 800 |
| Quesnel, BC | CKCQ | Cariboo Central Interior Radio Inc., 160 Front St., Quesnel BC V2J 2K1 – 250/992-7046; Fax: 250/992-2354 | 920 |
| Red Deer, AB | CKGY | Shaw Radio Ltd., PO Bag 5339, Red Deer AB T4N 6W1 – 403/343-1170; Fax: 403/346-1230 | 1170 |
| Red Deer, AB | CKRD | Monarch Broadcasting Ltd., 2840 Bremner Ave., PO Box 5700, Red Deer AB T4N 6V5 – 403/343-0700; Fax: 403/343-2573 | 700 |
| Red Lake, ON | CKDR-5 | *See* Dryden (CKDR) | 1340 |
| Regina, SK | CJME | RAWLCO Communications Ltd., #210, 2401 Saskatchewan Dr., Regina SK S4P 4H8 – 306/569-1300; Fax: 306/347-8557 | 1300 |
| Regina, SK | CKCK | Craig Broadcast Systems, 1922 Park St., Regina SK S4N 7M4 – 306/569-6200; Fax: 306/936-8329; Email: ckck.radio@sasknet.sk.ca | 620 |
| Regina, SK | CKRM | Harvard Communications Ltd., 2060 Halifax St, PO Box 9800, Regina SK S4P 1T7 – 306/566-9800; Fax: 306/781-7338 | 980 |
| Regina, SK | CKUR | University of Regina, Student Service Centre, Regina SK S4S 0A2 – 306/588-8812 | closed circuit; 760 |
| Regina, SK | *CBK | CBC, 2440 Broad St., PO Box 540, Regina SK S4P 4A1 – 306/347-9540; Fax: 306/347-9493 | 540 |
| Regina, SK | *†CBKF | Société Radio-Canada, 2440 Broad St., Regina SK S4P 4A1 – 306/347-9540; Fax: 306/347-9493 | |
| Revelstoke, BC | CKCR | *See* Salmon Arm (CKXR) | 1340 |
| Richmond, BC | CISL | Standard Radio Inc., #20, 11151 Horseshoe Way, Richmond BC V7A 4S5 – 604/272-6500; Fax: 604/272-0917; Email: cisl@uniserve.com | 650 |
| Rimouski, QC | †CAJT | CEGEP de Rimouski, a/s Agecor inc., 60, rue de l'Évéché ouest, Rimouski QC G5L 4H6 – 418/723-1880, ext.2265; Fax: 418/724-4961 | closed circuit |
| Rimouski, QC | †CFLP | Power Broadcasting Inc., 875, boul St-Germain ouest, CP 3875, Rimouski QC G5L 3T9 – 418/723-2323; Fax: 418/722-7508 | 1000 |
| Rimouski, QC | *†CJBR | Société Radio-Canada, 273, rue St-Jean Baptiste ouest, Rimouski QC G5L 4J8 – 418/723-2217; Fax: 418/723-4730 | 900 |
| Roberval, QC | †CHRL | Radio Roberval inc., 568, boul St-Joseph, Roberval QC G8H 2K6 – 418/275-1831; Fax: 418/275-2475 | 910 |

| LOCATION | CALL | *CBC Stations/Affiliates †French Language Stations | FREQ. |
|---|---|---|---|
| Roberval, QC | †CFED | Groupe Radio Antenne 6 inc., 568, boul St-Joseph, Roberval QC G8H 2K6 – 418/275-1831; Fax: 418/275-2475 | 1340 |
| Rosetown, SK | CJYM/CFYM | Dace Broadcasting Corp., PO Box 490, Rosetown SK S0L 2V0 – 306/882-2686; Fax: 306/882-3037 | 1330 |
| Rouyn-Noranda, QC | †CKRN | Radio Nord inc., 380, av Murdoch, CP 70, Rouyn-Noranda QC J9X 1G5 – 819/762-0741; Fax: 819/762-2280 | 1400 |
| Ste-Anne-des-Monts, QC | †CJMC | Radio du Golfe inc., 170, boul Ste-Anne est, CP 820, Ste-Anne-des-Monts QC G0E 2G0 – 418/763-5522; Fax: 418/763-7211 | 1490 |
| St. Catharines, ON | CHSC | Coultis Broadcasting Ltd., 36 Queenston St., St. Catharines ON L2R 2Y9 – 905/682-6691; Fax: 905/682-9434 | 1220 |
| St. Catharines, ON | CKTB | Standard Radio Inc., PO Box 610, St. Catharines ON L2R 6X7 – 905/684-1174; Fax: 905/684-4800; URL: http://www.htzfm.com | 610 |
| Ste-Foy, QC | CHRC | *See* Québec (CHRC) | 800 |
| St-Georges-de-Beauce, QC | †CKRB | Radio Beauce inc., 170, rue 120, St-Georges-de-Beauce QC G5Y 5C4 – 418/228-5535; Fax: 418/228-0096 | 1460 |
| St-Hyacinthe, QC | †CKBS | Radio St-Hyacinthe (1978) ltée, 855, rue Ste-Marie, St-Hyacinthe QC J2S 4R9 – 514/774-6486; Fax: 514/774-7785 | 1240 |
| Saint John, NB | CFBC | Fundy Cable Ltd./Ltée, Oldies 93, PO Box 930, Saint John NB E2L 4E2 – 506/658-2330; Fax: 506/658-2320; Email: www.radio@fundy.ca; URL: http://www.radio.fundy.ca | 930 |
| Saint John, NB | CHSJ | New Brunswick Broadcasting Ltd., PO Box 2000, Saint John NB E2L 3T4 – 506/632-3323; Fax: 506/632-3485; Email: chsj@nb.sympatico.ca | 700 |
| St. John's, NF | CKVO | VOCM Radio Newfoundland Ltd., PO Box 8590, St. John's NF A1B 3P5 – 709/726-5590; Fax: 709/726-4633 | 710 |
| St. John's, NF | CJYQ | NewCap Broadcasting, 208 Kenmount Rd., PO Box 8010, Stn A, St. John's NF A1B 3M7 – 709/753-4040; Fax: 709/753-4420; Email: q93@thezone.net | 930 |
| St. John's, NF | VOCM | VOCM Radio Newfoundland Ltd., PO Box 8-590, Stn A, St. John's NF A1B 3P5 – 709/726-5590; Fax: 709/726-4633 | 590 |
| St. John's, NF | VOWR | VOWR Radio Board, PO Box 7430, St. John's NF A1E 3Y5 – 709/579-9233; Fax: 709/579-9232 | 800 |
| St. John's, NF | *CBN | CBC, 344 Duckworth St., PO Box 12010, Stn A, St. John's NF A1B 3T8 – 709/576-5514; Fax: 709/576-5205 | 640 |
| Ste-Marie-de-Beauce, QC | †CJVL | Radio Beauce inc., 1360, rue Notre-Dame sud, Ste-Marie-de-Beauce QC G6E 2W9 – 418/387-1360; Fax: 418/387-3757 | 1360 |
| St-Pamphile, QC | †CHAL | *See* La Pocatière (CHOX) | 1350 |
| St. Paul, AB | CHLW | NorNet Broadcasting Ltd., #201, 4341 - 50 Ave., St. Paul AB T0A 3A3 – 403/645-4425; Fax: 403/645-2383; Email: nn07@west-teq.net | 1310 |
| St. Stephen, NB | WQDY | International Radio, PO Box 305, St. Stephen NB E3L 2X2 – 506/465-0989; Fax: 207/454-3062 | 1230 |
| Salmon Arm, BC | CKXR | Copper Island Broadcasting Co., PO Box 69, Salmon Arm BC V1E 4N2 – 250/832-2161; Fax: 250/832-2240 | 580 |
| Salmon Arm, BC | CKIR | Copper Island Broadcasting Co., PO Box 69, Salmon Arm BC V1E 4N2 – 250/832-2161; Fax: 250/832-2240 | 870 |
| Sarnia, ON | CHOK | Sarnia Broadcasters (1993) Ltd., 148 North Front St., PO Box 1070, Sarnia ON N7T 7K5 – 519/336-1070; Fax: 519/336-7523; Email: chok@icis.on.ca; URL: http://www.chok.com | 1070 |
| Sarnia, ON | CKTY | Blackburn Radio Inc., 1415 London Rd., Sarnia ON N7S 1P6 – 519/332-5500; Fax: 519/542-1520 | 1110 |
| Saskatoon, SK | CJWW | Radio One (Saskatoon) Corp., 345 - 4 Ave. South, Saskatoon SK S7K 5S5 – 306/244-1975; Fax: 306/665-7730; Email: cjww.radio@sasknet.sk.ca; URL: http://www.sasknet.com/cjww/ | 600 |
| Saskatoon, SK | CKOM | RAWLCO Communications Ltd., 3333 - 8 St. East, Saskatoon SK S7H 0W3 – 306/955-6595; Fax: 306/938-8329 | 650 |
| Saskatoon, SK | †CBKF-2 | *See* Regina (CBKF) | 860 |
| Saskatoon, SK | *CBK | CBC, CN Tower, 5th Fl., Saskatoon SK S7K 1J5 – 306/956-7400; Fax: 306/956-7488 | 540 |
| Scarborough, ON | CKCC | Centennial College, 651 Warden Ave., Scarborough ON M1L 3Z6 – 416/694-3033; Fax: 416/694-2664 | closed circuit |
| Sept-Îles, QC | †CKCN | Radio Sept-Îles inc., 437, av Arnaud, Sept-Îles QC G4R 3B3 – 418/962-3838; Fax: 418/968-6662 | 560 |
| Sherbrooke, QC | †CHLT | Télémedia Communications inc., 25, rue Bryant, Sherbrooke QC J1J 3Z5 – 819/563-6363; Fax: 819/566-4222 | 630 |
| Sherbrooke, QC | †CFLX | Radio Communautaire de l'Estrie, #400, 244, rue Dufferin, Sherbrooke QC J1H 4M4 – 819/566-2787; Fax: 819/566-7331 | 1300 |
| Simcoe, ON | CHNR | 600 Norfolk North, Simcoe ON N3Y 4K8 – 519/426-7700; Fax: 519/426-8574 | 1600 |
| Sioux Lookout, ON | CKDR-2 | *See* Dryden (CKDR) | 1400 |
| Slave Lake, AB | CKWA | Nor-Net Communications Ltd., PO Box 2470, Slave Lake AB T0G 2A0 – 403/849-2577; Fax: 403/849-4833; Email: ckwa@incentre.net | 1210 |
| Smithers, BC | CFBV | Cariboo Central Interior Radio Inc., PO Box 335, Smithers BC V0J 2N0 – 250/847-2277; Fax: 250/847-9411 | 870 |
| Smiths Falls, ON | CJET | Rideau Broadcasting, PO Box 630, Smiths Falls ON K7A 4T4 – 613/562-4630; Fax: 613/283-7243 | 630 |
| Steinbach, MB | CHSM | Golden West Broadcasting Ltd., 250 Main St., Steinbach MB R0A 2A0 – 204/326-3737; Fax: 204/324-8918 | 1250 |
| Stephenville, NF | CFSX | Humber Valley Broadcasting Co. Ltd., 30 Oregon Dr., Stephenville NF A2N 2X9 – 709/643-2191; Fax: 709/643-5025 | 870 |
| Stettler, AB | CKSQ | Nor-Net Broadcasting Ltd., 4703 - 58 St., Stettler AB T0C 2L1 – 403/742-2930; Fax: 403/742-0660 | 1400 |
| Stratford, ON | CJCS | Telemedia Communications Ontario Inc., 178 Ontario St., PO Box 904, Stratford ON N5A 6W3 – 519/271-2450; Fax: 519/271-3102 | 1240 |
| Sudbury, ON | CHNO | Pelmorex Radio, 295 Victoria St., Sudbury ON P3C 1K5 – 705/674-6401; Fax: 705/674-7322 | 550 |
| Sudbury, ON | †CHYC | Pelmorex Radio, 295 Victoria St., Sudbury ON P3C 1K5 – 705/674-6401; Fax: 705/674-7322 | 900 |
| Sudbury, ON | CIGM | Telemedia Communications Ontario Inc., 880 LaSalle Blvd., Sudbury ON P3A 1X5 – 705/566-4480; Fax: 705/560-7232 | 790 |
| Summerland, BC | CHOR | Okanagan Radio Ltd., PO Box 1170, Summerland BC V0H 1Z0 – 250/494-0333 | 1450 |
| Summerside, PE | CJRW | Gulf Broadcasters Co. Ltd., 763 Water St. East, Summerside PE C1N 4J3 – 902/436-2201; Fax: 902/436-8573; Email: cjrw@atcon.com; URL: http://www.icondata.com/cjrw/index.htm | 1240 |
| Sussex, NB | CJCW | Maritime Broadcasting System Ltd., PO Box 5900, Sussex NB E0E 1P0 – 506/432-2529; Fax: 506/433-4900; Email: cjcw@nbnet.nb.ca | 590 |
| Swift Current, SK | CKSW | Frontier City Broadcasting Co. Ltd., 134 Central Ave. North, Swift Current SK S9H 0L1 – 306/773-4605; Fax: 306/773-6390 | 570 |
| Swift Current, SK | CJSN | Frontier City Broadcasting Co. Ltd., 134 Central Ave. North, Swift Current SK S9H 0L1 – 306/773-4605; Fax: 306/773-6390 | 1490 |
| Sydney, NS | CJCB | Celtic Broadcasting Ltd., Radio Bldg., 318 Charlotte St., Sydney NS B1P 6K2 – 902/564-5596; Fax: 902/564-1057 | 1270 |
| Sydney, NS | CHER | Bras d'Or Broadcasting Ltd., PO Box 1201, Sydney NS B1P 6J9 – 902/539-8500; Fax: 902/562-5720 | 950 |
| Sydney, NS | *CBI | CBC, 285 Alexandra St., Sydney NS B1S 2E8 – 902/539-5050; Fax: 902/563-4170 | 1140 |
| Terrace, BC | CFTK | Okanagan Skeena Group Ltd., 4625 Lazelle Ave., Terrace BC V8G 1S4 – 250/635-6316; Fax: 250/638-6320; Email: info@osg.net; URL: http://www.osg.net | 590 |
| The Pas, MB | CJAR | Arctic Radio (1982) Ltd., PO Box 2980, The Pas MB R9A 1R7 – 204/623-5307; Fax: 204/623-5337; Email: oj1240@mts.net | 1240 |
| Thetford-Mines, QC | †CKLD | Radio-Mégantic ltée, CP 69, Thetford-Mines QC G6G 5S3 – 418/335-7533; Fax: 418/335-9009 | 1330 |
| Thompson, MB | CHTM | Arctic Radio (1982) Ltd., 201 Hayes Rd., Thompson MB R8N 1M5 – 204/778-7361; Fax: 204/778-5252 | 610 |
| Thunder Bay, ON | CKPR | CJSD Inc., 87 North Hill St., Thunder Bay ON P7A 5V6 – 807/346-2580; Fax: 807/345-4671 | 580 |
| Tillsonburg, ON | CKOT | Tillsonburg Broadcasting Co. Ltd., PO Box 10, Tillsonburg ON N4G 4H3 – 519/842-4281; Fax: 519/842-4284 | 1510 |
| Timmins, ON | CKGB | Telemedia Communications Ontario Inc., PO Box 1046, Timmins ON P4N 7H8 – 705/264-2351; Fax: 705/264-2984 | 750 |
| Toronto, ON | CFRB | Standard Radio Inc., 2 St. Clair Ave. West, Toronto ON M4V 1L6 – 416/924-5711; Fax: 416/323-6830 | 1010 |

| LOCATION | CALL | *CBC Stations/Affiliates †French Language Stations | FREQ. |
|---|---|---|---|
| Toronto, ON | CFTR | Rogers Broadcasting Ltd., 36 Victoria St., Toronto ON M5C 1H3 – 416/864-2000; Fax: 416/864-2116; Email: 680news@rci.rogers.com; URL: http://www.canoe.ca/680news | 680 |
| Toronto, ON | CHIN | Radio 1540 Ltd., 622 College St., Toronto ON M6G 1B6 – 416/531-9991; Fax: 416/531-5274; Email: chin@istar.ca; URL: http://www.chinradio.com | 1540 |
| Toronto, ON | CHOG | Westcom Radio Group Ltd., #1400, 5255 Yonge St., Toronto ON M2N 6P4 – 416/221-6400; Fax: 416/512-4810; Email: dhuszar@inforamp.net; URL: http://www.talk640.com | 640 |
| Toronto, ON | CHUM | CHUM Ltd., 1331 Yonge St., Toronto ON M4T 1Y1 – 416/925-6666; Fax: 416/926-4026; Email: chumam@1050chum.com | 1050 |
| Toronto, ON | CJCL | Telemedia Communications Ontario Inc., 40 Holly St., 9th Fl., Toronto ON M4S 3C3 – 416/482-0590; Fax: 416/488-1845; Email: thefan@telemedia.org | 590 |
| Toronto, ON | CHWO | *See* Oakville (CHWO) | |
| Toronto, ON | CIAO | *See* Brampton (CIAO) | |
| Toronto, ON | CKCC | *See* Scarborough (CKCC) | |
| Toronto, ON | CRSC | *See* North York (CRSC) | |
| Toronto, ON | *CBL | CBC, PO Box 500, Stn A, Toronto ON M5W 1E6 – 416/205-3311; Fax: 416/205-6336 | 740 |
| Toronto, ON | *†CJBC | Société Radio-Canada, CP 500, Succ A, Toronto ON M5W 1E6 – 416/205-2522; Fax: 416/205-5622 | 860 |
| Trail, BC | CFKC | Kootenay Broadcasting System Ltd., 1560 Second Ave., Trail BC V1R 1M4 – 250/428-5311; Fax: 250/368-8471 | 1340 |
| Trail, BC | CKKC | Kootenay Broadcasting System Ltd., 1560 Second Ave., Trail BC V1R 1M4 – 250/352-5510; Fax: 250/368-8471 | 880 |
| Trenton, ON | CJTN | Quinte Broadcasting Co. Ltd., 31 Quinte St., PO Box 9, Trenton ON K8V 5R1 – 613/392-1237; Fax: 613/394-6430 | 1270 |
| Trois-Rivières, QC | †CHLN | Télémedia Communications inc., 3550, boul Royal, Trois-Rivières QC G9A 5G8 – 819/374-3556; Fax: 819/374-3222 | 550 |
| Truro, NS | CKCL | Radio Atlantic (CKCL) Ltd., 187 Industrial Ave., Truro NS B2N 6V3 – 902/893-6060; Fax: 902/893-7771; Email: ckcl@atcon.com; URL: http://www.truroradio.ca | 600 |
| Val-d'Or, QC | †CKVD | Radio Nord inc., 1729 - 3e av, Val-d'Or QC J9P 1W3 – 819/825-9994; Fax: 819/825-6741 | 900 |
| Vancouver, BC | CFUN | CHUM Ltd., #300, 380 West 2nd Ave., Vancouver BC V5Y 1C8 – 604/871-9000; Fax: 604/871-2901; Email: cfunmail@cfun.com; URL: http://www.cfun.com | 1410 |
| Vancouver, BC | CHMB | Mainstream Braodcasting Corp., #100, 1200 West 73 Ave., Vancouver BC V6P 6G5 – 604/263-1320; Fax: 604/263-0320; Email: chmb@am1320.com; URL: http://www.am1320.com | 1320 |
| Vancouver, BC | CJVB | Firchild Radio Group, #101, 814 Richards St., Vancouver BC V6B 3A7 – 604/688-9931; Fax: 604/688-6559 | 1470 |
| Vancouver, BC | CKBD | Great Pacific Industries Inc., 1401 - 8 Ave. West, Vancouver BC V6H 1C9 – 604/731-6111; Fax: 604/731-0493 | 600 |
| Vancouver, BC | CKLG | Shaw Radio Ltd., 1006 Richards St., Vancouver BC V6B 1S8 – 604/681-7511; Fax: 604/681-9134 | 730 |
| Vancouver, BC | CKST | Radio One, #100, 856 Homer St., Vancouver BC V6B 2W5 – 604/669-1040; Fax: 604/684-6949; Email: comments@am1040.com; URL: http://www.am1040.com | 1040 |
| Vancouver, BC | CKWX | Rogers Broadcasting Ltd., 2440 Ash St., Vancouver BC V5Z 4J6 – 604/873-2599; Fax: 604/877-4494 | 1130 |
| Vancouver, BC | CISL | *See* Richmond (CISL) | 650 |
| Vancouver, BC | *CBU | CBC, 700 Hamilton St., PO Box 4600, Vancouver BC V6B 4A2 – 604/662-6920; Fax: 604/662-6088 | 690 |
| Vanderhoof, BC | CIVH | Cariboo Central Interior Radio Inc., 150 West Columbia St., PO Box 1370, Vanderhoof BC V0J 3A0 – 250/567-4914; Fax: 250/567-4982; Email: tbulmar@hwy16.com | 1340 |
| Verdun, QC | CIQC | Mount Royal Broadcasting Inc., 211, av Gordon, Verdun QC H4G 2R2 – 514/767-9250; Fax: 514/766-9569 | 600 |
| Verdun, QC | †CKVL | Radio Futura Ltée., 211, av Gordon, Verdun QC H4G 2R2 – 514/766-2311; Fax: 514/766-2122 | 850 |
| Vernon, BC | CICF | Okanagan Radio Ltd., 2800 - 31 St., Vernon BC V1T 5H4 – 250/545-9222; Fax: 250/549-8375; URL: http://www.mix105.com | 1050 |
| Vernon, BC | CJIB | Rogers Broadcasting Ltd., 3313 - 32 Ave., Vernon BC V1T 2E1 – 250/545-2141; Fax: 250/545-9008 | 940 |
| Victoria, BC | CFAX | Seacoast Communications Group Inc., 825 Broughton St., Victoria BC V8W 1E5 – 250/386-1070; Fax: 250/386-5775; Email: cfax@islandnet.com; URL: http://www.cfax1070.com | 1070 |
| Victoria, BC | CJVI | Rogers Broadcasting Ltd., 817 Fort St., Victoria BC V8W 1H6 – 250/382-0900; Fax: 250/382-4358; Email: asimpson@rci.rogers.com | 900 |
| Victoria, BC | CKXM | OK Radio Group Ltd., 3795 Carey Rd., Victoria BC V8Z 6T8 – 250/475-6611; Fax: 250/475-6626; URL: http://www.ckxm.com | 1200 |
| Victoriaville, QC | †CFDA | Radio Victoriaville Ltée, 55, rue St-Jean Baptiste, CP 490, Victoriaville QC G6P 6T3 – 819/752-5545; Fax: 819/752-7552 | 1380 |
| Ville-Marie, QC | *†CKVM | Radio-Témiscamingue inc., CP 3000, Ville-Marie QC J0Z 3W0 – 819/629-2710; Fax: 819/622-0716 | 710 |
| Wabush, NF | CFCB | 4 Grenfell Dr., PO Box 6000, Wabush NF A0R 1B0 – 709/282-3602; Fax: 709/282-5543 | 1340 |
| Wainwright, AB | CKKY | Nor-Net Communications Ltd., 1037 - 2nd Ave., Wainwright AB T9W 1K7 – 403/875-9153; Fax: 403/842-4636 | 830 |
| Waterloo, ON | CKKW | CHUM Ltd., 255 King St. North, Waterloo ON N2J 4V2 – 519/884-4470; Fax: 519/884-6482 | 1090 |
| Wawa, ON | CJWA | Pelmorex Radio, 55 Broadway Ave., Wawa ON P0S 1K0 – 705/856-4555; Fax: 705/856-1520 | 1240 |
| Welland, ON | CHOW | R.B. Communications, RR#23, Welland ON L3B 5R6 – 905/732-4433; Fax: 905/372-4780 | 1470 |
| Welland, ON | CRNC | Niagara College, PO Box 1005, Welland ON L3B 5S2 – 905/735-2211, ext.7434; Fax: 905/735-7987 | closed circuit |
| Westlock, AB | CFOK | Nornet Broadcasting Ltd., 9701 - 99 St., Westlock AB T7P 1Y5 – 403/349-4421; Fax: 403/349-6259; Email: cfok@west-teq.net | 1370 |
| Wetaskiwin, AB | CKJR | Nor-Net Communications Ltd., 5220 - 51 Ave., Wetaskiwin AB T9A 3E2 – 403/352-0144; Fax: 403/352-0606 | 1440 |
| Weyburn, SK | CFSL | Golden West Broadcasting Ltd., PO Box 340, Weyburn SK S4H 2K2 – 306/848-1190; Fax: 306/842-2720 | 1190 |
| Whitehorse, YT | CKRW | Klondike Broadcasting Co.Ltd., #203, 4102 - 4 Ave., Whitehorse YT Y1A 1H6 – 867/-668-6100; Fax: 867/668-4209 | |
| Whitehorse, YT | *CFWH | CBC, 3103 - 3rd Ave., Whitehorse YT Y1A 1E5 – 867/668-8400; Fax: 867/668-8408; Email: cbcyukon@whitehorse.cbc.ca | 570 |
| Williams Lake, BC | CKWL | Cariboo Central Interior Radio Inc., 83 South 1 Ave., Williams Lake BC V2G 1H4 – 250/392-6551; Fax: 250/392-4142; Email: wlamfm@netshop.net | 570 |
| Windsor, NS | CFAB | *See* Kentville (CKEN) | 1450 |
| Windsor, ON | CKLW | CHUM Ltd., 1640 Ouellette Ave., Windsor ON N8X 1L1 – 519/258-8888; Fax: 519/258-0182 | 800 |
| Windsor, ON | CKWW | CHUM Ltd., 1640 Ouellette Ave., Windsor ON N8X 1L1 – 519/258-8888; Fax: 519/258-0182 | 580 |
| Windsor, ON | *CBE | CBC, 825 Riverside Dr. West, Windsor ON N9A 5K9 – 519/255-3411; Fax: 519/255-3443 | 1550 |
| Windsor, ON | *†CBEF | Société Radio-Canada, 825 Riverside Dr. West, Windsor ON N9A 5K9 – 519/255-3411; Fax: 519/255-3573 | 540 |
| Wingham, ON | CKNX | Blackburn Radio Inc., 215 Carling Terrace, Wingham ON N0G 2W0 – 519/357-1310; Fax: 519/357-1897 | 920 |
| Winnipeg, MB | CIFX | CHUM Ltd., 1445 Pembina Hwy., Winnipeg MB R3T 5C2 – 204/477-5120; Fax: 204/453-8777; URL: http://www.1290talk.com | 1290 |
| Winnipeg, MB | CJOB | WIC Radio Ltd., 930 Portage Ave., Winnipeg MB R3G 0P8 – 204/786-2471; Fax: 204/783-4512; Email: cjob@xpressnet.com; URL: http://www.power97.com | 680 |
| Winnipeg, MB | CKJS | CKJS Ltd., 520 Corydon Ave., Winnipeg MB R3L 0P1 – 204/477-1221; Fax: 204/453-8244; Email: ckjs@magic.mb.ca | 810 |
| Winnipeg, MB | CKY | Rogers Broadcasting, Polo Park, Winnipeg MB R3G 0L7 – 204/788-3400; Fax: 204/788-3401 | 580 |

| LOCATION | CALL | *CBC Stations/Affiliates †French Language Stations | FREQ. |
|---|---|---|---|
| Winnipeg, MB | CMOR | Red River Community College, #DM20, 2055 Notre Dame Ave., Winnipeg MB R3H 0J9 – 204/632-2475; Fax: 204/632-7896; Email: jwalber@rrcc.mb.ca | closed circuit |
| Winnipeg, MB | *†CKSB | Société Radio-Canada, CP 160, Winnipeg MB R3C 2H1 – 204/788-3236; Fax: 204/788-3245 | 1050 |
| Winnipeg, MB | *CBW | CBC, 541 Portage Ave., PO Box 160, Winnipeg MB R3C 2H1 – 204/788-3222; Fax: 204/788-3225 | 990 |
| Woodstock, NB | *CJCJ | Carleton-Victoria Broadcasting Co. Ltd., 131 Queen St., PO Box 920, Woodstock NB E0J 2B0 – 506/325-3030; Fax: 506/325-3031 | 920 |
| Yarmouth, NS | CJLS | Radio CJLS Ltd., #201, 328 Main St., Yarmouth NS B5A 1E4 – 902/742-7175; Fax: 902/742-3143; Email: cjls@atcon.com. | 1340 |
| Yellowknife, NT | CJCD | CJCD Radio Ltd., PO Box 218, Yellowknife NT X1A 2N2 – 867/920-4636; Fax: 867/920-4033 | 1240 |
| Yellowknife, NT | *CFYK | CBC, PO Box 160, Yellowknife NT X1A 2N2 – 867/920-5400; Fax: 867/920-5440 | 1340 |
| Yorkton, SK | CJGX | Yorkton Broadcasting Co. Ltd., 120 Smith St. East, PO Box 9400, Yorkton SK S3N 3V3 – 306/782-2256; Fax: 306/783-4994; Email: cjgx@sk.sympatico.ca | 940 |

## FM BROADCASTING STATIONS

| LOCATION | CALL | *CBC Stations/Affiliates †French Language Stations | FREQ. |
|---|---|---|---|
| Ajax, ON | CJKX-FM | Durham Radio Inc., #201, 339 Westney Rd. South, Ajax ON L1S 7J6 – 905/428-9600; Fax: 905/686-2444; Email: kx96fm@hazel.com; URL: http://www.hazel.com/kx96fm | 95.9 |
| Baie-Comeau, QC | CHLC-FM | COGECO Radio-Télévision Inc., 399, rue de Puyjalon, Baie-Comeau QC G5C 1M4 – 418/589-3771; Fax: 418/589-9086 | 97.1 |
| Barrie, ON | CFJB-FM | Rock 95 (Barrie Orillia) Ltd., #205, 400 Bayfield St., PO Box 95, Barrie ON L4M 5A1 – 705/721-1291; Fax: 705/721-7842 | 95.7 |
| Barrie, ON | CHAY-FM | Shaw Radio Ltd., PO Box 937, Barrie ON L4M 4Y6 – 705/737-3511; Fax: 705/737-0603; Email: chayinfo@chayfm.com | 93.1 |
| Barrie, ON | CIQB-FM | Power Broadcasting Inc., 129 Ferris Lane, PO Box 101, Barrie ON L4M 4V1 – 705/726-1011; Fax: 705/726-0022; Email: talkback@b101fm.com; URL: http://www.b101fm.com | 101.1 |
| Belleville, ON | CJLX-FM | Loyalist College Radio Inc., PO Box 4200, Belleville ON K8N 5B9 – 613/969-0923; Fax: 613/966-1993; Email: cjix@loyalistc.on.ca | closed circuit; 92.3 |
| Belleville, ON | CIGL-FM | Quinte Broadcasting Co. Ltd., 10 Front St. South, PO Box 488, Belleville ON K8N 5B2 – 613/969-5555; Fax: 613/969-0288 | 97.1 |
| Belleville, ON | CJOJ-FM | 354 Pinnacle St., Belleville ON K8N 3B4 – 613/966-0955; Fax: 613/967-2565 | 95.5 |
| Bracebridge, ON | CFBG-FM | Telemedia Communications Ontario Inc., 50 Balls Dr., Bracebridge ON P1L 1T5 – 705/645-2218; Fax: 705/645-6957; Email: moose@muskoka.com | 100.9 |
| Brampton, ON | CIDC-FM | Dufferin Communications Inc., #20, 50 Kennedy Rd. South, Brampton ON L6W 3R7 – 416/213-1035 | 103.5 |
| Brandon, MB | CKX-FM | Craig Broadcast Systems Inc., 2940 Victoria Ave., Brandon MB R7B 0N2 – 204/728-1150; Fax: 204/727-2505 | 96.1 |
| Brantford, ON | CKPC-FM | Telephone City Broadcast Ltd., 571 West St., Brantford ON N3T 5P8 – 519/759-1000; Fax: 519/753-1470 | 92.1 |
| Brockville, ON | CHXL-FM | St. Lawrence Broadcasting Co. Ltd., PO Box 666, Brockville ON K6V 5V9 – 613/345-1666; Fax: 613/342-2438; Email: river@theriverrolls.com; URL: http://www.theriverrolls.com | 103.7 |
| Burlington, ON | CING-FM | Burlington Broadcasting Inc., 4144 South Service Rd., Burlington ON L7L 4X5 – 905/681-1079; Fax: 905/681-1758; URL: http://www.energy108.ca | 107.9 |
| Burnaby, BC | CJSF-FM | Simon Fraser Campus Radio, TC216, Simon Fraser University, Burnaby BC V5A 1S6 – 604/291-3727; Fax: 604/291-3695; Email: cjsf@sfu.ca; URL: http://www.sfu.ca/~cjsf | 93.9 |
| Burnaby, BC | CFML-FM | BC Institute of Technology, 2700 Willingdon Ave., Burnaby BC V5G 3H2 – 604/432-8510; Fax: 604/432-1792; Email: bcitbcst@bcit.bc.ca; URL: http://www.bcit.bc.ca | 104.5; cable |
| Calgary, AB | CMRC | Mount Royal College, 4825 Richard Rd. SW, Calgary AB T3E 6K6 – 403/240-6119; Fax: 403/240-6563 | cable; 107.5 |
| Calgary, AB | CKIS-FM | Rawlco Communications Ltd., 2723 - 37 Ave. NE, Calgary AB T1Y 5R8 – 403/291-9695; Fax: 403/250-5037 | 96.9 |
| Calgary, AB | CBR-FM | *See* Calgary (CBR) | 102.1 |
| Calgary, AB | CHFM-FM | Rogers Broadcasting Ltd., 3320 - 17 Ave. SW, Calgary AB T3E 6X6 – 403/246-9696; Fax: 403/246-6660; URL: http://www.chfm.com | 95.9 |
| Calgary, AB | CJAY-FM | Standard Radio Inc., PO Box 2750, Stn M, Calgary AB T2P 4P8 – 403/240-5850; Fax: 403/240-5801; URL: http://www.cjay92.com | 92.1 |
| Calgary, AB | CJSW-FM | University of Calgary, #127, MacEwan Hall, Calgary AB T2N 1N4 – 403/220-3904 | 90.9 |
| Calgary, AB | CKIK-FM | CKIK-FM Ltd., #1900, 125 - 9 Ave. SE, Calgary AB T2G 0P6 – 403/237-0770; Fax: 403/265-7807 | 107.3 |
| Calgary, AB | CKRY-FM | Shaw Radio Ltd., #500, 1121 Centre St. North, Calgary AB T2E 7K6 – 403/276-6105; Fax: 403/230-4343; Email: feedback@country105.com; URL: http://www.country105.com | 105.1 |
| Camrose, AB | CLCR | Augustana University College, 4901 - 46 Ave., Camrose AB T4V 2R3 – 403/672-2999 | closed circuit |
| Cap-aux-Meules, QC | †CFIM-FM | Diffusion Communautaire des Îles inc., CP 490, Cap-aux-Meules QC G0B 1K0 – 418/986-5233; Fax: 418/986-5319 | 92.7 |
| Carleton, QC | †CIEU-FM | Diffusion Communautaire-Baie des Chaleurs inc., 1645, boul Perron est, CP 3000, Carleton QC G0C 1J0 – 418/364-7094; Fax: 418/364-3150 | 94.9 |
| Charlottetown, PE | CHLQ-FM | Maritime Broadcasting Ltd., 141 Kent St., Charlottetown PE C1A 7M7 – 902/566-5550; Fax: 902/566-1338 | 93.1 |
| Charlottetown, PE | *†CBCT-FM | CBC, 430 University Ave., CP 2230, Charlottetown PE C1A 8B9 – 902/629-6400; Fax: 902/629-6518; URL: http://www.isn.net/cbc/ | 96.1 |
| Chatham, ON | CKSY-FM | Bea-Ver Communications Inc., 117 Keil Dr., PO Box 100, Chatham ON N7M 5K1 – 519/354-2200; Fax: 519/354-2880; Email: cksyfm@mnsi.net; URL: http://www.mnsi.net~cksyfm | 95.1 |
| Chicoutimi, QC | †CJAB-FM | Radiomutuel inc., 121, rue Racine est, CP 1090, Chicoutimi QC G7H 5G4 – 418/545-9450; Fax: 418/545-9186 | 94.5 |
| Chicoutimi, QC | *†CBJ-FM | *See* Chicoutimi (CBJ) | 100.9 |
| Chilliwack, BC | CKSR-FM | Star-FM Radio Inc., PO Box 386, Chilliwack BC V2P 6J7 – 604/795-7827; Fax: 604/795-6643; URL: http://www.fraservalley.com | 104.9/107.5 |
| Clearwater, BC | CFJC-FM-1 | *See* Kamloops (CFJC) | 102.9 |
| Cobourg, ON | CFMX-FM | *See* Toronto (CFMX-FM) | 96.3 |
| Collingwood, ON | CKCB | Collingwood Radio Ltd.., 1400 Hwy. 26 East, Collingwood ON L9Y 4W2 – 705/446-9510; Fax: 705/444-6776; Email: fm95.1@thepeak.georgian.net | 95.1 |
| Cornwall, ON | CFLG-FM | Tri-Co Broadcasting Ltd., 237 Water St. East, PO Box 969, Cornwall ON K6H 5V1 – 613/932-5180; Fax: 613/938-0355; Email: cflgradio@cnwl.igs.net | 104.5 |
| Cornwall, ON | CKON-FM | Akwesasne Communications Society, PO Box 1496, Cornwall ON K6H 5V5 – 613/575-2100; Fax: 613/575-2935 | 97.3 |
| Cornwall, ON | †CHOD-FM | Radio communautaire Cornwall-Alexandria inc., #202, 1111 Montreal Rd., Cornwall ON K6H 1E1 – 613/936-2463; Fax: 613/936-2568; Email: chod.fm@glen-net.ca; URL: http://www.3dbiz.com/chod | 92.1 |

| LOCATION | CALL | *CBC Stations/Affiliates †French Language Stations | FREQ. |
|---|---|---|---|
| Cranbrook, BC | CKKR-FM | Columbia Kootenay Broadcasting Co. Ltd., 19 - 9 Ave. South, Cranbrook BC V1C 2L9 – 250/426-2224; Fax: 250/426-5520 | 104.7 |
| Deer Lake, NF | CFDL-FM | *See* Corner Brook (CFCB) | 97.9 |
| Dégelis, QC | †CFVD | Radio Dégelis inc., Mix 95, 654 - 6e rue, Dégelis QC G5T 1Y1 – 514/853-3370; Fax: 514/853-3321 | 95.5 |
| Digby, NS | CJLS-FM-2 | *See* Yarmouth (CJLS) | 93.5 |
| Drayton Valley, AB | CIBW-FM | Big West Communications Corp., #3, 5606 - 55 St., PO Box 929, Drayton Valley AB T7A 1V3 – 403/542-9290; Fax: 403/542-9319; Email: big-west@telusplanet.net | 92.9 |
| Drummondville, QC | †CHRD | 2070, St-Georges, Drummondville QC J2C 5G6 – 819/475-1480; Fax: 819/475-5180 | 105.3 |
| Drummondville, QC | †CJDM-FM | Diffusion Power inc., #203, 412, rue Hériot, Drummondville QC J2B 1B5 – 819/474-1892; Fax: 819/474-6610; URL: http://www.cjdm.qc.ca | 92.1 |
| Edmonton, AB | CKUA-FM | CKUA Radio Foundation, 10526 Jasper Ave., 4th Fl., Edmonton AB T5J 1Z7 – 403/428-7595; Fax: 403/428-7624; Email: ckua@oanet.com; URL: http://www.ckua.org | 94.9 |
| Edmonton, AB | CFMG-FM | Telemedia Communications Inc., #700, 5241 Calgary Trail South, Edmonton AB T6H 5G8 – 403/458-1200; Fax: 403/460-9671; Email: cfmg@plant.eon.net | 104.9 |
| Edmonton, AB | CKER | CKER Radio Ltd., 6005 - 103 St., Edmonton AB T6H 2H3 – 403/438-1480; Fax: 403/437-5129 | 101.9 |
| Edmonton, AB | CFBR-FM | Standard Radio Inc., #100, 18520 Stony Plain Rd., Edmonton AB T5S 2E2 – 403/486-2800; Fax: 403/444-6927 | 100.3 |
| Edmonton, AB | CIRK-FM | Radio One Edmonton Corp., 10250 - 108 St., Edmonton AB T5J 2X3 – 403/428-8597; Fax: 403/428-7168 | 97.3 |
| Edmonton, AB | CISN-FM | Shaw Radio Ltd., 10550 - 102 St., Edmonton AB T5H 2T3 – 403/428-1104; Fax: 403/426-6502; Email: cisn@compusmart.ab.ca | 103.9 |
| Edmonton, AB | CKNG-FM | WIC Radio Ltd., 5204 - 84 St., Edmonton AB T6E 5N8 – 403/469-6992; Fax: 403/469-5937; Email: bigdog@power92.com | 92.5 |
| Edmonton, AB | CKRA-FM | NewCap Inc., 4752 - 99 St., Edmonton AB T6E 5H5 – 403/437-4996; Fax: 403/436-9803 | 96.3 |
| Edmonton, AB | CJSR-FM | First Alberta Campus Radio Association, #224 SUB, Edmonton AB T6G 2J7 – 403/492-5244; Fax: 403/492-3121; Email: cjsrfm@gpu.scv.ualberta ca; URL: http://www.ualberta.ca/~cjcrfm/ | |
| Edmonton, AB | *CBX-FM | *See* Edmonton (CBX) | 90.9 |
| Egmont, BC | CIEG-FM | *See* Squamish (CISQ-FM) | 107.5 |
| Elliot Lake, ON | CKNR | North Channel Broadcasters Inc., 15 Charles Walk, Elliot Lake ON P5A 2A2 – 705/848-3608; Fax: 705/848-1378; Email: cknr@cancom.net | 94.1 |
| Etobicoke, ON | CKHC-FM | Humber College, 205 Humber College Blvd., Etobicoke ON M9W 5L7 – 416/675-5046 | closed circuit |
| Fermont, QC | †CFMF-FM | Radio Communautaire Fermont inc., 20, Place Daviault, CP 280, Fermont QC G0G 1J0 – 418/287-5147; Fax: 418/287-5776 | 103.1 |
| Fort-Coulonge, QC | †CHIP-FM | La Radio du Pontiac inc., 33, rue Romain, CP 820, Fort-Coulonge QC J0X 1V0 – 819/683-3155; Fax: 819/683-3211 | 94.5 |
| Fort McMurray, AB | CKYX-FM | OK Radio Group Ltd., 9912 Franklin Ave., Fort McMurray AB T9H 2K5 – 403/743-2246; Fax: 403/791-7250 | 97.9 |
| Fox Creek, AB | CFFC-FM | *See* Peace River (CKYL) | 92.1 |
| Fredericton, NB | CKHJ-FM | Radio One Ltd., 206 Rookwood Ave., Fredericton NB E3B 2M2 – 506/451-9111; Fax: 506/452-2345 | 105.3 |
| Fredericton, NB | CHSR-FM | CHSR Broadcasting Inc., PO Box 4400, Fredericton NB E3B 5A3 – 506/453-4985; Fax: 506/453-4958; Email: chsr@mi.net; URL: http://www.unb.ca/web/chsr | 97.9 |
| Fredericton, NB | CIBX-FM | Radio One Ltd., 206 Rookwood Ave., Fredericton NB E3B 2M2 – 506/455-1069; Fax: 506/452-2345 | 106.9 |
| Gaspé, QC | †CJRG-FM | Radio Gaspé inc., 162, rue Jacques Cartier, CP 380, Gaspé QC G0C 1R0 – 418/368-3511; Fax: 418/368-1663 | 94.5 |
| Gold River, BC | CJGR-FM | *See* Campbell River (CFWB) | 101.1 |
| Grande Prairie, AB | CFGP | CFGP Radio, Division of OK Radio Group Ltd., #200, 9835 - 101 Ave., Grande Prairie AB T8V 5V4 – 403/532-9700; Fax: 403/532-1600; Email: cfgp@ccinet.ab.ca; http://www.terranet.ab.ca/sunfm | 97.7 |
| Guelph, ON | CFRU-FM | Radio Gryphon, University Centre, Level 2, University of Guelph, Guelph ON N1G 2W1 – 519/824-4120, ext.6919; Fax: 519/763-9603; Email: cfru@tdg.uoguelph.ca; URL: http://tdg.uoguelph.ca/~cfru | 93.3 |
| Guelph, ON | CIMJ-FM | Power Broadcasting Inc., 75 Speedvale Ave. East, Guelph ON N1E 6M3 – 519/824-7000; Fax: 519/824-4118; Email: power@in.on.ca | 106.1 |
| Halifax, NS | CHFX-FM | Maritime Broadcasting Co. Ltd., PO Box 400, Halifax NS B3J 2R2 – 902/422-1651; Fax: 902/422-5330 | 101.9 |
| Halifax, NS | CIEZ-FM | Sun Radio Ltd., #800, 1550 Bedford Hwy., Halifax NS B4A 1E6 – 902/835-6100; Fax: 902/835-1511 | 96.5 |
| Halifax, NS | CIOO-FM | CHUM Ltd., 2900 Agricola St., PO Box 1653, Halifax NS B3J 2Z4 – 902/453-2524; Fax: 902/453-3132; Email: c100@newedge.ca; URL: http://www.newedge.ca/c100 | 100.1 |
| Halifax, NS | CKDU-FM | Dalhousie University, Student Union Bldg., 6136 University Ave., Halifax NS B3H 4J2 – 902/494-6479; Fax: 902/494-1110; Email: ckdufm@ac.dal.ca; URL: http://is2.dal.ca/~ckdufm/ | 97.5 |
| Halifax, NS | *CBH-FM | CBC, 5600 Sackville St., PO Box 3000, Halifax NS B3J 3E9 – 902/420-8311; Fax: 902/420-4429 | 102.7 |
| Halifax, NS | *CBHA-FM | CBC, 5600 Sackville St., PO Box 3000, Halifax NS B3J 3E9 – 902/420-8311; Fax: 902/420-4429 | 90.5 |
| Hamilton, ON | CFMU-FM | McMaster University, Room 301, Hamilton Hall, McMaster University, Hamilton ON L8S 4K1 – 905/525-9140, ext.27208; Fax: 905/529-3208; Email: cfmu@freenet.hamilton.on.ca; URL: http://www.freenet.hamilton.on.ca/~ip007/cfmu.html | 93.3 |
| Hamilton, ON | CHMR-FM | Mohawk College, 135 Fennell Ave., PO Box 2034, Hamilton ON L8N 3T2 – 905/575-2175; Fax: 905/575-2385 | closed circuit/cable; 91.7 |
| Hamilton, ON | CJXY-FM | WIC Radio Ltd., #900, 875 Main St. West, Hamilton ON L8S 4R1 – 905/521-0953; Fax: 905/521-2306 | 95.3 |
| Hamilton, ON | CKLH-FM | Radiocorp Inc., #401, 883 Upper Wentworth St., Hamilton ON L9A 4Y6 – 905/574-1150; Fax: 905/574-6429; Email: klite@radiocorp.ca; URL: http://www.radiocorp.ca | 102.9 |
| Happy Valley, NF | *CFGB-FM | CBC, PO Box 1270, Happy Valley NF A0P 1E0 – 709/896-2911; Fax: 709/896-8900 | 89.5 |
| Hawkesbury, ON | †CHPR-FM | Radio Fusion Inc., #37, 151 Main St. East, Hawkesbury ON K6A 1A1 – 613/632-1119; Fax: 613/562-1902 | 102.1 |
| Hearst, ON | †CINN-FM | Radio de l'Epinette Noire inc., CP 2648, Hearst ON P0L 1NO – 705/372-1011; Fax: 705/362-7411; Email: cinn@nt.net | 94.1 |
| Hull, QC | †CIMF-FM | Télémedia Communications inc., 150, rue Edmonton, Hull QC J8Y 3S6 – 819/770-2463; Fax: 819/770-9338 | 94.9 |
| Huntsville, ON | CFBK-FM | Muskoka-Parry Sound Broadcasting, 15 Main St. East, PO Box 1055, Huntsville ON P0A 1K0 – 705/789-4461; Fax: 705/789-1269 | 105.5 |
| Joliette, QC | CJLM-FM | Coopérative de Radiodiffusion MF 103,5 de Lanaudière, 540, rue St-Thomas, Joliette QC J6E 3R4 – 514/756-1035; Fax: 514/756-8097 | 103.5 |
| Jonquière, QC | †CHOC-FM | Radio Communautaire du Saguenay inc., CP 306, Jonquière QC G7X 7W1 – 418/542-2265; Fax: 418/547-5356 | 92.5 |
| Kahnawake, QC | CKRK-FM | Kahnawake Broadcasting Service, PO Box 1050, Kahnawake QC J0L 1B0 – 514/638-1313; Fax: 514/638-4009 | 103.7 |
| Kamloops, BC | CIFM-FM | Jim Pattison Group, 460 Pemberton Terrace, Kamloops BC V2C 1T5 – 250/372-3322; Fax: 250/374-0445; URL: http://www.cifm.com | 98.3 |
| Kamloops, BC | CKRV-FM | NL Broadcasting, 611 Lansdowne St., Kamloops BC V2C 1Y6 – 250/372-2197; Fax: 250/372-0682 | 97.5 |
| Kamloops, BC | CFJC-FM | *See* Kamloops (CFJC) | 99.5 |

| LOCATION | CALL | *CBC Stations/Affiliates †French Language Stations | FREQ. |
|---|---|---|---|
| Kelowna, BC | CILK-FM | SILK-FM Broadcasting Ltd., 1598 Pandosy St., Kelowna BC V1Y 1P4 – 250/860-1010; Fax: 250/860-0505 | 101.5 |
| Kelowna, BC | CKLZ-FM | Seacoast Communications Group Inc., 3805 Lakeshore Rd., Kelowna BC V1W 3K6 – 250/763-1047; Fax: 250/762-2141; Email: cklz-fm@awmc.com; URL: http://www.cklz.com | 104.7 |
| Kelowna, BC | CKBL-FM | Okanagan Radio Ltd., 2419 Hwy. 97 North, Kelowna BC V1X 4J2 – 250/860-8600; Fax: 250/860-8856 | 99.9 |
| Kelowna, BC | *CBTK-FM | CBC, 243 Lawrence Ave., Kelowna BC V1Y 6L2 – 250/861-3781; Fax: 250/861-6644 | 88.9 |
| Kentville, NS | CKWM-FM | Annapolis Valley Radio, PO Box 310, Kentville NS B4N 1H5 – 902/678-2111; Fax: 902/678-9894 | 97.7 |
| Kingston, ON | CFLY-FM | St. Lawrence Broadcasting Co. Ltd., 99 Brock St., PO Box 1380, Kingston ON K7L 4Y5 – 613/544-1380; Fax: 613/546-9751 | 98.3 |
| Kingston, ON | CFMK-FM | Power Broadcasting Inc., 479 Counter St., Kingston ON K7M 7J3 – 613/549-1911; Fax: 613/549-7974; URL: http://www/spiritofkingston.com | 96.3 |
| Kingston, ON | CFRC-FM | Queen's University, Carruthers Hall, Kingston ON K7L 3N6 – 613/545-2121; Fax: 613/545-6049 | 101.9 |
| Kitchener, ON | CHYM-FM | Rogers Broadcasting Ltd., 305 King St. West, Kitchener ON N2G 4E4 – 519/743-2611; Fax: 519/743-7510 | 96.7 |
| Kitchener, ON | CFCA-FM | *See* Waterloo (CFCA-FM) | 105.3 |
| Kivalliq, NT | *CBQR-FM | CBC, Kivalliq NT X0C 0G0 – 867/645-2632 | 105.1 |
| La Pocatière, QC | †CHOX | CHOX FM Inc., 1000 - 6e av, CP 550, La Pocatière QC G0R 1Z0 – 418/856-1310; Fax: 418/856-3747 | 97.5 |
| La Pocatière, QC | †CHOX-FM | Radio La Pocatiére Ltée, 1000 - 6 av, CP 550, La Pocatière QC G0R 1Z0 – 418/856-1310; Fax: 418/856-3747 | 97.5 |
| La Ronge, SK | *CBKA-FM | CBC, PO Box 959, La Ronge SK S0J 1L0 – 306/425-3324; Fax: 306/425-2270 | 105.9 |
| Lac-Mégantic, QC | †CFJO-FM | *See* Thetford-Mines (CFJO-FM) | 101.7 |
| Laval, QC | †CFGL-FM | Cogeco Radio-Télévision inc., 2830, boul St-Martin est, Laval QC H7E 5A9 – 514/664-1500; Fax: 514/664-1651 | 105.7 |
| Leamington, ON | CHYR-FM | KEY Radio, 100 Talbot St. East, Leamington ON N8H 1L3 – 519/326-6171; Fax: 519/322-1110 | 96.7 |
| Lennoxville, QC | CJMQ | Radio Bishop's University, 112, Mountain House, CP 2135, Lennoxville QC J1M 1Z7 – 819/822-9689; Fax: 819/822-9747; URL: http://www.cyniska.vbishops.ca/cjmo/ | 88.9; 103.9 |
| Lethbridge, AB | CHLB | Monarch Broadcasting Ltd., 401 Mayor McGrath Dr. South, Lethbridge AB T1J 3L8 – 403/329-0955; Fax: 403/329-0195; Email: rxta@mail.telusplanet.net | 95.5 |
| Lethbridge, AB | CFRV-FM | Rogers Broadcasting Ltd., PO Box 820, Lethbridge AB T1J 3Z9 – 403/328-1077; Fax: 403/327-5879 | 107.7 |
| Lévis, QC | †CFLS-FM | Radio Etchemin inc., 5637, boul de la Rive sud, Lévis QC G6V 4Y5 – 418/833-2151; Fax: 418/833-4462 | 102.9 |
| Liverpool, NS | CKBW-FM-1 | *See* Bridgewater (CKBW) | 94.5 |
| London, ON | CFPL-FM | Blackburn Radio Inc., 369 York St., PO Box 2580, London ON N6A 4H3 – 519/438-8391; Fax: 519/438-2415; Email: daubrey@cfplradio.com; URL: http://www.mediawb.com | 95.9 |
| London, ON | CHRW-FM | University of Western Ontario, #250, UCC Bldg., London ON N6A 3K7 – 519/661-3601; Fax: 519/661-3372; URL: http://www.usc.uwo.ca/media/chrw | 94.7 |
| London, ON | CIQM-FM | Telemedia Communications Ontario Inc., 380 Wellington Rd., PO Box 1410, London ON N6A 5J2 – 519/661-2000; Fax: 519/667-2175 | 97.5 |
| London, ON | CIXX-FM | Radio Fanshawe Inc., Fanshawe College, 1460 Oxford St. East, London ON N5B 5H1 – 519/453-2810; Fax: 519/452-3139 | 106.9 |
| London, ON | CJBX-FM | Radio Corp., 743 Wellington Rd. South, London ON N6C 4R5 – 519/686-2525; Fax: 519/686-9067; Email: bx93@odyssey.on.ca | 92.7 |
| London, ON | CFRL-FM | Fanshawe College, 1460 Oxford St. East, London ON N5W 5H1 – 519/453-2810; Fax: 519/452-3139 | closed circuit |
| Longueuil, QC | †CIEL-FM | Radio MF CIEL (1981) inc., 89, St-Charles ouest, Longueuil QC J4H 1C5 – 514/527-8321; Fax: 514/646-9405 | 98.5 |
| Magog, QC | †CIMO-FM | Energie CIMO 1061, #100, 1750 rue Sherbrooke, Magog QC J1X 2T3 – 819/843-1414; Fax: 819/843-7769 | 106.1 |
| Maniwaki, QC | †CHGA-FM | Radio communautaire FM de la Haute Gatineau, 163, rue Laurier, Maniwaki QC J9E 2K6 – 819/449-3959; Fax: 819/449-7331 | 97.3 |
| Marathon, ON | CFNO-FM | North Superior Broadcasting Ltd., 93 Evergreen Dr., PO Box 1000, Marathon ON P0T 2E0 – 807/229-1010; Fax: 807/229-1686; Email: sbell@marathon.lakeheadu.ca | 93.1 |
| Matane, QC | †CHOE-FM | Communications Matane inc., 800, av du Phare ouest, CP 605, Matane QC G4W 1V7 – 418/562-8181; Fax: 418/562-0778; Email: choefm@quebectel.com | 95.3 |
| Merritt, BC | CFJC-FM | *See* Kamloops (CFJC) | 99.5 |
| Midland, ON | KICX-FM | Telemedia Communications Ontario Inc., 355 Cranston Cres., PO Box 609, Midland ON L4R 4L3 – 705/526-2268; Fax: 705/526-3060 | 104.1 |
| Mississauga, ON | CFRE-FM | Erindale College, University of Toronto, 3359 Missisauga Rd., Mississauga ON L5L 1C6 – 905/828-5310 | closed circuit |
| Moncton, NB | CFQM-FM | Maritime Broadcasting System, 1000 St. George Blvd., Moncton NB E1E 4M7 – 506/858-1039; Fax: 506/858-1209 | 103.9 |
| Moncton, NB | CJMO-FM | Atlantic Stereo Ltd., 27 Arsenault Court, Moncton NB E1E 4J8 – 506/858-5525; Fax: 506/858-5539 | 103.1 |
| Moncton, NB | †CKUM-FM | Université de Moncton, 159, av Massey, Moncton NB E1A 3E9 – 506/858-4485; Fax: 506/858-4524; Email: ckum@umoncton.ca | 105.7 |
| Moncton, NB | *CBA-FM | *See* Moncton (CBA) | 95.5 |
| Moncton, NB | *†CBAF-FM | Société Radio-Canada, 250 Archibald St., CP 950, Moncton NB E1C 8N8 – 506/853-6661; Fax: 506/853-6739 | 88.5, 98.3 |
| Moncton, NB | *†CBAL-FM | Société Radio-Canada, 250 Archibald St., CP 950, Moncton NB E1C 8N8 – 506/853-6657; Fax: 506/853-6661 | 98.3 |
| Mont Laurier, QC | CFLO | Sonème inc., 332, rue de la Madone, Mont Laurier QC J9L 1R9 – 819/623-6610; Fax: 819/623-7406 | 104.7 |
| Montréal, QC | CHOM-FM | CHUM Ltd., 1310, av Greene, Montréal QC H3Z 2B5 – 514/937-2466; Fax: 514/931-3977 | 97.7 |
| Montréal, QC | †CIBL-FM | Radio communautaire francophone de Montréal, #201, 1691, boul Pie-IX, Montréal QC H1V 2C3 – 514/526-2581; Fax: 514/526-3583; Email: cibl@generation.net | 101.5 |
| Montréal, QC | CITE-FM | Télémedia Communications inc., #602, 1411, rue Peel, Montréal QC H3A 1S5 – 514/845-2483; Fax: 514/288-1073 | 107.3 |
| Montréal, QC | CJFM-FM | Standard Radio Inc., 1411, rue du Fort, Montréal QC H3H 2R1 – 514/989-2536; Fax: 514/989-2525; URL: http://www.themix.com | 95.9 |
| Montréal, QC | †CKMF-FM | Radiomutuel inc., #120, 1717, boul René-Lévesque est, Montréal QC H2L 4T9 – 514/529-3229; Fax: 514/529-9308 | 94.3 |
| Montréal, QC | CKUT-FM | Radio McGill, 3647, rue University, Montréal QC H3A 2B3 – 514/398-6787; Fax: 514/398-8261 | 90.3 |
| Montréal, QC | CRSG | Concordia University, #647, 1455, boul de Maisonneuve ouest, Montréal QC H3G 1M8 – 514/848-7401; Fax: 514/848-7450 | 88.9 |
| Montréal, QC | †CFGL-FM | *See* Laval (CFGL-FM) | 105.7 |
| Montréal, QC | CFZZ-FM | *See* St-Jean-sur-Richelieu (CFZZ) | 104.1 |
| Montréal, QC | CKOI-FM | *See* Verdun (CKOI-FM) | 96.9 |
| Montréal, QC | *†CBF-FM | *See* Montréal (CBF) | 100.7 |
| Montréal, QC | *CBM-FM | *See* Montréal (CBM) | 93.5 |
| Nanaimo, BC | CKWV-FM | Central Island Broadcasting Ltd., 4550 Wellington Rd., Nanaimo BC V9T 2H3 – 250/758-1131; Fax: 250/758-4644 | |
| Nepean, ON | CKDJ-FM | Radio Algonquin, Algonquin College, 1385 Woodroffe Ave., Nepean ON K2G 1V8 – 613/727-4723, ext.7740; Fax: 613/727-7689; URL: http://www.ckdj.comnet.ca | 96.9; closed circuit |

| LOCATION | CALL | *CBC Stations/Affiliates †French Language Stations | FREQ. |
|---|---|---|---|
| Newmarket, ON | CKDX-FM | 1093641 Ontario Ltd., #402, 465 Davis Dr., Newmarket ON L3Y 2P1 – 905/898-1100; Fax: 905/853-4433; Email: ckdx@idirect.com | 88.5 |
| Niagara Falls, ON | CJRN-FM | CJRN 710 Inc., PO Box 710, Niagara Falls ON L2E 6X7 – 905/356-6710; Fax: 905/356-0696 | 101.0 |
| North Bay, ON | CKAT | Telemedia Communications Ontario Inc., 743 Main St. East, PO Box 3000, North Bay ON P1B 8K8 – 705/474-2000; Fax: 705/474-7761 | 101.9 |
| North Bay, ON | CRFM-FM | Canadore Radio, Canadore College, 100 College Dr., PO Box 5001, North Bay ON P1B 8K9 – 705/474-7601; Fax: 705/474-2384 | 89.9 |
| Oakville, ON | CORS | CORS Radio Sheridan, Sheridan College, 1430 Trafalgar Rd., Oakville ON L6H 2L1 – 905/845-9430, ext.2302; Fax: 905/815-4043 | closed circuit |
| Orillia, ON | CICX-FM | Telemedia Communications Ontario Inc., 7 Progress Dr., Orillia ON L3V 5C9 – 705/326-3511; Fax: 705/326-1816 | 105.9 |
| Oshawa, ON | CKGE-FM | Power Broadcasting Inc., 360 King St. West, Oshawa ON L1J 2K2 – 905/571-1350; Fax: 905/571-1150 | 94.9 |
| Ottawa, ON | CHEZ-FM | CHEZ-FM Inc., 134 York St., Ottawa ON K1N 5T5 – 613/562-1061; Fax: 613/562-1515; Email: chezmail@chez106.com; URL: http://www.chez106.com | 106.1 |
| Ottawa, ON | CHUO-FM | Radio Ottawa Inc., University of Ottawa, #227, 85 University Ave., Ottawa ON K1N 6N5 – 613/562-5965; Fax: 613/562-5848; Email: chuofm@uottawa.ca | 89.1 |
| Ottawa, ON | CJMJ-FM | RAWLCO Communications Ltd., 1575 Carling Ave., Ottawa ON K1Z 7M3 – 613/798-2565; Fax: 613/729-9829 | 100.3 |
| Ottawa, ON | CKQB-FM | Standard Radio Inc., 1504 Merivale Rd., Ottawa ON K2E 6Z5 – 613/225-1069; Fax: 613/226-3381; Email: thebear@magi.com; URL: http://www.thebear.net | 106.9 |
| Ottawa, ON | CKBY-FM | Rogers Broadcasting Ltd., #1900, Tower B, Place de Ville, 112 Kent St., Ottawa ON K1P 6J1 – 613/238-7482; Fax: 613/236-5382; Email: y105@ottawa.net; URL: http://www.ottawa.net/~105/ | 105.3 |
| Ottawa, ON | CKCU-FM | Radio Carleton, Unicentre, Carleton University, #517, 1125 Colonel By Dr., Ottawa ON K1S 5B6 – 613/520-2898; Fax: 613/520-4060 | 93.1 |
| Ottawa, ON | CKKL-FM | CHUM Ltd., 1900 Walkley Rd., Ottawa ON K1H 8P4 – 613/526-9393; Fax: 613/739-4040; Email: mailbox@koolcfra.com; URL: http://www.worldlink.ca/koolcfra | 93.9 |
| Ottawa, ON | †CIMF-FM | *See* Hull (CIMF-FM) | 94.9 |
| Ottawa, ON | CBRT-FM | *See* Nepean (CKDJ-FM) | |
| Ottawa, ON | *CBO | CBC, PO Box 3220, Stn C, Ottawa ON K1Y 1E4 – 613/562-8400; Fax: 613/562-8408 | 91.5 |
| Ottawa, ON | *†CBOF-FM | Société Radio-Canada, CP 3220, Succ C, Ottawa ON K1Y 1E4 – 613/562-8400; Fax: 613/562-8447 | 90.7 |
| Ottawa, ON | *CBOQ-FM | *See* Ottawa (CBO) | 103.3 |
| Ottawa, ON | *†CBOX-FM | *See* Ottawa (CBOF-FM) | 102.5 |
| Owen Sound, ON | CIXK-FM | Bayshore Broadcasting Corp., 270 - 9 St. East, PO Box 280, Owen Sound ON N4K 5P5 – 519/376-2030; Fax: 519/371-4242; Email: bayshore@radioowensound.com; URL: http://www.radioowensound.com | 106.5 |
| Parksville, BC | CKWV-FM-1 | *See* Nanaimo (CKWV-FM) | 99.9 |
| Parry Sound, ON | CKLP-FM | Playland Broadcasting Ltd., 4 Miller St., Parry Sound ON P2A 1S8 – 705/746-2163; Fax: 705/746-4292; URL: http://www.cklp.com | 103.3 |
| Pemberton, BC | CISP-FM | *See* Squamish (CISQ-FM) | 104.5 |
| Pembroke, ON | CHVR | Pelmorex Radio, 595 Pembroke St. East, Pembroke ON K8A 3L7 – 613/735-9670; Fax: 613/735-7748; Email: star96@fox.nstn.ca | 96.7 |
| Pender Harbour, BC | CIPN-FM | *See* Squamish (CISQ-FM) | 104.7 |
| Penticton, BC | CIGV-FM | Great Valleys Radio Ltd., 125 Nanaimo Ave. West, Penticton BC V2A 1N7 – 250/493-6767; Fax: 250/493-0098; Email: rhopson@mail.awinc.com; URL: http://www.pentonline.com | 100.7 |
| Penticton, BC | CJMG-FM | Okanagan Radio Ltd., 33 Carmi Ave., Penticton BC V2A 3G4 – 250/492-2800; Fax: 250/493-0370 | 97.1 |
| Peterborough, ON | CFFF-FM | Trent Radio, Trent University, Peterborough ON K9J 7B5 – 705/748-1777; Fax: 705/748-1795; Email: trent_radio@trentu.ca; URL: http://www.trentu.ca/trentradio | 96.3 |
| Peterborough, ON | CKQM-FM | CHUM Ltd., PO Box 177, Peterborough ON K9J 6Y8 – 705/742-8844; Fax: 705/742-1417; Email: radio@ckqm.com | 105.1 |
| Peterborough, ON | CKWF-FM | Power Broadcasting Inc., 1925 Television Rd., PO Box 4150, Peterborough ON K9J 6Z9 – 705/742-6101; Fax: 705/742-7274 | 101.5 |
| Pohénégamook, QC | †CFVD-FM-2 | *See* Dégelis (CFVD) | 104.9 |
| Port-Cartier, QC | †CIPC-FM | Radio régionale 99.1 FM Côte-Nord, 52, Elie-Rochefort, Port-Cartier QC G5B 1N3 – 418/766-6868; Fax: 418/766-6870 | 99.1 |
| Prince Albert, SK | CFMM-FM | Central Broadcasting Co. Ltd., PO Box 900, Prince Albert SK S6V 7R4 – 306/763-7421; Fax: 306/764-1850 | 99.1 |
| Prince George, BC | CKKN-FM | Monarch Broadcasting Ltd., 1220 - 6 Ave., Prince George BC V2L 3M8 – 250/564-8861; Fax: 250/562-8768; Email: benny@mindlink.net; http://www.pgonline.com/benny | 101.3 |
| Prince George, BC | CIRX-FM | Cariboo Central Interior Radio Inc., 1940 - 3 Ave., Prince George BC V2M 1G7 – 250/564-2524; Fax: 250/562-6611; Email: cjci@solution-4u.com; URL: http://www.cirx.com | 94.3 |
| Prince George, BC | *CBYG-FM | CBC, 1268 - 5 Ave., Prince George BC V2L 3L2 – 250/562-6701; Fax: 250/562-4777; Email: daybreak@netbistro.com | 91.5 |
| Québec, QC | †CHIK-FM | Radiomutuel inc., #105, 1245, ch Ste-Foy, Québec QC G1S 4P2 – 418/687-9900; Fax: 418/687-3106 | 98.9 |
| Québec, QC | †CHOI-FM | Les Entreprises de Radiodiffusion de la Capitale inc., 2136, ch Ste-Foy, Québec QC G1V 1R8 – 418/687-9810; Fax: 418/682-8427; URL: http://www.choifm.com | 98.1 |
| Québec, QC | †CITF-FM | Telemedia Communications Inc., #250, 580, Grande-Allée est, Québec QC G1R 2K2 – 418/525-4545; Fax: 418/525-6399 | 107.5 |
| Québec, QC | †CJMF-FM | COGECO Radio-Télévision inc., 600, rue Belvedère, Québec QC G1S 3E5 – 418/687-9330; Fax: 418/687-0211 | 93.3 |
| Québec, QC | †CKIA-FM | Radio Basse-Ville Inc., 600, côte d'Abraham, Québec QC G1R 1A1 – 418/529-9026; Fax: 418/529-4156 | 96.1 |
| Québec, QC | †CKRL-FM | Laval Campus, 47, rue Ste-Ursule, Québec QC G1R 4E4 – 418/692-2575; Fax: 418/692-5581 | 89.1 |
| Québec, QC | *†CBV-FM | *See* Québec (CBV) | 95.3 |
| Québec, QC | *CBVE-FM | CBC, #100, 900, Place d'Youville, Québec QC G1R 3P7 – 418/691-3620; Fax: 418/691-3610 | 104.7 |
| Red Deer, AB | CIZZ-FM | Shaw Radio Ltd., PO Bag 5339, Red Deer AB T4P 2N7 – 403/342-7655; Fax: 403/346-1230 | 98.9 |
| Regina, SK | CHMX-FM | Harvard Communications., 2060 Halifax St., PO Box 9200, Regina SK S4P 1T7 – 306/525-9195; Fax: 306/781-7338 | 92.1 |
| Regina, SK | CIZL-FM | RAWLCO Communications Ltd., #210, 2401 Saskatchewan Dr., Regina SK S4P 4H8 – 306/359-9936; Fax: 306/347-8557 | 98.9 |
| Regina, SK | CKIT-FM | Craig Broadcast Systems Inc., 1922 Park St., PO Box 6200, Regina SK S4N 7M4 – 306/569-6200; Fax: 306/936-8329 | 104.9 |
| Regina, SK | *†CBKF-FM | Société Radio-Canada, 2440 Broad St., CP 540, Regina SK S4P 4A1 – 306/347-9540; Fax: 306/347-9493 | 97.7 |
| Richmond, BC | CKZZ-FM | Standard Radio Inc., #20, 11151 Horseshoe Way, Richmond BC V7A 4S5 – 604/241-0953; Fax: 604/272-0917; Email: zinfo@z95.com; URL: http://www.z95.com | 95.3 |
| Rimouski, QC | †CIKI-FM | Diffusion Power Inc., 875, boul St-Germain ouest, Rimouski QC G5L 3T9 – 418/724-8833; Fax: 418/722-7508 | 98.7 |
| Rimouski, QC | CKMN-FM | Radio Communautaire du Comté, 570, boul St-Germaine ouest, Rimouski QC G5L 3R2 – 418/725-7137; Fax: 418/724-9650 | 96.5 |

| LOCATION | CALL | *CBC Stations/Affiliates †French Language Stations | FREQ. |
|---|---|---|---|
| Rimouski, QC | *†CJBR-FM | *See* Rimouski (CJBR) | 101.5 |
| Rivière-du-Loup, QC | †CJFP | Radio CJFP (1986) ltée, 64, Hotel de Ville, Rivière-du-Loup QC G5R 1L5 – 418/862-8241; Fax: 418/862-7704 | 103,7 |
| Rivière-du-Loup, QC | †CIBM-FM | 64, rue Hôtel-de-Ville, Rivière-du-Loup QC G5R 1L5 – 418/867-1071; Fax: 418/862-7704 | 107.1 |
| Rouyn-Noranda, QC | †CHOA-FM | Radio Nord inc., CP 70, Rouyn-Noranda QC J9X 5A5 – 819/762-0741; Fax: 819/762-2280; URL: http://www.rock-detente.com | |
| Sackville, NB | CHMA-FM | Mount Allison University, #315, University Centre, Sackville NB E0A 3C0 – 506/364-2221; Fax: 506/364-2233; Email: cradio@bigmac.mta.ca; URL: http://www.aci.mta.ca/theumbrella/chma | 106.9 |
| Ste-Adèle, QC | †CIME-FM | Diffusion Laurentides inc., CP 1260, Ste-Adèle QC J0R 1L0 – 514/229-2995; Fax: 514/229-7557 | 99.5 |
| St. Albert, AB | CFMG-FM | Balsa Broadcasting Corp., #602, 22 Sir Winston Churchill Ave., St. Albert AB T8N 1B4 – 403/458-1200; Fax: 403/460-9671; Email: cfmg@plant.cor.net | 104.9 |
| St. Andrews, NF | CFCV-FM | *See* Port aux Basques (CFGN) | 97.7 |
| St. Anthony, NF | CFNN-FM | *See* Corner Brook (CFCB) | 97.9 |
| St. Catharines, ON | CHRE-FM | Redmond Broadcasting Inc., 80 King St., St. Catharines ON L2R 7G1 – 905/688-1057; Fax: 905/688-3377; Email: light.fm@vaxxine.com; URL: http://www.lightfm.com/rock | 105.7 |
| St. Catharines, ON | CHTZ-FM | Standard Radio Inc., 12 Yates St., PO Box 977, St. Catharines ON L2R 6Z4 – 905/688-0977; Fax: 905/684-4800 | 97.7 |
| St-Georges-de-Beauce, QC | †CHJM-FM | Radio Beauce Inc., 170, rue 120 est, St-Georges-de-Beauce QC G5Y 5C4 – 418/227-0997; Fax: 418/228-0096 | 99.7 |
| St-Hilarion, QC | †CIHO-FM | Radio MF Charlevoix Inc., 315, ch Cartier nord, CP 160, St-Hilarion QC G0A 3V0 – 418/457-3333; Fax: 418/457-3518 | 96.3 |
| St-Hyacinthe, QC | †CFEI-FM | Radio St-Hyacinthe Ltée, 855, rue Ste-Marie, St-Hyacinthe QC J2S 4R9 – 514/774-6486; Fax: 514/774-7785 | 106.5 |
| St-Jean-sur-Richelieu, QC | †CFZZ | Diffusion Power inc., 104, rue Richelieu, St-Jean-sur-Richelieu QC J3B 6X3 – 514/346-0104; Fax: 514/348-2274 | 104.1 |
| Saint John, NB | CIOK-FM | CIOK Broadcasting Ltd., 400 Main St. North, Saint John NB E2K 1J4 – 506/658-5100; Fax: 506/658-5116 | 100.5 |
| Saint John, NB | CJYC-FM | Fundy Broadcasting Co. Ltd., PO Box 930, Saint John NB E2K 4S9 – 506/658-2330; Fax: 506/658-2320; Email: info@radio.fundy.ca; URL: http://www.radio.fundy.ca | 98.9 |
| Saint John, NB | *CBD-FM | CBC, 560 Main St., PO Box 2358, Saint John NB E2L 3V6 – 506/632-7710; Fax: 506/632-7761 | 91.3 |
| Saint John, NB | *†CBZF-FM | *See* Moncton (CBAF-FM) | 102.3 |
| St. John's, NF | CHOZ-FM | Newfoundland Broadcasting Co. Ltd., 446 Logy Bay Rd., PO Box 2050, St. John's NF A1C 5R6 – 709/726-2922; Fax: 709/726-3300; URL: http://www.ozfm.com | 94.7 |
| St. John's, NF | CKIX-FM | NewCap Broadcasting, PO Box 8010, St. John's NF A1B 3M7 – 709/753-4040; Fax: 709/753-6984 | 99.1 |
| St. John's, NF | VOCM-FM | VOCM Radio Newfoundland Ltd., PO Box 80590, Stn A, St. John's NF A1B 3P5 – 709/726-5590; Fax: 709/726-4633 | 97.5 |
| St. John's, NF | *CBN-FM | *See* St. John's (CBN) | 106.9 |
| St. Regis, ON | CKON-FM | *See* Cornwall (CKON-FM) | 97.3 |
| St. Stephen, NB | WQDY | International Radio, PO Box 305, St. Stephen NB E3L 2X2 – 506/465-0989; Fax: 506/484-3062 | 92.7 |
| St. Thomas, ON | CFHK-FM | CFHK Radio Ltd., 133 Curtis St., St. Thomas ON N5P 4H5 – 519/637-1572; Fax: 519/631-4693; Email: thehawk@icis.on.ca; URL: http://www.thehawk.on.ca | 103.0 |
| Sarnia, ON | CFGX-FM | Blackburn Radio, 1415 London Rd., Sarnia ON N7S 1P6 – 519/332-5500; Fax: 519/542-1520 | 99.9 |
| Saskatoon, SK | CFCR-FM | Community Radio Society of Saskatoon Inc., PO Box 7544, Saskatoon SK S7K 4L4 – 306/664-6678; Fax: 306/933-0038 | 90.5 |
| Saskatoon, SK | CFMC-FM | RAWLCO Communications Ltd., 3333 - 8 St. East, Saskatoon SK S7H 0W3 – 306/955-9500; Fax: 306/373-7587 | 95.1 |
| Saskatoon, SK | CHSN-FM | High-Line Broadcasting, #219, 3501 - 8th St. East, Saskatoon SK S7H 0W5 – 306/668-1021; Fax: 306/664-2090 | 102.1 |
| Saskatoon, SK | CFQC-FM | Forvest Broadcasting Corp., 345 - 4th Ave. South, Saskatoon SK S7K 5S5 – 306/244-1975; Fax: 306/665-7730; Email: cjww.radio@sasknet.sk.ca; URL: http://www.sasknet.com/cjww/ | 92.9 |
| Saskatoon, SK | *CBKS-FM | CBC, CN Tower, Midtown Plaza, 5th Fl., Saskatoon SK S7K 1J5 – 306/956-7400; Fax: 306/956-7417 | 105.5 |
| Sault Ste. Marie, ON | CHAS-FM | Telemedia Communications Ontario Inc., 642 Great Northern Rd., Sault Ste. Marie ON P6B 4Z9 – 705/759-9200; Fax: 705/942-6549; Email: mix100@soonet.ca | 100.5 |
| Sault Ste. Marie, ON | CJQM-FM | Pelmorex Radio, 642 Great Northern Rd., Sault Ste. Marie ON P6B 4Z9 – 705/759-9200; Fax: 705/946-3575; Email: q104@soonet.ca | 104.3 |
| Scarborough, ON | CSCR-FM | Scarborough College, University of Toronto, 1265 Military Trail, Scarborough ON M1C 1A4 – 416/287-7051; Fax: 416/287-7041; Email: cscr@fissure.scar.utoronto.ca | cable; 90.5 |
| Sechelt, BC | CISE-FM | *See* Squamish (CISQ-FM) | 104.7 |
| Selkirk, MB | CFQX-FM | Forvest Broadcasting, 701 Greenwood Ave., PO Box 400, Selkirk MB R1A 2B3 – 204/785-2929; Fax: 204/482-7853 | 104.1 |
| Senneterre, QC | †CIBO-FM | Radio Communautaire de Senneterre, 121, rue Première est, CP 1150, Senneterre QC J0Y 2M0 – 819/737-2222; Fax: 819/737-2221 | 100.5 |
| Sept-Îles, QC | *†CBSI-FM | Société Radio-Canada, #30, 350, rue Smith, Sept-Îles QC G4R 3X2 – 418/968-0720; Fax: 418/968-9219 | 98.1 |
| Shelburne, NS | CJLS-FM-1 | *See* Yarmouth (CJLS) | 96.3 |
| Shelburne, NS | CKBW-FM-2 | *See* Bridgewater (CKBW) | 93.1 |
| Sherbrooke, QC | †CITE-FM | Télémedia Communications Inc., 25, rue Bryant, Sherbrooke QC J1J 3Z5 – 819/566-6655; Fax: 819/566-1011; Email: cite@multimedias.ca | 102.7 |
| Simcoe, ON | CHCD | Redmond Broadcasting Inc., 600 Norfolk St. North, PO Box 1600, Simcoe ON N3Y 4K8 – 519/426-7700; Fax: 519/426-8574; Email: cd106@kwic.com | 106.7 |
| Sioux Lookout, ON | WRN-FM | Wawatay Radio Network, 16 - 5 Ave., PO Box 1180, Sioux Lookout ON P8T 1B7 – 807/737-2951; Fax: 807/737-3224 | 89.1, 106.7 |
| Smiths Falls, ON | CFMO-FM | Rideau Broadcasting, PO Box 630, Smiths Falls ON K7A 4T4 – 613/283-4630; Fax: 613/283-7243 | 101.1 |
| Sorel, QC | †CJSO-FM | Radio Diffusion Sorel-Tracy Inc., 100, boul Couillard Després, Sorel QC J3P 5C1 – 514/743-2772; Fax: 514/743-0293 | 101.7 |
| Squamish, BC | CISQ-FM | Rogers Broadcasting Ltd., PO Box 1068, Squamish BC V0N 3G0 – 604/892-1021; Fax: 604/892-6383; Email: mountainfm@mountain-inter.net | 107.1 |
| Sudbury, ON | CFLR | Laurentian Student & Community Radio Corp., Laurentian University, 935 Ramsey Rd., Sudbury ON P3E 2C6 – 705/675-1151, ext.2405; Fax: 705/675-4878; Email: mail@cflr.isys.ca; URL: http://www.cflr.isys.ca | cable; 106.7 |
| Sudbury, ON | CJMX-FM | Pelmorex Radio, 295 Victoria St., Sudbury ON P3C 1K5 – 705/674-6401; Fax: 705/674-7322; Email: mix105@sudburyradio.com; URL: http://www.sudburyradio.com | 105.3 |
| Sudbury, ON | CJRQ-FM | Telemedia Communications Ontario Inc., 880 Lasalle Blvd., Sudbury ON P3A 1X5 – 705/566-4480; Fax: 705/560-7232; Email: q92@cwconnect.com | 92.7 |
| Sudbury, ON | *CBCS-FM | CBC Northern Ontario Radio, 15 MacKenzie St., Sudbury ON P3C 4Y1 – 705/688-3200; Fax: 705/688-3220; Email: norontradio@sudbury.cbc.ca; URL: http://www.radio.cbc.ca | 99.9 |
| Sudbury, ON | *†CBON-FM | Société Radio-Canada, 15 MacKenzie St., Sudbury ON P3C 4Y1 – 705/688-3200; Fax: 705/688-3220 | 98.1 |
| Sydney, NS | CKPE-FM | Celtic Broadcasting Ltd., 318 Charlotte St., Sydney NS B1P 6K2 – 902/564-5596; Fax: 902/564-1057 | 94.9 |
| Sydney, NS | *†CBI-FM | *See* Sydney (CBI) | 105.1 |
| Sydney, NS | *†CBAF-FM | *See* Moncton (CBAF-FM) | 92.1 |
| Temiscaming, QC | †CKVM-FM | *See* Ville-Marie (CKVM) | 92.1 |

| LOCATION | CALL | *CBC Stations/Affiliates †French Language Stations | FREQ. |
|---|---|---|---|
| Terrace, BC | CJFW-FM | Skeena Broadcasters, Division of Okanagan Skeena Group Ltd., 4625 Lazelle Ave., Terrace BC V8G 1S4 – 250/635-6316; Fax: 250/638-6320; Email: info@osg.net; URL: http://www.osg.net | 103.1 |
| Thetford-Mines, QC | †CFJO-FM | Réseau des Appalaches (FM) Ltée, 327, rue Labbé, CP 69, Thetford-Mines QC G6P 6T3 – 418/338-1009; Fax: 418/338-0386; Email: cfjo@ivic.qc.ca | 103.3 |
| Thompson, MB | CINC-FM | Native Communications Inc., 76 Severn Cres., Thompson MB R8N 1M6 – 204/778-8343; Fax: 204/778-6559 | 96.3 |
| Thompson, MB | *CBWK-FM | CBC, 7 Selkirk St., Thompson MB R8N 0M4 – 204/677-2307; Fax: 204/677-9517 | 100.9 |
| Thunder Bay, ON | CJLB | NewCap Broadcasting Inc., KIXX 105 FM, 87 North Hill St., Thunder Bay ON P7A 5V6 – 807/346-2660; Fax: 807/345-6814; Email: kixx@radiotb.com | 105.3 |
| Thunder Bay, ON | CCSR-FM | Confederation College, PO Box 398, Thunder Bay ON P7C 4W1 – 807/475-6226; Fax: 807/623-6230 | |
| Thunder Bay, ON | CJSD-FM | CJSD Inc., 87 North Hill St., Thunder Bay ON P7A 5V6 – 807/346-2594; Fax: 807/345-4671 | 94.3 |
| Thunder Bay, ON | *CBQ-FM | CBC, 213 Miles St. East, Thunder Bay ON P7C 1J5 – 807/625-5000; Fax: 807/625-5035 | 88.3 |
| Tillsonburg, ON | CKOT-FM | Tillsonburg Broadcasting Co. Ltd., PO Box 20, Tillsonburg ON N4G 4H3 – 519/842-4281; Fax: 519/842-4284 | 101.3 |
| Timmins, ON | CJQQ-FM | Telemedia Communications Ontario Inc., 260 Second Ave., PO Box 1046, Timmins ON P4N 7H8 – 705/264-1316; Fax: 705/264-2984 | 92.1 |
| Toronto, ON | CFMX-FM | #101, 468 Queen St. East, Toronto ON M5A 1T7 – 416/367-5353; Fax: 416/367-1742 | 96.3/103.1 |
| Toronto, ON | CFNY-FM | Shaw Radio Ltd., #1600, 1 Dundas St. West, PO Box 14, Toronto ON M5G 1Z3 – 416/408-3343; Fax: 416/408-5400; Email: edge@passport.ca; URL: http://www.edge.passport.ca | 102.1 |
| Toronto, ON | CHFI-FM | Rogers Broadcasting Ltd., 36 Victoria St., Toronto ON M5C 1H3 – 416/864-2070; Fax: 416/864-2119; URL: http://www.rogers.com | 98.1 |
| Toronto, ON | CHIN-FM | Radio 1540 Ltd., 622 College St., Toronto ON M6G 1B6 – 416/531-9991; Fax: 416/531-5274; Email: chin@istar.ca; URL: http://www.chinradio.com | 100.7 |
| Toronto, ON | CHRY-FM | CHRY Community Radio Inc., York University, 258A Vanier College, 4700 Keele St., Toronto ON M3J 1P3 – 416/736-5293; Fax: 416/650-8052; Email: chry@yorku.ca; URL: http://www.chry.yorku.ca | 105.5 |
| Toronto, ON | CHUM-FM | CHUM Ltd., 1331 Yonge St., Toronto ON M4T 1Y1 – 416/925-6666; Fax: 416/926-4026 | 104.5 |
| Toronto, ON | CILQ-FM | Westcom Radio Group, #1400, 5255 Yonge St., Toronto ON M2N 6P4 – 416/221-0107; Fax: 416/512-4810; URL: http://www.q107.com | 107.1 |
| Toronto, ON | CIRV-FM | CIRC Radio Inc., 1087 Dundas St. West, Toronto ON M6J 1W9 – 416/537-1088; Fax: 416/537-2463 | 88.9 |
| Toronto, ON | CISS-FM | RAWLCO Communications, 49 Ontario St., 4th Fl., Toronto ON M5A 2V1 – 416/368-2000; Fax: 416/368-1036 | 92.5 |
| Toronto, ON | CIUT-FM | University of Toronto Community Radio, 91 St. George St., Toronto ON M5S 2E8 – 416/595-0909; Fax: 416/978-8182 | 89.5 |
| Toronto, ON | CJEZ-FM | Telemedia Communications Ontario Inc., 40 Eglinton Ave. East, 6th Fl., Toronto ON M4P 3B6 – 416/480-2097; Fax: 416/480-0688 | 97.3 |
| Toronto, ON | CJRT-FM | CJRT-FM INC., 150 Mutual St., Toronto ON M5B 2M1 – 416/595-0404; Fax: 416/595-9413 | 91.1 |
| Toronto, ON | CKFM-FM | Standard Radio Inc., 2 St. Clair Ave. West, Toronto ON M4V 1L6 – 416/922-9999; Fax: 416/323-6800 | 99.9 |
| Toronto, ON | CKLN-FM | CKLN Radio Inc., Ryerson Polytechnical Institute, 380 Victoria St., Toronto ON M5B 1W7 – 416/595-1477; Fax: 416/595-0226; Email: ckln@web.apc.org | 88.1 |
| Toronto, ON | CBFM-FM | George Brown College, 200 King St. East, Toronto ON M5A 3W8 – 416/867-2455; Fax: 416/867-2302 | closed circuit |
| Toronto, ON | CSCR-FM | *See* Scarborough (CSCR-FM) | |
| Toronto, ON | CFRE-FM | *See* Mississauga (CFRE-FM) | |
| Toronto, ON | *CBL-FM | *See* Toronto (CBL) | 94.1 |
| Trail, BC | CJAT | Kootenay Broadcasting System Ltd., 1560 Second Ave., Trail BC V1R 1M4 – 250/368-5510; Fax: 250/368-8471 | 95.7 |
| Trois-Rivières, QC | †CHEY-FM | Telemedia Communications Inc., 3550, boul Royale, Trois-Rivières QC G9A 5G8 – 819/374-3556; Fax: 819/374-3222 | 94.7 |
| Trois-Rivières, QC | †CIGB-FM | CIGB-FM, 1350, rue Royal, 12e étage, Trois-Rivières QC G9A 4J4 – 819/378-1023; Fax: 819/378-1360 | 102.3 |
| Truro, NS | CKTO-FM | Radio Atlantic (CKCL) Ltd., 187 Industrial Ave., PO Box 788, Truro NS B2N 6V3 – 902/893-6060; Fax: 902/893-7771; Email: themix.ckcl.ca; URL: http://www.themix.ckcl.ca | 100.9 |
| Valleyfield, QC | CKOD-FM | Radio Express Inc., 249, rue Victoria, Valleyfield QC J6T 1A9 – 514/373-0103; Fax: 514/373-4297 | 103.1 |
| Vancouver, BC | CFMI Rock 101 | CFMI, #2000, 700 West Georgia St., Vancouver BC V7Y 1K9 – 604/331-2808; Fax: 604/331-2727; Email: info@rock101.com; URL: http://www.rock101.com | 101.1 |
| Vancouver, BC | CFOX-FM | Shaw Radio Ltd., 1006 Richards St., Vancouver BC V6B 1S8 – 604/684-7221; Fax: 604/681-9134; URL: http://www.cfox.com | 99.3 |
| Vancouver, BC | CFRO-FM | Vancouver Co-operative Radio, 337 Carrall St., Vancouver BC V6B 2J4 – 604/684-8494; URL: http://vcr.bc.ca/cfro/welcome.html | 102.7 |
| Vancouver, BC | CHQM-FM | CHUM Ltd., #300, 380 West 2nd Ave., Vancouver BC V5Y 1C8 – 604/871-9000; Fax: 604/871-2901; Email: qmfmmail@qmfm.com; URL: http://www.qmfm.com | 103.5 |
| Vancouver, BC | CITR-FM | UBC, #233, 6138 Sub Blvd., Vancouver BC V6T 1Z1 – 604/882-3017; Fax: 604/882-9364; Email: citr@unixg.ubc.ca; URL: http://www.ans.ubc.ca/citr/citr.htm | 101.9 |
| Vancouver, BC | CJJR-FM | Great Pacific Industries Inc., 1401 West 8 Ave., Vancouver BC V6H 1C9 – 604/731-7772; Fax: 604/731-6111 | 93.7 |
| Vancouver, BC | CKKS-FM | Rogers Broadcasting Ltd., 2440 Ash St., Vancouver BC V5Z 4J6 – 604/872-2557; Fax: 604/873-0877; Email: kissfrog@rci.rogers.com; URL: http://www.97kissfm.com | 96.9 |
| Vancouver, BC | *CBU-FM | *See* Vancouver (CBU) | 105.7 |
| Vancouver, BC | *†CBUF-FM | Société Radio-Canada, 700 Hamilton St., CP 4600, Vancouver BC V6B 2R5 – 604/662-6169; Fax: 604/662-6161; URL: http://www.radio-canada.com/radioam | 97.7 |
| Vanderhoof, BC | CIRX-FM-1 | *See* Prince George (CIRX-FM) | 95.9 |
| Verdun, QC | †CKOI-FM | Radio Futura Inc., 211, av Gordon, Verdun QC H4G 2R2 – 514/766-2311; Fax: 514/761-2474 | 96.9 |
| Victoria, BC | CFUV-FM | University of Victoria Student Radio Society, PO Box 3035, Victoria BC V8W 3P3 – 250/721-8702; Fax: 250/721-7111 | 101.9 |
| Victoria, BC | CKKQ-FM | OK Radio Group Ltd., 3795 Carey Rd., Victoria BC V8Z 6T8 – 250/475-0100; Fax: 250/475-3299; URL: http://www.100.3theq.com/q | 100.3 |
| Victoria, BC | CKMO-FM | Camosun College, 3100 Foul Bay Rd., Victoria BC V8P 5J2 – 250/370-3658; Fax: 250/370-3660; Email: lalonde@camosun.bc.ca | |
| Victoriaville, QC | †CFJO-FM | Réseau des Appalaches (FM) Ltée, 55, rue St-Jean-Baptiste, Victoriaville QC G6P 6T3 – 819/752-2785; Fax: 819/752-3182; Email: cfjo@ivic.qc.ca | 103.3 |
| Waterloo, ON | CFCA-FM | CHUM Ltd., 255 King St. North, Waterloo ON N2J 4V2 – 519/884-4470; Fax: 519/884-6482 | 105.3 |
| Waterloo, ON | CKMS-FM | Radio Waterloo Inc., University of Waterloo, Bauer Warehouse, 200 University Ave. West, Waterloo ON N2L 3G1 – 519/886-2567; Fax: 519/884-3530; Email: ckmsfm@web.net | 100.3 |
| Waterloo, ON | CKWR-FM | Wired World Inc., 56 Regina St., Waterloo ON N2J 3A3 – 519/886-9870; Fax: 519/886-0090; Email: ckwr@worldchat.com | 98.7 |
| Whistler, BC | CISW-FM | *See* Squamish (CISQ-FM) | 102.1 |

| LOCATION | CALL | *CBC Stations/Affiliates †French Language Stations | FREQ. |
|---|---|---|---|
| Whitehorse, YT | CHON-FM | Northern Native Broadcasting, 4228A - 4 Ave., Whitehorse YT Y1A 1K1 – 867/668-6629; Fax: 867/668-6612 | 98.1 |
| Williams Lake, BC | CFFM-FM | Cariboo Central Interior Radio, 83 South First Ave., Williams Lake BC V2G 1H4 – 250/398-2336; Fax: 250/392-4142; Email: wlamfm@netshop.net. | 97.5, 94.9 |
| Windsor, ON | CIMX-FM | CHUM Ltd., 1640 Ouellette Ave., Windsor ON N8X 1L1 – 519/258-8888; Fax: 519/258-0182 | 88.7 |
| Windsor, ON | CJAM-FM | University of Windsor, 401 Sunset Ave., Windsor ON N9B 3P4 – 519/971-3606; Fax: 519/973-3605; Email: cjam@uwindsor.ca | 91.5 |
| Windsor, ON | CIDR-FM | CHUM Ltd., 1640 Ouellette Ave., Windsor ON N8X 1L1 – 519/258-8888; Fax: 519/258-0182 | 93.9 |
| Windsor, ON | *CBE-FM | *See* Windsor (CBE) | 89.9 |
| Wingham, ON | CKNX-FM | Blackburn Radio Group, 215 Carling Terrace, Wingham ON N0G 2W0 – 519/357-1310; Fax: 519/357-1897 | 101.7 |
| Winnipeg, MB | CKRC | Celtic Communications, #1630, 155 Carlton St., Winnipeg MB R3C 3H8 – 204/988-9999; Fax: 204/988-2118 | 99.9 |
| Winnipeg, MB | CHIQ-FM | CHUM Ltd., 1445 Pembina Hwy., Winnipeg MB R3T 5C2 – 204/477-5120; Fax: 204/453-0815 | 94.3 |
| Winnipeg, MB | CITI-FM | Rogers Broadcasting Ltd., Polo Park, Winnipeg MB R3G 0L7 – 204/788-3400; Fax: 204/788-3401 | 92.1 |
| Winnipeg, MB | CKMM-FM | Craig Broadcast Systems Inc., #1700, 155 Carlton St., Winnipeg MB R3C 3H8 – 204/942-1031; Fax: 204/943-7687; URL: http://www.star103.com | 103.1 |
| Woodstock, ON | CKDK-FM | Shaw Radio Ltd., 290 Dundas St., PO Box 100, Woodstock ON N4S 7W7 – 519/539-1040; Fax: 519/539-7479; Email: k104@saturn.execulink.com; http://www.saturn.execulink.com/~k104 | 103.9 |
| Yellowknife, NT | CKLB-FM | Native Communications Society of Western N.W.T., 5120 - 49 St., PO Box 1919, Yellowknife NT X1A 2P4 – 867/920-2277; Fax: 867/920-4205 | 101.9 |

## TELEVISION STATIONS

| LOCATION | CALL | *CBC Stations/Affiliates †French Language Stations | CHANNEL |
|---|---|---|---|
| Alert Bay, BC | CBUT-TV-16 | *See* Vancouver (CBUT-TV) | 11 |
| Alexis Creek, BC | CHIL-TV-1 | *See* Kamloops (CFJC-TV) | 8 |
| Alexis Creek, BC | CIAC-TV | *See* Burnaby (CHAN-TV) | 11 |
| Alma, QC | CBJET-TV-1 | *See* Montréal (CBMT-TV) | 32 |
| Alta Lake, BC | CHWM-TV-1 | *See* Victoria (CHEK-TV) | 7 |
| Anahim Lake, BC | CIAL-TV-1 | *See* Burnaby (CHAN-TV) | 5 |
| Annapolis Valley, NS | CJCH-TV-1 | *See* Halifax (CJCH-TV) | 10 |
| Anse-aux-Gascons, QC | CIVK-TV | *See* Montréal (CIVM-TV) | 32 |
| Antigonish, NS | CJCB-TV-2 | *See* Sydney (CJCB-TV) | 9 |
| Argentia, NF | CJAP-TV | *See* St. John's (CJON-TV) | 3 |
| Ashcroft, BC | CHAC-TV-2 | *See* Burnaby (CHAN-TV) | 2 |
| Ashcroft, BC | CJAC-TV-2 | *See* Kamloops (CFJC-TV) | 5 |
| Ashmont, AB | CFRN-TV-4 | *See* Edmonton (CFRN-TV) | 12 |
| Athabasca, AB | CBXT-TV-1 | *See* Edmonton (CBXT-TV) | 8 |
| Atikokan, ON | CBWCT-TV-1 | *See* Winnipeg (CBWT-TV) | 7 |
| Avola, BC | CJVO-TV | *See* Burnaby (CHAN-TV) | 13 |
| Baie-Comeau, QC | CBMIT-TV | *See* Montréal (CBMT-TV) | 28 |
| Baie-Trinité, QC | CIVF-TV | *See* Montréal (CIVM-TV) | 12 |
| Baie Verte, NF | CBNAT-TV-1 | *See* St. John's (CBNT-TV) | 3,12 |
| Banff, AB | CFCN-TV-2 | *See* Calgary (CFCN-TV) | 7 |
| Banff, AB | CBRT-TV-1 | *See* Calgary (CBRT-TV) | 5 |
| Barrie, ON | CKVR-TV | CKVR Channel 3, Division of CHUM Ltd., PO Box 519, Barrie ON L4M 4T9 – 705/734-3300; Fax: 705/733-0302 | 3 |
| Barriere, BC | CKTV-TV-1 | *See* Kamloops (CFJC-TV) | 12 |
| Barriere, BC | CKTV-TV-2 | *See* Burnaby (CHAN-TV) | 7 |
| Bassano, AB | CFCN-TV-7 | *See* Calgary (CFCN-TV) | 10 |
| Battle River, AB | CBXAT-TV-6 | *See* Edmonton (CBXT-TV) | 9 |
| Bay Bulls, NF | CJON-TV | *See* St. John's (CJON-TV) | 10 |
| Bay L'Argent, NF | CBNT-TV-27 | *See* St. John's (CBNT-TV) | 8 |
| Bay St. Lawrence, NS | CBIT-TV-17 | *See* Sydney (CBIT-TV) | 13 |
| Bay St. Lawrence, NS | CJCB-TV-5 | *See* Sydney (CJCB-TV) | 7 |
| Beaton, BC | CHBC-TV | *See* Kelowna (CHBC-TV) | 8 |
| Beauval, SK | CBKBT-TV | *See* Saskatoon (CBKST-TV) | 7 |
| Bellegarde, NF | †CBKFT-TV-9 | *See* St. John's (CBNT-TV) | 7 |
| Bellevue, AB | CBRT-TV-10 | *See* Calgary (CBRT-TV) | 57 |
| Big River, SK | CKBI-TV-5 | *See* Prince Albert (CKBI-TV) | 9 |
| Big Trout Lake, ON | CBWT-TV-1 | *See* Winnipeg (CBWT-TV) | 13 |
| Blackville, NB | CKAM-TV-3 | *See* Moncton (CKCW-TV) | 9 |
| Blanc Sablon, QC | CBMAST-TV | *See* Montréal (CBMT-TV) | 5 |
| Boiestown, NB | CHSJ-TV-3 | *See* Saint John (CHSJ-TV) | 13 |
| Bonavista, NF | CJWB-TV | *See* St. John's (CJON-TV) | 10 |
| Bonnington, BC | CBUDT-TV | *See* Vancouver (CBUT-TV) | 13 |
| Bonnyville, AB | CKSA-TV-2 | *See* Lloydminster (CKSA-TV) | 9 |
| Boston Bar, BC | CFJC-TV-1 | *See* Kamloops (CFJC-TV) | 5 |
| Bowen Island, BC | CBUT-TV-4 | *See* Vancouver (CBUT-TV) | 13 |
| Bowen Island, BC | CHAN-TV-2 | *See* Burnaby (CHAN-TV) | 3 |
| Brackendale, BC | CBUT-TV-34 | *See* Vancouver (CBUT-TV) | 35 |
| Brackendale, BC | CHAN-TV-5 | *See* Burnaby (CHAN-TV) | 9 |
| Brandon, MB | CKYB-TV | *See* Winnipeg (CKY-TV) | 4 |
| Brandon, MB | *CKX-TV | Craig Broadcast Systems Inc., 2940 Victoria Ave., PO Box 1180, Brandon MB R7B 0N2 – 204/728-1150; Fax: 204/727-2505 | 5,9,11 |
| Brent's Cove, NF | CBNAT-TV-18 | *See* St. John's (CBNT-TV) | 10 |
| Bridgetown, NS | CJCH-TV-4 | *See* Halifax (CJCH-TV) | 13 |
| Bridgewater, NS | CIHF-TV-6 | *See* Dartmouth (CIHF-TV) | 9 |

| LOCATION | CALL | *CBC Stations/Affiliates †French Language Stations | FREQ. |
|---|---|---|---|
| Brighton, ON | CKWS-TV-2 | *See* Kingston (CKWS-TV) | 66 |
| Brooks, AB | CFCN-TV-3 | *See* Calgary (CFCN-TV) | 9 |
| Buchans, NF | CBNAT-TV-2 | *See* St. John's (CBNT-TV) | 13 |
| Buffalo Narrows, SK | CBKDT-TV | *See* Saskatoon (CBKST-TV) | 11 |
| Bullhead Mountain, BC | CJDC-TV-2 | *See* Dawson Creek (CJDC-TV) | 8 |
| Burmis, AB | CBRT-TV-8 | *See* Calgary (CBRT-TV) | 47 |
| Burmis, AB | CFCN-TV-4 | *See* Calgary (CFCN-TV) | 5 |
| Burnaby, BC | CHAN-TV | Western International Communications Inc., 7850 Enterprise St., PO Box 4700, Burnaby BC V5A 1V7 – 604/420-2288; Fax: 604/421-9427 | 7 |
| Burnaby, BC | *BCTV-TV | WIC Television, 7850 Enterprise St., Burnaby BC V6B 4A3 – 604/420-2288; Fax: 604/421-9427 | 8 |
| Burns Lake, BC | CBCH-TV-2 | *See* Terrace (CFTK-TV) | 4 |
| Burns Lake, BC | CKHS-TV | *See* Burnaby (CHAN-TV) | 13 |
| Cache Creek, BC | CHAC-TV-1 | *See* Burnaby (CHAN-TV) | 12 |
| Cache Creek, BC | CJAC-TV-1 | *See* Kamloops (CFJC-TV) | 10 |
| Calgary, AB | CICT-TV | Calgary Television Ltd., Division of Westcom Television Group Ltd., 222 - 23 St. NE, Calgary AB T2E 7N2 – 403/235-7777; Fax: 403/248-0252; URL: http://www.cict.com | 2 |
| Calgary, AB | CFCN-TV | CFCN Communications Ltd., PO Box 7060, Stn E, Calgary AB T3C 3L9 – 403/240-5600; Fax: 403/240-5773; Email: channel3promo@cfcn.ca; URL: http://www.cfcn.ca | 3 |
| Calgary, AB | †CBRFT-TV | *See* Edmonton (CBXFT-TV) | 16 |
| Calgary, AB | *CBRT-TV | CBC, 1724 Westmount Blvd. NW, PO Box 2640, Calgary AB T2P 2M7 – 403/521-6000; Fax: 403/521-6007 | 9 |
| Campbell River, BC | CBUT-TV-8 | *See* Vancouver (CBUT-TV) | 3,82 |
| Campbellton, NB | CKCD-TV | *See* Moncton (CKCW-TV) | 7 |
| Canal Flats, BC | CBUBT-TV-1 | *See* Vancouver (CBUT-TV) | 12 |
| Canoe, BC | CHBC-TV-8 | *See* Kelowna (CHBC-TV) | 6 |
| Cape Broyle, NF | CJBL-TV-13 | *See* St. John's (CJON-TV) | 13 |
| Cardston, AB | CBRT-TV-12 | *See* Calgary (CBRT-TV) | 2 |
| Carleton, QC | †CHAU-TV | Télévision de la Baie des Chaleurs, CP 100, Carleton QC G0C 1J0 – 418/364-3344; Fax: 418/364-7168 | 5 |
| Carleton, QC | †CIVK-TV | *See* Montréal (CIVM-TV) | 15 |
| Cartwright, NF | CBNT-TV-21 | *See* St. John's (CBNT-TV) | 9 |
| Castlegar, BC | CBUAT-TV-2 | *See* Vancouver (CBUT-TV) | 3 |
| Castlegar, BC | CKTN-TV-1 | *See* Burnaby (CHAN-TV) | 5 |
| Causapscal, QC | †CBGAT-TV-5 | Causapscal QC | 9 |
| Celista, BC | CHBC-TV-6 | *See* Kelowna (CHBC-TV) | 3 |
| Chapais, QC | †CBFAT-TV-1 | *See* Montréal (CBFT-TV) | 12 |
| Chapeau, QC | †CIVP-TV | *See* Montréal (CIVM-TV) | 23 |
| Charlottetown, PE | CKCW-TV-1 | *See* Moncton (CKCW-TV) | 8 |
| Charlottetown, PE | *CBCT-TV | CBC, 430 University Ave., PO Box 2230, Charlottetown PE C1A 8B9 – 902/629-6400; Fax: 902/629-6518 | 13 |
| Charlottettetown, PE | †CBAFT-TV-5 | *See* Moncton (CBAFT-TV) | 31 |
| Chase, BC | CHSH-TV-2 | *See* Burnaby (CHAN-TV) | 13 |
| Chase, BC | CHSH-TV-1 | *See* Burnaby (CHAN-TV) | 7 |
| Chase, BC | CFJC-TV-8 | *See* Kamloops (CFJC-TV) | 11 |
| Chateh, AB | CBXAT-TV-7 | *See* Edmonton (CBXT-TV) | 5 |
| Chatham, NB | CKAM-TV-2 | *See* Moncton (CKCW-TV) | 10 |
| Chatham, ON | CBLN-TV-3 | *See* Toronto (CBLT-TV) | 64 |
| Cherryville, BC | CJCC-TV | *See* Burnaby (CHAN-TV) | 13 |
| Cherryville, BC | CJWR-TV-1 | *See* Kelowna (CHBC-TV) | 10 |
| Cheticamp, NS | CBIT-TV-2 | *See* Sydney (CBIT-TV) | 2 |
| Chetwynd, BC | CBCD-TV-2 | *See* Dawson Creek (CJDC-TV) | 7 |
| Chibougamau, QC | †CBFAT-TV | *See* Montréal (CBFT-TV) | 5 |
| Chibougamau, QC | CBMCT-TV | *See* Montréal (CBMT-TV) | 4 |
| Chicoutimi, QC | †CJPM-TV | Télé-Metropole inc., CP 600, Chicoutimi QC G7H 5G3 – 418/549-2576; Fax: 418/549-1130; Email: cjpm@saglac.qc.ca | 6 |
| Chicoutimi, QC | CBJET-TV | *See* Montréal (CBMT-TV) | 58 |
| Chilliwack, BC | CBUT-TV-2 | *See* Vancouver (CBUT-TV) | 3 |
| Chilliwack, BC | CHAN-TV-1 | *See* Burnaby (CHAN-TV) | 11 |
| Christina Lake, BC | CBUAT-TV-7 | *See* Vancouver (CBUT-TV) | 13 |
| Churchill, MB | CHFC-TV | *See* Winnipeg (CBWT-TV) | 8 |
| Clarenville, NF | CBNT-TV-10 | *See* St. John's (CBNT-TV) | 7 |
| Clarenville, NF | CJCN-TV-10 | *See* St. John's (CJON-TV) | 10 |
| Clearwater, BC | CHCW-TV-1 | *See* Kamloops (CFJC-TV) | 2 |
| Clearwater, BC | CHCW-TV-2 | *See* Burnaby (CHAN-TV) | 10 |
| Clinton, BC | CFJC-TV-4 | *See* Kamloops (CFJC-TV) | 9 |
| Clinton, BC | CHTS-TV-1 | *See* Burnaby (CHAN-TV) | 13 |
| Coachman's Cove, NF | CBNAT-TV-16 | *See* St. John's (CBNT-TV) | 8 |
| Coal Harbour, BC | CBUT-TV-20 | *See* Vancouver (CBUT-TV) | 8 |
| Coleman, AB | CBRT-TV-11 | *See* Calgary (CBRT-TV) | 17 |
| Conche, NF | CBNAT-TV-8 | *See* St. John's (CBNT-TV) | 13 |
| Corner Brook, NF | CJWN-TV | *See* St. John's (CJON-TV) | 10 |
| Corner Brook, NF | *CBYT-TV | CBC, 162 Premier Dr., PO Box 610, Corner Brook NF A2H 6G1 – 709/634-3141; Fax: 709/634-8506 | 5 |
| Courtenay, BC | CHAN-TV-4 | *See* Burnaby (CHAN-TV) | 13 |
| Courtenay, BC | CBUT-TV-1 | *See* Vancouver (CBUT-TV) | 9 |
| Coutts, AB | CBRT-TV-16 | *See* Calgary (CBRT-TV) | 4 |
| Cowley, AB | CBRT-TV-15 | *See* Calgary (CBRT-TV) | 27 |
| Cranbrook, BC | CBUBT-TV-7 | *See* Vancouver (CBUT-TV) | 65 |
| Crawford Bay, BC | CBUCT-TV-1 | *See* Vancouver (CBUT-TV) | 5 |
| Crescent Valley, BC | CBUCT-TV-4 | *See* Vancouver (CBUT-TV) | 33 |
| Creston, BC | CBUCT-TV-2 | *See* Vancouver (CBUT-TV) | 3 |

| LOCATION | CALL | *CBC Stations/Affiliates †French Language Stations | CHANNEL |
|---|---|---|---|
| Creston, BC | CKTN-TV-4 | *See* Burnaby (CHAN-TV) | 12 |
| Cross Lake, MB | CBWNT-TV | *See* Winnipeg (CBWT-TV) | 12 |
| Cumberland House, SK | CBWIT-TV | *See* Winnipeg (CBWT-TV) | 9 |
| Cypress Hills, SK | *CBCP-TV-2 | *See* Swift Current (CJFB-TV) | 2 |
| Dartmouth, NS | CIHF-TV | Global Communications Ltd., 14 Akerley Blvd., Dartmouth NS B3B 1J3 – 902/481-7400; Fax: 902/468-2154 | 20, 9, 18, 8, 45, 10, 34, 11, 6 |
| Dauphin, MB | CKYD-TV | Craig Broadcast Systems Inc., 28 Second Ave. NE, PO Box 628, Dauphin MB R7N 3B3 – 204/638-3116; Fax: 204/638-4071 | 12 |
| Dawson Creek, BC | CJDC-TV | Mega Communications Ltd., 901 - 102 Ave., Dawson Creek BC V1G 2B6 – 250/782-3341; Fax: 250/782-1809; Email: cjdctv@pris.bc.ca; URL: http://www.pris.bc.ca/cjdc-tel | 5 |
| Deer Lake, NF | CJLW-TV-7 | *See* St. John's (CJON-TV) | 7 |
| Digby, NS | CBHT | *See* Halifax (CBHT-TV) | 52 |
| Dingwall, NS | CBIT-TV-16 | *See* Sydney (CBIT-TV) | 12 |
| Dingwall, NS | CJCB-TV-3 | *See* Sydney (CJCB-TV) | 9 |
| Doaktown, NB | CHSJ-TV-2 | *See* Saint John (CHSJ-TV) | 8 |
| Doaktown, NB | CKAM-TV-4 | *See* Moncton (CKCW-TV) | 10 |
| Donald Station, BC | CBUBT-TV-4 | *See* Vancouver (CBUT-TV) | 3 |
| Drumheller, AB | CFCN-TV-6 | *See* Calgary (CFCN-TV) | 10 |
| Dryden, ON | CBWDT-TV | *See* Winnipeg (CBWT-TV) | 8 |
| Ear Falls, ON | CBWJT-TV | *See* Winnipeg (CBWT-TV) | 13 |
| Eastend, SK | CJFB-TV-1 | *See* Swift Current (CJFB-TV) | 2 |
| Easterville, MB | CBWHT-TV-2 | *See* Winnipeg (CBWT-TV) | 11 |
| Edmonton, AB | †CBXFT-TV | Société Radio-Canada, 8861 - 75 St., CP 555, Edmonton AB T5J 2P4 – 403/468-7500; Fax: 403/468-7792 | 11 |
| Edmonton, AB | CFRN-TV | Sunwapta Broadcasting, Division of Electrohome Ltd., 18520 Stony Plain Rd., PO Box 5030, Stn E, Edmonton AB T5P 4C2 – 403/483-5405; Fax: 403/486-5121; Email: cfrntv@worldgate.com | 3 |
| Edmonton, AB | CITV-TV | ITV, A Division of Westcom TV Group Ltd., 5325 Allard Way, Edmonton AB T6H 5B8 – 403/436-1250; Fax: 403/438-8448; Email: itv@ccinet.ab.ca; URL: http://www.itv.ca | 13 |
| Edmonton, AB | *CBXT-TV | CBC, 8861 - 75 St., PO Box 555, Edmonton AB T5J 2P4 – 403/468-7000; Fax: 403/468-7897 | 5 |
| Edmundston, NB | CBAFT-TV-2 | *See* Moncton (CBAFT-TV) | 13 |
| Edmundston, NB | CHCN-TV | *See* Saint John (CHSJ-TV) | 6 |
| Elliston, NF | CBNT-TV-7 | *See* St. John's (CBNT-TV) | 4 |
| Elrose, SK | CKEL-TV-1 | *See* Swift Current (CJFB-TV) | 7 |
| Enderby, BC | CFEN-TV-2 | *See* Burnaby (CHAN-TV) | 11 |
| Enderby, BC | CFEN-TV-1 | *See* Kelowna (CHBC-TV) | 4 |
| Erie, BC | CBUAT-TV-4 | *See* Vancouver (CBUT-TV) | 13 |
| Etzikom, AB | CHAT-TV-5 | *See* Medicine Hat (CHAT-TV) | 12 |
| Exshaw, AB | CBRT-TV | *See* Calgary (CBRT-TV) | 6, 34 |
| Fairford, MB | CBWGT-TV-2 | *See* Winnipeg (CBWT-TV) | 7 |
| Falkland, BC | CFAW-TV | *See* Burnaby (CHAN-TV) | 12 |
| Falkland, BC | CFWS-TV-1 | *See* Kelowna (CHBC-TV) | 10 |
| Fermeuse, NF | CBNT-TV-5 | *See* St. John's (CBNT-TV) | 11 |
| Fermeuse, NF | CJFR-TV-12 | *See* St. John's (CJON-TV) | 12 |
| Fernie, BC | CBUBT-TV-9 | *See* Vancouver (CBUT-TV) | 8 |
| Ferryland, NF | CBNT-TV-38 | *See* St. John's (CBNT-TV) | 4 |
| Field, BC | CBUBT-TV-13 | *See* Vancouver (CBUT-TV) | 11 |
| Fisher Branch, MB | CBWGT-TV | *See* Winnipeg (CBWT-TV) | 10 |
| Fisher Branch, MB | CKYA-TV | *See* Winnipeg (CKY-TV) | 8 |
| Fleur-de-Lys, NF | CBNAT-TV-20 | *See* St. John's (CBNT-TV) | 5 |
| Flin Flon, MB | CBWBT-TV | *See* Winnipeg (CBWT-TV) | 10 |
| Flin Flon, MB | CKYF-TV | *See* Winnipeg (CKY-TV) | 13 |
| Fogo Island, NF | CBNAT-TV-6 | *See* St. John's (CBNT-TV) | 2 |
| Fort Frances, ON | CBWCT-TV | *See* Winnipeg (CBWT-TV) | 5 |
| Fort Fraser, BC | CBCB-TV-2 | *See* Prince George (CKPG-TV) | 6 |
| Fort McMurray, AB | CBXT-TV-6 | *See* Edmonton (CBXT-TV) | 9 |
| Fort Nelson, BC | CBUGT-TV | *See* Vancouver (CBUT-TV) | 8 |
| Fort Qu'Appelle, SK | CBKT-TV-3 | *See* Regina (CBKT-TV) | 4 |
| Fort St. James, BC | CFFS-TV | *See* Burnaby (CHAN-TV) | 10 |
| Fort St. James, BC | CBCB-TV-3 | *See* Prince George (CKPG-TV) | 8 |
| Fort St. John, BC | CBCD-TV-3 | *See* Dawson Creek (CJDC-TV) | 9 |
| Fort Vermilion, AB | CBXAT-TV-5 | *See* Edmonton (CBXT-TV) | 11 |
| Fortune, NF | CBNT-TV-33 | *See* St. John's (CBNT-TV) | 9 |
| Fountain, BC | CFDF-TV-1 | *See* Burnaby (CHAN-TV) | 5 |
| Fox Creek, AB | CBXT-TV-7 | *See* Edmonton (CBXT-TV) | 5 |
| Fox Harbour, NF | CBNAT-TV-10 | *See* St. John's (CBNT-TV) | 7 |
| Fox Lake, AB | CBXAT-TV-10 | *See* Edmonton (CBXT-TV) | 9 |
| Foxwarren, MB | CKX-TV-1 | *See* Brandon (CKX-TV) | |
| Fraser Lake, BC | CFFL-TV-1 | *See* Burnaby (CHAN-TV) | 9 |
| Fraser Lake, BC | CFFL-TV-2 | *See* Prince George (CKPG-TV) | 6 |
| Fredericton, NB | †CBAFT-TV-10 | *See* Moncton (CBAFT-TV) | 19 |
| Fredericton, NB | *CBAT-TV | CBC, 1160 Regent St., PO Box 2200, Fredericton NB E3B 5G4 – 506/451-4000; Fax: 506/451-4003 | 4 |
| Fruitvale/Montrose, BC | CBUAT-TV-3 | *See* Vancouver (CBUT-TV) | 9 |
| Gillam, MB | CBWLT-TV | *See* Winnipeg (CBWT-TV) | 8 |
| Glovertown, NF | CBNT-TV-13 | *See* St. John's (CBNT-TV) | 3 |
| Gods Lake Narrows, MB | CBWXT-TV | *See* Winnipeg (CBWT-TV) | 13 |
| Gold Bridge, BC | CJGB-TV-1 | *See* Burnaby (CHAN-TV) | 6 |
| Gold River, BC | CBUT-TV-12 | *See* Vancouver (CBUT-TV) | 7 |

| LOCATION | CALL | *CBC Stations/Affiliates †French Language Stations | CHANNEL |
|---|---|---|---|
| Golden, BC | CBUBT-TV-2 | *See* Vancouver (CBUT-TV) | 13 |
| Goose Bay, NF | *CFLA-TV | CBC, 171 Hamilton River Rd., PO Box 1270, Goose Bay NF A0P 1E0 – 709/896-2911; Fax: 709/896-8900 | 8 |
| Grand Bank, NF | CJOX-TV | *See* St. John's (CJON-TV) | 2 |
| Grand Falls, NB | †CBAFT-TV-4 | *See* Moncton (CBAFT-TV) | 12 |
| Grand Falls, NF | CBNAT-TV | *See* St. John's (CBNT-TV) | 11 |
| Grand Falls, NF | CJCN-TV | *See* St. John's (CJON-TV) | 4 |
| Grand-Fonds, QC | †CIVB-TV | *See* Montréal (CIVM-TV) | 31 |
| Grand Forks, BC | CKSR-TV-1 | *See* Burnaby (CHAN-TV) | 7 |
| Grand Forks, BC | CBUT-TV-37 | *See* Vancouver (CBUT-TV) | 5 |
| Grand Rapids, MB | CBWHT-TV | *See* Winnipeg (CBWT-TV) | 8 |
| Grande Prairie, AB | CBXAT-TV | *See* Edmonton (CBXT-TV) | 10 |
| Grande Prairie, AB | CFRN-TV-1 | *See* Edmonton (CFRN-TV) | 13 |
| Grande Vallée, QC | †CBGAT-TV-3 | Grande Vallée QC | 6 |
| Granisle, BC | CIGR-TV-1 | *See* Burnaby (CHAN-TV) | 7 |
| Gravelbourg, SK | †CBKFT-TV-6 | *See* Winnipeg (CBWFT-TV) | 39 |
| Gravelbourg, SK | CKGT-TV | *See* Regina (CBKT-TV) | |
| Greenwater Lake, SK | CKBI-TV-3 | *See* Prince Albert (CKBI-TV) | 4 |
| Greenwood, BC | CBUT-TV-31 | *See* Vancouver (CBUT-TV) | 13 |
| Grinrod, BC | CHBC-TV | *See* Kelowna (CHBC-TV) | 72 |
| Gros Morne, QC | †CBGAT-TV-9 | Gros Morne QC | 4 |
| Hagensborg, BC | CBUIT-TV-4 | *See* Vancouver (CBUT-TV) | 11 |
| Halifax, NS | CJCH-TV | Atlantic Television System, PO Box 1653, Halifax NS B3J 2Z4 – 902/453-4000; Fax: 902/454-3302; URL: http://www.atv.ca | 5 |
| Halifax, NS | CIHF-TV | *See* Dartmouth (CIHF-TV) | 8 |
| Halifax, NS | *CBHT-TV | CBC, 1840 Bell St., PO Box 3000, Halifax NS B3J 3E9 – 902/420-8311; Fax: 902/420-4010; URL: http://www.halifax.cbc.ca | 3 |
| Hamilton, ON | CHCH-TV | Niagara Television Ltd., 163 Jackson St. West, PO Box 2230, Stn A, Hamilton ON L8N 3A6 – 905/522-1101; Fax: 905/546-1057; URL: http://www.ontv.ca | 11 |
| Hampden, NF | CBNAT-TV-23 | *See* St. John's (CBNT-TV) | 13 |
| Hand Hills, AB | CFCN-TV-1 | *See* Calgary (CFCN-TV) | 12 |
| Harbour Breton, NF | CBNT-TV-22 | *See* St. John's (CBNT-TV) | 13 |
| Harbour Breton, NF | CBNT-TV | *See* St. John's (CBNT-TV) | 13 |
| Harbour Mile, NF | CBNT-TV-29 | *See* St. John's (CBNT-TV) | 13 |
| Harbour Round, NF | CBNAT-TV-19 | *See* St. John's (CBNT-TV) | 12 |
| Harrington Harbour, BC | CBMUT-TV | *See* Montréal (CBMT-TV) | 8 |
| Harrison Hot Springs, BC | CBUT-TV-23 | *See* Vancouver (CBUT-TV) | 13 |
| Harvie Heights, AB | CBRT-TV-13 | *See* Calgary (CBRT-TV) | 61 |
| Hazelton, BC | CFTK-TV | *See* Terrace (CFTK-TV) | 9 |
| Hendrix Lake, BC | CIHL-TV | *See* Burnaby (CHAN-TV) | 12 |
| Hermitage, NF | CBNT-TV-24 | *See* St. John's (CBNT-TV) | 4 |
| Hickman's Harbour, NF | CBNT-TV-18 | *See* St. John's (CBNT-TV) | 4 |
| High Level, AB | CBXAT-TV-4 | *See* Edmonton (CBXT-TV) | 8 |
| High Prairie, AB | CBXAT-TV-2 | *See* Edmonton (CBXT-TV) | 2 |
| Hinton, AB | CBXT-TV-3 | *See* Edmonton (CBXT-TV) | 8 |
| Hixon, BC | CKPG-TV-1 | *See* Prince George (CKPG-TV) | 10 |
| Holberg, BC | CBUT-TV-21 | *See* Vancouver (CBUT-TV) | 2 |
| Hope, BC | CBUT-TV-6 | *See* Vancouver (CBUT-TV) | 9 |
| Houston, BC | CFHO-TV | *See* Burnaby (CHAN-TV) | 8 |
| Houston, BC | CBCH-TV-1 | *See* Terrace (CFTK-TV) | 2 |
| Hudson Bay, SK | CKOS | *See* Yorkton (CKOS-TV) | 9 |
| Hudson Hope, BC | CJDC | *See* Dawson Creek (CJDC-TV) | 11 |
| Hull, QC | †CFGS-TV | Radio Nord Inc., 171, rue Jean-Proulx, Hull QC J8Z 1W5 – 819/776-4949; Fax: 819/770-0272 | 49 |
| Hull, QC | †CHOT-TV | Radio Nord Inc., 171, rue Jean-Proulx, Hull QC J8Z 1W5 – 819/770-1040; Fax: 819/770-0272 | 40 |
| Hull, QC | CBOT-TV | *See* Ottawa (CBOT-TV) | 4 |
| Hull, QC | CIVO-TV | *See* Montréal (CIVM-TV) | 30 |
| Ignace, ON | CBWDT-TV-2 | *See* Winnipeg (CBWT-TV) | 13 |
| Ile a la Crosse, SK | CBKCT-TV | *See* Saskatoon (CBKST-TV) | 9 |
| Ingonish, NS | CBIT-TV-15 | *See* Sydney (CBIT-TV) | 2 |
| Invermere, BC | CBUBT-TV-3 | *See* Vancouver (CBUT-TV) | 2 |
| Inverness, NS | CJCB-TV-1 | *See* Sydney (CJCB-TV) | 6 |
| Island Falls, SK | CBWBT-TV-2 | *See* Winnipeg (CBWT-TV) | 7 |
| Jackhead, MB | CBWGT-TV-1 | *See* Winnipeg (CBWT-TV) | 5 |
| Jasper, AB | CBXT-TV-4 | *See* Edmonton (CBXT-TV) | 5 |
| Jean Cote, AB | CBXAT-TV-13 | *See* Edmonton (CBXT-TV) | 31 |
| Jean D'Or, AB | CBXAT-TV-9 | *See* Edmonton (CBXT-TV) | 13 |
| Jonquière, QC | †CFRS-TV | Radio Saguenay Ltée, 2303, rue Sir Wilfrid Laurier, Jonquière QC G7X 7X3 – 418/542-4551; Fax: 418/542-7217; Email: rstelevision@cybernaut.com | 4 |
| Jonquière, QC | †CJPM-TV | *See* Chicoutimi (CJPM-TV) | |
| Jonquière, QC | †CIVO-TV | *See* Montréal (CIVM-TV) | |
| Jonquière, QC | †CIVV-TV | Société de Radio-Télévision du Québec, CP 23041, Jonquière QC G7X 9Z8 – 418/695-8152; Fax: 418/695-8155 | 8 |
| Jonquiere, QC | *†CKRS-TV | Radio Saguenay Ltée, 2303, rue Sir Wilfrid Laurier, Jonquiere QC G7X 7X3 – 418/542-4551; Fax: 418/542-7217; Email: rstelevision@cyberhaute.com | 12 |
| Kamloops, BC | CFJC-TV | Jim Pattison Group, 460 Pemberton Terrace, Kamloops BC V2C 1T5 – 250/372-3322; Fax: 250/374-0445 | 4 |
| Kamloops, BC | CHKM-TV | *See* Burnaby (CHAN-TV) | 6 |
| Kedgwick, NB | †CBAFT-TV-9 | *See* Moncton (CBAFT-TV) | 44 |

| LOCATION | CALL | *CBC Stations/Affiliates †French Language Stations | CHANNEL |
|---|---|---|---|
| Kelowna, BC | CHBC-TV | Okanagan Valley Television, Div. of WIC Television Ltd., 342 Leon Ave., Kelowna BC V1Y 6J2 – 250/762-4535; Fax: 250/860-2422; Email: comments@chbc.wic.ca | 2 |
| Kelowna, BC | CHKL-TV | *See* Burnaby (CHAN-TV) | 5 |
| Kemano, BC | CFTK-TV | *See* Terrace (CFTK-TV) | |
| Kenora, ON | CJBN-TV | Norcom Telecommunications Ltd., PO Box 1810, Kenora ON P9N 3X8 – 807/547-2852; Fax: 807/547-2236 | 13 |
| Kenora, ON | CBWT-TV-7 | *See* Winnipeg (CBWT-TV) | 8 |
| Keremeos, BC | CHBC-TV | *See* Kelowna (CHBC-TV) | 4 |
| Kildala, BC | CFTK-TV | *See* Terrace (CFTK-TV) | 5 |
| Kingston, ON | CKWS-TV | Power Broadcasting Inc., 170 Queen St., Kingston ON K7K 1B2 – 613/544-2340; Fax: 613/544-5508 | 11 |
| Kitchener, ON | CKCO-TV | CAP Communications, 864 King St. West, Kitchener ON N2G 4E9 – 519/578-1313; Fax: 519/578-8375 | 13 |
| Kitchener, ON | CBLN-TV-1 | *See* Toronto (CBLT-TV) | 56 |
| Kitwanga, BC | CFTK-TV | *See* Terrace (CFTK-TV) | 13 |
| La Loche, SK | CBKDT-TV-2 | *See* Saskatoon (CBKST-TV) | 13 |
| La Ronge, SK | CBKST-TV-2 | *See* Saskatoon (CBKST-TV) | 12 |
| La Scie, NF | CBNAT-TV-21 | *See* St. John's (CBNT-TV) | 9 |
| La Tabatière, QC | CBMLT-TV | *See* Montréal (CBMT-TV) | 10 |
| La Tûque, QC | CBMET-TV | *See* Montréal (CBMT-TV) | 9 |
| Labrador City, NF | *CBNLT-TV | CBC, PO Box 576, Labrador City NF A2V 2L3 – 709/944-3616; Fax: 709/944-5472 | 13 |
| Lac-Bonnet, MB | CBWT-TV-2 | *See* Winnipeg (CBWT-TV) | 4 |
| Lac La Biche, AB | CFRN-TV-5 | *See* Edmonton (CFRN-TV) | 2 |
| Lac La Biche, AB | CBXT-TV-5 | *See* Edmonton (CBXT-TV) | 10 |
| Lake Louise, AB | CBRT-TV-4 | *See* Calgary (CBRT-TV) | |
| Lake Louise, AB | CFLL-TV-1 | *See* Calgary (CFCN-TV) | 6 |
| Lamaline, NF | CBNT-TV-35 | *See* St. John's (CBNT-TV) | 18 |
| Lawn, NF | CBNT-TV-36 | *See* St. John's (CBNT-TV) | 6 |
| Lawn, NF | CJLN-TV | *See* St. John's (CJON-TV) | 10 |
| Leaf Rapids, MB | CBWQT-TV | *See* Winnipeg (CBWT-TV) | 13 |
| Leoville, SK | CBKST-TV-3 | *See* Saskatoon (CBKST-TV) | 12 |
| Lethbridge, AB | CISA-TV | Lethbridge Television, Div. of WIC Television Ltd., 1401 - 28 St. North, Lethbridge AB T1H 6H9 – 403/327-1521; Fax: 403/320-2620; Email: cisa@cisa.wic.ca; URL: http://www.cisatv.com | 7 |
| Lethbridge, AB | CBRT-TV-6 | *See* Calgary (CBRT-TV) | 85 |
| Lethbridge, AB | CFCN-TV-5 | *See* Calgary (CFCN-TV) | 13 |
| Lillooet, BC | CFMZ-TV-1 | *See* Kamloops (CFJC-TV) | 2 |
| Lillooet, BC | CFDF-TV-2 | *See* Burnaby (CHAN-TV) | 13 |
| Little Fort, BC | CKTV-TV-1 | *See* Kamloops (CFJC-TV) | 12 |
| Liverpool, NS | CBHT-TV-1 | *See* Halifax (CBHT-TV) | 12 |
| Lloydminster, AB | CITL-TV | MidWest Television Ltd., 5026 - 50th St., Lloydminster AB T9V 1P3 – 403/875-3321; Fax: 403/875-4704 | 4 |
| Lloydminster, AB | CKSA-TV | MidWest Television Ltd., 5026 - 50th St., Lloydminster AB T9V 1P3 – 403/875-3321; Fax: 403/875-4704 | 2 |
| Lochaber, NS | CBLT-TV-12 | *See* Sydney (CBIT-TV) | 33 |
| Logan Lake, BC | CHLK-TV-2 | *See* Burnaby (CHAN-TV) | 13 |
| Logan Lake, BC | CFJC-TV | *See* Kamloops (CFJC-TV) | 11 |
| London, ON | CFPL-TV | South West Ontario Television Inc., PO Box 2880, Stn A, London ON N6A 4H9 – 519/686-8810; Fax: 519/668-3288 | 10 |
| Loos, BC | CBUHT-TV-2 | *See* Vancouver (CBUT-TV) | 6 |
| Lord's Cove, NF | CBNT-TV-34 | *See* St. John's (CBNT-TV) | 9 |
| Lougheed, AB | CFRN-TV-7 | *See* Edmonton (CFRN-TV) | 7 |
| Lumby, BC | CHID-TV-2 | *See* Burnaby (CHAN-TV) | 9 |
| Lumsden, NF | CBNT-TV-20 | *See* St. John's (CBNT-TV) | 12 |
| Lynn Lake, MB | CBWRT-TV | *See* Winnipeg (CBWT-TV) | 6 |
| Lytton, BC | CHWS-TV-1 | *See* Kamloops (CFJC-TV) | 11 |
| Lytton, BC | CILY-TV-2 | *See* Burnaby (CHAN-TV) | 8 |
| Mabel Lake, BC | CHPL-TV-1 | *See* Burnaby (CHAN-TV) | 13 |
| Mabel Lake, BC | CHPP-TV-1 | *See* Kelowna (CHBC-TV) | 8 |
| Mabou, NS | CBIT-TV-4 | *See* Sydney (CBIT-TV) | 10 |
| Mackenzie, BC | CKPG-TV-4 | *See* Prince George (CKPG-TV) | 6 |
| Mackenzie, BC | CIMK-TV-1 | *See* Burnaby (CHAN-TV) | 9 |
| Mafeking, MB | CBWYT-TV | *See* Winnipeg (CBWT-TV) | 2 |
| Malakwa, BC | CFFI-TV-1 | *See* Kelowna (CHBC-TV) | 4 |
| Malakwa, BC | CFFI-TV-2 | *See* Burnaby (CHAN-TV) | 11 |
| Manigotagan, MB | CBWGT-TV-3 | *See* Winnipeg (CBWT-TV) | 22 |
| Manning, AB | CBXAT-TV-3 | *See* Edmonton (CBXT-TV) | 12 |
| Maple Creek, SK | CHAT-TV-2 | *See* Medicine Hat (CHAT-TV) | |
| Margaree, NS | CBIT-TV-5 | *See* Sydney (CBIT-TV) | 8 |
| Marinette, NS | CJCH-TV-8 | *See* Halifax (CJCH-TV) | 23 |
| Marsoui, QC | †CBGAT-TV-8 | Marsoui QC | 12 |
| Marten Mtn./Slave Lake, AB | CBXAT-TV-11 | *See* Edmonton (CBXT-TV) | 11 |
| Marystown, NF | CBNT-TV-3 | *See* St. John's (CBNT-TV) | 5 |
| Marystown, NF | CJMA-TV-11 | *See* St. John's (CJON-TV) | 11 |
| Masset, BC | CHMH-TV-1 | *See* Terrace (CFTK-TV) | 8 |
| Matane, QC | †CBGA-TV | Société Radio-Canada, 155, rue St-Sacrement, CP 2000, Matane QC G4W 3P7 – 418/562-0290; Fax: 418/562-3555 | 6 |
| McBride, BC | CBUHT-TV-3 | *See* Vancouver (CBUT-TV) | 2 |
| McCreary, MB | CKX-TV-3 | *See* Brandon (CKX-TV) | 11 |
| McCusker Lake, MB | CBWUT-TV | *See* Winnipeg (CBWT-TV) | 10 |
| Meadow Lake, SK | CBCS-TV-1 | *See* Lloydminster (CKSA-TV) | 8 |
| Medicine Hat, AB | CHAT-TV | Monarch Broadcasting Co. Ltd., PO Box 1270, Medicine Hat AB T1A 7H5 – 403/529-1270; Fax: 403/529-1292; Email: ddietric@mlc.awinc.com | 6 |
| Medicine Hat, AB | CFCN-TV-8 | *See* Calgary (CFCN-TV) | 8 |

| LOCATION | CALL | *CBC Stations/Affiliates †French Language Stations | CHANNEL |
|---|---|---|---|
| Melfort, SK | CKBQ-TV | *See* Prince Albert (CKBI-TV) | |
| Melita, MB | CKX-TV-2 | *See* Brandon (CKX-TV) | |
| Merritt, BC | CFJC-TV-3 | *See* Kamloops (CFJC-TV) | 8 |
| Middleton, NS | CBHT-TV-6 | *See* Halifax (CBHT-TV) | 8 |
| Midway, BC | CBUT-TV-32 | *See* Vancouver (CBUT-TV) | 7 |
| Millertown, NF | CBNAT-TV-5 | *See* St. John's (CBNT-TV) | 9 |
| Ming's Bight, NF | CBNAT-TV-14 | *See* St. John's (CBNT-TV) | 10 |
| Minnedosa, MB | CKND-TV-2 | *See* Winnipeg (CKND-TV) | |
| Minto, BC | CFMT-TV-3 | *See* Kamloops (CFJC-TV) | 3 |
| Moncton, NB | CKCW-TV | CKCW-TV, Division of CHUM Ltd., 191 Halifax St., Moncton NB E1C 8R6 – 506/857-2600; Fax: 506/857-2618; URL: http://www.atv.ca | 2 |
| Moncton, NB | CHMT-TV | *See* Saint John (CHSJ-TV) | 7 |
| Moncton, NB | CIHF-TV-3 | *See* Dartmouth (CIHF-TV) | 27 |
| Moncton, NB | *CBAFT-TV | Radio-Canada Atlantique, 250 Archibald St., Moncton NB E1C 8N8 – 506/853-6666; Fax: 506/853-6739 | 7 |
| Mont-Climont, QC | †CBGAT-TV-1 | Mont-Climont QC | 13 |
| Mont-Laurier, QC | †CBFT-TV-2 | *See* Montréal (CBFT-TV) | 3 |
| Mont-Louis, QC | †CBGAT-TV-4 | Mont-Louis QC | 2 |
| Mont-Louis-Haut, QC | †CBGAT-TV-10 | Mont-Louis-Haut QC | 19 |
| Mont St-Michel, QC | †CBFT-TV-9 | *See* Montréal (CBFT-TV) | 16 |
| Mont-Tremblant, QC | †CBFT-TV-1 | *See* Montréal (CBFT-TV) | 11 |
| Montréal, QC | CFCF-TV | CFCF Inc., 405, av Ogilvy, Montréal QC H3N 1M4 – 514/273-6311; Fax: 514/276-9399 | 12 |
| Montréal, QC | †CFJP-TV | Télévision Quatre Saisons Inc.(TQS), 405, av Ogilvy, Montréal QC H3N 2Y4 – 514/271-3535; Fax: 514/271-6047 | 35 |
| Montréal, QC | †CFTM-TV | Télé-Métropole Inc., 1600, boul de Maisonneuve est, Montréal QC H2L 4P2 – 514/526-9251; Fax: 514/526-9208 | 10 |
| Montréal, QC | †CIVM-TV | Radio-Québec, 800, rue Fullum, Montréal QC H2K 3L7 – 514/521-2424; Fax: 514/873-7464 | 17 |
| Montréal, QC | *†CBFT-TV | Société Radio-Canada, 1400, boul René-Lévesque est, CP 6000, Montréal QC H3C 3A8 – 514/597-5970; Fax: 514/597-5551 | 2 |
| Montréal, QC | *CBMT-TV | CBC, 1400, boul René-Lévesque est, CP 6000, Montréal QC H3C 3A8 – 514/597-5970; Fax: 514/597-4596 | 6 |
| Montreal Lake, SK | CBKST-TV | *See* Saskatoon (CBKST-TV) | 11 |
| Moose Jaw, SK | CBKT-TV-1 | *See* Regina (CBKT-TV) | 4 |
| Moose Lake, MB | CBWIT-TV-1 | *See* Winnipeg (CBWT-TV) | 10 |
| Mount Hamilton, BC | CFHM-TV-1 | *See* Kamloops (CFJC-TV) | 7 |
| Mount McDonald, BC | CBUT-TV-27 | *See* Vancouver (CBUT-TV) | 59 |
| Moyie, BC | CBUBT-TV-14 | *See* Vancouver (CBUT-TV) | 6 |
| Mulgrave, NS | CBHT-TV-11 | *See* Sydney (CBIT-TV) | 12 |
| Murdochville, QC | †CBGAT-TV-2 | Murdochville QC | 10 |
| Murdochville, QC | CBMMT-TV | *See* Montréal (CBMT-TV) | 21 |
| Musgrave Harbour, NF | CBNAT-TV-11 | *See* St. John's (CBNT-TV) | 9 |
| Musgravetown, NF | CBNT-TV-17 | *See* St. John's (CBNT-TV) | 9 |
| Nakusp, BC | CJNP-TV-1 | *See* Kelowna (CHBC-TV) | 2 |
| Nakusp, BC | CJNP-TV-3 | *See* Burnaby (CHAN-TV) | 7 |
| Narrows Inlet, BC | CHNI-TV | *See* Victoria (CHEK-TV) | 10 |
| Natal, BC | CBUBT-TV-10 | *See* Vancouver (CBUT-TV) | 11 |
| Nelson, BC | CKTN-TV-3 | *See* Burnaby (CHAN-TV) | 3 |
| Nelson, BC | CBUCT-TV | *See* Vancouver (CBUT-TV) | 9 |
| Nelson House, MB | CBWPT-TV | *See* Winnipeg (CBWT-TV) | 11 |
| New Denver, BC | CHJV-TV | *See* Burnaby (CHAN-TV) | 13 |
| New Denver, BC | CBUCT-TV-6 | *See* Vancouver (CBUT-TV) | 17 |
| New Glasgow, NS | CBHT-TV-5 | *See* Halifax (CBHT-TV) | 4 |
| New Glasgow, NS | CJCB-TV-4 | *See* Sydney (CJCB-TV) | 2 |
| Newcastle, NB | CKAM-TV-1 | *See* Moncton (CKCW-TV) | 10 |
| Newcastle Ridge, BC | CFKB-TV-1 | *See* Victoria (CHEK-TV) | 7 |
| Nicola Valley, BC | CFJC-TV-12 | *See* Kamloops (CFJC-TV) | 10 |
| Nimpkish, BC | CFNV-TV-2 | *See* Victoria (CHEK-TV) | 6 |
| Noranda Mines, BC | CFJC-TV | *See* Kamloops (CFJC-TV) | 7 |
| Norquay, SK | CKOS-TV-1 | *See* Yorkton (CKOS-TV) | 13 |
| North Battleford, SK | CKBI-TV-2 | *See* Prince Albert (CKBI-TV) | 7 |
| North Bay, ON | CHNB-TV | MCTV-Mid Canada Communications Corp., 245 Oak St. East, PO Box 3220, North Bay ON P1B 8P8 – 705/476-3111; Fax: 705/495-4474; Email: northbaynews@baton.com | 4 |
| North Bay, ON | CKNY-TV | MCTV-Mid Canada Communications Corp., 245 Oak St. East, PO Box 3220, North Bay ON P1B 8P8 – 705/476-3111; Fax: 705/495-4474; Email: northbaynews@baton.com | 10 |
| Northeast Margaree, NS | CBIT-TV-6 | *See* Sydney (CBIT-TV) | 13 |
| Northwest Brook, NF | CBNT-TV-11 | *See* St. John's (CBNT-TV) | 4 |
| Norway House, MB | CBWOT-TV | *See* Winnipeg (CBWT-TV) | 9 |
| Notre-Dame-Laus, QC | †CBOFT-TV-3 | *See* Montréal (CBFT-TV) | 10 |
| Olalla, BC | CHKC-TV-5 | *See* Burnaby (CHAN-TV) | 11 |
| Old Fort Bay, QC | CBMVT-TV | *See* Montréal (CBMT-TV) | 13 |
| Oliver, BC | CHBC-TV-3 | *See* Kelowna (CHBC-TV) | 8 |
| 100 Mile House, BC | CFJC-TV-6 | *See* Kamloops (CFJC-TV) | 5 |
| Osnaburgh, ON | CBWDT-TV-4 | *See* Winnipeg (CBWT-TV) | 13 |
| Ottawa, ON | CHOT-TV | *See* Hull (CHOT-TV) | |
| Ottawa, ON | CHRO-TV | Baton Broadcasting Inc., 10 Kimway Cres., Ottawa ON K2E 6Z6 – 613/236-2476 | 5 |
| Ottawa, ON | CJOH-TV | Baton Broadcasting Inc., PO Box 5813, Stn Merivale, Ottawa ON K2C 3G6 – 613/224-1313; Fax: 613/274-4215; URL: http://www.baton.com | 13 |
| Ottawa, ON | *†CBOFT-TV | Société Radio-Canada, CP 3220, Succ C, Ottawa ON K1Y 1E4 – 613/724-1200; Fax: 613/724-5233 | 9 |
| Ottawa, ON | *CBOT-TV | CBC, PO Box 3220, Stn C, Ottawa ON K1Y 1E4 – 613/724-1200; Fax: 613/724-5512 | 4 |
| Oxford House, MB | CBWVT-TV | *See* Winnipeg (CBWT-TV) | 8 |

| LOCATION | CALL | *CBC Stations/Affiliates †French Language Stations | CHANNEL |
|---|---|---|---|
| Oyen, AB | CFON-TV-1 | *See* Calgary (CFCN-TV) | 2 |
| Oyen, AB | CHAT-TV-3, -4 | *See* Medicine Hat (CHAT-TV) | 4,6 |
| Pacquet, NF | CBNAT-TV-17 | *See* St. John's (CBNT-TV) | 6 |
| Palmbere Lake, SK | CBKDT-TV-1 | *See* Saskatoon (CBKST-TV) | 8 |
| Peace River, AB | CBXAT-TV-1 | *See* Edmonton (CBXT-TV) | 7 |
| Peace River, AB | CFRN-TV-2 | *See* Edmonton (CFRN-TV) | 3 |
| Peachland, BC | CHPT-TV-1 | *See* Kelowna (CHBC-TV) | 4 |
| Peachland, BC | CIPL-TV | *See* Burnaby (CHAN-TV) | 9 |
| Pelican Narrows, SK | CBWBT-TV-3 | *See* Winnipeg (CBWT-TV) | 5 |
| Pemberton, BC | CBUPT-TV | *See* Vancouver (CBUT-TV) | 4 |
| Pemberton, BC | CHPV-TV-1 | *See* Victoria (CHEK-TV) | 9 |
| Pembroke, ON | CHRO-TV | Baton Broadcasting Inc., PO Box 1010, Pembroke ON K8A 7T3 – 613/735-1036; Fax: 613/735-0022 | 5 |
| Penticton, BC | CHBC-TV-1 | *See* Kelowna (CHBC-TV) | 13 |
| Penticton, BC | CHKL-TV-1 | *See* Burnaby (CHAN-TV) | 10 |
| Percé, QC | CIVK-TV-2 | *See* Montréal (CIVM-TV) | 40 |
| Peterborough, ON | CHEX-TV | Power Broadcasting Inc., 1925 Television Rd., PO Box 4150, Peterborough ON K9J 6Z9 – 705/742-0451; Fax: 705/742-7274 | 12 |
| Petty Harbour, NF | CBNT-TV-37 | *See* St. John's (CBNT-TV) | 13 |
| Phoenix, BC | CBUT-TV-30 | *See* Vancouver (CBUT-TV) | 15 |
| Pickle Lake, ON | CBWDT-TV-5 | *See* Winnipeg (CBWT-TV) | 9 |
| Pikangikum, ON | CBWDT-TV-6 | *See* Winnipeg (CBWT-TV) | 7 |
| Pincher Creek, AB | CBRT-TV-9 | *See* Calgary (CBRT-TV) | 15 |
| Pincher Creek, AB | CHPC-TV-2 | *See* Calgary (CFCN-TV) | 11 |
| Pinehouse Lake, SK | CBKST-TV-6 | *See* Saskatoon (CBKST-TV) | 10 |
| Pitt River, BC | CIPT-TV | *See* Victoria (CHEK-TV) | 10 |
| Placentia, NF | CBNT-TV-2 | *See* St. John's (CBNT-TV) | 12 |
| Pleasant Bay, NS | CBIT-TV-3 | *See* Sydney (CBIT-TV) | 8 |
| Pointe-au-Père, QC | CFER-TV | 465, boul Ste-Anne, Pointe-au-Père QC G5M 1G1 – 418/722-6011; Fax: 418/724-7810 | 11 |
| Ponteix, SK | *CBCP-TV-3 | *See* Swift Current (CJFB-TV) | 3 |
| Port Alberni, BC | CHEK-TV-3 | *See* Victoria (CHEK-TV) | 11 |
| Port Alberni, BC | CBUT-TV-3 | *See* Vancouver (CBUT-TV) | 4 |
| Port Alice, BC | CBUT-TV-17 | *See* Vancouver (CBUT-TV) | 10 |
| Port Blandford, NF | CBNT-TV-32 | *See* St. John's (CBNT-TV) | 6 |
| Port Hardy, BC | CBUT-TV-19 | *See* Vancouver (CBUT-TV) | 6 |
| Port Hope Simpson, NF | CBNAT-TV-12 | *See* St. John's (CBNT-TV) | 12 |
| Port McNeill, BC | CBUT-TV-18 | *See* Vancouver (CBUT-TV) | 2 |
| Port Renfrew, BC | CJTV-TV-1 | *See* Burnaby (CHAN-TV) | 11 |
| Port Rexton, NF | CBNT-TV-1 | *See* St. John's (CBNT-TV) | 13 |
| Portage La Prairie, MB | CHMI-TV | Craig Broadcast Systems Inc., 350 River Rd., PO Box 13000, Portage La Prairie MB R1N 3V3 – 204/239-1113; Fax: 204/239-5794; Email: promo@opnet.net | 13 |
| Pouce Coupe, BC | CBCD-TV-1 | *See* Dawson Creek (CJDC-TV) | 7 |
| Prince Albert, SK | CIPA-TV | Shamrock Television System Inc., Prince Albert Division, 22 - 10 St. West, Prince Albert SK S6V 3A5 – 306/922-6066; Fax: 306/763-3041 | 9 |
| Prince Albert, SK | CKBI-TV | Shamrock Television System Inc., Prince Albert Division, 22 - 10 St. West, Prince Albert SK S6V 3A5 – 306/922-6066; Fax: 306/763-3041 | 5 |
| Prince George, BC | CKPG-TV | Monarch Broadcasting Ltd., 1220 - 6th Ave., Prince George BC V2L 3M8 – 250/564-8861; Fax: 250/562-8768; Email: ckpgmail@ckpg.bc.ca; URL: http://www.ckpg.ca | 2 |
| Prince George, BC | CIFG-TV | *See* Burnaby (CHAN-TV) | 12 |
| Prince Rupert, BC | CFTK-TV-1 | *See* Terrace (CFTK-TV) | 6 |
| Princeton, BC | CHNJ-TV-1 | *See* Burnaby (CHAN-TV) | 11 |
| Pritchard, BC | CFJC-TV-19 | *See* Kamloops (CFJC-TV) | 5 |
| Pritchard, BC | CHKM-TV-1 | *See* Burnaby (CHAN-TV) | 9 |
| Provost, AB | CKSA-TV-4 | *See* Lloydminster (CKSA-TV) | 12 |
| Pukatawagan, MB | CBWBT-TV-1 | *See* Winnipeg (CBWT-TV) | 11 |
| Purden, BC | CBUHT-TV-1 | *See* Vancouver (CBUT-TV) | 10 |
| Québec, QC | †CFAP-TV | Télévision Quatre Saisons inc., 500, rue Bouvier, CP 17500, Succ Terminus, Québec QC G1K 7X2 – 418/624-2222; Fax: 418/624-3099; Email: nouvelles@tqs-qc.com; URL: http://www.tqs-qc.com | 2 |
| Québec, QC | †CFER-TV-2 | *See* Pointe-au-Père (CFER-TV) | 5 |
| Québec, QC | †CIVQ-TV | *See* Montréal (CIVM-TV) | 15 |
| Queen Charlotte City, BC | CFTK-TV | *See* Terrace (CFTK-TV) | 4 |
| Quesnel, BC | CFJC-TV-11 | *See* Kamloops (CFJC-TV) | 7 |
| Quesnel, BC | CKPG-TV-5 | *See* Prince George (CKPG-TV) | 13 |
| Quesnel, BC | CITM-TV-2 | *See* Burnaby (CHAN-TV) | 8 |
| Radium Hot Springs, BC | CBUBT-TV-5 | *See* Vancouver (CBUT-TV) | 77 |
| Rainbow Lake, AB | CBXAT-TV-8 | *See* Edmonton (CBXT-TV) | 11 |
| Ramea, NF | CBNT-TV-25 | *See* St. John's (CBNT-TV) | 13 |
| Random Island, NF | CBNT-TV-19 | *See* St. John's (CBNT-TV) | 43 |
| Rapides-des-Joachims, QC | †CBOFT-TV-2 | *See* Ottawa (CBOFT-TV) | 31 |
| Red Deer, AB | CKRD-TV | RDTV, Division of Westcom TV Group Ltd., 2840 Bremner Ave., Red Deer AB T4R 1M9 – 403/346-2573; Fax: 403/346-9980; URL: http://www.rdtv.com | 6 |
| Red Deer, AB | CFRN-TV-6 | *See* Edmonton (CFRN-TV) | 8 |
| Red Lake, ON | CBWET-TV | *See* Winnipeg (CBWT-TV) | 10 |
| Red Rocks, NF | CJRF-TV-11 | *See* St. John's (CJON-TV) | 11 |
| Regina, SK | CKCK-TV | TV West Inc., PO Box 2000, Regina SK S4P 3E5 – 306/569-2000; Fax: 306/522-0090 | 2 |
| Regina, SK | CFSS-TV | *See* Yorkton (CKOS-TV) | 3 |
| Regina, SK | CFRE-TV | CanWest Television Inc., 370 Hoffer Dr., Regina SK S4N 7A4 – 306/775-4000; Fax: 306/721-4817 | 11 |

| LOCATION | CALL | *CBC Stations/Affiliates †French Language Stations | CHANNEL |
|---|---|---|---|
| Regina, SK | *†CBKFT-TV | Société Radio-Canada, 2440 Broad St., Regina SK S4P 4A1 – 306/347-9540; Fax: 306/347-9493 | 13 |
| Regina, SK | *CBKT-TV | CBC, 2440 Broad St., PO Box 540, Regina SK S4P 4A1 – 306/347-9540; Fax: 306/347-9493 | 9 |
| Revelstoke, BC | CHRP-TV-2 | *See* Burnaby (CHAN-TV) | |
| Revelstoke, BC | CHRP-TV-1 | *See* Kelowna (CHBC-TV) | 7 |
| Rimouski, QC | †CIVB-TV | Radio-Télévision du Québec, 79, rue de l'Évêché est, Rimouski QC G5L 1X7 – 418/727-3743; Fax: 418/727-3814 | 22 |
| Rimouski, QC | †CJPC-TV | *See* Montréal (CFJP-TV) | 18 |
| Rimrock, BC | CKRR-TV-1 | *See* Kamloops (CFJC-TV) | 9 |
| Rimrock, BC | CKRR-TV-2 | *See* Burnaby (CHAN-TV) | 11 |
| Riverhurst, SK | CJFB-TV-3 | *See* Swift Current (CJFB-TV) | 10 |
| Rivière-du-Loup, QC | †CFTF-TV | Télévision MBS, #100, 1298, boul Thériault, Rivière-du-Loup QC G5R 4C2 – 418/867-1341; Fax: 418/862-9752 | 29 |
| Rivière-du-Loup, QC | †CIMT-TV | Télé Inter-Rives Ltée, 15, rue de la Chute, Rivière-du-Loup QC G5R 5B7 – 418/867-1341; Fax: 418/867-4710 | 9 |
| Rivière-du-Loup, QC | *†CKRT-TV | Télé Inter-Rives Ltée, 15, rue de la Chute, Rivière-du-Loup QC G5R 5B7 – 418/867-1341; Fax: 418/867-4710 | 7 |
| Rivière-Paul, QC | CBMPT-TV | *See* Montréal (CBMT-TV) | 11 |
| Rock Creek, BC | CBUT-TV-33 | *See* Vancouver (CBUT-TV) | 33 |
| Rocky Mountain House, AB | CFMH-TV-2 | *See* Edmonton (CFRN-TV) | 12 |
| Roddickton, NF | CBNAT-TV-22 | *See* St. John's (CBNT-TV) | 11 |
| Rosemary, AB | CBRT-TV-5 | *See* Calgary (CBRT-TV) | 11 |
| Rouyn-Noranda, QC | †CFEM-TV | Radio Nord Inc., 380, rue Murdoch, Rouyn-Noranda QC J9X 1G5 – 819/762-0741; Fax: 819/762-2280 | 13 |
| Rouyn-Noranda, QC | †CKRN-TV | Radio Nord inc., 380, rue Murdoch, Rouyn-Noranda QC J9X 1G5 – 819/762-0741; Fax: 819/762-2280 | 4 |
| Rouyn-Noranda, QC | †CIVN-TV | *See* Montréal (CIVM-TV) | 8 |
| Ruby Creek, BC | CBUT-TV-26 | *See* Vancouver (CBUT-TV) | 25 |
| St. Albans, NF | CBNT-TV-4 | *See* St. John's (CBNT-TV) | 9 |
| St. Albans, NF | CJST-TV-13 | *See* St. John's (CJON-TV) | 13 |
| Ste-Anne-des-Monts, QC | †CBGAT-TV-11 | Ste-Anne-des-Monts QC | 8 |
| St. Anthony, NF | CBNAT-TV-4 | *See* St. John's (CBNT-TV) | 6 |
| St-Augustin-Saguenay, QC | CBMXT-TV | *See* Montréal (CBMT-TV) | 7 |
| St. Bernards, NF | CBNT-TV-30 | *See* St. John's (CBNT-TV) | 6 |
| St. Edward, PE | †CBAFT-TV-6 | *See* Moncton (CBAFT-TV) | 9 |
| Ste-Foy, QC | †CFCM-TV | Télé-Métropole Inc., 1000, av Myrand, CP 2026, Ste-Foy QC G1V 2W3 – 418/688-9330; Fax: 418/681-4239 | 4 |
| Ste-Foy, QC | CKMI-TV | Télé-Métropole Inc., 1000, av Myrand, CP 2026, Ste-Foy QC G1V 2W3 – 418/688-9330; Fax: 418/681-4239 | 5 |
| Ste-Foy, QC | *†CBVT-TV | Société Radio-Canada, 2505, boul Laurier, Ste-Foy QC G1V 2X2 – 418/654-1341; Fax: 418/654-3299 | 11 |
| Saint John, NB | CKLT-TV | ATV, Division of CHUM Ltd., 251 Bayside Dr., Saint John NB E2J 1A7 – 506/658-0100; Fax: 506/658-1208 | 9 |
| Saint John, NB | †CBAFT-TV-1 | *See* Moncton (CBAFT-TV) | 5 |
| Saint John, NB | CIHF-TV-2 | *See* Dartmouth (CIHF-TV) | 12 |
| Saint John, NB | *CBAT-TV | CBC, 560 Main St., PO Box 2358, Saint John NB E2L 3V6 – 506/632-7710; Fax: 506/632-7761 | 4 |
| St. John's, NF | CJON-TV | Newfoundland Broadcasting Co. Ltd., 446 Logy Bay Rd., PO Box 2020, St. John's NF A1C 5S2 – 709/722-5015; Fax: 709/726-5107 | 6 |
| St. John's, NF | *CBNT-TV | CBC, 95 University Ave., PO Box 12010, Stn A, St. John's NF A1B 3T8 – 709/576-5000; Fax: 709/576-5144 | 8 |
| St. Jones Within, NF | CBNT-TV-12 | *See* St. John's (CBNT-TV) | 9 |
| St. Lawrence, NF | CBNT-TV-28 | *See* St. John's (CBNT-TV) | 12 |
| St. Lawrence, NF | CJXL-TV-10 | *See* St. John's (CJON-TV) | 10 |
| St. Mary's, NF | CBNT-TV-6 | *See* St. John's (CBNT-TV) | 10 |
| St-Michel-des-Saints, QC | †CBFT-TV-3 | *See* Montréal (CBFT-TV) | 7 |
| St. Quentin, NB | †CBAFT-TV-8 | *See* Moncton (CBAFT-TV) | 21 |
| St. Vincent's, NF | CBNT-TV-26 | *See* St. John's (CBNT-TV) | 7 |
| Salmo, BC | CBUAT-TV-5 | *See* Vancouver (CBUT-TV) | 10 |
| Salmon Arm, BC | CHBC-TV-4 | *See* Kelowna (CHBC-TV) | 9 |
| Salmon Arm, BC | CFSA-TV-1 | *See* Burnaby (CHAN-TV) | 13 |
| Sandy Lake, ON | CBWDT-TV-7 | *See* Winnipeg (CBWT-TV) | 10 |
| Santa Rosa, BC | CKSR-TV | *See* Burnaby (CHAN-TV) | 83 |
| Sarnia, ON | CBLN-TV-2 | *See* Toronto (CBLT-TV) | 34 |
| Saskatoon, SK | CFQC-TV | TV West Inc., 216 - 1 Ave. North, Saskatoon SK S7K 3W3 – 306/665-8600; Fax: 306/664-0450 | 8 |
| Saskatoon, SK | CFSK-TV | CanWest Television Inc., 218 Robin Cres., Saskatoon SK S7L 7C3 – 306/665-6969; Fax: 306/665-6069 | 4 |
| Saskatoon, SK | †CBKFT-TV | *See* Regina (CBKFT-TV) | 13 |
| Saskatoon, SK | *CBKST-TV | CBC, CN Tower, Midtown Plaza, 5th Fl., Saskatoon SK S7K 1J5 – 306/956-7400; Fax: 306/956-7417 | 11 |
| Sault Ste. Marie, ON | CHBX-TV | MCTV-Mid-Canada Communications (Canada) Corp., 119 East St., PO Box 370, Sault Ste. Marie ON P6A 5M2 – 705/759-8232; Fax: 705/759-778 | 2 |
| Sault Ste. Marie, ON | CJIC-TV | MCTV-Mid-Canada Communications (Canada) Corp., 119 East St., PO Box 370, Sault Ste. Marie ON P6A 5M2 – 705/759-8232; Fax: 705/759-7783 | 5 |
| Savant Lake, ON | CBWDT-TV-3 | *See* Winnipeg (CBWT-TV) | 8 |
| Savona, BC | CFSC-TV-2 | *See* Burnaby (CHAN-TV) | 13 |
| Savona, BC | CFSC-TV-1 | *See* Kamloops (CFJC-TV) | 8 |
| Sayward, BC | CBUT-TV-10 | *See* Vancouver (CBUT-TV) | 4 |
| Scarborough, ON | CFTO-TV | BBS Ontario Inc., PO Box 9, Stn O, Scarborough ON M4A 2M9 – 416/299-2000; Fax: 416/299-2266; Email: programming@baton.com; URL: http://www.baton.com | 9 |
| Seal Cove, NF | CBNAT-TV-15 | *See* St. John's (CBNT-TV) | 7 |
| Sept-Îles, QC | †CIVG-TV | *See* Montréal (CIVM-TV) | 9 |
| Sept-Îles, QC | CBSET-TV | *See* Montréal (CBMT-TV) | 3 |
| Shalalth, BC | CJBT-TV-2 | *See* Burnaby (CHAN-TV) | 11 |
| Shalalth, BC | CJBT-TV-1 | *See* Kamloops (CFJC-TV) | 5 |
| Shaunavon, SK | *CBCP-TV-1 | *See* Swift Current (CJFB-TV) | 7 |
| Sheet Harbour, NS | CBHT-TV-4 | *See* Halifax (CBHT-TV) | 11 |
| Sheet Harbour, NS | CJCH-TV-5 | *See* Halifax (CJCH-TV) | 2 |
| Shelburne, NS | CBHT-TV-2 | *See* Halifax (CBHT-TV) | 7 |
| Sherbrooke, NS | CBHT-TV-16 | *See* Sydney (CBIT-TV) | 4 |
| Sherbrooke, QC | CFKS-TV | COGECO Inc., 3720, boul Industriel, Sherbrooke QC J1L 1Z9 – 819/565-9999; Fax: 819/822-4205 | 30 |

| LOCATION | CALL | *CBC Stations/Affiliates †French Language Stations | CHANNEL |
|---|---|---|---|
| Sherbrooke, QC | †CHLT-TV | Pathonic Communications Inc., 3330, rue King ouest, Sherbrooke QC J1L 1C9 – 819/565-7777; Fax: 819/563-0141 | 7 |
| Sherbrooke, QC | †CIVS-TV | *See* Montréal (CIVM-TV) | 24 |
| Sherbrooke, QC | CBMT-TV-3 | *See* Montréal (CBMT-TV) | 50 |
| Sherbrooke, QC | *†CKSH-TV | COGECO Inc., 3720 boul Industriel, Sherbrooke QC J1L 1Z9 – 819/565-9999; Fax: 819/822-4205 | 9 |
| Shoulder Mtn., BC | CFTK-TV | *See* Terrace (CFTK-TV) | 9 |
| Sioux Lookout, ON | CBWDT-TV-1 | *See* Winnipeg (CBWT-TV) | 12 |
| Sioux Narrows, ON | CBWAT-TV-1 | *See* Winnipeg (CBWT-TV) | 4 |
| 16 Mile House, BC | CHCS-TV-1 | *See* Burnaby (CHAN-TV) | 7 |
| Skaha Lake, BC | CHBC-TV-7 | *See* Kelowna (CHBC-TV) | 7 |
| Slave Lake, AB | CKHP-TV-1 | *See* Edmonton (CFRN-TV) | 4 |
| Slocan, BC | CBUCT-TV-5 | *See* Vancouver (CBUT-TV) | 39 |
| Smithers, BC | CFHO-TV-1 | *See* Burnaby (CHAN-TV) | 13 |
| Snow Lake, MB | CKYS-TV | *See* Winnipeg (CKY-TV) | 11 |
| Snow Lake, MB | CBWKT-TV | *See* Winnipeg (CBWT-TV) | 8 |
| Soda Creek, BC | CKSC-TV-1 | *See* Kamloops (CFJC-TV) | 4 |
| Soda Creek, BC | CKSC-TV-2 | *See* Burnaby (CHAN-TV) | 2 |
| Sooke, BC | CBUT-TV-28 | *See* Vancouver (CBUT-TV) | 3 |
| Southend, SK | CBKST-TV-8 | *See* Saskatoon (CBKST-TV) | 13 |
| Spencerville, ON | CKWS-TV-2 | *See* Kingston (CKWS-TV) | 26 |
| Spence's Bridge, BC | CJNA-TV-1 | *See* Kamloops (CFJC-TV) | 3 |
| Spence's Bridge, BC | CJNA-TV-2 | *See* Burnaby (CHAN-TV) | 7 |
| Spillimacheen, BC | CBUBT-TV-6 | *See* Vancouver (CBUT-TV) | 69 |
| Spiritwood, SK | CKBI-TV-6 | *See* Prince Albert (CKBI-TV) | 2 |
| Springdale, NF | CBNAT-TV-13 | *See* St. John's (CBNT-TV) | 13 |
| Squamish, BC | CHAN-TV-3 | *See* Burnaby (CHAN-TV) | 7 |
| Squamish, BC | CBUT-TV-5 | *See* Vancouver (CBUT-TV) | 11 |
| Stanley Mission, SK | CBKST-TV-4 | *See* Saskatoon (CBKST-TV) | 8 |
| Stewart, BC | CFTK-TV | *See* Terrace (CFTK-TV) | 11 |
| Stranraer, SK | CBKST-TV-1 | *See* Saskatoon (CBKST-TV) | 9 |
| Sudbury, ON | CICI-TV | MCTV-Mid-Canada Communications (Canada) Corp., 699 Frood Rd., Sudbury ON P3C 5A3 – 705/674-8301; Fax: 705/674-2706 | 5 |
| Sudbury, ON | CKNC-TV | Baton Broadcasting Inc., 699 Frood Rd., Sudbury ON P3C 5A3 – 705/674-8301 | 9 |
| Sunnybrae, NS | CBHT-TV-17 | *See* Sydney (CBIT-TV) | 6 |
| Swift Current, NF | CBNT-TV-31 | *See* St. John's (CBNT-TV) | 5 |
| Swift Current, NF | CJSC-TV-10 | *See* St. John's (CJON-TV) | 10 |
| Swift Current, SK | CJFB-TV | Swift Current Telecasting Co. Ltd., PO Box 160, Swift Current SK S9H 3V7 – 306/773-7266; Fax: 306/773-0123 | 5 |
| Sydney, NS | CJCB-TV | ATV, Division of CHUM Ltd., PO Box 4690, Sydney NS B1P 6H5 – 902/562-5511; Fax: 902/564-0495 | 4 |
| Sydney, NS | *CBIT-TV | CBC, 285 Alexandra St., Sydney NS B1S 2E8 – 902/539-5050; Fax: 902/562-7547 | 5 |
| Tabor Mountain, BC | CBUHT-TV | *See* Vancouver (CBUT-TV) | 78 |
| Taghum, BC | CKTN-TV-2 | *See* Burnaby (CHAN-TV) | 23 |
| Tahsis, BC | CBUT-TV-14 | *See* Vancouver (CBUT-TV) | 9 |
| Tasu, BC | CFTK-TV | *See* Prince George (CKPG-TV) | 11 |
| Tatla Lake, BC | CIAL-TV-2 | *See* Burnaby (CHAN-TV) | 9 |
| Taylor, BC | CBCD-TV-4 | *See* Dawson Creek (CJDC-TV) | 7 |
| Telkwa, BC | CFTK-TV-2 | *See* Terrace (CFTK-TV) | 7 |
| Temiscaming, QC | CIVK-TV | *See* Montréal (CIVM-TV) | 8 |
| Terrace, BC | CFTK-TV | Skeena Broadcasters, Division of Okanagan Skeena Group, 4625 Lazelle Ave., Terrace BC V2L 2M8 – 250/635-6316; Fax: 250/638-6320; Email: info@osg.net; URL: http://www.osg.net | 3 |
| Tête Jaune, BC | CBUHT-TV-4 | *See* Vancouver (CBUT-TV) | 10 |
| The Pas, MB | CKYP-TV | *See* Winnipeg (CKY-TV) | 12 |
| Thetford Mines, QC | CBMT-TV-4 | *See* Montréal (CBMT-TV) | 32 |
| Thompson, MB | CKYT-TV | *See* Winnipeg (CKY-TV) | 9 |
| Thunder Bay, ON | CKPR-TV | Thunder Bay Electronics Ltd., 87 North Hill St., Thunder Bay ON P7A 5V6 – 807/346-2600; Fax: 807/345-0932; Email: tbt@tbtv.com | 2 |
| Thunder Bay, ON | CHFD-TV | Thunder Bay Electronics Ltd., 87 North Hill St., Thunder Bay ON P7A 5V6 – 807/346-2600; Fax: 807/345-0932; Email: tbt@tbtv.com | 4 |
| Timmins, ON | CFCL-TV | MCTV-Mid-Canada Communications (Canada) Corp., PO Box 620, Timmins ON P4N 7G3 – 705/264-4211; Fax: 705/264-3266 | 6 |
| Timmins, ON | CITO-TV | MCTV-Mid-Canada Communications (Canada) Corp., PO Box 620, Timmins ON P4N 7G3 – 705/264-4211; Fax: 705/264-3266 | 3 |
| Tisdale, SK | CKBI-TV-6 | *See* Prince Albert (CKBI-TV) | 13 |
| Tofino, BC | CBUT-TV-22 | *See* Vancouver (CBUT-TV) | 10 |
| Topley Landing, BC | CHAN-TV | *See* Burnaby (CHAN-TV) | |
| Toronto, ON | CFMT-TV | Canada's First Multilingual Television, Rogers Broadcasting Ltd., 545 Lakeshore Blvd. West, Toronto ON M5V 1A3 – 416/260-0047; Fax: 416/260-3621; Email: cfmt@rci.rogers.com | 47 |
| Toronto, ON | TVOntario | TVO/TFO Network, 2180 Yonge St., PO Box 200, Stn Q, Toronto ON M4T 2T1 – 416/484-2600; Fax: 416/484-2725, 2867; URL: http://www.tvo.org | 19 |
| Toronto, ON | CIII-TV | Global Television Network, 81 Barber Greene Rd., Toronto ON M3C 2A2 – 416/446-5311; Fax: 416/446-5546 | 41 |
| Toronto, ON | CITY-TV | City TV, Division of CHUM Ltd., 299 Queen St. West, Toronto ON M5V 2Z5 – 416/591-5757; URL: http://www.citytv.com | 57 |
| Toronto, ON | CFTO-TV | *See* Scarborough (CFTO-TV) | 9 |
| Toronto, ON | *CBLT-TV | CBC, PO Box 500, Stn A, Toronto ON M5W 1E6 – 416/205-3311; Fax: 416/205-3453 | 5 |
| Toronto, ON | *†CBLFT-TV | Société Radio-Canada, CP 500, Succ A, Toronto ON M5W 1E6 – 416/205-3311; Fax: 416/205-5622 | 25 |
| Tors Cove, NF | CJON-TV-5 | *See* St. John's (CJON-TV) | 2 |
| Trail, BC | CBUAT-TV-6 | *See* Vancouver (CBUT-TV) | 11 |
| Trail, BC | CKTN-TV | *See* Burnaby (CHAN-TV) | 8 |

| LOCATION | CALL | *CBC Stations/Affiliates †French Language Stations | CHANNEL |
|---|---|---|---|
| Trepassey, NF | CJTP-TV-10 | *See* St. John's (CJON-TV) | 10 |
| Trinity-Wareham, NF | CBNT-TV-16 | *See* St. John's (CBNT-TV) | 2 |
| Trois-Rivières, QC | †CHEM-TV | TéléMétropole Multi-Régions inc., 3625, boul Chanoine-Moreau, Trois-Rivières QC G8Y 5N6 – 819/376-8880; Fax: 819/376-2906 | 8 |
| Trois-Rivières, QC | †CKTM-TV | COGECO Inc., 4141, boul St-Jean, CP 277, Trois-Rivières QC G9A 5G3 – 819/377-1441; Fax: 819/377-5442 | 13 |
| Trois-Rivières, QC | CFKM-TV | *See* Trois-Rivières (CKTM-TV) | 29 |
| Trois-Rivières, QC | CBMT-TV-1 | *See* Montréal (CBMT-TV) | 28 |
| Truro, NS | CBHT-TV-8 | *See* Halifax (CBHT-TV) | 55 |
| Truro, NS | CJCH-TV-2 | *See* Halifax (CJCH-TV) | 12 |
| Ucluelet, BC | CBUT-FM-7 | *See* Vancouver (CBUT-TV) | 7 |
| Ucluelet, BC | CKUP-TV-1 | *See* Burnaby (CHAN-TV) | 6 |
| Val-d'Or, QC | †CFVS-TV | Radio Nord Inc., 1729, av 3, Val-d'Or QC J9P 1W3 – 819/825-0010; Fax: 819/825-6741 | 29 |
| Val-d'Or, QC | CJDG-TV | *See* Rouyn-Noranda (CFEM-TV) | 10 |
| Val d'Or, QC | †CFVS-TV-1 | Radio Nord Inc., 1729, 3e av, Val d'Or QC J9P 1W3 – 819/825-0010; Fax: 819/825-7313 | 20 |
| Val d'Or, QC | †CIVA-TV | Société de Radio-Télévision du Québec, 689, 3e av, Val d'Or QC J9P 1S7 – 819/874-5132; Fax: 819/824-2431 | 8 |
| Val Marie, SK | CJFB-TV-2 | *See* Swift Current (CJFB-TV) | 2 |
| Valemount, BC | CBUHT-TV-5 | *See* Vancouver (CBUT-TV) | 6 |
| Vancouver, BC | CKVU-TV | Canwest Television Inc., 180 West 2nd St., Vancouver BC V5Y 3T9 – 604/876-1344; Fax: 604/874-8225 | 10 |
| Vancouver, BC | *†CBUFT-TV | Société Radio-Canada, 700 Hamilton St., CP 4600, Vancouver BC V6B 4A2 – 604/662-6000; Fax: 604/662-6161 | 26 |
| Vancouver, BC | *CBUT-TV | CBC, 700 Hamilton St., PO Box 4600, Vancouver BC V6B 4A2 – 604/662-6000; Fax: 604/662-6414 | 2 |
| Vanderhoof, BC | CBCB-TV-1 | *See* Prince George (CKPG-TV) | 18 |
| Vanderhoof, BC | CKIN-TV-1 | *See* Burnaby (CHAN-TV) | 8 |
| Vavenby, BC | CKVA-TV-1 | *See* Burnaby (CHAN-TV) | 8 |
| Vernon, BC | CHBC-TV-2 | *See* Kelowna (CHBC-TV) | 7 |
| Vernon, BC | CHKL-TV-2 | *See* Burnaby (CHAN-TV) | 12 |
| Victoria, BC | CHEK-TV | CHEK, Division of Westcom TV Group Ltd., 780 Kings Rd., Victoria BC V8T 5A2 – 250/383-2435; Fax: 250/384-7766; URL: http://www.chek6.com | 6 |
| Wabasca, AB | CBXAT-TV-12 | *See* Edmonton (CBXT-TV) | 7 |
| Wabowden, MB | CBWMT-TV | *See* Winnipeg (CBWT-TV) | 10 |
| Wainwright, AB | CKSA-TV-3 | *See* Lloydminster (CKSA-TV) | 8 |
| Wakeman Sound, BC | CJWS-TV | *See* Victoria (CHEK-TV) | 7 |
| Waterton Park, AB | CBRT-TV-7 | *See* Calgary (CBRT-TV) | 4 |
| Waterton Park, AB | CJWP-TV-2 | *See* Calgary (CFCN-TV) | 6 |
| Wellington/Hare Bay, NF | CBNT-TV-15 | *See* St. John's (CBNT-TV) | 24 |
| Wells/Barkerville, BC | CKWB-TV | *See* Burnaby (CHAN-TV) | 11 |
| Wesleyville, NF | CBNT-TV-9 | *See* St. John's (CBNT-TV) | 5 |
| Westwold, BC | CHBC-TV | *See* Kelowna (CHBC-TV) | 12 |
| Whistler, BC | CBUWT-TV | *See* Vancouver (CBUT-TV) | 13 |
| Whitecourt, AB | CFRN-TV-3 | *See* Edmonton (CFRN-TV) | 12 |
| Whitecourt, AB | CBXT-TV-2 | *See* Edmonton (CBXT-TV) | 8 |
| Wiarton, ON | CBLN-TV-5 | *See* Toronto (CBLT-TV) | 20 |
| Williams Lake, BC | CFJC-TV-5 | *See* Kamloops (CFJC-TV) | 8 |
| Williams Lake, BC | CITM-TV-1 | *See* Burnaby (CHAN-TV) | 13 |
| Willow Bunch, SK | CBKT-TV-2 | *See* Regina (CBKT-TV) | 10 |
| Windsor, ON | CHWI-TV | Baton Broadcasting Inc., 75 Riverside Dr. West, Windsor ON N9A 7C4 – 519/977-7432; Fax: 519/977-0564 | 16 |
| Windsor, ON | CKCO-TV | *See* Kitchener (CKCO-TV) | 42 |
| Windsor, ON | *CBET-TV | CBC, 825 Riverside Dr. West, PO Box 1609, Windsor ON N9A 1K7 – 519/255-3411; Fax: 519/255-3403 | 9 |
| Windsor, ON | *†CBEFT-TV | Société Radio-Canada, 825 Riverside Dr. West, CP 1609, Windsor ON N9A 1K7 – 519/255-3411; Fax: 519/255-3573 | 54 |
| Wingham, ON | CBLN-TV-4 | *See* Toronto (CBLT-TV) | 45 |
| Wingham, ON | CKNX-TV | South West Ontario Television Inc., 215 Carling Terrace, PO Box 100, Wingham ON N0G 1W0 – 519/357-4438; Fax: 519/357-4398 | 8 |
| Winlaw, BC | CBUCT-TV-3 | *See* Vancouver (CBUT-TV) | 12 |
| Winnipeg, MB | CKND-TV | CanWest Television Inc., 603 St. Mary's Rd., Winnipeg MB R2M 3L8 – 204/233-3304; Fax: 204/233-5615 | 9 |
| Winnipeg, MB | CKY-TV | Moffat Communications Ltd., Polo Park, Winnipeg MB R3G 0L7 – 204/788-3300; Fax: 204/788-3399 | 7 |
| Winnipeg, MB | CHMI-TV | Craig Broadcast Systems Inc., #100, 167 Lombard Ave., Winnipeg MB R3B 0T6 – 204/947-9613; Fax: 204/956-0811 | 13 |
| Winnipeg, MB | *CBWT-TV | CBC, 541 Portage Ave., PO Box 160, Winnipeg MB R3C 2H1 – 204/788-3222; Fax: 204/788-3167 | 6 |
| Winnipeg, MB | *†CBWFT-TV | Société Radio-Canada, 541 Portage Ave., CP 160, Winnipeg MB R3C 2H1 – 204/788-3141; Fax: 204/788-3639 | 3 |
| Wynyard, SK | CHSS-TV | *See* Yorkton (CKOS-TV) | 6 |
| Yarmouth, NS | CJCH-TV-7 | *See* Halifax (CJCH-TV) | 40 |
| Yarmouth, NS | CBHT-TV-3 | *See* Halifax (CBHT-TV) | 11 |
| Yellowknife, NT | CABL-TV | Northwestel Cable Inc., PO Box 1469, Yellowknife NT X1A 2P1 – 867/669-5469; Fax: 867/920-2331 | 2 |
| Yellowknife, NT | *CFYK-TV | CBC, PO Box 160, Yellowknife NT X1A 2N2 – 867/920-5400; Fax: 867/920-5489 | 8 |
| Yorkton, SK | CKOS-TV | Baton Broadcasting Inc., 95 East Broadway, Yorkton SK S3N 0L1 – 306/783-3685; Fax: 306/782-3433 | 5 |
| Yorkton, SK | CICC-TV | Baton Broadcasting Inc., 95 East Broadway, Yorkton SK S3N 0L1 – 306/783-3685; Fax: 306/782-3433 | 10 |

## SPECIALTY & PAY SERVICES

A&E Television Networks, 235 East 45 St., New York NY 10017 USA – 212/210-9104; Fax: 212/210-1303

Access - The Education Station, 3720 - 76 Ave., Edmonton AB T6B 2N9 – 403/440-7777; Fax: 403/440-8899; Email: access@incentre.net

Arts et Divertissement, 2100, rue Ste-Catherine ouest, Montréal QC H3H 2T3 – 514/939-3150; Fax: 514/939-3151

Asian Television Network, 130 Pony Dr., Newmarket ON L3Y 7B6 – 905/836-6460; Fax: 905/853-5212

Bravo!, The New Style Arts Channel, 299 Queen St. West, Toronto ON M5V 2Z5 – 416/591-5757; Fax: 416/340-7005; Email: bravospeakers@bravo.ca

Broadcast News Ltd., 36 King St. East, Toronto ON M5C 2L9 – 416/364-3172; Fax: 416/364-8896

C-SPAN (National Cable Satellite Corporation), #650, 400 North Capitol St. NW, Washington DC 20001 USA – 202/737-3220; Fax: 202/737-3323

Canadian Home Shopping Network (CHSN), 1400 Castlefield Ave., Toronto ON M6B 4H8 – 416/785-3500; Fax: 416/785-1300

Canadian Satellite Communications Ltd. (CANCOM), 50 Burnhamthorpe Rd. West, 10th Fl., Mississauga

ON L5B 3C2 – 416/272-4960; Fax: 416/272-3399; Email: pdumas@cancom.ca

Canal D, #800, 2100, rue Sainte-Catherine ouest, Montréal QC H3H 2T3 – 514/939-3150; Fax: 514/939-3151; Email: rpc@rpchoix.com

Canal Famille, #800, 2100, rue Ste-Catherine ouest, Montréal QC H3H 2T3 – 514/939-3150; Fax: 514/939-3151; Email: rpc@rpchoix.com

Canal Indigo, #900, 2100, rue Ste-Catherine ouest, Montréal QC H3H 2T3 – 514/939-5090; Fax: 514/939-5098

Canal Vie, 1717, boul René-Lévesque est, Montréal QC H2L 4E8 – 514/529-3210; Fax: 514/529-3219

CBC Newsworld, PO Box 500, Stn A, Toronto ON M5W 1E6 – 416/205-2950; Fax: 416/205-6080; Email: nwonline@toronto.cloc.ca

The Classic Channel, BCE Place, #100, 181 Bay St., PO Box 707, Toronto ON M5J 2T3 – 416/965-2010; Fax: 416/965-2015

CNN (Cable News Network), 1 CNN Center, Atlanta GA 30348-5366 USA – 404/827-2039; Fax: 404/827-2478; http://www.cnn.com

The Comedy Network, , Stn OToronto ON M4A 2M9 – 416/299-2000; Fax: 416/299-2653

Country Music Television, 49 Ontario St., 5th Fl, Toronto ON M5A 2V1 – 416/360-4626; Fax: 416/360-6263

The Discovery Channel, #100, 2225 Sheppard Ave. East, North York ON M2J 5C2 – 416/494-2929; Fax: 416/490-7067; Email: comments@discovery.ca

Fairchild Television Ltd., 35 East Beaver Creek Rd., Richmond Hill ON L4B 1B3 – 905/889-8090; Fax: 905/882-7120

The Family Channel Inc., BCE Place, 181 Bay St., PO Box 787, Toronto ON M5J 2T3 – 416/956-2030; Fax: 416/956-2035; Email: info@familychannel.ca

Headline Sports, #304, 370 King St. West, Toronto ON M5V 1J9 – 416/977-6787; Fax: 416/977-0238

HGTV Canada, 1155 Leslie St., Toronto ON M3C 2J6 – 416/444-9494; Fax: 416/444-0018

History Television Inc., #200, 121 Bloor St. East, Toronto ON M4W 3M5 – 416/967-0022; Fax: 416/967-0044

House of Commons Broadcasting Service, 180 Wellington St., PO Box 1036, Ottawa ON K1A 0A6 – 613/995-3490; Fax: 613/995-1496

Kaledioscope - America's Disability Channel, #300, 1777 NE Loop 410, San Antonio TX 78217 USA – 210/824-7446; Fax: 210/829-1388; TDD: 210/824-1666

Le Canal Nouvelles, 1600, boul de Maisonneuve est, Montréal QC H2L 4P2 – 514/526-9251; Fax: 514/598-6071

Le réseau de l'information (RDI), 1400, boul René-Lévesque est, Montréal QC H2L32C 3A8 – 514/597-7734; Fax: 514/597-5977

Le Reseau des Sports (RDS), #300, 1755, boul René-Lévesque est, Montréal QC H2K 4P6 – 514/599-2244; Fax: 514/599-2299

The Learning Channel, 7700 Wisconsin Ave., Bethesda MD 20814 USA – 301/986-0444; Fax: 301/986-4829

Les Réseaux Premier Choix, #800, 2100, rue Ste-Catherine ouest, Montréal QC H3H 2T3 – 514/939-3150; Fax: 514/939-3151; Email: rpc@rpchoix.xom

Life Network, 1155 Leslie St., Toronto ON M3C 2J6 – 416/444-9494; Fax: 416/444-0018; Email: info@lifenet.ca

MétéoMédia, #251, 1755, boul René-Lévesque est, Montréal QC H2K 4P6 – 514/597-1700; Fax: 514/597-0428

MovieMax, Division of Allarcom Pay Television Ltd., #200, 5324 Calgary Trail, Edmonton AB T6H 4J8 – 403/430-2800; Fax: 403/437-3188

MOVIEPIX (TMN Networks Inc., Astral Communications Company), 181 Bay St., PO Box 787, Toronto ON M5J 2T3 – 416/956-2010; Fax: 416/956-2012; Email: tmnpix@tmn.ca

MuchMusic Network, 299 Queen St. West, Toronto ON M5V 2Z5 – 416/591-5757; Fax: 416/340-7005

Musiqueplus, 209, rue Ste-Catherine est, Montréal QC H2X 1L2 – 514/284-7587; Fax: 514/284-1889

The Nashville Network (TNN), c/o Group Satellite Communications, 250 Harbor Dr., Stamford CT 06904-2210 USA – 203/965-6000; Fax: 203/965-6315

Odyssey, 437 Danforth Ave., Toronto ON M4K 1P1 – 416/465-1112; Fax: 416/465-6592

Ontario Parliament Network Broadcast & Recording Service, Legislative Assembly, Queen's Park, Toronto ON M7A 1A2 – 416/325-7900; Fax: 416/325-7916

Outdoor Life, , Stn OToronto ON M4A 2M9 – 416/299-2000; Fax: 416/299-2653

Premier Choix Networks Inc., 2100, rue Ste-Catherine ouest, Montréal QC H3H 2T3 – 514/939-3150; Fax: 514/939-3151

Prime, 81 Barber Greene Rd., Don Mills ON M3C 2A2 – 416/446-5311; Fax: 416/446-5544

RadioTélévision des débats de l'Assemblée nationale, #2.14, Édifice Pamphile-Le May, Québec QC G1A 1A3 – 418/643-9448; Fax: 418/646-8498

Report on Business Television (ROBTv), 50 Burnhamthorpe Rd., 10th Fl., Mississauga ON L5B 3C2 – 905/272-4960; Fax: 905/272-3399

Saskatchewan Legislative Assembly Broadcast Services, #123 Legislative Bldg., Regina SK S4S 0B3 – 306/787-2181; Fax: 306/787-1558

Showcase Television Inc., #200, 121 Bloor St. East, Toronto ON M4W 3M5 – 416/967-0022; Fax: 416/967-0044; Email: drama@showcase.ca

The Sports Network (TSN), #100, 2225 Sheppard Ave. East, North York ON M2J 5C2 – 416/494-1212; Fax: 416/490-7040

Sportscope Television Network, #104, 590 Alden Rd., Markham ON L3R 8N2 – 905/477-6787; Fax: 905/477-5547

Super Écran, #800, 2100, rue Sainte-Catherine ouest, Montréal QC H3H 2T3 – 514/939-3150; Fax: 514/939-3151; Email: rpc@rpchoix.com

Superchannel, Division of Allarcom Pay Television Ltd., #200, 5324 Calgary Trail, Edmonton AB T6H 4J8 – 403/430-2800; Fax: 403/437-3188

Talentvision TV, #B8, 525 West Broadway, Vancouver BC V5Z 4K5 – 604/708-1328; Fax: 604/708-1333

Talk TV, , Stn OToronto ON M4A 2M9 – 416/299-2000; Fax: 416/299-2653

Telelatino Network Inc., 5125 Steeles Ave. West, North York ON M9L 1R5 – 416/744-8200; Fax: 416/744-0966

TELETOON, BCE Place, 181 Bay St., Toronto ON M5J 2T3 – 416/956-2060; Fax: 416/956-2070

TMN The Movie Network, BCE Place, #100, 181 Bay St., PO Box 787, Toronto ON M5J 2T3 – 416/956-2010; Fax: 416/956-2018; Email: tmnpix@tmn.ca

TV5, La Télévision Internationale, #101, 1755, boul René-Lévesque est, Montréal QC H2K 4P6 – 514/522-5322; Fax: 514/522-6572; Email: tv5@tv5.org

Viewer's Choice Canada, BCE Place, 181 Bay St., PO Box 787, Toronto ON M5J 2G3 – 416/956-2010; Fax: 416/956-5399

Vision TV (Canada's Faith Network), 80 Bond St., Toronto ON M5B 1X2 – 416/368-3194; Fax: 416/368-9774

The Weather Network, #200, 186 Robert Speck Pkwy., Mississauga ON L4Z 3G1 – 905/566-9511; Fax: 905/566-7012

Women's Television Network (WTN), #300, 1661 Portage Ave., Winnipeg MB R3J 3T7 – 204/783-5116; Fax: 204/774-3227; Email: wtn@web.apc.org

YTV Canada Inc., #18, 64 Jefferson Ave., Toronto ON M6K 3H3 – 416/534-1191; Fax: 416/533-0346; Email: info@ytv.ca

## CABLE STATIONS

### BY TRANSMITTING LOCATION

Abbotsford, BC . . . . . . . . . . . . . . . . Rogers Cablesystems, 31450 Marshall Rd., PO Box 2125, Stn Clearbrook, Abbotsford BC V2T 3X8 – 604/858-0776; Fax: 604/850-2517
Acadieville, NB . . . . . . . . . . . . . . . . *See* Fundy Cable TV Ltd./ltée, Newcastle
Acton, ON. . . . . . . . . . . . . . . . . . . . . Halton Cable Systems Inc., 21 Main St. North, Acton ON L7J 1V9 – 519/853-1270; Fax: 519/853-1731; Email: info@western.on.ca
Acton, ON. . . . . . . . . . . . . . . . . . . . . *See* Western Co-Axial Limited, Hamilton
Albanel, QC . . . . . . . . . . . . . . . . . . . Télécâble Albanel inc., 95, rue Industrielle, Albanel QC G0W 1A0 – 418/279-5702; Fax: 418/279-3113
Albert Bridge, NS . . . . . . . . . . . . . . *See* Seaside Cable TV (1984) Ltd., Glace Bay
Alberton, PE. . . . . . . . . . . . . . . . . . . *See* Island Cablevision Ltd., Charlottetown
Alexandria, ON . . . . . . . . . . . . . . . . *See* Rogers Cablesystems Ottawa, Ottawa
Alfred, ON . . . . . . . . . . . . . . . . . . . . *See* Rogers Cablesystems Ottawa, Ottawa
Allan, SK. . . . . . . . . . . . . . . . . . . . . . *See* Shaw Cable Saskatoon, Saskatoon
Allanburg, ON . . . . . . . . . . . . . . . . . *See* Cogeco Cable Solutions, Niagara Falls
Allardville, NB . . . . . . . . . . . . . . . . . *See* Cable 2000 Inc., Bathurst
Allenford, ON . . . . . . . . . . . . . . . . . *See* Shaw Cable, Port Elgin
Alma, QC . . . . . . . . . . . . . . . . . . . . . Câblovision Alma inc., 590, rue Collard ouest, Alma QC G8B 1N2 – 418/668-3310; Fax: 418/668-0938
Alma, ON . . . . . . . . . . . . . . . . . . . . . *See* Saugeen Telecable Ltd., Hanover
Alouette, QC . . . . . . . . . . . . . . . . . . CFB Bagotville, Alouette QC G0V 1A0 – 418/693-2513; Fax: 418/693-2185
Altona, MB. . . . . . . . . . . . . . . . . . . . *See* Valley Cable Vision Ltd., Selkirk
Alvinston, ON . . . . . . . . . . . . . . . . . *See* AGI Cablevision Inc., Simcoe
Amos, QC. . . . . . . . . . . . . . . . . . . . . Télédistribution Amos inc., 27, rue Principale nord, Amos QC J9T 2K7 – 819/732-5570; Fax: 819/732-9282; Email: dufresne@leiro.com
Angers/Masson, QC. . . . . . . . . . . . . *See* Télécâble Laurentien inc., Hull
Arnprior, ON . . . . . . . . . . . . . . . . . . *See* Rogers Cablesystems Ottawa, Ottawa
Assiniboia, SK . . . . . . . . . . . . . . . . . *See* Shaw Cable Moose Jaw., Moose Jaw

Atikokan, ON ................. Videon, 120 Marks St., PO Box 1840, Atikokan ON P0T 1C0 – 807/597-6050; Fax: 807/597-4554
Atikokan, ON ................. *See* Videon CableSystems Inc., Winnipeg
Aurora, ON ................... Aurora Cable TV Ltd., 350 Industrial Pkwy. South, PO Box 547, Aurora ON L4G 3H3 – 905/727-1981; Fax: 905/727-7407
Aylmer, ON.................... *See* AGI Cablevision Inc., Simcoe
Ayton, ON..................... *See* Saugeen Telecable Ltd., Hanover
Baddeck, NS .................. *See* Seaside Cable TV (1984) Ltd., Glace Bay
Baie-St-Paul, QC.............. *See* Vidéo Dery ltée, La Baie
Baie-Ste-Anne, NB............. *See* Fundy Cable TV Ltd./ltée, Newcastle
Bancroft, ON.................. *See* Shaw Cable, Smiths Falls
Banff, AB..................... *See* Monarch Cable TV, Canmore
Barrys Bay, ON................ *See* Shaw Cable, Smiths Falls
Bathurst, NB ................. *See* Fundy Cable Ltd./ltée, Saint John
Bathurst, NB ................. Cable 2000 Inc., PO Box 2000, Bathurst NB E2A 4W4 – 506/547-8877; Fax: 506/548-8208
Beachburg, ON................. *See* Rogers Cablesystems Ottawa, Ottawa
Bearn, QC .................... *See* Câblotem inc., Ville-Marie
Beausejour, MB................ *See* Interlake Cable TV Ltd., Selkirk
Beaverbank, NB ............... *See* Fundy Cable TV Ltd./ltée, Newcastle
Beaverlodge, AB............... Small Community TV Inc., PO Box 510, Beaverlodge AB T0H 0C0 – 403/354-2510; Fax: 403/354-8780
Beebe, QC .................... *See* Vidéotron ltée, Sherbrooke
Belgrave, ON.................. *See* Kincardine Cable TV Ltd., Kincardine
Belleville, ON ............... Cablevue (Quinte) Ltd., 10 Front St. South, PO Box 149, Belleville ON K8N 4Z9 – 613/966-3226; Fax: 613/966-8329
Bellevue, AB ................. *See* Shaw Cable, Cranbrook
Bellfond, NB ................. *See* Fundy Cable TV Ltd./ltée, Newcastle
Bengough, SK ................. *See* Shaw Cable Moose Jaw., Moose Jaw
Benito, MB.................... *See* Westman Cable TV, Brandon
Big Cove, NB.................. *See* Fundy Cable TV Ltd./ltée, Newcastle
Binscarth, MB ................ *See* Westman Cable TV, Brandon
Birch River, MB .............. *See* Westman Cable TV, Brandon
Birtle, MB ................... *See* Westman Cable TV, Brandon
Blackville, NB ............... *See* Fundy Cable TV Ltd./ltée, Newcastle
Block House, NS............... Bragg Communications Inc., PO Box 84, Block House NS B0J 1E0 – 902/624-8305; Fax: 902/543-6582
Blyth, ON..................... *See* Mitchell-Seaforth Cable TV Ltd., Dryden
Boissevain, MB ............... *See* Westman Cable TV, Brandon
Borden, PE.................... *See* Island Cablevision Ltd., Charlottetown
Bothwell, ON.................. *See* AGI Cablevision Inc., Simcoe
Botwood, NF .................. *See* Cable Atlantic Inc., St. John's
Bourget, ON .................. *See* Rogers Cablesystems Ottawa, Ottawa
Bowsman, MB................... *See* Westman Cable TV, Brandon
Brampton, ON.................. Rogers Community 10, 13 Hansen Rd. South, Brampton ON L6W 3H6 – 905/457-3270; Fax: 905/456-1067
Brandon, MB................... Westman Cable TV, 1906 Park Ave., Brandon MB R7B 0R9 – 204/725-4300; Fax: 204/728-9288; Email: cathcart@wmcl.com
Brantford, ON................. *See* Rogers Cablesystems, Oshawa
Brechin, ON................... Bayshore Village Association Cable TV, Hayloft Lane, RR#3, Brechin ON L0K 1B0 – 705/484-0754
Bredenbury, SK................ *See* North Eastern Cablevision Ltd., Yorkton
Brockville, ON................ Brockville Cable, 205 King St. West, Brockville ON K6V 3R7 – 613/342-2640
Brownsville, ON .............. *See* AGI Cablevision Inc., Simcoe
Bruno, SK..................... *See* Shaw Cable Saskatoon, Saskatoon
Brussels, ON ................. *See* Mitchell-Seaforth Cable TV Ltd., Dryden
Buckingham, QC................ *See* Télécâble Laurentien inc., Hull
Buctouche, NB ................ *See* Fundy Cable TV Ltd./ltée, Newcastle
Burnaby, BC .................. West Coast Cablevision Ltd., 6665 Hastings St. East, Burnaby BC V5B 1S4 – 604/291-6691; Fax: 604/291-2944
Burnt Islands, NF ............ *See* Cable Atlantic Inc., St. John's
Caledon, ON .................. *See* Shaw Cable, Orangeville
Calgary, AB................... Shaw Cable, 2001 - 27 Ave. NE, PO Box 90, Stn J, Calgary AB T2A 6T9 – 403/250-8080; Fax: 403/291-0880
Calgary, AB................... Calgary Cable TV/FM, PO Box 90, Stn J, Calgary AB T2A 6T9 – 403/250-8080; Fax: 403/291-0880
Calgary, AB................... Rogers Cable TV, 3003 Macleod Trail SW, Calgary AB T2G 2P8 – 403/261-4200; Fax: 403/263-6076
Cambridge, NS ................ *See* Cross Country TV Ltd., Canning
Campbell River, BC............ Campbell River TV Association, 500 Robron Rd., Campbell River BC V9W 5Z2 – 250/923-8899; Fax: 250/923-7796; Email: forsyth@cr.iscanv.net
Campbell's Bay, QC............ Pontiac Cable Co. Inc., CP 217, Campbell's Bay QC J0X 1W7 – 819/648-2005; Fax: 819/648-5778
Canmore, AB................... Monarch Cable TV, 715 Railway Ave., PO Box 1989, Canmore AB T0L 0M0 – Fax: 403/678-5286
Canning, NS................... Cross Country TV Ltd., PO Box 310, Canning NS B0P 1H0 – 902/582-3328; Fax: 902/582-7499
Canora, SK.................... *See* North Eastern Cablevision Ltd., Yorkton
Cap-de-la-Madeleine, QC ...... Vidéotron ltée, #101, 190, rue Fusey, Cap-de-la-Madeleine QC G8T 2V8 – 819/375-7742; Fax: 819/375-8950
Cap-Lumière, NB .............. *See* Fundy Cable TV Ltd./ltée, Newcastle
Carberry, MB.................. *See* Westman Cable TV, Brandon
Cardiff, ON .................. *See* Village Cablesystems Ltd., Tweed
Carman, MB ................... *See* Valley Cable Vision Ltd., Selkirk
Carmanville, NF .............. *See* Cable Atlantic Inc., St. John's
Caroline, AB ................. *See* Monarch Cable TV, Canmore
Carp, ON ..................... *See* Rogers Cablesystems Ottawa, Ottawa
Carstairs, AB ................ *See* Monarch Cable TV, Canmore
Casselman, ON ................ Casselman Cable Co. Inc., PO Box 499, Casselman ON K0A 1M0 – 613/764-3420; Fax: 613/764-5631
Castlegar, BC................. Castlegar Shaw Cable Systems (B.C.) Ltd., 1951 Columbia Ave., Castlegar BC V1N 2W8 – 250/365-3122; Fax: 250/365-2676
Catalone, NS ................. *See* Seaside Cable TV (1984) Ltd., Glace Bay
Central Butte, SK ............ *See* Shaw Cable Moose Jaw., Moose Jaw
Chapais, QC................... *See* Vidéotron ltée, Chicoutimi
Chapleau, ON ................. Superior TV System, 17 Lorne St., Chapleau ON P0M 1K0 – 705/864-1462; Fax: 705/864-1341
Charlesbourg, QC.............. *See* Coopérative de Câblodistribution de l'Arrière-pays, Charlesbourg

Charlesbourg, QC . . . . . . . . . . . . . Coopérative de Câblodistribution de l'Arrière-pays, 860, av Notre-Dame, Charlesbourg QC G2N 1P7 – 819/849-7125; Fax: 819/849-7128; Email: arriere.pays@videotron.ca
Charlottetown, PE . . . . . . . . . . . . . Island Cablevision Ltd., 100 Cable Ct., Charlottetown PE C1B 1A9 – 902/569-4101; Fax: 902/569-4731; Email: islcable@peinet.pe.ca
Chatham, ON . . . . . . . . . . . . . . . . . Cogeco Cable, 491 Richmond St., Chatham ON N7M 1R2 – 519/352-8270; Fax: 519/352-8274; Email: chathamcableII@ciaccess.com
Chesley, ON . . . . . . . . . . . . . . . . . *See* Saugeen Telecable Ltd., Hanover
Cheticamp, NS . . . . . . . . . . . . . . . . Acadian Communications Ltd., PO Box 308, Cheticamp NS B0E 1H0 – 902/224-3204; Fax: 902/224-3000
Chibougamau, QC . . . . . . . . . . . . . *See* Vidéotron ltée, Chicoutimi
Chicoutimi, QC . . . . . . . . . . . . . . . Vidéotron ltée, 21, rue Racine ouest, CP 700, Chicoutimi QC G7H 5E1 – 418/693-9366; Fax: 418/545-6455
Chilliwack, BC . . . . . . . . . . . . . . . . *See* Lethbridge Cablenet, Lethbridge
Chilliwack, BC . . . . . . . . . . . . . . . . Chilliwack Cablenet, 9275 Nowell St., Chilliwack BC V2P 7G7 – 604/793-9944; Fax: 604/792-0966
Chipman, NB . . . . . . . . . . . . . . . . . *See* Fundy Cable Ltd. ltée, Fredericton
Churchbridge, SK. . . . . . . . . . . . . . *See* North Eastern Cablevision Ltd., Yorkton
Chute-aux-Outardes, QC . . . . . . . . Télécâble Côte-Nord inc., 113, Vallilee, Chute-aux-Outardes QC G0H 1C0 – 418/567-8404; Fax: 418/567-2106
Clarence Creek, ON . . . . . . . . . . . *See* Rogers Cablesystems Ottawa, Ottawa
Clarksburg, ON . . . . . . . . . . . . . . . *See* Rogers Cablesystems, Collingwood
Clinton, ON . . . . . . . . . . . . . . . . . . Bluewater TV Cable, RR#2, Clinton ON N0M 1L0 – 519/482-9233; Fax: 519/482-7098
Cobbs Hill, PE . . . . . . . . . . . . . . . . *See* Island Cablevision Ltd., Charlottetown
Cobden, ON . . . . . . . . . . . . . . . . . . *See* Rogers Cablesystems Ottawa, Ottawa
Cobourg, ON . . . . . . . . . . . . . . . . . Northumberland Cable TV, 9 Albert St., Cobourg ON K9A 2P7 – 905/372-2274; Fax: 905/372-2472
Collingwood, ON . . . . . . . . . . . . . . Rogers Cablesystems, 4 Sandford Fleming Dr., Collingwood ON L9Y 4V9 – 705/445-3400; Fax: 705/445-9949
Comox, BC . . . . . . . . . . . . . . . . . . . *See* Lethbridge Cablenet, Lethbridge
Consort, AB . . . . . . . . . . . . . . . . . . Progressive Cable Television Ltd., PO Box 250, Consort AB T0C 1B0 – 403/577-3550; Fax: 403/577-3503
Corner Brook, NF . . . . . . . . . . . . . *See* Cable Atlantic Inc., St. John's
Cornwall, ON . . . . . . . . . . . . . . . . . Cogeco Cable Solutions, 517 Pitt St., Cornwall ON K6J 3R4 – 613/932-5966; Fax: 613/932-3176
Courtenay, BC . . . . . . . . . . . . . . . . Comox Valley Cablenet Ltd., 1591 McPhee Ave., Courtenay BC V9N 3A6 – 250/334-0888; Fax: 250/334-3640
Courtland, ON . . . . . . . . . . . . . . . . *See* AGI Cablevision Inc., Simcoe
Cranberry Portage, MB. . . . . . . . . *See* Videon CableSystems Inc., Winnipeg
Cranbrook, BC. . . . . . . . . . . . . . . . Shaw Cable, 133 - 8 Ave. South, Cranbrook BC V1C 2K6 – 250/426-3341; Fax: 250/334-8900
Crapaud, PE . . . . . . . . . . . . . . . . . . *See* Island Cablevision Ltd., Charlottetown
Creemore, ON . . . . . . . . . . . . . . . . *See* Rogers Cablesystems, Collingwood
Cremona, AB . . . . . . . . . . . . . . . . . *See* Monarch Cable TV, Canmore
Creston, BC . . . . . . . . . . . . . . . . . . *See* Shaw Cable, Cranbrook
Crystal Beach, ON. . . . . . . . . . . . . *See* Cogeco Cable Solutions, Niagara Falls
Cudworth, SK. . . . . . . . . . . . . . . . . *See* Shaw Cable Saskatoon, Saskatoon
Dalmeny, SK. . . . . . . . . . . . . . . . . . *See* Shaw Cable Saskatoon, Saskatoon
Dartmouth, NS. . . . . . . . . . . . . . . . Access Cable Television Ltd., 190 Victoria Rd., PO Box 1011, Dartmouth NS B2Y 4A4 – 902/469-9540; Fax: 902/466-6482; Email: acc-cbl@fox.nstn.ca
Dauphin, MB . . . . . . . . . . . . . . . . . *See* Westman Cable TV, Brandon
Deer Lake, NF . . . . . . . . . . . . . . . . *See* Cable Atlantic Inc., St. John's
Delisle, SK . . . . . . . . . . . . . . . . . . . *See* Shaw Cable Saskatoon, Saskatoon
Deloraine, MB . . . . . . . . . . . . . . . . *See* Westman Cable TV, Brandon
Delta, BC . . . . . . . . . . . . . . . . . . . . Delta Cable Communications Ltd., 5381 - 48 Ave., Delta BC V4K 1W7 – 604/946-1144; Fax: 604/946-5627; Email: admin@deltacable.com
Digby, NS . . . . . . . . . . . . . . . . . . . . Access Cable Television Ltd., 88 Warwick St., Digby NS B0V 1A0 – 902/245-2519; Fax: 902/245-6511
Doaktown, NB . . . . . . . . . . . . . . . . *See* Fundy Cable Ltd. ltée, Fredericton
Dolbeau, QC. . . . . . . . . . . . . . . . . . *See* Vidéotron ltée, Chicoutimi
Drayton, ON. . . . . . . . . . . . . . . . . . *See* Saugeen Telecable Ltd., Hanover
Drummondville, QC . . . . . . . . . . . Drummondville Câblestrie inc., 1960, boul Lemire, Drummondville QC J2B 6X5 – 819/477-8687; Fax: 819/474-5313
Dryden, ON . . . . . . . . . . . . . . . . . . *See* Videon, Atikokan
Dryden, ON . . . . . . . . . . . . . . . . . . Dryden Video Cable, 75 Queen St., Dryden ON P8N 1A1 – 807/223-5525; Fax: 807/223-4445
Dryden, ON . . . . . . . . . . . . . . . . . . *See* Videon CableSystems Inc., Winnipeg
Dublin, ON. . . . . . . . . . . . . . . . . . . Mitchell-Seaforth Cable TV Ltd., 123 Ontario St., Dryden ON N0K 1E0 – 519/345-2341; Fax: 519/345-2873
Durham, ON. . . . . . . . . . . . . . . . . . *See* Saugeen Telecable Ltd., Hanover
Earlton, ON . . . . . . . . . . . . . . . . . . Earlton Cable Vision Ltd., 7 - 12th Ave. South, Earlton ON P0J 1E0 – 705/563-2698
Edmonton, AB. . . . . . . . . . . . . . . . Regional Cable TV (Western) Inc., 3552 - 78th Ave., Edmonton AB T6B 2X9 – 403/440-2525; Fax: 403/440-2828; Email: wrct@oanet.com
Edmonton, AB. . . . . . . . . . . . . . . . Shaw Cablesystems (Alberta) Ltd., 7633 - 50 St., Edmonton AB T6B 2W9 – 403/468-7115; Fax: 403/465-6405
Edmonton, AB. . . . . . . . . . . . . . . . Videotron Communications Ltd., 10450 - 178 St., Edmonton AB T5S 1S2 – Fax: 403/483-1732
Edmundston, NB . . . . . . . . . . . . . . *See* Fundy Cable Ltd./ltée, Saint John
Elie, MB . . . . . . . . . . . . . . . . . . . . . *See* Videon CableSystems Inc., Winnipeg
Elkhorn, MB. . . . . . . . . . . . . . . . . . *See* Westman Cable TV, Brandon
Elliot Lake, ON . . . . . . . . . . . . . . . *See* Northern Cable Holdings Ltd., Sudbury
Elmsdale, PE . . . . . . . . . . . . . . . . . *See* Island Cablevision Ltd., Charlottetown
Elmwood, ON. . . . . . . . . . . . . . . . . *See* Saugeen Telecable Ltd., Hanover
Embro, ON . . . . . . . . . . . . . . . . . . . *See* AGI Cablevision Inc., Simcoe
Erickson, MB . . . . . . . . . . . . . . . . . *See* Westman Cable TV, Brandon
Esterhazy, SK . . . . . . . . . . . . . . . . *See* North Eastern Cablevision Ltd., Yorkton
Estevan, SK. . . . . . . . . . . . . . . . . . *See* Lethbridge Cablenet, Lethbridge
Exshaw, AB . . . . . . . . . . . . . . . . . . *See* Monarch Cable TV, Canmore
Fabre, QC . . . . . . . . . . . . . . . . . . . . *See* Câblotem inc., Ville-Marie
Faro, YT . . . . . . . . . . . . . . . . . . . . . *See* Northern Television Systems Ltd., Whitehorse
Fenelon Falls, ON . . . . . . . . . . . . . Cable Cable Inc., RR#3, Fenelon Falls ON K0M 1M0 – 705/887-4563; Fax: 705/887-2580; Email: tonyfior@kawartha.net
Fenelon Falls, ON . . . . . . . . . . . . . Bobcaygeon Cable Inc., RR#3, Fenelon Falls ON K0M 1N0 – 705/887-6433; Fax: 705/887-2580
Fenwick, ON. . . . . . . . . . . . . . . . . . *See* Cogeco Cable Solutions, Niagara Falls
Fergus, ON . . . . . . . . . . . . . . . . . . . Fergus-Elora Cable TV Ltd., 475 St. Patrick St. West, Fergus ON N1M 1M2 – 519/843-3700; Fax: 519/843-2312
Fergus, ON . . . . . . . . . . . . . . . . . . . *See* Western Co-Axial Limited, Hamilton
Fleurimont, QC . . . . . . . . . . . . . . . Transvision Paré inc., 2175, ch Champigny, Fleurimont QC J1H 5H2 – 819/821-2021; Fax: 819/821-0231
Flin Flon, ON . . . . . . . . . . . . . . . . . *See* Videon CableSystems Inc., Winnipeg
Fonthill, ON . . . . . . . . . . . . . . . . . . *See* Cogeco Cable Solutions, Niagara Falls
Fort Erie, ON . . . . . . . . . . . . . . . . . *See* Cogeco Cable Solutions, Niagara Falls

Fort Frances, ON .............. *See* Videon CableSystems Inc., Winnipeg
Fort McMurray, AB ............ Shaw Cable, #200, 208 Beaconhill Dr., Fort McMurray AB T9H 2R1 – 403/743-3717; Fax: 403/790-1193
Fredericton, NB................ *See* Fundy Cable Ltd./ltée, Saint John
Fredericton, NB................ Fundy Cable Ltd. ltée, PO Box 1569, Fredericton NB E3B 5B1 – 506/453-1000; Fax: 506/452-2846
Gander, NF ................... *See* Cable Atlantic Inc., St. John's
Ganges, BC ................... Saltspring Cablevision (1981) Ltd., PO Box 300, PO Ganges, Salt Spring Island BC V8K 2V9 – 250/537-5550; Fax: 250/537-5550
Gaspé, QC .................... Câblo Distribution G. inc., 494, montée Wakeham, CP 1720, Gaspé QC G0C 1R0 – 418/368-3636; Fax: 418/368-7759
Georgetown, ON............... *See* Halton Cable Systems Inc., Acton
Georgetown, PE ............... *See* Island Cablevision Ltd., Charlottetown
Geraldton, ON................. Astrocom Cablevision Inc., 112 - 3 Ave. NE, PO Box 910, Geraldton ON P0T 1M0 – 807/854-1569; Fax: 807/854-2169
Gibsons, BC................... Coast Cable Communications Ltd., PO Box 218, Sechelt BC V0N 3A0 – 604/885-3224; Fax: 604/885-3203
Gilbert Plains, MB ............ *See* Westman Cable TV, Brandon
Glace Bay, NS ................. Seaside Cable TV (1984) Ltd., 1318 Grand Lake Rd., PO Box 279, Glace Bay NS B1A 5V4 – 902/539-6250; Fax: 902/539-2597; Email: hwoodman@highlander.cbnet.ns.ca
Gladstone, MB ................ *See* Westman Cable TV, Brandon
Glen Valley, PE................ *See* Island Cablevision Ltd., Charlottetown
Glenboro, MB ................. *See* Westman Cable TV, Brandon
Glencoe, ON .................. *See* AGI Cablevision Inc., Simcoe
Glovertown, NF................ Glovertown Cable TV Ltd., PO Box 131, Glovertown NF A0G 2L0 – 709/533-2377; Fax: 709/533-2702
Gorrie, ON.................... *See* Kincardine Cable TV Ltd., Kincardine
Granby, QC ................... Maxi Transvision inc., 210, St-Urbain, CP 10000, Granby QC J2G 9H7 – 514/378-7905; Fax: 514/372-5464
Grand Bend, ON............... *See* Mitchell-Seaforth Cable TV Ltd., Dryden
Grand Falls-Windsor, NF........ *See* Cable Atlantic Inc., St. John's
Grandview, MB ................ *See* Westman Cable TV, Brandon
Gravenhurst, ON............... Gravenhurst Cable System Ltd., 205 Jones Rd., Gravenhurst ON P1P 1M8 – 705/687-2256; Fax: 705/687-4789
Grimsby, ON .................. *See* Western Co-Axial Limited, Hamilton
Guelph, ON ................... Rogers Cablesystems, 18 Macdonnell St., Guelph ON N1H 6M1 – 519/824-2030; Fax: 519/824-4210
Guigues, QC .................. *See* Câblotem inc., Ville-Marie
Halifax, NS.................... Halifax Cable Ltd., PO Box 8660, Stn A, Halifax NS B3K 5M3 – 902/453-2800; Fax: 902/454-9159
Hamilton, ON ................. Rogers Cablesystems, #105, 135 James St. South, Hamilton ON L8P 2Z6 – 905/522-0123; Fax: 905/522-2420
Hamilton, ON ................. Mountain Cablevision Ltd., 141 Hester St., Hamilton ON L9A 2N9 – 905/389-1347; Fax: 905/574-6330; Email: jking@mountain.wave.ca
Hamilton, ON ................. Rogers Cablesystems, 695 Lawrence Rd., Hamilton ON L8K 6P1 – 905/547-7836; Fax: 905/547-5237
Hamilton, ON ................. TV Hamilton, 150 Dundurn St. South, Hamilton ON L8P 4K3 – 905/523-1414; Fax: 905/523-8141; Email: cable14@interlynx.net
Hamilton, ON ................. *See* Western Co-Axial Limited, Hamilton
Hamilton, ON ................. Western Co-Axial Limited, 1603 Main St. West, Hamilton ON L8S 1E6 – 905/522-3012; Fax: 905/522-1044; Email: info@western.on.ca
Hamiota, MB.................. *See* Westman Cable TV, Brandon
Hanover, ON.................. Saugeen Telecable Ltd., 111 - 7 Ave., Hanover ON N4N 2G8 – 519/364-2131; Fax: 519/364-4380
Happy Valley-Goose Bay, NF.... Northern Television Services Ltd., PO Box 879, Stn B, Happy Valley-Goose Bay NF A0P 1E0 – 709/896-5519; Fax: 709/896-0239
Happy Valley-Goose Bay, NF.... CF Cable, PO Box 148, Stn A, Happy Valley-Goose Bay NF A0P 1S0 – 709/896-2888; Fax: 709/989-7371
Harbour Grace, NF............. Andromeda Cablevision Ltd., PO Box 500, Harbour Grace NF A0A 2M0 – 709/596-7302; Fax: 709/596-2440
Harbour Grace, NF............. Community Cable Ltd., 410 Harvey St., PO Box 500, Harbour Grace NF A0A 2M0 – 709/596-7302; Fax: 709/596-2440
Harmony Junction, PE.......... *See* Island Cablevision Ltd., Charlottetown
Hawkesbury, ON............... Cogeco Cable Canada Inc., 1444 Aberdeen St., Hawkesbury ON K6A 1K7 – 613/632-2514; Fax: 613/632-8531
Hazelton, BC.................. *See* Skeena Cablevision, Terrace
Headingley, MB ............... *See* Videon CableSystems Inc., Winnipeg
Hensall, ON................... *See* Mitchell-Seaforth Cable TV Ltd., Dryden
High Prairie, AB ............... KBS TV, PO Box 1222, High Prairie AB T0G 1E0 – 403/523-3223; Fax: 403/523-3411
Hillsburgh, ON ................ *See* Shaw Cable, Orangeville
Holland Gardens, MB .......... *See* Valley Cable Vision Ltd., Selkirk
Holstein, ON .................. *See* Saugeen Telecable Ltd., Hanover
Hope, BC..................... Hope Cable Television, 380 Wallace St., PO Box 489, Hope BC V0X 1L0 – 604/869-2616; Fax: 604/869-9393
Houston, BC .................. *See* Skeena Cablevision, Terrace
Hull, QC...................... Télécâble Laurentien inc., 190, rue Edmonton, Hull QC J8Y 3S6 – 819/771-7717; Fax: 819/770-6112
Hunter River, PE .............. *See* Island Cablevision Ltd., Charlottetown
Huntsville, ON................. Huntsville Cable Services Ltd., 20 West St. South, Huntsville ON P1H 1P2 – 705/789-9801; Fax: 705/789-2331
Ile a la Crosse, SK.............. Bellanger Communications Inc., PO Box 304, Ile a la Crosse SK S0M 1C0 – 306/833-2173; Fax: 306/833-2132
Ile des Chenes, MB............. *See* Valley Cable Vision Ltd., Selkirk
Imperial, SK................... Imperial Cable System, PO Box 90, Imperial SK S0G 2J0 – 306/963-2220
Inuvik, NT ................... Inuvik TV Ltd., PO Box 2338, Inuvik NT X0E 0T0 – 867/979-2111; Fax: 867/979-3412
Isles-aux-Morts, NF ........... *See* Cable Atlantic Inc., St. John's
Kamloops, BC................. Kamloops Cablenet, 180 Briar Ave., Kamloops BC V2B 1C1 – 250/376-8888; Fax: 250/376-2544
Kamsack, SK .................. *See* North Eastern Cablevision Ltd., Yorkton
Kapuskasing, ON .............. *See* Northern Cable Holdings Ltd., Sudbury
Kaslo, BC..................... Kaslo Cable Ltd., PO Box 637, Kaslo BC V0G 1M0 – 250/353-2547
Kelowna, BC .................. Shaw Cablesystems (B.C.) Ltd., 2350 Hunter Rd., Kelowna BC V1X 7H6 – 250/762-4433; Fax: 250/762-7997
Kemptville, ON................ *See* Shaw Cable, Smiths Falls
Kenora, ON .................. Norcom Telecommunications Ltd., PO Box 1810, Kenora ON P9N 3X8 – 807/547-2853; Fax: 807/547-2236
Killarney, MB ................ *See* Westman Cable TV, Brandon
Kincardine, ON................ Kincardine Cable TV Ltd., 223 Bruce Ave., Kincardine ON N2Z 2P2 – 519/396-7802; Fax: 519/396-2599
Kingston, ON.................. Kingston Cablenet, 170 Colborne St., PO Bag 5500, Kingston ON K7L 5M7 – 613/544-6311; Fax: 613/545-0169
Kinistino, SK .................. Kinistino Cable TV Ltd., PO Box 10, Kinistino SK S0J 1H0 – 306/864-2461; Fax: 306/864-2880
Kitchener, ON................. Rogers Cablesystems, 85 Grand Crest Pl., PO Box 488, Kitchener ON N2G 4A8 – 519/893-2101; Fax: 519/893-7857
Kitimat, BC .................. *See* Skeena Cablevision, Terrace
La Baie, QC................... Vidéo Dery ltée, 524, rue Albert, La Baie QC G7B 3P3 – 418/544-3358; Fax: 418/544-0187
La Dore, QC .................. *See* Vidéotron ltée, Chicoutimi
La Pocatière, QC............... Câblodistribution de la Côte du Sud inc., 88, av 11e, CP 500, La Pocatière QC G0R 1Z0 – 418/856-2253; Fax: 418/856-4772
La Ronge, SK ................. Cable Ronge Inc., PO Box 1397, La Ronge SK S0J 1L0 – 306/425-2276; Fax: 306/425-2042
La Tûque, QC ................. Electro-Vision (La Tûque) inc., 333, rue St-Joseph, La Tûque QC G9X 1L3 – 819/523-3737; Fax: 819/523-3506

Labrador City, NF .............. Community Recreation Rebroadcasting Service Association/CRRS TV, Carol Lake Shopping Centre, Labrador City NF A2V 1L1 – 709/944-7676; Fax: 709/944-7675
Lac Beauport, QC .............. *See* Coopérative de Câblodistribution de l'Arrière-pays, Charlesbourg
Lac Delage, QC .............. *See* Coopérative de Câblodistribution de l'Arrière-pays, Charlesbourg
Lac Megantic, QC .............. Megantic Transvision inc., 5084, rue Frontenac, Lac-Megantic QC G6B 1H3 – 819/583-0432; Fax: 819/583-0454
Lac St-Charles, QC .............. *See* Coopérative de Câblodistribution de l'Arrière-pays, Charlesbourg
Lachenaie, QC .............. Télécâble des Mille-Îles inc., 940, montée Masson, Lachenaie QC J6W 2C9 – 514/471-2710; Fax: 514/471-5811
Lachute, QC .............. Communi-Cable inc., 330, rue Bethany, Lachute QC J8H 2N2 – 514/562-4059; Fax: 514/562-2213
Lafleche, SK .............. *See* Shaw Cable Moose Jaw., Moose Jaw
Lakefield, ON .............. *See* Shaw Cable, Smiths Falls
Lanark, ON .............. *See* Shaw Cable, Smiths Falls
Lancaster, ON .............. *See* Rogers Cablesystems Ottawa, Ottawa
Langton, ON .............. *See* AGI Cablevision Inc., Simcoe
L'Ardoise, NS .............. *See* Seaside Cable TV (1984) Ltd., Glace Bay
Leamington, ON .............. Trillium Cable Communications, 94 Talbot St. East, Leamington ON N8H 1L3 – 519/326-4423; Fax: 519/326-5666
Lethbridge, AB .............. Lethbridge Cablenet, 1232 - 3 Ave. South, Lethbridge AB T1J 0J9 – 403/328-2002; Fax: 403/329-4482
Limoges, ON .............. *See* Rogers Cablesystems Ottawa, Ottawa
Lindsay, ON .............. Lindsay Comcable, 55 George St. West, Lindsay ON K9V 4V6 – 705/878-9000; Fax: 705/328-2511; Email: comcable@lindsaytown.org
Lion's Head, ON .............. *See* Shaw Cable, Port Elgin
Liverpool, NS .............. Able Cablevision Ltd., 212 Main St., PO Box 449, Liverpool NS B0T 1K0 – 902/354-3424; Fax: 902/354-2246
London, ON .............. Rogers Cablesystems, 499 MacGregor Ave., London ON N6J 2K9 – 519/433-0141; Fax: 519/433-0157
London, ON .............. *See* Rogers Cablesystems, Oshawa
London, ON .............. *See* Rogers Cablesystems, Oshawa
Lorette, MB .............. *See* Valley Cable Vision Ltd., Selkirk
Louisbourg, NS .............. *See* Seaside Cable TV (1984) Ltd., Glace Bay
Lower Post, BC .............. *See* Lower Post First Nation, Watson Lake
Lucknow, ON .............. *See* Kincardine Cable TV Ltd., Kincardine
Lyons, ON .............. *See* AGI Cablevision Inc., Simcoe
Madoc, ON .............. Hastings Cable Vision Ltd., 37 Durham St. South, Madoc ON K0K 2K0 – 613/473-2839; Fax: 613/473-4853
Main-à-Dieu, NS .............. *See* Seaside Cable TV (1984) Ltd., Glace Bay
Manitou, MB .............. *See* Valley Cable Vision Ltd., Selkirk
Marion Bridge, NS .............. *See* Seaside Cable TV (1984) Ltd., Glace Bay
Masset, BC .............. Masset Haida Television Society, 1656 Main St., PO Box 602, Masset BC V0T 1M0 – 250/626-3994; Fax: 250/626-3941
Maxville, ON .............. *See* Rogers Cablesystems Ottawa, Ottawa
McCreary, MB .............. *See* Westman Cable TV, Brandon
McLennan, AB .............. *See* Small Community TV Inc., Beaverlodge
Medicine Hat, AB .............. Ralston Community Cable System, CFB Suffield, PO Box 6000, Medicine Hat AB T1A 8K8 – 403/544-4405; Fax: 403/544-4433
Medicine Hat, AB .............. Monarch Cable TV, 101 Carry Dr. SE, Medicine Hat AB T1B 3M6 – 403/527-5586; Fax: 403/527-4770
Melfort, SK .............. *See* Image Cable Systems Ltd., Yorkton
Melita, MB .............. *See* Westman Cable TV, Brandon
Melville, SK .............. *See* North Eastern Cablevision Ltd., Yorkton
Merritt, BC .............. Shaw Cablesystems (B.C.) Ltd., 2350 Hunter Rd., Kelowna BC V1X 7H6 – 250/762-4433; Fax: 250/762-7997
Miami, MB .............. *See* Valley Cable Vision Ltd., Selkirk
Midland, ON .............. Rogers Cablesystems Georgian Bay Ltd., PO Box 489, Midland ON L4R 4L3 – 705/526-5031; Fax: 705/526-0682
Millbrook, ON .............. *See* Shaw Cable, Smiths Falls
Milton, ON .............. *See* Halton Cable Systems Inc., Acton
Milverton, ON .............. *See* Saugeen Telecable Ltd., Hanover
Miminigash, PE .............. *See* Island Cablevision Ltd., Charlottetown
Minden, ON .............. Haliburton/Minden Cable TV, PO Box 10, Minden ON K0M 2K0 – 613/767-2675; Fax: 613/694-4006; Email: minden@cancom.net
Minitonas, MB .............. *See* Westman Cable TV, Brandon
Minnedosa, MB .............. *See* Westman Cable TV, Brandon
Minto, NB .............. *See* Fundy Cable Ltd. ltée, Fredericton
Miramichi, NB .............. *See* Fundy Cable Ltd./ltée, Saint John
Mississauga, ON .............. Rogers Cablesystems, 3573 Wolfedale Rd., Mississauga ON L5C 1V8 – 905/273-8000; Fax: 905/273-9661
Mistassini, QC .............. *See* Vidéotron ltée, Chicoutimi
Moncton, NB .............. Fundy Cable Ltd., 90 Driscoll Cres., Moncton NB E1E 3R8 – 506/857-8700; Fax: 506/857-8406
Montague, PE .............. *See* Island Cablevision Ltd., Charlottetown
Montréal, QC .............. CF Cable TV inc., #200, 405, av Ogilvy, Montréal QC H3N 2Y1 – 514/277-7133; Fax: 514/277-1823
Montréal, QC .............. Sorel-O-Vision, #500, 1420, rue Sherbrooke ouest, Montréal QC H3G 1K5 – 514/849-3711; Fax: 514/849-1855
Montréal, QC .............. Vidéotron ltée, 2000, rue Berri, Montréal QC H2L 4V7 – 514/281-1232; Fax: 514/985-8794; Email: communic@videotron.ca
Moose Jaw, SK .............. Shaw Cable Moose Jaw, 201 Manitoba St. East, Moose Jaw SK S6H 0A4 – 306/693-8585; Fax: 306/692-4859
Morden, MB .............. *See* Valley Cable Vision Ltd., Selkirk
Morell, PE .............. *See* Island Cablevision Ltd., Charlottetown
Morris, MB .............. *See* Valley Cable Vision Ltd., Selkirk
Mount Brydges, ON .............. *See* AGI Cablevision Inc., Simcoe
Mount Stewart, PE .............. *See* Island Cablevision Ltd., Charlottetown
Murray River, PE .............. *See* Island Cablevision Ltd., Charlottetown
Murray Roler, PE .............. *See* Island Cablevision Ltd., Charlottetown
Musgrave Harbour, NF .............. *See* Cable Atlantic Inc., St. John's
Musgravetown, NF .............. BMC Cablevision Co. Ltd., PO Box 16, Musgravetown NF A0C 1Z0 – 709/467-5306; Fax: 709/467-2489
Nanaimo, BC .............. Shaw Cablesystems (B.C.) Ltd., 711 Poplar St., Nanaimo BC V9S 5L8 – 250/754-5571; Fax: 250/754-3504
Nanticoke, ON .............. *See* Nor-Del Cablevision Ltd., Norwich
Neepawa, MB .............. *See* Westman Cable TV, Brandon
Neustadt, ON .............. *See* Saugeen Telecable Ltd., Hanover
New Germany, NS .............. New Germany Cablevision Ltd., RR#2, New Germany NS B0R 1E0 – 902/644-2358
New Glasgow, NS .............. Shaw Cable, PO Box 157, New Glasgow NS B2H 5E2 – 902/752-0310; Fax: 902/755-2236
New Liskeard, ON .............. *See* Northern Cable Holdings Ltd., Sudbury
Newcastle, NB .............. Fundy Cable TV Ltd./ltée, 454 King George Hwy., Newcastle NB E1V 1M1 – 506/622-9120; Fax: 506/622-3712

Newmarket, ON ............... Rogers Cable TV Ltd., 20 Gladman Ave., Newmarket ON L3Y 2N2 – 905/895-1731; Fax: 905/898-7577
Niagara Falls, ON ............. *See* Cogeco Cable Solutions, Niagara Falls
Niagara on the Lake, ON........ *See* Cogeco Cable Solutions, Niagara Falls
Niverville, MB................. *See* Valley Cable Vision Ltd., Selkirk
Norquay, SK .................. *See* North Eastern Cablevision Ltd., Yorkton
North Bay, ON ................ Rogers Cablesystems North Bay Ltd., 240 Fee St., PO Box 3170, North Bay ON P1B 8S4 – 705/472-6580; Fax: 705/472-7854
North Bay, ON ................ Cogeco Cable North Bay Ltd., PO Box 3170, North Bay ON P1B 8S4 – 705/472-6580; Fax: 705/472-7854
North Rustico, PE.............. *See* Island Cablevision Ltd., Charlottetown
Norway House, MB ............ Norway House Cree Nation Communications, PO Box 250, Norway House MB R0B 1B0 – 204/359-4683; Fax: 204/359-6191
Norwich, ON .................. Nor-Del Cablevision Ltd., PO Box 340, Norwich ON N0J 1P0 – 519/468-3116
Notre Dame de Lourdes, MB .... *See* Valley Cable Vision Ltd., Selkirk
Nottawa, ON .................. *See* Rogers Cablesystems, Collingwood
Oakville, ON .................. O1 Cablesystems Inc., 1173 North Service Rd. West, Unit 6, Oakville ON L6M 1V9 – 905/847-1132
Oakville, ON .................. Cable 1 Ontario Inc., #52, 635 Fourth Line, Oakville ON L6L 5W4 – 905/338-2378; Fax: 905/338-0174
O'Leary, PE................... *See* Island Cablevision Ltd., Charlottetown
Oliver, BC .................... OTV Cablevision, 9502 - 348th Ave., PO Box 790, Oliver BC V0H 1T0 – 250/498-3630; Fax: 250/498-8810; Email: otv@cablelan.net
One Hundred Mile House, BC ... *See* Shaw Cablesystems (B.C.) Ltd., Prince George
Orangeville, ON ............... Shaw Cable, 70 C-Line Rd., PO Box 56, Orangeville ON L9W 2Z5 – 519/941-4030; Fax: 519/941-6091
Oshawa, ON................... Rogers Cablesystems, 301 Marwood Dr., Oshawa ON L1H 1J4 – 905/436-4141; Fax: 905/579-5559
Ottawa, ON ................... Rogers Cablesystems Ottawa, 475 Richmond Rd., PO Box 6315, Stn J, Ottawa ON K2A 3Y8 – 613/759-8505; Fax: 613/722-8680
Owen Sound, ON .............. Rogers Cablesystems, 1040 - 20 St. East, PO Box 440, Owen Sound ON N4K 5P7 – 519/376-5195; Fax: 519/376-5216
Oxford Mills, ON .............. *See* Shaw Cable, Smiths Falls
Paisley, ON ................... *See* Shaw Cable, Port Elgin
Pakenham, ON ................ *See* Rogers Cablesystems Ottawa, Ottawa
Pangnirtung, NT ............... Pangnirtung Cable Television Ltd., 5120 - 49th St., PO Box 1469, Yellowknife NT X1A 2P1 – Fax: 867/920-3690
Panorama, BC ................. *See* Shaw Cable, Cranbrook
Parksville, BC ................. *See* Shaw Cablesystems (B.C.) Ltd., Nanaimo
Pasadena, NF.................. *See* Cable Atlantic Inc., St. John's
Pembroke, ON................. Cogeco Cable Solutions, 185 Lake St., Pembroke ON K8A 5M1 – 613/735-6819; Fax: 613/735-6177
Pender Harbour, BC............ *See* Coast Cable Communications Ltd., Sechelt
Penetanguishene, ON........... *See* Rogers Cablesystems Georgian Bay Ltd., Midland
Perkinsfield, ON ............... *See* Rogers Cablesystems Ottawa, Ottawa
Perth, ON..................... *See* Shaw Cable, Smiths Falls
Peterborough, ON.............. Rogers Cablesystems, 685 Queensway, PO Box 2290, Peterborough ON K9J 7Y8 – 705/742-9264; Fax: 705/742-3563
Pinawa, MB ................... *See* Videon CableSystems Inc., Winnipeg
Pine Falls, MB ................. Winnipeg River CATV, PO Box 659, Pine Falls MB R0E 1M0 – 204/367-2858; Fax: 204/367-4991
Plum Coulee, MB .............. *See* Valley Cable Vision Ltd., Selkirk
Pointe-Sapin, NB............... *See* Fundy Cable TV Ltd./ltée, Newcastle
Pond Inlet, NT................. P.I. Cable TV, Pond Inlet NT X0A 0S0 – 867/899-8887; Fax: 867/899-8849
Port Alberni, BC............... Ucluelet Video Services Ltd., PO Box 47, Ucluelet BC V0R 3A0 – 250/726-7792; Fax: 250/726-4373
Port Alberni, BC............... Shaw Cable, 3744 - 3 Ave., Port Alberni BC V9Y 4G1 – 250/723-6295; Fax: 250/723-4024
Port-aux-Basques, NF........... *See* Cable Atlantic Inc., St. John's
Port Bruce/Copenhagen, ON .... *See* AGI Cablevision Inc., Simcoe
Port Burwell/Vienna, ON ....... *See* AGI Cablevision Inc., Simcoe
Port Colborne, ON ............. *See* Cogeco Cable Solutions, Niagara Falls
Port Elgin, ON................. Shaw Cable, 1119 Goderich St. North, PO Box 1330, Port Elgin ON N0H 2C0 – 519/832-6297; Fax: 519/389-4096
Port McNicoll, ON ............. *See* Rogers Cablesystems Georgian Bay Ltd., Midland
Port Perry, ON ................ Compton Cable TV Ltd., Lot 7, Con. 5, PO Box 73, Port Perry ON L9L 1A2 – 905/985-8171; Fax: 905/985-0010
Port Robinson, ON............. *See* Cogeco Cable Solutions, Niagara Falls
Port Rowan, ON ............... *See* AGI Cablevision Inc., Simcoe
Portage la Prairie, MB .......... Portage Community Cablevision Ltd., PO Box 146, Portage La Prairie MB R1N 3B2 – 204/857-6623; Fax: 204/857-6665
Powell River, BC............... Powell River Cablenet, 4706 Ewing Place, Powell River BC V8A 2N5 – 604/485-4410; Fax: 604/485-6030
Prince Albert, SK .............. Shaw Cable Prince Albert, 2290 Second Ave. West, Prince Albert SK S6V 7E9 – 306/922-0202; Fax: 306/922-7122
Prince George, BC ............. Shaw Cablesystems (B.C.) Ltd., 470 - 3rd Ave., Prince George BC V2L 3B9 – 250/562-1345; Fax: 250/563-9222
Prince Rupert, BC.............. *See* Skeena Cablevision, Terrace
Queenston, ON ................ *See* Cogeco Cable Solutions, Niagara Falls
Quesnel, BC................... *See* Shaw Cablesystems (B.C.) Ltd., Prince George
Ramea, NF.................... Ramea Broadcasting Co., PO Box 23, Ramea NF A0M 1N0 – 709/625-2618; Fax: 709/625-2048
Red Deer, AB ................. Shaw Cablesystems, 6123 - 48th Ave., Red Deer AB T4N 5Z9 – 403/346-6633; Fax: 403/346-3962
Reef's Harbour, NF ............ Clearview Cable Ltd., PO Box 10, Reef's Harbour NF A0K 4L0 – 709/847-7441; Fax: 709/847-7100
Renfrew, ON .................. *See* Rogers Cablesystems Ottawa, Ottawa
Revelstoke, BC ................ Revelstoke Cable TV Ltd., 416 - 2nd St. West, PO Box 651, Revelstoke BC V0E 2S0 – 250/837-5246; Fax: 250/837-2900; Email: rctv@cablelan.net
Richibucto, NB ................ *See* Fundy Cable TV Ltd./ltée, Newcastle
Richmond Hill, ON............. Classic Communications Ltd., 244 Newkirk Rd., Richmond Hill ON L4C 3S5 – 905/884-8111; Fax: 905/884-8151
Ridgeville, ON................. *See* Cogeco Cable Solutions, Niagara Falls
Ridgeway, ON................. *See* Cogeco Cable Solutions, Niagara Falls
Riondel, BC................... Riondel Community Cable & Video Society, PO Box 59, Riondel BC V0B 2B0 – 250/225-3272; Fax: 250/225-3272
River Bourgeois, NS............ *See* Seaside Cable TV (1984) Ltd., Glace Bay
Rivers, MB.................... *See* Westman Cable TV, Brandon
Rivière-du-Loup, QC ........... Le Cable de Rivière-du-Loup ltée, 279A, rue Lafontaine, CP 1390, Rivière-du-Loup QC G5R 4L9 – 418/867-1478; Fax: 418/867-2829
Rivière-du-Loup, QC ........... Télédistribution Cablouis inc., 279A, rue Lafontaine, CP 1390, Rivière-du-Loup QC G5R 4L9 – 418/854-2453; Fax: 418/867-2829
Robe Blanche, NF.............. *See* Cable Atlantic Inc., St. John's
Roblin, MB ................... *See* Westman Cable TV, Brandon
Rock Island, QC ............... *See* Vidéotron ltée, Sherbrooke
Rockglen, SK.................. *See* Shaw Cable Moose Jaw., Moose Jaw
Rockwood, ON ................ *See* Halton Cable Systems Inc., Acton
Rocky Mountain House, AB..... Ram River Cable TV Ltd., 4712 - 49 Ave., PO Box 2010, Rocky Mountain House AB T0M 1T0 – 403/845-4940; Fax: 403/845-4797

Rocky Point, PE................*See* Island Cablevision Ltd., Charlottetown
Rogersville, NB................*See* Fundy Cable TV Ltd./ltée, Newcastle
Rossburn, MB..................*See* Westman Cable TV, Brandon
Rouleau, SK...................Rouleau Cable TV Association Inc., PO Box 250, Rouleau SK S0G 4H0 – 306/776-2270; Fax: 306/776-2482
Russell, MB....................*See* Westman Cable TV, Brandon
Rycroft, AB...................*See* Small Community TV Inc., Beaverlodge
Ste-Adèle, QC.................Télédiffusion Ste-Adèle inc., 605, ch Ste-Marguerite, CP 1375, Ste-Adèle QC J0R 1L0 – 514/229-7666; Fax: 514/229-7910
St. Adolphe, MB...............*See* Valley Cable Vision Ltd., Selkirk
Ste-Agathe-des-Monts, QC......Cable Laurentides ltée, 5, rue Laroque, CP 265, Ste-Agathe-des-Monts QC J8C 3A3 – 819/326-5572
Ste. Anne, MB.................*See* Valley Cable Vision Ltd., Selkirk
Ste-Anne-de-Kent, NB..........*See* Fundy Cable TV Ltd./ltée, Newcastle
St-Antoine, NB................*See* Fundy Cable TV Ltd./ltée, Newcastle
Ste-Brigitte-de-Laval, QC........*See* Coopérative de Câblodistribution de l'Arrière-pays, Charlesbourg
St Catharines, ON.............*See* Cogeco Cable Solutions, Niagara Falls
Ste-Catherine-de-la-Jacques-Cartier, QCCooperative de Cablodistribution Ste-Catherine-Fossambault, 8, rue Jolicoeur, CP 386, Ste-Catherine-de-la-Jacques-Cartier QC G0A 3M0 – 418/875-1118
St. Claude, MB................*See* Valley Cable Vision Ltd., Selkirk
St-Cyrille-de-Wendover, QC.....Transvision Weedon, 235, rue Nathalie, St-Cyrille-de-Wendover QC J1Z 1W6 – 819/477-4305; Fax: 819/477-4305
St. David's, ON...............*See* Cogeco Cable Solutions, Niagara Falls
St-Édouard, NB................*See* Fundy Cable TV Ltd./ltée, Newcastle
St. Eustache, MB..............*See* Videon CableSystems Inc., Winnipeg
St-Évariste, QC...............La Gaudeloupe Télévision inc., 430, rue Principale, St-Évariste QC G0M 1S0 – 418/459-6844
St-Évariste, QC...............Télé-Câble Labonté inc., 430, rue Principale, St-Évariste QC G0M 1S0 – 418/459-6844
St-Felicien, QC...............*See* Vidéotron ltée, Chicoutimi
St-Georges-de-Beauce, QC......Beauce Vidéo ltée, 11197 - 2e av, St-Georges-de-Beauce QC G5Y 1VP – 418/228-2755; Fax: 418/228-3015
St-Ignace, NB.................*See* Fundy Cable TV Ltd./ltée, Newcastle
St. Isidore, ON...............*See* Rogers Cablesystems Ottawa, Ottawa
St. Jean Baptiste, MB..........*See* Valley Cable Vision Ltd., Selkirk
Saint John, NB................Fundy Cable Ltd./ltée, 199 Chesley Dr., Saint John NB E2K 4S9 – 506/634-5800; Fax: 506/634-5019; Email: info@fundycbl.com
St. John's, NF................Cable Atlantic Inc., PO Box 8596, St. John's NF A1B 3P2 – 709/753-7583; Fax: 709/722-8384
St. John's, NF................Regional Cable TV (Atlantic) Inc., PO Box 12155, Stn A, St. John's NF A1B 4L1 – 709/754-3775; Fax: 709/754-3883
St-Laurent, QC................Fonex Data Systems Inc., 9410 Trans Canada Hwy., St-Laurent QC H4S 1R7 – 514/333-6639; Fax: 514/333-6635
St. Lazare, MB................*See* Westman Cable TV, Brandon
St-Marc-des-Carrière, QC.......Télé-Câble St-Marc-des-Carrières inc., 448, rue Sauvageau, St-Marc-des-Carrière QC G0A 4B0 – 418/268-5453; Fax: 418/268-5131
Ste-Marie-de-Beauce, QC........Télécâble Lac-Etchemin inc., 166, rue Notre-Dame nord, CP 1570, Ste-Marie-de-Beauce QC G6E 3C6 – 418/464-4416; Fax: 418/387-6915
Ste-Marie-de-Kent, NB.........*See* Fundy Cable TV Ltd./ltée, Newcastle
St. Peter's, NS...............*See* Seaside Cable TV (1984) Ltd., Glace Bay
St. Pierre Jolys, MB...........*See* Valley Cable Vision Ltd., Selkirk
St-Prime, QC..................*See* Vidéotron ltée, Chicoutimi
St-Raymond, QC................*See* Vidéo Dery ltée, La Baie
Ste-Rose-du-Lac, MB...........*See* Westman Cable TV, Brandon
Ste-Thérèse-de-Colombier, QC...*See* Télécâble Côte-Nord inc., Chute-aux-Outardes
St. Thomas, ON................Till Cable TV Ltd., PO Box 582, St. Thomas ON N5P 4B1 – 519/842-5242; Fax: 519/631-3253
St. Thomas, ON................Shaw Cable, PO Box 582, St. Thomas ON N5P 4B1 – 519/631-5060; Fax: 519/631-3253
St. Williams/Booth's Harbour, ON *See* AGI Cablevision Inc., Simcoe
Saltcoats, SK.................*See* North Eastern Cablevision Ltd., Yorkton
Sandy Lake, MB................*See* Westman Cable TV, Brandon
Sarnia, ON....................Rogers Cablesystems, 1421 Confederation St., PO Box 218, Sarnia ON N7T 7J1 – 519/332-8439
Saskatoon, SK.................Shaw Cable Saskatoon, 2326 Hanselman Ave., PO Box 1950, Saskatoon SK S7K 3S5 – 306/664-1007; Fax: 306/244-0105
Sauble Beach, ON..............*See* Shaw Cable, Port Elgin
Sault Ste. Marie, ON...........Rogers Cablesystems, 23 Manitou Dr., Sault Ste. Marie ON P6B 6GN – 705/946-2234; Fax: 705/946-4773
Schreiber, ON.................Morrill's Cable TV Ltd., 224 Park St., Schreiber ON P0T 2S0 – 807/824-2619
Sechelt, BC...................Coast Cable Communications Ltd., PO Box 218, Sechelt BC V0N 3A0 – 604/885-3224; Fax: 604/885-3203
Selkirk, MB...................Interlake Cable TV Ltd., PO Box 243, Selkirk MB R1A 2B2 – 204/785-8701; Fax: 204/785-8749
Selkirk, MB...................Valley Cable Vision Ltd., 186 Main St., PO Box 243, Selkirk MB R1A 2B2 – 204/785-8701; Fax: 204/785-8749
Shannon, QC...................Shannon Vision inc., 75, ch Gosford, Shannon QC G0A 4N0 – 418/844-3849; Fax: 418/844-2111
Shediac, NB...................Cable 2000 Inc., 79 Sackville St., PO Box 1317, Shediac NB E0A 3G0 – 506/532-6215
Shelburne, NS.................Seabreeze Cablevision Ltd., PO Box 1090, Shelburne NS B0T 1W0 – 902/875-4438; Fax: 902/875-4219
Sherbrooke, QC................Vidéotron ltée, 2830, rue Galt ouest, Sherbrooke QC J1K 2V8 – 819/822-6812; Fax: 819/822-6821
Shilo, MB.....................Shilo Cable TV, PO Box 40, Stn CFB, Shilo MB R0K 2A0 – 204/765-2586; Fax: 204/765-3093
Shoal Lake, MB................*See* Westman Cable TV, Brandon
Simcoe, ON....................AGI Cablevision Inc., 121 Donly Dr. South, PO Box 327, Simcoe ON N3Y 4L2 – 519/426-7360; Fax: 519/426-0162; Email: agicable@amtelecom.ca
Smithers, BC..................*See* Skeena Cablevision, Terrace
Smiths Falls, ON...............Shaw Cable, 207 Brockville St., Smiths Falls ON K7A 3Z3 – 613/283-6150; Fax: 613/283-1526
Snow Lake, MB.................*See* Videon CableSystems Inc., Winnipeg
Souris, MB....................*See* Westman Cable TV, Brandon
Southampton, ON...............*See* Shaw Cable, Port Elgin
Southern Kings, PE............*See* Island Cablevision Ltd., Charlottetown
Southey, SK...................Southey Cable, PO Box 248, Southey SK S0G 4P0 – 306/726-2202; Fax: 306/726-2202
Spirit River, AB...............*See* Small Community TV Inc., Beaverlodge
Springhill, PE................*See* Island Cablevision Ltd., Charlottetown
Springside, SK................*See* North Eastern Cablevision Ltd., Yorkton
Stanstead, QC.................*See* Vidéotron ltée, Chicoutimi
Stayner, ON...................*See* Rogers Cablesystems, Collingwood
Steinbach, MB.................*See* Valley Cable Vision Ltd., Selkirk
Stewart, BC...................*See* Skeena Cablevision, Terrace
Stoneham, QC..................*See* Coopérative de Câblodistribution de l'Arrière-pays, Charlesbourg

Stonewall, MB ................ *See* Interlake Cable TV Ltd., Selkirk
Straffordville, ON .............. *See* AGI Cablevision Inc., Simcoe
Strathclair, MB ................ *See* Westman Cable TV, Brandon
Sturgeon Falls, ON ............. *See* Northern Cable Holdings Ltd., Sudbury
Sudbury, ON .................. Northern Cable Holdings Ltd., #15, 500 Barrydowne Rd., PO Box 4500, Sudbury ON P3A 5W1 – 705/560-1560; Fax: 705/560-4752
Sundre, AB ................... *See* Monarch Cable TV, Canmore
Surrey, BC .................... Rogers Cablesystems Ltd., 10445 - 138 St., Surrey BC V3T 4X3 – 604/588-1229; Fax: 604/588-3404
Sussex, NB .................... Kings County Cable Ltd., 500 Main St., PO Box 1428, Sussex NB E0E 1P0 – 506/432-1000; Fax: 506/432-6330
Swan River, MB ............... *See* Westman Cable TV, Brandon
Swift Current, SK .............. *See* Shaw Cable Moose Jaw., Moose Jaw
Swift Current, SK .............. Shaw Cablesystems, 15 Dufferin St. West, Swift Current SK S9H 5A1 – 306/773-7218; Fax: 306/773-6421
Sydney, NS .................... Cape Breton Cablevision Ltd., 61 Melody Lane, Sydney NS B1P 3K4 – 902/562-5600; Fax: 902/564-5428
Taber, AB .................... Monarch Cable TV Ltd., PO Box 1448, Taber AB T0K 2G0 – 403/223-3331; Fax: 403/527-4770
Tara, ON ..................... *See* Shaw Cable, Port Elgin
Teeswater, ON ................. *See* Kincardine Cable TV Ltd., Kincardine
Terrace, BC ................... Skeena Cablevision, 4625 Lazelle Ave., Terrace BC V8G 1S4 – 250/635-6316; Fax: 250/638-6320; Email: info@osg.net
Teulon, MB ................... *See* Interlake Cable TV Ltd., Selkirk
The Pas, MB .................. *See* Videon CableSystems Inc., Winnipeg
The Rapids, NB ................ *See* Fundy Cable TV Ltd./ltée, Newcastle
Theodore, SK .................. *See* North Eastern Cablevision Ltd., Yorkton
Thetford-Mines, QC ............ Thetford Vidéo inc. 37, rue St-Joseph ouest, CP 274, Thetford-Mines QC G6G 5T1 – 418/335-6622; Fax: 418/335-9125
Thompson, MB ................. Videon Cable TV, 50 Selkirk Ave., Thompson MB R8N 0M7 – 204/778-7321; Fax: 204/677-9953
Thompson, MB ................. Native Communications Inc., 76 Severn Cres., Thompson MB R8N 1M6 – 204/778-8343; Fax: 204/778-6559; Email: nci@norcom.mb.ca
Thompson, MB ................. *See* Videon CableSystems Inc., Winnipeg
Thornbury, ON ................ *See* Rogers Cablesystems, Collingwood
Thorold, ON .................. *See* Cogeco Cable Solutions, Niagara Falls
Thunder Bay, ON .............. Shaw Cablesystems, 1635 Paquette Rd., PO Box 3450, Thunder Bay ON P7B 5E5 – 807/767-4422; Fax: 807/767-7211
Tignish, PE .................... *See* Island Cablevision Ltd., Charlottetown
Timmins, ON .................. *See* Northern Cable Holdings Ltd., Sudbury
Toronto, ON .................. Rogers Cablesystems, 35 Scarlett Rd., Toronto ON M6N 4J8 – 416/762-2777; Fax: 416/762-0380
Toronto, ON .................. Rogers Community 10 Etobicoke, 80 Worcester Rd., Etobicoke ON M9W 1K7 – 416/675-5930, ext.297; Fax: 416/675-4254
Toronto, ON .................. Newton Cable Communications Ltd., 78 Martin Ross Ave., North York ON M3J 2L4 – 416/661-5000; Fax: 416/661-7892
Toronto, ON .................. Rogers Cable TV, 855 York Mills Rd., Don Mills ON M3B 1Z1 – 416/446-6500; Fax: 416/446-6003
Toronto, ON .................. Shaw Cablesystems Ltd., #1, 700 Progress Ave., Scarborough ON M1H 2Z7 – 416/290-6222; Fax: 416/439-9978
Treherne, MB ................. *See* Valley Cable Vision Ltd., Selkirk
Trois-Rivières, QC ............. COGECO Câble inc., #200, 1630 - 6e rue, Trois-Rivières QC G8Y 5B2 – 819/372-9292; Fax: 819/372-3318
Truro, NS ..................... North Nova Cable Ltd., 361 Prince St., Truro NS B2N 1E4 – 902/895-1515; Fax: 902/893-2256
Tumbler Ridge, BC ............. North East Cable TV Ltd., PO Box 2050, Tumbler Ridge BC V0C 2W0 – 250/242-4300; Fax: 250/242-4840
Tweed, ON .................... Village Cablesystems Ltd., 36 Metcalfe St., PO Box 616, Tweed ON K0K 3J0 – 613/478-5766; Fax: 613/478-2192; Email: tgr@blvl.igs.net
Val-d'Or, QC .................. Cablevision du Nord de Québec inc., 45, boul Hôtel de Ville, Val-d'Or QC J9P 2M5 – 819/825-5133; Fax: 819/825-8710
Vananda, BC .................. Texada Community TV Association, PO Box 158, Vananda BC V0N 3K0 – 604/486-7640
Vernon, BC ................... Shaw Cable, 2924 - 28 Ave., Vernon BC V1T 8W6 – 250/542-2220; Fax: 250/542-2928
Victoria, BC ................... Rogers Cablesystems, 861 Cloverdale Ave., Victoria BC V8X 4S7 – 250/381-5050; Fax: 250/381-4190
Victoria, BC ................... Royal Oak Cablevision Ltd., 4500 West Saanich Rd., Victoria BC V8Z 3G2 – 250/479-8611; Fax: 250/479-8421
Victoria, BC ................... Shaw Cablesystems (B.C.) Ltd., 2614 Sooke Rd., Victoria BC V9B 1Y2 – 250/474-2111; Fax: 250/474-5005
Victoria Harbour, ON .......... *See* Rogers Cablesystems Georgian Bay Ltd., Midland
Ville-Marie, QC ................ Câblotem inc., 981, rte 101 nord, CP 9, Ville-Marie QC J0Z 3W0 – 819/629-3458; Fax: 819/622-0044
Virden, MB ................... *See* Westman Cable TV, Brandon
Virgil, ON ..................... *See* Cogeco Cable Solutions, Niagara Falls
Wallaceburg, ON ............... *See* Rogers Cablesystems, Sarnia
Wardsville/Newbury, ON ........ *See* AGI Cablevision Inc., Simcoe
Wasaga Beach, ON ............. *See* Rogers Cablesystems, Collingwood
Watson Lake, YT .............. Lower Post First Nation, PO Box 489, Watson Lake YT Y0A 1C0 – 250/779-3161; Fax: 250/779-3371; Email: lowerpost@watson.net
Welland, ON .................. *See* Cogeco Cable Solutions, Niagara Falls
Welland, ON .................. *See* Rogers Cablesystems, Sarnia
Wembley, AB ................. *See* Small Community TV Inc., Beaverlodge
Wesleyville, NF ................ *See* Cable Atlantic Inc., St. John's
Wetaskiwin, AB ............... Cable TV of Wetaskiwin Inc., 5001A - 51 Ave., Wetaskiwin AB T9A 0T9 – 403/352-3666; Fax: 403/352-7755
Weyburn, SK .................. Weyburn Cablenet, PO Box 1210, Weyburn SK S4H 2L5 – 306/842-0032; Fax: 306/842-3465
Whale Cove, NT ............... Hamlet of Whale Cove, Whale Cove NT X0C 0J0 – 867/896-9961; Fax: 867/896-9109
Whistler, BC .................. Whistler Cable Television Ltd., PO Box 630, Whistler BC V0N 1B0 – 604/932-1111; Fax: 604/932-1852
White City, SK ................. *See* Shaw Cable Moose Jaw., Moose Jaw
Whitehorse, YT ................ Northern Television Systems Ltd., #203, 4103 - 4 Ave., Whitehorse YT Y1A 1H6 – 867/667-4247; Fax: 867/667-4217
Whitney, ON .................. *See* Shaw Cable, Smiths Falls
Wiarton, ON .................. *See* Shaw Cable, Port Elgin
Williams Lake, BC ............. *See* Shaw Cablesystems (B.C.) Ltd., Prince George
Windsor, NS ................... Windsor Cable, 19 Nelson St., PO Box 640, Windsor NS B0N 2T0 – 902/798-8313; Fax: 902/798-4426
Windsor, ON .................. Shaw Cable, 2525 Dougall Ave., Windsor ON N8X 5A7 – 519/972-6677; Fax: 519/972-6688; Email: windsorcable11@wincom.net
Winkler, MB .................. *See* Valley Cable Vision Ltd., Selkirk
Winnipeg, MB ................. AML Wireless Systems Inc., 260 Saulteaux Cres., Winnipeg MB R3J 3T2 – 204/949-2400; Fax: 204/889-1268
Winnipeg, MB ................. Videon CableSystems Inc., 22 Scurfield Blvd., Winnipeg MB R3Y 1S5 – 204/287-4530; Fax: 204/287-8068; Email: videon@videon.ca
Winnipeg, MB ................. Shaw Cablesystems Manitoba Ltd., 930 Nairn Ave., Winnipeg MB R2L 0X8 – 204/780-8888; Fax: 204/667-4665
Witless Bay, NF ................ *See* Cable Atlantic Inc., St. John's
Woodlawn, ON ................ Constance Bay Cable Television Ltd., PO Box 310, Woodlawn ON K0A 3M0 – 613/832-3470; Fax: 613/832-2889
Woodstock, ON ................ Shaw Cablesystems (Ontario) Ltd., 21 Ridgeway Circle, PO Box 1208, Woodstock ON N4S 8P6 – 519/539-8101; Fax: 519/539-7731
Wynndel, BC .................. Wynndel Community TV Society, PO Box 5, Wynndel BC V0B 2N0 – 250/866-5542
Yarmouth, NS ................. *See* Halifax Cable Ltd., Halifax
Yellowknife, NT ............... Northwestel Cable Inc., PO Box 1469, Yellowknife NT X1A 2P1 – 867/920-2929; Fax: 867/920-2331

Yorkton, SK .................... Image Cable Systems Ltd., PO Box 280, Yorkton SK S3N 2V9 – 306/783-1322; Fax: 306/786-7686; Email: talk2us@imagecable.com
Yorkton, SK .................... North Eastern Cablevision Ltd., PO Box 550, Yorkton SK S3N 0X5 – 306/783-1566; Fax: 306/782-1952
Young, SK...................... Village of Young, PO Box 359, Young SK S0K 4Y0 – 306/259-2242
Zurich, ON ..................... *See* Mitchell-Seaforth Cable TV Ltd., Dryden

## ONLINE SERVICE PROVIDERS

The following listings include information on connection speeds & phone lines for online service providers. Many of the companies that responded to our request for information pointed out that the industry is changing rapidly; access, in terms of connection speed, number of users, etc. changes with demand. Contact the company directly for up-to-date information.

### ALBERTA

Alberta Supernet - Div. of Cyberion Networking Corp.
Pacific Plaza, #1660, 10020 - 101A Ave., Edmonton AB T5J 2G3
403/441-3663; Fax: 403/424-0743
http://www.supernet.ab.ca
Technical Sales Manager, Kelly Marples
Connection speed to Internet: T1
Users' top connection speed: 28.8K, 256K
Number of phone lines: 250

CADVision Development Corp.
#1810, 300 - 5th Ave. SW, Calgary AB T2P 3C4
403/777-1300; Fax: 403/777-1319
Email: info@cadvision.com; URL: http://www.cadvision.com
President, Geoffrey Shmigelsky
Connection speed to Internet: 155 Mbps
Users' top connection speed: 7 Mbps
Number of phone lines: 3,000+

Canada Connect Corp.
#403, 1300 - 8th St. SW, PO Box 2621, Stn M, Calgary AB T2P 3C1
403/777-2025; Fax: 403/777-2026
Email: sales@canuck.com; URL: http://www.xcite.com

Lexicom Ltd.
238 - 11 Ave. SE, Calgary AB T2G 0X8
403/262-6610; Fax: 403/640-2138
Email: rae@lexicom.ab.ca; URL: http://www.lexicom.ab.ca
Contact, Michael Rae
Connection speed to Internet: T1
Users' top connection speed: 56K
Number of phone lines: 160

Netmatrix Internet Company Inc.
#36001, 6449 Crowchild Trail SW, Calgary AB T3E 7C6
403/686-1169; Fax: 403/686-1193
Email: brian.simpson@netmatrix.com; URL: http://www.netmatrix.com
President, Brian Simpson
Connection speed to Internet: 10 Mbps
Users' top connection speed: 56K
Number of phone lines: 32

Nucleus Information Service
1835B - 10 Ave. SW, Calgary AB T3C 0K2
403/209-0000; Fax: 403/541-9474
Email: info@nucleus.com; URL: http://www.nucleus.com
Administration Manager, Cheryl McDonald
Connection speed to Internet: 10 Mbps
Users' top connection speed: 128K
Number of phone lines: 313

OA Internet Inc.
4907 - 99 St., Edmonton AB T6E 4Y1
403/430-0811; Fax: 403/436-9963
Email: info@oanet.com; URL: http://www.oanet.com
Manager, David Papp
Connection speed to Internet: 20 Mbps
Users' top connection speed: 10 Mbps
Number of phone lines: 500

SmartNet Internet Services
16810 - 104A Ave., Edmonton AB T5P 4J6
403/429-4388; Fax: 403/426-7110
Email: support@compusmart.ab.ca; URL: http://www.compusmart.ab.ca

Spots InterConnect Inc.
#400, 604 - 1st St. SW, Calgary AB T2P 1M7
403/571-7768; Fax: 403/571-7766
Email: info@spots.ab.ca; URL: http://www.spots.ab.ca
Vice-President, Operations, Jason Marshall
Connection speed to Internet: T1
Users' top connection speed: 128K

TELUS PLAnet Internet Service
10020 - 100 St., 22nd Fl., Edmonton AB T5J ON5
403/423-4638; Fax: 403/493-4277
Email: webmaster@telusplanet.net; URL: http://telusplanet.net
Director, Myron Borys
Connection speed to Internet: T1
Users' top connection speed: 7 Mbps

TIC Internet
PO Box 4041, Edmonton AB T6E 4S8
403/944-6941; Fax: 403/944-6942
Email: info@tic.ab.ca; URL: http://www.tic.ab.ca
CEO, Harm Gerding
Connection speed to Internet: 256K
Users' top connection speed: 33.6K
Number of phone lines: 14

WorldGate Inc.
#575, 10123 - 99 St., Edmonton AB T5J 3H1
403/413-1910; Fax: 403/421-4929
Email: sales@worldgate.com; info@worldgate.com; URL: http://www.worldgate.com

### BRITISH COLUMBIA

Axion Internet Communications Inc.
#600, 1380 Burrard St., Vancouver BC V6Z 2H3
604/687-8030; Fax: 604/687-8130
Email: info@axionet.com; URL: http://www.axionet.com
Retail Sales Coordinator, Heather Fulcher
Connection speed to Internet: 55 Mbps
Users' top connection speed: 33.6K

BC TEL Advanced Communications
#2600, 4270 Kingsway, Burnaby BC V5H 4N2
604/454-5100; Fax: 604/454-5199
Email: info@bctel.net; URL: http://www.bctel.net
Users' top connection speed: 155 Mbps

Fairview Technology Centre Ltd.
Route 1, Site 24, Conc. 9, Oliver BC V0H 1T0
250/498-4316; Fax: 250/498-3214
Email: bwklatt@ftcnet.com; URL: http://www.ftcnet.com
Partner, Bernard Klatt
Users' top connection speed: 33.6K, 56K
Number of phone lines: 15

Imaginet Communications Group Inc.
#200, 425 Carrall St., Vancouver BC V6B 6E3
604/662-8332; Fax: 604/662-3624
Email: info@imag.net; URL: http://www.express.ca

Internet Portal Services Inc.
#201, 2525 Manitoba St., Vancouver BC V5Y 3A7
604/257-9400; Fax: 604/257-9401
Email: info@portal.ca; URL: http://www.portal.ca
President, Larry Tolton
Connection speed to Internet: 10 Mbps
Users' top connection speed: 56K, 64K

Island Internet Inc.
#3, 57 Skinner St., Nanaimo BC V9R 5G9
250/753-1139; Fax: 250/753-8542
Email: support@island.net; URL: http://www.island.net
Owner, Jim Bourne
Connection speed to Internet: 10 Mbit
Users' top connection speed: 128K
Number of phone lines: 480

iSTAR Internet Inc.
#590, 601 West Hastings, Vancouver BC V6B 5A6
604/668-0600; Fax: 604/668-0601
http://www.istar.ca/

Pacific Interconnect Enterprises Inc.
4252 Commerce Circle, Victoria BC V8Z 4M2
250/953-2680; Fax: 250/953-2659
Email: sales@csp.net; URL: http://pinc.com/pi/

West Kootenay Powerlink
#249, 1290 Esplanade, Trail BC V1R 4T2
250/368-5773; Fax: 250/368-5386
Email: powerlink@awinc.com; URL: http://www.wkpowerlink.com
Owner, Peter Fulcher
Connection speed to Internet: T1
Users' top connection speed: 33.6K
Number of phone lines: 74

World Tel
#810, 675 West Hastings St., Vancouver BC V6B 1N2
604/685-3877; Fax: 604/687-0688
Email: info@worldtel.com; URL: http://www.worldtel.com
President, Barclay Hambrook
Connection speed to Internet: T1
Users' top connection speed: 33.6K
Number of phone lines: 14:1

### MANITOBA

Internet Solutions Inc.
490 Des Meurons St., 2nd Fl., Winnipeg MB R2H 2P5
204/982-1060; Fax: 204/982-1070
Email: info@solutions.net; URL: http://www.solutions.net
Director, Jason L.M. Remillard
Connection speed to Internet: T1
Users' top connection speed: 28.8K, 33.6K
Number of phone lines: 10:1 user/modem ratio

MBnet
c/o MBnet Networking Inc., University of Manitoba, Winnipeg MB R3T 2N2
204/474-7325; Fax: 204/275-5420
Email: info@mbnet.mb.ca; URL: http://www.mbnet.mb.ca
Manager, Ron Dallmeier
Connection speed to Internet: ATM
Users' top connection speed: 28.8K
Number of phone lines: 120

PCS Internet
1388 Spruce St., Winnipeg MB R3E 2V7
204/988-3236; Fax: 204/783-3185
Email: info@pcs.mb.ca; URL: http://www.pcs.mb.ca
Systems Manager, Wayne Tichon
Users' top connection speed: 33.6K

XpressNet
#1, 1325 Markham Rd., Winnipeg MB R3T 4J6
204/992-2469
Email: info@xpressnet.com; URL: http://www.xpressnet.com

### NOVA SCOTIA

Auracom Internet Services
#400, 3845 Dutch Village Rd., Halifax NS B3L 4H9

902/429-4747; Fax: 902/429-9003
http://www.auracom.com

NewEdge InterAccess
#1508, 1505 Agricola St., Halifax NS B3J 3K5
902/425-4222; Fax: 902/425-4433
Email: nesales@newedge.net; URL: http://www.newedge.net

North Shore Internet Services
#407, 169 Provost St., New Glasgow NS B2H 2P9
902/928-0565; Fax: 902/755-3126
Email: sales@nsis.com; URL: http://www.nsis.com
President, David Hayward
Connection speed to Internet: T1
Users' top connection speed: 128K

**NORTHWEST TERRITORIES**

Nunanet Worldwide Communications
PO Box 2049, Iqaluit NT X0A 0H0
867/979-0772; Fax: 867/979-1513
Email: webmaster@nunanet.com; URL: http://apa.nunanet.com/

**ONTARIO**

Access Route Canada Online Systems
5415 Dundas St. West, Etobicoke ON M9B 1B5
416/234-5345; Fax: 416/222-9453
Email: sysop@arcos.org; URL: http://www.arcos.net
Network Engineer, Mitch Tindale
Users' top connection speed: 33.6
Number of phone lines: 272

Barrie Connex Inc.
#606, 55 Cedar Pointe Dr., Barrie ON L4N 5R7
705/725-0819; Fax: 705/725-1287
Email: sales@bconnex.net; URL: http://www.bconnex.net
President, Dennis Simpson
Connection speed to Internet: T1
Users' top connection speed: 28.8K, 33.6K
Number of phone lines: 500

Burlington Network Services
140 Plains Rd. East, Burlington ON L7T 2C3
905/632-3977; Fax: 905/632-3536
Email: webmaster@bserv.com; URL: http://www.bserv.com
General Manager, Dave Cairney
Connection speed to Internet: T1
Users' top connection speed: 256K

Comnet Communications
#200, 102 Bank St., Ottawa ON K1P 5N4
613/233-5555; Fax: 613/233-2266
Email: info@comnet.ca; URL: http://www.comnet.ca

CoreLAN Communications Inc.
#5835, 1 First Canadian Place, Toronto ON M5X 1E3
416/362-1700; Fax: 416/362-5451
Email: webmaster@corelan.com; URL: http://www.corelan.com
Contact, Sales, Lorraine McNeil
Connection speed to Internet: T1

Cyberlink Online
444 Yonge St., PO Box 46021, Stn College Park, Toronto ON M5B 2L8
416/410-0111; Fax: 416/929-4434
Email: info@clo.com; URL: http://www.clo.com
Vice-President, Peter Van Leeuwen
Connection speed to Internet: T1
Users' top connection speed: 33.6K, 128K
Number of phone lines: 55+

Cyberus Online Inc.
#2, 99 Fifth Ave., Ottawa ON K1S 5P5
613/233-1215; Fax: 613/233-0292
Email: info@cyberus.ca; URL: http://www.cyberus.ca
Connection speed to Internet: 10 Mbps
Users' top connection speed: 33.6K, 28.8K, 64K

Durham.Net Inc.
Motor City Computers, 306 King St. West, Oshawa ON L1J 2J9
905/725-7980; Fax: 905/427-1381
Email: sales@durham.net; URL: http://www.durham.net
President, Dean Forester
Vice-President, George Ramos
Connection speed to Internet: T1
Users' top connection speed: 28.8K
Number of phone lines: 100

Ezenet Inc.
#940, 90 Eglinton Ave. East, Toronto ON M4P 2Y3
416/482-3037; Fax: 416/482-0707
Email: webmaster@ezenet.com; URL: http://www.ezenet.com
Vice-President, Kasra Meshkin
Connection speed to Internet: T1
Users' top connection speed: 128K, 28.8K
Number of phone lines: 200

HookUp Communications
#207, 1075 North Service Rd., Oakville ON L6M 2G2
905/847-8000; Fax: 905/847-8420
Email: info@hookup.net; URL: http://www.hookup.net
Regional Sales Administrator, Sara Mansell
Connection speed to Internet: T1
Users' top connection speed: 128K

iCOM Internet Services
#200, 7 Mary St., Hamilton ON L8R 1J6
905/522-1220
Email: sales@icom.ca; URL: http://www.icom.ca
Manager, Denise Zammit
Connection speed to Internet: T1
Users' top connection speed: 56K
Number of phone lines: 5:1 user/modem

Inasec Inc.
#320, 29 Beechwood Ave., Ottawa ON K1M 1M2
613/746-3200; Fax: 613/747-2046
Email: hcarter@inasec.ca; URL: http://www.inasec.ca
Contact, Helene Carter

Information Gateway Services Belleville
#113, 199 Front St., Belleville ON K8N 5H5
613/969-7458; Fax: 613/969-8499
Email: info@blvl.igs.net; URL: http://www.blvl.igs.net
General Manager, Al Freeland
Connection speed to Internet: 192K
Users' top connection speed: 33.6K
Number of phone lines: 50

Information Gateway Services Kingston
Canada Trust Bldg., #201, 181 Wellington St., Kingston ON K7L 3E3
613/544-4220; Fax: 613/544-1550
Email: info@king.igs.net; URL: http://www.king.igs.net
Manager, Ian Duchesne
Connection speed to Internet: T1
Users' top connection speed: 33.6K
Number of phone lines: 110+

Information Gateway Services Peterborough
#100, 223 Aylmer St., Peterborough ON K9J 3K3
705/876-9158; Fax: 705/876-9599
Email: info@ptbo.igs.net; URL: http://www.ptbo.igs.net
Owner, Sandra Macklin
Connection speed to Internet: T1
Users' top connection speed: 33.6K, 56K
Number of phone lines: 135

Inline Information Services Inc.
7305 Rapistan Ct., Mississauga ON L5N 5Z4
905/813-8800; Fax: 905/813-8286
Email: info@inline.net; URL: http://www.inline.net
President, Russ Cobbe
Connection speed to Internet: T1
Users' top connection speed: 28.8K
Number of phone lines: 5

Interhop Network Services Inc.
#500, 150 Consumers Rd., North York ON M2J 1P9
416/494-1603; Fax: 416/494-3788
Email: sales@interhop.net; URL: http://www.interhop.net
Manager, Operations, Jordi McLaughlin
Connection speed to Internet: 2 x T1
Users' top connection speed: 128 - 384K, 33.6K

InterLog Internet Services
#904, 1075 Bay St., Toronto ON M7A 2B1
416/920-2655; Fax: 416/975-9639
Email: sales@interlog.com; URL: http://www.interlog.com
Support Manager, Robert Rivers
Connection speed to Internet: T3
Users' top connection speed: 128K
Number of phone lines: 2,500

InterNet Kingston
Jackson Press Bldg., #302, 177 Wellington St., Kingston ON K7L 3E3
613/547-6939; Fax: 613/547-5436
Email: info@adan.kingston.net; URL: http://www.kingston.net
CEO, Margaret Row
Connection speed to Internet: T1
Users' top connection speed: 28.8K, 33.6K, 64K, 128K
Number of phone lines: 101

Internex Online Inc.
#1625, 20 Bay St., Toronto ON M5J 2N8
416/363-8424; Fax: 416/363-8713
Email: info@io.org; URL: http://www.io.org

Intranet Technologies Inc.
#330, 220 Laurier Ave. West, Ottawa ON K1P 5Z9
613/233-7455; Fax: 613/233-7535
Email: info@intranet.on.ca; URL: http://www.intranet.on.ca
Marketing Manager, Robert Menzies
Connection speed to Internet: 3 x T1
Users' top connection speed: 56K, 256K

Kingston Online Services
#309, 303 Bagot St., Kingston ON K7K 5W7
613/549-8667; Fax: 613/549-0642
Email: support@kos.net; URL: http://www.kos.net/
Administrator, Steve Cole
Connection speed to Internet: Dual T1
Users' top connection speed: 64K

Managed Network Systems Inc.
870 University Ave. West, Windsor ON N9A 5R9
519/258-2333; Fax: 519/258-3009
Email: info@mnsi.net; URL: http://www.mnsi.net
Contact, Clayton Zekelman
Connection speed to Internet: 4 x T1
Users' top connection speed: 48K
Number of phone lines: 1,000

MicroAge Internet Access
871B Tungsten St., Thunder Bay ON P7B 6H2
807/343-4490; Fax: 807/346-4963
Email: lhintikk@microage-tb.com; URL: http://www.microage-tb.com/

Myna Communications Inc.
#505, 151 Front St. West, PO Box 14, Toronto ON M5J 2N1
416/362-7000; Fax: 416/362-7001
Email: sales@myna.com; URL: http://www.myna.com/

National Online
Waterloo ON
519/725-0606
Email: info@nonline.net; URL: http://www.canweb.net/nonline/

NETinc
#206, 20 Jackson St. West, Hamilton ON L8P 3K9
905/525-4555; Fax: 905/525-3222
Email: sales@netinc.ca; URL: http://www.netinc.ca

Networx Internet System
#LL101, 154 Jackson St. East, Hamilton ON L8N 1L4

905/528-4638; Fax: 905/525-8473
Email: sales@networx.on.ca; URL: http://www.networx.on.ca/
NovaTech Computer Careers
857 Norwest Rd., Kingston ON K7P 2N2
613/384-7959; Fax: 613/384-1358
Email: burkey@cyberschool.com; URL: http://www.novatech.on.ca
ONRAMP Network Services Inc.
#18, 570 Hood Rd., Markham ON L3R 4G7
905/470-4064; Fax: 905/470-6484
Email: sales@onramp.ca; URL: http://www.onramp.ca
Sales Manager, Karim Mitha
Connection speed to Internet: 10 Mbps
Users' top connection speed: T1
Pathway Communications Inc.
#2205, 1 Yonge St., Toronto ON M5E 1E5
416/214-6363; Fax: 416/214-6238
Email: info@pathcom.com; URL: http://www.pathcom.com
Connection speed to Internet: T1-T3
Users' top connection speed: 33.6K
Number of phone lines: 1,100+
Sentex Communications Corp.
240D Holiday Inn Dr., Cambridge ON N3C 3X4
519/651-3400; Fax: 519/651-2215
Email: support@sentex.net; URL: http://www.sentex.net
Owner, Keith Winter
Connection speed to Internet: T1
Users' top connection speed: 128K
Number of phone lines: fewer than 100
Spectranet Connections Inc.
#46, 220 Wyecroft Rd., Oakville ON L6K 3V1
905/338-3552; Fax: 905/338-7549
Email: mailbox@spectranet.ca; URL: http://www.spectranet.ca
General Manager, Adam Kulchyski
Connection speed to Internet: T1
Users' top connection speed: 56K
Number of phone lines: 150
Travel-Net Communications Inc.
292 Montréal Rd., Ottawa ON K1L 6B7
613/744-3000; Fax: 613/744-2602
Email: info@travel-net.com; URL: http://www.travel-net.com
Users' top connection speed: 64K, 128K
UUNET Canada Inc.
#1910, 20 Bay St., Toronto ON M5J 2N8
416/368-6621; Fax: 416/368-1350
Email: info@uunet.ca; URL: http://www.uunet.ca
Connection speed to Internet: T3, T1
Users' top connection speed: 64K, 128K
ViaNet Internet Solutions
128 Larch St., Sudbury ON P3E 5J8
705/675-0400; Fax: 705/675-0404
Email: info@vianet.on.ca; URL: http://www.vianet.on.ca
Owner/CEO, Will Gasteiger
Connection speed to Internet: T1
Users' top connection speed: 33.6K, 64K
Number of phone lines: 100
WINCOM (Windsor Information Network Company)
#835, 4510 Rhodes Dr., Windsor ON N8W 5K5
519/945-9462; Fax: 519/945-9777
Email: sales@wincom.net; URL: http://www.wincom.net
President, Morris Whatmore
Connection speed to Internet: 2 x T1
Number of phone lines: 600
WorldCHAT
3018 New St., Burlington ON L7N 1M5
905/637-9111; Fax: 905/637-0140
Email: jhoskin@worldchat.com; URL: http://www.worldchat.com
President, John A. Hoskin
Connection speed to Internet: 10 Mbps
Users' top connection speed: T1
Worldwide Data Communications Inc.
#900, 383 Richmond St., London ON N6A 3C4
519/642-1411
http://www.wwdc.com/

**PRINCE EDWARD ISLAND**

Island Services Network
Home Building, #303, 129 Kent St., Charlottetown PE C1A 1N4
902/892-4476; Fax: 902/894-6012
Email: info@isn.net; URL: http://www.isn.net
President, Kevin O'Brien
Users' top connection speed: 33.6K

**QUÉBEC**

AEI Internet Services
2124, rue Drummond, Montréal QC H3H 2R2
514/284-4452; Fax: 514/294-4995
Email: info@aei.ca; URL: http://www.aei.ca
Directeur, Denis Raymond
Connection speed to Internet: T3
Users' top connection speed: 56K
Atréide Communications
500, boul Greber, Gatineau QC J8T 7W3
819/243-1414; Fax: 819/243-2754
Email: tech@atreide.net; URL: http://www.atreide.net
Technicien, Daniel Bolduc
Connection speed to Internet: 1.54 Mbps
Users' top connection speed: 33.6K
Number of phone lines: 125
Axess Communications
CP 4822, St-Laurent QC H4L 1G9
514/337-2002; Fax: 514/337-2061
Email: support@axess.com; URL: http://www.axess.com
Office Manager, Susan Tress
Connection speed to Internet: T1
Users' top connection speed: 33.6K, 56.6K
Number of phone lines: 7:1 ratio
Babillard Synapse Inc.
22, rue Beloeil, Gatineau QC J8T 7G3
819/561-1697; Fax: 819/561-9304
Email: info@synapse.net; URL: http://www.synapse.net
President, Daniel Coulombe
Connection speed to Internet: T1
Users' top connection speed: 128K, 56K
Number of phone lines: 160
CitéNet Telecom Inc.
1155, rue René-Lévesque ouest, Montréal QC H3B 3T6
514/861-5050; Fax: 514/861-5953
Email: info@citenet.net; URL: http://www.citenet.net
Connection speed to Internet: T3
Users' top connection speed: 28.8K
Communications Accessibles Montréal
#050, 1205, rue Papineau, Montréal QC H2K 4R2
514/529-3000; Fax: 514/529-3300
Email: info@cam.org; URL: http://www.cam.org
General Manager, George Subirana
Connection speed to Internet: T1
Number of phone lines: 560
Concepta Communications Inc.
2425, boul des Récollets, Trois-Rivières QC G8Z 4G1
819/378-8362; Fax: 819/378-7335
Email: support@concepta.com; URL: http://www.concepta.com
Administrateur de reseau, Patrice Boucher
Connection speed to Internet: 1.54 Mbps
Users' top connection speed: 33.6K
Number of phone lines: 112
Le groupe Médiom
74, rue Jacques Cartier, Québec QC G1L 3S1
418/640-7474; Fax: 418/640-0515
Email: groupe@mediom.qc.ca; URL: http://www.mediom.qc.ca
Director, Richard Maheux
Connection speed to Internet: T1
Users' top connection speed: 33.6K
Number of phone lines: 132
Internet Global Info-Access
#2A, 2360, ch Lucerne, Mont-Royal QC H3R 2J8
514/737-2091; Fax: 514/737-0133
Email: info@globale.net; URL: http://globale.net
President, Nagib Tajdin
Connection speed to Internet: T1
ITI Inc.
2816, rue Beriot, Boisbriand QC J7E 4H4
514/895-3877; Fax: 514/437-4063
Email: info@iti.qc.ca; URL: http://www.iti.qc.ca/iti
President, Mario Lavallee
Connection speed to Internet: 512K
Users' top connection speed: 64K
Number of phone lines: 26
MicroAge Internet Services
#700, 5160, boul Decarie, Montréal QC H1J 1Y8
514/483-6040
http://www.microage.ca
Montréal Internet Inc.
1070, rue Beaulac, St-Laurent QC H4R 1R7
514/337-1985; Fax: 514/337-3401
Email: admin@montrealnet.ca; URL: http://www.montrealnet.ca
President, Saul Dragunas
Connection speed to Internet: 512 Kbps
Number of phone lines: 60
MPACT Immedia Corp.
#2250, 1155, rue René-Lévesque ouest, Montréal QC H3B 4T3
514/397-9747; Fax: 514/398-9340
Email: service@immedia.ca; URL: http://www.mpact.ca
Director, Communications, John Davidson
NetAxis Inc.
#360, 5160, boul Decarie, Montréal QC H3W 3C3
514/482-8989; Fax: 514/483-6718
Email: admin@netaxis.ca; URL: http://www.netaxis.ca
Coordinator, Helda Belik
Connection speed to Internet: T1
Odyssée Internet
85, rue de la Commune est, 3e étage, Montréal QC H2Y 1J1
514/861-3432; Fax: 514/861-6599
Email: info@odyssee.net; URL: http://www.odyssee.net
Point Net Communications Inc.
1852, rue Rachel est, Montréal QC H2H 1P4
514/524-3187; Fax: 514/524-2831
Email: info@point-net.com; URL: http://www.point-net.com
CEO, Francois Laprade
Connection speed to Internet: T1
Users' top connection speed: 56.6K
Number of phone lines: 100
PubNIX Montréal
CP 147, Côte-St-Luc QC H4V 2Y3
514/990-5911; Fax: 514/990-9443
Email: info@pubnix.net; URL: http://www.pubnix.net
Contact, Customer Service, Shelagh Webster
Connection speed to Internet: T1
Users' top connection speed: 128K
Number of phone lines: 30
Réseau Interordinateurs Scientifique Québécois
#800, 1801, rue McGill College, Montréal QC H3A 2N4
514/840-1234; Fax: 514/840-1244
Email: info-cirisq@risq.qc.ca; URL: http://www.risq.qc.ca
Project Manager, Mario Cantin
Connection speed to Internet: 155 Mbps, 622 Mbps

Users' top connection speed: Ethernet
St-Jean InterNet Inc.
18, rue Carmen, Iberville QC J2X 4J3
514/358-5074; Fax: 514/346-7770
Email: info@stjeannet.ca; URL: http://www.stjeannet.ca
Services Internet ABACOM
#240, 780, rue King ouest, Sherbrooke QC J1H 1R7
819/820-2929; Fax: 819/820-8866
Email: info@abacom.com; URL: http://www.abacom.com
President, Alain Parsons
Connection speed to Internet: T1
Users' top connection speed: 56K
UPC Communications Internet
CP 9004, Ste-Foy QC G1V 4A8
418/656-0090; Fax: 418/656-6981
Email: info@upc.qc.ca; URL: http://www.upc.qc.ca
Contact, Steve Paradis

**SASKATCHEWAN**
Data Link Canada
12 Gardiner Ave., Regina SK S4P 4P6
306/585-0362; Fax: 306/352-6450
Email: jim.nickel@dlcwest.com; URL: http://www.dlcwest.com
President, Jim Nickel
Connection speed to Internet: T1
Number of phone lines: 250
WBM Office Systems
414 McDonald St., Regina SK S4N 6E1
306/791-1300; Fax: 306/791-1301
Email: lblackwe@wbm.ca; URL: http://www.wbm.ca
General Manager, Lynn Blackwell
Connection speed to Internet: T1
Users' top connection speed: 128K

**UNITED STATES**
America On-Line
8619 Westwood Center Dr., Vienna VA 22185-2285
Toll Free: 1-800-827-6364
CompuServe Inc.
5000 Arlington Center Blvd., PO Box 20212, Columbus OH 43220
http://www.compuserve.com
President & CEO, Robert J. Massey

## FREENETS

Community Access Canada: http://cnet.unb.ca/

**ALBERTA**
Calgary Free-Net, Calgary AB: http://www.freenet.calgary.ab.ca/
Edmonton Free-Net, Edmonton AB: http://www.freenet.edmonton.ab.ca/

**BRITISH COLUMBIA**
Campbell River Community Network, Campbell River BC: http://www.cn.camriv.bc.ca/
Canada Home Town Page: http://netbistro.com/~jgrogan/
CIAO, Trail BC: http://www.ciao.trail.bc.ca/
CivicNet B.C.: http://www.civicnet.gov.bc.ca
Mount Arrowsmith Community Network: http://macn.bc.ca/
Nanaimo SchoolsNET, Nanaimo BC: http://www.sd68.nanaimo.bc.ca
NANO, Vanderhoof BC: http://www.nano.bc.ca
Sea to Sky Free-Net: http://sea-to-sky.net
Sunshine Coast Community Network: http://www.sunshine.net/sunshine.html
Valley Net, Abbotsford BC: http://mindlink.net/paul_kurucz/vnet.htm
Vancouver CommunityNet, Vancouver BC: http://www.vcn.bc.ca
Victoria Telecommunity Network , VictoriaBC: http://freenet.victoria.bc.ca/vifa.html

**MANITOBA**
Blue Sky Freenet: http://www.freenet.mb.ca/
EASTMAN FreeNet: http://wtp1.eastman.freenet.mb.ca/

**NEW BRUNSWICK**
Fredericton Area Network, Fredericton NB: http://fan1.csd.unb.ca/cfn/info/Home.html
Saint John Free-Net, Saint John NB: http://www.sjfn.nb.ca/

**NEWFOUNDLAND**
St. John's InfoNET, St. John's NF: http://www.InfoNET.st-johns.nf.ca/

**NOVA SCOTIA**
Antigonish Community Network, Antigonish NS: http://www.grassroots.ns.ca/
Cape Breton Community Network: http://highlander.cbnet.ns.ca/cbnet/mainmenu.html
Chebucto FreeNet, Halifax NS: http://www.ccn.cs.dal.ca/

**ONTARIO**
Brant FreeNet, Brantford ON: http://www.bfree.on.ca/
FLORA Community Web, Ottawa ON: http://www.flora.ottawa.on.ca
National Capital Free-Net, Ottawa ON: http://www.ncf.carleton.ca
Niagara's Electronic Village: http://freenet.npiec.on.ca/
Social Development Network: http://www.web.apc.org/sdn/
Toronto Free-Net, TorontoON: http://www.torfree.net
Wellington FreeSpace: http://www2freespace.net/

**QUÉBEC**
Nouveau Libertel: http://www.nouveau.qc.ca/

**SASKATCHEWAN**
Great Plains Free-Net, Regina SK: http://www.gpfn.sk.ca
Saskatoon Free-Net, Saskatoon SK: http://www.sfn.saskatoon.sk.ca/

## WEBSITE DIRECTORY

### ARTS & CULTURE

ABC CANADA ............ http://www.abc-canada.org
Academy of Canadian Cinema & Television............ http://www.academy.ca
Aero Space Museum of Calgary ............ http://www.lexicom.ab.ca/~aerospace/aerospace.html
Agnes Etherington Art Centre ............ http://www.queensu.ca/ageth/
Agriculture Museum............ http:www.agriculture.nmstc.ca
Alberta Aviation Museum ............ http://www.discoveredmonton.com/AviationMuseum/
Alberta Playwrights' Network............ http://www.nucleus.com/~apn
Alberta Railway Museum ............ http://www.discoveredmonton.com/railwaymuseum/
Alliance Québec ............ http://www.aq.qc.ca
The Anne Murray Centre............ http://www.grtplaces.com/ac/anne
Antigonish Heritage Museum ............ http://www.grassroots.ns.ca/tour/ahm.htm
Antiquarian Booksellers' Association of Canada............ http://206.217.21.64/ca/index.html
Aquatic Hall of Fame & Museum of Canada Inc.. ............ http://www.mbnet.mb.ca/city/parks/recserv/aquahall/INDEX.HTM
Archives Association of British Columbia............ http://www.harbour.com/AABC/
Archives Association of Ontario............ http://www.fis.utoronto.ca/groups/aao/
Archives Society of Alberta............ http://www.glenbow.org/asa/home.htm
Archives de la Ville de Québec............ http://www.webquebec.com/villege/villeqc/vilarch.html
Archives nationales du Québec............ http://www.anq.gouv.qc.ca
Archives of Ontario ............ http://www.gov.on.ca/MCZCR/archives
Art Cannon Gallery ............ http://www.artcannon.com
Art Gallery of Greater Victoria ............ http://vvv.com/aggv/
Art Gallery of Hamilton............ http://www.culturenet.ca/agh
Art Gallery of Newfoundland & Labrador ............ http://www.mun.ca/agnl/
Art Gallery of Nova Scotia ............ http://www.agns.ednet.ns.ca
Art Gallery of Ontario ............ http://www.AGO.on.ca
The Art Gallery of Southwestern Manitoba ............ http://www.docker.com/~agsm
Art Gallery of Sudbury............ http://www.ags-gas.on.ca
Art Gallery of York University............ http://www.yorku.ca/admin/agyu
Art Libraries Society of North America............ http://caroline.eastlib.ufl.edu/arlis/
Asian Canadian Writers' Workshop of Canada ............ http://www.asian.ca

| | |
|---|---|
| Associated Designers of Canada | http://www.ffa.ucalgary.ca/adc/indexadc.htm |
| Association Museums New Brunswick | http://www.amnb.nb.ca |
| Association culturelle franco-canadienne de la Saskatchewan | http://www.dlcwest.com/~acfc/ |
| Association des archivistes du Québec | http://www.archives.ca/aaq/ |
| Association for Canadian Theatre Research | http://www.unb.ca/web/english/candrama/candrama.htm |
| Association for the Export of Canadian Books | http://aecb.org |
| Association nationale des éditeurs de livres | http://www.cam.org/~anel/index.htm |
| Association of Book Publishers of British Columbia | http://www.books.bc.ca |
| Association of Canadian Archivists | http://www.archives.ca/aca/ |
| Association of Canadian Map Libraries & Archives | http://www.sscl.uwo.ca/assoc/acml/acmla.html |
| Association of Canadian Orchestras | http://home.ican.net/~assoc |
| Association of Canadian Publishers | http://www.publishers.ca |
| Association of Newfoundland & Labrador Archives | http://www.infonet.st-johns.nf.ca/providers/anla/anlahome.html |
| Association québécoise des marionnettistes | http://www.aei.ca/~aqm/ |
| BC Archives & Records Service | http://www.bcarchives.gov.bc.ca/index.htm |
| Ballet British Columbia | http://www.discovervancouver.com/balletbc/ |
| Banff Centre Archives | http://www.banffcentre.ab.ca |
| Banff Park Museum | http://www.worldweb.com/ParksCanada-Banff/museum.html |
| Beaton Institute Archives | http://eagle.uccb.ns.ca/beaton/beaton.html |
| Benares Historic House & Visitor Centre | http://www.city.mississauga.on.ca |
| Bethune Memorial House National Historic Site | http://parkscanada.pch.gc.ca/parks/ontario/bethune_memorialhouse |
| Bibliographical Society of Canada | http://www.library.utoronto.ca/~bsc |
| Black Cultural Centre for Nova Scotia | http://www.nstn.ca/bccns/bcc.html |
| Bradley Museum | http://www.city.mississauga.on.ca |
| British Columbia Drama Association | http://www.culturenet.ca/theatrebc/ |
| British Columbia Library Association | http://www.interchg.ubc.ca/bcla |
| British Columbia Museums Association | http://www.MuseumsAssn.bc.ca/~bcma/ |
| Bruce County Museum & Archives | http://www.swbi.net/bruce_county_museum.htm |
| Burlington Art Centre | http://www.BurlingtonArtCentre.on.ca |
| Calgary & Edmonton (1891) Railway Museum | http://www.discoveredmonton.com/RailMuseum/ |
| Calgary Highlanders Museum & Archives | http://db.nucleus.com/highmus/default.htm |
| Calgary Opera Association | http://www.lexicom.ab.ca/~calopera |
| Calgary Philharmonic Society | http://www.tiger.ab.ca/cpo/ |
| Campbell House | http://www.advsoc.on.ca/campbell/index.html |
| Canada's National History Society | http://www.cyberspc.mb.ca/~otmw/cnhs/cnhs.html |
| Canada's Sports Hall of Fame | http://www.inforamp.net/~cshof |
| The Canadian Business Hall of Fame | http://www.jacan.org |
| Canadian Academy of Recording Arts & Sciences | http://www.juno-awards.ca |
| Canadian Architectural Archives | http://www.ucalgary.ca/library/CAA/index.html |
| Canadian Arts Presenting Association | http://www.culturenet.ca/capacoa/ |
| Canadian Association for Music Therapy | http://www.bmts.com/~smacnay/camt/camt.html |
| Canadian Association of Journalists | http://www.eagle.ca/caj/ |
| Canadian Association of Music Libraries, Archives & Documentation Centres Inc. | http://www.caml.yorku.ca/ |
| Canadian Association of Professional Dance Organizations | http://www.culturenet.ca/capdo/ |
| Canadian Association of Public Libraries | http://www.cla.amlibs.ca |
| Canadian Authors Association | http://www.CanAuthors.org/national.html |
| Canadian Catholic Historical Association - English Section | http://www.umanitoba.ca/colleges/st_pauls/ccha/ccha.html |
| Canadian Centre for Architecture | http://cca.qc.ca/ |
| The Canadian Children's Book Centre | http://www.lglobal.com/~ccbc/ |
| Canadian Conference of the Arts | http://www.culturenet.ca |
| Canadian Council of Archives | http://www.CdnCouncilArchives.ca |
| Canadian Country Music Association | http://www.ccma.org |
| Canadian Craft & Hobby Association | http://www.cdncraft.org |
| Canadian Esperanto Youth | http://www.engcorp.com/kea/jek.html |
| Canadian Film Centre | http://www.cdnfilmcentre.com |
| Canadian Friends Historical Association | http://home.interhop.net/~aschrauwe/ |
| Canadian Heritage Information Network | http://www.chin.gc.ca |
| Canadian Institute for Theatre Technology | http://www.ffa.ucalgary.ca/citt/index.html |
| Canadian Institute of the Arts for Young Audiences | http://www.wimsey.com/Youngarts/ |
| Canadian Library Association | http://www.cla.amlibs.ca |
| Canadian Linguistic Association | http://www.ucs.mun.ca/~cla-acl |
| The Canadian Museum of Civilization | http://www.civilization.ca |
| Canadian Museum of Contemporary Photography | http://cmcp.gallery.ca |
| Canadian Museum of Health and Medicine | http://www.cmhm.org |
| Canadian Museum of Nature | http://www.nature.ca |
| Canadian Museum of Rail Travel - Cranbook | http://www.cyberlink.bc.ca/~camal/index.html |
| Canadian Museums Association | http://www.museums.ca |
| Canadian Music Centre | http://www.culturenet.ca/cmc |
| Canadian Music Educators' Association | http://www.ucs.mun.ca/~cmea/ |
| Canadian Musical Reproduction Rights Agency | http://www.cmrra.ca |
| Canadian National Aboriginal Tourism Association | http://www.v1i.ca/clients/abc/cnata/cnata3.htm |
| Canadian Opera Company | http://www.coc.ca |
| Canadian Postal Museum | http://www.cmcc.muse.digital.ca/cpm.html |
| Canadian Publishers' Council | http://www.pubcouncil.ca |
| Canadian Quilters Association | http://www.nt.net/~giselef/cqaacc1.htm |
| Canadian Science Writers' Association | http://www.interlog.com/~cswa |
| Canadian Society for the Study of Names | http://GeoNames.NRCan.gc.ca/english/CSSN.html |

Canadian Society of Children's Authors, Illustrators & Performers .... http://www.interlog.com/~canscaip
Canadian University Music Society .... http://www.utoronto.ca/cums/
Canadian Warplane Heritage Museum .... http://www.warplane.com
The Canadian Wildlife & Wilderness Art Museum .... http://intranet.ca/cawa/
Canso Museum/Whitman House .... http://www.schoolnet.ca/collections/canso/index.htm
Cape Breton Regional Library .... http://www.nshpl.library.ns.ca/regionals/cbr/
Carleton University Art Gallery .... http://www.carleton.ca/gallery
Centre culturel franco-manitobain .... http://francoculture.ca/ccfm
Centre d'interpretation Le Vieux-Poste .... http://www.bbsi.net/mrcu/
Centre des auteurs dramatiques .... http://globale.net/~cead
Centre for Mennonite Brethren Studies .... http://www.cdnmbconf.ca/mb/cmbs.htm
Centre international de recherche en aménagement linguistique .... http://www.ciral.ulaval.ca
City of Richmond Archives .... http://www.city.richmond.bc.ca/archives/archives.html
City of Vancouver Archives .... http://www.city.vancouver.bc.ca/ctyclerk/archives/index.html-ssi
City of Victoria Archives & Records Division .... http://www.city.victoria.bc.ca/archives/index.htm
Colchester Historical Society Museum .... http://www.shelburne.nscc.ns.ca/nsgna/col/col_main.htm
Contemporary Dancers Canada .... http://www.escape.ca/~cesmb/wcd/wcdhome.htm
Council of Nova Scotia Archives .... http://Fox.nstn.ca/~cnsa/
Courtenay & District Museum .... http://www.courtenaymuseum.bc.ca
The Crime Writers of Canada .... http://www.swifty.com/cwc/cwchome.htm
Currency Museum of the Bank of Canada .... http://www.bank-banque-canada.ca
Dance Ontario Association .... http://www.icomm.ca/danceon
DanceArts Vancouver .... http://www.mcsquared.com/DanceArts/
Dancemakers .... http://www.interlog.com/~dncemkrs/
DeLeon White Gallery .... http://www.eco-art.com/deleon/
The Delta Mill .... http://www.web.canlink.com/kwatson/delta/stonemill.html
Design Exchange .... http://www.hyperm.com/dxsite
Early Music Vancouver .... http://mindlink.net/earlymusic/
Earth Sciences Museum .... http://www.science.uwaterloo.ca/earth/museum/museum.html
Eastern Counties Regional Library .... http://www.library.ns.ca/regionals/ecr
Edinburgh Square Heritage & Cultural Centre .... http://www.headstartcomp.on.ca/heritage/square
Editors' Association of Canada .... http://www.web.net/eac-acr
Edmonton Jazz Society .... http://www.ualberta.ca/edmonton/jazz
Edmonton Public Schools Archives & Museum .... http://www.discoveredmonton.com/SchoolMuseum/
Edmonton Symphony Orchestra .... http://www.tgx.com/eso
Electrical Engineering Museum .... http://www.unb.ca
Embroiderers' Association of Canada, Inc. .... http://www.eac.ca/embroidery/
Energeum .... http://www.eub.gov.ab.ca
Esperanto Association of Canada .... http://www.engcorp.com/kea/indexa.html
Fédération culturelle canadienne-française .... http://francoculture.ca/fccf/
Federation of British Columbia Writers .... http://www.swifty.com/bcwa/index.html
Federation of Canadian Music Festivals .... http://www.planet.eon.net/~tuckey/NATIONAL.HTML
Fieldcote Memorial Park & Museum .... http://www.currentthinking.com/fieldcote
Fisheries Museum of the Atlantic .... http://www.ednet.ns.ca/educ/museum/fma/
Fort Edmonton Park .... http://www.gov.edmonton.ab.ca/fort/
Fort Henry .... http://forthenry.kingston.net
Fort Langley National Historic Site .... http://fas.sfu.ca/canheritage
Fort Point Museum .... http://www.lunco.com/heritage/fortpoint.htm
Fort Saskatchewan Museum .... http://www.fortsaskinfo.com/museum/
Fort Steele Heritage Town .... http://www.MuseumsAssn.bc.ca/~bcma/museums/fsht/
Fundy Geological Museum .... http://207.134.69.10/nova-scotia/fundygeomuseum/
Galerie d'art de L'Université de Moncton .... http://www.umoncton.ca/gaum/hp_luc8.html
Gallery 1.1.1. .... http://www.umanitoba.ca/schools/art/info/gallery.html
Gallery 44, Centre for Contemporary Photography .... http://www.interlog.com/~g44/
Gallery Arcturus .... http://www.arcturus.ca
Gallery Gachet .... http://www.info-mine.com/gachet
Glenbow Museum, Art Gallery, Library & Archives .... http://www.glenbow.org
Grand Forks Art Gallery .... http://www.islandnet.com/~bcma/museums/gfag/gfag.html
Grande Prairie Museum .... http://www.telusplanet.net/public/amassee/gpmuseum.html
Greater Vancouver International Film Festival Society .... http://viff.org/viff/
Gros Morne National Park Visitor Reception Centre .... http://www.parkscanada.pch.gc.ca/parks
Group of Ten Artists Gallery .... http://www.artword.net/ten
Guelph Civic Museum .... http://www.freespace.net/~museum/welcome.html
HMCS Haida Naval Museum .... http://www3.sympatico.ca/hrc/haida/
Halton County Radial Railway .... http://www.nl-marketing.com/hcrr/
Harbour Gallery .... http://www.designerinfolink.com/resource/harbgly.html
Harbourfront Centre .... http://www.harbourfront.on.ca
Head-Smashed-In Buffalo Jump .... http://www.head-smashed-in.com
Heraldry Society of Canada .... http://www.hsc.ca/
Heritage Foundation of Newfoundland & Labrador .... http://www.avalon.nf.ca/heritage
Heritage House Museum, a Victorian restoration, c.1867 .... http://www.town.smiths.falls.on.ca
Heritage North Museum .... http://www.mysterynet.mb.ca/museum/index.html
Historic Fort York .... http://www.torontohistory.on.ca
Historic Hat Creek Ranch .... http://www.hatcreekranch.com
Hockey Hall of Fame .... http://www.hhof.com
Independent Film & Video Alliance .... http://www.ffa.ucalgary.ca/
Interior Designers Institute of British Columbia .... http://www.designsource.bc.ca
International Council on Monuments & Sites Canada .... http://www.icomos.org/canada

| | |
|---|---|
| Inuit Art Foundation | http://www.inuitart.org |
| Inverarden Regency Cottage Museum | http://www.cnwl.igs.net/~slm/index.html |
| Italian Cultural Institute | http://www.iicto-ca.org |
| Japanese Canadian National Museum & Archives Society | http://www.shinnova.com/part/86-jcma/jcma10-e.htm |
| Jasper-Yellowhead Museum & Archives | http://www.discoverjasper.com/JasperMuseum/ |
| The Justina M. Barnicke Gallery | http://www.utoronto.ca/gallery/ |
| Kings Landing Historical Settlement | http://www.grtplaces.com/ac/landing/ |
| Kitimat Centennial Museum | http://www.kitimat.sno.net/kitmuse |
| L'Institut canadien de Québec | http://www.icqbdq.qc.ca |
| L'Opéra de Montréal | http://www.operademontreal.qc.ca |
| La Have Island Marine Museum | http://www.lunco.com/heritage/lehaveisl.htm |
| La La La Human Steps | http://www.bart.nl/~xipe/lalala.htm |
| La Société des musées québécois | http://www.uqam.ca/musees/ |
| Laubach Literacy Canada | http://www.nald.ca/llc.htm |
| Law Society of Upper Canada Archives | http://www.lsuc.on.ca/about/history/about_archives.html |
| The League of Canadian Poets | http://www.swifty.com/lc/ |
| Lieu historique national du Parc-de-L'Artillerie | http://www.upc.qc.ca/pch/artillerie |
| The Literary Press Group of Canada | http://www.lpg.ca |
| London Museum of Archaeology & Iroquoian Village Site | http://www.uwo.ca/museum/index.html |
| Lord Strathcona's Horse (Royal Canadians) Regimental Museum | http://www.nucleus.com/~rdennis/ |
| MacKenzie Art Gallery | http://www.uregina.ca/~macken// |
| Macaulay Heritage Park | http://www.pec.on.ca/macaulay |
| Maltwood Art Museum & Gallery | http://www.maltwood.uvic.ca |
| Manitoba Agricultural Museum | http://www.ag-museum.mb.ca |
| Manitoba Amateur Radio Museum Inc. | http://www.mbnet.mb.ca/~donahue/austin.html |
| Manitoba Arts Council | http://www.infobahn.mb.ca/mac |
| Manitoba Association of Architects | http://cad9.cadlab.umanitoba.ca/MAA.html |
| Manitoba Heritage Federation Inc. | http://www.mts.net/~mhf |
| Manitoba Library Association | http://www.mbnet.mb.ca/cm |
| Manitoba Museum of Man & Nature | http://www.mbnet.mb.ca/ManitobaMuseum |
| Manitoba Sports Hall of Fame & Museum Inc. | http://www.sport.mb.ca |
| Manitoba Theatre Centre | http://www.mtc.mb.ca |
| Manitoba Writers' Guild | http://www.mbwriter.mb.ca |
| Marine Museum of the Great Lakes at Kingston | http://www.marmus.ca |
| Mariposa Folk Foundation | http://www.eagle.ca/mariposa |
| Maritime History Archive | http://www.mun.ca/mha/ |
| Maritime Museum of British Columbia | http://www.vicnet.net/~mmbc/ |
| Maritime Museum of the Atlantic | http://www.ednet.ns.ca/educ/museum/mma/ |
| McCord Museum of Canadian History | http://www.mccord-museum.qc.ca |
| McCrae House | http://www.freespace.net/~museum/welcome.html |
| McGill University Archives | http://www.archives.mcgill.ca |
| The McMichael Canadian Art Collection | http://www.mcmichael.com |
| Meewasin Valley Authority | http://www.lights.com/meewasin |
| Mendel Art Gallery & Civic Conservatory | http://www.mendel.saskatoon.sk.ca |
| Mercer Union, A Centre for Contemporary Visual Art | http://www.interlog.com/~mercer |
| Metropolitan Toronto Archives & Records Centre | http://www.metrotor.on.ca/services/departments/clerk.html#archives |
| Metropolitan Toronto Police Museum & Discovery Centre | http://www.ntps.on.ca |
| Mildred M. Mahoney Silver Jubilee Dolls' House Gallery | http://www.angelfire.com/biz/DollHouseGallery/index.html |
| Miller Museum of Mineralogy & Geology | http://geol.queensu.ca/museum/museum.html |
| Moose Jaw Art Museum & National Exhibition Centre | http://www.chin.gc.ca/ |
| Morris & Helen Belkin Art Gallery | http://web.arts.ubc.ca/belkin/gallery.htm |
| Musée Acadien | http://www.umoncton.ca/maum/maum.html |
| Musée J. Armand Bombardier | http://www.ucctech.com/museejab |
| Musée d'art contemporain de Montréal | http://Media.MACM.qc.ca |
| Musée de l'Amerique française | http://www.mcq.org |
| Musée de la civilisation | http://www.mcq.org |
| Musée des arts décoratifs de Montréal | http://www.madm.org |
| Musée des beaux arts de Montréal | http://www.mbam.qc.ca, http://www.mmfa.qc.ca |
| Musée du Bas-St-Laurent | http://ucctech.com/museejab/ |
| Musée du Québec | http://www.mdq.org |
| Museum & Archive of Games | http://www.uwaterloo.ca/~museum |
| Museum at Campbell River | http://www.island.net/~crm_chin |
| The Museum of Industry | http://www.ednet.ns.ca/educ/museum/moi/index.htm |
| Museum for Textiles | http://www.interlog.com/~gwhite/ttt/tttintro.html |
| Museum of the Regiments | http://www.lexicom.ab.ca/~regiments/ |
| Music for Young Children | http://www.myc.com |
| Muskoka Pioneer Village & Museum | http://www.pioneervillage.org |
| Muttart Public Art Gallery | http://www.culturenet.ca/muttart |
| Nanaimo Community Archives | http://bbs.sd68.nanaimo.bc.ca/nol/community/nca.htm |
| Nanton Lancaster Society & Air Museum | http://www.lexicom.ab.ca/~nanton/nanton.html |
| National Archives of Canada | http://www.archives.ca |
| National Aviation Museum | http://www.aviation.nmstc.ca |
| National Ballet of Canada | http://www.national.ballet.ca |
| National Gallery of Canada | http://national.gallery.ca |
| The National Library of Canada | http://www.nlc-bnc.ca/ |
| National Museum of Science & Technology | http://www.science-tech.nmstc.ca |
| National Screen Institute - Canada | http://www.nsi-canada.ca |
| Native Earth Performing Arts Inc. | http://www.io.org/~naterth/naterth.htm |

|  |  |
|---|---|
| Naval Museum of Alberta | http://www.lexicom.ab.ca/~navalmuseum/navalmuseum.html |
| Newfoundland Historical Society | http://www.infonet.st-johns.nf.ca/nfldhist/ |
| Newfoundland Museum | http://calvin.stemnet.nf.ca/~cshea/ |
| Newfoundland Provincial Resource Library | http://www.stemnet.nf.ca/Community/PublicLibrary/ |
| Newfoundland Symphony Youth Orchestra | http://www.engr.mun.ca/~whitt/nsyo/nsyo.html |
| The Nickle Arts Museum | http://www.ucalgary.ca |
| North Vancouver Museum & Archives | http://www.district.north-van.bc.ca/nvma |
| Northwest Territories Archives | http://tailpipe.learnnet.nt.ca/pwnhc/nwta.htm |
| Nova Scotia Centre for Craft & Design | http://WWW.EDnet.NS.Ca/educ/heritage/crafts/ |
| Nova Scotia Highland Village | http://www.ednet.ns.ca/educ/museum/other_ns/highland_village/ |
| Nova Scotia Library Association | http://www.library.ns.ca/nsla |
| Nova Scotia Museum | http://www.ednet.ns.ca/educ/museum/ |
| Oakville Museum | http://www.town.oakville.on.ca |
| Odon Wagner Gallery | http://www.owgalery.com |
| Ojibway Nature Centre | http://www.city.windsor.on.ca/parkrec/ojibway.htm |
| Old Fort William | http://www.oldfortwilliam.on.ca |
| Old Kings Courthouse Museum | http://www.go.ednet.ns.ca/~ip960031 |
| Old Strathcona Model & Toy Museum | http://www.discoveredmonton.com/ToyMuseum/ |
| Ontario Association of Art Galleries | http://www.culturenet.ca/oaag/ |
| Ontario Crafts Council | http://www.craft.on.ca/occ |
| Ontario Folk Dance Association | http://www.web.net/~ofda |
| Ontario Library Association | http://www.ola.amlibs.ca |
| Ontario Museum Association | http://www.museumassn.on.ca |
| Orchestras Ontario | http://home.ican.net/~assoc |
| Ordre des architectes du Québec | http://www.oaq.com |
| Ordre des traducteurs et interprètes agréés du Québec | http://www.otiaq.org |
| Owen Sound Marine-Rail Museum | Http://www.geocities.com/Athens/Delphi/6265 |
| Owens Art Gallery | http://www.mta.ca/owens/ |
| Pacific Opera Victoria | http://www.islandnet.com/~opera/ |
| Parkdale-Maplewood Community Museum | http://www.ednet.ns.ca/educ/museum/other_ns/parkdale/museum1.html |
| Perfume Factory & Museum | http://www.tourismniagara.com/perfumefactory/ |
| Photo Marketing Association International - Canada | http://www.pmai.org |
| Photographic Historical Society of Canada | http://web.onramp.ca/phsc |
| Pier 21 Society | http://pier21.ns.ca |
| Playwrights Union of Canada | http://www.puc.ca |
| Point Pelee National Park Visitor Centre (Natural History Museum) | http://parkscanada.pch.gc.ca |
| Pointe-à-Callière, Museum of Archaeology & History | http://www.musee-Pointe-a-Calliere.qc.ca |
| Portage Plains Regional Library | library@freenet.mb.ca |
| The Power Plant | http://www.culturenet.ca/powerplant |
| Presqu'ile Provincial Park Museum | presquil@parks.kosone.com |
| Prince Albert National Park Nature Centre | http://www.parkscanada.pch.gc.ca |
| Prince Edward Island Crafts Council | gopher://gopher.well.sf.ca.us/00/Art/PEI.Crafts.Council |
| Prince Edward Island Museum & Heritage Foundation | http://www.peisland.com/peimuseum/welcome.htm |
| Prince Edward Island Potato Museum | http://www.worldsites.net/peipotatomuseum/ |
| Prince of Wales Northern Heritage Centre | http://pwnhc.nt.ca |
| Professional Association of Canadian Theatres | http://webhome.idirect.com/~pact/ |
| Professional Opera Companies of Canada | http://www.operademontreal.qc.ca |
| Provincial Archives of Alberta | http://www.gov.ab.ca/~mcd/mhs/paa/paa.htm |
| Provincial Archives of Manitoba | http://www.gov.mb.ca/chc/archives/index.html |
| Provincial Archives of New Brunswick | http://www.gov.nb.ca/supply/archives |
| Provincial Museum of Alberta | http://www.pma.edmonton.ab.ca |
| Public Archives & Records Office | http://www.gov.pe.ca/educ/archives/archives_index.asp |
| Queen's University Archives | http://stauffer.queensu.ca/webarch/ |
| Queens County Museum | http://www.geocities.com/Paris/2669/ |
| Quesnel & District Museum & Archives | http://www.sd28.bc.ca/museum/ |
| Réseau des archives du Québec | http://www.raq.qc.ca |
| Rassemblement des bibliothèques publiques du Lac-Saint-Jean et Saguenay | http://www.crsbpslsj.biblio.qc.ca/regroupement.html |
| Reactor Gallery | http://www.reactor.ca |
| Redpath Museum | http://www.mcgill.ca/Redpath |
| Remington-Alberta Carriage Centre | http://www.remingtoncentre.com |
| Revelstoke Railway Museum | http://www.railwaymuseum.com |
| Reynolds-Alberta Museum | http://www.gov.ab.ca/~mcd/mhs/ram/ram.htm |
| Right Hon. John G. Diefenbaker Centre for the Study of Canada | http://library.usask.ca/remate.html |
| The Robert McLaughlin Gallery | http://www.rmg.on.ca |
| Royal Architectural Institute of Canada | http://www.aecinfo.com/raic/index.html |
| Royal British Columbia Museum | http://rbcm1.rbcm.gov.bc.ca/index.html |
| Royal Canadian College of Organists | http://www.capitalnet.com/~rjewell/rcco.html |
| Royal Canadian Mint | http://www.rcmint.ca |
| Royal Canadian Mounted Police Centennial Museum | http://rbcm1.rbcm.gov.bc.ca |
| Royal London Wax Museum | http://www.waxworld.com |
| Royal Ontario Museum | http://www.rom.on.ca |
| Royal Saskatchewan Museum | http://www.gov.sk.ca/govt/munigov/cult&rec/rsm/ |
| The Royal Society of Canada | http://www.rsc.ca |
| Royal Tyrrell Museum of Palaeontology | http://tyrrell.magtech.ab.ca |
| Rutherford House Provincial Historic Site | http://www.gov.ab.ca/~mcd/mcd.htm |
| Saskatchewan Archives Board | http://www.gov.sk.ca/govt/archives/ |
| Saskatchewan Council of Archives | http://www.usask.ca/archives/sca.html |
| Saskatchewan Council of Cultural Organizations | http://www.sasknet.com/~SCCO/ |

| | |
|---|---|
| Saskatchewan Crafts Council | http://www.ffa.ucalgary.ca/scco/scc.html; http://www.sasknet.sk.ca/SCCO/SCC.html |
| Saskatchewan Library Association | http://www.lib.sk.ca/sla/ |
| Saskatchewan Motion Picture Association | http://midxpress.com/midxpress/smpia/main.htm |
| Saskatchewan Music Festival Association Inc. | http://www.ffa.ucalgary.ca/scco/smea.html |
| Saskatchewan Playwrights Centre | http://bailey2.unibase.com/~grain/SPC_Homepage.html |
| Saskatchewan Writers Guild Inc. | http://www.sasknet.com/~skwriter |
| Sculptor's Society of Canada | http://www.lglobal.com/sculpcan/Welcome.html |
| Sharon Temple Museum | http://www.interhop.net/museum/sharon.html |
| Shaw Festival | http://shawfest.sympatico.ca |
| Simon Fraser University Archives | http://www.sfu.ca/archives/index.htm |
| Simon Fraser University Museum of Archaeology & Ethnology | http://www.sfu.ca/archaeology |
| Sir Wilfred Grenfell College Art Gallery | http://www.swgc.mun.ca |
| Société Pro Musica Inc. | http://www.apexdigital.com/promusica |
| Société de développement des périodiques culturels québécois | http://www3.sympatico.ca/sodep/ |
| Société québécoise d'espéranto | http://www.cam.org/~mmaerten/esk.html |
| Society of Composers, Authors & Music Publishers of Canada | http://www.socan.ca |
| Songwriters Association of Canada | http://www.goodmedia.com/sac/ |
| Southern Alberta Art Gallery | http://upanet.uleth.ca/~saag |
| Spencer Entomological Museum | http://www.insecta.com |
| Springhill Miners Museum | http://www.grtplaces.com/ac/mine |
| Stationhouse Gallery | http://sos-connect.com/station/ |
| Stephansson House Provincial Historic Site | http://www.gov.ab.ca/~mcd/mhs/steph/stephans.htm |
| Stephen Leacock Museum | http://www.transdata.ca/leacock/leacock.html |
| Steveston Museum | http://www.netlink2000.com/villager |
| Stratford Festival | http://www.ffa.ucalgary.ca/stratford/home.htm |
| Sun Ergos, A Company of Theatre & Dance | http://www.sunergos.com |
| Symphony Hamilton | http://www.netaccess.on.ca/~artset |
| Symphony New Brunswick | http://www.discribe.ca/snb |
| Tafelmusik Baroque Orchestra | http://www.tafelmusik.org |
| Théâtre français de Toronto | http://francoculture.ca/theatre/tft/ |
| The Toronto Symphony Orchestra | http://www.tso.on.ca |
| Thomas McCulloch Museum | http://is.dal.ca/~sfry/museum1.htm/ |
| Tom Thomson Memorial Art Gallery | http://www.tomthomson.org |
| Toronto Aerospace Museum | http://tor-pw1.netcom.ca/~n.flight/small.html |
| Toronto Dance Theatre | http://www.tdt.com |
| Toronto International Film Festival | http://www.bell.ca/filmfest |
| Toronto Theatre Alliance | http://www.ffa.ucalgary,ca/tta/ |
| Trinity Square Video | http://www.modworld.com/tsv |
| Two Turtle Iroquois Fine Art Gallery | http://wchat.on.ca/tom/2turtle.htm |
| U'Mista Cultural Centre & Society | http://www.swifty.com/umista/ |
| Ukrainian Museum of Canada | http://www.saskstar.sk.ca/umc |
| Union des écrivaines et écrivains québécois | http://www.uneq.qc.ca |
| United Church of Canada BC Conference Archives | http://www.interchange.ubc.ca/bstewart/index.html |
| United Church of Canada/Victoria University Archives | http://www.vicu.utoronto.ca/archives/archives.htm |
| Univers Maurice Rocket Richard Universe | http://www.Rocket9.org |
| University of Alberta - Museums & Collections Services | http://www.ualberta.ca/MUSEUMS |
| University of Alberta Archives | http://www.ualberta.ca/ARCHIVES/ |
| University of British Columbia Archives | http://www.library.ubc.ca/spcoll/general.html |
| University of Western Ontario Symphony Orchestra | http://www.uwo.ca/music |
| Upper Canada Village | http://www.parks.on.ca |
| Uxbridge-Scott Museum & Archives | http://www.uxbridge.com/museum |
| The Vancouver Art Gallery | http://www.vanartgallery.bc.ca |
| Vancouver Cultural Alliance | http://www.culturenet.ca/vca |
| Vancouver Independent Dance Agency | http://www.vkool.com/dancentre |
| The Vancouver Maritime Museum Society | http://www.vmm.bc.ca |
| The Vancouver Museum | http://www.vanmuseum.bc.ca |
| Vancouver New Music | http://www.newmusic.org/VNMS |
| Vancouver Opera | http://www.vanopera.bc.ca |
| Vancouver Police Historical Society & Centennial Museum | http://www.city.vancouver.bc.ca/police/museum/ |
| Vancouver Symphony Society | http://www.culturenet.ca/vso/ |
| Vancouver Youth Symphony Orchestra | http://www.vcn.bc.ca/vyso |
| Visual Arts Nova Scotia | http://www.cfn.cs.dal.ca/Culture/VANS/index.html |
| VU centre de diffusion et de production de la photographie | http://www2.zone.ca/~vuphoto |
| Walter Phillips Gallery | http://www-nmr.banffcentre.ab.ca/WPG |
| Wellington Community Historical Museum | http://www.lookupontario.com |
| West Vancouver Memorial Library | http://www.wvml.jeslacs.bc.ca |
| Western Canada Aviation Museum Inc. | http://www.wcam.mb.ca |
| Western Development Museum | http://www.sfn.saskatoon.sk.ca/arts/wdm/ |
| Westfield Heritage Centre | http://www.worldchat.com/public/westfield/westf1.htm |
| Wheatland Regional Library | http://www.wheatland.lib.sk.ca |
| Whyte Museum of the Canadian Rockies | http://www.cadvision.com/db/wmer |
| Wilfrid Laurier University Symphony Orchestra | http://www.wlu.ca/~wwwmusic/ |
| Windsor's Community Museum | http://www.city.windsor.on.ca/wpl/museum.htm |
| The Winnipeg Art Gallery | http://www.wag.mb.ca |
| Winnipeg Symphony Orchestra Inc. | http://www.aroundmanitoba.com/wso/ |
| Women in View | http://www.ffa.ucalgary.ca/vca/wmnvie.htm |
| Writers Guild of Alberta | http://www.rtt.ab.ca/rtt.writers |
| Writers' Alliance of Newfoundland & Labrador | http://www.infonet.st-johns.nf.ca/providers/writers/writers.html |

Writers' Federation of New Brunswick .......... http://www.sjfn.nb.ca/community_hall/W/Writers_Federation_NB/index.htm
Writers' Federation of Nova Scotia .......... http://www.chebucto.ns.ca/Culture/WFNS/
The Writers' Union of Canada .......... http://www.swifty.com/twuc
Yarmouth County Museum & Historical Research Archives.......... http://www.ycn.library.ns.ca/museum/yarcomus.htm
Yellowhead Regional Library System .......... http://www.ccinet.ab.ca/yrl/
York University Archives .......... http://www.library.yorku.ca/depts/asc/archives.htm
Yukon Council of Archives.......... http://moondog.usask.ca/cca/yuk1.html

## BUSINESS & FINANCE

AGF Funds Inc.......... http://www.agf.com
AIC Limited .......... http://www.aicfunds.com/
ASEAN-Canada Business Council.......... http://www.chamber.ca
Admax Regent International Management Ltd. .......... http://www.admaxregent.com
Aetna Life Insurance Company of Canada.......... http://www.aetna.ca
Affiliated FM Insurance Company.......... http://www.allendale.com
Aim Funds Group Canada Inc.......... http://www.aimfunds.com
Alberta Association of the Appraisal Institute of Canada .......... http://www.cyberpage.com/appraisal/alberta/appraisal.html
The Alberta Stock Exchange.......... http://www.albertastock.com
Alberta Treasury Branches .......... http://www.atb.com
Allendale Mutual Insurance Company .......... http://www.allendale.com
Altamira Investment Services Inc. .......... http://www.altamira.com
Amex Bank of Canada.......... http://www.americanexpress.com/canada/
Appraisal Institute of Canada .......... http://www.aicanada.org
Arthur & District Chamber of Commerce .......... http://www.freespace.net/~arthur
Arthur Andersen & Co.......... http://www.arthurandersen.com
Asia Pacific Foundation of Canada .......... http://www.apfc.ca
Association de planification fiscale et financière .......... http://www.apff.org
Association of Canadian Advertisers Inc.......... http://www3.sympatico.ca/aca/
Association of Municipal Tax Collectors of Ontario .......... http://www.intranet.ca/amtco/
Association of Professional Recruiters of Canada .......... http://www.hrtoday.com
Assurances Générales des Caisses Desjardins Inc.. .......... http://www.insurance_canada.ca/insurcan/desjard.nt
Atlantic Provinces Chamber of Commerce.......... http://www.apcc.ca/chamber
Atlantic Provinces Economic Council .......... http://ttg.sba.dal.ca/apec/
Atlas Asset Management Inc.......... http://www.atlasfunds.ca
Avery Cooper & Co.. .......... http://www.averyco.nt.ca
BDO Dunwoody.......... http://www.bdo.ca
Banca Commerciale Italiana of Canada.......... http://www.bcibank.ca
Bank of Montreal Investment Management Ltd.......... http://www.fcfunds.bomil.ca/
Bank of Montreal .......... http://www.bmo.com
The Bank of Nova Scotia.......... http://www.scotiabank.ca
Beallor & Partners .......... http://www.beallor.com
Belleville & District Chamber of Commerce .......... http://www.city.belleville.on.ca/chamber/
Better Business Bureau of Mainland BC.......... http://www.bbbmbc.com
Better Business Bureau of Nova Scotia.......... http://www.bbbns.com/bbbns
Better Business Bureau of Windsor & Southern Ontario.......... http://www.wincom.net/wbbb/
Bissett & Associates Investment Management Ltd.. .......... http://www.bissett.com
British Columbia & Yukon Chamber of Mines .......... http://www.bc-mining-house.com/chamber
British Columbia Chamber of Commerce.......... http://www.bcchamber.org
British Columbia Real Estate Association .......... http://www.bcrea.bc.ca
Building Owners & Managers Association of the Greater Toronto Area .......... http://www.bomatoronto.org
Business Development Bank of Canada .......... http://www.bdc.ca/
Business Documents & Systems Association .......... http://www.bdsa.ca
C.D. Howe Institute .......... http://www.cdhowe.org
CIBC Securities Inc.......... http://www.cibc.com/products/investment/mfunds/
CIBC Wood Gundy .......... http://www.woodgundy.com/
CIGNA Insurance Company of Canada .......... http://www.cigna.com
CT Securities International Inc. .......... http://www.ctsecurities.com
Campbell River & District Chamber of Commerce.......... http://www.vquest.com/crchamber/
Canaccord Capital Corporation .......... http://www.canaccord.com
Canada China Business Council .......... http://www.ccbc.com
Canada-India Business Council.......... http://www.canada-indiabusiness.ca
Canada Life Casualty Insurance Company .......... http://www.canadalife.com/casualty
The Canada Life Assurance Company.......... http://www.canadalife.com
Canada Trust Company .......... http://www.canadatrust.com
Canada West Foundation.......... http://www.cwf.ca
Canadian Association for Business Economics, Inc. .......... http://www.cabe.ca
Canadian Association of Career Educators & Employers .......... http://www.cacee.com/workweb
Canadian Association of Family Enterprise .......... http://www.cafe-uc.on.ca/
The Canadian Association of Financial Planners.......... http://www.cafp.org/
Canadian Association of Mutual Insurance Companies .......... http://www.camic.ca
Canadian Bankers Association .......... http://www.cba.ca
Canadian Board of Marine Underwriters .......... http://www.webcom.com/cbmu/
The Canadian Chamber of Commerce.......... http://www.chamber.ca
Canadian Co-operative Association.......... http://www.coopcca.com
Canadian Commercial Corp.......... http://www.ccc.ca
Canadian Council for Public-Private Partnerships.......... http://www.inforamp.net/~partners
Canadian Direct Marketing Association .......... http://www.cdma.org
Canadian Economics Association.......... http://pacific.commerce.ubc.ca/cea/

|  |  |
|---|---|
| Canadian Federation of Business & Professional Women's Clubs | http://www.bpwcanada.com |
| Canadian Federation of Independent Business | http://www.cfib.ca |
| Canadian Finance & Leasing Association | http://www.inforamp.net/~mreid/cfla.html |
| Canadian Franchise Association | http://www.cfa.ca |
| Canadian Imperial Bank of Commerce | http://www.cibc.com |
| Canadian Importers Association Inc. | http://www.importers.ca |
| Canadian Institute for Organization Management | http://www.chamber.ca |
| Canadian Institute of Actuaries | http://www.actuaries.ca/CIA/CIA.html |
| Canadian Institute of Chartered Accountants | http://www.cica.ca/ |
| Canadian International Mutual Funds | http://www.cifunds.com |
| Canadian Junior Chamber | http://web.idirect.com/~canadajc/ |
| Canadian Labour Market & Productivity Centre | http://www.clmpc.ca |
| Canadian Life & Health Insurance Association Inc. | http://www.inforamp.net/~clhia/ |
| Canadian Manufacturers of Chemical Specialties Association | http://www.cmcs.org |
| Canadian Meat Importers Committee | http://www.importers.ca |
| Canadian Office Products Association | http://www.copa.ca |
| The Canadian Payroll Association | http://www.payroll.ca |
| Canadian Professional Sales Association | http://www.cpsa.com |
| Canadian Property Tax Association, Inc. | http://www.cpta.org |
| The Canadian Public Relations Society, Inc. | http://www.cprs.ca/ |
| The Canadian Real Estate Association | http://www.mls.ca |
| Canadian Society of Customs Brokers | http://www.cscb.ca |
| Canadian Sporting Goods Association | http://www.globalsports.com/csga |
| Canadian Standards Association | http://www.csa.ca/ |
| Canadian Tax Foundation | http://www.ctf.ca |
| Canadian Venture Capital Association | http://www.cvca.ca |
| Canadian Western Bank | http://www.cwbank.com |
| Canadian Youth Business Foundation | http://www.cybf.ca |
| Capital Alliance Ventures Inc. | http://www.cavi.com |
| Centre de recherche et développement en économique | http://tornade.ere.umontreal.ca/crde/ |
| Certified General Accountants Association of Alberta | http://www.cga-canada.org/alberta/ |
| Certified General Accountants Association of British Columbia | http://www.cga-bc.org |
| Certified General Accountants Association of Canada | http://www.cga-canada.org |
| Certified General Accountants Association of Ontario | http://www.cga-ontario.org |
| Certified General Accountants Association of Saskatchewan | http://www.cga-canada.org/saskatchewan |
| Certified Management Accountants Society of British Columbia | http://www.cmabc.com |
| Chambre de Commerce du Québec | http://www.ccq.ca |
| Chambre de Commerce et d'industrie du Québec métropolitain | http://www.cciqm.qc.ca |
| Chambre de commerce du Montréal métropolitain | http://www.ccmm.qc.ca |
| The Chemical Institute of Canada | http://www.chem-inst-can.org |
| Chubb Insurance Company of Canada | http://www.chubbinsurance.ca |
| Citizens Bank of Canada | http://www.citizens.com |
| Citizens Trust Company | http://www.citizenstrust.ca |
| Clean Environment Mutual Funds | http://www.cleanenvironment.com |
| Co-operators General Insurance Company | http://www.cooperators.ca |
| Cobourg & District Chamber of Commerce | http://marlo.eagle.ca/cobourg/chamber/ |
| Collins Barrow Chartered Accountants | http://www.collinsbarrow.com |
| Confédération des caisses populaires et d'économie desjardins du Québec | http://www.desjardins.com |
| The Conference Board of Canada | http://www.conferenceboard.ca/nbec |
| Conseil des assurances de dommages | http://www.conseilad.qc.ca |
| Conseil québécois du commerce de détail | http://www.cqcd.com |
| Coopers & Lybrand | http://www.ca.coopers.com |
| Cornerstone 52 Foundation | http://www.cornerstone52.org/ |
| Corporate-Higher Education Forum | http://www.work.org/C-HEF/ |
| Credit Institute of Canada | http://www.creditedu.org |
| Credit Union Central of Canada | http://www.cucentral.ca |
| Crosson Voyer Chartered Accountants | http://www.crossonvoyer.bc.ca/ |
| Crown Life Insurance Company | http://www.crownlife.ca |
| Cyr Mortgage & Investment Corp. | http://www.cyrmortgages.com. |
| Dai-Ichi Kangyo Bank (Canada) | http://www.infoweb.or.jp/dkb/index-e.html |
| Deloitte & Touche | http://www.deloitte.ca |
| Desjardins Trust Inc. | http://www.desjardins.com/ |
| Desjardins-Laurentian Life Assurance Company Inc. | http://www.avdl.com |
| Doane Raymond | http://www.drgt.ca |
| Dryden District Chamber of Commerce | http://www.dryden.nor-ont.ca |
| Dynamic Mutual Funds | http://www.dynamic.ca |
| Economic Developers Council of Ontario Inc. | http://www.edco.on.ca |
| Edmonton Chamber of Commerce | http://www.tnc.com/ecc/ |
| Edward D. Jones & Co. | http://www.edwardjones.com/Canada_HTML/home.shtml |
| Electronic Commerce Canada | http://www.ecc.ca |
| Elliott & Page Limited | http://www.fundlib.com/ellpag.html |
| Elliott, Tulk, Pryce, Anderson | http://www.etpa.bc.ca |
| Equion Securities Canada Limited | http://www.equion.com |
| Equisure Financial Network Inc. | http://www.equisure.ca |
| The Equitable Life Insurance Company of Canada | http://www.equitable.ca |
| Ernst & Young | http://www.eycan.com |
| Evancic Perrault Robertson | http://www.epr.ca |
| F.C.G. Securities Corporation | http://www.fcg.ca |

Federal Insurance Company ............ http://www.chubbinsurance.ca
Fidelity Investments Canada Limited ............ http://www.fidelity.ca
First American Title Insurance Company ............ http://www.firstam.com
First Marathon Securities Limited ............ http://www.fmarathon.com
The Fraser Institute ............ http://www.fraserinstitute.ca
Friedberg Mercantile Group ............ http://www.friedberg.com
Friends of the Environment Foundation ............ http://www.fef.ca/
GT Global ............ http://www.gtglobal.ca
The General Accident Assurance Company of Canada ............ http://www.genacc.ca
General American Life Insurance Company ............ http://www.genam.com
Georgia Pacific Securities Corporation ............ http://www.gpsec.bc.ca/contact.html
Global Securities Corporation ............ http://www.globalsec.com
Great Pacific Management Co. Ltd. ............ http://www.gpmc.com
The Great-West Life Assurance Company ............ http://www.gwl.ca
Greater Victoria Chamber of Commerce ............ http://vvv.com/Chamber
The Guardian Group of Funds Limited ............ http://www.guardianfunds.com/
The Halifax Insurance Company ............ http://www.halifaxinsurance.com
Hamilton & District Chamber of Commerce ............ http://www.hamilton-cofc.on.ca
Hartford Insurance Company of Canada ............ http://www.thehartford.com
Hong Kong-Canada Business Association ............ http://www.hkcba.com
Hongkong Bank of Canada ............ http://www.hkbc.com
Horwath Orenstein Chartered Accountants ............ http://www.hto.com/
Howson Tattersall Investment Counsel Ltd. ............ http://www.saxonfunds.com/~saxon
Human Resources Professionals Association of Ontario ............ http://www.hrpao.org
ING Trust Company of Canada ............ http://www.ingdirect.ca
Information Technology Association of Canada ............ http://www.itac.ca/
Institute of Canadian Advertising ............ http://www.goodmedia.com/ica/
Institute of Canadian Bankers ............ http://www.icb.org
Institute of Certified Management Consultants of Canada ............ http://www.cmc-consult.org
Institute of Chartered Accountants of Alberta ............ http://www.icaa.ab.ca
Institute of Chartered Accountants of British Columbia ............ http://www.ica.bc.ca
Institute of Chartered Accountants of Ontario ............ http://www.icao.on.ca
The Institute of Internal Auditors ............ http://www.theiia.org
Insurance Bureau of Canada ............ http://www.ibc.ca
Insurance Corporation of British Columbia ............ http://www.icbc.com
International Association of Business Communicators/Toronto ............ http://www.iabctoronto.com
International Special Events Society - Toronto Chapter ............ http://www.ndgphoenix.com/ises.html
Investment Funds Institute of Canada ............ http://www.mutfunds.com/ific
Investors Group Inc. ............ http://www.investorsgroup.com
Italian Chamber of Commerce in Canada ............ http://www.italchamber.qc.ca
Kemptville & District Chamber of Commerce ............ http://www.cyberus.ca/~chamberk
L'Entraide Assurance-Vie, Compagnie Mutuelle ............ http://www.lentraide.com
Lévesque Securities Inc. ............ http://www.lsi.ca
Laurentian Bank of Canada ............ http://www.laurentianbank.com
Le Publicité club de Montréal ............ http://www.pcm.montreal.qc.ca/
Leduc & District Chamber of Commerce ............ http://www.tnc.com/commerce
Life Underwriters Association of Canada ............ http://www.luac.com
Loewen, Ondaatje, McCutcheon Limited ............ http://www.lomrsch.com
London Guarantee Insurance Company ............ http://www.londonguarantee.com
London Life Insurance Company ............ http://www.londonlife.com
MFQ-Vie, Corporation d'Assurance ............ http://www.mfq.qc.ca
Mackenzie Financial Corporation ............ http://www.fundlib.com/mackenzie.html
Manitoba Real Estate Association ............ http://www.manitobarealestate.com
The Manufacturers Life Insurance Company ............ http://www.manulife.com
Manulife Bank of Canada ............ http://www.manulife.com
The Maritime Life Assurance Company ............ http://www.maritimelife.ca
Mawer Investment Management ............ http://www.mawer.com/
Melfort & District Chamber of Commerce ............ http://www.nlnet.melfort.sk.ca/mcc/
Meloche Monnex Inc. ............ http://www.meloche-monnex.com
Merit Investment Corporation ............ http://www.meritinvestment.com
Merrill Lynch Canada Inc. ............ http://www.merrill-lynch.com
Midland Walwyn Capital Inc. ............ http://www.midwal.ca
Mississauga Board of Trade ............ http://www.mbot.com
Montréal Exchange ............ http://www.me.org
Motor Dealers' Association of Alberta ............ http://www.compusmart.ab.ca/mdaalta
The Mutual Group ............ http://www.themutualgroup.com/
Mutual Investco Inc. ............ http://www.themutualgroup.com/
NN Life Insurance Company of Canada ............ http://www.ingfin.com
National Advertising Benevolent Society ............ http://www.nabs.org
National Bank of Canada ............ http://www.nbc.ca/
National Quality Institute ............ http://www.nqi.com
National Society of Fund Raising Executives ............ http://www.nsfre.org/
Native Investment & Trade Association ............ http://www.native-invest-trade.com
Navigator Fund Company Ltd. ............ http://www.navigator.ca
Northwest Territories Chamber of Commerce ............ http://www.ssimicro.com/~nwtcofc
Northwestern Ontario Associated Chambers of Commerce ............ http://www.tb-chamber.on.ca
Okanagan Skeena Group Ltd. ............ http://www.osg.net
Ontario Chamber of Commerce ............ http://www.occ.on.ca

Ontario Public Buyers Association, Inc. .......... http://vaxxine.com/opba
Ordre des comptables agréés du Québec .......... http://www.uquebec.ca/comptables/agrees
Ordre des comptables généraux licenciés du Québec .......... http://www.cga-quebec.org
Pacific Corporate Trust Company .......... http://www.pctc.com
Pacific International Securities Inc. .......... http://www.pi-securities.com
Peace Hills Trust Company .......... http://www.peacehills.com/
Peoples Trust Company .......... http://www.peoplestrust.com
Perigee Investment Counsel Inc. .......... http://www.perigeeinvest.com
Peter Cundill & Associates Ltd. .......... http://www.cundill.com
Petroleum Accountants Society of Canada .......... http://www.cadvision.com/pasc
Phillips, Hager & North Investment Management Ltd. .......... http://www.phn.ca/
Progressive Casualty Insurance Company of Canada .......... http://www.auto-insurance.com
Project Management Institute .......... http://www.pmi.org
Promotional Products Association of Canada Inc. .......... http://www.promotionalproducts.com/ppac
Protection Mutual Insurance Company .......... http://www.promutual.com
Purchasing Management Association of Canada .......... http://www.pmac.ca
Qualicum Beach Chamber of Commerce .......... http://nanaimo.ark.com/~qualicum/
RBC Dominion Securities Inc. .......... http://www.rbcds.com/
RGA Life Reinsurance Company of Canada .......... http://www.rgare.com
Real Estate Institute of Canada .......... http://www.reic.ca
Reinsurance Research Council .......... http://www.collinscan.com/~collins/clientspgs/rrc.html
Renaissance Capital Inc. .......... http://www.rcican.com
Retail Council of Canada .......... http://www.retailcouncil.org
The R-M Trust Company .......... http://www.rmtrust.ca
Royal Bank of Canada .......... http://www.royalbank.com
Royal Mutual Funds Inc. .......... http://www.royalbank.com/english/fund/index.html
Sagit Investment Management Ltd. .......... http://www.sagit.com/funds
Salomon Brothers Canada Inc .......... http://www.salomon.com
Scotia Securities Inc. .......... http://www.scotiabank.ca
ScotiaMcLeod Inc. .......... http://www.scotiacapital.com
Scudder Canada Investor Services Ltd. .......... http://www.scudder.ca
Société des relationnistes du Québec inc. .......... http://www.planetecom.net/srq/
Society of Management Accountants of Alberta .......... http://www.cmaab.com
Society of Management Accountants of Canada .......... http://www.cma-canada.org
Society of Management Accountants of Ontario .......... http://www.cma-ontario.org
Spectrum United Mutual Funds Inc. .......... http://www.fundlib.com/specbull.html
Spectrum United Mutual Funds Inc. .......... http://www.spectrumunited.ca/
Standard Life Mutual Funds Limited .......... http://www.standardlife.ca
State Farm Life Insurance Company .......... http://www.statefarm.com
Strategic Leadership Forum .......... http://www.slf-canada.org
Sun Life Trust Company .......... http://www.sunlife.com
Surrey Chamber of Commerce .......... http://www.surreycoc.com/cip/CHAMBER.HTML
TD Asset Management .......... http://www.tdbank.ca/tdbank/mutual/index.html
TD Trust Company .......... http://www.tdbank.ca
Talvest Fund Management Inc. .......... http://www.talvest.com
Templeton Management Limited .......... http://www.templeton.ca
The Toronto-Dominion Bank .......... http://www.tdbank.ca
Thunder Bay Chamber of Commerce .......... http://www.tb-chamber.on.ca
Tobermory & District Chamber of Commerce .......... http://www.tobermory.org
Tradex Management Inc. .......... http://www.tradex.ca
Treasury Management Association of Canada .......... http://www.tmac.ca
Trimark Financial Corporation .......... http://www.trimark.com
Trimark Investment Management Inc. .......... http://www.trimark.com/
Trimark Trust .......... http://www.trimarktrust.com
UNUM CANADA .......... http://www.unum.com
University Avenue Financial .......... http://www.fundlib.com/univers.html
Valley Real Estate Board Inc. .......... http://www.valleyboard.ca
The Vancouver Stock Exchange .......... http://www.vse.com
Vermilion & District Chamber of Commerce .......... http://www.agt.net/public/townvrml/index.htm
Versus Brokerage Services Inc. .......... http://www.canada.etrade.com
West Shore Chamber of Commerce .......... http://westshore.bc.ca
Whistler Chamber of Commerce .......... http://www.whistler.net/coc/index.html
White Rock & South Surrey Chamber of Commerce .......... http://www.our-town.bc.ca
Whitehorse Chamber of Commerce .......... http://www.yukon.net/wcc
Winnipeg Chamber of Commerce .......... http://www.winnipegchmbr.mb.ca
Winnipeg Real Estate Board .......... http://www.mls.ca
The Winnipeg Stock Exchange .......... http://www.wse.ca
World Trade Centre Montréal .......... http://www.wtc-mtl.com
Yield Management Group Inc. .......... http://www.ymg.ca
Yukon Chamber of Commerce .......... http://www.yukonweb.com/business/ycc/

## CANADIANS & SOCIETY

Affiliation of Multicultural Societies & Service Agencies of BC .......... http://www.amssa.org
AFS Interculture Canada .......... http://www.afs.org
Alberta Civil Liberties Research Centre .......... http://www.FreeNet.Calgary.ab.ca/populati/communit/acl/aclrc.html
Alberta Family History Society .......... http://www.freenet.calgary.ab.ca/science/afhs.html
Alberta Native Friendship Centres Association .......... http://www.nativecentres.org
Alliance Québec .......... http://www.aq.qc.ca

|  |  |
|---|---|
| Amnistie internationale, Section canadienne (Francophone) | http://www.amnistie.qc.ca |
| Assemblée internationale des parlementaires de langue française | http://www.regionamerique.aiplf.org |
| Assembly of First Nations | http://www.afn.ca |
| Association canadienne-française de l'Alberta | http://francalta.ab.ca |
| Association canadienne-française de l'Ontario | http://www.franco.ca/acfo |
| Association culturelle franco-canadienne de la Saskatchewan | http://www.dlcwest.com/~acfc/ |
| Association franco-yukonnaise | http://francoculture.ca/afy |
| Black Cultural Centre for Nova Scotia | http://www.nstn.ca/bccns/bcc.html |
| B'nai Brith Canada | http://www.bnaibrith.ca |
| British Columbia Genealogical Society | http://www.npsnet.com/bcgs |
| Canada's National History Society | http://www.cyberspc.mb.ca/~otmw/cnhs/cnhs.html |
| Canadian Alliance in Solidarity with the Native Peoples | http://www.pathcom.com/~casnp/ |
| Canadian Association for the Advancement of Women & Sport & Physical Activity | http://infoweb.magi.com/~wmnsport/index.html |
| Canadian Association of Retired Persons | http://www.fifty-plus.net/ |
| Canadian Association on Gerontology | http://www.cagacg.ca |
| Canadian Catholic Historical Association - English Section | http://www.umanitoba.ca/colleges/st_pauls/ccha/ccha.html |
| Canadian Congress for Learning Opportunities for Women | http://www.nald.ca/cclow.htm |
| Canadian Council for International Co-operation | http://www.web.net/ccic-ccci |
| Canadian Ethnocultural Council | http://www.web.net/~cec/ |
| Canadian Federation of Business & Professional Women's Clubs | http://www.bpwcanada.com |
| Canadian Foundation for the Americas | http://www.focal.ca |
| Canadian Friends Historical Association | http://home.interhop.net/~aschrauwe/ |
| The Canadian Grey Panthers Advocacy Network | http://www.panthers.net |
| Canadian Heritage Information Network | http://www.chin.gc.ca |
| Canadian Institute for Historical Microreproductions | http://www.nlc-bnc.ca/cihm/ |
| Canadian Institute of International Affairs | http://www.trinity.utoronto.ca/ciia/ |
| Canadian Jewish Congress | http://www.cjc.ca |
| Canadian Lesbian & Gay Archives | http://www.clga.ca/archives |
| Canadian National Aboriginal Tourism Association | http://www.v1i.ca/clients/abc/cnata/cnata3.htm |
| Canadian Women in Communications | http://www.citytv.com/cwc/ |
| Canadian Women's Foundation | http://www.cdnwomen.org |
| CARE Canada | http://www.care.ca |
| Centre culturel franco-manitobain | http://francoculture.ca/ccfm |
| Chinese Information & Community Services of Greater Toronto | http://www.ipoline.com/cics |
| Citizens for Public Justice | http://www.web.net/~cpj |
| CODE | http://www.web.net/~code |
| Cornerstone 52 Foundation | http://www.cornerstone52.org/ |
| Couchiching Institute on Public Affairs | http://www.couch.ca |
| The Council of Canadians | http://www.web.net/coc |
| The CRB Foundation | http://www2.excite.sfu.ca/default.html |
| Elderhostel Canada | http://www.elderhostel.org |
| Fédération canadienne pour l'alphabétisation en français | http://www.franco.ca/alpha/ |
| Fédération culturelle canadienne-française | http://francoculture.ca/fccf/ |
| Fédération de la jeunesse canadienne-française inc. | http://www.franco.ca/fjcf |
| Fédération des communautés francophones et acadienne du Canada | http://www.franco.ca/fcfa |
| Fédération des francophones de Terre-Neuve et du Labrador | http://www.franco.ca/fftnl/index.htm |
| Fédération québécoise des sociétés de généalogie | http://www.gouv.qc.ca/francais/minorg/mccq/dpm/organis/fqsg/fqsg.htm |
| Genealogical Association of Nova Scotia | http://www.ccn.cs.dal.ca/Recreation/GANS/gans_homepage.html |
| Goethe-Institut Toronto | http://www.goethe.de/uk/tor |
| Goethe-Institut/German Cultural Centre (Vancouver) | http://www.goethe.de/uk/van |
| Grand Council of the Crees | http://www.gcc.ca |
| The Great Lakes Marine Heritage Foundation | http://www.marmus.ca |
| Heraldry Society of Canada | http://www.hsc.ca/ |
| Heritage Foundation of Newfoundland & Labrador | http://www.avalon.nf.ca/heritage |
| Icelandic National League | http://www.helix.net/~rasgeirs/ |
| International Centre for Human Rights & Democratic Development | http://www.ichrdd.ca |
| International Council on Monuments & Sites Canada | http://www.icomos.org/canada |
| International Development Education Resource Association | http://www.vcn.bc.ca/idera |
| Inuit Art Foundation | http://www.inuitart.org |
| Italian Cultural Institute | http://www.iicto-ca.org |
| The Jewish Federation of Greater Toronto | http://www.feduja.org/ |
| Le Conseil pour l'unité canadienne | http://www.ccu-cuc.ca/ |
| League for Human Rights of B'nai Brith Canada | http://www.bnaibrith.ca/league_f.htm |
| Macedonian Human Rights Movement of Canada | http://www.mhrmc.on.ca |
| Makivik Corporation | http://www.accent.net/adst/MakWeb/Index.html |
| Manitoba Association for Rights & Liberties | http://www.winnipeg.freenet.mb.ca/marl/marl_hm.html |
| Manitoba Council for International Cooperation | http://www.escape.ca/~mcic |
| Manitoba Heritage Federation Inc. | http://www.mts.net/~mhf |
| Manitoba Indian Cultural Education Centre | http://www.schoolnet.ca/ext/aboriginal/micec/index.html |
| MediaWatch | http://www.myna.com/~mediawat/ |
| Monarchist League of Canada | http://www.monarchist.ca |
| Multicultural Association of Nova Scotia | http://fox.nstn.ca/~multicul/ |
| Nancy's Very Own Foundation | http://www.coolwomen.org |
| National Association of Women in Construction | http://www.nawic.org |
| National Society of Fund Raising Executives | http://www.nsfre.org/ |
| Native Counselling Services of Alberta | http://www.compusmart.ab.ca/ncsa/home.html |
| Native Investment & Trade Association | http://www.native-invest-trade.com |

| | |
|---|---|
| New Brunswick Genealogical Society | http://degaulle.hil.unb.ca/genealogy/society.html |
| Newfoundland & Labrador Genealogical Society Inc. | http://infonet.st-johns.nf.ca/Community/Providers/NLGS/nlgs.html |
| Ontario Council for International Cooperation | http://www.web.net/~ocic/ |
| Ontario Genealogical Society | htpp://www.interlog.com/~dreed/ogs_home.htm |
| Ontario Metis Aboriginal Association | http://www.omaa.org |
| Organization of Professional Immigration Consultants | http://opic.org |
| Ottawa-Carleton Immigrant Services Organization | http://www.ncf.carleton.ca/freeport/social.services/cis/ociso/menu |
| Oxfam-Canada | http://www.oxfam.ca |
| Peace Brigades International (Canada) | http://www.ncf.carleton.ca/pbi |
| Physicians for Global Survival (Canada) | http://www.web.net/~pgs/ |
| Polonia Przyszlosci - Polonia for the Future | http://www.pol-net.com/polonia/ |
| Prince Edward Island Museum & Heritage Foundation | http://www.peisland.com/peimuseum/welcome.htm |
| Project Ploughshares | http://watserv1.uwaterloo.ca/~plough/ |
| Québec Family History Society | http://www.cam.org/~qfhs/index.html |
| The Royal Society of Canada | http://www.rsc.ca |
| Saskatchewan Genealogical Society | http://www.regina.ism.ca/orgs/sgs/index.htm |
| Saskatchewan Indian Cultural Centre | http://www.lights.com/sicc/ |
| Servas Canada | http://servas.org |
| Société des acadiens et acadiennes du Nouveau-Brunswick | http://www.rbmulti.nb.ca/saanb/saanb.htm |
| Société franco-manitobaine | http://www.franco-manitobain.org |
| Société généalogique canadiénne-française | http://www.sgcf.com |
| Society for Canadian Women in Science & Technology | http://www.harbour.sfu.ca/scwist/ |
| Ten Days for Global Justice | http://www.web.net/~tendays/ |
| Union of British Columbia Indian Chiefs | http://www.indigenous.bc.ca |
| United Nations Association in Canada | http://www.unac.org |
| Urban Alliance on Race Relations | http://www.uarr.org |
| West Coast Railway Association | http://www.wcra.org |
| The Women & Environments Education & Development Foundation | http://www.web.net/~weed/ |
| Woodland Cultural Centre | http://www.ciphermedia.com/WOODLAND/MM.HTML |
| World University Service of Canada | http://www.wusc.ca |

## COMMUNICATIONS

| | |
|---|---|
| ASM International | http://www.asm-intl.org |
| Actualisation | http://www.actualisation.com |
| Ad Astra Books | http://www.aero.com/adastra/ |
| Addiction Research Foundation | http://www.arf.org |
| Addison-Wesley Publishers Ltd. | http://www.aw.com/canada |
| Aldergrove Star | http://www.aldstar.com |
| Almark & Co. - Booksellers | http://www.75711.2144@compuserve.com |
| Alpel Publishing | http://www.accent_net/alpelie/ |
| Alter Ego Editions | http://www.alterego.montreal.qc.ca |
| The Alternate Press | http://www.life.ca |
| Althouse Press | http://www.uwo.ca/edu/press |
| The Amherstburg Echo Community News | http://www.bowesnet.com/amherstburgecho |
| Angel Publications | http://www.magi.com/~angelpub/ |
| Anson-Cartwright Editions | http://www.interlog.com/~hac |
| Aquila Communications Ltd. | http://www.generation.net/~aquila |
| Ariane Editions Inc. | http://www.mlink.net/~ariane |
| Arnold Publishing Ltd. | http://www.arnold.ca |
| Asian Educational Services (Canada) Ltd. | http://www.travel-net.com/~educa/aesmain.htm |
| Association des agences de publicité du Québec | http://www.aapq.qc.ca |
| Association nationale des éditeurs de livres | http://www.cam.org/~anel/index.htm |
| Association of Book Publishers of British Columbia | http://www.books.bc.ca |
| Association of Canadian Publishers | http://www.publishers.ca |
| Association of Records Managers & Administrators | http://www.arma.org/hq/ |
| Association pour l'avancement des sciences et des techniques de la documentation | http://www.asted.org |
| The Aurora | http://www.14wing.qrwd.dnd.ca |
| Aviation Publishers Co. Ltd. | http://www.aviationpublishers.com |
| BBM Bureau of Measurement | http://www.bbm.ca/ |
| BC Advanced Systems Institute | http://www.asi.bc.ca/asi/ |
| Banff Centre Press | http://www.banffcentre.ab.ca |
| Battle Street Books | http://www.llnetpage.bc.ca/battlestreetbooks |
| Beach Holme Publishers Limited | http://www.swifty.com |
| Beacon Distributing/Cook Communications | http://www.cook.ca |
| Beacon | http://www.rb.nf.ca/beacon |
| Ben-Simon Publications | http://www.simon-sez.com |
| Bendall Books | http://www.islandnet.com/bendallbooks |
| Between the Lines | http://www.btl.on.ca |
| Black Rose Books | http://www.webnet/blackrosebooks |
| Blizzard Publishing Ltd. | http://www.blizzard.mb.ca/catalog |
| Boissevain Recorder | http://www.techplus.com/recorder.recorderhome.htm |
| Boston Mills Press | http://www.boston-mills.on.ca |
| Breakwater Books Ltd. | http://www.nfld.com/~krose/breakw.htm |
| Bridgewater Bulletin | http://fox.nstn.ca/~lighthse/ |
| British Columbia Association of Broadcasters | http://www.bcab.org |
| Broadview Press | http://www.broadviewpress.com |
| Broquet inc. | http://www.stjeannet.ca/broquet |

Bungalo Books ........ http://www.bungalobooks.com
Butterworths Canada Ltd. ........ http://www.butterworths.ca
C.D. Howe Institute ........ http://www.cdhowe.org
CANARIE Inc. ........ http://www.canarie.ca
CCH Canadian Limited ........ http://www.ca.cch.com/
COACH, Canada's Health Informatics Association ........ http://www.telusplanet.net/public/coachorg/
Cable Television Standards Foundation ........ http://ctsc.ca
Callawind Publications Inc. ........ http://www.callawind.com
Camrose Booster ........ http://www.ifpa.com
Canada Communications Group Publishing ........ http://www.ccg.gcc.ca
Canada Law Book Inc. ........ http://www.canadalawbook.ca
Canada's Coalition for Public Information ........ http://www.canarie.ca/cpi
Canadian Almanac & Directory Publishing Company ........ http://www.canadainfo.com
Canadian Association of Broadcasters ........ http://www.cab-acr.ca
Canadian Association of Ethnic (Radio) Broadcasters ........ http://www.chinradio.com
Canadian Association of Photographers & Illustrators in Communications ........ http://www.capic.org
Canadian Association of Research Libraries ........ http://www.uottawa.ca/library/carl
Canadian Book Review Annual ........ http://www.interlog.com/~cbra
Canadian Booksellers Association ........ http://www.cbabook.org
Canadian Business Telecommunications Alliance ........ http://www.telecon.ca
Canadian Cable Television Association ........ http://www.ccta.ca
Canadian Community Newspapers Association ........ http://www.sentex.net/~ccna
Canadian Farm Writers' Federation ........ http://www.uoguelph.ca/Research/cfwf
Canadian Heritage Information Network ........ http://www.chin.gc.ca
Canadian Information & Image Management Society ........ http://www.ciims.ca
Canadian Information Processing Society ........ http://www.cips.ca
Canadian Institute for Historical Microreproductions ........ http://www.nlc-bnc.ca/cihm/
Canadian Institute for Telecommunications Research ........ http://www.citr.ee.mcgill.ca
Canadian Magazine Publishers Association ........ http://www.cmpa.ca/
Canadian Newspaper Association ........ http://www.cna-acj.ca/
The Canadian Press ........ http://www.xe.com/canpress/
Canadian Publishers' Council ........ http://www.pubcouncil.ca
Canadian Satellite Users Association ........ http://www.bbande.com
Canadian Telecommunications Consultants Association ........ http://www.ctca.ca
Canadian University Press ........ http://www.interlog.com/~cup/
Canadian Wireless Telecommunications Association ........ http://www.cwta.ca
Captus Press ........ http://www.captus.com
The Carillon ........ http://www/derksenprinters.com
Carswell ........ http://www.carswell.com/carswell.home
Cavendish Books Inc. ........ http://www.gardenbooks.com
Centax Books & Distribution ........ http://www.printwest.com/centax
Centre international pour le développement de l'inforoute en français ........ http://www.cidif.org/
The Charlton Press ........ http://www.charltonpress.com
The Chessnut Press ........ http://www.odyssee.net/~drknight
Clinton News-Record ........ http://www.bowesnet.com/newsrecord
Coach House Books ........ http://www.chbooks.com
The Coast Guard ........ http://www.klis.com/fundy/coastguard
Collingwood Enterprise-Bulletin ........ http://www.eb.georgian.net
Colombo & Company ........ http://www.inforamp.net/~JRC
Commonwealth Publications Inc. ........ http://www.commonwealthpub.com
Communications Information Technology Ontario ........ http://www.itrc.on.ca/
Communications, Energy & Paperworkers Union of Canada (CLC) ........ http://www.cep.ca/cep/
Community Information Centre of Metropolitan Toronto ........ http://www.web.net/~cicmt/
Company's Coming Publishing Limited ........ http://www.companyscoming.com
Connexions Information Sharing Services ........ http://www.connexions.org
Continental Records Co. Ltd. ........ http://www.gocontinental.com
Corporation des maîtres photographes du Québec inc. ........ http://www.intertower.com/cmpq.html
Coteau Books/Thunder Creek Publishing Cooperative ........ http://www.coteau.unibase.com
Crabtree Publishing Co. Ltd. ........ http://www.crabtree-pub.com
Crown Publications Inc. ........ http://www.com/crownpub/
Culture Concepts Inc. ........ http://www3.sympatico.ca/cultureconcepts
Delhi News-Record ........ http:www.swopp.com/delhi-records
Development Press ........ http://www.cibbir,bc,ca/~connor
Doubleday Canada Ltd. ........ http://www.bold.com
Dryden Observer ........ http://www.awc/on.ca.observer
The Drum ........ http://www.nnsl.com
ECW Press ........ http://www.ecw.ca/press
EDIMAG inc. ........ http://www.edimag.com
Earthscan Canada ........ http://www.nextcity.com/earthscan/pubearth.htm
Editions du Bois-de-Coulonge ........ http://www.ebc.qc.ca
Electronic Frontier Canada Inc. ........ http://insight.mcmaster.ca/org/efc/efc.html
Emond Montgomery Publications Ltd. ........ http://www.emp.on.ca
Les Éditions du Blé ........ http://www.magic.mb.ca/~alexis
Éditions Centre FORA ........ http://www.centrefora.on.ca
Éditions Doberman inc. ........ http://www.qui.qc.ca/clients/doberman
Les Éditions Flammarion Ltée ........ http://www.flammarion.qc.ca
Éditions FM ........ http://www.beauchemin.qc.ca
Les Éditions le Griffon d'argile ........ http://www.griffondargile.com

| | |
|---|---|
| Les Éditions l'Image de l'art | http://www.beauchemin.qc.ca |
| Éditions Logiques | http://www.logique.com |
| Éditions Multimondes | http://multim.com |
| Les Éditions de la nouvelle plume, coopérative ltée | http://www.dicwest.com/~acfc/Associations/Nouvelleplume/nouvelleplume.html |
| Éditions Reynald Goulet | http://www.goulet.ca |
| Éditions de la paix | http://www.netgraphe.qc.ca/editpaix |
| Éditions la Pensée inc. | http://www.lidec.qc.ca |
| Les Éditions Transcontinental inc. | http://www.logique.com |
| Exportlivre | http://www.cyberglake.net/users/exportlivre |
| Fairview Post | http://www.Bowesnet.com/Fairview |
| Fisher House Publishing | http://www.ocii.com/~fisher/shp.htm |
| Fitzhenry & Whiteside Limited | http://www.fitzhenry.ca |
| Fort Frances Times | http://www.fftimes.com |
| The Fraser Institute | http://www.fraserinstitute.ca |
| The Freelancer | http://www.bowesnet.com/mayerthorpe |
| Friends of Canadian Broadcasting | http://friendscb.org |
| Garamond Press | http://www.garamond.ca/garamond |
| Golden Books Publishing | http://www.senetex.net~goldenbk |
| Goose Lane Editions | http://www.cygnus.nb.ca/bookstr/glane/glogo.html |
| Gordon Soules Book Publishers Ltd. | http://www.gordonsoules.com |
| Groupe Beauchemin, éditeur ltée | http://www.beauchemin.qc.ca |
| Guernica Editions Inc. | http://ourworld.compuserve.com/hompages/guernica |
| Guidance Centre | http://www.utor.ca/guidance |
| Gulf Islands Driftwood | http://www.driftwood.bc.ca |
| Gutter Press | http://www.salzmann.com/gutter |
| HMS Press | http://www.mirror.org/commerce/hmspress |
| Harcourt Brace & Company Canada, Ltd. | http://www.harcourtbrace-canada.com |
| Harlequin Enterprises Ltd. | http://www.romance.net |
| HarperCollins Canada Ltd. | http://www.harpercollins.com |
| Heritage House Publishing Co. Ltd. | http://www.island.net/~herhouse |
| Highway Book Shop | http://www.onlink.net/cybermail/bookshop/index.htm |
| The Hill Times | http://www.thehilltimes.ca |
| Hinterland Publishers | http://www.hinterland.mb.ca |
| Hogrefe & Huber Publishers | http://www/hhpub.com |
| House of Anansi Press | http://www.irwin-pub.com/irwin/anansi/ |
| Hushion House Publishing Ltd. | http://www.hushion.com |
| ICURR Press | http://www.icurr.org/icurr/ |
| IDRC Books/Les Éditions du CRDI | http://www.idrc.ca/ |
| ITMB Publishing Ltd. | http:/www.nas.com/travelmaps |
| ITP Nelson | http://www.nelson.com/nelson.html |
| Inclusion Press International | http://www.inclusion.com |
| Indexing & Abstracting Society of Canada | http://tornade.ere.umontreal.ca/~turner/iasc/home.html |
| Information Resource Management Association of Canada | http://www.irmac.ca |
| Information Technology Association of Canada | http://www.itac.ca/ |
| Information Technology Industry Alliance of Nova Scotia | http://www.seimac.com/~ITANS/ |
| Inner City Books | http://www.inforamp.net/~icb |
| Insomniac Press | http://www.insomniacpress.com |
| The Institute for Research on Public Policy | http://www.irpp.org |
| Interactive Multimedia Arts & Technologies Association | http://www.imat.ca/ |
| International Interactive Communications Society - Toronto Chapter | http://www.tayson.com/iics/ |
| International Press Publications Inc. | http://www.interlog.com/~ipp |
| International Special Events Society - Toronto Chapter | http://www.ndgphoenix.com/ises.html |
| Irwin Publishing | http://www.irwin-pub.com/irwin/ |
| J & L Macpherson Educational Services Ltd. | http://www.fichther.com/envirocan |
| J.L.H. Law Books Ltd. | http://www.lawbookstores.com |
| Jeux de mots | http://www.jeuxdemots.qc.ca |
| The Jewish Post & News | http://www.jewishpost.mb.ca |
| John Coutts Library Services Ltd. | http://wizbang.coutts.on.ca |
| John Wiley & Sons Canada Ltd. | http://www/wiley.com |
| Keng Seng Enterprises | http://www.kengseng.com |
| Key Porter Books Limited | http://www/keyporter.com |
| Kindred Productions | http://www.mbconf.org/mbc/kp/kindred.htm |
| Kitchener News Company Ltd. | http://www.kitnews.com |
| Knowbuddy Resources | http://www.knowbuddyresources.com |
| Kugh Enterprises | http://www.yukon.web.com/tourism/kugh |
| L'Impact | http://www.belin.qc.ca/impact |
| La Liberté | http://www.presse.ouest.mb.ca |
| The Lakeshore Advance | http://www.bowesnet.com/ladvance/ |
| Lancelot Press Ltd. | http://www.atcon.com/lancelot |
| Le Goût de Vivre | http://www.bconnex.net/~legout |
| Le Madawaska | http://www.terra-tech.nb.ca/madawaska |
| Leamington Post & News | http://www.bowenet.com |
| Leduc & County This Week | http://www.compusmart.ab.ca/thisweek |
| Leduc Representative | http://www.bowesnet.com/leduc |
| Les Presses de l'Université de Montréal | http://www.pum.umontreal.ca/pum/ |
| Library Bound | http://www.librarybound.com |
| Literary Press Group of Canada | http://www.lpg.ca |
| Little Brick Schoolhouse Inc. | http://www.littlebrick.com |

Lone Pine Publishing .......... http://www.lonepinepublishing.com
Lost Moose, The Yukon Publishers .......... http://www.yukonweb.com/business/lost_moose
Louise Courteau, éditrice inc. .......... http://club-culture.com/club/
Lugus Publications Ltd. .......... http://www.travel-net.com/blochfd/lugus.html
Malin Head Press .......... http://www.magi.com/~shearonj
Manitoba Community Newspapers Association .......... http://mcna.com
Marginal Distribution .......... http://www.ptbo.igs.net/~marginal
McGill-Queen's University Press .......... http://www.mcgill.ca/mqupress
McGraw-Hill Ryerson Limited .......... http://www.mcgrawhill.ca
MediaWatch .......... http://www.myna.com/~mediawat/
The Merritt News .......... http://www.merritt-news.bc.ca
Michelin North America (Canada) Inc. .......... http://www.michelin-travel.com
Micromedia Limited .......... http://www.mmltd.com
Milestone Publications Inc. .......... http://www.milestonepub.com
Minnedosa Tribune .......... http://www.techplus.com/trib/index.htm
Miramichi Weekend .......... http://www.mibe.nb
moonprint .......... http://www/escape/ca/~elle
Moosomin World-Spectator .......... http://www.world-spectator.com
Moulin Publishing Ltd. .......... http://www.moulinpub.com
The Mountaineer .......... http://www.rmhnet.com/mountaineer/index
Munsey Music .......... http://www.digiserve.com/stoneman/
National Advertising Benevolent Society .......... http://www.nabs.org
National Book Service .......... http://www.nbs.com
National Capital FreeNet .......... http://www.ncf.carleton.ca/
Neepawa Banner .......... http://www.techplus.com/banner
New Society Publishers .......... http://www.newsociety.com
Newfoundland & Labrador Alliance of Technical Industries .......... http://www.netfx.iom.net/nati/
The News .......... http://www.bowesnet.com/spnews/
News/North .......... http://www.nnsl.com
North Peace Express .......... http://www.sterlingnews.com/Alaska
North Shore News .......... http://www.nsnews.com
Nunatsiaq News .......... http://www.nunanet.com/~nunat
OZ New Media .......... http://www.newmedia.com
Oliver Chronicle .......... http://www.img.net/oliver
Ontario Community Newspapers Association .......... http://www.ocna.org
Orangeville Citizen .......... http://www.headwaters.com/citizen/citizen.html
Orca Book Publishers Ltd. .......... http://www.swifty.com/orca/index.htm
Orleans Community Weekly Journal .......... http://www.ocwj.on.ca
Owl Books .......... http://www.owl.on.ca
Oxford University Press .......... http://www.oupcan.com
Oyen Echo .......... http://www.inter.ab.ca/oyen
Pacific Edge Publishing .......... http://www.schoolnet.ca/vp/cdncont/
Pauline Books & Media .......... http://www.netrover.com/~pauline
Pemmican Publications .......... http://fox.nstn.ca/~pemmican
Penguin Books Canada Ltd. .......... http://www.penguin.ca
Photo Marketing Association International - Canada .......... http://www.pmai.org
Photographic Historical Society of Canada .......... http://web.onramp.ca/phsc
Playwrights Canada Press .......... http://www.puc.ca
Polyscience Publications Inc. .......... http://www.ietc.ca/polysci/
Powell River Peak .......... http://www.windspirit.com/peak/
Power Engineering Books Ltd. .......... http://powerengbooks.com
Prentice-Hall Canada Inc. .......... http://prenhall.com/
Press Gang Publishers Feminist Co-operative .......... http://www.pressgang.bc.ca
Prosveta Inc. .......... http://www.prosveta.com
Québec dans le Monde .......... http://www.total.net/~quebecmonde
Quon Editions .......... http://www.quoned.com
R.G. Mitchell Family Books Inc. .......... http://www.rgm.ca
Radio Amateurs of Canada .......... http://www.rac.ca/
Radio Television News Directors' Association (Canada) .......... http://www.vvv.com/~rtnda/
Random House of Canada Ltd. .......... http://www.randomhouse.com
Rebel Publishing .......... http://www.oncomdis.on.ca/bounty.htm
Reference Press .......... http://www.wcl.on.ca/~refpress
Regroupement québécois pour le sous-titrage inc. .......... http://www.surdite.org/
Reidmore Books .......... http://www.reidmore.com
Renouf Publishing Co. Ltd. .......... http://www.renoufbooks.com
Robert Davies Multimedia Publishing .......... http://www.rdppub.com
Rocky Mountain Books .......... http://www.rmbooks.com
Ronsdale Press .......... http://www.ronsdalepress.com
Roussan Publishers Inc./Roussan éditeur inc. .......... http://www.magnet.ca/roussan
SBF Media Limited .......... http://www.sbfmedia.com
Sackville Tribune-Post .......... http://www.media.medianet.ca/trib/
Saunders Book Co. .......... http://www.saundersbook.ca
Scholarly Book Services Inc. .......... http://www.globalserve.net/~sbookscan
Scholastic Canada Ltd. .......... http://www.scholastic.ca
SchoolNet National Advisory Board .......... http://www.schoolnet.ca/snab; http://www.rescol.ca/ccnr
Script Publishing Inc. .......... http://www.ioe-design.com/script/
Seaforth Huron Expositor .......... http://www.bowesnet.com/expositor
Self-Counsel Press Ltd. .......... http://www.self-counsel.com

Services Documentaires Multimedia Inc. .... http://www.sdm.qc.ca
Sherwood Park This Week .... http://www.compusmart.ab.ca/thisweek
Shoreline/Littoral .... http://www.total.net/~bookline
Slave River Journal .... http://www.auroranet.nt.casrj
Société de développement des périodiques culturels québécois .... http://www3.sympatico.ca/sodep/
Society of Television Lighting Directors Canada .... http://web.idirect.com/~stld
Somerville House Books Limited .... http://www.goodmedia.com/somervillehouse
Sono Nis Press .... http://www.islandnet.com/~sononis/
Sound And Vision Publishing Ltd. .... http://www.soundandvision.com
Southam Magazine & Information Group .... hhtp://www.southam.com
Special Libraries Association .... http://www.sla.org/
St. Albert Gazette .... http://www.greatwest.ca
Stanstead Journal .... http://www.tomifobia.com
Statistics Canada .... http://www.statcan.ca
Stoddart Publishing Co. Limited .... http://www.genpub.com/stoddart/index.html
Sun-Scape Enterprises Ltd. .... http://www.sun-scape.com
TUNS Press .... http://www.tuns.ca/press
Talmage Book Centre .... http://www.terraport.net/tbc/tbc.htm
Talon Books Ltd. .... http://www.swifty.com/talon
Telecommunications Research Institute of Ontario .... http://www.trio.ca
Television Bureau of Canada, Inc.. .... http://www.tvb.ca
The Times .... http://www.mindentimes.on.ca
The Times .... http://www.rannie.com
Thistledown Press Ltd. .... http://www.thistledown.sk.ca
Thunder Bay Post .... http://www.tbsource.com
Tikka Books .... http://www.accent.net/alpelie/
Tofield Mercury .... http://www@tofieldmercury.com
Trifolium Books Inc. .... http://www.pubcouncil.ca/trifolium
Trilobyte Press .... http://www.successatschool.com
Tuesday Times-Reformer .... http://www.swopp.com/reformer
Ulverscroft Large Print (Canada) Ltd. .... http://dspace.dial.pipex.com/town/plaza/hfss/
Ulysses Books & Maps Distribution .... http://www.ulysse.ca
Umbrella Press .... http://www.interlog.com/~umbpress
United Church Publishing House .... http://www.@uccan.org
University Extension Press .... http://www.extension.usask.ca/
University of Alberta Press .... http://www.ualberta.ca/~uap
University of British Columbia Press .... http://www.ubcpress.ubc.ca
University of Calgary Press .... http://www.ucalgary.ca/UCPress
University of Manitoba Press .... http://www.umanitoba.ca/publications.uofmpress
University of Ottawa Press .... http://www.uopress.uottawa.ca
University of Toronto Press .... http://www.library.utoronto.ca/www/utpress/depthome.htm
Véhicule Press .... http://www.cam.org/~vpress
Vancouver Echo .... http://www.vannet.com/vanecho
Vermilion Standard .... http://www/bowesnet.com/Vermilion
Veteran Eagle .... http://www.geocities.com/Eureka/8053
Virden Empire Advance .... http://www.techplus.com/empire/homepage.htm
Wetaskiwin Times Advertiser .... http://www.bowesnet/wtimes
The Whistler Question .... http://www.whistlerquestion.com
White Wolf Publishers .... http://www.tdimports.com
Whitecap Books Ltd. .... http://www.whitecap.ca
Wilfrid Laurier University Press .... http://www.wlu.ca/~wwwpress/
Wilson et Lafleur .... http://www.wilsonlafleur.com
Windflower Communications. .... http://www.infobahn.mb.ca/brandtfamily
Wingham Advance-Times .... http://www.eedy.com/advancetimes/
Women in Film & Television - Toronto .... http://www.goodmedia.com/wift/
Wuerz Publishing Ltd. .... http://www.mbnet.mb.ca/~swuerz

## EDUCATION

ABCDEF Canada .... http://www.refer.qc.ca/ABCDEF/
AFS Interculture Canada .... http://www.afs.org
Academy Canada Career College .... http://www.academycanada.com
Academy of Learning .... http://www.academyol.com
Acadia University .... http://www.acadiau.ca; gopher://gopher.acadiau.ca
Agence francophone pour l'enseignement supérieur et la recherche .... http://www.refer.qc.ca
Albert College .... http://www.telos.ca/quinta/albertc
Alberta Fire Training School .... http://www.gov.ab.ca/~lab/afts/aftindex.html
Alberta Teachers' Association .... http://www.teachers.ab.ca
Alberta Vocational College .... http://www.avcedm.ges.ab.ca
Algonquin College .... http://www.algonquinc.on.ca/
Architectural Institute of British Columbia .... http://www.aibc.bc.ca
Asia-Pacific International Graduate School of Management .... http://www.apiu.edu
Assiniboine Community College .... http://www.assiniboinec.mb.ca/
Association canadienne d'éducation de langue française .... http://www.acelf.ca
Association canadienne des professeurs d'immersion .... http://www.sfu.ca/cprf/acpi/
Association des institutions d'enseignement secondaire .... http://www.cadre.qc.ca
Association for Canadian Studies .... http://www.er.uqam.ca/nobel/c1015/
Association for Canadian Theatre Research .... http://www.unb.ca/web/english/candrama/candrama.htm
Association for Media & Technology in Education in Canada .... http://www.camosun.bc.ca/~amtec/

Association for the Promotion & Advancement of Science Education ........... http://www.apase.bc.ca
Association francophone internationale des directeurs d'établissements scolaires ........ http://grics.qc.ca/afides
Association of Canadian Community Colleges ........ http://www.accc.ca
Association of Canadian Medical Colleges ........ http://www.acmc.ca
Association of Canadian Universities for Northern Studies ........ http://www.geog.mcgill.ca/northern/acunhome.html
Association of Colleges of Applied Arts & Technology of Ontario ........ gopher://info.senecac.on.ca:2000/
Association of Universities & Colleges of Canada ........ http://www.aucc.ca
Association pour l'avancement des sciences et des techniques de la documentation ........ http://www.asted.org
Association québécoise des commissions scolaires ........ http://www.login.net/qsba
Association québécoise du personnel de direction des écoles ........ http://grics.qc.ca/aqpde/
Athabasca University ........ http://www.athabascau.ca
Atlantic Business College ........ http://www.abc.nb.ca
Augustana University College ........ gopher://gopher/augustana.ab.ca:70/1
Automotive Training Centre ........ http://www.trionline.com/tri/atc
BC Institute of Technology ........ http://www.bcit.bc.ca/
The Banff Centre ........ http://www-nmr.banffcentre.ab.ca
Bishop's University ........ http://www.ubishops.ca
Brandon University ........ http://www.brandonu.ca; gopher://gopher.brandonu.ca
British Columbia Confederation of Parent Advisory Councils ........ http://www.discoverlearning.com
British Columbia Institute of Technology ........ http://www.bcit.bc.ca/
British Columbia Teachers' Federation ........ http://www.bctf.bc.ca
Brock University ........ http://www.brocku.ca
CDI College of Business & Technology ........ http://www.cdicollege.com
CTI Counsellor Training Institute Ltd. ........ http://home.istar.ca/~cti
Cambrian College ........ http://www.cambrianc.on.ca
Camosun College ........ http://www.camosun.bc.ca/
Campion College ........ http://www.uregina.ca/calendar/fedcoll/html#camp
Canadian Alliance of Student Associations ........ http://www.casa.ca
Canadian Asian Studies Association ........ http://tornade.ere.umontreal.ca/~denm/casa.htm
Canadian Association for Co-operative Education ........ http://www.sfu.ca/cafce
Canadian Association for Distance Education ........ http://www.cade-aced.ca
Canadian Association for Graduate Studies ........ http://www.uottawa.ca/associations/cags-acea/
Canadian Association for Pastoral Practice & Education ........ http://www3.ns.sympatico.ca/cappe/home.htm
Canadian Association for University Continuing Education ........ http://www.tile.net/tile/listserv/caucel.html
Canadian Association of Career Educators & Employers ........ http://www.cacee.com/workweb
Canadian Association of College & University Libraries ........ http://www.cla.amlibs.ca
Canadian Association of Research Libraries ........ http://www.uottawa.ca/library/carl
Canadian Association of Second Language Teachers ........ http://www2.tvo.org/education/caslt
Canadian Association of University Teachers ........ http://www.caut.ca
Canadian Bureau for International Education ........ http://www.cbie.ca
Canadian Council for Multicultural & Intercultural Education ........ http://www.intranet.on.ca/~ccmie/
Canadian Council for the Advancement of Education ........ http://www.stmarys.ca/partners/ccae/ccae.htm
Canadian Education Association ........ http://www.acea.ca
Canadian Emergency Preparedness College ........ http://hoshi.cic.sfu.ca/epc/
Canadian Evaluation Society ........ http://www.unites.uqam.ca/ces/ces-sce.html
Canadian Federation of Students ........ http://www.cfs-fcee.ca
Canadian Film Centre ........ http://www.cdnfilmcentre.com
Canadian Home & School Federation ........ http://cnet.unb.ca/cap/partners/chsptf/
Canadian Institute of Financial Planning ........ http://www.mutfunds.com/cifp
Canadian Institute of Gemmology ........ http://www.deepcove.com/cig
Canadian Institute of Strategic Studies ........ http://www.ciss.ca
Canadian Interuniversity Athletic Union ........ http://www.ciau.ca
Canadian Investment Funds Course ........ http://www.mutfunds.com/ific
Canadian Mathematical Society ........ http://camel.math.ca
Canadian Music Educators' Association ........ http://www.ucs.mun.ca/~cmea/
Canadian Philosophical Association ........ http://www.uwindsor.ca/cpa
Canadian Political Science Association ........ http://www.sfu.ca/igs/CPSA.html
Canadian Research Institute for the Advancement of Women ........ http://www3.sympatico.ca/criaw
Canadian School Boards Association ........ http://www.cdnsba.org/
Canadian Society for Eighteenth-Century Studies ........ http://tornade.ere.umontreal.ca/~melancon/csecs.tdm.html
The Canadian Society for Mesopotamian Studies ........ http://www.chass.utoronto.ca/nmc/rim/csms.html
Canadian Society for Nondestructive Testing, Inc. ........ http://www.csndt.org
Canadian Society for the Study of Names ........ http://GeoNames.NRCan.gc.ca/english/CSSN.html
Canadian Teachers' Federation ........ http://www.ctf-fce.ca
Canadian University Music Society ........ http://www.utoronto.ca/cums/
Canadian Vocational Association ........ http://www.cva.ca
Canadore College of Applied Arts & Technology ........ http://www.canadorec.on.ca/index.html
Canadore College ........ http://www.canadorec.on.ca/
Capilano College ........ http://www.capcollege.bc.ca/
The Career Academy ........ http://www.careeracademy.com
Career Blazers Learning Centre ........ http://www.muskoka.com/busmall/cblazers
Carleton University ........ http://www.carleton.ca/
Centennial College ........ http://www.cencol.on.ca
Central Newfoundland Regional College ........ http://www.cnrcoll.nf.ca/
Centre d'animation de développement et de recherche en éducation ........ http://www.cadre.qc.ca
Centre international de recherche en aménagement linguistique ........ http://www.ciral.ulaval.ca

Classical Association of Canada ... http://137.122.12.15/Docs/Societies/ClassAc/Classic.Assoc.html
Collège Boréal ... http://www.borealc.on.ca
Collège des Grands Lacs ... http://grandslacs.on.ca/
Collège universitaire de Saint-Boniface ... http://www.ustboniface.mb.ca/
College of New Caledonia ... http://www.cnc.bc.ca/
College of the Rockies ... http://www.cotr.bc.ca/
Comenius Institute ... http://www.uniserve.com/comenius
The Commonwealth of Learning ... http://www.col.org
Community Legal Education Association (Manitoba) Inc. ... http://www.acjnet.org/white/clea.html
Complections International - The Make-Up School ... http://www.complectionsmake-up.com
Concordia University ... http://www.concordia.ca
Conestoga College ... http://www.conestogac.on.ca
Conférence des recteurs et des principaux des universités du Québec ... http://www.crepuq.qc.ca
Confederation College ... http://www.confederationc.on.ca/
Confederation of Alberta Faculty Associations ... http://www.ualberta.ca/~cafa/
Continuing Legal Education Society of BC ... http://www.cle.bc.ca
Corporate-Higher Education Forum ... http://www.work.org/C-HEF/
Council of Ontario Universities ... http://www.cou.on.ca
Council of Prairie & Pacific University Libraries ... http://library.usask.ca/coppul
DalTech ... http://www.tuns.ca/index.html
Dalhousie University ... http://www2.dal.ca
Dawson College ... http://www.dawsoncollege.qc.ca
Douglas College ... http://www.douglas.bc.ca/
Durham College ... http://durham.durhamc.on.ca
École des Hautes Études Commerciales ... http://www.hec.ca
École Polytechnique ... http://www.polymtl.ca
Emily Carr Institute of Art & Design ... http://www.eciad.bc.ca/
Erickson College ... http://www.erickson.edu
Erindale College ... http://www.erin.utoronto.ca/
Fédération des cégeps ... http://www.fedecegeps.qc.ca
Fédération des commissions scolaires du Québec ... http://grics.qc.ca/fcsq/accueil.htm
Fanshawe College ... http://www.fanshawec.on.ca/
Federation of Women Teachers' Associations of Ontario ... http://www.fwtao.on.ca
Fields College International ... http://www.fieldscollege.com/~esl
Forest Engineering Research Institute of Canada ... http://www.feric.ca
Foundation for Educational Exchange Between Canada & the USA ... http://www.usis-canada.usia.gov/fulbrigh.htm
George Brown College ... http://www.gbrownc.on.ca/
Georgian College ... http://www.georcoll.on.ca
The Glenn Gould Professional School of the Royal Conservatory of Music ... http://www.rcmusic.ca
Grande Prairie Regional College ... http://www.gprc.ab.ca
Grant MacEwan Community College ... http://www.gmcc.ab.ca/
Granton Institute of Technology ... http://www.grantoninstitute.com/
Herbert Marshall McLuhan Foundation ... http://www.mcluhan.ca/mcluhan/foundation.html
Herzing Institute of Montréal ... http://www.herzing.edu
Humanist Association of Canada ... http://magi.com/~hac/hac.html
Humanities & Social Sciences Federation of Canada ... http://www.hssfc.ca
Humber College ... http://www.humberc.on.ca/
ICS Canadian Ltd. ... http://www.ics-canada.com
Institut National de la Recherche Scientifique (INRS) ... http://www.inrs.uquebec.ca/
Institut Superieur d'Electronique ... http://www.institut.com
Institut national de la recherche scientifique ... http://www.inrs-urb.uquebec.ca
Institute of Indigenous Government ... http://www.indigenous.bc.ca
Interactive Multimedia Arts & Technologies Association ... http://www.imat.ca/
International Academy of Merchandising & Design Ltd. ... http://www.iaod.com
International Academy of Natural Health Sciences (Canada) ... http://www.health4all.com
International Council for Adult Education ... http://www.web.net/icae/
International Council for Canadian Studies ... http://www.iccs-ciec.ca
International Development Education Resource Association ... http://www.vcn.bc.ca/idera
International Federation of Institutes for Advanced Study ... http://www.ifias.ca/
Keewatin Community College ... http://www.keewatincc.mb.ca
Kemptville College of Agricultural Technology ... http://home.istar.ca/~kcat
Keyano College ... http://www.keyanoc.ab.ca/
Keyin Technical College ... http://www.keyin.com
King's College ... http://www.kingsu.ab.ca
Kwantlen University College ... http://www.kwantlen.bc.ca
La Cité Collégiale ... http://www.lacitec.on.ca
Lakehead University ... http://www.lakeheadu.ca/
Lakeland College ... http://www.lakelandc.ab.ca/
Lambton College ... http://www.lambton.on.ca/
Langara College ... http://www.langara.bc.ca
Laubach Literacy Canada ... http://www.nald.ca/llc.htm
Laurentian University ... http://www.laurentian.ca/
Le Réseau d'enseignement francophone à distance du Canada ... http://www.franco.ca/refad/
Learning Disabilities Association of Canada ... http://edu-ss10.educ.queensu.ca/~lda/
Lester B. Pearson College of the Pacific ... http://www.pearson-college.uwc.ca/pearson
Lethbridge Community College ... http://www.lethbridgec.ab.ca
London, Board of Education for the City of ... http://www.lbe.edu.on.ca
Loyalist College ... http://www.loyalistc.on.ca/

| | |
|---|---|
| Magi Learning Centre | http://magi.ns.ca |
| Malaspina University College | http://www.mala.bc.ca |
| Manitoba Teachers' Society | http://www.mts.net/teachers/ |
| Maritime Forest Ranger School | http://www.webcom.com/forestry/MFRS/ |
| McGill University | http://www.mcgill.ca |
| McMaster University | http://www.mcmaster.ca/index.html |
| Memorial University of Newfoundland | http://www.mun.ca |
| Mensa Canada Society | http://www.rohcg.on.ca/mensa/mensa.html |
| Mohawk College | http://www.mohawkc.on.ca |
| Mount Allison University | http://www.mta.ca/ |
| Mount Royal College | http://www.mtroyal.ab.ca/ |
| Mount Saint Bernard College | http://www.stfx.ca/msbresid/ |
| Mount Saint Vincent University | http://www.msvu.ca/ |
| Movement for Canadian Literacy | http://www.nald.ca/mcl/mcl2.htm |
| NDE Institute of Canada | http://www.vaxxine.com/ndeinst |
| National Screen Institute | http://www.nsi-canada.ca |
| Natural Resources Canada | http://www.emr.ca/home/nrcanhpe.htm |
| New Brunswick Community College (Saint John) | http://www.saintjohn.nbcc.nb.ca |
| New Brunswick Community Colleges | http://www.gov.nb.ca/ael/nbcc/ |
| Newfoundland & Labrador Home & School Federation | http://www.stemnet.nf.ca/Organizations/NLHSF/ |
| Newfoundland & Labrador Teachers' Association | http://www.stemnet.nf.ca/Organizations/NLTA/ |
| Niagara College | http://www.niagarac.on.ca/ |
| Nipissing University | http://www.unipissing.ca/ |
| North Island College | http://www.nic.bc.ca |
| The North-South Institute | http://www.nsi-ins.ca |
| North West Regional College | http://www.nwrc.sk.ca |
| Northern Alberta Institute of Technology | http://www.nait.ab.ca/ |
| Northern College of Applied Arts & Technology | http://www.northernc.on.ca |
| Northern College | http://www.northernc.on.ca/ |
| Northern Lights College | http://www.nlc.bc.ca |
| Northwest Community College | http://www.nwcc.bc.ca |
| Northwest Territories Teachers' Association | http://www.nwtta.nt.ca |
| Nova Scotia Agricultural College | http://www.nsac.ns.ca |
| Nova Scotia Teachers Union | http://www.nstu.ns.ca |
| Okanagan University College | http://www.ouc.bc.ca/ |
| Olds College | http://www.oldscollege.ab.ca/ |
| Ontario Alliance of Christian Schools | http://www.oacs.org |
| Ontario Public School Boards Association | http://www.opsba.org/ |
| Ontario Public School Teachers' Federation | http://www.nt.net/~torino/opstf.htm |
| Ontario Secondary School Teachers' Federation | http://www.osstf.on.ca |
| Open Learning Agency | http://www.ola.bc.ca |
| Ottawa School of Art | http://infoweb.magi.com/~osa/ |
| Pathfinder Business College | http://www.pathfindercollege.com |
| Pitman Business College | http://www.pitmancollege.com |
| Providence College & Seminary | http://www.providence.mb.ca |
| Queen's University | http://info.queensu.ca/ |
| RCC School of Electronics Engineering Technology | http://www.rcc.on.ca |
| Red Deer College | http://www.rdc.ab.ca/rdc/index.html |
| Red River Community College | http://www.rrcc.mb.ca/ |
| Richmond School of Hairdressing | http://www.ontimeprint.com/hairschool |
| Robertson College Inc. | http://www.robertsoncollege.com |
| Royal Canadian Institute | http://www.psych.utoronto.ca/people/vislab/RCI.html |
| Royal Military College of Canada | http://www.rmc.ca/ |
| Royal Roads University | http://www.royalroads.ca |
| Ryerson Polytechnic University | http://www.ryerson.ca/ |
| Saint Mary's University | http://www.stmarys.ca |
| Saskatchewan Indian Federated College | http://www.uregina.ca/calendar/fedcoll.html#sifc |
| Saskatchewan Institute of Applied Science & Technology | http://www/siast.sk.ca |
| Saskatchewan Teachers' Federation | http://www.stf.sk.ca |
| The Sault College | http://www.saultc.on.ca/ |
| Scarborough College | http://www.scar.utoronto.ca/ |
| SchoolNet National Advisory Board | http://www.schoolnet.ca/snab; http://www.rescol.ca/ccnr |
| Selkirk College | http://www.selkirk.bc.ca |
| Seneca College | http://www.senecac.on.ca/ |
| Shaw College | http://www.shaw-college.com |
| Sheridan College | http://www.sheridanc.on.ca |
| Simon Fraser University | http://www.sfu.ca/ |
| Sir Sandford Fleming College | http://www.flemingc.on.ca/ |
| Société pour la promotion de l'enseignement de l'anglais au Québec | http://cyberscol.qc.ca/partenaires/speaq/speaq.htm |
| Society for the Study of Egyptian Antiquities | http://www.geocities.com/TheTropics/1456/ |
| St. Augustine's Seminary of Toronto | http://www.canxsys.com/staugust.htm |
| St. Clair College | http://www.stclairc.on.ca/ |
| St. Francis Xavier University | http://www.stfx.ca |
| St. Lawrence College | http://www.stlawrencec.on.ca |
| St. Thomas University | http://www.stthomasu.ca |
| The Southern Alberta Institute of Technology | http://www.sait.ab.ca/ |
| Télé-Université | http://www.teluq.uquebec.ca |
| TESL Canada Federation | http://www.tesl.ca/ |

Technical University of Nova Scotia .......... http://www.tuns.ca/index.html
TeleLearning Network of Centres of Excellence .......... http://www.telelearn.ca
Toronto Baptist Seminary & Bible College .......... http://www.tbs.edu
Toronto Institute of Pharmaceutical Technology .......... http://www.tipt.com
Tourism Training Institute .......... http://www.axionet.com/tourism
Trend College Hospitality Management Institute .......... http://www.trend.bc.ca/homepage
Trent University .......... http://www.trentu.ca
Trinity Western University .......... http://www.twu.ca
United World Colleges .......... http://www.pearson-college.uwc.ca/pearson/
Université Laval .......... http://www.ulaval.ca/index.html
Université Sainte Anne .......... http://ustanne-59.ustanne.ednet.ns.ca/
Université de Moncton .......... http://www.umoncton.ca
Université de Montréal .......... http://www.umontreal.ca
Université du Québec à Chicoutimi .......... http://www.uqac.uquebec.ca/
Université du Québec à Hull .......... http://www.uqah.uquebec.ca/
Université du Québec à Montréal .......... http://www.uqam.ca/
Université du Québec à Rimouski .......... http://www.uqar.uquebec.ca/
Université du Québec en Abitibi-Témiscamingue .......... http://www.uqat.uquebec.ca/
Université du Québec .......... http://www.uquebec.ca/
The University of Calgary .......... http://www.ucalgary.ca/
University College of Cape Breton .......... http://www.uccb.ns.ca
University College of the Cariboo .......... http://www.cariboo.bc.ca
University College of the Fraser Valley .......... gopher://gopher.ucfv.bc.ca/
University of Alberta .......... http://web.cs.ualberta.ca/ualberta.html
University of British Columbia .......... http://www.ubc.ca
University of Calgary .......... http://www.ucalgary.ca
University of Guelph .......... http://www.uoguelph.ca/
University of King's College .......... http://www.ukings.ns.ca
University of Lethbridge .......... http://www.uleth.ca
University of Manitoba .......... http://www.umanitoba.ca
University of Manitoba .......... http://www.umanitoba.ca; gopher://gopher.cc.umanitoba.ca
University of New Brunswick .......... http://www.unb.ca/
University of Northern British Columbia .......... http://www.unbc.edu; http://quarles.unbc.edu/keen/welcome.html
University of Ottawa .......... http://www.uottawa.ca
University of Prince Edward Island .......... http://www.upei.ca
University of Saskatchewan .......... http://www.usask.ca
University of Toronto .......... http://www.utoronto.ca/
University of Victoria .......... http://www.uvic.ca
University of Waterloo .......... http://www.uwaterloo.ca/
University of Western Ontario .......... http://www.uwo.ca/
University of Windsor .......... http://www.uwindsor.ca/
University of Winnipeg .......... http://www.uwinnipeg.ca
Vancouver Community College .......... http://www.vcc.bc.ca
Vancouver School of Theology .......... http://www.interchg.ubc.ca/vst/
Waterloo Region Roman Catholic Separate School Board .......... http://www.watrc.edu.on.ca
Wilfrid Laurier University .......... http://www.wlu.ca
Willis College of Business & Technology .......... http://www.willis-training.com/
World University Service of Canada .......... http://www.wusc.ca
York University .......... http://www.yorku.ca
Yukon College .......... http://www.yukoncollege.yk.ca

## GOVERNMENT & PUBLIC ADMINISTRATION

### Government of Canada

Canadian Government Homepage .......... http://canada.gc.ca
Governor General & Commander-in-Chief of Canada .......... http://www.gg.ca
Office of the Prime Minister (Lib.) .......... http://pm.gc.ca/
The Cabinet/Canadian Ministry .......... http://canada.gc.ca/howgoc/cab/cabind_e.html
Privy Council Office .......... http://canada.gc.ca/depts/agencies/pcoind_e.html
The Senate of Canada .......... http://www.parl.gc.ca/36/senmemb/senate/bio-e/bio-e.htm
House of Commons .......... http://www.parl.gc.ca
Office of the Leader of the Opposition, Reform Party .......... http://www.reform.ca
Agriculture & Agri-Food Canada .......... http://aceis.agr.ca
Atlantic Canada Opportunities Agency .......... http://www.acoa.ca/
Atomic Energy Control Board .......... http://www.gc.ca/aecb/
Atomic Energy of Canada Limited .......... http://www.aecl.ca
Auditor General of Canada .......... http://www.oag-bvg.gc.ca/
Bank of Canada .......... http://www.bank-banque-canada.ca/english/intro-e.htm
Business Development Bank of Canada .......... http://www.bdc.ca/
Canada Centre for Remote Sensing .......... http://www.ccrs.nrcan.gc.ca/
Canada Council for the Arts .......... http://www.canadacouncil.ca
Canada Deposit Insurance Corporation .......... http://www.cdic.ca
Canada Investment & Savings .......... http://www.cis-pec.gc.ca/
Canada Lands Company .......... http://www.clc.ca
Canada Mortgage & Housing Corporation .......... http://www.cmhc-schl.gc.ca
Canada Ports Corporation .......... http://canada.gc.ca/depts/agencies/cpoind_e.html
Canada Post Corporation .......... http://www.mailposte.ca
Canadian Broadcasting Corporation .......... http://www.cbc.ca/

| Organization | Website |
|---|---|
| Canadian Business Service Centre | http://www.cbsc.org/ |
| Canadian Centre for Occupational Health & Safety | http://www.ccohs.ca |
| Canadian Centre on Substance Abuse | http://www.ccsa.ca |
| Canadian Commercial Corporation | http://www.ccc.ca |
| Canadian Council for International Co-operation | http://www.web.net/ccic-ccci |
| Canadian Council of Ministers of the Environment | http://www.ccme.ca/ccme |
| Canadian Food Inspection Agency | http://www.cfia-acia.agr.ca |
| Canadian General Standards Board | http://www.pwgsc.gc.ca/cgsb |
| Canadian Grain Commission | http://www.cgc.ca |
| Canadian Heritage | http://www.pch.gc.ca/ |
| Canadian Human Rights Commission | http://www.chrc.ca/chrc.html |
| Canadian International Development Agency | http://www.acdi.cida.gc.ca |
| Canadian International Grains Institute | http://www.cigi.mb.ca |
| Canadian International Trade Tribunal | http://canada.gc.ca/depts/agencies/cttind_e.html |
| Canadian Polar Commission | http://www.polarcom.gc.ca/ |
| Canadian Radio-Television & Telecommunications Commission | http://www.crtc.gc.ca/ |
| Canadian Security Intelligence Service | http://www.csis-scrs.gc.ca |
| Canadian Space Agency | http://www.space.gc.ca/ |
| Canadian Tourism Commission | http://xinfo.ic.gc.ca/Tourism/ |
| Canadian Transportation Agency | http://www.cta-otc.gc.ca |
| Canadian Wheat Board | http://canada.gc.ca/depts/agencies/cwbind_e.html |
| Citizenship & Immigration Canada | http://cicnet.ingenia.com/english/index.html |
| Correctional Service Canada | http://www.csc-scc.gc.ca |
| Defence Construction Canada | http://canada.gc.ca/depts/agencies/dccind_e.html |
| Elections Canada | http://www.elections.ca/ |
| Emergency Preparedness Canada | http://hoshi.cic.sfu.ca/epc |
| Enquiries Canada | http://canada.gc.ca |
| Environment Canada | http://www.ec.gc.ca |
| Export Development Corporation | http://www.edc.ca |
| Farm Credit Corporation Canada | http://www.fcc-sca.com |
| Federal Office of Regional Development (Québec) | http://www.bfdrq-fordq.gc.ca |
| Finance Canada | http://www.fin.gc.ca/fin-eng.html |
| Fisheries & Oceans Canada | http://www.ncr.dfo.ca/home_e.htm |
| Foreign Affairs & International Trade Canada | http://www.dfait-maeci.gc.ca |
| Geological Survey of Canada | http://www.emr.ca/gsc/ |
| Hazardous Materials Information Review Commission | http://canada.gc.ca/depts/agencies/hmiind_e.html |
| Health Canada | http://www.hwc.ca/links/english.html |
| Human Resources Development Canada | http://www.hrdc-drhc.gc.ca |
| Immigration & Refugee Board | http://www.irb.gc.ca |
| Indian & Northern Affairs Canada | http://www.inac.gc.ca/ |
| Industry Canada | http://info.ic.gc.ca; Strategis Website: http://strategis.ic.gc.ca |
| Information Commissioner of Canada | http://infoweb.magi.com/~accessca/index.html |
| International Development Research Centre | http://www.idrc.ca |
| Justice Canada | http://canada.justice.gc.ca/ |
| Medical Research Council of Canada | http://wwwmrc.hwc.ca/ |
| National Advisory Council on Aging | http://www.hc-sc.gc.ca/seniors-aines |
| National Advisory Council on Science & Technology | http://xinfo.ic.gc.ca/opengov/nabst/nabst.html |
| National Archives of Canada | http://www.archives.ca/ |
| National Capital Commission | http://canada.gc.ca/depts/agencies/nccind_e.html |
| National Crime Prevention Council | http://crime-prevention.org/ncpc |
| National Defence (Canada) | http://www.debbs.ndhq.dnd.ca/dnd.htm |
| National Energy Board | http://www.neb.gc.ca |
| National Film Board of Canada | http://www.nfb.ca/ |
| National Parole Board | http://canada.gc.ca/depts/agencies/npbind_e.html |
| National Research Council Canada | http://www.nrc.ca/ |
| National Round Table on the Environment & Economy | http://www.nrtee-trnee.ca |
| National Search & Rescue Secretariat | http://www.nss.gc.ca |
| Natural Resources Canada | http://www.NRCan.gc.ca/ |
| Natural Sciences & Engineering Research Council of Canada | http://www.nserc.ca |
| North American Wetlands Conservation Council (Canada) | http://www.wetlands.ca |
| Northern Pipeline Agency Canada | http://canada.gc.ca/depts/agencies/npaind_e.html |
| Office of the Commissioner of Official Languages | http://ocol-clo.gc.ca |
| Office of the Superintendent of Financial Institutions | http://www.osfi-bsif.gc.ca/english.htm |
| Parks Canada | http://parkscanada.pch.gc.ca/ |
| Passport Office | http://www.dfait-maeci.gc.ca/passport/pass.htm |
| Prairie Farm Rehabilitation Administration | http://www.agr.ca/pfra |
| Privacy Commissioner of Canada | http://infoweb.magi.com/~privcan/ |
| Public Service Commission of Canada | http://www.psc-cfp.gc.ca |
| Public Works & Government Services Canada | http://www.pwgsc.gc.ca |
| Revenue Canada | http://www.rc.gc.ca |
| Royal Canadian Mint | http://www.rcmint.ca |
| Royal Canadian Mounted Police | http://www.rcmp-grc.gc.ca/html/rcmp2.htm |
| Security Intelligence Review Committee | http://www.sirc-csars.gc.ca/main_e.html |
| Social Sciences & Humanities Research Council of Canada | http://www.sshrc.ca |
| Solicitor General Canada | http://www.sgc.gc.ca |
| St. Lawrence Seaway Authority | http://www.seaway.ca |
| Standards Council of Canada | http://www.scc.ca/indexe.html |
| Statistics Canada | http://www.statcan.ca |

| | |
|---|---|
| Status of Women Canada | http://canada.gc.ca/depts/agencies/swcind_e.html |
| Telefilm Canada | http://www.telefilm.gc.ca |
| Transport Canada | http://www.tc.gc.ca |
| Transportation Safety Board of Canada | http://bst-tsb.gc.ca |
| Treasury Board of Canada | http://www.tbs-sct.gc.ca |
| Western Economic Diversification Canada | http://www.wd.gc.ca |

**Government of Alberta**

| | |
|---|---|
| Alberta Government Homepage | http://www.gov.ab.ca/ |
| Premier's Office | http://www.gov.ab.ca/gov/prem/premier.html |
| Legislative Assembly | http://www.assembly.ab.ca/ |
| Alberta Office of the Auditor General | http://www.assembly.ab.ca/auditor.gen/auditor.htm |
| Alberta Science & Research Authority | http://www.gov.ab.ca/~sra/ |
| Alberta Advanced Education & Career Development | http://www.gov.ab.ca/dept/aecd.html |
| Alberta Agriculture, Food & Rural Development | http://www.agric.gov.ab.ca/ |
| Alberta Community Development | http://www.gov.ab.ca/~mcd/mcd.htm |
| Alberta Economic Development & Tourism | http://www.edt.gov.ab.ca |
| Alberta Education | http://ednet.edc.gov.ab.ca |
| Alberta Energy | http://www.energy.gov.ab.ca |
| Alberta Environmental Protection | http://www.gov.ab.ca/~env/ |
| Alberta Family & Social Services | http://www.gov.ab.ca/dept/fss.html |
| Alberta Federal & Intergovernmental Affairs | http://www.gov.ab.ca/dept/figa.html |
| Alberta Health | http://www.health.gov.ab.ca/ |
| Alberta Justice | http://www.gov.ab.ca/dept/just.html |
| Alberta Labour | http://www.gov.ab.ca/dept/lbr.html |
| Alberta Municipal Affairs | http://www.gov.ab.ca/dept/ma.html |
| Alberta Public Works, Supply & Services | http://www.gov.ab.ca/~pwss/ |
| Alberta Research Council | http://www.arc.ab.ca |
| Alberta Transportation & Utilities | http://www.gov.ab.ca/ZXtu/ext.htm |

**Government of British Columbia**

| | |
|---|---|
| British Columbia Government Homepage | http://www.gov.bc.ca/ |
| Legislative Assembly | http://www.legis.gov.bc.ca/ |
| British Columbia Securities Commission | http://www.bcsc.bc.ca/ |
| British Columbia Environmental Assessment Office | http://www.eao.gov.bc.ca/ |
| British Columbia Hydro & Power Authority | http://www.bchydro.bc.ca |
| British Columbia Provincial Emergency Program | http://hoshi.cic.sfu.ca/~pep/ |
| Elections British Columbia | http://vvv.com/~electionsbc/ |
| Financial Institutions Commission | http://www.fic.gov.bc.ca/ |
| Institute of Ocean Sciences | http://www.ios.bc.ca/ |
| Ministry of Aboriginal Affairs | http://www.aaf.gov.bc.ca/aaf/ |
| Ministry of Agriculture, Fisheries & Food | http://www.agf.gov.bc.ca/ |
| Ministry of Children & Families | http://www.ssrv.gov.bc.ca/ |
| Ministry of Education, Skills & Training | http://www.est.gov.bc.ca/ |
| Ministry of Employment & Investment | http://www.ei.gov.bc.ca/ |
| Ministry of Environment, Lands & Parks | http://www.env.gov.bc.ca/ |
| Ministry of Finance & Corporate Relations | http://www.fin.gov.bc.ca/ |
| Ministry of Forests | http://www.for.gov.bc.ca |
| Ministry of Health | http://www.hlth.gov.bc.ca |
| Ministry of Human Resources | http://www.mhr.gov.bc.ca |
| Ministry of Labour | http://www.labour.gov.bc.ca/welcome.htm |
| Ministry of Municipal Affairs & Housing | http://www.marh.gov.bc.ca/ |
| Ministry of Small Business, Tourism & Culture | http://www.tbc.gov.bc.ca/homepage.html |
| Ministry of Women's Equality | http:www.weq.gov.bc.ca |
| Office of the Auditor General | http://www.aud.gov.bc.ca/ |
| Office of the Information & Privacy Commissioner | http://www.oipcbc.org |
| Office of the Ombudsman | http://www.ombud.gov.bc.ca/ |
| Science Council of British Columbia | http://www.scbc.org/ |
| Workers' Compensation Board of British Columbia | http://www.wcb.bc.ca/ |

**Government of Manitoba**

| | |
|---|---|
| Manitoba Government Homepage | http://www.gov.mb.ca/ |
| Premier's Office | http://www.gov.mb.ca/text/quotepg1.html |
| Legislative Assembly | http://www.gov.mb.ca/leg-asmb/index1.html |
| Economic Innovation & Technology Council | http://www.eitc.mb.ca/eitc.html |
| Manitoba Agriculture | http://www.gov.mb.ca/agriculture/ |
| Manitoba Culture, Heritage & Citizenship | http://www.gov.mb.ca/manitoba/chc/immsettl/citz_hom.html |
| Manitoba Education & Training | http://www.gov.mb.ca/educate/index.html |
| Manitoba Energy & Mines | http://www.gov.mb.ca/em/index.html |
| Manitoba Environment | http://www.gov.mb.ca/environ/index.html |
| Manitoba Family Services | http://www.gov.mb.ca/fs/first/ffindex.html |
| Manitoba Finance | http://www.gov.mb.ca/finance/ |
| Manitoba Health | http://www.gov.mb.ca/health/index.html |
| Manitoba Hydro | http://www.hydro.mb.ca |
| Manitoba Labour | http://www.gov.mb.ca/labour/ |
| Manitoba Natural Resources | http://www.gov.mb.ca/natres/index.html |
| Manitoba Telecom Services | http://www.mts.mb.ca/ |
| Workplace Safety & Health Division | http://www.gov.mb.ca/labour/safety/index.html |

**Government of New Brunswick**

New Brunswick Government Homepage .......... http://www.gov.nb.ca/
Legislative Assembly .......... http://www.gov.nb.ca/legis/index.htm
Department of Advanced Education & Labour .......... http://www.gov.nb.ca/ael/index.htm
Department of Agriculture & Rural Development .......... http//www.gov.nb.ca/agricult/index.htm
Department of Economic Development & Tourism .......... http://www.gov.nb.ca/edt/index.htm
Department of Education .......... http://www.gov.nb.ca/education/index.htm
Department of Finance .......... http://www.gov.nb.ca/finance/index.htm
Department of Fisheries & Aquaculture .......... http://www.gov.nb.ca/dfa/index.htm
Department of Health & Community Services .......... http://www.gov.nb.ca/hcs/
Department of Human Resources Development .......... http://inter.gov.nb.ca/hrd/
Department of Intergovernmental & Aboriginal Affairs .......... http://www.gov.nb.ca/iga/home1_e.htm
Department of Justice .......... http://www.gov.nb.ca/justice/index.htm
Department of Municipalities, Culture & Housing .......... http://www.gov.nb.ca/mch/index.htm
Department of Natural Resources & Energy .......... http://www.gov.nb.ca/dnre/index.htm
Department of the Environment .......... http://www.gov.nb.ca/environ/index.htm
Department of the Solicitor General .......... http://www.gov.nb.ca/solgen/index.htm
Department of Supply & Services .......... http://www.gov.nb.ca/supply/index.htm
New Brunswick Emergency Measures Organization .......... http://www.gov.nb.ca/pss/emo.htm
New Brunswick Research & Productivity Council .......... http://www.rpc.unb.ca
Premier's Council on the Status of Disabled Persons .......... http://www.gov.nb.ca/pcsdp/english/index.htm
Regional Development Corporation .......... http://www.gov.nb.ca/rdc/home_e.htm
Workplace Health, Safety & Compensation Commission .......... http://www.gov.nb.ca/whscc/index.htm

**Government of Newfoundland & Labrador**

Newfoundland & Labrador Government Homepage .......... http://www.gov.nf.ca/
Premier's Office .......... http://www.gov.nf.ca/exec/premier/premier.htm
Executive Council .......... http://www.gov.nf.ca/exec/start.htm
House of Assembly .......... http://www.gov.nf.ca/house/hoa_ovr.htm
Department of Development & Rural Renewal .......... http://www.gov.nf.ca/dev.htm
Department of Education .......... http://www.gov.nf.ca/edu/startedu.htm
Department of Environment & Labour .......... http://www.gov.nf.ca/envlab.htm
Department of Finance & Treasury Board .......... http://www.gov.nf.ca/fin/
Department of Fisheries & Aquaculture .......... http://www.gov.nf.ca/fishaq.htm
Department of Forest Resources & Agrifoods .......... http://www.gov.nf.ca/forest.htm
Department of Government Services & Lands .......... http://www.gov.nf.ca/gsl/startgsl.htm
Department of Health .......... http://www.gov.nf.ca/health/starthel.htm
Department of Human Resources & Employment .......... http://www.gov.nf.ca/hre/startdos.htm
Department of Industry, Trade & Technology .......... http://www.gov.nf.ca/itt/startitt.htm
Department of Justice & Attorney General .......... http://www.gov.nf.ca/just/startjus.htm
Department of Mines & Energy .......... http://www.gov.nf.ca/mines.htm
Department of Municipal & Provincial Affairs .......... http://www.gov.nf.ca/mpa/startmpa.htm
Department of Tourism, Culture & Recreation .......... http://public.gov.nf.ca/tcr/
Department of Works, Services & Transportation .......... http://public.gov.nf.ca/wst/
Newfoundland & Labrador Housing Corporation .......... http://www.gov.nf.ca/nlhc/nlhc.htm
Treasury Board Secretariat .......... http://www.gov.nf.ca/exec/Presiden/presiden.htm

**Government of Northwest Territories**

Northwest Territories Government Homepage .......... http://www.ssmicro.com/~xpsognwt/Net/index.html
Legislative Assembly .......... http://www.ssimicro.com/~epsognwt/Net/departments/assembly/Gov.html
Department of Education, Culture & Employment .......... http://siksik.learnnet.nt.ca
Department of Finance .......... http://www.fin.gov.nt.ca
Department of Health & Social Services .......... http://www.hlthss.gov.nt.ca/
Department of Justice .......... http://pingo.gov.nt.ca/Phone/Dept/dep0013.htm#Il
Department of Municipal & Community Affairs .......... http://www.maca.gov.nt.ca
Department of Public Works & Services .......... http://www.gov.nt.ca/pws
Department of Resources, Wildlife & Economic Development .......... http://www.edt.gov.nt.ca/
Department of Transportation .......... http://www.gov.nt.ca/Transportation

**Government of Nova Scotia**

Nova Scotia Government Homepage .......... http://www.gov.ns.ca/
Premier's Office .......... http://www.gov.ns.ca/govt/prem/
Legislative House of Assembly .......... http://www.gov.ns.ca/legi/house.htm
Advisory Council on the Status of Women .......... http://www.gov.ns.ca/govt/staw/
Department of Agriculture & Marketing .......... http://www.nsac.ns.ca/nsdam/
Department of Business & Consumer Services .......... http://www.gov.ns.ca/bacs/
Department of Education & Culture .......... http://www.ednet.ns.ca/
Department of Finance .......... http://www.gov.ns.ca/fina/
Department of Fisheries .......... http://www.gov.ns.ca/fish/
Department of Health .......... http://www.gov.ns.ca/heal
Department of Housing & Municipal Affairs .......... http://www.gov.ns.ca/homa/
Department of Human Resources .......... http://www.gov.ns.ca/humr/
Department of Justice .......... http://www.gov.ns.ca/just/
Department of Labour .......... http://www.gov.ns.ca/labr/
Department of Natural Resources .......... http://www.gov.ns.ca/natr/
Department of the Environment .......... http://www.gov.ns.ca/envi/
Nova Scotia Innovation Corporation .......... http://www.innovacorp.ns.ca
Nova Scotia Economic Renewal Agency .......... http://www.gov.ns.ca/ecor/

| | |
|---|---|
| Nova Scotia Emergency Measures Organization | http://www.gov.ns.ca/envi/dept/emo |
| Nova Scotia Human Rights Commission | http://www.gov.ns.ca/just/humanrts/ |
| Nova Scotia Technology & Science Secretariat | http://www.gov.ns.ca/tss/ |
| Office of the Auditor General | http://www.gov.ns.ca/legi/audg/ |
| Workers' Compensation Board of Nova Scotia | http://www.pixelmotion.ns.ca/wcb/home.html |

**Government of Ontario**

| | |
|---|---|
| Ontario Government Homepage | http://www.gov.on.ca/ |
| Lieutenant Governor's Office | http://ontla.on.ca/assemsrv/lg.htm |
| Premier's Office | http://www.gov.on.ca/premier/office/html |
| Executive Council | http://ontla.on.ca/members/exec.htm |
| Legislative Assembly | http://www.ontla.on.ca |
| Information & Privacy Commissioner of Ontario | http://www.ipc.on.ca |
| Ministry of Agriculture, Food & Rural Affairs | http://www.gov.on.ca/OMAFRA/english/ag.html |
| Ministry of Community & Social Services | http://www.gov.on.ca/CSS/ |
| Ministry of Consumer & Commercial Relations | http://www.ccr.gov.on.ca/mccr/welcome.htm |
| Ministry of Economic Development, Trade & Tourism | http://www.gov.on.ca |
| Ministry of Education & Training | http://www.edu.gov.on.ca |
| Ministry of Environment & Energy | http://www.ene.gov.on.ca/ |
| Ministry of Finance | http://www.gov.ca/FIN/hmpage.html |
| Ministry of Health | http://www.gov.on.ca/health |
| Ministry of Labour | http://www.gov.on.ca/LAB/main.htm |
| Ministry of Municipal Affairs & Housing | http://nrserv.mmah.gov.on.ca/ |
| Ministry of Natural Resources | http://www.mnr.gov.on.ca/mnr/ |
| Ministry of Northern Development & Mines | http://www.gov.on.ca/MNDM |
| Ministry of Transportation | http://www.gov.on.ca/MTO/ |
| Ontario Provincial Police | http://www.gov.on.ca/opp/ |
| Ontario Hydro | http://www.hydro.on.ca |
| Ontario Womens Directorate | http://www.gov.on.ca/owd |
| Workers' Compensation Board | http://www.wcb.on.ca/ |

**Government of Prince Edward Island**

| | |
|---|---|
| Prince Edward Island Government Homepage | http://www.gov.pe.ca/ |
| Lieutenant Governor's Office | http://www.gov.pe.ca/lg/index.html |
| Premier's Office | http://www.gov.pe.ca/premier/index.html |
| Executive Council | http://www.gov.pe.ca/ec/index.html |
| Legislative Assembly | http://www.gov.pe.ca/leg.index.html |
| Department of Agriculture & Forestry | http://www.gov.pe.ca/daff/index.html |
| Department of Community Affairs & Attorney General | http://www.gov.pe.ca/paag/index.html |
| Department of Economic Development & Tourism | http://www.gov.pe.ca/edt/index.html |
| Department of Education | http://www.gov.pe.ca/educ/ |
| Department of Fisheries & Environment | http://www.gov.pe.ca/env/index.html |
| Department of Health & Social Services | http://www.gov.pe.ca/hss/index.html |
| Department of Transportation & Public Works | http://www.gov.pe.ca/tpw/index.html |
| Department of the Provincial Treasury | http://www.gov.pe.ca/pt/index.html |
| Enterprise PEI | http://www.gov.pe.ca/edt/epei.html |
| Food Technology Centre | http://www.gov.pe.ca/ftc/index.html |
| Tourism PEI | http://www.gov.pe.ca |

**Government of Québec**

| | |
|---|---|
| Québec Government Homepage | http://www.gouv.qc.ca/ |
| Cabinet du premier ministre | http://www.premier.gouv.qc.ca |
| Conseil exécutif | http://www.cex.gouv.qc.ca |
| Assemblée nationale | http://www.assnat.qc.ca |
| Conseil de la science et de la technologie | http://www.cst.gouv.qc.ca/cst/cst_mandatE.html |
| Conseil du trésor | http://www.riq.qc.ca/scthtml/sct.htm |
| L'Inspecteur général des Institutions financières | http://www.igif.gouv.qc.ca/ |
| Ministère de l'Emploi et de la Solidarité | http://www.msr.gouv.qc.ca/ |
| Ministère de l'Agriculture, des Pêcheries et de l'Alimentation | http://www.agr.gouv.qc.ca/mapaq/ |
| Ministère de l'Éducation | http://www.gouv.qc.ca/francais/minorg/medu/medu_intro.html |
| Ministère de l'Environnement et de la Faune | http://www.mef.gouv.qc.ca |
| Ministère de l'Industrie, du commerce, de la Science et de la technologie | http://www.gouv.qc.ca/francais/minorg/micst/micst_intro.html |
| Ministère de la Culture et des Communications | http://www.mcc.gouv.qc.ca |
| Ministère de la Justice | http://www.gouv.qc.ca/francais/minorg/mjust/mjust_intro.html |
| Ministère de la Métropole | http://www.metropole.gouv.qc.ca |
| Ministère de la Santé et des services sociaux | http://www.msss.gouv.qc.ca |
| Ministère de la Sécurité publique | http://www.secpub.gouv.qc.ca/ |
| Ministère des Relations avec les citoyens et de l'Immigration | http://www.immq.gouv.qc.ca/ |
| Ministère des Affaires Municipales | http://www.mam.gouv.qc.ca |
| Ministère des Finances | http://www.finances.gouv.qc.ca/ |
| Ministère des Relations Internationales | http://www.mri.gouv.qc.ca |
| Ministère des Ressources Naturelles | http://www.mrn.gouv.qc.ca |
| Ministère des Transports | http://www.gouv.qc.ca/francais/minorg/mtrans/mtrans_intro.html |
| Ministère du Travail | http://www.travail.gouv.qc.ca/ |
| Protecteur du Citoyen | http://www.ombuds.gouv.qc.ca |
| Secrétariat à la famille | http://www.gouv.qc.ca/gouv/francais/minorg/sfamille/const.html |
| Secrétariat aux affaires autochtones | http://www.gouv.qc.ca/gouv/francais/minorg/saa/index.html |
| Secrétariat aux affaires intergouvernementales canadiennes | http://www.gouv.qc.ca/francais/minorg/maig/maig_intro.html |

Tourisme Québec ........ http://www.tourisme.gouv.qc.ca
Vérificateur général du Québec ........ http://www.sgo.gouv.qc.ca/vgq

**Government of Saskatchewan**

Saskatchewan Government Homepage ........ http://www.gov.sk.ca/
Premier's Office ........ http://www.sasknet.sk.ca
Executive Council ........ http://www.gov.sk.ca/execcoun/cabinet.htm#nillson
Legislative Assembly ........ http://www.legassembly.sk.ca/
Provincial Auditor (Saskatchewan) ........ http://www.legassembly.sk.ca/ProvAud/default.htm
Saskatchewan Human Rights Commission ........ http://www.gov.sk.ca/govt/hrc/
Saskatchewan Opportunities Corporation ........ http://www.gov.sk.ca/soco/
Saskatchewan Agriculture & Food ........ http://www.gov.sk.ca/agfood/
Saskatchewan Crown Investments Corporation ........ http://www.gov.sk.ca/govt/crowninv/
Saskatchewan Economic & Co-operative Development ........ http://www.gov.sk.ca/econdev/
Saskatchewan Education ........ http://www.sasked.gov.sk.ca
Saskatchewan Energy & Mines ........ http://www.gov.sk.ca/enermine/
Saskatchewan Environment & Resource Management ........ http://www.gov.sk.ca/govt/environ/
Saskatchewan Finance ........ http://www.gov.sk.ca/govt/finance/
Saskatchewan Health ........ http://www.gov.sk.ca/govt/health/
Saskatchewan Highways & Transportation ........ http://www.gov.sk.ca/govt/highways/
Saskatchewan Indian & Metis Affairs Secretariat ........ http://www.gov.sk.ca/govt/indmet/
Saskatchewan Intergovernmental Affairs ........ http://www.gov.sk.ca/govt/intergov/
Saskatchewan Justice ........ http://www.gov.sk.ca/govt/justice/
Saskatchewan Labour ........ http://www.gov.sk.ca/govt/labour/
Saskatchewan Municipal Government ........ http://www.gov.sk.ca/govt/munigov/
Saskatchewan Post-Secondary Education & Skills Training ........ http://www.gov.sk.ca
Saskatchewan Public Service Commission ........ http://www.gov.sk.ca/psc/
Saskatchewan Research Council ........ http://www.src.sk.ca
Saskatchewan Social Services ........ http://www.gov.sk.ca/govt/socserv/
Saskatchewan Telecommunications (SaskTel) ........ http://www.sasktel.com/

**Municipal & Regional Government**

Annapolis County ........ http://www.tartannet.ns.ca/~munofann/
Brant ........ http://www.bfree.on.ca/comdir/brantcounty/brantco.htm
City of Abbotsford ........ http://www.city.abby.bc.ca.abby
City of Barrie ........ http://www.city.barrie.on.ca/citymin.htm
City of Belleville ........ http://www.city.belleville.on.ca/
City of Brampton ........ http://www.city.brampton.on.ca/
City of Brantford ........ http://207.61.52.13:80/brantford/
City of Brockville ........ http://www.brockville.com
City of Burlington ........ http://worldchat.com/cob
City of Calgary ........ http//www.gov.calgary.ab.ca/
City of Camrose ........ http://www.camrose.com/
City of Charlottetown ........ http://www.munisource.org/charlottetown/welcome.html
City of Chatham ........ http://www.wincom.net/CHATHAM/
City of Coquitlam ........ http://www.gov.coquitlam.bc.ca/
City of Cornwall ........ http://www.city.cornwall.on.ca
City of Cranbrook ........ http://city.cranbrook.bc.ca/~cityhall/index.htm
City of Edmonton ........ http://www.gov.edmonton.ab.ca/
City of Elliot Lake ........ http://www.cityofelliotlake.com/
City of Etobicoke ........ http://www.busdev.city.etobicoke.on.ca
City of Fredericton ........ http://www.city.fredericton.nb.ca
City of Gloucester ........ http://www.city.gloucester.on.ca/
City of Grande Prairie ........ http://www.ccinet.ab.ca/city-of-gp/homepage.htm
City of Kingston ........ http://www.city.kingston.on.ca
City of Kitchener ........ http://www.oceta.on.ca/city.kitchener
City of Lethbridge ........ http://www.city.lethbridge.ab.ca
City of London ........ http://www.city.london.on.ca
City of Mississauga ........ http://www.city.mississauga.on.ca
City of Nanaimo ........ http://www.city.nanaimo.bc.ca/
City of Nepean ........ http://www.city.nepean.on.ca
City of Niagara Falls ........ http://www.niagara.com/city.niagara-falls
City of North Bay ........ http://www.city.north-bay.on.ca/northbay.htm
City of Orillia ........ http://www.city.orillia.on.ca/
City of Ottawa ........ http://city.ottawa.on.ca
City of Red Deer ........ http://www.city.red-deer.ab.ca/
City of Regina ........ http://www.cityregina.com
City of Richmond ........ http://www.city.richmond.bc.ca
City of Saint John ........ http://www.city.saint-john.nb.ca
City of Sault Ste. Marie ........ http://www.sault-canada.com
City of Scarborough ........ http://www.city.scarborough.on.ca/
City of St. Albert ........ http://www.city.st-albert.ab.ca
City of Sudbury ........ http://www.city.sudbury.on.ca
City of Surrey ........ http://www.city.surrey.bc.ca/
City of Thorold ........ http://www.thorold.com/mayor.html
City of Toronto ........ http://www.city.toronto.on.ca/
City of Vancouver ........ http://www.city.vancouver.bc.ca/
City of Vaughan ........ http://www.city.vaughan.on.ca

City of Victoria .......... http://www.city.victoria.bc.ca/
City of Waterloo .......... http://www.city.waterloo.on.ca
City of Whitehorse .......... http://www.city.whitehorse.yk.ca
City of Windsor .......... http://www.city.windsor.on.ca/
City of Winnipeg .......... http://www.city.winnipeg.mb.ca/city
City of Yellowknife .......... http://www.city.yellowknife.nt.ca
City of York .......... http://www.city.york.on.ca
Clarington .......... http://www.municipality.clarington.on.ca
Coaticook .......... http://www.multi-medias.ca/Mrc_Coaticook/
Communauté urbaine de Montréal .......... http://www.cum.qc.ca
Dist. of Chilliwack .......... http://www.gov.chilliwack.bc.ca/
Dist. of Maple Ridge .......... http://district.maple-ridge.bc.ca
Dist. of Mission .......... http://www.city.mission.bc
Dist. of North Vancouver .......... http://www.district.north-van.bc.ca/
Kootenay Boundary Regional District .......... http://www.rdkb.com
Oxford .......... http://www.hometown.on.ca
Regional Municipality of Halifax .......... http://www.region.halifax.ns.ca/
Regional Municipality of Halton .......... http://www.region.halton.on.ca
Regional Municipality of Metropolitan Toronto .......... http://www.metrotor.on.ca/
Regional Municipality of Niagara .......... http://www.regional.niagara.on.ca
Regional Municipality of Ottawa-Carleton .......... http://www.rmoc.on.ca (English) http://www.rmoc.on.ca/Bienvenue.html (French)
Regional Municipality of Peel .......... http://www.region.peel.on.ca
Regional Municipality of Sudbury .......... http://www.region.sudbury.on.ca
Regional Municipality of Waterloo .......... http://www.oceta.on.ca/region.waterloo/
Regional Municipality of York .......... http://www.region.york.on.ca
Saint John .......... http://www.sjport.com
Town of Flamborough .......... http://www.town.flamborough.on.ca
Town of Fort Frances .......... http://www.ff.lakeheadu.ca/rrfdc/ff-title
Town of Grand Bay-Westfield .......... http://www.town.grandbay.nb.ca/
Town of Kincardine .......... http://www.town.kincardine.on.ca/
Town of Listowel .......... http://www.micro-man.com/listowel
Town of Markham .......... http://www.city.markham.on.ca
Town of Orangeville .......... http://www.headwaters.com/orangeville/
Town of Pickering .......... http://www.town.pickering.on.ca
Town of Ridgetown .......... http://www.ciaccess.com/chatl/rcat.ridge.ridge.htm
Town of Tillsonburg .......... http://oxford.net/~tburg
Town of Wallaceburg .......... http://www/kent.net/wallaceburg
Town of Whitby .......... http://town.whitby.on.ca
Twp. of Cumberland .......... http://www.municipality.cumberland.on.ca
Twp. of Goulbourn .......... http://www.twp.goulbourn.on.ca/welcome.htm
Twp. of Norwich .......... http://www.oxford.net/~twpnor/ns2/
Twp. of Ramsay .......... http://www.ott.igs.net/~pakenham/ramsay
Twp. of West Nissouri .......... http://www.twp.est-nissouri-on.ca
Twp. of Yonge, Front of .......... http://www.mulberry.com/~fofyonge/
Village of Port Burwell .......... http://www.kanservu.ca/burwell/
Ville de Brossard .......... http://www.ville.brossard.qc.ca
Ville de Gatineau .......... http://gamma.omnimage.ca/clients/gatineau/
Ville de Jonquière .......... http://ville.jonquiere.qc.ca
Ville de Lachine .......... http://sun2.cum.qc.ca/LACHINE/
Ville de Laval .......... http://www.ville.laval.qc.ca/
Ville de Montréal .......... http://www.ville.montreal.qc.ca/
Ville de Québec .......... http://www.megatoon.com/web-quebec
Ville de Sherbrooke .......... http://ville.sherbrooke.qc.ca

**Miscellaneous Government**

Air Force Association of Canada .......... http://www.airforce.ca
Alberta Urban Municipalities Association .......... http://www.auma.ab.ca
Association of Municipalities of Ontario .......... http://www.amo.on.ca
Canadian Foundation for the Americas .......... http://www.focal.ca
Canadian Institute of Cultural Affairs .......... http://www.web.net/~icacan/
Canadian Institute of International Affairs .......... http://www.trinity.utoronto.ca/ciia/
Canadian Institute of Strategic Studies .......... http://www.ciss.ca
Canadian Urban Institute .......... http://www.interlog.com/~cui
Defence Associations National Network .......... http://www.sfu.ca/~dann
Federation of Canadian Municipalities .......... http://www.fcm.ca
Institute of Ocean Sciences .......... http://www.ios.bc.ca/
Institute of Public Administration of Canada .......... http://www.ipaciapc.ca
Institute on Governance .......... http://www.igvn.ca
Intergovernmental Committee on Urban & Regional Research .......... http://www.icurr.org/icurr/
Lester B. Pearson Canadian International Peacekeeping Training Centre .......... http://www.cdnpeacekeeping.ns.ca
National Water Research Institute .......... http://www.cciw.ca/nwri/intro.html
Ontario Professional Planners Institute .......... http://www.interlog.com/~oppi
Ontario Public Interest Research Group .......... http://www.campuslife.utoronto.ca/groups/opirg/
Planning Institute of British Columbia .......... http://www.pibc.bc.ca
Princess Patricia's Canadian Light Infantry Association .......... http://www.nucleus.com/ppcli
Professional Association of Foreign Service Officers (Ind.) .......... http://www.pafso.com
Purchasing Management Association of Canada .......... http://www.pmac.ca
Science for Peace .......... http://www.math.yorku.ca/sfp/

Social Sciences & Humanities Research Council of Canada.................... http://www.sshrc.ca
TeleLearning Network of Centres of Excellence .............................. http://www.telelearn.ca
The Naval Officers Association of Canada .................................. http://www.naval.ca
Union des municipalités régionales de comté et des municipalités locales du Québec.................. http://www.umrcq.qc.ca
Union of Nova Scotia Municipalities ....................................... http://www.munisource.org/unsm
United Nations Association in Canada ...................................... http://www.unac.org
Urban Development Institute of Canada ..................................... http://www.udi.bc.ca

## HEALTH & MEDICAL

AboutFace .................................................................. http://www.interlog.com/~abtface/
Acupuncture Foundation of Canada Institute ................................. http://www.afcinstitute.com/afci.html
Addiction Research Foundation.............................................. http://www.arf.org
Addictions Foundation of Manitoba ......................................... http://afm.mb.ca
Against Drunk Driving...................................................... http://www.netmediapro.com/add/
AIDS Vancouver ............................................................. http://mindlink.net/aids_vancouver/
Alberta Medical Association................................................ http://www.amda.ab.ca
Alzheimer Society of Canada ............................................... http://www.alzheimer.ca
Amyotrophic Lateral Sclerosis Society of Canada............................ http://www.als.ca
The Arthritis Society ...................................................... http://www.arthritis.ca
Association des conseils des médecins, dentistes et pharmaciens du Québec....... http://www.acmdp.qc.ca
Association des denturologistes du Québec .................................. http://www.adq-qc.com
Association of Canadian Medical Colleges.................................... http://www.acmc.ca
Association of Local Public Health Agencies................................. http://www.alphaweb.org
Association of Ontario Health Centres ...................................... http://www.aohc.org
Association québécoise de l'épilepsie ...................................... http://www.cam.org/~aqe/
Breast Cancer Action........................................................ http://infoweb.magi.com/~bcanet/
British Columbia Association of Optometrists................................ http://www.optometrists.bc.ca
British Columbia Cancer Agency.............................................. http://www.bccancer.bc.ca
British Columbia Cancer Foundation ......................................... http://www.bccancer.bc.ca
British Columbia Health Association......................................... http://www.HINETBC.org/BCHA/BCHAhome.html
British Columbia Medical Association........................................ http://www.bcma.org
Calgary General Hospital ................................................... http://www.crha-health.ab.ca
Calgary Regional Health Authority........................................... http://www.crha-health.ab.ca
Canadian Abortion Rights Action League ..................................... http://www.interlog.com/~caral
Canadian AIDS Society....................................................... http://www.cdnaids.ca
Canadian Association for Music Therapy ..................................... http://www.bmts.com/~smacnay/camt/camt.html
Canadian Association for Quality in Health Care ............................ http://highlander.cbnet.ns.ca/cbnet/healthca/caqhc/
Canadian Association for Suicide Prevention................................. http://www3.sympatico.ca/masecard/index.html
Canadian Association of Critical Care Nurses ............................... http://www.execulink.com/~caccn
The Canadian Association of Emergency Physicians............................ http://unixg.ubc.ca:780/~grunfeld/caep.html
Canadian Association of Optometrists ....................................... http://fox.nstn.ca/~eyedocs/caoorg.html
Canadian Association of Speech-Language Pathologists & Audiologists.......... http://www.caslpa.ca
Canadian Association on Gerontology ........................................ http://www.cagacg.ca
Canadian Bacterial Diseases Network......................................... http://www.cbdn.ca
Canadian Centre for Occupational Health & Safety ........................... http://www.ccohs.ca
Canadian Centre on Substance Abuse.......................................... http://www.ccsa.ca
Canadian Chiropractic Association .......................................... http://www.inforamp.net/~ccachiro
Canadian Coordinating Office for Health Technology Assessment .............. http://www.ccohta.ca
Canadian Council for Tobacco Control........................................ http://www.ccsh.ca
Canadian Council on Health Services Accreditation........................... http://www.cchsa.ca
Canadian Cystic Fibrosis Foundation......................................... http://www.ccff.ca/~cfwww/index.html
Canadian Dental Association ................................................ http://www.cda-adc.ca
Canadian Diabetes Association .............................................. http://www.diabetes.ca/
Canadian Foundation for the Study of Infant Deaths ......................... http://www.sidscanada.org/sids.html
Canadian Genetic Diseases Network........................................... http://data.ctn.nrc.ca/bc/content/type12/org319/parent.htm
Canadian Health Record Association ......................................... http://www.chra.ca
Canadian Healthcare Association............................................. http://www.canadian-healthcare.org
Canadian HIV/AIDS Legal Network............................................. http://www.odyssee.net/~jujube
Canadian Institute of Child Health.......................................... http://www.cich.ca
Canadian Intravenous Nurses Association .................................... http://web.idirect.com/~csotcina
Canadian Liver Foundation................................................... http://www.liver.ca
Canadian Lung Association................................................... http://www.lung.ca
Canadian Massage Therapist Alliance......................................... http://www.collinscan.com/~collins/clientspgs/cmtai.html
Canadian Medical Association ............................................... http://www.cma.ca
Canadian Memorial Chiropractic College...................................... http://www.cmcc.ca
Canadian Network of Toxicology Centres...................................... http://www.uoguelph.ca/cntc
Canadian Ophthalmological Society .......................................... http://eyesite.ca
Canadian Paediatric Society ................................................ http://www.cps.ca
Canadian Pharmaceutical Association......................................... http://www.cdnpharm.ca
Canadian Physiotherapy Association.......................................... http://www.physiotherapy.ca
Canadian Play Therapy Institute ............................................ http://www.playtherapy.org/
Canadian Psychiatric Association............................................ http://medical.org
Canadian Psychological Association ......................................... http://www.cpa.ca
Canadian Public Health Association ......................................... http://www.cpha.ca
The Canadian Red Cross Society ............................................. http://www.redcross.ca
Canadian Rheumatology Association .......................................... http://www.arthritis.ca/cra/index.html
Canadian Schizophrenia Foundation........................................... http://www.orthomed.org

| | |
|---|---|
| Canadian Sleep Society | http://bisleep.medsch.ucla.edu/CSS/css.html |
| Canadian Society for International Health | http://www.csih.org/csihmem.html |
| Canadian Society of Aerospace Medicine | http://www.casi.ca |
| Canadian Society of Clinical Neurophysiologists | http://www.ccns.org |
| Canadian Society of Hospital Pharmacists | http://www.cshp.ca/~cshp |
| Canadian Society of Laboratory Technologists | http://www.cslt.com |
| Canadian Society of Orthopaedic Technologists | http://web.idirect.com/~csotcina/csot.html |
| Canadian Society of Plastic Surgeons | http://www.plasticsurgery.ca |
| Canadian Spinal Research Organization | http://www.csro.com |
| Canadian Thoracic Society | http://www.lung.ca/thorax/index.html |
| Canadian Urological Association | http://www.cua.org |
| Canadian Wholesale Drug Association | http://www.cwda.com |
| Cancer Research Society Inc. | http://www.cancer-research-society.ca |
| Candlelighters Childhood Cancer Foundation Canada | http://www.candlelighters.ca |
| Catholic Health Association of Canada | http://www.net-globe.com/chac/ |
| Centre hospitalier de St. Mary | http://www.smhc.qc.ca |
| Centre hospitalier régional du Suroît | http://www.rocler.qc.ca/chrs/chrs.html |
| Child & Parent Resource Institute | http://www.hometown.on.ca/cpri/ |
| Childbirth By Choice Trust | http://web.idirect.com/~cbctrust/ |
| Clarke Institute of Psychiatry | http://www.theClarke-inst.on.ca |
| COACH, Canada's Health Informatics Association | http://www.telusplanet.net/public/coachorg/ |
| Collège des médecins du Québec | http://www.cmq.org |
| College of Family Physicians of Canada | http://www.cfpc.ca |
| College of Physicians & Surgeons of Alberta | http://www.cpsa.ab.ca |
| College of Physicians & Surgeons of Manitoba | http://www.umanitoba.ca/colleges/cps |
| College of Physicians & Surgeons of New Brunswick | http://www.cpsnb.org |
| Crohn's & Colitis Foundation of Canada | http://www.ccfc.ca |
| Dairy Nutrition Council of Alberta | http://www.dnca.ab.ca |
| Deer Lodge Centre Inc. | http://www.mbnet.mb.ca/cvm/health/deerlod2.html |
| Dept. of Health & Community Services | http://www.gov.nb.ca/hcs/ |
| DES Action Canada | http://www.web.net/~desact |
| Dr. Everett Chalmers Hospital | http://www.gov.nb.ca/hospital/region3/ |
| Endometriosis Association, Inc. | http://www.endometriosisassn.org |
| Epilepsy Canada | http://www.epilepsy.ca |
| Epilepsy Ontario | http://www.epilepsy.org |
| Fédération des médecins omnipraticiens du Québec | http://www.sante.qc.ca/synapses/fmoq.htm |
| Fédération québécoise des massothérapeutes | http://www.globale.com/data/fqm.htm |
| Glenrose Rehabilitation Hospital | http://www.grhosp.ab.ca |
| Halton District Health Council | http://cwhweb.mcmaster.ca |
| Health Action Network Society | http://www.hans.org/ |
| Health Evidence Application & Linkage Network | http://hiru.mcmaster.ca/nce |
| Heart & Stroke Foundation of Alberta | http://www.hsfacal.org/ |
| Hôpital de l'Enfant-Jésus | http://hej.clic.net:8000/email/ |
| L'Hôpital de réadaptation Lindsay | http://www.hopital-lindsay.qc.ca |
| Hôpital Maisonneuve-Rosemont | http://alize.ere.umontreal.ca/~beauprea/dept_md/ |
| Hôpital neurologique de Montréal | http://www.mni.mcgill.ca/mni/aboutmnh.html |
| Institut Philippe Pinel de Montréal | http://brise.ere.umontreal/ca/~beaudetn/index.html |
| Institut universitaire de gériatrie de Sherbrooke | http://www.usherb.ca/Iugs/iugs.html |
| International Association for Medical Assistance to Travellers | http://www.sentex.net/~iamat |
| Klinic Community Health Centre | http://www.klinic.ma.ca |
| Leprosy Mission Canada | http://www.tlmcanada.org |
| London Health Sciences Centre | http://www.lhsc.on.ca |
| Manitoba Cancer Treatment & Research Foundation | http:pwc.mctrf.mb.ca |
| M.E. Association of Canada | http://www.mecan.ca |
| The Medical Council of Canada | http://www.mcc.ca |
| Mental Health Centre Penetanguishene | http://www.mhcvc.on.ca/m1mhcp.htm |
| The Michener Institute for Applied Health Sciences | http://www.michener.on.ca |
| The Migraine Association of Canada | http://www.migraine.ca |
| Misericordia Hospital (Caritas Health Group) | http://www.caritas.ab.ca |
| Multiple Sclerosis Society of Canada | http://www.mssoc.ca |
| Muscular Dystrophy Association of Canada | http://www.mdac.ca |
| Myasthenia Gravis Association of British Columbia | http://home.istar.ca/ntnc |
| National Association of Pharmacy Regulatory Authorities | http://www.napra.org |
| National Institute of Nutrition | http://www.hwc.ca:8080/nin |
| North American Chronic Pain Association of Canada | http://www3.sympatico.ca/nacpac/ |
| North Central Health District | http://www.nlnet.melfort.sk.ca/muh/ncdhb |
| Nova Scotia Chiropractic Association | http://www.medianet.ca/nsca/ |
| Nurses Association of New Brunswick | http://www.nanb.nb.ca |
| Ontario Association of Children's Mental Health Centres | http://www.oacmhc.org |
| Ontario Association of Directors of Volunteer Services in Healthcare | http://www.interlog.com/~odvh/ |
| The Ontario Cancer Treatment & Research Foundation | http://www.octrf.on.ca |
| Ontario College of Pharmacists | http://www.ocpharma.com |
| Ontario Dental Association | http://www.oda.on.ca/ |
| Ontario Hospital Association | http://www.oha.com |
| Ontario Lung Association | http://www.on.lung.ca |
| Ontario Medical Association | http://www.oma.org |
| Ontario Nurses' Association | http://www.ona.org/ |
| Ordre des dentistes du Québec | http://www.odq.qc.ca/ |

Ordre des infirmières et infirmiers du Québec ........ http://www.oiiq.org
Ordre professionnel des diététistes du Québec ........ http://www.opdq.org
Orillia Soldiers' Memorial Hospital ........ http://www.barint.on.ca/osmh/osmh.html
Parents of Multiple Births Association of Canada Inc. ........ http://www.pomba.org
Peninsulas Health Care Corporation ........ http://www.phcc.nf.net
Perth Community Care Centre Inc. ........ http://www.dignicare.com
Pharmaceutical Manufacturers Association of Canada ........ http://www.pmac-acim.org
Pharmacological Society of Canada ........ http://www.pmcol.ualberta.ca/psc/
Physicians for Global Survival (Canada) ........ http://www.web.net/~pgs/
Prince Edward Island Lung Association ........ http://www.lung.ca
Protein Engineering Network of Centres of Excellence ........ http://www.pence.ualberta.ca
Provincial Mental Health Advisory Board ........ http://www.pmhab.ab.ca
Registered Nurses Association of British Columbia ........ http://www.rnabc.bc.ca
Registered Psychiatric Nurses Association of Manitoba ........ http://www.psychiatricnurses.mb.ca/rpnam/index.html
Respiratory Health Network of Centres of Excellence ........ http://www.meakins.mcgill.ca/Inspiraplex/index.html
The Roeher Institute ........ http://indie.ca/roeher/
The Royal College of Physicians & Surgeons of Canada ........ http://rcpsc.medical.org
Saint John Regional Hospital ........ http://www.ahsc.health.nb.ca
The Salvation Army Grace Hospital ........ http://www.grace.ottawa.on.ca
Sarnia & District Children's Treatment Centre ........ http://www.sarnia.com/groups/sdctc
Saskatchewan Lung Association ........ http://www.sk.lung.ca
Schizophrenia Society of Canada ........ http://www.schizophrenia.ca
Simcoe County District Health Council ........ http://www.dhc.simcoe.on.ca
Society of Obstetricians & Gynaecologists of Canada ........ http://www.medical.org/sogc_docs/SOGC.html
Spina Bifida & Hydrocephalus Association of Canada ........ http://www.sbhac.ca
St. Boniface General Hospital ........ http://bison.umanitoba.ca
St. Joseph's Auxiliary Hospital ........ http://www.stjosephs.ab.ca
St. Mary's of the Lake Hospital ........ http://www.canlink.com/pccc
St. Michael's Extended Care Centre ........ http://www.connect.ab.ca/~smeccs/
Thyroid Foundation of Canada ........ http://home.ican.net/~thyroid/Canada.html
Victorian Order of Nurses for Canada ........ http://www.von.ca
West Park Hospital ........ http://www.westpark.org
York Region District Health Council ........ http://www.counselinc.com/yorkdhc

## INDUSTRY

Accommodation Motel Ontario Association ........ http://www.motelsontario.on.ca
Agricultural Groups Concerned About Resources & the Environment ........ http://www.agcare.org
Agricultural Institute of Canada ........ http://www.aic.ca
Air & Waste Management Association ........ http://www.awma.org
Alberta Association of Architects ........ http://www.aaa.ab.ca
Alberta Conservation Tillage Society ........ http://www.actsagtec.com
Alberta Hotel Association ........ http://www.albertahotels.ab.ca
Alberta Ready-Mixed Concrete Association ........ http://www.constructworld.com/armca/
Alberta Society of Engineering Technologists ........ http://aset.worldgate.com
Alberta Wheat Pool ........ http://www.awp.com/
Alliance of Manufacturers & Exporters Canada ........ http://www.palantir.ca/the-alliance//
Applied Science Technologists & Technicians of British Columbia ........ http://www.asttbc.org
Architectural Institute of British Columbia ........ http://www.aibc.bc.ca
The Asbestos Institute ........ http://www.asbestos-institute.ca
Associated Designers of Canada ........ http://www.ffa.ucalgary.ca/adc/indexadc.htm
Association des agences de publicité du Québec ........ http://www.aapq.qc.ca
Association des chefs de services d'incendie du Québec ........ http://www.acsiq.qc.ca
Association des fournisseurs d'hôtels et restaurants inc. ........ http://www.afhr.com
L'Association des hôteliers du Québec ........ http://www.destinationquebec.com
Association des industries forestières du Québec ltée ........ http://www.aifq.qc.ca
Association des manufacturiers de bois de sciage du Québec ........ http://www.sciage-lumber.qc.ca
Association for the Export of Canadian Books ........ http://aecb.org
Association nationale des éditeurs de livres ........ http://www.cam.org/~anel/index.htm
Association of Architectural Technologists of Ontario ........ http://www.aato.on.ca
Association of Book Publishers of British Columbia ........ http://www.books.bc.ca
Association of Canadian Publishers ........ http://www.publishers.ca
Association of Canadian Travel Agents ........ http://www.acta.net
Association of Consulting Engineers of Canada ........ http://www.acec.ca
Association of Consulting Engineers of Manitoba Inc. ........ http://www.tetres.ca/acem/index.html
Association of Engineering Technicians & Technologists of Newfoundland ........ http://www.cabot.nf.ca/aettn
Association of Professional Engineers & Geoscientists of British Columbia ........ http://www.apeg.bc.ca
Association of Professional Engineers & Geoscientists of Newfoundland ........ http://www.apegn.nf.ca
Association of Professional Engineers & Geoscientists of Saskatchewan ........ http://www.apegs.sk.ca
Association of Professional Engineers, Geologists & Geophysicists - Alta. ........ http://www.apegga.com
Association of Professional Engineers, Geologists & Geophysicists - NWT ........ http://www.napegg.nt.ca
Association of Professional Engineers of New Brunswick ........ http://www.apenb.nb.ca
Association of Professional Engineers of Nova Scotia ........ http://www.apens.ca
Association of Professional Engineers of Prince Edward Island ........ http://www.isn.net/virtual/apepei/
Association touristique de Chaudière-Appalaches ........ http://www.chaudapp.qc.ca
Association touristique de la Gaspésie ........ http://www.tourisme-gaspesie.qc.ca
Association touristique de Lanaudière ........ http://tourisme-lanaudiere.qc.ca
Association touristique de l'Outaouais ........ http://www.achilles.net/~ato/
Association Touristique des Cantons-de-l'Est ........ http://www.tourisme-estrie.qc.ca

Association touristique des Îles-de-la-Madeleine .... http://www.ilesdelamadeleine.com/tourisme.htm
Association touristique du Bas-Saint-Laurent .... http://www.tourismebas-st-laurent.com
Association touristique du Saguenay-Lac-Saint-Jean .... http://www.atrsaglac.d4m.com
Association Touristique Régionale de Duplessis .... http://www.bbsi.net/atrd/
Atlantic Building Supply Dealers Association .... http://Fox.nstn.ca/~absda/
Automotive Industries Association of Canada .... http://www.aftmkt.com
Automotive Parts Manufacturers' Association .... http://www.capma.com
Ayrshire Breeders Association of Canada .... http://www.ayrshire-canada.com
BBM Bureau of Measurement .... http://www.bbm.ca/
Béton Canada .... http://www.usherb.ca/beton/
Brewers Association of Canada .... http://www.brewers.ca
British Columbia & Yukon Chamber of Mines .... http://www.bc-mining-house.com/chamber
British Columbia & Yukon Hotels Association .... http://www.fleethouse.com/fhcanada/bc-acco.htm
British Columbia Construction Association .... http://www.bccassn.com
British Columbia Federation of Agriculture .... http://www.bcfa.bc.ca/bcfa
British Columbia Marine Trades Association .... http://bcmarine.com
British Columbia Safety Council .... http://www.safetycouncil.bc.ca
British Columbia Technology Industries Association .... http://www.bctia.org
Business Documents & Systems Association .... http://www.bdsa.ca
Cable Television Standards Foundation .... http://ctsc.ca
Canada Grains Council .... http://www.canadagrainscouncil.ca
Canada Safety Council .... http://www.safety-council.org
Canadian Academy of Recording Arts & Sciences .... http://www.juno-awards.ca
Canadian Advanced Technology Association .... http://www.cata.ca/
Canadian Air Cushion Technology Society .... http://www.casi.ca/
Canadian Alarm & Security Association .... http://www.canasa.org
Canadian Association for Composite Structures & Materials .... http://www.cacsma.ca
Canadian Association of Career Educators & Employers .... http://www.cacee.com/workweb
Canadian Association of Certified Planning Technicians .... http://www.networx.on.ca/~cacpt
Canadian Association of Drilling Engineers .... http://www.lexicom.ab.ca/~cade
Canadian Association of Fish Exporters .... http://www.seafood.ca
Canadian Association of Home Inspectors .... http://www.bconnex.net/~jmlueck/cahi.html
Canadian Association of Internet Providers .... http://www.caip.ca/
Canadian Association of Oilwell Drilling Contractors .... http://www.caodc.ca/
Canadian Association of Petroleum Producers .... http://www.capp.ca
Canadian Booksellers Association .... http://www.cbabook.org
Canadian Cattlemen's Association .... http://www.cattle.ca
Canadian Centre for Occupational Health & Safety .... http://www.ccohs.ca
Canadian Charolais Association .... http://www.charolais.com
Canadian Chemical Producers' Association .... http://www.ccpa.ca
Canadian Construction Association .... http://www.cca-acc.com
Canadian Consulting Agrologists Association .... http://www.igw.ca/ccaa
Canadian Council for Human Resources in the Environment Industry .... http://www.chatsubo.com/cchrei
Canadian Council of Professional Engineers .... http://www.ccpe.ca
Canadian Council of Technicians & Technologists .... http://www.cctt.ca/
Canadian Egg Marketing Agency .... http://www.canadaegg.ca
Canadian Electricity Association .... http://www.canelect.ca
Canadian Energy Pipeline Association .... http://www.cepa.com
Canadian Environment Industry Association .... http://www.ceia.org
Canadian Environment Industry Association - British Columbia .... http://www.ceia-bc.com/
Canadian Federation of Agriculture .... http://www.cfa-fca.ca
Canadian Federation of Chefs & Cooks .... http://www.cybersmith.net/cfcc/
Canadian Food Brokers Association .... http://web.idirect.com/~cfba
Canadian Geotechnical Society .... http://www.inforamp.net/~cgs
Canadian Gift & Tableware Association .... http://www.cgta.org
Canadian Hardwood Plywood Association .... http://www.lumberweb.com/chpa/
Canadian Honey Packers' Association .... http://www.worldexport.com/labonte/
Canadian Independent Record Production Association .... http://www.cmrra.ca/cirpa
Canadian Industrial Innovation Centre .... http://www.innovationcentre.ca
Canadian Institute of Cultural Affairs .... http://www.web.net/~icacan/
Canadian Institute of Forestry .... http://www.cif-ifc.org/
Canadian Institute of Gemmology .... http://www.deepcove.com/cig/
Canadian Institute of Mining, Metallurgy & Petroleum .... http://www.cim.org
Canadian Institute of Plumbing & Heating .... http://www.ciph.com
Canadian Institute of Quantity Surveyors .... http://www.ciqs.org
Canadian Institute of Steel Construction .... http://www.cisc-icca.ca
Canadian Institute of Travel Counsellors of Ontario .... http://www.citcontario.com
Canadian Kitchen Cabinet Association .... http://www.kitchenweb.com/ckca/en/
Canadian Livestock Records Corporation .... http://www.clrc.on.ca
Canadian Lumbermen's Association .... http://www.lumberweb.com/cla/en/
Canadian Magazine Publishers Association .... http://www.cmpa.ca/
Canadian Marine Manufacturers Association .... http://www.cmma.ca
Canadian Meat Importers Committee .... http://www.importers.ca
Canadian Mineral Analysts .... http://www.info-mine.com/assoc-inst/cma/
Canadian Morgan Horse Association Inc. .... http://www.osha.igs.net/~cmha/.index.htm
Canadian National Aboriginal Tourism Association .... http://www.v1i.ca/clients/abc/cnata/cnata3.htm
Canadian Office Products Association .... http://www.copa.ca
Canadian Pallet Council .... http://www.cpcpallet.com

|  |  |
|---|---|
| Canadian Pharmaceutical Association | http://www.cdnpharm.ca |
| Canadian Plastics Industry Association | http://www.plastics.ca |
| Canadian Pork Council | http://www.canpork.ca |
| Canadian Port & Harbour Association | http://www.newswire.ca/cpha/cpha1.htm |
| Canadian Portland Cement Association | http://www.buildingweb.com/cpca/index.html |
| Canadian Prestressed Concrete Institute | http://www.buildingweb.com/cpci/ |
| Canadian Produce Marketing Association | http://www.cpma.ca |
| Canadian Professional Logistics Institute | http://www.loginstitute.ca |
| Canadian Publishers' Council | http://www.pubcouncil.ca |
| Canadian Pulp & Paper Association | http://www.open.doors.cppa.ca/ |
| Canadian Sanitation Supply Association | http://www.cssa.com |
| Canadian Seed Trade Association | http://www.hookup.net/~csta/ |
| Canadian Society for Chemical Engineering | http://www.chem-inst-can.org |
| Canadian Society for Chemistry | http://www.chem-inst-can.org |
| Canadian Society for Civil Engineering | http://www.csce.ca |
| Canadian Society for Mechanical Engineering | http://home.istar.ca/~csocme/index.htm |
| Canadian Society for Nondestructive Testing, Inc. | http://www.csndt.org |
| Canadian Society of Agricultural Engineering | http://www.engr.usask.ca/societies/csae/ |
| Canadian Society of Extension | http://tdg.uoguelph.ca/cse |
| Canadian Society of Petroleum Geologists | http://www.cspg.org |
| Canadian Society of Safety Engineering, Inc. | http://www.csse.org |
| Canadian Soft Drink Association | http://www.softdrink.ca |
| Canadian Sphagnum Peat Moss Association | http://www.peatmoss.com |
| Canadian Sporting Goods Association | http://www.globalsports.com/csga |
| Canadian Standardbred Horse Society | http://home.ican.net/~troton |
| Canadian Standards Association | http://www.csa.ca/ |
| Canadian Steel Producers Association | http://www.canadiansteel.ca |
| Canadian Tooling & Machining Association | http://www.ctma.com |
| Canadian Turkey Marketing Agency | http://www.canturkey.ca |
| Canadian Welding Bureau | http://www.cwbgroup.com |
| Canadian Well Logging Society | http://www.canpic.ca/CWLS |
| Canadian Wholesale Drug Association | http://www.cwda.com |
| Canadian Window & Door Manufacturers Association | http://www.windoorweb.com/cwdma |
| Canadian Wood Council | http://cwc.metrics.com/cwc.html |
| CANARIE Inc. | http://www.canarie.ca |
| Canola Council of Canada | http://www.canola-council.org |
| Certified Technicians & Technologists Association of Manitoba | http://www.cctt.ca/members/manitoba.htm |
| Christian Farmers Federation of Ontario | http://www.christianfarmers.org |
| Christmas Tree Growers' Association of Ontario Inc. | http://www.christmastrees.on.ca |
| Co-op Atlantic | http://www.co-op-atlantic.ca |
| The Coal Association of Canada | http://www.coal.ca |
| Comité canadien des éléctrotechnologies | http://www.cce.qc.ca |
| Conseil québécois du commerce de détail | http://www.cqcd.com |
| Construction Specifications Canada | http://www.csc-dcc.ca |
| Consulting Engineers of Alberta | http://www.caisnet.com/cea/ |
| Continental Automated Buildings Association | http://www.caba.org |
| Convention & Visitors Bureau of Windsor | http://www.city.windsor.on.ca/cvb |
| Coopérative fédérée du Québec | http://www.coopfed.qc.ca |
| Crop Protection Institute of Canada | http://www.cropro.org |
| Dairy Farmers of Ontario | http://www.milk.org |
| Design Exchange | http://www.hyperm.com/dxsite |
| Electronic Commerce Canada | http://www.ecc.ca |
| Electronics & Information Association of Manitoba | http://www.mbnet.mb.ca/~eiam/ |
| The Engineering Institute of Canada | http://www.eic-ici.ca |
| Environmental Services Association of Alberta | http://www.esaa.org |
| Flax Council of Canada | http://www.flaxcouncil.ca |
| Food & Consumer Products Manufacturers of Canada | http://www.fcpmc.com |
| Food Institute of Canada | http://foodnet.fic.ca/fic/fic.html |
| Forest Engineering Research Institute of Canada | http://www.feric.ca |
| Groupe LACTEL, Société en commandite | http://www.lactel.com |
| Heating, Refrigerating & Air Conditioning Institute of Canada | http://www.hrai.ca |
| Holstein Association of Canada | http://www.holstein.ca/ |
| Industrial Accident Prevention Association Ontario | http://www.iapa.on.ca |
| Industrial Gas Users Association | http://www.hypernet.on.ca/igua/ |
| Industrial Research & Development Institute | http://www.irdi.on.ca |
| Information Technology Association of Canada | http://www.itac.ca/ |
| Information Technology Industry Alliance of Nova Scotia | http://www.seimac.com/~ITANS/ |
| Institute of Electrical & Electronics Engineers Canada | http://www.ieee.ca |
| Instrument Society of America | http://www.isa.org |
| Interior Designers Institute of British Columbia | http://www.designsource.bc.ca |
| International Institute for Sustainable Development | http://iisd1.iisd.ca/ |
| Jersey Canada | http://www.jerseycanada.com |
| Jubilee Centre for Agricultural Research | http://www.christianfarmers.org |
| Klondike Visitors Association | http://www.dawsoncity.com |
| Kootenay Country Tourist Association | http://travel.bc.ca/region/kootenay/index.html |
| Landscape Ontario Horticultural Trades Association | http://www.hort-trades.com |
| Machinery & Equipment Manufacturers' Association of Canada | http://www.memac.org |
| Major Industrial Accidents Council of Canada | http://hoshi.cic.sfu.ca/miacc/ |

Manitoba Association of Architects ........ http://cad9.cadlab.umanitoba.ca/MAA.html
Manitoba Environmental Industries Association Inc. ........ http://www.canpay.com/meia/
Maritime Lumber Bureau ........ http://www.mlb.ca
Master Brewers Association of The Americas ........ http://www.mbaa.com
Metropolitan Toronto Convention & Visitors Association ........ http://www.tourism-toronto.com
Mining Association of British Columbia ........ http://www.info-mine.com/assoc-inst/mabc/
Mining Association of Canada ........ http://www.mining.ca
Motor Dealers' Association of Alberta ........ http://www.compusmart.ab.ca/mdaalta
Muskoka Tourism ........ http://www.muskoka.com/tourism/
NACE - International ........ http://www.nace.org
National Aboriginal Forestry Association ........ http://sae.ca/nafa
National Association of Women in Construction ........ http://www.nawic.org
National Farmers Union ........ http://www.wbm.ca/users/farmers
National Optics Institute ........ http://www.ino.qc.ca
New Brunswick Federation of Agriculture ........ http://personal.nbnet.nb.ca/nbfa/nbfa.htm
Newfoundland & Labrador Alliance of Technical Industries ........ http://www.netfx.iom.net/nati/
Newfoundland & Labrador Construction Association ........ http://www.netfx.iom.net/nlca/
Newfoundland Environmental Industry Association ........ http://www.webpage.ca/neia/
Niagara Falls, Canada Visitor & Convention Bureau ........ http://www.tourismniagara.com/nfcvcb/
North of Superior Tourism Association ........ http://www.nosta.on.ca
Northern Ontario Tourist Outfitters Association ........ http://www.virtualnorth.com/noto/
Nova Scotia Environmental Industry Association ........ http://www.isisnet.com/nseia/
Nova Scotia Institute of Agrologists ........ http://www.nsac.ns.ca/nsdam/nsia/
Nunavut Tourism ........ http://www.nunatour.nt.ca
Office des congrès et du tourisme du Grand Montréal ........ http://www.cum.qc.ca/octgm/Welcome.html
Office du tourisme de Laval ........ http://www.tourismelaval.qc.ca
Office du tourisme et des congrès de la communauté urbaine de Québec ........ http://www.quebec-region.cuq.qc.ca
Okanagan Similkameen Tourism Association ........ http://www.travel.bc.ca/region/ok
Ontario Association of Architects ........ http://www.oaa.on.ca
Ontario Beekeepers' Association ........ http://www.tdg.ca/ontag/bee
Ontario Community Newspapers Association ........ http://www.ocna.org
Ontario Concrete Pipe Association ........ http://www.ccpa.com
The Ontario Farm Animal Council ........ http://www.milk.org/ofac.htm
Ontario Federation of Agriculture ........ http://www.ofa.on.ca
Ontario Fruit & Vegetable Growers' Association ........ http://www.tdg.ca/ontag/ofvga
Ontario Hotel & Motel Association ........ http://www.ohma.com
Ontario Institute of Agrologists ........ http://www.freespace.net/~oia
Ontario Maple Syrup Producers' Association ........ http://www.tdg.ca/ontag/omspa/
Ontario Professional Planners Institute ........ http://www.interlog.com/~oppi
Ontario Safety League ........ http://www.osl.org
Ontario's Sunset Country Travel Association ........ http://www.ontariossunsetcountry.ca
Ordre des architectes du Québec ........ http://www.oaq.com
Ordre des ingénieurs du Québec ........ http://www.oiq.qc.ca
Ottawa Tourism & Convention Authority ........ http://www.tourottawa.org
PEI Roadbuilders & Heavy Construction Association ........ http://www3.sympatico.ca/pei.roadbuilders/
Petroleum Communication Foundation ........ http://www.pcf.ab.ca
Petroleum Recovery Institute ........ http://www.pri.com
Petroleum Services Association of Canada ........ http://www.psac.ca
Petroleum Society of CIM ........ http://www.canpic.ca/PETSOC/
Pharmaceutical Manufacturers Association of Canada ........ http://www.pmac-acim.org
Pictou County Tourist Association ........ http://www.animax.com/pcta
PIJAC Canada ........ http://www.pijaccanada.com
Planning Institute of British Columbia ........ http://www.pibc.bc.ca
Prairie Implement Manufacturers Association ........ http://www.pima.ca
Professional Association of Canadian Theatres ........ http://webhome.idirect.com/~pact/
Professional Engineers Ontario ........ http://www.peo.on.ca
Propane Gas Association of Canada Inc. ........ http://www.propanegas.ca
Prospectors & Developers Association of Canada ........ http://www.pdac.ca
Recreation Vehicle Dealers Association of Alberta ........ http://www.rvda-alberta.com
Recreation Vehicle Dealers Association of Canada ........ http://www.rvda.ca
Resorts Ontario ........ http://www.resorts-ontario.com
Restaurant & Foodservices Association of British Columbia & the Yukon ........ http://www.yes.net/RFABCY/
Retail Council of Canada ........ http://www.retailcouncil.org
Roofing Contractors Association of British Columbia ........ http://www.rcabc.org
Royal Agricultural Winter Fair Association ........ http://www.royalfair.org
Royal Architectural Institute of Canada ........ http://www.aecinfo.com/raic/index.html
Saskatchewan Association of Architects ........ http://cad9.cadlab.umanitoba.ca/SAA.html
Saskatchewan Motion Picture Association ........ http://midxpress.com/midxpress/smpia/main.htm
SHAD International ........ http://www.shad.ca
Society of Graphic Designers of Canada ........ http://www.swifty.com/gdc/
Society of Motion Picture & Television Engineers ........ http://www.smpte.org/
Strategic Leadership Forum, The International Society for Strategic Management/Toronto Chapter ........ http://www.slf-canada.org
Structural Board Association ........ http://www.sba-osb.com/
TeleLearning Network of Centres of Excellence ........ http://www.telelearn.ca
Tourism Industry Association of PEI ........ http://www.gov.pe.ca/conv/tiapei.html
Tourism Saskatoon ........ http://www.city.saskatoon.sk.ca/tourism
Tourism Vancouver/Greater Vancouver Convention & Visitors Bureau ........ http://www.tourism-vancouver.org

Tourism Victoria/Greater Victoria Visitors & Convention Bureau .......... http://travel.victoria.bc.ca/
Tourism Winnipeg .......... http://www.tourism.winnipeg.mb.ca
Tourisme Jeunesse .......... http://www.tourismej.qc.ca
Travel Alberta .......... http://www.atp.ab.ca/
Union des producteurs agricoles .......... http://www.upa.qc.ca/
Urban Development Institute of Canada .......... http://www.udi.bc.ca
Used Car Dealers Association of Ontario .......... http://www.ucda.org
Vancouver Coast & Mountains Tourism Region .......... http://travel.bc.ca
Winnipeg Construction Association .......... http://www.wpgca.com/
Wool Bureau of Canada .......... http://www.woolmark.com

## LABOUR & TRADES

Alberta Federation of Labour .......... http://www.afl.org
Alberta Ready-Mixed Concrete Association .......... http://www.constructworld.com/armca/
Alberta Teachers' Association .......... http://www.teachers.ab.ca
American Federation of Labor & Congress of Industrial Organizations .......... http://www.aflcio.org
Arbitration & Mediation Institute of Saskatchewan Inc. .......... http://www.saskstar.sk.ca/amis/
The Asbestos Institute .......... http://www.asbestos-institute.ca
Association of Professional Recruiters of Canada .......... http://www.hrtoday.com
British Columbia Construction Association .......... http://www.bccassn.com
British Columbia Federation of Labour .......... http://www.bcfed.com
British Columbia Marine Trades Association .......... http://bcmarine.com
British Columbia Safety Council .......... http://www.safetycouncil.bc.ca
British Columbia Teachers' Federation .......... http://www.bctf.bc.ca
Canada Safety Council .......... http://www.safety-council.org
Canadian Air Traffic Control Association (Ind.) .......... http://www.catca.ca
Canadian Association of Fish Exporters .......... http://www.seafood.ca
Canadian Association of Labour Media .......... http://www.calm.ca
Canadian Centre for Occupational Health & Safety .......... http://www.ccohs.ca
Canadian Committee on Labour History .......... http://www.mun.ca/cclh/
Canadian Compensation Association .......... http://www.assn-office.com/cca
Canadian Construction Association .......... http://www.cca-acc.com
Canadian Council for Human Resources in the Environment Industry .......... http://www.chatsubo.com/cchrei
Canadian Federation of Chefs & Cooks .......... http://www.cybersmith.net/cfcc/
Canadian Injured Workers Alliance .......... http://indie.ca/ciwa/
Canadian Institute of Plumbing & Heating .......... http://www.ciph.com
Canadian Sanitation Supply Association .......... http://www.cssa.com
Canadian Union of Public Employees (CLC) .......... http://www.cupe.ca
Canadian Welding Bureau .......... http://www.cwbgroup.com
CAW Canada (CLC) .......... http://www.caw.ca/caw/
Centrale de l'enseignement du Québec .......... http://ceq.qc.ca
Comité canadien des éléctrotechnologies .......... http://www.cce.qc.ca
Communications, Energy & Paperworkers Union of Canada (CLC) .......... http://www.cep.ca/cep/
Confédération des syndicats nationaux .......... http://www.accent.net/csn/
Construction Specifications Canada .......... http://www.csc-dcc.ca
Corporation des bibliothécaires professionnels du Québec .......... http://www.cbpq.qc.ca
Federation of Women Teachers' Associations of Ontario .......... http://www.fwtao.on.ca
Human Resources Professionals Association of Ontario .......... http://www.hrpao.org
Industrial Accident Prevention Association Ontario .......... http://www.iapa.on.ca
Institute of Electrical & Electronics Engineers Canada .......... http://www.ieee.ca
International Brotherhood of Boilermakers (AFL-CIO) .......... http://www.boilermakers.org
Major Industrial Accidents Council of Canada .......... http://hoshi.cic.sfu.ca/miacc/
National Association of Women in Construction .......... http://www.nawic.org
National Hockey League Players' Association (Ind.) .......... http://www.nhlpa.com
National Union of Public & General Employees .......... http://www.nupge.ca
Native Brotherhood of British Columbia (Ind.) .......... http://www.nq.com/native/
Newfoundland & Labrador Construction Association .......... http://www.netfx.iom.net/nlca/
Ontario Federation of Labour .......... http://www.ofl-fto.on.ca
Ontario Public Service Employees Union .......... http://www.inforamp.net/~opseu/
Ontario Safety League .......... http://www.osl.org
L'Ordre professionnel des conseillers en relations industrielles du Québec .......... http://www.opcriq.qc.ca
PEI Roadbuilders & Heavy Construction Association .......... http://www3.sympatico.ca/pei.roadbuilders/
Professional Association of Foreign Service Officers (Ind.) .......... http://www.pafso.com
Public Service Alliance of Canada (CLC) .......... http://www.psac.com/
Research Council Employees' Association (Ind.) .......... http://ftn.net/~rcea/
Roofing Contractors Association of British Columbia .......... http://www.rcabc.org
Society of Graphic Designers of Canada .......... http://www.swifty.com/gdc/
Society of Ontario Hydro Professional & Administrative Employees .......... http://www.society.on.ca
United Steelworkers of America (AFL-CIO/CLC) .......... http://www.uswa.org
Winnipeg Construction Association .......... http://www.wpgca.com/

## LAW & JUSTICE

A.B. Cameron .......... http://wwwebster.ab.ca/camlaw
Acheson & Co. .......... http://www.achesonco.com
Advocacy Resource Centre for the Handicapped .......... http://www.indie.ca/arch
Aikins, MacAulay & Thorvaldson .......... http://www.aikins.com
Alan Pratt .......... http://www.hookup.net/~apratt
Alberta Civil Liberties Research Centre .......... http://www.FreeNet.Calgary.ab.ca/populati/communit/acl/aclrc.html

Alberta Civil Trial Lawyers' Association .......... http://www.actla.com
Alepin Gauthier .......... http://www.alepin.com
Amicus Law Centre .......... http://www.islandnet.com/~amicus
Andriessen & Associate .......... http://ourworld.compuserve.com/homepages/andriessen_and_associates
B.J. Donnelly .......... http://www.netcom.ca~jbd.lawtml
Baker & McKenzie .......... http://www.bakerinfo.com
Baker Newby .......... http://www.bakernewby.com
Balfour Moss .......... http://www.dlcwest.com/~balfourmoss
Barreau du Québec .......... http://www.barreau.qc.ca
Barrigar & Moss .......... http://www.barrmoss.com
Bartley & von Cramon .......... http://www.bvc-law.com
Bassett & Company .......... http://www.oklawyers.com
Beatrice A. Havlovic .......... http://www.linguanet.ns.ca
Bell Spagnuolo Legal Offices .......... http://www.bellspag.com
Bennett Best Burn .......... http://www.bbburn.com
Bereskin & Parr .......... http://www.bereskinparr.com
Bishop & McKenzie .......... http://www.tgx.com/bishop-mckenzie
Blake, Cassels & Graydon .......... http://www.blakes.ca
Blaney, McMurtry, Stapells, Friedman .......... http://www.blaney.com
Borden & Elliot .......... http://www.borden.com
Boyne Clarke .......... http://www.boyneclarke.ns.ca
Braithwaite Boyle .......... http://www.edmonton.com/web/injurylaw/
Bratty & Partners .......... http://www.bratty.com
Brent & Greenhorn .......... http://broadwaynet.com/~bandglaw
Brimage, Tyrrell, Van Severen & Homeniuk .......... http://www.brimage.com
Bruce E. Walker .......... home.istar.ca/~bwalker/
Buset & Partners .......... http://www.buset.on.ca
C.N. Karbaliotis .......... http://www.techne.com
Calvin Martin, Q.C. .......... http://fox.nstn.ca/~duc14/law.html
Canadian Association of Law Libraries .......... http://www.kingston.net/iknet/call
Canadian Association of Legal Assistants .......... http://www.dyedurham.ca/cala/
Canadian Bar Association .......... http://cba.org/abc
Canadian Copyright Licensing Agency .......... http://cancopy.com/
Canadian HIV/AIDS Legal Network .......... http://www.odyssee.net/~jujube
Canadian Institute for the Administration of Justice .......... http://www.acjnet.org/CIAJ-ICAJ/
Canadian Law & Society Association .......... http://www.juris.uqam.ca/rcds/INDEX_EN.HTM
Canadian Musical Reproduction Rights Agency .......... http://www.cmrra.ca
Carr & Company .......... http://www.carrco.com
Carr, Stevenson & MacKay .......... http://www.peinet.pe.ca/csm
Cassels Brock & Blackwell .......... http://www.casselsbrock.com/
Chait Amyot .......... http://www.chait-amyot.ca
Chambre des notaires du Québec .......... http://www.cdnq.org
Chauhan & Associates .......... http://www.io.org/~chauhan
Chown, Cairns .......... http://www.chown-cairns.com/northland/cc
Cleveland & Doan .......... http://www.meridian-com.com/clevdoan
Cohen Highley Vogel & Dawson .......... http://www.chvd.on.ca/lawyers
Community Legal Education Association (Manitoba) Inc. .......... http://www.acjnet.org/white/clea.html
Continuing Legal Education Society of BC .......... http://www.cle.bc.ca
Cox Downie .......... http://www.coxdownie.ns.ca
Crosbie, Ches Barristers .......... http://www.chescrosbie.com
Cunningham, Swan, Carty, Little & Bonham .......... http://www.cswan.com
D'Arcy Hiltz .......... http://www.pathcom.com/-hiltzlaw
David & Touchette .......... http://www.masc-web.com/dvdtct/
David L. Zifkin .......... http://www.zifkin.com
Davies, Ward & Beck .......... http://www.dwb.com
Davis & Company .......... http://www.davis.ca
Dawson, Wood & Company .......... http://www.intouch.bc.ca/pub/dawson.wood
Desjardins Ducharme Stein Monast .......... http://www.ddsm.ca
Dianne Saxe .......... http://www.envirolaw.com
Duncan & Craig .......... http://www.duncanandcraig.com
Durocher Simpson .......... http://www.tgx.com/durocher
Environmental Law Centre .......... http://www.web.net/~elc
Eric P. Polten .......... http://www.poltenhodder.com/~ph
Farano, Green .......... http://www.inforamp.net/~goldfarb/
Fasken Campbell Godfrey .......... http://www.fasken.com/
Federation of Law Societies of Canada .......... http://www.flsc.ca/
Feller Drysdale .......... http://www.feller_drysdale.com
Ferguson Gifford .......... http://www.fergif.com
Field Atkinson Perraton .......... http://www.fieldlaw.com/
Filion, Wakely & Thorup .......... http://www.filion.on.ca
Fortier & Gladu .......... http://oracle.dsuper.net/~gladu/fg_com.html
Fraser & Beatty .......... http://www.fraserbeatty.ca
Galbraith Law Office .......... http://www.connect.ab.ca/~glo
Gardiner, Blumberg .......... http://www.blumberg-law.com
Gaston Lafleur .......... http://www.cgcd.com
George Paul Smith .......... http://www.peelbarristers.com
Goldberg, Shinder, Gardner & Kronick .......... http://www.gsgk.com
Goodman & Carr .......... http://www.goodmancarr.com

| | |
|---|---|
| Gordon & Velletta | http://www.vvv.com/~gordvell |
| Gordon R. Baker, Q.C. | http://www.myna.com/~gbaker/ |
| Gounden & Miller | http://www.discovervancouver/goundenmiller |
| Gowlings | http://www.gowlings.com |
| Grosman, Grosman & Gale | http://www.grosman.com |
| Guberman, Garson | http://www.gubermangarson.com |
| Hanson, Hashey | http://hansonhashey.nb.ca |
| Heelis, Williams & Little | http://www.14churchstlawoffice.com |
| Howard, Mackie | http://howardmackie.com |
| Hughes & Young | http://www.hugheslaw.on.ca |
| Hughes, Amys | http://www.hughesamys.com |
| IGRG Inc. (The Industry Government Relations Group) | http://home.istar.ca/~igrgadm |
| International Environmental Liability Management Association | http://www.magic.ca/ielma/IELMA.html |
| Irvin H. Sherman, Q.C. | http://www.home.ican.net/~irv |
| Jacques Gauthier | http://www.legal.info.ca |
| James F.C. Rose | http://www.members.aol.com/rosecruise/wills.htm |
| Jamieson Bains | http://www.jblawyers.com |
| Jaques Law Office | http://www.dlcwest.com/~jaques.law/ |
| Jerome Stanleigh | http://www.stanleigh.com |
| Karas & Associates | http://www.karas.ca |
| Keyser Mason Ball | http://www.kmblaw.com |
| Kiedrowski & Associates | http://www3.sympatico.ca/john.kiedrowski |
| Kitchen, Kitchen, Simeson & McFarlane | http://www.kksm.com |
| Kloppenburg & Kloppenburg | http://www.lexsask.com |
| Koskie & Company | http://www.sk.sympatico.ca/tkoskie |
| Koskie & Minsky | http://www.koskieminsky.com |
| Lackman, Firestone Law Offices | http://www.tor.shaw.wave.ca/~lackman |
| Lacroix, Forest & Del Frate | http://www.sudburylaw.com |
| Ladner Downs | http://www.ladner.com/ladner |
| Lafleur Brown | http://www.login.net/lafleurbrown |
| Lancaster, Mix & Welch | http://www.lmw.com |
| Lapointe Rosenstein | http://www.lapros.qc.ca |
| Larson Suleman Sohn Boulton | http://www.lssb.com |
| Laveaux, Franck | http://www.laveaux.com |
| Lavery, de Billy | http://www.laverydebilly.com |
| Law Society of Alberta | http://www.law.ualberta.ca/lawsociety |
| Law Society of Upper Canada | http://www.lsuc.on.ca/Welcome.html |
| Lawlor Rochester | http://www.glaholt.com |
| Leanne M. Chahley | leannec@worldgate.com |
| Legal Education Society of Alberta | http://www.law.ualberta.ca/lesa/ |
| Lerner & Associates | http://www.lerner.ca |
| Levine Associates | http://www.interlog.com/~levlaw/ |
| Lewis, Day | http://www.lewisday.nf.ca |
| Linda H. Kolyn | http://www.pathcom.com/~dadey/homepage.htm |
| Lindsay Kenney | http://www.lindsaykenney.bc.ca |
| Lloyd A. Hackett | http://www.rims.org |
| Lon Hall Attorneys | http://ourworld.compuserve.com/homepages/lha_ent_law |
| Lorne S. Jackson | http://web.idirect.com/~kid |
| Low, Glenn & Card | http://www.canfind.com/index.html |
| MacDonald & Associates | http://www.ssimicro.com/~sevente/flycolor/hayriver/business/macdonald |
| MacLachlan McNab Hembroff | http://www.virco.net |
| MacTavish, de Lint, Hamersfeld | http://www.inforamp.net/~mdlh |
| Macaulay McColl | http://www.macaulay.com |
| Maguire & Company | http://www.islandnet.com/~magco |
| Maitland & Company | http://www.maitland.com |
| Major, Caron | majorcaron.com |
| Mannella & Associs | http://www.mannella.com |
| Martineau, Walker | http://www.fasken.com/offices.html |
| Marusyk Bourassa Miller & Swain | http://www.mbm-law.com |
| McCarthy Ttrault | http://www.mccarthy.ca |
| McCuaig Desrochers | http://www.mccuaig.com |
| McDonald & Hayden | http://www.mchayden.on.ca |
| McInnes Cooper & Robertson | http://fax.nstn.ca/~mcrhfx |
| McKenzie Nash Bryant | http:///www.mnblawyers.com |
| McLellan Associates | http://www.thelawstore.com |
| McLellan Herbert | http://www.mclellanherbert.com |
| McMillan Binch | http://www.mcbinch.com |
| McNamee Law Office | http://www.mcnamee-law.com |
| Meighen Demers | http://www.meighendemers.com |
| Michael P. Reilly | http://www.oak.net/reilly |
| Michael W. Kelly | http://www.hookup.net/~mikelly |
| Miller Thomson | http://wwa.millerthomson.ca |
| Milner Fenerty | http://www.milfen.com |
| Morrie Sacks Law Corp. | sackslaw.bc.ca |
| Murphy Collette Murphy | http://www.discribe.ca/marco |
| Nova Scotia Barristers' Society | http://home.istar.ca/~nsbs/ |
| Osler, Hoskin & Harcourt | http://www.osler.com |
| Owen, Dickey | http://www.bconnex.net/~odlaw/ |

Pallett Valo .......... http://www.pallettvalo.com
Parlee McLaws .......... http://www.parlee.com
Paterson, MacDougall .......... http://www.pmlaw.com
Paul E. Harte .......... http://www.hartelaw.com
Paul Lee & Associates .......... http://www.paullee.com
Pavey, Law .......... http://www.paveylaw.com
Perley-Robertson, Panet, Hill & McDougall .......... http://www.perlaw.ca
Pink Breen Larkin .......... http://www.labour-law.com
Pink, Murray, Graham .......... http://www.criminaldefence.com
Pitblado & Hoskin .......... http://www.mts.net/~lawyers/index.html
Plaskacz & Associates .......... http://www.plaskacz.com
Poole Milligan .......... http://www.poolemilligan.com
Poole, A.F.N., Q.C. .......... http://web.idirect.com:80/~poole/
Pouliot L'Ecuyer .......... http://www.droit.com
The Public Interest Advocacy Centre .......... http://www.web.net/piac/
Public Legal Education Association of Saskatchewan, Inc. .......... http://www.sfn.saskatoon.sk.ca/education/pleasask/index.html
R. Geoffrey Newbury .......... http://www.io.org/~newbury
R.E. Lauder .......... http://www.norlink.net/~rlauder/
R.O. Kallio, City Solicitor .......... http://www.niagara.com/city.niagara-falls
Rancourt, Legault, Boucher & Godbout .......... http://www.rocler.qc.ca/rancourt
Reid, McNaughton .......... http://reidlaw.com/lawyers
Reynolds, Mirth, Richards & Farmer .......... http://www.ualberta.ca/~law/firms/reynolds/
Richards Buell Sutton .......... http://www.rbs.com
Rimer & Company .......... http://rimart.com/rimer
Robert D. Mcintyre, Q.C. .......... http://www.ontlaw.com
Robertson Stromberg .......... http://www.robertsonstromberg.com
Ron Jourard .......... http://www.defencelaw.com
Rosenblatt Associates .......... http://www.immigrate.net
Rotfleisch & Samulovitch .......... http://www.taxpage.com
Russell & DuMoulin .......... http://rdcounsel.com/rd
S.G.R. MacMillan .......... http://www.sgrm.com
Salloum Doak .......... http://www.awinc.com/salloum
Sarlo O'Neill .......... http://www.soonet.ca/sarlo-oneill
Shepherd Grenville-Wood .......... http://www.sgwmiss.com
Shtabsky & Tussman .......... http://www.stlaw.com
Sim, Hughes, Ashton & McKay .......... http://www.simbas.com
Simpson, Wigle .......... http://www.ads-online.on.ca/
Singleton Urquhart Scott .......... http://www.singleton.com
Smith Lyons .......... http://www.smithlyons.ca
Smith, Byck & Grant .......... http://www.nt.net/sbg/sbg1.html
Society of Composers, Authors & Music Publishers of Canada .......... http://www.socan.ca
Somerville & Company .......... http://www.boundary.bc.ca/Business/PSLC
Sotos, Karvanis .......... http://www.sotoskarvanis.com
Speigel Nichols Fox .......... http://www.ontlaw.com
Stanley Kershman Law Office .......... http://www.bankruptlaw.com
Stephen J. Lautens .......... http://beachnet.org/sjl
Stewart McKelvey Stirling Scales .......... http://www.nstn.ca/smss
Stringam Denecky .......... http://www.dtmn.com/sd
Swinton & Company .......... http://www.swinton.ca
Szabo & Company .......... http://www.thelawyers.com
Taylor & Company .......... http://www.taylor-co.com/info
Thomas & Davis .......... http://www.thomasanddavis.com
Vandor & Company .......... http://www.vandorco.ca
Wardlaw, Mullin, Carter & Thwaites .......... http://www.beeline.ca//wardlaw
Weir & Foulds .......... http://www.weirfoulds.com
Wheatley Sadownik .......... http://www.wheatleysadownik.com
White, Ottenheimer & Baker .......... http://www.wob.nf.ca
Wilder Wilder & Langtry .......... http://www.wilderwilder.com
Wilf K. Backhaus .......... http://wildrose.net/backhaus/strlw1.htm
William B. Horkins .......... http://www.interlog.com/~horkins
Willms & Shier .......... http://www.willmsshier.com
Woloshyn Mattison .......... http://www.sasklaw.com
Zalapski & Pahl .......... http://www.tnc.com/zap/

## PUBLIC SERVICES

Air Cadet League of Canada .......... http://www.isisnet.com/smacdouga/rcac.html
The Army Cadet League of Canada .......... http://ww2.isys.ca/army/index.html
Association of Community Information Centres in Ontario .......... http://www.web.apc.org/acico/
Association of Professional Recruiters of Canada .......... http://www.hrtoday.com
BC Council for Families .......... http://www.bccf.bc.ca
Bereaved Families of Ontario .......... http://www.inforamp.net/~bfo
Big Brothers of Canada .......... http://www.bbsc.ca
Boys & Girls Clubs of Canada .......... http://www.bgccan.com
Canadian Association for Community Living .......... http://indie.ca/cacl/index.htm
Canadian Association of Elizabeth Fry Societies .......... http://www.web.apc.org/~kpate
Canadian Association of Retired Persons .......... http://www.fifty-plus.net/
Canadian Association of Social Workers .......... http://www.intranet.ca/~casw-acts/
Canadian Association on Gerontology .......... http://www.cagacg.ca

Canadian Avalanche Association ........ http://www.avalanche.ca/snow
Canadian Career Development Foundation ........ http://infoweb.magi.com/~ccdffcac
Canadian Centre for Philanthropy ........ http://www.web.net/imagine/
The Canadian Corps of Commissionaires ........ http://www.comnet.ca/~cccnhq/commish.htm
Canadian Council for Refugees ........ http://www.web.net/~ccr/
Canadian Council on Rehabilitation & Work ........ http://www.ccrw.org
Canadian Public Health Association ........ http://www.cpha.ca
The Canadian Red Cross Society ........ http://www.redcross.ca
Canadian Youth Foundation ........ http://www.cyf.ca
Child Find Canada Inc. ........ http://www.childfind.ca
Child Welfare League of Canada ........ http://infoweb.magi.com/~cwlc/
The Children's Wish Foundation of Canada ........ http://www.childrenswish.ca
Chinese Information & Community Services of Greater Toronto ........ http://www.ipoline.com/cics
Co-operative Housing Federation of BC ........ http://www.vcn.bc.ca/chfbc/
Confédération des organismes familiaux du Québec inc. ........ http://www.odyssee.net/~cofaq3ci/cofaq
Couchiching Institute on Public Affairs ........ http://www.couch.ca
Council of Canadians with Disabilities ........ http://www.pcs.mb.ca/~ccd/
Dying with Dignity ........ http://www.web.net/dwd
The Easter Seal Society (Ontario) ........ http://www.easterseals.org
Edmonton Social Planning Council ........ http://www.compusmart.ab.ca/espc
Elderhostel Canada ........ http://www.elderhostel.org
Family Service Canada ........ http://www.familyforum.com/fsc/index.htm
Girl Guides of Canada ........ http://www.girlguides.ca
Guelph & Wellington United Way Social Planning Council ........ http://www.unitedway.well-guelph.org/
Habitat for Humanity Canada ........ http://www.sentex.net/~hfhc/
Human Resources Professionals Association of Ontario ........ http://www.hrpao.org
The John Howard Society of Canada ........ http://www.nald.ca/jhs.htm
Kids Help Phone ........ http://kidshelp.sympatico.ca
Kinsmen & Kinette Clubs of Canada ........ http://nucleus.com/~gedwards/kinsmen.html
Kinsmen Rehabilitation Foundation of British Columbia ........ http://mindlink.net/kinsmen_rehab/
Knights of Columbus ........ http://www.kofc-supreme-council.org
Lifesaving Society ........ http://www.lifesaving.ca
Missing Children Society of Canada ........ http://www.childcybersearch.org/mcsc/
National Anti-Poverty Organization ........ http://www.napo-onap.ca
One Parent Families Association of Canada ........ http://www.tcn.net/~oneparent/
Ontario Association of Children's Aid Societies ........ http://www.oacas.org
Ontario Association of Directors of Volunteer Services in Healthcare ........ http://www.interlog.com/~odvh/
Ontario Funeral Service Association Inc. ........ http://www.ofsa.org
Ontario March of Dimes ........ http://www.omod.org
Parent Finders of Canada ........ http://www2.portal.ca/~reunion
Réseau enfants retour Canada ........ http://www.alliance9000.com/E/MCNC/11.html
The Right to Die Society of Canada ........ http://www.islandnet.com/~deathnet
Royal Canadian Legion ........ http://www.legion.ca
Samaritan's Purse - Canada ........ http://www.samaritan.org
Saskatchewan Association for Community Living ........ http://www.usask.ca/education/SACL/
Scouts Canada ........ http://www.scouts.ca
St. John Ambulance ........ http://www/sja.ca
Suicide Information & Education Centre ........ http://www.siec.ca
United Way of Barrie/South Simcoe ........ http://www.bconnex.net/~uwbss
United Way of Canada ........ http://www.uwc-cc.ca
United Way of Greater Toronto ........ http://www.uwgt.org
United Way of Sarnia-Lambton ........ http://www.sarnia.com/groups/unitedway/
United Way/Centraide Ottawa-Carleton ........ http://www.unitedwayoc.on.ca
Vanier Institute of The Family ........ http://www.cfc-efc.ca/vif/
Variety Club of British Columbia, Tent 47 ........ http://www.variety.bc.ca
Vocational & Rehabilitation Research Institute ........ http://www.vrri.org
The War Amputations of Canada ........ http://www.waramps.ca

## RECREATION

Active Living Alliance for Canadians with a Disability ........ http://www.activeliving.ca/alliance/alliance.html
Alberta Schools' Athletic Association ........ http://www.afternet.com/ASAA/
Alpine Club of Canada ........ http://www.culturenet.ca/acc/
American & Canadian Underwater Certification Inc. ........ http://www.acuc.es/
Appaloosa Horse Club of Canada ........ http://www.agt.net/public/appaloos/
Association de golf du Québec ........ http://www.memocard.com/QGA/
L'Association des hôteliers du Québec ........ http://www.destinationquebec.com
Association of Canadian Mountain Guides ........ http://www.acmg.com
Association of Canadian Travel Agents ........ http://www.acta.net
Association of Canadian Travel Agents - Alberta ........ http://www.acta.ab.ca
Athletics Canada ........ http://canoe2.canoe.ca/athcan/
Badminton Canada ........ http://www.badminton.ca/
Baseball Canada ........ http://www.cdnsport.ca/baseball
Basketball Alberta ........ http://www.basketballalberta.ab.ca
Basketball Canada ........ http://www.cdnsport.ca/basketball/
Basketball New Brunswick ........ http://www.nbi.ca/bnb
BC Snowmobile Federation ........ http://www.bcsf.org/sledding
Bobsleigh Canada ........ http://www.cdnsport.ca/bobcan
British Columbia & Yukon Hotels Association ........ http://www.fleethouse.com/fhcanada/bc-acco.htm

|  |  |
|---|---|
| British Columbia Automobile Association | http://www.bcaa.bc.ca |
| British Columbia Golf Association | http://www.bcga.org |
| The Bruce Trail Association | http://www.brucetrail.org/ |
| Calgary Convention & Visitors Bureau | http://www.visitor.calgary.ab.ca/ |
| Camping Association of Nova Scotia | http://www.kidscamps.com/canadian-camping |
| Canadian Adult Recreational Hockey Association | http://www.carha.ca |
| Canadian Amateur Boxing Association | http://www.boxing.ca |
| Canadian Amateur Diving Association Inc. | http://www.diving.ca/diving/cada.html |
| Canadian Amateur Speed Skating Association | http://www.speedskating-canada.ca |
| Canadian Amateur Wrestling Association | http://www.cdnsport.ca/wrestling/ |
| Canadian Association for Health, Physical Education, Recreation & Dance | http://www.activeliving.ca/activeliving/cahperd/indexfr.html |
| Canadian Automobile Association | http://www.caa.ca |
| Canadian Automobile Association Québec | http://www.caa-quebec.qc.ca |
| Canadian Automobile Sport Clubs - Ontario Region Inc. | http://www3.sympatico.ca/casc.or/ |
| Canadian Bridge Federation | http://www.cbf.ca/CBFHome.html |
| Canadian Canoe Association | http://www.openface.ca/paddle/ |
| Canadian Centre for Ethics in Sport | http://www.cces.ca |
| Canadian Craft & Hobby Association | http://www.cdncraft.org |
| Canadian Curling Association | http://www.curling.ca |
| Canadian Fencing Federation | http://www.fencing.ca |
| Canadian Figure Skating Association | http://www.cfsa.ca/ |
| Canadian Fitness & Lifestyle Research Institute | http://activeliving.ca/activeliving/cflri.html |
| Canadian Football League | http://www.cfl.ca/ |
| Canadian Freestyle Ski Association | http://infoweb.magi.com/freestyl/ |
| Canadian Hockey Association | http://www.canadianhockey.ca |
| Canadian In-Line & Roller Skating Association | http://www.io.org/~cirsa/cirsa.html |
| Canadian Institute of Travel Counsellors of Ontario | http://www.citcontario.com |
| Canadian Interuniversity Athletic Union | http://www.ciau.ca |
| Canadian Intramural Recreation Association | http://www.cdnsport.ca/activeliving/cira.html |
| Canadian Iris Society | http://www.netcom.ca/~cris/CIS.html |
| Canadian Lacrosse Association | http://www.lacrosse.ca/ |
| Canadian Marine Manufacturers Association | http://www.cmma.ca |
| Canadian Numismatic Association | http://home.ican.net/~nunetcan/ |
| Canadian Parks & Wilderness Society | http://www.afternet.com/~tnr/cpaws/cpaws.html |
| Canadian Parks/Recreation Association | http://activeliving.ca/activeliving/cpra.html |
| Canadian Power & Sail Squadrons (Canadian Headquarters) | http://www.cps-ecp.ca |
| Canadian Professional Rodeo Association | http://www.rodeocanada.com |
| Canadian Quilters Association | http://www.nt.net/~giselef/cqaacc1.htm |
| Canadian Recreational Canoeing Association | http://www.crca.ca/ |
| Canadian Ski Council | http://www.skicanada.org |
| Canadian Soccer Association | http://www.canoe.ca/SoccerCanada/home.html |
| Canadian Society for Horticultural Science | http://www.aic.ca/members/cshs.html |
| Canadian Society for Psychomotor Learning & Sport Psychology | http://www.scapps.org |
| Canadian Special Olympics Inc. | http://www.incontext.ca/cso/index.html |
| Canadian Sport & Fitness Administration Centre | http://www.cdnsport.ca/ |
| Canadian Sport Parachuting Association | http://www.islandnet.com/~murrays/cspa.html |
| Canadian Sporting Arms & Ammunition Association | http://www.eagle.ca/showgun |
| Canadian Tennis Association | http://www.tenniscanada.com |
| Canadian Wheelchair Basketball Association | http://www.cwba.ca/ |
| Canadian Wheelchair Sports Association | http://indie.ca/cwsa/ |
| Canadian Yachting Association | http://www.cdnsport.ca/~smorrow |
| Chess Federation of Canada | http://www.globalx.net/cfc/ |
| Coaching Association of Canada | http://www.coach.ca/ |
| Embroiderers' Association of Canada, Inc. | http://www.eac.ca/embroidery/ |
| Fédération des clubs de motoneigistes du Québec | http://www.fcmq.qc.ca |
| Fédération du plongeon amateur du Québec | http://www.cigp.com/atlanta/federati/plongeon/ |
| Fédération québécoise des échecs | http://WWW.CAM.ORG/~fqechec |
| Fédération québécoise des jeux récréatifs | http://www.fqjr.qc.ca/ |
| Field Hockey Canada | http://www.cyberus.ca/~fieldhockey/ |
| Gymnastics Canada Gymnastique | http://www.capitalnet.com/~chiug/cangym.html |
| Hostelling International - Canada | http://www.HostellingIntl.ca/ |
| International Computer Chess Association (Canada) | http://www.cs.unimaas.nl/ |
| Judo Canada | http://www.ccn.cs.dal.ca/SportFit/JNS/judocan.html |
| Manitoba Recreational Canoeing Association | http://130.179.24.217/mrca/mrca.html |
| Model Aeronautics Association of Canada Inc. | http://www.maac.ca |
| National Association of Watch & Clock Collectors | http://www.nawcc.org |
| National Firearms Association | http://www.nfa.ca |
| National Hockey League Players' Association (Ind.) | http://www.nhlpa.com |
| Ontario Camping Association | http://www.ontcamp.on.ca |
| Ontario Electric Railway Historical Association | http://www.hcry.org |
| Ontario Federation of Snowmobile Clubs | http://www.transdata.ca/~ofsc/~ofsc.htm |
| Ontario Golf Association | http://www.oga.org |
| Ontario Horticultural Association | http://www.interlog.com/~onthort |
| Ontario Minor Hockey Association | http://www.omhahockey.com |
| Ontario Parks Association | http://www.hookup.net/~opa |
| Ontario Private Campground Association | http://www.campgrounds.org |
| Ontario Recreation Facilities Association | http://www.pathcom.com/~orfa/ |
| Ontario Trails Council | http://www.csp.trentu.ca/gomrm/otc.html |

Outdoor Recreation Council of British Columbia .... http://mindlink.net/outrec_council/outrec.htm
Outward Bound Western Canada.... http://www.infinity.ca/outwardbound/
Radio Amateurs of Canada.... http://www.rac.ca/
Recreation Vehicle Dealers Association of Alberta .... http://www.rvda-alberta.com
Recreation Vehicle Dealers Association of Canada .... http://www.rvda.ca
Régie de la sécurité dans les sports du Québec.... http://www.rssq.gouv.qc.ca
Resorts Ontario.... http://www.resorts-ontario.com
Ringette Canada .... http://www.ringette.ca/
Royal Canadian Golf Association .... http://www.rcga.org
The Royal Philatelic Society of Canada.... http://www.interlog.com/~rpsc
Saskatchewan Baseball Association.... http://www.dlcwest.com/~skbaseball/
Saskatchewan Crafts Council .... http://www.ffa.ucalgary.ca/scco/scc.html; http://www.sasknet.sk.ca/SCCO/SCC.html
Ski Jumping Canada.... http://www.cdnsport.ca/jump
Soaring Association of Canada.... http://www.sac.ca/
Softball Canada.... http://www.cdnsport.ca/softball/
Sport BC.... http://www.sport.bc.ca/SportBC/
Sport Manitoba .... http://www.sport.mb.ca
Sport Nova Scotia .... http://fox.nstn.ca/~sportns/
Swimming/Natation Canada .... http://www.swimming.ca
Tennis BC .... http://www.tennis.bc.ca
Tennis Manitoba.... http://www.escape.ca/~tennismb
Trail Riders of the Canadian Rockies .... http://www.canuck.com/~trcr
Travel Alberta.... http://www.atp.ab.ca/
Vancouver Coast & Mountains Tourism Region .... http://travel.bc.ca
Vélo-Québec .... http://www.velo.qc.ca
Vintage Locomotive Society Inc. .... http://www.winnipeg.freenet.mb.ca/pdc/
Water Polo Canada.... http://www.waterpolo.ca
Water Ski Canada.... http://www.utoronto.ca/ski/water/ca/index.html
WorldHomes Holiday Exchange .... http://www.homelink.org

## RELIGION

Apostolic Church of Pentecost of Canada Inc.... http://www.illuminart.com/acop/
Associated Gospel Churches of Canada .... http://www.agcofcanada.com/home/
Atlantic School of Theology .... http://novanet.ns.ca/ast/homepage.html
Baptist Convention of Ontario & Québec.... http://www.baptist.ca
Baptist General Conference of Canada.... http://www.datanet.ab.ca/users/bgcc/
The Bible League of Canada.... http://www.worldchat.com/public/bibleag/
Briercrest Bible College.... http://www.briercrest.ca
Canadian Association for Pastoral Practice & Education.... http://www3.ns.sympatico.ca/cappe/home.htm
Canadian Baptist Ministries.... http://www.cbmin.org
Canadian Bible Society .... http://www.canbible.ca
Canadian Chapter of the International Council of Community Churches .... http://www.angelfire.com/biz/saterio/index.html
Canadian Conference of Catholic Bishops .... http://www.cam.org/~cccb
Canadian Conference of Mennonite Brethren Churches .... http://www.cdnmbconf.ca/mb/mbdoc.htm
The Canadian Council of Christians & Jews.... http://www.interlog.com/~cccj/
The Canadian Council of Churches .... http://www.web.net/~ccchurch
Canadian Council of Muslim Women .... http://www.qucis.queensu.ca/home/fevens/ccmw.html
Canadian Religious Conference .... http://www.crc.ca/crcn/
Canadian Unitarian Council .... http://www.web.net/~cuc
Centre for Mennonite Brethren Studies .... http://www.cdnmbconf.ca/mb/cmbs.htm
Christian Aid Mission.... http://www.christianaid.ca
Christian Reformed World Relief Committee of Canada.... http://www.kingsu.ab.ca/~jake/crwrc.htm
ChristianWeek.... http://www.christianweek.org
Compass: A Jesuit Journal.... http://www.io.org/~gvanv/compass/comphome.html
Congregational Christian Churches in Canada.... http://www.cccc.ca
Evangelical Fellowship of Canada .... http://www.efc-canada.com
Evangelical Lutheran Church in Canada.... http://info.wlu.ca/~wwwsem/elcic/ehome.html
Fondation Père-Eusèbe-Ménard.... http://www.odyssee.net/~fondatio/
Free Methodist Church in Canada .... http://www.fmc-canada.org
Habitat for Humanity Canada.... http://www.sentex.net/~hfhc/
Inter-Varsity Christian Fellowship of Canada.... http://www.dar.com/ivcf/
The Jewish Tribune.... http://www.canada_ibm.net/bnaibrith/
Mennonite Brethren Herald .... http://www.cdnmbconf.ca/mb/mbherald.htm
Mennonite Central Committee Canada.... http://www.mennonitecc.ca/mcc
Ontario Alliance of Christian Schools .... http://www.oacs.org
Organisation catholique canadienne pour le développement et la paix .... http://www.devp.org
Orthodox Missionary Church of Canada.... http://phobos.astro.uwo.ca/~arenburg/omcc.html
Presbyterian Church in Canada .... http://www.presbycan.ca/index.html
Presbyterian Record.... http://www.presbyterian.ca
Providence College & Seminary.... http://www.providence.mb.ca
Redeemer College .... http://www.redeemer.on.ca
The Salvation Army in Canada.... http://www.sallynet.org
Séminaire de Sherbrooke.... http://www.login.net/semsherb
Shalom .... http://www3.ns.sympatico.ca/ajc.halifax/main.html
Society for the Propagation of the Faith for Canada .... http://www.eda.net~missions
St. Peter's Abbey & College .... stpetes@orion.sk.sympatico.ca
The Society of Saint Peter the Apostle .... http://www.eda.net/~missions/peter.htm
The United Church Observer .... http://www.ucobserver.org

## SCIENCE & NATURE

Aerospace Industries Association of Canada ........ http://www.aiac.ca
Agricultural Groups Concerned About Resources & the Environment ........ http://www.agcare.org
Agricultural Institute of Canada ........ http://www.aic.ca
Air & Waste Management Association ........ http://www.awma.org
Alberta Conservation Tillage Society ........ http://www.actsagtec.com
Alberta Institute of Agrologists ........ http://www.aia.ab.ca
Alberta Society of Professional Biologists ........ http://www.ccinet.ab.ca/aspb/
Animal Alliance of Canada ........ http://www.inforamp.net/~aac/
Applied Science Technologists & Technicians of British Columbia ........ http://www.asttbc.org
Arctic Institute of North America ........ http://www.ucalgary.ca/aina/
Association des industries forestières du Québec ltée ........ http://www.aifq.qc.ca
Association des microbiologistes du Québec ........ http://www.iaf.uquebec.ca/amq/
Association for the Promotion & Advancement of Science Education ........ http://www.apase.bc.ca
Association of Canadian Universities for Northern Studies ........ http://www.geog.mcgill.ca/northern/acunhome.html
Association of Professional Engineers & Geoscientists - BC ........ http://www.apeg.bc.ca
Association of Professional Engineers & Geoscientists - Nfld. ........ http://www.apegn.nf.ca
Association of Professional Engineers, Geologists & Geophysicists - Alta. ........ http://www.apegga.com
Association of Professional Engineers, Geologists & Geophysicists - NWT ........ http://www.napegg.nt.ca
Atlantic Salmon Federation ........ http://www.flyfishing.com/asf/
Avicultural Advancement Council of Canada ........ http://www.islandnet.com/~aacc
Ayrshire Breeders Association of Canada ........ http://www.ayrshire-canada.com
BC Advanced Systems Institute ........ http://www.asi.bc.ca/asi/
Biophysical Society of Canada ........ http://www.ibd.nrc.ca/~bsc
British Columbia Federation of Agriculture ........ http://www.bcfa.bc.ca/bcfa
British Columbia Institute of Agrologists ........ http://www.bcia.com
CSR: Corporations Supporting Recycling ........ http://www.csr.org
Calgary Science Centre ........ http://www.calgaryscience.ca
Canadian Advanced Technology Association ........ http://www.cata.ca/
Canadian Association for Composite Structures & Materials ........ http://www.cacsma.ca
Canadian Association for Environmental Analytical Laboratories ........ http://www.caeal.ca
Canadian Association of Fish Exporters ........ http://www.seafood.ca
Canadian Association of Palynologists ........ http://gpu.srv.ualberta.ca/~abeaudoi/cap/cap.html
Canadian Association of Petroleum Producers ........ http://www.capp.ca
Canadian Association of Physicists ........ http://www.cap.ca
Canadian Astronomical Society ........ http://www.astro.queensu.ca/~casca/
Canadian Avalanche Association ........ http://www.avalanche.ca/snow
Canadian Bacterial Diseases Network ........ http://www.cbdn.ca
Canadian Centre for Pollution Prevention ........ http://c2p2.sarnia.com
Canadian Consulting Agrologists Association ........ http://www.igw.ca/ccaa
Canadian Council of Ministers of the Environment ........ http://www.ccme.ca/ccme
Canadian Council of Technicians & Technologists ........ http://www.cctt.ca/
Canadian Earth Energy Association ........ http://www.earthenergy.org
Canadian Energy Pipeline Association ........ http://www.cepa.com
Canadian Energy Research Institute ........ http://www.ucalgary.ca/UofC/Others/CERI/index.htm
Canadian Environment Industry Association - British Columbia ........ http://www.ceia-bc.com/
Canadian Environment Industry Association ........ http://www.ceia.org
Canadian Federation of Agriculture ........ http://www.cfa-fca.ca
Canadian Federation of Biological Societies ........ http://www.fermentas.com/cfbs/
Canadian Gas Association ........ http://www.cga.ca
Canadian Gas Research Institute ........ http://www.hookup.net/~cgri/
Canadian Genetic Diseases Network ........ http://data.ctn.nrc.ca/bc/content/type12/org319/parent.htm
Canadian Geophysical Union ........ http://www.cg.nrcan.gc.ca/cgu/cgu.html
Canadian Geoscience Council ........ http://www.science.uwaterloo.ca/earth/cgc/cgc.html
Canadian Geotechnical Society ........ http://www.inforamp.net/~cgs
Canadian Honey Packers' Association ........ http://www.worldexport.com/labonte/
Canadian Hydrographic Association ........ http://www.cciw.ca/dfo/chs/cha/cha-home.html
Canadian Institute for Environmental Law & Policy ........ http://www.web.net/cielap
Canadian Institute of Biotechnology ........ http://www.biotech.ca
Canadian Institute of Forestry ........ http://www.cif-ifc.org/
Canadian Institute of Mining, Metallurgy & Petroleum ........ http://www.cim.org
Canadian Mathematical Society ........ http://camel.math.ca
Canadian Medical & Biological Engineering Society Inc. ........ http://www.bcit.bc.ca/~sohs/cmbes.htm
Canadian Meteorological & Oceanographic Society ........ http://www.meds.dfo.ca/cmos/
Canadian Nature Federation ........ http://www.web.net/~cnf
Canadian Network of Toxicology Centres ........ http://www.uoguelph.ca/cntc
Canadian Nuclear Association ........ http://www.cna.ca/weare.html
Canadian Operational Research Society ........ http://www.ncf.carleton.ca/freeport/prof.assoc/cors/menu
Canadian Phytopathological Society ........ http://res.agr.ca/lond/pmrc/cps/cpshome.html
Canadian Renewable Fuels Association ........ http://www.greenfuels.org
Canadian Science & Technology Historical Association ........ http://www.physics.uoguelph.ca/hist/CSTHA.html
Canadian Society for Chemical Engineering ........ http://www.chem-inst-can.org
Canadian Society for Chemical Technology ........ http://www.chem-inst-can.org
Canadian Society for Chemistry ........ http://www.chem-inst-can.org
Canadian Society for Computational Studies of Intelligence ........ http://cscsi.sfu.ca
Canadian Society for Horticultural Science ........ http://www.aic.ca/members/cshs.html
Canadian Society of Agricultural Engineering ........ http://www.engr.usask.ca/societies/csae/
Canadian Society of Animal Science ........ http://tdg.res.uoguelph.ca/~aic/csas.html

|  |  |
|---|---|
| Canadian Society of Exploration Geophysicists | http://www.geo.ucalgary.ca:80/cseg |
| Canadian Society of Extension | http://tdg.uoguelph.ca/cse |
| Canadian Society of Laboratory Technologists | http://www.cslt.com |
| Canadian Society of Landscape Architects | http://www.clr.utoronto.ca/ORG/CSLA/ |
| Canadian Society of Petroleum Geologists | http://www.cspg.org |
| Canadian Society of Safety Engineering, Inc. | http://www.csse.org |
| Canadian Society of Soil Science | http://www.umanitoba.ca/CSSS |
| Canadian Solar Industries Association Inc. | http://www.newenergy.org/newenergy/cansia.html |
| Canadian Sphagnum Peat Moss Association | http://www.peatmoss.com |
| Canadian Veterinary Medical Association | http://www.upei.ca/~cvma/ |
| Canadian Water & Wastewater Association | http://www.cwwa.ca |
| Canadian Water Resources Association | http://www.cwra.org/cwra |
| Canadian Well Logging Society | http://www.canpic.ca/CWLS |
| Canadian Wind Energy Association Inc. | http://keynes.fb12.tu-berlin.de/luftraum/konst/canwea.html |
| Canadian Wood Council | http://cwc.metrics.com/cwc.html |
| The Chemical Institute of Canada | http://www.chem-inst-can.org |
| The Clean Nova Scotia Foundation | http://www.ccn.cs.dal.ca/Environment/CNSF/cnsf.html |
| The Composting Council of Canada | http://www.compost.org |
| Crop Protection Institute of Canada | http://www.cropro.org |
| Ducks Unlimited Canada | http://www.ducks.ca |
| Edmonton Space & Science Centre | http://www.ee.ualberta.ca/essc |
| Electronic Commerce Canada | http://www.ecc.ca |
| Energy Council of Canada | http://www.energy.ca |
| Energy Pathways Inc. | http://www.epi.ca/home.htm |
| Energy Probe Research Foundation | http://www.nextcity.com/EnergyProbe/ |
| Enviro-Accès Inc. | http://www.enviroaccess.ca/ |
| Environment Probe | http://www.nextcity.com/EnvironmentProbe/ |
| Environmental Services Association of Alberta | http://www.esaa.org |
| The Evergreen Foundation | http://www.evergreen.ca/ |
| Fédération québécoise de la faune | http://www.fqf.qc.ca |
| Federation of Alberta Naturalists | http://www.connect.ab.ca/~fan |
| Federation of BC Naturalists | http://www.nq.com/land4nature/ |
| Federation of Nova Scotia Naturalists | http://ccn.cs.dal.ca/Environment/FNSN/hp-fnsn.html |
| Federation of Ontario Naturalists | http://www.web.net/fon |
| Food Institute of Canada | http://foodnet.fic.ca/fic/fic.html |
| Forest Alliance of British Columbia | http://www.forest.org |
| Forest Engineering Research Institute of Canada | http://www.feric.ca |
| Friends of the Environment Foundation | http://www.fef.ca/ |
| Geological Association of Canada | http://www.esd.mun.ca/~gac/ |
| Greenpeace Canada | http://www.greenpeacecanada.org/ |
| Harmony Foundation of Canada | http://www.harmonyfdn.bc.ca/~harmony |
| Heritage Foundation of Newfoundland & Labrador | http://www.avalon.nf.ca/heritage |
| Industrial Biotechnology Association of Canada | http://www.biotech.ca/members/ibac.htm |
| Industrial Research & Development Institute | http://www.irdi.on.ca |
| Institut national de la recherche scientifique | http://www.inrs-urb.uquebec.ca |
| Institute for Aerospace Studies | http://www.utias.utoronto.ca/ |
| Institute for Robotics & Intelligent Systems | http://www.precarn.ca |
| Institute for Space & Terrestrial Science | http://www.ists.ca |
| Intergovernmental Committee on Urban & Regional Research | http://www.icurr.org/icurr/ |
| International Association of Science & Technology for Development | http://www.iasted.com/ |
| International Environmental Liability Management Association | http://www.magic.ca/ielma/IELMA.html |
| International Institute for Sustainable Development | http://iisd1.iisd.ca/ |
| International Society of Indoor Air Quality & Climate | http://www.cyberus.ca/~dsw/ |
| Jubilee Centre for Agricultural Research | http://www.christianfarmers.org |
| Manitoba Environmental Industries Association Inc. | http://www.canpay.com/meia/ |
| Manitoba Institute of Agrologists | http://www.mia.mb.ca |
| National Aboriginal Forestry Association | http://sae.ca/nafa |
| National Energy Conservation Association | http://www.mbnet.mb.ca/~neca/ |
| National Optics Institute | http://www.ino.qc.ca |
| Nature Saskatchewan | http://www.unibase.com/~naturesk |
| NeuroScience Network | http://www.cns.ucalgary.ca/nce |
| Newfoundland & Labrador Construction Association | http://www.netfx.iom.net/nlca/ |
| Newfoundland Environmental Industry Association | http://www.webpage.ca/neia/ |
| Nova Scotia Environmental Industry Association | http://www.isisnet.com/nseia/ |
| Nova Scotia Institute of Agrologists | http://www.nsac.ns.ca/nsdam/nsia/ |
| Nova Scotian Institute of Science | http://www.ccn.cs.dal.ca/Science/NSIS/Home.html |
| Ocean Voice International, Inc. | http://www.ovi.ca |
| Ontario Centre for Environmental Technology Advancement | http://www.oceta.on.ca |
| Ontario Environmental Network | http://www.web.net/~oen |
| Ontario Institute of Agrologists | http://www.freespace.net/~oia |
| Ontario Kinesiology Association | http://www.interlog.com/~oka |
| Ontario Science Centre | http://www.osc.on.ca |
| Pacific Space Centre | http://pacific-space-centre.bc.ca |
| The Pembina Institute for Appropriate Development | http://www.piad.ab.ca |
| Petroleum Communication Foundation | http://www.pcf.ab.ca |
| Petroleum Recovery Institute | http://www.pri.com |
| Petroleum Services Association of Canada | http://www.psac.ca |
| Petroleum Society of CIM | http://www.canpic.ca/PETSOC/ |

Pitch-In Canada ........ http://www.pitch-in.ca/
Pollution Probe Foundation ........ http://www.web.net/~pprobe/
Propane Gas Association of Canada Inc. ........ http://www.propanegas.ca
Protein Engineering Network of Centres of Excellence ........ http://www.pence.ualberta.ca
Recycling Council of British Columbia ........ http://www.rcbc.bc.ca
Recycling Council of Ontario ........ http://www.web.net/rco
Respiratory Health Network of Centres of Excellence ........ http://www.meakins.mcgill.ca/Inspiraplex/index.html
The Roberta Bondar Earth & Space Centre ........ http://www.senecac.on.ca/bondar/planet.htm
Royal Astronomical Society of Canada ........ http://www.rasc.ca
SHAD International ........ http://www.shad.ca
Saskatchewan Environmental Society ........ http://www.lights.com/ses/
Saskatchewan Land Surveyors' Association ........ http://www.gov.sk.ca/spmc/sgd/sls/slsahome.htm
Saskatchewan Soil Conservation Association Inc. ........ http://paridss.usask.ca/consgroups/ssca/sscahome.htm
Science Alberta Foundation ........ http://www.FreeNet.Calgary.ab.ca/science/sciencab.html
Science World British Columbia ........ http://www.scienceworld.bc.ca
Science for Peace ........ http://www.math.yorku.ca/sfp/
Sea Shepherd Conservation Society ........ http://www.seashepherd.org
Société québécoise d'assainissement des eaux ........ http://www.sqac.gouv.qc.ca
Society for Canadian Women in Science & Technology ........ http://www.harbour.sfu.ca/scwist/
Society of Toxicology of Canada ........ http://meds-ss10.meds.queensu.ca/stcweb/
Solar Energy Society of Canada Inc. ........ http://www.newenergy.org/newenergy/sesci.html
Solid Waste Association of North America ........ http://www.swana.org
Statistical Society of Canada ........ http://mast.queensu.ca/~ssc/en/welcome.html
United Nations Environment Programme ........ http://www.unep.org
Water Environment Association of Ontario ........ http://www.oww.org
Western Canada Water & Wastewater Association ........ http://www.wcwwa.ca
Western Canada Water Environment Association ........ http://www.wcwwa.ca
Western Canada Wilderness Committee ........ http://www.web.net/wcwild/
The Women & Environments Education & Development Foundation ........ http://www.web.net/~weed/
World Society for the Protection of Animals ........ http://www.way.net/wspa/
World Wildlife Fund - Canada ........ http://www.wwfcanada.org

## TRANSPORTATION

Aerospace Industries Association of Canada ........ http://www.aiac.ca
Air Canada ........ http://www.aircanada.ca
Air Transport Association of Canada ........ http://www.atac.ca
Alberta Trucking Association ........ http://www.albertatrucking.com
Algoma Central Railway Inc. ........ http://www.mcs.net/~dsdawdy/Canpass/acr/soo_her.html
American Airlines Inc. ........ http://www.amrcorp.com
Atlantic Provinces Transportation Commission ........ http://www.aptc.nb.ca
BC Rail Ltd. ........ http://www.bcrail.com/bcr/index.htm
British Columbia Automobile Association ........ http://www.bcaa.bc.ca
British Columbia Marine Trades Association ........ http://bcmarine.com
Canadian Aeronautics & Space Institute ........ http://www.casi.ca
Canadian Air Traffic Control Association (Ind.) ........ http://www.catca.ca
Canadian Airlines International Ltd. ........ http://www.cdnair.ca
Canadian Automobile Association ........ http://www.caa.ca
Canadian Automobile Association Québec ........ http://www.caa-quebec.qc.ca
Canadian Council of Motor Transport Administrators ........ http://www.ccmta.ca/
Canadian Institute of Traffic & Transportation ........ http://www.citt.ca
Canadian International Freight Forwarders Association, Inc. ........ http://www.ciffa.com/ciffa/
Canadian National Railway Company ........ http://www.cn.ca
Canadian Owners & Pilots Association ........ http://www.copanational.org
Canadian Port & Harbour Association ........ http://www.newswire.ca/cpha/cpha1.htm
Canadian Regional Airlines ........ http://www.cdnair.ca
Canadian Shipowners Association ........ http://www.shipowners.ca
Canadian Transportation Research Forum ........ http://www.venax.ca/ctrf/
Canadian Trucking Association ........ http://www.cta.ca
Canadian Warplane Heritage ........ http://www.warplane.com
Chartered Institute of Transport in North America ........ http://www.cit.ca
Czech Airlines ........ http://www.baxter.net/csa
Electric Vehicle Association of Canada ........ http://ww.evac.ca
GO Transit ........ http://www.mcs.net/~dsdawdy/Canpass/go/go_top.html
Icelandair ........ http://www.centrum.is/icelandair
Institute for Aerospace Studies ........ http://www.utias.utoronto.ca/
International Civil Aviation Organization ........ http://www.cam.org/~icao/
International Industry Working Group ........ http://www.iata.org
Northwest Airlines ........ http://www.nwa.com
Ontario Electric Railway Historical Association ........ http://www.hcry.org
Ontario Northland Transportation Commission ........ http://www.mcs.net/~dsdawdy/Canpass/onr/onr.html
Ontario Trucking Association ........ http://www.ontruck.org
Private Motor Truck Council of Canada ........ http://www.pmtc.ca
Québec North Shore & Labrador Railway Company ........ http://www.mcs.net/~dsdawdy/Canpass/qnsl/qnsl.html
The Railway Association of Canada ........ http://www.railcan.ca
SEDS - Canada ........ http://www.seds.ca
Via Rail Canada Inc. ........ http://www.mcs.net/~dsdawdy/Canpass/via/via.html
Vintage Locomotive Society Inc. ........ http://www.winnipeg.freenet.mb.ca/pdc/
West Coast Railway Association ........ http://www.wcra.org

# SECTION 6

## ARTS & CULTURE DIRECTORY



**See ADDENDA at the back of this book for late changes & additional information.**

## MUSEUMS & SCIENCE CENTRES

**The Canadian Museum of Civilization/Musée canadien des civilisations (CMC)**
100 Laurier St., PO Box 3100, Stn B, Hull QC J8X 4H2
819/776-7000; Fax: 819/776-8300
URL: http://www.civilization.ca
The Canadian Museum of Civilization conducts research in Canadian studies & collects, preserves & displays objects which reflect Canada's cultural heritage. Its activities extend across the country through field research programs, publications & loans to various groups & institutions. Through permanent & changing exhibitions, public programs, film & theatre programs, the museum unfolds the stories of Canada's prehistory, native cultures, explorers, settlers & multicultural heritage. The Canadian War Museum, an affiliated museum of the Canadian Museum of Civilization, houses an extensive collection depicting Canada's military history; The Canadian Postal Museum, a division of CMC, is responsible for a collection depicting postal history.
President & Executive Director, Dr. George MacDonald
Vice-President, Public Affairs, Pierre Pontbriand

**CANADIAN WAR MUSEUM/MUSÉE CANADIEN DE LA GUERRE**
350 Sussex Dr., ON K1A OM8
URL: http://www.cmcc.muse.digital.ca/cwm/cwmeng/cwmeng.html

**Canadian Museum of Contemporary Photography/Musée canadien de la photographie contemporaine (CMCP/MCPC)**
1 Rideau Canal, PO Box 465, Stn A, Ottawa ON K1N 9N6
613/990-8257; Fax: 613/990-6542; Email: cmcp@ngc.chin.gc.ca
URL: http://cmcp.gallery.ca
The CMCP collects, interprets & disseminates contemporary Canadian photography as an art form & as a form of social documentation. Thematic & solo exhibitions are organized & presented quarterly at the museum's galleries & circulated across Canada & abroad through travelling exhibitions. Education programs & publications; boutique; theatre; collection storage; an affiliate of the National Gallery of Canada.
Director, Martha Hanna
Associate Curator, Pierre Dessureault
Asst. Curator, Carol Payne
Manager, Exhibitions, Publications & Communications, Maureen McEvoy
Administration Officer, Lise Krueger

**Canadian Museum of Nature/Musée canadien de la nature**
PO Box 3443, Stn D, Ottawa ON K1P 6P4
613/566-4700; Fax: 613/954-5958; Email: enquiries@mus_nature.ca
URL: http://www.nature.ca
The CMN conducts research, maintains collections & presents educational programs across Canada. At the Victoria Memorial Museum Bldg. in Ottawa there are seven permanent exhibit halls on the Earth, Life Through the Ages, Birds in Canada, Mammals in Canada, Animals in Nature, Plant Life & the Viola MacMillan Mineral Gallery as well as three special exhibits areas. The Museum is the repository of some eight million specimens, with approximately 100,000 new items being added every year. These collections, although used in exhibits, are more for research than display & are open to study by qualified students & others. Museum expertise is available for consultation or project co-ordination.
Interim President, Colin Eades
Executive Vice-President, Dr. Patrick Colgan – 613/953-5357
Vice-President, Public Programs, Leslie Patten – 613/998-4972
Director, Capital Projects, Colin Eades – 613/991-2264
Director, Arctic Program, Mark Araham – 613/998-0247
Director, Origins Program, Gerald Fitzgerald – 613/954-0358
Director, Biodiversity Program, Robert McFetridge – 613/998-9486
Director, Business Initiatives Bureau, Maryse Brunet-Lalonde – 613/998-5673

**Currency Museum of the Bank of Canada/Musée de la monnaie**
245 Sparks St., Ottawa ON K1A 0G9
613/782-8914; Fax: 613/782-8874
URL: http://www.bank-banque-canada.ca
The most complete collection of Canadian notes & coins in the world, plus representative collections of world coins & paper money, including whales' teeth, glass pearls, elephant-hair bracelets, shells & copper axes.
Chief Curator & Head of Museum, J. Graham Esler
Director, Museum Programming, Louise O'Neill
Coordinator, Public Relations, Laurette Bergeron

**National Aviation Museum/Musée national de l'aviation**
11 Aviation Pkwy., PO Box 9724, Stn T, Ottawa ON K1G 5A3
613/993-2010; Fax: 613/990-3655; Email: Lucas@istar.ca; TDD: 613/990-7530
URL: http://www.aviation.nmstc.ca
Follow the "Walkway of Time" which tells the story of aviation from Canada's first powered flight in 1909 to the jet age through most of the 118 aircraft in our collection. Stars include the A.E.G. G.IV, the only WWI German twin-engine aircraft in existence; the Lancaster Bomber, built & flown by Canadians; the 1947 prototype of the world famous bush plane, the Beaver; & the Messerschmitt Me 163B, the first rocket airplane. Don't miss our Virtual Reality Hang-Glider Simulator or our new exhibit, "Pushing the Envelope: Advances in Aviation Technology", featuring the Avro Arrow, Jetliner, CL-84 & the Twin Otter. Café, boutique, free parking.
Director General, Christopher Terry
Curator Emeritus, A.J. Shortt
A/Director, Public Programmes, Francine Poirier
Communications Officer, Christina Lucas – 613/993-4243
Junior Communications Officer, Julie Têtu – 613/991-3834

**National Museum of Science & Technology/Musée national des sciences et de la technologie (NMST/MNST)**

1867 St. Laurent Blvd., PO Box 9724, Ottawa ON K1G 5A3

613/991-3044; Fax: 613/990-3654; Email: slitech@istar.ca; TTY: 613/991-9207

URL: http://www.science-tech.nmstc.ca

Hands-on exhibits in the areas of ground transportation, marine technology, communications, space, agriculture, industrial & domestic technologies, physics, computer science, printing & astronomy, from early times to the present. Automobiles, locomotives, music boxes & telephones make up some of the museum's many collections. The National Aviation Museum, located at Rockcliffe Airport, is affiliated with the National Museum of Science & Technology. Public programs at the Central Experimental Farm include farm animals, "A Barn of the 1920s" & "The Amazing Potato" exhibits, horse-drawn wagon rides, the Sheep Shearing Festival in May & the Fall Harvest Celebration in Oct.

Advertising & Promotion Officer, Leeanne Akehurst
Director, NMST Corporation, Dr. Geneviève Sainte-Marie
Director General, National Aviation Museum, Christopher Terry
Director General, Public Programmes, Dr. Paul Donahue
Director General, Collection & Research, David Richeson
Director General, Management Services, Graham Parsons
Director, Curatorial Services, Geoff Rider
Curator, Communications, Bryan Dewalt
Senior Curator, Industrial & Domestic Technology, Thierry Ruddel
Senior Curator, Energy, Louise Trottier
Senior Curator, Physical Sciences & Space, Randall Brooks
Curator, Land Transportation, David Monaghan
Curator, Marine Transportation, Garth Wilson
Curator, Aviation History, Reynald Fortir
Director, Agriculture Museum, Michelle Dondo-Tardiff
Coordinator, Public Programming (Agric. Museum), Tamara Tarasoff
Director, Exhibit Development & Production, Ginette Bériault
Director, Interpretation & Visitor Services Division, Claude Faubert
Director, Communications & Promotion, Marion Grobb
Advertising & Promotion Officer, Cynthia Jolly
Media Relations Officer, Jean-Guy Monette

## ALBERTA

**Glenbow Museum, Art Gallery, Library & Archives**

130 - 9 Ave. SE, Calgary AB T2G 0P3

403/268-4100; Fax: 403/265-9769; Email: glenbow@glenbow.org

URL: http://www.glenbow.org

Glenbow documents the settlement of Western Canada with exhibits tracing the lives & traditions of native peoples, the development of the railway, ranching, farming & growing up in the West. A large art gallery highlights historical & contemporary art from Glenbow's own collections as well as from national & international collections. Books, maps, photographs & manuscripts relating to southern Alberta history are available for study in the extensive Library & Archives.

Vice-President, Collections Management, Patricia Ainslie
Vice-President, Glenbow Enterprises, Sharon Gutruth
Director, Library & Archives, Lynette Walton
President & CEO, Dr. Robert Janes
Chief Financial Officer & Vice-President, Central Services, Joe Konrad
Vice-President, Program & Exhibit Development, Donna Livingstone

**Provincial Museum of Alberta**

12845 - 102 Ave., Edmonton AB T5N 0M6

403/453-9100; Fax: 403/454-6629

URL: http://www.pma.edmonton.ab.ca

Major collections & exhibits of Alberta's natural & human history, including habitat groups, geology, palaeontology, native cultures, archaeology & western Canadian history; presentations from major museums around the world & an annual natural history exhibition; museum shop, cafeteria, publications information service, films, lectures, live demonstrations & cultural performances; special programs for schools & other groups; discovery room.

Director, Dr. Philip H.R. Stepney
Manager, Operations, Tim Willis
Manager, Exhibits & Visitor Services, Don Clevett
Manager, Archaeology & Ethnology, Dr. J.W. Ives
Manager, Curatorial & Collections Administration, Dr. Bruce McGillivray
Communications Co-ordinator, Kathleen Thurber

**Royal Tyrrell Museum of Palaeontology**

c/o Midland Provincial Park, PO Box 7500, Drumheller AB T0J 0Y0

403/823-7707; Fax: 403/823-7131; Email: rtmp@dns.magtech.ab.ca

URL: http://tyrrell.magtech.ab.ca

Operated by Alberta Community Development; the 11,200 sq.m. facility includes a public gallery which features dramatic murals, interactive displays, computer games, mini-theatres & some 800 fossil specimens, including more than 35 complete dinosaur skeletons & 100s of fossil reptiles. A Paleoconservatory houses semi-tropical plants, aquaria, interpreted trails, a cafeteria & giftshop. The museum conducts major field based research in Western Canada & abroad.

Director, Dr. Bruce Naylor

**FIELD STATION**

Dinosaur Provincial Park, PO Box 60, AB T0J 0Y0

403/378-4342; Fax: 403/378-4247

The satellite Field Station exhibits the knowledge of local ancient environments & contains on-site preparation & research facilities to support annual fieldwork programs.

**Other Museums & Science Centres in Alberta**

Airdrie: Nose Creek Valley Museum, PO Box 3351, Airdrie AB T4B 2B6 – 403/948-6685 – Curator, Julian Fell – Open year round

Alberta Beach: Garden Park Farm Museum, PO Box 639, Alberta Beach AB T0E 0A0 – 403/924-3391 – David Oselies

Alix Wagon Wheel Regional Museum, PO Box 157, Alix AB T0C 0B0 – 403/747-2708 – Curator, Alice Whitfield – Local history; open year round

Alliance & District Museum, PO Box 101, Alliance AB T0B 0A0 – President, Rose Barnes – Pioneer & farm life; open year round

Andrew & District Local History Museum, PO Box 180, Andrew AB T0B 0C0 – 403/365-3606 – Verna Topolinsky – Open year round

Banff Park Museum, PO Box 900, Banff AB T0L 0C0 – 403/762-1558; Fax: 403/762-3229; Email: hsmanager@pksbnp.dots.ddg.ca; URL: http://www.worldweb.com/ParksCanada-Banff/museum.html – Historic Sites Manager, Maureen Peniuk – Open year round; winter closed Tues. & Wed.

Banff: Luxton Museum of the Plains Indian, c/o Buffalo Nations Cultural Society, 1 Birch Ave., PO Box 850, Banff AB T0L 0C0 – 403/762-2388; Fax: 403/760-2803; Email: luxton@telusplanet.net – Executive Director, Pete Brewster – Plains Indians artifacts; open year round

Banff: Whyte Museum of the Canadian Rockies, PO Box 160, Banff AB T0L 0C0 – 403/762-2291; Fax: 403/762-8919; Email: wmcr@banff.net; URL: http://www.cadvision.com/db/wmer – Director, Edward J. Hart – Open year round

Barrhead & District Centennial Museum, PO Box 4122, Barrhead AB T7N 1A1 – 403/674-5203 – Curator, Mabel Gravel – Open daily in summer; winter by appt.

Beaverlodge: South Peace Centennial Museum, PO Box 493, Beaverlodge AB T0H 0C0 – 403/354-8869 – President, Gordon McLean – Pioneer equipment & buildings; open mid-May - Oct. 1

Blairmore: The Frank Slide Interpretive Centre (FSIC), PO Box 959, Blairmore AB T0K 0E0 – 403/562-7388; Fax: 403/562-8635 – Area Supervisor, Monica Field – Site of the 1903 rockslide avalanche; open June 1 - Labour Day, 9 am - 8 pm; 10 am - 4 pm remainder of year

Blairmore: Leitch Collieries Provincial Historic Site, PO Box 959, Blairmore AB T0K 0E0 – 403/562-7388; Fax: 403/562-8635 – Area Supervisor, Monica Field – Open May 15 - Labour Day

Bellevue Underground Mine, PO Box 959, AB T0K 0E0 – 403/562-7388; Fax: 403/562-8635 – Area Supervisor, Monica Field – Open daily May 15 - Labour Day

Bowden Pioneer Museum, PO Box 576, Bowden AB T0M 0K0 – 403/224-2122 – Curator, Bill Henderson

Brooks & District Museum, PO Box 2078, Brooks AB T1R 1C7 – 403/362-5073 – Open May 1 - Aug. 31

Calgary: Aero Space Museum of Calgary, Hangar #10, 4629 McCall Way NE, Calgary AB T2E 7H1 – 403/250-3752; Fax: 403/250-8399; Email: aerospace@lexicom.ab.ca; URL: http://www.lexicom.ab.ca/~aerospace/aerospace.html – Executive Director, Everett L. Bunnell – Open year round

Calgary: Alberta Sports Hall of Fame & Museum, #100, 635 - 6 Ave. SW, Calgary AB T2P 0T5 – 403/269-6000; Fax: 403/297-6669 – Curator, Janice Smith – Open year round

Calgary Chinese Cultural Centre, 197 - 1 St. SW, Calgary AB T2P 4M4 – 403/262-5071; Fax: 403/232-6387 – Administrator, Stephen Lee – Open year round

Calgary Highlanders Museum & Archives, 4520 Crowchild Trail SW, Calgary AB T3E 1T8 – 403/974-2855; Fax: 403/974-2855; URL: http://db.nucleus.com/highmus/default.htm – Curator, Brian King

Calgary Police Service Interpretive Centre & Archives, 133 - 6 Ave. SE, Calgary AB T2G 4Z1 – 403/268-4565; Fax: 403/974-0508 – Curator/Administrator, Janet Pieschel – Open year round

Calgary Science Centre (CSC), #73, 701 - 11 St. SW, PO Box 2100, Stn M, Calgary AB T2P 2M5 – 403/221-3700; Fax: 403/237-0186; Email: discover@calgaryscience.ca; URL: http://www.calgaryscience.ca – Executive Director, William T. Peters – Open year round.

Calgary: Energeum, 640 - 5 Ave. SW, Calgary AB T2P 3G4 – 403/297-4293; Fax: 403/297-3757; Email: gassee@mail.eub.gov.ab.ca; URL: http://www.eub.gov.ab.ca – Curator, Ellen Gasser – Alberta's energy resources; hands-on displays; computer games; school programs; tours; open year round; free

Calgary: Fort Calgary Historic Park (FCPS), #106, 750 - 9th Ave. SE, PO Box 2100, Stn M, Calgary AB T2P 2M5 – 403/290-1875; Fax: 403/265-6534 – Executive Director, Don S. Hardy – 40 acre park; interpretive centre; 1875 fort reconstruction project; guided tours; open May 1 - Thanksgiving

Calgary: Heritage Park Historical Village, 1900 Heritage Dr. SW, Calgary AB T2V 2X3 – 403/259-1900; Fax: 403/252-3528 – Manager, Historical

Operations, W.D. Parama; General Manager, R.R. Smith – Pre-1914 western Canadian history in an authentic life setting; open May - Oct.

Calgary: Lord Strathcona's Horse (Royal Canadians) Regimental Museum, 4520 Crowchild Trail SW, Calgary AB T3E 1T8 – 403/242-6610; Fax: 403/974-2854; Email: rdennis@nucleus.com; URL: http://www.nucleus.com/~rdennis/ – Curator, Rick Dennis – Open year round

Calgary: Museum of the Regiments, CFB Calgary, 4520 Crowchild Trail SW, Calgary AB T3E 1Y8 – 403/240-7057; Fax: 403/240-7190; Email: regiments@lexicom.ab.ca; URL: http://www.lexicom.ab.ca/~regiments/ – Depicts the history of the four regiments of Calgary; art gallery

Calgary: Naval Museum of Alberta, 1820 - 24 St. SW, Calgary AB T2T 0G6 – 403/242-0002; URL: http://www.lexicom.ab.ca/~navalmuseum/navalmuseum.html

Calgary: The Nickle Arts Museum (NAM), c/o The University of Calgary, 2500 University Dr. NW, Calgary AB T2N 1N4 – 403/220-7234; Fax: 403/282-4742; Email: nickle@acs.ucalgary.ca; URL: http://www.ucalgary.ca – Director, Dr. Ann Davis – Founded in 1979 through a donation from Sam Nickle & a Province of Alberta grant; champions contemporary Western Canadian art & numismatics; changing exhibitions & programs

Calgary: Olympic Hall of Fame & Museum/Temple Olympique de la Renommée, Canada Olympic Park, 88 Canada Olympic Rd. SW, Calgary AB T3B 5R5 – 403/247-5454; Fax: 403/286-7213 – Curator, J. Thomas West – Three floors of exhibits on Winter Olympic history & the XV Olympic Winter Games in Calgary; Olympic Volunteer Theatre; Bobsleigh & Ski Jump simulators

Calgary: Princess Patricia's Canadian Light Infantry Regimental Museum & Archives, 4520 Crowchild Trail SW, Calgary AB T2T 5J4 – 403/974-2860; Fax: 403/974-2864; Email: ppcli@nucleus.com – Curator, Capt. R. Raidt, MMM, CD – Artifacts relating to history & traditions of the PPCLI; PPCLI primary source documents, letters & papers; also a small, unique library

Calgary: Sam Livingston Fish Hatchery & Rearing Station, 1440 - 17A St. SE, Calgary AB T2G 4T9 – 403/297-6561; Fax: 403/297-2839 – Superintendent, W. Schenk – Open year round

Calgary: Sarcee People's Museum, 3700 Anderson Rd. SW, Calgary AB T2W 3C4 – 403/238-2677

Calgary: University of Calgary Museum of Zoology, 2500 University Dr., Calgary AB T2N 1N4 – 403/220-5269; Fax: 403/289-9311; Email: fitch@acs.ucalgary.ca – Curator, Dr. H.I. Rosenberg – Teaching museum used for zoology & ecology courses

Camrose & District Centennial Museum, PO Box 1622, Camrose AB T4V 1X6 – 403/672-3298 – Volunteer Curator, Angela Johnson – Open May - Sept., otherwise by appt.

Canmore: Centennial Museum of Canmore, 907 - 7th Ave., Canmore AB T1W 2A9 – 403/678-2462; Fax: 403/678-2216 – President, Royal McKellar – Open year-round; extended summer hours.

Cardston: Brooks Aqueduct National/Provincial Historic Site, c/o Remington Alberta Carriage Centre, PO Box 1649, Cardston AB T0K 0K0 – 403/653-5139; Summer: 362-4451; Fax: 403/653-5160; Email: brooks@mcd.gov.ab.ca – Aqueduct Supervisor, Heather MacAulay

Cardston: C.O. Card Home & Court House Museum, PO Box 1830, Cardston AB T0K 0K0 – 403/653-4322 – Curator, Leo S. Stutz – Open June 1-Aug. 31, Mon.-Sat.; archives open year round on Wed. or by appt.

Cardston: Remington-Alberta Carriage Centre, 623 Main St., PO Box 1649, Cardston AB T0K 0K0 – 403/653-5139; Fax: 403/653-5160; Email: info@remingtoncentre.com; URL: http://www.remingtoncentre.com – Facility Manager, Chris Williams – Over 200 carriages, wagons & sleighs

Carstairs: Roulston Museum, PO Box 1067, Carstairs AB T0M 0N0 – 403/337-3710 – President, Patricia Barr; Curator, Betty Ayers – Main collection housed in the hall of Knox Presbyterian Church, a registered historic site; church records; pictures & artifacts of local life from early settlement to present; McQuaig House (1901); archives

Castor & District Museum, PO Box 864, Castor AB T0C 0X0 – 403/882-3409 – President, Marjorie Marshall

Cereal Prairie Pioneer Museum, PO Box 131, Cereal AB T0J 0N0 – 403/326-3899 – Director, F. Adams

Claresholm Museum, PO Box 397, Claresholm AB T0L 0T0 – 403/625-3131 – Curator, Mae Weber

Cochrane Ranch Historic Site, PO Box 1522, Cochrane AB T0L 0W0 – 403/932-2902; Fax: 403/932-2578; Email: cochrane@mcd.gov.ab.ca – Area Manager, Ken Carson – Alberta's first large-scale ranch; open May 15 - Labour Day; hiking & picnic areas open year round

Cochrane: Riding Mountain Historical Society & Pinewood Museum, PO Box 339, Cochrane AB T0L 0W0 – President, Marilyn Whittle

Cochrane: Stephansson House Provincial Historic Site, c/o Historic Sites & Archives Service, PO Box 1522, Cochrane AB T0W 0W0 – 403/728-3929; URL: http://www.gov.ab.ca/~mcd/mhs/steph/stephans.htm – Area Manager, Frank Milligan – Icelandic poet's pioneer home; open May 15 - Labour Day

Coleman: Crowsnest Museum, PO Box 306, Coleman AB T0K 0M0 – 403/563-5434 – Curator, Laura Johnston – Open year round

Coutts: Belmore's Museum, PO Box 176, Coutts AB T0K 0N0 – 403/344-3888 – Director, Belmore Schultz – Open summer

Czar: Prairie Panorama Museum, PO Box 60, Czar AB T0B 0Z0 – 403/857-2155 – Curator, Helena Lawrason

DeBolt & District Pioneer Museum, PO Box 447, DeBolt AB T0H 1B0 – 403/957-3957; Fax: 403/957-2934 – Curator, Fran Moore – Open summer

Delburne: Anthony Henday Museum, PO Box 374, Delburne AB T0M 0V0 – 403/749-2711 – President, Audrey Nicholson

Donalda & District Museum, PO Box 40, Donalda AB T0B 1H0 – 403/883-2345 – Director, Georgina Brown

Drumheller Dinosaur & Fossil Museum, PO Box 2135, Drumheller AB T0J 0Y0 – 403/823-2593 – Curator, Dorothy Farmer

Drumheller: Homestead Antique Museum, PO Box 3154, Drumheller AB T0J 0Y0 – 403/823-2600 – Curator, Robert Llewellyn – Open summer

East Coulee School Museum, PO Box 539, East Coulee AB T0J 1B0 – 403/822-3970; Fax: 403/822-2111 – Manager, Andy DeJong – Open year round

Edmonton: 408 Tactical Helicopter Squadron Museum, CFB Edmonton, Edmonton AB T0A 2H0 – 403/973-4381

Edmonton: AGT Vista 33: View Gallery & Museum, 10020 - 100 St., 33rd Fl., Edmonton AB T5J 0N5 – 403/493-3333; Fax: 403/493-3006 – Technician/Restoration & Fabrication Specialist, R. Foster – Telephone industry artifacts; open year round

Edmonton: Alberta Aviation Museum, 11410 Kingsway Ave., Edmonton AB T5G 0X4 – 403/453-1078; Fax: 403/453-1885; URL: http://www.discoveredmonton.com/AviationMuseum/

Edmonton: Alberta Railway Museum, PO Box 70014, Edmonton AB T5C 3R6 – 403/472-6229; Fax: 403/487-8705; URL: http://www.discoveredmonton.com/railwaymuseum/ – General Manager, Herb Dixon – Open Victoria to Labour day, 10 am - 6 pm

Edmonton: Beaver House, c/o Alberta Culture & Multiculturalism, 10158 - 103 St., 3rd Fl., Edmonton AB T5J 0X6 – 403/427-2031; Fax: 403/422-9132

Edmonton: Calgary & Edmonton (1891) Railway Museum, 10447 - 86 Ave., Edmonton AB T6E 2M4 – 403/433-9739; Email: tuckwelc@supernet.ab.ca; URL: http://www.discoveredmonton.com/RailMuseum/

Edmonton Police Museum & Archives, 9620 - 103A Ave., Edmonton AB T5H 0H7 – 403/421-2274; Fax: 403/421-2341; Email: EPS@whet.gov.edmonton.ab.ca – Curator/Director, Anne Lindsay – Open Mon. - Sat., 9 am - 3 pm

Edmonton Public Schools Archives & Museum, 10425 - 99 Ave., Edmonton AB T5K 0E5 – 403/422-1970; URL: http://www.discoveredmonton.com/SchoolMuseum/ – Supervisor, Catherine Luck

Edmonton Radial Railway Society, PO Box 45040, Stn Lansdowne Peel, Edmonton AB T6H 5Y1 – 403/457-1269; Fax: 403/457-9315 – President, Harvey Bradley – Restored streetcar rides for visitors to Fort Edmonton Park

Edmonton Space & Science Centre, 11211 - 142 St. NW, Edmonton AB T5M 4A1 – 403/451-334, 452-9100; Fax: 403/455-5882; Email: essc@planet.eon.net; URL: http://www.ee.ualberta.ca/essc – Director, Les G. Young; Director, Development, George Smith – IMAX theatre; planetarium; exhibit galleries; Challenger Learning Centre; observatory; giftshop; café; Ham Radio Station

Edmonton: Father Lacombe Chapel/La Chapelle du Père Lacombe, c/o Historic Sites Service, 8820 -112 St., Edmonton AB T6G 2P8 – 403/427-3995; Fax: 403/422-4288; Email: lacombe@mcd.gov.ab.ca – Area Manager, Catherine Whalley – Located on St. Vital Ave., St. Albert; open May 15 - Labour Day; admission fee

Edmonton: Fort Edmonton Park, c/o City of Edmonton Community Services, PO Box 2359, Edmonton AB T5J 2R7 – 403/496-8787; Fax: 403/496-8797; URL: http://www.gov.edmonton.ab.ca/fort/ – Director, Bryan Monaghan – Canada's largest living history park; more than 70 period buildings & a complete fur-trading fort set in four time eras; costumed interpreters; steam train & street car; giftshops & restaurants

Edmonton: John Walter Museum, Edmonton Parks & Recreation, PO Box 2359, Edmonton AB T5J 2R7 – 403/496-7275; URL: http://www.discoveredmonton.com/JohnWalter/ – Director, Gary Dewar

Edmonton: Old Strathcona Model & Toy Museum, 8603 - 104 St., Edmonton AB T6E 4G6 – 403/433-4512; Email: Bobbell@connect.ab.ca; URL: http://www.discoveredmonton.com/ToyMuseum/ – Director, Gerry Bell; Director, Bob Bell

Edmonton: Rutherford House Provincial Historic Site, 11153 Saskatchewan Dr., Edmonton AB T6G 2S1 – 403/427-3995; Fax: 403/422-4288; URL: http://www.gov.ab.ca/~mcd/mcd.htm – Area Manager, Catherine Whalley – Home of Alberta's first premier; gift shop, tea room, tours & special events; open year round

Edmonton: Strathcona Archaeological Centre in Strathcona Science Park, c/o Historic Sites & Archives Service, 8820 - 112 St., Edmonton AB T6G 2P8

Edmonton: The Telephone Historical Centre (THC), 10437 - 83 Ave., PO Box 4962, Edmonton AB T6E 4T5 – 403/441-2077; Fax: 403/433-4068; Email: thc@planet.eon.net; URL: http://www.discoveredmonton.com/telephonemuseum/ – Executive Director, Bert Yeudall – Open year round

Edmonton: Ukrainian Canadian Archives & Museum, 9543 - 110 Ave., Edmonton AB T5H 1H3 – 403/424-7580 – Director, Harry Yopyk

Edmonton: Ukrainian Catholic Women's League of Canada Arts & Crafts Museum, 10825 - 97th St., Edmonton AB T5H 2M4 – 403/466-7210 – President, Ann Burtnik – Open year round

Edmonton: Ukrainian Cultural Heritage Village, c/o Historic Sites & Archives Service, 8820 - 112 St., Edmonton AB T6G 2P8 – 403/662-3640; Fax: 403/662-3273; Email: uchv@ncd.gov.ab.ca – Manager, Barry Manchak – Located 25 minutes east of Edmonton on Hwy.16; open May 15 - Thanksgiving

Edmonton: Ukrainian Museum of Canada (Alberta Branch), 10611 - 110 Ave., Edmonton AB T5H 1H7 – 403/483-5932; Fax: 403/423-6738 – President, N. Seniw

Edmonton: University of Alberta - Museums & Collections Services, Ring House #1, Edmonton AB T6G 2E2 – 403/492-5834; Fax: 403/492-6185; Email: museums@gpu.srv.ualberta.ca; URL: http://www.ualberta.ca/MUSEUMS – Director, Janine Andrews, Email: Janine.Andrews@ualberta.ca; Curator, Central Collection of Art & Historic Artifacts, Jim Corrigan, Email: j.corrigan@ualberta.ca; Manager, Collections Program, Leslie Latta-Guthrie, Email: l.latta-guthrie@ualberta.ca; Manager, Communication Program, Frannie Blondheim, Email: Frannie.Blondheim@ualberta.ca – A central service & coordinating unit for the University of Alberta's 40 teaching & research collections, which include natural & applied science, human history & art

Edmonton: University of Alberta Dental Museum, Dentistry Pharmacy Centre, University of Alberta, Edmonton AB T6G 2N8 – 403/492-5194; Fax: 403/492-1624; Email: gsperber@gpu.srv.ualberta.ca – Curator, Dr. G. Sperber

Elk Point: Fort George Museum, PO Box 66, Elk Point AB T0A 1A0 – 403/724-3654 – Director, Steve Andrishak – Open May 15 - Labour Day

Evansburg: Pembina Lobstick Historical Museum, PO Box 85, Evansburg AB T0E 0T0 – 403/727-3861; Fax: 403/727-3861 – President, Hazel B. Fausak; Secretary, Lois M. Jenkins

Fairview: RCMP Centennial Celebration Museum, PO Box 326, Fairview AB T0H 1L0 – 403/835-2467 – Curator, Viola Evans – Original barracks; open summer

Fort Macleod: The Fort Museum, PO Box 776, Fort Macleod AB T0L 0Z0 – 403/553-4703; Fax: 403/553-3451; Email: ftmuseum@telusplanet.net; URL: http://www.discoveralberta.com/fortmuseum/ – Curator, Carla Niers – Tells the story of the arrival of the NWMP into Western Canada, and the Natives and Pioneers of that time

Fort Macleod: Head-Smashed-In Buffalo Jump, PO Box 1977, Fort Macleod AB T0L 0Z0 – 403/553-2731; Fax: 403/553-3141; Email: info@head-smashed-in.com; URL: http://www.head-smashed-in.com – Facility Manager, Chris Williams – Designated World Heritage Site; open year round

Fort McMurray Oil Sands Interpretive Centre, 515 MacKenzie Blvd., Fort McMurray AB T9H 4X3 – 403/743-7167; Fax: 403/791-0710; Email: fmosic@mcd.gov.ab.ca – Manager, Marsha Regensburg – Open year round

Fort McMurray: Historic Dunvegan, c/o Oil Sands Interpretive Centre, 515 MacKenzie Blvd., Fort McMurray AB T9H 4X3 – 403/864-2266; Fax: 403/835-5525; Email: dunvegan@mcd.gov.ab.ca – Manager, Marsha Regensburg – Fur & provision post; open May 15 - Labour Day

Fort Saskatchewan Museum, 10104 - 101 St., Fort Saskatchewan AB T8L 1V9 – 403/998-1750; Email: museum@fortsaskinfo.com; URL: http://www.fortsaskinfo.com/museum/ – Curator, Kris Nygren

Fort Vermilion: Rocky Lane School Museum, PO Box 9000, Fort Vermilion AB T0H 1N0 – 403/927-3297; Fax: 403/927-4344 – Director, M. Nugent

Girouxville: Musée Girouxville Museum, PO Box 276, Girouxville AB T0H 1S0 – 403/323-4252 – Administrator, Estelle Girard

Grande Prairie Museum, Pioneer Museum Society of Grande Prairie & District, PO Box 687, Grande Prairie AB T8V 3A8 – 403/532-5482; Fax: 403/831-7371; URL: http://www.telusplanet.net/public/amassee/gpmuseum.html – Administrator/Curator, Peter Goertzen – Dinosaur bones; arrowheads; wildlife exhibits; pioneer artifacts; heritage village; open daily May-Sept. 30, 10-6

Hanna Pioneer Village Archives & Museum, PO Box 1528, Hanna AB T0J 1P0 – 403/854-4244; Fax: 403/854-3279 – President, Bill McFalls; Curator, George Patzer

High Prairie & District Museum & Historical Society, PO Box 1442, High Prairie AB T0G 1E0 – 403/523-2601 – Curator, M. Rose Lizee

High River: Museum of the Highwood, 129 - 3rd Ave. SW, High River AB T1V 1M9 – 403/652-7156; Fax: 403/652-2396 – Director, Lynn Cartwright

Hines Creek: End of Steel Heritage Museum & Park, PO Box 686, Hines Creek AB T0H 2A0 – 403/494-3522 – President, Wilson Coon – Northern Alberta Railway

Hinton: Alberta Forest Service Museum, 1176 Switzer Dr., Hinton AB T7V 1V3 – 403/865-8200; Fax: 403/865-8266 – Director, Terry Smith

Iddesleigh: Rainy Hills Historical Society Pioneer Exhibits (RHHS), Iddesleigh AB T0J 1T0 – 403/898-2443; Fax: 403/898-2443 – Sec.-Treas., Michele Olson – Community museum exhibiting homestead items including furnishings, clothing, farm equipment & photographs. Also features a blacksmith shop, school room, general store, an old-time kitchen & the original Iddlesleigh Alberta Wheat Post Office building.

Innisfail Historical Village, 52nd Ave. & 42nd St., Innisfail AB T0M 1A0 – 403/227-2906 – Curator, L. Boyd

Islay: Morrison Museum of the Country School, PO Box 120, Islay AB T0B 2J0 – Director, Allen Ronaghan

Jasper-Yellowhead Museum & Archives, PO Box 42, Jasper AB T0E 1E0 – 403/852-3013; Fax: 403/852-3240; Email: jymachir@telusplanet.net – Museum Manager, Kathy Glenn – Open year round

Leduc: Dr. Woods House Museum, PO Box 5201, Leduc AB T9E 6L6 – 403/986-1517 – Director, Rev. N. Quigley – Open year round, Tues.-Thurs., 1-4 pm

Lethbridge: Fort Whoop-Up, PO Box 1074, Lethbridge AB T1J 4A2 – 403/329-0444; Fax: 403/329-0645 – Director, Richard Shockley – Located in Indian Battle Park, west end of 3rd Ave. South; open year round

Lethbridge: Sir Alexander Galt Museum, c/o Community Services Dept., 910 - 4 Ave. South, Lethbridge AB T1J 0P6 – 403/320-3898; Fax: 403/329-4958 – Coordinator/Curator, Cecile McCleary

Longview: Bar U Ranch National Historic Site, PO Box 168, Longview AB T0L 1H0 – 403/395-2212; Fax: 403/395-2331

Lougheed: Iron Creek Museum, PO Box 294, Lougheed AB T0B 2V0 – 403/386-3984 – President, Thomas Clouston; Secretary, Irene Potter – Two, one-room school houses; church; blacksmith & shoe repair shop; artifacts

Medicine Hat Museum & Art Gallery (MHM&AG), 1302 Bomford Cres. SW, Medicine Hat AB T1A 5E6 – 403/527-6266; Fax: 403/528-2464 – Director, T.A. Willock

Mirror & District Museum, PO Box 246, Mirror AB T0B 3C0 – 403/788-3828 – President, Clara Klink – Local history museum; St. Monica's Anglican Church historic site

Mundare: Basilian Fathers Museum, PO Box 379, Mundare AB T0B 3H0 – 403/764-3887 – Ukrainian culture & religion

Nanton Lancaster Society & Air Museum, PO Box 1051, Nanton AB T0L 1R0 – 403/646-2270; Fax: 403/646-2270; Email: nanton@lexicom.ab.ca; URL: http://www.lexicom.ab.ca/~nanton/nanton.html – Curator, Bob Evans; Sec.-Treas., Dave Birrell

Olds: Mountain View Museum, PO Box 3882, Olds AB T4H 196 – 403/556-8464 – Director, Daniel Harder – Open 9 a.m. to 5 p.m. Monday to Friday from July to September; off-season, Tuesday, Wednesday, Thursday from 1 p.m. to 5 p.m.

Oyen: Crossroads Museum, PO Box 477, Oyen AB T0J 2J0 – 403/664-3850 – President, Nellie Eaton

Peace River Centennial Museum & Archives (PRMCAA), 10302 - 99 St., Peace River AB T8S 1K1 – 403/624-4261; Fax: 403/624-4270; Email: prmcaa@ccinet.ca – Executive Director/Curator, Victoria Barsalou; Chairperson, Arlene Staicesku

Pincher Creek Museum & Kootenai Brown Historical Park, PO Box 1226, Pincher Creek AB T0K 1W0 – 403/627-3684 – President, Ernie Kettles – Open year round

Plamondon & District Museum, PO Box 75, Plamondon AB T0A 2T0 – 403/798-3883 – Director, Marie Bourassa

Ponoka: Fort Ostell Museum, 5320 - 54 St., Ponoka AB T4J 1L8 – 403/783-5224 – Director, Connie Pugh

Red Deer: Fort Normandeau Historic Site & Interpretive Centre, 6300 - 45 Ave., Red Deer AB T4N 3M4 – 403/347-7550; Fax: 403/347-2550 – Head of Interpretation, J. Robertson

Red Deer & District Museum & Archives, PO Box 800, Red Deer AB T4N 5H2 – 403/343-6844; Fax: 403/342-6644 – Director, Wendy Martindale

Redcliff Historical & Museum Society, PO Box 758, Redcliff AB T0J 2P0 – 403/548-6260 – President, Chuck Watkins; Vice-President, Dwight Kilpatrick – Exhibits showing the commercial & recreational aspect of Redcliff citizens. Extensive drug store, domestic, school, toy & organizational exhibits; open 9-5 May-Aug. Tue.-Sat., Sundays 2-4, Oct.-Apr. by appt.

Redwater & District Museum, PO Box 114, Redwater AB T0A 2W0 – 403/942-3552 – Anne Key

Rimbey: Pas-Ka-Poo Historical Park, Rimbey AB T0C 2J0 – 403/843-2084 – Secretary, Charles F. Plank

Rocky Mountain House National Historic Park, PO Box 2130, Rocky Mountain House AB T0M 1T0 – 403/845-2412; Fax: 403/845-5320 – Area Supt., Dan Gaudet – Site of fur trading posts; open spring & summer

Rosebud Centennial Museum, PO Box 601, Rosebud AB T0J 2T0 – 403/677-2208; Fax: 403/677-2065 – Chairman, George Comstock – A collection of pioneer tools, etc. that have been donated to the museum

Rowley: Yester-Year Artifacts Museum, Rowley AB T0J 2X0 – 403/368-3816 – President, Heather McKee

Sangudo: Lac Ste-Anne Pioneer Museum, PO Box 525, Sangudo AB T0E 2A0 – 403/785-2398 – Archivist, Marian Dinwoodie

Seba Beach: All Saints Heritage Place, Seba Beach AB T0E 2B0 – 403/420-6704 – Lorna Cowley

St. Albert: Musée Héritage Museum & Archives, 5 Ste-Anne St., St. Albert AB T8N 3Z9 – 403/459-1528; Fax: 403/459-1546; Email: museum@compusmart.ab.ca – Acting Director/Curator, Karen Korchinski

St. Paul: Fort George & Buckingham House Provincial Historic Site (FGBH), Provincial Bldg., #318, 5025 - 49 Ave., St. Paul AB T0A 3A4 – 403/645-6256; Fax: 403/645-4760; Email: FtGeorge@mcd.gov.ab.ca – Facility Manager, Karen L. Doyle

– Archaeological remains of 2 fur trade forts; interpretive centre & gift shop; open May 15 - Labour Day

St. Paul: Musée Historique de St. Paul, PO Box 1925, St. Paul AB T0A 3A0 – 403/645-4800 – Présidente, Germaine Champagne

St. Paul: Victoria Settlement Provincial Historic Site, Provinical Bldg., #318, 5025 - 49 Ave., St. Paul AB T0A 3A4 – 403/645-6256; Fax: 403/645-4760 – Facility Manager, Karen L. Doyle – Hudson Bay Company post & settlement; open May 15-Labour Day

Stettler Town & Country Museum, PO Box 2118, Stettler AB T0C 2L0 – 403/742-4534 – Curator, Catherine Anderson

Stony Plain: Multicultural Heritage Centre, PO Box 2188, Stony Plain AB T7Z 1X7 – 403/963-2777; Fax: 403/963-0233 – Executive Director, Judy Unterschultz

Strome: Sodbuster Archives Museum, PO Box 151, Strome AB T0B 4H0 – 403/376-3688 – Sec.-Treas., Joan Brockhoff

Sundre Historical Museum & Pioneer Village, PO Box 314, Sundre AB T0M 1X0 – 403/638-3233 – Manager, Sheilagh MacGregor – Open summer

Three Hills: Kneehill Historical Museum, PO Box 653, Three Hills AB T0M 2A0 – 403/443-5348 – Muriel Park

Tofield Historical Museum, Tofield AB T0B 4J0 – 403/662-2542 – President, Harold Schultz

Trochu & District Museum, PO Box 538, Trochu AB T0M 2C0 – 403/442-2334 – Curator, George O. Braham

Viking Historical Museum, PO Box 270, Viking AB T0B 4N0 – 403/336-3066 – Director, J.H. Roddick – Open summer

Wainwright Museum, PO Box 2994, Wainwright AB T9W 1S9 – 403/842-3115; Fax: 403/842-4910 – President, Battle River Historical Society, Erika Foley

Wanham: Grizzly Bear Prairie Museum, PO Box 68, Wanham AB T0H 3P0 – 403/694-3933 – Curator, Stanley Sather

Wetaskiwin: Alberta Central Railway Museum, RR#2, Wetaskiwin AB T9A 1W9 – 403/352-2257; Fax: 403/352-2257 – Operations Manager, W.G. Wilson; Curatorial Manager, Ellen Wilson – CPR rolling stock

Wetaskiwin: Canada's Aviation Hall of Fame, PO Box 6360, Wetaskiwin AB T9A 2G1 – 403/361-1351; Fax: 403/361-1239 – Curator, Jennifer Romanko

Wetaskiwin: Reynolds-Alberta Museum (RAM), PO Box 6360, Wetaskiwin AB T9A 2G1 – 403/361-1351; Fax: 403/361-1239; Email: ram@mcd.gov.ab.ca; 1-800-661-4726; URL: http://www.gov.ab.ca/~mcd/mhs/ram/ram.htm – Facility Manager, Bill Casey – Museum of transportation, agriculture & industry; home to Canada's Aviation Hall of Fame; open year round

Wetaskiwin: Reynolds Aviation Museum, c/o Reynolds Museum, 4118 - 57 St., Wetaskiwin AB T9A 2B6 – 403/352-5201; Fax: 403/352-4666 – President, Stanley G. Reynolds; Curator, Byron Reynolds – Antique & military aircraft & related articles

Wetaskiwin & District Museum, 5010 - 53 Ave., Wetaskiwin AB T9A 0Y7 – 403/352-0227; Fax: 403/352-0226 – Director, Sylvia Larson – Located in Wetaskiwin's original Electric Light Building (c1908); artifacts interpreting history & settlement of people in Wetaskiwin & surrounding area; curriculum-based school programs; guided tours upon request

Willingdon: Historic Village & Pioneer Museum, PO Box 102, Willingdon AB T0B 4R0 – 403/367-2445 – Curator, Nancy Hawrelak; President, Nick P. Hawrelak – Ukrainian & Romanian artifacts; open summer

## BRITISH COLUMBIA

### Museum of Anthropology

University of British Columbia, 6393 Marine Dr. NW, Vancouver BC V6T 1Z2
604/822-5087; Fax: 604/822-2974; Email: jenwebb@unixg.ubc.ca
Art & objects from around the world, with emphasis on First Nations cultures of the Northwest Coast; displayed in architect Arthur Erickson's award-winning building overlooking Howe Sound.
Director, Dr. Michael M. Ames

### Royal British Columbia Museum

PO Box 9815, Stn Prov Gvt, Victoria BC V8W 9W2
250/387-3701; Fax: 250/356-8197
URL: http://rbcm1.rbcm.gov.bc.ca/index.html
Founded in 1886, the RBCM specializes in the natural and human history of British Columbia.
Executive Director, Bill Barkley
Director, Curatorial Services, Grant Hughes
Director, Operations, Pauline Rafferty
Director, Public Programmes, Brent Cooke
Manager, Policy & Planning, Gayle Tomlinson
Chief, Marketing Services, Vacant
Chief, Publishing, Gerry Truscott
Chief, Exhibits, Doug Sage
Chief, Biological Collections, Jim Cosgrove
Chief, Conservation Services, Val Thorp
Chief, Anthropological Collections, Vacant
Manager, History, Jim Wardrop
Chief, Library Services, Frederike Verspoor
Manager, Natural History Research, Rob Cannings
Section Chief, Botany, Richard Hebda
Head, Vertebrate Zoology, Alex Peden
Head, Invertebrate Zoology, Phil Lambert
Manager, Anthropology, Alan Hoover
Head, History, Bob Griffin

### The Vancouver Museum

1100 Chestnut St., Vancouver BC V6J 3J9
604/736-4431; Fax: 604/736-5417
URL: http://www.vanmuseum.bc.ca
Established in 1894. Collections include Vancouver civic history, First Nations, Asian decorative arts. Special programming, gift shop; open year round.
Executive Director, Greg Evans

### Other Museums & Science Centres in British Columbia

Alert Bay: U'Mista Cultural Centre & Society, PO Box 253, Alert Bay BC V0N 1A0 – 250/974-5403; Fax: 250/974-5499; Email: umista@north.island.net; URL: http://www.swifty.com/umista/ – Administrator, Linda Manz – Kwakwaka'wakw museum contains potlach collection returned by the National Museum of Man & the Royal Ontario Museum

Armstrong-Spallumcheen Museum & Art Society, PO Box 308, Armstrong BC V0E 1B0 – 250/546-8318

Ashcroft Museum & Archives, PO Box 129, Ashcroft BC V0K 1A0 – 250/453-9232; Fax: 250/453-9664 – Curator, Helen Forster – Open 5 days a week, April - Nov.

Atlin Historical Museum (AHS), PO Box 111, Atlin BC V0W 1A0 – 250/651-7522; Fax: 250/651-7522 – President, Carrie Knickerbocker – Open daily May 15 - Sept. 15 & by appt.

Barkerville Historic Town, PO Box 19, Barkerville BC V0K 1B0 – 250/994-3332; Fax: 250/994-3435; Email: can-bht@immedia.ca – Manager, Jim Worton; Curator, William Quackenbush – Restored Cariboo Gold Rush town; Cottonwood House Historic Site; Blessing's Grave; McLeod Lake Post; Richfield Court House; open year round

Barriere: North Thompson Museum, PO Box 228, Barriere BC V0E 1E0 – 250/672-5583; Fax: 250/672-9311 – President, Heritage Society, Fran Wagstaff

Bella Coola Museum, PO Box 726, Bella Coola BC V0T 1C0 – 250/799-5767; Fax: 250/982-2328; Email: rmorton@belco.bc.ca

Black Creek: Miracle Beach Provincial Park Nature House, PO Box 71, Black Creek BC V9G 1K8 – 250/337-8181; Fax: 250/337-5720 – Manager, Heather Robinson – Open July - Aug., M-D, 10 am - 6 pm

Britannia Beach: British Columbia Museum of Mining, PO Box 188, Britannia Beach BC V0N 1J0 – 604/688-8735, 896-2233; Fax: 604/896-2260 – Curator/Manager, Sherry Elchuk; General Manager, Terry Johnson – Guided underground tours with live mining demonstrations; gift shop; gold recovery; mining house; open May - Oct. & by appt.

Burnaby Village Museum, 6501 Deer Lake Ave., Burnaby BC V5G 3T6 – 604/293-6500; Fax: 604/293-6525 – Manager, Cultural Services, Denis Nokony – Open daily Apr. - Sept. & Christmas

Burnaby: Simon Fraser University Museum of Archaeology & Ethnology, c/o Dept. of Archaeology, Simon Fraser University, Burnaby BC V5A 1S6 – 604/291-3325; Fax: 604/291-4727; URL: http://www.sfu.ca/archaeology – Curator, Barbara Winter – Major emphasis on the Pacific Northwest coast; open year round

Burns Lake: Lakes District Museum Society, PO Box 266, Burns Lake BC V0J 1E0 – 250/692-7450 – President, Ronnice Gelz

Cache Creek: Historic Hat Creek Ranch, PO Box 878, Cache Creek BC V0K 1H0 – 250/457-9722; Fax: 250/457-9311; Email: explore@hatcreekranch.com; URL: http://www.hatcreekranch.com – General Manager, Dan Meakes – Early ranching & transportation history; native interpretation program; trail, wagon & stage coach rides; gift shop; grounds open year round; visitor services open mid-May - mid-Oct.

Campbell River Optical Maritime Museum, #102, 250 Dogwood St., Campbell River BC V9W 2X9 – 250/287-2052 – Curator, Robert Somerville – Open year round

Campbell River: Museum at Campbell River (MCR), 470 Island Hwy., PO Box 70, Stn A, Campbell River BC V9W 4Z9 – 250/287-3103; Fax: 250/286-0109; Email: crm_chin@island.net; URL: http://www.island.net/~crm_chin – Director, James Tirrul-Jones – Exhibits include First Nations ceremonial masks & regalia, coastal logging history & settler development; Archives & Research Centre; gift shop

Castlegar & District Heritage Society, 400 - 13th Ave., Castlegar BC V1N 1G2 – 250/365-8215 – Zuckerberg Island Heritage Park; CPR Museum; BC Provincial Jail

Castlegar: Doukhobor Village Museum, PO Box 3081, Castlegar BC V1N 3H4 – 250/365-6622 – President, Elmer Verigan – Open daily May -Sept.

Chase: Shuswap Lake Provincial Park Nature House, RR#1, Chase BC V0E 1M0 – 250/955-2217 – Zone Manager, P.V. Rathbone

Chetwynd: Little Prairie Heritage Museum, PO Box 1777, Chetwynd BC V0C 1J0 – 250/788-3358 – President, Shirley Weeks; Sec.-Treas., Bobbie Larsen – Open July & Aug.

Chilliwack Museum, 45820 Spadina Ave., Chilliwack BC V2P 1T3 – 604/795-5210; Fax: 604/795-5291 – Director, Ron Denman – Open year round

Chilliwack Museum & Archives, 9291 Corbould St., Chilliwack BC V2P 4A6 – 604/795-9255; Fax: 604/795-5291 – Archivist, Kelly Stewart – Open year round

Clearbrook: Fraser Valley Antique Farm Machinery Association, PO Box 2234, Clearbrook BC V2T 3X8 – 604/859-4979 – President, Jake Woelk

Clearbrook: Mennonite Historical Society Museum of BC, PO Box 2032, Clearbrook BC V2T 3T8 – Curator, Anna Wiens

Clearwater: Yellowhead Museum, RR#1, PO Box 1778, Clearwater BC V0E 1N0 – 250/674-3660 – Curator, Ida Dekelver – Closed due to flooding

Clinton: South Cariboo Historical Museum Society, 1419 Cariboo Hwy., Clinton BC V0K 1K0 – 250/459-2442 – President, Loraine Huestis – Open daily May - Oct.

Courtenay & District Museum, c/o Cultural & Natural Heritage of the Comox Valley, 360 Cliffe Ave., Courtenay BC V9N 2H9 – 250/334-3611; Fax: 250/334-4277; Email: museum@mail.island.net; URL: http://www.courtenaymuseum.bc.ca – Curator, Deborah Griffiths – Includes archives; open year round

Cranbrook: Aasland Museum Taxidermy, 220 Kimberley Hwy. NE, Cranbrook BC V1C 4H4 – 250/426-3566 – Director, Odd Aasland

Cranbrook: Canadian Museum of Rail Travel - Cranbook, 1 Van Horne St., PO Box 400, Cranbrook BC V1C 4H9 – 250/489-3918; Fax: 250/489-5744; Email: camal@cyberlink.bc.ca; URL: http://www.cyberlink.bc.ca/~camal/index.html – Executive Director, Garry W. Anderson; Associate Director, Mark McDonald

Cranbrook: St. Eugene Mission Development Project, Site 15, SS#3, Comp. 14, Cranbrook BC V1C 6H3 – 250/489-2372; Fax: 250/489-5760 – Manager, Helder Ponte – Open June - Labour Day, Mon.-Fri.

Creston & District Museum, PO Box 1123, Creston BC V0B 1G0 – 250/428-9262; Fax: 250/428-9262 – President, Fred Ryckman – Open spring, summer, fall; in winter by appt.

Creston Valley Wildlife Management Area (CVWMA), PO Box 640, Creston BC V0B 1G0 – 250/428-3259; Fax: 250/428-3276 – Area Manager, Brian Stushnoff

Crofton: Old Crofton School Museum Society, PO Box 159, Crofton BC V0R 1R0 – 250/246-3804 – President, John Fransen

Cumberland Museum & Archives, 2680 Dunsmuir Ave., PO Box 258, Cumberland BC V0R 1S0 – 250/336-2445; Fax: 250/336-2321; Email: cma_chin@island.net – Curator, Barbara Lemky – Open year round

Dawson Creek Station Museum, 900 Alaska Ave., Dawson Creek BC V1G 4T6 – 250/782-9595; Fax: 250/782-9538 – President, Day Roberts – Open year round

Dawson Creek: Walter Wright Pioneer Village, c/o Dawson Creek Station Museum, 900 Alaska Ave., Dawson Creek BC V1G 4T6

Delta Museum & Archives, 4858 Delta St., Delta BC V4K 2T8 – 604/946-9322; Fax: 604/946-5791; Email: dmachin@van.hookup.net – Director/Curator, Donna Bryman; Archivist, Rita Wong

Denman Island Museum, PO Box 28, Denman Island BC V0R 1T0 – 250/335-0880 – Curator, Jean Brooks

Duncan: British Columbia Forest Museum, 2892 Drinkwater Rd., RR#4, Trans Canada Hwy, Duncan BC V9L 3W8 – 250/715-1113; Fax: 250/715-1170; Email: 103436.3520@compuserve.com – Manager, Michael Osborn

Duncan: Cowichan & Chemainus Valleys Ecomuseum, PO Box 491, Duncan BC V9L 4T8 – 250/746-1611; Fax: 250/748-3509 – Executive Director, Wilma Wood

Duncan: Cowichan Bay Maritime Centre, PO Box 787, Duncan BC V9L 3Y1 – 250/746-4955; Fax: 250/746-4955 – Executive Director, Cowichan Wooden Boat Society, Paul Mitchell; Curator, Eric Sandilands

Duncan: Cowichan Valley Museum, PO Box 1014, Duncan BC V9L 2W3 – 250/746-6612; Fax: 250/748-4818; Email: cvm@islandnet.com – Curator/Manager, Priscilla Davis – Includes archives; open year round

Enderby & District Museum Society, PO Box 367, Enderby BC V0E 1V0 – 250/838-7170; Fax: 250/838-0123 – Curator, Joan Cowan – Open year round

Fernie & District Historical Society Museum, PO Box 1527, Fernie BC V0B 1M0 – 250/423-7016 – Sec.-Treas., Ella A. Verkerk – Coal mining history museum; local history & early families research

Fort Langley: BC Farm Machinery & Agricultural Museum Association, PO Box 279, Fort Langley BC V1M 2R8 – 604/888-2273 – President, Tom Burton – Open daily mid-Mar. - Thanksgiving; in winter by appt.

Fort Langley National Historic Site/Lieu historique national Fort-Langley (FLNHS), PO Box 129, Fort Langley BC V1M 2R5 – 604/888-4424; Fax: 604/888-2577; Email: fort_langley@pch.gc.ca; URL: http://fas.sfu.ca/canheritage – Area Supt., Janet Weatherston; Chief, Heritage Communications, Terence McCalmont – Birthplace of British Columbia; partially reconstructed Hudson's Bay Co. trading post, c.1858; open year round (phone for seasonal detail)

Fort Langley: Langley Centennial Museum & National Exhibition Centre, PO Box 800, Fort Langley BC V1M 2S2 – 604/888-3922; Fax: 604/888-7291; Email: can-lconnec@immedia.ca – Arts & Heritage Supervisor, Sue Morhun – Open year round

Fort Nelson Heritage Museum, PO Box 716, Fort Nelson BC V0C 1R0 – 250/774-3536; Fax: 250/774-3536 – Curator, Marlin Brown – Artifacts related to the construction of the Alaska Highway; open mid-May - mid-Sept.

Fort St. James National Historic Site, PO Box 1148, Fort St. James BC V0J 1P0 – 250/996-7191; Fax: 250/966-8566 – Superintendent, Steve Langdon – Historic buildings from 1890s fur trading era; open mid-May - Aug.

Fort St. John-North Peace Museum, 9323 - 100 St., Fort St. John BC V1J 4N4 – 250/787-0430; Fax: 250/787-0405 – President, Larry Evans – Open year round

Fort Steele Heritage Town, Fort Steele BC V0B 1N0 – 489/489-3351; Fax: 489/489-2624; URL: http://www.MuseumsAssn.bc.ca/~bcma/museums/fsht/ – Regional Manager, Martin J.E. Ross – Restored 1890's mining boom town of the East Kootenay; open year round

Fraser Lake Museum, PO Box 430, Fraser Lake BC V0J 1S0 – 250/699-6257; Fax: 250/699-6469 – Municipal Clerk, Angus Davis – Open summer

Ganges: Salt Spring Island Farmer's Institute & Museum, PO Box 961, Ganges BC V0S 1E0 – 250/537-9567 – President, Perry Booth

Garibaldi Heights: Squamish Valley Museum, PO Box 166, Garibaldi Heights BC V0N 1T0 – 604/898-3273 – President, Doug Fenton – Open summer

Gibsons: Elphinstone Pioneer Museum & Society, PO Box 766, Gibsons BC V0N 1V0 – 604/886-8232; Email: elphinstone-pioneer_museum@sunshine.net – President, Lola Westell – The culture & history of the Sunshine Coast; resource library; archives;thousands of historical photographs

Gold Bridge: Bralorne Pioneer Museum, SS#1 - Bralorne, Gold Bridge BC V0K 1P0 – 250/238-2240, 2519 – Director, Gail Goudry – Open summer

Golden & District Museum, 1302 - 11 Ave., PO Box 992, Golden BC V0A 1H0 – 250/344-5169; Fax: 250/344-5169 – Curator, Colleen Torrence – Open Apr. - Sept.

Grand Forks: Boundary Museum Society, 7370 - 5th St., PO Box 817, Grand Forks BC V0H 1H0 – 250/442-3737 – Manager, Joan Miller – Open year round

Grand Forks: Chain Saw Museum, PO Box 1180, Grand Forks BC V0H 1H0 – 250/442-3518 – Director, Michael Acres

Grand Forks: Mountain View Doukhobor Museum, Hardy Mountain Rd., PO Box 1235, Grand Forks BC V0H 1H0 – 250/442-8855 – Open June-Sept.

Greenwood Museum, PO Box 399, Greenwood BC V0H 1J0 – 250/445-6355; Fax: 250/445-6166 – Chairman, Wally Duerksen – Old jail, supreme court

Groundbirch: Bruce Groner Museum, PO Box 149, Groundbirch BC V0C 1T0 – 250/780-2383; Fax: 250/780-2248 – Director, Olga Lineham – Open summer

Harrison Mills: Kilby Historic Store & Farm, 215 Kilby Rd., PO Box 55, Harrison Mills BC V0M 1L0 – 604/796-9576; Fax: 604/796-9592; Email: khsfchin@ntoaline.com – Site Manager, Jamea Lister – Open daily May - Oct., 10 am - 5 pm, & by appt.

Hazelton: 'Ksan Historical Village, PO Box 326, Hazelton BC V0J 1Y0 – 250/842-5544; Fax: 250/842-6533 – Executive Director, Laurel Mould – Replica Gitskan Indian Village; open year round

Hope Museum, 919 Water Ave., PO Box 26, Hope BC V0X 1L0 – 604/869-7322; Fax: 604/869-2160 – Manager, Inge Wilson – Open summer; off-season tours by request

Hope: John Weaver Sculpture Museum, PO Box 1723, Hope BC V0X 1L0 – 604/869-5312; Fax: 604/869-5117 – Curator, Henry Weaver

Hope: Remember When Doll Museum, RR#2, PO Box 6, Hope BC V0X 1L0 – 604/869-2923

Horsefly: Jack Lynn Memorial Museum, c/o Horsefly Historical Society, PO Box 148, Horsefly BC V0L 1L0 – 250/620-3304 – Curator, Harriette Erickson

Hudson's Hope Museum & Historical Society, PO Box 98, Hudson's Hope BC V0C 1V0 – 250/783-5735 – Curator, Lisa Hildebrandt; President, Gord McDonald – Museum is the Hudson's Bay Company store of 1942; archives; fossil collection; Aboriginal display; North West & Hudson's Bay Company artifacts; North West Mounted Police, trapping, coal mining, gold mining, pioneer, logging & World War memorabilia & photographic history of W.A.C. Bennett dam

Invermere: Windermere Valley Museum, PO Box 2315, Invermere BC V0A 1K0 – 250/342-9769 – Archivist, Jaryl McIsaac; Curator, Dorothy Blunden – Open June - Sept.

Kamloops Museum Association & Archives, 207 Seymour St., Kamloops BC V2C 2E7 – 250/828-3576; Fax: 250/828-3578 – Archivist/Curator, Elisabeth Duckworth – Open year round

Kamloops: Rocky Mountain Rangers Museum & Archives, 1221 McGill Rd., PO Box 3250, Kamloops BC V2C 6B8 – 604/327-7424; Fax: 604/374-1063 – W.C. Robertson

Kamloops: Secwepemc Cultural Education Society (SCES), 355 Yellowhead Hwy., Kamloops BC V2H 1H1 – 250/828-9801; Fax: 250/372-1127 – Museum Coordinator, Ken Favrholdt – Traditional culture of the Shuswap people; museum open year round

Kaslo City Hall, 413 - 4th St., PO Box 576, Kaslo BC V0G 1M0 – 250/353-2311; Fax: 250/353-7767 – Designated National Historic Site; open Mon. - Fri.

Kaslo: S.S. Moyie National Historic Site, PO Box 537, Kaslo BC V0G 1M0 – 250/353-2525; Fax: 250/353-2525 – President, Jack Morris; Manager, Ken Butler – Oldest intact passenger sternwheeler in the world; gift shop; operated by the Kootenay Lake Historical Society; open daily mid-May to mid-Sept.

Kelowna: BC Orchard Industry Museum, 1304 Ellis St., Kelowna BC V1Y 1Z8 – 250/763-0433; Fax: 250/763-5722; Email: kelowna.museum@cyberstore.ca – Director, U. Surtees; Curator, W. Wilson

Kelowna: Benvoulin Heritage Church, 2279 Benvoulin Rd., Kelowna BC V1W 2C8 – 250/762-6911 – Open daily in summer; in winter by appt.

Kelowna: Father Pandosy Mission, 3685 Benvoulin Rd., Kelowna BC V1Y 8R3 – 250/860-8369 – Caretaker/Manager, Judy Toms – Oblate Mission, 1859; open daily Easter - Thanksgiving

Kelowna: Guisachan House, 1060 Cameron Ave., PO Box 1055, Stn A, Kelowna BC V1Y 7P7 – 250/862-9368

Kelowna Centennial Museum & National Exhibition Centre, 470 Queensway, Kelowna BC V1Y 6S7 – 250/763-2417; Fax: 250/763-5722; Email: kelowna.museum@cyberstore.ca – Curator/

Director, Kelowna Museum Association, Ursula Surtees; Assistant Director, Dan Bruce; Assistant Curator, Wayne Wilson

Kelowna: Silver Lake Forestry Centre, #105 - 2417 Hwy. 97 North, Kelowna BC V1X 4J2 – 250/860-6410; Fax: 250/604/860-8856 – Regional Manager, Heather Rice – Logging artifacts

Keremeos: The Grist Mill at Keremeos, Upper Bench Rd., RR#1, Keremeos BC V0X 1N0 – 250/499-2888; Fax: 250/499-2434 – Designated British Columbia Heritage Site; open May - Oct.

Keremeos: South Similkameen Museum, PO Box 135, Keremeos BC V0X 1N0 – 250/499-5445 – Custodian, Doreen Smith – Open May - Aug.

Kimberley Heritage Musuem, PO Box 144, Kimberley BC V1A 2Y5 – 250/427-7510 – Curator, Marie Stang – Early Kimberley History; outdoor mining display; open year round; free

Kitimat Centennial Museum, 293 City Centre, Kitimat BC V8C 1T6 – 250/632-7022; Fax: 250/632-7429; Email: ishaw@kitimat.sno.net, kitmuse@kitimat.sno.net; URL: http://www.kitimat.sno.net/kitmuse – Curator, Louise Shaw – Natural history; homesteader & Haisla histories; Kemano-Kitimat Project history; temporary exhibitions; giftshop; open year round

Kitwanga: Meanskinisht Village Historical Association & Museum, PO Box 183, Kitwanga BC V0J 2A0 – 250/849-5732 – Director, Mary G. Dalen

Ladysmith: Black Nugget Museum, 12 Gatacre St., PO Box 1449, Ladysmith BC V0R 2E0 – 250/245-4846; Fax: 250/246-2441 – Curator, Kurt Guilbride – Open daily May - Sept.

Ladysmith Railway Historical Society & Museum, PO Box 777, Ladysmith BC V0R 2E0 – 250/245-4454 – President, Vincent J. Herkel

Lake Cowichan: Kaatza Station Museum & Archives, PO Box 135, Lake Cowichan BC V0R 2G0 – 250/749-6142; Fax: 250/749-3900 – Curator, Barbara Simkins – Open year round

Langley: Canadian Museum of Flight & Transportation (CMFT), #200, 5333 - 216th St., Langley BC V3A 4R1 – 604/532-0035; Fax: 604/532-0056 – Curator, George Proulx – Historic aircraft & other artifacts; research library & photo collections; open daily, year round

Lazo: Comox Airforce Museum (CAFM), CFB Comox, Lazo BC V0R 2K0 – 250/339-8162; Fax: 250/339-8162; Email: camuseum@mars.ark.com – Chairman, Major Joel Clarkston; Curator, Corky Hansen – History of CFB Comox & West coast aviation

Lillooet District Historical Society & Museum, PO Box 441, Lillooet BC V0K 1V0 – 250/256-4308; Fax: 250/256-4288 – Curator, Hilda Bryson – Open daily May - Oct.

Mackenzie Museum, PO Box 934, Mackenzie BC V0J 2C0 – 250/997-4323 – President, Christopher Johansen

Manning Park Visitor Centre, PO Box 3, Manning Park BC V0X 1H0 – 250/804-8836 – Area Supervisor, Jim Wiebe

Maple Ridge Museum & Archives, 22520 - 116th Ave., Maple Ridge BC V2X 0S4 – 604/463-5311; Email: vcp@istar.ca – Curator, Val Patenaude – Open year round

Maple Ridge: Thomas Haney House, 11012 - 224 St., Maple Ridge BC V2X 5Z7 – 604/463-1377 – Open Wed.-Sun, 1-4 pm

Mayne Island Agricultural Society & Museum, Mayne Island BC V0N 2J0 – 250/539-2283 – Director, M.W. Haggart

McBride: Valley Museum & Archives Society, PO Box 775, McBride BC V0J 2E0 – 250/569-2411 – Trustee, Matthew Wheeler – Displays within McBride & District Public Library

Merritt: Nicola Valley Museum & Archives, 2202 Jackson Ave., PO Box 1262, Merritt BC V1K 1B8 – 250/378-4145; Fax: 250/378-4145 – Office Manager, Bette Sulz – Craigmont, Judge Henry Castillou, ranching & mining displays; James Teit Gallery; open year round

Midway: Kettle River Museum, PO Box 149, Midway BC V0H 1M0 – 250/449-2614; Fax: 250/449-2614 – Secretary, T. Freeman; Treasurer, M. Johnson; Chairman, R. Roylance – CPR Station, Mile "O" Kettle Valley Railway

Mission: Fraser River Heritage Park, 7494 Mary St., PO Box 3341, Mission BC V2V 4J5 – 604/826-0277 – Former site of St. Mary's Mission & Indian Residential School; open daily Victoria Day - Labour Day

Mission District Historical Society & Museum, 33201 - 2nd Ave., Mission BC V2V 1J9 – 604/826-1011 – Curator, Kim Allen – Local & Native Indian history

Nakusp Museum, c/o Arrow Lakes Historical Society, PO Box 584, Nakusp BC V0G 1R0 – 250/265-3323 – Curator, Milton Parent – Open June - Sept.

Nanaimo: The Bastion, #211, 450 Stewart Ave., Nanaimo BC V9S 4C6 – 250/754-6195 – Director, W. Stannard – 1853 Hudson's Bay Co. log fortification

Nanaimo District Museum (NDM), 100 Cameron Rd., Nanaimo BC V9R 2X1 – 250/753-1821; Fax: 250/753-1777; Email: ndmuseum@island.net – Director/Curator, Debra Bodner – Open year round

Naramata Museum, S5, C41, RR#1, Naramata BC V0H 1N0 – 250/496-5567 – Director, Phil Rounds

Nelson Museum, 402 Anderson St., Nelson BC V1L 3Y3 – 250/352-9813; Fax: 250/352-5721; Email: alowrey@awinc.com – Director, Mrs. Shawn Lamb; President, Alan R. Ramsden – Small boats; archives - extensive local newspapers, Notre Dame University Collection; Doukhobor & Kooteniana Collection; local artists in Mildred Erb Gallery

New Denver: Sandon Museum, PO Box 52, New Denver BC V0G 1S0 – Fax: 250/358-2607 – President, R. Kenneth Williams – Historic site & silver mining history; open daily May 20 - Oct. 15; in winter by appt.

New Denver: Silvery Slocan Museum, 202 Main St., PO Box 301, New Denver BC V0G 1S0 – 250/358-2201; Fax: 250/358-7251 – Open daily June - Thanksgiving

New Westminster: Canadian Lacrosse Hall of Fame, 302 Royal Ave., New Westminster BC V3L 1H7 – 604/527-4640; Fax: 604/527-4641; Email: amiller@city.new-westminster.bc.ca – Curator, Archie W. Miller

New Westminster: Irving House Historic Centre & New Westminster Museum & Archives, 302 Royal Ave., New Westminster BC V3L 1H7 – 604/521-7656; Fax: 604/521-2079; Email: can-nwm@immedia.ca – Curator, Archie W. Miller – Open year round

New Westminster: Museum of the Royal Westminster Regiment Historical Society, The Armouries, 530 Queens Ave., New Westminster BC V3L 1K3 – 604/526-5116; Fax: 604/666-4042 – Curator, Lt.Col. B.V. Morgan, (Ret'd); Chair, Brig. H.E. Hamm, C.D., (Ret'd)

New Westminster: Samson V Maritime Museum, 302 Royal Ave., New Westminster BC V3L 1H7 – 604/527-4640; Fax: 604/527-4641; Email: vfrancis@city.new-westminster.bc.ca – Curator, Archie W. Miller – Moored on the Fraser River at the Westminster Quay Public Market

North Vancouver: Lynn Canyon Ecology Centre, 3663 Park Rd., North Vancouver BC V7J 3G3 – 604/981-3103; Fax: 604/981-3154 – Chief Naturalist, Kevin M. Bell

North Vancouver Museum & Archives, 209 West 4th St., North Vancouver BC V7M 1H8 – 604/987-5618; Fax: 604/987-5600; Email: nvmchin@jumppoint.com; URL: http://www.district.north-van.bc.ca/nvma – Director, Robin Inglis – Celebrates & preserves North Vancouver's social, industrial & cultural history; WWII shipbuilding; P.G.E. Railway; logging

Okanagan Falls: Bassett House Museum, 1145 Main St., Okanagan Falls BC V0H 1R0 – 250/497-5308; Fax: 250/497-5358 – Open May - Sept.

Okanagan Falls Heritage Place, c/o Okanagan Falls Heritage & Museum Society, PO Box 323, Okanagan Falls BC V0H 1R0 – 250/497-8734 – President, Paul Mallory

Oliver Heritage Society Museum & Archives, PO Box 847, Oliver BC V0H 1T0 – 250/498-4027; Fax: 250/498-4027 – Archivist, Laura Klassen – Open year round; Archives: M-R, 9 am -4 pm; Museum: May 15th - Sept.15, T-D, 10 am - 5 pm

Osoyoos Museum & Archives, PO Box 791, Osoyoos BC V0H 1V0 – 250/495-2582 – Treasurer, Dan H. Zuk – Wide range of displays, including dioramas & murals; open daily July - Sept.

Parksville: Craig Park & Museum, PO Box 1452, Parksville BC V0R 2S0 – 250/248-6966 – Museum Manager, M. Leffler; Archives, P. Cardwell – Open mid-May - Labour Day

Peachland Museum, 5890 Beach Ave., Peachland BC V0H 1X0 – 250/767-3441 – Open June - Aug.

Pemberton Museum, PO Box 267, Pemberton BC V0N 2L0 – 604/894-6274 – Curator, Margaret Fougberg

Penticton (R.N. Atkinson) Museum & Archives, 785 Main St., Penticton BC V2A 5E3 – 250/490-2451; Fax: 250/492-0440; Historic Ships: 604/492-0403 – Curator/Director, R.S. Manuel; Administrator, Marlene Trenholm – The historic CPR steamships S.S. Sicamous & S.S. Naramata are part of the museum; open Mon. - Sat. year round

Pitt Meadows Heritage & Museum Society, 19235 Davison Rd., Pitt Meadows BC V3Y 1A2 – 604/465-5238 – President, Sandra Caddo

Port Clements Museum, PO Box 417, Port Clements BC V0T 1R0 – 250/557-4576 – Historical Coordinator, Kathleen E. Dalzell – Logging, mining, marine & pioneering artifacts; open year round, reduced hours in winter

Port Alberni: Alberni Valley Museum, 4255 Wallace St., Port Alberni BC V9Y 3Y6 – 250/723-2181; Fax: 250/723-1035; Email: avmuseum@city.port-alberni.bc.ca – Director, Jean McIntosh; Education/Extension, Shelley Harding; Curator, Jacqueline Gijssen

Port Edward: North Pacific Cannery Museum, 1889 Skeena Dr., Port Edward BC V0V 1G0 – 250/628-3538 – Manager, Dr. Nancy Oliver – Open year round

Port Hardy Museum & Archives, PO Box 2126, Port Hardy BC V0N 2P0 – 250/949-8143 – Curator, William F. Reeve – Local museum; exhibits include natural history; archeology; settler history & local industries

Port Moody Station Museum, 2734 Murray St., Port Moody BC V3H 1X2 – 604/939-1648 – Director, Al Sholund; President, A. McNeil

Pouce Coupe Museum, 5006 - 49th Ave., PO Box 293, Pouce Coupe BC V0C 2C0 – 250/786-5555; Fax: 250/786-5257 – Open May 15 - Sept. 15

Powell River Historical Museum & Archives Association, PO Box 42, Powell River BC V8A 4Z5 – 604/485-2222; Email: museum@prcn.org – Coordinator, Teedie Gentine – Open June-Sept.

Prince George: Fraser-Fort George Regional Museum (FFGRM), PO Box 1779, Prince George BC V2L 4V7 – 250/562-1612; Fax: 250/562-6395; Email: ffgrmuseum@solutions-4u.com – Director, George Phillips – Natural history, transportation, town development, photo archives; McGregor Model Forest Info Centre; hands-on science & technology exhibit; open year round

Prince George Railway & Forest Industry Museum, PO Box 2408, Prince George BC V2N 2S6 – 250/563-7351; Fax: 250/561-1776 – President, Roy Smith

Prince Rupert: Kwinitsa Station Railway Museum, PO Box 669, Prince Rupert BC V8J 3S1 – 250/627-1915 (summer), 627-3207 (winter); Fax: 250/627-8009; Email: smarsden@citytel.net – Director, Susan Marsden – Railway & early Prince Rupert history; museum is a restored train station; open June - Sept.

Prince Rupert: Museum of Northern British Columbia, & Ruth Harvey Art Gallery, PO Box 669, Prince Rupert BC V8J 3S1 – 250/624-3207; Fax: 250/627-0999 – Curator, Elaine Moore – Northwest coast native artifacts; open year round

Prince Rupert Fire Museum, 200 - 1st Ave. West, Prince Rupert BC V8J 1A8 – 250/624-2211; 627-4475; Fax: 250/624-3407 – Director, Brian Hadland; President, Marvin Kristoff – Firefighting in Prince Rupert since 1908; restored 1925 fire engine; BC Police display; open year round

Princeton & District Museum & Archives Society, 167 Vermillion Ave., PO Box 281, Princeton BC V0X 1W0 – 250/295-7588 – Director, Margaret Stoneberg – Museum open mid-June - Aug.; archives open year round

Quathiaski Cove: Kwagiulth Museum & Cultural Centre, PO Box 8, Quathiaski Cove BC V0P 1N0 – 250/285-3733; Fax: 250/285-2400 – Director, Gina Robertson – Potlatch collection of Kwagiulth ceremonial artifacts

Queen Charlotte: Kitwanga Fort National Historic Site, c/o Gwaii Haanas National Park Reserve, PO Box 37, Queen Charlotte BC V0T 1S0 – 250/559-8818; Fax: 250/559-8366; Email: gwaiicom@island.net – Commemorates the culture of the Tsimshian people & their history; located near an important native trade route between the Skeena & Nass Rivers

Quesnel & District Museum & Archives (QDMA), 405 Barlow Ave., Quesnel BC V2J 2C3 – 250/992-9580; Fax: 250/992-9680; Email: can-qdm@immedia.ca; URL: http://www.sd28.bc.ca/museum/ – Curator, Ruth Stubbs – Open year round

Revelstoke Court House, 1100 - 2nd St. West, Revelstoke BC V0E 2S0 – 250/837-7636; Fax: 250/836-7640

Revelstoke Museum & Archives, PO Box 1908, Revelstoke BC V0E 2S0 – 250/837-3067, 2898; Fax: 250/837-4930 – Curator, Cathy English – Open year round

Revelstoke Railway Museum (RRM), 719 Track St. West, PO Box 3018, Revelstoke BC V0E 2S0 – 250/837-6060; Fax: 250/837-3732; Email: railway@junction.net; URL: http://www.railwaymuseum.com – Director, Martin Fransen

Revelstoke: Rogers Pass Centre, Glacier National Park, PO Box 350, Revelstoke BC V0E 2S0 – 250/837-6274; Fax: 250/837-9696 – Superintendent, Roger Beardmore – Open daily in summer; contact for winter hours

Revelstoke: Three Valley Gap, PO Box 860, Revelstoke BC V0E 2S0 – 250/837-2109 – Historic frontier ghost town

Richmond Museum, #180, 7700 Minoru Gate, Richmond BC V6Y 1R9 – 604/231-6440; Fax: 604/231-6423; Email: museum@city.richmond.bc.ca – Curator/Director, Lana Panko – Holdings include archaeology, ethnology, textiles, furnishings & items significant to agriculture, fishing, transportation, recreation, communications, business & technology; public & education programs; art gallery, library & archives also form part of the Centre

Richmond: Steveston Museum, 3811 Moncton St., Richmond BC V7E 3A0 – 604/271-6868; URL: http://www.netlink2000.com/villager – Chairman, E. Turner – Housed in a 1905 bank building

Richmond: The Trev Deeley Motorcycle Museum, 13500 Verdun Pl., Richmond BC V6V 1V4 – 604/273-5421; Fax: 604/273-2029 – Over 240 antique motorcycles

Rossland: BC Firefighters Museum, PO Box 789, Rossland BC V0G 1Y0 – 250/362-5514 (summer); 362-9531 (winter) – President, M. Pickering; Manager, K. Thatcher – Open June -Sept.

Rossland Historical Museum, PO Box 26, Rossland BC V0G 1Y0 – 250/362-7722; Fax: 250/362-5379 – Manager, Joyce Austin – Local pioneer & mining history; Western Canada Ski Hall of Fame; open daily mid-May - mid-Sept.; in winter by appt.

Saanichton Historical Artifacts Society (SHAS), 7321 Lochside Dr., RR#3, Saanichton BC V8M 1W4 – 250/652-5522; Fax: 250/652-5654; Email: shas@horizon.bc.ca – President, Archie Millar

Salmo Museum, 104 - 4th St., PO Box 69, Salmo BC V0G 1Z0 – 250/357-2200 – Curator, Gloria Currie

Salmon Arm Museum Heritage Association (SAM), PO Box 1642, Salmon Arm BC V1E 4P7 – 250/832-5243; Fax: 250/832-5291 – Curator, Deborah Chapman; Manager, Ted McTaggart – Open June - Sept.

Sayward: Link & Pin Logging & Pioneer Museum, Sayward BC V0P 1R0 – 250/287-9421 – Director, Frances Duncan – Open June-Sept.

Shawnigan Lake Historical Society Museum, PO Box 331, Shawnigan Lake BC V0R 2W0 – 250/748-5707; Fax: 250/748-2493 – President, Tom Paterson – Open daily July & Aug., weekends in winter

Sicamous: Eagle Valley Museum & Heritage Society, PO Box 944, Sicamous BC V0E 2V0 – 250/836-4635 – President, Adelaide Simpson

Sidney: A.N.A.F. Vets Sidney No. 302 Museum Unit, PO Box 2051, Sidney BC V8L 3S3 – 250/656-2051; Fax: 250/656-6410 – Director, Don Mann – Military artifacts

Sidney: BC Aviation Museum, Victoria Airport, 1910 Norseman Rd., Sidney BC V8L 5V5 – 250/655-3300

Sidney: James Island Museum, #3, 10084 - 3rd St., Sidney BC V8L 3B3 – 250/656-1868 – President, S. Beatrice Bond

Sidney Marine Mammal & Historical Museum, 9801 Seaport Pl., Sidney BC V8L 1Y2 – 250/656-1322; Fax: 250/655-4508; Email: can-smmhm@immedia.ca – Manager, Calvor Palmateer

Sidney: West Coast Museum of Flying, 10137 West Saanich Rd., Sidney BC V8L 5T6 – 250/656-9339; Fax: 250/655-3993

Skidegate: Queen Charlotte Islands Museum, PO Box 1373, Skidegate BC V0T 1S1 – 250/559-4643; Fax: 250/559-4662; Email: muse@island.net – Curator, Nathalie Macfarlane

Smithers: Adams Igloo Wildlife Museum, Site 9, Comp. 1, RR#1, Smithers BC V0J 2N0 – 250/847-3188

Smithers: Bulkley Valley Museum, PO Box 2615, Smithers BC V0J 2N0 – 250/847-5322; Fax: 250/847-3337 – Curator, Lillian Weedmark – Open year round

Sooke Region Museum, Art Gallery & Historic Moss Cottage, PO Box 774, Sooke BC V0S 1N0 – 250/642-6351; Fax: 250/642-7089 – Executive Director, Terry Malone – Open year round

Stewart Historical Museum, PO Box 402, Stewart BC V0T 1W0 – 250/636-2568; Fax: 250/636-2568 – President, Karin Hanhart

Summerland Museum & Heritage Society, 9521 Wharton St., PO Box 1491, Summerland BC V0H 1Z0 – 250/494-9395; Fax: 250/494-9326; Email: smchschin@vip.net – Curator, Ursula Richardson – Open year round

Surrey: Historic Stewart Farmhouse, 13723 Crescent Rd., Surrey BC V4A 2W3 – 604/574-5744; Fax: 604/574-7338 – Director, B.A. Sommer – 1894 historic farm; open mid-Feb. - mid-Dec.

Surrey Museum & Archives, 6022 - 176 St., Surrey BC V3S 4E7 – 604/543-3456; Fax: 604/543-3457 – Manager, Heritage Services, Beverly Sommer – Community history; open Tues. - Sat. year round

Terrace Heritage Park Museum, PO Box 246, Terrace BC V8G 4A6 – 250/635-2508 – President, Mamie Kerby – Open April - Sept. & by appt.

Tofino: West Coast Maritime Museum, PO Box 249, Tofino BC V0R 2Z0 – 250/725-3346 – Curator, Olivia Mal

Trail Museum, 1051 Victoria St., PO Box 405, Trail BC V1R 4L7 – 250/364-1262; Fax: 250/364-0830 – Curator, Jamie Forbes – Open June - Aug.

Valemount & Area Museum & Archives, PO Box 850, Valemount BC V0E 2Z0 – 250/566-4177, 4336; Fax: 250/566-8411; Email: museum@cancom.net – Open May - Oct.; off-season by appt.

Vancouver: 15th Field Artillery Regiment Museum & Archives Society, 2025 - 11th Ave. West, Vancouver BC V6J 2C7 – 604/666-4370; Fax: 604/666-4083 – Director, Victor Stevenson

Vancouver: BC Medical Association Archives & Museum, 1665 Broadway West, Vancouver BC V6J 1X1 – 604/736-5551 – C.W. Fraser

Vancouver: BC Sugar Museum, 123 Rogers St., PO Box 2150, Vancouver BC V6B 3V2 – 604/253-1131; Fax: 604/253-2517 – Museum Co-ordinator, Joanne Denton – Open year round; closed weekends & holidays

Vancouver: Biblical Museum of Canada, 5800 University Blvd., PO Box 27090, Stn Collingwood, Vancouver BC V5R 6A8 – 604/432-6122; Fax: 604/435-8181 – Curator, Rev. Frederick W. Metzger

Vancouver: British Columbia Museum of Medicine, Academy of Medicine Bldg., 1807 - 10 Ave. West, Vancouver BC V6J 2A9 – Director, Dr. C. McDonnel

Vancouver: British Columbia Regiment Museum & Society, 620 Beatty St., Vancouver BC V6B 2L9 – 604/666-4368 – Curator, W.D. Edgar

Vancouver: British Columbia Sports Hall of Fame & Museum, BC Place Stadium, 777 Pacific Blvd. South, Vancouver BC V6B 4Y8 – 604/687-5520; Fax: 604/687-5510 – General Manager, Don Taylor; Curator, Bob Graham

Vancouver: Canadian Craft Museum (CCM), 639 Hornby St., Vancouver BC V6C 2G3 – 604/687-8266; Fax: 604/684-7174 – Administrative Director, Giovanni Festa – Dedicated to Canadian & international craft, craftsmanship & design, both contemporary & historical

Vancouver: Cowan Vertebrate Museum, Dept. of Zoology, University of British Columbia, 6270 University Blvd., Vancouver BC V6T 2A9 – 604/228-4665 – Director, G. Scudder

Vancouver: M.Y. Williams Geological Museum, Dept. of Geological Sciences, University of British Columbia, 6339 Stores Rd., Vancouver BC V6T 1Z4 – 604/228-5586; Fax: 604/228-6088 – Curator, Joe Nagel – Includes mounted dinosaur

Vancouver: Old Hastings Mill Store Museum, 1575 Alma Rd., Vancouver BC V6R 3P3 – 604/228-1213

Vancouver: Pacific Space Centre (PSC), 1100 Chestnut St., Vancouver BC V6J 3J9 – 604/738-7827; Fax: 604/736-5665; Email: ddodge@pacific-space-centre.bc.ca; URL: http://pacific-space-centre.bc.ca – Managing Director, John Dickenson; Programme Director, Paul Deans

Vancouver: The P.G.E. Station, c/o North Vancouver Museum, 209 -4th St. West, Vancouver BC V7M 1H8 – 604/987-5618; Fax: 604/987-5609; Email: nvmchin@jumppoint.com; URL: http://www.district.north-van.bc.ca/nvmd – Director, Robin Inglis – Recently restored to present community displays & the history of Pacific Great Eastern Railway

Vancouver: Science World British Columbia, 1455 Quebec St., Vancouver BC V6A 3Z7 – 604/268-6363; 443-7440 (Admin.); Fax: 604/682-2923; Email: mcotic@scienceworld.bc.ca; URL: http://www.scienceworld.bc.ca – Director, Sales & Marketing, Ray Lord; Director, Development,

Marion Northcott; Director, Community Extensions, Patti Leigh; Director, Operations, Bill Economos; Director, Guest Services, Maryann Rankin

Vancouver: Seaforth Highlanders Regimental Museum, Seaforth Armoury, 1650 Burrard St., Vancouver BC V6J 3G4 – 604/738-9510

Vancouver: Spencer Entomological Museum (SEM), Dept. of Zoology, University of British Columbia, 6270 University Blvd., Vancouver BC V6T 1Z4 – 604/822-3379; Fax: 604/822-2416; Email: needham@zoology.ubc.ca; URL: http://www.insecta.com – Curator, K. Needham; Director, G.G.E. Scudder – Largest collection of B.C. insects in the world containing 600,000 specimens

Vancouver: The Vancouver Maritime Museum Society (VMM), 1905 Ogden Ave., Vancouver BC V6J 1A3 – 604/257-8300; Fax: 604/737-2621; URL: http://www.vmm.bc.ca – Executive Director, James P. Delgado – Includes National Historic Site St. Roch, RCMP Schooner

Vancouver Police Historical Society & Centennial Museum, 240 Cordova St. East, Vancouver BC V6A 1L3 – 604/665-3346; Fax: 604/665-5078; URL: http://www.city.vancouver.bc.ca/police/museum/ – Curator, Eudon Rhymer

Vanderhoof Community Museum, c/o Nechako Valley Historical Society, PO Box 1515, Vanderhoof BC V0J 3A0 – 250/567-2991; Fax: 250/567-2991 – Curator, Michael Fryatt; President, Doris Stewart – Community museum, 1920 café & nine-building Heritage Village; seasonal

Vernon: Greater Vernon Museum & Archives, 3009 - 32 Ave., Vernon BC V1T 2L8 – 250/542-3142; Fax: 250/542-5358; Email: vm-chin@junction.net – Curator, Ron Candy – Open year round

Vernon: O'Keefe Ranch & Interior Heritage Society, PO Box 955, Vernon BC V1T 6M8 – 250/542-7868; Email: can-orihs@immedia.ca – Manager/Curator, Ken Mather; Visitor Services Manager, Dave Sayer – Open May - Thanksgiving

Victoria: The Canadian Scottish Regiment (Princess Mary's) Regimental Museum, Bay Street Armoury, 715 Bay St., Victoria BC V8T 1R1 – 250/363-8753; Fax: 250/363-3593 – Director, Geoffrey D. Curry; Director, John R. Wigmore – Items of historical significance to the regiment; located in the Bay Street Armoury, a National Historic Site built in 1915

Victoria: Canadiana Costume Museum & Archives of BC, 2818 Aldwynd Rd., Victoria BC V9B 3S7 – 250/478-7564 – President, Iris Emerson; Secretary, Gloria Simmons – Storage facilities for preservation purposes; reference library by appt.

Victoria: Carr House, c/o Ministry of Small Business, Tourism & Culture, 207 Government St., Victoria BC V8V 2K8 – 250/383-5843; Fax: 250/383-5843; Email: ch.chin@island.net – Curator, Jan Ross – Birthplace of Emily Carr

Victoria: CFB Esquimalt Naval Museum & Military Museum, PO Box 17000, Stn Station Forces, Victoria BC V9A 7N2 – 250/363-4312, 5655; Fax: 250/363-4252 – Curator, Richard Dawe; Asst. Curator, D. Towell – Open year round Mon-Fri, 10-3:30

Victoria: The Craigdarroch Castle Historical Museum Society, 1050 Joan Cres., Victoria BC V8S 3L5 – 250/592-5323; Fax: 250/592-1099 – Executive Director, Bruce W. Davies

Victoria: Craigflower Heritage Site, 110 Island Hwy., Victoria BC V9B 1E9 – 250/387-3067 – Director, Colin K. Campbell

Victoria: Fort Rood Hill & Fisgard Lighthouse National Historic Sites, 501 Belmont Rd., Victoria BC V9C 1B5 – 250/380-4662 – Turn of the century coastal defence gun batteries & first permanent lighthouse on Canada's west coast; open daily

Victoria: Goldstream Region Museum Society, #2, 697 Goldstream Ave., Victoria BC V9B 2X2 – 250/474-6113 – President, Phyllis Griffiths

Victoria: Helmcken House Pioneer Doctor's Residence, 638 Elliott St., Victoria BC V8W 1W1 – 250/387-4697; Fax: 250/387-5129 – Manager, John D. Adams – Open June - Sept.

Victoria: Maritime Museum of British Columbia, 28 Bastion Sq., Victoria BC V8W 1H9 – 250/385-4222; Fax: 250/382-2869; Email: mmbc@vicnet.com; URL: http://www.vicnet.net/~mmbc/ – Director, Guy Mathias

Victoria: Metchosin School Museum, 4475 Happy Valley Rd., Victoria BC V9C 4B1 – 250/478-3451 – Curator, Ron Bradley

Victoria: Point Ellice House Museum, 2616 Pleasant St., Victoria BC V8T 4V3 – 250/385-3837 – Curator, Michael Zarb – Open June - Sept.

Victoria: Royal London Wax Museum, 470 Belleville St., Victoria BC V8V 1W9 – 250/388-4461; Fax: 250/388-4493; Email: khl@pinc.com; URL: http://www.waxworld.com – President, Dr. Arne H. Lane; Managing Director, Ken H. Lane – Open daily

Wells Museum (WHS), Wells Historical Society, PO Box 244, Wells BC V0K 2R0 – 250/994-3422 – Curator, Judy Campbell – Open May - Labour Day

White Rock Museum/Archives, 15322 Buena Vista Ave., White Rock BC V4B 1Y6 – Curator, Lorraine M. Ellenwood

Williams Lake Museum, RR#2, Williams Lake BC V2G 2C8 – 250/392-5573; Fax: 250/392-7404 – President, June Eckert

Yale: Historic Yale Museum, 31179 Douglas St., PO Box 74, Yale BC V0K 2S0 – 604/863-2324 – President, Verna Shilson

Ymir Arts & Museum Society, PO Box 65, Ymir BC V0G 2K0 – 250/357-9600 – Chairperson, Doug Blake – Heritage 2-room schoolhouse with small historical collection (photos & artifacts of Ymir); monthly coffee houses featuring local musicians.

## MANITOBA

### Manitoba Museum of Man & Nature/Musée de l'homme et de la nature du Manitoba

190 Rupert Ave., Winnipeg MB R3B 0N2
204/956-2830; Fax: 204/942-3679; Email: info@museummannature.mb.ca; Info Line: 204/943-3139
URL: http://www.mbnet.mb.ca/ManitobaMuseum

Seven permanent galleries & Alloway Hall which houses temporary & travelling exhibitions. Permanent galleries are: Orientation (in which the main theme of the Museum is explained), Earth History, Grasslands, Urban (a section of Winnipeg, reconstructed as it might have been in 1920), Nonsuch (a replica of the 17th-century Ketch), Arctic-Subarctic & Boreal Forest. The Planetarium provides educational & entertaining programs for the general public & school groups in the 287-seat Star Theatre; feature presentations touch all aspects of astronomy, science fact/science fiction, as well as present day space programs & technology. The Science Centre is a hands-on education centre dealing with the ways in which the universe is perceived by the five senses. The Education & Programs Departments provide special activities for schools & other groups. Live demonstrations & performances; lectures.

Director, Programs, G. Wurtak
Director, Operations, T. Nickle
Chief, Marketing, K. Roos Pavlik
Producer, Planetarium, E. Barker
Manager, Joyce Moroz

### Other Museums & Science Centres in Manitoba

Arrow River: Clegg's Museum of Horse-Drawn Vehicles, Arrow River MB R0M 2H0 – 204/562-3648 – Director, R.E. Clegg

Ashern Pioneer Museum, PO Box 642, Ashern MB R0C 0E0 – 204/768-3147 – Chairperson, Emma Geisler – Open July & Aug.

Austin: Manitoba Agricultural Museum, PO Box 10, Austin MB R0H 0C0 – 204/637-2354; Fax: 204/637-2395; Email: info@ag-museum.mb.ca; URL: http://www.ag-museum.mb.ca – Administrator, Terry Farley – Pioneer artifacts; homesteaders' village, annual Thresherman's Reunion & Stampede; Open Victoria Day - Oct. 1

Beausejour: Pioneer Village Museum, PO Box 310, Beausejour MB R0E 0C0 – 204/268-3048 – President, Peter H. Kozyra – Open July & Aug.

Belmont & District Museum, PO Box 69, Belmont MB R0K 0C0 – 204/537-2252, 2430

Belmont: Evergreen Firearms Museum Inc., Belmont MB R0K 0C0 – 204/537-2647 – Military & sporting firearms; open by appt.

Birtle: Birdtail Country Museum, PO Box 508, Birtle MB R0M 0C0 – 204/842-3363, 5219 – President, G. Huberdeau – Open May 23 - Sept. & by appt.

Boissevain: Beckoning Hills Museum Inc., 425 Mill Rd. South, PO Box 389, Boissevain MB R0K 0E0 – 204/534-6544 – President, Ken Patterson; Secretary, E. Brake – Pioneer & native artifacts; Open end of May - Sept.

Boissevain: Moncur Gallery, Civic Centre, Boissevain MB R0K 0E0 – 204/534-2433, 6478; Fax: 204/534-6085; Email: gmay@mail.techplus.com; URL: http://www.techplus.com/boissevain/moncur/galleryhtm – Sec.-Treas., Gerald May – Open Mon. - Sat.; Sun. by appt.

Brandon: 26th Field Artillery Regiment Museum, 116 Victoria Ave., Brandon MB R7A 1B2 – 204/728-2559 – Mr. Ross – Open Sun.

Brandon: B.J. Hales Museum of Natural History, McMaster Hall Concourse, Brandon University, #270 - 18th St., Brandon MB R7A 6A9 – 204/727-7307; Fax: 204/728-7346 – Curator, Maureen Rodgers

Brandon Mental Health Centre Museum & Archives, PO Box 420, Brandon MB R7A 5Z5 – 204/726-2725; Fax: 204/726-4157 – Curator, Jessie Little

Brandon: Chapman Museum, RR#2, PO Box 43, Brandon MB R7A 5Y2 – 204/728-7396 – Director, A.T. Chapman – 16 historic buildings containing artifacts of the past

Brandon: Commonwealth Air Training Plan Museum, Group 520, PO Box 3, RR#5, Brandon MB R7A 5Y5 – 204/727-2444 – President, Archie Londry

Brandon: Daly House Museum & Steve Magnacca Research Centre, 122 - 18 St., Brandon MB R7A 5A4 – 204/727-1722 – Curator, Sandra Head – Period home of the 1890s; 1903 grocery store; 1882 council chambers; open daily in the summer; Wed. to Sun. winter

Brandon: Manitoba Amateur Radio Museum Inc. (MARM), 25 Queens Cres., Brandon MB R7B 1G1 – 204/728-2463; Fax: 204/728-2463; Email: dsnydal@mb.sympatico.ca; URL: http://www.mbnet.mb.ca/~donahue/austin.html – Curator, Dave Snydal – Canada's only amateur radio museum

Carberry Plains Museum, 520 - 4 Ave., PO Box 130, Carberry MB R0K 0H0 – 204/834-2195, 3295 – Chairman, Marjorie Baron – Open mid-June - mid-Sept.

Carberry: The Seton Centre, 116 Main St., PO Box 508, Carberry MB R0K 0H0 – 204/834-2059 – Materials by & about Ernest Thompson Seton; open June - Thanksgiving

Carberry: Spruce Woods Provincial Heritage Park, Visitor Services Information Centre & Museum, PO Box 900, Carberry MB R0K 0H0 – 204/827-2543; Fax: 204/834-2614 – Interpreter, Lisa Mandziak – Northwest Co. fur-trading artifacts

Carman: Dufferin Historical Museum, PO Box 426, Carman MB R0G 0J0 – Chairman, L.G. Budd – Open Victoria Day - Labour Day

Carman: Heaman's Antique Autorama, Hwy. 3, PO Box 105, Carman MB R0G 0J0 – 204/745-2981

Cartwright: Badger Creek Museum, PO Box 9, Cartwright MB R0K 0L0 – 204/529-2363; Fax: 204/529-2288 – Colleen Mullin

Churchill: Eskimo Museum, PO Box 10, Churchill MB R0B 0E0 – 204/675-2030; Fax: 204/675-2140 – Curator, Lorraine Brandson – Open Mon. - Sat.

Churchill: Parks Canada, Wapusk National Park and Manitoba North National Historic Sites, PO Box 127, Churchill MB R0B 0E0 – 204/675-8863; Fax: 204/675-8863; Email: wapusk_np@pch.gc.ca – Area Superintendent, Pam Doyle

Churchill: Prince of Wales Fort & Cape Merry National Historic Site, PO Box 127, Churchill MB R0B 0E0 – 204/675-8863

Crystal City Community Museum, 218 Broadway, Crystal City MB R0K 0N0 – 204/873-2293 – Fully operational print shop started by Thomas Greenway (7th premier of Manitoba) in 1881

Darlingford School Heritage Museum, Darlingford MB R0G 0L0 – 204/246-2026, 2137

Dauphin: Cross of Freedom Historical Site & Museum, 121 - 7 Ave. SE, Dauphin MB R7N 2E3 – 204/638-9641, 9607; Fax: 204/638-5424 – President, John Slobodzian – The history & culture of Ukrainian pioneers

Dauphin: Fort Dauphin Museum, 140 Jackson Ave., PO Box 181, Dauphin MB R7N 2V1 – 204/638-6630 – Sec.-Treas., Bob MacKenzie; Administrator, Gladys Fendick; President, Ray Storozinski – Replica of Northwest Co. Trading Post, plus numerous artifacts & an archeaological lab; open mid-May - mid-Sept. & by appt.

Dufresne: Aunt Margaret's Museum of Childhood Inc., Trans-Canada Hwy., Dufresne MB R0A 0J0 – 204/422-8426

Dugald: Cook's Creek Heritage Museum, Grp. 22, Box 6, RR#2, Dugald MB R0E 0N0 – 204/853-2166; Fax: 204/444-4448 – Curator, Erazm Kowalski – Open Daily May - Oct. & by appt.

Dugald Costume Museum & Pioneer Home, PO Box 38, Dugald MB R0E 0K0 – 204/853-2166; Fax: 204/853-2077 – Curator, Monique Brandt; Development, Diana Hart; Education Director, Glenda Peterson; Administrator, Kim Reid – Over 30,000 artifacts spanning 400 years; collection of costume, textiles & related accessories

Eddystone: Village Site Museum, Eddystone MB R0L 0S0 – 204/448-2040

Elkhorn: Manitoba Automobile Museum Foundation, PO Box 477, Elkhorn MB R0M 0N0 – 204/845-2604 – Sec.-Treas., Garth Mitchell – 70 restored antique automobiles 1908-1930, pioneer & Indian artifacts; open May - Sept.

Erickson: The Parsonage & Nedrob School, Erickson MB R0J 0P0 – 204/636-2431

Eriksdale Museum, PO Box 71, Eriksdale MB R0C 0W0 – 204/739-2621, 5273 – Chair, Donna Smith; Secretary, Eileen McLelland – Open mid-May - Sept., 1:30 pm - 4:30 pm, excluding Thurs. & Sun.

Flin Flon Museum, PO Box 100, Flin Flon MB R8A 1M6 – 204/687-7511; Fax: 204/687-5133 – Director, Brenda Russell – Mining, transportation & culture; open daily May - mid-Sept.

Gardenton: Ukrainian Museum, Park & Village, Gardenton MB R0A 0M0 – 204/425-3501 – President, Linda Shewchuk – Clothing, icons & many articles from the early settlers; an exhibit of churches & photos of early pioneer life

Gimli Historical Museum, PO Box 1197, Gimli MB R0C 1B0 – 204/642-5317

Gladstone & District Museum, PO Box 651, Gladstone MB R0J 0T0 – 204/385-2551 – President, O.E. Whitten

Grandview: The Watson Crossley Community Museum, PO Box 396, Grandview MB R0L 0Y0 – 204/546-2661 – President, Gerald Morran – Historical, agricultural & antique cars; open daily mid-June - Labour Day

Hamiota Pioneer Club Museum, PO Box 577, Hamiota MB R0M 0T0 – 204/764-2222, 2434 – President, John L. Rankin – Open Sundays in July & Aug. & by appt.

Hartney: Hart-Cam Museum, PO Box 323, Hartney MB R0M 0X0

Inglis: St. Elie 1908 Pioneer Church Museum, Inglis MB R0J 0X0 – 204/564-2228; Fax: 204/564-2643 – President, Barry Sawchuk – Designated provincial historic site

Killarney: J.A. Victor David Municipal Museum, 414 Williams Ave., PO Box 584, Killarney MB R0K 1G0 – 204/523-7325 – Director, Gwen Powell

La Broquerie: Musée Saint Joachim, PO Box 66, La Broquerie MB R0A 0W0 – 204/424-5232 – Directrice, Laura Gallant

La Rivière: Archibald Historical Museum, PO Box 97, La Rivière MB R0G 1A0 – 204/242-2825, 2554 – President, R.K. Wallcraft – 1878 log house furnished as it was during Nellie McClung's residency; open mid-May - Labour Day or beyond by appt

Ladywood: Atelier Ladywood Museum, RR#3, PO Box 14, Ladywood MB R0E 0C0 – 204/265-3226 – Director, Lenard Anthony

Lundar Museum Society, PO Box 265, Lundar MB R0C 1Y0 – 204/762-5689 – Director, Sigfus Johannson – Open mid-June - Sept.

Melita: Antler River Historical Society Museum, PO Box 155, Melita MB R0M 1L0 – 204/522-8289 – President, J. McRae – Open June 15 - Sept. 15

Miami Museum, PO Box 38, Miami MB R0G 1H0 – 204/435-2245 – President, John Andrews

Miniota Municipal Museum Inc., PO Box 189, Miniota MB R0M 1M0 – 204/567-3675, 3789 – Chairman, Vernon Rollo – Open May - Oct.

Minnedosa & District Co-operative Museum, 49 - 2 Ave. NW, PO Box 1453, Minnedosa MB R0J 1E0 – 204/867-3444; Fax: 204/867-5171 – President, Margret Shorrock – Open July 1 - Labour Day

Moosehorn Heritage Museum Inc., PO Box 28, Moosehorn MB R0C 2E0 – 204/768-2087 – President, Lois Metner, 204/768-2087; Secretary, Marlene Metner, 204/768-2052 – May 15 - Aug. 30 & by appt.

Morden & District Museum of Palaeontology & Pioneer Artifacts, c/o Morden Recreation Centre, 111-B Gilmore Ave., PO Box 1529, Morden MB R6M 1N9 – 204/822-3406 – Director, John Wan – Open seven days a week from 1 p.m. to 5 p.m.

Morris & District Centennial Museum Inc., PO Box 344, Morris MB R0G 1K0 – 204/746-2528 – Director, W.M. Schellenberg

Neepawa: Beautiful Plains Museum, PO Box 1732, Neepawa MB R0J 1H0 – 204/476-3896 – President, Lorna Smith – Open daily in summer

Neepawa: The Margaret Laurence Home, 312 First Ave., PO Box 2099, Neepawa MB R0J 1H0 – 204/476-3612

Notre Dame de Lourdes: Museum Dom Benoît & Chapel Ste. Thérèse, Notre Dame de Lourdes MB R0G 1M0 – 204/248-2372, 2105 – 1,000 artifacts on pioneer life; open daily May 15 - Oct. 15

Pilot Mound: Marringhurst Pioneer Park Museum, RR#2, Pilot Mound MB R0G 1P0 – 204/825-2697 – Jeannie Neustaedter

Pilot Mound Centennial Museum, Centennial Bldg., Broadway St., Pilot Mound MB R0G 1P0

Plum Coulee & District Museum, PO Box 36, Plum Coulee MB R0G 1R0 – 204/829-3419; Fax: 204/829-3436 – Director, Kim Porte – Mennonite pioneer artifacts

Portage la Prairie: The Fort-La-Reine Museum & Pioneer Village, PO Box 744, Portage la Prairie MB R1N 3C2 – 204/857-3259 – Manager, Vic P. Edwards – Twenty-three different venues including main museum building, Fort la Reine & the William Van Horne Railway business car

Rapid City Museum, PO Box 271, Rapid City MB R0K 1W0 – 204/826-2597 – Curator, J.W. Northam – Open July & Aug.

Reston & District Museum, PO Box 292, Reston MB R0M 1X0 – 204/877-3960 – Curator, Art Smith – Open July - Aug.

Rivers: The Clack Bros. Museum, Rivers MB R0K 1X0 – Open May - Nov.

Riverton: Hecla Island Heritage Home Museum, c/o Hecla Provincial Park, PO Box 70, Riverton MB R0C 2R0 – 204/279-2056, 378-2945 – Icelandic homestead

Roblin: Keystone Pioneer Museum, Hwy. 5, PO Box 10, Roblin MB R0L 1P0 – 204/937-2935 – President, Art McIntyre

Sainte-Anne des Chênes: Musée Pointe des Chênes, #70, 210, Villa Youville inc., Sainte-Anne des Chênes MB R5H 1C9 – 204/422-5624; Fax: 204/422-5842 – Responsable, Florentine Beriault

Sandy Lake: Ukrainian Cultural Heritage Museum, Sandy Lake MB R0J 1X0 – 204/585-2168, 2636 – 1899 Ukrainian settlement

Selkirk: Kennedy House, 1 Keystone Dr., Selkirk MB R1A 2H5 – 204/334-2498 (Summer); 204/785-5080 (Off-Season) – 19th-century home owned by Hudson Bay Co. fur trader & Arctic explorer

Selkirk: Lower Fort Garry National Historic Site, Group 343, RR#3, PO Box 37, Selkirk MB R1A 2A8 – 204/785-6050; Fax: 204/482-5887; Visitor Info: 204/949-3600 – Site Coordinator, Bob Andrews; Elena Vandale – 1830s Hudson's Bay Co.; open mid-May - Labour Day

Selkirk: Marine Museum of Manitoba Inc., PO Box 7, Selkirk MB R1A 2B1 – 204/482-7761; Fax: 204/785-2452 – Chairperson, Ted Francis – Open May - Sept.

Selkirk: St. Andrews' Rectory National Historic Park, Group 343, RR#3, PO Box 37, Selkirk MB R1A 2A8 – 204/949-3600; Fax: 204/482-5887 – Open daily mid-May - Labour Day & weekends in Sept.

Seven Sisters Falls: Nutimik Lake Museum, c/o Whiteshell Provincial Park, Seven Sisters Falls MB R0E 1Y0 – 204/348-2203

Seven Sisters Falls: Whiteshell Natural History Museum, c/o Dept. of Natural Resources, Seven Sisters Falls MB R0E 1Y0 – 204/348-2846; Fax: 204/348-7141 – Park Manager, Mark Clarke

Shilo: Royal Canadian Artillery Museum, CFB Shilo, Shilo MB R0K 2A0 – 204/765-3534; Fax: 204/765-3095 – Curator, J.A. Eskritt – Two permanent galleries & one hall; research library; archives; war diary rooms; outdoor display area; over 150 major pieces of equipment; over 10,000 military articles; open year round

Shoal Lake: Police & Pioneer Museum, PO Box 315, Shoal Lake MB R0J 1Z0 – 1870s & 1880s NWMP & pioneer artifacts; open by appt.

Snowflake: Star Mound School Museum Park, Snowflake MB R0G 2K0 – 204/876-4749 – President, Alvin Findlay – One-room country school c. 1886

Souris: Hillcrest Museum, PO Box 1287, Souris MB R0K 2C0 – 204/483-2008, 3245 – President, Anne Rose – Includes agricultural museum & CPR caboose; open May - Sept.

St-Georges: Musée St-Georges, CP 171, St-Georges MB R0E 1V0 – 204/367-8801, 2927 – Conservateur, Jean Dupont – Open May - Sept.

St-Joseph: Musée St-Joseph Museum Inc., PO Box 47, St-Joseph MB R0G 2C0 – 204/737-2241 – Président, Jean-Louis Perron – Domestic & agricultural artifacts; open May 15 - Sept. 15

St-Malo: Musée Le Pionnier, St-Malo MB R0A 1T0 – 204/347-5767 – Director, Maurice Comeault

St-Pierre-Jolys: Musée de St-Pierre-Jolys Inc., 432, rue Joubert, CP 321, St-Pierre-Jolys MB R0A 1V0 – 204/433-7226; Fax: 204/433-7181 – President, Gerald Fontaine – Religious & early settlement artifacts; tea room; open July & Aug. & by appt.

St. Claude Museum, PO Box 131, St. Claude MB R0G 1Z0 – 204/379-2405 – President, Henri Bellec – 1,500 artifacts relating to French history of the area; open summer & by request

Steinbach: Mennonite Heritage Village, PO Box 1136, Steinbach MB R0A 2A0 – 204/326-9661; Fax: 204/326-5046 – Executive Director, Harv Klassen – Includes J.J. Reimer Historical Library & Archives; open year round

Stonewall Quarry Park, PO Box 250, Stonewall MB R0C 2Z0 – 204/467-5354; Fax: 204/467-9129 – Manager, Carl Martin

Strathclair Museum, Strathclair MB R0J 2C0 – 204/365-5202, 5201 – Sec.-Treas., Helga Gerrard – Open mid-May - mid-Sept.

Swan Valley Museum, PO Box 2078, Swan River MB R0L 1Z0 – 204/734-3585 – President, Glynn Donaldson; Receptionist, Laura Lafrance – Open mid-May - mid-Sept.

Teulon & District Museum, PO Box 197, Teulon MB R0C 3B0 – 204/886-2792 – Secretary, Mary Revel

The Pas: The Sam Waller Museum, 306 Fischer Ave., PO Box 185, The Pas MB R9A 1K4 – 204/623-3802; Fax: 204/623-5506 – Director, Laura MacLean

Thompson: Heritage North Museum, 163 Princeton Dr., Thompson MB R8N 2A4 – 204/677-2313; Fax: 204/677-3434; Email: museum@mysterynet.mb.ca; URL: http://www.mysterynet.mb.ca/museum/index.html – Curator, Paul Legault – Geology, natural history, archaeology, community history, travelling exhibits, pioneer artifacts; open year round

Treherne Museum, PO Box 30, Treherne MB R0G 2V0 – 204/723-2621 (Museum), 2044 (Civic Centre) – Chairperson, Lorraine Darling

Victoria Beach: Ateah Homestead, Victoria Beach MB R0E 2C0 – 204/754-2357 – Director, Sam Ateah

Virden: Currahee Military Museum, PO Box 729, Virden MB R0M 2C0 – 204/748-2454; Fax: 204/748-1805 – Director, John Hipwell – Open year round

Virden: Pioneer Home Museum of Virden & District, 390 King St. West, PO Box 2001, Virden MB R0M 2C0 – 204/748-1659 – President, Shelley Davies – Open summer 9-6 daily

Virden: River Valley School Museum, PO Box 729, Virden MB R0M 2C0 – 204/748-2454 – President, Pat Hipwell

Wabowden Historical Museum Inc., Wabowden MB R0B 1S0 – 204/689-2362, 2269; Fax: 204/689-2355 – Sec-Treas., Cindy Jonasson; President, Carol Sanoffsky; Vice-President, Brenda Tozer – Open in summer & by appt.

Wasagaming: Pinewood Museum, 154 Wasagaming Dr., Wasagaming MB R0J 2H0 – 204/735-2205, 848-7622 – Open daily June - Labour Day

Wasagaming: Riding Mountain National Park (RMNP), General Delivery, Wasagaming MB R0J 2H0 – 204/848-7275; Fax: 204/848-7272 – Communications Officer, Rosemarie Peloquin

Waskada Museum, Waskada MB R0M 2E0 – 204/673-2533 – Sec.-Treas., E.V. Dow – Open summer

Wawanesa: Sipiweske Museum, Wawanesa MB R0K 2J0 – 204/824-2244

Whitemouth Municipal Museum, PO Box 294, Whitemouth MB R0E 2G0 – 204/348-2576 – President, Harvey Pischke – Open June 1 - Sept. 30

Winkler: Pembina Threshermen's Museum Inc., PO Box 1103, Winkler MB R6W 4B2 – 204/822-5369, 325-7497; Fax: 204/325-8450 – Bill Reimer – Antique machinery tools, household effects & accessories used by pioneers who settled in the Pembina Valley

Winnipeg: Aquatic Hall of Fame & Museum of Canada Inc., 25 Poseidon Bay, Winnipeg MB R3M 3E4 – 204/957-1700; Fax: 204/942-2325; URL: http://www.mbnet.mb.ca/city/parks/recserv/aquahall/INDEX.HTM – Director, Vaughan L. Baird – Open daily year round

Winnipeg: Clothing & Textiles Museum, Human Ecology Bldg., University of Manitoba., 35 Chancellor's Circle, Winnipeg MB R3T 2N2 – 204/474-8138; Fax: 204/275-7592; Email: turnbull@ms.umanitoba.ca – Dr. Susan Turnbull Caton

Winnipeg: Crafts Museum at the Crafts Guild of Manitoba, 183 Kennedy St., Winnipeg MB R3C 1S6 – 204/943-1190

Winnipeg: Dalnavert Museum, 61 Carlton St., Winnipeg MB R3C 1N7 – 204/943-2835; Fax: 204/943-2565 – Curator, Tim Worth – 1895 restored Victorian home of Hugh John Macdonald, son of Sir John A. Macdonald

Winnipeg: Forest Sandilands Centre & Museum, c/o Manitoba Forestry Association, 900 Corydon Ave., Winnipeg MB R3M 0Y4 – 204/453-3182 – Program Director, William Baker

Winnipeg: Fort Garry Horse Regimental Museum & Archives Inc., c/o McGregor Armoury, 551 Machray Ave., Winnipeg MB R2W 1A8 – 204/586-6298; Fax: 204/582-0370 – Chairman, L. Lajeunesse

Winnipeg: Fort Whyte Centre for Environmental Education, 1961 McCreary Rd., PO Box 124, Winnipeg MB R3Y 1G5 – 204/989-8350

Winnipeg: Grant's Old Mill, 3310 Portage Ave., PO Box 2002, Stn A, Winnipeg MB R3K 2E5 – 204/986-5613 – Miller, Archibald McLachlan – Open June - Aug.

Winnipeg: Historical Museum of St. James-Assiniboia, 3180 Portage Ave., Winnipeg MB R3K 0Y5 – 204/888-8706 – Curator, Grant Tyler – Open year round

Winnipeg: Ivan Franko Museum, 595 Pritchard Ave., Winnipeg MB R2W 2K4 – 204/589-4397; Fax: 204/589-3404 – Director, Zenovy Nykolyshyn

Winnipeg: J.B. Wallis Museum of Entomology, Dept. of Entomology, Entomology Bldg., University of Manitoba, 424 University Centre, Winnipeg MB R3T 2N2 – 204/474-6023, 6024; Fax: 204/275-0402 – Curator, Dr. R.E. Roughley – 250,000 species of insects

Winnipeg: Le Musée de St-Boniface Museum, 494, av Taché, Winnipeg MB R2H 2B2 – 204/237-4500; Fax: 204/986-7964 – Curator, Pierrette Boily; Administrator, Dr. Philippe R. Mailhot – Open year round

Winnipeg: Living Prairie Museum, 2795 Ness Ave., Winnipeg MB R3J 3S4 – 204/832-0167; Fax: 204/986-4172; Email: prairie@mbnet.mb.ca; URL: http://www.city.winnipeg.mb.ca/city/parks/envserv/interp/living.html – Nature centre & one of the last remaining examples of Tall Grass Prairie in a 12-hectare outdoor museum

Winnipeg: Manitoba Children's Museum, The Forks, 45 Forks Market Rd., Winnipeg MB R3C 4T6 – 204/956-1888 – Executive Director, Jane Eisbrenner – Hands-on exhibits; open daily year round

Winnipeg: Manitoba Sports Hall of Fame & Museum Inc. (MSHOF), Offices, #210, 200 Main St., Winnipeg MB R3C 4M2 – 204/925-5735; Fax: 204/925-5792; URL: http://www.sport.mb.ca – Executive Director, Rick D. Brownlee

Winnipeg: Miami Station Museum, PO Box 1855, Winnipeg MB R3C 3R1 – 204/942-4632 – Director, Peter Lacey – National historic site; 1889 Northern Pacific & Manitoba Railway station; open weekends & holidays during summer & by appt.

Winnipeg: Ogniwo Polish Museum, 1417 Main St., Winnipeg MB R2W 3V3 – 204/586-5070 – Chairperson, Christine Tabernor

Winnipeg: Oseredok Ukrainian Cultural & Educational Centre, Art Gallery & Museum, 184 Alexander Ave. East, Winnipeg MB R3B 0L6 – 204/942-0218 – Curator, Shawna Balas – Open Tues. - Sat.

Winnipeg: Queen's Own Cameron Highlanders of Canada Regimental Museum Inc., Rm. 230, Minto Armoury, 969 St. Matthew's Ave., Winnipeg MB R3G 0J7 – 204/786-4330 – Curator, Sgt. Grant Tyler

Winnipeg: Riel House National Historic Site/Lieu historique national de la Maison-Riel, 330 River Rd., Winnipeg MB R2M 3Z8 – 204/257-1783 (summer), 233-4888 (winter); Fax: 204/233-4888 – Directrice, Janelle Reynolds – Open daily mid-May - Labour Day

Winnipeg: Ross House Museum, 61 Carlton St., Winnipeg MB R3C 1N7 – 204/943-2835, off-season; 204/943-3958, summer – Curator, Tim Worth – Western Canada's first post office, built 1854; open summer

Winnipeg: Royal Canadian Mint, 520 Lagimodiere Blvd., Winnipeg MB R2J 3E7 – 204/257-3359; Fax: 204/255-5203; URL: http://www.rcmint.ca – Director, Roy Yogasingan – Open May - Sept.

Winnipeg: Royal Winnipeg Rifles Regimental Museum, Minto Armoury, #208, 969 St. Matthews Ave., Winnipeg MB R3G 0J7 – 204/786-4350 (Orderly Room) – Archivist, Win Anders; Archivist, Bruce Tascona – Open Tues. & Sat. & by appt.; closed Sat. in Jun-Aug

Winnipeg: Seven Oaks House Museum, 1650 Main St., PO Box 25176, Winnipeg MB R2V 4C8 – 204/339-7429 – S. Hupe – Home of John Inkster, c.1851; open end May - Labour Day

Winnipeg: St. Volodymyr Ukranian Catholic Centre Museum, 418 Aberdeen Ave., Winnipeg MB R2W 1V7 – 204/582-1940 – Chairperson, Jean Michalishyn

Winnipeg: University of Manitoba Museums, c/o Fort Garry Campus, 424 University Centre, Winnipeg MB R3T 2N2 – Director, Dale Amundson – Gallery III; Janet Ian Gallery; Mineralogy Museum; Zoology Museum; Planetarium

Winnipeg: UVAN Historical Museum & Archives, #205, 456 Main St., Winnipeg MB R3B 1B6 – 204/942-5095; Fax: 204/947-3882 – Curator, Prof. M. Tarnawesky

Winnipeg: Western Canada Aviation Museum Inc./Musée de l'aviation de l'ouest du Canada (WCAM), Hangar T-2, 958 Ferry Rd., Winnipeg MB R3H 0Y8 – 204/786-5503; Fax: 204/775-4761; Email: info@wcam.mb.ca; URL: http://www.wcam.mb.ca – Executive Director, George W. Elliott

Winnipeg Police Department Museum, 130 Allard Ave., Winnipeg MB R3K 0T4 – 204/986-3976; Fax: 204/986-6101 – Curator, Jack Templeman

Winnipeg Beach Ukranian Homestead, PO Box 396, Winnipeg Beach MB R0C 3G0 – 204/389-4079 – F. Domitruk – Artifacts of Ukrainian origin & tradition; historic house with furnishings; clay-bake oven; grist mill

Winnipegosis Museum, Winnipegosis MB R0L 2G0 – 204/656-4791 – President, Stephen Lytwyn – Housed in former CNR Railway Station (c.1897); 65-foot freighter, the "Myrtle M"; artifacts; CNR historical material; War Memorial items; Native handiwork

Woodlands Pioneer Museum, Woodlands MB R0C 3H0 – 204/383-5584 – Director, Opal Langrell – Open mid-May - August or by appt.

## NEW BRUNSWICK

### Kings Landing Historical Settlement

Transcanada, Exit 259, Prince William NB E0H 1S0
506/363-5090; Fax: 506/363-5757
URL: http://www.grtplaces.com/ac/landing/
Vibrant historical settlement along the banks of the St. John River, depicting rural life from the Loyalist to the Victorian eras (1784-1890).

### Musée Acadien (MAUM)

c/o Université de Moncton, Moncton NB E1A 3E9
506/858-4088; Fax: 506/858-4043; Email: leblanna@umoncton.ca
URL: http://www.umoncton.ca/maum/maum.html

AKA: Musée acadien de l'Université de Moncton
Directeur, Bernard LeBlanc

**New Brunswick Museum/Musée du Nouveau-Brunswick (NBM/MNB)**
277 Douglas Ave., Saint John NB E2K 1E5
506/643-2300; Fax: 506/643-2360
Collections include human history, marine & technology, prints, fine & decorative arts, botany, zoology, geology; provincial museum of New Brunswick, established in 1842; full range of exhibitions & programs offered daily; closed Christmas Day and Good Friday.
Director, Frank Milligan

**Other Museums & Science Centres in New Brunswick**

Bathurst: Herman J. Good V.C. Memorial Museum, c/o Royal Canadian Legion Branch 18, 575 St. Peters Ave., Bathurst NB E2A 2Y5 – 506/546-3135 – Director, Cy Comeau

Blackville Historical Society Museum, Rte. 8, Blackville NB E0C 1C0 – 506/843-7761

Boiestown: Central New Brunswick Woodmen's Museum, PO Box 7, Boiestown NB E0H 1A0 – 506/369-7214; Fax: 506/369-9081 – Museum Manager, Jane Gibson

Caraquet: Le Musée Acadien/Acadian Historical Village, 15, boul St-Pierre est, CP 420, Caraquet NB E0B 1K0 – 506/727-1713; Fax: 506/727-7719 – Président-directeur, Léopold Chaisson – 1780 to early 1900's recreated Acadian settlement

Chatham: Miramichi Natural History Museum, 149 Wellington St., PO Box 162, Chatham NB E1N 3A5 – 506/773-7305 – Curator, Carl Landry

Chatham: St. Michael's Historical Museum, 12 Alexandra St., Chatham NB E1N 1V2 – 506/773-3277 – Curator, John Connell

Chatham: W.S. Loggie Cultural Centre & Loggie House, 222 Wellington St., Chatham NB E1N 1M9 – 506/773-7645 – President, Joan Cripps

Clair: Le Petit Musée, PO Box 401, Clair NB E0L 1B0 – 506/992-3637 – Présidente, Blanche Long

Clifton Royal: John Fisher Memorial Museum, c/o Peninsula Heritage Inc., RR#1, Clifton Royal NB E0G 1N0 – 506/763-2101 – Director, Judith Baxter

Dalhousie: Musée Restigouche Regional Museum, 437 George St., PO Box 1717, Dalhousie NB E0K 1B0 – 506/684-4685 – Manager, Andrew Blackadar

Doaktown: Doak Historic Park & Doak House, Rte. 8, Doaktown NB E0C 1G0 – 506/365-4363

Doaktown: Miramichi Atlantic Salmon Museum, PO Box 38, Doaktown NB E0C 1G0 – 506/365-7787; Fax: 506/365-7359 – General Manager, Isabelle Loughead

Dorchester Properties Committee, c/o Westmorland Historical Society, PO Box 166, Dorchester NB E0A 1M0 – 506/379-6633 – Chair, Sylvia Yeoman – Operating: The Keillor House (Westmorland Centennial Museum, c. 1813), 506/379-6633; open June - Sept. or by appt.; Bell Inn (c.1811), 506/379-6633; open April - Dec.; St. James Presbyterian Church Museum, 506/379-2580; Beachkirk Collection (c. 1884); open June-Sept. or by appt.; The Maritime Penetentiary Museum, 506/379-6633; open June-Sept.

Douglastown: MacDonald Farm Historic Park, Douglastown NB E0C 1H0 – 506/778-6085; Fax: 506/778-6101 – H. Blair Carter – c. 1815-20

Douglastown: Rankin House Museum, Rte. 8, Douglastown NB E0C 1H0 – 506/773-3448 – Archivist, Edith MacAllister

Edmundston: Musée Historique du Madawaska, 165, boul Hébert, Edmundston NB E3V 2S8 – 506/735-8804; Fax: 506/739-5373 – Curator, Richard Therrien

Fredericton: Brydone Jack Observatory Museum, c/o University of New Brunswick, PO Box 4400, Fredericton NB E3B 5A3 – 506/453-4723

Fredericton: Electrical Engineering Museum, University of New Brunswick, Dept. of Electrical Engineering, PO Box 4400, Fredericton NB E3B 5A3 – 506/453-4561; Fax: 506/453-3589; Email: eeoffice@unb.ca; URL: http://www.unb.ca – Chair, Dr. Eugene Lewis

Fredericton: House of International Dolls, 214 Cedar Ave., Fredericton NB E3A 2C6 – 902/658-2449 – D.J. Sparling – Open mid-June - Labour Day

Fredericton: New Brunswick Power Electricity Museum, 515 Queen St., PO Box 2000, Fredericton NB E3B 1B9 – 506/458-6805; Fax: 506/458-3060

Fredericton: New Brunswick Sports Hall of Fame/Temple de la renommée sportive du Nouveau-Brunswick, 503 Queen St., PO Box 6000, Fredericton NB E3B 5H1 – 506/453- 3747; Fax: 506/459-0481; Email: deborahw@gov.nb – Executive Director, Kathy Meagher

Fredericton: Old Government House/Ancienne Résidence du Gouvernement, PO Box 6000, Fredericton NB E3B 5H1 – 506/453-2324; Fax: 506/453-2416; Email: cynthiaw@gov.nb.ca; URL: http://www.gov.nb.ca/mch/culaff/heritage/ – Manager, Cynthia Wallace-Casey

Fredericton: York-Sunbury Historical Society Museum, PO Box 1312, Fredericton NB E3B 5C8 – 506/455-6041 – Assistant Curator, Bruce Lynch; Administrator/Program Officer, Lynn Frizzell – Military & local history

Fredericton Junction: Currie House, Fredericton Junction NB E0G 1T0 – 506/368-2818 – President, Arline Landry

Gagetown: Queens County Museum, The Tilley House, Gagetown NB E0G 1V0 – 506/488-2966 – Curator, Jean Shannon – Birthplace of Sir Leonard Tilley, Father of Confederation

Grand Falls Museum/Musée de Grand-Sault, PO Box 1572, Grand Falls NB E0J 1M0 – 506/473-5265; Fax: 506/473-7160 – Director, Patrick McCooey

Grand Manan Museum & Walter B. McLaughlin Marine Gallery, PO Box 66, Grand Harbour NB E0G 1X0 – 506/662-3524 – Curator, Wendy Dathan – Open June - Sept.; in winter by appt.

Grand-Anse: Musée des Papes, 184 Acadie St., PO Box 60, Grand-Anse NB E0B 1R0 – 506/732-3003; Fax: 506/732-5491 – Directeur, Edmond Landry

Hampton: Kings County Historical Society Museum, c/o Kings County Historical & Archival Society Inc., PO Box 5001, Hampton NB E0G 1Z0 – 506/832-6009; Fax: 506/832-6007 – Archives Curator, A. Faye Pearson – Artifacts include textiles, clothing, china, guns, glassware, military, royalty, art & archival material

Hillsborough Railway Museum, PO Box 70, Hillsborough NB E0A 1X0 – 506/734-3195 – Director, John N. Whitmore

Hillsborough: Hon. William Henry Steeves House, 24 Mill St., PO Box 148, Hillsborough NB E0A 1X0 – 506/734-3102 – Administrator, Alvin Edgett

Hopewell Cape: Albert County Museum, PO Box 3, Hopewell Cape NB E0A 1Y0 – 506/734-2003 – President, Dawn Kinnie – County Jail, c.1846; County Court House, c.1904; Agricultural Exhibit Building; open June 15-Sept. 15

Kedgwick Forestry Museum Inc./Musée Forestier de Kedgwick Inc., Rte. 17, Kedgwick NB E0K 1C0 – 506/284-3138 – President, Romuald Coulombe – Tree-clad hills & clear running streams

Masionnette: Oyster Museum, Rte. 303, Masionnette NB E0B 1X0 – 506/727-2004

Minto Museum, 71 Main St., Minto NB E0E 1J0 – 506/327-3383

Moncton: Free Meeting House, c/o Moncton Museum, 20 Mountain Rd., Moncton NB E1C 2J8 – 506/853-3003 – Director, Jim Roper – Open summer

Moncton: Lutz Mountain Meeting House, 3030 Mountain Rd., Moncton NB E1G 2W8 – 506/384-7719 – President, Eleanor Weldon – Museum located at 3143 Mountain Rd.

Moncton Museum/Musée de Moncton, 20 Mountain Rd., Moncton NB E1C 2J8 – 506/853-3003; Fax: 506/853-7558 – Director, Jim Roper – Open year round

New Denmark Memorial Museum, c/o New Denmark Historical Society, New Denmark NB E0J 1T0 – 506/553-6464 – President, Sterling Jensen

Oromocto: CFB Gagetown Military Museum/Musée militaire de la BFC Gagetown, A-5, PO Box 17000, Stn Station Forces, Oromocto NB E2V 4J5 – 506/422-1304; Fax: 506/422-1304 – Curator, M. Richard – Open year round

Perth-Andover: Southern Victoria Historical Society Museum, Main St., Perth-Andover NB E0J 1V0 – 506/273-6750

Petit-Rocher: New Brunswick Mining & Mineral Interpretation Centre, Rte. 134, Petit-Rocher NB E0B 2E0 – 506/783-8714

Plaster Rock Museum, Rte. 109, Plaster Rock NB E0J 1W0 – 506/356-6077; Fax: 506/356-6081 – Danny Braun

Rexton: Richibucto River Historical Society & Museum, PO Box 211, Rexton NB E0A 2L0 – 506/523-4408 – President, Dr. John McCleave

Robichaud: Sportsmans Museum Reg'd., PO Box 9, Robichaud NB E0A 2S0 – 506/532-4750 – Owner/Operator, Clorice Landry

Sackville: Acadian Odyssey National Historic Site/Lieu historique national de l'odyssée acadienne, c/o Fort Beauséjour National Historic Site, RR#3, Sackville NB E0A 3C0 – 506/758-9783; Fax: 506/536-4399 – Manager, Pierrette Robichaud

Sackville: Fort Beauséjour National Historic Site, RR#3, Sackville NB E0A 3C0 – 506/364-6080; Fax: 506/536-4399; Email: fort_beausejour@pch.gc.ca – Manager, Pierrette Robichaud

Sackville: Struts Centre, 5 Willow Place, Sackville NB E0A 3C0 – 506/536-1211 – Director, Christopher Lawlor

Saint John: Barbour's General Store, PO Box 1971, Saint John NB E2L 4L1 – 506/658-2939; Fax: 506/632-6118 – Tourist Officer, Shirley Elliott

Saint John: Loyalist House Museum, 120 Union St., Saint John NB E2L 1A3 – 506/652-3590 – Museum Manager, Steve McNeil

Saint John: Partridge Island Museum, PO Box 6326, Saint John NB E2L 4R7 – 506/693-2598; Fax: 506/693-2598; Email: hew@mi.net – Executive Director, Harold E. Wright; President, Michael H. Bamford

Saint John Firefighters Association Museum, 24 Sydney St., Saint John NB E2L 2L3 – 506/633-1840

Saint John Jewish Historical Museum, 29 Wellington Row, Saint John NB E2L 3H4 – 506/633-1833; Fax: 506/633-1833 – Director, Marcia Koven – Collects, displays & preserves articles related specifically to the Saint John Jewish community; provides a research facility for genealogists, historians & religious scholars; 7 display areas

Saint John Sports Hall of Fame, PO Box 1971, Saint John NB E2L 4L1 – 506/658-2909; Fax: 506/658-2902 – Chair, Betty MacMillan – Located in Harbour Station

Saint John: Tel & Telephone Pioneer Museum, Saint John NB E2L 4K2 – Community Relations Officer, D.E. Trueman

Saint-François-de Madawaska: Connors Museum, 3614 Rte. 205, Saint-François-de Madawaska NB E7A 1S3 – 506/992-2500 – Director, Suzie Bernier – Items used in general store; blacksmith shop; Victorian mansion

Shediac: Maison Pascal-Poirier, 259, rue Principale, Shediac NB E0A 3G0 – 506/532-9726

Shippagan: Historic Society Nicolas-Denys Documentation Centre, Rte. 113, Shippagan NB E0B 2P0 – 506/336-2346

St-Basile Chapel Museum, PO Box 150, St-Basile NB E0L 1H0 – 506/266-5971 – Director, Rev. Napoléon Michaud

St-Isidore Museum Inc., Rte. 160, St-Isidore NB E0B 2L0 – 506/358-6344

St-Jacques: Musée Automobile Museum, CP 1567, St-Jacques NB E7B 1H3 – 506/735-2525; Fax: 506/735-7262 – Conservateur, Gilles S. Landry

St. Andrews: The Henry Phipps Ross & Sarah Juliette Ross Memorial Museum, 188 Montague St., PO Box 603, St. Andrews NB E0G 2X0 – 506/529-1824; Fax: 506/529-3383 – Director, Margot Magee Sackett – Decorative arts museum in one of St. Andrews' finest early houses; open June - Oct.

St. Martins: Quaco Museum & Library, Rte. 111, St. Martins NB E0G 2Z0 – 506/833-4740 (July & Aug.), 833-4768 (off-season) – Curator, Barbara McIntyre; Librarian, Elizabeth Thibodeau

St. Stephen: Charlotte County Museum, 443 Milltown Blvd., St. Stephen NB E3L 1J9 – 506/466-3295; Fax: 506/466-7701 – Director, Irene Ritch – Exhibits on 3 floors of the 1864 James Murchie Home; collection includes china, hand-crafted articles, quilts, samplers, costumes, early tools & furniture; theme rooms portray area from the late 18th - early 20th century

Sussex: Agricultural Museum of New Brunswick, Rte. 1, Sussex NB E0E 1P0 – 506/433-6799

Tabusintac Centennial Memorial Library & Museum, Rte. 11, Tabusintac NB E0C 2A0 – 506/779-9261 – Bertha Stymiest; Bertha Wishart

Tracadie-Sheila: Musée Historique de Tracadie, #399, 222, rue du Couvent, Tracadie-Sheila NB E1X 1E1 – 506/395-1500; Fax: 506/395-1504 – S. Dorina Frigault

Village de Barachois: L'Église historique Saint-Henri-de Barachois, RR#1, Village de Barachois NB E0A 2S0 – 506/532-2976 – Contremaître, Armand Landry

Welshpool: Campobello Island Public Library & Museum, Welshpool NB E0G 3H0 – 506/752-2268 – President, Dale Calder

Welshpool: Roosevelt Campobello International Park, PO Box 9, Welshpool NB E0G 3H0 – 506/752-2922 – A/Executive Secretary & Superintendent, Henry W. Stevens – Summer home of Franklin Delano Roosevelt

Woodstock: Old Carleton County Court House, c/o Carleton County Historical Society, 128 Connell St., PO Box 898, Woodstock NB E0J 2B0 – 506/328-9706 – President, John Glass

## NEWFOUNDLAND

### Newfoundland Museum/Musée de Terra Nova

285 Duckworth St., PO Box 8700, St. John's NF A1B 4J6

709/729-2329; Fax: 709/729-2179

URL: http://calvin.stemnet.nf.ca/~cshea/

Holdings include artifacts, prints & watercolours relating to the province in the areas of Archaeology, Ethnology, Natural History & History (large collection of folk furniture & military artifacts).

Director, Michael Clair

Chief Curator, Dr. Bernard Ransom

Curator, Museum Education Services, Allan Clarke

### Other Museums & Science Centres in Newfoundland

Bonne Bay: Wiltondale Pioneer Village, c/o Bonne Bay Development Association, Woody Point, PO Box 159, Bonne Bay NF A0K 1P0 – 709/453-2470; Fax: 709/453-7214 – Curator, Colleen Howell – Recreated turn-of-the-century logging community; museum; one-room schoolhouse; church; log barn; general store, craft store & tearoom.

Botwood Heritage Centre, PO Box 490, Botwood NF A0H 1E0 – 709/257-2839; Fax: 709/257-3330 – Director, Ed Evans

Burin Heritage House, PO Box 326, Burin NF A0E 1E0 – 709/891-2217 – President, Jessie Shave

Carbonear Railway Station, PO Box 64, Carbonear NF A0A 1T0 – 709/596-2267 – President, Bobbie Hatch

Carbonear: Shades of the Past, PO Box 496, Carbonear NF A0A 1T0 – 709/596-1977 – Director, Stan Deering

Channel-Port-aux-Basques Museum, 118 Main St., PO Box 1299, Channel-Port-aux-Basques NF A0M 1C0 – 709/695-7604, 2460 – Maitland Strangemore – Maritime artifacts; open daily in summer

Corner Brook: Humber-Bay of Islands Museum Society, 65 Central St., Corner Brook NF A2H 2M7 – 709/634-7907; Fax: 709/634-7907 – Acting President, Philip Greenacre; Sec.-Treas., George Rose

Corner Brook: Sticks & Stones House, 12 Riverhead Rd., Corner Brook NF A2H 1J6 – 709/634-3275 – Director, Ruby MacDonald

Cow Head: Tête de Vache Community Museum, PO Box 47, Cow Head NF A0K 2A0 – 709/243-2023 – Curator, Glenda Reid-Bavis, 709/243-2466; Curator, Elizabeth Payne, 709/243-2521

Deer Lake: Humber Valley Heritage Museum, c/o Humber Valley Development Association, PO Box 989, Deer Lake NF A0K 2E0 – 709/635-3861 – Coordinator, Glenda Garnier – Open June-Aug. & by appt.

Durrell Museum, Durrell NF A0G 1Y0 – 709/884-2613 – Curator, David Burton – Open summer

Ferryland: Historic Ferryland Museum & Shoreline Crafts, Ferryland NF A0A 2H0 – 709/432-2711 – Curator, Maxine Dunne

Flat Rock Museum, 663 Windgap Rd., Flat Rock NF A1K 1C7 – 709/437-6312; Fax: 709/437-6311 – Treasurer, Rita Farrell – Open July - Sept. or by appt.

Fogo Island: Bleakhouse Museum, Fogo, Fogo Island NF A0G 2B0 – 709/266-2237 – c.1816; Schoolhouse Museum, c.1888; open July - Aug.

Gander: North Atlantic Aviation Museum, PO Box 234, Gander NF A1V 1W6 – 709/256-2923; Fax: 709/256-2124

Goose Bay: Northern Lights Military Museum, PO Box 188, Goose Bay NF A0P 1C0 – 709/896-5939 – Curator, Bruce Haynes

Grand Bank: Southern Newfoundland Seamen's Museum (SNSM), Marine Dr., PO Box 1109, Grand Bank NF A0E 1W0 – 709/832-1484; Fax: 709/832-2053 – Museum Curator, Gerald Crews

Grand Falls-Windsor: Beothuck Village, St. Catherine St., Grand Falls-Windsor NF A2A 1W9 – 709/489-9629 – Open June - Sept.

Grand Falls-Windsor: Mary March Regional Museum, 22 St. Catherine St., Grand Falls-Windsor NF A2A 1W9 – 709/292-4523; Fax: 709/292-4526 – Curator, Clifford O. Evans

Greenspond Museum, PO Box 100, Greenspond NF A0G 2N0 – 709/269-4111 – Director, Derrick Bragg – Open July & Aug.

Griquet: Port aux Choix National Historic Park, PO Box 70, Griquet NF A0K 2X0 – 709/623-2608, 861-3522 – Supt., Bruce Bradbury

Happy Valley: Labrador Heritage Society & Museum, Main Branch, PO Box 719, Stn B, Happy Valley NF A0P 1E0 – 709/896-2762 – Director, Elsie Johnson – Open summer

Happy Valley: Them Days, PO Box 939, Stn B, Happy Valley NF A0P 1E0 – Archivist & Business Manager, Gilliam H. Brown

Harbour Grace: Conception Bay Museum, PO Box 298, Harbour Grace NF A0A 2M0 – 709/596-5465, 596-1309 (winter) – Curator, Peggy Fahey – Open June - Aug; off season by appt.

Jerseyside: Castle Hill National Historic Park, PO Box 10, Jerseyside NF A0B 2G0 – 709/227-2401; Fax: 709/227-2452 – Officer-in-Charge, Ann Smith – 17th & 18th century remains of French & English fortifications

L'Anse au Loup: Labrador Straits Museum, PO Box 98, L'Anse au Loup NF A0K 3L0 – 709/927-5659 – President, Margaret Buckle

Lewisporte: Bye the Bay Museum, Women's Institute Bldg., PO Box 291, Lewisporte NF A0G 3A0 – 709/535-2844, 8787 – Committee Secretary, Joy Freake – Twenty-eight ft. hooked rug depicting Lewisporte's history; artifacts; spinning wheel; craft shop

Marystown Museum, PO Box 688, Marystown NF A0E 2M0 – 709/279-1507, 1462 – Chairman, Albert Dober – Open daily mid-June - Aug.

Moreton's Harbour Museum, PO Box 28, Moreton's Harbour NF A0G 3H0 – 709/684-2355 – Chair, Women's Institute, Margaret Knight – Open in summer & by appt.

Musgrave Harbour: Fishermen's Museum, 4 Marine Dr., Musgrave Harbour NF A0G 3J0 – 709/655-2162 – Curator, Roland W. Abbott – Open daily in summer

Nain: Piulimatsivik - Nain Museum, PO Box 247, Nain NF A0P 1L0 – 709/922-2821 – Supervisor, Rev. Renatus Hunter – Inuit & Moravian artifacts

Old Perlican: Howard House of Artifacts, PO Box 100, Old Perlican NF A0A 3G0 – 709/587-2022 – Owner, Jerome Howard – Located 3 miles from Old Perlican on Shore Line country road at Daniel's Cove; 19th century artifacts

Placentia Area Museum, O'Reilly House, 48 Riverside Dr., PO Box 233, Placentia NF A0B 2Y0 – 709/227-5568 – Chairperson, Barbara Bailey – Restored to 1902

Placentia Bay: St. Bartholomew's Church, c/o Mt. Arlington Hts., PO Box 25, Placentia Bay NF A0B 2L0 – 709/228-2394 – Supervisor, Mary Jane Keating

Port Union Museum, PO Box 98, Port Union NF A0C 2J0 – 709/464-3315, 469-2728 – Manager, Linda Clarke; Curator, Gail Doody – Open mid June - September; small admission fees apply

Port aux Basques: Gulf Museum, c/o South West Coast Historical Society, PO Box 1299, Port aux Basques NF A0M 1C0 – 709/695-7604 – President, The South West Coast National Society, Henry K. Gibbons

Port de Grave: Fishermen's Museum & Porter House, Port de Grave NF A0A 3J0 – 709/786-3912 – Curator, Herman Porter

Pouch Cove Museum, PO Box 59, Pouch Cove NF A0A 3L0 – 709/335-2848; Fax: 709/335-2840 – Curator, Terry White

Red Bay Interpretation Centre, Red Bay NF A0K 4K0 – 709/920-2197 – Community Clerk, Josie Moore – Archaeological remains of world's largest 16th-century whaling port; open June 15 - Sept. & by request

Rocky Harbour: Gros Morne National Park Visitor Reception Centre, PO Box 130, Rocky Harbour NF A0K 4N0 – 709/458-2417; Fax: 709/458-2059; URL: http://www.parkscanada.pch.gc.ca/parks – Chip Bird

Salvage Fishermens' Museum, Salvage NF A0G 3X0 – 709/677-2414 – Marion Heffern – Open daily Mon-Sun 9:30-7:30

Springdale: Harvey Grant Heritage Centre Community Museum, PO Box 57, Springdale NF A0J 1T0 – 709/673-4313; Fax: 709/673-4969 – Greg Hillier – Open Tues.-Sat. in summer

St. Anthony: Grenfell House Museum, PO Box 93, St. Anthony NF A0K 4S0 – 709/454-3333; Fax: 709/454-3171 – Sir Wilfred Grenfell Home; open May - Sept.

St. John's: Anglican Cathedral Museum, 68 Queen's Rd., St. John's NF A1C 2A8 – 709/726-5677; Fax: 709/726-2053 – Very Rev. William J. Bellamy

St. John's: Beothuck Provincial Park, Dept. of Tourism, Culture & Recreation, Parks & Natural Areas, PO Box 8700, St. John's NF A1B 4J6 – 709/489-9832; Fax: 709/729-1100; Email: dhustins@tourism.gov.nf.ca – Director, D. Hustins

St. John's: Boyd's Cove Beothuk Interpretation Centre, Newfoundland Historic Resources Division, PO Box 8700, St. John's NF A1B 4J6 – 709/729-0592; Fax: 709/729-0870; Email: lbadcock@tourism.gov.nf.ca; Interpretation Centre: 709/656-3114 – Historic Sites Officer, Linda Badcock – Exhibits on Beothuk life c. 1700; preserved archaeological site; walking trails; open daily in summer

St. John's: Cape Bonavista Lighthouse Provincial Historic Site, Newfoundland Historic Resources Division, PO Box 8700, St. John's NF A1B 4J6 – 709/729-0592; Fax: 709/729-0870; Email: lbadcock@tourism.gov.nf.ca; Lighthouse: 709/468-7444 – Historic Sites Officer, Linda Badcock – Restored to 1870 period; open daily in summer & in winter by appt.

St. John's: Cape Spear National Historic Site/Lieu historique national du Cap-Spear, PO Box 1268, St. John's NF A1C 5M9 – 709/772-5367; Fax: 709/772-6302; Operational Season: 709/772-4210 – Head, Client Services, Robert Sheldon – 1835 lighthouse; most Easterly point North America

St. John's: CBC Radio Museum, 344 Duckworth St., St. John's NF A1B 3T8 – 709/737-4207; Fax: 709/737-4954 – Director, John F. O'Mara

St. John's: Commissariat House Provincial Historic Site, c/o Newfoundland Historic Resources Division, PO Box 8700, St. John's NF A1B 4J6 – 709/729-0592, House: 709/729-6730; Fax: 709/729-0820; Email: lbadcock@tourism.gov.nf.ca – Historic Sites Officer, Linda Badcock – Restored to 1830; open daily in summer & in winter by appt.

St. John's: Heart's Content Cable Station Provincial Historic Site, Newfoundland Historic Resources Division, PO Box 8700, St. John's NF A1B 4J6 – 709/729-0592; Site: 709/583-2160; Fax: 709/729-0870; Email: lbadcock@tourism.gov.nf.ca – Historic Sites Officer, Linda Badcock – Site of the first successful transatlantic telegraph cable landing, 1866; open daily in summer

St. John's: Hiscock House Provincial Historic Site, c/o Newfoundland Historic Resources Division, PO Box 8700, St. John's NF A1B 4J6 – 709/729-0592; Fax: 709/729-0870; Email: lbadcock@tourism.gov.nf.ca; Historic Site: 709/464-2042 – Historic Sites Officer, Linda Badcock – Restored to 1910; open daily mid-June to mid-Oct.

St. John's: James J. O'Mara Pharmacy Museum, Apothecary Hall, 488 Water St., St. John's NF A1E 1B3 – 709/753-5877; Fax: 709/753-8615; Email: npha@nf.sympatico.ca – Secretary-Registrar, Donald F. Rowe – Drug store c. 1895; open mid-June - mid-Sept. or by appt.

St. John's: Lester-Garland Premises Provincial Historic Site, c/o Newfoundland Historic Resources Division, PO Box 8700, St. John's NF A1B 4J6 – 709/729-0592; Fax: 709/729-0870; Email: lbadcock@tourism.gov.nf.ca; Historic Site: 709/464-2042 – Historic Sites Officer, Linda Badcock – Mercantile bldg. including counting house restored to 1820 & retail shop restored to 1910; open daily mid-June to mid-Oct.

St. John's: MockBeggar Property Provincial Historic Site, c/o Newfoundland Historic Resources Division, PO Box 8700, St. John's NF A1B 4J6 – 709/729-0592; Fax: 709/729-0870; Email: lbadcock@tourism.gov.nf.ca; Historic Site: 709/468-7300; Fax: 709/468-7444 – Historic Sites Officer, Linda Badcock – Home of Newfoundland statesman, Senator F. Gordon Bradley; restored to 1939; open daily mid-June to mid-Oct.

St. John's: Newfoundland & Labrador Sports Hall of Fame, c/o Sport Newfoundland & Labrador, Bldg. 25, Torbay, PO Box 8700, St. John's NF A1B 4J6 – 709/576-4932; Fax: 709/576-7493 – General Manager, Glenn Normore

St. John's: Newfoundland Freshwater Resource Centre, PO Box 5, St. John's NF A1B 2Z2 – 709/754-3474; Fax: 709/754-5947 – Executive Director, Patricia Buchanan

St. John's: Newfoundland Transport Museum in Pippy Park, 212 Mount Scio Rd., PO Box 21059, St. John's NF A1A 5B2 – Chairman, Clement Durachko – Series of exhibits on transport themes of historic importance; open Canada Day to Labour Day

St. John's: Point Amour Lighthouse Provincial Historic Site, Newfoundland Historic Resources Division, PO Box 8700, St. John's NF A1B 4J6 – 709/729-0592; Fax: 709/729-0870; Email: lbadcock@tourism.gov.nf.ca; Lighthouse: 709/927-5825; Fax: 709/927-5833 – Historic Sites Officer, Linda Badcock – Exhibits on the history of the Labrador Straits & on lighthouses; open daily in the summer

St. John's: Quidi Vidi Battery Provincial Historic Site, Newfoundland Historic Resources Division, PO Box 8700, St. John's NF A1B 4J6 – 709/729-0592; Battery: 709/729-2977; Fax: 709/729-0870; Email: lbadcock@tourism.gov.nf.ca – Historic Sites Officer, Linda Badcock – Restored to 1812; open daily in summer

St. John's: Regatta Museum, PO Box 214, St. John's NF A1C 5J3 – 709/753-9448 – Director, Gail Malone

St. John's: Royal Newfoundland Constabulary Museum, PO Box 7247, St. John's NF A1E 3Y4 – 709/729-8151; Fax: 709/729-8214; Email: gbrownw@rnc.gov.nt.ca – Deputy Chief, Gary F. Browne; Sgt. R. Morgan – North America's oldest police force

St. John's: Signal Hill National Historic Site, PO Box 1268, St. John's NF A1C 5M9 – 709/772-5367; Fax: 709/772-2940 – Area Interpretive Officer, Ray Troke

St. John's: St. Thomas' Old Garrison Church Museum, 8 Military Rd., St. John's NF A1C 2C4 – 709/722-2632 – Curator, Dr. John Netten – c. 1836

St. John's: Trinity Interpretation Centre, Newfoundland Historic Resources Division, PO Box 8700, St. John's NF A1B 4J6 – 709/729-0592; Fax: 709/729-0870; Email: lbadcock@tourism.gov.nf.ca; Interpretation Centre: 709/464-2042 – Historic Sites Officer, Linda Badcock – Exhibits on the commercial & social history of Trinity; open daily in summer

St. John's: Victoria Hydro Electric Plant, 55 Kenmount Rd., St. John's NF A1B 3P6 – 709/737-5614; Fax: 709/737-5832 – Director, R.F. Gosine – 1904 hydro electric plant

St. Lawrence Miner's Museum, PO Box 128, St. Lawrence NF A0E 2V0 – 709/873-2222; Fax: 709/873-3352 – Curator, Leo Slaney – Open daily in summer

St. Lunaire-Griquest: Hopedale Mission, c/o Area Supt., Canadian Parks Service, PO Box 70, St. Lunaire-Griquest NF A0K 2X0 – 709/623-2601 – Collection spans 200+ years of European Moravian Mission as well as artifacts from early Inuit/Eskimo cultures

St. Lunaire-Griquest: L'Anse aux Meadows National Historic Site, Canadian Parks Service, PO Box 70, St. Lunaire-Griquest NF A0K 2X0 – 709/623-2601 – Park Supt., Bruce Bradbury – UNESCO World Heritage Site depicting first authenticated European presence in North America; Visitor centre open mid-June - Labour Day

Stephenville: Port au Bay/Bay St. George Heritage Association, PO Box 314, Stephenville NF A2N 2Z5 – 709/643-9042 – Chair, Gilbert Higgins – Regional archive & exhibition centre

Torbay Museum, PO Box 190, Torbay NF A1K 1E3 – 709/437-6571 – Curator, Jerri Pellegrinetti – Open daily in summer & in winter by appt.

Trepassey Area Museum, PO Box 13, Trepassey NF A0A 4B0 – 709/438-2465 – President, Stella Devereaux – Open July & Aug.

Trinity Museum & Archives, PO Box 32, Trinity NF A0C 2S0 – 709/464-3706; Fax: 709/464-3706 – Curator, David White – Open daily mid-June - mid-Sept. Operates: The Green Family Forge Blacksmith Museum & Trinity archives

Twillingate Museum, General Delivery, Twillingate NF A0G 4M0 – 709/884-2825 – Curator, Lorna Stuckless – Open mid-June - mid-Sept.

Wesleyville: Bonavista North Regional Museum, PO Box 48, Wesleyville NF A0G 4R0 – 709/536-2402 – Curator, Rev. Naboth Winsor – Open daily in summer

Whitbourne Museum, Whitbourne NF A0B 3K0 – 709/759-2345; Fax: 709/759-2242 – Curator, Judy Gosse – Open July - Labour Day

## NOVA SCOTIA

### Fisheries Museum of the Atlantic

Lunenburg Waterfront, PO Box 1363, Lunenburg NS B0J 2C0

902/634-4794; Fax: 902/634-8990; Email: nsmfma@chin.cycor.ca

URL: http://www.ednet.ns.ca/educ/museum/fma/

Fishing heritage of the Atlantic coast; includes fishing vessels, aquarium, theatre & reference library; part of the Nova Scotia Museum.

Curator, Heather Getson

Curator, Education, Ralph Getson

General Manager, Jim Tupper

### Maritime Museum of the Atlantic/Musée Martime d'Atlantique (MMA)

1675 Lower Water St., Halifax NS B3J 1S3

902/429-7490; Fax: 902/424-0612; Email: murraymr@gov.ns.ca

URL: http://www.ednet.ns.ca/educ/museum/mma/

Marine history branch of the Nova Scotia Museum; on waterfront; marine artifacts, memorabilia from the Titanic, Halifax explosion exhibit, restored ship chandlery, extensive small craft collection; library & gift shop; Vessel CSS Acadia at museum wharf along with schooner Bluenose II.

Manager, Michael Murray

### Nova Scotia Museum

1747 Summer St., Halifax NS B3H 3A6

902/424-6471; Fax: 902/424-0560

URL: http://www.ednet.ns.ca/educ/museum/

Established in 1868, the Nova Scotia Museum consists of 25 museums across the province: Nova Scotia Museum of Natural History, Halifax; Maritime Museum of the Atlantic, Halifax; Haliburton House, Windsor; Uniacke Estate Park Museum, Mount Uniacke; Prescott House, Starr's Point; Lawrence House, Maitland; Balmoral Grist Mill, Balmoral; Sutherland Steam Mill, Denmark; Fishermen's Life Museum, Jeddore; Shand House, Windsor; Nova Scotia Museum of Industry, Stellarton; Fisheries Museum of the Atlantic, Lunenburg; Wile Carding Mill, Bridgewater; Perkins House, Liverpool; Ross-Thomson House, Shelburne; Dory Shop, Shelburne; Old Meeting House, Barrington; Barrington Woolen Mill, Barrington; Firefighters' Museum of Nova Scotia, Yarmouth; North Hills Museum, Granville Ferry; McCulloch House, Pictou; Sherbrooke Village, Sherbrooke; Cossit House, Sydney; Ross Farm, New Ross; Fundy Geological Museum, Parrsboro.

**Other Museums & Science Centres in Nova Scotia**

Annapolis Royal: North Hills Museum, PO Box 503, Annapolis Royal NS R0S 1A0 – 902/532-2168 – Executive Director, Annapolis Historic Restoration Society, John Kirby

Annapolis Royal: Port Royal National Historic Site/ Lieu historique national de Port-Royal, PO Box 9, Annapolis Royal NS B0S 1A0 – 902/532-2898; Fax: 902/532-2232 – Area Supt., Lilian Stewart – Replica French settlement 1605-1613; home of the Order of Good Cheer; open May 15 - Oct. 15

Antigonish Heritage Museum, 20 East Main St., Antigonish NS B2G 2B2 – 902/863-6160; URL: http://www.grassroots.ns.ca/tour/ahm.htm – Manager, Jocelyn Gillis

Arichat: Le Noir Forge, General Delivery, Arichat NS B0E 1A0 – 902/226-9364; Fax: 902/226-1919 – Vice-President, Jean Bonin; President, Donna Boudrot; Treasurer, Joel Brown; Secretary, Leann Paon – Community museum; local artifacts; local artisan blacksmith

Baddeck: Alexander Graham Bell National Historic Site/Lieu historique national Alexander-Graham-Bell, PO Box 159, Baddeck NS B0E 1B0 – 902/295-2069; Fax: 902/295-3496; Email: agbellhs@auracom.com – Field Unit Supt., B. Villeneuve; Site Manager, Aynsley MacFarlane – Collection concentrates on Bell's work in Baddeck

Baddeck: Grassy Island National Historic Site/Lieu historique national de l'Île-Grassy, c/o Alexander Graham Bell National Historic Site, PO Box 159, Baddeck NS B0E 1B0 – 902/295-2069; Fax: 902/295-3496; Email: agbellhs.@auracom.com – Field Unit Supt., B. Villeneuve; Site Manager, Aynsley MacFarlane – Open June 1 - Sept. 15

Baddeck: The Great Hall of the Clans, Highland Pioneers Museum, PO Box 9, Baddeck NS B0E 1B0 – 902/295-3411 – Executive Director, Jim MacAulay

Baddeck: Marconi National Historic Site/Lieu historique national Marconi, c/o Alexander Graham Bell National Historic Site, PO Box 159, Baddeck NS B0E 1B0 – 902/295-2069; Fax: 902/295-3496; Email: agbellhs@auracom.com – Field Unit Supt., B. Villeneuve; Site Manager, Aynsley MacFarlane

Baddeck: Victoria County Archives & Museum, PO Box 75, Baddeck NS B0E 1B0 – 902/295-3397 – Curator, Margot MacAulay; Curator, Donald MacAulay – Open summer

Barrington: Cape Sable Historical Society Centre, Barrington NS B0W 1E0 – 902/637-2185 – Executive Director, Candace Stevenson – Local history & archives; operates: Old Meeting House, c.1765, oldest nonconformist church in Canada; Woolen Mill, c.1884; Seal Island Lighthouse Museum.

Barss Corner: Parkdale-Maplewood Community Museum, 3005 Barss Corner Rd., RR#1, Barss Corner NS B0R 1A0 – 902/644-3288; Fax: 902/644-3422; Email: rosmith@fox.nstn.ns.ca; URL: http://www.ednet.ns.ca/educ/museum/other_ns/parkdale/museum1.html – Administrator, Donna M. Smith; Curator, Barbara Veinot; Sec.-Treas., Wendy Looke

Bear River: Riverview Ethnographic Museum, 18 Chute Rd., RR#1, Box 3, Bear River NS B0S 1B0 – 902/467-3762; Fax: 902/467-3762 – Owner & Curator, Sarah Elizabeth Glover – Folk costumes & early Americana, open year round

Bedford: Atlantic Canada Aviation Museum/Musée D'aviation des provinces Atlantique (ACAM), 1658 Bedford Hwy., PO Box 44006, Bedford NS B4A 4J7 – 902/873-3773 – Curator, David McMahon – A collection of planes, artifacts & biographies related to aviation history in the Atlantic provinces.

Bridgetown: James House Museum, c/o Bridgetown & Area Historical Society, PO Box 373, Bridgetown NS B0S 1C0 – 902/665-4530, 4215 – President, Ken Nye

Bridgetown: Tupperville School Museum, RR#3, Bridgetown NS B0S 1C0 – 902/665-2004 – Chairperson, Marion Inglis – Open daily mid-May - mid-Sept.

Bridgewater: DesBrisay Museum & Exhibition Centre, 130 Jubilee Rd., PO Box 353, Bridgewater NS B4V 2W9 – 902/543-4033; Fax: 902/543-4713 – Director, Gary Selig – Home of famed porcupine quill-decorated cradle; parkland & trails; open year round

Bridgewater: Wile Carding Mill, 242 Victoria Rd., PO Box 353, Bridgewater NS B4V 2W9 – 902/543-8233; Fax: 902/543-4713 – Director, Gary Selig – Last surviving plant of a 19th century water-powered industrial park; part of Nova Scotia Museum; open June - Sept.

Canso Museum/Whitman House, Union St., PO Box 128, Canso NS B0H 1H0 – 902/366-2170; Fax: 902/366-3093; URL: http://www.schoolnet.ca/collections/canso/index.htm – Chairman, Joseph Walsh; Curator, Martha Kavanaugh – c.1885

Cheticamp: Musée Acadien, CP 98, Cheticamp NS B0E 1H0 – 902/224-2170 – Directrice, Diane Poirier

Church Point: Le Musée Sainte-Marie, PO Box 28, Church Point NS B0W 1M0 – 902/769-2832 – Présidente, Marguerite Leblanc – Largest wooden church in North America; open June - Oct.

Church Point: Musée du centre Acadien de L'Université Sainte-Anne, Church Point NS B0W 1M0 – 902/769-2114, poste 159 – Directeur, Neil Boucher

Clark's Harbour: Archelaus Smith Museum & Historical Society, PO Box 291, Clark's Harbour NS B0W 1P0 – 902/745-3361, 3227; Email: timkins@atcon.com; URL: http://www.bmhs.ednet.ns.ca/tourism/smith.htm – President, Heather Atkinson – History of Cape Sable Island including fishing techniques & gear, the Cape Island boat, shipwrecks, lives of sea captains, items from old kitchens, paintings by local artists, geneological & other historical records

Cole Harbour Heritage Farm Museum, 471 Poplar Dr., Cole Harbour NS B2W 4L2 – 902/434-0222; Fax: 902/434-0222 – Elizabeth Corser – Open year round

Dartmouth: Evergreen Historic House, 26 Newcastle St., Dartmouth NS B2Y 3M5 – 902/464-2301; Fax: 902/464-8210 – Curator, Betty-Ann Aaboe-Milligan – Open June, July & Aug.

Dartmouth: Quaker Whalers House, 59 Ochterloney St., Dartmouth NS B2Y 1C3 – 902/464-2253; Fax: 902/464-8210 – Director, Dartmouth Municipal Heritage Museum, Richard H. Field, 902/464-2356 – c. 1785; Nantucket whalers

Dartmouth: Shubenacadie Canal Commission, Fairbanks Centre, 54 Locks Rd., Dartmouth NS B2X 2W7 – 902/462-1826; Fax: 902/434-6787 – General Manager, Peter Latta

Deep Brook: Old St. Edwards Loyalist Church, Clementsport, Nova Scotia, Deep Brook NS B0S 1J0 – 902/638-8554 – Contact, Kathleen Cox – Original Loyalist church consecrated 1797; open summer afternoons or by appt.

Digby: Admiral Digby Museum, 95 Montague Row, PO Box 1644, Digby NS B0V 1A0 – 902/245-6322 – President, Nola Jeffrey – Open June - Sept. & by appt.

Dingwall: North Highland Community Museum, RR#1, Dingwall NS B0C 1G0 – 902/383-2051 – Director, Heather Morrison

Glace Bay: Cape Breton Miners' Museum, 42 Birkley St., Glace Bay NS B1A 5T8 – 902/849-4522; Fax: 902/849-8022 – Vice-Chair, Bill Corbett; Secretary, Marg Graham; Chairman, Dr. Terry MacLean; Treasurer, Carole MacLeod; Director, Tom Miller

Grand Pré: Fort Edward National Historic Site, c/o Grand Pré National Historic Site, PO Box 150, Grand Pré NS B0P 1M0 – 902/542-3631

Grand-Pré National Historic Site, PO Box 150, Grand Pré NS B0P 1M0 – 902/542-3631 – Superintendent, Barbara LeBlanc – Bilingual guides interpret history of the Acadians; open daily May 15 - Oct. 15

Guysborough: Old Court House Museum, PO Box 232, Guysborough NS B0H 1N0 – 902/533-4008 – Curator, Kim Avery – Open June - Oct.

Halifax: Fisherman's Life Museum (FLM), Jeddore, Oyster Ponds, 58 Navy Pool Loop, Halifax NS B0J 1W0 – 902/889-2053; Fax: 902/889-2053 – Chief Guide, Eleanor Keeping; Caretaker, Martha Monk – Open June-October 15

Halifax Citadel National Historic Site, PO Box 9080, Stn A, Halifax NS B3K 5M7 – 902/426-5080; Fax: 902/426-4228

Halifax Police Museum, 1975 Gottingen St., Halifax NS B3J 2H1 – 902/421-6840; Email: hpd@atcon.com – Curator, Sgt. Dan Young

Halifax: HMCS Sackville, 1675 Lower Water St., Halifax NS B3K 3B4 – 902/429-5600, 427-0550, ext.2837; Email: nstn1674@fox.nstn.ca; URL: http://www.fox.nstn.ca:80/~nstn1674/navy3.html – Chairman, Capt. Hal Davies; Commanding Officer, Lcdr. Sherry Richardson – World War II ship & interpretation centre; open summer

Halifax: Lawrence House, c/o Curator, Branch Museums, Nova Scotia Museum, 1747 Summer St., Halifax NS B3H 3A6 – c.1865 home of William D. Lawrence, shipwright; open daily May 15 - Oct.

Halifax: Maritime Command Museum/Musée du Commandement Maritime, Admiralty House, PO Box 99000, Stn Forces, Halifax NS B3K 5X5 – 902/427-0550, ext.8250; Fax: 902/427-8541 – Director, Marilyn Gurney – Open year round

Halifax: Nova Scotia Sport Heritage Centre, World Trade & Convention Centre, #403, 1800 Argyle St., Halifax NS B3J 3N8 – 902/421-1266; Fax: 902/425-1148 – Executive Director, Bill Robinson – Open year round

Halifax: Prescott House, c/o Curator, Branch Museums, Nova Scotia Museum, 1747 Summer St., Halifax NS B3H 3A6 – 902/542-3984; Fax: 902/542-3984 – Nancy Morton – c.1814, open June - Oct. 15

Halifax: Prince of Wales Martello Tower National Historic Site, PO Box 9080, Stn A, Halifax NS B3K 5M7 – 902/426-5080; Fax: 902/426-4228

Halifax: Sutherland Steam Mill, c/o Curator, Branch Museums, Nova Scotia Museum, 1747 Summer St., Halifax NS B3H 3A6 – 902/657-3365

Halifax: Thomas McCulloch Museum, Biology Dept., Dalhousie University, 1355 Oxford St., Halifax NS B3H 4J1 – 902/494-3530, 3515; Fax: 902/494-3736; Email: biology@dal.ca; URL: http://is.dal.ca/~sfry/museum1.htm/ – Chief Curator, Stephen Fry – Collection of mounted birds, artifacts, Lorenzen ceramic mushrooms, shells & insects; occasional temporary exhibits; open 8:30-4:40 weekdays; free admission

Halifax: Uniacke House, c/o Curator, Branch Museums, Nova Scotia Museum, 1747 Summer St., Halifax NS B3H 3A6 – c.1813; open June - Oct. 15

Halifax: York Redoubt National Historic Site, PO Box 9080, Stn A, Halifax NS B3K 5M7 – 902/426-5080

Hantsport: Churchill House & Marine Memorial Room Museum, PO Box 399, Hantsport NS B0P 1P0 – 902/684-3461 – Administrator, Norma MacLeod

Inverness Miners Museum, PO Box 161, Inverness NS B0E 1N0 – 902/258-2097 – Director, T. MacDonald

Iona: Nova Scotia Highland Village, PO Box 58, Iona NS B0A 1L0 – 902/725-2272; Fax: 902/725-2227; Email: nshviona@fox.nstn.ca; URL: http://www.ednet.ns.ca/educ/museum/other_ns/highland_village/ – Manager, Rodney Chaisson

Kentville: Blair House Museum, Kentville Agricultural Centre, Kentville NS B4N 1J5 – 902/678-1093; Fax: 902/678-1567 – Manager, Janice Lutz

Kentville: Old Kings Courthouse Museum, 37 Cornwallis St., Kentville NS B4N 2E2 – 902/678-

6237; Fax: 902/679-0066; Email: khs@glinx.com; URL: http://www.go.ednet.ns.ca/~ip960031 – Curator, Bria Stokesbury; Assistant-Curator, Cathy Margeson – Social & natural history of Kings County; Parks Canada commemorative exhibit to the New England Planters

La Have Island Marine Museum, RR#1, La Have NS B0R 1C0 – 902/688-2565; URL: http://www.lunco.com/heritage/lehaveisl.htm – President, Wade Hirtle – Historical treasures from a community that derived its life & livelyhood from the sea

Lahave: Fort Point Museum, c/o Lunenburg County Historical Society, PO Box 99, Lahave NS B0R 1C0 – 902/688-2696 (summer); Email: ftpt@auracom.com; URL: http://www.lunco.com/heritage/fortpoint.htm – President, Jean Gaudet – On site of Fort Ste. Marie de Grâce, 1632

Liverpool: Milton Heritage Society & Blacksmith Shop Museum, PO Box 10, Liverpool NS B0T 1K0 – 902/354-5663 – Curator, Christine Tupper

Liverpool: Perkins House, Queen's County Museum, 105 Main St., PO Box 1078, Liverpool NS B0T 1K0 – 902/354-4058 – Curator, Linda Rafuse – Connecticut style cottage built by merchant & diarist Simeon Perkins; open June - Oct. 15

Liverpool: Queens County Museum, PO Box 1078, Liverpool NS B0T 1K0 – 902/354-4058; URL: http://www.geocities.com/Paris/2669/ – Curator, Linda Rafuse

Lockeport: Little School Museum, Lockeport NS B0T 1L0 – 902/656-2238 – Secretary, Heather Suttle – Replica of a former school room & a marine room; historical artifacts of local area

Louisbourg: Atlantic Statiquarium Marine Museum, PO Box 316, Louisbourg NS B0A 1M0 – 902/733-2721 – Director, Alex Storm

Louisbourg: The Fortress of Louisbourg National Historic Site/Forteresse-de-Louisourg, Lieu historique nationale, PO Box 160, Louisbourg NS B0A 1M0 – 902/733-2280; Fax: 902/733-2362; Email: bill_oshea@pch.qc.ca – Field Unit Manager, Parks Canada, Cape Breton District, Bernard Villeneuve

Louisbourg: The Rectory, PO Box 396, Louisbourg NS B0Z 1M0 – President, William O'Shea – Open year round

Louisbourg: S&L (Sydney & Louisburg) Railway Museum, PO Box 225, Louisbourg NS B0A 1M0 – 902/733-2720 – President, William Bussy – Open June 1 - Oct. 15.

Mabou: An Drochaid/The Bridge, PO Box 175, Mabou NS B0E 1X0 – 902/945-2311

Mahone Bay: Settlers' Museum & Culture Centre, 578 Main St., PO Box 583, Mahone Bay NS B0J 2E0 – 902/624-6263 – Curator, Wilma Stewart – Open May 15 - Sept.

Maitland: East Hants Historical Museum, RR#1, Maitland NS B0N 1T0 – 902/261-2627 – President, Roy Rhyno

Meteghan: La Vieille Maison, CP 10, Meteghan NS B0W 2J0 – 902/645-2322; Fax: 902/645-3032 – Director, Eddie Comeau

Middleton: Annapolis Valley Macdonald Museum, 21 School St., PO Box 925, Middleton NS B0S 1P0 – 902/825-6116 – Executive Director, Cathy Bezanson – Open year round

Mount Uniacke: South Rawdon Museum, RR#1, Mount Uniacke NS B0N 1Z0 – 902/757-2344 – Curator, Helen Haley – Artifacts housed in the former Sons of Temperance Hall built in 1867; exhibits profile the community's history, industries, homes & families. Open daily, June - Labour Day, Sept. by appt.

Musquodoboit Railway Museum, PO Box 303, Musquodoboit Harbour NS B0J 2L0 – 902/889-2689 – Director, Ena Rowlings – Open May 16 - Oct.

New Glasgow: MacPherson's Mill & Farm Homestead, PO Box 403, New Glasgow NS B2H 5E5 – 902/752-7828 – Director, Dr. H. Locke – c. 1857

New Glasgow: Pictou County Historical Museum, 86 Temperance St., New Glasgow NS B2H 3A7 – 902/752-5583 – President, Graham Holman – Open July & Aug.

New Ross: Ross Farm Museum, New Ross NS B0J 2M0 – 902/689-2210; Fax: 902/689-2264 – Branch Director, A. Hiltz – Ross family farm 1817

North East Margaree: Margaree Salmon Museum, North East Margaree NS B0E 2H0 – 902/248-2848 – Curator, Frances Hart

North East Margaree: Museum of Cape Breton Heritage, North East Margaree NS B0E 2H0 – 902/248-2551

Parrsboro: Fundy Geological Museum, 6 Two Island Rd., PO Box 640, Parrsboro NS B0M 1S0 – 902/254-3814; Fax: 902/254-3666; Email: fundyg@ns.sympatico.ca; URL: http://207.134.69.10/nova-scotia/fundygeomuseum/ – Director/Curator, Kenneth Admans; Education Officer, Marilyn Smith – Open year round

Parrsboro: Mineral & Gem Geological Museum, PO Box 297, Parrsboro NS B0M 1S0 – 902/254-2627 – Curator, Marilyn Smith

Pictou: Loch Broom Log Church, RR#2, Pictou NS B0K 1H0

Pictou: McCulloch House Museum (MCH), Old Haliburton Rd., PO Box 1210, Pictou NS B0K 1H0 – 902/485-4563, (open season) 485-1150 – Chief Interpreter, Katherine Chaisson – Open Jun. 1 - Oct. 15

Pictou: Northumberland Fisheries Museum (NFM), PO Box 494, Pictou NS B0K 1H0 – 902/485-4972 – Chair, Dwight MacDonald – Located in the historic C.N. Station; fishing artifacts from the late 1800's to present day; original fisherman's Bunkhouse; The "Silver Bullet"; photographs

Port Hastings Museum & Archives, PO Box 115, Port Hastings NS B0E 2T0 – 902/625-1295 – Curator, Beryl MacDonald

Port Hood: Chestico Museum & Historical Society, PO Box 144, Port Hood NS B0E 2W0 – 902/787-2244 – President, Susan Mailette – Artifacts from the local community; house histories, historical events, people, etc. of the Port Hood area

River Hebert: King Seaman School Museum, c/o Minudie Tourist Council, RR#2, River Hebert NS B0L 1G0 – 902/251-2041 – Open daily July - Labour Day

Riverport: Ovens Natural Park & Museum, PO Box 38, Riverport NS B0J 2W0 – 902/766-4621; Fax: 902/766-4344 – Director, Angela Chapin

Sackville: Fultz Corner Restoration Society, Fultz House Museum, PO Box 124, Sackville NS B0J 2S0 – 902/865-3794 – Director, A. Ruth Auld

Shag Harbour: Chapel Hill Museum, Shag Harbour NS B0W 3B0 – 902/723-2830 – President, Eric Shand; Secretary, Cindy Nickerson; Treasurer, Kaye Ross

Shearwater Aviation Museum, CFB Shearwater, Shearwater NS B0J 3A0 – 902/460-1083; Fax: 902/460-1449 – Director, Lt.-Col. J. Hincke; Curator, Gordon McLauchlan – Open May - Oct.

Shelburne: John C. Williams Dory Shop, PO Box 39, Shelburne NS B0T 1W0 – 902/875-3219; Fax: 902/875-4141 – Coordinator, Emma Harris – Restored dory factory, est. 1880; open June 1 - Sept. 30

Shelburne: Ross Thomson House, c/o Chief Guide, PO Box 39, Shelburne NS B0T 1W0 – 902/875-3141; Fax: 902/875-4141 – Coordinator, Emma Harris – 1785 Loyalist house & garden; 18th century store & chandler; 19th century military artifacts

Shelburne County Museum, Dock St. & Maiden Lane, PO Box 39, Shelburne NS B0T 1W0 – 902/875-3219 – Curator, Finn Bower – Open year round

Sherbrooke Restoration, PO Box 295, Sherbrooke NS B0J 3C0 – 902/522-2400 – Project Director, Craig MacDonald – 20 buildings, 1860-1890, on original sites; open June - Oct. 15

Smith's Cove Historical Museum, RR#1, Smith's Cove NS B0S 1S0 – President, Dorothy Gray

Springhill: The Anne Murray Centre, Main St., PO Box 610, Springhill NS B0M 1X0 – 902/597-8614; Fax: 902/597-2001; URL: http://www.grtplaces.com/ac/anne – Executive Director, Shelagh F. Rayworth – Pays tribute to the achievements of Springhill's internationally acclaimed singing superstar; Open May - Oct., otherwise by appt.

Springhill Miners Museum, Black River Rd., PO Box 610, Springhill NS B0M 1X0 – 902/597-3449 (summer); 902/597-8614; Fax: 902/597-2001; URL: http://www.grtplaces.com/ac/mine – Acting Director, Shelagh Rayworth – Tours of the Springhill coal mine, famous in song & legend; gift shop & picnic area; open May - Oct.

St. Peter's: Nicolas Denys Museum, PO Box 249, St. Peter's NS B0E 3B0 – 902/535-2175 – Curator, Jessie MacDonald – Micmac, Acadien, Scottish & Irish artifacts

Stellarton: The Museum of Industry, PO Box 2590, Stellarton NS B0K 1S0 – 902/755-5425; Fax: 902/755-7045; Email: educnsm.mcnabbada@gov.ns.ca; URL: http://www.ednet.ns.ca/educ/museum/moi/index.htm – Branch Director, Debra McNabb – Atlantic Canada's largest museum; chronicles the impact of industrialization on the people, economy & landscape of Nova Scotia; features Canada's oldest steam locomotives, an historic model railway layout, a belt-driven working machine shop & a collection of Nova Scotia's Trenton glass

Sydney: Cape Breton Centre for Heritage & Science, 225 George St., Sydney NS B1P 1J5 – 902/539-1572; Fax: 902/539-1572 – Curator, Janet Maltby – Operates Cossit House, c.1787, open June - Oct. 15; St. Patrick's Church Museum, open summer & fall

Tatamagouche: Balmoral Grist Mill, RR#4, Tatamagouche NS B0K 1V0 – 902/657-3016 – Supt., John E. Taylor

Tatamagouche: Sunrise Trail Museum, Main St., Tatamagouche NS B0K 1V0 – 902/657-2433 – Director, Ellen Millard – Open daily mid-June - mid-Sept.

Truro: Colchester Historical Society Museum, 29 Young St., PO Box 412, Truro NS B2N 5C5 – 902/895-6284; Fax: 902/895-9530; Email: chmusarc@atcon.com; URL: http://www.shelburne.nscc.ns.ca/nsgna/col/col_main.htm – Curator, Ira E. Creelman; Archivist, Nan Harvey – Open year round

Truro: The Little White Schoolhouse, c/o Nova Scotia Teachers College, PO Box 810, Truro NS B2N 5G5 – 902/895-5347; Fax: 902/893-5610; Email: Tiwana@n.s.sympatico.ca – President, Eric Bent; Curator, Harvey W. MacPhee

West Bay: Marble Mountain Community Museum, RR#1, West Bay NS B0E 3K0 – 902/756-2638 – Curator, Jean McNicol

West Pubnico: Musée acadien de Pubnico-Ouest, CP 92, West Pubnico NS B0W 3S0 – 902/762-2039 – Président, Elaine Surette

Westphal: Black Cultural Centre for Nova Scotia, 1149 Main St., Westphal NS B2Z 1A8 – 902/434-6223; Fax: 902/434-2306; Email: blackcc@fox.nstn.ca; URL: http://www.nstn.ca/bccns/bcc.html – Chief Curator, Henry Bishop – History & culture dating back to the 1600s; open year round

Windsor: Shand House, Clifton Ave., PO Box 2683, Windsor NS B0N 2T0 – 902/798-8213

Windsor: Thomas Chandler Haliburton House, PO Box 2683, Windsor NS B0N 2T0 – 902/798-2915 – Open June 1 - Oct. 15

Windsor: West Hants Historical Society, 281 King St., Windsor NS B0N 2T0 – 902/798-5265 – President, Veronica Connelly – June - Sept 30

Wolfville: Randall House Museum, 171 Main St., PO Box 38, Wolfville NS B0P 1X0 – 902/542-9775 –

Director, Heather A. Davidson – c. 1808; open daily June 15 - Sept. 15

Yarmouth: Firefighters' Museum of Nova Scotia & National Exhibition Centre, Nova Scotia Museum Complex, 451 Main St., Yarmouth NS B5A 1G9 – 902/742-5525; Fax: 902/742-5525 – Curator, David Darby – Artifacts date to the early 1800s; open year round

Yarmouth County Museum & Historical Research Archives, c/o Yarmouth County Historical Society, 22 Collins St., Yarmouth NS B5A 3C8 – 902/742-5539; Fax: 902/749-1120; Email: ycn0056@ycn.library.ns.ca; URL: http://www.ycn.library.ns.ca/museum/yarcomus.htm – Director/Curator, E.J. Ruff; Archivist, Laura Bradley – Also operates the Pelton-Fuller House in Yarmouth, the historic summer home of A.C. Fuller, the Fuller Brush Man

## NORTHWEST TERRITORIES

### Prince of Wales Northern Heritage Centre (PWNHC)

PO Box 1320, Yellowknife NT X1A 2L9
867/873-7551; Fax: 867/873-0205;
Email: charles_arnold@ece.learnet.nt.ca
URL: http://pwnhc.nt.ca

Archeological, ethnological, historical & fine arts collections from the Arctic & Subarctic regions of the NWT; comparative faunal collections of indigenous animals; NWT Archives contain 7,000 books, newspapers & periodicals; historical photo collection; research centre.

Director, Charles D. Arnold
Territorial Achivist, Richard Valpy
Curator, Joanne Bird

### Other Museums & Science Centres in Northwest Territories

Fort Smith: Northern Life Museum & National Exhibition Centre, PO Box 420, Fort Smith NT X0E 0P0 – 867/872-2349; Fax: 867/872-4345 – Director, Boris Atamanenko; Curator, Gina Sydenham – Collection, preservation & presentation of NWT culture & history - Open year round

Fort Smith: Wood Buffalo National Park Visitor Reception Centre, PO Box 750, Fort Smith NT X0E 0P0 – 867/872-2349; Fax: 867/872-4345 – Community Liaison Officer, Tamar Vandenberghe

Hamlet of Arctic Bay: Sod House Museum, c/o Innumarit Committee, Hamlet of Arctic Bay NT X0A 0A0 – 867/439-9918

Holman Museum, General Delivery, Holman NT X0A 0S0 – 867/396-3141 – Curator, Alan Sim

Iqaluit: Nuantta Sunaqutangit Museum, PO Box 605, Iqaluit NT X0A 0H0 – 867/979-5537; Fax: 867/979-4533 – Curator, Denise Kekkema

Norman Wells: Colville Lake Museum, Norman Wells NT X0E 0V0 – Curator, Bern Will Brown

Norman Wells Historical Centre, PO Box 56, Norman Wells NT X0E 0V0 – 867/587-2415; Fax: 867/587-2469 – Manager, Warren Schmitke

Pangnirtung: Auyuittuq National Park Reserve (ANPR), Parks Canada, Nunavut District, PO Box 353e, Pangnirtung NT X0A 0R0 – 867/473-8828; Email: nunavut_info@pch.gc.ca; URL: http://www.parkscanada.pch.gc.ca/parks/nwtw/auynit/ug/auyu:huge.htm – Yves Bossé

Pangnirtung: Sipalaseequtt Museum Society, Angmarlik Centre, Pangnirtung NT X0E 0R0 – 867/473-8756 – Manager, Simeonie Akpalialuk

Sachs Harbour Museum, c/o Hamlet Council, Sachs Harbour NT X0E 0Z0 – 867/690-4361

## ONTARIO

### Canadian Football Hall of Fame & Museum

58 Jackson St. West, Hamilton ON L8P 1L4
905/528-7566; Fax: 905/528-9781

Exhibits profile the history & progression of football in Canada; interactive education programs, unique collections, a library/archives & the Grey Cup trophy; gift shop & mail order.

Managing Director, Janice Smith

### Hockey Hall of Fame/Le Temple de la Renommée du Hockey (HHOF)

BCE Place, 30 Yonge St., Toronto ON M5E 1X8
416/360-7765; Fax: 416/360-1501
URL: http://www.hhof.com

Opened in June 1993; films, photos, memorabilia.

Chairman, Board of Directors, Scotty (Ian) Morrison

### Ontario Science Centre/Centre des sciences de l'Ontario

770 Don Mills Rd., North York ON M3C 1T3
416/429-4100; Fax: 416/696-3124
URL: http://www.osc.on.ca

Over 800 interactive exhibits on the environment, technology, food, chemistry, communications, sport & space; exhibits, programs, demonstrations, workshops & films for the public; special programs for school groups, children, adults & senior citizens; gift shops & restaurant; Ontario's only OMNIMAX Theatre featuring a 24-metre dome screen with wrap-around sound; open year round.

Director General & CEO, Dr. Sid A. Katz

### Royal Ontario Museum (ROM)

100 Queen's Park, Toronto ON M5S 2C6
416/586-5549; Fax: 416/586-5863; Info Line: 416/586-8000
URL: http://www.rom.on.ca

The Royal Ontario Museum is Canada's largest museum & is a major research institution consisting of curatorial departments in the fields of art, archaeology & science & a number of other departments dealing with education, communication & administration. The ROM continues to develop new galleries after completing an extensive renovation & expansion project. On display are Far Eastern, Greek, Roman & Egyptian artifacts & textiles, European art, life science specimens, invertebrate fossils & dinosaurs. Also featured are special exhibitions. Notable galleries include the S.R. Perfen Gem & Gold Room, which showcases nearly 1,000 gems & 70 gold specimens, the Dinosaur Gallery, the Bat Cave Gallery & a hands-on Gallery, the Discovery Centre; the Canadian Heritage Floor, which includes the Sigmund Samuel Canadiana Gallery, shows the fine & decorative art achievements of early French & English settlers. The museum offers a variety of programs & activities including special exhibitions, concerts, lectures, film, & gallery tours & field trips. Education Services: The department organizes school tours, produces learning resource materials, & provides professional development courses for Ontario teachers. For school bookings, call 416/586-5801. Outreach Services: The department offers circulating & modular exhibitions to local museums, libraries, shopping centres, schools & service organizations throughout the province & the country (416/586-5682). Public Services: Free guided gallery tours; walking tours during summer.

Director, Lindsay Sharp

### Other Museums & Science Centres in Ontario

Almonte: Mill of Kintail, RR#1, Almonte ON K0A 1A0 – 613/256-3610; Fax: 613/259-3468 – Curator, Carol Munden

Almonte: Mississippi Valley Textile Museum, PO Box 784, Almonte ON K0A 1A0 – 613/256-3754; Fax: 613/256-3754 – President, Mary K. Hugessen – Information on the early mills & their owners; displays of period offices; artifacts & machinery related to the beginnings of the textile industry

Almonte: North Lanark Regional Museum, PO Box 218, Almonte ON K0A 1A0 – 613/256-1805 – Curator, Dawn Leduc

Ameliasburgh Historical Museum, PO Box 67, Ameliasburgh ON K0K 1A0 – 613/968-9678; Fax: 613/962-1514 – Curator, Marion Casson

Amherstburg: Fort Malden National Historic Site/Lieu historique national du Fort-Malden (FMNHS), 100 Laird Ave., PO Box 38, Amherstburg ON N9V 2Z2 – 519/736-5416; Fax: 519/736-6603; Email: Bob_Garcia@pch.gc.ca – Resource Centre Specialist, Bob Garcia; Site Manager, Rob Watt

Amherstburg: North American Black Historical Museum Inc., 277 King St., Amherstburg ON N9V 2C7 – 519/736-5433; Fax: 519/736-5433 – Curator, Elise Harding-Davis – Open April - Nov.

Amherstburg: Park House Museum, 214 Dalhousie St., Amherstburg ON N9V 1W4 – 519/736-2511 – Curator, Valerie Buckle

Ancaster: Fieldcote Memorial Park & Museum, 64 Sulphur Springs Rd., PO Box 81123, Ancaster ON L9G 4X1 – 905/648-8144; Fax: 905/648-8144; Email: bradleyj.@currentthinking; URL: http://www.currentthinking.com/fieldcote

Ancaster: Hermitage Gatehouse Museum, Hamilton Region Conservation Authority, PO Box 7099, Ancaster ON L9G 3L3 – 905/648-4427; Fax: 905/648-4622 – Director, Community Relations, Joan Bell

Ancaster: Ingledale, c/o Hamilton Region Conservation Authority, PO Box 7099, Ancaster ON L9G 3L3 – 416/643-2103 – Superintendent, Bruce Mackenzie – c. 1812 home of Inglehart family

Ancaster: Sulpher Springs Station/Dundas Valley Trail Centre, c/o Hamilton Region Conservation Authority, PO Box 7099, Ancaster ON L9G 3L3 – 905/648-4427 – Supt., Paul Piett

Ancaster: Valens Log Cabin/Valens Conservation Area, c/o Hamilton Region Conservation Authority, PO Box 7099, Ancaster ON L9G 3L3 – 905/659-7715 – Curator, Scott Hanville

Appin: Ekfrid Township Museum, Appin ON N0L 1A0 – 519/289-2016 – President, Margot Dargatz

Arnprior & District Museum/Musée d'Arnprior et Région, 35 Madawaska St., Arnprior ON K7S 1R6 – 613/623-4902; Fax: 613/623-8091 – Curator, Helen Golding

Astra: RCAF Memorial Museum/ARC Musée Commémoratif, 8 Wing Trenton, PO Box 1000, Stn Forces, Astra ON K0K 3W0 – 613/965-2140; 2208; Fax: 613/965-7532 – Executive Director, Jeffrey Brace; Curator, Earl Hewison – Social history museum dedicated to the airmen & airwomen who served in Canada's Air Forces; features world's only complete Mark VII Halifax bomber, 14 aircraft, commemorative cairns & more than 2,200 "AD ASTRA" granite stones; artifacts; memorabilia; gift shop

Atikokan Centennial Museum, Civic Centre, PO Box 849, Atikokan ON P0T 1C0 – 807/597-6585 – Manager/Curator, Lorraine Stromberg

Aurora Museum, 22 Church St., Aurora ON L4G 1G4 – 905/727-8991 – Curator, Jacqueline Stuart – Local history museum: exhibits, events, reference library

Aurora: Hillary House & the Koffler Museum of Medicine, 15372 Yonge St., Aurora ON L4G 1N8 – 905/727-4015 – Site Manager, John MacIntyre

Aylmer & District Museum, 14 East St., Aylmer ON N5H 1W2 – 519/773-9723 – Curator, Patricia Zimmer – Changing historical exhibits, local archives, tourist centre

Aylmer: Ontario Police College Museum, PO Box 1190, Aylmer ON N5H 2T2 – 519/773-5361; Fax: 519/773-5762 – Curator, M. Brown

Bancroft Mineral Museum, c/o Bancroft & District Chamber of Commerce, PO Box 539, Bancroft ON K0L 1C0 – 613/332-1513; Fax: 613/332-2119; Email: chamber@commerce.bancroft.on.ca – Curator, Chris Fouts – 350 locally collected mineral specimens; mineral collecting field trips; open year round

Bancroft: North Hastings Heritage Museum, PO Box 239, Bancroft ON K0L 1C0 – 613/332-1884 – Chair, Vilma Walker

Bath: Loyalist Cultural Centre, Adolphustown Park, Bath ON K0H 1G0 – 613/373-2196; Fax: 613/373-0043; Email: staples@ihorizons.net – Katherine Staples – Artifacts; military display; genealogical resources; open Victoria to Labour Day & by appt.

Beachville District Museum, 584371 Beachville Rd., PO Box 6, Beachville ON N0J 1A0 – 519/423-6497; Fax: 519/423-6126 – Curator, Sue Fletcher

Beaver River Museum, 284 Simcoe St., PO Box 314, Beaverton ON L0K 1A0 – 705/426-9641 – Curator, Julienne Everett – 1840s stone jail, settler's log cabin, working man's brick house; local archives; Meeting Place (Beaverton Thorah Eldon Historical Society)

Belleville: Glanmore National Historic Site, 257 Bridge St. East, Belleville ON K8N 1P4 – 613/962-2329; Fax: 613/962-6340; Email: glanmorehcm@suckercreek.on.ca – Curator/Manager, Rona Rustige

Belleville: O'Hara Mill Museum, c/o Moira River Conservation Authority, PO Box 698, Belleville ON K8N 5B3 – 613/968-8240

Blind River: Timber Village Museum, PO Box 628, Blind River ON P0R 1B0 – 705/356-7544; Fax: 705/962-6340 – Secretary, Linda Rainville

Bloomfield: Quinte Educational Museum & Archives, 1 Stanley St., PO Box 220, Bloomfield ON K0K 1G0 – 613/393-3166, ext.254 – Curator, Jennifer Weymark – Extensive collection of educational memorabilia

Bobcaygeon: Kawartha Settlers' Village, 85 Dunn St., Bobcaygeon ON K0M 1A0 – 705/738-6163 – President, Judy Muzzi; Vice-President, George Truss – Historic homes & buildings collected on former Kawartha farm; regional arts & heritage centre

Bolton: Canadian Museum of Animal Art, PO Box 500, Bolton ON L7E 5T4 – 905/859-0651 – J.M. James – Animal art in all its forms

Bothwell: Fairfield Museum, RR#3, Bothwell ON N0P 1C0 – 519/692-4397 – Curator, Archie McIntyre – Site of Moravian Delaware mission, est. 1792, destroyed 1813 by US soldiers; artifacts from burnt village

Bowmanville Museum, 37 Silver St., PO Box 188, Bowmanville ON L1C 3K9 – 905/623-2734; Fax: 905/623-5684 – Curator, Charles Taws – Restored 1847 house depicting way of life of a wealthy merchant family; antique doll gallery; Marion Wiseman Gallery

Bracebridge: Woodchester Villa, PO Box 2231, Bracebridge ON P1L 1W1 – 705/645-8111 – Curator, Elene J. Freer

Bracebridge: Woodmere Logging Museum, PO Box 2001, Bracebridge ON P0B 1C0 – 705/767-3303 – Jim Wood – Open July - Aug.

Brampton: Region of Peel Archives & Museum, 9 Wellington St. East, Brampton ON L6W 1Y1 – 905/451-9051; Fax: 905/451-9051; Email: somersd@region.peel.on.ca – Regional Archivist, Sharon Larade; Curator, Exhibitions, David Somers

Brantford: Bell Homestead & Henderson Home, 94 Tutela Heights Rd., Brantford ON N3T 1A1 – 519/756-6220; Fax: 519/759-5975 – Curator, Brian Wood – Family home of Alexander Graham Bell

Brant County Museum, 57 Charlotte St., Brantford ON N3T 2W6 – 519/752-2483; Email: can-bcma-b@immedia.ca – Curator, Susan Twist

Brantford: Myrtleville House Museum, 34 Myrtleville Dr., Brantford ON N3V 1C2 – 519/752-3216; Fax: 519/752-9550; Email: myrtleville@bfree.on.ca; Tourism Brantford: 1-800-265-6299; URL: http://www.bfree.on.ca/comdir/musgal/myrtle/ – Executive Director/Curator, Susan E. Sager

Brighton: Presqu'ile Provincial Park Museum, RR#4, Brighton ON K0K 1H0 – 613/475-4324; Fax: 613/475-4324; Email: parkpr@epo.gov.on.ca; URL: presquil@parks.kosone.com – Park Supt, Tom Mates – One of Ontario's oldest provincial parks (1922); displays & programs of early history of the area; working lighthouse

Brighton: Proctor House Museum (SOHO), 96 Young St., PO Box 578, Brighton ON K0K 1H0 – 613/475-2144 – President, Tom Cunningham

Brockville Museum, 5 Henry St., Brockville ON K6V 6M4 – 613/342-4397; Fax: 613/342-7345; Email: bm-chin@mulberry.com – Director, Bonnie Burke – Committed to the preservation & promotion of Brockville; artifacts; archives

Bruce Mines Museum, Taylor St., Hwy. #17, Bruce Mines ON P0R 1C0 – 705/785-3426; Fax: 705/785-3170 – Curator, Tina Peppler – Referred to as "The Church of the Rock"; thousands of local artifacts; archives; tourist information; giftshop

Burgessville: Oxford County Museum School, PO Box 37, Burgessville ON N0J 1C0 – 519/424-9964 – Curator, Judy A. Livingstone; Chairperson, Barry Tate – Set in historic 1905 school house; collection includes educational materials & children's toys from the 1880's to the 1960's; tours & educational programs

Burlington: Ireland House Museum, 2168 Guelph Line, Burlington ON L7P 4M3 – 905/332-9888

Burlington: Joseph Brant Museum, 1240 North Shore Blvd. East, Burlington ON L7S 1C5 – 905/634-3556; Fax: 905/634-4498 – Collection housed in reconstruction of Chief Brant's home

CFB Borden: Borden Military Museum & Archives/Musée commémoratif et archives de la Borden, CFB Borden ON L0M 1C0 – 705/423-3531; Fax: 705/423-3531 – Curator, Keith Lawson; Asst. Curator, Jim Sadlier

Caledonia: Edinburgh Square Heritage & Cultural Centre, 80 Caithness St. East, PO Box 2056, Caledonia ON N3W 2G6 – 905/765-3134; Fax: 905/765-3009; Email: eschin@interlynx.com; URL: http://www.headstartcomp.on.ca/heritage/square – Director/Curator, Barbra Lang Walker – Local history museum & cultural centre located in the former town hall built in 1857; special events

Callander: North Himsworth Twp. Museum, PO Box 100, Callander ON P0H 1H0 – 705/752-2282; Fax: 705/752-3116 – Curator, Carol Anne Pretty; Curator, Carol Anne Pretty – Former home & office of Dr. A.R. Dafoe, physician to the Dionne quintuplets

Cambellcroft: Dorothy's House Museum (EDHS), 3632 Ganaraska Rd., Cambellcroft ON L0A 1B0 – 905/797-1170; Fax: 905/797-3379; Email: edhs@nhb.com; URL: http://www.nhb.com/edhs.htm

Campbellford-Seymour Heritage Centre, 113 Front St. North, PO Box 1294, Campbellford ON K0L 1L0 – 705/653-2634 – Jean Tilney – Displays on a theme basis several times a year. Open every Wednesday year round; June - September, Tuesday - Saturday 10-4. Also has an active archives & research centre.

Cannington & Area Historical Society, Centennial Museum, PO Box 196, Cannington ON L0E 1E0 – 705/432-2558 – Curator, Edna Eastman

Carleton Place: Victoria School Museum, 267 Edmund St., Carleton Place ON K7C 3E8 – 613/253-1395

Cayuga: Haldimand County Museum, 8 Echo St., PO Box 38, Cayuga ON N0A 1E0 – 905/772-5880 – Curator, Merle Knight

Chapleau Centennial Museum, PO Box 129, Chapleau ON P0M 1K0 – 705/864-1330; Fax: 705/864-0761 – Open May 15 - Oct. 15

Chatham-Kent Museum, 75 William St. North, Chatham ON N7M 4L4 – 519/354-8338; Fax: 519/354-4170; Email: can-ccg@immedia.ca – Curator, David Benson

Chatham Railroad Museum, PO Box 434, Chatham ON N7M 5K5 – 519/352-3097 – Gary Shurgold – Located in a C.N. baggage car built in 1955, it was removed from active service in 1982 & was resurrected in its present form in 1989. It contains early railroad equipment such as switches, lanterns, a caboose stove, several model trains & other memorabilia.

Chatham: Firefighting Museum, c/o Chatham Fire Department,, 5 Second St., Chatham ON K7M 5X2 – 519/436-3295; Fax: 519/352-8620

Chatham: Milner Heritage House, c/o Chatham-Kent Museum, 75 William St. North, Chatham ON N7M 4L4 – 519/354-8338; Fax: 519/354-4170; Email: can-ccc@immedia.ca – Curator, David Benson – Open by appt. only

Cheltenham: The Great War Flying Museum, Brampton Airport, RR#1, Cheltenham ON L0P 1C0 – 905/838-1400

Clarksburg: Beaver Valley Military Museum, Marsh St., PO Box 40, Clarksburg ON N0H 1J0 – 519/599-3031; Fax: 519/599-2474 – Curator, Muriel Hewgill – WWI & WWII; open summer

Cloyne Pioneer Museum, PO Box 228, Cloyne ON K0H 1K0 – 613/336-8712 – Curator, Frances Watt – Open July - Sept.

Cobalt's Northern Ontario Mining Museum, 24 Silver St., PO Box 215, Cobalt ON P0J 1C0 – 705/679-8301; Fax: 705/679-5050; Email: cnomchin@nt.net – Sec.-Treas., Anne Fraboni

Cochrane Railway & Pioneer Museum, 210 Railway St., PO Box 490, Cochrane ON P0L 1C0 – 705/272-4361; Fax: 705/272-6068 – Curator, Paul Latondress

Coldwater Canadiana Heritage Museum, PO Box 125, Coldwater ON L0K 1E0 – 705/835-5032; Email: billing@bconnex.net – President, Gary Brandon; Vice-President, Harold Greenwood; Sec.-Treas., Alan Billington – 1840s log house + other buildings

Collingwood: The Collingwood Museum, Hwy. 26 & St. Paul St., PO Box 556, Collingwood ON L9Y 4B2 – 705/445-4811; Fax: 705/445-9004 – Curator, Tracy Marsh

Comber: Tilbury West Agricultural Museum, PO Box 158, Comber ON N0P 1J0 – 519/687-2240 – Curator, Myrtle Frankfurth

Combermere: Madonna House Pioneer Museum, Combermere ON K0J 1L0 – 613/756-0103 – Director, Linda Lambeth

Commanda General Store Museum, Commanda ON P0H 1J0 – 705/729-2113 – Chair, Richard Jeffrey

Cornwall: Inverarden Regency Cottage Museum, 3332 Montréal Rd., PO Box 773, Cornwall ON K6H 5T5 – 613/938-9585; Fax: 613/938-9585; Email: slm@cnwl.igs.net; URL: http://www.cnwl.igs.net/~slm/index.html – Curator, Ian Bowering – Open daily Apr. - Nov.; closed Monday

Cornwall: United Counties Museum, 731 Second St. West, PO Box 773, Cornwall ON K6H 5T5 – 613/932-2381; Fax: 613/830-8741 – Curator, Marie Lacabanne – Open daily Apr. - Oct.

Cornwall Island: Museum of the North American Indian Travelling College, RR#3, Cornwall Island ON K6H 5R7 – 613/932-9454; Fax: 613/932-0092; Email: nnatc@glen-net.ca – Executive Director, Barbara Barnes

Cumberland Heritage Village Museum, 2940 Queen St., PO Box 159, Cumberland ON K4C 1E6 – 613/833-3059; Fax: 613/830-3061; Email: chumchin@cyberplus.ca

Delhi: Ontario Tobacco Museum & Heritage Centre, 200 Talbot Rd., Delhi ON N4B 2A2 – 519/582-0278; Fax: 519/582-0122; Email: otmchin@simcom.on.ca – Curator/Director, Myles G. Cowan

Delhi: Tobacco Museum & Heritage Centre, 200 Talbot Rd., Delhi ON N4B 2A2 – 519/582-0278; Fax: 519/582-0122 – Operations Co-Ordinator, Mary E. Baruth

Delhi: Windham Township Pioneer Museum, c/o Ontario Tobacco Museum & Heritage Centre, 200 Talbot Rd., Delhi ON N4B 2A2 – 519/582-0278; Fax: 519/582-0122 – Curator, Mary E. Baruth

Delta: The Delta Mill/The Old Stone Mill Museum (DMS), PO Box 172, Delta ON K0E 1G0 – 613/924-2658; URL: http://www.web.canlink.com/kwatson/delta/stonemill.html – President, A. Shaw – Stone mill c. 1810

Dresden: Uncle Tom's Cabin Historic Site (UTCHS), RR#5, Dresden ON N0P 1M0 – 519/683-2978; Fax: 519/683-1256; Email: parkway@ebtech.net – Curator, Barbara Carter – Original home of the Rev. Josiah Henson

Dryden & District Museum, 15 Van Horne Ave., Dryden ON P8N 2A5 – 807/223-4671; Fax: 807/223-3999 – Director/Curator, Edna Libbus Boon

Dundas Historical Society Museum, 139 Park St. West, Dundas ON L9H 5G1 – 905/627-7412; Fax: 905/223-3999 – Curator, Olive Newcombe

Dunvegan: The Glengarry Pioneer Museum, PO Box 27, Dunvegan ON K0C 1J0 – 613/527-5230 – Curator, Ruth McIntosh – 1840 log inn; miniature cheese factory; 1869 municipal hall; carriage shed & log barn

Ear Falls District Museum, PO Box 309, Ear Falls ON P0V 1T0 – 807/222-3198 – Curator, J. Appel

Elgin: Jones Falls Defensible Lockmaster's House & Blacksmith Shop, PO Box 10, Elgin ON K0G 1E0 – 613/359-5377; Fax: 613/354-6042 – Sector Supervisor, Sandy Haining – Lockmaster's house c. 1841; blacksmith shop produces hardware c. 1843

Elgin: Kingston Mills Blockhouse, PO Box 10, Elgin ON K0G 1E0 – 613/359-5377; Fax: 613/359-6042 – Sector Supervisor, A.J. "Sandy" Haining – 1840s animated militia barracks

Elk Lake Museum & Heritage Centre, c/o Corporation of Township of James, PO Box 70, Elk Lake ON P0J 1G0 – 705/678-2237 – Chairman, M.D. Giles – History of area, in particular, mining, lumbering, agriculture

Elliot Lake Nuclear & Mining Museum, Municipal Offices, 45 Hillside Dr. North, Elliot Lake ON P5A 1X5 – 705/461-7233; Fax: 705/461-7244 – Curator, Robert E. Manuel – Logging & wildlife display, art gallery; open year round

Emo: Rainy River District Women's Institute Museum, PO Box 511, Emo ON P0W 1E0 – 807/482-2792 – Curator, Tina Visser – Small pioneer museum

Englehart & Area Historical Museum, 69 - 6th Ave., PO Box 444, Englehart ON P0J 1H0 – 705/544-2400; Fax: 705/544-8737 – Curator, Susan Noakes – Open May 1 - Dec. 1

Essex: Bicentennial Museum, Township of Maidstone & Area, 1095 Puce Rd., RR#3, Essex ON N8M 2X7 – 519/727-6668, ext.39 – President, Sue Sylvester

Essex: John R. Park Homestead, c/o Essex Region Conservation Authority, 360 Fairview Ave. West, Essex ON N8M 1Y6 – 519/738-2029; Fax: 519/776-8688; Email: erca@wincom.net; URL: http://www.wincom.net/~erca – Curator, Janet Cobban – Living history museum; open year round

Etobicoke: The Canadian Business Hall of Fame/Le Temple de la renommée de l'entreprise canadienne, c/o Junior Achievement of Canada, 1 Westside Dr., Etobicoke ON M9C 1B2 – 416/622-4602; Fax: 416/622-6861; Email: ghabib@jacan.org; URL: http://www.jacan.org – President & CEO, George Habib – Located in The Galleria, BCE Place

Etobicoke: Montgomery's Inn, 4709 Dundas St. West, Etobicoke ON M9A 1A8 – 416/394-8113; Fax: 416/394-6027 – Heritage Coordinator/Director, U. Ernest Buchner

Exeter: Arkona Lion's Museum & Information Centre, c/o Ausable-Bayfield Conservation Authority, RR#3, Exeter ON N0M 1S5 – 519/828-3071; Fax: 519/235-1963; Email: abca@execulink – General Manager, Tom Prout – Native artifacts, fossils & minerals; open May - Oct.

Fenelon Falls Museum, 50 Oak St., PO Box 667, Fenelon Falls ON K0M 1N0 – 705/887-1044; Fax: 705/887-4337 – Chairman of Museum Board, Malcolm Fleck; Sec.-Treas., Evelyn Fleck; Curator, Naomi Struik

Fergus: Wellington County Museum & Archives, RR#1, Fergus ON N1M 2W3 – 519/846-0916; Fax: 519/846-9630 – Director, Ellen Langlands – National Historic Site; English, Irish & Scottish heritage of the area; museum housed in an 1877 limestone House of Industry & Refuge; open year round

Flesherton: Frontier Village, c/o Archie Bernard, RR#2, Flesherton ON N0C 1E0 – 519/924-3250; Fax: 519/924-3330

Flesherton: South Grey Museum & Historical Library, PO Box 299, Flesherton ON N0C 1E0 – 519/924-2843 – Curator, Catherine Carmichael – Open daily

Forest-Lambton Museum, 59 Broadway Ave., RR#1, Forest ON N0N 1J0 – 519/786-5884 – Curator, E.M. Powell

Fort Erie: Mildred M. Mahoney Silver Jubilee Dolls' House Gallery, 657 Niagara Blvd., Fort Erie ON L2A 3H9 – 905/871-5833; Email: yvonne@iaw.on.ca; URL: http://www.angelfire.com/biz/DollHouseGallery/index.html – Curator, June Spear; Assistant Curator, Yvonne Hopkins

Fort Frances Museum & Cultural Centre, 259 Scott St., Fort Frances ON P9A 1G8 – 807/274-7891; Fax: 807/274-8479 – Curator, Pam Hawley – Operates: Logging Tugboat Hallett; Tower Lookout Historical Museum & Fort St. Pierre, Pither's Point Park; open summer

Frankford: Orval Berry Museum, 22 Belleville St., Frankford ON K0K 2C0 – 613/398-6531 – Orval Berry; Peggy Berry – Open year round, Sat., Sun. & holidays

Frankville: Montgomery House, Kitley Historical Association, RR#1, Frankville ON K0E 1H0 – 613/275-2025 – President, Grant Montgomery

Gananoque Historical Museum, 10 King St. East, PO Box 158, Gananoque ON K7G 2T7 – 613/382-4024; Fax: 613/382-8587 – Curator, Lynette McLellan – Open mid-June - mid-Sept., Mon. - Sat.

Glenburnie: Polliwog Castle/Antique Doll & Toy Museum, Division St. North, RR#1, Glenburnie ON K0H 1S0 – 613/548-4702 – Open daily Victoria Day - Labour Day & weekends in winter

Gloucester: Canadian Basketball Hall of Fame, c/o Basketball Canada, 1600 James Naismith Dr., Gloucester ON K1B 5N4

Gloucester: Curling Hall of Fame & Museum of Canada Inc., 1600 James Naismith Dr., Gloucester ON K1B 5N4 – Curator, Tom Fisher

Gloucester Museum, 4550 Bank St., RR#6, Gloucester ON K1G 3N4 – 613/822-2076

Goderich: Huron County Museum & Archives, 110 North St., Goderich ON N7A 2T8 – 519/524-2686; Fax: 519/524-5677 – Director, Claus Breede – Operates the Marine Museum, South Harbour

Huron Historical Gaol, 181 Victoria St., ON N7A 2S9 – 524-2686; Fax: 524-5677 – Curator, Harold Erb

Golden Lake Algonquin Museum, PO Box 28, Golden Lake ON K0J 1X0 – 613/625-2027 – Curator, Philip Commanda

Gore Bay Museum, Western Manitoulin Historical Society, c/o Town Clerk, PO Box 298, Gore Bay ON P0P 1H0 – 705/282-2420

Gormley: Whitchurch-Stouffville Museum, 14732 Woodbine Ave., Gormley ON L0H 1G0 – 905/727-8954; Fax: 905/727-8954 – Curator, Dorie Billich

Gowganda & Area Museum, Gowganda ON P0J 1J0 – 705//624-3171 – Director, David Ford – Open mid-May - mid-Sept.

Grafton: Barnum House Museum, PO Box 161, Grafton ON K0K 2G0 – 416/349-2656; Fax: 416/349-2656 – Patrick Archer; Lorraine Oliver; Douglas Sifton – Open year round

Grand Bend: Lambton Heritage Museum, RR#2, Grand Bend ON N0M 1T0 – 519/243-2600 – Curator, Robert Tremain

Gravenhurst: Bethune Memorial House National Historic Site, 235 John St. North, Gravenhurst ON P1P 1G4 – 705/687-4261; Fax: 705/687-4935; Email: ont_bethune@pch.gc.ca; URL: http://parkscanada.pch.gc.ca/parks/ontario/bethune_memorialhouse – Site Manager, Maryellen Corcelli – Birthplace of Dr. Norman Bethune; tours of restored 1890 Presbyterian mansion; open year round

Gravenhurst: Muskoka Steamship & Historical Society, PO Box 1283, Gravenhurst ON P0C 1G0

Grimsby: The Grimsby Museum, 6 Murray St., PO Box 244, Grimsby ON L3M 4G5 – 905/945-5292; Fax: 905/945-0715 – Curator, Janet Cannon

Guelph Civic Museum, Guelph Museums, 6 Dublin St. South, Guelph ON N1H 4L5 – 519/836-1221; Fax: 519/836-5280; Email: gcmchin@wat.hookup.net; URL: http://www.freespace.net/~museum/welcome.html – Director, Laurence Grant; Curator, Bev Dietrich; Coordinator of Public Programs, Val Harrison

Guelph: McCrae House, c/o Guelph Museums, 6 Dublin St. South, Guelph ON N1H 4L5 – 519/836-1482; Fax: 519/836-5280; Email: gcmchin@wat.hookup.net; URL: http://www.freespace.net/~museum/welcome.html – Director, Laurence Grant; Curator, Bev Dietrich; Coordinator of Public Programs, Val Harrison – 1872 birthplace of John McCrae, author of "In Flanders Fields"; located at 108 Water St.

Haliburton Highlands Museum, PO Box 535, Haliburton ON K0M 1S0 – 705/457-2760 – Director, Thomas Ballantine

Hamilton: Dundurn Castle, Dundurn Park, York Blvd., Hamilton ON L8R 3H1 – 905/522-5313; Fax: 905/522-4535 – Curator, Bill Nesbitt

Hamilton Children's Museum, 1072 Main St. East, Hamilton ON L8M 1N6 – 905/546-4848; Fax: 905/546-4851 – Curator, Diane Collins

Hamilton Military Museum/Le musée militaire de Hamilton, Dundurn Park, York Blvd., Hamilton ON L8R 3H1 – 905/546-4974; Fax: 905/546-2016; Email: can-hmm@immedia.ca – Curator, Brenda Brownlee

Hamilton: The Hamilton Museum of Steam & Technology, 900 Woodward Ave., Hamilton ON L8H 7N2 – 905/549-5225; Fax: 905/549-1156 – Curator, Ian Kerr-Wilson – Two Gartshore steam powered beam engines housed in 1859 Hamilton Pumping Station

Hamilton Psychiatric Hospital Museum, PO Box 585, Hamilton ON L8N 3K7 – 905/575-6022; Fax: 905/575-6038 – Mary Ann McNamara – Preserves the history of psychiatric care & treatment in Ontario with an emphasis on events at the Hamilton Psychiatric Hospital & in the regions it serves.

Hamilton-Scourge Project, City Hall, 71 Main St. West, Hamilton ON L8P 4Y5 – 905/546-3967; Fax: 905/546-2338 – Manager, Cultural Services, Marilynn Havelka – Two 1812 schooners

Hamilton: McMaster Museum of Art (MMA), 1280 Main St. West, Hamilton ON L8S 4L6 – 905/525-

9140, ext.23081; Fax: 905/527-4548; Email: museum@mcmail.cis.mcmaster.ca – Director & Curator, Kim G. Ness; Manager, Collections & Operations, Gerrie Loveys; Head, Information, Rose Anne Prevec

Hamilton: Mohawk Trail School Museum, 141 Reno Ave., Hamilton ON L8T 2S6 – 905/527-5092 – Director, Walter Moir – 1882 schoolhouse

Hamilton: Royal Hamilton Light Infantry Heritage Museum, John Weir Foote VC Armoury, 200 James St. North, Hamilton ON L8R 2L1 – 905/572-2742; Fax: 905/528-5443 – Curator, D. Wentworth

Hamilton: Whitehern, McQuesten Residence, 41 Jackson St. West, Hamilton ON L8P 1L3 – 905/546-2018; Fax: 905/546-4933 – Curator, Ania Latoszek

Harrow: Southwestern Ontario Heritage Village, PO Box 221, Harrow ON N0R 1G0 – 519/776-6909; Fax: 519/776-8321 – Curator, Georgia Klym-Skeates

Holland Centre: Comber Pioneer Village, Rte. 3, Holland Centre ON N0H 1R0 – 519/794-3467 – Director, Robert James Comber

Huntsville: Muskoka Pioneer Village & Museum, 88 Brunel Rd., Huntsville ON P1H 1R1 – 705/789-7576; Fax: 705/789-6169; Email: village@vianet.on.ca; URL: http://www.pioneervillage.org – General Manager, John Finley

Ignace Heritage Centre, 36 Hwy. #17 West, PO Box 480, Ignace ON P0T 1T0 – 807/934-2280; Fax: 807/934-6452 – CEO, C. Penney – Open year round

Ingersoll Cheese Factory Museum/Musée de la fabrique de fromage d'Ingersol, PO Box 340, Ingersoll ON N5C 3V3 – 519/485-0120, 485-5510 (summer); Fax: 519/485-3543 – Curator, Shirley Lovell – 5 buildings including cheese factory museum, blacksmith shop, barn & community museum; Ingersoll Sports Hall of Fame houses Harold Wilson's Miss Canada IV Speedboat; "Pathway of the Giants" woodcarved scene; open daily July - Aug; weekends May - Labour Day

Iron Bridge Historical Museum, PO Box 460, Iron Bridge ON P0R 1H0

Iroquois: Carman House Museum, c/o Municipal Clerk, Carman Rd. South, PO Box 249, Iroquois ON K0E 1K0 – 613/-652-4422; Fax: 613/652-4636 – Brenda Millard; Sandy Decker

Iroquois Falls Pioneer Museum, PO Box 448, Iroquois Falls ON P0K 1E0 – 705/258-3730; Fax: 705/258-3694 – Curator, Nancy Renwick – Open June 15 - Aug. 31

Jordan: Ball's Falls Historical Park & Conservation Area, 6th Ave., RR#1, Jordan ON L0R 1S0 – 905/562-5235; Fax: 905/227-2998 – Curator, Christine Hayward

Jordan Historical Museum of the Twenty, PO Box 39, Jordan ON L0R 1S0 – 905/562-5242 – Curator/Director, Diane O'Neill

Kakabeka Falls: Hymers Museum, RR#1, Kakabeka Falls ON P0T 1W0 – Curator, M. Petryshyn

Kapuskasing: Ron Morel Memorial Museum, 88 Riverside Dr., Kapuskasing ON P5N 1B3 – 705/335-5443, 2341; Fax: 705/337-1741

Kenora: Lake of the Woods Museum, 300 Main St. South, PO Box 497, Kenora ON P9N 3X5 – 807/467-2105 – Director, Reg Reeve

Keswick: Georgina Village Museum, Civic Centre Rd., RR#2, Keswick ON L4P 3E9 – 905/476-4301; Fax: 905/476-7492 – Open June - Labour Day

Killarney Centennial Museum, 32 Commissioners St., Killarney ON P0M 2A0 – 705/287-2424; Fax: 705/287-2660 – Howard Beauvais; Emil Zamlska

King Township Historical Society Museum, PO Box 136, King City ON L0G 1K0 – 905/727-6322 – Director, Helen Poulis

Kingston: Bellevue House National Historic Site/La Villa-Bellevue (BHNHS), 35 Centre St., Kingston ON K7L 4E5 – 613/545-8666; Fax: 613/545-8721; Email: bellevue_house@pch.gc.ca; TDD-545-8668 – Supt., John H. Grenville – Home of Sir John A. Macdonald, restored to late 1840s period; videos in English, French, Cantonese, Japanese & German

Kingston: Canadian Forces Communications & Electronics Museum, CFB Kingston, Stn Vimy, Kingston ON K7K 5L0 – 613/541-5395; Fax: 613/546-0908 – Director, Capt. J.A. MacKenzie

Kingston: Correctional Service of Canada Museum/Musée du service correctionnel du Canada (CSCM/MSCC), 440 King St. West, Kingston ON K7L 4V7 – 613/530-3122; Fax: 613/545-8698 – Curator, Dave St. Onge

Kingston: Fort Henry, PO Box 213, Kingston ON K7L 4V8 – 613/542-7388; Fax: 613/542-3054; Email: can-fh@immedia.ca; URL: http://forthenry.kingston.net – Manager, John Robertson – The Citadel of Upper Canada, brought to life by the Fort Henry Guard; restaurant; gift stores; children's muster parades

Kingston: Frontenac County Schools Museum, 559 Bagot St., Kingston ON K7K 3E1 – 613/544-9113 – Curator, Beth Hogan; Association President, Gwendolyn Thorburn – One-room rural schoolhouse

Kingston: International Hockey Hall of Fame & Museum Inc., PO Box 82, Kingston ON K7L 4V6 – 613/544-2355, 546-5687 – Executive Director, Doug Nichols – Hockey from its organized beginning in Kingston, 1855, to now; Bobby Hull collection

Kingston Archaeological Centre, c/o Cataraqui Archaeological Research Foundation, 370 King St. West, Kingston ON K7L 2X4 – 613/542-3483; Fax: 613/542-3483; Email: carf@kos.net – Displays depicting the 8000-year history of human occupation of the Kingston region; research library; special collections

Kingston Fire Department Museum, 271 Brock St., Kingston ON K7L 1S5 – 613/542-9727

Kingston: MacLachlan Woodworking Museum, Grass Creek Park, 2993 Hwy. 2, PO Box 966, Kingston ON K7L 4X8 – 613/542-0543; Fax: 613/546-0908 – Director, Matthew Turner

Kingston: Marine Museum of the Great Lakes at Kingston, 55 Ontario St., Kingston ON K7L 2Y2 – 613/542-2261; Fax: 613/542-0043; Email: mmuseum@stauffer.queensu.ca; URL: http://www.marmus.ca – Executive Director, Maurice D. Smith – Audrey E. Rushbrook Library and Archives open year round, appts. preferred.

Kingston: Miller Museum of Mineralogy & Geology, Miller Hall, Queen's University, Kingston ON K7L 3N6 – 613/545-6767; Fax: 613/545-6592; Email: badham@geolserv.geol.queensu.ca; URL: http://geol.queensu.ca/museum/museum.html – Curator, Mark Badham

Kingston: Murney Tower Museum, PO Box 54, Kingston ON K7L 4V6 – 613/544-9925 – c. 1846 Martello Tower; open daily Victoria Day - Labour Day

Kingston: Pump House Steam Museum, 23 Ontario St., Kingston ON K7L 2Y2 – 613/546-4696; Fax: 613/542-0043; Email: mmuseum@stauffer.queensu.ca; URL: http://www.marmus.ca – Director, Maurice Smith – 19th Century building housing Kingston's first water-pumping statio; numerous steam engines, a working model train set & the steam yacht "Phoebe"

Kingston: The Royal Military College Museum/Le musée du Collège militaire royal du Canada, Kingston ON K7K 5L0 – 613/541-6000, ext.6664; Fax: 613/542-3565 – Committee Chair, Dr. J.G. Pike; Curator, Ross McKenzie – Open daily July - Labour Day

Kingsville: Jack Miner Museum, c/o The Jack Miner Migratory Bird Foundation, Kingsville ON N9Y 2E8 – 519/733-4034 – Curator, Beth Shaughnessy

Kirkland Lake: Museum of Northern History at the Sir Harry Oakes Chateau, 2 Chateau Dr., PO Box 1148, Kirkland Lake ON P2N 3M7 – 705/568-8800; Fax: 705/567-6611; Email: museumkl@nt.net – Director/Curator, Lydia Alexander

Kitchener: Doon Heritage Crossroads, RR#2, Kitchener ON N2G 3W5 – 519/748-1914; Fax: 519/748-0009; Email: rtom@region.waterloo.on.ca; URL: http://www.region.waterloo.on.ca/doon – Curator, Interpretations & Programmes, Wendy Connell; Curator/Manager, Thomas A. Reitz – Turn of the century living history village; open daily May - Dec.

Kitchener: Joseph Schneider Haus Museum, 466 Queen St. South, Kitchener ON N2G 1W7 – 519/742-7752; Fax: 519/742-0089 – Manager/Curator, Susan Burke

Kitchener: Woodside National Historic Site/Lieu historique nationale de Woodside, 528 Wellington St. North, Kitchener ON N2H 5L5 – 519/742-5273; Fax: 519/742-0561; Email: ont_woodside@pch.gc.ca; TTY: 519/742-5273 – Supt., Kim Seward-Hannam – Boyhood home of William Lyon Mackenzie King, 1891; open May - Dec.

Kleinburg Doll Museum, 10489 Islington Ave. North, Kleinburg ON L0J 1C0 – 905/893-1358 – Open year round

Komoka Railway Museum Inc., 133 Queen St., PO Box 22, Komoka ON N0L 1R0 – 519/657-1912 – President, John Kanakos; Curator, Ron Davis

Lakefield: Christ Church Museum, 33 Colborne St., PO Box 926, Lakefield ON K0L 2H0 – 705/652-3614 – Chairman, Charles McDermott

Lanark: Middleville Museum, RR#2, Lanark ON K0G 1K0 – 613/259-5462 – Chairperson, Alice Borrowman

Latchford: House of Memories, PO Box 82, Latchford ON P0J 1N0 – 705/676-2417; Fax: 705/676-2121 – Curator, Helen LaRose

Leamington: Point Pelee National Park Visitor Centre (Natural History Museum), RR#1, Leamington ON N8H 3V4 – 519/322-2365; Fax: 519/322-1277; URL: http://parkscanada.pch.gc.ca – Chief, Visitor Activities, Lily J. Meleg

Limehouse: Canadian Military Studies Museum, RR#1, Limehouse ON L0P 1H0 – 905/877-6522 – Director, Frank F. Grant

Lindsay: Victoria County Historical Society Museum, 322 Kent St. West, PO Box 74, Lindsay ON K9V 4R8 – 705/799-6672 – President, Lorraine Petzold

Lively: Anderson Farm Museum, 25 Black Lake Rd., Lively ON P3Y 1J3 – 705/692-4448; Fax: 705/692-3225 – Curator, James Fortin – Open year round

London: Fanshawe Pioneer Village (FPV), 2609 Fanshawe Park Rd. East, London ON N5X 4A1 – 519/457-1296; Fax: 519/457-3364 – Executive Director, Dr. William Finlayson; Manager, Luanne Ollivier

London: First Hussars: Citizen Soldiers Museum, 399 Ridout St. North, London ON N6A 2P1 – 519/471-1538 – Director, Alastair Neely

London: Grosvenor Lodge, 1017 Western Rd., London ON N6G 1G5 – 519/645-2845; Fax: 519/645-0981

London: Guy Lombardo Museum, 205 Wonderland Rd. South, London ON N6K 2T3 – 519/473-9003; Fax: 519/473-9003 – Managing-Director, John Noubarian; Chairman, Gino Nicodemo

London Museum of Archaeology & Iroquoian Village Site, Lawson-Jury Bldg., University of Western Ontario, 1600 Attawandaron Rd., London ON N6G 3M6 – 519/473-1360; Fax: 519/473-1363; Email: brigutto@julian.uwo.ca; URL: http://www.uwo.ca/museum/index.html – Director General, Dr. William Finlayson; Manager, Barb Rigutto – Wilfrid Jury collection; museum open year round

London Regional Art & Historical Museums (LRAHM), 421 Ridout St. North, London ON N6A 5H4 – 519/672-4580; Fax: 519/660-8397 – Executive Director, Ted Fraser; Business Manager, Finance, Brenda Fleming – Operates: Eldon House

Eldon House, 481 Ridout St. North, ON N6A 2P8 – 519/672-4580; Fax: 519/660-8397 – House & contents exemplify family life in the London area from 1834 to the present

London Regional Children's Museum, 21 Wharncliffe Rd. South, London ON N6J 4G5 – 519/434-5726; Fax: 519/434-1443 – Executive Director, Leigh-Anne Stradeski

London: The Royal Canadian Regiment Museum, Wolseley Barracks, London ON N5Y 4T7 – 519/660-5102; Fax: 519/660-5344; Email: rhq.thercr@onlinesys.com – Curator, Maj. A.F. Butlers; Asst. Curator, M.Cpl. G.H. Johnson

Lucan: Donnelly Homestead, 34937 Roman Line, RR#3, Lucan ON N0M 2J0 – 519/227-1244 – Contact, Robert Salts

Magnetawan Historical Museum, PO Box 130, Magnetawan ON P0A 1P0 – 705/387-3308 – Curator, Gloria Monahan

Mallorytown: Interpretive Centre & Brown's Bay Wreck/Centre d'acceuil & l'Épave de la baie Brown, St. Lawrence Islands National Park, RR#3, 2 Country Rd. 5, Mallorytown ON K0E 1R0 – 613/923-5261; Fax: 613/923-2229; Email: ont_sli@pch.gc.ca – Park Liaison, Ken Robinson – Natural & human history of 1,000 Islands; 1812 gunboat raised from the river

Manitowaning: Assiginack Museum, Mill Complex & SS Norisle Heritage Park, PO Box 238, Manitowaning ON P0P 1N0 – 705/859-3905 – Curator, Jeanette Allen

Manotick: Swords & Ploughshares Museum, PO Box 520, Manotick ON K0A 2N0 – 613/837-0149

Manotick: Watson's Mill, PO Box 145, Manotick ON K4M 1A2 – 613/692-2500; Fax: 613/692-0831 – Chair, Ian MacDonald

Markham District Historical Museum, 9350 Hwy. 48, Markham ON L3P 3J3 – 905/294-4576; Fax: 905/294-4590 – Manager, Birgitta MacLeod – Open year round

Marten River Logging Museum, c/o Marten River Provincial Park, Marten River ON P0H 1T0 – 705/892-2200 – Park Supt., C.J. Osborne

Massey Area Museum, 160 Sauble St., PO Box 237, Massey ON P0P 1P0 – 705/865-2266 – Curator, Carolyn Hein – Eleven-room museum featuring exhibits of turn-of-the-century logging; Aboriginal & Fort Lacloche artifacts, minerals, farming & model rooms; collection of family trees of 55 local pioneer families

Matheson: Thelma Miles Museum, PO Box 329, Matheson ON P0K 1N0 – 705/273-2325; Fax: 705/273-2140 – Director/Curator, Karen Barber

Mattawa & District Museum, PO Box 9, Mattawa ON P0H 1V0 – 705/744-5495 – President of Board, Marjorie Wall – Open May - Oct.

Mattawa: Voyageur Heritage Centre/Le Centre Ou Patrimoine Du Voyageur, Samuel de Champlain Provincial Park, PO Box 147, Mattawa ON P0H 1V0 – 705/744-2276; Fax: 705/744-0587 – Park Supt., J. Drechsler – Hands-on interpretation of Native, Explorer & Voyageur themes; 3 authentic birchbark canoes; replica of a 12-metre trade canoe; theatre with videos

Meaford Museum, 111 Bayfield St., Meaford ON N4L 1H1 – 519/538-5974 – Curator, Freda MacDonnell – Open daily May -Sept.

Meldrum Bay: Mississagi Strait Lighthouse Museum, General Delivery, Meldrum Bay ON P0P 1R0 – 705/283-3011; Fax: 705/283-3209 – Peggy Mullen – Open mid-May - Sept.

Meldrum Bay: The Net Shed Museum, Water St., Meldrum Bay ON P0P 1R0 – 705/283-3385 – Director, Dawn McKinlay – Open June - Labour Day

Merrickville: The Blockhouse Museum, c/o Secretary, Merrickville & District Historical Society, PO Box 29, Merrickville ON K0G 1N0 – Community museum depicting Upper Canada in the 1860s

Midland: Huronia Museum, PO Box 638, Midland ON L4R 4P4 – 705/526-2844; Fax: 705/527-6622; Email: can-hm@immedia.ca – Director/Curator, Jamie Hunter – Recreated Huron Village represents one of hundreds that existed in the Georgian Bay area, representing a unique & sophisticated society which lasted nearly 1,000 years; Canada's first recreated Native village

Midland: Martyrs' Shrine, Midland ON L4R 4K5 – 705/526-3788; Fax: 705/526-1546 – Director, Rev. Donald F. Beaudois

Midland: Sainte-Marie among the Hurons/Sainte-Marie-au-Pays-des-Hurons (SMATH), c/o Economic Development, Trade & Tourism, Huronia Historical Parks, PO Box 160, Midland ON L4R 4K8 – 705/526-7838; Fax: 705/526-9193 – General Manager, John Barrett-Hamilton; Site Manager, Pierre Lafaive

Midland: Wye Marsh Wildlife Centre, PO Box 100, Midland ON L4R 4K6 – 705/526-7809 – Executive Director, Robert Whittam

Milford: Mariners' Park Museum, PO Box 54, Milford ON K0K 2P0 – 613/476-4695; Fax: 613/476-8392 – Chair, Judy Zeleny

Milton: Halton Region Museum, RR#3, Milton ON L9T 2X7 – 905/875-2200; Fax: 905/876-4322 – Manager, Heritage Services, Paul H. Attack

Milton: Ontario Agricultural Museum, PO Box 38, Milton ON L9T 2Y3 – 905/878-8151, 876-4530 – General Manager, John Wiley

Minden: Kanawa International Museum of Canoes, Kayaks & Rowing Craft, RR#2, Minden ON K0M 2K0 – 705/489-2644 – Curator, Michael Ketemer

Minesing: Simcoe County Museum, RR#2, Minesing ON L0L 1Y0 – 705/728-3721; Fax: 705/728-9130 – Curator, Gloria Taylor

Mississauga: Benares Historic House & Visitor Centre, 1507 Clarkson Rd. North, Mississauga ON L5J 2W8 – 905/615-3277; 822-2061; Fax: 905/822-5372; URL: http://www.city.mississauga.on.ca – Facility Supervisor, Scott Gillies – Restored to reflect the way the Harris family of Benares, Clarkson, lived in 1918; local connection to world-famous "Jalna" novels written by Canadian author, Mazo de la Roche

Mississauga: Bradley Museum, 1620 Orr Rd., Mississauga ON L5J 4T2 – 905/822-1569; Fax: 905/823-3591; URL: http://www.city.mississauga.on.ca – Program Development Supervisor, Annemarie Hagan – Restored 1830s Loyalist farmhouse; period gardens; displays & gift shop in 1830s Regency cottage; Sunday Tea Room; special events throughout the year

Moore Museum, 94 Moore Line, Mooretown ON N0N 1M0 – 519/867-2020 – Curator, Laurie Mason – Open year round; Jan. - Feb. by appt.

Moose Factory Centennial Museum, Moose Factory ON P0L 1W0 – 705/658-4605 – Director, Ivan Gravel

Moosonee: Revillon Frères Museum, c/o Moosonee Development Area Board, PO Box 127, Moosonee ON P0L 1Y0 – 705/336-2933, 2497 – Recreation Director, Robin Langille – Open June - Labour Day

Morpeth: Rondeau Provincial Park Visitor Centre, c/o Ministry of Natural Resources, RR#1, Morpeth ON N0P 1X0 – 519/674-1772; Fax: 519/674-1755 – Director, Pamela E. Burns

Morrisburg: Upper Canada Village, RR#1, Morrisburg ON K0C 1X0 – 613/543-3704; Fax: 613/543-4098; URL: http://www.parks.on.ca – Manager, Barry Hughes – Representation of 1860s riverfront community with over 30 homes, trade shops & operating mills; children's activities; open daily from Victoria Day weekend to Thanksgiving Monday

Mount Brydges: Ska-Nah-Doht Indian Village, RR#1, Mount Brydges ON N0L 1W0 – 519/264-2420 – Curator, Andrea French

Mount Hope: Canadian Warplane Heritage Museum (CWH), Hamilton Airport, 9280 Airport Rd., Mount Hope ON L0R 1W0 – 905/679-4183; Fax: 905/679-4186; Email: museum@warplane.com; URL: http://www.warplane.com – Curator, Darlene McKinnon; Vice-President, R.J. Franks

Napanee: Allan Macpherson House, 180 Elizabeth St., PO Box 183, Napanee ON K7R 3M3 – 613/354-5982 – Director/Curator, Elizabeth Hunter

Napanee: Lennox & Addington County Museum & Archives, 97 Thomas St. East, PO Bag 1000, Napanee ON K7R 3S9 – 613/354-3027; Fax: 613/354-3112; Email: museum@fox.nstn.ca – Manager, Jane Foster; Archivist, Jennifer Bunting

Napanee: Old Hay Bay Church, RR#2, Napanee ON K7R 3K7 – 613/373-2232; Fax: 613/373-0043; Email: staples@ihorizons.net – Secretary, K.J. Crawford; K. Staples – Circa 1792, oldest exisiting Methodist Church in Canada; open daily July 1 - Labour Day & by appt.

Nepean: Algonquin College Museum, Museum Technology Program, Algonquin College, 1385 Woodroffe Ave., Nepean ON K2G 1V8 – 613/727-7612; Fax: 613/727-7684 – Director, Patrick Wohler

Nepean: The Log Farm/La Vieille Ferme, 670 Cedarview Rd., Nepean ON K2R 1E5 – 613/825-4352, 239-5188

Nepean Museum Inc., 16 Rowley Ave., Nepean ON K2G 1L9 – 613/723-7936; Fax: 613/723-7936 – Director, Dan Hoffman

New Liskeard: Little Claybelt Homesteaders Museum, PO Box 1718, New Liskeard ON P0J 1P0 – 705/647-9575 – Chairperson, Dorothy Greenwood

Newmarket: Elman W. Campbell Museum, 134 Main St. South, Newmarket ON L3Y 3Y7 – 905/953-5314; Fax: 905/898-2083 – Curator, Elizabeth Sinyard

Niagara Falls: Guinness Museum of World Records, 4943 Clifton Hill, Niagara Falls ON L2G 3N5 – 905/356-2299 – Open year round

Niagara Falls: Louis Tussaud's Waxworks, 4915 Clifton Hill, Niagara Falls ON L2G 3N5 – 905/374-6601 – General Manager, Rick Blanchard

Niagara Falls: Lundy's Lane Historical Museum, 5810 Ferry St., Niagara Falls ON L2G 1S9 – 905/358-5082 – Curator, Margaret Anne Tabaka – 1874 museum located on the site of the Battle of Lundy's Lane; first floor interprets the early settlement & tourism of Niagara Falls & features War of 1812 & Fenian Raid militaria; second floor holds a Victorian parlour, an early kitchen, toys & dolls, photographs & a gallery of seasonal displays & travelling exhibits

Niagara Falls: McFarland House, c/o Niagara Parks Commission, PO Box 150, Niagara Falls ON L2E 6T2 – 905/356-2241; Fax: 905/354-6041 – Community Services Officer, April Petrie – Early 1800s Loyalist home which served as a hospital during the War of 1812; now houses Tea Room with home baking & Niagara Wines

Niagara Falls: Movieland Wax Museum, 4950 Clifton Hill, Niagara Falls ON L2G 3N4 – 905/358-3061; Fax: 905/358-9456 – General Manager, Guy Paone – Open year round

Niagara Falls Museum, Est. 1827, 5651 River Rd., PO Box 960, Niagara Falls ON L2E 6V8 – 905/356-2151; Email: nfmuseum@aol.com; USA tel: 716/285-4898 – Director, Jacob Sherman – 700,000 artifacts; 9 Egyptian mummies; dinosaur fossils; minerals; Daredevil Hall of Fame

Niagara Falls: Oak Hall, PO Box 150, Niagara Falls ON L2E 6T2 – 905/356-2241; Fax: 905/354-6041 – Chairman, Gary F. Burroughs; General Manager, Robert W. Tytaneck – Administrative offices for the Niagara Parks Commission

Niagara Falls: Old Fort Erie, Niagara Parks Commission, PO Box 150, Niagara Falls ON L2E 6T2 – 905/871-0540 – Manager, J. Saunders

Niagara Falls: Ripley's Believe It or Not Museum, 4960 Clifton Hill, Niagara Falls ON L2G 3N4 – 905/356-2238 – General Manager, Rick Blanchard

Niagara Falls: Willoughby Twp. Historical Museum, 9935 Niagara Pkwy., RR#3, Niagara Falls ON L2E 6S6 – 905/295-4036 – Curator, Emma Chambers – Located in a rural school house; displays dating from late 1700s to 1970s; household, agricultural, municipal, library & military artifacts; magnito switchboard

Niagara Fire Museum, PO Box 498, Niagara on the Lake ON L0S 1J0 – 905/468-7279 – Asst. Curator, Michele Stewart

Niagara Historical Society Museum, 43 Castlereagh St., PO Box 208, Niagara on the Lake ON L0S 1J0 – 905/468-3912; Fax: 905/468-1728 – Curator/Director, William Severin – Ontario's first purpose-built museum

Niagara National Historic Sites, Parks Canada, PO Box 787, Niagara on the Lake ON L0S 1J0 – 905/468-4257; 905/468-4638; Fax: 905/468-4638; Email: daler@pksnia.dots.doe.ca – Supt., R. Dale; Chief, Visitor Activities, D. Webb; Chief, Historic Resource Conservation, D. Greenall – Includes Fort George, Navy Hall, Brock's Monument & Butler's Barracks

Niagara on the Lake: Perfume Factory & Museum, 393 York Rd., Niagara on the Lake ON L0S 1J0 – 905/685-6666; Fax: 905/984-8226; URL: http://www.tourismniagara.com/perfumefactory/ – Eddie Youssoufian – Open Feb. - Dec.

Niagara Apothecary, 5 Queen St., Niagara-on-the-Lake ON L0S 1J0 – 905/468-3845, 962-4861 (off-season) – Curator, Ernst Stieb

Nipigon Museum, PO Box 208, Nipigon ON P0T 2J0 – 807/887-2727 – Curator, Roland Choiselat

Nipissing Twp. Museum, Twp. of Nipissing Office, Nipissing ON P0H 1W0 – 705/724-2938 – Curator, Joe Steele

North Bay: Dionne Homestead Museum, c/o Chamber of Commerce, PO Box 747, North Bay ON P1B 8J8 – 705/472-8480; Fax: 705/472-8027 – Director, Sharon Clark-Bedard – Open Victoria Day - Thanksgiving

North Bay & Area Museum, 171 Main St. West, PO Box 628, North Bay ON P1B 8J5 – 705/476-2323 – Curator, Pamela Handley – Exhibits on local history as well as special exhibits from the Royal Ontario Museum & other national & provinical museums

North Bay: Ontario Northland Transportation Commission Archives & Museum, 555 Oak St. East, North Bay ON P1B 8L3 – 705/472-4500 – Archivist, Janet Calcaterra

North Buxton: Raleigh Township Centennial Museum, PO Box 53, North Buxton ON N0P 1Y0 – 519/352-4799 – Curator, Alice Newby

North York: Black Creek Pioneer Village, 1000 Murray Ross Pkwy., North York ON M3J 2P3 – 416/736-1733; Fax: 416/661-6610 – Manager, Marty Brent

North York: Gibson House Museum, 5172 Yonge St., North York ON M2N 5P6 – 416/395-7432; Fax: 416/395-7442 – Curator, Karen Edwards

North York: History of Contraception Museum, c/o Ortho Pharmaceutical (Canada) Ltd., 19 Green Belt Dr., North York ON M3C 1L9 – 416/449-9444 – Curator, Heather Bennett

North York: Irving E. & Ray Kanner Heritage Museum, 3560 Bathurst St., North York ON M6A 2E1 – 416/789-2500, ext.2802; Fax: 416/785-2378 – Coordinator, Pat Dickinson

North York: The Roberta Bondar Earth & Space Centre, 1750 Finch Ave. East, North York ON M2J 2X5 – 416/491-5050; Email: 2thesky@learn.senecac.on.ca; URL: http://www.senecac.on.ca/bondar/planet.htm – Curator, Robert Hudek – 60-seat star theatre featuring 2000 visible stars, 5 planets, sun & moon; accessory projectors provide simulations of aurorae, meteor showers, bolides & solar & lunar eclipses

North York: Toronto Aerospace Museum (TAM), 65 Carl Hall Rd., North York ON M3K 2B6 – 416/638-6078; Fax: 416/638-5509; Email: n.flight@netcom.ca; URL: http://tor-pw1.netcom.ca/~n.flight/small.html – Project Manager, Robin D. Murray; Director, Richard Banigan; Director, Brendon Nunes; Building Manager, Fred Rol; Engineer, Monique Sapineo; Director, Educational Services, Bill Turner

Norwich & District Museum & Archives, RR#3, Norwich ON N0J 1P0 – 519/863-3101 (Museum); 863-3638 (Archives) – Curator, Ian Bell; Archivist, Lisa Miettinen – 1889 Quaker Meeting House

Oakville: Canadian Golf Hall of Fame, 1333 Dorval Dr., Oakville ON L6J 4Z3 – 905/849-9700; Fax: 905/845-7040; Email: golfhouse@rcga.org – Curator, Karen E. Hewson – History of golf in Canada; theatre, giftshop, research facilities (by appt.); open year round

Oakville Museum, 8 Navy St., Oakville ON L6J 2Y5 – 905/338-4400; Fax: 905/815-5973; Email: iknight@town.oakville.on.ca; URL: http://www.town.oakville.on.ca – Manager/Curator, Irene Knight – Museum buildings: Custom House, Chisholm Family Home & Old Post Office

Odessa: Historic Babcock Mill, 100 Bridge St., PO Box 70, Odessa ON K0H 2H0 – 613/389-8314

Ohsweken: Chiefswood Museum, PO Box 5000, Ohsweken ON N0A 1M0 – 519/752-5005; Fax: 519/752-9578 – Curator, Paula Whitlow – Birthplace of poet E. Pauline Johnson; plans to open fully restored for summer, 1998

Oil Springs: Oil Museum of Canada, PO Box 16, Oil Springs ON N0N 1P0 – 519/834-2840; Fax: 519/834-2840 – Manager, Donna McGuire – Open daily May - Oct. 31; Nov. - Apr., Mon. - Fri.

Orillia: Stephen Leacock Museum, PO Box 625, Orillia ON L3V 6K5 – 705/326-9357; Fax: 705/326-9357; Email: leacock@mail.translate.ca; URL: http://www.transdata.ca/leacock/leacock.html – Director/Curator, Daphne Mainprize

Orono: Clarke Museum & Archives, Municipality of Clarington, PO Box 152, Orono ON L0B 1M0 – 905/983-9243; Email: can-cma-mc@immedia.ca – Curator, Mark Jackman

Oshawa: Canadian Automotive Museum, 99 Simcoe St. South, Oshawa ON L1H 4G7 – 905/576-1222 – Curator/Manager, Michael Foley

Oshawa Sydenham Museum, Lakeview Park, 7 Henry St., PO Box 2303, Oshawa ON L1H 7V5 – 905/436-7624 – Director, Laura Suchan – Henry House; Robinson House; Guy House

Oshawa: Parkwood Estate, 270 Simcoe St. North, Oshawa ON L1G 4T5 – 905/433-4311; Fax: 905/721-4765 – Curator, Brian Malcolm – Once home to R.S. McLaughlin, founder of General Motors of Canada; tours of 55-room mansion highlighting original furnishings; garden Teahouse; garden Tearoom

Ottawa: Agriculture Museum/Musée de l'agriculture, Bldg. 88, Central Experimental Farm, PO Box 9724, Stn T, Ottawa ON K1G 5A3 – 613/991-3044; Fax: 613/947-2374; URL: http:www.agriculture.nmstc.ca – Director, Michelle Dondo-Tardiff; Head, Interpretation & School Services, Tamara Tarasoff

Ottawa: The Billings Estate Museum/Musée du domaine Billings, 2100 Cabot St., Ottawa ON K1H 6K1 – 613/247-4830; Fax: 613/247-4832; Email: bemchin@ott.hookup.net – Curator/Manager, Lynn Villeneuve – Home & property of Braddish & Lamira Billings, two of Ottawa's earliest settlers, c. 1828; exhibits highlight 5 generations of family & community history

Ottawa: Bytown Historical Museum/Musée Bytown, PO Box 523, Stn B, Ottawa ON K1P 5P6 – 613/234-4570; Fax: 613/234-4846; Email: ah294@freenet.carleton.ca – Director/Curator, Lana Shaw

Ottawa: Governor General's Foot Guards Museum, Drill Hall, Cartier Sq., Ottawa ON K1A 0K2 – 613/990-0620 – Curator, Martin J. Lane, CD – Regimental museum; brief history of regiment from 1872 to present by way of artifacts

Ottawa: Laurier House National Historic Site, 335 Laurier Ave. East, Ottawa ON K1N 6R4 – 613/992-8142

Ottawa: Mackenzie King Estate/Domaine Mackenzie-King, National Capital Commission, #202, 40 Elgin St., Ottawa ON K1P 1C7 – 809/827-2711, ext.124; Fax: 809/827-3337 – Coordinator, Denis Messier – Located in Gatineau Park

Ottawa: Museum of Canadian Scouting, 1345 Baseline Rd., PO Box 5151, Stn F, Ottawa ON K2C 3G7 – 613/224-5131; Fax: 613/224-3571 – Executive Director, Bob Hallett

Ottawa Sports Hall of Fame/Temple de la renomée des sports d'Ottawa, Civic Centre, 1015 Bank St., Ottawa ON K1S 3W7 – 613/564-1485; Fax: 613/564-1619 – Chairman, James A. Durrell

Owen Sound: Billy Bishop Heritage Museum, 948 - 3rd Ave. West, Owen Sound ON N4K 4P6 – 519/371-0031 – Childhood home of Canada's most-decorated serviceman, William Avery Bishop, VC ; photographs, documents & artifacts

Owen Sound: County of Grey-Owen Sound Museum, 975 - 6th St. East, Owen Sound ON N4K 1G9 – 519/376-3690; Fax: 519/376-7970; Email: museum@greycounty.on.ca; URL: http://www.greycounty.on.ca/museum/index.html – Director, A.W. Landen – Collects, preserves, restores, documents, interprets & displays the material culture of Grey County & the Owen Sound, c. 1815 - present; 3 display galleries open year round; 5 period buildings open seasonally

Owen Sound Marine-Rail Museum, 1165 First Ave. West, Owen Sound ON N4K 4K8 – 519/371-3333; URL: Http://www.geocities.com/Athens/Delphi/6265 – Acting Curator, Orris Hull – Displays & exhibits detail the transportation history & local industry of Owen Sound

Parry Sound: West Parry Sound District Museum (WPSDM), 17 George St., PO Box 337, Parry Sound ON P2A 2X4 – 705/746-5365; Fax: 705/746-8775; Email: can-wpsdm@immedia.ca – Director/Curator, Craig E. D'Arcy

Pelee Island Heritage Centre, c/o Pelee Island Municipal Office, Pelee Island ON N0R 1M0

Pembroke: Champlain Trail Museum, 1032 Pembroke St. East, PO Box 985, Pembroke ON K8A 7M5 – 613/735-0517 – Curator/Manager, Susan Corbett-Cyr

Penetanguishene: Discovery Harbour/Havre de la Découverte, PO Box 1800, Penetanguishene ON L0K 1P0 – 705/549-8064; Fax: 705/549-4858 – General Manager, John Barrett-Hamilton

Penetanguishene Centennial Museum, 13 Burke St., Penetanguishene ON L9M 1C1 – 705/549-2150; Fax: 705/549-3749 – Curator, Angela Dyck

Perth: Innisville & District Museum, c/o Arnie Jackson, Carleton Place, PO Box 1165, Perth ON K7C 4L1 – 613/257-1527 – Arnie Jackson – Country-style museum

Perth: The Perth Museum, 80 Gore St. East, Perth ON K7H 1H9 – 613/267-1947; Fax: 613/267-7351 – Curator, Douglas M. McNichol – 1840 stone home of Senator Matheson; open year round

Petawawa: Canadian Forces Base Petawawa Military Museum, Canadian Forces Base Petawawa, Petawawa ON K8H 2X3 – 613/588-5239 – Base Museologist, Dennis Lavoie

Peterborough: Hope Water Powered Saw Mill, c/o Otonabee Region Conservation Authority, #200, 380 Armour Rd., Time Sq., Peterborough ON K9H 7L7 – 705/745-5791; Fax: 705/745-7488 – Operations

Manager, John Williams; General Manager, Dan White

Peterborough: Hutchison House Museum, 270 Brock St., Peterborough ON K9H 2P9 – 705/743-9710 – Curator, Stephanie Ford Forrester

Peterborough: Lang Pioneer Village, 470 Water St., Peterborough ON K9H 3M3 – 705/295-6694; Fax: 705/295-6644 – Manager, Angela Chittick

Peterborough: Lang Water Powered Grist Mill, c/o Otonabee Region Conservation Authority, #200, Time Sq., 380 Armour Rd., Peterborough ON K9H 7L7 – 705/745-5791; Fax: 705/745-7488 – Operations Manager, John Williams; General Manager, Dan White

Peterborough Centennial Museum & Archives, PO Box 143, Peterborough ON K9J 6Y5 – 705/743-5180 – Manager, Ken Doherty

Peterborough Lift Lock Visitor Centre, c/o Trent Severn Waterway, PO Box 567, Peterborough ON K9J 6Z6 – 705/750-4950; Fax: 705/750-4958 – Manager, F. Irons – Open Apr. - mid-Oct.

Peterborough: Trent-Severn Waterway/Voie navigable Trent-Severn (TSW), PO Box 567, Peterborough ON K9J 6Z6 – 705/742-9267; Fax: 705/742-9644 – Supt., John Lewis; Director of Canal Operations, Fred Alyea; Chief Engineer, Wayne Pacey

Pickering Museum Village, c/o Town of Pickering, One The Esplanade, Pickering ON L1V 6K7 – 905/420-4620 (winter), 683-8401 (summer); Fax: 905/420-2596 – Program Supt., Sharon Milton

Picton: Macaulay Heritage Park, PO Box 2150, Picton ON K0K 2T0 – 613/476-3833; Fax: 613/476-8356; URL: http://www.pec.on.ca/macaulay – Curator, Allyson Kelly – Administers Prince Edward County Museum; Macaulay House

Picton: Mariners' Museum Lighthouse Park, RR#3, Picton ON K0K 2T0 – 613/476-8392; Fax: 613/476-6771 (Call first) – Preserves the history of sailors & fisherman of Prince Edward County; over 6,000 artifacts

Picton: North Marysburgh Museum, The Rose House, Prince Edward County, RR#4, Picton ON K0K 2T0 – 613/476-4436 (winter), 5439 (summer) – Curator, Kimmberley L. Hart – Early settlers home furnished with 19th-century artifacts

Port Carling: Muskoka Lakes Museum, PO Box 432, Port Carling ON P0B 1J0 – 705/765-5367; Fax: 705/765-6271; Email: musklake@muskoka.com – Director, Lindsay Hill

Port Colborne Historical & Marine Museum, 280 King St., PO Box 572, Port Colborne ON L3K 5X8 – 905/834-7604 – Director/Curator, Virginia Anger

Port Dover: City of Nanticoke Museum Board, Clerk's Department, 230 Main St., Port Dover ON N0A 1N0

Port Dover Harbour Museum, 44 Harbour St., PO Box 1298, Port Dover ON N0A 1N0 – 519/583-2660; Email: RNET: can-pdhm@immedia.ca – Curator, Sylvia Crossland

Port Perry: Scugog Shores Historical Museum, 16210 Island Rd., RR#3, Port Perry ON L9L 1B4 – 905/985-3589; Fax: 905/985-3492; Email: can-sshm@immedia.ca – Curator/Director, Daniel Robert

Port Rowan: Backus Heritage Village & Conservation Education Centre (BHCA), RR#3, Port Rowan ON N0E 1M0 – 519/586-2201; Fax: 519/586-7333; Email: lpadmin@nornet.on.ca; URL: http://www.nornet.on.ca/~lprca/

Prescott: Fort Wellington National Historic Site/Lieu historique national du Fort-Wellington, PO Box 479, Prescott ON K0E 1T0 – 613/925-2896; Fax: 613/925-1536 – Area Supt., D.J. Delaney

Prescott: The Forwarders' Museum, PO Box 2179, Prescott ON K0E 1T0 – 613/925-5788 – Curator, Marg Solomatenko – Tells of the development & operation of the "Forwarding Trade"

Queenston: Laura Secord Homestead, PO Box 1812, Queenston ON L0S 1L0 – 905/357-4020, 262-4851 – District Manager, Sandra Theal

Queenston,: Mackenzie House, Heritage Printery, PO Box 1824, Queenston, ON L0S 1L0 – 905/262-5676

Red Lake Museum, PO Box 64, Red Lake ON P0V 2M0 – 807/727-3006

Renfrew: McDougall Mill Museum, PO Box 544, Renfrew ON K7V 4B1 – 613/432-2129 – Curator, Marie Henderson – 1855 mill on the Bonnechere River

Richards Landing: Fort St. Joseph National Historic Site, PO Box 220, Richards Landing ON P0R 1J0 – 705/246-2664(summer); 942-6262 (winter) – Winter mailing: c/o Ken B. McMillan, Soo Ship Canal, 1 Canal Dr., Sault Ste. Marie, ON P6A 6W4.

Richards Landing: St. Joseph Island Museum Complex, RR#2, Richards Landing ON P0R 1J0 – 705/246-2672; Winter: 705/246-2482 – Curator, Gayle Tisdall – Six artifact buildings represent the pioneer era (1820-1880) & the settlement era after the Homestead Act of 1868; over 5,000 artifacts; farming, lumbering, maple syruping & early navigation displays; 2 schools, a church, a store, a barn & an 1880 log cabin

Richmond: Goulbourn Museum, PO Box 1065, Richmond ON K0A 2Z0 – 613/831-2393

Ridge House Museum, 53 Erie St. South, Ridgetown ON N0P 2C0 – 519/674-2223; Fax: 519/674-0660 – Director, Elsie Reynolds – Open May - Dec.

Ridgeway: Fort Erie Historical Museum, c/o Fort Erie Museum Board, 402 Ridge Rd., PO Box 339, Ridgeway ON L0S 1N0 – 905/894-5322; Fax: 905/894-6851 – Curator, Jane Davies – Open daily mid-June - Labour Day; otherwise by appt.

Ridgeway: Fort Erie Historical Railroad Museum, PO Box 339, Ridgeway ON L0S 1N0 – 905/871-1412 – Curator, Jane Davies – Located on Central Ave.; open daily Victoria Day - Labour Day

Ridgeway Battlefield Park, c/o Fort Erie Museum Board, PO Box 339, Ridgeway ON L0S 1N0 – 905/894-5322 – Curator, Jane Davies

Rockton: Westfield Heritage Centre (WHC), Rockton ON L0R 1X0 – 519/621-8851; Fax: 519/621-6897; Email: westfld@worldchat.com; URL: http://www.worldchat.com/public/westfield/westf1.htm – Manager, Rondalyn Brown; Program Officer, Rob Winninger – 33 historic buildings; special programs include Christmas, Maple Syrup, American Civil War Re-enactment; guided tours & rental facilities available

Rockwood: Halton County Radial Railway, RR#2, Rockwood ON N0B 2K0 – 519/856-9802; Fax: 519/856-1399; Email: streetcar@hcry.org; URL: http://www.nl-marketing.com/hcrr/ – Curator, Joan Johns

Rosemont: Dufferin County Museum & Archives, PO Box 120, Rosemont ON L0N 1R0 – 705/435-1881; Fax: 705/435-9876; Email: dcmchin@planeteer.com – Curator, Wayne Townsend

Sarnia: Pilot House Museum, 2012 Wayne Ave. South, RR#4, Sarnia ON N7T 7H5 – 519/344-6136 – Director, Malcolm McRae – Centre castle of Great Lakes tanker SS Imperial Hamilton

Sault Ste. Marie: Ermatinger Old Stone House, c/o Historic Sites Board, PO Box 580, Sault Ste. Marie ON P6A 5N1 – 705/759-5443; Fax: 705/759-6605; Email: can-eosh@immedia.ca – Curator, Daphne Poirier

Sault Ste. Marie Canal National Historic Site, Sault Ste. Marie ON P6A 6W4 – 705/941-6262; Fax: 705/941-6206; Email: pkssc.dots.doe.ca@igw – Acting Supt., Fred Howe

Sault Ste. Marie Museum, 690 Queen St. East, Sault Ste. Marie ON P6A 2A4 – 705/759-7278; Fax: 705/759-3058; Email: ssmmchin@adss.on.ca – Curator/Administrator, Judy McGonigal

Sault Ste. Marie: St. Mary's River Marine Centre, PO Box 23099, Stn Mall, Sault Ste. Marie ON P6A 6W6 – 705/942-2919; Fax: 705/942-6368 – President, Udo Rauk

Scarborough Historical Museum, Thomson Memorial Park, 1007 Brimley Rd., Scarborough ON M1P 3E8 – 416/431-3441; Fax: 416/431-3441 – Manager/Curator, Madeleine Callaghan – Includes Cornell House, McCowan Log Cabin & Hough Carriage Works

Seaforth: The Van Egmond House, PO Box 1033, Seaforth ON N0K 1W0 – 519/522-0413 – Chairman, Phil Malcolm – Restored & furnished with antiques representative of the period prior to Confederation

Selkirk: Wilson P. MacDonald Memorial School Museum, Selkirk ON N0A 1P0 – 416/776-3319 – Curator, Dana B. Stavinga

Sharon Temple Museum, 18974 Leslie St., PO Box 331, Sharon ON L0G 1V0 – 905/478-2389; Fax: 905/895-9277; URL: http://www.interhop.net/museum/sharon.html – Site Director, Ruth Mahoney – National historic site, the Sharon Temple of the Children of Peace, 8 related buildings & museum

Sheguiandah: Little Current-Howland Centennial Museum, Sheguiandah ON P0P 1W0 – 705/368-2367 – Curator, Eva Skipper

Simcoe: Eva Brook Donly Museum, 109 Norfolk St. South, Simcoe ON N3Y 2W3 – 519/426-1583 – Curator, William Yeager

Sioux Lookout Museum, PO Box 158, Sioux Lookout ON P0V 2T0 – 807/737-1562

Smiths Falls: Heritage House Museum, a Victorian restoration, c.1867/Musée de la maison du patrimoine, Old Slys Rd., PO Box 695, Smiths Falls ON K7A 4T6 – 613/283-8560; Fax: 613/283-4764; Email: hhmchin@falls.igs.net; URL: http://www.town.smiths.falls.on.ca – Curator, Susan McNichol – Open year round, 11 am - 4:30 pm

Smiths Falls: Industrial Heritage Complex, c/o Rideau Canal, Parks Canada, 34A Beckwith St. South, Smiths Falls ON K7A 2A8 – 613/283-5170; Fax: 613/283-0677 – Visitor Services, Simon Lunn – 19th century development of Rideau Canal at Merrickville

Smiths Falls Railway Museum Association Inc. - Rideau Valley Division, PO Box 962, Smiths Falls ON K7A 5A5 – 613/283-5696 – President, Ross Robinson; Archivist, Bill Lesurf; Curator, Julia Brady – Former CNoR/CNR Station

Sombra Township Museum, PO Box 76, Sombra ON N0P 2H0 – 519/892-3982, 3631 – Curator, Sandy Broad

Southampton: Bruce County Museum & Archives, 33 Victoria St. North, PO Box 180, Southampton ON N0H 2L0 – 519/797-3644, 2080; Fax: 519/797-2191; Email: museum@swbi.net; URL: http://www.swbi.net/bruce_county_museum.htm – Director/Curator, Barbara Ribey

St Catharines: Mountain Mills Museum, c/o Parks & Recreation Dept., City of St Catharines, PO Box 3012, St Catharines ON L2R 7C2

St Catharines: St. Catharines Museum, 1932 Government Rd., PO Box 3012, St Catharines ON L2R 7C2 – 905/984-8880; Fax: 905/984-6910; Email: muslk3@niagara.com – Chief Museum Complex Officer, Virginia Hatch Stewart

St. George: Adelaide Hunter-Hoodless Homestead, 359 Blue Lake Rd., RR#1, St. George ON N0E 1N0 – 519/448-1130; Fax: 519/448-1130 – Curator, Suzanne Doiron – Birthplace of Adelaide Hunter-Hoodless, founder of the first Women's Institute

St. Jacobs: The Maple Syrup Museum, Princess St., St. Jacobs ON N0B 2N0 – 519/669-2423; Fax: 519/669-4230 – Albert Martin – Open year round

St. Marys Museum, 177 Church St. South, PO Box 98, St. Marys ON N4X 1A9 – 519/284-3556; Fax: 519/284-2881; Email: can-stmm@immedia.ca – Curator, Mary Smith

St. Thomas: Elgin County Pioneer Museum, 32 Talbot St., St. Thomas ON N5P 1A3 – 519/631-6537 – Curator/Director, Deborah Herkimer

St. Thomas: The Elgin Military Museum, 30 Talbot St., St. Thomas ON N5P 1A3 – 519/633-7641 – Curator, Sterling Ince

Stoney Creek: Battlefield House Museum, 77 King St. West, PO Box 66561, Stoney Creek ON L8G 5E5 – 905/662-8458; Fax: 905/662-0529; Email: bhmchin@binatech.on.ca – Curator, Susan Ramsay – Historic Battlefield House commemorates the Battle of Stoney Creek & depicts the life of the Gage family in the early 1800s; 32 acres of parkland

Stoney Creek: Erland Lee (Museum) Home, 552 Ridge Rd., Stoney Creek ON L8J 2Y6 – 905/662-2691 – Curator, Mary Kneebone

Stratford: Brocksden Country School Museum, 87 Nile St., Stratford ON N5A 4C7

Stratford: Fryfogel Inn, PO Box 462, Stratford ON N5A 5S4 – 1850s country inn

Stratford: Minnie Thomson Memorial Museum, 138 Vivian St., Stratford ON N5A 5E1 – 519/271-1138

Stratford: Perth Regiment Museum, c/o Stratford Armoury, 80 Waterloo St. South, Stratford ON N5A 4A9 – Curator, John Blue

Strathroy: A.W. Campbell House Museum, c/o St. Clair Region Conservation Authority, 205 Mill Pond Cres., Strathroy ON N7G 3P9 – 519/245-3710 – Community Relations Supervisor, Rick Battson

Strathroy Middlesex Museum, 84 Oxford St., Strathroy ON N7G 3A5 – 519/245-0492 – Director, Muriel Kew

Sturgeon Falls: Musée Sturgeon River House Museum, PO Box 1390, Sturgeon Falls ON P0H 2G0 – 705/753-4716; Fax: 705/753-5476 – Chief Officer, Denis Arseneau

Sudbury: Art Gallery of Sudbury/Galerie d'art de Sudbury, 453 Ramsey Rd., Sudbury ON P3E 2Z7 – 705/675-4871; Fax: 705/674-3065; Email: ags@ags-gas.on.ca; URL: http://www.ags-gas.on.ca – Director/Curator, Pierre Arpin; Coordinator of Services, Michelle Landry

Sudbury: Centre franco-ontarien de folklore (CFOF), Maison d'Youville, 38, rue Xavier, Sudbury ON P3C 2B9 – 705/675-8986; Fax: 705/675-5809 – Directeur de la recherche, folkloriste, Rév. P. Germain Lemieux, S.J.

Sudbury: Copper Cliff Museum, Leisure Services Dept., PO Bag 5000, Stn A, Sudbury ON P3A 5P3 – 705/674-3141, ext.457; Fax: 705/671-8145 – Rick Sleaver

Sudbury: Flour Mill Museum, 514 Notre Dame St., Bag 5000, Stn A, Sudbury ON P3A 5P3 – 705/674-2391; Fax: 705/671-8145 – Curator, Peter Philipon

Sudbury: Science North, 100 Ramsey Lake Rd., Sudbury ON P3E 5S9 – 705/522-3701; Fax: 705/522-4954 – CEO, Jim Marchbank; Marketing Manager, Leslie Standford – Includes Solar Observatory

Sundridge Maple Sugar House & Museum, Art Gallery, & Pioneer Home, Sundridge ON P0A 1Z0 – 705/384-7764 – Open year round

Sutton West: Georgina Village Museum, PO Box 495, Sutton West ON L0E 1R0 – 905/476-4301; Fax: 905/476-8100 – President, Eric Lamaus; Treasurer, Marg Godfrey

Sutton West: Eildon Hall Sibbald Memorial Museum, Sibbald Point Provincial Park, RR#2, Sutton West ON L0E 1R0 – 905/722-3268 – Chief Volunteer, Mary Brown

Tehkummah Township Little Schoolhouse and Museum, c/o Municipal Office, Tehkummah ON P0P 2C0 – 705/859-3293 – Curator, John Novak

Thunder Bay: 1910 Logging Museum, c/o Parks Division Victoria Ville Civic Centre, 111 Syndicate Ave. South, Thunder Bay ON P7E 6S4 – 807/625-2351; Fax: 807/625-3528 – Dan Gillies

Thunder Bay: Northwestern Ontario Sports Hall of Fame, 2203 Moodie St. East, Thunder Bay ON P7C 5N4 – 807/622-2852; Fax: 807/622-2736 – Executive Director, Diane Imrie

Thunder Bay: Old Fort William (OFW), Vickers Heights PO, Thunder Bay ON P0T 2Z0 – 807/577-8461; Fax: 807/473-2327; URL: http://www.oldfortwilliam.on.ca – Managing Director, Ronald D. Zizman

Thunder Bay: Paipoonge Historical Museum, RR#6, Thunder Bay ON P7C 5N5 – 807/939-1262; Fax: 807/939-1550 – Curator, Lois Garrity

Thunder Bay Museum, 425 East Donald St., Thunder Bay ON P7E 5V1 – 807/623-0801; Fax: 807/622-6880; Email: tbhms@tbaytel.net – Curator, Tory Tronrud; Director, Dorette Carter

Tillsonburg Museum, 30 Tillson Ave., Tillsonburg ON N4G 2Z8 – 519/842-2294; Fax: 519/842-9431 – Curator, Rita Corner

Timmins Museum: National Exhibition Centre/Musée de Timmins: Centre national d'exposition, City of Timmins, 220 Algonquin Blvd. East, Timmins ON P4N 1B3 – 705/235-5066; Fax: 705/235-9631; Email: can-tmnec@immedia.ca – Director/Curator, Karen Bachmann

Tobermory: The Peninsula & St. Edmunds Township Museum, PO Box 70, Tobermory ON N0H 2R0 – 519/596-2479 – Curator, Marjorie Munn

Toronto: The Bata Shoe Museum (BSM), 327 Bloor St. West, Toronto ON M5S 1W7 – 416/979-7799; Fax: 416/979-0078 – Director, Sharon McDonald; Chair, Sonja Bata

Toronto: Beth Tzedec Reuben & Helene Dennis Museum, 1700 Bathurst St., Toronto ON M5P 3K3 – 416/781-3511; Fax: 416/781-0150 – Curator, Dorion Liebgett

Toronto: Campbell House, 160 Queen St. West, Toronto ON M5H 3H3 – 416/597-0227; Fax: 416/597-1588; URL: http://www.advsoc.on.ca/campbell/index.html – Curator, Carol Martin; Chair, Tom Carey

Toronto: Canada's Sports Hall of Fame/Temple de la Rénommée des Sports du Canada (CSHOF), Exhibition Place, Toronto ON M6K 3C3 – 416/260-6789; Fax: 416/260-9347; Email: cshof@inforamp.net; URL: http://www.inforamp.net/~cshof – Executive Director, Allan Stewart – Three floors of exhibits & touchscreen videos; tells the story of Canada's great sport heritage; open Mon.-Fri., 10 am - 4:30 pm; free

Toronto: Canadian Baseball Hall of Fame, c/o Ontario Place, 955 Lake Shore Blvd. West, Toronto ON M6K 3B9 – 416/965-7917; Fax: 416/598-0056 – Open May - Labour Day

Toronto: Canadian Museum of Health and Medicine (CMHM), The Toronto Hospital, 101 College St., Toronto ON M5G 2C4 – 416/603-5444; Fax: 416/603-5863; Email: fpope@torhosp.toronto.on.ca; URL: http://www.cmhm.org – Director/Curator, Felicity Pope – New museum being developed at The Toronto Hospital will focus on the health experiences of Canadians from 1600 to the present; opening in the year 2000.

Toronto: Casa Loma, 1 Austin Terrace, Toronto ON M5R 1X8 – 416/923-1171; Fax: 416/923-5734; Email: info@casaloma.org – CEO, Virginia Cooper – Former home of industrialist Sir Henry Pellatt; open for tours daily

Toronto: CBC Museum, 250 Front St. West, PO Box 500, Stn A, Toronto ON M5W 1E6 – 416/205-5574; Fax: 416/205-7583 – Curator, Ivan Harris; Coordinator, Faye Blum

Toronto: Century Schoolhouse, 502 Sammon Ave., Toronto ON M4C 2V3 – 416/396-2074; Fax: 416/396-2238 – Evelyn Wilson

Toronto: City of York Museum, c/o City Clerk, 2700 Eglinton Ave. West, Toronto ON M6M 1V1 – 416/394-2513; Fax: 416/394-2803 – Curator, Bernard J. Thompson

Toronto: Colborne Lodge, c/o Heritage Toronto, 205 Yonge St., Toronto ON M5B 1N2 – 416/392-6827; Fax: 416/392-0375; URL: http://www.torontohistory.on.ca – Site Manager, Cheryl Hart

Toronto: The Enoch Turner Schoolhouse (1848), 106 Trinity St., Toronto ON M5A 3C6 – 416/863-0010 – Executive Officer, Dean Malloy – One of Toronto's oldest institutions & the city's first free school

Toronto: Fire Fighting Museum, Toronto Fire Academy, 895 Eastern Ave., Toronto ON M4L 1A2

Toronto: George R. Gardiner Museum of Ceramic Art, 111 Queen's Park, Toronto ON M5S 2C7 – 416/586-8000; Fax: 416/586-8085 – Director/Curator, Meredith Chilton

Toronto: The Grange, Art Gallery of Ontario, 317 Dundas St. West, Toronto ON M5T 1G4 – 416/977-0414

Toronto: Historic Fort York, c/o Heritage Toronto, 205 Yonge St., Toronto ON M5B 1N2 – 416/392-6907; Fax: 416/392-6917; URL: http://www.torontohistory.on.ca – Site Manager, Ken Purvis – Birthplace of the City of Toronto; largest collection of original War of 1812 buildings in Canada; accessible at Strachan & Fleet Sts., on Garrison Rd., or by TTC on Bathrst south of Front

Toronto: HMCS Haida Naval Museum/NCSM Haida Musée Navale, Ontario Place, 955 Lakeshore Blvd. West, Toronto ON M6K 3B9 – 416/314-9755; Fax: 416/314-9878; Email: hnmchin@planeteer.com; URL: http://www3.sympatico.ca/hrc/haida/ – Manager, Sheila Shaver; Site Coordinator, Carla Morse

Toronto: Latvian History Museum, 125 Broadview Ave., Toronto ON M4M 2E9 – 416/889-0472 – Curator, Andrew Brumelis

Toronto: Mackenzie House, c/o Heritage Toronto, 205 Yonge St., Toronto ON M5B 1N2 – 416/392-6827; Fax: 416/392-6834; Email: info@torontohistory.on.ca; URL: http://www.torontohistory.on.ca – Managing Director, George Waters – Located at: 82 Bond St., Toronto

Toronto: Marine Museum of Upper Canada, c/o Toronto Historical Board, 205 Yonge St., Toronto ON M5B 1N2 – 416/392-1765; Fax: 416/392-1767 – Curator, John Summers – Located in Exhibition Place, next to the Automotive Bldg.

Toronto: Metropolitan Toronto Police Museum & Discovery Centre, 40 College St., Toronto ON M5G 2J3 – 416/808-7020; Fax: 416/808-7052; URL: http://www.ntps.on.ca – Historian, Sharon McDonald – Interactive displays portray the diverse aspects of policing, past & present

Toronto: Museum for Textiles, 55 Centre Ave., Toronto ON M5G 2H5 – 416/599-5321; Fax: 416/599-2911; URL: http://www.interlog.com/~gwhite/ttt/tttintro.html – Executive Director, Sarah Holland

Toronto: Museum of Childhood (MOC), 55 Mill St., Toronto ON M5A 3C4 – 416/368-2866; Fax: 416/964-2716 – President, Loet Vos – Extensive collection of childhood toys, clothes, furniture, books; opening date before year 2000; educational presentations & traveling exhibits available

Toronto: Museum of Mental Health Services, 1001 Queen St. West, Toronto ON M6J 1H4 – 416/535-8501

Toronto: Museum of Promotional Arts, Toronto, PO Box 400, Stn Adelaide, Toronto ON M5C 2J5 – President/CEO, Frances E.M. Johnston

Toronto: The Queen's Own Rifles of Canada Regimental Museum, Casa Loma, 1 Austin Terrace, Toronto ON M5R 1X8 – 905/826-6138 – Curator, Capt. Peter Simundson, CD – Display artifacts pertinent to the history of the regiment from 1860-present

Toronto: Queen's York Rangers Museum, 660 Fleet St., Toronto ON M5V 1A9 – 416/973-3265 – Acting Curator, Maj. S.H. Bull

Toronto: Redpath Sugar Museum, 95 Queen's Quay East, Toronto ON M5E 1A3 – 416/366-3561; Fax: 416/366-7550 – Corporate Archivist, Richard Feltoe

Toronto: Royal Canadian Military Institute Museum, 426 University Ave., Toronto ON M5G 1S9 – 416/597-0286 – Curator, Gregory Loughton

Toronto: Royals Museum, Fort York Armoury, c/o W. Bennett, 54 Meighen Ave., Toronto ON M4B 2G9 – 416/757-3955; 369-3677 – Curator, Capt. W. Bennett

Toronto: The Salvation Army George Scott Railton Heritage Centre, 2130 Bayview Ave., Toronto ON M4N 3K6 – 416/481-4441; Fax: 416/481-6096 – Director, Major Paul Murray

Toronto: Scadding Cabin, c/o York Pioneers & Historical Society, 2482 Yonge St., PO Box 45026, Toronto ON M4P 3E3 – 416/481-8648

Toronto: Sesquicentennial Museum, Records & Archives, Toronto Board of Education, 155 College St., Toronto ON M5T 1P6 – 416/591-8202; Fax: 416/591-8375 – Curator, Gail Gregory

Toronto: Spadina Historic House Museum, c/o Heritage Toronto, 205 Yonge St., Toronto ON M5B 1N2 – 416/392-6827; Fax: 416/392-6834; Email: info@torontohistory.on.ca; URL: http://www.torontohistory.on.ca – Managing Director, George Waters – Located at: 285 Spadina Rd., Toronto

Toronto: Taras H. Shevchenko Museum, 1614 Bloor St., Toronto ON M6P 1A7 – 416/534-8662 – President, Wm. Harasym – Ethnographic

Toronto: Todmorden Mills Heritage Museum & Art Centre, 850 Coxwell Ave., Toronto ON M4C 5R1 – 416/396-2819; Fax: 416/466-4170; Email: tmmchin@planeteer.com – Curator/Administrator, Susan Hughes – Located at 67 Pottery Rd.

Toronto Scottish Regimental Museum, Fort York Armoury, 660 Fleet St., Toronto ON M5V 1A9

Toronto's First Post Office (TFPO), 260 Adelaide St. East, Toronto ON M5A 1N1 – 416/865-1833; Fax: 416/865-9414; URL: http://www.web-sights.com/tfpo – Curator, Victoria von Schilling

Toronto: Ukrainian Museum of Canada, 620 Spadina Ave., Toronto ON M5S 2H4 – 416/923-3318; Fax: 416/923-8266; Email: svi@stvladimir.on.ca – Curator, Halya Kluchko – Open Thursdays from 10 a.m to 1:30 p.m.

Tweed & Area Heritage Centre, 40 Victoria St. North, PO Box 665, Tweed ON K0K 3J0 – 613/478-3989 – Curator, E. Morton

Uxbridge: Thomas Foster Memorial Temple, c/o Uxbridge-Scott Museum, PO Box 1301, Uxbridge ON L9P 1N5 – 905/852-5854; Email: museum@uxbridge.com – Curator, Allan McGillivray – Built by former mayor of Toronto, Thomas Foster, in 1935/36 as a memorial to the local pioneers

Uxbridge-Scott Museum & Archives, PO Box 1301, Uxbridge ON L9P 1N5 – 905/852-5854; Email: museum@uxbridge.com; URL: http://www.uxbridge.com/museum – Curator, Allan McGillivray – Displays of artifacts & photos that help to tell the story of the Uxbridge area

Vernon: Osgoode Twp. Historical Society & Museum, PO Box 74, Vernon ON K0A 3J0 – 613/821-4062 – Archivist/Curator, Donna Bowen – Exhibits furniture, quilts, toys, household implements & artifacts that reflects township history; The Museum annex: early agricultural implements, tools & industrial artifacts

Verona: Bell Rock Mill Museum, Verona ON K0H 2W0 – 613/374-1458; After Hours: 613/478-1195 – Owner/Curator, Richard Tosswill – Water-powered working milling technology, publicly & freely accessed; eastern white cedar shingles, heritage quality, available

Wasaga Beach: Nancy Island Historic Site, c/o Wasaga Beach Provincial Park, PO Box 183, Wasaga Beach ON L0L 2P0 – 705/429-2728; Fax: 705/429-7983

Waterford: Spruce Row Museum, 159 Nichol St., Waterford ON N0E 1Y0 – 519/443-4211 – Curator, Priscilla Ivey – History of the Waterford & Townsend area; displays; tours; audio-visual presentations; educational programming & hands-on demonstrations

Waterloo: Brubacher House Museum, c/o Conrad Grebel College, Waterloo ON N2L 3G6 – 519/886-3855 – Director, Nelson Scheifele

Waterloo: Earth Sciences Museum, Biology Bldg., University of Waterloo, Waterloo ON N2L 3G1 – 519/888-4567, ext.2469; Fax: 519/746-7484; Email: esmuseum@sciborg.uwaterloo.ca; URL: http://www.science.uwaterloo.ca/earth/museum/museum.html – Director, Dr. Jocelyne Legault; Curator, Peter Russell

Waterloo: Museum & Archive of Games, Burt Matthews Hall, University of Waterloo, Waterloo ON N2L 3G1 – 519/888-4424; Fax: 519/746-6776; Email: museum@healthy.uwaterloo.ca; URL: http://www.uwaterloo.ca/~museum – Curator, Dr. Ronald Johnson; Assistant Curator, Prof. Rhonda Ryman

Waterloo: Museum of Visual Science & Optometry, University of Waterloo, Waterloo ON N2L 3G1 – 519/885-1211, ext.3405; Fax: 519/725-0784 – Curator, Prof. E. Fisher

Welland Historical Museum, 65 Hooker St., Welland ON L3C 5G9 – 905/732-2215 – Curator/Director, Mac Swackhammer

Wellington Community Historical Museum, Main St., PO Box 160, Wellington ON K0K 3L0 – 613/399-5015; URL: http://www.lookupontario.com – Curator, Diane Wenn

Westport: Rideau District Museum, PO Box 305, Westport ON K0G 1X0 – 613/273-2502 – Chairperson, Janice Steele – Housed in 1850s blacksmith & carriage shop with forges & bellows intact

White Lake: Waba Cottage Museum, PO Box 167, White Lake ON K0A 3L0 – 613/623-4341 – Chairperson, V. Miller – Situated in an 8-acre park amongst heritage buildings and a boat launch

Whitney: Algonquin Visitor Centre & Algonquin Logging Museum, PO Box 219, Whitney ON K0J 2M0 – 613/637-2828; Fax: 613/637-2138 – Natural Heritage Education Leader, Dan Strickland; Natural Heritage Education Program Manager, Rick Stronks; Group Education Coordinator, Naturalist Colin Jones

Williamstown: The Nor'Westers & Loyalist Museum, PO Box 69, Williamstown ON K0C 2J0 – 613/347-3547 – Chair, Joan P. MacDonald – Housed in a Georgian-style building; stories of loyalist pioneers & partners of the Northwest Fur Company

Windsor: Ojibway Nature Centre, c/o Dept. of Parks & Recreation, 2450 McDougall, Windsor ON N8X 3N6 – 519/966-5852; Fax: 519/966-9658; Email: ojibway@city.windsor.on.ca; URL: http://www.city.windsor.on.ca/parkrec/ojibway.htm – Director, Paul Pratt

Windsor: Serbian Heritage Museum of Windsor (SHM), 6770 Tecumseh Rd. East, Windsor ON N8T 1E6 – 519/944-4884; Fax: 519/974-3963 – Director, Svetlana Miskovic

Windsor: Willistead Manor, 1899 Niagara St., Windsor ON N8Y 1K3 – 519/255-6545

Windsor's Community Museum, 254 Pitt St. West, Windsor ON N9A 5L5 – 519/253-1812; Fax: 519/253-0919; Email: wcmchin@win.hookup.net; URL: http://www.city.windsor.on.ca/wpl/museum.htm – Curator, Janet Cobban; Assistant Curator, Madelyn Della Valle

Wingham & District Historical Museum, 275 Josephine St., PO Box 1522, Wingham ON N0G 2W0 – 519/357-3550

Woodstock Museum, 466 Dundas St., City Square, Woodstock ON N4S 1C4 – 519/537-8411; Fax: 519/539-3275 – Curator, Sheila A. Johnson

## PRINCE EDWARD ISLAND

### Prince Edward Island Museum & Heritage Foundation/Le Musée patrimoine de l'Île-du-Prince-Édouard

2 Kent St., Charlottetown PE C1A 1M6
902/368-6600; Fax: 902/368-6608; Email: peimhf@cycor.ca
URL: http://www.peisland.com/peimuseum/
Executive Director, Christopher Severance

#### BASIN HEAD FISHERIES MUSEM

PE C0B 2B0
902/357-2966
Site Director, Boyde Beck

#### BEACONSFIELD HISTORIC HOUSE

2 Kent St., PE C1A 1M6
902/368-6606
Site Director, Tracey MacLeod

#### ELMIRA RAILWAY MUSEUM

PE C0A 1K0
902/357-2481
Site Director, Chris Severance

#### EPTEK NATIONAL EXHIBITION CENTRE

Waterfront Properties, 130 Water St., PE C1N 1A9
902/888-8373
Site Director, Susan Rodgers

#### GREEN PARK SHIPBUILDING MUSEUM & YEO HOUSE

Tyne Valley, RR#1, PE C0B 1T0
Site Director, Linda Arsenault

#### LE MUSÉE ACADIEN

PO Box 159, PE C0B 1T0
902/432-2880
Site Director, Cécile Gallant

#### ORWELL CORNER HISTORIC VILLAGE

PE C0A 2E0
902/651-2013
Site Director, Wendell Boyle

### Other Museums & Science Centres in Prince Edward Island

Charlottetown: Fort Amherst/Port La Joye National Historic Site, c/o Canadian Parks Service, PO Box 487, Charlottetown PE C1A 7L1 – 902/675-2220; Fax: 902/675-2220 – First European settlement on the Island; open June - Labour Day

Charlottetown: Green Gables House, PEI National Park, PO Box 487, Charlottetown PE C1A 7L1 – 902/672-2211; Fax: 902/672-3154 – District Chief, Visitor Activities, Philip Michael – Open May 14 - Oct. 31

Charlottetown: Province House National Historic Site, c/o Canadian Heritage, 165 Richmond St., Charlottetown PE C1A 1J1 – 902/566-7626; Fax: 902/566-7226 – Site Coordinator, Sharon Larter – Includes Confederation Chamber, the site of historic discussions regarding union of the BNA colonies; remains the Legislative Bldg. for PEI; open year round

Charlottetown: Spoke Wheel Car Museum, RR#3, Charlottetown PE C1A 7J7 – Director, Clarence Foster

Hunter River: Royal Atlantic Wax Museum, Rte. 6, Cavendish Beach, Hunter River PE C0A 1N0 – 902/

963-2350 – Marjorie Evans; Allan Evans – 109 life-sized wax figures in period costume

Kensington: Anne of Green Gables Museum at Silver Bush, PO Box 491, Kensington PE C0B 1M0 – 902/436-1787; Fax: 902/436-7329 – Director, George Campbell – Open June, Sept. & Oct.

Kensington: The Keir Memorial Museum, PO Box 177, Kensington PE C0B 1M0 – 902/836-3054 – Treasurer, Kathy Murphy – Open July - Sept.

Kensington: Lucy Maud Montgomery Birthplace, RR#6, Kensington PE C0B 1M0 – 902/886-2596 – Curator, Merle Cole – Open May - Thanksgiving

Kensington: Veterans' Memorial Military Museum, Legion Branch 9, Kensington PE C0B 1M0 – 902/836-3600 – Col. E.W. Johnstone – Open June 15 - Sept. 15

Miscouche: Le Musée Acadien de l'Ile-du-Prince-Édouard, 23 Main Dr. East, CP 159, Miscouche PE C0B 1T0 – 902/436-6237 – Directrice, Cécile Gallant

Montague: Garden of the Gulf Museum, PO Box 1237, Montague PE C0A 1R0 – 902/838-2467 – Curator, Mary Brydon – Pioneer history; open mid-June - Sept.

Murray Harbour: Log Cabin Museum, Murray Harbour PE C0A 1V0 – 902/962-2201 – Director, Preston Robertson – Open July - Labour Day

Murray River: Northumberland Mill & Museum, Murray River PE C0A 1W0 – President, Linda Lidstone-Reynolds

O'Leary: Prince Edward Island Potato Museum, 22 Parkview Dr., PO Box 602, O'Leary PE C0B 1V0 – 902/859-2039; URL: http://www.worldsites.net/peipotatomuseum/ – President, Dr. L. George Dewar – Community museum, little red schoolhouse, a heritage chapel & log barn; open June 1 - Oct. 15

O'Leary: West Point Lighthouse Museum, RR#2, O'Leary PE C0B 1V0 – 902/859-3605; Fax: 902/859-3117 – Manager, Carol Livingstone

Richmond: Les Maisons de Bouteilles/The Bottle Houses, CP 72, Richmond PE COB 1Y0 – 902/854-2987; URL: http://www.isn.net/acadie/Bouteill.htm – Réjeanne Arsenault – Three fantasy-like buildings made of over 25,000 vari-coloured bottles, creating a symphony of light and colour within; located in Cape Egmont; flower gardens

Summerside: International Fox Hall of Fame Museum, 286 Fitzroy St., Summerside PE C1N 1J2 – 902/436-2400 – Chairman, Andrew Walker – Located at historic Holman Homestead & Gardens; museum tells the story of the PEI silver fox industry heyday between 1894 & WWII

Tyne Valley: Ellerslie Shellfish Museum Association, PO Box 24, Tyne Valley PE C0B 2C0 – 902/831-2933 – Director, Nan Kernaghan

Wellington: Musée d'Art religieux, Rte 11, 802 Water St. East, Wellington PE C1N 4J6 – 902/854-2260 – Director, Ulric Poirier

Wood Islands: Ripley's Believe It or Not Museum, c/o Thomas MacMillan, PO Belle River, Wood Islands PE C0A 1B0 – 902/963-2242; Fax: 902/962-2017 – Open June - Sept.

## QUÉBEC

### Canadian Centre for Architecture/Centre Canadien d'Architecture (CCA)

1920, rue Baile, Montréal QC H3H 2S6
514/939-7000; Fax: 514/939-7020; Email: ref@cca.qc.ca
URL: http://cca.qc.ca/
Museum & study centre devoted to the art of architecture & its history. Four major research collections: (Library of over 160,000 vols.); prints & drawings (some 22,000 works); archives (over 250,000) items; photographs (some 50,000 images); Facilities include seven main galleries, octagonal gallery, theatre, library, scholars' wing, bookstore, meeting & reception area, park & garden.
Director, Phyllis Lambert
Associate Director, Robert Spickler
Chief Curator, Nicholas Olsberg
Associate Librarian, Rosemary Haddad
Assistant Director, Museum Services, Wendy Owens
Head, Communications, Hélène Panaiote

### McCord Museum of Canadian History/Musée McCord d'histoire canadienne

690, rue Sherbrooke ouest, Montréal QC H3A 1E9
514/398-7100; Fax: 514/398-5045; Email: info@mccord.lan.mcgill.ca
URL: http://www.mccord-museum.qc.ca
Costumes & textiles; ethnology & archaeology; photographic archives; decorative arts; paintings, prints & drawings; archives & library. Open year round.
Executive Director, Claude Benoit
Director, Communications, Wanda Palma
Director, Development, Elizabeth Kennell
Director, Marketing, Michel Pelletier
Director, Finance & Administration, Philip Leduc
Director, Curatorial & Research Services, Moira McCaffrey
Director, Collection Management & Access Services, Nicole Vallières
Director, Building & Security, William Misuirak

### Musée de la civilisation

85, rue Dalhousie, CP 155, Succ B, Québec QC G1K 7A6
418/643-2158; Fax: 418/646-9705; Email: mcqweb@mcq.org
URL: http://www.mcq.org
Located in Quebec City's Old Port, near Place Royale; the Museum offers more than ten theme-oriented exhibitions simultaneously, of which three are permanent: Memoirs (The history of Québec); Objects of Civilization; LaBarque (a 250 year-old boat, found on the site of the Museum); temporary & international exhibitions reflect human adventure & experiences from societies around the world; French & English texts; tours in French & English.
Directeur général, Roland Arpin
Directrice, Communications, Julie Gagnon

### Musée de l'Amerique française (MAF)

9, rue de l'Université, CP 460, Succ Haute-Ville, Québec QC G1R 4R7
418/692-2843; Fax: 418/692-5206; Email: mcqweb@mcq.org
URL: http://www.mcq.org
Collections of paintings by European & Canadian artists, scientific works, rare & ancient books; numismatic collection; ethnological collection; historical archives; open year round.
Directeur, Roland Arpin
Directrice, Communications, Julie Gagnon

### Musée des arts décoratifs de Montréal/Montréal Museum of Decorative Arts (MDAM/MMDA)

2200, rue Crescent, CP 1200, Succ A, Montréal QC H3C 2Y9
514/284-1252; Fax: 514/284-0123
URL: http://www.madm.org
Founded in 1979, collections date from 1935 to the present; the Lilliane & David M. Stewart Collection is considered one of the foremost collections of decorative arts & industrial design in North America; international exhibitions on furniture, glass, textiles, ceramics, graphic arts; open year round.
Directeur, Luc d'Iberville-Moreau
Information Officer, Claire Thériault

### Musée du Québec

Parc des Champs-de-Bataille, Québec QC G1R 5H3
418/643-2150; Fax: 418/646-3330; Email: webmdq@mdq.org
URL: http://www.mdq.org
Prestigious collections of 17th-, 18th- & 19th-century art; collection of contemporary art; library, bookstore & educational service; varied temporary exhibitions; situated on the Plains of Abraham; open year round.
Director, Dr. John R. Porter
Chief Librarian, Louise Allard

### Pointe-à-Callière, Museum of Archaeology & History

Angle de la Commune, 350, place Royale, Montréal QC H2Y 3Y5
514/872-9150; Fax: 514/872-9151; Email: info@musee-Pointe-a-Calliere.qc.ca
URL: http://www.musee-Pointe-a-Calliere.qc.ca
AKA: Pointe-Callière
Overlooking the St-Lawrence River, this museum is a key attraction in the historical quarter of Old Montréal; collection comprises artifacts & architectural remains relating to the founding of the city; includes the Old Customs House (150, rue Saint-Paul); program activities can be adapted to the needs of the general public, school groups, students or anyone with an interest in archaeology or history; multimedia show, permanent & temporary exhibits.
Directrice générale, Francine Lelièvre
Directrice, Communications/Marketing, Marilyne Desrochers Benson
Directrice, Recherche/Conservation/Diffusion, Sylvie Dufresne
Directrice, Animation/Éducation, Ginette Cloutier
Directeur, Commercialisation, Guy Brisebois
Directrice, Administration Finances, Johane Freenette

### Other Museums & Science Centres in Québec

Asbestos: Musée minéralogique d'Asbestos/Asbestos Mineralogical Museum, 104, rue Letendre, Asbestos QC J1T 1E3 – 819/879-6444, 5308 – Directeur, A.J. Millen – Minerals from the Jeffrey Mine; local mining history & exploration of survey instruments; workshops; free admission

Aylmer: The Canadian Golf Museum & Historical Institute, The Kingsway Golf & Country Club, 1461 Mountain Rd., RR#2, Aylmer QC J9H 5E1 – 819/827-0330 – Director, W. Lyn Stewart

Aylmer: Musée d'Aymer Museum Inc., PO Box 311, Aylmer QC J9H 5E6 – 819/682-0291 – Curator, Paul George

Baie Comeau: La Musée de Baie-Comeau, 43, rue Mance, PO Box 273, Baie Comeau QC G4Z 2H1 – 418/296-9690 – Président, Raphael Hovington

Batiscan: Musée, Vieux Presbytère de Batiscan, 340, rue Principale, PO Box 76, Batiscan QC G0X 1A0 – 418/362-2051 – Responsable, Claire Grandbois

Beaumont: Moulin de Beaumont, 2, route du Fleuve, Beaumont QC G0R 1C0 – 418/833-1867 – Directeur, Gilles Sheedy

Berthierville: Musée Gilles-Villeneuve, Formule No. 27, Berthierville QC J0K 1A0 – 514/836-2714 – Superviseur, Alain Bellehumeur

Berthierville: Village du Défricheur, 1497, Grande Côte, Route 138, Berthierville QC J0K 1A0 – 514/836-4539

Bonaventure: Musée acadien du Québec, 95, av Port-Royal, CP 730, Bonaventure QC G0C 1E0 – 418/534-4000; Fax: 418/534-4105 – Directeur, Jean-Claude Cyr

Boucherville: Maison Louis-Hippolyte Lafontaine, 566, Marie Victorin, Boucherville QC J4B 1X1 – 514/449-8347; Fax: 514/449-4709 – Directeur, Daniel Marineau

Château-Richer: Musée de l'Abeille, 8862, boul Sainte-Anne, Château-Richer QC G0A 1N0 – 418/824-4411; Fax: 418/824-4411 – Vice-President, Redmond Hayes – Bee museum

Chambly: Lieu historique du Fort-Chambly, 2, rue Richelieu, PO Box 115, Chambly QC J3L 2B9 – 514/658-1585 – Régisseur, Claude Picher

Chicoutimi: La Pulperie de Chicoutimi, 300, rue Dubuc, Chicoutimi QC G7J 4M1 – 418/698-3100; Fax: 418/698-3158; URL: http://www.reseau.qc.ca/pulperie.htm – Yolande Racine

Coaticook: Musée Beaulne, 96, rue Union, Coaticook QC J1A 1Y9 – 819/849-6560; Fax: 819/849-9519 – Directeur, Pierre Jean

Cookshire: Compton County Historical Museum Society, Cookshire QC J0B 1M0 – 819/875-5256 – Curator, M. Owens

Coteau-du-Lac: Lieu historique national de Coteau-du-Lac, 308a, ch du Fleuve, CP 550, Coteau-du-Lac QC J0P 1B0 – 514/763-5631; Fax: 514/763-1654

Desbiens: Centre d'interpretation de la Métabetchouane, 243, rue Hébert, CP 266, Desbiens QC G0W 1N0 – 418/346-5341 – Présidente, Gisèle Gagnon-Plourde

Drummondville: Le Village Québecois d'Antan, 1425, rue Montplaisir, Drummondville QC J2B 7T5 – 819/478-1441; Fax: 819/478-8155 – Reconstitution d'un village canadien-français du siècle dernier (1810-1910).

Gaspé: Centre d'interpretation du Parc National Forillon/Forillon National Park Interpretation Centre, CP 1220, Gaspé QC G0C 1R0 – 418/892-5572; Fax: 418/368-6837 – Chef, section de l'interpretation, Maxime St-Amour

Gaspé: Musée de la Gaspésie, 80, boul Gaspé, CP 680, Gaspé QC G0C 1R0 – 418/368-5710; Fax: 418/368-5715 – Directeur général, Jean-Marie Fallu

Havre-Aubert, Îles-de-la-Madeleine: Musée de la Mer Inc., CP 69, Havre-Aubert, Îles-de-la-Madeleine QC G0B 1J0 – 418/937-5711 – Directeur, Frédéric Landry

Hull: Canadian Postal Museum/Musée Canadien de la Poste (CPM/MCP), Canadian Museum of Civilization, 100 Laurier St., PO Box 3100, Stn B, Hull QC J8X 4H2 – 819/776-8200; Fax: 819/776-7062; Email: francine.brousseau@cmcc.muse.digital.ca; URL: http://www.cmcc.muse.digital.ca/cpm.html – Director, Francine Brousseau

Joliette: Musée d'art de Joliette, 145, rue Wilfrid-Corbeil, Joliette QC J6E 4T4 – 514/756-0311; Fax: 514/756-6511 – Directrice, France Gascon

Kahnawake: Musée Kateri Tekakwitha, PO Box 70, Kahnawake QC J0L 1B0 – 514/632-6030 – Directeur/Conservateur, Léon Lajoie

Kamouraska: Musée de Kamouraska, 69, av Morel, PO Box 99, Kamouraska QC G0L 1M0 – 418/492-3144, 9783 – Directrice générale, Yvette Raymond

Knowlton: Brome County Historical Museum, Archives & Historical Society (BCHS), PO Box 690, Knowlton QC J0E 1V0 – 514/243-6782 – Archivist, Marion L. Phelps – Museum open mid-May - mid-Sept.; archives by appt.

La Baie: Musée du Fjord, 3346, boul de la Grande-Baie sud, La Baie QC G7B 1G2 – 418/544-7394; Fax: 418/544-1764 – Directrice, Guylaine Simard

La Guadeloupe: Écomusée de la Haute-Beauce, Musée Territoire, 325, rue Principale, rte 108, St-Evariste, PO Box 595, La Guadeloupe QC G0M 1G0 – 418/459-3195; Fax: 418/459-3122 – Directrice, Nicole Lamontagne

La Pocatière: Musée François-Pilote, 100, av Painchaud, La Pocatière QC G0R 1Z0 – 418/856-3145; Fax: 418/856-5611 – Directeur général, Paul-André Leclerc

La Prairie: Société historique de la Prairie de la Magdeleine, 249, rue Sainte-Marie, CP 131, La Prairie QC J5R 3Y2 – 514/659-1393 – Président, Jean L'Heureux

La Sarre: Musée d'histoire et d'Archéologie, av Principale, CP 115, La Sarre QC J9X 2X4 – 514/333-2512 – Directeur, Dominique Godbout

Lac-à-la-Croix: Musée Jules Lamy de Lac-à-la-Croix, 301, av du Musée, CP 40, Lac-à-la-Croix QC G0W 1W0 – 418/349-3633; Fax: 418/349-8724

Lachine: Lieu historique national du commerce de la fourrure à Lachine/The Fur Trade in Lachine National Historic Site, 1255, St-Joseph, Lachine QC H8S 2M2 – 514/637-7433; Fax: 514/637-5325

Lachine: Musée de la Ville de Lachine, 110, ch de LaSalle, Lachine QC H8S 2X1 – 514/634-3471; Fax: 514/634-8164 – Directeur, Jacques Toupin

Lachine: Musée des Soeurs de Sainte-Anne, 1950, rue Provost, Lachine QC H8S 1P7 – 514/637-3783; Fax: 514/637-5400 – Conservatrice, Sr. Colette Masson

Lachute: Musée régional d'Argenteuil/Argenteuil Regional Museum, 50, rue Principale, PO Box 5, Lachute QC J8H 3X2 – 514/387-3861 – Registrar, Noreen Lowe – Historical exhibitions: 8 exhibition rooms

Laurentides: Lieu historique national Sir Wilfrid Laurier, PO Box 70, Laurentides QC J0R 1C0 – 514/439-3702; Fax: 514/439-5721 – Récoisseur, Thomas Piché

Laval: Maison André-Benjamin-Papineau, 5475, boul St-Martin ouest, Laval QC H7T 1C6 – 514/681-1157

Laval: Musée Écologique - (C.J.N.) Vanier, 3995, boul Lévesque, Laval QC H7E 2R3 – 514/661-9320 – Directeur, Alfred Rioux

Lévis: Musée du College de Lévis, 9, rue Mgr Gosselin, Lévis QC G6V 5K1 – 418/837-8600 – Directeur/conservateur, Loic Bernard

Lévis: Société historique Alphonse-Desjardins (SHAD), 6, rue du Mont-Marie, Lévis QC G6V 1V9 – 418/835-2090; Fax: 418/835-9173 – Administrative Assistant, Esther Normand – Résidence du fondateur de la première caisse populaire en Amérique du Nord (c. 1882); ouverte à l'année; entrée gratuite

Longueuil: Musée historique Charles Le Moyne, 4, rue St-Charles est, Longueuil QC J4H 1A9

Longueuil: Musée Marie-Rose Durocher/Lieux historiques S.N.J.M., a/s 80, rue St-Charles est, Longueuil QC J4H 1A9 – 514/651-8104; Fax: 514/651-8636; Email: SNJMGA@connectino.com – Directrice, Stella Plante – Congregation des Soeurs des Saints Noms de Jésus et de Marie

Loretteville: Musée Kio-Warini, Village Huron, Loretteville QC G2B 3W5 – 418/843-5515 – Directeur, François Vincent

Malartic: Musée régional des Mines et des arts de Malartic, 650, rue de la Paix, PO Box 4227, Malartic QC J0Y 1Z0 – 819/757-4677 – Directeur, Jean Massiscotte

Maniwaki: Château Logue, 8, rue Comeau, Maniwaki QC J9E 2R8 – 819/449-7999, 5102; Fax: 819/449-7078 – Director, François Ledoux – Interpretative centre focusing on the history & evolution of fire prevention; open May - Oct.

Matane: Musée du Vieux-Phare, 968, av du Phare ouest, CP 608, Matane QC G4W 1V7 – 418/562-9766 – Directeur, Dr. Robert Fournier

Melbourne: Richmond County Historical Society Museum, PO Box 280, Melbourne QC J0B 2B0 – 819/845-2303 – President, Agnes Keenan

Mont St-Hilaire Nature Conservation Centre, 422, rue des Moulins, Mont St-Hilaire QC J3G 4S6 – 514/467-1755 – Michel Drew

Montebello: Lieu Historique National Du Manoir-Papineau, 500, Notre-Dame, CP 444, Montebello QC J0V 1L0 – 819/423-6965; Fax: 819/423-6455 – Régisseur, Lorraine Neault – 1846 Papineau family home restored to period style; open May - Oct.

Montmagny: Maison de l'accordéon, 301, boul Taché est, CP 71, Montmagny QC G5V 3S3 – 418/248-9196 – Research centre & collection of accordians; open June 24 - Labour Day

Montréal: Alcan Museum & Archives, 1188, rue Sherbrooke ouest, Montréal QC H3A 3G2 – 514/848-8187; Fax: 514/848-8116 – Chief Librarian, Lucie Dion

Montréal: Biodôme de Montréal, 4777, av Pierre-de-Coubertin, Montréal QC H1V 1B3 – 514/868-3000; Fax: 514/868-3065 – Directeur adjoint, Jean-Pierre Doyon – Écosystemes: forêt tropicale, forêt laurentienne, Saint-Laurent marine, monde polaire

Montréal: Black Watch of Canada Regimental Memorial Museum, 2067, Bleury St., Montréal QC H3A 2K2 – 514/842-5045; Fax: 514/496-2759 – Curator, Johanna Douglas-O'Neill

Montréal: Canadian Olympic Hall of Fame/Temple de la renommée olympique du Canada, c/o Canadian Olympic Association, 2380, av Pierre Dupuy, Montréal QC H3C 3R4 – 514/861-3371; Fax: 514/861-2896 – Director, Corporate Affairs, Kathleen Giguère

Montréal: Chapelle Nôtre-Dame de Bon-Secours-Musée Marguerite Bourgeoys, 400, rue St-Paul est, Montréal QC H2Y 1H4 – 514/282-8670; Fax: 514/282-8672 – Directress General, Danielle Dubois – Open spring of 1998; exhibits will interpret the history of the chapel & its role in Montréal from its foundation in 1657 to the present day; life & work of Marguerite Bourgeoys; Amerindian firepits & traces of the stakes of the wooden stockade of 1709; artifacts

Montréal: Écomusée de la Maison du Fier Monde, 2349, rue de Rouen, PO Box 1048, Stn C, Montréal QC H2L 4V3 – 514/598-8185; Fax: 514/598-8185 – Coordinnateur de muséologie, René Binette

Montréal: Gallery of the Saidye Bronfman Centre for the Arts, 5170, Côte Sainte-Catherine, Montréal QC H3W 1M7 – 514/739-2301; Fax: 514/739-9340 – Asst. Director/Curator, Katia Meir; Director/Curator, David Liss

Montréal: Insectarium de Montréal, 4581, rue Sherbrooke est, Montréal QC H1X 2B1 – 514/872-0663; Fax: 514/872-0662; Email: insects@rcip.cycor.ca – Founder, Georges Brossard

Montréal: Le Musée David M. Stewart au Fort de l'Île Sainte-Hélène/The David M. Stewart Museum at the Fort Île Sainte-Hélène, CP 1200, Succ A, Montréal QC H3C 2Y9 – 514/861-6701; Fax: 514/284-0123 – Directeur, Bruce D. Bolton; Conservateur, Guy Vadeboncoeur

Montréal: Lieu historique national de Sir George-Etienne Cartier, 458, Notre-Dame est, Montréal QC H2Y 1C8 – 514/283-2282; Fax: 514/283-5560 – Régisseur, Thomas Piché

Montréal: Maison de la poste/Post Office Houe, 1035, rue St-Jacques, Montréal QC H3C 1H0 – 514/283-4602

Montréal: Maison Saint-Gabriel, 2146, Place Dublin, Montréal QC H3K 2A2 – 514/935-8136; Fax: 514/935-5692; Email: msgrcip@globetrotter.gc.ca – Directrice, Madeleine Juneau, CND

Montréal: Marguerite d'Youville Museum, 1185, rue St-Mathieu, Montréal QC H3H 2H6 – 514/932-7724

Montréal History Centre/Centre d'histoire de Montréal, 335, Place d'Youville, Montréal QC H2Y 3T1 – 514/872-3207; Fax: 514/872-9645 – Anne Marie Collins

Montréal: The Montréal Holocaust Memorial Centre/Le Centre Commémoratif de l'Holocauste à Montréal, 5151, Côte Sainte-Catherine, Montréal QC H3W 1M6 – 514/345-2605; Fax: 514/344-2651; Email: mhmc@accent.net – Executive Director, Bill A. Surkis

Montréal: Musée de la Banque de Montréal/Bank of Montreal Museum, 129, rue St-Jacques, CP 6002, Montréal QC H2Y 1L6 – 514/877-6810; Fax: 514/877-1140 – Archivist, Yolaine Toussaint – Recreated office of the first cashier in Canada's oldest banking institution; open year round

Montréal: Musée de l'Église Notre-Dame, 426, rue Saint-Sulpice, Montréal QC H2Y 2V5 – 514/842-2925; Fax: 514/842-3370 – Yolande Tremblay

Montréal: Musée de l'Oratoire Saint-Joseph/Saint Joseph Oratory Museum, 3800, ch Reine-Marie, Montréal QC H3V 1H6 – 514/733-8211; Fax: 514/733-9735 – Directeur, André Bergeron

Montréal: Musée des Soeurs Grises de Montréal, 1185, rue Saint-Mathieu, Montréal QC H3H 2H6 – 514/937-9501, ext.335; Fax: 514/937-0503 – Directrice, Sr. Jeanne Laporte

Montréal: Musée du Château Ramezay/Château Ramezay Museum, 280, rue Notre-Dame est, Montréal QC H2Y 1C5 – 514/861-7182; Fax: 514/861-8317 – Directeur, André J. Delisle

Montréal: Musée du Cinéma/cinémathèque québécoise, 335, boul de la Maisonneuve ouest, Montréal QC H2X 1K1 – 514/842-9763; Fax: 514/842-1816; Email: http://www.cinematheque.qc.ca – Directeur à la conservation, Robert Daudelin

Montréal: Musée Juste pour rire, 2111, boul St-Laurent, Montréal QC H2X 2T5 – 514/845-4000; Fax: 514/845-4140

Montréal: Musée Marc-Aurèle Fortin, 118, rue St-Pierre, Montréal QC H2Y 2L7 – 514/845-6108 – Directeur, René Buisson

Montréal: Redpath Museum/Musée Redpath, McGill University, 859, rue Sherbrooke ouest, Montréal QC H3A 2K6 – 514/398-4086; Fax: 514/398-3185; URL: http://www.mcgill.ca/Redpath – Director, Dr. Graham Bell

Montréal: Royal Canadian Ordnance Corps Museum/Le Musée du Corps des Magasins Militaires Royal Canadien, 6560, rue Hochlega, CP 4000, Succ K, Montréal QC H1N 3R9 – 514/252-2241 – Curator, Maj. Ivan Burch, (Ret'd)

Montréal: Saint-Laurent Art Museum, 615, av Ste-Croix, Montréal QC H4L 3X6 – 514/747-7367; Fax: 514/747-8892 – Director, Johane Canning-Lacroix – Housed in the Neo-Gothic chapel of Coll@'ge de Saint-Laurent; over 6,000 artifacts reflecting French-Canadian culture, including the tools used by the artists & artisans of the past next to their creations; permanent exhibition contains a large selection of ancient artifacts

Montréal: Univers Maurice Rocket Richard Universe, 2800, rue Viau, Montréal QC H1V 3J3 – 514/251-9930; URL: http://www.Rocket9.org

New Richmond: Gaspesian British Heritage Centre, 351, boul Perron ouest, New Richmond QC G0C 2B0 – 418/392-4487 – Michael Todd Duguay; Joan Dow – Loyalist era from 1760 to 1900s; June - Sept.

Nicolet: Musée des religions, 900, boul Louis-Fréchette, Nicolet QC J3T 1V5 – 819/293-6148; Fax: 819/293-4161; Email: Musée_des_Religions@itr.qc.ca – Directrice, Michèle Paradis

Odanak: Musée des Abénakis d'Odanak, Société historique d'Odanak, 108, Waban-Aki, Odanak QC J0G 1H0 – 514/568-2600; Fax: 514/568-5959; Email: Abenaki@Enter-Net.com – Directrice, Nicole O'Bomsawin

Paspébiac: Site historique du Banc-de-Paspébiac, 3e rue, rte du Banc, CP 430, Paspébiac QC G0C 2K0 – 418/752-6229; Fax: 418/752-6408 – Directrice générale, Sylvie Bond – Sea heritage & traditional trades; tours; gift shop; restaurant "L'Ancre" serves fresh Gaspé seafood; open June - Oct.

Péribonka: Musée Louis-Hémon, 700, Maria-Chapdelaine, Péribonka QC G0W 2G0 – 418/374-2177; Fax: 418/374-2516 – Directrice, Lynn Boisselle

Percé: Centre d'interprétation du Parc de l'Île-Bonaventure-et-du-rocher-Percé, CP 310, Percé QC G0C 2L0 – 418/782-2721 – Natural heritage & history; saltwater aquariums; open June - mid-Oct.

Percé: Musée Le Chafaud, 145, rte 132, Percé QC G0C 2L0 – 418/782-5100 – Open June - mid-Oct.

Pointe-au-Père: Musée de la Mer de Rimouski, 1034, du Phare, Pointe-au-Père QC G5M 1L8 – 418/724-6214 – Directeur, Serge Guay

Pointe-au-Pic: Musée de Charlevoix, 1, ch du Hâvre, CP 549, Pointe-au-Pic QC G0T 1M0 – 418/665-4411; Fax: 418/665-4560; Email: ncpprcip@cite.net – Directrice, Nicole Desjardins

Québec: Centre d'interprétation du Vieux-Port-de-Québec/Old Port of Québec Interpretation Centre, 2, rue d'Auteuil, CP 2474, Succ Terminus, Québec QC G1K 7R3 – 418/648-3300; Fax: 418/648-3678 – Régisseure, Nicole Ouellet

Québec: Lieu historique national Cartier-Brébeuf, 2, rue d'Auteuil, CP 2474, Succ Terminus, Québec QC G1L 7R3 – 418/648-4038 – Régisseure, Eve Bardou – Reproduction grandeur nature du vaisseau amiral de Jacques Cartier, "La Grande Hermine"

Québec: Lieu historique national des Fortifications-de-Québec/Fortifications of Québec National Historic Site, 2, rue d'Auteuil, CP 2474, Succ Terminus, Québec QC G1K 7R3 – 418/648-7016; Fax: 418/648-4825 – Supt., Pierre-Denis Cloutier

Québec: Lieu historique national du Fort-Numéro-Un de-la-pointe-de-Lévy/Fort No. 1 at Pointe-de-Lévy National Historic Site, 41, ch du Gouvernement, a/s 2, rue d'Auteuil, CP 2474, Succ Terminus, Québec QC G1K 7R3 – 418/835-5182; Fax: 418/835-5443 – Interpretive Technician, Nicole Boucher

Québec: Lieu historique national du Parc-de-L'Artillerie/Artillery Park National Historic Site, 2, rue d'Auteuil, CP 2474, Succ Terminus, Québec QC G1K 7R3 – 418/648-4205; Fax: 418/648-4825; URL: http://www.upc.qc.ca/pch/artillerie (Français); http://www.upc.qc.ca/pch/artillery (English) – Supt., Pierre-Denis Cloutier

Québec: Musée des Augustines de l'Hôtel-Dieu de Québec, 32, rue Charlevoix, Québec QC G1R 5C4 – 418/692-2492; Fax: 418/692-2668 – Directrice du Musée, S. Nicole Perron, AMJ – A rich patrimony of art and ethnology gathered by the Augustines for over 3 centuries; medical instrument display from the 17th century to the present; open year round

Québec: Musée des Ursulines de Québec, 12, rue Donnacona, PO Box 760, Stn Haute-Ville, Québec QC G1R 4T1 – 418/694-0694 – Directrice, Soeur Gabrielle Dagnault, o.s.u. – Ursuline heritage under the French regime (1639 - 1759), art gallery, chapel; open Jan. - Nov.

Québec: Musée du Royal 22e Régiment, La Citadelle, CP 6020, Succ Haute-Ville, Québec QC G1R 4V7 – 418/648-3563 – Conservateur, Maj. Robert Girard

Québec: Place-Royale, a/s Ministère des Affaires culturelles, Secteur Place-Royale, 225, Grande-Allée est, Bloc C, Québec QC G1R 5K5 – 418/643-9314 – Directeur, André Couture – Grande concentration de bâtiments des XVII et XVIIIe siècles

Rimouski: Musée régional de Rimouski, 35, rue Saint-Germain ouest, Rimouski QC G5L 4B4 – 418/724-2272 – Directeur général, François Lachapelle

Rimouski: Site historique de la Maison Lamontagne, 540, rue St-Germain est, Rimouski QC G5L 1E9 – 418/722-4038; Fax: 418/722-0226 – Directeur, Robert Malenfant

Rivière-Du-Loup: Musée du Bas-St-Laurent, 300, rue St-Pierre, Rivière-Du-Loup QC G5R 3V3 – 418/862-7547; Fax: 418/862-3019; URL: http://ucctech.com/museejab/ – Directeur, Pierre Rastoul

Roberval: Village Historique de Val-Jalbert, PO Box 34, Roberval QC G8H 2N4 – 418/275-3132; Fax: 418/275-5875 – Directeur, Philippe Auguste Morin

Rouyn-Noranda: La Maison Dumulon, CP 242, Rouyn-Noranda QC J9X 5C3 – 819/797-7125; Fax: 819/762-3367 – Directrice, Diane Tremblay

Saint-Constant: Canadian Railway Museum/Musée ferroviaire canadien, 120, rue St-Pierre, Saint-Constant QC J5A 2G9 – 514/638-1522; Fax: 514/638-1563 – Françine St-Jean

Saint-Hyacinthe: Musée du Séminaire de Saint-Hyacinthe, 650, rue Girouard est, CP 370, Saint-Hyacinthe QC J2S 7B7 – 514/774-0203; Fax: 514/774-7101 – Directeur, Jean-Nöl Dion – Museum of natural sciences, archeology, ethnology, religious heritage & works of art

Saint-Jean-sur-Richelieu: Musée du Fort Saint-Jean, Collège Militaire Royal Saint-Jean, Saint-Jean-sur-Richelieu QC J0J 1R0 – 514/346-2131 – Directeur, Capt. D. Landry – Histoire du Fort Saint-Jean de 1666 à aujourd'hui

Saint-Jean-sur-Richelieu: Musée régional du Haut-Richelieu, 182, Jacques-Cartier nord, Saint-Jean-sur-Richelieu QC J3B 7W3 – 514/347-0649; Fax: 514/357-2285 – Directeur, Michel Roy

Saint-Joseph-de-Beauce: Musée Marius Barbeau, PO Box 1081, Saint-Joseph-de-Beauce QC G0S 2V0 – 418/397-4039 – Animatrice, Johanne Lessard

Saint-Lambert: Musée Marsil/Marsil Museum, 349, Riverside, Saint-Lambert QC J4P 1A8 – 514/671-3098; Fax: 514/465-8694; Email: mars@quebectel.com – Directrice, Louise Séguin; Curator of Costume, Cynthia Cooper – Original exhibitions exploring costume, textiles & fibre; permanent collection of costumes (19th & 20th century) & textiles

Sept-Îles: Centre d'interpretation Le Vieux-Poste, 500, boul Laure, Sept-Îles QC G4R 1X7 – 418/968-2070; Fax: 418/968-8323; Email: mrcn@bbsi.net; URL: http://www.bbsi.net/mrcu/ – Directeur, Guy Tremblay – Open 9-5 daily from Jun. 22 to mid-Aug.

Sept-Îles: Musée Régional de la Côte-Nord, 500, boul Laure, PO Box 725, Sept-Îles QC G4R 4K9 – 418/968-2070; Fax: 418/968-8323 – Directeur, Guy Tremblay – L'Exposition permanente, "Un rivage sans fin," trace un portrait socio-économique de cette région; centre de documentation; ateliers multidisciplinaires; visites guidées

Sherbrooke: Centre d'interpretation de l'histoire de Sherbrooke, 275, rue Dufferin, Sherbrooke QC J1H 4M5 – 819/821-5406; Fax: 819/821-5417 – Directrice, Johanne Lacasse – Heritage of Sherbrooke & the Eastern Townships; open year round

Sherbrooke: Musée de Séminaire de Sherbrooke, Musée de la Tour, Centre d'exposition Léon Marcotte, 222, rue Frontenac, Sherbrooke QC J1H 1J9 – 819/564-3200; Fax: 819/564-7388 – Directeur général, Charles Farrar; Directeur, Marketing, Michel Rodrigue

Sherbrooke: Musée des beaux-arts de Sherbrooke, 174, rue Palais, Sherbrooke QC J1H 4P9 – 819/821-2115 – Directeur/conservateur, Michel Forest

Sillery: Domaine Cataraqui, 2141, ch St-Louis, Sillery QC G1T 1P9 – 418/681-3010; Fax: 418/681-3865 – Conservateur, Eric Lord – Exhibition centre, historic gardens & official house of the Government of Québec

Sillery: Villa Bagatelle, 1563 ch St-Louis, Sillery QC G1S 1G1 – 418/688-8074; Fax: 418/681-3865 – Conservateur, Eric Lord – Exhibition Centre & garden

St-Eustache: Moulin Légaré, 232, rue St-Eustache, St-Eustache QC J7R 2L7 – 514/472-4440, poste 433 – 1762 flour mill; open mid-April - mid-Dec.

St-Eustache: Musée Jean-Hotte, 405, Grande-Côté, St-Eustache QC J7P 1H6 – 514/473-4370 – 15,000 artifacts; toys, antique cars, trains; open March 15 - Nov.

St-Jean-Port-Joli: Musée des Anciens Canadiens, 332, av de Gaspé ouest, St-Jean-Port-Joli QC G0R 3G0 – 418/598-3392; Fax: 418/598-3392 – Jean-Guy Desjardin; Camile Michaud; Denis Michaud – Woodcarving, arts & crafts traditions, 15-minute video on wood, stone & ice-carving techniques; open year round

St-Jean-Port-Joli: Musée les Retrouvailles, 248, av de Gaspé est, St-Jean-Port-Joli QC G0R 3G0 – 418/598-3531 – Weaving looms, spinning wheels, agricultural & domestic artifacts; open June 24 - Labour Day

St-Ulric: Le Musée La Gare de Rivière Blanche, 235, boul Joseph Roy, PO Box 57, St-Ulric QC G0J 3H0 – 418/737-4708 – Responsable, Chantal Frégeot

Stanbridge East: Missisquoi Museum/Musée de Missisquoi, PO Box 186, Stanbridge East QC J0J 2H0 – 514/248-3153; Fax: 514/248-0420 – Executive Secretary, Pamela Realffe; Curator, Heather Darch; Archivist, Judy Antle – Cornell Mill, Hodge's Store & Bill's Barn.; Missisquoi County Archives

Stanstead Historical Society/Société Historique de Stanstead, 35, rue Dufferin, PO Box 268, Stanstead QC J0B 3E0 – 819/876-7322; Fax: 819/876-7936; Email: mccrcip@interlink.qc.ca – Director/Curator, Hervé Gagnon – Operates the Colby Curtis Museum & Carrollcroft Property

Ste-Foy: Le Centre muséographique de l'Université Laval, Pavillon Louis-Jacques-Casault, Université Laval, Ste-Foy QC G1K 7P4 – 418/656-7111; Fax: 418/656-7925; Email: centre.museographique@cmus.ulaval.ca – Directrice, Nicole Brindle

Ste-Foy: Maison Hamel-Bruneau, 2608, ch St-Louis, CP 218, Ste-Foy QC G1V 4E1 – 418/654-4325; Fax: 418/654-4151 – Built in 1858; temporary exhibitions & cultural events

Ste-Foy: Musée de Géologie, Université Laval, Pavillon Pouliot, 4e étage, Ste-Foy QC G1K 7P4 – 418/656-2193 – Conservateur, André Lévesque

Sutton: Eberdt Museum of Communications, PO Box 430, Sutton QC J0E 2K0 – 514/538-2649 – Director/Curator, E. Eberdt

Tadoussac: Chapelle des Indiens, CP 69, Tadoussac QC G0T 2A0 – 418/235-4324 – Curé, Yvon Cholette

Thetford Mines: Musée minéralogique et minier de Thetford Mines, PO Box 462, Thetford Mines QC G6G 5T3 – 418/335-2123; Fax: 418/335-5605; Email: mmmra@tm.megantic.net – Directeur, François Cinq-Mars

Tourelle: Halte touristique Menoum, 22, boul Perron ouest, Tourelle QC G0E 2J0 – 418/763-7446 – Traditional fishery methods; open June-Sept.

Trois-Rivières: Lieu historique national des forges du Saint-Maurice/Forges du Saint-Maurice National Historic Site, 10 000, boul des Forges, Trois-Rivières QC G9C 1B1 – 819/378-5116; Fax: 819/378-0887 – Régisseure, Carmen Desfossés LePage

Trois-Rivières: Musée d'archaéologie de l'Université du Québec à Trois-Rivières, 3351, boul des Forges, Trois-Rivières QC G9A 5H7 – 819/376-5032 – Conservateur, René Ribes

Trois-Rivières: Musée Pierre Boucher, Séminaire Saint-Joseph, 858, rue Laviolette, Trois-Rivières QC G9A 5S3 – 819/376-4459; Fax: 819/378-0607 – Directrice, Françoise Chainé

Val d'Or: Village Minier de Bourlamaque, 90, av Perreault, CP 212, Val d'Or QC J9P 4P3 – 819/825-7616; Fax: 819/825-9853 – Directeur, Pierre Dufour

Valcourt: Musée J. Armand Bombardier, 1001, av J.A. Bombardier, CP 370, Valcourt QC J0E 2L0 – 514/532-5300; Fax: 514/532-2260; URL: http://www.ucctech.com/museejab – Directrice générale, France Bissonnette; Conservateur, Carl F. Eisan

Valleyfield: Écomusée des deux-rives, 111, rue Ellice, Valleyfield QC J6T 1E7 – 514/371-6772 – Présidente, Yolande Latour

Vaudreuil: Musée régional de Vaudreuil-Soulanges (MRVS), 431, av St-Charles, Vaudreuil QC J7V 2N3 – 514/455-2092; Fax: 514/455-6782 – Directeur, Daniel Bissonnette

Victoriaville: Musée Laurier, 16, rue Laurier ouest, Victoriaville QC G6P 6P3 – 819/357-8655; Fax: 819/357-8655 – Directeur/Conservateur, Richard Pedneault – Résidence de Sir et Lady Laurier.

Wendake: Musée Arouane, 10, rue Alexandre-Duchesneau, Wendake QC G0A 4V0 – 418/845-1241

l'Islet-sur-Mer: Musée maritime Bernier, 55, rue des Pionniers est, l'Islet-sur-Mer QC G0R 2B0 – 418/247-5001; Fax: 418/247-5002 – Directrice générale, Sonia Chassé

## SASKATCHEWAN

### Royal Saskatchewan Museum

Wascana Park, College & Albert, Regina SK S4P 3V7
306/787-2815, 2810; Fax: 306/787-2820
URL: http://www.gov.sk.ca/govt/munigov/cult&rec/rsm/

Major collections & exhibits of Saskatchewan's natural & human history, including archaeology, entomology, botany, natural history, paleontology & geology. First Nations Gallery opened June 1993. Life Sciences Gallery under development. Earth Sciences Gallery, Paleo Pit interactive gallery for children & Megamunch, a half-size robotic Tyrannosaurus. Publication of informational booklets & nature notes, giftshop, research library, information services, films, teachers' workshops, educational programs.

Director, Ron Borden
Curator, Life Sciences, David Baron
Curator, Aboriginal History, Margaret Hanna
Curator, Entomology, Keith Roney
Curator, Archaeology, Ian Brace
Supervisor, Exhibits, Ron Tillie
Supervisor, Education & Extension, Paula Hill

### Western Development Museum (WDM)

Curatorial Centre, 2935 Melville St., Saskatoon SK S7J 5A6
306/934-1400; Fax: 306/934-4467; Email: wdm@sfn.saskatoon.sk.ca
URL: http://www.sfn.saskatoon.sk.ca/arts/wdm/
Executive Director, David Klatt
Marketing Director, Jan Olsen
Director, Administration, Gary Carlson

#### 1910 BOOMTOWN

2610 Lorne Ave. South, SK S7J 0S6
306/931-1910; Fax: 306/934-0525
Manager, Tom Waiser

#### HERITAGE FARM & VILLAGE

PO Box 183, SK S9A 2Y1
306/445-8033; Fax: 306/445-7211
Manager, Wayne Fennig

#### HISTORY OF TRANSPORTATION

50 Diefenbaker Dr., PO Box 185, SK S6H 4N8
306/693-5989; Fax: 306/691-0511
Manager, Lyn Johnson

#### STORY OF PEOPLE

Hwy. #16 West, PO Box 98, SK S3N 2V6
306/783-8361; Fax: 306/782-1027
Manager, Susan Manziuk

### Other Museums & Science Centres in Saskatchewan

Alida: Gervais Wheels Museum, PO Box 40, Alida SK S0C 0B0 – 306/443-2303 – Director, Alex Gervais

Arcola Museum, PO Box 279, Arcola SK S0C 0G0 – 306/455-2480 – President, JoAnne Martin

Assiniboia & District Historical Museum, Assiniboia SK S0H 0B0 – 306/642-3003, 4216 – 1912 stores & offices; open year round

Avonlea: Heritage House & Avonlea District Museum, PO Box 401, Avonlea SK S0H 0C0 – 306/868-2101; Fax: 306/868-2221 – President, Garry Erdelyan – A display of local pioneer artifacts

Battleford: Fort Battleford National Historic Site, PO Box 70, Battleford SK S0M 0E0 – 306/937-2621; Fax: 306/937-3370 – A/Supt., Glen Ebert – NWMP post, c. 1886; open May - Oct.

Battleford: Fred Light Museum, PO Box 40, Battleford SK S0M 0E0 – 306/937-7111; Fax: 306/937-2450 – Supervisor, Bernadette Leslie – Pioneer artifacts, gun collection, military artifacts; open May - Sept.

Beauval: Frazer's Museum, PO Box 64, Beauval SK S0M 0G0 – Director, John Frazer

Big Beaver Nature Centre & Museum, c/o Big Muddy Guided Tour Association, Big Beaver SK S0H 0G0 – 306/267-6017

Biggar Museum & Gallery, 202 - 3rd Ave. West, PO Box 1598, Biggar SK S0K 0M0 – 306/948-3451 – Curator, Diane LaRouche

Biggar: Homestead Museum, PO Box 542, Biggar SK S0K 0M0 – 306/948-3427 – Director, Roger Martin

Blaine Lake Museum, PO Box 10, Blaine Lake SK S0J 0J0 – Town Administrator, Eleanora Boyko

Bracken Community Museum, PO Box 35, Bracken SK S0N 0G0 – 306/293-2878 – Laura C. Wright – 8 rooms, fully furnished with stores, office equipment, kitchen items, period furniture & many miscellaneous items

Broadview Museum, c/o Broadview Historical & Museum Association Inc., PO Box 556, Broadview SK S0G 0K0 – 306/696-2612 – Archivist, Iva Galbraith – Pioneer displays, CPR Station & caboose, Sod house, Indian & military artifacts

Bulyea: Lakeside Museum, PO Box 101, Bulyea SK S0G 0L0 – 306/725-4558 – Director, Robert Swanston

Cadillac Historical Society & Museum, Cadillac SK S0N 0K0 – 306/785-2128 – Sec.-Treas., Alta Legros

Canwood Museum, Village of Canwood, Canwood SK S0J 0K0 – 306/468-2616 – Terry Lofstrom

Carlyle: Rusty Relics Museum Inc., PO Box 840, Carlyle SK S0C 0R0 – 306/453-2266 – President, Roy Olmstead – 1943 Canadian Pacific caboose, Canadian National motor car, CN tool shed; open daily 10-5 from mid-June to Labour Day weekend

Climax Community Museum Inc., PO Box 59, Climax SK S0N 0N0 – 306/293-2051 – President/Curator, Victor Van Allen – Pioneer collection - domestic, tools, military, hospital & sports

Coronach District Museum, PO Box 449, Coronach SK S0H 0Z0 – 306/267-5724 – Chairman, Judy Greenwood – Features historical displays, records, photos & artifacts representing the lives of pioneers of the area

Craik: Prairie Pioneer Museum, PO Box 157, Craik SK S0G 0V0 – 306/734-2480 – Director, R. Meshke

Cut Knife: Clayton McLain Memorial Museum, PO Box 335, Cut Knife SK S0M 0N0 – 306/398-2590

Denare Beach: Northern Gateway Museum, PO Box 70, Denare Beach SK S0P 0B0 – 306/362-2054 – Director, Brenda Avison; Director, Maxine Gunn

Dinsmore: Yester-Years Community Museum, PO Box 216, Dinsmore SK S0L 0T0 – 306/846-2139 – President, Helyn Tru

Dodsland Museum, Dodsland SK S0L 0V0 – Director, Jocelyn Sipley

Duck Lake Regional Interpretive Centre, PO Box 328, Duck Lake SK S0K 1J0 – 306/467-2057; Fax: 306/467-2257 – Executive Director, Mariette Forseille

Duff Community Heritage Museum, PO Box 57, Duff SK S0A 0S0 – 306/728-3592 – Sec.-Treas., Norman Schick

Eastend Museum & Cultural Centre, PO Box 214, Eastend SK S0N 0T0 – 306/295-3819 – Secretary, Glen Duke – Open May - Sept.

Edam: Harry S. Washbrook Museum, PO Box 182, Edam SK S0M 0V0 – 306/397-2260 – Director, Harry Washbrook

Elbow Museum & Historical Society, PO Box 207, Elbow SK S0H 1J0 – 306/854-2285 – President, Lewis Webster

Elrose Heritage Society, PO Box 556, Elrose SK S0L 0Z0 – 306/378-2213 – President, Betty Rudd

Esterhazy Community Museum, Esterhazy SK S0A 0X0 – 306/745-6761, 2988 – A.M. Provick – Potash mine; fall-out shelter; first Bohemian Band instruments

Esterhazy: Kaposvar Historic Site, PO Box 115, Esterhazy SK S0A 0X0 – 306/745-6761 – Secretary, Jean Pask – 1907 church & rectory; Annual Pilgrimage in August

Estevan National Exhibition Centre, 118 - 4th St., Estevan SK S4A 0T4 – 306/634-7644; Fax: 306/634-2490 – NWMP barracks, local artifacts, travelling exhibitions; open year round

Eston: Prairie West Historical Centre & Society, PO Box 910, Eston SK S0L 1A0 – 306/962-3772 – Programme Coordinator, Pat Rooke

Foam Lake Museum, PO Box 1041, Foam Lake SK S0A 1A0 – 306/272-4292 – Sec.-Treas., Inge Helgason

Fort Qu'Appelle Museum, PO Box 544, Fort Qu'Appelle SK S0G 1S0 – 306/332-6033 – Secretary, Nellie Hiebert – 1864 Hudson Bay Co. post; open July - Sept.

Frenchman Butte Museum, PO Box 114, Frenchman Butte SK S0M 0W0 – 306/344-4478 – President, Gordon Howard; Curator, Gwen Zweifel

Frobisher Threshermen's Museum, PO Box 194, Frobisher SK S0C 0Y0 – 306/486-2162 – Sec.-Treas., S. Stobart

Glen Ewen Community Antique Centre, Glen Ewen SK S0C 1C0 – 306/925-2221 – Director, Arne Hansen

Glentworth Museum, PO Box 174, Glentworth SK S0H 1V0 – Secretary, Sonia Falconer

Goodsoil Historical Museum, PO Box 57, Goodsoil SK S0M 1A0 – 306/238-2084 – Secretary, Minnie Hofer

Grenfell Community Museum, PO Box 1156, Grenfell SK S0G 2B0 – 306/697-2431; Fax: 306/697-2500 – Secretary, Jean Kerr

Hague: Saskatchewan River Valley Museum, PO Box 630, Hague SK S0K 1X0 – Receptionist, Shirley Fisher

Hazenmore: Heritage Hazenmore Inc., PO Box 103, Hazenmore SK S0N 1C0 – 306/264-5105 – President, Roberta McKeith – Artifacts from early 1900's forward which were once used by the community.

Herbert: Klassen's Homestead Museum, PO Box 28, Herbert SK S0H 2A0 – 306/784-2915 – Director, Peter Klassen

Hodgeville Community Museum, Hodgeville SK S0H 2B0 – 306/677-2693 – President, Faye Rister – Eight rooms depicting an early homestead

Hudson Bay Museum, PO Box 931, Hudson Bay SK S0E 0Y0 – 306/865-2170 – Curator, Barbara Demasson

Humboldt & District Museum & Gallery, PO Box 2349, Humboldt SK S0K 2A0 – 306/682-5226; Fax: 306/682-3144; Email: hblt.museum@sk.sympatico.ca – Curator, J. Hoesgen

Imperial & District Museum, PO Box 269, Imperial SK S0G 2J0 – 306/963-2280 – Chairman, Fred Grigg

Imperial: Nels Berggren Museum, PO Box 125, Imperial SK S0G 2J0 – 306/963-2033 – Director, Nels Berggren

Indian Head Museum, PO Box 566, Indian Head SK S0G 2K0 – 306/695-2556 – President, Lloyd Pearon

Ituna Cultural & Historical Museum, PO Box 282, Ituna SK S0A 1N0

Kamsack & District Museum, PO Box 991, Kamsack SK S0A 1S0 – 306/542-4415 – President, John Barisow – Open May - Sept.

Kerrobert & District Museum, PO Box 401, Kerrobert SK S0L 1R0 – 306/834-2744 – Secretary, Mary Andrews

Kincaid Museum, PO Box 177, Kincaid SK S0H 2J0 – 306/264-3910 – Chairperson, Val Wurmlinger

Kindersley Plains Museum Inc., 903 - 11th Ave. East, PO Box 599, Kindersley SK S0L 1S0 – 306/463-6620 – Secretary, Cecil Campbell; President, Cecilia Pincemin – Open 9-6 daily, May 15-Aug.31

Kinistino District Pioneer Museum Inc., PO Box 10, Kinistino SK S0J 1H0 – 306/864-2474; Fax: 306/864-3465 – Treasurer, Shirley Jackson

Kipling District Museum, Kipling SK S0G 2S0 – 306/736-2488 – Treasurer, Alvin Cunningham

Kisbey Museum, 291 Ross St., PO Box 190, Kisbey SK S0C 1L0 – 306/462-2027 – President, Velma Hale – 1,000+ objects; open Thursdays through July & Aug. & by request

La Ronge: Mistasinihk Place Interpretive Centre, c/o Saskatchewan Family Foundation, PO Box 5000, La Ronge SK S0J 1L0 – 306/425-4350; Fax: 306/425-2580 – Sport & Recreation Consultant, Dennis Moore

Lancer Centennial Museum, PO Box 3, Lancer SK S0N 1G0 – 306/689-2925; Fax: 306/689-2890 – Cliff Murch

Lashburn Centennial Museum, PO Box 343, Lashburn SK S0M 1H0 – 306/285-3860

Lloydminster: Barr Colony Heritage Cultural Centre, 5011 - 49 Ave., Lloydminster SK S9V 0T8 – 306/825-5655; Fax: 306/825-7170 – Includes Barr Colony Museum, Imhoff & Berghammer Art Collections, Fuch's Wildlife

Loon Lake: Big Bear Trails Museum, PO Box 219, Loon Lake SK S0M 1L0 – 306/837-2070 – Director, John W. Simpson

Lumsden Heritage Museum, Qu'Appelle Dr., Lumsden SK S0G 3C0 – 306/731-2905 – President, B. McGill – Qu'Appelle Valley history; John Deere tractor display, town history & picnic area; open May - Sept.

Main Centre Heritage Museum, PO Box 42, Main Centre SK S0H 2V0 – 306/784-3272 – Chairman, Dora Wall

Maple Creek: Antique Tractor Museum & Frontier Village, Maple Creek SK S0N 1N0 – 306/667-2964 – Director, John Stewart

Maple Creek: Fort Walsh National Historic Site, PO Box 278, Maple Creek SK S0N 1N0 – 306/662-2645; Fax: 306/662-2711 – Site Coordinator, Monica Wawryk – NWMP & trading post; open May - Oct.

Maple Creek: Old Timers Museum Inc., PO Box 1540, Maple Creek SK S0N 1N0 – 306/662-2474 – Treasurer, Cindy Drury – Open year round

Maryfield Museum, PO Box 262, Maryfield SK S0G 3K0 – 306/646-2201

McCord & District Museum, PO Box 30, McCord SK S0H 2T0 – 306/478-2522 – Secretary, Audrey J. Wilson – CPR station bldg., caboose & historic church tell of prairie pioneers & the rise & decline of a railway prairie town

Meadow Lake Museum, PO Box 610, Meadow Lake SK S0M 1V0 – 306/236-3622 – Director, Vincent Huffman

Melfort & District Museum, 401 Melfort St. West, PO Box 3222, Melfort SK S0E 1A0 – 306/752-5870; Fax: 306/752-5556; Email: melfort.museum@sk.sympatico.ca – Curator, Frances Westlund – Archives, community museum, log house, blacksmith shop, one-room school & agricultural displays

Melville Heritage Museum Inc., PO Box 2528, Melville SK S0A 2P0 – 306/728-2070 – Curator, Marj Redenbach; President, Joe Miller

Melville Railway Museum, PO Box 2863, Melville SK S0A 2P0 – 306/728-4177; Fax: 306/728-5911 – Chairperson, Adeline Kolooziejak; General Manager, Eileen Farough

Middle Lake Museum, PO Box 157, Middle Lake SK S0K 2X0 – Curator, Susan Bauer

Milden Community Museum, Milden SK S0L 2L0 – 306/935-2163 – President, Margy Reid – A community museum holding local artifacts including those of an old-time school, hospital & bedroom

Moose Jaw Art Museum & National Exhibition Centre, Crescent Park, Moose Jaw SK S6H 0X6 – 306/692-4471; Fax: 306/694-8016; Email: mjamchin@sk.sympatico.ca; URL: http://www.chin.gc.ca/ – Curator, Heather Smith – Art, history & science exhibits; 3,000 artifacts; open year round

Moose Jaw: Sukanen Ship Pioneer Village & Museum of Saskatchewan, PO Box 2071, Moose Jaw SK S6H 7T2 – 306/693-3506 – President, R. Jones; Secretary, A. Giesbretch

Moosomin: Jamieson Museum, 306 Gertie St. North, PO Box 236, Moosomin SK S0G 3N0 – 306/435-3156 – President, Tim Jamieson – Open May - Oct.

Morse Museum & Cultural Centre, PO Box 308, Morse SK S0H 3C0 – 306/629-3230; Fax: 306/629-3230 – President, Darlene Nicholson

Mossbank & District Museum Inc., PO Box 278, Mossbank SK S0H 3G0 – 306/354-2889 – President, Roy Tollefson

Muenster: St. Peter's College Museum, PO Box 10, Muenster SK S0K 2Y6 – 306/682-3373 – Curator, Rev. Rudolph Novecosky

Naicam Museum, PO Box 93, Naicam SK S0K 2Z0 – 306/874-2173 – Secretary, Helen Sandsbraaten

Neudorf Historical Museum, PO Box 12, Neudorf SK S0A 2T0 – 306/748-2519 – Curator, Norman Miller

Nipawin & District Living Forestry Museum, Hwy. 35 West, PO Box 1917, Nipawin SK S0E 1E0 – 306/862-9299; Fax: 306/862-4717 – Curator, Mike Mochoruk – Open May - Sept.

Nokomis & District Museum & Heritage Co-op, PO Box 56, Nokomis SK S0G 3R0 – 306/528-2080 – Director, R.F. Edwards

North Battleford: Saskatchewan Baseball Hall of Fame & Museum, 121 - 20th St., PO Box 1388, North Battleford SK S0M 0E0 – 306/445-8485; Fax: 306/446-0509 – President, David W. Shury, Q.C.

Oxbow: Ralph Allen Memorial Museum, 802 Railway Ave., Oxbow SK S0C 2B0 – 306/483-2400, 5065 – President, N. Black – Open May - Sept.

Paynton: Bresaylor Heritage Museum Association Inc., PO Box 33, Paynton SK S0M 2J0 – 306/895-4813 – Curator, Velma Foster – Artifacts from the Bresaylor Settlement established in 1882, the main settlement era after the railway arrived in 1906 & subsequent decades up to the 1960s

Pelly: Fort Pelly & Livingston Museum, PO Box 363, Pelly SK S0A 2Z0 – 306/595-2030 – President, Mabel Campbell

Plenty: Carscadden's Museum, PO Box 149, Plenty SK S0L 2R0 – 306/932-2226 – Director, William Olson

Porcupine Plain & District Museum, PO Box 148, Porcupine Plain SK S0E 1H0 – 306/278-2317 – Curator/Director, Joyce Logan

Prairie River Museum, PO Box 9, Prairie River SK S0E 1J0 – 306/889-4220; Fax: 306/889-4220 – President, Edward G. Suwinski – Housed in 1919 CN Railway Station; artifacts reflect the early lumbering & agricultural industries of the Prairie River region; Native artifacts

Prelate: St. Angela's Museum & Archives, PO Box 220, Prelate SK S0N 2B0 – 306/673-2200; Fax: 306/673-2635 – Director, Sister Philomena Marte

Prince Albert: John & Olive Diefenbaker House, 246 - 19th St. West, Prince Albert SK S6V 4C6 – 306/922-9641 – Director, Stan Hanson – Open May - Sept.

Prince Albert Historical Museum, PO Box 531, Prince Albert SK S6V 4V5 – 306/764-2992, 1394 – Manager/Curator, R.E.G. Smith – Photos, documents & artifacts on the history of Prince Albert; open May 15 - Sept. 5

Raymore Pioneer Museum Inc., PO Box 453, Raymore SK S0A 3J0 – Sec.-Treas., Wayne Focht

Regina: Diefenbaker Homestead, c/o Wascana Centre Authority, 2900 Wascana Dr., PO Box 7111, Regina SK S4P 3S7 – 306/522-3661; Fax: 306/565-2742; Email: wca@sasknet.sk.ca – Public Relations Officer, Irene Pisula – Open May - Sept.

Regina: Fort Carlton Provincial Historic Park, 3211 Albert St., Regina SK S4S 5W6 – 306/467-4512 (summer), 787-9571 (winter); Fax: 306/787-7000 –

Located on the junction of the overland route to Fort Garry & the water routes to Hudson Bay which was the distribution centre for moving trade goods & furs in and out of the North West

Regina: Government House Historic Property (GH), 4607 Dewdney Ave., Regina SK S4P 3V7 – 306/787-5717; Fax: 306/787-5714 – Acting Manager, Paula Hill

Regina Plains Museum, 1801 Scarth St., 4th Fl., Regina SK S4P 2G9 – 306/780-9435; Fax: 306/565-2979; Email: rp.museum@sk.sympatico.ca – Curator, Sandra Massey – Regina's civic museum

Regina: Royal Canadian Mounted Police Centennial Museum/Musée de la GRC, PO Box 6500, Regina SK S4P 3J7 – 306/780-5838; Fax: 306/780-6349; URL: http://rbcm1.rbcm.gov.bc.ca – Director, W.A.F. MacKay

Regina: Saskatchewan Pharmacy Museum, #700, 4010 Pasqua St., Regina SK S4S 6S4 – 306/584-2292; Fax: 306/584-9695; Email: saskpharm@sk.sympatico.ca – President, C. Choplan

Regina: Saskatchewan Science Centre, Wascana Centre, College & Albert, Regina SK S4P 3V7 – 306/791-7900 – Over 70 hands-on exhibits; open year-round

Regina: Wood Mountain Post Provincial Historic Park, 3211 Albert St., Regina SK S4K 5W6 – 306/266-4322 (summer), 787-9571 (winter); Fax: 306/787-7000 – NWMP detachment patrolled the border from 1874-1918 regulating whiskey traders, horse thieves & cattle rustlers; the post became involved in a major international incident when Sitting Bull & the Lakota arrived in 1877

Riverhurst: F.T. Hill Museum, Riverhurst SK S0H 3P0 – 306/353-2112 – Curator, Winnie Hockman – Gun collection, Indian artifacts, pioneer items; open June - Sept. & by appt.

Rocanville & District Museum Society Inc., PO Box 490, Rocanville SK S0A 3L0 – 306/645-2113, 2605; Fax: 306/645-4492 – Sec.-Treas., Phyllis Ore

Rose Valley & District Heritage Museum, PO Box 232, Rose Valley SK S0E 1M0 – 306/322-2034 – Sec.-Treas., Irene Martinson

Rosetown Museum & Art Centre, Centennial Library, Rosetown SK S0L 2V0 – 306/882-3566 – Director, Frank Glass

Rosthern: Batoche National Historic Park/Lieu national historique Batoche (BNHS), PO Box 999, Rosthern SK S0K 3R0 – 306/423-6227; Fax: 306/423-5400

Rosthern: Mennonite Heritage Museum, PO Box 546, Rosthern SK S0K 3R0 – 306/232-5353; Fax: 306/232-5518 – Chairman, Ed Roth

Saskatoon: Geological Museum, Dept. of Geological Sciences, University of Saskatchewan, Saskatoon SK S7N 0W0 – 306/966-5683; Fax: 306/966-8593 – Head/Geological Sciences, J. Oliphant

Saskatoon: Meewasin Valley Authority (MVA), 402 - 3rd Ave. South, Saskatoon SK S7K 3G5 – 306/665-6888; Fax: 306/665-6117; Email: meewasin@thelink.ca; URL: http://www.lights.com/meewasin – Acting Executive Director, Gwen Charman

Saskatoon: Museum of Antiquities, University of Saskatchewan, Murray Bldg., Rm. 237, 3 Campus Dr., Saskatoon SK S7N 5A4 – 306/966-7818 – Administrator, Catherine F. Gunderson

Saskatoon: Natural Science Museum, Dept. of Biology & Natural Science, University of Saskatchewan, Saskatoon SK S7N 0W0 – 306/966-4400 (bio); 966-5684 (geo); Fax: 306/966-4461 – Head/Biology Dept., Dr. R.J.F. Smith

Saskatoon: Right Hon. John G. Diefenbaker Centre for the Study of Canada, University of Saskatchewan, 101 Diefenbaker Place, Saskatoon SK S7N 5B8 – 306/966-8382; Fax: 306/966-6207; Email: aikenhead@admin.usask.ca; URL: http://library.usask.ca/remate.html – Director, R. Bruce Shepard – Public museum, archives & centre for Canadian Studies

Saskatoon: Ukrainian Museum of Canada (UMC), 910 Spadina Cres. East, Saskatoon SK S7K 3H5 – 306/244-3800; Fax: 306/652-7620; Email: ukrmuse@ks.sympatico.ca; URL: http://www.saskstar.sk.ca/umc – Registrar, Randal Badnaryk; Director, Marie Kishchuk

Sceptre: Great Sandhills Museum, PO Box 29, Sceptre SK S0N 2H0 – 306/623-4345; Fax: 306/623-4612 – President, Gertrude Hale

Shaunavon: Grand Coteau Heritage & Cultural Centre, Centre St., PO Box 966, Shaunavon SK S0N 2M0 – 306/297-3882; Fax: 306/297-3668; Email: gchcc@sk.sympatico.ca – Curator, Ingrid Cazakoff – Natural history museum, heritage museum, art gallery, public library; open year round

Spalding: Reynold Rapp Museum, PO Box 308, Spalding SK S0K 4C0 – 306/872-2164 – President, Ruth Briggs; Secretary, Garth Ulrich

Spruce Home: Buckland Heritage Museum, Hwy. 2, Spruce Home SK S0J 2N0 – 306/764-8470 – Open June - Sept.

Spy Hill: Wolverine Hobby & Historical Society Museum, PO Box 191, Spy Hill SK S0A 3W0 – 306/534-4534 – Secretary, Jean Olson

St. Brieux: Musée St. Brieux Museum, 300 Barbier Dr., CP 224, St. Brieux SK S0K 3V0 – 306/275-2123 – Curator, Lilianne Leray – Documentation au sujet de la vie des pionniers, de leurs origines, des missions environnantes et de l'église catholique pré-Vatican II; des tournées en français ou en anglais sont offertes

St. Victor: McGillis Pioneer Home, St. Victor SK S0H 3T0 – 306/642-3155 – Co-Director, L. Bissonnette

St. Walburg & District Historical Museum Inc., PO Box 336, St. Walburg SK S0M 2T0 – 306/248-3359 – President, J.F. Schmitz

Star City: Our Heritage Museum, PO Box 38, Star City SK S0E 1P0 – 306/863-2309; Fax: 306/863-2277 – Sec.-Treas., Jean Jacklin; Chairman, Audrey Tkachuk – A collection of pioneer artifacts used by the early settlers to this area

Stoughton & District Museum, 327 Main St., PO Box 381, Stoughton SK S0G 4T0 – 306/457-2662 – Committee Chairperson, Betty Wright

Strasbourg & District Museum, PO Box 446, Strasbourg SK S0G 4VO – 306/725-3372 – Director, Albert Keyser

Sturgis Station House Museum, PO Box 255, Sturgis SK S0A 4A0 – 306/548-5565; Fax: 306/548-2948 – Artifacts from the community & surrounding area from pre-pioneer days to the present

Swift Current Museum, 105 Chaplin St. East, Swift Current SK S9H 1H9 – 306/778-2775; Fax: 306/778-2194 – Director, Hugh Henry – Natural & human history museum; open year round

Swift Current: Wright Historical Museum, PO Box 712, Swift Current SK S9H 3W7 – 306/773-8733 – Director, Andrew Wright

Tompkins Museum, PO Box 393, Tompkins SK S0N 2S0 – 306/622-2024 – Owner, Stanley A. Dimmock

Unity & District Heritage Museum, PO Box 591, Unity SK S0K 4L0 – 306/228-3864 – President, Bev Smith – Open May 20 - Sept. 5

Val Marie: Perrault's Museum, PO Box 216, Val Marie SK S0N 2T0 – 306/298-2241 – Directrice, Lise Perrault

Vanguard Centennial Museum, Vanguard SK S0N 2V0 – 306/582-2244 – Librarian, Doris Burns

Verigin: National Doukhobour Heritage Village, PO Box 99, Verigin SK S0A 4H0 – 306/542-4441; Fax: 306/542-2017 – Manager, Philip Perepelkin – Eleven buildings make up the Heritage Village Museum Complex; thousands of Doukhobour artifacts, photos, handicrafts, clothing, hand tools; barns, a blacksmith shop & agricultural equipment

Verwood Community Museum, Verwood SK S0H 4G0 – 306/642-5767 – Secretary, Helen Domes

Wakaw: John G. Diefenbaker Replica Law Office, PO Box 760, Wakaw SK S0K 4P0 – 306/233-5157 – Curator, William Kindrachuk

Wakaw Heritage Society Museum, PO Box 475, Wakaw SK S0K 4P0 – 306/233-4257 – President, Celestine Boehm

Waskesiu Lake: Prince Albert National Park Nature Centre, Waskesiu Lake SK S0J 2Y0 – 306/663-4512; Fax: 306/663-5424; Email: panp_info@pch.gc.ca; URL: http://www.parkscanada.pch.gc.ca – Chief Client Services, Dawn Bronson – Participatory exhibits & displays on boreal forest; park features

Wawota & District Museum, Wawota SK S0G 5A0 – 306/739-2110 – Chairman, Tom Wayling

Webb: Prairie Wildlife Interpretation Centre, PO Box 10, Webb SK S0N 2X0 – 306/674-2287 – Manager, Russell Wall

Weekes: Dunwell & Community Museum, Weekes Recreation Centre, PO Box 120, Weekes SK S0E 1V0 – 306/278-2906

Weyburn: Soo Line Historical Museum, 411 Industrial Lane, PO Box 1016, Weyburn SK S4H 2L2 – 306/842-2922 – Curator/Manager, Lavine Stepp – Old power house

Weyburn: Turner Curling Museum, PO Box 370, Weyburn SK S4H 2K6 – 306/848-3217; Fax: 306/842-2001 – Don Turner – Open Sat. & Sun., 2-5 pm, year round; tours by appt.

White Fox Museum, PO Box 68, White Fox SK S0J 3B0 – 306/276-2170

Whitewood: Old George's Authentic Collectibles, PO Box 118, Whitewood SK S0G 5C0 – 306/735-2255; Fax: 306/735-4399 – Owner/Curator, George C. Chopping – Collection of over 20,000 artifacts

Whitewood Historical Museum, PO Box 752, Whitewood SK S0G 5C0 – 306/735-4388 – Sec.-Treas., Carole Armstrong

Wilkie & District Museum, PO Box 868, Wilkie SK S0K 4W0 – 306/843-2717 – Sec.-Treas., Frances Lowe

Willow Bunch Museum, 8 - 5th St. East, Willow Bunch SK S0H 4K0 – 306/473-2806; Fax: 306/473-2245 – President, Marguerite Campagne; Secretary, Louise Boisvert

Wolseley & District Museum, Wolseley SK S0G 5H0 – Director, Harold Olive

Wood Mountain Rodeo-Ranch Museum, PO Box 53, Wood Mountain SK S0H 4L0 – 306/266-4539 – President, Pat Fitzpatrick; Coordinator, Lois Todd

Wynard & District Museum, PO Box 743, Wynard SK S0A 4T0 – 306/554-2898; Fax: 306/554-3224 – Director, Dave Cross

## YUKON

### MacBride Museum

1st Ave. & Wood St., PO Box 4037, Whitehorse YT Y1A 3S9

867/667-2709; Fax: 867/633-6607

Museum of cultural & natural history. Yukon heritage from pre-history to present. Natural history, archeological & paleontological specimens; ethnographic artifacts, historic artifacts, photographs & archival materials; large industrial & transportation artifacts. Includes outdoor displays, two heritage buildings, 450 sq. m. of exhibits. Open May 15 to Sept. 15 & by appointment.

Director/Curator, Clifford Evans

### Other Museums & Science Centres in Yukon

Destruction Bay: Kluane Museum of Natural History, Mile 1093, Alaska Hwy., General Delivery, Destruction Bay YT Y0B 1H0 – 867/841-4541 – Manager, Iris Wilson – Wildlife display, native handicrafts; open Victoria Day - Labour Day

Haines Junction: Klukshu National Park, PO Box 5309, Haines Junction YT Y0B 1L0 – 867/634-2251; Fax: 867/634-2686 – Traditional salmon fishing & processing as done by Southern Tutchone people; open mid-May - Sept.

Keno City Mining Museum, General Delivery, Keno City YT Y0B 1J0 – 867/995-2792 summer, 995-3103 winter; Fax: 867/995-2730 – Mike Mancini – Open Victoria Day - Labour Day

Teslin: George Johnston Tlingit Indian Museum, Mile 804, Alaska Hwy., PO Box 146, Teslin YT Y0A 1B0 – 867/390-2550; Fax: 867/390-2828 – Open Victoria Day - Labour Day

Whitehorse: Fort Selkirk, c/o Tourism Yukon, Heritage Branch, PO Box 2703, Whitehorse YT Y1A 2C6 – 867/667-5386; Fax: 867/667-8844; Email: dolynyk@gov.yk.ca – Historic Sites Coordinator, Yukon Heritage Branch, Doug Olynyk – Accessible only by boat or plane; contact Selkirk First Nation, Pelly Crossing, YK Y0B 1P0; 403/537-3331; Fax: 403/537-3902; Attn: Chief Pat Van Bibber; open mid-May - mid-Sept.

Whitehorse: LePage Park, c/o Yukon Historical & Museums Association, PO Box 4357, Whitehorse YT Y1A 3T5 – 867/667-4704; Fax: 867/667-4506 – President, Brent Slobodin – Walking tours by interpreters in period costume, June - Aug.; open year round

Whitehorse: Old Log Church Museum, 3rd Ave. & Elliot St., PO Box 5956, Whitehorse YT Y1A 5L7 – 867/668-2555; Fax: 867/668-2555 – Curator, Clare McDowell – Open May - Labour Day

Whitehorse: Yukon Transportation Museum, PO Box 5867, Whitehorse YT Y1A 5L6 – 867/668-4792; Fax: 867/633-5547 – Curator, Shannon Prentice Poelman; Giftshop Manager, Jocelyn Laveck; President, Harry Lowry – Transporation displays depicting the first commercial aircraft in the Yukon; construction of the Alaska Highway, the White Pass & Yukon Route Railway; open daily, Victoria Day - mid-Sept.

# ARCHIVES

### National Archives of Canada/Archives nationales du Canada

395 Wellington St., Ottawa ON K1A 0N3

613/995-5138; Fax: 613/995-6274

URL: http://www.archives.ca

Private papers, public records, machine-readable archives, maps, paintings, photographs, films & sound recordings. Research services & facilities.

Assistant National Archivist & Acting National Archivist, D.L. McDonald – 613/992-0660

### Alberta

Athabasca: Alice B. Donahue Library & Archives, PO Box 2099, Athabasca AB T9S 2B6 – 403/675-2735; Fax: 403/675-5933 – Archivist, Marilyn Moll

Athabasca University - Thomas A. Edge Archives, One University Dr., PO Box 10,000, Athabasca AB T9S 1A1 – 403/675-6271; Fax: 403/675-6477; Email: eileen@admin.athabascau.ca – Eileen Hendy

Banff Centre Archives, PO Box 1020, Banff AB T0L 0C0 – 403/762-6440; Fax: 403/762-6236; Email: elizabeth_cameron@banffcentre.ab.ca; URL: http://www.banffcentre.ab.ca – Elizabeth Kundert-Cameron

Calgary: Canadian Architectural Archives, 2500 University Dr. NW, Calgary AB T2N 1N4 – 403/220-7420; Fax: 403/282-6837; Email: zimon@acs.ucalgary.ca; URL: http://www.ucalgary.ca/library/CAA/index.html – Curator, Kathy Zimon

Calgary: City of Calgary Archives, 313 - 7 Ave. SE, Calgary AB T2P 2M5 – 403/268-8180; Fax: 403/268-2362; Email: ccarch@gov.calgary.ab.ca

Calgary: Legal Archives Society of Alberta, 919 - 11 Ave. SW, 5th Fl., Calgary AB T2R 1P3 – 403/244-5510; Fax: 403/228-1728; Email: klumpenr@cadvision.com – Richard Klumpenhouwer

Calgary: University of Calgary Archives, 2500 University Dr. NW, Calgary AB T2N 1N4 – 403/220-7271; Fax: 403/282-6837; Email: jgafuik@ucdasvm1.admin.ucalgary.ca – University Archivist, Jo-Ann Munn Gafuik

Edmonton: Alberta Community Development, 901 Standard Life Centre, 10405 Jasper Ave., Edmonton AB T5J 4R7 – 403/427-6315; Fax: 403/422-9132 – Director, Clive Padfield

Edmonton: City of Edmonton Archives, 10440 - 108 Ave., Edmonton AB T5H 3Z9 – 403/496-8710; Fax: 403/496-8732; Email: bibsen@gov.edmonton.ab.ca – City Archivist, Bruce Ibsen

Edmonton: Lutheran Historical Institute, 7100 Ada Blvd., Edmonton AB T5B 4E4 – 403/474-8156; Fax: 403/477-9829 – Director, Norman J. Threinen; Archivist, Karen Baron – Open year round

Edmonton: Provincial Archives of Alberta/Archives provinciales d'Alberta (PAA), 12845 - 102 Ave., Edmonton AB T5N 0M6 – 403/427-1750; Fax: 403/427-4646; Email: paa@mcd.gov.ab.ca; URL: http://www.gov.ab.ca/~mcd/mhs/paa/paa.htm – Director & Provincial Archivist, Dr. Sandra Thomson

Edmonton: University of Alberta Archives, University of Alberta, Ring House #1, Edmonton AB T6G 2E2 – 403/492-0531; Fax: 403/492-6185; Email: archives@library.ualberta.ca; URL: http://www.ualberta.ca/ARCHIVES/ – Chief Archivist, Bryan Corbett, Email: bcorbett@library.ualberta.ca; Associate Archivist, Brian Hobbs, 403/466-6123; Archives Assistant, Kevan Warner, 403/466-6118

Lethbridge: City of Lethbridge Archives, 910 - 4 Ave. South, Lethbridge AB T1J 0P6 – 403/329-7302; Fax: 403/329-4958; Email: archives@city.lethbridge.ab.ca – City Archivist, Greg Ellis

St. Albert: Oblate Archives - Grandin Province/Archives Oblates - Province Grandin, 3 St. Vital Ave., St. Albert AB T8N 1K1 – 403/459-5072 – Archivist, Dr. Gaston J. Montmigny., O.M.I.

Wetaskiwin: City of Wetaskiwin Archives, 4904 - 51 St., Wetaskiwin AB T9A 1L2 – 403/352-3344; Fax: 403/352-0930 – Archivist, Carolyn Hill

### British Columbia

Castlegar: Selkirk College Archives & Local History Collection, PO Box 1200, Castlegar BC V1N 3J1 – 250/365-7292; Fax: 250/365-7259; Email: johnmans@selkirk.bc.ca – Chief Librarian, John Mansbridge – West Kootenay area & the Doukhobors

Kaslo: Kootenay Lake Archives, PO Box 537, Kaslo BC V0G 1M0 – 250/353-2563, 2525; Fax: 250/353-2563 – Volunteer Archivist, Elizabeth Scarlett – Operated by the Kootenay Lake Historical Society to preserve information on the history of Kaslo & its immediate area, in particular, the S.S. Moyie & other sternwheelers of Kootenay Lake

Mission Community Archives, 33215 - Second Ave., PO Box 3522, Mission BC V2V 4L1 – 604/820-2621; Fax: 604/820-2621; Email: mca@city.mission.bc.ca – Archivist & Records Manager, Valerie Billesberger

Nanaimo Community Archives, c/o Nanaimo District Museum, 100 Cameron Rd., 3rd Fl., Nanaimo BC V9R 2X1 – 250/753-4462; Fax: 250/753-1777; Email: nca@nanaimo.ark.com; URL: http://bbs.sd68.nanaimo.bc.ca/nol/community/nca.htm – Community Archivist, Diane Foster

Prince Rupert City & Regional Archives, PO Box 1093, Prince Rupert BC V8J 4H6 – 250/624-3326; Fax: 250/624-3706; Email: archives@citytel.net – Archivist, Barbara Sheppard

Richmond: City of Richmond Archives, 7700 Minoru Gate, Richmond BC V6Y 1R9 – 604/231-6431; Email: archives@city.richmond.bc.ca; URL: http://www.city.richmond.bc.ca/archives/archives.html

Trail: Cristoforo Colombo Lodge Archives, 830 Bell Place, Trail BC V1R 3K1 – 250/368-3280 – Curator, Anne Gagliani – Italians in Trail

Vancouver: Anglican Diocese of New Westminster Archives, 6000 Iona Dr., Vancouver BC V6T 1L4 – 604/822-9583; Fax: 604/822-9212; Email: anglican_archives@skybus.com – Archivist, Doreen Stephens

Vancouver: Archives of the Roman Catholic Archdiocese of Vancouver, 150 Robson St., Vancouver BC V6B 2A7 – 604/683-0281 – Archivist, Rev. J. Hanrahan, CSB

Vancouver: City of Vancouver Archives, 1150 Chestnut St., Vancouver BC V6J 3J9 – 604/736-8561; Fax: 604/736-0626; Email: archives@.city.vancouver.bc.ca; URL: http://www.city.vancouver.bc.ca/ctyclerk/archives/index.html-ssi – City Archivist, Sue Baptie, Email: sue_baptie@city.vancouver.bc.ca

Vancouver: Japanese Canadian National Museum & Archives Society (JCNMAS), 511 East Broadway, Vancouver BC V5T 1X4; URL: http://www.shinnova.com/part/86-jcma/jcma10-e.htm – Archivist, Shane Foster

Vancouver: United Church of Canada BC Conference Archives, 6000 Iona Dr., Vancouver BC V6T 1L4 – 604/822-9589; Fax: 604/822-9212; Email: bstewart@unixg.ubc.ca; URL: http://www.interchange.ubc.ca/bstewart/index.html – Archivist, Bob Stewart

Vancouver: University of British Columbia Archives, Old Main Library, 1956 Main Mall, Vancouver BC V6T 1Z1 – 604/822-2521; Fax: 604/822-9587; URL: http://www.library.ubc.ca/spcoll/general.html – Division Head, Brenda Peterson, Email: brendap@unixg.ubc.ca; University Archivist, Chris Hives, Email: chives@unixg.ubc.ca

Victoria: BC Archives & Records Service (BCARS), 655 Belleville St., Victoria BC V8V 1X4 – 250/387-5885; Fax: 250/387-2072; Email: access@bcars.gs.gov.bc.ca; URL: http://www.bcarchives.gov.bc.ca/index.htm – Provincial Archivist, John A. Bovey; Deputy Provincial Archivist, Gary A. Mitchell, CRM

Victoria: City of Victoria Archives & Records Division (CVARD), 1 Centennial Sq., Victoria BC V8W 1P6 – 250/361-0375; Fax: 250/361-0348; Email: careyp@ch.city.victoria.bc.ca; URL: http://www.city.victoria.bc.ca/archives/index.htm – Archives Manager, James Burrows

Victoria: Saanich Municipal Archives, 770 Vernon Ave., Victoria BC V8X 2W7 – 250/475-1775; Fax: 250/475-5400 – Archivist, Geoffrey Castle

Williams Lake: Cariboo Chilcotin Archives, Williams Lake Library, 110 Oliver St., Williams Lake BC V2G 1L8 – 250/392-3630; Fax: 250/392-3518 – Librarian, Lillian Mack

### Manitoba

Carberry Plains Archives, 115 Main St., PO Box 581, Carberry MB R0K 0H0 – 204/834-3043

Winnipeg: Archives des Soeurs de la Charité de Montréal, Soeurs Grises, Province Saint-Boniface, 151, rue Despins, Winnipeg MB R2H 0L7 – 204/237-8941; Fax: 204/237-3466

Winnipeg: Centre for Mennonite Brethren Studies (CMBS), #1, 169 Riverton Ave., Winnipeg MB R2L 2E5 – 204/669-6575; Fax: 204/654-1865; Email: CmbsArchives@Cdn.MBConf.ca; URL: http://www.cdnmbconf.ca/mb/cmbs.htm – Director, Abe Dueck; Archivist, Alfred Redekopp, Email: aredek@mbnet.mb.ca

Winnipeg: Jewish Historical Society of Western Canada Archives, #116, 123 Doncaster St., Winnipeg MB R3B 2K3 – 204/942-4822; Fax: 204/477-7460 – Executive Secretary, Esther Slater; President, Roz Usiskin; Archivist, Bonnie Tregobov

Winnipeg: Manitoba Gay/Lesbian Archive, #1, 222 Osborne St. South, PO Box 1661, Winnipeg MB R3C 2Z6 – 204/945-6660; Fax: 204/478-1160 – Chris Vogel

Winnipeg: Mennonite Heritage Centre Gallery & Archives, 600 Shaftesbury Blvd., Winnipeg MB R3P 0M4 – 204/888-6781; Fax: 204/831-5675; Email: lkippen@mbnet.mb.ca – Historian/Archivist, Lawrence Klippenstein; Assistant Archivist, Alf Redekopp – Western Canadian, Russian & Prussian Mennonite manuscripts, documents, photographs, etc.; open Mon. - Fri., 8:30 am - 5 pm

Winnipeg: Provincial Archives of Manitoba (PAM), 200 Vaughan St., Winnipeg MB R3C 1T5 – 204/945-3971; Fax: 204/948-2008; Email: pam@chc.gov.mb.ca; URL: http://www.gov.mb.ca/chc/archives/index.html – Provincial Archivist, Peter Bower, Email: pbower@chc.gov.mb.ca

## New Brunswick

Fredericton: Provincial Archives of New Brunswick/Archives provinciales du Nouveau-Brunswick (PANB), PO Box 6000, Fredericton NB E3B 5H1 – 506/453-2122; Fax: 506/453-3288; Email: mbeyea@gov.nb.ca; URL: http://www.gov.nb.ca/supply/archives – Director, Marion Beyea

## Newfoundland

St. John's: Maritime History Archive, Henrietta Harvey Bldg., Memorial Univeristy, St. John's NF A1C 5S7 – 709/737-8428; Fax: 709/737-4569; Email: mha@morgan.ucs.mun.ca; URL: http://www.mun.ca/mha/ – Archivist, Heather Wareham

St. John's: Memorial University of Newfoundland Folklore & Language Archive (MUNFLA), Hickman Bldg., Memorial University, St. John's NF A1B 3X8 – 709/737-8401; Fax: 709/737-2345; Email: munfla@kean.ucs.mun.ca – Director, Martin Lovelace; Archivist, Philip Hiscock – Collections of folklore/folklife, oral history & popular culture, primarily pertaining to Newfoundland & Labrador

St. John's: Provincial Archives of Newfoundland & Labrador, Colonial Bldg., Military Rd., St. John's NF A1C 2C9 – 709/729-3065; Fax: 709/729-0578 – Acting Provincial Archivist, Paul Kenney

## Nova Scotia

Halifax: Public Archives of Nova Scotia, 6016 University Ave., Halifax NS B3H 1W4 – 902/424-6060; Fax: 902/424-0628 – Provincial Archivist, W. Brian Speirs – Open year round

Sydney: Beaton Institute Archives, PO Box 5300, Sydney NS B1P 6L2 – 902/563-1329; Fax: 902/562-8899; Email: cmacleod@caper2.uccb.ns.ca; URL: http://eagle.uccb.ns.ca/beaton/beaton.html – Archivist, Dr. R. Morgan

## Ontario

Fonthill: Pelham Historical Resource Centre, PO Box 903, Fonthill ON L0S 1E0 – Collection Coordinator, Mary Lamb

Hamilton: Canadian Baptist Archives (CBA), c/o McMaster Divinity College, McMaster University, Hamilton ON L8S 4K1 – 905/525-9140, ext.23511; Fax: 905/577-4782; Email: colwellj@mcmail.cls.mcmaster.ca – Archivist, Judith Colwell

Kingston: Anglican Diocese of Ontario Archives (ADOA), 90 Johnson St., Kingston ON K7L 1X7 – 613/544-4774; Fax: 613/547-3745; Email: archive@dioceseofontario.on.ca; URL: http://www.ontario.anglican.ca – Diocesan Archivist, Paul Banfield

Kingston: Queen's University Archives, Kathleen Ryan Hall, Queen's University, Kingston ON K7L 3N6 – 613/545-2378; Fax: 613/545-6403; Email: archives@post.queensu.ca; URL: http://stauffer.queensu.ca/webarch/ – University Archivist, Donald S. Richan

Maple: City of Vaughan Archives (CVA), 2141 Major Mackenzie Dr., Maple ON L6A 1T1 – 905/832-2281; Fax: 905/832-8535 – Corp. Archivist, Dan Zelenyj

Minesing: Simcoe County Archives (SCA), RR#2, Minesing ON L0L 1Y0 – 705/726-9300, ext.287; Fax: 705/725-5341 – County Archivist, Bruce Beacock – SCA manages the permanent corporate & municipal records of the County of Simcoe & of the municipalities which comprise the County; also collects information on all media which documents the history of the County of Simcoe

North York: The Ontario Jewish Archives (OJA), 4600 Bathurst St., North York ON M2R 3V2 – 416/635-2883, ext.170; Fax: 416/635-1408 – Director, Dr. Stephen Speisman

North York: York University Archives, Scott Library, #305, 4700 Keele St., North York ON M3J 1P3 – 416/736-5442; Fax: 416/650-8039; Email: archives@yorku.ca; URL: http://www.library.yorku.ca/depts/asc/archives.htm – University Archivist, Kent M. Haworth – Preserves & makes available the archival records of York University & private research collections in support of Canadian Studies programs

Orillia: Huronia Regional Centre Archives/Museum, Ontario Ministry of Community & Social Services, 700 Memorial Ave., PO Box 1000, Orillia ON L3V 6L2 – 705/326-7361, ext.2704; Fax: 705/326-3445 – Secretary, Margaret de Munnik; Chair, HRC Archives/Museum Committee, Hugh Duncan

Oshawa Community Archives, 1450 Simcoe St. South, Oshawa ON L1H 8S8 – 905/436-7624; Fax: 905/436-7625 – Archivist, Tammy Robinson

Ottawa: Archives de l'Université d'Ottawa/University of Ottawa Archives, 100 Marie-Curie, salle 012, Ottawa ON K1N 6N5 – 613/562-5750; Fax: 613/562-5198; Email: archives@uottawa.ca – Archiviste en chef de l'Université, Michel Prévost, Email: prevost@uottawa.ca

Ottawa: Archives de l'Université Saint-Paul, Edifice Deschâtelets, 175 Main St., Ottawa ON K1S 1C3 – 613/237-0580 – Pére Roland Leclaire – Saint-Paul University founded in 1965

Ottawa: City of Ottawa Archives/Archives municipales d'Ottawa, 174 Stanley Ave., Ottawa ON K1M 1P1 – 613/742-5014; Fax: 613/742-5113 – City Archivist, Louise Roy-Brochu; Assistant Archivist, David Bullock

Ottawa: Department of National Defence - Directorate of History & Heritage/Défense nationale - Directeur - Histoire et Patrimoine, Major-General George R. Pearkes Bldg., 101 Colonel By Dr., Ottawa ON K1A 0K2 – 613/998-7058; Fax: 613/990-8579 – Director, Dr. Serge Bernier

Peterborough: Trent University Archives, Peterborough ON K9J 7B8 – 705/748-1413; Fax: 705/748-1315; Email: bdodge@trentu.ca – University Archivist, Bernadine Dodge

Prescott: Grenville County Historical Society, PO Box 982, Prescott ON K0E 1T0 – 613/925-0489 – Treasurer, Bea Hemsley; President, Betty Ring; Secretary, Valerie Schultz – Resource Centre with a minimal user fee; open June-Aug. 10-4, Mon.-Fri.; Sept.-June, Tues. from 10-4 or by appt.

Scarborough Archives & Historical Collection, 730 Scarborough Golf Club Rd., Scarborough ON M1G 1H7 – 416/396-6930 – Archivist, Richard Schofield – Research material about Scarborough & education in Scarborough

Stratford Festival Archives, PO Box 520, Stratford ON N5A 6V2 – 519/271-4040, ext. 278; Fax: 519/271-1040; Email: archives@stratford-festival.on.ca – Archivist, Lisa Brant

Stratford-Perth Archives, 24 St. Andrew St., Stratford ON N5A 1A3 – 519/273-0399; Fax: 519/271-6265 – Archivist-Administrator, Lutzen Riedstra – Archives for the municipalities of Stratford & Perth County; municipal & school records; family & organizational records; photographs; maps, architectural drawings, posters, & documentary artwork; open 9-5 Mon.-Sat.

Toronto: Anglican Church of Canada General Synod Archives, 600 Jarvis St., Toronto ON M4Y 2J6 – 416/924-9192; Fax: 416/968-7983; Email: tthompson@national.anglican.ca – Archivist, Terry Thompson; Archivist, Records Management, Dorothy Kealey

Toronto: Anglican Diocese of Toronto Archives, Synod Office, 135 Adelaide St. East, Toronto ON M5C 1L8 – 416/363-6021; Fax: 416/363-7678; URL: http://www.toronto.anglican.ca – Archivist, Mary-Anne Nicholls

Toronto: Archives of the Institute of the Blessed Virgin Mary in North America (ANA-ibvm), 101 Mason Blvd., Toronto ON M5M 3E2 – 416/487-5543; Fax: 416/485-9884 – General Archivist, Juliana Dusel

Toronto: Archives of Ontario, #300, 77 Grenville St., Toronto ON M5S 1B3 – 416/327-1600; Fax: 416/327-1999; Email: sommerc@archives.gov.on.ca; URL: http://www.gov.on.ca/MCZCR/archives – Archivist of Ontario, Ian E. Wilson

Toronto: Archives of the Roman Catholic Archdiocese of Toronto (ARCAT), #505, 1155 Yonge St., Toronto ON M4T 1W2 – 416/934-3400, ext.501; Fax: 416/934-3444 – Archivist, Marc F. Lerman

Toronto: Archives Society of Jesus, Upper Canada (ASJUC), 15 St. Mary St., Toronto ON M4Y 2R5 – 416/922-5474; Fax: 416/922-2898 – Director, Rev. P. Boyle, S.J.

Toronto: Canadian Lesbian & Gay Archives, #201, 56 Temperance St., PO Box 639, Stn A, Toronto ON M5W 1G2 – 416/921-6310; Fax: 416/777-2755 – President, Ray Brillinger

Toronto: City of Toronto Archives, City Hall, 100 Queen St. West, Toronto ON M5H 2N2 – 416/392-7483; Fax: 416/392-1558 – City Archivist, David Whorley – Keeps historical records created by the municipal government dating backto Toronto's incorporation in 1834 & documents the City's physical, social, cultural & political history; reading room hours: Mon.-Fri., 8:30-4:30

Toronto: Dance Collection Danse, 145 George St., Toronto ON M5A 2M6 – 416/365-3233; Fax: 416/365-3169 – Co-Director, Lawrence Adams; Co-Director, Miriam Adams – Canadian dance history; database; publishing; education

Toronto: General Archives of the Basilian Fathers (GABF), 81 St. Mary St., Toronto ON M5S 1J4 – 416/926-7279; Fax: 416/920-3413 – Archivist, Rev. Kevin Kirley

Toronto: The Joan Baillie Archives of the Canadian Opera Company, 227 Front St. East, Toronto ON M5A 1E8 – 416/363-6671; Fax: 416/363-5584 – Archivist, Birthe Joergensen

Toronto: Law Society of Upper Canada Archives, Osgoode Hall, 130 Queen St. West, Toronto ON M5H 2N6 – 416/947-7600, ext.2220; Fax: 416/947-3991; Email: archref@lsuc.on.ca; URL: http://www.lsuc.on.ca/about/history/about_archives.html – Manager, Archives, Ann-Marie Langois – Records relating to the Ontario legal profession & the Law Society since its origins in 1797

Toronto: Metropolitan Toronto Archives & Records Centre, 255 Spadina Rd., Toronto ON M5R 2V3 – 416/397-5000; Fax: 416/392-9685; Email: archives@metrodesk.metrotor.on.ca; URL: http://www.metrotor.on.ca/services/departments/clerk.html#archives – Manager, Archives & Outreach, Michael Moir

Toronto: The National Ballet of Canada Archives, 470 Queens Quay West, Toronto ON M5V 3K4 – 416/

345-9686; Fax: 416/345-8323; Email: info@national.ballet.ca; URL: http://www.national.ballet.ca – Archivist, Sharon Vanderlinde

Toronto: The Presbyterian Church in Canada Archives, #104, 11 Soho St., Toronto ON M5T 1Z6 – 416/595-1277 – Archivist/Records Administrator, Kim Arnold

Toronto: Ryerson Polytechnic University Archives, 350 Victoria St., Toronto ON M5B 2K3 – 416/979-5000, ext.7027; Fax: 416/979-5215; Email: cdoucet@acs.ryerson.ca – Archivist, Claude Doucet

Toronto Harbour Commission Archives, 60 Harbour St., Toronto ON M5J 1B7 – 416/863-2008; Fax: 416/863-4830; Email: mdale@torontoport.com – Archivist, Michele Dale

Toronto: Trinity College Archives, 6 Hoskin Ave., Toronto ON M5S 1H8 – 416/978-2019; Fax: 416/978-2797; Email: pilon@epas.utoronto.ca – Archivist, Henri Pilon

Toronto: Trinity Square Video, 172 John St., 4th Fl., Toronto ON M5T 1X5 – 416/593-1332; Fax: 416/593-0958; Email: tsv@magic.ca; URL: http://www.modworld.com/tsv

Toronto: United Church of Canada/Victoria University Archives, 73 Queen's Park Cres. East, Toronto ON M5S 1K7 – 416/585-4563; Fax: 416/585-4584; Email: uccvu.archives@utoronto.ca; URL: http://www.vicu.utoronto.ca/archives/archives.htm – Chief Archivist, Jean Dryden

Toronto: University College Archives, University of Toronto, 15 King's College Circle, Toronto ON M5S 3H5 – 416/978-8154; Fax: 416/971-2059 – Archivist, Douglas Richardson – Publications, manuscripts, photographs, artifacts, works of art, etc. relating to the history, buildings & traditions of University College & its predecessor, King's College, Toronto

Toronto: University of Toronto Archives, Thomas Fisher Rare Book Library, 120 Saint George St., Toronto ON M5S 1A5 – 416/978-5344; Fax: 416/978-1667; Email: wells@library.utoronto.ca – University Archivist, Garron Wells

Waterloo: Evangelical Lutheran Church in Canada, Eastern Canada Synod Archives, 75 University Ave. West, Waterloo ON N2L 3C5 – 519/886-9770 – Archivist, Erich Schultz

Waterloo: Mennonite Archives of Ontario, Conrad Grebel College, Waterloo ON N2L 3G6 – 519/885-0220, ext.238; Email: steiner@library.uwaterloo.ca – Archivist, Samuel Steiner

Waterloo: Wilfrid Laurier University Archives, 75 University Ave. West, Waterloo ON N2L 3C5 – 519/884-1970, ext.3825; Fax: 519/884-8023; Email: jmmitche@mach1.wlu.ca – Archives Librarian, Joan Mitchell

### Prince Edward Island

Charlottetown: Public Archives & Records Office (PARO), PO Box 1000, Charlottetown PE C1A 7M4 – 902/368-4290; Fax: 902/368-5544; Email: htholman@gov.pe.ca; URL: http://www.gov.pe.ca/educ/archives/archives_index.asp – Provincial Archivist, H.T. Holman; Historic Records Archivist, Marilyn Bell

### Québec

Beauport: Archives de la Maison Généralice des Soeurs de la Charité de Québec, 2655, rue Le Pelletier, Beauport QC G1C 3X7 – 418/628-8860; Fax: 418/628-6052 – Archiviste, Gemma Gastonguay

Chicoutimi: Archives de la Société historique du Saguenay, CP 456, Chicoutimi QC G7H 5C8 – 418/549-2805; Fax: 418/545-8240 – Archiviste, Roland Bélanger

Gaspé: Centre d'archives de la Gaspésie, 80, boul Gaspé, Gaspé QC G0L 1R0 – 418/368-1534; Fax: 418/368-1535 – Archiviste, André Ruest

Montréal: Archives de la Province du Canada: Oblats de Marie-Immaculée, 3456, av du Musée, Montréal QC H3G 2C7 – 514/844-1924; Fax: 514/285-2248 – Archiviste, Normand Martel

Montréal: Archives de l'Archevêché de Montréal/Archives of the Archdiocese of Montréal, 2000, rue Sherbrooke ouest, Montréal QC H3H 1G4 – 514/931-7311; Fax: 514/931-3432; Email: chanc@cam.org – Archivist, Mgr Michel Parent

Montréal: Archives des Soeurs Grises de Montréal, 138, rue Saint-Pierre, Montréal QC H2Y 2L7 – 514/842-9411; Fax: 514/842-7855 – Gadtane Chevrier, s.g.m.

Montréal: Bell Canada Telephone Historical Collection/Le service de la documentation historique de Bell Canada, #820, 1050, Côte du Beaver Hall, Montréal QC H2Z 1S4 – 514/870-5214; Fax: 514/875-2537 – Director, Historical/IRC, Stephanie Sykes

Montréal: Canadian Jewish Congress National Archives, 1590, av Dr. Penfield, Montréal QC H3G 1C5 – 514/931-7531 – A/Director, Janice Rosen

Montréal: Canadian Pacific Archives/Archives Canadien Pacifique, PO Box 6042, Stn Centre-Ville, Montréal QC H3C 3E4 – 514/395-5135; Fax: 514/395-5132 – Archivist, Judith L. Nefsky

Montréal: Concordia University Archives/Service des archives de l'Université Concordia, 1455, boul de Maisonneuve ouest, Montréal QC H3G 1M8 – 514/848-7775; Fax: 514/848-2857; Email: archive@vax2.concordia.ca – Director, Nancy Marrelli

Montréal: Corporate Archives, Royal Bank of Canada, Mezzinine-2, 1, Place Ville-Marie, PO Box 6001, Montréal QC H3C 3A9 – 514/874-2104; Fax: 514/874-2445 – Corporate Archivist, Gordon Rabchuk

Montréal: Division des archives de l'Université de Montréal (DAUM), 2700, boul Édouard-Montpetit, CP 6128, Succ Centre-Ville, Montréal QC H3C 3J7 – 514/343-6023; Fax: 514/343-2239; Email: archives@ere.umontreal.ca – Directeur, Jean-Yves Rousseau

Montréal: McGill University Archives (MUA), 3459, rue McTavish, Montréal QC H3A 1Y1 – 514/398-3772; Fax: 514/398-8456; Email: gordie@archive.lan.mcgill.ca; URL: http://www.archives.mcgill.ca – University Archivist, Gordon Burr

Montréal: Service des archives et de gestion des documents, Université du Québec à Montréal, 1430, rue Saint-Denis, CP 8888, Succ Centre-Ville, Montréal QC H3C 3P8 – 514/987-6130; Fax: 514/987-8487 – Directrice, Christiane Huot

Montréal: Ville de Montréal - Gestion de documents et des archives, #113, 275, rue Notre-Dame est, Montréal QC H2Y 1C6 – 514/872-2678; Fax: 514/872-3475 – Chef de division, Diane Charland

Québec: Archives de la Ville de Québec (AVQ), 350, rue Saint-Joseph est, 4e étage, Québec QC G1K 3B2 – 418/691-6371; Fax: 418/691-7894; URL: http://www.webquebec.com/villeqc/villeqc/vilarch.html – Archiviste, Ginette Noël

Ste-Foy: Archives nationales du Québec, 1210, av du Séminaire, CP 10450, Ste-Foy QC G1V 4N1 – 418/643-4376; Fax: 418/646-0868; Email: ANQ@mcc.gouv.qc.ca; URL: http://www.anq.gouv.qc.ca – Directeur général, Robert Garon

- Centre d'archives de Montréal, 1945, rue Mullins, QC H3K 1N9 – 514/873-3065; Fax: 514/873-2980; Email: ANQ_Montreal@mcc.gouv.qc.ca – Directrice, Lucille Vachon
- Centre d'archives de Québec, Pavillon Louis-Jacques-Casault, 1210, av du Séminaire, PO Box 10450, QC G1V 4N1 – 418/643-8904; Fax: 418/646-0868; Email: ANQ.Quebec@mcc.gouv.qc.ca – Directeur, Jean-Pierre Therrien
- Centre d'archives de l'Abitibi-Témiscamingue et du Nord-du-Québec, 27, rue du Terminus ouest, QC J9X 2P3 – 819/762-4484; Fax: 819/764-6480; Email: ANQ_Rouyn@mccq.gouv.qc.ca – Archiviste régionale, Louise-Hélène Audet
- Centre d'archives de l'Estrie, 740, rue Galt ouest, Bur. 11, rez-de-chaussée, QC J1H 1Z3 – 819/820-3010; Fax: 819/820-3930; ANQ_Sherbrooke@mccq.gouv.qc.ca – Archiviste régional, Gilles Durand
- Centre d'archives de l'Outaouais, 170, rue de l'Hôtel-de-Ville, QC J8X 4C2 – 819/772-3010; Fax: 819/772-3950; Email: ANQ_Hull@mccq.qc.ca – Archiviste régionale, Hélène Cadieux
- Centre d'archives de la Côte-Nord, #190-2, 700, boul Laure, QC G4R 1Y1 – 418/964-8434; Fax: 418/964-8500; Email: ANQ_Sept-Iles@mccq.gouv.qc.ca
- Centre d'archives de la Mauricie - Bois-Francs, 225, rue des Forges, QC G9A 2G7 – 819/371-6015; Fax: 819/371-6158; Email: ANQ_Trois-Rivieres@mccq.gouv.qc.ca – Archiviste régional, Yvon Martin
- Centre d'archives du Bas-Saint-Laurent et de la Gaspésie - Îles-de-la-Madeleine, 337, rue Moreault, QC G5L 1P4 – 418/727-3500; Fax: 418/727-3739; Email: ANQ.Rimouski@mcc.gouv.qc.ca – Archiviste régional, Donald O'Farrell
- Centre d'archives du Saguenay - Lac-Saint-Jean, 930, rue Jacques-Cartier est, local C-103, QC G7H 2A9 – 418/698-3516; Fax: 418/698-3758; Email: ANQ.Chicoutimi@mccq.gouv.qc.ca – Archiviste régional, Jacques Thibeault

### Saskatchewan

Regina: University of Regina Archives, University of Regina Library, Room 627, Regina SK S4S 0A2 – 306/585-5314; Fax: 306/586-9862; Email: archives@max.cc.uregina.ca – Fay Hutchinson

Saskatoon: City of Saskatoon Archives, 88 - 24th St. East, Saskatoon SK S7K 0K4 – 306/975-7811; Fax: 306/975-2612; Email: aa393@sfn.saskatoon.sk.ca – Erik Anderson

Saskatchewan Archives Board, University of Saskatchewan, Murray Bldg., 3 Campus Dr., Saskatoon SK S7N 5A4 – 306/933-5832; Fax: 306/933-7305; Email: sabsktn@sk.sympatico.ca; URL: http://www.gov.sk.ca/govt/archives/ – Provincial Archivist, Trevor Powell; Chief Archivist, Nadine Small

Saskatoon: University of Saskatchewan Archives, Murray Bldg., Room 301, 3 Campus Dr., Saskatoon SK S7N 5A4 – 306/966-6028; Fax: 306/966-6040; Email: avery@sklib.usask.ca – Cheryl Avery

### Yukon

Whitehorse: Yukon Archives, PO Box 2703, Whitehorse YT Y1A 2C6 – 867/667-5321; Fax: 867/393-6253; Email: yarchive@gov.yk.ca – Director of Libraries & Archives, Linda Johnson; Assistant Territorial Archivist, Diane Chisholm; Archives Librarian, Peggy D'Orsay; Accession Archivist, Clara Rutherford; Government Records Archivist, Blair Taylor; Reference Coordinator, Heather Jones

## ART GALLERIES

### National Gallery of Canada/Musée des beaux-arts du Canada (NGC/MBAC)

380 Sussex Dr., PO Box 427, Stn A, Ottawa ON K1N 9N4

613/990-1985; Fax: 613/993-4385; Email: info@gallery.ca

URL: http://national.gallery.ca

The permanent collection of the National Gallery comprises paintings, sculpture, prints & drawings, photographs, film & video art from the Canadian, European, American & Asian schools. Special exhibitions as well as permanent installations of the gallery's collections are on display. The gallery also sends its exhibitions on tour across the country & participates in international exhibitions. Services provided to the public include lectures, talks, tours, films, workshops, concerts & a bookstore.

Director, Dr. Shirley Thomson
Deputy Director, Yves Dagenais
Chief Librarian, Murray Waddington
Assistant Director, Exhibitions & Installations, Daniel Amadei
Head, Restoration & Conservation Laboratory, Marian Barclay
Registrar, Delphine Bishop
Curator, Prints & Drawings, Mimi Cazort
Chief, Education, Mary Ellen Herbert
Curator, Canadian Art, Charles Hill
Curator, European Art, Catherine Johnston
Assistant Director, Communications & Marketing, Helen Murphy
Curator, Contemporary Art, Diana Nemiroff
Assistant Director, CCVA, G.V. Shepherd
Chief, Publications, Serge Thériault
Acting Curator, Photographs, Anne Thomas

## ALBERTA

### The Edmonton Art Gallery (EAG)

2 Sir Winston Churchill Sq., Edmonton AB T5J 2C1
403/422-6223; Fax: 403/426-3105

Collections include: Canadian & international contemporary & historical paintings, sculpture, photography & graphic art. Research fields: western Canadian art, historical & contemporary art; painting; sculpture; photography; graphics. Activities: Guided tours; lectures; films; gallery talks; art rental & sales gallery; studio art classes for children & adults; docent program workshops & seminars; tour exhibitions across Canada. Facilities: 10 exhibition areas; 158-seat auditorium; classrooms; members' lounge. Art books; handicrafts; ceramics, prints & reproductions for sale in gallery shop.

Director, Vincent J. Varga
Communications Manager, John Tuckwell

### Other Art Galleries in Alberta

Banff: Walter Phillips Gallery (WPG), PO Box 1020, Banff AB T0L 0C0 – 403/762-6281; Fax: 403/762-6659; URL: http://www-nmr.banffcentre.ab.ca/WPG – Director/Curator, Catherine Crowston – Contemporary, fine & decorative arts; open year round, closed Mondays

Brocket: Oldman River Cultural Centre, PO Box 70, Brocket AB T0K 0H0 – 403/965-3939 – Director, Jo-Ann Yellow Horn – Open year round

Calgary: Illingworth Kerr Gallery (IKG), Alberta College of Art & Design, 1407 - 14 Ave. NW, Calgary AB T2N 4R3 – 403/284-7632; Fax: 403/289-6682; Email: ron.moppett@acad.ab.ca – Asst. Curator, Richard Gordon; Director/Curator, Ron Moppett – Contemporary art exhibitions, publications, lectures, screenings & related events

Calgary: Mount Royal College Gallery, 4825 Richard Rd. SW, Calgary AB T3E 6K6 – 403/246-6344

Calgary: Muttart Public Art Gallery, 1221 - 2nd St. SW, Calgary AB T2R 0W5 – 403/266-2764; Fax: 403/264-8077; URL: http://www.culturenet.ca/muttart – Director/Curator, Kathryn Burns; President, Board of Directors, Thomas E. Lester

Edmonton: Front Gallery, 12306 Jasper Ave., Edmonton AB T5N 3K5 – 403/488-2952

Edmonton: Horizon Art Galleries, 10114 - 123 St., Edmonton AB T5N 1N2 – 403/482-2011

Edmonton: West End Gallery, 12308 Jasper Ave., Edmonton AB T5N 3K5 – 403/488-4892

Grande Prairie: Prairie Gallery, 10209 - 99 St., Grande Prairie AB T8V 2H3 – 403/532-8111; Fax: 403/539-1991 – Director/Curator, Elizabeth Ginn

Lethbridge: Southern Alberta Art Gallery (SAAG), 601 - 3 Ave. South, Lethbridge AB T1J 0H4 – 403/327-8770; Fax: 403/328-3913; Email: SAAG@upanet.uleth.ca; URL: http://upanet.uleth.ca/~saag – Director/Curator, Joan Stebbins

Lethbridge: University of Lethbridge Art Gallery, 4401 University Dr., Lethbridge AB T1K 3M4 – 403/329-2690; Fax: 403/329-2022 – Director, Jeffrey Spalding

## BRITISH COLUMBIA

### The Vancouver Art Gallery

750 Hornby St., Vancouver BC V6Z 2H7
604/662-4700; Fax: 604/682-1086; Admin. tel.: 604/682-4668
URL: http://www.vanartgallery.bc.ca
Director, Alf Bogusky
Public Relations, Donna Call

### Other Art Galleries in British Columbia

Burnaby Art Gallery, 6344 Deer Lake Ave., Burnaby BC V5G 2J3 – 604/291-9441; Fax: 604/291-6776; Email: can-bag-bb@immedia.can – Director/Curator, Karen Henry

Burnaby: The Simon Fraser Gallery, AQ 3004, Simon Fraser University, Burnaby BC V5A 1S6 – 604/291-4266; Fax: 604/291-3029 – Director, Dr. E.M. Gibson; Registrar of the Collection, Janet Menzies

Canyon: The Alfoldy Gallery, PO Box 57, Canyon BC V0B 1C0 – 250/428-7473 – Elaine & Andy Alfoldy – Open Wed., Fri. - Sun.; July, Aug. & Sept. open daily 11 am - 5:30 pm

Castlegar: Kootenay Gallery of Art, History & Science, RR#1, Site 2, Comp. 10, Castlegar BC V1N 3H7 – 250/365-3337; Fax: 250/365-3822; Email: kgal@netidea.com – Co-Director, Gail Oglow; Co-Director, Myrna Cobb – Exhibits on art, history & science, from international to local sources; open year round

Dawson Creek Art Gallery, #101, 816 Alaska Ave., Dawson Creek BC V1G 4T6 – 250/782-2601; Fax: 250/782-3352 – Manager, Loris Martin – Open year round

Grand Forks Art Gallery, PO Box 2140, Grand Forks BC V0H 1H0 – 250/442-2211; Fax: 250/442-0099; Email: can-gfag@immedia.ca; URL: http://www.islandnet.com/~bcma/museums/gfag/gfag.html – Director, Richard Reid – Historical & contemporary works by established & emerging regional, national & international artists

Hazelton: Northwestern National Exhibition Centre, PO Box 333, Hazelton BC V0J 1Y0 – 250/842-5723 – Director, Eve Hope – 'Ksan permanent collection of artifacts; art, history displays; open year round

Kamloops Art Gallery Society, 207 Seymour St., Kamloops BC V2C 2E7 – 250/828-3543; Fax: 250/828-0662; Email: can-kag-kl@immedia.ca – Director/Curator, Jann L.M. Bailey

Kaslo: The Artery Gallery of Photography, PO Box 1102, Kaslo BC V0G 1M0 – 250/353-2575

Kaslo: Langham Cultural Centre Galleries, PO Box 1000, Kaslo BC V0G 1M0 – 250/353-2661

Kelowna Art Gallery, 1315 Water St., Kelowna BC V1Y 9P4 – 250/762-2226 – Director, Carolyn Vesely – Historical & contemporary fine art; gift shop; open year round

Maple Ridge Art Gallery Society, 11995 Haney Pl., Maple Ridge BC V2X 6G2 – 604/467-5855 – President, Jo Moncur

Nakusp: Bonnington Arts Centre, 6th Ave. West & 4th St. North, Nakusp BC V0G 1R0 – 250/265-4234; Fax: 250/265-3808 – Open Sept. -Jun.

Nanaimo Art Gallery & Exhibition Centre, c/o Malaspina College, 900 - 5 St., Nanaimo BC V9R 5S5 – 250/755-8790; Fax: 250/755-8725 – Director, Jane Cole

New Westminster: Amelia Douglas Gallery, PO Box 2503, New Westminster BC V3L 5B2 – 604/527-5528 – Representative, Ulrike Ebeling

North Vancouver: Bernadette's Galleries, 1321 Pemberton Ave., North Vancouver BC V7P 2R6 – 604/980-7216; Fax: 604/983-9978; Email: bernadette@xl.ca – Bernadette Johnson – Open year round

North Vancouver: Presentation House Gallery, 333 Chesterfield Ave., North Vancouver BC V7M 3G9 – 604/986-1351; Fax: 604/986-5380 – Director/Curator, Karen Love

Oliver: Vaseaux Lake Galleries, Hwy. 97 North, RR#2, Oliver BC V0H 1T0 – 250/498-3522; Fax: 250/498-3546

Osoyoos Art Gallery, 89 St. & Main, Osoyoos BC V0H 1V0 – 250/495-2800

Penticton: Art Gallery of the South Okanagan (AGSO), 11 Ellis St., Penticton BC V2A 1H3 – 250/493-2928; Fax: 250/493-3992; Email: agso@vip.net – Director, Geraldine Parent

Port Alberni: Rollin Art Centre, 3061 - 8th Ave., Port Alberni BC V9Y 2K5 – 250/724-3412; Fax: 250/724-3472 – Administrator, Margi Kristensen; Director, Communications, Gina Sufrin

Port Moody: Mountain View Gallery, 2720 St. Johns St., Port Moody BC V3H 2B7 – 604/936-3472 – Chief Officer, Noreen De Jong

Prince George Art Gallery, 2820 - 15th Ave., Prince George BC V2M 1T1 – 250/563-6447; Fax: 250/563-3211; Email: pgag@vortex.netbistro.com – Director/Curator, Julia Whittaker – Open Tues. - Sun.

Qualicum Beach: The Old School House Gallery & Arts Centre (TOSH), 122 Fern Rd. West, PO Box 1791, Qualicum Beach BC V0R 2T0 – 250/752-6133; Fax: 250/752-2600 – President, Brad Wylie

Smithers Gallery Association & Public Art Gallery, Central Park Bldg., PO Box 122, Smithers BC V0J 2N0 – 250/847-3898, 2996 – President, Marjory Then – Open summer

Surrey Art Gallery, Surrey Arts Centre, 13750 - 88 Ave., Surrey BC V3W 3L1 – 250/501-5566; Fax: 250/501-5581; Email: artgallery@city.surrey.bc.ca; http://www.surreyartgallery.com – Curator, Exhibitions, Liane Davison; Curator, Visual Arts Programs, Ingrid Kolt – Promotes contemporary BC & Canadian artists; exhibitions & public programs encourage community appreciation of contemporary visual art; open year round

Vancouver: Charles H. Scott Gallery, Emily Carr College of Art & Design, 1399 Johnston St., Granville Island, Vancouver BC V6H 3R9 – 604/844-3809; Fax: 604/844-3801 – Curator, Greg Bellerby

Vancouver: Circle Craft Gallery, #1, 1666 Johnston St., Vancouver BC V6H 3S2 – 604/669-8021; Fax: 604/669-8585 – Contact, Helen Wennerstrom

Vancouver: Contemporary Art Gallery, 555 Hamilton St., Vancouver BC V6B 2R1 – 604/681-2700; Fax: 604/681-2710 – Director/Curator, Keith Wallace

Vancouver: Exposure Gallery (VAPA), 851 Beatty St., Vancouver BC V6B 2M6 – 604/688-6853; Fax: 604/688-6853; Email: exposuregallery@bc.sympatico.ca – Director/Curator, Ian McGuffie

Vancouver: Gallery Gachet, 88 East Cordova St., Vancouver BC V6A 1K2 – 604/687-2468; Fax: 604/687-1196; Email: gachet@cafe.net; URL: http://www.info-mine.com/gachet – General Manager, Mary Ann Anderson; Promotions Director, April Porter

Vancouver: Gallery of BC Ceramics, 1359 Cartwright St., Vancouver BC V6H 3R7 – 604/669-5645; Fax: 604/669-5627

Vancouver: grunt gallery, #116, 350 - 2nd Ave. East, Vancouver BC V5T 4R8 – 604/875-9516; Fax: 604/877-0073 – Director, Glenn Alteen

Vancouver: Heffel Gallery Limited, 2247 Granville St., Vancouver BC V6H 3G1 – 604/732-6505; Fax: 604/732-4245

Vancouver: Marion Scott Gallery, 481 Howe St., Vancouver BC V6C 2X6 – 604/685-1934; Fax: 604/685-1890 – Director, Judy Kardosh

Vancouver: Morris & Helen Belkin Art Gallery, University of British Columbia, 1825 Main Mall, Vancouver BC V6T 1Z2 – 604/822-2759; Fax: 604/822-6689; URL: http://web.arts.ubc.ca/belkin/gallery.htm – Publicity/Public Events, Naomi Saurada; Preparator, Owen Sopotiuk; Director/Curator, Scott Watson; Administrator, Mary Williams

Vancouver: Raymond Chow Art Gallery, 1618 West 75th Ave., Vancouver BC V6P 6G2 – 604/263-5439; Fax: 604/263-1568 – Freda Ling

Vancouver: Sidney & Gertrude Zack Gallery, 950 West 41st Ave., Vancouver BC V5Z 2N7 – 604/257-5111; Fax: 604/257-5121

Vancouver: Wickaninnish Gallery, #14, 1166 Johnston Rd., Vancouver BC V6H 3S2 – 604/681-1057

Vernon Public Art Gallery (VPAG), 3228 - 31st Ave., Vernon BC V1T 2H3 – 250/545-3173; Fax: 250/545-9096 – Director, Susan Brandoli – Community programming; local, regional, national & international exhibitions; gift shop; art & video rentals; group tours

Victoria: Art Gallery of Greater Victoria (AGGV), 1040 Moss St., Victoria BC V8V 4P1 – 250/384-4101; Fax: 250/361-3995; Email: wboyer@pine.com; URL: http://vvv.com/aggv/ – Director, Patricia E. Bovey; Head, Public Affairs, Wendy Boyer – Canadiana 1860 to present; permanent exhibition of work of Emily Carr

Victoria: Maltwood Art Museum & Gallery (MAMAG), PO Box 3025, Victoria BC V8W 3P2 – 250/721-8298; Fax: 250/721-8997; Email: msegger@uvic.ca; URL: http://www.maltwood.uvic.ca – Director, Martin Segger

Victoria: Open Space Arts Society, 510 Fort St., Victoria BC V8W 1E6 – 250/383-8833; Fax: 250/380-1999; Email: openarc@islandnet.com

Wells: Island Mountain Gallery, PO Box 65, Wells BC V0K 2R0 – 250/994-3466 – Executive Director, Dorothea Funk; Treasurer, Marilyn Rummel

West Vancouver: Ferry Building Gallery, 1414 Argyle Ave., West Vancouver BC V7T 1C2 – 604/925-7290; Fax: 604/925-5913

White Rock: Arnold Mikelson Mind & Matter Gallery, 13743 -16 Ave., White Rock BC V4A 1P7 – 604/536-6460; Fax: 604/536-7117 – Owner/Director, Mary Mikelson – Wood sculptures of the late Arnold Mikelson

Williams Lake: Image Gallery, #3, 85 South 3rd Ave., Williams Lake BC V2G 1J1 – 250/392-6360; Fax: 250/392-6188

Williams Lake: Stationhouse Gallery, BC Rail Station, 1 North Mackenzie Ave., Williams Lake BC V2G 1N4 – 250/392-6113; Fax: 250/392-6184; URL: http://sos-connect.com/station/ – President, Bev Pemberton; Treasurer, Elizabeth Robertson; Secretary, Sheila Wyse; Gallery Coordinator, Susan Lacourciere – Monthly exhibitions; gift shop

## MANITOBA

### The Winnipeg Art Gallery (WAG)

300 Memorial Blvd., Winnipeg MB R3C 1V1

204/786-6641; Fax: 204/788-4998; 204/775-7297 (24hr.)

URL: http://www.wag.mb.ca

Founded in 1912 & opened in its present location in 1971. A permanent collection of almost 20,000 works of art with emphasis on Canadian & Manitoba artists. Also includes traditional & contemporary decorative arts, photography & European art. Highlights include the largest collection of contemporary Inuit art in the world, & the Gort Collection of Northern Gothic & late Renaissance paintings & altar panels. Facilities: 120,000 sq. ft. building with 9 major galleries; 25,000 sq. ft. rooftop sculpture garden; 325 seat Muriel Richardson Auditorium; 8,000 sq. ft. rooftop restaurant; 12,000 sq. ft. studio bldg.; gift shop, art rental & sales; lecture & seminar rooms; Clara Lander Library (24,000 volumes, 100 subscriptions, 10,000 artist biographies, 20,000 slides, misc. archives).

Chief Curator, Tom Smart

Director, Michel V. Cheff

Associate Director, Education & Public Programs, Claudette Lagimodière

Manager, Finance & Administration, Judy Murphy

Marketing & Communications Manager, Chris Brown

### Other Art Galleries in Manitoba

Leaf Rapids National Exhibition Centre, PO Box 220, Leaf Rapids MB R0B 1W0 – 204/473-8682; Fax: 204/473-2707 – Director, Denise Desjarlais – Open year round; offers new exhibitions every month; general interest courses; performances; special programs for children

Portage & District Arts Council (PDAC), 160 Saskatchewan Ave. West, Portage la Prairie MB R1N 0M1 – 204/239-6029; Fax: 204/239-1472; Email: pdac@portage.net – Executive Director, Eveline Mauws – Tues. - Sat., 11 am - 5 pm; new gallery exhibition each month; gift shop

Winnipeg: Ace Art Inc., 2nd 290 McDermot Ave., Winnipeg MB R3B 2A2 – 204/944-9763; Fax: 204/944-9763; Email: aceart@escape.ca – Director, Sigrio Dahle; Director, Grant Guy

Winnipeg: Centre culturel franco-manitobain (CCFM), 340, boul Provencher, Winnipeg MB R2H 0G7 – 204/233-8972; Fax: 204/233-3324 – Directeur, Alain Boucher

Winnipeg: The Floating Gallery, #218, 100 Arthur St., Winnipeg MB R3B 1H3 – 204/942-8183; Fax: 204/942-1555; Email: floatgal@pangea.ca – Director/Curator, Charles Shilliday – An art gallery for photography.

Winnipeg: Gallery 1.1.1., 211 FitzGerald Bldg., School of Art, University of Manitoba, Winnipeg MB R3T 2N2 – 204/474-9322; Fax: 204/275-3148; URL: http://www.umanitoba.ca/schools/art/info/gallery.html – Gallery Director, Prof. Dale Amundson, Email: amundsn@bldgumsu.lan1.umanitoba.ca; Gallery Assistant, Donalda Johnson, Email: djohnso@bldgumsu.lan1.umanitoba.ca

Winnipeg: Site Gallery, #2, 55 Arthur St., Winnipeg MB R3B 1H1 – 204/942-1618; Fax: 204/943-7980 – President, Keith Oliver – T-D, 11 am - 4 pm by appt.

Winnipeg: Upstairs Gallery, 266 Edmonton St., Winnipeg MB R3C 1R9 – 204/943-2734; Fax: 204/949-0793 – Director, Faye Settler

## NEW BRUNSWICK

### Owens Art Gallery

c/o Mount Allison University, York St., Sackville NB E0A 3C0

506/364-2574; Fax: 506/364-2575; Email: gkelly@mta.ca

URL: http://www.mta.ca/owens/

Permanent collection of over 2500 works, dating from the 18th century; 30 exhibitions yearly.

Director, Gemey Kelly

### Other Art Galleries in New Brunswick

Florenceville: Andrew & Laura McCain Gallery, PO Box 270, Florenceville NB E0J 1K0 – 506/392-5249; Fax: 506/392-6143

Fredericton: Beaverbrook Art Gallery/La galerie d'art Beaverbrook, 703 Queen St., PO Box 605, Fredericton NB E3B 5A6 – 506/458-8545, 8546; Fax: 506/459-7450; Email: bag@nbnet.nb.ca – Director, Ian G. Lumsden

Fredericton: Gallery Connexion, PO Box 696, Fredericton NB E3B 5B4 – 506/454-1433; Fax: 506/454-1401; Email: connex@nbnet.nb.ca – Coordinator, Sarah Maloney

Fredericton: UNB Art Centre, Memorial Hall, University of New Brunswick, PO Box 4400, Fredericton NB E3B 5A3 – 506/453-4623; Fax: 506/453-4599; Email: mem@unb.ca – Director, Marie Maltais

Moncton: Atelier IMAGO, 140 Botsford St., Moncton NB E1C 4X5 – 506/388-1431

Moncton: Galerie d'art de L'Université de Moncton (GAUM), Édifice Clément-Cormier, Université de Moncton, Moncton NB E1A 3E9 – 506/858-4088; Fax: 506/858-4043; Email: charetl@umoncton.ca; URL: http://www.umoncton.ca/gaum/hp_luc8.html – Directeur-conservateur, Luc A. Charette

Moncton: Galerie Georges-Goguen SRC, 250 Archibald St., CP 950, Moncton NB E1C 5K3 – 506/853-6666 – Daniel Fournier – Primarily promotes the works of Atlantic artists

Moncton: Galerie Sans Nom Coop Ltée, #16, 140 Botsford St., Moncton NB E1C 4X4 – 506/854-5381; Fax: 506/857-2064 – Président, Paul Bossé

Sackville: Struts Gallery An Artist-Run Centre, 7 Lorne St., Sackville NB E0A 3C0 – 506/536-1211; Fax: 506/536-4565; Email: gelgstrand@mta.ca – Coordinator, Gregory Elgstrand – Presenting local, regional & national contemporary artist-initiated activities: expositions, performances, demonstrations, workshops, symposia, residencies

Saint John: City of Saint John Gallery, Aitken Bicentennial Exhibition Centre, 20 Hazen Ave., Saint John NB E2L 3G8 – 506/649-6040; Fax: 506/632-6118 – Bernard J. Cormier – First municipally funded art gallery in Atlantic Canada; features monthly exhibitions of local & regional art works

St. Andrews: Sunbury Shores Arts & Nature Centre, 139 Water St., PO Box 100, St. Andrews NB E0G 2X0 – 506/529-3386 – Director, Ray Peterson

St. Stephen: St. Croix Library Gallery, 1 Budd Ave., St. Stephen NB E3L 1E8 – 506/466-7529; Fax: 506/466-7574

## NEWFOUNDLAND

### Art Gallery of Newfoundland & Labrador

Arts and Cultural Centre, Memorial University of Newfoundland, PO Box 4200, St. John's NF A1C 5S7

709/737-8210; Fax: 709/737-2007; Email: agnl@morgan.ucs.mun.ca; Info Line: 709/737-8209

URL: http://www.mun.ca/agnl/

Regularly changing exhibitions of all media, chiefly contemporary Canadian, with some international, historic Canadian & Newfoundland folk art & traditional crafts; permanent collection of contemporary Canadian art in many media, with strong holdings of Newfoundland work; art slide library. Extensive public programming & special projects with emphasis on collaboration with professional artists & performers; education activities; travelling exhibitions organized & circulated nationally & through APAGA; open year round.

Director, Patricia Grattan – Email: pgrattan@morgan.ucs.mun.ca

#### Other Art Galleries in Newfoundland

Grand Falls-Windsor: Central Newfoundland Visual Arts Society, PO Box 898, Grand Falls-Windsor NF A2A 2P7 – President, Alice Dicks

St. John's: Eastern Edge Art Gallery, PO Box 2641, Stn C, St. John's NF A1C 6K1 – 709/739-1882; Fax: 709/579-1636 – Bonnie Leyton

## NOVA SCOTIA

#### Art Gallery of Nova Scotia (AGNS)

1741 Hollis St., PO Box 2262, Halifax NS B3J 3C8

902/424-7542; Fax: 902/424-7359; Email: riordb@gov.ns.ca

URL: http://www.agns.ednet.ns.ca

Housed in 1868 heritage building.

Director, Bernard Riordon

#### Other Art Galleries in Nova Scotia

Halifax: Anna Leonowens Gallery, Nova Scotia College of Art & Design, 5163 Duke St., Halifax NS B3J 3J6 – 902/494-8184; Fax: 902/425-3997; Email: jessica@nscad.ns.ca – Administrative Director, Jessica Kerrin

Halifax: Centre for Art Tapes, #104, 5663 Cornwallis St., Halifax NS B3K 1B6 – 902/429-7299 – Director, Catherine Phoenix

Halifax: Dalhousie Art Gallery (DAG), 6101 University Ave., Halifax NS B3H 3J5 – 902/424-2403; Fax: 902/494-2890 – Director, Mern O'Brien – Open year round

Halifax: Eye Level Gallery, 1672 Barrington St., Halifax NS B3J 2A2 – 902/425-6412; Fax: 902/425-6412; Email: ak593@ccn.cs.dal.ca – Gallery Coordinator, Moritz Gaede

Halifax: MSVU Art Gallery, Mount Saint Vincent University, Seton Academic Centre, Mount Saint Vincent University, Halifax NS B3M 2J6 – 902/457-6160; Fax: 902/457-2447; Email: art.gallery@msvu.ca – Director, Ingrid Jenkner; Secretary, Traci Scanlan – Open daily except Mondays; exhibition program emphasizes women as cultural subjects & producers, new Nova Scotia artists, & themes relevant to the university's academic programs

Halifax: Nova Scotia Centre for Craft & Design (NSCCD), J.W. Johnston Bldg., 1683 Barrington St., Halifax NS B3J 1Z9 – 902/424-4062; Fax: 902/424-0670; Email: hlfxjohn.coms.tylercd@gov.ns.ca; URL: http://WWW.EDnet.NS.Ca/educ/heritage/crafts/ – Head, C.D. Tyler – Includes the Mary E. Black Gallery, a craft showroom, an info centre, & 5 studios; open year round

Cape Breton Regional Centre for Craft & Design, 225 George St., PO Box 1686, NS B1P 6T7 – 902/539-7491; Fax: 539-4807 – Director, Patricia McClelland

Halifax: Saint Mary's University Art Gallery, Saint Mary's University, Halifax NS B3H 3C3 – 902/420-5445, ext.5444; Email: gordon.laurin@stmarys.ca – Director/Curator, Gordon Laurin – Contemporary visual arts by artists within & outside the region; lectures, publications & performing arts program; maintains a media production centre; permanent collection of over 1,150 works

Lunenburg Art Gallery (L.A.G.8), 19 Pelham St., PO Box 1418, Lunenburg NS B0J 2C0 – 902/634-3305; Fax: 902/634-9544; Email: aloha@tallships.istar.ca – President, Josephine Eisenhauer – Meldrum collection by the late Earl Bailly; open year round

Pictou: Hector Exhibit Centre, PO Box 1210, Pictou NS B0K 1H0 – 902/485-4563 – Society President, Doris MacMillan – Genealogical & historical archives for Pictou County

Sydney: University College of Cape Breton Art Gallery, PO Box 5300, Sydney NS B1P 6L2 – 902/539-5300, ext.311 – Director, Barry Gabriel

Wolfville: Acadia University Art Gallery, Wolfville NS B0P 1X0 – 902/585-1373; Fax: 902/558-1070; Email: fran.kruschen@acadiau.ca – Director, Franziska Kruschen – Open year round

## ONTARIO

#### Art Gallery of Hamilton (AGH)

123 King St. West, Hamilton ON L8P 4S8

905/527-6610; Fax: 905/577-6940; Email: agh@netaccess.on.ca

URL: http://www.culturenet.ca/agh

Collection of 7,500 art objects; holds one of Canada's most comprehensive collections of Canadian historical, modernist & contemporary art; British, American & European works

Director, Ted Pietrzak

#### Art Gallery of Ontario (AGO)

317 Dundas St. West, Toronto ON M5T 1G4

416/979-6648; Fax: 416/204-2713

URL: http://www.AGO.on.ca

One of the largest art museums in North America, with 50 new & renovated galleries. Collection of more than 16,000 works, from 15th-century European to contemporary, reflects 600 years of creativity; more than half of the collection comprises Canadian & Inuit art. The Gallery's Henry Moore Sculpture Centre contains the world's largest public collection of Moore's work. Other services include the Anne Tannenbaum Gallery School, the Edward P. Taylor Audio-Visual Centre, Reference Library & Archives, the Marvin Gelber Print & Drawing Study Centre, the Dr. Mariano Elia Hands-On Centre, the Gallery Shop, restaurant & café. A visit to The Grange, an historic home restored to the 1830s, is included with admission.

Director, Dr. Maxwell Anderson

#### Art Gallery of Windsor (AGW)

3100 Howard Ave., Windsor ON N8X 3Y8

519/969-4494; Fax: 519/969-3732

One of the larger, non-government run galleries in Ontario; focus is on Canadian art in an international context; permanent collection of 2,500 paintings & sculptures; resource centre & gift shop; closed Mondays.

Director, Nataley Nagy

Curator, Contemporary Art, Helga Pakasaar

Curator, Historical Art, Robert McKaskell

Curator, Education, Christine Goodchild

#### The McMichael Canadian Art Collection

10365 Islington Ave., Kleinburg ON L0J 1C0

905/893-1121; Fax: 905/893-2588; Email: info@mcmichael.com

URL: http://www.mcmichael.com

The collection features works of art created by First Nations & Inuit artists, the artists of the Group of Seven & their contemporaries, & other artists who have contributed to the development of Canadian art. Comprehensive education program at kindergarten, elementary & secondary school levels; guided group tours by appointment; extension program & temporary exhibition program. Also programs for adults & special interest groups.

Executive Director/CEO, Barbara A. Tyler

Chief Curator, Jean Blodgett

Chairman, Board of Trustees, G. Joan Goldfarb

Manager, Marketing, Neil Beaudry

Director, Marketing & Visitor Services, Vicki Lymburner

Group & Travel Industry Sales Coordinator, Phil Brace

Librarian/Archivist, Linda Morita

#### Other Art Galleries in Ontario

Barrie: MacLaren Art Centre, 147 Toronto St., Barrie ON L4N 1V3 – 705/721-9696; Email: maclaren@mcw.on.ca – Open year round

Bracebridge: Chapel Gallery, c/o Muskoka Arts & Crafts Inc., 15 King St., PO Box 376, Bracebridge ON P1L 1T7 – 705/645-5501; Fax: 705/645-0385 – Curator, Elene J. Freer – Open Tues. - Sat.

Bracebridge: Ziska Gallery - Muskoka, Ziska Rd., RR#1, Bracebridge ON P1L 1W8 – 705/645-2587 – Curator, Jack MacCallum – The beauty of nature in paintings & sculpture

Brampton: Art Gallery of Peel, 9 Wellington St. East, Brampton ON L6W 1Y1 – 905/454-5441; Email: somersd@region.peel.on.ca – Curator, David Somers

Brantford: Glenhyrst Art Gallery of Brant, 20 Ava Rd., Brantford ON N3T 5G9 – 519/756-5932; Fax: 519/756-5910 – Gallery Director, Stephen Robinson

Buckhorn: The Gallery On the Lake ... Buckhorn, Hwy. #36, PO Box 10, Buckhorn ON K0L 1J0 – 705/657-3296; Fax: 705/657-8766 – President & CEO, Edwin H. Matthews; Vice-President, Barbara J. Matthews – Largest privately owned gallery in Canada; open daily, 9 am - 5 pm, year round

Burlington Art Centre (BAC), 1333 Lakeshore Rd., Burlington ON L7S 1A9 – 905/632-7796; Fax: 905/632-0278; Email: info@BurlingtonArtCentre.on.ca; URL: http://www.BurlingtonArtCentre.on.ca – Executive Director, MFA Ian D. Ross; Director of Programs, MA George Wale; Director of Development, Barbara Smith; Curator of Collection, MFA Jonathan Smith

Caledon East: Yaneff International Art, 18949 Centreville CRK. Rd., Caledon East ON L0N 1E6 – 905/584-9569; Fax: 905/584-9569; Email: posters@yaneff.com; URL: http://www.yaneff.com – Director/Curator, Chris Yaneff

Cambridge: The Library & Gallery (Cambridge Galleries), 20 Grand Ave. North, Cambridge ON N1S 2K6 – 519/621-0460; Fax: 519/621-2080 – Gallery Director, Mary Misner – 20 exhibitions per year reflect a range of local to international developments in contemporary & historical visual arts; includes a collection of contemporary fibre art & studio courses for all ages.

Chatham: Thames Art Gallery (TAG), Chatham Cultural Centre, 75 William St. North, Chatham ON N7M 4L4 – 519/354-8338; Fax: 519/436-3237; Email: cccchin@cha.hookup.net – Curator, Carl L. Lavoy

Cobourg: Art Gallery of Northumberland, 55 King St. West, Cobourg ON K9A 2M2 – 416/372-0333; Fax: 416/372-1587 – Director/Curator, Heather Ardies

Cornwall Regional Art Gallery/Galerie régionale des arts de Cornwall (CRAG), 164 Pitt St., PO Box 1822, Cornwall ON K6H 6N6 – 613/938-7387; Fax: 613/937-3399 – Executive Director, Sylvie Lizotte

Curve Lake: Whetung Craft Centre & Art Gallery, Curve Lake ON K0L 1R0 – 705/657-3661; Fax: 705/657-3412 – Owner, Michael Whetung – Open year round

Durham Art Gallery, PO Box 1021, Durham ON N0G 1R0 – 519/369-3692 – Director, Bear Epp

Etobicoke: The Art Gallery, Neilson Park Creative Centre, 56 Neilson Dr., Etobicoke ON M9C 1V7 – 416/622-5294; Fax: 416/622-0892 – Administrator, Lorre Hand; President, Board of Directors, Kathleen Havshalter – Provides a community focus for creative visual arts; variety of exhibitions with strong emphasis on local & contemporary artists

Grimsby Public Art Gallery, 25 Adelaide St., Grimsby ON L3M 1X2 – 905/945-3246; Fax: 905/945-4442 – Director, Mary A. Rashleigh – Permament collection of 1,000 works; exhibitions & programmes

Guelph: Macdonald Stewart Art Centre (MSAC), 358 Gordon St., Guelph ON N1G 1Y1 – 519/837-0010; Fax: 519/767-2661 – Director, Judith Nasby, Email: Jnasby@uoguelph.ca; Curator, Nancy Campbell, Email: Ngcampbe@uoguelph.ca

Haileybury: Temiskaming Art Gallery, 545 Lakeshore Rd., PO Box 1090, Haileybury ON P0J 1K0 – 705/672-3707; Fax: 705/672-5966 – Director/Curator, Maureen Steward – Public gallery; open year round

Haliburton: Rails' End Gallery, PO Box 912, Haliburton ON K0M 1S0 – 705/457-2330; Fax: 705/457-2338 – Curator, Pamela Kinney; Book Keeper & Gallery Asst., Ginny Urquhart – Open April 1st to December 1st.

Kingston: Agnes Etherington Art Centre/Centre d'art Agnes Etherington (AEAC), Queen's University, Kingston ON K7L 3N6 – 613/545-2190; Fax: 613/545-6765; Email: agnes@post.queensu.ca; URL: http://www.queensu.ca/ageth/ – Director, David McTavish – Contemporary & historical art exhibitions; open year round

Kingston: Edward Day Gallery, 253 Ontario St., Kingston ON K7L 2Z4 – 613/547-0774; Fax: 613/547-2757; Email: eddaygal@fox.nstn.ca – Donald Day; Mary Sue Rankin

Edward Day Gallery, 33 Hazelton Ave., ON M5R 2E3 – 416/921-6540; Fax: 416/921-6624

Kingston: St. Lawrence College Art Gallery, Portsmouth Ave., Kingston ON K7L 5A6 – Director, D. Gordon

Kitchener: Homer Watson House & Gallery, 1754 Old Mill Rd., Kitchener ON N2P 1H7 – 519/748-4377; Fax: 519/748-6808 – Curator, Gretchen McCulloch – Open Jan. - Dec.

Kitchener-Waterloo Art Gallery (KWAG), 101 Queen St. North, Kitchener ON N2H 6P7 – 519/579-5860; Fax: 519/578-0740 – Director, Brad Blain – Open year round

Leamington: The Art Centre, c/o South Essex Arts Association, 72 Talbot St. North, Leamington ON N8H 1M4 – 519/326-2711; Fax: 519/322-4959 – President, Stuart Miller – Open year round

Lindsay: The Lindsay Gallery, 8 Victoria Ave. North, Lindsay ON K9V 4E5 – 705/324-1780 – Director, Rodney Malham

London: Gibson Gallery, 181 King St., London ON N6A 1C9 – 519/439-0451

London: McIntosh Gallery, University of Western Ontario, London ON N6A 3K7 – 519/661-3181; Fax: 519/661-3059; Email: mciamk@uwoadmin.uwo.ca – Director, Arlene Kennedy

Minden: Agnes Jamieson Gallery, PO Box 648, Minden ON K0M 2K0 – 705/286-3763 – Administrator, Alice Don

Mississauga: Art Gallery of Mississauga (AGM), 300 City Centre Dr., Mississauga ON L5B 3C1 – 905/896-5088; Fax: 905/615-4167 – Vice-President, David Callander; President, Ron Starr; Executive Director, Fred Troughton; Treasurer, Jack Wade

Mississauga: Blackwood Gallery, Erindale College, University of Toronto, 3359 Mississauga Rd. North, Mississauga ON L5L 1C6 – 905/828-3789; Fax: 905/828-5202; Email: nhazelgrove@credit.erin.utoronto.ca – Curator, Nancy Hazelgrove; Administrator, Dean Catherine Rubincam, Ph.D.

Mississauga: The Gallery, 1900 Dundas St. West, Mississauga ON L5K 1P9 – 905/823-7323

Mississauga: Harbour Gallery, 1697 Lakeshore Rd. West, Mississauga ON L5J 1J4 – 905/822-5495; Fax: 905/822-5578; URL: http://www.designerinfolink.com/resource/harbgly.html – Director, Jacqueline Bryant; Assistant Director, Indira Roy Choudhury

Mississauga: Springbank Visual Arts Centre, c/o Mississauga Visual Arts, 3057 Mississauga Rd. North, Mississauga ON L5L 1C8 – 905/828-9151 – President, Norm Reid

Niagara Falls Art Gallery, Kurelek Collection, 8058 Oakwood Dr., RR#2, Niagara Falls ON L2E 6S5 – 905/356-1514 – Director/Curator, Brian Smylski

Niagara on the Lake: Samuel E. Weir Collection & Library of Art, RR#1, Niagara on the Lake ON L0S 1J0 – 905/262-4510; Fax: 905/262-4477 – Curator, Shiava Alwis – Open Victoria Day - Thanksgiving

North Bay: White Water Gallery, 226 Main St. West, PO Box 1491, North Bay ON P1B 8K6 – 705/476-2444 – Director, Martin Karch-Ackerman; Director, Michele Karch-Ackerman

North Bay: W.K.P. Kennedy Gallery of the North Bay Arts Centre, 150 Main St. East, PO Box 911, North Bay ON P1B 8K1 – 705/474-1944; Fax: 705/474-8431 – Director/Curator, Dennis Geden

North York: Art Gallery of North York, Ford Centre for the Performing Arts, 5040 Yonge St., North York ON M2N 6R8 – 416/395-0067; Fax: 416/395-7598; Email: beyre@city.north-york.on.ca – Director, Glen E. Cumming – Six exhibitions a year of contemporary art being produced in Canada from painting & sculpture to photography & installation art; free admission; wheelchair accessible

North York: Art Gallery of York University (AGYU), Ross Bldg. N145, 4700 Keele St., North York ON M3J 1P3 – 416/736-5169; Fax: 416/736-5985; Email: AGYU@yorku.ca; URL: http://www.yorku.ca/admin/agyu – Director/Curator, Loretta Yarlow

North York: Glendon Gallery/Galerie Glendon, Glendon College, York University, 2275 Bayview Ave., North York ON M4N 3M6 – 416/487-6721; Fax: 416/487-6779; Email: gallery@glendon.yorku.ca – Gallery Coordinator, Tiffany Moore – University-affiliated public art gallery that focuses on contemporary Canadian art of merit with an added interest in francophone artistic expression; literature in French & English; guided tours & lectures

North York: Koffler Gallery, 4588 Bathurst St., North York ON M2R 1W6 – 416/636-2145; Fax: 416/636-1536 – Director, Jane Mahut

Oakville Galleries, Gairloch Gallery, 1306 Lakeshore Rd. East, Oakville ON L6L 1G2 – 905/844-4402 – Director, Steven Pozel

Centennial Gallery, 120 Navy St., ON L6J 2Z4

Ohsweken: Two Turtle Iroquois Fine Art Gallery, RR#1, Ohsweken ON N0A 1M0 – 519/751-2774; Email: twoturtl@wchat.on.ca; URL: http://wchat.on.ca/tom/2turtle.htm

Orton: Burdette Gallery Ltd., RR#2, Orton ON L0N 1N0 – 519/928-5547 – Open year round

Oshawa: The Robert McLaughlin Gallery, Civic Centre, Oshawa ON L1H 3Z3 – 905/576-3000; Fax: 905/576-9774; Email: communications@rmg.on.ca; URL: http://www.rmg.on.ca – Director, Joan Murray

Ottawa: Artists' Centre d'Artistes Ottawa Inc., (Gallery 101), 319 Lisgar St., Ottawa ON K2P 0E1 – 613/230-2799 – Managing Director, Diane Shantz

Ottawa: The Canadian Wildlife & Wilderness Art Museum/Musée canadien d'art naturaliste (CWWAM), 150 MacLaren St., PO Box 98, Stn B, Ottawa ON K1P 6C3 – 613/237-1581; Fax: 613/237-1581; Email: cawa@intranet.ca; URL: http://intranet.ca/cawa/ – Director, Gary Slimon

Ottawa: Carleton University Art Gallery (CUAG), Carleton University, St. Patrick's Bldg., 1125 Colonel By Dr., Ottawa ON K1S 5B6 – 613/520-2120; Fax: 613/520-4409; Email: mbell@ccs.carleton.ca; URL: http://www.carleton.ca/gallery – Director, Michael Bell – 10,000 works in contemporary Canadian art, European prints & drawings from the 16th to 19th centuries, Inuit prints & sculpture

Ottawa: Galerie SAW Video, 67 Nicholas St., Ottawa ON K1N 7B9 – 613/236-6181; Fax: 613/564-4428; Video: 613/238-7648 – Garry Mainprize

Ottawa: Gallery 101 Centre d'Artistes, An Artist-Run Centre for Contemporary Visual Art, 319 Lisgar St., Ottawa ON K2P 0E1 – 613/230-2799; Fax: 613/230-3253; Email: oneoone@web.net – Artistic Director, Tim Dallett; Managing Director, Kevin Aaron Gibbs

Owen Sound: Tom Thomson Memorial Art Gallery, 840 - 1 Ave. West, Owen Sound ON N4K 4K4 – 519/376-1932; Fax: 519/376-3037; Email: ttm-chin@bmts.com; URL: http://www.tomthomson.org – Director, Brian Meehan

Peterborough: Art Gallery of Peterborough, 2 Crescent St., Peterborough ON K9J 2G1 – 705/743-9179; Fax: 705/743-8168 – Director, Illi-Maria Tamplin

Peterborough: Artspace Strike 3 Gallery, 129A Hunter St. West, PO Box 1748, Peterborough ON K9J 7X6 – 705/748-3883; Fax: 705/748-3224 – Artistic Director, Andrea Fatona

Peterborough: Hunter West Gallery, 131 Hunter St. West, Peterborough ON K9H 2K7 – 705/876-9623

Peterborough: The Russell Gallery of Fine Art, 138 Simcoe St., Peterborough ON K9H 2H5 – 705/743-0151; Fax: 705/743-8010 – Bruce Rapp; Sally Rapp

Sarnia: Gallery Lambton, 124 South Christina St., Sarnia ON N7T 2M6 – 519/337-3291 – Director, Howard Ford

Sault Ste. Marie: The Art Gallery of Algoma, 10 East St., Sault Ste. Marie ON P6A 3C3 – 705/949-9067; Fax: 705/949-6261 – Director, Michael Burtch

Simcoe: Lynnwood Arts Centre, 21 Lynnwood Ave., PO Box 67, Simcoe ON N3Y 4K8 – 519/428-0540; Fax: 519/428-0787 – Director, Susan J. Lowery

St Catharines: Rodman Hall Arts Centre, 109 St. Paul Cres., St Catharines ON L2S 1M3 – 905/684-2925; Fax: 905/682-4733 – Director, David Aurandt

St. Thomas: Art Gallery St. Thomas-Elgin, 301 Talbot St., St. Thomas ON N5P 1B5 – 519/631-4040; Fax: 519/631-4040 – Executive Director, Rick Nixon; Administrator, Diane Dobson

Stouffville: The Latcham Gallery, 6240 Main St., Stouffville ON L4A 1E2 – 905/640-2395 – Art Director, D. Vanessa Perry

Stratford: The Gallery/Stratford, 54 Romeo St., Stratford ON N5A 4S9 – 519/271-5271; Fax: 519/271-1642 – Director, Robert Freeman – A non-profit, public art gallery open year round with a schedule of exhibitions offering a wide range of Canadian art and educational programmes

Thunder Bay Art Gallery, 1080 Keewatin St., PO Box 1193, Stn F, Thunder Bay ON P7C 4X9 – 807/577-6427; Fax: 807/577-3781 – Director, Sharon Godwin; Curator, Janet Clark

Toronto: A Space, #110, 401 Richmond St. West, Toronto ON M5T 2R7 – 416/979-9633; Fax: 416/979-9683; Email: aspace@interlog.com; URL: http://www.interlog.com/~aspace/

Toronto: Academy of Spherical Arts, 38 Hanna Ave., Toronto ON M6K 1X5 – 416/532-2782; Fax: 416/532-3075

Toronto: Angell Gallery, 890 Queen St. West, Toronto ON M6J 1G3 – 416/530-0444; Email: angellgallery@gncom.com

Toronto: Annex Art Centre Gallery, 1073 Bathurst St., Toronto ON M5R 3G8 – 416/516-0110 – Curator, Deborah Harris – Open Mon.-Thurs

Toronto: Art at 80, #313, 80 Spadina Ave., Toronto ON M5V 2J3 – 416/366-3690; Fax: 416/348-9058

Toronto: Art Dialogue Gallery, 31 Dundonald St., Toronto ON M4Y 1L3 – 416/928-5904

Toronto: Art Metropole, 788 King St. West, Toronto ON M5V 1N6 – 416/703-4400; Fax: 416/703-4404; Email: ART_Metropole@intacc.web.net – Director, A.A. Bronson; President, Ann Webb; Manager, Bookstore, Ann Dean

Toronto: Artia Russian Fine Art, 620 Richmond St. West, Toronto ON M5V 1Y9 – 416/703-1255

Toronto: Bau-Xi Gallery, 340 Dundas St. West, Toronto ON M5T 1G5 – 416/977-0600

Toronto: Bay of Spirits Gallery, 156 Front St. West, 1st Fl., Toronto ON M5J 2L6 – 416/971-5190; Fax: 416/971-5938

Toronto: Christopher Cutts Gallery, #204, 21 Morrow Ave., Toronto ON M6R 2H9 – 416/532-5566; Fax: 416/532-7272

Toronto: Cold City Gallery, 686 Richmond St. West, Toronto ON M6J 1C3 – 416/504-6681; Fax: 416/504-9680

Toronto: Cygnet Gallery, 80 Scollard St., Toronto ON M5R 1G2

Toronto: DeLeon White Gallery, 455 King St. West, Toronto ON M5V 1K4 – 416/597-9466; Fax: 416/597-8466; Email: white@eco-art.com; URL: http://www.eco-art.com/deleon/

Toronto: Drabinsky Gallery, 86 Scollard St., Toronto ON M5R 1G2 – 416/324-5766

Toronto: Gallery 44, Centre for Contemporary Photography, #120, 401 Richmond St. West, Toronto ON M5V 3A8 – 416/979-3941; Fax: 416/340-8458; Email: G44@interlog.com; URL: http://www.interlog.com/~g44/ – Open Tues.-Sat., 11-5

Toronto: Gallery 7, 33 Hazelton Ave., Toronto ON M5R 2E3 – 416/968-6247; Fax: 416/968-7231

Toronto: Gallery Arcturus, 80 Gerrard St. East, Toronto ON M5B 1G6 – 416/977-1077; Fax: 416/977-1066; URL: http://www.arcturus.ca

Toronto: Gallery Gabor Ltd., 587 Markham St., Toronto ON M6G 2L7 – 416/534-1839 – Director/Curator, Gabor P. Mezei

Toronto: Gallery Louise Smith, 33 Prince Arthur Ave., Toronto ON M5R 1B2 – 416/924-1096; Fax: 416/924-3918

Toronto: Gallery Moos Ltd., 622 Richmond St. West, Toronto ON M5V 1Y9 – 416/504-5445; Fax: 416/504-5446

Toronto: Gallery One, 121 Scollard St., Toronto ON M5R 1G4 – 416/929-3103

Toronto: Gallery Phillip, 939 Lawrence Ave. East, Toronto ON M3C 1P8 – 416/447-1301

Toronto: Gallery Sheila Roth, 276 Avenue Rd., Toronto ON M4V 2G7 – 416/920-0112

Toronto: Gallery TPW, #310, 80 Spadina Ave., Toronto ON M5V 2J4 – 416/504-4242; Fax: 416/504-6510; Email: gllerytpw@interlog.com – Director, Gary Hall; Program Coordinator, Kim Fullerton

Toronto: Garnet Press, 580 Richmond St. West, Toronto ON M5V 1Y9 – 416/504-5012

Toronto: Group of Ten Artists Gallery, Queen's Quay Terminal, 207 Queen's Quay West, 2nd Level, Toronto ON M5J 1A7 – 416/203-6940; Fax: 416/444-4505; URL: http://www.artword.net/ten – President, D.D. Gadjanski; Secretary, Ita Pechenick; Treasurer, Pamela Portanier-Tong; Director, Margaret Roseman – Founded by a group of award-winning artists broadly; each artist is available at the gallery to talk to, demonstrate & explain their technique to interested viewers

Toronto: Illuminary Art Gallery, #606, 96 Spadina Ave., Toronto ON M5V 2J6 – 416/703-6500

Toronto: The Isaacs/Innuit Gallery, 9 Prince Arthur Ave., Toronto ON M5R 1B2 – 416/921-9985; Fax: 416/921-9530; Email: inuitgal@istar.ca – A. Isaacs; K. Williamson – Contemporary Inuit art, Inuit antiquities & early North American Indian art

Toronto: Jane Corkin Gallery, #302, 179 John St., Toronto ON M5T 1X4 – 416/979-1980

Toronto: John B. Aird Gallery, MacDonald Block, 900 Bay St., Main Fl., Toronto ON M7A 1Y5 – 416/928-6772

Toronto: Joseph D. Carrier Art Gallery, 901 Lawrence Ave. West, Toronto ON M6A 1C3 – 416/789-7011

Toronto: The Justina M. Barnicke Gallery, Hart House, University of Toronto, 7 Hart House Circle, Toronto ON M5S 3H3 – 416/978-8398; Fax: 416/978-8387; Email: judi.schwartz@utoronto.ca; URL: http://www.utoronto.ca/gallery/ – Director/Curator, Judith Schwartz

Toronto: Kaspar Gallery, 86 Scollard St., Toronto ON M5R 1G2 – 416/968-2536; Fax: 416/968-2537 – Co-Owner, Draha Kasper; Co-Owner, Emerich Kasper

Toronto: Knight Galleries International, 643 Yonge St., 2nd Fl., Toronto ON M4Y 1Z9 – 416/923-0836; Fax: 416/923-8985; Email: knight@knightgall.com; URL: http://www.knightgall.com

Toronto: La Parete Gallery, 1086 Bathurst St., Toronto ON M5R 3G9 – 416/533-8292; Fax: 416/533-4632

Toronto: Linda Genereux Gallery, 21 Morrow Ave., Toronto ON M6R 2H9 – 416/588-0430; Fax: 416/588-6843

Toronto: Marianne Friedland Gallery, 122 Scollard St., Toronto ON M5R 1G2 – 416/324-5766; Fax: 416/324-5770

Toronto: The Market Gallery, South St. Lawrence Market, 95 Front St. East, Toronto ON M5E 1C2 – 416/392-7604; Fax: 416/392-0572 – Curator, Pamela Wachna – A focus on the art & history of Toronto

Toronto: Maslak-McLeod Gallery, 25 Prince Arthur Ave., Toronto ON M5R 1B2 – 416/944-2577

Toronto: Mercer Union, A Centre for Contemporary Visual Art, 439 King St. West, Toronto ON M5V 1R5 – 416/977-1412; Fax: 416/977-8622; Email: mercer@interlog.com; URL: http://www.interlog.com/~mercer – Co-Director, Anette Larsson; Co-Director, Kelly McCray

Toronto: Mira Godard Gallery, 22 Hazelton Ave., Toronto ON M5R 2E2 – 416/964-8197

Toronto: The Mitchell Gallery, 112 Scollard St., Toronto ON M5R 1G2 – 416/515-7246; Fax: 416/515-7568

Toronto: Odon Wagner Gallery, 196 Davenport Rd., Toronto ON M5R 1J2 – 416/962-0438; Fax: 416/962-1581; Email: odon@owgalery.com; URL: http://www.owgalery.com

Toronto: Olga Korper Gallery, 17 Morrow Ave., Toronto ON M6R 2H9 – 416/538-8220; Fax: 416/538-8772 – Olga Korper – Established in 1973, the gallery is committed to the exhibition & promotion of Canadian & International contemporary art

Toronto: Open Studio, 468 King St. West, 3rd Fl., Toronto ON M5V 1L8 – 416/504-8238

Toronto: Painted City, 236 Queen St. East, Toronto ON M5A 1S3 – 416/364-0269; Fax: 416/364-1446

Toronto: The Power Plant, 231 Queen's Quay West, Toronto ON M5J 2G8 – 416/973-4949; Fax: 416/973-4933; Email: powerplant@harbourfront.on.ca; URL: http://www.culturenet.ca/powerplant – Director, Steven Pozel

Toronto: Prime Gallery, 52 McCaul St., Toronto ON M5T 1V9 – 416/593-5750

Toronto: Propeller Gallery, Darling Bldg., #303, 96 Spadina Ave., Toronto ON M5V 2J6 – 416/504-7142; Fax: 416/763-2627

Toronto: Reactor Gallery, 51 Camden St., Toronto ON M5V 1V2 – 416/703-1913; Fax: 416/362-6356; Email: inquiry@reactor.ca; URL: http://www.reactor.ca

Toronto: The Red Head Gallery, Darling Bldg., 96 Spadina Ave., 8th Fl., Toronto ON M5V 2J6 – 416/504-5654

Toronto: Sable-Castelli Gallery, 33 Hazelton Ave., Toronto ON M5R 2E3 – 416/961-0011; Fax: 416/961-9908 – Jared Sable – Canadian contemporary art

Toronto: S.L. Simpson Gallery, 515 Queen St. West, Toronto ON M5V 2B4 – 416/504-3738; Fax: 416/504-7979

Toronto: Stephen Bulger Gallery, 700 Queen St. West, Toronto ON M6J 1E7 – 416/504-0575; Fax: 416/504-8929; Email: sbulger@interlog.com – Exhibition & sale of Canadian & international photography, with an emphasis on social documentation; bookstore, museum framing services, & archival supplies

Toronto: Susan Hobbs Gallery, 137 Tecumseth St., Toronto ON M6J 2H2 – 416/504-3699; Fax: 416/504-8064 – Susan Hobbs

Toronto: Teodora Art Gallery, 45 Avenue Rd., Toronto ON M5R 2G3 – 416/515-0450; Fax: 416/656-1063; Email: 102341,1772@compuserve.com; URL: http://www.starcitysearch.teodoragallery.com – Teodora Pica – Features approximately 10 solo exhibitions & two group shows per year; committed to contemporary Canadian art

Toronto: Thebes Gallery, 613 King St. West, Toronto ON M5V 1M5 – 416/504-3956

Toronto Centre for Contemporary Art, 155A Roncesvalles Ave., Toronto ON M6R 2L3 – 416/536-6220 – Director, Kazimir Glaz

Toronto Dominion Gallery of Inuit Art, Aetna Tower, Ground Level, T-D Centre, PO Box 1, Stn Toronto Dom, Toronto ON M5K 1A2 – 416/982-8473

Toronto: University of Toronto Art Centre, University of Toronto, 15 King's College Circle, Toronto ON M5S 3H7 – 416/978-1838; Fax: 416/971-2059 – Director, Prof. Ken Bartlett, 585-4590; Malcove Curator, Dr. Sheila Campbell, 978-6596; Curator, University College Art Collection, Douglas Richardson, 978-8154; Univerity of Toronto Art Curator, Liz Wylie, 946-3029 – Housing galleries with exhibitions from 3 art collections: the Malcove Collection, the University College Art Collection & the University of Toronto Art Collection

Toronto: Wynick/Tuck Gallery, 80 Spadina Ave., 4th Fl., Toronto ON M5V 2J3 – 416/504-8716

Toronto: Ydessa Hendeles Art Foundation (YHAF), PO Box 757, Stn F, Toronto ON M4Y 2N6 – 416/413-9400; Fax: 416/969-9889; Email: ydessa@yhaf.org – Ydessa Hendeles – Located at 778 King St. West

Toronto: YYZ Artists' Outlet, 401 Richmond St. West, Toronto ON M5V 3A8 – 416/410-8851; Fax: 416/410-8851; Email: yyz@interlog.com; URL: http://www.interlog.com/~yyz/ – Co-Director, Melinda Sato

Waterloo: Aaron Galleries Inc., 25 Young St. East, Waterloo ON N2J 2L4 – ; Email: aelpo@sentex.net; URL: http://www.sentex.net/~aelpo/aarongal.html – Director, Mario Stocco

Waterloo: Arts Centre Gallery, University of Waterloo, Waterloo ON N2L 3G1 – 519/885-1211, ext.2442 – Curator, Earl W. Stieler

Waterloo: Canadian Clay & Glass Gallery/Galerie Canadienne de la Céramique et du Verre, 25 Caroline St. North, Waterloo ON N2L 2Y5 – 519/746-1882; Fax: 519/746-6396 – Chair, Board of Directors, Lori Brien

Waterloo: Enook Galleries, 29 Young St. East, PO Box 335, Waterloo ON N2J 4A4 – 519/884-3221 – President, Norman Socha – Canadian Inuit & Indian art: prints, sculptures, original paintings, craft items

Waterloo: Robert Langen Gallery, Wilfrid Laurier University, Waterloo ON N2L 3C5 – 519/884-1970, ext.3801; Email: thranka@mach1.wlu.ca – Curator/Art Gallery Coordinator, Teri Hranka

Whitby Arts Incorporated "The Station Gallery", PO Box 124, Whitby ON L1N 5R7 – 905/668-4185 – Director/Curator, Linda Paulocik

Woodstock Art Gallery (WAG), 447 Hunter St., Woodstock ON N4S 4G7 – 519/539-6761; Fax: 519/539-2564 – Curator, Anna-Marie Larsen

## PRINCE EDWARD ISLAND

**Confederation Centre Art Gallery & Museum/Le Musée d'Art du Centre de la Confédération (CCAG&M)**
145 Richmond St., Charlottetown PE C1A 1J1
902/628-6111; Fax: 902/566-4648
Critical inquiry into 200 years of Canadian art; 28 annual exhibitions; 15,000 work collection.
Director, Terry Graff

## QUÉBEC

### Musée d'art contemporain de Montréal (MACM)

185, rue Ste-Catherine ouest, Montréal QC H2X 1Z8
514/847-6212; Fax: 514/847-6290; 847-6226 (administration)
URL: http://Media.MACM.qc.ca

Collection of over 5,000 works dating from 1939 by artists from Québec, Canada & around the world; a specialized reference centre is available for research; various performances, lectures & educational programs are offered by the museum throughout the year; restaurant, boutique & bookstore.

Directeur, Marcel Brisebois
Curator-in-Chief, Paulette Gagnon

### Musée des beaux arts de Montréal/Montréal Museum of Fine Arts

1379-1380, rue Sherbrooke ouest, PO Box 3000, Stn H, Montréal QC H3G 2T9
514/285-1600; Fax: 514/844-6042; Email: webmbam@cam.org
URL: http://www.mbam.qc.ca, http://www.mmfa.qc.ca

Oldest art museum in Canada (1860); 65 rooms house important collections of engravings, drawings, sculptures, paintings, furniture, silverware & porcelain; open year round.

Directeur, Pierre Théberge
Head, Public Relations, Maurice Boucher

### Other Art Galleries in Québec

Amos: Centre d'exposition d'Amos, 222, 1ère av est, Amos QC J9T 1H3 – 819/732-6070; Fax: 819/732-3242; Email: exposition@ville.amos.qc.ca; URL: http://www.ville.amos.qc.ca – Directrice, Marianne Trudel

Aylmer: Centre d'exposition l'imagier, 9, rue Front, Aylmer QC J9H 4W8 – 819/684-1445 – Directrice, Yvette Debain

Baie-Saint-Paul: Centre d'Art, 4, boul Fafard, CP 789, Baie-Saint-Paul QC G0A 1B0 – 418/435-3681

Beauport: Galerie des Sculptures, 907, boul Rochette, Beauport QC G1C 1C7

Carleton: Centre d'Artistes Vaste et Vague, 756, boul Perron, CP 877, Carleton QC G0C 1J0 – 418/364-3123

Chicoutimi: Espace Virtuel, 534, rue Jacques-Cartier, Chicoutimi QC G7H 5B7 – 418/549-3618 – Présidente, Diane Landry

Drummondville: Galerie d'art l'Union-Vie du Centre Culturel de Drummondville, 175, rue Ringuet, Drummondville QC J2C 2P7 – 819/477-5416; Fax: 819/477-5723 – Directeur, Normand Blanchette

Hull: Axe Néo-7 Art Contemporain, 205, rue Montcalm, Hull QC J8Y 3B7 – 819/771-2122 – Coordonnateur, Jean-Yves Vigneau

Hull: Galerie Montcalm, Maison du Citoyen, 25, rue Laurier, Hull QC J8X 4C8 – 819/595-7488; Fax: 819/595-7425 – Directrice, Jacqueline Tardiff

Jonquière: Centre national d'exposition, 4160, rue du Vieux Pont, CP 605, Succ A, Jonquière QC G7X 7W4 – 418/546-2177; Fax: 418/546-2180 – Directrice, Jacqueline Caron

Laval: Cercle d'Art, Complexe Alfred Dallaire, 2159, boul St-Martin est, Laval QC H7E 4X6 – 514/384-2551

Laval: Galerie d'art Mayfair, 1550, boul des Laurentides, Laval QC H7M 2N8 – 514/662-0555

Laval: Galerie de l'Atelier, 74, av du Pacifique, Laval QC H7N 3X7 – 514/662-1513

Laval: Salle Alfred Pellan, Maison des arts de Laval, 1395, boul de la Concorde ouest, Laval QC H7N 5W1 – 514/662-4440

Lévis: Centre d'Art de Lévis, 33, rue Wolfe, Lévis QC G6V 8T2 – 418/833-8831

Lennoxville: Bishop's University Artists' Centre/Centre d'Artistes de l'Université Bishop's, Bishop's University, Lennoxville QC J1M 1Z7 – 819/822-9000, ext.2687; Fax: 819/822-9661 – Gallery Coordinator, Chantal Groleau

Matane: Galerie d'art de Matane, 616, rue St-Rédempteur, Matane QC G4W 1L1 – 418/562-1240, poste 2250; Fax: 418/566-2115 – Président, Delphis Bélanger

Mont-Laurier: Centre d'exposition Mont-Laurier, 385, rue Du Pont, PO Box 323, Mont-Laurier QC J9L 3N7 – 819/623-2441; Fax: 819/623-7262; Email: orcentex@sympatico.ca – Directrice, Reine Charbonneau

Montréal: Art Cannon Gallery, 4885, av Parc, Montréal QC H2V 4E7 – 514/274-9118; Email: art@artcannon.com; URL: http://www.artcannon.com – Director, Misha Gostick – Offers electronic portfolios, artists agents & consultation services

Montréal: Atelier d'historie Hochelaga-Maisonneuve, 1691, boul Pie IX, Montréal QC H1V 2C3 – 514/523-5930 – Directeur, Ghyslaine Teller

Montréal: Galerie de l'UQAM, 1400, rue Berri, CP 8888, Succ Centre-ville, Montréal QC H3C 3P8 – 514/987-6150; Fax: 514/987-3009 – Directrice par intérim, Chantal Bouthat

Montréal: Galerie Dominion, 1438, rue Sherbrooke ouest, Montréal QC H3G 1K4 – 514/845-7833

Montréal: Galerie l'Industrielle-alliance, 680, rue Sherbrooke ouest, Montréal QC H3A 2S6 – 514/499-3768; Fax: 514/284-2655 – Directrice, Danielle Brunelle

Montréal: La Centrale (Galerie Powerhouse), #311D, 279, rue Sherbrooke ouest, Montréal QC H2X 1Y2 – 514/844-3489 – Coordinator, Elaine Frigon

Montréal: Leonard & Bina Ellen Art Gallery/Galerie d'art Leonard & Bina Ellen, Concordia University, 1400, boul de Maisonneuve ouest, Montréal QC H3G 1M8 – 514/848-4750; Fax: 514/848-4751; Email: jennyc@vax2.concordia.ca – Director/Curator, Karen Antaki

Pointe-Claire: Stewart Hall Art Gallery, 176, rue Lakeshore, Pointe-Claire QC H9S 4J7 – 514/630-1254; Fax: 514/630-1259 – Open year round; exhibitions from local, national & international sources; paintings, photographs, sculptures, graphics & theme exhibitions; free admission; wheelchair access

Québec: Galerie Municipale au Palais Montcalm, Bureau des arts et de la culture, Palais Montcalm, 995, place D'Youville, Québec QC G1R 3P1 – Chargée d'interpretation, Henriette Thériault

Québec: VU centre de diffusion et de production de la photographie, 523, Saint-Vallier est, Québec QC G1K 3P9 – 418/640-2585; Fax: 418/640-2586; Email: vuphoto@microtec.ca; URL: http://www2.zone.ca/~vuphoto – Directeur, Gaétan Gosselin

Rouyn-Noranda: Centre d'exposition de Rouyn-Noranda inc., 425, boul du Collège, CP 415, Rouyn-Noranda QC J9X 5C4 – 819/762-6600 – Directrice, Céline Rivard

Saint-Georges: Centre d'Art de St-Georges, 250, 18e rue ouest, Saint-Georges QC G5Y 4S9 – 418/228-2027 – Jacqueline Ferland – Open year round

Saint-Hyacinthe: Expression, Centre d'exposition de Saint-Hyacinthe, 405, av Saint-Simon, Saint-Hyacinthe QC J2S 5C3 – 514/773-4209 – Directeur, Michel Groleau

Saint-Lambert: Galarie du Centre, 250, rue Saint-Laurent, CP 555, Saint-Lambert QC J4P 3R8 – 514/672-4772 – Directrice, Jacqueline Beaudry Dion

Saint-Léonard: Galerie Port-Maurice, 8420, boul Lacordaire, Saint-Léonard QC H1R 3G5 – 514/328-8585 – Coordonnatrice, Louise Cayer

Shawinigan: Centre d'exposition de Shawinigan, 2100, boul Des Hêtres, PO Box 400, Shawinigan QC G9N 6V3 – 819/539-1888; Fax: 819/539-2400; Email: CASOI@login.net – Directeur, Robert Y. Desjardins

St-Laurent: Musée d'Art de St-Laurent (MASL), 615, av Ste-Croix, St-Laurent QC H4L 3X6 – 514/747-7367; Fax: 514/747-8892 – Directrice, Johane Canning-Lacroix

Trois-Rivières: Galerie d'art du Parc Inc., Manoir de Tonnancour, 864, rue des Ursulines, CP 871, Trois-Rivières QC G9A 5J9 – 819/374-2355; Fax: 819/374-1758; Email: galerie_art.duparc@tr.cgocable.ca – Directrice, Christiane Simoneau

Val d'Or: Centre d'exposition de Val d'Or inc., 600, 7e rue, Val d'Or QC J9P 3P3 – 819/825-0942 – Directrice, Lise Gagné

Verdun: Centre culturel de Verdun, 5955, rue Bannantyne, Verdun QC H4H 1H6 – 514/765-7170; Fax: 514/765-7167 – Directeur, Claude Vadeboncoeur

## SASKATCHEWAN

### MacKenzie Art Gallery (MAG)

3475 Albert St. South, Regina SK S4S 6X6
306/522-4242; Fax: 306/569-8191
URL: http://www.uregina.ca/~macken//

Historical & contemporary Canadian, American & European works; special emphasis on western Canadian art; works on paper, contemporary photography, major touring exhibits; facilities include learning centre, studios, theatre, gift shop; sculpture court; open daily year round.

Director, Kate Davis
Communications, Kathy Weisshaar

### Mendel Art Gallery & Civic Conservatory (MAG)

950 Spadina Cres. East, PO Box 569, Saskatoon SK S7K 3L6
306/975-7610; Fax: 306/975-7670; Email: mendel@mendel.saskatoon.sk.ca
URL: http://www.mendel.saskatoon.sk.ca

Historical & contemporary Canadian & international art; 3,500 works; open daily year round.

Director, Terry Fenton

### Other Art Galleries in Saskatchewan

North Battleford: The Chapel Gallery, PO Box 460, North Battleford SK S9A 2Y6 – 306/445-7266 – Curator, Unafred Ann Shiplett

Prince Albert: Grace Campbell Gallery, c/o John M. Cuelenaere Public Library, 125 - 12 St. East, Prince Albert SK S6V 1B7 – 306/763-8496; Fax: 306/763-3816; Email: gray@jmc.panet.pa.sk.ca – Gallery Coordinator, Janet Gray, Email: gray@panet.panet.pa.sk.ca; Library Director, Eleanor Acorn

Regina: Assiniboia Gallery, 2429 - 11th Ave., Regina SK S4P 0K4 – 306/522-0997 – Contemporary Canadian art; open year round

Regina: Dunlop Art Gallery, 2311 - 12th Ave., PO Box 2311, Regina SK S4P 3Z5 – 306/777-6040; Fax: 306/352-5550; Email: hmarzolf@rpl.regina.sk.ca – Director, Helen Marzolf; Curator, Vera Lemecha

Regina: Gallery on the Roof, Saskatchewan Power Corp., 2025 Victoria Ave., Regina SK S4P 0S1 – 306/566-3176 – Curator, Dale Kilbride

Regina: McIntyre Street Gallery, 2347 McIntyre St., Regina SK S4P 2S3 – 306/757-4323; Fax: 306/359-0280 – Director, Louise Durnford – Contemporary Saskatchewan art; open year round

Regina: Rosemont Art Gallery, 2420 Elphinstone St., PO Box 1790, Regina SK S4P 3C8 – 306/522-5940 – Director/Curator, Karen Schoonover

Saskatchewan Craft Gallery (SCC), 813 Broadway Ave., Saskatchewan SK S7N 1B5 – 306/653-3616; Fax: 306/244-2711

Saskatoon: A.K.A. Gallery, 12 - 23rd St. East, 3rd Fl., Saskatoon SK S7K 0H5 – 306/652-0044; Fax: 306/652-9924; Email: aa/82@SFN.Saskatoon.sk.ca – Administrative Co-ordinator, Susan Bustin

Saskatoon: Gordon Snelgrove Art Gallery, 191 Murray Bldg., University of Saskatchewan, Saskatoon SK S7N 5A4 – 306/966-4208; Fax: 306/966-4266; Email: gyoung@duke.usask.ca – Coordinator, Gary Young – Teaching gallery in support of department of art & art history.

Saskatoon: Photographers Gallery (TPG), 12 - 23rd St. East, 2nd Fl., Saskatoon SK S7K 0H5 – 306/244-8018; Fax: 306/665-6568; Email: acolo@sfn.saskatoon.sk.ca

Saskatoon: St. Thomas Moore Art Gallery, 1437 College Dr., Saskatoon SK S7N 0W6 – 306/966-8900 – Director, Colleen Fitzgerald

Swift Current National Exhibition Centre, 411 Hebert St. East, Swift Current SK S9H 1M5 – 306/778-2736; Fax: 306/778-2198 – Director, David Humphries

Weyburn: Allie Griffin Art Gallery (AGAG), PO Box 1178, Weyburn SK S4H 0H9 – 306/848-3278; Fax: 306/848-3220 – Gallery Curator, Helen Mamer; Arts Director, Alice Neufeld – Located at 45 Bison Ave.

Weyburn: Prairie Gallery, Signal Hill Arts Centre, 424 - 10th Ave. South, 2nd Fl., Weyburn SK S4H 2A1

Yorkton Arts Council, Yorkton Arts Council, 49 Smith St. East, Yorkton SK S3N 0H4 – 306/783-8722; Fax: 306/786-7667 – President, Lori Glauser; Coordinator, Ken Kohlert

# PERFORMING ARTS

## THEATRE

### The Actors' Fund of Canada/La Caisse des acteurs du Canada inc. (1957)
#860, 10 Saint Mary St., Toronto, ON M4Y 1P9
416/975-0304, Fax: 416/975-0306
President, V. Harwood

### Alberta Playwrights' Network (APN) (1985)
1134 - 8 Ave. SW, 2nd Fl., Calgary, AB T2P 1J5
403/269-8564, Fax: 403/269-8564, Toll Free: 1-800-268-8564
Email: apn@nucleus.com, URL: http://www.nucleus.com/~apn
President, Sherring Amsden
Administrator, Liz Portier
Publications: Rave Review, bi-m.
Affiliates: Theatre Alberta

### Association for Canadian Theatre Research/Association de recherches théâtrales au Canada (ACTR) (1976)
90 Beauvista Dr., Sherwood Park, AB T8A 3X1
403/464-0703, Fax: 403/467-6731, Toll Free: 1-800-269-7037
Email: annen@cs.athabascau.ca, URL: http://www.unb.ca/web/english/candrama/candrama.htm
President, Ches Skinner
Treasurer, Anne Nothof
Secretary, Louise Forsyth
Publications: ACTR/ARTC Newsletter, s-a.; Theatre Research in Canada

### Association québécoise des critiques de théâtre (AQCT) (1984)
54, av Helmwood, Montréal, QC H2V 2E4
514/278-5764
Président, Michel Vais

### Association québécoise des marionnettistes (AQM) (1981)
**Union internationale de la marionnette - Canada**
Centre UNIMA au Québec, CP 7, Succ De Lorimier, Montréal, QC H2H 2N6
514/499-0875
Courrier électronique: aqm@aei.ca, URL: http://www.aei.ca/~aqm/
Président, Benoît Dubois
Publications: La Marionnette en manchette, 5 fois par an

### Association québécoise du théâtre amateur inc. (AQTA) (1958)
6, rue de l'Exposition, CP 977, Victoriaville, QC G6P 8Y1
819/752-2501, Téléc: 819/758-4466
Directrice générale, Jocelyne Lévis
Publications: Trac, 10 fois par an

### Association of Summer Theatres 'Round Ontario (ASTRO) (1985)
#1500, 415 Yonge St., Toronto, ON M5B 2E7
416/408-4556, Fax: 416/408-3402
Email: thon@interlog.com,
President, Alex Mustakas
Publications: Guide to Summer Theatres, a.

### Bard on the Beach Shakespeare Festival
1101 West Broadway, Vancouver, BC V6H 1G2
604/737-0625; Box Office: 604/739-0559, Fax: 604/737-0425
Artistic Director, Christopher Gaze
General Manager, Marilyn Navarro Leiton

### British Columbia Drama Association (1933)
**Theatre BC**
#307, 1005 Broad St., Victoria, BC V8W 2A1
250/381-2443, Fax: 250/381-4419
Email: theatrebc@pacificcoast.net, URL: http://www.culturenet.ca/theatrebc/
Executive Director, Jim Harding
Publications: Theatre BC News, q.
Affiliates: BC Touring Council; Assembly of BC Arts Councils; CultureNet

### Buddies in Bad Times Theatre
12 Alexander St., Toronto, ON M4Y 1B4
416/975-9130; Box Office: 416/975-8555, Fax: 416/975-9293
Artistic Director, Sky Gilbert
General Manager, Tim Jones

### Canadian Institute for Theatre Technology (CITT) (1989)
2500 University Dr. NW, Calgary, AB T2N 1N4
403/220-4905, Fax: 403/282-7751
Email: citt@cnetmail.ffa.ucalgary.ca, URL: http://www.ffa.ucalgary.ca/citt/index.html
Office Manager, Kathy Watson
Publications: Sightlines, 10 pa; Theatre Design & Technology
Affiliates: United States Institute for Theatre Technology

### Canadian Popular Theatre Alliance (CPTA)
c/o Concrete Theatre, 10920 - 88 Ave., Edmonton, AB T6G 0Z1
403/439-3905, Fax: 403/433-4782
Coordinator, Mieko Ouchi

### The Canadian Stage Company
26 Berkeley St., Toronto, ON M5A 2W3
416/367-8243; Box Office: 416/368-3110, Fax: 416/367-1768
Email: canthe@idirect.com,
Managing Director & Producer, Martin Bragg
Artistic Director, Bob Baker
Director of Communications & Development, Celia Smith

### Canadian Theatre Critics Association/Association des critiques de théâtre du Canada (CTCA) (1979)
#700, 250 Dundas St. West, Toronto, ON M5T 2Z5
416/367-8896, Fax: 416/367-5992
Founding President, Jeniva Berger
Publications: CTCA Newsletter, q.
Affiliates: Capital Critics Association; Association québécoise des critiques de théâtre

### Caravan Stage Society
349 Wellington St., PO Box 1995, Kingston, ON K7K 6E1
613/531-8390, Fax: 613/531-8391
Artistic Director, Paul Kirby
Administrator, Ted Worth

### Centre des auteurs dramatiques (CEAD) (1965)
3450, rue St. Urbain, Montréal, QC H2X 2N5
514/288-3384, Téléc: 514/288-7043
Courrier électronique: cead@globale.net, URL: http://globale.net/~cead
Directrice général, Jacques Vézina
Présidente, Carole Fréchette
Publications: Dramaturgies/Nouvelles, semi-annuel; Théâtre Québec

### Le Cercle Molière (1925)
340, boul Provencher, CP 1, Winnipeg, MB R2H 3B4
204/233-8053; Box Office: 204/233-8972, Téléc: 204/233-2373
Directeur artistique, Roland Mahé

### Conseil québécois du théâtre (CQT)
#4120, 5505, boul Saint-Laurent, Montréal, QC H2T 1S6
514/278-9208, Téléc: 514/278-9239
Courrier électronique: cqt@cam.org,
Directrice générale, Dominique Violette

### Council of Drama in Education (CODE)
#1106, 360 Watson St., Whitby, ON L1N 9G2
905/666-4408, Fax: 905/723-7024
Liaison Officer, Lisa Taylor
Publications: CODE Journal, a.; CODE Newsletter

### Evergreen Theatre Society (1983)
984 West Broadway, PO Box 53541, Vancouver, BC V5Z 1K7
604/876-4200, Fax: 604/876-4200
Email: patnjohn@smartt.com,
Artistic Manager, Patricia Andrew-Keith

### First Vancouver Theatrespace Society
18 - 2414 Main St., Vancouver, BC V5T 3E3
604/873-3646, Fax: 604/873-4231
Executive Director, Joanna Maratta

### Fringe of Toronto Festival
#303, 720 Bathurst St., Toronto, ON M5S 2R4
416/534-5919, Fax: 416/534-6021
Producer, Nancy Webster
General Manager, Linda Keyworth

### Globe Theatre Society (1966)
1801 Scarth St., Regina, SK S4P 2G9
306/525-9553, Fax: 306/352-4194
Email: globetheatre@sk.sympatico.ca,
Artistic Director, Susan Ferley
Affiliates: Canadian Actors' Equity

### Gryphon Theatre Foundation (1969)
PO Box 454, Barrie, ON L4M 4T7

705/728-4634; Box Office: 705/728-4613, Fax: 705/728-4623
Producer, Uwe Meyer
Administrator, Barbara Aoki

### Harbourfront Centre
#100, 410 Queens Quay West, Toronto, ON M5V 2Z3
416/973-4600, Fax: 416/973-6055
Email: publicity@harbourfront.on.ca, URL: http://www.harbourfront.on.ca
Artistic Director, Don Shipley
General Manager, Bill Boyle
Director, Marketing & Development, Ann Brookes

### International Theatre Institute - Canadian Centre (1979)
**Canadian Centre of the ITI**
Acadia University, PO Box 1441, Wolfville, NS B0P 1X0
902/542-1932, Fax: 902/542-1526
Administrator, Andria Hill
Publications: ITI Newsletter, q.
Affiliates: Organisation internationale des scenographes, architectes et techniciens de théâtre

### Intrepid Theatre Co. Society
510 Fort St., Victoria, BC V8W 1E6
250/383-2663, Fax: 250/380-1999
Email: intrepid@bc.sympatico.ca,
Executive Director, Janet Munsil

### Manitoba Association of Playwrights (MAP) (1979)
#503, 100 Arthur St., Winnipeg, MB R3B 1H3
204/942-8941, Fax: 204/942-1555
Coordinator, Rory Runnells
Publications: Ellipsis, 4-5 pa

### Manitoba Theatre Centre (MTC) (1957)
174 Market Ave., Winnipeg, MB R3B 0P8
204/956-1340, Fax: 204/947-3741
Email: mtc@mb.sympatico.ca, URL: http://www.mtc.mb.ca
Artistic Director, Steven Schipper
General Manager, Zaz Bajon
Publications: Ovation, bi-m.

### Native Earth Performing Arts Inc. (NEPA) (1983)
#302, 720 Bathurst St., Toronto, ON M5S 2R4
416/531-1402, Fax: 416/531-6377
URL: http://www.io.org/~naterth/naterth.htm
Artistic Director, Drew Hayden Taylor
General Manager, Eva Nell Harin
Publications: Native Earth Performing Arts Newsletter, q.

### Neptune Theatre Foundation
#B24, 1903 Barrington St., Halifax, NS B3J 3L7
902/429-7300, Fax: 902/429-1211
General Manager, Bruce Klinger
Artistic Director, Linda Moore

### New West Theatre Society
c/o Yates Centre, 910 - 4th Ave. South, Lethbridge, AB T1J 0P6
403/381-9378; Box Office: 403/329-7328, Fax: 403/380-4694
Email: parkinson@uleth.ca,
Artistic/Managing Director, Brian C. Parkinson

### Nova Scotia Drama League
#901, 1809 Barrington St., Halifax, NS B3J 3K8
902/425-3876, Fax: 902/422-0881
Executive Director, Eva Moore

### Nova Scotia Professional Theatre Alliance (NSPTA)
c/o Two Planks & a Passion Theatre, PO Box 413, Canning, NS B0P 1H0
902/582-3073, Fax: 902/582-7943
Email: twoplanx@auracom.com,
President, Ken Schwartz
Administrator, Chris O'Neill
Publications: NSPTA News, m.

### Ontario Puppetry Association
Box 180, #0116, 65 Front St. West, Toronto, ON M5J 1E6
General Manager, Sara Meurling
President, Tom Vandenberg
Publications: Opal, bi-m.
Affiliates: UNIMA International; Theatre Ontario; North York Arts Council
Office: #306, 56 The Esplanade, Toronto, ON M5E 1A7, 416/861-0202
Ontario Centre for Puppetry Arts: 116 Cornelius Pkwy., North York, ON M6L 2K5, 416/246-9222, Fax: 416/246-0922 (call first)

### PACT Communications Centre (PCC) (1985)
#1500, 415 Yonge St., Toronto, ON M5B 2E7
416/595-6455, Fax: 416/595-6450, Toll Free: 1-800-263-7228
Email: pact@idirect.com, URL: http://webhome.idirect.com/~pact
Executive Director, Pat Bradley
Chair, Liz Palmieri
Publications: Artsboard, m.; The Theatre Listing
Affiliates: Charitable Wing of Professional Association of Canadian Theatres

### Performing Arts Sponsors Organization of Nova Scotia (PASONS)
PO Box 3150, Windsor, NS B0N 2T0
902/798-3893, Fax: 902/798-0557
Executive Director, Pamela Kinsman

### Phoenix Theatre Society
10330 - 84 Ave., Edmonton, AB T6E 2G9
403/434-4015, Fax: 403/438-4016
Email: phoenix@freenet.edm.ab.ca,
General Manager, Laurie Blakeman

### Playwrights Theatre Centre
1405 Anderson St., Vancouver, BC V6H 3R5
604/685-6228, Fax: 604/685-7451
Email: ptcplays@cyberstore.ca,
General Manager, Jan Carley

### Playwrights Union of Canada (PUC) (1972)
54 Wolseley St., 2nd Fl., Toronto, ON M5T 1A5
416/703-0201, Fax: 416/703-0059, Toll Free: 1-800-561-3318
Email: cdplay@interlog.com, URL: http://www.puc.ca
Executive Director, Angela Rebeiro
Publications: CanPlay, bi-m.; Directory of Members

### Popular Theatre Alliance of Manitoba (PTAM) (1984)
Portage Place, #Y300, 393 Portage Ave., Winnipeg, MB R3B 3H6
204/957-5425, Fax: 204/942-1774
Artistic Director, Debbie Patterson
Publications: PTAM News, bi-a.

### Prairie Theatre Exchange (PTE) (1972)
Portage Place, #Y300, 393 Portage Ave., Winnipeg, MB R3B 3H6
204/942-7291, Fax: 204/942-1774
General Manager, Cherry Karpyshin
President, Janice Penner

### Professional Association of Canadian Theatres (PACT) (1976)
#1500, 415 Yonge St., Toronto, ON M5B 2E7
416/595-6455, Fax: 416/595-6450, Toll Free: 1-800-263-7228
Email: pact@idirect.com, URL: http://webhome.idirect.com/~pact/
Executive Director, Pat Bradley
President, Jerry Doiron
Publications: Impact, q.
Affiliates: PACT Communications Centre; Canadian Centre of the International Theatre Institute; Canadian Conference of the Arts

### Saskatchewan Drama Association
#203, 2135 Albert St., Regina, SK S4P 2V1
306/525-0151, Fax: 306/525-6277
Executive Director, Catherine Anderson

### Saskatchewan Playwrights Centre (SPC)
PO Box 3092, Saskatoon, SK S7K 3S9
306/665-7707, Fax: 306/665-7707
Email: sk.playwrights@sk.sympatico.ca, URL: http://bailey2.unibase.com/~grain/SPC_Homepage.html
Dramaturge, Angus Ferguson

### Shaw Festival (1963)
**Shaw Festival Theatre Foundation**
PO Box 774, Niagara on the Lake, ON L0S 1J0
905/468-2153, Fax: 905/468-5438, Toll Free: 1-800-511-7429
URL: http://shawfest.sympatico.ca
Artistic Director, Christopher Newton
Administrative Director, Colleen Blake
Publications: PSHAW, 3 pa
Affiliates: Canadian Institute for Theatre Technology

### Société québécoise d'études théâtrales (SQET) (1976)
CP 459, Succ. Outremont, Montréal, QC H2V 4N3
514/237-7466
Contact, Claude Larouche
Publications: L'Annuaire théâtral, semi-annuel

### Stratford Festival (1952)
PO Box 520, Stratford, ON N5A 6V2
705/271-4040; Box Office: 273-1600, Fax: 705/271-2734, Toll Free: 1-800-567-1600
Email: dprosser@stratford_festival.on.ca, URL: http://www.ffa.ucalgary.ca/stratford/home.htm
Artistic Director, Richard Monette
General Manager, Mary Hofstetter

### Theatre Alberta Society (1985)
11759 Groat Rd., 3rd Fl., Edmonton, AB T5M 3K6
403/422-8162, Fax: 403/422-2663
Email: theatreab@oanet.com,
Executive Director, Kathy Classen
Publications: TA News, q.

### Theatre Calgary
220 - 9 Ave. SE, Calgary, AB T2G 5C4
403/294-7440; Box Office: 403/294-7447, Fax: 403/294-7493
Email: schniedm@cadvision.com,
Executive Producer, Brian Rintoul
Production/Facility Manager, Monty Schnieder

### Théâtre français de Toronto
#303, 219 Dufferin St., Toronto, ON M6K 1Y9
416/534-7303; Box Office: 416/534-6604, Téléc: 416/534-9087
URL: http://francoculture.ca/theatre/tft/
Directeur administrative, Greg Brown

### Theatre Network (1975) Society (1975)
10708 - 124 St., Edmonton, AB T5M 0H1
403/453-2440, Fax: 403/453-2596

Artistic Director, Ben Henderson
General Manager, David Hennessey
Affiliates: Edmonton Professional Arts Council

### Theatre New Brunswick (TNB) (1967)
The Playhouse, PO Box 566, Fredericton, NB E3B 5A6
506/458-8345, Fax: 506/459-6206
Executive Producer, Walter Learning
General Manager, Nancy Coy

### Theatre Newfoundland Labrador
PO Box 655, Corner Brook, NF A2H 6G1
709/639-7238, Fax: 709/639-1006
Artistic Director, Jerry Etienne
Administrator, Gaylene Buckle

### Theatre Ontario (1971)
#1500, 415 Yonge St., Toronto, ON M5B 2E7
416/408-4556, Fax: 416/408-3402
Executive Director, Sandra Tulloch
Publications: Theatre Ontario News, 5 pa

### Theatre Prince Edward Island (1980)
550 University Ave., Charlottetown, PE C1A 4P3
902/566-0321, Fax: 902/566-0420
Administrator, Daphne Harker
Artistic Director, Ron Irving
Associate Artistic Director, Rob MacLean
Publications: Newsletter
Affiliates: PEI Council of the Arts

### Theatre Terrific Society (1985)
4397 West 2nd Ave., Vancouver, BC V6R 1K4
604/222-4020, Fax: 604/222-4024
General Manager, Tanya Babalow
Publications: Theatre Terrific Update, 3 pa

### Théâtres associés inc. (TAI)
1501, rue Jeanne-Mance, Montréal, QC H2X 1Z9
514/842-6361, Téléc: 514/842-9730
Secrétaire général, Jacques Cousineau

### Théâtres unis enfance jeunesse (TUEJ) (1986)
CP 627, Succ. Desjardins, Montréal, QC H5B 1B7
514/446-4863, Téléc: 514/467-1982
Président, Stéphane Lavoie
Coordonnatrice, Andrée Garon
Organisation(s) affiliée(s): Conseil québécois du Théâtre

### Toronto Theatre Alliance (TTA) (1980)
#403, 720 Bathurst St., Toronto, ON M5S 2R4
416/536-6468, Fax: 416/536-3463, Toll Free: 1-800-541-0499
Email: tta@idirect.com, URL: http://www.ffa.ucalgary,ca/tta/
Executive Director, Jessica Fraser
Publications: TTA Reports, bi-m.
Affiliates: Professional Association of Canadian Theatres (PACT)

### Vancouver Professional Theatre Alliance (VPTA)
#2, 2414 Main St., Vancouver, BC V5T 3E3
604/879-2999, Fax: 604/876-5114
Administrator, Amanda Spottiswoode

### Vancouver Youth Theatre Society
#200, 275 East 8th Ave., Vancouver, BC V5T 1R9
604/877-0678, Fax: 604/876-7100
Artistic Director, Judith Hogan
Business Manager, Craig Laven

### Women in View
314 Powell St., Vancouver, BC V6A 1G4
604/685-6684, Fax: 604/685-6649
URL: http://www.ffa.ucalgary.ca/vca/wmnvie.htm
Executive Director, Dawn Brennan

### Young People's Theatre (YPT)
165 Front St. East, Toronto, ON M5A 3Z4
416/363-5131; Box Office: 416/862-2222, Fax: 416/363-5136
Artistic Director, Maja Ardal
General Manager, Catherine Smalley

## MUSIC

### Académie de musique du Québec (AMQ) (1870)
1231, rue Panet, CP 818, Succ. C, Montréal, QC H2L 4L6
514/528-1961, Téléc: 514/526-7572
Présidente, Françoise Bertrand
Vice-Présidente, Gertrude Perreault
Secrétaire, Serge Montreuil
Publications: Accord, 3 fois par an

### Alberta Choral Federation (ACF) (1972)
#209, 14218 Stony Plain Rd., Edmonton, AB T5N 3R3
403/488-7464, Fax: 403/488-4132
Executive Director, Robin John King
Publications: Quires, q.

### Alberta Recording Industries Association (ARIA) (1984)
#1205, 10109 - 106 Street, Edmonton, AB T5J 3L7
403/428-3372, Fax: 403/426-0188, Toll Free: 1-800-465-3117
President, R. Harlan Smith
Publications: Notes, m.

### Alliance for Canadian New Music Projects/ Alliance pour des projets de musique canadienne nouvelle (ACNMP) (1978)
**Contemporary Showcase**
Canadian Music Centre, 20 St. Joseph St., 3rd Fl., Toronto, ON M4Y 1J9
416/963-5937, Fax: 416/961-7198
General Manager, Colleen Perrin
President, Jill Kelman
Publications: Contempo, q.; Contemporary Showcase Syllabus

### Alliance Chorale Manitoba
340 Provencher Blvd., Winnipeg, MB R2H 0G7
204/233-8972, Téléc: 204/233-3324
Contact, Gilles Landry

### Alliance des chorales du Québec (ACQ)
4545, av Pierre-de-Coubertin, CP 1000, Succ. M, Montréal, QC H1V 3R2
514/252-3020, Téléc: 514/252-3222
Directrice générale, Christine Dumas

### Association of Canadian Choral Conductors/ Association des chefs de choeur canadiens (ACCC) (1980)
49, rue de Tracy, Blainville, QC J7C 4B7
514/430-5573, Fax: 514/430-4999
Executive Director, Patricia Abbott
President, Dr. Malcolm V. Edwards
Publications: Anacrusis, q.; Membership/Professional Directory; Repertoire Lists
Affiliates: Canadian Conference of the Arts; International Federation for Choral Music

### Association of Canadian Orchestras/Association des orchestres canadiens (ACO) (1972)
#311, 56 The Esplanade, Toronto, ON M5E 1A7
416/366-8834, Fax: 416/366-1780
Email: assoc@ican.net, URL: http://home.ican.net/~assoc
Executive Director, Betty Webster
Publications: Orchestra Canada/Orchestres Canada, bi-m.; The Directory of Canadian Orchestras & Youth Orchestras
Affiliates: American Symphony Orchestra League; International Alliance of Orchestra Associations
Member Orchestras
Brandon University Orchestra: Director, Nándor Szederkényi; Dr. Earl Davey, School of Music, Brandon University, 270 - 18th St., Brandon, MB R7A 6A9, 204/728-9520, Fax: 204/728-6839, Email: music@brandonu.ca
Brantford Symphony Orchestra Association Inc.: President, John Canning; General Manager, Andrea Bodkin; Music Director, Stanley Saunders, 185 King George Rd., PO Box 24012, Brantford, ON N3R 7X3, 519/759-8781, Fax: 519/759-8431
Calgary Philharmonic Society: Executive Director, Leonard D. Stone; Director, Finance & Administration, John M. Partridge; Executive Assistant, Joyce Van Halderen, 205 - 8 Ave. SE, Calgary, AB T2G 0K9, 403/571-0270, Fax: 403/294-7424, URL: http://www.tiger.ab.ca/cpo/
Calgary Youth Orchestra: Music Director, Glenn Price, Mount Royal College, 4825 Richard Rd. SW, Calgary, AB T3E 6K6, 403/240-5978, Fax: 403/240-6594
Cathedral Bluffs Symphony Orchestra of Scarborough: President, Neil Blair; Music Director, Clifford Poole, 37 Eglinton Sq., PO Box 51074, Scarborough, ON M1L 4T0, 905/509-5857, Fax: 905/509-5883
Chebucto Symphony Orchestra: President, Moreah Staven; Music Director, Christoph Both, 902/542-2200, PO Box 24025, Dartmouth, NS B3A 4T4
Concerts symphoniques de Sherbrooke inc.: Présidente, Marie-Josée Trottier Lagassé; Directeur artistique, Gilles Auger, #201, 32, rue Wellington nord, Sherbrooke, QC J1H 5B7, 819/821-0227, Téléc: 819/562-5411
Counterpoint Community Orchestra: President, Paul T. Willis; Music Director, Judy Yan, 600 Church St., Toronto, ON M4Y 2E7, 416/926-9806
Deep River Symphony Orchestra: President, Blair Smith; Music Director, Peter Morris, PO Box 1496, Deep River, ON K0J 1P0
Delta Youth Orchestra: President, Ann Bates, PO Box 131, Delta, BC V4K 3N6, 604/943-9663, Fax: 604/986-8805
East York Symphony Orchestra: President, Bruce Tidd; Music Director, Douglas Sanford, 110 Rumsey Rd., East York, ON M4G 1P2, 416/467-7142, Fax: 416/467-7142
Eastern Ontario Concert Orchestra: President, Debbie Shaw; Music Director, Gordon Craig, PO Box 23087, Belleville, ON K8P 5J3, Fax: 613/394-1447, Email: davies@quinte.net
Edmonton Philharmonic Society: President/General Manager, John D'Haese, 403/481-2711; Music Director, George Naylor, 186 Oeming Rd. NW, Edmonton, AB T6R 2G2
Edmonton Symphony Orchestra: President, Audrey Luft; Managing Director, W.R. McPhee; Music Director, Grzegorz Nowak, 10160 - 103 St., Edmonton, AB T5J 0X6, 403/428-1108, Fax: 403/425-0167, Email: eso@oanet.com, URL: http://www.tgx.com/eso
Edmonton Youth Orchestra Association: General Manager, Eileen Lee, PO Box 66041, RPO Heritage, Edmonton, AB T6J 6T4, 403/436-7932, Fax: 403/436-7932
Ensemble contemporain de Montréal: Président, Laurent Wermenlinger, #302, 1908, rue Panet, Montréal, QC H2L 3A2, 514/524-0173, Téléc: 514/524-0323
Esprit Orchestra: President, Paul Mingay; Music Director, Alex Pauk, #410, 35 McCaul St., Toronto, ON M5T 1V7, 416/599-7880, Fax: 416/599-1344
Etobicoke Philharmonic Orchestra: President, Peggy Pinkerton; Music Director, Tak-Ng Lai, 19 Hilldowntree Rd., Etobicoke, ON M9A 2Z4, 416/233-5665

Fraser Valley Symphony Society: Music Director, David Rushton; President, Heather Beckett, 250/853-5878, PO Box 122, Abbotsford, BC V2S 4N8

Georgian Bay Symphony: President, Bert Hood; Music Director, John Barnum, PO Box 133, Owen Sound, ON N4K 5P1, 519/372-0212, Email: gbs@log.on.ca

Greater Hamilton Symphony Association: Manager, Sandra E. Motta; President, Sandi Sherk, 991 King St. West, PO Box 89007, Hamilton, ON L8S 4R5, 905/526-6690, Fax: 905/526-1050

Greater Victoria Youth Orchestra: Associate Manager, Diana MacDonald; President, Dr. John Money, 1611 Quadra St., Victoria, BC V8W 2L5, 250/360-1121, Fax: 250/381-3573, Info Line: 250/360-1121, Email: GVYO@bc.sympatico.ca

Guelph Youth Orchestra Association: Manager, James Bruder, PO Box 31072, Guelph, ON N1H 8K1, 519/824-1642, Fax: 519/856-1666

Halton Youth Symphony: Manager, Cindy Steele, PO Box 494, Stn Main, Oakville, ON L6J 5A8, 905/681-0442

Hamilton Philharmonic Youth Orchestra: Music Director, Glenn Mallory, PO Box 57134, Stn Jackson, Hamilton, ON L8P 4W9

Hart House Orchestra: President, Susan Wilson; Music Director, Errol Gay, University of Toronto, 7 Hart House Circle, Toronto, ON M5S 1A1, 416/978-0537

Huronia Symphony Orchestra: President, C. Jane MacLaren; Music Director, Rosemary Thomson, PO Box 904, Barrie, ON L4M 4Y6, 705/721-4752

International Symphony Orchestra of Sarnia & Port Huron: General Manager, Anne M. Brown; Music Director, Zdzislaw Kopac, 774 London Rd., Sarnia, ON N7T 4Y1, 519/337-7775, Fax: 519/337-1822

Kamloops Intermediate Orchestra: Music Director, Kathleen Hogan, PO Box 1387, Kamloops, BC V2C 6L7, 250/825-2234

Kamloops Symphony Orchestra: General Manager, Kathy Humphreys, PO Box 57, Kamloops, BC V2C 5K3, 250/372-5000, Fax: 250/372-5089

Kingston Symphony Association: General Manager, Tricia Baldwin; President, James Coles; Music Director, Glen Fast, 77 Brock St., PO Box 1616, Kingston, ON K7L 5C8, 613/546-9729, Fax: 613/546-8580

Kingston Youth Orchestra: Music Director, Gordon Craig, 894 Plainview Place, Kingston, ON K7P 2K3, 613/545-2066

Kitchener-Waterloo Chamber Orchestra: President, Dale Gellatly; Music Director, Graham Coles, PO Box 34015, RPO Highland Hills, Kitchener, ON N2N 3G2, 519/744-3828, Fax: 519/747-1284

Kitchener-Waterloo Symphony Orchestra Association Inc.: General Manager, Mark Jamison; Music Director, Chosei Komatsu, 101 Queen St. North, Kitchener, ON N2H 6P7, 519/745-4711, Fax: 519/745-4474, Email: kwsymph@worldchat.com

Kitchener-Waterloo Symphony Youth Orchestra: Manager, Heather Bean, 101 Queen St. North, Kitchener, ON N2H 6P7, 519/745-4711, Fax: 519/745-4474

Korean-Canadian Symphony Orchestra: President, Lucas Yoo; Music Director, Sung-Soon Kim, #203, 703 Bloor St. West, Toronto, ON M6G 1L5, 416/229-4271

Lethbridge Symphony Orchestra: President, James A.P. Day; Music Director, Claude Lapalme, PO Box 1101, Lethbridge, AB T1J 4A2, 403/328-6808, Fax: 403/380-4418

London Community Orchestra: President, Malcolm Morham; Music Director, Mariusz Debich; Manager, Margaret Whitby, 1551 Ryersie Rd., London, ON N6G 2S2, 519/432-4461, Fax: 519/858-4982

London Youth Symphony: General Manager, P. Austin, PO Box 553, Stn B, London, ON N6A 4W8, 519/472-2606

Manitoba Chamber Orchestra: General Manager, Rita Menzies, #202, 1317A Portage Ave., Winnipeg, MB R3G 0V3, 204/783-7377

Medicine Hat Symphonic Society: President, James Vandersloot, PO Box 1295, Medicine Hat, AB T1A 7N1, 403/529-6813

Mississauga Chamber Players: President, Megan Pallett, 7781 Tremaine Rd., RR#6, Milton, ON L9T 2Y1, 905/273-3300

Mississauga Symphony: President, Graham Fox; Music Director, John Barnum, 161 Lakeshore Rd. West, Mississauga, ON L5H 1G3, 905/274-1571, Fax: 905/274-7770

Mississauga Youth Orchestra: President, Karen MacPherson, PO Box 247, Stn A, Mississauga, ON L5A 2Z7

National Arts Centre Orchestra of Canada: Managing Director, Christopher Deacon; Art Director, Trevor Pinnock, 53 Elgin St., PO Box 1534, Stn B, Ottawa, ON K1P 5W1, 613/947-7000, ext. 361, Fax: 613/943-1400

National Youth Orchestra Association of Canada: President, Victor Ujimoto; General Manager, Hubert C. Meyer, 1032 Bathurst St., Toronto, ON M5R 3G7, 416/532-4470, Fax: 416/532-6879

New Brunswick Youth Orchestra: Administrator, Don Rayment, Email: Rayment@nbnet.nb.ca, 38 Cliff St., Saint John, NB E2L 3A7, 506/657-1498

New Hamilton Orchestra: General Manager, Jack Nelson, Hamilton Place, #705, 25 Main St. West, Hamilton, ON L8P 1H1, 905/526-1677, Fax: 905/526-1606

Newfoundland Symphony Orchestra Association: President, Keith Wellon; Office Manager, Wendy Stevenson, Arts & Culture Centre, Prince Philip Dr., PO Box 1854, St. John's, NF A1C 5P9, 709/753-6492, Fax: 709/753-0561

Newfoundland Symphony Youth Orchestra: President, Janet Martin, PO Box 72, Goulds, NF A1S 1G3, 709/726-1575, Fax: 709/726-0610, URL: http://www.engr.mun.ca/~whitt/nsyo/nsyo.html

Niagara Symphony Association: President, Laura A. Bruce, #104, 73 Ontario St., St Catharines, ON L2R 5J5, 905/687-4993, Fax: 905/687-1149

Niagara Youth Orchestra Association: President, John Veeneman; Music Director, Stan Kopac, Ridley Sq., #148, 111 Fourth Ave., St Catharines, ON L2S 3P5, 905/704-0559, Fax: 905/704-0558

North Bay Symphony Orchestra: General Manager, Rex Hiscock; President, Nori Sugimoto; Music Director, Victor Sawa, #106, 269 Main St. West, North Bay, ON P1B 2T8, 705/494-7744, Fax: 705/494-7663

North York Concert Orchestra: President, Colin Bantin, 6 Apsely Rd., North York, ON M5M 2X8, 416/481-1406, Fax: 416/481-7379

North York Symphony Association: Executive Director, Al Kowalenko, CAE; Music Director, Kerry Stratton, #109, 1210 Sheppard Ave. East, North York, ON M2K 1E3, 416/499-2204, Fax: 416/490-9739

North York Symphony Youth Orchestra: President, Harry Cogill, #109, 1210 Sheppard Ave. East, North York, ON M2K 1E3, 416/499-2204, Fax: 416/490-9739

Northumberland Orchestra Society: President, Barbara Birney; Music Director, Matthew Jaskiewicz, PO Box 1012, Cobourg, ON K9A 4W4, 905/885-2782, Fax: 905/885-1779

Nova Scotia Youth Orchestra: President, Ian Mann; Music Director, Gregory Burton, #200, 1541 Barrington St., Halifax, NS B3J 1Z5, 902/423-5984, Fax: 902/423-5984

Oakville Chamber Ensemble: President, Peter H. Miller; Music Director, Charles Demuynck, 1703 Pilgrim's Way, Oakville, ON L6M 2G5, 905/827-5277

Oakville Symphony Orchestra Inc.: General Manager, Jeannine Filippini, 297 Lakeshore Rd. East, Oakville, ON L6J 1J3, 905/844-7984, Fax: 905/844-0823

Okanagan Symphony Society: Executive Director, Bill Woodward; President, Fred Miles, PO Box 1120, Stn A, Kelowna, BC V1Y 7P8, 250/763-7544, Fax: 250/763-3553

Orchestra London Canada Inc.: President, Robert C. Rienzo; Music Director, Mark Laycock, 520 Wellington St., London, ON N6A 3R1, 519/679-8558, Fax: 519/679-8914, Email: orchestra.london@icis.on.ca, URL: http://www.icis.on.ca/orchestra

Orchestre de chambre de Montréal: President, Theresa Skladanowski; Music Director, Wanda Kaluzny, #1100, 1200, av McGill College, Montréal, QC H3B 4G7, 514/871-1224, Téléc: 514/393-9069

Orchestre de jeunes de la Montérégie: President, Jean Martel, 496, Pierre Germain, St-Hilaire, QC G3H 5L2, 514/460-7101, Téléc: 514/464-2794

Orchestre symphonique de l'Estrie: General Manager, Annie Lévesque, CP 1512, Rimouski, QC G5L 8M4, 418/725-5354

Orchestre symphonique des jeunes de Joliette: Président, Gilles Tessier, CP 105, Joliette, QC J6E 3Z3, 514/755-6766

Orchestre symphonique des jeunes Laval-Laurentides: Président, Michel Viau, PO Box 274, Ste-Rose-de-Laval, QC H7K 4T3, 514/435-3608

Orchestre symphonique des jeunes de Lévis: Président, Christine Caron, CP 46024, Succ. Galeries Chagnon, Lévis, QC G6V 8S3

Orchestre symphonique des jeunes de la Montérégie: Présidente, Louise Hedon, 496, rue Pierre-Germain, St-Hilaire, QC J3H 5L2

Orchestre symphonique des jeunes de Montréal: Président, Anne-Marie Lizotte; Directeur artistique, Louis Lavigueur, CP 418, Succ. Youville, Montréal, QC H2P 2V6, 514/878-9411

Orchestre symphonique des jeunes Philippe-Fillion: Présidente, Charlotte Lecours, 2100, rue des Hêtres, Shawanigan, QC G9N 6V3, 819/539-6000, Téléc: 819/539-2400

Orchestre symphonique des jeunes du Saguenay Lac St-Jean: Directeur musique, Jacques Clément, 202, rue Jacques-Cartier est, Chicoutimi, QC G7H 6R8, 418/545-3409, Téléc: 418/545-8287

Orchestre symphonique des jeunes de Sherbrooke: Président, Pierre Massé, CP 1536, Sherbrooke, QC J1H 5M4, 819/566-1888

Orchestre symphonique des jeunes du West Island: Présidente, Aline Blain, 100, av Douglas Shand, Pointe Claire, QC H9R 4V1, 514/630-1218, Téléc: 514/630-1261

Orchestre symphonique de Laval: Président, André Pilon, #410, 1, Place Laval, Laval, QC H7N 1A1, 514/662-7222, Téléc: 514/629-2972

Orchestre symphonique de Montréal: Directrice générale, Michèle Courchesne; Musicothécaire, Giulio Masella; Directeur artistique, Charles Dutoit, 260, boul de Maisonneuve, Montréal, QC H2X 1Y9, 514/842-3402, Téléc: 514/842-0728

Orchestre symphonique de Québec: Directeur général, Gilles Moisan, 130, av Grande-Allée ouest, Québec, QC G1R 2G7, 418/643-5598, Téléc: 418/646-9665

Orchestre symphonique régional d'Abitibi-Témiscamingue: Présidente, Patrice Perron; Directrice générale, Madeleine Perron, CP 2305, Rouyn-Noranda, QC J9X 5A9, 819/762-0043, Téléc: 819/762-0043

Orchestre symphonique du Saguenay Lac St-Jean: Président, André Filion; Directeur général, Gilles Larouche, 202, rue Jacques-Cartier est, Chicoutimi, QC G7H 6R8, 418/545-3409, Téléc: 418/545-8287

Orchestre symphonique de Trois-Rivières: Président, Pierre Kirouac; Directeur artistique, Gilles Bellemare, CP 1281, Trois-Rivières, QC G9A 5K8, 819/373-5340, Téléc: 819/373-6693

Orillia Youth Symphony Orchestra: Manager, Grace Miller, 52 Elmer Ave., Orillia, ON L3V 2S7, 705/326-7548, 325-3209

Oshawa-Durham Symphony Orchestra: Executive Director, Bob Johnston; Chairman, Alice Sheffield, PO Box 444, Oshawa, ON L1H 7L5, 905/579-6711

Ottawa Symphony Orchestra Inc.: General Manager, Marian Pickering; Music Director, David Currie, #309, 1390 Prince of Wales Dr., Ottawa, ON K2C 3N6, 613/224-4982, Fax: 613/224-4982

Ottawa Youth Orchestra: Music Director, John Gomez, 604 Queen Elizabeth Driveway, Ottawa, ON K1S 3N5, 613/860-0378

Pembroke Symphony Orchestra: President, Paul Schwartzentruber, PO Box 374, Pembroke, ON K8A 6X6, 613/732-8837

Peterborough Symphony Orchestra: General Manager, Sigrid Rishor, PO Box 1135, Peterborough, ON K9J 7H4, 705/742-1992, Fax: 705/742-2077

Philharmonie des jeunes d'Ottawa-Carleton: President, Joan Walsh Lefaivre, #95, 2111 Montréal Rd., Gloucester, ON K1J 8M8, 613/781-4397

Prince Edward Island Symphony Society: General Manager, John Clement; Executive Secretary, Maryanne E. Palmer, PO Box 185, Charlottetown, PE C1A 7K4, 902/894-3566, Fax: 902/892-5637, Email: clement@pei.sympatico.ca

Prince George Symphony Orchestra Society: General Manager, Wendy Dawson; Co-President, Les Waldie; Co-President, Rachael Donovan; Music Director, Paul Andreas Mahr, 2880 - 15 Ave., Prince George, BC V2M 1T1, 250/562-0800, Fax: 250/562-0844

Pro Arte Orchestra: President, Joseph Macerollo; Music Director, Victor Di Bello, 1692 Danforth Ave., Toronto, ON M4C 1H8, 416/466-4515

Red Deer Symphony Orchestra: President, Richard D. McDonell; Music Director, Claude Lapalme, PO Box 1116, Red Deer, AB T4N 6S5, 403/340-2948, Fax: 403/340-2948

Regina Symphony: Executive Director, Pat Middleton; President, Mel Weisbart, 200 Lakeshore Dr., Regina, SK S4P 3V7, 306/586-9555, Fax: 306/586-2133

Richmond Community Orchestra & Chorus: President, Ray Haynes, #130, 10691 Shellbridge Way, Richmond, BC V6X 2W8, 604/276-2747

Royal Conservatory Orchestra: General Manager, Shannon Paterson; Music Director, Rennie Regehr, 273 Bloor St. West, Toronto, ON M5S 1W2, 416/408-2824, Fax: 416/408-3096

Saskatchewan Orchestral Association: Administrator, Kathy Butler; President, Lola Mae Crawley, 23 Quincy Dr., Regina, SK S4S 6L7, 306/586-6879, Fax: 306/585-3701

Saskatoon Symphony Society: General Manager, Sigrid-Ann Thors, #703, 601 Spadina Cres. East, Saskatoon, SK S7K 3G8, 306/665-6414, Fax: 306/652-3364

Saskatoon Youth Orchestra: Music Director, Wayne Toews, 1610 Morgan Ave., Saskatoon, SK S7H 2S1, 306/955-6336, Fax: 306/955-6336

Sault Symphony Association: Conductor/Director, John Wilkinson; Chairman, Doris Clarke; Manager, Patti Gardi, #2, 121 Brock St., Sault Ste Marie, ON P6A 3B6, 705/945-5337, Fax: 705/945-5337

Scarborough Philharmonic Orchestra: General Manager, Ann Brokelman, 128 Sylvan Ave., Scarborough, ON M1M 1K3, 416/261-0380, Fax: 416/261-0652

Scotia Chamber Players: Managing & Artistic Director, Christopher Wilcox, #317, 1541 Barrington St., Halifax, NS B3J 1Z5, 902/429-9467, Fax: 902/425-6785

South Saskatchewan Youth Orchestra: Music Director, Alan Denike, 101 Leopold Cres., Regina, SK S4T 6N5, 306/586-3007, Fax: 306/586-2133

Sudbury Symphony Orchestra Association Inc.: Executive Director, Marg Barry; Artistic Director, Dr. Metro Kozak, St. Andrew's Place, 111 Larch St., 3rd Fl., Sudbury, ON P3E 4T5, 705/673-1280, Fax: 705/673-1434

Sudbury Youth Orchestra Inc.: President, Nora Mirabelli, PO Box 2241, Stn A, Sudbury, ON P3A 4S1

Surrey Youth Orchestra: Music Director, Lucille Lewis, PO Box 9060, Surrey, BC V3T 5P8, 604/572-9225

Symphony Hamilton: President, Sandi Sherk; Music Director, James R. McKay, 59 Oxford St., Hamilton, ON L8R 2W9, 905/526-6690, Fax: 905/526-1050, URL: http://www.netaccess.on.ca/~artset

Symphony of the Kootenays: President, Laura Wilson; General Manager/Music Director, Ronald Edinger, PO Box 512, Cranbrook, BC V1C 4J1, 250/426-2924, Fax: 250/489-2101

Symphony New Brunswick: Music Director, Nurhan Arman, 32 King St., Saint John, NB E2L 1G3, 506/634-8379, Fax: 506/634-0843, Toll Free: 1-800-848-3311, Email: symphony@nbnet.nb.ca, URL: http://www.discribe.ca/snb

Symphony Nova Scotia: General Manager, Barbara Richman; Music Director, Leslie B. Dunner, Park Lane, #301, 5657 Spring Garden Rd., PO Box 218, Halifax, NS B3J 3R4, 902/421-1300, Fax: 902/422-1209

Tafelmusik Baroque Orchestra: Managing Director, Ottie Lockey; Music Director, Jeanne Lamon, 427 Bloor St. West, PO Box 14, Toronto, ON M5S 1X7, 416/964-9562, Fax: 416/964-2782, Email: info@tafelmusik.org, URL: http://www.tafelmusik.org

Te Deum Orchestra & Singers: Artistic Director, Dr. Richard Birney-Smith, 105 Victoria St., Dundas, ON L9H 2C1, 905/628-4533; Box Office: 416/205-5555, Fax: 905/628-9204, Toll Free: 1-800-263-0320

Thunder Bay Symphony Orchestra Association: President, Michael Comuzzi; General Manager, Clint Kuschak; Executive Assistant, Brenda Gilham, PO Box 24036, Thunder Bay, ON P7A 7A9, 807/345-4331, Fax: 807/345-8915

Thunder Bay Symphony Youth Orchestra: President, Donna Mercer, 428 Brown St., Thunder Bay, ON P7E 2K2, 807/475-8535

Timmins Symphony Orchestra: President, Roger E. Fennell, PO Box 1365, Timmins, ON P4N 7N2, 705/267-1006

Timmins Youth Orchestra: Music Director, Geoffrey Lee, c/o Timmins Symphony, PO Box 1365, Timmins, ON P4N 7N2, 705/267-1006, Fax: 705/267-1006

Toronto Chinese Philharmonic Orchestra: President, Winston Man; Music Director, Tak-Ng Lai, 2 Fern Ave., Richmond Hill, ON L4B 3R7, Fax: 905/882-7645

Toronto Chinese Youth Orchestra: Music Director, Tak-Ng Lai, 2 Fern Ave., Richmond Hill, ON L4B 3R7, 905/882-0241, Fax: 905/882-7645

Toronto Sinfonietta: President, Krzysztof Liebert; Music Director, Matthew Jaskiewicz, 588 Spadina Ave., Toronto, ON M5E 2H2, 416/488-0191, Fax: 416/488-0191

The Toronto Symphony Orchestra: Managing Director, Stan Shortt; President, Robert Martin; Music Director, Jukka-Pekka Saraste, 212 King St. West, 5th Fl., Toronto, ON M5H 1K5, 416/593-7769, Fax: 416/977-2912, Email: tso@clo.com, URL: http://www.tso.on.ca

Toronto Symphony Youth Orchestra: Manager, Colin Clarke, #550, 212 King St. West, Toronto, ON M5H 1K5, 416/593-7769, ext.372, Fax: 416/593-6788

University of Toronto Symphony Orchestra: Music Director, Dwight Bennett; President, Dean David Beach, Faculty of Music, University of Toronto, 80 Queen's Park Cres., Toronto, ON M5S 2C5, 416/978-3733, Fax: 416/978-5771

University of Western Ontario Symphony Orchestra: Director, Jerome David Summers, Faculty of Music, University of Western Ontario, 1151 Richmond St. North, London, ON N6A 3K7, 519/661-2043, Fax: 519/661-3531, Email: music@uwo.ca, URL: http://www.uwo.ca/music

Vancouver Island Symphony: General Manager, Marion V. Watkins, Email: mwatkins@island.net; Music Director, Marlin Wolfe, PO Box 661, Nanaimo, BC V9R 5L9, 250/754-0177, Fax: 250/753-3665

Vancouver Philharmonic Orchestra: President, Janet Gabites, PO Box 27503, Stn Oakridge, Vancouver, BC V5Z 4M4

Vancouver Symphony Society: President & General Manager, Barry McArton; Director, Finance & Administration, Mark Zimmerman, 601 Smithe St., Vancouver, BC V6B 5G1, 604/684-9100, Fax: 604/684-9264, Email: reachus@vansymphony.ca, URL: http://www.culturenet.ca/vso/

Vancouver Youth Symphony Orchestra: Manager, Charlotte Epp, 3214 - 10th Ave. West, Vancouver, BC V6K 2L2, 604/737-0714, Fax: 604/731-4133, Email: vyso@vcn.bc.ca, URL: http://www.vcn.bc.ca/vyso

Victoria Symphony: General Manager, C. Stephen Smith; Administrative Assistant, Lynn Mesher; President, Joan Banister, 846 Broughton St., Victoria, BC V8W 1E4, 250/385-9771, Fax: 250/385-7767

Wilfrid Laurier University Symphony Orchestra: General Manager, Jerzy Kaplanek; Music Director, Janez Govednik, Faculty of Music, 75 University Ave. West, Waterloo, ON N2L 3C5, 519/884-1970, ext.2692, Fax: 519/747-9129, URL: http://www.wlu.ca/~wwwmusic/

Windsor Symphony Society: Executive Director, Tim Dawkins; Music Director, Susan Haig, 198 Pitt St. West., Windsor, ON N9A 5L4, 519/973-1238, Fax: 519/973-0764

Winnipeg Symphony Orchestra Inc.: Executive Director, Howard Jang; Artistic Director, Bramwell Tovey, #101, 555 Main St., Winnipeg, MB R3B 1C3, 204/949-3950; Box Office: 949-3999, Fax: 204/956-4271, URL: http://www.aroundmanitoba.com/wso/

Winnipeg Youth Orchestra: Music Director, Carlisle Wilson, PO Box 273, Winnipeg, MB R3C 2G9, 204/253-0637, Fax: 204/254-1396

York Symphony Orchestra Inc.: General Manager, Ralph Markham; Music Director, Roberto De Clara, PO Box 355, Richmond Hill, ON L4C 4Y6, 416/460-0860, Fax: 416/884-3787

York Symphony Youth Orchestra: Music Director, June Miller, PO Box 355, Richmond Hill, ON L4C 4Y6, 416/410-0860

Youth Orchestra of Durham: Music Director, John Beaton, 212 Woodlea Cres., Oshawa, ON L1J 3J3, 905/579-2401

Youth Orchestra of Toronto: Music Director, Ann Cooper Gay, 276 MacPherson Ave., Toronto, ON M4V 1A3, 416/929-1119

### Bach Elgar Choral Society (1905)

**Bach Elgar Choir**

10 MacNab St. South, Hamilton, ON L8P 4Y3

905/527-5995, Fax: 905/527-5088

Publications: Voice of the City, q.

Affiliates: Ontario Choral Federation; Hamilton & Region Arts Council; Council for Business & the Arts in Canada; Canadian Conference of the Arts

### Calgary Early Music Society (CEMS) (1976)

PO Box 157, Stn M, Calgary, AB T2P 2H6

403/286-0023

President, Alan Jessop

Publications: Newsletter, q.

**Calgary Opera Association (1972)**
The Burns Bldg., #601, 237 - 8th Ave. SE, Calgary, AB T2G 5C3
403/262-7286, Fax: 403/263-5428
Email: calopera@lexicom.ab.ca, URL: http://www.lexicom.ab.ca/~calopera
General Director, David Speers
Publications: Bravo, q.
Affiliates: Actors Equity Association

**Canadian Academy of Recording Arts & Sciences/Académie canadienne des arts et des sciences de l'enregistrement (CARAS) (1975)**
124 Merton St., 3rd Fl., Toronto, ON M4S 2Z2
416/485-3135, Fax: 416/485-4978
URL: http://www.juno-awards.ca
Executive Director, Daisy C. Falle
Publications: CARAS News, q.

**Canadian Amateur Musicians/Musiciens amateurs du Canada (CAMMAC) (1953)**
#2509, 1751, rue Richardson, Montréal, QC H3K 1G6
514/932-8755, Fax: 514/932-9811
Executive Director, Danièle Rhéaume
Publications: The Amateur Musician/Le musicien amateur, s-a.

**Canadian Association for Music Therapy/ Association de musicothérapie du Canada (CAMT) (1974)**
Wilfrid Laurier University, 75 University Ave. West, Waterloo, ON N2L 3C5
519/884-1970, ext.6828, Fax: 519/884-8853, Toll Free: 1-800-996-2268
Email: ltracy@mach1.wlu.ca, URL: http://www.bmts.com/~smacnay/camt/camt.html
President, Kevin Kirkland
Administrative Coordinator, Lynda Tracy
Publications: CAMT Newsletter, 3 pa; Canadian Journal of Music Therapy

**Canadian Band Association/Association canadienne des harmonies (CBA) (1934)**
2345 Orchard Dr., Abbotsford, BC V3G 2B5
604/850-1413, Fax: 604/888-4324
President, Allan Hicks
Publications: The Canadian Band Journal, q.; Canadian Band Association Directory

**ALBERTA BAND ASSOCIATION (ABA)**
#808, 10136 - 100 St., Edmonton, AB T5J 0P1
403/429-0482, Fax: 403/429-0559
Executive Director, Raymond Baril
Publications: Musicom, q.

**FÉDÉRATION DES HARMONIES DU QUÉBEC (FHQ) (1927)**
4545, av Pierre-de-Coubertin, CP 1000, Succ. M, Montréal, QC H1V 3R2
514/252-3026, Téléc: 514/251-8038
Coordonnatrice, Chantal Isabelle
Président, Claude St-Amand
Publications: Harmonie-Québec, trimestriel
Organisation(s) affiliée(s): Fédération des associations de musiciens éducateurs du Québec

**MANITOBA BAND ASSOCIATION (1987)**
15 Pinecrest Bay, Winnipeg, MB R2G 1W2
204/663-1226
Executive Director, Ken Epp
Publications: BandNews, 3 pa

**NEW BRUNSWICK BAND ASSOCIATION**
PO Box 32, Florenceville, NB E3B 6J6
506/392-5115
Secretary, Sonja Sproull

**NOVA SCOTIA BAND ASSOCIATION**
210 Kaulback St., Truro, NS B2N 3T9
902/895-1015, Fax: 902/328-6220
Secretary, Jean McKenzie

**ONTARIO BAND ASSOCIATION (1934)**
Canadian Forces, School of Music, CFB Borden, Borden, ON L0M 1C0
613/993-2016
Executive Secretary, Benjamin Trowell
Publications: CBA Newsletter, q.

**SASKATCHEWAN BAND ASSOCIATION (SBA) (1983)**
1840 McIntyre St., Regina, SK S4P 2P9
306/522-2263, Fax: 306/656-2177
Email: sask.band@sk.sympatico.ca,
Executive Director, Holly Wildeman
Publications: SBA Journal, q.
Affiliates: Saskatchewan Pipe Band Association

**Canadian Bureau for the Advancement of Music (CBAM) (1917)**
Exhibition Place, Toronto, ON M6K 3C3
416/260-7795
CAO, Nancy Manning

**Canadian Children's Opera Chorus (CCOC) (1968)**
Opera Centre, #215, 227 Front St. East, Toronto, ON M5A 1E8
416/366-0467, Fax: 416/363-5584
Manager, Nina Draganic
Publications: Keynotes, s-a.

**Canadian Country Music Association/ Association de la musique country canadienne (CCMA) (1976)**
#127, 3800 Steeles Ave. West, Woodbridge, ON L4L 4G9
905/850-1144, Fax: 905/850-1330
Email: ccma@sprynet.com, URL: http://www.ccma.org
Executive Director, Sheila Hamilton
Publications: Canada Country, q.

**Canadian Disc Jockey Association (CDJA) (1977)**
#300, 3148 Kingston Rd., Scarborough, ON M1M 1P4
416/755-3898, Fax: 416/287-8817
Executive Director, Dennis E. Hampson
National Vice-President, James Griffin
National Membership Director, Blain Davis
National Secretary, Dan Shantz
Publications: CDJA Newsletter, m.
Affiliates: American DJ Association

**Canadian Independent Record Production Association (CIRPA) (1975)**
#614, 214 King St. West, Toronto, ON M5H 3S6
416/593-1665, Fax: 416/593-7563
Email: cirpa@interlog.com, URL: http://www.cmrra.ca/cirpa
President, Brian Chater
Research Director, Donna Murphy
Membership/Communications, Sharon Hookway
International Trade Shows, Mary Vrantsidis
Publications: CIRPA Newsletter, m.

**Canadian League of Composers**
c/o Canadian Music Centre, 20 St. Joseph St., Toronto, ON M4Y 1J9
416/964-1364
President, Dr. Rodney Sharman

**Canadian Music Centre/Centre de musique canadienne (CMC) (1959)**
Chalmers House, 20 St. Joseph St., Toronto, ON M4Y 1J9
416/961-6601, Fax: 416/961-7198
Email: cmc@interlog.com, URL: http://www.culturenet.ca/cmc
Executive Director, Simone Auger
President, Timothy Maloney
Publications: Directory of Associate Composers; Acquisitions; CMCDS Catalogue; Canadian Choral Music Catalogue; Canadian Orchestral Music Catalogue
Affiliates: International Association of Music Information Centres; Canadian Music Libraries Association

**Canadian Music Competitions Inc./Concours de musique du Canada inc.**
#705, 1030, rue Saint-Alexandra, Montréal, QC H2Z 1P3
514/879-1959, Fax: 514/979-1835
Founder, Claude Deschamps
Acting General Director, Louis Dallaire

**Canadian Music Educators' Association/ Association canadienne des éducateurs de musique (CMEA) (1959)**
43 Victoria Hill, Sydney, NS B1R 1N9
902/567-2398, Fax: 902/564-0123
Email: efavaro@fox.nstn.ca, URL: http://www.ucs.mun.ca/~cmea/
President, Eric Favaro
Publications: Canadian Music Educator, Newsletter Edition, 3 pa; Canadian Music Educator
Affiliates: International Society for Music Education

**Canadian Music Festival Adjudicators' Association (1960)**
1671 Lakeshore Rd., RR#5, Sarnia, ON N7T 7H6
519/542-4572, Fax: 519/542-4854
President, Gwen Beamish
Vice-President, Kathleen Keple
Vice-President, Ireneus Zuk
Publications: CMFAA Newsletter, 3 pa

**Canadian Musical Heritage Society/Société pour le patrimoine musical canadien (CMHS) (1982)**
50 Rideau St., PO Box 53161, Ottawa, ON K1N 1C5
613/520-2600, ext.8265, Fax: 613/520-6677
Email: cford@ccs.carleton.ca,
Executive Secretary, Clifford Ford
Publications: News from the Canadian Musical Heritage/Nouvelles de la société pour le patrimoine musical canadien

**Canadian Opera Company/Compagnie d'opéra canadienne (COC) (1950)**
227 Front St. East, Toronto, ON M5A 1E8
416/363-6671, Fax: 416/363-5584, Toll Free: 1-800-250-4653
Email: info@coc.ca, URL: http://www.coc.ca
Artistic Director, Richard Bradshaw
General Manager, Elaine Calder
Publications: Prelude
Affiliates: The Canadian Opera Foundation; Canadian Opera Women's Committee

**Canadian Recording Industry Association/ Association de l'industrie canadienne de l'enregistrement (CRIA)**
#400, 1250 Bay St., Toronto, ON M5R 2B1
416/967-7272, Fax: 416/967-9415
President, W. Brian Robertson
Office Manager, Brenda Gaze

**Canadian Society for Traditional Music (CSTM) (1956)**
PO Box 4232, Stn C, Calgary, AB T2T 5N1
403/230-0340
Director, John Leeder
Publications: Canadian Folk Music Journal; Canadian Folk Music Bulletin

### Canadian University Music Society/Société de musique des universités canadiennes (CUMS) (1979)
c/o Becker Associates, PO Box 507, Stn Q, Toronto, ON M4T 2M5
416/483-7282, Fax: 416/489-1713
Email: jbecker@interlog.com, URL: http://www.utoronto.ca/cums/
President, Dr. Maureen Volk, 709/737-7486, Email: mvolk@morgan.ucs.mun.ca
Vice-President, Dr. Tom Gordon, Email: tgordon@ubishops.ca
Secretary, Dr. Joanne Rivest, 514/523-4327, Email: rivestjo@dsuper.net
Publications: Canadian University Music Society Review, s-a.; CUMS Newsletter; CUMS Directory
Affiliates: Social Sciences & Humanities Research Council of Canada

### Country Music Foundation of Canada Inc. (1987)
8607 - 128 Ave., Edmonton, AB T5E 0G3
403/476-8230, Fax: 403/472-2584
Chairman, William Maxim

### Early Music Vancouver (1970)
**Vancouver Society for Early Music**
1254 - 7 Ave. West, Vancouver, BC V6H 1B6
604/732-1610, Fax: 604/732-1602
Email: earlymusic@mindlink.bc.ca, URL: http://mindlink.net/earlymusic/
Executive Director, José Verstappen
Publications: Musick, q.

### Edmonton Jazz Society (EJS) (1973)
**Yardbird Suite**
10203 - 86 Ave., Edmonton, AB T6E 2M2
403/432-0428, Fax: 403/433-3773
Email: yardbird@istar.ca, URL: http://www.ualberta.ca/edmonton/jazz
Publications: Newsletter, 5-6 pa

### Edmonton Opera Association (1963)
#320, 10232 - 112 St., Edmonton, AB T5K 1M4
403/424-4040; Box Office: 429-1000, Fax: 403/429-0600
Artistic Director, Irving Guttman, C.M.
General Manager, Nejolla B. Korris
Publications: About Opera, 3 pa

### Festival Chorus of Calgary
The Calgary Centre for Performing Arts, 205 - 8 Ave. SE, Calgary, AB T2G 0K9
403/294-7400

### Foundation to Assist Canadian Talent on Records (FACTOR) (1982)
125 George St., 2nd Fl., Toronto, ON M5A 2N4
416/368-8678
Executive Director, Heather Ostertag
Publications: Canadian Record Catalogue/de disques canadiens

### Friends of Chamber Music (1948)
PO Box 74636, RPO Kits, Vancouver, BC V6K 4P4
604/437-5716, Fax: 604/437-4769
Program Chairman, Eric Wilson

### Kiwanis Music Festival Association of Greater Toronto
3315 Yonge St., 2nd Fl., Toronto, ON M4N 2L9
416/487-5885, Fax: 416/487-5784
Email: kiwanismusicfest.toronto@sympatico.ca,
General Manager, Eileen Keown

### Manitoba Composers' Association Inc. (MCA) (1982)
#407, 100 Arthur St., Winnipeg, MB R3B 1H3
204/942-6152, Fax: 204/942-1555
President, Paul Sparling

### Manitoba Opera Association Inc. (1969)
Portage Place, #393, Portage Ave., PO Box 31027, Winnipeg, MB R3B 3K9
204/942-7479, Fax: 204/949-0377
President, James Astwood
Publications: House Programs, 3 pa
Affiliates: Opera America; Canadian Actor's Equity

### Mariposa Folk Foundation (1961)
1436 Queen St. West, PO Box 90026, Toronto, ON M6K 1L0
416/588-3655, Fax: 416/536-4021
URL: http://www.eagle.ca/mariposa
President, Doug Baker
Publications: Mariposa Notes, q.

### Music & Entertainment Industry Educators Association (MEIEA) (1978)
c/o Trebas Institute, 451, rue St-Jean, Montréal, QC H2Y 2R5
514/845-4141
Director, David P. Leonard
Publications: MEIEA Notes, q.

### Music Industries Association of Canada/Association canadienne des industries de la musique (MIAC) (1971)
#109, 1210 Sheppard Ave. East, North York, ON M2K 1E3
416/490-1871, Fax: 416/490-9739
Executive Director, Al Kowalenko, CAE
Publications: MIAC Statistics Report, a.; MIAC Newsletter
Affiliates: Music Distributors Association - USA; National Association of Music Merchants - USA

### Music for Young Children/Musique pour les jeunes enfants (MYC) (1980)
39 Leacock Way, Kanata, ON K2K 1T1
613/592-7565, Fax: 613/592-9353, Toll Free: 1-800-561-1692
Email: myc@myc.com, URL: http://www.myc.com
International Director, Frances M. Balodis, M.Ed., A.R.C.T.
Business Manager, Gunars Balodis
Administrator, Dianne Markle
Publications: MYC from C to C/Gofrit, m.; MY YOU Communicate

### Musicaction (1985)
#209, 455, rue Saint-Antoine ouest, Montréal, QC H2Z 1J1
514/861-8444, Téléc: 514/861-4423
Directrice générale, Nicole Payette

### The National Music Festival/Festival national de musique (1972)
1034 Chestnut Ave., Moose Jaw, SK S6H 1A6
306/693-7087, Fax: 306/693-7087
Executive Director, Sharon L. Penner
Chairman, J. Alexander Clark
Publications: Official Regulations & Syllabus, a.
Affiliates: Federation of Canadian Music Festivals

### National Shevchenko Musical Ensemble Guild of Canada (1972)
626 Bathurst St., Toronto, ON M5S 2R1
416/533-2725, Fax: 416/533-6348
Administrator, Ginger Kautto
Publications: Bulletin, s-a.

### New Brunswick Competitive Festival of Music Inc. (1936)
PO Box 2022, Saint John, NB E2L 3T5
506/652-8581
President, Shirley Dysart
Executive Secretary, Colleen Arseneau
Affiliates: New Brunswick Federation of Music Festivals; Canadian Federation of Music Festivals

### Nova Scotia Kiwanis Music Festival (1935)
PO Box 1623, Stn Central Halifax, Halifax, NS B3J 2Z1
902/423-6147, Fax: 902/423-6147
Executive Director, Sharon Harland
Publications: Syllabus, a.; Program
Affiliates: Federation of Music Festivals of Nova Scotia; Federation of Canadian Music Festivals; CIBC National Festival of Music

### Ontario Choral Federation
100 Richmond St. East, Toronto, ON M5C 1P9
416/363-7488, Fax: 416/363-8236
Executive Director, Bev Jahnke

### Opera Canada (1960)
#434, 366 Adelaide St. East, Toronto, ON M5A 3X9
416/363-0395, Fax: 416/363-0396, Toll Free: 1-800-331-6014
Publications: Opera Canada, q.
Affiliates: Professional Opera Companies of Canada

### L'Opéra de Montréal (L'OdM) (1980)
260, boul de Maisonneuve ouest, Montréal, QC H2X 1Y9
514/985-2222, Téléc: 514/985-2219, Infoligne: 514/282-6732
Courrier électronique: adm@total.net, URL: http://www.operademontreal.qc.ca
Directeur général et artistique, Bernard Uzan
Administrateur artistique, Michel Beaulac
Directeur, Communications et marketing, Patrick-Jean Poirier
Directrice, Développement et financement, Elise Côté
Directrice, Atelier Lyrique, Chantal Lambert, 514/596-0223
Directeur, Production, Michel Gagnon
Directeur, Technique, Olivier Gascon
Président, Conseil d'administration, Roger D. Landry

### Opera Ontario (1980)
**Kitchener Waterloo Opera; Opera Hamilton**
Stelco Tower, #200, 100 King St. West, Hamilton, ON L8P 1A2
905/527-7627, Box Office: 526-6556, Fax: 905/527-0014
General Director, Kenneth D. Freeman
Publications: High Notes, q.; Kudos

### Orchestras Ontario (1955)
#311, 56 The Esplanade, Toronto, ON M5E 1A7
416/366-8834, Fax: 416/366-1780
Email: assoc@ican.net, URL: http://home.ican.net/~assoc
Executive Director, Betty Webster

### Organization of Canadian Symphony Musicians/L'Organisation des musiciens d'orchestres symphonique du Canada (OCSM) (1981)
#6, 445, rue Gerard-Morrisset, Québec, QC G1S 4V5
418/688-0801
President, Evelyne Robitaille
Publications: Una Voce, q.
Affiliates: Association of Canadian Orchestras; Canadian Conference of the Arts

### Pacific Opera Victoria (POV) (1975)
1316B Government St., Victoria, BC V8W 1Y8
250/385-0222, Fax: 250/382-4944, Info Line: 250/382-1641
Email: opera@islandnet.com, URL: http://www.islandnet.com/~opera/
Artistic Director, Timothy Vernon
Manager, Ticket Services & Artistic Administration, Barbara Newton

**Professional Opera Companies of Canada (1980)**
c/o L'Opéra de Montréal, 260, boul de Maisonneuve ouest, Montréal, QC H2X 1Y9
514/985-2222, Fax: 514/985-2219
Email: odm@total.net, URL: http://www.operademontreal.qc.ca
General Artistic Director, Bernard Uzan

**Raag-Mala Music Society of Toronto**
63 Cassis Dr., Etobicoke, ON M9V 4Z4
905/472-0937
President, Dinesh Gandhi

**Royal Canadian College of Organists/Collège royal canadien des organistes (RCCO) (1909)**
#302, 112 St. Clair Ave. West, Toronto, ON M4V 2Y3
416/929-6400, Fax: 416/929-6400
Email: rjewell@capitalnet.com, URL: http://www.capitalnet.com/~rjewell/rcco.html
Executive Director, Peter Nikiforuk
Publications: Yearbook; Organ Canada/Orgue Canada; The American Organist

**Saskatoon Opera Association (1977)**
PO Box 414, Stn Sub 6, Saskatoon, SK S7N 0W0
306/374-1630
General Manager, Marilyn Harrison
Publications: Newsletter

**Société Pro Musica Inc./Pro Musica Society Inc. (1948)**
3450, rue St-Urbain, Montréal, QC H2X 2N5
514/845-0532, Téléc: 514/845-1500
Courrier électronique: promusica@apexdigital.com, URL: http://www.apexdigital.com/promusica
Directeur général, Monique Dubé
Directeur artistique, Pierre Rolland

**Society for the Preservation & Encouragement of Barber Shop Quartet Singing in America Inc. (1938)**
c/o Harmony Hall, 6315 Third Ave., Kenosha, WI 53140 USA
414/654-9111, 653-8440, Fax: 414/654-4048
Executive Director, Joe Liles
Publications: The Harmonizer, bi-m.

**Songwriters Association of Canada/Association des auteurs-compositeurs canadiens**
#400, 1235 Bay St., Toronto, ON M5R 3K4
416/924-7664, Fax: 416/924-5228
Email: sac@goodmedia.com, URL: http://www.goodmedia.com/sac/
Executive Director, Donna Murphy
Publications: The Bridge, q.

**The Toronto Mendelssohn Choir (1894)**
60 Simcoe St., Toronto, ON M5J 2H5
416/598-0422, Fax: 416/598-2992
General Manager, Donna White

**Vancouver New Music (VNMS) (1973)**
**Vancouver New Music Society**
#400, 873 Beatty St., Vancouver, BC V6B 2M6
604/606-6440, Fax: 604/606-6442
Email: newmusic@cyberstore.ca, URL: http://www.newmusic.org/VNMS
General Manager, Randy Smith
President, Michael Shea
Artistic Director, Owen Underhill
Affiliates: Canadian Music Centre

**Vancouver Opera (VO) (1958)**
**Vancouver Opera Association**
#500, 845 Cambie St., Vancouver, BC V6B 4Z9
604/682-2871; Box Office: 604/683-0222, Fax: 604/682-3981
Email: info@vanopera.bc.ca, URL: http://www.vanopera.bc.ca
General Director, Robert J. Hallam
Publications: House Program, 5 pa; On Stage
Affiliates: Canadian Actors' Equity Association; IATSE; AFM

**Western Board of Music (WBM) (1934)**
11044 - 90 Ave., Edmonton, AB T6G 1A7
403/492-3264, Fax: 403/492-0200, Toll Free: 1-800-263-9738
Executive Director, Leslie Vermeer
Publications: WB News/Bulletin, 3-4 pa

**Winnipeg Music Competition Festival**
#206, 180 Market Ave. East, Winnipeg, MB R3B 0P7
204/947-0184, Fax: 204/957-1132
Executive Director, Bill Muir

**Youth & Music Canada/Jeunesses musicales du Canada (YMC)**
305, av Mont-Royal est, Montréal, QC H2T 1P8
514/845-4108; Toronto: 416/535-0660
Executive Director, Nicolas Desjardins

## DANCE

**Alberta Ballet (1966)**
Nat Christie Centre, 141 - 18 Ave. SW, Calgary, AB T2S 0B8
403/245-4222, Fax: 403/245-6573
Artistic Director, Ali Pourfarrokh
Executive Director, Greg Epton
Publications: Balletin, q.
Alberta Ballet School of Dance: West Annex, 2nd Fl., 906 - 12th Ave. SW, Calgary, AB T2R 1K7, 403/245-2274, Fax: 403/245-2293
Edmonton Branch Office: #201, 10310 Jasper Ave., Edmonton, AB T5J 2W4, 403/428-6839, Fax: 403/428-4589

**Alberta Dance Alliance (ADA) (1984)**
11759 Groat Rd., 2nd Fl., Edmonton, AB T5M 3K6
403/422-8107, Fax: 403/422-8161, Toll Free: 1-888-422-8107
Email: abdance@incentre.ab.ca,
Executive Director, Bobbi Westman
Publications: Dancelines, q.

**Anjali Cultural Horizons Inc.**
#174, 11 Dufferin Rd., Ottawa, ON K1M 2A6
613/745-1368, Fax: 613/745-0299
Artistic Director, Anne-Marie Gaston

**Ballet British Columbia (1986)**
#102, 1101 West Broadway, Vancouver, BC V6H 1G2
604/732-5003, Fax: 604/732-4417
Email: balletbc@discovervancouver.com, URL: http://www.discovervancouver.com/balletbc/
Artistic Director, John Alleyne
General Manager, Howard R. Jang
Publications: Back Stage with the Ballet, s-a.

**Ballet Creole**
428C Queen St. East, Toronto, ON M5A 1T4
416/861-3048, Fax: 416/214-0620
Artistic Director, Patrick Parson

**Ballet Jörgen**
213B Glebeholme Blvd., Toronto, ON M4J 1S8
416/461-5045, Fax: 416/751-8388
Artistic Director, Bengt Jörgen
Administrator, Susan Bodie

**Ballet North**
12245 - 131 St., Edmonton, AB T5L 1M8
403/455-8407, Fax: 403/454-0137
Artistic Director, Paula Groulx
General Manager, Paul Reich

**Ballet Ouest**
CP 85, Beaconsfield, QC H9W 5T6
514/990-7729, Téléc: 514/398-8241
Artistic Director, Margaret Mehuys
Secretary, Suzanne Watt

**Les Ballets Jazz de Montréal (1972)**
3450, rue St-Urbain, Montréal, QC H2X 2N5
514/982-6771, Téléc: 514/982-9145
Courrier électronique: bjazzmtl@interlink.net,
Directeur artistique, Yvan Michaud
Directrice générale, Caroline Salbaing

**birtz & co dance institute**
579 - 3rd St. SE, Medicine Hat, AB T1A 0H2
403/526-4485
Email: jbirtz@mlc.awinc.com,
Artistic Director, Joanne Birtz
General Manager, Louise Plante

**Brian Webb Dance Co.**
c/o Grant MacEwan College, PO Box 1796, Edmonton, AB T5J 2P2
403/497-4416, Fax: 403/497-4330
Artistic Director, Brian Webb
Administrative Assistant, Daisy Kaiser

**Brouhaha danse**
5277, rue St-Denis, Montréal, QC H2J 2M4
514/273-8221, Téléc: 514/528-5842
Directrice artistique, Hélène Langevin

**Canadian Association of Professional Dance Organizations/Association canadienne des organisations professionnelles de danse (CAPDO) (1978)**
3790 Farmview Rd., RR#1, Kinburn, ON K0A 2H0
613/832-0397, Fax: 613/832-1321
Email: capdo@magi.com, URL: http://www.culturenet.ca/capdo/
Executive Director, Ellen Busby
Publications: Membership Directory; Fax News Bulletin
Affiliates: Member Companies: Alberta Ballet Company, Edmonton; Anna Wyman Dance Theatre, Vancouver; Ballet British Columbia, Vancouver; Contemporary Dancers, Winnipeg; Dancemakers, Toronto; Dancevision/Dansevision, Toronto; Danny Grossman Dance Company, Toronto; Les Grands Ballets Canadiens, Montréal; Le Groupe de la Place Royale, Ottawa; The National Ballet of Canada, Toronto; The National Ballet School, Toronto; Royal Winnipeg Ballet, Winnipeg; Theatre Ballet of Canada, Ottawa; Toronto Dance Theatre, Toronto

**Canadian Children's Dance Theatre**
509 Parliament St., Toronto, ON M4X 1P3
416/924-5657, Fax: 416/924-4141
Artistic Director, Deborah Lundmark
Managing Director, Michael Smith

**Canadian Dance Teachers Association/Association canadienne des professeurs de danse (CDTA) (1949)**
#38, 6033 Shawson Dr., Mississauga, ON L5T 1H8
905/564-2139
President, Irene Collins
Office Manager, Joan Amodeo
Publications: Newsletter, s-a.

**Carousel Theatre Society (1974)**
1411 Cartwright St., Vancouver, BC V6H 3R7
604/669-3410; Box Office: 604/685-6217, Fax: 604/669-3817

Artistic & Managing Director, Elizabeth Ball
Publications: The Carousel, q.
Affiliates: Professional Association of Canadian Theatres (PACT)

**Carré des Lombes**
#514, 3575, boul St-Laurent, Montréal, QC H2X 2T7
514/287-9339, Téléc: 514/287-9415
Directrice artistique, Danièle Desnoyers

**Cash & Company Dance**
925 Longfellow Ave., Mississauga, ON L5H 2X9
416/274-5057
Artistic Director, Susan Cash

**Catalyst Theatre Society of Alberta**
8529 - 103 St., Edmonton, AB T6E 6P3
403/431-1750, Fax: 403/433-3060
Email: catalyst@compusmart.ab.ca,
Co-Artistic Director, Jonathan Christenson
Co-Artistic Director, Joey Tremblay
General Manager, Heather Redfern

**Cercle d'expression artistique Nyata Nyata**
4374, boul St-Laurent, 3e étage, Montréal, QC H2W 1Z5
514/849-9781, Téléc: 514/849-9781
Directeur artistique, Zab Maboungou
Directeur général, Paul Miller

**Cercle virtueux dansethéâtre**
3772, rue de Bullion, Montréal, QC H2W 2C8
514/499-0678
Directrice artistique, Dulcinea Langfelder

**Compagnie de Brune**
CP 656, Succ. Desjardins, Montréal, QC H5B 1B7
514/525-0663, Téléc: 514/525-2052
Directrice artistique, Lynda Gaudreau

**Compagnie de Danse ethnique Migrations**
CP 8892, Ste-Foy, QC G1V 4N7
418/522-0539
Directeur artistique, Richard Turcotte
Directrice générale, Yvette Michelin

**La Compagnie Danse Partout**
#214, 310, boul Langelier, Québec, QC G1K 5N3
418/649-8312, Téléc: 418/649-4702
Directeur artistique, Luc Tremblay
Responsable, Administration, Jean-Pierre Parent

**Compagnie Marie Chouinard**
#615, 3981, boul St-Laurent, Montréal, QC H2W 1Y5
514/843-9036, Téléc: 514/849-7616
Directrice artistique, Marie Chouinard
Directeur général, Pierre Des Marais

**Contemporary Dancers Canada (1964)**
**Winnipeg's Contemporary Dancers**
109 Pulford St., Winnipeg, MB R3L 1X8
204/452-0229, Fax: 204/287-8618
Email: mwq250@freenet.mb.ca,
URL: http://www.escape.ca/~cesmb/wcd/wcdhome.htm
Artistic Director, Tom Stroud
General Manager, Alanna M. Keefe

**Création Isis**
760, av Walker, Montréal, QC H4C 2H4
514/933-4571, Fax: 514/933-2680
Co-Artistic Director, Jo Lechay
Co-Artistic Director, Eugene Lion
Administrator, Robert Byron Hutchings

**Dance Collective**
671 Walker Ave., Winnipeg, MB R3L 1C6
204/284-4886
Artistic Director, Ruth Cansfield
General Manager, Hugh Conacher

**Dance Manitoba Inc.**
#204, 180 Market Ave. East, Winnipeg, MB R3B 0P7
204/943-7116, Fax: 204/986-4400
Administrator, Heather Guest

**Dance Nova Scotia (DANS)**
#901, 1809 Barrington St., Halifax, NS B3J 3K8
902/422-1749, Fax: 902/422-0881
Email: dance@fox.nstn.ca,
Executive Director, Dianne Milligan
Publications: DANS News, q.; Quarterly Report

**Dance Ontario Association/Association Ontario Danse**
179 Richmond St. West, Toronto, ON M5V 1V3
416/204-1083, Fax: 416/204-1085, Toll Free: 1-800-363-6087
Email: danceont@iComm.ca,
URL: http://www.icomm.ca/danceon
Executive Director, Mimi Beck
General Manager, Rosslyn Jacob-Edwards
Publications: Headlines, bi-m.
Affiliates: Canadian Alliance of Dance Artists

**Dance Oremus Danse (DOD) (1983)**
#6, 510 Jarvis St., Toronto, ON M4Y 2H6
416/928-0208, Fax: 416/925-2543
Artistic Director, Paul Dwyer
General Manager, Peter Stadnyk

**Dance Saskatchewan (1979)**
152 - 2nd Ave. North, PO Box 8789, Saskatoon, SK S7K 6S6
306/931-8480, Fax: 306/244-1520,
Toll Free: 1-800-667-8480
Email: dancesask@sk.sympatico.ca,
Executive Director, Jill Reid
Publications: Footnotes, 5 pa; Youthline; Dance Directory

**Dance Umbrella of Ontario**
#201, 490 Adelaide St. West, Toronto, ON M5V 1Y2
416/504-6429, Fax: 416/504-8702
Email: duodance@interlog.com,
Executive Director, Myles Warren

**DanceArts Vancouver**
#402, 873 Beatty St., Vancouver, BC V6B 2M6
604/606-6425, Fax: 604/606-6432
URL: http://www.msquared/DanceArts/
Artistic Director, Judith Marcuse
Executive Director, Andrew Wilhelm-Boyles
Acting Manager, Kathrin Lake

**Dancecorps**
399 West 5th Ave., Vancouver, BC V5Y 1J6
604/877-1910, Fax: 604/877-1910
Co-Artistic Director, Harvey Meller
Co-Artistic Director, Cornelius Fisher-Credo
General Manager, Jim Smith

**Dancemakers (1974)**
927 Dupont St., Toronto, ON M6H 1Z1
416/535-8880, Fax: 416/535-8929
Email: dncemkrs@interlog.com,
URL: http://www.interlog.com/~dncemkrs/
Artistic Director, Serge Bennathan
General Manager, K. George Wolf
Administrator, Lisanne Gavigan
Publications: Dancemakers News, s-a.

**Dancer Transition Resource Centre/Centre de Ressources pour Danseurs en Transition (1985)**
#202, 66 Gerrard St. East, Toronto, ON M4Y 2R3
416/595-5655, Fax: 416/595-0009
Executive Director, Joysanne Sidimus
President, Karen Kain
Chair, Lynda Hamilton Bronfman
Membership Coordinator, Lisa Frye
Administrator, Janet Sandor
Publications: Dancer Transition Resource Centre Newsletter; Connections: Networking Directory; Dance Life
Affiliates: Canadian Association of Professional Dance Organizations; The Ontario Dance Network; Le Regroupement québécois de la Danse

**Dancer's Studio West**
2007 - 10th Ave. SW, Calgary, AB T3C 0K4
403/244-0950, Fax: 403/243-5178
Artistic Director, Elaine Bowman
Director General, Peter Hoff

**Danny Grossman Dance Company**
511 Bloor St. West, Toronto, ON M5S 1Y4
416/531-8350, Fax: 416/531-1791
Email: dgdance@interlog.com,
Artistic Director, Danny Grossman
General Manager, Jane Marsland

**Danse actuelle Martine Époque**
986, rue Fabre, Longueuil, QC J4J 5A8
514/282-7063
Directrice artistique, Martine Époque

**Danse-Cite inc. (1982)**
#2220, 840, rue Cherrier est, Montréal, QC H2L 1H4
514/525-3595, Téléc: 514/525-6632
Directeur artistique, Daniel Soulières

**Danse Imédia**
1204, Mont-Royal est, Montréal, QC H2J 1Y1
514/526-2201
Directeur artistique, Rafik Sabbagh

**Danse Kalashas**
#27, 6186, av Notre-Dame de Grâce, Montréal, QC H4B 1K8
514/484-3508
Chorégraphe, Richard Tremblay

**Danse Trielle**
CP 1433, Succ. St-Martin, Laval, QC H7V 3P7
514/629-4514
Directrice artistique, Sylvie Samson
Administrateur, Richard Beaupré

**Danstabat**
2456 Pandora St., Vancouver, BC V5K 1V6
604/255-2930
Artistic Director, Chick Snipper
General Manager, Louise Bentall

**Decidedly Jazz Danceworks**
1514 - 4 St. SW, Calgary, AB T2R 0Y4
403/245-3533, Fax: 403/245-3584
Artistic Director, Vicki Adams Willis
General Manager, Kathi Sundstrom

**Desrosiers Dance Theatre (1980)**
#103, 219 Broadview Ave., Toronto, ON M4M 2G3
416/463-5341, Fax: 416/463-4770
Artistic Director, Robert Desrosiers
Publications: Correspondance

**EDAM Performing Arts Society (EDAM)**
303 East 8th Ave., Vancouver, BC V5T 1S1
604/876-9559, Fax: 604/876-9559
Email: edam@bc.sympatico.ca,

Artistic Director, Peter Bingham
General Manager, Mona Hamill
Affiliates: Canadian Association of Professional Dance Organizations

**Fijiwara Dance Inventions**
66 Humewood Dr., Toronto, ON M6C 2W5
416/654-8426
Artistic Director, Denise Fujiwara

**Fondation Jean-Pierre Perreault (1984)**
2022, rue Sherbrooke est, Montréal, QC H2K 1B9
514/525-2464, Téléc: 514/525-0172
Courrier électronique: fjpp@cam.org,
Directeur artistique et chorégraphe, Jean-Pierre Perreault
Directrice générale, Louise Laplante

**Formation de danse Howard Richard**
551, Mont-Royal est, 3e étage, Montréal, QC H2J 1W6
514/527-7770, Téléc: 514/527-7621
Directeur artistique, Howard Richard
Directeur administratif, Charles St-Onge

**Fortier Danse-Création**
CP 605, Succ. C, Montréal, QC H2L 4L5
514/529-8158, Téléc: 514/525-0172
Directeur artistique, Paul-André Fortier
Directeur administratif, Gilles Savary

**Gina Lori Riley Dance Enterprises (1979)**
3277 Sandwich St., Windsor, ON N9C 1A9
519/977-5438, Fax: 519/977-8218
Artistic Director, Gina Lori Riley
Publications: Newsletter, s-a.

**Goh Ballet Society**
2345 Main St., Vancouver, BC V5T 3C9
604/872-4014, Fax: 604/872-4011
Artistic Director, Choo Chiat Goh

**Les Grands Ballets Canadiens (1956)**
Maison de la Danse, 4816, rue Rivard, Montréal, QC H2J 2N6
514/849-8681, Téléc: 514/849-0098
Directeur artistique, Lawrence Rhodes
Directrice général, Alain Dancyger

**Le Groupe de la Place Royale**
#2, 2 Daly St., Ottawa, ON K1N 6E2
613/235-1492, Fax: 613/235-1651
Email: bj581@freenet.carleton.ca,
Artistic Director, Peter Boneham
General Manager & Associate Director, Katherine Watson

**Intempco**
**New Dance Horizons**
#202, 1808 Smith St., Regina, SK S4P 2N4
306/525-5393, Fax: 306/569-4649
Artistic Director, Robin Poitras
Administrative/Production Coordinator, Michael Toppings

**Jocelyne Montpetit Danse**
a/s Gestion artistique Badeaux, 4387, av Christophe-Colomb, Montréal, QC H2J 3G4
514/521-5850, Téléc: 514/521-7157
Directrice artistique, Jocelyne Montpetit

**Julie West Dance Foundation**
#3, 88 MacLaren St., Ottawa, ON K2P 0K6
613/234-4310, Fax: 613/594-8705
Artistic Director, Julie West

**Jumpstart Performance Society (1984)**
6450 Deer Lake Ave., Burnaby, BC V5G 2J3
604/299-4522, Fax: 604/299-7635
Email: jumpsav@netcom.ca,
Artistic Director, Lee Eisler
Office Manager, Jean Hart

**Karen Jamieson Dance Company**
221 East 16th Ave., Vancouver, BC V5T 2T5
604/872-5658, Fax: 604/872-7932
Artistic Director, Karen Jamieson
Managing Director, Jay Rankin, Email: jay_rankin@mindlink.bc.ca

**Kinesis Dance Society**
1773 East 4th Ave., Vancouver, BC V5N 1J9
604/872-0233
Artistic Director, Paras Terezakis

**Kokora Dance Theatre Society**
314 Powell St., Vancouver, BC V6A 1G4
604/662-7441, Fax: 604/683-6649
Artistic Director, Barbara Bourget
Executive Director, Jay Hirabayashi

**Kompany Dance**
#810, 10136 - 100 St., Edmonton, AB T5J 0P1
403/944-9115
Artistic Director, Darold Roles
Artistic Director, Ron Schuster
General Manager, Colette Switzer

**La La La Human Steps**
#206, 5655, av du Parc, Montréal, QC H2V 4H2
514/277-9090, Téléc: 514/277-0862
URL: http://www.bart.nl/~xipe/lalala.htm
Directeur artistique, Édouard Lock
Co-directrice, Marie-Andrée Roussel
Co-directeur, Gilles Pelletier

**Lola MacLaughlin Dance**
#103, 1014 Homer St., Vancouver, BC V6B 2W9
604/683-8240
Artistic Director, Lola MacLaughlin

**Louise Bédard Danse**
a/s de La Femme 100 Têtes, #304, 150, rue Grant, Longueuil, QC J4H 3H6
514/646-6248, Téléc: 514/646-7619
Directrice artistique, Louise Bédard
Directrice générale, Yolaine Gervais

**Lucie Grégoire Danse**
a/s de Diagramme gestion culturelle, #4140, 5505, boul St-Laurent, Montréal, QC H2T 1S6
514/273-7785, Fax: 514/273-8051
Email: diagram@cam.org,
Directrice artistique, Lucie Grégoire

**Manitoba Independent Choreographers Association**
131 Salme Dr., Winnipeg, MB R2M 1Y9
204/255-1048, Fax: 204/255-6499
Gail Petursson-Hiley
Patti Caplette

**Margie Gillis Dance Foundation/Fondation de danse Margie Gillis**
#502, 3575 boul St-Laurent, Montréal, QC H2X 2T7
514/845-3115, Fax: 514/845-3424
Email: lindafoy@oikyinter.com,
Artistic Director, Margie Gillis
Administrative Director, Linda Foy
Publications: Margie Gillis Newsletter, 3 pa

**Mascall Dance**
1130 Jervis St., Vancouver, BC V6E 2C7
604/689-9339, Fax: 604/689-9399
Artistic Director, Jennifer Mascall
General Manager, Jim Smith, Email: jgsmith@wimsey.com

**Menaka Thakkar & Company**
c/o DUO, #201, 490 Adelaide St. West, Toronto, ON M5V 1T2
416/360-6429, Fax: 416/363-8702
Artistic Director, Menaka Thakkar

**Mile Zero Dance Company**
#112, 2315 - 119 St., Edmonton, AB T6G 4E2
403/437-5907, Fax: 403/437-5907
Artistic Director, Deborah Shantz

**Montréal Danse**
300, boul de Maisonneuve est, Montréal, QC H2X 3X6
514/845-2031, Téléc: 514/845-5376
Directrice artistique, Kathy Casey
Directrice générale, Raymonde Gazaille

**Movements**
10053 - 111 St., 6th Fl., Edmonton, AB T5K 2H8
403/488-6745, Fax: 403/488-8713
Artistic Director, Sharlene Thomas
Administrator, Gail Graham

**National Ballet of Canada**
Walter Carsen Centre, 470 Queens Quay West, Toronto, ON M5V 3K4
416/345-9686, Fax: 416/345-8323
Email: info@national.ballet.ca, URL: http://www.national.ballet.ca
Artistic Director, James Kudelka
Executive Director, Valerie Wilder
General Manager, Robert Johnston

**O Vertigo Danse**
4455, de Rouen, Montréal, QC H1V 1H1
514/251-9177, Téléc: 514/251-7358
Directrice artistique, Ginette Laurin
Directrice administrative, Mireille Martin

**Ontario Ballet Theatre**
1133 St. Clair Ave. West, Toronto, ON M6E 1B1
416/656-9568, Fax: 416/651-4803
Executive Director, Sarah Lockett
Artistic Director, Raymond Smith
General Manager, Kally Lloyd-Jones

**Ontario Folk Dance Association (OFDA) (1969)**
22 Latimer Ave., Toronto, ON M5N 2L8
416/489-3566, Info Line: 416/489-1621
Email: kbudd@web.net, URL: http://www.web.net/~ofda
President, Diane Gladstone
Publications: Ontario Folkdancer, 7 pa

**Opéra Atelier (1986)**
**Atelier Theatre Society**
Hazelton Lanes, 87 Avenue Rd., PO Box 343, Toronto, ON M5R 3R9
416/925-3767, Fax: 416/925-4895
Co-Artistic Director, Marshall Pynkoski
Co-Artistic Director, Jeannette Zingg
General Manager, Joan Bosworth

**Paula Moreno Spanish Dance Co.**
c/o DUO, #201, 490 Adelaide St. West, Toronto, ON M5V 1T2
416/504-6429, Fax: 416/504-8702
Artistic Director, Paula Moreno

**Les Productions DancEncorps (1979)**
#13, 140, rue Botsford, Moncton, NB E1C 4X4
506/855-0998, Téléc: 506/852-3401
Courrier électronique: rondupui@nbnet.nb.ca,
Directrice artistique, Chantal Cadieux
Directrice exécutive, Louise Olivier
Publications: JasEncorps, trimestriel

**Red Thunder Cultural Society**
Chadi K'Azi Company
3700 Anderson Rd. SW, PO Box 81, Calgary, AB T2W 3C4
403/281-8410, Fax: 403/281-8460
Artistic Director, Lee Crowchild

**Regroupement québécois de la danse (RQD) (1984)**
#818, 3575, boul St-Laurent, Montréal, QC H2X 2T7
514/849-4003, Téléc: 514/849-3288
Directeur général, Gaétan Patenaude
Publications: Bulletin, semi-annuel; Bulletin Express
Organisation(s) affiliée(s): Agora de la danse; Regroupement québécois des créateurs professionnels

**Royal Academy of Dancing/Canada**
#404, 3284 Yonge St., Toronto, ON M4N 2L6
416/489-2813, Fax: 416/489-3222
Administrator, Jan Garvey

**The Royal Scottish Country Dance Society (RSCDS)**
12 Coates Cres., Edinburgh EH3 7AF Scotland
031/225-3854, Fax: 031/225-7783
Secretary, G.S. Parker
Office Manager, E. Watt

**Royal Winnipeg Ballet (1939)**
380 Graham Ave., Winnipeg, MB R3C 4K2
204/956-0183, Fax: 204/943-1994
Executive Director, Andrew Wilhelm-Boyles
President, Susan J. Glass
School Director, David Moroni
Artistic Director, André Lewis
Publications: Backstage Pass, q.; Ballet-Hoo; Souvenir Program
Affiliates: Canadian Association of Professional Dance Organizations; Association of Performing Arts Presenters; International Society of Performing Arts Administrators

**Les Sortilèges**
6560, rue Chambord, Montréal, QC H2G 3B9
514/274-5655, Téléc: 514/274-7418
Directeur artistique, Jimmy Di Genova
Administratrice, Carmen Millette

**Springboard Dance Collective**
#1420, 700 - 4 Ave. SW, Calgary, AB T2P 3J4
403/237-7452, Fax: 403/237-7452
Artistic Director, Alison Bonney-Gregson
General Manager, Laurie Montemurro

**Square & Round Dance Federation of Nova Scotia (1983)**
RR#1, Cambridge Station, NS B0P 1G0
902/538-9513
Email: buttons@fox.nstn.ca,
Publicity, Harold Redden
Publications: Between Tips, irreg.; Newsletter
Affiliates: Dance Nova Scotia

**Sun Ergos, A Company of Theatre & Dance (1977)**
#2205, 700 - 9th St. SW, Calgary, AB T2P 2B5
403/264-4621, Fax: 403/245-5613, Toll Free: 1-800-743-3351
Email: waltermoke@sunergos.com, URL: http://www.sunergos.com
Artistic Director, Robert Greenwood
Artistic Director, Dana Luebke

**Sursaut inc.**
CP 1591, Sherbrooke, QC J1H 5M4
819/822-8912
Directrice artistique, Francine Châteauvert
Administratrice, Lucie Boulay

**Sylvain Émard Danse**
a/s Diagramme gestion culturelle, #4140, 5505, boul St-Laurent, Montréal, QC H2T 1S6
514/273-7785, Téléc: 514/273-8051
Directeur artistique, Sylvain Émard

**Toronto Dance Theatre (TDT) (1969)**
80 Winchester St., Toronto, ON M4X 1B2
416/967-1365, Fax: 416/963-4379
Email: tdt@interlog.com, URL: http://www.tdt.com
Artistic Director, Christopher House
General Manager, Jini Stolk
Publications: Toronto Dance Theatre Newsletter, q.

**Toronto & District Square & Round Dance Association (1951)**
c/o Ed & Kitty Giles, RR#2, Burnt River, ON K0M 1C0
705/488-2973, Info Line: 416/510-1811
President, Ed Calhoun
Secretary, Ed Giles
Publications: Topics, 10 pa
Affiliates: Canadian Square & Round Dance Society

**Two Planks & a Passion Theatre Association (TP&aP) (1992)**
1212 Main St., PO Box 413, Canning, NS B0P 1H0
902/582-3073, Fax: 902/582-7943
Email: twoplanx@auracom.com,
President, Richard Owen
Vice-President, Susan Wolfraim
Treasurer, Ken Schwartz
Publications: Passion Pages, s-a.
Affiliates: Playwrights Union of Canada

**Vancouver Independent Dance Agency (1985)**
Dance Centre
#400, 873 Beatty St., Vancouver, BC V6B 2M6
604/606-6413, Fax: 604/606-6401
Email: dancentre@vkool.com, URL: http://www.vkool.com/dancentre
Coordinator, Ruth Norgaard
Director, Denis Bergeron
Administrator, Bernard Sauvé
Publications: Dance Central, m.

**Vancouver Moving Theatre (1983)**
523 Main St., PO Box 88270, Vancouver, BC V6A 4A5
604/254-6911, Fax: 604/254-6911
Email: thunter@istar.ca,
Artistic Director, Savannah Walling
General Manager, Terry Hunter

**Vinok Folkdance Ensemble (1988)**
PO Box 4867, Edmonton, AB T6E 5G7
403/454-3739, Fax: 403/454-3436
Email: vinok@planet.eon.net,
Artistic Director, Doyle Marko
Artistic Director, Leanne Koziak

**Wild Excursions Movement Theatre**
#1, 1306 East 18th Ave., Vancouver, BC V5N 1H6
604/873-1631
Artistic Director, Conrad Alexandrowicz

**Zone animée**
5426, rue Casgrain, Montréal, QC H2T 1X2
514/274-3721
Chorégraphe, Nathalie Lamarche
Chorégraphe, Danielle Lecourtois
Chorégraphe, Daniel Éthier

# FLORA & FAUNA

## WILDLIFE, ZOOS & OUTDOOR EDUCATION CENTRES

### Alberta

Calgary Zoo, Botanical Garden & Prehistoric Park, St. George's Island, 1300 Zoo Rd. NE, PO Box 3036, Stn B, Calgary AB T2M 4R8 – 403/232-9300; Fax: 403/237-7582, URL: http://www.cadvision.com/Home_Pages/accounts/calzoo/ – Executive Director, Ian Gray – 136 acres + 320 acre off-site breeding & conservation facility; educational & adopt-an-animal programs; gift shop; open year round

Edmonton: Valley Zoo, PO Box 2359, Edmonton AB T5J 2R7 – 403/496-6912; Fax: 403/944-7529 – Director, Linda D.M. Cochrane

Patricia: Dinosaur Provincial Park, PO Box 60, Patricia AB T0J 2K0 – 403/378-4342; Fax: 403/378-4247, URL: http://www.gov.ab.ca/~env/nrs/dinosaur/

Rocky Mountain House: Sleepy Valley Game Farm, RR#1, Rocky Mountain House AB T0M 1T0 – 403/845-6357 – Open July & Aug.

### British Columbia

Aldergrove: Vancouver Game Farm, 5048 - 264th St., Aldergrove BC V4W 1N7 – 604/856-6825; Fax: 604/857-9008; Info Line: 604/857-9005 – C. Kwon

Duncan: Cowichan & Chemainus Valleys Ecomuseum, PO Box 491, Duncan BC V9L 4T8 – 250/746-1611; Fax: 250/748-3509 – Executive Director, Wilma Wood

Kamloops Wildlife Park, PO Box 698, Kamloops BC V2C 5L7 – 250/573-3242; Fax: 250/573-2406; Email: wildlife@kamloops.net – General Manager, Rob Purdy – Vertebrate collection; conservation, education & recreation

Kelowna: Speedwell Bird Sanctuary, PO Box 144, Kelowna BC V1Y 7N3 – 250/766-2081; Fax: 250/766-0617 – Dan Bruce

North Vancouver: Maplewood Farm, 405 Seymour River Pl., North Vancouver BC V7H 1S6 – 250/929-5610; Fax: 250/929-9341; Email: johnstoa@worksyard.district.north-van.bc.ca

Penticton: Okanagan Game Farm, PO Box 100, Penticton BC V2A 6J9 – 250/497-5405; Fax: 250/497-6145

Vancouver: Stanley Park Wildlife Services Dept., 2099 Beach Ave., Vancouver BC V6G 1Z4 – 604/257-8528; Fax: 604/257-8378 – Manager, Wildlife Services, Mike Mackintosh

### Manitoba

Rennie: Alfred Hole Goose Sanctuary, Rennie MB R0E 1R0 – 204/369-5470 (summer); 369-5258 (winter); Fax: 204/369-5341 – Park Manager, Mark Clarke – Visitor Centre interprets the history of the site as well as the biology of geese; summer program features hands-on activities

Thompson Recreation Zoo, 275 Thompson Dr. North, Thompson MB R8N 0C3 – 204/677-7982; Fax: 204/677-4854 – Ray Johnson – Open year round

Winnipeg: Assiniboine Park Zoo, 2355 Corydon Ave., Winnipeg MB R3P 0R5 – 204/986-6921; Fax: 204/832-5420; Email: apzoowpg@escape.ca, URL: http://www.mbnet.mb.ca./city/parks/envserv/zoo/zoo.html – Director, Douglas Ross

### New Brunswick

Edmundston: Ferme Aqua Zoo, St-Jacques, RR#3, Edmundston NB E3V 3K5 – 506/739-9149

Lamèque Zoo, Lamèque NB E0B 1V0 – 506/344-7214, 7343

Moncton: Magnetic Hill Zoo, c/o City of Moncton, Community Services Dept., 655 Main St., Moncton

NB E1C 1E8 – 506/384-9381; Fax: 506/853-3569; Email: bruce.dougan@moncton.org – Manager, Bruce Dougan

Saint John: Cherry Brook Zoo, Sandy Point Rd., RR#1, Saint John NB E2L 3W2 – 506/634-1440; Fax: 506/634-0717

Upper Kingsclear: Woolastook Recreation Park, 5171 Rt. 2, Upper Kingsclear NB L3E 1P4 – 506/363-5410; Fax: 506/363-5406; Email: woola@nbnet.nb.ca – Stephan Bartlett – Recreational park: campground nightly & seasonally, waterslides, hiking & biking trails, mini golf, picnic park

### Newfoundland

Glovertown: Terra Nova National Park, Glovertown NF A0G 2L0 – 709/533-2801; Fax: 709/533-2706; Email: christine_pike@pch.gc.ca – Supt., Heather Maclellan

Holyrood: Salmonier Nature Park, PO Box 190, Holyrood NF A0A 2R0 – 709/729-6974; Fax: 709/229-7888

### Nova Scotia

Aylesford: Oaklawn Farm, Aylesford NS B0P 1C0 – 902/847-9790 – Open Easter - autumn

### Ontario

Bowmanville Zoological Park, 340 King St. East, Bowmanville ON L1C 3K5 – 905/623-5655; Fax: 905/623-9675 – Co-Director, Leslie Pon Tell – Canada's oldest operating zoo, featuring Animal Kingdom shows, elephant rides, restaurant & gift shop; open May - Sept.

Cambridge: African Lion Safari & Game Farm, RR#1, Cambridge ON N1R 5S2 – 519/623-2620; Fax: 519/623-9542, URL: http://www.lionsafari.com/ – General Manager, Mike Takacs – Open Apr. - Oct.

Cherry Valley: The Exotarium, c/o The Reptile Breeding Foundation, PO Box 17, Cherry Valley ON K0K 1P0 – 613/476-7710 (May - Oct.); Email: tomhuff@blvl.igs.net – Owner, Tom Huff – Rare & endangered reptiles, amphibians & invertebrates

Earlton Zoo, PO Box 430, Earlton ON P0J 1E0 – 705/563-8300; Fax: 705/563-2200 – Pierre Belanger – Over 40 species represented; petting zoo; playground; guided tours; snack bar; open May - Oct.

Gananoque: 1000 Islands Wild Kingdom, 855 Stone St. North, Gananoque ON K7G 1Z6 – 613/382-7141

Guelph: Kortright Waterfowl Park, 305 Niska Rd., Guelph ON N1H 6J3 – 519/824-6729 – Open March - Oct. on weekends & statutory holidays

Kingsville: Jack Miner's Bird Sanctuary, PO Box 39, Kingsville ON N9Y 2E8 – 519/733-4034

Morrisburg: Upper Canada Migratory Bird Sanctuary, Parks of the St. Lawrence, RR#1, Morrisburg ON K0C 1X0 – 613/543-3704; Fax: 613/543-2847 – Parks Operations Coordinator, Rod Davidson

North York: Kortright Centre for Conservation, c/o Metro Region Conservation Authority, 5 Shoreham Dr., North York ON M3N 1S4 – 416/832-2289; Fax: 416/832-8238; Email: kcc@interlog.com, URL: http://www.kortright.org – Multimedia Coordinator, Bryan L. Davies

Orono: Jungle Cat World Inc., 3667 Conc. 6, RR#1, Orono ON L0B 1M0 – 905/983-5016; Fax: 905/983-9858; Email: jungle@netrover.com, URL: http://www.jungle.com – President, Wolfram H. Klose

Peterborough: Riverview Park & Zoo, Peterborough Utilities Commission, PO Box 4125, Peterborough ON K9J 6Z5 – 705/748-9300, ext.303; Fax: 705/745-6866

Scarborough: Metro Toronto Zoo, 361A Old Finch Ave., Scarborough ON M1B 5K7 – 416/392-5900; Fax: 416/392-5934, URL: http://www.torontozoo.com – General Manager, Calvin J. White – Open year round

St Catharines: Happy Rolph Bird Sanctuary & Children's Farm, c/o St Catharines Parks & Recreation Dept., PO Box 3012, St Catharines ON L2R 7C2 – 905/937-7210

Thunder Bay: Chippewa Park Zoo, c/o Parks & Recreation Dept., 950 Memorial Ave., Thunder Bay ON P7B 4A2 – 807/623-3463, 625-2351

Toronto: High Park Menagerie, c/o Parks & Recreation, City Hall, Toronto ON M5H 2N2 – 416/392-7251

Toronto: Riverdale Farm, Riverdale Park, c/o Dept. of Parks & Recreation, City Hall, 201 Winchester St., Toronto ON M5H 2N2 – 416/392-7251

Toronto Islands Park Farm, c/o Metro Toronto Parks & Culture, 55 John St., 24th Fl., Toronto ON M5V 3C6 – 416/392-8196; Fax: 416/392-8379

### Québec

Bonaventure: Jardin Zoologique de Bonaventure, CP 428, Bonaventure QC G0C 1E0 – 418/534-3410 – Director, Bernard Arsenault

Charlesbourg: Jardin Zoologique du Québec, 9300, av de la Faune, Charlesbourg QC G1G 4G4 – 418/622-0313; Fax: 418/644-9004, URL: http://www.spsnq.qc.ca/zoo.html – Biologiste, Christian Potvin – Open year round

Granby: Jardin Zoologique de Granby, 525, rue St-Hubert, Granby QC J2G 5P3 – 514/372-9113; Fax: 514/372-5531; Email: zoo@granby.mtl.net, URL: http://www.econoroute.com/montreal/granby/zoo.htm – Directeur Général, Mario Limoges – Open mid-May - Oct. (Thanksgiving Day)

Hemmingford: Parc Safari Africain (Québec) Inc., 850, rte 202, Hemmingford QC J0L 1H0 – 514/247-2727

Maskinongé: Zoo de St. Édouard-Maskinongé, 3381, rte 248 ouest, Maskinongé QC J0K 2H0 – 819/268-5150; Fax: 819/268-5150

Sherbrooke: Parc Plateau, av du Parc/Terrill, CP 610, Sherbrooke QC J1H 5H9 – 819/821-5500

St-Félicien: Jardin Zoologique de St-Félicien, 2230, boul du Jardin, CP 90, St-Félicien QC G8K 2P8 – 418/679-0543; Fax: 418/679-3647 – Directeur général, Martin Laforge

Ste-Anne-de-Bellevue: Ecomuseum, 21125, ch Sainte-Marie, Ste-Anne-de-Bellevue QC H9X 3L2 – 514/457-9449; Fax: 514/457-0769; Email: ecomus@total.net – Open year round

### Saskatchewan

Regina: Ipsco Wild Life Park & Pool, PO Box 1670, Regina SK S4P 3C7 – 306/949-4360 – Park Manager, Fred Hannah

Regina: Wascana Waterfowl Park, Wascana Centre, Lakeshore Dr., PO Box 7111, Regina SK S4P 3S7 – 306/522-3661; Fax: 306/565-2742 – Executive Director, J.B. Paterson

Saskatoon: Forestry Farm Park & Zoo, 1903 Forest Dr., Saskatoon SK S7S 1G9 – 306/975-3382 – Open year round

## AQUARIA

### British Columbia

Cowichan Bay: Marine Ecology Station, RR#1, Cowichan Bay BC V0R 1N0 – 250/748-4522; Fax: 250/748-4410; Email: mareco@island.net, URL: http://www.island.net/~mareco/ – Director, Dr. Bill Austin

Vancouver Aquarium, Stanley Park, PO Box 3232, Vancouver BC V6B 3X8 – 604/685-3364; Fax: 604/631-2529; Email: communications@vanaqua.org; Info Line: 604/682-1118, URL: http://www.vancouver-aquarium.org – Executive Director, Dr. John Nightingale

Victoria: Pacific Undersea Gardens, 490 Belleville St., Victoria BC V8V 1W9 – 250/382-5717; Fax: 250/382-5210 – Manager, Maxine Becker

Victoria: Undersea Gardens of Victoria, Inner Harbour, 490 Belleville St., Victoria BC V8V 1W9 – 250/382-5717; Fax: 250/598-1361

### Manitoba

Winnipeg: Resolute Bay Aquarium, c/o H. Welch, Fisheries & Oceans Canada, 501 University Cres., Winnipeg MB R3T 2N6 – 204/983-5132; Fax: 204/984-2404 – Open summers

### New Brunswick

Shippagan: Aquarium et Centre Marin de Shippagan, CP 1010, Shippagan NB E0B 2P0 – 506/336-3013; Fax: 506/336-3057; Email: aquarium@gov.nb.ca – Directeur, Clarence LeBreton

St. Andrews: Huntsman Marine Science Centre, Brandy Cove Road, St. Andrews NB E0G 2X0 – 506/529-1200; Fax: 506/529-1212; Email: huntsman@nbnet.nb.ca, URL: http://www.unb.ca/web/huntsman – Executive Director, Dr. John H. Allen – Founded in 1969 with the cooperation of universities & the federal government; includes a public aquarium/museum with local flora & fauna, & the Atlantic Reference Centre which houses a zoological & botanical museum reference collection; research & teaching in marine sciences & coastal biology; marine education courses for elementary, high school & university groups

### Newfoundland

St. John's: The Fluvarium, Nagle's Place, Box 5, St. John's NF A1B 2Z2 – 709/754-FISH; Fax: 709/754-5947 – Executive Director, Pamela Karasek

### Ontario

Niagara Falls: Marineland, 7657 Portage Rd., Niagara Falls ON L2E 6X8 – 905/356-8250; Fax: 905/374-6652 – President, John Heler – Open April 1 - Oct. 15

### Prince Edward Island

Charlottetown: PEI Marine Aquarium Ltd., 68 Queen St., Charlottetown PE C1A 7K7 – 902/892-2203 – V.E. Williams – Open June - Sept.

### Québec

Ste-Flavie: Centre d'Interpretation du Saumon Atlantique, 900, rte de la Mer, Ste-Flavie QC G0J 2L0 – 418/775-2969; Fax: 418/775-9466 – Jean Marc Vincent – Open June - mid-Oct.

Ste-Foy: Aquarium du Québec, 1675, av des Hôtels, Ste-Foy QC G1W 4S3 – 418/659-5266; Fax: 418/646-9238 – Directeur, André Martel – Open year round

### Saskatchewan

Fort Qu'Appelle: Fish Culture Station, PO Box 190, Fort Qu'Appelle SK S0G 1S0 – 306/332-3200 – R. Kidd

## BOTANICAL GARDENS

### Alberta

Brooks: Golden Prairie Arboretum, Alberta Agriculture, Food & Rural Development, SS#4, Brooks AB T1R 1E6 – 403/362-1300; Fax: 403/362-1306; Email: murray@agric.gov.ab.ca – Dr., Christine Murray – Collection of deciduous trees & shrubs

Calgary: Devonian Gardens, Level 4, Toronto-Dominion Square, 317 - 7 Ave. SW, Calgary AB T2P 2Y9 – 403/221-4560; Fax: 403/221-4581; Email: dkroeker@gov.calgary.ab.ca – Supervisor, David Kroeker – 2.5 acre indoor park; 138 varieties of greenery; available for private functions; open daily 9 am - 9 pm; admission free

Edmonton: Devonian Botanic Garden of the University of Alberta, University of Alberta, Edmonton AB T6G 2E1 – 403/987-3054; Fax: 403/987-4141, URL: http://www.discoveredmonton.com/devonian/dbg.html – Director, Dr. Dale Vitt – 80 acres of cultivated gardens & 110 acres of natural area; native & alpine plants, ecological reserves, the Kurimoto Japanese Garden & a Butterly House; picnic area, concession & gift shop; open daily May - mid-Oct.

Edmonton: Muttart Conservatory, 98 Ave. & 96A St., Edmonton AB T6C 3Z8 – 403/496-8755; Fax: 403/496-8747 – Director, David Schneider – Four pyramids house flora of different climates, including arid, temperate, & tropical environments; 2,000 species of orchids; outdoor trial gardens in summer

Glenevis: George Pegg Botanic Garden, General Delivery, Glenevis AB T0E 0X0 – 403/785-2421 – President, R. Peterson

High Level: Boreal Botanic Garden, PO Box 1106, High Level AB T0H 1Z0 – 403/926-4697; Fax: 403/926-3442 – Jorden Johnston

Lethbridge: Nikka Yuko Japanese Gardens, c/o Lethbridge & District Japanese Garden Society, PO Box 751, Lethbridge AB T1J 3Z6 – 403/328-3511; Fax: 403/328-0511 – General Manager, Denise B. Stephen – Open spring, summer, fall

Olds College Arboretum, Olds College, Olds AB T0M 1P0

Trochu Arboretum & Gardens, PO Box 340, Trochu AB T0M 2C0 – 403/442-2111; Fax: 403/442-2528 – President, Henrietta Peterson – Open Victoria Day to Thanksgiving

## British Columbia

100 Mile House Demonstration Forest, c/o South Cariboo Chamber of Commerce, 422 Cariboo Hwy. 97 South, PO Box 2312, 100 Mile House BC V0K 2E0 – 250/395-5353; Fax: 250/395-4085; Email: sccofc@netshop.net, URL: http://www.netshop.net/~100mile/sccofc/html – Manager, Kathy McKenzie

Burnaby: Simon Fraser University Arboretum, Dept. of Biological Sciences, Simon Fraser University, Burnaby BC V5A 1S6

Chilliwack: Minter Gardens, 52892 Bunker Rd., Rosedale, PO Box 40, Chilliwack BC V2P 6H7 – 604/794-7191; Fax: 604/792-8893; Email: bminter@minter.org, URL: http://www.minter.org – Brian & Faye Minter – Open Apr. - Oct.

Kimberley: Cominco Gardens, PO Box 144, Kimberley BC V1A 2Y5 – 250/428-5311; Fax: 250/427-5252

Nanaimo: Grant Ainscough Arboretum & McMillan Bloedell Restoration Centre, 65 Front St., Nanaimo BC V9R 5H9 – 250/755-3467; Fax: 250/755-3464 – Liz Kline – Open year round

North Vancouver: Park & Tilford Gardens, Park & Tilford Centre, #440, 333 Brookbank Ave., North Vancouver BC V7J 3S8 – 604/984-8200; Fax: 604/984-6099 – Garden Director, Todd Major

Prince George: David Douglas Botanical Garden Society, PO Box 1305, Prince George BC V2M 2S3

Richmond: Fantasy Garden World, 10800 No. 5 Rd., Richmond BC V7A 4E5

Surrey: Green Timbers, 9800A - 140th St., Surrey BC V3T 4M5 – 604/582-7170

Vancouver: Bloedel Conservatory, Queen Elizabeth Park, c/o Sunset Nursery, 290 - 51 Ave. East, Vancouver BC V5X 1C5 – 604/257-8584; Fax: 604/257-2412 – Manager, Alex M. Downie – Canada's largest single-structure tropical conservatory featuring over 500 species in simulated rain-forest, subtropic & desert environments; also features tropical birds, parrots & a Japanese Koi fish collection

Vancouver: Dr. Sun Yat-Sen Classical Chinese Garden, 578 Carrall St., Vancouver BC V6B 5K2 – 604/662-3207; Fax: 604/682-4008; Email: sunyatsen@bc.sympatico.ca, URL: http://www.discovervancouver.com/sun – Executive Director, Heather O'Hagan – The first authentic, full-scale Chinese garden built outside China

Vancouver: Nitobe Memorial Garden, University of British Columbia, 1903 West Mall, Vancouver BC V6T 1Z4 – 604/822-6038; Fax: 604/822-2016; Email: blaine@unixg.ubc.ca, URL: http://www.hedgerows.com – Director, Bruce Macdonald – Authentic Japanese tea & stroll garden; cherry blossoms; Japanese Irises, Japanese Maples; Koi; lanterns & much more

Vancouver: Queen Elizabeth Arboretum, 2099 Beach Ave., Vancouver BC V6G 1Z4 – 604/873-1133 – Trades Foreman, T. Mathot

Vancouver: UBC Botanical Garden, University of British Columbia, 6804 Southwest Marine Dr., Vancouver BC V6T 1W5 – 604/822-4208, 6038; Fax: 604/822-2016; Email: blaine@unixg.ubc.ca, URL: http://www.hedgerows.com – Director, Bruce Macdonald – Living museum of plants in 70 acres; over 10,000 assorted trees, shrubs, flowers; divided into various components

Vancouver: VanDusen Botanical Garden, 5251 Oak St., Vancouver BC V6M 4H1 – 604/878-9274; Fax: 604/266-4326 – Curator, Roy Forster – Open year round

Victoria: The Butchart Gardens Ltd., PO Box 4010, Victoria BC V8X 3X4 – 250/652-4422; Fax: 250/652-3883; Email: email@butchartgardens.bc.ca; Info line: 604/652-2422, URL: http://butchartgardens.bc.ca/ – The Butchart/Ross family – Open year round

Victoria: The Crystal Garden, 713 Douglas St., Victoria BC V8W 2B4 – 250/381-1213, 1277; Fax: 250/383-1218; Email: crystal@islandnet.com – Open year round

Victoria: Douglas Fir Arboretum, c/o Research Division, BC Forest Service, Victoria BC V8V 1X5

Victoria: Horticulture Centre of the Pacific, 505 Quayle Rd., Victoria BC V8X 3X1

## Manitoba

Boisevain: International Peace Garden, PO Box 419, Boisevain MB R0K 0E0 – 204/534-2510; Fax: 204/701/263-4390

Morden Arboretum, Agriculture Canada Research Centre, Unit 100-101, Rte. 100, Morden MB R6M 1Y5 – 204/822-4471; Fax: 204/822-6841; Email: cdavidson@em.agr.ca – Dr. Campbell G. Davidson

Portage La Prairie: Island Park Arboretum, Parks Division, 97 Saskatchewan Ave. East, Portage La Prairie MB R1N 0L8

Winnipeg: Assiniboine Park, 2799 Roblin Blvd., Winnipeg MB R3R 0B8 – 204/986-2675; Fax: 204/832-7134, URL: http://www.mbnet.mb.ca/city/parks/ – Manager of Park & Open Space, City of Winnipeg Parks & Recreation, Don Budinsky – Includes Conservatory, English Garden, 280 ha forest

Winnipeg: Woody Plant Test Arboretum, Dept. of Plant Science, University of Manitoba, Winnipeg MB R3T 2N2

## New Brunswick

Fredericton Botanic Garden, PO Box 57, Stn A, Fredericton NB E3B 4Y2

Saint-Jacques: New Brunswick Botanical Gardens, Main St., Saint-Jacques NB E0L 1K0 – 506/739-6335 – Opened 1993; 22 acres

## Newfoundland

St. John's: The Memorial University Botanical Garden at Oxen Pond, c/o Memorial University, St. John's NF A1C 5S7 – 709/737-8590; Fax: 709/737-8596; Email: mbishop@morgan.ucs.mun.ca, URL: http://www.mun.ca/botgarden – Director, Dr. K. Wilf Nicholls – Open May - Nov.

## Nova Scotia

Annapolis Royal Historic Gardens, 441 Saint George St., PO Box 278, Annapolis Royal NS B0S 1A0 – 902/532-7018 – Theme gardens, collections & displays reflect historical periods - Open May - Oct.

Halifax Public Gardens, c/o Parks, Natural Services, Halifax Regional Municipality, PO Box 1749, Stn Armdale, Halifax NS B3S 3A5 – 902/421-6551 – General Manager, Parks, Natural Services, Stephen King – Formal Victorian Garden, located at Summer St. & Spring Garden Rd.

## Ontario

Guelph: The Arboretum, University of Guelph, Guelph ON N1G 2W1 – 519/824-4120, ext. 2113; Fax: 519/763-9598; Email: bhealy@uoguelph.ca, URL: http://www.uoguelph.ca/~arboretu – Director, Prof. Alan Watson Email: awatson@uoguelph.ca – Environmental education activities; plant collections; evaluation of flora

Hamilton: Centre for Canadian Historical Horticultural Studies, Royal Botanical Gardens, PO Box 399, Hamilton ON L8N 3H8 – 905/527-1158; Fax: 905/577-0375; Email: brownlee@rbg.ca – Contact, Linda Brownlee 905/527-1158, ext.246

Hamilton: Royal Botanical Gardens, PO Box 399, Hamilton ON L8N 3H8 – 905/527-1158; Fax: 905/577-0375 – Director, Sharilyn Ingram

Kakabeka Falls: Lauber Arboretum, RR#1, Kakabeka Falls ON P0T 1W0 – 807/475-5330 – Laura Sitch – 20+ species of trees, mostly near natives

London: Sherwood Fox Arboretum, University of Western Ontario, Richmond St. North, London ON N6A 5B7 – 519/679-2111, ext. 6506 – James B. Phipps

Miller Lake: Larkwhistle Garden, RR#1, Miller Lake ON N0H 1Z0

Mississauga: Eridale College Arboretum, Erindale College, Mississauga Rd. North, Mississauga ON L5L 1C6

Niagara Parks Botanical Gardens & School of Horticulture, c/o Niagara Parks Commission, PO Box 150, Niagara Falls ON L2E 6T2 – 905/356-8554; Fax: 905/356-5488, URL: http://www.npbg.org – Director, Deborah Whitehouse – Includes the Niagara Parks Butterfly Conservatory

North York: Edwards Gardens, Civic Garden Centre, 777 Lawrence Ave. E, North York ON M3C 1P2 – 416/397-1340; Fax: 416/397-1354 – The garden information centre

Rexdale: Humber Arboretum, 205 Humber College Blvd., Rexdale ON M9W 5L7 – 416/675-6622, ext.4661; Fax: 416/675-9730; Email: bodwort@admin.humberc.on.ca – Director, Stephen Bodsworth

Ridgetown: J.J. Neilson Arboretum, Ridgetown College, University of Guelph, Ridgetown ON N0P 2C0 – 519/674-1628; Fax: 519/674-1600; Email: knentwig@ridgetownc.uoguelph.ca, URL: http://www.ridgetownc.on.ca/arboretum – Coordinator, Ken Nentwig – Includes upwards of 500 taxa., including Carolinian trees & shrubs, & collections of Viburnum & Dogwood, along with perennial & annual displays, & theme landscape areas

Ruthven: Colasanti Tropical Gardens & Petting Farm, PO Box 40, Ruthven ON N0P 2G0 – 519/326-3287; Fax: 519/322-2302; Email: colasanti@mnsi.net – Joe Colasanti – Over 10 greenhouses filled with tropical plants; outdoor maze & cactus garden

Sault Ste Marie: Great Lakes Forestry Centre Arboretum, Canadian Forest Service, PO Box 490, Sault Ste Marie ON P6A 5M7 – 705/949-9461;

Fax: 705/759-5700; Email: dkennington@fcor.glfc.forestry.ca – Arboretum Manager, D.J. Kennington

Sebringville: Brickman Botanical Garden, RR#1, Sebringville ON N0K 1X0

St Catharines: Walker Botanic Garden, Rodman Hall Arts Centre, 109 St. Paul Cres., St Catharines ON L2S 1M3

Sudbury: Laurentian University Arboretum, Ramsey Lake Rd., Sudbury ON P3E 2C6

Thunder Bay: Centennial Conservatory, c/o Parks & Recreation Dept., 1601 Dease St. North, Thunder Bay ON P7B 4A2 – 807/662-7036; Fax: 807/622-7602 – Open year round, 1-4 daily

Thunder Bay: International Friendship Garden, Parks Division, Victoriaville Civic Centre, 111 South Syndicate Ave., Thunder Bay ON P7E 6S4 – 807/625-3166; Fax: 807/625-3258 – Coordinator, Parks Services, Don Vezina

Thunder Bay: Lakehead University Arboretum, c/o Lakehead University, 955 Oliver Rd., Thunder Bay ON P7B 5E1 – 807/343-8624; Fax: 807/343-8116 – Nancy Luckai – Open year round

Toronto: Allan Gardens Conservatory, 19 Horticultural Ave., Toronto ON M5A 2P2 – 416/392-7288; Fax: 416/392-0318; Email: ckennedy@city.toronto.on.ca, URL: http://www.city.toronto.on.ca – Supt., Chris Kennedy

Whitby: Cullen Gardens, RR #2, 300 Taunton Rd. West, Whitby ON L1N 5R5 – 416/294-7965, 668-6606

Windsor: Fogolar Furlan Botanic Garden, 1800 E.C. Row, North Service Rd., Windsor ON N8W 1Y3

Windsor: Jackson Park Queen Elizabeth II Garden, c/o Parks & Recreation Dept., 2450 McDougall Rd., Windsor ON N8X 3N6 – 519/255-6276; Fax: 519/255-7990, URL: http://www.city.windsor.on.ca – Commissioner, Lloyd Burridge

## Prince Edward Island

Kensington: Malpeque Gardens, RR#1, Blue Heron Dr., Kensington PE C0B 1M0 – George MacKay – Open June 15 - Aug. 15

## Québec

Mont-Joli: Les Jardins de Métis, PO Box 242, Mont-Joli QC G5H 3L1 – 418/775-2221; Fax: 418/775-6201 – Directeur, Alexander Reford

Montréal: Jardin botanique de Montréal, 4101, rue Sherbrooke est, Montréal QC H1X 2B2 – 514/872-1400; Fax: 514/872-3765 – Director, Gilles Vincent – Collection of 21,000 plant species & varieties, 10 exhibition greenhouses & 30 thematic gardens from around the world; centre covers 75 hectares

Otter Lake: Belle Terre Botanic Garden & Arboretum, Otter Lake QC J0X 2P0

Ste-Anne-de-Bellevue: Morgan Arboretum, Macdonald College, McGill University, PO Box 500, Ste-Anne-de-Bellevue QC H8X 3Z9 – 514/398-7811 – Director, Eric R. Thompson

Ste-Foy: Jardin Roger-Van den Hende, Universite Laval, Pavillon de L'Envirotron, Ste-Foy QC G1K 7P4 – 418/656-3410; Fax: 418/656-7871; Email: patrice.belanger@crh.u/aua/.ca – Open April - Oct.; free admission

## Saskatchewan

Estevan: Shand Greenhouse, PO Box 280, Estevan SK S4A 2A3 – 306/634-5413; Fax: 306/634-6682; Email: shand.greenhouse@awinc.com – Manager, Debbie Nielsen – Greenhouse, shade houses, nursery, display area; uses by-products of energy generation from the Shand Power Station - Open year round

Indian Head: Prairie Farm Rehabilitation Administration, Hwys. 1 & 56, PO Box 940, Indian Head SK S0G 2K0 – 306/695-2284; Fax: 306/695-2568; Email: pf21802@pfra.gc.ca – Manager, Dr. J.A.G. Howe – Arboretum, nursery, horticultural displays - Open daily

Saskatoon: Patterson Garden, Dept. of Horticulture Science, University of Saskatchewan, 51 Campus Dr., Saskatoon SK S7N 5A8 – 306/966-5855; Fax: 306/966-8106, URL: http://www.ag.usask.ca/cofa/depts/hlsc.html – M.D. Devine

# SECTION 7

## BUSINESS & FINANCE DIRECTORY




**See ADDENDA at the back of this book for late changes & additional information.**


## DOMESTIC BANKS

**See Index for Bank of Canada, and the Federal Business Development Bank, which are Crown Corporations, listed in the Government Section.**

Chartered banks in Canada are incorporated by letters patent and are governed by the Bank Act which establishes the legislative framework for Canada's banking system.

The Bank Act provides for the incorporation of two classes of banks. Schedule I banks are those banks in which no one shareholder or group of associated shareholders owns more than 10 per cent of any class of shares of the bank. Schedule II banks are closely held by foreign banks or other eligible financial institutions. Schedule I and Schedule II banks have the same general powers, restrictions and obligations under the Bank Act.

Foreign banks are permitted to incorporate "foreign bank subsidiaries" under the Bank Act, and to commence business in Canada on the basis of reciprocal treatment for Canadian banks. Foreign bank subsidiaries are Schedule II banks under the Bank Act.

The Bank Act provides that banks have the power of a natural person and may engage in or carry on the business of banking, including the authority to provide any financial service; lend money, and make advances, with or without security; issue subordinated debentures, subject to terms and conditions; hold and deal with real property; take and set conditions for realization on security; pay interest on a debt payable to a bank and charge interest on a loan, advance or any debt or liability of the bank; and subject to terms and conditions, engage in financial leasing and factoring, venture capital and data processing.

The Bank Act embodies many provisions designed for the protection of creditors and shareholders including requirements related to minimum capital adequacy, shareholders' audits by public accountants and government inspection.

### Office of the Superintendent of Financial Institutions/Bureau du Surintendant des Institutions Financières

Kent Sq., 255 Albert St., Ottawa ON K1A 0H2
613/990-7788; Fax: 613/952-8219; Toll Free: 1-800-385-8647
Superintendent, John Palmer

### Canadian Banking Ombudsman

#1602, 4950 Yonge St., North York ON M2N 6K1
416/287-2877; Toll Free: 1-888-451-4519; Toll Free Fax: 1-888-422-2865; Email: canadianbankingombudsman@sympatico.ca
Ombudsman, Michael Lauber

### SCHEDULE I BANKS

Bank of Montreal/Banque de Montréal
129, rue St-Jacques ouest, Montréal QC H2Y 1L6
514/877-1285; Fax: 514/877-6922; Toll Free: 1-800-555-3000
URL: http://www.bmo.com
CEO, Matthew W. Barrett
Toronto Executive Offices: First Canadian Place, 100 King St. West, Toronto ON M5X 1A1: 416/867-5000; Fax: 416/927-2710: Email: info@bmo.com
Revenue: $1,700,000,000; Assets: $185,900,000,000 (January 31, 1997)
Number of Branches: 1,292

The Bank of Nova Scotia/La Banque de Nouvelle-Écosse
Scotia Plaza, 44 King St. West, Toronto ON M5H 1H1
416/866-6161; Fax: 416/866-3750; Telex: WUI6719400
Email: email@Scotiabank.ca; URL: http://www.scotiabank.ca
CEO, Peter C. Godsoe
Revenue: $5,400,000,000; Assets: $168,700,000,000 (January 31, 1997)
Number of Branches: 1,146

Canadian Imperial Bank of Commerce/Banque de commerce canadienne imperiale
Commerce Court, PO Box 1, Stn Commerce Court, Toronto ON M5L 1A2
416/980-2211; Fax: 416/368-8843
URL: http://www.cibc.com
CEO, A.L. Flood
Revenue: $14,800,000,000; Assets: $199,000,000,000 (1996)

Canadian Western Bank/Banque Canadienne de l'Ouest
#2300, 10303 Jasper Ave., Edmonton AB T5J 3X6
403/423-8888; Fax: 403/423-8897
URL: http://www.cwbank.com
President/CEO, Larry M. Pollock
Revenue: $145,000,000; Assets: $1,800,000,000 (October 31, 1996)
Number of Branches: 21

National Bank of Canada/Banque Nationale du Canada
600, rue de La Gauchetière ouest, Montréal QC H3B 4L2
514/394-5000; Fax: 514/394-8434
URL: http://www.nbc.ca/
Chair/CEO, André Bérard
Toronto Administrative Offices: #200, 150 York St., Toronto ON M5H 3A9: 416/864-9080; Fax: 416/864-7819
Revenue: $4,200,000,000; Assets: $53,100,000,000 (October 31, 1996)
Number of Branches: 632

Royal Bank of Canada
1, Place Ville Marie, CP 6001, Succ A, Montréal QC H3C 3A9
514/874-2110; Fax: 514/874-6582; Telex: 055-61086
URL: http://www.royalbank.com
Chair/CEO, John E. Cleghorn
Toronto Executive Offices: Royal Bank Plaza, Lower Concourse, PO Box 1, Stn Royal Bank, Toronto ON M5J 2J5: 416/974-5151; Fax: 416/974-0135; Toll Free: 1-800-263-9191
Assets: $234,400,000,000 (January 31, 1997)
Number of Branches: 1,487

The Toronto-Dominion Bank
TD Centre, PO Box 1, Stn Toronto-Dominion, Toronto ON M5K 1A2
416/982-8222; Toll Free 1-800-387-2092; Telex: 06524267
Email: tdinfo@tdbank.ca; URL: http://www.tdbank.ca
President/CEO, A.C. Bailie
Revenue: $9,100,000,000; Assets: $125,600,000,000 (1996)
Number of Branches: 953

## SCHEDULE II BANKS

Citizens Bank of Canada
#401, 815 West Hastings St., Vancouver BC V6C 1B4
604/682-7171; Fax: 604/708-7858; Toll Free: 1-888-708-7800
Email: service@citizensbank.ca; URL: http://www.citizens.com
CEO, Linda C. Crompton

Laurentian Bank of Canada/Banque Laurentienne du Canada
#1585, 1981, av McGill College, Montréal QC H3A 3K3
514/284-3921; Fax: 514/284-2426
URL: http://www.laurentianbank.com
President/CEO, Henri-Paul Rousseau
Revenue: $429,600,000; Assets: $12,500,000,000 (October 31, 1996)
Number of Branches: 246

Manulife Bank of Canada
500 King St. North, Waterloo ON N2J 4C6
519/747-7000; Fax: 519/747-2112
URL: http://www.manulife.com
Sr. Vice-President, J.R. Fedchyshyn
Number of Branches: 2

## FOREIGN BANK SUBSIDIARIES IN CANADA

**Address shown is that of the Canadian head office.**

ABN AMRO Bank Canada
Aetna Tower, Toronto-Dominion Centre, #1500, 79 Wellington St. West, 15th Fl., PO Box 55, Stn Toronto-Dominion, Toronto ON M5K 1E7
416/867-1019; Fax: 416/867-9410
President/CEO, Willem Veger

Amex Bank of Canada
American Express Place, 101 McNabb St., Markham ON L3R 4H8
905/474-8000; Fax: 905/474-8561
URL: http://www.americanexpress.com/canada/
President/General Manager, A. Stark

Banca Commerciale Italiana of Canada
#1800, 130 Adelaide St. West, PO Box 100, Toronto ON M5H 3P5
416/366-8101; Fax: 416/214-2555; Toll Free: 1-800-224-5596
Email: barnettl@bcibank.ca; URL: http://www.bcibank.ca
President/CEO, Gennaro Stammati
Number of Branches: 12

Banco Central Hispano-Canada
#340, 141 Adelaide St. West, Toronto ON M5H 3L5
416/365-7070; Fax: 416/365-7850
Exec. Vice-President/CEO, John Estruch
Revenue: $14,200,000; Assets: $198,700,000 (December 31, 1996)

Bank of America Canada
#2700, 200 Front St. West, Toronto ON M5V 3L2
416/349-4100; Fax: 416/349-4277
President/CEO, Alfred P. Buhler
Assets: $3,000,000,000 (December 31, 1996)

Bank of China (Canada)
Canada Trust Tower, BCE Place, #3740, 161 Bay St., PO Box 612, Toronto ON M5J 2S1
416/362-2991, 4958; Fax: 416/362-3047
President/CEO, L. Gu

The Bank of East Asia (Canada)
East Asia Centre, #102-103, 350 Hwy. 7 East, Richmond Hill ON L4B 3N2
905/882-8182; Fax: 905/882-0253
General Manager/CEO, Cedric C.K. Ng

Bank of Tokyo-Mitsubishi (Canada)
#2100, Royal Bank Plaza, South Tower, PO Box 42, Toronto ON M5J 2J1
416/865-0220; Fax: 416/865-9511, 0196
President/CEO, Hirochi Degawa
Revenue: $121,400,000; Assets: $1,400,000,000 (October 31, 1995)

Banque Nationale de Paris (Canada)
1981, av McGill College, Montréal QC H3A 2W8
514/285-6000; Fax: 514/285-6278
President/CEO, André Chaffringeon

BT Bank of Canada/Banque BT du Canada
North Tower, #1700 Royal Bank Plaza, PO Box 100, Stn Royal Bank, Toronto ON M5J 2J2
416/865-0770; Fax: 416/941-9587
President/CEO, Harvey S. Naglie
Number of Branches: 1

The Chase Manhattan Bank of Canada/Banque Chase Manhattan du Canada
First Canadian Place, 100 King St. West, PO Box 6900, Stn 1st Can. Place, Toronto ON M5X 1A4
416/216-4100; Fax: 416/216-4166
President/CEO, Dale G. Blue
Revenue: $37,963,000; Assets: $1,497,151 (October 31, 1996)

Cho Hung Bank of Canada
#1100, 2 Sheppard Ave. East, North York ON M2N 5Y7
416/590-9500; Fax: 416/590-9550
President/CEO, Chee Kwan
Revenue: $12,300,000; Assets: $187,200,000 (October 31, 1996)

Citibank Canada
Citibank Place, #1900, 123 Front St. West, Toronto ON M5J 2M3
416/947-5500; Fax: 416/947-5813
Chair & CEO, Paul Labbé
Revenue: $405,000,000; Assets: $6,300,000,000 (1996)

Crédit Lyonnais Canada
Centre ManuVie, 2000, rue Mansfield, 18e étage, Montréal QC H3A 3A6
514/288-4848; Fax: 514/288-5679; Telex: 05-25245
Vice-President, Louis A. Bastien, Administration
Revenue: $145,400,000; Assets: $2,400,000,000 (1996)
Number of Branches: 3

Crédit Suisse Canada
#1300, 525 University Ave., Toronto ON M5G 2K6
416/351-3500; Fax: 416/351-3630
President/CEO, K.P. Kuebel

Dai-Ichi Kangyo Bank (Canada)
#5025, Commerce Court West, PO Box 295, Stn Commerce Court, Toronto ON M5L 1H9
416/365-9666; Fax: 416/365-7314; Telex: 06-22604; Toll Free: 1-800-668-5917
URL: http://www.infoweb.or.jp/dkb/index-e.html
Chair, President/CEO, H. Ikeda
Revenue: $51,875,000; Assets: $784,431,000 (October 31, 1996)

Deutsche Bank Canada
#1200, 222 Bay St., PO Box 196, Toronto ON M5K 1H6
416/682-8400; Fax: 416/682-8484
President/CEO, Stephen von Romberg-Droste
Assets: $5,400,000,000 (1996)

Dresdner Bank Canada
#1700, 2 First Canadian Place, PO Box 430, Stn 1st Can Place, Toronto ON M5X 1E3
416/369-8300; Fax: 416/369-8362
President/CEO, David N. Brandt
Revenue: $60,200,000; Assets: $899,600,000 (1996)

First Chicago NBD Bank, Canada
BCE Place, #4240, 161 Bay St., PO Box 613, Toronto ON M5J 2S1
416/865-0466; Fax: 416/363-7574; Telex: 06-218722
Chair/Sr. Vice-President, James W. McNamee, II, First Chicago Bank NBD Corporation, Chicago, Ill.
Assets: $591,000,000 (December 31, 1996)
Number of Branches: 1

Fuji Bank Canada
Canada Trust Tower, BCE Place, #2800, 161 Bay St., PO Box 609, Toronto ON M5H 2S1
416/865-1020; Fax: 416/865-9618
President/CEO, Kenichiro Tanaka
Assets: $1,100,000,000 (October 31, 1996)

Hanil Bank Canada
36 Lombard St., Toronto ON M5C 2X3
416/214-1111; Fax: 416/214-1112
President/CEO, C.K. Choe

Hongkong Bank of Canada
#300, 885 Georgia St. West, Vancouver BC V6C 3E9
604/685-1000; Fax: 604/641-1909
URL: http://www.hkbc.com
President/CEO, W.R.P. Dalton
Assets: $23,100,000,000 (May 27, 1997)

The Industrial Bank of Japan (Canada)
#1102, 100 Yonge St., PO Box 29, Toronto ON M5C 2W1
416/365-9550; Fax: 416/367-3452
Email: ibjc@tor.hookup.net
President/CEO, Mitsuo Iwamoto
Revenue: $59,857,000; Assets: $808,192,000 (October 31, 1996)

International Commercial Bank of Cathay (Canada)
#910, 150 York St., PO Box 4037, Toronto ON M5H 3S5
416/947-2800; Fax: 416/947-9964
President/CEO, H.H.B. Tai

Israel Discount Bank of Canada
#M100, 150 Bloor St. West, Toronto ON M5S 2Y5
416/926-7200; Fax: 416/926-0090
CEO/Chief General Manager, Manfred H. Gerstung

Korea Exchange Bank of Canada
#600, 2345 Yonge St., Toronto ON M4P 2E5
416/932-1234; Fax: 416/932-1235; Telex: 0623274
President/CEO, Jai Hak Roh
Assets: $378,500,000 (1996)
Number of Branches: 6

Mellon Bank Canada
Toronto-Dominion Centre, #3200, Royal Trust Tower, Toronto ON M5K 1K2
416/860-0777
President, Tom C. MacMillan

Morgan Bank of Canada
#2200, Royal Bank Plaza, South Tower, PO Box 80, Stn Royal Bank, Toronto ON M5J 2J2
416/981-9200; Fax: 416/865-1641
President/CEO, Geoff Gouinlock

National Bank of Greece (Canada)/Banque Nationale de Grèce (Canada)
1170, Place du Frère André, Montréal QC H3B 3C6
514/954-1522; Fax: 514/954-1224
CEO, N. Avgoustakis
Revenue: $31,400,000; Assets: $374,200,000 (1996)
Number of Branches: 8

National Westminster Bank of Canada
#2060, Royal Bank Plaza, South Tower., 200 Bay St., PO Box 10, Stn Royal Bank, Toronto ON M5J 2J1
416/865-0170; Fax: 416/865-0934
President/CEO, Alex Constandse
Assets: $929,000,000 (October 31, 1996)

Paribas Bank of Canada
#4100, TD Centre, Royal Trust Tower, PO Box 31, Stn Toronto-Dominion, Toronto ON M5K 1N8
416/365-9600; Fax: 416/947-0086
President/CEO, Edward Speal

Republic National Bank of New York (Canada)/ Banque République Nationale de New York (Canada)
1981, av McGill College, Montréal QC H3A 3A9
514/288-5551; 416/367-1710 (Toronto); Fax: 514/286-4577
President/CEO, Allan Schouela
Assets: $894,000,000 (December 31, 1996)

Sakura Bank (Canada)
#3601, Commerce Court West, PO Box 59, Stn Commerce Court, Toronto ON M5L 1B9
416/369-8531; Fax: 416/369-0268
President/CEO, Naoaki Yokota

Sanwa Bank Canada
Canada Trust Tower, BCE Place, Box 525, #4400, 161 Bay St., Toronto ON M5J 2S1
416/366-2583; Fax: 416/366-8599
President/CEO, K. Sakurai

Société Générale (Canada)
#1800, 1501, av McGill College, Montréal QC H3A 3M8
514/841-6000; Fax: 514/841-6250
Président, Alain Clot

Sottomayor Bank Canada
1102 Dundas St. West, Toronto ON M6J 1X2
416/588-9819; Fax: 416/588-1416; Toll Free: 1-800-641-7962; Telex: 06-22692
Email: Sotto@istar.ca
Chair, Luis de Mello Champalimaud
Number of Branches: 3

State Bank of India (Canada)
1600 Royal Bank Plaza, North Tower, PO Box 81, Stn Royal Bank, Toronto ON M5J 2J2
416/865-0414; Fax: 416/865-1735; Toll Free: 1-800-668-8947
President/CEO, N.K. Puri
Revenue: $5,400,000; Assets: $85,400,000 (October 1996)
Number of Branches: 2

The Sumitomo Bank of Canada
#1400, Ernst & Young Tower, Toronto-Dominion Centre, PO Box 172, Stn Toronto Dominion, Toronto ON M5K 1H6
416/368-4766; Fax: 416/367-3565
President/CEO, Osamu Okahashi

Swiss Bank Corporation (Canada)/Société de Banque Suisse (Canada)
#780, 207 Queen's Quay West, PO Box 103, Toronto ON M5J 1A7
416/203-2180; Fax: 416/203-4303
Exec. Director/CEO, Beat Guldimann

Tokai Bank Canada
Sun Life Centre, #2401, 150 King St. West, PO Box 84, Toronto ON M5H 1J9
416/597-2210; Fax: 416/591-7415
President/CEO, R. Kurihara
Revenue: $23,236,000; Assets: $336,374,000 (October 31, 1996)

Union Bank of Switzerland (Canada)
154 University Ave., Toronto ON M5H 3Z4
416/343-1800; Fax: 416/343-1900
President/CEO, Max P. Strebel

United Overseas Bank (Canada)
Vancouver Centre, #310, 650 Georgia St. West, PO Box 11616, Vancouver BC V6B 4N9
604/662-7055; Fax: 604/662-3356
Director/General Manager, Terence Tong

### SAVINGS BANKS IN CANADA

Alberta Treasury Branches
ATB Plaza, #1200, 9925 - 109 St., Edmonton AB T5K 2J8
403/493-7309; Fax: 403/422-4178
URL: http://www.atb.com
CEO & Superintendent, Paul G. Haggis
Revenue: $810,000,000; Assets: $8,818,567,000 (March 1996)
Number of Branches: 147 branches; 131 agencies

Province of Ontario Savings Office/Caisse d'épargne de l'Ontario
33 King St. West, 2nd Fl., Oshawa ON L1H 8H5
905/433-5788; Fax: 905/433-6519; Toll Free: 1-888-283-8333
Chair, Michael L. Gourley
Revenue: $164,800,000; Assets: $2,400,000,000 (March 31, 1996)
Number of Branches: 23

## TRUST COMPANIES

Trust companies are incorporated under the federal Trust and Loan Companies Act and/or corresponding provincial legislation. The business of trust companies falls into two distinct activities - financial intermediary (banking) and fiduciary functions. As a financial intermediary, a trust company borrows funds from the public in the form of guaranteed investment certificates or savings deposits and invests them in mortgages, securities and other loans.

The fiduciary or trustee functions are unique to trust companies. In their fiduciary functions, trust companies serve as administrators of estates, trusts and agencies and do not have ownership of the assets under their administration. The estate, trust and agency activities of trust companies are governed by provincial legislation. Trust companies also act as agents and registrars for various types of stocks and as trustees for corporate bond issues; real estate managers and real estate agents; investment managers or counsellors; managers of sinking funds; custodians; and agents for personal services.

Aetna Trust Company
Park Place, #2230, 666 Burrard St., Vancouver BC V6C 2X8
604/685-1208; Fax: 604/685-9997
President, Arnold E. Miles-Pickup

AGF Trust Company
Toronto-Dominion Centre, #2006, 77 King St. West, Toronto ON M5K 1E9
416/216-5353; Fax: 416/216-5350; Toll Free: 1-888-754-1133
Email: tiger@agf.com; URL: http://www.agf.com/agftrust/
President/Chief Operating Officer, D.R. Doherty

All Nations Trust Company
#208, Yellowhead Hwy., Kamloops BC V2H 1H1
604/828-9770; Fax: 604/372-2585
President, Ruth Williams

The Bank of Nova Scotia Trust Company
Scotia Plaza, 44 King St. West, Toronto ON M5H 1H1
416/866-6161
President/CEO, J. Rory MacDonald

Bankers' Trust Company (Canada)
#1700, 200 Bay St., PO Box 100, Toronto ON M5J 2J2
416/865-0770; Fax: 416/865-0779
CEO, Harvey Naglie

Bonaventure Trust Inc.
#200, 1245, rue Sherbrooke ouest, Montréal QC H3G 1G3
514/841-6335; Fax: 514/841-6340; Toll Free: 1-800-363-6337
President, Claude A. Garcia

Canada Trust Company
Canada Trust Tower, BCE Place, 161 Bay St., 35th Fl., Toronto ON M5J 2T2
416/361-8000; Fax: 416/361-8253; Toll Free: 1-800-668-8888
Email: ctmailbox@canadatrust.com; URL: http://www.canadatrust.com
President/CEO, W. Edmund Clark
Assets: $246,000,000,000 (December 31, 1996)
Number of Branches: 421

The Canadian Depository for Securities Limited
Stock Exchange Tower, 609 Granville St., 8th Fl., PO Box 10338, Vancouver BC V7Y 1J8
604/631-6000; Fax: 604/688-9658
Retail Director, Glenn Knowles

Canadian Italian Trust Company/Fiducie Canadienne Italienne
6999, boul St-Laurent, Montréal QC H2S 3E1
514/270-4124; Fax: 514/270-2247
President, Giuseppe Di Battista

Canadian Western Trust
#2230, 666 Burrard St., Vancouver BC V6C 2Y8
604/685-1208; Fax: 604/685-9997; Toll Free: 1-800-663-1124
President/CEO, Larry Pollock
Revenue: $6,100,000; Assets: $288,700,000 (October 31, 1996)

Capital Trust Corporation
600, boul René-Lévesque ouest, Montréal QC H3B 1N4
514/393-7233; Fax: 514/393-1736
President, Robert Beutel

CIBC Trust Corporation
#900, 55 Yonge St., Toronto ON M5E 1S4
416/861-7000; Fax: 416/862-2272; Toll Free: 1-800-668-7389
President/CEO, P. Jane Bazarkewich

Citizens Trust Company
#401, 815 West Hastings St., Vancouver BC V6C 1B4
604/682-7171; Fax: 604/708-7790
URL: http://www.citizenstrust.ca
President/CEO, Linda Crompton
Number of Branches: 5

Co-Operative Trust Company of Canada
333 - 3rd Ave. North, Saskatoon SK S7K 2M2
306/956-1800; Fax: 306/652-7614; Toll Free: 1-800-472-4857
Email: ctec.king@co-operativetrust.ca
President/CEO, Myrna J Bentley
Revenue: $86,300,000; Assets: $955,400,000 (1996)
Number of Branches: 10

Community Trust Company Ltd.
2271 Bloor St. West, 3rd Fl., Toronto ON M6S 1P1
416/763-2291; Fax: 416/763-2444; Toll Free: 1-800-268-1576
President, C.E. . Zulian
Revenue: $15,000,000; Assets: $163,000,000 (1996)
Number of Branches: 1

Connor Clark Private Trust
Scotia Plaza, #4714, 40 King St. West, Toronto ON M5H 3Y2
416/867-1716; Fax: 416/867-9771
Chief Operating Officer, Mark Damelin, C.A.
Assets: $473,000,000 (December 31, 1996)

Desjardins Trust Inc./Fiducie Desjardins Inc.
1, Complexe Desjardins, CP 34, Succ Desjardins, Montréal QC H5B 1E4
514/286-9441; Fax: 514/286-3184; Toll Free: 1-800-361-6840
URL: http://www.desjardins.com/
President/CEO, Jean Landry, FCA
Revenue: $11,800,000; Assets: $1,600,000,000 (1996)

The Effort Trust Company
242 Main St. East, Hamilton ON L8N 1H5
905/528-8956; Fax: 905/528-8182
President/CEO, Thomas J. Weisz
Revenue: $25,000,000; Assets: $153,000,000 (1996)
Number of Branches: 2

The Equitable Trust Company
#700, 30 St. Clair Ave. West, Toronto ON M4V 3A1
416/515-7000
President, Geoffrey Bledin
Revenue: $14,000,000; Assets: $210,000,000 (December 31, 1996)

Evangeline Trust Company/Société de Fiducie Évangeline
535 Albert St., Windsor NS B0N 2T0

902/798-8326; Fax: 902/798-3656
Chair & CEO, Barbara D. Hughes, Q.C.
Family Trust Corporation
4 Main St. North, Markham ON L3P 1X2
FirstLine Trust Company
#700, 33 Yonge St., Toronto ON M5E 1G4
416/865-1511; Fax: 416/865-1566
President, Brendan Calder
Fortis Trust Corporation
139 Water St., PO Box 767, St. John's NF A1E 3Y3
709/726-7992; Fax: 709/726-1839
President, Stanley Marshall
HongKong Bank Trust Company
#2700, 10303 Jasper Ave. NW, Edmonton AB T5J 3N6
403/421-2020; Fax: 403/421-2022
President/CEO, Brian Robertson
Household Trust Company
#500, 101 Duncan Mill Rd., North York ON M3B 1Z3
416/443-3600; Fax: 416/443-1428
President/CEO, Tom Arndt
ING Trust Company of Canada
111 Gordon Baker Rd., North York ON M2H 3R1
416/497-5157; Fax: 416/758-5215; Toll Free: 1-800-ING-DIRECT
Email: clientservices@ingdirect.ca; URL: http://www.ingdirect.ca
President/CEO, Arkadi Kuhlmann
Inland Trust & Savings Corporation Ltd.
#201, One Forks Market Rd., Winnipeg MB R3C 4L9
204/949-4800; Fax: 204/949-4848; Toll Free: 1-800-665-8897
President, Ken Cooper
Investors Group Trust Co. Ltd./La Compagnie de Fiducie du Groupe Investors Ltée
One Canada Centre, 447 Portage Ave., Winnipeg MB R3C 3B6
204/943-0361; Fax: 204/949-1340
URL: http://www.investorsgroup.com
President/CEO, Wayne Stanley Walker
Revenue: $110,000,000; Assets: $28,000,000,000 (1996)
Laurentian Trust of Canada Inc.
425, boul de Maisonneuve ouest, 1e étage, Montréal QC H3A 3G5
514/284-7000; Fax: 514/284-3210
President/CEO, Henri-Paul Rousseau
Revenue: $62,300,000; Assets: $1,500,000,000 (October 31, 1996)
London Trust & Savings Corporation
#200, 4950 Yonge St., North York ON M2N 6K1
416/229-6700; Fax: 416/229-2478
President, S. Goldfarb
Mennonite Trust Limited
3005 Central St., PO Box 40, Waldheim SK S0K 4R0
306/945-2080; Fax: 306/945-2225
Manager, Timothy Redekopp
Montreal Trust
Place Montréal Trust, 1800, av McGill College, 15e étage, CP 1900, Succ B, Montréal QC H3A 3K9
514/982-7000; Fax: 514/982-7069
President/CEO, Robert W. Chisholm
MRS Trust Company
#305, 150 Bloor St. West, Toronto ON M5S 3B5
416/926-0221; Fax: 416/413-9790
President, Allan Warren
The Municipal Trust Company
70 Collier St., PO Box 147, Barrie ON L4M 4S9
705/734-7500; Fax: 705/734-7600
Chair/CEO, Maxwell L. Rotstein
Mutual Trust Company
#400, 70 University Ave., PO Box 17, Toronto ON M5J 2M4
416/598-2665; Fax: 416/598-7837
President/CEO, R. Doré
Natcan Trust Company/Société de Fiducie Natcan
National Bank Bldg., 600, rue de la Gauchetière ouest, Montréal QC H3B 4L2
514/394-8494; Fax: 514/394-6987
President, Richard Carter
National Trust Company
1 Adelaide St. East, Toronto ON M5C 2W8
416/361-3611
CEO, Robert Chisholm
Northern Trust Company, Canada
BCE Place, #4540, 161 Bay St., Toronto ON M5J 2S1
416/365-7161; Fax: 416/365-9484
Oxford Trust Company Ltd.
First Alberta Place, #1500, 777 - 8 Ave. SW, Calgary AB T2P 3R5
403/262-9889
President, Carl Cheverie
Pacific & Western Trust Corporation
#950, 410 - 22nd St. East, Saskatoon SK S7K 5T6
306/244-1868; Fax: 306/244-4649
President, David R. Taylor
Pacific Corporate Trust Company
#830, 625 Howe St., Vancouver BC V6C 3B8
604/689-9853; Fax: 604/689-8144
Email: pacific@pctc.com; URL: http://www.pctc.com
President, John Andrew Halse
Number of Branches: 2
Peace Hills Trust Company
Kensington Place, 10011 - 109 St., 10th Fl., Edmonton AB T5J 3S8
403/421-1606; Fax: 403/426-6568
Email: pht@peacehills.com; URL: http://www.peacehills.com/
President/CEO, W.W. Hannay
Peoples Trust Company
888 Dunsmuir St., 14th Fl., Vancouver BC V6C 3K4
604/683-2881; Fax: 604/683-8798
Email: people@peoplestrust.com; URL: http://www.peoplestrust.com
President/CEO, Frank A. Renou
Revenue: $23,000,000; Assets: $260,000,000
The R-M Trust Company
393 University Ave., 5th Fl., Toronto ON M5G 2M7
416/813-4500; Fax: 416/813-4555
URL: http://www.rmtrust.ca
President/CEO, Julian Clark
Number of Branches: 8
The Royal Trust Corporation of Canada
Royal Trust Tower, 77 King St. West, 3rd Fl., PO Box 7500, Stn A, Toronto ON M5W 1P9
416/974-1400; Fax: 416/861-9658; Toll Free: 1-800-668-1990
President/CEO, Anthony A. Webb
Assets: $685,000,000,000 (1996)
Sherbrooke Trust
75, rue Wellington nord, CP 250, Sherbrooke QC J1H 5J2
819/563-4011; Fax: 819/563-9340
Sun Life Trust Company
225 King St. West, 5th Fl., Toronto ON M5V 3C5
416/943-6532; Toll Free: 1-800-668-7283
URL: http://www.sunlife.com
President/CEO, Gary Corsi
Swiss Bank Corporation Trust (Canada)/Trust Société de Banque Swisse
207 Queens Quay West, Toronto ON M5J 1A7
416/203-4220; Fax: 416/203-4303
Asst. Secretary, Glen McBurney, Information Services
TD Trust Company
Commercial Union Tower, 4th Fl., Toronto ON M5K 1A2
416/982-2638; Fax: 416/345-5227; Toll Free: 1-800-268-7878
URL: http://www.tdbank.ca
President, Charles Macfarlane
Trimark Trust/Fiducie Trimark
#5300, First Canadian Place, PO Box 114, Stn 1st Can Place, Toronto ON M5X 1A4
416/362-6900; Fax: 416/364-0626; Toll Free: 1-800-387-4553
Email: trust@trimarktrust.com; URL: http://www.trimarktrust.com
President/Chief Operating Officer, Harry Enchin
Revenue: $90,500,000; Assets: $500,000,000 (March 31, 1997)
Number of Branches: 8
The Trust Company of Bank of Montreal
302 Bay St., 7th Fl., Toronto ON M5X 1A1
416/867-5688; Fax: 416/956-2363
President, A. Donald C. Mutch
The Trust Company of London Life
#304, 255 Queen's Ave., London ON N6A 5R8
519/432-4037; Fax: 519/532-5948; Toll Free: 1-800-511-2222
President/CEO, R. Lillyman
Trust Général du Canada
1100, rue University, Montréal QC H3B 2G7
514/871-7100; Fax: 514/871-7525
President/CEO, Michel W. Petit
Trust La Laurentienne du Canada Inc./Laurentian Trust of Canada Inc.
425, boul de Maisonneuve ouest, Montréal QC H3A 3G5
514/284-7000; Fax: 514/284-3210; Toll Free: 1-800-363-9560
President, Paul Tardif
Revenue: $62,307,000; Assets: $1,514,378,000 (October 31, 1996)
Number of Branches: 2
Trust Prêt et Revenu/Savings & Investment Trust
#700, 850, Place d'Youville, Québec QC G1K 7P3
418/692-1221; Fax: 418/692-1675
Chair/President/CEO, Paul Tardif
Western Pacific Trust Company
#200, 455 Granville St., Vancouver BC V6C 1T1
604/683-0455; Fax: 604/669-6978
Manager, Alison Alfer, Communications

# INVESTMENT FUND MANAGERS IN CANADA

**Funds marked with an * are RRSP eligible.**

ABC Funds
#500, 8 King St. East, Toronto ON M5C 1B5
416/365-9696; Fax: 416/365-9705
President, Irwin Michael
Mutual Funds:
ABC: American Value Fund
ABC: Fully-Managed Fund*
ABC: Fundamental-Value Fund*
Acadia Investment Funds/Fonds de placement Acadie
295, boul St-Pierre ouest, CP 5554, Caraquet NB E1W 1B7
506/727-1345; Fax: 506/727-1344; Toll Free: 1-800-351-1345
President/CEO, Amédée Haché
Mutual Funds:
Acadia: Balanced fund
Acadia: Bond Fund
Acadia: Money Market Fund
Acadia: Mortgage Fund
AGF Funds Inc.
Toronto-Dominion Bank Tower, 31st Fl., PO Box 50, Stn Toronto-Dominion, Toronto ON M5K 1E9
416/367-3981; Toll Free: 1-800-268-8583
Email: tiger@agf.com; URL: http://www.agf.com
Sr. Vice-President, Allen Clarke

Mutual Funds:
AGF: Canada Fund
AGF: RSP Global Bond Fund*
AGF: Special U.S. Fund
AIC Limited
1375 Kearns Rd., Burlington ON L7P 4V7
905/331-9900; Fax: 905/331-1321; 1-800-263-2144
Email: info@aicfunds.com; URL: http://www.aicfunds.com/
Chair & CEO, Michael Lee-Chen
Mutual Funds:
AIC: American Advantage Fund
AIC: Canadian Advantage Fund*
AIC: Diversified Canada Fund*
AIC: Emerging Markets Fund
AIC: Income Equity Fund*
AIC: Money Market Fund*
AIC: Value Fund
AIC: World Equity Fund
Aim Funds Group Canada Inc.
#1802, 150 King St. West, Toronto ON M5H 1J9
416/408-2222; Fax: 416/408-3735
Email: aimfunds@istar.ca; URL: http://www.aimfunds.com
President/CEO, Milan J. Voticky
Mutual Funds:
Admax: American Performance Fund
Admax: American Select Growth Fund
Admax: Asset Allocation Fund*
Admax: Canadian Performance Fund*
Admax: Canadian Select Growth Fund*
Admax: Cash Performance Fund*
Admax: Global Health Sciences Fund
Aim: Aggressive Growth Fund
Regent: Dragon 888 Fund
Regent: Europa Performance Fund
Regent: International Fund*
Regent: Korea Fund
Regent: Nippon Fund*
Regent: Tiger Fund*
Regent: World Income Fund*
All-Canadian Management Inc.
PO Box 7320, Ancaster ON L9G 3N6
905/648-2025; Fax: 905/648-5422
President, Michael A. Parente
Mutual Funds:
All-Canadian: Capital Fund*
All-Canadian: Compound Fund*
All-Canadian: Consumer Fund*
Altamira Investment Services Inc./Placements Altamira Inc.
#200, 250 Bloor St. East, Toronto ON M4W 1E6
416/925-1623; Fax: 416/925-5352
Email: advice@altamira.com; URL: http://www.altamira.com
President, Philip Armstrong
Mutual Funds:
Altamira: AltaFund Investment Corp.*
Altamira: Asia Pacific Fund*
Altamira: Balanced Fund*
Altamira: Bond Fund*
Altamira: Capital Growth Fund Limited*
Altamira: Dividend Fund Inc.*
Altamira: Equity Fund*
Altamira: European Equity Fund*
Altamira: Global Bond Fund*
Altamira: Global Discovery Fund
Altamira: Global Diversified Fund*
Altamira: Global Small Company Fund*
Altamira: Growth & Income Fund*
Altamira: Income Fund*
Altamira: Japanese Opportunity Fund*
Altamira: North American Recovery Fund*
Altamira: Precious & Strategic Metal Fund*
Altamira: Resource Fund*
Altamira: Science & Technology Fund*
Altamira: Select American Fund*
Altamira: Short Term Canadian Income Fund
Altamira: Short Term Global Income Fund*
Altamira: Short Term Government Bond Fund*
Altamira: Special Growth Fund*
Altamira: Speculative High Yield Bond Fund*
Altamira: T-Bill Fund
Altamira: US Larger Company Fund*
Atlas Asset Management Inc.
#500, 110 Yonge St., Toronto ON M5C 1T4
416/369-7672; Fax: 416/369-7756; General Inquiries: 416/862-8527; Fax: 416/943-5962
Email: atlas.funds@atlasfunds.ca; URL: http://www.atlasfunds.ca
President, Susan Dabarno
Mutual Funds:
Atlas American: Advantage Value Fund
Atlas American: Large Cap Growth Fund
Atlas American: RSP Index Fund*
Atlas Canadian: Balanced Fund*
Atlas Canadian: Bond Fund*
Atlas Canadian: Dividend Growth Fund*
Atlas Canadian: Emerging Growth Fund*
Atlas Canadian: High Yield Bond Fund*
Atlas Canadian: Large Cap Growth Fund*
Atlas Canadian: Large Cap Value Fund*
Atlas Canadian: Small Cap Growth Fund*
Atlas Canadian: Small Cap Value Fund*
Atlas International: Emerging Markets Growth Fund
Atlas International: European Value Fund
Atlas International: Global Value Fund
Atlas International: Large Cap Growth Fund
Atlas International: Latin American Value Fund
Atlas International: Pacific Basin Value Fund
Atlas International: RSP Index Fund*
Atlas International: World Bond Fund*
Atlas Money Market: American Money Market Fund*
Atlas Money Market: Canadian Money Market Fund*
Atlas Money Market: Canadian T-Bill Fund*
Hercules: Emerging Market Debt Fund
Hercules: European Value Fund
Hercules: Global Short-Term Fund
Hercules: Latin American Fund
Hercules: Pacific Basin Value Fund
Hercules: World Bond Fund*
Bank of Montreal Investment Management Ltd.
55 Bloor St. West, 15th Fl., Toronto ON M4W 3N5
416/867-5000; Fax: 416/956-2363; 1-800-665-7700
URL: http://www.fcfunds.bomil.ca/
President, Terry A. Jackson
Mutual Funds:
First Canadian Aggressive Growth Funds: Emerging Markets Fund
First Canadian Aggressive Growth Funds: Far East Growth Fund
First Canadian Aggressive Growth Funds: Global Science & Technology Fund
First Canadian Aggressive Growth Funds: Latin American Fund
First Canadian Aggressive Growth Funds: Precious Metals Fund
First Canadian Aggressive Growth Funds: Resource Fund*
First Canadian Aggressive Growth Funds: Special Growth Fund*
First Canadian Aggressive Growth Funds: US Special Growth Fund
First Canadian Growth Funds: Asset Allocation Fund*
First Canadian Growth Funds: Equity Index Fund*
First Canadian Growth Funds: European Growth Fund
First Canadian Growth Funds: Growth Fund*
First Canadian Growth Funds: International Growth Fund
First Canadian Growth Funds: Japanese Growth Fund
First Canadian Growth Funds: NAFTA Advantage Fund
First Canadian Growth Funds: US Equity Index Fund*
First Canadian Growth Funds: US Growth Fund
First Canadian Growth Funds: US Value Fund
First Canadian Income Funds: Bond Fund*
First Canadian Income Funds: Dividend Income Fund
First Canadian Income Funds: International Bond Fund
First Canadian Income Funds: Mortgage Fund*
First Canadian Security Funds: Money Market Fund*
First Canadian Security Funds: T-Bill Fund*
BNP (Canada) Valeurs Mobilières Inc./BNP (Canada) Securities Inc.
1981, av McGill College, 5e étage, Montréal QC H3A 2W8
514/285-7597; Fax: 514/285-7598
President, Michel Landriault
Mutual Funds:
Fonds d'obligations BNP (Canada)*
Fonds marché monétaire BNP (Canada)*
BPI Capital Management Corporation
Canada Trust Tower, BCE Place, #3900, 161 Bay St., Toronto ON M5J 2S1
416/861-9811; Fax: 416/861-9415; 1-800-263-2427
President/CEO, James L. McGovern
Mutual Funds:
BPI: American Equity Value Fund
BPI: American Small Companies Fund
BPI: Asia Pacific Fund
BPI: Canadian Balanced Fund*
BPI: Canadian Bond Fund*
BPI: Canadian Equity Value Fund*
BPI: Canadian Mid-Cap Fund*
BPI: Canadian Resource Fund Inc.*
BPI: Canadian Small Companies Fund
BPI: Dividend Income Fund
BPI: Emerging Markets Fund
BPI: Global Balanced RSP Fund
BPI: Global Equity Value Fund
BPI: Global RSP Bond Fund
BPI: Global Small Companies Fund
BPI: High Income Fund*
BPI: Income & Growth Fund*
BPI: International Equity Value Fund
BPI: T-Bill Fund*
BPI: US Money Market Fund
Burgeonvest Investment Counsel Ltd.
Commerce Place, One King St. West, 11th Fl., Hamilton ON L8N 3P6
905/528-6505
Mutual Funds:
Dolphin: Growth Fund*
Dolphin: Income Fund*
Marlborough: Canadian Balanced Fund
Marlborough: International Balanced Fund
Canada Trust Mutual Funds
BCE Place, 161 Bay St., 3rd Fl., Toronto ON M5J 2T2
416/361-8000; Fax: 416/361-5333; Toll Free: 1-800-386-3757
URL: http://www.canadatrust.com/mutual/index.html
President, Alan D. Wolfson
Mutual Funds:
Canada Trust: Amerigrowth Fund*
Canada Trust: Asiagrowth Fund*
Canada Trust: Balanced Fund*
Canada Trust: Bond Fund*
Canada Trust: Dividend Income Fund*
Canada Trust: Emerging Markets Fund
Canada Trust: Eurogrowth Fund*
Canada Trust: Global Growth Fund*
Canada Trust: International Bond Fund*
Canada Trust: International Equity Fund

Canada Trust: Money Market Fund*
Canada Trust: Mortgage Fund*
Canada Trust: North American Fund
Canada Trust: Premium Money Market Fund
Canada Trust: Short Term Bond Fund
Canada Trust: Special Equity Fund*
Canada Trust: Stock Fund*
Canada Trust: US Equity Fund

Canadian International Mutual Funds
151 Yonge St., 7th Fl., Toronto ON M5C 2Y1
416/364-1145; Fax: 416/364-2969; Toll Free 1-800-268-9374
URL: http://www.cifunds.com
Sr. Vice-President, William Holland
Mutual Funds:
C.I.: American Fund
C.I.: American RSP Fund*
C.I.: Canadian Balanced Fund*
C.I.: Canadian Bond Fund*
C.I.: Canadian Growth Fund*
C.I.: Canadian Income Fund
C.I.: Covington Fund*
C.I.: Emerging Markets Fund
C.I.: Global Bond RSP Fund*
C.I.: Global Equity RSP Fund*
C.I.: Global Fund
C.I.: High Yield Income Fund
C.I.: International Balanced Fund
C.I.: International Balanced RSP Fund
C.I.: Latin American Fund
C.I.: Money Market Fund*
C.I.: Pacific Fund
C.I.: US Money Market Fund
C.I.: World Bond Fund
C.I. Sector Fund Limited: Canadian Sector Shares
C.I. Sector Fund Limited: Global Consumer Products Sector Shares
C.I. Sector Fund Limited: Global Financial Services Sector Shares
C.I. Sector Fund Limited: Global Health Sciences Sector Shares
C.I. Sector Fund Limited: Global Resources Sector Shares
C.I. Sector Fund Limited: Global Technology sector Shares
C.I. Sector Fund Limited: Global Telecommunications Sector Shares
C.I. Sector Fund Limited: Short Term Sector Shares*
Hansberger Value Series Shares: Asian Fund
Hansberger Value Series Shares: Developing Markets Fund
Hansberger Value Series Shares: European Fund
Hansberger Value Series Shares: Global Small Cap Fund
Hansberger Value Series Shares: International Fund
Harbour: Harbour Fund*
Harbour: Harbour Growth & Income Fund*
Monarch: Canadian Fund*
Monarch: Canadian Resource Fund*
Monarch: Dividend Fund*

Capital Alliance Ventures Inc.
#600, 60 Queen St., Ottawa ON K1P 5Y7
613/567-3225; Fax: 613/567-3979; Toll Free 1-800-304-2330
Email: info@cavi.com; URL: http://www.cavi.com
President, Richard Charlebois

Century DJ Fund
819 Belhaven Cres., Burlington ON L7T 2J7
905/608-0727
Mutual Funds:
Century DJ Mutual Fund

Chou Associates Management Inc.
70 Dragoon Cres., Scarborough ON M1V 1N4
416/299-6749; Fax: 416/299-6749
President, Francis Chou
Mutual Funds:
Chou Associates Fund
Chou RRSP Fund*

CIBC Securities Inc.
200 King St. West, 7th Fl., PO Box 51, Stn Commerce Court, Toronto ON M5H 4A8
416/351-4444; Fax: 416/351-4455; Toll Free: 1-800-465-3863
URL: http://www.cibc.com/products/investment/mfunds/
President/CEO, Donald J. Rolfe
Mutual Funds:
CIBC: Balanced Fund*
CIBC: Canadian Bond Fund*
CIBC: Canadian Equity Fund
CIBC: Canadian Index Fund
CIBC: Canadian Resources Fund*
CIBC: Canadian Short-Term Bond Fund
CIBC: Canadian T-Bill Fund*
CIBC: Capital Appreciation Fund
CIBC: Dividend Fund
CIBC: Emerging Economies Fund
CIBC: Energy Fund
CIBC: European Equity Fund
CIBC: Far East Prosperity Fund
CIBC: Financial Services Fund
CIBC: Global Bond Fund
CIBC: Global Equity Fund
CIBC: Global Technology Fund
CIBC: International Index RRSP Fund
CIBC: Japanese Equity Fund
CIBC: Latin American Fund
CIBC: Money Market Fund*
CIBC: Mortgage Fund*
CIBC: North American Demographics Fund
CIBC: Precious Metals Fund
CIBC: Premium Canadian T-Bill Fund*
CIBC: US Dollar Money Market Fund
CIBC: US Equity Fund
CIBC: US Index RRSP Fund
CIBC: US Opportunities Fund

Clean Environment Mutual Funds
#1800, 65 Queen St. West, Toronto ON M5H 2M5
416/366-9933; Fax: 416/366-2568; Toll Free: 1-800-461-4570
URL: http://www.cleanenvironment.com
President, Ian Ihnatowycz, MBA, CFA
Mutual Funds:
Clean Environment: Balanced Fund*
Clean Environment: Equity Fund*
Clean Environment: Income Fund*
Clean Environment: International Equity Fund*

Dominion Equity Resource Fund Inc.
Bow Valley Square II, #1710, 205 - 5 Ave. SW, Calgary AB T2P 2V7
403/531-2657; Fax: 403/264-5844
President, Ron B. Coleman
Mutual Funds:
Dominion Equity Resource Fund Inc.

Dynamic Mutual Funds/Fonds d'Investissement Dynamique
Scotia Plaza, 40 King St. West, 55th Fl., Toronto ON M5H 4A9
416/365-5100; Fax: 416/365-2558; 1-800-268-8186
Email: invest@dynamic.ca; URL: http://www.dynamic.ca
President, Terence Buie
Mutual Funds:
Asset Allocation Funds: Dynamic Global Partners Fund
Asset Allocation Funds: Dynamic Partners Fund*
Asset Allocation Funds: Dynamic Team Fund*
Equity Funds: Dynamic Americas Fund
Equity Funds: Dynamic Canadian Growth Fund*
Equity Funds: Dynamic Canadian Real Estate Fund
Equity Funds: Dynamic Dividend Growth Fund*
Equity Funds: Dynamic Europe Fund
Equity Funds: Dynamic Far East Fund
Equity Funds: Dynamic Fund of Canada Ltd.*
Equity Funds: Dynamic Global Millennia Fund
Equity Funds: Dynamic Global Precious Metals Fund
Equity Funds: Dynamic Global Resource Fund
Equity Funds: Dynamic International Fund
Equity Funds: Dynamic Precious Metals Fund*
Equity Funds: Dynamic Quebec Fund
Equity Funds: Dynamic Real Estate Equity Fund*
Income Funds: Dynamic Dividend Fund*
Income Funds: Dynamic Global Bond Fund*
Income Funds: Dynamic Global Income & Growth Fund
Income Funds: Dynamic Government Income Fund*
Income Funds: Dynamic Income Fund*
Income Funds: Dynamic Money Market Fund*

Elliott & Page Limited
#1120, 120 Adelaide St. West, Toronto ON M5H 1V1
416/365-8300; Fax: 416/365-2143, 2156
URL: http://www.fundlib.com/ellpag.html
President/CEO, Jim Crysdale
Mutual Funds:
Elliott & Page: American Growth Fund*
Elliott & Page: Asian Growth Fund
Elliott & Page: Balanced Fund*
Elliott & Page: Bond Fund*
Elliott & Page: Emerging Markets Fund
Elliott & Page: Equity Fund*
Elliott & Page: Global Balanced Fund
Elliott & Page: Global Bond Fund
Elliott & Page: Global Equity Fund
Elliott & Page: Money Fund*
Elliott & Page: T-Bill Fund

Ethical Funds Inc.
#510, 815 West Hastings St., Vancouver BC V6C 1B4
604/331-8350; Fax: 604/331-8399; 1-800-267-5019
President, John A. Linthwaite
Mutual Funds:
Ethical: Balanced Fund*
Ethical: Global Bond Fund
Ethical: Growth Fund*
Ethical: Income Fund*
Ethical: Money Market Fund*
Ethical: North American Equity Fund
Ethical: Pacific Rim Fund
Ethical: Special Equity Fund*

Fidelity Investments Canada Limited
Ernst & Young Tower, #900, 222 Bay St., PO Box 90, Toronto ON M5K 1P1
416/307-5300; Fax: 416/307-5523; 1-800-263-4077
URL: http://www.fidelity.ca
CEO, John H. Simpson
Mutual Funds:
American Funds: Growth America Fund
American Funds: North American Income Fund
American Funds: Small Cap America Fund
American Funds: U.S. Money Market Fund
Canadian Funds: Canadian Asset Allocation Fund*
Canadian Funds: Canadian Bond Fund
Canadian Funds: Canadian Growth Company Fund
Canadian Funds: Canadian Income Fund
Canadian Funds: Canadian Short Term Asset Fund
Canadian Funds: Capital Builder Fund*
Canadian Funds: RSP Global Bond Fund*
Canadian Funds: True North Fund*
International Funds: Asset Manager Fund
International Funds: Emerging Markets Bond Fund
International Funds: Emerging Markets Portfolio Fund
International Funds: European Growth Fund
International Funds: Far East Fund
International Funds: International Portfolio Fund
International Funds: Japanese Growth Fund
International Funds: Latin American Growth Fund

First Marathon Securities Limited . The Exchange Tower, #3200, 2 First Canadian Place, PO Box 21, Toronto ON M5X 1J9
416/869-3707; Fax: 416/869-0089; Toll Free: 1-800-661-3863
URL: http://www.fmarathon.com
President/Chief Financial Officer, Lawrence S. Bloomberg
Mutual Funds:
Marathon: Equity Fund*
Marathon: Resource Fund
Fonds Ficadre/Ficadre Fund
625, rue Saint-Amable, Québec QC G1R 2G5
418/643-3884; Fax: 418/528-0457; 1-800-667-7643
Directrice, Vivianne Drolet
Mutual Funds:
Fonds Ficadre: Fond d'actions*
Fonds Ficadre: Fond d'obligations*
Fonds Ficadre: Fond équilibré
Fonds Ficadre: Fond marché monetaire*
Fonds de Placement Acadie Inc./Acadia Investment Funds Inc.
295 St. Pierre Blvd. West, PO Box 5554, Caraquet NB E1W 1B7
506/727-1345; Fax: 506/727-1344; 1-800-461-1318
President/CEO, Amédéee Haché
Mutual Funds:
Acadia: Balanced Fund*
Acadia: Bond Fund*
Acadia: Money Market Fund*
Acadia: Mortgage Fund*
Fonds Trust Général du Canada
1100, rue University, Montréal QC H3B 2G7
514/871-7100; Fax: 514/871-8525
Mutual Funds:
Trust Général d'actions Americaines
Trust Général fonds d'actions Canadiennes*
Trust Général fonds d'hypothèques
Trust Général fonds d'obligations*
Trust Général fonds de croissance*
Trust Général fonds équilibre
Trust Général fonds international*
Trust Général fonds marché monétaire*
Friedberg Mercantile Group
BCE Place, #250, 181 Bay St., PO Box 866, Toronto ON M5J 2T3
416/364-2700; Fax: 416/364-0572; Toll Free: 1-800-461-2700
Email: fmgtor@inforamp.net; URL: http://www.friedberg.com
Albert D. Friedberg
Mutual Funds:
Friedberg: Currency Fund
Friedberg: Diversified
Friedberg: Double Gold Plus Fund*
Friedberg: Foreign Bond Fund
Global Strategy Financial Inc.
#1600, 33 Bloor St. East, Toronto ON M4W 3T8
416/966-3676; Fax: 416/927-9168; Toll Free: 1-800-387-1229
President, Richard Wernham
Mutual Funds:
Global Strategy: Asia Fund
Global Strategy: Bond Fund*
Global Strategy: Canada Growth Fund*
Global Strategy: Canadian Small Cap Fund
Global Strategy: Diversified Americas Fund*
Global Strategy: Diversified Asia Fund*
Global Strategy: Diversified Bond Fund*
Global Strategy: Diversified Europe Fund*
Global Strategy: Diversified Foreign Bond Fund*
Global Strategy: Diversified Gold Plus Fund*
Global Strategy: Diversified Growth Fund*
Global Strategy: Diversified Japan Plus Fund
Global Strategy: Diversified Latin American Fund*
Global Strategy: Diversified Short-Term Income Fund*
Global Strategy: Diversified World Equity*
Global Strategy: Europe Plus Fund
Global Strategy: Foreign Bond Fund
Global Strategy: Income Plus Fund*
Global Strategy: Japan Fund*
Global Strategy: Latin American Fund
Global Strategy: Real Estate Securities Fund
Global Strategy: T-Bill Savings Fund*
Global Strategy: US Equity Fund*
Global Strategy: US Growth Fund
Global Strategy: US Savings Fund
Global Strategy: World Fund
Greystone Capital Management Inc.
#300, 1230 Blackfoot Dr., Regina SK S4S 7G4
306/779-6400; Fax: 306/585-1570
President/CEO, Donald W. Black
Mutual Funds:
Greystone: Managed Global Fund
Greystone: Managed Wealth Fund*
Groupe Financier Concorde
850, Place d'Youville, Québec QC G1R 3P6
418/694-0000; Fax: 418/692-1679; 1-800-363-0598
President/CEO, Michel Fragasso
Mutual Funds:
Concorde Balanced Fund*
Concorde Fonds Dividende*
Concorde International Fund
Fonds d'hypothèques Concorde*
Fonds de croissance Concorde*
Fonds de revenu Concorde*
Fonds du marché monetaire Concorde
GT Global
Royal Trust Tower, TD Centre, #4001, 77 King St. West, PO Box 297, Toronto ON M5K 1K2
416/594-4300; Fax: 416/594-0656; Toll Free 1-800-588-5684
Email: glbcan@inforamp.net; URL: http://www.gtglobal.ca
Vice-President, Finance & Administration, David Warren
Mutual Funds:
GT Global: Canada Fund Inc. - Canada Growth Class
GT Global: Canada Money Market Fund
GT Global: Growth & Income Fund
GT Global: World Bond Fund
GT Global Canada Fund Inc.: Canada Income Class
GT Global Fund Inc.: American Growth Class
GT Global Fund Inc.: Global Health Care Class
GT Global Fund Inc.: Global Infrastructure Class
GT Global Fund Inc.: Global Natural Resources Class
GT Global Fund Inc.: Global Telecommunications Class
GT Global Fund Inc.: Global Theme Class
GT Global Fund Inc.: Latin America Growth Class
GT Global Fund Inc.: Pacific Growth Class
GT Global Fund Inc.: Short-Term Income Class
The Guardian Group of Funds Limited
#3100, Commerce Court West, PO Box 201, Toronto ON M5L 1E8
416/947-4099; Fax: 416/947-0601; Toll Free 1-800-668-5613
URL: http://www.guardianfunds.com/
President/Chief Operating Officer, Harold Hillier
Mutual Funds:
Guardian: American Equity Fund Ltd.
Guardian: Asia Pacific Fund
Guardian: Canadian Balanced Fund*
Guardian: Canadian Income Fund*
Guardian: Canadian Money Market Fund*
Guardian: Emerging Markets Fund
Guardian: Enterprise Fund*
Guardian: Foreign Income Fund*
Guardian: Global Equity fund
Guardian: Growth & Income Fund*
Guardian: Growth Equity Fund*
Guardian: International Balanced Fund*
Guardian: International Income Fund*
Guardian: Monthly Dividend Fund Ltd.*
Guardian: Monthly High Income Fund
Guardian: US Money Market Fund*
Hodgson Roberton Laing
#2300, One Queen St. East, Toronto ON M5C 2Y5
416/364-4444; Fax: 416/955-4878; Toll Free 1-800-268-9622
Mutual Funds:
Hodgson Roberton Laing: Balanced Fund*
Hodgson Roberton Laing: Bond Fund*
Hodgson Roberton Laing: Canadian Fund*
Hodgson Roberton Laing: Instant $$ Fund*
Hodgson Roberton Laing: Overseas Growth Fund
Hongkong Bank Securities Inc.
1066 West Hastings St., 25th Fl., Vancouver BC V6E 3X1
604/257-4842; Fax: 604/257-4867
President, Steve Wilson
Mutual Funds:
Hongkong Bank Americas Fund
Hongkong Bank Asian Growth Fund
Hongkong Bank Balanced Fund
Hongkong Bank Canadian Bond Fund
Hongkong Bank Dividend Income Fund
Hongkong Bank Emerging Markets Fund
Hongkong Bank Equity Fund*
Hongkong Bank European Growth Fund
Hongkong Bank Global Fund
Hongkong Bank Money Market Fund*
Hongkong Bank Mortgage Fund*
Hongkong Bank Small Cap Growth Fund
Howson Tattersall Investment Counsel Ltd.
Cadillac Fairview Tower, #1904, 20 Queen St. West, PO Box 95, Toronto ON M5H 3R3
416/979-1818; Fax: 416/979-7424; Toll Free: 1-888-287-2966
Email: saxon@saxonfunds.com; URL: http://www.saxonfunds.com/~saxon
President, Robert Tattersall
Mutual Funds:
Saxon Funds: Balanced Fund*
Saxon Funds: Small Cap Fund*
Saxon Funds: Stock Fund*
Saxon Funds: World Growth Fund
Investors Group Inc.
One Canada Centre, 447 Portage Ave., PO Box 5000, Winnipeg MB R3C 3B6
204/943-0361; Fax: 204/956-1446
URL: http://www.investorsgroup.com
President/CEO, H. Sanford Riley
Jones Heward Investment Management Inc.
#4200, 77 King St. West, Toronto ON M5K 1J5
416/359-5000; Fax: 416/359-5040; Toll Free: 1-800-361-1392
President/CEO, John P. Donnelly
Mutual Funds:
Jones Heward: American Fund
Jones Heward: Bond Fund*
Jones Heward: Canadian Balanced Fund
Jones Heward: Jones Heward Fund*
Jones Heward: Money Market Fund*
Leon Frazer & Associates Ltd.
#2001, 8 King St. East, Toronto ON M5C 1B6
416/864-1120; Fax: 416/864-1491
Chair, G.L. Frazer
Mutual Funds:
Associate Investors Limited*
London Fund Management Ltd.
255 Dufferin Ave., London ON N6A 4K1
519/432-2000; Toll Free 1-888-462-9986
President, Roger Lillyman
Mutual Funds:
Maxxum: American Equity Fund
Maxxum: Canadian Balanced Fund*
Maxxum: Canadian Equity Growth Fund*
Maxxum: Dividend Fund*
Maxxum: Global Equity Fund*
Maxxum: Money Market Fund*

Maxxum: Natural Resource Fund*
Maxxum: Precious Metals Fund*
Mackenzie Financial Corporation
#400, 150 Bloor St. West, Toronto ON M5S 2X9
416/922-5322; Fax: 416/922-9194; 1-800-387-0614
URL: http://www.fundlib.com/mackenzie.html
President/CEO, Alexander Christ
Mutual Funds:
Industrial: American Fund
Industrial: Balanced Fund*
Industrial: Bond Fund*
Industrial: Cash Management Fund*
Industrial: Dividend Fund Limited*
Industrial: Equity Fund Limited*
Industrial: Future Fund*
Industrial: Growth Fund*
Industrial: Horizon Fund*
Industrial: Income Fund*
Industrial: Mortgage Securities Fund*
Industrial: Pension Fund*
Industrial: Short Term Fund*
Ivy: Canadian Fund
Ivy: Enterprise Fund
Ivy: Foreign Equity Fund
Ivy: Growth & Income Fund
Ivy: Mortgage Fund
Mackenzie: Sentinel Canada Equity Fund*
Mackenzie: Sentinel Global Fund
Universal: Americas Fund
Universal: Canadian Growth Fund Limited*
Universal: Canadian Resource Fund*
Universal: European Opportunities Fund
Universal: Far East Fund
Universal: Growth Fund
Universal: Japan Fund
Universal: US Emerging Growth Fund
Universal: US Money Market Fund
Universal: World Asset Allocation Fund*
Universal: World Balanced RRSP Fund*
Universal: World Emerging Growth Fund*
Universal: World Equity Fund
Universal: World Growth RRSP Fund
Universal: World Income RRSP Fund
Universal: World Precious Metals Fund
Universal: World Tactical Bond Fund
Majendie Charlton Ltd.
Waterfront Centre, #320, 200 Burrard St., Vancouver BC V6C 3L6
604/682-6446; Fax: 604/662-8594; Toll Free: 1-800-822-6446
President/CEO, Arnie Miles-Pickup
Mutual Funds:
Top 50 Equity Fund*
Top 50 T-Bill/Bond Fund*
Top 50 US Equity Fund
Manulife Securities International Ltd./Placements Manuvie Internationale Ltée
500 King St. North, Waterloo ON N2J 4C6
519/747-7000; Fax: 519/747-6968; Toll Free 1-800-265-7401
President/CEO, John A. Vivash
Mutual Funds:
Manulife Cabot: Blue Chip Fund*
Manulife Cabot: Canadian Equity Fund*
Manulife Cabot: Canadian Growth Fund*
Manulife Cabot: Diversified Bond Fund*
Manulife Cabot: Emerging Growth Fund*
Manulife Cabot: Global Equity Fund
Manulife Cabot: Money Market Fund*
Mawer Investment Management
#600, 603 - 7th Ave. SW, Calgary AB T2P 2T5
403/262-4673; Fax: 403/262-4099; Toll Free: 1-800-889-6248
Email: mawerwebmaster@mawer.com; URL: http://www.mawer.com/
Gerald A. Cooper-Key
Mutual Funds:
Mawer Canadian Balanced Retirement Savings Fund*
Mawer Canadian Bond Fund*
Mawer Canadian Diversified Investment Fund
Mawer Canadian Equity Fund*
Mawer Canadian Equity Money Market Fund*
Mawer Canadian Income Fund
Mawer High Yield Bond Fund
Mawer New Canada Fund*
Mawer US Equity Fund
Mawer World Investment Fund
MD Management Limited/Gestion MD Limitée
1867 Alta Vista Dr., Ottawa ON K1G 5W8
613/731-4552; Fax: 613/526-1352; 1-800-267-4022
President/CEO, F.R. Hewett
Mutual Funds:
Balanced Fund: MD Balanced Fund*
Canadian Equity Funds: MD Equity Fund*
Canadian Equity Funds: MD Select Fund*
Foreign Equity Funds: MD Emerging Markets Fund
Foreign Equity Funds: MD Growth Fund Ltd.
Foreign Equity Funds: MD US Equity Fund
Group Deferred Annuity Contract: MD Income Fund*
Income Funds: MD Bond & Mortgage Fund*
Income Funds: MD Bond Fund*
Income Funds: MD Dividend Fund*
Income Funds: MD Global Bond Fund
Income Funds: MD Money Fund*
M.K. Wong & Associates Ltd.
#2520, 1066 Hastings St. West, Vancouver BC V6E 3X1
604/257-1000; Fax: 604/669-8420; Toll Free: 1-800-665-9360
Email: pryan@cyberstore.ca
CEO, Milton Wong
Mutual Funds:
Lotus Group: Balanced Fund*
Lotus Group: Bond Fund*
Lotus Group: Canadian Equity Fund*
Lotus Group: Income Fund
Lotus Group: International Bond Fund
Lotus Group: International Equity Fund
MOF Management Ltd.
Pacific Centre, #2020, 609 Granville St., PO Box 10379, Vancouver BC V7Y 1G6
604/643-7414; Fax: 604/643-7733; 1-800-663-6370
CEO, Donald D. MacFayden
Mutual Funds:
Multiple Opportunities Fund*
Special Opportunities Fund Ltd.
Mutual Investco Inc.
227 King St. South, Waterloo ON N2J 4C5
519/888-3900; Fax: 519/888-2990
URL: http://www.themutualgroup.com/
Chair, Barry Triller
Mutual Funds:
Mutual Alpine: Asian Fund
Mutual Alpine: Equity Fund
Mutual Alpine: Resources Fund
Mutual Leader: Amerifund
Mutual Leader: Bond Fund*
Mutual Leader: Diversifund 40*
Mutual Leader: Equifund*
Mutual Premier: American Fund
Mutual Premier: Blue Chip Fund*
Mutual Premier: Bond Fund*
Mutual Premier: Diversified Fund*
Mutual Premier: Emerging Markets Fund
Mutual Premier: Growth Fund*
Mutual Premier: International Fund*
Mutual Premier: Money Market Fund
Mutual Premier: Mortgage Fund*
Mutual Summit: Dividend Growth Fund
Mutual Summit: Equity Fund
Mutual Summit: Foreign Equity Fund
Mutual Summit: Growth & Income Fund
National Bank Securities Inc./Placements banque nationale inc.
1100, rue University, 7e étage, Montréal QC H3B 2G7
514/394-6900; Fax: 514/394-8204; Toll Free: 1-888-293-6637
CEO, Jacques Daoust
Mutual Funds:
General Trust: Balanced Fund*
General Trust: Bond Fund*
General Trust: Canadian Equity Fund*
General Trust: Growth Fund*
General Trust: International Fund*
General Trust: Money Market Fund*
General Trust: Mortgage Fund*
General Trust: US Equity Fund*
InvesNat: Blue Chip American Equity
InvesNat: Canadian Bond Fund*
InvesNat: Canadian Equity Fund*
InvesNat: Corporate Cash Management Fund*
InvesNat: Dividend Fund*
InvesNat: European Equity Fund
InvesNat: Far East Equity Fund
InvesNat: International RSP Bond Fund*
InvesNat: Japanese Equity Fund
InvesNat: Money Market Fund*
InvesNat: Mortgage Fund*
InvesNat: Retirement Balanced Fund*
InvesNat: Short-Term Government Bond Fund*
InvesNat: Treasury Bill Plus Fund*
InvesNat: US Money Market Fund
National Trust Mutual Funds
One Financial Place, One Adelaide St. East, Toronto ON M5C 2W8
416/361-3863; Fax: 416/361-5563; Toll Free: 1-800-563-4683
Vice-President, Tammy Murray, Retail Deposits & Mutual Funds
Mutual Funds:
National Trust: American Equity Fund
National Trust: Balanced Fund*
National Trust: Canadian Bond Fund*
National Trust: Canadian Equity Fund*
National Trust: Dividend Fund*
National Trust: Emerging Markets Fund
National Trust: International Equity Fund
National Trust: International RSP Bond Fund
National Trust: Money Market Fund*
National Trust: Mortgage Fund*
National Trust: Special Equity Fund*
Navigator Fund Company Ltd.
#1120, 444 St. Mary Ave., Winnipeg MB R3C 3T1
204/942-7788; Fax: 204/947-1665; Toll Free 1-800-665-1667
URL: http://www.navigator.ca
President/CEO, Wes Gibson, FCA
Mutual Funds:
Navigator: American Value Investment Fund
Navigator: Asia-Pacific Fund
Navigator: Canadian Income Fund*
Navigator: Latin-American Fund
Navigator: Value Investment Retirement Fund*
O'Donnell Investment Management Corporation
#601, 4100 Yonge St., PO Box 17, North York ON M2P 2B5
416/221-2800; Fax: 416/221-5200
President/CEO & Secretary, James F. O'Donnell
OHA Investment Management Limited
#2501, 200 Front St. West, Toronto ON M5V 3L1
416/205-1455; Fax: 416/205-1440; 1-800-268-9597
President, R. Hutcheon
Mutual Funds:
OHA: Balanced Fund*
OHA: Bond Fund*
OHA: Canadian Equity Fund*
OHA: Foreign Equity Fund*
OHA: Short-Term Fund*

Ontario Teachers' Group Investment Fund
57 Mobile Dr., Toronto ON M4A 1H5
416/752-9410; Fax: 416/752-6649; Toll Free 1-800-263-9541
General Manager, John Elder
Mutual Funds:
OTG: Balanced Section*
OTG: Diversified Section*
OTG: Fixed Value Section*
OTG: Global Value Fund*
OTG: Growth Section*
OTG: Mortgage Income Section*

Perigee Investment Counsel Inc.
#1400, 320 Bay St., PO Box 9, Toronto ON M5H 4A6
416/860-0616; Fax: 416/860-0628
Email: fundinfo@perigreeinvest.com; URL: http://www.perigeeinvest.com
Sr. Principal, D. Alex WilsonChair
Mutual Funds:
Perigee: Accufund
Perigee: Aurora Bond Fund
Perigee: Axis Fund
Perigee: Calibrator Equity Fund
Perigee: Diversifund
Perigee: Hemisphere Equity Fund
Perigee: Meridian Bond Fund
Perigee: Proton Income Fund
Perigee: Quadrant Equity Fund
Perigee: Sequent Bond Fund
Perigee: Sphere Equity Fund
Perigee: Symmetry Balanced Fund
Perigee: T-Plus Fund
Perigee: Trajectory Equity Fund
Perigee: Vector US Fund

Peter Cundill & Associates Ltd.
Sun Life Plaza, #1200, 1100 Melville St., Vancouver BC V6E 4A6
604/685-4231; Fax: 604/689-9532; Toll Free: 1-800-663-0156
URL: http://www.cundill.com
President/CEO, Mark C. Stevens
Mutual Funds:
Cundill: Security Fund*
Cundill: Value Fund

Phillips, Hager & North Investment Management Ltd.
#1700, 1055 West Hastings St., Vancouver BC V6E 2H3
604/691-6781; Fax: 604/685-5712; 1-800-661-6141
URL: http://www.phn.ca/
President, Tony Gage
Mutual Funds:
Phillips, Hager & North: Balanced Fund*
Phillips, Hager & North: Bond Fund*
Phillips, Hager & North: Canadian Equity Fund*
Phillips, Hager & North: Canadian Equity Plus Fund*
Phillips, Hager & North: Canadian Money Market Fund*
Phillips, Hager & North: Dividend Income Fund
Phillips, Hager & North: International Equity Fund
Phillips, Hager & North: North American Equity Fund
Phillips, Hager & North: Short-Term Bond & Mortgage Fund
Phillips, Hager & North: U.S. Equity Fund
Phillips, Hager & North: Vintage Fund*

Pursuit Financial Management Corp.
#402, 1200 Sheppard Ave. East, North York ON M2K 2S5
416/502-9300; Fax: 416/502-9394; Toll Free: 1-800-253-9619
Mutual Funds:
Pursuit: American Fund
Pursuit: Canadian Equity Fund*
Pursuit: Global Bond Fund
Pursuit: Global Equity Fund
Pursuit: Income Fund*
Pursuit: Money Market Fund*

Royal Mutual Funds Inc.
Royal Trust Tower, TD Centre, 5th Fl., PO Box 7500, Stn A, Toronto ON M5W 1P9
416/955-3618; Fax: 416/955-3630; Toll Free: 1-800-463-3863; Toll Free Fax: 1-888-323-2223
Email: funds@www.royalbank.com; URL: http://www.royalbank.com/english/fund/index.html
President/CEO, Simon Lewis
Mutual Funds:
Royal: $U.S. Money Market Fund
Royal: Asian Growth Fund
Royal: Balanced Fund*
Royal: Bond Fund*
Royal: Canadian Equity Fund*
Royal: Canadian Growth Fund*
Royal: Canadian Money Market Fund
Royal: Canadian Small Cap Fund*
Royal: Canadian T-Bill Fund*
Royal: Dividend Fund*
Royal: Energy Fund*
Royal: European Growth Fund
Royal: Global Bond Fund*
Royal: International Equity Fund
Royal: Japanese Stock Fund
Royal: Latin American Fund
Royal: Life Science & Technology Fund
Royal: Monthly Income Fund
Royal: Mortgage Fund*
Royal: Precious Metals Fund*
Royal: U.S. Equity Fund
Royal Trust: Advantage Balanced Fund*
Royal Trust: Advantage Income Fund*
Zweig: Global Managed Assets
Zweig: Strategic Growth Fund

Sagit Investment Management Ltd.
#900, 789 Pender St. West, Vancouver BC V6C 1H2
604/685-3193; Fax: 604/681-7536; Toll Free: 1-800-663-1003
Email: client@sagit.com; URL: http://www.sagit.com/funds
President, Raoul Tsakok
Mutual Funds:
Cambridge: American Growth Fund
Cambridge: Americas Fund
Cambridge: Balanced Fund*
Cambridge: China Fund
Cambridge: Global Fund
Cambridge: Growth Fund*
Cambridge: Pacific Fund
Cambridge: Resource Fund*
Cambridge: Special Equity Fund*
Trans-Canada: Bond Fund*
Trans-Canada: Dividend Fund*
Trans-Canada: Money Market Fund*
Trans-Canada: Pension Fund*
Trans-Canada: Value Fund*

Sceptre Investment Counsel Limited
#1200, 26 Wellington St. East, Toronto ON M5E 1W4
416/601-9898; Fax: 416/367-5938; 1-800-265-1888
President/CEO, Michael J. Wiggan
Mutual Funds:
Sceptre Asian Growth Fund
Sceptre Balanced Growth Fund*
Sceptre Bond Fund*
Sceptre Equity Growth Fund*
Sceptre International Fund
Sceptre Money Market Fund*

Scotia Securities Inc.
Scotia Plaza, 40 King St., 5th Fl., Toronto ON M5H 1H1
416/866-6563; Fax: 416/866-2018; Toll Free: 1-800-268-9269
URL: http://www.scotiabank.ca
President/CEO, Andrew Scipio del Campo
Mutual Funds:
Scotia: Global Bond Fund
Scotia CanAm: Growth Fund*
Scotia CanAm: Income Fund*
Scotia Excelsior: American Equity Growth Fund
Scotia Excelsior: Balanced Fund*
Scotia Excelsior: Canadian Blue Chip Fund*
Scotia Excelsior: Canadian Growth Fund*
Scotia Excelsior: Defensive Income Fund*
Scotia Excelsior: Dividend Fund*
Scotia Excelsior: Government of Canada T-Bill Fund
Scotia Excelsior: Income Fund*
Scotia Excelsior: International Fund
Scotia Excelsior: Latin American Fund
Scotia Excelsior: Money Market Fund*
Scotia Excelsior: Mortgage Fund*
Scotia Excelsior: Pacific Rim Fund
Scotia Excelsior: Precious Metals Fund*
Scotia Excelsior: Premium T-Bill Fund*
Scotia Excelsior: Total Return Fund*

Scudder Canada Investor Services Ltd.
BCE Place, 161 Bay St., PO Box 712, Toronto ON M5J 2S1
416/941-9393; Fax: 416/350-2018; Toll Free: 1-800-850-3863
Email: canada_mail@scudder.com; URL: http://www.scudder.ca
President/CEO, Gale K. Caruso
Mutual Funds:
Scudder: Canadian Bond Fund*
Scudder: Canadian Equity Fund*
Scudder: Canadian Money Market Fund
Scudder: Canadian Short Term Bond Fund*
Scudder: Emerging Markets Fund
Scudder: Global Fund
Scudder: Greater Europe Fund
Scudder: Pacific Fund
Scudder: US Growth & Income Fund

Spectrum United Mutual Funds Inc.
145 King St. West, 3rd Fl., Toronto ON M5H 1J8
416/352-3100; Fax: 416/352-3239; Toll Free: 1-800-263-1851
Email: info@spectrumunited.ca; URL: http://www.spectrumunited.ca/
President, Allen C. Marple
Mutual Funds:
Spectrum United: American Equity Fund
Spectrum United: American Growth Fund
Spectrum United: Asian Dynasty Fund
Spectrum United: Asset Allocation Fund*
Spectrum United: Canadian Equity Fund*
Spectrum United: Canadian Growth Fund*
Spectrum United: Canadian Investment Fund*
Spectrum United: Canadian Portfolio of Funds*
Spectrum United: Canadian Resource Fund*
Spectrum United: Canadian Stock Fund*
Spectrum United: Canadian T-Bill Fund*
Spectrum United: Diversified Fund*
Spectrum United: Dividend Fund*
Spectrum United: Emerging Markets Fund
Spectrum United: European Growth Fund
Spectrum United: Global Bond Fund
Spectrum United: Global Diversified Fund
Spectrum United: Global Equity Fund
Spectrum United: Global Growth Fund
Spectrum United: Global Telecommunications Fund
Spectrum United: Long-Term Bond Fund*
Spectrum United: Mid-Term Bond Fund*
Spectrum United: Optimax USA Fund
Spectrum United: RRSP International Bond Fund*
Spectrum United: Short-Term Bond Fund*
Spectrum United: US Dollar Money Market Fund

Standard Life Mutual Funds Limited
1245, rue Sherbrooke ouest, 19e étage, Montréal QC H3G 1G3
514/499-4476; Fax: 514/499-4466
URL: http://www.standardlife.ca/

President, Claude Garcia
Mutual Funds:
Standard Life: Balanced Fund*
Standard Life: Bond Fund*
Standard Life: Canadian Dividend Mutual Fund*
Standard Life: Equity Fund*
Standard Life: Growth Equity Mutual Fund*
Standard Life: International Bond Mutual Fund*
Standard Life: International Equity Mutual Fund
Standard Life: Money Market Fund*
Standard Life: Natural Resource Mutual Fund*
Standard Life: US Equity Mutual Fund

Stone & Co. Limited
#710, 155 University Ave., Toronto ON M5H 3B7
416/364-9188; Fax: 416/364-8456; 1-800-336-9528
Managing Director, Richad G. Stone
Mutual Funds:
Flagship: Growth & Income Fund*
Flagship: Money Market Fund*
Flagship: Stock Fund Canada*

Strategic Value Corp.
95 St. Clair Ave. West, 7th Fl., Toronto ON M4V 1N7
416/860-9100; Fax: 416/860-9090; Toll Free: 1-800-408-2311
Email: strategicvalue.funds@sympatico.ca
Chair, Mark S. Bonham
Mutual Funds:
Strategic Value: American Equity Fund
Strategic Value: American Equity Value Fund
Strategic Value: Asia Pacific Fund
Strategic Value: Canadian Balanced Fund*
Strategic Value: Canadian Equity Fund*
Strategic Value: Canadian Equity Value Fund
Strategic Value: Canadian Small Companies Fund*
Strategic Value: Commonwealth Fund Ltd.
Strategic Value: Dividend Fund Ltd.*
Strategic Value: Emerging Markets Fund
Strategic Value: Europe Fund
Strategic Value: Global Balanced Fund
Strategic Value: Global Balanced RSP Fund
Strategic Value: Global Equity Fund
Strategic Value: Government Bond Fund*
Strategic Value: Income Fund*
Strategic Value: International Fund Ltd.
Strategic Value: Strategic Value Fund

Talvest Fund Management Inc./Gestion financière Talvest Inc.
#3200, 1000, rue de la Gauchetière ouest, Montréal QC H3B 4W5
514/875-9090; Fax: 514/875-9304; Toll Free 1-800-268-8258
Email: talvest@marketing.com; URL: http://www.talvest.com
Chair, Jean-Guy Desjardins
Mutual Funds:
Canadian Medical Discoveries Fund Inc.*
Canadian Science & Technology Growth Fund Inc.*
Hyperion: Asian Fund
Hyperion: Canadian Equity Growth Fund*
Hyperion: European Fund
Hyperion: Global Health Care Fund
Hyperion: Global Science & Technology Fund
Hyperion: High Yield Bond Fund*
Hyperion: Small Cap Canadian Equity Fund*
Hyperion: Value Line U.S. Equity Fund
Talvest: Bond Fund*
Talvest: Canadian Asset Allocation Fund*
Talvest: Canadian Equity Value Fund
Talvest: Dividend Fund*
Talvest: Foreign Pay Cdn. Bond Fund*
Talvest: Global Asset Allocation Fund
Talvest: Global RRSP Fund*
Talvest: Income Fund*
Talvest: Money Fund*
Talvest: New Economy Fund*

TD Asset Management
Toronto-Dominion Tower, Toronto-Dominion Centre, PO Box 100, Stn Toronto-Dominion, Toronto ON M5K 1G8
416/982-6432; Fax: 416/982-6625; Toll Free: 1-800-268-8166
Email: funderman@tdbank.ca; URL: http://www.tdbank.ca/tdbank/mutual/index.html
President, J. Mark Wettlaufer
Mutual Funds:
Green Line: Asian Growth Fund
Green Line: Balanced Growth Fund*
Green Line: Balanced Income Fund*
Green Line: Blue Chip Equity Fund*
Green Line: Canadian Bond Fund*
Green Line: Canadian Equity Fund*
Green Line: Canadian Government Bond Fund*
Green Line: Canadian Index Fund*
Green Line: Canadian Money Market Fund*
Green Line: Canadian T-Bill Fund*
Green Line: Dividend Fund
Green Line: Emerging Markets Fund
Green Line: Energy Fund*
Green Line: European Growth Fund*
Green Line: Global Government Bond Fund
Green Line: Global RSP Bond Fund*
Green Line: Global Select Fund
Green Line: Health Sciences Fund
Green Line: International Equity Fund
Green Line: Japanese Growth Fund
Green Line: Latin American Growth Fund
Green Line: Mortgage Fund*
Green Line: Mortgage-Backed Fund*
Green Line: North American Growth Fund
Green Line: Precious Metal Fund*
Green Line: Real Return Bond Fund*
Green Line: Resource Fund*
Green Line: Science & Technology Fund
Green Line: Short-Term Income Fund*
Green Line: U.S. Blue Chip Equity Fund
Green Line: U.S. Index Fund
Green Line: U.S. Money Market Fund*
Green Line: Value Fund*

Templeton Management Limited
#2101, One Adelaide St. East, Toronto ON M5C 3B8
416/957-6000; Fax: 416/364-4708; Toll Free: 1-800-387-0830
URL: http://www.templeton.ca
President/CEO, Donald F. Reed, CFA, CIC
Mutual Funds:
Templeton: Balanced Fund*
Templeton: Canadian Asset Allocation Fund*
Templeton: Canadian Bond Fund*
Templeton: Canadian Stock Fund*
Templeton: Emerging Markets Fund
Templeton: Global Balanced Fund
Templeton: Global Bond Fund
Templeton: Global Smaller Companies Fund
Templeton: Growth Fund, Ltd.
Templeton: International Balanced Fund
Templeton: International Stock Fund
Templeton: Treasury Bill Fund*

Tradex Management Inc./Gestion Tradex Inc.
#1610, 45 O'Connor St., Ottawa ON K1P 1A4
613/233-3394; Fax: 613/233-8191; 1-800-567-3863
Email: tradex@fox.nstn.ca
President, Andrew Billingsley
Mutual Funds:
Tradex Bond Fund*
Tradex Emerging Markets Country Fund
Tradex Equity Fund Limited*

Trimark Investment Management Inc.
#5600, One First Canadian Place, PO Box 487, Toronto ON M5X 1E5
416/362-7181; Fax: 416/362-8515; Toll Free: 1-800-387-9845
Email: invest@trimark.com; URL: http://www.trimark.com/
President, Bradley J. Badeau
Mutual Funds:
The Americas Fund
Trimark Advantage Bond Fund*
Trimark Canadian Bond Fund*
Trimark Canadian Fund*
Trimark Discovery Fund
Trimark Fund
Trimark Government Income Fund*
Trimark Income Growth Fund*
Trimark Indo-Pacific Fund
Trimark Interest Fund*
Trimark RSP Equity Fund*
Trimark Select Balanced Fund*
Trimark Select Canadian Growth Fund*
Trimark Select Growth Fund

University Avenue Financial
40 University Ave., Main Fl., Toronto ON M5J 1T1
416/351-1617; Fax: 416/351-8225; Toll Free: 1-800-465-1812
URL: http://www.fundlib.com/univers.html
President/CEO, Andrew M. Roblin
Mutual Funds:
University Avenue: Bond Fund*
University Avenue: Canadian Fund*
University Avenue: Growth Fund*
University Avenue: Money Fund

Yield Management Group Inc.
#2300, One Queen St. East, Toronto ON M5C 2W5
416/364-3711; Fax: 416/955-4877
Email: marketing@ymg.fnt.net; URL: http://www.ymg.ca
President/CEO, Greg Edwards
Mutual Funds:
YMG: Balanced Fund*
YMG: Emerging Companies Fund*
YMG: Growth Fund*
YMG: Hedge Fund*
YMG: Income Fund*
YMG: International Fund*
YMG: Money Market Fund*

# STOCK EXCHANGES

## The Alberta Stock Exchange

Stock Exchange Tower, 300 - 5 Ave. SW, 21st Fl., Calgary AB T2P 3C4 1996 Volume: 4.1 billion shares ($6 billion)
403/974-7400; Fax: 403/237-0450
Email: info@ase.ca;
URL: http://www.albertastock.com

#### Executives

President & Chief Operating Officer, T.A. Cumming
Exec. Vice-President, G.A. Romanzin
Chair, J. Cranston

#### Board of Governors

W. Auch
C.O.G. Baptist
I.D. Beddis
I.S. Brown
Public Governor, J.S. Burns, Q.C.
J.W. Cranston
T.A. Cumming
B.A. Fiell
Public Governor, R.W. Laidlaw
J.L McLaws
M.G. Prew
Public Governor, J.G. Rennie
Jim G. Sorenson
J.H. Wells
John B. Zaozirny, Q.C.

**MEMBER FIRMS & CORPORATIONS**
**with member seatholder**

Brenark Securities Ltd., 905/332-5222; Fax: 905/332-5855, 1100 Burloak Dr., 6th Fl., Burlington ON L7L 6B2

Brink, Hudson & Lefever Ltd., 604/688-0133; Fax: 604/682-2574, Bentall Centre, #1200, 595 Burrard St., PO Box 49135, Vancouver BC V7X 1J1 — P.J. Jennings

Bunting Warburg Inc., 416/364-3293; Fax: 416/364-1976, BCE Place, #4100, 161 Bay St., PO Box 617, Toronto ON M5J 2S1

Canaccord Capital Corporation, 604/643-7300; Fax: 604/643-7606; Toll Free: 1-800-663-1899, Pacific Centre, #2200, 609 Granville St., PO Box 10337, Vancouver BC V7Y 1H2 — Dennis N. Burdett

CIBC Wood Gundy Securities Inc., 403/260-0525, Bankers Hall, 309 - 8th Ave. SW, 2nd Fl., Calgary AB T2P 1C6

C.M. Oliver & Company Limited, 403/263-6133; Fax: 403/233-8835, #1205, 855 - 2nd St. SW, Calgary AB T2P 3N4 — J. Ross

CT Securities International Inc., 416/947-7200; Fax: 416/947-7213, #950, 70 York St., Toronto ON M5J 1S9

CT Securities Services Inc., 416/981-5000; Fax: 416/981-1339, 70 York St., 8th Fl., Toronto ON M5J 1S9 — R.A. Cosburn

Deutsche Morgan Grenfell Canada Ltd., 416/682-8000; Fax: 416/368-0085, Ernst & Young Tower, TD Centre, #1100, 222 Bay St., PO Box 64, Toronto ON M5K 1E7

DPM Securities Inc., 514/630-7500; Fax: 514/630-7347, #602, 755, boul St-Jean, Pointe-Claire QC H9R 5M9

Eagle & Partners Inc., 416/365-2440; Fax: 416/365-2449, Scotia Plaza, #3912, 40 King St. West, PO Box 506, Toronto ON M5H 3Z7

First Marathon Securities Limited, 403/290-0809; Fax: 403/269-7099, Bankers Hall, #4100, 855 - 2nd St. SW, Calgary AB T2P 4J8 — C.M. Stuart

FirstEnergy Capital Corp., 403/262-0600; Fax: 403/262-0644, #1600, 333 - 7th Ave. SW, Calgary AB T2P 2Z1 — W. Brett Wilson

Friedberg Mercantile Group, 416/364-2700; Fax: 416/364-0572; Toll Free: 1-800-461-2700, BCE Place, #250, 181 Bay St., PO Box 866, Toronto ON M5J 2T3

Georgia Pacific Securities Corporation, 604/668-1800; Fax: 604/668-1816, Two Bentall Centre, 555 Burrard St., 16th Fl., Vancouver BC V7X 1S6 — R. Brian Ashton

Global Securities Corporation, 604/689-5400; Fax: 604/689-5401, Royal Centre, #2900, 1055 West Georgia St., PO Box 11190, Vancouver BC V6E 3R5 — David.S. Chernoff

Goepel Shields & Partners Inc., 403/297-0434; Fax: 403/297-0430, Canada Place, #730, 407 - 2 St. SW, Calgary AB T2P 2Y3 — T.A. Budd

Golden Capital Securities Limited, 604/688-1898; Fax: 604/682-8874, #168, 1177 West Hastings St., Vancouver BC V6B 2K3

Gordon Capital Corporation, 403/261-3790; Fax: 403/269-5897, Bankers Hall, #3450, 855 - 2nd St. SW, Calgary AB T2P 4J8 — John Lloyd-Price

Gordon Capital Corporation, 416/868-7800; Fax: 416/364-6514, #5300, Toronto-Dominion Centre, PO Box 67, Stn Toronto-Dominion, Toronto ON M5K 1E7

Griffiths McBurney & Partners Ltd., 416/367-8600; Fax: 416/943-6175, #1100, 145 King St. West, Toronto ON M5H 1J8

Groome Capital Advisory Inc., 416/861-3080; Fax: 416/861-0418, 90 Adelaide St. West, Toronto ON M5H 3V9

Haywood Securities Inc., 604/643-1100; Fax: 604/643-1199, Commerce Place, #1100, 400 Burrard St., Vancouver BC V6C 3A6 — J.P.P. Tognetti

HSBC James Capel Canada Inc., 403/531-0545; Fax: 403/531-0540; Toll Free: 1-800-308-6671, #2200, 777 - 8 Ave. SW, Calgary AB T2P 3R5 — J.M. Romanchuk

Jennings Capital Inc., 403/292-0970; Fax: 403/292-0979, #2600, 520 - 5 Ave. SW, Calgary AB T2P 3R7 — Robert G. Jennings

Jones, Gable & Company Limited, 416/362-5454; Fax: 416/365-8037, #600, 110 Yonge St., Toronto ON M5C 1T6 — Don M. Ross

Lévesque Beaubien Geoffrion Inc., 403/531-8400; Fax: 403/531-8413, #2150, 421 - 7 Ave. SW, Calgary AB T2P 4K9 — K. Bannister

Loewen, Ondaatje, McCutcheon Limited, 416/964-4455; Fax: 416/964-4492, Hazelton Lanes, East Tower, 55 Avenue Rd., Toronto ON M5R 3L2 — Garrett Herman

Majendie Charlton Limited, 403/262-5542; Fax: 403/265-9655, #2710, 140 - 4 Ave. SW, Calgary AB T2P 3N3 — W.W. Charlton

Marleau, Lemire Securities Inc., 416/595-5500; Fax: 416/595-0996, #2000, 150 King St. West, Toronto ON M5H 1J9

McDermid St. Lawrence Securities Ltd., 403/221-0333; Fax: 403/221-0350, #2600, 700 - 9 Ave. SW, Calgary AB T2P 3V4 — I.S. Brown

Merit Investment Corporation, 416/867-6000; Fax: 416/867-6137; Toll Free: 1-800-616-8858, #1000, 55 University Ave., Toronto ON M5J 2P8 — L. Kieselstein

Merrill Lynch Canada Inc., 416/586-6000; Fax: 416/586-6616, Merrill Lynch Canada Tower, 200 King St. West, Toronto ON M5H 3W3 — George B. Dunn

Midland Walwyn Capital Inc., 403/266-0123; Fax: 403/264-1030, #900, 350 - 7th Ave. SW, Calgary AB T2P 3N9 — B.J. Geisler

Midland Walwyn Capital Inc., 416/369-7400; Fax: 416/369-8172, Bay Wellington Tower, BCE Place, #400, 181 Bay St., Toronto ON M5J 2V8

Nesbitt Burns Inc., 403/260-9300; Fax: 403/260-9356, Bankers Hall East, #4000, 855 - 2 St. SW, Calgary AB T2P 4N2 — G.E. Perron

Nesbitt Burns Inc., 416/359-4000; Fax: 416/359-4311, #5000, First Canadian Place, PO Box 150, Stn 1st Canadian Place, Toronto ON M5X 1H3

Odlum Brown Limited, 604/669-1600; Fax: 604/681-8310, Pacific Centre, #1800, 609 Granville St., PO Box 10012, Vancouver BC V7Y 1A3 — S.R. Sherwood

Pacific International Securities Inc., 604/664-2900; Fax: 604/664-2649, #1900, 666 Burrard St., Vancouver BC V6C 3N1 — Lawrence H. McQuid

Perry Securities Ltd., 403/532-7717; Fax: 403/538-0600, 10135 - 101 Ave., Grande Prairie AB T8V 0Y4 — K.G. Perry

Peters & Co. Limited, 403/261-4850; Fax: 403/266-4116, #2500, 350 - 7th Ave. SW, Calgary AB T2P 4N1 — H.F. Osler

RBC Dominion Securities Inc., 403/299-7000; Fax: 403/298-1601, 707 - 7 Ave. SW, 3rd Fl., Calgary AB T2P 3H6

Research Capital Corporation, 403/265-7400; Fax: 403/237-5951, #1330, 140 - 4 Ave. SW, Calgary AB T2P 3M3 — I.G. Griffin

Roche Securities Limited, 403/424-5131; Fax: 403/429-1874, Oxford Tower, #1202, 10235 - 101st St., Edmonton AB T5J 3G1

Rogers & Partners Securities Inc., Fax: 403/265-6039; 1-800-430-6999, First Alberta Place, #2300, 777 - 8 Ave. SW, Calgary AB T2P 3R5 — J.V. Rogers

ScotiaMcLeod Inc., 403/298-4000; Fax: 403/298-4099, #920, 401 - 9th Ave. SW, Calgary AB T2P 3C5 — J.W. Cranston

Sprott Securities Limited, 403/266-4240; Fax: 403/266-4250; Toll Free: 1-800-461-9491, #1900, 355 - 4th Ave. SW, Calgary AB T2P 0J1 — E.S. Sprott

StephenAvenue Securities Inc., 403/777-2442; Fax: 403/777-2469, Lancaster Bldg., #701, 304 - 8th Ave. SW, Calgary AB T2P 1C2 — P.E. Pullam

TD Securities Inc., 416/982-6160; Fax: 416/983-3176, Ernst & Young Tower, Toronto-Dominion Centre, 222 Bay St., 20th Fl., Toronto ON M5K 1A2 — Keith Gray

Union Securities Ltd., 604/687-2201; Fax: 604/684-6307, Pacific Centre, #900, 609 Granville St., PO Box 10341, Vancouver BC V7Y 1H4 — Norman F. Thompson

Versus Brokerage Services Inc., 416/214-1960; Fax: 416/864-3918, BCE Place, #3810, 181 Bay St., PO Box 751, Toronto ON M5J 2T3

W.D. Latimer Co. Limited, 416/363-5631; Fax: 416/363-8022, #2508, Toronto-Dominion Centre, PO Box 96, Stn Toronto-Dominion, Toronto ON M5K 1G8 — C.M. Bracken

Whalen Béliveau & Associés Inc., 514/844-5443; Fax: 514/844-5216, #600, 1010, rue Sherbrooke ouest, Montréal QC H3A 2R7

Wolverton Securities Ltd., 604/688-3477; Fax: 604/662-5205, 777 Dunsmuir St., 17th Fl., PO Box 10115, Vancouver BC V7Y 1J5

Yorkton Securities Inc., 403/260-8400; Fax: 403/269-7870, #4400, 400 - 3 Ave. SW, Calgary AB T2P 4H2 — B.N. Wolverton

Yorkton Securities Inc., 416/864-3500; Fax: 416/864-9134, #3100, BCE Place, 181 Bay St., PO Box 830, Toronto ON M5J 2T3 — M.G. Prew

## Montréal Exchange/Bourse de Montréal

Tour de la Bourse, 800, Victoria Sq., PO Box 61, Montréal QC H4Z 1A9 1996 Volume: 4,304,504,842 shares ($50,166,152,424)

514/871-2424; Fax: 514/871-3553

Email: info@me.org; URL: http://www.me.org

**Executives**

Chair, René G. Jarry, Governing Committee

President/CEO, Gérald A. Lacoste

Sr. Vice-President, Elaine C. Phénix, Capital Development

Interim Exec., Giovanni Giarrusso, Markets

Sr. Vice-President, Joan S. Paiement, Finance, Technology & Administration

**MEMBER FIRMS & CORPORATIONS**
**with member seatholder**

Altamira Securities Inc., 416/925-2512; Fax: 416/925-5352, #200, 250 Bloor St. East, Toronto ON M4W 1E6

Beacon Securities Limited, 902/423-1260; Fax: 902/425-5237, 1707 Grafton St., Halifax NS B3J 2C6

BLC Securities Inc., 514/350-2800; Fax: 514/250-2899, Tour de la Banque Laurentienne, #1985, 1981, av McGill College, Montréal QC H3K 3A3

Brockhouse & Cooper Inc., 514/932-7171; Fax: 514/932-8288, #4025, 1250, boul René-Lévesque ouest, Montréal QC H3B 4W8

Bunting Warburg Inc., 416/364-3293; Fax: 416/364-1976, BCE Place, #4100, 161 Bay St., PO Box 617, Toronto ON M5J 2S1

Canaccord Capital Corporation, 604/643-7300; Fax: 604/643-7606; Toll Free: 1-800-663-1899, Pacific Centre, #2200, 609 Granville St., PO Box 10337, Vancouver BC V7Y 1H2

Casgrain & Compagnie Limitée, 514/871-8080; Fax: 514/871-1943, #1625, 500, boul René-Lévesque ouest, Montréal QC H2Z 1W7

Chouinard, McNamara Inc., 514/393-3430; Fax: 514/393-1110, #1300, 1100, boul René-Lévesque ouest, Montréal QC H3B 4N4

CIBC Wood Gundy Securities Inc., 416/594-7000; Fax: 416/594-7067, BCE Place, #700, 161 Bay St., Toronto ON M5J 2S1

C.M. Oliver & Company Limited, 604/668-6700; Fax: 604/681-8964, 750 West Pender St., 2nd Fl., Vancouver BC V6C 1B5

Commission Direct Inc., 416/941-5622; Fax: 416/941-5626, #1010, 121 King St. West, PO Box 11, Toronto ON M5H 3T9

Credifinance Securities Limited, 416/955-0159; Fax: 416/364-1522, #3303, 130 Adelaide St. West, Toronto ON M5H 3P5

Credit Suisse First Boston Canada Inc., 416/351-1600; Fax: 416/351-3639, #1300, 525 University Ave., Toronto ON M5G 2K6

CT Securities Services Inc., 416/981-5000; Fax: 416/981-1339, 70 York St., 8th Fl., Toronto ON M5J 1S9

CTI Capital inc., 514/861-3500; Fax: 514/861-3230, #1635, 1, Place Ville-Marie, Montréal QC H3B 2B6

D&B Internat Securities Inc., 514/842-4111; Fax: 514/842-3600, #1702, 1115, rue Sherbrooke ouest, Montréal QC H3A 1H3

Deacon Capital Corp., 416/350-3250; Fax: 416/350-3201, 320 Bay St., 9th Fl., PO Box 3, Toronto ON M5H 4A6

Demers Conseil inc., 514/879-1702; Fax: 514/879-5977, #1120, 615, boul René-Lévesque ouest, Montréal QC H3B 1P5

Desjardins Securities Inc., 514/987-1749; Fax: 514/842-3137; 1-800-361-4342, Tour de l'Est, 2, complexe Desjardins, 15e étage, CP 394, Succ Desjardins, Montréal QC H5B 1J2

Deutsche Morgan Grenfell Canada Ltd., 416/682-8000; Fax: 416/368-0085, Ernst & Young Tower, TD Centre, #1100, 222 Bay St., PO Box 64, Toronto ON M5K 1E7

Dlouhy Investments Inc., 514/845-8111; Fax: 514/845-0200, #1200, 1350, rue Sherbrooke ouest, Montréal QC H3G 1J1

DPM Securities Inc., 514/630-7500; Fax: 514/630-7347, #602, 755, boul St-Jean, Pointe-Claire QC H9R 5M9

Dubeau Capital & Compagnie ltée, 418/628-5533; Fax: 418/628-7844, #530, 5600, boul des Galeries, Québec QC G2K 2H6

Edward D. Jones & Co., 905/273-8400; Fax: 905/273-8424, Sussex Centre, #902, 90 Burnhamthorpe Rd. West, Mississauga ON L5B 3C3

Fairvest Securities Corporation, 416/364-9000; Fax: 416/364-6710, #700, 8 King St. East, Toronto ON M5C 1B5

F.C.G. Securities Corporation, 416/364-8600; Fax: 416/364-3581, #2750, 145 King St. West, Toronto ON M5H 1J8

Fimat Produits Dérivés Canada Inc., 514/841-6200; Fax: 514/841-6254, #1800, 1501 av McGill College, Montréal QC H3A 3M8

First Marathon Securities Limited, 416/869-3707; Fax: 416/869-0089; Toll Free: 1-800-661-3863, The Exchange Tower, #3200, 2 First Canadian Place, PO Box 21, Toronto ON M5X 1J9

Fortune Financial Corporation, 416/291-4400; Fax: 416/291-4457, One Corporate Plaza, #608, 2075 Kennedy Rd., Scarborough ON M1T 3V3

Friedberg Mercantile Group, 416/364-2700; Fax: 416/364-0572; Toll Free: 1-800-461-2700, BCE Place, #250, 181 Bay St., PO Box 866, Toronto ON M5J 2T3

Georgia Pacific Securities Corporation, 604/668-1800; Fax: 604/668-1816, Two Bentall Centre, 555 Burrard St., 16th Fl., Vancouver BC V7X 1S6

Goepel Shields & Partners Inc., 416/594-1000; Fax: 416/594-1008, #1600, 150 York St., Toronto ON M5H 3S5

Golden Capital Securities Limited, 604/688-1898; Fax: 604/682-8874, #168, 1177 West Hastings St., Vancouver BC V6B 2K3

Goldman Sachs Canada, 416/343-8900; Fax: 416/343-8792, #1201, 150 King St. West, Toronto ON M5H 1J9

Gordon Capital Corporation, 416/868-7800; Fax: 416/364-6514, #5300, Toronto-Dominion Centre, PO Box 67, Stn Toronto-Dominion, Toronto ON M5K 1E7

Great Pacific Management Co. Ltd., 604/669-1143; Fax: 604/669-0310, 1125 Howe St., 4th Fl., Vancouver BC V6Z 2K8

Griffiths McBurney & Partners Ltd., 416/367-8600; Fax: 416/943-6175, #1100, 145 King St. West, Toronto ON M5H 1J8

Le Groupe Option Retraite inc., 514/861-0777; Fax: 514/861-1976, #201, 455, rue St-Antoine ouest, Montréal QC H2Z 1J1

HSBC James Capel Canada Inc., 416/947-2700; Fax: 416/947-2730, #1200, 105 Adelaide St. West, Toronto ON M5H 1P9

J. Pasztor & Associates Inc., 416/922-1326; Fax: 416/922-1110, 19 Shorncliffe Ave., Toronto ON M4V 1S9

Jones, Gable & Company Limited, 416/362-5454; Fax: 416/365-8037, #600, 110 Yonge St., Toronto ON M5C 1T6

Lafferty, Harwood & Partners Limited, 514/287-7306; Fax: 514/287-7123, #1920, 2020, rue University, Montréal QC H3A 2A5

Leduc & Associés valeurs mobilières inc., 514/499-1066; Fax: 514/499-1071, #2300, 2020, rue University, Montréal QC H3A 2A5

Lévesque Beaubien Geoffrion Inc., 514/879-2222; Fax: 514/879-5142, Édifice Sun Life, 1155, rue Metcalfe, 5e étage, Montréal QC H3B 4S9

Loewen, Ondaatje, McCutcheon Limited, 416/964-4455; Fax: 416/964-4492, Hazelton Lanes, East Tower, 55 Avenue Rd., Toronto ON M5R 3L2

MacDougall MacDougall & MacTier Inc., 514/394-3000; Fax: 514/871-1481, Place du Canada, #2000, 1010, rue de la Gauchetière ouest, Montréal QC H3B 4J1

MacDougall, Meyer inc., 514/288-8823; Fax: 514/288-3272, #1500, 2050, rue Mansfield, Montréal QC H3A 1Y9

Maison Placements Canada Inc., 514/879-1662; Fax: 514/879-1673, #2230, Place du Canada, Montréal QC M3B 2N2

Marleau, Lemire Securities Inc., 416/595-5500; Fax: 416/595-0996, #2000, 150 King St. West, Toronto ON M5H 1J9

Maxima Capital inc., 514/878-2525; Fax: 514/878-2393, 266, rue St-Paul est, Montréal QC H2Y 1G9

Merit Investment Corporation, 416/867-6000; Fax: 416/867-6137; Toll Free: 1-800-616-8858, #1000, 55 University Ave., Toronto ON M5J 2P8

Merrill Lynch Canada Inc., 416/586-6000; Fax: 416/586-6616, Merrill Lynch Canada Tower, 200 King St. West, Toronto ON M5H 3W3

Midland Walwyn Capital Inc., 416/369-7400; Fax: 416/369-8172, Bay Wellington Tower, BCE Place, #400, 181 Bay St., Toronto ON M5J 2V8

Morgan Stanley Canada Ltd., 416/943-8400; Fax: 416/368-0796, #3700, 181 Bay St., PO Box 776, Toronto ON M5J 2T3

National Bank Securities Inc., 514/394-6900; Fax: 514/394-8204; Toll Free: 1-888-293-6637, 1100, rue University, 7e étage, Montréal QC H3B 2G7

Nesbitt Burns Inc., 514/286-7200; Fax: 514/286-7262, #3200, 1501, av McGill College, Montréal QC M3A 3MB

Nesbitt Burns Inc., 416/359-4000; Fax: 416/359-4311, #5000, First Canadian Place, PO Box 150, Stn 1st Canadian Place, Toronto ON M5X 1H3

Newcrest Capital Inc., 416/862-9160; Fax: 416/862-8053, #1200, 55 Yonge St., Toronto ON M5E 1J4

Odlum Brown Limited, 604/669-1600; Fax: 604/681-8310, Pacific Centre, #1800, 609 Granville St., PO Box 10012, Vancouver BC V7Y 1A3

Pensec Inc., 613/724-5434; Fax: 613/724-5489, #1204, 99 Metcalfe St., Ottawa ON K1P 6L7

Pictet (Canada) & Company Limited, 514/288-8161; Fax: 514/288-5473, #2900, 1800, av McGill College, Montréal QC H3A 3J6

Pollitt & Co. Inc., 416/365-3313; Fax: 416/368-0141, Commerce Court North, #1101, 25 King St. West, PO Box 94, Toronto ON M5L 1B9

RBC Dominion Securities Inc., 416/842-2000; Fax: 416/842-5360, Royal Bank Plaza, South Tower, 200 Bay St., PO Box 50, Toronto ON M5J 2W7

Refco Futures (Canada) Limited, 416/862-7000; Fax: 416/862-0576, Canada Trust Tower, BCE Place, #3630, 161 Bay St., PO Box 702, Toronto ON M5J 2S1

Research Capital Corporation, 416/860-7600; Fax: 416/860-7674, Ernst & Young Tower, TD Centre, 15th Fl., PO Box 265, Toronto ON M5K 1J5

ScotiaMcLeod Inc., 416/863-7411; Fax: 416/863-7751, Scotia Plaza, 40 King St. West, PO Box 4085, Stn A, Toronto ON M5W 1H8

Société Générale Securities Inc., 514/954-2300; Fax: 514/875-8136, #709, 1155, av University, Montréal QC H3B 3A7

Sprott Securities Limited, 416/362-7485; Fax: 416/943-6499, South Tower, Royal Bank Plaza, #3450, 200 Bay St., PO Box 63, Stn Royal Bank, Toronto ON M5J 2J2

Tassé & Associés, limitée, 514/879-2100; Fax: 514/879-3903, Maison Trust Royal, #1200, 630, boul René-Lévesque ouest, Montréal QC H3B 1S6

Thomson Kernaghan & Co. Ltd., 416/860-8800; Fax: 416/367-8055, 365 Bay St., 2nd Fl., Toronto ON M5H 2V2

Versus Brokerage Services Inc., 416/214-1960; Fax: 416/864-3918, BCE Place, #3810, 181 Bay St., PO Box 751, Toronto ON M5J 2T3

W.D. Latimer Co. Limited, 416/363-5631; Fax: 416/363-8022, #2508, Toronto-Dominion Centre, PO Box 96, Stn Toronto-Dominion, Toronto ON M5K 1G8

Whalen Béliveau & Associés Inc., 514/844-5443; Fax: 514/844-5216, #600, 1010, rue Sherbrooke ouest, Montréal QC H3A 2R7

Yamaichi International (Canada) Limited, 514/499-1110; Fax: 514/499-1113, #2300, 600, boul de Maisonneuve ouest, Montréal QC H3A 3J2

Yorkton Securities Inc., 416/864-3500; Fax: 416/864-9134, #3100, BCE Place, 181 Bay St., PO Box 830, Toronto ON M5J 2T3

## The Toronto Stock Exchange

The Exchange Tower, 2 First Canadian Place, Toronto ON M5X 1J2 1996 Volume: 298,104,277 shares ($6,492,525,613)
416/947-4700; Fax: 416/947-4585
Email: info@tse.com

#### Executives

President/CEO, Rowland W. Fleming
Sr. Vice-President, John W. Carson, Market Regulation
Sr. Vice-President, Susan E. Crocker, Equities
Sr. Vice-President, Brian C. Harding, Information Systems & Trading Services
Vice-President, Keith E. Boast, Q.C., External Affairs
Vice-President, Irene A. Boychuk, Human Resources
Vice-President, J. Adam Conyers, Finance & Administration, Treasurer
Vice-President, Leonard P. Petrillo, General Counsel & Secretary
Vice-President, Stephen Rive, Derivative Markets

#### Board of Governors

Chair, Barbara G. Stymicst
Vice-Chair, Daniel F. Sullivan
Board Member, Rowland W. Flemming
Board Member, G. F. Kym Anthony
Board Member, Paul K. Bates

Public Governor, Diana Bennett Gale
Public Governor, William H. Broadhurst
Public Governor, W. Robert Farquharson
Board Member, Wayne C. Fox
Board Member, Helen M. Kearns
Public Governor, John P. Mulvihill
Board Member, Richard W. Nesbitt
Board Member, Gary D. Reamey
Board Member, L. Rodney Sim

**MEMBER FIRMS & CORPORATIONS**
**with member seatholder**

Altus Securities Inc., 416/369-9211; Fax: 416/369-9268, #1100, 55 Yonge St., Toronto ON M5E 1J4 — B.B. Kizemchuk

Brant Securities Limited, 416/486-2200; Fax: 416/486-3907, #1000, 2200 Yonge St., Toronto ON M4S 2C6 — Reuben Brant

Brawley Cathers Limited, 416/363-5821; Fax: 416/947-1310, #600, 141 Adelaide St. West, Toronto ON M5H 3L9 — D.M. Stovel

Brenark Securities Ltd., 905/332-5222; Fax: 905/332-5855, 1100 Burloak Dr., 6th Fl., Burlington ON L7L 6B2 — Ronald W. Smith

Brink, Hudson & Lefever Ltd., 604/688-0133; Fax: 604/682-2574, Bentall Centre, #1200, 595 Burrard St., PO Box 49135, Vancouver BC V7X 1J1 — Brian D. Graves

Brockhouse & Cooper Inc., 514/932-7171; Fax: 514/932-8288, #4025, 1250, boul René-Lévesque ouest, Montréal QC H3B 4W8 — Richard L. Cooper

Bunting Warburg Inc., 416/364-3293; Fax: 416/364-1976, BCE Place, #4100, 161 Bay St., PO Box 617, Toronto ON M5J 2S1 — J.M. Estey

BZW Canada Limited, 416/350-3200; Fax: 416350-3201, 304 Bay St., 9th Fl.,Toronto ON M5H 4A5— John Plaxton

Caldwell Securities Ltd., 416/862-7755; Fax: 416/862-2498; Toll Free: 1-800-387-0859, #1710, 150 King St. West, PO Box 47, Toronto ON M5H 1J9 — B.T.N. Caldwell

Canaccord Capital Corporation, 416/869-7368; Fax: 416/869-7356; Toll Free: 1-800-382-9280, #1200, 320 Bay St., PO Box 6, Toronto ON M5H 4A6 — W.H. McMahon

Cassels Blaikie & Co. Limited, 416/941-7500; Fax: 416/867-9821; Toll Free: 1-800-463-6931, One Financial Place, #200, 1 Adelaide St. East, Toronto ON M5C 2W8 — J. Alan Brown

CIBC Wood Gundy Securities Inc., 416/594-7000; Fax: 416/594-7067, BCE Place, #700, 161 Bay St., Toronto ON M5J 2S1 — Wayne C. Fox

C.M. Oliver & Company Limited, 604/668-6700; Fax: 604/681-8964, 750 West Pender St., 2nd Fl., Vancouver BC V6C 1B5 — C.M. O'Brian

Commission Direct Inc., 416/941-5622; Fax: 416/941-5626, #1010, 121 King St. West, PO Box 11, Toronto ON M5H 3T9 — T.R. Green

Connor, Clark & Company Ltd., 416/360-0006; Fax: 416/360-8380, Scotia Plaza, #5110, 40 King St. West, PO Box 125, Toronto ON M5H 3Y2 — J.C. Clark

Correspondent Network, 416/869-8509; Fax: 416/869-7548, The Exchange Tower, #3220, 2 First Canadian Place, PO Box 470, Toronto ON M5X 1E4 — L.S. Bloomberg

Credifinance Securities Limited, 416/955-0159; Fax: 416/364-1522, #3303, 130 Adelaide St. West, Toronto ON M5H 3P5 — G. Benarroch

Credit Suisse First Boston Canada Inc., 416/351-1600; Fax: 416/351-3639, #1300, 525 University Ave., Toronto ON M5G 2K6 — K.W. Redpath

CT Securities International Inc., 416/947-7200; Fax: 416/947-7213, #950, 70 York St., Toronto ON M5J 1S9 — P.A. Ruys de Perez

CT Securities Services Inc., 416/981-5000; Fax: 416/981-1339, 70 York St., 8th Fl., Toronto ON M5J 1S9 — R.A. Cosburn

Deacon Capital Corp., 416/350-3250; Fax: 416/350-3201, 320 Bay St., 9th Fl., PO Box 3, Toronto ON M5H 4A6 — J.L. Easson

Desjardins Securities Inc., 514/987-1749; Fax: 514/842-3137; 1-800-361-4342, Tour de l'Est, 2, complexe Desjardins, 15e étage, CP 394, Succ Desjardins, Montréal QC H5B 1J2 — Réjean Duguay

Deutsche Morgan Grenfell Canada Ltd., 416/682-8000; Fax: 416/368-0085, Ernst & Young Tower, TD Centre, #1100, 222 Bay St., PO Box 64, Toronto ON M5K 1E7 — E.A. Pennock

Dlouhy Investments Inc., 514/845-8111; Fax: 514/845-0200, #1200, 1350, rue Sherbrooke ouest, Montréal QC H3G 1J1 — P. Dlouhy

Dominick & Dominick Securities Inc., 416/363-0201; Fax: 416/366-8279, #1714, 150 York St., 17th Fl., Toronto ON M5H 3S5 — J.S. Jenkins

Eagle & Partners Inc., 416/365-2440; Fax: 416/365-2449, Scotia Plaza, #3912, 40 King St. West, PO Box 506, Toronto ON M5H 3Z7 — B.S. Gordon

Edward D. Jones & Co., 905/273-8400; Fax: 905/273-8424, Sussex Centre, #902, 90 Burnhamthorpe Rd. West, Mississauga ON L5B 3C3 — G.D. Reamey

Equion Securities Canada Limited, 416/216-6500; Fax: 416/216-6510, #1100, 320 Bay St., PO Box 15, Toronto ON M5H 4A6 — Michael Nairne

Fairvest Securities Corporation, 416/364-9000; Fax: 416/364-6710, #700, 8 King St. East, Toronto ON M5C 1B5 — W. R. Riedl

First Delta Securities Inc., 416/364-4001; Fax: 416/364-6603; Toll Free: 1-800-206-7448, #400, 350 Bay St., Toronto ON M5H 2S6 — Geordie Trusler

First Marathon Securities Limited, 416/869-3707; Fax: 416/869-0089; Toll Free: 1-800-661-3863, The Exchange Tower, #3200, 2 First Canadian Place, PO Box 21, Toronto ON M5X 1J9 — Lawrence S. Bloomberg

FirstEnergy Capital Corp., 403/262-0600; Fax: 403/262-0644, #1600, 333 - 7th Ave. SW, Calgary AB T2P 2Z1 — W. Brett Wilson

Forbes & Walker Securities Limited, 416/925-3555; Fax: 416/925-5633, #400, 30A Hazelton Ave., Toronto ON M5R 2E2 — J.D. Hamilton

Foster & Associates Financial Services Inc., 416/369-1980; Fax: 416/369-1070; Toll Free: 1-800-559-8853, #500, 10 King St. East, Toronto ON M5C 1C3 — Briar Foster

Friedberg Mercantile Group, 416/364-2700; Fax: 416/364-0572; Toll Free: 1-800-461-2700, BCE Place, #250, 181 Bay St., PO Box 866, Toronto ON M5J 2T3 — Albert D. Friedberg

Georgia Pacific Securities Corporation, 604/668-1800; Two Bentall Centre, 555 Burrard St., 16th Fl., Vancouver BC V7X 1S6 — R. Brian Ashton

Global Securities Corporation, 604/689-5400; Fax: 604/689-5401, Royal Centre, #2900, 1055 West Georgia St., PO Box 11190, Vancouver BC V6E 3R5 — David.S. Chernoff

Goepel Shields & Partners Inc., 416/594-1000; Fax: 416/594-1008, #1600, 150 York St., Toronto ON M5H 3S5 — D.E. Roberts

Golden Capital Securities Limited, 604/688-1898; Fax: 604/682-8874, #168, 1177 West Hastings St., Vancouver BC V6B 2K3 — P.K.M. Chu

Gordon Capital Corporation, 416/868-7800; Fax: 416/868-5450, #5300 Toronto-Dominion Centre, PO Box 67, Stn Toronto-Dominion, Toronto, ON M5K 1E7— Peter A. Bailey

Gordon Private Client Corporation, 416/350-2828; Fax: 416/350-2820; Toll Free: 1-800-603-6086, Royal Trust Tower, Toronto Dominion Centre, #4300, PO Box 47, Toronto ON M5K 1B7 — Peter L. Wallace

Griffiths McBurney & Partners Ltd., 416/367-8600; Fax: 416/943-6175, #1100, 145 King St. West, Toronto ON M5H 1J8 — B.D. Griffiths

G.W. Welkin Capital Corp. of Canada, 905/886-0312; Fax: 905/886-0200, #312, 15 Wertheim Ct., Richmond Hill ON L4B 3H7 — G.T.H. Wong

Haywood Securities Inc., 604/643-1100; Fax: 604/643-1199, Commerce Place, #1100, 400 Burrard St., Vancouver BC V6C 3A6 — J.P.P. Tognetti

HSBC James Capel Canada Inc., 416/947-2700; Fax: 416/947-2730, #1200, 105 Adelaide St. West, Toronto ON M5H 1P9 — D.C. Pangman

Independent Trading Group, 416/363-6229; Fax: 416/363-1635, The Exchange Tower, 2 First Canadian Place, 3rd Fl., PO Box 84, Toronto ON M5X 1J2 — J.F. Taugher

Instinet Canada Limited, 416/368-2211; Fax: 416/368-2562, #2100, 2 First Canadian Place, Toronto ON M5X 1E3 — J.P. Watts

IPO Capital Corporation, 905/890-7800; Fax: 905/890-3891, 5889 Coopers Ave., 2nd Fl., Mississauga ON L4Z 1P9 — R.J. Emerson

Jones, Gable & Company Limited, 416/362-5454; Fax: 416/365-8037, #600, 110 Yonge St., Toronto ON M5C 1T6 — Don M. Ross

Kearns Capital Limited, 416/361-6032; Fax: 416/361-6050, #1604, 141 Adelaide St. West, Toronto ON M5H 3L5 — Helen M. Kearns

Kingwest & Company, 416/927-7740; Fax: 416/927-9264, 86 Avenue Rd., Toronto ON M5R 2H2 — R.L. Fogler

Lafferty, Harwood & Partners Limited, 514/287-7306; Fax: 514/287-7123, #1920, 2020, rue University, Montréal QC H3A 2A5 — N. Trudeau

Lévesque Beaubien Geoffrion Inc., 416/865-7400; Fax: 416/865-7605, #600, 121 King St. West, Toronto ON M5H 3T9 — P. Brunet

Lévesque Securities Inc., 416/865-7400; Fax: 416/865-7604, #600, 121 King St. West, Toronto ON M5H 3T9 — P. Brunet

Loewen, Ondaatje, McCutcheon Limited, 416/964-4455; Fax: 416/964-4492, Hazelton Lanes, East Tower, 55 Avenue Rd., Toronto ON M5R 3L2 — Garrett Herman

MacDougall MacDougall & MacTier Inc., 514/394-3000; Fax: 514/871-1481, Place du Canada, #2000, 1010, rue de la Gauchetière ouest, Montréal QC H3B 4J1 — B.H. MacDougall

Maison Placements Canada Inc., 416/947-6040; Fax: 416/947-6046, #906, 130 Adelaide St. West, PO Box 99, Toronto ON M5H 3P5 — J.R. Ing

Majendie Charlton Ltd., 604/682-6446; Fax: 604/662-8594; Toll Free: 1-800-822-6446, Waterfront Centre, #320, 200 Burrard St., Vancouver BC V6C 3L6 — N.L. Majendie

Marleau, Lemire Securities Inc., 416/595-5500; Fax: 416/595-0996, #2000, 150 King St. West, Toronto ON M5H 1J9 — Howard S. Eisen

McDermid St. Lawrence Securities Ltd., 416/777-7000; Fax: 416/777-7020, #1300, 151 Yonge St., Toronto ON M5C 3A2 — J.A. Chisholm

Merit Investment Corporation, 416/867-6000; Fax: 416/867-6137; Toll Free: 1-800-616-8858, #1000, 55 University Ave., Toronto ON M5J 2P8 — Barry H. Kasman

Merrill Lynch Canada Inc., 416/586-6000; Fax: 416/586-6616, Merrill Lynch Canada Tower, 200 King St. West, Toronto ON M5H 3W3 — George B. Dunn

Midland Walwyn Capital Inc., 416/369-7400; Fax: 416/369-8172, Bay Wellington Tower, BCE Place, #400, 181 Bay St., Toronto ON M5J 2V8 — L. Rodney Sim

MMI Group Inc., 416/363-3050; Fax: 416/368-4330, 135 King St. East, Main Fl., Toronto ON M5C 1G6 — C.H. Bayles

Morgan Stanley Canada Ltd., 416/943-8400; Fax: 416/368-0796, #3700, 181 Bay St., PO Box 776, Toronto ON M5J 2T3 — Peter J. Dey

Moss, Lawson & Co. Limited, 416/864-2700; Fax: 416/864-2756; Toll Free: 1-800-268-9733, #410, One Toronto St., Toronto ON M5C 2W3 — B.H. Pryce

NBC Clearing Services Inc., 514/879-5363; Fax: 514/879-2520, 1155, rue Metcalfe, 5e étage, Montréal QC H3B 4S9 — G. Ostiguy
Nesbitt Burns Inc., 416/359-4000; Fax: 416/359-4311, #5000, First Canadian Place, PO Box 150, Stn 1st Canadian Place, Toronto ON M5X 1H3 — P.E. Norris
Newcrest Capital Inc., 416/862-9160; Fax: 416/862-8053, #1200, 55 Yonge St., Toronto ON M5E 1J4 — R.J. O'Leary
The Nikko Securities Co. Canada, Ltd., 416/366-2600; Fax: 416/364-4110, #3808, Toronto-Dominion Bank Tower, Toronto-Dominion Centre, PO Box 84, Stn Toronto-Dominion, Toronto ON M5K 1G8
Nomura Canada Inc., 416/868-1683; Fax: 416/359-8956, #5830, One First Canadian Place, PO Box 434, Toronto ON M5X 1E3 — Thomas K. Wu
Octagon Capital Canada Corporation, 416/368-3322; Fax: 416/368-3811, Guardian of Canada Tower, #406, 181 University Ave., Toronto ON M5H 3M7 — L.P. Haughton
Odlum Brown Limited, 604/669-1600; Fax: 604/681-8310, Pacific Centre, #1800, 609 Granville St., PO Box 10012, Vancouver BC V7Y 1A3 — R.G. Sutherland
Pacific International Securities Inc., 604/664-2900; Fax: 604/664-2649, #1900, 666 Burrard St., Vancouver BC V6C 3N1 — Max Meier
Pensec Inc., 613/724-5434; Fax: 613/724-5489, #1204, 99 Metcalfe St., Ottawa ON K1P 6L7 — A.E. Smith
Peters & Co. Limited, 403/261-4850; Fax: 403/266-4116, #2500, 350 - 7th Ave. SW, Calgary AB T2P 4N1 — R.G. Peters
Polar Securities Inc., 416/367-4364; Fax: 416/367-0564, 350 Bay St., 13th Fl., Toronto ON M5H 2S6 — J.P. Sabourin
Pollitt & Co. Inc., 416/365-3313; Fax: 416/368-0141, Commerce Court North, #1101, 25 King St. West, PO Box 94, Toronto ON M5L 1B9 — M.H. Pollitt
Pope & Company, 416/593-5535; Fax: 416/593-5099, 15 Duncan St., Toronto ON M5H 3P9 — F. Pope
Porthmeor Securities Inc., 416/361-1511; Fax: 416/361-1099, #1207, 79 Wellington St. West, Toronto ON M5K 1H6 — Paul K. Bates
RBC Dominion Securities Inc., 416/842-2000; Fax: 416/842-5360, Royal Bank Plaza, South Tower, 200 Bay St., PO Box 50, Toronto ON M5J 2W7 — P.W. Hand
Research Capital Corporation, 416/860-7600; Fax: 416/860-7674, Ernst & Young Tower, TD Centre, 15th Fl., PO Box 265, Toronto ON M5K 1J5 — D.C. Hetherington
St. James Securities Inc., 416/214-9550; Fax: 416/214-9554, #1814, 150 York St., Toronto ON M5H 3S5 — Rodger Gray
Salman Partners Inc., 604/685-2450; Fax: 604/685-2471, #2230, 885 West Georgia St., Vancouver BC V6C 3E8 — T.K. Salman
ScotiaMcLeod Inc., 416/863-7411; Fax: 416/863-7751, Scotia Plaza, 40 King St. West, PO Box 4085, Stn A, Toronto ON M5W 1H8 — Brian J. Porter
Sprott Securities Limited, 416/362-7485; Fax: 416/943-6499, South Tower, Royal Bank Plaza, #3450, 200 Bay St., PO Box 63, Stn Royal Bank, Toronto ON M5J 2J2 — Eric S. Sprott
Standard Securities Capital Corporation, 416/515-0505; Fax: 416/515-0477, 35A Hazelton Ave., Toronto ON M5R 2E3 — G.R. Winthrope
Sun Life Securities Inc., 416/408-7978; Fax: 416/408-3885; Toll Free: 1-800-835-0812, 225 King St. West, 5th Fl., Toronto ON M5V 3C5 — G. Corsi
Tassé & Associés, limitée, 416/868-6200; Fax: 416/868-1566, #1118, 181 University Ave., Toronto ON M5H 3M7 — H. Tassé
Taurus Capital Markets Ltd., 416/361-2000; Fax: 416/364-0971, Scotia Plaza, #3000, 40 King St. West, Toronto ON M5H 3Y2 Taurus Capital Markets Ltd., Toronto — Lorne J. Levy
TD Securities Inc., 416/982-6160; Fax: 416/983-3176, Ernst & Young Tower, Toronto-Dominion Centre, 222 Bay St., 20th Fl., Toronto ON M5K 1A2 — Keith Gray
Thomson Kernaghan & Co. Ltd., 416/860-8800; Fax: 416/367-8055, 365 Bay St., 2nd Fl., Toronto ON M5H 2V2 — E.J. Kernaghan
Union Securities Ltd., 604/687-2201; Fax: 604/684-6307, Pacific Centre, #900, 609 Granville St., PO Box 10341, Vancouver BC V7Y 1H4 — Norman F. Thompson
Versus Brokerage Services Inc., 416/214-1960; Fax: 416/864-3918, BCE Place, #3810, 181 Bay St., PO Box 751, Toronto ON M5J 2T3 — D.M. Lay
Watt Carmichael Inc., 416/864-1500; Fax: 416/864-0883, Commercial Union Tower, #1402, Toronto-Dominion Centre, PO Box 60, Toronto ON M5K 1E7 — H.J.W. Carmichael
W.D. Latimer Co. Limited, 416/363-5631; Fax: 416/363-8022, #2508, Toronto-Dominion Centre, PO Box 96, Stn Toronto-Dominion, Toronto ON M5K 1G8 — C.M. Bracken
Whalen Béliveau & Associés Inc., 416/362-2813, #901, 141 Adelaide St. West, Toronto ON M5H 3L5 — W.R. Whalen
Wolverton Securities Ltd., 604/688-3477; Fax: 604/662-5205, 777 Dunsmuir St., 17th Fl., PO Box 10115, Vancouver BC V7Y 1J5 — E.C. Paterson
Yamaichi International (Canada) Limited, 514/499-1110; Fax: 514/499-1113, #2300, 600, boul de Maisonneuve ouest, Montréal QC H3A 3J2 — T. Shoji
Yorkton Securities Inc., 416/864-3500; Fax: 416/864-9134, #3100, BCE Place, 181 Bay St., PO Box 830, Toronto ON M5J 2T3 — G.S. Paterson

## The Vancouver Stock Exchange

Stock Exchange Tower, 609 Granville St., PO Box 10333, Vancouver BC V7Y 1H1 1996 Volume: 8,319,590,669 shares ($11,986,187,377)
604/689-3334; Fax: 604/688-6051
Email: information@vse.ca; URL: http://www.vse.com

#### Executives

President/CEO, Michael E. Johnson
Vice-President, Mary K. Beck, Compliance
Vice-President, John E. Boddie, Marketing
Vice-President & Chief Financial Officer, Lloyd Costley
Vice-President, Heather Dalcourt, Human Resources
Vice-President, John M. Forbes, Corporate Affairs & Secretary
Vice-President, Marc A. Foreman, Trading & Market Information Services
Vice-President, Warren H. Funt, Corporate Finance Services
Director, Glenn Knowles, Depository, Clearing & Settlement Services
Vice-President, Dave D. Ross, Technology
Director, G. Halfnights, Applications Development
Director, J. Sutherland, Communications
Director, S.M. de Stein, Market Information Services
Director, D.A. Gordon, Marketing
General Counsel, D.A. Armour
Controller, L.S. Liau

#### Board of Governors

Chair, D. Bradstreet-Daughney
Vice-Chair, M. Meier
Honorary Sec.-Treas., J.C. Lay
R.B. Ashton
D.N. Burdett
M-Y. Chan
G.M. Medland
P. Reid
Norman F. Thompson
M.E. Johnson
F.M. Banducci
B.S. Bassett
T.Y.C. Chan
K.R. Cory
L.J. McFadden
N.M. McKinstry
D.A. Risling
D.J. Yea
B. Brink
M.B. Couvelier
R. Kunin
L. Rubin

#### MEMBER FIRMS & CORPORATIONS

**with member seatholder**

Brink, Hudson & Lefever Ltd., 604/688-0133; Fax: 604/682-2574, Bentall Centre, #1200, 595 Burrard St., PO Box 49135, Vancouver BC V7X 1J1 — J.L. Mathers
Bunting Warburg Inc., 604/682-0791; Fax: 604/681-4220, Bentall Centre, #3314, 1055 Dunsmuir St., PO Box 49332, Vancouver BC V7X 1L4 — P.D. Ayriss
Canaccord Capital Corporation, 604/643-7300; Fax: 604/643-7606; Toll Free: 1-800-663-1899, Pacific Centre, #2200, 609 Granville St., PO Box 10337, Vancouver BC V7Y 1H2 — Peter M. Brown
CIBC Wood Gundy Securities Inc., 604/661-2300, #2100, 885 West Georgia St., Vancouver BC V6C 3E8 — J.C. Lay
C.M. Oliver & Company Limited, 604/668-6700; Fax: 604/681-8964, 750 West Pender St., 2nd Fl., Vancouver BC V6C 1B5 — C.M. O'Brian
Connor, Clark & Company Ltd., 604/689-0006; Fax: 604/688-1406, Cathedral Place, #1100, 925 Georgia St. West, Vancouver BC V6C 3L2 — G.P. Reid
Correspondent Network, 416/869-8509; Fax: 416/869-7548, The Exchange Tower, #3220, 2 First Canadian Place, PO Box 470, Toronto ON M5X 1E4
CT Securities International Inc., 604/685-3809; Fax: 604/681-1722, Oceanic Plaza, #1980, 1066 West Hastings St., Vancouver BC V6E 3X1 — G.J. Handley
Deacon Capital Corp., 416/350-3250; Fax: 416/350-3201, 320 Bay St., 9th Fl., PO Box 3, Toronto ON M5H 4A6
Dominick & Dominick Securities Inc., 416/363-0201; Fax: 416/366-8279, #1714, 150 York St., 17th Fl., Toronto ON M5H 3S5
DPM Securities Inc., 514/630-7500; Fax: 514/630-7347, #602, 755, boul St-Jean, Pointe-Claire QC H9R 5M9
Eagle & Partners Inc., 416/365-2440; Fax: 416/365-2449, Scotia Plaza, #3912, 40 King St. West, PO Box 506, Toronto ON M5H 3Z7 — B.S. Gordon
First Marathon Securities Limited, 604/682-6351; Fax: 604/681-7538, Commerce Place, #2000, 400 Burrard St., Vancouver BC V6C 3A6 — R.J. Disbrow
Friedberg Mercantile Group, 416/364-2700; Fax: 416/364-0572; Toll Free: 1-800-461-2700, BCE Place, #250, 181 Bay St., PO Box 866, Toronto ON M5J 2T3
Georgia Pacific Securities Corporation, 604/668-1800; Fax: 604/668-1816, Two Bentall Centre, 555 Burrard St., 16th Fl., Vancouver BC V7X 1S6 — R. Brian Ashton
Global Securities Corporation, 604/689-5400; Fax: 604/689-5401, Royal Centre, #2900, 1055 West Georgia St., PO Box 11190, Vancouver BC V6E 3R5 — David S. Chernoff
Goepel Shields & Partners Inc., 604/661-1777; Fax: 604/661-1790, #1100, 701 West Georgia St., PO Box 1011, Vancouver BC V7Y 1K8 — Ruston E.T. Goepel
Golden Capital Securities Limited, 604/688-1898; Fax: 604/682-8874, #168, 1177 West Hastings St., Vancouver BC V6B 2K3 — D.Y.H. Siu

Gordon Capital Corporation, 604/669-9555; Fax: 604/669-8848, Commerce Place, #2100, 400 Burrard St., Vancouver BC V6C 3A6 — D.C. Gordon
Great Pacific Management Co. Ltd., 604/669-1143; Fax: 604/669-0310, 1125 Howe St., 4th Fl., Vancouver BC V6Z 2K8 — S. Russell Isaac
Haywood Securities Inc., 604/643-1100; Fax: 604/643-1199, Commerce Place, #1100, 400 Burrard St., Vancouver BC V6C 3A6 — J.P.P. Tognetti
HSBC James Capel Canada Inc., 604/687-8557; Fax: 604/687-8566, #1110, 885 West Georgia St., Vancouver BC V6C 3E8 — A.M.B. Olivier
Jones, Gable & Company Limited, 604/685-1481; Fax: 604/685-3761, #400, 700 West Pender St., Vancouver BC V6C 1C1 — J.D. Gunther
Lévesque Beaubien Geoffrion Inc., 604/643-2800; Fax: 604/643-2792, Montreal Trust Centre, 510 Burrard St., 7th Fl., Vancouver BC V6C 3A8 — P. Brunet
Lévesque Securities Inc., 416/865-7400; Fax: 416/865-7604, #600, 121 King St. West, Toronto ON M5H 3T9 — P. Brunet
Loewen, Ondaatje, McCutcheon Limited, 416/964-4455; Fax: 416/964-4492, Hazelton Lanes, East Tower, 55 Avenue Rd., Toronto ON M5R 3L2
Majendie Charlton Ltd., 604/682-6446; Fax: 604/662-8594; Toll Free: 1-800-822-6446, Waterfront Centre, #320, 200 Burrard St., Vancouver BC V6C 3L6 — N.L. Majendie
Marleau, Lemire Securities Inc., 604/668-7900; Fax: 604/683-7127, #500, 999 Hastings St. West, Vancouver BC V6C 2W7 — H. Eisen
McDermid St. Lawrence Securities Ltd., 604/654-1111; Fax: 604/654-1224, #1000, 601 West Hastings St., PO Box 90, Vancouver BC V6B 5E2 — K.N. Aune
Merit Investment Corporation, 416/867-6000; Fax: 416/867-6137; Toll Free: 1-800-616-8858, #1000, 55 University Ave., Toronto ON M5J 2P8 — L. Kieselstein
Merrill Lynch Canada Inc., 604/687-2663; Fax: 604/687-3663, #2080, 200 Burrard St., Vancouver BC V6C 3L6 — G.B. Dunn
Midland Walwyn Capital Inc., 604/688-2111; Fax: 604/661-7700, Three Bentall Centre, #1100, 595 Burrard St., PO Box 49020, Vancouver BC V7X 1C3 — G.G. Fabbro
Moss, Lawson & Co. Limited, 416/864-2700; Fax: 416/864-2756; Toll Free: 1-800-268-9733, #410, One Toronto St., Toronto ON M5C 2W3 — B.H. Pryce
Nesbitt Burns Inc., 604/669-7424; Fax: 604/631-2658, Park Place, #2500, 666 Burrard St., Vancouver BC V6C 2X8 — P.J. Powell
Odlum Brown Limited, 604/669-1600; Fax: 604/681-8310, Pacific Centre, #1800, 609 Granville St., PO Box 10012, Vancouver BC V7Y 1A3 — S.R. Sherwood
Pacific International Securities Inc., 604/664-2900; Fax: 604/664-2649, #1900, 666 Burrard St., Vancouver BC V6C 3N1 — Max Meier
Peters & Co. Limited, 403/261-4850; Fax: 403/266-4116, #2500, 350 - 7th Ave. SW, Calgary AB T2P 4N1 — R.G. Peters
RBC Dominion Securities Inc., 604/257-7000; Fax: 604/257-7138, Park Place, #2100, 666 Burrard St., Vancouver BC V6C 3B1 — M.L. Cullen
Research Capital Corporation, 604/669-7122; Fax: 604/669-5034, Bentall Centre, #564, 1055 Dunsmuir St., PO Box 49356, Vancouver BC V7X 1L4
Salman Partners Inc., 604/685-2450; Fax: 604/685-2471, #2230, 885 West Georgia St., Vancouver BC V6C 3E8 — T.K. Salman
ScotiaMcLeod Inc., 604/661-7400; Fax: 604/661-7432, #1100, 609 Granville St., PO Box 10342, Vancouver BC V7Y 1H6 — D.M. Rodger
Sprott Securities Limited, 604/681-7344; Fax: 604/681-7322; Toll Free: 1-800-667-7344, #1560, 200 Burrard St., Vancouver BC V6C 3L6
Taurus Capital Markets Ltd., 416/361-2000; Fax: 416/364-0971, Scotia Plaza, #3000, 40 King St. West, Toronto ON M5H 3Y2
TD Securities Inc., 604/654-3700; Fax: 604/654-3757, Pacific Centre, #1800, 700 Georgia St. West, PO Box 10001, Vancouver BC V7Y 1A2 — W.K. Gray
Thomson Kernaghan & Co. Ltd., 416/860-8800; Fax: 416/367-8055, 365 Bay St., 2nd Fl., Toronto ON M5H 2V2 — E.J. Kernaghan
Union Securities Ltd., 604/687-2201; Fax: 604/684-6307, Pacific Centre, #900, 609 Granville St., PO Box 10341, Vancouver BC V7Y 1H4 — Norman N. Thompson
Versus Brokerage Services Inc., 604/257-7676; Fax: 604/257-7699, Park Place, #730, 666 Burrard St., Vancouver BC V6C 2X8 — Douglas E. Steiner
W.D. Latimer Co. Limited, 416/363-5631; Fax: 416/363-8022, #2508, Toronto-Dominion Centre, PO Box 96, Stn Toronto-Dominion, Toronto ON M5K 1G8 — C.M. Bracken
West Coast Securities Ltd., 604/681-1286; Fax: 604/688-7145, #509, 700 West Pender St., Vancouver BC V6C 1G8 — J.D. Thomas
Whalen Béliveau & Associés Inc. Park Place, #3210, 666 Burrard St. West, Vancouver BC V6C 2X8
Wolverton Securities Ltd., 604/688-3477; Fax: 604/662-5205, 777 Dunsmuir St., 17th Fl., PO Box 10115, Vancouver BC V7Y 1J5 — B.N. Wolverton
Yorkton Securities Inc., 604/640-0400; Fax: 604/640-0300, Bentall Centre, #1000, 1055 Dunsmuir St., PO Box 49333, Vancouver BC V7X 1L4 — F. Giustra

## The Winnipeg Stock Exchange

#620, One Lombard Place, Winnipeg MB R3B 0X3
1996 Volume: Industrials - 40,921 shares ($575,751)
204/987-7070; Fax: 204/987-7079
Email: info@wse.ca; URL: http://www.wse.ca

#### Executives

Chair, Thomas D.A. Waitt
Vice-Chair, Gordon J. Wimble
President, Ken Cooper
Corporate Secretary, Joyce C. Fieting

#### Board of Governors

Guy N. Bieber
Vincent W. Catalano
Ronald L. Coke
Alan S. Dunnett
Kelly A. Jacob
Duncan D. Jessiman, Jr.
Edward G.A. Percival
Donald H. Penny
Charles D. Spiring
Philip A. Taylor

#### MEMBER FIRMS & CORPORATIONS
**with member seatholder**

Bank of Montreal Investor Services Inc., 416/867-5503; Fax: 416/867-4728, First Canadian Place, 20th Fl., Toronto ON M5X 1A1 — Alan C. Joudrey
Bieber Securities Inc., 204/946-0297; Fax: 204/956-0747, #801, 400 St. Mary Ave., Winnipeg MB R3C 4K5 — Guy N. Bieber
CIBC Investor Services Inc., 416/351-4331; Fax: 416/351-4333, 200 King St. West, 16th Fl., PO Box 51, Toronto ON M5L 1A2 — Jack Verkruysse
CIBC Wood Gundy Securities Inc., 204/958-4300, Winnipeg Square, #2600, 360 Main St., Winnipeg MB R3C 3Z3 — Gordon J. Wimble
Correspondent Network, 416/869-8509; Fax: 416/869-7548, The Exchange Tower, #3220, 2 First Canadian Place, PO Box 470, Toronto ON M5X 1E4 — B. David Burnes
Credential Securities Inc., 604/730-5163; Fax: 604/730-5166, 1441 Creekside Dr., Vancouver BC V6J 4S7 — D. Kevin Whelley
CT Securities International Inc., 416/947-7200; Fax: 416/947-7213, #950, 70 York St., Toronto ON M5J 1S9 — P.A. Ruys de Perez
Edward D. Jones & Co., 905/273-8400; Fax: 905/273-8424, Sussex Centre, #902, 90 Burnhamthorpe Rd. West, Mississauga ON L5B 3C3 — G.D. Reamey
Friedberg Mercantile Group, 416/364-2700; Fax: 416/364-0572; Toll Free: 1-800-461-2700, BCE Place, #250, 181 Bay St., PO Box 866, Toronto ON M5J 2T3 — Albert D. Friedberg
Gordon Private Client Corporation, 204/942-7711; Fax: 204/942-0047; Toll Free: 1-800-545-4069, Commodity Tower, #2070, 360 Main St., Winnipeg MB R3C 3Z3 — Patrick M. Cooney
Hongkong Bank Discount Trading Inc., 416/868-6800; Fax: 416/868-6249, #1680, 70 York St., Toronto ON M5J 1S9 — Peter J. Hickman
Investors Group Securities Inc., 204/956-8667; Fax: 204/944-8985, One Canada Centre, 447 Portage Ave., 2nd Fl., Winnipeg MB R3C 3B6 — Philip A. Taylor
Lévesque Securities Inc., 204/942-8942; Fax: 204/942-1597, #890, 360 Main St., Winnipeg MB R3C 3Z3 — Edward G.A. Percival
Majendie Charlton Ltd., 604/682-6446; Fax: 604/662-8594; Toll Free: 1-800-822-6446, Waterfront Centre, #320, 200 Burrard St., Vancouver BC V6C 3L6 — N.L. Majendie
MD Management Limited, 613/731-4552; Fax: 613/526-1352; 1-800-267-4022, 1867 Alta Vista Dr., Ottawa ON K1G 5W8 — Ronald P. Bannerman
Merrill Lynch Canada Inc., 416/586-6000; Fax: 416/586-6616, Merrill Lynch Canada Tower, 200 King St. West, Toronto ON M5H 3W3 — George B. Dunn
Midland Walwyn Capital Inc., 204/947-0612; Fax: 204/947-0623, #1010, 447 Portage Ave., Winnipeg MB R3B 3H5 — D. Mark Schiefner
Nesbitt Burns Inc., 204/949-2500; Fax: 204/947-3415, #1300, 360 Main St., Winnipeg MB R3C 3Z3 — Thomas D.A. Waitt
RBC Dominion Securities Inc., 204/934-5311; Fax: 204/942-8276, #2900, One Lombard Place, PO Box 278, Winnipeg MB R3B 0Y2 — Alan S. Dunnett
Royal Bank Action Direct Inc., 905/764-5227; Fax: 905/764-0430, #200, 260 East Beaver Creek Rd., Richmond Hill ON L4B 3N3 — Michael A. Bastian
Scotia Discount Brokerage Inc., 416/866-2021; Fax: 416/866-2018, Scotia Plaza, 40 King St. West, 5th Fl., Toronto ON M5H 1H1 — Andrew H. Scipio del Campo
ScotiaMcLeod Inc., 204/944-0025; Fax: 204/946-9236, #501, 200 Portage Ave., Winnipeg MB R3C 3X2 — Edward R. Griffith
TD Securities Inc., 204/988-2200; Fax: 204/988-2875, #1709, 201 Portage Ave., Winnipeg MB R3C 3E7 — James A. Coldwell
TD Securities Inc., 204/988-2641; Fax: 204/943-2094, #1617, 201 Portage Ave., PO Box 7700, Winnipeg MB R3C 3E7 — Kelly A. Jacob
Wellington West Capital Inc., 204/925-2250; Fax: 204/942-6194; Toll Free: 1-800-461-6314, #3106, 201 Portage Ave., Winnipeg MB R3B 3K6 — Charles D. Spiring

# INSURANCE COMPANIES

Insurance companies are registered to conduct business under the federal Insurance Companies Act and/or corresponding provincial legislation. Life insurance companies are registered to underwrite life insurance, accident and sickness insurance and annuity business. Property and casualty insurance companies are registered to provide insurance other than life insurance. The companies may either be stock companies owned by shareholders, or mutual companies which are owned by their policyholders.

For provincially incorporated companies (marked *) not listed below, contact the Superintendent of Insurance, each province (see "Insurance" in the Government Quick Reference, Section 4).

#### CLASSES OF INSURANCE

Classes of insurance indicated below may be one or more of the following: Accident, Aircraft, Auto, Boiler & Machinery, Credit, Fidelity, Fire, Hail & Crop, Legal Expense, Liability, Life, Personal Accident & Sickness, Property, Surety, & Theft.

*Acadie Vie/Acadia Life
295, boul St. Pierre ouest, CP 5554, Caraquet NB E1W 1B7
506/727-1300; Fax: 506/727-1338
Amédée Haché
Classes of Insurance: Personal Accident & Sickness; Life

*Additional Municipal Hail Ltd.
2100 Cornwall St., Regina SK S4P 2K7
306/569-1852

Aetna Casualty & Surety Company of Canada
#1070, 36 Toronto St., Toronto ON M5C 2C5
416/368-5750; Fax: 416/864-3888
President/CEO, Brian Divell
Classes of Insurance: Auto; Aircraft; Boiler & Machinery; Fidelity; Liability; Property; Surety

Aetna Life Insurance Company of Canada
Aetna Tower, TD Centre, 79 Wellington St. West, PO Box 120, Toronto ON M5K 1N9
416/864-8000; Fax: 416/864-1270; Toll Free: 1-800-361-7979
URL: http://www.aetna.ca
President/CEO, Nick P. Villani
Classes of Insurance: Personal Accident & Sickness; Life

Affiliated FM Insurance Company
#202, 155 Gordon Baker Rd., North York ON M2H 3N7
416/494-7111; Fax: 416/494-7598
URL: http://www.allendale.com
President/CEO, Shivan S. Subramaniam
Classes of Insurance: Boiler & Machinery; Fire; Property

*AFLAC Insurance Company of Canada
#300, 5915 Airport Rd., Mississauga ON L4V 1T1
905/678-7800; Fax: 905/673-5995; Toll Free: 1-800-263-6188
President, Denis R. Scodellaro
Classes of Insurance: Personal Accident & Sickness; Life

*Alberta Motor Association Insurance Co.
10310 G.A. MacDonald Ave., PO Box 8180, Stn South, Edmonton AB T6H 5X9
403/430-5600; Fax: 403/430-5599
Email: gwentworth@ama.ab.ca
General Manager, Gord Wentworth
Classes of Insurance: Auto; Fire; Personal Accident & Sickness; Property

Alexander Hamilton Life Insurance Company of America
#1000, 100 Sheppard Ave. East, North York ON M2N 6N7
Chief Agent, Paul F. Palmer
Classes of Insurance: Personal Accident & Sickness; Life

Allendale Mutual Insurance Company
#202, 155 Gordon Baker Rd., North York ON M2H 3N7
416/494-7111; Fax: 416/494-7598
URL: http://www.allendale.com
President/CEO, Shivan S. Subramaniam
Classes of Insurance: Boiler & Machinery; Fire; Property

Allianz Insurance Company of Canada
#200, 425 Bloor St. East, Toronto ON M4W 3R5
416/961-5015; Fax: 416/961-8874; Toll Free: 1-800-387-5601
President/CEO, Robert E. Maynard
Classes of Insurance: Auto; Fire; Personal Accident & Sickness; Property

Allianz Life Insurance Company of North America
10 Allstate Pkwy., Markham ON L3R 5P8
905/470-4780; Fax: 905/477-6447; Toll Free: 1-800-328-5601
Chief Agent, Doreen Johnston
Classes of Insurance: Personal Accident & Sickness; Life

Allstate Insurance Company of Canada
10 Allstate Pkwy., Markham ON L3R 5P8
905/477-6900; Fax: 905/475-4991
Chair/CEO, Ed Young
Classes of Insurance: Auto; Property

*L'Alpha, Compagnie d'Assurances Inc.
430, rue Saint-Georges, Drummondville QC J2C 4H4
819/474-7958; Fax: 819/478-1736
Président, Michel Verrier
Classes of Insurance: Auto; Liability; Property; Surety

American Bankers Insurance Company of Florida
#1700, 5001 Yonge St., North York ON M2N 6T7
416/733-3360; Fax: 416/733-7826
Vice-President/Chief Agent, John Leslie
Classes of Insurance: Credit; Personal Accident & Sickness; Liability; Property

American Bankers Life Assurance Company of Florida
#1700, 5001 Yonge St., North York ON M2N 6T7
416/733-3360; Fax: 416/733-7826
Vice-President/Chief Agent, John Leslie
Classes of Insurance: Personal Accident & Sickness; Life

American Credit Indemnity Company
#800, 1010, rue De Serigny, Longueuil QC J4K 5G7
514/646-1515; Fax: 514/646-4170; Toll Free: 1-800-361-3367
Chief Agent, R. Labelle
Classes of Insurance: Credit

American Home Assurance Company
145 Wellington St. West, 14th Fl., Toronto ON M5J 1H8
416/596-3000; Fax: 416/977-2743
Chief Agent, Gary A. McMillan
Classes of Insurance: Auto; Personal Accident & Sickness; Property

American Income Life Insurance Company
c/o McLean & Kerr, #2800, 130 Adelaide St. West, Toronto ON M5H 3P5
416/364-5371; Fax: 416/366-8571
Chief Agent, R.B. Cumine, Q.C.
Classes of Insurance: Personal Accident & Sickness; Life

American International Assurance Life Company Ltd.
145 Wellington St. West, Toronto ON M5J 1H8
416/596-3900
President/CEO, James C.K. Wong
Classes of Insurance: Personal Accident & Sickness; Life

American National Fire Insurance Company
Scotia Plaza, #2100, 40 King St. West, Toronto ON M5H 3C2
416/488-3601
Chief Agent, J. Brian Reeve
Classes of Insurance: Auto; Fire; Personal Accident & Sickness; Property

American Re-Insurance Company
#1902, 20 Queen St. West, PO Box 65, Toronto ON M5H 3R3
416/591-8668; Fax: 416/591-8830; Toll Free: 1-800-387-2959
Chief Agent, Stephen Halfpenny
Classes of Insurance: Auto; Personal Accident & Sickness; Property

Amex Life Assurance Company
#403, 60 Bloor St. West, Toronto ON M4W 3L8
416/969-9216; Fax: 416/969-9407
Chief Agent, Judy Ha
Classes of Insurance: Personal Accident & Sickness; Life

*Anglo-Canada General Insurance Company
217 York St., 4th Fl, London ON N6A 5P9
519/679-9440
Chair/CEO, Jean-Denis Talon
Classes of Insurance: Auto; Fire; Personal Accident & Sickness; Property

Antigonish Farmers' Mutual Fire Insurance Company
188 Main St., PO Box 1535, Antigonish NS B2G 2L8
902/863-3544; Fax: 902/863-0664
President, P.A. Macintosh
Classes of Insurance: Fire

Arkwright Mutual Insurance Company
#4, 1101 Nicholson Rd., Newmarket ON L3Y 7V1
905/853-0858; Fax: 905/853-0183
Chief Agent, Alan R. Hayes
Classes of Insurance: Property

Assicurazioni Generali S.P.A.
#500, 1000, rue de la Gauchetière ouest, Montréal QC H3B 4W5
514/875-5790; Fax: 514/875-9769
Chief Agent, W.J. Green
Classes of Insurance: Auto; Property

*Association Independante d'Entraide des Israelites de Montréal
1705, Rodolphe-Bédard, Saint-Laurent QC H4L 2P7
514/748-9954
Président, M.J. Bernstein

*Association Protectrice des Policiers Municipaux de Québec
275, rue Gignac, Québec QC G1K 8W5
418/691-6170
Président, Jean-Marie Angers

*Assumption Mutual Life Insurance Company/ Assomption Compagnie Mutuelle d'Assurance-Vie
770 Main St., PO Box 160, Moncton NB E1C 1E7
506/853-6040; Fax: 506/853-5421
Denis Losier
Classes of Insurance: Personal Accident & Sickness; Life

*L'Assurance Mutuelle des Fabriques de Montréal
1071, rue de la Cathédrale, Montréal QC H3B 2V4
514/395-4969; Fax: 514/861-8921; Toll Free: 1-800-567-6586
Directeur général, Serge Léonard
Classes of Insurance: Property

*L'Assurance Mutuelle des Fabriques de Québec
Archevêché de Québec, 2, rue Port Dauphin, Québec QC G1R 5K5
418/687-2564; Fax: 418/687-1056
Directeur général, Jean-Guy Dupont
Classes of Insurance: Fire; Property

*Assurance-Vie Banque Nationale, Compagnie d'Assurance-Vie
600, rue de la Gauchetière ouest, 4e étage, Montréal QC H3B 4L2
514/394-6080; Fax: 514/394-6601
Directeur général, Pierre Desbiens

*Assurances Générales des Caisses Desjardins Inc.
6300, boul de la Rive-Sud, CP 3500, Lévis QC G6V 6P9
418/835-4771; Fax: 418/835-5599; Toll Free: 1-800-463-4850
President/CEO, Jude Martineau
Classes of Insurance: Auto; Fire; Property

*Atlantic Insurance Company Ltd.
64 Commonwealth Ave., Mount Pearl NF A1N 1W8
709/364-5209
President, David Woolley

Avemco Insurance Company
#500, 140 Allstate Pkwy., Markham ON L3P 5Y8
905/470-1414; Fax: 905/470-1737
Chief Agent, Donald G. Smith
Classes of Insurance: Aircraft

Aviation & General Insurance Company Limited
c/o British Aviation Insurance Group (Canada) Ltd., #100, 100 Renfrew Dr., Markham ON L3R 9R6
905/479-2244; Fax: 905/479-0751
Chief Agent, Peter S. May
Classes of Insurance: Miscellaneous

*AXA Assurances
#600, 2020, rue University, Montréal QC H3A 2A5
514/282-1914; Fax: 514/982-9588
CEO, Jean-Denis Talon
Classes of Insurance: Auto; Personal Accident & Sickness; Life; Property

AXA Boréal Assurances Inc.
1100, boul René-Lévesque ouest, Montréal QC H3B 4P4
514/392-6000; Fax: 514/392-6328
CEO, Jean-Denis Talon

*AXA Boreal Farm Insurance/AXA Boréal Assurances Agricoles Inc.
1100, boul René-Lévesque ouest, 16e étage, Montréal QC H3B 4P4
514/392-6000; Fax: 514/392-7777
CEO, Jean-Denis Talon

AXA Canada
#600, 2020, av University, Montréal QC H3A 2A5
514/282-1914
President, Jean-Denis Talon

*AXA Insurance (Canada)
#1400, 5700 Yonge St., North York ON M2M 4K2
416/250-1992; Fax: 416/250-5833
CEO, Jean-Denis Talon
Classes of Insurance: Auto; Fire; Personal Accident & Sickness; Life; Property

AXA Pacific Insurance Company
999 Hastings West St., 2nd Fl., PO Box 22, Vancouver BC V6C 2W2
604/669-4247; Fax: 604/682-6693
CEO, Jean-Denis Talon
Classes of Insurance: Auto; Aircraft; Boiler & Machinery; Credit; Fidelity; Hail & Crop; Personal Accident & Sickness; Liability; Property; Surety

AXA Réassurances
#1930, 1800, av McGill College, Montréal QC H3A 3J6
514/842-9262; Fax: 514/842-5311
President & Chief Agent, Claire Gariépy
Classes of Insurance: Auto; Aircraft; Boiler & Machinery; Fidelity; Hail & Crop; Personal Accident & Sickness; Liability; Life; Property; Surety

Balboa Insurance Company
201 Queens Ave., PO Box 5071, Stn A, London ON N6A 4M5
519/672-1070; Fax: 519/672-2623
Chief Agent, Anthony W. Miles
Classes of Insurance: Personal Accident & Sickness; Property

The Baloise Insurance Company Ltd./La Baloîse, Compagnie d'Assurances
#1703, 155 University Ave., Toronto ON M5H 3B6
416/366-3012; Fax: 416/366-3465
Chief Agent, Patrick J. King

Bankers Life & Casualty Company
Scotia Plaza, #2100, 40 King St. West, Toronto ON M5H 3C2
416/869-5300; Fax: 416/360-8877; Toll Free: 1-800-257-9228
Chief Agent, J. Brian Reeve
Classes of Insurance: Personal Accident & Sickness; Life

*Barreau du Québec
#550, 445, boul Saint-Laurent, Montréal QC H2Y 3T8
514/954-3452
Président, Sébastien Allard

*Blue Cross of Atlantic Canada
644 Main St., PO Box 220, Moncton NB E1C 8L3
506/853-1811; Fax: 506/853-4651; Toll Free: 1-800-667-4511
President/CEO, L.R. Furlong
Classes of Insurance: Accident; Personal Accident & Sickness; Life

The Boiler Inspection & Insurance Company of Canada
18 King St. East, Toronto ON M5C 1C4
416/363-5491; Fax: 416/363-0538
Email: ho@biico.ccmail.compuserve.com
President, Normand Mercier
Classes of Insurance: Boiler & Machinery; Property

British Aviation Insurance Group (Canada) Ltd.
#200, 100 Renfrew Dr., Markham ON L3R 9R6
905/479-2244; Fax: 905/479-0751
President, Peter May
Classes of Insurance: Accident; Aircraft

*British Columbia Insurance Company
#1800, 777 Hornby St., Vancouver BC V6Z 1S4
604/688-1541; Fax: 604/688-5978; Toll Free: 1-800-663-0597
President, Yvon Trépanier
Classes of Insurance: Auto; Fire; Property

*British Columbia Life & Casualty Company
2025 Broadway West, PO Box 9300, Vancouver BC V6B 4G3
604/737-5700
Classes of Insurance: Personal Accident & Sickness; Life

Bureau du Fondé de Pouvoir du Canada pour les Souscripteurs du Lloyd's/Office of the Attorney In Fact in Canada for Lloyd's Underwriters
#1540, 1155, rue Metcalfe, Montréal QC H3B 2V6
514/861-8361; Fax: 514/861-0470
Attorney In Fact in Canada, M.J. Oppenheim
Classes of Insurance: Auto; Fire; Personal Accident & Sickness; Property

Business Men's Assurance Company of America
c/o McLean & Kerr, #2800, 130 Adelaide St. West, Toronto ON M5H 3P5
416/364-5371; Fax: 416/366-8571
Chief Agent, R.B. Cumine, Q.C.
Classes of Insurance: Personal Accident & Sickness; Life

*CAA Insurance Company (Ontario)
60 Commerce Valley Dr. East, Thornhill ON L3T 7P9
905/771-3000; Fax: 905/771-3410; Toll Free: 1-800-268-3750
Vice-President & Chief Financial Officer, Nicholas J. Parks
Classes of Insurance: Auto; Personal Accident & Sickness; Property; Surety

Calvert Insurance Company
#500, 36 King St. East, Toronto ON M5C 1E5
416/361-1728; Fax: 416/361-6113
Chief Agent, Philip H. Cook
Classes of Insurance: Auto; Fire; Property

The Canada Life Assurance Company/La Compagnie d'Assurance du Canada sur la Vie
330 University Ave., Toronto ON M5G 1R8
416/597-1456; Fax: 416/597-6215
Email: info@canadalife.com; URL: http://www.canadalife.com
President/CEO, David A. Nield
Classes of Insurance: Personal Accident & Sickness; Life

Canada Life Casualty Insurance Company
330 University Ave., Toronto ON M5G 1R8
416/597-2640; Fax: 416/597-9783; Toll Free: 1-800-310-7990
Email: home_auto@canadalife.com; URL: http://www.canadalife.com/casualty
President/Chief Operating Officer, D.V. Newton
Classes of Insurance: Auto; Legal Expense; Property

*Canada West Insurance Company
Canada Place, #400, 9777 - 102 Ave. NW, PO Box 1520, Edmonton AB T5J 2N7
403/497-3000; Fax: 403/429-4659; Toll Free: 1-800-661-5636
President/CEO, Barbara Addie
Classes of Insurance: Auto; Fire; Property

Canadian Direct Insurance Incorporated
#217, 610 - 6th St., New Westminster BC V3L 3C2
604/525-2115; Fax: 604/517-3214; Toll Free: 1-888-225-5234
Email: insurancegeneral@canadiandirect.com
President/CEO, Guy Cloutier
Classes of Insurance: Auto; Miscellaneous; Property

*Canadian General Insurance Company
2206 Eglinton Ave. East, Toronto ON M1L 4S8
416/289-1800; Fax: 416/288-9756

Canadian General Insurance Group Limited
#500, 2206 Eglinton Ave. East, Scarborough ON M1L 4S8
416/288-1800; Fax: 416/288-9756; Toll Free: 1-800-387-4518
President/CEO, R. Lewis Dunn
Classes of Insurance: Auto; Accident; Fire; Liability; Property; Surety

Canadian Group Underwriters Insurance Company
#502, 6733 Mississauga Rd., Mississauga ON L5N 6J5
905/819-2030; Fax: 905/819-2117
President, J.P. McCarthy
Classes of Insurance: Auto; Personal Accident & Sickness; Property

*Canadian Lawyers Insurance Association
#600, 919 - 11th Ave. SW, Calgary AB T2R 1P3
403/229-4716; Fax: 403/228-1728
Chair, Daniel Campbell

*Canadian Millers' Mutual Insurance Company
40 George St. North, Cambridge ON N1S 2M8
519/621-4060; Fax: 519/740-3490; Toll Free: 1-800-665-3682
President, John Koslowsky
Classes of Insurance: Boiler & Machinery; Fire; Liability; Property

Canadian Northern Shield Insurance Company
#1900, 555 Hastings St. West, PO Box 12133, Vancouver BC V6B 4N6
604/662-2911; Fax: 604/662-5698; Toll Free: 1-800-663-1953
Chief Operating Officer, T. Michael Porter
Classes of Insurance: Auto; Boiler & Machinery; Fidelity; Personal Accident & Sickness; Liability; Property; Surety

Canadian Premier Life Insurance Company
#500, 80 Tiverton Ct., Markham ON L3R 0G4
905/479-7500; Fax: 905/948-2100
Vice-President/CEO, Aaron Hill
Classes of Insurance: Personal Accident & Sickness; Life

The Canadian Surety Company
#1200, 2200 Yonge St., Toronto ON M4S 2C6
416/487-7195; Fax: 416/482-6176; Toll Free: 1-800-268-7397
President/CEO, Barbara Addie
Classes of Insurance: Auto; Accident; Aircraft; Boiler & Machinery; Fire; Liability; Property; Theft

*Canadian Trinity Life Insurance Company
288 Lakeshore Rd. East, Oakville ON L6J 1J2
905/844-9413; Fax: 905/844-5274
President, Richard G. Bruce
Classes of Insurance: Personal Accident & Sickness; Life

Canadian Union Insurance Company
2475, boul Laurier, Sillery QC G1T 1C4
Classes of Insurance: Miscellaneous
*Canassurance, Compagnie d'Assurance-Vie Inc.
#160, 550, rue Sherbrooke ouest, Montréal QC H3A 1B9
514/286-8400; Fax: 514/286-8475
Directeur général, Claude Ferron
Classes of Insurance: Life
*Canassurance, Compagnie d'Assurances Générales Inc./Canassurance General Insurance Company Inc.
#160, 550, rue Sherbrooke ouest, Montréal QC H3A 1B9
514/286-8400; Fax: 514/286-8475
Directeur général, Pierre Julien
Classes of Insurance: Property
*La Capitale, Compagnie d'Assurance Générale
525, boul René-Lévesque est, 6e étage, Québec QC G1K 7X2
418/528-5525; Fax: 418/646-5960; Toll Free: 1-800-561-7279
Président/Directeur général, Réal Circé
Classes of Insurance: Auto; Legal Expense; Property
*Carleton Mutual Fire Insurance Company
PO Box 154, Florenceville NB E0J 1K0
506/392-6041
Elaine Hunter
Classes of Insurance: Property
Centennial Insurance Company
c/o Focus Group Inc., #500, 36 King St. East, Toronto ON M5C 1E5
416/361-1728; Fax: 416/361-6113
Chief Agent, Philip H. Cook
Classes of Insurance: Auto; Accident; Boiler & Machinery; Fire; Property; Theft
*Chambre des Notaires du Québec
#2650, 630, boul René-Lévesque ouest, Montréal QC H3B 1T6
514/879-1793
Michel A. Charland
Chicago Title Insurance Company
#1006, 141 Adelaide St. West, Toronto ON M5H 3L5
416/955-9496; Fax: 416/955-9492
Director, J. Donald Bergeron, Canadian Operations
Chubb Insurance Company of Canada/Chubb du Canada Compagnie d'Assurance
One Financial Place, One Adelaide St. East, Toronto ON M5C 2V9
416/863-0550; Fax: 416/863-5010
Email: chubb.tor@chubbinsurance.ca; URL: http://www.chubbinsurance.ca
President, Janice M. Tomlinson
Classes of Insurance: Auto; Fire; Personal Accident & Sickness; Property
CIBC General Insurance Company Limited
5150 Spectrum Way, Mississauga ON L4W 5G8
905/206-6000; Fax: 905/206-6090
President/Chief Operating Officer, Kevin McNeil
Classes of Insurance: Auto; Personal Accident & Sickness; Life; Property
CIBC Life Insurance Company Limited
5150 Spectrum Way, Mississauga ON L4W 5G8
905/206-6000; Toll Free: 1-800-565-6010
President/Chief Operating Officer, Gabor Kalmar
Classes of Insurance: Personal Accident & Sickness; Life
CIGNA Insurance Company of Canada
The Exchange Tower, 2 First Canadian Place, 12th Fl., PO Box 185, Stn 1st Can Pl, Toronto ON M5X 1A6
416/368-2911; Fax: 416/594-2600
URL: http://www.cigna.com
President/CEO, Samuel B. Cupp, Jr.
Classes of Insurance: Auto; Aircraft; Boiler & Machinery; Fidelity; Fire; Hail & Crop; Personal Accident & Sickness; Liability; Property; Surety
CIGNA Life Insurance Company of Canada
#1400, 250 Yonge St., Toronto ON M5B 2L7
416/591-1225; Fax: 416/591-7488
President, Brendan McCormick
Classes of Insurance: Personal Accident & Sickness; Life
The Citadel General Assurance Company
1075 Bay St., Toronto ON M5S 2W5
416/928-8500; Fax: 416/928-1553
President/CEO, William H. Gleed, C.L.U.
Classes of Insurance: Auto; Personal Accident & Sickness; Property
Clare Mutual Insurance Company
Belliveau Cove NS B0W 1J0
902/837-4597; Fax: 902/837-7745
President, Aldaige Comeau
Classes of Insurance: Fire; Theft
*Co-operative Hail Insurance Company Ltd.
2709 - 13th Ave., PO Box 777, Regina SK S4P 3A8
306/522-8691; Fax: 306/352-9130
President, W. Bruce Lutz
Classes of Insurance: Hail & Crop
Co-operators General Insurance Company
Priory Square, Guelph ON N1H 6P8
519/824-4400; Fax: 519/824-0599
URL: http://www.cooperators.ca
President/CEO, G. Terry Squire
Classes of Insurance: Auto; Personal Accident & Sickness; Property
*Coachman Insurance Company
802 The Queensway, Stn ., Toronto ON M8Z 1N5
416/255-3417; Fax: 416/255-1454
President, David Rooney
Classes of Insurance: Auto
Cologne Life Reinsurance Company
2 St. Clair Ave. East, 6th Fl., Toronto ON M4T 2V6
416/960-3601; Fax: 416/960-5291
Chief Agent, John M. Kosiancic
Classes of Insurance: Personal Accident & Sickness; Life
Cologne Reinsurance Company (Koelnische Rueckversicherungs-Gesellschaft Ag)
#201, 3650 Victoria Park Ave., Scarborough ON M2H 3P7
416/496-1148; Fax: 416/496-1089
Chief Agent, V. Lorraine Williams
Classes of Insurance: Auto; Aircraft; Boiler & Machinery; Credit; Fidelity; Hail & Crop; Liability; Property; Surety
COLONIA Life Insurance Company
2 St. Clair Ave. East, 6th Fl., Toronto ON M4T 2V6
416/960-3601; Fax: 416/960-5291
President/CEO, J.M. Kosiancic
Classes of Insurance: Personal Accident & Sickness; Life
*Colonial Fire & General Insurance Company Ltd.
PO Box 13370, St. John's NF A1B 4B7
709/753-3069
President/CEO, Godfrey J. Wedgwood
Combined Insurance Company of America/ Compagnie d'Assurance Combined d'Amerique
#300, 7300 Warden Ave., Markham ON L3R 0X3
905/305-1922; Fax: 905/305-8600
Chief Agent, Dan C. Evans
Classes of Insurance: Personal Accident & Sickness; Life
The Commerce Group Insurance Company/Le Groupe Commerce Compagnie d'Assurances
2450, rue Girouard ouest, St-Hyacinthe QC J2S 3B3
514/773-9701; Fax: 514/773-6773
President/Chief Operating Officer, Claude Dussault
Classes of Insurance: Auto; Personal Accident & Sickness; Property
Commercial Union Assurance Company of Canada
Commercial Union Tower, Toronto-Dominion Centre, #1700, 100 Wellington St. West, Toronto ON M5K 1L9
416/361-2500; Fax: 416/361-2617
Chair, President/CEO, Gerry S. Stafford
Classes of Insurance: Auto; Personal Accident & Sickness; Property
Commercial Union Assurance Company plc
350 Albert St.., Ottawa ON K1R 1A4
613/786-2000; Fax: 613/238-7448
Chief Agent, D. Shillington
Classes of Insurance: Property
Commercial Union Life Assurance Company of Canada
#300, Consilium Place, PO Box 370, Stn A, Scarborough ON M1K 5C3
416/296-0700; Fax: 416/296-1705
President/CEO, Frank J. Crowley
Classes of Insurance: Personal Accident & Sickness; Life
Commonwealth Insurance Company
Bentall Three, #1500, 595 Burrard St., PO Box 49115, Vancouver BC V7X 1G4
604/683-5511; Fax: 604/683-8968
President/CEO, John B.O. Watson
Classes of Insurance: Liability; Marine; Property
*La Compagnie d'Assurance Belair Inc./Belair Insurance Company Inc.
5455, rue St-André, Montréal QC H2J 4A9
514/270-1700; Fax: 514/270-9809
Président, Jacques Valotaire
Classes of Insurance: Auto; Property
Compagnie Transcontinentale de Réassurance
1080, côte du Beaver Hall, 19e étage, Montréal QC H2Z 1S8
514/878-2600; Fax: 514/878-9309; Toll Free: 1-800-363-6800
Chief Agent, Jacques Mailloux
Classes of Insurance: Auto; Fire; Personal Accident & Sickness; Property
CompCorp Life Insurance Company
#1600, One Queen St. East, Toronto ON M5C 2X9
416/359-2001; Fax: 416/955-9688
President/CEO, Alan E. Morson
Classes of Insurance: Personal Accident & Sickness; Life
Connecticut General Life Insurance Company
#1400, 250 Yonge St., PO Box 14, Toronto ON M5B 2L7
416/591-1225; Fax: 416/591-7488
Chief Agent, Eman Hassan
Classes of Insurance: Personal Accident & Sickness; Life
Continental Assurance Company
105 Adelaide St. West, Toronto ON M5H 1P9
416/354-4400
Chief Agent, Byron G. Messier
Classes of Insurance: Accident; Personal Accident & Sickness; Life
Continental Casualty Company
105 Adelaide St. West, Toronto ON M5H 1P9
416/350-4400; Fax: 416/350-4412
Chief Agent, Byron G. Messier
Classes of Insurance: Auto; Accident; Aircraft; Boiler & Machinery; Credit; Fidelity; Fire; Hail & Crop; Legal Expense; Liability; Property; Surety; Theft
The Continental Insurance Company
105 Adelaide St. West, Toronto ON M5H 1P9
416/350-4400; Fax: 416/350-4412
Chief Agent, Byron G. Messier
Classes of Insurance: Auto; Aircraft; Boiler & Machinery; Credit; Fidelity; Fire; Hail & Crop; Legal Expense; Liability; Property; Surety; Theft
*Coronation Insurance Company, Limited
Royal Trust Tower, #3426, 77 King St. West, PO Box 284, Toronto ON M5K 1K2
416/360-8183; Fax: 416/360-8267
President, Robert E. Taylor
Classes of Insurance: Property

*La Corporation d'Assurance de Personnes la Laurentienne
500, rue Grande Allée est, Québec QC G1R 7E3
418/647-5222; Fax: 418/647-5119
Directeur général, Humberto Santos

Coseco Insurance Company
Priory Square, Guelph ON N1H 6P8
519/824-4400; Fax: 519/822-4173
President/CEO, G. Terry Squire
Classes of Insurance: Auto; Liability; Property

Crown Life Insurance Company
1901 Scarth St., Regina SK S4P 4L4
306/751-6000; Fax: 306/751-6001; Toll Free: 1-800-827-6965
URL: http://www.crownlife.ca
President/CEO, Brian A. Johnson
Classes of Insurance: Personal Accident & Sickness; Life

*CUMBA
562 Eglinton Ave. East, Toronto ON M4P 1B9
416/487-5451; Fax: 416/487-3379
General Manager, D. Tripp
Classes of Insurance: Personal Accident & Sickness

CUMIS General Insurance Company
PO Box 5065, Burlington ON L7R 4C2
905/632-1221; Fax: 905/632-9412; Toll Free: 1-800-263-9120
President/CEO, T. Michael Porter
Classes of Insurance: Auto; Accident; Boiler & Machinery; Credit; Fidelity; Fire; Personal Accident & Sickness; Life; Property; Surety

CUMIS Life Insurance Co.
PO Box 5065, Burlington ON L7R 4C2
905/632-1221; Fax: 905/632-9412; Toll Free: 1-800-263-9122
President/CEO, T. Michael Porter
Classes of Insurance: Personal Accident & Sickness; Life

*Desjardins-Laurentian Life Assurance Company Inc./Assurance vie Desjardins-Laurentienne inc.
200, av des Commandeurs, Lévis QC G6V 6R2
418/838-7870; Fax: 418/833-5985; Toll Free: 1-800-463-7870
Email: info@avdl.com; URL: http://www.avdl.com
CEO, Michel Thérien
Classes of Insurance: Credit; Personal Accident & Sickness; Life

*Dome Insurance Corp. Ltd.
#800, 240 Graham Ave., Winnipeg MB R3C 0J7
204/947-2835
Chief Agent, Richard R. Bracken
Classes of Insurance: Auto; Fire

The Dominion of Canada General Insurance Company/Compagnie d'assurance générale dominion du Canada
165 University Ave., Toronto ON M5H 3B9
416/362-7231; Fax: 416/362-9918
President/CEO, George L. Cooke
Classes of Insurance: Auto; Boiler & Machinery; Liability; Property; Surety

Eagle Star Insurance Company Ltd.
c/o Focus Group Inc., #500, 36 King St. East, Toronto ON M5C 1E5
416/361-1728; Fax: 416/361-6113
Chief Agent, P.H. Cook
Classes of Insurance: Auto; Aircraft; Boiler & Machinery; Fidelity; Personal Accident & Sickness; Liability; Property; Surety

Eastern Marine Underwriters
60 Yonge St., Toronto ON M5E 1H5
416/362-2961; Fax: 416/362-7281
President, Gerry Giroux
Classes of Insurance: Fire; Personal Accident & Sickness; Property

Ecclesiastical Insurance Office plc/Société des Assurances Écclésiastiques
#502, 2300 Yonge St., PO Box 2401, Toronto ON M4P 1E4
416/484-4555; Fax: 416/484-6352
Chief Agent, Stephen M. Oxley
Classes of Insurance: Marine; Property

Economical Mutual Insurance Company
111 Westmount Rd. South, PO Box 2000, Waterloo ON N2J 4S4
519/570-8200; Fax: 519/570-8389
President/CEO, Noel Walpole, F.I.I.C.
Classes of Insurance: Auto; Accident; Boiler & Machinery; Fidelity; Fire; Personal Accident & Sickness; Liability; Property; Surety; Theft

Elite Insurance Company
#500, 2206 Eglinton Ave. East, Scarborough ON M1L 4S8
416/288-1800; Fax: 416/288-9756

The Empire Life Insurance Company/L'Empire Compagnie d'Assurance-Vie
259 King St. East, Kingston ON K7L 3A8
613/548-1881; Fax: 613/548-4584
President/CEO, Christopher H. McElvaine, F.S.A., F.C.I.A.
Classes of Insurance: Life

Employers Insurance of Wausau - a Mutual Company/Société d'Assurance Mutuelle des Employeurs de Wausau
c/o D.M. Williams & Associates Ltd., #201, 3650 Victoria Park Ave., North York ON M2H 3P7
416/496-1148; Fax: 416/496-1089
Chief Agent, V.L. Williams
Classes of Insurance: Auto; Aircraft; Boiler & Machinery; Fidelity; Personal Accident & Sickness; Liability; Property; Surety

Employers Reinsurance Corporation
The Aetna Tower, Toronto-Dominion Centre, #1402, 79 Wellington St. West, PO Box 311, Stn Toronto-Dominion, Toronto ON M5K 1K2
416/941-6050; Fax: 416/941-6072
Resident Vice-President & Chief Agent, Peter Borst
Classes of Insurance: Auto; Personal Accident & Sickness; Property

*L'Entraide Assurance-Vie, Compagnie Mutuelle/L'Entraide Mutual Life Insurance Company
#100, 1195, rue de Lavigerie, CP 9636, Ste-Foy QC G1V 4C2
418/658-0663; Fax: 418/658-5065
Email: service@lentraide.com; URL: http://www.lentraide.com
Président, Gaétan GagnéChef de la direction
Classes of Insurance: Personal Accident & Sickness; Life

The Equitable Life Assurance Society of the United States
#1400, 250 Yonge St., PO Box 14, Toronto ON M5B 2L7
Chief Agent, M.E. Hassan
Classes of Insurance: Personal Accident & Sickness; Life

The Equitable Life Insurance Company of Canada
One Westmount Rd. North, Waterloo ON N2J 4C7
519/886-5110; Fax: 519/886-5314
Email: head-office@equitable.ca; URL: http://www.equitable.ca
President/CEO, Ronald D. Beaubien
Classes of Insurance: Life

Everest Reinsurance Company
Scotia Plaza, #5001, 40 King St. West, Toronto ON M5H 3Y2
416/862-1228; Fax: 416/366-5899; Toll Free: 1-800-461-9241
Chief Agent, T.D. MacKenzie
Classes of Insurance: Auto; Aircraft; Boiler & Machinery; Credit; Fidelity; Hail & Crop; Personal Accident & Sickness; Liability; Property; Surety

*L'Excellence Compagnie d'Assurance-Vie
#202, 5055, boul Métropolitain est, Montréal QC H1R 1Z7
514/327-0020; Fax: 514/327-6242
Directeur général, Louis Gosselin
Classes of Insurance: Personal Accident & Sickness; Life

*L'Exclusive, Compagnie d'Assurances Générales
#207, 1305, boul Lebourgneuf, Québec QC G2K 2E4
418/621-9393; Fax: 418/621-9333; Toll Free: 1-888-621-9393

*Family Insurance Corporation
#2000, 1040 Georgia St. West, Vancouver BC V6E 4H1
604/681-6123
Classes of Insurance: Auto; Property

*Farm Mutual Reinsurance Plan Inc.
1305 Bishop St. North, PO Box 3428, Cambridge ON N3H 4T3
519/740-6415; Fax: 519/740-8852
President, John A. Harper
Classes of Insurance: Auto; Property

Federal Insurance Company/Compagnie d'Assurances Federale
One Financial Place, One Adelaide St. East, Toronto ON M5C 2V9
416/863-0550; Fax: 416/863-6945
URL: http://www.chubbinsurance.ca
Chief Agent, Janice M. Tomlinson
Classes of Insurance: Auto; Boiler & Machinery; Fidelity; Personal Accident & Sickness; Liability; Surety

Federated Insurance Company of Canada
717 Portage Ave., PO Box 5800, Winnipeg MB R3C 3C9
204/786-6431; Fax: 204/779-2643; Toll Free: 1-800-665-1934
President, John M. Paisley
Classes of Insurance: Auto; Boiler & Machinery; Fidelity; Fire; Liability; Property; Surety; Theft

Federated Life Insurance Company of Canada
717 Portage Ave., PO Box 5800, Winnipeg MB R3C 3C9
204/786-6431; Fax: 204/783-6913; Toll Free: 1-800-665-1934
President, John Paisley
Classes of Insurance: Personal Accident & Sickness; Life

Federation Insurance Company of Canada/La Fédération Compagnie d'Assurances du Canada
#500, 1000, de la Gauchetière ouest, Montréal QC H3B 4W5
514/875-5790; Fax: 514/875-9769
President/CEO, W.J. Green
Classes of Insurance: Auto; Boiler & Machinery; Fidelity; Fire; Hail & Crop; Legal Expense; Liability; Property; Surety

Financial Life Assurance Company of Canada
10 Four Seasons Pl., 10th Fl., PO Box 335, Etobicoke ON M9C 4V3
416/626-7002; Fax: 416/626-0657
President/CEO, Hugh D. Haney
Classes of Insurance: Personal Accident & Sickness; Life

First American Title Insurance Company
#801, 1290 Central Pkwy. West, Mississauga ON L5C 4R3
905/566-8675; Fax: 905/566-8676; Toll Free: 1-800-663-6777; Toll Free Fax: 1-800-705-0006
Email: ddavies@firstam.com; URL: http://www.firstam.com
Regional Vice-President, International Operations, Thomas H. Grifferty
Classes of Insurance: Property

*First Canadian Insurance Corporation
10727 - 82 Ave., Edmonton AB T6E 2B1
Classes of Insurance: Personal Accident & Sickness; Life

First Canadian Title Company Limited
#801, 1290 Central Pkwy. West, Mississauga ON L5C 4R3

905/566-0425; Fax: 905/566-8613; Toll Free: 1-800-307-0370
President, Patrick J. Chetcuti

First North American Insurance Company
5650 Yonge St., North York ON M2M 4G4
416/229-4515; Fax: 416/229-3040
President/CEO, Domenic D'Alessandro
Classes of Insurance: Auto; Personal Accident & Sickness; Property

Folksamerica Reinsurance Company
#1202, 80 Bloor St. West, Toronto ON M5S 2V1
416/961-0400; Fax: 416/961-5797
Sr. Vice-President & Chief Agent, Jim M. Willis
Classes of Insurance: Auto; Fidelity; Hail & Crop; Liability; Property; Surety

Forethought Life Insurance Company
3380 South Service Rd., Burlington ON L7N 3J5
905/681-0094; Fax: 905/681-2756
Chief Agent, J. Brian Reeve
Classes of Insurance: Life

Frankona Ruckversicherungs - Aktien - Gesellschaft
#330, 20 Richmond St. East, Toronto ON M5C 2R9
416/777-0066; Fax: 416/777-0365
Chief Agent & Manager, David E. Wilmot, Canadian Operations
Classes of Insurance: Auto; Aircraft; Boiler & Machinery; Credit; Fidelity; Fire; Hail & Crop; Personal Accident & Sickness; Liability; Life; Property; Surety

*Fundy Mutual Fire Insurance Company
700 Main St., PO Box 730, Sussex NB E0E 1P0
506/432-1535; Fax: 506/433-6788; Toll Free: 1-800-222-9550
General Manager, Jim Wilson
Classes of Insurance: Property

GAN Canada Insurance Company
649 North Service Rd. West, PO Box 5012, Burlington ON L7R 4L5
905/681-4903; Fax: 905/681-4944
Chair/President, Robert J. Lever
Classes of Insurance: Auto; Property

GAN General Insurance Company
649 North Service Rd. West, PO Box 5012, Burlington ON L7R 4L5
905/681-4901; Fax: 905/681-4951; Toll Free: 1-800-565-7090
Chair, President/CEO, Robert Lever
Classes of Insurance: Auto; Personal Accident & Sickness; Property

GAN VIE, Compagnie Française d'Assurances sur la Vie
#1200, 425, boul de Maisonneuve ouest, Montréal QC H3A 3G5
514/938-1313
Chief Agent, Eric L. Clark
Classes of Insurance: Life

GE Capital Casualty Co.
#510, 154 University Ave., Toronto ON M5H 3Y9
President/CEO, Ian Wright
Classes of Insurance: Property

GE Capital Mortgage Insurance Company (Canada)
2300 Meadowvale Blvd., Mississauga ON L5N 5P9
905/858-5422; Fax: 905/858-5423
President/CEO, Brian L. Hurley

The General Accident Assurance Company of Canada
#2600, 2 First Canadian Place, PO Box 410, Stn 1st Can Place, Toronto ON M5X 1J1
416/368-4733; Fax: 416/368-9039
URL: http://www.genacc.ca
President/CEO, Howard Moran
Classes of Insurance: Auto; Personal Accident & Sickness; Property

General American Life Insurance Company
c/o RGA Life Reinsurance Company of Canada, #2220, 1501, av McGill College, Montréal QC H3A 3M8
514/985-5260; Fax: 514/985-3066; Toll Free: 1-800-985-GEAM
Email: mail@rga-reinsurance.com; URL: http://www.genam.com
Chief Agent, André St-Amour
Classes of Insurance: Personal Accident & Sickness; Life

General Reinsurance Corporation
#5705, 1 First Canadian Place, PO Box 471, Toronto ON M5X 1E4
416/869-0490; Fax: 416/360-2020; Toll Free: 1-800-268-9671
Chief Agent, Gerald A. Wolfe
Classes of Insurance: Auto; Personal Accident & Sickness; Property

*Gerling Global General Insurance Company
480 University Ave., Toronto ON M5G 1V6
416/598-4651; Fax: 416/598-9507
President, Andreas H. Henke, M.A., F.I.I.C.
Classes of Insurance: Boiler & Machinery; Liability; Property

*Gerling Global Life Insurance Company/La Gerling Globale, Compagnie d'Assurance-Vie
480 University Ave., 15th Fl., Toronto ON M5G 1V6
416/598-4677; Fax: 416/598-3901
President, Peter L. Schaefer
Classes of Insurance: Personal Accident & Sickness; Life

*Gerling Global Reinsurance Company
480 University Ave., Toronto ON M5G 1V6
416/598-4688; Fax: 416/598-9507
President, Andreas H. Henke, M.A., F.I.I.C.

*Germania Mutual Insurance Company
217 Kaiser William Ave., PO Box 40, Langenburg SK S0A 2A0
306/743-5363

Gore Mutual Insurance Company
252 Dundas St., PO Box 70, Cambridge ON N1R 5T3
519/623-1910; Fax: 519/623-8348; Toll Free: 1-800-265-8600
Chair/CEO, Robert J. Collins-Wright
Classes of Insurance: Auto; Boiler & Machinery; Fire; Personal Accident & Sickness; Liability; Property; Theft

Grain Insurance & Guarantee Company
#1240, One Lombard Pl., Winnipeg MB R3B 0V9
204/943-0721; Fax: 204/943-6419
President/General Manager, Ralph N. Jackson
Classes of Insurance: Fidelity; Liability; Property; Surety

Great American Insurance Company
#2100, 40 King St. West, Toronto ON M5H 3C2
416/869-5300; Fax: 416/360-8877
Chief Agent, J. Brian Reeve
Classes of Insurance: Auto; Personal Accident & Sickness; Property

The Great-West Life Assurance Company/Great-West, Compagnie d'Assurance Vie
100 Osborne St. North, PO Box 6000, Winnipeg MB R3C 3A5
204/946-1190; Fax: 204/946-7838
URL: http://www.gwl.ca
President/CEO, Raymond L. McFeetors
Classes of Insurance: Life

Green Shield Canada
5001 Yonge St., North York ON M2N 6P5
416/221-7001
Classes of Insurance: Personal Accident & Sickness

*Groupe Promutuel, Fédération de sociétés mutuelles d'assurance générale
#300, 1091, ch Saint-Louis, Sillery QC G1S 1E2
418/683-1212; Fax: 418/683-3303
President, Normand Fontaine
Classes of Insurance: Auto; Personal Accident & Sickness; Property

The Guarantee Company of North America/La Garantie, Compagnie d'Assurance de l'Amérique du Nord
Place du Canada, #1560, 1010, rue de la Gauchetière ouest, Montréal QC H3B 2R4
514/866-6351; Fax: 514/866-0157; Toll Free: 1-800-361-8603
President/CEO, Jules Quenneville, C.A.
Classes of Insurance: Auto; Accident; Boiler & Machinery; Fidelity; Fire; Hail & Crop; Personal Accident & Sickness; Legal Expense; Liability; Property; Surety; Theft

Guardian Insurance Company of Canada
181 University Ave., Toronto ON M5W 3M7
416/941-5050; Fax: 416/941-9791
President/CEO, Henry J. Curtis, M.A., F.C.I.I.
Classes of Insurance: Auto; Fire; Personal Accident & Sickness; Property

The Halifax Insurance Company
75 Eglinton Ave. East, Toronto ON M4P 3A4
416/440-1000; Fax: 416/440-0799
URL: http://www.halifaxinsurance.com
President/CEO, Donald K. Lough
Classes of Insurance: Auto; Accident; Boiler & Machinery; Fidelity; Fire; Personal Accident & Sickness; Liability; Property; Surety

Hannover Ruckversicherungs - Aktiengesellschaft
c/o D.M. Williams & Assoc. Ltd., #201, 3650 Victoria Park Ave., North York ON M2H 3P7
416/496-1148; Fax: 416/496-1089
Chief Agent, V.L. Williams
Classes of Insurance: Auto; Aircraft; Boiler & Machinery; Fidelity; Hail & Crop; Personal Accident & Sickness; Liability; Property; Surety

The Hartford Fire Insurance Company
20 York Mills Rd., North York ON M2P 2C2
416/733-1777; Fax: 416/733-1463; Toll Free: 1-800-268-6660
General Manager & Chief Agent for Canada, Gray G. Davis
Classes of Insurance: Auto; Fire; Personal Accident & Sickness

Hartford Insurance Company of Canada
20 York Mills Rd., North York ON M2P 2C2
416/733-1777; Fax: 416/733-1463
Email: lifeinfo@thehartford.com; URL: http://www.thehartford.com
President/CEO, Gray G. Davis
Classes of Insurance: Auto; Fire; Personal Accident & Sickness; Property

Helvetia Swiss Insurance Company Limited/Helvetia Compagnie Suisse d'Assurances
#500, 1000, rue de la Gauchetière ouest, Montréal QC H3B 4W5
514/875-5790; Fax: 514/875-9769
Chief Agent, W.J. Green
Classes of Insurance: Auto; Fire; Marine; Property

*Heritage General Insurance Company
#M101, 401 Bay St., Toronto ON M5H 2Y4
416/861-6991; Fax: 416/861-6989
President, Robert N.D. Hogan
Classes of Insurance: Personal Accident & Sickness

The Home Insurance Company
c/o The Focus Group Inc., #500, 36 King St. East, Toronto ON M5C 1E5
416/361-1728; Fax: 416/361-6113
Chief Agent, Philip H. Cook
Classes of Insurance: Auto; Aircraft; Boiler & Machinery; Fidelity; Personal Accident & Sickness; Liability; Property; Surety

Household Life Insurance Company/Compagnie d'Assurance-Vie Household
#100, 5100, rue Sherbrooke est, Montréal QC H1V 3M3
Chief Agent, Gaétan Toupin
Classes of Insurance: Personal Accident & Sickness; Life

*Hutterian Brethren General Insurance Corporation
#208, 62 Hargrave St., Winnipeg MB R3C 1N1
204/947-3849
Chief Agent, David J. Miller

*Hutterian Brethren Mutual Insurance Corporation
c/o H.B. Farm Agencies Ltd., #208, 62 Hargrave St., Winnipeg MB R3C 1N1
204/943-1565; Fax: 204/956-9380
Chief Agent, David J. Miller
Classes of Insurance: Property

The Imperial Life Assurance Company of Canada/ L'Impériale, Compagnie d'Assurance-Vie
95 St. Clair Ave. West, Toronto ON M4V 1N7
416/926-2600; Fax: 416/923-1599
President/CEO, Marcel Pepin
Classes of Insurance: Personal Accident & Sickness; Life

*L'Industrielle-Alliance Compagnie d'Assurance sur la Vie/Industrial-Alliance Life Insurance Company
1080, ch Saint-Louis, Sillery QC G1K 7M3
418/684-5000; Fax: 418/683-5663
Email: source@inalco.com
Chair, President/CEO, Raymond Garneau
Classes of Insurance: Personal Accident & Sickness; Life

The Insurance Company
#4, 1101 Nicholson Rd., Newmarket ON L3Y 7V1
905/853-0858; Fax: 905/853-0183
Chief Agent, Colleen Sexsmith
Classes of Insurance: Auto; Personal Accident & Sickness; Property

*Insurance Company of Prince Edward Island
125 Pownal St., PO Box 666, Charlottetown PE C1A 7L3
902/566-5666

*Insurance Corporation of British Columbia
151 Esplanade West, North Vancouver BC V7M 3H9
604/661-2800; Fax: 604/661-2244; Toll Free: 1-800-663-3051
URL: http://www.icbc.com
President/CEO, T.M. Thompson
Classes of Insurance: Auto

*Insurance Corporation of Newfoundland Ltd.
187 Kenmount Rd., PO Box 8485, St. John's NF A1B 3N9
709/758-5650; Fax: 709/579-4500
Chair, Maxwell De Koven
Classes of Insurance: Property

*The International Life Insurance Company/ L'Internationale, Compagnie d'Assurance-Vie
#1514, 1010, rue Sherbrooke ouest, Montréal QC H3A 2R7
514/842-3905
Présidente et Directrice générale, Yolande Blouin
Classes of Insurance: Personal Accident & Sickness; Life

ITT Hartford Life Insurance Company of Canada/ ITT Hartford du Canada, Compagnie d'Assurance Vie
3027 Harvester Rd., Burlington ON L7N 3G9
905/639-6200; Fax: 905/639-7763
Email: hartford@ftn.net
President/CEO, Mark Sylvia
Classes of Insurance: Personal Accident & Sickness; Life

J.C. Penney Life Insurance Company
#500, 80 Tiverton Ct., Markham ON L3R 0G4
905/479-7500
Chief Agent, Aaron Hill
Classes of Insurance: Personal Accident & Sickness; Life

Jevco Insurance Company/La Compagnie d'Assurances Jevco
#1150, 2021, rue Union, Montréal QC H3A 2S9
514/284-9340, 9350; Fax: 514/284-3390
President/CEO, William G. Star
Classes of Insurance: Auto; Liability; Property; Surety

John Hancock Mutual Life Insurance Company
c/o McLean & Kerr, #2800, 130 Adelaide St. West, Toronto ON M5H 3P7
416/364-5371; Fax: 416/366-8571
Chief Agent, Robin B. Cumine, Q.C.
Classes of Insurance: Personal Accident & Sickness; Life

Kemper Reinsurance Company
#201, 3650 Victoria Park Ave., North York ON M2H 3P7
416/496-1148; Fax: 416/496-1089
Chief Agent, V.L. Williams
Classes of Insurance: Auto; Aircraft; Boiler & Machinery; Fidelity; Hail & Crop; Personal Accident & Sickness; Liability; Property; Surety

The Kings Mutual Insurance Company
PO Box 10, Berwick NS B0P 1E0
902/538-3187; Fax: 902/538-7271; Toll Free: 1-800-565-7220
President, J.J. Ueffing
Classes of Insurance: Property

Kingsway Financial Services Inc.
#200, 5310 Explorer Dr., Mississauga ON L4W 5H8
905/629-7888; Fax: 905/629-5008
President, William G. Star

*Kingsway General Insurance Company
5310 Explorer Dr., Mississauga ON L4W 5H8
905/629-7888; Fax: 905/629-5008; Toll Free: 1-800-265-5458
President/CEO, William G. Star
Classes of Insurance: Auto; Fidelity; Fire; Liability; Property; Surety

Laurier Life Insurance Company
304 The East Mall, 9th Fl., Etobicoke ON M9B 6E2
416/234-9700; Fax: 416/234-9764
President, Van M. Campbell
Classes of Insurance: Personal Accident & Sickness; Life

*Lawyers' Professional Indemnity Company
Osgoode Hall, 130 Queen St. West, Toronto ON M5H 2N6
416/947-3431; Fax: 416/599-8341
President, Edwin J. Anderson

Lawyers Title Insurance Corporation
65 Queen St. West, 17th Fl., Toronto ON M5H 2M5
416/368-4611; Fax: 416/367-2502
Chief Agent, David L. Gibson

*Les Assurances Funeraires Rousseau et Frère Limitée
445, rue des Volontaires, CP 213, Trois-Rivières QC G9A 5G1
819/374-6225
Président, Arthur Rousseau

*Liberty Health
3500 Steeles Ave. East, Markham ON L3R 0X4
905/946-4050; Fax: 905/946-4929; Toll Free: 1-800-268-3743
President, Gery Barry
Classes of Insurance: Personal Accident & Sickness; Life

Liberty Life Assurance Company of Boston
#3320, 181 Bay St., Toronto ON M5J 2T3
416/365-7587; Fax: 416/365-9302
Chief Agent, B.G. Johnston
Classes of Insurance: Personal Accident & Sickness; Life

Liberty Mutual Fire Insurance Company
#3320, 181 Bay St., Toronto ON M5J 2T3
416/365-7587; Fax: 416/365-9302; Toll Free: 1-800-461-5079
Chief Agent, Gery Barry
Classes of Insurance: Auto; Aircraft; Boiler & Machinery; Fidelity; Personal Accident & Sickness; Liability; Property; Surety

Liberty Mutual Insurance Company
#3320, 181 Bay St., Toronto ON M5J 2T3
416/365-7587; Fax: 416/365-9302
Chief Agent, Gery Barry
Classes of Insurance: Auto; Aircraft; Boiler & Machinery; Fidelity; Personal Accident & Sickness; Liability; Property; Surety

Life Insurance Company of North America
#1400, 250 Yonge St., PO Box 14, Toronto ON M5B 2L7
416/591-1225; Fax: 416/591-7488
Chief Agent, Eman Hassan
Classes of Insurance: Personal Accident & Sickness; Life

Life Investors Insurance Company of America
c/o John Milnes & Associates, 68 Scollard St., 2nd Fl., Toronto ON M5R 1G2
416/964-0067; Fax: 416/964-3338
Chief Agent, John R. Milnes
Classes of Insurance: Personal Accident & Sickness; Life

Life Reassurance Corporation of America
c/o Deloitte & Touche, #1400, 181 Bay St., PO Box 12, Toronto ON M5J 2V1
416/601-6188
Chief Agent, Wayne Musselman
Classes of Insurance: Personal Accident & Sickness; Life

The Lincoln National Life Insurance Company
#1700, 151 Yonge St., Toronto ON M5C 2W7
416/777-2500; Fax: 416/777-2499
Chief Agent, Brenda Buckingham, Q.C.
Classes of Insurance: Personal Accident & Sickness; Life

Lloyd's
#1540, 1155, rue Metcalfe, Montréal QC H3B 2V6
514/861-8361; Fax: 514/861-0470; Toll Free: 1-800-565-5693
Director, David Gittings, Regulatory Division
Classes of Insurance: Auto; Accident; Aircraft; Boiler & Machinery; Credit; Fidelity; Fire; Hail & Crop; Personal Accident & Sickness; Legal Expense; Liability; Marine; Property; Theft

Lombard General Insurance Company of Canada
105 Adelaide St. West, Toronto ON M5H 1P9
416/350-4400; Fax: 416/350-4412
President/CEO, Byron G. Messier
Classes of Insurance: Auto; Aircraft; Boiler & Machinery; Credit; Fidelity; Fire; Hail & Crop; Legal Expense; Liability; Property; Surety; Theft

Lombard Insurance Company
105 Adelaide St. West, Toronto ON M5H 1P9
416/350-4400; Fax: 416/350-4412
President/CEO, Bryon G. Messier
Classes of Insurance: Auto; Aircraft; Boiler & Machinery; Credit; Fidelity; Fire; Hail & Crop; Legal Expense; Liability; Property; Surety; Theft

London & Midland General Insurance Company
201 Queens Ave., PO Box 5071, London ON N6A 4M5
519/672-1070; Fax: 519/672-2623
Vice-President/General Manager, A.W. Miles
Classes of Insurance: Accident; Personal Accident & Sickness; Property

The London Assurance
#630, 48 Yonge St., Toronto ON M5E 1G6
416/363-0814; Fax: 416/363-0459
Chief Agent, R.J. Gunn

London Guarantee Insurance Company
#342B, 77 King St. West, PO Box 284, Toronto ON M5K 1K2
416/360-8183; Fax: 416/360-8267
Email: rtaylor@londonguarantee.com; URL: http://www.londonguarantee.com
President/CEO, Robert E. Taylor
Classes of Insurance: Boiler & Machinery; Fidelity; Liability; Property; Surety

London Life Insurance Company/London Life, Compagnie d'Assurance-Vie
255 Dufferin Ave., London ON N6A 4K1
519/432-5281; Fax: 519/679-3518
URL: http://www.londonlife.com
President/CEO, Fredric J. Tomczyk
Classes of Insurance: Personal Accident & Sickness; Life

*The Loyalist Insurance Company
#106, 911 Golf Links Rd., Ancaster ON L9K 1H9
905/648-1722; Fax: 905/648-7399
Chair, James D. Coon

Lumbermens Mutual Casualty Company
320 Front St. West, 6th Fl., Toronto ON M5V 3B6
416/593-6626; Fax: 416/351-2502; Toll Free: 1-800-387-2934
Email: kemperto@interramp.com
Chief Agent, D.E. Aitchison
Classes of Insurance: Auto; Accident; Aircraft; Boiler & Machinery; Fidelity; Fire; Hail & Crop; Liability; Property; Surety

*Manitoba Mennonite Mutual Insurance Company
85 Hwy. 12 North, PO Box 3550, Steinbach MB R0A 2A0
204/326-6468; Fax: 204/326-1865
President, Delbert F. Plett, Q.C.
Classes of Insurance: Property

*Manitoba Motor Club Insurance Co. Inc.
PO Box 1400, Winnipeg MB R3C 2Z3
204/987-6161
Chief Agent, Michael R. Mager

*Manitoba Public Insurance
731 - 1 St., Brandon MB R7A 6C3
204/729-9400; Fax: 204/727-3261
President/General Manager, Jack W. Zacharias
Classes of Insurance: Auto

The Manufacturers Life Insurance Company
200 Bloor St. East, Toronto ON M4W 1E5
416/926-0100; Fax: 416/926-5454
URL: http://www.manulife.com
President/CEO, Dominic D'Alessandro
Classes of Insurance: Life

Marine Indemnity Insurance Company of America
#1200, 48 Yonge St., Toronto ON M5E 1G6
416/364-5485; Fax: 416/364-9068
Chief Agent, Peter T. Perkins
Classes of Insurance: Liability; Property

Maritime Insurance Company Limited
60 Yonge St., Toronto ON M5E 1H5
416/362-2961; Fax: 416/362-7281
President, G.J. Giroux
Classes of Insurance: Marine; Property

The Maritime Life Assurance Company
Maritime Life Bldg., 2701 Dutch Village Rd., PO Box 1030, Halifax NS B3J 2X5
902/453-4300; Fax: 902/453-7041
Email: bblack@maritimelife.ca; URL: http://www.maritimelife.ca
President/CEO, William A. Black
Classes of Insurance: Life

Markel Insurance Company of Canada
105 Adelaide St. West, 7th Fl., Toronto ON M5H 1P9
416/364-7800; Fax: 416/364-1625
President, Mark Ram
Classes of Insurance: Auto

Maryland Casualty Company/Compagnie Maryland Casualty
1, Place Ville-Marie, 40e étage, Montréal QC H3B 4M4
514/871-1522; Fax: 514/871-8977
Classes of Insurance: Auto; Aircraft; Boiler & Machinery; Fidelity; Personal Accident & Sickness; Liability; Property; Surety

Massachusetts Mutual Life Insurance Company
c/o McLean & Kerr, #2800, 130 Adelaide St. West, Toronto ON M5H 3P5
416/364-5371; Fax: 416/366-8571
Chief Agent, R.B. Cumine, Q.C.
Classes of Insurance: Personal Accident & Sickness; Life

Meloche Monnex Inc.
50, Place Crémazie, 12 étage, Montréal QC H2P 1B6
514/382-6060; Fax: 514/385-2162
URL: http://www.meloche-monnex.com
President/Chief Operating Officer, Raymond A. Décarie, Client Services
Classes of Insurance: Auto; Fire; Personal Accident & Sickness; Life; Property

*Mennonite Mutual Insurance Co. (Alberta) Ltd.
76 Skyline Cres. NE, Calgary AB T2K 5X7
403/275-6996; Fax: 403/275-3711
General Manager, Larry L. Jantzi
Classes of Insurance: Auto; Fidelity; Liability; Property

*Metro General Insurance Corporation Ltd.
PO Box 548, St. John's NF A1C 5K9
709/726-1922
President & Sec.-Treas., Kevin Hutchings

Metropolitan Life Insurance Company of Canada/Compagnie d'Assurance-Vie La Métropolitan du Canada
99 Bank St., Ottawa ON K1P 5A3
613/560-7446; Fax: 613/560-7668
President/CEO, William R. Prueter
Classes of Insurance: Personal Accident & Sickness; Life

*MFQ-Vie, Corporation d'Assurance
625, rue Saint-Amable, Québec QC G1R 2G5
418/643-3884; Fax: 418/528-0457; Toll Free: 1-800-463-5549
URL: http://www.mfq.qc.ca
Chair/CEO, Alphé Poiré
Classes of Insurance: Life

MIC Life Insurance Corporation
#400, 8500 Leslie St., PO Box 6000, Thornhill ON L3T 4S5
905/882-3900; Fax: 905/882-3955
Chief Agent, C.W. Hastings
Classes of Insurance: Personal Accident & Sickness; Life

*Midwest Insurance Inc.
301 - 4th Ave. North, Saskatoon SK S7K 2L8
306/653-2233

The Minnesota Mutual Life Insurance Company
c/o McLean & Kerr, #2800, 130 Adelaide St. West, Toronto ON M5H 3P5
416/364-5371; Fax: 416/366-8571
Chief Agent, R.B. Cumine, Q.C.
Classes of Insurance: Life

Mitsui Marine & Fire Insurance Company, Ltd.
c/o D.M. Williams & Assoc. Ltd., #201, 3650 Victoria Park Ave., North York ON M2H 3P7
416/496-1148; Fax: 416/496-1089
Chief Agent, V.L. Williams
Classes of Insurance: Auto; Personal Accident & Sickness; Property

Motors Insurance Corporation
#400, 8500 Leslie St., PO Box 6000, Thornhill ON L3T 4S5
905/882-3900; Fax: 905/882-3955
Chief Agent, C.W. Hastings
Classes of Insurance: Auto; Property

Munich Reinsurance Company
390 Bay St., 22nd Fl., Toronto ON M5H 2Y2
416/366-9206; Fax: 416/366-4330; Toll Free: 1-800-444-5321
Chief Agent, Property & Casualty, John P. Phelan
Classes of Insurance: Auto; Aircraft; Boiler & Machinery; Credit; Fidelity; Hail & Crop; Personal Accident & Sickness; Liability; Life; Property; Surety

Munich Reinsurance Company of Canada
390 Bay St., 22nd Fl., Toronto ON M5H 2Y2
416/366-9206; Fax: 416/366-4330; Toll Free: 1-800-268-9705
President, John P. Phelan
Classes of Insurance: Auto; Aircraft; Boiler & Machinery; Credit; Fidelity; Hail & Crop; Personal Accident & Sickness; Property; Surety

*The Municipal Insurance Association of British Columbia
#710, 1090 Pender St. West, Vancouver BC V6E 2N7
604/683-6266

*The Mutual Fire Insurance Company of British Columbia
#105, 10334 - 152A St., Surrey BC V3R 7P8
Classes of Insurance: Auto; Fire; Property

The Mutual Group
227 King St. South, Waterloo ON N2J 4C5
519/888-2290; Fax: 519/888-2990
URL: http://www.themutualgroup.com/
President/CEO, Robert M. Astley
Classes of Insurance: Personal Accident & Sickness; Life

Mutual of Omaha Insurance Company
500 University Ave., Toronto ON M5G 1V8
416/598-4321; Fax: 416/598-5356
Exec. Vice-President & Chief Agent for Canada, David R. Lafayette
Classes of Insurance: Personal Accident & Sickness; Life

La Mutuelle du Mans Assurances I.A.R.D.
c/o Mutuelles du Mans Management Ltd., #1000, 20 Queen St. West, Toronto ON M5H 3R3
416/598-1084; Fax: 416/598-1980
Chief Agent, L.R. Quintal
Classes of Insurance: Auto; Fire; Personal Accident & Sickness; Property

La Mutuelle du Mans Assurances Vie
2475, boul Laurier, Sillery QC G1T 1C4
Chief Agent, Normand Brunet
Classes of Insurance: Personal Accident & Sickness; Life

*La Mutuelle d'Église de l'Inter-ouest
180, boul Mont-Bleu, Hull QC J8Z 3J5
819/595-0708
Président, Jean Levert

NAC Reinsurance Corporation
#300, 211 Consumers Rd., North York ON M2J 4G8
416/498-9822; Fax: 416/498-1465
Chief Agent, T.P. Flynn
Classes of Insurance: Auto; Fire; Personal Accident & Sickness; Property

*National Frontier Insurance Company
#200, 147 McIntyre St. West, North Bay ON P1B 2Y5
705/476-4814; Fax: 705/476-8694
Vice-President/Chief Operating Officer, David Liddle
Classes of Insurance: Auto; Fire; Personal Accident & Sickness; Property

The National Life Assurance Company of Canada
522 University Ave., Toronto ON M5G 1Y7
416/598-2122; Fax: 416/598-2195; Toll Free: 1-800-387-4326
President/Chief Operating Officer, V.P. Tonna
Classes of Insurance: Life

Nationwide Mutual Insurance Company
c/o John Milnes & Associates, 68 Scollard St., 2nd Fl., Toronto ON M5R 1G2
416/964-0630; Fax: 416/964-3338
Chief Agent, John R. Milnes
Classes of Insurance: Auto; Personal Accident & Sickness; Miscellaneous; Property

New Hampshire Insurance Company
145 Wellington St. West, Toronto ON M5J 1H8
416/596-3000; Fax: 416/977-2743
Chief Agent, Gary A. McMillan
Classes of Insurance: Auto; Boiler & Machinery; Fire; Liability; Property

New York Life Insurance Company/Compagnie d'Assurances New York Life
#2100, Scotia Plaza, 40 King St. West, Toronto ON M5H 3C2
416/960-4500; Fax: 416/968-0901

Chief Agent, J. Brian Reeve
Classes of Insurance: Personal Accident & Sickness; Life

Niagara Fire Insurance Company
One Adelaide St. East, PO Box 219A, Toronto ON M5W 1B6
416/350-4400; Fax: 416/350-4412
Chief Agent in Canada, Byron G. Messier
Classes of Insurance: Auto; Aircraft; Boiler & Machinery; Credit; Fidelity; Fire; Hail & Crop; Legal Expense; Liability; Property; Surety; Theft

Nippon Fire & Marine Insurance Company Ltd.
c/o Canadian General Insurance Company, #500, 2206 Eglinton Ave. East, Scarborough ON M1L 4S8
416/288-1800; Fax: 416/288-9756
Chief Agent, R. Lewis Dunn
Classes of Insurance: Auto; Fire; Property

NN Life Insurance Company of Canada/NN Compagnie d'Assurance-Vie du Canada
One Concorde Gate, North York ON M3C 3N6
416/391-2200; Fax: 416/391-1585
Email: cwalker@interlog.com; URL: http://www.ingfin.com
President/CEO, Frederick C. Wolfe
Classes of Insurance: Personal Accident & Sickness; Life

*Norfolk Mutual Fire Insurance Company
37 Kent St. South, Simcoe ON N3Y 2X7
519/426-1294; Fax: 519/426-7594
Manager, Carrol E. Lambert
Classes of Insurance: Auto; Fire; Property

The North Waterloo Farmers Mutual Insurance Company
100 Erb St. East, Waterloo ON N2J 2L5
519/886-4530; Fax: 519/746-0222
GM, Robert L. Monte
Classes of Insurance: Auto; Hail & Crop; Liability; Property

The North West Life Assurance Company of Canada
#800, 1040 West Georgia St., Vancouver BC V6E 4H1
604/689-1211; Fax: 604/682-2013
Vice-President & Secretary, Arthur W. Putz
Classes of Insurance: Life

Northern Indemnity Inc.
#2210, 120 Adelaide St. West, Toronto ON M5H 1T1
416/214-1878; Fax: 416/214-1875
President, Robert Lamendola
Classes of Insurance: Fidelity; Surety

The Norwich Union Life Company Canada
60 Yonge St., Toronto ON M5E 1H5
416/362-2961; Fax: 416/362-4077
Chief Agent, Guy S. Pentelow
Classes of Insurance: Life

Old Republic Insurance Company of Canada/L'Ancienne Republique Compagnie d'Assurance du Canada
100 King St. West, PO Box 557, Hamilton ON L8N 3K9
905/523-5936; Fax: 905/523-1471
President/CEO, Anthony Chmiel
Classes of Insurance: Auto; Property

*Ontario Mutual Insurance Association
1305 Bishop St. North, PO Box 3187, Cambridge ON N3H 4S6
519/622-9220; Fax: 519/622-9227
President, Glen Johnson
Classes of Insurance: Auto; Personal Accident & Sickness; Property

*Optimum Assurance Agricole Inc./Optimum Farm Insurance Inc.
#250, 1500, rue Royale, Trois-Rivières QC G9A 6E6
819/373-2040; Fax: 819/373-2801; Toll Free: 1-800-567-9369
President, Yvon Trépanier
Classes of Insurance: Auto; Fire; Property

*Ordre des Architectes du Québec
#301, 360, rue Notre-Dame ouest, Montréal QC H2Y 1T9
514/842-4979
Président, Bernard McNamara

*Ordre des Dentistes du Québec
625, boul René-Lévesque ouest, 15e étage, Montréal QC H3B 1R2
514/875-8511
Président, Robert Salois

*Pacific Coast Fishermen's Mutual Marine Insurance Company
#200, 4259 Canada Way, Burnaby BC V5G 1H7
604/438-4240

*Palliser Insurance Corp.
#103, 3502 Taylor St. East, Saskatoon SK S7H 5H9
306/955-1330

The Paul Revere Life Insurance Company/Paul Revere Compagnie d'Assurance-Vie
5420 North Service Rd., PO Box 5044, Burlington ON L7R 4C1
905/319-9501; Fax: 905/319-9490
Chief Agent, J.P. Charlebois
Classes of Insurance: Personal Accident & Sickness; Life

*Peace Hills General Insurance Company
#902, 10011 - 109 St. NW, Edmonton AB T5J 3S8
403/424-3986; Fax: 403/424-0396; Toll Free: 1-800-272-5614
President/CEO, Diane Strashok, A.I.I.C.
Classes of Insurance: Auto; Fire; Hail & Crop; Property

*Pembridge Inc.
#400, 1243 Islington Ave., Etobicoke ON M8X 2Y3
416/231-1300; Fax: 416/231-2612; Toll Free: 1-800-557-7232
President/CEO, Douglas E. McIntyre
Classes of Insurance: Auto; Accident; Boiler & Machinery; Credit; Fidelity; Fire; Hail & Crop; Personal Accident & Sickness; Legal Expense; Liability; Property; Theft

Penncorp Life Insurance Company
#400, 90 Dundas St. West, Mississauga ON L5B 2T5
905/272-0210
President/CEO, J. Paul Edmondson
Classes of Insurance: Personal Accident & Sickness; Life

The Personal Insurance Company of Canada
703 Evans Ave., Toronto ON M9C 5A7
416/621-6000; Fax: 416/620-3911
President/Chief Operating Officer, Kevin McNeil
Classes of Insurance: Auto; Property

*La Personnelle-Vie Corporation d'Assurance
625, rue Saint-Amable, Québec QC G1R 2G5
418/644-4229; Fax: 418/528-0457; Toll Free: 1-800-463-5549
Chair/CEO, Alphé Poiré
Classes of Insurance: Life

Phoenix Home Life Mutual Insurance Company
Scotia Plaza, #2100, 40 King St. West, Toronto ON M5H 3C2
416/869-5300; Fax: 416/360-8877
Chief Agent, J. Brian Reeve
Classes of Insurance: Personal Accident & Sickness; Life

The Phoenix Insurance Company
Scotia Plaza, #2100, 40 King St. West, Toronto ON M5H 3C2
416/869-5300; Fax: 416/360-8877
Chief Agent, J. Brian Reeve
Classes of Insurance: Auto; Fire; Property

Pictou County Farmers' Mutual Fire Insurance Company
PO Box 130, Pictou NS B0K 1H0
902/485-4542; Fax: 902/485-5136
President, Reg Holman
Classes of Insurance: Liability; Property

Pierce National Life Insurance
#4, 1101 Nicholson Rd., Newmarket ON L3Y 7V1
905/853-0858; Fax: 905/853-0183
Chief Agent, Colleen Sexsmith
Classes of Insurance: Life

*Pinnacle Insurance Corp.
637 Main St. North, PO Box 967, Moose Jaw SK S6H 4P6
306/694-1797

Pool Insurance Company
#1007, 220 Portage Ave., Winnipeg MB R3C 0A5
204/942-0658; Fax: 204/989-2235
President, Charles H. Swanson
Classes of Insurance: Property

The Portage La Prairie Mutual Insurance Company
PO Box 340, Portage La Prairie MB R1N 3B8
204/857-3415; Fax: 204/239-6655
President, Hugh G. Owens
Classes of Insurance: Auto; Fire; Legal Expense; Liability; Property; Theft

*Premier Insurance Company
5905 Campus Rd., Mississauga ON L4V 1P9
905/676-1240; Fax: 905/676-9318
President, R.V. McCarron

Primerica Life Insurance Company of Canada
#301, 350 Burnhamthorpe Rd. West, PO Box 2500, Stn Malton, Mississauga ON L4T 4J4
905/848-7731; Fax: 905/270-7096
President/CEO, Glen Williams
Classes of Insurance: Personal Accident & Sickness; Life

Primmum Insurance Company
50, Place Crémazie, 5e étage, Montréal QC H2P 1B6
514/382-6060; Fax: 514/385-2162
Classes of Insurance: Auto; Personal Accident & Sickness; Property

*Prince Edward Island Mutual Insurance Company
201 Water St., Summerside PE C1N 1B4
902/436-2185; Fax: 902/436-0148; Toll Free: 1-800-565-5441
General Manager, Malcolm MacFarlane
Classes of Insurance: Fire; Property

Principal Mutual Life Insurance Company
c/o John Milnes & Associates, 68 Scollard St., 2nd Fl., Toronto ON M5R 1G2
416/964-0630; Fax: 416/964-3338
Chief Agent, John R. Milnes
Classes of Insurance: Personal Accident & Sickness; Life

Progressive Casualty Insurance Company of Canada
200 Yorkland Blvd., 5th Fl., North York ON M2J 5C1
416/499-9947; Fax: 416/499-4322; Toll Free: 1-800-268-3278
URL: http://www.auto-insurance.com
Product Manager, William J. Conner
Classes of Insurance: Auto

*Promutuel Réassurance
#300, 1091, ch Saint-Louis, Sillery QC G1S 1E2
418/683-1212; Fax: 418/683-3303
Directeur général, Jacques Douville
Classes of Insurance: Auto; Property

*Promutuel Vie Inc.
134, rue St-Charles, St-Jean-Sur-Richelieu QC J3B 2C3
514/346-5041; Fax: 514/346-0224
General Manager, Michel Tardif
Classes of Insurance: Personal Accident & Sickness; Life

Protection Mutual Insurance Company
Ennisclare Office Centre, #810, 1275 North Service Rd. West, Oakville ON L6M 3G4
905/827-9000; Fax: 905/827-9008
URL: http://www.promutual.com
Chief Agent, J. Gray
Classes of Insurance: Boiler & Machinery; Fidelity; Property

Protective Insurance Company
68 Scollard St., 2nd Fl., Toronto ON M5R 1G2
416/964-0067; Fax: 416/964-3338
Chief Agent, John R. Milnes
Classes of Insurance: Auto; Property

Providence Washington Insurance Company
#1703, 155 University Ave., Toronto ON M5H 3B7
416/366-3012; Fax: 416/366-3465
Chief Agent, Jack G. Dovey
Classes of Insurance: Marine; Property

Provident Life & Accident Insurance Company
5420 North Service Rd., Burlington ON L7R 4C1
905/319-9501; Fax: 905/319-6518
Classes of Insurance: Personal Accident & Sickness

*Provincial Health Authorities of Alberta Liability Protection Plan
#200, 10044 - 108 St., Edmonton AB T5J 3S7
403/426-8502; Fax: 403/424-4309

Québec Assurance Company/Compagnie d'Assurance du Québec
#800, 2, place Alexis-Nihon, Montréal QC H3Z 3C1
514/932-1157; Fax: 514/932-5046
President, R.J. Gunn
Classes of Insurance: Auto; Fire; Property

*Red River Valley Mutual Insurance Company
245 Centre Ave. East, PO Box 940, Altona MB R0G 0B0
204/324-6434, 284-0684 (Winnipeg); Fax: 204/324-1316
CEO, H.G. Heinrichs
Classes of Insurance: Auto; Property

Reliable Life Insurance Company/La Reliable Compagnie d'Assurance Vie
100 King St. West, PO Box 557, Hamilton ON L8N 3K9
905/523-5587; Fax: 905/528-4685
Chair/CEO, A.T. Chmiel
Classes of Insurance: Personal Accident & Sickness; Life

Reliance Insurance Company
#1906, 200 King St. West, Toronto ON M5H 3T4
416/581-0101; Fax: 416/581-1109
First Vice-President, Paul Primiani, Underwriting
Classes of Insurance: Auto; Boiler & Machinery; Fidelity; Fire; Liability; Property

ReliaStar Life Insurance Company
c/o D.M. Williams & Assoc. Ltd., #201, 3650 Victoria Park Ave., North York ON M2H 3P7
416/496-1148; Fax: 416/496-1089
Chief Agent, V.L. Williams
Classes of Insurance: Personal Accident & Sickness; Life

RGA Life Reinsurance Company of Canada/RGA, Compagnie de Réassurance-Vie du Canada
#1200, 55 University Ave., Toronto ON M5J 2H7
416/682-0000
Email: mail@rga-reinsurance.com; URL: http://www.rgare.com
President/CEO, André St-Amour
Classes of Insurance: Life

Royal Insurance Company of Canada/La Royale du Canada, Compagnie d'Assurance
10 Wellington St. East, Toronto ON M5E 1L5
416/366-7511; Fax: 416/367-9869
President/CEO, R.J. Gunn
Classes of Insurance: Auto; Personal Accident & Sickness; Property

Royal Life Insurance Company of Canada Ltd.
277 Lakeshore Rd. East, Oakville ON L6J 1H9
905/842-6200; Fax: 905/842-6294; Toll Free: 1-800-263-1747
President/CEO, Clive S. Smith
Classes of Insurance: Life

Royale Belge
#1200, 425, boul de Maisonneuve ouest, Montréal QC H3A 3G5
514/288-1900; Fax: 514/288-8099
Chief Agent, Harvey Campbell
Classes of Insurance: Life

SAFR Société Anonyme Française de Réassurances
1080, Côte du Beaver Hall, 19e étage, Montréal QC H2Z 1S8
514/878-2600; Fax: 514/878-9309; Toll Free: 1-800-363-6800
Chief Agent, Jacques Mailloux, C.A.
Classes of Insurance: Auto; Personal Accident & Sickness; Life; Property

*Saskatchewan Auto Fund
2260 - 11 Ave., Regina SK S4O 0J9
306/751-1200; Fax: 306/565-8666
President, Larry Fogg
Classes of Insurance: Auto

*Saskatchewan Motor Club Insurance Company Ltd.
200 Albert St. North, Regina SK S4R 5E2
306/791-4321

Saskatchewan Mutual Insurance Company
279 - 3 Ave. North, Saskatoon SK S7K 2H8
306/653-4232; Fax: 306/664-1957; Toll Free: 1-800-667-3067
President/CEO, R.W. Trost
Classes of Insurance: Auto; Fire; Property

SCOR Canada Reinsurance Company
BCE Place, #5000, 161 Bay St., Toronto ON M5J 2S1
416/869-3670; Fax: 416/365-9393
President/CEO, Laurent Thabault
Classes of Insurance: Auto; Personal Accident & Sickness; Property

SCOR Reinsurance Company
c/o SCOR Services Canada Inc., #5000, 161 Bay St., Toronto ON M5J 2S1
416/869-3670; Fax: 416/365-9393
Chief Agent, Jaya Narayan
Classes of Insurance: Auto; Fire; Property

SCOR Vie
BCE Place, Canada Trust Tower, #5000, 161 Bay St., Toronto ON M5J 2S1
416/869-3670; Fax: 416/365-9393
Chief Agent, Jaya Narayan
Classes of Insurance: Personal Accident & Sickness; Life

Scotia General Insurance Company
#400, 100 Yonge St., Toronto ON M5H 1H1
President/CEO, Oscar Zimmerman
Classes of Insurance: Auto; Personal Accident & Sickness; Life; Property

Scotia Life Insurance Company
Scotia Plaza, 44 King St. West, Toronto ON M5H 1H1
President/CEO, Oscar Zimmerman
Classes of Insurance: Personal Accident & Sickness; Life

*Scottish & York Insurance Co. Limited
2206 Eglinton Ave. East, Scarborough ON M1L 4S8
416/288-1800; Fax: 416/288-5888
Classes of Insurance: Auto; Property

Seaboard Life Insurance Company
2165 West Broadway, PO Box 5900, Vancouver BC V6B 5H6
604/734-1667; Fax: 604/734-8221
President/CEO, Robert T. Smith
Classes of Insurance: Personal Accident & Sickness; Life

Seaboard Surety Company of Canada
#1500, 2 Bloor St. West, Toronto ON M4W 3E2
416/925-9360; Fax: 416/925-5336
President/Chief Operating Officer, Les Kanic
Classes of Insurance: Property; Surety

*La Securité, Assurances Générales Inc.
6300, boul de la Rive-Sud, Lévis QC G6V 6P9
418/835-4771; Fax: 418/835-5599

*Security Life Insurance Company
2206 Eglinton Ave. East, Scarborough ON M1L 4S8
416/494-2497; Fax: 416/494-4616
General Manager, George Mejury

Security National Insurance Company/La Sécurité Nationale compagnie d'assurances
50, Place Crémazie, 12e étage, Montréal QC H2P 1B6
514/382-6060; Fax: 514/385-2162; Toll Free: 1-800-361-3821
Classes of Insurance: Auto; Fire; Personal Accident & Sickness; Property

Sentry Insurance - a Mutual Company
#600, 133 Richmond St. West, Toronto ON M5H 2L3
416/363-6103; Fax: 416/363-7454
Chief Agent, Donald G. Smith
Classes of Insurance: Auto; Property

*SGI Canada
2260 - 11th Ave., Regina SK S4P 0J9
306/751-1200; Fax: 306/565-8666
President, Larry Fogg
Classes of Insurance: Auto; Fire; Personal Accident & Sickness; Property

Skandia Insurance Company Ltd.
c/o D.M. Williams & Associates Ltd., #201, 3650 Victoria Park Ave., North York ON M2H 3P7
416/496-1148; Fax: 416/496-1089
Chief Agent, V. Lorraine Williams
Classes of Insurance: Auto; Aircraft; Boiler & Machinery; Fidelity; Liability; Property; Surety

*SMDA Insurance Corporation
#330, 3303 Hillsdale St., Regina SK S4S 6W9
306/721-2920; Fax: 306/721-2200
President, Ben R. Holden
Classes of Insurance: Personal Accident & Sickness; Life

*La Société Cooperative de Frais Funeraires Inc.
160, boul Graham, Montréal QC H3P 3H9
514/735-2025
Président, Pierre Bourgie

*Société Nationale d'Assurance Inc./National Insurance Company
#1500, 425, boul de Maisonneuve ouest, Montréal QC H3A 3G5
514/288-8711; Fax: 514/288-8269; Toll Free: 1-800-361-7653
President, Yvon Trépanier
Classes of Insurance: Auto; Fire; Property

Société de Réassurance des Assurances Mutuelles Agricoles
#1520, 70 York St., Toronto ON M5J 1S9
416/364-3048; Fax: 416/364-1788
Chief Agent, Angus Ross
Classes of Insurance: Auto; Personal Accident & Sickness; Property

*Société de Secours Mutuels des Citoyens de Casacalenda
519, av 76e, Montréal QC H8R 2P8
514/363-6718
Président, Bino Romano

*Société de Secours Mutuels de St-Zacharie
652, rue 15e, St-Zacharie QC G0M 2C0
418/593-3109
Président, Gilles Couture

*Southeastern Mutual Fire Insurance Company
115 Queen St., Moncton NB E1C 1K6
506/386-3325
Raymond White
Classes of Insurance: Property

The Sovereign General Insurance Company
#2200, 855 - 2 Ave. SW, Calgary AB T2P 4J8
403/298-4200; Fax: 403/298-4217
President/CEO, G. Terry Squire
Classes of Insurance: Auto; Accident; Boiler & Machinery; Fidelity; Fire; Personal Accident & Sickness; Liability; Property; Surety; Theft

*Sphere Drake Insurance Public Limited Company
3200 Erin Mills Pkwy., PO Box 67051, Stn Millway, Mississauga ON L5L 5W9
905/828-4951; Fax: 905/828-3453
Chief Agent, Taro Asnani

*SSQ, Société d'Assurance Générales Inc.
#440, 1245, ch Ste-Foy, Québec QC G1S 4P2
418/683-0554; Fax: 418/683-5603; Toll Free: 1-800-463-2343
President/Directeur général, René Hamel
Classes of Insurance: Auto; Fire; Legal Expense; Property

*SSQ, Société d'Assurance-Vie Inc.
2525, boul Laurier, CP 10500, Ste-Foy QC G1V 4H6
418/651-7000; Fax: 418/652-2739; Toll Free: 1-800-463-5525
Email: sbussier@riq.qc.ca
President/CEO, Pierre Genest, F.S.A., F.C.I.A.
Classes of Insurance: Personal Accident & Sickness; Life

*St-Laurent, Compagnie de Réassurance
#1200, 425, boul de Maisonneuve ouest, Montréal QC H3A 3G5
514/288-1900; Fax: 514/288-8099
President, Mario Georgiev
Classes of Insurance: Life

*La St-Maurice, Compagnie d'Assurance
2450, rue Girouard ouest, St-Hyacinthe QC J2S 3B3
514/288-8241
Président, Gilles Clark

St. Paul Fire & Marine Insurance Company/La Compagnie d'Assurance Saint Paul
#1200, 121 King St. West, Toronto ON M5H 3T9
416/366-8301; Fax: 416/366-0846; Toll Free: 1-800-268-8481
President, Charles T. Wilson
Classes of Insurance: Auto; Personal Accident & Sickness; Property

The Standard Life Assurance Company/Compagnie d'Assurance Standard Life
1245, rue Sherbrooke ouest, Montréal QC H3G 1G3
514/284-6711; Fax: 514/499-4908; Toll Free: 1-888-841-6633
Email: information@standardlife.ca; URL: http://www.standardlife.ca
President, Claude A. Garcia, Canadian Operations
Classes of Insurance: Life

*Stanley Mutual Insurance Company
PO Box 70, Stanley NB E0H 1T0
506/367-2273
James F. Pinnock
Classes of Insurance: Property

State Farm Fire & Casualty Company
#102, 100 Consilium Pl., Scarborough ON M1H 3G9
416/290-4100; Fax: 416/290-4337
URL: http://www.statefarm.com
Chief Agent, Robert J. Cooke
Classes of Insurance: Property

State Farm Life Insurance Company
#102, 100 Consilium Pl., Scarborough ON M1H 3G9
416/290-4100; Fax: 416/290-4438
URL: http://www.statefarm.com
Chief Agent, Robert J. Cooke
Classes of Insurance: Life

State Farm Mutual Automobile Insurance Company
#102, 100 Consilium Pl., Scarborough ON M1H 3G9
416/290-4100; Fax: 416/290-4337
URL: http://www.statefarm.com
Chief Agent, Robert J. Cooke
Classes of Insurance: Auto

Stewart Title Guaranty Company
c/o Encon Insurance Managers Inc., #700, 350 Albert St.., Ottawa ON KIR 1A4
613/786-2000; Fax: 613/786-2001
Chief Agent, Denis J. Shillington
Classes of Insurance: Liability

The Sumitomo Marine & Fire Insurance Co., Ltd./Compagnie d'Assurance Maritime et Incendie Sumitomo, Ltée
One Financial Place, One Adelaide St. East, Toronto ON M5C 2V9
416/863-0550; Fax: 416/863-9488
Chief Agent, Janice M. Tomlinson
Classes of Insurance: Auto; Fire; Property

Sun Life Assurance Company of Canada
150 King St. West, Toronto ON M5H 1J9
416/979-9966; Fax: 416/585-9546
URL: http://www.sunlife.com
President/Chief Operating Officer, Donald A. Stewart
Classes of Insurance: Personal Accident & Sickness; Life

*La Survivance, Compagnie Mutuelle d'Assurance-Vie
1555, rue Girouard ouest, Saint-Hyacinthe QC J2S 2Z6
514/773-6051; Fax: 514/773-6470
Directeur général, Jean Bouchard
Classes of Insurance: Personal Accident & Sickness; Life

Swiss Reinsurance Company Canada
99 Yorkville Ave., 3rd Fl., Toronto ON M5R 3K5
416/972-0272; Fax: 416/972-1644; Toll Free: 1-800-268-7116
President/CEO, M. Albers
Classes of Insurance: Auto; Fire; Property

Swiss Reinsurance Company Canada - Life & Health Branch
#3000, 161 Bay St., Toronto ON M5J 2T6
416/947-3800
Chief Agent, Peter B. Patterson
Classes of Insurance: Personal Accident & Sickness; Life

Swiss Union General Insurance Company Limited/Union Suisse Compagnie Générale d'Assurances
#500, 1000, rue de la Gauchetière ouest, Montréal QC H3B 4W5
514/875-5790; Fax: 514/875-9769
Chief Agent, William J. Green
Classes of Insurance: Auto; Boiler & Machinery; Fidelity; Hail & Crop; Liability; Life; Property; Surety

Terra Nova Insurance Company Limited
#740, 70 York St., Toronto ON M5J 1S9
416/864-0500; Fax: 416/864-1030
Chief Agent, J. Brian Reeve
Classes of Insurance: Auto; Personal Accident & Sickness; Property

TIG Insurance Company
c/o Canadian Insurance Consultants Inc., #600, 133 Richmond St. West, Toronto ON M5H 2L3
416/363-6103; Fax: 416/363-7454
Chief Agent, Donald G. Smith
Classes of Insurance: Auto; Personal Accident & Sickness; Liability; Property

TIG Reinsurance Company
c/o Canadian Insurance Consultants Inc., #600, 133 Richmond St. West, Toronto ON M5H 2L3
416/363-6103; Fax: 416/831-6345
Chief Agent, Donald G. Smith
Classes of Insurance: Property

The Tokio Marine & Fire Insurance Company, Limited
105 Adelaide St. West, Toronto ON M5H 1P9
416/350-4400; Fax: 416/350-4412
Chief Agent in Canada, Byron G. Messier
Classes of Insurance: Auto; Accident; Aircraft; Boiler & Machinery; Credit; Fidelity; Fire; Hail & Crop; Legal Expense; Liability; Property; Surety; Theft

Toronto-Dominion General Insurance Company
Commercial Union Tower, 6th Fl., PO Box 307, Toronto ON M5K 1A2
416/307-1319; Fax: 416/960-0082
Classes of Insurance: Auto; Property

Toronto-Dominion Life Insurance Company
Commercial Union Tower, 6th Fl., Toronto ON M5K 1A2
President/CEO, Dunbar Russel
Classes of Insurance: Personal Accident & Sickness; Life

Toronto Mutual Life Insurance Company
112 St. Clair Ave. West, Toronto ON M4V 2Y3
416/960-3463; Fax: 416/960-0531
President, John T. English
Classes of Insurance: Personal Accident & Sickness; Life

Trade Indemnity plc
#707, 331 Cooper St., Ottawa ON K2P 0G5
613/235-9511; Fax: 613/235-0329; Toll Free: 1-800-267-7697
Chief Agent, Tom Leonard
Classes of Insurance: Credit

Traders General Insurance Company
2206 Eglinton Ave. East, Scarborough ON M1L 4S8
416/288-1800; Fax: 416/288-9756
President/CEO, Lewis Dunn
Classes of Insurance: Auto; Property

Trafalgar Insurance Company of Canada
#200, 425 Bloor St. East, Toronto ON M4W 3R5
416/961-5015; Fax: 416/961-8874; Toll Free: 1-800-387-5601
President/CEO, Robert E. Maynard
Classes of Insurance: Auto; Fire; Personal Accident & Sickness; Property

Transamerica Life Insurance Company of Canada
300 Consilium Pl., Scarborough ON M1H 3G2
416/290-6221; Fax: 416/290-2883
President/CEO, George A. Foegele
Classes of Insurance: Personal Accident & Sickness; Life

Transatlantic Reinsurance Company
145 Wellington St. West, Toronto ON M5J 1H8
416/596-0366; Fax: 416/971-8782
Chief Agent, Gary A. McMillan
Classes of Insurance: Auto; Aircraft; Boiler & Machinery; Fidelity; Hail & Crop; Personal Accident & Sickness; Liability; Property; Surety

The Travelers Indemnity Company
c/o CAS Accounting for Insurance Inc., #4, 1101 Nicholson Rd., Newmarket ON L3Y 7V1
905/853-0858; Fax: 905/853-0183
Chief Agent, Brian Divell
Classes of Insurance: Auto; Fire; Property

The Travelers Insurance Company
Scotia Plaza, #2100, 40 King St. West, Toronto ON M5H 3C2
416/869-5300; Fax: 416/360-8877
Chief Agent, J. Brian Reeve
Classes of Insurance: Personal Accident & Sickness; Life

Trygg-Hansa Reinsurance Company of Canada
#1402, 18 King St. East, Toronto ON M5C 1C4
416/361-0056; Fax: 416/361-0147
President, Robert W. Easton
Classes of Insurance: Auto; Personal Accident & Sickness; Property

Underwriters Insurance Company
c/o Fasken, Campbell, Godfrey, Toronto-Dominion Centre, PO Box 20, Stn Toronto-Dominion, Toronto ON M5K 1N6
416/366-8381; Fax: 416/364-7813
Chief Agent in Canada, Robert W. McDowell
Classes of Insurance: Auto; Property

Unifund Assurance Company
95 Elizabeth Ave., St. John's NF A1B 1R7
709/737-1500; Fax: 709/737-1580
CEO, Paul Johnson
Classes of Insurance: Auto; Personal Accident & Sickness; Property

*Union du Canada Assurance-Vie/Union of Canada Life Insurance
325 Dalhousie St., PO Box 717, Ottawa ON K1P 5P8
613/241-3660; Fax: 613/241-4627

President/CEO, Gérard Desjardins
Classes of Insurance: Personal Accident & Sickness; Life

Union Fidelity Life Insurance Company
PO Box 4081, Stn A, Toronto ON M4W 1M7
416/922-1922; Fax: 416/922-1914
Chief Agent, Dan C. Evans
Classes of Insurance: Personal Accident & Sickness; Life

*L'Union-Vie, Compagnie Mutuelle d'Assurance/The Union Life, Mutual Assurance Company
142, rue Hériot, Drummondville QC J2B 6W9
819/478-1315; Fax: 819/474-1990; Toll Free: 1-800-567-0988
Président/Directeur général, Jacques Desbiens, F.S.A., F.I.C.A.
Classes of Insurance: Personal Accident & Sickness; Life

Unione Italiana di Riassicurazione S.P.A.
#2220, 1501, av McGill College, Montréal QC H3A 3M8
514/985-5260; Fax: 514/985-3066; Toll Free: 1-800-985-GEAM
Email: mail@rga-reinsurance.com
Chief Agent, Life, André St-Amour
Classes of Insurance: Life

*L'Unique, Compagnie d'Assurances Générales
925, ch St-Louis, Québec QC G1S 1C1
418/683-2711; Fax: 418/688-9684; Toll Free: 1-800-463-4800
President, William H. Gleed, C.L.U.
Classes of Insurance: Auto; Fire

United American Insurance Company
145 King St. West, Toronto ON M5H 3X6
416/366-0800; Fax: 416/367-1954
Chief Agent, Connie Vaccaro
Classes of Insurance: Personal Accident & Sickness; Life

*United General Insurance Corporation
190 Prospect St. West, Suite A, Fredericton NB E3B 2T8
506/459-5121; Toll Free: 1-800-563-9363
Wally Jarvis
Classes of Insurance: Property

UNUM CANADA
#1000, 18 King St. East, Toronto ON M5C 2Z5
416/594-3700; Toll Free: 1-800-387-1555
URL: http://www.unum.com
President, Jean-Pierre Charlebois
Classes of Insurance: Personal Accident & Sickness; Life

Utica Mutual Insurance Company
c/o Focus Group Inc., #500, 36 King St. East, Toronto ON M5C 1E5
416/361-1728; Fax: 416/361-6113
Chief Agent, Philip H. Cook
Classes of Insurance: Auto; Boiler & Machinery; Fidelity; Liability; Property

*La Vigilance, Société de Secours Mutuels
27, rue des Neiges, Beauport QC G1E 5T7
418/667-6100
Président, Claude DesRoches

Virginia Surety Company, Inc.
#300, 7300 Warden Ave., Markham ON L3R 0X3
905/305-1922; Fax: 905/305-8600
Chief Agent, Dan C. Evans
Classes of Insurance: Auto; Property

Voyageur Insurance Company
#403, 44 Peel Centre Dr., Brampton ON L6T 4M8
905/791-8700; Fax: 905/791-4600; Toll Free: 1-800-668-4342
CEO, David R. Cooper
Classes of Insurance: Personal Accident & Sickness; Property

*WASA Insurance Company Ltd.
2669 Deacon St., Abbotsford BC V2T 6H3
604/850-9272

Waterloo Insurance Company
111 Westmount Rd. South, PO Box 2000, Waterloo ON N2J 4S4
519/570-8200; Fax: 519/570-8389
President/CEO, Noel G. Walpole, F.I.I.C.
Classes of Insurance: Auto; Accident; Fire; Liability; Property

The Wawanesa Life Insurance Company
191 Broadway, Winnipeg MB R3C 3P1
204/985-3940; Fax: 204/985-3872
President/CEO, G.J. Hanson
Classes of Insurance: Personal Accident & Sickness; Life

The Wawanesa Mutual Insurance Company
191 Broadway, Winnipeg MB R3C 3P1
204/985-3811; Fax: 204/942-7724
President/CEO, G.J. Hanson, C.A., F.I.I.C., F.L.M.I.
Classes of Insurance: Auto; Fire; Life; Property

Westbury Canadian Life Insurance Company
PO Box 2918, Hamilton ON L8N 3R5
905/528-6766; Fax: 905/526-3127; Toll Free: 1-800-263-9241
President/CEO, W. Grant Hardy
Classes of Insurance: Personal Accident & Sickness; Life

*Western Agricultural Insurance Corp.
339 Main St. North, Moose Jaw SK S6H 4N7
306/694-5959

Western Assurance Company
10 Wellington St. East, Toronto ON M5E 1L5
416/366-7511; Fax: 416/367-9869
President, R.J. Gunn
Classes of Insurance: Auto; Fire; Property

Western Surety Company
PO Box 527, Regina SK S4P 2G8
306/777-0600; Fax: 306/359-0929
President/CEO, Leo C. Ell
Classes of Insurance: Surety

*Western Union Insurance Company
333 - 5 Ave. SW, 15th Fl., Calgary AB T2P 4W7
403/269-7961; Fax: 403/265-7754; Toll Free: 1-800-668-8384
President/Chief Operating Officer, Derek Iles
Classes of Insurance: Auto; Property

Winterthur Reinsurance Corporation of America
#830, 1075 Bay St., Toronto ON M5S 2W5
416/928-8542; Fax: 416/928-3041
Chief Agent, Douglas M. Fernandes
Classes of Insurance: Auto; Personal Accident & Sickness; Property

The Yasuda Fire & Marine Insurance Company, Limited
2 First Canadian Pl, 12th Fl., Toronto ON M5X 1A6
416/368-4011; Fax: 416/594-3051
Chief Agent, Cynthia Santiago
Classes of Insurance: Auto; Property

Zurich Indemnity Company of Canada
400 University Ave., Toronto ON M5G 1S7
416/586-3600; Fax: 416/586-2525
President/CEO, Stephen R. Smith
Classes of Insurance: Auto; Personal Accident & Sickness; Property

Zurich Insurance Company
400 University Ave., Toronto ON M5G 1S7
416/586-3000; Fax: 416/586-2858
Chief Agent, Stephen R. Smith
Classes of Insurance: Auto; Personal Accident & Sickness; Property

Zurich Life Insurance Company of Canada
400 University Ave., Toronto ON M5G 1S7
416/586-3000; Fax: 416/586-2525
Sr. Vice-President, Nigel H. Ayers, Corporate Development
Classes of Insurance: Personal Accident & Sickness; Life

# ACCOUNTING FIRMS

Albert L. Stal & Co.
#301, 1370 Don Mills Rd., North York ON M3B 3N7
416/449-0130; Fax: 416/444-7363
Managing Partner, Albert L. Stal, CA, CFP

Altman, Tran, Villemaire, St-Aubin
#525, 1440, rue St-Catherine ouest, Montréal QC H3G 1R8
514/874-0988; Fax: 514/874-0911

Arthur Andersen & Co.
#1900, 79 Wellington St. West, PO Box 29, Stn Toronto-Dominion, Toronto ON M5K 1B9
416/863-1540; Fax: 416/947-7878
URL: http://www.arthurandersen.com
Canadian Director, William Quan, Administration

Avery Cooper & Co.
Laurentian Bldg., 4918 - 50 St., PO Box 1620, Stn Main, Yellowknife NT X1A 2P2
403/873-3441; Fax: 403/873-2353; Toll Free: 1-800-661-0787
Email: avery@averyco.nt.ca; URL: http://www.averyco.nt.ca
Managing Partner, Gerald Avery, FCGA

BDO Dunwoody
Royal Bank Plaza, PO Box 32, Toronto ON M5J 2J8
416/865-0111; Fax: 416/367-3912
Email: info@national.bdo.ca; URL: http://www.bdo.ca
CEO, Peter E. Held

Beallor & Partners
28 Overlea Blvd., Toronto ON M4H 1B6
416/423-0707; Fax: 416/423-7000
Email: beallor@beallor.com; URL: http://www.beallor.com

Bennett Gold
#302, 1 Concorde Gate, Toronto ON M3C 3N6
416/449-2249; Fax: 416/449-4133
Email: rygold@bennettgold.ca; URL: http://www.bennettgold.ca

Bing C. Wong & Associates Ltd.
124 East Pender St., 3rd Fl., Vancouver BC V6A 1T3
604/682-7561; Fax: 604/682-7665
President, Bing C. Wong

Campbell Saunders Ltd.
1200 - 650 W Georgia, Vancouver BC V6A 2A1
604/681-5500; Fax: 604/685-7100
Email: campbell saunders@bc.sympatico.ca
President, Harold Saunders

Chapman & Riendeau, Chartered Accountants
#201, 32 Tupper St. North, Portage La Prairie MB R1N 1W8
204/857-6861; Fax: 204/239-6226

Clarke Starke & Diegel
871 Victoria St. North, Kitchener ON N2B 3S4
519/579-5520; Fax: 519/570-3611

Clarkson Rouble & Partners
5190 Shuttle Dr., Mississauga ON L4W 4J8
905/629-4047; Fax: 905/629-3070

Collins Barrow Chartered Accountants
#1400, 777 - 8 Ave. SW, Calgary AB T2P 3R5
403/298-1500; Fax: 403/298-5814
Email: calgary@collinsbarrow.com; URL: http://www.collinsbarrow.com
Managing Partner, Laurie Glans, CA

Coopers & Lybrand
145 King St. West, Toronto ON M5H 1V8
416/869-1130; Fax: 416/863-0926
URL: http://www.ca.coopers.com

C.R. Barclay, C.A.
245 Yorkland Blvd., 3rd Fl., North York ON M2J 4W9
416/497-8946; Fax: 416/497-9925
Sole Practitioner, Colin Barclay, RFP, CFP

Crosson Voyer Chartered Accountants
#300, 1122 Mainland St., Vancouver BC V6B 5L1

604/684-3371; Fax: 604/684-9832
URL: http://www.crossonvoyer.bc.ca/

Cyna & Co.
#339, 200 Finch Ave. West, North York ON M2R 3W4
416/225-9991

Dan McNeill & Co.
#303, 1268 - 5th Ave., Prince George BC V2L 3L2
250/563-7812; Fax: 250/563-4115
Email: dan_mcneill@bc.sympatico.ca
President, Dan McNeill, CGA

Deloitte & Touche
800 Sun Life Tower, 150 King St. West, Toronto ON M5H 1J9
416/599-5399; Fax: 416/599-5462
URL: http://www.deloitte.ca
Managing Partner/CEO, Colin Taylor

Doane Raymond
Royal Bank Plaza, North Tower, 200 Bay St., 10th Fl., PO Box 55, Toronto ON M5J 2P9
416/366-0100; Fax: 416/360-4944
Email: doaneraymond@drgt.ca; URL: http://www.drgt.ca
Exec. Partner/CEO, David A. Hope

Donald Bain Macaskill R.F.P.
#107, 2545 Bloor St. West, Toronto ON M6S 1S1
416/763-2437; Fax: 416/763-2437
Owner, Donald Bain Macaskill, R.F.P.

Elliott, Tulk, Pryce, Anderson
#1101, 750 West Pender St., Vancouver BC V6C 2T8
604/684-5357; Fax: 604/684-0187
Email: etpa@cycor.ca; URL: http://www.etpa.bc.ca

Ernst & Young
Ernst & Young Tower, Toronto-Dominion Centre, 222 Bay St., Toronto ON M5K 1J7
416/864-1234; Fax: 416/864-1174
URL: http://www.eycan.com
Chair/CEO, Ronald G. Gage

Evancic Perrault Robertson
National Administration Office, PO Box 187, Maple Ridge BC V2X 7G1
604/467-4165; Fax: 604/467-1219
Email: eprmr@istar.ca; URL: http://www.epr.ca
Administrator, Verle Spindor

Fine & Associés/Fine & Associates
5101, rue Buchan, Montréal QC H4P 1S4
514/731-0761; Fax: 514/731-4639

Flood & Company
#910, 800 - 6 Ave. SW, Calgary AB T2P 3G3
403/263-1523; Fax: 403/263-1524
Email: flood_co@telusplanet.net

Gagnon, Roy, Brunet & Associés
#105, 3925, rue Rachel est, Montréal QC H1X 3G8
514/255-1001; Fax: 514/255-1002
Director, Pierre St-Louis

Galano, Enzo & Associates
#508, 20 Jackson St. West, Hamilton ON L8P 1L2
905/528-0144; Fax: 905/528-0144
Proprietor, Enzo Galano

Gardner, Zuk Dessen
258 Wilson Ave., North York ON M3H 1S6
416/631-9800
Leonard Zuk

Gaviller & Company
PO Box 460, Owen Sound ON N4K 5P7
519/376-5850

Horwath Orenstein Chartered Accountants
#300, 595 Bay St., Toronto ON M5G 2C2
416/596-1711; Fax: 416/596-7894
Email: info@hto.com; URL: http://www.hto.com/

Huxham & Co.
#201, 990 Cedar St., Campbell River BC V9W 7Z8
250/287-2131; Fax: 250/287-2134
Email: huxhamcr@cr.island.net; URL: http://www.vquest.com/huxham/

Jacques, Davis, Lefaivre & Associés s.e.n.c.
1080, Côte du Beaver Hall, 19e étage, Montréal QC H2Z 1S8
514/878-2600; Fax: 514/866-6860; 1-800-363-6800
Email: jdlass@login.net

Kahale Wong Leung & Wood
50 Richmond St. East, 4th Fl., Toronto ON M5C 1N7
416/862-8181; Fax: 416/862-8313
Email: hleung@ipo.com

Kentner, Kelly & Wilson
15 Barrie Blvd., St. Thomas ON N5P 4B9
519/631-6360; Fax: 519/631-2198

Kenway Mack Slusarchuk Stewart
#220, 333 - 11 Ave. SW, Calgary AB T2R 1L9
403/233-7750; Fax: 403/266-5267
Email: info@kmss.ca

Kestenberg, Rabinowicz & Partners
2797 John St., Markham ON L3R 2Y8
905/946-1300; Fax: 905/946-9797
Sr. Partner, Harvey Kestenberg, CFP, CA

King & Company
1201 Energy Square, 10109 - 106 St., Edmonton AB T5J 3L7
403/423-2437; Fax: 403/426-5861
Edward King

Kingston Ross Pasnak
#2760, 10180 - 101 St. NW, Edmonton AB T5J 3S7
403/425-0636; Fax: 403/429-4817
Email: krp@planet.eon.net; URL: http://www.kingston-ross-pasnak.com/

Koster, Spinks & Koster
4 Glengrove Ave. West, Toronto ON M4R 1N4
416/489-8100; Fax: 416/489-9194

KPMG
Box 122, Scotia Plaza, #5400, 40 King St. West, PO Box 122, Toronto ON M5H 3Z2
416/777-8500; Fax: 416/777-8818
Email: webmaster@kpmg.ca; URL: http://www.kpmg.ca
Chair/CEO, J. Spencer Lanthier

Laberge Lafleur
#2960, 2600, boul Laurier, Ste-Foy QC G1V 4M6
418/659-7265; Fax: 418/659-5937

Lazer Grant & Company
167 Lombard Ave, Stn 710, Winnipeg MB R3B 0V3
204/942-0300; Fax: 204/957-5611
Email: lgcadmin@lazergrant.ca; URL: http://www.lazergrant.ca

Lindquist Avey Macdonald Baskerville Inc.
One Adelaide St. East, 30th Fl., Toronto ON M5C 2V9
416/777-2440; Fax: 416/777-2441
Email: sdann@lindavey.com

MacIsaac Younker Roche Soloman
16 Garfield St., Charlottetown PE C1A 6A5
902/566-5633
Email: macisac.younker@pei.sympatico.ca

MacKay & Partners
Highfield Place, #705, 10010 - 106th St., Edmonton AB T5J 3L8
403/420-0626; Fax: 403/425-8780

McDonald & Company
#301, 2955 Gladwin Rd., Abbotsford BC V2T 5T4
604/853-2264; Fax: 604/853-3189
Donald L. McDonald, R.F.P.

McIntyre & McLarty, Chartered Accountants
#310, 666 Kirkwood Ave., Ottawa ON K1Z 5X9
613/729-1110; Fax: 613/729-4477
Email: bhiscoe@mcintyremclarty.com

Meyers Norris Penny & Co.
160 - 14th St., Brandon MB R7A 7K1
204/727-0661; Fax: 204/726-1543
URL: http://www.mnp.ca
Managing Partner, D.H. Penny, FCA

Millard Rouse & Rosebrugh
96 Nelson St., Brantford ON N3T 2N1
519/759-3511; Fax: 519/759-7961
Email: millards@bis.on.ca

Mintz & Partners
#100, 1446 Don Mills Rd., North York ON M3B 3N6
416/391-2900; Fax: 416/391-2748
Email: info@mintzca.com; URL: http://www.mintzca.com
Managing Partner, Harley Mintz

Moore Stephens Hyde Houghton Chartered Accountants
295 The West Mall, Toronto ON M9C 4Z4
416/622-6251; Fax: 416/622-9672
Email: info@tor.mshh.com; URL: http://www.interlog.com/~hyde/

Moquin Ménard Giroux & Associés
#500, 101, boul Roland Therrien, Longueuil QC J4H 4B9
514/670-9615; Fax: 514/866-1887

Mount Real Corporation
2500, rue Allard, Montréal QC H4E 2L4
514/762-2500; Fax: 514/762-6535
URL: http://www.mountreal.com
President/CEO, Lino P. Matteo

Norman Thackeray, Chartered Accountant
4922 - 52nd St., Red Deer AB T4N 2C8
403/342-2950; Fax: 403/341-5440
Proprietor, Norman L. Thackeray, B.Ed., CFP, CA

Nova Financial Services Limited
PO Box 426, Welland ON L3B 5R2
905/732-1640; Fax: 905/732-1397

Oehler & Associates Financial Management Limited
#300, 2631 - 28th Ave., Regina SK S4S 6X3
306/775-5200; Fax: 306/775-5215
Email: boehler@cableregina.com
President, Terry L. Oehler, RFP

Perreault Wolman Grzywacz & Cie
#814, 5250, rue Ferrier, Montréal QC H4P 2N7
514/731-7987; Fax: 514/731-8782

Peter Norton
#201, 1929 West Broadway, Vancouver BC V6J 1Z3
604/736-8358; Fax: 604/736-8359
Email: Peter_Norton@mindlink.bc.ca
Principal, Peter Norton, CFP, RFP

Powell Jones
121 Anne St. South, Barrie ON L4N 7B6
705/728-7461; Fax: 705/728-8317

Prapavessis Jasek
#203, 1001 Champlain Ave., Burlington ON L7L 5Z4
905/336-5338; Fax: 905/336-3449

Ptack Schnarch Basevitz
#400, 3333, boul Graham, Montréal QC H3R 3L5
514/341-5511; Fax: 514/342-0589
Email: info@psb.qc.ca
Managing Partner, Morton Ptack, FCA

Raymond C.S. Liu Professional Corp.
First Edmonton Place, #410, 10665 Jasper Ave., Edmonton AB T5J 3S9
403/429-1047; Fax: 403/424-9035
Sr. Partner, Raymond Liu, RFP

Richter Usher & Vineberg
#700, 90 Eglinton Ave. East, Toronto ON M4P 2Y3
416/932-8000; Fax: 416/932-6200
Email: info@richter.net; URL: http://www.richter.ca

Robinson, Lott & Brohman
15 Lewis Rd., PO Box 744, Stn Main, Guelph ON N1H 1E9
519/822-9933; Fax: 519/822-9212
URL: http://www.rlb.ca

Romanovsky & Associates
9913 - 112 St. NW, Edmonton AB T5K 1L6
403/447-5830; Fax: 403/451-6291
Email: nbronsch@oanet.com
Selwyn Romanovsky, CA

Rooney Greig Whitrod Filion & Associés
#250, 315, boul Brunswick, Pointe-Claire QC H9R 5M7
514/694-5775; Fax: 514/694-8405

Roth Mosey & Partners
1574 Lincoln Rd., Windsor ON N8Y 2J4

519/977-6410; Fax: 519/977-7083
Email: rmp@roth-mosey.com

Savage & Moles Chartered Accountants
#S300, 197 County Court Blvd., Brampton ON L6W 4P6
905/451-4034

Scarrow & Donald
#100, 5 Donald St., Winnipeg MB R3L 2T4
204/982-9800; Fax: 204/474-2886

Schlesinger Newman Goldman
#1600, 625, boul René-Lévesque ouest, Montréal QC H3B 1R2
514/866-8553; Fax: 514/866-8469
Email: sng@cam.org

Schurman Sudsbury & Associates Ltd.
189 Water St., Summerside PE C1N 1B2
902/436-2171; Fax: 902/436-0960

Schwartz Levitsky Feldman
1980, rue Sherbrooke ouest, Montréal QC H3H 1E8
514/937-6392; Fax: 514/933-9710
Email: harry.feldman@slf.ca; URL: http://www.slf.ca
Managing Partner, Sydney M. Levitsky, CA

Schwartz Levitsky Feldman (Toronto)
1167 Caledonia Rd., Toronto ON M6A 2X1
416/785-5353; Fax: 416/785-5663
Email: saul.muskat@slf.ca

Sharma, V.B., CA
#200, 3390 Midland Ave., Scarborough ON M1V 5K3
416/292-4431; Fax: 416/292-7247
Owner, V.B. Sharma, CA, CPA

Shurtleff Savage McIlquham
27 Place D'Armes, PO Box 1450, Kingston ON K7L 5C7
613/549-7781; Fax: 613/549-7553

Soberman Isenbaum & Colomby
#1100, 2 St. Clair Ave. East, Toronto ON M4T 2T5
416/964-7633; Fax: 416/964-6454
Managing Partner, John Colomby

Soden & Co.
25 Campbell St., Belleville ON K8N 1S6
613/968-3495; Fax: 613/968-7359
Email: soden@blvl.igs.net

Sone & Rovet
#512, 1200 Sheppard Ave. East, Toronto ON M2K 2S5
416/498-7200; Fax: 416/498-6877
Email: s-r@oak.net; URL: http://www.oak.net/sone

Stanley Kwan & Company
#910, 4950 Yonge St., North York ON M2N 6K1
416/226-6668; Fax: 416/226-6862

Stevenson & Lehocki
310 Plains Rd. East, Burlington ON L7T 4J2
905/632-0640; Fax: 905/632-0645

Todd Associates
85 Davisbrook Blvd., Toronto ON M1T 2J3
416/493-1104; Fax: 416/494-5092
Email: jimtodd@netcom.ca
Owner, James H. Todd, CFP, RFP

Transport Financial Services Ltd.
105 Bauer Pl., Waterloo ON N2L 6B5
519/886-8070; Fax: 519/886-5214
Email: tfs@tfsgroup.com; URL: http://www.tfsgroup.com
President, Richard G. Bennett

Truster Zweig
#210, 111 Granton Dr., Richmond Hill ON L4B 1L5
416/222-5555; Fax: 416/707-1322
Email: tzcas@netcom.ca

Walters Hoffe
PO Box 348, Gander NF A1V 1W7
709/651-4100; Fax: 709/256-2957

Watson Aberant & Arnold
4212 - 98th St., Edmonton AB T6E 6A1
403/438-5969; Fax: 403/437-3918

Weiler & Company
512 Woolwich St., Guelph ON N1H 3X7
519/837-3111; Fax: 519/837-1049
Email: dweiler@weiler.ca
Dennis Weiler

Wilson Administrative Services Ltd.
6451 Telford Ave., Burnaby BC V5H 2Y8
604/437-5716

Young, Parkyn, McNab & Co.
#100, 530 - 8 St. South, Lethbridge AB T1J 2J8
403/382-6800; Fax: 403/327-8990
Email: wrj@ypm.ab.ca; URL: http://www.ypm.ab.ca

Zeifman & Company
201 Bridgeland Ave., Toronto ON M6A 1Y7
416/256-4000; Fax: 416/256-4001
Email: zeifman@zeifman.ca; URL: http://www.zeifman.ca

# BOARDS OF TRADE & CHAMBERS OF COMMERCE IN CANADA

## INTERNATIONAL CHAMBERS & BUSINESS COUNCILS

ASEAN-Canada Business Council, c/o Canadian Chamber of Commerce, #501, 350 Sparks St., Ottawa ON K1R 7S8 – 613/238-4000; Fax: 613/238-7643; Email: info@chamber.ca; URL: http://www.chamber.ca

Brazil-Canada Chamber of Commerce, Carleton Tower, #720, 2 Carleton St., Toronto ON M5B 1J3 – 416/596-0992; Fax: 416/596-1257 – General Manager, Beth L. Wolff

British Canadian Chamber of Trade & Commerce, #305, 7100 Woodbine Ave., Markham ON L3R 5J2 – 905/475-3896; Fax: 905/475-0311; Email: bcctc@sympatico.ca – Executive Director, John Archer

Canada-Arab Business Council, #501, 350 Sparks St., Ottawa ON K1R 7S8 – 613/238-4000; Fax: 613/238-7643 – Chairman, J. Lambert Toupin, QC

Canada China Business Council, #802, 110 Yonge St., Toronto ON M5C 1T4 – 416/954-3800; Fax: 416/954-3806; Email: ccbc@istar.ca; URL: http://www.ccbc.com – Executive Director, David Mulroney

Canada China Business Council--Beijing Office, CITIC Bldg., #18-2, 19 Jianguomenwai St., Beijing 100 04 – (86 10) 6512-6120, ext.1820, 1821, 1822; Fax: (86 10) 6512-6125; Email: ccbc@chinaonline.com.cn.net

Canada China Business Council--Shanghai Office, Flat 1801A, Bldg. C, New Century Plaza, 48 Xing Yi Rd., Shanghai 200 35 – (86 21) 6270-2948; Fax: 6219-3118; Email: ccbcsh@chinaonline.com.cn.net

Canada China Business Council--Western Canada Office, SFU at Harbour Centre, #2600, 515 West Hastings St., Vancouver BC V6B 5K3 – 604/291-5190; Fax: 604/291-5039; Email: Alison_Winters@sfu.ca

Canada Czech Republic Chamber of Commerce, Exchange Tower, 14th Fl., 2 First Canadian Place, PO Box 198, Toronto ON M5X 1A6 – 416/367-3432; Fax: 416/367-3492 – Managing Director, Lubomir J. Novotny

Canada-Finland Chamber of Commerce, #604, 1200 Bay St., Toronto ON M5R 2A5 – 416/964-7400; Fax: 416/964-1524 – President, John Hylton

Canada-India Business Council, Heritage Bldg., 181 Bay St., PO Box 818, Ottawa ON M5J 2T3 – 416/868-6415; Fax: 416/868-0189; Email: admin.c-ibc@sympatico.ca; URL: http://www.canada-indiabusiness.ca – Executive Director, Murray Jans

Canada-Indonesia Business Council, 260 Adelaide St. East, PO Box 110, Toronto ON M5A 1N1 – 416/366-8490; Fax: 416/947-1534 – Contact, Peter Dawes

Canada-Israel Chamber of Commerce, #1100, 48 St. Clair Ave. West, Toronto ON M4V 2Z2 – 416/961-7302 – President, David Goldstein

Canada-Japan Trade Council, #903, 75 Albert St., Ottawa ON K1P 5E7 – 613/233-4047; Fax: 613/233-2256; Email: cjtc@magi.com – President, Klaus Pringsheim

Canada-Netherlands Chamber of Commerce, #1100, 34 King St. East, Toronto ON M5C 2X8 – 416/368-0350; Fax: 416/368-7231; Email: 103123.2740@compuserve.com – Manager/International Trade Advisor, Nico Fernhout

Canada-Netherlands Chamber of Commerce--Atlantic Canada Chapter, #2100, 1801 Hollis St., Halifax NS B3J 2X6 – 902/429-4111; Fax: 902/429-8215 – Darlene Jameson

Canada-Netherlands Chamber of Commerce--Québec Chapter, #304, 300, rue St-Sacrement, Montréal QC H2Y 1X4 – 514/847-2223; Fax: 514/288-9183 – Secretary, Virginie Sondermeyer

Canada-Netherlands Chamber of Commerce--Western Canada Chapter, #1007, 470 Granville St., Vancouver BC V6C 1V5 – 604/688-5017; Fax: 604/684-7194 – Contact, Herman Suttorp

Canada-Pakistan Business Council, 4329, av King Edward, Montréal QC H4B 2H4 – 514/488-3979; Fax: 514/488-3979; Email: 75323.2252@compuserve.com – President, Werner R. Strub

Canada-Russia Business Council, #812, 330 Bay St., Toronto ON M5H 2S8 – 416/862-2821; Fax: 416/862-2820 – Executive Director, Susan Santiago

Canada-Sri Lanka Business Council, 30A Hazelton Ave., Toronto ON M5R 2E2 – 416/846-1214; Fax: 416/849-4823

Canada-United Kingdom Chamber of Commerce, 3 Regent St., London SW1 4N – (0171) 930-7711; Fax: (0171) 930-9703 – Executive Director, Geoffrey F. Bacon

Canadian Armenian Business Council Inc., #200, 12291, boul Laurentian, Montréal QC H4K 1N5 – 514/333-7655; Fax: 514/333-7280 – President, Harry Markarian

Canadian Council for the Americas, #300, 360 Bay St., Toronto ON M5H 2V6 – 416/367-4313; Fax: 416/367-5460; Email: cca@ibm.net – President, Halina Ostrovki

Canadian German Chamber of Industry & Commerce Inc., #1410, 480 University Ave., Toronto ON M5G 1V2 – 416/598-3355; Fax: 416/598-1840; Email: germanchambertoronto@netaxis.ca – President & CEO, Uwe Harnack

Canadian German Chamber of Industry & Commerce Inc.--Montréal, #1604, 1010, rue Sherbrooke ouest, Montréal QC H3A 2R7 – 514/844-3051; Fax: 514/844-1473

Canadian German Chamber of Industry & Commerce Inc.--Vancouver, #617, 1030 West Georgia St., Vancouver BC V6E 2Y3 – 604/681-4469; Fax: 604/681-4489

Canadian/Romanian Council of Trade & Commerce, #203, 2525 St. Laurent Blvd., Ottawa ON K1H 8P5 – 613/737-2922; Fax: 613/733-9501 – Chair, Robert De Valk

Chamber of Commerce for Belgium & Luxembourg in Canada, Tour de la Bourse, PO Box 528, Montréal QC H4Z 1J8 – 514/845-4650 – President, Albert Van Herck

Chamber of Commerce of Spain in Canada, #832, 150 Bloor St. West, Toronto ON M5S 2X9 – 416/927-8787; Fax: 416/927-7888 – President, Ronald H. Rumble

Chambre de Commerce Canada-Maroc, 390, rue Notre-Dame ouest, 5e étage, Montréal QC H2Y 1T9

Chambre de Commerce Canado-Tunisienne, #312, 5255, boul Henri-Bourassa ouest, St-Laurent QC H4R 1K4 – Adel Berrais

Chambre de Commerce française du Canada, 360, rue Saint-Francois-Xavier, Montréal QC H2Y 2S8 – 514/281-1246; Fax: 514/289-9594; Email: ccfc.mtl@sympatico.ca – Président, Pierre Lapointe

Chambre de commerce française du Canada--Ontario, #406, 347 Bay St., Toronto ON M5H 2R7 – 416/777-9658; Fax: 416/777-9659 – Président, Michel Finance

Chambre de Commerce Lao du Canada, #2, 6420, rue Victoria, Montréal QC H3W 2S7

Chambre de Commerce sud-africaine à Montréal, 770, rue Sherbrooke ouest, 13e étage, Montréal QC H3A 1G1 – Directeur, Charles Bédard

Conseil d'affaires tchèque du Québec, 8480, boul St-Laurent, Montréal QC H2P 2M6 – Directrice exécutive, Dora Romano

Danish Canadian Chamber of Commerce, #403, 15 Wertheim Court, Richmond Hill ON L4B 3H7 – 905/882-9901; Fax: 905/882-5472 – Vice-Chairman, Secretary, Knud Westergaard

The Estonian-Canadian Chamber of Commerce, 958 Broadview Ave., Toronto ON M4K 2R6 – 416/606-3825; Fax: 416/461-0448; Email: estcancofc@neocom.ca

International Chamber of Commerce, 38, Cours Albert 1er, Paris F-7 008 – (33 1) 49 53 28 28; Fax: (33 1) 42 25 86 63; Telex: 650770F; Email: icclib@ibnet.com – Contact, J.C. Rouher

Ireland-Canada Chamber of Commerce, #1600, 2020, rue University, Montréal QC H3A 2A5 – 514/288-5705; Fax: 514/288-6629 – President, Helen Carrigy-McCaffrey

Italian Chamber of Commerce in Canada, #680, 550, rue Sherbrooke ouest, Montréal QC H3A 1B9 – 514/844-4249; Fax: 514/844-4875; Toll Free: 1-800-263-4372; Email: camit@magnet.ca; URL: http://www.italchamber.qc.ca – Executive Director, Marianna Simeone

Italian Chamber of Commerce of Toronto, #306, 901 Lawrence Ave. West, Toronto ON M6A 1C3 – 416/789-7169; Fax: 416/789-7160 – Managing Director, C. Valeri

Scandinavian Canadian Chamber of Commerce, #822, 602 West Hastings St., Vancouver BC V6B 1P2 – 604/669-4428; Fax: 604/669-4420 – Executive Director, Peter Nielsen

Slovak Canadian Chamber of Commerce, 34 Leading Rd., Toronto ON M9V 3S9 – 416/749-8447; Fax: 416/740-1453; URL: http://www.neocom.ca/~weinwurm/sccc.htm

The Swedish-Canadian Chamber of Commerce, #1504, 2 Bloor St. West, Toronto ON M4W 3E2 – 416/925-8661; Fax: 416/929-8639 – General Manager, Jeanette Kristensson

Swiss Canadian Chamber of Commerce (Montréal) Inc., 1572, av Dr. Penfield, Montréal QC H3G 1C4 – 514/937-5822

Swiss Canadian Chamber of Commerce (Ontario) Inc., 6795 Steeles Ave. West, Etobicoke ON M9V 4R9 – 416/741-2256; Fax: 416/741-0140 – Executive Officer, A. Mettler

## CHAMBERS OF MINES

Alberta Chamber of Resources, Oxford Tower, #1410, 10235 - 101 St., Edmonton AB T5J 3G1 – 403/420-1030,1031; Fax: 403/425-4623 – Managing Director, Donald Currie

British Columbia & Yukon Chamber of Mines, 840 Hastings St. West, Vancouver BC V6C 1C8 – 604/681-5328; Fax: 604/681-2363; Email: chamber@bc-mining-house.com; URL: http://www.bc-mining-house.com/chamber – Managing Director, Jack Patterson

Chamber of Mineral Resources of Nova Scotia, #1720, 1801 Hollis St., Halifax NS B3J 3N4 – 902/422-5806; Fax: 902/422-9563 – Managing Director, Dick Smyth

Chamber of Mines of Eastern British Columbia, 215 Hall St., Nelson BC V1L 5X4 – 250/352-5242; Fax: 250/352-7227 – President, Bruce Doyle

Northwest Territories Chamber of Mines, PO Box 2818, Yellowknife NT X1A 2R1 – 867/873-5281; Fax: 867/920-2145 – General Manager, Tom W. Hoefer, M.Sc., P.Geol.

Yukon Chamber of Mines, PO Box 4427, Whitehorse YT Y1A 3T5 – 867/667-2090; Fax: 867/668-7127 – Managing Director, Dave Austin

## CANADIAN BOARDS OF TRADE & CHAMBERS OF COMMERCE

The Canadian Chamber of Commerce, #501, 350 Sparks St., Ottawa ON K1R 7S8 – 613/238-4000; Fax: 613/238-7643; Email: info@chamber.ca; URL: http://www.chamber.ca – National President, Timothy Reid

The Canadian Chamber of Commerce--Québec Regional Office, #1430, 1080, Côte du Beaver Hall, Montréal QC H2Z 1T2 – 514/866-4334; Fax: 514/866-7296

The Canadian Chamber of Commerce--Toronto Office, Heritage Bldg., BCE Place, Box 818, 181 Bay St., PO Box 818, Toronto ON M5J 2T3 – 416/868-6415; Fax: 416/868-0189

Canadian Junior Chamber, #303, 3100 Steeles Ave. East, Markham ON L3R 8T3 – 905/948-0048; Fax: 905/948-0047; URL: http://web.idirect.com/~canadajc/ – President, Darren Flagg

Chamber of Maritime Commerce, #704A, 350 Sparks St., Ottawa ON K1R 7S8 – 613/233-8779; Fax: 613/232-6211; Email: grickma@ibm.net; URL: http://www.oceanwide.com/cmc/ – President, J.D. Smith

Jeune chambre de commerce de Montréal, #509, 625, av du Président-Kennedy, Montréal QC H3A 1K2 – 514/845-4951; Fax: 514/845-0587 – Directrice générale, Annemarie Dubost

## PROVINCIAL & TERRITORIAL BOARDS OF TRADE & CHAMBERS OF COMMERCE

Alberta Chamber of Commerce, Edmonton Centre, #2105, TD Tower, Edmonton AB T5J 2Z1 – 403/425-4180; Fax: 403/429-1061; Toll Free: 1-800-272-8854 – Executive Director, Norman S. Leach, CAE

Atlantic Provinces Chamber of Commerce, #110, 236 George St., Moncton NB E1C 1W1 – 506/857-3980; Fax: 506/859-6131; Email: apcc@atcon.com; URL: http://www.apcc.ca/chamber – Chairman, Brendan Fahey

British Columbia Chamber of Commerce, #1607, 700 West Pender St., Vancouver BC V6C 1G8 – 604/683-0700; Fax: 604/683-0416; URL: http://www.bcchamber.org – President, John Winter

Chambre de Commerce du Québec, #3030, 500, place d'Armes, Montréal QC H2Y 2W2 – 514/844-9571; Fax: 514/844-0226; URL: http://www.ccq.ca – Président, Michel Audet

Manitoba Chamber of Commerce, #167, 167 Lombard Ave. East, Winnipeg MB R3B 0V6 – 204/942-2561; Fax: 204/942-2227 – Executive Vice-President, Lance A. Norman

Northwest Territories Chamber of Commerce, PO Box 2544, Yellowknife NT X1A 2P8 – 403/920-9505; Fax: 403/873-4174; Email: nwtcofc@ssimicro.com; URL: http://www.ssimicro.com/~nwtcofc – President, David Connelly

Northwestern Ontario Associated Chambers of Commerce, 857 North May St., Thunder Bay ON P7C 3S2 – 807/622-5858; Fax: 807/622-7752; Email: chamber@tb-chamber.on.ca; URL: http://www.tb-chamber.on.ca – President, Dave Barker

Ontario Chamber of Commerce, #808, 2345 Yonge St., Toronto ON M4P 2E5 – 416/482-5222; Fax: 416/482-5879; Email: info@occ.on.ca; URL: http://www.occ.on.ca – Executive Director, Douglas Robson

Saskatchewan Chamber of Commerce, Chateau Tower, #1630, 1920 Broad St., Regina SK S4P 3V2 – 306/352-2671; Fax: 306/781-7084; Email: skchamber@dlcwest.com – Executive Director, Mary Ann McFadyen

Yukon Chamber of Commerce, #201, 208 Main St., Whitehorse YT Y1A 2A9 – 867/667-2000; Fax: 867/667-4507; Toll Free: 1-800-661-0500; Email: ycc@yknet.yk.ca; URL: http://www.yukonweb.com/business/ycc/ – President, John Carroll

## BY PROVINCE & TERRITORY

### ALBERTA

Airdrie CC, PO Box 3661, AB T4B 2B8 – 403/948-4412; Fax: 403/948-3141 – Executive Director, Jan Peterson

Alberta Beach & District CC, PO Box 280, AB T0E 0A0 – 403/924-3421; Fax: 403/924-3421 – President, Brian Eyres

Alix CC, PO Box 145, AB T0C 0B0 – 403/747-2405; Fax: 403/747-2403 – President, Clarence Verveda

Andrew & District CC, PO Box 454, AB T0B 0C0

Athabasca & District CC, c/o Town Office, 4705A - 49 St., AB T9S 1B7 – 403/675-3999; Fax: 403/675-3038 – President, Kelly Olson

Banff CC, Banff Centre, PO Box 1020, AB T0L 0C0 – 403/762-6155; Fax: 403/762-6116 – Gery Frey

Barrhead & District CC, PO Box 4524, AB T7N 1A4 – 403/674-2338; Fax: 403/674-5648 – Executive Director, Sonny Rajoo

Bassano & District CC, PO Box 849, AB T0J 0B0 – 403/641-3512; Fax: 403/641-3981 – President, George Longmuir

Beaumont & District CC, 4901 - 55 Ave., PO Box 6, AB T4X 1M9 – 403/929-8000; Fax: 403/929-2547 – President, Greg Bowen

Beaverlodge & District CC, PO Box 303, AB T0H 0C0 – 403/354-8785; Fax: 403/354-2101 – President, Michael Walker

Beiseker CC, PO Box 277, AB T0M 0G0 – 403/947-2356 – President, Derilynn Woldan

The Bentley & District CC, PO Box 777, AB T0C 0J0 – 403/748-3500; Fax: 403/748-3120 – President, Pat Jorgensen

Bently CC, PO Box 777, AB T0C 0J0 – 403/748-3120; Fax: 403/748-3390 – Treasurer, Barb Carson, 403/748-3000

Berwyn & District CC, PO Box 144, AB T0H 0E0 – Fax: 403/338-2100 – President, Gail Sandboe

Blackfalds CC, PO Box 249, AB T0M 0J0 – 403/885-2976; Fax: 403/885-2655 – President, Richard Hursh

Bluffton & District CC, PO Box 38, AB T0C 0M0 – 403/843-6302; Fax: 403/843-3392 – President, Helen Karlstrom

Bon Accord & District CC, PO Box 688, AB T0A 0K0 – 403/921-3468; Fax: 403/921-3919 – President, Lou Mandruskiak

Bonnyville & District CC, PO Box 6054, AB T9N 2G7 – 403/826-3252; Fax: 403/826-4525 – President, Trent Law

Bow Island/Burdett & District CC, PO Box 569, AB T0K 0G0 – 403/545-2939; Fax: 403/545-2574 – President, Terry Butterwick

Bowden & District CC, PO Box 629, AB T0M 0K0 – 403/224-3332; Fax: 403/224-2432 – President, Ralph Beggs

Boyle & District CC, PO Box 496, AB T0A 0M0 – 403/689-4180; Fax: 403/689-3998 – President, Barry Sawka

Bragg Creek CC, PO Box 216, AB T0L 0K0 – 403/949-2599; Fax: 403/949-3254 – President, Gerry Miller

Breton & District CC, PO Box 243, AB T0C 0P0 – 403/696-2427; Fax: 403/696-3797 – President, Coreena Van de Cappelle

* BT - Board of Trade; BC - Bureau de commerce; CC - Chamber of Commerce/Chambre de commerce

Brooks & District CC, PO Box 400, AB T1R 1B4 – 403/362-7641; Fax: 403/362-6893 – President, Pete Falkenberg, 403/362-3300

Bruderheim & District CC, PO Box 512, AB T0B 0S0 – 403/796-2163; Fax: 403/796-3560 – President, Pat Sarazin

Calgary CC, 517 Centre St. South, AB T2G 2C4 – 403/750-0400; Fax: 403/266-3413 – President, Murray Mikulak

Calmar & District CC, PO Box 392, AB T0C 0V0 – 403/985-3112; Fax: 403/985-3039 – President, Nancy Nakark

Camrose CC, 5402 - 48 Ave., AB T4V 0J7 – 403/672-4217; Fax: 403/672-1059 – Executive Director, Pat Twomey

Canmore/Kananskis CC, 801 - 8th St., PO Box 1178, AB T0L 0M0 – 403/678-4094; Fax: 403/678-3455 – President, Carmen Colborne

Cardston & District CC, PO Box 1212, AB T0K 0K0 – 403/653-2798 – President, Ron Johnson

Caroline & District CC, PO Box 90, AB T0M 0M0 – 403/722-4066; Fax: 403/722-4002; Email: dhovind@mail.incentre.net – President, Leonard Hemphill

Carstairs CC, PO Box 1030, AB T0M 0N0 – 403/337-1403; Fax: 403/337-2999 – Mark Ketter

Cereal & District BT, PO Box 131, AB T0J 0N0 – 403/326-3817; Fax: 403/326-3817 – President, Mary Waterhouse

Coaldale CC, PO Box 1117, AB T1M 1M9 – 403/345-2358; Fax: 403/345-5888 – President, Kim Craig

Cochrane & District CC, PO Box 1416, AB T0L 0W0 – 403/932-6810; Fax: 403/932-3591 – President, Hank Biesbroek

Cold Lake Regional CC, PO Box 454, AB T9M 1P1 – 403/594-4747; Fax: 403/594-3711 – Office Administrator, Tracy Anderson

Coronation & District CC, PO Box 960, AB T0C 1C0 – 403/578-2422; Fax: 403/578-3020 – President, Barry Clampitt, 403/578-3695

Cremona Watervalley & District CC, PO Box 356, AB T0M 0R0 – 403/637-3752; Fax: 403/637-3900 – President, Mabel Maxim

Crowsnest Pass CC, PO Box 706, Blairmore AB T0K 0E0 – 403/562-2813; Fax: 403/562-2815 – President, Ken Sorensen

Devon CC, PO Box 837, AB T0C 1E0 – 403/987-5177; Fax: 403/987-2220 – President, Gary Thomson, 403/420-6850

Diamond Valley CC, PO Box 61, Turner Valley AB T0L 2A0 – 403/933-4954; Fax: 403/933-4360 – President, Ian MacGregor, 403/933-7878

Didsbury CC, PO Box 176, AB T0M 0W0 – 403/335-3066; Fax: 403/335-3591; Toll Free: 1-800-863-4872 – George Anderson

Drayton Valley & District CC, PO Box 5318, AB T7A 1R5 – 403/542-7578; Fax: 403/542-9211 – Executive Director, Karen Kirkwood

Drumheller Regional Chamber of Development & Tourism, PO Box 999, AB T0J 0Y0 – 403/823-8100; Fax: 403/823-4469 – General Manager, Cory Campbell

Eckville & District CC, PO Box 609, AB T0M 0X0 – 403/746-2231; Fax: 403/746-2005 – President, Gordon Ebden

Edgerton & District CC, PO Box 303, AB T0B 1K0 – 403/755-3747; Fax: 403/755-2084 – President, Jean Sawchuk

Edmonton CC, #600, 10123 - 99 St., AB T5J 3G9 – 403/426-4620; Fax: 403/424-7946; URL: http://www.tnc.com/ecc/ – President, Pat Adams

Edson & District CC, 5433 - 3 Ave., AB T7E 1L5 – 403/723-4918; Fax: 403/723-5545 – President, Mike Dion

Elk Point CC, PO Box 639, AB T0A 1A0 – 403/724-4087; Fax: 403/724-4211 – President, Vicki Brooker

Evansburg & Entwistle CC, PO Box 598, AB T0E 0T0 – 403/727-2757; Fax: 403/727-3526 – President, Carol Cardinal

Fairview & District CC, PO Box 1034, AB T0H 1L0 – 403/835-3483; Fax: 403/835-3483 – President, Jim Backus, 403/835-4440

Falher CC, PO Box 814, AB T0H 1M0 – 403/837-2364; Fax: 403/837-2647 – Sec./Manager, Cindy Levesque

Foremost & District CC, PO Box 272, AB T0K 0X0 – 403/867-2174; Fax: 403/867-3579 – P. Reyner

Fort MacLeod & District CC, PO Box 757, AB T0L 0Z0 – 403/553-4955; Fax: 403/553-2656 – President, Joyce Bonertz

Fort McMurray CC, 200 Professional Bldg., 9908 Franklin Ave., AB T9H 2K5 – 403/743-3100; Fax: 403/790-9757 – Executive Director, Carolyn Baikie

Fort Saskatchewan CC, 10030 - 99 Ave., PO Box 3072, AB T8L 2T1 – 403/998-4355; Fax: 403/998-1515 – President, Doug Chettleborough

Fort Vermilion & Area BT, PO Box 456, AB T0H 1N0 – 403/927-4563; Fax: 403/927-3380 – President, Martin Braat

Fox Creek CC, PO Box 774, AB T0H 1P0 – 403/622-3821; Fax: 403/622-2878 – President, Vaughn Nelson

Gibbons & District CC, PO Box 38, AB T0A 1N0 – 403/923-2129; Fax: 403/923-3826 – President, Chris MacDonald

Girouxville CC, PO Box 57, AB T0H 1S0 – 403/323-3090; Fax: 403/323-4110 – President, Norm Doucette

Glendon & District Chamber, PO Box 249, AB T0A 1P0 – 403/635-4263; Fax: 403/635-3838 – President, Rick Lotsberg

Grande Cache CC, PO Box 1342, AB T0E 0Y0 – 403/827-2062; Fax: 403/827-2062 – President, Bud Lovegren

Grande Prairie & District CC, 10011 - 103 Ave., AB T8V 1B9 – 403/532-5340; Fax: 403/532-2926 – Executive Director, Trenton Perrott

Hanna CC, PO Box 2248, AB T0J 1P0 – 403/854-4659; Fax: 403/854-4917 – President, Adrian Mohl, 403/854-4659

Hardisty & District CC, PO Box 159, AB T0B 1V0 – 403/888-3786; Fax: 403/888-2408 – President, Colleen Munn

High Level & District CC, PO Box 202, AB T0H 1Z0 – 403/926-2470; Fax: 403/926-3289 – President, Gerry Hosey

High Prairie & District CC, PO Box 519, AB T0G 1E0 – 403/523-3505; Fax: 403/523-4810 – President, Judy Shybunia

High River CC, PO Box 5244, AB T1V 1M4 – 403/652-3336; Fax: 403/652-7660 – Executive Director, Susan Cooper

Hinton & District CC, 309 Gregg Ave., AB T7V 2A7 – 403/865-2777; Fax: 403/865-1062 – Manager, Cyndy Mork

Hythe CC, PO Box 404, AB T0C 2C0 – 403/356-2990 – President, Norma Hujdic

Innisfail CC, PO Box 6031, AB T4G 1S7 – 403/227-1177; Fax: 403/227-6749 – Manager, Susan Rombs

Jasper Park CC, 632 Connaught Dr., PO Box 98, AB T0B 1E0 – 403/852-3858; Fax: 403/852-4932 – General Manager, Brian Rode

Killam & District CC, PO Box 272, AB T0B 2L0 – 403/385-3949; Fax: 403/385-2129 – President, Terry Hamilton

La Crete CC, PO Box 1088, AB T0H 2H0 – 403/928-3771; Fax: 403/928-3875 – President, Jake Fehr

Lac La Biche CC, PO Box 804, AB T0A 2C0 – 403/623-2818; Fax: 403/623-2671 – Executive Director, Russ Ledger

Lacombe & District CC, 5036 - 51 St., AB T4L 1W2 – 403/782-4300; Fax: 403/782-4302 – Manager, Mickey Penhale

Leduc & District CC, 6420 - 50 St., AB T9E 7K9 – 403/986-5454; Fax: 403/986-8108; Email: commerce@tnc.com; URL: http://www.tnc.com/commerce – President, Bill Emmerzael

Legal & District CC, PO Box 338, AB T0G 1L0 – 403/961-3241; Fax: 403/961-3453 – President, Bill Mchellan

Lethbridge CC, #200, 529 - 6 St. South, AB T1J 2E1 – 403/327-1586; Fax: 403/327-1001 – General Manager, Jody Nilsson

Lloydminster CC, Meridian Bldg., 4420 - 50 Ave., AB T9V 0W2 – 403/875-9013; Fax: 403/875-0755 – President, Kathy Harvey

Lloydminster CC, c/o Coldwell Banker/Cityside RLT, 5021 - 50th St., AB T9V 0L9 – 403/875-3343; Fax: 403/875-8631 – President, Kathy Harvey

Mallaig CC, PO Box 144, AB T0A 2K0 – 403/635-3887 – President, Don Emerson

Manning & District BT, PO Box 130, AB T0H 2M0 – 403/836-2033; Fax: 403/823-2275 – President, Beverly Kleinschroth

Mannville & District CC, PO Box 54, AB T0B 2W0 – 403/763-3800; Fax: 403/763-2110 – Executive Director, Ev Maron

Marwayne & District CC, PO Box 183, AB T0B 2X0 – 403/847-4636; Fax: 403/847-2177 – President, Dawn Miller

Mayerthorpe & District CC, PO Box 1279, AB T0E 1N0 – 403/786-2535; Fax: 403/786-2780 – President, Doug McDermid, 403/786-2141

McLennan CC, PO Box 90, AB T0H 2L0 – 403/324-2164; Fax: 403/324-3932 – President, Bruce Brulotte

Medicine Hat & District CC, 413 - 6th Ave. SE, AB T1A 2S7 – 403/527-5214; Fax: 403/527-5182 – General Manager, Craig Couillard

Millet & District CC, PO Box 389, AB T0C 1Z0 – 403/387-4571; Fax: 403/387-5588 – President, Joe Green Wood

Morinville & District CC, PO Box 3130, AB T8R 1S1 – 403/939-2885; Fax: 403/939-2885 – President, Brent Melville

Pigeon Lake Regional CC, General Delivery, Mulhurst Bay AB T0C 2C0 – 403/389-3854; Fax: 403/389-3854 – President, Norm Froom

Nanton & District CC, PO Box 548, AB T0L 1R0 – 403/646-2736; Fax: 403/646-5554 – President, Larry Wynnyk

Nordegg CC, General Delivery, AB T0M 2H0 – 403/721-2208; Fax: 403/721-2208 – Cheri Adolph

Okotoks & District CC, PO Box 1053, AB T0L 1T0 – 403/938-2848; Fax: 403/938-5441 – President, Cheryl Pedscalny, 403/938-2008

Olds & District CC, PO Box 4210, AB T4H 1P8 – 403/556-7070; Fax: 403/556-1515 – President, Allan Entwhistle, 403/556-7827

Onoway & District CC, PO Box 723, AB T0E 1V0 – 403/967-3435; Fax: 403/967-3435 – President, Ian Abbott

Oyen & District CC, PO Box 420, AB T0J 2J0 – 403/664-3622; Fax: 403/664-3622; Email: oyenecho@agt.net; URL: http://www.inter.ab.ca/oyen/ – President, Diana Walker, 403/664-3622

Peace River BT, PO Box 6599, AB T8S 1S4 – 403/624-3535; Fax: 403/624-4663 – President, Mike Mathew

Picture Butte & District CC, PO Box 540, AB T0K 1V0 – 403/732-4623; Fax: 403/732-4703 – President, Jon Stevens

Pincher Creek & District Chamber of Economic Development, PO Box 2287, AB T0K 1W0 – 403/627-5199; Fax: 403/627-5850; Email: pcinfo@canuck.com – Vice-President, Alastair MacLean

Ponoka & District CC, PO Box 4188, AB T4J 1R6 – 403/783-3888; Fax: 403/783-3434 – President, Linda Steinmann

Provost & District CC, PO Box 637, AB T0B 3S0 – 403/753-2748; Fax: 403/453-6060 – President, Terry Tucker

Rainbow Lake CC, PO Box 273, AB T0H 2Y0 – 403/956-3123; Fax: 403/956-3649 – President Elect, Dale Lederer

Raymond CC, PO Box 918, AB T0K 2S0 – 403/752-4226; Fax: 403/752-3936 – President, Ron Hancock

Red Deer CC, 3017 - 50th Ave., AB T4N 5Y6 – 403/347-4491; Fax: 403/343-6188; Email: rdchamber@cnnet.com; URL: http://chamber.reddeer.net/ – Executive Director, Pat Henry

Redwater & District CC, PO Box 322, AB T0A 2W0 – 403/942-3012; Fax: 403/942-2036 – President, Tom Wilkinson

Rimbey CC, PO Box 87, AB T0C 2J0 – 403/843-4445; Fax: 403/843-3055 – President/Secretary, Kevin Lentz

Rocky Mountain House & District CC, PO Box 1374, AB T0M 1T4 – 403/845-5450; Fax: 403/845-7764 – Manager, Cheryl Munro

St. Albert CC, 71 St. Albert Rd., St Albert AB T8N 6L5 – 403/458-2833; Fax: 403/458-6515 – Executive Director, Natalie Zigarlick

St. Paul & District CC, 4537 - 50 Ave., PO Box 887, AB T0A 3A0 – 403/645-6800; Fax: 403/645-6059; Email: stpaulcc@incentre.net – Executive Director, Rhea Labrie

Sedgewick CC, PO Box 625, AB T0B 4C0 – 403/384-3636 – President, Chris Forster

Sexsmith & District CC, PO Box 146, AB T0H 3C0 – 403/568-4031; Fax: 403/568-2833 – President, Linda Sodergren

Sherwood Park & District CC, PO Box 3103, AB T8A 2A6 – 403/464-0801; Fax: 403/449-3581; Email: chamber1@telusplanet.net; URL: http://www.telusplanet.net/public/chamber1/ – President, Al Peterson

Slave Lake & District CC, PO Box 190, AB T0G 2A0 – 403/849-3222; Fax: 403/849-5977 – President, Ken Giblin

Smoky Lake & District CC, PO Box 654, AB T0A 30C – 403/656-4347 – President, Ed Shaske

Spirit River & District CC, PO Box 930, AB T0H 3G0 – 403/864-3600; Fax: 403/864-4506 – Treasurer, Shenda Janis

Spruce Grove & District CC, PO Box 4210, AB T7X 3B4 – 403/962-2561; Fax: 403/962-4417; Email: sgcc@tnc.com; URL: http://superhorse.tnc.com/sgcc/ – Business Manager, Pam Brace

Stettler & District CC, PO Box 58, AB T0C 2L0 – 403/742-3181; Fax: 403/742-3123 – President, Judy Hagel

Stony Plain & District CC, PO Box 2300, AB T7Z 1X7 – 403/963-4545; Fax: 403/963-4542 – Manager, Sharon Dumont

Strathmore CC, PO Box 2222, AB T1P 1K2 – 403/934-2959; Fax: 403/934-6492 – President, Cloude Gaugvin

Sundre CC, PO Box 1085, AB T0M 1X0 – 403/638-4749; Fax: 403/638-3733 – President, Dan Church

Upper Red Deer River CC, PO Box 570, Sundre AB T0M 1X0 – 403/637-2229 – President, Cy Cynewsham

Swan Hills CC, PO Box 540, AB T0G 2C0 – 403/333-2224; Fax: 403/333-4201 – Manager, Jean McKeever

Sylvan Lake CC, PO Box 9003, AB T4S 1S6 – 403/887-5050; Fax: 403/887-4944 – President, Matt Toonders

Taber & District CC, 4702 - 50 St., AB T1G 2B6 – 403/223-2265; Fax: 403/223-2291 – President, Bryce Bennett

Thorhild CC, PO Box 384, AB T0A 3J0 – 403/398-3550; Fax: 403/398-2010 – President, Wayne Lannon, 403/398-3550

Thorsby & District CC, PO Box 270, AB T0C 2P0 – 403/789-2100; Fax: 403/789-2155 – President, Clarence Kruger

Three Hills & District CC, PO Box 277, AB T0M 2A0 – 403/433-2471 – President, Brad Luijkx

Tofield CC, c/o Rob Gillrie, General Delivery, AB T0B 4J0 – 403/662-4046; Fax: 403/662-3993 – President, Bruce Kleavey

Trochu CC, PO Box 86, AB T0M 2C0 – 403/442-2345; Fax: 403/442-4213 – Phil Frere

Two Hills & District CC, PO Box 225, AB T0B 4K0 – 403/657-3759 – President, Robert Hargreves

Valleyview CC, PO Box 1020, AB T0H 3N0 – 403/524-3904; Fax: 403/524-4535 – President, Jim Bates

Vegreville & District CC, 4500 Volodymyr Dr., PO Box 877, AB T9C 1R9 – 403/632-2771; Fax: 403/632-6958 – President, Dan Beaudette

Vermilion & District CC, 5011 - 50 Ave., AB T9X 1A7 – 403/853-6593; Fax: 403/853-1740; Email: townvrml@agt.net; URL: http://www.agt.net/public/townvrml/index.htm – Manager, Margaret Holt

Vulcan & District CC, PO Box 1161, AB T0L 2B0 – 403/485-2996; Fax: 403/485-2878; Email: vulcaned@agt.net – President, Sue Williams

Wainwright & District CC, PO Box 2997, AB T9W 1S9 – 403/842-4910; Fax: 403/842-4910 – President, Doug Morgan, 403/842-3145

Waskatenau & District CC, PO Box 54, AB T0A 3P0 – 403/358-2616; Fax: 403/358-2662 – President, Richard Ronaghan

Westlock & District CC, 9936 - 107 St., AB T7P 2K6 – 403/349-4444; Fax: 403/349-5551 – President, Deborah Stasiuk, 403/349-5900

Wetaskiwin Chamber of Economic Development & Tourism, 4910 - 55A St., AB T9A 2R7 – 403/352-1679; Fax: 403/352-4640 – CEO, Bob Jeffery

Whitecourt & District CC, PO Box 1011, AB T7S 1N9 – 403/778-5363; Fax: 403/778-2351 – Executive Director, Irma Edgell

Willow Creek CC, PO Box 1092, Claresholm AB T0L 0T0 – 403/625-4250; Fax: 403/625-4774 – President, David Mulholland

Worsley CC, PO Box 181, AB T0H 3W0 – President, Doug Allen

**BRITISH COLUMBIA**

Abbotsford CC, 2462 McCallum Rd., BC V2S 3P9 – 604/859-9651; Fax: 604/850-6880; Email: acoc@bc.sympatico.ca – Manager, Leona Klingspon

Armstrong-Spallumcheen CC, PO Box 118, BC V0E 1B0 – 250/546-8155; Fax: 250/546-8868 – President, Myrna Christianson

Ashcroft & District CC, PO Box 183, BC V0K 1H0 – 250/453-2642 – Secretary, Sandra Bennett

Atlin BT, PO Box 365, BC V0W 1A0 – President, George Holman

Bamfield CC, PO Box 5, BC V0R 1B0 – 250/728-3006 – President, David Payne

Barriere CC, PO Box 1190, BC V0E 1E0 – 250/672-9966; Fax: 250/672-9864 – President, Laura Christianson

Bella Coola District BT, PO Box 371, BC V0T 1C0 – 250/799-5349; Fax: 250/799-5450 – President, Doug Pelton

Bowen Island CC, PO Box 102, BC V0N 1G0 – 604/947-2838 – President, Robert Wiltshire

Burnaby CC, #149, 9855 Austin Ave., BC V3J 1N4 – 604/421-0084; Fax: 604/421-3630; URL: http://beta4.island.net – Manager, Abby Anderson

Burns Lake & District CC, PO Box 339, BC V0J 1K0 – 250/692-3773; Fax: 250/692-3493 – Manager, Susan Schienbein

Cache Creek CC, PO Box 460, BC V0K 1H0 – 250/457-9566; Fax: 250/457-9192

Campbell River & District CC, 1235 Shoppers Row, PO Box 400, BC V9W 5B6 – 250/287-4636; Fax: 250/286-6490; Email: crchambr@vquest.com; URL: http://www.vquest.com/crchamber/ – Manager, Heather Pate

Castlegar & District CC, 1995 - 6 Ave., BC V1N 4B7 – 250/365-6313; Fax: 250/365-5778; Email: cdcoc@knet.kootenay.net – Manager, Marlene Krueckl

Central Coast CC, PO Box 40, Bella Bella BC V0T 1B0 – 250/957-2609 – President, Tracy MacDonald

Chase & District CC, PO Box 592, BC V0E 1M0 – 250/679-8432; Fax: 250/679-3120 – Manager, Eileen McKinnon

Chemainus & District CC, PO Box 575, BC V0R 1K0 – 250/246-3944; Fax: 250/246-3251 – Manager, Dyan Freer

Chetwynd & District CC, 5217 North Access Rd., PO Box 1000, BC V0C 1J0 – 250/788-3345; Fax: 250/788-7843 – Manager, Valerie Simpson Bulmer

Christina Lake CC, Hwy. 3 & Kimura Rd., BC V0H 1E2 – 250/447-6161; Fax: 250/447-6161 – President, Valerie Sampson

Clearwater & District CC, RR#1, PO Box 1988, BC V0E 1N0 – 250/674-2646; Fax: 250/674-3693 – Manager, Marie Cornell

Clinton & District CC, PO Box 256, BC V0K 1K0 – 250/459-2535 – President, Martin Schinkel

Cloverdale BT, #201, 17687 - 57A Ave., PO Box 505, BC V3S 1G4 – 604/574-9802; Fax: 604/574-6457 – President, Anne Sharkey

Columbia Valley CC, PO Box 1019, Invermere BC V0A 1K0 – 250/342-2844; Fax: 250/342-3261; Email: columbia.valley.chamber@rockies.net – President, Allen Miller

Comox Valley CC, 2040 Cliffe Ave., Courtenay BC V9N 2L3 – 250/334-3234; Fax: 250/334-4908; Email: chmbr@mars.ark.com; URL: http://www.vquest.com:80/cvchamber/ – Manager, Barry Wood

CC Serving Coquitlam, Port Coquitlam, Port Moody, #3, 1180 Pinetree Way, BC V3B 7L2 – 604/464-2716; Fax: 604/464-6796 – Executive Director, Elizabeth Voigt

Cranbrook CC, PO Box 84, BC V1C 4H6 – 250/426-5914; Fax: 250/426-3873; Email: cbkchamber@cyberlink.bc.ca; URL: http://www.cyberlink.bc.ca/chamber/cranbrook/index.html – President, Bill Bennett

Kootenay Lake CC, PO Box 96, Crawford Bay BC V0B 1E0 – 250/227-9226; Fax: 250/227-9220 – President, Steve Smith

Creston CC, 1711 Canyon St., PO Box 268, BC V0B 1G0 – 250/428-4342; Fax: 250/428-9411; Email: crescofc@awinc.com – Manager, Bonnie Karountzos

Cumberland CC, PO Box 250, BC V0R 1S0 – 250/336-8313; Fax: 250/336-2455 – Manager, Sandy Baird

Dawson Creek & District CC, #300, 1323 - 102 Ave., BC V1G 3W2 – 250/782-4868; Fax: 250/782-2371; Email: dawsoncreek.chamber@neonet.bc.ca – Manager, Lynda Tidder-Martin

Tahltan CC, PO Box 338, Dease Lake BC V0C 1L0 – 250/771-3700; Fax: 250/771-3702 – Manager, Stu Pike

Delta CC, 6201 - 60 Ave., BC V4K 4E2 – 604/946-4232; Fax: 604/946-5285 – Executive Director, Denny Gooch

Duncan-Cowichan CC, 381 Trans-Canada Hwy., BC V9L 3R5 – 250/746-4636; Fax: 250/746-8222 – Manager, Diane Colman

Elkford CC, 4A Front St., PO Box 220, BC V0B 1H0 – 250/865-4614; Fax: 250/865-2442; Email: ecofc@titianlink.com – Manager, Sue Sundstrom

Enderby & District CC, 700 Railway St., PO Box 1000, BC V0E 1V0 – 250/838-6727; Fax: 250/838-0123; Email: enderbychamber@jetstream.net; URL: http://www.jetstream.net/enderby/chamber.html – Manager, Maureen Bressler

Esquimalt CC, 1153 Esquimalt Rd., PO Box 36019, Victoria BC V9A 7J5 – 250/384-3228; Fax: 250/384-5772 – President, Mark Eraut

Falkland CC, PO Box 69, BC V0E 1W0 – 250/379-2939; Fax: 250/545-0437 – President, Erica Britton

Fernie CC, Hwy. 3 & Dicken Rd., BC V0B 1M0 – 250/423-6868; Fax: 250/423-3811 – Manager, David Keiver

Fort Fraser CC, General Delivery, BC V0J 1N0 – 250/690-7477 – President, Gilbert Sholty

Fort Langley & District CC, 9167 Glover Rd., BC V1M 2R4 – 604/888-1477; Fax: 604/888-2657 – Manager, Michele Coleman

* BT - Board of Trade; BC - Bureau de commerce; CC - Chamber of Commerce/Chambre de commerce

Fort Nelson CC, PO Box 196, BC V0C 1R0 – 250/774-2956; Fax: 250/774-2958; Email: fncc@cancom.net – Executive Director, Shannon Matchett

Fort St. John & District CC, 9323 - 100 St., BC V1J 4N4 – 250/785-6037; Fax: 250/785-7181 – Executive Director, Trudy Eklund Dorie

Fort St. James CC, PO Box 1164, Fort St James BC V0J 1P0 – 250/996-7023; Fax: 250/996-7047 – Manager, Linda Baird

Fraser Lake CC, PO Box 1059, BC V0J 1S0 – 604/699-6219; Fax: 604/699-6496

Gabriola CC, PO Box 249, Gabriola Island BC V0R 1X0 – 250/247-9332; Fax: 250/247-9332; Email: gabriola@island.net; URL: http://www.island.net/~gabriola – President, Steve Wohlleben

Galiano Island CC, RR#1, BC V0N 1P0 – 250/539-5779; Fax: 250/539-5779 – President, Dave Hutton

Gibsons & District CC, PO Box 1190, BC V0N 1V0 – 604/886-2325; Fax: 604/886-2379 – Manager, Emily Perry

Bridge River Valley CC, General Delivery, Gold Bridge BC V0K 1P0 – 250/238-2457; Fax: 250/238-2457 – President, John Courchesne

Gold River CC, PO Box 39, BC V0P 1G0 – 250/283-2972 – President, David Cyr

Golden & District CC, PO Box 1320, BC V0A 1H0 – 250/344-7125; Fax: 250/344-6688 – Manager, Sandra Ross

Grand Forks & Districts CC, PO Box 1086, BC V0H 1H0 – 250/442-2833; Fax: 250/442-5688 – Manager, Marion Ashby

Greenwood & District BT, PO Box 430, BC V0H 1J0 – 250/445-6323; Fax: 250/445-6166 – Manager, Marilyn Walker

Harrison Hot Springs CC, PO Box 255, BC V0M 1K0 – 604/796-3425; Fax: 604/769-3188 – Manager, Bob Bell

The Hazeltons & District CC, PO Box 1, New Hazelton BC V0J 2J0 – 250/842-6006; Fax: 250/842-6340 – President, Colin Smith

Hope & District CC, PO Box 370, BC V0X 1L0 – 604/869-2021; Fax: 604/869-2160 – Manager, Inge Wilson

Houston & District CC, 3289 Hwy. 16, PO Box 396, BC V0J 1Z0 – 250/845-7640; Fax: 250/845-3682; Email: chamberh@mail.netshop.net – Manager, Cheryl Kelley

Hudson's Hope CC, c/o District Office, PO Box 330, BC V0C 1V0 – Manager, Faye Lavallee

West Shore CC, 697 Goldstream Ave., Victoria BC V9B 2X2 – 250/478-1130; Fax: 250/478-1584; Email: chamber@westshore.bc.ca; URL: http://westshore.bc.ca – Manager, R.J. Cowie

Greater Kamloops CC, 1290 Trans Canada Hwy. West, BC V2C 6R3 – 250/372-7722; Fax: 250/828-9500 – Manager, Maureen Freeman

Kamloops CC, 1290 West Trans Canada Hwy., BC V2C 6R3 – 250/372-7722; Fax: 250/828-9500 – President, John Dormer

Kaslo CC, PO Box 329, BC V0G 1M0 – 250/353-2992; Fax: 250/353-7141 – President, Gordon Page

Kelowna CC, 544 Harvey Ave., BC V1Y 6C9 – 250/861-1515; Fax: 250/861-3624 – Executive Director, Bonnie Bates Gibbs

Keremeos & District CC, PO Box 490, BC V0X 1N0 – 250/499-5225; Fax: 250/499-2252 – Manager, Ken Randle

Kimberley Bavarian Society CC, 350 Ross St., BC V1A 2Z9 – 250/427-3666; Fax: 250/427-5378 – Manager, Hazel Liebscher

Kitimat CC, PO Box 214, BC V8C 2G7 – 250/632-6294; Fax: 250/632-4685 – Manager, Gail Guise

Kitsilano CC, PO Box 34369, Stn D, Vancouver BC V6J 4P3 – 604/731-4454; Fax: 604/731-0097 – President, Patricia Tracy

Ladysmith CC, PO Box 598, BC V0R 2E0 – 250/245-2112; Fax: 250/245-3798 – President, Adrienne Lait

Lake Cowichan & District CC, PO Box 824, BC V0R 2G0 – 250/749-3244; Fax: 250/749-0187

Langley CC, #1, 5761 Glover Rd., BC V3A 8M8 – 604/530-6656; Fax: 604/530-7066 – Manager, Lynn Whitehouse

Lillooet & District CC, PO Box 650, BC V0K 1V0 – 250/256-4364; Fax: 250/256-7262 – Manager, Brenda Ryks

Logan Lake CC, PO Box 1090, BC V0K 1W0 – 250/523-6504; Fax: 250/523-6504 – President, Lauchlan McDonald

Lumby & District CC, PO Box 534, BC V0E 2G0 – 250/547-2300; Fax: 250/547-2300; URL: http://www.monashee.com – Manager, Lorrie Pelletier

Lytton & District CC, PO Box 460, BC V0K 1Z0 – 250/455-2523; Fax: 250/455-6669 – Manager, Peggy Chute

Mackenzie CC, PO Box 880, MacKenzie BC V0J 2C0 – 250/997-5459; Fax: 250/997-6117; Email: markay@perf.bc.ca; URL: http://www.perf.bc.ca – Manager, Margaret Grant

Pender Harbour & Egmont CC, PO Box 265, Madeira Park BC V0N 2H0 – 604/883-2561; Fax: 604/883-2561 – Secretary, Michael C. Crowe

Maple Ridge CC, 22238 Lougheed Hwy., BC V2X 2T2 – 604/463-3366; Fax: 604/463-3201 – Manager, Helen Secco

Charlotte Islands CC, PO Box 38, Massett BC V0T 1M0 – 250/626-3300; Fax: 250/626-3434 – President, Gordon Feyer

Mayne Island Community CC, PO Box 2, BC V0N 2J0 – 250/539-2327 – President, Christine Starkey

McBride & District CC, PO Box 2, BC V0J 2E0 – 250/569-3366; Fax: 250/569-3394 – President, Cathy Wiltsie

Merritt & District CC, PO Box 1649, BC V0K 2B0 – 250/378-5634; Fax: 250/378-6561 – Manager, Kelly Reid

Mission Regional CC, 34033 Lougheed Hwy., BC V2V 4J5 – 604/826-6914; Fax: 604/826-5916 – Manager, Loretta White

Nakusp CC, PO Box 387, BC V0G 1R0 – 250/265-4234; Fax: 250/265-3808 – Manager, Shannon Roberts

Greater Nanaimo CC, 777 Poplar St., BC V9S 2H7 – 250/753-1191; Fax: 250/754-5186; Email: chamber@island.net; URL: http://www.island.net/~chamber/ – Executive Director, Jane Hutchins

Nelson & District CC, 225 Hall St., BC V1L 5X4 – 250/352-3433; Fax: 250/352-6355 – Manager, Howard Dirks

New Westminster CC, 601 Queens Ave., BC V3M 1L1 – 604/521-7781; Fax: 604/521-0057; Email: nwcc@newwestchamber.com – Executive Director, Marjorie Steeves Campbell

North Shuswap CC, PO Box 101, Celesta BC V0E 1L0 – 250/955-2113; Fax: 250/955-0770 – Manager, Jay Simpson

Okanagan Falls CC, PO Box 246, BC V0H 1R0 – 250/497-8800; Fax: 250/497-8822 – Secretary, Charles Hayes

Oliver & District CC, PO Box 460, BC V0H 1T0 – 250/498-6321; Fax: 250/498-3156 – Manager, Joan Thompson

Osoyoos CC, PO Box 277, BC V0H 1V0 – 250/495-7142; Fax: 250/495-6161 – Manager, Bonnie Dancey

Parksville & District CC, 1275 East Island Hwy., PO Box 99, BC V9P 2G3 – 250/248-3613; Fax: 250/248-5210; Email: parksvil@nanaimo.ark.com; URL: http://nanaimo.ark.com/~parksvil/ – Manager, Lou Biggemann

Pemberton CC, PO Box 370, BC V0N 2L0 – 604/894-6175; Fax: 604/932-1279 – Secretary, Judy Lemke

Penticton CC, 185 Lakeshore Dr. West, BC V2A 1B7 – 250/492-4103; Fax: 250/492-6119; URL: http://www.penticton.org – Executive Director, James Pearmain

Pitt Meadows CC, 12492 Harris Rd., BC V3Y 2J4 – 604/465-7820; Fax: 604/465-1106 – Manager, Norah Wilsdon

Alberni Valley CC, RR#2, Site 215, C-10, Port Alberni BC V9Y 7L6 – 250/724-6535; Fax: 250/724-6560 – Manager, Elverna Baker

Port Hardy & District CC, PO Box 249, BC V0N 2P0 – 250/949-7622; Fax: 250/949-6653 – Manager, Heather Overy

Port McNeill & District CC, PO Box 129, BC V0N 2R0 – 250/956-4033; Fax: 250/956-4977 – Manager, Kathleen Kinley

Port Renfrew CC, 62 Parkinson St., BC V0S 1K0 – 250/647-5443 – President, Bob Corteau

Powell River CC, 6807 Wharf St., BC V8A 1T9 – 604/485-4051; Fax: 604/485-4272 – Manager, CouLynn Carlson

Prince George CC, 770 Brunswick St., BC V2L 2C2 – 250/562-2424; Fax: 250/562-6510 – Executive Director, Sherry Sethen

Prince Rupert & District CC, 111 - 3rd St., BC V8J 4C4 – 250/624-2296; Fax: 250/624-6105 – Manager, Lily Stewart

Princeton & District CC, PO Box 540, BC V0X 1W0 – 250/295-3103; Fax: 250/295-3255 – Manager, Christiane Gosselin

Qualicum Beach CC, 2711 West Island Hwy., BC V9K 2C4 – 250/752-9532; Fax: 250/752-2923; Email: qualicum@nanaimo.ark.com; URL: http://nanaimo.ark.com/~qualicum/ – Manager, Georgia MacLean

Queen Charlotte Islands CC, PO Box 38, Masset BC V0T 1M0 – 250/626-3300; Fax: 250/626-3300 – Manager, Annette Fields

Quesnel & District CC, 703 Carson Ave., BC V2J 2B6 – 250/992-8716; Fax: 250/992-9606 – Manager, Marnie Greening

Radium Hot Springs CC, PO Box 225, BC V0A 1M0 – 250/347-9331; Fax: 250/347-9127 – Manager, Leona Young

Revelstoke CC, PO Box 490, BC V0E 2S0 – 250/837-5345; Fax: 250/837-4223; Email: cocrev@mindlink.bc.ca; URL: http://www.revelstokecc.bc.ca/mountns – Manager, Adelheid Bender

Richmond CC, #150, 5890 No. 3 Rd., BC V6X 3P6 – 604/278-2822; Fax: 604/278-2972; Email: richmond@jumppoint.com; URL: http://www.rpl.richmond.bc.ca/community/chamber/index.html – Executive Director, Shelley Leonhardt

Rossland CC, PO Box 1385, BC V0G 1Y0 – 250/362-5666; Fax: 250/362-5399 – Manager, Lorraine Duske

Saanich Peninsula CC, 9768 Third St., Sidney BC V8L 3A4 – 250/656-3616; Fax: 250/656-7111; Email: saanpcoc@octonet.com; URL: http://www.octonet.com/saanpcoc – Executive Director, Gary R. MacPherson

Salmo & District CC, PO Box 400, BC V0G 1Z0 – 250/357-2596 – Manager, Heather Street

Salmon Arm & District CC, PO Box 999, BC V1E 4P2 – 250/832-6247; Fax: 250/832-8382 – Manager, Rosella Hillson

Salt Spring Island CC, 127 Lower Ganges Rd., BC V8K 2T1 – 250/537-4223; Fax: 250/537-4276; Email: chamber@saltspring.com; URL: http://www.saltspringisland.bc.ca – Manager, Melva Geldreich

Chilliwack CC, 44150 Luckakuck Way, RR#1, Sardis BC V2R 4A7 – 604/858-8121; Fax: 604/858-0157 – Executive Director, Brenda Dehn

Sechelt & District CC, PO Box 360, BC V0N 3A0 – 604/885-0662; Fax: 604/885-0691 – Manager, Colleen Clark

Seton Shalath District CC, PO Box 2067, Seton Portage BC V0N 3B0 – 250/259-8318; Fax: 250/259-8218 – President, George Prosick

South Cowichan CC, RR#1, Mill Bay BC V0R 2P0 – 250/743-3566; Fax: 250/743-5332 – Manager, June Painter

Sicamous & District CC, PO Box 346, BC V0E 2V0 – 250/836-3313; Fax: 250/836-4368 – Manager, Doreen Favel

Slocan District CC, PO Box 488, New Denver BC V0G 1S0 – 250/358-2544; Fax: 250/358-7998 – President, Gordon Brookfield

Smithers District CC, PO Box 2379, BC V0J 2N0 – 250/847-5072; Fax: 250/847-3337 – Manager, Rosemary Madden

Sooke-Jordan River CC, 6697 Sooke Rd., PO Box 18, BC V0S 1N0 – 250/642-6112; Fax: 250/642-3066; URL: http://www.sookenet.com/sooke/chamber/homepage.html – Manager, Heidi Griffith

Sorrento District CC, PO Box 7, BC V0E 2W0 – 250/675-3515 – President, Mark McIvity

South Cariboo CC, PO Box 2312, 100 Mile House BC V0K 2E0 – 250/395-5353; Fax: 250/395-4085; Email: sccofc@netshop.net; URL: http://www.netshop.net/~100mile/sccofc.html – Manager, Kathy McKenzie

Sparwood & District CC, Aspen Dr., PO Box 1448, BC V0B 2G0 – 250/425-2423; Fax: 250/425-7130; Email: sparwood.chamber@mail.rmin.net – Manager, Brian Knox

Squamish & Howe Sound CC, PO Box 1009, BC V0N 3G0 – 604/892-9244; Fax: 604/892-2034; Email: cocsqhs@mountain_inter.net – Manager, Wendy Magee

Stewart-Hyder International CC, PO Box 306, BC V0T 1W0 – 250/636-9224; Fax: 250/636-2199; Email: shcofc@kermode.net – President, Ann Burton

Summerland CC, PO Box 1075, BC V0H 1Z0 – 250/494-2686; Fax: 250/494-4039 – Manager, Alan Forsdick

Surrey CC, 15105A - 105 Ave., BC V3R 7G9 – 604/581-7130; Fax: 604/588-7549; URL: http://www.surreycoc.com/cip/CHAMBER.HTML – Executive Director, Patsy Schell

Tahsis CC, PO Box 278, BC V0P 1X0 – 250/934-6667; Fax: 250/934-6515 – President, Cathy Daynes

Terrace & District CC, 4511 Keith Ave., BC V8G 1K1 – 250/635-2063; Fax: 250/635-2573 – Manager, Bobbie Phillips

Tofino-Long Beach CC, PO Box 476, BC V0R 2Z0 – 250/725-3414; Fax: 250/725-3296 – Manager, Bob Nixon

Trail District CC, 843 Rossland Ave., BC V1R 4S8 – 250/368-3144; Fax: 250/368-6427 – Manager, Michele Cherot

District of Tumbler Ridge CC, PO Box 606, BC V0C 2W0 – 250/242-4702; Fax: 250/242-5159 – Manager, April Moi

Ucluelet CC, PO Box 428, BC V0R 3A0 – 250/726-4641; Fax: 250/726-4611 – President, Skip Rowland

Valemount CC, PO Box 298, BC V0E 2Z0 – 250/566-4887; Fax: 250/566-4333 – President, Bill Armstrong

North Vancouver CC, 131 - 2 St. East, BC V7L 1C2 – 604/987-4488; Fax: 604/987-8272 – Manager, Judi Ainsworth

Vancouver BT, #400, 999 Canada Place, BC V6C 3C1 – 604/681-2111; Fax: 604/681-0437 – Managing Director, Darcy Rezac

Vanderhoof District CC, PO Box 126, BC V0J 3A0 – 250/567-2124; Fax: 250/567-3316 – Manager, Paula Walbauer

Greater Vernon CC, 3700 - 33 St., BC V1T 5T6 – 250/545-0771; Fax: 250/545-3114 – Manager, Kathryn Arkell

Greater Victoria CC, 525 Fort St., BC V8W 1E8 – 250/383-7191; Fax: 250/385-3552; Email: gterrell@pinc.com; URL: http://vvv.com/Chamber – President, Myrna Borleske

Wells - Barkerville CC, PO Box 26, BC V0K 2R0 – 250/994-2332; Fax: 250/994-3451 – President, Claire Kujundzie

West Vancouver CC, 775 - 15th St., BC V7T 2S9 – 604/926-6614; Fax: 604/926-6436 – Manager, Janice Hlynski

Westbank & District CC, 2375 Pamela Rd., PO Box 26022, BC V4T 2G3 – 250/768-3378; Fax: 250/768-3465 – Manager, Trish Sol

Whistler CC, PO Box 181, BC V0N 1B0 – 604/932-5528; Fax: 604/932-3755; URL: http://www.whistler.net/coc/index.html – Manager, Thelma Johnstone

White Rock & South Surrey CC, 15150 Russell Ave., BC V4B 2P5 – 604/536-6844; Fax: 604/536-4994; Email: whiterock@chambernet.bc.ca; URL: http://www.our-town.bc.ca – President, Bill Reid

Williams Lake & District CC, 1148 Broadway South, BC V2G 1A4 – 250/392-5025; Fax: 250/392-4214; Email: wldcc@stardate.bc.ca – President, Ken Wilson

Zeballos BT, PO Box 208, BC V0P 2A0 – 250/761-4090; Fax: 250/761-4097 – President, Tom Weston

**MANITOBA**

Arborg CC, PO Box 415, MB R0C 0A0 – 204/376-5233; Fax: 204/376-5234 – President, Herman Palsson

Ashern CC, PO Box 582, MB R0C 0E0 – 204/768-2899; Fax: 204/768-2046 – Manager, Shelley Bjornson

Beausejour CC, PO Box 224, MB R0E 0C0 – 204/268-1906; Fax: 204/268-3531 – President, Reg Black

Birtle & District CC, PO Box 278, MB R0M 0C0 – 204/842-5250; Fax: 204/842-3349 – President, Woody Langford

Boissevain CC, PO Box 953, MB R0K 0E0 – 204/534-6400; Fax: 204/534-7188 – President, Murray Fingus

Brandon CC, 1043 Rosser Ave., MB R7A 0L5 – 204/727-5431; Fax: 204/727-2040 – General Manager, Lee Jebb

Carberry CC, PO Box 101, MB R0K 0H0 – 204/834-2353; Fax: 204/834-3073 – President, Mary-Ann Baron

Carman & Community CC, PO Box 249, MB R0G 0J0 – 204/745-3741; Fax: 204/745-6348 – Manager, Ron Funk

Churchill CC, PO Box 176, MB R0B 0E0 – 204/675-8881; Fax: 204/675-2643 – President, Bob Penwarden

Crystal City CC, PO Box 56, MB R0K 0N0 – 204/873-2499; Fax: 204/873-2450 – President, Henry Harms

Dauphin CC, 21C - 3 Ave. NE, MB R7N 1C1 – 204/638-4838; Fax: 204/638-08795790 – Manager, Darlene Pushkarenico

Deloraine CC, PO Box 748, MB R0M 0M0 – 204/747-2003; Fax: 204/747-2927 – President, Craig Adams

Elie CC, PO Box 175, MB R0H 0H0 – 204/353-2543; Fax: 204/353-2286 – President, Colin Vann

Emerson CC, Town Hall, PO Box 339, MB R0A 0L0 – 204/373-2732; Fax: 204/373-2599 – President, Menno Zacharias

Erickson CC, PO Box 188, MB R0J 0P0 – 204/636-2925; Fax: 204/636-7789 – President, Bev Turnball

Eriksdale & District CC, PO Box 434, MB R0C 0W0 – 204/739-5563; Fax: 204/739-2073 – President, Al Kelner

Falcon/West Hawk CC, Falcon Beach MB R0E 0N0 – Fax: 204/349-8450

Flin Flon & District CC, 84 Church St., PO Box 806, MB R8A 0A6 – 204/687-4518; Fax: 204/687-4456 – President, Darren Laval

Gladstone CC, PO Box 563, MB R0J 0T0 – 204/385-3125; Fax: 204/385-2860 – President, Richard Beastall

Grunthal CC, PO Box 451, MB R0A 0R0 – 204/434-6270; Fax: 204/434-6970 – President, Jake Friesen

Hamiota CC, PO Box 430, MB R0M 0T0 – 204/764-2801; Fax: 204/764-2568 – President, Shirley Dale

Hartney & District CC, PO Box 224, MB R0M 0X0 – 204/858-2277; Fax: 204/858-2340 – President, Brenda Hicks

Headingley CC, 5434 Portage Ave., MB R4H 1G2 – 204/889-5074; Fax: 204/897-5277 – Office Manager, Audrey Hedley

Killarney CC, PO Box 809, MB R0K 1C0 – 204/523-4236; Fax: 204/523-7117 – President, Bill Janz

La Broquerie CC, PO Box 309, MB R0A 0W0 – 204/424-5551; Fax: 204/424-5552 – President, Annette Tetrault

La Salle & District CC, PO Box 603, MB R0G 1B0 – 204/736-4134; Fax: 204/736-4576 – President, Terrance Petty

Lac du Bonnet & District CC, PO Box 598, MB R0E 1A0 – 204/345-6846; Fax: 204/345-8694 – President, Rita Lansard

Leaf Rapids CC, PO Box 26, MB R0B 1W0 – 204/473-2423; Fax: 204/473-2288 – President, Barbara Bloodworth

Lorette CC, PO Box 87, MB R0A 0Y0 – 204/878-2458; Fax: 204/878-9596 – President, Robert Plett

Lynn Lake CC, PO Box 900, MB R0B 0W0 – 204/356-8444; Fax: 204/356-2940 – President, Cathie Watson

MacGregor CC, PO Box 357, MB R0H 0R0 – 204/685-2862; Fax: 204/685-2631 – Executive Director, Clare Tarr

Melita CC, PO Box 666, MB R0M 1L0 – 204/522-3215; Fax: 204/522-3176 – President, Irv Skelton

Morris CC, PO Box 98, MB R0G 1K0 – 204/746-2391; Fax: 204/746-2243 – President, Del Stevenson

Neepawa & District CC, PO Box 726, MB R0J 1H0 – 204/476-5292; Fax: 204/476-5231; Email: neepawa@mail.techplus.com – Manager, Angela Pearen

Notre Dame CC, PO Box 107, Notre Dame de Lourdes MB R0G 1M0 – 204/248-2332; Fax: 204/248-2281 – President, Maurice Boisvert, Jr.

Pansy CC, General Delivery, Zhoda MB R0A 2P0 – 204/425-3434 – President, Jake Wall

Pilot Mound CC, PO Box 356, MB R0G 1P0 – 204/825-2313; Fax: 204/825-2313 – President, E.J. Collins

Portage & District CC, 11 - 2nd St. NE, Portage La Prairie MB R1N 1R8 – 204/857-7778; Fax: 204/857-4095; Email: plpchamb@cpnet.net – President, Barry Greenberg

Rivers & District CC, PO Box 795, MB R0K 1X0 – 204/328-7491; Fax: 204/328-7944 – President, Wally Hillier

Roblin CC, PO Box 729, MB R0L 1P0 – 204/937-2248; Fax: 204/937-8302 – President, Larry Mills

Rossburn & District CC, PO Box 579, MB R0G 1V0 – 204/859-2636; Fax: 204/859-2696 – President, Darrell Drul

Russell CC, PO Box 155, MB R0J 1W0 – 204/773-2456; Fax: 204/773-3235 – Secretary-Manager, Viola Coulter

Assiniboia CC, PO Box 42122, RPO Ferry Rd., Winnipeg MB R3J 3X7 – 204/774-4154; Fax: 204/774-4201; Email: st.chamber@accel.ca – President, Doug Sewell

Ste Rose & District CC, PO Box 688, Ste Rose du Lac MB R0L 1S0 – 204/447-2621; Fax: 204/447-2442; Email: ececchin@mb.sympatico.ca – President, Gil Dion

Selkirk CC, 200 Eaton, PO Box 89, MB R1A 2B1 – 204/482-7176; Fax: 204/482-5448 – President, George Hacking

Shoal Lake & District CC, PO Box 511, MB R0J 1Z0 – 204/759-2340; Fax: 204/759-2835 – President, Dan Szwaluk

Somerset CC, PO Box 187, MB R0G 1L0 – 204/744-2171; Fax: 204/744-2836

Souris & Glenwood CC, PO Box 939, MB R0K 2C0 – 204/483-2155 – President, Shelley Ross

St. Boniface CC, #2, 157 Provencher Blvd., Winnipeg MB R2H 0G2 – 204/235-1406; Fax: 204/233-8122 – President, Gabriel L. Forest

* BT - Board of Trade; BC - Bureau de commerce; CC - Chamber of Commerce/Chambre de commerce

St Claude CC, PO Box 334, MB R0G 1Z0 – 204/379-2413; Fax: 204/379-2413 – President, Giles Chappelaz

St Pierre CC, 515 Jolys Ave. East, St Pierre Jolys MB R0A 1V0 – 204/433-7911; Fax: 204/433-7621 – President, Lucien Nayet

Starbuck CC, PO Box 117, MB R0G 2P0 – 204/735-2462; Fax: 204/735-2748 – President, Mark Morse

Steinbach CC, PO Box 1795, MB R0A 2A0 – 204/326-9566; Fax: 204/326-4171 – Manager, Linda Burdett

Stonewall CC, PO Box 762, MB R0C 2Z0 – 204/467-8377; Fax: 204/467-2265 – President, Shelley Stewart

Swan River CC, PO Box 1540, MB R0L 1Z0 – 204/734-3102; Fax: 204/734-4342 – President, Kevin Neely

The Pas & District CC, PO Box 996, MB R9A 1L1 – 204/623-7256; Fax: 204/623-7256 – President, Jeff Russenholt

Thompson CC, 162 Princeton Dr., MB R8N 2A4 – 204/677-4155; Fax: 204/677-3434 – Manager, Paul Legault

Treherne CC, PO Box 344, MB R0G 2V0 – 204/723-2610; Fax: 204/723-2050 – President, Shayne Gibson

Teulon CC, PO Box 353, MB R0C 3B0 – 204/886-2084; Fax: 204/886-2315 – President, Chris Dawson

Virden CC, PO Box 899, MB R0M 2C0 – 204/747-3955; Fax: 204/748-2501 – President, Larry Wright

Wasagaming CC, PO Box 222, MB R0J 2H0 – 204/848-2742; Fax: 204/848-2149 – President, Bev Gowler

Waskada CC, PO Box 160, MB R0M 2E0 – 204/673-2522; Fax: 204/673-2535 – President, Gary Williams

Whitemouth CC, PO Box 189, MB R0E 2G0 – 204/348-7631; Fax: 204/348-7150 – President, Brian McDougald

Winkler CC, #335, 185 Main St., MB R6W 4B1 – 204/325-9758; Fax: 204/325-5915 – President, Robert Jones

Pinawa CC, PO Box 698, Winnipeg MB R0E 1L0 – 204/753-2674 – President, Allan Cassidy

Winnipeg CC, #500, 167 Lombard Ave., MB R3B 3E5 – 204/944-8484; Fax: 204/944-8492; Email: wcoc@escape.ca; URL: http://www.winnipegchmbr.mb.ca – President, Shelley Morris

#### NEW BRUNSWICK

Baie-Ste-Anne CC, RR#2, NB E0C 1A0 – 506/228-4405; Fax: 506/228-3711 – Director, Alphonse Turbide

Bath CC, PO Box 87, NB E0J 1E0 – 506/278-5213; Fax: 506/278-5963 – Director, Michael Blanchard

Bathurst CC, 275 Main St., NB E2A 1A9 – 506/548-8498; Fax: 506/548-1127 – President, Vern Card, 506/545-6416, Fax: 506/546-5205, Email: d2000@dige2000.com

Beresford CC, PO Box 599, NB E0B 1H0 – 506/546-4902; Fax: 506/542-1880 – President, Gilberte Pitre, 506/542-9406

CC de Bertrand, NB E0B 1J0 – President, Yves Thériault, 506/727-7494

CC de Bertrand, NB E0B 1J0 – Président, Yves Thériault

Blackville CC, PO Box 208, NB E0C 1C0 – President, Leroy Stewart, 506/843-6609, Fax: 506/843-6737

Bouctouche CC, PO Box 338, Buctouche NB E0A 1G0 – 506/743-2411; Fax: 506/743-8991 – President, Jacques Bourque, 506/743-5622

Campbellton CC, PO Box 234, NB E3N 3G4 – 506/753-7856; Fax: 506/759-7557 – Executive Director, Suzanne Matte

CC de la région de Cap-Pelé, CP 699, NB E0A 1J0 – 506/577-6704; Fax: 506/577-2880 – Président, Hector Doiron, Email: doiron@atcon.com

CC de Caraquet, 138, boul St-Pierre ouest, NB E1W 1B6 – Président, Claudette Gingras, 506/727-3162, Fax: 506/727-4117

Centreville CC, PO Box 147, NB E0J 1H0 – President, Randy McDougall, 506/276-4567, Fax: 506/276-4380

Greater Miramichi CC, PO Box 250, Chatham NB E1N 3A5 – 506/622-2345; Fax: 506/622-0917 – President, Roy Innes

CC de Cocagne & Notre-Dame, RR#1, Boite 19, Site 1, NB E0A 1K0 – 506/576-6126 – Président, Adrien Léger

Collette CC, RR#3, Boite 9, Site 18, Rogersville NB E0A 2T0 – Président, Maurice DesRoches, 506/622-0752, Fax: 506/622-0477

Dalhousie Region CC, PO Box 1295, NB E0K 1B0 – President, Dr. Marc Levesque, 506/684-2747

East Regional CC, PO Box 149, Dalhousie NB E0K 1B0 – President, Paul Hayes, 506/684-3337, Fax: 506/684-4717

Eastern Charlotte CC, General Delivery, St. George NB E0G 1Y0 – President, Irene Wright, 506/456-3951, Fax: 506/456-2509

Eastern New Brunswick CC, PO Box 1030, Newcastle NB E1V 3V5 – 506/855-8579; Fax: 506/862-8351 – President, Claude Babineau

Edmundston CC, 74, ch Canada, NB E3V 1V5 – 506/737-1866; Fax: 506/737-1862 – Executive Director, Joanne Bérubé-Gagné

Kennebecassis Village CC, 115 Old Hampton Rd., Fairvale NB E2E 2P9 – President, Mike Cole, 506/849-1790, Fax: 506/849-1851

Florenceville CC, PO Box 236, NB E0J 1K0 – 506/392-5590; Fax: 506/392-6819 – President, Marg Hunter-Papineau

Fredericton CC, PO Box 275, NB E3B 4Y9 – 506/458-8006; Fax: 506/451-1119; Email: fchamber@nbnet.nb.ca; URL: http://www.discribe.ca/chamber/ – General Manager, Krista A. Hamilton

Gagetown CC, PO Box 194, NB E0G 1V0 – President, Ron Samuels, 506/488-2249, Fax: 506/488-3188

Grand Falls & District CC, PO Box 1509, NB E3Z 1C8 – 506/473-1905; Fax: 506/473-9091 – President, Sylvie Daigle, 506/473-3276

Grand Manan CC, PO Box 110, Grand Harbour NB E0G 1X0 – 506/662-3432 – President, John Large

Grand-Digue CC, Grande-Digue NB E0A 2S0 – Secrétaire, Anne-Marie Bourque

Hampton Area CC, PO Box 329, NB E0G 1Z0 – President, Guy Bernard, 506/832-7042, Fax: 832-3353

Inkerman CC, CP 119, NB E0B 1S9 – 506/336-8540 – Présidente, Edith Robichaud

Lameque CC, CP 113, NB E0B 1V0 – 506/344-2217; Fax: 506/344-5380 – Président, Roger Noel

CC de Maisonnette, CP 261, NB E0B 1X0 – Président, Yves Godin

McAdam-Harvey CC, PO Box 411, NB E0H 1K0 – 506/784-3575; Fax: 506/784-3575 – President, Bernadette Lam

Miramichi BT, Boiestown NB E0H 1A0 – 506/369-7127 – President, Cal Copeland

Greater Moncton CC, #100, 910 Main St., NB E1C 1G6 – 506/853-1970; Fax: 506/853-8454 – President, Levi Clain, Q.C.

CC de Neguac, NB E0C 1S0 – Président, Arthur Savoie

Oromocto & Area CC, PO Box 21009, NB E2V 2G5 – President, Robin L. Hanson, 506/446-6824, Fax: 506/446-6828

Perth-Andover CC, PO Box 896, NB E0J 1V0 – 506/273-2276; Fax: 506/273-2033 – President, Danny McCarthy, 506/273-4663, Fax: 506/273-4351

CC de Petite Rivière de l'Île, CP 108, Shippagan NB E0B 2P0 – 506/336-8357 – Présidente, Emilia Lanteigne

Plaster Rock Regional CC, NB E0G 1W0 – 506/356-8522 – President, Molly Ashworth

CC de Pointe-Sapin, General Delivery, NB E0A 2A0 – 506/876-3855 – President, Anne Kelly

Richibucto CC, PO Box 670, NB E0A 2M0 – 506/523-4342; Fax: 506/523-6362 – Président, Robert Robichaud

River Valley CC, PO Box 707, Grand Bay NB E0G 1W0 – 506/738-8666; Fax: 506/738-3697 – President, Diane Bormke

CC de Rivière-du-Portage, CP 127, NB E0C 1Y0 – Président, Alice Thibodeau, 506/395-5208

CC de Rogersville, CP 168, NB E0A 2T0 – 506/775-6738; Fax: 506/775-6002; Email: cormierc@nbnet.nb.ca – Président, Cyrille Cormier

Greater Sackville CC, 22A Lansdowne St., NB E0A 3C0 – 506/364-8911; Fax: 506/364-8082; Email: gscc@nbnet.nb.ca – Executive Director, Diane Fullerton

St. Andrews CC, PO Box 89, NB E0G 2X0 – 506/529-3555; Fax: 506/529-8095; Email: townsrch@nbnet.nb.ca – Executive Director, Susan Corbyn

CC de Sainte-Anne-de-Madawaska, CP 390, NB E0L 1G0 – 506/445-2275; Fax: 506/445-2045 – Président, Reynald Roy

CC de Saint-Antoine, 218, rue Principale, Saint-Antoine-de-Kent NB E0A 2X0 – 506/525-2768; Fax: 506/523-9131 – President, Gilles Lemieux

CC de Saint-François, CP 378, Saint-François-de-Madawaska NB E7A 1G4 – 506/992-3362; Fax: 506/992-3930 – Président, Serge Boulet

Saint John BT, PO Box 6037, NB E2L 4R5 – 506/634-8111; Fax: 506/632-2008; Email: sjbtrade@nbnet.nb.ca – President, Tom Creamer, 506/634-8787, Fax: 506/634-0565

CC régionale de St-Léonard, 725, rue Principale, NB E0L 1M0 – 506/423-7847 – Président, Paul Abud

CC de Saint-Louis-de-Kent, NB E0A 1Z0 – 506/743-2422; Fax: 506/743-1033 – Présidente, Bernard Landry

CC de Saint-Quentin Inc., CP 1116, NB E0K 1J0 – 506/235-3666; Fax: 506/235-1804 – Président, Florent Pelletier

CC de St-Raphaël/Pigeon Hill, CP 117, St-Raphaël-sur-Mer NB E0B 2N0 – 506/336-2329 – Secrétaire, Humbert Savoie

CC de St-Simon, École des pêches, NB E0B 1L0 – 506/727-6531 – Président, Édard Albert

St. Stephen Area CC, PO Box 206, NB E3L 2X3 – 506/466-6292; Fax: 506/466-3577 – President, Maria Kulcher, 506/466-5519, Fax: 506/466-5558

Shediac & Area BT, c/o Frenette's Funeral Home, 248 Main St., NB E0A 3G0 – 506/532-3297 – President, Ives Frenette

CC de Shippagan, CP 201, NB E0B 2P0 – Président, Ivan Robichaud

Sussex & District CC, PO Box 1317, NB E0E 1P0 – 506/433-3429; Fax: 506/433-3623 – President, Pam Folkins

Campobello CC, General Delivery, Wilsons Beach NB E0G 3L0 – President, Gordon Phillips, 506/752-2233

Woodstock CC, PO Box 26, NB E0J 2B0 – President, Rob Van Dien, 506/328-4873, Fax: 506/328-4894

York North CC, PO Box 695, Nackawic NB E0H 1P0 – 506/575-9622; Fax: 506/575-2075; Email: ryansgre@nbnet.nb.ca – President, Greg MacFarlane

#### NEWFOUNDLAND

Argentia Area CC, PO Box 272, Placentia NF A0B 2Y0 – 709/227-5396; Fax: 709/227-5731 – President, Gary Hynes

Arnold's Cove & Area CC, PO Box 204, NF A0B 1A0 – 709/463-8505; Fax: 709/463-2499 – President, Keith Wareham

Baccalieu Trails CC, PO Box 29, Winterton NF A0B 3M0 – 709/749-6206; Fax: 709/583-2093 – General Manager, Peter Hiscock

Baie Verte CC, PO Box 578, NF A0K 1B0 – President, Kevin Thistle, 709/532-4646, Fax: 709/532-8310

Bay d'Espoir CC, PO Box 66, St Albans NF A0H 2E0 – 709/538-3552; Fax: 709/538-3439 – President, Tracey Perry

Bay St. George CC, PO Box 478, Stephenville NF A2N 3A3 – 709/643-5629 – President, Reginald Dawson

Bell Island CC, General Delivery, NF A0A 4H0 – 709/488-2912 – Secretary, Brian Burke

Bishop's Falls CC, PO Box 940, NF A0H 1C0 – 709/258-5404; Fax: 709/258-5404 – President, Tom MacDonald

Botwood CC, PO Box 1000, NF A0H 1E0 – 709/257-3656; Fax: 709/257-2628 – President, Brian Flood

Channel-Port-aux-Basques CC, PO Box 1389, NF A0M 1C0 – 709/695-3688; Fax: 709/695-7925 – President, Gary O'Brien

Clarenville Area CC, PO Box 834, NF A0E 1J0 – 709/466-3296; Fax: 709/466-1373 – President, Gary Decker, 709/466-2394, Fax: 709/466-2569

Conception Bay South CC, PO Box 951, Manuels NF A1W 1N4 – President, Richard Smith, 709/834-3838, Fax: 709/834-1437

Corner Brook CC, PO Box 475, NF A2H 6E6 – 709/634-5831; Fax: 709/639-9792; Email: cbcc@atcon.com – Executive Director, C. Whiteway

Deer Lake CC, PO Box 57, NF A0K 2E0 – 709/635-2451; Fax: 709/635-5857 – President, Charles McCarthy

Exploits Regional CC, PO Box 272, Grand Falls-Windsor NF A2A 2J7 – 709/489-7512; Fax: 709/489-7532 – Executive Director, Sean Cooper, Email: cooper@thezone.net

Gander & Area CC, 109 Trans Canada Hwy., NF A1V 1P6 – 709/256-7110; Fax: 709/256-4080 – General Manager, Gerald L. Gray

Harbour Breton CC, PO Box 102, NF A0H 1P0 – 709/885-2317; Fax: 709/885-2317 – President, Doreen Vallis

Harbour Grace BT, PO Box 284, NF A0A 2M0 – 709/596-5192; Fax: 709/579-4304 – President, David Weeks, 709/596-2171, Fax: 709/596-4304

Labrador West CC, PO Box 273, Labrador City NF A2V 2K5 – 709/944-3723; Fax: 709/944-5383 – President, Dr. Frank Manstan

Labrador North CC, PO Box 460, Stn B, Happy Valley-Goose Bay NF A0P 1E0 – 709/896-2421; Fax: 709/896-5028 – President, Peter Woodward

Lewisporte & Area CC, PO Box 953, NF A0G 3A0 – 709/535-2840; Fax: 709/535-2482; Email: lacc@cancom.net – President, Cluney Sheppard, 709/535-8691, Fax: 709/535-2133

Marystown-Burin Area CC, PO Box 728, NF A0E 2M0 – 709/279-2080; Fax: 709/279-2080 – President, Russel J. Murphy

Mount Pearl CC, 64 Commonwealth Ave., NF A1N 1WB – 709/364-8513; Fax: 709/364-8500; Email: mtpchmber@nlnet.nf.ca – President, Cheryl Rodd, 709/745-3929

St. John's BT, 66 Kenmount Rd., PO Box 5127, NF A1C 5V5 – 709/726-2961; Fax: 709/726-2003 – General Manager, Bruce J. Tilley

Springdale CC, PO Box 37, NF A0J 1T0 – President, John Warr, 709/673-3925, Fax: 709/673-3920

St. Anthony CC, PO Box 191, St Anthony NF A0K 4S0 – President, Berry Bromley, 709/454-2191, Fax: 709/454-3718, Email: bebbltd@terra.nlnet.nf.ca

**NORTHWEST TERRITORIES**

Keewatin CC, PO Box 238, Baker Lake NT X0C 0A0 – 819/793-2319; Fax: 819/793-2310 – President, Glenn McLean

Nunavut CC, PO Box 238, Baker Lake NT X0C 0A0 – 819/793-2319; Fax: 819/793-2310 – President, Glenn McLean

Kitikmeot CC, PO Box 92, Cambridge Bay NT X0E 0C0 – 403/983-2331; Fax: 403/983-2043 – President, Lyle Hawkins

Fort Simpson CC, PO Box 563, NT X0E 0N0 – 403/695-3555; Fax: 403/695-3313 – Economic Development Officer, Sean Whelly

Fort Smith CC, PO Box 121, NT X0E 0P0 – 403/872-2155; Fax: 403/872-5311 – President, Geoff Stock

Hay River CC, 10K Gagnier St., NT X0E 1G1 – 403/874-5248; Fax: 403/874-5251 – President, Andrew Nelson

Beaufort Delta Board of Tourism & Trade, PO Box 2600, Inuvik NT X0E 0T0 – 403/979-2705; Fax: 403/979-3090 – President, Robert Cook

Baffin Regional CC, PO Box 59, Iqaluit NT X0A 0H0 – 819/979-2802; Fax: 819/979-0164 – President, Rhoda Arreak

Iqaluit CC, PO Box 1107, NT X0A 0H0 – 819/979-3400; Fax: 819/979-3400 – President, Alain Carriere

Kugluktuk CC, PO Box 277, NT X0E 0E0 – 403/982-3001; Fax: 403/982-3021 – President, Randy Mulder

Norman Wells CC, PO Box 400, NT X0E 0V0 – 403/587-2559; Fax: 403/587-2821 – President, Kevin Diebold

Yellowknife CC, #6, 4807 - 49 St., NT X1A 3T5 – 403/920-4944; Fax: 403/920-4640 – Executive Director, Cheryl Best

**NOVA SCOTIA**

Amherst CC, PO Box 283, NS B4H 3Z4 – 902/667-8186; Fax: 902/667-4490; Email: amchmbr@atcon.com – President, Steve Hatcher, 902/667-7358, Fax: 902/667-8180

Annapolis Royal BT, PO Box 2, NS B0S 1A0 – 902/532-7404; Fax: 902/532-7346 – President, John Stevens

Annapolis Valley Affiliated Boards of Trade, PO Box 1149, Middleton NS B0S 1P0 – 902/825-4344; Fax: 902/825-4634 – President, Marc Blinn, 902/769-3300, Fax: 1-800-769-0109

Antigonish CC, PO Box 1626, NS B2G 2L8 – 902/863-6308; Fax: 902/863-6308 – President, Joeanne Mahoney, 902/863-4754, Fax: 902/863-1805

Barrington Area CC, PO Box 110, NS B0W 1E0 – 902/745-2109; Fax: 902/745-1309 – President, Bruce M. Atkinson

Bear River BT, General Delivery, NS B0S 1B0 – 902/467-3808; Fax: 902/467-3808 – President, Brian Reynolds

Berwick & District BT, PO Box 664, NS B0P 1E0 – 902/538-9373; Fax: 902/847-3139 – President, Ken Pineo

Bridgetown BT, PO Box 467, NS B0S 1C0 – 902/665-2825 – President, Joanne Acker

Bridgewater & Area CC, PO Box 100, NS B4V 2W8 – 902/543-4263; Fax: 902/688-2399; Email: bwaterch@atcon.com – President, Peter Bessey, 902/543-8176, Fax: 902/543-1548

Canso & Area BT, PO Box 235, NS B0H 1H0 – 902/533-2197; Fax: 902/533-3822 – President, Frank X. Fraser

Industrial Cape Breton BT, 140 Pitt St., PO Box 131, Sydney NS B1P 6G9 – 902/564-6453; Fax: 902/539-7487 – President, Avvie Druker

Chester Municipal CC, PO Box 831, NS B0J 1J0 – 902/457-7786; Fax: 902/275-2125 – President, Ross DeMont

CC de Clare, CP 35, Church Point NS B0W 1M0 – 902/769-2040; Fax: 902/645-2861 – Présidente, Elaine Thimot, Email: jodrey@marina.istar.ca

Digby & Area BT, PO Box 641, NS B0V 1A0 – 902/245-5558; Fax: 902/245-6525 – President, Geraldine Costa

East Hants CC, PO Box 76, Milford Station NS B0N 1Y0 – 902/758-4257; Fax: 902/758-4257 – President, Paul Roderick

Grand Narrows & District BT, PO Box 149, Iona NS B0A 1L0 – 902/725-2843 – President, Fonce Farrell

Metropolitan Halifax CC, PO Box 8990, NS B3K 5M6 – 902/468-7111; Fax: 902/468-7333 – President, Bill Black, 902/453-7045, Fax: 902/453-7060

Kentville & Area BT, PO Box 314, NS B4N 3X1 – 902/678-2157; Fax: 902/678-9455 – President, Alan T. Tufts

Lunenburg BT, PO Box 1300, NS B0J 2C0 – 902/634-8800; Fax: 902/634-9499 – President, Edgar Blinn

United Mosers River BT, RR#2, NS B0J 2K0 – 902/347-2039; Fax: 902/347-2498 – President, Dennis Sharpe

Mulgrave & Area CC, PO Box 3, Port Hawkesbury NS B0E 2G0 – 902/625-0803 – Secretary, Ray Carpenter

Musquodoboit Harbour & District BT, PO Box 64, NS B0T 1B0 – 902/889-2752; Fax: 902/889-2362 – President, Robert Stevens

Pictou County CC, East River Plaza, 980 East River Rd., New Glasgow NS B2H 3S5 – 902/755-3463; Fax: 902/755-2848; Email: pccc@north.nsis.com; URL: http://www.nsis.com/CofC – Executive Director, Barrie MacMillan

North Queens BT, PO Box 183, Caledonia NS B0T 1B0 – 902/682-2535 – President, David Crooker

Northside CC, 84 Pleasant St., North Sydney NS B2A 1L6 – 902/736-1211 – President, Stephen MacAdam

Parrsboro & District BT, PO Box 297, NS B0M 1S0 – 902/254-3266; Fax: 902/254-2822 – President, Rick Brodie, 902/254-3881, Fax: 902/254-2588

Strait Area CC, PO Box 441, Port Hawkesbury NS B0E 2V0 – 902/625-1588; Fax: 902/625-5985; Email: sacoc@atcon.com; URL: http://www.atcon.com/~sacoc/ – Executive Director, Ellen Cecchetto

Preston & Area BT, PO Box 3412, Dartmouth NS B2W 5G3 – 902/435-7211; Fax: 902/434-4615 – President, Spencer Colley, 902/464-2610

Riverport & District BT, c/o Deli Seafoods, NS B0J 2R0 – 902/766-4820 – President, Lynn Boone

Sheet Harbour BT, PO Box 239, NS B0J 3B0 – 902/885-2147 – President, Reg Dooks, 902/885-3477, Fax: 902/885-3488

Shelburne & Area CC, PO Box 189, NS B0T 1W0 – 902/875-1133; Fax: 902/875-4199 – President, Sharon Christie, 902/875-1515, Fax: 902/875-2187

South Queens CC, PO Box 1378, Liverpool NS B0T 1K0 – 902/354-7105; Fax: 902/354-2424 – President, Dan Swansburg, Email: sqchambr@atcon.com

Springhill CC, PO Box 1030, NS B0M 1X0 – 902/597-2429; Fax: 902/597-2967 – President, Robert Gilroy

Northumberland CC, PO Box 279, Tatamagouche NS B0K 1V0 – 902/657-2223; Fax: 902/657-3600 – President, Marjorie Mattatall

Tiverton & District BT, PO Box 694, NS B0V 1G0 – 902/839-2687 – President, W. Outhouse

Truro & District CC, PO Box 54, NS B2N 5B6 – 902/895-6328; Fax: 902/897-6641; Email: tdcoc@atcon.com – Managing Director, Bob Baxter

Windsor & District BT, PO Box 2188, NS B0N 2T0 – 902/798-4461; Fax: 902/798-0021 – President, Brian Watling, 902/798-8666, Fax: 902/798-8686

Yarmouth CC, PO Box 532, NS B5A 4B4 – 902/742-3074; Fax: 902/749-1383; Email: ycc@atcon.com – President, Andy Nickerson

**ONTARIO**

Ajax-Pickering BT, #223, 1099 Kingston Rd., ON L1V 1B5 – 905/837-6638; Fax: 905/837-1629 – Board Secretary, Lesley Whyte

Alliston & District CC, PO Box 32, ON L9R 1W5 – 705/435-7921; Fax: 705/435-1106 – General Manager, D. Gaston

Angus CC, PO Box 792, ON L0M 1B0 – 705/424-2424 – Sec.-Treas., L. Kremer

Arthur & District CC, PO Box 519, ON N0G 1A0 – 519/848-5603; Fax: 519/848-3849; Email: arthur@freespace.net; URL: http://www.freespace.net/~arthur – Past President, Brian Cooper

Athens District CC, PO Box 543, ON K0E 1B0 – 613/924-9141; Fax: 613/924-9901 – Kathryn Hudson

Atwood & District CC, 217 Main St., PO Box 10, ON N0G 1B0 – 519/356-2216; Fax: 519/356-2832 – Manager, Neil Cockwell

* BT - Board of Trade; BC - Bureau de commerce; CC - Chamber of Commerce/Chambre de commerce

Aurora CC, Aurora Shopping Centre, 14483 Yonge St., PO Box 28539, ON L4G 6S6 – 905/727-7262; Fax: 905/841-6217 – General Manager, Rosalyn Gonsalves

Baden & District CC, PO Box 130, ON N0B 1G0 – Sec.-Treas., H. Schmidt

Bancroft & District CC, PO Box 539, ON K0L 1C0 – 613/332-1513; Fax: 613/332-2119; Email: chamber@commerce.bancroft.on.ca; URL: http://www.commerce.bancroft.on.ca – General Manager, Gordon MacKey

Greater Barrie CC, 89 Dunlop St. East, ON L4M 1A7 – 705/721-5000; Fax: 705/726-0973 – Executive Director, Wanda D. Collison

Beaver Valley CC, PO Box 477, Thornbury ON N0H 2P0 – 519/599-5591; Fax: 519/599-2055 – Secretary, Patricia Irish

Beaverton District CC, 412 Bay St., PO Box 699, ON L0K 1A0 – 705/426-9061; Fax: 705/426-4378 – President, J. Hudson

Belleville & District CC, 5 Moira St., PO Box 726, ON K8N 5B3 – 613/962-4597; Fax: 613/962-3911; Email: chamber@city.belleville.on.ca; URL: http://www.city.belleville.on.ca/chamber/ – General Manager, R. Broadbridge

Black River-Matheson CC, 365 MacDougal Ave., PO Box 494, ON P0K 1N0 – 705/273-2475; Fax: 705/273-2340 – President, J. Barber

Blenheim & District CC, 35 Talbot St., PO Box 1353, ON N0P 1A0 – Administrative Secretary, B. Gander

Blind River CC, PO Box 9, ON P0R 1B0 – 705/356-1579

Bobcaygeon & Area CC, 123 East St. South, PO Box 388, ON K0M 1A0 – 705/738-2202; Fax: 705/738-1534; Toll Free: 1-800-318-6173 – Office Manager, Cindy Snider

Bracebridge CC, 1-1 Manitoba St., ON P1L 1S4 – 705/645-5231; Fax: 705/645-7592; Email: bracecha@muskoka.com – General Manager, Leslie E. Talbot

Bradford & District CC, PO Box 59, ON L3Z 2A7 – 905/775-3037; Fax: 905/775-6752 – General Manager, C. Servant

The Brampton BT, #504, 8 Nelson St. West, ON L6X 4J2 – 905/451-1122; Fax: 905/450-0295; URL: http://www.bramptonbot.com – General Manager, E. Moyer

Brantford Regional CC, 77 Charlotte St., PO Box 1294, ON N3T 5T6 – 519/753-2617; Fax: 519/753-0921 – Executive Vice-President, Anne Buchanan

Brockville & District CC, Block House Island, PO Box 1341, ON K9V 5Y6 – 613/342-6553; Fax: 613/342-6849 – Executive Director, P. Dunn

Burlington CC, 3385 Harvester Rd., ON L7N 3N2 – 905/639-0174; Fax: 905/333-3956; Email: bcc@wchat.on.ca; URL: http://www.worldchat.com/commercial/commerce/ – Executive Director, Scott McCammon

Caledon CC, Courtyards of Caledon, 33 King St. West, PO Box 626, Bolton ON L7E 5T5 – 905/857-7393; Fax: 905/857-7405 – General Manager, P. Pasanen

Caledonia Regional CC, PO Box 2035, ON N3W 2G6 – 905/765-0377; Fax: 905/765-4409 – President, D. Britton

Cambridge CC, 531 King St. East, ON N3H 3N4 – 519/653-1424; Fax: 519/653-1734 – Executive Director, K.M. Thompson

Carleton Place & District CC, 175 Bridge St., PO Box 301, ON K7C 3P4 – 613/257-1976; Fax: 613/257-8170; Email: carlpl@fox.nstn.ca; URL: http://www.town.carleton-place.on.ca – Manager, Jackie Cowlin

Cayuga & District CC, PO Box 118, ON N0A 1E0 – 905/772-3978; Fax: 905/772-3037 – Secretary, M. Hanrath

Chatham & District CC, 235 King St. West, ON N7M 1E6 – 519/352-7540; Fax: 519/352-8741; URL: http://www.ciaccess.com/~chat11/cdcc/homepage.htm – General Manager, G.A. Antaya

Cobourg & District CC, Dressler House, 212 King St. West, ON K9A 2N1 – 905/372-5831; Fax: 905/372-2411; Toll Free: 1-800-262-6874; Email: cobourg-cofc@eagle.ca; URL: http://marlo.eagle.ca/cobourg/chamber/ – Manager, Carol A. Farren

Cochrane BT, PO Box 1468, ON P0L 1C0 – 705/272-4926; Fax: 705/272-3026 – Sec.-Treas., Lynne Duquette

Collingwood CC, 155 Hurontario St., ON L9Y 2M1 – 705/445-0221; Fax: 705/445-6858 – President, P. Morrocco

Cornwall CC, #102, 132 - 2 St. East, PO Box 338, ON K6H 5T1 – 613/933-4004; Fax: 613/933-8466; Email: strasser@chamber.cornwall.on.ca; URL: http://www.chamber.cornwall.on.ca – General Manager, Lezlie Strasser

Cumberland CC (Ontario) Inc., PO Box 49011, Orleans ON K1C 7E4 – 613/824-9137; Fax: 613/834-8398 – Executive Director, W. Shields

Delhi District CC, PO Box 11, ON N4B 2W8 – Fax: 582-3870 – Secretary, H. Brown

Dryden District CC, 284 Government Rd., PO Box 725, ON P8N 2Z4 – 807/223-2622; Fax: 807/223-2626; Toll Free: 1-800-667-0935; Email: chamber@moosenet.net; URL: http://www.dryden.nor-ont.ca – Manager, Barb Lyotier

Dunnville CC, 106 Main St. West, PO Box 124, ON N1A 2X1 – 905/774-3183; Fax: 905/774-9281 – Administrator, Karen Bernard

Durham & District CC, PO Box 800, ON N0G 1R0 – 519/369-5750; Fax: 519/369-5750 – Secretary, Jean Hutcheson

Dutton-Dunwich CC, PO Box 211, ON N0L 1J0 – 519/762-3128 – Sec.-Treas., Mike Gardiner

East Gwillimbury CC, PO Box 606, Sharon ON L0G 1V0 – 905/478-8142; Fax: 905/478-8074 – Secretary, Hanni Staheli

Elliot Lake & District CC, Hwy. 108 Civic Centre, ON P5A 2T1 – 705/848-3974; Fax: 705/848-2987 – Executive Assistant, R. Alger

Elmira & Woolwich CC, 5 First St. East, ON N3B 2E3 – 519/669-2605; Fax: 519/669-8251 – Executive Director, N. Lucier

Elmwood & District CC, RR#2, ON N0G 1S0 – President, M. Hamel

Elora & District CC, 1 MacDonald Sq., PO Box 814, ON N0B 1S0 – 519/846-9841; Fax: 519/846-2074 – Administrator, S. Clarke

Englehart & District CC, PO Box 171, ON P0J 1H0 – 705/544-2658; Fax: 705/544-2658 – Manager, P. Woollings

Espanola & District CC, PO Box 5085, ON P5E 1S1 – R.S. Molly

Etobicoke CC, #100, 701 Evans Ave., ON M9C 1A3 – 416/622-5557; Fax: 416/622-4544 – Executive Director, Donald E. Overholt

Fenelon Falls North Kawartha District CC, PO Box 28, ON K0M 1N0 – 705/887-3409; Fax: 705/887-9259 – Office Manager, L. Matthews

Flamborough CC, #8, Hwy. 5 West, PO Box 1030, Waterdown ON L0R 2H0 – 905/689-7650; Fax: 905/689-1313 – Administrator, Jim Chambers

Flesherton & District CC, PO Box 292, ON N0C 1E0 – 519/924-3687 – President, Colleen Boer

Greater Fort Erie CC, #4, 427 Garrison Rd., ON L2A 1N1 – 905/871-3803; Fax: 905/871-1561 – Manager, C. Montana

Fort Frances CC, 474 Scott St., ON P9A 1H2 – 807/274-5773; Fax: 807/274-8706; Toll Free: 1-800-820-3678; Email: thefort@ff.lakeheadu.ca; URL: http://fort-frances.lakeheadu.ca/~glandher/fort_fra.html – Office Manager, Heather Herbert

1,000 Islands Gananoque & District CC, 2 King St. East, ON K7G 1E6 – 613/382-3250; Fax: 613/382-1585; Toll Free: 1-800-561-1595; Email: chamber@gananoque.com; URL: http://www.gananoque.com – Sylvia Fletcher

Georgina BT, PO Box 133, Keswick ON L4P 3E1 – 905/476-7870; Fax: 905/476-6700; Toll Free: 1-888-436-7462 – Administrative Assistant, Ron J. Brooks

Geraldton District CC, PO Box 156, ON P0T 1M0 – 807/854-1281; Fax: 807/854-1252 – President, P. Kyro

Gloucester CC, #53, 5450 Canotek Rd., ON K1J 9G3 – 613/745-3578; Fax: 613/745-8575 – Executive Director, Jim Anderson

Goderich & District CC, PO Box 414, ON N7A 4C7 – 519/524-1172 – Secretary/Business Manager, Laura Johnston

The Gogama CC, 921 Woodward Ave., Milton ON L9T 3X2 – 705/894-2788 – Chairman, John F. Rich

Grand Bend & Area CC, #1, 81 Crescent St., PO Box 248, ON N0M 1T0 – 519/238-2001; Fax: 519/238-8302 – Secretary, Pamela Reid

Gravenhurst CC/Visitors Bureau, Gravenhurst Opera House, #295, One Muskoka Rd. South, ON P1P 1J1 – 705/687-4432; Fax: 705/687-4382 – Executive Director, Ann Zangari

Grimsby & District CC, #2, 76 Main St. West, ON L3M 1R6 – 905/945-8319; Fax: 905/945-1615 – Manager, Jinny Day

Guelph CC, 485 Silvercreek Pkwy. North, PO Box 1268, ON N1H 6N6 – 519/822-8081; Fax: 519/822-8451; Email: gchamber@mgl.ca; URL: http://www.mgl.ca/~gchamber/ – General Manager, Gary Nadalin

Hagersville & District CC, PO Box 243, ON N0A 1H0 – 905/768-5979 – Sec.-Treas., Ted Heinrichs

Haliburton Highlands CC, PO Box 147, Minden ON K0M 2K0 – 705/286-1760; Fax: 705/286-6016; Toll Free: 1-800-461-7677 – Office Manager, B. Dean

Halton Hills CC, 170 Guelph St., Georgetown ON L7G 4A7 – 905/877-7119; Fax: 905/873-5117 – Executive Director, Anne Sidebottom

Hamilton & District CC, 555 Bay St. North, ON L8L 1H1 – 905/522-1151; Fax: 905/522-1154; Email: hdcc@Hamilton-CofC.on.ca; URL: http://www.hamilton-cofc.on.ca

Hanover CC, #1, 214 - 10th St., ON N4N 1N7 – 519/364-5777; Fax: 519/364-6949 – President, I. Cruickshank

Harriston-Minto & District CC, PO Box 864, ON N0G 1Z0 – 519/338-3034; Fax: 519/338-3520 – Vice-President, R.A. Weiss

Hawkesbury CC, 1575 Tupper St., PO Box 798, ON K6A 3C9 – 613/632-8066; Fax: 613/632-3324; Email: chamber@hawknet.ca; URL: http://www.glen-net.ca/chamber/ – Coordinator, Francine Fournier

Huntsville/Lake of Bays CC, #1, 8 West St. North, ON P1H 2B6 – 705/789-4771; Fax: 705/789-6191; Email: hchamber@muskoka.com – General Manager, Brenda Caskenette

Ingersoll District CC, 128 Duke St., PO Box 400, ON N5C 3V3 – 519/485-7333; Fax: 519/485-6183 – Promoter/Manager, B. Wallace

Innisfil CC, c/o Gibson & Adams, PO Box 262, Stroud ON L0L 2M0 – 705/436-1701; Fax: 705/436-1710 – President, G. MacKenzie

Iroquois Falls & District CC, 727 Synagogue Ave., PO Box 840, ON P0K 1G0 – 705/232-4656; Fax: 705/232-4656 – Office Manager, Rose-Marie Purdy-Peever

Kanata CC, #109, 275 Michael Cowpland Dr., ON K2M 2G2 – 613/592-8343; Fax: 613/592-1157 – Administrator, S. Cramm

Kapuskasing & District CC, 100 Government Rd., ON P5N 3H8 – 705/335-2332; Fax: 705/335-2359 – Secretary, D. Bliss

Kemptville & District CC, PO Box 1047, ON K0G 1J0 – 613/258-4838; Fax: 613/258-4322; Email: chamberk@cyberus.ca; URL: http://www.cyberus.ca/~chamberk – Manager, Valerie Paterson

Kenora & District CC, PO Box 471, ON P9N 3X5 – 807/467-4646; Fax: 807/468-4760 – Executive Assistant, Heather Grant

Kincardine & District CC, PO Box 115, ON N2Z 2Y6 – 519/396-9333; Fax: 519/396-5529 – President, Ken Jackson

King City CC, PO Box 502, ON L0G 1K0 – 905/833-0869; Fax: 905/833-2553 – Secretary, E.L. Hinder

Greater Kingston CC, 209 Wellington St., ON K7K 2Y6 – 613/548-4453; Fax: 613/548-4743; Email: chamber@limestone.kosone.com; URL: http://www.canlink.com/chamber – General Manager, Gail Logan

Kirkland Lake & District CC, PO Box 966, ON P2N 2E6 – 705/567-5444; Fax: 705/567-1666; Email: klcofc@nt.net – Manager, Eleanor Newton

CC of Kitchener & Waterloo, 80 Queen St. North, PO Box 2367, Stn B, ON N2H 6L4 – 519/576-5000; Fax: 519/742-4760; Email: admin@kiwatchamber.on.ca; URL: http://www.kitwatchamber.on.ca – Acting Executive Director, Mary Sue Fitzpatrick

Lakefield & District CC, Water St., PO Box 537, ON K0L 2H0 – 705/652-3141; Fax: 705/652-6963; Email: info@lakefield-district.com; URL: http://www.lakefield-district.com

Land O'Lakes CC, PO Box 135, Northbrook ON K0H 2G0 – 613/336-9460; Fax: 613/336-9460 – Acting Secretary, Susanne Lauper

Land-of-Nipigon CC, PO Box 760, ON P0T 2J0 – 807/887-1493 – Secretary, Gina Barnes

Leamington District CC, #303B, 33 Princess St., PO Box 321, ON N8H 3W3 – 519/326-2721; Fax: 519/326-3204 – General Manager, Chris Chopchik

Lincoln CC, 4800 South Service Rd., PO Box 1000, Beamsville ON L0R 1B0 – 905/563-5044; Fax: 905/563-6566 – Secretary/Manager, Cathy McNiven

Lindsay & District CC, 4 Victoira Ave. North, ON K9V 4E5 – 705/324-2393; Fax: 705/324-2473; Email: coc@lindsaytown.org – General Manager, Brenda Caskenette

Listowel CC, PO Box 232, ON N4W 3H4 – 519/291-1590 – President, M. Tremblay

Manitoulin CC, PO Box 915, Little Current ON P0P 1K0 – 705/282-0713; Fax: 705/282-2989 – President, B. Barfoot

London CC, 244 Pall Mall St., PO Box 3295, ON N6A 5P6 – 519/432-7551; Fax: 519/432-8063; Email: lcoc.info@chamber.london.on.ca; URL: http://www.chamber.london.on.ca – General Manager, Gerry MacCartney

Longlac CC, PO Box 877, ON P0T 1A0 – 807/876-2273; Fax: 807/876-4337 – President, L. Tucker

Lucknow & District CC, PO Box 313, ON N0G 2H0 – 519/528-3436; Fax: 519/528-3436; Email: rosy@hurontel.on.ca – President, P. McKillop

Lyndhurst Seeleys Bay & District CC, PO Box 89, ON K0E 1N0 – 613/387-3847 – Treasurer, C. Shaw

Manitouwadge CC, PO Box 2030, ON P0T 2C0 – 807/826-3227, ext.240; Fax: 807/826-4592 – Managing Director, Terese Bullough

Marathon & District CC, PO Box 988, ON P0T 2E0 – 807/229-2112; Fax: 807/229-2112 – President, Sandra Svenkeson

Markdale CC, PO Box 177, ON N0C 1H0 – 519/986-3677 – Sec.-Treas., Ian Drummond

Markham BT, #210, 3780 - 14th Ave., ON L3R 9Y5 – 905/474-0730; Fax: 905/474-0685 – Executive Director, Ruth Burkholder

Maryborough Township CC, PO Box 143, Moorefield ON N0G 2K0 – 519/638-3441; Fax: 519/638-5856 – President, D. Campbell

Maxville CC, PO Box 279, ON K0C 1T0 – 613/527-3131; Fax: 613/527-1119 – Secretary, J. Scott

Meaford & District CC, PO Box 4836, ON N4L 1X6 – 519/538-4020; Fax: 519/538-5295 – Executive Secretary, V. Mullin

Merrickville & District CC, PO Box 571, ON K0G 1N0 – 613/269-2229; Fax: 613/269-3713 – President, Judy Clarke

Midland CC, 208 King St., ON L4R 3L9 – 705/526-7884; Fax: 705/526-1744; Email: midland@cryston.ca; URL: http://www.southerngeorgianbay.on.ca – General Manager/Economic Development Commissioner, Joyce A. Campbell, Ec.D.

Milton CC, PO Box 52, ON L9T 2Y3 – 905/878-0581; Fax: 905/878-4972 – General Manager, Sandy Martin

Mississauga BT, #100, 3 Robert Speck Pkwy., ON L4Z 2G5 – 905/273-6151; Fax: 905/273-4937; URL: http://www.mbot.com – Executive Director, David A. Gordon

Morrisburg & District CC, PO Box 288, ON K0C 1X0 – 613/543-3443; Fax: 613/543-4387 – Secretary, Linda Bowers

Mount Forest District CC, 521 Main St. North, PO Box 1493, ON N0G 2L0 – 519/323-4480 – Manager, Carol Teston

Napanee & District CC, PO Box 431, ON K7R 3P5 – 613/354-2331; Fax: 613/354-5114; URL: http://chamber.napanee.on.ca – President, P. Veltheer

Nepean CC, #201, 28 Thorncliff Pl., ON K2H 6L2 – 613/828-5556; Fax: 613/828-8022 – President, Buck Arnold

New Hamburg BT, PO Box 457, ON N0B 2G0 – 519/662-3000; Fax: 519/662-2601 – Secretary, Sam Lucibello

Newmarket CC, 78 Main St. South, ON L3Y 3Y6 – 905/898-5900; Fax: 905/853-7271 – Manager, Robert T. Carter

CC Niagara Falls, 4394 Queen St., ON L2E 2L3 – 905/374-3666; Fax: 905/374-2972; Email: nfchamber@vaxxine.com; URL: http://www.nflschamber.com – Executive Director, Glenn Gandy

Niagara on the Lake CC, 153 King St., PO Box 1043, ON L0S 1J0 – 905/468-4263; Fax: 905/468-4930; Email: notlinfo@niagaraonthelake.com; URL: http://www.niagara-on-the-lake.com – General Manager, N.G. Rumble

North Bay & District CC, 1375 Seymour St., PO Box 747, ON P1B 8J8 – 705/472-8480; Fax: 705/472-8027; URL: http://www.city.north-bay.on.ca/chamber.htm – Manager, G. DeVuono

North York CC, #200, 298 Sheppard Ave. West, ON M2N 1N5 – 416/226-9345; Fax: 416/590-1729 – General Manager, Tracy Blyth

Norwich Township CC, PO Box 128, ON N0J 1P0 – 519/863-2689; Fax: 519/863-2469 – President, D.M. Buck

Oakville CC, 170 Country Squire Lane, ON L6J 4Z3 – 905/845-6613; Fax: 905/845-6475 – Executive Vice-President, Brenda Kempel

Orangeville & District CC, PO Box 101, ON L9W 2Z5 – 519/941-0490; Fax: 519/941-0492 – Manager, Catherine Callum

Orillia & District CC, 150 Front St. South, ON L3V 4S7 – 705/326-4424; Fax: 705/327-7841 – Managing Director, Susan Lang

Township of Osgoode CC, PO Box 558, ON K0A 2W0 – 613/826-0661 – President, J. Bath

Oshawa/Clarington CC, 50 Richmond St. East, ON L1G 7C7 – 905/728-1683; Fax: 905/432-1259 – Executive Director, Peter Mitchell

Ottawa-Carleton BT, #1710, 350 Albert St., ON K1R 1A4 – 613/230-3631; Fax: 613/236-7498; URL: http://www.board-of-trade.org – President, W. Bagnell

Owen Sound & District CC, PO Box 1028, ON N4K 6K6 – 519/376-6261; Fax: 519/376-5647 – President, N. Osborne

Parry Sound & Area CC, 70 Church St., ON P2A 1Y9 – 705/746-4213; Fax: 705/746-6537; Toll Free: 1-800-461-4261 – Administrator/Manager, Jan Hanna

Pembroke & Area CC, 2 International Dr., ON K8A 6W5 – 613/735-5381; Fax: 613/735-2738 – Treasurer, G. Gybulski

Penetanguishene-Tiny CC, Town Docks, End of Hwy. 93, 2 Main St., ON L9M 1T1 – 705/549-2232; Fax: 705/549-6640; Email: ptcc@webgate.net; URL: http://www.huronet.com/chamb_commerce/ – General Manager, Patricia Belfrey

Perth CC, 80 Gore St. East, ON K7H 1H9 – 613/267-3200; Fax: 613/267-6797 – General Manager, Marion Crawford

Greater Peterborough CC, 175 George St. North, ON K9J 3G6 – 705/748-9771; Fax: 705/743-2331; Email: commerce@knet.flemingc.on.ca; URL: http://www.ptbo.igs.net/~chamber – General Manager, Don Frise

Prince Edward CC, 116 Main St., PO Box 893, Picton ON K0K 2T0 – 613/476-2421; Fax: 613/476-7461 – Secretary/Manager, Babbs Welsh

Pointe-au-Baril CC, Hwy. 69, PO Box 67, Pointe-au-Baril-Station ON P0G 1K0 – 705/366-2331; Fax: 705/366-2331 – Manager, Roxie McPhee

Port Colborne-Wainfleet CC, 76 Main St. West, ON L3K 3V2 – 905/834-9765; Fax: 905/834-1542 – Office Manager, D. Panetta

Port Dover BT, 225 Main St., PO Box 239, ON N0A 1N0 – ; URL: http://www.nornet.on.ca/portdover/ – President, L. Varey

Port Elgin & District CC, 515 Goderich St., ON N0H 2C4 – 519/832-2332; Fax: 519/389-3725; Toll Free: 1-800-387-3456 – General Manager, Connie Barker

Port Hope & District CC, 35 & 37 John St., ON L1A 2Z3 – 905/885-5519; Fax: 905/885-1142 – Manager, Debbie McQueen

Port Rowan-Long Point CC, Main St., PO Box 357, ON N0E 1M0 – President, P. Steiner

Port Sydney & Area CC, PO Box 1000, ON P0B 1L0 – 705/385-0162; Fax: 705/385-0163 – President, A. Lenze

Prescott & District CC, PO Box 2000, ON K0E 1T0 – 613/925-2257; Fax: 613/925-1585 – Executive Manager, Mike Boyles

Red Lake District CC, PO Box 430, ON P0V 2M0 – 807/727-3722; Fax: 807/727-3285 – Treasurer, T. Patrick

Renfrew & Area CC, PO Box 220, ON K7V 4A3 – 613/432-7015 – Manager, B. Mayhew

Richmond Hill CC, 376 Church St. South, ON L4C 9V8 – 905/884-1961; Fax: 905/884-1962 – General Manager, Barbara Scollick

Rideau Township CC, PO Box 817, Manotick ON K4M 1A7 – 613/489-0228; Fax: 613/489-2928 – President, D. Watchorn

Ridgetown & District CC, PO Box 522, ON N0P 2C0 – 519/674-0766; Fax: 519/674-0763 – President, H.J. Cole

Rodney Aldborough CC, RR#1, ON N0L 2C0 – Chairman, J. Fisher

Russell CC, PO Box 218, ON K4R 1C8 – 613/445-5308; Fax: 613/445-3140 – President, M. Ion

St Thomas & District CC, 555 Talbot St., ON N5P 1C5 – 519/631-1981; Fax: 519/631-0466; Email: chamber@ccia.st-thomas.ca; URL: http://www.mts-inc.com/chamber/ – President/CEO, Bob Hammersley

Sarnia Lambton CC, 224 North Vidal St., ON N7T 5Y3 – 519/336-2400; Fax: 519/336-2085 – General Manager, Gerry Macartney

Sauble Beach CC, General Delivery, ON N0H 2G0 – 519/422-1051 – Secretary, M. Husak

Sault Ste. Marie CC, 334 Bay St., Sault Ste Marie ON P6A 1X1 – 705/949-7152; Fax: 705/759-8166; Email: ssmcoc@age.net; URL: http://www.sault-canada.com – General Manager, Gene Nori

Scarborough/Metro East CC, #216, 1200 Markham Rd., ON M1H 3C3 – 416/439-4140; Fax: 416/439-4147 – Executive Director, D. Smyth

* BT - Board of Trade; BC - Bureau de commerce; CC - Chamber of Commerce/Chambre de commerce

Schomberg CC, General Delivery, ON L0G 1T0 – President, B. Conzelmann

Scugog CC, 269 Queen St., PO Box 1282, Port Perry ON L9L 1B1 – 905/985-4971; Fax: 905/986-1049; URL: http://web.idirect.com/~haertel/chamber/chamber.html – 1st Vice-President, B. McIntosh

Simcoe & District CC, 76 Kent St. South, ON N3Y 2Y1 – 519/426-5867; Fax: 519/428-7718; URL: http://www.kwic.com:80/~chamber – General Manager, Yvonne Di Pietro

Sioux Lookout CC, PO Box 577, ON P8T 1A8 – 807/737-1937; Fax: 807/737-1778 – Executive Administrator, Linda Adduono

Smiths Falls & District CC, Town Hall, 77 Beckwith St. North, ON K7A 2B8 – 613/283-1334; Fax: 613/283-4764; Toll Free: 1-800-257-1334 – Manager, Victoria Ash

South River & Area CC, PO Box 600, ON P0A 1X0 – 705/386-0005 – Secretary/Manager, E. Innes

Southampton CC, Southampton Tourist Information Centre, 33 Victoria St. North, PO Box 261, ON N0H 2L0 – 519/797-2215; Fax: 519/797-2191; Email: southampton@sunsets.com; URL: http://www.sunsets.com/southampton – President, T. Thomas

St Catharines & District CC, 11 King St., PO Box 940, ON L2R 6Z4 – 905/684-2361; Fax: 905/684-2100; Email: kdrewitt@stc-chamber.com – Interim Office Manager, Kathy Bissell

Stratford & District CC, #1, 121 Ontario St., 2nd Fl., ON N5A 3H1 – 519/273-5250; Fax: 519/273-2229 – General Manager, Nancy Bomasuit

Sudbury & District CC, 166 Douglas St., ON P3E 1G1 – 705/673-7133; Fax: 705/673-2944; Email: cofc@sudbury.com – Executive Director, Debbi Nicholson

Tavistock CC, PO Box 670, ON N0B 2R0 – 519/655-3303; Fax: 519/655-3591 – President, J. Buffham

Thornbury & District CC, PO Box 477, ON N0H 2P0 – 519/599-3223 – President, M. Douglas

Thorold CC, 3 Front St. North, ON L2V 3Y7 – 905/680-4233; Fax: 905/680-6612 – Office Manager, Terry M. Dow

Thunder Bay CC, 857 May St. North, ON P7C 3S2 – 807/622-9642; Fax: 807/622-7752; Email: chamber@tb-chamber.on.ca; URL: http://www.tb-chamber.on.ca – President, Rebecca Johnson

Tilbury & District CC, PO Box 1355, ON N0P 2L0 – 519/682-1766; Fax: 519/682-1766 – Secretary, S. Blain

Tillsonburg District CC, PO Box 113, ON N4G 4H3 – 519/842-5571; Fax: 519/842-2941; Email: matt@oxford.net – Sec.-Treas., Matthew Scholtz

Timmins CC, PO Box 985, ON P4N 7H6 – 705/360-1900; Fax: 705/360-1193 – Manager, Roberta Carey

Tobermory & District CC, PO Box 250, ON N0H 2R0 – 519/596-2452; Fax: 519/596-2452; Email: chamber@log.on.ca; URL: http://www.tobermory.org – Coordinator, Gayle Golz

BT of Metropolitan Toronto, One First Canadian Place, PO Box 60, ON M5X 1C1 – 416/366-6811; Fax: 416/366-4906 – President & CEO, M. Elyse Allan

Trenton & District CC, 97 Front St., ON K8V 4N6 – 613/392-7635; Fax: 613/392-8400 – Manager, J. Kingston

Tri-Town & District CC, #78, Hwy. 11B, PO Box 811, New Liskeard ON P0J 1P0 – 705/647-5771; Fax: 705/647-8633 – Office Manager, T. Nagy-Thisdelle

Uxbridge & District CC, PO Box 640, ON L9P 1N1 – 905/852-7683 – Secretary, Lois Bushell

Vaughan CC, #101, 8 Director Ct., Woodbridge ON L4L 3Z5 – 905/850-0024; Fax: 905/850-2441; Email: jjn@istar.ca – General Manager, Jennifer Nicholson

Walkerton & District CC, 7 Victoria St., PO Box 1344, ON N0G 2V0 – 519/881-3413; Fax: 519/881-4009 – Manager, Nicole Schnurr

Wallaceburg & District CC, PO Box 20048, ON N8A 5G1 – 519/627-1443; Fax: 519/627-9231 – General Manager, D. Keeler

Wasaga Beach CC, 35 Dunkerron St., PO Box 394, ON L0L 2P0 – 705/429-2247; Fax: 705/429-1407 – Office Manager, Lorie Coyle

The Welland/Pelham CC, 32 East Main St., ON L3B 3W3 – 905/732-7515; Fax: 905/732-7175 – Executive Director, Dolores Fabiano

West Carleton District CC, PO Box 179, Carp ON K0A 1L0 – 613/839-5327; Fax: 613/839-0056 – Secretary, R. Lyall

West Lincoln CC, PO Box 555, Smithville ON L0R 2A0 – 905/957-1606; Fax: 905/957-0088 – President, M. Van Spronsen

West Muskoka CC, PO Box 536, Bala ON P0C 1A0 – 705/762-3214; Fax: 705/762-0791 – Allan Turnbull

Whitby CC, 128 Brock St. South, ON L1N 4J8 – 905/668-4506; Fax: 905/668-1894 – General Manager, Debra Cullis-Filip

Whitchurch-Stouffville CC, PO Box 1500, ON L4A 8A4 – 905/642-4227; Fax: 905/642-8966 – Office Manager, Barbara St. John

Windsor & District CC, 2575 Ouellette Place, ON N8X 1L9 – 519/966-3696; Fax: 519/966-0603 – President, Larry E. Sandre, C.A.

Wingham & Area CC, PO Box 368, ON N0G 2W0 – 519/357-1522; Fax: 519/357-1551 – Secretary, Andy Beninger

Woodstock District CC, 18 Wellington St. North, ON N4S 6P2 – 519/539-9411; Fax: 519/539-5433 – General Manager, A.A. Mowat

Belmore CC, RR#1, PO Box 21, Wroxeter ON N0G 2X0 – 519/392-8010 – Sec.-Treas., Ruth Knight

Zurich & District CC, PO Box 189, ON N0M 2T0 – 519/236-4982 – Secretary, Delores Schilbe

### PRINCE EDWARD ISLAND

Greater Charlottetown CC, 127 Kent St., PO Box 67, PE C1A 7K2 – 902/628-2000; Fax: 902/368-3570; Email: charcham@atcon.com – President, John Ives, 902/566-2121, Fax: 902/566-9203

South Shore Chamber pf Commerce, RR#1, Crapaud PE C0A 1J0 – 902/658-2781; Fax: 902/964-3377 – President, Scott Dawson, 902/566-2628, Fax: 902/892-4008

Eastern Kings Regional CC, PO Box 328, Souris PE C0A 2B0 – 902/687-2055; Fax: 902/687-3424 – President, Alice Winterhalder

Kensington & Area CC, PO Box 234, PE C0B 1M0 – 902/836-3209; Fax: 902/836-5659; Email: kennet@atcon.com – President, Winston Cousins, 902/836-3824

Montague & District CC, PE C0A 1R0 – 902/838-2323 – President, Cameron McLean

Greater Summerside CC, #10, 263 Harbour Dr., PE C1N 5P1 – 902/436-9651; Fax: 902/436-8320; Email: gscc@atcon.com – President, Marilyn Waugh-Arsenault

West Prince CC, Alberton PE C0B 1B0 – 902/853-2297; Fax: 902/853-3822 – President, Paul Arsenault

### QUÉBEC

CC de l'Abitibi-Ouest, #100, 6 - 8e av est, La Sarre QC J9Z 1N6

CC de la Région d'Acton, CP 1448, Acton Vale QC J0H 1A0 – 514/546-7642

CC d'Alma, 200, av des Pins ouest, QC G8B 6P9

CC d'Amiante, CP 572, Thetford-Mines QC G6G 5T6 – 418/335-3441

CC d'Amos-Région, 102, av de la Gare, CP 93, QC J9T 3A5

CC d'Amqui, CP 2317, QC G0J 1B0

CC d'Anse-au-Griffon, CP 62, QC G0E 1A0 – 418/892-5259

CC d'Arundel, Barkmere, Huberdeau, Montcalm, CP 183, QC J0T 1G0

Cercle des affaires de la région d'Asbestos, CP 176, QC J1T 3M9

CC de Baie-Comeau, 63, Place Lasalle, QC G4Z 1J8 – 418/296-2010

CC de Barraute, CP 217, QC J0Y 1A0

CC de Bas St-François, CP 293, Pierreville QC J0G 1J0 – 514/568-3540

CC de Basse Côte-Nord, Secteur Est, CP 399, Lourdes-du-Blanc-Sablon QC G0G 1W0

CC de Beauceville, 595, 9e av de Léry, CP 782, Beauceville-Est QC G0S 1A0 – 418/774-2322; Fax: 418/774-6485 – Président, Christian Duval

CC de Beauport-Cote de Beaupré, 589, av Royale, QC G1E 1Y5

CC de Bécancour, CP 531, St-Grégoire QC G0X 1G0

CC de la région de Berthier, 145, ch de la Traverse, St-Ignace-de-Loyola QC J0K 2P0

CC de Bic et St-Valérien, CP 437, QC G0L 1B0

CC de Bois-des-Filion-Lorraine, CP 72012, QC J6Z 4N9

CC de Bois-Francs, 122, rue Acqueduc, CP 641, Victoriaville QC G6P 6V7

CC région Bolton, 858, route Missisquoi, Bolton Centre QC JOE 1G0 – 514/292-4217 – Président, Richard Clinton

CC de Bonaventure, CP 848, QC G0C 1E0

CC de Brandon, 117, rue Pacifique, CP 778, St-Gabriel-de-Brandon QC J0K 2N0 – 514/835-2105; Fax: 514/835-2105 – Secrétaire, France Brisebois

CC de Cacouna, CP 324, QC G0L 1G0

CC de Cap-St-Ignace, CP 115, QC G0R 1H0

CC de Cap-de-la-Madeleine, 170, rue des Cheneaux, CP 183, QC G8T 7W2

CC de Cap-des-Rosiers, 1127, Cap-des-Rosiers, QC G0E 1E0

CC de Carleton, CP 209, QC G0C 1J0

CC de Causapscal, 5, rue St-Jacques sud, QC G0J 1J0

CC de Châteauguay, #106, 265, boul d'Anjou, QC J6J 5J9

CC du bassin de Chambly, 1101, boul Brassard, CP 209, QC J3L 5R4

CC de Chapais, CP 99, QC G0W 1H0

CC de Charlesbourg-Chauveau, #295, 8500, rue Henri-Bourassa, CP 7008, QC G1G 5E1 – 418/626-5514; Fax: 418/626-5485

CC de Charlevoix-Est, #200, 130, boul de Comporté, La Malbaie QC G5A 1P7

CC de Charlevoix-Ouest, 11, rue St-Jean-Baptiste, CP 1900, Baie-St-Paul QC G0A 1B0

CC de Chibougamau, 550, 3e rue, CP 600, QC G8P 2Y8

CC de Chicoutimi, 31, rue Racine Ouest, CP 1162, QC G7H 5G4

CC de la région de Coaticook, CP 243, QC J1A 2T7

CC de Contrecoeur, 525, rue St-Antoine, QC J0L 1C0 – 514/587-2353; Fax: 514/587-2353

CC de Cookshire, CP 75, QC J0B 1M0

CC de Cowansville et région, 500, rue Sud, QC J2K 2X8

CC de Delisle, CP 83, QC G0W 1L0

CC Denis-Riverin, CP 422, Ste-Anne-des-Monts QC G0E 2G0

CC des Moulins, #305, 1025, Montée Masson, Lachenaie QC J6W 5H9

CC de Disraéli, 817, av Champlain, QC G0N 1E0

CC de Dolbeau, CP 26, QC G8L 2P9 – 418/276-7073; Fax: 418/276-9518

CC de Donnacona, Cap-Santé, CP 358, QC G0A 1T0

CC de Drummond, 405, rue St-Jean, CP 188, Drummondville QC J2B 6V7

CC de Duparquet, CP 70, QC J0Z 1W0

CC de East-Angus, CP 490, East Angus QC J0B 1R0

CC East Broughton, CP 209, QC G0N 1G0 – Président, Michel Bastille

CC de Farnham et Région, #102, 477, rue de l'Hôtel de Ville, QC J2N 2H3

CC Ferme-Neuve, CP 715, QC J0W 1C0 – 819/587-3882; Fax: 819/587-3861

CC de Forestville, CP 1030, QC G0T 1E0
CC de Frampton, CP 127, QC G0R 1M0
CC de Gaspé, CP 66, QC G0C 1R0
CC de Gaspésie Centrale, CP 160, Grande-Vallée QC G0E 1K0 – Présidente, Denise Mirville, 418/393-2808
CC du Coeur de la Gatineau, RR#1, Gracefield QC J0X 1W0
CC du district de Granby - Bromont, #200, 328, rue Principale, CP 907, QC J2G 2W4
CC et d'industrie de Grand-Mère, CP 322, QC G9T 5L1
CC de Grande-Rivière, CP 145, QC G0C 1V0 – 418/385-3088 – Président, Jean-Guy Boudreau, 418/385-3224
CC de Grenville et Canton, CP 219, QC J0V 1J0
CC de Haut St-Maurice, 1525, ch de la Rivière Croche, La Tûque QC G9X 3N7
CC Hauts-Reliefs, 1047, route 263, St-Fortunat QC G0P 1G0
CC de Haut-Richelieu, 31, rue Frontenac, St-Jean-sur-Richelieu QC J3B 2K1
CC Haute Matawinie, 721, rue Brassard, St-Michel-des-Saints QC J0K 3B0
CC de Hemmingford, CP 295, QC J0L 1H0 – 514/247-3310; Fax: 514/247-2389
CC d'Îles-de-la-Madeleine, CP 307, Cap-aux-Meules QC G0B 1B0 – 418/986-4112
CC du Grand Joliette, 500, rue Dollar, QC J6E 4M4
CC de Jonquière, 3791, rue de la Fabrique, CP 211, QC G7X 7V9
CC de L'Assomption, CP 3027, QC J5W 4M9 – 514/589-2405; Fax: 514/589-9213
CC de l'Érable, CP 341, Plessisville QC G6L 2Y8
CC L'Isle-Verte, 115, rue St-Jean Baptiste, QC G0L 1K0
CC et d'industrie de l'Outaouais, #300, 166, rue Varennes, Gatineau QC J8T 8G4
CC et d'industrie de Ville de La Baie, 1226, 6e av, CP 1416, QC G7B 3P5
CC de la Pocatière, CP 2080, La Pocatière QC G0R 1Z0
CC de Labelle, 7404, boul du Curé Labelle, CP 630, QC J0T 1H0 – 819/686-2708; Fax: 819/686-2606 – Directrice générale, Marie-Emma Rabellins
CC de Lac Brôme, CP 723, Knowlton QC J0E 1V0
CC de Lac des Deux-Montagnes, #400, 190 - 41e av, Pointe-Calumet QC J0N 1G2 – 819/473-2708 – Président, Rosaire Morin
CC région de Mégantic, 3620, rue St-Adolphe, Lac Mégantic QC G6B 1M4 – 819/583-4662; Fax: 819/583-5476; Toll Free: 1-888-383-4662
CC de Lac Robertson, La Tabatière QC G0G 1T0 – Sec.-Trés., G. Organ
CC Lac du Cerf, 141, ch du Lac Mallone, Lac-du-Cerf QC J0W 1S0
CC de Lachute, CP 517, QC J8H 3Y1
CC et d'industrie de Laval, #200, 1555, boul Chomedey, QC H7V 3Z1
CC de Lavaltrie, CP 691, QC J0K 1H0
CC Le Gardeur, 333, boul Lacombe, QC J5Z 1N2
CC Les Escoumins, CP 758, QC G0T 1K0
CC de St-Côme-Linière, CP 827, QC G0M 1J0
CC et d'industrie de Magog-Orford, CP 233, QC J1X 3W8
CC de Malartic, CP 368, QC J0Y 1Z0
CC de Maniwaki, CP 5, QC J9E 3B3
CC de Maria, CP 1098, QC G0C 1Y0
CC de Marieville, #2, 491, rue Ste-Marie, CP 1502, QC J3M 1N2
CC de Mascouche, #240, 2822, ch Ste-Marie, QC J7K 1N4 – 514/966-1536; Fax: 514/966-1531
CC région de Matane, 968, du Phare Ouest, CP 518, QC G4W 3P5
CC de Mirabel, 13 479, boul du Curé Labelle, QC J7J 1H1
CC de Mistassini, CP 1330, QC G0W 2C0
CC de la région de Mont-Joli, CP 183, QC G5H 3K9
CC de Mont-Laurier, 177, boul A. Paquette, QC J9L 1J2 – 819/623-3642; Fax: 819/623-5220 – Directeur général, Luc Brunet Beaudry
Mount Royal Business Centre, #110, 4480, Côte de Liesse, Mont-Royal QC H4N 2R1 – 514/733-8600; Fax: 514/733-6343
CC de Mont-Tremblant, 140A, rue du Couvent, CP 248, QC J0T 1Z0
CC de Montmagny, 37, rue Ste-Marie, QC G5V 2R6
CC du Montréal métropolitain, Niveau plaza, #12500, 5, Place Ville-Marie, QC H3B 4Y2 – 514/871-4000; Fax: 514/871-1255; Email: info@ccmm.qc.ca; URL: http://www.ccmm.qc.ca – Vice-président exécutif, Luc Lacharité
CC du Sud-Ouest de l'Île de Montréal, 530, rue de l'Église, CP 308, Verdun QC H4G 3E9 – Directeur général, Marc Snyder
CC de Montréal-Nord, Place Levasseur, #19, 5600, boul Henri-Bourassa est, QC H1G 2T3 – 514/329-4453; Fax: 514/329-5373 – Directrice générale, France Huneault
CC Rive-Sud de Montréal, #100, 1000, rue de Serigny, Longueuil QC J4H 5B1 – 514/463-2121
CC des Monts, CP 422, Ste-Anne-des-Monts QC G0E 2G0
CC de la région de Napierville, 210, St-Nicolas, QC J0J 1L0
CC de Nicolet, 30, rue Notre-Dame, QC J3T 1G1 – 819/293-4537; Fax: 819/293-4537
CC du secteur de Normandin, 1048, rue St-Cyrille, CP 1080, QC G0W 2E0 – 418/274-2004; Fax: 418/274-7171
CC de Notre-Dame-du-Lac, CP 147, QC G0L 1X0
CC de Notre-Dame-du-Nord, CP 517, QC J0Z 3B0
CC d'Oka, CP 310, QC J0N 1E0
CC d'Outremont, #209, 40, rue Bates, QC H2V 4T5
CC du Grand Paspébiac, 172, rte St-Pie-IX, QC G0C 2K0
CC de Percé, CP 431, QC G0C 2L0
CC de Piedmont, 100, rue de la Gare, QC J0R 1K0
CC de Pont-Rouge, CP 744, QC G0A 2X0
CC de Port-Cartier, CP 82, QC G5B 2G7
CC de Princeville, CP 430, QC G0P 1E0
CC et d'industrie du Québec métropolitain--Centre de commerce international de l'Est du Québec, 17, rue Saint-Louis, QC G1R 3Y8 – 418/694-0225; Fax: 418/694-2286 – Directeur, Frédéric Couttet
CC et d'industrie du Québec métropolitain, 17, rue St-Louis, QC G1R 3Y8 – 418/692-3853; Fax: 418/694-2286; Email: cciqm@megatoon.com; URL: http://www.cciqm.qc.ca – Directeur général, Alain Kirouac
CC Rive-Sud de Québec, 4950, boul de la Rive-Sud, CP 312, Lévis QC G6V 4Z6
CC de Radisson, CP 901, QC J0Y 2X0
CC de Rawdon, 3588, rue Metcalfe, QC J0K 1S0
CC de Repentigny, CP 140, QC J6A 2T7
CC de la région de Richmond, CP 339, QC J0B 2H0
CC de Rimouski, #201B, 125, boul René Lepage, CP 1296, QC G5L 8M2
CC de Rivière St-Augustin, Pointe-à-la-Croix QC G0C 2R0 – 418/947-2721
CC de Rivière-au-Renard, CP 54, QC G0E 2A0
CC du Transcontinental, CP 157, Rivière-Bleue QC G0L 2B0
CC de Rivière-des-Prairies, #200, 9708 - 4e rue, QC H1C 1T2 – 514/494-8916 – Président, Louis Pelletier
CC de Rivière-du-Loup, 37, rue St-Louis, QC G5R 2V3 – 418/862-5243; Fax: 418/862-5136
CC de Roberval, CP 115, Succ Bureau chef, QC G8H 2N4
CC de Rock-Forest, Saint-Élie, Deauville, CP 6265, Rock Forest QC J1N 3C9
CC de Rougemont, 11, ch Marieville, QC J0L 1M0
CC et d'industrie du Rouyn-Noranda régional, CP 634, QC J9X 5C6 – 819/797-2000; Fax: 819/762-3091 – Vice-président exécutif, Julie Bouchard
CC de Sainte-Adèle, 333, boul Sainte-Adèle, QC J0R 1L0 – 514/229-2644
CC de St-Adolphe-d'Howard, CP 390, QC J0T 2B0
CC du Grand de Sainte-Agathe-des-Monts, CP 323, QC J8C 3C6 – 819/326-3731; Fax: 819/326-3936 – Directeur général, Francis Duff
CC de St-Anicet, 1529, rte 132, local 233, QC J0S 1M0
CC de St-Anselme Honfleur Inc., CP 28, QC G0R 2N0 – 418/885-4540; Fax: 418/885-9089
CC de Saint-Basile-le-Grand, CP 1064, QC J3N 1M5
CC de St-Boniface, 1515, boul Trudel est, St-Boniface-de-Shawinigan QC G0X 2L0
CC de Ste-Brigitte-de-Laval, CP 196, QC G0A 3K0
CC de Saint-Bruno, 1377, rue Hillside, QC J3V 3L3 – 514/653-2861
CC de St-Camille-de-Bellechasse, 77, Route 204, QC G0R 2S0 – 418/595-2451; Fax: 418/595-2451 – Président, Claude Campagna
CC Jacques-Cartier, CP 53, Ste-Catherine-de-la-J. Cartier QC G0A 3M0
CC de Saint-Césaire, 1201, av St-Paul, QC J0L 1T0
CC de Ste-Claire, CP 728, QC G0R 2V0
CC de Saint-Côme, 1240, rue Principale, QC J0K 2B0
CC de Ste-Croix, CP 488, QC G0S 2H0
CC de St-Donat, CP 129, St-Donat-de-Montcalm QC J0T 2C0 – 819/424-2833; Fax: 819/424-3809
CC de St-Ephrem-de-Beauce, CP 268, St-Éphrem-de-Beauce QC G0M 1R0
CC Les Grès, CP 177, St-Étienne-des-Grès QC G0X 2P0
CC de St-Esprit, 24, rue Principale, QC J0K 2L0
CC de St-Eugène-de-Guigues, CP 1018, QC J0Z 3L0
CC de la région de Saint-Eustache, 192, boul Industriel, St-Eustache QC J7R 5C2 – 514/491-1991
CC de St-Faustin, Lac Carré, Lac Supérieur, CP 341, QC J0T 2G0
CC de St-Félicien, CP 34, QC G8K 2P8
Association de développement économique de Valois, CP 869, St-Félix-de-Valois QC J0K 2M0
CC régionale de Ste-Foy, #610, 2700, boul Laurier, QC G1V 2L8 – ; URL: http://www.riq.qc.ca/ccrsf
CC de St-Frédéric, 196, rue Principale, QC G0N 1P0
CC de St-Gédéon, CP 118, QC G0M 1T0
CC de St-Georges-de-Beauce, 12435, 1re av est, QC G5Y 2E3 – 418/228-7879; Fax: 418/228-8074 – Directrice générale, Jeanne Bizier
CC de Ste-Germaine - Lac Etchemin, CP 128, Lac-Etchemin QC G0R 1S0
CC de St-Hubert, CP 86, St-Hubert-de-Témiscouata QC G0L 3L0
CC du district de Saint-Hyacinthe, #260, 2685, boul Casavant ouest, QC J2S 8B8
CC de St-Jérôme métropolitain, 324, rue Labelle, QC J7Z 5L3
CC de St-Jean-de-Dieu, CP 392, QC G0L 3M0
CC de St-Jean-de-Matha, 180, rue Ste-Louise, QC J0K 2S0
CC et d'industrie de Saint-Joseph-de-Beauce, CP 507, St-Joseph-de-Beauce QC G0S 2V0
CC de St-Jovite, CP 67, QC J0T 2H0
CC de Ste-Julienne, CP 429, Sainte-Julienne QC J0K 2T0 – 819/831-3551; Fax: 819/831-3551
CC de Ste-Justine, 167, Route 204, QC G0R 1Y0
CC de St-Laurent, #105, 9900, boul Cavendish, QC H4M 2V2 – 514/333-5222; Fax: 514/333-0937; Email: admin@chambr.saint-laurent.qc.ca; URL: http://www.cibus.ca/stlaurent – Directeur général, Alex Harper
CC de St-Léonard, #202, 4875, boul Metropolitain est, QC H1R 3J2 – 514/325-4232; Fax: 514/325-8980 – Président, Roberto Colavecchio
CC de St-Léonard-d'Aston, CP 520, QC J0C 1M0
CC de St-Léonard-de-Portneuf, 530, rue Lefebvre, QC G0A 4A0 – 418/337-4469
CC de Saint-Lin, 457, rue St-Isidore, CP 250, QC J0R 1C0
CC de St-Marc-des-Carrières, CP 579, QC G0A 4B0
CC de Ste-Marguerite du Lac Masson - Estérel, CP 480, Lac-Masson QC J0T 1L0
CC de Sainte-Marie de Beauce, CP 684, QC G6E 3B9

* BT - Board of Trade; BC - Bureau de commerce; CC - Chamber of Commerce/Chambre de commerce

CC de Saint-Martin de Beauce, CP 31, QC G0M 1B0
CC de Ste-Perpétue, 589, rue Principale, Ste-Perpétue-de-l'Islet QC G0R 3Z0 – 418/359-2226
CC d'Île d'Orléans, 490, Côte du Pont, St-Pierre-d'Orléans QC G0A 4E0
CC de Fugèreville, 490, Côte du Pont, St-Pierre-d'Orléans QC G0A 4E0
CC de St-Prosper, CP 519, QC G0M 1Y0
CC de St-Raymond, CP 238, QC G0A 4G0
CC de Saint-Rémi, CP 918, QC J0L 2L0
CC de Thérèse de Blainville, CP 465, Ste-Thérèse-de-Blainville QC J7E 4J8
CC de la région de Salaberry-de-Valleyfield, #200, 185, rue Victoria, QC J6T 1A7
CC de Senneterre, CP 747, QC J0Y 2M0 – 819/737-2694; Fax: 819/737-2694 – Président, Guylaine Taillefer
CC de Sept-Îles, #204, 700, boul Laure, QC G4R 1Y1 – 418/968-3488; Fax: 418/968-3432
CC de Shawinigan et Shawinigan-Sud, Hôtel de Ville, CP 397, QC G9N 6V1 – 819/536-5197; Fax: 819/536-4478
CC de la région Sherbrookoise, 390, rue King ouest, CP 1356, Sherbrooke QC J1H 5L9
CC de Sorel-Tracy métropolitain, CP 568, QC J3P 5N9
CC de Témiscaming-Kipawa, CP 304, QC J0Z 3R0
CC de Tring Jonction, 17, rue St-Michel, QC G0N 1X0
CC de Trois-Pistoles, CP 876, QC G0L 4K0
CC du district de Trois-Rivières, CP 1045, QC G9A 5K4 – 819/375-9628; Fax: 819/375-9083 – Directeur général, Mario Côté
CC de Val-d'Or, 400, 3e av, QC J9P 1R9
CC de Valcourt et Région, CP 900, QC J0E 2L0
CC de Vallée de la Petite Nation, CP 590, St-André-Avellin QC J0V 1W0
CC de Vallée du Richelieu, #304, 220, rue Brébeuf, Beloeil QC J3G 5P3
CC et d'industrie de Varennes, CP 61, QC J3X 1P9
CC de Vaudreuil-Dorion, #200, 417, av Roche, QC J7V 2M9
CC Soulanges et Région, CP 122, Dorion QC J7V 5W1 – 514/424-4190
CC de Ville Dégelis, CP 722, QC G5T 2C9
CC de Ville-Marie, CP 308, QC J0Z 3W0 – 819/629-2193; Fax: 819/622-0716
CC de Villebois, 3070, Villebois rang 6, QC J0Z 3V0
CC de Waterloo, CP 309, QC J0E 2N0 – 819/539-1102
CC de la région de Weedon, CP 400, QC J0B 3J0
CC de West-Island, #201, 1870, boul des Sources, Pointe-Claire QC H9R 5N4 – 514/697-4228; Fax: 514/697-2562 – Directrice générale, Hélène Carrier
CC de Windsor et région, CP 115, QC J1S 2L7

**SASKATCHEWAN**

Arborfield BT, c/o Arborfield Credit Union, PO Box 265, SK S0E 0A0 – 306/769-8581; Fax: 306/769-4114 – President, Alvin Alyeh, 306/769-8687
Aylsham & District BT, c/o Ken Rae Farms, PO Box 21, SK S0E 0C0 – 306/862-4849; Fax: 306/862-4506 – President, Glen Gray, 306/862-3028, Fax: 306/862-5306
Battlefords CC, Hwy. 40 & 16E, PO Box 1000, North Battleford SK S9A 3E6 – 306/445-6226; Fax: 306/445-6633 – President, David Odishaw, 306/445-3888, Fax: 445-8088
Big River CC, c/o Third & Main, 300 Main St., PO Box 473, SK S0J 0E0 – 306/469-4488 – President, Wanda Watier
Biggar & District CC, c/o Advance AG & Industrial, Hwy. 4, PO Box 879, SK S0K 0M0 – 306/948-5262; Fax: 306/948-5263 – President, Mike Messer
Blaine Lake & District CC, c/o Macleods-True Value, 113 Main St., PO Box 178, SK S0J 0J0 – 306/497-2461; Fax: 306/497-2293 – President, Barbara Woytuik
Broadview CC, c/o Eckland Gates, 528 Edmonton St., PO Box 700, SK S0G 0K0 – 306/696-3272; Fax: 306/696-2508 – President, Gary Ecklund
Candle Lake CC, c/o Brassard's Service Ltd., PO Box 68, SK S0J 3E0 – 306/929-2233; Fax: 306/929-2220 – President, Stella Brassard
Canora & District CC, c/o Jaz Inc., 110 - 1st St. West, PO Box 2007, SK S0A 0L0 – 306/563-5886; Fax: 306/563-6743 – President, Juliet A. Zbijniff
Carlyle CC, c/o Skyline Motor Inn, Hwy. 13, PO Box 385, SK S0C 0R0 – 306/453-6745; Fax: 306/453-2702 – President, Ron Wiebe
Carrot River & District BT, c/o Carrot River Agencies Ltd., 19 Main St., PO Box 340, SK S0E 0L0 – 306/768-2533; Fax: 306/768-3491 – President, Perry C. Cavanaugh
Choiceland & District CC, c/o Grow Plan Fertilizers Ltd., 155 Railway Ave. West, PO Box 339, SK S0J 0M0 – 306/428-2300; Fax: 306/428-2424 – President, Frank H. Bond
Coronach Community CC, c/o Curran's Esso Service, One Railroad Ave. East, PO Box 57, SK S0H 0Z0 – 306/267-3251; Fax: 306/267-3234 – President, Bob Paisley, 306/267-5747, Fax: 306/267-2230
Cut Knife CC, c/o Cut Knife Agencies, 200 Street St., PO Box 400, SK S0M 0N0 – 306/398-4901; Fax: 306/306/398-4909 – President, Todd Schwindt
Debden & District CC, c/o Little Country Grill, PO Box 100, SK S0J 2X0 – 306/724-4487 – Acting President, Denise Sirois
Eastend CC, c/o Eastend Pharmacy, 112 Maple Ave. South, PO Box 534, SK S0N 0T0 – 306/295-3233; Fax: 306/295-3887 – President, Laurie McCuaig, 306/295-3218
Eatonia & District CC, c/o Hansen's Agency Ltd., 216 Main St., PO Box 460, SK S0L 0Y0 – 306/967-2201; Fax: 306/967-2302 – President, Bruce Cooke
Edam & District BT, c/o Day's Electric Ltd., Main St., PO Box 86, SK S0M 0V0 – 306/397-2332 – President, Cameron R. Day
Esterhazy & District CC, c/o E & M Parts, PO Box 778, SK S0A 0X0 – 306/745-2667; Fax: 306/745-2446 – President, Barry Hassler, 306/745-3965, Fax: 306/745-3965
Estevan CC, 1102 - 4th St., SK S4A 0W7 – 306/634-2828; Fax: 306/634-6729 – Executive Director, Linda Mack
Eston BT, c/o Eston Flowers, 113 Main St. South, PO Box 1000, SK S0L 1A0 – 306/962-3717; Fax: 306/962-4445 – President, Audrey Tumback
Foam Lake CC, c/o Lee Agencies Ltd., 320 Main St., PO Box 238, SK S0A 1A0 – 306/272-3242; Fax: 306/272-4294 – President, Rod M. Lee
Fort Qu'Appelle & District CC, c/o Country Plaza Motors, 121 Soiux Ave. South, PO Box 1273, SK S0G 1S0 – 306/332-5603; Fax: 306/332-5460 – President, Larry Schultz, 306/332-5533, Fax: 306/332-5535
Fox Valley CC, c/o Double L. Farms, PO Box 133, SK S0N 0V0 – 306/666-4447; Fax: 306/666-4448 – President, Lester Lodoen
Goodsoil & District CC, c/o Goodsoil Credit Union, Main St., PO Box 88, SK S0M 1A0 – 306/238-2033; Fax: 306/238-4441 – President, Lucille Martin, 306/238-2112, Fax: 306/238-4544
Grenfell CC, c/o Greg Watkins CMA, PO Box 219, SK S0G 2B0 – 306/697-3510; Fax: 306/697-3431 – President, Greg Watkins
Gull Lake & District CC, c/o Pioneer Co-op Farm Supply, 625 Proton Ave., PO Box 262, SK S0N 1A0 – 306/672-4105 – President, Casey Vaskevicius
Herbert & District CC, c/o Country Corner Crafts, 519 Herbert Ave., PO Box 190, SK S0H 2A0 – 306/784-2401; Fax: 306/784-2966 – President, Ronda Ens, 306/784-2424, Fax: 306/784-3246
Hudson Bay & District CC, c/o Northeast Service, PO Box 130, SK S0E 0Y0 – 306/865-3808; Fax: 306/865-2251 – President, Neil Hardy
Humboldt & District CC, c/o Yuen's Family Clothing, 503 Main St., PO Box 3009, SK S0K 2A0 – 306/682-2166; Fax: 306/682-3262 – President, Danny Yuen
Ituna & District CC, PO Box 609, SK S0A 1N0 – 306/795-3188; Fax: 306/795-3636 – President, Alfred W. Moore
Kamsack & District CC, PO Box 817, SK S0A 1S0 – 306/542-3078; Fax: 306/542-3068 – President, Craig Clearwater
Kelvington & District CC, c/o Kelvington Radio, 107 Main St., PO Box 1077, SK S0A 1W0 – 306/327-4656 – President, Linda Donais, 306/327-5200, Fax: 306/327-4947
Kenaston & District CC, c/o Boehmer's Garage, 701 - 3rd St., PO Box 302, SK S0G 2N0 – 306/252-2171 – President, John Boehmer
Kerrobert CC, 521 Atlantic Ave., PO Box 454, SK S0L 1R0 – 306/834-2461; Fax: 306/834-5445 – President, Robert Aellen
Kindersley CC, 608 - 12th Ave. East, PO Box 1537, SK S0L 1S0 – 306/463-2320; Fax: 306/463-4607 – President, Rick Hertz, 306/463-6408
Kinistino & District CC, c/o Tom's Radio & TV, 202 Dixon Ave., SK S0J 1H0 – 306/864-2244 – President, Tom Dewing
Kipling CC, c/o Graham Dayle Chartered Accountant, 507 Main St., PO Box 700, SK S0G 2S0 – 306/736-8211; Fax: 306/736-8295 – President, Scott Kearns, 306/736-2535, Fax: 306/736-8445
La Ronge & District CC, PO Box 286, SK S0J 1L0 – 306/425-3055; Fax: 306/425-3883
Langenburg & District CC, c/o Wardale Farm Equipment Ltd., Hwy. 16 West, PO Box 190, SK S0A 2A0 – 306/743-2312; Fax: 306/743-2953 – President, Dale Kotzer
Leader BT, c/o M & P Construction, 111 - 7th St. West, SK S0N 1H0 – 306/628-3347 – President, Barry Miller
Macklin CC, c/o Royal Bank of Canada, 4816 Herald St., PO Box 642, SK S0L 2C0 – 306/753-2045; Fax: 306/753-2339 – President, Gary Thompson
Maidstone & District CC, PO Box 461, SK S0M 1M0 – 306/893-2273; Fax: 306/893-2909 – President, Connie McCulloch
Maple Creek CC, PO Box 1865, SK S0N 1N0 – 306/662-2811; Fax: 306/662-4131; Email: mccedc@sk.sympatico.ca – Co-Chair, Johanna Drury
Meadow Lake & District CC, PO Box 1168, SK S0M 1V0 – 306/236-5939
Melfort & District CC, c/o Chamber Office, 620 Saskatchewan Ave., PO Box 2002, SK S0E 1A0 – 306/752-4636; Fax: 306/752-9505; URL: http://www.nlnet.melfort.sk.ca/mcc/ – Manager, Corinna Stevenson
Melville & District CC, c/o Chamber Office, 420 Main St., PO Box 429, SK S0A 2P0 – 306/728-4177; Fax: 306/728-5911 – Manager, Eileen Farough
Moose Jaw CC, 88 Sask St. East, PO Box 1359, SK S6H 4R3 – 306/692-6414; Fax: 306/692-6463; Email: rmclean@focalpoint.net – President, Brian Martynook, 306/692-7536, Fax: 306/692-2343
Moosomin CC, c/o McKay Publications Ltd., 624 Main St., PO Box 250, SK S0G 3N0 – 306/435-2445; Fax: 306/435-3969 – President, Don Osman, 306/435-3851
Nipawin & District CC, PO Box 177, SK S0E 1E0 – 306/862-5252; Fax: 306/862-5350 – Manager, Tracey Senger
Norquay CC, c/o Norquay Co-op, 13 Hwy. 49 East, PO Box 340, SK S0A 2V0 – 306/594-2215 – Secretary, Christine Sokulski, 306/594-2228
Outlook & District CC, c/o Lutheran Collegiate, PO Box 459, SK S0L 2N0 – 306/867-8344; Fax: 306/867-9947 – President, Daniel A. Haugen
Pangman CC, c/o Western Canadian Farm & Ranch Supply Ltd., PO Box 38, SK S0C 2C0 – 306/442-4449; Fax: 306/442-2064 – President, Harry Sheppard

Pierceland & District CC, c/o Beaver River Banner, PO Box 555, SK S0M 2K0 – 306/839-4496; Fax: 306/839-2306 – President, Lillian Mein
Porcupine Plain & District CC, c/o Porcupine Opportunties, PO Box 666, SK S0E 1H0 – 306/278-3017; Fax: 306/278-3150 – Co-President, Carl Kwiatkowski
Prince Albert CC, 3700 - 2 Ave. West, SK S6W 1A2 – 306/764-6222; Fax: 306/922-4727; Email: pachamber@sk.sympatico.ca; URL: http://www.thechamberofcom.com – President, Gerry Stroshein, 306/763-4646, Fax: 306/763-8199
Radville CC, c/o Eldene's Music, 110 Main St., PO Box 22, SK S0G 2G0 – 306/869-2729 – President, Laurie Nuspl, 306/869-2610
Regina CC, 2145 Albert St., SK S4P 2V1 – 306/757-4658; Fax: 306/757-4668; Email: regina.chamber@sk.sympatico.ca; URL: http://www.wcw.net/sk/regina.chamber/ – Executive Director, Deanna Dalla-Vicenza
Rosetown & District CC, c/o Prairie Centre Credit Union, PO Box 940, SK S0L 2V0 – 306/882-2899; Fax: 306/882-3326 – President, George Leith
Rosthern CC, c/o L & L Meats Inc., 1005 - 6th St., PO Box 96, SK S0K 3R0 – 306/232-4221 – Chairman, Les Neufeld
St. Brieux & District CC, c/o Bourgault Air Seeder, Hwy. 368, PO Box 130, SK S0K 3V0 – 306/275-2300; Fax: 306/275-2307 – President, Lorraine Perault
St Walburg CC, c/o Kim's Service, 110 - 2nd St. East, PO Box 303, SK S0M 2T0 – 306/248-3421 – President, Kim Rendle, 306/248-3421
Saskatoon CC, 345 - 3 Ave. South, SK S7K 1M6 – 306/244-2151; Fax: 306/244-8366 – Executive Director, Kent Smith-Windsor
Shaunavon CC, c/o Gallery of Gold, 370 Centre St., PO Box 1450, SK S0N 2M0 – 306/297-2385; Fax: 306/297-2241 – President, Leslie Goldstein
South Shore CC, c/o Alexander's Welding, PO Box 459, Regina Beach SK S0G 4C0 – 306/729-2327 – President, Morley Alexander
Spiritwood CC, c/o Spiritwood New & Used, 109 Main St., PO Box 365, SK S0J 2M0 – 306/883-2266; Fax: 306/884-3738 – President, Bruce Rogers
Star City BT, c/o Canada Post Corp., 112 - 4th St., PO Box 142, SK S0E 1P0 – 306/863-2509 – President, Carol Pederson
Stoughton CC, PO Box 476, SK S0G 4T0 – 306/457-3188 – President, Thomas Sangster
Swift Current CC, Route 35, Mobile Delivery, SK S9H 3V6 – 306/773-7268; Fax: 306/773-5686 – Executive Director, Marlene Arndt
Tisdale & District CC, c/o Crawford Studios, 1014 - 100th St., PO Box 657, SK S0E 1T0 – 306/873-3277 – President, Margaret Crawford
Unity & District CC, c/o Michael's Photography, 372 - 5th Ave. East, PO Box 1205, SK S0K 4L0 – 306/228-2701; Fax: 306/228-4221 – President, Michael Soloski
Vonda CC, c/o My Florist, PO Box 181, SK S0K 4N0 – 306/258-2110; Fax: 306/258-2035 – President, Leanne Holynski
Wadena & District CC, PO Box 962, SK S0A 4J0 – 306/338-2561; Fax: 306/338-3621 – President, Pat Casement
Waskesiu CC, PO Box 216, Waskesiu Lake SK S0J 2Y0 – 306/663-5898; Fax: 306/663-5448 – President, Myrna Nagy
Watrous & District CC, PO Box 280, SK S0K 4T0 – 306/946-3955; Fax: 306/946-3966 – President, Earl Amendt
Watson & District CC, c/o Sask Liquor & Gaming, PO Box 356, SK S0K 4V0 – 306/287-3511; Fax: 306/287-3319 – President, Neil Bryce
Weyburn CC, 411 Industrial Lane, PO Box 1300, SK S4H 3J9 – 306/842-4738; Fax: 306/842-0520 – Manager, Lois Benneweis
Wolseley & District CC, PO Box 519, SK S0G 5H0 – 306/698-2244 – President, Shirley Harris
Wynyard & District CC, c/o Wynyard Pharmacy, 225 Bosworth St., PO Box 309, SK S0A 4T0 – 306/554-2571; Fax: 306/554-3990 – President, Walter Peterson
Yorkton CC, PO Box 1051, SK S3N 2X3 – 306/783-4368; Fax: 306/786-6978 – Manager, John McPake
Zenon Park BT, c/o Zenon Park Credit Union, 735 Main St., PO Box 250, SK S0E 1W0 – 306/767-2434 – President, Allen Georget

#### YUKON TERRITORY

Whitehorse CC, #101, 302 Steele St., YT Y1A 2C5 – 867/667-7545; Fax: 867/667-4507; Email: wcc@yukon.net; URL: http://www.yukon.net/wcc – President, Rick Nielsen

## CONSULTANT LOBBYISTS

Consultant lobbyists are individuals who, for payment and on behalf of a client, communicate with a public office holder in attempts to influence government decisions. They must register when they lobby for the making, developing or amending of legislative proposals, bills or resolutions, regulations, policies or programs; and the awarding of federal grants, contributions or contracts.

The Lobbyists Registration Act, which came into force on January 31, 1996, requires lobbyists to report their clients and employers, the parent and subsidiary companies of corporations that benefit from the lobbying, the organizational members of coalition groups that lobby, which government departments or agencies are contacted, and the specific subject matters of lobbying activities.

The Canadian Almanac listing of consultant lobbyists is based on information submitted to the Lobbyists Registration Branch. For further information, consult the Lobbyists Registry under Marketplace Services through Strategis, Industry Canada's gateway to the Internet at the following address: http://strategis.ic.gc.ca.

### ALBERTA

#### CALGARY

Bennett Jones Verchere, Bankers Hall East, #4500, 855 - 2 St. SW, Calgary AB T2P 4K7 – 403/298-3100; Fax: 403/265-7219
C. Michael Ryer
John R. Crawford & Associates, 6 Hawthorne Cres. NW, Calgary AB T2N 3V4 – 403/284-9733; Fax: 403/284-9733
John R. Crawford
Felesky Flynn, First Canadian Centre, #3400, 350 - 7 Ave SW, Calgary AB T2P 3N9 – 403/260-3300; Fax: 403/263-9649; Email: felesky@mail.cycor.ca
Brian A. Felesky, Q.C.
D. Blair Nixon
F. Brenton Perry
Leslie E. Skingle
Donald H. Watkins
GSI Grants Consultants Canada Inc., 17003 Sunvale Rd. SE, Calgary AB T2X 2S5 – 403/256-1989; Fax: 403/256-2180
Robert Dann, Email: rob@agt.net
Howard, Mackie, Canterra Tower, #1000, 400 - 3 Ave. SW, Calgary AB T2P 4H2 – 403/232-9523; Fax: 403/266-1395; Email: postmaster@howardmackie.com; URL: http://howardmackie.com
Colin P. MacDonald
KPMG, #1200, 205 - 5th Ave. SW, Calgary AB T2P 4B9 – 403/691-8421; Fax: 403/691-8008; Email: rbrown@kpmg.ca
Robert A. Brown
Macleod Dixon, Canterra Tower, #3700, 400 - 3 Ave. SW, Calgary AB T2P 4H2 – 403/267-8222; Fax: 403/264-5973; Email: md@lexcom.ab.ca
E.A. Heakes
J.G. McKee
J. Cameron Millikin Consulting Ltd., 3803 - 8A St. SW, Calgary AB T2T 3B6 – 403/243-2970; Fax: 403/287-1023
John Cameron Millikin
Milner Fenerty, Fifth Ave. Place, 30th Floor, 237 - 4th Ave. SW, Calgary AB T2P 4X7 – 403/268-7000; Fax: 403/268-3100; Email: milfen@milfen.com; URL: http://www.milfen.com
Gerald D. Chipeur
Francis M. Saville, Q.C.
Osler, Hoskin & Harcourt, #1900, 333 - 7th Ave. SW, Calgary AB T2P 2Z1 – 403/260-7044; Fax: 403/260-7024
Jack A. Silverson
Price Waterhouse, #1200, 425 - 1 Ave. SW, Calgary AB T2P 3V7 – 403/267-1277; Fax: 403/264-4745
Laurie Pare
Peter Wallis Consulting Ltd., 3617 - 7th St. SW, Calgary AB T2T 2Y2 – 403/287-3634; Fax: 403/287-3634; Email: wallisp@cadvision
Peter C. Wallis
Waymar Energy Inc., #400, 550 - 5th Ave. SW, Calgary AB T2P 3Y6 – 403/281-6467; Fax: 403/281-5151
Wayne I. Bobye

#### EDMONTON

Canadian Corporate Consultants Ltd., #1202, 10109 - 106 St., Edmonton AB T5J 3L7 – 403/429-4488; Fax: 403/425-3575
Barry Strauss
Government Policy Consultants (GPC), Canada Trust Tower, #1100, 10104 - 103 Ave., Edmonton AB T5J 0H8 – 403/944-0696; Fax: 403/441-9849
James V. Campbell
Hill & Knowlton, Royal LePage, #990, 10130 - 103 St., Edmonton AB T5J 3N9 – 403/428-6459; Fax: 403/420-1230
Brian Wik
Milner Fenerty, Manulife Pl., #2900, 10180 - 101 St., Edmonton AB T5J 3V5 – 403/423-7100; Fax: 403/423-7276; Email: milfen@milfen.com; URL: http://www.milfen.com
T.W. Wakeling
Parlee McLaws, Manulife Pl., #1500, 10180 - 101 St., Edmonton AB T5J 4K1 – 403/423-8500; Fax: 403/423-2870; Email: lawyers@parlee.com; URL: http://www.parlee.com
B.D. Hirsche

### BRITISH COLUMBIA

#### LIONS BAY

Ellen M. Gunn, PO Box 101, Lions Bay BC V0N 2E0 – 604/921-1135; Fax: 604/921-1293
Ellen M. Gunn

#### SIDNEY

Alexander C. Phillips, #27, 2353 Harbour Rd., Sidney BC V8L 3X8 – 250/655-1952; Fax: 250/655-1952
Alexander C. Phillips

#### SURREY

Concise Consulting Ltd., 8881 - 160 St., Surrey BC V4N 2X8 – 604/951-0500; Fax: 604/951-8899
Prem S. Vinning

#### VANCOUVER

Acres International Limited, 845 Cambie St., 4th Fl., Vancouver BC V6B 2P4 – 604/683-9141; Fax: 604/683-9148
Scott R. Hanna
Michael A. Bailey & Associates, Bentall Centre, Box: 49104, #1753, 595 Burrard St., Vancouver BC

* BT - Board of Trade; BC - Bureau de commerce; CC - Chamber of Commerce/Chambre de commerce

V7X 1G4 – 604/684-2228; Fax: 604/683-6345; Email: bailhoff@axionet.com

Bailey Michael A.

Canadian Public Affairs Consulting Group Inc., 1028 Hamilton St., Vancouver BC V6B 2R9 – 604/688-0753; Fax: 604/688-8239

Paul Daniell

Charles Kelly

Farris, Vaughan, Wills & Murphy, Pacific Centre South, 700 West Georgia St., PO Box 10026, Vancouver BC V7Y 1B3 – 604/684-9151; Fax: 604/661-9349; Email: info@farris.com

A. Keith Mitchell, Q.C.

Koffman Birnie & Kalef, 885 West Georgia St., 19th Fl., Vancouver BC V6C 3H4 – 604/891-3688; Fax: 604/891-3788

David A.G. Birnie

Lang Michener Lawrence & Shaw, Three Bentall Centre, #2500, 595 Burrard St., PO Box 49200, Vancouver BC V7X 1L1 – 604/689-9111; Fax: 604/685-7084

Peter Botz

Francois E.J. Tougas

Robertson Rozenhart Inc., #270, 1075 West Georgia St., Vancouver BC V6E 3C9 – 604/664-7640; Fax: 604/688-3105

Donald E. McDonald

Catherine J. Robertson

Rosenbloom & Aldridge, #1300, 355 Burrard St., Vancouver BC V6C 2G8 – 604/605-5555; Fax: 604/684-6402; Email: rosenbloom_aldridge@bc.sympatico.ca

James R. Aldridge

Marcus Bartley

Donald J. Rosenbloom

Schorn Consulting Ltd., Box: 1078, #1500, 885 West Georgia St., Vancouver BC V6C 3E8 – 604/684-6125; Fax: 604/488-0319

Elden Schorn

Stikeman, Elliott, Park Pl., #1700, 666 Burrard St., Vancouver BC V6C 2X8 – 604/631-1300; Fax: 604/681-1825

Eugene Hsiad Yu Kwan

Thomas & Davis, #1310, 1111 West Georgia St., Vancouver BC V6E 4M3 – 604/689-7522; Fax: 604/689-7525

J. Christopher Thomas

Thorsteinssons, Three Bentall Centre, 595 Burrard St., 27th Fl., PO Box 49123, Vancouver BC V7X 1J2 – 604/689-1261; Fax: 604/688-4711

Michael J. O'Keefe, Q.C.

## MANITOBA

### BRANDON

Meyers, Norris, Penny & Co., 160 - 14th St., Brandon MB R7A 7K1 – 204/727-0661; Fax: 204/726-1543

Scott Dickson

Jerry Lupkowski

Daryl L. Ritchie

### WINNIPEG

Fillmore & Riley, Winnipeg Sq., #1700, 360 Main St., Winnipeg MB R3C 3Z3 – 204/957-8321; Fax: 204/957-0516

Wayne D. Leslie

Taylor McCaffrey, 400 St. Mary Ave., 9th Fl., Winnipeg MB R3C 4K5 – 204/949-1312; Fax: 204/957-0945; Email: taylorm@mbnet.mb.ca

Stephen D. Lerner

## NEWFOUNDLAND

### ST. JOHN'S

Atlantic Perspectives Inc., 146 Waterford Bridge Rd., St. John's NF A1E 1C9 – 709/738-4001; Fax: 709/738-4005

Gary Anstey

WB Holdings Ltd., 54 Hyde Park Dr., St. John's NF A1A 5G3 – 709/738-3957; Fax: 709/754-3032

R. Winston Baker

## NOVA SCOTIA

### BEDFORD

Angel Consulting Service, #310, 15 Dartmouth Rd., Bedford NS B4A 3X6 – 902/832-7114; Fax: 902/832-7115

John R. Angel

### YARMOUTH

Pink Macdonald Harding, 379 Main St., PO Box 398, Yarmouth NS B5A 4B3 – 902/742-7861; Fax: 902/742-0425

Coline M. Campbell

## ONTARIO

### BRANTFORD

Neumann Consulting Services, PO Box 1505, Brantford ON N3T 5V2 – 519/759-7885; Fax: 519/759-7885

David E. Neumann

### BURLINGTON

HH Environmental Inc., 4192 Inglewood Dr., Burlington ON L7L 1E2 – 905/639-2787; Fax: 905/639-4388

Hugh H. Eisler

Michael Vollmer Yacht Design Inc., 1399 Birch Ave., Burlington ON L7S 1J2 – 905/681-8778; Fax: 905/637-6712

Michael Vollmer

### CUMBERLAND

Murray R. Ramsbottom Enterprises Inc., 1666 Marronier Ct., Cumberland ON K4C 1C2 – 613/769-1444

R. Murray Ramsbottom

### GLOUCESTER

BJV Consulting, 3207 Treetop Ct., Gloucester ON K1T 3P7 – 613/523-9579; Fax: 613/523-9195

Brian J. Veinot

John S. Klenavic, 62 Southpark Dr., Gloucester ON K1B 3B3 – 613/824-3053; Fax: 613/824-3053; Email: klenavic@trytel.com

John S. Klenavic

### KANATA

Ducharme & Associates, 35 Balding Cres., Kanata ON K2K 2L3 – 613/591-0302; Fax: 613/591-0302

Edward Ducharme

### MANOTIK

The Weston Group, 5638 South River Dr., Manotik ON K4M 1J4 – 613/692-4803; Fax: 613/692-3516

William Weston

### MARKHAM

N. Wilson Consulting Inc., 93 Fincham Ave., Markham ON L3P 4E2 – 905/472-8782; Fax: 905/472-4449; Email: newilson@platinum1.com

Nancy E. Lum-Wilson

### MISSISSAUGA

Affiliated Customs Brokers Ltd., 6470 Northam Dr., Mississauga ON L4V 1H9 – 905/676-3936; Fax: 905/672-5335

Sydney Martin

Arthur Andersen & Co., #1200, 2 Robert Speck Pkwy., Mississauga ON L4Z 1H8 – 905/949-3900; Fax: 905/949-3911

Tony Ancimer

Craig Cowan

Derek George

Commodity Tax Services, 2373 Basswood Cres., Mississauga ON L5L 1Y2 – 905/828-1339; Fax: 905/896-1263

Barry P. Korchmar

Brian Kelly Consulting, #102, 3050 Orleans Rd., Mississauga ON L5L 5P7 – 905/569-6994

Brian Kelly

McMillan Binch, #800, 3 Robert Speck Pkwy., Mississauga ON L4Z 2G5 – 905/566-2003; Fax: 905/566-2029

John Armstrong, Email: jarmstrong@mcbinch.com

David Butler

Price Waterhouse, #1100, 1 Robert Speck Pkwy., Mississauga ON L4Z 3M3 – 905/272-1200; Fax: 905/272-3937

Morley P. Hirsch

Peter F. Kila

Barry Smith, #117, 377 Burnhamthorpe Rd. East, Mississauga ON L5A 3Y1 – 905/276-9701; Fax: 905/276-1973

Barry Smith

### NEPEAN

Robert Bowen Associates Ltd., 8 Solva Dr., Nepean ON K2H 5R5 – 613/828-6219; Fax: 613/828-6684

Robert R. Bowen

Gary Brooks, 17 Cimarron Cr., Nepean ON K2G 6E1 – 613/723-2695; Fax: 613/723-3503

Gary C. Brooks

JL Consulting, 142F Valley Stream Dr., Nepean ON K2H 9C6 – 613/721-8904; Fax: 613/721-8918

Jean L.J. Lamoureux

George MacFarlane, #220, 2 Gurdwara Rd., Nepean ON K2E 1A2 – 613/226-8588; Fax: 613/226-7103

George MacFarlane

Garry Rolston Associates, 9 Kane Terrace, Nepean ON K2J 2A5 – 613/825-3250; Fax: 613/825-7640; Email: grolston@israr.ca

Garry Rolston

Peter Allan Staruch, 31 Mohawk Cres., Nepean ON K2H 7G7 – 613/828-7266

Peter Allan Staruch

Thrust Line International, 34 Farlane Blvd., Nepean ON K2E 5H4 – 613/225-1869; Fax: 613/235-0784

A. Sean Henry

### OAKVILLE

Lloyd A. Hackett, 1310 Ingledene Dr., Oakville ON L6H 2J4 – 905/845-8226; Fax: 905/845-9578; Email: cdrims@globalserve.net; URL: http://www.rims.org

Lloyd A. Hackett

### ORLEANS

Henault Enterprises Inc., 1204 St-Moritz Ct., Orleans ON K1C 2B3 – 613/824-2184; Fax: 613/824-2184

Philippe G. Henault

Michael M. Johnson & Associates Inc., 1647 Sunview Dr., Orleans ON K1C 5C6 – 613/841-6685; Fax: 613/841-6686; Email: mmjohnson@sympatico.ca

Michael M. Johnson

Waldrum & Associates, 6608 Windsong Ave., Orleans ON K1C 6N1 – 613/830-7229; Fax: 613/841-0371; Email: waldrum@magi.com

Alexander Waldrum

**OTTAWA**

Alphalink, 221 Remic Ave., Ottawa ON K1P 6L2 – 613/563-3972; Fax: 613/563-2025
J. Brian Linklater

C.D. Arthur & Associates Inc., #1004, 275 Sparks St., Ottawa ON K1R 7X9 – 613/236-5581; Fax: 613/238-0368
Douglas C. Arthur

Association House, #800, 55 Metcalfe St., Ottawa ON K1P 6L5 – 613/567-3080; Fax: 613/232-7148
James S. Deacey
John Gorman
Brian Guest
Jan Lounder
Les McIlroy
Brian P. Metcalfe
Paul Pellegrini
Art Silverman
Jean-Paul Sirois
Ken Winchcomb

Paul-Andre Baril, #311, 225 Metcalfe St., Ottawa ON K2P 1P9 – 613/238-1269; Fax: 613/238-2501
Paul-Andre Baril

Barrows & Associates, #1300, 55 Metcalfe St., Ottawa ON K1P 6L5 – 613/238-4371; Fax: 613/238-8642
Gil Barrows

BCI Regulatory Policy, #202, 2301 Carling Ave., Ottawa ON K2B 7G3 – 613/596-0257; Fax: 613/596-5040
Doug D. Blair

Leonard Belaire, 17 St. Andrew St., Ottawa ON K1N 5E8 – 613/241-2896; Fax: 613/241-8633
Leonard Belaire

Jean Belanger, 2230 Quinton St., Ottawa ON K1H 6V3 – 613/731-6362; Fax: 613/731-6199
Jean Belanger

Gerald Berger Consulting Inc., 384 Hamilton Ave. South, Ottawa ON K1Y 1C7 – 613/728-6177; Fax: 613/728-5827
Gerald Arthur Berger

T.J. Bindon Consulting Inc., #2102, 500 Laurier Ave. West, Ottawa ON K1R 5E1 – 613/234-7376; Fax: 613/234-7562
Thomas J. Bindon

Blake, Cassels & Graydon, World Exchange Plaza, 45 O'Connor St., 20th Fl., Ottawa ON K1P 1A4 – 613/788-2200; Fax: 613/788-2247; Email: ottawa@blakes.ca; URL: http://www.blakes.ca
Nancy Brooks
Gord Cameron, Email: gkc@blakes.ca

Brogan Consulting, #202, 2301 Carling Ave., Ottawa ON K2B 7B9 – 613/596-5042; Fax: 613/596-5040
Thomas P. Brogan

P.J. Burman Consultant, 2340 Hoddington Cres., Ottawa ON K1H 8J4 – 613/733-3028; Fax: 613/733-9531
Pannalal J. Burman

Canadian Public Affairs Consulting Group Inc., #1000, 100 Sparks St., Ottawa ON K1P 5B7 – 613/238-7400; Fax: 613/563-7671
Craig Oliver
G. Peter Smith

Caparim International, 37 Linden Terrace, Ottawa ON K1S 1Z1 – 613/563-3292; Fax: 613/230-3560
Richard H. Bower

Capello Consulting, 37 Claudet Cres., Ottawa ON K1G 4R4 – 613/738-7224; Fax: 613/738-7440
Gerald G. Capello

Capital Hill Group/Groupe Capital Hill, #300, 66 Queen St., Ottawa ON K1P 5C6 – 613/235-0221; Fax: 613/235-9694; Email: info@capitalhill.ca
David Angus
Steven Dover
David Dyer
Philippe Gervais
Herb Metcalfe
Jean-Francois Thibault
Nanci Woods

Arthur Carew & Company, 40 Signal St., Ottawa ON K2L 1B9 – 613/831-1816; Fax: 613/831-4697
Arthur V. Carew

CFN Consultants, #1502, 222 Queen St., Ottawa ON K1P 5V9 – 613/232-1576; Fax: 613/238-5519
John Allan
Barry L. Code
Eldon J. Healey
William R. Oldford
George D. Simpson
Raymond N. Sturgeon

Conexus Research Group Inc., #300, 55 Murray St., Ottawa ON K1N 5M3 – 613/234-7099; Fax: 613/563-7239
Paul C. Larocque

Corporation House Ltd., #1400, 60 Queen St., Ottawa ON K1P 5Y7 – 613/238-5678; Fax: 613/238-5391
Samuel F. Hughes
Ronald Lefebvre
Robert Morton
Douglas B. Wurtele

Douglas Coupar & Associates, #210, 151 Metcalfe St., Ottawa ON K2P 1N8 – 613/565-7106; Fax: 613/565-7554
Dougals Coupar

Paul W. Couse, #1001, 275 Slater St., Ottawa ON K1P 5H9 – 613/563-2525; Fax: 613/236-3333
Paul W. Couse

Craven Associates, #1003, 275 Slater St., Ottawa ON K1P 5H9 – 613/236-4451; Fax: 613/230-8707
Geoff Craven

Creedy Associates, 500 Besserer St., Ottawa ON K1N 6C4 – 613/789-1657; Fax: 613/237-4061
Graham Creedy

Robert W. Cunningham, #406, 201 MacLeod St., Ottawa ON K2P 0Z9 – 613/567-1609; Fax: 613/567-5015
Robert W. Cunningham

De Kemp & Associates Ltd., #1127, 90 Sparks St., Ottawa ON K1P 5B4 – 613/235-7336; Fax: 613/235-5866
Philip A. De Kemp

De Valk Consulting Inc., #203, 2525 St. Laurent Blvd., Ottawa ON K1H 8P5 – 613/739-7850; Fax: 613/733-9501; Email: fppac@sympatico.ca
Erina De Valk
Robert G. De Valk

Deacey Public Affairs Consultants Inc., #800, 55 Metcalfe St., Ottawa ON K1P 6L5 – 613/567-3080; Fax: 613/232-7148
James Deacey

T.M. Denton Consultants, 37 Heney St., Ottawa ON K1N 5V6 – 613/789-5397; Fax: 613/789-5398; Email: tmdenton@ftn.net
Timothy M. Denton

Fred Doucet Consulting International Inc. (FDCI), #360, 440 Laurier Ave. West, Ottawa ON K1R 7X6 – 613/782-2336; Fax: 613/782-2428
Alfred (Fred) Doucet
Jaffray Wilkins

Duralex Management Inc., 45 O'Connor St., 20th Fl., Ottawa ON K1P 5H9 – 613/236-3882; Fax: 613/230-6429
Leo Duguay

Earnscliffe Strategy Group Inc., #1002, 275 Sparks St., Ottawa ON K1R 7X9 – 613/563-4455; Fax: 613/236-6173
Harry J. Near
Scott Reid
Michael W. Robinson

Evans Strategic Policy Inc., #1001, 350 Sparks St., Ottawa ON K1R 7S8 – 613/563-3205; Fax: 613/235-3111
John L. Evans

Flavell Kubrick & Lalonde, #1700, 280 Slater St., Ottawa ON K1P 1C2 – 613/230-6030; Fax: 613/230-6969
C.J. Michael Flavell
Geoffrey C. Kubrick
Paul M. Lalonde

Jason P. Flint Consulting, 236 St. Andrew, Ottawa ON K1N 5G8 – 613/241-6186; Fax: 613/563-8850
Jason P. Flint

Fraser & Beatty, #1200, 180 Elgin St., Ottawa ON K2P 2K7 – 613/783-9611; Fax: 613/563-7800; URL: http://www.fraserbeatty.ca
Richard J. Mahoney

Global Public Affairs Inc., World Exchange Plaza, #1640, 45 O'Connor St., Ottawa ON K1P 1A4 – 613/782-2336; Fax: 613/782-2428
Edmond Chiasson
Gerry Doucet
Maurice Lafontaine
Victor Little
Randy Pettipas
Kenneth D. Taylor
Jaffray Wilkins

Government Policy Consultants (GPC), #1600, 350 Albert St., PO Box 74, Ottawa ON K1R 1A4 – 613/238-2090; Fax: 613/238-9380
Leah Anderson
Claude Bechard
Gerald A. Berger
Michael Brooks
Remi Bujold
Jeremy Byatt
James V. Campbell
Robert Carman
Pelino Colaiacovo
James Crossland
Dwight Dibben
Julie E. Dickson
Bruce R. Drysdale
Alison German
John G. Harding
Stewart Lindale
Wes Muir
Andy Orr
Bruce Rawson
Faye Roberts
Patrice Ryan
Melissa Tamblyn
William Tretiak
Laura E. Tupper
Michael Von Herff

Government Policy Research Associates Inc., #1127, 90 Sparks St., Ottawa ON K1P 5B4 – 613/235-5360; Fax: 613/235-5866
Gordon A. Harrison

Gowlings, #2600, 160 Elgin St., PO Box 466, Stn D, Ottawa ON K1P 1C3 – 613/233-1781; Fax: 613/563-9869; Email: marketing@gowlings.com; URL: http://www.gowlings.com
James H. Buchan
Hy Calof, Q.C.
Richard G. Dearden
Ronald D. Lunau
Terry D. McEwan
Sean Moore
Joel B. Taller

Grey, Clark, Shih & Associates Ltd., #1004, 275 Sparks St., Ottawa ON K1R 7X9 – 613/238-7743; Fax: 613/238-0368
Peter J. Clark
Chandra Gibbs
Chris Hines

GVI Consultants Inc., PO Box 1226, Stn B, Ottawa ON K1P 5R3 – 819/827-1112; Fax: 819/827-8242
Gilles Verret, Email: gverret@cyberus.ca

Hendin, Hendin & Lyon, #726, 50 O'Connor St., Ottawa ON K1P 6L2 – 613/563-4804; Fax: 613/563-3878
Stuart E. Hendin, Q.C.

Hession, Neville & Associates, #700, 99 Bank St., Ottawa ON K1P 6B9 – 613/232-2842; Fax: 613/238-6096

Ross Christensen
Peter C. Connolly
J. Paul Hession
Raymond V. Hession
William J. Musgrove
William H. Neville

Hill & Knowlton, #1300, 55 Metcalfe St., Ottawa ON K1P 6L5 – 613/238-4371; Fax: 613/238-8642
Carl Baltare
Gil Barrows
Robert Bruchet
Glenn Chadwell
Graham Hardman
Mike McNaney
Brian L. Mersereau
David B. Miller
Gordon O'Connor
Peter Rutherford
Jeff Smith

E.E. Hobbs & Associates Ltd., 162 Glebe Ave., Ottawa ON K1S 2C5 – 613/230-6999; Fax: 613/230-2674
Ernest E. Hobbs

Hooper Lefebvre Consultants, #1400, 60 Queen St., Ottawa ON K1P 5Y7 – 613/238-5678; Fax: 613/238-5391
Ronald Charles Lefebvre

Humphreys Public Affairs Group Inc., #1620, 130 Albert St.., Ottawa ON K1P 5G4 – 613/230-3155; Fax: 613/236-2556
Jennifer A. Hartley
David L. Humphreys
James L. Lorimer

IGRG Inc. (The Industry Government Relations Group), #1110, 350 Sparks St., Ottawa ON K1R 7S8 – 613/232-1413; Fax: 613/232-9554; URL: http://home.istar.ca/~igrgadm
Gary Leroux
David MacDonald
Robert M. Mill
Scott Proudfoot
Michael G. Teeter
Ramsey M. Withers

Inter/Sect Alliance Inc., #1127, 90 Sparks St., Ottawa ON K1P 5B4 – 613/235-5385; Fax: 613/235-5866; Email: intersec@worldlink.ca
Gordon Harrison
Jill Maase
Barry L. Smith

InterCon Consultants, #1003, 275 Slater St., Ottawa ON K1P 5H9 – 613/236-4451; Fax: 613/230-8707
Peter Cameron
Ross Campbell
Geoffrey Hugh Craven
Ernest B. Creber

J.S.L. Consulting Services Ltd., #709, 99 Bank St., Ottawa ON K2P 6B9 – 613/827-2844; Fax: 613/827-5337
John S. Legate

Ken James & Associates, #906, 75 Albert St., Ottawa ON K1P 5E7 – 613/236-2966; Fax: 613/236-8169
Ken A. James

Don Jarvis Consultants, #1127, 90 Sparks St., Ottawa ON K1P 5B4 – 613/238-7809; Fax: 613/235-5866
Donald M. Jarvis

J.R. Jenkins Consultants Inc., 1052 Cromwell Dr., Ottawa ON K1V 6K5 – 613/733-3159
John Robert Jenkins

Johnston & Buchan, #1700, 275 Slater St., Ottawa ON K1P 5H9 – 613/236-3882; Fax: 613/230-6423; Email: johnbuch@magi.com
Robert J. Buchan
Laurence J.E. Dunbar

Michael A. Kelen, #700, 99 Bank St., Ottawa ON K1P 6B9 – 613/232-6272; Fax: 613/238-6096
Michael A. Kelen

Kiedrowski & Associates, 74 Iona St., Ottawa ON K1Y 3L8 – 613/724-3857; Fax: 613/724-3891; Email: john.kiedrowski@sympatico.ca; URL: http://www3.sympatico.ca/john.kiedrowski
John S. Kiedrowski

Livingston Trade Services, #1409, 130 Albert St., Ottawa ON K1P 5G4 – 613/235-7359; Fax: 613/563-1074
Kenneth H. Sorensen

Ludgate Group, #1110, 350 Sparks St., Ottawa ON K1R 7S8 – 613/232-1413; Fax: 613/232-9554
Robert Bolduc

Philip H. MacNeill, #1200, 155 Queen St., Ottawa ON K1P 6L1 – 613/232-9096; Fax: 613/232-2283; Email: office@brewers.ca
Philip H. MacNeill

Marcotte Consulting, 443 Kintyre Private, Ottawa ON K2C 3M9 – 613/727-1469; Fax: 613/727-8541
Michelle L. Marcotte

Metcalfe & Associates, #800, 55 Metcalfe St., Ottawa ON K1P 6L5 – 613/567-3080; Fax: 613/232-7148
Brian P. Metcalfe

Midpoint Consultants, #1015, 50 O'Connor St., Ottawa ON K1P 6L2 – 613/230-2727; Fax: 613/230-2934
Scott G. Walker

Moorcroft Quaiattini Inc., #200, 155 Queen St., Ottawa ON K1P 6L1 – 613/751-4493; Fax: 613/751-4496
Rick Moorcroft
Gordon Quaiattini

S.A. Murray Consulting Inc. (SAMCI), 81 Metcalfe St., 10th Fl., Ottawa ON K1P 6K7 – 613/236-3383; Fax: 613/236-4184; Email: samci@inasec.ca
Michelle Bishop
Margo Craig-Garrison
Jim Everson
Andrew Jones
Rick A. Moorcroft
Don Moors
Dominique O'Rourke
Greg Owen
Gordon Quaiattini
Jan Ramsay
Teresa Sarkesian
Gordon Shields
Gilles Verret
Susan Whitney

National Public Relations, #450, 55 Metcalfe St., Ottawa ON K1P 6L5 – 613/233-1699; Fax: 613/233-2431; Email: ggarner@ottawa.nationalpr.com
Gordon E. Garner
Howard Mains

Ogilvy Renault, #1600, 45 O'Connor St., Ottawa ON K1P 1A4 – 613/780-8661; Fax: 613/230-5459; Email: info@ogilvyrenault.com
Brenda C. Swick-Martin

Osler, Hoskin & Harcourt, #1500, 50 O'Connor St., Ottawa ON K1P 6L2 – 613/235-7234; Fax: 613/235-2867; Email: jsomers@osler.com; URL: http://www.osler.com
Glen A. Bloom
Kenneth L. Boland
Martha Healey
J. François Lemieux
Michael L. Phelan
David K. Wilson

Parallax Public Affairs Inc., #800, 55 Metcalfe St., Ottawa ON K1P 6L5 – 613/230-5939; Fax: 613/238-6096
Mark Resnick

Perley-Robertson, Panet, Hill & McDougall, #400, 90 Sparks St., Ottawa ON K1P 1E2 – 613/238-2022; Fax: 613/238-8775; 1-800-268-8292; Email: lawyers@perlaw.ca; URL: http://www.perlaw.ca
Howard P. Knopf
A. de Lotbinière Panet, Q.C.

Policy Insights Inc., #402, 222 Queen St., Ottawa ON K1P 5V9 – 613/563-8078; Fax: 613/563-4284
Ken J.I. MacKay

Prospectus Associates in Corporate Development Inc., 346 Waverley St., Ottawa ON K2P 0W5 – 613/231-2727; Fax: 613/237-7666
Thomas Creary
Robert Evershed
William J. Pristanski

Public Sector Company Ltd. (PSC), #200, 440 Laurier Ave., Ottawa ON K1R 7X6 – 613/782-2467; Fax: 613/782-2284
Bruce H.E. Maynard
John McGill
Peter Woods

Rawson Group Initiatives Inc., #300, 222 Argyle Ave., Ottawa ON K2P 1B9 – 613/236-7960; Fax: 613/230-6597
Bruce Rawson

RCG Remillard Consulting Group, 47 Langevin Ave., Ottawa ON K1M 1G1 – 613/746-5530; Fax: 613/562-0097
Richard Remillard

Berel Rodal Associates, 525 Hillcrest Ave., Ottawa ON K2A 2N1 – 613/725-2683; Fax: 613/729-9478; Email: rodal@imti.com
Berel Rodal

Sanders & Associates Inc., 1020 Grenon Ave., Ottawa ON K2B 8L8 – 613/829-8836; Fax: 613/829-9874; Email: jasanders@dtol.com
Joseph Sanders

C.G. Smallridge & Associates, #1109, 130 Albert St., Ottawa ON K1P 5G4 – 613/563-2194; Fax: 613/563-2196
Colin G. Smallridge

Smith Lyons, #1700, 45 O'Connor St., Ottawa ON K1P 1A4 – 613/230-3988; Fax: 613/230-7085; Email: slottawa@magi.com
J.J.M. Shore

Stikeman, Elliott, #914, 50 O'Connor St., Ottawa ON K1P 6L2 – 613/234-4555; Fax: 613/230-8877
Mirko Bibic
Randall Hofley
Lawson A.W. Hunter, Q.C.
T. Gregory Kane, Q.C.
Donald A. Kubesh
Stuart C. McCormack

Strategex Consultants Inc., #205, 541 Sussex Dr., Ottawa ON K1N 6Z6 – 613/562-3686; Fax: 613/562-3688
Robert Landry

Strategico Inc., 45 O'Connor St., 20th Fl., Ottawa ON K1P 6L2 – 613/235-0260; Fax: 613/235-7012
Gordon Ritchie

Summa Strategies Canada Inc., #900, 100 Sparks St., Ottawa ON K1P 5B7 – 613/235-1400; Fax: 613/235-1444
John F. Phillips
Douglas Young
Paul Zed

Tactix Government Consulting Inc., #600, 99 Bank St., Ottawa ON K1P 6B9 – 613/566-7053; Fax: 613/233-9527
Sonja C. MacDonald
Anthony Stikeman

Temple Scott Associates Inc., #201, 8 York St., Ottawa ON K1N 5S6 – 613/241-6000; Fax: 613/241-6001; Email: tsa@globalx.net
Ian Anderson

Thorington Corporation, 333 Preston St., 11th Fl., Ottawa ON K1S 5N4 – 613/236-5156; Fax: 613/236-5142
Randal R. Goodfellow

Thornley Fallis Inc., #606, 90 Sparks St., Ottawa ON K1P 5B4 – 613/231-3355; Fax: 613/231-4515; Email: pennefather@thornleyfallis.com
Joan Pennefather

Ian Watson Consulting, 60 Queen St., 14th Fl., Ottawa ON K1P 5Y7 – 613/241-5678; Fax: 613/238-5391
Ian Watson

**ROCKCLIFFE**

John A.M. Wilson, 17 Bittern Ct., Rockcliffe ON K1L 8K9 – 613/741-4605; Fax: 613/741-0007
John A.M. Wilson

**THORNHILL**

David M. Sherman Tax Author & Consultant, 53 Bevshire Circle, Thornhill ON L4J 5B4 – 905/889-7658; Fax: 905/889-3246; Email: dave@1suc.on.ca
David M. Sherman

**TORONTO**

Advance Planning & Communications Inc., #1605, 95 St. Clair Ave. West, Toronto ON M4V 1N6 – 416/967-3702; Fax: 416/967-6414; Email: advance@interlog.com
Amanda Walton

Anstey & Associates, #1901, 77 Bloor St. West, Toronto ON M5S 1M2 – 416/920-7950; Fax: 416/920-6409
Sandra Anstey

Apco Associates, 1881 Yonge St., Toronto ON M4S 3C4 – 416/486-7229; Fax: 416/486-9783
Pamela Heneault, Email: pamela_heneault@acicanada.com
Perry Martin
Chris Ward

Appleton & Associates, 129 Yorkville Ave., 3rd Fl., Toronto ON M5R 1C4 – 416/966-8800; Fax: 416/966-8801; Email: fcappell@appletonlaw.com
Franklyn Cappell

Argyle Communications Inc., South Tower, #1007, 175 Bloor St. East, Toronto ON M4W 3R8 – 416/968-7311
Ray Argyle

Baker & McKenzie, #2100, 181 Bay St., PO Box 874, Toronto ON M5J 2T3 – 416/865-6941; Fax: 416/863-6275; URL: http://www.bakerinfo.com
Kevin B. Coon
Roy K. Kusano
Brian D. Segal

Gordon R. Baker, Q.C., Exchange Tower, Box: 426, #1470, 2 First Canadian Place, Toronto ON M5X 1E3 – 416/365-7203; Fax: 416/365-7204; Email: gordbaker@myna.com; URL: http://www.myna.com/~gbaker/
Gordon R. Baker

BDO Dunwoody, PO Box 32, Stn Royal Bank, Toronto ON M5J 2J8 – 416/369-3064; Fax: 416/865-0887
Owen A. Anderson
Bruce D. McLachlin
Raymond J. Pare

Blake, Cassels & Graydon, Commerce Court West, 28th Fl., PO Box 25, Toronto ON M5L 1A9 – 416/863-2400; Fax: 416/863-2653, 4250; Email: toronto@blakes.ca; URL: http://www.blakes.ca
J.J. Forgie, Email: jjf@blakes.ca

Blaney, McMurtry, Stapells, Friedman, Cadillac Fairview Tower, #1400, 20 Queen St. West, Toronto ON M5H 3R3 – 416/593-1221; Fax: 416/593-5437; Email: info@blaney.com; URL: http://www.blaney.com
Larry S. Grossman

Borden & Elliot, Scotia Plaza, #4400, 40 King St. West, Toronto ON M5H 3Y4 – 416/367-6000; Fax: 416/367-6749; Email: info@borden.com; URL: http://www.borden.com
Jeffrey S. Graham, Email: jgraham@borden.com
R. Andrew G. Harrison, Email: aharriso@borden.com
John D. Hylton, Q.C., Email: jhylton@borden.com
Eva M. Krasa, Email: ekrasa@borden.com
J. Fraser Mann, Email: fmann@borden.com
Geoffrey B. Morawetz, Email: gmorawet@borden.com
Simon B. Scott, Q.C., Email: sscott@borden.com
Terrance A. Sweeney, Email: tsweeney@borden.com
John J. Tobin, Email: jtobin@borden.com
Laura M. White, Email: lmwhite@borden.com
Gordon J. Zimmerman, Email: gzimmerm@borden.com

Bresver, Grossman, Scheininger & Davis, #2800, 390 Bay St., Toronto ON M5H 2Y2 – 416/869-0366; Fax: 416/869-0321; Email: bgsdlaw.com
Lester L. Scheininger

Burstyn Jeffery Inc., #1240, 155 University Ave., Toronto ON M5H 3B7 – 416/361-1475; Fax: 416/361-1652; Email: pjeffery@burstynjeffery.com
Pamela Jeffery
Catherine McKellar

C.G. Management & Communications Inc., One First Canadian Place, #780, PO Box 5100, Toronto ON M5X 1A9 – 416/362-8744; Fax: 416/362-5344
Utilia M. Amaral
Nancy P. Coldham
Donald P. Gracey
Lisa Parr

Cadesky & Associates, Atria III, Box: 126, #903, 2225 Sheppard Ave. East, Toronto ON M2J 5C2 – 416/498-9500; Fax: 416/498-9501
Howard S. Berglas

Cassels Brock & Blackwell, Scotia Plaza, #2100, 40 King St. West, Toronto ON M5H 3C2 – 416/869-5300; Fax: 416/360-8877; Email: postmaster@casselsbrock.com; URL: http://www.casselsbrock.com/
Stephen R. LeDrew

Coopers & Lybrand, 5160 Yonge St., Toronto ON M2N 6L3 – 416/229-3102; Fax: 416/229-3184
Harold A. Burke
Kevin Dancey
Douglas Magnusson
Israel H. Mida
Bradley A. Sakich

Corecon, #385, 401 Richmond St. West, Toronto ON M5V 3A8 – 416/593-1020; Fax: 416/593-2639
Sara L. Levinson

Davies, Ward & Beck, #4400, 1 First Canadian Place, 44th Fl., PO Box 63, Toronto ON M5X 1B1 – 416/863-0900; Fax: 416/863-0871; Email: info@dwb.com; URL: http://www.dwb.com
K.A. Siobhan Monaghan
David W. Smith, Q.C.

Deloitte & Touche, BCE Place, #1400, 181 Bay St., Toronto ON M5J 2V1 – 416/601-6270; Fax: 416/601-6151
Anna Diminno
Andrew W. Dunn
Mary Esteves
John Stacey
James M. Vincze

G.W. Doucet Associates Ltd., #20013, 4839 Leslie St., Willowdale ON M2J 5E3 – 416/498-1994
Gerald J. Doucet

Dworkin Communications Inc., #300, 2255 Sheppard Ave., Toronto ON M2J 4Y1 – 416/496-5075; Fax: 416/496-6160
Lawrence Dworkin

Edelman Public Relations Worldwide, #1120, 40 University Ave., Toronto ON M5J 1T1 – 416/979-1120; Fax: 416/979-0176; Email: edelman@spectranet.ca
Charles A. Fremes
Murray D. Krantz

Ernst & Young, Ernst & Young Tower, Toronto-Dominion Centre, PO Box 251, Stn Toronto Dominion, Toronto ON M5K 1J7 – 416/864-1234; Fax: 416/864-1174
Denis Brown
John Haag
Satya N. Poddar
Rosemary Schmidt

Fasken Campbell Godfrey, #3600, 66 Wellington St. West, Toronto ON M5K 1N6 – 416/366-8381; Fax: 416/364-7813; Email: firstname_lastname@fasken.com; URL: http://www.fasken.com/
D.A. Cannon
S.K. D'Arcy
R.E. Nobrega
J.M. Robinson, Q.C.
S.S. Ruby
D.J. Steadman

Finkelstein & Associates, 437 Spadina Rd., PO Box 23016, Toronto ON M5P 2W3 – 416/487-2353; Fax: 416/487-1245
Michael J. Finkelstein

FPM Group Ltd., 90 Floral Pkwy., 2nd Fl., Toronto ON M6L 2B9 – 416/242-9363
Joseph Ragusa

Fraser & Beatty, One First Canadian Place, 100 King St. West, PO Box 100, Toronto ON M5X 1B2 – 416/863-4511; Fax: 416/863-4592; Email: webmaster@fraserbeatty.ca; URL: http://www.fraserbeatty.ca
R.J. Mahoney

Fraser & Beatty, Madison Centre, #2300, 4950 Yonge St., North York ON M2N 6K1 – 416/733-3300; Fax: 416/221-5254; URL: http://www.fraserbeatty.ca
Jules L. Lewy
Riccardo C. Trecroce

Genest Murray DesBrisay Lamek, #700, 130 Adelaide St. West, Toronto ON M5H 4C1 – 416/368-8600; Fax: 416/360-2625
Bruce B. Campbell
John C. Murray

Goodman Phillips & Vineberg, #2400, 250 Yonge St., Toronto ON M5B 2M6 – 416/979-2211; Fax: 416/979-1234
Neil H. Harris
Jon R. Johnson
Bob Rae
Carrie B.E. Smit

Allan E. Gotlieb, #5300, Commerce Court West, PO Box 85, Toronto ON M5L 1B9 – 416/869-5664; Fax: 416/947-0866
Allan E. Gotlieb

Gottlieb & Pearson, #1800, 4950 Yonge St., North York ON M2N 6K1 – 416/250-1550; Fax: 416/250-7889
Darrel H. Pearson

Gowlings, #4900, Commerce Court West, PO Box 438, Stn Commerce Court, Toronto ON M5L 1J3 – 416/862-7525; Fax: 416/862-7661; URL: http://www.gowlings.com/toronto.htm
Steven Gaon
Gary Graham
Emma Grell
Mark L. Madras
Dean Saul

Hazzard & Hore, #1002, 141 Adelaide St. West, Toronto ON M5H 3L5 – 416/868-0074; Fax: 416/868-1468
Edward Hore

Hill & Knowlton, #800, 1 Eglinton Ave. East, Toronto ON M4P 3A1 – 416/483-5228; Fax: 416/483-4111
Michael E. Coates

Hon. Robert P. Kaplan, Q.C., #301, 55A Avenue Rd., Toronto ON M5R 2G3 – 416/922-4444; Fax: 416/964-2584
Hon. Robert P. Kaplan, P.C., Q.C.

Don Kerr Consulting, 110 MacPherson Ave., Toronto ON M5R 1W8 – 416/920-8114; Fax: 416/920-4905
Donald Kerr

Koskie & Minsky, #900, 20 Queen St. West, PO Box 52, Toronto ON M5H 3R3 – 416/977-8353; Fax: 416/977-3316; URL: http://www.koskieminsky.com
Raymond Koskie, Q.C., Email: rkoskie@koskieminsky.com

Lang Michener, BCE Pl., #2500, 181 Bay St., PO Box 747, Toronto ON M5J 2T7 – 416/360-8600; Fax: 416/365-1719; Email: debbies@toronto.langmichener.ca

Gerald D. Courage
Gordon M. Farquharson, Q.C.
Pierre Richard

**TORONTO**

Lee Associates, #506, 44 Charles St. West, Toronto ON K1P 6K7 – 416/960-8881; Fax: 416/967-0572
Andrea L. Vincent

**TORONTO**

MacBain Public Affairs Inc., 59A Hannaford St., Toronto ON M4E 3G8 – 416/699-2337; Fax: 416/699-6613
Robert W. MacBain

W.A. MacDonald Associates Inc., BCE Place, #3720, 161 Bay St., PO Box 621, Toronto ON M5J 2S1 – 416/865-7091; Fax: 416/865-7934
William A. MacDonald

Macleod Dixon, BCE Place, #4520, 181 Bay St., PO Box 792, Toronto ON M5J 2T3 – 416/360-8511; Fax: 416/360-8277; Email: 75143.2536@compuserve.com
Edward A. Heakes

McCarthy Tétrault, Toronto-Dominion Bank Tower, #4700, PO Box 48, TD Centre, Toronto ON M5K 1E6 – 416/362-1812; Fax: 416/868-0673; URL: http://www.mccarthy.ca
Thomas B. Akin
Neil E. Bass
John W. Boscariol
Danielle M. Bush
Bradley Crawford, Q.C.
Riyaz Dattu
Peter S. Grant
Hon. Donald S. Macdonald, P.C.

McDonald & Hayden, #1500, 1 Queen St. East, Toronto ON M5C 2Y3 – 416/364-3100; Fax: 416/601-4100; Email: ddouglas@mchayden.on.ca; URL: http://www.mchayden.on.ca
Clifford M. Goldlist

McIlroy & McIlroy Inc., #2725, 25 King St. West, PO Box 228, Toronto ON M5L 1E8 – 416/777-0447; Fax: 416/777-0136
James P. McIlroy

McMillan Binch, South Tower, #3800, Royal Bank Plaza, Toronto ON M5J 2J7 – 416/865-7000; Fax: 416/865-7048; 1-888-622-4624; URL: http://www.mcbinch.com
D.J. Albrecht
A.N. Campbell
P.G. Cathcart, Q.C.
R.S.G. Chester
K.S.M. Hanly
J.A. Kazanjian
T. O'Sullivan
J.W.F. Rowley
G.W. Scott, Q.C.
D.G. Wentzell
M.M. Yaksich

Morris, Rose, Ledgett, Canada Trust Tower, BCE Pl., #2700, 161 Bay St., Toronto ON M5J 2S1 – 416/981-9400; Fax: 416/863-9500
Stuart F. Bollefer
Michael K. Eisen

Norditrade Inc., 33 Laird Dr., Toronto ON M4G 3S9 – 416/467-8438; Fax: 416/467-0429; Email: norditde@interlog.com
Lars Henriksson

Osler, Hoskin & Harcourt, PO Box 50, One First Canadian Place, Toronto ON M5X 1B8 – 416/362-2111; Fax: 416/862-6666; Email: counsel@osler.com; URL: http://www.osler.com
S. Firoz Ahmed
David R. Allgood
Ronald G. Atkey, Q.C.
Lyndon A.J. Barnes
Monica E. Biringer
Eugene A.G. Cipparone
Peter H.G. Franklyn
Peter L. Glossop
Douglas T. Hamilton
Philip J.B. Heath
Andrew H. Kingissepp
Julie Y. Lee
Norman C. Loveland
John H. Macfarlane
David S. McFarlane
Andrew McGuffin
Blake M. Murray
Jack A. Silverson
David T. Tetreault
Richard G. Tremblay

Paragon Reputation Management (Canada) Inc., #1010, 6 Adelaide St. East, Toronto ON M5C 1H6 – 416/363-3111; Fax: 416/363-3944
Douglas B. Hay

Susan J. Peacock Consulting, 153 Madison Ave., Toronto ON M5R 2S8 – 416/961-1888; Fax: 416/968-1016
Susan J. Peacock

Victor Peters, TD Centre, 79 Wellington St. West, PO Box 189, Toronto ON M5K 1N2 – 416/865-7300; Fax: 416/814-3120
Victor Peters

Policy Concepts, #410, 60 Bloor St. West, Toronto ON M4W 3B8 – 416/922-6156; Fax: 416/922-4295
Peter S. Regenstreif

Price Waterhouse, #1900, 5700 Yonge St., North York ON M2M 4K7 – 416/218-1403; Fax: 416/218-1499
Bruce Harris

Public Perspectives Inc., #900, 20 Queen St. West, PO Box 52, Toronto ON M5H 3R3 – 416/971-8726; Fax: 416/581-1528; Email: ppi@koskieminsky.com
Darrell L. Brown
Raymond Koskie
Peter Landry

Purden Communications, 160 Bloor St. East, Toronto ON M4W 3P7 – 416/413-1218; Fax: 416/413-1550
Carolyn Purden

Thomas Robson Communications & Public Affairs, #400, 1235 Bay St., Toronto ON M5R 3K4 – 416/515-0535; Fax: 416/515-0950
Tom W. Robson

Mary A. Ross Hendriks, #1000, 145 King St. West, Toronto ON M5H 1J8 – 416/368-2351; Fax: 416/368-5193
Mary A. Ross Hendriks

Rothschild & Co. Ltd., 240 MacPherson Ave., Toronto ON M4V 1A2 – 416/801-9701; Fax: 416/533-8013
Eric W. Rothschild

Rudolph & Associates, 57 Grandview Ave., Toronto ON M4K 1J1 – 416/463-7599; Fax: 416/463-7636
Mark S. Rudolph

Joseph Schmidt & Associates, 8 Totteridge Rd., Toronto ON M9A 1Z1 – 416/237-9353; Fax: 416/237-9369
Joseph Schmidt

Smith Lyons, Scotia Plaza, #5800, 40 King St. West, Toronto ON M5H 3Z7 – 416/369-7200; Fax: 416/369-7250; Email: rmconnelly@smithlyons.ca; URL: http://www.smithlyons.ca
H.B. Mayer, Q.C.
R.C. Owens
R.M. Richler
J.J. Shore

Stikeman, Elliott, #5300, Commerce Court West, PO Box 85, Toronto ON M5L 1B9 – 416/869-5500; Fax: 416/947-0866; Email: info@tor.stikeman.com
Allan E. Gotlieb
Margaret E. Grottenthaler

Strategy Corp. Inc., TD Bank Tower, TD Centre, #3908, PO Box 122, Toronto ON M5K 1H1 – 416/864-7112; Fax: 416/864-7117
John R. Duffy

Tiendale Ltd., #2000, 390 Bay St., Toronto ON M5H 2Y2 – 416/351-0394; Fax: 416/860-0580
Michael Homsi

Tory Tory DesLauriers & Binnington, #3000, Aetna Tower, Toronto-Dominion Centre, PO Box 270, Stn Toronto Dominion, Toronto ON M5K 1N2 – 416/865-0040; Fax: 416/865-7380
Stephen P. Billion
John Unger
James W. Welkoff

Tom Trbovich & Associates, #812, 35 Church St., Toronto ON M5E 1T3 – 416/364-2607; Fax: 416/364-0963
Tom Trbovich

Veritas Communications Inc., #704, 161 Eglinton Ave. East, Toronto ON M4P 1J5 – 416/482-2248; Fax: 416/482-2292
David W. McLaughlin

Warren Group Inc., Box: 24, #5900, 1 First Canadian Place, Toronto ON M5X 1K2 – 416/360-7337; Fax: 416/367-3316
Robert M. Warren

Michael Wilson International Inc., #2378, 181 Bay St., PO Box 875, Toronto ON M5J 2T3 – 416/842-4000; Fax: 416/842-4001
Michael Wilson

Kathleen Winn & Associates, 911 Carlaw Ave., Toronto ON M4K 3L4 – 416/461-8874; Fax: 416/461-2525
Kathleen J. Winn

Eileen Wykes Communications, #700, 1 Eglinton Ave. East, Toronto ON M4P 3A1 – 416/921-1894; Fax: 416/921-1894
Eileen Wykes

**WINDSOR**

Belowus Easton English Holmes, 100 Ouellette Ave., 7th Fl., Windsor ON N9A 6T3 – 519/973-1900; Fax: 519/973-0225
R. Bruck Easton, Q.C.

## QUÉBEC

**GATINEAU**

Kehoe, Blais, Major & Parent, #200, 344, boul Maloney est, Gatineau QC J8P 7A6 – 819/663-2439; Fax: 819/663-4816
Claude Grant

Le Groupe Cortan, 771, boul St-Rene est, Gatineau QC J8P 1T2 – 819/663-0961; Fax: 819/782-2428
Denis Tanguay

**HULL**

Lawrence Cannon et Associés, 116, rue Marcel Chaput, Hull QC J9A 3B2 – 819/771-4035; Fax: 819/771-1765; Email: lcannon@istar.ca
Lawrence Cannon

Teledesic Corporation, 80, rue Belleau, Hull QC J9A 1H1 – 819/770-8088; Fax: 819/770-2361
Marc Dupuis

**MONTRÉAL**

Byers Casgrain, #3900, 1, Place Ville-Marie, Montréal QC H3B 4M7 – 514/878-8811; Fax: 514/866-2241
Jean-Claude Bachand
Jean Bazin, Q.C.
William S. Grodinsky
John Hurley

Canvin Consultants Inc., #110, 3300, Cote-Vertu ouest, St-Laurent QC H4R 2B7 – 514/695-2113; Fax: 514/695-3027
Harold J. Canvin

CEF Ganesh Corporation, #82, 1227, rue Sherbrooke ouest, Montréal QC H3G 1G1 – 514/868-7396; Fax: 514/868-7492; Email: ceforget@teleglobe.ca
Claude E. Forget

Robert Church, 82, boul William, Verdun QC H3E 1R6 – 514/765-8903; Fax: 514/765-3472
Robert Church

Desjardins Ducharme Stein Monast, Tour de la Banque Nationale, #2400, 600, rue de la Gauchetière ouest, Montréal QC H3B 4L8 – 514/878-9411; Fax: 514/878-9092; 1-800-670-0102; Email: avocat@ddsm.ca; URL: http://www.ddsm.ca
Guy J.H. Lord
Eckler Partners Limited, #1245, 2020, rue University, Montréal QC H3A 2A5 – 514/848-9077; Fax: 514/848-9079
Nicholas Bauer
Forum Communications Affaires Publiques Inc., #300, 1176, rue Bishop, Montréal QC H3G 2E3 – 514/954-1080; Fax: 514/954-1868
Marc K. Parson
Gervais Gagnon Covington & Associes Inc., #200, 606, rue Cathcart, Montréal QC H3B 1K9 – 514/393-9500; Fax: 514/393-9324
Graham A. Covington
Jean-Rene Gagnon
Richard Gervais
Goodman Phillips & Vineberg, 1501 McGill College Ave., 26th Fl., Montréal QC H3A 3N9 – 514/841-6000; Fax: 514/841-6499; 1-888-841-6400
Mark D. Brender
Alan J. Shragie
Groupe Declic, #160, 1515, boul Chomeday, Laval QC H7V 3Y7 – 514/688-1500; Fax: 514/688-9899
Paulin G.P. Grenier
Heenan Blaikie, #2500, 1250, boul René-Lévesque ouest, Montréal QC H3B 4Y1 – 514/846-1212; Fax: 514/846-3427
Norman S. Bacal
André Bureau
Forrest C. Hume, #1100, 1200, av McGill College, Montréal QC H3B 4G7 – 514/874-0722; Fax: 514/393-9069
Forrest Clyde Hume
Insercor, #2A, 202 Elgar St., Nuns Island QC H3E 1C8 – 514/762-1292; Fax: 514/762-3736
John Welch
Keenan Lehrer, #1500, 1 Westmount Sq., Montréal QC H3Z 2P9 – 514/935-6222; Fax: 514/935-2314
John T. Keenan
Lavery, de Billy, #4000, 1, Place Ville-Marie, Montréal QC H3B 4M4 – 514/871-1522; Fax: 514/871-8977; Email: info@lavery.qc.ca; URL: http://www.laverydebilly.com
John Mavridis
Martineau, Walker, a/s Fasken Martineau, Stock Exchange Tower, #3400, 800, Place-Victoria, CP 242, Montréal QC H4Z 1E9 – 514/397-7400; Fax: 514/397-7600; 1-800-361-6266; URL: http://www.fasken.com/offices.html
Hon. Francis Fox, P.C., Q.C.
Stephen S. Heller
Eric M. Maldoff
Epiphane Mawussi, 13, ch Bord du Lac, Pointe-Claire QC H9S 4G9 – 514/697-3712; Fax: 514/281-9887
Epiphane Ayi Mawussi
Robert D. Murray & Associates, 630, boul René-Lévesque ouest, 3e étage, CP 10, Montréal QC H3C 2R3 – 514/397-6236; Fax: 514/397-6109
Robert Daniel Murray
Ogilvy Renault, #1100, 1981, McGill College Ave., Montréal QC H3A 3C1 – 514/847-4747; Fax: 514/286-5474; Email: info@ogilvyrenault.com
Thomas S. Gillespie
Pierre Laflamme
Wilfrid Lefebvre, Q.C.
Simon V. Potter
Paquette Gadler Avocats, #B10, 300, Place d'Youville, Montréal QC H2Y 2B6 – 514/849-0771; Fax: 514/849-4817
Paul Martin
Ramco Enterprises, #762, 1077, rue St-Mathieu, Montréal QC H3H 2S4 – 514/989-9057; Fax: 514/935-3785
Richard A. Morgan
Raymond, Chabot, Martin, Pare, #1900, 600, rue de la Gauchetière ouest, Montréal QC H3B 4L8 – 514/878-2691; Fax: 514/878-2127
Marc-Andre Morin
Robinson Sheppard Shapiro, Tour Stock Exchange, #4700, 800, Place Victoria, CP 322, Montréal QC H4Z 1H6 – 514/878-2631; Fax: 514/878-1865
Jacques J.R. Bouchard
J.J. Schneiderman Consultants, 3489, av Vendome, Montréal QC H4A 3M6 – 514/481-4900; Fax: 514/489-2905; Email: jj@accent.net
Jonathan J. Schneiderman
Stikeman, Elliott, #3900, 1155, boul René-Lévesque ouest, Montréal QC H3B 3V2 – 514/397-3000; Fax: 514/397-3222; Email: info@mtl.stikeman.com
Marc Lalonde, P.C., O.C., Q.C.
John W. Leopold
H. Heward Stikeman, O.C., Q.C.
Techsortia CAI Corporate Affairs International, #3030, 1000, rue de la Gauchetière ouest, Montréal QC H3B 4W5 – 514/861-9595; Fax: 514/861-9596
Steven Jast
Jean Leblond
Francoise Lyon
Douglas J. McConnachie
Howard Silverman
Towers Perrin, 1800, rue McGill College, 22e étage, Montréal QC H3A 3J6 – 514/982-2010; Fax: 514/982-9269
Robert Blais

#### QUEBEC

Aubut Chabot, #600, 900, boul René-Lévesque est, CP 910, Québec QC G1R 4T4 – 418/524-5131; Fax: 418/524-1717; Email: aubuchab@microtec.net
Marcel Aubut, Q.C.
Boily Morency, #230, 70, rue Dalhousie, Québec QC G1K 4B2 – 418/694-0704; Fax: 418/694-2140
Jean-Paul B. Boily

#### STE-FOY

Hill & Knowlton, 2876, de la Promenade, Ste-Foy QC G1W 2J1 – 418/659-6887; Fax: 418/659-2798
Dennis Dawson

## SASKATCHEWAN

#### SASKATOON

Gauley & Co., 701 Broadway Ave., PO Box 638, Saskatoon SK S7K 3L7 – 306/653-1212; Fax: 306/652-1323; Email: gauleyco@eagle.wbm.ca
J.J. Dierker, Q.C.
McKercher McKercher & Whitmore, 374 - 3rd Ave. South, Saskatoon SK S7K 1M5 – 306/653-2000; Fax: 306/244-7335; Email: mckerche@eagle.wbm.ca
D.B. Richardson

# SECTION 8

## HEALTH DIRECTORY



**See ADDENDA at the back of this book for late changes & additional information.**

### GOVERNMENT DEPARTMENTS IN CHARGE

ALBERTA: Dept. of Health, Minister's Office, 228 Legislature Bldg., Edmonton AB T5K 2B6 – 403/427-3665; Fax: 403/429-5954

Dept. of Health - Communications Branch, 10025 Jasper Ave., 18th Fl., PO Box 2222, Edmonton AB T5J 2P4 – 403/427-7164; Fax: 403/427-1171

BRITISH COLUMBIA: Ministry of Health, Minister's Office, Parliament Bldgs., 306 Legislative Bldg., Victoria BC V8V 1X4 – 250/387-5394, 952-1297 (info. line); Fax: 250/387-3696

MANITOBA: Manitoba Health, Community & Mental Health Services Division, Hospital Services, 599 Empress St., PO Box 925, Winnipeg MB R3C 2T6 – 204/786-7324; Fax: 204/772-2943

NEW BRUNSWICK: Dept. of Health & Community Services - Communications, PO Box 5100, Fredericton NB E3B 5G8 – 506/453-2536; Fax: 506/444-4697

NEWFOUNDLAND: Dept. of Health, West Block, Confederation Bldg., PO Box 8700, St. John's NF A1B 4J6 – 709/729-3127; Fax: 709/729-0121

NORTHWEST TERRITORIES: Dept. of Health & Social Services, PO Box 1320, Yellowknife NT X1A 2L9 – 867/920-6173; Fax: 867/873-0266

NOVA SCOTIA: Dept. of Health, Joseph Howe Bldg., PO Box 488, Halifax NS B3J 2R8 – 902/424-5818; Fax: 902/424-0506

ONTARIO: Ministry of Health, Institutional Health Division, 5700 Yonge St., North York ON M2M 4K5 – 416/327-7126; Fax: 416/327-7763

PRINCE EDWARD ISLAND: Dept. of Health and Social Services, 16 Garfield St., PO Box 2000, Charlottetown PE C1A 7N8 – 902/368-6130; Fax: 902/368-6136

QUÉBEC: Ministère de la santé et des services sociaux, Service de l'infocentre, 1005, ch Ste-Foy, 4e étage, Québec QC G1S 4N4 – 418/643-6209; Fax: 418/528-1630

SASKATCHEWAN: Saskatchewan Health - Corporate Information & Technology Branch, 3475 Albert St., Regina SK S4S 6X6 – 306/787-4636; Fax: 306/787-7589

YUKON TERRITORY: Health & Social Services, PO Box 2703, Whitehorse YT Y1A 2C6 – 867/667-3673; Fax: 867/667-3096

## ALBERTA

### REGIONAL HEALTH AUTHORITIES

Calgary Regional Health Authority, 1035 - 7 Ave. SW, Calgary AB T2R 3E9 – 403/541-3670; Fax: 403/541-3681, 2644; EMail: kenora.warden@crha-health.ab.ca – Authority responsible for 1,815 beds – CEO, Paul Rushforth

Camrose: East Central Regional Health Authority 7, 4703 - 53 St., Camrose AB T4V 1Y8 – 403/672-8800; Fax: 403/672-5023 – CEO, Larry Odegard

Devon: WestView Regional Health Authority, c/o Devon General Hospital Admin. Office, #A, 101 Erie St. South, Devon AB T9G 1A6 – 403/987-8204; Fax: 403/987-8233 – CEO, Larry Smook

Drumheller: Regional Health Authority 5, 515 Hwy. 10 East, PO Box 429, Drumheller AB T0J 0Y0 – 403/823-5245; Fax: 403/823-7589 – CEO, Jim H. Ramsbottom

Edmonton: Alberta Cancer Board, 9707 - 110 St., 6th Fl., Edmonton AB T5K 2L9 – 403/482-9300; Fax: 403/488-7809 – Pres. & CEO, J.M. Turc, M.D.

Edmonton: Capital Health Authority, 1J2 Walter C. Mackenzie Centre, 8440 - 112 St., Edmonton AB T6G 2B7 – 403/492-5000; Fax: 403/492-4257 – CEO, Sheila Weatherill

Edmonton: Provincial Mental Health Advisory Board, 10025 Jasper Ave., PO Box 1360, Edmonton AB T5J 2N3 – 403/422-2233; Fax: 403/422-2472 – Responsible for 872 beds – Exec. Dir., Nancy Reynolds, 403/422-2439

Fort McMurray: Northern Lights Regional Health Authority, 7 Hospital St., Fort McMurray AB T9H 1P2 – 403/791-6024; Fax: 403/791-6029 – CEO, Dalton M. Russell

Grande Prairie: Mistahia Regional Health Authority, Provincial Bldg., 2nd Fl., #2101, 10320 - 99 St., Grande Prairie AB T8V 6J4 – 403/538-5387; Fax: 403/538-5455 – CEO, Bernie McCallion

High Level: Northwestern Regional Health Authority, #200, 10106 - 100 Ave., PO Box 10000, High Level AB T0H 1Z0 – 403/926-4388; Fax: 403/926-4149 – CEO, Rod Mohr

High Prairie: Keeweetinok Lakes Regional Health Authority #15, 5226 - 53 Ave., PO Box 874, High Prairie AB T0G 1E0 – 403/523-6641; Fax: 403/523-6642; EMail: blangein@ccinet.ab.ca – Responsible for 110 beds – CEO, Brenda Langevin

High River: Headwaters Health Authority, 560 - 9 Ave. West, High River AB T1V 1B3 – 403/652-0104; Fax: 403/652-0190 – CEO, Dwight Nelson

Lethbridge: Chinook Health Region, 960 - 19 St. South, Lethbridge AB T1J 1W5 – 403/382-6009; Fax: 403/382-6011 – CEO, G.J. Tourigny

Medicine Hat: Palliser Health Authority, 666 - 5 St. SW, Medicine Hat AB T1A 4H6 – 403/529-8042; Fax: 403/529-8998 – Pres., Tom Seaman

Peace River: Peace Regional Health Authority, 10015 - 98 St., PO Box 6178, Peace River AB T8S 1S2 – 403/624-7260; Fax: 403/618-3405 – CEO, Brian Hrab

Red Deer: David Thompson Health Region, #602, 4920 - 51 St., PO Box 5026, Red Deer AB T4N 6A1 – 403/341-8622; Fax: 403/341-8632 – Responsible for 426 acute care, 23 psychiatric & 821 long term care beds – CEO, Al Martin

Smoky Lake: Lakeland Regional Health Authority, 210 Provincial Bldg., PO Box 248, Smoky Lake AB T0A 3C0 – 403/656-2030; Fax: 403/656-2033; EMail: bbell@telusplanet.net – Responsible for 712 beds – CEO, W.C. (Bill) Bell

Westlock: Aspen Regional Health Authority #11, Provincial Bldg., PO Box 2308, Westlock AB T0G 2L0 – 403/349-8705; Fax: 403/349-4879 – CEO, Robert Cable

Wetaskiwin: Crossroads Regional Health Authority, 5610 - 40 Ave., PO Box 6627, Wetaskiwin AB T9A 2G3 – 403/361-4333; Fax: 403/361-4336 – CEO, Peter Langelle

## GENERAL HOSPITALS

Athabasca Healthcare Centre, 3100 - 49 Ave., Athabasca AB T9S 1M9 – 403/675-6000; Fax: 403/675-7050 – 35 acute care, 23 long term care beds – Aspen Regional Health Authority #11

Banff Mineral Springs Hospital, PO Box 1050, Banff AB T0L 0C0 – 403/762-2222; Fax: 403/762-4193 – 20 acute care, 20 continuing care beds – Headwaters Health Authority – Senior Community Health Dir., West, Tom Novak

Barrhead Healthcare Centre, 4815 - 51 Ave., Barrhead AB T7N 1M1 – 403/674-2221, 424-6178; Fax: 403/674-6773, 6503 – 35 acute care, 15 long term care, 100 nursing home beds – Aspen Regional Health Authority #11 – Dir., Bob Keenan

Bassano General Hospital, PO Box 120, Bassano AB T0J 0B0 – 403/641-3520; Fax: 403/641-2157 – 10 acute care, 7 continuing care beds – Palliser Health Authority – Dir., Health Services, L. Ferguson

Beaverlodge Municipal Hospital, PO Box 480, Beaverlodge AB T0H 0C0 – 403/354-2136; Fax: 403/354-8355 – 18 acute care beds – Mistahia Regional Health Authority – Site Coord., Judy White

Black Diamond: Oilfields General Hospital, PO Box 1, Black Diamond AB T0L 0H0 – 403/933-2222; Fax: 403/933-2031 – 8 acute care, 28 continuing care beds – Headwaters Health Authority – Site Suprv., Emily Brookwell

Blairmore: Crowsnest Pass Health Care Centre, 2001 - 107 St., PO Box 510, Blairmore AB T0K 0E0 – 403/562-2831; Fax: 403/562-8992 – 16 acute care, 60 continuing care beds – Chinook Health Region – Exec. Dir., Donna Stelmachovich

Bonnyville Health Centre & Auxiliary Centre, PO Box 1008, Bonnyville AB T9N 2J7 – 403/826-3311; Fax: 403/826-6187 – 24 acute care, 30 long term care beds – Lakeland Regional Health Authority – Adm., Clement Johnson

Bow Island Health Centre, PO Box 3990, Bow Island AB T0K 0G0 – 403/545-2211; Fax: 403/545-2281 – 10 acute care, 20 continuing care beds – Palliser Health Authority – Pres., Tom Seaman

Boyle Healthcare Centre, 1004 Lakeview Rd., PO Box 330, Boyle AB T0A 0M0 – 403/689-3731; Fax: 403/689-3951 – 20 acute care beds – Aspen Regional Health Authority #11 – Site Suprv., Donna Larson

Breton Health Centre, PO Box 340, Breton AB T0C 0P0 – 403/696-4700; Fax: 403/696-4747 – 21 long term care beds – Crossroads Regional Health Authority

Brooks Health Centre, 440 - 3rd St. East, PO Box 300, Brooks AB T1R 1B3 – 403/362-3456; Fax: 403/362-6039 – 40 acute care, 75 continuing care beds – Palliser Health Authority – Dir. of Health Servs., Leonna Ferguson

Calgary General Hospital - Peter Lougheed Centre, 3500 - 26th Ave. NE, Calgary AB T1Y 6J4 – 403/291-8555; Fax: 403/291-8888 – 461 acute care beds – Calgary Regional Health Authority – Adm., Jeanette Pick, 403/670-1401, Fax: 403/670-1533

Calgary: Alberta Children's Hospital, 1820 Richmond Rd. SW, Calgary AB T2T 5C7 – 403/229-7211; Fax: 403/229-7221 – 115 beds – Calgary Regional Health Authority – Adm., Jeanette Pick

Calgary: Foothills Medical Centre, 1403 - 29 St. NW, Calgary AB T2N 2T9 – 403/670-1110; Fax: 403/670-2400 – 692 acute care, 180 continuing care beds – Calgary Regional Health Authority – Adm., Jeanette Pick

Camrose: St. Mary's Hospital, 4607 - 53 St., Camrose AB T4V 1Y5 – 403/679-6100; Fax: 403/679-6198 – 76 acute care beds – East Central Regional Health Authority 7 – Exec. Dir., Michael Shea

Canmore Hospital, PO Box 130, Canmore AB T0L 0M0 – 403/678-5536; Fax: 403/678-9874 – 12 acute care, 23 continuing care beds – Headwaters Health Authority – Site Suprv., Barb Shellian

Cardston Hospital, 144 - 2nd St. West, PO Box 1440, Cardston AB T0K 0K0 – 403/653-4411; Fax: 403/653-4399, 4115 – 25 acute care, 72 continuing care beds – Chinook Health Region – Exec. Dir., Roger N. Walker

Castor: Our Lady of the Rosary Hospital, PO Box 329, Castor AB T0C 0X0 – 403/882-3434; Fax: 403/882-2751 – 5 acute care, 20 continuing care beds – East Central Regional Health Authority 7 – Exec. Dir., Marilyn Weber

Cereal Municipal Hospital, PO Box 130, Cereal AB T0J 0N0 – 403/326-3838; Fax: 403/326-3730 – 5 long term care beds, 11 alternate living beds – Regional Health Authority 5 – Dir. of Health Servs., Stan Faupel, 403/854-3331

Claresholm General Hospital, PO Box 610, Claresholm AB T0L 0T0 – 403/625-3344; Fax: 403/625-3862 – 16 acute care beds – Headwaters Health Authority – Site Suprv., Brian Popp

Coaldale Health Care Centre, 2100 - 11 St., Coaldale AB T1M 1L2 – 403/345-3075; Fax: 403/345-2681 – 47 continuing care beds – Chinook Health Region – CEO, Bob Petrashewsky

Cold Lake Health Centre, 314 - 25 St., Cold Lake AB T9M 1G6 – 403/639-3322; Fax: 403/639-2255 – 29 acute care, 25 long term care beds – Lakeland Regional Health Authority – Coord., Heather Armstrong

Consort Municipal Hospital, PO Box 310, Consort AB T0C 1B0 – 403/577-3555; Fax: 403/577-3950 – 5 acute care, 15 continuing care beds – East Central Regional Health Authority 7 – Health Care Coord., Sissel Bray

Coronation Health Centre, PO Box 500, Coronation AB T0C 1C0 – 403/578-3803; Fax: 403/578-3474 – 10 acute care, 23 continuing care beds – East Central Regional Health Authority 7 – Health Care Coord., Carol Funnell

Daysland Health Centre, PO Box 27, Daysland AB T0B 1A0 – 403/374-3746; Fax: 403/374-2111 – 16 acute care beds, 10 long term care beds – East Central Regional Health Authority 7 – Health Care Coord., Mariann Wolbeck

Devon General Hospital, 101 Erie St. South, PO Box 438, Devon AB T0C 1E0 – 403/987-3376; Fax: 403/987-4614 – 10 acute care beds – WestView Regional Health Authority – Area Team Leader, Joy Myskin

Didsbury District Health Services, PO Box 130, Didsbury AB T0M 0W0 – 403/335-9393; Fax: 403/335-4816 – 15 acute care beds, 80 continuing care beds – Regional Health Authority 5 – Dir. of Health Servs., Dennis Stabbler

Drayton Valley Health Centre, 4550 Madsen Ave., Drayton Valley AB T0E 0M0 – 403/621-4841; Fax: 403/621-4966 – 40 acute care, 50 continuing care beds – Crossroads Regional Health Authority – Site Coord., Wendy Schneider

Drumheller District Health Services, PO Box 4500, Drumheller AB T0J 0Y0 – 403/823-6500; Fax: 403/823-5076 – 56 acute care, 110 continuing care beds – Regional Health Authority 5 – Regional Dir., Acute Care, Linda L. Stanger

Edmonton: Grey Nuns Community Hospital & Health Centre, 1100 Youville Dr. West, Edmonton AB T6L 5X8 – 403/450-7000; Fax: 403/450-7500; EMail: sfynn@caritas.ab.ca – 160 acute care beds – Capital Health Authority – Site Adm., Beverley Rachwalski

Edmonton: Misericordia Hospital (Caritas Health Group), 16940 - 87 Ave., Edmonton AB T5R 4H5 – 403/930-5611; Fax: 403/930-5774 – 157 acute care beds – Capital Health Authority – Site Adm., Ellen Pekeles

Edmonton: Royal Alexandra Hospital, 10240 Kingsway Ave., Edmonton AB T5H 3V9 – 403/477-4111; Fax: 403/477-4777 – 519 beds, 52 bassinets – Capital Health Authority – Senior Operating Officer, Leslee Thompson

Edmonton: Walter C. Mackenzie Health Sciences Centre, 8440 - 112 St., Edmonton AB T6G 2B7 – 403/492-8822; Fax: 403/492-4990 – 560 acute care beds – Capital Health Authority – Site Adm., Lynn Cook

Edson & District Health Care Centre, 4716 - 5 Ave., Edson AB T7E 1S8 – 403/723-3331; Fax: 403/723-7787 – 10 acute care, 50 continuing care beds – WestView Regional Health Authority – Area Team Leader, Laurel Becker

Elk Point Health Centre, PO Box 3, Elk Point AB T0A 1A0 – 403/724-3847; Fax: 403/724-3085 – 10 acute care, 25 long term care beds – Lakeland Regional Health Authority – Coord., Clinical Health Services, Barbara Kaufman

Empress Health Centre, PO Box 159, Empress AB T0J 1E0 – 403/565-3777; Fax: 403/565-3002 – 15 beds – Palliser Health Authority – Area Unit Mgr., Lynne Baisley

Fairview Health Complex, PO Box 2201, Fairview AB T0H 1L0 – 403/835-6100; Fax: 403/835-5789 – 25 acute care, 75 long term care beds – Mistahia Regional Health Authority – Site Coord., Lisa Weston

Fort Macleod Health Care Centre, 744 - 26 St., PO Box 520, Fort Macleod AB T0L 0Z0 – 403/553-4487; Fax: 403/553-4567 – 12 acute care beds – Chinook Health Region – Adm., William Ayotte

Fort McMurray: Northern Lights Regional Health Centre, 7 Hospital St., Fort McMurray AB T9H 1P2 – 403/791-6161; Fax: 403/791-6042 – 86 acute care, 30 long term care beds – Northern Lights Regional Health Authority – Pres., Donald M. Ford

Fort Saskatchewan General Hospital, 9430 - 95 St., Fort Saskatchewan AB T8L 1R8 – 403/998-2256; Fax: 403/992-1532 – 30 beds – Lakeland Regional Health Authority – Coord., Mary Ann Iatz

Fort Vermilion: St. Theresa General Hospital, PO Box 128, Fort Vermilion AB T0H 1N0 – 403/927-3761; Fax: 403/927-4271 – 26 acute care, 10 long term care beds – Northwestern Regional Health Authority – Assistant Exec. Dir., Bill Dainard

Fox Creek Healthcare Centre, 600 - 3 St., PO Box 990, Fox Creek AB T0H 1P0 – 403/622-3545; Fax: 403/622-3474 – 4 acute care beds – Aspen Regional Health Authority #11 – Site Suprv., Carrie Howe

Grande Cache General Hospital, PO Box 629, Grande Cache AB T0E 0Y0 – 403/827-3701; Fax: 403/827-2859 – 15 acute care beds – Mistahia Regional Health Authority – Site Coord., Julie Wakefield

Grande Prairie: Queen Elizabeth II Hospital, 10409 - 98 St., Grande Prairie AB T8V 2E8 – 403/538-7100; Fax: 403/538-7501 – 150 acute care, 117 long term beds – Mistahia Regional Health Authority – Pres., Kenneth J. Fox

Grimshaw/Berwyn & District Hospital, PO Box 648, Grimshaw AB T0H 1W0 – 403/332-1155; Fax: 403/332-1177 – 15 acute care beds – Mistahia Regional Health Authority – Site Coord., Sharon Thurston

Hanna District Health Services, PO Box 730, Hanna AB T0J 1P0 – 403/854-3331; Fax: 403/854-3253 – 15 acute care beds – Regional Health Authority 5 – Dir. of Health Servs., Stan Faupel

Hardisty Health Centre, PO Box 269, Hardisty AB T0B 1V0 – 403/888-3742; Fax: 403/888-2427 – 5 acute care, 15 continuing care beds – East Central Regional Health Authority 7 – Health Care Coord., Sissel Bray

High Level General Hospital, PO Box 400, High Level AB T0H 1Z0 – 403/926-3791; Fax: 403/926-2944 – 20 acute care, 5 long term care beds – Northwestern Regional Health Authority – Adm., Gina Halliwell

High Prairie Health Complex, PO Box 1, High Prairie AB T0G 1E0 – 403/523-3341; Fax: 403/523-3888 – 25 acute care beds – Keeweetinok Lakes Regional Health Authority #15 – Team Mgr. Institutional Servs., David Allen

High River General Hospital, 560 - 9th Ave. West, High River AB T1V 1B3 – 403/652-2222; Fax: 403/652-0199 – 37 acute care, 75 continuing care beds – Headwaters Health Authority – Site Suprv., Emily Brookwell

Hinton General Hospital, 1280 Switzer Dr., Hinton AB T7V 1V2 – 403/865-3333; Fax: 403/865-1099 – 17 beds – WestView Regional Health Authority – Area Team Leader, Donna Grier

Innisfail Health Centre, 5023 - 42nd St., Innisfail AB T4G 1A9 – 403/227-3381; Fax: 403/227-4160 – 20 acute care, 80 continuing care beds – David Thompson Health Region – Vice-Pres., South, Candace Spurrell

Jasper: Seton Hospital Jasper, 518 Robson St., PO Box 310, Jasper AB T0E 1E0 – 403/852-3344; Fax: 403/852-3413 – 10 acute care, 16 long term care beds – WestView Regional Health Authority – Area Team Leader, Patricia Breakey

Killam Health Centre, PO Box 40, Killam AB T0B 2L0 – 403/385-3741; Fax: 403/385-3904 – 5 acute care, 40 continuing care beds – East Central Regional Health Authority 7 – Exec. Dir., Alice Stafinski

Lac La Biche: William J. Cadzow Health Centre, PO Box 507, Lac La Biche AB T0A 2C0 – 403/623-4404; Fax: 403/623-5904 – 30 acute care, 41 long term care beds – Lakeland Regional Health Authority – Coord., Allan Sinclair

Lacombe Hospital, 5430 - 47 Ave., Lacombe AB T4L 1G8 – 403/782-3336; Fax: 403/782-2818 – 20 acute care, 75 long term care beds – David Thompson Health Region – Vice-Pres., North, Lou Davidson

Lamont Health Care Centre - General & Extended Care, 5216 - 53 St., Lamont AB T0B 2R0 – 403/895-2211; Fax: 403/895-7305 – 10 acute care, 81 long term care beds – Lakeland Regional Health Authority – Exec. Dir., Harold James

Leduc Health Centre, 4210 - 48 St., Leduc AB T9E 5Z3 – 403/986-7711; Fax: 403/980-4490 – 37 acute care beds – Crossroads Regional Health Authority – Site Coord., Lynda Callioux

Lethbridge Regional Hospital, 960 - 19 St. South, Lethbridge AB T1J 1W5 – 403/382-6009; Fax: 403/382-6011 – 266 beds – Chinook Health Region

Manning General Hospital, PO Box 1250, Manning AB T0H 2M0 – 403/836-3391; Fax: 403/836-3410 – 10 acute care, 15 long term care beds – Peace Regional Health Authority – Acting Adm., Joyce Halliday

Mannville Health Centre, PO Box 1000, Mannville AB T0B 2W0 – 403/763-3621; Fax: 403/763-3678 – 6 acute care, 18 continuing care beds – East Central Regional Health Authority 7 – Health Care Coord., Audrey Cusack

Mayerthorpe Healthcare Centre, 4417 - 45 St., PO Box 30, Mayerthorpe AB T0E 1N0 – 403/786-2261, 2645; Fax: 403/786-2023 – 25 acute care, 30 long term care beds – Aspen Regional Health Authority #11 – Site Suprv., Heather Thompson

McLennan Sacred Heart Community Health Centre, PO Box 2000, McLennan AB T0H 2L0 – 403/324-3730; Fax: 403/324-2267 – 20 acute care, 45 long term care beds – Peace Regional Health Authority – CEO, Peace Regional Health Authority, Brian Hrab

Medicine Hat Regional Hospital, 666 - 5 St. SW, Medicine Hat AB T1A 4H6 – 403/529-8000; Fax: 403/529-8949 – 175 acute care, 135 continuing care beds – Palliser Health Authority – Exec. Dir., T.A. Seaman

Milk River: Border Counties General Hospital, 517 Centre Ave. East, PO Box 90, Milk River AB T0K 1M0 – 403/647-3500; Fax: 403/647-2197 – 8 acute care, 21 continuing care beds – Chinook Health Region – Unit Mgr., Lorraine Dobrocane

Mundare Mary Immaculate Health Care Centre, PO Box 349, Mundare AB T0B 3H0 – 403/764-3730; Fax: 403/764-3039 – 23 long term care beds – Lakeland Regional Health Authority – Exec. Dir., Sr. Eugenia Stefaniuk

Olds General Hospital, 3901 - 57th Ave., Olds AB T4H 1T4 – 403/556-3381; Fax: 403/556-2199 – 31 acute care, 50 continuing care beds – David Thompson Health Region – Vice-Pres., South, Candace Spurrell

Oyen Big Country Hospital Hospital, 312 - 3rd Ave. East, PO Box 150, Oyen AB T0J 2J0 – 403/664-3526; Fax: 403/664-2074 – 10 acute care, 30 continuing care beds – Palliser Health Authority – Dir. of Health Servs., Lynne Baisley

Peace River Community Health Centre, PO Box 400, Peace River AB T8S 1T6 – 403/624-7500; Fax: 403/624-9667 – 29 acute care, 75 long term care beds – Peace Regional Health Authority – Acting Adm. & Dir. of Patient Care, Grace Williams

Picture Butte Municipal Hospital, 301 Cowan Ave., PO Box 430, Picture Butte AB T0K 1V0 – 403/732-4611; Fax: 403/732-5567 – 16 continuing care, 3 observation beds – Chinook Health Region – Adm., vacant

Pincher Creek Municipal Hospital, 1222 Mill Ave., PO Box 968, Pincher Creek AB T0K 1W0 – 403/627-3333; Fax: 403/627-5275 – 16 acute care, 31 continuing care beds – Chinook Health Region – Site Adm., Terese Fleming

Ponoka General Hospital, 5800 - 57th Ave., Ponoka AB T4J 1P1 – 403/783-3341; Fax: 403/783-6907 – 30 acute care, 30 continuing care beds – David Thompson Health Region – Vice-Pres., North, Lou Davidson

Provost Health Centre, PO Box 270, Provost AB T0B 3S0 – 403/753-2291; Fax: 403/753-6132 – 15 acute care, 37 continuing care beds, 11 alternative housing – East Central Regional Health Authority 7 – Health Care Coord., Val Sorby

Raymond General Hospital, PO Box 599, Raymond AB T0K 2S0 – 403/752-4561; Fax: 403/752-3554 – 12 acute care, 35 continuing care beds – Chinook Health Region – Adm., F. Bruce Romeike

Red Deer Regional Hospital Centre, 3942 - 50A Ave., PO Box 5030, Red Deer AB T4N 4E7 – 403/343-4422; Fax: 403/343-4433 – 285 beds – David Thompson Health Region – Vice-Pres., Central, Gord Birbeck

Redwater General Hospital, PO Box 39, Redwater AB T0A 2W0 – 403/942-3932; Fax: 403/942-2373; EMail: redh2ohc@telusplanet.net – 10 acute care beds – Lakeland Regional Health Authority – Coord., Betty Kolewaski

Rimbey General Hospital, 5228 - 50 Ave., PO Box 440, Rimbey AB T0C 2J0 – 403/843-2271; Fax: 403/843-2506 – 15 acute care, 85 continuing care beds – David Thompson Health Region – Vice-Pres., West, Bryan Judd

Rocky Mountain House General Hospital, 5016 - 52 Ave., Rocky Mountain House AB T0M 1T3 – 403/845-3347; Fax: 403/845-7030 – 31 acute care – David Thompson Health Region – Vice-Pres., West, Bryan Judd

St. Albert: Sturgeon Community Health Centre, 201 Boudreau Rd., St. Albert AB T8N 6C4 – 403/460-6200; Fax: 403/460-6262 – 73 acute care beds – Capital Health Authority – Community Health Network Adm., Wendy Hill

St. Paul: Ste. Therese Health Centre, 4713 - 48 Ave., St. Paul AB T0A 3A3 – 403/645-3331; Fax: 403/645-1809 – 40 acute care, 30 long term care beds – Lakeland Regional Health Authority – Exec. Dir., Kevin Bestby

Slave Lake Hospital, 309 - 6 St. NE, Slave Lake AB T0G 2A2 – 403/849-3732; Fax: 403/849-5141 – 25 acute care, 15 long term care beds – Keeweetinok Lakes Regional Health Authority #15 – Team Mgr., Institutional Services, Andrea Taylor

Smoky Lake: George McDougall Memorial Health Centre, PO Box 340, Smoky Lake AB T0A 3C0 – 403/656-3034; Fax: 403/656-3010 – 10 acute care, 56 long term care beds – Lakeland Regional Health Authority – Coord., Clinical/Health Services, Grace Regnier

Spirit River: Central Peace General Hospital, PO Box 339, Spirit River AB T0H 3G0 – 403/864-3993; Fax: 403/864-3495 – 16 acute care beds – Mistahia Regional Health Authority – Site Coord., Karen Osborne

Stettler Health Centre, PO Box 500, Stettler AB T0C 2L0 – 403/742-7400; Fax: 403/742-1244 – 25 acute care, 92 continuing care beds – East Central Regional Health Authority 7 – Health Care Coord., Marie Owen

Stony Plain Municipal Hospital, 4800 - 55 Ave., Stony Plain AB T7Z 1P9 – 403/963-2241; Fax: 403/963-7192 – 10 acute care beds – WestView Regional Health Authority – Area Team Leader, Myrene Couves

Strathmore District Health Services, 200 Brent Blvd., Strathmore AB T1P 1J9 – 403/934-4204; Fax: 403/934-3948 – 19 acute care, 26 continuing care beds – Regional Health Authority 5 – Dir. of Health Servs., Reginald McRae

Sundre General Hospital, 709 - 1 St. NE, PO Box 3, Sundre AB T0M 1X0 – 403/638-3033; Fax: 403/638-4971 – 13 acute care, 15 continuing care beds – David Thompson Health Region – Vice-Pres., South, Candace Spurrell

Swan Hills Healthcare Centre, 29 Freeman Dr., PO Box 266, Swan Hills AB T0G 2C0 – 403/333-7000, 429-7062; Fax: 403/333-7009 – 4 acute care beds – Aspen Regional Health Authority #11 – Facility Suprv., Karen Bouman

Taber & District Health Care Complex, 4326 - 50 Ave., PO Box 939, Taber AB T0K 2G0 – 403/223-4461; Fax: 403/223-1703 – 25 acute care, 70 continuing care beds – Chinook Health Region – Adm., Bob Stratychuk

Three Hills District Health Services, PO Box 340, Three Hills AB T0M 2A0 – 403/443-2444; Fax: 403/443-5565; EMail: hospadmin@kneehill.com – 19 acute care, 23 continuing care beds – Regional Health Authority 5 – Adm., vacant

Tofield Health Centre, PO Box 300, Tofield AB T0B 4J0 – 403/662-3263; Fax: 403/662-3835 – 16 acute care, 50 continuing care beds – East Central Regional Health Authority 7 – Health Care Coord., Betty Perras

Trochu-St. Mary's Health Care Centre, 451 DeChauney Ave., PO Box 100, Trochu AB T0M 2C0 – 403/442-3955; Fax: 403/442-3945 – 28 continuing care beds – David Thompson Health Region – Adm., Peter Verhesen

Two Hills Health Care Centre & Nursing Home, 4401 - 53rd Ave., PO Box 160, Two Hills AB T0B 4K0 – 403/657-3344; Fax: 403/657-2508 – 16 acute care, 60 long term care beds – Lakeland Regional Health Authority – Adm., Val Sebree

Valleyview Health Complex, PO Box 358, Valleyview AB T0H 3N0 – 403/524-3356; Fax: 403/524-4462 – 15 acute care, 15 long term care beds – Mistahia Regional Health Authority – Site Coord., Ann Polard

Vegreville: St. Joseph's General Hospital, PO Box 490, Vegreville AB T9C 1R5 – 403/632-2811; Fax: 403/632-6177 – 30 acute care beds – Lakeland Regional Health Authority – Adm., Eugene Rudyk

Vermilion Health Centre, PO Box 1050, Vermilion AB T0B 4M0 – 403/853-5305; Fax: 403/853-4786 – 25 acute care, 65 continuing care beds – East Central Regional Health Authority 7 – Health Care Coord., Jan Scott

Viking Health Centre, PO Box 60, Viking AB T0B 4N0 – 403/336-4786; Fax: 403/336-4983 – 16 acute care beds – East Central Regional Health Authority 7 – Health Care Coord., Kathryn Miskew

Vilna: Our Lady's Health Centre, PO Box 160, Vilna AB T0A 3L0 – 403/636-3599; Fax: 403/636-3633 – 8 long term care beds – Lakeland Regional Health Authority

Vulcan Community Health Centre, PO Box 299, Vulcan AB T0L 2B0 – 403/485-3333; Fax: 403/485-2336 – 8 acute care, 15 long term care beds – Headwaters Health Authority – Site Suprv., Brian Popp

Wabasca/Desmarais General Hospital, PO Box 450, Wabasca AB T0G 2K0 – 403/891-3007; Fax: 403/891-

3784 – 10 acute care, 5 long term care beds – Keeweetinok Lakes Regional Health Authority #15 – Team Mgr., Health Services, Linda Shea

Wainwright Health Centre, 530 - 6 Ave., Wainwright AB T9W 1R6 – 403/842-3324; Fax: 403/842-2887, 4290 – 20 acute care, 70 continuing care beds – East Central Regional Health Authority 7 – Health Care Coord., Cheryl Huxley

Westlock Healthcare Centre, 10220 - 93 St., PO Box 1590, Westlock AB T0G 2L0 – 403/349-3301, 423-2238; Fax: 403/349-6973 – 40 acute care, 22 long term care beds – Aspen Regional Health Authority #11 – Facility Suprv., Joyce Nadeau

Wetaskiwin Health Centre, 6910 - 47 St., Wetaskiwin AB T9A 3N3 – 403/361-7100; Fax: 403/361-4107 – 83 acute care, 105 long term care beds – Crossroads Regional Health Authority – Site Coord., Bruce Finkel

Whitecourt Healthcare Centre, 20 Sunset Blvd., Whitecourt AB T7S 1M8 – 403/778-2285, 424-7856; Fax: 403/778-5161 – 24 acute care beds – Aspen Regional Health Authority #11 – Site Suprv., Wilf Pruden

Willingdon: Mary Immaculate Hospital, 5222 - 51 St., PO Box 179, Willingdon AB T0B 4R0 – 403/367-2288; Fax: 403/367-2733 – 20 long term care beds – Lakeland Regional Health Authority – Exec. Dir., Sr. Eugenia Stefaniuk

## AUXILIARY HOSPITALS/HEALTH CARE CENTRES

Athabasca Healthcare Centre, *see* General Hospitals listings

Banff Mineral Springs Hospital, *see* General Hospitals listings

Barrhead Healthcare Centre, *see* General Hospitals listings

Bashaw Community Health Centre, 5308 - 53 St., PO Box 449, Bashaw AB T0B 0H0 – 403/372-3731; Fax: 403/372-4050 – 29 beds – David Thompson Health Region – Vice-Pres., North, Lou Davidson

Bassano General Hospital, *see* General Hospitals listings

Bentley Care Centre, 4834 - 52 Ave., PO Box 30, Bentley AB T0C 0J0 – 403/748-4115; Fax: 403/748-2727 – 16 beds – David Thompson Health Region – Adm., West, Bryan Judd

Black Diamond: Oilfields General Hospital, *see* General Hospitals listings

Blairmore: Crowsnest Pass Health Care Centre, *see* General Hospitals listings

Bonnyville Health Centre & Auxiliary Centre, *see* General Hospitals listings

Bow Island Health Centre, *see* General Hospitals listings

Breton Health Centre, *see* General Hospitals listings

Brooks Health Centre, *see* General Hospitals listings

Calgary: Bethany Care Society, Calgary, 1001 - 17th St. NW, Calgary AB T2N 2E5 – 403/284-0161; Fax: 403/284-1992 – Administrative office for Bethany Care Centres in Airdrie, Cochrane & Calgary; also operates Bethany Lifeline an emergency help line serving the elderly & handicapped in Southern Alberta, Saskatchewan & B.C. – Calgary Regional Health Authority – CEO, R. Greer Black

Calgary: Bethany Care Society, Calgary - Bethany Care Centre - Calgary, 916 - 18A St. NW, Calgary AB T3A 4N2 – 403/284-6014; Fax: 403/284-6085 – 470 beds – Calgary Regional Health Authority – Adm., Paul Moore

Calgary: Carewest Cross Bow Auxiliary Hospital, 1011 Centre Ave. East, Calgary AB T2E OA3 – 403/267-2950; Fax: 403/267-2995 – 98 beds – Calgary Regional Health Authority – Site Leader, Margaret Marlin

Calgary: Carewest Dr. Vernon Fanning Extended Care Centre, 722 - 16 Ave. NE, Calgary AB T2E 6V7 – 403/276-8551; Fax: 403/230-6902 – 294 beds – Calgary Regional Health Authority – Site Leader, Joan Gilmore

Calgary: Carewest Glenmore Park Auxiliary Hospital, 6909 - 14 St. SW, Calgary AB T2V 1P6 – 403/258-7650; Fax: 403/258-7676 – 170 beds – Calgary Regional Health Authority – Site Leader, Iris Neuman

Calgary: Carewest Sarcee Auxiliary Hospital, 3504 - 29 St. SW, Calgary AB T3E 2L3 – 403/686-8100; Fax: 403/686-8104 – 175 beds – Calgary Regional Health Authority – Site Leader, Jim Townend

Calgary: Colonel Belcher Auxiliary Hospital, 1213 - 4 St. SW, Calgary AB T2R 0X7 – 403/541-3600; Fax: 403/237-8251 – 135 beds – Calgary Regional Health Authority – Site Leader, Mary Sangha

Calgary: Foothills Medical Centre, *see* General Hospitals listings

Calgary: Rockyview General Hospital, 7007 - 14th St. SW, Calgary AB T2V 1P9 – 403/541-3000; Fax: 403/541-3434 – 507 beds – Calgary Regional Health Authority – Adm., Jeanette Pick

Camrose: Rosehaven Care Center (The Bethany Group), 4612 - 53 St., Camrose AB T4V 1Y6 – 403/679-3000; Fax: 403/679-3001 – 139 beds – East Central Regional Health Authority 7 – Exec. Dir., John Grant

Canmore Hospital, *see* General Hospitals listings

Cardston Hospital, *see* General Hospitals listings

Carmangay: Little Bow Auxiliary Hospital, PO Box 160, Carmangay AB T0L 0N0 – 403/643-3522; Fax: 403/643-3554 – 20 beds – Headwaters Health Authority – Suprv., Plant Maintenance, Pete Shersta-betoff

Claresholm: Willow Creek Auxiliary Hospital & Nursing Home, 4251 - 8 St. West, PO Box 700, Claresholm AB T0L 0T0 – 403/625-3361; Fax: 403/625-3822 – 100 beds – Headwaters Health Authority – Site Suprv., Pat Manderville

Coaldale Health Care Centre, *see* General Hospitals listings

Cold Lake Health Centre, *see* General Hospitals listings

Coronation Health Centre, *see* General Hospitals listings

Didsbury District Health Services, *see* General Hospitals listings

Drayton Valley Health Centre, *see* General Hospitals listings

Drumheller District Health Services, *see* General Hospitals listings

Edmonton General Hospital & Continuing Care Centre (Caritas Health Group), 11111 Jasper Ave., Edmonton AB T5K 0L4 – 403/482-8111; Fax: 403/482-8035 – 278 continuing care beds – Capital Health Authority – Program Adm., Ken Pickard

Edmonton: Capital Care Dickinsfield, 14225 - 94 St., Edmonton AB T5E 6C6 – 403/496-3300; Fax: 403/476-4585 – 289 beds – Capital Health Authority – Vice-Pres., Operations, Susan Paul

Edmonton: Capital Care Grandview, 6215 - 124 St., Edmonton AB T6H 3V1 – 403/496-7100; Fax: 403/496-7150 – 195 beds – Capital Health Authority – Adm., Helen Lantz

Edmonton: Good Samaritan Auxiliary Hospital, 9649 - 71 Ave., Edmonton AB T6E 5J2 – 403/431-3600; Fax: 403/431-3699 – 200 beds – Capital Health Authority

Edmonton: Mewburn Veterans Centre, 11440 University Ave., Edmonton AB T6G 1Z1 – 403/496-7160; Fax: 403/496-7199 – 140 beds – Capital Health Authority – Pres., Sheila Weatherill

Edmonton: St. Joseph's Auxiliary Hospital, 10707 - 29 Ave., Edmonton AB T6J 6W1 – 403/430-9110; Fax: 403/430-9777 – 204 beds – Capital Health Authority – CEO, Mike Ripko

Elk Point Health Centre, *see* General Hospitals listings

Elnora Community Health Centre, 425 - 8th Ave., PO Box 659, Elnora AB T0M 0Y0 – 403/773-3636; Fax: 403/773-3949 – David Thompson Health Region

Empress Health Centre, *see* General Hospitals listings

Fairview Health Complex, *see* General Hospitals listings

Fort McMurray: Northern Lights Regional Health Centre, *see* General Hospitals listings

Galahad Health Care Centre, PO Box 88, Galahad AB T0B 1R0 – 403/583-3788; Fax: 403/583-2105 – 20 continuing care beds – East Central Regional Health Authority 7 – Health Care Coord., Sheila Fossey

Grande Prairie: Queen Elizabeth II Hospital, *see* General Hospitals listings

High Prairie Health Complex, *see* General Hospitals listings

Islay Health Centre, PO Box 55, Islay AB T0B 2J0 – 403/744-3795; Fax: 403/744-3922 – 12 continuing care beds – East Central Regional Health Authority 7 – Health Care Coord., Audrey Cusack

Jasper: Seton Hospital Jasper, *see* General Hospitals listings

Lac La Biche: William J. Cadzow Health Centre, *see* General Hospitals listings

Lacombe Community Health Centre, 5010 - 51 St., Lacombe AB T4L 1W2 – 403/782-3218; Fax: 403/782-2866 – 75 beds – David Thompson Health Region – VP, Community Health Services, Denise McBain

Lamont Health Care Centre - General & Extended Care, *see* General Hospitals listings

Leduc Health Centre, *see* General Hospitals listings

Lloydminster: Dr. Cooke Extended Care Centre, PO Box 1007, Lloydminster AB T9V 0Z7 – 403/875-2291; Fax: 403/875-3505 – 106 beds – East Central Regional Health Authority 7 – CEO, Brian Heidt

Manning General Hospital, *see* General Hospitals listings

Mannville Health Centre, *see* General Hospitals listings

Mayerthorpe Healthcare Centre, *see* General Hospitals listings

McLennan Sacred Heart Community Health Centre, *see* General Hospitals listings

Medicine Hat Regional Hospital, *see* General Hospitals listings

Milk River: Border Counties General Hospital, *see* General Hospitals listings

Mundare Mary Immaculate Health Care Centre, *see* General Hospitals listings

Myrnam Health Centre, PO Box 220, Myrnam AB T0B 3K0 – 403/366-3870; Fax: 403/366-3919 – outpatient health centre – Lakeland Regional Health Authority – Suprv., Nursing, R. Langden

Oyen Big Country Hospital Hospital, *see* General Hospitals listings

Peace River Community Health Centre, *see* General Hospitals listings

Picture Butte Municipal Hospital, *see* General Hospitals listings

Pincher Creek Municipal Hospital, *see* General Hospitals listings

Ponoka General Hospital, *see* General Hospitals listings

Provost Health Centre, *see* General Hospitals listings

Radway Health Care Centre, PO Box 70, Radway AB T0A 2V0 – 403/736-3740; Fax: 403/736-2353 – 23 beds – Lakeland Regional Health Authority – Coord., Betty Kolewaski

Raymond General Hospital, *see* General Hospitals listings

Red Deer: Dr. Richard Parsons Auxiliary Hospital, 3929 - 52 Ave., PO Box 5030, Red Deer AB T4N 4J8 – 403/343-4422; Fax: 403/420-1605 – 100 beds – David Thompson Health Region – Pres., Gerry Vanhooren

Rimbey General Hospital, *see* General Hospitals listings

Rocky Mountain House Community Health Centre, 4934 - 50 St., PO Box 340, Rocky Mountain House AB T0M 1T0 – 403/845-3030; Fax: 403/845-4975 – 30 continuing care beds – David Thompson Health Region

St. Paul: Ste. Therese Health Centre, *see* General Hospitals listings

Smoky Lake: George McDougall Memorial Health Centre, *see* General Hospitals listings

Strathmore District Health Services, *see* General Hospitals listings

Taber & District Health Care Complex, *see* General Hospitals listings

Three Hills District Health Services, *see* General Hospitals listings

Tofield Health Centre, *see* General Hospitals listings

Trochu-St. Mary's Health Care Centre, *see* General Hospitals listings

Two Hills Health Care Centre & Nursing Home, *see* General Hospitals listings

Valleyview Health Complex, *see* General Hospitals listings

Vermilion Health Centre, *see* General Hospitals listings

Vilna: Our Lady's Health Centre, *see* General Hospitals listings

Vulcan Community Health Centre, *see* General Hospitals listings

Wainwright Health Centre, *see* General Hospitals listings

Westlock Healthcare Centre, *see* General Hospitals listings

Westlock Long Term Care Centre, 9732 - 100 Ave., PO Box 1100, Westlock AB T0G 2L0 – 403/349-3306; Fax: 403/429-3502 – 102 beds – Aspen Regional Health Authority #11 – Site Suprv., Mona Theriault

Wetaskiwin Health Centre, *see* General Hospitals

## FEDERAL HOSPITALS

Cardston: Blood Indian Hospital, PO Box 490, Cardston AB T0K 0K0 – 403/653-3351; Fax: 403/653-4824 – Head Adm., Dr. Charles Weasel

Medley: Canadian Forces Base Medical Squadron, Four Wing Cold Lake, General Delivery, Medley AB T0A 2M0 – 403/840-8000, ext.8749

## HOME CARE OFFICES/COMMUNITY HEALTH CARE OFFICES

Andrew Community Health Services, c/o Andrews Lodge, PO Box 450, Andrew AB T0B 0C0 – 403/365-3591 – Lakeland Regional Health Authority

Athabasca Health Services, 3401 - 48 Ave., Athabasca AB T9S 1M7 – 403/675-2231; Fax: 403/675-3111 – Aspen Regional Health Authority #11

Banff National Park Health Unit Office, PO Box 1266, Banff AB T0L 0C0 – 403/762-2990; Fax: 403/762-5570 – Headwaters Health Authority – Pat Brooks

Barrhead Health Services, PO Box 4131, Barrhead AB T7N 1A1 – 403/674-3408; Fax: 403/674-3941 – Aspen Regional Health Authority #11

Beaumont Health Unit, 5005 - 50 Ave., Beaumont AB T4X 1E7 – 403/929-2454; Fax: 403/929-2001 – Crossroads Regional Health Authority

Beaverlodge/Hythe District Home Care Office, 412 - 10A St., Beaverlodge AB T0H 0C0 – 403/354-2647; Fax: 403/354-1550 – Mistahia Regional Health Authority

Black Diamond Health Unit, 128 Centre Ave. NW, PO Box 34, Black Diamond AB T0L 0H0 – 403/933-4335; Fax: 403/933-2031 – Headwaters Health Authority – Janet Melbourne, 403/652-0139

Blairmore Community & Wellness Site, 12501 - 20 Ave., PO Box 67, Blairmore AB T0K 0E0 – 403/562-7378; Fax: 403/562-7379 – Chinook Health Region

Bonnyville Community Health Services, 5102 - 51 St., PO Box 5244, Bonnyville AB T9N 2G4 – 403/826-3381; Fax: 403/826-6470 – Lakeland Regional Health Authority

Boyle Health Services, PO Box 201, Boyle AB T0A 0M0 – 403/689-2677; Fax: 403/689-2835 – Aspen Regional Health Authority #11

Brooks Community Health Services, PO Box 894, Brooks AB T1R 1B7 – 403/362-3388; Fax: 403/362-8126 – Palliser Health Authority

Calgary: Bowness Community Health Centre, 6328 - 35th Ave. NW, Calgary AB T3B 1S4 – 403/288-7774 – Calgary Regional Health Authority

Calgary: East Health Centre, 112 - 28 St. SE, Calgary AB T2A 5J9 – 403/248-8868; Fax: 403/282-0399 – Calgary Regional Health Authority

Calgary: Forest Lawn District Office, 3810 - 17 Ave. SE, Calgary AB T2A 0S4 – 403/248-6228; Fax: 403/248-0429 – Calgary Regional Health Authority

Calgary: Haysboro District Office, 12 Haddon Rd. SW, Calgary AB T2V 2X6 – 403/252-3534; Fax: 403/253-5129 – Calgary Regional Health Authority

Calgary: Northwest Health Centre, #109. 1829 Ranchlands Blvd. NW, Calgary AB T3G 2A7 – 403/239-6600; Fax: 403/239-6056 – Calgary Regional Health Authority

Calgary: Scarboro District Office, c/o Alberta Children's Hospital, 1820 Richmond Rd. SW, Calgary AB T2T 5C7 – 403/244-2484; Fax: 403/245-1746 – Calgary Regional Health Authority

Calgary: Shaganappi District Office, 3415 - 8 Ave. SW, Calgary AB T3C 0E8 – 403/242-0210; Fax: 403/246-0326 – Calgary Regional Health Authority

Calgary: South Health Centre, 240 Midway Park SE, Calgary AB T2X 1N4 – 403/256-7191; Fax: 403/256-7987 – Calgary Regional Health Authority

Calgary: Thornhill District Office, 6617 Centre St. North, Calgary AB T2K 4Y5 – 403/274-4515; Fax: 403/275-9064 – Calgary Regional Health Authority

Calgary: Village Square District Office, 2623 - 56 St. NE, Calgary AB T1Y 6E7 – 403/280-9816; Fax: 403/285-6304 – Calgary Regional Health Authority

Calling Lake Health Services, General Delivery, Calling Lake AB T0G 0K0 – 403/331-3760; Fax: 403/331-2200 – Aspen Regional Health Authority #11

Canmore Health Unit Office, PO Box 428, Canmore AB T0L 0M0 – 403/678-5656; Fax: 403/678-5068 – Headwaters Health Authority – Elaine Spencer

Cardston Community & Wellness Site, Provincial Bldg., 576 Main St., PO Box 1590, Cardston AB T0K 0K0 – 403/653-4981; Fax: 403/653-4985 – Chinook Health Region

Castor Community Health Office, PO Box 94, Castor AB T0C 0X0 – 403/882-3404 – East Central Regional Health Authority 7

Claresholm Health Unit, 5221 - 2nd St. West, PO Box 1391, Claresholm AB T0L 0T0 – 403/625-4061; Fax: 403/625-4062 – Headwaters Health Authority – Janet Melbourne, 403/652-0139

Coaldale Community & Wellness Site (18th St.), 2018 - 18 St., PO Box 1000, Coaldale AB T1M 1M8 – 403/327-6507; Fax: 403/345-2043 – Chinook Health Region

Consort Community Health Services, PO Box 146, Consort AB T0C 1B0 – 403/577-3770; Fax: 403/577-2235 – East Central Regional Health Authority 7

Coronation Community Health Services, PO Box 338, Coronation AB T0C 1C0 – 403/578-3200 – East Central Regional Health Authority 7

Devon Health Unit, Suite C, 101 Erie St., Devon AB T9G 1A6 – 403/987-8224; Fax: 403/987-8232 – WestView Regional Health Authority – Area Team Leader, Joy Myskiw

Didsbury Health Unit Office, 1601 - 15 Ave. SW, PO Box 17, Didsbury AB T0M 0W0 – 403/335-3233; Fax: 403/335-8361 – Regional Health Authority 5

Drayton Valley Health Unit, 5136 - 51 Ave., Drayton Valley AB T7A 1R4 – 403/542-4415; Fax: 403/621-4998 – Crossroads Regional Health Authority

Drumheller Health Unit Office, 601 - 7th St. East, Drumheller AB T0J 0Y5 – 403/823-3341; Fax: 403/823-6657 – Regional Health Authority 5

Eckville Community Health Centre, 5120 - 51 Ave. West, Eckville AB T0M 0X0 – 403/746-2201; Fax: 403/746-2185 – 20 beds – David Thompson Health Region – Adm., Kevin McEntee

Edmonton: Capital Health Home Care, #402, 1026 - 24 St., Edmonton AB T5N 4A3 – 403/413-3660; Fax: 403/488-3401 – Capital Health Authority – Dir., Gloria Mohr

Edmonton: Casteldowns Health Centre, #34 Lake Beaumaris Mall, 153333 Castledowns Rd., Edmonton AB T5X 3Y7 – 456/-9394 – Capital Health Authority

Edmonton: Clareview Health Centre, 14023 Claireview Village Centre, 139 Ave. & Victoria Trail, Edmonton AB T5Y 2B6 – 403/473-1224 – Capital Health Authority

Edmonton: Duggan Health Centre, 5035 - 108A St., Edmonton AB T6H 2Z9 – 403/435-9209 – Capital Health Authority

Edmonton: Eastwood Health Centre, 7919 - 118 Ave., Edmonton AB T5B 0R5 – 403/474-8266 – Capital Health Authority

Edmonton: Home Care Administration, #402, 10216 - 124 St., Edmonton AB T5N 4A3 – 403/482-1965; Fax: 403/482-4194 – Capital Health Authority – Dir., Community Care, Jean Kipp

Edmonton: St. Albert Health Centre, 23 Sir Winston Churchill Ave., PO Box 174, Edmonton AB T8N 1N3 – 403/459-6671 – Capital Health Authority

Edmonton: West Jasper Place Health Centre, 9720 - 182 St., Edmonton AB T5T 3T9 – 403/489-4982 – Capital Health Authority

Edmonton: Woodcroft Health Centre, 1340 - 114 Ave., Edmonton AB T5M 2Y5 – 403/453-3571 – Capital Health Authority

Edson Health Unit, 5028 - 3rd Ave., PO Box 6240, Edson AB T7E 1X4 – 403/723-4421; Fax: 403/723-6299 – WestView Regional Health Authority

Elk Point Community Health Services, c/o Elk Point Hospital, PO Box 442, Elk Point AB T0A 1A0 – 403/724-3532; Fax: 403/724-2867 – Lakeland Regional Health Authority

Elnora: Delburne Community Health Centre, PO Box 659, Elnora AB T0M 0Y0 – 403/749-3660; Fax: 403/749-2710 – David Thompson Health Region – Adm., Yvonne Hoppins, 403/773-3636

Empress Community Health Services, Empress Hospital, PO Box 159, Empress AB T0J 1E0 – 403/565-3795; Fax: 403/565-3890 – Palliser Health Authority

Fairview District Home Care Office, PO Box 552, Fairview AB T0H 1M0 – 403/835-4951; Fax: 403/835-3879 – Mistahia Regional Health Authority

Falher Community Health Services, PO Box 636, Falher AB T0H 1M0 – 403/837-2145; Fax: 403/837-8368 – Peace Regional Health Authority

Fishing Lake Settlement Community Health Services, General Delivery, Stn Sputinow, Fishing Lake AB T0A 3G0 – 403/943-2202 – Lakeland Regional Health Authority

Fort Macleod Community & Wellness Site, 521 - 26 St., PO Box 727, Fort Macleod AB T0L 0Z0 – 403/553-4451; Fax: 403/553-2333 – Chinook Health Region

Fort McMurray Community Health Services, 9921 Main St., Fort McMurray AB T9H 4Y5 – 403/743-3232; Fax: 403/743-8506 – Northern Lights Regional Health Authority

Fort Saskatchewan Community Health Services, 9821 - 108 St., 3rd Fl., Fort Saskatchewan AB T8L 2J2 – 403/998-3366; Fax: 403/998-7404 – Lakeland Regional Health Authority

Fort Vermilion Community Health Services, PO Box 68, Fort Vermilion AB T0H 1N0 – 403/927-3391; Fax: 403/927-4440 – Adm., Jenny Radsma

Fox Creek Health Services, PO Box 430, Fox Creek AB T0H 1P0 – 403/622-3730; Fax: 403/622-4169 – Aspen Regional Health Authority #11

Gibbons Community Health Services, Central Medical Clinic, 5018 - 48 St., Gibbons AB T0A 1N0 – 403/923-3700 – Lakeland Regional Health Authority

Glendon Health Centre, PO Box 570, Glendon AB T0A 1P0 – 403/635-3861; Fax: 403/635-4213 – Lakeland Regional Health Authority – Adm., Donald E. Cole

Grande Centre Community Health Services, 4720 - 55 St., Grande Centre AB T0A 1T1 – 403/594-4404; Fax: 403/594-2404 – Lakeland Regional Health Authority

Grande Centre: Elizabeth Settlement Community Health Services, PO Box 1800, Grande Centre AB T0A 1T0 – 403/594-3383 – Lakeland Regional Health Authority

Grande Prairie: South Peace Health Unit, 10320 - 99 St., Grande Prairie AB T8V 6J4 – 403/532-4441; Fax: 403/532-1550

Hanna Health Unit Office, 401 - 3 ave. & Centre St. East, PO Box 279, Hanna AB T0J 1P0 – 403/854-3325; Fax: 403/854-4850 – Regional Health Authority 5

High Level Health Centre, 9806 - 100 Ave., 2nd Fl., PO Box 2000, High Level AB T0H 1Z0 – 403/926-7000; Fax: 403/926-7001 – Northwestern Regional Health Authority – Adm., D. Hampel

High Level: Paddle Prairie Community Health Services, c/o High Level Community Health Services, PO Box 2000, High Level AB T0H 1Z0 – 403/981-2188; Fax: 403/926-7001 – Northwestern Regional Health Authority – Adm., Jenny Radsma

High Prairie: Keeweetinok Lakes Community Health Services, PO Box 33, High Prairie AB T0G 1E0 – 403/523-4434; Fax: 403/523-5946 – Keeweetinok Lakes Regional Health Authority #15 – Team Mgr. Health Servs., Valerie Beynon

High River: Foothills Health Unit, 310 MacLeod Trail, PO Box 5638, High River AB T1V 1M7 – 403/652-3297; Fax: 403/652-2537 – Headwaters Health Authority – Lori Anderson, 403/652-0142

Hinton Health Unit, 1280A Switzer Dr., Hinton AB T7V 1T5 – 403/865-2277; Fax: 403/865-3727 – WestView Regional Health Authority – Area Team Leader, Donna Grier

Hughenden Community Health Services, PO Box 25, Hughenden AB T0B 2E0 – 403/856-3655 – East Central Regional Health Authority 7

Innisfail Community Health Centre, 4904 - 50 St., PO Box 6094, Innisfail AB T0M 1A0 – 403/227-3636; Fax: 403/227-4170 – David Thompson Health Region – VP, Community Health Services, Denise McBain

Jasper Health Unit, PO Box 1740, Jasper AB T0E 1E0 – 403/852-4759; Fax: 403/852-4752 – WestView Regional Health Authority

Kinuso Community Health Services, PO Box 208, Kinuso AB T0G 1K0 – 403/775-3501; Fax: 403/775-3944 – Keeweetinok Lakes Regional Health Authority #15

Kitscoty Community Health Services, PO Box 508, Kitscoty AB T0B 2P0 – 403/846-2824; Fax: 403/846-2731 – East Central Regional Health Authority 7

La Crete Health Centre, 295, La Crete AB T0H 2H0 – 403/928-3242; Fax: 403/928-3080 – Northwestern Regional Health Authority – Adm., Jenny Radsma

Lac La Biche Community Health Services, 9503 Beaverhill Rd., PO Box 869, Lac La Biche AB T0A 2C0 – 403/623-4471; Fax: 403/623-2615 – Lakeland Regional Health Authority

Lamont Community Health Services, PO Box 65, Lamont AB T0B 2R0 – 403/895-2248; Fax: 403/895-2200 – Lakeland Regional Health Authority

Leduc Health Unit, 5007 - 49 Ave., Leduc AB T9E 6M6 – 403/986-2222; Fax: 403/986-1424 – Crossroads Regional Health Authority

Lethbridge Community Health Site (Train Stn.), 801 - 1st Ave. South, Lethbridge AB T1J 4L5 – 403/327-2166; Fax: 403/328-5934; EMail: phassel@lhr.ab.ca – Chinook Health Region – CEO, Gil Tourigny

Magrath Community & Wellness Site, 135 West Civic Ave., PO Box 126, Magrath AB T0K 1J0 – 403/758-3331; Fax: 403/758-3332 – Chinook Health Region

Manning Community Health Services, PO Box 95, Manning AB T0H 2M0 – 403/836-3765; Fax: 403/836-2918 – Peace Regional Health Authority

Mayerthorpe Health Services, General Delivery, Mayerthorpe AB T0E 1N0 – 403/786-4198; Fax: 403/786-2383 – Aspen Regional Health Authority #11

Medicine Hat Community & Wellness Site, 770 First St. SE, Medicine Hat AB T1A 0B4 – 403/527-1136; Fax: 403/526-8229 – Palliser Health Authority

Morinville Health Services, #103, 10008 - 107 St., Morinville AB T8R 1L3 – 403/939-1200; Fax: 403/939-7126, 1216 – Aspen Regional Health Authority #11

Nanton Health Unit, 2214 - 20 St., PO Box 812, Nanton AB T0L 1R0 – 403/646-2277; Fax: 403/646-3046 – Headwaters Health Authority – Lori Anderson, 403/652-0142

Okotoks Health Unit, 22 Elizabeth St., PO Box 758, Okotoks AB T0L 1T3 – 403/938-4911; Fax: 403/938-2783 – Headwaters Health Authority – Dir., Community Care Services, Janet Melbourne, 403/652-0139

Olds Community Health Centre, 5030 - 50 St., PO Box 459, Olds AB T0M 1P0 – 403/556-8441; Fax: 403/556-6842 – David Thompson Health Region – VP, Community Health Services, Denise McBain

Oyen Community Health Services, PO Box 296, Oyen AB T0J 2J0 – 403/854-3325; Fax: 403/854-4850 – Palliser Health Authority

Peace River Community Health Services, PO Box 6178, Peace River AB T8S 1S2 – 403/624-3611; Fax: 403/624-3169 – Peace Regional Health Authority

Peerless Lake: Northern Lakes Health Serivces, PO Box 90, Peerless Lake AB T0G 2W0 – 403/869-3930; Fax: 403/869-2053 – Keeweetinok Lakes Regional Health Authority #15

Picture Butte Community & Wellness Site, 301 Cowan Ave., PO Box 652, Picture Butte AB T0K 1V0 – 403/732-4762, 4020 (home care); Fax: 403/732-5062 – Chinook Health Region

Pincher Creek Community & Wellness Site, 782 Main St., PO Box 1685, Pincher Creek AB T0K 1W0 – 403/627-3266; Fax: 403/627-2771 – Chinook Health Region

Ponoka Community Health Centre, 5900 Hwy. 2A, PO Box 1143, Ponoka AB T0C 2H0 – 403/783-4491; Fax: 403/783-3825 – David Thompson Health Region – VP, Community Health Services, Denise McBain

Provost Community Health Services, PO Box 729, Provost AB T0B 3S0 – 403/753-6180 – East Central Regional Health Authority 7

Rainbow Lake Health Centre, PO Box 177, Rainbow Lake AB T0H 2Y0 – 403/956-3646; Fax: 403/926-3338 – Northwestern Regional Health Authority – Adm., Jenny Radsma

Raymond Community & Wellness Site, 200 N. - 2nd Ave. West, PO Box 251, Raymond AB T0K 2S0 – 403/752-3303; Fax: 403/752-4655 – Chinook Health Region

Red Deer Community Health Centre, 2845 Bremner Ave., Red Deer AB T4R 1S2 – 403/341-2100; Fax: 403/341-2196 – David Thompson Health Region – Vice-Pres., Community Health Services, Denise McBain

Red Earth Creek: Northern Lakes Health Services, General Delivery, Red Earth Creek AB T0G 1X0 – 403/649-2242; Fax: 403/649-2029 – Keeweetinok Lakes Regional Health Authority #15

Redwater Community Health Services, 4715 - 50 Ave., PO Box 57, Redwater AB T0A 2W0 – 403/942-3801; Fax: 403/942-2024 – Lakeland Regional Health Authority

Rimbey Community Health Centre, 4709 - 51 Ave., PO Box 464, Rimbey AB T0C 2J0 – 403/843-2288; Fax: 403/843-3050 – David Thompson Health Region – Adm., Denise McBain

St. Paul Community Health Services, 5610 - 50 Ave., St. Paul AB T0A 3A1 – 403/645-3396; Fax: 403/645-6609 – Lakeland Regional Health Authority

Sherwood Park: Home Care Strathcona Office, 2 Brower Dr., Sherwood Park AB T8H 1V4 – 403/467-5549; Fax: 403/449-1476 – Capital Health Authority

Slave Lake: Keeweetinok Lakes Community Health Services, 405 - 6 Ave. SW, Slave Lake AB T0G 2A4 – 403/849-3947; Fax: 403/849-3083 – Keeweetinok Lakes Regional Health Authority #15 – Team Mgr., Gail Robertson

Smith Health Services, PO Box 68, Smith AB T0G 2B0 – 403/829-3758; Fax: 403/829-3830 – Aspen Regional Health Authority #11

Smith: Flatbush Health Services, c/o Smith Office, PO Box 68, Smith AB T0G 2B0 – 403/681-3980; Fax: 403/681-3940 – Aspen Regional Health Authority #11

Smoky Lake Community Health Services, 108 Wheatland Ave., PO Box 127, Smoky Lake AB T0A 3C0 – 403/656-3595; Fax: 403/656-2242

Spirit River District Home Care Office, PO Box 187, Spirit River AB T0H 3G0 – 403/864-3063; Fax: 403/864-4187 – Mistahia Regional Health Authority

Spruce Grove Health Unit, 315 Jespersen Ave., PO Box 4323, Spruce Grove AB T7X 1B5 – 403/962-4072; Fax: 403/962-4994 – WestView Regional Health Authority – Senior Public Health Inspector, Doug Drysdale

Stettler Community Health Services, 5911 - 50 Ave., PO Box 550, Stettler AB T0C 2L0 – 403/742-3326; Fax: 403/742-1353 – East Central Regional Health Authority 7

Stony Plain Health Unit, 4905 - 47 Ave., Stony Plain AB T7Z 1S3 – 403/963-8000; Fax: 403/963-7612 – WestView Regional Health Authority

Stony Plain Home Care Office, #203, 4709 - 44 Ave., Stony Plain AB T7Z 1N4 – 403/963-3366; Fax: 403/963-9267 – WestView Regional Health Authority – Dir., Judy Tait

Strathmore Health Unit Office, 650 Winchester Rd., Strathmore AB T1P 1J9 – 403/934-3454; Fax: 403/934-3827 – Regional Health Authority 5

Sundre Community Health Centre, 212 - 6th Ave., PO Box 101, Sundre AB T0M 1X0 – 403/638-4063; Fax: 403/638-4460 – David Thompson Health Region

Swan Hills Health Services, PO Box 261, Swan Hills AB T0G 2C0 – 403/333-7077; Fax: 403/333-7009 – Aspen Regional Health Authority #11

Sylvan Lake Community Health Centre, Lakview Heights Mall, #4, One Sylvan Dr., Sylvan Lake AB T0M 1Z0 – 403/887-2241; Fax: 403/887-2610 – David Thompson Health Region

Taber Community & Wellness Site, 5009 - 56 St., Taber AB T1G 1M8 – 403/223-4403; Fax: 403/223-8733 – Chinook Health Region

Thorhild Community Health Services, County Office, 801 - 1st St., Thorhild AB T0A 3J0 – 403/398-3879 – Lakeland Regional Health Authority

Thorsby Health Unit, 4825 Hankin St., Thorsby AB T0C 2P0 – 403/789-3031; Fax: 403/789-3747 – Crossroads Regional Health Authority

Three Hills District Health Unit, PO Box 95, Three Hills AB TOM 2A0 – 403/443-5355; Fax: 403/443-2207 – Regional Health Authority 5

Tofield Community Health Services, General Delivery, 5218 - 50 St., Tofield AB T0B 4J0 – 403/662-3984; Fax: 403/662-3355 – East Central Regional Health Authority 7

Trout Lake: Northern Lakes Health Services, General Delivery, Trout Lake AB T0G 1X0 – 403/869-3922; Fax: 403/869-2054 – Keeweetinok Lakes Regional Health Authority #15

Valleyview District Home Care Office, 5112 - 50 Ave., PO Box 756, Valleyview AB T0H 3N0 – 403/524-

3338; Fax: 403/524-3153 – Mistahia Regional Health Authority

Vauxhall Community & Wellness Site, General Delivery, 408 - 1st Ave., Vauxhall AB T0K 2K0 – 403/654-2232, 2151 (home care); Fax: 403/654-2134 – Chinook Health Region

Vegreville Community Health Services, 5318 - 50 St., PO Box 99, Vegreville AB T0B 4L0 – 403/632-3331; Fax: 403/632-4334 – Lakeland Regional Health Authority

Vermilion Community Health Services, #1, 4701 - 52 St., Vermilion AB T9X 1J9 – 403/853-5270; Fax: 403/853-7362 – East Central Regional Health Authority 7

Vulcan Health Unit, Vulcan Community Health Centre, PO Box 214, Vulcan AB T0L 2B0 – 403/485-2285; Fax: 403/485-2639 – Headwaters Health Authority – Dir., Public Health Services, Lori Anderson, 403/652-0142

Wabasca: Keeweetinok Lakes Community Health Services, PO Box 9, Wabasca AB T0G 2K0 – 403/891-3931; Fax: 403/891-3011 – Keeweetinok Lakes Regional Health Authority #15 – Team Mgr., Linda Shea

Wainwright Community Health Services, PO Box 716, Wainwright AB T0B 4P0 – 403/842-4077; Fax: 403/842-3151 – East Central Regional Health Authority 7

Warner Community & Wellness Site, 300 County Rd., PO Box 8, Warner AB T0K 2L0 – 403/642-3737, 327-5578; Fax: 403/642-3944 – Chinook Health Region

Westlock Health Services, 10724 - 101 St., PO Box 274, Westlock AB T0G 2L0 – 403/349-3316; Fax: 403/349-5725 – Aspen Regional Health Authority #11

Wetaskiwin Health Unit, 5610 - 40 Ave., Wetaskiwin AB T9A 3E4 – 403/361-4333; Fax: 403/361-4335 – Crossroads Regional Health Authority – Adm., Peter Langelle

Whitecourt Health Services, 163 Provincial Bldg., Whitecourt AB T7S 1N2 – 403/778-5555, 5558; Fax: 403/778-3852 – Aspen Regional Health Authority #11

Winfield Health Unit, PO Box 114, Winfield AB T0C 2X0 – 403/682-3731; Fax: 403/682-3734 – Crossroads Regional Health Authority

## MENTAL HEALTH HOSPITALS & COMMUNITY FACILITIES

Airdrie Mental Health Clinic, PO Box 5205, Airdrie AB T4B 2B3 – 403/948-3878 – Provincial Mental Health Advisory Board

Athabasca Mental Health Clinic, #130, 4903 - 50 St., Athabasca AB T95 1E2 – 403/675-5404; Fax: 403/675-3994 – Provincial Mental Health Advisory Board

Barrhead Mental Health Clinic, 6203 - 49 St., Barrhead AB T0G 0E0 – 403/674-8243; Fax: 403/674-8352 – Provincial Mental Health Advisory Board

Blairmore Mental Health Clinic, 12501 - 20 Ave., PO Box 870, Blairmore AB T0K 0E0 – 403/562-2966; Fax: 403/562-3226 – Provincial Mental Health Advisory Board

Bonnyville Mental Health Clinic, PO Box 6917, Bonnyville AB T9N 2H1 – 403/826-2404; Fax: 403/826-6114 – Provincial Mental Health Advisory Board

Brooks Mental Health Clinic, 440 -3t. East, PO Box 1775, Brooks AB T1R 1C5 – 403/362-1252; Fax: 403/362-1223 – Provincial Mental Health Advisory Board

Calgary: Central Calgary Community Mental Health Clinic, #200, 1000 - 8th Ave. SW, Calgary AB T2P 3M7 – 403/297-7311; Fax: 403/297-5354 – Provincial Mental Health Advisory Board – Clinic Mgr., Ellen Maddison

Calgary: Northeast Calgary Community Mental Health Clinic, #130, 920 - 36 St. NE, Calgary AB T2A 6L8 – 403/297-7196; Fax: 403/297-7160 – Provincial Mental Health Advisory Board

Calgary: Northwest Calgary Community Mental Health Clinic, #280, 1620 - 29th St. NW, Calgary AB T2N 4L7 – 403/297-7345; Fax: 403/297-4543 – Provincial Mental Health Advisory Board

Camrose Mental Health Clinic, Aspen Business Park, 4911A - 47 St., Camrose AB T4V 1J9 – 403/679-1241; Fax: 403/679-1740 – Provincial Mental Health Advisory Board

Canmore Mental Health Clinic, 800 Access Rd., PO Box 1029, Canmore AB T0L 0M0 – 403/678-4696; Fax: 403/678-1951 – Joseph Greene

Claresholm Care Centre, PO Box 2198, Claresholm AB T0L 1T0 – 403/625-1495; Fax: 403/625-4177 – 100 beds – Provincial Mental Health Advisory Board – Chief Operating Officer, Don Ehman

Claresholm/Raymond Care Centre, PO Box 490, Claresholm AB T0L 0T0 – 403/625-8500; Fax: 403/625-4318 – 18 beds – Provincial Mental Health Advisory Board – CEO, Lori Kilbank

Cochrane Mental Health Clinic, PO Box 807, Cochrane AB T0L 0W0 – 403/932-3455; Fax: 403/932-2971 – Provincial Mental Health Advisory Board

Didsbury Mental Health Clinic, c/o Victoria Square Mall, 1210 -20 Ave., PO Box 130, Didsbury AB T0M 0W0 – 403/335-7285; Fax: 403/335-7227 – Provincial Mental Health Advisory Board

Drayton Valley Mental Health Clinic, PO Box 7276, Drayton Valley AB T0E 0M0 – 403/542-3140; Fax: 403/542-4426 – Provincial Mental Health Advisory Board

Drumheller Mental Health Clinic, PO Box 2086, Drumheller AB T0J 0Y0 – 403/823-1652; Fax: 403/823-1623 – Provincial Mental Health Advisory Board

Edmonton Mental Health Clinic, 108 St. Bldg., 5th Fl., 9942 - 108 St., Edmonton AB T5K 2J5 – 403/427-4444; Fax: 403/427-0424 – Provincial Mental Health Advisory Board

Edmonton: Alberta Hospital Edmonton, 17480 Fort Rd., PO Box 307, Edmonton AB T5J 2J7 – 403/472-5200; Fax: 403/472-5445 – 404 beds – Provincial Mental Health Advisory Board – CEO, Nancy Reynolds

Edson Mental Health Clinic, #100, Provincial Bldg., 111 - 54 St., Edson AB T7E 1T2 – 403/723-8294; Fax: 403/723-8297 – Provincial Mental Health Advisory Board

Fairview Mental Health Clinic, PO Box 2201, Fairview AB T0H 1L0 – 403/835-6149; Fax: 403/835-5789 – Provincial Mental Health Advisory Board

Fort McMurray Mental Health Clinic, Provinical Bldg., 9th Fl., 9915 Franklin Ave., Fort McMurray AB T9H 2K4 – 403/743-7450; Fax: 403/743-7466 – Provincial Mental Health Advisory Board

Fort Saskatchewan Mental Health Clinic, #301, 9821 - 108 St., Fort Saskatchewan AB T8L 2J2 – 403/998-5225; Fax: 403/998-7828 – Provincial Mental Health Advisory Board

Grande Cache Mental Health Clinic, 702 Pine Plaza, Grande Cache AB T0E 0X0 – 403/827-4998; Fax: 403/827-4787 – Provincial Mental Health Advisory Board

Grande Prairie Mental Health Clinic, #600, 10014 - 99 St., Grande Prairie AB T8V 3N4 – 403/538-5160; Fax: 403/538-6279 – Provincial Mental Health Advisory Board

Hanna Mental Health Clinic, Provincial Bldg., 401 McRae Dr., PO Box 1000, Hanna AB T0J 1P0 – 403/854-5585; Fax: 403/854-5517 – Provincial Mental Health Advisory Board

High Prairie Mental Health Clinic, Provincial B;dg., 2nd Fl., PO Box 967, High Prairie AB T0G 1E0 – 403/523-6700; Fax: 403/523-6701

High River Mental Health Clinic, Andrell Bldg., 2nd Fl., 309 First St. West, High River AB T0L 1B0 – 403/652-8340; Fax: 403/652-1456 – Provincial Mental Health Advisory Board – Donavon Bentz

Hinton Mental Health Clinic, 131 Market St., PO Box 2659, Hinton AB T7V 2A2 – 403/865-8247; Fax: 403/865-8327 – Provincial Mental Health Advisory Board

Innisfail Mental Health Clinic, Provincial Bldg., 4904 - 50 St., Innisfail AB T0M 1A0 – 403/227-4601; Fax: 403/227-5683 – Provincial Mental Health Advisory Board

Lac La Biche Mental Health Clinic, 9503 Beaver Hill Rd., PO Box 297, Stn Courier Box 3, Lac La Biche AB T0A 2C0 – 403/623-5230; Fax: 403/623-6232; EMail: mhc-lacl@telusplanet.net – Provincial Mental Health Advisory Board

Lacombe Mental Health Clinic, Agriculture Financing Serv. Corp., Courier Bag 16, 5033 - 52 St., 2nd Fl., Lacombe AB T4L 2A6 – 403/782-3413; Fax: 403/782-3878 – Provincial Mental Health Advisory Board

Leduc Mental Health Clinic, Leduc General Hospital, NE Annex, 4210 - 48 St., PO Box 5006, Leduc AB T9E 5Z3 – 403/986-2660; Fax: 403/986-9292 – Provincial Mental Health Advisory Board

Lethbridge Mental Health Clinic, 200 - 5 Ave. South, Lethbridge AB T1J 4C7 – 403/381-5260; Fax: 403/382-4518 – Provincial Mental Health Advisory Board

Lloydminster: Mental Health Services, 4815 - 50 St., Lloydminster AB S9V 0M8 – 306/825-6410; Fax: 306/825-6419 – Provincial Mental Health Advisory Board – Dir. of Community Programs, Trevor Lloyd, 306/880-6181

Medicine Hat Mental Health Clinic, #2 Provincial Bldg., 346 - 3 St. SE, Medicine Hat AB T1A 0G7 – 403/529-3500; Fax: 403/529-3562 – outpatient community-based mental health facility – Provincial Mental Health Advisory Board – Adm., Ed Hall

Olds Mental Health Clinic, Provinicial Bldg., 2nd Fl., 5025 - 50 St., Olds AB T4H 1R9 – 403/556-4204; Fax: 403/556-4265 – Provincial Mental Health Advisory Board

Peace River Mental Health Clinic, 9715 - 100 St., PO Box 900-8, Peace River AB T8S 1J7 – 403/624-6151; Fax: 403/624-6565 – Provincial Mental Health Advisory Board

Pincher Creek Mental Health Clinic, 782 Main St., PO Box 2105, Pincher Creek AB T0K 1W0 – 403/627-1121; Fax: 403/627-1145 – Provincial Mental Health Advisory Board

Ponoka Mental Health Clinic, PO Box 4244, Ponoka AB T4J 1R6 – 403/783-7903; Fax: 403/783-7926 – Provincial Mental Health Advisory Board

Ponoka: Alberta Hospital Ponoka, PO Box 1000, Ponoka AB T4J 1R8 – 403/783-7667; Fax: 403/783-7860 – 172 beds – Provincial Mental Health Advisory Board – Exec. Dir., Ken Sheehan

Provost Mental Health Clinic, Provincial Bldg., 5419 - 44 St., Provost AB T0B 3S0 – 403/753-2575; Fax: 403/753-6132 – Provincial Mental Health Advisory Board

Red Deer Mental Health Centre, #209, 4920 - 51 St., Red Deer AB T4N 6K8 – 403/340-5466; Fax: 403/340-4874 – Provincial Mental Health Advisory Board – Adm., Ron St. Dennis

Rimbey Mental Health Centre, Provincial Bldg., 5025 - 55 St., Rimbey AB T0C 2J0 – 403/843-2406; Fax: 403/843-2337 – Provincial Mental Health Advisory Board – Adm., Ron St. Dennis

Rocky Mountain House Mental Health Clinic, 4919 - 51 St., Rocky Mountain House AB T0M 1T0 – 403/845-8300; Fax: 403/845-8575 – Provincial Mental Health Advisory Board

St. Albert Mental Health Clinic, 30 St. Winston Churchill Ave., St. Albert AB T8N 3A3 – 403/459-2820; Fax: 403/460-7152 – Provincial Mental Health Advisory Board

St. Paul Mental Health Clinic, #202, Provincial Bldg., 5025 - 49 Ave., St. Paul AB T0A 3A0 – 403/645-6307;

Fax: 403/645-6293 – Provincial Mental Health Advisory Board

Sherwood Park Mental Health Clinic, Strathcona Place, 340 Sioux Rd., Sherwood Park AB T8A 3X6 – 403/467-6562; Fax: 403/464-3705 – Provincial Mental Health Advisory Board

Slave Lake Mental Health Clinic, 113 - 6 Ave. NW, Slave Lake AB T0G 2A1 – 403/849-7242; Fax: 403/849-7284 – Provincial Mental Health Advisory Board

Stettler Mental Health Clinic, 4835 - 50 St., PO Box 600, Stettler AB T0C 2L0 – 403/742-7591; Fax: 403/742-7916 – Provincial Mental Health Advisory Board

Stony Plain Mental Health Clinic, Provincial Bldg., 4709 - 44 Ave., Stony Plain AB T7Z 1N4 – 403/963-6151; Fax: 403/963-7186 – Provincial Mental Health Advisory Board

Strathmore Mental Health Clinic, Hilton Plaza, 209 Third St., PO Box 2002, Strathmore AB T1P 1K2 – 403/934-5174; Fax: 403/934-2685 – Provincial Mental Health Advisory Board

Swan Hills Mental Health Clinic, 29 Freeman Dr., PO Box 261, Swan Hills AB T0G 2C0 – 403/333-7077; Fax: 403/333-7009 – Provincial Mental Health Advisory Board

Taber Mental Health Services Clinic, 5011 - 49 Ave., PO Box 1749, Taber AB T0K 2G0 – 403/223-7932; Fax: 403/223-7902 – Provincial Mental Health Advisory Board

Vegreville Mental Health Clinic, Husky Plaza Mall, E341 - 50 Ave., Vegreville AB T9C 1P8 – 403/632-5449; Fax: 403/632-5496 – Provincial Mental Health Advisory Board

Vermilion Mental Health Clinic, 4701 - 52 St., PO Box 1228, Vermilion AB T0B 2M0 – 403/853-8168; Fax: 403/853-8279 – Provincial Mental Health Advisory Board

Wainwright Mental Health Clinic, Provincial Bldg., 810 - 14th Ave., PO Box 20, Wainwright AB T9W 1R2 – 403/842-7522; Fax: 403/842-7520 – Provincial Mental Health Advisory Board

Westlock Mental Health Clinic, PO Box 723, Westlock AB T0G 2L0 – 403/349-5246; Fax: 403/349-5846 – Provincial Mental Health Advisory Board

Wetaskiwin Community Mental Health Centre, Dykes Bldg., 2nd Fl., 5108 - 51 Ave., Wetaskiwin AB T9A 0S6 – 403/361-1245; Fax: 403/361-1387 – Provincial Mental Health Advisory Board

Whitecourt Mental Health Clinic, Provincial Bldg., 2nd Fl., 5020 - 52 Ave., Whitecourt AB T0E 2L0 – 403/778-7147; Fax: 403/778-7212 – Provincial Mental Health Advisory Board

## NURSING HOMES/LONG TERM CARE FACILITIES

Airdrie: Bethany Care Society, Calgary - Bethany Care Centre - Airdrie, 1736 - 1st Ave. NW, Airdrie AB T4B 2C4 – 403/948-6022; Fax: 403/948-3897 – 74 beds – Calgary Regional Health Authority – Adm., Peggy Mollerup

Athabasca Extendicare, 4517 - 53 St., Athabasca AB T9S 1K4 – 403/675-2291; Fax: 403/675-3833 – 50 beds – Aspen Regional Health Authority #11 – Adm., Joan Cody

Barrhead Healthcare Centre, *see* General Hospitals listings

Barrhead: Keir Care Centre, 5115 - 45 St., PO Box 1330, Barrhead AB T0G 0E0 – 403/674-4506; Fax: 403/674-3003 – 100 beds – Aspen Regional Health Authority #11 – Site Suprv., Leslie Penny

Bentley Care Centre, *see* Auxiliary Hospitals/Health Care Centres listings

Blairmore: Crowsnest Pass Health Care Centre, *see* General Hospitals listings

Bonnyville: Extendicare Bonnyville, 4602 - 47 Ave., Bonnyville AB T9N 2E8 – 403/826-3341; Fax: 403/826-4890 – 50 beds – Lakeland Regional Health Authority – Adm., Donna Densmore

Breton Health Centre, *see* General Hospitals listings

Brooks Health Centre, *see* General Hospitals listings

Calgary: Bethany Care Society, Calgary, *see* Auxiliary Hospitals/Health Care Centres listings

Calgary: Bethany Care Society, Calgary - Bethany Care Centre - Calgary, *see* Auxiliary Hospitals/Health Care Centres listings

Calgary: The Beverly Centre Inc., 1729 - 90th Ave. SW, Calgary AB T2V 4S1 – 403/253-8806; Fax: 403/252-7771 – 220 beds – Calgary Regional Health Authority – Adm., Sharon Cornick

Calgary: Bow-Crest Nursing Home, 5927 Bowness Rd. NW, Calgary AB T3B 0C7 – 403/288-2373; Fax: 403/247-2120 – 150 beds – Calgary Regional Health Authority – Adm., Jitu Patel

Calgary: Bow View Manor, 4628 Montgomery Blvd. NW, Calgary AB T3B 0K7 – 403/288-4446; Fax: 403/288-8522 – 174 beds – Calgary Regional Health Authority – Adm., Norma Jackson

Calgary: Brentwood Nursing Home, 2727 Trans Canada NW, Calgary AB T2N 3Y6 – 403/289-2576; Fax: 403/282-7027 – 120 beds – Calgary Regional Health Authority – Ruth Simpson

Calgary: Carewest George Boyack Nursing Home, 1203 Centre Ave. NE, Calgary AB T2P 0A5 – 403/267-2750; Fax: 403/267-2757 – 221 beds – Calgary Regional Health Authority – Site Leader, Marg Marlin

Calgary: Carewest Sarcee Auxiliary Hospital, *see* Auxiliary Hospitals/Health Care Centres listings

Calgary: Central Park Lodge Nursing Home, 1813 - 9th St. SW, Calgary AB T2T 3C2 – 403/244-8994; Fax: 403/244-5939 – 123 beds – Calgary Regional Health Authority – Adm., Patricia Hull

Calgary: Chinook Nursing Home, 1261 Glenmore Trail SW, Calgary AB T2V 4Y8 – 403/252-0141; Fax: 403/253-0292 – 149 beds – Calgary Regional Health Authority – Senior Adm., Darlene Kadonaga

Calgary: Extendicare Cedars Villa Nursing Homes, 3330 - 8th Ave. SW, Calgary AB T3C 0E7 – 403/249-8915; Fax: 403/246-7561 – 248 beds – Calgary Regional Health Authority – Adm., Lori Young

Calgary: Extendicare Hillcrest Nursing Home, 1512 - 8th Ave. NW, Calgary AB T2N 1C1 – 403/289-0236; Fax: 403/289-2350 – 112 beds – Calgary Regional Health Authority – Adm., Jean Jantzon

Calgary: Extendicare Scottish Nursing Home, 610 - 25 Ave. SW, Calgary AB T2S 0L6 – 403/228-5352; Fax: 403/228-2496 – 46 beds – Calgary Regional Health Authority – Adm., Pierre Poirier

Calgary: Father Lacombe Nursing Home, 332 - 146 Ave. SE, Calgary AB T2X 2A3 – 403/256-4641; Fax: 403/256-1669 – 110 beds – Calgary Regional Health Authority – Exec. Dir., Hilda Anderson

Calgary: Forest Grove Care Centre Ltd., 4726 - 8th Ave. SE, Calgary AB T2A 0A8 – 403/272-9831; Fax: 403/248-5788 – 225 beds – Calgary Regional Health Authority – Adm., Barbara Kerr

Calgary: Glamorgan Cedars Villas Nursing Home, 105 Galbraith Dr. SW, Calgary AB T3V 4Z5 – 403/242-5911; Fax: 403/242-7613 – 55 beds – Calgary Regional Health Authority – Joyce Spiers

Calgary: Mayfair Nursing Home, 8240 Collicut St. SW, Calgary AB T2V 2X1 – 403/252-4445; Fax: 403/253-6216 – 142 beds – Calgary Regional Health Authority – Pres., Carl Bond

Calgary: Rockyview General Hospital, *see* Auxiliary Hospitals/Health Care Centres listings

Calgary: Southwood Nursing Home, 211 Heritage Dr. SE, Calgary AB T2H 1M9 – 403/252-1194; Fax: 403/253-0393 – 120 beds – Calgary Regional Health Authority – Pat Rowe

Camrose: Bethany Long Term Care Centre, 4501 - 47 St., Camrose AB T4V 1H9 – 403/679-1000; Fax: 403/679-1020 – 149 beds – East Central Regional Health Authority 7 – Exec. Dir., Elvira Pain

Cardston: Grandview Nursing Home, 990 Main St., PO Box 1440, Cardston AB T0K 0K0 – 403/653-4054; Fax: 403/653-3771 – 40 beds – Chinook Health Region – Exec. Dir., Roger N. Walker

Carvel: Everglades Lodge, RR#1, Carvel AB T0E 0H0 – 403/963-6066 – 66 beds – Adm., Jae Jeung

Castor: Our Lady of the Rosary Hospital, *see* General Hospitals listings

Cereal Municipal Hospital, *see* General Hospitals listings

Claresholm: Willow Creek Auxiliary Hospital & Nursing Home, *see* Auxiliary Hospitals/Health Care Centres listings

Cochrane: Bethany Care Society, Calgary - Bethany Care Centre - Cochrane, 302 Quigly Dr., Cochrane AB T0C 1C0 – 403/932-6422; Fax: 403/932-4617 – 78 beds – Calgary Regional Health Authority – Adm., Jacqueline Copple

Cold Lake Health Centre, *see* General Hospitals listings

Consort Municipal Hospital, *see* General Hospitals listings

Didsbury District Health Services, *see* General Hospitals listings

Drayton Valley Health Centre, *see* General Hospitals listings

Drumheller District Health Services, *see* General Hospitals listings

Edmonton General Hospital & Continuing Care Centre (Caritas Health Group), *see* Auxiliary Hospitals/Health Care Centres listings

Edmonton: Allen Gray Continuing Care Centre, 7510 - 89 St., Edmonton AB T6C 3J8 – 403/469-2371; Fax: 403/465-2073 – 52 beds – Capital Health Authority – CEO, G. Yaremko

Edmonton: Capital Care Dickinsfield, *see* Auxiliary Hospitals/Health Care Centres listings

Edmonton: Capital Care Grandview, *see* Auxiliary Hospitals/Health Care Centres listings

Edmonton: Capital Care Lynnwood, 8740 - 165 St., Edmonton AB T5R 2R8 – 403/483-2500; Fax: 403/484-8089 – 316 beds – Capital Health Authority – VP, Operations, Robert McKim

Edmonton: Capital Care Norwood, 10410 - 111 Ave., Edmonton AB T5G 3A2 – 403/496-3200; Fax: 403/474-9806 – 307 beds – Capital Health Authority – Vice-Pres., Operations, Marilyn Snow

Edmonton: Capital Care Norwood - Mount Pleasant Site, 10530 - 56 Ave., Edmonton AB T6H 0X7 – 403/496-3221; Fax: 403/496-3222 – Capital Health Authority

Edmonton: Central Park Lodge, 5905 - 112 St., Edmonton AB T6H 3J4 – 403/434-1451; Fax: 403/436-4300 – 134 beds – Capital Health Authority

Edmonton: Extendicare North, 13210 - 114 St., Edmonton AB T5E 5E2 – 403/454-8616; Fax: 403/447-5906 – 117 beds – Capital Health Authority

Edmonton: Extendicare South, 9510 - 80 St., Edmonton AB T6C 2T1 – 403/469-1307; Fax: 403/469-5196 – 80 beds – Capital Health Authority

Edmonton: Good Samaritan Auxiliary Hospital, *see* Auxiliary Hospitals/Health Care Centres listings

Edmonton: Good Samaritan Millwoods Centre, 101 Youville Dr., Edmonton AB T6L 7A4 – 403/413-3501; Fax: 403/462-8850 – Assisted living centre – 60 beds – Capital Health Authority – Co-Adm., Ellen Ayles

Edmonton: Good Samaritan Mount Pleasant Care Centre, 10530 - 56 Ave., Edmonton AB T6H 0X7 – 403/431-3902; Fax: 403/431-3949 – 46 beds – Capital Health Authority – Dir., Maintenance, H. Boles

Edmonton: Good Samaritan Southgate Care Centre, 4225 - 107th St., Edmonton AB T6J 2P1 – 403/436-2720; Fax: 403/438-2395 – 225 beds – Capital Health Authority

Edmonton: Good Samaritan Wedman House, 10525 - 19 Ave., Edmonton AB T6H 5A2 – 403/438-1030;

Fax: 403/435-8435 – Assisted living centre – 30 beds – Capital Health Authority

Edmonton: Hardisty Nursing Home Inc., 6240 - 101 Ave., Edmonton AB T6A 0H5 – 403/466-9267; Fax: 403/465-9457 – 204 beds – Capital Health Authority – Adm., Debbie Hoffman

Edmonton: Jasper Place Central Park Lodge, 8903 - 168th St., Edmonton AB T5R 2V6 – 403/489-4931; Fax: 403/489-5435 – 100 beds – Capital Health Authority – Adm., Lynda Doll

Edmonton: Jubilee Lodge Nursing Home, 10333 -76 St., Edmonton AB T6A 3A8 – 403/469-4456; Fax: 403/466-3799 – 156 beds – Capital Health Authority – Adm., Blaine Turner

Edmonton: Laurier House, 16815 - 88 Ave., Edmonton AB T5R 5Y7 – 403/413-4712 – 10 beds – Capital Health Authority

Edmonton: Mewburn Veterans Centre, *see* Auxiliary Hospitals/Health Care Centres listings

Edmonton: Millwoods Shepherd's Care Centre, 6620 - 28 Ave., Edmonton AB T6K 2R1 – 403/463-9810; Fax: 403/462-1643 – 147 beds – Capital Health Authority – Exec. Dir., Herbert Haut

Edmonton: St. Joseph's Auxiliary Hospital, *see* Auxiliary Hospitals/Health Care Centres listings

Edmonton: St. Michael's Extended Care Centre, 7404 - 139 Ave., Edmonton AB T5C 3H7 – 403/473-5621; Fax: 403/472-4506; EMail: smeccs@connect.ab.ca – 225 beds – Capital Health Authority – Exec. Dir., B. Shulakewych

Edmonton: Venta Nursing Home, 13525 - 102 St., Edmonton AB T5E 4K3 – 403/476-6633; Fax: 403/476-6943 – 88 beds – Capital Health Authority – Adm., Ausma Birzgalis

Edson & District Health Care Centre, *see* General Hospitals listings

Elk Point Health Centre, *see* General Hospitals listings

Fort Macleod Special Development Unit, 744 - 26 St., Fort Macleod AB T0L 0Z0 – 403/553-4482; Fax: 403/553-4567 – 31 continuing care beds – Chinook Health Region

Fort Macleod: Extendicare Ltd. - Fort Macleod, 654 - 29 St., PO Box 189, Fort Macleod AB T0L 0Z0 – 403/553-3955; Fax: 403/553-2812 – 50 beds – Chinook Health Region – Adm., Greg Guyn

Fort McMurray: Northern Lights Regional Health Centre, *see* General Hospitals listings

Fort Saskatchewan: Rivercrest Lodge Nursing Home, 10104 - 101 Ave., Fort Saskatchewan AB T8L 2A5 – 403/998-2425; Fax: 403/998-5350 – 84 beds – Lakeland Regional Health Authority – Adm., Don McLeod

Grande Prairie Care Centre, 10039 - 98 St., Grande Prairie AB T8V 2E7 – 403/532-3525; Fax: 403/532-6504 – 60 beds – Mistahia Regional Health Authority – Dir. of Nursing, Myrna Wendall

Grande Prairie: Queen Elizabeth II Hospital, *see* General Hospitals listings

High Prairie: J.B. Wood Nursing Home, High Prairie Health Complex, PO Box 1, High Prairie AB T0G 1E0 – 403/523-4732; Fax: 403/523-3888 – 30 beds – Keeweetinok Lakes Regional Health Authority #15 – Coord. Regional Long Term Care, Ruth Hampton

High River General Hospital, *see* General Hospitals listings

Hythe Nursing Home, PO Box 100, Hythe AB T0H 2C0 – 403/356-3818; Fax: 403/356-3633 – 31 beds – Mistahia Regional Health Authority – Site Coord., Molly Mummert

Innisfail Health Centre, *see* General Hospitals listings

Islay Health Centre, *see* Auxiliary Hospitals/Health Care Centres listings

Lacombe Hospital, *see* General Hospitals listings

Lamont Health Care Centre - General & Extended Care, *see* General Hospitals listings

Leduc: Salem Manor Nursing Home, 4419 - 46 St., Leduc AB T9E 6L2 – 403/986-8654; Fax: 403/986-4130 – 100 beds – Crossroads Regional Health Authority – Adm., Ed Fuellbrandt

Lethbridge: Edith Cavell Care Centre, 1255 - 5 Ave. South, Lethbridge AB T1J 0V6 – 403/328-6631; Fax: 403/320-9061 – 100 beds – Chinook Health Region – Adm., Marian Teierle

Lethbridge: Extendicare Ltd. - Lethbridge, 1821 - 13 St. North, Lethbridge AB T1H 2V4 – 403/328-6664; Fax: 403/327-8909 – 120 beds – Chinook Health Region – Adm., Joyce Adachi

Lethbridge: St. Michael's Health Centre - Southland Nursing Home, 1511 - 15 Ave. North, Lethbridge AB T1H 1W2 – 403/382-6439; Fax: 403/320-1645 – 125 beds – Chinook Health Region – Adm., Romeo Paulhus

Lethbridge: St. Michael's Health Centre Administration, 608 - 5th Ave. South, Lethbridge AB T1J 4G9 – EMail: exec1@agt.net – Chinook Health Region – Exec. Dir., Romeo H. Paulhus, 403/382-6400, Fax: 604/382-6433

Lethbridge: St. Michael's Health Centre Palliative Care Program, 935 - 17 St. South, Lethbridge AB T1J 3E4 – 403/382-6494; Fax: 403/320-1698 – 6 beds – Chinook Health Region – Adm., Romeo Paulhus

Linden Nursing Home, PO Box 220, Linden AB T0M 1J0 – 403/546-3966; Fax: 403/546-4061 – 37 beds – Regional Health Authority 5 – Adm., Gary Barkman

Magrath Hospital, 37E 2nd Ave. North, PO Box 550, Magrath AB T0K 1J0 – 403/758-3371; Fax: 403/758-3698 – 23 beds – Chinook Health Region – Coord., Bill Ayotte

Mayerthorpe Extendicare, 4706 - 54 St., PO Box 569, Mayerthorpe AB T0E 1N0 – 403/786-2211; Fax: 403/786-2274 – 50 beds – Aspen Regional Health Authority #11 – Adm., Viola Oskoboiny

McLennan Sacred Heart Community Health Centre, *see* General Hospitals listings

McLennan Sacred Heart Community Health Centre - Our Lady of the Lake Nursing Home, McLennan AB – 403/324-3740; Fax: 403/324-3950 – 45 beds

Nanton Mountainview Estates, PO Box 176, Nanton AB T0L 1R0 – 403/646-5491; Fax: 403/684-3804 – Dir./Owner, Donella Sewell

Olds General Hospital, *see* General Hospitals listings

Peace River Community Health Centre, *see* General Hospitals listings

Ponoka: Northcott Care Centre, 4209 - 48 Ave., PO Box 1740, Ponoka AB T4J 1P4 – 403/783-4764; Fax: 403/783-6420 – 72 beds – Adm., Art Ulveland

Provost Health Centre, *see* General Hospitals listings

Radway Health Care Centre, *see* Auxiliary Hospitals/Health Care Centres listings

Red Deer Nursing Home, 4736 - 30th St., Red Deer AB T4N 5H8 – 403/343-4458; Fax: 403/341-4988 – 118 beds – David Thompson Health Region – Pres., Gerry Vanhooren

Red Deer: Valley Park Manor Nursing Home, 5505 - 60th Ave., Red Deer AB T4N 4W2 – 403/343-4722; Fax: 403/341-5938 – 100 beds – David Thompson Health Region – Vice-Pres., Gord Birbeck

Red Deer: West Park Lodge, 5715 - 41 St. Crescent, Red Deer AB T4N 1B3 – 403/343-7471; Fax: 403/343-3424 – David Thompson Health Region

Rimbey General Hospital, *see* General Hospitals listings

St. Albert: Youville Home, 9 St. Vital Ave., St. Albert AB T8N 1K1 – 403/460-6900; Fax: 403/459-4139 – 162 beds – Capital Health Authority – Adm., Ken Pickard

St. Paul: Extendicare Nursing Home - St. Paul, 4614 - 47 Ave., St. Paul AB T0A 3A3 – 403/645-3375; Fax: 403/645-4290 – 75 beds – Lakeland Regional Health Authority – Adm., Steve Krim

Sherwood Park Care Centre, 2020 Brentwood Blvd., Sherwood Park AB T8A 0X1 – 403/467-2281; Fax: 403/449-1529 – 75 beds – Capital Health Authority – Exec. Dir., L. Dunfield

Sherwood Park: Strathcona Care Centre, 12 Brower Dr., Sherwood Park AB T8H 1V3 – 403/467-3366; Fax: 403/467-4095 – 100 beds – Capital Health Authority – Adm., Mary Ann Platz

Slave Lake Hospital, *see* General Hospitals listings

Smoky Lake: George McDougall Memorial Health Centre, *see* General Hospitals listings

Stettler Health Centre, *see* General Hospitals listings

Stony Plain: Good Samaritan Care Centre Stony Plain, 5600 - 50th St., Stony Plain AB T7Z 1P8 – 403/963-2261, 6066; Fax: 403/963-5156 – 90 beds – WestView Regional Health Authority – Pres., Phil Gaudet

Strathmore District Health Services, *see* General Hospitals listings

Taber & District Health Care Complex, *see* General Hospitals listings

Three Hills District Health Services, *see* General Hospitals listings

Tofield Health Centre, *see* General Hospitals listings

Trochu-St. Mary's Health Care Centre, *see* General Hospitals listings

Vegreville Long Term Care Centre, 5225 - 43 St., PO Box 959, Vegreville AB T9C 1S1 – 403/632-2871; Fax: 403/632-6680 – 90 beds – Lakeland Regional Health Authority – Coord., Pearl Babiuk

Vermilion Health Centre, *see* General Hospitals listings

Viking: Extendicare - Viking, 5020 - 57th Ave., PO Box 430, Viking AB T0B 4N0 – 403/336-4790; Fax: 403/336-4004 – 60 beds – East Central Regional Health Authority 7 – Adm., Lorie Little

Vulcan Community Health Centre, *see* General Hospitals listings

Vulcan Extendicare, 715 - 2 Ave. South, PO Box 810, Vulcan AB T0L 2B0 – 403/485-2022; Fax: 403/485-2879 – 46 beds – Headwaters Health Authority – Adm., Dianne Harder

Wainwright Health Centre, *see* General Hospitals listings

Westlock Long Term Care Centre, *see* Auxiliary Hospitals/Health Care Centres listings

Wetaskiwin Health Centre, *see* General Hospitals listings

## NURSING STATIONS

Chateh Hay Lakes: Hay Lakes Nursing Station, General Delivery, Chateh Hay Lakes AB T0H 1B0 – 403/495-2705 – Nurse in Charge, Louise Stacey

Fort Chipewyan Nursing Station, General Delivery, Fort Chipewyan AB T0P 1B0 – 403/697-3650; Fax: 403/697-3763 – Nurse in Charge, Lorri Frank

Fox Lake Nursing Station, General Delivery, Fox Lake AB T0H 1R0 – 403/659-3730; Fax: 403/659-3960 – Nursing Suprv., Christopher Ryan

Worsley Health Centre, General Delivery, Worsley AB T0H 3W0 – 403/685-3752; Fax: 403/685-2007

## PRIVATE HOSPITALS

Medicine Hat: Central Park Lodge, 603 Prospect Dr. SW, Medicine Hat AB T1A 4C2 – 403/527-5531; Fax: 403/527-5533 – 158 beds – Palliser Health Authority – Adm., David Dennis

Medicine Hat: Sunnyside Nursing Home, 1720 Bell St. SW, Medicine Hat AB T1A 5G1 – 403/527-3838 – 104 beds – Palliser Health Authority – Mgr., S. Greenstein

## SPECIAL TREATMENT CENTRES

(Includes: Abortion Clinics, Cancer Clinics, Rehabilitation Centres, Treatment Centres)

Calgary: Alberta Cancer Board/Tom Baker Cancer Centre, 1331 - 29th St. NW, Calgary AB T2N 4N2 – 403/670-1711; Fax: 403/283-1651 – cancer treatment – Dir., Dr. Gavin Stuart

Calgary: Grace Women's Health Centre, 1441 - 29 St. NW, Calgary AB T2N 4JB – 403/670-2200; Fax: 403/670-2190 – Calgary Regional Health Authority – Pres., Mary Cullen

Calgary: Kensington Clinic, 2431 - 5th Ave. NW, Calgary AB T2W 0T3 – 403/283-9117; Fax: 403/283-9139 – abortion clinic

Calgary: Southern Alberta Clinic, #120, 1040 - 7 Ave. SW, Calgary AB T2P 3G9 – 403/262-4460; Fax: 403/290-0933 – breast screening clinic

Canmore Pain Clinic Inc., PO Box 130, Canmore AB T0L 0M0 – 403/678-7200; Fax: 403/678-7201 – Dir., Dr. Michael Wuitchik

Edmonton: Alberta Cancer Board/Cross Cancer Institute, 11560 University Ave. NW, Edmonton AB T6G 1Z2 – 403/432-8771; Fax: 403/432-8411 – cancer treatment – 44 beds – Dir., Dr. A.L.A. Fields

Edmonton: Children's Health Centre of Northern Alberta, #4100, Education & Development Centre, 8308 - 114th St., Edmonton AB T6G 2V2 – 403/492-9997; Fax: 403/492-3535 – 225 beds – Pres., Brian C. Lemon

Edmonton: Glenrose Rehabilitation Hospital, 10230 - 111 Ave., Edmonton AB T5G 0B7 – 403/471-2262; Fax: 403/474-8863; EMail: pschoenb@cha.ab.ca – rehabilitation centre – 240 beds – Capital Health Authority – Patient Care Dir. & Acting Site Dir., Linda Youell

Edmonton: Good Samaritan Wedman Village Homes, 1603/1609 Bearspaw Dr. East, Edmonton AB T6J 5E2 – 403/435-5072; Fax: 403/435-8435 – Alzheimer care centre – Capital Health Authority

Edmonton: McConnell Place North, 9113 - 144 Ave., Edmonton AB T5E 6K2 – 403/496-2575; Fax: 403/472-6699 – Alzheimer care centre; opening in 1998 McConnell West (36 additional beds) – 36 beds – Capital Health Authority

Edmonton: Morgentaler Clinic of Edmonton, 10141 - 150th St., Edmonton AB T5P 1P2 – 403/484-1124; Fax: 403/489-3379 – abortion clinic – Exec. Dir., Susan Fox

Edmonton: Northern Alberta Clinic, 311 Kingsway Garden Mall, Edmonton AB T5G 3A6 – 403/474-4300; Fax: 403/477-8418 – breast screening clinic

Fort McMurray Cancer Clinic, c/o Fort McMurray Regional Hospital, 7 Hospital St., Fort McMurray AB T9H 1P2 – 403/791-6161 – cancer treatment

Grande Prairie Cancer Clinic, 10409 - 98th St., Grande Prairie AB T8V 2E8 – 403/538-7588; Fax: 403/532-9120 – cancer treatment – Dir., Dr. Claudia Strehlke

Lethbridge Cancer Clinic, c/o Lethbridge Regional Hospital, #2H209, 960 - 19th St. South, Lethbridge AB T1J 1W5 – 403/329-0633; Fax: 403/320-0508 – cancer treatment – Dir., Dr. Thomas Melling

Lethbridge: Children's Centre, Room A252, 2nd Fl., 200 - 5th Ave. South, Lethbridge AB T1J 4C7 – 403/381-5255; Fax: 403/381-5336 – children's assessment, rehabilitation & education centre – Chinook Health Region

Medicine Hat Cancer Clinic, 666 - 5th St. SW, Medicine Hat AB T1A 4H6 – 403/529-8817; Fax: 403/529-8007 – cancer treatment – Dir., Dr. A.R. McClelland

Peace River Cancer Clinic, c/o Peace River Auxiliary Hospital, PO Box 400, Peace River AB T0H 2X0 – 403/624-7500 – Suprv., Physical Plant, Don Kennedy

Red Deer: Central Alberta Cancer Centre, 3942 - 50A Ave., PO Box 5030, Red Deer AB T4N 6R2 – 403/343-4526; Fax: 403/346-1160 – cancer treatment – Dir., Dr. Neil Graham

# BRITISH COLUMBIA

## REGIONAL HEALTH AUTHORITIES

Abbotsford: Fraser Valley Health Region, 34194 Marshall Rd., Abbotsford BC V2S 5E4 – 604/556-5060, 5064; Fax: 604/556-5077 – CEO, Larry Tokarchuk

Armstrong: North Okanagan/Columbia Shuswap Regional Health Board, 2740 Haugen Ave., PO Box 388, Armstrong BC V0E 1B0 – 250/546-2917; Fax: 250/546-6593 – CEO, George Wellwood

Kamloops: Thompson Regional Health Bd., 311 Columbia St., Kamloops BC V2C 2T1 – 250/314-2784; Fax: 250/314-2765 – Chair, Sharon Frisseli

Kelowna: Okanagan Similkameen Health Region, 2180 Ethel St., Kelowna BC V1Y 3A1 – 250/862-4010; Fax: 250/862-4201 – CEO, Murray Ramsden

Nanaimo: Central Vancouver Island Health Region, #610, 495 Dunsmuir St., Nanaimo BC V9R 6B9 – 250/741-5500; Fax: 250/741-5507 – Responsible for 1,000+ beds – CEO, Grant Roberge

New Westminster: Simon Fraser Health Region, 260 Sherbrooke St., New Westminster BC V3L 3M2 – 604/520-4200; Fax: 604/520-4827 – Responsible for 1,000 acute care & 1,000 long term care beds – Pres. & CEO, Jim Fair

North Vancouver: North Shore Health Region, #210, 171 West Esplanade, North Vancouver BC V7M 3J9 – 604/984-3841; Fax: 604/984-3840; EMail: fgaudet@lgh.hnet.bc.ca – CEO, Dr. Inge Schamborzki

Prince George: Northern Interior Regional Health Board, #708, 299 Victoria St., Prince George BC V2L 5B8 – 250/565-6920; Fax: 250/565-6514 – CEO, Dave Richardson

Surrey: South Fraser Health Region, Surrey Memorial Hospital Annex, 13750 - 96th Ave., Surrey BC V3V 1Z2 – 604/585-5680; Fax: 604/585-5688 – CEO, Pat Zanon

Vancouver/Richmond Health Board, #3, 1060 West 8th Ave., Vancouver BC V6H 1C4 – 604/775-1866; Fax: 604/775-1804 – CEO, John Tegenfeldt

Victoria: Capital Health Region, 2101 Richmond Ave., Victoria BC V8R 4R7 – 250/370-8877; Fax: 250/370-8750 – Responsible for 1,421 beds – CEO, Ken Fyke

## COMMUNITY HEALTH COUNCILS

Arras: South Peace Community Health Council, General Delivery, Arras BC V0C 1B0 – 250/782-8501; Fax: 250/784-7301 – CEO, Rick Robinson

Campbell River/Nootka Community Health Council, 427 - 10th Ave., Campbell River BC V9W 4E4 – 250/287-4844; Fax: 250/287-9326 – CEO, Doug Marrie

Castlegar & District Health Council, 709 - 10th St., Castlegar BC V1N 2H7 – 250/365-7711; Fax: 250/365-2298 – CEO, Ken Talarico

Courtenay: Comox Valley Community Health Council, #101, 1509 Cliffe Ave., Courtenay BC V9N 2K6 – 250/338-5453; Fax: 250/338-5415 – Senior Health Adm., Don Brown

Cranbrook Health Council, 13 - 24th Ave. North, Cranbrook BC V1C 3H9 – 250/489-6473; Fax: 250/426-5285 – CEO, Gerry Vanhooren

Creston & District Health Council, PO Box 5000, Creston BC V0B 1G0 – 250/428-2283; Fax: 250/428-7244 – CEO, Ray Mabbett

Fernie: Elk Valley & South Country Health Council, c/o Fernie District Hopsital Admin., PO Box 670, Fernie BC V0B 1M0 – 250/423-4453; Fax: 250/423-3732 – CEO, John McAuley

Fort Nelson-Liard Community Health Council, PO Box 60, Fort Nelson BC V0C 1R0 – 250/774-6916; Fax: 250/774-3731 – Exec. Dir., Bryan Redford

Fort St. John: North Peace Health Council, 9636 - 100th Ave., Fort St. John BC V1J 1Y3 – 250/262-5296; Fax: 250/262-5294 – CEO, Andrew Neuner

Golden Health Council, PO Box 1260, Golden BC V0A 1H0 – 250/344-5271; Fax: 250/344-2511 – CEO, Peter White

Grand Forks: Boundary Health Council, 7474 - 3rd St., PO Box 2647, Grand Forks BC V0H 1H0 – 250/442-8200; Fax: 250/442-8311 – CEO, Garth Burnell

Hagensborg: Bella Coola Valley & District Community Health Council, PO Box 71, Hagensborg BC V0T 1H0 – 250/982-2725; Fax: 250/799-5635 – Chair, Jack McKinnon

Hazelton: Upper Skeena Health Council, c/o Wrinch Memorial Hospital, PO Box 100, Hazelton BC V0J 1Y0 – 250/842-5211; Fax: 250/842-5865 – CEO, Phil Muir

Houston: Bulkley Valley Health Council, c/o Houston Health Centre, PO Box 538, Houston BC V0J 1Z0 – 250/845-2294; Fax: 250/845-2005 – Acting CEO, Hanna White

Invermere: Columbia Valley Health Council, PO Box 5001, Invermere BC V0A 1K0 – 250/342-9201; Fax: 250/342-2319 – Acting CEO, Tom Crump

Kimberley Community Health Council, PO Box 37, Kimberley BC V1A 2Z8 – 250/427-4807; Fax: 250/427-2616 – CEO, Paul Vermeulen

Kitimat & Area Health Council, c/o Kitimat General Hospital, 899 Lahakas Blvd., Kitimat BC V8C 1E7 – 250/632-8322; Fax: 250/632-3044 – CEO, Linda Coles

Masset: Queen Charlotte Islands/Haida Gwaii Community Health Council, PO Box 619, Masset BC V0T 1M0 – 250/559-4300; Fax: 250/559-4312 – Acting CEO, Elio Azzara

Nelson & Area Health Council, 3 View St., Nelson BC V1L 2V1 – 250/354-2340; Fax: 250/354-2320 – CEO, George Gillies

New Aiyansh: Nisga'a Community Health Council, 256 Tait Ave., PO Box 234, New Aiyansh BC V0J 1A0 – 250/633-2212; Fax: 250/633-2512 – Exec. Dir., Reg Percival

New Denver: Arrow Lakes/Upper Slocan Valley Community Health Council, 401 Galena Ave., PO Box 129, New Denver BC V0G 1S0 – 250/358-7911; Fax: 250/358-7117 – CEO, Judy Cameron

100 Mile House: South Cariboo Community Health Council, PO Box 399, 100 Mile House BC V0K 2E0 – 250/395-2202; Fax: 250/395-2662 – CEO, William Marshall

Port McNeil: Mount Waddington Community Health Council, 2750 Kingcome Pl., PO Box 548, Port McNeil BC V0N 2R0 – 250/956-3655; Fax: 250/956-3653 – CEO, Dora Nicinski

Powell River Community Health Council, c/o Powell River General Hospital, 5000 Joyce Ave., Powell River BC V8A 5R3 – 604/485-3207; Fax: 604/485-3266 – CEO, Bill Crysler

Prince Rupert: North Coast Community Health Council, c/o Prince Rupert Regional Hospital, 1305 Summit Ave., Prince Rupert BC V8J 2A6 – 205/624-0233; Fax: 205/624-2195 – CEO, Roger Walker

Quesnel & District Community Health Council, 543 Front St., Quesnel BC V2K 2K7 – 250/249-5746; Fax: 250/992-5277

Sechelt: Sunshine Coast Community Health Council, PO Box 133, Sechelt BC V0N 3A0 – 604/885-8631; Fax: 604/885-8633 – CEO, Wendy Turner

Squamish: Sea to Sky Community Health Council, 38140 Behrner St., Squamish BC V0N 3G0 – 604/892-6030; Fax: 604/892-9417 – CEO, Brian Kines, 604/892-6014

Stewart: Snow Country Health Council, PO Box 8, Stewart BC V0T 1W0 – 250/636-2221; Fax: 250/636-2715 – Acting CEO, Lynda Hyde

Terrace & Area Health Council, 4720 Haugland Ave., Terrace BC V8G 2W7 – 250/638-4021; Fax: 250/635-7639; EMail: maleisin@bcsc02.gov.bc.ca – CEO, Michael Leisinger

Trail: Greater Trail Health Council, 1200 Hospital Bench, Trail BC V1R 4M1 – 250/364-3419; Fax: 250/364-3422 – CEO, Paul Caraca

Waglisla: Central Coast Community Health Council, c/o R.W. Lange Memorial Hospital, Waglisla BC V0T 1Z0 – 250/957-2314; Fax: 250/957-2612 – Interim CEO, Wendy McDonald

Williams Lake: Central Cariboo Chilcotin Health Council, PO Box 2000, Williams Lake BC V2G 2P3 – 250/392-8202; Fax: 250/392-4460 – CEO, Martin Oets

## GENERAL HOSPITALS

Abbotsford: Matsqui-Sumas-Abbotsford General Hospital, 2179 McCallum Rd., Abbotsford BC V2S 3P1 – 604/853-2201; Fax: 604/853-0734 – 352 beds – Pres./CEO, Larry Tokarchuk

Alert Bay: St. George's Hospital, 182 Fir St., PO Box 223, Alert Bay BC V0N 1A0 – 250/974-5585; Fax: 250/974-5422 – 14 beds – CEO, Dora Nicinski, 250/956-3655, Fax: 250/956-3653

Ashcroft & District General Hospital, PO Box 488, Ashcroft BC V0K 1A0 – 250/453-2211; Fax: 250/453-9685 – 24 beds – Thompson Regional Health Bd. – Adm., Sylvia Gerwien

Bella Coola General Hospital, Mackay St., PO Box 220, Bella Coola BC V0T 1C0 – 250/799-5311; Fax: 250/799-5635 – 15 beds – Adm., Anne Toupin

Burnaby Hospital, 3935 Kincaid St., Burnaby BC V5G 2X6 – 604/434-4211; Fax: 604/431-4708 – 466 beds – CEO, Dr. John Blatherwick, 604/775-2146, Fax: 604/775-2144

Burns Lake: Lakes District Hospital & Health Centre, 741 Centre St., PO Box 479, Burns Lake BC V0J 1E0 – 250/692-3181; Fax: 250/692-3633 – 26 beds – Public Adm., Doug Marrie

Campbell River & District General Hospital, 375 - 2 Ave., Campbell River BC V9W 3V1 – 250/287-7111; Fax: 250/287-8889 – 115 beds – CEO, Brian MacLure

Castlegar & District Hospital, 709 - 10 St., Castlegar BC V1N 2H7 – 250/365-7711; Fax: 250/365-2298 – 90 beds – Adm., Ken A. Talarico

Chetwynd General Hospital, PO Box 507, Chetwynd BC V0C 1J0 – 250/788-2236; Fax: 250/788-2145 – 18 beds – Interim CEO, Meribel Miller

Chilliwack General Hospital, 45600 Menholm Rd., Chilliwack BC V2P 1P7 – 604/795-4141; Fax: 604/795-4110 – 412 beds – CEO, Etta Richmond

Clearwater: Dr. Helmcken Memorial Hospital, RR#1, Clearwater BC V0E 1N0 – 250/674-2244; Fax: 250/674-2477 – 10 beds – Adm., Linda K. Basran

Comox: St. Joseph's General Hospital, 2137 Comox Ave., Comox BC V9N 4B1 – 250/339-1402; Fax: 250/339-1432 – Exec. Dir., Michael Pontus

Cranbrook Regional Hospital, 13 - 24th Ave. North, Cranbrook BC V1C 3H9 – 250/426-5281; Fax: 250/426-5285 – Exec. Dir., Merlen W. Hokanson

Creston Valley Hospital, 312 - 15 Ave., Creston BC V0B 1G0 – 250/428-2286; Fax: 250/428-5959 – 32 acute care, 20 extended care beds – Acting Exec. Dir., Jackie Malone

Dawson Creek & District Hospital, 11100 - 13th St., Dawson Creek BC V1G 3W8 – 250/782-8501; Fax: 250/784-7301 – 57 beds – CEO, Rick Robinson

Delta Hospital, 5800 Mountain View Blvd., Delta BC V4K 3V6 – 604/946-1121; Fax: 604/946-3086 – 158 beds – South Fraser Valley Regional Health Board – Exec. Dir., David C. Richardson

Duncan: Cowichan District Hospital, 3045 Gibbins Rd., Duncan BC V9L 1E5 – 250/746-4141; Fax: 250/746-4247 – 118 beds – Public Adm., Robert J. Smith

Enderby & District Memorial Hospital, 500 George St., PO Box 340, Enderby BC V0E 1V0 – 250/546-6131; Fax: 250/546-9943 – 28 beds – Transition Mgr., Brian Kines, 250/838-6441, Fax: 250/838-9530

Fernie District Hospital, 1501 - 5 Ave., PO Box 670, Fernie BC V0B 1M0 – 250/423-4453; Fax: 250/423-3732 – 50 beds – CEO, John McAulay

Fort Nelson General Hospital, PO Box 60, Fort Nelson BC V0C 1R0 – 250/774-6916; Fax: 250/774-3731 – 41 beds – Adm., Bryan Redford

Fort St. John General Hospital, 9636 - 100 Ave., PO Box 1, Fort St. John BC V1J 1Y3 – 250/785-6611; Fax: 250/785-4060 – 45 beds – CEO, Chris Wenzel

Golden & District General Hospital, 9th Ave., PO Box 1260, Golden BC V0A 1H0 – 250/344-5271; Fax: 250/344-2511 – Adm., Peter White

Grand Forks: Boundary Hospital, 7649 - 22 St., PO Box 189, Grand Forks BC V0H 1H0 – 250/442-8211; Fax: 250/442-3922 – 70 beds – Adm., Garth Burnell

Hazelton: Wrinch Memorial Hospital, Hazelton BC V0J 1Y0 – 250/842-5211; Fax: 250/842-5865 – Adm., Dr. Philip A. Muir

Hope: Fraser Canyon Hospital, 1275 - 7 Ave., RR#2, Hope BC V0X 1L0 – 604/869-5656; Fax: 604/869-7710 – 61 beds – Fraser Valley Regional Health Board – CEO, Ray Marshall

Invermere & District Hospital, PO Box 5001, Invermere BC V0A 1K0 – 250/342-9201; Fax: 250/342-2319 – 30 beds – Adm., Milton Crawford

Kamloops: Royal Inland Hospital, 311 Columbia St., Kamloops BC V2C 2T1 – 250/374-5111; Fax: 250/314-2333 – 260 beds – Thompson Regional Health Bd. – Public Adm., Paul Chapin

Kaslo: Victorian Hospital of Kaslo, PO Box 607, Kaslo BC V0G 1M0 – 250/353-2211; Fax: 250/353-7772 – 5 beds – Nelson & Area Health Council – Adm., Margaret Milner

Kelowna General Hospital, 2268 Pandosy St., Kelowna BC V1Y 1T2 – 250/862-4000; Fax: 250/862-4020 – 731 beds – CEO, Murray Ramsden

Kimberley & District Hospital, 260 - 4th Ave., Kimberley BC V1A 2R6 – 250/427-2215; Fax: 250/427-4342 – 53 beds – Adm., Joan Poweska

Kitimat General Hospital, 899 Lahakas Blvd., Kitimat BC V8C 1E7 – 250/632-2121; Fax: 250/632-3044 – 69 beds – CEO, Linda Coles

Ladysmith & District General Hospital, 1111 - 4th Ave., PO Box 10, Ladysmith BC V0R 2E0 – 250/245-2221; Fax: 250/245-3238 – 42 beds – Central Vancouver Island Regional Health Board – Adm., Donald U. Brown

Langley Memorial Hospital, 22051 Fraser Hwy., Langley BC V3A 4H4 – 604/534-4121; Fax: 604/534-6411 – 451 beds – Pres., Pat Zanon

Lillooet District Hospital, 951 Murray St., PO Box 249, Lillooet BC V0K 1V0 – 250/256-4233; Fax: 250/256-4746 – 31 beds – Adm., Raelene Shea

Lytton: St. Bartholomew's Hospital, 844 Main St., PO Box 99, Lytton BC V0K 1Z0 – 250/455-2221; Fax: 250/455-6621 – 20 beds – Adm., Doug Calder

Mackenzie & District Hospital, PO Box 249, Mackenzie BC V0J 2C0 – 250/997-3263; Fax: 250/997-3940 – 12 beds – Adm., Janice Blackmore

Maple Ridge: Ridge Meadows Hospital & Health Care Centre, 11666 Laity St., PO Box 5000, Maple Ridge BC V2X 7G5 – 604/463-4111; Fax: 604/463-1888 – 250 beds – Pres., Jim Fair, 604/520-4840, Fax: 604/520-4827

Masset: Queen Charlotte Islands General Hospital - Masset Division, PO Box 319, Masset BC V0T 1M0 – 205/626-8343 – Queen Charlotte Islands/Haida Gwaii Community Health Council – Adm., Alio Azzara

McBride & District Hospital, 594 King St., PO Box 128, McBride BC V0J 2E0 – 250/569-2251; Fax: 250/569-3369 – 16 beds – Northern Interior Regional Health Board – Adm., Victor Chicoine

Merritt: Nicola Valley General Hospital, Hwy. 5 North, RR#1, Merritt BC V0K 2B0 – 250/378-2242; Fax: 250/378-3287 – 25 beds – Exec. Dir., Terry Frizzell

Mission Memorial Hospital, 7324 Hurd St., Mission BC V2V 3H5 – 604/826-6261; Fax: 604/826-9513 – 135 beds – Fraser Valley Regional Health Board – Adm., Randy Wong

Nakusp: Arrow Lakes Hospital, PO Box 87, Nakusp BC V0G 1R0 – 250/265-3622; Fax: 250/265-4435 – 17 beds – Acting Adm., Barb Chwachka

Nanaimo Regional General Hospital, 1200 Dufferin Cr., Nanaimo BC V9S 2B7 – 250/754-2141; Fax: 250/755-7633 – 409 beds – Central Vancouver Island Regional Health Board – Pres., E.E. (Gene) Freeborn

Nelson: Kootenay Lake District Hospital, 3 View St., Nelson BC V1L 2V1 – 250/352-3111; Fax: 250/354-2320 – 57 beds – Adm., Jack J. Miller

New Denver: Slocan Community Hospital & Health Care Centre, 401 Galena Ave., PO Box 129, New Denver BC V0G 1S0 – 250/358-7911; Fax: 250/358-7117 – 40 beds – Adm., Judy Cameron

New Westminster: Royal Columbian Hospital, 330 Columbia St. East, New Westminster BC V3L 3W7 – 604/520-4253; Fax: 604/520-3842 – 375 beds – Pres., Jim Fair, 604/520-4840, Fax: 604/520-4827

New Westminster: Saint Mary's Hospital, 220 Royal Ave., New Westminster BC V3L 1H6 – 604/521-1881; Fax: 604/527-3358 – 96 beds – CEO, Bernard Bilodeau

North Vancouver: Lions Gate Hospital, 231 East 15 St., North Vancouver BC V7L 2L7 – 604/988-3131; Fax: 604/984-5838 – 650 beds – CEO, Inge Schamborzki, 604/984-3840, Fax: 604/984-3841

Oliver: South Okanagan General Hospital, McKinney Rd., PO Box 760, Oliver BC V0H 1T0 – 250/498-3474; Fax: 250/498-6851 – 105 beds – Exec. Dir., Ken Doepker

100 Mile District General Hospital, 555 Cedar Ave., PO Box 399, 100 Mile House BC V0K 2E0 – 250/395-2202; Fax: 250/395-2662 – 60 beds – CEO, Bill Marshall

Penticton Regional Hospital, 550 Carmi Ave., Penticton BC V2A 3G6 – 250/492-4000; Fax: 250/492-9025 – 179 acute care, 100 extended care beds – South Okanagan/Similkameen Regional Health Board – Exec. Dir., Ken Burrows, Email: ken-burrows@prh.hosp.gov.bc.ca

Port Alberni: West Coast General Hospital, 3841 - 8 Ave., Port Alberni BC V9Y 4S1 – 250/723-2135; Fax: 250/724-8805 – 53 beds – Vancouver/Richmond Health Board – Adm., Ron Mustard

Port Alice Hospital, 1090 Marine Dr., PO Box 69, Port Alice BC V0N 2N0 – 250/284-3555; Fax: 250/284-6163; EMail: kportalicehospital@capescott.net – 3 beds – Mount Waddington Community Health Council – Site Mgr., Nancy Lee Deslauriers

Port Hardy Hospital, Park Dr., PO Box 790, Port Hardy BC V0N 2P0 – 250/949-6161; Fax: 250/949-7000 – 17 beds – Site Mgr., Isabel Savignac

Port McNeill & District Hospital, PO Box 790, Port McNeill BC V0N 2R0 – 250/956-4461; Fax: 250/956-4823 – CEO, Dora Nickinski, 250/956-3655, Fax: 250/956-3653

Port Moody: Eagle Ridge Hospital, 475 Guildford Way, Port Moody BC V3H 3W9 – 604/461-2022; Fax: 604/461-9972 – 175 beds – Pres., Jim Fair, 604/520-4840, Fax: 604/520-4827

Powell River General Hospital, 5000 Joyce Ave., Powell River BC V8A 5R3 – 604/485-3211; Fax: 604/485-3245 – 125 beds – Adm., Ed Marion

Prince George Regional Hospital, 2000 - 15 Ave., Prince George BC V2M 1S2 – 250/565-2000; Fax: 250/565-2343 – 219 beds – Exec. Dir., Ken Doepker

Prince Rupert Regional Hospital, 1305 Summit Ave., Prince Rupert BC V8J 2A6 – 250/624-2171; Fax: 250/624-2195 – 41 acute care, 23 extended care beds – North Coast Community Health Council – CEO, Roger Walker

Princeton General Hospital, 98 Ridgewood Ave., PO Box 610, Princeton BC V0X 1W0 – 250/295-3233; Fax: 250/295-3344 – 30 beds – Adm., Dorothy Cobb

Queen Charlotte Islands General Hospital - Queen Charlotte City Divison, PO Box 9, Queen Charlotte

City BC V0T 1S0 – 250/559-8466; Fax: 250/559-4312 – 21 beds – Queen Charlotte Islands/Haida Gwaii Community Health Council – Adm., Elio Azzara

Quesnel: G.R. Baker Memorial Hospital, 543 Front St., Quesnel BC V2J 2K7 – 250/992-2181; Fax: 250/992-5652 – 44 beds – Adm., Kenneth T. Last

Revelstoke: Queen Victoria Hospital, PO Box 5000, Revelstoke BC V0E 2S0 – 250/837-2131; Fax: 250/837-4788 – 57 beds – Adm., James Vaillancourt

The Richmond Hospital, 7000 Westminster Hwy., Richmond BC V6X 1A2 – 604/278-9711; Fax: 604/244-5191 – 470 beds – Co-Chair, Kirk Mitchell

Rossland: Mater Misericordiae Health Care Facility, 1961 Georgia St., PO Box 1239, Rossland BC V0G 1Y0 – 250/362-7344; Fax: 250/362-7366 – 41 beds – CEO, C.F. (Rick) Riley

Saanichton: Saanich Peninsula Hospital, 2166 Mount Newton Cross Rd., Saanichton BC V8M 2B2 – 250/652-3911; Fax: 250/652-6920 – 226 beds – Capital Health Region – Adm., Robert Myers

Salmon Arm: Shuswap Lake General Hospital, PO Box 520, Salmon Arm BC V1E 4N6 – 250/833-3600; Fax: 250/833-3611 – Exec. Dir., Eugene M. Casavant

Salt Spring Island: The Lady Minto Gulf Islands Hospital, 135 Crofton Rd., Salt Spring Island BC V8K 1T1 – 250/537-5545; Fax: 250/537-1475 – 50 beds – Capital Health Region – CEO, Karen Davies

Sechelt: St. Mary's Hospital, PO Box 7777, Sechelt BC V0N 3A0 – 604/885-8614; Fax: 604/885-8628; EMail: brown.carol@SMSH.hnet.bc.c a – 83 beds – Interim CEO, Carol Brown

Smithers: Bulkley Valley District Hospital, 3950 - 8 Ave., PO Box 370, Smithers BC V0J 2N0 – 250/847-2611; Fax: 250/847-2446 – 32 beds – Public Adm., Dr. Lorne Klippert

Sparwood General Hospital, PO Box 9, Sparwood BC V0B 2G0 – 250/425-6212; Fax: 250/425-2313 – 12 beds – Adm., Lynn Noble

Squamish General Hospital, 38140 Clarke Dr., PO Box 6000, Squamish BC V0N 3G0 – 604/892-5211; Fax: 604/892-9417 – 94 beds – Adm., John R. Dillabough

Summerland General Hospital, PO Box 869, Summerland BC V0H 1Z0 – 250/494-6811; Fax: 250/494-8755 – 71 beds – South Okanagan/Similkameen Regional Health Board – CEO, Robert Heise

Surrey Memorial Hospital, 13750 - 96th Ave., Surrey BC V3V 1Z2 – 604/581-2211; Fax: 604/588-3320 – 656 beds – Pres., Bernie Blais

Terrace: Mills Memorial Hospital, 4720 Haugland Ave., Terrace BC V8G 2W7 – 250/635-2211; Fax: 250/635-7639 – 52 beds – CEO, Michael A. Leisinger

Tofino General Hospital, 261 Neill St., PO Box 190, Tofino BC V0R 2Z0 – 250/725-3212; Fax: 250/725-3324 – 21 beds – Public Adm., Robert J. Smith

Trail Regional Hospital, 1200 Hospital Bench, Trail BC V1R 4M1 – 250/368-3311; Fax: 250/364-3422 – 135 beds – Acting CEO, Ron L. Parisotto

Vancouver Hospital & Health Sciences Centre, 855 - 12 Ave. West, Vancouver BC V5Z 1M9 – 604/875-4111; Fax: 604/875-4686 – 1,500 beds – Vancouver/Richmond Health Board – Pres. & CEO, Murray T. Martin, 604/875-4999

Vancouver: British Columbia Children's Hospital, 4480 Oak St., Vancouver BC V6H 3V4 – 604/875-2345; Fax: 604/875-3456 – pediatric hospital – 242 beds – Vancouver/Richmond Health Board – Interim Pres., Anne Sutherland Boal

Vancouver: Mount Saint Joseph Hospital, 3080 Prince Edward St., Vancouver BC V5T 3N4 – 604/874-1141; Fax: 604/875-8733 – 230 beds – Vancouver/Richmond Health Board – CEO, Dianne Doyle

Vancouver: St. Paul's Hospital, 1081 Burrard St., Vancouver BC V6Z 1Y6 – 604/682-2344; Fax: 604/631-5135 – 448 beds – Acting Pres. & CEO, Dr. Tom Ward

Vancouver: St. Vincent's Hospital Heather, 749 - 33rd Ave. West, Vancouver BC V5Z 2K4 – 604/876-7171; Fax: 604/876-6729 – 192 beds – Vancouver/Richmond Health Board – Adm., Dianne Doyle

Vancouver: Sunny Hill Health Centre for Children, 3644 Slocan St., Vancouver BC V5M 3E8 – 604/434-1331; Fax: 604/436-1743 – 28 beds – Pres., Ron Lindstrom

Vancouver: UBC Health Sciences Centre Hospital, 2211 Wesbrook Mall, Vancouver BC V6T 2B5 – 604/822-7121; Fax: 604/822-7186 – Pres. & CEO, Murray Martin, 604/875-4999

Vanderhoof: St. John Hospital, RR#2, Vanderhoof BC V0J 3A0 – 250/567-2211; Fax: 250/567-9713 – 33 beds – Northern Interior Regional Health Board – CEO, Ben L. Gumm

Vernon Jubilee Hospital, 2101 - 32nd St., Vernon BC V1T 5L2 – 250/545-2211; Fax: 250/545-5602 – 161 beds – Exec. Dir., Bruce Swan

Victoria General Hospital, 35 Helmcken Rd., Victoria BC V8Z 6R5 – 250/727-4212; Fax: 250/386-9119 – 464 beds – Capital Health Region – Pres., Patricia Coward, 250/370-8699

Victoria: Aberdeen Hospital, 1450 Hillside Ave., Victoria BC V8T 2B7 – 250/595-4321; Fax: 250/595-8412 – 600 beds – Capital Health Region – Adm., Peter McAllister

Victoria: The Gorge Road Hospital, 63 Gorge Rd. East, Victoria BC V9A 1L2 – 250/386-2464; Fax: 250/386-9119 – 332 beds – Capital Health Region – Pres./CEO, Patricia Coward, 250/370-8699

Victoria: Queen Alexandra Centre for Children's Health, 2400 Arbutus Rd., Victoria BC V8N 1V7 – 250/477-1826; Fax: 250/721-6837 – 50 beds – Pres., Cheryl Craver

Victoria: Royal Jubilee Hospital, 1900 Fort St., Victoria BC V8R 1J8 – 250/370-8000; Fax: 250/370-8750 – 634 beds – Capital Health Region – Pres., Patricia Coward, 250/370-8699

Waglisla: R.W. Large Memorial Hospital, Waglisla BC V0T 1Z0 – 250/957-2314; Fax: 250/957-2612 – 21 beds – Adm., Wendy MacDonald

White Rock: Peace Arch Hospital, 15521 Russell Ave., White Rock BC V4B 2R4 – 604/531-5512; Fax: 604/531-0726 – 177 acute care, 375 extended care beds – South Fraser Valley Regional Health Board – Acting CEO, Betty Ann Busse

Williams Lake: Cariboo Memorial Hospital, 517 - 6 Ave. North, Williams Lake BC V2G 2G8 – 250/392-4411; Fax: 250/392-2157 – 76 beds – Exec. Dir., Martin Oets

## AUXILIARY HOSPITALS/HEALTH CARE CENTRES

Armstrong: Pleasant Valley Health Centre, 3800 Patten Dr., PO Box 460, Armstrong BC V0E 1B0 – 250/546-3035; Fax: 250/546-8834 – 40 long term care beds – Dir., Nursing, Sue Gubbels

Barriere & District Health Centre, PO Box 659, Barriere BC V0E 1E0 – 250/672-9731; Fax: 250/672-5144 – Adm., Linda Comazzetto

Chase & District Health Centre, 825 Thompson St., PO Box 1099, Chase BC V0E 1M0 – 250/679-3312; Fax: 250/679-5329 – 4 beds – Adm., Gerri Rintoul

Chemainus Health Care Centre, 9909 Esplanade St., PO Box 499, Chemainus BC V0R 1K0 – 250/246-3291; Fax: 250/246-3844 – 75 beds – Public Adm., Robert J. Smith

Cumberland Health Care Centre, PO Box 400, Cumberland BC V0R 1S0 – 250/336-8531; Fax: 250/336-2100 – 76 intermediate care beds – Adm., vacant

Gold River Health Clinic, PO Box 580, Gold River BC V0P 1G0 – 250/283-2626; Fax: 250/283-7561 – Adm., Rosemary Alexander

Houston Health Centre, PO Box 538, Houston BC V0J 1Z0 – 250/845-2294; Fax: 250/845-2005 – Adm., Hanne White

Logan Lake Health Centre, PO Box 1089, Logan Lake BC V0K 1W0 – 250/523-9414; Fax: 250/523-6869 – Adm., Lea Doran

New Aiyansh: James Samuel Gosnell Memorial Health Centre, 256 Tait Ave., PO Box 234, New Aiyansh BC V0J 1A0 – 250/633-2212; Fax: 250/633-2512 – 4 beds – Nisga'a Valley Health Board – Adm., Floyd Davis

Pemberton & District Health Centre, PO Box 310, Pemberton BC V0N 2L0 – 604/894-6633; Fax: 604/894-6918; EMail: pemhlth@pop.gov.bc.ca – Health Servs. Coord., Cathy McLeod

Qualicum Beach: Eagle Park Health Care Facility, 777 Jones St., Qualicum Beach BC V9K 2L1 – 250/752-7075; Fax: 250/752-8316 – Adm., Pat Chern

Stewart Community Health Centre, 9 St. & Brightwell St., PO Box 8, Stewart BC V0T 1W0 – 250/636-2221; Fax: 250/636-2715 – 3 beds – CEO, Linda Hyde

Tahsis Health Centre, 1085 Maquinna Dr., PO Box 399, Tahsis BC V0P 1X0 – 250/934-6322; Fax: 250/934-6404 – 3 holding beds – Campbell River/Nootka Community Health Council – Adm., Pamela Seitz

Telegraph Creek: Stikine Regional Health Centre, PO Box 100, Telegraph Creek BC V0C 2W0 – 250/771-5801; Fax: 250/771-3439 – Public Adm., Doug Marrie

Terrace: James Samuel Gosnell Memorial Health Centre, PO Box 724, Terrace BC V8G 4C1 – 250/633-2212; Fax: 250/633-2512 – Adm., Floyd Davis

Tumbler Ridge Health Care Centre, 220 Front St., PO Box 80, Tumbler Ridge BC V0C 2W0 – 250/242-5271; Fax: 250/242-3889 – Adm., Dennis Hickey

Valemount Health Centre, PO Box 697, Valemount BC V0E 2Z0 – 250/566-9138; Fax: 250/566-4319; EMail: health@uis.bc.ca – outpatient health centre – Northern Interior Regional Health Board – Adm., Marilyn Harkness

Victoria: Fairfield Health Centre, 841 Fairfield Rd., Victoria BC V8V 3B6 – 250/389-6300; Fax: 250/727-4221 – Capital Health Region – Pres., Ken Fyke

## FEDERAL HOSPITALS

Masset: Canadian Forces Station Hospital Masset, PO Box 2000, Masset BC V0T 1M0 – 250/626-3902; Fax: 250/626-3902 – Senior Medical Officer, 250/626-3902, ext.303

## HOME CARE OFFICES/COMMUNITY HEALTH CARE OFFICES

Castlegar: Central Kootenay Community Health Services Society, 813 - 10th St., Castlegar BC V1N 2H7 – 250/365-4320; Fax: 250/365-4303 – Interim Senior Mgr., Dr. Nelson Ames

Courtenay: Upper Island Central Coast Community Health Services Society, 480 Cumberland Rd., Courtenay BC V9N 2C4 – 250/334-1141; Fax: 250/384-1182 – Medical Health Officer/Exec. Dir., Dr. Brian Emerson

Cranbrook: East Kootenay Community Health Services Society, 1212 - 2nd St. North, Cranbrook BC V1C 4T6 – 250/426-1355; Fax: 250/426-1324 – CEO, Glen Timbers

Dawson Creek: Peace Liard Community Health Services Society, 1001 - 110th Ave., Dawson Creek BC V1G 4X3 – 250/784-2400; Fax: 250/784-2413 – Interim Senior Mgr., Dr. Kelly Bernard

Gibson: Coast Garibaldi Community Health Services Society, 494 South Fletcher Rd., PO Box 78, Gibson BC V0N 1V0 – 604/886-5620; Fax: 604/886-2250 – Interim Senior Mgr., Dr. Paul Martiquet

Terrace: North West Community Health Services Society, 3412 Kalum St., Terrace BC V8G 4T2 – 250/638-2272; Fax: 250/638-2264 – Interim Senior Mgr., Dave Dennis

Williams Lake: Cariboo Community Health Services Society, 540 Borland St., 3rd Fl., Williams Lake BC V2G 1R8 – 250/398-4627; Fax: 250/398-4249 – Exec. Dir., Allison Ruault

## NURSING HOMES/LONG TERM CARE FACILITIES

Abbotsford: Menno Hospital, 32945 Marshall Rd., Abbotsford BC V2S 1K1 – 604/859-7631; Fax: 604/859-6931 – Adm., Gerald Neufeld

Armstrong: Pleasant Valley Health Centre, *see* Auxiliary Hospitals/Health Care Centres listings

Burnaby: Fellburn Care Centre, 6050 Hastings St. East, Burnaby BC V5B 1R6 – 604/299-7471; Fax: 604/299-1015 – 110 beds – Simon Fraser Health Region – Site Adminstrator, Cathie Speers, 604/525-0911, Fax: 604/517-8651

Burnaby: St. Michael's Centre Extended Care Hospital, 7451 Sussex Ave., Burnaby BC V5J 5C2 – 604/434-1323; Fax: 604/434-6469 – 168 beds – Exec. Dir., Gerald Herkel

Fort St. James: Stuart Lake Hospital, Stuart Dr., PO Box 1060, Fort St. James BC V0J 1P0 – 250/996-8201; Fax: 250/996-8777 – Adm., Ben. L. Gumm

Fort St. John: Peace Lutheran Extended Care Centre, 9908 - 108th Ave., Fort St. John BC V1J 2R3 – 250/785-8941; Fax: 250/785-2296 – Adm., Willy Olesen

Kamloops: Overlander Extended Care Hospital, 953 Southill St., Kamloops BC V2B 7Z9 – 250/554-2323; Fax: 250/554-3403 – 200 beds – Thompson Regional Health Bd. – Adm., E. Karen McClelland

Langley Lodge, 5451 - 204th St., Langley BC V3A 5M9 – 640/530-2305; Fax: 640/532-4205 – 151 beds – Adm., Werner Pauls

Nelson: Mount St. Francis Hospital, 1300 Gordon Rd., Nelson BC V1L 3M5 – 250/352-3531; Fax: 250/352-6942 – Adm., Sheila Hart

New Westminster: Queen's Park Hospital, 315 McBride Blvd., New Westminster BC V3L 5E8 – 604/525-0911; Fax: 604/525-9712 – Pres. & CEO, Jim Fair

Parksville: Trillium Lodge, 401 Moilliet St., PO Box 940, Parksville BC V9P 2G9 – 250/248-8353; Fax: 250/248-8388 – Adm., Jim Banks

Pouce Coupe Care Home, PO Box 98, Pouce Coupe BC V0C 2C0 – 250/786-5791; Fax: 250/786-5492 – Interim CEO, Mike McPhail

Vancouver: Louis Brier Hospital, 1055 - 41st Ave. West, Vancouver BC V6M 1W9 – 604/261-9376; Fax: 604/266-8712 – 217 beds – Vancouver/Richmond Health Board – Adm., Ken Levitt

Vancouver: Normandy Private Hospital, 4505 Valley Dr., Vancouver BC V6L 2L1 – 604/261-4292 – 180 beds – Adm., Lynn Tomyk

Vancouver: St. Vincent's Hospital Arbutus, 6650 Arbutus St., Vancouver BC V6P 5S5 – 604/266-4166; Fax: 604/876-6729 – 75 beds – Vancouver/Richmond Health Board – Adm., Dianne Doyle

Vancouver: St. Vincent's Hospital Langara, 255 - 62nd Ave. West, Vancouver BC V5X 2C9 – 604/325-4116; Fax: 604/877-3081 – 150 beds – Vancouver/Richmond Health Board – Adm., Dianne Doyle

Vancouver: Trout Lake Manor, 3490 Porter St., Vancouver BC V5N 4H2 – 604/874-2803 – 100 beds – Adm., Verna Merrifield

Victoria: Central Park Lodge - Glenwarren Lodge, 1230 Balmoral Rd., Victoria BC V8T 1B3 – 250/383-2323 – 130 beds – Adm., Thom Murray

Victoria: Juan de Fuca Hospitals (Aberdeen, Glengarry, Mount Tolmie, Priory), 1450 Hillside Ave., Victoria BC V8T 2B7 – 250/595-5722; Fax: 250/595-8412 – 512 beds – Capital Health Region – CEO, Jeanette Funke-Furber

Victoria: Mount St. Mary Hospital, 999 Burdett Ave., Victoria BC V8V 3G7 – 250/384-7158; Fax: 250/384-7631 – CEO, Colleen Black

Victoria: Oak Vay Kiwanis Pavillon, 3034 Cedarhill Rd., Victoria BC V8T 3J2 – 250/598-2022; Fax: 250/598-0023 – 121 beds – Exec. Dir., Erna Jacobs

Victoria: Wayside House, 550 Foul Bay Rd., Victoria BC V8S 4H1 – 250/598-4521 – 18 beds – Adm., Connie Martin

West Vancouver Care Centre, 1675 - 27th St., West Vancouver BC V7V 4K9 – 604/925-1247 – 75 beds – Adm., Georgina Buchanan

West Vancouver: Beacon Hill Lodge, 525 Clyde Ave., West Vancouver BC V7T 1C4 – 604/926-6856 – 73 beds – Adm., Jane Robinson

## NURSING STATIONS

Burnaby: The Canadian Red Cross Society - BC - Yukon Division, #400, 4710 Kingsway, Burnaby BC V5H 4M2 – 604/431-4200; Fax: 604/431-4275 – Responsible for Red Cross Outpost Nursing Stations in: Alexis Creek; Atlin; Bamfield; Blue River; Edgewood, & Kyuquot – Mgr., Outpost Hospitals, Nancy Laframboise

## PRIVATE HOSPITALS

Burnaby: Carlton Private Hospital, 4125 Canada Way, Burnaby BC V5G 1G9 – 604/438-8224 – 75 beds – Adm., Gary Bell

Burnaby: Deer Lake Private Hospital, 6907 Elwell St., Burnaby BC V5E 1K3 – 604/522-5447; Fax: 604/522-2310 – 37 beds – Simon Fraser Health Region – Admin. Coord., Annamae Clarke

Burnaby: Willingdon Private Hospital, 4435 Grange St., Burnaby BC V5H 1P4 – 604/433-2455; Fax: 604/433-5804 – 95 beds – Adm., A.L. Bennewith

Coquitlam: Como Lake Private Hospital, 657 Gatensbury St., Coquitlam BC V3J 5G9 – 604/939-9277 – 89 beds – Adm., Gary Bell

Coquitlam: Dufferin Care Centre, 1131 Dufferin St., Coquitlam BC V3B 7X5 – 604/552-1166; Fax: 604/552-3116 – 125 beds – Simon Fraser Health Region – Site Adm., Gloria Hunter

Delta: Ladner/Deltaview Private Hospital, 9321 Burns Dr., Delta BC V4K 3N3 – 604/596-8814, 8842 – 144 beds – Adm. & Supt., Salim Devji

Fort Langley: Simpson Private Hospital, 8838 Glover Rd., Fort Langley BC V0X 1J0 – 250/383-7814 – 56 beds – Adm., Richard Haliburton

Kelowna: Still Waters Private Hospital, 1450 Sutherland Ave., Kelowna BC V1Y 5Y5 – 250/860-2216 – 78 beds – Adm., Greg Kornell

Maple Ridge: Holyrood Manor, 22710 - 117th Ave., Maple Ridge BC V2X 3E6 – 604/467-8831; Fax: 604/467-8262 – 106 beds – Simon Fraser Health Region – General Mgr., Richard Haliburton

Nelson: Willowhaven Private Hospital, RR#1, Site 18, Comp. 1, Nelson BC V1L 5P4 – 250/825-4411 – 84 beds – Co-Adm., Altaf Jina

North Vancouver: North Shore Private Hospital, 1070 Lynn Valley Rd., North Vancouver BC V7J 1Z8 – 604/988-4181 – 50 beds – Adm., Medi Sherkat

Prince George: Simon Fraser Lodge, 2410 Laurier Cres., Prince George BC V2M 2B3 – 250/563-3413 – 116 beds – Adm./Supt., Kathy Giene

Vancouver: Amherst Private Hospital, 375 - West 59th Ave., Vancouver BC V5X 1X3 – 604/321-6777 – 75 beds – Adm., Joan Stewart

Vancouver: Braddan Private Hospital, 2450 West 2nd Ave., Vancouver BC V6X 1J6 – 604/731-2127 – 50 beds – Adm., Maureen McIntosh

Vancouver: Carlsbad Private Hospital, 2423 Cornwall Ave., Vancouver BC V6X 1B9 – 604/733-7133 – 47 beds – Adm., T. McDonald, 604/731-2273

Vancouver: Edith Cavell Private Hospital, 2855 Sophia St., Vancouver BC V5T 3L2 – 604/874-9321 – 62 beds – Adm., Kevin Svoboda

Vancouver: Kensington Private Hospital, 750 West 41st Ave., Vancouver BC V5Z 2N3 – 604/261-8108 – 78 beds – Adm., Nujin Rana

Vancouver: Lakeside Place, 3499 Porter St., Vancouver BC V5N 4H2 – 604/874-3558; Fax: 604/874-3587 – 65 beds – Adm., Verna Merrifield

Vancouver: Royal Ascot Care Centre, 2455 East Broadway, Vancouver BC V5M 1Y1 – 604/254-5559, ext.28 – 78 beds – Vancouver/Richmond Health Board – Adm., Stan Dubas

Vancouver: Southpines Private Hospital, 325 West 59th Ave., Vancouver BC V5X 1X3 – 604/321-0214 – 34 beds – Adm., D. McDonald, 604/736-6460

Victoria: Sandringham Private Hospital, 1650 Fort St., Victoria BC V8R 1H9 – 250/595-2313 – 85 beds – General Mgr., Richard Haliburton

West Vancouver: Inglewood Private Hospital, 725 Inglewood Ave., West Vancouver BC V7T 1X5 – 604/922-9394; Fax: 604/922-2709 – 231 beds – North Shore Health Region – Managing Dir., David Ail

## SPECIAL TREATMENT CENTRES

(Includes: Abortion Clinics, Cancer Clinics, Rehabilitation Centres, Treatment Centres)

Elkford & District Diagnostic & Treatment Centre, PO Box 640, Elkford BC V0B 1H0 – 250/865-2247; Fax: 250/865-2797 – Adm., Wendy Timmerman

Fraser Lake Diagnostic & Treatment Centre, PO Box 1000, Fraser Lake BC V0J 1S0 – 250/699-7742; Fax: 250/699-6987 – Public Adm., Doug Marrie

Hudson's Hope Gething Diagnostic & Treatment Centre, PO Box 599, Hudson's Hope BC V0C 1V0 – 250/783-9991; Fax: 250/783-9125 – Adm., Heather M. Wilson

Keremeos Diagnostic & Treatment Centre, PO Box 579, Keremeos BC V0X 1N0 – 250/499-5518; Fax: 250/499-2559 – Adm., Anne Ardiel

Vancouver: The Arthritis Centre of B.C., 895 West 10th Ave., Vancouver BC V5Z 1L7 – 604/879-7511; Fax: 604/871-4500 – Exec. Dir., Mike Mahony

Vancouver: B.C. Drug & Poison Information Centre, c/o St. Paul's Hospital, 1081 Burrard St., Vancouver BC V6Z 1Y6 – 604/682-2344, ext.2126; Fax: 604/631-5262 – Managing Dir., Derek E. Daws, B.Sc.

Vancouver: BC Rehab - George Pearson Centre, 700 - 57th St. West, Vancouver BC V6P 1S1 – 604/321-3231; Fax: 604/321-7833; EMail: bcrehab.bc.ca – treatment centre – 180 beds – Vancouver/Richmond Health Board – Adm., Dr. John Higenbottam

Vancouver: BC Rehab - G.F. Strong Centre, 4255 Laurel St., Vancouver BC V5Z 2G9 – 604/734-1313; Fax: 604/737-6359; EMail: bcrehab.bc.ca – treatment centre – 112 beds – Vancouver/Richmond Health Board – Adm., Dr. John Higenbottam

Vancouver: British Columbia Cancer Agency, 600 - 10th Ave. West, Vancouver BC V5Z 4E6 – 604/877-6000; Fax: 604/872-4596 – cancer treatment – 36 beds – CEO, Dr. Donald Carlow

Vancouver: British Columbia's Women's Hospital & Health Centre, 4500 Oak St., Vancouver BC V6H 3N1 – 604/875-3060; Fax: 604/875-3136 – Interim Pres. & CEO, Ron McKerrow

Vancouver: Elizabeth Bagshaw Woman's Clinic, #40, 3195 Granville St., Vancouver BC V6H 3K1 – 604/736-7878; Fax: 604/736-8081 – abortion clinic – Adm., Cheryl Davies

Vancouver: Everywoman's Health Centre, 2005 - 44th St. East, Vancouver BC V5P 1N1 – 604/322-6692 – abortion clinic

Vancouver: Holy Family Hospital, 7801 Argyle St., Vancouver BC V5P 3L6 – 604/321-2661; Fax: 604/321-2696 – rehabilitation & extended care hospital – 222 beds – Vancouver/Richmond Health Board – Pres., W.T. Frier

Victoria: British Columbia Cancer Agency - Victoria Clinic, Royal Jubilee Hospital, 1900 Fort St., Victoria BC V8R 1J8 – 250/370-8228; Fax: 250/370-8750 – cancer treatment

Whistler Diagnostic & Treatment Centre, 4380 Lorimer Rd., Whistler BC V0N 1B4 – 604/932-4911; Fax: 604/932-4992 – Acting Adm., Bill Crysler

# MANITOBA

## REGIONAL HEALTH AUTHORITIES

Brandon Regional Health Authority, #201, 340 - 9th St., Brandon MB R7B 6C2 – 204/729-2204; Fax: 204/726-6536 – CEO, Earl Backman

Carman: Regional Health Authority - Central Manitoba Inc., 40 - 2nd St. NE, PO Box 1819, Carman MB R0G 0J0 – 204/745-6677; Fax: 204/745-5050 – CEO, Gary Buchanan

Churchill Regional Health Authority Inc., Churchill Health Centre, General Delivery, Churchill MB R0B 0E0 – 204/675-8318; Fax: 204/675-2243 – CEO, Linda DuBick

Dauphin: Parkland Regional Health Authority Inc., Dauphin Village Mall, #112, 27 - 2 Ave. SW, Dauphin MB R7N 3E5 – 204/622-6222; Fax: 204/622-6232; EMail: prha@mb.sympatico.ca – CEO, Andre Remillard

Flin Flon: Nor-Man Regional Health Authority Inc., 84 Church St., PO Box 130, Flin Flon MB R8A 1M7 – 204/687-1302; Fax: 204/687-6405 – CEO, Gerry Hildebrand

La Broquerie: South Eastman Health/Santé Sud-est inc., PO Box 470, La Broquerie MB R0A 0W0 – 204/424-5880; Fax: 204/424-5888 – CEO, Reg Toews

Pinawa: North Eastman Health Association Inc., W.B. Lewis School, Aberdeen Ave. & Burrows Rd., PO Box 339, Pinawa MB R0E 1L0 – 204/753-2012; Fax: 204/753-2015 – CEO, Kevin Beresford

Selkirk: Interlake Regional Health Authority Inc., 825 Manitoba Ave., PO Box 9600, Selkirk MB R1A 2B5 – 204/785-5500; Fax: 204/785-2750; EMail: Irha@mb.sympatico.ca – CEO, Tom Novak

Shoal Lake: Marquette Regional Health Authority Inc., 512 - 4th Ave., PO Box 9, Shoal Lake MB R0J 1Z0 – 204/759-3441; Fax: 204/759-3127 – CEO, Sandra Delorme

Souris: South Westman Regional Health Authority Inc., PO Box 579, Souris MB R0K 2C0 – 204/483-5000; Fax: 204/483-5005 – CEO, Earl Backman

Thompson: Burntwood Regional Health Authority Inc., 867 Thompson Dr. South, Thompson MB R8N 1Z4 – 204/677-6502; Fax: 204/677-7299 – CEO, Calvin Tant

## GENERAL HOSPITALS

Altona Community Memorial Health Centre, PO Box 660, Altona MB R0G 0B0 – 204/324-6411; Fax: 204/324-1299 – 22 beds – Exec. Dir., Peter Elias

Arborg & District Health Centre, PO Box 10, Arborg MB R0C 0A0 – 204/376-5247; Fax: 204/376-5669 – 16 beds – Exec. Dir., Tannis Erikson

Ashern: Lakeshore General Hospital, PO Box 110, Ashern MB R0C 0E0 – 204/768-2461; Fax: 204/768-2337 – 16 beds – Lakeshore Hospital/Lakeshore District Health System – Adm., Wayne Lavallee

Ashern: Lakeshore Hospital/Lakeshore District Health System, PO Box 110, Ashern MB R0C 0E0 – 204/768-2461; Fax: 204/768-2337 – 20 beds – Adm., Lakeshore District Health System, Wayne Lavallee

Boissevain Health Centre District, PO Box 899, Boissevain MB R0K 0E0 – 204/534-2451; Fax: 204/534-6487 – 12 acute care, 20 continuing care beds – South Westman Regional Health Authority Inc. – Adm., F.J. Woodmass

Brandon General Hospital, 150 McTavish Ave. East, Brandon MB R7A 2B3 – 204/726-1122; Fax: 204/726-1394; EMail: AizenmanA@Docker.com – 319 beds – Brandon Regional Health Authority – CEO, vacant

Carberry Plains District Health Centre, PO Box 1, Carberry MB R0K 0H0 – 204/834-2144; Fax: 204/834-3333 – 27 beds – Adm., Dale Aitken

Carman Memorial Hospital, PO Box 610, Carman MB R0G 0J0 – 204/745-2021; Fax: 204/745-2756 – 30 beds – Exec. Dir., René Comte

Cartwright & District Hospital, PO Box 118, Cartwright MB R0K 0L0 – 204/529-2452; Fax: 204/529-2562 – 10 beds – Tri-Lake Health District – CEO, Miriam Nichol

Churchill Health Centre, Churchill Town Centre, General Delivery, Churchill MB R0B 0E0 – 204/675-8381; Fax: 204/675-2243 – 31 beds – Churchill Regional Health Authority Inc. – CEO, Linda DJuBick

Crystal City: Rock Lake Hospital/Rock Lake Health District, PO Box 130, Crystal City MB R0K 0N0 – 204/873-2132; Fax: 204/873-2185 – 16 beds – Regional Health Authority - Central Manitoba Inc. – Exec. Dir., Rock Lane Health District, Terrance Hills

Dauphin Regional Health Centre, 625 - 3 St. SW, Dauphin MB R7N 1R7 – 204/638-3010; Fax: 204/638-3183 – 83 beds – Parkland Regional Health Authority Inc. – Exec. Dir., vacant

Deloraine Health Centre, PO Box 447, Deloraine MB R0M 0M0 – 204/747-2745; Fax: 204/747-2160; EMail: delhealthmpr@techplus.com – 18 beds – South West Health District – Exec. Dir., John Rekai

Emerson Hospital, PO Box 428, Emerson MB R0A 0L0 – 204/373-2109; Fax: 204/373-2748 – 8 beds – Exec. Dir., Helmut Klassen

Erickson District Health Centre, PO Box 25, Erickson MB R0J 0P0 – 204/636-7777; Fax: 204/636-2471 – 12 beds – Adm., Mike Kufflick

Eriksdale: Elizabeth M. Crowe Memorial Hospital, PO Box 130, Eriksdale MB R0C 0W0 – 204/739-2611; Fax: 204/739-2065 – 17 beds – Lakeshore Hospital/Lakeshore District Health System – Adm., Wayne Lavallee

Fisher Branch Medical Facilities Inc., PO Box 370, Fisher Branch MB R0C 0Z0 – 204/372-6258; Fax: 204/372-6554 – Dir. of Nursing, June Caldwell

Flin Flon General Hospital & Personal Care Home, PO Box 340, Flin Flon MB R8A 1N2 – 204/687-7591; Fax: 204/687-8494; EMail: ffghlib@mb.sympatico.ca – 83 acute, 30 long term care beds – Nor-Man Regional Health Authority Inc. – Exec. Dir., Sandra Gummrson

Gillam Hospital Inc., PO Box 2000, Gillam MB R0B 0L0 – 204/652-2600; Fax: 204/652-2536 – 10 beds – CEO, Neil McMartin

Gimli: Johnson Memorial Hospital, PO Box 250, Gimli MB R0C 1B0 – 204/642-5116; Fax: 204/642-5860 – 35 beds – Gimli Hospital District No.39 – Exec. Dir., Dawna Suchy

Gladstone: Seven Regions Health Centre, PO Box 1000, Gladstone MB R0J 0T0 – 204/385-2968; Fax: 204/385-2663 – 20 beds – Exec. Dir., Garry Mattin

Grandview District Hospital, PO Box 339, Grandview MB R0L 0Y0 – 204/546-2425; Fax: 204/546-3269 – 18 beds – Adm./Dir. of Nursing, Glenis Pacak

Hamiota District Health Centre, 177 Birch Ave., Hamiota MB R0M 0T0 – 204/764-2412; Fax: 204/764-2049 – 22 beds – Adm., Vaughn Wilson

Killarney: Tri-Lake Health Centre/Tri-Lake Health District, PO Box 4000, Killarney MB R0K 1G0 – 204/523-4661; Fax: 204/523-8948 – 26 beds – South Westman Regional Health Authority Inc. – CEO, Tri-Lake Health District, Miriam Nichol

Lynn Lake District Hospital No. 38, PO Box 2030, Lynn Lake MB R0B 0W0 – 204/356-2474; Fax: 204/356-8023 – 25 beds – Nurse Mgr., Brenda Neufeld

McCreary/Alonsa Health Centre, PO Box 250, McCreary MB R0J 1B0 – 204/835-2482; Fax: 204/835-2713 – 13 beds – Adm., Brenda Williams

Melita Health Centre, PO Box 459, Melita MB R0M 1L0 – 204/522-8197; Fax: 204/522-3161 – 11 beds – South West Health District – Acting CEO, John Rakai

Minnedosa Hospital/Minnedosa Health District, PO Box 960, Minnedosa MB R0J 1E0 – 204/867-2701; Fax: 204/867-2239 – 27 beds – Adm., Minnedosa Health District, Mike Kufflick

Morris General Hospital, PO Box 519, Morris MB R0G 1K0 – 204/746-2301; Fax: 204/746-2197 – 27 beds – Regional Health Authority - Central Manitoba Inc. – Exec. Dir., Helmut Klassen

Neepawa District Memorial Hospital, PO Box 1240, Neepawa MB R0J 1H0 – 204/476-2394, 5855 (Admin.); Fax: 204/476-5007, 3765 (Admin.) – 38 beds – Exec. Dir., Eric Gustafson

Norway House Hospital, Norway House MB R0B 1B0 – 204/359-6731; Fax: 204/359-6599 – 16 beds – Adm., Leonard T. York

Pinawa Hospital, PO Box 220, Pinawa MB R0E 1L0 – 204/753-2334; Fax: 204/753-2219 – 17 beds – Winnipeg River Health District – Adm., Linda West

Pine Falls Health Complex, PO Box 2000, Pine Falls MB R0E 1M0 – 204/367-4441; Fax: 204/367-8981 – 26 beds – North Eastman Health Association Inc. – Exec. Dir., Susan Derk

Portage District General Hospital, 524 - 5 St. SE, Portage la Prairie MB R1N 3A8 – 204/239-2211; Fax: 204/239-6039 – 128 beds – Exec. Dir., Garry Mattin

Rossburn District Health Centre, PO Box 40, Rossburn MB R0J 1V0 – 204/859-2413; Fax: 204/859-2526 – 10 beds – Adm./Dir. of Nursing, Patti Chegwin

Russell District Hospital, Bag Service 2, Russell MB R0J 1W0 – 204/773-2125; Fax: 204/773-2142 – 38 beds – Exec. Dir./Dir. of Nursing, Marguerite Kendell

Ste Anne Hospital, 52 St. Gerard St., PO Box 10, Ste Anne MB R0A 1R0 – 204/422-8837; Fax: 204/422-9929 – 21 beds – Exec. Dir., F. Labossiere

St. Claude Hospital, PO Box 400, St. Claude MB R0G 1Z0 – 204/379-2585; Fax: 204/379-2655 – 12 beds – Exec. Dir., Ardith Rothwell

Ste Rose General Hospital, PO Box 60, Ste Rose du Lac MB R0L 1S0 – 204/447-2131; Fax: 204/447-2250 – 60 beds – Exec. Dir., John J.M. Kelly

Selkirk & District General Hospital, 100 Easton Dr., PO Box 5000, Selkirk MB R1A 2M2 – 204/482-5800; Fax: 204/785-9113 – 75 beds – Interlake Regional Health Authority Inc. – Exec. Dir., Tom Novak

Shoal Lake - Strathclair Health Centre, PO Box 490, Shoal Lake MB R0J 1Z0 – 204/759-2336; Fax: 204/759-2480 – 19 beds – Acting Exec. Dir., Rowena Kominko

Swan Lake: Lorne Memorial Hospital, PO Box 40, Swan Lake MB R0G 2S0 – 204/836-2132; Fax: 204/836-2044 – 21 beds – Exec. Dir., René Comte

Swan River Valley Hospital, PO Box 1450, Swan River MB R0L 1Z0 – 204/734-3441; Fax: 204/734-9081 – 77 beds – Exec. Dir., Todd Stepanuik

Teulon Hospital/Tuelon-Hunter Memorial Health District, PO Box 89, Teulon MB R0C 3B0 – 204/886-2433; Fax: 204/886-2653 – 20 beds – Interlake Regional Health Authority Inc. – Exec. Dir., Teulon-Hunter Memorial Health District, Tannis Erickson

The Pas Health Complex Inc., PO Box 240, The Pas MB R9A 1K4 – 204/623-6431; Fax: 204/623-5372 – 60 beds – Exec. Dir., Don Solar

Thompson General Hospital, 871 Thompson Dr. South, Thompson MB R8N 0C8 – 204/677-5300; Fax: 204/778-8298 – 72 beds – Exec. Dir., Vic Wiebe

Winkler: Bethel Hospital, 133 - 6th St., PO Box 1070, Winkler MB R6W 4B1 – 204/325-4354; Fax: 204/325-5944 – 53 beds – Exec. Dir., Ray Racette

Winnipeg: Concordia Hospital, 1095 Concordia Ave., Winnipeg MB R2K 3S8 – 204/667-1560; Fax: 204/667-1049 – 196 beds – Exec. Dir., Bill Patmore, 204/661-7144

Winnipeg: Health Sciences Centre, 820 Sherbrook St., Winnipeg MB R3A 1R9 – 204/774-6511; Fax: 204/787-3912 – teaching hospital – 854 beds – Pres., A. Rodney Thorfinnson, 204/787-7346

Winnipeg: Misericordia General Hospital, 99 Cornish Ave., Winnipeg MB R3C 1A2 – 204/774-6581; Fax: 204/783-6052 – 224 beds – Pres., Ted Bartman, 204/788-8361

Winnipegosis General Hospital, PO Box 280, Winnipegosis MB R0L 2G0 – 204/656-4881; Fax: 204/656-4402 – 18 beds – Exec. Dir., Paul Quennelle

Winnipeg: Riverview Health Centre, One Morley Ave., Winnipeg MB R3L 2P4 – 204/452-3411; Fax: 204/452-3246 – 319 beds – Pres., Norman R. Kasian, 204/478-6212

Winnipeg: St. Boniface General Hospital, 409 Tache Ave., Winnipeg MB R2H 2A6 – 204/233-8563; Fax: 204/231-0640 – teaching hospital – 557 beds – Pres. & CEO, Kenneth Tremblay

Winnipeg: The Salvation Army Grace General Hospital, 300 Booth Dr., Winnipeg MB R3J 3M7 – 204/837-8311; Fax: 204/885-7909 – 261 beds – Pres. & CEO, Capt. John McFarlane, 204/837-0143, Fax: 204/831-0029

Winnipeg: Seven Oaks General Hospital, 2300 McPhillips St., Winnipeg MB R2V 3M3 – 204/632-7133; Fax: 204/697-2106 – 290 beds – Acting Pres., T. Woodward, 204/632-3327

Winnipeg: Victoria General Hospital, 2340 Pembina Hwy., Winnipeg MB R3T 2E8 – 204/269-3570; Fax: 204/261-0223 – 221 beds – Pres. & CEO, Marion Suski, 204/477-3376

## AUXILIARY HOSPITALS/HEALTH CARE CENTRES

Baldur Health Centre/Baldur Health District, PO Box 128, Baldur MB R0K 0B0 – 204/535-2373; Fax: 204/535-2116 – 14 beds – South Westman Regional Health Authority Inc. – Exec. Dir., Baldur Health District, R.J. Westwood

Beauséjour Hospital/Beauséjour Hospital District No. 29, PO Box 1178, Beauséjour MB R0E 0C0 – 204/268-1076; Fax: 204/268-1207 – 30 beds – North Eastman Health Association Inc. – Adm., Carolyn Shaw

Birtle Health Centre/Birtle Health Services District No. 10, PO Box 10, Birtle MB R0M 0C0 – 204/842-3317; Fax: 204/842-3375 – 19 beds – Marquette Regional Health Authority Inc. – Area Mgr., Birth Health Services District No.10, Gerrie Berry

Deloraine: South West Health District, PO Box 447, Deloraine MB R0M 0M0 – 204/747-2745; Fax: 204/747-2160 – Exec. Dir., John Rekai

Emerson: Red River Valley Health District, PO Box 428, Emerson MB R0A 0L0 – 204/373-2109; Fax: 204/373-2748 – Exec. Dir., Helmut Klassen

Gimli Hospital/Gimli Hospital District No.39, PO Box 250, Gimli MB R0C 1B0 – 204/642-5116; Fax: 204/642-5860 – Exec. Dir., Dawn Suchy

Glenboro Health Centre/Glenboro Health District, PO Box 310, Glenboro MB R0K 0X0 – 204/827-2438; Fax: 204/827-2199 – 14 beds – Parkland Regional Health Authority Inc. – CEO, R.J. Westwood

Hartney Medical Nursing Unit, PO Box 280, Hartney MB R0M 0X0 – 204/858-2078; Fax: 204/483-2310 – 9 beds – Souris Health District – Adm., F.J. Woodmass

Lac du Bonnet District Health Centre, *see* Winnipeg River Health District, Auxiliary Hospitals/Health Care Centres listings

Lac du Bonnet: Winnipeg River Health District, PO Box 1030, Lac du Bonnet MB R0E 1A0 – 204/345-8647; Fax: 204/345-8609 – Chairman District Board, Laurie Pilon

Leaf Rapids Health Centre, PO Box 370, Leaf Rapids MB R0B 1W0 – 204/473-2441; Fax: 204/473-8273 – 8 beds – Nurse Mgr., Norma Charriere

MacGregor & District Health Centre, PO Box 250, MacGregor MB R0H 0R0 – 204/685-2850; Fax: 204/685-2529 – 6 beds – Exec. Dir., Garry Mattin

Manitou: Pembina Health Centre/Pembina-Manitou Health District, PO Box 129, Manitou MB R0G 1G0 – 204/248-2092; Fax: 204/248-2499 – Regional Health Authority - Central Manitoba Inc. – Exec. Dir., Pembina-Manitou Health District, René Comte

Morden Hospital District, 30 Stephen St., Morden MB R6M 1X8 – 204/822-4411; Fax: 204/822-4520 – 58 beds – Regional Health Authority - Central Manitoba Inc. – Exec. Dir., Ray Racette

Notre Dame Medical Nursing Unit, PO Box 130, Notre Dame de Lourdes MB R0G 1M0 – 204/248-2112, 2092 (Admin.); Fax: 204/248-2499 – 10 beds – Exec. Dir., René Comte

Reston District Health Centre, PO Box 250, Reston MB R0M 1X0 – 204/877-3925; Fax: 204/877-3998 – 17 beds – Health District No. 10 – Adm., John Rakai

Rivers: Riverdale Health Centre/Riverdale Health Services District, PO Box 428, Rivers MB R0K 1X0 – 204/328-5321; Fax: 204/328-7130 – 16 beds – Marquette Regional Health Authority Inc. – Area Mgr., Riverdale Health Services District, Glenda Hutchinson

Roblin Health District, PO Box 940, Roblin MB R0L 1P0 – 204/937-2142; Fax: 204/937-8892 – 25 beds – Parkland Regional Health Authority Inc. – Adm., C. Clearwater

St. Pierre-Jolys: Centre Medico-Social DeSalaberry District Health Centre, PO Box 320, St. Pierre-Jolys MB R0A 1V0 – 204/433-7611; Fax: 204/433-7466 – 18 beds – Adm. & Dir. of Nursing, Suzanne Nicolas

Snow Lake Medical Nursing Unit, PO Box 453, Snow Lake MB R0B 1M0 – 204/358-2300; Fax: 204/358-7310 – 4 beds – Adm., Gerry Hildebrand

Souris Health District, PO Box 10, Souris MB R0K 2C0 – 204/483-2121; Fax: 204/483-2310 – 30 beds – South West Health District – CEO, Paul Brackstone

Steinbach: Bethesda Health & Social Services, PO Box 939, Steinbach MB R0A 2AO – 204/326-6411; Fax: 204/326-6931 – 80 beds – Exec. Dir., Wilmar Chopyk

Stonewall & District Health Centre, 385 - 3rd St. West, PO Box 2000, Stonewall MB R0C 2Z0 – 204/467-5514; Fax: 204/467-9194 – 15 beds – Exec. Dir., Kevin Beresford

Treherne: Tiger Hills Health Centre/Tiger Hills Health District, PO Box 130, Treherne MB R0G 2V0 – 204/723-2133; Fax: 204/723-2869 – 18 beds – South Westman Regional Health Authority Inc. – Exec. Dir., Tiger Hills Health District, R.J. Westwood

Virden Hospital/Health District No. 10, PO Box 400, Virden MB R0M 2C0 – 204/748-1230; Fax: 204/748-2053 – 24 beds – South Westman Regional Health Authority Inc. – Adm., Health District No.10, John Rakai

Vita District Health Centre Inc., 217 First Ave. West, Vita MB R0A 2K0 – 204/425-3804; Fax: 204/425-3545 – 10 beds – Adm., K.P. Aujlay

Wawanesa & District Memorial Health Centre, PO Box 309, Wawanesa MB R0K 2G0 – 204/824-2335; Fax: 204/824-2148 – 9 beds – CEO, Jim Westwood

Whitemouth District Health Centre, PO Box 160, Whitemouth MB R0E 2G0 – 204/348-7191; Fax: 204/348-7911 – 6 beds – Adm., Therese Conroy

Winnipeg: Clinique Youville Clinic Inc., 33 Marion St., Winnipeg MB R2H 0S8 – 204/233-0262; Fax: 204/233-1520 – Exec. Dir., Claire Betker

Winnipeg: Health Action Centre - Health Sciences Centre, 425 Elgin Ave., Winnipeg MB R3A 1P2 – 204/947-1626; Fax: 204/942-7828; EMail: healthac@mb.sympatico.ca – Exec. Dir., Jeanette Edwards

Winnipeg: Hope Centre Health Care Inc., 240 Powers St., Winnipeg MB R2W 5L1 – 204/589-8354; Fax: 204/586-4260 – Exec. Dir., Giselle Lamy

Winnipeg: Klinic Community Health Centre, 870 Portage Ave., Winnipeg MB R3G 0P1 – 204/784-4090; Fax: 204/772-7998 – Exec. Dir., Karen Ingebrigson

Winnipeg: M.F.L. Occupation Health Centre, #102, 275 Broadway, Winnipeg MB R3C 4M6 – 204/949-0811; Fax: 204/956-0848 – Exec. Dir., Judy Cook

Winnipeg: Mount Carmel Clinic, 886 Main St., Winnipeg MB R2W 5L4 – 204/582-2311; Fax: 204/582-1341 – Exec. Dir., Thomas Kean

Winnipeg: Nor'west Health & Social Service Centre Inc., #103, 61 Tyndall Ave., Winnipeg MB R2X 2T4 – 204/633-5955; Fax: 204/632-4666 – Exec. Dir., Cheryl Susinski

Winnipeg: Village Clinic, 668 Corydon Ave., Winnipeg MB R3M 0X7 – 204/453-0045; Fax: 204/453-5214 – Exec. Dir., Patricia. Stewart

Winnipeg: Women's Health Clinic Inc., 419 Graham St., 3rd Fl., Winnipeg MB R3C 0M3 – 204/947-1517; Fax: 204/943-3844 – Exec. Dir., Barbara Wiktorowicz

## FEDERAL HOSPITALS

Hodgson: Percy E. Moore Hospital, PO Box 190, Hodgson MB R0C 1N0 – 204/372-8444; Fax: 204/372-6991 – 16 beds – Adm., Elaine Kennedy

Norway House Hospital, Norway House MB R0B 1B0 – 204/359-6731; Fax: 204/359-6080 – Adm., B. Rowden

## HOME CARE OFFICES/COMMUNITY HEALTH CARE OFFICES

Beausejour: Community & Mental Health Services, 20 - 1st St. South, Beausejour MB R0E 0C0 – 204/268-6114; Fax: 204/268-3890 – North Eastman Health Association Inc. – Regional Dir., Gerhard Suss

Brandon: Community & Mental Health Services, 340 - 9th St., Brandon MB R7A 6C2 – 204/726-6294; Fax: 204/726-6536 – Brandon Regional Health Authority – Regional Dir., Carmel Olson

Dauphin: Community & Mental Health Services, 27 - 2nd Ave. SW, Dauphin MB R7N 3E5 – 204/622-2035; Fax: 204/638-3278 – Parkland Regional Health Authority Inc. – Regional Dir., Yvonne Hrynkiw

Portage la Prairie: Community & Mental Health Services, 25 Tupper St. South, Portage la Prairie MB R1N 3K1 – 204/239-3101; Fax: 204/239-3148 – Regional Health Authority - Central Manitoba Inc. – Regional Dir., Sheldon Hiltz

Selkirk: Community & Mental Health Services, Administration Bldg., 3rd Fl., PO Box 9600, Selkirk MB R1A 2B5 – 204/785-5160; Fax: 204/785-5210 – Interlake Regional Health Authority Inc. – Regional Dir., Pat Kinrade

The Pas: Community & Mental Health Services, 115 - 3rd St. East, PO Box 2550, The Pas MB R9A 1M4 – 204/627-8240; Fax: 204/623-5792 – Nor-Man Regional Health Authority Inc. – Regional Dir., John Karpan

Thompson: Community & Mental Health Services, 867 Thompson Dr. South, Thompson MB R8N 1Z4 – 204/677-7293; Fax: 204/677-6517 – Burntwood Regional Health Authority Inc. – Acting Regional Dir., Debbie Nelson

Winnipeg: Community & Mental Health Services - Winnipeg Region, #5, 189 Evanson St., Winnipeg MB R3G 0N9 – 204/945-4505; Fax: 204/945-1735 – Acting Regional Dir., Peter Dubienski

Winnipeg: Independent Living Resource Centre, #201, 294 Portage Ave., Winnipeg MB R3C 0B9 – 204/947-0194

## MENTAL HEALTH HOSPITALS & COMMUNITY FACILITIES

Selkirk Mental Health Centre, 825 Manitoba Ave. West, PO Box 9600, Selkirk MB R1A 2B5 – 204/482-3810; Fax: 204/785-8936 – CEO, Marcia Thomson

Winkler: Eden Health Care Services, 204 Main St., PO Box 129, Winkler MB R6W 4A4 – 204/325-5355; Fax: 204/325-8742; EMail: edencare@web4.net – Exec. Dir., Ken Loewen

Winkler: Eden Mental Health Centre, 1500 Pembina Ave., Winkler MB R6W 1T4 – 204/325-4325; Fax: 204/325-8429 – 40 beds – Adm., Dennis Driedger

## NURSING HOMES/LONG TERM CARE FACILITIES

Altona & District Personal Care Home, PO Box 660, Altona MB R0G 0B0 – 204/324-6411; Fax: 204/324-1299 – 25 beds – Adm., P. Elias

Altona: The Ebenezer Home for the Aged, 235 - 5th St. NE, PO Box 900, Altona MB R0G 0B0 – 204/324-6486; Fax: 204/324-8917 – 44 beds – Exec. Dir., Peter Elias

Arborg: Pioneer Health Services Inc., PO Box 10, Arborg MB R0C 0A0 – 204/376-5226; Fax: 204/376-5669 – 40 beds – Adm., T. Erikson

Ashern Personal Care Home, *see* Lakeshore Hospital/Lakeshore District Health System, General Hospitals listings

Baldur Manor, PO Box 128, Baldur MB R0K 0B0 – 204/535-2456; Fax: 204/535-2116 – 20 beds – Baldur Health Centre/Baldur Health District – Charge Nurse, Joyce Wilson

Bayside Personal Care Home Inc., *see* Tri-Lake Health Centre/Tri-Lake Health District, General Hospitals listings

Beausejour: East-Gate Lodge Inc., 646 James Ave., PO Box 1690, Beausejour MB R0E 0C0 – 204/268-1029; Fax: 204/268-3225 – 60 beds – Dir., G. Boonstra

Benito Health Centre, PO Box 490, Benito MB R0L 0C0 – 204/539-2815; Fax: 204/539-2482 – 25 beds – Exec. Dir., T. Stepanuik

Birtle Personal Care Home Inc., PO Box 10, Birtle MB R0M 0C0 – 204/842-3317; Fax: 204/842-3375 – 20 beds

Boissevain: Evergreen Place, PO Box 899, Boissevain MB R0K 0E0 – 204/534-2451; Fax: 204/534-6487 – 20 beds – Nurse in Charge, Susan Nay

Brandon: Central Park Lodges Ltd., 3015 Victoria Ave., Brandon MB R7B 2K2 – 204/728-2030; Fax: 204/729-8351 – 89 beds – Mgr./Adm., Teresa Kindrat

Brandon: Dinsdale Personal Care Home, 510 - 6th St., Brandon MB R7A 3N9 – 204/727-3636; Fax: 204/727-2103 – 60 beds – Adm., Capt. Leslie Russell

Brandon: Fairview Home Inc., 1351 - 13th St., Brandon MB R7A 4S5 – 204/728-6696; Fax: 204/727-7616 – 248 – A/Exec. Dir., Janet Wilcox-McKay

Brandon: Hillcrest Place, 930 - 26th St., Brandon MB R7B 2B8 – 204/728-6690; Fax: 204/726-0089 – 100 beds – Adm., Kathy Sutherland

Brandon: Rideau Park Personal Care Home, 525 Victoria Ave. East, Brandon MB R7A 6S9 – 204/727-1734; Fax: 204/726-6690 – 98 beds – Adm., Larry Sage

Carberry Personal Care Home, 1st Ave., Carberry MB R0K 0H0 – 204/834-2076; Fax: 204/834-3333 – 30 beds – Adm., Dale Aitken

Carman: Boyne Lodge, PO Box 910, Carman MB R0G 0J0 – 204/745-6715; Fax: 204/745-6152 – 70 beds – Regional Health Authority - Central Manitoba Inc. – Dir., V. Droedger

Dauphin Personal Care Home Inc., 625 Third St. SW, Dauphin MB R7N 1R7 – 204/638-3010; Fax: 204/638-3183 – 90 beds – Parkland Regional Health Authority Inc. – Dir. of Resident Servs., Arlene Olynick

Dauphin: St. Paul's Home, 703 Jackson St., Dauphin MB R7N 2N2 – 204/638-3129; Fax: 204/638-9294 – 70 beds – Exec. Dir., Sr. Jean Zemliak

Deloraine Health Centre - Delwynda Court Personal Care Home Inc., PO Box 447, Deloraine MB R0M 0M0 – 204/747-2864; Fax: 204/747-2160; EMail: delhealthmpr@techplus.com – 16 beds – Adm., C. Olson

Deloraine: Bren-Del-Win Lodge, PO Box 527, Deloraine MB R0M 0M0 – 204/747-2119; Fax: 204/747-2160 – 30 beds – CEO, John Rakai

Elkhorn: Elkwood Manor, PO Box 70, Elkhorn MB R0M 0N0 – 204/845-2575; Fax: 204/845-2371 – 24 beds – Health District No. 10 – Adm., John Rakai

Emerson Personal Care Home (Red River Valley Lodge), PO Box 428, Emerson MB R0A 0L0 – 204/373-2208 – 20 beds – Exec. Dir., Helmuth Klassen

Emerson: Red River Valley Lodge (Emerson), PO Box 428, Emerson MB R0A 0L0 – 204/373-2109; Fax: 204/373-2748 – 20 beds – Dir. of Care, M. Fitchett

Erickson Personal Care Home, PO Box 25, Erickson MB R0J 0P0 – 204/636-7777; Fax: 204/636-2471 – 14 beds – Adm., Mike Kufflick

Eriksdale Personal Care Home, 1st St. NE, PO Box 130, Eriksdale MB R0C 0W0 – 204/739-2611; Fax: 204/739-2065 – 20 beds – Lakeshore Hospital/Lakeshore District Health System – Adm., Wayne Lavallee

Flin Flon General Hospital & Personal Care Home, *see* General Hospitals listings

Flin Flon: Northern Lights Manor Inc., PO Box 340, Flin Flon MB R8A 1N2 – 204/687-7591; Fax: 204/687-8494 – 30 beds – Unit Mgr., Gail Friesen

Gilbert Plains Health District, PO Box 368, Gilbert Plains MB R0L 0X0 – 204/548-2161; Fax: 204/548-2516 – 30 beds – Adm., Jerry Mrozowich

Gimli: Betel Home Foundation, PO Box 10, Gimli MB R0C 1B0 – 204/642-5004; Fax: 204/642-7243 – 80 beds – Interlake Regional Health Authority Inc. – Exec. Dir., Brenna Raemer

Gladstone: Third Crossing Manor Inc., PO Box 539, Gladstone MB R0J 0T0 – 204/385-2474; Fax: 204/385-2163 – 50 beds – Dir. of Personal Care, Donna Cymbalist

Glenboro Personal Care Home, *see* Glenboro Health Centre/Glenboro Health District, Auxiliary Hospitals/Health Care Centres listings

The Grandview Personal Care Home Inc., 308 Jackson St., PO Box 130, Grandview MB R0L 0Y0 – 204/546-2769; Fax: 204/546-2207 – 40 beds – Exec. Dir., Jerry Mrozowich

Grunthal: Menno Home for the Aged, PO Box 280, Grunthal MB R0A 0R0 – 204/434-6496; Fax: 204/434-9131 – 40 beds – Exec. Dir., Frank Klassen

Hamiota Personal Care Home, *see* Hamiota District Health Centre, General Hospitals listings

Killarney: Lakeview Senior Citizens Home, PO Box 730, Killarney MB R0K 1G0 – 204/523-4661 – 35 beds – Tri-Lake Health District – Head Nurse, L. Blixhavn

Lac du Bonnet Personal Care Home, PO Box 1030, Lac du Bonnet MB R0E 1A0 – 204/345-8675; Fax: 204/345-8609 – 30 beds – Winnipeg River Health District – Dir. of Res. Servs., Judy Coleman

Lundar Personal Care Home, 1st St. South, PO Box 296, Lundar MB R0C 1Y0 – 204/762-5663, 5866; Fax: 204/762-5164 – 20 beds – Lakeshore Hospital/Lakeshore District Health System – Adm., W. Lavallee

MacGregor Personal Care Home, PO Box 250, MacGregor MB R0H 0R0 – 204/685-2850; Fax: 204/685-2529 – 20 beds

McCreary/Alonsa Personal Care Home Inc., *see* McCreary/Alonsa Health Centre, General Hospitals listings

Melita & Area Personal Care Home Inc., 147 Summit St., Melita MB R0M 1L0 – 204/522-3975; Fax: 204/522-3161 – 20 beds – Charge Nurse, J. Vanbeselaere

Minnedosa & District Personal Care Home, *see* Minnedosa Hospital/Minnedosa Health District, General Hospitals listings

Morden: Tabor Home, Morden MB R0M 1Y3 – 204/822-4848; Fax: 204/822-5289 – 60 beds – Exec. Dir., L. Thiessen

Morris: Red River Valley Lodge Inc., PO Box 507, Morris MB R0G 1K0 – 204/746-2394; Fax: 204/746-2123 – 40 beds – Regional Health Authority - Central Manitoba Inc. – Dir. of Care, Julie Blouin

Morris: The Rosenort Eventide Home Inc., RR#1, PO Box 75, Morris MB R0G 1K0 – 204/746-8455; Fax: 204/746-6288 – 26 – Exec. Dir., L. Friesen

Neepawa: East View Lodge, PO Box 1240, Neepawa MB R0J 1H0 – 204/476-2383; Fax: 204/476-3645 – 123 beds – Exec. Dir., Eric Gustafson

Norway House: Pinaow Wachi Inc., PO Box 98, Norway House MB R0B 1B0 – 204/359-6606 – 26 beds – Adm., Brian Rowden

Notre Dame de Lourdes: Foyer Notre Dame Inc., PO Box 190, Notre Dame de Lourdes MB R0G 1M0 – 204/248-2092; Fax: 204/248-2499 – 61 beds – Regional Health Authority - Central Manitoba Inc. – Exec. Dir., R. Comte

Notre Dame de Lourdes: Pembina-Manitou Health Centre, PO Box 190, Notre Dame de Lourdes MB R0G 1M0 – 204/242-2744; Fax: 204/248-2499 – 8 beds – Exec. Dir., René Comte

Pilot Mound: Prairie View Lodge, PO Box 269, Pilot Mound MB R0G 1P0 – 204/825-2717 – 30 beds – Rock Lake Hospital/Rock Lake Health District – Charge Nurse, C. Yake

Pilot Mound: Rock Lake Personal Care Home Inc., PO Box 269, Pilot Mound MB R0G 1P0 – 204/825-2246 – 24 beds – Rock Lake Hospital/Rock Lake Health District – Charge Nurse, C. Yake

Pine Falls: Sunnywood Manor, PO Box 2000, Pine Falls MB R0E 1M0 – 204/367-8201 – 20 beds – North Eastman Health Association Inc. – Community Health Mgr., Susan Derk

Portage la Prairie: Douglas Campbell Lodge, 150 - 9th St. SE, Portage la Prairie MB R1N 3T6 – 204/239-6006; Fax: 204/239-0055 – 60 beds – Personal Care Home Dir., Mary Thomas

Portage la Prairie: Lions Prairie Manor, 24 - 9th St. SE, Portage la Prairie MB R1N 3V4 – 204/857-7864; Fax: 204/857-8207 – 151 beds – Regional Health Authority - Central Manitoba Inc. – Exec. Dir., M. Graham

Reston: Willowview Personal Care Home, PO Box 250, Reston MB R0M 1X0 – 204/877-3925; Fax: 204/877-3998 – 20 beds – South Westman Regional Health Authority Inc. – Facility Coord., D. Obach

Rivers: Riverdale Personal Care Home Inc., 512 Québec St., PO Box 428, Rivers MB R0K 1X0 – 204/328-5321; Fax: 204/328-7130 – 20 beds – Riverdale Health Services District – CEO, G.P. Worthington

Roblin & District Personal Care Home, *see* Roblin Health District, Auxiliary Hospitals/Health Care Centres listings

Roblin: Crocus Court Personal Care Home, 15 Hospital St., PO Box 940, Roblin MB R0L 1P0 – 204/937-2149; Fax: 204/937-8892 – 60 beds – Parkland Health District – Dir. of Patient Servs., C. Jerome

Rossburn Personal Care Home Inc., *see* Rossburn District Health Centre, General Hospitals listings

Russell & District Personal Care Home Inc., PO Box 400, Russell MB R0J 1W0 – 204/773-2731; Fax: 204/773-2232 – 40 beds – Exec. Dir., E. Nernberg

St. Adolphe Nursing Home Ltd., PO Box 40, St. Adolphe MB R5A 1A1 – 204/883-2181 – 42 beds – Adm., D. Brousseau

Ste. Anne: Villa Youville Inc., 208 Central Ave., Ste. Anne MB R5H 1C9 – 204/422-5624; Fax: 204/422-5842 – 66 beds – South Eastman Health/Santé Sud-est inc. – Exec. Dir., Claude Lachance

St. Claude: Manoir de St. Claude inc., PO Box 400, St. Claude MB R0G 1Z0 – 204/379-2585; Fax: 204/379-2655 – 18 beds – Adm., Claude Lachance

St-Pierre-Jolys: Respos Jolys inc., PO Box 320, St-Pierre-Jolys MB R0A 1V0 – 204/433-7611; Fax: 204/433-7466 – 16 beds – Charge Nurse, D. Murray

Ste. Rose du Lac: Dr. Gendreau Memorial Personal Care Home Inc., PO Box 420, Ste. Rose du Lac MB R0L 1S0 – 204/447-2019; Fax: 204/447-2267 – 40 beds – Exec. Dir., B.H. Kardoes

Sandy Lake Medical Nursing Home Inc., PO Box 7, Sandy Lake MB R0J 1X0 – 204/585-2107; Fax: 204/585-5352 – 36 beds – Exec. Dir., Linda Earl

Selkirk: Betel Home Foundation, 212 Manchester Ave., Selkirk MB R1A 0B6 – 204/482-7933; Fax: 204/482-4651 – 92 beds – Interlake Regional Health Authority Inc. – Exec. Dir., Brenna Raemer

Selkirk: Red River Place, 133 Manchester Ave., Selkirk MB R1A 0B5 – 204/482-3036; Fax: 204/482-9499 – 104 beds – Exec. Dir., M.S. Fages

Selkirk: Tudor House Personal Care Home, 800 Manitoba Ave., Selkirk MB R1A 2C9 – 204/482-6601; Fax: 204/482-4369 – 76 beds – Adm., P.A. Martyniw

Shoal Lake: Morley House of Shoal Lake, PO Box 490, Shoal Lake MB R0J 1Z0 – 204/759-2118; Fax: 204/759-2230 – 40 beds – Exec. Dir., Garry Dunits

Souris Health District - Souris District Personal Care Home, *see* South West Health District, Auxiliary Hospitals/Health Care Centres listings

Souris: Victoria Park Lodge, PO Box 940, Souris MB R0K 2C0 – 204/483-2487; Fax: 204/483-3805 – 20 beds – Exec. Dir., F.J. Woodmass

Steinbach: Bethesda Personal Care Home Inc., PO Box 939, Steinbach MB R0A 2A0 – 204/326-6411; Fax: 204/326-6931 – 60 beds

Steinbach: Rest Haven Nursing Home, 185 Woodhaven Ave., Steinbach MB R0A 2A0 – 204/326-2206; Fax: 204/326-3521 – 60 beds – Exec. Dir., L. Penner

Stonewall: Rosewood Lodge Inc., 385 - 3rd St. West, Stonewall MB R0C 2Z0 – 204/467-5514; Fax: 204/467-9194 – 30 beds – Charge Nurse, D. Shura

Swan River Valley Hospital - Swan Valley Lodge, PO Box 1450, Swan River MB R0L 1Z0 – 204/734-3441; Fax: 204/734-9081 – 70 beds – Dir. of Nursing, Pam Mullin

Swan River Valley Personal Care Home Inc., 334 - 8th Ave. South, PO Box 1390, Swan River MB R0L 1Z0 – 204/734-4521; Fax: 204/734-9081 – 60 beds – Dir. of Resident Servs., M.A. Swojanovsk

Teulon: Goodwin Lodge Inc., PO Box 89, Teulon MB R0C 3B0 – 204/886-2108 – 20 beds – Teulon Hospital/Tuelon-Hunter Memorial Health District – Head Nurse, Ann Heinrichs

The Pas: St. Paul's Residence, PO Box 240, The Pas MB R9A 1K4 – 204/623-9226 – 66 beds – Assistant Dir. of Nursing, M. Smith

Treherne: Tiger Hills Manor Inc., PO Box 130, Treherne MB R0G 2V0 – 204/723-2023; Fax: 204/723-2869 – 22 beds – Charge Nurse, K. Robinson

Virden: The Sherwood Home, PO Box 2000, Virden MB R0M 2C0 – 204/748-1546; Fax: 204/748-2822 – 50 beds – South Westman Regional Health Authority Inc. – Adm., G. Rakai

Virden: West-Man Nursing Home Inc., PO Box 1630, Virden MB R0M 2C0 – 204/748-2709; Fax: 204/748-3432 – 50 beds – Exec. Dir., M. Sangster

Vita District Health Centre Inc. - Vita & District Personal Care Home, 217 First Ave. West, Vita MB R0A 2K0 – 204/425-3804; Fax: 204/425-3545 – 44 beds

Wawanesa Personal Care Home, PO Box 309, Wawanesa MB R0K 2G0 – 204/824-2335; Fax: 204/824-2148 – 20 beds – Charge Nurse, Val Zoerb

Whitemouth Personal Care Home Inc., PO Box 160, Whitemouth MB R0E 2G0 – 204/348-7191; Fax: 204/348-7911 – 20 beds

Winkler: Salem Home Inc., 165 - 15 St., Winkler MB R6W 1T8 – 204/325-4316; Fax: 204/325-5442 – 125 beds – Exec. Dir., S. Janzen

Winnipeg: Beacon Hill Lodge, 190 Fort St., Winnipeg MB R3C 1C9 – 204/942-7541; Fax: 204/944-0136 – 175 beds – Adm., Phyllis Boryskiewich

Winnipeg: Bethania Mennonite Personal Care Home Inc., 1045 Concordia Ave., Winnipeg MB R2K 3S7 – 204/667-0795; Fax: 204/667-7078 – 149 beds – Exec. Dir., H. Epp

Winnipeg: Central Park Lodges of Canada Ltd. (#1), 440 Edmonton St., Winnipeg MB R3B 2M4 – 204/942-5291; Fax: 204/947-1969 – 277 beds – Adm., A. Solar

Winnipeg: Central Park Lodges of Canada Ltd. (#2), 70 Poseidon Bay, Winnipeg MB R3M 3E5 – 204/452-6204; Fax: 204/474-2173 – 218 beds – Mgr., Joanne Kuharski

Winnipeg: Centre Taché Nursing Centre, 185 Despins St., Winnipeg MB R2H 2B3 – 204/233-3692; Fax: 204/233-6803 – 314 beds – Exec. Dir., Francis LaBassière

Winnipeg: Concordia Hospital, 1095 Concordia Ave., Winnipeg MB R2K 3S8 – 204/661-7154; Fax: 204/667-1049 – 60 beds – Exec. Dir., Bill Patmore

Winnipeg: The Convalescent Home of Winnipeg, 276 Hugo St. North, Winnipeg MB R3M 2N6 – 204/475-1987; Fax: 204/453-7149 – 84 beds – Exec. Dir., A.L. (Tony) Fraser

Winnipeg: Deer Lodge Centre Inc., 2109 Portage Ave., Winnipeg MB R3J 0L3 – 204/837-1301; Fax: 204/885-4983 – 461 beds – Exec. Dir., J. Currie

Winnipeg: Donwood Manor, 171 Donwood Dr., Winnipeg MB R2G 0V9 – 204/668-4410; Fax: 204/663-5429 – 121 beds – Exec. Dir., Herta Janzen

Winnipeg: Fort Garry Care Centre Ltd., 1776 Pembina Hwy., Winnipeg MB R3T 2G2 – 204/269-6939; Fax: 204/275-2192 – 64 beds – Exec. Dir., G. Kalef

Winnipeg: Foyer Valade Inc., 450 River Rd., Winnipeg MB R2M 5M4 – 204/254-3332; Fax: 204/254-0329 – 115 beds – Exec. Dir., Francis LaBossière

Winnipeg: Fred Douglas Lodge, 1275 Burrows Ave., Winnipeg MB R2X 0B8 – 204/586-8541; Fax: 204/589-0110 – 137 beds – Exec. Dir., George Ralph

Winnipeg: Golden Door Geriatric Centre, 1679 Pembina Hwy., Winnipeg MB R3T 2G6 – 204/269-6308; Fax: 204/269-5626 – 78 beds – Adm., M.E. Lutz

Winnipeg: Golden Links Lodge, c/o PO Box 248, Stn St Vital, Winnipeg MB R2M 4A5 – 204/257-9947; Fax: 204/257-2405 – 88 beds – Exec. Dir., D.A. Buys-Holowachuk

Winnipeg: Golden West Centennial Lodge, 811 School Rd., Winnipeg MB R2Y 0S8 – 204/888-3311; Fax: 204/831-0544 – 116 beds – Exec. Dir., Maj. Wm. Loveless

Winnipeg: Heritage Lodge Personal Care Home Inc., 3555 Portage Ave., Winnipeg MB R3K 0X2 – 204/888-7940; Fax: 204/832-6544 – 86 beds – Adm., Linda Norton

Winnipeg: Holiday Haven Nursing Home, 5501 Roblin Blvd., Winnipeg MB R3R 0G8 – 204/888-3363; Fax: 204/896-4763 – 155 beds – Adm., R. Beaudin

Winnipeg: Holy Family Nursing Home, 165 Aberdeen Ave., Winnipeg MB R2W 1T9 – 204/589-7381; Fax: 204/589-8605 – 284 beds – Exec. Dir., J.N. Kisil

Winnipeg: Kildonan Personal Care Centre Inc., 1970 Henderson Hwy., Winnipeg MB R2G 1P2 – 204/334-4633; Fax: 204/204-334-4632 – 120 beds – Adm., Rick Kordalchuk

Winnipeg: Lions Manor, 320 Sherbrook St., Winnipeg MB R3B 2W6 – 204/784-1240; Fax: 204/784-1241 – 63 beds – Exec. Dir., A. Davies

Winnipeg: Luther Home, 1081 Andrews St., Winnipeg MB R2V 2G9 – 204/338-4641; Fax: 204/338-4643 – 80 beds

Winnipeg: Manitoba Odd Fellows' Home Inc., 4025 Roblin Blvd., Winnipeg MB R3R 0E3 – 204/832-1612; Fax: 204/832-0523 – 43 beds – Exec. Dir., M. Schultz

Winnipeg: Maples Personal Care Home, 500 Mandalay Dr., Winnipeg MB R2P 1V4 – 204/632-8570; Fax: 204/697-0249 – 200 beds – Adm., Robert G. Beaudin

Winnipeg: Meadowood Manor, 577 St. Anne's Rd., Winnipeg MB R2M 5B2 – 204/257-2394; Fax: 204/254-5402 – 88 beds – Exec. Dir., Charles Kunze

Winnipeg: Metropolitan Kiwanis Courts, 2300 Ness Ave., Winnipeg MB R3J 1A2 – 204/885-7700; Fax: 204/831-1022 – 47 beds – Exec. Dir., H. Ritchie

Winnipeg: The Middlechurch Home of Winnipeg, 280 Balderstone Ave., RR#1B, Winnipeg MB R3C 2E5 – 204/339-1947; Fax: 204/338-3498 – 197 beds – Exec. Dir., L. Holgate

Winnipeg: Oakview Place, 2395 Ness Ave., Winnipeg MB R3J 1A5 – 204/888-3005; Fax: 204/831-8101 – 245 beds – Adm., Debra Senychych

Winnipegosis-Mossey River Personal Care Home Inc., PO Box 280, Winnipegosis MB R0L 2G0 – 204/656-4676; Fax: 204/656-4402 – 20 beds

Winnipeg: Park Manor Personal Care Home Inc., 301 Redonda St., Winnipeg MB R2C 1L7 – 204/222-3251; Fax: 204/222-3237 – 100 beds – Exec. Dir., C.L. Toop

Winnipeg: River East Personal Care Home Ltd., 1375 Molson St., Winnipeg MB R2K 4K8 – 204/668-7460; Fax: 204/668-7459 – 120 beds – Acting Adm., Patricia Stephenson

Winnipeg: St. Joseph's Residence Inc., 1149 Leila Ave., Winnipeg MB R2P 1S6 – 204/697-8031; Fax: 204/697-8075 – 100 beds – Exec. Dir., Sr. G. Pura

Winnipeg: St. Norbert Nursing Home, 50 St. Pierre St., Winnipeg MB R3V 1J6 – 204/269-4538; Fax: 204/269-8150 – 91 beds – Adm., David Brousseau

Winnipeg: The Sharon Home Inc., 146 Magnus Ave., Winnipeg MB R2W 2B4 – 204/586-9781; Fax: 204/589-7560 – 229 beds – Exec. Vice-Pres., Daniel Ruth

Winnipeg: Tache Nursing Centre - Hospitalier Tache inc., 185 Despins St., Winnipeg MB R2H 2B3 – 204/233-3692; Fax: 204/233-6803 – 314 beds – Exec. Dir., Francis M. LaBossière

Winnipeg: Tuxedo Villa, 2060 Corydon Ave., Winnipeg MB R3P 0N3 – 204/889-2650; Fax: 204/896-0258 – 213 beds – Adm., Sydney Moffitt

Winnipeg: Vista Park Lodge, 144 Novavista Dr., Winnipeg MB R2N 1P8 – 204/257-6688; Fax: 204/257-0446 – 100 beds – Adm., J. McKee

Winnipeg: West Park Manor, 3199 Grant Ave., Winnipeg MB R3R 1X2 – 204/889-3330; Fax: 204/832-9555 – 150 beds – Exec. Dir., E.A. Gallant

## NURSING STATIONS

Winnipeg: Health & Welfare Canada - Medical Services Branch, 303 Main St., 5th Fl., Winnipeg MB R3C 0H4 – 204/983-4199 – Nursing stations are located at: Garden Hill (2 beds), Ste. Therese (2 beds), God's Lake Narrows (3 beds), Oxford House (3 beds), Cross Lake (4 beds), Little Grand & Rapids (2 beds), Poplar River (2 beds), Pukatawagon (2 beds), Nelson House (2 beds), Shamattawa (5 beds), Split Lake (4 beds), Brochet (3 beds), South Indian Lake (3 beds), Berens River (3 beds), Bloodvien (2 beds), Wassagamack (2 beds), Red Sucker Lake (2 beds), Lac Brochet (2 beds), God's River (1 bed), Tadoule Lake (2 beds) & York Landing (2 beds)

## SPECIAL TREATMENT CENTRES

(Includes: Abortion Clinics, Cancer Clinics, Rehabilitation Centres, Treatment Centres)

Winnipeg: Community Therapy Services Inc., 35 King St., 5th Fl., Winnipeg MB R3B 1H4 – 204/949-0533; Fax: 204/942-1428 – Exec. Dir., I. Corobow

Winnipeg: Deaf Centre Manitoba Inc., 285 Pembina Hwy., Winnipeg MB R3L 2E1 – 204/284-0802; Teletype phone: 204/475-0702; Fax: 204/474-0073 – 22 beds – Exec. Dir., Doug Momotiuk

Winnipeg: Manitoba Adolescent Treatment Centre Inc., 120 Tecumseh St., Winnipeg MB R3E 2A9 – 204/477-6391; Fax: 204/783-8948 – drug rehabilitation centre – 25 beds – Exec. Dir., Paul Leveille

Winnipeg: Manitoba Cancer Treatment & Research Foundation, 100 Olivia St., Winnipeg MB R3E 0V9 – 204/787-2142, 2197; Fax: 204/787-1184, 783-6875; EMail: brent.schacter@mctrf.mb.ca – cancer treatment – Pres. & CEO, Dr. Brent A. Schacter, 204/787-2241

Winnipeg: Manitoba Cardiac Institute (Refit Centre), 1390 Taylor Ave., Winnipeg MB R3M 3V8 – 204/488-8023; Fax: 204/488-4819 – rehabilitation centre – Exec. Dir., Don Fletcher

Winnipeg: Morgantaler Clinic, 883 Corydon Ave., Winnipeg MB R3M 0W7 – abortion clinic

Winnipeg: Rehabilitation Centre for Children, 633 Wellington Cres., Winnipeg MB R3M 0A8 – 204/452-4311; Fax: 204/477-5547 – rehabilitation centre – Exec. Dir., Heather Mutcheson

## NEW BRUNSWICK

### REGIONAL HEALTH AUTHORITIES

Bathurst: Corporation hospitalière de la région 6/Nor-East Health Network, a/s Hôpitalregional Chaleur, 1750, dr Sunset, Bathurst NB E2A 4L7 – 506/548-8961; Fax: 506/547-0016 – Responsible for 310 beds – Dir. gen. par interim, Conrad Pichette

Campbellton: Region 5 Hospital Corporation, c/o Campbellton Regional Hospital, PO Box 910, Campbellton NB E3N 3H3 – 506/789-5000; Fax: 506/789-5025 – CEO, Dan Arseneau

Edmundston: Corporation hospitalière de la région 4, 275, boul Hébert, PO Box 100, Edmundston NB E3V 4E4 – 506/739-2211; Fax: 506/739-2238 – Dir. gen., Gilbert St-Onge

Fredericton: Region 3 Hospital Corporation, 700 Priestman St., PO Box 9000, Fredericton NB E3B 5N5 – 506/452-5678; Fax: 506/452-5670; EMail: region3@gov.nb.ca – Pres., John McGarry

Miramichi: Region 7 Hospital Corporation, c/o Miramichi Regional Hospital, 500 Water St., Miramichi NB E1V 3G5 – 506/623-3000; Fax: 506/623-3465 – Responsible for 173 beds – CEO, John R. Tucker

Moncton: Corporation hospitalière de la région 1 (Beauséjour), a/s Hôpital Docteur Georges-L. Dumont, 330, rue Archibald, Moncton NB E1C 2Z3 – 506/862-4210; Fax: 506/862-4213 – Président, Pierre LeBouthillier, 506/862-4210, Fax: 506/862-4213

Moncton: Region 1 Hospital Corporation (Southeast), c/o The Moncton Hospital, 135 MacBeath Ave., Moncton NB E1C 6Z8 – 506/857-5757; Fax: 506/857-5545 – CEO, Ginette Gagné-Koch

Saint John: Atlantic Health Sciences Corporation (Region 2 Hospital Corp.), c/o Saint John Regional Hospital, PO Box 5200, Saint John NB E2L 4L4 – 506/648-6000; Fax: 506/648-6364 – CEO, David Carlin

### GENERAL HOSPITALS

Bath: Northern Carleton Hospital, Hospital St., Bath NB E0J 1E0 – 506/278-2400; Fax: 506/278-2449 – 23 beds – Adm., Dean C. Cummings

Bathurst: Chaleur Regional Hospital, 1750 Sunset Dr., Bathurst NB E2A 4L7 – 506/548-8961; Fax: 506/545-1428 – 270 beds – Corporation hospitalière de la région 6/Nor-East Health Network – Facility Mgr., Diane Seperich

Campbellton Regional Hospital, PO Box 880, Campbellton NB E3N 3H3 – 506/789-5000; Fax: 506/789-5025 – 175 beds – Region 5 Hospital Corporation – Adm., Dan Arseneau

Caraquet: Centre hospitalier de l'Enfant-Jésus, 1, boul St-Pierre ouest, PO Box 900, Caraquet NB E1W 1B6 – 506/726-2166; Fax: 506/726-2188 – 50 lits – Corporation hospitalière de la région 6/Nor-East Health Network – Adm. d'établissement, Fernand Rioux

Dalhousie: Hôpital St-Joseph, 270, rue Victoria, Dalhousie NB E0K 1B0 – 506/684-7000; Fax: 506/684-4751 – 60 beds – Adm. d'établissement, Diane Leger, 506/684-3391

Edmundston: Hôpital régional d'Edmundston/Edmundston Regional Hospital, 275, boul Hébert, PO Box 100, Edmundston NB E3V 4E4 – 506/739-2211; Fax: 506/739-2248 – 222 lits – Corporation hospitalière de la région 4 – Adm., Gilbert St-Onge

Fredericton: Dr. Everett Chalmers Hospital, PO Box 9000, Fredericton NB E3B 5N5 – 506/452-5400; Fax: 506/452-5500; EMail: region3@gov.nb.ca – 430 beds – Region 3 Hospital Corporation – Pres., Region 3 Hospital Corporation, John McGarry

Grand-Sault: Hôpital général de Grand-Sault inc., 625, boul Evérard H. Daigle, PO Box 1200, Grand-Sault NB E3Z 1C6 – 506/473-7555; Fax: 506/473-7530 – 50 lits – Dir. des services adm., Solange Bossé

Lamèque: Centre hospitalier de Lamèque, Lamèque NB E0B 1V0 – 506/344-3400; Fax: 506/344-3403 – 12 lits – Corporation hospitalière de la région 6/Nor-East Health Network – Responsable de l'établissement/DSI, Roseline Hébert

McAdam: MacLean Memorial Hospital, PO Box 311, McAdam NB E0H 1K0 – 506/784-6300; Fax: 506/784-6306 – 4 observation beds

Minto: Queens North Health Complex, PO Box 309, Minto NB E0E 1J0 – 506/327-7800; Fax: 506/327-7812 – 15 beds – Dir. of Operations, John Di Paola

Miramichi Regional Hospital, 500 Water St., Miramichi NB E1V 3G5 – 506/623-3000; Fax: 506/623-3465 – 210 beds – Region 7 Hospital Corporation – CEO, John R. Tucker

Moncton Hospital, 135 MacBeath Ave., Moncton NB E1C 6Z8 – 506/857-5111; Fax: 506/857-5545; EMail: mctnhosp@nbnet.nb.ca – 547 beds – Region 1 Hospital Corporation (Southeast) – COO, Ruth Duffey

Moncton: Hôpital Dr. Georges L. Dumont, 330, rue Archibald, Moncton NB E1C 2Z3 – 506/862-4000; Fax: 506/862-4256 – 383 lits – Corporation hospitalière de la région 1 (Beauséjour) – Président et Dir. gen., Pierre J. LeBouthillier

Newcastle Hospital, 673 King George Hwy., PO Box 420, Newcastle NB E1V 3M5 – 506/627-7000; Fax: 506/627-7029 – 114 beds – Facility Mgr., Phyllis Mossman

North Head: Grand Manan Hospital Ltd., PO Box 219, North Head NB E0G 2M0 – 506/662-8411; Fax: 506/662-8819 – 14 beds – Adm., Julie Green

Oromocto Public Hospital, 103 Winnebago St., Oromocto NB E2V 1C6 – 506/357-4700; Fax: 506/357-4735 – 65 beds – Facility Mgr., John McGarry

Perth-Andover: Hôtel-Dieu de Saint-Joseph, 500 East Riverside Dr., PO Box 187, Perth-Andover NB E0J 1V0 – 506/273-7100; Fax: 506/273-7200 – 55 beds – Dir. of Nursing, Joy Van Tassel

Plaster Rock: Tobique Valley Hospital Inc., Plaster Rock NB E0J 1W0 – 506/356-6600; Fax: 506/356-6618 – 15 beds – Adm., Dean P. Cummings

The Sackville Memorial Hospital, Main St. West, PO Box 1170, Sackville NB E0A 3C0 – 506/364-4100; Fax: 506/536-1983 – 21 beds – Region 1 Hospital Corporation (Southeast) – Liaison Coord., Audrey Hicks

Ste-Anne-de-Kent: Hôpital Stella Maris de Kent, PO Box 09, Ste-Anne-de-Kent NB E0A 2V0 – 506/743-7800; Fax: 506/743-7813 – 20 beds – Corporation hospitalière de la région 1 (Beauséjour) – Dir. d'établ., Adrien Babineau

Saint John Regional Hospital, PO Box 2100, Saint John NB E2L 4L2 – 506/648-6093; Fax: 506/648-6799; EMail: thoch@reg2.health.nb.ca – 705 beds – Atlantic Health Sciences Corporation (Region 2 Hospital Corp.) – Adm., Cherry Thorne

Saint John: Ridgewood Veterans Wing, PO Box 2100, Saint John NB E2L 4L2 – 506/635-2420; Fax: 506/635-2425 – Coord., Bonnie Lambert

Saint John: St. Joseph's Hospital, 130 Bayard Dr., Saint John NB E2L 3L6 – 506/632-5555; Fax: 506/632-5551 – 120 beds – Atlantic Health Sciences Corporation (Region 2 Hospital Corp.) – Adm., Cherry Thorne

St-Quentin: Hôtel-Dieu Saint-Joseph de St-Quentin, 9, rue Canada, St-Quentin NB E0K 1J0 – 506/235-2300; Fax: 506/235-7202 – 20 lits – Adm. d'établissement, Réal Thériault

St. Stephen: The Charlotte County Hospital, 4 Garden St., St. Stephen NB E3L 2L9 – 506/465-4444; Fax: 506/465-4418 – 80 beds – Atlantic Health Sciences Corporation – Facility Mgr., Arlene Haddon

Sussex Health Centre, Leonard Dr., PO Box 5006, Sussex NB E0E 1P0 – 506/432-3100; Fax: 506/432-3106; EMail: secll@reg2.health.nb.ca – 36 beds – Atlantic Health Sciences Corporation – Facility Mgr., Lloyd D. Secord, 506/432-3207

Tracadie-Sheila: Centre hospitalier de Tracadie, PO Box 3180, Stn Bur. chef, Tracadie-Sheila NB E1X 1G5 – 506/394-3001; Fax: 506/394-3034 – 70 lits – Corporation hospitalière de la région 6/Nor-East Health Network – Dir. d'établissement, Conrad Pichette

Woodstock: The Carleton Memorial Hospital, 785 Main St., PO Box 6000, Woodstock NB E0J 2B0 – 506/325-6700; Fax: 506/325-6765 – 80 beds – Adm., Dean P. Cummings

### AUXILIARY HOSPITALS/HEALTH CARE CENTRES

Albert County Hospital, PO Box 28, Albert NB E0A 1A0 – 506/882-3100; Fax: 506/882-3101 – Region 1 Hospital Corporation (Southeast) – Facility Mgr., Ann Dowe

Baie Ste-Anne Health Centre, PO Box 38, Baie Ste-Anne NB E0C 1A0 – 506/228-4859; Fax: 506/228-3884 – Facility Mgr., Brenda McFarlane

Black's Harbour: Fundy Health Centre, Black's Harbour NB E0G 1H0 – 506/456-4200; Fax: 506/456-2537 – 4 observation beds – Atlantic Health Sciences Corporation (Region 2 Hospital Corp.) – Acting Adm., Shirley Hatt

Blackville Health Centre, PO Box 10, Blackville NB E0C 1C0 – 506/843-6446; Fax: 506/843-6485 – Facility Mgr., Brenda McFarlane

Boiestown: Upper Miramichi Health Services Centre, PO Box 245, Boiestown NB E0H 1J0 – 506/369-2700; Fax: 506/369-2664

Campobello Health Centre, Campobello NB E0G 3H0 – 506/752-2491; Fax: 506/752-2654 – Facility Adm., Arlene Haddon

Chipman Health Centre, Chipman NB E0E 1J0 – 506/339-7650; Fax: 506/339-7652 – Health Centre Nurse, Mildred Dale

Dalhousie: East Restigouche Community Health Care Centre, RR#1, Site 10, PO Box 1, Dalhousie NB E0K 1B0 – 506/684-8455; Fax: 506/684-4751 – Facility Mgr., Diane Léger

Deer Island Health Centre, Deer Island NB E0G 1R0 – 506/747-2394; Fax: 506/747-2417 – Facility Adm., Arlene Haddon

Doaktown Health Centre, 8 Miramichi St., Doaktown NB E0C 1G0 – 506/365-6100; Fax: 506/365-6104 – Adm., Lorri Amos

Fredericton Junction Health Centre, Fredericton Junction NB E0G 1T0 – 506/368-6505; Fax: 506/368-6502 – Nurse Coord., Anne Walsh

Harvey Station: Harvey Community Hospital Ltd., Harvey Station NB E0H 1H0 – 506/366-6400; Fax: 506/366-6403 – Nurse Coord., Anne Walsh

Jacquet River Health Centre, Jacquet River NB E0B 1T0 – 506/237-2215; Fax: 506/684-4751 – Facility Mgr., Diane Légère

Neguac Health Centre, PO Box 34, Neguac NB E0C 1S0 – 506/776-5638; Fax: 506/778-1011 – Facility Mgr., Brenda McFarlane

Paquetville: Centre de santé-Paquetville, PO Box 130, Paquetville NB E0B 2B0 – 506/764-2424; Fax: 506/764-2425 – Adm. d'établissement, Edwidge Cormier

Petitcodiac Health Centre, PO Box 88, Petitcodiac NB E0A 2H0 – 506/756-3351; Fax: 506/756-3406 – Region 1 Hospital Corporation (Southeast) – Nurse Mgr., Heather Steeves

Pointe Verte: Centre de santé Pointe Verte, PO Box 238, Pointe Verte NB E0B 2H0 – 506/783-2001; Fax: 506/783-8623 – Corporation hospitalière de la région 6/Nor-East Health Network – Adm. d'établissement, Roxanne Tarjan

Rexton Community Health Centre, PO Box 158, Rexton NB E0A 2L0 – 506/523-7940; Fax: 506/79499547 – Region 1 Hospital Corporation (Southeast) – Nurse Mgr., Lucille Cormier

Rogersville Community Health Centre, PO Box 418, Rogersville NB E0A 2T0 – 506/775-6108; Fax: 506/775-6298 – Facility Mgr., Brenda McFarlane

Ste-Anne-de-Madawaska: Centre de santé de Ste-Anne-de-Madawaska, 1, rue de la Clinique, Ste-Anne-de-Madawaska NB E7E 1B9 – 506/445-2348; Fax: 506/735-0880 – Adm. d'établissement, Gilbert St-Onge

Shediac: Centre médical régional de Shediac, 419, rue Main, Shediac NB E0A 3G0 – 506/533-2700; Fax: 506/533-2710 – Adm. d'établissement par intérim, Adrien Babineau

Stanley Health Centre, PO Box 130, Stanley NB E0H 1T0 – 506/367-7730; Fax: 506/367-7738 – Nurse Coord., Anne Walsh

## HOME CARE OFFICES/COMMUNITY HEALTH CARE OFFICES

Caraquet: Centre de Bénévolat de la Péninsule Acadienne Inc., PO Box 397, Caraquet NB E0B 1K0

Chipman Outreach, Chipman NB E0E 1C0

Fredericton: Comcare, 384 Queen St., Fredericton NB E3B 1B2 – 506/451-1303; Fax: 506/452-8565 – Mgr., Shirley Clayton

Fredericton: Olsten Kimberley Quality Care, 142 Brunswick St., Fredericton NB E3B 1G6 – 506/458-9934; Fax: 506/458-9963 – Branch Dir., Louise Billings

Fredericton: People Care, #1, Victoria Health Centre, 65 Brunswick St., Fredericton NB E3B 1G5

Fredericton: Private Care, PO Box 20116, Fredericton NB E3B 5H0 – 506/459-1888; Fax: 506/454-8707

Fredericton: Victorian Order of Nurses, Fredericton Branch, 65 Brunswick St., Fredericton NB E3B 1G5 – 506/458-8365; Fax: 506/459-2899

Harvey Outreach, Harvey NB E0H 1H0 – 506/366-3017; Fax: 506/366-2927 – Adm., Bev Werbs

McAdam Outreach for Seniors, Wauklehegan Manor Inc., McAdam NB E0H 1K0 – 506/784-6308; Fax: 506/784-6306 – Adm., Mary Grant

Minto Services to Seniors, Queens North Health Complex, Minto NB E0E 1J0

Saint John: Hospice Saint John, 116 Coburg St., Saint John NB E2K 3K1

St. Stephen: Home Support Services Inc., PO Box 293, St. Stephen NB E3L 2X2

Stanley: Paradise Lodge, Stanley NB E0H 1T0

Westfield: Senior Watch Inc., 98 Nerepis Rd., RR#2, Westfield NB E0G 3J0 – 506/757-8706; Fax: 506/757-2992; EMail: senior@nbnet.nb.ca – Adm., Jean Porter

## MENTAL HEALTH HOSPITALS & COMMUNITY FACILITIES

Campbellton: Restigouche Hospital Centre Inc., PO Box 10, Campbellton NB E3N 3G2 – 506/789-7000; Fax: 506/789-7065 – 195 beds – Adm., Claudette Redstone

Saint John: Centracare of Saint John Inc., PO Box 3220, Stn B, Saint John NB E2M 4H7 – 506/635-7550; Fax: 506/635-2500 – 145 beds – Adm., Cherry Thorne

## NURSING HOMES/LONG TERM CARE FACILITIES

Albert: Forest Dale Home Inc., Riverside, PO Box 4, Albert NB E0A 1A0 – 506/882-2281; Fax: 506/882-0118 – 40 beds – Adm., Ethel Duffy

Baker Brook: Foyer Ste. Elizabeth Inc., 25, rue des Ormes, Baker Brook NB E7A 2J6 – 506/258-3020; Fax: 506/258-3010 – 50 beds – Dir. gen. par intérim, Pierre Gignac

Bath: River View Manor Inc., Hospital Rd., Bath NB E0J 1E0 – 506/278-6030; Fax: 506/278-5962 – 40 beds – Adm., Sharon Eagan

Bathurst: Le Foyer Notre-Dame de Lourdes Inc., 2055 Vallée-Lourdes, Bathurst NB E2A 4P8 – 506/549-5085; Fax: 506/548-9818 – 100 lits – Dir. gen., Claude Desrosiers, 506/549-5052

Bathurst: Villa Chaleur, DVA Unit, 795, rue Champlin, Bathurst NB E2A 4M8 – 506/548-3338; Fax: 506/548-4196 – 10 lits – Adm., Lucie Fournier

Black's Harbour: Fundy Nursing Home, Black's Harbour NB E5H 1C2 – 506/456-4213; Fax: 506/456-4259 – 20 beds – Adm., Shirley Hatt

Boiestown: Central New Brunswick Nursing Home Inc., PO Box 249, Boiestown NB E0H 1A0 – 506/369-7262; Fax: 506/369-2331 – 30 beds – Adm., Manley Black

Bouctouche: Manoir Saint-Jean Baptiste Inc., 5, av Richard, PO Box 296, Bouctouche NB E0A 1G0 – 506/743-7344; Fax: 506/743-7343 – 50 lits – Dir. gen., Donald Daigle

Campbellton Nursing Home Inc., 101 Dover St., PO Box 850, Campbellton NB E3N 3H3 – 506/789-7800; Fax: 506/789-7808 – 100 beds – Adm., Ken Murray

Campobello Lodge Inc., Welsh Pool, Campobello NB E0G 3H0 – 506/752-7101; Fax: 506/752-7105; EMail: cmplodge@campnet.nb.ca – 30 beds – Adm., Sherry Johnston

Caraquet: Villa Beauséjour Inc., PO Box 5608, Caraquet NB E1W 1B7 – 506/726-2744; Fax: 506/726-2745 – 62 lits – Dir. gen., Roger Landry

Dalhousie Nursing Home Inc./Le Foyer Dalhousie inc., 300 Victoria St., PO Box 1689, Dalhousie NB E0K 1B0 – 506/684-7800; Fax: 506/684-7832 – 105 beds – Adm., Gilles Richard

Edmundston: Villa Des-Jardins Inc., 50, rue Queen, Edmundston NB E3V 3N4 – 506/735-2112; Fax: 506/735-2462 – 30 lits – Dir., Cécile Paillard

Fredericton Junction: White Rapids Manor Inc., Fredericton Junction NB E0G 1T0 – 506/368-6508; Fax: 506/368-6502 – Adm., Barb Smith

Fredericton: Pine Grove, 521 Woodstock Rd., Fredericton NB E3B 2J2 – 506/444-3400; Fax: 506/444-3409; EMail: pine@nb.net.ca – 70 beds – Adm., Barbara Gregan

Fredericton: York Manor Inc., 100 Sunset Dr., Fredericton NB E3A 1A3 – 506/444-3880; Fax: 506/444-3544 – 198 beds – Adm., Kerry Wolstenholme

Gagetown Nursing Home Inc., PO Box 130, Gagetown NB E0G 1V0 – 506/488-2328; Fax: 506/488-2888 – 38 beds – Adm., Kathy Hamilton

Grand Falls Manor Inc./Manoir de Grand-Sault Inc., PO Box 2000, Grand Falls NB E3Z 1E2 – 506/473-7726; Fax: 506/473-7849 – 72 beds – Dir. gen., Maurice Richard

Hampton: Dr. V.A. Snow Centre Inc., RR#4, Hampton NB E0G 1Z0 – 506/832-6210; Fax: 506/832-7674 – 50 beds – Adm., Judy Paquet

Hartland: Central Carleton Nursing Home Inc., 139 Rockland Rd., RR#4, Hartland NB E0J 1N0 – 506/375-3033; Fax: 506/375-3035 – 30 beds – Adm., Gwen Cullins-Jones

Harvey: Swan Haven Nursing Home Ltd., Harvey NB E0H 1H0 – 506/366-2950 – 21 beds – Owner, Frances P. Ward

Inkerman: Les Résidences Inkerman Inc., PO Box 156, Inkerman NB E0B 1S0 – 506/336-3910; Fax: 506/336-3912 – 30 lits – Dir. gen., Paul Arseneau

Lamèque: Les Résidences Lucien Saindon Inc., PO Box 480, Lamèque NB E0B 1V0 – 506/344-3232; Fax: 506/344-3240 – 54 lits – Dir. gen., Gaëtan Haché

McAdam: Waulkehegan Manor Inc., McAdam NB E0H 1K0 – 506/784-6300; Fax: 506/784-6306 – 36 beds – Adm., Mary Grant

Minto: W.G. Bishop Nursing Home, PO Box 309, Minto NB E0E 1J0 – 506/327-7853; Fax: 506/327-7812 – 30 beds – CEO, Lisa Allard

Miramichi Senior Citizens Home Inc., 1400 Water St., Miramichi NB E1N 1A4 – 506/773-5801; Fax: 506/773-7069 – 81 beds – Adm., Shirley MacDonald

Miramichi: Mount Saint Joseph of Chatham N.B., 51 Lobban Ave., Miramichi NB E1N 3W4 – 506/778-6550; Fax: 506/778-0193 – 133 beds – Adm., R.B. Stewart

Moncton: Kenneth E. Spencer Memorial Home, 35 Atlantic Baptist Ave., Moncton NB E1E 4N3 – 506/858-7870; Fax: 506/858-9674 – 200 beds – Adm., Steven Campbell

Moncton: Villa du Repos Inc., 474 Elmwood Dr., Moncton NB E1A 2X3 – 506/857-3560; Fax: 506/859-1619 – 126 lits – Dir. gen., Paul Williams

Néguac: Le Foyer Saint-Bernard Ltée, PO Box 161, Néguac NB E0C 1S0 – 506/776-3774 – 24 lits – Propriétaire, Diane Mazerolle

North Head: Grand Manan Nursing Home Inc., PO Box 189, North Head NB E0G 2M0 – 506/662-7111; Fax: 506/662-7117 – 30 beds – Adm., Sharon Urquhart

Paquetville: Manoir Edith B. Pinet Inc., PO Box 99, Paquetville NB E0B 2B0 – 506/764-3270; Fax: 506/764-2451 – 30 lits – Dir. gen., Marthe Robichaud

Perth-Andover: Victoria Glen Manor Inc., Beech Glen Rd., Perth-Andover NB E0J 1V0 – 506/273-4885; Fax: 506/273-4975 – 65 beds – Adm., Dawn Bishop

Plaster Rock: Tobique Valley Manor Inc., PO Box 99, Plaster Rock NB E0J 1W0 – 506/356-6040; Fax: 506/356-6041 – 30 beds – Adm., Eric Haddad

Port Elgin: Westford Nursing Home, 57 West Main St., PO Box 119, Port Elgin NB E0A 2K0 – 506/538-2307; Fax: 506/538-7293 – 30 beds – Adm., Judith White

Rexton Lions Nursing Home Inc., PO Box 70, Rexton NB E0A 2L0 – 506/523-7720; Fax: 506/523-7933 – 30 beds – Adm., Dianne Robichard

River Glade: Jordan Memorial Home, The Glades, Sanatorium Rd., River Glade NB E0A 2P0 – 506/756-3355; Fax: 506/756-2081 – 100 beds – Adm., G.A. Hollingsworth

Riverview: The Salvation Army Lakeview Manor, 50 Suffolk St., Riverview NB E1B 4K6 – 506/387-2012; Fax: 506/387-7200 – 50 beds – Exec. Dir., Maj. Reginald Pell

Robertville: La Villa Sormany Inc., PO Box 250, Robertville NB E0B 2K0 – 506/542-2736; Fax: 506/542-2733 – 40 beds – Dir. gen., Lucie Marteau

Rogersville: Foyer Assomption, PO Box 296, Rogersville NB E0A 2T0 – 506/775-2040; Fax: 506/775-2053 – 50 lits – Dir. gen., Willie Robichaud

Sackville: Drew Nursing Home, 165 Main St., Sackville NB E0A 3C0 – 506/364-4900; Fax: 506/364-4921 – 130 beds – Adm., Ann Johnson

St. Andrews: Passamaquoddy Lodge Inc., PO Box 370, St. Andrews NB E0G 2X0 – 506/529-5240; Fax: 506/529-5258 – 60 beds – Adm., Faith Keith

Saint Antoine: Foyer Saint-Antoine, PO Box 300, Saint Antoine NB E0A 2X0 – 506/525-2229; Fax: 506/525-1013 – 30 lits – Dir. gen., Gilles C. Ouellette

Saint-Basile: Le Foyer Saint-Joseph de Saint-Basile Inc., 475, rue Principale, Saint-Basile NB E7C 1J2 –

506/263-5561; Fax: 506/263-4101 – 126 lits – Dir. gen., Sr. Claudette Ouellet

Saint John: Carleton Kirk Lodge, 3 Carleton Kirk Pl., Saint John NB E2M 5B8 – 506/635-7040; Fax: 506/635-7038 – 70 beds – Adm., Tim Stevens

Saint John: The Church of St. John & St. Stephen Home Inc., 130 University Ave., Saint John NB E2K 4K3 – 506/634-6001; Fax: 506/634-6126 – 80 beds – Adm., Judy Heffern

Saint John: Kennebec Manor, 475 Woodward Ave., Saint John NB E2K 4N1 – 506/634-1333; Fax: 506/658-9376 – 70 beds – Adm., Jacob Hiebert

Saint John: Loch Lomond Villa, 185 Loch Lomond Rd., Saint John NB E2J 3S3 – 506/643-7175; Fax: 506/643-7198 – 201 beds – Adm., Tom Jarrett, 506/643-7170

Saint John: Rocmaura Inc., 10 Park St., Saint John NB E2K 4P1 – 506/634-7050; Fax: 506/636-7053 – 150 beds – Adm., Sr. Anita Holmes

Saint John: Turnbull Home, 240 Wentworth St., Saint John NB E2L 2T6 – 506/648-7200; Fax: 506/648-9786 – 40 beds – Adm., Elizabeth Crouchman

Saint Joseph: Le Foyer St Thomas de la Vallée de Memramcook inc., 589, rue Centrale, PO Box 120, Saint Joseph NB E0A 2Y0 – 506/758-2110; Fax: 506/758-9489 – 30 lits – Dir. gen., Pierre Landry

Saint-Léonard: Foyer Notre-Dame de Saint-Léonard Inc., PO Box 190, Saint-Léonard NB E7E 2H5 – 506/423-3151; Fax: 506/423-3152 – 35 lits – Dir. gen., Michel Fournier

Saint-Louis-de-Kent: Villa Maria Inc., PO Box 40, Saint-Louis-de-Kent NB E0A 2Z0 – 506/876-2402; Fax: 506/876-2868 – 73 lits – Dir. gen., Laurie Vautour

Saint-Quentin: Résidence Mgr Melanson Inc., 40, rue Canada, RR#1, Saint-Quentin NB E0K 1J0 – 506/235-6030; Fax: 506/235-6075 – 42 lits – Dir. gen., Louiselle V. Cormier

St. Stephen Nursing Home Inc., RR#4, Hwy 3, St. Stephen NB E3L 2Y2 – 506/466-1868; Fax: 506/466-6081 – 29 beds – Owner, Raymond Lee Disher

St. Stephen: Lincourt Manor Inc., 1 Chipman St., St. Stephen NB E3L 2W9 – 506/466-3007; Fax: 506/466-3845 – 60 beds – Adm., Jane Lyons

Shédiac: Villa Providence Shédiac Inc., 273, rue Main, PO Box 340, Shédiac NB E0A 3G0 – 506/532-4484; Fax: 506/532-8189 – 204 lits – Dir. gen., Paul Williams

Shippagan: Les Résidences Mgr Chiasson Inc., PO Box 368, Shippagan NB E0B 2P0 – 506/336-3266; Fax: 506/336-3099 – 100 lits – Dir. gen., Octave Haché

Shippagan: Villa Beau Rivage Ltée, PO Box 444, Shippagan NB E0B 2P0 – 506/336-8988 – 29 lits – Propriétaire, Gisèle Duguay

Stanley: Nashwaak Villa Inc., Stanley NB E0H 1T0 – 506/367-7731; Fax: 506/367-7745 – 30 beds – Adm., Penny Higgs

Sussex: Kiwanis Nursing Home Inc., 11 Bryant St., PO Box 5002, Sussex NB E0E 1P0 – 506/432-3118; Fax: 506/432-3104 – 70 beds – Adm., Lloyd Secord

Tabusintac Nursing Home Inc., 14 Manse Rd., PO Box 99, Tabusintac NB E0C 2A0 – 506/779-8228; Fax: 506/779-8149 – 30 beds – Adm., Betty Blake

Tracadie-Sheila: Villa Saint-Joseph Inc., PO Box 2500, Tracadie-Sheila NB E1X 1G7 – 506/395-4800; Fax: 506/395-4826 – 64 lits – Bureau chef, Wilfred Robichaud

Woodstock: Carleton Manor Inc., PO Box 6000, Woodstock NB E0J 2B0 – 506/328-4373; Fax: 506/328-9672 – 89 beds – Adm., Patricia MacNeil

Youngs Cove Road: Mill Cove Nursing Home Inc., PO Box 518, Youngs Cove Road NB E0E 1S0 – 506/488-3033; Fax: 506/488-3037 – 75 beds – Adm., Patricia Hamilton

### SPECIAL TREATMENT CENTRES

(Includes: Abortion Clinics, Cancer Clinics, Rehabilitation Centres, Treatment Centres)

Fredericton: Morgentaler Clinic Abortion Services, 88 Ferry Ave., Fredericton NB E3A 1R8 – 506/451-9060; Fax: 506/451-9062; EMail: righters@nbnet.nb.ca – Adm., Allison Brewer

Fredericton: Stan Cassidy Centre for Rehabilitation, 180 Woodbridge St., Fredericton NB E3B 4R3 – 506/452-5225; Fax: 506/452-5190 – rehabilitation centre – 20 beds – Dir. of Specialized Rehab. Servs., Janice Eloway

Saint John West: Ridgewood Addiction Services, PO Box 3566, Stn B, Saint John West NB E2M 4Y1 – 506/674-4300; Fax: 506/674-4374; EMail: naisha@nbnet.nb.ca – 93 beds – Atlantic Health Sciences Corporation – Exec. Dir., Bonnie Lambert

Saint John: Workers' Rehabilitation Centre, Workplace Health Safety and Compensation Commission of N.B., PO Box 3067, Stn B, Saint John NB E2M 4X7 – 506/738-8411; Fax: 506/738-3470 – Vice-Pres., Prevention & Rehabilitation, Dr. Dow Dorcas

St. Stephen: Valley View Manor Inc., RR#1, St. Stephen NB E3L 2Y2 – 506/466-1234 – Special care home – Owner, Wanda Higgins

## NEWFOUNDLAND

### REGIONAL HEALTH AUTHORITIES

Carbonear: Avalon Health Care Institutions Board, 86 Highroad South, Carbonear NF A1Y 1A4 – 709/945-5155; Fax: 709/945-5158 – CEO, George Butt

Clarenville: Peninsulas Health Care Corporation, PO Box 2800, Clarenville NF A0E 1J0 – 709/466-5339; Fax: 709/466-1623 – Responsible for 310 beds at 7 sites – Acting CEO, Pat Coish

Corner Brook: Western Health Care Corporation, c/o Western Memorial Regional Hospital, PO Box 2005, Corner Brook NF A2H 6J7 – 709/637-5000; Fax: 709/634-2649 – Interim CEO, Rob Kenny

Gander: Central East Health Care Institutions Board, 125 Trans Canada Hwy., Gander NF A1V 1P7 – 709/256-5530; Fax: 709/256-7800 – CEO, David Lewis

Grand Falls-Windsor: Central West Health Care Institutions Board, Union St., Grand Falls-Windsor NF A2A 2E1 – 709/292-2138; Fax: 709/292-2249 – CEO, Donald Keats

Happy Valley-Goose Bay: Health Labrador Corporation, PO Box 190, Stn A, Happy Valley-Goose Bay NF A0P 1S0 – 709/896-7171; Fax: 709/896-4032 – CEO, Keith Sansford

St Anthony: Grenfell Regional Health Services Board, St Anthony NF A0K 4S0 – 705/454-3333; Fax: 705/454-2052 – CEO, John Budgell

St. John's Nursing Home Board, 29-31 Pippy Place, 2nd Fl., St. John's NF A1B 3X2 – 709/579-8537; Fax: 709/579-0580 – CEO, Allan Bradley

St. John's: Health Care Corporation of St. John's, South Wing, Waterford Hospital, Waterford Bridge Rd., St. John's NF A1E 4J8 – 709/758-1300; Fax: 709/758-1302; EMail: hcc.stob@hccsj.nf.ca – Responsible for 1,259 beds – Pres. & CEO, Elizabeth M. Davis, RSM

### GENERAL HOSPITALS

Burin Peninsula Health Centre, PO Box 340, Burin NF A0E 1E0 – 709/891-1040; Fax: 709/891-3375 – 47 acute care beds – Peninsulas Health Care Corporation – CEO, P. Coish

Carbonear General Hospital, 86 Highroad South, Carbonear NF A1Y 1A4 – 709/945-5111; Fax: 709/945-5158 – 80 acute care beds – Avalon Health Care Institutions Board – Exec. Dir., G. Butt

Clarenville: Dr. G.B. Cross Memorial Hospital, PO Box 1300, Clarenville NF A0E 1J0 – 709/466-3411; Fax: 709/466-3300; EMail: greid@phcc.nf.net – 48 acute care, 7 continuing care beds – Peninsulas Health Care Corporation – VP, Planning, Information & Resource Development, G. Reid

Corner Brook: Western Memorial Regional Hospital, PO Box 2005, Corner Brook NF A2H 6J7 – 709/637-5000; Fax: 709/634-2649 – 209 beds – Western Health Care Corporation – CEO, L. Birmingham

Gander: James Paton Memorial Hospital, 125 TransCanada Hwy., Gander NF A1V 1P7 – 709/651-2500; Fax: 709/256-7800 – 92 acute care beds – Central East Health Care Institutions Board – CEO, E. Forward

Grand Falls-Windsor: Central Newfoundland Regional Health Centre, 50 Union St., Grand Falls-Windsor NF A2A 2E1 – 709/292-2500; Fax: 709/292-2249 – 142 acute care beds – Central West Health Care Institutions Board – CEO, H. Hynes

Happy Valley-Goose Bay: Melville Hospital, Postal Station A, Happy Valley-Goose Bay NF A0P 1S0 – 709/896-2417; Fax: 709/896-8966 – 34 acute care beds – Health Labrador Corporation – CEO, B. Rowe

Labrador City: Captain William Jackman Memorial Hospital, 410 Booth Ave., Labrador City NF A2V 2K1 – 709/944-2632; Fax: 709/944-6045 – 29 acute care, 6 continuing care beds – Health Labrador Corporation – Exec. Dir., M. Condon

St Anthony: Charles S. Curtis Memorial Hospital, West St., PO Box 1-628, St Anthony NF A0K 4S0 – 709/454-3333; Fax: 709/454-2052 – 67 acute care beds – Grenfell Regional Health Services Board – CEO, John Budgell

St. John's: The General Hospital/Health Sciences Centre, 300 Prince Philip Dr., St. John's NF A1B 3V6 – 709/758-1308; Fax: 709/737-6770 – teaching hospital – 307 acute care beds – Health Care Corporation of St. John's – CEO, Dr. E. Parsons

St. John's: Janeway Child Health Centre, 710 Janeway Pl., St. John's NF A1A 1R8 – 709/778-4428; Fax: 709/778-4446 – teaching hospital – 103 acute care beds – Health Care Corporation of St. John's – CEO, M. Pardy

St. John's: St. Clare's Mercy Hospital, 154 Lemarchant Rd., St. John's NF A1C 5B8 – 709/758-1317; Fax: 709/738-1216 – teaching hospital – 217 acute care beds – Health Care Corporation of St. John's – CEO, L. Jones

St. John's: Salvation Army Grace General Hospital, 241 Lemarchant Rd., St. John's NF A1E 1P9 – 709/758-1306; Fax: 709/778-6640 – teaching hospital – 204 acute care beds – Health Care Corporation of St. John's – CEO, G. Tilley

Stephenville: Sir Thomas Roddick Hospital, 89 Ohio Dr., Stephenville NF A2N 2V6 – 709/643-5111; Fax: 709/643-3104 – 56 acute care beds – Western Health Care Corporation – Exec. Dir., Y. Noseworthy

### AUXILIARY HOSPITALS/HEALTH CARE CENTRES

Badger's Quay: Bonavista North Health Care Complex, PO Box 209, Badger's Quay NF A0G 1B0 – 709/536-2160, 2405; Fax: 709/536-3334 – 12 acute care, 45 continuing care beds – Central East Health Care Institutions Board – CEO, W. Winsor

Baie Verte Peninsula Health Centre, Baie Verte NF A0K 1B0 – 709/532-4281; Fax: 709/532-4939 – 4 acute care, 19 continuing care beds – Central West Health Care Institutions Board – CEO, Wayne Vincent

Bell Island: Dr. Walter Templeman Community Health Centre, PO Box 580, Bell Island NF A0A 4H0 – 709/488-2821; Fax: 709/488-2600 – 6 acute care, 14 continuing care beds – Health Care Corporation of St. John's – CEO, T. O'Brien

Bonavista Community Health Centre, PO Box 1, Bonavista NF A0C 1B0 – 709/468-7881; Fax: 709/468-7223 – 10 acute care, 73 continuing care beds – Peninsulas Health Care Corporation – CEO, A. Croucher

Burgeo: Calder Health Care Centre, Burgeo NF A0M 1A0 – 709/886-3350; Fax: 709/886-3382 – 4 acute care, 18 continuing care beds – Western Health Care Corporation – CEO, R. Staples-Payne

Churchill Falls Clinic, PO Box 100, Churchill Falls NF A0R 1A0 – 709/925-3381; Fax: 709/925-3246 – Health Labrador Corporation – Florence Rogers

Fogo Island Hospital, PO Box 9, Fogo NF A0G 2B0 – 709/266-2221; Fax: 709/266-2409 – 12 beds – Central East Health Care Institutions Board – Facility Mgr., Ann Green

Forteau: Labrador South Health Centre, Forteau NF A0K 2P0 – 709/931-2450; Fax: 709/931-2000 – Grenfell Regional Health Services Board

Grand Bank Community Health Centre, PO Box 310, Grand Bank NF A0E 1W0 – 709/832-2500 – Peninsulas Health Care Corporation – CEO, J. Penney

Harbour Breton Hospital, Harbour Breton NF A0H 1P0 – 709/885-2359; Fax: 709/885-2358 – 5 acute care, 10 continuing care beds – CEO, D. Johnston

Norris Point: Bonne Bay Health Centre, Norris Point NF A0K 3V0 – 709/458-2201; Fax: 709/458-2074 – 5 acute care, 15 continuing care beds – Western Health Care Corporation – Adm., Meta Carpenter

Northwest River Clinic, Northwest River NF A0P 1M0 – 709/497-8351; Fax: 709/497-8521 – Health Labrador Corporation – Adm., Joanne Montague

Old Perlican: Dr. A.A. Wilkinson Memorial Health Centre, PO Box 70, Old Perlican NF A0A 3G0 – 709/587-2200; Fax: 709/587-2275 – 6 beds – Nurse in Charge, Maureen Oliver

Placentia & Area Health Care Complex, PO Box 480, Placentia NF A0B 2Y0 – 709/227-2013; Fax: 709/227-5476 – 10 acute care, 75 continuing care beds – Avalon Health Care Institutions Board – Facility Mgr., Diane Reid

Port aux Basques: Dr. Charles L. LeGrow Health Centre, PO Box 250, Port aux Basques NF A0M 1C0 – 709/695-2175; Fax: 709/695-3118 – 20 acute care, 30 continuing care beds – Western Health Care Corporation – CEO, R. Graham

Port Saunders: Rufus Guinchard Health Care Centre, PO Box 40, Port Saunders NF A0K 4H0 – 709/861-3533; Fax: 709/861-3772 – 8 acute care, 11 continuing care beds – Western Health Care Corporation – CEO, D. Brown

St. Lawrence: US Memorial Community Health Centre, PO Box 398, St. Lawrence NF A0E 2V0 – 709/873-2330; Fax: 709/873-2390 – 30 beds – Peninsulas Health Care Corporation – Site Coord., Betty Ann Collins

Springdale: Green Bay Community Health Centre, PO Box 280, Springdale NF A0J 1T0 – 709/673-3911, 3936; Fax: 709/673-3186 – 125 continuing care beds – Central West Health Care Institutions Board – Adm., Wayne Vincent

Twillingate: Notre Dame Bay Memorial Health Centre, PO Box 1-748, Twillingate NF A0G 4M0 – 709/884-2131; Fax: 709/884-2586 – 18 acute care, 27 continuing care beds – Central East Health Care Institutions Board – Exec. Dir., C. Herridge

Whitbourne: Dr. Wm. H. Newhook Community Health Centre, Whitbourne NF A0B 3K0 – 709/759-2300; Fax: 709/759-2387 – CEO, L. English

## HOME CARE OFFICES/COMMUNITY HEALTH CARE OFFICES

Corner Brook: Community Health - Western, PO Box 156, Corner Brook NF A2H 6C7 – 709/637-5243; Fax: 709/637-5159 – Exec. Dir., Dr. Minnie Wasmeier

Gander: Community Health - Central, 143 Bennett Dr., Gander NF A1V 2E6 – 709/256-7969; Fax: 709/651-3556 – Exec. Dir., A. Neal Ludlow

Holyrood: Community Health - Eastern, PO Box 70, Holyrood NF A0A 2R0 – 709/229-4855; Fax: 709/229-4005 – Exec. Dir., Calvin Kinden

St. John's: Community Health - St. John's Region, PO Box 13122, Stn A, St. John's NF A1B 4A4 – 709/738-4831; Fax: 709/738-4832; EMail: hcc.scodo@hccsj.nf.ca – Health Care Corporation of St. John's – Exec. Dir., Brenda Fitzgerald

## MENTAL HEALTH HOSPITALS & COMMUNITY FACILITIES

St. John's: Waterford Hospital, 306 Waterford Bridge Rd., St. John's NF A1E 4J8 – 709/364-0111; Fax: 709/364-0464 – 87 acute care, 159 continuing care beds – Health Care Corporation of St. John's – CEO, C. Simms, 709/758-3320

## NURSING HOMES/LONG TERM CARE FACILITIES

Badger's Quay: Bonnews Lodge, PO Box 209, Badger's Quay NF A0G 1B0 – 709/536-2160; Fax: 709/536-3334 – 45 beds – Facility Mgr., Marie Parsons

Bonavista: Golden Heights Manor, Postal Service 1, Bonavista NF A0C 1B0 – 709/468-2043; Fax: 709/468-7223 – 61 beds – Adm., vacant

Botwood: Dr. Hugh Twomey Health Centre, PO Box 250, Botwood NF A0H 1E0 – 709/257-2874; Fax: 709/257-4613 – 82 beds – Central West Health Care Institutions Board – Adm., Wayne Vincent

Buchans: A.M. Guy Memorial Health Centre, PO Box 10, Buchans NF A0H 1G0 – 709/672-3326; Fax: 709/672-3390 – 18 beds – Central West Health Care Institutions Board – CEO, W. Vincent

Carbonear: Harbour Lodge Nursing Home, 86 High Rd. South, Carbonear NF A1Y 1A4 – 709/596-7002; Fax: 709/596-1956 – 127 beds – Avalon Health Care Institutions Board – CEO, George Butt

Carbonear: Interfaith Citizens Home, 41 Water St., Carbonear NF A1Y 1B1 – 709/596-5101; Fax: 709/596-0041 – 55 beds – Avalon Health Care Institutions Board – Facility Mgr., Deborah Farrell

Clarke's Beach: Pentecostal Senior Citizen's Home, PO Box 130, Clarke's Beach NF A0A 1W0 – 709/786-2993; Fax: 709/786-2759 – 89 beds – St. John's Nursing Home Board – Facility Mgr., Beverley Bellefleur

Corner Brook: Dr. J.I. O'Connell Centre, PO Box 2005, Corner Brook NF A2H 6J7 – 709/637-5000; Fax: 709/634-2649 – 140 beds – Western Health Care Corporation – CEO, M. Powell

Corner Brook: Inter Faith Home for Senior Citizens, Churchill St., Corner Brook NF A2H 5L8 – 709/639-9247; Fax: 709/639-1126 – 106 beds – Western Health Care Corporation – Adm., Max Powell

Gander: Lakeside Homes Ltd., 95 Airport Blvd., Gander NF A1V 2L7 – 709/256-8850; Fax: 709/256-4259 – 118 beds – Central East Health Care Institutions Board – Adm., Noel Anthony

Grand Bank: Blue Crest Nursing Home, PO Box 160, Grand Bank NF A0E 1W0 – 709/832-1660; Fax: 709/832-2103 – 80 beds – Peninsulas Health Care Corporation – CEO, Joan Penney

Grand Falls-Windsor: Carmelite House Senior Citizens' Home, 21 Carmelite Rd., Grand Falls-Windsor NF A2A 1Y4 – 709/489-2274; Fax: 709/489-5778 – 94 beds – Central West Health Care Institutions Board – Adm., P. Mitchell

Happy Valley-Goose Bay: Harry L. Paddon Memorial Home, PO Box 766, Happy Valley-Goose Bay NF A0P 1E0 – 709/896-2469; Fax: 709/896-5241 – 53 beds – Health Labrador Corporation – Adm., D. Saunders

Lewisporte: North Haven Manor Senior Citizens' Home, PO Box 880, Lewisporte NF A0G 3A0 – 709/535-6726; Fax: 709/535-8383 – 68 beds – Central West Health Care Institutions Board – Exec. Dir., D. Jphnston

Mount Pearl: Masonic Park Senior Citizen's Home, Administration Office, Mount Pearl NF A1N 3K5 – 709/368-6081; Fax: 709/368-4129 – 41 beds – St. John's Nursing Home Board – Adm., Marie Evans

Paradise: Murphy's Shady Rest Lodge Ltd., PO Box 159, Paradise NF A1L 1C5 – 709/895-6786 – 18 beds – Adm., Cavell Murphy

Placentia & Area Health Care Complex, *see* Auxiliary Hospitals/Health Care Centres listings

St. Anthony Interfaith Home, PO Box 69, St. Anthony NF A0K 4S0 – 709/454-3506; Fax: 709/454-4134 – 49 beds – Grenfell Regional Health Services Board – CEO, Rosari Patey

St. John's: Agnes Pratt Home, 239 Topsail Rd., St. John's NF A1E 2B4 – 709/579-0185; Fax: 709/739-5457 – 136 beds – St. John's Nursing Home Board – Adm., Don Green

St. John's: Dr. Leonard A. Miller Centre, 1 - 100 Forest Rd., St. John's NF A1A 1E5 – 709/737-6555; Fax: 709/737-6969 – 153 continuing care beds – Health Care Corporation of St. John's – CEO, L. Jones

St. John's: Glenbrook Lodge, 105 Torbay Rd., St. John's NF A1A 2G9 – 709/726-1969; Fax: 709/726-0610; EMail: glenbrook@thezone.net – 145 beds – St. John's Nursing Home Board – Adm., Aux. Capt. Donald Cummings

St. John's: Hoyles-Escasoni Complex, 10 Escasoni Pl., St. John's NF A1A 3R6 – 709/570-2311; Fax: 709/753-9620 – 400 beds – St. John's Nursing Home Board – AED - Resident Servs., Janice Pike

St. John's: Saint Luke's Home, 24 Deluxe Rd., St. John's NF A1E 5C3 – 709/579-0052; Fax: 709/579-7317 – 127 beds – Adm., Margaret Boone

St. John's: St. Patrick's Mercy Home, 146 Elizabeth Ave., St. John's NF A1B 1S5 – 709/726-2687; Fax: 709/726-0722 – 214 beds – St. John's Nursing Home Board – Adm., Katherine Turner

Springdale: Valley Vista Senior Citizens Home, PO Box 130, Springdale NF A0J 1T0 – 709/673-3936; Fax: 709/673-3186 – Adm., D. Vincent

Stephenville Crossing: Bay St. George Senior Citizens Home, PO Box 250, Stephenville Crossing NF A0N 2C0 – 709/646-5800; Fax: 709/646-2375 – 126 beds – Western Health Care Corporation – A.C.E.D., Long Term Care, Catherine MacDonald

## NURSING STATIONS

Black Tickle Nursing Station, Black Tickle NF A0K 1N0 – 709/471-8832; Fax: 709/471-8893 – Health Care Corporation of St. John's – Adm., Glendene Snook

Cartwright Nursing Station, Cartwright NF A0K 1V0 – 709/938-7285; Fax: 709/938-7286 – Health Care Corporation of St. John's – Adm., Leela Subramanian

Charlottetown Nursing Station, Charlottetown NF A0K 5Y0 – 709/949-0259; Fax: 709/949-0259 – Grenfell Regional Health Services Board

Davis Inlet Nursing Station, Davis Inlet NF A0P 1A0 – 709/478-8842; Fax: 709/478-8817 – Health Labrador Corporation – Adm., Delrose Gordon

Flower's Cove: Strait of Belle Isle Health Centre, Flower's Cove NF A0K 2N0 – 709/456-2401; Fax: 709/456-2562

Harbour Deep Nursing Station, Harbour Deep NF A0K 2Z0 – 709/843-3291; Fax: 709/843-4103 – Grenfell Regional Health Services Board

Hopedale Nursing Station, Hopedale NF A0P 1G0 – 709/933-3857; Fax: 709/933-3744 – Health Labrador Corporation – Adm., Ann McElligott

Makkovik Nursing Station, Makkovik NF A0P 1J0 – 709/923-2229; Fax: 709/923-2428 – Health Labrador Corporation – Jennifer McGrath

Mary's Harbour Nursing Station, Mary's Harbour NF A0K 3P0 – 709/921-6228; Fax: 709/921-6975 – Grenfell Regional Health Services Board

Nain Nursing Station, Nain NF A0P 1L0 – 709/922-2912; Fax: 709/922-2103 – Health Labrador Corporation – Adm., Claudine Foster

Port Hope Simpson Nursing Station, Port Hope Simpson NF A0K 4E0 – 709/960-0271; Fax: 709/960-0392 – Grenfell Regional Health Services Board

Postville Nursing Station, Postville NF A0P 1N0 – 709/479-9851; Fax: 709/479-9715 – Health Labrador Corporation – Lynda Laidler

Rigolet Nursing Station, Rigolet NF A0P 1P0 – 709/947-3386; Fax: 709/947-3401 – Health Labrador Corporation – Helen Michelin

Roddickton: White Bay Central Health Centre, Roddickton NF A0K 4P0 – 709/457-2215; Fax: 709/457-2076 – Grenfell Regional Health Services Board

St. Lewis Nursing Station, St. Lewis NF A0K 4W0 – 709/939-2230; Fax: 709/939-2342 – Grenfell Regional Health Services Board – Nurse-in-charge, Woodrow Burden

### SPECIAL TREATMENT CENTRES

(Includes: Abortion Clinics, Cancer Clinics, Rehabilitation Centres, Treatment Centres)

St. John's: Children's Rehabilitation Centre, Janeway Place, St. John's NF A1A 1R8 – 709/778-4222; Fax: 709/778-4333 – rehabilitation centre – 11 beds – Health Care Corporation of St. John's – Adm., Lynn Crosby, 709/778-4427

St. John's: Dr. H. Bliss Murphy Cancer Centre, Newfoundland Cancer Treatment & Research Foundation, 300 Prince Philip Dr., St. John's NF A1B 3V6 – 709/737-6480; Fax: 709/753-0927 – CEO, Bertha Paulse

## NORTHWEST TERRITORIES

### REGIONAL HEALTH AUTHORITIES

Cambridge Bay: Kitikmeot Health Board, PO Box 200, Cambridge Bay NT X0E 0C0 – 867/983-7328; Fax: 867/983-2253; EMail: experson@assmicro.com – Exec. Dir., Alice Isnor

Hay River Community Health Board, 3 Gaetz Dr., Hay River NT X0E 0R8 – 867/874-6512; Fax: 867/874-3377 – CEO, David Mathews

Inuvik Regional Health Board, PO Box 2, Inuvik NT X0E 0T0 – 867/979-2955; Fax: 867/979-2422 – Responsible for one hospital, 44 beds, 9 community health centres & 2 satelite stations – Acting CEO, Frank Russell

Iqaluit: Baffin Regional Health Board, PO Box 200, Iqaluit NT X0A 0H0 – 867/979-7600; Fax: 867/979-7609 – CEO, Patricia Kermeen

Rankin Inlet: Keewatin Regional Health Board, PO Box 298, Rankin Inlet NT X0C 0G0 – 867/645-2171; Fax: 867/645-2409 – Exec. Dir., James Egan

Yellowknife: Stanton Regional Health Board, PO Box 10, Yellowknife NT X1A 2N1 – 867/669-4102; Fax: 867/669-4128 – CEO, Dennis Cleaver

### GENERAL HOSPITALS

Fort Simpson Hospital, PO Box 246, Fort Simpson NT X0E 0N0 – 867/695-2291; Fax: 867/695-2117 – 14 beds – Adm., Muriel Davison

Hay River: H.H. Williams Memorial Hospital, 3 Gaetz Dr., Hay River NT X0E 0R8 – 867/-874-6512; Fax: 867/974-3449 – 45 beds – Hay River Community Health Board – Exec. Dir., David Matthews

Inuvik Regional Hospital, PO Box 2, Inuvik NT X0E 0T0 – 867/979-2955; Fax: 867/979-2422 – 44 beds – Inuvik Regional Health Board – CEO, vacant

Iqaluit: Baffin Regional Hospital, PO Box 200, Iqaluit NT X0A 0H0 – 867/979-5231; Fax: 867/979-4514 – CEO, Patricia Kermeen

Yellowknife: Stanton Regional Hospital, PO Box 10, Yellowknife NT X1A 2N1 – 867/873-2254; Fax: 867/873-4382 – 102 beds – Stanton Regional Health Board – CEO, Dennis Cleaver

### AUXILIARY HOSPITALS/HEALTH CARE CENTRES

Fort Smith Health Centre, PO Box 1080, Fort Smith NT X0E 0P0 – 867/872-6200; Fax: 867/872-6275 – 25 beds – Acting Exec. Dir., Lorraine Tordiff

### HOME CARE OFFICES/COMMUNITY HEALTH CARE OFFICES

Fort Resolution: Deninu Community Health & Social Services Board, General Delivery, Fort Resolution NT X0E 0M0 – 867/394-4511; Fax: 867/394-3117 – Gail Beaulieu

Fort Simpson: Deh Cho Health & Social Services, PO Box 240, Fort Simpson NT X0E 0N0 – 867/695-3815; Fax: 867/695-2920 – CEO, Kathy Tsetso

Lutselk'e Health and Social Services, PO Box 28, Lutselk'e NT X0E 1A0 – 867/370-3151; Fax: 867/370-3813 – Betty Kendall-Haskins

Rae-Edzo: Dogrib Community Services Board, PO Box 1, Rae-Edzo NT X0E 0Y0 – 867/371-3006; Fax: 867/371-3053 – Gerriann Donahue

Yellowknife Health & Social Services, PO Box 608, Yellowknife NT X1A 2N5 – 867/873-7276; Fax: 867/873-0289 – Acting Exec. Dir., Carolyn Mandrusiak

### NURSING HOMES/LONG TERM CARE FACILITIES

Fort Smith: Northern Lights Special Care Home, PO Box 1319, Fort Smith NT X0E 0P0 – 867/872-5403; Fax: 867/872-5404 – 21 beds – Adm., Cheryl Comin

Hay River: Woodland Manor, 52A Woodland Dr., Hay River NT X0E 0R8 – 867/874-2493; Fax: 867/874-3717 – Adm., Jennifer Seeley

Yellowknife: Aven Seniors' Centre, PO Box 1564, Yellowknife NT X1A 2P2 – 867/920-2443; Fax: 867/873-9915 – 29 beds – Exec. Dir., Catherine Praamsma

## NOVA SCOTIA

### REGIONAL HEALTH AUTHORITIES

Clementsport: Western Regional Health Board, PO Box 74, Clementsport NS B0S 1E0 – 902/638-3452; Fax: 902/638-8170 – CEO, Victor Maddalena

Halifax: Central Regional Health Board, Scotia Sq., #1401, 5251 Duke St., Halifax NS B3J 1P3 – 902/420-8825; Fax: 902/420-8820 – CEO, Barry MacMillan

North Sydney: Eastern Regional Health Board, 65 Memorial Dr., North Sydney NS B2A 3S8 – 902/794-6030; Fax: 902/794-6022 – CEO, John Breen

Truro: Northern Regional Health Board, #6, 44 Inglis Place, Truro NS B2N 4B4 – 902/897-6265; Fax: 902/893-0250 – CEO, Wayne Tucker

### GENERAL HOSPITALS

Advocate Harbour: Bayview Memorial Health Centre, Advocate Harbour NS B0M 1A0 – 902/392-2859; Fax: 902/392-2625 – 10 beds – Site Mgr., Connie Ells

Amherst: Highland View Regional Hospital, 110 East Pleasant St., Amherst NS B4H 1N6 – 902/667-3361; Fax: 902/667-6306 – 83 beds – Exec. Dir., David Turner

Antigonish: St. Martha's Regional Hospital, 25 Bay St., Antigonish NS B2G 2G5 – 902/863-2830; Fax: 902/863-1176 – 84 beds – Eastern Region District Health Board – Facility Mgr., Liz Isenor

Baddeck: Victoria County Memorial Hospital, PO Box 220, Baddeck NS B0E 1B0 – 902/295-2760; Fax: 902/295-3432 – 12 beds – Site Mgr., Ann Robertson

Bridgewater: Health Services Association of the Shouth Shore - South Shore Regional Hospital, 90 Glen Allen Dr., Bridgewater NS B4V 3S6 – 902/543-4603; Fax: 902/543-4719 – 110 beds – General Mgr., Jerry Fraser

Canso: Eastern Memorial Hospital, PO Box 10, Canso NS B0H 1H0 – 902/366-2794; Fax: 902/366-2740 – 11 beds – Site Mgr., Rose Richardson

Cheticamp: Sacred Heart Hospital, Main St., PO Box 129, Cheticamp NS B0E 1H0 – 902/224-4020; Fax: 902/224-2903 – 10 beds – Adm., Yolande LeVert

Cleveland: Strait-Richmond Hospital, RR#1, Cleveland NS B0E 1J0 – 902/625-3100; Fax: 902/625-3804 – Site Mgr., Debbie Cotton

Dartmouth General Hospital, 325 Pleasant St., Dartmouth NS B2Y 4G8 – 902/465-8300; Fax: 902/465-8537 – 126 beds – Exec. Dir., Donald Peters, 902/465-8353

Digby General Hospital, Warwick St., PO Box 820, Digby NS B0V 1A0 – 902/245-2501; Fax: 902/245-5517 – 29 beds – Western Region District Health Board – Clinical Site Mgr., Lynda Casey

Glace Bay Health Care Corp. (General), 300 South St., Glace Bay NS B1A 1W5 – 902/849-5511; Fax: 902/842-9775 – 70 acute care, 46 veterans, 24 long term care beds – CEO, Barry MacMillan

Guysborough Memorial Hospital, PO Box 170, Guysborough NS B0H 1N0 – 902/533-3702; Fax: 902/533-4066 – 10 beds – Eastern Region District Health Board – Facility Mgr., Freda Kennedy

Halifax: IWK-Grace Health Centre for Children, Women & Families, 5980 University Ave., Halifax NS B3H 4N1 – 902/420-6600; Fax: 902/422-3009 – CEO, Richard Nurse

Halifax: Queen Elizabeth II Health Sciences Centre (New Halifax Infirmary), 1796 Summer St., Halifax NS B3H 4A7 – 902/473-2222; Fax: 902/473-3368 – 651 beds – CEO, Donald P. Schurman, 902/428-2240

Halifax: Queen Elizabeth II Health Sciences Centre (Victoria General Hospital), 1278 Tower Rd., Halifax NS B3H 2Y9 – 902/473-2222; Fax: 902/473-7052 – 1,100 beds – CEO, Donald P. Schurman, 902/428-2240

Inverness Consolidated Hospital, PO Box 610, Inverness NS B0E 1N0 – 902/258-2100; Fax: 902/258-3025 – Site Mgr., Claire MacQuarie

Kentville: Valley Regional Hospital, 150 Exhibition St., Kentville NS B4N 5E3 – 902/678-7381; Fax: 902/679-1904 – 145 beds – Western Region District Health Board – General Mgr., Gary Slauenwhite

Liverpool: Queens General Hospital, PO Box 370, Liverpool NS B0T 1K0 – 902/354-3436; Fax: 902/354-2018 – Clinical Site Mgr., Clare MacNeil

Lunenburg: Health Services Association of the Shouth Shore - Fishermen's Memorial Hospital, PO Box 1180, Lunenburg NS B0J 2C0 – 902/634-8801; Fax: 902/634-3668 – 82 beds – General Mgr., Jerry Fraser

Middle Musquodoboit: Musquodoboit Valley Memorial Hospital, Middle Musquodoboit NS B0N 1X0 – 902/384-2220; Fax: 902/384-3310 – 12 beds – Adm., Joan Murray

Middleton: Soldiers' Memorial Hospital, PO Box 730, Middleton NS B0S 1P0 – 902/825-3411; Fax: 902/825-4811 – 86 beds – Western Regional Health Board – Clinical Site Mgr., Jill Ambler

Musquodoboit Harbour: Twin Oaks Memorial Hospital, RR#1, PO Box 309, Musquodoboit Harbour NS B0J 2L0 – 902/889-2200; Fax: 902/889-2470 – 12 beds – Central Regional Health Board – Adm., Janet Crowell

Neil's Harbour: Buchanan Memorial Hospital, Neil's Harbour NS B0C 1N0 – 902/336-2200; Fax: 902/336-2399 – 13 beds – Site Mgr., Pauline Chubbs

New Glasgow: Aberdeen Hospital, 835 East River Rd., New Glasgow NS B2H 3S6 – 902/752-7600; Fax: 902/755-2356; EMail: lib.abh@north.nsis.com – 119 beds – CEO, Patrick Flinn

New Waterford Consolidated Hospital, 716 King St., New Waterford NS B1H 3Z5 – 902/862-6411; Fax: 902/862-8277 – 28 acute care, 21 chronic care beds – CEO, John Malcolm

North Sydney: Northside Harbour View Hospital Corporation, Purves St., PO Box 399, North Sydney NS B2A 3M4 – 902/794-8521; Fax: 902/794-3355 – 136 beds – CEO, John Malcolm

Pictou: Sutherland-Harris Memorial Hospital, 20 Haliburton Rd., PO Box 1059, Pictou NS B0K 1H0 – 902/485-4324; Fax: 902/485-8835 – 32 beds – Adm., Norman Ferguson

Pugwash: North Cumberland Memorial Hospital, 260 Church St., PO Box 242, Pugwash NS B0K 1L0 – 902/243-2521; Fax: 902/243-2941 – Adm., Beryl MacLean

Sheet Harbour: Eastern Shore Memorial Hospital, 22737 Route #7, Sheet Harbour NS B0J 3B0 – 902/885-2554; Fax: 902/885-3200 – 20 beds – Adm., A. Donald Batstone

Shelburne: Roseway Hospital, PO Box 610, Shelburne NS B0T 1W0 – 902/875-3011; Fax: 902/875-1580 – 26 beds – Western Regional Health Board – Clinical Site Mgr., Nanette Holden

Sherbrooke: St. Mary's Memorial Hospital, PO Box 279, Sherbrooke NS B0J 3C0 – 902/522-2882; Fax: 902/522-2556 – 8 beds – Adm., Shirley Bowen

Springhill: All Saint's Hospital, 10 Princess St., PO Box 700, Springhill NS B0M 1X0 – 902/597-3773; Fax: 902/597-3440 – 20 beds – Site Mgr., Fran McMillan

Sydney: Cape Breton Health Care Complex, 1482 George St., Sydney NS B1P 1P3 – 902/567-8000; Fax: 902/567-7878 – 311 beds – CEO, John Malcolm

Tatamagouche: Lillian Fraser Memorial Hospital, 110 Blair Ave., PO Box 40, Tatamagouche NS B0K 1V0 – 902/657-2382; Fax: 902/657-3745 – 15 beds – CEO, Douglas Cunningham

Truro: Colchester Regional Hospital, 207 Willow St., Truro NS B2N 5A1 – 902/893-5557; Fax: 902/893-5559 – 133 beds – CEO, Brenda Payne

Windsor: Hants Community Hospital, PO Box 520, Windsor NS B0N 2T0 – 902/798-8351; Fax: 902/798-6002 – CEO, Donn Peters

Yarmouth Regional Hospital, 60 Vancouver St., Yarmouth NS B5A 2P5 – 902/742-3541; Fax: 902/742-0369 – 135 beds – Western Region District Health Board – General Mgr., Anthony Muise

## AUXILIARY HOSPITALS/HEALTH CARE CENTRES

Annapolis Community Health Centre, 821 St. George St., PO Box 426, Annapolis Royal NS B0S 1A0 – 902/532-2381; Fax: 902/532-2113; EMail: ceo@achc.ns.ca – 7 beds – Western Region District Health Board – Clinical Site Mgr., Fran Duggan

Arichat: St. Anne Community & Nursing Care Centre, PO Box 30, Arichat NS B0E 1A0 – 902/226-2826; Fax: 902/226-1529 – 29 beds – Acting Adm., Judy Breau

Berwick: Western Kings Memorial Health Centre, 121 Orchard St., PO Box 490, Berwick NS B0P 1E0 – 902/538-3111; Fax: 902/538-9590 – Adm., John Dow

Lower Sackville: Cobequid Multi-Service Centre, 70 Memory Lane, Lower Sackville NS B4C 5A1 – 902/865-5750; Fax: 902/865-6814 – Central Regional Health Board – Exec. Dir., Margaret Merlin

Parrsboro: South Cumberland Community Care Centre, PO Box 489, Parrsboro NS B0M 1S0 – 902/254-2540; Fax: 902/254-2504 – 16 beds – Northern Regional Health Board – Site Mgr., Connie Ells

Wolfville: Eastern Kings Community Health Centre, PO Box 1180, Wolfville NS B0P 1X0 – 902/542-2266; Fax: 902/542-4619 – Western Region District Health Board

## HOME CARE OFFICES/COMMUNITY HEALTH CARE OFFICES

Halifax: Central Region Home Care Services, #309, 6061 Young St., Halifax NS B2K 2A3 – 902/424-2688; Fax: 902/424-0765 – Dir., David Chadwick

Lunenburg: Western Region Home Care Services, 14 High St., PO Box 1180, Lunenburg NS B0J 2C0 – 902/634-7500, 7501; Fax: 902/634-7507 – Dir., Alice Middleton

Sydney: Eastern Region Home Care Services, 77 King's Rd., Sydney NS B1S 1A2 – 902/563-3701; Fax: 902/563-5602 – Dir., Claire Nyiti

Truro: Northern Region Home Care Services, PO Box 295, Truro NS B2N 5C1 – 902/893-6277; Fax: 902/893-5839 – Dir., Eleanor MacDougall

## MENTAL HEALTH HOSPITALS & COMMUNITY FACILITIES

Antigonish: St. Martha's Regional Hospital, see General Hospital listings

Bridgewater: Health Services Association of the South Shore-South Shore Regional Hospital, see General Hospital listings

Dartmouth: Nova Scotia Hospital, 300 Pleasant St., PO Box 1004, Dartmouth NS B2Y 3Z9 – 902/464-3111; Fax: 902/464-4825; EMail: nshp.ldmcmast@gov.ns.ca – 166 beds – Exec. Dir., Anne McGuire

Halifax: Queen Elizabeth II Health Sciences Centre (Abbie J. Lane Memorial Bldg.), 5109 Jubilee Rd., Halifax NS B3H 2E2 – Pres. & CEO, Donald P. Schurman

Inverness Consolidated Hospital, see General Hospital listings

Kentville: Valley Regional Hospital, see General Hospital listings

New Glasgow: Aberdeen Hospital, see General Hospital listings

Sydney: Cape Breton Health Centre Complex, see General Hospital listings

Truro: Colchester Regional Hospital, see General Hospitals

Windsor: Hants Community Hospital, see General Hospital listings

Yarmouth Regional Hospital, see General Hospital listings

## NURSING HOMES/LONG TERM CARE FACILITIES

Advocate Harbour: Bayview Memorial Nursing Care Unit, Advocate Harbour NS – 902/392-2859; Fax: 902/392-2625 – Site Mgr., Connie Ells

Amherst: Gables Lodge, c/o Mr. & Mrs. S. Hussain, 260 Church St., Amherst NS B4H 3C9 – 902/667-3501; Fax: 902/667-3533 – 95 beds – Adm., Kathy Maltby

Annapolis Royal Nursing Home, St. George St., RR#2, Annapolis Royal NS B0S 1A0 – 902/532-2240; Fax: 902/532-7151 – Linda Bailey

Annapolis Royal: Northhills Nursing Home Ltd., PO Box 220, Annapolis Royal NS B0S 1A0 – 902/532-5555; Fax: 902/532-7449 – Adm., Frankie Sheehy

Antigonish: R.K. MacDonald Nursing Home, 64 Pleasant St., Antigonish NS B2G 1W7 – 902/863-2578; Fax: 902/863-4437 – 106 beds – Eastern Region District Health Board – Adm., Evelyn Lindsey

Arichat: St. Anne Community & Nursing Care Centre, *see* Auxiliary Hospitals/Health Care Centres listings

Armdale: Glades Lodge, 25 Alton Dr., Armdale NS B3N 1M1 – 902/477-1777; Fax: 902/477-8174 – 123 beds – Adm., Jan White

Baddeck: Alderwood Home for the Aged, PO Box 218, Baddeck NS B0E 1B0 – 902/295-2644; Fax: 902/295-1698 – 70 beds – Adm., Marcella Roberts

Beaverbank: Scotia Nursing Homes Ltd., 125 Knowles Cres., Beaverbank NS B4G 1E7 – 902/865-6364; Fax: 902/865-3582 – 210 beds – Adm., Stephen Pace

Berwick: Grand View Manor, PO Box 309, Berwick NS B0P 1E0 – 902/538-3118; Fax: 902/538-3998 – Adm., Graham Hardy

Bridgetown: Mountain Lea Lodge, RR#1, Church St., Bridgetown NS B0S 1C0 – 902/665-4489; Fax: 902/665-2900 – 1 respite, 112 long term care beds – Adm., Larry Masters

Bridgewater: Hillside Pines, 77 Exhibition Dr., Bridgewater NS B4V 3K6 – 902/543-1525; Fax: 902/543-8083 – 50 beds – Adm., Sheila MacKinnon

Caledonia: North Queens Nursing Home, PO Box 181, Caledonia NS B0T 1B0 – 902/682-2553; Fax: 902/682-2602 – Exec. Dir., Norma Lenco

Canso Seaside Manor, PO Box 70, Canso NS B0H 1H0 – 902/366-3030; Fax: 902/366-3093 – Adm., Darren Bennett

Chester: Shoreham Village, 3777 North St., RR#1, Chester NS B0J 1J0 – 902/275-5631; Fax: 902/275-2586 – 83 beds – Adm., Brian Selig

Cheticamp: Foyer Père Fiset, 754, rue Main, PO Box 219, Cheticamp NS B0E 1H0 – 902/224-2087; Fax: 902/224-1188 – 60 lits – Adm., Betty Ann Aucoin

Dartmouth: Oakwood Terrace, 10 Mount Hope Ave., Dartmouth NS B2Y 4K1 – 902/469-3702; Fax: 902/469-3824 – 111 beds – Adm., Glen Griffin

Digby: Tideview Terrace, PO Box 1120, Digby NS B0V 1A0 – 902/245-4718; Fax: 902/245-6674 – 89 beds – Adm., Gary Burlingham

Eastern Passage: Oceanview Manor, 1909 Caldwell Rd., PO Box 130, Eastern Passage NS B3G 1M4 – 902/465-6020; Fax: 902/465-4929 – 184 beds – Adm., Keith Menzies

Glace Bay Health Care Corp., 197 Main St., Glace Bay NS B1A 4Z8 – 902/849-5531; Fax: 902/849-2287 – Dir., Site Services, Mary MacIsaac

Glace Bay: Seaview Manor, 275 South St., Glace Bay NS B1A 1W6 – 902/849-7300; Fax: 902/849-7401 – 101 beds – Adm., Catherine Power

Glace Bay: Victoria Haven Nursing Home, 429A Third St., Glace Bay NS B1A 4G6 – 902/849-8826 – Adm., Deborah MacLeod

Glenwood: Nakile Home for the Aged, RR#1, Glenwood NS B0W 1W0 – 902/643-2707; Fax: 902/643-2862 – Adm., Bertha Brannen

Guysborough: Milford Haven Corporation, PO Box 300, Guysborough NS B0H 1N0 – 902/533-2828; Fax: 902/533-4066 – 50 beds – Adm., Mary Jurcina-Taylor

Halifax: Armview Estates, 126 Purcell's Cove Rd., Halifax NS B3P 1B5 – 902/477-8051; Fax: 902/477-5726 – 255 beds – Adm., Melanie Ray

Halifax: Colonial Nursing Home, 1019 Lucknow St., Halifax NS B3H 2T2 – 902/420-0697; Fax: 902/492-3936 – Deborah Morgan-Downey

Halifax: Fairview Villa, 245 Main Ave., Halifax NS B3M 1B7 – 902/443-1971; Fax: 902/443-9037 – 207 beds – Central Regional Health Board – Adm., Carol Ann Gallant

Halifax: Melville Lodge, 50 Shoreham Lane, Halifax NS B3P 2R3 – 902/479-1030; Fax: 902/477-1663 – Adm., Dorothy Redmond

Halifax: Northwoodcare Inc., 2615 Northwood Terrace, Halifax NS B3K 3C6 – 902/454-8311; Fax: 902/455-6408 – 596 beds – Adm., Lloyd Brown

Halifax: Saint Vincent Guest Home, 2080 Windsor St., Halifax NS B3K 5B1 – 902/429-0550; Fax: 902/492-3703 – 160 beds – Adm., Kristin Schmitz

Inverness Memorial Nursing Care Unit, PO Box 610, Inverness NS B0E 1N0 – 902/258-2100; Fax: 902/258-3025 – Interim Facility Mgr., Clare MacQuarrie

Inverness: Inverary Manor, Maple St., PO Box 460, Inverness NS B0E 1N0 – 902/258-2581, 2842; Fax: 902/258-3865 – Joan MacLellan

Kentville: Evergreen Home for Special Care, 655 Park St., Kentville NS B4N 3V7 – 902/678-7355; Fax: 902/678-5996 – 120 beds – Western Region District Health Board – Adm., Fred Houghton

Liverpool: Queens Manor, PO Box 1283, Liverpool NS B0T 1K0 – 902/354-3451; Fax: 902/354-5383 – 59 beds – Adm., Norma Lenco

Lockeport: Surf Lodge Nursing Home, 73 Howe St., PO Box 160, Lockeport NS B0T 1L0 – 902/656-2014; Fax: 902/656-2026 – Adm., Margaret Coates

Lunenburg: Harbour View Haven, 25 Blockhouse Hill Rd., PO Box 1480, Lunenburg NS B0J 2C0 – 902/634-8836; Fax: 902/634-8792 – 127 beds – Adm., G.W. Crouse

Mahone Bay: Mahone Nursing Home, PO Box 320, Mahone Bay NS B0J 2E0 – 902/624-8341; Fax: 902/624-6338 – 57 long term care, 4 respite beds – Adm., Anne Kennedy

Meteghan: Villa Acadienne, PO Box 248, Meteghan NS B0W 2K0 – 902/645-2065; Fax: 902/645-3899; EMail: villa.acadienne@marina.istar.ca – 84 beds, 2 respite – Adm., Lucille Maillet

Musquodoboit Harbour: The Birches Twin Oaks Senior Citizens Assocation, RR#2, Halifax County, Musquodoboit Harbour NS B0J 2L0 – 902/889-3474; Fax: 902/889-2271 – 40 beds – Adm., Janet Crowell

Neil's Harbour: Highland Manor, PO Box 48, Stn Cape Breton, Neil's Harbour NS B0C 1N0 – 902/336-2895 – 20 beds – Adm., Donna Rideout

New Germany: Rosedale Home, RR#2, PO Box 8, New Germany NS B0R 1E0 – 902/644-2008; Fax: 902/644-3260 – 20 beds – Adm., Henry Saulnier

New Glasgow: Glen Haven Manor, 739 East River Rd., New Glasgow NS B2H 5E9 – 902/752-2588; Fax: 902/752-0053 – 212 beds – Adm., James Ferguson

New Waterford: Maple Hill Manor, 700 King St., New Waterford NS B1H 3Z5 – 902/862-6495; Fax: 902/862-9294 – 50 beds – Adm., Cathy MacPhee

North Sydney: Northside Community Guest Home, 11 Queen St., PO Box 100, North Sydney NS B2A 1A2 – 902/794-4733; Fax: 902/794-9021 – 90 beds – Adm., Lucy MacEachern

Parrsboro: South Cumberland Community Care Centre, *see* Auxiliary Hospitals/Health Care Centres listings

Pictou: Maritime Odd Fellows Home (IOOF), PO Box 850, Pictou NS B0K 1H0 – 902/485-5492; Fax: 902/485-9233 – 41 beds – Adm., Janet Johnston

Pictou: Shiretown Nursing Home (Edward Mortimer Place), Haliburton Rd., PO Box 250, Pictou NS B0K 1H0 – 902/485-4341; Fax: 902/485-9203 – Adm., Katherine V. Sullivan

Port Hawkesbury Nursing Home, PO Box 2105, Port Hawkesbury NS B0E 2V0 – 902/625-1460; Fax: 902/625-3232 – Adm., Fran Payne

Pugwash: East Cumberland Lodge, PO Box 250, Pugwash NS B0K 1L0 – 902/243-2504; Fax: 902/243-3375 – 65 beds – Adm., Diane Reid

St. Peter's: Richmond Villa, PO Box 250, St. Peter's NS B0E 3B0 – 902/535-3030; Fax: 902/535-2256 – 73 beds – Adm., Isabelle Johnston

Sandy Point: Roseway Manor Inc., PO Box 518, Sandy Point NS B0T 1W0 – 902/875-4707; Fax: 902/875-4105 – 65 beds – Adm., Karl White

Sheet Harbour: Duncan MacMillan Home for the Aged, Sheet Harbour NS B0J 3B0 – 902/885-2545; Fax: 902/885-3289 – 25 beds – Adm., Janet Crowell

Sherbrooke: High Crest Sherbrooke, Sherbrooke NS B0J 3C0 – 902/522-2147; Fax: 902/522-2628 – Adm., Marion Carroll

Springhill: Highcrest Springhill Nursing Home, 7 Sproul St., PO Box 2170, Springhill NS B0M 1X0 – 902/597-2797; Fax: 902/597-8339 – 55 beds – Adm., Mildred Carr-Shrum

Stellarton: Valley View Villa, RR#1, Stellarton NS B0K 1S0 – 902/755-5780; Fax: 902/755-3104 – Adm., David Lank

Sydney Mines: Miner's Memorial Manor, 15 Lorne St., Sydney Mines NS B1V 3B9 – 902/736-1992; Fax: 902/736-0667 – Adm., Harry Blinkhorn

Sydney: Breton Bay Nursing Home, 70 St. Anthony Dr., Sydney NS B1S 2R5 – 902/539-4560; Fax: 902/567-6234 – Adm., Ellen Stoddard

Sydney: Cape Breton Healthcare Complex - Northside Harbourview Nursing Care Unit, 1482 George St., Sydney NS B1P 1P3 – 902/567-8000; Fax: 902/567-7878 – Dir. of Nursing, Frances MacCormack

Sydney: The Cove Guest Home, 320 Alexander St., Sydney NS B1S 2G1 – 902/539-5267; Fax: 902/539-7565 – 108 beds – Adm., Archie MacKeigan

Sydney: MacGillivray Guest Home, 25 Xavier Dr., Sydney NS B1S 2R9 – 902/539-6110; Fax: 902/567-0437 – 74 beds – Adm., Jack Coffey

Tatamagouche: Willow Lodge, Blair Ave., PO Box 249, Tatamagouche NS B0K 1V0 – 902/657-3101; Fax: 902/657-3859 – 51 beds – Adm., Douglas Cunningham

Truro: Glenview Lodge, RR#3, East Prince St., Truro NS B2N 5B2 – 902/895-8715; Fax: 902/897-1903 – Adm., Donna VanKroonenburg

Truro: Hillcrest Manors Ltd., Manor Dr., PO Box 1210, Truro NS B2N 5H1 – 902/895-2891; Fax: 902/893-2361 – Adm., Kim Power

Windsor Elms, 590 King St., Windsor NS B0N 2T0 – 902/798-2251; Fax: 902/798-0914 – 116 beds – Adm., Rev. Ross MacDonald

Windsor: Dykeland Lodge, 124 Cottage St., Windsor NS B0N 2T0 – 902/798-8346; Fax: 902/798-8312 – 110 beds – Adm., W.R. Brooks

Windsor: Hants Community Hospital - Haliburton Place, PO Box 520, Windsor NS B0N 2T0 – 902/798-8351; Fax: 902/798-6002 – Adm., Carol Harvey

Wolfville Nursing Home, RR#2, 346 Main St., Wolfville NS B0P 1X0 – 902/542-2429; Fax: 902/542-2761 – Adm., Deanna MacDonald

Yarmouth: Tidal View Manor, 60 Vancouver St., Yarmouth NS B5A 2P5 – 902/742-7853; Fax: 902/742-0369 – 103 beds – Adm., Sandra Boudreau

Yarmouth: Villa St. Joseph du Lac, RR#1, Lakeside, PO Box 810, Yarmouth NS B5A 4A5 – 902/742-7128; Fax: 902/749-1342 – Adm., Roy Smith

## SPECIAL TREATMENT CENTRES

(Includes: Abortion Clinics, Cancer Clinics, Rehabilitation Centres, Treatment Centres)

Halifax: Nova Scotia Breast Screening Clinic, Halifax Shopping Centre, #103, Tower 1, 7001 Mumfod Rd., Halifax NS B3L 4H6 – 902/496-3956; Fax: 902/496-3959 – Mgr., Marie Peek

Halifax: Nova Scotia Cancer Centre, 5820 University Ave., Halifax NS B3H 1V7 – 902/428-4200; Fax: 902/428-4277 – cancer treatment – Clinic Mgr., Maureen MacIntyre

Halifax: Nova Scotia Hearing & Speech Clinic, Fenwich Place, 5599 Fenwick St., 32nd Fl., Halifax NS B3H 1R2 – 902/423-7354; Fax: 902/423-0981 – Dir., Dr. Brad Stach

Halifax: Queen Elizabeth II Health Sciences Centre (Camp Hill Veterans' Memorial Bldg.), 5955 Jubilee Rd., Halifax NS B3H 2E1 – 175 beds – Pres. & CEO, Donald P. Schurman

Halifax: Queen Elizabeth II Health Sciences Centre (Nova Scotia Rehabilitation Centre), 1341 Summer St., Halifax NS B3H 4K4 – 902/422-1787; Fax: 902/425-6466 – rehabilitation centre – 66 beds – CEO, Donald P. Schurman, 902/428-2240

Waterville: Kings Regional Health & Rehabilitation Centre, PO Box 128, Waterville NS B0P 1V0 – 902/538-3103; Fax: 902/538-7022 – 113 beds – Interim Adm., Eleanor Newton

# ONTARIO

## REGIONAL HEALTH AUTHORITIES

Barrie: Simcoe County District Health Council, #216, Victoria Sq., 11 Victoria St., Barrie ON L4N 6T3 – 705/734-9960; Fax: 705/734-9987; EMail: scdhc@dhc.simcoe.on.ca – Exec. Dir., Floyd Dale

Belleville: Hastings & Prince Edward Counties District Health Council, #101, 375 Dundas St. West, Belleville ON K8P 1B3 – 613/962-4660; Fax: 613/962-5130 – Exec. Dir., Steve Elson

Brampton: Peel District Health Council, #220, Plaza II, 350 Rutherford Rd. South, Brampton ON L6W 4N6 – 905/455-4856; Fax: 905/455-5285 – Exec. Dir., Bob Youtz

Brantford: Brant District Health Council, #304, 233 Colborne St., Brantford ON N3T 2H4 – 519/756-1330; Fax: 519/756-6013 – Exec. Dir., Catherine Knipe

Chatham: Kent County District Health Council, 75 Thames St., Chatham ON N7L 1S4 – 519/351-1162; Fax: 519/351-6583 – Exec. Dir., Ron Shaw

Cornwall: DHC of Eastern Ontario, #301, 132 Second St., Cornwall ON K6H 1Y4 – 613/933-9585; Fax: 613/933-3977; EMail: info@eo-dhc.hip.on.ca – Exec. Dir., Rita Busat

Fonthill: Niagara District Health Council, 1428 Pelham St. South, PO Box 1220, Fonthill ON L0E 1E0 – 905/892-5771; Fax: 905/892-1593 – Exec. Dir., Gary Zalot

Guelph: Wellington-Dufferin District Health Council, Woodlawn Sq., Units 217 & 218, 251 Woodlawn Rd. West, Guelph ON N1H 8J1 – 519/836-7440; Fax: 519/836-7177 – Exec. Dir., James Whaley

Hamilton-Wentworth District Health Council, #301, 10 George St., Hamilton ON L8P 1C8 – 905/570-1441; Fax: 905/570-1202 – Exec. Dir., Susan Goodman

Huntsville: East Muskoka/Parry Sound District Health Council, #202, 36 Chaffey St., Huntsville ON P1H 1J4 – 705/789-4429; Fax: 705/789-6943 – Exec. Dir., Peter Deane

Keewatin: Kenora-Rainy River District Health Council, 104 Government Rd., PO Box 379, Keewatin ON P0K 1C0 – 807/547-2028; Fax: 807/547-2094 – Exec. Dir., Joe Brown

Kingston, Frontenac & Lennox & Addington District Health Council, #400, 471 Counter St., Kingston ON K7M 8S8 – 613/549-5253; Fax: 613/542-9223 – Exec. Dir., Elizabeth McIver

London: Thames Valley District Health Council, The Gordon J. Mogenson Bldg., #105, 100 Collip Circle, London ON N6G 4X8 – 519/858-5015; Fax: 519/858-5016 – Exec. Dir., Paul Huras

Mitchell: Huron-Perth District Health Council, 235 St. George St., Mitchell ON N0K 1N0 – 519/348-4498; Fax: 519/348-4300 – Exec. Dir., Fraser Bell

Newmarket: York Region District Health Council, #300, 1091 Gorham St., Newmarket ON L3Y 7V1 – 905/830-9899; Fax: 905/830-9903; EMail: yorkdhc@istar.ca – Exec. Dir., Graham Constantine

North Bay: Nipissing-Timiskaming District Health Council, 310 Algonquin Ave., North Bay ON P1B 4W2 – 705/494-9126; Fax: 705/494-9127; EMail: ntdhc@onlink.net – Exec. Dir., Shehnaz Alidina

Oakville: Halton District Health Council, #510, 700 Dorval Dr., Oakville ON L6K 3V3 – 905/842-2120; Fax: 905/842-7131; EMail: haltdhcgen1@world-chat.com – Exec. Dir., Linda Rothney

Ottawa-Carleton Regional Health Council, #350, 955 Green Valley Cres., Ottawa ON K2C 3V4 – 613/723-1440; Fax: 613/723-5162 – Exec. Dir., Anna Telner Wex

Owen Sound: Grey-Bruce District Health Council, 733 Ninth Ave. East, Unit 4, Owen Sound ON N4K 3E6 – 519/376-6691; Fax: 519/376-3074; EMail: gbdhc@srhip.on.ca – Exec. Dir., Karen Levenick

Parry Sound: West Muskoka Parry Sound District Health Council, 17 James St., 2nd Fl., Parry Sound ON P2A 1T4 – 705/746-2123; Fax: 705/746-8156 – Exec. Dir., Peter Deane

Pembroke: Renfrew County District Health Council, 12 International Dr., RR#4, Pembroke ON K8A 6W5 – 613/732-2335; Fax: 613/732-8719; EMail: dhc_renfrew@moh.gov.on.ca – Exec. Dir., Lynn Bowering

Peterborough: Haliburton, Kawartha & Pine Ridge District Health Council, #210, 849 Alexander Ct., PO Box 544, Peterborough ON K9J 7H8 – 705/748-2992; Fax: 705/748-9600 – Exec. Dir., Marshall Elliott

Sarnia: Lambton District Health Council, #401, 265 North Front St., Sarnia ON N7T 7X1 – 519/337-5485; Fax: 519/337-9293 – Exec. Dir., Frank Chalmers

Sault Ste. Marie: Algoma District Health Council, #405, 123 March St., Sault Ste. Marie ON P6A 2Z5 – 705/942-0200; Fax: 705/942-7579 – Exec. Dir., Anthony Ubaldi

Smith Falls: Rideau Valley District Health Council, 1 Abel St., PO Box 487, Smith Falls ON K7A 4T4 – 613/283-6980; Fax: 613/283-3177 – Exec. Dir., Peter N.T. Roberts

Sudbury: Manitoulin & Sudbury District Health Council, #300, 336 Pine St., Sudbury ON P3C 1X8 – 705/675-5654; Fax: 705/675-2870; EMail: MSDHC@age.net – Exec. Dir., Terry Tilleczek

Thunder Bay District Health Council, 1093 Barton St., Thunder Bay ON P7B 5N3 – 807/623-6131; Fax: 807/623-0355 – Exec. Dir., Celso Teixeira

Timmins: Cochrane District Health Council, #203, 119 Pine St. South, Timmins ON P4N 2K3 – 705/264-9539; Fax: 705/264-8620 – Exec. Dir., Anne Vincent

Toronto: Metropolitan Toronto District Health Council, #200, 4141 Yonge St., Willowdale ON M2P 2A8 – 416/222-6522; Fax: 416/222-5587 – Exec. Dir., Lorne Zon

Townsend: Haldimand-Norfolk District Health Council, 101 Nanticoke Creek Pkwy., PO Box 5081, Townsend ON N0A 1S0 – 519/587-2231; Fax: 519/587-5112 – Exec. Dir., Sally Campeau

Waterloo Region District Health Council, #218, 75 King St. South, Waterloo ON N2J 1P2 – 519/884-6390; Fax: 519/884-0445 – Exec. Dir., Gavin Grimson

Whitby: Durham Region District Health Council, #218, 1614 Dundas St. East, Whitby ON L1N 8Y8 – 905/433-4262; Fax: 905/433-2307 – Exec. Dir., Lynda Hessey

Windsor: Essex County District Health Council, 4510 Rhodes Dr., Unit 720, Windsor ON N8W 5K5 – 519/944-5888; Fax: 519/944-0619; EMail: lpaolatto@srhip.on.ca – Exec. Dir., Hume Martin

## GENERAL HOSPITALS

Ajax & Pickering General Hospital, 580 Harwood Ave. South, Ajax ON L1S 2J4 – 905/683-2320; Fax: 905/683-2618 – 116 beds – Durham Region District Health Council – Adm., Bruce W. Cliff

Alexandria: Glengarry Memorial Hospital, Hwy. 43, Alexandria ON K0C 1A0 – 613/525-2222; Fax: 613/525-4515 – 48 beds – DHC of Eastern Ontario – Chief Administrative Officer, Kurt Pristanski

Alliston: Stevenson Memorial Hospital, 200 Fletcher Cr., PO Box 4000, Alliston ON L9R 1W7 – 705/435-6281; Fax: 705/435-2327 – 43 beds – Simcoe County District Health Council – Exec. Dir., Edward Takacs

Almonte General Hospital, 75 Spring St., PO Box 940, Almonte ON K0A 1A0 – 613/256-2500; Fax: 613/256-4889 – 52 beds – Rideau Valley District Health Council – Exec. Dir., Ray Timmons

Arnprior & District Memorial Hospital, 350 John St. North, Arnprior ON K7S 2P6 – 613/623-3166; Fax: 613/623-8488 – 54 beds – Renfrew County District Health Council – CEO, Ron Kedrosky

Atikokan General Hospital, 120 Dorothy St., Atikokan ON P0T 1C0 – 807/597-4215; Fax: 807/597-1210 – 15 acute care, 26 chronic care beds – Kenora-Rainy River District Health Council – Exec. Dir., Bruce Villella

Barrie: The Royal Victoria Hospital, 76 Ross St., Barrie ON L4N 1G4 – 705/728-9802; Fax: 705/728-2408 – 297 beds – Simcoe County District Health Council – Pres., E. Long

Barry's Bay: St. Francis Memorial Hospital, Siberia Rd., PO Box 129, Barry's Bay ON K0J 1B0 – 613/756-3044; Fax: 613/756-0106 – 36 beds – Renfrew County District Health Council – Adm., Keray O'Reilly

Belleville General Hospital, 265 Dundas St. East, PO Box 428, Belleville ON K8N 5A9 – 613/969-5511; Fax: 613/968-8234 – 261 beds – Hastings & Prince Edward Counties District Health Council – Pres. & CEO, Brian Steinberg

Blind River: St. Joseph's Health Centre, 525 Causley St., PO Box 970, Blind River ON P0R 1B0 – 705/356-2265; Fax: 705/356-1220 – 36 beds – Algoma District Health Council – CEO, Paul Davies

Bowmanville: Memorial Hospital, 47 Liberty St. South, Bowmanville ON L1C 2N4 – 905/623-3331; Fax: 905/623-0681 – 106 beds – Durham Region District Health Council – Pres., Thomas Schonberg

Bracebridge: South Muskoka Memorial Hospital, 75 Anne St., PO Box 1570, Bracebridge ON P1L 1R6 – 705/645-4404; Fax: 705/645-4594 – 80 beds – East Muskoka Parry Sound District Health Council – CEO, Blaise MacNeil

Brampton: Peel Memorial Hospital, 20 Lynch St., Brampton ON L6W 2Z8 – 905/796-4066; Fax: 905/451-5552 – 418 beds – Peel District Health Council – Pres. & CEO, Bruce Harber

The Brantford General Hospital, 200 Terrace Hill St., Brantford ON N3R 1G9 – 519/752-7871; Fax: 519/752-0098 – 220 beds – Brant District Health Council – Pres., Richard B. Woodcock

Brantford: St. Joseph's Hospital, 99 Wayne Gretzky Pkwy., Brantford ON N3S 6T6 – 519/753-8641; Fax: 519/753-1468 – 101 beds – Brant District Health Council – Exec. Dir., Romeo Cercone

Brockville General Hospital, 75 Emma St., Brockville ON K6V 1S8 – 613/345-5645; Fax: 613/345-2529 – 149 beds – Rideau Valley District Health Council – Exec. Dir., Jim Merkley

Brockville: St. Vincent de Paul Hospital, 42 Garden St., Brockville ON K6V 2C3 – 613/342-4461; Fax: 613/342-54461 – 59 beds – Rideau Valley District Health Council – Exec. Dir., Tom Harrington

Burlington: Joseph Brant Memorial Hospital, 1230 North Shore Blvd., Burlington ON L7R 4C4 – 905/632-3730; Fax: 905/336-6480 – 240 beds – Halton District Health Council – Pres. & CEO, Don Scott

Cambridge Memorial Hospital, 700 Coronation Blvd., Cambridge ON N1R 3G2 – 519/621-2330; Fax: 519/740-4938 – 296 beds – Waterloo Region District Health Council – CEO, Helen Wright

Campbellford Memorial Hospital, 146 Oliver Rd., Campbellford ON K0L 1L0 – 705/653-1140; Fax: 705/653-4371 – 69 beds – Haliburton, Kawartha & Pine Ridge District Health Council – Pres. & CEO, Richard N. Quesnel

Carleton Place & District Memorial Hospital, 211 Lake Ave. East, Carleton Place ON K7C 1J4 – 613/257-2200; Fax: 613/257-8849 – 26 beds – Rideau Valley District Health Council – Exec. Dir., Robert Dahl

Chapleau: Services de santé de Chapleau Health Services - Chapleau General Hospital, Broomhead Rd., PO Box 757, Chapleau ON P0M 1K0 – 705/864-1520; Fax: 705/864-0449 – 30 beds – Manitoulin & Sudbury District Health Council – Interim CEO, Bonnie-Jean Wilson

Chatham-Kent Health Alliance - Public General Campus, 106 Emma St., Chatham ON N7L 1A8 – 519/352-6400; Fax: 519/436-2536 – 156 beds – Kent County District Health Council – Exec. Dir., Bernie Blais

Chatham-Kent Health Alliance - St. Joseph's Campus, 519 King St. West, Chatham ON N7M 1G8 – 519/352-2500; Fax: 519/352-5261 – 76 beds – Kent County District Health Council – Exec. Dir., Bernie Blais

Chesley & District Memorial Hospital, 39 Second St. SE, Chesley ON N0G 1L0 – 519/363-2340; Fax: 519/363-2340 – 20 beds – Grey-Bruce District Health Council – Exec. Dir., Michael Jackson

Clinton Public Hospital, 98 Shipley St., Clinton ON N0M 1L0 – 519/482-3447; Fax: 519/482-5960 – 42 beds – Huron-Perth District Health Council – Exec. Dir., Allan Halls

Cobourg: Northumberland Health Care Corp., 176 Chapel St., PO Box 140, Cobourg ON K9A 4K9 – 905/372-6811; Fax: 905/372-4243 – 118 beds – Haliburton, Kawartha & Pine Ridge District Health Council – Exec. Dir., Roderic Potter

Cochrane: The Lady Minto Hospital at Cochrane, 241 - 8 St., PO Box 4000, Cochrane ON P0L 1C0 – 705/272-7200; Fax: 705/272-5486 – 58 beds – Cochrane District Health Council – Exec. Dir., Daniel O'Mara

Collingwood General & Marine Hospital, 459 Hume St., Collingwood ON L9Y 1W9 – 705/445-2550; Fax: 705/444-2679 – 74 beds – Simcoe County District Health Council – CEO, Paul W. Darby

Cornwall General Hospital, 510 Second St. East, Cornwall ON K6H 1Z6 – 613/932-3300; Fax: 613/936-4605 – 100 beds – DHC of Eastern Ontario – CEO, Murray Halkett

Cornwall: Hôtel-Dieu Hospital, 840 McConnell Ave., Cornwall ON K6H 5S5 – 613/938-4240; Fax: 613/938-4067 – 103 acute care, 80 chronic care beds – DHC of Eastern Ontario – Exec. Dir., John Haslehurst

Deep River & District Hospital, 1 McElligott St., Deep River ON K0J 1P0 – 613/584-3333; Fax: 613/584-4920 – 24 beds – Renfrew County District Health Council – Adm., Jennifer McDougall

Dryden District General Hospital, 58 Goodall St., PO Box 3003, Dryden ON P8N 2Z6 – 807/223-5261; Fax: 807/223-2370 – 67 beds – Kenora-Rainy River District Health Council – CEO, Andrew Skene

Dunnville: Haldimand War Memorial Hospital, 206 John St., Dunnville ON N1A 2P7 – 905/774-7431; Fax: 905/774-8672 – 65 beds – Metropolitan Toronto District Health Council – CEO, P.L. Mailloux

Durham Memorial Hospital, 320 College St., PO Box 638, Durham ON N0G 1R0 – 519/369-2340; Fax: 519/369-6180; EMail: dmhosp@wcl.on.ca – 32 beds – Grey-Bruce District Health Council – CEO, Roxy Edwards

Elliot Lake: St. Joseph's General Hospital, 70 Spine Rd., Elliot Lake ON P5A 1X2 – 705/848-7181; Fax: 705/848-1758 – 81 beds – Algoma District Health Council – CEO, Sr. Sarah Quackenbush

Englehart & District Hospital, 61 - 5 St., PO Box 69, Englehart ON P0J 1H0 – 705/544-2301; Fax: 705/544-8600 – 35 beds – Nipissing-Timiskaming District Health Council – CEO, Tim Gerkre

Espanola General Hospital, 825 McKinnon Dr., Espanola ON P5E 1R4 – 705/869-1420; Fax: 705/869-2608 – 59 beds – Manitoulin & Sudbury District Health Council – Exec. Dir., Paul Davies

Exeter: South Huron Hospital Association, 24 Huron St. West, Exeter ON N0M 1S2 – 519/235-2700; Fax: 519/235-3405 – 38 beds – Huron-Perth District Health Council – CEO, Don Currell

Fergus: Groves Memorial Community Hospital, 235 Union St. East, Fergus ON N1M 1W3 – 519/843-2010; Fax: 519/843-7420 – 72 beds – Exec. Dir., Graham Clark

Fort Erie: Douglas Memorial Hospital, 230 Bertie St., Fort Erie ON L2A 1Z2 – 905/871-6600; Fax: 905/871-7765 – 64 beds – Niagara District Health Council – Adm., John Candeloro

Fort Frances: Riverside Health Care Facilities Inc., 110 Victoria Ave., Fort Frances ON P9A 2B7 – 807/274-

3261; Fax: 807/274-2898; EMail: riverside@fort-frances.lakeheadu.ca – 97 beds – Kenora-Rainy River District Health Council – Exec. Dir., Paul Brown

Georgetown & District Memorial Hospital, One Princess Anne Dr., Georgetown ON L7G 2B8 – 905/873-0111; Fax: 905/873-9653 – 80 beds – Halton District Health Council – CEO, Ron Noble

Geraldton District Hospital, 500 Hogarth Ave., Geraldton ON P0T 1M0 – 807/854-1862; Fax: 807/854-1568 – 60 beds – Thunder Bay District Health Council – Adm., W. Harvey Harris

Goderich: Alexandra Marine & General Hospital, 120 Napier St., Goderich ON N7A 1W5 – 519/524-8323; Fax: 519/524-5579 – 78 beds – Huron-Perth District Health Council – Exec. Dir., K.T. Engelstad

Grimsby: West Lincoln Memorial Hospital, 169 Main St. East, Grimsby ON L3M 1P3 – 905/945-2253; Fax: 905/945-0504 – 78 beds – Niagara District Health Council – Exec. Dir., Gordon D. Gibson

Guelph General Hospital, 115 Delhi St., Guelph ON N1E 4J4 – 519/822-5350; Fax: 519/822-2170; EMail: sbone@sentex.net – 101 beds – Wellington-Dufferin District Health Council – CEO, Richard Ernst

Guelph: St. Joseph's Hospital & Home, 80 Westmount Rd., Guelph ON N1H 5H8 – 519/824-2620; Fax: 519/763-0264 – 85 acute care, 101 continuing care, 124 nursing home beds – Wellington-Dufferin District Health Council – Pres./CEO, Sr. Margaret Myatt

Hagersville: West Haldimand General Hospital, 75 Parkview Rd., Hagersville ON N0A 1H0 – 416/768-3311; Fax: 416/768-1820 – 42 beds – Haldimand-Norfolk District Health Council – Exec. Dir., Edmund Palmeroy

Haliburton Highlands Health Services Corp. - Haliburton Hospital, PO Box 115, Haliburton ON K0M 1S0 – 705/457-1392; Fax: 705/457-2398 – 40 beds – Charge Nurse, Lynne Johnston

Hamilton Health Sciences Corp. - Chedoke-McMaster Site, 1200 Main St. West, PO Box 2000, Hamilton ON L8N 3Z5 – 905/521-2100; Fax: 905/521-5090 – 588 beds – Hamilton-Wentworth District Health Council – Pres. & CEO, Cott Rowand

Hamilton Health Sciences Corp. - Hamilton Civic Hospital, 237 Barton St. East, Hamilton ON L8L 2X2 – 905/527-0271; Fax: 905/546-1861 – 704 beds – Hamilton-Wentworth District Health Council – Pres. & CEO, Dr. Scott Rowand

Hamilton: Hamilton Health Sciences Corp. - Henderson Division, 711 Concession St., Hamilton ON L8V 1C3 – 905/389-4411; Fax: 905/575-2662 – Pres. & CEO, Scott Rowand

Hamilton: St. Joseph's Hospital, 50 Charlton Ave. East, Hamilton ON L8N 4A6 – 905/522-4941; Fax: 905/521-6067 – 484 beds – Hamilton-Wentworth District Health Council – Pres. & CEO, Allan J. Greve

Hamilton: St. Peter's Hospital, 88 Maplewood Ave., Hamilton ON L8M 1W9 – 905/549-6525; Fax: 905/549-2242 – 284 beds – Hamilton-Wentworth District Health Council – CEO, Peter Carruthers

Hanover & District Hospital, 90 - 7 Ave., Hanover ON N4N 1N1 – 519/364-2340; Fax: 519/364-6602 – 80 beds – Grey-Bruce District Health Council – Exec. Dir., Peter Fabricius

Hawkesbury & District General Hospital, 1111 Ghislain St., Hawkesbury ON K6A 3G5 – 613/632-1111; Fax: 613/632-6450 – 68 beds – DHC of Eastern Ontario – Pres. & CEO, Michel Lalonde

Hearst: Hôpital Nôtre-Dame Hospital, 1405 Edward St., PO Box 8000, Hearst ON P0L 1N0 – 705/362-4291; Fax: 705/372-1957 – 60 lits – Cochrane District Health Council – CEO, R.G. Lafleur

Hornepayne Community Hospital, 278 Front St., PO Box 190, Hornepayne ON P0M 1Z0 – 807/868-2442; Fax: 807/868-2697 – 13 beds – Algoma District Health Council – Acting Adm., Lisa Verrino

Huntsville District Memorial Hospital, 354 Muskoka Rd. #3 North, Huntsville ON P1H 1H7 – 705/789-2311; Fax: 705/789-0557 – 75 beds – East Muskoka/Parry Sound District Health Council – CEO, Bruce E. Laughton

Ingersoll: Alexandra Hospital, 29 Noxon St., Ingersoll ON N5C 3V6 – 519/485-1700; Fax: 519/485-7002 – 35 beds – Thames Valley District Health Council – Site Adm., Sandy Whittall

Iroquois Falls: Anson General Hospital, 58 Anson Dr., Iroquois Falls ON P0K 1E0 – 705/258-3911; Fax: 705/258-3221 – 40 beds – Cochrane District Health Council – CEO, Daniel O'Mara

Kapuskasing: Sensenbrenner Hospital, 101 Progress Cres., Kapuskasing ON P5N 3H5 – 705/337-6111; Fax: 705/335-6902 – 78 beds – Cochrane District Health Council – CEO, Allan Yarush

Kemptville District Hospital, Concession Rd., PO Box 2007, Kemptville ON K0G 1J0 – 613/258-3435; Fax: 613/258-4997 – 52 beds – Rideau Valley District Health Council – Exec. Dir., Lynne Budgell

Kenora: Lake of the Woods District Hospital, 21 Sylvan St. West, Kenora ON P9N 3W7 – 807/468-9861; Fax: 807/468-3939 – 109 beds – Kenora-Rainy River District Health Council – Adm., Robert Muir

Kincardine & District General Hospital, 43 Queen St., PO Box 4000, Kincardine ON N2Z 2Z2 – 519/396-3331; Fax: 519/396-3699 – 57 beds – Grey-Bruce District Health Council – Exec. Dir., Mike Jackson

Kingston General Hospital, 76 Stuart St., Kingston ON K7L 2V7 – 613/548-3232; Fax: 613/548-6042 – 393 beds – Kingston, Frontenac & Lennox & Addington District Health Council – Pres. & CEO, Dr. Peter Glynn

Kingston: Hôtel-Dieu Hospital, 166 Brock St., Kingston ON K7L 5G2 – 613/544-3310; Fax: 613/544-7175 – 186 beds – Kingston, Frontenac & Lennox & Addington District Health Council – Exec. Dir., Hugh C. Graham

Kingston: St. Mary's of the Lake Hospital, Providence Continuing Care Centre, 340 Union St. West, PO Box 3600, Kingston ON K7L 5A2 – 613/544-5220; Fax: 613/544-6655; EMail: pcccf@king.igs.net – 195 beds – Kingston, Frontenac & Lennox & Addington District Health Council – Pres. & CEO, Cathy Dunne

Kirkland & District Hospital, 145 Government Rd. East, Kirkland Lake ON P2N 3P4 – 705/567-5251; Fax: 705/568-2102 – 62 beds – Nipissing-Timiskaming District Health Council – Exec. Dir., J. William C. Lewis

Kitchener: Grand River Hospital, Kitchener-Waterloo Health Centre, PO Box 9056, Kitchener ON N2G 1G3 – 519/749-4322; Fax: 519/749-4208 – 705 beds – Waterloo Region District Health Council – Pres. & CEO, Al Collins

Kitchener: St. Mary's General Hospital, 911 Queens Blvd., Kitchener ON N2M 1B2 – 519/744-3311; Fax: 519/749-6426 – 221 beds – Pres. & CEO, Bruce M. Antonello

Leamington District Memorial Hospital, 194 Talbot St. West, Leamington ON N8H 1N9 – 519/322-2501; Fax: 519/322-5584 – Expanding to accommodate 625 beds – 88 beds – Essex County District Health Council – Acting Exec. Dir., Warren Chant

Lindsay: Ross Memorial Hospital, 10 Angeline St. North, Lindsay ON K9V 4M8 – 705/324-6111; Fax: 705/328-2817 – 174 beds – Haliburton, Kawartha & Pine Ridge District Health Council – Pres. & CEO, Anthony Vines

Listowel Memorial Hospital, 255 Elizabeth St. East, Listowel ON N4W 2P5 – 519/291-3120; Fax: 519/291-5440 – 73 beds – Huron-Perth District Health Council – Adm., James Van Camp

Little Current: Manitoulin Health Centre, 11 Meredith St., PO Box 640, Little Current ON P0P 1K0 – 705/368-2300; Fax: 705/368-3603 – 55 beds – Manitoulin & Sudbury District Health Council – Exec. Dir., Bruce Cunningham

London Health Sciences Centre - University Campus, 339 Windermere Rd., London ON N6A 5A5 – 519/663-3300; Fax: 519/663-3876 – Thames Valley District Health Council – Pres. & CEO, Tony Dagnone

London Health Sciences Centre - Victoria Campus - Westminister Site, 800 Commissioners Rd. East, PO Box 5375, London ON N6A 4G5 – 519/685-8500; Fax: 519/685-8127 – 948 beds, 40 bassinets – Thames Valley District Health Council – Pres. & CEO, Dr. Tony Dagnone

London: Parkwood Hospital, 801 Commissioners Rd. East, London ON N6C 5J1 – 519/685-4292; Fax: 519/685-4052 – 432 beds – Thames Valley District Health Council – Pres. & CEO, Michael Boucher

London: St. Joseph's Health Centre, 268 Grosvenor St., London ON N6A 4V2 – 519/646-6000; Fax: 519/646-6054 – To be changed to an ambulatory care, outpatient services, day surgery & low-risk obstetrical services facility by Dec. 31, 1999 – 368 beds – Thames Valley District Health Council – Pres. & CEO, Philip C. Hassen

London: St. Joseph's Health Centre - St. Mary's Hospital, 35 Grosvenor St., London ON N6A 4G5 – 519/646-6000; Fax: 519/646-6054 – 110 beds – Thames Valley District Health Council – Pres. & CEO, Philip C. Hassen

Manitouwadge General Hospital, Manitou Rd., Manitouwadge ON P0T 2C0 – 807/826-3251; Fax: 807/826-4216 – 18 beds – Thunder Bay District Health Council – Adm., Judith C. Harris

Marathon: Wilson Memorial General Hospital, 28 Peninsula Rd., Marathon ON P0T 2E0 – 807/229-1740; Fax: 807/229-1721 – 25 beds – Thunder Bay District Health Council – Exec. Dir., Paul Paradis

Markdale: Centre Grey General Hospital, 55 Isla St., PO Box 406, Markdale ON N0C 1H0 – 519/986-3040; Fax: 519/986-4562 – 38 beds – Grey-Bruce District Health Council – Adm., Michael Mazza

Markham-Stouffville Hospital, 381 Church St., PO Box 1800, Markham ON L3P 7P3 – 905/472-7097; Fax: 905/472-7086 – 195 beds – York Region District Health Council – Pres., Marilyn J. Bruner

Matheson: Bingham Memorial Hospital, PO Box 70, Matheson ON P0K 1N0 – 705/273-2424; Fax: 705/273-2515 – 40 beds – Cochrane District Health Council – Adm., Daniel O'Mara

Mattawa General Hospital, 215 Third St., PO Box 70, Mattawa ON P0H 1V0 – 705/744-5511; Fax: 705/744-0466; EMail: jbmathos@neilnet.com – 19 beds – Nipissing-Timiskaming District Health Council – Exec. Dir., Jerry T. Betik

Meaford General Hospital, 229 Nelson St. West, PO Box 340, Meaford ON N0H 1Y0 – 519/538-1311; Fax: 519/538-5500 – 56 beds – Grey-Bruce District Health Council – Exec. Dir., Charles F. Robinson

Midland: Huronia District Hospital, 1 St. Andrews Dr., PO Box 760, Midland ON L4R 1N6 – 705/526-3751; Fax: 705/526-2007 – 106 beds – Simcoe County District Health Council – Adm., Gordon A. Key

Milton District Hospital, 30 Derry Rd. East, Milton ON L9T 2X5 – 905/878-2383; Fax: 905/878-0498 – 85 beds – Waterloo Region District Health Council – Exec. Dir., Brian D. Brady

Mindemoya: Manitoulin Health Centre - Mindemoya Hospital, Mindemoya ON P0P 1S0 – 705/377-5311; Fax: 705/377-5799 – 14 beds – Patient Care Coord., M. Watson

Minden: Haliburton Highlands Health Services Corp., PO Box 569, Minden ON K0M 2K0 – 705/286-4997; Fax: 705/286-4819; EMail: floucks@halhi.net.on.ca – 10 beds – Haliburton, Kawartha & Pine Ridge District Health Council – Exec. Dir., Foster Loucks

Mississauga Hospital, 100 Queensway West, Mississauga ON L5B 1B8 – 905/848-7100; Fax: 905/848-7139 – 444 beds – Peel District Health Council – Pres., Dennis Egan

Mississauga: The Credit Valley Hospital, 2200 Eglinton Ave. West, Mississauga ON L5M 2N1 – 905/813-2200; Fax: 905/813-4444 – 280 beds – Peel District Health Council – Pres., Dean Sane

Moosonee: James Bay General Hospital, PO Box 370, Moosonee ON P0L 1Y0 – 705/336-2947; Fax: 705/336-2637 – 33 beds – Cochrane District Health Council – Exec. Dir., Brent Woodford

Mount Forest: Louise Marshall Hospital, 630 Dublin St., PO Box 190, Mount Forest ON N0G 2L0 – 519/323-2210; Fax: 519/323-3741 – 37 beds – Wellington-Dufferin District Health Council – Adm., R.G. Emmerson

Napanee: Lennox & Addington County General Hospital, 8 Park Dr., Napanee ON K7R 2Z4 – 613/354-3301; Fax: 613/354-7157 – 42 beds – Kingston, Frontenac & Lennox & Addington District Health Council – Exec. Dir., W.A. Ronald

Nepean: Queensway-Carleton Hospital, 3045 Baseline Rd., Nepean ON K2H 8P4 – 613/721-2000; Fax: 613/721-4770 – 193 beds – Ottawa-Carleton Regional Health Council – Pres. & CEO, Robert Devitt

New Liskeard: Temiskaming Hospital, Shepherdson Rd., PO Box T, New Liskeard ON P0J 1P0 – 705/647-8121; Fax: 705/647-5800 – 99 beds – Nipissing-Timiskaming District Health Council – Exec. Dir., Wayne Coveyduck

Newbury: The Four Counties General Hospital, RR#3, Newbury ON N0L 1Z0 – 519/693-4441; Fax: 519/693-7084 – 31 beds – Thames Valley District Health Council – Exec. Dir., Janak Jass

Newmarket: York County Hospital, 596 Davis Dr., Newmarket ON L3Y 2P9 – 905/853-2209; Fax: 905/853-2220 – 246 beds – York Region District Health Council – Pres., Daniel Carriere

Niagara Falls: Greater Niagara General Hospital, 5546 Portage Rd., PO Box 1018, Niagara Falls ON L2E 6X2 – 905/358-0171; Fax: 905/358-8437 – 250 beds – Niagara District Health Council – Pres. & CEO, John H. Carter

Niagara-on-the-Lake Hospital, 176 Wellington St., PO Box 1270, Niagara-on-the-Lake ON L0S 1J0 – 905/468-4284; Fax: 905/468-7690 – 20 beds – Niagara District Health Council – Chief Adm., Robert Lawler

Nipigon District Memorial Hospital, 125 Hogan Rd., PO Box 37, Nipigon ON P0T 2J0 – 807/887-3026; Fax: 807/887-2800 – 37 beds – Thunder Bay District Health Council – CEO, Donald E. Ross

North Bay General Hospital, 750 Scollard St., North Bay ON P1B 5A4 – 705/474-8600; Fax: 705/495-7960; EMail: mhurst@nbgh.on.ca – 215 beds – Nipissing-Timiskaming District Health Council – Pres., Mark Hurst

North Bay General Hospital - McLaren Site, 720 McLaren St., North Bay ON P1B 3L9 – 705/474-8600; Fax: 705/495-7960 – Pres., Mark Hurst

Oakville-Trafalgar Memorial Hospital, 327 Reynolds St., Oakville ON L6J 3L7 – 905/338-4616; Fax: 905/338-4636 – 274 beds – Halton District Health Council – Pres. & CEO, John Oliver

Orangeville: Dufferin-Caledon Health Care Corporation - Dufferin Area, 32 First St., Orangeville ON L9W 2E1 – 519/941-2410; Fax: 519/942-0482 – 113 active care, 26 chronic care beds – Wellington-Dufferin District Health Council – Exec. Dir., Nancy Ross

Orillia Soldiers' Memorial Hospital, 170 Colborne St. West, Orillia ON L3V 2Z3 – 705/325-2201; Fax: 705/325-7953 – 168 beds – Simcoe County District Health Council – Exec. Dir., Glen H. Penwarden

Oshawa General Hospital, 24 Alma St., Oshawa ON L1G 2B9 – 905/576-8711; Fax: 905/433-4338 – 487 beds – Durham Region District Health Council – Acting Pres. & CEO, Patricia Adolphus

Ottawa Civic Hospital, 1053 Carling Ave., Ottawa ON K1Y 4E9 – 613/761-4000; Fax: 613/761-5393 – 600 beds – Ottawa-Carleton Regional Health Council – Pres., Ambrose Hearn, 613/761-4201

Ottawa General Hospital, 501 Smyth Rd., Ottawa ON K1H 8L6 – 613/737-7777; Fax: 613/737-8934 – 489 beds – Ottawa-Carleton Regional Health Council – Pres., Jacques Labelle, 613/737-8449

Ottawa: Children's Hospital of Eastern Ontario, 401 Smyth Rd., Ottawa ON K1H 8L1 – 613/737-7600; Fax: 613/738-3216 – 150 beds – Ottawa-Carleton Regional Health Council – CEO, Gary Cardiff

Ottawa: Hôpital Montfort, 713, ch Montréal, Ottawa ON K1K 0T2 – 613/746-4621; Fax: 613/748-4947 – To become an ambulatory-care centre with some in-patient programs – 180 beds – Ottawa-Carleton Regional Health Council – Exec. Dir., Gérald Savoie

Ottawa: Riverside Hospital of Ottawa, 1967 Riverside Dr., Ottawa ON K1H 7W9 – 613/738-7100; Fax: 613/738-8522 – Scheduled to be closed by 1999 – 204 beds – Exec. Dir., D. Wayne Fyffe

Ottawa: The Salvation Army Grace Hospital, 1156 Wellington St., Ottawa ON K1Y 2Z4 – 613/728-4611; Fax: 613/724-4628 – specialized hospital; scheduled to be closed by 1999 – 65 beds – Ottawa-Carleton Regional Health Council – Pres., Major Malcolm D. Robinson

Ottawa: Sisters of Charity of Ottawa Hospital - Saint-Vincent Pavilion, 60 Cambridge St. North, Ottawa ON K1R 7A5 – 613/233-4041; Fax: 613/782-2785 – 464 beds – Ottawa-Carleton Regional Health Council – Pres. & CEO, Michel Bilodeau

Ottawa: Sisters of Charity of Ottawa Hospital - Élisabeth Bruyère Pavilion, 43 Bruyère St., Ottawa ON K1N 5C8 – 613/562-0050; Fax: 613/562-6367 – 225 beds – Ottawa-Carleton Regional Health Council – Pres. & CEO, Michel Bilodeau

Owen Sound: The Grey Bruce Regional Health Centre, 1400 - 8th St. East, PO Box 1400, Owen Sound ON N4K 6M9 – 519/376-2121; Fax: 519/376-9760 – 272 beds – Grey-Bruce District Health Council – Pres. & CEO, Garth Pierce

Palmerston & District Hospital, 500 White's Rd., PO Box 130, Palmerston ON N0G 2P0 – 519/343-2022; Fax: 519/343-3821 – 35 beds – Adm. & CEO, R.G. Emmerson

Paris: The Willett Hospital, 238 Grand River St. North, Paris ON N3L 2N7 – 519/442-2251; Fax: 519/442-1641 – 62 beds – Brant District Health Council – Exec. Dir., Mary Sylver

Parry Sound: West Parry Sound Health Centre, 10 James St., Parry Sound ON P2A 1T3 – 705/746-9321; Fax: 705/746-7364 – 66 acute care, 64 chronic care beds – West Muskoka Parry Sound District Health Council – CEO, Norman Maciver

Pembroke General Hospital, 705 MacKay St., Pembroke ON K8A 1G8 – 613/732-2811; Fax: 613/732-9986 – 104 beds – Renfrew County District Health Council – Exec. Dir., Sheila Schultz

Penetanguishene General Hospital, 25 Jeffery St., Penetanguishene ON L9M 1K6 – 705/549-7442; Fax: 705/549-4031 – 52 beds – Simcoe County District Health Council – Exec. Dir., Doris Shirriff

Peterborough Civic Hospital, 1 Hospital Dr., Peterborough ON K9J 7C6 – 705/743-2121; Fax: 705/876-5120; EMail: info@pch.org – 303 beds – Haliburton, Kawartha & Pine Ridge District Health Council – Acting Exec. Dir., Dean McDonald

Peterborough: St. Joseph's General Hospital, 384 Rogers St., Peterborough ON K9H 7B6 – 705/743-4251; Fax: 705/740-8345 – 162 beds – Haliburton, Kawartha & Pine Ridge District Health Council – Exec. Dir., Mary Ann Shill

Petrolia: Charlotte Eleanor Englehart Hospital, 447 Greenfield St., Petrolia ON N0N 1R0 – 519/882-1170; Fax: 519/882-3711 – 72 beds – Lambton District Health Council – CEO, Wayne Woods

Picton: Prince Edward County Memorial Hospital, Main Street East, PO Box 1900, Picton ON K0K 2T0 – 613/476-2181; Fax: 613/476-8600; EMail: mboultbee@pecmh.net – 46 beds – Hastings & Prince Edward Counties District Health Council – Exec. Dir., D. Monty Boultbee

Port Colborne General Hospital, 260 Sugarloaf St., Port Colborne ON L3K 2N7 – 905/834-4501; Fax: 905/834-0404 – 115 beds – Niagara District Health Council – Exec. Dir., Barry Lockhart

Port Hope: Northumberland Health Care Centre - Port Hope & District Hospital, 53 Wellington St., Port Hope ON L1A 2M6 – 905/885-6371; Fax: 905/885-1948 – Adm., Enos Stewart

Port Perry: North Durham Health Services, 451 Paxton St., Port Perry ON L9L 1A8 – 905/985-7321; Fax: 905/985-0739 – 42 beds – Durham Region District Health Council – CEO, Guy Kirvan

Rainy River: Riverside Health Care Facilities - Rainy River Hospital, Rainy River ON P0W 1L0 – 807/852-3232; Fax: 807/852-3565 – 15 beds – Kenora-Rainy River District Health Council – Exec. Dir., Paul Brown

Red Lake Margaret Cochenour Memorial Hospital, PO Box 5005, Red Lake ON P0V 2M0 – 807/727-2231; Fax: 807/727-2923 – 34 beds – Kenora-Rainy River District Health Council – Adm., Hal Fjeldsted

Renfrew Victoria Hospital, 499 Raglan St. North, Renfrew ON K7V 1P6 – 613/432-4851; Fax: 613/432-8649 – 65 beds – Renfrew County District Health Council – Exec. Dir., Randy Penney

Richards Landing: Sault Area Hospitals - Matthews Memorial Hospital, PO Box 188, Richards Landing ON P0R 1J0 – 705/246-2570; Fax: 705/246-2569 – 9 beds – Adm., Ruth Clavet

Richmond Hill: York Central Hospital, 10 Trench St., Richmond Hill ON L4C 4Z3 – 905/883-2020; Fax: 905/883-2455 – 247 beds – York Region District Health Council – Pres. & CEO, Frank J. Lussing

St Catharines General Hospital, 142 Queenston St., St Catharines ON L2R 7C6 – 905/684-7271; Fax: 905/684-1468 – 303 beds – Niagara District Health Council – Pres. & CEO, T. Robert M. Lawler

St Catharines: Hôtel-Dieu Hospital, 155 Ontario St., St Catharines ON L2R 5K3 – 905/682-6411; Fax: 905/682-0663 – 124 beds – Niagara District Health Council – Exec. Dir., Frank Vetrano

St Catharines: The Shaver Hospital, 541 Glenridge Ave., PO Box 158, St Catharines ON L2R 6S5 – 905/685-1381; Fax: 905/687-4871 – 124 beds – Niagara District Health Council – Exec. Dir., K.S. Johnston

St. Marys Memorial Hospital, 267 Queen St. West, PO Box 940, St. Marys ON N4X 1B6 – 519/284-1332, ext.305; Fax: 519/284-4631; EMail: smmh@mgl.ca – 27 beds – Huron-Perth District Health Council – CEO, Terry Fadelle

St. Thomas Elgin General Hospital, 189 Elm St., PO Box 2007, St. Thomas ON N5P 3W2 – 519/631-2020; Fax: 519/631-1825 – 288 beds – Huron-Perth District Health Council – Pres. & CEO, Terry J. Kondrat

Sarnia General Hospital, 220 North Mitton St., Sarnia ON N7T 6H6 – 519/464-4500; Fax: 519/464-4501 – 166 beds – Lambton District Health Council – CEO, Michel Gagné

Sarnia: St. Joseph's Health Centre of Sarnia, 89 Norman St., Sarnia ON N7T 6S3 – 519/464-4466; Fax: 519/336-8780 – 260 beds – Lambton District Health Council – Exec. Dir., Donald McDermott

Sault Ste Marie: Sault Area Hospitals, 969 Queen St. East, Sault Ste Marie ON P6A 2C4 – 705/759-3601; Fax: 705/759-3640 – 393 beds – Algoma District Health Council – Pres. & CEO, Manu Malkani

Seaforth Community Hospital, 24 Centennial Dr., PO Box 99, Seaforth ON N0K 1W0 – 519/527-1650; Fax: 519/527-2665 – 41 beds – Huron-Perth District Health Council – CEO, Bill Thibert

Shelburne: Dufferin-Caledon Health Care - Shelburne District, PO Box 190, Shelburne ON L0N 1S2 – 519/925-3340; Fax: 519/925-2130 – Wellington-Dufferin District Health Council – Exec. Dir., Nancy Ross

Simcoe: Norfolk General Hospital, 365 West St., Simcoe ON N3Y 1T7 – 519/426-0750; Fax: 519/426-

8542 – 131 beds (46 chronic care beds) – Haldimand-Norfolk District Health Council – Exec. Dir., Harold Shantz

Sioux Lookout District Health Centre, Fifth St. South, PO Box 909, Sioux Lookout ON P8T 1B4 – 807/737-3700; Fax: 807/737-3454 – 49 beds – Kenora-Rainy River District Health Council – Exec. Dir., Mark Balcaen

Smiths Falls: The Perth & Smiths Falls District Hospital, 60 Cornellia St. West, Smiths Falls ON K7A 2H9 – 613/283-2330; Fax: 613/283-8990 – 111 beds – Renfrew County District Health Council – CEO, Caroline Manley

Smooth Rock Falls Hospital, 107 Kelly Rock, PO Box 219, Smooth Rock Falls ON P0L 2B0 – 705/338-2781; Fax: 705/338-4410 – 32 beds – Cochrane District Health Council – Exec. Dir., Thomas H. Boyd

Southampton: Saugeen Memorial Hospital, 340 High St., PO Box 310, Southampton ON N0H 2L0 – 519/797-3230; Fax: 519/797-2442 – 39 beds – Grey-Bruce District Health Council – Adm., Carl Crymble

Stratford General Hospital, 46 General Hospital Dr., Stratford ON N5A 2Y6 – 519/272-8202; Fax: 519/271-7173 – 169 beds – Huron-Perth District Health Council – CEO, Bernard Schmidt

Strathroy Middlesex General Hospital, 395 Carrie St., Strathroy ON N7G 3C9 – 519/245-1550; Fax: 519/245-5438 – 97 beds – Thames Valley District Health Council – Exec. Dir., Thomas M. Enright

Sturgeon Falls: The West Nipissing General Hospital, 111 Coursol Rd., Sturgeon Falls ON P0H 2G0 – 705/753-3110; Fax: 705/753-0210 – 66 beds – Nipissing-Timiskaming District Health Council – Exec. Dir., Yves Campeau

Sudbury General Hospital of the Immaculate Heart of Mary, 700 Paris St., Sudbury ON P3B 3B5 – 705/674-3181; Fax: 705/675-4769 – 230 beds – Manitoulin & Sudbury District Health Council – Exec. Dir., Carl Roy

Sudbury Memorial Hospital, 865 Regent St. South, Sudbury ON P3E 3Y9 – 705/671-1000; Fax: 705/671-5656 – 189 beds – Manitoulin & Sudbury District Health Council – Exec. Dir., Esko Vainio

Sudbury: Laurentian Hospital, 41 Ramsey Lake Rd., Sudbury ON P3E 5J1 – 705/522-2200; Fax: 705/523-7041; EMail: lhlib@vianet.on.ca – 308 beds – Manitoulin & Sudbury District Health Council – CEO, Janice Skot

Terrace Bay: The McCausland Hospital, 2 Cartier Dr., Terrace Bay ON P0T 2W0 – 807/825-3273; Fax: 807/825-9623 – 23 beds – Thunder Bay District Health Council – CEO, C.M. Fewer

Thunder Bay Regional Hospital - South Site (Mckellar Site), 325 South Archibald St., Thunder Bay "F" ON P7E 1G6 – 807/343-7123; Fax: 807/343-7165 – 267 beds – Thunder Bay District Health Council – Interim Pres. & CEO, Scott Potts

Thunder Bay Regional Hopsital - North Site (Port Arthur), 460 North Court St., Thunder Bay "P" ON P7A 4X6 – 807/343-6622; Fax: 807/345-9975 – 176 beds – Thunder Bay District Health Council – Interim Pres. & CEO, Scott Potts

Thunder Bay: Hogarth-Westmount Hospital, 300 North Lillie St., Thunder Bay ON P7C 4Y7 – 807/625-1110; Fax: 807/625-1155 – 198 beds – Thunder Bay District Health Council – CEO, Carl White

Thunder Bay: St. Joseph's Care Group, 35 North Algoma St., PO Box 3251, Thunder Bay ON P7B 5G7 – 807/343-2431; Fax: 807/345-4994 – 148 beds – Thunder Bay District Health Council – Exec. Dir., Carl White

Tillsonburg District Memorial Hospital, 167 Rolph St., Tillsonburg ON N4G 3Y9 – 519/842-3611; Fax: 519/842-6733; EMail: tdmh@oxford.net – 79 beds – Thames Valley District Health Council – Pres., James Spencer

Timmins & District Hospital, 700 Ross Ave. East, Timmins ON P4N 8P2 – 705/267-2131; Fax: 705/267-6311 – 190 beds – Cochrane District Health Council – Exec. Dir., Irene Krys

Toronto East General & Orthopaedic Hospital, 825 Coxwell Ave., Toronto ON M4C 3E7 – 416/469-6005; Fax: 416/469-6106; EMail: teg@library.utoronto.ca – 387 beds – Metropolitan Toronto District Health Council – Pres., Gail Paech

The Toronto Hospital Corporation - Toronto General & Toronto Western Divisions, 585 University Ave., Bell Wing #658, Toronto ON M5G 2C4 – 416/340-3300; Fax: 416/340-3179 – 1,093 beds – Metropolitan Toronto District Health Council – Pres. & CEO, Alan R. Hudson

Toronto: Baycrest Centre for Geriatric Care, 3560 Bathurst St., Toronto ON M6A 2E1 – 416/785-2500; Fax: 416/785-2464 – 372 beds – Metropolitan Toronto District Health Council – Pres. & CEO, Stephen W. Herbert

Toronto: Bloorview Macmillan Health Centre - Bloorview Site, 25 Buchan Court, Willowdale ON M2J 4S9 – 416/494-2222; Fax: 416/494-9985 – 87 beds – Metropolitan Toronto District Health Council – COO, Sheila Jarvis

Toronto: Centenary Health Centre, 2867 Ellesmere Rd., Scarborough ON M1E 4B9 – 416/284-8131; Fax: 416/281-7323 – 437 beds – Metropolitan Toronto District Health Council – Pres., Allan Whiting

Toronto: The Doctors' Hospital, 45 Brunswick Ave., Toronto ON M5S 2M1 – 416/923-5411; Fax: 416/923-5445 – Scheduled to close by 1998; programs transferred to The Toronto Hospital, Western Division – 77 beds – Metropolitan Toronto District Health Council – Pres., R.J. Brian McFarlane

Toronto: The Etobicoke General Hospital, 101 Humber College Blvd., Etobicoke ON M9V 1R8 – 416/747-3466; Fax: 416/747-8608; EMail: egh-comrel@naccess.com – 241 beds – Metropolitan Toronto District Health Council – Pres. & CEO, Leo Steven

Toronto: The Hospital for Sick Children, 555 University Ave., Toronto ON M5G 1X8 – 416/813-5707; Fax: 416/813-5393 – 421 beds – Metropolitan Toronto District Health Council – Pres., Michael J. Strofolino

Toronto: Humber River Regional Hospital, 2111 Finch Ave. West, Downsview ON M3N 1N1 – 416/747-3821; Fax: 416/747-3882 – 218 beds – Metropolitan Toronto District Health Council – CEO, Darlene Barnes

Toronto: Humber River Regional Hospital - Church St. Site, 200 Church St., Weston ON M9N 1N8 – 416/249-8111; Fax: 416/243-4511 – 208 beds – Metropolitan Toronto District Health Council – Pres. & CEO, Scott Dudgeon

Toronto: Lyndhurst Hospital, 520 Sutherland Dr., Toronto ON M4G 3V9 – 416/422-5551; Fax: 416/422-5216 – 79 beds – Metropolitan Toronto District Health Council – Pres. & CEO, Randy F. Swan

Toronto: Mount Sinai Hospital, 600 University Ave., Toronto ON M5G 1X5 – 416/596-4200; Fax: 416/586-8787 – 392 beds – Metropolitan Toronto District Health Council – Pres. & CEO, Theodore Freedman

Toronto: North York Branson Hospital, 555 Finch Ave. West, Willowdale ON M2R 1N5 – 416/635-2563; Fax: 416/635-2537 – Scheduled to close by 1999; may become an ambulatory care facility – 258 beds – Metropolitan Toronto District Health Council – Pres., J.A. Gallop

Toronto: North York General Hospital, 4001 Leslie St., Willowdale ON M2K 1E1 – 416/756-6000; Fax: 416/756-6384 – 345 beds – Metropolitan Toronto District Health Council – Pres., D. Murray MacKenzie

Toronto: Northwestern General Hospital, 2175 Keele St., Toronto ON M6M 3Z4 – 416/243-4555 – Scheduled to close by end of 1999, programs being going to Humber River Regional Hospital sites – 186 beds – Metropolitan Toronto District Health Council – Pres., Brent Chambers

Toronto: Queensway General Hospital, 150 Sherway Dr., Etobicoke ON M9C 1A5 – 416/253-2935; Fax: 416/253-2505 – 200 beds – Metropolitan Toronto District Health Council – Pres., Kenneth W. White

Toronto: The Runnymede Chronic Care Hospital, 274 St. Johns Rd., Toronto ON M6P 1V5 – 416/762-7316; Fax: 416/762-3836 – Scheduled to close by 1999 – 114 beds – Metropolitan Toronto District Health Council – Pres., Normand A. Allaire

Toronto: St. Joseph's Health Centre, 30 The Queensway, Toronto ON M6R 1B5 – 416/530-6008; Fax: 416/530-6835 – 439 beds – Metropolitan Toronto District Health Council – Pres. & CEO, Marilyn Bruner

Toronto: St. Michael's Hospital, 30 Bond St., Toronto ON M5B 1W8 – 416/864-5617; Fax: 416/864-5669 – 377 beds – Metropolitan Toronto District Health Council – Pres. & CEO, Jeffrey Lozon

Toronto: The Salvation Army Scarborough Grace General Hospital, 3030 Birchmount Rd., Scarborough ON M1W 3W3 – 416/495-2400; Fax: 416/495-2432 – 255 beds – Metropolitan Toronto District Health Council – Pres. & CEO, Lt.-Col. Irene Stickland

Toronto: The Salvation Army Toronto Grace General Hospital, 650 Church St., Toronto ON M4Y 2G5 – 416/925-2251; Fax: 416/925-6360 – Scheduled to close by 1999 – 119 beds – Metropolitan Toronto District Health Council – Pres., Capt. Dennis Brown

Toronto: Scarborough General Hospital, 3050 Lawrence Ave. East, Scarborough ON M1P 2V5 – 416/438-2911; Fax: 416/431-8204; EMail: rbodrug@netrover.com – 437 beds – Metropolitan Toronto District Health Council – Pres., Ronald Bodrug

Toronto: Sunnybrook Health Science Centre, 2075 Bayview Ave., North York ON M4N 3M5 – 416/480-4111; Fax: 416/480-6033; EMail: sunnybrook.utoronto.ca – 1,000 beds – Pres. & CEO, Tom Closson

Toronto: The Wellesley Central Hospital - Sherbourne Site, 333 Sherbourne St., Toronto ON M5A 2S5 – 416/969-4111; Fax: 416/969-4183 – Scheduled to change to an ambulatory care facility by 1999 – 16 beds – Metropolitan Toronto District Health Council – Exec. Dir., William Louth

Toronto: The Wellesley Central Hospital - Wellesley Site, 160 Wellesley St. East, Toronto ON M4Y 1J3 – 416/926-7002; Fax: 416/926-4908 – Scheduled to close by 1999; programs to be transferred to St. Michael's & Sunnybrook – 299 beds – Metropolitan Toronto District Health Council – Acting Pres. & CEO, Dr. Sandra Jelenich

Toronto: Women's College Hospital, 76 Grenville St., Toronto ON M5S 1B2 – 416/323-7706; Fax: 416/323-7311 – Scheduled to close by 1999; programs to be transferred to Sunnybrook Health Sciences Centre with ambulatory care women's health programs being provided at a downtown facility – 226 beds – Metropolitan Toronto District Health Council – Acting CEO, Patricia Campbell

Trenton Memorial Hospital, 242 King St., Trenton ON K8V 5S6 – 613/392-2541; Fax: 613/392-3749 – 84 beds – Hastings & Prince Edward Counties District Health Council – Pres. & CEO, Peter O'Brien

Uxbridge: North Durham Health Services, 4 Campbell Dr., PO Box 5003, Uxbridge ON L9P 1S4 – 905/649-2223; Fax: 905/852-7844 – Durham Region District Health Council – CEO, Guy Kirvan

Walkerton: County of Bruce General Hospital, 21 McGivern St., Walkerton ON N0G 2V0 – 519/881-1220; Fax: 519/881-2848 – 45 beds – Grey-Bruce District Health Council – Exec. Dir., Michael Jackson

Wallaceburg: Sydenham District Hospital, 325 Margaret Ave., Wallaceburg ON N8A 2A7 – 519/627-1461; Fax: 519/627-0898 – 45 beds – Kent County District Health Council – Exec. Dir., Lou Emery

Wawa: North Algoma Health Organization - The Lady Dunn General Hospital, Government Rd., PO Box 179, Wawa ON P0S 1K0 – 705/856-2335; Fax: 705/

856-7533 – 31 beds – Algoma District Health Council – CEO, Frank Buerkle

Welland County General Hospital, 65 Third St., Welland ON L3B 4W6 – 905/732-6111; Fax: 905/732-2628 – 398 beds – CEO & Pres., Timothy Wright

The Whitby General Hospital, 300 Gordon St., Whitby ON L1N 5T2 – 905/668-6831; Fax: 905/430-3421 – 81 beds – Durham Region District Health Council – CEO, Elizabeth Woodbury

Wiarton: Bruce Peninsula Health Services, 369 Mary St., PO Box 250, Wiarton ON N0H 2T0 – 519/534-1260; Fax: 519/534-4450 – 26 beds – Grey-Bruce District Health Council – Exec. Dir., Gwen Morris

Winchester District Memorial Hospital, 566 Louise St., Winchester ON K0C 2K0 – 613/774-2420; Fax: 613/774-0453 – 84 beds – DHC of Eastern Ontario – Pres. & CEO, vacant

The Windsor Regional Hospital - Western Campus, 1453 Prince Rd., Windsor ON N9C 3Z4 – 519/257-5100; Fax: 519/257-5244 – 483 beds – Essex County District Health Council – Pres./CEO, Lloyd W. Preston

The Windsor Regional Hospital - Metropolitan Campus, 1995 Lens Ave., Windsor ON N8W 1L9 – 519/254-5577, ext.627; Fax: 519/254-3150 – 627 beds – Essex County District Health Council – Pres. & CEO, Lloyd W. Preston

Windsor: Hôtel Dieu Grace Hospital, 1030 Ouellette Ave., Windsor ON N9A 1E1 – 519/973-4430; Fax: 519/973-0803 – 589 beds – Essex County District Health Council – Exec. Dir., Frank Bagatto

Wingham & District Hospital, 270 Carling Terrace, Wingham ON N0G 2W0 – 519/357-3210; Fax: 519/357-2931 – 86 beds – Huron-Perth District Health Council – Exec. Dir., Lloyd Koch

Woodstock General Hospital, 270 Riddell St., Woodstock ON N4S 6N6 – 519/421-4244; Fax: 519/537-8369 – 100 beds – Thames Valley District Health Council – Pres. & CEO, Natasa Veljovic

## AUXILIARY HOSPITALS/HEALTH CARE CENTRES

Emo Health Centre, PO Box 390, Emo ON P0W 1E0 – 807/482-2881; Fax: 807/482-2493 – 23 beds – Kenora-Rainy River District Health Council – Adm., Peggy Mason

Kitchener: Grand River Hospital Corp. - Freeport Health Centre, 3570 King St. East, Kitchener ON N2A 2W1 – 519/893-2710; Fax: 519/893-8342 – Pres. & CEO, Al Collins

Sault Ste. Marie & District Group Health Association, 240 McNabb St., Sault Ste. Marie ON P6B 1Y5 – 705/759-1234; Fax: 705/759-5528; Tollfree: 1-800-461-2407; EMail: group.health.centre@sympatico.ca – Multi-specialty, ambulatory care facility with diagnostic services – Pres. & CEO, John Harwood

## FEDERAL HOSPITALS

Moose Factory General Hospital, PO Box 34, Moose Factory ON P0L 1W0 – 705/658-4544; Fax: 705/658-4452 – 58 beds – Adm., Meryl Huff

Ottawa: National Defence Medical Centre, 1745 Alta Vista Dr., Ottawa ON K1A 0K6 – 613/945-6600; Fax: 613/998-8093 – Commandant, Capt. R. Climie

Ottawa: Rideau Veterans Home, 363 Smyth Rd., Ottawa ON K1A 5A1 – 613/998-8198 – Adm., R. Giroux

Sioux Lookout Zone Hospital, 7th Ave. North, PO Box 1500, Sioux Lookout ON P8T 1C2 – 807/737-3030; Fax: 807/737-1724 – 37 beds – Adm., Marjorie Y. Johnson

## HOME CARE OFFICES/COMMUNITY HEALTH CARE OFFICES

Barrie: Community Care Access Centre - Simcoe County, 15 Sperling Dr., Barrie ON L4M 6K9 – 705/721-7444; Fax: 705/722-5237; Tollfree: 1-888-721-2222 – CEO, Robert Morton

Belleville: Hastings & Prince Edward Counties Home Care Program, c/o Belleville General Hospital, 265 Dundas St. East, PO Box 428, Belleville ON K8N 5A9 – 613/966-3530, 969-7400, ext.2206; Fax: 613/969-0996 – Dir., Elizabeth Temple

Brantford: Brant Community Care Access Centre, 274 Colborne St., Brantford ON N3T 2H5 – 519/759-7752; Fax: 519/759-7130; EMail: branthcp@world-chat.com – Exec. Dir., Pat Davies, 519/759-7040, ext.223

Brockville: Leeds, Grenville & Lanark Home Care Program, c/o Leeds, Grenville & Lanark District Health Unit, 458 Laurier Blvd., Brockville ON K6V 7A3 – 613/345-0060; Fax: 613/345-3294; Tollfree: 1-800-267-4403 – Dir., Judy Killoran

Burlington: Halton Region Home Care Program, 460 Brant St., Burlington ON L7R 4B6 – 905/639-5228; Fax: 905/639-5320 – Dir., Sandra Shadwick

Chatham: Kent Chatham Home Care Program, 220 Riverview Dr., PO Box 306, Chatham ON N7M 5K4 – 519/351-9780; Fax: 519/352-1373, 351-5842 – Dir., E. Merilyn Allison

Clinton: Huron County LTC Division/Home Care Program, 80 Mary St., PO Box 458, Clinton ON N0M 1L0 – 519/482-3411; Fax: 519/482-7231 – Dir., Karen Lehnen

Cornwall: Community Care Access Centre for the Eastern Counties, 1000 Pitt St., Cornwall ON K6J 5T1 – 613/936-1171; Fax: 613/933-9916 – CEO, Jocelyne Contant

Gloucester: Ottawa-Carleton Region Home Care Program, 1223 Michael St. North, Gloucester ON K1J 7T2 – 613/745-5525; Fax: 613/745-6984 – Dir., Catherine Danbrook

Guelph: Community Care Access Centre of Wellington-Dufferin - Placement services office, 176 Speedvale Ave., Guelph ON N1H 1C3 – 519/824-5021; Fax: 519/824-3327 – Exec. Dir., Ross Kirkconnell

Guelph: Community Care Access Centre of Wellington-Dufferin, #205, 2 Quebec St., Guelph ON N1H 2T3 – 519/823-2550; Fax: 519/823-8682 – Exec. Dir., Ross Kirkconnell

Hamilton-Wentworth Home Care Program, 414 Victoria Ave. North, Hamilton ON L8L 5G8 – 905/523-8600; Fax: 905/528-1883 – Dir., Betty Muggah

Huntsville: Muskoka-East Parry Sound Home Care Program, 354 Muskoka Rd. 3 North, PO Box 1, Huntsville ON P1H 1H7 – 705/789-6451; Fax: 705/789-1982; Tollfree: 1-800-263-2805 – Dir., Vaughn Adamson

Kenora: Community Care Access Centre for Kenora & Rainy River Districts, 21 Wolsley St., Kenora ON P9N 3W7 – 807/468-6491; Fax: 807/468-1437 – Exec. Dir., Dave Murray

Kingston, Frontenac & Lennox & Addington Community Care Access Centre, 471 Counter St., Kingston ON K7M 3L5 – 613/544-7090; Fax: 613/544-1494 – CEO, Nancy Sears, Email: nsears@kfla-cc.org

Kirkland Lake: Timiskaming Home Care Program, 31 Station Rd. North, PO Box 98, Kirkland Lake ON P2N 3M6 – 705/567-9355, 9350, ext.203; Fax: 705/567-5476 – Dir., Susan Donaldson

Lindsay: Haliburton, Kawartha, Pine Ridge District Home Care Program, 108 Angeline St. South, Lindsay ON K9V 3L5 – 705/324-9165; Fax: 705/324-0884; Tollfree: 1-800-347-0285 – Dir., Marg Plaunt

London: Middlesex-London Home Care Program, 50 King St., London ON N6A 5L7 – 519/663-5410; Fax: 519/432-1645 – Acting Dir., Hal Finlayson, 519/663-5332, ext.2420

Mississauga: Peel Region Home Care Program, #202, 2227 South Millway, Mississauga ON L5L 3R6 – 905/791-7800, ext.7309; Fax: 905/820-3368 – Dir., Home Care & Community Services, Linda Instance

Newmarket: Community Care Access Centre of York Region, 1100 Gorham St., Unit 1, Newmarket ON L3Y 7V1 – 905/895-1240, 722-4223; Fax: 905/853-6297 – Pres. & CEO, Bill Innes

North Bay & District Home Care Program, The Thomson Bldg., 101 McIntyre St. West, PO Box 450, North Bay ON P1B 8J1 – 705/474-1400; Fax: 705/474-0080 – Dir., Yvonne Weir

Ohsweken: Six Nations Home Care Program, Ohsweken ON N0A 1M0 – 519/445-2201; Fax: 519/445-4914 – Dir. of Operations, Ken Jacobs

Orangeville: Community Care Access Centre of Wellington-Dufferin - Dufferin Office, 55 Fourth Ave., Orangeville ON L9W 1G7 – 519/941-4123; Fax: 519/941-9841 – Exec. Dir., Ross Kirkconnell

Owen Sound: Grey-Bruce Community Care Access Centre, #301, 920 - 1st St., Owen Sound ON N4K 4K5 – 519/371-2112; Fax: 519/371-5612; EMail: eb-ccac@bmts.com – Exec. Dir., Judy Chalmers

Parry Sound Home Care Program, 50B Seguin St., Parry Sound ON P2A 1B4 – 705/746-9351; Fax: 705/746-4812 – Adm., Dodie Kernohan

Pembroke: Renfrew Home Care Program, Renfrew County & District Health Unit, 7 International Dr., Pembroke ON K8A 6W5 – 613/735-4133; Fax: 613/732-8752 – Acting Dir., Dr. Michael Corriveau

Peterborough Home Care Program, 10 Hospital Dr., Peterborough ON K9J 8M1 – 705/743-2212; Fax: 705/743-9559 – Dir., Ann Payne

St Catharines: Niagara Region Home Care Program, 573 Glenridge Ave., St Catharines ON L2T 4C2 – 905/684-9441; Fax: 905/684-8463, 2297 – Dir., Wanda Yarmoshuk

St. Thomas: Elgin Community Care Access Centre, 99 Edward St., St. Thomas ON N5P 1Y8 – 519/631-9907; Fax: 519/631-2236 – CEO, Nancy Fazackerley

Sarnia-Lambton Community Care Access Centre, Bldg. #1040, 1086 Modeland Rd., PO Box 244, Stn DOW Bldg., Sarnia ON N7T 7S6 – 519/336-1000; Fax: 519/336-1419; Tollfree: 1-800-461-9196 – Adm., Peter Fitzsimons

Sault Ste. Marie: Algoma Home Care Program, #1, 369 Queen St. East, Sault Ste. Marie ON P6A 1Z4 – 705/949-1650; Fax: 705/949-1663 – Adm., Pierrette Brown

Simcoe: Haldimand-Norfolk Home Care Program, 76 Victoria St., Simcoe ON N3Y 1L5 – 519/426-7400, 7320, ext.3301/2; Fax: 519/426-7622 – Dir., Mary Anne Baker

Stratford: Perth District Home Care Program, 653 West Gore St., Stratford ON N5A 1L4 – 519/273-2010; Fax: 519/273-2847 – Dir., Jennifer Allen

Sudbury: Manitoulin-Sudbury Community Care Access Centre, 1760 Regent St. South, Sudbury ON P3E 3Z8 – 705/522-3460; Fax: 705/522-3855 – CEO, Robert Knight

Thunder Bay Home Care Program, #220, 1139 Alloy Dr., Thunder Bay ON P7B 6M8 – 807/344-0012; Fax: 807/345-3476 – Dir., Donna Opie

Timmins: Porcupine Home Care Program, 12 Elm St. North, Timmins ON P4N 6A1 – 705/267-7766; Fax: 705/267-7795; Tollfree: 1-800-890-6566 – Acting Dir., Jackie Gerrie

Toronto: Home Care Program for Metropolitan Toronto, 45 Sheppard Ave. East, Willowdale ON M2N 5W9 – 416/229-2929; Fax: 416/224-0908 – Pres., Marian Walsh, 416/229-2929, ext.5376, Fax: 416/229-1274

Two Hill Community Health Services, PO Box 458, Two Hills ON T0B 4K0 – 403/657-3361; Fax: 403/657-2928 – Lakeland Regional Health Authority

Waterloo Home Care Program, 99 Regina St. South, PO Box 1612, Waterloo ON N2J 4G6 – 519/883-2210; Fax: 519/883-2234 – Dir., Kevin Mercer

Whitby: Durham Region Home Care Program, 605 Brock St. North, Whitby ON L1N 4J3 – 905/430-3308; Fax: 905/430-3297 – Dir., Barbara Olsen

Windsor-Essex Home Care Program, 3000 Temple Dr., Windsor ON N8W 5J6 – 519/974-3022, ext.225; Fax: 519/974-1746 – Dir., Shirley Quick

Woodstock: Oxford County Home Care Program, 410 Buller St., Woodstock ON N4S 8A3 – 519/539-1284; Fax: 519/539-0065 – Dir., Kathy Desai

## MENTAL HEALTH HOSPITALS & COMMUNITY FACILITIES

Brockville Psychiatric Hospital, Prescott Rd., PO Box 1050, Brockville ON K6V 5W7 – 613/345-1461; Fax: 613/342-6194 – Scheduled to be closed by Dec. 31, 1999 – 295 beds – Rideau Valley District Health Council – Adm., David Hunter

Guelph: Community Mental Health Clinic, 147 Delhi St., Guelph ON N1E 4J8 – 519/821-2060 – Wellington-Dufferin District Health Council – Exec. Dir., Dr. Vernon Leditt

Guelph: Homewood Health Centre, 150 Delhi St., Guelph ON N1E 4J8 – 519/824-1010; Fax: 519/824-1827 – Wellington-Dufferin District Health Council – CEO, Dr. Ed Perez

Hamilton Psychiatric Hospital, 100 - 5th St. West, PO Box 585, Hamilton ON L8L 2B3 – 905/388-2511; Fax: 905/575-6038 – 245 beds – Hamilton-Wentworth District Health Council – Adm., Mary Sutherland

Kingston Psychiatric Hospital, 752 King St. West, PO Box 603, Kingston ON K7L 4X3 – 613/546-1101; Fax: 613/548-5577 – 317 beds – Kingston, Frontenac & Lennox & Addington District Health Council – Adm., Wayne Barnett

Leamington District Memorial Hospital, see General Hospital listngs

London Psychiatric Hospital, 850 Highbury Ave., PO Box 2532, London ON N6A 4H1 – 519/455-5110; Fax: 519/455-3712 – Scheduled to be closed by Dec. 31, 1999 – 346 beds – Thames Valley District Health Council – Adm., Robert Cunningham

North Bay Psychiatric Hospital, PO Box 3010, North Bay ON P1B 8L1 – 705/474-1200; Fax: 705/472-1694 – 307 beds – Nipissing-Timiskaming District Health Council – Adm., Dave J. Barker

Ottawa: Royal Ottawa Hospital, 1145 Carling Ave., Ottawa ON K1Z 7K4 – 613/722-6521; Fax: 613/722-4577 – Ottawa-Carleton Regional Health Council – Associate Exec. Dir., Rita Notarandrea

Penetanguishene: Mental Health Centre Penetanguishene, 500 Church St., Penetanguishene ON L9M 1G3 – 705/549-3181; Fax: 705/549-3446; EMail: mhcpen@mhcp.on.ca – 296 beds – Simcoe County District Health Council – Adm., George Kytayko

St. Thomas Psychiatric Hospital, 467 Sunset Dr., PO Box 2004, St. Thomas ON N5P 3V9 – 519/631-8510; Fax: 519/631-2681 – Scheduled to be closed by Dec. 31, 1999 – 289 beds – Huron-Perth District Health Council – Adm., Robert Cunningham

Sudbury: The Community Mental Health Group - Network North, 680 Kirkwood Dr., Sudbury ON P3E 1X3 – 705/675-9192; Fax: 705/675-3501 – 117 beds – Manitoulin & Sudbury District Health Council – CEO, Michael S. Park

Thunder Bay: Lakehead Psychiatric Hospital, 580 Algoma St. North, PO Box 2930, Thunder Bay ON P7B 5G4 – 807/343-4341; Fax: 807/343-4373 – 137 beds – Thunder Bay District Health Council – Adm., Ron Saddington

Toronto: Clarke Institute of Psychiatry, 250 College St., Toronto ON M5T 1R8 – 416/979-2221; Fax: 416/979-6902 – 103 beds – Pres. & CEO, Dr. P. Garfinkel

Toronto: C.M. Hinks Treatment Centre, 440 Jarvis St., Toronto ON M4Y 2H4 – 416/924-1164; Fax: 416/924-8208 – Mental health facility for children 0-18 years – 30 beds – Exec. Dir., Dr. Freda Martin

Toronto: Queen Street Mental Health Centre, 1001 Queen St. West, Toronto ON M6J 1H4 – 416/535-8501; Fax: 416/583-4307 – 474 beds – Metropolitan Toronto District Health Council – Adm., Allison Stuart

Whitby Mental Health Centre, 700 Gordon St., PO Box 613, Whitby ON L1N 5S9 – 905/668-5881; Fax: 905/430-4032 – 287 beds – Durham Region District Health Council – Adm., Ron Ballantyne

## NURSING HOMES/LONG TERM CARE FACILITIES

Ailsa Craig: Craigholme Nursing Home, 221 Main St. East, PO Box 130, Ailsa Craig ON N0M 1A0 – 519/293-3215; Fax: 519/293-3704 – 83 beds – Thames Valley District Health Council – Adm., Brent Martin

Ajax: Ballycliffe Lodge Nursing Home, 70 Station St., Ajax ON L1S 1R9 – 905/683-7321; Fax: 905/427-5846 – 100 beds – Durham Region District Health Council – Adm., Carol McIlveen

Alexandria: Community Nursing Home, 92 Centre St., Alexandria ON K0C 1A0 – 613/525-2022; Fax: 613/525-2023 – 70 beds – DHC of Eastern Ontario – Adm., Terry Dube

Alliston: Good Samaritan Nursing Home, 481 Victoria St. East, Alliston ON L9R 1J8 – 705/435-5722; Fax: 705/435-7982 – 55 beds – Simcoe County District Health Council – Adm., Lynda Weaver

Almonte Country Haven, 333 Country St., Almonte ON K0A 1A0 – 613/256-3095; Fax: 613/256-3096 – 82 beds – Rideau Valley District Health Council – Adm., Patricia Watson

Almonte: Fairview Manor, 95 Spring St., PO Box 1360, Almonte ON K0A 1A0 – 613/256-3113; Fax: 613/256-5780 – 100 beds – Rideau Valley District Health Council – Adm., G. McFarlane

Amherstburg: Richmond Terrace, 89 Rankin St., Amherstburg ON N9V 1E7 – 519/736-4295; Fax: 519/736-2995 – 115 beds – Essex County District Health Council – Adm., Victoria Iler

Amherstview: Helen Henderson Nursing Home, 343 Amherst Dr., Amherstview ON K7N 1X3 – 613/384-4585; Fax: 613/384-9407 – 70 beds – Kingston, Frontenac & Lennox & Addington District Health Council – Adm., Larry Gibson

Arnprior: The Grove Arnprior & District Nursing Home, 275 Ida St. North, Arnprior ON K7S 3M7 – 613/623-6547; Fax: 613/623-4844 – 60 beds – Renfrew County District Health Council – Adm., Ronald J. Kedrosky

Arthur: Caressant Care Arthur Nursing Home, 215 Eliza St., Arthur ON N0G 1A0 – 519/848-3795; Fax: 519/848-2273 – 80 beds – Wellington-Dufferin District Health Council – Adm., Gwen Good

Athens: Maple View Lodge, PO Box 100, Athens ON K0E 1B0 – 613/924-2696; Fax: 613/924-2123 – 41 beds – Rideau Valley District Health Council – Adm., P. Donovan

Atikokan General Hospital, *see* General Hospitals listings

Aurora Resthaven Extended Care & Convalesance, 32 Mill St., Aurora ON L4G 2R9 – 905/727-1939; Fax: 905/727-6299 – 176 beds – York Region District Health Council – Adm., Sheila Hoinkes

Aurora: The Willows Estate Nursing Home, 13837 Yonge St., Aurora ON L4G 3G8 – 905/727-0128; Fax: 905/841-0454 – 84 beds – York Region District Health Council – Adm., Susan Jackson

Aylmer: Chateau Gardens Aylmer Nursing Home, 465 Talbot St. West, Aylmer ON N5H 1K8 – 519/773-3423; Fax: 519/765-2573 – 60 beds – Thames Valley District Health Council – Adm., Mary Walker

Aylmer: Terrace Lodge, 475 Talbot St. East, Aylmer ON N5H 3A5 – 519/773-9205; Fax: 519/765-2667 – 100 beds – Thames Valley District Health Council – Adm., F.J. Boyes

Bancroft: Hastings Centennial Manor, 36 Maple St., PO Box 758, Bancroft ON K0L 1C0 – 613/332-2070; Fax: 613/332-2837 – 104 beds – Hastings & Prince Edward Counties District Health Council – Adm., Rob McLaughlin

Barrie: Coleman Health Care Centre, 140 Cundles Rd. West, Barrie ON L4M 4S4 – 705/726-8691; Fax: 705/726-5085 – 112 beds – Simcoe County District Health Council – Adm., Françoise Bouchard

Barrie: Grove Park, 234 Cook St., PO Box 460, Barrie ON L4M 4T7 – 705/726-1003; Fax: 705/726-1076 – 93 beds – Simcoe County District Health Council – Adm., D.M. Johnson

Barrie: I.O.O.F. Senior Citizen Homes Inc., 10 Brooks St., Barrie ON L4M 3H7 – 705/728-2364; Fax: 705/728-6024 – 155 beds – Simcoe County District Health Council – Adm., Nick Manherz

Barrie: Leisureworld/Barrie, 130 Owen St., Barrie ON L4M 3H7 – 705/726-8621; Fax: 705/726-0821 – 57 beds – Simcoe County District Health Council – Adm., Diane Greene

Barry's Bay: Valley Manor Nursing Home, Mintha St., Lot 177, PO Box 490, Barry's Bay ON K0J 1B0 – 613/756-2643; Fax: 613/756-7601 – 70 beds – Renfrew County District Health Council – Adm., Linda Shulist

Beamsville: Albright Manor, 5035 Mountain St., Beamsville ON L0R 1B0 – 905/563-8252; Fax: 905/563-5223 – 231 beds – Niagara District Health Council – Adm., John Buma

Beamsville: Nipponia Home, 4505 Thirty Rd., Beamsville ON L0R 1B0 – 905/563-8312; Fax: 905/563-8312 – 20 beds – Niagara District Health Council – Adm., Shinichi Sawada

Beaverton: Lakeview Manor, 133 Main St., Beaverton ON L0K 1A0 – 705/426-7388; Fax: 705/426-4218 – 149 beds – Waterloo Region District Health Council – Adm., Elizabeth Powell

Beeton: Simcoe Manor, Main St. East, Beeton ON L0G 1A0 – 905/729-2267; Fax: 905/729-4350 – 126 beds – Simcoe County District Health Council – Adm., Brenda Urbanski

Belleville: Belcrest Nursing Home, 431 Dundas St. West, Belleville ON K8P 1B6 – 613/968-4434; Fax: 613/968-6910 – 60 beds – Hastings & Prince Edward Counties District Health Council – Adm., James A. Clegg

Belleville: Hastings Manor, 476 Dundas St. West, Belleville ON K8N 5B2 – 613/968-6467; Fax: 613/967-0128 – 251 beds – Hastings & Prince Edward Counties District Health Council – Adm., Claudette Dignard-Remillard

Belleville: Montgomery Lodge Nursing Home, 145 Farley Ave., Belleville ON K8N 4L1 – 613/968-8835; Fax: 613/968-3207 – 59 beds – Hastings & Prince Edward Counties District Health Council – Adm., James Clegg

Belleville: Westgate Lodge Nursing Home, 37 Wilkie St., Belleville ON K8P 4E4 – 613/966-1323; Fax: 613/966-5126 – 88 beds – Hastings & Prince Edward Counties District Health Council – Adm., Elizabeth McGrath

Blenheim Community Village, 10 Mary Ave., Blenheim ON N0P 1A0 – 519/676-8119; Fax: 519/676-0610 – 65 beds – Kent County District Health Council – Adm., Ruth A. McDougall

Blind River: Golden Birches Terrace, c/o St. Joseph's Health Centre, 525 Causley St., Blind River ON P0R 1B0 – 705/356-2265; Fax: 705/356-1220 – 20 beds – Algoma District Health Council – Adm., Paul Davies

Bobcaygeon: Case Manor Nursing Home, 28 Boyd St., PO Box 670, Bobcaygeon ON K0M 1A0 – 705/738-2374; Fax: 705/738-3821 – 80 beds – Haliburton, Kawartha & Pine Ridge District Health Council – Adm., Dale G. Ross

Bobcaygeon: Pinecrest Nursing Home, Lot 12, Concession 19, Bobcaygeon ON K0M 1A0 – 705/738-2366;

Fax: 705/889-8127 – 58 beds – Haliburton, Kawartha & Pine Ridge District Health Council – Adm., Karen White

Bolton: King Nursing Home, 49 Sterne St., Bolton ON L0P 1A0 – 905/857-4117; Fax: 905/857-5181 – 86 beds – Peel District Health Council – Adm., Janice L. King

Bolton: Vera M. Davis Community Care Centre, 80 Allan Dr., Bolton ON L7E 1P7 – 905/857-0975; Fax: 905/857-7872 – 64 beds – Peel District Health Council – Adm., Carolyne Clubine

Bourget Nursing Home, 2279 Laval St., Bourget ON K0A 1E0 – 613/487-2331; Fax: 613/487-3464 – 50 beds – DHC of Eastern Ontario – Adm., Louise Dion

Bowanville: Strathaven Lifecare Centre, 264 King St. East, Bowanville ON L1C 1P9 – 905/623-2553; Fax: 905/623-1374 – 199 beds – Waterloo Region District Health Council – Adm., Jane Noble

Bowmanville: Marnwood Lifecare Centre, 26 Elgin St., Bowmanville ON L1C 3C8 – 905/623-5731; Fax: 905/623-4497 – 60 beds – York Region District Health Council – Adm., Catherine Luby

Bracebridge: The Pines, 42 Pine St., Bracebridge ON P1L 1N5 – 705/645-4488; Fax: 705/645-6857 – 105 beds – East Muskoka/Parry Sound District Health Council – Adm., Steve O'Neil

Bradford Place, 136 Barrie St., Bradford ON L3Z 2A9 – 905/775-8118; Fax: 905/773-0263 – 90 beds – Simcoe County District Health Council – Adm., Nana Rosenberger

Brampton: Faith Manor Nursing Home, 7900 McLaughlin Rd. South, Brampton ON L6V 3N2 – 905/459-3333; Fax: 905/459-8667 – 120 beds – Peel District Health Council – Adm., John Kalverda

Brampton: Peel Manor, 525 Main St. North, Brampton ON L6X 1N9 – 905/453-4140; Fax: 905/453-7802 – 177 beds – Peel District Health Council – Adm., Inga Mazuryk

Brampton: Tullamore Nursing Home, 133 Kennedy Rd. South, Brampton ON L6W 3G3 – 905/459-2324; Fax: 905/459-2329 – 159 beds – Peel District Health Council – Adm., Geoffrey Doff

Brantford: John Noble Home, 97 Mount Pleasant St., Brantford ON N3T 1T5 – 519/756-2920; Fax: 519/756-7942 – 361 beds – Brant District Health Council – Adm., J. Mills

Brantford: Leisureworld/Brantford Centre, 389 West St., Brantford ON N3R 3V9 – 519/759-4666; Fax: 519/759-0200 – 90 beds – Brant District Health Council – Adm., Mary Ann Owens

Brantford: Versa-Care Centre, Brantford, 425 Park Rd. North, Brantford ON N3R 7G5 – 519/759-1040; Fax: 519/759-5343 – retirement community; 79 long term care beds, retirement lodge 93 beds, apartments accommodating 121 – Brant District Health Council – Adm., Marilyn Robson

Brighton: Maplewood, 14 Maplewood Ave., Brighton ON K0K 1H0 – 613/475-2442; Fax: 613/475-2445 – 49 beds – Haliburton, Kawartha & Pine Ridge District Health Council – Adm., Mary Chester

Brockville: Fulford Home, 280 King St. East, Brockville ON K6V 1E2 – 613/342-7380; Fax: 613/342-2997 – 34 beds – Rideau Valley District Health Council – Adm., Betty Macdougall

Brockville: St. Lawrence Lodge, 1803 Prescott Rd. East, PO Box 1130, Brockville ON K6V 5W2 – 613/345-0255; Fax: 613/345-1029 – 240 beds – Rideau Valley District Health Council – Adm., William Luker

Brockville: Sherwood Park Manor, 1814 Highway 2 East, Brockville ON K6V 5T1 – 613/342-5531; Fax: 613/342-3767 – 75 beds – Rideau Valley District Health Council – Adm., Henry Bloemen

Brunner Nursing Home, Lot 76, Concession 1W, Brunner ON N0K 1C0 – 519/595-8903; Fax: 519/595-8272 – 26 beds – Huron-Perth District Health Council – Adm., Joanne Ross

Brussels: Huronlea Home for the Aged, Turnberry St. South, Brussels ON N0G 1H0 – 519/887-9267; Fax: 519/482-5263 – 64 beds – Huron-Perth District Health Council – Adm., Cathy Brown

Burlington: Brantwood Lifecare Centre, 802 Hager Ave., Burlington ON L7S 1X2 – 905/637-3481; Fax: 905/637-7514 – 138 beds – Halton District Health Council – Adm., Mary Scott

Burlington: Cama Woodlands Nursing Home, 159 Panin Rd., Burlington ON L7V 1A1 – 905/681-6441; Fax: 905/681-2678 – 60 beds – Halton District Health Council – Adm., Andrea Pomeroy

Burlington: Maple Villa Long Term Care Centre, 441 Maple Ave., Burlington ON L7S 1L8 – 905/639-2264; Fax: 905/639-3034 – 93 beds – Halton District Health Council – Adm., Barbara Goetz

Cambridge Country Manor, 3680 Speedsville Rd., Cambridge ON N3H 4R6 – 519/650-0100; Fax: 519/650-1697 – 79 beds – Waterloo Region District Health Council – Adm., Lynne Lawson

Cambridge: Fairview Mennonite Home, 799 Concession Rd., Cambridge ON N3H 4L1 – 519/653-5719; Fax: 519/650-1242 – 84 beds – Waterloo Region District Health Council – Adm., T. Kennel

Cambridge: Golden Years Nursing Home, 704 Eagle St. North, PO Box 3277, Cambridge ON N1R 2J2 – 519/653-5493; Fax: 519/650-1495 – 88 beds – Waterloo Region District Health Council – Adm., Nancy Kauffman-Lambert

Cambridge: Hilltop Manor Nursing Home, 42 Elliott St., Cambridge ON N1R 2J2 – 519/621-3067; Fax: 519/621-3443 – 89 beds – Waterloo Region District Health Council – Adm., John Heutinck

Cambridge: Riverbend Place, 650 Coronation Blvd., Cambridge ON N1R 7S6 – 519/740-3820; Fax: 519/740-0961 – 53 beds – Waterloo Region District Health Council – Adm., Marg Dykeman

Cambridge: Saint Luke's Place, A Place for Seniors, 1624 Franklin Blvd., Cambridge ON N3C 3P4 – 519/658-5183; Fax: 519/658-2991 – provides long term care, retirement home & apartments – 114 long term care beds – Waterloo Region District Health Council – Adm., John Kauffman

Campbellford: Burnbrae Gardens, 320 Burnbrae Rd. East, Campbellford ON K0L 1L0 – 705/653-4100; Fax: 705/653-2598 – 43 beds – Haliburton, Kawartha & Pine Ridge District Health Council – Adm., Mary Anne Greco

Cannifton: E.J. McQuigge Lodge, Black Diamond Rd., Lot 5 & 6, PO Box 68, Cannifton ON K0K 1K0 – 613/966-7717; Fax: 613/966-7646 – 56 beds – Hastings & Prince Edward Counties District Health Council – Adm., Anita Garland

Cannington: Bon-Air Nursing Home, 131 Laidlaw St. South, Cannington ON L0E 1E0 – 705/432-2385; Fax: 705/432-3331 – 55 beds – Durham Region District Health Council – Adm., Lynne Disik

Carleton Place: Versa-Care Centre, 256 High St., Carleton Place ON K7C 1X1 – 613/257-4355; Fax: 613/253-2190 – 60 beds – Rideau Valley District Health Council – Adm., Ken Herrington

Chapleau: Cedar Grove Lodge, 101 Pine St., Chapleau ON P0M 1K0 – 705/864-1616 – 18 beds – Manitoulin & Sudbury District Health Council – Adm., Bonnie J. Wilson

Chatham: Copper Terrace LTC Facility, 91 Tecumseh Rd., Chatham ON N7M 1B3 – 519/354-5442; Fax: 519/354-2089 – 151 beds – Kent County District Health Council – Adm., Carolee Milliner

Chatham: Meadow Park Nursing Home, 110 Sandys St., Chatham ON N7L 4X3 – 519/351-1330; Fax: 519/351-7933 – 97 beds – Kent County District Health Council – Acting Adm., Debbie Lashbrook

Chatham: Thamesview Lodge, 475 Grand Ave. West, Chatham ON N7L 4R5 – 519/352-4823; Fax: 519/352-2891 – 230 beds – Kent County District Health Council – Adm., Shirley Clark

Chatham: Victoria Residence, 190 Stanley Ave., Chatham ON N7M 3J9 – 519/354-0610; Fax: 519/354-7741 – 90 beds – Kent County District Health Council – Acting Adm., Greg Keating

Chatsworth: Versa-Care Centre, Chatsworth, RR#3, Chatsworth ON N0H 1G0 – 519/794-2244; Fax: 519/794-2597 – 34 beds – Grey-Bruce District Health Council – Adm., Catherine Hollister

Chesley: Elgin Abbey Nursing Home, 380 First Ave. North, PO Box 200, Chesley ON N0G 1L0 – 519/363-3195; Fax: 519/363-2747 – 27 beds – Grey-Bruce District Health Council – Adm., Elizabeth Elvidge

Chesley: Parkview Manor Health Care Centre, 98 - 3rd St. SE, PO Box 298, Chesley ON N0G 1L0 – 519/363-2416; Fax: 519/363-2171 – 34 beds – Grey-Bruce District Health Council – Adm., Carole Woods

Clarence Creek: Centre d'accueil Roger Séguin, 435 Lemay St., PO Box 160, Clarence Creek ON K0A 1N0 – 613/488-2053; Fax: 613/488-2274 – 110 beds – DHC of Eastern Ontario – Adm., Paul Mathieu

Clinton: Huronview, Lot 50, Consession 1, Tuckersmith Township, PO Box 219, Clinton ON N0M 1L0 – 519/482-3451; Fax: 519/482-5263 – 120 beds – Huron-Perth District Health Council – Adm., Cathy Brown

Cobden: Lakeview Nursing Home, 49 Pembroke St., Hwy. 17, Cobden ON K0J 1K0 – 613/646-2109; Fax: 613/646-2182 – 55 beds – Renfrew County District Health Council – Adm., Vallerie Pellerin

Cobourg: Golden Plough Lodge, 983 Burnham St., Cobourg ON K9A 4J7 – 416/372-8759; Fax: 416/372-8525 – 161 beds – Haliburton, Kawartha & Pine Ridge District Health Council – Adm., Carol Shaw

Cobourg: Streamway Villa, 19 James St. West, Cobourg ON K9A 2J8 – 416/372-0163; Fax: 416/372-0581 – 59 beds – Haliburton, Kawartha & Pine Ridge District Health Council – Adm., Caroline Tompkins

Cochenour: Owen J. Matthews, Hwy 125, PO Box 160, Cochenour ON P0V 1L0 – 807/662-3281; Fax: 807/662-2037 – 22 beds – Kenora-Rainy River District Health Council – Adm., Kevin Queen

Cochrane: Extendicare/Cochrane, 411 - 11th Ave. North, PO Box 280, Cochrane ON P0L 1C0 – 705/272-4144; Fax: 705/272-4155 – 37 beds – Cochrane District Health Council – Acting Adm., Lise Rivard

Collingwood Nursing Home Ltd., 250 Campbell St., Collingwood ON L9Y 4J9 – 705/445-3991; Fax: 705/445-5060 – 60 beds – Simcoe County District Health Council – Adm., Peter Zober

Collingwood: Bay Haven Nursing Home, 499 Hume St., Collingwood ON L9Y 4H8 – 705/445-6501; Fax: 705/445-6506 – 60 beds – Simcoe County District Health Council – Adm., Karen Milligan

Collingwood: Sunset Manor, Raglan St., Collingwood ON L9Y 3Z4 – 705/445-4499; Fax: 705/445-9742 – 150 beds – Simcoe County District Health Council – Adm., Tim Sandell

Corbeil: Nipissing Manor Nursing Care Centre, RR#1, Corbeil ON P0H 1K0 – 705/752-1100; Fax: 705/752-2570 – 120 beds – Nipissing-Timiskaming District Health Council – Adm., W.E. Graham

Cornwall: Glen-Stor-Dun Lodge, 1900 Montréal Rd., Cornwall ON K6H 5T1 – 613/933-3384; Fax: 613/933-7214 – 132 beds – DHC of Eastern Ontario – Adm., F. Lafave

Cornwall: Parisien Manor Nursing Home, 439 Second St. East, Cornwall ON K6H 1Z2 – 613/933-2592; Fax: 613/933-3839 – 65 beds – DHC of Eastern Ontario – Adm., Johneen Rennie

Cornwall: St. Joseph's Villa (Cornwall), 14 York St., Cornwall ON K6J 3Y6 – 613/933-6040; Fax: 613/933-9429 – 100 beds – DHC of Eastern Ontario – Adm., John Haslehurst

Cornwall: Sandfield Place, 220 Emma St., Cornwall ON K6J 5V8 – 613/933-6972; Fax: 613/938-2261 – 53 beds – DHC of Eastern Ontario – Adm., Joyce Kinnear

Cornwall: Tsi Ion Kwa Nonh So:Te, RR#3, Cornwall Island, Cornwall ON K6H 5R7 – 613/932-1409; Fax: 613/932-8845 – 30 beds – DHC of Eastern Ontario – Adm., Bonnie Cole

Cornwall: Versa-Care Centre, Cornwall, 201 - 11th St. East, Cornwall ON K6H 2Y6 – 613/933-7420; Fax: 613/933-2759 – 118 beds – DHC of Eastern Ontario – Adm., Barbara Fraser

Courtland: Sacred Heart Villa, Hwy. 59, PO Box 279, Courtland ON N0J 1E0 – 519/688-0710; Fax: 519/688-0052 – 54 beds – Haldimand-Norfolk District Health Council – Adm., Linda Hare

Creemore: Creedan Valley Nursing Home, 143 Mary St., Creemore ON L0M 1G0 – 705/466-3437; Fax: 705/466-3063 – 92 beds – Simcoe County District Health Council – Adm., Dianne Greene

Deep River: North Renfrew Long-Term Care Centre, 47 Ridge Rd., Deep River ON K0J 1P0 – 613/584-1900; Fax: 613/584-9183; EMail: nrltcsinc@intranet.ca – 21 beds – Renfrew County District Health Council – Adm., Ann Aikens

Delaware: Middlesex Terrace, RR#1, Delaware ON N0L 1E0 – 519/652-3483; Fax: 519/652-6915 – 105 beds – Thames Valley District Health Council – Adm., Janice McAskill

Delhi Nursing Home, 750 Gilbraltar St., Delhi ON N4B 3B3 – 519/582-3400; Fax: 519/582-0300 – 60 beds – Haldimand-Norfolk District Health Council – Adm., Janet Krolouski

Deseronto: Friendly Manor Nursing Home, Hwy. 2, Lot 1, Concession 1, PO Box 305, Deseronto ON K0K 1X0 – 613/396-3438; Fax: 613/396-2729 – 58 beds – Kingston, Frontenac & Lennox & Addington District Health Council – Administration, Joan Watt

Dryden District General Hospital, *see* General Hospitals listings

Dundas: Blackadar Nursing Home, 101 Creighton Rd., Dundas ON L9H 3B7 – 905/627-5465; Fax: 905/628-2044 – 80 beds – Hamilton-Wentworth District Health Council – Adm., D. Dean Blackadar

Dundas: St. Joseph's Villa (Dundas), 56 Governor's Rd., Dundas ON L9H 5G7 – 905/627-3541; Fax: 905/628-0825 – 378 beds – Exec. Dir., Paul O'Krafka

Dundas: Wentworth Lodge, 41 South St. West, Dundas ON L9H 4C4 – 905/628-6359; Fax: 905/628-3788 – 210 beds – Hamilton-Wentworth District Health Council – Adm., Judith Evans

Dunnville: Grandview Lodge/Dunnville, 657 Lock St. West, Dunnville ON N1A 1V9 – 416/774-7548; Fax: 416/774-1440 – 206 beds – Haldimand-Norfolk District Health Council – Adm., Arlene Lawlor

Durham: Rockwood Terrace, 575 Sadler St. East, Durham ON N0G 1R0 – 519/369-6035; Fax: 519/369-6736 – 100 beds – Grey-Bruce District Health Council – Adm., John Flick

Dutton: Bobier Convalescent Home, 265 Shackleton St., Dutton ON N0L 1J0 – 519/762-2417; Fax: 519/762-2361 – 57 beds – Thames Valley District Health Council – Adm., Fred Boyes, 519/631-0620

Elmira: Chateau Gardens (Elmira) Nursing Home, 11 Herbert St., Elmira ON N3B 2B8 – 519/669-2921; Fax: 519/669-3027 – 48 beds – Waterloo Region District Health Council – Adm., Joan Norris

Elmvale: Sara Vista Nursing Centre, 59 Simcoe St., Elmvale ON L0L 1P0 – 705/322-2182; Fax: 705/322-8326 – 60 beds – Simcoe County District Health Council – Adm., Anitta Robertson

Elora: Wellington Terrace, Wellington Dr., PO Box 70, Elora ON N0B 1S0 – 519/846-5359; Fax: 519/846-9192 – 176 beds – Wellington-Dufferin District Health Council – Adm., Peter Barnes

Embrun: St. Jacques Nursing Home, 915 Notre Dame St., Embrun ON K0A 1W0 – 613/443-3442; Fax: 613/443-1716 – 60 beds – DHC of Eastern Ontario – Adm., Louise Gaudreau

Englehart: Northview Nursing Home, 7 River Rd., Englehart ON P0J 1H0 – 705/544-8191; Fax: 705/544-8255 – 48 beds – Nipissing-Timiskaming District Health Council – Adm., Carol-Ann Poan

Espanola Nursing Home, 799 Queensway Ave., Espanola ON P5E 1R3 – 705/ 869-1420; Fax: 705/869-2068 – 30 beds – Manitoulin & Sudbury District Health Council – CEO, Paul Davies

Essex Health Care Centre, 111 Iler Ave., Essex ON N8M 1T6 – 519/776-5243; Fax: 519/776-4450 – 142 beds – Essex County District Health Council – Adm., Geraldine Picken

Exeter Villa, 155 John St. East, Exeter ON N0M 1S1 – 519/235-1581; Fax: 519/235-3219 – 47 beds – Huron-Perth District Health Council – Adm., Mary Jane MacDougall

Fergus: Caressant Care Fergus Nursing Home, 450 Queen St. East, Fergus ON N1M 2Y7 – 519/843-2400; Fax: 519/843-2200 – 87 beds – Wellington-Dufferin District Health Council – Adm., Marilyn Jacobi

The Fordwich Village Nursing Home, 63 Adelaide St., Fordwich ON N0G 1V0 – 519/335-3168 – 33 beds – Huron-Perth District Health Council – Adm. & Dir. of Care, Catherine Weber

Forest: North Lambton Rest Home, 39 Morris St., Forest ON N0N 1J0 – 519/786-2151; Fax: 519/786-2156 – 88 beds – Lambton District Health Council – Acting Adm., Kevin McIver

Fort Erie: Crescent Park Lodge, 4 Hagey Ave., Fort Erie ON L2A 5M5 – 905/871-8330; Fax: 905/871-9212 – 68 beds – Niagara District Health Council – Adm., Rosemary Turner

Fort Erie: Gilmore Lodge, 50 Gilmore Rd., Fort Erie ON L2A 2M1 – 905/871-6160; Fax: 905/871-0435 – 80 beds – Niagara District Health Council – Adm., Carrie Kaye

Fort Frances: Rainycrest Home for the Aged, 550 Osborne St., Fort Frances ON P9A 3T2 – 807/274-9858; Fax: 807/274-7368 – 168 beds – Kenora-Rainy River District Health Council – Adm., Kevin Queen

Gananoque: Carveth Care Centre, 375 James St., Gananoque ON K7G 2A1 – 613/382-4752; Fax: 613/382-8514 – 93 beds – Rideau Valley District Health Council – Adm., Tim Gibson

Garson Manor Nursing Home, 219 O'Neil Dr. East, PO Box 10, Garson ON P3L 1S5 – 705/693-2734; Fax: 705/693-5031 – 80 beds – Manitoulin & Sudbury District Health Council – Adm., Erkki Leinala

Geraldton District Hospital, *see* General Hospitals listings

Glenburnie: Fairmount Home, 2069 Battersea Rd., RR#1, Glenburnie ON K0H 1S0 – 613/546-4264; Fax: 613/546-0489 – 96 beds – Kingston, Frontenac & Lennox & Addington District Health Council – Adm., M.J. McCarthy

Gloucester: Extendicare/Laurier Manor, 1715 Montréal Rd., Gloucester ON K1J 6N4 – 613/741-5122; Fax: 613/741-8432 – 240 beds – Ottawa-Carleton Regional Health Council – Adm., William Smith

Gloucester: St. Louis Residence, 879, ch Parc Hiawatha, Gloucester ON K1C 2Z6 – 613/824-1720; Fax: 613/824-8064 – 196 beds – Ottawa-Carleton Regional Health Council – Adm., Sr. Diane Albert

Goderich: Versa-Care Centre, Goderich, 290 South St., Goderich ON N7A 4G6 – 519/524-7324; Fax: 519/524-8739 – 91 beds – Huron-Perth District Health Council – Adm., Dana Livingstone

Gore Bay: Manitoulin Lodge, 3 Main St., PO Box 360, Gore Bay ON P0P 1H0 – 705/282-2007; Fax: 705/282-3422 – 61 beds – Manitoulin & Sudbury District Health Council – Adm., Linda J. Williams

Gravenhurst: Leisureworld/Muskoka, 200 Kelly Dr., Gravenhurst ON P1P 1P3 – 705/687-3444; Fax: 705/687-6319 – 71 beds – East Muskoka/Parry Sound District Health Council – Adm., Azmina Drummond

Grimsby: Deer Park Villa, 150 Central Ave., Grimsby ON L3M 4Z3 – 905/945-4164; Fax: 905/945-7774 – 39 beds – Niagara District Health Council – Adm., Cornelia Tank

Grimsby: Kilean Lodge, 81-83 Main St. East, Grimsby ON L3M 1N6 – 905/945-9243; Fax: 905/945-1126 – 50 beds – Niagara District Health Council – Adm., Margaret Wasslen

Grimsby: Shalom Manor, 12 Bartlett Ave., Grimsby ON L3M 4N5 – 905/945-9631; Fax: 905/945-1211 – 132 beds – Niagara District Health Council – Adm., Melis Koomans

Guelph: Eden House Nursing Home, RR#2, Guelph ON N1H 6H8 – 519/856-4622; Fax: 519/856-7412 – 58 beds – Wellington-Dufferin District Health Council – Adm., John Bouwmeester

Guelph: The Elliott Group, 170 Metcalfe St., Guelph ON N1E 4Y3 – 519/822-0491; Fax: 519/822-5658 – nursing home & retirement complex – 250 beds – Wellington-Dufferin District Health Council – CEO, David Hicks

Guelph: Lapointe-Fisher Nursing Home, 271 Metcalfe St., Guelph ON N1E 4Y8 – 519/821-9030; Fax: 519/821-6021 – 92 beds – Wellington-Dufferin District Health Council – Adm., Ann Root

Guelph: St. Joseph's Home, 325 Edinburgh Rd. North, Guelph ON N1H 1E3 – 519/824-2620; Fax: 519/767-3434 – 136 beds – Wellington-Dufferin District Health Council – Adm., Sr. Margaret Myatt

Guelph: St. Joseph's Hospital & Home, *see* General Hospitals listings

Hagersville: Norcliffe Lifecare Centre, 85 Main St. North, Hagersville ON N0A 1H0 – 416/768-1641; Fax: 416/768-1538 – 60 beds – Haldimand-Norfolk District Health Council – Adm., Ben Bernardo

Haileybury: Extendicare/Tri-Town Nursing Home, 143 Bruce St., PO Box 999, Haileybury ON P0J 1K0 – 705/672-2151; Fax: 705/672-5348 – 60 beds – Nipissing-Timiskaming District Health Council – Adm., Ghislaine Julien

Haileybury: Temiskaming Lodge, 100 Bruce St., Haileybury ON P0J 1K0 – 705/672-2123; Fax: 705/672-5734 – 80 beds – Nipissing-Timiskaming District Health Council – Adm., Edith Schultz

Haliburton: Extendicare/Haliburton Nursing Home, Park St., PO Box 780, Haliburton ON K0M 1S0 – 705/457-1722; Fax: 705/457-3914 – 60 beds – Haliburton, Kawartha & Pine Ridge District Health Council – Adm., Jane Rosenberg

Hamilton Convalescent Centre, 125 Wentworth St. South, Hamilton ON L8N 2Z1 – 905/527-1482; Fax: 905/527-0679 – 64 beds – Hamilton-Wentworth District Health Council – Adm., Lorraine Preston-Orchard

Hamilton: Grace Villa (Hamilton) Nursing Home, 45 Lockton Cres., Hamilton ON L8V 4V5 – 905/387-4812; Fax: 905/387-4814 – 184 beds – Hamilton-Wentworth District Health Council – Adm., David Baker

Hamilton: Idlewyld Manor, 449 Sanatorium Rd., Hamilton ON L9C 2A7 – 905/574-2000; Fax: 905/574-0139 – 101 beds – Hamilton-Wentworth District Health Council – Adm., Beverley Preuss

Hamilton: Macassa Lodge, 701 Upper Sherman Dr., Hamilton ON L8V 3M7 – 905/546-2800; Fax: 905/546-4989 – 270 beds – Hamilton-Wentworth District Health Council – Adm., Bob Malloy

Hamilton: Parkview Nursing Centre, 545 King St. West, Hamilton ON L8P 3M7 – 905/525-5903; Fax: 905/525-5907 – 126 beds – Hamilton-Wentworth District Health Council – Adm., Sandra Smith

Hamilton: St. Olga's Lifecare Centre, 570 King St. West, Hamilton ON L8P 1C2 – 905/522-8572; Fax: 905/577-0644 – 90 beds – Hamilton-Wentworth District Health Council – Adm., Shona Taylor

Hamilton: Shalom Village Nursing Home, 60 Macklin St. North, Hamilton ON L8S 3S1 – 905/529-1613; Fax: 905/529-7542 – 60 beds – Hamilton-Wentworth District Health Council – Adm., Patricia Morden

Hamilton: Townsview Lifecare Centre, 39 Mary St., Hamilton ON L8R 3L8 – 905/523-6427; Fax: 905/528-0610 – 219 beds – Hamilton-Wentworth District Health Council – Adm., Walter Sguazzin

Hamilton: Versa-Care Centre, Hamilton, 330 Main St. East, Hamilton ON L8N 3T9 – 905/523-7134; Fax: 905/523-7137 – 248 beds – Hamilton-Wentworth District Health Council – Adm., Brad Lawrence

Hamilton: Victoria Nursing Home, 176 Victoria Ave. North, Hamilton ON L8L 5G1 – 905/527-9111; Fax: 905/526-1871 – 75 beds – Hamilton-Wentworth District Health Council – Adm., Ranka Stipancic, RN

Hamilton: The Wellington Nursing Home, 1430 Upper Wellington St., Hamilton ON L9A 5H3 – 905/385-2111; Fax: 905/385-2110 – 102 beds – Hamilton-Wentworth District Health Council – Adm., Mary Reid

Hanover Care Centre, 700 - 19th Ave., Hanover ON N4N 3S6 – 519/364-3700; Fax: 519/364-7194 – 41 beds – Grey-Bruce District Health Council – Adm., Sharon Garcia

Hanover: Versa-Care Centre, Hanover, 101 - 10th St., Hanover ON N4N 1M9 – 519/364-4320, 364-2620; Fax: 519/364-6953 – 70 long term care beds, 62 retirement, 132 retirement apartments – Grey-Bruce District Health Council – Adm., Michael O'Keeffe

Harriston: Geri-Care Nursing Home, 24 Louise St., PO Box 250, Harriston ON N0G 1Z0 – 519/338-3700; Fax: 519/338-2744 – 89 beds – Wellington-Dufferin District Health Council – Adm., Mary T. Haid

Hawkesbury: Prescott & Russell Residence, 1020 Cartier Blvd., Hawkesbury ON K6A 1W7 – 613/632-2755; Fax: 613/632-4056 – 146 beds – DHC of Eastern Ontario – Adm., Pierre Arsenault

Hearst: Foyer des Pionniers, 1317 Edward St., PO Box 1538, Hearst ON P0L 1N0 – 705/362-5825; Fax: 705/362-5519 – 61 beds – Cochrane District Health Council – Adm., Elizabeth Howe

Hensall: Queensway Nursing Home, 100 Queen St. East, Hensall ON N0M 1X0 – 519/262-2830; Fax: 519/262-3403 – 40 beds – Huron-Perth District Health Council – Adm., Edward Underwood

Hornepayne Community Hospital, *see* General Hospitals listings

Huntsville: Fairvern Nursing Home, 14 Mill St., Huntsville ON P0A 1K0 – 705/789-4476; Fax: 705/789-1371 – 76 beds – East Muskoka/Parry Sound District Health Council – Adm., Bruce Laughton

Ingersoll: Oxford Regional Nursing Home, 263 Wonham St. South, Ingersoll ON N5C 3P6 – 519/485-3920; Fax: 519/485-6497 – 80 beds – Thames Valley District Health Council – Acting Adm., Gloria McKibbin

Iroquois Falls: South Centennial Manor, 240 Fyfe St., PO Box 610, Iroquois Falls ON P0K 1E0 – 705/258-3836; Fax: 705/258-3694 – 69 beds – Cochrane District Health Council – Adm., Ken Wollan

Jasper: Rosebridge Manor, 131 Roses Bridge Rd., RR#2, Jasper ON K0G 1G0 – 613/283-5471; Fax: 613/283-9012 – 78 beds – Rideau Valley District Health Council – Adm., Nelly Hobbs

Kapuskasing: Extendicare/Kapuskasing, 45 Ontario St., PO Box 460, Kapuskasing ON P5N 2Y5 – 705/335-6633; Fax: 705/337-6051 – 60 beds – Cochrane District Health Council – Adm., Louise Gaulin

Kapuskasing: North Centennial Manor, 2 Kimberley Dr., Kapuskasing ON P5N 1L5 – 705/335-6125; Fax: 705/337-1091 – 71 beds – Cochrane District Health Council – Adm., Gil Dionne

Kemptville: Bayfield Manor Nursing Home, 100 Elvira St., Kemptville ON K0G 1J0 – 613/258-7484; Fax: 613/258-3838 – 66 beds – Rideau Valley District Health Council – Adm., Michael J. Hall

Kenora: Birchwood Terrace Nursing Home, 237 Lakeview Dr., Kenora ON P9N 3X8 – 807/468-8625; Fax: 807/468-4060 – 96 beds – Kenora-Rainy River District Health Council – Adm., Denise Miault

Kenora: Pinecrest, 1220 Valley Dr., Kenora ON P9N 2W7 – 807/468-3165; Fax: 807/468-6346 – 161 beds – Kenora-Rainy River District Health Council – Adm., Kevin Queen

Keswick: Cedarvale Lodge, 121 Morton Dr., Keswick ON L4P 2M5 – 905/476-2656; Fax: 905/476-5689 – nursing home with 40 bed retirement home attached – 60 beds – York Region District Health Council – Adm., Wynanda Rosenberger

Kilworthy: Balmoral Lodge Nursing Home, RR#1, Kilworthy ON P0E 1G0 – 705/689-2029; Fax: 705/689-5844 – 42 beds – East Muskoka/Parry Sound District Health Council – Acting Adm., Glenys Heskamp

Kincardine: Versa-Care Trillium Court, 550 Philip Pl., Kincardine ON N2Z 3A6 – 519/396-4400; Fax: 519/396-9092 – 40 long term care beds, 64 retirement suites – Grey-Bruce District Health Council – Adm., Robert Millar

King City Lodge Nursing Home, 146 Fog Rd., King City ON L7B 1A3 – 905/833-5037; Fax: 905/833-5925 – 36 beds – York Region District Health Council – Adm., Linda Albert James

Kingston: Extendicare/Kingston, 309 Queen Mary Rd., Kingston ON K7M 6P4 – 613/549-5010; Fax: 613/549-7347 – 150 beds – Kingston, Frontenac & Lennox & Addington District Health Council – Adm., Marilyn C. Benn

Kingston: Providence Manor, 275 Sydenham St., Kingston ON K7K 1G7 – 613/549-4164; Fax: 613/549-7472 – 223 beds – Kingston, Frontenac & Lennox & Addington District Health Council – Acting Adm., Cathy Dunne

Kingston: Rideaucrest Home, 175 Rideau St., Kingston ON K7K 3H6 – 613/547-6792; Fax: 613/531-9107 – 170 beds – Kingston, Frontenac & Lennox & Addington District Health Council – Adm., J.D. Smith

Kingston: Trillium Ridge, 800 Edgar St., Kingston ON K7M 8S4 – 613/547-0040; Fax: 613/547-3734 – 90 beds – Kingston, Frontenac & Lennox & Addington District Health Council – Adm., Ray Jourdain

Kirkland Lake: Extendicare/Kirkland Lake, 155 Government Rd. East, PO Box 3900, Kirkland Lake ON P2N 3P4 – 705/567-3268; Fax: 705/567-4638 – 100 beds – Nipissing-Timiskaming District Health Council – Adm., Margaret Orr

Kirkland Lake: Teck Pioneer Residence, 38 Churchill Dr., Kirkland Lake ON P2N 1V1 – 705/567-3257; Fax: 705/567-3737 – 74 beds – Nipissing-Timiskaming District Health Council – Adm., Debra Stivrins

Kitchener: A.R. Goudie Eventide Home (Salvation Army), 369 Frederick St., Kitchener ON N2H 2P1 – 519/744-5182; Fax: 519/744-3887 – 79 beds – Waterloo Region District Health Council – Adm., Ed Hiscock

Kitchener: Central Park Lodge, 60 Westheights Dr., Kitchener ON N2N 2A8 – 519/576-3320; Fax: 519/745-3227 – 240 beds – Waterloo Region District Health Council – Adm., Dianne O'Rourke

Kitchener: Sunnyside Home, 247 Franklin St. North, Kitchener ON N2A 1Y5 – 519/893-8482; Fax: 519/893-4450 – 263 beds – Waterloo Region District Health Council – Adm., Gail Carlin

Kitchener: Trinity Village Care Centre, 2727 Kingsway Dr., Kitchener ON N2C 1A7 – 519/893-6320; Fax: 519/893-3432 – 150 beds – Waterloo Region District Health Council – Adm., Arthur Schelter

Kitchener: Winston Park Nursing Home, 695 Blockline Rd., Kitchener ON N2E 3K1 – 519/576-2430; Fax: 519/576-8990 – 95 beds – Adm., James Schlegel

Komoka: Country Terrace, 10072 Oxbow Dr., RR#3, Komoka ON N0L 1R0 – 519/657-2955; Fax: 519/657-8516 – 120 beds – Thames Valley District Health Council – Adm., Mary Raithby

Lancaster: Chateau Gardens (Lancaster) Nursing Home, 303 Military Rd., Lancaster ON K0C 1N0 – 613/347-3016; Fax: 613/347-1680 – 60 beds – DHC of Eastern Ontario – Adm., Diane Morin

Leamington Mennonite Home, 22 Garrison Ave., Leamington ON N8H 2P2 – 519/326-6109; Fax: 519/326-3595 – 72 beds – Essex County District Health Council – Adm., Jean Marie Drummond

Leamington Nursing Home, 24 Franklin Rd., Leamington ON N8H 4B7 – 519/326-3289; Fax: 519/326-0102 – 120 beds – Essex County District Health Council – Adm., Roxanne Belli

Leamington: Sun Parlor Home for Senior Citizens, 175 Talbot St. East, Leamington ON N8H 1L9 – 519/326-5731; Fax: 519/326-8952 – 206 beds – Essex County District Health Council – Adm., Karl Samuelson

Limoges: Foyer St-Viateur Nursing Home, 1003 Limoges Rd. South, PO Box 119, Limoges ON K0A 2M0 – 613/443-5751; Fax: 613/443-5950 – 57 beds – DHC of Eastern Ontario – Adm., Richard R. Marleau

Lindsay: Caressant Care Lindsay Nursing Home, 240 Mary St. West, Lindsay ON K9V 5K5 – 705/324-1913; Fax: 705/328-3283 – 60 beds – Haliburton, Kawartha & Pine Ridge District Health Council – Adm., Julia Chamberlain

Lindsay: Frost Manor, 225 Mary St. West, Lindsay ON K9V 5K3 – 705/324-8333; Fax: 705/878-5840 – 62 beds – Haliburton, Kawartha & Pine Ridge District Health Council – Adm., Kay Davis

Lindsay: Victoria Manor Home for the Aged, 220 Angeline St. South, Lindsay ON K9V 4R2 – 705/324-3558; Fax: 705/324-8607 – 166 beds – Haliburton, Kawartha & Pine Ridge District Health Council – Adm., Alan Cavell

Lion's Head: Golden Dawn Nursing Home, 80 Main St., PO Box 129, Lion's Head ON N0H 1W0 – 519/793-3716; Fax: 519/793-4503 – 45 beds – Grey-Bruce District Health Council – Adm., Frank Walker

Listowel: Caressant Care Listowel Nursing Home, 710 Reserve Ave. South, Listowel ON N4W 2L1 – 519/291-1041; Fax: 519/291-5420 – 52 beds – Huron-Perth District Health Council – Adm., Eleanor MacEwen

Little Current: Manitoulin Centennial Manor, 70 Robinson St. West, PO Box 460, Little Current ON P0P 1K0 – 705/368-2710; Fax: 705/368-2694 – 60 beds – Manitoulin & Sudbury District Health Council – Adm., Barbara Eadie

London: Chateau Gardens (Queens) Nursing Home, 518 Queens Ave., London ON N6B 1Y7 – 519/434-2727; Fax: 519/679-3482 – 63 beds – Thames Valley District Health Council – Acting Adm., Donna Heffron

London: Chelsey Park (Oxford) Nursing Home, 310 Oxford St. West, London ON N6H 4N6 – 519/432-1855; Fax: 519/679-7324 – 247 beds – Thames Valley District Health Council – Adm., Jane Boudreau-Bailey

London: Dearness Home for Senior Citizens, 710 Southdale Rd. East, London ON N6E 1R8 – 519/681-4400; Fax: 519/681-0714 – 375 beds – Thames Valley District Health Council – Adm., Doug Goodman

London: Extendicare/London, 860 Waterloo St., London ON N6A 3W6 – 519/433-6658; Fax: 519/642-1711 – 170 beds – Thames Valley District Health Council – Adm., Jill Knowlton

London: Kensington Village, 1340 Huron St., London ON N5V 3R3 – 519/455-3910; Fax: 519/455-1570 – 108 beds – Thames Valley District Health Council – Acting Adm., Carol Drudge

London: Marian Villa, 200 College Ave., London ON N6A 1Y1 – 519/646-6000; Fax: 519/646-6148 – 247 beds – Thames Valley District Health Council – Adm., Phillip Hassen

London: The McCormick Home for the Aged, 230 Victoria St., London ON N6A 2C2 – 519/432-2648; Fax: 519/645-6982 – 141 beds – Thames Valley District Health Council – Adm., Terry Guzyk

London: Meadow Park Nursing Home, 1210 Southdale Rd. East, London ON N6E 1B4 – 519/686-0484; Fax: 519/686-9932 – 122 beds – Thames Valley District Health Council – Adm., Shirley Hodgson

London: Mount Hope Centre for Long Term Care, 21 Grosvenor St., London ON N6A 1Y1 – 519/646-6000; Fax: 519/646-6148 – 147 beds – Adm., Mary Collins

London: Versa-Care Centre, Lambeth, 848 Gideon Dr., RR#32, London ON N6KP 1P2 – 519/472-1270; Fax: 519/472-0228 – 157 beds – Thames Valley District Health Council – Adm., Shirley Nugent

London: Versa-Care Elmwood Place, 46 Elmwood Pl., London ON N6J 1J2 – 519/433-7259; Fax: 519/660-4778 – 60 beds – Thames Valley District Health Council – Adm., Mary Heppelle

Long Sault: Woodland Villa, 30 Milles Roches Rd., RR#1, Long Sault ON K0C 1P0 – 613/534-2276; Fax: 613/534-8559 – 111 beds – DHC of Eastern Ontario – Adm., Norm Quenneville

L'Orignal: Pleasant Rest Nursing Home, 428 Front Rd., L'Orignal ON K0B 1K0 – 613/675-4617; Fax: 613/675-1374 – 60 beds – DHC of Eastern Ontario – Adm., Jean-Pierre Paquette

Lucknow: Pinecrest Manor Nursing Home, 399 Bob St., Lucknow ON N0G 2H0 – 519/528-2820; Fax: 519/528-2377 – 61 beds – Grey-Bruce District Health Council – Adm., Brenda Koornneef

Markdale: Grey Owen Lodge, 206 Toronto St., Markdale ON N0C 1H0 – 519/986-3010; Fax: 519/986-4644 – 41 beds – Grey-Bruce District Health Council – Adm., John Flick

Markham: Markhaven, 54 Parkway Ave., Markham ON L3P 2G4 – 905/294-2233; Fax: 905/294-5740 – 75 beds – York Region District Health Council – Adm., A. Jennings

Markham: Versa-Care Centre, Markham, 6824 Highway 7, Markham ON L6B 1A8 – 905/294-0511; Fax: 905/471-0750 – 50 beds – York Region District Health Council – Acting Adm., George Tsapoitis

Marmora: Caressant Care Marmora, 58 Bursthall St., Marmora ON K0K 2M0 – 613/472-3130; Fax: 613/472-5388 – 84 beds – Hastings & Prince Edward Counties District Health Council – Adm., Deborah J. Warren

Maryhill Extended Care Centre, 60 Church St. North, Maryhill ON N0B 2B0 – 519/648-2117; Fax: 519/648-2570 – 31 beds – Waterloo Region District Health Council – Adm., Ralph Link

Matheson: The Rosedale Centre Extended Care Unit, 507 - 8th Ave., Matheson ON P0K 1N0 – 705/273-2424; Fax: 705/273-2515 – 20 beds – Cochrane District Health Council – Adm., Dan O'Mara

Mattawa: Algonquin Nursing Home, 231 Tenth St., Mattawa ON P0H 1V0 – 705/744-2202; Fax: 705/744-2787 – 72 beds – Nipissing-Timiskaming District Health Council – Adm., Zena Monestime

Maxville Manor, 80 Mechanic St. West, Maxville ON K0C 1T0 – 613/527-2170; Fax: 613/527-3130 – 125 beds – DHC of Eastern Ontario – Exec. Dir., Craig Munro

Meaford Nursing Home, 135 William St., Meaford ON N4L 1T4 – 519/538-1010; Fax: 519/538-5699 – 77 beds – Grey-Bruce District Health Council – Adm., Doris Bilitz

Merrickville: Hilltop Manor Nursing Home, 1005 St. Lawrence St., Merrickville ON K0G 1N0 – 613/269-4707; Fax: 613/269-3534 – 60 beds – Rideau Valley District Health Council – Adm., Bernard Bouchard

Metcalfe: Township of Osgoode Care Centre, 7650 Snake Island Rd., Metcalfe ON K0A 2P0 – 613/821-1034; Fax: 613/821-0070 – 70 beds – Ottawa-Carleton Regional Health Council – Adm., Murray B. Munro

Midland: St. Andrew's Centennial Manor, 340 Dominion Ave., Midland ON L4R 4S5 – 705/526-3781; Fax: 705/526-5656 – 70 beds – Simcoe County District Health Council – Adm., Walter Ens

Midland: The Villa Care Centre, 689 Yonge St., Midland ON L4R 2E1 – 705/526-4238; Fax: 705/526-0490 – 109 beds – Simcoe County District Health Council – Adm., Olivia Rettinger

Milton: Allendale, 185 Ontario St., Milton ON L9T 2M4 – 905/878-4141; Fax: 905/878-8797 – 300 beds – Halton District Health Council – Adm., M. Strecker

Milton: Mount Nemo Lodge, RR#2, Milton ON L9T 2X6 – 905/335-3636; Fax: 905/335-3699 – 60 beds – Halton District Health Council – Adm., Allen Sybersma

Milverton: Knollcrest Lodge, 50 William St., Milverton ON N0K 1M0 – 519/595-8121; Fax: 519/595-8199 – 75 beds – Huron-Perth District Health Council – Adm., Susan Rae

Minden: Hyland Crest Senior Citizen's Home, PO Box 30, Minden ON K0M 2K0 – 705/286-2140; Fax: 705/286-6384 – 62 beds – Haliburton, Kawartha & Pine Ridge District Health Council – Adm., Gary McKnight

Mississauga Lifecare Centre, 55 The Queensway West, Mississauga ON L5B 1B5 – 905/270-0170; Fax: 905/270-3234 – 202 beds – Peel District Health Council – Adm., Myrna Simms

Mississauga Nursing Home, 26 Peter St. North, Mississauga ON L5H 2G7 – 905/278-2213; Fax: 905/278-1311 – 55 beds – Peel District Health Council – Adm., Novak Bajin

Mississauga: Carmel Heights Home for the Aged, 1720 Sherwood Forest Circle, Mississauga ON L5K 1R1 – 905/822-5298 – 63 beds – Pres., Sr. Mary Rita

Mississauga: Chelsey Park (Streetsville) Nursing Home, 1742 Bristol Rd. West, Mississauga ON L5M 1X9 – 905/826-3045; Fax: 905/826-9978 – 118 beds – Peel District Health Council – Adm., Wendy Shelley

Mississauga: Chesley Park (Mississauga) Nursing Home, 2250 Hurontario St., Mississauga ON L5B 1M8 – 905/270-0411; Fax: 905/270-1749 – 237 beds – Peel District Health Council – Adm., Dr. Debys Symons

Mississauga: Erin Mills Lodge Nursing Home, 2132 Dundas St. West, Mississauga ON L5K 2K7 – 905/823-6700; Fax: 905/823-2410 – 86 beds – Peel District Health Council – Adm., Anne Helm

Mississauga: Sheridan Villa, 2460 Truscott Dr., Mississauga ON L5J 3Z8 – 905/823-1160; Fax: 905/823-7971 – 236 beds – Peel District Health Council – Adm., Verena Steger

Mississauga: Tyndall Nursing Home, 1060 Eglinton Ave. East, Mississauga ON L4W 1K3 – 905/624-1511; Fax: 905/629-9346 – 151 beds – Peel District Health Council – Adm., B.D. Jolly

Mitchell Nursing Home, 184 Napier St., Mitchell ON N0K 1N0 – 519/348-8861; Fax: 519/348-4214 – 48 beds – Huron-Perth District Health Council – Adm., Cathy Wight

Mitchell: Ritz Lutheran Villa, RR#5, Mitchell ON N0K 1N0 – 519/348-8612; Fax: 519/348-4420 – 83 beds – Huron-Perth District Health Council – Adm., Doreen M. Saunders

Mount Forest: Birmingham Lodge, 356a Birmingham St. East, Mount Forest ON N0G 2L2 – 519/323-4019; Fax: 519/323-3005 – retirement home – 96 beds – Adm., Ilonka van Willigen

Mount Forest: Saugeen Valley Nursing Centre, 465 Dublin St., Mount Forest ON N0G 2L0 – 519/323-2140; Fax: 519/323-3540 – 87 beds – Wellington-Dufferin District Health Council – Adm., Harold Lebold

Mount Pleasant: Brucefield Manor Nursing Home, 612 Mount Pleasant, Mount Pleasant ON N0E 1K0 – 519/484-2500; Fax: 519/484-2590 – 59 beds – Brant District Health Council – Acting Adm., Millie Chrisite

Napanee: Carewell Quinte Beach Nursing Home, Hwy. 2, Napanee ON K7R 3K7 – 613/396-3438; Fax: 613/396-2729 – 78 beds – Adm., Joan Watt

Napanee: Lenadco Home for the Aged, 310 Bridge St. West, Napanee ON K7R 2G4 – 613/354-3306; Fax: 613/354-7387 – 160 beds – Kingston, Frontenac & Lennox & Addington District Health Council – Adm., Richard Williams

Nepean: Carleton Lodge, 55 Lodge Rd., Nepean ON K2C 3H1 – 613/825-3763; Fax: 613/825-0245 – 161 beds – Ottawa-Carleton Regional Health Council – Adm., H. Lokhat

Nepean: Extendicare/Starwood, 114 Starwood Rd., Nepean ON K2G 3N5 – 613/224-3960; Fax: 613/224-9309 – 192 beds – Ottawa-Carleton Regional Health Council – Adm., Lynda Welch

New Hamburg: Northview Nursing Home, 200 Boulee St., New Hamburg ON N0B 2G0 – 519/662-2280; Fax: 519/662-1090 – 97 beds – Waterloo Region District Health Council – Adm., Ray Schlegel

Newcastle: Versa-Care Centre, Newcastle, 330 King St. West, Newcastle ON L1B 1G9 – 905/987-4702; Fax: 905/987-3621 – 88 beds – Waterloo Region District Health Council – Adm., Stephanie Sanborn

Newmarket: Arbor Living Centres, 581 Davis Dr., Newmarket ON L3Y 2P6 – 905/895-7661; Fax: 905/895-2138 – 182 beds – York Region District Health Council – Adm., Helen Lockie

Newmarket: Greenacres, 194 Eagle St., Newmarket ON L3Y 1J6 – 905/895-2381; Fax: 905/895-5368 – 179 beds – York Region District Health Council – Adm., Shawn Turner

Newmarket: Versa-Care Centre, Newmarket, 329 Eagle St., Newmarket ON L3Y 1K3 – 905/895-5187; Fax: 905/895-2645 – 70 beds – York Region District Health Council – Adm., Gwen Bate

Newmarket: Versa-Care Lodge, Newmarket, 52 George St., Newmarket ON L3Y 4V3 – 905/853-3242; Fax: 905/895-5139 – 93 beds – York Region District Health Council – Adm., Deena-Kay Irwin-Froese

Niagara Falls: Dorchester Manor, 6350 Dorchester Rd., Niagara Falls ON L2G 5T5 – 905/356-7430; Fax: 905/356-2199 – 98 beds – Niagara District Health Council – Adm., A. Whalen

Niagara Falls: Oakwood Park Lodge, 6747 Oakwood Dr., Niagara Falls ON L2E 6S5 – 905/356-8732; Fax: 905/356-2122 – 153 beds – Niagara District Health Council – Adm., Lori Turcotte

Niagara Falls: R.H. Lawson Eventide Home, 5050 Jepson St., Niagara Falls ON L2E 1K5 – 905/356-1221; Fax: 905/356-9609 – 100 beds – Niagara District Health Council – Adm., Maj. Harold Rideout

Niagara Falls: Valley Park Lodge, 6400 Valley Way, Niagara Falls ON L2E 7E3 – 905/358-3277; Fax: 905/358-3012 – 65 beds – Niagara District Health Council – Adm., Jennifer Kennedy

Niagara-on-the-Lake: Chateau Gardens (Niagara) Nursing Home, 120 Wellington St., Niagara-on-the-Lake ON L0S 1J0 – 905/468-2111; Fax: 905/468-4463 – 124 beds – Niagara District Health Council – Adm., Susan Norton

Niagara-on-the-Lake: Upper Canada Lodge, 272 Wellington St., Niagara-on-the-Lake ON L0S 1J0 – 905/468-4208; Fax: 905/468-0520 – 79 beds – Niagara District Health Council – Adm., Patrick O'Neill

Nipigon District Memorial Hospital, *see* General Hospitals listings

North Bay: Cassellholme, 400 Olive St., North Bay ON P1B 6J4 – 705/474-4250; Fax: 705/474-6129 – 240 beds – Nipissing-Timiskaming District Health Council – Adm., Gordon Shields

North Bay: Leisureworld North Bay Centre, 401 William St., North Bay ON P1A 1X5 – 705/476-2602; Fax: 705/476-1624 – 148 beds – Nipissing-Timiskaming District Health Council – Adm., Brenda Prieur

Northbrook: Pine Meadow Nursing Home, Lloyd St., PO Box 100, Northbrook ON K0H 2G0 – 613/336-9120; Fax: 613/336-9144 – 60 beds – Kingston, Frontenac & Lennox & Addington District Health Council – Adm., Colleen M. Haley-Wicklam

Norwich: Norvilla Nursing Home, 11 Elgin St. East, Norwich ON N0J 1P0 – 519/863-2717 – 40 beds – Thames Valley District Health Council – Adm., Maureen Sinden

Norwood: Pleasant Meadow Manor, 105 Alma St., Norwood ON K0L 2V0 – 705/639-5308; Fax: 705/639-5309 – 60 beds – Haliburton, Kawartha & Pine Ridge District Health Council – Adm., Jane Adams-Taylor

Oakville Lifecare Centre, 599 Lyons Lane, Oakville ON L6J 2Y2 – 905/845-9933; Fax: 905/845-9950 – 205 beds – Halton District Health Council – Adm., Stephen Picott

Ohsweken: Iroquois Lodge Nursing Home, Chiefswood Rd., Ohsweken ON N0A 1M0 – 519/445-2224; Fax: 519/445-4180 – 50 beds – Brant District Health Council – Adm., Belva M. Monture

Orangeville: Avalon Care Centre & Retirement Lodge, 355 Broadway Ave., Orangeville ON L9W 3Y3 – 519/941-5161; Fax: 519/941-9532 – 137 beds – Wellington-Dufferin District Health Council – Adm., David K. Holwell

Orillia: Al-Mar Nursing Home, 327 Muskoka Rd., Orillia ON L3V 4G5 – 705/326-6038; Fax: 705/327-5373 – 38 beds – Simcoe County District Health Council – Adm., Jacqueline Payne

Orillia: Hillcrest Lodge, 86 Cedar St., Orillia ON L3V 2V5 – 705/326-3181; Fax: 705/326-7867 – 48 beds – Adm., Sharon Turner

Orillia: Sunset Lodge (Salvation Army), 127 Peter St. North, Orillia ON L3V 4Z4 – 705/325-5715; Fax: 705/329-0860 – 31 beds – Simcoe County District Health Council – Adm., Maj. N. Janes

Orillia: Trillium Manor Home for the Aged, 12 Grace Ave., Orillia ON L3V 2K2 – 705/325-1504; Fax: 705/325-7661 – 122 beds – Simcoe County District Health Council – Adm., Sharon Turner

Orillia: Versa-Care Centre, Orillia, 291 Mississauga St. West, Orillia ON L3V 3B9 – 705/325-2289; Fax: 705/325-7178 – 94 beds – Simcoe County District Health Council – Adm., Mary Bullock

Orleans: Madonna Nursing Home, 1533 St. Joseph Blvd., Orleans ON K1C 1S9 – 613/824-2040; Fax: 613/824-5151 – 75 beds – Ottawa-Carleton Regional Health Council – Adm., Jacques Lemieux

Oshawa: Extendicare/Oshawa, 82 Park Rd. North, Oshawa ON L1J 4L1 – 905/579-0011; Fax: 905/579-1733 – 175 beds – Waterloo Region District Health Council – Adm., Linda Grills

Oshawa: Hillsdale Manor, 600 Oshawa Blvd. North, Oshawa ON L1G 5T9 – 905/579-1777; Fax: 905/579-3911 – 435 beds – Waterloo Region District Health Council – Adm., Fred Fountain

Oshawa: Versa-Care Centre, Oshawa, 186 Thornton Rd. South, Oshawa ON L1J 5Y2 – 905/576-5181; Fax: 905/576-0078 – 104 beds – Waterloo Region District Health Council – Adm., Arlene Inkster

Ottawa: Bronson Place, 950 Bank St., Ottawa ON K1S 5G6 – 613/238-2727; Fax: 613/238-4643 – 70 beds – Ottawa-Carleton Regional Health Council – Adm., Susan LeConte

Ottawa: Extendicare/Medex, 1865 Baseline Rd., Ottawa ON K2C 3K6 – 613/225-5650; Fax: 613/225-0960 – 192 beds – Ottawa-Carleton Regional Health Council – Adm., Maureen Dillon

Ottawa: Extendicare/New Orchard Lodge, 99 New Orchard Ave., Ottawa ON K2B 5E6 – 613/820-2110; Fax: 613/820-6380 – 111 beds – Ottawa-Carleton Regional Health Council – Adm., Susan Reed

Ottawa: Extendicare/West End Villa, 2179 Elmira Dr., Ottawa ON K2C 3S1 – 613/829-3501; Fax: 613/829-3504 – 240 beds – Ottawa-Carleton Regional Health Council – Adm., Helen Pinel

Ottawa: Hillel Lodge, 125 Wurtemburg St., Ottawa ON K1N 8L9 – 613/789-7132; Fax: 613/789-1371 – 48 beds – Ottawa-Carleton Regional Health Council – Adm., Stephen Schneiderman

Ottawa: Island Lodge, 1 Porter's Island, Ottawa ON K1N 5M2 – 613/789-5100; Fax: 613/789-3704 – 331 beds – Ottawa-Carleton Regional Health Council – Adm., J. Chene

Ottawa: Maycourt Convalescent Home, 114 Cameron Ave., Ottawa ON K1S 0X1 – 613/733-0760; Fax: 613/730-7903 – 50 beds – Ottawa-Carleton Regional Health Council – Adm., Marjorie Rogers

Ottawa: The Perley and Rideau Veterans' Health Centre, 1750 Russell Rd., Ottawa ON K1G 5Z6 – 613/526-7171; Fax: 613/526-7172 – 450 beds – Ottawa-Carleton Regional Health Council – Exec. Dir. & CEO, Greg Fougère

Ottawa: St. Patrick's Home, 2865 Riverside Dr., Ottawa ON K1V 8N5 – 613/731-4660; Fax: 613/731-4056 – 202 beds – Ottawa-Carleton Regional Health Council – Adm., Sr. Mona Martin

Ottawa: Versa-Care Lodge, Ottawa, 2330 Carling Ave., Ottawa ON K2B 7H1 – 613/820-9328; Fax: 613/820-9774 – 326 beds – Ottawa-Carleton Regional Health Council – Adm., Chris Sandes

Ottawa: Villa Marguerite, 75 Bruyere St., Ottawa ON K1N 5C8 – 613/562-6369; Fax: 613/562-6367 – 71 beds – Ottawa-Carleton Regional Health Council – Adm., Sr. Diane Albert

Owen Sound: Lee Manor, 875 Sixth St. East, Owen Sound ON N4K 5W5 – 519/376-4420; Fax: 519/371-5406 – 150 beds – Grey-Bruce District Health Council – Adm., Al Wood

Owen Sound: Versa-Care Georgian Heights, 1115 - 10th St. East, Owen Sound ON N4K 6B1 – 519/371-1441; Fax: 519/371-1092 – 40 beds – Grey-Bruce District Health Council – Adm., Tracee Givens

Owen Sound: Versa-Care Maple View, 1029 - 4th Ave. West, Owen Sound ON N4K 4W1 – 519/376-2522; Fax: 519/371-3304 – 29 beds – Grey-Bruce District Health Council – Adm., Tracee Givens

Owen Sound: Versa-Care Summit Place, 850 - 4th St. East, Owen Sound ON N4K 6A3 – 519/376-3212; Fax: 519/371-0923 – 119 beds – Grey-Bruce District Health Council – Adm., Nan Dunbar

Palmerston: Royal Terrace, 600 Whites Rd., PO Box 640, Palmerston ON N0G 2P0 – 519/343-2611; Fax: 519/343-2860 – 67 beds – Wellington-Dufferin District Health Council – Adm., P.K. Ramchandani

Paris: Park Lane Terrace, 295 Grand River St. North, Paris ON N3L 2N9 – 519/442-2753; Fax: 519/442-3696 – 60 beds – Brant District Health Council – Adm., Beth South

Paris: Versa-Care Telfer Place, 245 Grand River St. North, Paris ON N3L 3G2 – 519/442-4411; Fax: 519/442-6724 – 45 beds – Brant District Health Council – Adm., Linda Ingham

Parkhill: Chateau Gardens (Parkhill) Nursing Home, 250 Tain St., PO Box 129, Parkhill ON N0M 2K0 – 519/294-6342; Fax: 519/294-0107 – 59 beds – Thames Valley District Health Council – Adm., Donna Heffron

Parry Sound: Belvedere Heights, 21 Belvedere Ave., Parry Sound ON P2A 2A2 – 705/746-9367; Fax: 705/746-7706 – 101 beds – West Muskoka Parry Sound District Health Council – Adm., Jack Agema

Pembroke: Marianhill, 600 Cecelia St., Pembroke ON K8A 7Z3 – 613/735-6838; Fax: 613/732-3934 – 131 beds – Renfrew County District Health Council – Adm., Kelly Isfan

Pembroke: Miramichi Lodge, 400 Bell St., Pembroke ON K8A 2K5 – 613/735-0175; Fax: 613/735-8061 – 186 beds – Renfrew County District Health Council – Adm., Brian Burbridge

Penetanguishene: Georgian Manor, 7 Harriett St., PO Box 129, Penetanguishene ON L9M 1K8 – 705/549-3166; Fax: 705/549-6062 – 107 beds – Simcoe County District Health Council – Adm., Robert Morton

Perth Community Care Centre Inc., Dignicare Inc., 55 Sunset Blvd., RR#4, Perth ON K7H 3C6 – 613/267-2506; Fax: 613/267-7060 – 120 beds – Rideau Valley District Health Council – Adm., Joyce Firlotte

Perth: Lanark Lodge, RR#4, Perth ON K7H 3C6 – 613/267-4225; Fax: 613/264-2668 – 163 beds – Rideau Valley District Health Council – Assistant Adm., Petrr Bennett

Peterborough: Anson House, 136 Anson St., Peterborough ON K9H 5R1 – 705/743-3172; Fax: 705/743-9028 – 42 beds – Haliburton, Kawartha & Pine Ridge District Health Council – Adm., Kevin Murphy

Peterborough: Extendicare/Peterborough, 80 Alexander Ave., Peterborough ON K9J 6B4 – 705/743-7552; Fax: 705/742-9664 – 212 beds – Haliburton, Kawartha & Pine Ridge District Health Council – Adm., Margaret Lazure

Peterborough: Fairhaven Home, 131 Langton St., Peterborough ON K9H 6K3 – 705/743-4265; Fax: 705/743-6292 – 253 beds – Haliburton, Kawartha & Pine Ridge District Health Council – Exectuive Dir., Patricia Knapp

Peterborough: Marycrest Home for the Aged, 200 St. Luke's Ave., Peterborough ON K9H 1E7 – 705/743-4744; Fax: 705/743-7532 – 156 beds – Haliburton, Kawartha & Pine Ridge District Health Council – Adm., Sr. Jacqueline Janisse

Peterborough: Riverview Manor Nursing Home, 1155 Water St., Peterborough ON K9H 3P8 – 705/748-6706; Fax: 705/748-5407 – 124 beds – Haliburton, Kawartha & Pine Ridge District Health Council – Adm., Barbara Payne

Peterborough: Springdale Country Manor, 1726 Hwy. 7A, RR#5, Peterborough ON K9J 6X6 – 705/742-8811; Fax: 705/742-8812 – 65 beds – Haliburton, Kawartha & Pine Ridge District Health Council – Adm., Jane Adams-Taylor

Petrolia: Fiddick's Nursing Home, 437 First Ave., Petrolia ON N0N 1R0 – 519/882-0370; Fax: 519/882-0375 – 60 beds – Lambton District Health Council – Adm., Michael Fiddick

Petrolia: Lambton Meadowview Villa, RR#4, Petrolia ON N0N 1R0 – 519/882-1470; Fax: 519/882-3600 – 125 beds – Lambton District Health Council – Adm., Doug Hutton

Pickering: Community Nursing Home, 1955 Valley Farm Rd., Pickering ON L1V 1X6 – 905/831-2522; Fax: 905/420-6030 – 169 beds – Waterloo Region District Health Council – Adm., Douglas Pember

Picton: Carewell Picton Manor Nursing Home, 9 Hill St., Picton ON K0K 2T0 – 613/476-6140; Fax: 613/476-5240 – 78 beds – Hastings & Prince Edward Counties District Health Council – Adm., Norma Bongard

Picton: Kentwood Park, 2 Ontario St., PO Box 1298, Picton ON K0K 2T0 – 613/476-5671; Fax: 613/476-3986 – 48 beds – Adm., Norma Bongard

Picton: McFarland (H.J.) Memorial Home, RR#2, Picton ON K0K 2T0 – 613/476-2138; Fax: 613/476-8356 – 84 beds – Hastings & Prince Edward Counties District Health Council – Adm., E. Gervais

Picton: Versa-Care Hallowell House, RR#1, Picton ON K0K 2T0 – 613/476-4444; Fax: 613/476-1566 – 101 beds – Hastings & Prince Edward Counties District Health Council – Adm., Janice Wilkes

Picton: West Lake, West Lake Rd., PO Box 2229, Picton ON K0K 2T0 – 613/393-2055; Fax: 613/393-2057 – 47 beds – Hastings & Prince Edward Counties District Health Council – Adm., Joan Watt

Plantagenet: Pinecrest Nursing Home, 101 Parent St., RR#1, PO Box 250, Plantagenet ON K0B 1L0 – 613/673-4835; Fax: 613/673-2675 – 60 beds – DHC of Eastern Ontario – Adm., Lyne Simoneau

Port Colborne: Northland Manor, 485 Northland Ave., Port Colborne ON L3K 4B3 – 905/835-2463; Fax: 905/835-6518 – 87 beds – Niagara District Health Council – Adm., Larry Jackson

Port Dover: Versa-Care Centre, Port Dover, 501 St. George St., Port Dover ON N0A 1N0 – 519/583-1422; Fax: 519/583-3197 – 70 beds – Haldimand-Norfolk District Health Council – Adm., Ellen Coffey

Port Hope: Community Nursing Home, 20 Hope St. South, Port Hope ON L1A 2M8 – 905/885-6367; Fax: 905/885-6368 – 97 beds – Haliburton, Kawartha & Pine Ridge District Health Council – Adm., Douglas Palmer

Port Hope: Regency Manor Nursing Home, 66 Dorset St. East, Port Hope ON L1A 1E3 – 905/885-4558; Fax: 905/885-7386 – 50 beds – Haliburton, Kawartha & Pine Ridge District Health Council – Adm., Cynthia Knight-Pocock

Port Perry: Community Nursing Home, 15941 Simcoe St. North, Port Perry ON L9L 1A6 – 905/985-3205; Fax: 905/985-3721 – 75 beds – Waterloo Region District Health Council – Adm., Edna Goss

Port Stanley: Extendicare/Port Stanley, 288 East St., Port Stanley ON N5L 1J6 – 519/782-3339; Fax: 519/782-4756 – 60 beds – Thames Valley District Health Council – Adm., Charles Marczinski

Powassan: Eastholme, 200 Big Bend Ave., PO Box 400, Powassan ON P0H 1Z0 – 705/724-2005; Fax: 705/724-5429 – 74 beds – East Muskoka/Parry Sound District Health Council – Adm., Steven Piekarski

Prescott: Wellington House Nursing Home, 970 Edward St. North, PO Box 401, Prescott ON K0E 1T0 – 613/925-2834; Fax: 613/925-5425 – 60 beds – Rideau Valley District Health Council – Adm., Bernadette Timco

Puslinch: Morriston Park Nursing Home, RR#2, Puslinch ON N0B 2J0 – 519/822-9179; Fax: 519/822-4459 – 28 beds – Wellington-Dufferin District Health Council – Adm., Alfred Urfey

Renfrew: Bonnechere Manor, 470 Albert St., Renfrew ON K7V 4L5 – 613/432-4873; Fax: 613/432-7138 – 180 beds – Renfrew County District Health Council – Adm., Brian Burbridge

Renfrew: Groves Park Lodge, 470 Raglan St. North, Renfrew ON K7V 1P5 – 613/432-5823; Fax: 613/432-5287 – 75 beds – Renfrew County District Health Council – Asst. Adm., Carol Haywood

Richmond Hill: Mariann Home, 9915 Yonge St., Richmond Hill ON L4C 1V1 – 905/884-9276; Fax: 905/884-1800 – 52 beds – York Region District Health Council – Adm., Sr. Mary Verhoeven

Ridgetown: Versa-Care Village, Ridgetown, 9 Myrtle St., Ridgetown ON N0P 2C0 – 519/674-5427; Fax: 519/674-2422 – 40 beds – Kent County District Health Council – Adm., Kathy Morningstar

Rockland: St. Joseph Nursing Home, 1615 Laurier St., Rockland ON K4K 1C8 – 613/446-5126; Fax: 613/446-1516 – 81 beds – DHC of Eastern Ontario – Adm., Jacqueline Brown

St Catharines: Extendicare/St. Catharines, 283 Pelham Rd., St Catharines ON L2S 1X7 – 905/688-3311; Fax: 905/688-5774 – 152 beds – Niagara District Health Council – Adm., Mary Britt

St Catharines: Heidehof, 600 Lake St., St Catharines ON L2N 4J4 – 905/935-3344; Fax: 905/935-0081 – 106 beds – Niagara District Health Council – Adm., Gordon Midgley

St Catharines: Ina Grafton-Gage Home (Niagara), 413 Linwell Rd., St Catharines ON L2M 2P3 – 905/935-6822; Fax: 905/935-6847 – 40 beds – Niagara District Health Council – Adm., D. Caughey

St Catharines: Linhaven, 403 Ontario St., St Catharines ON L2N 1L5 – 905/934-3364; Fax: 905/934-6975 – 226 beds – Niagara District Health Council – Adm., Dan Oettinger

St Catharines: Tabor Manor, 1 Tabor Dr., St Catharines ON L2N 1V9 – 905/934-2548; Fax: 905/934-6467 – 80 beds – Niagara District Health Council – Adm., Rudy Siemens

St Catharines: Tufford Nursing Home, 312 Queenston Rd., St Catharines ON L2P 2X4 – 905/682-0503; Fax: 905/682-2770 – 64 beds – Niagara District Health Council – Adm., Cecilia Osczypko

St Catharines: Versa-Care Centre, St. Catharines, 168 Scott St., St Catharines ON L2N 1H2 – 905/934-3321; Fax: 905/934-9011 – 200 beds – Niagara District Health Council – Adm., Sandra Fredericks

St Catharines: West Park Health Centre, 103 Pelham Rd., St Catharines ON L2S 1S9 – 905/688-1031; Fax: 905/688-9646 – 122 beds – Niagara District Health Council – Adm., Michael Walter

St Jacobs: Derbecker's Heritage House, 54 Eby St., St Jacobs ON N0B 2N0 – 519/664-2921; Fax: 519/664-2380 – 72 beds – Waterloo Region District Health Council – Adm., Pamela Derbecker

St Marys: Kingsway Lodge Nursing Home, 310 Queen St. East, St Marys ON N0M 2V0 – 519/284-2921; Fax: 519/284-4468 – 35 beds – Huron-Perth District Health Council – Adm., Scott A. Mackay

St Marys: Wildwood Care Centre, 100 Ann St., St Marys ON N4X 1A1 – 519/284-3628; Fax: 519/284-0575 – 60 beds – Huron-Perth District Health Council – Adm., Lynn Walsh

St Thomas: Caressant Care St. Thomas Nursing Home, 15 Bonnie Pl., St Thomas ON N5R 5T8 – 519/633-6493; Fax: 519/633-9329 – 116 beds – Thames Valley District Health Council – Adm., Marlene Powner

St Thomas: Elgin Manor, RR#1, St Thomas ON N5P 3S5 – 519/631-0620; Fax: 519/633-0475 – 90 beds – Thames Valley District Health Council – Adm., Fred Boyes

St Thomas: Rest Haven Nursing Home, 4 May Bucke St., St Thomas ON N5R 5J6 – 519/633-3164; Fax: 519/631-8362 – 60 beds – Thames Valley District Health Council – Adm., Ann Stansell

St Thomas: Valleyview Home for the Aged, 29 Elysian St., St Thomas ON N5P 1R5 – 519/633-1030; Fax: 519/633-7295 – 136 beds – Thames Valley District Health Council – Adm., Michael Carroll

Sarnia: Marshall Gowland Manor, 1000 London Rd., Sarnia ON N7S 1N7 – 519/336-3720; Fax: 519/336-3734 – 126 beds – Lambton District Health Council – Acting Adm., Vicki Lucas

Sarnia: Trillium Villa Nursing Home, 1221 Michigan Ave., Sarnia ON N7S 3Y3 – 519/542-5520; Fax: 519/542-5953 – 152 beds – Lambton District Health Council – Adm., Jean Kimmerly

Sarnia: Versa-Care Centre, Sarnia, 1464 Blackwell Rd., Sarnia ON N7S 5M4 – 519/542-3421; Fax: 519/542-3604 – 100 beds – Lambton District Health Council – Adm., Ann Currie

Sarnia: Vision Nursing Home, 229 Wellington St., Sarnia ON N7T 1G9 – 519/336-6551; Fax: 519/336-5878 – 60 beds – Lambton District Health Council – Adm., Bernard Bax

Sarsfield: Versa-Care Centre, Sarsfield, 2861 Colonial Rd., PO Box 130, Sarsfield ON K0A 3E0 – 613/835-2977; Fax: 613/835-2982 – 46 beds – Ottawa-Carleton Regional Health Council – Adm., Conny Menger

Sault Ste Marie: Extendicare/Tendercare, 770 Great Northern Rd., Sault Ste Marie ON P6A 5K7 – 705/949-3611; Fax: 705/945-6303 – 119 beds – Algoma District Health Council – Adm., Laureanne Ryan

Sault Ste Marie: Extendicare/Van Daele, 39 Van Daele St., Sault Ste Marie ON P6B 4V3 – 705/949-7934; Fax: 705/945-0968 – 149 beds – Algoma District Health Council – Adm., Bill Lonergan

Sault Ste Marie: F.J. Davey Home, 860 Great Northern Rd., Sault Ste Marie ON P6A 5K7 – 705/942-2204; Fax: 705/942-2234 – 184 beds – Algoma District Health Council – Adm., Peter MacLean

Sault Ste Marie: Mauno Kaihla Koti, 725 North St., Sault Ste Marie ON P6B 5Z3 – 705/945-9987; Fax: 705/945-1217 – 60 beds – Algoma District Health Council – Exec. Dir., Lewis Massad

Sault Ste. Marie: Pathways Retirement Residence, 375 Trunk Rd., Sault Ste. Marie ON P6A 3S9 – 705/759-1079; Fax: 705/759-1211 – 150 beds – CEO, Len Barnett

Seaforth Manor, 100 James St., Seaforth ON N0K 1W0 – 519/527-0030; Fax: 519/527-2862 – 63 beds – Huron-Perth District Health Council – Adm., Ruth Hilderbrand

Selby: The Village Green Nursing Home, PO Box 94, Selby ON K0K 2Z0 – 613/388-2693; Fax: 613/388-2694 – 66 beds – Ottawa-Carleton Regional Health Council – Adm., Linda Pierce

Shelburne Residence, 200 Robert St., Shelburne ON L0N 1S0 – 519/925-3746; Fax: 519/925-1476 – 60 beds – Wellington-Dufferin District Health Council – Adm., Colin McDavid

Shelburne: Dufferin Oaks, 151 Centre St., Shelburne ON L0N 1S4 – 519/925-2140; Fax: 519/925-5067 – 165 beds – Wellington-Dufferin District Health Council – Adm., Melvin H. Lloyd

Simcoe: Cedarwood Village, 500 Queensway West, Simcoe ON N3Y 4R5 – 519/426-8305; Fax: 519/426-2511 – 90 beds – Haldimand-Norfolk District Health Council – Adm., Marlene Vanham

Simcoe: The Norfolk Hospital Nursing Home, 365 West St., Simcoe ON N3Y 1T7 – 519/426-0750; Fax: 519/426-3326 – 80 beds – Haldimand-Norfolk District Health Council – Adm., Harold Shantz

Simcoe: Norview Lodge, 510 Queensway West, PO Box 604, Simcoe ON N3Y 4L8 – 519/426-0902; Fax: 519/426-9867 – 179 beds – Haldimand-Norfolk District Health Council – Adm., Kim Jenereaux

Sioux Lookout: William A. (Bill) George Extended Care, 75 Fifth Ave., Sioux Lookout ON P8T 1K9 – 807/737-1364; Fax: 807/737-2449 – 20 beds – Kenora-Rainy River District Health Council – CEO, Mark Balcaen

Smiths Falls: Broadview Nursing Home, 210 Brockville St., Smiths Falls ON K7A 3Z4 – 613/283-1845; Fax: 613/283-7073 – 75 beds – Rideau Valley District Health Council – Adm., Leonard Parsons

Smooth Rock Falls Hospital, *see* General Hospitals listings

Southampton Care Centre, 140 Grey St., Southampton ON N0H 2L0 – 519/797-3220; Fax: 519/797-5487 – 84 beds – Grey-Bruce District Health Council – Adm., Carol Warner

Stayner Nursing Home, 244 Main St., Stayner ON L0M 1S0 – 705/428-3614; Fax: 705/428-0537 – 49 beds – Simcoe County District Health Council – Adm., Lorraine Baker

Stayner: Sweetbriar Lodge Nursing Home, RR#2, Stayner ON L0M 1S0 – 705/428-3613; Fax: 705/428-3311 – 50 beds – Simcoe County District Health Council – Adm., Nancy Archdekin

Stirling Manor Nursing Home, 218 Edward St., Stirling ON K0K 3E0 – 613/395-2596; Fax: 613/395-0930 – 75 beds – Hastings & Prince Edward Counties District Health Council – Adm., Judith Norlock

Stoney Creek Lifecare Centre, 199 Glover Rd., Stoney Creek ON L8E 5P9 – 905/643-1795; Fax: 905/643-1085 – 45 beds – Hamilton-Wentworth District Health Council – Adm., Stacey Best

Stoney Creek: Clarion Nursing Home, 337 Hwy. 8, Stoney Creek ON L8G 1E7 – 905/664-2281; Fax: 905/664-2966 – 100 beds – Hamilton-Wentworth District Health Council – Adm., Michael Janjic

Stoney Creek: Heritage Green Nursing Home, 353 Isaac Brock Dr., Stoney Creek ON L8J 1Y1 – 905/573-7177; Fax: 905/573-7151 – 112 beds – Hamilton-Wentworth District Health Council – Adm., Kenneth D. Reimche

Stoney Creek: Pine Villa Nursing Home, 490 Hwy. 8, Stoney Creek ON L8G 1G6 – 905/662-5033; Fax: 905/662-6336 – 38 beds – Hamilton-Wentworth District Health Council – Adm., Augustus Thomas

Stouffville: Green Gables Manor Nursing Home, 9th Line Rd., RR#2, Stouffville ON L4A 7X3 – 905/640-1310; Fax: 905/640-2231 – 37 beds – York Region District Health Council – Adm., Kathleen Szela

Stouffville: Parkview Home, 481 Rupert Ave., Stouffville ON L4A 1T7 – 905/640-1911; Fax: 905/640-4051 – 109 beds – York Region District Health Council – Adm., Wallace Kribs

Stratford: Greenwood Court, 90 Greenwood Ct., Stratford ON N5A 7W5 – 519/273-4662 – 45 beds –

Huron-Perth District Health Council – Adm., Victoria Stuart

Stratford: People Care Centre, 198 Mornington St., Stratford ON N5A 5G3 – 519/271-4440; Fax: 519/271-4446 – 60 beds – Huron-Perth District Health Council – Adm., Pat Kelly

Stratford: Spruce Lodge, 643 West Gore St., Stratford ON N5A 1L4 – 519/271-4090; Fax: 519/271-5862 – 128 beds – Huron-Perth District Health Council – Adm., Marilyn Herman

Stratford: Versa-Care Centre, Stratford, RR#5, Stratford ON N5A 6S6 – 519/393-5132; Fax: 519/393-5130 – 90 beds – Huron-Perth District Health Council – Adm., Deanne Roussell

Strathroy: Sprucedale Care Centre, 150 Fraser St., Strathroy ON N7G 4C3 – 519/245-2808; Fax: 519/245-1767 – 62 beds – Thames Valley District Health Council – Adm., Darren Micallef

Strathroy: Strathmere Lodge, Albert St. West, Strathroy ON N7G 3J3 – 519/245-2520; Fax: 519/245-5711 – 175 beds – Thames Valley District Health Council – Adm., Larry Hills

Sturgeon Falls: Au Château, 106 Michaud St., Sturgeon Falls ON P0H 2G0 – 705/753-1550; Fax: 705/753-3135 – 162 beds – Nipissing-Timiskaming District Health Council – Adm., Wayne Foisy

Sudbury: Extendicare/Falconbridge, 281 Falconbridge Rd., Sudbury ON P3A 5K4 – 705/566-7980; Fax: 705/566-3300 – 234 beds – Manitoulin & Sudbury District Health Council – Acting Adm., Keith Clement

Sudbury: Extendicare/York, 333 York St., Sudbury ON P3E 5J3 – 705/674-4221; Fax: 705/674-4281 – 288 beds – Manitoulin & Sudbury District Health Council – Acting Adm., Dennis Boschetto

Sudbury: Pioneer Manor, 960 Notre Dame Ave., Sudbury ON P3A 2T4 – 705/566-4270; Fax: 705/524-1767 – 349 beds – Manitoulin & Sudbury District Health Council – Adm., Catherine Sandblom

Sutton West: River Glen Haven Nursing Home, 160 High St., Sutton West ON L0E 1R0 – 905/722-3631; Fax: 905/722-8638 – 119 beds – York Region District Health Council – Adm., Susan Williams

Tavistock: Bonnie Brae Health Care Centre, 55 Woodstock St. North, Tavistock ON N0B 2R0 – 519/655-2420; Fax: 519/655-3432 – 80 beds – Thames Valley District Health Council – Adm., Joyce Penney

Tavistock: The Maples Home for Seniors, 94 William St. South, PO Box 400, Tavistock ON N0B 2R0 – 519/655-2344; Fax: 519/655-2851 – 43 beds – Thames Valley District Health Council – Adm., Lois Riehl

Tavistock: People Care Tavistock, 28 William St. North, PO Box 460, Tavistock ON N0B 2R0 – 519/655-2031; Fax: 519/655-3583 – 100 beds – Thames Valley District Health Council – Adm., O'Derald Gingerich

Tecumseh: Brouillette Manor Nursing Home, 11900 Brouillette Ct., Tecumseh ON N8N 1S3 – 519/735-9810; Fax: 519/735-8569 – 60 beds – Essex County District Health Council – Adm., Donald Hewitt

Tecumseh: Versa-Care Place Tecumseh, 1400 Banwell Rd., Tecumseh ON N8N 2M4 – 519/735-3204; Fax: 519/735-1836 – 142 beds – Essex County District Health Council – Adm., Patricia Pacuta

Terrace Bay: Birchwood Terrace, Hwy. 17, PO Box 250, Terrace Bay ON P0T 2W0 – 807/825-3748; Fax: 807/825-3859 – 23 beds – Thunder Bay District Health Council – Adm., Michael Yakamovich

Thessalon: Algoma Manor, 1 Owen St., Thessalon ON P0R 1L0 – 705/842-2840; Fax: 705/842-2650 – 108 beds – Algoma District Health Council – Adm., Peter MacLean

Thornbury: Errinrung Nursing Home, 67 Bruce St., PO Box 69, Thornbury ON N0H 2P0 – 519/599-2737; Fax: 519/599-3410 – 42 beds – Grey-Bruce District Health Council – Adm., Jeanne Lune

Thunder Bay: Bethammi Nursing Home, 63 Carrie St., Thunder Bay ON P7A 4J2 – 807/767-6263; Fax: 807/767-1672 – 109 beds – Thunder Bay District Health Council – Adm., Sr. Bonnie A. MacLellan

Thunder Bay: Central Park Lodge, 315 South Syndicate Ave., Thunder Bay ON P7E 1E2 – 807/623-6919; Fax: 807/623-8499 – 107 beds – Adm., Valerie Gosse

Thunder Bay: Dawson Court, 523 North Algoma St., Stn P, Thunder Bay ON P7A 5C2 – 807/625-2926; Fax: 807/345-8854 – 150 beds – Thunder Bay District Health Council – Adm., Mike Kennedy

Thunder Bay: Grandview Lodge/Thunder Bay, 200 Lillie St., Thunder Bay ON P7E 2V6 – 807/625-2923; Fax: 807/623-4075 – 150 beds – Thunder Bay District Health Council – Adm., Donald Holmstrom

Thunder Bay: Pinewood Court, 445 James St. South, Thunder Bay ON P7E 2V6 – 807/577-1127; Fax: 807/475-9455 – 75 beds – Thunder Bay District Health Council – Adm., Michael Yakamovich

Thunder Bay: Pioneer Ridge, 750 Tungsten St., Thunder Bay ON P7B 6R1 – 807/346-3910; Fax: 807/346-3916 – 150 beds – Thunder Bay District Health Council – Adm., Joyce Green

Thunder Bay: Versa-Care Centre, Thunder Bay, 135 South Vickers St., Thunder Bay ON P7E 1J2 – 807/623-9511; Fax: 807/623-6992 – 161 beds – Thunder Bay District Health Council – Adm., Gail Henry

Tilbury Manor Nursing Home, 16 Fort St., Tilbury ON N0P 2L0 – 519/682-0243; Fax: 519/682-2358 – 85 beds – Kent County District Health Council – Adm., Gwen Waddick

Tillsonburg: Maple Manor Nursing Home, 73 Bidwell St., Tillsonburg ON N4G 3T8 – 519/842-3563; Fax: 519/842-4901 – 101 beds – Thames Valley District Health Council – Adm., George Kanuik

Timmins: Extendicare/Timmins, 15 Hollinger Lane, Timmins ON P0N 1G0 – 705/360-1913; Fax: 705/268-3975 – 119 beds – Cochrane District Health Council – Adm., Sharon Chevrier

Timmins: Golden Manor, 481 Melrose Blvd., Timmins ON P4N 5H3 – 705/264-5375; Fax: 705/267-4662 – 177 beds – Cochrane District Health Council – Adm., Heather Bozzer

Toronto: Albion Lodge, 111 Kendleton Dr., Etobicoke ON M9V 1V2 – 416/392-2349; Fax: 416/392-4528 – 98 beds – Metropolitan Toronto District Health Council – Adm., Wayne Fotty

Toronto: Altamont Nursing Home, 92 Island Rd., Scarborough ON M1C 2P5 – 416/284-4781; Fax: 416/284-3634 – 159 beds – Metropolitan Toronto District Health Council – Adm., Gladys Brett

Toronto: Anglican Houses - Cana Place, 3333 Finch Ave. East, Scarborough ON M1W 2R9 – 416/497-4770; Fax: 416/497-9069 – 50 beds – Metropolitan Toronto District Health Council – Adm., Jim McMinn

Toronto: Barton Place Nursing Home, 914 Bathurst St., Toronto ON M5R 3G5 – 416/533-9473; Fax: 416/538-2685 – 254 beds – Metropolitan Toronto District Health Council – Adm., Derrick Hoare

Toronto: Baycrest Centre for Geriatric Care - Jewish Home for the Aged, 3560 Bathurst St., Toronto ON M6A 2E1 – 416/785-2500; Fax: 416/785-2464 – 372 beds – Metropolitan Toronto District Health Council – Adm., Stephen Herbert

Toronto: Belmont House, 55 Belmont St., Toronto ON M5R 1R1 – 416/964-9231; Fax: 416/964-1448 – 296 beds – Metropolitan Toronto District Health Council – Adm., M.J. Large

Toronto: Bendale Acres, 2920 Lawrence Ave. East, Scarborough ON M1P 2T8 – 416/397-7000; Fax: 416/397-7067 – 300 beds – Metropolitan Toronto District Health Council – Adm., Shirley Barnes

Toronto: Carefree Lodge, 306 Finch Ave. East, North York ON M2N 4S5 – 416/397-1500; Fax: 416/397-1501 – 127 beds – Metropolitan Toronto District Health Council – Adm., Vilma Kalu

Toronto: Casa Verde Health Centre, 3595 Keele St., North York ON M3J 1M7 – 416/633-3431; Fax: 416/633-6736 – 231 beds – Metropolitan Toronto District Health Council – Adm., Karen Kapadia

Toronto: Castleview Wychwood Towers, 351 Christie St., Toronto ON M6G 2C3 – 416/392-5700; Fax: 416/392-4157 – 437 beds – Metropolitan Toronto District Health Council – Adm., Cathy Renwick

Toronto: Central Park Lodge, 1145 Albion Rd., Etobicoke ON M9V 4J7 – 416/745-4800; Fax: 416/745-0445 – 290 beds – Metropolitan Toronto District Health Council – Adm., Tamara Christie

Toronto: Cheltenham Nursing Home, 5935 Bathurst St., North York ON M2R 1Y8 – 416/223-4050; Fax: 416/223-4159 – 170 beds – Metropolitan Toronto District Health Council – Adm., Yvonne Tolton

Toronto: Chester Village, 717 Broadview Ave., Toronto ON M4K 2P5 – 416/466-2173; Fax: 416/466-6781 – 174 beds – Metropolitan Toronto District Health Council – Adm., Paul Klamer

Toronto: Christie Gardens, 600 Melita Cres., Toronto ON M6G 3Z4 – 416/530-1330; Fax: 416/530-1686 – 88 beds – Metropolitan Toronto District Health Council – Adm., Catherine Belmore

Toronto: Copernicus Lodge, 66 Roncesvalles Ave., Toronto ON M6R 3A7 – 416/536-7122; Fax: 416/536-8242 – 108 beds – Metropolitan Toronto District Health Council – Adm., Barbara Nytko

Toronto: Craiglee Nursing Home, 102 Craiglee Dr., Scarborough ON M1N 2M7 – 416/264-2260; Fax: 416/267-8176 – 94 beds – Metropolitan Toronto District Health Council – Adm., Doris McDougall

Toronto: Cummer Lodge, 205 Cummer Ave., North York ON M2M 2E8 – 416/392-9500; Fax: 416/392-9499 – 414 beds – Metropolitan Toronto District Health Council – Adm., Leah Walters

Toronto: Dom Lipa Nursing Home, 52 Neilson Dr., Etobicoke ON M9C 1V7 – 416/621-3820; Fax: 416/621-9773 – 30 beds – Metropolitan Toronto District Health Council – Adm., Patricia King

Toronto: Drs. Paul & John Rekai Centre, 345 Sherbourne St., Toronto ON M5A 2S3 – 416/964-1599; Fax: 416/964-3907 – 126 beds – Metropolitan Toronto District Health Council – Adm., Mary Hoare

Toronto: Ehatare Nursing Home, 40 Old Kingston Rd., Scarborough ON M1E 3J5 – 416/284-0828; Fax: 416/284-5595 – 32 beds – Metropolitan Toronto District Health Council – Adm., Marika Boujoff

Toronto: Elmgrove Living Centre, 35 Elm Grove Ave., Toronto ON M6K 2J2 – 416/537-2465; Fax: 416/537-2468 – 123 beds – Metropolitan Toronto District Health Council – Adm., Tara Singh

Toronto: Extendicare/Bayview, 550 Cummer Ave., North York ON M2K 2M2 – 416/226-1331; Fax: 416/226-2745 – 205 beds – Metropolitan Toronto District Health Council – Adm., Susan Schendel

Toronto: Extendicare/Guildwood, 60 Guildwood Pkwy., Scarborough ON M1G 1R6 – 416/266-7711; Fax: 416/269-5123 – 169 beds – Metropolitan Toronto District Health Council – Adm., Kathy Suma

Toronto: Extendicare/North York, 1925 Steeles Ave. East, North York ON M2H 2H3 – 416/493-4666; Fax: 416/493-4886 – 288 beds – Metropolitan Toronto District Health Council – Adm., Sheilagh Tasson

Toronto: Extendicare/Scarborough, 3830 Lawrence Ave. East, Scarborough ON M1G 1R6 – 416/439-1243; Fax: 416/439-4818 – 154 beds – Metropolitan Toronto District Health Council – Adm., Chris Robinson

Toronto: Fairview Nursing Home, 14 Cross St., Toronto ON M6J 1S8 – 416/534-8820; Fax: 416/538-1658 – 108 beds – Metropolitan Toronto District Health Council – Adm., Herbert Chambers

Toronto: Fudger House, 439 Sherbourne St., Toronto ON M4X 1K6 – 416/392-5252; Fax: 416/392-4174 – 250 beds – Metropolitan Toronto District Health Council – Adm., Anne Evans

Toronto: Garden Court Nursing Home, 1 Sand Beach Rd., Etobicoke ON M8V 2W2 – 416/259-6172; Fax:

416/259-7925 – 45 beds – Metropolitan Toronto District Health Council – Adm., Dean Davey

Toronto: Harold & Grace Baker Centre, 1 Northwestern Ave., Toronto ON M6M 2J7 – 416/654-2889; Fax: 416/654-0217 – 235 beds – Metropolitan Toronto District Health Council – Adm., Richard Mirabelli

Toronto: Hellenic Care for Seniors, 215 Tyrrel Ave., Toronto ON M6G 4A9 – 416/654-3904; Fax: 416/654-4988 – 78 beds – Metropolitan Toronto District Health Council – Adm., Vania Sakelaris

Toronto: The Heritage Nursing Home, 1195 Queen St. East, Toronto ON M4M 1L6 – 416/461-8185; Fax: 416/461-5472 – 201 beds – Metropolitan Toronto District Health Council – Adm., Melba Graham

Toronto: Highbourne Lifecare Centre, 420 The East Mall, Etobicoke ON M9B 3Z9 – 416/621-8000; Fax: 416/621-0671 – 255 beds – Metropolitan Toronto District Health Council – Adm., Evelyn MacDonald

Toronto: Ina Grafton-Gage Home (Toronto), 2 O'Connor Dr., Toronto ON M4K 2K1 – 416/422-4891; Fax: 416/422-1613 – 110 beds – Metropolitan Toronto District Health Council – Adm., Gordon Blowes

Toronto: Ivan Franko Home (Etobicoke), 767 Royal York Rd., Etobicoke ON M8Y 2T3 – 416/239-7364; Fax: 416/239-5102 – 85 beds – Metropolitan Toronto District Health Council – Adm., Maria Kiebalo

Toronto: Kennedy Lodge Nursing Home, 1400 Kennedy Rd., Scarborough ON M1P 2L7 – 416/752-8282; Fax: 416/752-0645 – 289 beds – Metropolitan Toronto District Health Council – Adm., Ginnette Taylor

Toronto: Kipling Acres, 2233 Kipling Ave., Etobicoke ON M9W 4L3 – 416/392-2300; Fax: 416/392-3360 – 335 beds – Metropolitan Toronto District Health Council – Adm., Brock Hall

Toronto: Lakeshore Lodge, 3197 Lakeshore Blvd. West, Etobicoke ON M8V 3X5 – 416/392-9400; Fax: 416/392-9401 – 150 beds – Metropolitan Toronto District Health Council – Adm., Lorraine Siu

Toronto: The Laughlen Centre, 110 Edward St., Toronto ON M5G 2A5 – 416/597-0373; Fax: 416/597-8234 – 215 beds – Metropolitan Toronto District Health Council – Exec. Dir., Anne Hayes

Toronto: Leisure World St. George Centre, 225 St. George St., Toronto ON M5R 2M2 – 416/967-3985; Fax: 416/967-3951 – 238 beds – Metropolitan Toronto District Health Council – Adm., Vicki Wootton

Toronto: Leisureworld Scarborough Centre, 130 Midland Ave., Scarborough ON M1N 4B2 – 416/264-2301; Fax: 416/264-3704 – 302 beds – Metropolitan Toronto District Health Council – Adm., Sharon Steele

Toronto: Lincoln Place Nursing Home, 429 Walmer Rd., Toronto ON M5P 2X9 – 416/967-6949; Fax: 416/928-1965 – 260 beds – Metropolitan Toronto District Health Council – Adm., Tulia Ferreira

Toronto: Maynard Nursing Home, 28 Halton St., Toronto ON M6J 1R3 – 416/533-5198; Fax: 416/533-3492 – 77 beds – Metropolitan Toronto District Health Council – Adm., Alan Bowman

Toronto: Metro Toronto Legion Village, 59 Lawson Rd., West Hill ON M1C 2J1 – 416/284-9235; Fax: 416/284-7169 – 100 beds – Metropolitan Toronto District Health Council – Adm., Catherine Hilge

Toronto: Mon Sheong Home for the Aged, 36 D'Arcy St., Toronto ON M5T 1J7 – 416/977-3762; Fax: 416/977-3231 – 65 beds – Metropolitan Toronto District Health Council – Adm., Anne Chan

Toronto: Nisbet Lodge, 740 Pape Ave., Toronto ON M4K 3S7 – 416/469-1105; Fax: 416/469-1107 – 103 beds – Metropolitan Toronto District Health Council – Adm., Barry Lee

Toronto: North Park Nursing Home, 450 Rustic Rd., North York ON M6L 1W9 – 416/247-0531; Fax: 416/247-6159 – 75 beds – Metropolitan Toronto District Health Council – Adm., Rebecca Wylie

Toronto: Norwood Nursing Home, 122 Tyndall Ave., Toronto ON M6K 2E2 – 416/535-3011; Fax: 416/535-6439 – 60 beds – Metropolitan Toronto District Health Council – Adm., Dr. Horst Sebald

Toronto: The O'Neill Centre, 33 Christie St., Toronto ON M6G 3B1 – 416/536-1116; Fax: 416/536-6941 – 162 beds – Metropolitan Toronto District Health Council – Adm., Ann-Marie Mohler

Toronto: Rockcliffe Nursing Home, 3015 Lawrence Ave. East, Scarborough ON M1P 2V7 – 416/264-3201; Fax: 416/264-2609 – 204 beds – Metropolitan Toronto District Health Council – Adm., Phyllis Jardine

Toronto: St. Clair O'Connor Community Nursing Home, 2703 St. Clair Ave. East, Toronto ON M4B 3M3 – 416/757-8757; Fax: 416/751-7315 – 25 beds – Metropolitan Toronto District Health Council – Adm., Grace Sweatman

Toronto: Seniors' Health Centre, 2 Buchan Ct., North York ON M2J 5A3 – 416/756-1040; Fax: 416/495-9738 – 150 beds – Metropolitan Toronto District Health Council – Adm., Dianne E. Anderson

Toronto: Seven Oaks, 9 Neilson Rd., Scarborough ON M1N 5E1 – 416/392-3500; Fax: 416/392-3579 – 249 beds – Metropolitan Toronto District Health Council – Adm., Karen Wallace

Toronto: Shepherd Lodge, 3760 Sheppard Ave. East, Agincourt ON M1S 3E2 – 416/609-5700; Fax: 416/293-6229 – 148 beds – Metropolitan Toronto District Health Council – Adm., Joyce Oliver

Toronto: Shepherd Terrace, 3758 Sheppard Ave. East, Toronto ON M1T 3K9 – 416/609-5700; Fax: 416/293-6229 – 60 beds – Metropolitan Toronto District Health Council – Adm., Joyce Oliver

Toronto: Spencer House, 36 Spencer Rd., Toronto ON M6K 2J6 – 416/531-5737; Fax: 416/531-4722 – 120 beds – Metropolitan Toronto District Health Council – Adm., Ivor Zagroev

Toronto: Suomi-Koti Toronto Nursing Home, 795 Eglinton Ave. East, Toronto ON M4G 4E4 – 416/425-4134; Fax: 416/425-6319 – 34 beds – Metropolitan Toronto District Health Council – Adm., Tellervo Varvas

Toronto: Tendercare Living Centre/McNicoll Manor, 1020 McNicoll Ave., Scarborough ON M1W 2J6 – 416/499-2020; Fax: 416/499-3379 – 254 beds – Metropolitan Toronto District Health Council – Adm., Francis Martis

Toronto: Thompson House, 1 Overland Dr., Toronto ON M3C 2C3 – 416/449-4474; Fax: 416/447-6364 – 136 beds – Metropolitan Toronto District Health Council – Adm., William Krever

Toronto: True Davidson Acres, 200 Dawes Rd., Toronto ON M4C 5M8 – 416/397-0400; Fax: 416/397-0401 – 281 beds – Metropolitan Toronto District Health Council – Adm., Sylvia Moreland

Toronto: Ukrainian Canadian Care Centre, 60 Richview Rd., Etobicoke ON M9A 5E4 – 416/243-7653; Fax: 416/243-7452 – 120 beds – Metropolitan Toronto District Health Council – Adm., Carol Jarman

Toronto: Van-Del Manor Nursing Home, 1673 Kingston Rd., Scarborough ON M1N 1S6 – 416/699-3244; Fax: 416/699-3245 – 58 beds – Metropolitan Toronto District Health Council – Adm., Stella Pinnock

Toronto: Versa-Care Centre, Etobicoke, 95 Humber College Blvd., Etobicoke ON M9V 5B6 – 416/746-7466; Fax: 416/740-5812 – 94 beds – Metropolitan Toronto District Health Council – Adm., Jane Odgen

Toronto: Versa-Care Centre, Toronto Main, 77 Main St., Toronto ON M4E 2V6 – 416/690-3001; Fax: 416/690-6866 – 150 beds – Metropolitan Toronto District Health Council – Adm., Barbara Beecroft

Toronto: Villa Colombo Homes for the Aged, 40 Playfair Ave., Toronto ON M6B 2P9 – 416/789-2113; Fax: 416/789-5986 – 268 beds – Metropolitan Toronto District Health Council – Adm., Terrence McBurney

Toronto: The Wexford, 1860 Lawrence Ave. East, Scarborough ON M1R 5B1 – 416/752-8877; Fax: 416/752-8414 – 166 beds – Metropolitan Toronto District Health Council – Adm., Luba Funston

Toronto: White Eagle Nursing Home, 138 Dowling Ave., Toronto ON M6K 3A6 – 416/533-7935; Fax: 416/537-0309 – 56 beds – Metropolitan Toronto District Health Council – Adm., Eileen Trevors

Toronto: Yee Hong Centre for Geriatric Care, 2311 McNicoll Ave., Scarborough ON M1V 5L3 – 416/321-6333; Fax: 416/321-6313 – Nursing home, seniors community centre, medical centre, rehabilitation centre, retirement homes – 90 beds – Metropolitan Toronto District Health Council – Exec. Dir., Florence Wong

Toronto: Yorkview Lifecare Centre, 2045 Finch Ave. West, North York ON M3N 1M9 – 416/745-0811; Fax: 416/745-0568 – 266 beds – Metropolitan Toronto District Health Council – Adm., Patrick Brown

Trenton: Crown Ridge Place, 106 Crown St., Trenton ON K8V 6R3 – 613/392-1289; Fax: 613/392-6939 – 84 beds – Hastings & Prince Edward Counties District Health Council – Adm., Fred R. Freeman

Trenton: Trent Valley Lodge Nursing Home, 195 Bay St., Trenton ON K8V 1H9 – 613/392-9235; Fax: 613/392-0688 – 70 beds – Hastings & Prince Edward Counties District Health Council – Adm., Bill Weaver Jr.

Trout Creek: Lady Isabelle Nursing Home, MacDonald St., Trout Creek ON P0H 2L0 – 705/723-5232; Fax: 705/723-5794 – 66 beds – East Muskoka/Parry Sound District Health Council – Adm., Sadie Newman

Unionville: Bethany Lodge, 23 Second St., Unionville ON L3R 2C2 – 905/477-3838; Fax: 905/477-2888 – 101 beds – York Region District Health Council – Adm., B. Stainton

Unionville: Union Villa, 4300 Hwy. 7, Unionville ON L3R 1L8 – 905/477-2822; Fax: 905/477-6080 – 162 beds – York Region District Health Council – Adm., Donna Barudzija

Uxbridge: Versa-Care Centre, Uxbridge, 130 Reach St., Uxbridge ON L0C 1K0 – 905/852-5191; Fax: 905/852-6467 – 100 beds – Waterloo Region District Health Council – Adm., Sharon Dickinson

Vanier: Centre d'accueil Champlain, 275 Perrier St., Vanier ON K1L 5C6 – 613/746-3543; Fax: 613/746-5572 – 116 beds – Ottawa-Carleton Regional Health Council – Adm., Jocelyn Wells

Vineland: United Mennonite Home, 3311 - 2nd St., Vineland ON L0R 2C0 – 905/562-7385; Fax: 905/562-3711 – 80 beds – Niagara District Health Council – Adm., Art Sieb

Virgil: Heritage Place, 1743 Four Mile Creek Rd., Virgil ON L0S 1T0 – 905/468-1111; Fax: 905/468-4384 – 36 beds – Niagara District Health Council – Adm., Rudy Siemens

Walkerton: Brucelea Haven, 41 McGivern St. West, Walkerton ON N0G 2V0 – 519/881-1570; Fax: 519/881-0231 – 144 beds – Grey-Bruce District Health Council – Adm., D.J. Moore

Wallaceburg: Lapointe-Fisher Nursing Home, 427 Nelson St., Wallaceburg ON N8A 4G9 – 519/627-1663 – 99 beds – Kent County District Health Council – Adm., Shona Outridge

Wardsville: Babcock Nursing Home, 196 Wellington St., Wardsville ON N0L 2N0 – 519/693-4415; Fax: 519/693-4876 – 60 beds – Thames Valley District Health Council – Adm., Joan Enns

Warkworth: Community Nursing Home, 97 Mill St., Warkworth ON K0K 3K0 – 705/924-2311; Fax: 705/924-2329 – 60 beds – Haliburton, Kawartha & Pine Ridge District Health Council – Adm., Myrna Ogden

Waterloo: Parkwood Mennonite Home Inc., 75 Cardinal Cres. South, Waterloo ON N2J 2E6 – 519/885-4810; Fax: 519/886-6720 – 58 beds – Waterloo Region District Health Council – Adm., Gloria Dirks

Waterloo: Pinehaven Nursing Home, 229 Lexington Rd., Waterloo ON N2K 2E1 – 519/885-6990; Fax: 519/885-4216 – 84 beds – Waterloo Region District Health Council – Adm., Connie Cox

Watford Nursing Home, 344 Victoria St., Watford ON N0M 2S0 – 519/876-2928; Fax: 519/876-2520 – 63 beds – Lambton District Health Council – Adm., Lynne-Anne Gallaway

Welland County General Hospital - Extended Care Unit, 65 Third St., Welland ON L3B 4W6 – 905/732-6111; Fax: 905/732-3268 – 75 beds – Niagara District Health Council – Adm., Susan Alexander

Welland: Foyer Richelieu Residence, 655 Tanguay St., Welland ON L3B 5W5 – 905/734-1400; Fax: 905/734-1386 – 62 beds – Niagara District Health Council – Adm., Dr. J. Harvey

Welland: Sunset Haven, 163 First Ave., Welland ON L3C 1Y5 – 905/735-1620; Fax: 905/735-2606 – 347 beds – Niagara District Health Council – Dir., Social Services & Senior Citizens Dept., Susan Reid

Whitby: Fairview Lodge, 632 Dundas St. West, PO Box 300, Whitby ON L1N 5S3 – 905/668-5851; Fax: 905/668-8934 – 198 beds – Waterloo Region District Health Council – Adm., Sharon Swain

Whitby: Sunnycrest Nursing Home, 1635 Dundas St. East, Whitby ON L1N 2K9 – 905/686-1061; Fax: 905/686-1061 – 136 beds – Waterloo Region District Health Council – Adm., Jean Forrest

Wiarton: Gateway Haven, 671 Frank St., Wiarton ON N0H 2T0 – 519/534-1113; Fax: 519/534-4733; EMail: bcgwh@bmts.com – 96 beds – Grey-Bruce District Health Council – Adm., Bob Moreton

Wikwemikong Nursing Home, PO Box 114, Wikwemikong ON P0P 2J0 – 705/859-3107; Fax: 705/859-2245 – 60 beds – Manitoulin & Sudbury District Health Council – Adm., Mark Manitowabi

Winchester: Dundas Manor Nursing Home, 533 Clarence St., PO Box 970, Winchester ON K0C 2K0 – 613/774-2293; Fax: 613/774-5507 – 98 beds – DHC of Eastern Ontario – Acting Adm., Ross Alguire

Windsor: Central Park Lodge, 3387 Riverside Dr. East, Windsor ON N8Y 1A8 – 519/948-5293; Fax: 519/948-3715 – 157 beds – General Mgr., Jean Piccinato

Windsor: Chateau Park Nursing Home, 2990 Riverside Dr. West, Windsor ON N9C 1A2 – 519/254-4341; Fax: 519/254-7931 – 59 beds – Essex County District Health Council – Adm., Patricia Bruckman

Windsor: Huron Lodge, 1475 Huron Church Rd., Windsor ON N9C 2K9 – 519/253-6060; Fax: 519/977-8027 – 256 beds – Essex County District Health Council – Acting Adm., Mary Bateman

Windsor: Malden Park Continuing Care Centre, 1453 Prince Rd., Windsor ON N9C 3Z4 – 519/257-5111; Fax: 519/257-5474 – 225 beds – Essex County District Health Council – Adm., Barry Brown

Windsor: Regency Park Nursing/Retirement Centre, 567 Victoria Ave., Windsor ON N9A 4N1 – 519/254-1141; Fax: 519/254-3759 – 60 beds – Essex County District Health Council – Adm., Patricia Bruckman

Windsor: Riverside Health Care Centre, 6475 Wyandotte St. East, Windsor ON N8S 1N9 – 519/948-4054; Fax: 519/974-6675 – 66 beds – Essex County District Health Council – Adm., Bonnie Reeves

Windsor: Versa-Care Windsor Place, 350 Dougall Ave., Windsor ON N9A 4P4 – 519/256-7868; Fax: 519/256-1991 – 244 beds – Essex County District Health Council – Acting Adm., Deborah Pidgeon

Windsor: Villa Maria, 2856 Riverside Dr. West, Windsor ON N9C 1A2 – 519/254-3763; Fax: 519/254-7657 – 120 beds – Essex County District Health Council – Adm., George Leamon

Wingham: Braemar Retirement Centre, RR#1, Wingham ON N0G 2W0 – 519/357-3430; Fax: 519/357-2303 – 69 beds – Huron-Perth District Health Council – Adm., Murdoch C. MacGowan

Woodbridge: Devonshire Pine Grove Inc., 8403 Islington Ave. North, Woodbridge ON L4L 1X3 – 905/850-3605; Fax: 905/850-3832 – 100 beds – York Region District Health Council – Adm., Juris Taurins

Woodbridge: Kristus Darzs Latvian Home, 11290 Pine Valley Dr., Woodbridge ON L4L 1A6 – 905/832-3300; Fax: 905/832-2029 – 100 beds – York Region District Health Council – Adm., Maris Inveiss

Woodslee: Country Village Health Care Centre, County Rd. 8, RR#2, Woodslee ON N0R 1V0 – 519/839-4812; Fax: 519/839-4813 – 104 beds – Essex County District Health Council – Acting Adm., Sue Aubin

Woodstock: Caressant Care Woodstock Nursing Home, 81 Fyfe Ave., Woodstock ON N4S 8A3 – 519/539-6461; Fax: 519/539-9601; EMail: agroulx@odyssey.on.ca – 95 beds – Thames Valley District Health Council – Adm., Annette Groulx

Woodstock: Woodingford Lodge, 423 Devonshire Ave., PO Box 308, Woodstock ON N4S 7X6 – 519/539-1245; Fax: 519/539-8937 – 228 beds – Thames Valley District Health Council – Adm., Bob Hines

Zurich: Bluewater Rest Home, PO Box 220, Zurich ON N0M 2T0 – 519/236-4373; Fax: 519/236-7685 – 65 beds – Huron-Perth District Health Council – Adm., Josef Risi

## NURSING STATIONS

Bearskin Lake Nursing Station, Bearskin Lake ON P0V 1E0 – Nurse in Charge, Heather Cameron

Big Trout Lake Nursing Station, Big Trout Lake ON P0V 1G0 – Nurse in Charge, Carol Rogers

Deer Lake: Oscar-Jeannette Lindokken Nursing Station, Deer Lake ON P0V 1N0 – Nurse in Charge, Catherine Mayers

Fort Albany: Kashechewan Nursing Station, Fort Albany ON P0L 1H0 – 705/275-4444; Fax: 705/275-1010 – Nurse in Charge, Mary Douhaniuk

Fort Hope: Kevin Sagutcheway Nursing Station, Fort Hope ON P0T 1L0 – Nurse in Charge, Norma Corrish

Kasabonika Nursing Station, Kasabonika Lake ON P0V 1Y0 – 807/535-1189; Fax: 807/535-1192 – Nurse in Charge, Gloria Bilyk

Lansdowne House Nursing Station, Lansdowne House ON P0T 1Z0 – 519/753-3153; Fax: 519/752-0249 – Exec. Dir., J. Renahan

New Osnaburg Nursing Station, New Osnaburg ON P0V 2H0 – 807/928-2298; Fax: 807/928-2767 – Nurse in Charge, Gabrielle Lynn

Pikangikum Nursing Station, via Red Lake GPO, Pikangikum ON P0V 2L0 – Nurse in Charge, Mary Bender

Round Lake: Sena Memorial Nursing Station, via Wegamow GPO, Round Lake ON P0V 2Y0 – Nurse in Charge, Kush Janmohammed

Sandy Lake Nursing Station, Sandy Lake ON P0V 1V0 – 807/774-3461; Fax: 807/774-1585 – Nurse in Charge, Florence Tarrant

Webequie Nursing Station, Webequie ON P0T 3A0 – Nurse in Charge, Joan Trusdale

## PRIVATE HOSPITALS

Burford: Sunridge Lodge Retirement Home, 86 King St., PO Box 119, Burford ON N0E 1A0 – 519/449-1019; Fax: 519/449-5478 – Retirement home & personal care/assisted living facility – 8 beds – Adm., Murray Charters

Cobourg: Sidbrook Private Hospital, 411 King St. East, Cobourg ON K9A 1M4 – 905/372-3411; Fax: 905/372-9532 – Haliburton, Kawartha & Pine Ridge District Health Council – Adm., Enos Stewart

Guelph: The Homewood Sanitarium, 150 Delhi St., Guelph ON N1E 6K9 – 519/824-1010; Fax: 519/824-1827 – Exec. Dir., Dr. R.A. Pond

Kingston: Institute of Psychotherapy Limited, 113 Lower Union St., PO Box 1237, Kingston ON K7L 4Y8 – 613/546-3116; Fax: 613/546-3119 – 18 beds – Adm., Dr. D. Scott

Lakefield Private Hospital, 1 Grant Ave., PO Box 489, Lakefield ON K0L 2H0 – 705/652-3421 – Haliburton, Kawartha & Pine Ridge District Health Council – Adm., Doreen Jolliffe

London: Grace Villa Private Hospital, 201 Riverside Dr., London ON N6H 1E5 – 519/438-7422; Fax: 519/438-9902 – Adm., Judith Abel

Penetanguishene: Beechwood Private Hospital, 58 Church St., PO Box 1090, Penetanguishene ON L0K 1P0 – 705/549-7473; Fax: 705/549-4326 – 20 beds – Simcoe County District Health Council – Adm., Larry Bellisle

Perth Community Care Centre Inc. - Perth Wiseman's Private Hospital, 55 Sunset Blvd., RR#4, Perth ON K7H 3C6 – 613/267-2506; Fax: 613/267-7060 – 17 beds – Adm., Joyce Firlotte

Thornhill: Shouldice Private Hospital, 7750 Bayview Ave., PO Box 370, Thornhill ON L3T 4A3 – 905/889-1125; Fax: 905/889-4216 – 89 beds – York Region District Health Council – Adm., A. O'Dell

Thorold: Maple Hurst Hospital, 14 St. David Rd. West, Thorold ON L2V 2K9 – 905/227-2301; Fax: 905/227-9632 – Pres., Basil Griffis

Toronto: Bellwood Health Services, 1020 McNicholl Ave., Scarborough ON M1W 2J5 – 416/495-0926; Fax: 416/495-7943 – Metropolitan Toronto District Health Council – Pres., Dr. Linda Bell

Toronto: Dewson Private Hospital, 47 Dewson St., Toronto ON M6H 1G6 – 416/536-5009; Fax: 416/536-2125 – Scheduled to close by 1999 – 31 beds – Metropolitan Toronto District Health Council – Adm., L.W. Freeman

Toronto: Don Mills Surgical Unit Ltd., 20 Wynford Dr., Don Mills ON M3C 1J4 – 416/441-1947; Fax: 416/441-2144 – Metropolitan Toronto District Health Council – Adm., Dr. Dennis Evans

Toronto: Institute of Traumatic Plastic & Restorative Surgery, 215 Victoria St., Toronto ON M5B 1Z3 – 416/364-5326; Fax: 416/921-9364 – Adm., Dr. J.E. Fenn

Toronto: St. Joseph's Morrow Park Infirmary & Private Hospital, 3377 Bayview Ave., Willowdale ON M2M 2S4 – 416/222-1101; Fax: 416/250-3117 – 35 beds – Metropolitan Toronto District Health Council – Adm., Sr. Catherine McDonough

Woodbridge: Cosmetic Surgery Hospital, 4650 Hwy. 7, Woodbridge ON L4L 1S7 – 905/851-1500; Fax: 905/856-4406 – York Region District Health Council – Adm., Dr. Lloyd Carlsen

Woodstock Private Hospital, 369 Huron St., Woodstock ON N4S 7A5 – 519/537-8162; Fax: 519/537-7204 – Adm., Irma C. Vander Zwaag

## SPECIAL TREATMENT CENTRES

(Includes: Abortion Clinics, Cancer Clinics, Rehabilitation Centres, Treatment Centres)

Brantford: Lansdowne Children's Centre, 21 Preston Blvd., Brantford ON N3T 5B1 – 519/753-3153; Fax: 519/753-5927 – Acting Exec. Dir., Diane Pick

Chatham: Kent County Children's Treatment Centre, 355 Lark St., Chatham ON N7L 1G9 – 519/354-0520; Fax: 519/354-7355 – Adm., Mary Anne McLean

Mississauga: Erinoak - Serving Young People with Physical Disabilities, 2277 South Millway Dr., Mississauga ON L5L 2M5 – 905/820-7111; Fax: 905/820-1333; EMail: dthomson@cepp.org – Out patient services only – Exec. Dir., Diana Thomson

Oshawa: Grandview Rehabilitation & Treatment Centre of Durham Region, 600 Townline Rd. South, Oshawa ON L1H 7K6 – 905/728-1673; Fax: 905/728-2961 – Exec. Dir., Linda Watson

The Ottawa Children's Treatment Centre, 395 Smyth Rd., PO Box 8469, Ottawa ON K1G 3H9 – 613/737-0871 – Exec. Dir., Ruth Koch-Schulter

Ottawa: Royal Ottawa Health Care Group - Rehabilitation Centre, 505 Smyth Rd., Ottawa ON K1H 8M2 – 613/722-6521; Fax: 613/722-4577 – 74 beds – Ottawa-Carleton Regional Health Council – Exec. Dir., George Langill

Parry Sound: West Parry Sound Health Centre - Church St. Site, 88 Church St., Parry Sound ON P2A 1Z3 – 705/746-2111; Fax: 705/746-6338 – chronic are unit – 114 beds – CEO, Norman Maciver

Peterborough: Five Counties Children's Treatment Centre, 872 Dutton Rd., Peterborough ON K9H 7G1 – 705/748-2221; Fax: 705/748-3526 – Exec. Dir., Phil Ogden

St Catharines: Niagara Rehabilitation Centre, 547 Glenridge Ave., St Catharines ON L2T 4C2 – 905/688-2980; Fax: 905/688-9591 – outpatient rehabilitation centre – Niagara District Health Council – Exec. Dir., Candace Paris

Sarnia & District Children's Treatment Centre, 1240 Murphy Rd., Sarnia ON N7S 2Y6 – 519/542-3471; Fax: 519/542-4115; EMail: sdctc@ebtech.net – Exec. Dir., Christine Murphy

Sault Ste. Marie Detoxification Unit, 911 Queen St. East, Sault Ste. Marie ON P6A 2B6 – 705/942-1872; Fax: 705/759-6369 – drug treatment centre – 15 beds – Dir., Carole Swan

Sault Ste Marie: Children's Rehabiliation Centre - Algoma, 74 Johnson Ave., Sault Ste Marie ON P6C 2V5 – 705/759-1131; Fax: 705/759-0783 – outpatient health services centre – Acting Exec. Dir., Susan Vanagas-Coté

Sudbury: Laurentian Hospital Children's Treatment Centre, 1204 St. Jerome St., Sudbury ON P3A 2V9 – 705/560-8000; Fax: 705/560-4273 – outpatient, community-based rehabilitation centre – Dir., Sally Spence

Thunder Bay: George Jeffrey Children's Treatment Centre, 507 North Lillie St., Thunder Bay ON P7C 4V8 – 807/623-4381; Fax: 807/623-6626 – Exec. Dir., Peggy Fulton

Toronto Eye Bank, c/o University of Toronto, 1 Spadina Cres., Toronto ON M5S 2J5 – 416/480-7465 – Scientific Dir., Dr. William Dixon

Toronto Rehabilitation Centre, 345 Rumsey Rd., Toronto ON M4G 1R7 – 416/425-6630; Fax: 416/425-0301 – Metropolitan Toronto District Health Council – Exec. Dir., Dr. T. Kavanagh

Toronto Rehabilitation Instutute of Toronto, 550 University Ave., Toronto ON M5G 2A2 – 416/597-5111; Fax: 416/597-6625 – 428 beds – Metropolitan Toronto District Health Council – CEO, Dr. Frank Markel

Toronto-Sunnybrook Regional Cancer Centre, 2075 Bayview Ave., North York ON M4N 3M5 – 416/488-5801; Fax: 416/480-6002 – cancer treatment centre

Toronto: Addiction Research Foundation, 33 Russell St., Toronto ON M5S 2S1 – 416/595-6000; Fax: 416/595-5017 – drug rehabilitation centre – Pres. & CEO, Dr. Terry Kendall

Toronto: Bloorview MacMillan Health Centre - Hugh MacMillan Site, 350 Rumsey Rd., Toronto ON M4G 1R8 – 416/425-6220; Fax: 416/425-6591 – 87 beds – Metropolitan Toronto District Health Council – COO, Sheila Jarvis

Toronto: Bob Rumball Centre for the Deaf, 2395 Bayview Ave., North York ON M2L 1A2 – 416/449-9651 – Exec. Dir., Rev. Rumball

Toronto: Cabbagetown Women's Clinic, 302 Gerrard St. East, Toronto ON M5A 2H7 – 416/323-0642; Fax: 416/323-3099 – abortion clinic – Exec. Dir., Dr. M. Burvaina

Toronto: Casey House Hospice, 9 Huntley St., Toronto ON M4Y 2K8 – 416/962-7600; Fax: 416/962-5147; EMail: info@caseyhouse.on.ca – Metropolitan Toronto District Health Council – Exec. Dir., John Flannery

Toronto: Choice in Health Clinic, #207, 597 Parliament St., Toronto ON M4X 1W3 – 416/975-9300; Fax: 416/975-0314 – abortion clinic – Dir., Margaret Hancock

Toronto: The Donwood Institute, 175 Brentcliffe Rd., Toronto ON M4G 3Z1 – 416/425-3930; Fax: 416/425-7896; EMail: info@donwood.org – 38 beds – Metropolitan Toronto District Health Council – Pres. & CEO, Dr. David Korn

Toronto: Downsview Rehabiliation Centre, Workers Compensation Board, 115 Torbarrie Rd., Downsview ON M3L 1G8 – 416/244-1761; Fax: 416/240-2083 – 125 beds – Exec. Dir., Dr. Deo Bodasing

Toronto: The Marvelle Koffler Breast Centre, Mount Sinai, 600 University Ave., 12th Fl., Toronto ON M5G 1X5 – 416/596-4200; Fax: 416/586-8847 – cancer treatment

Toronto: The Morgentaler Clinic, 727 Hillsdale Ave. East, Toronto ON M4S 1V4 – 416/932-0446; Fax: 416/932-0837 – abortion clinic – Dir., Dr. Henry Morgentaler

Toronto: The Ontario Cancer Institute - The Princess Margaret Hospital, 610 University Ave., Toronto ON M5G 2M9 – 416/946-2000; Fax: 416/946-6547 – 103 beds – Metropolitan Toronto District Health Council – Pres. & CEO, Dr. Alan R. Hudson

Toronto: The Ontario Cancer Treatment & Research Foundation, 620 University Ave., 15th Fl., Toronto ON M5G 2L7 – 416/971-9800; Fax: 416/971-6888; EMail: jirwin@octrf.on.ca – Pres. & CEO, Dr. Charles Hollenberg

Toronto: Orthopaedic & Arthritic Hospital, 43 Wellesley St. East, Toronto ON M4Y 1H1 – 416/967-8500; Fax: 416/967-8593 – Scheduled to close by 1999 – 84 beds – Metropolitan Toronto District Health Council – Pres., Roger Sharman

Toronto: Providence Centre Home for the Aged, Chronic Care & Rehabilitation Hospital, 3276 St. Clair Ave. East, Scarborough ON M1L 1W1 – 416/759-9321; Fax: 416/285-3758 – 577 beds – Metropolitan Toronto District Health Council – Pres. & CEO, Marian J. Leslie

Toronto: Rehabilitation Instutute of Toronto, 47 Austin Terrace, Toronto ON M5R 1Y8 – 416/537-3421; Fax: 416/537-8628 – May close in 1999 – 85 beds – Metropolitan Toronto District Health Council – Pres. & CEO, Dr. Frank Markel

Toronto: The Riverdale Hospital, 14 St. Matthews Rd., Toronto ON M4M 2B5 – 416/461-8251; Fax: 416/461-1670; EMail: Linda_Davis.The_Riverdale_Hospital@mail.trh.toronto.on.ca – Chronic care & rehabilitation hospital; scheduled to close by 1999 – 590 beds – Metropolitan Toronto District Health Council – Acting Pres. & CEO, Linda Davis

Toronto: St. Bernard's Rehabilitation, 683 Finch Ave. West, Willowdale ON M2R 1P2 – 416/635-8422; Fax: 416/635-8507 – Scheduled to close by 1999 – 59 beds – Metropolitan Toronto District Health Council – Adm., Sr. Norbert Wind

Toronto: St. John's Rehabilitation Hospital, 285 Cummer Ave., North York ON M2M 2G1 – 416/226-6780; Fax: 416/226-6265 – 185 beds – Metropolitan Toronto District Health Council – Adm., Miriam Lowi

Toronto: The Scott Clinic, 157 Gerrard St. East, Toronto ON M5A 2E4 – 416/962-4108, 5771 – abortion clinic – Medical Dir., Dr. R.H. Scott

Toronto: West Park Hospital, 82 Buttonwood Ave., Toronto ON M6M 2J5 – 416/243-3600; Fax: 416/243-8947 – Rehabiliation & chronic care facility – 316 beds – Metropolitan Toronto District Health Council – CEO, Barry Monaghan

Windsor: Children's Rehabilitation Centre of Essex County, 3945 Matchette Rd., Windsor ON N9C 4C2 – 519/252-7281; Fax: 519/252-5873 – Exec. Dir., Ross H. Byron

# PRINCE EDWARD ISLAND

## REGIONAL HEALTH AUTHORITIES

Alberton: West Prince Regional Health Authority, PO Box 10, Alberton PE C0B 1B0 – 902/853-2330; Fax: 902/853-4046 – CEO, Jeannita Bernard

Charlottetown: Queens Region Health & Community Services, PO Box 2000, Charlottetown PE C1A 7N8 – 902/368-6061; Fax: 902/368-6169 – CEO, Wayne Hooper

Montague: Southern Kings Health Region, PO Box 3000, Montague PE C0A 1R0 – 902/838-0945; Fax: 902/838-0940 – CEO, Gordon MacKay

Souris: Eastern Kings Health, PO Box 640, Souris PE C0A 2B0 – 902/687-7150; Fax: 902/687-7175 – CEO, Susan Birt

Summerside: East Prince Health Authority, 109 Water St., Summerside PE C1N 5L2 – 902/888-8028; Fax: 902/888-8023 – CEO, Peter Ramsay

## GENERAL HOSPITALS

Alberton: Western Hospital, PO Box 10, Alberton PE C0B 1B0 – 902/853-8650; Fax: 902/853-8651 – 25 beds – West Prince Regional Health Authority – Adm., Kenneth Ezard, 902/853-8660

Charlottetown: Queen Elizabeth Hospital, PO Box 6600, Charlottetown PE C1A 8T5 – 902/894-2111; Fax: 902/894-2146 – 282 beds – Queens Region Health & Community Services – Adm., Cecil Villard

Montague: King's County Memorial Hospital, 409 McIntyre Ave., Montague PE C0A 1R0 – 902/838-0777; Fax: 902/838-0770 – 30 beds – Southern Kings Health Region – Adm., Susan MacLeod

O'Leary Community Hospital, MacKinnon Dr., PO Box 160, O'Leary PE C0B 1V0 – 902/859-3110; Fax: 902/859-2489 – 8 acute care beds – West Prince Regional Health Authority – Adm., Ken Ezeard

Souris Hospital, PO Box 339, Souris PE C0A 2B0 – 902/687-7150; Fax: 902/687-7175 – 17 beds – Eastern Kings Health – Regional Mgr., Susan Bert

Summerside: Prince County Hospital, 259 Beattie Ave., Summerside PE C1A 2A9 – 902/436-9131; Fax: 902/888-3659 – 113 beds – East Prince Health Authority – Exec. Dir., Peter Ramsay, 902/888-8029

Tyne Valley: Stewart Memorial Hospital, PO Box 10, Tyne Valley PE C0B 2C0 – 902/831-2718; Fax: 902/831-3074 – 4 acute care beds – East Prince Health Authority – Adm., Kay Lewis

## HOME CARE OFFICES/COMMUNITY HEALTH CARE OFFICES

Charlottetown: Community & Residential Services, c/o Beach Grove Home, PO Box 2000, Charlottetown PE C1A 7N8 – 902/368-4790; Fax: 902/368-4858

Montague: Community & Residential Services, Riverview Manor, PO Box 820, Montague PE C0A 1R0 – 902/838-0772; Fax: 902/838-0774

O'Leary: Community & Residential Services, PO Box 8, O'Leary PE C0B 1V0 – 902/859-8730; Fax: 902/859-8701

Souris: Community & Residential Services, Souris Hospital, Souris PE C0A 2B0 – 902/687-7096; Fax: 902/687-7175

Summerside: Community & Residential Services, 310 Brophy Ave., Summerside PE C1N 5N4 – 902/888-8440; Fax: 902/888-8439

## MENTAL HEALTH HOSPITALS & COMMUNITY FACILITIES

Charlottetown: The Hillsborough Hospital & Special Care Centre, PO Box 1929, Charlottetown PE C1A 7N5 – 902/368-5400; Fax: 902/368-5467 – 197 beds –

Queens Region Health & Community Services – Adm., Cecil Villard

## NURSING HOMES/LONG TERM CARE FACILITIES

Alberton: Maplewood Manor, PO Box 400, Alberton PE C0B 1B0 – 902/853-8610; Fax: 902/853-8616 – 48 beds – West Prince Regional Health Authority – Dir., Nursing, Erna Glydon

Belfast: Dr. John Gillis Memorial Lodge, Eldon Belfast PO, Belfast PE C0A 1A0 – 902/659-2337 – Donald MacDonald

Charlottetown: Andrews Residence, Malpeque Rd., Charlottetown PE C1A 7J9 – 902/368-2790

Charlottetown: Beach Grove Home, PO Box 3500, Charlottetown PE C1A 7N9 – 902/368-4190 – Queens Region Health & Community Services

Charlottetown: Frogmore Lodge, 92 Longworth Ave., Charlottetown PE C1A 5A7 – 902/892-7607

Charlottetown: Garden Home, 310 North River Rd., Charlottetown PE C1A 3M4 – 902/892-4131

Charlottetown: Langille House, 212-214 Kent St., Charlottetown PE C1A 1P2 – 902/628-8228

Charlottetown: Lennox Nursing Home, 140 Water St., Charlottetown PE C1A 1A7 – 902/894-4968

Charlottetown: MacMillan Lodge, 230 Richmond St., Charlottetown PE C1A 1J5 – 902/894-7173 – 17 beds – Adm., Claudette MacMillan

Charlottetown: McQuaid Lodge, 36 Kent St., Charlottetown PE C1A 1M8 – 902/892-0791

Charlottetown: Old Rose Lodge, 319 Queen St., Charlottetown PE C1A 4C4 – 902/368-8313

Charlottetown: Park West Lodge, 22 Richmond St., Charlottetown PE C1A 1H4 – 902/566-2260

Charlottetown: PEI Atlantic Baptist Home, 16 Centennial Dr., Charlottetown PE C1A 5C5 – 902/566-5975

Charlottetown: Prince Edward Home, 5 Brighton Rd., Charlottetown PE C1A 8T6 – 902/368-4440; Fax: 902/368-5946 – 143 beds – Queens Region Health & Community Services – Adm., Carolyn Villard

Charlottetown: Sherwood, Corrigan Home, 22 Hemlock Ct., Charlottetown PE C1A 8E3 – 902/894-9686 – Queens Region Health & Community Services

Charlottetown: Sunset Lodge, 78 Walthen Dr., Charlottetown PE C1A 4T8 – 902/894-7217; Fax: 902/894-7036 – 65 beds – Adm., Maj. Diane May

Charlottetown: Tenderwood Lodge, 15 Hawthorne Ave., Charlottetown PE C1A 5X8 – 902/566-5174

Charlottetown: Whisperwood Villa, 160 St. Peters Rd., Charlottetown PE C1A 5P8 – 902/566-5556

Crapaud: South Shore Villa, PO Box 24, Crapaud PE C0A 1N0 – 902/658-2228

Hunter River: Rosewood Residence, Hunter River PE C0A 1N0 – 902/964-2456

Kensington: Clinton View Lodge, Clinton RR#6, Kensington PE C0B 1W0 – 902/885-2276

Lower Montague: Shady Rest, RR#2, Lower Montague PE C0A 1R0 – 902/838-4298

Miscouche Villa, Miscouche PE C0B 1T0 – 902/436-1946

Montague: Fraser Valley Inn, Main St., PO Box 233, Montague PE C0A 1R0 – 902/838-2673

Montague: MacKinnon Pines, 505 Campbellton St., Montague PE C0A 1R0 – 902/838-2656

Montague: Riverview Manor, Montague PE C0A 1R0 – 902/838-0772; Fax: 902/838-0774 – 50 beds – Southern Kings Health Region – Adm., Susan NacLeod

New Glasgow: River View Rest Home, New Glasgow PE C0A 1N0 – 902/964-2795

O'Leary: Lady Slipper Villa, PO Box 40, O'Leary PE C0B 1V0 – 902/859-3544

Sherwood: Corrigan Lodge, 9 Valhalla Dr., Sherwood PE C1A 8N4 – 902/894-5858 – 33 beds – Adm., Noreen Corrigan

Souris: Bayview Lodge, 22 Washington St., Souris PE C0A 2B0 – 902/687-3122

Souris: Colville Manor, PO Box 640, Souris PE C0A 2B0 – 902/687-2380 – Eastern Kings Health

Summerside: MacDonald Rest Home, 197 Cambridge St., Summerside PE C1N 1N1 – 902/436-7359; Fax: 902/854-2625

Summerside: Summerset Manor, 205 Lefurgey Ave., Summerside PE C1N 2L9 – 902/888-8318; Fax: 902/888-8338 – 88 beds – East Prince Health Authority – Adm., Joan Hubley

Summerside: Wedgewood Manor, 310 Brophy St., Summerside PE C1N 5N4 – 902/888-8340; Fax: 902/888-8369 – 76 beds – East Prince Health Authority – Dir., Joan Hubley

Tignish: David Lodge, Tignish PE C0B 2B0 – 902/882-3721

Tyne Valley: Murphy's Country Lodge, Tyne Valley PE C0B 2C0 – 902/ 831-2213

Wellington: La Cooperative le Chez Nous Ltée, 64 Sunset Dr., Wellington PE C0B 2E0 – 902/854-3426

## SPECIAL TREATMENT CENTRES

(Includes: Abortion Clinics, Cancer Clinics, Rehabilitation Centres, Treatment Centres)

Charlottetown: Special Care Unit, 65 McGill Ave., Charlottetown PE C1A 2K1 – 902/368-4720

# QUÉBEC

## DISTRICTS HOSPITALIERS/BUREAUX DE SANTÉ

Baie Comeau: Régie régionale de la santé et des services sociaux de la Côte-nord, 691, rue Jalbert, Baie Comeau QC G5G 2A1 – 418/589-9845; Fax: 418/589-8574 – Dir. gen. (par intérim), Ivo di Piazza

Chibougamau: Regie régionale de la santé et des services sociaux du Nord-du-Québec, 179, 5e av, Chibougamau QC G8P 3A7 – 418/748-7741; Fax: 418/748-6391 – Dir. gen., Bernard Fortin

Chicoutimi: Régie régionale de la santé et des services sociaux du Saguenay-Lac-Saint-Jean, 930, rue Jacques Cartier est, Chicoutimi QC G7H 7K9 – 418/545-4980; Fax: 418/545-8791 – Dir. gen., Louis-Philippe Thibault

Chisasibi: Conseil cri de la santé et des services sociaux de la Baie-James, CP 250, Chisasibi QC J0M 1E0 – 819/855-2844; Fax: 819/855-2867 – Responsible for 32 beds – Dir. gen., James Bobbish

Gaspé: Régie régionale de la santé et des services sociaux de la Gaspésie-Îles-de-la-Madeleine, 144, boul Gaspé, CP 5002, Gaspé QC G0G 1R0 – 418/368-2349; Fax: 418/368-4942 – Dir. gen., Denis Loiselle

Hull: Régie régionale de la santé et des services sociaux de l'Outaouais, 104, rue Lois, Hull QC J8Y 3R7 – 819/770-7747; Fax: 819/771-8632 – Dir. gen., Armand Boudreau

Kuujjuaq: Regie régionale de la santé et des services sociaux du Nanavik, CP 900, Kuujjuaq QC J0M 1C0 – 819/964-2222; Fax: 819/964-2888 – Dir. gen., Lizzie Epoo-York

Longueuil: Régie régionale de la santé et des services sociaux de la Montérégie, 1255, rue Beauregard, Longueuil QC J4K 2M3 – 514/679-6772; Fax: 514/679-6443 – Dir. gen., Claude Boily

Montréal: Regie régionale de la santé et des services sociaux de Laval, 800, boul Chomedey, 2e étage, Laval QC H7N 3Y4 – 514/978-2000 – Dir. gen., Michele Auclair

Montréal: Regie régionale de la santé et des services sociaux de Montréal-centre, 3725, rue St-Denis, Montréal QC H2X 3L9 – 514/286-6500; Fax: 514/286-5669 – Dir. gen., Marcel Villeneuve

Québec: Regie régionale de la santé et des services sociaux de la region de Québec, 525, boul Wilfrid Hamel, Québec QC G1M 2S8 – 418/529-5311; Fax: 418/529-4463 – Dir. gen. par intérim, Claude Boisjoli

Rimouski: Centre régional de la santé et des services sociaux du Bas-St-Laurent, #140, 288, Pierre-Saindon, 1er étage, Rimouski QC G5L 9A8 – 418/724-7085; Fax: 418/722-0356 – Dir. gen., Pierre-André Bernier

Rouyn-Noranda: Régie régionale de la santé et des services sociaux de l'Abitibi-Temiscamingue, 1, 9e rue, Rouyn-Noranda QC J9X 2A9 – 819/797-3264; Fax: 819/797-1947 – Dir. gen. (par intérim), Daniel Fortin

Saint-Charles-Borromée: Regie régionale de la santé et des services sociaux de Lanaudière, 1000, boul Ste-Anne, Saint-Charles-Borromée QC G6E 6J2 – 514/759-1157; Fax: 514/759-0023 – Dir. gen., Raynald Bergeron

Saint-Jerome: Régie régionale de la santé et des services sociaux des Laurentides, #210, 100, rue Labelle, Saint-Jerome QC J7Z 5N6 – 514/436-8622; Fax: 514/436-2530 – Dir. gen., Michel Leger

Ste-Marie: Régie régionale de la santé et des services sociaux de Chaudière-Appalaches, 363, rte Cameroun, Ste-Marie QC G6E 3E2 – 418/386-3363; Fax: 418/386-3361 – Dir. gen., Lionel Chouinard

Sherbrooke: Régie régionale de la santé et des services sociaux de l'Estrie, 2424, rue King ouest, Sherbrooke QC J1J 2E8 – 819/566-7861; Fax: 819/569-8894 – Dir. gen., Jean-Pierre Duplantie

Trois-Rivières: Régie régionale de la santé et des services sociaux de la Mauricie-Bois-Francs, 550, rue Bonaventure, 3e étage, Trois-Rivières QC G9A 2B5 – 819/693-3636; Fax: 819/373-1627 – Dir. gen., Paulin Dumas

## CENTRES HOSPITALIERS

Alma: Hôtel-Dieu d'Alma, 300, boul Champlain sud, Alma QC G8B 5W3 – 418/662-3421; Fax: 418/668-9691 – 225 lits – Dir. gen., Gabriel Collard

Amos: Centre hospitalier Hôtel-Dieu, 622, 4e rue ouest, Amos QC J9T 2S2 – 819/732-3341; Fax: 819/732-0425 – 145 lits – Régie régionale de la santé et des services sociaux de l'Abitibi-Temiscamingue – Dir. gen., Michel Michaud

Amqui: Centre hospitalier d'Amqui, 135, rue de l'Hôpital, Amqui QC G0J 1B0 – 418/629-2211; Fax: 418/629-4498 – 71 lits – Centre régional de la santé et des services sociaux du Bas-St-Laurent – Dir. gen., Alain Paquet

Asbestos: Centre hospitalier d'Asbestos, 475, 3e av, Asbestos QC J1T 1X6 – 819/879-7151; Fax: 819/879-7433 – 35 lits – Dir. gen., Paul-Aime Jacques

Baie-Comeau: Centre hospitalier régional - Pavillon Boisvert, 70, av Mance, Baie-Comeau QC G4Z 1M9 – 418/296-2281 – 62 lits – Dir. gen., Jacques A. Levesque

Baie Comeau: Centre hospitalier régional - Pavillon Le Royer, 635, boul Joliet, Baie Comeau QC G5C 1P1 – 418/589-3701; Fax: 418/589-9654 – 155 lits – Régie régionale de la santé et des services sociaux de la Côte-nord – Dir. gen., Denis Boudreau

Baie-Saint-Paul: Centre hospitalier de Charlevoix, 74, rue Ambroise-Fafard, CP 5000, Baie-Saint-Paul QC G0A 1B0 – 418/435-5150; Fax: 418/435-3315 – 243 lits – Dir. gen., Robert Vallières

Beauport: Hôpital de l'Enfant-Jésus (Centre St-Augustin), 2135, Terrasse Cadieux, Beauport QC G1C 1Z2 – 418/667-3910; Fax: 418/667-4094 – 326 lits – Dir. gen., Gaston Pellan

Beloeil: Réseau Santé Richelieu-Yamaska - Pavillon Villa Beauséjour, 80, rue Richelieu, Beloeil QC J3G 4N5 – Régie régionale de la santé et des services sociaux de la Montérégie – Dir. gen., Rodrique Blanchette

Bernierville: Hôpital St-Julien, 220, rue Principale, Bernierville QC G0N 1N0 – 418/428-3771; Fax: 418/428-9601 – 615 lits – Dir. gen., René Houle

Buckingham: Centre hospitalier de Buckingham, 500, rue Bélanger, Buckingham QC J8L 2M4 – 819/986-3341; Fax: 819/986-4000 – 134 lits – Régie régionale de la santé et des services sociaux de l'Outaouais – Dir. gen., Jacques Prud'homme

Cap-aux-Meules: Centre hospitalier de l'Archipel, 430, rue Principale, CP 730, Cap-aux-Meules QC G0B 1B0 – 418/986-2121; Fax: 418/986-6845 – 64 lits – Dir. gen., Gaétan Doré

Cap-de-la-Madeleine: Hôpital Cloutier, 155, rue Toupin, CP 218, Cap-de-la-Madeleine QC G8T 7W3 – 819/370-2100; Fax: 819/379-6511 – 130 lits – Dir. gen., Reynald Dessureault

Chandler: Centre hospitalier de Chandler, 451, rue Monseigneur Ross est, CP 3300, Chandler QC G0C 1K0 – 418/689-2261; Fax: 418/689-5551 – 131 lits – Dir. gen., Denis Caron

Charny: Complexe de santé et CLSC Paul-Gilbert, 9330, boul du Centre-Hospitalier, Charny QC G6X 1L6 – 418/832-2993; Fax: 418/832-9041 – 135 lits – Dir. gen., Paul Bergeron

Châteauguay: Centre hospitalier Anna-Laberge, 200, boul Brisebois, Châteauguay QC J6K 4W8 – 514/699-2425; Fax: 514/699-2525 – 250 lits – Régie régionale de la santé et des services sociaux de la Montérégie – Dir. gen., Jacques Cotton

Chibougamau: Hôpital Chibougamau ltée, 51, 3e rue, Chibougamau QC G8P 1N1 – 418/748-2676; Fax: 418/748-3662 – 71 lits – Dir. gen., Régis de Roy

Chicoutimi: Complexe hospitalier de la Sagamie, 305, av Saint-Vallier, CP 5006, Chicoutimi QC G7H 5H6 – 418/549-2195; Fax: 418/549-7081 – 628 lits – Dir. gen., Lucien Martel, 418/541-1090

Chicoutimi: Pavillon Roland Saucier, 150, rue Pinel, CP 2250, Chicoutimi QC G7G 3W4 – 418/549-5474; Fax: 418/549-8143 – 68 lits – Dir. gen., Lucien Martel

Chisasibi: Centre hospitalier régional Chisasibi, Chisasibi QC J0M 1E0 – 819/855-2844; Fax: 819/855-2098 – 25 lits – Dir. gen., James Bobbish

Cowansville: Hôpital Brôme-Missisquoi-Perkins, 950, rue Principale, Cowansville QC J2K 1K3 – 514/266-4342; Fax: 514/263-8669 – 140 lits – Régie régionale de la santé et des services sociaux de la Montérégie – Dir. gen., Mario Cyr

Cowansville: Hôpital St-Louis de Cowansville inc., 133, rue Larouche, Cowansville QC J2K 1T2 – 514/263-2220; Fax: 514/263-3401 – 28 lits – Dir. gen., Claude Codère

Des Ruisseaux: Centre de Mont-Laurier, 2561, ch de Lievre sud, Des Ruisseaux QC J9L 3G3 – 819/623-1234; Fax: 819/44-4299 – 80 lits – Régie régionale de la santé et des services sociaux des Laurentides – Dir. gen., Pierre Pagé

Dolbeau: Centre de santé Maria-Chapdelaine, 2000, boul Sacré-Coeur, Dolbeau QC G8L 2R5 – 418/276-1420; Fax: 418/276-5137 – 125 lits – Régie régionale de la santé et des services sociaux du Saguenay-Lac Saint-Jean – Dir. gen., Rodrigue Gagnon

Drummondville: Hôpital Ste-Croix, 570, rue Heriot, Drummondville QC J2B 1C1 – 419/478-6464; Fax: 419/478-6455 – 323 lits – Régie régionale de la santé et des services sociaux de la Mauricie-Bois-Francs – Dir. gen., Joaquin Bastida

Fleurimont: Centre hospitalier universitaire santée de l'Estrie - site Fleurimont, 3001, 12e av nord, Fleurimont QC J1H 5N4 – 819/563-5555; Fax: 819/820-6417 – 388 lits – Dir. gen., Normand Simoneau

Gaspé: Centre hospitalier hôtel-dieu de Gaspé, 215, boul York ouest, CP 120, Gaspé QC G0C 1S0 – 418/368-3301; Fax: 418/368-6850 – 56 lits – Régie régionale de la santé et des services sociaux de la Gaspésie-Îles-de-la-Madeleine – Dir. gen., Louis-Philippe Ste-Croix

Gaspé: Centre hospitalier Mgr Ross, 150, rue Mgr Ross, CP 800, Gaspé QC G0C 1R0 – 418/368-2291; Fax: 418/368-6730 – 241 lits – Dir. gen., Lewis Fitzpatrick

Gatineau: Centre hospitalier de Gatineau, 909, boul de la Verendrye ouest, CP 2000, Gatineau QC J8P 7H2 – 819/561-8100; Fax: 819/561-8306 – 289 lits – Régie régionale de la santé et des services sociaux de l'Outaouais – Dir. gen., Jean Laporte

Granby: Centre hospitalier de Granby, 205, boul Leclerc, Granby QC J2G 1T7 – 514/372-5491; Fax: 514/372-7197 – 227 lits – Dir. gen., Lucie Wiseman

Grand-Mère: Centre hospitalier Laflèche-Grand-Mère, 1650, 6e av, Grand-Mère QC G9T 2K4 – 819/533-2500; Fax: 819/538-7640 – 167 lits – Dir. gen., Guy d'Anjou

Greenfield Park: Hôpital Charles Lemoyne, 121, boul Taschereau, Greenfield Park QC J4V 2H1 – 514/466-5000; Fax: 514/466-5779 – 571 lits – Régie régionale de la santé et des services sociaux de la Montérégie – Dir. gen., Jean-Pierre Montpetit

Havre-Saint-Pierre: Centre de santé Saint-Jean-Eudes, 1035, Promenade des Anciens, CP 190, Havre-Saint-Pierre QC G0G 1P0 – 418/538-2212; Fax: 418/538-3066 – 39 lits – Dir. gen., Bill Noel

Hull: Centre hospitalier régional de l'Outaouais, 116, boul Lionel-Emond, Hull QC J8Y 1W7 – 819/595-6000; Fax: 819/595-6306 – 369 lits – Régie régionale de la santé et des services sociaux de l'Outaouais – Dir. gen., Paul Moreau

Jonquière: Centre hospitalier Jonquière, 2230, rue de l'Hôpital, CP 1200, Jonquière QC G7X 7X2 – 418/695-7700; Fax: 418/695-7715 – 201 lits – Dir. gen., Jacqueline St-Cyr

Kuujjuaq: Centre de santé Tulattavik de l'Ungava, CP 149, Kuujjuaq QC J0M 1C0 – 819/964-2905; Fax: 819/964-2653 – 22 lits – Dir. gen., Minnie Grey

La Baie: Hôpital de la Baie des Ha Ha , 100, rue Docteur-Desgagné, La Baie QC G7B 3P9 – 418/544-3381; Fax: 418/544-0770 – 102 lits – Dir. gen., Marcel Harvey

La Malbaie: Centre hospitalier St-Joseph, 303, rue Saint-Etienne, CP 340, La Malbaie QC G0T 1J0 – 418/665-3711; Fax: 418/665-4672 – 56 lits – Regie régionale de la santé et des services sociaux de la region de Québec – Dir. gen., Jacques Tremblay

La Peche: Centre hospitalier Gatineau Memorial, CP 160, Succ Wakefield, La Peche QC J0X 3G0 – 819/459-2342; Fax: 819/459-3947 – 26 lits – Régie régionale de la santé et des services sociaux de l'Outaouais – Dir. gen., Bernard Piché

La Pocatière: Hôpital de Nôtre-Dame-de-Fatima, 1201, 6e av, CP 460, La Pocatière QC G0R 1Z0 – 418/856-3540; Fax: 418/856-4737 – 49 lits – Dir. gen., Robert Leclerc

La Sarre: Centre hospitalier La Sarre, CP 6000, La Sarre QC J9Z 2X7 – 819/333-2311; Fax: 819/333-4316 – 49 lits – Régie régionale de la santé et des services sociaux de l'Abitibi-Temiscamingue – Dir. gen., Daniel Fortin

La Tûque: Centre hospitalier Saint-Joseph de La Tûque, 885, boul Ducharme, La Tûque QC G9X 3C1 – 819/523-4581; Fax: 819/523-7992 – 160 lits – Régie régionale de la santé et des services sociaux de la Mauricie-Bois-Francs – Dir. gen., Guy Lemieux

Lac-Etchemin: Le Sanatorium Begin, 331, place du Sanatorium, Lac-Etchemin QC G0R 1S0 – 418/625-3101; Fax: 418/625-3109 – 273 lits – Dir. gen., Jean-Yves Julien

Lac-Mégantic: Centre hospitalier Lac-Mégantic, 3569, rue Laval, Lac-Mégantic QC G6B 1A5 – 819/583-0330; Fax: 819/583-4674 – 105 lits – Régie régionale de la santé et des services sociaux des Laurentides – Dir. gen., Yves Rivard

Lachute: Hôpital d'Argenteuil, 145, boul de la Providence, Lachute QC J8H 4C7 – 514/562-3761; Fax: 514/562-9209 – 121 long term care, 59 short term care beds – Régie régionale de la santé et des services sociaux des Laurentides – Dir. gen., René Giard

L'Annonciation: CH Laurentides et centre réadaptation Hautes-Vallees, 1525, rue Principale nord, L'Annonciation QC J0T 1T0 – 819/275-2118; Fax: 819/275-2564 – 258 lits – Dir. gen., Jean-Pierre Massicotte

Lévis: Hôtel-Dieu de Lévis, 143, rue Wolfe, Lévis QC G6V 3Z1 – 418/835-7121; Fax: 418/835-7143 – 492 lits – Régie régionale de la santé et des services sociaux de Chaudière-Appalaches – Dir. gen., Hervé Moysan

Longueuil: Centre hospitalier Pierre-Boucher, 1333, boul Jacques-Cartier est, Longueuil QC J4M 2A5 – 514/468-8111; Fax: 514/468-8188 – 362 lits – Régie régionale de la santé et des services sociaux de la Montérégie – Dir. gen., Gilles Dufault

Longueuil: Réseau Santé Richelieu-Yamaska - Pavillon Saint-Charles, 125, boul Ste-Foy, Longueuil QC J4J 1W7 – 514/679-6772; Fax: 514/679-6443 – Régie régionale de la santé et des services sociaux de la Montérégie

Loretteville: Centre hospitalier Chauveau, 29, rue de l'Hôpital, Loretteville QC G2A 2T7 – 418/842-3651; Fax: 418/842-8660 – 76 lits – Regie régionale de la santé et des services sociaux de la region de Québec – Dir. gen., Michel Marcotte

Louiseville: Regroupement de la Santé et des Services sociaux de la MRC de Maskinogné, 41, boul Comtois, Louiseville QC J5V 2H8 – 819/228-2731; Fax: 819/228-2973 – 10 lits – Dir. gen., Gerard Desaulniers

Magog: Centre hospitalier et d'hébergement de Memphrémagog, 50, rue Saint-Patrice est, Magog QC J1X 3X3 – 819/843-3381; Fax: 819/843-8262 – 168 lits – Dir. gen., Donald Langlais

Malartic: Centre hospitalier Malartic, 1141. rue Royale, CP 800, Malartic QC J0Y 1Z0 – 819/757-4342; Fax: 819/757-4330 – 49 lits – Dir. gen., Christiane Glaçon

Maniwaki: Centre hospitalier de Maniwaki, 309, boul Desjardins, Maniwaki QC J9E 2E7 – 819/449-2300; Fax: 819/449-6137 – 94 lits – Régie régionale de la santé et des services sociaux de l'Outaouais – Dir. gen., Paul Charbonneau

Maria: Centre hospitalier Baie-des-Chaleurs, 419, boul Perron, Maria QC G0C 1Y0 – 418/759-3443; Fax: 418/759-5063 – 183 lits – Dir. gen., Bernard Nadeau

Matane: Centre hospitalier de Matane, 333, rue Thibault, Matane QC G4W 2W5 – 418/562-3135; Fax: 418/562-9374 – 123 lits – Régie régionale de la santé et des services sociaux de la Gaspésie-Îles-de-la-Madeleine – Dir. gen., Charles Sénéchal

Montmagny: Hôtel-Dieu de Montmagny, 350, boul Taché ouest, Montmagny QC G5V 3R8 – 418/248-0630; Fax: 418/248-0820 – 150 lits – Régie régionale de la santé et des services sociaux de Chaudière-Appalaches – Dir. gen., Yves Lachapelle

Montréal: Centre hospitalier Angrignon - Pavillon LaSalle, 8585, Terrasse Champlain, Lasalle QC H8P 1C1 – 514/365-1510; Fax: 514/595-2227 – 241 lits – Regie régionale de la santé et des services sociaux de Montréal-centre – Dir. gen., Jacques Maynard

Montréal: Centre hospitalier Angrignon, 4000, boul Lasalle, Verdun QC H4G 2A3 – 514/765-8121; Fax: 514/765-7306 – 547 lits – Regie régionale de la santé et des services sociaux de Montréal-centre – Dir. gen., Jacques Maynard

Montréal: Centre hospitalier Catherine Booth, 4375, av Montclair, Montréal QC H4B 2J5 – 514/481-0431; Fax: 514/481-0029 – 84 lits – Regie régionale de la santé et des services sociaux de Montréal-centre – Dir. gen., Joanne Davison

Montréal: Centre hospitalier Côte-des-Neiges, 4565, ch de la Reine Marie, Montréal QC H3W 1W5 – 514/340-3517; Fax: 514/340-3500 – 327 lits – Dir. gen., Colette Tracyk

Montréal: Centre hospitalier de Lachine, 650, 16e av, Lachine QC H8S 3N5 – 514/637-2351; Fax: 514/637-1632 – 129 lits – Dir. gen., André Marcoux

Montréal: Centre hospitalier de Saint-Laurent, 1275, ch Cote-Vertu, Saint-Laurent QC H4L 4V2 – 514/

747-4771; Fax: 514/747-8809 – 124 beds – Dir. gen., Jean-Pierre Massicotte

Montréal: Centre hospitalier de St. Mary, 3830, av Lacombe, Montréal QC H3T 1M5 – 514/345-3511; Fax: 514/734-2636; EMail: sys/smhc@smh.qc.ca – 414 lits – Regie régionale de la santé et des services sociaux de Montréal-centre – Chef opérations et directeur gen. par intérim, Sean Harty

Montréal: Centre hospitalier de l'Univeristé de Montréal - Pavillon Hôtel-Dieu, 3840, rue St-Urbain, Montréal QC H2W 1T8 – 514/843-2611; Fax: 514/843-3065 – 570 lits – Regie régionale de la santé et des services sociaux de Montréal-centre – Dir. gen., Michel Larivière

Montréal: Centre hospitalier de l'Université de Montréal - Pavillon Notre-Dame, 1560, rue Sherbrooke est, Montréal QC H2L 4M1 – 514/876-6421; Fax: 514/876-7129 – 911 lits – Regie régionale de la santé et des services sociaux de Montréal-centre – Dir. gen., David Levine

Montréal: Centre hospitalier de l'Université de Montréal - Pavillon Saint-Luc, 1058, rue St-Denis, Montréal QC H2X 3J4 – 514/281-2121, 3200; Fax: 514/281-4056 – 716 lits – Regie régionale de la santé et des services sociaux de Montréal-centre – Dir. gen., Jean Leblanc

Montréal: Centre hospitalier Fleury, 2180, rue Fleury est, Montréal QC H2B 1K3 – 514/381-9311; Fax: 514/383-5086 – 252 lits – Regie régionale de la santé et des services sociaux de Montréal-centre – Dir. gen., Lucien Hervieux

Montréal: Centre hospitalier Gouin-Rosemont, 1970, boul Rosemont, Montréal QC H2G 1S8 – 514/273-3681; Fax: 514/273-7645 – 43 lits – Dir. gen., Juliette P. Bailly

Montréal: Centre hospitalier J. Henri Charbonneau, 3095, rue Sherbrooke est, Montréal QC H1W 1B2 – 514/523-1173; Fax: 514/523-4196 – 213 lits – Regie régionale de la santé et des services sociaux de Montréal-centre – Dir. gen., Marcellin Dallaire

Montréal: Centre hospitalier Jacques Viger, 1051, rue St-Hubert, Montréal QC H2L 3Y5 – 514/842-7181; Fax: 514/842-7689 – 347 lits – Dir. gen., Damien Dallaire

Montréal: Centre hospitalier Mont-Sinai, 5690, boul Cavendish, Côte-Saint-Luc QC H4W 1S7 – 514/369-2222; Fax: 514/369-2225 – 107 lits – Regie régionale de la santé et des services sociaux de Montréal-centre – Dir. gen., Joseph Rothbart

Montréal: Cité de la santé de Laval, 1755, boul René-Laennec, CP 440, Laval QC H7M 3L9 – 514/668-1010; Fax: 514/975-5545 – 452 lits – Dir. gen., Daniel Adam, 514/975-5598

Montréal: Hôpital Champlain de Verdun, 1325, rue Crawford, Verdun QC H4H 2N6 – 514/766-8513; Fax: 514/766-3731 – 228 lits – Dir. gen., Ghislain Girard

Montréal: Hôpital de Montréal pour enfants, 2300, rue Tupper, Montréal QC H3H 1P3 – 514/934-4400; Fax: 514/934-4477 – 186 lits – Regie régionale de la santé et des services sociaux de Montréal-centre – Dir. gen., Elisabeth Riley

Montréal: Hôpital du Sacré-Coeur de Montréal, 5400, boul Gouin ouest, Montréal QC H4J 1C5 – 514/338-2222; Fax: 514/338-2384 – 605 lits – Regie régionale de la santé et des services sociaux de Montréal-centre – Dir. gen., Kiem-Thien Dao

Montréal: L'Hôpital général de Lachine, 3320, rue Notre-Dame, Lachine QC H8T 1W8 – 514/637-1161; Fax: 514/637-7851 – 147 lits – Dir. gen., Roland J. Saint-Arnaud

Montréal: Hôpital général de Montréal/The Montréal General Hospital, 1650, av Cedar, Montréal QC H3G 1A4 – 514/937-6011; Fax: 514/937-2455; EMail: postiguy@is.mgh.mcgill.ca – 672 lits – Regie régionale de la santé et des services sociaux de Montréal-centre – Dir. gen., Gérard Douville

Montréal: Hôpital général du Lakeshore, 160, ch Stillview, Pointe-Claire QC H9R 2Y2 – 514/630-2225; Fax: 514/630-3302 – 257 lits – Régie régionale de la santé et des services sociaux de la Montérégie – Dir. gen., Gilles Lanteigne, 514/630-2107

Montréal: Hôpital général Juif Sir Mortimer B. Davis/Sir Mortimer B. Davis Jewish General Hospital, 3755, ch Côte Ste-Catherine, Montréal QC H3T 1E2 – 514/340-8222; Fax: 514/340-7530 – 605 lits – Dir. gen., Henri Elbaz

Montréal: Hôpital Jean-Talon, 1385, rue Jean-Talon est, Montréal QC H2E 1S6 – 514/495-6767; Fax: 514/495-6734 – 340 lits – Dir. gen., Pierre Ledoux

Montréal: Hôpital Maisonneuve-Rosemont, 5415, boul de l'Assomption, Montréal QC H1T 2M4 – 514/252-3591; Fax: 514/252-3827 – 780 lits – Dir. gen., André Ducharme

Montréal: Hôpital Marie Enfant, 5200, rue Belanger est, Montréal QC H1T 1C9 – 514/374-1710; Fax: 514/374-7944 – 100 lits – Regie régionale de la santé et des services sociaux de Montréal-centre – Dir. gen., Michel Brunet

Montréal: Hôpital Mont-Sinai, 5690, boul Cavendish, Cote-Saint-Luc QC H4W 1S7 – 514/369-2222; Fax: 514/369-2225 – 107 lits – Dir. gen., vacant

Montréal: Hôpital neurologique de Montréal, 3801, rue Université, Montréal QC H3A 2B4 – 514/398-1944; Fax: 514/398-8540 – 135 lits – Regie régionale de la santé et des services sociaux de Montréal-centre – Associate directeur gen., Jim Gates

Montréal: Hôpital Nôtre-Dame de la Merci, 555, boul Gouin ouest, Montréal QC H3L 1K5 – 514/331-3020; Fax: 514/331-5827 – 392 lits – Regie régionale de la santé et des services sociaux de Montréal-centre – Dir. gen., Michel Bouffard, 514/331-3025

Montréal: Hôpital Reddy Memorial, 4039, rue Tupper, Westmount QC H3Z 1T5 – 514/933-7511 – 201 beds – Dir. gen., Réjean Plante

Montréal: Hôpital Royal Victoria, 687, av des Pins ouest, Montréal QC H3A 1A1 – 514/842-1231; Fax: 514/842-2271 – 610 lits – Regie régionale de la santé et des services sociaux de Montréal-centre – Dir. gen., Phillip P. Aspinall

Montréal: Hôpital St-Charles Borromée, 66, boul René-Lévesque est, Montréal QC H2X 1N3 – 514/861-9331; Fax: 514/861-8385 – 275 lits – Dir. gen., Gilbert Gagnon

Montréal: Hôpital Saint-Joseph de la Providence, 11844, av Bois-de-boulogne, Montréal QC H3M 2X7 – 514/334-3120; Fax: 514/334-5881 – 139 lits – Regie régionale de la santé et des services sociaux de Montréal-centre – Dir. gen., Mathieu Lafrance

Montréal: Hôpital Sainte-Jeanne d'Arc de Montréal, 3570, rue St-Urbain, Montréal QC H2X 2N8 – 514/282-5000; Fax: 514/282-9206 – 318 lits – Regie régionale de la santé et des services sociaux de Montréal-centre – Dir. gen., François Savard

Montréal: Hôpital Sainte-Justine, 3175, ch de la Côte Ste-Catherine, Montréal QC H3T 1C5 – 514/345-4665; Fax: 514/345-4808 – 592 lits – Regie régionale de la santé et des services sociaux de Montréal-centre – Dir. gen., Jean-Pierre Chicoine

Montréal: Hôpital Santa Cabrini, 5655, rue St-Zotique est, Montréal QC H1T 1P7 – 514/252-6000; Fax: 514/252-6453 – 417 lits – Regie régionale de la santé et des services sociaux de Montréal-centre – Dir. gen., Irene Giannetti

Montréal: Institut de cardiologie de Montréal, 5000, rue Bélanger est, Montréal QC H1T 1C8 – 514/376-3330; Fax: 514/593-2540 – 171 lits – Dir. gen., Raymond Carignan

Montréal: Institut thoracique de Montréal, 3650, rue St-Urbain, Montréal QC H2X 2P4 – 514/849-5201; Fax: 514/849-2180 – 124 lits – Regie régionale de la santé et des services sociaux de Montréal-centre – Dir. gen., Phillip P. Aspinall

Montréal: Jewish Rehabilitation Hospital/Hôpital juif de réadaptation, 3205, Place Alton-Goldbloom, Laval QC H7V 1R2 – 514/688-9550; Fax: 514/688-3673 – 120 lits – Dir. gen., Rosyln Cabot

Montréal: Pavillon Albert Prevost, 6555, boul Gouin ouest, Montréal QC H4K 1B3 – 514/333-4237; Fax: 514/338-4352 – 132 lits – Dir. gen., Khien-Thien Dao

Nicolet: Hôpital du Christ-Roi, 675, rue St-Jean-Baptiste, Nicolet QC J3T 1S4 – 819/293-2071; Fax: 819/293-6160 – 95 lits – Dir. gen., Ginette Simard-Montplaisir

Notre-Dame-du-Lac: Hôpital Notre-Dame-du-Lac, 58, rue de l'Eglise, CP 310, Notre-Dame-du-Lac QC G0L 1X0 – 418/899-6751; Fax: 418/899-2809 – 78 lits – Centre régional de la santé et des services sociaux du Bas-St-Laurent – Dir. gen. (interim), Michel Samson

Ormstown: Hôpital Barrie Memorial, 28, rue Gale, CP 200, Ormstown QC J0S 1K0 – 514/829-2321; Fax: 514/829-3582 – 61 lits – Dir. gen., Guy Rho

Povungnituk: Centre hospitalier de la Baie d'Hudson, Povungnituk QC J0M 1P0 – 819/988-2802; Fax: 819/988-2796 – 15 lits – Dir. gen., Michel Garcia

Québec: Centre hospitalier universitaire de Québec - Hôtel-Dieu de Québec, 11, Côte du Palais, Québec QC G1R 2J6 – 418/691-5257; Fax: 418/691-5205 – 476 lits – Dir. gen., Dr Robert Busilacchi

Québec: Centre hospitalier universitaire de Québec - Pavillon St-François-d'Assise, 10, rue de l'Espinay, Québec QC G1L 3L5 – 418/525-4303; Fax: 418/525-4426 – 666 lits – Dir. gen., Gerard Roy

Québec: Hôpital général de Québec, 260, boul Langelier, Québec QC G1K 5N1 – 418/529-0931; Fax: 418/529-4088 – 377 lits – Regie régionale de la santé et des services sociaux de la region de Québec – Dir. gen., Roger Corriveau

Québec: L'Hôpital Jeffery Hale, 1250, ch Ste-Foy, Québec QC G1S 2M6 – 418/683-4471; Fax: 418/683-8471 – 116 lits – Regie régionale de la santé et des services sociaux de la region de Québec – Dir., Services administratifs, Clément Lacroix

Québec: Pavillon Saint-Sacrement, 1050, ch Ste-Foy, Québec QC G1S 4L8 – 418/682-7511; Fax: 418/682-7972 – 441 lits – Regie régionale de la santé et des services sociaux de la region de Québec – Dir. gen., Gaston Pellan

Repentigny: Centre hospitalier Le Gardeur, 135, boul Claude David, Repentigny QC J6A 1N6 – 514/654-7525; Fax: 514/585-5939 – 258 lits – Régie régionale de la santé et des services sociaux des Laurentides – Dir. gen., Giséle Boyer

Rimouski: Centre hospitalier Régional de Rimouski, 150, av Rouleau, Rimouski QC G5L 5T1 – 418/723-7851, 724-8442; Fax: 418/724-8616 – 344 lits – Centre régional de la santé et des services sociaux du Bas-St-Laurent – Dir. gen., Julie Doyon-Proulx

Rivière-du-Loup: Centre hospitalier régional du Grand-Portage, 75, rue St-Henri, Rivière-du-Loup QC G5R 2A4 – 418/868-1000; Fax: 418/868-1032 – 173 lits – Centre régional de la santé et des services sociaux du Bas-St-Laurent – Dir. gen., Raymond April

Roberval: Hôtel-Dieu de Roberval, 450, rue Brassard, Roberval QC G8H 1B9 – 418/275-0110; Fax: 418/275-6202 – 361 lits – Régie régionale de la santé et des services sociaux du Saguenay-Lac Saint-Jean – Dir. gen., André-Guy Cloutier

Rouyn-Noranda: Centre hospitalier Rouyn-Noranda, 4, 9e rue, Rouyn-Noranda QC J9X 2B2 – 819/764-5131; Fax: 819/764-4211 – 219 lits – Régie régionale de la santé et des services sociaux de l'Abitibi-Temiscamingue – Dir. gen., Nelson Laflamme

Ste-Agathe-des-Monts: Centre hospitalier Laurentien, 234, rue St-Vincent, Ste-Agathe-des-Monts QC J8C 2B8 – 819/324-4000; Fax: 819/324-4010 – 98 lits – Régie régionale de la santé et des services sociaux des Laurentides – Dir. gen., Jacques Gaudette

Ste-Anne-de-Beaupré: Hôpital Sainte-Anne-de-Beaupré, 9974, rue Royale, Ste-Anne-de-Beaupré QC G0A 3C0 – 418/827-3726; Fax: 418/827-6107 – 35 lits – Regie régionale de la santé et des services sociaux de la region de Québec – Dir. gen., Jean-Yves Simard, 418/827-3791

Ste-Anne-des-Monts: Hôpital des Monts, 50, rue Belvedere, CP 790, Ste-Anne-des-Monts QC G0E 2G0 – 418/763-2261; Fax: 418/763-7460 – 65 lits – Centre régional de la santé et des services sociaux du Bas-St-Laurent – Dir. gen., Robert Deschenes

Saint-Charles Borromée: Centre hospitalier regional Delanaudière, 1000, boul Sainte-Anne, Saint-Charles Borromée QC J6E 5B5 – 514/759-8222; Fax: 514/759-7969 – 725 lits – Dir. gen., Maurice Blais

St-Eustache: Centre hospitalier St-Eustache, 520, boul Arthur-Sauve, CP 153, St-Eustache QC J7R 5B1 – 514/473-6811; Fax: 514/473-6966 – 190 lits – Régie régionale de la santé et des services sociaux des Laurentides – Dir. gen., Jean-Guy Nadeau

Ste-Foy: Centre hospitalier de l'Université de Québec, 2705, boul Laurier, Ste-Foy QC G1V 4G2 – 418/656-4141; Fax: 418/654-2762 – 410 lits – Dir. gen., Gérard Roy

Ste-Foy: Hôpital Laval, 2725, ch Ste-Foy, Ste-Foy QC G1V 4G5 – 418/656-4880; Fax: 418/656-4829 – 370 lits – Regie régionale de la santé et des services sociaux de la region de Québec – Dir. gen., Gilles Lagacé

St-Georges: Centre hospitalier Beauce-Etchemin, 1515, 17e rue, St-Georges QC G5Y 4T8 – 418/228-2031; Fax: 418/227-3825 – 155 lits – Dir. gen. interim, Michel Bernard

Saint-Hyacinthe: Réseau Santé Richelieu-Yamaska - Pavillon Hôtel-Dieu, 1800, rue Dessaulles, Saint-Hyacinthe QC J2S 2T2 – 514/774-6495; Fax: 514/774-0947 – 609 lits – Régie régionale de la santé et des services sociaux de la Montérégie – Dir. gen., Rodrique Blanchette

Saint-Hyacinthe: Réseau Santé Richelieu-Yamaska - Pavillon Honoré-Mercier, 2750, boul Laframboise, Saint-Hyacinthe QC J2S 4Y8 – 514/771-3333 – 834 lits – Régie régionale de la santé et des services sociaux de la Montérégie – Dir. gen., Rodrique Blanchette

St-Jean-sur-Richelieu: Hôpital du Haut-Richelieu, 920, boul du Séminaire, St-Jean-sur-Richelieu QC J3A 1B7 – 514/359-5000; Fax: 514/359-5251 – 309 lits – Régie régionale de la santé et des services sociaux de la Montérégie – Dir. gen., André Trottier

St-Jérôme: Hôtel-Dieu de St-Jérôme, 290, rue Montigny, St-Jérôme QC J7Z 5T3 – 514/431-8200; Fax: 514/431-8244 – 444 lits – Régie régionale de la santé et des services sociaux des Laurentides – Dir. gen., Claude Guimont

Salaberry-de-Valleyfield: Centre hospitalier régional du Suroît, 150, rue St-Thomas, Salaberry-de-Valleyfield QC J6T 6C1 – 514/371-9925; Fax: 514/371-3607; EMail: chrsbout@rocler.qc.ca – 314 lits – Régie régionale de la santé et des services sociaux de la Montérégie – Dir. gen., Paul-Henri Boutin

Sept-Iles: Centre hospitalier régional de Sept-Iles, 45, rue Père Divet, Sept-Iles QC G4R 3N7 – 418/962-9761; Fax: 418/962-2701 – 226 lits – Régie régionale de la santé et des services sociaux de la Côte-nord – Dir. gen., Daniel Petit

Shawinigan-Sud: Centre hospitalier régional de la Mauricie, 50, 118e rue, Shawinigan-Sud QC G9P 4E7 – 819/536-7500; Fax: 819/536-7658 – 250 lits – Dir. gen., vacant

Shawinigan: Centre hospitalier Sainte-Thérèse, 1705, av Georges, Shawinigan QC G9N 2N1 – 819/537-9351; Fax: 819/537-4737 – 90 lits – Dir. gen., Jacques Veilletta

Shawville: Centre hospitalier du Pontiac, 200, rue Argue, CP 280, Shawville QC J0X 2Y0 – 819/647-2211; Fax: 819/647-2409 – 81 lits – Dir. gen., Gilles Lanteigne

Sherbrooke: Centre hospitalier, 375, rue Argyle, Sherbrooke QC J1J 3H5 – 819/569-3661; Fax: 819/569-4688 – 137 lits – Dir. gen., Marie Trousdell

Sherbrooke: Centre universitaire de santé de l'Estrie - site Bowen, 580, rue Bowen sud, Sherbrooke QC J1G 2E8 – 819/569-2551; Fax: 819/822-6766 – 322 lits – Dir. gen., Albert Painchaud

Sherbrooke: Centre universitaire de santé de L'Estrie - site King, 300, rue King est, Sherbrooke QC J1G 1B1 – 819/563-2366; Fax: 819/563-5201 – 284 lits – Régie régionale de la santé et des services sociaux de l'Estrie – Dir. gen., Normand Légault

Sherbrooke: Institut universitaire de gériatrie de Sherbrooke, 1036, rue Belvédère sud, Sherbrooke QC J1H 4C4 – 819/821-5100; Fax: 819/821-2065; EMail: institut@login.net – 487 lits – Régie régionale de la santé et des services sociaux de l'Estrie – Dir. gen., Daniel Bergeron

Sorel: Hôtel-Dieu de Sorel, 400, av Hôtel-Dieu, Sorel QC J3P 1N5 – 514/746-6000; Fax: 514/746-2782 – 241 lits – Régie régionale de la santé et des services sociaux de la Montérégie – Dir. gen., Pierre-Yves Desjardins, 514/746-6226

Thetford Mines: Centre hospitalier de la région de l'Amiante, 1717, rue Notre-Dame nord, Thetford Mines QC G6G 2V4 – 418/338-7777; Fax: 418/335-7616 – 299 lits – Régie régionale de la santé et des services sociaux de Chaudière-Appalaches – Dir. gen., Jean-Claude Gagné

Trois-Rivières: Centre hospitalier Sainte-Marie - Pavillon Sainte-Marie, 1991, boul du Carmel, Trois-Rivières QC G8Z 3R9 – 819/378-9700; Fax: 819/378-9850 – 310 lits – Régie régionale de la santé et des services sociaux de la Mauricie-Bois-Francs – Dir. gen., Mathieu Vaillancourt

Trois-Rivières: Pavillon St-Joseph, 731, rue Ste-Julie, Trois-Rivières QC G9A 1Y1 – 819/372-3557; Fax: 819/372-3581 – 275 lits – Régie régionale de la santé et des services sociaux de la Mauricie-Bois-Francs – Dir. gen., Claude Blais

Val-d'Or: Centre hospitalier de Val d'Or, 725, 6e rue, Val-d'Or QC J9P 3Y1 – 819/825-6711; Fax: 819/825-4615 – 173 lits – Régie régionale de la santé et des services sociaux de l'Abitibi-Temiscamingue – Dir. gen., Gaetan Gratton

Victoriaville: Centre d'hébergement de la MRC d'Arthabaska, 61, av de l'Ermitage, Victoriaville QC G6P 6X4 – 819/758-7511; Fax: 819/758-4852 – 232 lits – Dir. gen., Gilles Perreault

Victoriaville: Hôtel-Dieu d'Arthabaska, 5, rue des Hospitalières, Victoriaville QC G6P 6N2 – 819/357-2030; Fax: 819/357-4314 – 289 lits – Dir. gen., Jean Bartkowiak

Ville-Marie: Centre de santé Sainte-Famille, 22, rue Notre-Dame, CP 2 000, Ville-Marie QC J0Z 3W0 – 819/629-2420; Fax: 819/629-3257 – 94 lits – Dir. gen., Pierre Larouche

Wakefield: Gatineau Memorial Hospital, 150 Burnside Ave., CP 160, Wakefield QC J0X 3G0 – 819/459-2342; Fax: 819/459-3947 – 25 beds – Exec. Dir., Bernard Piché

Waterloo: C.H.S.L.D. Horace-Boivin, 5300, av Courville, CP 1230, Waterloo QC J0E 2N0 – 514/539-5512; Fax: 514/539-1830; EMail: centrehb@enDirect.qc.ca – 40 lits – Dir. gen., Bernard Fournelle

## HÔPITAUX AUXILIAIRES/CENTRES DE SOINS DE SANTÉ

Acton Vale: CLSC la Chenaie, 1266, rue Lemay, CP 370, Acton Vale QC J0H 1A0 – 514/546-3225; Fax: 514/546-4981 – Dir. gen., Fernand Filion

Aguanish: Dispensaire-Aguanish (CS St-Jean Eudes), Aguanish QC G0G 1A0 – 418/533-2301 – Dir. gen., Denis R. Boudreau

Alma: CLSC Le Norois, Edifice complexe J.-Gagnon, 100, ave Saint-Joseph, Alma QC G8B 7A6 – 418/668-4563; Fax: 418/668-5403 – Dir. gen., Jacques Levesque

Amos: CLSC de l'Elan, 1242, route 111 est, CP 729, Amos QC J9T 3X3 – 819/732-3271; Fax: 819/732-1282 – Dir. gen., Jacques Guimond

Asbestos: CLSC le Chaumiere, 601, boul Simoneau, Asbestos QC J1T 4G7 – 819/879-7181; Fax: 819/879-4005 – Dir. gen., Raynald Dodier

Aupaluk: Dispensaire d'Aupaluk, Aupaluk QC J0M 1X0 – 819/491-7077 – Dir. gen., Minnie Grey

Aylmer: CLSC Grande-Rivière, 425, rue le Guerrier, Aylmer QC J9H 6N8 – 819/684-2251; Fax: 819/684-2541 – Dir. gen., Pierre Paquin

Baie-Johan-Beetz: Dispensaire-Baie-Johan-Beetz (CS de la Minganie), Baie-Johan-Beetz QC G0C 1B0 – 418/539-0169 – Dir. gen., Denis R. Boudreau

Beloeil: CLSC le Vallée des Patriotes, 347, rue Duvernay, Beloeil QC J3G 5S8 – 514/467-0157; Fax: 514/467-2269 – Dir. gen., Jean-Yves Leblanc

Berthierville: CLSC d'Autray, 761, rue Notre-Dame, CP 1470, Berthierville QC J0K 1A0 – 514/836-7011; Fax: 514/836-1545 – Dir. gen., Norman Blackburn

Boucherville: CLSC des Seigneuries, 160, boul de Montarville, Boucherville QC J4B 6S2 – 514/652-2917; Fax: 514/652-9902 – Dir. gen., André Foisy

Brossard: CLSC Samuel de Champlain, Complex Taschereau, #100, 5811, boul Taschereau, Brossard QC J4Z 1A5 – 514/445-4452; Fax: 514/445-5535 – Dir. gen., Michel Lapointe

Buckingham: CLSC de la Vallée de la Lievre, 578, boul Cité des Jeunes, Buckingham QC J8L 2W1 – 819/986-3359; Fax: 819/986-5671 – Dir. gen., Jacques Parenteau

Candiac: CLSC Kateri, 90, boul Marie-Victorin, Candiac QC J5R 1C1 – 514/659-7661; Fax: 514/444-6260 – Dir. gen., André J. Coté

Cap-aux-Meules: CLSC des Iles, 420, ch Principale, CP 670, Cap-aux-Meules QC G0B 1B0 – 418/986-5323; Fax: 418/986-4911 – Dir. gen., Germain Chevarie

Cap-de-Madeleine: CLSC du Rivage, 20, rue Notre-Dame, Cap-de-Madeleine QC G8T 7W1 – 819/378-4163 – Dir. gen., Vital Gaudet

Causapscal: CLSC la Vallée, 558, rue Saint-Jacques nord, Causapscal QC G0J 1J0 – 418/756-3451; Fax: 418/756-3038 – Dir. gen., Liza Chamberland

Chandler: CLSC la Saline, 633, av Daignault, CP 1090, Chandler QC G0C 1K0 – 418/689-2572; Fax: 418/689-4707 – Dir. gen., Clement Michel

Chapais: CLSC des Grands Bois, 32, 3e av, CP 1300, Chapais QC G0W 1H0 – 418/745-2591; Fax: 418/745-3240 – Dir. gen., René Ricard

Charlesbourg: CLSC La Source, 280, av Notre-Dame, Charlesbourg QC G2M 1K9 – 418/849-2572; Fax: 418/849-0661 – Dir. gen., Louis Blanchette

Chateauguay: CLSC Chateauguay, 101, rue Lauzon, Chateauguay QC J6K 1C7 – 514/691-7410; Fax: 514/691-6202 – Dir. gen., André Racine

Chertsey: CLSC de Matawinie, 8161, route 125, RR#1, Chertsey QC J0K 3K0 – 514/882-2488; Fax: 514/882-9072 – Dir. gen., Philippe Lupien

Chicoutimi: CLSC des Coteaux, 326, rue des Saguenens, CP 5150, Chicoutimi QC G7H 6J6 – 418/545-1262; Fax: 418/693-0049 – Dir. gen., Helene Gobeil

Chicoutimi: CLSC Saguenay-nord, 222, rue Saint-Ephrem, Chicoutimi QC G7G 2W5 – 418/545-1575; Fax: 418/545-7293 – Dir. gen., Carroll Malenfant

Coaticook: Carrefour de la Santé et des Services sociaux CLSC et CHSLD de la MRC de Coaticook, 138, rue Jeanne-Mance, Coaticook QC J1A 1W3 – 819/849-4876; Fax: 819/849-6735 – 115 beds – Dir. gen., Rémi Lavigne

Drummondville: CLSC Drummond, 350, rue Saint-Jean, Drummondville QC J2B 5L4 – 819/474-2572; Fax: 819/474-2828 – Dir. gen., Gaetan Mercure

Fermont: Centre de santé de l'Hematite, 1, rue Aquilon, CP 550, Fermont QC G0G 1J0 – 418/287-5461; Fax: 418/287-5281 – 5 lits – Dir. gen., Micheline Rioux

Forestville: CLSC de Forestville, 2, 7e rue, CP 790, Forestville QC G0T 1E0 – 418/587-2212; Fax: 418/587-2865 – 15 lits – Dir. gen., Lucien Lessard

Fortierville: CLSC les Bles d'Or, 216, rue Principale, Fortierville QC G0S 1J0 – 819/287-4442; Fax: 819/287-4605 – Dir. gen., vacant

Gaspé: CLSC de la Pointe, 154, boul Renard est, CP 220, Gaspé QC G0E 2A0 – 418/269-3391; Fax: 418/269-5294 – Dir. gen., Jean-Claude Plourde

Gatineau: CLSC des Draveurs, 80, av Gatineau, Gatineau QC J8T 4J3 – 819/561-2550; Fax: 819/561-3034 – Dir. gen., Gilles Gelinas

Gatineau: CLSC le Moulin, 510, boul Maloney est, Gatineau QC J8P 1E7 – 819/663-9214; Fax: 819/663-2326 – Dir. gen., Robert Allard

Granby: CLSC de la Haute Yamaska, 294, rue Deragon, Granby QC J2G 5J5 – 514/375-1442; Fax: 514/375-5666 – Dir. gen., Francois Blais

Grande-Vallée: CLSC l'Estran, 71, rue Saint-Francois-Xavier, CP 190, Grande-Vallée QC G0E 1K0 – 418/393-2001; Fax: 418/393-2952 – Dir. gen., Harry Lachance

Hull: CLSC de Hull, 85, rue Saint-Redempteur, Hull QC J8X 4E6 – 819/770-6900; Fax: 819/770-8707 – Dir. gen., Pierre Ippersiel

Huntingdon: Centre hospitalier du Comté de Huntingdon, 198, rue Châteauguay, CP 6000, Huntingdon QC J0S 1H0 – 514/264-6111; Fax: 514/264-4923 – 60 lits – Dir. gen., Guy Deschenes

Huntingdon: CLSC Huntingdon, 220, rue Chateauguay, CP 820, Huntingdon QC J0S 1H0 – 514/264-6108; Fax: 514/264-6801 – Dir. gen., Guy Deschenes

Iberville: CLSC Vallée des Forts, 874, rue Champlain, Iberville QC J2X 3W9 – 514/358-2572; Fax: 514/347-3275 – Dir. gen., Mario Lafreniere

Joilette: CLSC de Joliette, 245, rue Curé-Majeau, Joilette QC J6E 8S8 – 514/755-2111; Fax: 514/755-4896 – Dir. gen., Pierre Boissonneault

Kangiqsualujjuaq: Dispensaire de Kangiqsualujjuaq, Kangiqsualujjuaq QC J0M 1N0 – 819/337-5312 – Dir. gen., Minnie Grey

Kangiqsujuaq: Dispensaire de Kangiqsujuaq, Kangiqsujuaq QC J0M 1K0 – 819/338-3303 – Dir. gen., Minnie Grey

Kangirsuk: Dispensaire de Kangirsuk, Kangirsuk QC J0M 1A0 – 819/935-4225 – Dir. gen., Minnie Grey

Kawawachikamach: Dispensaire de Kawawachikamach, CP 5114, Kawawachikamach QC G0G 2Z0 – 418/585-3664

La Baie: CLSC du Fjord, 80, rue Aime-Gravel, La Baie QC G7B 2M4 – 418/544-7316; Fax: 418/544-0292 – Dir. gen., André Carrier

La Guadeloupe: CLSC la Guadeloupe, 763, 14e av, La Guadeloupe QC G0M 1G0 – 418/459-3441; Fax: 418/459-3289 – Dir. gen., Claude Lemieux

La Malbaie: CLSC Charlevoix, 600, boul de Comporte, La Malbaie QC G5A 1S8 – 418/665-6413; Fax: 418/665-6413 – Dir. gen., Alain Ouellet

La Sarre: CLSC des Auroles Boreales, 285, 1re rue est, La Sarre QC J9Z 3K1 – 819/333-2534; Fax: 819/333-3111 – Dir. gen., Michel Coté

La Tuque: CLSC du Haunt Saint-Maurice, 350, av Brown, La Tuque QC G9X 2W4 – 819/523-6171; Fax: 819/523-6176 – Dir. gen., Mario Morand

Lac-Etchemin: CLSC des Etchemins, 201, rue Claude-Bilodeau, CP 428, Lac-Etchemin QC G0R 1S0 – 418/625-8001; Fax: 418/625-3009 – Dir. gen., Bernard Lamy

Lac-Megantic: CLSC Maria-Thibault, 3700, rue Laval, Lac-Megantic QC G6B 1A4 – 819/583-2572; Fax: 819/583-5364 – Dir. gen., Jocelyn Ouellet

Lachute: CLSC d'Argenteuil, 551, rue Berry, Lachute QC J8H 1S4 – 415/562-8581; Fax: 415/562-2111 – Dir. gen., Suzanne Gourgeon

L'Ancienne-Lorette: Point de services Ancienne-Lorette, 1305, rue de la Hutte, L'Ancienne-Lorette QC G2E 3M9 – 418/877-7578 – 30 places – Dir. gen., Gilles Proulx

Laurier-Station: CLSC Arthur Caux, 135, rue de la Station, CP 189, Laurier-Station QC G0S 1N0 – 418/728-3435; Fax: 418/728-3477 – Dir. gen., Paul-Emile Coulombe

Le Gardeur: CLSC Le Meandre, 193, rue Notre-Dame, Le Gardeur QC J5Z 3C4 – 514/654-9012; Fax: 514/654-0262 – Dir. gen., Suzanne Roy

Lebel-Sur-Quevillon: Centre de santé Lebel, 950, boul Quevillon nord, CP 5000, Lebel-Sur-Quevillon QC J0Y 1X0 – 819/755-4881; Fax: 819/755-3581 – 14 lits – Dir. gen., O'Neil Durocher

Les Escoumins: Centre de santé de la Haute Côte-Nord, 4, rue de l'Hôpital, CP 1000, Les Escoumins QC G0T 1K0 – 418/233-2931; Fax: 418/233-2608 – 44 lits – Dir. gen., Fernand Boutin

L'Ile-d'Anticosti: Dispensaire-Port-Meneir, Anticosti (CS de la Minganie), L'Ile-d'Anticosti QC G0G 2Y0 – 418/535-0176 – Dir. gen., Denis R. Beaudreau

Longueuil: CLSC Longueuil-Est, 388, rue Lamarre, Longueuil QC J4J 1T2 – 514/463-2850; Fax: 514/646-7552 – Dir. gen., Lise Latreille-Zaman

Longueuil: CLSC Longueuil-Ouest, 291, boul Curé-Poirier ouest, Longueuil QC J4J 2G4 – 514/651-9830; Fax: 514/651-4606 – Dir. gen., Luc Genest

Lourdes-Du-Blanc-Sablon: Centre de santé de la Basse Côte Nord, CP 130, Lourdes-Du-Blanc-Sablon QC G0G 1W0 – 418/461-2144; Fax: 418/461-2731 – 48 lits – Dir. gen., Rémy Beaudoin

Low: CLSC de la Vallée de la Gatineau, Route 105, CP 63, Low QC J0X 2C0 – 819/422-3548; Fax: 819/422-3568 – Dir. gen., Louis-Maurice Dionne

Magog: CLSC Alfred-Desrochers, 1750, rue Sherbrooke, Magog QC J1X 2T3 – 819/843-2572; Fax: 819/843-2940 – Dir. gen., Jean Lavigne

Maniwaki: CLSC de la Rivière Desert, 186, rue King, Maniwaki QC J9E 3M1 – 819/449-2513; Fax: 819/449-4102 – Dir. gen., Serge Boucher

Matagami: Centre de santé Isle-Dieu, 130, boul Matagami, CP 790, Matagami QC J0Y 2A0 – 819/739-2515; Fax: 819/739-4777 – 15 lits – Dir. gen., Louisette Pilotte

Matane: CLSC de Matane, 349, av Saint-Jerome, Matane QC G4W 3A8 – 418/562-5741; Fax: 418/562-9236 – Dir. gen., René Lepage

Matapedia: CLSC Malauze, 14, boul Perron, CP 190, Matapedia QC G0J 1V0 – 418/865-2221; Fax: 418/865-2317 – Dir. gen., Pierre Portelance

Mistassini: CLSC des Chutes, 201, boul des Peres, Mistassini QC G0W 2C0 – 418/276-5452; Fax: 418/276-5575 – Dir. gen., Rodrigue Gagnon

Moffet: Point de service Moffet, CP 38, Moffet QC J0Z 2W0 – 819/747-4171 – Dir. gen., Pierre Larouche

Mont-Laurier: CLSC des Hautes-Laurentides, 515, boul Albiny Paquette, Mont-Laurier QC J9L 1K8 – 819/623-1228; Fax: 819/623-1311 – Dir. gen., Denis Bouchard

Montréal: Centre d'accueil - CLSC de Rosemont, 3245, boul Saint-Joseph est, Montréal QC H1Y 2B6 – 514/374-8660 – Dir. gen., Lise Langevin

Montréal: Centre hospitalier St-Michel, 8040, 9e av., Montréal QC H1Z 2Y9 – 514/722-2571; Fax: 514/725-0785 – 192 lits – Dir. gen., Bertrand Girard

Montréal: CLSC Ahuntsic, 1165, boul Henri-Bourassa est, Montréal QC H2C 3K2 – 514/381-4221; Fax: 514/389-1361 – Dir. gen., Daniel Corbeil

Montréal: CLSC Bordeaux-Cartierville, 12060, av de Bois-de-Boulogne, Montréal QC H3M 2X9 – 514/331-2572 – Dir. gen., Mathieu Lafrance

Montréal: CLSC Cote-des-Neiges, 5700, ch de la Cote-des-Neiges, Montréal QC H3T 2A8 – 514/731-8531; Fax: 514/731-4012 – Dir. gen., Jacques Lorion

Montréal: CLSC des Faubourgs, 1250, rue Sanguinet, Montréal QC H2X 3E7 – 514/527-2361; Fax: 514/847-0728 – Dir. gen., Renée Spain

Montréal: CLSC des Mill-Iles, 4731, boul Levesque est, Laval QC H7C 1M9 – 514/661-5370; Fax: 514/661-6177 – Dir. gen., Gilbert Cadieux

Montréal: CLSC du Plateau Mont-Royal, 4689, av Papineau, Montréal QC H2H 1V4 – 514/521-7663; Fax: 514/521-1886 – Dir. gen., Marie Montpetit

Montréal: CLSC du Vieux la Chine, 1900, rue Notre-Dame, Lachine QC H8S 2G2 – 514/636-0164 – Dir. gen., Leonard Vincent

Montréal: CLSC Hochelaga-Maisonneuve, 1620, av de Lasalle, Montréal QC H1V 2J8 – 514/253-2181; Fax: 514/253-1239 – Dir. gen., Paul Leguerrier

Montréal: CLSC J. Octave Roussin, 13926, rue Notre-Dame est, Montréal QC H1A 1T5 – 514/642-4050; Fax: 514/498-7507 – Dir. gen., Monique Corbeil

Montréal: CLSC Lac St-Louis, 180, av Cartier, Pointe-Claire QC H9S 4S1 – 514/697-4110; Fax: 514/697-6341 – Dir. gen., Sandra Golding

Montréal: CLSC Lasalle, 7475, boul Newman, 2e étage, Lasalle QC H8N 1X3 – 514/364-2572 – Dir. gen., Jean-Paul Bouchard

Montréal: CLSC Mercier-est/Anjou, 9403, rue Sherbooke est, Montréal QC H1L 6P2 – 514/356-2572; Fax: 514/356-2571 – Dir. gen., André Lemelin

Montréal: CLSC Metro, #500, 1801, boul de Maisonneuve ouest, Montréal QC H3H 1J9 – 514/934-0354; Fax: 514/934-3776 – Dir. gen., Gary Furlong

Montréal: CLSC Montréal-nord, 11441, boul Lacordaire, Montréal QC H1G 4J9 – 514/327-0400; Fax: 514/327-1275 – Dir. gen., Pierre Ouimet

Montréal: CLSC Norman-Bethune, 1655, rue du Couvent, Laval QC H7W 3A8 – 514/687-5690; Fax: 514/687-5998 – Dir. gen., Richard Rivest

Montréal: CLSC Notre-Dame-de-Grace/Montréal-ouest, #110, 2525, boul Cavendish, Montréal QC H4B 2Y4 – 514/485-1670; Fax: 514/485-6406 – Dir. gen., Terry Kaufman

Montréal: CLSC Olivier-Guimond, 5455, rue Chauveau, Montréal QC H1N 1G8 – 514/255-2365; Fax: 514/255-1443 – Dir. gen., Renée Audy

Montréal: CLSC Parc Extension, 469, rue Jean-Talon ouest, Montréal QC H3N 1R4 – 514/273-9591; Fax: 514/273-8954 – Dir. gen., Richard Vezina

Montréal: CLSC la Petit Patrie, 6520, rue de Saint-Vallier, Montréal QC H2S 2P7 – 514/273-4508; Fax: 514/272-6278 – Dir. gen., Yves Poirier

Montréal: CLSC Pierrefonds, 13800, boul Gouin est, Pierrefonds QC H8Z 3H6 – 514/626-2572; Fax: 514/626-6514 – Dir. gen., Mariette le Brun-Bohemier

Montréal: CLSC Rene-Cassin, #600, 5800, boul Cavendish, Cote-St-Luc QC H4W 2T5 – 514/488-9163; Fax: 514/485-1612 – Dir. gen., Leon Ouaknine

Montréal: CLSC Rivière-des-Prairies, 8655, boul Perras, Montréal QC H1E 4M7 – 514/648-4963; Fax: 514/648-8565 – Dir. gen., Jean-Pierre Deschenes

Montréal: CLSC St-Henri, 3833, rue Notre-Dame ouest, Montréal QC H4C 1P8 – 514/933-7541; Fax: 514/933-1740 – Dir. gen., Louis-Paul Thauvette

Montréal: CLSC Saint-Leonard, 5540, rue Jarry est, Saint-Leonard QC H1P 1T9 – 514/328-3460; Fax: 514/328-2976 – Dir. gen., Robert Chalifoux

Montréal: CLSC St-Louis du Parc, 155, boul Saint-Joseph est, Montréal QC H2T 1H4 – 514/286-9657; Fax: 514/286-9706; EMail: czd5@musica.mcgill.ca – Dir. gen., Saul Panofsky

Montréal: CLSC Saint-Michel, 7950, boul Saint-Michel, Montréal QC H1Z 3E1 – 514/374-8223; Fax: 514/374-9180 – Dir. gen., Pierre Durocher

Montréal: CLSC Ste-Rose de Laval, 280, boul Roi-du-nord, Laval QC H7L 4L2 – 514/622-5110; Fax: 514/622-4150 – Dir. gen., Marie Beauchamp

Montréal: CLSC Verdun/Côte St-Paul, 400, av de l'Eglise, Verdun QC H4G 2M4 – 514/766-0546; Fax: 514/762-4139 – Dir. gen., Robert Capistran

Montréal: CLSC Villeray, 1425, rue Jarry est, Montréal QC H2E 1A7 – 514/376-4141; Fax: 514/722-3758 – Dir. gen., Gyslaine Samson-Saulnier

Montréal: CLSC/CHSLD du Marigot, 1351, boul des Laurentides, Laval QC H7M 2Y2 – 514/668-1803; Fax: 514/668-4988; EMail: hbradet@total.net – 100 lits – Regie régionale de la santé et des services sociaux de Laval – Dir. gen., Henri Bradet

Montréal: Santé au travail et info-santé, 75, rue de Port-Royal, Montréal QC H3H 1J9 – 514/853-2460; Fax: 514/858-6568; EMail: sst~o@login.net – Dir. gen., Pierre Ouimet

Murdochville: Centre de santé des Hauts Bois, 600, av Dr. William May, Murdochville QC G0E 1W0 – 418/784-2572; Fax: 418/784-3629 – 3 lits – Dir. gen., Robert Lapointe, 418/784-3333

Natashquan: Dispensaire-Natashquan (CS de la Minganie), Natashquan QC G0G 2E0 – 418/726-3387 – Dir. gen., Denis R. Boudreau

Paspebiac: CLSC Chaleurs, 145, route 132, CP 7000, Paspebiac QC G0C 2K0 – 418/752-6611; Fax: 418/752-6734 – Dir. gen., Jean-Marie le Brasseur

Plessisville: CLSC-CHSLD de l'Erable, 1331, rue Saint-Calixte, Plessisville QC G6L 1P4 – 819/362-6301; Fax: 819/362-6300 – 40 lits – Dir. gen., Remi Moisan

Pohenegamook: CLSC des Frontières, 1922, rue St-Vallier, CP 70, Pohenegamook QC G0L 2T0 – 418/859-2450; Fax: 418/859-3484 – 25 lits – Dir. gen., Armand Demers

Port Cartier: Centre de santé de Port-Cartier, 103, boul des Rochelois, Port Cartier QC G5B 1K5 – 418/766-2715; Fax: 418/766-5229 – 10 lits – Dir. gen., Jean-Marc Maloney

Quaqtaq: Dispensaire de Quaqtaq, Quaqtaq QC J0M 1J0 – 819/492-9977 – Dir. gen., Minnie Grey

Québec: CLSC Haute-Ville, 55, ch Ste-Foy, Québec QC G1R 1S9 – 418/641-2572 – Dir. gen., Gaetan Garon

Radisson: Centre hospitalier La Grande Rivière, CP 800, Radisson QC J0Y 2X0 – 819/638-8240; Fax: 819/638-7496 – 5 lits – Dir. gen., Jules Pelletier

Remigny: Point de service Remigny, Remigny QC J0Z 3H0 – 819/761-3491 – Dir. gen., Pierre Larouche

Richelieu: CLSC du Richelieu, 633, 12e av, Richelieu QC J3L 4V5 – 514/658-7561; Fax: 514/658-7568 – Dir. gen., Julien Tremblay

Richmond: CLSC du Val Saint-Francois, 110, rue Barlow, CP 890, Richmond QC J0B 2H0 – 819/826-3781; Fax: 819/826-3867 – Dir. gen., Gary Furlong

Rimouski: CLSC de l'Estuaire, 165, rue des Gouverneurs, Rimouski QC G5L 7R2 – 418/724-7204; Fax: 418/724-7743 – Dir. gen., Gilles Giasson, 418/727-5419

Rivière-au-Tonnerre: Dispensaire-Rivière-au-Tonnerre (CS de la Minganie), Rivière-au-Tonnerre QC G0G 2N0 – 418/465-2146 – Dir. gen., Denis R. Boudreau

Rivière-Saint-Jean: Dispensaire-Rivière-St-Jean (CS St-Jean-Eudes), Rivière-Saint-Jean QC G0G 2N0 – 418/949-2020 – Dir. gen., Denis R. Beaudreau

Roberval: Le Claire Fontaine, 835, rue Roland, Roberval QC G8H 3J5 – 418/275-1360; Fax: 418/275-6211 – Dir. gen., Laurent Bouillon

Rouyn-Noranda: CLSC le partage des eaux, 19, rue Perreault ouest, Rouyn-Noranda QC J9X 2T3 – 819/762-8144; Fax: 819/762-1057 – Dir. gen., Roger Dumais

Saint-Andre-Avellin: CLSC de la Petite Nation, 12, rue Saint-Andre, CP 120, Saint-Andre-Avellin QC J0V 1W0 – 819/983-7341; Fax: 819/983-7708 – Dir. gen., Michel Audra

Saint-Clement: CLSC des Basques, 25, rue Saint-Pierre, Saint-Clement QC G0L 2N0 – 418/963-2933 – Dir. gen., Raymond LeBlond

Saint-Esprit: CLSC Montcalm, 110, rue Saint-Isidore, Saint-Esprit QC J0K 2L0 – 514/839-3676; Fax: 514/839-6603 – Dir. gen., Paul-Yvon de Billy

Saint-Eustache: CLSC Jean-Oliver-Chenier, 29, ch Oka, Saint-Eustache QC J7R 1K6 – 514/491-1233; Fax: 514/491-3424 – Dir. gen., Gylaine Boucher

Saint-Fabien-de-Panet: CLSC Antoine-Rivard, 10, rue Alphonse, CP 39, Saint-Fabien-de-Panet QC G0R 2J0 – 418/249-2572; Fax: 418/249-2507 – Dir. gen., Pierre Thibaudeau

Saint-Felicien: CLSC des Pres-Bleus, 1228, boul Sacre-Coeur, CP 10, Saint-Felicien QC G8K 2P8 – 418/679-5270; Fax: 418/679-3510 – Dir. gen., Michel Bernard

Saint-Hubert: CLSC St-Hubert, 6800, boul Cousineau, Saint-Hubert QC J3Y 8Z4 – 514/443-7400; Fax: 514/676-4645 – Dir. gen., Michele Laverdure

Saint-Hyacinthe: CLSC des Maskoutains, 2650, rue Morin, Saint-Hyacinthe QC J2S 8H1 – 514/778-1144; Fax: 514/778-1899 – Dir. gen., Denis Blanchard

Saint-Hyacinthe: Réseau Santé Richelieu-Yamaska - Pavillon Honoré-Mercier, *see* Centres hospitaliers listings

St-Jean-Port-Joli: CLSC des Trois-Saumons, 430, rue Jean Leclerc, St-Jean-Port-Joli QC G0R 3G0 – 418/598-3355; Fax: 418/598-9800 – 40 lits – Dir. gen., Jean-Marc Bourgault

Saint-Jerome: CLSC Arthur-Buies, 430, rue Labelle, Saint-Jerome QC J7Z 5L3 – 514/431-2221; Fax: 514/431-6538 – Dir. gen., Georges Legal

Saint-Joseph-de-Beauce: CLSC Beauce-Centre, 1125, ave du Palais, CP 790, Saint-Joseph-de-Beauce QC G0S 2V0 – 418/397-5722; Fax: 418/397-2457 – Dir. gen., Claude Jobin

Saint-Jovite: CLSC des Trois Vallées, 352, rue Leonard, Saint-Jovite QC J0T 2H0 – 819/425-3771; Fax: 819/425-2695 – Dir. gen., Christine Lessard

Saint-Lazare: CLSC de Bellechasse, 100, rue Monseigneur Bilodeau, Saint-Lazare QC G0R 3J0 – 418/883-2227; Fax: 418/887-6400 – Dir. gen., Michel Girard

St-Marc-des-Carrieres: CLSC de Portneuf, 1045, av Bona Dussault, St-Marc-des-Carrieres QC G0A 4B0 – 418/268-3571; Fax: 418/268-6248 – Dir. gen., Jocelyn Richard

Saint-Maxime-du-Mont-Louis: CLSC des Berges, 19, 1re ave ouest, CP 100, Saint-Maxime-du-Mont-Louis QC G0E 1T0 – 418/797-2744; Fax: 418/797-5122 – Dir. gen., Michelle Arcand

St-Pamphile: CLSC - Centre d'accueil des Appalaches, 103, rue du Foyer nord, CP 580, St-Pamphile QC G0R 3X0 – 418/356-3393; Fax: 418/356-2756 – Dir. gen., Bernard Lamy

Saint-Paulin: CLSC Valentine-Lupien, 2841, rue Lafleche, Saint-Paulin QC J0K 3G0 – 819/268-2572; Fax: 819/268-2505 – Dir. gen., Henri-Paul Picotte

Saint-Remi: CLSC Jardin du Québec, 2, rue Sainte-Famille, Saint-Remi QC J0L 2L0 – 514/454-4671; Fax: 514/454-4538 – Dir. gen., Gilles Charest

Saint-Romuald: CLSC Chutes-de-la-Chaudière-Desjardins, 2055, boul de la Rive sud, Saint-Romuald QC G6W 2S5 – 418/835-3400 – Dir. gen., Celine L. Morin

Saint-Tîte: CLSC Normandie, 750, rue du Couvent, CP 430, Saint-Tîte QC G0X 3H0 – 418/365-7555; Fax: 418/365-6009 – Dir. gen., Donat Gingras

Sainte-Adele: CLSC des Pays-d'en-Haut, 1390, boul Sainte-Adele, CP 2130, Sainte-Adele QC J0R 1L0 – 514/229-6601; Fax: 514/229-7220 – Dir. gen., Gilles Morin

Sainte-Anne-de-Beaupre: CLSC Orleans, 9500, boul Sainte-Anne, CP 278, Sainte-Anne-de-Beaupre QC G0A 3C0 – 418/827-5241; Fax: 418/827-6107 – Dir. gen., Jean-Guy Trottier

Sainte-Genevieve-de-Batiscan: CLSC des Chenaux, 90, route Rivière-á-Veillette, RR#4, Sainte-Genevieve-de-Batiscan QC G0X 2R0 – 418/362-2727; Fax: 418/362-3125 – Dir. gen., vacant

Sainte-Marie: CLSC Nouvelle-Beauce, 1133, boul Vachon nord, CP 1630, Sainte-Marie QC G6E 3C6 – 418/387-8181; Fax: 418/387-8188 – Dir. gen., Marc Tanguay

Sainte-Monique: CLSC Nicolet-Yamaska, 390, rue Principale, Sainte-Monique QC J0G 1N0 – 819/289-2255; Fax: 819/289-2982 – Dir. gen., Marcel Nolet

Sainte-Therese: CLSC Therese-de-Blainville, 55, rue Saint-Joseph, Sainte-Therese QC J7E 4Y5 – 514/430-4553; Fax: 514/430-0140 – Dir. gen., Micheline Vallières Joly

Salaberry-de-Valleyfield: CLSC Seigneurie de Beauharnois, 71, rue Maden, Salaberry-de-Valleyfield QC J6S 3V4 – 514/371-0143; Fax: 514/371-7682 – Dir. gen., Jean Cloutier

Schefferville: Dispensaire de Schefferville, 326-328, rue A.P. Low, CP 1059, Schefferville QC G0G 2T0 – 418/585-2645

Senneterre: Centre de santé le Minordet, 961, rue de la Clinique, CP 4000, Senneterre QC J0Y 2M0 – 819/737-2243; Fax: 819/737-8425 – 4 lits – Dir. gen., Sylvie Desmarais

Sept-Iles: CLSC des Sept Iles, 405, av Brochu, Sept-Iles QC G4R 2W9 – 418/962-2572; Fax: 418/962-1858 – Dir. gen., André Tremblay

Shawinigan: CLSC du centre de la Mauricie, 1600, boul Biermans, Shawinigan QC G9N 8L2 – 819/539-8371; Fax: 819/539-8853 – Dir. gen., Renald Turcotte

Sherbrooke: CLSC Gaston-Lessard, 1200, rue King est, Sherbrooke QC J1G 1E4 – 819/563-0144; Fax: 819/563-9912 – Dir. gen., Denis Lalumiere

Sherbrooke: CLSC SOC, 50, rue Camirand, Sherbrooke QC J1H 4J5 – 819/565-1330; Fax: 819/565-4411 – Dir. gen., Jaime Borja

Sorel: CLSC du Havre, 201, rue du Havre, CP 590, Sorel QC J3P 7N7 – 514/746-4545; Fax: 514/746-7296 – Dir. gen., Claire Roussey

Tasiujaq: Dispensaire de Tasiujaq, Tasiujaq QC J0M 1T0 – 819/633-9977 – Dir. gen., Minnie Grey

Temiscaming: Centre de santé de Témiscaming, 180, rue Anvik, CP 760, Temiscaming QC J0Z 3R0 – 819/627-3385; Fax: 819/627-3629 – 20 lits – Dir. gen., Gilbert Ladouceur

Terrebonne: CLSC Lamater, 4625, boul des Seigneurs, Terrebonne QC J6W 5B1 – 514/471-2881; Fax: 514/471-7134 – Dir. gen., Helene Gobeil

Thetford Mines: CLSC Frontenac, 17, rue Notre-Dame sud, Thetford Mines QC G6G 1J1 – 418/338-3511; Fax: 418/338-1668 – Dir. gen., Normand Baker

Trois-Rivieres: CLSC Les Forges, 500, rue Saint-Georges, Trois-Rivieres QC G9A 2K8 – 819/379-7131; Fax: 819/373-7726 – Dir. gen., Laurent Pare

Val-Belair: CLSC de la Jacques-Cartier, 1465, rue de l'Etna, Val-Belair QC G3K 1Y8 – 418/843-2572; Fax: 418/842-4662 – Dir. gen., Claude Soucy

Vaudreuil-Dorion: CLSC le Presqu'ile, 490, boul Harwood, Vaudreuil-Dorion QC J7V 7H4 – 514/455-6171; Fax: 514/455-9086 – Dir. gen., Guy Dufresne

Victoriaville: CLSC Suzor-Cote, 100, rue de l'Ermitage, Victoriaville QC G6P 9N2 – 819/758-7281; Fax: 819/758-5009 – Dir. gen., Richard Desrochers

Weedon: CLSC Fleur de Lys, 460, 2e av, Weedon QC J0B 3J0 – 819/877-3434; Fax: 819/877-3714 – Dir. gen., Guy Dufresne

Wemindji: Dispensaire de Wemindji, Wemindji QC J0M 1L0 – 819/978-0225 – Dir. gen., James Bobbish

## HÔPITAUX PSYCHIATRIQUES ET ASSISTANCE COMMUNAUTAIRE

Alma: Villa des Lys - SAHT, 825, av Tanguay, Alma QC G8B 5Y2 – 30 places – Dir. gen., Laurent Bouillon

Alma: Villa des Lys inc., 400, boul Champlain sud, Alma QC G8B 5W1 – 418/662-3447; Fax: 418/662-7860 – 37 beneficiaires – Dir. gen., Laurent Bouillon

Aylmer: Centre Mgr-Proulx, 151, rue Broad, Aylmer QC J9H 3L7 – 819/684-1022; Fax: 819/684-8153 – 88 beneficiaires – Dir. gen., Danielle Lessard

Baie-Saint-Paul: SAHT St-Placide, 86, RR#4, Baie-Saint-Paul QC G0A 1B0 – 418/435-2980 – 50 places – Dir. gen., Robert Vallieres

Beauport: Centre hospitalier Robert Giffard, 2601, rue de la Canardière, Beauport QC G1J 2G3 – 418/663-5966; Fax: 418/666-0427; EMail: dsthchrg@qbc.clic.net – 1,413 lits – Dir. gen., Réjean Cantin

Beauport: Clinique Roy Rousseau, 2579, ch de la Canardière, Beauport QC G1J 2G2 – 418/663-5711; Fax: 418/663-5727 – 140 lits – Dir. gen., Jacques Garneau

Brossard: Les Ateliers Horizon inc. (St-Lambert), 3530, rue Isabelle, Brossard QC J4Y 2R3 – 514/444-5588 – 100 places – Dir. gen., Jean-Pierre Picard

Chambly: Le SAHT de Chambly, 2135, boul Industriel, Chambly QC J3L 4C5 – 514/658-5687 – 35 places – Dir. gen., Jean-Pierre Picard

Charlesbourg: Centre de réadaptation la Triade, 9080, boul du Jardin, Charlesbourg QC G1G 4B3 – 418/626-3244; Fax: 418/626-7773 – Dir. gen., Gilles Proulx

Chicoutimi: Centre de réadaptation du Saguenay, 766, rue du Cenacle, Chicoutimi QC G7H 2J2 – 418/549-4003; Fax: 418/549-5281 – 56 beneficiaires – Dir. gen., Normand Dionne

Fatima: Centre de réadaptation des Iles, CP 580, Fatima QC G0T 1G0 – 418/986-3590; Fax: 418/986-5778 – 25 places – Dir. gen., Micheline Decoste

Gatineau: Services Gatineau (Pavillon du Parc inc.), 811, boul St-René ouest, Gatineau QC J8R 2S4 – 819/243-4443 – 40 places – Dir. gen., Danielle Lessard

Hull: Centre hospitalier Pierre Janet, 20, rue Pharand, Hull QC J9A 1K7 – 819/771-7761; Fax: 819/771-2908 – 99 lits – Régie régionale de la santé et des services sociaux de l'Outaouais – Dir. gen., Pierre Gagnon

Hull: Services Hull (Pavillon du Parc inc.), 178, rue Jean Proulx, Hull QC J8Z 1V3 – 819/777-2944 – 36 places – Dir. gen., Danielle Lessard

La Malbaie: Service d'Apprentissage aux habitudes de travail La Malbaie, 100, rue Nairn, La Malbaie QC G5A 1L8 – 418/665-7121 – 50 places – Dir. gen., Robert Vallieres

Lac-Etchemin: SAHT Etchemins, 102, rue Giguere, Lac-Etchemin QC G0R 1S0 – 418/625-3420 – 30 places – Dir. gen., Pierre Maheu

Lafontaine: Pavillon Ste-Marie inc., 45, rue du Pavillon, Lafontaine QC J7Y 3R6 – 514/438-3583; Fax: 514/438-7481 – 130 beneficiaires – Dir. gen., Francyne Jolicoeur

L'Assomption: Centre de réadaptation l'Envol inc., 391, rue Saint-Etienne, CP 29, L'Assomption QC J0K 1G0 – 514/589-2213; Fax: 514/589-4581 – Dir. gen., Claude Ouellet

Longueuil: Centre d'accueil de Longueuil, 600, rue Prefontaine, Longueuil QC J4K 3V6 – 514/670-3220 – 54 beneficiaires – Dir. gen., Jean-Pierre Picard

Malartic: Centre hospitalier de Malartic, 1141, rue Royale, CP 800, Malartic QC J0Y 1Z0 – 819/757-4342; Fax: 819/757-4330 – 49 lits – Dir. gen., Christiane Glacon

Montréal: Centre de réadaptation Gabrielle Major, 6455, rue Jean Talon est, 6e étage, Saint-Leonard QC H1S 3E8 – 514/255-4025; Fax: 514/255-7620 – 48 beneficiaires – Dir. gen., Helene Duval

Montréal: Centre de réadaptation Lisette-Dupras, 8000, rue Notre-Dame ouest, Saint-Pierre QC H8R 1H2 – 514/274-5571; Fax: 514/274-8905 – 88 beneficiaires – Dir. gen., John Aung-Thwin

Montréal: Centre Louise Vachon Enr., 4390, boul Saint-Martin ouest, Laval QC H7T 1C3 – 514/687-2970; Fax: 514/687-4184 – Dir. gen., Rolande Sabourin

Montréal: Hôpital Douglas, 6875, boul Lasalle, Verdun QC H4H 1R3 – 514/761-6131; Fax: 514/888-4067; EMail: dredea@douglas.mcgill.ca – Centre hospitalier de soins pyschiatriques (195 lits) & centre d'hébergement et de soins de longue durée (455 lits) – 600 beds – Regie régionale de la santé et des services sociaux de Montréal-centre – Dir. gen., Jacques Hendlisz

Montréal: Hôpital Louis-H. Lafontaine, 7401, rue Hochelaga, Montréal QC H1N 3M5 – 514/251-4000, poste 4030; Fax: 514/251-0856 – 1,070 lits – Regie régionale de la santé et des services sociaux de Montréal-centre – Dir. gen., Albert Painchaud

Montréal: Hôpital Rivière-des-Prairies, 7070, boul Perras, Montréal QC H1E 1A4 – 514/323-7260; Fax: 514/323-8622 – 523 lits – Dir. gen., Dr Jacques Mackay

Montréal: Institut Philippe Pinel de Montréal, 10905, boul Henri-Bourassa est, Montréal QC H1C 1H1 – 514/648-8461; Fax: 514/494-4406 – 295 lits – Regie régionale de la santé et des services sociaux de Montréal-centre – Dir. gen., Lionel Beliveau

Montréal: Point de service centre de jour, 4211, rue Hochelaga, Montréal QC H1V 1B8 – 514/252-0133 – 40 places – Dir. gen., Helene Duval

Montréal: Point de service Champ d'Eau, #106, 9125, rue Pascal Gagnon, Saint-Leonard QC H1P 1Z4 – 514/327-3028 – 35 places – Dir. gen., Helene Duval

Québec: Hôtel Dieu du Sacré-Coeur de Jésus de Québec, 1, av du Sacré-Coeur, Québec QC G1N 2W1 – 418/529-6851; Fax: 418/529-2971 – 49 lits – Dir. gen., Gaetan Caron

Repentigny: Centre Hospitalier Le Gardeur, see Centres hospitaliers listings

Roberval: Centre psychiatrique de Roberval, 483, av Bouchard, Roberval QC G8H 1K2 – 418/274-1360; Fax: 418/275-6211 – 275 lits – Dir. gen., P.A. Lambert

Saint-Charles-Borromée: Centre hospitalier régional Delanaudière, see Centres hospitaliers listings

Saint-Wenceslas: Centre l'Aubier inc., 1170, rue Sainte-Therese, CP 27, Saint-Wenceslas QC G0Z 1J0 – 819/224-7669; Fax: 819/224-7712 – 50 beneficiaires – Dir. gen., Francine P. Lampron

Sainte-Marguerite-du-Lac-Masson: Residence Ste-Marguerite inc., 88, ch Masson, Sainte-Marguerite-du-Lac-Masson QC J0T 1L0 – 514/228-2877; Fax: 514/228-4212 – 60 beneficiaires – Dir. gen., Jean-Paul Gohier

Sorel: L'Atelier Riverain, 15, rue Albert, Sorel QC J3P 3T9 – 514/743-1213 – 60 places – Dir. gen., Ronald Creary

Victoriaville: Centre d'accueil Nor-Val, 26, rue Saint-Jean-Baptiste, Victoriaville QC G6P 4C7 – 819/758-6272; Fax: 819/758-4448 – 298 lits – Dir. gen., Paul-Antoine Ouellet

## CENTRES D'ACCUEIL ET D'HÉBERGEMENT

Acton Vale: Centre d'accueil d'Acton Vale, 1268, rue Ricard, CP 850, Acton Vale QC J0H 1A0 – 514/546-3234; Fax: 514/546-4811 – 80 lits – Dir. gen., Maurice Coutu

Albanel: Foyer St-Joseph d'Albanel Inc., 320, rue de l'Eglise, Albanel QC G0W 1A0 – 418/279-5202; Fax: 418/279-5939 – 24 lits – Dir. gen., Gisele Duchesne Leboeuf

Alma: Foyer Normandie d'Alma Inc., 50, ch du Foyer nord, CP 220, Alma QC G8B 5V6 – 418/668-8313; Fax: 418/668-2453 – 59 lits – Dir. gen., Alain Gaudreault

Amos: Foyer Harricana inc., 632, 1e rue ouest, Amos QC J9T 2N2 – 819/732-6521; Fax: 819/732-7526 – 91 lits – Dir. gen., Paul-Emile Doré

Asbestos: Centre hospitalier d'Asbestos, *see* Centres hospitaliers listings

Asbestos: Le Foyer d'Asbestos, 225, rue Saint-Jean-Baptiste, Asbestos QC J1T 2C3 – 819/879-5475; Fax: 819/879-6736 – 47 lits – Dir. gen., Jean-Yves Poisson

Aylmer: CHSLD Aylmer, 216, ch Fraser, Aylmer QC J9H 2H8 – 819/684-5316; Fax: 819/684-3936 – 65 lits – Dir. gen., Vincenzo Simonetta

Aylmer: CLSC et CHSLD Island Rivière, 445, boul Wilfrid-Lavigne, Aylmer QC J9H 6H9 – 819/684-1101; Fax: 819/684-0261 – 75 lits – Régie régionale de la santé et des services sociaux de l'Outaouais – Dir. gen., Aurele Dufour

Baie-Comeau: Centre hospitalier régional - Pavillon Boisvert, *see* Centres hospitaliers listings

Baie-Saint-Paul: Centre d'accueil Pierre-Dupre, 10, rue Boivin, CP 1779, Baie-Saint-Paul QC G0A 1B0 – 418/435-5562 – 75 lits – Dir. gen., Robert Vallieres

Baie-Saint-Paul: Centre hospitalier de Charlevoix, *see* Centres hospitaliers listings

Baie-Trinite: Centre d'accueil Trinite, 3, rue Saint-Joseph, Baie-Trinite QC G0H 1A0 – 418/939-2251 – 15 lits – Dir. gen., Gaetan Gauthier

Beauceville: Centre hospitalier de Beauceville, 253, 108e rue, Beauceville QC G0M 1A0 – 418/774-3304; Fax: 418/774-2304 – 162 places – Dir. gen., Gilles Morin

Beauharnois: Centre d'accueil le Vaisseau d'Or, 55, rue Saint-Andre, Beauharnois QC J6N 3G7 – 514/429-6403; Fax: 514/429-6602 – 86 lits – Dir. gen., Lise Belanger

Beauport: Centre Yvonne Sylvain, 3365, rue Guimont, Beauport QC G1E 2H1 – 418/663-8171 – 116 lits – Dir. gen., Gaston Pellan

Beauport: Hôpital de l'Enfant-Jesus (Centre du Fargy), 700, boul des Chutes, Beauport QC G1E 2B7 – 418/663-9934 – 60 lits – Dir. gen., Gaston Pellan

Beauport: Hôpital de l'Enfant-Jésus (Centre St-Augustin), *see* Centres hospitaliers listings

Beaupre: L'Accueil de Notre-Dame de Beaupre, 1, rue des Erables, CP 280, Beaupre QC G0A 1E0 – 418/827-3738 – 39 lits – Dir. gen., Jean-Yves Simard

Beaupre: Foyer Beaupre Enr., 11280, av Royale, Beaupre QC G0A 1E0 – 418/827-5345 – 15 lits – Dir. gen., Jeanne-D'Arc Fortin

Bedford: Centre hospitalier de Bedford, 34, rue St-Joseph, CP 1140, Bedford QC J0J 1A0 – 514/248-4304; Fax: 514/248-4676 – 42 places – Dir. gen., Georges Robitaille

Beloeil: Centre d'hébergement Champlain-Beloeil, 221, rue Brunelle, Beloeil QC J3G 2M9 – 514/467-3356; Fax: 514/467-3357 – 57 lits – Dir. gen., Guy Joly

Beloeil: Centre Marguerite-Adam, 425, rue Hubert, Beloeil QC J3G 2T1 – 514/467-1631 – 70 lits – Dir. gen., Ghislain Lavergne

Beloeil: Villa Beausejour, 80, boul Richelieu, Beloeil QC J3G 4N5 – 514/467-7594 – 23 places – Dir. gen., Robert Busilacchi

Bernierville: Maison du Sacré-coeur, 230, rue Principale, Bernierville QC G0N 1N0 – 418/428-3444 – 47 lits – Dir. gen., René Houle

Bernierville: Pavillon Morisset Huppe, 290, route 165, CP 370, Bernierville QC G0N 1N0 – 418/428-3568; Fax: 418/428-3021 – 14 places – Dir. gen., Lucie Morisset-Huppé

Berthierville: Centre hospitalier le Château de Berthier inc., 730, rue Frontenac, CP 240, Berthierville QC J0K 1A0 – 514/836-6241; Fax: 514/836-4013 – 41 lits – Dir. gen., Guy Ducharme

Berthierville: CHSLD Berthier, 400, rue Frontenac, Berthierville QC J0K 1A0 – 514/836-3756; Fax: 514/836-1319 – 81 lits – Dir. gen., Vincenzo Simonetta

Berthierville: Foyer Sacré-coeur de Berthierville inc., 1010, rue Montcalm, CP 30, Berthierville QC J0K 1A0 – 514/836-3759 – 42 lits – Dir. gen., Michel Lapierre

Bishopton: La Villa du Repos, CP 124, Bishopton QC J0B 1G0 – 819/884-5568 – 17 places – Dir. gen., Albert Kratzenberg

Black Lake: Foyer du Lac Noir inc., 1, rue Du Foyer, CP 40, Black Lake QC G0N 1A0 – 418/423-7508; Fax: 418/423-5250 – 26 lits – Dir. gen., André Rodrigue

Black Lake: Pavillon Yves et Suzanne Boutin, 868, rue Saint-Desire, Black Lake QC G0N 1A0 – 418/423-2945 – 13 places – Dir. gen., André Rodrigue

Boucherville: Centre d'accueil Jeanne Crevier, 151, rue de Muy, Boucherville QC J4B 4W7 – 514/641-0590; Fax: 514/641-3082 – 59 lits – Dir. gen., Robert Sabino

Boucherville: Residence de Boucherville inc., 782, boul Marie-Victorin, Boucherville QC J4B 1Y3 – 514/655-8045 – 18 places – Dir. gen., Robert Sabino

Bromptonville: Foyer de Bromptonville inc., 15, rue de la Croix sud, CP 460, Bromptonville QC J0B 1H0 – 819/846-2708; Fax: 819/846-4328 – 38 lits – Dir. gen., Real Jacques

Brossard: Centre d'accueil Marcelle Ferron Inc., 8600, boul Marie Victorin, Brossard QC J4X 1A1 – 514/923-1430; Fax: 514/923-1805 – 175 lits – Dir. gen., Zeff Guiducci

Buckingham: Centre d'accueil de Buckingham, 111, rue Lucerne, Buckingham QC J8L 3C9 – 819/986-1043; Fax: 819/986-5671 – 79 – Dir. gen., Bernard Guidon

Campbell's Bay: Manoir St-Joseph, rue Reid, CP 430, Campbell's Bay QC J0X 1K0 – 819/648-5852; Fax: 819/648-2378 – 39 lits – Dir. gen., Michel Pigeon

Cap-aux-Meules: Villa Plaisance, 506, ch Principal, CP 970, Cap-aux-Meules QC G0B 1B0 – 418/986-3645; Fax: 418/986-2746 – 50 lits – Dir. gen., Gaetan Doré

Cap-Chat: CHSLD de Cap-Chat, 41, rue Nicholas, CP 400, Cap-Chat QC G0J 1E0 – 418/786-5523; Fax: 418/786-5421 – 82 lits – Dir. gen., André Jalbert

Cap-de-la-Madeleine: Centre d'accueil Luc Desilets, 145, rue Toupin, Cap-de-la-Madeleine QC G8T 3Z8 – 819/379-8441 – 32 lits – Dir. gen., Reynald Dessureault

Cap-de-la-Madeleine: Foyer Pere Frederic inc., 80, ch du Passage, Cap-de-la-Madeleine QC G8T 2M2 – 819/375-4849 – 120 lits – Dir. gen., Vital Gaudet

Cap-de-la-Madeleine: Pavillon Nazareth du Cap (1985) inc., 317, boul Loranger, Cap-de-la-Madeleine QC G8T 3V8 – 819/375-6274 – 24 places – Dir. gen., Vital Gaudet

Cap-St-Ignace: Centre d'accueil St-Ignace, 91, rue du Manoir est, Cap-St-Ignace QC G0R 1H0 – 418/246-5644 – 43 lits – Dir. gen., Jean-Paul Lacroix

Caplan: Pavillon Manoir St-Charles de Caplan, 101, boul Perron, CP 188, Caplan QC G0C 1H0 – 418/388-5648 – 25 places – Dir. gen., Vilmont Moreau

Chambly: Manoir Soleil inc., 125, rue Daigneault, Chambly QC J3L 1G7 – 514/658-4441; Fax: 514/658-6521 – 44 lits – Dir. gen., Suzanne Gaudet

Chambly: Residence St-Joseph de Chambly, 100, rue Martel, Chambly QC J3L 1V3 – 514/658-6271 – 39 lits – Dir. gen., Michel Desnoyers

Chandler: Centre hospitalier de Chandler, *see* Centres hospitaliers listings

Chandler: Villa Pabos, 75, av des Cedres, CP 1088, Chandler QC G0C 1K0 – 418/689-6621; Fax: 418/689-4860 – 62 lits – Dir. gen., Louisette Langlois

Charlesbourg: Centre d'accueil St-François, 600, 60e rue est, Charlesbourg QC G1H 3A9 – 418/623-1515 – 22 lits – Dir. gen., Aline Clouthier

Charlesbourg: Centre d'hébergement St-Joseph inc., 1430, av Notre-Dame, Charlesbourg QC G2N 1S1 – 418/849-1891; Fax: 418/849-1892 – 30 lits – Dir. gen., Yvonette Cote-Letourneau

Charlesbourg: Centre hospitalier St-Jean-Eudes inc., 6000, 3e av ouest, Charlesbourg QC G1H 7J5 – 418/627-1124; Fax: 418/627-4995 – 64 lits – Dir. gen., Clemence Boucher

Charlesbourg: Le Foyer de Charlesbourg inc., 7150, boul Cloutier, Charlesbourg QC G1H 5V5 – 418/628-0456; Fax: 418/622-8676 – 91 lits – Dir. gen., Gratien Tardif

Charlesbourg: Pension Marie-Chantal, 8320, 1e av, Charlesbourg QC G1G 4C2 – 418/628-7563 – 31 places – Dir. gen., Jacques Garneau

Charny: Complexe de santé et CLSC Paul-Gilbert, *see* Centres hospitaliers listings

Châteauguay: Centre d'hébergement Champlain-Châteauguay, 210, rue Salaberry sud, Châteauguay QC J6K 3M9 – 514/699-1694 – 96 lits – Dir. gen., Guy Joly

Châteauguay: Le Foyer de Châteauguay inc., 95, rue Haute-Rivière, Châteauguay QC J6K 3P1 – 514/692-8231; Fax: 514/692-7920 – 74 lits – Dir. gen., Gaetan Roy

Chatham: Villa d'Argenteuil inc., 21, rue Renaud (1er et 2e étage), Chatham QC J0V 2A0 – 514/562-8738 – 22 places – Dir. gen., René Giard

Chicoutimi: Le Foyer Delage, 257, rue St-Armand, CP 10, Chicoutimi QC G7G 1S4 – 418/549-3941; Fax: 418/549-5444 – 53 lits – Dir. gen., Benoit Duplessis

Chicoutimi: Foyer St-Francois inc., 293, av Sainte-Famille, Chicoutimi QC G7H 4J5 – 418/549-3727; Fax: 418/543-2038 – 44 lits – Dir. gen., Sonia Bergeron

Chicoutimi: Pavillon Roland Saucier, *see* Centres hospitaliers listings

Clermont: Foyer de Clermont inc., 6, rue du Foyer, CP 520, Clermont QC G0T 1C0 – 418/439-4684; Fax: 418/439-4062 – 42 lits – Dir. gen., Jacques Tremblay

Cleveland: Foyer Wales, 506, rte 243, Cleveland QC J0B 2H0 – 819/826-3266; Fax: 819/826-2549 – 222 lits – Dir. gen., Roderick MacIver

Coaticook: Centre hospitalier de Coaticook, 138, rue Jeanne-Mance, Coaticook QC J1A 1W3 – 819/849-4876; Fax: 819/849-6735 – 67 lits – Dir. gen., Rémi Lasigne

Coaticook: Pavillon Boiscastel, 399, rue Court, Coaticook QC J1A 1L7 – 819/849-4876 – 48 lits – Dir. gen., Remi Lavigne

Contrecoeur: Centre d'accueil Contrecoeur, 4700, rue Marie-Victorin, CP 1120, Contrecoeur QC J0L 1C0 – 514/587-2492; Fax: 514/587-8411 – 50 lits – Dir. gen., Robert Sabino

Côte-Nord-du-Golfe-St-Laurent: Pavillon Dr. Donald G. Hodd, c/o Mrs. A. Roberts, Harringon Harbour, Côte-Nord-du-Golfe-St-Laurent QC G0G 1N0 – 514/795-3353; Fax: 418/795-3361 – 14 lits – Dir. gen., Remy Beaudoin

Coteau-du-Lac: Maison de la Providence, Coteau-du-Lac, 341, ch du Fleuve, Coteau-du-Lac QC J0P 1B0 – 514/763-5951 – 71 lits – Dir. gen., Claude-Yves de Repentigny

Coteau-du-Lac: Pavillon Denise Enr., 29, Route 338, Coteau-du-Lac QC J0P 1B0 – 514/763-5543 – 29 lits – Dir. gen., Yvan LaFontaine

Coteau-du-Lac: Pavillon Laura Ferguson, 60, ch du Fleuve, CP 339, Coteau-du-Lac QC J0P 1B0 – 514/267-3379 – 15 places – Dir. gen., Paul-Henri Boutin

Coteau-Landing: Hôpital Nôtre-Dame-de-Coteau-Landing ltée, 37, rue Principale, CP 180, Coteau-Landing QC J0P 1C0 – 514/267-3581; Fax: 514/267-9263 – 44 lits – Dir. gen., Pierre Perrier

Cowansville: Centre d'accueil de Cowansville, 200, rue Principale, Cowansville QC J2K 1J2 – 514/263-5142; Fax: 514/263-5114 – 72 lits – Dir. gen., Lucien Rioux

Crabtree: Pavillon Racette, 180, 8e rue, Crabtree QC J0K 1B0 – 514/754-2804 – 14 places – Dir. gen., Maurice Blais

Danville: Centre d'hebergement de Danville, 114, rue Daniel Johnson, CP 690, Danville QC J0A 1A0 – 819/839-2760; Fax: 819/839-3813 – 55 lits – Dir. gen., Jean-Bernard Breault

Deauville: Centre d'accueil Deauville inc., 168, rue Dion, CP 330, Deauville QC J1N 3H2 – 819/864-6631 – 16 lits – Dir. gen., Claudette Gregoire

Degelis: Residence Degelis inc., 587, 6e rue, Degelis QC G0L 1H0 – 418/853-3919 – 24 places – Dir. gen., Rejean Pelletier

Delisle: Le Domaine du Bel Age de Saint-Coeur de Marie, 4750, av Grande-Decharge, CP 157, Delisle QC G0W 1L0 – 418/347-3394 – 35 lits – Dir. gen., Alain Gaudreault

Des Ruisseaux: Pavillon Cloutier et St-Louis Enr., 4700, ch de la Lievre nord, Des Ruisseaux QC J9L 3G4 – 819/623-5371 – 20 places – Dir. gen., Gilles Huberdeau

Deschaillons-sur-Saint-Laurent: Foyer Deschaillons, 1045, rue Marie-Victorin, CP 219, Deschaillons-sur-Saint-Laurent QC G0S 1G0 – 819/292-2262; Fax: 819/292-3046 – 44 lits – Dir. gen., Gisele Marquis

Deux-Montagnes: CHSLD Deux-Montagnes inc., 2700, ch Oka, Deux-Montagnes QC J7R 4K1 – 514/473-5111; Fax: 514/491-4309 – 32 lits – Dir. gen., Louis-Henri Fournier

Deux-Montagnes: Manoir Grand Moulin inc., 2, Croissant Grand-Moulin, Deux-Montagnes QC J7R 6B4 – 514/473-7360; Fax: 514/473-5941 – 58 lits – Dir. gen., Denis Renaud

Disraeli: Foyer de Disraeli inc., 260, av Champlain, CP 698, Disraeli QC G0N 1E0 – 418/449-2020; Fax: 418/449-4006 – 47 lits – Dir. gen., André Rodrigue

Dolbeau: Pavillon Maison du Bel Age, 2020, rue Provencher, Dolbeau QC G8L 2B4 – 418/276-1866 – 30 places – Dir. gen., Jacques Turcotte

Donnacona: Centre régional d'hébergement et de santé de Portneuf - Centre d'hébergement Donnacona, 250, boul Gaudreau, CP 370, Donnacona QC G0A 1T0 – 418/285-3025 – 81 lits – Dir. gen., Fernand Morasse

Drummondville: Centre Frederick-George-Heriot, 75, rue St-Georges, Drummondville QC J2C 4G6 – 819/477-0544; Fax: 819/477-3888 – 362 lits – Dir. gen., Nagui Habashi

Drummondville: Pavillon Marie-Reine des Coeurs, 1145, boul Mercure, Drummondville QC J2B 3L7 – 819/477-3455 – 19 places – Dir. gen., Nagui Habashi

Drummondville: Villa du Boise, 100, rue Laforest, Drummondville QC J2B 6X1 – 819/478-1292 – 34 places – Dir. gen., Nagui Habashi

East Angus: Le CHSLD de la mrc du Haunt-Saint-François, 120, rue Rosseau, CP 550, East Angus QC J0B 1RO – 819/832-2487; Fax: 819/832-2676 – 55 lits – Dir. gen., Albert Kratzenberg

East Broughton: Foyer Sacré-coeur de Jésus d'East Broughton, 272, rue Principale, East Broughton QC G0N 1G0 – 418/427-2068 – 33 lits – Dir. gen., André Rodrigue

Farnham: Les Foyers Farnham inc., 800, rue Saint-Paul nord, Farnham QC J2N 2K6 – 514/293-3168; Fax: 514/293-7878 – 62 lits – Dir. gen., Claude Codere

Fleurimont: Centre d'accueil Shermont inc., 3220, 12e av nord, Fleurimont QC J1H 5H2 – 819/820-8900; Fax: 819/820-8902 – 52 lits – Dir. gen., Jean Sevigny

Fortierville: CHSLD les Seigneuries, 521, av du Foyer, Fortierville QC G0S 1J0 – 819/287-4686 – 44 lits – Dir. gen., Raymond Dion

Garthby: Manoir Aylmer inc., 9, rue Albert, CP 70, Garthby QC G0Y 1B0 – 418/458-2172; Fax: 418/458-2777 – 32 lits – Dir. gen., Real Paquette

Gaspé: Foyer Notre-Dame de Gaspé, 50, rue Bosse, CP 40, Gaspé QC G0C 1R0 – 418/368-2125; Fax: 418/368-2315 – 29 places – Dir. gen., Léo Ste-Croix

Gatineau: Centre d'accueil de Gatineau, 134, rue Maple, Gatineau QC J8P 7C3 – 819/663-2886; Fax: 819/663-2953 – 100 lits – Dir. gen., Paul-André Gervais

Gatineau: Centre d'hébergement Champlain-Gatineau, 176, rue Brian, Gatineau QC J8P 4S1 – 819/663-9228; Fax: 819/663-9229 – 42 lits – Dir. gen., Jean-Charles Gignac

Gatineau: Centre d'hébergement Champlain-Templeton, 18, rue Hamel, Gatineau QC J8P 1V9 – 819/663-5425 – 44 lits – Dir. gen., Guy Joly

Granby: Centre d'accueil Marie-Berthe Couture, 230, av des Erables Ouest, Granby QC J2G 9B1 – 514/375-8003; Fax: 514/372-7197 – 75 lits – Dir. gen., Lucie Wiseman

Granby: Le Centre d'accueil Regina Mundi, 200, boul Robert, Granby QC J2G 8C7 – 514/372-5125; Fax: 514/372-2828 – 24 lits – Dir. gen., Armand Gagne

Granby: Centre hospitalier de Granby, *see* Centres hospitaliers listings

Granby: Centre Notre-Dame de Granby, 363, rue Notre-Dame, Granby QC J2G 3L4 – 514/372-7302; Fax: 514/372-5404 – 39 lits – Dir. gen., Bernard Fournelle

Granby: CHSLD Horace-Boivin, 71, rue Court, Granby QC J2G 4Y7 – 514/372-2419; Fax: 514/372-7617 – 55 lits – Dir. gen., Bernard Fournelle, 514/776-5222

Grand-Mère: CHSLD du Centre Mauricie, 1650, 6e av, Grand-Mère QC G9T 2K4 – 819/533-2500; Fax: 819/538-7640 – 75 lits – Dir. gen., vacant

Grand-Mère: Foyer Grand'Mère inc., 690, 7e av, CP 400, Grand-Mère QC G9T 2B4 – 819/538-1681; Fax: 819/538-5353 – 53 lits – Dir. gen., Raymond Guilbert

Grand-Metis: Pavillon Metis inc., 412, Rte. 132, Grand-Metis QC G0J 1Z0 – 418/775-7032 – 16 places – Dir. gen., Ronald Anctil

Grandes-Bergeronnes: Foyer Monseigneur Gendron inc., 450, rue de la Mer, CP 68, Grandes-Bergeronnes QC G0T 1G0 – 418/232-6224; Fax: 418/232-6771 – 42 lits – Dir. gen., Francis Bouchard

Ham-Nord: Foyer Saints-Anges, 493, rue Principale, CP 69, Ham-Nord QC G0P 1A0 – 819/344-2940; Fax: 819/344-2584 – 38 lits – Dir. gen., Real Lavertu

Havre-Saint-Pierre: Foyer de Havre Saint-Pierre, 933, rue Boreale, CP 490, Havre-Saint-Pierre QC G0G 1P0 – 418/538-2006; Fax: 418/538-3642 – 51 lits – Dir. gen., Maurice Jomphe

Herbertville: Foyer le Pionnier d'Hebertville, 640, rue Villeneuve, Herbertville QC G0W 1S0 – 418/344-1911 – 39 lits – Dir. gen., Alain Gaudreault

Hull: Pavillon de l'Ile, 35, rue Saint-Jacques, Hull QC J8X 2Y4 – 819/771-9176 – 23 places – Dir. gen., Jean-Pierre Allard

Hull: Pavillon du Portage, 310, rue Notre-Dame, Hull QC J8X 3V2 – 819/776-5757 – 29 places – Dir. gen., Jean-Pierre Allard

Hull: Residence foyer du Bonheur, 125, boul Lionel Emond, Hull QC J8Y 5S8 – 819/770-1880; Fax: 819/770-8624 – 319 lits – Dir. gen., Jean-Pierre Allard

Hull: Residence la Pieta, 273, rue Laurier, Hull QC J8X 3W8 – 819/771-1112; Fax: 819/771-3710 – 151 lits – Dir. gen., Jean-Pierre Allard

Iberville: Residence Champagnat d'Iberville inc., 370, 5e av, CP 52, Iberville QC J2X 1V1 – 514/347-3769; Fax: 514/347-3892 – 102 lits – Dir. gen., Jacques Gemme

Ile-d-Orléans: Villa Alphonse Bonenfant, 1199, ch Royal, Ile-d-Orléans QC G0A 4E0 – 418/828-9114; Fax: 418/828-1127 – 50 lits – Dir. gen., Ronald Blais

Île-Perrot: Centre d'accueil Laurent-Bergevin, 200, boul Perrot, Île-Perrot QC J7V 7M7 – 514/453-5860; Fax: 514/453-8939 – 80 lits – Dir. gen., Lise Belanger

Joliette: Le Centre d'accueil St-Eusèbe, 585, boul Manseau, Joliette QC J6E 3E5 – 514/759-8222; Fax: 514/759-1579 – 158 lits – Dir. gen., Maurice Blais

Joliette: Le Foyer Notre-Dame, 144, rue Saint-Joseph, Joliette QC J6E 5C4 – 514/756-8728 – 25 lits – Dir. gen., Rejeanne Marois

Jonquière: Residence des Annees d'or, 1900, rue Fortier, Jonquière QC G7X 4L3 – 418/547-4738 – 66 lits – Dir. gen., Jacqueline St-Cyr

Jonquière: Residence Georges Hebert, 2841, rue Faraday, CP 1490, Jonquière QC G7S 4L1 – 418/695-7800 – 75 lits – Dir. gen., Jacqueline St-Cyr

Jonquière: Residence Ste-Marie, 2184, rue Perrier, Jonquière QC G7X 9C9 – 418/547-4738; Fax: 418/547-1134 – 68 lits – Dir. gen., Jacqueline St-Cyr

Kingsey Falls: Foyer de Kingsey Falls inc., 2, rue Saint-Aime, CP 60, Kingsey Falls QC J0A 1B0 – 819/363-2243; Fax: 819/363-2345 – 57 lits – Dir. gen., Gilles Perreault

La Baie: Foyer St-Joseph de La Baie inc., 2002, rue Alexis-Simard, La Baie QC G7B 2K9 – 418/544-2865; Fax: 418/544-0770 – 55 lits – Dir. gen., Marcel Harvey

La Doré: Centre d'accueil de La Doré, 4921, rue des Peupliers, La Doré QC G8J 1E7 – 418/256-3851; Fax: 418/256-3852 – 21 lits – Dir. gen., Claude J.Y. Theberge

La Guadeloupe: Le Pavillon Notre-Dame inc., 437 - 15e rue ouest, CP 490, La Guadeloupe QC G0M 1G0 – 418/459-3476; Fax: 418/459-6428 – 49 lits – Dir. gen., Richard Busque

La Malbaie: Accueil Bellerive (1970) Inc., 367, rue Saint-Etienne, CP 490, La Malbaie QC G5A 1M3 – 418/665-3724; Fax: 418/665-2249 – 57 lits – Dir. gen., Jacques Tremblay

La Pêche: Centre d'accueil de la Basse-Gatineau, 9, ch Passe-Partout, CP 59, La Pêche QC J0X 2W0 – 819/456-3863 – 32 lits – Dir. gen., Louis-Philippe Mayrand

La Peche: Le Foyer d'accueil de Gracefield, CP 59, La Peche QC J0X 2W0 – 819/456-3863; Fax: 819/456-4531 – 31 lits – Dir. gen., Louis-Philippe Mayrand

La Pocatière: Centre d'accueil Sainte-Anne-de-la-Pocatière, 402, 1e rue, CP 460, La Pocatière QC G0R 1Z0 – 418/856-3118 – 37 lits – Dir. gen., Robert Leclerc

La Prairie: Centre d'accueil La Prairie, 500, boul Balmoral, La Prairie QC J5R 4N5 – 514/659-9148; Fax: 514/659-9989 – 131 lits – Dir. gen., Gaetan Roy

La Prairie: Foyer Notre-Dame de LaPrairie inc., 444, rue Leon Bloy est, La Prairie QC J5R 3G6 – 514/659-5828; Fax: 514/659-0753 – 28 lits – Dir. gen., Robert Legault

La Sarre: Le Foyer de l'age d'or inc., 22, 1e av est, La Sarre QC J9Z 1C4 – 819/333-5525; Fax: 819/333-4903 – 27 lits – Dir. gen., Camil Dion

Labelle: Pavillon LeTourneau, 13411, rue Cure Labelle, Labelle QC J0T 1H0 – 819/686-3484 – 15 places – Dir. gen., Pierre Page

Labelle: Residence de LaBelle, 50, rue de l'Eglise, CP 38, Labelle QC J0T 1H0 – 819/686-2372 – 48 lits – Dir. gen., Yvan Lachaine

Lac-au-Saumon: Residence Marie-Anne Ouellet, 6, rue Turbide, Lac-au-Saumon QC G0J 1M0 – 418/778-5816 – 96 lits – Dir. gen., Alain Paquet

Lac-Bouchette: Le Foyer de Lac-Bouchette inc., 99, rte de l'Ermitage, Lac-Bouchette QC G0W 1V0 – 418/348-6313; Fax: 418/348-6342 – 32 lits – Dir. gen., Claude J.Y. Theberge

Lac-Etchemin: Foyer Lac-Etchemin, 227, 1e av, CP 369, Lac-Etchemin QC G0R 1S0 – 418/625-6661; Fax: 418/625-6661 – 78 lits – Dir. gen., Jean-Yves Julien

Lac-Etchemin: Le Sanatorium Begin, *see* Centres hospitaliers listings

Lac-Kenogami: Pavillon St-Dominique Enr., 3528, rue Fortin, Lac-Kenogami QC G7X 1B7 – 418/547-5289 – 19 places – Dir. gen., Guy St-Onge

Lac-Megantic: La Maison Paternelle, 3675, rue du Foyer, Lac-Megantic QC G6B 2K2 – 819/583-4222; Fax: 819/583-0900 – 48 lits – Dir. gen., Raymonde Lapointe-Lagueux

Lac-Nominingue: Pavillon Lachaine & Lajeunesse Enr., 237, rue Martineau, CP 452, Lac-Nominingue QC J0W 1R0 – 819/278-4529 – 15 places – Dir. gen., Pierre Page

Lac-Nominingue: Pavillon St-Louis Enr., 2188, ch Tour du Lac, Lac-Nominingue QC J0W 1R0 – 819/278-3774 – 18 places – Dir. gen., Pierre Page

Lac-Norminingue: Pavillon Thibault Enr., 330, rue des Merles, CP 164, Lac-Norminingue QC J0W 1R0 – 819/278-4257 – 14 places – Dir. gen., Pierre Page

Lachute: Hôpital d'Argenteuil, *see* Centres hospitaliers listings

Lachute: La Residence de Lachute, 377, rue Principale, Lachute QC J8H 1Y1 – 514/562-5203; Fax: 514/562-4156 – 52 lits – Dir. gen., Jane Thomson

Lachute: Residence Robitaille Enr., 350, rue Bethany, CP 458, Lachute QC J8H 3X9 – 514/562-2862 – 39 lits – Dir. gen., René Giard

Lacolle: Pavillon d'accueil Lacolle, 71, rue de l'Eglise nord, Lacolle QC J0J 1J0 – 514/246-2602 – 26 lits – Dir. gen., Fernand Tremblay

Lambton: Le Castel des Aieux, 310, rue Principale, CP 490, Lambton QC G0M 1H0 – 418/486-7417 – 41 lits – Dir. gen., Raymonde Lapointe-Lagueux

L'Annonciation: CH Laurentides et centre réadaptation Hautes-Vallees, *see* Centres hospitaliers listings

Lanoraie-d'Autray: Centre Alphonse Rondeau, 419, rue Faust, Lanoraie-d'Autray QC J0K 1E0 – 514/887-2343 – 75 lits – Dir. gen., Yvon Poirier

L'Assomption: Centre de l'Assomption, 410, boul l'Ange Gardien, CP 890, L'Assomption QC J0K 1G0 – 514/589-2101 – 160 lits – Dir. gen., Yvon Poirier

Laurentides: Centre d'accueil St-Antoine de Padoue, 521, rue Saint-Joseph, CP 219, Laurentides QC J0R 1C0 – 514/439-3217 – 110 lits – Dir. gen., Jacques Beaupre

Le Gardeur: Centre Alexandre Archambeault, 37, rue Notre-Dame, Le Gardeur QC J5Z 1R3 – 514/582-8704 – 48 lits – Dir. gen., Yvon Poirier

Lennoxville: Foyer Grace Christian, 1501, rue Campbell, RR#2, Lennoxville QC J1M 2A3 – 819/842-2164 – 49 lits – Dir. gen., John Degrace

Lévis: Centre d'accueil Saint-Joseph de Lévis inc., 107, rue Saint-Louis, CP 1188, Lévis QC G6V 6R9 – 418/833-3414; Fax: 418/833-3417 – 125 lits – Dir. gen., Pierre Paradis

Lévis: Pavillon Bellevue inc., 543, rue Saint-Joseph est, Lévis QC G6V 1G9 – 418/833-3490; Fax: 418/833-6874 – 50 lits – Dir. gen., Claude Talbot

Lévis: Villa Mon Domaine inc., 109, av Mont-Marie, Lévis QC G6V 8B4 – 418/837-6408 – 57 lits – Dir. gen., Jean-Noel Begin

L'Islet-sur-Mer: Foyer Bon-Secours inc., 125, Rte. des Pionniers ouest, L'Islet-sur-Mer QC G0R 2B0 – 418/247-5149 – 33 lits – Dir. gen., Pierrette D. Guimond

Longueuil: Centre d'accueil le Manoir Trinite, 15, rue Pratt est, Longueuil QC J4H 3S9 – 514/674-4948 – 115 lits – Dir. gen., France Larin

Longueuil: Centre d'accueil Mgr-Coderre, 2761, rue Beauvais, Longueuil QC J4M 2A1 – 514/468-1516 – 100 lits – Dir. gen., France Larin

Longueuil: Centre d'accueil St-Laurent inc., 675, boul Quinn, Longueuil QC J4H 2N6 – 514/670-5480; Fax: 514/670-9874 – 22 lits – Dir. gen., Marc-André Domingue

Longueuil: Les CHSLD de Longueuil, 40, rue Lévis, Longueuil QC J4H 1S5 – 514/670-5110; Fax: 514/670-0599 – 105 lits – Dir. gen., France Larin

Longueuil: CHSLD René-Lévesque, 1901, rue Claude, Longueuil QC J4G 1Y5 – 514/651-2210; Fax: 514/670-7731 – 224 lits – Dir. gen., France Larin

Longueuil: CHSLD St-Felix de Longueuil inc., 650, ch Chambly, Longueuil QC J4H 3L8 – 514/677-5253; Fax: 514/677-5384 – 54 lits – Dir. gen., Vincenzo Simonetta

Longueuil: Pavillon Marie-Victorin, 1500, boul Marie-Victorin est, Longueuil QC J4G 1A4 – 514/646-1011; Fax: 514/928-3054 – 36 lits – Dir. gen., Kevin Shemie

Longueuil: Pavillon Renaissance, 2381, av Dieppe, Longueuil QC J4L 2K3 – 514/679-5826 – 16 places – Dir. gen., France Larin

Longueuil: Pavillon St-Patrick, 90, boul Guimond, Longueuil QC J4G 1L5 – 514/677-8414 – 25 places – Dir. gen., Robert Sabino

Longueuil: Réseau Santé Richelieu-Yamaska - Pavillon Saint-Charles, *see* Centres hospitaliers listings

Lorretteville: Foyer de Loretteville inc., 165, rue Lessard, Lorretteville QC G2B 2V9 – 418/842-9191; Fax: 418/842-4472 – 66 lits – Dir. gen., Michel Marcotte

Lotbinière: Le Foyer de Lotbinière, 7472, rue Marie-Victorin, CP 87, Lotbinière QC G0S 1S0 – 418/796-2015 – 38 lits – Dir. gen., André Paquet

Louiseville: Regroupement de la Santé et des Services sociaux de la MRC de Maskinongé, *see* Centres hospitaliers listings

Louisville: Centre d'accueil de Louisville inc., 181, av Choisy, Louisville QC J5V 1V3 – 819/228-2706; Fax: 819/228-9944 – 129 lits – Dir. gen., Micheline Bonner Lesage

Luceville: Pavillon de Luceville inc., 48, boul Saint-Pierre, Luceville QC G0K 1E0 – 418/739-4905 – 24 places – Dir. gen., Ronald Anctil

Luceville: Pavillon Therese Lepage, 52, rue Saint-Antoine, Luceville QC G0K 1E0 – 418/739-3901 – 18 places – Dir. gen., Ronald Anctil

Lyster: Foyer de Lyster, 2180, rue Becancour, Lyster QC G0S 1V0 – 819/389-5923; Fax: 819/389-5969 – 35 lits – Dir. gen., Michel Lauzon

Macamic: Centre hospitalier St-Jean, 169, 7e av est, Macamic QC J0Z 2S0 – 819/782-4661; Fax: 819/782-2400 – 222 lits – Dir. gen., Camil Dion

Magog: Centre hospitalier et d'hébergement de Memphrémagog, *see* Centres hospitaliers listings

Magog: Pavillon Place Victoria, 147, rue Victoria, Magog QC J1X 2J7 – 819/843-7333 – 18 places – Dir. gen., Donald Langlais

Magog: Residence Ste-Marguerite Marie, 64, rue St-Pierre, Magog QC J1X 3A2 – 819/843-0202; Fax: 819/843-9518 – 47 lits – Dir. gen., Serge Lacourse

Malartic: Villa St-Martin inc., 701, rue de la Paix, CP 639, Malartic QC J0Y 1Z0 – 819/757-3663; Fax: 819/757-3309 – 51 lits – Dir. gen., Jean-Pierre Cote

Maniwaki: Foyer Père Guinard, 177, rue des Oblats, Maniwaki QC J9E 1G5 – 819/449-4900; Fax: 819/449-2079 – 77 lits – Dir. gen., Louis-Philippe Mayrand

Manseau: Pavillon Robert Morin, 305, Moose Park, CP 122, Manseau QC G0X 1Y0 – 418/356-2455 – 15 places – Dir. gen., Raymond Dion

Maria: Centre hospitalier Baie-des-Chaleurs, *see* Centres hospitaliers listings

Maria: Residence Saint-Joseph, 491, Rte. 132, CP 10, Maria QC G0C 1Y0 – 418/759-3458; Fax: 418/759-5103 – 125 lits – Dir. gen., Bernard Nadeau

Marieville: Centre Rouville, 300, rue du Docteur Poulin, Marieville QC J3M 1L7 – 514/460-4475; Fax: 514/460-4104 – 245 lits – Dir. gen., Julien Tremblay

Martinville: Pavillon St-Gabriel Enr., 213, ch de l'Eglise, Martinville QC J0B 2A0 – 819/835-5355 – 15 places – Dir. gen., Real Jacques

Mascouche: Pavillon des Pins, 1151, ch Pincourt, Mascouche QC J7L 2X8 – 514/474-4772 – 16 places – Dir. gen., Joyce Boillat

Mashteuiatsh: Centre Tshishemishk, 410, rue Amish, Mashteuiatsh QC G0W 2H0 – 418/275-5535 – 20 lits – Dir. gen., Edouard Robertson

Massueville: Foyer Familial St-Aime (1986) inc., 201, rue Cartier, Massueville QC J0G 1K0 – 514/788-2223; Fax: 514/788-2223 – 65 lits – Dir. gen., Serge Cournoyer

Matane: Foyer d'accueil de Matane, 150, av Saint-Jerome, Matane QC G4W 3A2 – 418/562-4154; Fax: 418/562-9281 – 106 lits – Dir. gen., Clement Gauthier

McMasterville: Pavillon McMasterville, 329, ch du Richelieu, McMasterville QC J3G 1T8 – 514/464-8827 – 14 places – Dir. gen., Raymond Carignan

Metabetchouan: Le CHSLD de Lac-Saint-Jean-Est, 40, rue de l'Hôpital, Metabetchouan QC G0W 2A0 – 418/349-2861; Fax: 418/349-2288 – 200 lits – Dir. gen., Alain Gaudreault

Metabetchouan: Pavillon Diane Enr., 27, rue Saint-Pierre, Metabetchouan QC G0W 2A0 – 418/349-8390; Fax: 418/349-8048 – 14 places – Présidente, Diane Lamontagne

Mirabel: Centre d'accueil de St-Benoit, 9100, rue Dumouchel, Mirabel QC J0N 1K0 – 514/258-2481; Fax: 514/258-4980 – 75 lits – Dir. gen., André C. Desuatels

Mistassini: CHSLD Maria-Chapdelaine, 116, av des Chutes, Mistassini QC G0W 2C0 – 418/276-1153; Fax: 418/276-4355 – 64 lits – Dir. gen., Jacques Turcotte

Mont-Joli: Foyer Ste-Bernadette inc., 1039, boul Jacques-Cartier, CP 292, Mont-Joli QC G5H 3L1 – 418/775-2241; Fax: 418/775-2242 – 24 lits – Dir. gen., Lucette Berube-Goyette

Mont-Joli: Hôpital de Mont-Joli inc., 800, ch du Sanatorium, Mont-Joli QC G5H 3L6 – 418/775-7261; Fax: 418/775-8607 – 364 lits – Dir. gen., Ronald Anctil

Mont-Joli: Pavillon Jacques-Cartier Enr., 1147, boul Jacques-Cartier nord, Mont-Joli QC G5H 2S5 – 418/775-5984 – 16 places – Dir. gen., Ronald Anctil

Mont-Joli: Pavillon Lamarre-Pinel Enr., 1049, boul Jacques-Cartier, Mont-Joli QC G5H 2S4 – 418/775-2727 – 17 places – Dir. gen., Ronald Anctil

Mont-Joli: Pavillon St-Joseph, 31, rue du Lac, Mont-Joli QC G5H 3P1 – 418/775-3041 – 20 places – Dir. gen., Roanld Anctil

Mont-Joli: La Residence de Mont-Joli inc., 75, av des Retraites, Mont-Joli QC G5H 1E7 – 418/775-4351; Fax: 418/775-6284 – 47 lits – Dir. gen., Ronald Anctil

Mont-Laurier: Centre d'accueil Sainte-Anne de Mont-Laurier, 411, rue de la Madone, Mont-Laurier QC J9L 1S1 – 819/623-5940; Fax: 819/623-7347 – 60 lits – Dir. gen., Gilles Huberdeau

Mont-Laurier: Pavillon Therrien inc., 278, rue de la Madone, Mont-Laurier QC J9L 1R5 – 819/623-6315 – 24 places – Dir. gen., Gilles Huberdeau

Mont-Louis: Centre d'accueil du Littoral inc., 10, 5e rue est, Mont-Louis QC G0E 1T0 – 418/797-2960; Fax: 418/797-2950 – 35 lits – Dir. gen., Michèle Lamarre

Montmagny: Foyer d'Youville, 168, rue Saint-Joseph, Montmagny QC G5V 1H8 – 418/248-0182; Fax: 418/248-4464 – 111 lits – Dir. gen., Jean-Paul Lacroix

Montmagny: Pavillon Goulet & Labrecque inc., 44, rue Saint-Thomas, Montmagny QC G5V 1L3 – 418/248-7268 – 18 places – Dir. gen., Jean-Paul Lacroix

Montmagny: Pavillon Labrie, 155, Place des Meuniers, Montmagny QC G5V 1M6 – 418/248-5577 – 15 places – Dir. gen., Jean-Paul Lacroix

Montréal: Assn Montréalaise pour les Aveugles - Res. Gilman, 7000, rue Sherbrooke ouest, Montréal QC H4B 1R3 – 514/489-8201; Fax: 514/489-3477; EMail: mabinfo@axess.com – 59 lits – Regie régionale de la santé et des services sociaux de Montréal-centre – Dir. gen., Paul Bareau

Montréal: C.A. Armand Lavergne, 3500, rue Chapleau, Montréal QC H2K 4N3 – 514/527-8921 – 188 lits – Dir. gen., Rolande Laurin-Dorval

Montréal: Les Cedres-Centre d'accueil pour personnes agée, 95, boul Gouin est, Montréal QC H3L 1A6 – 514/389-1023; Fax: 514/389-0581 – 22 lits – Dir. gen., Diane Chaunt

Montréal: Centre Biermans, 7905, rue Sherbrooke est, Montréal QC H1L 1A4 – 514/351-9891; Fax: 514/351-1556 – 242 lits – Dir. gen., Jacques Hould

Montréal: Centre Le Cardinal inc., 12900, rue Notre-Dame est, Montréal QC H1A 1R9 – 514/645-2766; Fax: 514/640-6267 – 204 lits – Dir. gen., André Groulx

Montréal: Centre d'accueil Alfred Desrochers, 5325, av Victoria, Montréal QC H3W 2P2 – 514/731-3891 – 125 lits – Dir. gen., Yves Jette

Montréal: Centre d'accueil Chevalier de Lorimer, 4625, av de Lorimier, Montréal QC H2H 2B4 – 514/526-2894; Fax: 514/526-9942 – 75 lits – Dir. gen., Jean-Louis Vaillancourt

Montréal: Centre d'accueil Chomedey, 4115, 9e rue, Laval QC H7W 1Y2 – 514/688-4393 – 23 lits – Dir. gen., Michel de Luca

Montréal: Centre d'accueil Dante, 6887, rue Chatelain, Montréal QC H1T 3X7 – 514/252-1535; Fax: 514/252-1096 – 104 lits – Regie régionale de la santé et des services sociaux de Montréal-centre – Dir. gen., Irene Giannetti

Montréal: Centre d'accueil de Lachine, 650, Place d'Accueil, Lachine QC H8S 3Z5 – 514/634-7161; Fax: 514/634-8751 – 211 lits – Dir. gen., Leonard Vincent

Montréal: Centre d'accueil Denis-Benjamin Viger, 3292, boul Cherrier est, Saint-Raphael-de-l'Ile-Bizard QC H9C 2C2 – 514/620-6310; Fax: 514/620-6553 – 125 lits – Dir. gen., Suzanne Lafortune

Montréal: Centre d'accueil Eloria Lepage, 3090, av de la Pepinière, Montréal QC H1N 3N4 – 514/252-1710 – 160 lits – Dir. gen., Gisele Besner

Montréal: Centre d'accueil Ernest Routhier, 2110, rue Wolfe, Montréal QC H2L 4V4 – 514/525-2546 – 96 lits – Dir. gen., Damien Dallaire

Montréal: Centre d'accueil Father Dowd/Father Dowd Home, 6565, ch Hudson, Montréal QC H3S 2T7 – 514/731-9601; Fax: 514/731-7253 – 135 lits – Dir. gen., John R. Walker

Montréal: Centre d'accueil Fernand Larocque, 5436, boul Lévesque est, Laval QC H7C 1N7 – 514/661-5440; Fax: 514/661-6554 – 96 lits – Dir. gen., Michel Briere

Montréal: Centre d'accueil Francois Seguenot, 13950, rue Notre-Dame est, Montréal QC H1A 1T5 – 514/642-7741 – 77 lits – Dir. gen., Monique Corbeil

Montréal: Centre d'accueil Gouin-Rosemont, 1970, boul Rosemont, Montréal QC H2G 1S8 – 514/273-3681; Fax: 514/273-7645 – 105 lits – Dir. gen., France Mailhot, 514/251-6011

Montréal: Centre d'accueil Henri Bradet, 6465, av Chester, Montréal QC H4V 2Z8 – 514/483-1380 – 125 lits – Dir. gen., Jean Michaud

Montréal: Centre d'accueil Heritage inc., 5716, ch de la Cote-Saint-Antoine, Montréal QC H4A 1R9 – 514/484-2645 – 15 lits – Dir. gen., Michael Pomilo

Montréal: Centre d'accueil Idola St-Jean, 250, boul Cartier ouest, Laval QC H7N 5S5 – 514/668-6750 – 100 lits – Dir. gen., Michel Briere

Montréal: Centre d'accueil Jean XXIII, 6900, 15e av, Montréal QC H1X 2V9 – 514/725-2190 – 24 lits – Dir. gen., Marie-Claire Lamontagne

Montréal: Centre d'accueil Jeannine Gingras, 6770, boul Pie IX, Montréal QC H1X 2C8 – 514/725-7757 – 20 lits – Dir. gen., Rita Bloutier

Montréal: Centre d'accueil Judith Jasmin, 8850, rue Bisaillon, Montréal QC H1K 4N2 – 514/354-5990 – 75 lits – Dir. gen., Claude Desjardins

Montréal: Centre d'accueil Juif, 5750, rue Lavoie, Montréal QC H3W 3H5 – 514/735-9999; Fax: 514/735-9094 – 160 lits – Dir. gen., Isaac Katofsky

Montréal: Centre d'accueil LaSalle, 8686, rue Centrale, LaSalle QC H8P 3N4 – 514/364-6700; Fax: 514/364-0484 – 202 lits – Dir. gen., Jean-Paul Bouchard

Montréal: Centre d'accueil Louis Riel, 2120, rue Augustin-Gantin, Montréal QC H3K 3G3 – 514/931-2263; Fax: 514/931-2299 – 100 lits – Dir. gen., Germain Harvey

Montréal: Centre d'accueil Marie-Rollet, 5003, rue Saint-Zotique est, Montréal QC H1T 1N6 – 514/729-5281 – 125 lits – Dir. gen., Michel Brunet

Montréal: Centre d'accueil Nazaire Piche, 150, 15e av, Lachine QC H8S 3L9 – 514/637-2326; Fax: 514/637-1224 – 100 lits – Dir. gen., Leonard Vincent

Montréal: Centre d'accueil la Piniere, 4895, rue Saint-Joseph, Laval QC H7C 1H6 – 514/661-3305 – 100 lits – Dir. gen., Michel Briere

Montréal: Centre d'accueil Real Morel, 3500, rue Wellington, Verdun QC H4G 1T3 – 514/761-5874; Fax: 514/761-7264 – 152 lits – Dir. gen., Germain Harvey

Montréal: Centre d'accueil St-Margaret/St. Margaret's Home, 50, av Hillside, Westmount QC H3Z 1V9 – 514/845-2141; Fax: 514/932-4379 – 96 lits – Dir. gen., John R. Walker

Montréal: Centre d'accueil Ste-Marie Inc., 4045, rue Prieur est, Montréal QC H1H 2M9 – 514/322-0650; Fax: 514/322-5176 – 30 lits – Dir. gen., Micheline Gauthier

Montréal: Centre de gerontologie Manoir Dorval inc., 2400, ch Herron, Dorval QC H9S 5W3 – 514/631-7288 – 60 lits – Dir. gen., Howard Modlin

Montréal: Le Centre de soins prolonges de Montréal, 5155, rue Ste-Catherine est, Montréal QC H1V 2A5 – 514/255-2833; Fax: 514/255-6275 – 280 lits – Dir. gen., Caroline Barbir

Montréal: Centre d'hébergement Champlain - Marie-Victorin, 7150, rue Marie-Victorin, Montréal QC H1G 2J5 – 514/324-2044; Fax: 514/324-4096 – 300 lits – Dir. gen., Guy Joly

Montréal: Centre d'hébergement Champlain-Villeray, 1640, rue Tillemont, Montréal QC H2E 1C2 – 514/725-9881; Fax: 514/725-9883 – 28 lits – Dir. gen., Guy Joly

Montréal: Centre d'hébergement Emilie Gamelin, Armand-Lavergne, 1440, rue Dufresne, Montréal QC H2K 3J3 – 514/527-8921 – 194 lits – Dir. gen., Rolande Laurin-Dorval

Montréal: Centre d'hébergement et de soins de longue durée Bourget inc., 11570, rue Notre-Dame est, Montréal QC H1B 2Z4 – 514/645-1673; Fax: 514/645-1673 – 112 lits – Dir. gen., Yvon Girard

Montréal: Centre d'hébergement et de soins de longue durée Gouin inc., 4445, boul Henri-Bourassa est, Montréal QC H1H 5M4 – 514/327-6209; Fax: 514/327-9912 – 93 lits – Dir. gen., Francesco Ieraci

Montréal: Centre d'hébergement le Royer, 7351, rue Jean Desprez, Anjou QC H1K 5A6 – 514/493-9397; Fax: 514/493-9103 – 96 lits – Dir. gen., Jean-Bernard Breault, 514/849-1357

Montréal: Centre d'hébergement St-Albert-le-Grand inc., 4357, av Charlemagne, Montréal QC H1X 2H2 – 514/259-6905; Fax: 514/259-8984 – 18 lits – Dir. gen., Johanne Pacquette

Montréal: Centre d'hébergement St-Francois inc., 4105, Montée Masson, Laval QC H0A 1G0 – 514/666-6541; Fax: 514/666-1601 – 53 lits – Dir. gen., Marie-Christine Moulin

Montréal: Centre d'hébergement St-Georges inc., 1205, rue Labelle, Montréal QC H2L 4C1 – 514/849-1357; Fax: 514/849-8465 – 280 lits – Dir. gen., Jean-Bernard Breault

Montréal: Centre d'Hébergement St-Vincent-Marie inc., 1175, ch Cote Vertu, St-Laurent QC H4L 5J1 – 514/744-1175; Fax: 514/744-0557 – 66 lits – Dir. gen., Mary Maley

Montréal: Centre Geriatrique le bel age de Fabre, 5200, 80e av, Laval QC H7R 1J9 – 514/627-7990; Fax: 514/627-7993 – 64 lits – Dir. gen., Kenneth Courville

Montréal: Centre hospitalier Côte-des-Neiges, *see* Centres hospitaliers listings

Montréal: Centre hospitalier de Lachine, *see* Centres hospitaliers listings

Montréal: Centre hospitalier de l'Université de Montréal - Pavillon Notre-Dame, *see* Centres hospitaliers listings

Montréal: Centre hospitalier gériatrique Maimonides, 5795, av Caldwell, Cote-Saint-Luc QC H4W 1W3 – 514/483-2121; Fax: 514/483-1561 – 352 lits – Dir. gen., vacant

Montréal: Centre hospitalier Jacques Viger, *see* Centres hospitaliers listings

Montréal: Centre Triest, 4900, boul Lapointe, Montréal QC H1K 4W9 – 514/353-1227 – 275 lits – Dir. gen., Jacques Hould

Montréal: Chateau sur le Lac, 16289, boul Gouin ouest, Sainte-Geneviève QC H9H 1E2 – 514/620-9794 – 50 lits – Dir. gen., B.S. Kachra

Montréal: Chateau Westmount, 4860, boul de Masionneuve ouest, Westmount QC H3Z 3G2 – 514/369-3000; Fax: 514/369-0014 – 112 lits – Dir. gen., Ginette Villeneuve

Montréal: C.H.S.L.D. Bayview inc., 27, ch Lakeshore, Pointe-Claire QC H9S 4H1 – 514/695-9384; Fax: 514/695-5723 – 128 lits – Dir. gen., George Guillon

Montréal: CHSLD Champlain - Manoir de Verdun, 5500, boul Lasalle, Verdun QC H4H 1N9 – 514/769-8801 – 215 lits – Dir. gen., Ghislain Girard

Montréal: CHSLD Dollard-des-Ormeaux, 197, rue Thornhill, Dollard-des-Ormeaux QC H9B 3H8 – 514/684-0173; Fax: 514/684-0179 – 160 lits – Dir. gen., Vincenzo Simonetta

Montréal: Les CHSLD du Plateau Mont-Royal, 4255, av Papineau, Montréal QC H2H 2P6 – 514/526-4981; Fax: 514/526-0645 – 312 lits – Regie régionale de la santé et des services sociaux de Montréal-centre – Dir. gen., Jean-Louis Vaillancourt

Montréal: CHSLD Jeanne-Leber, 7445, Hochelaga, Montréal QC H1N 3V2 – 514/251-6000 – 400 lits – Dir. gen., Juliette P. Bailly

Montréal: CHSLD Maire-Claret inc., 3345, boul Henri-Bourassa est, Montréal-Nord QC H1H 1H6 – 514/322-4380 – 78 lits

Montréal: CHSLD Mont Royal, 275, av Brittany, Mont-Royal QC H3P 3C2 – 514/739-5593 – 260 lits – Dir. gen., Vincenzo Simonetta

Montréal: CHSLD l'oasis de Laval inc., 300, Place Juge-Desnoyers, Laval QC H7G 4R1 – 514/629-9395; Fax: 514/629-2145 – 25 lits – Dir. gen., Francoise Cadieux-Boucher

Montréal: CHSLD Pierrefonds, 14775, boul Pierrefonds, Pierrefonds QC H9H 4Y1 – 514/620-1220; Fax: 514/620-0024 – 64 lits – Dir. gen., Vincenzo Simonetta

Montréal: CHSLD Ste-Germaine Cousin, 14241, av Victoria, Montréal QC H1A 1P2 – 514/642-5341; Fax: 514/642-5343 – 46 lits – Dir. gen., Vincenzo Simonetta

Montréal: CHSLD Ville-Emard, 6935, rue Hamilton, Montréal QC H4E 3C8 – 514/769-3812; Fax: 514/769-7581 – 53 lits – Dir. gen., Vincenzo Simonetta

Montréal: Foyer Dorval, 225, av de la Presentation, Dorval QC H9S 3L7 – 514/631-9094; Fax: 514/631-4420 – 100 lits – Dir. gen., Leonard Vincent

Montréal: Foyer pour personnes agées Saint-Laurent inc., #18, 1055, ch Cote-Vertu, Saint-Laurent QC H4L 1Y8 – 514/744-4981; Fax: 514/744-0895 – 144 lits – Dir. gen., Mariette Lebrun-Bohemier

Montréal: Foyer Rousselot, 5655, rue Sherbrooke est, Montréal QC H1N 1A4 – 514/254-9421; Fax: 514/254-3967 – 157 lits – Dir. gen., Robert Boucher

Montréal: Foyer St-Marc, 3300, boul Cremazie est, Montréal QC H2A 1A3 – 514/374-2420; Fax: 514/288-7076 – 64 lits – Dir. gen., Michel Duchesne

Montréal: Foyer Senneville, 55, ch Senneville, Senneville QC H9X 1C1 – 514/457-2440 – 220 lits – Dir. gen., Richard Watkins

Montréal: Les Foyers Presbyteriens de St-Andrew inc., 3350, boul Cavendish, Montréal QC H4B 2M7 – 514/489-8190; Fax: 514/489-7253 – 70 lits – Dir. gen., John R. Walker

Montréal: Griffith McConnell Home Residence, 5790, av Parkhaven, Côte-Saint-Luc QC H4W 1Y1 – 514/482-0590; Fax: 514/482-2643 – 136 lits – Exec. Dir., Davis F. Walls

Montréal: L'Hôpital Chinois de Montréal, 7500, rue St-Denis, Montréal QC H2R 2E6 – 514/273-9154; Fax: 514/273-2446 – 108 lits – Dir. gen., Pierre Lalonde

Montréal: Hôpital du Sacré-Coeur de Montréal, *see* Centres hospitaliers listings

Montréal: Hôpital général Juif Sir Mortimer B. Davis/Sir Mortimer B. Davis Jewish General Hospital, *see* Centres hospitaliers listings

Montréal: Hôpital Grace Dart Hospital, 6085, rue Sherbrooke est, Montréal QC H1N 1C2 – 514/256-9021; Fax: 514/251-2391 – 101 beds – Regie régionale de la santé et des services sociaux de Montréal-centre – Exec. Dir., Caroline Barbir

Montréal: Hôpital Jean-Talon, *see* Centres hospitaliers listings

Montréal: Hôpital Maisonneuve-Rosemont, *see* Centres hospitaliers listings

Montréal: Hôpital St-Denis, 2870, boul Rosemont, Montréal QC H1Y 1L7 – 514/727-8173; Fax: 514/465-7017 – 19 lits – Dir. gen., Gisèle Désilets

Montréal: Hôpital Ste-Rita, 11720, av Desy, Montréal QC H1G 4C3 – 514/323-5210; Fax: 514/323-2136 – 50 lits – Dir. gen., Vincenzo Simonetta

Montréal: Hôpital Sainte-Anne, 305, boul des Anciens-Combattants, Sainte-Anne-de-Bellevue QC H9X 1Y9 – 514/457-3440; Fax: 514/457-5741 – 910 lits – Dir. gen., Richard Watkins

Montréal: Hôpital La Visitation, 161, boul Henri-Bourassa ouest, Montréal QC H3L 1N2 – 514/331-2220; Fax: 514/331-8572 – 70 lits – Dir. gen., Michel Bouffard

Montréal: Iakhihsohtha Lodge, CP 40, Akwesasne QC H0M 1A0 – 613/575-2507 – 30 lits – Dir. gen., Michael Mitchell

Montréal: Institut Canadien-Polonais du Bien-Etre inc., 5655, rue Belanger est, Montréal QC H1T 1G2 – 514/259-2551; Fax: 514/259-9948 – 126 lits – Dir. gen., Anna Brychcy

Montréal: Jewish Hospital of Hope Centre/Centre hospitalier Juif de l'espérance, 5725, av Victoria, Montréal QC H3W 3H6 – 514/738-4500; Fax: 514/738-2611 – 160 beds – Exec. Dir., Isaac Katofsky

Montréal: Ma Maison St-Joseph, 5605, rue Beaubien est, Montréal QC H1T 1X4 – 514/254-4991; Fax: 514/257-1742 – 93 lits – Dir. gen., Sr. Therese

Montréal: Maison de santé Woodlawn Enr., 1391, rue du College, Saint-Laurent QC H4L 2L4 – 514/747-1433 – 13 lits – Dir. gen., Fernand Tremblay

Montréal: Manoir l'Age-d'Or, 3430, rue Jeanne-Mance, Montréal QC H2X 2J9 – 514/842-1147; Fax: 514/842-1146 – 212 lits – Dir. gen., Gilbert Gagnon

Montréal: Manoir Beaconsfield, 34, av Woodland, Beaconsfield QC H9W 4V9 – 514/694-2000 – 23 lits – Dir. gen., Annie Maffre

Montréal: Manoir Cartierville, 12235, rue Grenet, Montréal QC H4J 2N9 – 514/337-7300; Fax: 514/337-4188 – 283 lits – Dir. gen., Francois Lamarre

Montréal: Manoir des Roseraies, 1050, av Gordon, Verdun QC H4G 2S2 – 514/768-6605 – 50 lits – Dir. gen., Jean-Claude Goyer

Montréal: Manoir Fleury Enr., 2145, rue Fleury est, Montréal QC H2B 1J8 – 514/388-1553; Fax: 514/388-4161 – 25 lits – Dir. gen., Mariana Lavoie

Montréal: Manoir Ile de l'ouest, 17725, boul Pierrefonds, Pierrefonds QC H9J 3L1 – 514/620-9850 – 63 lits – Dir. gen., John Karakas

Montréal: Manoir Pierrefonds inc., 18465, boul Gouin ouest, Pierrefonds QC H9K 1A6 – 514/626-6651; Fax: 514/626-6415 – 100 lits – Dir. gen., Ginette Villeneuve

Montréal: Manoir St-Patrice inc., 3615, boul Perron, Laval QC H7V 1P4 – 514/681-5854; Fax: 514/681-6120 – 132 lits – Dir. gen., Elmer Carey

Montréal: Manoir Verdun, 5500, boul Lasalle, Verdun QC H4N 1N9 – 514/769-8801 – 215 lits – Dir. gen., Alain Gaudreault

Montréal: Pavillon Auclair, 6910, rue Boyer, Montréal QC H3W 2M4 – 514/272-3011 – 160 lits – Dir. gen., André Paquette

Montréal: Pavillon Bruchesi, 225, rue Rachel est, Montréal QC H2H 1R4 – 514/528-1603 – 83 lits – Dir. gen., Jean Leblanc

Montréal: Pavillon Chomedey, 3825, boul Lévesque ouest, Laval QC H7V 1G6 – 514/682-3388; Fax: 514/682-6129 – 50 lits – Dir. gen., Marie Beauchamps

Montréal: Pavillon des Seigneurs, 1800, rue Saint-Jacques ouest, Montréal QC H3J 2R5 – 514/935-4681; Fax: 514/935-6189 – 192 lits – Dir. gen., André Paquette

Montréal: Pavillon Duguay Enr., 3934, ch du Souvenir, Laval QC H7W 1A8 – 514/688-9053 – 21 places – Dir. gen., Michel Brière

Montréal: Pavillon Fabre, 943, 40e av, Laval QC H7R 4X4 – 514/627-4612 – 29 places – Dir. gen., Pierre Marson

Montréal: Pavillon Laurendeau Enr., 19, av Laurendeau, Montréal QC H1B 4X9 – 514/645-3782 – 19 places – Dir. gen., Raymond Carignan

Montréal: Pavillon Louis Riel inc., 201, av Broadway, Montréal QC H1B 5A4 – 514/645-6802 – 29 places – Dir. gen., Raymond Carignan

Montréal: Pavillon Morand inc., 12412, rue Notre-Dame est, Montréal QC H1B 2Z1 – 514/640-5353 – 29 places – Dir. gen., Jean Leblanc

Montréal: Pavillon Omer inc., 1505, rue de Beaurivage, Montréal QC H1L 5V3 – 514/353-5467 – 20 places – Dir. gen., Raymond Carignan

Montréal: Pavillon Rejean Longpre enr., 13952, rue de Montigny, Montréal QC H1A 1J6 – 514/642-1841 – 20 places – Dir. gen., Raymond Carignan

Montréal: Pavillon Saint-Clement, 549, rue Theodore, Montréal QC H1V 3B1 – 514/433-2421 – 27 places – Dir. gen., Jean Leblanc

Montréal: Pavillon St-Henri, 5205, rue Notre-Dame ouest, Montréal QC H4C 3L2 – 514/931-0851; Fax: 514/931-2993 – 237 lits – Dir. gen., André Paquette

Montréal: Pavillon St-Hubert, Sherbrooke inc., 2047-2049, rue Saint-Hubert, Montréal QC H2L 3Z6 – 514/526-7941 – 21 places – Dir. gen., Jean Leblanc

Montréal: Pavillon Suzanne Blanchard inc., 1919, 9e av, Montréal QC H1B 4E7 – 514/645-3204 – 29 places – Dir. gen., Raymond Carignan

Montréal: Pavillon Yolande et Gilles inc., 3655, rue Sherbrooke est, Montréal QC H1W 1E3 – 514/529-7897 – 29 places – Dir. gen., Claude Desjardins

Montréal: Residence Angelica inc., 3435, boul Gouin est, Montréal QC H1H 1B1 – 514/324-6110; Fax: 514/324-9332 – 400 lits – Dir. gen., Sr. Anne-Marie Marolo

Montréal: Residence Berthiaume-duTremblay, 1635, boul Gouin est, Montréal QC H2C 1C2 – 514/381-1841; Fax: 514/381-1090 – 248 lits – Dir. gen., Gaston Bouchard

Montréal: Residence a la Bonne Étoile inc., 7401, av Churchill, Verdun QC H4H 2L5 – 514/767-4739 – 29 places – Dir. gen., Joyce Boillat

Montréal: Residence Claude & Claire, 12650, 41e av, Montréal QC H1E 2E7 – 514/494-0935 – 20 places – Dir. gen., Jacques Mackay

Montréal: Residence Dandurand, 3841, rue Dandurand, Montréal QC H1X 1P3 – 514/729-5902; Fax: 514/729-5902 – 18 lits – Dir. gen., Guy Gauthier

Montréal: Residence Dorion, 1360, rue Jean-Talon est, Montréal QC H2E 1S2 – 514/270-9271; Fax: 514/270-6779 – 147 lits – Dir. gen., Gilles Saint-Pierre

Montréal: Residence du Bonheur Enr., 5855, rue Boulard, Laval QC H0A 1G0 – 514/666-1567 – 50 lits – Dir. gen., Linda Sirois

Montréal: Residence Fleur de Lys, 15304, rue Notre-Dame est, Montréal QC H1A 1S6 – 514/642-3317; Fax: 514/642-8688 – 29 places – Dir. gen., Albert Painchaud

Montréal: La Residence Fulford, 1221, rue Guy, Montréal QC H3H 2K8 – 514/933-7975; Fax: 514/933-3773 – 39 lits – Dir. gen., Ingrid Leuzy

Montréal: Residence Legare, 1615, av Emile Journault, Montréal QC H2M 2G3 – 514/384-5490 – 100 lits – Dir. gen., André Soucy

Montréal: Residence Louvain, 9600, rue Saint-Denis, Montréal QC H2M 1P2 – 514/381-7256 – 155 lits – Dir. gen., André Soucy

Montréal: Residence Maison Neuve, 2300, rue Nicolet, Montréal QC H1W 3L4 – 514/527-2161 – 228 lits – Dir. gen., Gisele Besner

Montréal: Residence Marie-Christine inc., 1487, boul des Laurentides, Laval QC H7M 2Y3 – 514/663-3901; Fax: 514/663-7916 – 38 lits – Dir. gen., Marie-Christine Moulin

Montréal: Residence Paul Lizotte, 6850, boul Gouin est, Montréal QC H1G 6L7 – 514/326-7140 – 126 lits – Dir. gen., Pierre Ouimet

Montréal: Residence Rive Soleil, 15150, rue Notre-Dame est, Montréal QC H1A 1W6 – 514/642-5509; Fax: 514/642-4120 – 50 lits – Dir. gen., Roger-G. Bergeron

Montréal: Residence Riviera inc., 3860, boul Lévesque ouest, Laval QC H7V 1G7 – 514/682-0111; Fax: 514/682-0154 – 84 lits – Dir. gen., Marilyn Nadon

Montréal: Residence Robert Cliche, 3730, rue de Bellechasse, Montréal QC H1X 3E5 – 514/374-8660 – 100 lits – Dir. gen., Michel Bourque

Montréal: Residence St-Maxime Inc., 3717, boul Lévesque ouest, Laval QC H7V 1G4 – 514/682-0414 – 46 lits – Dir. gen., Madeleine Bourbeau

Montréal: Residence Sainte-Claire inc., 8950, rue Sainte-Claire est, Montréal QC H1L 1Z1 – 514/351-3877; Fax: 514/352-5956 – 38 lits – Dir. gen., Marcel Daniel

Montréal: Residence Sainte-Dorothée, 350, boul Samson, Laval QC H7X 1J4 – 514/689-0933; Fax: 514/689-3147 – 280 lits – Dir. gen., Lise Groleau

Montréal: Residence Villeray, 6767, rue Cartier, Montréal QC H2G 3G2 – 514/270-9271 – 95 lits – Dir. gen., Gilles Saint-Pierre

Montréal: Residence Yvon-Brunet, 6250, av Newman, Montréal QC H4E 4K4 – 514/765-8000; Fax: 514/765-8064 – 191 lits – Dir. gen., Germain Harvey

Montréal: Les Residences Laurendeau, 1725, boul Gouin est, Montréal QC H2C 3H6 – 514/384-2020; Fax: 514/384-4245 – 300 lits – Dir. gen., André Soucy

Montréal: Residences Marois ttée, 14, boul Daniel-Johnson, Laval QC H7V 2C2 – 514/681-2100; Fax: 514/681-7494 – 39 lits – Dir. gen., Normand Goyette

Montréal: Villa Belle Rive inc., 5320, boul Gouin est, Montréal QC H1G 1B4 – 514/321-1367 – 27 lits – Dir. gen., Francoise Chapleau

Montréal: Villa Ste-Genevieve (1986) inc., 5002, boul Saint-Charles, Pierrefonds QC H9H 3G1 – 514/620-8780; Fax: 514/626-3010 – 42 lits – Dir. gen., Dr. Lambros Chaniotis

New Carlisle: Centre d'accueil de la Baie, 108, rue Principale, CP 577, New Carlisle QC G0C 1Z0 – 418/752-3386; Fax: 418/752-6483 – 75 lits – Dir. gen., Vilmont Moreau

Nicolet: Foyer de Nicolet, 175, rue Marguerite d'Youville, Nicolet QC J3T 1T3 – 819/293-2142; Fax: 819/293-8590 – 215 lits – Dir. gen., Rejeanne Letendre

Nicolet: Hôpital du Christ-Roi, *see* Centres hospitaliers listings

Normandin: Foyer St-Cyrille de Normandin inc., 1153, av des Ecoles, CP 490, Normandin QC G0W 2E0 – 418/274-3416; Fax: 418/274-5679 – 23 lits – Dir. gen., Jacques Turcotte

Normandin: Pavillon Ghislain Genest, 1162, av des Ecoles, CP 369, Normandin QC G0W 2E0 – 418/274-2993 – 18 places – Dir. gen., Jacques Turcotte

North Hatley: Foyer Connaught, 77 Main St., CP 629, North Hatley QC J0B 2C0 – 819/842-2164; Fax: 819/842-2667 – 49 lits – Dir. gen., John Degrace

North Hatley: La Maison Blanche de North Hatley inc., 977, rue Massawippi, CP 298, North Hatley QC J0B 2C0 – 819/842-2478; Fax: 819/842-2470 – 60 lits – Dir. gen., Gisele Croteau

Notre-Dame-du-Bon-Conseil: L'Accueil Bon-Conseil, 91, rue Saint-Thomas, CP 90, Notre-Dame-du-Bon-Conseil QC J0C 1A0 – 819/336-2122; Fax: 819/336-2453 – 57 lits – Dir. gen., Nagui Habashi

Notre-Dame-du-Mont-Carmel: Pavillon Valmont inc., Lac Doucet, 260, 3e rue, Notre-Dame-du-Mont-Carmel QC G0X 3J0 – 819/375-8744 – 18 places – Dir. gen., Vital Gaudet

Notre-Dame-du-Nord: Pavillon Tête du Lac inc., 15, rue Ontario, CP 550, Notre-Dame-du-Nord QC J0Z 3B0 – 418/723-2787 – 21 places – Dir. gen., Nicole Landry

Oka: Manoir Oka inc., 2083, ch Oka, CP 567, Oka QC J0N 1E0 – 514/479-6447; Fax: 514/479-6447 – 34 lits – Dir. gen., Robert Fournier

Ormstown: Le Centre d'accueil Ormstown-Huntingdon, 65, rue Hector, Ormstown QC J0S 1K0 – 514/829-2346 – 72 lits – Dir. gen., Claude-Yves de Repentigny

Palmarolle: Le Foyer Mgr Halde, 136, rue Principale est, CP 70, Palmarolle QC J0Z 3C0 – 819/787-2612; Fax: 819/787-3293 – 27 lits – Dir. gen., Fabiola Pelletier

Pierreville: Foyer Lucien Shooner inc., 50, rue Paul-Comtois, CP 220, Pierreville QC J0G 1J0 – 514/568-2712; Fax: 514/568-3658 – 59 lits – Dir. gen., Pierre Levasseur

Plessisville: Foyer des Bois-Francs, 1450, av Trudelle, Plessisville QC G6L 1T9 – 819/362-3558; Fax: 819/362-9266 – 40 lits – Dir. gen., Michel Lauzon

Pointe-a-la-Croix: Pavillon Ste-Helene, 41, rue Sarto, CP 69, Pointe-a-la-Croix QC G0C 1L0 – 418/788-5654 – 20 places – Dir. gen., Martin Savoie

Pointe-au-Pic: Villa des Erables, 54, rue Principale, Pointe-au-Pic QC G0T 1M0 – 418/665-2542 – 13 places – Dir. gen., Jacques Tremblay

Povungnituk: Centre hospitalier de la Baie d'Hudson, *see* Centres hospitaliers listings

Price: Pavillon de Price, 4, rue du Centre, Price QC G0J 1Z0 – 418/775-2882 – 22 places – Dir. gen., Ronald Anctil

Price: Pavillon Lavoie Chouinard Enr., 26, rue de la Gare, Price QC G0J 1Z0 – 418/775-3544 – 19 places – Dir. gen., Ronald Anctil

Princeville: Foyer St-Eusebe inc., 435, rue Saint-Jacques est, CP 610, Princeville QC G0P 1E0 – 819/364-2355; Fax: 819/362-9266 – 27 lits – Dir. gen., Michel Lauzon

Québec: Centre d'accueil le Faubourg, 925, av Turnbull, Québec QC G1R 2X6 – 418/524-2463 – 96 lits – Dir. gen., Gerard Roy

Québec: Le Centre d'accueil Nazareth inc., 715, rue des Glacis, Québec QC G1R 3P8 – 418/694-0492; Fax: 418/694-9452 – 75 lits – Dir. gen., Louise Gaudreault

Québec: Centre d'accueil St-Antoine, 1451, boul Pere-Lelievre, Québec QC G1M 1N8 – 418/683-2516 – 283 lits – Dir. gen., Gerard Roy

Québec: Centre de services Notre-Dame-de-Lourdes, 105, rue Hermine, Québec QC G1K 1Y5 – 418/529-2501; Fax: 418/529-1693 – 226 lits – Dir. gen., Robert Laroche

Québec: Centre de services Saint-Charles, 850, rue de Beaujeu, Québec QC G1J 2R6 – 418/529-6571 – 93 lits

Québec: Centre d'hébergement Champlain-Limoilou, 220, rue de la Sapinière Dorion est, Québec QC G1L 1P5 – 418/623-1824; Fax: 418/623-1824 – 32 lits – Dir., Soins infirmiers, Janine Turgeon

Québec: Centre hospitalier St-François inc., 1604, 1re av, Québec QC G1L 3L6 – 418/524-6033; Fax: 418/524-9542 – 29 lits – Dir. des soins, Josée Gosselin

Québec: Centre hospitalier universitaire de Québec - Pavillon St-François-d'Assise, *see* Centres hospitaliers listings

Québec: Centre Louis-Hebert, 1550, rue de la Pointe-aux-Lievres nord, Québec QC G1L 4M8 – 418/524-2496; Fax: 418/529-3450 – 52 lits – Dir. gen. par interim, Richard Rousseau

Québec: La Champenoise, 990, rue Gerard Moriseet, Québec QC G1S 1X6 – 418/681-4637 – 20 lits – Dir. gen., André la Roche

Québec: Habitation Grande Allee, 1175, rue Turnbull, Québec QC G1R 5L5 – 418/522-3979; Fax: 418/522-7870 – 78 lits – Dir. gen., Michel Baumont, 418/691-2352

Québec: Hôpital de l'Enfant-Jésus (Centre Maizerets), 2480, ch de la Canardiére, Québec QC G1J 2G1 – 418/663-3518; Fax: 418/663-8501 – 54 lits – Dir. gen., Gaston Pellan

Québec: Pavillon la Residence Langelier, 350, boul Langelier, Québec QC G1K 5N3 – 418/524-1477 – 26 places – Dir. gen., Robert Laroche

Québec: Pavillon Saint-Sacrement, *see* Centres hospitaliers listings

Québec: La Residence Grande-Allee, 1175, rue Turnbull, Québec QC G1R 5L5 – 418/522-3979 – 29 places – Dir. gen., Robert Laroche

Rawdon: Centre d'accueil Heather II, 3468, 3e av, Rawdon QC J0K 1S0 – 514/834-2512; Fax: 514/834-5805; EMail: klein1@total.net – 40 lits – Regie régionale de la santé et des services sociaux de Lanaudière – Dir. gen., Paul Arbec

Rawdon: CHSLD Heather I, 3931 Lakeshore Dr., Rawdon QC J0K 1S0 – 514/834-2512 – 76 lits

Repentigny: Centre le Gardeur, 60, boul Aubert, Repentigny QC J6A 4N8 – 514/585-5933 – 78 lits – Dir. gen., Yvon Poirier

Repentigny: Pavillon LeBlanc - Longpre Enr., 14, rue Leonie, Repentigny QC J6A 3A8 – 514/585-4206 – 24 places – Dir. gen., Yvon Poirier

Repentigny: Pavillon-Ste-Therese, 697, rue Notre-Dame, Repentigny QC J6A 2W9 – 514/581-6143 – 21 places – Dir. gen., Claude Desjardins

Richmond: Foyer Richmond inc., 980, rue McGauran, CP 860, Richmond QC J0B 2H0 – 819/826-3711; Fax: 819/826-5724 – 64 lits – Dir. gen., Nicole Corbin

Rigaud: Foyer de Rigaud inc., 5, rue d'Amour, Rigaud QC J0P 1P0 – 514/453-5860; Fax: 514/451-6370 – 66 lits – Régie régionale de la santé et des services sociaux de la Montérégie – Dir. gen., Lise Belisle Bélanger

Rimouski: Le Foyer de Rimouski inc., 645, boul Saint-Germain, Rimouski QC G5L 3S2 – 418/724-4111; Fax: 418/724-0604 – 242 lits – Dir. gen., Gilles Gauvreau

Rimouski: Manoir de Caroline inc., 280, rue Belzile, Rimouski QC G5L 8K7 – 418/723-0611; Fax: 418/723-0615 – 85 lits – Dir. gen., Claude Talbot

Ripon: Centre d'accueil de Ripon, 46, rue Principale, CP 70, Ripon QC J0V 1V0 – 819/983-6173; Fax: 819/983-1494 – 42 lits – Dir. gen., Denise Bergevin

Rivière-Beaudette: Pavillon Ste-Anne Enr., 990, ch Sainte-Claire, Rivière-Beaudette QC J0P 1R0 – 514/269-2167 – 22 places – Dir. gen., Paul-Henri Boutin

Rivière-Bleue: Villa de la Rivière, 45, rue du Foyer, CP 98, Rivière-Bleue QC G0L 2B0 – 418/893-5511; Fax: 418/893-7151 – 43 lits – Dir. gen., Rejean Pelletier

Rivière-du-Loup: Hôpital Saint-Joseph, 28, rue Joly, Rivière-du-Loup QC G5R 3H2 – 418/862-6385; Fax: 418/862-1986 – 142 lits – Dir. gen., Gilles Paradis

Rivière-du-Loup: Villa Fraserville inc., 70, rue Saint-Henri, Rivière-du-Loup QC G5R 2A1 – 418/862-7251; Fax: 418/862-2902 – 39 lits – Dir. gen., Raymond April

Rivière-Ouelle: Centre d'accueil Therese Martin, 100, ch de la Petite Anse, Rivière-Ouelle QC G0L 2C0 – 418/856-4433; Fax: 418/856-4381 – 126 lits – Dir. gen., Jean-Claude Rousseau

Roberval: Le Domaine du Bon Temps, 400, av Bergeron, Roberval QC G8H 1K8 – 418/275-3623 – 63 lits – Dir. gen., Bernard Fortin

Roberval: Pavillon Ferland, 992, boul Saint-Joseph, Roberval QC G8H 2L9 – 418/275-4376 – 23 places – Dir. gen., Laurent Bouillon

Rouyn-Noranda: Centre d'accueil Youville, 3, 9e rue, Rouyn-Noranda QC J9X 2A9 – 819/764-3281 – 75 lits – Dir. gen., Gerard Marinovich

Rouyn-Noranda: Maison Pie XII, 512, av Richard, Rouyn Noranda QC J9X 4M1 – 819/762-0908; Fax: 819/764-5036 – 82 places – Dir. gen., Daniel Bergeron

Rouyn-Noranda: Pavillon Claude Larouche, 30, rue Monseigneur Tessier est, Rouyn-Noranda QC J9X 3B9 – 819/764-4706 – 29 places – Dir. gen., Daniel Bergeron

Ste-Agathe-des-Monts: Centre hospitalier Laurentien - Foyer Ste-Agathe, 21, rue Godon ouest, Ste-Agathe-des-Monts QC J8C 1E5 – 819/326-1141 – 55 lits – Dir. gen., Jacques Gaudette

Ste-Agathe-des-Monts: Centre hospitalier Laurentien - Pavillon Grignon, 2, rue Préfontaine ouest, Ste-Agathe-des-Monts QC J8C 1C3 – 514/326-3551; Fax: 514/324-4010 – 32 lits – Dir. gen., Jacques Gaudette

Ste-Agathe-des-Monts: Centre hospitalier Laurentien - Pavillon Sinai, 100, ch Mont Sinai, Ste-Agathe-des-Monts QC J8C 3A4 – 819/326-2303 – 67 lits – Dir. gen., Jacques Guadette

Saint-Alexandre: Foyer Villa Maria inc., 404, av du Foyer, Saint-Alexandre QC G0L 2G0 – 418/495-2914; Fax: 418/495-2829 – 78 lits – Dir. gen., Jean-Claude Rousseau

Saint-André-Avellin: Centre d'accueil la Petite Nation, 76, rue Saint-André, CP 230, Saint-André-Avellin QC J0V 1W0 – 819/983-2731; Fax: 819/983-7812 – 71 lits – Dir. gen., André Dupuis

Ste-Anne-de-la-Pérade: Foyer de la Pérade inc., 60, rue de la Fabrique, CP 217, Ste-Anne-de-la-Pérade QC G0X 2J0 – 418/325-2313; Fax: 418/325-2313 – 47 lits – Dir. gen., Gilles Cossette

Saint-Anselme: Pavillon de l'age d'or St-Anselme inc., 40, rue Saint-Marc, Saint-Anselme QC G0R 2N0 – 418/885-4482 – 48 lits – Dir. gen., Yvan de Blois

Saint-Antoine-sur-Richelieu: Accueil du Rivage inc., 1008, rue du Rivage, CP 60, Saint-Antoine-sur-Richelieu QC J0L 1R0 – 514/787-3163; Fax: 514/787-1156 – 36 lits – Dir. gen., J. André Bergeron

Saint-Antonin: Le Foyer de St-Antonin inc., 286, rue Principale, Saint-Antonin QC G0L 2J0 – 418/862-7993; Fax: 418/862-5278 – 39 lits – Dir. gen., Raymond April

Saint-Apollinaire: La Lignée Lotbinière, 32, rue Industrielle, CP 310, Saint-Apollinaire QC G0S 2E0 – 418/881-3982; Fax: 418/881-3482 – 40 lits – Dir. gen., André Paquet

St-Augustin-De-Desmaures: CHSLD St-Augustin, 4954, rue Marie Le Franc, St-Augustin-De-Desmaures QC G3A 1V5 – 418/871-1232; Fax: 418/871-0744 – 87 lits – Dir. gen., Vincenzo Simonetta

St-Augustin-de-Desmaures: Jardins du Haut Saint-Laurent (1992) enr., 4770, rue Saint-Felix, St-Augustin-de-Desmaures QC G3A 1B1 – 418/872-4936; Fax: 418/872-4245 – 110 lits – Dir. gen., Nathalie Côté

Saint-Basile: Pavillon Saint-Basile, 329, rue de l'Eglise, Saint-Basile QC G0A 3G0 – 418/329-2066 – 21 places – Dir. gen., Fernand Morasse

Ste-Béatrix: Pavillon Ste-Béatrix Enr., #1100-1102, rang Sainte-Cecile, Ste-Béatrix QC J0K 1Y0 – 514/883-8405 – 14 places – Dir. gen., Maurice Blais

St-Benoît-Labre: Pavillon Baillargeon inc., 357, Rte 271, St-Benoît-Labre QC G0M 1P0 – 418/228-9141 – 28 places – Dir. gen., Richard Busque

Saint-Bernard-de-Lacolle: Residence Florence Groulx inc., 7, rang Saint-Louis, Saint-Bernard-de-Lacolle QC J0J 1V0 – 514/246-2232; Fax: 514/246-4111 – 50 lits – Dir. gen., André Gaudette

St-Boniface-de-Shawinigan: Pavillon St-Boniface inc., 50, rue Principale, St-Boniface-de-Shawinigan QC G0X 2L0 – 819/535-3223 – 16 places – Dir. gen., Jacques Veillette

Saint-Bruno: Centre Montarville, 265, boul Seigneuriale ouest, Saint-Bruno QC J3V 2H4 – 514/461-2650 – 150 lits – Dir. gen., Ghislain Lavergne

St-Casimir: Centre régional d'hébergement et de santé de Portneuf - Centre d'hébergement Saint-Casimir, 605, ruc Fleury, CP 10, St-Casimir QC G0A 3L0 – 418/339-2861 – 63 lits – Dir. gen., Fernand Morasse

Ste-Cecile: Pavillon Ste-Cecile, 4581, rue Principale, Ste-Cecile QC G0Y 1J0 – 819/583-0400 – 15 places – Dir. gen., Raymonde Lapointe-Lagueux

St-Célestin: Foyer de St-Célestin, 475, rue Houde, CP 90, St-Célestin QC J0C 1G0 – 819/229-3617; Fax: 819/229-1165 – 52 lits – Dir. gen. (par intérim), Pierre Levasseur

St-Césaire: Residence Val-Joli, 1425, rue Notre-Dame, St-Césaire QC J0L 1T0 – 514/469-3194 – 39 lits – Dir. gen., Michel Desnoyers

Ste-Claire: Villa Prevost inc., 84, boul Begin sud, CP 490, Ste-Claire QC G0R 2V0 – 418/883-3357; Fax: 418/883-4204 – 51 lits – Dir. gen., Yvan Deblois

Ste-Croix: Centre d'accueil de Ste-Croix, 6245, rue Principale, Ste-Croix QC G0S 2H0 – 418/926-3247 – 48 lits – Dir. gen., André Paquet

St-Cyprien: Foyer St-Cyprien inc., 175, rue Principale, CP 118, St-Cyprien QC G0L 2P0 – 418/963-2018; Fax: 418/963-2499 – 46 lits – Dir. gen., Robert Gagnon

St-David: Centre d'accueil St-David inc., 10, rue Rivière, St-David QC J0G 1L0 – 514/789-2033; Fax: 514/789-2994 – 45 lits – Dir. gen., Mohammed Settouche

St-Donat: Foyer de St-Donat inc., 430, rue Bellevue, CP 250, St-Donat QC J0T 2C0 – 819/424-2503; Fax: 819/424-5639 – 41 lits – Dir. gen., Jean-Jacques Lamarche

St-Édouard-de-Frampton: Les CHSLD Nouvelle-Beauce-Frampton, 148, rue Principale, St-Édouard-de-Frampton QC G0R 1M0 – 418/479-2970 – 33 lits – Dir. gen., Benoit Guillemette

Ste-Élisabeth: Centre d'accueil Ste-Élisabeth, 2410, rue Principale, Ste-Élisabeth QC J0K 2J0 – 514/759-8355; Fax: 514/759-9750 – 108 lits – Dir. gen. par interim, Paul Parent

Ste-Élisabeth: Residence Ste-Élisabeth Enr., 250, rue Principale, Ste-Élisabeth QC J0A 1M0 – 819/358-2771 – 17 places – Dir. gen., Gilles Perreault

St-Éphrem-de-Beauce: Foyer Ste-Famille inc., 1, rue Plante, CP 310, St-Éphrem-de-Beauce QC G0M 1R0 – 418/484-2121; Fax: 418/484-2144 – 36 lits – Dir. gen., Real Roy

St-Eugene: Centre d'accueil de St-Eugene de l'Islet Inc., 24, rue Commerciale, St-Eugene QC G0R 1X0 – 418/247-3927; Fax: 418/247-3928 – 36 lits – Dir. gen., Pierrette D. Guimond

St-Eustache: Centre d'accueil l'Ermitage, 112, 25e av, St-Eustache QC J7P 2V2 – 514/473-5961; Fax: 514/491-1847 – 111 lits – Dir. gen., Kevin Shemie

St-Eustache: Manoir St-Eustache, 55, rue Chenier, St-Eustache QC J7R 4Y8 – 514/472-0013; Fax: 514/472-0016 – 74 lits – Dir. gen., Denis Renaud

St-Eustache: Pavillon St-Louis inc., 154, rue St-Louis, St-Eustache QC J7R 1Y2 – 514/472-9002 – 23 places – Dir. gen., Denis Renaud

Saint-Fabien-de-Panet: Centre d'accueil de Saint-Fabien-de-Panet, 19, rue Principale, Saint-Fabien-de-Panet QC G0R 2J0 – 418/249-4051; Fax: 418/249-2371 – 45 lits – Dir. gen., Jean-Paul Lacroix

St-Félicien: Le Foyer de la Paix inc., 1229, boul Sacre-Coeur, CP 400, St-Félicien QC G8K 1A5 – 418/679-1585; Fax: 418/679-2376 – 44 lits – Dir. gen., Claude J.Y. Theberge

St-Félicien: Pavillon de l'Amitie, 996, 1e rue, St-Félicien QC G8K 1Y4 – 418/679-1777 – 20 places – Dir. gen., Claude J.Y. Theberge

Ste-Félicité: Pavillon Marie-Anna, 170, boul Perron, CP 188, Ste-Félicité QC G0J 2K0 – 418/733-4851 – 16 places – Dir. gen., Clement Gauthier

St-Flavien: Le Foyer de St-Flavien, 82, rue Principale, St-Flavien QC G0S 2M0 – 418/728-2727 – 41 lits – Dir. gen., André Paquet

Ste-Foy: Foyer Notre-Dame de Foy inc., 2580, ch Sainte-Foy, Ste-Foy QC G1V 1T9 – 418/653-3626; Fax: 418/654-9307 – 18 lits – Dir. gen., Jean-René Desmarais

Ste-Foy: Pavillon Hélène-de-Champlain, 809, rue du Chanoine Scott, Ste-Foy QC G1V 3N5 – 418/656-6957 – 23 places – Dir. gen., Jacques Garneau

Ste-Foy: Residence Paul Triquet, 789, rue de Belmont, Ste-Foy QC G1V 4V2 – 418/657-6890 – 64 lits – Dir. gen., Gérard Roy

Saint-François de Sales: Pavillon St-François de Sales, 306, rue du Foyer, CP 28, Saint-François de Sales QC G0W 1M0 – 418/348-6798 – 20 places – Dir. gen., Claude J.-Y. Theberge

St-Gabriel-de-Brandon: Centre d'accueil Desy inc., 90, rue Maskinonge, CP 840, St-Gabriel-de-Brandon QC J0K 2N0 – 514/835-4712; Fax: 514/835-7606 – 54 lits – Dir. gen., Real Naud

St-Gabriel-de-Brandon: Pavillon Laurette Boucher, 200, rue Saint-Gabriel, St-Gabriel-de-Brandon QC J0K 2N0 – 514/835-5083 – 13 places – Dir. gen., Real Naud

St-Gabriel-de-Brandon: Pavillon Ma-Mi Enr., 156, rue Dequoy, St-Gabriel-de-Brandon QC J0K 2N0 – 514/835-4969 – 15 places – Dir. gen., Real Naud

St-Gabriel-de-Brandon: Pavillon St-Gabriel Enr., 179, rue Maskinonge, St-Gabriel-de-Brandon QC J0K 2N0 – 514/835-5309 – 14 places – Dir. gen., Maurice Blais

St-Gabriel-de-Brandon: Residence Chez Maman Enr., 1780, rang 6, St-Gabriel-de-Brandon QC J0K 2N0 – 514/835-5123 – 20 lits – Dir. gen., Guylaine Comtois-Lavoie

St-Gabriel-de-Rimouski: Pavillon Fortin Enr., 309, rue Principale, CP 130, St-Gabriel-de-Rimouski QC G0K 1M0 – 418/798-8888 – 25 places – Dir. gen., Ronald Anctil

Saint-Georges Est: L'Accueil de Ville Saint-Georges Inc., 11515, 8e av, Saint-Georges Est QC G5Y 1J5 – 418/228-2021 – 50 lits – Dir. gen., Richard Busque

Saint-Georges: Centre d'accueil St-Louis Inc., 16705, 1e av, Saint-Georges QC G5Y 2G6 – 418/228-2041; Fax: 418/228-9365 – 45 lits – Dir. gen., Gerard Gendreau

Saint-Georges: Le Foyer Saint-Georges de Beauce Inc., 405, 18e rue, Saint-Georges QC G5Y 4T2 – 418/228-2081 – 55 lits – Dir. gen., Richard Busque

Saint-Georges: Residence du Bon Pasteur, 300, 18e rue, Saint-Georges QC G5Y 4S9 – 418/228-9015 – 29 places – Dir. gen., Richard Busque

St-Gérard: Pavillon St-Gérard, 339, rue Roy nord, St-Gérard QC G0Y 1K0 – 819/877-2032 – 17 places – Dir. gen., Albert Kratsenberg

St-Gervais: Foyer St-Gervais inc., 70, rue Saint-Etienne, St-Gervais QC G0R 3C0 – 418/887-3387; Fax: 418/887-3388 – 37 lits – Dir. gen., Yvan Deblois

Ste-Hénédine: Les CHSLD Nouvelle-Beauce-Ste-Hénédine, 104, Rte Langevin, CP 40, Ste-Hénédine QC G0S 2R0 – 418/935-3658 – 47 lits – Dir. gen., Benoit Guillemette

St-Honoré-de-Beauce: Centre d'accueil St-Honoré, 452, rue Principale, CP 160, St-Honoré-de-Beauce QC G0M 1V0 – 418/485-6357; Fax: 418/485-6232 – 33 lits – Dir. gen., Richard Busque

Saint-Hubert: CHSLD Montérégie, 2042, boul Marie, Saint-Hubert QC J4T 2B4 – 514/671-5596; Fax: 514/671-5079 – 90 lits – Dir. gen., Vincenzo Simonetta

Saint-Hubert: Pavillon Residence Saint-Hubert, 5160, montee Saint-Hubert, Saint-Hubert QC J3Y 1V7 – 514/676-8411 – 38 places – Dir. gen., Jean-Pierre Montpetit

Saint-Hubert: Pavillon St-Hubert, 3823, rue Grand Boulevard, Saint-Hubert QC J4T 2M3 – 514/445-3598; Fax: 514/462-0838 – 32 lits – Dir. gen., Kevin Shemie

St-Hyacinthe: Pavillon Girouard, 2320, rue Girouard, St-Hyacinthe QC J2S 3B1 – 514/774-9022 – 30 places – Dir. gen., Ghislaine Lavergne

St-Hyacinthe: Residence Gaucher-Heroux inc., 2935, rue St-Pierre ouest, St-Hyacinthe QC J2T 1R7 – 514/774-1927 – 29 lits – Dir. gen., Yvon St-Laurent

St-Hyacinthe: Villa des Frenes Inc., 2755, av Raymond, St-Hyacinthe QC J2S 5W8 – 514/773-4688; Fax: 514/467-4210 – 77 lits – Dir. gen., Ghislaine Lavergne

St-Isidore-de-Dorchester: Les CHSLD Nouvelle-Beauce-St-Isidore, 102, rue Saint-Albert, St-Isidore-de-Dorchester QC G0S 2S0 – 418/882-5601 – 45 lits – Dir. gen., Benoit Guillemette

St-Jacques: Foyer St-Jacques, 30, rue Sainte-Anne, St-Jacques QC J0K 2R0 – 514/839-2695 – 55 lits – Dir. gen., Jacques Beaupre

Saint-Jean-de-Boischatel: Pavillon des Chutes, 5500, boul Sainte-Anne, Saint-Jean-de-Boischatel QC G0A 1H0 – 418/822-2578 – 29 places – Dir. gen., Robert Laroche

St-Jean-de-Dieu: Villa Dube inc., 20, rue de la Villa, CP 10, St-Jean-de-Dieu QC G0L 3M0 – 418/963-2713; Fax: 418/963-2493 – 42 lits – Dir. gen., Donald Gagnon

St-Jean-sur-Richelieu: Centre Georges Phaneuf, 230, rue Jacques-Cartier nord, St-Jean-sur-Richelieu QC J3B 6T4 – 514/346-1133; Fax: 514/346-2199 – 135 lits – Dir. gen., André Trottier

St-Jean-sur-Richelieu: Centre Gertrude Lafrance, 150, boul St-Luc, St-Jean-sur-Richelieu QC J3A 1G2 – 514/348-4941; Fax: 514/348-7693 – 211 lits – Dir. gen., André Trottier

St-Jérôme: L'Auberge (St-Jérôme) Inc., 66, rue Danis, St-Jérôme QC J7Y 2R3 – 514/436-3131; Fax: 514/436-4139 – 81 lits – Dir. gen., Germain Beauséjour

Saint-Jérôme: Centre d'Youville, 531, rue Laviolette, Saint-Jérôme QC J7Y 2T8 – 514/436-3061; Fax: 514/436-8328 – 128 lits – Dir. gen., Germain Beauséjour

St-Jérôme: Foyer Soleil inc., 225, ch du Lac Bertrand, RR#2, St-Jérôme QC J7Z 5T5 – 514/438-1704; Fax: 514/438-6594 – 53 lits – Dir. gen., Richard Parisien

St-Joseph-de-Beauce: Foyer Mgr O. Roy, 755, rue Sainte-Christine, St-Joseph-de-Beauce QC G0S 2V0 – 418/397-6817; Fax: 418/397-6642 – 78 lits – Dir. gen., Richard Busque

St-Joseph-de-Coleraine: Pavillon Coulombe, 212, av Proulx, St-Joseph-de-Coleraine QC G0N 1B0 – 418/423-4527 – 20 places – Dir. gen., André Rodrigue

St-Jovite: Residence St-Jovite, 925, rue Ouimet, CP 910, St-Jovite QC J0T 2H0 – 819/425-2793 – 56 lits – Dir. gen., Yvan Lachaine

Ste-Justine: Foyer Ste-Justine, 100, rue du Foyer, CP 129, Succ Langevin, Ste-Justine QC G0R 1Y0 – 418/383-3413 – 28 lits – Dir. gen., Jean-Yves Julien

Saint-Lambert: CHSLD de la MRC de Champlain, 831, av Notre-Dame, Saint-Lambert QC J4R 1S1 – 514/672-3320; Fax: 514/672-3370 – 281 lits – Dir. gen., Jean-Denis Godbout

St-Lazare-de-Bellechasse: Pavillon V. Audet, 121, rue Principale, St-Lazare-de-Bellechasse QC G0R 3J0 – 418/883-2384 – 14 places – Dir. gen., Yvan Deblois

St-Liguori: Foyer St-Liguori, 771, rue Principale, St-Liguori QC J0K 2X0 – 514/753-7062 – 44 lits – Dir. gen., Jacques Beaupre

St-Louis-du-Ha-Ha: Foyer Beausejour inc., 25, rue Saint-Philippe, St-Louis-du-Ha-Ha QC G0L 3S0 – 418/854-2631; Fax: 418/854-0430 – 54 lits – Dir. gen., Rejean Pelletier

Ste-Luce: Pavillon Ste-Luce, 51, rte du Fleuve ouest, CP 166, Ste-Luce QC G0K 1P0 – 418/739-3555 – 16 places – Dir. gen., Ronald Anctil

St-Ludger: Pavillon St-Ludger inc., 210, rue de la Salle, CP 99, St-Ludger QC G0M 1W0 – 819/548-5551; Fax: 819/548-5553 – 34 lits – Dir. gen., Raymonde Lapointe-Lagueux

St-Magloire: Foyer St-Magloire inc., 15, rue de la Caisse Populaire, CP 39, St-Magloire QC G0R 3M0 – 418/257-2881; Fax: 418/257-2187 – 33 lits – Dir. gen., Jean-Yves Julien

St-Magloire: Pavillon Lefrance Enr., 104, rue Principale, St-Magloire QC G0R 3M0 – 418/257-2951 – 14 places – Dir. gen., Jean-Yves Julien

St-Marc-des-Carrières: Centre régional d'hébergement et de santé Portneuf - Centre d'hébergement Saint-Marc-des-Carrières, 444, rue Beauchamps, CP 220, St-Marc-des-Carrières QC G0A 4B0 – 418/268-3511 – 53 lits – Dir. gen., Fernand Morasse

Saint-Methode-de-Frontenac: Foyer Valin inc., 28, rue des Erables, CP 160, Saint-Methode-de-Frontenac QC G0N 1S0 – 418/422-2362; Fax: 418/422-2448 – 72 lits – Dir. gen., André Rodrigue

St-Michel-de-Bellechasse: CHSLD Notre-Dame de Lourdes, 80, rue Principale, CP 10, St-Michel-de-Bellechasse QC G0R 3S0 – 418/884-2811; Fax: 418/884-3714 – 80 lits – Dir. gen., Giovanni Simonetta

St-Michel-des-Saints: Centre d'accueil Brassard inc., 390, rue Brassard, CP 309, St-Michel-des-Saints QC J0K 3B0 – 514/833-6331; Fax: 514/833-6093 – 35 lits – Dir. gen. par intérim, Jean-Jacques Lamarche

Saint-Michel-du-Squatec: Hôpital Saint-Michel-du-Squatec, 10, rue Saint-Andre, CP 177, Saint-Michel-du-Squatec QC G0L 4H0 – 418/855-2442; Fax: 418/855-2357 – 23 lits – Dir. gen., Réjean Pelletier

St-Narcisse: Centre d'accueil de St-Narcisse inc., 361, rue du College, St-Narcisse QC G0X 2Y0 – 418/328-3351; Fax: 418/328-4140 – 37 lits – Dir. gen., Gilles Cossette

St-Odilon: Villa St-Odilon, 377, rue Langevin, CP 160, St-Odilon QC G0S 3A0 – 418/464-4731; Fax: 418/464-4732 – 28 lits – Dir. gen., Richard Busque

Saint-Pacôme: CHSLD Regroupement Kamouraska, Centre Anjou, 127, rue Galarneau, Saint-Pacôme QC G0L 3X0 – 418/852-2281; Fax: 418/852-3230 – 72 lits – Dir. gen., Jean-Claude Rousseau

Saint-Pamphile: Residence Bellevue, 88, rue du Foyer, Saint-Pamphile QC G0R 3X0 – 418/356-3843 – 33 lits – Dir. gen., Bernard Lamy

Saint-Pascal: Villa Saint-Pascal inc., 575, av Martin, CP 520, Saint-Pascal QC G0L 3Y0 – 418/492-2342; Fax: 418/492-1793 – 82 lits – Dir. gen., Jean-Claude Rousseau

St-Paulin: Pavillon St-Paulin inc., 2680, rang Saint-Louis, St-Paulin QC J0K 3G0 – 819/268-5202 – 30 places – Dir. gen., Jacques Veillette

Ste-Perpétue-de-L'Islet: Residence du Bonheur, 8, av du Foyer, Ste-Perpétue-de-L'Islet QC G0R 3Z0 – 418/359-2247 – 40 lits – Dir. gen., Bernard Lamy

St-Pierre-D'Orléans: Hôpital de l'Enfant-Jésus (Villa Alphonse Bonenfant), 1199, ch Royal, St-Pierre-D'Orléans QC G0A 4E0 – 418/828-9114 – 50 lits – Dir. gen., Gaston Pellan

St-Pierre-les-Becquets: Foyer Romain Becquet Inc., 255, Rte. Marie-Victorin, St-Pierre-les-Becquets QC G0X 2Z0 – 819/263-2245; Fax: 819/263-2636 – 40 lits – Dir. gen., Raymond Dion

St-Prosper-de-Dorchester: Pavillon de l'hospitalité, 2770, 20e av, St-Prosper-de-Dorchester QC G0M 1Y0 – 418/594-8174 – 46 lits – Dir. gen., Jean-Yves Julien

St-Raphaèl-de-Bellechasse: Foyer St-Raphael Inc., 84, rue du Foyer, St-Raphaèl-de-Bellechasse QC G0R 4C0 – 418/243-2855; Fax: 418/243-2990 – 59 lits – Dir. gen., Yvan Deblois

Saint-Raymond: Centre régional d'hébergement et de santé de Portneuf - Centre d'hébergement Saint-Raymond, 324. rue Saint-Joseph, CP 490, Saint-Raymond QC G0A 4G0 – 418/337-4661 – 64 lits – Dir. gen., Fernand Morasse

St-Rémi: Centre d'accueil Pierre-Remi-Narbonne, 110, rue du College, St-Rémi QC J0L 2L0 – 514/454-4694; Fax: 514/454-3614 – 56 lits – Dir. gen., Gaetan Roy

St-Romuald: Le Foyer Chanoine Audet inc., 2155, ch du Sault, St-Romuald QC G6W 2K7 – 418/839-8845; Fax: 418/839-2800 – 55 lits – Dir. gen., Marcel Bernard

St-Romuald: Villa Beausejour, 2230, boul Rive sud, St-Romuald QC G6W 2S4 – 418/839-7801 – 38 places – Dir. gen., Marcel Bernard

St-Sauveur-des-Monts: Villa du Vieux Sapin inc., 55, rue Hochard, St-Sauveur-des-Monts QC J0R 1R0 – 514/227-2241; Fax: 514/227-6186 – 34 lits – Dir. gen., Colette Desjardins

St-Siméon: Foyer de Notre-Dame du Sacré-Coeur de St-Simeon, 371, rue Saint-Laurent, CP 7, St-Siméon QC G0T 1X0 – 418/638-2414; Fax: 418/638-2470 – 38 lits – Dir. gen., Benoit Guerin

Ste-Sophie: Centre d'hébergement Jaclo Inc., 2319, rue Sainte-Marie, CP 129, Ste-Sophie QC J0R 1S0 – 514/436-5627; Fax: 514/436-6663 – 31 lits – Dir. gen., Claude Briere

St-Stanislas-de-Champlain: Centre d'accueil St-Stanislas inc., 255, rue Principale, CP 99, St-Stanislas-de-Champlain QC G0X 3E0 – 418/328-3142; Fax: 418/328-4172 – 43 lits – Dir. gen., Paul Sills

St-Sulpice: Pavillon St-Sulpice, 1625, rue Notre-Dame, St-Sulpice QC J0K 3J0 – 514/581-7141 – 14 places – Dir. gen., Yvon Poirier

St-Sylvestre: Le Foyer de St-Sylvestre Inc., 828, rue Principale, St-Sylvestre QC G0S 3C0 – 418/596-2217; Fax: 418/596-2218 – 31 lits – Dir. gen., Germain Leblond

St-Sylvestre: Pavillon Michel Blais inc., 53, rang Sainte-Catherine, St-Sylvestre QC G0S 3C0 – 418/596-2764 – 14 places – Dir. gen., Germain Leblond

St-Thecle: Foyer de Saint-Thecle inc., 651, rue Saint-Jacques, CP 246, St-Thecle QC G0X 3G0 – 418/289-2114; Fax: 418/289-3538 – 48 lits – Dir. gen., Gilles Cossette

Ste-Thérèse: Centres Drapeau et Deschambault, 100, rue Chanoine Lionel Groulx, Ste-Thérèse QC J7E 5E1 – 514/437-4267; Fax: 514/437-0788 – 228 lits – Dir. gen., André Poirier

Ste-Thérèse: Pavillon Marie-Thérèse Inc., 44, rue Dagenais, Ste-Thérèse QC J7E 3C8 – 514/435-0451 – 12 places – Dir. gen., André Poirier

St-Thomas-de-Joliette: Centre d'accueil St-Thomas - Siege Social, 791, rue Principale, St-Thomas-de-Joliette QC J0K 3L0 – 514/759-1513 – 32 lits – Dir. gen., Paul-Yves Laviolette

St-Timothée: La Maison des Aine(e)s, 1, rue des Aines, St-Timothée QC J6S 6M8 – 514/377-3925; Fax: 514/377-3490 – 38 lits – Dir. gen., Denis Charland

St-Tite-des-Caps: Centre d'accueil St-Tite-des-Caps, 97, av de la Montagne, St-Tite-des-Caps QC G0A 4J0 – 418/823-2440 – 86 lits – Dir. gen., Jean-Yves Simard

St-Tite: Foyer Mgr Paquin inc., 580, rue du Couvent, CP 400, St-Tite QC G0X 3H0 – 418/365-5107; Fax: 418/365-7914 – 63 lits – Dir. gen., Gilles Cossette

St-Urbain-de-Charlevoix: Pavillon le Gite, 1070, rue Saint-Edouard, St-Urbain-de-Charlevoix QC G0A 4K0 – 418/439-3362 – 20 places – Dir. gen., Robert Vallieres

Ste-Véronique: Pavillon Michel et Liliane Heafey, 1808, Rte. 117, CP 323, Ste-Véronique QC J0W 1X0 – 819/275-3116 – 16 places – Dir. gen., Pierre Page

St-Zacharie: Pavillon Garant, 668, 12e av, St-Zacharie QC G0M 2C0 – 418/593-3267 – 26 places – Dir. gen., Jean-Yves Julien

Sainte-Agathe-des-Monts: Foyer Sainte-Agathe, 21, rue Godon ouest, Sainte-Agathe-des-Monts QC J8C 1E5 – 819/326-1141 – 55 lits – Dir. gen., Jacques Gaudette

Sainte-Anne-de-Beaupré: Pavillon Sainte-Anne, 10632, boul Sainte-Anne, Sainte-Anne-de-Beaupré QC G0A 3C0 – 418/827-5093 – 16 places – Dir. gen., Rejean Cantin

Sainte-Marguerite-du-Lac-Masson: Manoir de la Pointe Blueue (1978), 428, av Baron Empain, RR#1, Sainte-Marguerite-du-Lac-Masson QC J0T 1L0 – 514/228-2503; Fax: 514/228-2503 – 91 lits – Dir. gen., Jacqueline Gagnon

Sainte-Marie: Les CHSLD Nouvelle-Beauce-Sainte-Marie, 40, boul Vachon, CP 99, Sainte-Marie QC G6E 3B4 – 418/387-5228; Fax: 418/387-3782 – 65 lits – Dir. gen., Marc Tanguay

Sainte-Marthe-du-Cap: Pavillon des Aines, 2460, rue Notre-Dame, Sainte-Marthe-du-Cap QC G8T 8B3 – 819/374-6551 – 31 places – Dir. gen., Vital Guadet

Salaberry-de-Valleyfield: Les Centres du Haut St-Laurent (CHSLD), 18, rue de la Fabrique, Salaberry-de-Valleyfield QC J6T 4G8 – 514/373-4013; Fax: 514/373-0325; EMail: chsl@rocler.qc.ca – 280 lits – Régie régionale de la santé et des services sociaux de la Montérégie – Dir. gen., Claude-Yves de Repentigny

Sayabec: Foyer Sainte-Marie de Sayabec, 1, rue Saindon, CP 130, Sayabec QC G0J 3K0 – 418/536-5456 – 31 lits – Dir. gen., Alain Paquet

Sept-Îles: Pavillon des Îles, 540, av Franquelin, Sept-Îles QC G4R 2M1 – 418/962-9801; Fax: 418/962-6420 – 60 lits – Dir. gen., Charlotte Audet

Shawinigan-Sud: Centre d'accueil de Shawinigan-Sud Inc., 80, 118e rue, CP 1160, Shawinigan-Sud QC G9P 4E8 – 819/537-0111; Fax: 819/537-1895 – 41 lits – Dir. gen., Raymond Guilbert

Shawinigan: Centre d'accueil les Chutes inc., 5000, av Albert-Tessier, Shawinigan QC G9N 6T6 – 819/533-5751; Fax: 819/539-5400 – 64 lits – Dir. gen., Jacques Moreau

Shawinigan: Centre d'accueil Dr. Joseph Garceau, 243, 1e rue, CP 4017, Shawinigan QC G9N 7Y5 – 819/537-5173 – 90 lits – Dir. gen., Raymond Guilbert

Shawinigan: Centre hospitalier Sainte-Thérèse, *see* Centres hospitaliers listings

Shawinigan: Foyer Dehauffe, 750, boul Saint-Maurice, Shawinigan QC G9N 1L6 – 819/536-5601; Fax: 819/536-4994 – 107 lits – Dir. gen., Raymond Guilbert

Shawville: Centre hospitalier du Pontiac, *see* Centres hospitaliers listings

Shawville: Pavillon Pontiac, 290, rue Marion, CP 2001, Shawville QC J0X 2Y0 – 819/647-5755; Fax: 819/647-2453 – 50 lits – Dir. gen., Michel Pigeon

Sherbrooke: Centre universitaire de santé de l'Estrie - site Bowen, *see* Centres hospitaliers listings

Sherbrooke: Le Foyer St-Joseph de Sherbrooke, 611, boul Queen nord, Sherbrooke QC J1H 3R6 – 819/564-6655; Fax: 819/564-6504 – 252 lits – Dir. gen., Benoit Mercier

Sherbrooke: Institut universitaire de gériatrie de Sherbrooke, *see* Centres hospitaliers listings

Sherbrooke: Maison Reine Marie inc., 1630, rue Galt ouest, Sherbrooke QC J1H 2B5 – 819/566-1414; Fax: 819/346-5081 – 48 lits – Dir. gen., Yoland Gregoire

Sherbrooke: Mont St-Dominique, 361, rue Moore, Sherbrooke QC J1H 1C1 – 819/346-5512; Fax: 819/563-5023 – 50 lits – Dir. gen., Matija Bojanic

Sherbrooke: Le Pavillon Catherine, 165, rue Moore, Sherbrooke QC J1H 1B8 – 819/567-7519 – 35 places – Dir. gen., Real Jacques

Sherbrooke: Pavillon Simon Cote Inc., 44, rue Kennedy sud, Sherbrooke QC J1G 2H6 – 819/563-2242 – 25 places

Sherbrooke: La Residence de l'Estrie de Sherbrooke Inc., 500, rue Murray, Sherbrooke QC J1G 2K6 – 819/569-5131; Fax: 819/822-4102 – 152 lits – Dir. gen., Real Jacques

Sillery: Pavillon Saint-Dominique, 1045, boul Saint-Cyrille ouest, Sillery QC G1S 1V3 – 418/681-3561; Fax: 418/687-9196 – 142 lits – Dir. gen., Jeanne Laliberte

Sillery: Saint Brigid's Home Inc., 1645, ch Saint-Louis, Sillery QC G1S 4M3 – 418/681-4689; Fax: 418/527-6882 – 162 lits – Dir. gen., Louis Hanrahan

Sorel: Foyer Richelieu inc., 40, rue de Ramesay, Sorel QC J3P 3Y7 – 514/742-5936 – 68 lits – Dir. gen., Yvan Rheault

Sorel: L'Hôpital général de Sorel, 151, rue George, Sorel QC J3P 1C8 – 514/746-5555; Fax: 514/746-4897 – 175 lits – Dir. gen., Jacques Blais

Sorel: Hôpital Richelieu Inc., 30, rue Ferland, Sorel QC J3P 3C7 – 514/743-5569; Fax: 514/743-1803 – 34 lits – Dir. gen., Jacques Blais

Sutton: Foyer Sutton, 50, rue Western, CP 719, Sutton QC J0E 2K0 – 514/538-3332; Fax: 514/538-0514 – 75 lits – Dir. gen., Claude Codere

Temiscaming: Pavillon de Temiscaming, 48, 5e rue, Temiscaming QC J0Z 3R0 – 819/627-3543 – 14 places – Dir. gen., Nicole Landry

Terrebonne: Centre d'accueil Lorrain inc., 834, rue Dupre, Terrebonne QC J6W 3K7 – 514/471-3303; Fax: 514/471-3498 – 24 lits – Dir. gen., Jacques Lorrain

Terrebonne: Centre d'hébergement des Moulins inc., 934, rue Saint-Sacrement, Terrebonne QC J6W 3G2 – 514/471-4885; Fax: 514/471-5095 – 55 lits – Dir. gen., Gerald Asselin

Terrebonne: Pavillon Longpre - Gravel, 575, rue Saint-Louis, Terrebonne QC J6W 1J3 – 514/471-8557 – 18 places – Dir. gen., Yvon Poirier

Thetford-Mines: Pavillon Jacques Boutin Enr., 736, boul Ouellet ouest, Thetford-Mines QC G6G 4X5 – 418/335-7681 – 26 places – Dir. gen., André Rodrigue

Thetford-Mines: Residence Denis Marcotte, 56, 9e rue est, Thetford-Mines QC G6G 5H5 – 418/338-4556; Fax: 418/338-6242 – 70 lits – Dir. gen., André Rodrigue

Tracy: Residence Sorel-Tracy inc., 4025, rue Frontenac, Tracy QC J3R 4G8 – 514/742-9427; Fax: 514/742-9668 – 64 lits – Dir. gen., Wilner Bien-Aimé

Trois-Pistoles: Centre hospitalier de Trois-Pistoles, 550, rue Nôtre-Dame est, Trois-Pistoles QC G0L 4K0 – 418/851-3301; Fax: 418/851-2934 – 125 lits – Dir. gen., Donald Gagnon

Trois-Rivières: Foyer Joseph-Denys Inc., 1274, rue Laviolette, Trois-Rivières QC G9A 1W4 – 819/378-4838; Fax: 819/374-6697 – 116 lits – Dir. gen., Gervais Morissette

Trois-Rivières: Pavillon la Cathedrale, 645, rue Bonaventure, Trois-Rivières QC G9A 2B8 – 819/373-9887 – 18 places – Dir. gen., Gervais Morissette

Trois-Rivières: Residence Cooke, 3450, rue Ste-Marguerite, Trois-Rivières QC G8Z 1X3 – 819/375-7713; Fax: 819/375-5659 – 153 lits – Dir. gen., Gervais Morissette

Trois-Rivières: Residence Louis Dennoncourt, 435, rue Saint-Roch, Trois-Rivières QC G9A 2L9 – 819/376-2566 – 75 lits – Dir. gen., Gervais Morissette

Upton: Domaine du Bel Age Enr., 906, rue Lanoi, Upton QC J0H 2E0 – 514/549-4405 – 9 lits – Dir. gen., Jacqueline Gosslin

Val-Brillant: Villa Mon Repos, 31, rue Saint-Pierre ouest, Val-Brillant QC G0J 3L0 – 418/742-3230 – 29 places – Dir. gen., Alain Paquet

Val-d'Or: Foyer de Val-d'Or Inc., 1212, av Brebeuf, Val-d'Or QC J9P 2C9 – 819/825-3093; Fax: 819/824-8745 – 96 lits – Dir. gen., Jean-Pierre Coté

Valcourt: Foyer de Valcourt inc., 1150, rue Champlain, CP 459, Valcourt QC J0E 2L0 – 514/532-3190; Fax: 514/532-3233 – 41 lits – Dir. gen., Nicole Corbin

Vallée-Jonction: Les CHSLD Nouvelle-Beauce-Vallée, 228, rue du Foyer, Vallée-Jonction QC G0S 3J0 – 418/253-5469 – 49 lits – Dir. gen., Benoit Guillemette

Vanier: Hôpital Christ-Roi, 300, boul Wilfrid-Hamel, Vanier QC G1M 2R9 – 418/682-1711; Fax: 418/682-5784 – 162 lits – Regie régionale de la santé et des services sociaux de la region de Québec – Dir. gen., Denis Carbonneau

Varennes: Foyer Lajemmerais, 60, rue d'Youville, CP 450, Varennes QC J3X 1T6 – 514/652-2995; Fax: 514/652-2998 – 82 lits – Dir. gen., Robert Sabino

Vaudreuil: Centre d'accueil Vaudreuil, 408, boul Roche, Vaudreuil QC J7V 7M9 – 514/453-5860; Fax: 514/455-1998 – 100 lits – Régie régionale de la santé et des services sociaux de la Montérégie – Dir. gen., Lise Belisle Bélanger

Vaudreuil: Manoir Harwood Enr., 170, rue Boileau, Vaudreuil QC J7V 8A3 – 514/424-6458; Fax: 514/424-2074 – 51 lits – Dir. gen., Denis Charland

Victoriaville: Centre d'accueil l'Ermitage, 45, av de l'Ermitage, Victoriaville QC G6P 6X4 – 819/758-7511 – 133 lits – Dir. gen., Gilles Perreault

Victoriaville: Centre hospitalier des Bois-Francs, 61, av de l'Ermitage, Victoriaville QC G6P 6X4 – 819/758-7511; Fax: 819/758-4852 – 100 lits – Dir. gen., Gilles Perreault

Victoriaville: Pavillon Bujold-Lefebvre enr., 60, rue Olivier, Victoriaville QC G6P 5G7 – 819/752-4411 – 28 places – Dir. gen., Gilles Perreault

Victoriaville: Pavillon Familial des Bois-Francs inc., 21, rue Marchand, Victoriaville QC G6P 4J5 – 819/752-9920 – 36 places – Dir. gen., Gilles Perreault

Ville-Marie: Centre d'accueil Duhamel, 37, rue Saint-Jean Bapiste sud, CP 3500, Ville-Marie QC J0Z 3W0 – 819/629-3027; Fax: 819/629-2805 – 61 lits – Dir. gen., Nicole Landry

Warwick: Foyer Étoiles d'Or inc., 10, rue l'Heureux, CP 610, Warwick QC J0A 1M0 – 819/358-6833; Fax: 819/358-6150 – 55 lits – Dir. gen., Gilles Perreualt

Waterville: Foyer de Waterville, 265, rue Compton est, CP 210, Waterville QC J0B 3H0 – 819/877-2500; Fax: 819/837-2916 – 20 lits – Dir. gen., Jeannette Delage

Weedon: Foyer de Weedon Inc., 245, rue Saint-Janvier, CP 250, Weedon QC J0B 3J0 – 819/877-2500; Fax:

819/877-3089 – 52 lits – Dir. gen., Albert Kratzenberg

Windsor: Hôpital St-Louis de Windsor inc., 23, rue Ambroise-Dearden, CP 2000, Windsor QC J1S 1G8 – 819/845-2751; Fax: 819/845-5834 – 36 lits – Dir. gen., Nicole Corbin

Wotton: Le Centre d'accueil de Wotton, 666, rue Saint-Jean, Wotton QC J0A 1N0 – 819/828-2251 – 32 lits – Dir. gen., Jean-Yves Poisson

Yamachiche: Foyer Ernest Jacob inc., 610, rue Sainte-Anne, Yamachiche QC G0X 3L0 – 819/296-3787; Fax: 819/296-2170 – 56 lits – Dir. gen., Micheline Bonner Lesage

## HÔPITAUX PRIVÉS

Greenfield Park: Centre hospitalier Rive-Sud Inc., 860, av Victoria, Greenfield Park QC J4V 1M8 – 514/465-7017; Fax: 514/465-7017 – 30 lits – Dir. gen., Benoit Desilets

Kahnawake: Kateri Memorial Hospital Centre/Centre hospitalier Kateri memorial, CP 10, Kahnawake QC J0L 1B0 – 514/638-3930; Fax: 514/638-4634 – 43 beds – Adm., Irene Tschernomor

Montréal: Centre hospitalier Guy Laporte, 30, boul St-Joseph est, Montréal QC H2T 1G9 – 514/845-4241; Fax: 514/845-4428 – 31 lits – Dir. gen., Jules Robert

Montréal: Centre métropolitain de Chirurgie Plastique Inc., 999, rue de Salaberry, Montréal QC H3L 1L2 – 514/332-7091; Fax: 514/382-5784 – 17 lits – Dir. gen., Marcel-A. Dion

Montréal: Clinique communautaire de Pointe St-Charles, 500, av Ash, Montréal QC H3K 2R4 – 514/937-9251; Fax: 514/937-3492 – Dir. gen., Jocelyne Bernier

Montréal: Hôpital Bellechasse, 3950, rue de Bellechasse, Montréal QC H1X 1J5 – 514/374-5500; Fax: 514/374-0858 – 183 lits – Président et Dir. gen., Dr Jean-Marc Dumas

Montréal: Hôpital Marie Clarac, 3530, boul Gouin est, Montréal QC H1H 1B7 – 514/322-8800; Fax: 514/326-8811 – 204 lits – Dir. gen., Louise Beaulac

Montréal: Hôpital Notre-Dame-de-Lourdes, 1870, boul Pie-IX, Montréal QC H1V 2C6 – 514/527-4595; Fax: 514/527-4475 – 162 lits – Dir. gen., Robert St-Pierre

Montréal: Hôpital Ste-Thérèse inc., 9307, boul La Salle, La Salle QC H8R 2M7 – 514/366-3556 – 47 lits – Dir. gen., Réjeanne Lemieux-Labbé

Montréal: Hôpital Shriners pour enfants (Québec) inc./Shriners Hospital for Crippled Children, 1529, av Cedar, Montréal QC H3G 1A6 – 514/842-4464; Fax: 514/842-7553 – 40 lits – Dir. gen., Allan D. Hicks

Montréal: Hôpital Ville-Marie Inc., 7015, boul Gouin est, Montréal QC H1E 5N2 – 514/955-8242; Fax: 514/955-4733 – 70 lits – Dir. gen., Louis Gariépy

Montréal: Villa Medica inc., 225, rue Sherbrooke est, Montréal QC H2X 1C9 – 514/288-8201; Fax: 514/288-7076 – 207 lits – Dir. gen., Michel Duchesne

Québec: Centre hospitalier Nôtre-Dame du Chemin Inc., 510, ch Ste-Foy, Québec QC G1S 2J5 – 418/681-7882; Fax: 418/681-5387 – 50 lits – Dir. gen., Antoine Pichette

Québec: Centre hospitalier St-Sacrement Ltée, 1165, ch Ste-Foy, Québec QC G1S 2M8 – 418/527-4836; Fax: 418/527-1743; EMail: chss@sumpatico.ca – 63 lits – Dir. gen., Jacques Pichette

Québec: Hôpital Ste-Monique (1988) inc., 4805, boul Wilfrid Hamel, Québec QC G1P 2J7 – 418/871-8701; Fax: 418/871-0105 – 58 lits – Dir. gen., Andrée Begin

Rawdon: Centre hospitalier Heather Inc., 3931 Lakeshore Dr., Rawdon QC J0K 1S0 – 514/834-2512; Fax: 514/834-5805; EMail: klein1@total.net – 76 lits – Regie régionale de la santé et des services sociaux de Lanaudière – Dir. gen., Paul Arbec

Saint-Georges: Centre hospitalier de l'Assomption Inc., 16750, boul Lacroix, Saint-Georges QC G5Y 2G4 – 418/228-2041; Fax: 418/228-9366 – 117 lits – Dir. gen., Gerard Gendreau

Sillery: La Maison Michel Sarrazin, 2101, ch St-Louis, Sillery QC G1T 2P5 – 418/688-0878; Fax: 418/681-8636 – 15 lits – Dir. gen., Louis Dionne

Waterloo: Centre gériatrique Courville Inc., 5305, av Courville, CP 580, Waterloo QC J0E 2N0 – 514/539-1821; Fax: 514/539-1937 – 32 lits – Dir. gen., Evelyn Courville

## CENTRES DE TRAITEMENTS SPÉCIALISÉS

(comprend: cliniques d'avortement, cliniques de soins aux cancéreux, centres de réadaptation professionnelle, centres de traitement)

Baie-Comeau: Centre N.-A.-Labrie, 659, boul Blance, Baie-Comeau QC G5C 2B2 – 418/589-5704; Fax: 418/589-6371 – centre de réadaptation des drogues – 63 lits – Dir. gen., Gaetan Gauthier

Chicoutimi: Maison d'accueil Doris Pineault, 2888, rue Roussel, Chicoutimi QC G7G 1Y9 – 418/549-5474 – 27 lits de néonatalogie – Dir. gen., Guy St-Onge

Hull: Centre de réadaptation la ressource, 325, rue Laramee, Hull QC J8Y 3A4 – 819/777-6261; Fax: 819/777-0073 – centre de réadaptation (déficience auditive, visuelle, & motrice) – Dir. gen., Jean-Pierre Blais

Hull: Pavillon Jellinek, 25, rue Saint-François, Hull QC J9A 1B1 – 819/776-5584; Fax: 819/776-0255 – centre de réadaptation des drogues – 26 beneficiaires – Dir. gen., Guy Charpentier

Joilette: Centre de réadaptation le Bouclier, 260, rue Lavaltrie sud, Joilette QC J6E 5X7 – 514/755-2741; Fax: 514/755-4895 – centre de réadaptation (déficience motrice) – Dir. gen., Lise Bolduc

Lemoyne: Clinique externe Foster, #200, 2475, rue St-Georges, Lemoyne QC J4R 2T4 – 514/466-7981 – centre de réadaptation des drogues – Dir. gen., Jean-Guy Poirier

Longueuil: Atelier Protege/Bibliotheque Braille, 1255, rue Beauregard, Longueuil QC J4K 2M3 – 514/463-1710 – centre de réadaptation (déficience visuelle)

Longueuil: Institut Nazareth et Louis-Braille, 1111, rue Saint-Charles ouest, Longueuil QC J4K 5G4 – 514/463-1710; Fax: 514/463-0243 – centre de réadaptation (déficience visuelle) – Dir. gen., Gabriel Collard

Montréal: Assn Montréalaise pour les Aveugles - Maison Penfield, 7000, rue Sherbrooke ouest, Montréal QC H4B 1R3 – 514/489-8201; Fax: 514/489-3477 – centre de réadaptation (déficience visuelle) – Dir. gen., John A. Sims

Montréal: Centre d'accueil Prefontaine, 3100, rue Rachel est, Montréal QC H1W 1A1 – 514/521-1280; Fax: 514/521-7854 – centre de réadaptation des drogues – 30 beneficiaires – Dir. gen., Pierre Lamarche

Montréal: Centre d'accueil Prefontaine II, 4055, av Papineau, Montréal QC H2K 4K2 – 514/521-8054 – centre de réadaptation des drogues – 18 beneficiaires – Dir. gen., Pierre Lamarche

Montréal: Centre de réadaptation alternatives, 10555, boul St-Laurent, Montréal QC H3L 2P5 – 514/385-6444; Fax: 514/385-5186 – centre de réadaptation des drogues – Dir. gen., Pierre Lamarche

Montréal: Centre de réadaptation Constance-Lethbridge, 7005, boul de Maisonneuve ouest, Montréal QC H4B 1T3 – 514/487-1770; Fax: 514/487-5494 – centre de réadaptation (déficience motrice) – Dir. gen., Howard G. Martin

Montréal: Centre de réadaptation Lucie-Bruneau, 2222, av Laurier est, Montréal QC H2H 1C4 – 514/527-4521; Fax: 514/527-0979 – centre de réadaptation (déficience motrice) – 60 beneficiaires – Dir. gen., Leon Lafleur, 514/527-4527

Montréal: Centre Hospitalier Richardson, 5425, av Bessborough, Montréal QC H4V 2S7 – 514/483-1380; Fax: 514/483-4596 – Ambulatory rehabilitation services – 42 lits – Dir. gen., Jean Michaud

Montréal: Centre Mackay, 3500, boul Decarie, Montréal QC H4A 3J5 – 514/482-0500; Fax: 514/482-4536 – centre de réadaptation (déficience motrice) – 35 beneficiaires – Dir. gen., John Spencer

Montréal: Domremy-Montréal, 15693, boul Gouin ouest, Sainte-Geneviève QC H9H 1C3 – 514/626-0220 – centre de réadaptation des drogues – 70 beneficiaires – Dir. gen., Pierre Lamarche

Montréal: L'Hôpital de réadaptation Lindsay, 6363, ch Hudson, Montréal QC H3S 1M9 – 514/737-3661; Fax: 514/737-0592; EMail: mbrunet@hopital-lindsay.qc.ca – hôpital de courte-durée spécialisé – 155 lits – Regie régionale de la santé et des services sociaux de Montréal-centre – Dir. gen., Michel A. Brunet

Montréal: Institut de réadaptation de Montréal, 6300, av Darlington, Montréal QC H3S 2J4 – 514/340-2085; Fax: 514/340-2149 – 104 lits – Dir. gen., Jacques R. Nolet

Montréal: Institut Raymond-Dewar, 3600, rue Berri, Montréal QC H2L 4G9 – 514/284-2581; Fax: 514/284-0699 – centre de réadaptation (déficience motrice) – Dir. gen., Pierre-Paul Lachapelle

Pointe-du-Lac: Domremy, 2931, rue Notre-Dame, CP 70, Pointe-du-Lac QC G0X 1Z0 – 819/377-2441; Fax: 819/377-2560 – centre de réadaptation des drogues – 24 beneficiaires – Dir. gen., Gratien Thibeault

Prevost: Centre d'accueil le Portage, 1790, ch du Lac Echo, RR#1, Prevost QC J0R 1T0 – 514/224-2944 – centre de réadaptation des drogues – 110 beneficiaires – Dir. gen., Peter Vamos

Québec: Centre de réadaptation en toxicomanie de Québec, 1, av du Sacre-Coeur, 5e étage est, Québec QC G1N 2W1 – 418/529-6851 – Dir. gen., Adrien Lacroix, 418/657-1668

Québec: Hôpital de l'Enfant-Jésus, 1401, 18e rue, Québec QC G1J 1Z4 – 418/649-0252; Fax: 418/649-5557 – centre hospitalier de soins aigus affilié à l'Université Laval spécialisé en sciences neurologiques et traumatologie – 517 lits – Regie régionale de la santé et des services sociaux de la region de Québec – Dir. gen., Gaston Pellan

Québec: Institut de réadaptation en déficience physique en Québec, 525, boul Wilfrid Hamel, Québec QC G1M 2S8 – 418/529-9141; Fax: 418/529-7318 – centre de réadaptation (déficience motrice) – 153 beneficiaires – Dir. gen., vacant

Rouyn-Noranda: SAHT de Rouyn-Noranda - Deficience Physique, 1, 9e rue, Rouyn-Noranda QC J9X 2A9 – 819/762-6592 – centre de réadaptation (déficience motrice) – 18 places – Dir. gen., Jean-Claude Beauchemin

Ste-Anne-des-Monts: Centre réadaptation pour personnes toxicomanes l'Escale, 145, 7e rue ouest, Ste-Anne-des-Monts QC G0E 2G0 – 418/763-2261; Fax: 418/763-7460 – centre de réadaptation des drogues – 16 beneficiaires – Dir. gen., Robert Deschenes

Ste-Foy: Centre Cardinal-Villeneuve, 2975, ch Saint-Louis, Ste-Foy QC G1W 1P9 – 418/653-8766 – centre de réadaptation (déficience motrice) – 34 beneficiaires – Dir. gen., Bernard Tremblay

Saint-Hubert: Centre de réadaptation Montergie, 5110, boul Cousineau, Saint-Hubert QC J3Y 7G5 – 514/443-2100; Fax: 514/443-4196 – centre de réadaptation des drogues – Dir. gen., Pierre Menard

Saint-Philippe: Pavillon Foster, 6, rue Foucreault, CP 119, Saint-Philippe QC J0L 2K0 – 514/659-8911; Fax: 514/659-7173 – centre de réadaptation des drogues – 20 beneficiaires – Dir. gen., Jean-Guy Poirier

Sherbrooke: Atelier Federal, 932, rue Federal, Sherbrooke QC J1H 5A7 – 819/346-8411 – centre de réadaptation (déficience motrice) – 40 places – Dir. gen., Gilles Servant

Sherbrooke: Centre de réadaptation Estrie inc., 1930, rue King ouest, Sherbrooke QC J1J 2E2 – 819/346-8411; Fax: 819/564-7670 – centre de réadaptation (déficience motrice) – 36 places – Dir. gen., Gilles Servant

Sherbrooke: Centre Jean-Patrice Chiasson, 1270, rue Galt ouest, Sherbrooke QC J1H 2A7 – 819/821-2500; Fax: 819/563-8322 – centre de réadaptation des drogues – 9 places; 4 beneficiaires – Régie régionale de la santé et des services sociaux de l'Estrie – Dir. gen., Héléne Desbiens

Sherbrooke: La Maison St-Georges (Sherbrooke) Inc., 433, rue Marquette, Sherbrooke QC J1H 1M5 – 819/562-1533 – centre de réadaptation des drogues – Dir. gen., Claude Dussault

Trois-Rivières: Centre de réadptation Interval, 4100, rue Jacques de Labadie, CP 1960, Trois-Rivières QC G9A 5M6 – 819/378-4083; Fax: 819/378-1354 – centre de réadaptation (déficience motrice) – Dir. gen., Raymond Beaudry

## SASKATCHEWAN

### REGIONAL HEALTH AUTHORITIES

Assiniboia: South Country Health District, PO Box 1120, Assiniboia SK S0H 0B0 – 306/642-5733; Fax: 306/642-5433 – CEO, Dale Schmeichel

Estevan: Southeast Health District, 1174 Nicholson Rd., Estevan SK S4A 2V3 – 306/634-7626; Fax: 306/634-7824 – CEO, Dan Florizone

Fort Qu'Appelle: Touchwood Qu'Appelle Health District, PO Box 850, Fort Qu'Appelle SK S0G 1S0 – 306/332-6431; Fax: 306/332-1824 – CEO, Royce Gill

Grenfell: Pipestone Health District, PO Box 970, Grenfell SK S0G 2B0 – 306/697-4000; Fax: 306/697-2686 – Responsible for 85 acute care & 315 long term care beds – CEO, Alvin Gallinger

Humboldt: Central Plains Health District, PO Box 690, Humboldt SK S0K 2A0 – 306/682-5526; Fax: 306/682-3596 – CEO, Gren Smith-Windsor

Kamsack: Assiniboine Valley Health District, PO Box 368, Kamsack SK S0A 1S0 – 306/542-3007; Fax: 306/542-2995 – CEO, Gary Johnson

Kindersley: Prairie West Health District, 1003 - 1st St. West, Kindersley SK S0L 1S2 – 306/463-2611; Fax: 306/463-3362 – CEO, Greg Hadvbiak

Lanigan: Living Sky Health District, PO Box 1060, Lanigan SK S0K 2M0 – 306/365-1430; Fax: 306/365-2099 – CEO, Andy Cebryk

Lloydminster Health District, 3820 - 43rd Ave., Lloydminster SK S9V 1Y5 – 306/820-6181; Fax: 306/825-9880 – CEO, Brian Heidt

Maidstone: Twin Rivers Health District Inc., PO Box 629, Maidstone SK S0M 1M0 – 306/893-4850; Fax: 306/893-4480 – CEO, Lloyd Bullock

Meadow Lake: Northwest Health District, 711 Centre St., Meadow Lake SK S9X 1E6 – 306/236-5777; Fax: 306/236-5801; EMail: nwhd@sk.sympatico.ca – CEO, Irene Denis

Melfort: North Central Health District, PO Box 1990, Melfort SK S0E 1A0 – 306/752-9600; Fax: 306/752-2276; EMail: nchd@sk.synmpatico.ca – Responsible for 192 beds – CEO, David Fan

Melville: North Valley Health District, 256 - 2nd Ave. West, PO Box 1090, Melville SK S0A 2P0 – 306/728-4762; Fax: 306/728-4925 – Acting CEO, S. Fox

Moose Jaw-Thunder Creek Health District, 455 Fairford St. East, Moose Jaw SK S6H 1H3 – 306/694-0295; Fax: 306/692-5596 – Interim CEO, Vern McClellands

Nipawin: North-East Health District, PO Box 389, Nipawin SK S0E 1E0 – 306/862-5900; Fax: 306/862-9310 – CEO, Rayann Ulvick

North Battleford: Battlefords Health District, 1092 - 197 St., 4th Fl., North Battleford SK S9A 1Z1 – 306/446-6606; Fax: 306/446-4114 – Responsible for 400 beds – Acting CEO, Ted King

Outlook: Midwest Health District, PO Box 1100, Outlook SK S0L 2N0 – 306/867-9700; Fax: 306/867-1877 – CEO, Doug Ball

Prince Albert Health District, 2345 - 10th Ave. West, PO Box 5700, Prince Albert SK S6V 7V6 – 306/953-0500; Fax: 306/763-1501 – CEO, Stan Rice

Regina Health District, 2180 - 23 Ave., Regina SK S4S 0A5 – 306/359-5287; Fax: 306/359-5222 – Pres. & CEO, Dr. Glenn S. Bartlett

Rosthern: Gabriel Springs Health District, PO Box 309, Rosthern SK S0K 3R0 – 306/232-4305; Fax: 306/232-5218 – CEO, Alex Horner

Saskatoon Health District, Royal University Hospital, 6th Fl., 103 Hospital Dr., Saskatoon SK S7N 0W8 – 306/655-1576; Fax: 306/655-1037 – Responsible for 830 beds – Pres., Jim Fergusson

Shaunavon: Southwest Health District, PO Box 339, Shaunavon SK S0N 2M0 – 306/297-2523; Fax: 306/297-3881 – CEO, Alan Ruetz

Spiritwood: Parkland Health District, 511 - 4 St. East, PO Box 427, Spiritwood SK S0J 2M0 – 306/883-3300; Fax: 306/883-3700 – CEO, C. Jean Morrison

Swift Current Health District, 429 - 4th Ave. SE, Swift Current SK S9H 2J9 – 306/778-5103; Fax: 306/773-9513 – CEO, Gordon A. Allsen

Swift Current: Rolling Hills Health District, #2, 1061 Central Ave. North, Swift Current SK S9H 4Y9 – 306/773-2224; Fax: 306/773-0033 – CEO, Marlene Weston

Tisdale: Pasquia Health District, PO Box 1780, Tisdale SK S0E 1T0 – 306/873-3100; Fax: 306/873-5994 – CEO, Gordon Denton

Unity: Greenhead Health District, PO Box 1538, Unity SK S0K 4L0 – 403/228-6330; Fax: 403/228-3860 – CEO, Michael Kukurudza

Wawota: Moose Mountain Health District, PO Box 61, Wawota SK S0G 5A0 – 306/739-2593; Fax: 306/739-2668 – CEO, Warren Wallin

Weyburn: South Central Health District, PO Box 2003, Weyburn SK S4H 2Z9 – 306/842-7211; Fax: 306/842-7237 – responsible for 69 acute care, 435 long term care, 11 respite, 1 observation, 8 multipurpose beds – CEO, Lee Spencer

Yorkton: East Central Health District, 270 Bradbrooke Dr., Yorkton SK S3N 2K6 – 306/786-3155; Fax: 306/786-3151; EMail: east-central-health-district@hmtnet.com – CEO, Dr. James Millar

### GENERAL HOSPITALS

Arcola Health Centre, Arcola SK S0C 0G0 – 306/455-2771; Fax: 306/455-2397 – 18 beds – Mgr., Health Services, Joanne Hollingshead

Assiniboia Union Hospital, Assiniboia SK S0H 0B0 – 306/642-3351; Fax: 306/642-3804 – 12 beds – Dir., Nursing, Betty Peterson

Balcarres Union Hospital, Balcarres SK S0G 0C0 – 306/334-2636; Fax: 306/334-2674 – 16 beds – Adm., Ann Barnsley

Big River Hospital, PO Box 100, Big River SK S0J 0E0 – 306/469-2220; Fax: 306/469-2237 – 10 beds – Parkland Health District – CEO, Jean Morrison

Biggar Union Hospital, Biggar SK S0K 0M0 – 306/948-3323; Fax: 306/948-2011 – 135 beds – Dir., Health Services, Ed Kryzanowski

Broadview Union Hospital, Broadview SK S0G 0K0 – 306/696-2441; Fax: 306/696-2611 – 16 beds – Pipestone Health District – Facility Mgr., Linda Beutler

Canora Hospital, Canora SK S0A 0L0 – 306/563-5621; Fax: 306/563-5571 – 33 beds – Nurse Adm., Mavis Bouey

Carrot River Hospital, Carrot River SK S0E 0L0 – 306/768-2722; Fax: 306/768-2734 – 18 beds – Community Coord., Lynda Blum

Central Butte Union Hospital, Central Butte SK S0H 0T0 – 306/796-2190; Fax: 306/796-4610 – 30 beds – Adm.-Coord., Myrna Peterson

Cudworth: St. Michael's Hospital, PO Box 220, Cudworth SK S0K 1B0 – 306/256-3443; Fax: 306/256-3311 – 10 acute care, 4 continuing care beds – Adm., Joseph P. Habetler

Davidson Union Hospital, Davidson SK S0G 1A0 – 306/567-2801; Fax: 306/567-4380 – 13 beds – Midwest Health District – Adm., James Thomson

Esterhazy: St. Anthony's Hospital, PO Box 280, Esterhazy SK S0A 0X0 – 306/745-3973; Fax: 306/745-3388 – 18 beds – Adm., Gordon Karpinka

Estevan: St. Joseph's Hospital, 1176 Nicholson Rd., Estevan SK S4A 0H3 – 306/634-0400; Fax: 306/634-8785 – Exec. Dir., Harvey Fox

Foam Lake Union Hospital, PO Box 190, Foam Lake SK S0A 1A0 – 306/272-3737 – Adm., Ray King

Fort Qu'Appelle Indian Hospital, PO Box 220, Fort Qu'Appelle SK S0G 1S0 – 306/332-5611; Fax: 306/332-4352 – Adm., Lillian Alexus

Gravelbourg: St. Joseph's Hospital, 216 Bettez St., Gravelbourg SK S0H 1X0 – 306/648-3185; Fax: 306/648-3440 – 9 acute care, 50 continuing care beds – Adm., Raymond Mulaire

Hafford Hospital & Special Care Centre, PO Box 130, Hafford SK S0J 1A0 – 306/549-2108; Fax: 306/549-4660 – 26 beds – Dir., Care, Linda Findelet

Hafford Hospital & Special Care Centre, PO Box 130, Hafford SK S0J 1A0 – 306/549-2108; Fax: 306/549-4660 – 25 beds – Parkland Health District – Dir. of Care, Linda E. Fendelet

Herbert-Morse Union Hospital, PO Box 220, Herbert SK S0H 2A0 – 306/784-2202; Fax: 306/784-3452 – 17 beds – Hospital Coord., Sharon Yeske

Hudson Bay Union Hospital, Hudson Bay SK S0E 0Y0 – 306/865-2219; Fax: 306/865-2429 – 10 acute care, 1 respite, 5 long term care – Pasquia Health District – Community Mgr., Garry Form

Humboldt: St. Elizabeth's Hospital, PO Box 10, Humboldt SK S0K 2A0 – 306/682-2603; Fax: 306/682-4046 – 40 beds – Central Plains Health District – Adm., Jim Ramsay

Ile a la Crosse: St. Joseph's Hospital, PO Bag 500, Ile a la Crosse SK S0M 1C0 – 306/833-2081; Fax: 306/833-2556 – 42 beds – Adm., Marie Adele Désjarlais

Indian Head Union Hospital, PO Box 340, Indian Head SK S0G 2K0 – 306/695-3878; Fax: 306/695-2525 – Adm., Kathy Grad

Kamsack Hospital, Kamsack SK S0A 1S0 – 306/542-2636; Fax: 306/542-4360 – Adm., P. Ratushny

Kelvington Union Hospital, PO Box 70, Kelvington SK S0A 1W0 – 306/327-4711; Fax: 306/327-5115 – Adm., Lawrence Wytrykusz

Kerrobert Union Hospital, PO Box 320, Kerrobert SK S0L 1R0 – 306/834-2646; Fax: 306/834-1007 – Adm., Todd Stepanuik

Kindersley Hospital, 1003 - 1st St. West, Kindersley SK S0L 1S0 – 306/463-2611; Fax: 306/463-4550 – 25 beds – Prairie West Health District – Adm., Audrey Steiert

Kinistino Union Hospital, PO Box 460, Kinistino SK S0J 1H0 – 306/864-2292; Fax: 306/864-2440 – Adm., Carol Pryznyk

Kipling Memorial Union Hospital, PO Box 420, Kipling SK S0G 2S0 – 306/736-2553; Fax: 306/736-8407 – Suprv., Physical Plant, A. Gall

La Ronge Hospital, PO Box 6900, La Ronge SK S0L 1L0 – 306/425-2422 – Suprv., Plant Maintenance, J. Hoeft

LaLoche: St. Martin's Hospital, LaLoche SK S0M 1G0 – 306/822-2011; Fax: 306/822-2112 – 12 beds – Adm., Violet Lemaigre

Lanigan Hospital, Lanigan SK S0K 2M0 – 306/365-1400; Fax: 306/365-3354 – 18 beds – Living Sky Health District – Adm., T. Andy Cebryk

Leader Union Hospital, Leader SK S0N 1H0 – 306/628-3343; Fax: 306/628-4413 – Adm., Helen Thorburn

Lestock: St. Joseph's Hospital, PO Box 280, Lestock SK S0A 2G0 – 306/274-2215; Fax: 306/274-2045 – 9 acute care, 6 long term care beds – Touchwood Qu'Appelle Health District – Exec. Dir., Pamela Heinrichs

Lloydminster Hospital, 3820 - 43 Ave., Lloydminster SK S9V 1Y5 – 306/820-6000; Fax: 306/825-9880 – Lloydminster Health District – CEO, Brian Heidt

Loon Lake Union Hospital & Special Care Home, PO Box 68, Loon Lake SK S0M 1L0 – 306/837-2114; Fax: 306/837-2268 – 12 beds – Sec.-Treas., Marlene Chapellaz

Maidstone Union Hospital, PO Box 160, Maidstone SK S0M 1M0 – 306/893-2622; Fax: 306/893-2922 – Adm., Greg Trotter

Maple Creek Union Hospital, Maple Creek SK S0N 1N0 – 306/662-2611; Fax: 306/662-3210 – Exec. Dir., Sheila Mulatz

Meadow Lake Union Hospital, PO Box 600, Meadow Lake SK S0M 1V0 – 306/236-3661; Fax: 306/236-3244 – Adm., Irene Denis

Melfort Union Hospital, PO Box 1480, Melfort SK S0E 1A0 – 306/752-2811; Fax: 306/742-5578 – Adm., Wilfred Veller

Melville: St. Peter's Hospital, PO Box 1810, Melville SK S0A 2P0 – 306/728-5407; Fax: 306/728-4870; EMail: sph1@spreda.sk.ca – 50 beds – North Valley Health District – CEO, Terri Hodges

Moose Jaw Union Hospital, 455 Fairford St. East, Moose Jaw SK S6H 1H3 – 306/694-1515; Fax: 306/692-5596 – Pres. & CEO, John Borody

Moosomin Union Hospital, PO Box 400, Moosomin SK S0G 3N0 – 306/435-3303; Fax: 306/435-3211 – Adm., Skuli Bjornson

Nipawin Union Hospital, PO Box 2104, Nipawin SK S0E 1E0 – 306/862-4643; Fax: 306/862-9310 – Adm., Rayaun Ulrich

North Battleford: Battlefords Union Hospital, 1092 - 107 St., North Battleford SK S9A 1Z1 – 306/446-7350; Fax: 306/446-7301 – Adm., Bob Miller

Outlook Union Hospital, Outlook SK S0L 2N0 – 306/867-8676; Fax: 306/867-9449 – Sec.-Treas., Mervin Dewing

Paradise Hill Hospital, Paradise Hill SK S0M 2G0 – 306/344-2255; Fax: 306/344-2277 – Adm., Brenda Rutherford

Porcupine-Carragana Union Hospital, PO Box 70, Porcupine Plain SK S0E 1H0 – 306/278-2233; Fax: 306/278-3088 – 9 beds – Pasquia Health District – Community Health Mgr., Christine Pohl

Preeceville Hospital, PO Box 469, Preeceville SK S0A 3B0 – 306/547-2102; Fax: 306/547-2223 – Adm., Thom Carnahon

Prince Albert: Holy Family Hospital, 675 - 15 St. West, Prince Albert SK S6V 3R8 – 306/922-2605, 953-1217 (admin.); Fax: 306/763-1882 – 90 beds – Prince Albert Health District – Exec. Dir., Sr. Margaret Vickers

Prince Albert: Victoria Union Hospital, 1200 - 24th St. West, Prince Albert SK S6V 5T4 – 306/764-1551; Fax: 306/763-2871 – Exec. Dir., David Fan

Redvers Health Centre, PO Box 30, Redvers SK S0C 2H0 – 306/452-3553; Fax: 306/452-3556 – 18 beds – Moose Mountain Health District – Mgr., Health Services, Murray Gores

Regina General Hospital, 1440 - 14 Ave., Regina SK S4P 0W5 – 306/766-4444; Fax: 306/766-4723 – 286 beds – Regina Health District – Pres. & CEO, Dr. Glenn S. Barlett

Regina: Pasqua Hospital, 4101 Dewdney Ave., Regina SK S4T 1A5 – 306/766-2222; Fax: 306/766-2751 – 256 beds – Regina Health District – Pres. & CEO, Dr. Glenn S. Barlett

Rosetown & District Health Centre, PO Box 850, Rosetown SK S0L 2V0 – 306/882-2672; Fax: 306/882-3335 – Adm., Robert Legoffe

Rosthern Union Hospital, Rosthern SK S0K 3R0 – 306/232-4811; Fax: 306/232-4887 – Adm., Nestor Yaganiski

Saskatoon City Hospital, 701 Queen St., Saskatoon SK S7K 0M7 – 306/655-8000; Fax: 306/655-8269 – Pres., John Malcolm

Saskatoon: Royal University Hospital, 103 Hospital Dr., Saskatoon SK S7N 0W8 – 306/655-1576; Fax: 306/655-1037 – 429 beds – Saskatoon Health District – Pres., Jim Fergusson

Saskatoon: St. Paul's Hospital, 1702 - 20 St. West, Saskatoon SK S7M 0Z9 – 306/655-5000; Fax: 306/655-5716 – Pres., Walter Podiluk

Shaunavon Union Hospital, PO Box 789, Shaunavon SK S0N 2M0 – 306/297-2644; Fax: 306/297-2502 – 15 beds – Program Coord., Gloria Illerbrun

Shellbrook Hospital, Shellbrook SK S0J 2E0 – 306/747-2603; Fax: 306/747-3004 – Adm., Clifford E. Skange

Spalding Community Health Centre, Spalding SK S0K 4C0 – 306/872-2022; Fax: 306/872-2186 – Sec.-Treas., Maria Leonard

Spiritwood Hospital, PO Box 69, Spiritwood SK S0J 2M0 – 306/883-2133; Fax: 306/883-2136 – Adm., David W. McLachlan

Swift Current Union Hospital, 499 - 4th Ave. NE, Swift Current SK S9H 2K1 – 306/778-9400; Fax: 306/778-0189 – Exec. Dir., Gordon A. Allsen

Tisdale Hospital, Tisdale SK S0E 1T0 – 306/873-2621; Fax: 306/873-5994 – 24 beds – Adm., Nancy Carter

Turtleford: Riverside Memorial Union Hospital, PO Box 10, Turtleford SK S0M 2Y0 – 306/845-2195; Fax: 306/845-2772 – Adm., Lionel Chabot

Unity Hospital, PO Box 741, Unity SK S0K 4L0 – 306/228-2666; Fax: 306/228-2292; EMail: greenhead.health@sk.sympatico.ca – 15 beds – Greenhead Health District – Adm., Kim Halter

Uranium City Hospital, Uranium City SK S0J 2W0 – 306/498-2412; Fax: 306/498-2577 – 28 beds – Adm., Ian Berg

Wadena Union Hospital, PO Box 10, Wadena SK S0A 4J0 – 306/338-2515; Fax: 306/338-2720 – 12 beds – Central Plains Health District – Adm., Eugene Kalenchuk

Wakaw Union Hospital, PO Box 309, Wakaw SK S0K 4P0 – 306/233-4611; Fax: 306/233-5990 – 21 beds – Gabriel Springs Health District – Care Team Mgr., Pat Taciuk

Watrous Hospital, Watrous SK S0K 4T0 – 306/946-3341; Fax: 306/946-2880 – Adm., Annita Romich

Wawota Health Centre, Wawota SK S0G 5A0 – 306/739-2244; Fax: 306/739-2802 – Sec./Mgr., Bruce Norsworthy

Weyburn General Hospital, 201 - 1st Ave. NE, Weyburn SK S4H 0N1 – 306/842-8400; Fax: 306/842-0737 – 50 acute care – South Central Health District – CEO, Lee Spencer

Wilkie Union Hospital, Wilkie SK S0K 4W0 – 306/843-2644; Fax: 306/843-3222 – Adm., Miles Sookocheff

Wolseley Memorial Union Hospital, PO Box 458, Wolseley SK S0G 5H0 – 306/698-2377; Fax: 306/698-2988 – Suprv., Plant Maintenance, W. McBride

Wynyard Hospital, Wynyard SK S0A 4T0 – 306/554-2586; Fax: 306/554-2247 – Adm., L. Haraasen

Yorkton Regional Health Centre, 270 Bradbrooke Dr., Yorkton SK S3N 2K6 – 306/782-2401; Fax: 306/782-3359 – 148 beds – East Central Health District – Pres./CEO, Dr. J. Millar

## AUXILIARY HOSPITALS/HEALTH CARE CENTRES

Arborfield Health Centre & Arborfield Special Care Lodge, PO Box 160, Arborfield SK S0E 0A0 – 306/769-8722; Fax: 306/769-8640 – Sec.-Treas., A. Lindsay

Beechy Health Centre, Beechy SK S0L 0C0 – 306/859-2118; Fax: 306/859-2206 – Midwest Health District – CEO, Doug Ball

Bengough Health Centre/Twilight Home Inc., PO Box 399, Bengough SK S0C 0K0 – 306/268-2848; Fax: 306/268-2046 – 26 long term care beds, 1 palliative, 1 respite – South Central Health District – Mgr., Community Health Services, Madonna L. Unteresner

Birch Hills Memorial Health Centre, PO Box 578, Birch Hills SK S0J 0G0 – 306/749-3331; Fax: 306/749-2440 – CEO, Karl Humeniuk

Borden Community Health Centre, Borden SK S0K 0N0 – 306/997-2110; Fax: 306/997-2114 – Adm., Monica Kohlhammer

Cabri: Prairie Health Care Centre, PO Box 79, Cabri SK S0N 0J0 – 306/587-2623; Fax: 306/587-2751 – 18 beds – CEO, Janet Little

Canora: Norquay Health Centre/Gateway Lodge Inc., c/o Canora, PO Box 1387, Canora SK S0A 0L0 – 306/594-2133; Fax: 306/594-2488 – Adm., Daniel Florizone

Climax: Border Community Health Centre, Climax SK S0N 0N0 – 306/293-2222; Fax: 306/293-2860 – Sec.-Treas., Michelle Balfour

Coronach & District Health Centre, PO Box 150, Coronach SK S0H 0Z0 – 306/267-2022; Fax: 306/267-2324 – 13 beds – South Central Health District – Mgr., Community Health Services, Judy Ludtke, 306/267-2123

Craik & District Health Centre, PO Box 208, Craik SK S0G 0V0 – 306/734-2288; Fax: 306/734-2248 – 15 beds – Moose Jaw-Thunder Creek Health District – Dir. of Care, Elaine M. Spencer

Cupar Health Centre, Cupar SK S0G 0Y0 – 306/723-4300; Fax: 306/723-4416 – Regina Health District – Adm., Richard Jensen

Cut Knife Health Complex, PO Box 220, Cut Knife SK S0M 0N0 – 306/398-4718; Fax: 306/398-2206 – Sec.-Treas., Sonja Pellerin

Delisle Community Health & Social Centre, Delisle SK S0L 0P0 – 306/493-2323

Dinsmore Health Care Centre, PO Box 219, Dinsmore SK S0L 0T0 – 306/846-2222; Fax: 306/846-2225 – 20 beds – Adm., Anne Rankin

Dodsland Health Centre, Dodsland SK S0L 0V0 – 306/356-2172; Fax: 306/356-2042

Eastend Wolf Willow Health Centre, PO Box 220, Eastend SK S0N 0T0 – 306/295-3534; Fax: 306/295-3223 – 24 beds – Adm., Barry Grant

Eatonia Health Care Centre, PO Box 400, Eatonia SK S0L 0Y0 – 306/967-2591; Fax: 306/967-2373 – 13 beds – Adm., C. Cooke

Edam: Lady Minto Health Care Centre, PO Box 178, Edam SK S0M 0V0 – 306/397-2222; Fax: 306/397-2225 – 2 acute care, 2 respite, 1 palliative, 14 long term care beds – Battlefords Health District – Adm., Caroll Sutton

Eston Health Centre, Eston SK S0L 1A0 – 306/962-3667; Fax: 306/962-3242 – Team Mgr., Care, Margaret Vogel

Fillmore Union Health Centre/Fillmore Special-Care Home Inc., PO Box 246, Fillmore SK S0G 1N0 – 306/722-3315; Fax: 306/722-3877 – 20 beds – Adm., Heather Haupstein

Gainsborough & Area Health Centre, Gainsborough SK S0C 0Z0 – 306/685-2277; Fax: 306/685-4636 – 14 beds – Adm., Laurie Cole

Goodsoil: L. Gervais Memorial Health Centre, PO Box 100, Goodsoil SK S0M 1A0 – 306/238-2100; Fax: 306/238-4449 – 14 beds – Sec.-Treas., Fred Puffer

Grenfell Health Centre, Grenfell SK S0G 2B0 – 306/697-2853; Fax: 306/697-3459 – Adm., Peter Rousay

Gull Lake Health Centre, Gull Lake SK S0N 1A0 – 306/672-4147; Fax: 306/672-4475 – Sec.-Treas., Theresa Moritz

Hodgeville Community Health & Social Centre, Hodgeville SK S0H 2B0 – 306/677-2292; Fax: 306/677-2466

Imperial: Long Lake Valley Integrated Facility, PO Box 180, Imperial SK S0G 2J0 – 306/963-2210; Fax: 306/963-2480 – 13 beds – Adm., Wanda Gustafson

Invermay Health Centre/Gateway Lodge Inc., Invermay SK S0A 0L0 – 306/593-2133; Fax: 306/593-4566

Ituna Health Centre, Ituna SK S0A 1N0 – 306/795-2622; Fax: 306/795-3592 – Adm., Sharon Henchert

Kincaid Health Centre, PO Box 179, Kincaid SK S0H 2J0 – 306/264-3233; Fax: 306/264-3878 – Sec.-Treas., Pat Williamson

Kyle & District Health Centre, PO Box 70, Kyle SK S0L 1T0 – 306/375-2251; Fax: 306/375-2422 – 19 beds – Sec.-Treas., Evelyn Mazzel

LaFleche & District Health Centre, LaFleche SK S0H 2K0 – 306/472-5230; Fax: 306/472-5405 – 13 beds – Sec.-Treas., Pauline Dumont

Lampman Community Health Centre, PO Box 238, Lampman SK S0C 1N0 – 306/487-2561; Fax: 306/487-3103 – 21 beds – Sec.-Treas., Linda Grimes

Langenburg Health Centre, PO Box 9, Langenburg SK S0A 2A0 – 306/743-2661; Fax: 306/743-2844 – Adm., Darwyn MacKenzie

LaRonge Health Centre, PO Box 6900, LaRonge SK S0J 1L0 – 306/425-2422; Fax: 306/425-3298 – Adm., Lionel Shabot

Leoville: Evergreen Health Centre, PO Box 160, Leoville SK S0J 1N0 – 306/984-2136; Fax: 306/984-2046 – 16 beds – CEO, Adrian Sakundiak

Leroy Community Health & Social Centre, Leroy SK S0K 2P0 – 306/286-3347

Lucky Lake Health Centre, PO Box 250, Lucky Lake SK S0L 1Z0 – 306/858-2133; Fax: 306/858-2312 – 19 beds – Sec.-Treas., Peggy M. Erickson

Macklin: St. Joseph's Health Centre, Macklin SK S0L 2C0 – 306/ 753-2115; Fax: 306/753-2181 – Adm., Deborah King

Mankota: Prairie View Health Centre, Mankota SK S0H 2W0 – 306/478-2200; Fax: 306/478-2462 – Adm., Sheila Gebhart

Maryfield Community Health & Social Centre, Maryfield SK S0G 3K0 – 306/646-2133

Midale: Mainprize Manor & Health Care Corporation, PO Box 239, Midale SK S0C 1S0 – 306/458-2446 – 16 beds – Adm., Arlice Adderley

Milden Health Centre, Milden SK S0L 2L0 – 306/935-2142; Fax: 306/935-2200 – Sec.-Treas., Doug Ball

Montmartre Health Centre, PO Box 206, Montmartre SK S0G 3M0 – 306/424-2222; Fax: 306/424-2227 – 14 beds – Adm., Peter Rousay

Moosomin: Whitewood Health Centre, PO Box 400, Moosomin SK S0G 3N0 – 306/735-2688; Fax: 306/435-2512 – Adm., Skuli Bjornson

Mossbank Community Health & Social Centre, Mossbank SK S0H 3G0 – 306/354-2300

Neilburg: Manitou Health Centre, PO Box 190, Neilburg SK S0M 2C0 – 306/823-4262; Fax: 306/823-4590 – Twin Rivers Health District Inc. – Sec.-Treas., Dale Demarais

Neudorf Community Health & Social Centre, Neudorf SK S0A 2T0 – 306/748-2566

Nokomis Health Centre/Pufer Special Care Home Corp., PO Box 98, Nokomis SK S0G 3R0 – 306/528-2114; Fax: 306/528-4655 – 16 beds – Sec.-Treas., T. Andy Cebryk

Oxbow: Galloway Health Centre, PO Box 268, Oxbow SK S0C 2B0 – 306/483-2956; Fax: 306/483-5178 – 14 beds – Adm., Mary Ackerman

Pangman Hospital, Pangman SK S0C 2C0 – 306/442-2044; Fax: 306/442-4416 – Sec.-Treas., Kathy Jacques

Ponteix Health Centre, Ponteix SK S0N 1Z0 – 306/625-3382; Fax: 306/625-3764 – 2 observation beds – Rolling Hills Health District – Health Centre Coord., Adele Boisjoli

Quill Lake Community Health & Social Centre, Quill Lake SK S0A 3E0 – 306/383-2266

Rabbit Lake Integrated Facility, PO Box 156, Rabbit Lake SK S0M 2L0 – 306/824-2020; Fax: 306/824-2011 – Sec.-Treas., Gwen Moore

Radville: Marian Health Centre, Radville SK S0C 2G0 – 306/869-2224; Fax: 306/869-2653 – Adm., Sheila Jubenville

Raymore Community Health & Social Centre, Raymore SK S0A 3J0 – 306/746-2231

Regina: Plains Health Centre, 4500 Wascana Pkwy., Regina SK S4S 5W9 – 306/766-6211; Fax: 306/766-6722 – 189 beds – Regina Health District – Pres. & CEO, Dr. Glenn S. Bartlett

Rockglen: Grasslands Health Centre, PO Box 19, Rockglen SK S0H 3R0 – 306/476-2030; Fax: 306/476-2534 – 13 beds – Sec.-Treas., Louise Todd

Rose Valley & District Integrated Care Facility, PO Box 310, Rose Valley SK S0E 1M0 – 306/322-2115 – 12 beds – Adm., Ian Begg

St. Walburg Helath Centre, St. Walburg SK S0M 2T0 – 306/248-3355; Fax: 306/248-3413 – Sec.-Treas., Linda English

Smeaton & District Health Centre, PO Box 59, Smeaton SK S0J 2J0 – 306/426-2051; Fax: 306/426-2229 – Sec.-Treas., Roni Jean Grunerud

Strasbourg & District Health Centre, Strasbourg SK S0G 4V0 – 306/725-3220

Theodore Health Centre, Theodore SK S0A 4C0 – 306/647-2115; Fax: 306/647-2238 – Adm., Gerald Hoffman

Vanguard Health Centre, Vanguard SK S0N 2V0 – 306/582-2044; Fax: 306/582-4833 – Sec.-Treas., R.W. Kehoe

Watson Community Health Centre & Quill Plains Lodge, PO Box 220, Watson SK S0K 4V0 – 306/287-3791; Fax: 306/287-3909 – Adm., Edna Favreau

Willow Bunch Community Health & Social Centre, Willow Bunch SK S0H 4K0 – 306/473-2310

Zenon Park Community Health & Social Centre, Zenon Park SK S0E 1W0 – 306/767-2221

## FEDERAL HOSPITALS

Fort Qu'appelle Indian Hospital, PO Box 220, Fort Qu'appelle SK S0G 1S0 – 306/332-5611 – Suprv., Plant Maintenance, Tony Kurtz

## MENTAL HEALTH HOSPITALS & COMMUNITY FACILITIES

North Battleford: Saskatchewan Hospital North Battleford, PO Box 39, North Battleford SK S9A 2X8 – 306/446-6800; Fax: 306/445-5392 – Adm., Moira Gautron

## NURSING HOMES/LONG TERM CARE FACILITIES

Arborfield Health Centre & Arborfield Special Care Lodge, *see* Auxiliary Hospitals/Health Care Centres listings

Assiniboia Pioneer Lodge Inc., PO Box 1388, Assiniboia SK S0H 0B0 – 306/642-3311 – 62 beds – Adm., James Larson

Assiniboia Pioneer Lodge Inc. (Ross Payant Nursing Home), PO Box 1388, Assiniboia SK S0H 0B0 – 306/642-3304 – 63 beds

Balcarres: Parkland Lodge Corporation, PO Box 488, Balcarres SK S0G 0C0 – 306/334-2677 – 35 beds – Adm., Elizabeth Jarocki

The Battlefords District Care Centre, PO Box 69, Battleford SK S0M 0E0 – 306/446-6900; Fax: 306/937-2258 – 158 beds – Battlefords Health District – Facility Mgr., Marlene Tarnowsky

Bengough Health Centre/Twilight Home Inc., *see* Auxiliary Hospitals/Health Care Centres listings

Big River: Lake-Wood Lodge Inc., PO Box 760, Big River SK S0J 0E0 – 306/469-2333 – 30 beds – Adm., Jack De Vlaming

Biggar: Diamond Lodge Co. Ltd., PO Box 340, Biggar SK S0K 0M0 – 306/948-3385 – 60 beds – Adm., Eugene Motruk

Birch Hills Memorial Health Centre, *see* Auxiliary Hospitals/Health Care Centres listings

Broadview & District Centennial Lodge Inc., PO Box 670, Broadview SK S0G 0K0 – 306/696-2459; Fax: 306/696-2577 – 36 beds – Pipestone Health District – Mgr., Linda Zinkhan

Cabri: Prairie Health Care Centre, *see* Auxiliary Hospitals/Health Care Centres listings

Canora: Gateway Lodge Inc., PO Box 1387, Canora SK S0A 0L0 – 306/563-5685 – 78 beds – Adm., J. Matsalla

Canora: Norquay Health Centre/Gateway Lodge Inc., *see* Auxiliary Hospitals/Health Care Centres listings

Canwood: Whispering Pine Place Inc., PO Box 418, Canwood SK S0J 0K0 – 306/468-2900 – 30 beds – Adm., Brenda Person

Carlye: Moose Mountain Lodge Company Inc., PO Box 729, Carlye SK S0C 0R0 – 306/453-2434 – 36 beds – Adm., Terry Steininger

Carnduff: The Border-Line Housing Co. (1975) Inc. (Sunset Haven), PO Box 250, Carnduff SK S0C 0S0 – 306/462-3424 – 68 beds – Adm., Clara Irwin

Carrot River: Pasquia Special Care Home, PO Box 250, Carrot River SK S0E 0L0 – 306/768-2725 – 38 beds – Adm., Wanda Kiteley

Central Butte & District Regency Manor Inc., PO Box 430, Central Butte SK S0H 0T0 – 306/796-4338 – 30 beds – Adm., Laurie Stephens

Coronach & District Health Centre, *see* Auxiliary Hospitals/Health Care Centres listings

Craik & District Health Centre, *see* Auxiliary Hospitals/Health Care Centres listings

Cudworth Nursing Home, PO Box 190, Cudworth SK S0K 1B0 – 306/256-3423 – 29 beds – Adm., Betty Lewandoski

Cupar & District Nursing Home Inc. (Shalom), PO Box 310, Cupar SK S0G 0Y0 – 306/723-4666 – 48 beds – Adm., Richard Jensen

Cut Knife Health Complex, *see* Auxiliary Hospitals/Health Care Centres listings

Dalmeny: Spruce Manor Special Care Home, PO Box 190, Dalmeny SK S0K 1E0 – 306/254-2162 – 36 beds – Adm., Jacob Frosse

Davidson: Arm River Housing Corporation (Prairie View Lodge), PO Box 756, Davidson SK S0G 1A0 – 306/567-3111; Fax: 306/567-4380 – 37 beds – Midwest Health District – Adm., James Thomson

Dinsmore Health Care Centre, *see* Auxiliary Hospitals/Health Care Centres listings

Duck Lake & District Nursing Home Inc., PO Box 370, Duck Lake SK S0K 1J0 – 306/467-4440 – 30 beds – Adm., Eric Goretzky

Eastend Wolf Willow Health Centre, *see* Auxiliary Hospitals/Health Care Centres listings

Eatonia Health Care Centre, *see* Auxiliary Hospitals/Health Care Centres listings

Edam: Lady Minto Health Care Centre, *see* Auxiliary Hospitals/Health Care Centres listings

Elrose Health Centre, PO Box 100, Elrose SK S0L 0Z0 – 306/378-2882; Fax: 306/378-2812 – 36 beds – Adm., Carolyn Torrance

Esterhazy: Centennial Special Care Home, PO Box 310, Esterhazy SK S0A 0X0 – 306/745-2323 – 60 beds – Adm., Sherrell Fox

Estevan Regional Nursing Home, 1921 Wallock Rd., Estevan SK S4A 2B5 – 306/634-2689 – 80 beds – Adm., Brenda Rabman

Estevan: Souris Valley Housing Company, 1028 Hillcrest Dr., Estevan SK S4A 1Y7 – 306/634-4154 – 27 beds – Adm., Norman Vall

Eston: Jubilee Lodge Inc., PO Box 667, Eston SK S0L 1A0 – 306/962-3215 – 35 beds – Adm., Carol Pryznyk

Fillmore Union Health Centre/Fillmore Special-Care Home Inc., *see* Auxiliary Hospitals/Health Care Centres listings

Foam Lake Jubilee Home, PO Box 460, Foam Lake SK S0A 1A0 – 306/272-4141 – 54 beds – Adm., Mervin Prystupa

Fort Qu'Appelle: Qu'Appelle Valley Housing Corp. (Echo Lodge), Fort Qu'Appelle SK S0G 1S0 – 306/332-4300 – 51 beds – Adm., Norm Zimmer

Gainsborough & Area Health Centre, *see* Auxiliary Hospitals/Health Care Centres listings

Goodsoil: L. Gervais Memorial Health Centre, *see* Auxiliary Hospitals/Health Care Centres listings

Gravelbourg: Foyer d'Youville, 216 Bettez St., Gravelbourg SK S0H 1X0 – 306/648-3185 – 50 beds – Adm., Raymond Mulaire

Grenfell & District Pioneer Home, PO Box 760, Grenfell SK S0G 2B0 – 306/697-2842 – 39 beds – Adm., Ernest C. Schmidt

Gull Lake & District Special Care Home Ltd., PO Box 539, Gull Lake SK S0N 1A0 – 306/672-3366 – 36 beds – Adm., Terry Hardy

Hafford Hospital & Special Care Centre, *see* General Hospitals listings

Herbert Heritage Manor, PO Box 10, Herbert SK S0H 2A0 – 306/784-3167; Fax: 306/784-3564 – 32 beds – Adm., Brian D. Penner

Herbert Nursing Home Inc., PO Box 520, Herbert SK S0H 2A0 – 306/784-2661 – 55 beds – Adm., Kenneth J. Isaak

Hudson Bay Pioneer Lodge, PO Box 940, Hudson Bay SK S0E 0Y0 – 306/865-2566; Fax: 306/865-2112 – 23 beds – Pasquia Health District – Community Health Mgr., Garry Form

Humboldt & District Housing Corp. (St. Mary's Villa), PO Box 1360, Humboldt SK S0K 2A0 – 306/682-3962 – 101 beds – Adm., Tom Ferguson

Imperial: Long Lake Valley Integrated Facility, *see* Auxiliary Hospitals/Health Care Centres listings

Indian Head: Golden Prairie Home, PO Box 250, Indian Head SK S0G 2K0 – 306/695-3636; Fax: 306/695-2698 – 47 beds – Pipestone Health District – Mgr., Penny L. Kerr

Invermay Health Centre/Gateway Lodge Inc., *see* Auxiliary Hospitals/Health Care Centres listings

Ituna & District Pioneer Lodge, PO Box 430, Ituna SK S0A 1N0 – 306/795-2683 – 36 beds – Adm., Murray McIntosh

Kamsack & District Nursing Home, PO Box 99, Kamsack SK S0A 1S0 – 306/542-3666 – 62 beds – Adm., Roger Zelinski

Kamsack Senior Housing Ltd. (Eaglestone Lodge), PO Box 1330, Kamsack SK S0A 1S0 – 306/542-2620 – 25 beds – Adm., Anita Dixon

Kelvington: Kelvindell Lodge Company, PO Box 280, Kelvington SK S0A 1W0 – 306/327-5151 – 46 beds – Adm., L. Wytrykusz

Kerrobert: Buena Vista Lodge, PO Box 440, Kerrobert SK S0L 1R0 – 306/834-2463 – 28 beds – Adm., Edward L. Kryzanowski

Kerrobert: Pioneer Haven Co. Ltd., PO Box 650, Kerrobert SK S0L 1R0 – 306/834-5255 – 30 beds – Adm., B. Ernie Tendler

Kindersley Senior Care Inc. (Heritage Manor), 901 - 1st St. West, Kindersley SK S0L 1S1 – 306/463-6401 – 80 beds – Adm., Brian Martin

Kinistino & District Housing Corporation (Jubilee Lodge), PO Box 370, Kinistino SK S0J 1H0 – 306/864-2851 – 36 beds – Adm., Carol Pryznyk

Kipling: Willowdale Lodge Care Home, PO Box 537, Kipling SK S0G 2S0 – 306/736-2218 – 26 beds – Adm., Murray Goeres

Kyle & District Health Centre, *see* Auxiliary Hospitals/Health Care Centres listings

La Ronge: La Ronge Hospital, *see* General Hospitals listings

LaFleche & District Health Centre, *see* Auxiliary Hospitals/Health Care Centres listings

Lampman Community Health Centre, *see* Auxiliary Hospitals/Health Care Centres listings

Langham Senior Citizens Home, PO Box 287, Langham SK S0K 2L0 – 306/283-4210 – 28 beds – Adm., Margaret Balzer

Lanigan: Central Parkland Lodge, PO Box 459, Lanigan SK S0K 2M0 – 306/365-3015 – 35 beds – Adm., Kathy Cole

Leader: Western Senior Citizens Home, PO Box 69, Leader SK S0N 1H0 – 306/628-3565 – 36 beds – Adm., Fenton Yeo

Leask: Wheatland Lodge Inc., PO Box 130, Leask SK S0J 1M0 – 306/466-4949; Fax: 306/466-2205 – 30 beds – Adm., Gail Cote

Leoville: Evergreen Health Centre, *see* Auxiliary Hospitals/Health Care Centres listings

Lestock: St. Joseph's Hospital, *see* General Hospitals listings

Lloydminster & District Senior Citizens Lodge (Jubilee Home), 3902 - 45th Ave., Lloydminster SK S9V 1Z2 – 403/825-2132 – 50 beds – Adm., Linda Graham

Loon Lake Union Hospital & Special Care Home, *see* General Hospitals listings

Lucky Lake Health Centre, *see* Auxiliary Hospitals/Health Care Centres listings

Lumsden & District Heritage Home Inc., PO Box 479, Lumsden SK S0G 3C0 – 306/731-2247 – 30 beds – Adm., Matthew A. Kalp

Macklin: Golden Twilight Lodge Incorporated, Macklin SK S0L 2C0 – 306/753-2217 – 25 beds – Adm., Mervin Dewing

Maidstone: Pine Island Lodge Ltd., PO Box 40, Maidstone SK S0M 1M0 – 306/893-2223 – 27 beds – Adm., Varn McClelland

Mankota: Prairie View Health Centre, *see* Auxiliary Hospitals/Health Care Centres listings

Maple Creek: Cypress Lodge Corp., PO Box 878, Maple Creek SK S0N 1N0 – 306/662-2671 – 61 beds – Adm., Bryce Wirachowsky

Meadow Lake: Northland Pioneers Lodge Inc., PO Box 40, Meadow Lake SK S0M 1V0 – 306/236-5812 – Adm., Floyd Gibb

Melfort & District Pioneer Lodge (Nirvana), PO Box 5000, Melfort SK S0E 1A0 – 306/752-2130 – 60 beds – Adm., Joe Rybinski

Melfort: Parkland Regional Care Centre, 302 Bemister Ave. East, PO Box 2260, Melfort SK S0E 1A0 – 306/752-2767 – 92 beds – Adm., Robert J. Duns

Melville: St. Paul Lutheran Home, PO Box 1390, Melville SK S0A 2P0 – 306/728-4591; Fax: 306/728-5471 – 144 beds – North Valley Health District – Adm., Don Whittmire

Midale: Mainprize Manor & Health Care Corporation, *see* Auxiliary Hospitals/Health Care Centres listings

Middle Lake: Bethany Pioneer Village Inc., PO Box 8, Middle Lake SK S0K 2X0 – 306/367-2033 – 36 beds – Adm., Glenn McDougall

Montmartre Health Centre, *see* Auxiliary Hospitals/Health Care Centres listings

Moose Jaw: Extendicare Ltd., 1151 Coteau St. West, Moose Jaw SK S6H 5G5 – 306/693-5191 – 127 beds – Adm., Tarry Vanbocquestal

Moose Jaw: Ina Grafton Gage Home, 200 Iriquois St. East, Moose Jaw SK S6H 4T3 – 306/692-4882, 4033; Fax: 306/692-3433 – 39 beds – Moose Jaw-Thunder Creek Health District – Adm., Dolores Willfong

Moose Jaw: Pioneer Housing Association of Moose Jaw, 1000 Albert St., Moose Jaw SK S6H 2Y2 – 306/692-6711 – 103 beds – Adm., Donald Campbell

Moosomin: Eastern Saskatchewan Pioneer Lodge Nursing Home, 405 Windover Ave., PO Box 858, Moosomin SK S0G 3N0 – 306/435-2100 Nursing Home, 435-2326 Lodge – 46 beds – Adm., Larry Signarowski

Nipawin District Nursing Home Inc. (Pineview Lodge), PO Box 2105, Nipawin SK S0E 1E0 – 306/862-9828 – 106 beds – Adm., Michael Kukurudza

Nokomis Health Centre/Pufer Special Care Home Corp., *see* Auxiliary Hospitals/Health Care Centres listings

North Battleford: The Battlefords River Heights Lodge Corporation, 2001 - 99th St., PO Box 657, North Battleford SK S9A 0S3 – 306/445-2497 – 142 beds – Adm., William H. Smith

North Battleford: Societe Joseph Breton Inc. (Villa Pascal), 1301 - 113th St., North Battleford SK S9A 3K1 – 306/445-8465 – 40 beds – Adm., Normand Poirier

Outlook & District Pioneer Home Inc., PO Box 396, Outlook SK S0L 2N0 – 306/867-8321 – 52 beds – Adm., Judy Jeska

Oxbow: Galloway Health Centre, *see* Auxiliary Hospitals/Health Care Centres listings

Ponteix: Foyer St-Joseph Nursing Home, PO Box 450, Ponteix SK S0N 1Z0 – 306/625-3366; Fax: 306/625-3918 – 30 beds – Adm., Sr. Marie Paule Béliveau, 306/625-3810

Ponteix: Rolling Hills Villa, PO Box 148, Ponteix SK S0N 1Z0 – 306/625-3511 – 18 beds – Adm., Roxanne Stringer

Porcupine Plain: Red Deer Nursing Home, PO Box 70, Porcupine Plain SK S0E 1H0 – 306/278-2469 – 50 beds – Adm., L. Merriman

Preeceville Lions Housing Corporation Ltd. (Lyons Lodge), PO Box 348, Preeceville SK S0A 3B0 – 306/547-3112 – 30 beds – Adm., Marlene Shapherd

Prince Albert: Mont St. Joseph Home Inc., 777 - 28th St. East, Prince Albert SK S6V 8C2 – 306/764-2856; Fax: 306/922-7475 – 120 beds – Prince Albert Health District – Exec. Dir., Karl Humeniuk

Prince Albert: Northern Housing Development Inc. (Herb Bassett Home), 1220 - 25th St. West, Prince Albert SK S6V 7P7 – 306/764-7777 – 144 beds

Prince Albert: Northern Housing Development Inc. (Pineview Terrace), 701 - 13th St. West, Prince Albert SK S6V 3E9 – 306/764-7777 – 53 beds

Rabbit Lake Integrated Facility, *see* Auxiliary Hospitals/Health Care Centres listings

Radville: Marian Home, PO Box 310, Radville SK S0M 2L0 – 306/869-2254 – 49 beds – Adm., Sheila Jubenville

Raymore: Silver Heights Special Care Home, PO Box 549, Raymore SK S0A 3J0 – 306/746-5744 – 30 beds – Touchwood Qu'Appelle Health District – Adm., Loralee Bailey

Redvers Centennial Haven, PO Box 399, Redvers SK S0C 2H0 – 306/452-3331 – 24 beds – Adm., Lori Hinz

Regina Lutheran Home, 1925 - 5th Ave. North, Regina SK S4R 8P6 – 306/543-4055 – 91 beds – Adm., Allan Hoffman

Regina Pioneer Village Ltd., 430 Pioneer Dr., Regina SK S4T 6L8 – 306/757-5646 – 405 beds – Adm., Ron Reavley

Regina: Extendicare Elmview, 4125 Rae St., Regina SK S4S 3A5 – 306/586-1787; Fax: 306/585-0255 – 65 beds – Regina Health District – Adm., Cathy Hauck

Regina: Extendicare Parkside, 4540 Rae St., Regina SK S4S 3B4 – 306/586-0220 – 228 beds – Adm., Shirley Van Moorleham

Regina: Extendicare Sunset, 260 Sunset Dr., Regina SK S4S 2S3 – 306/586-3355 – 152 beds – Adm., Marian Ogrodnick

Regina: Martin Luther Housing Corporation - Martin Luther Place, 46 Rogers Pl., Regina SK S4S 6S1 – 306/584-9107 – Managing Dir., Lorne Wettstein, 306/543-0288, Fax: 306/545-3211

Regina: The Qu'Appelle Diocesan Housing Company, 1425 College Ave., Regina SK S4P 1B4 – 306/522-0335 – 34 beds – Adm., Lucille Meaney

Regina: The Salvation Army William Booth Special Care Home, 50 Angus Rd., Regina SK S4R 6P6 – 306/543-0655 – 83 beds – Interim Adm., Maj. H. Thornhill

Regina: Santa Maria Senior Citizens Home, 4215 Regina Ave., Regina SK S4S 0J5 – 306/584-5566 – 162 beds – Adm., Beverly Olineck

Rockglen: Grasslands Health Centre, *see* Auxiliary Hospitals/Health Care Centres listings

Rosetown & District Health Centre, *see* General Hospitals listings

Rosetown: Wheatbelt Centennial Lodge Inc., PO Box 250, Rosetown SK S0L 2V0 – 306/882-3567 – 28 beds – Adm., Robert LeGoffe

Rosthern: Mennonite Nursing Home Inc., PO Box 370, Rosthern SK S0K 3R0 – 306/232-4861; Fax: 306/232-5611 – 86 beds – Adm., David Ratzlaff

St Brieux: Chateau Providence Inc., PO Box 340, St Brieux SK S0K 3V0 – 306/275-2227 – 30 beds – Adm., Wendy Smith

St Walburg: Lakeland Lodge Inc., PO Box 70, St Walburg SK S0M 2T0 – 306/248-3677 – 28 beds – Adm., Maryanne Hill

Saltcoats: Lakeside Manor Care Home Inc., PO Box 340, Saltcoats SK S0A 3R0 – 306/744-2353 – 30 beds – Adm., Dorothy Dawson

Saskatoon Convalescent Home, 101 - 31st St. West, Saskatoon SK S7L 0P6 – 306/244-7155 – 60 beds – Adm., Nathaniel Swaan

Saskatoon: Central Haven Special Care Home Inc., 1020 Avenue I North, Saskatoon SK S7L 2H7 – 306/665-6180 – 60 beds – Adm., Clarence Sawatzky

Saskatoon: Circle Drive Special Care Home Inc., 3055 Preston Ave. South, PO Box 60020, Saskatoon SK S7K 7L2 – 306/955-4800 – 50 beds – Adm., Leonard Enns

Saskatoon: Convent of Sion, 333 Acadia Dr., Saskatoon SK S7H 3V5 – 306/374-9566; Fax: 306/374-6648 – 16 beds – Saskatoon Health District – Adm., Sr. Beth Linthicum

Saskatoon: Del Haven Lodge, 316 - 4th Ave. North, Saskatoon SK S7K 2L7 – 306/653-2867 – 52 beds – Adm., Jean Neudorf, R.P.N.

Saskatoon: Elmwood Residences Inc. (Kinsmen Elmwood Lodge), 2012 Arlington Ave., Saskatoon SK S7J 2H5 – 306/374-5151 – 50 beds – Adm., Richard Baxter

Saskatoon: Extendicare Preston, 2225 Preston Ave., Saskatoon SK S7J 2E7 – 306/374-2242 – 82 beds – Adm., Pat Amos

Saskatoon: Jubilee Residences Inc. (Porteous), 833 Ave. P North, Saskatoon SK S7L 2W5 – 306/382-2626 – 117 beds – Adm., Ivan Kresak

Saskatoon: Jubilee Residences Inc. (Stensrud), 2202 McEown Ave., Saskatoon SK S7L 3L6 – 306/373-5580 – 100 beds – Adm., Heather Anderson

Saskatoon: Lutheran Sunset Home, Lutheran Sunset Home Foundation, 1212 Osler St., Saskatoon SK S7N 0T9 – 306/664-0300; Fax: 306/664-0311 – The foundation provides: special care home, housing for independent elderly, low-cost family housing, group living homes & day care for elderly – 129 beds – Saskatoon Health District – Exec. Dir., Harold Hesje

Saskatoon: Oliver Lodge, 1405 Faulkner Cres., Saskatoon SK S7L 3R5 – 306/382-4111 – 121 beds – Saskatoon Health District – Adm., M. Mitchell

Saskatoon: Parkridge Centre, 110 Gropper Cres., Saskatoon SK S7M 5N9 – 306/655-3800; Fax: 306/655-3801 – 238 beds – Saskatoon Health District – Resident Care Servs., Karen Knelsen

Saskatoon: St. Ann's Senior Citizens Village Corporation, 2910 Louise St., Saskatoon SK S7J 3L8 – 306/374-8900 – 80 beds – Adm., L.J. Moxness

Saskatoon: St. Joseph's Home for the Aged, 33 Valans Dr., Saskatoon SK S7L 3S2 – 306/382-6306 – 85 beds – Adm., Sr. Theodosia

Saskatoon: The Salvation Army Eventide Home, 2221 Adelaide St. East, Saskatoon SK S7J 0J6 – 306/374-5737 – 60 beds – Adm., Maj. Travis S. Wagner

Saskatoon: Sherbrooke Community Centre, 301 Acadia Dr., Saskatoon SK S7H 2E7 – 306/374-7955 – 286 beds – Adm., E. Marleau

Saskatoon: Sunnyside Nursing Home, 2200 St. Henry Ave., Saskatoon SK S7M 0P5 – 306/653-1267 – 106 beds – Adm., Desmond Dobroskay

Saskatoon: Ursuline Sisters of St. Angela's Convent, 1212 College Dr., Saskatoon SK S7N 0W4 – 306/653-2134 – 5 beds

Shaunavon Special Care Inc., 632 - 2nd St. East, Shaunavon SK SON 2M0 – 306/297-2245 Lodge, 297-2353 Nursing Home – 23 beds – Adm., Shannon Pomeroy

Shellbrook: Parkland Housing Company, Parkland Terrace, PO Box 670, Shellbrook SK S0J 2E0 – 306/747-2639 – 36 beds – Adm., Faith Mazurek

Spiritwood: Idylwild Senior Citizens Lodge, PO Box 159, Spiritwood SK S0J 2M0 – 306/883-2267 – 36 beds – Adm., Ted Boddy

Stoughton: Newhope Pioneer Lodge Incorporated, PO Box 38, Stoughton SK S0G 4T0 – 306/457-2552 – 30 beds – Adm., Edith Raiwet

Strasbourg: Last Mountain Pioneer Home, PO Box 549, Strasbourg SK S0G 4V0 – 306/725-3342 – 43 beds – Adm., Maxine Flotre

Swift Current: Chantelle Management Ltd., Swift Current Centre, 700 Aberdeen St. SE, Swift Current SK S9H 3E3 – 306/773-9371 – 70 beds – Adm., Vera Hyde

Swift Current: Palliser Regional Care Centre, PO Box 1420, Swift Current SK S9H 3G6 – 306/773-8307 – 105 beds – Adm., Keith Dalby

Swift Current: Prairie Pioneers Lodge, 300 Central Ave. South, Swift Current SK S9H 3G3 – 306/773-7524 – 58 beds – Adm., Esther Wall

Theodore Health Centre, *see* Auxiliary Hospitals/Health Care Centres listings

Tisdale & District Housing Company (Newmarket Manor), PO Box 2620, Tisdale SK S0E 1T0 – 306/873-5828; Fax: 306/873-4822 – 40 beds – Adm., Gordon Denton

Tisdale & District Housing Company (Sasko Park Lodge), PO Box 1330, Tisdale SK S0E 1T0 – 306/873-4585; Fax: 306/873-2404 – 33 beds – Pasquia Health District – Adm., Gordon Denton

Turtleford: Turtle River Nursing Home, PO Box 10, Turtleford SK S0M 2Y0 – 306/845-2195 – 15 beds – Adm., Vern McClelland

Unity: Unimac Pioneers Lodge, PO Box 970, Unity SK S0K 4L0 – 306/228-2744 – 43 beds – Adm., Mervin Dewing

Wadena: Pleasant View Care Home, Wadena SK S0A 4J0 – 306/338-3275 – 46 beds – Adm., Mike Koval

Wakaw: Lakeview Pioneer Lodge Housing Company, PO Box 189, Wakaw SK S0K 4P0 – 306/233-4621; Fax: 306/233-5225 – 50 beds – Adm., Claudia Vachon, R.N.

Waldheim: Menno Home of Saskatchewan, PO Box 130, Waldheim SK S0K 4S0 – 306/965-2070 – 43 beds – Adm., Marlin Roth

Warman Mennonite Special Care Home, Warman SK S0K 4S0 – 306/933-2011; Fax: 306/933-2782 – 31 beds – Saskatoon Health District – Adm., John Friesen

Watrous: Manitou Lodge, PO Box 10, Watrous SK S0K 4T0 – 306/946-3718 – 36 beds – Adm., John Knoch

Watson Community Health Centre & Quill Plains Lodge, *see* Auxiliary Hospitals/Health Care Centres listings

Wawota & District Special Care Home Inc., PO Box 99, Wawota SK S0G 5A0 – 306/739-2400 – 30 beds – Adm., Aaron Fornwald

Weyburn & District Special Care Homes Corporation, 704 - 5th St. NE, Weyburn SK S4H 1A3 – 306/842-4455 – 110 beds – Adm., Alex Horner

Weyburn: Souris Valley Regional Care Centre, PO Box 2001, Weyburn SK S4H 2L7 – 306/842-7481 – 241 beds – Adm., Warren Wallin

Whitewood & District Nursing Home Inc., PO Box 699, Whitewood SK S0G 5C0 – 306/735-2634 – 30 beds – Adm., Dan Shiplack

Wilkie & District Centennial Nursing Home, PO Box 459, Wilkie SK S0K 4W0 – 306/843-2668 – 30 beds – Adm., Bryce Martin

Wolseley: Lakeside Home, PO Box 10, Wolseley SK S0G 5H0 – 306/698-2573 – 80 beds – Adm., Arthur Colclough

Wynyard & District Housing Corporation (Golden Acres), PO Box 190, Wynyard SK S0A 4T0 – 306/554-3312 – 51 beds – Adm., Gary Hilderman

Yorkton & District Nursing Home Corporation, 200 Bradbrooke Dr., Yorkton SK S3N 2K5 – 306/782-2117 – 160 beds – Adm., Glen Kozak

Yorkton: Anderson Lodge, 150 Independent St., Yorkton SK S3N 0S7 – 306/783-4911 – 61 beds – Adm., Kerry Bodnarchuk

## SPECIAL TREATMENT CENTRES

(Includes: Abortion Clinics, Cancer Clinics, Rehabilitation Centres, Treatment Centres)

Moose Jaw: Providence Place for Holistic Health, 100 Second Ave. NE, Moose Jaw SK S6H 1B8 – 306/694-8081; Fax: 306/694-8804 – 188 beds – Exec. Dir., Bill Bell

Regina: Wascana Rehabilitation Centre, 2180 - 23 Ave., Regina SK S4S 0A5 – 306/766-5100; Fax: 306/766-5222 – rehabilitation centre, long term care centre – 303 inpatient, 44 hostel beds – Regina Health District – Pres. & CEO, Dr. Glenn S. Bartlett

# YUKON TERRITORY

## GENERAL HOSPITALS

Watson Lake Hospital, PO Box 500, Watson Lake YT Y0A 1C0 – 867/536-4444; Fax: 867/536-7302 – 10 beds – Nurse in Charge, Sue Rudd

Whitehorse General Hospital, 5 Hospital Rd., Whitehorse YT Y1A 3H7 – 867/667-8700; Fax: 867/667-2451 – CEO, Marny Willis

## AUXILIARY HOSPITALS/HEALTH CARE CENTRES

Beaver Creek Health Centre, General Delivery, Beaver Creek YT Y0B 1A0 – 867/862-4444; Fax: 867/862-7909

Carcross Health Centre, PO Box 27, Carcross YT Y0A 1B0 – 867/821-4444; Fax: 867/821-3909

Carmacks Health Centre, General Delivery, Carmacks YT Y0B 1C0 – 867/863-4444; Fax: 867/863-6612 – 2 beds

Destruction Bay Health Centre, General Delivery, Destruction Bay YT Y0B 1H0 – 867/841-4444; Fax: 867/841-5274

Haines Junction Health Centre, General Delivery, Haines Junction YT Y0B 1L0 – 867/634-4444; Fax: 867/634-2733

Pelly Crossing Health Centre, General Delivery, Pelly YT Y0B 1P0 – 867/537-4444; Fax: 867/537-3611

Ross River Health Centre, General Delivery, Ross River YT Y0B 1S0 – 867/969-4444; Fax: 867/969-2014

Teslin Health Centre, General Delivery, Teslin YT Y0A 1B0 – 867/390-4444; Fax: 867/390-2217

Watson Lake Health Centre, PO Box 500, Watson Lake YT Y0A 1C0 – 867/-536-4444; Fax: 867/536-7302

Whitehorse Health Centre, #300, 211 Main St., Whitehorse YT Y1A 2B3 – 867/667-6371; Fax: 867/667-2707

Whitehorse: Mt. McIntyre Native Health Centre, PO Box 1217, Whitehorse YT Y1A 5A5 – 867/668-7289; Fax: 867/633-6095

## MENTAL HEALTH HOSPITALS & COMMUNITY FACILITIES

Whitehorse: Mental Health Services, Hospital Rd., Whitehorse YT Y1A 3H8 – 867/667-8346; Fax: 867/667-8372

## NURSING STATIONS

Dawson City Nursing Station, PO Box 10, Dawson YT Y0B 1G0 – 867/993-4444; Fax: 867/993-5811

Faro Nursing Station, PO Box 99, Faro YT Y0B 1K0 – 867/994-4444; Fax: 867/994-3457

Mayo Nursing Station, PO Box 98, Mayo YT Y0B 1M0 – 867/996-4444; Fax: 867/996-2018

Old Crow Nursing Station, General Delivery, Old Crow YT Y0B 1N0 – 867/996-4444; Fax: 867/966-3614

# SECTION 9

## EDUCATION DIRECTORY



**See ADDENDA at the back of this book for late changes & additional information.**

## ALBERTA

### Alberta Advanced Education & Career Development

10155 - 102 St., 7th Fl., Edmonton AB T5J 4L5
403/422-4488; Fax: 403/422-5126

### Alberta Education

Communications Branch, Devonian Bldg., 11160 Jasper Ave., Edmonton AB T5K 0L2
403/427-2285; Fax: 403/427-0591

#### CURRICULUM INFORMATION

Director, Curriculum Branch, Keith Wagner, 403/427-2984; Fax: 422-3745

#### LEARNING TECHNOLOGIES BRANCH

Box 4000, Barrhead AB T7N 1P4
403/674-5333; Fax: 403/674-6561
Director, Garry Popowich

**For detailed departmental listings, see Index: "Education, Depts."**

### PUBLIC SCHOOL BOARDS & DIVISIONS IN ALBERTA

Includes counties, francophone educational regions, public school districts, Roman Catholic public school districts, regional divisions, regional school districts & school divisions, charter schools.

Aspen View Regional Division #19
3602 - 48 Ave., Athabasca AB T9S 1M8
403/675-2273; Fax: 403/675-5512 – Supt., John Ord; Asst. Sec.-Treas., Maurice Gushta

Battle River Regional Division #31
5402 - 48A Ave., Camrose AB T4V 0L3
403/672-6131; Fax: 403/672-6137 – Supt., Merle A. Stover; Sec.-Treas., Bill Schulte

Black Gold Regional Division #18
Nisku Centre, #301, 1101 - 5 St., Nisku AB T9E 7N3
403/955-6025; Fax: 403/955-6050 – Supt., Lowell Throndson; Sec.-Treas., Gordon Handke

Buffalo Trail Regional Division #28
1041 - 10A St., Wainwright AB T9W 2R4
403/842-6144; Fax: 403/842-3255 – Supt., Terry Pearson; Sec.-Treas., Vince Rodgers

Calgary School District #19
Education Centre Bldg., 515 Macleod Trail SE, Calgary AB T2G 2L9
403/294-8100; Fax: 403/294-8336 – Chief Supt., Donna Michaels; Supt. & Treas., Finance, Ursula Mergny

Canadian Rockies Regional Division #12
PO Box 748, Banff AB T0L 0C0
403/762-5581; Fax: 403/762-8271 – Supt., Brian Callaghan; Sec.-Treas., David Mackenzie

Chinook's Edge Regional Division #5
4904 - 50 St., PO Box 6080, Innisfail AB T4G 1W4
403/227-4272; Fax: 403/227-3652 – Supt., Altha Neilson; Treas., Susan Roy

Clearview Regional Division #24
PO Box 1420, Stettler AB T0C 2L0
403/742-3331; Fax: 403/742-1388 – Supt., Gillian Bushrod; Sec.-Treas., Robert Dick

East Central Francophone Education Region #3
PO Box 249, St. Paul AB T0A 3A0
403/645-3888; Fax: 403/645-2045 – Supt., Donald Michaud; Sec.-Treas., Yvan Beaubien

Edmonton School District #7
Centre for Education, One Kingsway, Edmonton AB T5H 4G9
403/429-8080; Fax: 403/429-8318 – Acting Supt., Emery Dosdall; Treas., Dean Power

Elk Island Public School Regional Division #14
2001 Sherwood Park Dr., Sherwood Park AB T8A 3W7
403/464-3477; Fax: 403/464-8056 – Supt., Terry Gunderson; Treas., Brian J. Smith

Foothills School Division #38
PO Box 5700, High River AB T1V 1M7
403/652-6522; Fax: 403/652-4204 – Supt., David Lynn; Sec.-Treas., Clair O. Belsher

Fort McMurray School District #2833
231 Hardin St., Fort McMurray AB T9H 2G2
403/799-7900; Fax: 403/743-2655 – Supt., John Waddell; Sec.-Treas., Randy Hoffman

Fort Vermilion School Division #52
PO Box 1, Fort Vermilion AB T0H 1N0
403/927-3766; Fax: 403/927-4625 – Supt., Michael Davenport; Sec.-Treas., Grant Mann

Golden Hills Regional Division #15
435A Hwy. #1, Strathmore AB T1P 1J4
403/934-5121; Fax: 403/934-5125 – Supt., Dr. G. McKinnon; Sec.-Treas., Wayne Bralin

Grande Prairie School District #2357
10213 - 99 St., Grande Prairie AB T8V 2H3
403/532-4491; Fax: 403/539-4265 – Supt., Derek Taylor; Sec.-Treas., Bob Leech

Grande Yellowhead Regional Division #35
3656 - 1 Ave., Edson AB T7E 1S8
403/723-4471; Fax: 403/723-2414 – Supt., Klaus Puhlmann; Sec.-Treas., Earl Trathen

Grasslands Regional Division #6
408 First St. West, Brooks AB T1R 0V8
403/362-2555; Fax: 403/362-8225 – Supt., Duncan Gillespie; Sec.-Treas., Leeann Woods

High Prairie School Division #48
PO Box 870, High Prairie AB T0G 1E0
403/523-3337; Fax: 403/523-4639 – Supt., Verne Evans; Sec.-Treas., Laurie Marston

Horizon School Division #67
6304 - 52 St., Taber AB T1G 1J7
403/223-3547; Fax: 403/223-2999 – Supt., Dr. Eric Johnson; Sec.-Treas., Viola Powell

Lethbridge School District #51
433 - 15 St. South, Lethbridge AB T1J 2Z5
403/380-5301; Fax: 403/327-4387 – Supt., Gary Kiernan; Sec.-Treas., Don Lussier

Livingstone Range School Division #68
PO Box 1959, Claresholm AB T0L 0T0
403/625-3356; Fax: 403/325-2424 – Supt., Lloyd Cavers; Treas., Don Olsen

Lloydminster Public School Division #1753
5017 - 46 St., Lloydminster AB T9V 1R4
403/875-5541; Fax: 403/875-7829 – Supt., Don Duncan; Treas., Beverley Henry

Medicine Hat School District #76
601 - 1 Ave. SW, Medicine Hat AB T1A 4Y7
403/528-6700; Fax: 403/529-5339 – Supt., Harold T. Storlien; Sec.-Treas., Doug Pudwell

North Central Francophone Education Region #4
8815D - 92 St., Edmonton AB T6C 3P9
403/468-6440; Fax: 403/440-1631 – Supt., Gerard Bissonnette; Sec.-Treas., Paulette Briand

Northeast Francophone Education Region #2
190 Tamarack Way, Fort Mcmurray AB T9K 1A1
403/791-7702; Fax: 403/791-5391 – Supt., Vacant; Sec.-Treas., Sandra Boudreault

Northern Gateway Regional Division #10
4104 Kepler St., Whitecourt AB T7S 1M8
403/778-2800; Fax: 403/778-6719 – Supt., L. Larson; Treas., Cody McClintock

Northern Lights School District #69
6005 - 50 Ave., Bonnyville AB T9N 2L4
403/826-3145; Fax: 403/826-4600 – Supt., Ed Wittchen; Sec.-Treas., Gary Krawchuk

Northland School Division #61
PO Bag 1400, Peace River AB T8S 1V2
403/624-2060; Fax: 403/624-5914 – Supt., Colin Kelly; Sec.-Treas., Fred deKleine

Northwest Francophone Education Region #1
PO Box 1220, St. Isidore AB T0H 3B0
403/624-8855; Fax: 403/624-8554 – Supt., Denise Bourassa; Sec.-Treas., Anita Belzile

Palliser Regional Division #26
#101, 905 - 4 Ave. South, Lethbridge AB T1J 0P4
403/328-4111; Fax: 403/380-6890 – Supt., John Bolton; Sec.-Treas., John J. Gleason

Parkland School Division #70
4603 - 48 St., Stony Plain AB T7Z 2A8
403/963-4010; Fax: 403/963-4169 – Supt., Dr. David Young; Sec.-Treas., Thomas Olson

Peace River School Division #10
PO Box 6960, Peace River AB T8S 1S7
403/624-3601; Fax: 403/624-5941 – Supt., David Van Tamelan; Sec.-Treas., Bruce Moltzan

Peace Wapiti Regional Division #33
8611A - 108 St., Grande Prairie AB T8V 4C5
403/532-8133; Fax: 403/532-4234 – Supt., R. Gerald Mazer; Sec.-Treas., Murray Donaghy

Pembina Hills Regional Division #7
5310 - 49 St., Barrhead AB T7N 1P3
403/674-8500; Fax: 403/674-3262 – Supt., Sig Schmold; Treas., Tracy Meunier

Prairie Land Regional Division #25
PO Box 1400, Hanna AB T0J 1P0
403/854-4481; Fax: 403/854-2803 – Supt., Robert Tredger; Sec.-Treas., Dennis Moss

Prairie Rose Regional Division #8
918 - 2 Ave., PO Box 204, Dunmore AB T0J 1A0
403/527-5516; Fax: 403/528-2264 – Supt., Keith Jones; Sec.-Treas., Patricia Cocks

Red Deer School District #104
4747 - 53 St., Red Deer AB T4N 2E6
403/342-3710; Fax: 403/347-8190 – Supt., David Blacker; Asst. Supt., Business Service, Ray Congdon

Rocky View School Division #41
2616 - 18 St. NE, Calgary AB T2E 7R1
403/250-1504; Fax: 403/250-3281 – Supt., Colleen Brownlee; Sec.-Treas., Darrell Couture

St. Paul Education Regional Division #1
4901 - 47 St., St. Paul AB T0A 3A3
403/645-3323; Fax: 403/645-5789 – Supt., Ted Cabaj; Sec.-Treas., Jean Champagne

South Central Francophone Education Region #6
#202, 1324 - 11 Ave. SW, Calgary AB T3C 0M6
403/228-2999; Fax: 403/228-9321 – Supt., Vacant; Sec.-Treas., Roger Lalonde

Southern Francophone Education Region #7
#202, 325 - 6 St. South, Lethbridge AB T1J 2C7
403/329-4189; Fax: 403/329-9132 – Supt., Vacant; Sec.-Treas., Hélène Bourgeois

Sturgeon School Division #24
9820 - 104 St., Morinville AB T8R 1L8
403/939-4341; Fax: 403/939-5520 – Supt., John Hogarth; Sec.-Treas., Murray R. Lloyd

Westwind Regional Division #9
PO Box 10, Cardston AB T0K 0K0
403/653-4991; Fax: 403/653-4641 – Supt., Dr. Mel Cottle; Sec.-Treas., Drew Chipman

Wetaskiwin Regional Division #11
4710 - 55 St., Wetaskiwin AB T9A 3B7
403/352-6018; Fax: 403/352-7886 – Supt., Hal Kluczny; Sec.-Treas., Donna Mogg

Wild Rose School Division #66
PO Box 8000, Rocky Mountain House AB T0M 1T0
403/845-3376; Fax: 403/845-3850 – Supt., Jim McLellan; Sec.-Treas., Alex Weber

Wolf Creek Regional Division #32
6000 Hwy. 2A, Ponoka AB T4J 1P6
403/783-3473; Fax: 403/783-3483 – Supt., Lyle Lorenz; Sec.-Treas., Joe Henderson

## PROTESTANT SEPARATE SCHOOL DISTRICTS

St. Albert Protestant Separate School District #6
60 Sir Winston Churchill Ave., St. Albert AB T8N 0G4
403/460-3712; Fax: 403/460-7686 – Supt., Ruth Leblanc; Sec.-Treas., Mel Poole

## ROMAN CATHOLIC SEPARATE SCHOOL DISTRICTS

Calgary Roman Catholic Separate School District #1
1000 - 5th Ave. SW, Calgary AB T2P 4T9
403/298-1411; Fax: 403/237-9694 – Chief Supt., Bill Dever; Sec.-Treas., Deborah Achen

Christ Redeemer Catholic Separate Regional Division #3
46 Elma St., Okotoks AB T0L 1T3
403/938-2659; Fax: 403/938-4575 – Supt., Ronald Wallace; Treas., Dennis Schneider

East Central Alberta Catholic Separate School Regional Division #16
223 - 10 St., Wainwright AB T9W 1N7
403/842-3992; Fax: 403/842-5322 – Supt., George Bunz; Treas., Marilyn Bachmann

Edmonton Roman Catholic Separate School District #7
9807 - 106 St., Edmonton AB T5K 1C2
403/441-6000; Fax: 403/425-8759 – Supt., Terry Fortin; Sec.-Treas., R. G. Bennett

Evergreen Catholic Separate Regional Division #2
PO Box 4265, Spruce Grove AB T7X 3B4
403/962-5627; Fax: 403/962-4664 – Supt., Jim Collins; Sec.-Treas., Gary Innes

Fort McMurray Roman Catholic Separate School District #32
9809 Main St., Fort McMurray AB T9H 1T7
403/799-5700; Fax: 403/799-5706 – Acting Supt., Dan McIsaac; Sec.-Treas., Vacant

Fort Saskatchewan Roman Catholic Separate School District #104
#124, 8818 - 111 St., Fort Saskatchewan AB T8L 3T4
403/998-4622; Fax: 403/998-1100 – Supt., James Sheasgreen; Sec.-Treas., Andrew Isbister

Good Shepherd Roman Catholic Regional Division #13
4921 - 43 St., Drayton Valley AB T7A 1P5
403/542-5267; Fax: 403/542-6060 – Supt., Bryce Knudson; Sec.-Treas., Joyce Murray

Grande Prairie Roman Catholic Separate School District #28
9902 - 101 St., Grande Prairie AB T8V 2P5
403/532-3013; Fax: 403/532-3430 – Supt., Lorne Radbourne; Sec.-Treas., Grant Burge

Greater St. Albert Catholic Regional Division #29
6 St. Vital Ave., St. Albert AB T8N 1K2
403/459-7711; Fax: 403/458-3213 – Supt., Lee Lucente; Sec.-Treas., Al Summers

Holy Family Catholic Separate Regional Division #17
PO Box 789, High Prairie AB T0G 1E0
403/523-3771; Fax: 403/523-4603 – Supt., Marcel Michaud; Sec.-Treas., Diana Hildebrand

Holy Spirit Roman Catholic Separate Regional Division #4
534 - 18 St. South, Lethbridge AB T1J 3E7
403/327-9555; Fax: 403/327-9595 – Supt., Frank Letain; Sec.-Treas., Karel Meulenbroek

Holy Trinity Catholic Regional Division #21
3804B - 47 St., Whitecourt AB T7S 1M8
403/778-5666; Fax: 403/778-2727 – Supt., Bryan Kulmatycki; Sec.-Treas., Frank Booth

Lakeland Roman Catholic Separate School District #150
4810 - 46 St., Bonnyville AB T9N 1B5
403/826-3235; Fax: 403/826-7576 – Supt., Henri Lemire; Sec.-Treas., Adele Coates

Lloydminster Roman Catholic Separate School District #89
5411 - 50 Ave., Lloydminster SK S9V 0R1
306/825-8911; Fax: 306/825-9855 – Dir., R.V. Mokelky; Sec.-Treas., Tom Schinold

Medicine Hat Catholic Separate School Regional Division #20
1251 - 1 Ave. SW, Medicine Hat AB T1A 8B4
403/527-2292; Fax: 403/529-0917 – Supt., Patrick Glashan; Sec.-Treas., Tony Giesinger

North Peace Roman Catholic Separate School District #43
10307 - 99 St., Peace River AB T8S 1R5
403/624-3956; Fax: 403/624-1154 – Supt., Wayne Doll; Sec.-Treas., Huguette Ropchan

Red Deer Roman Catholic Separate School District #17
3827 - 39 St., Red Deer AB T4N 0Y6
403/343-1055; Fax: 403/347-6410 – Supt., Lloyd Baumgarten; Sec.-Treas., Richard M. Dornstauder

St. Thomas Aquinas Regional Division #22
5108A - 47 St., Leduc AB T9E 6Y9
403/986-2500; Fax: 403/986-8620 – Supt., Eugene Miller; Sec.-Treas., Ron Beakhouse

Sherwood Park Catholic Separate School District #105
2017 Brentwood Blvd., Sherwood Park AB T8A 0X2
403/467-8896; Fax: 403/467-5469 – Supt., Patrick Maguire; Sec.-Treas., Alberta M. Hutchings

Slave Lake Roman Catholic Separate School District #364
109 - 6 Ave. SE, Slave Lake AB T0G 2A3
403/849-3020; Fax: 403/849-5900 – Supt., Michel Beaudoin; Sec.-Treas., Noel Moriyama

Sundance Catholic Separate Regional Division #10
#203, 211 Pembina Ave., Hinton AB T7V 2B3
403/865-3811; Fax: 403/865-5633 – Supt., Joffre Plaquin; Sec.-Treas., Cheryl Freeman

Vegreville Catholic Separate School District #16
5121 - 52 Ave., Vegreville AB T9C 1M2
403/632-6821; Fax: 403/632-3448 – Supt., Bernard McCracken; Sec.-Treas., Daniel Dubuc

## CHARTER SCHOOLS

Action for Bright Children School – Gr. 1-9
414 - 10A St. NE, Calgary AB T2E 4P2
403/234-9612 – Supt., Vacant; Sec.-Treas., Stan Doherty

Almadina School Society
#563, 3545 - 32 Ave. NE, Calgary AB T1Y 6M6
403/590-1633; Fax: 403/530-5073

Aurora School Ltd.
8755 - 170 St., Edmonton AB T5R 5Y6
403/930-5502; Fax: 403/930-5598

Boyle Street Service Society – Gr. 1-12
10116 - 105 Ave., Edmonton AB T5H 0K2
403/425-4106; Fax: 403/425-2205 – Supt., Emery Dosball; Sec.-Treas., Deanna Bright

Centre for Academic & Personal Excellence – Gr. 1-9
51 - 6 St. SE, Medicine Hat AB T1A 8N1
403/528-2983; Fax: 403/528-3048 – Supt., Teresa Bimimmo; Sec.-Treas., Judy Herring

Education for the Gifted Society – Gr. Pre.-9
#103, 1604 Sherwood Dr., Sherwood Park AB T8A 0Z2
403/467-6409 – Supt., Vacant; Treas., Greg Paton

Global Learning Academy
315 - 86 Ave. SE, Calgary AB T2H 1Z2
403/543-7050

Society for Talent Education – Gr. Pre.-6
7211 - 96A Ave., Edmonton AB T6B 1B5
403/468-2598 – Administrator, Loretta Isaac

## NATIVE SCHOOLS

(Jurisdiction of Indian & Northern Affairs Canada.)

#### BANDS, BOARDS OF EDUCATION

Alexander Band, PO Box 1440, Morinville AB T0G 1P0 – 403/939-3868; Fax: 403/939-3991 – Adm., E. Arcand – Gr. 1-12

Alexis Band, PO Box 27, Glenevis AB T0E 0X0 – 403/967-5919; Fax: 403/967-2671 – Adm., Roderick Alexis – Gr. 1-12

Beaver Lake Tribe #131, PO Box 960, Lac La Biche AB T0A 2C0 – 403/623-4548; Fax: 403/623-4659 – Adm., D. Kirby

Bigstone Education Authority Society, General Delivery, Desmarais AB T0G 0T0 – 403/891-3825 – Gr. 1-6

Cree Band #461, c/o Sturgeon Lake Band School, PO Box 5, Valleyview AB T0H 3N0 – 403/524-4590; Fax: 403/524-3696 – Adm., Nareen Narayan – Gr. 1-12

Dene Tha Band, PO Box 118, Chateh AB T0H 0S0 – 403/321-3842 – Supt., Education, Russell Lahti – Gr. 1-9

Driftpile Band, General Delivery, Driftpile AB T0G 0V0 – 403/355-3615 – Dir. of Ed., Steven Kulmatycki – Gr. 1-12

Ermineskin Band, General Delivery, Hobbema AB T0C 1N0 – 403/585-3931; Fax: 403/585-2001 – Adm., Don Sinclaire

Ermineskin Smallboy Band, General Delivery, Robb AB T0E 1X0 – 403/794-3784 – Adm., Melvin Nadeau – Gr. 1-9

Federally Administered Schools, c/o Indian & Inuit Affairs, #630, 9700 Jasper Ave., Edmonton AB T5J 4G2 – 403/594-3733; Fax: 403/594-5845

Frog Lake Band, General Delivery, Frog Lake AB T0A 1M0 – 403/943-3918 – Dir., Clarence Faithfull – Gr. 10-12

Heart Lake Band, PO Box 447, Lac La Biche AB T0A 2C0 – 403/623-2600; Fax: 403/623-3505 – Adm., Sidney Rodnunsky

Horse Lake First Nation, PO Box 303, Hythe AB T0H 2C0 – 403/356-2248; Fax: 403/356-3666

Kainaiwa Board of Education, PO Box 240, Standoff AB T0L 1Y0 – 403/737-3966; Fax: 403/737-2361 – Gr. 7-12

Kehewin Band, PO Box 6218, Bonnyville AB T8N 2G8 – 403/826-6200; Fax: 403/826-6265 – Adm., Victor John

Kiseputinow Education Dept., PO Box 130, Hobbema AB T0C 1N0 – 403/585-3979; Fax: 403/585-3799 – Gr. 1-6

Kitaskinaw Education Authority, PO Box 90, Enoch AB T7X 3Y3 – 403/470-5657; Fax: 403/470-5687 – Gr. 1-9

Little Red River Board of Education, PO Box 1830, High Level AB T0H 1Z0 – 403/759-3810 – Supt., Marvin Fyten – Gr. 1-12

Montana Community School, PO Box 129, Hobbema AB T0C 1N0 – 403/585-2000; Fax: 403/585-2022 – Gr. Pre.-9

O'chiese Education Authority, PO Box 337, Rocky Mountain House AB T0M 1T0 – 403/989-2000; Fax: 403/989-2122 – Gr. 1-9

Paul Band Education Authority, PO Box 89, Duffield AB T0E 0N0 – 403/892-2691 – Gr. Pre.-6

Peigan Band, PO Box 130, Brochet AB T0K 0H0 – 403/965-3910; Fax: 403/965-3713 – Dir., Ben Kawaguchi

Saddle Lake Education Authority, PO Box 70, Saddle Lake AB T0A 3T0 – 403/726-3730 – Gr. 10-12

Samson Band, PO Box 658, Hobbema AB T0C 1N0 – 403/585-2211; Fax: 403/585-3857 – Adm., Grace Buffalo

Sarcee Band, 3700 Anderson Rd. SW, PO Box 131, Calgary AB T2W 3C4 – 403/251-1600; Fax: 403/251-9961

Siksika Board of Education, PO Box 1099, Siksika AB T0J 3W0 – 403/734-5220 – Dir., Robert Breaker

Stoney Band, PO Box 40, Morley AB T0L 1N0 – 403/881-3966

Sunchild First Nation Band, PO Box 747, Rocky Mountain House AB T0M 1T0 – 403/989-3787

Swan River First Nation, PO Box 270, Kinuso AB T0G 1K0 – 403/775-3536; Fax: 403/775-3796 – Gr. 7-12

Tallcree Band, PO Box 310, Fort Vermilion AB T0H 1N0 – 403/927-4381 – Adm., Michael J. Campbell – Gr. 1-6

Whitefish Lake Educational Authority, PO Box 274, Goodfish AB T0A 1R0 – 403/428-9501 – Gr. Pre.-9

Whitefish Lake First Nation, General Delivery, Atikameg AB T0G 0C0 – 403/767-3914; Fax: 403/767-3814 – Gr. 1-12

Woodland Cree First Nation, General Delivery, Cadotte Lake AB T0H 0N0 – 403/629-3803; Fax: 403/629-3898 – Gr. 1-12

Yellowhead Tribal Council, 17304 - 105 Ave., 3rd Fl., Edmonton AB T5S 1G4 – 403/484-0303; Fax: 403/481-7275 – Dir. of Ed., Jim Brule – Gr. 10-12

## UNIVERSITIES

### Athabasca University

1 University Dr., Athabasca AB T9S 3A3
Fax: 403/675-6145; Toll Free: 1-800-788-9041
URL: http://www.athabascau.ca
Registrar, Joan Fraser, B.A., M.Ed.
President, Dominique Abrioux, Ph.D.
Vice-President, Academic, Alan Davis, Ph.D.
Vice-President, Finance, Art Nutt, C.A.
Manager, Learning Services, C. Nelson, B.A., B.Ed.
Director, Library Services, Steven Schafer
Executive Director, Student Services, Judith Hughes, Ph.D.

#### SCHOOLS WITH CHAIRS

Centre for Computing, Information Systems & Mathematics, Peter Holt, B.Sc.
Centre for Distance Education, R. Spencer, B.A., M.A., Ph.D.
Centre for Economics, Industrial Relations & Organizational Studies, John Newark, B.A., M.A., Ph.D.
Centre for Global & Social Analysis, Jeremy Mouat, B.A., M.A., Ph.D.
Centre for Information & Communication Studies, Andrew Woudstra, B.A., B.Comm., M.B.A., C.M.A.
Centre for Innovative Management, Jane Borland, B.A., M.B.A.
Centre for Language & Literature, Joseph J. Pivato, B.A., M.A., Ph.D.
Centre for Learning Accreditation, Ken Collier, B.A., M.S.W., Ph.D.
Centre for Natural & Human Science, Dietmar Kennepohl, B.Sc., Ph.D.
Centre for Nursing & Health Studies, Roberta L. Carey, R.N., B.A., M.A., Ph.D.
Centre for Psychology, Lyle Grant, B.A., M.A., Ph.D.
Centre for State & Legal Studies, Anwar (Andy) N. Khan, Dip.Ed., B.A., M.A., LL.B., M.A., Fil.
Centre for Work & Community Services, Bruce Spencer, Cert.Ed., B.Sc., M.A., Ph.D.

### Augustana University College

4901 - 46 Ave., Camrose AB T4V 2R3
403/679-1100; Fax: 403/679-1129
URL: gopher://gopher/augustana.ab.ca:70/1
President, Rev. Richard Husfloen
Chair, Board of Regents, Sandra Anderson
Dean & Vice-President, Academic Affairs, Janet Wright
Registrar, Raymond Blacklock
Librarian, Nancy Goebel
Manager, Bookstore, Elaine Duchscherer

### University of Alberta

26 University Campus NW, Edmonton AB T6G 2E8
403/492-3111, 2325; Fax: 403/492-2997
Email: public.affairs@ualberta.ca; URL: http://web.cs.ualberta.ca/ualberta.html
Chancellor, L. Hyndman, O.C., LL.B.
President, R. Fraser, Ph.D.
Chair, Board of Governors, J. Ferguson, B.Comm.
Vice-President, Academic, D. Owram, Ph.D.
Vice-President, Finance & Administration, G. Harris, M.A.Sc.
Acting Vice-President, Research & External Affairs, R. Smith, Ph.D.
Assoc. Vice-President & Executive Director, External Relations, T.R. Flannigan, Ph.D.
Comptroller & Assoc. Vice-President, N. Merali, C.M.A.
Registrar & Assoc. Vice-President, B.J. Silzer, M.Ed.
Director, Public Affairs, J.A. Myers, LL.B.
Director, Materials Management, R.A. Bennett, M.B.A.
Manager, Bookstore, J. Picheca, B. Com.
Director, School of Library & Information Studies, S. Bertram, Ph.D.
Director, School of Native Studies, J. Dempsey, M.A.
Dean, Students, J. Newton, Ph.D.

#### FACULTIES WITH DEANS

Agriculture, Forestry & Home Economics, I.N. Morrison, Ph.D.
Arts, P. Clements, D.Phil.
Business, M. Percy, Ph.D.
Education, L. Beauchamp, Ph.D.
Engineering, D. Lynch, Ph.D.
Extension, R. Garrison, Ph.D.
Faculté Saint-Jean, Claudette Tardif, Ph.D.
Graduate Studies & Research, M. Gray, Ph.D.
Law, L. Klar, LL.M.
Medicine & Oral Health Sciences, D.L. Tyrrell, Ph.D.
Nursing, M. Wood, Ph.D.
Pharmacy & Pharmaceutical Sciences, R.E. Moskalyk, Ph.D.
Physical Education & Recreation, A. Quinney, Ph.D.
Rehabilitation Medicine, A. Cook, Ph.D.
Science, R.E. Peter, Ph.D.

#### AFFILIATED COLLEGES

Canadian Union College, PO Box 430, College Heights AB T0C 0Z0 – 403/782-3381; Fax: 403/782-3170; Toll Free: 1-800-661-8129 – President, Victor Fitch

Concordia University College, 7128 Ada Blvd., Edmonton AB T5B 4E4 – 403/479-8481; Fax: 403/474-1933

King's College, 10766 - 97 St., Edmonton AB T5H 2M1 – 403/465-3500; Fax: 403/425-8166; URL: http://www.kingsu.ab.ca – Chair, Board of Governors, William Wildeboer

North America Baptist College, 11525 - 23rd Ave., Edmonton AB T6J 4T3 – 403/437-1960

St. Joseph's College, c/o University of Alberta, Edmonton AB T6G 2J5 – 403/492-7681 – President, Rev. R.J. Barringer, C.S.B., D.Phil.

St. Stephen's College, c/o University of Alberta, Edmonton AB T6G 2J5 – 403/439-7311 – Principal, Dr. G.I. Mundle, D.Min.

### The University of Calgary

2500 University Dr. NW, Calgary AB T2N 1N4
403/220-5110; Fax: 403/282-7298

URL: http://www.ucalgary.ca/
Chancellor, M.A. McCaig, B.Ed.
Chair, Board of Governors, J.E. Newall, B.Comm.
President & Vice-Chancellor, T. White, B.Sc., M.A., Ph.D.
Registrar, G.J.P. Krivy, B.Ed., M.Ed., Ph.D.
Vice-President, Academic, J.D. Calkin, B.Sc.N., M.Sc.N., Ph.D.
Vice-President, Finance & Services, G.K. Winter, B.Sc., M.Sc., Ph.D.
Vice-President, Research, C.H. Langford, A.B., Ph.D.
Director, Information Services, A.H. MacDonald, B.A., B.L.S., A.L.I.A.A.
Director, Libraries, T.M. Eadie, B.A., M.A., M.L.S.
Director, University Secretariat, R. Williams, B.A. (Hons.)
Executive Director, External Relations, S. Reid, B.Sc.

#### FACULTIES WITH DEANS

Continuing Education, T.P. Keenan, M.S., Ed.M.
Education, I. Winchester, D.Phil.
Engineering, S.C. Wirasinghe, Ph.D., P.Eng.
Environmental Design, R.J.D. Page, B.A., M.A., D.Phil.
Fine Arts, Maurice Yacowar, Ph.D.
General Studies, M.J. McMordie, B.Arch., Ph.D.
Graduate Studies, D.J. Bercuson, B.A., M.A., Ph.D., F.R.S.C.
Humanities, R.B. Bond, B.A., M.A., Ph.D., A.R.C.T., A.R.C.C.O.
Kinesiology, W.L. Veale, B.Sc., M.Sc., Ph.D., F.R.S.C.
Law, M. Wylie, B.A., LL.B., B.C.L.(Oxon)
Management, P.M. Maher, B.E., M.B.A., Ph.D., P.Eng.
Medicine, E.R. Smith, M.D., FRCP(C) (F.R.C.P.C)
Acting Dean, Nursing, Carol Rogers, R.N., M.H.Sc.
Science, E.J.M. Kendall, B.Sc., M.Sc., Ph.D.
Social Sciences, S.J. Randall, B.A., M.A., Ph.D.
Social Work, R.J. Thomlison, B.Sc., B.S.W., M.S.W., Ph.D.

### University of Lethbridge

4401 University Dr., Lethbridge AB T1K 3M4
403/320-5700; Fax: 403/329-5159
URL: http://www.uleth.ca
President, H.E. Tennant
Director, Development, Charlotte Caton
Vice-President, Academic, Seamus O'Shea
Assoc. Vice-President, Academic, L. Stebbins
Assistant Vice-President, Students, Wilma Winter
Director, Research Services, R. McHugh
Manager, Materials Management, Barry Kimery
Manager, Bookstore, Donna Kampen

#### FACULTIES WITH DEANS

Arts & Science, Bhagwan Dua
Education, Laurie Walker
Management, Ali Dastmalchian

#### SCHOOLS WITH DIRECTORS

Dean, Fine Arts, Vondis Miller
Dean, Nursing, Una Ridley

## INSTITUTES OF TECHNOLOGY

#### THE NORTHERN ALBERTA INSTITUTE OF TECHNOLOGY

11762 - 106 St., Edmonton AB T5G 2R1
403/471-7400; Fax: 403/471-8583
URL: http://www.schoolfinder.com/profiles/colleges/nait.htm
President, Stan G. Souch

#### THE SOUTHERN ALBERTA INSTITUTE OF TECHNOLOGY

1301 - 16 Ave. NW, Calgary AB T2M 0L4
403/284-8581; Fax: 403/281-8940
URL: http://www.sait.ab.ca/
President, Dale Landry, Email: dale.landry@sait.ab.ca

## PUBLIC COLLEGES

#### FAIRVIEW COLLEGE

PO Box 3500, Fairview AB T8S 1V9
403/835-6600; Fax: 403/835-6670
Email: sroy@fairviewc.ab.ca
President, Fred Trotter

#### GRANDE PRAIRIE REGIONAL COLLEGE

10726 - 106 Ave., Grande Prairie AB T8V 4C4
403/539-2024; Fax: 403/539-2749
President, Gordon Gilgan

#### GRANT MACEWAN COMMUNITY COLLEGE

c/o Administration Office, City Centre Campus, 10700 - 104 Ave., Edmonton AB T5J 4S2
403/497-5401; Fax: 403/497-5405
URL: http://www.gmcc.ab.ca/
President, Dr. Paul Byrne, Email: byrnep@admin.gmcc.ab.ca
City Centre Campus, 10700 - 104 Ave., Edmonton AB T5J 4S2 – 403/497-5040; Fax: 403/497-5045
Jasper Place Campus, 10045 - 156 St., Edmonton AB T5P 2P7 – 403/497-4340; Fax: 403/497-4300
Mill Woods Campus, 7319 - 29 Ave., Edmonton AB T6K 2P1 – 403/497-4040; Fax: 403/497-4045

#### KEYANO COLLEGE

8115 Franklin Ave., Fort McMurray AB T9H 2H7
403/791-4800; Fax: 403/791-1555; Toll Free: 1-800-251-1408
URL: http://www.keyanoc.ab.ca
President, Dr. Douglas MacRae

#### LAKELAND COLLEGE

c/o Corporate Offices, 5707 - 47 Ave. West, Vermilion AB T9X 1K6
403/853-8400; Fax: 403/853-7355
President, Dr. Steve Pawlak
Lloydminster Campus, Bag 6600, Lloydminster SK S9V 1Z3 – 403/871-5700; Fax: 403/875-5136

#### LETHBRIDGE COMMUNITY COLLEGE

3000 College Dr. South, Lethbridge AB T1K 1L6
403/320-3335; Fax: 403/329-0530
Email: pr@lethbridgec.ab.ca; URL: http://www.lethbridgec.ab.ca
President, Donna Allan

#### MEDICINE HAT COLLEGE

299 College Dr. SE, Medicine Hat AB T1A 3Y6
403/529-3801; Fax: 403/526-7750
President, D. Ralph Weeks, Ph.D., Email: weeks@acd.mhc.ab.ca

#### MOUNT ROYAL COLLEGE

4825 Richard Rd. SW, Calgary AB T3E 6K6
403/240-6111; Fax: 403/240-5938
Email: dkoop@mtroyal.ab.ca; URL: http://www.mtroyal.ab.ca/
President, Thomas L. Wood

#### OLDS COLLEGE

4500 - 50th St., Olds AB T4H 1R6
403/556-8365; Fax: 403/556-4692
President, Robert Turner

#### PRAIRIE BIBLE COLLEGE & GRADUATE SCHOOL

PO Box 4000, Three Hills AB T0M 2N0
403/443-5511; Fax: 403/443-5540; Toll Free: 1-800-661-2425
President, Paul W. Ferris
Chancellor, Ted S. Rendall

#### RED DEER COLLEGE

56 Ave. & 32 St., PO Box 5005, Red Deer AB T4N 5H5
403/342-3215; Fax: 403/340-8940
President, Dan Cornish

## POST-SECONDARY & SPECIALIZED INSTITUTIONS

#### ACADEMY OF LEARNING

15628 Stony Plain Rd., Edmonton AB T5P 3Z4
403/496-9428; Fax: 403/944-9341
Email: academy@freenet.edmonton.ab.ca
Computer & business skills training

#### ACADEMY OF PROFESSIONAL HAIR DESIGN

4929 - 49 St., Red Deer AB T4N 1Z1
403/347-2018
Esthetics

#### ALBERTA COLLEGE OF ART & DESIGN

1407 - 14 Ave. NW, Calgary AB T2N 4R3
403/284-7600; Fax: 403/289-6682
President, Arthur Greenblatt

#### THE BANFF CENTRE

PO Box 1020, Stn 1, Banff AB T0L 0C0
403/762-6100; Fax: 403/762-6444
URL: http://www-nmr.banffcentre.ab.ca
Director, Communications & Development, Jon Bjorgum
President/CEO, Dr. Graeme D. McDonald

#### THE CAREER COLLEGE

#200, 206 - 7th Ave. SW, Calgary AB T2P 0W7
403/266-0966; Fax: 403/265-7679
Career training

#### THE CAREER COLLEGE

10310 Jasper Ave., 7th Fl., Edmonton AB T5J 2W4
403/424-6650; Fax: 403/425-3263
Career training

#### CHAPALE BUSINESS COLLEGE

#600, 10089 Jasper Ave., Edmonton AB T5J 1V1
403/429-0036; Fax: 403/420-0425
Business, accounting, legal, medical programs

#### CHIT BROADCASTING SCHOOL

PO Box 929, Drayton Valley AB T7A 1V3
403/542-9290; Fax: 403/542-9319

#### GRANTON INSTITUTE OF TECHNOLOGY

#1840, 10123 - 99th St., Edmonton AB T2J 3J1
403/421-4433
Distance education

#### MAYFAIR COLLEGE

#315, 9804 - 100 Ave., Grande Prairie AB T8V 0T8
403/539-5090; Fax: 403/539-7089
Computer training

#### NATIONAL SCREEN INSTITUTE

10022 - 103 St., 3rd Fl., Edmonton AB T5J 0X2
403/421-4084; Fax: 403/425-8098
Email: filmhero@nsi-canada.ca; URL: http://www.nsi-canada.ca

#### PETROLEUM INDUSTRY TRAINING SERVICE

#13, 2115 - 27 Ave. NE, Calgary AB T2E 7E4
403/250-9606; Fax: 403/291-9408
Executive Director, Paul Schoenhals

#### REEVES BUSINESS & CAREER COLLEGE

5012 - 49 St., PO Box 51, Lloydminster AB S9V 0X9
403/875-3308; Fax: 403/875-9209
Secretarial, accounting training

## VOCATIONAL CENTRES

#### ALBERTA VOCATIONAL COLLEGE

Downtown Campus, 10215 - 108 St., Edmonton AB T5J 1L6
403/427-2823; Fax: 403/427-4211

Email: info@edma.avc.calgary.ab.ca; URL: http://www.avcedm.ges.ab.ca
President, Irene Lewis, Email: ilewis@edma.avc.calgary.ab.ca
Lynn Lauren Campus, 5606 - 47 St., Wetaskiwin AB T9A 2A2 – 403/352-6009; Fax: 403/352-7092
Winnifred Stewart Campus, 11140 - 131 St., Edmonton AB T5M 1C1 – 403/422-9061

**ALBERTA VOCATIONAL COLLEGE (CALGARY)**
332 - 6 Ave. SE, Calgary AB T2G 4S6
403/297-3930; Fax: 403/297-4081
Email: info@avc.calgary.ab.ca
President, Sharon Carry

**ALBERTA VOCATIONAL COLLEGE (LAC LA BICHE)**
PO Box 417, Lac La Biche AB T0A 2C0
403/623-5551; Fax: 403/623-5639
Director, William Lieshoff

**ALBERTA VOCATIONAL COLLEGE (LESSER SLAVE LAKE)**
1201 Main St. SE, Slave Lake AB T0G 2A3
403/849-8611; Fax: 403/849-2570
Email: neidig@grda.avc.calgary.ab.ca
President, Dan Vandermeulen
Acting Vice-President, Rick Neidig

## INDEPENDENT & PRIVATE SCHOOLS

**Schools listed alphabetically by city.**

Airdrie Koinonia Christian School, Big Hill Springs Rd., RR#1, Airdrie AB T4B 2A3 – 403/948-5100; Fax: 403/948-5563 – Gr. Pre.-12
Banff International College, PO Box 1020, Stn 3, Banff AB T0L 0C0 – 403/762-6430; Fax: 403/762-8423 – Gr. 7-12
Bellis Christian Academy, PO Box 116, Bellis AB T0A 0J0 – 403/636-3547; Fax: 403/636-3430 – Gr. Pre.-12
Bluffton: Echo Valley Christian School, PO Box 12, Bluffton AB T0C 0M0 – 403/843-4555 – Gr. 1-9
Bow Island: Cherry Coulee Christian Academy, PO Box 1037, Bow Island AB T0K 0G0 – 403/542-2107; Fax: 403/542-2107 – Gr. Pre.-12; Special Ed.
Brant Christian School, PO Box 130, Brant AB T0L 0L0 – 403/684-3752; Fax: 403/684-3894 – Gr. Pre.-9
Brooks: Newell Christian School, PO Box 2063, Brooks AB T1R 1C7 – 403/378-4448; Fax: 403/378-3991 – Gr. Pre.-12
Buffalo Head Mennonite School Society, PO Box 25, Buffalo Head Prairie AB T0H 4A0 – 403/928-2623 – Gr. 2 schools
Calgary: Academic Excellence Inc., 108 Lake Lucerne Close SW, Calgary AB T2P 3N8 – 403/225-2682
Calgary: Accord International School, #207, 197 First St. SW, Calgary AB T2P 4M4 – 403/262-5071; Fax: 403/232-6387
Calgary: Akiva Academy, 140 Haddon Rd. SW, Calgary AB T2V 2Y3 – 403/258-1312; Fax: 403/258-3812 – Gr. Pre.-6
Calgary: Alberta Charitable Society St. Pius X, 401 - 8 St. NE, Calgary AB T2E 4G8 – 403/233-0031; Fax: 403/266-1998
Calgary: Apostolic Christ Training School, 615 Northmount Dr. NW, Calgary AB T2K 3J6 – 403/289-7570; Fax: 403/289-8356 – Gr. Pre.-12
Calgary: Association for Christian Schooling, Calgary AB T2W 5G6 – 403/251-2884; Fax: 403/251-2884 – Gr. Pre.-10
Calgary: Banbury Crossroads Private School, #101, 1410 - 1st St. SW, Calgary AB T2R 0V8 – 403/269-5261 – Gr. 1-12; Special Ed.
Calgary: Banff Mountain Academy, 550 - 6 Ave. SE, Calgary AB T2P 0S2 – 403/262-7387 – Gr. 10-12
Calgary: Bethel Christian Academy, #142, 3359 - 27 St. NE, Calgary AB T1Y 5E4 – 403/250-1342
Calgary Academy, Site 2, SS #3, PO Box 103, Calgary AB T3C 3N9 – 403/686-6444; Fax: 403/240-3427 – Gr. 1-12; Special Ed.; Evening Credit
Calgary Chinese Alliance School, 150 Beddington Blvd. NE, Calgary AB T3K 2E2 – 403/274-6925
Calgary Chinese Private School, #239, 197 First St. SW, Calgary AB T2P 4M4 – 403/264-2233; Fax: 403/282-7327 – Gr. 10-12
Calgary Christian High School, 5029-26 Ave. SW, Calgary AB T3E 0R5 – 403/242-2896; Fax: 403/686-1281 – Gr. 7-12; Special Ed.
Calgary Christian School, 2839 - 49 St. SW, Calgary AB T3E 3X9 – 403/242-2896; Fax: 403/242-6682 – Gr. Pre.-6; Special Ed.
Calgary: The Calgary French School, 6304 Larkspur Way SW, Calgary AB T3E 5P7 – 403/240-1500; Fax: 403/249-5899 – Gr. Pre.-6
Calgary International College, #1100, 833 - 4 Ave. SW, Calgary AB T2P 3T5 – 403/233-2982; Fax: 403/269-7568 – Gr. Pre.; 7-12
Calgary Islamic Private School, 225 - 28 St. SE, Calgary AB T2A 5K4 – 403/248-2773; Fax: 403/569-6654 – Gr. Pre.-6
Calgary Jewish Academy, 6700 Kootenay St. SW, Calgary AB T2V 1P7 – 403/253-3992; Fax: 403/255-0842 – Gr. Pre.-12
Calgary Montessori School, c/o Clem Gardner Elementary School, 5915 Lewis Dr. SW, Calgary AB T3E 5Z4 – 403/246-2275 – Gr. Pre.-12
Calgary Waldorf School, 1915 - 36 Ave. SW, Calgary AB T2T 2G6 – 403/287-1868; Fax: 403/287-3414 – Gr. Pre.-9
Calgary: Canadian Choral Music School, 305 - 10 Ave. SE, Calgary AB T2G 0W9 – 403/241-8836; Fax: 403/571-5049 – Gr. 1-9
Calgary: Christopher Robin School, 1011 Beverley Blvd. SW, Calgary AB T2V 2C4 – 403/252-6063 – Gr. Pre.-6
Calgary: Clearwater Academy, #102, 1509 Centre St. SW, Calgary AB T2G 2E6 – 403/278-0216 – Gr. 1-9
Calgary: Columbia College, 805 Manning Rd. NE, Calgary AB T2E 7N8 – 403/235-9309; Fax: 403/272-3805 – Gr. 1-12; Special Ed.
Calgary: Delta West Academy, #307, 1111 - 11 Ave. SW, Calgary AB T2R 0G5 – 403/228-4746; Fax: 403/228-4748 – Gr. 1-12; Special Ed.
Calgary: Educere Learning Centre, #430, 910 - 7 Ave., Calgary AB T2P 3N8 – 403/266-2355; Fax: 403/263-8766 – Gr. 10-12
Calgary: Equilibrium Inter-Educational Institute, #360, 703 - 6 Ave. SW, Calgary AB T2P 0T9 – 403/237-7239; Fax: 403/237-7239 – Gr. 10-12; Evening Credit
Calgary: Foothills Academy, 745 - 37 St. NW, Calgary AB T2N 4T1 – 403/270-9400; Fax: 403/270-9438 – Gr. 1-12; Special Ed.
Calgary: Froebel's Garden of Children, 2523 - 56 St. NE, Calgary AB T1Y 6E7 – 403/280-4855 – Gr. Pre.-6
Calgary: GCA, 16520 - 24 St., Calgary AB T2J 5G5 – 403/254-9050; Fax: 403/256-9695 – Gr. Pre.-9; Special Ed.
Calgary: German Language School of Calgary, #201, 3112 - 11 St. NE, Calgary AB T2E 7J1 – 403/291-3514; Fax: 403/433-4789 – Gr. 10-12
Calgary: Grace Christian Campus, 4932 Brisebois Dr., Calgary AB T2L 2G5 – 403/282-1656; Fax: 403/282-1696 – Gr. 1-9
Calgary: Greek Community School, 1 Tamarac Cres. SW, Calgary AB T3C 3B7 – 403/282-0322; Fax: 403/246-4553 – Gr. 10-12
Calgary: Henderson College of Business, #450, 401 - 9 Ave. SW, Calgary AB T2P 3C5 – 403/237-6911; Fax: 403/234-7942 – Gr. 10-12
Calgary: Heritage Christian School, 155 Falconridge Cres. NE, Calgary AB T3J 1Z9 – 403/280-4800; Fax: 403/280-4817 – Gr. Pre.-12
Central Campus, 2020 - 6 St. NW, Calgary AB T2M 3G3 – 403/289-8213; Fax: 403/282-5878
Northwest Campus, 5300 - 53 Ave. NE, Calgary AB T3A 2G8 – 403/247-1314; Fax: 403/286-9933
Calgary: Italian School of Calgary, 24 Beddington Way NE, Calgary AB T3K 1N9 – 403/246-2399; Fax: 403/246-2399 – Gr. 1-12; Evening Credit
Calgary: Lang School - German Canadian Club, 3127 Bowwood Dr. NW, Calgary AB T3B 2E7 – 403/286-8649; Fax: 403/286-8649 – Gr. 10-12
Calgary: Learning Experience Society, 567 Parkridge Dr. SE, Calgary AB T2J 5C5 – 403/278-0356; Fax: 403/256-4346 – Gr. 1-6
Calgary: Lycée Louis Pasteur, 4416 - 16 St. SW, Calgary AB T2T 4H9 – 403/243-5420; Fax: 403/287-2245 – Gr. Pre.-9
Calgary: Lycee Louis Pasteur, 4416 - 16 St. SW, Calgary AB T2T 4H9 – 403/243-5420; Fax: 403/287-2245 – Gr. Pre.-9
Calgary: Menno Simons School, 307 - 55 Ave. SW, Calgary AB T2H 0A3 – 403/531-0745; Fax: 403/531-0747 – Gr. Pre.-9
Calgary: Montessori Elementary School, 2105 Cliff St. SW, Calgary AB T2S 2G4 – 403/229-0386; Fax: 403/229-2669 – Gr. Pre.-6
Calgary: North Calgary Christian Academy, 719 - 44 Ave. NW, Calgary AB T2K 0J5 – 403/282-3405; Fax: 403/220-0326 – Gr. Pre.-12
Calgary: Prince of Peace Lutheran School, RR#7, Box 10, Site 17, Calgary AB T1X 1E1 – 403/285-2288; Fax: 403/285-2855 – Gr. Pre.-9
Calgary: Renert Centre, MacEwan Student Centre, Univ. of Calgary, Calgary AB T2N 1N4 – 403/974-8600 – Gr. 10-12
Calgary: Renfrew Educational Services, PO Box 52013, Edmonton Trail RPO, Calgary AB T2E 8K9 – 403/276-2211; Fax: 403/286-9875 – Gr. Pre.-6
Calgary: Rundle College, 2612 - 37 Ave. NE, Calgary AB T1Y 5L2 – 403/291-3866; Fax: 403/250-7184
Calgary: St. John Bosco Private School, 235 - 8 St. NE, Calgary AB T2E 4G6 – 403/233-0031
Calgary: Tyndale Christian School, 414 - 11A St. NE, Calgary AB T2E 4P3 – 403/262-7554; Fax: 403/262-7554 – Gr. 1-12
Calgary: West Island College, 7410 Blackfoot Trail SE, Calgary AB T2H 1M5 – 403/255-5300; Fax: 403/252-1434 – Gr. 7-12
Calgary: Western Baptist Academy, 4324 - 19 Ave. NW, Calgary AB T3B 0R7 – 403/247-2107
Cardston: Red Crow Community College, PO Box 1258, Cardston AB T0K 0K0 – 403/737-2400; Fax: 403/737-2361 – Gr. 1-12
Caroline: Living Faith Christian School, PO Box 100, Caroline AB T0M 0M0 – 403/722-2225; Fax: 403/722-2459 – Gr. 1-12
Champion: Hope Christian School, PO Box 235, Champion AB T0L 0R0 – 403/897-3019; Fax: 403/897-2392 – Gr. 1-12
Coaldale Christian School, 2008 - 8 St., Coaldale AB T1M 1L1 – 403/345-4055; Fax: 403/345-6436 – Gr. Pre.-9; Special Ed.
Cold Lake: Lakeland Christian Academy, PO Box 8397, Cold Lake AB T0A 0V0 – 403/639-2077; Fax: 403/639-3815 – Gr. 1-12
College Heights Adventist Junior Academy, 185 College Ave., College Heights AB T4L 1Z6 – 403/782-6212; Fax: 403/782-7507 – Gr. Pre.-9
Devon Christian School, PO Box 960, Devon AB T0C 1E0 – 403/987-4157; Fax: 403/987-3331 – Gr. Pre.-9
Dewberry: Lakeland Country School, PO Box 25, Dewberry AB T0B 1G0 – 403/847-2292 – Gr. 1-9
Didsbury: Koinonia Christian Education Society, PO Box 1405, Didsbury AB T0M 0W0 – 403/335-9587; Fax: 403/335-9286 – Gr. 2 schools; Gr. 1-9
Edberg: Countryside Christian School, PO Box 113, Edberg AB T0B 1J0 – 403/877-2654
Edmonton: Alberta College, 10050 MacDonald Dr., Edmonton AB T5J 2B7 – 403/428-1851; Fax: 403/424-6371 – Gr. 10-12
Edmonton: The Bilingual Montessori Learning Centre, 7200 - 156 St., Edmonton AB T5R 1X3 – 403/484-4796; Fax: 403/489-7548 – Gr. 1-9

Edmonton: Centennial Montessori School, 6755 - 88 St., Edmonton AB T6E 4Y4 – 403/439-0872; Fax: 403/405-5752 – Gr. Pre.-12
Edmonton: Concordia College, 7128 Ada Blvd., Edmonton AB T5B 4E4 – 403/479-8481; Fax: 403/474-1933 – Gr. 10-12; Lutheran
Edmonton: Concordia College of Continuing Education, 9359 - 67A St., Edmonton AB T6B 1R7 – 403/466-6633; Fax: 403/466-9394 – Gr. 10-12; Evening Credit
Edmonton: Connections Canada Inc., #1000, 10089 Jasper Ave., Edmonton AB T5J 1V1 – 403/428-8145
Edmonton: Dante Alighieri Italian School, c/o St. Alphonsus School, 11624 - 81 St., Edmonton AB T5B 2S2 – 403/474-1787 – Gr. 10-12
Edmonton: Diaspora Continuing Education, #211, 8204 - 104 St., Edmonton AB T6E 4E6 – 403/944-0506; Fax: 403/944-0506 – Gr. 10-12
Edmonton Academy, 10231 - 120 St., Edmonton AB T5K 2A4 – 403/482-5449; Fax: 403/482-0902 – Gr. 1-12; Spec. Ed.
Edmonton Bible Heritage Christ School, 13054 - 112 St., Edmonton AB T5E 5S9 – 403/454-3672; Fax: 403/488-3672 – Gr. 1-12
Edmonton Christian High School, 14304 - 109 Ave., Edmonton AB T5N 1H6 – 403/454-0791; Fax: 403/454-0793 – Gr. 10-12
Edmonton Islamic School, 13070 - 113 St., Edmonton AB T5E 5A8 – 403/454-4573; Fax: 403/452-1243 – Gr. Pre.-6; Special Ed.
Edmonton Menorah Academy, 10735 - 144 St., Edmonton AB T5N 3L1 – 403/451-1848; Fax: 403/451-2254 – Gr. Pre.-12
Edmonton: Faith Lutheran School, 8540 - 69 Ave., Edmonton AB T6B 0R6 – 403/496-9302; Fax: 403/496-9829 – Gr. Pre.-9
Edmonton: German Canadian Association of Alberta, 15403 - 92 Ave., Edmonton AB T5R 5C1 – 403/484-1469; Fax: 403/48356776 – Gr. 10-12
Edmonton: German Saturday School, 10014 - 81 Ave., Edmonton AB T6E 1W8 – 403/433-1604; Fax: 403/433-6623 – Gr. 10-12
Edmonton: Gil Vincente School, 9578 - 118 Ave., Edmonton AB T5G 0P1 – 403/474-9391 – Gr. 10-12
Edmonton: Hellenic Community Heritage School, 10450 - 116 St., Edmonton AB T5K 2S4 – 403/454-2382 – Gr. 10-12
Edmonton: Heritage School, 8540 - 69 Ave., Edmonton AB T6E 0R6 – 403/469-6689; Fax: 403/465-7181
Edmonton: Hispanic Saturday School, 14403 - 117 St., Edmonton AB T5X 1N3 – 403/472-0532
Edmonton: Islamic Institute for Education, 7532 Meridian St., Edmonton AB T6P 1R5 – 403/463-8913; Fax: 403/463-8915 – Gr. 7-12
Edmonton: Manning Adult Learning Centre, 21611 Meridian St., PO Box 2290, Edmonton AB T5J 3H7 – 403/472-6052; Fax: 403/495-6036 – Gr. 10-12
Edmonton: Meadowlark Christian School, 9825 - 158 St., Edmonton AB T5P 2X4 – 403/483-6480; Fax: 403/487-8992 – Gr. Pre.-9
Edmonton: Millwoods Christian School, 8704 Millwoods Rd., Edmonton AB T6K 3J3 – 403/462-2627; Fax: 403/462-9322 – Gr. Pre.-12; Special Ed.
Edmonton: North Edmonton Christian School, 13470 Fort Rd., Edmonton AB T5A 1Z5 – 403/476-6281; Fax: 403/478-1728 – Gr. Pre.-9
Edmonton: Opportunity Avenues Program, #301, 10526 Jasper Ave., Edmonton AB T5J 1Z7 – 403/428-7590; Fax: 403/425-1549
Edmonton: Parkland Immanuel Christian School, 21304 - 35 Ave. NW, Edmonton AB T6M 2P6 – 403/444-6443; Fax: 403/444-6448 – Gr. Pre.-12
Edmonton: Progressive Academy, 12245 - 131 St., Edmonton AB T5L 1M8 – 403/455-8344; Fax: 403/455-8344 – Gr. Pre-12; Special Ed.
Edmonton: St. Emeric Hungarian School, 12960 - 112 St., Edmonton AB T5E 6J1 – 403/454-5105 – Gr. 10-12
Edmonton: St. George's Hellenic Language School, 10831 - 124 St., Edmonton AB T5M 0H4 – 403/452-1455; Fax: 403/452-1455 – Gr. 10-12
Edmonton: St. John's Institute Ukrainian School, 11024 - 82 Ave., Edmonton AB T6G 0T2 – 403/439-2320; Fax: 403/439-0989
Edmonton: St. Luke's College, 10419 - 159 St., Edmonton AB T5P 3A6 – 403/486-7422; Fax: 403/486-7423 – Gr. 7-12
Edmonton: Solomon Learning Institute Ltd., Campus Tower, #307, 8625 - 112 St., Edmonton AB T6G 1K8 – 403/431-1515
Edmonton: Tempo School, 5603 - 148 St., Edmonton AB T6H 4T7 – 403/434-1190; Fax: 403/430-6209 – Gr. 1-12
Edmonton: Victory Christian School, 11520 Ellerslie Rd. SW, Edmonton AB T6W 1A2 – 403/413-0322; Fax: 403/988-6323 – Gr. Pre.-12
Edmonton: West Edmonton Christian School, 14345 McQueen Rd., Edmonton AB T5N 3L5 – 403/455-8515; Fax: 403/452-5669 – Gr. Pre.-9
Edson: Yellowhead Christian School, 4711 - 9 Ave., Edson AB T7E 1E2 – 403/723-3850; Fax: 403/723-7566 – Gr. Pre.-12
Fairview Christian School, c/o Pentecostal Church, 11804 - 104 Ave., Fairview AB T0H 1L0 – 403/835-2706 – Gr. 1-9
Fort MacLeod: Little Pony Private Institute of Fine Arts, 622 - 12 St., Fort MacLeod AB T0L 0Z0 – 403/553-4440; Fax: 403/553-4440 – Gr. 1-12
Fort McMurray: Almont Rose Centre for Learning, 9919 Manning Ave., Fort McMurray AB T9H 2B8 – 403/743-4990; Fax: 403/743-5417 – Gr. 10-12
Fort McMurray Christian School, 101 Tundra Dr., Fort McMurray AB T9H 5A4 – 403/743-1079 – Gr. 1-6
Fort McMurray: Genesis Christian School, PO Box 5634, Fort McMurray AB T9H 3G6 – 403/743-8729
Fort McMurray: Moberly Hall School, 194B Grenfell Cres., Fort McMurray AB T9H 2M6 – 403/743-8409; Fax: 403/743-9407 – Gr. 1-12
Fort McMurray: Seapotakinum School, PO Box 6130, Fort McMurray AB T9H 4W1 – 403/334-2293; Fax: 403/334-2457 – Gr. 10-12
Fort Saskatchewan Christ School, 9935 - 93 Ave., Fort Saskatchewan AB T8L 1N5 – 403/998-7044; Fax: 403/998-7388 – Gr. Pre.-9; Special Ed.
Fort Vermilion: Vermilion Peace School, PO Box 211, Fort Vermilion AB T0H 1N0 – 403/927-4540
Fox Creek: Maranatha Christian Academy Fellowship, PO Box 369, Fox Creek AB T0H 1P0 – 403/622-2393 – Gr. Pre.-9
Grand Centre: Trinity Christian School, 6015 - 51 St. Ave., Grand Centre AB T0A 1T2 – 403/594-2205; Fax: 403/594-0190 – Gr. 1-12
Grande Centre: Masakhane College, 4910 - 50 Ave., Grande Centre AB T0A 1T0 – 403/594-0001; Fax: 403/594-2268 – Gr. 10-12
Grande Prairie Christian School, 8202 - 110 St., Grande Prairie AB T8V 1M3 – 403/539-4566; Fax: 403/539-4748 – Gr. Pre.-12
Grande Prairie: Hillcrest Christian School, 10306 - 102 St., Grande Prairie AB T8V 2W3 – 403/539-9161; Fax: 403/532-3244 – Gr. Pre.-9
Grande Prairie: Machitawin Centre, 10105 - 97 Ave., Grande Prairie AB T8V 0N5 – 403/532-8261; Fax: 403/532-8261 – Gr. 10-12
Hines Creek: Cleardale Mennonite School, PO Box 597, Hines Creek AB T0H 2A0 – 403/685-2674
Hobbema: Maskwachees Cultural School, PO Box 360, Hobbema AB T0C 1N0 – 403/585-3925; Fax: 403/585-2080 – Gr. 10-12
Hythe: Living Springs Christian School, PO Box 672, Hythe AB T0H 2C0 – 403/356-3322; Fax: 403/356-2822
Innisfail: Buffalo Creek Learning Centre, PO Box 6000, Innisfail AB T4G 1V1 – 403/227-3391; Fax: 403/227-6022 – Gr. 1-12
Joussard: North Country School, Bag 1, Joussard AB T0G 1J0 – 403/776-2215 – Gr. 1-12
Kingman: Cornerstone Christian Academy, PO Box 99, Kingman AB T0B 2M0 – 403/672-7197; Fax: 403/672-7197 – Gr. Pre.-12; Special Ed.
La Crete: Peace Mennonite School, PO Box 640, La Crete AB T0H 2H0 – 403/928-2453
Lacombe: Central Alberta Christian High School, 22 Eagle Rd., Lacombe AB T4L 1G7 – 403/782-4535; Fax: 403/782-5425 – Gr. 10-12
Lacombe Christian School, 5206 - 58 St., Lacombe AB T4L 1G9 – 403/782-6531; Fax: 403/782-5760 – Gr. Pre.-9
Lacrete: Wilson Prairie Mennonite School, PO Box 988, Lacrete AB T0H 2H0 – 403/928-2242
Leduc: Covenant Christian School, PO Box 3827, Leduc AB T9E 6M7 – 403/986-8353; Fax: 403/986-8360 – Gr. Pre.-9; Special Ed.
Lethbridge: Edu-Cater Skills Centre, PO Box 1446, Lethbridge AB T1J 4K2 – 403/381-7768 – Gr. 1-12; Special Ed.
Lethbridge: Immanuel Christian School, 802 - 6 Ave. North, Lethbridge AB T1H 0S1 – 403/328-4783; Fax: 403/328-4082 – Gr. Pre.-12; Special Ed.
Lethbridge Christian School, 2010 - 5 Ave. North, Lethbridge AB T1H 0N5 – 403/320-0677; Fax: 403/320-0828 – Gr. Pre.-9
Lethbridge Montessori Kindergarten Society, 915 - 6 St. South, Lethbridge AB T1J 2E9 – 403/327-5271 – Gr. 1-6
Lethbridge: Providence Christian School, 1100 - 40 Ave. North, Lethbridge AB T1H 6B7 – 403/381-4418 – Gr. Pre.-12
Lethbridge: Taber Christian School, 802 - 6 Ave. North, Lethbridge AB T1H 0S1 – 403/327-4223 – Gr. Pre.-9
Linden: Kneehill Christian School, PO Box 370, Linden AB T0M 1J0 – 403/546-3781 – Gr. 1-9
Mayerthorpe Academy of Christian Learning, PO Box 277, Mayerthorpe AB T0E 1N0 – 403/786-2670
Medicine Hat: Cornerstone Christian School, PO Box 1599, Medicine Hat AB T1A 7Y5 – 403/529-6169 – Gr. Pre.-9
Medicine Hat Christian School, 68 Rice Dr. SE, Medicine Hat AB T1B 3X2 – 403/526-3246; Fax: 403/528-9048 – Gr. Pre.-9
Monarch: Calvin Christian School, PO Box 40, Monarch AB T0L 1M0 – 403/381-3030; Fax: 403/381-4241 – Gr. Pre.-12; Special Ed.
Morinville Christian School, 10515 - 100 Ave., Morinville AB T8R 1A2 – 403/939-2987 – Gr. 1-12
Neerlandia: Covenant Canadian Reformed School, PO Box 67, Neerlandia AB T0G 1R0 – 403/674-4774; Fax: 403/674-4774 – Gr. 1-11; Special Ed.
Okotoks: Edison School, 5 Elizabeth St., PO Box 21, Okotoks AB T0L 1T0 – 403/938-7670; Fax: 403/938-7224 – Gr. Pre.-9
Okotoks: Strathcona-Tweedsmuir School, RR#2, Okotoks AB T0L 1T0 – 403/938-4431; Fax: 403/938-4492 – Gr. 1-12
Olds Koinonia Christian School, PO Box 4039, Olds AB T4H 1P7 – 403/556-4038; Fax: 403/556-4038 – Gr. Pre.-12
Pincher Creek: Chief Mountain School, PO Box 1630, Pincher Creek AB T0K 1W0 – 403/627-2383; Fax: 403/626-3033 – Gr. 1-9
Pincher Creek: Rockyview Christian School, PO Box 1387, Pincher Creek AB T0K 1W0 – 403/627-2466
Ponoka Christian School, 6300 - 50 St., Ponoka AB T4J 1E6 – 403/783-6563; Fax: 403/783-6687; URL: http://www.gospel.com.net:80/csi/directory/canada/homepages/central/ponoka.html – Gr. Pre.-9
Raymond: Prairie Christian School, PO Box 631, Raymond AB T0K 2S0 – 403/756-3636
Raymond: Stirling Mennonite Day School, PO Box 768, Raymond AB T0K 2S0 – 403/756-2277 – Gr. 1-9
Red Deer: Alberta Conference 7th Day Adventist Academy, 37541 Hwy. 2, Red Deer AB T4E 1B1 – 403/342-5044; Fax: 403/343-1523 – Gr. Pre.-12

Red Deer: Koinonia Christ School of Red Deer, 6014 - 57 Ave., Red Deer AB T4N 4S9 – 403/346-1818; Fax: 403/347-3013 – Gr. Pre.-12

Red Deer: Parkland School Special Education, 6016 - 45 Ave., Red Deer AB T4N 3M4 – 403/347-3911; Fax: 403/342-2677 – Special Ed.

Red Deer Christian School, 5210 - 61 St., Red Deer AB T4N 6N8 – 403/346-5795; Fax: 403/347-3003 – Gr. Pre.-9

Red Deer: Word of Life School Society, RR#4, Site 4, PO Box 30, Red Deer AB T4N 5E4 – 403/343-6510; Fax: 403/343-8480 – Gr. Pre.-12

Rimbey Christian School, PO Box 90, Rimbey AB T0C 2J0 – 403/843-3904; Fax: 403/843-3904 – Gr. Pre.-12; Special Ed.

Rocky Christian School, 5204 - 54 Ave., Rocky Mountain House AB T0M 1T3 – 403/845-3516; Fax: 403/845-4370 – Principal, William Slofstra – Gr. Pre.-9; Spec. Ed.

Saddle Lake Full Gospel School, PO Box 69, Saddle Lake AB T0A 3T0 – 403/636-3736; Fax: 403/636-3994 – Gr. Pre.-9

St. Albert: Elmar Samuel School, 1 Gate Ave., St. Albert AB T8N 0R4 – 403/460-1776; Fax: 403/460-1213 – Gr. 1-9

St. Paul: Blue Quills First Nations College, PO Box 279, St. Paul AB T0A 3A0 – 403/645-4455; Fax: 403/645-5215 – Gr. 10-12

St. Paul: Life Values School, PO Box 1453, St. Paul AB T0A 3A0 – 403/645-4490; Fax: 403/726-2119 – Gr. 1-12

Sherwood Park: Boscoe Homes, PO Box 4100, Sherwood Park AB T8A 2A7 – 403/449-3333; Fax: 403/449-3344 – Gr. 1-12

Sherwood Park: Strathcona Christian Academy, 1011 Cloverbar Rd., Sherwood Park AB T8A 4V7 – 403/464-7127; Fax: 403/467-1454 – Gr. Pre.-12

Siksika: Old Sun Community College, PO Box 1250, Siksika AB T0J 3W0 – 403/264-9658; Fax: 403/734-5110 – Gr. 10-12; Evening Credit

Spirit River: Northern Lights School, RR#1, Site 4, Box 19, Spirit River AB T0H 3G0 – 403/351-2242

Spruce Grove: Living Waters Christian Academy, 5 Grove Dr. West, Spruce Grove AB T7X 3X8 – 403/962-3331; Fax: 403/962-3958 – Gr. Pre.-9

Standoff: Chief Shot Both Sides School, PO Box 85, Standoff AB T0L 1Y0 – 403/737-2203; Fax: 403/737-2622 – Gr. Pre.-12

Stettler: Lakeview Christian School, PO Box 1057, Stettler AB T0C 2L0 – 403/742-4840 – Gr. 1-9

Stony Plain: Alberta Centre for Chinese Studies, PO Box 2104, Stony Plain AB T7Z 1X6 – 403/463-2255; Fax: 403/963-7857 – Gr. 10-12

Stony Plain: St. John's School of Alberta, RR#5, Stony Plain AB T0E 2G0 – 403/429-4140 – Gr. 7-12

Stony Plain: St. Matthew Lutheran School, PO Box 939, Stony Plain AB T0E 2G0 – 403/963-2715; Fax: 403/963-7324 – Gr. Pre.-9

Sundre: Olds Mountain View Christian School, RR#1, Site 4, Box 5, Sundre AB T0M 1X0 – 403/556-1116 – Gr. 1-12

Sylvan Lake: Lighthouse Christian School, PO Box 907, Sylvan Lake AB T0M 1Z0 – 403/887-2166 – Gr. Pre.-6

Three Hills: Prairie Bible Institute, PO Box 4000, Three Hills AB T0M 2N0 – 403/443-5511; Fax: 403/443-5540 – Gr. Pre.-12; Special Ed.

Tilley: Duchess Bethel Mennonite School, PO Box 150, Tilley AB T0J 3K0 – 403/378-4855

Vegreville: Ivan Franko Ukrainian School, 5234 - 45B Ave., Vegreville AB T9C 1L3 – 403/632-4907 – Gr. 10-12

Warburg: Lucy Baker School, RR#1, Warburg AB T0C 2T0 – 403/848-2568; Fax: 403/848-2568 – Gr. 7-12

* indicates enrollment figure.

# BRITISH COLUMBIA

## Ministry of Education, Skills & Training

Parliament Bldgs., PO Box 9150, Stn Prov Govt, Victoria BC V8V 9H1
250/356-2500; Fax: 250/356-5945
URL: http://www.est.gov.bc.ca/
Minister, Hon. Paul Ramsey

### EDUCATION PROGRAMS DIVISION

Director, Technology & Distance Education Branch, Dr. B. Carbol, 250/356-2326; Fax: 250/387-5515
Director, Curriculum & Resources Branch, Jerry Mussio, 250/356-7269; Fax: 250/356-2316

**For detailed departmental listings, see Index: "Education, Depts."**

## SCHOOL DISTRICTS

Elections for school trustees are held in November throughout the Province. Enrollment figures shown below are from the 1996/97 academic year. Included in the school district figures are students at containment centres (institutions operating under the Ministry of the Attorney General); students in provincial resource programs (provide services to students with special needs); alternate programs offered at facilities such as rehabilitation centres; correspondence regional schools.

**Districts with an enrollment of more than 10,000 are in bold print.**

**Abbotsford School District #34**
2790 Tims St., Clearbook BC V2T 4M7
604/859-4891; Fax: 604/852-8587
*18,209
Supt., Dr. Robin Arden
Sec.-Treas., Leonard Archer

Alberni School District #70 – *6,193
4690 Roger St., Port Alberni BC V9Y 3Z4
250/723-3565; Fax: 250/723-0318 – Supt., Harry Janzen; Sec.-Treas., Robert Kanngiesser

Arrow Lakes School District #10 – *940
PO Box 340, Nakusp BC V0G 1R0
250/265-3638; Fax: 250/265-3701 – Supt., Dan Russell; Sec.-Treas., Vic Pirie

Boundary School District #51 – *2,343
PO Box 640, Grand Forks BC V0H 1H0
250/442-8258; Fax: 250/442-8800 – Supt., Denny Kemprud; Sec.-Treas., Woody Kehler

Bulkley Valley School District #54 – *2,986
PO Box 758, Smithers BC V0J 2N0
250/847-3261; Fax: 250/847-4276 – Supt., A.W. Cooper; Sec.-Treas., Jim Floris

**Burnaby School District #41**
5325 Kincaid St., Burnaby BC V5G 1W2
604/664-8441; Fax: 604/664-8382
*24,152
Supt., Dr. George Miller
Sec.-Treas., Robert Ingram

Campbell River School District #72 – *7,931
425 Pinecrest Rd., Campbell River BC V9W 3P2
250/830-2300; Fax: 250/287-2616 – Supt., Brendan Croskery; Sec.-Treas., Murray Ruehlen

Cariboo-Chilcotin School District #27 – *9,510
350 - 2 Ave. North, Williams Lake BC V2G 1Z9
250/398-3800; Fax: 250/392-3600 – Supt., Brian Butcher; Sec.-Treas., Andrew Sullivan

Central Coast School District #49 – *412
PO Box 130, Hagensborg BC V0T 1H0
250/982-2691; Fax: 250/982-2319 – Supt., Walter Robinson; Sec.-Treas., Duncan Morgan

**Central Okanagan School District #23**
1940 Haynes Rd., Kelowna BC V1X 5X7
250/860-8888; Fax: 250/860-9799
*22,463
Supt. of Schools, Ron Rubadeau
Sec.-Treas., Paul Durose

**Chilliwack School District #33**
46361 Yale Rd. East, Chilliwack BC V2P 2P9
604/792-1321; Fax: 604/792-9665
*10,952
Supt., Phil Halladay
Sec.-Treas., Don Murray

Coast Mountains School District #82 – *7,853
3211 Kenney St., Terrace BC V8G 3E9
250/635-4931; Fax: 250/635-4287 – Supt., F.M. Hamilton; Sec.-Treas., Barry Piersdorff

**Comox Valley School District #71**
607 Cumberland Rd., Courtenay BC V9N 7G5
250/334-5500; Fax: 250/334-4472
*10,444
Supt., Clyde Woolman
Sec.-Treas., William A. Burns

**Coquitlam School District #43**
550 Poirier St., Coquitlam BC V3J 6A7
604/939-9201; Fax: 604/939-7828
*31,276
Supt., Tom Harris
Sec.-Treas., Peter Boyle

**Cowichan School District #79**
2557 Beverly St., Duncan BC V9L 2X3
250/749-6636; Fax: 250/749-3543
*11,062
Supt., Geoff Johnson
Sec.-Treas., William Brown

**Delta School District #37**
4585 Harvest Dr., Delta BC V4K 5B4
604/946-4101; Fax: 604/946-3910
*18,496
Supt., Dr. Rod A. Wickstrom
Sec.-Treas., Steven Pillar

Fort Nelson School District #81 – *1,283
PO Box 87, Fort Nelson BC V0C 1R0
250/774-2591; Fax: 250/774-2598 – Supt. & Sec.-Treas., Anne Cooper

Francophone Education Authority Schools – *1,666
#229, 1555 - 7 Ave. West, Vancouver BC V6J 1S1
604/736-5030; Fax: 604/736-5028

Fraser Cascade School District #78 – *1,634
PO Bag 3200, Hope BC V0X 1L0
604/869-2411; Fax: 604/869-7400 – Supt., Keith Lanphear; Sec.-Treas., Ken Campbell

Gold Trail School District #74 – *2,262
PO Box 250, Ashcroft BC V0K 1A0
250/453-9101; Fax: 250/453-2425 – Supt., James Despot; Sec.-Treas., Alan Franks

**Greater Victoria School District #61**
PO Box 700, Victoria BC V8W 2R1
250/475-4100; Fax: 250/475-4110
*23,854
Supt., Dr. Keith Cameron
Sec.-Treas., Robert Whitmore

Gulf Islands School District #64 – *1,812
112 Rainbow Road, Salt Spring Island BC V8K 2K0
250/537-5548; Fax: 250/537-4200 – Supt., Dr. Andrew Duncan; Sec.-Treas., Rod Scotvold

Haida Gwaii - Queen Charlotte School District #50 – *1,103
PO Box 69, Queen Charlotte City BC V0T 1S0
250/559-8471; Fax: 250/559-8849 – Supt., Dr. Linda Rossler; Sec.-Treas., Peter Edwards

Howe Sound School District #48 – *4,601
PO Box 250, Squamish BC V0N 3G0
604/892-5228; Fax: 604/892-1038 – Supt., Douglas Courtice; Sec.-Treas., Nancy Edwards

**Kamloops-Thompson School District #73**
1383 - 9 Ave., Kamloops BC V2C 3X7
250/374-0679; Fax: 250/372-1183
*18,430
Supt., T.D. Grieve
Sec.-Treas., Jim Sheldon

Kootenay-Columbia School District #20 – *6,202
2079 Columbia Ave., Trail BC V1R 1K7
250/368-6434; Fax: 250/364-2470 – Supt., Pat Dooley; Sec.-Treas., Bill Babakaiff

Kootenay Lake School District #8 – *6,878
308 Anderson St., Nelson BC V1L 3Y2
250/352-6681; Fax: 250/352-6686 – Acting Sec.-Treas., Dave Douglas; Supt., Don Truscott

**Langley School District #35**
4875 - 222 St., Langley BC V3A 3Z7
604/534-7891; Fax: 604/530-4973
*20,824
Supt., Richard Bulpitt
Sec.-Treas., Don Dunaway

**Maple Ridge School District #42**
22225 Brown Ave., Maple Ridge BC V2X 8N6
604/463-4200; Fax: 604/463-4181
*14,335
Supt., D. Therrien
Sec.-Treas., Adam Andruschak

Mission School District #75 – *7,357
33046 - 4 Ave., Mission BC V2V 1S5
604/826-6286; Fax: 604/826-4517 – Supt., Nancy Wells; Sec.-Treas., Guy Bonnefoy

**Nanaimo-Ladysmith School District #68**
395 Wakesiah Ave., Nanaimo BC V9R 3K6
250/754-5521; Fax: 250/741-5309
*17,325
Supt., Jim Dyck
Sec.-Treas., Dean Cooper

Nechako Lakes School District #91 – *6,054
PO Drawer 129, Vanderhoof BC V0J 3A0
250/567-2284; Fax: 250/567-4639 – Supt. & Sec.-Treas., Louise Burgart

New Westminster School District #40 – *6,313
821 - 8th St., New Westminster BC V3M 3S9
604/517-6240; Fax: 604/517-6390 – Supt., Tom Rothney; Sec.-Treas., Charles T. Condon

Nicola-Similkameen School District #58 – *3,135
PO Box 4100, Merritt BC V1K 1B8
250/378-5156; Fax: 250/378-6263 – Supt., Mike Henderson; Sec.-Treas., H. Bruce Tisdale

Nisga'a School District #92 – *589
2500 Tait Ave., PO Box 240, New Aiyansh BC V0J 1A0
250/633-2228; Fax: 250/633-2425 – Supt., Alvin McKay; Sec.-Treas., Alvin Azak

North Okanagan-Shuswap School District #83 – *9,191
PO Box 129, Salmon Arm BC V1E 4N2
250/832-2157; Fax: 250/832-9428 – Supt., Doug Pearson; Sec.-Treas., Bernard Dogterom

**North Vancouver School District #44**
721 Chesterfield Ave., North Vancouver BC V7M 2M5
604/987-8141; Fax: 604/987-7154
*18,552
Supt., Dr. Robin Brayne
Sec.-Treas., Leonard Berg

Okanagan Similkameen School District #53 – *3,517
Bag 5000, Oliver BC V0H 1T0
250/498-3481; Fax: 250/498-4070 – Supt., Hart Doerksen; Sec.-Treas., Terry P. Killough

Okanagan Skaha School District #67 – *8,175
425 Jermyn Ave., Penticton BC V2A 1Z4
250/770-7700; Fax: 250/770-7730 – Supt., Dr. Larry Thomas; Sec.-Treas., Frank Regehr

Peace River North School District #60 – *5,106
9803 - 102 St., Fort St. John BC V1J 4B3
250/262-6000; Fax: 250/262-6046 – Supt., Wayne Cheesman; Sec.-Treas., Edna Barber

Peace River South School District #59 – *6,099
10105 - 12A St., Dawson Creek BC V1G 3V7
250/782-8571; Fax: 250/782-3204 – Supt., C.G. Parslow; Sec.-Treas., Cathy Esselink

Powell River School District #47 – *3,551
4351 Ontario Ave., Powell River BC V8A 1V3
604/485-6271; Fax: 604/485-6435 – Supt., Mike Heron; Sec.-Treas., E.A. Byng

**Prince George School District #57**
1894 - 9 Ave., Prince George BC V2M 1L7
250/561-6800; Fax: 250/561-6801
*19,517
Supt., Phil Redmond
Sec.-Treas., Bryan Mix

Prince Rupert School District #52 – *4,586
634 - 6 Ave. East, Prince Rupert BC V8J 1X1
250/624-6717; Fax: 250/624-6517 – Supt., Bob David; Sec.-Treas., Walt Dallamore

Qualicum School District #69 – *4,625
499 West Island Hwy., PO Box 430, Parksville BC V9P 2G5
250/248-4241; Fax: 250/248-5767 – Supt., John C. Moss; Sec.-Treas., Daniel Whiting

Quesnel School District #28 – *5,555
401 North Star Rd., Quesnel BC V2J 5K2
250/992-8802; Fax: 250/992-7652 – Supt., Ed Napier; Sec.-Treas., Tim Klotz

Revelstoke School District #19 – *1,813
PO Bag 5800, Revelstoke BC V0E 2S0
250/837-2101; Fax: 250/837-9335 – Supt., Tom Williams; Sec.-Treas., Bruce Buchannon

**Richmond School District #38**
7811 Granville Ave., Richmond BC V6Y 3E3
604/668-6000; Fax: 604/668-6006
*24,491
Supt., Chris Kelly
Sec.-Treas., K.L. Morris

Rocky Mountain School District #6 – *5,018
PO Box 430, Invermere BC V0A 1K0
250/342-9243; Fax: 250/342-6966 – Supt., Dick Chambers; Sec.-Treas., Cameron Dow

Saanich School District #63 – *8,656
2125 Keating Cross Rd., Saanichton BC V8M 2A5
250/652-7300; Fax: 250/652-6421 – Supt., Jack Fleming; Sec.-Treas., Bruce Hunt

Sooke School District #62 – *9,334
3143 Jacklin Rd., Victoria BC V9B 5R1
250/474-9800; Fax: 250/474-9825 – Supt., Leo J. Chaland; Sec.-Treas., David Lockyer

Southeast Kootenay School District #5 – *4,694
940 Industrial Rd. No. 1, Cranbrook BC V1C 4C6
250/426-4201; Fax: 250/489-5460 – Supt., Roy McLean; Sec.-Treas., Robert Norum

Stikine School District #87 – *389
PO Box 190, Dease Lake BC V0C 1L0
250/771-4440; Fax: 250/771-4441 – Supt. & Sec.-Treas., Garry Roth

Sunshine Coast School District #46 – *4,523
PO Box 220, Gibsons BC V0N 1V0
604/886-8811; Fax: 604/886-4652 – Supt., Clifford Smith; Sec.-Treas., Tim Anderson

**Surrey School District #36**
14225 - 56 Ave., Surrey BC V3X 3A3
604/596-7733; Fax: 604/597-0191
*55,244
Supt., Dr. Fred Renihan
Sec.-Treas., Wayne Jefferson

Vancouver Island North School District #85 – *2,883
PO Box 90, Port Hardy BC V0N 2P0
250/949-6618; Fax: 250/949-8792 – Supt., Larry Naidoo; Sec.-Treas., John R. Martin

Vancouver Island West School District #84 – *923
PO Box 100, Gold River BC V0P 1G0
250/283-2241; Fax: 250/283-7352 – Supt., Andris Freimanis; Sec.-Treas., Kevin Cormack

**Vancouver School District #39**
1595 - 10 Ave. West, Vancouver BC V6J 1Z8
604/713-5000; Fax: 604/713-5049
*61,263
Supt., Donald Goodridge
Sec.-Treas., Dave Yuen

**Vernon School District #22**
1401 - 15 St., Vernon BC V1T 8S8
250/542-3331; Fax: 250/549-9200
*10,477
Supt., Michael McAvoy
Sec.-Treas., David Greenan

West Vancouver School District #45 – *6,792
1075 - 21 St., West Vancouver BC V7V 4A9
604/981-1000; Fax: 604/981-1001 – Acting Sec.-Treas., Phil Turin; Supt., Doug Player

## CORRESPONDENCE SCHOOLS

Central Interior Distance Education, 1788 Diefenbaker Ave., PO Box 7400, Prince George BC V2N 4V7 – 250/563-1818; Fax: 250/563-1150 – Principal, Harry Hufty – *459

Distance Education School - Kootenays, 570 Johnstone Rd., RR#1, Nelson BC V1L 5P4 – 250/354-4311; Fax: 250/354-6629 – Principal, Bob McLure – *691

Fraser Valley Distance Education, 49520 Prairie Central Rd., Chilliwack BC V2P 6H3 – 604/794-7310; Fax: 604/795-8480 – Principal, Eric Dombierer – *940

Greater Vancouver Distance Education, 530 - 41st Ave. East, Vancouver BC V5W 1P3 – 604/660-7947; Fax: 604/660-5042 – Principal, Judy Dallas – *2,009

North Coast Distance Education, 3211 Kenney St., PO Box 5000, Terrace BC V8G 5K2 – 250/635-7944; Fax: 250/638-3649 – Principal, Joe Vander Kwaak – *338

North Island Distance Education, 2080 Wallace Ave., Comox BC V9M 1W9 – 250/339-6119; Fax: 250/339-5555 – Principal, John Anderson – *842

Northern BC Distance Education, 10704 - 97th Ave., Fort St. John BC V1J 6L7 – 250/785-1333; Fax: 250/785-1188 – Principal, Chuck Froese – *445

South Central Distance Education, 2475 Merritt Ave., PO Box 4700, Merritt BC V1K 1B8 – 250/378-4254; Fax: 250/378-1447 – Principal, Paul Montgomery – *1,573

South Island Distance Education, 4575 Wilkinson Rd., Victoria BC V8Z 7E8 – 250/479-6839; Fax: 250/479-9870 – Principal, Gregory Bunyan – *1,198

## SCHOOL FOR THE HEARING IMPAIRED

Provincial School for the Deaf, c/o Burnaby South Secondary School, 5455 Rumble St., Burnaby BC V5J 2B7 – 604/664-8560; Fax: 604/664-8561 – Principal, Provincial Program for the Deaf, John Anderson – *120

## UNIVERSITIES

### Royal Roads University
2005 Sooke Rd., Victoria BC V9B 5Y2
250/391-2511; Fax: 250/391-2500; Toll Free: 1-800-788-8028
URL: http://www.royalroads.ca
President, Gerald Kelly
Exec. Asst. to President/Board Secretary, Lyla Smith
Vice-President, Administration, Nick Rubidge

### Simon Fraser University
Burnaby BC V5A 1S6
604/291-4641; Fax: 604/291-4860
Email: http://www.sfu.ca; URL: http://www.sfu.ca/
Chancellor, Joseph Segal, LL.D.
President & Vice-Chancellor, John O. Stubbs, B.A., M.Sc., D.Phil.
Vice-President, Academic & Provost, David P. Gagan, B.A., M.A., Ph.D.
Vice-President, Finance & Administration, Roger Ward, B.Sc., M.Sc., Ph.D.
Vice-President, Research, Bruce P. Clayman, B.Sc., M.Sc., Ph.D.
Vice-President, Harbour Centre & Continuing Studies, Jack P. Blaney, B.Ed., M.Ed., Ed.D.
Assoc. Vice-President, Academic, Judith Osborne, LL.B., M.A., LL.M.
Executive Director, External Relations, Gregg Macdonald, B.A., M.A.
Executive Director, University Development, Meg Clarke, B.A., M.A.
Registrar & Dean, Student Services, W. Ronald Heath, B.S.A.

University Librarian, Theodore (Ted) C. Dobb, B.A., B.L.S.
Manager, Purchasing Services, R. Szczotko
Director, Bookstore, Biff Savoie, B.A.

**FACULTIES WITH DEANS**

Applied Sciences, Ronald Marteniuk, B.P.E., M.A., Ph.D.
Arts, John T. Pierce, B.A., M.A., Ph.D.
Business Administration, John H. Waterhouse, B.Sc., M.B.A., Ph.D.
Education, Robin Barrow, B.A., Cert.Ed., Ph.D.
Graduate Studies, Bruce P. Clayman, B.Sc., Ph.D.
Science, Colin H.W. Jones, B.Sc., Ph.D.

## Trinity Western University

7600 Glover Rd., Langley BC V2Y 1Y1
604/888-7511; Fax: 604/888-5336
URL: http://www.twu.ca
Director, Admissions, Cam Lee
Director, Finance, Harvey Ouellette
Director, Libraries, David A. Twiest, B.A., M.A., M.R.E.
President, R. Neil Snider, B.A., B.Ed., M.Ed., Ph.D.
Registrar, Lawrence Van Beek, M.A., B.Th.
Vice-President & Dean, Academic Affairs, Donald Page, B.A., M.A., Ph.D.
Assoc. Academic Dean, Deane E.D. Downey, B.A., M.A., Ph.D.
Vice-President, University Advancement, Ron Kuehl, B.A.
Vice-President, Student Life, Thomas F. Bulick, Th.B., M.A., Ph.M.
Vice-President, Strategic Planning, Guy S. Saffold, B.Sc., M.Div., Ed.D.
Executive Assistant & University Secretary, Glen C. Forrester, B.Sc., M.Sc.
Vice-President, University Enterprises, Lou Sawchenko, B.R.E., M.A., Ph.D.

**FACULTIES WITH DEANS**

Arts & Religious Studies, Philip Wiebe, B.A., M.A., Ph.D.
Business & Economics, John Sutherland, B.Comm., M.B.A., M.A.
Graduate Studies, Donald Page, B.A., M.A., Ph.D
Natural & Applied Sciences, John D. Van Dyke, B.Sc., Ph.D.
Social Sciences & Education, Harro Van Brummelen, B.Sc., M.Ed., Ed.D.

**AFFILIATED COLLEGES**

The Associated Canadian Theological Schools of Trinity Western University, 7600 Glover Rd., Langley BC V3A 6H4 – 604/888-7511; Fax: 604/888-5729 – Coordinator, Guy Saffold, B.Sc., M.Div., Ed.D.
Canadian Baptist Seminary, 7600 Glover Rd., Langley BC V3A 6H4 – 604/888-1265; Fax: 604/888-5729 – President, Barrie Palfreyman, B.Ed., M.Ed., M.Min., Ed.D.
Canadian Pentecostal Seminary, West Campus, 21277 - 56 Ave., Langley BC V2Y 1M3 – 905/542-7400; Fax: 905/542-7313 – National Director, William Griffin
Northwest Baptist Theologic College & Seminary, PO Box 790, Langley BC V3A 8B8 – 604/888-3310 – President, Larry McCullough, B.A., Th.M., Th.D.
Trinity Western Seminary, 7600 Glover Rd., Langley BC V3A 6H4 – 604/888-6158; Fax: 604/888-5729 – President, R.N. Snider, B.A., B.Ed., M.Ed., Ph.D
Western Pentecostal Bible College, PO Box 1700, Abbotsford BC V2S 7E7 – 604/853-7491; Fax: 604/853-8951 – President, James G. Richards, Ph.D.

## University of British Columbia

Vancouver BC V6T 1Z2
604/822-2211
URL: http://www.ubc.ca
Visitor, The Hon. David C. Lam, Lt. Governor of British Columbia
Chancellor, William L. Sauder, B.Comm., LL.D.
President & Vice-Chancellor, Martha Piper, B.S., M.A., Ph.D.
Vice-President, Academic & Provost, Daniel Birch, B.A., M.A., Ph.D.
Vice-President, Administration & Finance, Terry E. Sumner, C.A.
Vice-President, External Affairs, Peter W. Ufford
Vice-President, Research, B.H. Bressler, B.Sc., M.Sc., Ph.D.
Vice-President, Student & Academic Services, M.M. Klawe, B.Sc., Ph.D.

**DIRECTORS & OTHER OFFICERS**

Registrar, R.A. Spencer, B.E., Ph.D., P.Eng.
Director, Athletics & Sport Services, Robert Philip, B.Ed., M.A.
Director, Bookstore, Debbie Harvey
Director, Centre for Continuing Education, Walter Uegama, Ph.D.
Director, Ceremonies & Community Relations, Charles E. Slonecker, D.D.S., Ph.D.
Director, Counselling & Resource Centre, Mary Stott
Director, Extra-sessional Studies, Kenneth Slade, M.Ed., Ph.D.
Director, Financial Services, Jacqueline Rice
Director, Purchasing, K. Bowler
Director, University Computing Services, J. Leigh, M.Sc., C.D.P.

**FACULTIES WITH DEANS**

Agricultural Sciences, Moura Quayle, B.L.A., M.L.A.
Applied Science, Michael Isaacson, M.A., Ph.D., P.Eng., F.A.S.C.E., F.C.S.C.E., M.E.I.C., M.I.A.H.R.
Arts, Shirley Neuman, B.A., M.A., Ph.D.
Acting Dean, Commerce & Business Administration, Derek Atkins, B.A., M.A., Ph.D.
Dentistry, Edwin H.K. Yen, D.D.S., Dip.Ortho., Ph.D.
Education, Nancy Sheehan, B.A., B.Ed., M.Ed., Ph.D.
Forestry, C.S. Binkley, A.B., M.S., Ph.D.
Graduate Studies, Frieda Granot, B.Sc., M.Sc., Ph.D.
Law, Joost Blom, B.A., LL.B., B.C.L., LL.M.
Medicine, John A. Cairns, M.D., F.R.C.P.C.
Pharmaceutical Sciences, Frank S. Abbott, B.S.P., M.S., Ph.D.
Science, B.C. McBride, M.Sc., Ph.D.

**SCHOOLS WITH DIRECTORS**

Architecture, Sanford Hirshen, A.B., B.Arch., M.Arch., F.A.I.A.
Audiology & Speech Sciences, Judith R. Johnston, B.A., M.A., Ph.D.
Community & Regional Planning, William E. Rees, B.Sc., Ph.D.
Acting Director, Family & Nutritional Sciences, Daniel Perlman, A.B., M.A., Ph.D.
Principal, Green College, Richard Ericson, B.A., M.A., Ph.D., Litt.D.
Library, Archival & Information Studies, Kenneth Haycock, B.A., M.Ed., A.M.L.S., Ed.D.
Music, Jesse Read, B.Mus., M.Mus.
Nursing, Kathryn May, B.S.N., M.S., D.NSc.
Physical Education & Recreation, Robert W. Schutz, B.P.E., M.Sc., Ph.D.
Rehabilitation Sciences, Anne Carswell, Dip. (O.T.), B.Sc., M.Sc., Ph.D.
Social Work, Elaine Stolar, B.A., M.S.W., M.A.
Principal, St. John's College, Grant Ingram, B.Sc., M.Sc., Ph.D.

**AFFILIATED COLLEGES**

Regent College, 5800 University Blvd., Vancouver BC V6T 2E T – 604/224-3245 – Walter C. Wright, Jr., B.A., M.Div., Ph.D.
St. Mark's College (Roman Catholic), 5935 Iona Dr., Vancouver BC V6T 1J7 – 604/822-4463 – Rev. Paul C. Burns, C.S.B., B.A., S.T.B., M.A., B.Litt., Ph.D.

## University of Northern British Columbia

3333 University Way, PO Box 1950, Prince George BC V2N 4Z9
250/960-5555; Fax: 250/960-5794
URL: http://www.unbc.edu; http://quarles.unbc.edu/keen/welcome.html
President, Geoffrey Weller
Vice-President, Academic, Ken Coates
Secretary to the Board of Governors, Wendy Fletcher
Director, Communications, Clive Keen
Director, University Development, Michael Hamer
University Librarian, Pat Appavoo

**FACULTIES WITH DEANS**

Arts & Sciences, Dr. Robin Fisher
Health & Human Sciences, Dr. David Fish
Management & Administration, Dr. Doug Nord
Natural Resources & Environmental Studies, Dr. Fred Gilbert
Research & Graduate Studies, Dr. Bill Morrison

## University of Victoria

PO Box 1700, Victoria BC V8W 2Y2
250/721-7211; Fax: 250/721-6223
URL: http://www.uvic.ca
Chancellor, Norma I. Mickelson, B.Ed., M.A., Ph.D.
President & Vice-Chancellor, David F. Strong, B.Sc., M.Sc., Ph.D., F.R.S.C.
Vice-President, Academic & Provost, Penelope W. Codding, B.S., Ph.D.
Vice-President, Finance & Operations, J. Donald Rowlatt, B.Comm., Ph.D., Bursar
University Secretary, Sheila Sheldon Collyer, B.A.
Administrative Registrar, D. Cledwyn Thomas, B.A.
Director, Public Relations & Information Services, Bruce Kilpatrick, B.A.

**FACULTIES WITH DEANS**

Business, Roger N. Wolff, B.Sc., M.B.A., D.B.A.
Education, Bruce L. Howe, Dip.Ed., B.S., M.S., Ph.D.
Engineering, D. Michael Miller, B.Sc., M.Sc., Ph.D.
Fine Arts, Anthony Welch, B.A., M.A., Ph.D.
Graduate Studies, Gordana Lazarevich, Artist & Licentiate Dip., B.Sc., M.Sc., Ph.D.
Human & Social Development, Anita E. Molzahn, B.Sc., M.N., Ph.D.
Humanities, G.R. Ian MacPherson, B.A., M.A., Ph.D.
Law, David S. Cohen, B.Sc., LL.B., LL.M.
Science, Dr. John T. Weaver, B.Sc., M.Sc., Ph.D.
Social Sciences, John A . Schofield, B.A., M.B.A., M.A., Ph.D.

# COMMUNITY COLLEGES

**CAMOSUN COLLEGE**

Lansdowne Campus, 3100 Foul Bay Rd., Victoria BC V8P 5J2
250/370-3000; Fax: 250/370-3660
URL: http://www.camosun.bc.ca
President, Dr. Elizabeth Ashton
Interurban Campus, 4461 Interurban Rd., RR#3, Victoria BC V8X 3X1 – Fax: 604/370-3750

**CAPILANO COLLEGE**

2055 Purcell Way, North Vancouver BC V7J 3H5
604/986-1911; Fax: 604/984-4985
Email: glee@capcollege.bc.ca; URL: http://www.capcollege.bc.ca/
President, Greg Lee, Ph.D.

**COLLEGE OF NEW CALEDONIA**

3330 - 22nd Ave., Prince George BC V2N 1P8
250/562-2131; Fax: 250/561-5816; Toll Free: 1-800-371-8111

* indicates enrollment figure.

Email: askcnc@cnc.bc.ca; URL: http://www.cnc.bc.ca
President, Dr. Terence Weninger
Lakes District Campus, Hwy. 16 West, PO Box 5000, Burns Lake BC V0J 1E0 – 250/692-1700; Fax: 250/692-1750
Mackenzie Campus, Evergreen Mall, PO Box 2110, Mackenzie BC V0J 2C0 – 250/997-4333; Fax: 250/997-3779
Nechako Campus, Hospital Rd., RR#2, Vanderhoof BC V0J 3A0 – 250/567-3200; Fax: 250/567-9584
Quesnel Campus, 488 McLean St., Quesnel BC V2J 2P2 – 250/997-7500; Fax: 250/991-7502

#### COLLEGE OF THE ROCKIES
PO Box 8500, Cranbrook BC V1C 5L7
250/489-2751; Fax: 250/489-1790
Email: info@cotr.bc.ca; URL: http://www.cotr.bc.ca
President, Wm. Berry Calder
Manager, Communications Services, Toni Eitzenberger
Creston Campus, PO Box 1978, Creston BC V0B 1G0
Fernie Campus, PO Box 1770, Fernie BC V0B 1M0
Golden Campus, PO Box 376, Golden BC V0A 1H0
Invermere Campus, PO Box 960, Invermere BC V0A 1K0

#### DOUGLAS COLLEGE
PO Box 2503, New Westminster BC V3L 5B2
604/527-5400; Fax: 604/527-5095
URL: http://www.douglas.bc.ca/
President, Susan R. Witter

#### KWANTLEN UNIVERSITY COLLEGE
12666 - 72 Ave., Surrey BC V3W 2M8
604/599-2100; Fax: 604/599-2068
URL: http://www.kwantlen.bc.ca/
President, G.B. (Gerry) Kilcup
Langley Campus, 20901 Langley Bypass, Langley BC V3A 8G9 – 250/599-2100; Fax: 250/599-3277
Newton Campus, 13479 - 77 Ave., Surrey BC V3W 6Y1 – 250/599-2100; Fax: 250/599-2975
Richmond Campus, 8771 Lansdowne Rd., Richmond BC V6X 3V8 – 250/599-2100; Fax: 250/599-2716
Surrey Campus, 12666 - 72 Ave., Surrey BC V3T 5H8 – 250/599-2100; Fax: 250/599-2068

#### MALASPINA UNIVERSITY COLLEGE
900 Fifth St., Nanaimo BC V9R 5S5
250/753-3245; Fax: 250/755-8725
URL: http://www.mala.bc.ca
President, Richard Johnston
Cowichan Campus, 222 Cowichan Way, RR#6, Duncan BC V9L 4T8 – 250/748-2591; Fax: 250/746-3529
Nanaimo Campus, 900 Fifth St., Nanaimo BC V9R 5S5 – 250/753-3245; Fax: 250/755-8725
Parksville-Qualicum Office, Box 42, 223 Mills St., Parksville BC V9P 2G3 – 250/248-9792
Powell River Campus, 3960 Selkirk, Powell River BC V8A 3C6 – 604/485-2878; Fax: 604/485-2868

#### NORTH ISLAND COLLEGE
2300 Ryan Rd., Courtenay BC V9N 8N6
250/334-5271; Fax: 250/334-5292
Email: nicad3.nic.bc.ca; URL: http://www.nic.bc.ca
President, Dr. M. Neil Murphy
Director, Communications & Community Liaison, Susan Toresdahl
Campbell River Regional Campus, 1681 South Dogwood, Campbell River BC V9W 8C1 – 250/286-8911; Fax: 250/286-8900
Comox Valley Regional Campus, 2300 Ryan Rd., Courtenay BC V9N 8N6 – 250/334-5000; Fax: 250/334-5018
Port Alberni Regional Campus, 3699 Roger St., Port Alberni BC V9Y 8E3 – 250/724-8711; Fax: 250/724-8700
Port Hardy Regional Campus, PO Box 901, Port Hardy BC V0N 2P0 – 250/949-7912; Fax: 250/949-2617

#### NORTHERN LIGHTS COLLEGE
11401 - 8 St., Dawson Creek BC V1G 4G2
250/782-5251; Fax: 250/782-5233
URL: http://www.nlc.bc.ca
Acting President, J. Birnie, Email: jbirnie@nlc.bc.ca
Director, Community Relations, C. Lorincz, 604/784-7513; Email: clorincz@nlc.bc.ca
Chetwynd Campus, PO Box 1180, Chetwynd BC V0C 1J0 – 250/788-2248; Fax: 250/788-9706 – Principal, Merlin Nichols
Dawson Creek Campus, 11401 - 8 St., Dawson Creek BC V1G 4G2 – 250/782-5251; Fax: 250/782-6069 – Principal, Carolyn Rochon
Fort Nelson Campus, PO Box 860, Fort Nelson BC V0C 1R0 – 250/774-2741; Fax: 250/774-2750 – Principal, John Boraas
Fort St. John Campus, 9820 - 120 St., PO Box 1000, Fort St. John BC V1J 6K1 – 250/785-6981; Fax: 250/785-1294 – Acting Principal, Helena Bastedo

#### NORTHWEST COMMUNITY COLLEGE
College Services, 5331 McConnell Ave., PO Box 726, Terrace BC V8G 4X2
250/635-6511; Fax: 250/635-3511
URL: http://www.nwcc.bc.ca
Acting President, Beth Davies
Hazelton Campus, Omenica St., PO Box 338, Hazelton BC V0J 2N0 – 250/842-5291; Fax: 250/842-5813
Houston Campus, 3221 - 14 St., PO Box 1277, Houston BC V0J 1Z0 – 250/845-7266; Fax: 250/845-3521
Kitimat Campus, 606 Mountainview Sq., Kitimat BC V8C 2N2 – 250/632-4766; Fax: 250/632-5069
Masset Campus, PO Box 289, Masset BC V0T 1M0 – 250/626-3627; Fax: 250/626-3699
Nass Campus, c/o Nisga'a Tribal Council, General Delivery, New Aiyansh BC V0J 1A0 – 250/633-2292; Fax: 250/633-2463
Prince Rupert Campus, 130 - 1 Ave. West, Prince Rupert BC V8J 1A8 – 250/624-6054; Fax: 250/624-4920
Queen Charlotte Islands Campus, PO Box 67, Queen Charlotte City BC V0T 1S0 – 250/559-8222; Fax: 250/559-8219
Smithers Campus, 3966 - 2 Ave., PO Box 3606, Smithers BC V0J 2N0 – 250/847-4461; Fax: 250/847-4568
Stewart Campus, c/o Stewart Secondary School, PO Box 919, Stewart BC V0T 1W0 – 250/636-9184; Fax: 250/636-2770
Terrace Campus, 5331 McConnell Ave., Terrace BC V8G 4X2 – 250/635-6511; Fax: 250/638-5432

#### OKANAGAN UNIVERSITY COLLEGE
3333 College Way, Kelowna BC V1V 1V7
250/762-5445; Fax: 250/862-5476
URL: http://www.okanagan.bc.ca/
President, Kathryn Bindon, Email: president@okanagan.bc.ca
Executive Director, University College Advancement, Dr. Karen Shaw
Penticton Campus, 583 Duncan Ave. West, Penticton BC V2A 8E1 – 250/492-4305; Fax: 250/492-5355 – Centre Director, Allan Markin
Salmon Arm Campus, PO Box 189, Salmon Arm BC V1E 4N3 – 250/832-2126; Fax: 250/492-3950 – Centre Director, Clyde Tucker
Vernon Campus, 7000 College Way, Vernon BC V1B 2N5 – 250/545-7291; Fax: 250/804-8850 – Centre Director, Whitney Buggey

#### SELKIRK COLLEGE
301 Frank Beinder Way, PO Box 1200, Castlegar BC V1N 3J1
250/365-7292; Fax: 250/365-3929
URL: http://www.selkirk.bc.ca/
President, Leo Perra, Email: perra@selkirk.bc.ca
Nelson Campus, 2001 Silver King Rd., Nelson BC V1L 1C8 – 250/352-6601; Fax: 250/352-3180
Trail Campus, 900 Helena St., Trail BC V1R 4S6 – 250/368-5236; Fax: 250/368-4983

#### UNIVERSITY COLLEGE OF THE CARIBOO
PO Box 3010, Kamloops BC V2C 5N3
250/828-5000; Fax: 250/828-5086
URL: http://www.cariboo.bc.ca/
President, A.J. Wright
100 Mile House Campus, Provincial Bldg., 572 South Birch Ave., PO Box 2109, 100 Mile House BC V0K 2E0 – 250/395-3115; Fax: 250/395-2894
Merritt Campus, 1600 Voght St., PO Box 4400, Merritt BC V0K 2B0 – 250/378-2967; Fax: 250/378-8231
Williams Lake Campus, 351 Hodgson Rd., Williams Lake BC V2G 3P7 – 250/392-8000; Fax: 250/392-4984

#### UNIVERSITY COLLEGE OF THE FRASER VALLEY
33844 King Rd., RR#2, Abbotsford BC V2S 4N2
604/853-7441; Fax: 604/853-7558
URL: gopher://gopher.ucfv.bc.ca/
President, Dr. Peter Jones

#### VANCOUVER COMMUNITY COLLEGE
1155 East Broadway, Vancouver BC V5N 5T9
604/871-7000; Fax: 604/871-7100
URL: http://www.vcc.bc.ca
President, J. Cruickshank
Vice-President, Education, D. Dorn
Vice-President, Educational Support Services, L. Martin
City Centre Campus, 250 West Pender St., Vancouver BC V6B 1S9 – 604/443-8300; Fax: 604/443-8588
King Edward Campus, 1155 East Broadway, Vancouver BC V5N 5T9 – 604/871-7000; Fax: 604/871-7100

## TECHNICAL & VOCATIONAL INSTITUTES

#### BC INSTITUTE OF TECHNOLOGY
3700 Willingdon Ave., Burnaby BC V5G 3H2
604/434-3304; Fax: 604/434-6243
URL: http://www.bcit.bc.ca/
Vice-President, Education, Brian Gillespie
Vice-President, Finance & Administration, Clayton E. McKinley
Vice-President, Student Services & Educational Support, Gerry Moss
President, John Watson
Burnaby Campus, 3700 Willingdon Ave., Burnaby BC V5G 3H2 – 604/434-5734
Downtown Campus, 555 Seymour St., Vancouver BC – 604/412-7777
Pacific Marine Training Campus, 265 West Esplanade, North Vancouver BC V7M 1A5 – 604/985-2862 – Associate Dean, Capt. Roman Piechocki
Sea Island Campus, #200, 5301 Airport Rd. South, Richmond BC V7B 1B5 – 604/278-4831

#### EMILY CARR INSTITUTE OF ART & DESIGN
1399 Johnston St., Vancouver BC V6H 3R9
604/844-3800; Fax: 604/844-3801
URL: http://www.eciad.bc.ca/
President, Dr. Ronald Burnett

#### JUSTICE INSTITUTE OF B.C.
715 McBride Blvd., New Westminster BC V3L 5T4
604/525-5422; Fax: 604/528-5518
President, Larry Goble

## POST-SECONDARY & SPECIALIZED INSTITUTIONS

#### ABC INDUSTRIAL EMERGENCY CARE TRAINING SCHOOL INC.
#303, 4211 Kingsway, Burnaby BC V5H 1Z6
604/435-7773; Fax: 604/435-7939
Industrial first aid

**ACADEMY OF EXCELLENCE**
1119 Fort St., Victoria BC V8V 3K9
604/386-3621

**ACADEMY OF LEARNING**
#300, 2030 Marine Dr., North Vancouver BC V7P 1V7
604/987-4277; Fax: 604/987-4213
Email: errol@info-mine.com; URL: http://www.academyol.com
Computer & business skills
Academy of Learning, 6531 Buswell St., Richmond BC V6Y 2G9

**THE ANNA WYMAN SCHOOL OF DANCE ARTS**
1457 Marine Dr., West Vancouver BC V7T 1B8
604/926-6535

**ASIA-PACIFIC INTERNATIONAL GRADUATE SCHOOL OF MANAGEMENT**
#A100, 355 Burrard St., Vancouver BC V6C 2G6
604/688-3115; Fax: 604/688-0252
Email: apigsm@direct.ca; URL: http://www.apiu.edu
International management

**ASPEN EDUCATIONAL**
109 Victoria St., Kamloops BC V2C 1Z4
250/374-2229; Fax: 250/374-8954; Toll Free: 1-800-746-1600
Email: aspen@mail.netshop.net

**AUTOMOTIVE TRAINING CENTRE**
#210, 13460 Smallwood Place, Richmond BC V6V 1W8
604/270-6121; Fax: 604/270-6123

**BARKEL BUSINESS SCHOOL LTD.**
#211, 3030 Lincoln Ave., Coquitlam BC V3B 6B4
604/464-8717; Fax: 604/464-4122
Secretarial, bookkeeping & computer training

**BC COLLEGE OF OPTICS**
#207, 2001 - 36th Ave. East, Vancouver BC V5P 1C9
604/327-4467; Fax: 604/327-2337
Opticianry

**BC SCHOOL OF ART THERAPY**
1931 Lee Ave., Victoria BC V8R 4W9
250/598-6434; Fax: 250/598-6434
Art therapy within a clinical setting

**BLANCHE MACDONALD INSTITUTE**
111 Smithe St., Vancouver BC V6B 4Z8
604/685-0347; Fax: 604/669-1415
Fashion, beauty, esthetics programs

**BM CHAN INTERNATIONAL SCHOOL OF HAIR DESIGN & ESTHETICS**
2951 Kingsway, Vancouver BC V5R 5J4
604/437-3109; Fax: 604/327-8088
Hair, esthetics & nail courses

**BURNABY COLLEGE**
#450, 4800 Kingsway, Burnaby BC V5H 4J2
604/437-5711; Fax: 604/437-8709
Desktop publishing, graphic design, computerized accounting & office training, medical office, hospitality, ESL

**CANADIAN ACUPRESSURE INSTITUTE INC.**
#301, 733 Johnson St., Victoria BC V8W 3C7
250/388-7475
Training in acupressure & shiatsu

**CANADIAN AVALANCHE ASSOCIATION**
PO Box 2759, Revelstoke BC V0E 2S0
250/837-2435; Fax: 250/837-4624
Email: canav@mindlink.bc.ca
Observing weather, snowpack conditions, forecasting snow stability

**CANADIAN BUSINESS ENGLISH INSTITUTE**
#400, 1130 West Pender St., Vancouver BC V6E 4A4
604/685-0291; Fax: 604/685-0294
ESL, TOEFL, international business, computer training

**CANADIAN COLLEGE OF BUSINESS & LANGUAGE**
16 Bastion Sq., Victoria BC V8W 1H9
250/383-3933; Fax: 250/383-2292

**CANADIAN ELECTROLYSIS COLLEGE LTD.**
#201, 13303 - 72nd Ave., Surrey BC V3W 2N5
604/597-1101; Fax: 604/597-1101

**CANADIAN FAMILY RESOURCE INSTITUTE**
Broadway Plaza, #L1, 601 West Broadway, Vancouver BC V5Z 4C2
604/879-2291
Nurse's aides training

**CANADIAN INSTITUTE OF GEMMOLOGY**
PO Box 57010, Vancouver BC V5K 5G6
604/530-8569; Fax: 604/530-8569
Email: wolf@kwantlen.bc.ca; URL: http://www.deepcove.com/cig
Diamond grading, jewellery, history & design, gem identification

**CANADIAN TRAVEL SCHOOL**
#501, 1755 West Broadway, Vancouver BC V6J 4S5
604/736-8000; Fax: 604/731-9819
Email: ctsyvr@axionet.com
Travel & tourism

**CANAPRO EMPLOYMENT TRAINERS**
#301, 68 - 2nd Ave. East, Vancouver BC V5T 1B1
604/875-0052; Fax: 604/875-0053
Career/job search counselling, ESL

**CAREERS 2000 COLLEGE & BUSINESS TRAINING CENTRE**
#260, 13711 - 72nd Ave., Surrey BC V3W 2P2
604/543-9000; Fax: 604/543-9000
Computer & business training

**CDI COLLEGE OF BUSINESS & TECHNOLOGY**
#200, 789 West Pender St., Vancouver BC V6C 1H2
604/685-8585; Fax: 604/685-2422
URL: http://www.cdicollege.com
Director, Claudia Adair
Network specialist training, programming, business applications, desktop publishing

**CHEMAINUS NATIVE COLLEGE**
12541 Trans Canada Hwy., PO Box 730, Ladysmith BC V0R 2E0
250/245-3522; Fax: 250/245-8263
Adult secondary program, business management & community economic development

**COLUMBIA ACADEMY OF RADIO, TELEVISION & RECORDING ARTS**
1295 West Broadway, Vancouver BC V6H 3X8
604/736-3316; Fax: 604/731-5458
M. Hasselbach

**COMENIUS INSTITUTE**
#2, 640 West Pender St., Vancouver BC V6B 1V8
604/689-9844
URL: http://www.uniserve.com/comenius
Design, graphic skills & construction theory

**COMOX VALLEY BEAUTY SCHOOL**
911 McPhee Ave., Courtenay BC V9N 3A1
604/338-9982; Fax: 604/338-0199

**COMPUCOLLEGE SCHOOL OF BUSINESS**
#200, 889 West Pender St., Vancouver BC V6C 3B2
604/682-6600; Fax: 604/687-0983
Email: steve@compucollege.ca
Secretarial, business, computer, travel & hospitality

**COSMETOLOGY SCHOOL OF CANADA LTD.**
#350, 789 West Pender St., Vancouver BC V6C 1H2
604/669-3319; Fax: 604/669-3318
Aesthetics, bodycare, spa treatments, electrolysis, make-up, modelling, etc.

**COWICHAN VALLEY TRADE SCHOOL LTD.**
81 Trunk Rd., Duncan BC V9L 2N7
250/748-6255; Fax: 250/748-4997
Service industry training

**CTI COUNSELLOR TRAINING INSTITUTE LTD.**
#405, 510 West Hastings St., Vancouver BC V6B 1L8
604/683-2442; Fax: 604/688-9001; Toll Free: 1-800-667-3272
Email: cti@istar.ca; URL: http://home.istar.ca/~cti
Counselling practice training

**DLR RESOURCES**
PO Box 322, Lion's Bay BC V0N 2E0
604/921-8191; Fax: 604/921-8191

**DUTOT & JAMESON CONSULTING**
#201, 1009 Belvedere St., Enderby BC V0E 1V0
250/838-7199; Fax: 250/838-6020
Life & employment skills

**ELIZABETH LESLIE LTD. COLLEGE OF FASHION MERCHANDISING, MODELLING & PERSONAL DEVELOPMENT**
#111, 2255 - 8th Ave. West, Vancouver BC V6K 2A6
604/738-6223
Fashion

**ERICKSON COLLEGE**
2021 Columbia St., Vancouver BC V5Y 3C9
604/879-5600; Fax: 604/879-7234; Toll Free: 1-800-665-6949
Email: info@erickson.edu; URL: http://www.erickson.edu
Psychotherapy & counselling, personal & professional empowerment & growth

**ESL TEACHER TRAINING CENTRE**
#105, 2412 Laurel St., Vancouver BC V5Z 3T2
604/872-1236; Fax: 604/872-1275

**FIELDS COLLEGE INTERNATIONAL**
3491 Shelbourne St., Victoria BC V8P 4J2
250/472-0323; Fax: 250/472-0324
URL: http://www.fieldscollege.com/~esl
English as a Second Language
Managing Director, Wanda Fields

**FINE-ART BARTENDING SCHOOL**
3516 Lakeshore Rd., Kelowna BC V1W 3L5
250/861-6699; Fax: 250/860-0998

**GATEWAY CAREERS INC.**
#270, 3355 West Broadway St., Vancouver BC V6R 2B1
604/738-0285; Fax: 604/738-0994
Long-term care aides, security guards, ESL

**GEN CANADA**
#380, 789 West Pender St., Vancouver BC V6C 1H2
604/689-1079; Fax: 604/689-1649

**GRANTON INSTITUTE OF TECHNOLOGY**
#404, 999 Canada Place, Vancouver BC V6C 3E2
604/685-8923
Distance education courses

**GRANVILLE BUSINESS COLLEGE**
#320, 885 Dunsmuir St., Vancouver BC V6C 1N5

* indicates enrollment figure.

604/683-8850; Toll Free: 1-800-661-9885
Office administration, computer training

**GREATER REGIONAL TECHNICAL COLLEGE**
6830 Burlington Ave., Burnaby BC V5J 4H1
604/439-1101; Fax: 604/439-1190
Employment training

**HARBOURSIDE COLLEGE**
555 West Hastings St., Vancouver BC V6B 4N4
604/688-4242; Fax: 604/688-2237
ESL, TOEFL

**HELEN LEFEAUX INC. SCHOOL OF FASHION DESIGN**
#100, 247 Abbott St., Vancouver BC V6B 2K7
604/687-3352; Fax: 604/687-3356
Fashion design

**HELM CAREER TRAINING & CONSULTATION**
1143 Sutherland Ave., Kelowna BC V1Y 5Y2
250/861-1898; Fax: 250/861-4055
Career training in health, human service, community support

**HILLTOP SECURITY ACADEMY**
#500, 990 Homer St., Vancouver BC V5B 2W4
604/930-8377; Fax: 604/930-8378

**HORIZONS WEST LANGUAGE SCHOOL**
#200, 9801 King George Hwy., Surrey BC V3T 5H5
604/951-0521; Fax: 604/951-8084

**INSTITUTE OF INDIGENOUS GOVERNMENT**
342 Water St., Vancouver BC V6B 1B6
604/602-9555; Fax: 604/602-3400
Email: iig@cyberstore.ca; URL: http://www.indigenous.bc.ca

**INTERNATIONAL TRAVEL ACADEMY**
Oakridge Centre, North Office Tower, #700, 650 - 41st Ave. West, Vancouver BC V5Z 2M9
604/266-3120; Fax: 604/266-3155; Toll Free: 1-800-420-2229
Email: knosko@sita.com
Travel, tourism, hospitality training

**ISLAND OFFICE TRENDS**
#101, 3939 Quadra St., Victoria BC V8X 1J5
250/727-7624; Fax: 250/727-2893
Email: iotrends3@pacificcoast.net; URL: http://www.pacificcoast.net/~iotrends
Computer & business skills training, desktop publishing, internet & web page design

**ISLAND SKILL DEVELOPMENT CENTRE**
#204, 190 Wallace St., Nanaimo BC V9R 5B1
604/754-3370

**ISLAND TAX SCHOOL INC.**
10 Esplanade, PO Box 250, Nanaimo BC V9R 5K9
250/753-7116; Fax: 250/753-7118
Tax laws, tax forms courses

**JENNINGS INSTITUTE FOR PERFORMING ARTISTS INC.**
1870 Sperling Ave., Burnaby BC V5B 4K5
604/420-3213; Fax: 604/420-3214
Representation & management of performers, training in dance, music, drama, speech arts & theoretical subjects

**JOJI'S HAIR ACADEMY**
1340 Commercial Dr., Vancouver BC V5L 3X6
604/255-5858; Fax: 604/255-5851

**JOSLIN GROUP**
#301, 1456 Johnston Rd., White Rock BC V4B 3Z5
604/538-1651; Fax: 604/538-9836
Computer systems consulting & training

**KAMLOOPS VOCATIONAL HEALTH SCIENCES**
346 Seymour St., Kamloops BC V2C 2G2
250/314-0670; Fax: 250/314-0671
Pharmacy technician, rehabilitation assistant, respite caregiver training

**KINGSTON COLLEGE**
6709 Heather St., Vancouver BC V6P 3P3
604/294-3288; Fax: 604/294-3323

**KINGSTON COLLEGE**
2286 Holdon Ave., Burnaby BC V5B 4Y5
604/294-8813

**LANGARA COLLEGE**
100 West 49th Ave., Vancouver BC V5Y 2Z6
604/323-5511; Fax: 604/323-5555
URL: http://www.langara.bc.ca
President, Linda Holmes

**LANGLEY COLLEGE OF TRADE & COMMERCE**
20381 - 66 Ave., Langley BC V2Y 1P3
604/530-8411; Fax: 604/530-4034

**LBD SCHOOL OF BUSINESS INC.**
#203, 301 Dogwood St., Campbell River BC V9W 2Y1
250/287-9850; Fax: 250/287-9850
Computer, office & entrepreneurship programs

**LESTER B. PEARSON COLLEGE OF THE PACIFIC**
650 Pearson College Dr., Victoria BC V9C 4H7
250/391-2411; Fax: 250/391-2412
President, Peter D. Bavinton

**LIFE SKILLS TRAINING CENTRES**
1367 - 128 St., Surrey BC V4A 3T5
604/535-2888; Fax: 604/572-8712

**MAGAS-MEYERS ENTERPRISES LTD.**
1019 Venture Way, PO Box 514, Gibsons BC V0N 1V0
604/886-3807; Fax: 604/886-3807

**MANTISSA TECHNICAL COLLEGE INC.**
225 - 2nd Ave. West, Vancouver BC V5Y 1C7
604/877-1402
Email: mantiss@deepcove.com
Computer aided design, drafting, graphics & animation

**MCKAY TECHNICAL INSTITUTE LTD.**
#228, 610 - 6th St., New Westminster BC V3L 3C2
604/517-1152; Fax: 604/517-0212
Email: bmanning@nw.byteshop.com
Computer graphic design, medical & dental office

**METRO TRAINING INSTITUTE**
#700, 333 Terminal Ave., Vancouver BC V6A 2L7
604/682-6020; Fax: 604/682-6468
Automotive & collision repair training, computer graphics, horticultural grounds maintenance & management
Surrey Campus, #310, 13281 - 78 Ave., Surrey BC V3W 5B9 – 604/599-3630; Fax: 604/599-7204

**NATIONAL COLLEGE INC.**
5350 Cambridge St., Burnaby BC V5B 1C5
604/299-1667; Fax: 604/299-2465

**NATIONWIDE TRAVEL COLLEGE**
#202, 6751 Westminster Hwy., Richmond BC V7C 4V4
604/276-8824; Fax: 604/276-2449; Toll Free: 1-800-336-9166
Travel & tourism

**NATIVE EDUCATION CENTRE**
285 - 5th Ave. East, Vancouver BC V5T 1H2
604/873-3761; Fax: 604/873-9152
Upgrading & occupational skills

**NEWCASTLE COLLEGE**
20179 - 56th Ave., Langley BC V3A 3Y6
604/530-4555; Fax: 604/533-6655
Bridging programs, ESL, vocational/counselling services

**ONE STOP CAREER CENTRES**
#2, 1890 Cooper Rd., Kelowna BC V1Y 8B7
250/861-8600; Fax: 250/717-4001; Toll Free: 1-888-717-7867
Private post-secondary institution

**OPEN LEARNING AGENCY**
4355 Mathissi Pl., Burnaby BC V5G 4S8
604/431-3000; Fax: 604/431-3333
URL: http://www.ola.bc.ca
President, Dr. Glen Farrell

**OUTWARD BOUND WESTERN CANADA**
109, 1367 West Broadway, Vancouver BC V6H 4A9
604/737-3093; Fax: 604/737-3109
Email: ob@uniserve.com
Executive Director, Andrew Orr

**PACIFIC GATEWAY INTERNATIONAL COLLEGE**
1155 Robson St., 3rd Fl., Vancouver BC V6E 1B5
604/687-3595; Fax: 604/687-3586

**PACIFIC VOCATIONAL COLLEGE LTD.**
4064 McConnell Dr., Burnaby BC V5A 3A8
604/421-5255; Fax: 604/421-7445
Piping trades

**PAUL DE COSTA INSTITUTE**
1402 Douglas St., Victoria BC V8W 2G1
604/386-7993; Fax: 604/386-7945

**PERSONAL GROWTH CONSULTING TRAINING CENTRE**
#5A, 319 Victoria St., Kamloops BC V2C 2A3
250/372-8071; Fax: 250/372-8270

**PIC CONSULTANTS LTD.**
1281 West Georgia St., 9th Fl., Vancouver BC V6E 3J7
604/669-3535; Fax: 604/689-8622

**PITMAN BUSINESS COLLEGE**
688 West Hastings, 3rd Fl., Vancouver BC V6B 1P1
604/685-7696; Fax: 604/685-9879
Email: pitman@pitmancollege.com; URL: http://www.pitmancollege.com

**PRO-SOFT TRAINING INSTITUTE INC.**
13575 King George Hwy., Surrey BC V3T 2V1
604/581-5017; Fax: 604/581-6229
Office courses, ESL

**PROCARE INSTITUTE INC.**
7087 Sierra Dr., Burnaby BC V5A 1A4
604/291-0030; Fax: 604/298-7789
Email: pjwhite@direct.ca
Health care aides

**RCABC ROOFING INSTITUTE**
9734 - 201st St., Langley BC V1M 3E8
604/882-9734; Fax: 604/882-1744
Email: roofing@rcabc.org; URL: http://www.rcabc.org
Roofing training

**RESOURCEWORKS TRAINING & DEVELOPMENT**
13579 Bentley Rd., Surrey BC V3R 5B8
604/582-9931; Fax: 604/582-9917
Caree & computer training

**RHODES & ASSOCIATES**
#710, 333 Terminal Ave., Vancouver BC V6A 2L7
604/669-7522; Fax: 604/669-7680

**RICHMOND SCHOOL OF HAIRDRESSING**
8057 Anderson Rd., Richmond BC V6Y 1S2
604/276-8202; Fax: 604/279-0225
Email: rshd@chatsubo.net; URL: http://www.ontimeprint.com/hairschool
Director, Nevin Middleton
Hairstyling courses

**RIDGE MEADOWS BUSINESS & TRAINING CENTRE**
22610 Dewdney Trunk Rd., Maple Ridge BC V2X 3J9
604/467-5163; Fax: 604/467-7548

**SASSY'S ACADEMY OF HAIR**
413 - 9th Ave. North, PO Box 1077, Golden BC V0A 1H0
604/344-2033

**SPECTRUM COLLEGE**
930 Sherwood Lane, West Vancouver BC V7V 3X9
604/922-8779

**SPROTT-SHAW COLLEGE OF BUSINESS**
#204, 10114 King George Hwy., Surrey BC V3T 2W4
604/583-1004; Fax: 604/589-5230
Email: cpurcell@uniserve.com

**STELLAR COLLEGE**
2485 Montrose Ave., Abbotsford BC V2S 3T2
604/527-0569
Job re-entry, life skills programs

**STENBERG & ASSOCIATES TRAINERS**
#B201, 20218 Fraser Hwy., Langley BC V3A 4E6
604/534-0611; Fax: 604/534-4133
Care & community support workers training, cooking courses

**SUNSHINE COAST COMPUTER COLLEGE**
5588B Inlet Ave., PO Box 2429, Sechelt BC V0N 3A0
604/885-3386; Fax: 604/885-7123
Email: betty-anne_pap@sunshine.net

**TOURISM TRAINING INSTITUTE**
1754 West Broadway, Vancouver BC V6J 1Y1
604/736-7008; Fax: 604/736-7723
Email: tourism@tourismti.bc.ca; URL: http://www.axionet.com/tourism
Travel & tourism

**TREBAS INSTITUTE**
#305, 112 East 3rd Ave., Vancouver BC V5T 1C8
604/872-2666; Fax: 604/872-3001
President, David P. Leonard, 514/845-4141
Audio engineering, music production, multimedia programs

**TREND COLLEGE HOSPITALITY MANAGEMENT INSTITUTE**
555 West Hastings St., PO Box 12022, Vancouver BC V6B 4N4
604/687-8830; Fax: 604/683-1446
Email: agilman@trend.bc.ca; URL: http://www.trend.bc.ca/homepage
Business management, hospitality, travel & tourism

**U-MEEK HUMAN RESOURCES DEVELOPMENT INC.**
#206, 14727 - 108 Ave., Surrey BC V3R 1V9
604/581-0267; Fax: 604/581-4267

**VANCOUVER ART THERAPY INSTITUTE**
#350, 1425 Marine Dr., West Vancouver BC V7T 1B9
604/926-9381; Fax: 604/926-5728

**VANCOUVER MAPLE LEAF LANGUAGE COLLEGE**
#250, 815 West Hastings St., Vancouver BC V6C 1B4
604/688-7942; Fax: 604/688-7985
Email: study@vlc-canada.com; URL: http://www.discovervancouver.com/vic_maple_leaf
English as a second language training, business, secretarial skills & hospitality management

**VANCOUVER SCHOOL OF THEOLOGY**
6000 Iona Dr., Vancouver BC V6T 1L4
604/822-9031; Fax: 604/822-9212
Email: fwhfld@unixg.ubc.ca; URL: http://www.interchg.ubc.ca/vst/
Director, Degree Programs, The Rev. Dr. James A. McCullum
Principal, The Rev. Dr. W.J. Phillips

**WAKINYAN CAREER COLLEGE**
#203, 96 Broadway East, Vancouver BC V5T 4N9
604/871-9933

**WEST COAST COLLEGE OF HEALTH CARE**
#1, 15355 - 102A Ave., Surrey BC V3R 7K1
604/951-6644; Fax: 604/951-6608
Email: wcc@planeteer.com
Pharmacy technician, rehabilitation assistant, veterinary assistant, health care aide, medical lab assistant, community support worker, home support worker, corrections officer courses

**WESTERN ACADEMY OF PHOTOGRAPHY**
755A Queens Ave., Victoria BC V8T 1M2
250/383-1522; Fax: 250/383-1534
Professional photography, journalism/photojournalism

**WESTERN MONTESSORI TEACHERS' COLLEGE**
#108, 135 Balmoral Dr., Port Moody BC V3H 1X7
604/461-7132; Fax: 604/469-2754

**WILBER ENTERPRISES LTD.**
9811 - 114th Ave., Fort St. John BC V1J 4R8
604/785-7192; Fax: 604/785-7192

## INDEPENDENT & PRIVATE SCHOOLS

**Schools with enrollment of 50 or more, listed alphabetically by city.**

Abbotsford Christian School, 35011 Old Clayburn Rd., Abbotsford BC V2S 7L7 – 604/850-5342; Fax: 604/859-2240 – Principal, Dwight L. Moodie – *1,227 – Gr. K.-12
Abbotsford: Cornerstone Christian School, 3970 Gladwin Rd., PO Box 520, Abbotsford BC V2S 5Z5 – 604/859-7867; Fax: 604/855-9367 – Principal, Ward McGowan – *205 – Gr. K.-12
Abbotsford: Dasmesh Punjabi School, 33094 South Fraser Way, Abbotsford BC V2S 2A9 – 604/852-8986; Fax: 604/852-8924 – Principal, Dalip Singh Gill – *210 – Gr. K.-7; Gen. & Sikh Studies
Abbotsford: Mennonite Educational Institute, #2240, 4081 Clearbrook Rd., Abbotsford BC V2T 3X8 – 604/859-9762; Fax: 604/859-9206 – Principal, Leo Regehr – *947 – Gr. K.-12
Abbotsford: St. James School, 2767 Townline Rd., Abbotsford BC V2S 6A9 – 604/852-1788; Fax: 604/850-5376 – Principal, Catherine Kraemer – *243 – Gr. K.-7
Abbotsford: St. John Brebeuf, 2747 Townline Rd., Abbotsford BC V2T 5E1 – 604/855-0571; Fax: 604/855-0572 – Principal, Wendell MacCormack – *292 – Gr. 8-12
Agassiz Christian School, 7571 Morrow Rd., PO Box 3230, Agassiz BC V0M 1A0 – 604/796-9310; Fax: 604/796-9519 – Principal, Henry Tuininga – *92 – Gr. K.-7
Agassiz: Seabird Island Community School, 5 Chowat Rd., PO Box 930, Agassiz BC V0M 1A0 – 604/796-3061; Fax: 604/796-3068 – Principal, Barbara Rose – *119 – Gr. K.-10
Ahousat: Maaqtusiis School, General Delivery, Ahousat BC V0R 1A0 – 250/670-9589; Fax: 250/670-9543 – Principal, Gregory Louie – *171 – Gr. K.-12
Aldergrove: Fraser Valley Adventist Academy, 26026 - 48 Ave., PO Box 249, Aldergrove BC V4W 2T8 – 604/856-7852; Fax: 604/856-1002 – Principal, Marjorie Fortney – *289 – Gr. K.-12
Alert Bay: T'lisalagi'lakw School, Front St., PO Box 50, Alert Bay BC V0N 1A0 – 250/974-5591; Fax: 250/974-2475 – Principal, John Anderson – *121 – Gr. K.-10
Burnaby: Columbia College, 6037 Marlborough Ave., Burnaby BC V5H 3L6 – 604/430-6422; Fax: 604/439-0548 – Principal, Michael Weiss – *159 – Sec.
Burnaby: Deer Lake SDA School, 5550 Gilpin St., Burnaby BC V5G 2H6 – 604/434-5844; Fax: 604/434-5845 – Principal, Murray Cooper – *180 – Gr. K.-10
Burnaby: Holy Cross School, 1450 Delta Ave., Burnaby BC V5B 3G2 – 604/299-3530; Fax: 604/299-3534 – Principal, Jennifer Gallivan – *230 – Gr. K.-7
Burnaby: John Knox Christian School, 8260 - 13 Ave., Burnaby BC V3N 2G5 – 604/522-1410; Fax: 604/522-4606 – Principal, Peter Valkenier – *218 – Gr. K.-7; Special Ed.
Burnaby: Kenneth Gordon School, 7855 Meadow Ave., Burnaby BC V3N 2V8 – 604/524-5224; Fax: 604/524-8297 – Principal, Ellen Baglot – *56 – Elem.
Burnaby: Kingston College, 2286 Holdom Ave., Burnaby BC V5B 4Y5 – 604/294-3288; Fax: 604/294-3323 – Principal, Seann Lyncaster – *127 – Gr. 11-12
Burnaby: Our Lady of Mercy School, 7481 - 10 Ave., Burnaby BC V3N 2S1 – 604/526-7121; Fax: 604/520-3194 – Principal, Colleen Burrell – *242 – Gr. K.-7
Burnaby: St. Francis de Sales School, 6656 Balmoral St., Burnaby BC V5E 1J1 – 604/435-5311; Fax: 604/434-4798 – Principal, Cecilia McLaren – *211 – Gr. K.-7
Burnaby: St. Helen's School, 3894 Triumph St., Burnaby BC V5C 1Y7 – 604/299-2234; Fax: 604/299-3565 – Principal, Waldemar Sambor – *269 – Gr. K.-7
Burnaby: St. Michael's School, 9387 Holmes St., Burnaby BC V3N 4C3 – 604/526-9768; Fax: 604/540-9799 – Principal, Ethel Jackson – *236 – Gr. K.-7
Burnaby: St. Thomas More Collegiate, 7450 - 12 Ave., Burnaby BC V3N 2K1 – 604/521-1801; Fax: 604/520-0725 – Principal, Hugh O'Neill – *569 – Gr. 8-12; Boys
Campbell River Christian School, 250 South Dogwood St., Campbell River BC V9W 6Y7 – 250/287-4266; Fax: 250/287-3130 – Principal, Gordon Wickens – *290 – Gr. K.-12
Chemainus: St. Joseph's School, 9735 Elm St., PO Box 900, Chemainus BC V0R 1K0 – 250/246-3191; Fax: 250/246-2921 – Principal, Eleanor Greveling – *204 – Gr. K.-7
Chilliwack Christian School, 9750 McNaught, PO Box 161, Chilliwack BC V2P 6J4 – 604/792-4171; Fax: 604/792-0640 – Principal, Doyle Smiens – *217 – Gr. K.-7
Chilliwack: Highroad Academy, 46641 Chilliwack Central Rd., Chilliwack BC V2P 1K3 – 604/792-4680; Fax: 604/792-2465 – Principal, Berne J. Watters – *276 – Gr. K.-12
Chilliwack: John Calvin School, 4268 Stewart Rd., Chilliwack BC V2R 5G3 – 604/823-6814; Fax: 604/823-6791 – Principal, Pieter H. Torenvliet – *257 – Gr. K.-7
Chilliwack: Mount Cheam Christian School, 48988 Yale Rd. East, Chilliwack BC V2P 6H4 – 604/794-3072; Fax: 604/794-3078 – Principal, Adrian Stoutjesdyk – *316 – Gr. K.-12
Chilliwack: St. Mary's School, 8909 Mary St., Chilliwack BC V2P 4J4 – 604/792-7715; Fax: 604/792-3013 – Principal, Shelley Macdonell – *232 – Gr. K.-7
Chilliwack: Timothy Christian School, 50420 Castleman Rd., Chilliwack BC V2P 6H4 – 604/794-7114; Fax: 604/794-3520 – Principal, Herb Krul – *409 – Gr. K.-12

* indicates enrollment figure.

Chilliwack: Valley Christian School, 8700 Young Rd., Chilliwack BC V2P 4P4 – 604/793-7997; Fax: 604/793-7991 – Principal, Philip Hills – *115 – Gr. K.-7

Cobble Hill: Evergreen Independent School, 3805 Cobble Hill Rd., PO Box 166, Cobble Hill BC V0R 1L0 – 250/743-2433; Fax: 250/743-2570 – Principal, Penny Pope – *53 – Gr. K.-6

Coquitlam: British Columbia Christian Academy, 2665 Runnel Dr., Coquitlam BC V3E 1S3 – 604/941-8426; Fax: 604/945-6455 – Principal, Ian Jarvie – *132 – Gr. K.-12

Coquitlam College, 516 Brookmere Ave., Coquitlam BC V3J 1W9 – 604/939-6633; Fax: 604/939-0336 – Principal, Roger Kopf – *196 – Gr. 10-12

Coquitlam: Our Lady of Fatima School, 315 Walker St., Coquitlam BC V3K 4C7 – 604/936-4228; Fax: 604/936-4403 – Principal, Robertson Wood – *239 – Gr. K.-7/French Immersion

Coquitlam: Queen of All Saints Elementary, 1405 Como Lake Ave., Coquitlam BC V3J 5K7 – 604/931-9071; Fax: 604/931-9089 – Principal, Christina Aldus – *219 – Gr. K.-7

Coquitlam: Traditional Learning Academy, 1189 Rochester Ave., Coquitlam BC V3K 2X3 – 604/931-7265; Fax: 604/931-7265 – Principal, Martin Dale – *92 – Gr. K.-12

Cranbrook: Ktunaxa Independent School, Mission Rd., S-15, SS3, C-122, Cranbrook BC V1C 6H3 – 250/489-5762; Fax: 250/489-2091 – Principal, K. Bailey-Romanko – *65 – Gr. K.-12

Cranbrook: St. Mary's Catholic Public School, 1701 - 5 St. South, PO Box 250, Cranbrook BC V1C 1K1 – 250/426-5017; Fax: 250/426-5076 – Principal, Douglas F. Mitchell – *324 – Gr. K.-7, Learning Assistance, French A.S.L.

Dawson Creek: Mountain Christian School, 11501 - 17th St., PO Box 2308, Dawson Creek BC V1G 4P2 – 250/782-9528; Fax: 250/782-5891 – Principal, Abram Born – *61 – Gr. K.-12

Dawson Creek: Notre Dame School, 925 - 104 Ave., Dawson Creek BC V1G 2H8 – 250/782-4923; Fax: 250/782-4388 – Principal, Eileen Materi – *162 – Gr. K.-7; Learning Assistance, Enrichment

Dawson Creek: Ron Pettigrew Christian School, PO Box 688, Dawson Creek BC V1G 4H7 – 250/782-4580; Fax: 250/782-9805 – Principal, Debbie Maddigan – *96 – Gr. K.-12

Delta Christian School, 4789 - 53 St., Delta BC V4K 2Y9 – 604/946-2514; Fax: 604/946-2589 – Principal, Jacob Lieuwen – *214 – Gr. K.-7

Delta: Immaculate Conception School, 8840 - 119 St., Delta BC V4C 6M4 – 604/596-6116; Fax: 604/596-4338 – Principal, Sr. Alexis Taphorn – *448 – Gr. K.-7

Delta: Sacred Heart School, 3900 Arthur Dr., PO Box 10, Delta BC V4K 3N5 – 604/946-2611; Fax: 604/946-4533 – Principal, Mary-Joyce Derouin – *258 – Gr. K.-7

Delta: Traditional Learning Academy, 10680 - 84th Ave., Delta BC V4C 2L2 – 604/582-7898; Fax: 604/582-7898 – Principal, Tom McRae – *98 – Gr. K.-7

Duncan Christian School, 5781 Chesterfield St., Duncan BC V9L 3M1 – 250/746-5341; Fax: 250/746-3615 – Principal, Jacoba M. Spyksma – *382 – Gr. K.-12; Special Ed.

Duncan: Queen of Angels School, RR#5, Duncan BC V9L 4T6 – 250/746-5919; Fax: 250/746-8689 – Principal, Ellen McMillan – *394 – Gr. K.-9

Duncan: Queen Margaret's School, 660 Brownsey Ave., Duncan BC V9L 1C2 – 250/746-4185; Fax: 250/746-4187 – Principal, Dr. Stephen Johnson – *199 – Gr. K.-12

Duncan: Sunrise Waldorf School, RR#7, 4344 Peters Rd., Duncan BC V9L 4W4 – 250/743-7253 – Principal, Peter Morris – *110 – Gr. K.-7

Enderby Christian School, 104 Meadow Cres., PO Box 339, Enderby BC V0E 1V0 – 250/838-6035; Fax: 250/838-6085 – Principal, Michael Wilson – *125 – Gr. K.-10

Fort James: St. Maria Goretti School, PO Box 1390, Fort James BC V0J 1P0 – 250/996-8441; Fax: 250/996-2229 – Principal, Simon Waltham-Smith – *83 – Gr. K.-7

Fort St. John: Christian Life School, 8923 - 112th Ave., Fort St. John BC V1J 5H8 – 250/785-1437; Fax: 250/785-4852 – Principal, Richard Flake – *149 – Gr. K.-12

Fort St. John: Immaculata Catholic School, 10011 - 96 St., Fort St. John BC V1J 1L2 – 250/785-3524; Fax: 250/785-0049 – Principal, Gary Boechler – *198 – Gr. K.-7; Special Ed.

Hazelton: Kispiox Elementary, 1279 Lax Seel St., PO Box 418, Hazelton BC V0J 1Y0 – 250/842-6148; Fax: 250/842-5720 – Principal, R. Steinbeisser – *119 – Gr. K.-7

Houston Christian School, Hillside Dr., PO Box 237, Houston BC V0J 1Z0 – 250/845-7736; Fax: 250/845-7738 – Principal, Jack Vanden Born – *154 – Gr. K.-12

Iskut: Klappan Independent Day School, PO Box 60, Iskut BC V0J 1K0 – 250/234-3561; Fax: 250/234-3562 – Principal, M. McMurray – *101 – Gr. K.-9

Kamloops Christian School, 685 Tranquille Rd., Kamloops BC V2B 3H7 – 250/376-6900; Fax: 250/376-6904 – Principal, Dean Whiteway – *580 – Gr. K.-12

Kamloops: Our Lady of Perpetual Help School, 235 Poplar St., Kamloops BC V2B 4B9 – 250/376-2343; Fax: 250/376-2361 – Principal, Sr. Mary Macdonald – *225 – Gr. K.-7

Kamloops: St. Ann's Academy, 205 Columbia St., Kamloops BC V2C 2S7 – 250/372-5452; Fax: 250/372-5257 – Principal, Br. Peter O'Loughlin – *621 – Gr. K.-12

Kelowna: Heritage Christian School, 295 Gerstmar Rd., Kelowna BC V1X 4A6 – 250/862-2377; Fax: 250/862-4943 – Principal, Don Irwin – *162 – Gr. K.-12

Kelowna: Immaculata Regional High School, 1493 KLO Rd., Kelowna BC V1W 3N8 – 250/762-2730; Fax: 250/861-3028 – Principal, John Campbell – *231 – Gr. 8-12

Kelowna Christian School, 3285 Gordon Dr., Kelowna BC V1W 3N4 – 250/861-3238; Fax: 250/861-4844 – Principal, Dr. Kenneth Penner – *573 – Gr. K.-12

Kelowna Waldorf School, PO Box 29093, RPO Okanagan Mission, Kelowna BC V1W 4A7 – 250/764-4130; Fax: 250/764-4130 – Principal, Lynn Wallace – *82 – Gr. K.-8

Kelowna: Okanagan Adventist Academy, 1035 Hollywood Rd., Kelowna BC V1X 4N3 – 250/860-5305; Fax: 250/868-9703 – Principal, Robert Richards – *195 – Gr. K.-12

Kelowna: St. Joseph Elementary School, 839 Sutherland Ave., Kelowna BC V1Y 5X4 – 250/763-3371; Fax: 250/763-2740 – Principal, Beverly Pulyk – *357 – Gr. K.-7; Learning Assistance

Kemano: Lord Alexander School, General Delivery, Kemano BC V0T 1K0 – 250/634-5577; Fax: 250/634-5441 – Principal, Jeannine Rowsell – *50 – Gr. K.-8

Kitimat: St. Anthony's School, 1750 Nalabila Blvd., Kitimat BC V8C 1E6 – 250/632-6313; Fax: 250/632-6313 – Principal, Ann M. Herz – *210 – Gr. K.-7

Kitwanga: Gitanyow Independent School, PO Box 369, Kitwanga BC V0J 2A0 – 250/849-5528; Fax: 250/849-5870 – Principal, Laura Derrick – *54 – Gr. K.-8

Ladner: Boundary Bay Montessori House School, 5008 - 47A Ave., Ladner BC V4K 1T9 – 604/940-9844; Fax: 604/943-7827 – Principal, Heather Main – *55 – Gr. 1-7

Langley: Credo Christian Elementary School, 21919 - 52 Ave., Langley BC V2Y 2M7 – 604/530-1131; Fax: 604/530-4268 – Principal, J.A. Roukema – *193 – Gr. K.-7/Spec. Ed.

Langley: Credo Christian High School, 21846 - 52 Ave., PO Box 3457, Langley BC V3A 4R8 – 604/530-5396; Fax: 604/530-8965 – Principal, Ed Vanderboom – *340 – Gr. 8-12

Langley: The King's School, 21783 - 76B Ave., Langley BC V0X 1T0 – 604/888-0969; Fax: 604/888-0977 – Principal, Robert Beck – *194 – Gr. K.-12

Langley Christian School, 21789 - 50 Ave., Langley BC V3A 3T2 – 604/533-2222; Fax: 604/533-7276 – Principal, Leo Smit – *597 – Gr. K.-10

Langley: St. Catherine's School, 20244 - 32 Ave., Langley BC V2Z 2C9 – 604/534-6564; Fax: 604/534-4871 – Principal, Patricia F. Delany – *234 – Gr. K.-7; Learning Assistance

Lister: Bountiful Elementary/Secondary School, 4702 Lyons Rd., PO Box 226, Lister BC V0B 1Y0 – 250/428-4679; Fax: 250/428-4789 – Principal, Merrill R. Palmer – *156 – Gr. K.-10

Lytton: Mestanta Technological Institute, PO Box 300, Lytton BC V0K 1Z0 – 250/455-2522; Fax: 250/455-2512 – Principal, Dr. Patricia Left – *231 – Gr. K.-12

Maple Ridge: Haney-Pitt Meadows Christian School, 12140 - 203 St., Maple Ridge BC V2X 4V5 – 604/465-4442; Fax: 604/465-1685 – Principal, Rodney Berg – *304 – Gr. K.-8

Maple Ridge: James Cameron School, PO Box 157, Maple Ridge BC V2X 7G1 – 604/465-8444; Fax: 604/465-4561 – Principal, Helen MacDonald – *52 – Gr. 3-7

Maple Ridge: Meadowridge School, 12224 - 240th St., Maple Ridge BC V4R 1N1 – 604/467-4444; Fax: 604/467-4989 – Principal, Otto Hookey – *437 – Gr. K.-12; University Prep.

Maple Ridge: St. Patrick's School, 22589 - 121 Ave., Maple Ridge BC V2X 3T5 – 604/467-1571; Fax: 604/467-2686 – Principal, Anne Kully – *244 – Gr. K.-7

Matsqui: Valley Christian School, 5930 Riverside St., PO Box 220, Matsqui BC V4X 3R2 – 604/826-1388; Fax: 604/826-2744 – Principal, Dorothy Peters – *682 – Gr. K.-11

Merritt: Maranatha Christian School, 2990 Vogt St., Merritt BC V1K 1C8 – 250/378-2626; Fax: 250/378-2408 – Principal, Norm Walker – *95 – Gr. K.-12

Merville: Comox Valley Christian School, 1050 Larkin Rd., PO Box 425, Merville BC V0R 2M0 – 250/337-5335; Fax: 250/337-5632 – Principal, Ron Gamache – *108 – Gr. K.-9

Mill Bay: Brentwood College School, PO Box 1000, Mill Bay BC V0R 2P0 – 250/743-5521; Fax: 250/743-2911 – Principal, William Ross – *402 – Gr. 8-12

Moricetown Elementary School, Site 15, RR#1, Beaver Rd., PO Box 25, Moricetown BC V0J 2N0 – 250/847-3166; Fax: 250/847-3813 – Principal, Sandra Martin – *80 – Gr. K.-6

Nanaimo Christian School, 198 Holland Rd., Nanaimo BC V9R 6W2 – 250/754-4512; Fax: 250/754-4271 – Principal, John Reems – *213 – Gr. K.-10; Special Ed.

Nanaimo Montessori School, 945 Waddington Rd., Nanaimo BC V9S 4V1 – 250/753-0649 – Principal, James Nelson – *53 – Gr. K.

Nanoose Bay: Parksville Christian School, Morello Rd., PO Box 53, Nanoose Bay BC V0R 2R0 – 250/468-9433; Fax: 250/468-7748 – Principal, Arend Bakker – *122 – Gr. K.-8

Nelson Waldorf School, PO Box 165, Nelson BC V1L 5P9 – 250/352-6919 – Principal, D. Oese-Lloyd – *154 – Gr. K.-8; Learning Assistance, French & German A.S.L.

Nelson: St. Joseph's School, 523 Mill St., Nelson BC V1L 4S2 – 250/352-3041; Fax: 250/352-9188 – Principal, Mary Gris – *165 – Gr. K.-6; Special. Ed.

North Vancouver: Holy Trinity Elementary School, 128 West 27 St., North Vancouver BC V7N 2H1 – 604/987-4454; Fax: 604/987-0360 – Principal, Chris Sumner – *245 – Gr. K.-7

North Vancouver: Mulgrave School, 1325 East Keith Rd., North Vancouver BC V7J 1J3 – 604/984-9030; Fax: 604/984-9034 – Principal, Linda Hamer – *110 – Gr. K.-5

North Vancouver: St. Edmund's School, 535 Mahon Ave., North Vancouver BC V7M 2R7 – 604/988-7364; Fax: 604/988-7350 – Principal, Pat Hamilton – *200 – Gr. K.-7

North Vancouver: St. Thomas Aquinas School, 541 West Keith Rd., North Vancouver BC V7M 1M5 – 604/987-4431; Fax: 604/987-7816 – Principal, Marilyn Williams – *435 – Gr. 8-12

North Vancouver: Vancouver Waldorf School, 2725 St. Christopher's Rd., North Vancouver BC V7K 2B6 – 604/985-7435; Fax: 604/985-4948 – Principal, Colin Dutson – *282 – Gr. K.-12

Penticton: Holy Cross Elementary School, 1299 Manitoba St., Penticton BC V2A 5Z9 – 250/490-4602; Fax: 250/493-0773 – Principal, Bernard Hopley – *124 – Gr. K.-7

Penticton Community Christian School, #102, 148 Roy Ave., PO Box 910, Penticton BC V2A 7G1 – 250/493-5233; Fax: 250/493-0773 – Principal, Alistair Jackson – *72 – Gr. K.-8

Port Alberni: Ha-Ho-Payuk, 5000 Mission Rd., PO Box 1279, Port Alberni BC V9Y 7M1 – 250/724-5542; Fax: 250/724-7335 – Principal, Mary Chambers – *95 – Gr. K.-6

Port Alberni Christian School, 4006 - 8th Ave., Port Alberni BC V9Y 4S4 – 250/723-2700; Fax: 250/723-5799 – Principal, W. Van Deventer – *63 – Gr. K.-9

Port Coquitlam: Archbishop Carney Secondary School, 1335 Dominion St., Port Coquitlam BC V3B 7M6 – 604/942-7465; Fax: 604/942-5289 – Principal, Peter Dawe – *312 – Gr. 8-10

Port Coquitlam: Our Lady of the Assumption School, 2255 Fraser Ave., Port Coquitlam BC V3B 6G8 – 604/942-5522; Fax: 604/942-8313 – Principal, John Van Der Pauw – *242 – Gr. K.-3

Port Hardy: Avalon Adventist Junior Academy, 4640 Byng Rd., PO Box 974, Port Hardy BC V0N 2P0 – 250/949-8243; Fax: 250/949-6770 – Principal, Anthony Oucharek – *102 – Gr. K.-10

Port Hardy: Gwa'sala-'nakwaxda'xw Band School, PO Box 1799, Port Hardy BC V0N 2P0 – 250/949-7743; Fax: 250/949-7422 – Principal, Rizwan Hemraj – *123 – Gr. K.

Powell River: Assumption School, 7091 Glacier St., Powell River BC V8A 1R8 – 604/485-9894; Fax: 604/485-7984 – Principal, Gregory Southwell – *230 – Gr. K.-8

Prince George: Cedars Christian School, 701 North Nechako Rd., Prince George BC V2K 1A2 – 250/564-0707; Fax: 250/564-0729 – Principal, Vic Wiens – *302 – Gr. K.-11

Prince George: Immaculate Conception School, Cathedral Ave., PO Box 1487, Prince George BC V2L 4V5 – 250/964-4362; Fax: 250/964-9465 – Principal, Luci Redmond – *199 – Gr. K.-7, Spec. Ed.

Prince George: O'Grady Catholic High School, O'Grady Rd., PO Box 8000, Prince George BC V2N 3Z2 – 250/964-4455; Fax: 250/964-4456 – Principal, H.L. Bucher – *355 – Gr. 8-12

Prince George Academy, 2055 - 20th Ave., Prince George BC V2L 4B9 – 250/563-8585; Fax: 250/564-6800 – Principal, Susan Steeves – *62 – Gr. K.-12

Prince George: Sacred Heart School, 785 Patricia Blvd., Prince George BC V2L 3V5 – 250/563-5201; Fax: 250/563-5283 – Principal, Terry Wilson – *201 – Gr. K.-7, Spec. Ed.

Prince George: St. Mary's School, 1088 Gillett St., Prince George BC V2M 2V3 – 250/563-7502; Fax: 250/563-7818 – Principal, Sr. Yvonne Jones – *211 – Gr. K.-7

Prince George: Westside Academy, SS#2, Site 10, Comp. 13, Prince George BC V2N 2K6 – 250/964-9600; Fax: 250/964-9604 – Principal, Marlo Johnson – *121 – Gr. K.

Prince Rupert: Annunciation School, 627 - 5 Ave. West, Prince Rupert BC V8J 1V1 – 250/624-5873; Fax: 250/627-4486 – Principal, Flora D'Angelo – *279 – Gr. K.-7

Quesnel: St. Ann's School, 150 Sutherland Ave., Quesnel BC V2J 2J5 – 250/992-6237 – Principal, Donald Murphy – *103 – Gr. K.-7

Richmond: Choice Learning Centre, 20451 Westminster Hwy., Richmond BC V6V 1B3 – 604/273-2418; Fax: 604/273-2419 – Principal, Lorraine Ford – *110 – Elem.

Richmond: Muslim School, 12300 Blundell Rd., Richmond BC V6W 1B3 – 604/270-2511; Fax: 604/270-2511 – Principal, Mohammed Ali – *346 – Gr. K.-9

Richmond Christian School, 5240 Woodwards Rd., Richmond BC V7E 1H1 – 604/272-5720; Fax: 604/272-7370 – Principal, Ian Codling – *581 – Gr. K.-12

Richmond International High School & College, 8671 Odlin Cres., Richmond BC V6X 1G1 – 604/244-0100; Fax: 604/244-0102 – Principal, Jindra Repa – *126 – Gr. 10-12

Richmond Jewish Day School, 9711 Geal Rd., Richmond BC V7E 1R4 – 604/275-3393; Fax: 604/275-9322 – Principal, Philip Moses – *139 – Gr. K.-7

Richmond: St. Joseph the Worker School, 4451 Williams Rd., Richmond BC V7E 1J7 – 604/277-1115; Fax: 604/272-5214 – Principal, Lesya Balsevich – *216 – Gr. K.-7

Richmond: St. Paul's School, 8251 St. Alban's Rd., Richmond BC V6Y 2L2 – 604/277-4487; Fax: 604/277-1810 – Principal, Frank Dragojevich – *212 – Gr. K.-7

Saltspring Centre School, 355B Blackburn Rd., Saltspring Island BC V8K 2B8 – 250/537-9130 – Principal, Frances Rautenbach – *70 – Gr. K.-9

Shawnigan Lake: Maxwell International Baha'i School, PO Box 1000, Shawnigan Lake BC V0R 2W0 – 250/743-7144; Fax: 250/743-3522 – Principal, Arini Beaumaris – *182 – Gr. 7-12

Shawnigan Lake School, RR#1, 1975 Renfrew Rd., Shawnigan Lake BC V0R 2W0 – 250/743-5516; Fax: 250/743-6200 – Principal, Simon Bruce-Lockhart – *360 – Gr. 8-12

Smithers: Bulkley Valley Christian School, PO Box 3635, Smithers BC V0J 2N0 – 250/847-4238; Fax: 250/847-3564 – Principal, Evert A. Vroon – *381 – Gr. K.-12

Smithers: Ebenezer Canadian Reformed School, PO Box 3700, Smithers BC V0J 2N0 – 250/847-3492; Fax: 250/847-3912 – Principal, Henk Vanbeelen – *125 – Gr. K.-12

Smithers: St. Joseph's School, 4054 Broadway Ave., PO Box 454, Smithers BC V0J 2N0 – 250/847-9414; Fax: 250/847-3221 – Principal, B. Brivuzoff – *202 – Gr. K.-7

Summerland: The Glenfir School, 9533 Main St., PO Box 1800, Summerland BC V0H 1Z0 – 250/494-0004; Fax: 250/494-0058 – Principal, Thomas Meredith – *93 – Gr. K.-9

Surrey: Bible Way Christian Academy, 18603 - 60th Ave., Surrey BC V3S 7P4 – 604/576-8188 – Principal, David Burns – *40 – Gr. K.-7

Surrey: Cloverdale Catholic School, 17511 - 59 Ave., Surrey BC V3S 1P3 – 604/574-5151; Fax: 604/574-5160 – Principal, Trudy Desjardine – *236 – Gr. K.-7/Learning Assistance

Surrey: Cornerstone Kindergarten, 14724 - 84 Ave., Surrey BC V3S 2M5 – 604/599-9918 – Principal, Rita Gausman – *54 – Gr. K.-2

Surrey: Diamond Elementary, 18620 - 56th Ave., Surrey BC V3S 1G1 – 604/576-1146; Fax: 604/574-9831 – Principal, Douglas Smith – *128 – Gr. K.-7

Surrey: Fraser Valley Christian High School, 15353 - 92 Ave., Surrey BC V3R 1C3 – 604/581-1033; Fax: 604/581-1712 – Principal, Al Boerema – *393 – Gr. 8-12; Special Ed.

Surrey: Heritage Christian School, 3487 King George Hwy., Surrey BC V4P 1B7 – 604/536-5967; Fax: 604/536-5967 – Principal, Brian Roodnick – *162 – Gr. K.-9

Surrey: Holy Cross Regional High School, 16193 - 88 Ave., Surrey BC V4N 1G3 – 604/581-3023; Fax: 604/583-4795 – Principal, Robert Dejulius – *780 – Gr. 8-12

Surrey: Khalsa School Surrey, 6933 - 124th St., Surrey BC V3W 3W6 – 604/591-2248; Fax: 604/591-3396 – Principal, Harchand Gill – *746 – Gr. K.-10

Surrey: Our Lady of Good Counsel School, 10504 - 139 St., Surrey BC V3T 4L5 – 604/581-3154 – Principal, Corina Meisl – *243 – Gr. K.-7

Surrey: Pacific Academy, 10238 - 168 St., Surrey BC V4N 1Z4 – 604/581-5353; Fax: 604/581-0087 – Principal, Raymond C. Sutton – *961 – Gr. K.-12

Surrey: Regent Christian Academy, 15100 - 66A Ave., Surrey BC V3S 2A6 – 604/599-8171; Fax: 604/597-9090 – Principal, Paul Johnson – *188 – Gr. K.-12

Surrey: Relevant High, 18620 - 56 Ave., Surrey BC V3S 1G1 – 604/574-4736; Fax: 604/574-9831 – Principal, Douglas Smith – *96 – Gr. 8-12

Surrey: Roots & Wings Montessori, 6962 - 124th St., Surrey BC V3W 3W7 – 604/590-2717; Fax: 604/590-2724 – Principal, Kristin Cassie – *91 – Gr. K.

Surrey: St. Bernadette School, 13130 - 65B Ave., Surrey BC V3W 9M1 – 604/596-1101; Fax: 604/597-9534 – Principal, Doreen Junk – *213 – Gr. K.-7

Surrey: South Ridge School, 2656 - 160 St., Surrey BC V4P 2M7 – 604/535-5056; Fax: 604/535-3676 – Principal, Alan Brown – *231 – Gr. K.-10

Surrey: Star of the Sea School, 15024 - 24 Ave., Surrey BC V4A 2H8 – 604/531-6316; Fax: 604/531-0171 – Principal, Rita Smith – *256 – Gr. K.-7

Surrey Christian School, 9115 - 160 St., Surrey BC V4N 2X7 – 604/581-2474; Fax: 604/581-5211 – Principal, Anthonie Jansen – *511 – Gr. K.-8

Surrey: White Rock Christian Academy, 2265 - 152 St., Surrey BC V4A 4P1 – 604/531-9186; Fax: 604/531-1727 – Principal, Susan Penner – *248 – Gr. K.-12

Surrey: William of Orange Christian School, 5790 - 175 St., PO Box 34090, Surrey BC V3S 8C4 – 604/576-2144 – Principal, Apko Nap – *111 – Gr. 1-7

Surrey: Zion Lutheran School, 5950 - 179 St., Surrey BC V3S 4J9 – 604/576-6313; Fax: 604/576-1399 – Principal, James Murray – *145 – Gr. K.-7/Learning Assistance

Terrace: Centennial Christian School, 3608 Sparks St., Terrace BC V8G 2V6 – 250/635-6173; Fax: 250/635-9385 – Principal, Frank Voogd – *251 – Gr. K.-10

Terrace: Veritas Catholic School, 4836 Straume Ave., Terrace BC V8G 4G3 – 250/635-3035; Fax: 250/635-7588 – Principal, Frances P. Nuyten – *209 – Gr. K.-7

Trail: St. Michael's Elementary School, 1329 - 4 Ave., Trail BC V1R 1S3 – 250/368-6151; Fax: 250/368-9962 – Principal, Maureen Johnson – *223 – Gr. K.-7

Vancouver: Blessed Sacrament School, 3020 Heather St., Vancouver BC V5Z 3K3 – 604/876-7211; Fax: 604/876-7280 – Principal, Pauline Teglasi – *203 – Gr. K.-7; French Immersion

Vancouver: Bodwell College, 2026 - West 12th Ave., Vancouver BC V6J 2G2 – 604/737-8221; Fax: 604/737-8213 – Principal, Dr. Lawrence Fast – *236 – Gr. 8-12

Vancouver: Corpus Christi School, 6344 Nanaimo St., Vancouver BC V5P 4K7 – 604/321-1117; Fax: 604/327-1410 – Principal, Marian McDermott – *217 – Gr. K.-7; Learning Assistance

Vancouver: Crofton House School, 3200 West 41 Ave., Vancouver BC V6N 3E1 – 604/263-3255; Fax: 604/263-4941 – Principal, Barbara Walker – *657 – Gr. 1-12; University Prep.

Vancouver: Dorset College, 200 City Square, 555 - 12th Ave. West, Vancouver BC V5Z 3X7 – 604/879-8686; Fax: 604/874-8686 – Principal, Margaret Misfeldt – *223 – Sec.

Vancouver: Fraser Academy, 2294 West 10 Ave., Vancouver BC V6K 2H8 – 604/736-5575; Fax: 604/736-5578 – Principal, Scott Armstrong – *146 – Gr. 1-12

Vancouver: Immaculate Conception School, 3745 West 28 Ave., Vancouver BC V6S 1S6 – 604/224-5012; Fax: 604/224-3721 – Principal, Mary Paetsch – *204 – Gr. K.-7

* indicates enrollment figure.

Vancouver: Kester Grant College, 2412 Laurel St., Vancouver BC V5Z 3T2 – 604/877-0355; Fax: 604/877-0375 – Principal, Ian Wakeford – *60 – Gr. 10-12

Vancouver: Khalsa School Vancouver, 5987 Prince Albert St., Vancouver BC V5W 3E2 – 604/321-1226 – Principal, Amar Dhaliwal – *133 – Gr. K.-7; Gen. & Sikh Studies

Vancouver: Little Flower Academy, 4195 Alexandra St., Vancouver BC V6J 4C6 – 604/738-9016; Fax: 604/738-5749 – Principal, Sr. Eileen Kelly – *434 – Gr. 8-12; Girls

Vancouver: Maimonides School, 5465 Baillie St., Vancouver BC V5Z 3M6 – 604/263-9700; Fax: 604/263-4848 – Principal, Edward Collins – *67 – Gr. 8-12

Vancouver: Notre Dame Regional Secondary School, 2855 Parker St., Vancouver BC V5K 2T8 – 604/255-5454; Fax: 604/255-2115 – Principal, Michael Cooke – *643 – Gr. 8-12

Vancouver: Our Lady of Perpetual Help School, 2550 Camosun St., Vancouver BC V6R 3W6 – 604/228-8811; Fax: 604/224-6822 – Principal, Maria Fasan – *346 – Gr. K.-7

Vancouver: Our Lady of Sorrows School, 575 Slocan St., Vancouver BC V5K 3X5 – 604/253-2434; Fax: 604/253-1523 – Principal, Anne Coulombe – *236 – Gr. K.-7

Vancouver: Royal Canadian College, 2236 - 12th Ave. West, Vancouver BC V6K 2N7 – 604/738-2221; Fax: 604/263-9078 – Principal, T. Kung – *67 – Gr. 9-12

Vancouver: St. Andrew's School, 450 - 47 Ave. East, Vancouver BC V5W 2B4 – 604/325-6317; Fax: 604/325-0920 – Principal, Ruth Cash – *223 – Gr. K.-7

Vancouver: St. Augustine's School, 2145 West 8 Ave., Vancouver BC V6K 2A5 – 604/731-8024; Fax: 604/739-1712 – Principal, Catherine Oberndorf – *212 – Gr. K.-7/Learning Assistance

Vancouver: St. Francis of Assisi School, 870 Victoria Dr., Vancouver BC V5L 4E7 – 604/253-7311; Fax: 604/253-7375 – Principal, Laila Maravillas – *205 – Gr. K.-7/Learning Assistance

Vancouver: St. Francis Xavier School, 884 East Pender St., Vancouver BC V6A 1W1 – 604/254-2714; Fax: 604/254-2514 – Principal, Therese Leung – *340 – Gr. K.-7

Vancouver: St. George's School, 4175 West 29 Ave., Vancouver BC V6S 1V6 – 604/224-1304; Fax: 604/224-5346 – Principal, Gordon Atkinson – *917 – Gr. 1-12; Boys

Vancouver: St. John's International, 1088 Homer St., Vancouver BC V6B 2W9 – 604/683-4572; Fax: 604/683-4679 – Principal, Dr. Rod Matheson – *100 – Gr. 8-12

Vancouver: St. John's School, 2215 West 10 Ave., Vancouver BC V6K 2J1 – 604/732-4434; Fax: 604/732-1074 – Principal, Christopher McGill – *174 – Gr. K.-12

Vancouver: St. Joseph's School, 3261 Fleming St., Vancouver BC V5N 3V6 – 604/872-5715; Fax: 604/872-5700 – Principal, Michael Boreham – *211 – Gr. K.-7/Spec. Ed.

Vancouver: St. Jude's School, 2953 East 15 Ave., Vancouver BC V5M 2K7 – 604/434-1633; Fax: 604/434-8677 – Principal, Maria Anzulovich – *223 – Gr. K.-7

Vancouver: St. Mary's School, 5239 Joyce St., Vancouver BC V5R 4G8 – 604/437-1312; Fax: 604/437-1193 – Principal, Sandra Marshall – *222 – Gr. K.-7

Vancouver: St. Patrick's Elementary School, 2850 Quebec St., Vancouver BC V5T 3A9 – 604/879-4411; Fax: 604/879-3737 – Principal, Sheila Roberts – *265 – Gr. K.-7

Vancouver: St. Patrick's Regional Secondary School, 115 East 11 Ave., Vancouver BC V5T 2C1 – 604/874-6422; Fax: 604/874-5176 – Principal, Eugene Luttrell – *468 – Gr. 8-12

Vancouver Christian School, 3496 Mons Dr., Vancouver BC V5M 3E6 – 604/435-3113; Fax: 604/430-1591 – Principal, Ronald Donkersloot – *348 – Gr. K.-10; Learning Assistance

Vancouver College, 5400 Cartier St., Vancouver BC V6M 3A5 – 604/261-4285; Fax: 604/261-2284 – Principal, Br. Kieran Murphy – *1,004 – Gr. K.-12; Learning Assistance

Vancouver Formosa Academy, 5621 Killarney St., Vancouver BC V5R 3W4 – 604/436-2332; Fax: 604/436-2331 – Principal, Milton Chen – *65 – Gr. 8-10

Vancouver Hebrew Academy, 5750 Oak St., Vancouver BC V6M 2V9 – 604/266-1245; Fax: 604/264-0648 – Principal, Shayndel Feuerstein – *116 – Gr. K.-7

Vancouver Montessori School, 8650 Barnard St., Vancouver BC V6P 5G5 – 604/261-0315 – Principal, Prasannata Runkel – *125 – Gr. K.

Vancouver Talmud Torah, 998 West 26 Ave., Vancouver BC V5Z 2G1 – 604/736-7307; Fax: 604/736-9754 – Principal, Solly Kaplinski – *397 – Gr. K.-7

Vancouver: York House School, 4176 Alexandra St., Vancouver BC V6J 2V6 – 604/736-6551; Fax: 604/736-6530 – Principal, G. Ruddy – *594 – Gr. K.-12; University Prep, French Program

Vanderhoof: Northside Christian School, RR#2, PO Box 1, Vanderhoof BC V0J 3A0 – 250/567-9335; Fax: 250/567-9332 – Principal, W. Shenk – *140 – Gr. 1-12

Vanderhoof: Rainbow Christian School, 448 Connaught, PO Box 1339, Vanderhoof BC V0J 3A0 – 250/567-3107; Fax: 250/567-3177 – Principal, Wilfred Loewen – *101 – Gr. K.-8

Vanderhoof: St. Joseph's School, PO Box 1429, Vanderhoof BC V0J 3A0 – 250/567-2794; Fax: 250/567-4564 – Principal, Claire Petrucci – *152 – Gr. K.-7; Learning Assistance

Vernon: Pleasant Valley Academy, 1802 - 45th Ave., Vernon BC V1T 3M7 – 250/545-7852; Fax: 250/545-9230 – Principal, Daniel Self – *78 – Gr. K.-10

Vernon: St. James School, 2700 - 28 Ave., Vernon BC V1T 1V7 – 250/542-4081; Fax: 250/542-5696 – Principal, Mary Manton – *296 – Gr. K.-10; Learning Assistance, Enrichment

Vernon Christian School, 6890 Pleasant Valley Rd., Vernon BC V1B 3R5 – 250/545-7345; Fax: 250/545-0254 – Principal, Elco Vandergrift – *234 – Gr. K.-8

Victoria: Cathedral School, 912 Vancouver St., Victoria BC V8V 3V7 – 250/383-5125; Fax: 250/386-4013 – Principal, Laura Heintzman – *75 – Gr. K.

Victoria: Crossroads Christian School, 3460 Shelbourne St., Victoria BC V8P 4G5 – 250/592-1335; Fax: 250/592-4945 – Principal, Alan Rich – *58 – Gr. K.-7

Victoria: Glenlyon-Norfolk School, 801 Bank St., Victoria BC V8S 4A8 – 250/598-2621; Fax: 250/598-4505 – Principal, David Brooks – *735 – Gr. K.-12; 3 schools

Victoria: Lighthouse Christian Academy, 1289 Parkdale Dr., Victoria BC V9B 4G9 – 250/474-5311; Fax: 250/474-5021 – Principal, Dorothy Spencelayh – *120 – Gr. K.-10

Victoria: Maria Montessori Academy, 4052 Wilkinson Rd., Victoria BC V8Z 5A5 – 250/479-4746; Fax: 250/479-1925 – Principal, Ann Stevens – *77 – Gr. K.-6

Victoria: Montessori Centre of Victoria, 1530 Lionel St., Victoria BC V8R 2X8 – 250/592-3414; Fax: 250/592-3446 – Principal, Karen L. Colussi – *110 – Gr. K.-7

Victoria: Pacific Christian School, 654 Agnes St., Victoria BC V8Z 2E6 – 250/479-4532; Fax: 250/479-3511 – Principal, John Messelink – *709 – Gr. K.-12

Victoria: St. Andrew's Regional High School, 880 MacKenzie Ave., Victoria BC V8X 3G5 – 250/479-1414; Fax: 250/479-5356 – Principal, Arthur Therrien – *329 – Gr. 8-12

Victoria: St. Andrew's School, 1002 Pandora Ave., Victoria BC V8V 3P5 – 250/382-3815; Fax: 250/385-3830 – Principal, James O'Reilly – *336 – Gr. K.-7; Learning Assistance, Enrichment

Victoria: St. Joseph's Catholic School, 757 West Burnside Rd., Victoria BC V8Z 1M9 – 250/479-1232; Fax: 250/479-1907 – Principal, Ken Leason – *203 – Gr. K.-7

Victoria: St. Margaret's School, 1080 Lucas Ave., Victoria BC V8X 3P7 – 250/479-7171; Fax: 250/479-8976 – Principal, Stephen Clayton – *386 – Gr. K.-12

Victoria: St. Michael's University School (Junior), 820 Victoria Ave., Victoria BC V8S 4N3 – 250/598-3922; Fax: 250/592-0783 – Principal, Sally Blyth – *161 – Gr. K.-5

Victoria: St. Michael's University School (Middle), 3400 Richmond Rd., Victoria BC V8P 4P5 – 250/592-3549; Fax: 250/592-3942 – Principal, Clifford. Yorath – *198 – Gr. 6-8

Victoria: St. Michael's University School (Senior), 3400 Richmond Rd., Victoria BC V8P 4P5 – 250/592-2411; Fax: 250/592-2812 – Principal, Peter Tongue – *491 – Gr. 9-12

Victoria: St. Patrick's School, 2368 Trent St., Victoria BC V8R 4Z3 – 250/592-6713; Fax: 250/592-6717 – Principal, Joseph Colistro – *398 – Gr. K.-7

Victoria: Trinity Christian School, 98 Cadillac Ave., Victoria BC V8Z 4T1 – 250/475-2977; Fax: 250/475-2988 – Principal, Mark Langley – *134 – Gr. K.-1

Victoria: West-Mont School, 1016 Marwood Rd., Victoria BC V9C 3C4 – 250/474-2626; Fax: 250/478-8944 – Principal, Patrick Micek – *79 – Gr. K.-6

Waglisla: Bella Bella Community School, General Delivery, Waglisla BC V0T 1Z0 – 250/957-2391; Fax: 250/957-2691 – Principal, Scott Benwell – *274 – Gr. K.-12

West Vancouver: Collingwood School, 70 Morven Dr., West Vancouver BC V7S 1B2 – 604/925-3331; Fax: 604/925-3373 – Principal, Graham M. Baldwin – *771 – Gr. K.-12

West Vancouver: St. Anthony's School, 595 Keith Rd., West Vancouver BC V7T 1L8 – 604/922-0011; Fax: 604/922-3196 – Principal, Geraldine Jang – *200 – Gr. K.-7/Learning Assistance

Westbank: Our Lady of Lourdes Elementary School, 2547 Hebert Rd., Westbank BC V4T 2J6 – 250/768-9008; Fax: 250/768-0168 – Principal, Roman Mahnic – *75 – Gr. K.-7

Williams Lake: Cariboo Adventist Academy, 1405 South Lakeside Dr., Williams Lake BC V2G 3A7 – 250/392-4741; Fax: 250/392-6583 – Principal, Daniel Carley – *154 – Gr. K.-12

Williams Lake: Sacred Heart Catholic School, 455 Pigeon Ave., Williams Lake BC V2G 4R5 – 250/398-7770; Fax: 250/398-7725 – Principal, Marlene Kosolofski – *87 – Gr. K.-5

## OVERSEAS STUDENT SELECTION OFFICES

Hong Kong: British Columbia Student Selection Office, International Education & Student Services Centre Ltd., #901, Hutchinson House, 10 Harcourt Rd., Hong Kong Hong Kong – 852-845-1155; Fax: 852-845-4114 – BC Education Officer, Mei Mei Yiu

Japan: British Columbia Student Selection Office, BC Trade Office, Place Canada 3F, 3-37, Akasaka 7-chome, Minato-ku, Tokyo 107 Japan – 813-3-408-6171; Fax: 813-3-408-6340 – BC Education Officer, Jean Maeda

Taiwan R.O.C.: British Columbia Student Selection Office, Kamsun Development Ltd., Room 2202, 22/F, #333, Keelung Rd., Sec. 1, Taipei Taiwan R.O.C. – 886-2-722-08; Fax: 886-2-757-6593 – BC Education Officer, Sherry Yuan

# MANITOBA

### Manitoba Education & Training

#168, 401 York Ave., Winnipeg MB R3C 0P8
204/945-4325; Fax: 204/945-1291
Email: minedu@leg.gov.mb.ca

**SCHOOL PROGRAMS DIVISION**

Acting Director, Program Implementation Branch, Erika Erika Kreis, Kreis, 204/945-1033; Fax: 204/945-5060

Pat, MacDonald, Director Program Development Branch, 204/945-0926; Fax: 204/945-5060

**For detailed departmental listings, see Index: "Education, Depts."**

## SCHOOL DIVISIONS & DISTRICTS

The Province of Manitoba is divided into 57 educational units: 48 School Divisions; 6 Remote School Districts; 3 Special Revenue School Districts. The 6 Remote School Districts, one Special Revenue District, & the 48 School Divisions are controlled by elected school boards. Elections are held in accordance with the Local Authorities Election Act.

Fifty-six educational units are responsible for the provision of elementary & secondary education; one for secondary technical education only.

**Boards with an enrollment of more than 10,000 are in bold print.**

Agassiz School Division #13 – *3,077
PO Box 1206, Beausejour MB R0E 0C0
204/268-2465; Fax: 204/268-4149 – Supt., Waldo Klassen

Antler River School Division #43 – *933
PO Box 370, Melita MB R0M 1L0
204/522-3292; Fax: 204/522-3776; Email: arsd@mail.techplus.com – Supt., Bob Bell

Assiniboine South School Division #3 – *6,589
3401 Roblin Blvd., Winnipeg MB R3R 0C6
204/889-5523; Fax: 204/896-0409; Email: assdnews@minet.gov.mb.ca – Supt., Steve Dvorak

Beautiful Plains School Division #31 – *1,721
PO Box 700, Neepawa MB R0J 1H0
204/476-2388; Fax: 204/476-3606; Email: bpsd@techplus.com – Supt., Dennis Wrightson

Birdtail River School Division #38 – *1,397
General Delivery, Crandall MB R0M 0H0
204/562-3677; Fax: 204/562-3634; Email: brsd38@mb.sympatico.ca – Supt., Ron Van Den Bussche

Boundary School Division #16 – *773
PO Box 1001, Dominion City MB R0A 0H0
204/427-2091; Fax: 204/427-2531; Email: rperron@ibm.net – Supt., Keith Bricknell

Brandon School Division #40 – *8,184
1031 - 6 St., Brandon MB R7A 4K5
204/729-3100; Fax: 204/727-2217; Email: info@brandonsd.mb.ca – Supt., Bob Swayze

Dauphin-Ochre School (Area #1) Division #33 – *2,036
505 Main St. South, Dauphin MB R7N 1L3
204/638-3001; Fax: 204/638-7250; Email: dosa3@mbnet.mb.ca – Supt., James Dalton

Duck Mountain School Division #34 – *860
PO Box 400, Winnipegosis MB R0L 2G0
204/656-4885; Fax: 204/656-4980; Email: duckmtn@minet.gov.mb.ca – Supt., Syl Didur

Evergreen School Division #22 – *1,834
PO Box 1200, Gimli MB R0C 1B0
204/642-5186; Fax: 204/642-7273; Email: esd@mts.net – Supt., James Daltow

Flin Flon School Division #46 – *1,697
30 Adams St., Flin Flon MB R8A 1A8
204/687-3413; Fax: 204/687-3517; Email: reagan@minet.gov.mb.ca – Supt., Dan Reagan

Fort la Bosse School Division #41 – *1,815
PO Box 1420, Virden MB R0M 2C0
204/748-2692; Fax: 204/748-2436;
Email: flbbdidluck@mail.techplus.com – Supt., Bonnie Thiessen

Fort Garry School Division #5 – *7,206
181 Henlow Bay, Winnipeg MB R3Y 1M7
204/488-1757; Fax: 204/488-2095; Email: fgsd@fgsd.winnipeg.mb.ca – Supt., Henry Izatt

Franco-Manitobaine Division Scolaire #49 – *4,413
485, ch Dawson, CP 204, Lorette MB R0A 0Y0
204/878-9399; Fax: 204/878-9407; Email: deny@dsfm.mb.ca – Acting Supt., Georges Druwè

Frontier School Division #48 – *5,916
1402 Notre Dame Ave., Winnipeg MB R3E 3G5
204/775-9741; Fax: 204/775-9940; Email: frontier@mbnet.mb.ca – Supt., Keven Van Camp

Garden Valley School Division #26 – *2,758
PO Box 3000, Winkler MB R6W 4C8
204/325-8335; Fax: 204/325-4132 – Supt., John A. Janzen

Hanover School Division #15 – *5,787
PO Box 2170, Steinbach MB R0A 2A0
204/326-6471; Fax: 204/326-9901 – Supt., Gilbert Unger

Interlake School Division #21 – *3,553
PO Box 4000, Stonewall MB R0C 2Z0
204/467-8485; Fax: 204/467-8334 – Acting Supt., Wendell Sparkes

Intermountain School Division #36 – *1,216
PO Box 160, Grandview MB R0L 0Y0
204/546-2068; Fax: 204/546-2770;
Email: howsmith@minet.gov.mb.ca – Supt., Howard Smith

Kelsey School Division #45 – *2,047
PO Box 4700, The Pas MB R9A 1R4
204/623-6421; Fax: 204/623-7704; Email: kelsey@minet.gov.mb.ca – Supt., Al Yaskiw

Lakeshore School Division #23 – *1,501
PO Box 100, Eriksdale MB R0C 0W0
204/739-2101; Fax: 204/739-2145 – Supt., Ronald Weston

Lord Selkirk School Division #11 – *4,778
205 Mercy St., Selkirk MB R1A 2C8
204/482-5942; Fax: 204/482-3000 – Supt., Gail Bagnall

Midland School Division #25 – *1,640
182 Main St. South, Carman MB R0G 0J0
204/745-2003; Fax: 204/745-3699 – Supt., Eugene Wiebe

Morris-MacDonald School Division #19 – *1,783
PO Box 400, Morris MB R0G 1K0
204/746-2317; Fax: 204/746-2785; Email: buzahora@sympatico.mb.ca – Supt., Larry McCrady

Mountain School Division #28 – *938
PO Box 160, Notre-Dame-de-Lourde MB R0G 1M0
204/248-2228; Fax: 204/248-2482 – Supt., Henri Bouvier

Norwood School Division #8 – *1,071
200 St. Mary's Rd., Winnipeg MB R2H 1H9
204/237-0212; Fax: 204/231-1912 – Supt., Alex Boyes

Pelly Trail School Division #37 – *1,053
PO Box 640, Russell MB R0J 1W0
204/773-3107; Fax: 204/773-3909;
Email: pelly.trail@ptsd.mb.ca – Supt., Marshall Draper

Pembina Valley School Division #27 – *854
PO Box 459, Manitou MB R0G 1G0
204/242-2797; Fax: 204/242-3275; Email: pvsd27@mb.sympatico.ca – Supt., Lorne Miller

Pine Creek School Division #30 – *1,484
PO Box 420, Gladstone MB R0J 0T0
204/385-2216; Fax: 204/385-2825; Email: pcsddo@cpnet.net – Supt., Ed Sklar

Portage la Prairie School Division #24 – *3,890
535 - 3 St. NW, Portage la Prairie MB R1N 2C4
204/857-8756; Fax: 204/239-5998; Email: mkristof@portage.net – Supt., Gary Little

Red River School Division #17 – *644
PO Box 219, St. Pierre-Jolys MB R0A 1V0
204/433-7815; Fax: 204/433-7102; Email: rperron@ibm.net – Supt., Ron Perron

Rhineland School Division #18 – *1,466
PO Box 390, Altona MB R0G 0B0
204/324-6491; Fax: 204/324-1664; Email: rsd@mb.sympatico.ca – Supt., Don Wiebe

**River East School Division #9**
589 Roch St., Winnipeg MB R2K 2P7
204/667-7130; Fax: 204/661-5618
Email: resd@mbnet.mb.ca
*13,345
Supt., George Wall
Asst. Supt., Dr. Bob Cross
Asst. Supt., Henry Kojima

Rolling River School Division #39 – *2,333
PO Box 1170, Minnedosa MB R0J 1E0
204/867-2754; Fax: 204/867-2037; Email: rrsd@rrsd.mb.ca – Supt., Neil Whitley

St. Boniface School Division #4 – *4,939
50 Monterey Rd., Winnipeg MB R2J 1X1
204/253-2681; Fax: 204/257-4805; Email: rfewing@minet.mb.ca – Supt., Jean-Yves Rochon

St. James-Assiniboia School Division #2 – *9,369
2574 Portage Ave., Winnipeg MB R3J 0H8
204/888-7951; Fax: 204/831-0859; Email: stjamesa@mbnet.mb.ca – Sec.-Treas. & Dir., Education, George Buchholz

St. Vital School Division #6 – *9,963
900 St. Mary's Rd., Winnipeg MB R2M 3R3
204/257-7827; Fax: 204/256-8553; Email: stvsdiv6@stvital.winnipeg.mb.ca – Supt., Norbert Philippe

Seine River School Division #14 – *4,074
192 Central Ave., Ste. Anne MB R5H 1C3
204/422-8807; Fax: 204/422-8141 – Supt., Roy Seidler

Seven Oaks School Division #10 – *9,312
830 Powers St., Winnipeg MB R2V 4E7
204/586-8061; Fax: 204/589-2504; Email: sevenoak@minet.gov.mb.ca – Supt., John Wiens

Souris Valley School Division #42 – *1,187
PO Box 820, Souris MB R0K 2C0
204/483-2128; Fax: 204/483-2296 – Supt., Lloyd Paulson

South Winnipeg Technical Centre School Division – *1,200
130 Henlow Bay, Winnipeg MB R3Y 1G5
204/989-6500; Fax: 204/488-4152

Swan Valley School Division #35 – *2,028
PO Box 995, Swan River MB R0L 1Z0
204/734-4531; Fax: 204/734-2273; Email: bschaf@swanvalley.freenet.mb.ca – Supt., William Schaffer

Tiger Hills School Division #29 – *1,258
PO Box 130, Glenboro MB R0K 0X0
204/827-2881; Fax: 204/827-2050; Email: tigerhil@cpnet.net – Supt., Ray Le Neal

Transcona-Springfield School Division #12 – *8,214
760 Kildare Ave. East, Winnipeg MB R2C 3Z4
204/958-6565; Fax: 204/224-2783 – Supt., Dr. Gerry Saleski

Turtle Mountain School Division #44 – *1,325
PO Box 280, Killarney MB R0K 1G0
204/523-7531; Fax: 204/523-7269 – Supt., Gary Maxwell

Turtle River School Division #32 – *1,015
PO Box 309, McCreary MB R0J 1B0
204/835-2067; Fax: 204/835-2426; Email: trsd@minet.gov.mb.ca – Supt., Joe Mudry

Western School Division #47 – *1,461
215 - 12th St., Morden MB R6M 1X4
204/822-4448; Fax: 204/822-4262; Email: western@minet.gov.mb.ca – Supt., Colin Jamieson

White Horse Plain School Division #20 – *1,071
PO Box 160, Elie MB R0H 0H0
204/353-2828; Fax: 204/353-2480 – Supt., Norbert Delaquis

**Winnipeg School Division #1**
1577 Wall St. East, Winnipeg MB R3E 2S5
204/775-0231; Fax: 204/783-0231
Email: adminofc@sbo.wsd1.winnipeg.mb.ca
*33,858
Chief Supt., Jack Smyth
Supt., Schools, Pauline Clarke
Supt., Schools, Al Krahn
Supt., Schools, Jan Schubert

* indicates enrollment figure.

#### SPECIAL REVENUE SCHOOL DISTRICTS

Pine Falls School District #2155 – *108
PO Box 190, Pine Falls MB R0E 1M0
204/367-2254; Fax: 204/367-8809

Whiteshell School District #2408 – *347
PO Box 130, Pinawa MB R0E 1L0
204/753-8366; Fax: 204/753-2237; Email: dougallg@eastman.freenet.mb.ca

#### REMOTE SCHOOL DISTRICTS

Churchill School District #2264 – *227
PO Box 338, Churchill MB R0B 0E0
204/675-2218; Fax: 204/675-2648

Leaf Rapids School District #2460 – *380
PO Box 697, Leaf Rapids MB R0B 1W0
204/473-2423; Fax: 204/473-2288; Email: lrsd@mail.concom.net

Lynn Lake School District #2312 – *245
PO Box 730, Lynn Lake MB R0B 0W0
204/356-8444; Fax: 204/356-2940

Mystery Lake School District #2355 – *3,707
408 Thompson Dr. North, Thompson MB R8N 0C5
204/677-6150; Fax: 204/677-9528

Snow Lake School District #2309 – *295
PO Box 220, Snow Lake MB R0B 1M0
204/358-7708; Fax: 204/358-2451

Sprague School District #2439 – *161
PO Box 69, Sprague MB R0A 1Z0
204/437-2175; Fax: 204/437-2893; Email: rossgray@minet.gov.mb.ca

## NATIVE SCHOOLS

#### BAND OPERATED SCHOOLS

Southeast Tribal Division for Schools Inc., #300, 208 Edmonton St., Winnipeg MB R3C 1R7 – 204/943-7412; Fax: 204/947-0082

#### INDIVIDUAL BAND OPERATED SCHOOLS

Abraham Beardy Memorial School, General Delivery, Shamattawa MB R0B 1K0 – 204/565-2022; Fax: 204/565-2122 – Gr. Pre.-10

Amos Okemow Memorial School, God's River MB R0B 0N0 – 204/366-2070; Fax: 204/366-2105 – Gr. Pre.-10

Anicinabe School, PO Box 219, Pine Falls MB R0E 1M0 – 204/367-2285; Fax: 204/367-9205 – Gr. Pre.-9

Birdtail Sioux N & K School, Beulah MB R0M 0B0 – 204/586-4634; Fax: 204/568-4687 – Gr. Pre.-K.

Charles Sinclair School, PO Box 1, Koostatak MB R0C 1S0 – 204/645-2206; Fax: 204/645-2614 – Gr. Pre.-12

Chemawawin School, PO Box 10, Easterville MB R0C 0V0 – 204/329-2115; Fax: 204/329-2214 – Gr. Pre.-10

Chief Clifford Lynxleg Anishinabe School, Valley River Reserve, Shortdale MB ROL 1W0 – 204/546-2641; Fax: 204/546-3120 – Gr. Pre.-9

Chief Sam Cook Mahmuwee Education Centre, Split Lake MB R0B 1P0 – 204/342-2134; Fax: 204/342-2139 – Gr. Pre.-12

Dakota Plains School, PO Box 110, Portage la Prairie MB R1N 3B2 – 204/252-2895; Fax: 204/252-2525 – Gr. Pre.-5

Dakota Tipi School, PO Box 841, Portage la Prairie MB R1N 3C3 – 204/857-7414; Fax: 204/239-6384 – Gr. K.-6

Dauphin River School, PO Box 140, Gypsumville MB R0C 1J0 – 204/659-5268; Fax: 204/659-4458 – Gr. 1-9

Donald Ahmo School, General Delivery, Crane River MB R0L 0M0 – 204/732-2548; Fax: 204/732-2596 – Gr. Pre.-8

Fox Lake Native Spiritual School, PO Box 279, Gillam MB R0B 0L0 – 204/486-2307; Fax: 204/486-2606 – Gr. K.-8

Garden Hill Elementary School, Island Lake MB R0B 0T0 – 204/456-2391; Fax: 204/456-2350

Garden Hill First Nations High School, Island Lake MB R0B 0T0 – 204/456-2886; Fax: 204/456-2894 – Gr. 7-12

George Knott School, Wasagamach Bay MB R0B 1Z0 – 204/457-2493; Fax: 204/457-2273 – Gr. Pre.-10

George Saunders Memorial School, York Landing MB R0B 2B0 – 204/341-2118; Fax: 204/341-2137 – Gr. Pre.-9

Ginew School, PO Box 10, Ginew MB R0A 2R0 – 204/427-2490; Fax: 204/427-2398 – Gr. Pre.-9

God's Lake Narrows First Nation School, God's Narrows MB R0B 0M0 – 204/335-2003; Fax: 204/335-2440 – Gr. Pre.-9

Indian Springs School (Swan Lake Band), PO Box 1, Mariapolis MB R0K 1K0 – 204/836-2332; Fax: 204/836-2317 – Gr. Pre.-8

Jackhead School, Dallas MB R0C 0S0 – 204/394-2378; Fax: 204/394-2104 – Gr. Pre.-9

Joe A. Ross School, Opasquiak Education Authority, PO Box 1078, The Pas MB R9A 1L1 – 204/623-4286; Fax: 204/623-4442 – Gr. Pre.-12

Keeseekoowenin School, PO Box 100, Elphinstone MB R0J 0N0 – 204/625-2062; Fax: 204/625-2418 – Gr. Pre.-8

Lake Manitoba School, General Delivery, Vogar MB R0C 3C0 – 204/768-2728; Fax: 204/768-2194 – Gr. Pre.-12

Lake St. Martin School, PO Box 2020, Gypsumville MB R0C 1J0 – 204/659-5774; Fax: 204/659-5739 – Gr. Pre.-9

Little Saskatchewan School, Gypsumville MB R0C 1J0 – 204/659-2672; Fax: 204/659-5763 – Gr. Pre.-8

Long Plain School, Long Plain Education Authority, Long Plain Reserve, Edwin MB R0H 0G0 – 204/252-2326; Fax: 204/252-2786 – Gr. Pre.-9

Mikisew Middle School, Cross Lake MB R0B 0J0 – 204/676-3030; Fax: 204/676-3796 – Gr. 5-8

Miskooseepi School, Bloodvein MB R0C 0J0 – 204/395-2012; Fax: 204/395-2189 – Gr. Pre.-9

Neil Dennis Kematch Memorial School, General Delivery, Pelican Rapids MB R0L 1L0 – 204/587-2045; Fax: 204/587-2341

Oak Lake Sioux School, PO Box 146, Pipestone MB R0M 1T0 – 204/854-2975; Fax: 204/854-2525

Otetiskewin Kiskinwamahtowekamik, Nelson House MB R0B 1A0 – 204/484-2242; Fax: 204/484-2002 – Gr. Pre.-12

Otter Nelson River, Cross Lake Education Authority, Cross Lake MB R0B 0J0 – 204/676-2050; Fax: 204/676-2464 – Gr. Pre.-12

Oxford House School, Oxford House MB R0B 1C0 – 204/538-2318; Fax: 204/538-2782 – Gr. Pre.-12

Peguis Central School, PO Box 670, Peguis MB R0C 3J0 – 204/645-2164; Fax: 204/645-2270 – Gr. Pre.-12

Peter Yassie Memorial School, Tadoule Lake MB R0B 2C0 – 204/684-2279; Fax: 204/684-2336

Petit Casimir Memorial School, Lac Brochet MB R0B 2E0 – 204/337-2278; Fax: 204/337-2078

Pinaymootang School, Fairford Reserve, Fairford MB R0C 0X0 – 204/659-2045; Fax: 204/659-4424 – Gr. Pre.-12

Pine Creek School, PO Box 160, Camperville MB R0L 0J0 – 204/524-2318; Fax: 204/524-2177 – Gr. Pre.-9

Pukatawagan School, Pukatawagan MB R0B 1G0 – 204/553-2163; Fax: 204/553-2225 – Gr. K.-10

Red Sucker Lake School, Red Sucker Lake MB R0B 1H0 – 204/469-5302; Fax: 204/469-5436 – Gr. Pre.-11

Sagkeeng Anicinabe High School, PO Box 1610, Pine Falls MB R0E 1M0 – 204/367-2243; Fax: 204/367-4566 – Gr. 9-12

Sagkeeng School, PO Box 1610, Pine Falls MB R0E 1M0 – 204/367-2588; Fax: 204/367-4410 – Gr. Pre.-8

St. Theresa Point School, St. Theresa Point MB R0B 1J0 – 204/462-2600; Fax: 204/462-2255 – Gr. Pre.-10

Sandy Bay School, Marius MB R0H 0T0 – 204/843-2407; Fax: 204/843-2269 – Gr. Pre.-12

Sergeant Tommy Prince School, Scanterbury MB R0E 1W0 – 204/766-2636; Fax: 204/766-2306 – Gr. Pre.-6

Sioux Valley School, Sioux Valley Reserve, PO Box 39, Griswold MB R0M 0S0 – 204/855-2536; Fax: 204/855-2023 – Gr. Pre.-9

Waywayseecappo Community School, Wayayseecappo Reserve, PO Box 40, Rossburn MB R0J 1S0 – 204/859-2811; Fax: 204/859-2992 – Gr. Pre.-8

Wuskwi Sipihk School, PO Box 307, Birch River MB R0L 0E0 – 204/236-4783; Fax: 204/236-4779 – Gr. Pre.-8

Yellowquill College, Crescent Rd. West, PO Box 1599, Portage la Prairie MB R1N 3P1 – 204/239-1570; Fax: 204/857-4272 – Gr. 10-12

## INSTITUTIONAL SCHOOLS

Agassiz Youth Centre, 2 River Rd., PO Box 1342, Portage la Prairie MB R1N 3A9 – 204/239-3028; Fax: 204/239-3025

Manitoba Development Centre, Portage la Prairie MB R1N 3C6 – 204/856-4200; Fax: 204/856-4258

Manitoba School for the Deaf, 242 Stradford St., Winnipeg MB R2Y 2C9 – 204/945-8934; Fax: 204/945-1767

Manitoba Youth Centre, 170 Doncaster St., Winnipeg MB R3N 1X9 – 204/475-2010; Fax: 204/945-3112

Marymound School, 442 Scotia St., Winnipeg MB R2V 1X4 – 204/338-7971; Fax: 204/334-1496

Pine Ridge School, 1035 - 1st St. North, Brandon MB R7A 7C6 – 204/726-2631; Fax: 204/726-7125

## UNIVERSITIES

### Brandon University

#270 - 18th St., Brandon MB R7A 6A9
204/728-9520; Fax: 204/726-4573
URL: http://www.brandonu.ca; gopher://gopher.brandonu.ca
Chancellor, Kevin Kavanagh, Q.C.
Purchasing Agent, Janet Chaboyer
President & Vice-Chancellor, C. Dennis Anderson
President, Academic & Research, Patrick Carrabré
Chief Administrative & Financial Officer, Scott Lamont
Executive Assistant to the President, Lee Clark
Manager, Book Store, Elaine Rust
Registrar (Pro Tem), Darcy Bower
Director, Development & External Relations, Bruce Shavers

#### FACULTIES WITH DEANS

Arts, R. Florida
Education, R. Common
Science, R. Smith
Student Services, D. Bower

#### SCHOOLS WITH DIRECTORS

Acting Dean, Music, R. Goddard

### University of Manitoba

#202, Admin. Building, Winnipeg MB R3T 2N2
204/474-8880
URL: http://www.umanitoba.ca; gopher://gopher.cc.umanitoba.ca
Chancellor, Arthur V. Mauro, O.C., LL.D.
President & Vice-Chancellor, Emoke Szathmary, B.A., Ph.D.
Executive Assistant to the President, W.F.W. Neville, B.A.(Hons), M.A.
Vice-President, Administration, Terry Falconer, C.A.
Vice-President, Academic & Provost, J. Gardner, B.Sc.(Hons), M.Sc., Ph.D.
Vice-President, Research & External Programs, T.P. Hogan, B.A., M.A., Ph.D.
Assoc. Vice-President, B.A. Fijal
Assoc. Vice-President, D. McCallum, B.Sc.
Assoc. Vice-President, Research, J. Kesselman, B.A., M.A., Ph.D.
Vice-Provost, Student Affairs, D.R. Morphy, B.A., M.A., Ph.D.

Vice-Provost, Staff Development, K. Ogden, A.B., M.A.T.
Vice-Provost, Programs, R.A. Johnson, B.Sc. (E.E.)
Admissions, D. Halstead
Director, Human Resources, C. Farr, B.A.
Director, Libraries, C. Presser, A.B., M.L.S.

**FACULTIES WITH DEANS**
Agricultural & Food Sciences, J. Elliot
Architecture, M.G. Cox
Arts, R. Currie
Acting Dean, Continuing Education, A. Percival
Dentistry, J. Wright
Education, R. Magsino
Engineering, D. Sheilds
Graduate Studies, K.R. Hughes
Human Ecology, R. Berry
Law, A. Braid
Interim Dean, Management, Jerry Gray
Medicine, N. Anthonisen
Nursing, J. Beaton
Pharmacy, W. Hindmarsh
Physical Education & Recreation Studies, H. Janzen
Science, J. Jamieson
Social Work, D. Fuchs

**SCHOOLS WITH DIRECTORS**
Art, D. Amundson
Dental Hygiene, E. Brownstone
Div. of Occupational Therapy, Ann D. Booth
Div. of Physical Therapy, B. Loveridge
Medical Rehabilitation, F. Stein
Music, R.B. Wedgewood

**AFFILIATED COLLEGES**
Collège universitaire de Saint-Boniface, 200, av de la Cathédrale, Winnipeg MB R2H 0H7 – 204/233-0210 – Rector, P. Ruest, B.A.Lat.(Phil.), B.Ed., M.Ed., Ph.D.
St. Andrew's College, 475 Dysart Rd., Winnipeg MB R3T 2M7 – 204/474-8895 – Principal, R. Yereniuk, B.A., M.A., Ph.D.
St. John's College, 400 Dysart Rd., Winnipeg MB R3T 2M5 – 204/474-8531 – Warden, M. McLean, B.A., L.Th., M.A., D.Phil.
St. Paul's College, 430 Dysart Rd., Winnipeg MB R3T 2M6 – 204/474-8575 – Rector, J. Stapleton, B.S., M.T.S., M.A., Ph.D.
University College, 500 Dysart Rd., Winnipeg MB R3T 2M8 – 204/474-9388 – Provost, C.C. Bigelow, B.A.Sc., M.Sc., Ph.D.

**APPROVED TEACHING CENTRES**
Canadian Mennonite Bible College, 600 Shaftesbury Blvd., Winnipeg MB R3P 0M4 – 204/888-6781 – President, Rev. J. Neufeld
Canadian Nazarene College, 1301 Lee Blvd., Winnipeg MB R3T 2P7 – 204/269-2120 – President, Dr. R. Coulter
Catherine Booth Bible College, 447 Webb Pl., Winnipeg MB R3B 2P2 – 204/947-6701, 6702, 6950 – President, Major Earl Robinson
Prairie Theatre Exchange, Unit Y, 300-393 Portage Ave., Winnipeg MB R3B 2H6 – 204/942-7291 – Artistic Director, M. Springate

### University of Winnipeg
515 Portage Ave., Winnipeg MB R3B 2E9
204/786-7811; Fax: 204/786-8983
Email: adm@uwinnipeg.ca; URL: http://www.uwinnipeg.ca
Chancellor, Carol Shields
Chair, Board of Regents, R. Purves
President, Marsha Hanen
Vice-President, Administration, G. Lane
Vice-President, Academic, George Tomlinson
Controller, H. McMullin
University Secretary, R. Kingsley
Executive Director, University Relations, J. Anderson
Purchasing Agent, B. Bater
Manager, Bookstore, Vacant
President, Menno Simons College, G. Richert

**SCHOOLS WITH DIRECTORS**
Dean, Arts & Science, Dr. Michael Zaworotko
Dean, Collegiate, D. Price
Dean, Continuing Education, C. Nordman
Dean, Theology, H. King

**ASSOCIATED INSTITUTION**
Concord College, 169 Riverton Ave., Winnipeg MB R2L 2ES – 204/669-6583

## COMMUNITY COLLEGES

**ASSINIBOINE COMMUNITY COLLEGE**
1430 Victoria Ave. East, Brandon MB R7A 2A9
204/726-6600; Fax: 204/726-6753
Email: info@adminet.assiniboinec.mb.ca; URL: http://www.assiniboinec.mb.ca
President, B. Cooke
Parkland Campus, 520 Whitmore Ave. East, PO Box 4000, Dauphin MB R7N 2V5 – 204/622-2023; Fax: 204/638-3941

**ÉCOLE TECHNIQUE ET PROFESSIONNELLE**
c/o Collège Universitaire de Saint-Boniface, 200, av de la Cathédrale, Saint-Boniface MB R2H 0H7
204/233-0210; Fax: 204/237-3240
Director, Raymonde Gagné, B.A., Cert.Ed., M.B.A.

**KEEWATIN COMMUNITY COLLEGE**
436 - 7 St. East, PO Box 3000, The Pas MB R9A 1M7
204/627-8500; Fax: 204/623-7316; Toll Free: 1-800-238-8508
URL: http://www.keewatincc.mb.ca
President, W.A. Sam Shaw, Email: sshaw@keewatincc.mb.ca

**RED RIVER COMMUNITY COLLEGE**
2055 Notre Dame Ave., Winnipeg MB R3H 0J9
204/632-2311; Fax: 204/632-9661
URL: http://rrcc.mb.ca

## POST-SECONDARY & SPECIALIZED INSTITUTIONS

**ACADEMY OF LEARNING - NORTH**
1109 Henderson Hwy., Winnipeg MB R2G 1L4
204/334-2121; Fax: 204/334-2129
Email: academyo@mts.net
Computer & business training
Academy of Learning - South: 106B Scurfied Blvd., Winnipeg MB R3Y 1G4 – 204/489-7684

**APPLIED MULTIMEDIA TRAINING CENTRES**
495 Portage Ave., Winnipeg MB R3B 2E4
204/772-4411; Fax: 204/772-2896
Multimedia & computer graphics

**CAMBRIAN COLLEGE**
909 - 24th St., Brandon MB R7B 1Y5
204/725-3492

**CANADIAN COLLEGE OF TAXIDERMY**
419 - 1st Ave., McCreary MB R0J 1B0
204/835-2639; Fax: 204/835-2764

**CANADIAN SCHOOL OF FLORAL ART**
569 St. Mary's Rd., Winnipeg MB R2M 3M6
204/233-2426

**CAREER DEVELOPMENT INSTITUTE**
#400, 393 Portage Ave., Winnipeg MB R3B 2H6
204/942-1773

**CDI COLLEGE OF BUSINESS & TECHNOLOGY**
#400, 393 Portage Ave., Winnipeg MB R3B 2H6
204/942-1773; Fax: 204/942-1134
Computer & business training

**COMPUTER MULTIMEDIA TECHNOLOGY CENTRE**
491 Portage Ave., Winnipeg MB R3B 2E4
204/772-4411

**EUROPEAN SCHOOL OF ESTHETICS**
#200, 241 Vaughan St., Winnipeg MB R3C 1T6
204/943-3440
Esthetics

**GRANTON INSTITUTE OF TECHNOLOGY**
177 Lombard Ave., 7th Fl., Winnipeg MB R3B 0W5
204/943-5655
Distance education

**HALLCREST CAREER COLLEGE**
Skywalk Level, #205, 400 St. Mary Ave., Winnipeg MB R3C 4K5
204/943-3555; Fax: 204/943-4555
Email: hallcrst@pangea.ca
Business, accounting, office, computer programs

**HERZING CAREER COLLEGE**
723 Portage Ave., Winnipeg MB R3G 0M8
204/775-8175

**MID-OCEAN RECORDING STUDIO**
1578 Erin St., Winnipeg MB R3E 2T1
204/774-3715

**NATIONAL INSTITUTE OF BROADCASTING**
1546 St. James St., Winnipeg MB R3H 0L2
204/775-8751; Fax: 204/772-6720

**NEW METHOD COLLEGE**
1189 Pembina Hwy., Winnipeg MB R3T 2A5
204/982-1870; Fax: 204/475-7427
Business & communications skills

**PANACHE AGENCY MODELS SCHOOL**
#106, 897 Corydon Ave., Winnipeg MB R3M 0W7
204/982-6150; Fax: 204/474-2687
Models training

**PATAL VOCATIONAL PREPARATION SCHOOLS LTD.**
#200, 220 Hespeler Ave., Winnipeg MB R2L 0L4
204/669-7102; Fax: 204/669-7106
Life skills, upgrading, computer training

**PROFESSIONAL TRANSPORT DRIVER TRAINING SCHOOL**
300 Oak Point Hwy., Winnipeg MB R2R 1V1
204/925-1580; Fax: 204/925-1587
Air brake licence training

**PROVIDENCE COLLEGE & SEMINARY**
Otterburne MB R0A 1G0
204/433-7488; Fax: 204/433-7158
Email: lwild@providence.mb.ca; URL: http://www.providence.mb.ca

**REIMER EXPRESS DRIVER TRAINING INSTITUTE INC.**
1216 Fife St., Winnipeg MB R2X 2N6
204/958-5100; Fax: 204/958-3034
Tractor trailer drivers training

**RIGHT CHOICE DRIVER TRAINING INC.**
985 Dugald Rd., Winnipeg MB R2J 0G8
204/989-5200; Fax: 204/989-5209
Comprehensive class 1-3 transport driver training

**ROBERTSON COLLEGE INC.**
696 Portage Ave., Winnipeg MB R3G 0M6
204/774-9444; Fax: 204/774-9345; Toll Free: 1-800-716-4301

* indicates enrollment figure.

Email: rcollege@escape.ca; URL: http://www.robertsoncollege.com
Registrar, Richard McDougall

**SCHOOL OF RECORDING ARTS OF MANITOBA**
275 Selkirk Ave., Winnipeg MB R2W 2L6
204/586-8057

**SCIENTIFIC-MARVEL SCHOOL OF HAIRSTYLING & ESTHETICS**
269 Kennedy St., Winnipeg MB R3C 1T2
204/943-2245
Skin care & hairstyling

**SUCCESS/COMPUCOLLEGE SCHOOL OF BUSINESS**
#215, 267 Edmonton St., Winnipeg MB R3C 1S2
204/942-6495; Fax: 204/944-0752; Toll Free: 1-888-522-0555

## INDEPENDENT & PRIVATE SCHOOLS

**Schools listed alphabetically by city.**

Arborg: Interlake Mennonite Fellowship School, PO Box 388, Arborg MB R0C 0A0 – 204/364-2328 – Gr. 1-10
Arborg: Lake Centre Mennonite Fellowship School, PO Box 417, Arborg MB R0C 0A0 – 204/364-2201 – Gr. 1-9
Arborg: Morweena Christian School, PO Box 1030, Arborg MB R0C 0A0 – 204/364-2466; Fax: 204/364-2218 – Gr. 1-12
Austin Christian School, PO Box 460, Austin MB R0H 0C0 – 204/637-2303 – Gr. 1-12
Austin Mennonite School, PO Box 267, Austin MB R0H 0C0 – 204/637-2008 – Gr. 1-10
Austin: Pine Creek School, Pine Creek Colony, PO Box 299, Austin MB R0H 0C0 – Gr. 1-8
Beausejour: Willow Grove School, PO Box 783, Beausejour MB R0E 0C0 – 204/268-3207 – Gr. 3-9
Birnie: Shady Oak Christian School, General Delivery, Birnie MB R0J 0J0 – 204/966-3477 – Gr. 1-9
Brandon: Christian Heritage School, 2025 - 26 St., Brandon MB R7B 3Y2 – 204/725-3209; Fax: 204/728-5487 – *87 – Gr. K.-9
Brandon: Early Years Development Centre, 911 - 26th St., Brandon MB R7B 2B7 – 204/728-3275; Fax: 204/727-2036 – Gr. Pre.-K.
Carman: Dufferin Christian School, Box 1450, Carman MB R0G 0J0 – 204/745-2278; Fax: 204/745-3441 – *156 – Gr. K.-12
Cartwright Community Independent School, General Delivery, Cartwright MB R0K 0L0 – 204/529-2357; Fax: 204/529-2455 – Gr. 10-12
Cartwright: Rock Lake School, PO Box 69, Cartwright MB R0K 0L0 – 204/529-2349 – Gr. 1-9
Dauphin: Western Christian College, PO Box 5000, Dauphin MB R7N 2V5 – 204/638-8801; Fax: 204/638-7054 – *83 – Gr. 7-12
Edwin: Grace Christian Academy, General Delivery, Edwin MB R0H 0G0 – 204/252-2217 – Gr. 1-12
Elma: Riverside School, PO Box 136, Elma MB R0E 0Z0 – 204/348-2686 – Gr. 1-9
Fort Whyte: McGillivray Montessori School, PO Box 99, Fort Whyte MB R0G 0G0 – 204/488-5046 – *88 – Gr. Pre.-6
Fort Whyte: Winnipeg South Academy, McGillivray Campus, 2290 McGillivray Blvd., Fort Whyte MB R3Y 1G5 – 204/488-5046; Fax: 204/895-0737
Grandview: Poplar Grove School, PO Box 70, Grandview MB R0L 0Y0 – 204/546-2691 – Gr. 1-9
Gretna: Mennonite Collegiate Institute, PO Box 250, Gretna MB R0G 0V0 – 204/327-5891; Fax: 204/327-5872 – *161 – Gr. 9-12
Horndean Christian Day School, PO Box 79, Horndean MB R0G 0Z0 – 204/829-3865; Fax: 204/325-5175 – Gr. 2-9
Île-des-Chênes: Blackmore Private School, Rainbow Colony, PO Box 310, Île-des-Chênes MB R0A 0T0 – 204/878-2428 – Gr. 4-12
Kenville: Emmanuel Fellowship Christian School, PO Box 9, Kenville MB R0L 0B0 – 204/734-2651; Fax: 204/734-3631 – Gr. 1-12
Kenville: Riverdale School, RR#1, Kenville MB R0L 0Z0 – 204/539-2660 – Gr. 1-9
Killarney Christian Academy, PO Box 1150, Killarney MB R0K 1G0 – 204/523-7318 – Gr. 1-12
Killarney: Lakeside Christian School, PO Box 894, Killarney MB R0K 1G0 – 204/523-8240; Fax: 204/523-8240 – Gr. K.-7
Kleefeld: New Hope Christian School, PO Box 120, Kleefeld MB R0A 0V0 – 204/377-4204 – Gr. 1-12
Kleefeld: Wild Rose School, PO Box 167, Kleefeld MB R0A 0V0 – 204/377-4778 – Gr. 1-8
Lorette: New Life Academy, PO Box 468, Lorette MB R0A 0Y0 – 204/878-2521 – Gr. 3-12
MacGregor: Baker Colony School, PO Box 490, MacGregor MB R0H 0R0 – 204/252-2645; Fax: 204/252-2178
Morden College, 514 Stephen St., Morden MB R6M 1T7 – 204/822-6156 – Gr. 10-12
Morris: Albright Private School, PO Box 819, Morris MB R0G 1K0 – 204/746-8933 – Gr. K.-8
Morris Christian Day School, PO Box 447, Morris MB R0G 1K0 – 204/746-8130 – Gr. 1-10
Neepawa: Living Hope School, PO Box 2158, Neepawa MB R0J 1H0 – 204/966-3274 – Gr. 1-10
Pine Falls: Christian Faith Academy, PO Box 459, Pine Falls MB R0E 1M0 – 204/367-2056 – Gr. 1-12
Plum Coulee: Prairie Mennonite School, PO Box 53, Plum Coulee MB R0G 1R0 – 204/829-3336 – Gr. 1-9
Portage Christian Academy, PO Box 1300, Portage la Prairie MB R1N 3L5 – 204/857-3780; Fax: 204/857-3780 – Gr. 2-12
Portage La Prairie: Westpark School, PO Box 91, Portage La Prairie MB R1N 3B2 – 204/857-3726; Fax: 204/239-6545 – *138 – Gr. K.-12
Rapid City: Potter's Wheel Christian School, PO Box 315, Rapid City MB R0K 1W0 – 204/826-2607 – Gr. 2-9
Riverton: Mennville Christian School, Box 448, Riverton MB R0C 2R0 – 204/378-5576 – *51 – Gr. K.-10
Roblin: Parkland Christian School, PO Box 480, Roblin MB R0L 1P0 – 204/937-2870 – Gr. 1-9
Roblin: St. Vladimir's College, PO Box 789, Roblin MB R0L 1P0 – 204/937-2173; Fax: 204/937-8265 – Gr. 10-12
Rosenort: Prairie View School, PO Box 117, Rosenort MB R0G 1W0 – 204/746-8837
Ste. Anne: Greenland School, RR#1, PO Box 224, Ste. Anne MB R0A 1R0 – 204/355-4922 – Gr. 1-9
Sinclair: Stony Creek School, PO Box 5, Sinclair MB R0M 2A0 – 204/662-4431 – Gr. 1-9
Steinbach: Church of God Holiness Academy, PO Box 20639, Steinbach MB R0A 2T2 – 204/326-4149
Steinbach: Country View School, PO Box 3910, Steinbach MB R0A 2A0 – 204/326-1481 – Gr. 1-9
Steinbach: Mennonite Christian Academy, PO Box 20749, Steinbach MB R0A 2T2 – 204/434-9315; Fax: 204/434-6624 – Gr. 1-10
Steinbach Christian Academy, PO Box 20629, Steinbach MB R0A 2T2 – 204/326-5553; Fax: 204/326-6908 – Gr. K.-10
Steinbach Christian High School, PO Box 1420, Steinbach MB R0A 2A0 – 204/326-3537 – *69 – Gr. 10-12
Swan River: Community Bible Fellowship Christian School, PO Box 1630, Swan River MB R0L 1Z0 – 204/734-2174 – Gr. K.-9
Tolstoi: Border View Christian Day School, PO Box 83, Tolstoi MB R0A 2E0 – 204/427-2932 – Gr. K-9
Winkler: Grace Valley Mennonite Academy, RR#1, PO Box 139, Grp.7, Winkler MB R6W 4A1 – 204/829-3301
Winkler: Valley Mennonite Academy, Grp. 7, RR#1, PO Box 139, Winkler MB R6W 4A1 – Gr. 1-12
Winnipeg: Alhijra Islamic School, 1551 Pembina Hwy., Winnipeg MB R3T 2E5 – 204/477-1343
Winnipeg: Balmoral Hall, 630 Westminster Ave., Winnipeg MB R3C 3S1 – 204/784-1600; Fax: 204/774-5534 – Head, Diane Bieber – *437 – Gr. K.-12
Winnipeg: Beautiful Savior Lutheran School, 1541 St. Mary's Rd., Winnipeg MB R2M 3V8 – 204/257-8534
Winnipeg: Calvin Christian School, 245 Sutton Ave., Winnipeg MB R2G 0T1 – 204/338-7981 – *307 – Gr. K.-9
Winnipeg: Children's House, 150 Pacific Ave., Winnipeg MB R3B 3K8 – 204/956-1622 – Gr. Pre.-K
Winnipeg: Christ the King School, 12 Lennox Ave., Winnipeg MB R2M 1A6 – 204/257-0027; Fax: 204/257-3325 – *164 – Gr. Pre.-6
Winnipeg: Faith Academy, 600 Jefferson Ave., Winnipeg MB R2V 0P2 – 204/338-6150; Fax: 204/338-1170 – *183 – Gr. K.-12
Winnipeg: Holy Cross School, 300 Dubuc St., Winnipeg MB R2H 1E4 – 204/237-4936; Fax: 204/237-7433 – *258 – Gr. K.-8
Winnipeg: Holy Ghost School, 333 Selkirk Ave., Winnipeg MB R2W 2L8 – 204/582-1053; Fax: 204/582-4870 – *225 – Gr. K.-8
Winnipeg: Immaculate Heart of Mary School, 650 Flora Ave., Winnipeg MB R2W 2S5 – 204/582-5698; Fax: 204/586-6698 – *188 – Gr. K.-8
Winnipeg: Immanuel Christian School, 215 Rougeau Ave., Winnipeg MB R2C 3Z9 – 204/661-8937; Fax: 204/669-7013 – *131 – Gr. K.-12
Winnipeg: Indian Metis Holiness School, 610 Selkirk Ave., Winnipeg MB R2W 2N1 – 204/949-0870; Fax: 204/586-9484 – Gr. 1-11
Winnipeg: Joseph Wolinsky Collegiate, 437 Matheson Ave., Winnipeg MB R2W 0E1 – 204/589-5345; Fax: 204/589-3075 – *256 – Gr. 7-12
Winnipeg: Keystone Christian School, 1770 King Edward St., Winnipeg MB R2R 0M5 – 204/987-8811; Fax: 204/633-1992 – Gr. K-12
Winnipeg: The King's School, 851 Panet Rd., Winnipeg MB R2K 4C9 – 204/989-6581; Fax: 204/989-6592 – *109 – Gr. K.-10
Winnipeg: The Laureate Academy, 367 Hampton St., Winnipeg MB R3J 1P7 – 204/831-7107; Fax: 204/885-3217 – Gr. 1-11
Winnipeg: Linden Christian School, 877 Wilkes Ave., Winnipeg MB R3P 1B8 – 204/989-6730; Fax: 204/488-6952 – *114 – Gr. K.-9
Winnipeg: Mennonite Brethren Collegiate Institute, 180 Riverton Ave., Winnipeg MB R2L 2E8 – 204/667-8210; Fax: 204/661-5091 – *508 – Gr. 7-12
Winnipeg: Montessori Learning Centres Inc., 170 Ashland Ave., Winnipeg MB R3L 1L1 – 204/475-1039 – Gr. Pre.-K.
Winnipeg: Msgr. James K. MacIsaac School, 249 Arnold Ave., Winnipeg MB R3L 0W5 – 204/452-7632; Fax: 204/453-3081 – *122 – Gr. K.-8
Winnipeg: Oholei Torah School, 2095 Sinclair St., Winnipeg MB R2V 3K2 – 204/339-8737; Fax: 204/586-0487 – Gr. Pre.-7
Winnipeg: Ramah Hebrew School, 705 Lanark St., Winnipeg MB R3N 1M4 – 204/488-4493; Fax: 204/488-4671 – *338 – Gr. Pre.-6
Winnipeg: Red River Valley Junior Academy, 56 Grey St., Winnipeg MB R2L 1V3 – 204/667-2383; Fax: 204/667-1396 – *76 – Gr. K.-10
Winnipeg: St. Aidan's Christian School, c/o 274 Campbell St., Winnipeg MB R3N 1B5 – 204/489-3390
Winnipeg: St. Alphonsus School, 343 Munroe Ave., Winnipeg MB R2K 1H2 – 204/667-6271; Fax: 204/663-4187 – *231 – Gr. K.-8
Winnipeg: St. Boniface Diocesan High School, 282 Dubuc St., Winnipeg MB R2H 1E4 – 204/987-1560; Fax: 204/237-9891 – *213 – Gr. 9-12
Winnipeg: St. Charles Academy, 331 St. Charles St., Winnipeg MB R3K 1T6 – 204/837-1520; Fax: 204/837-2326 – *185 – Gr. K.-8
Winnipeg: St. Edward's School, 836 Arlington St., Winnipeg MB R3E 2E4 – 204/774-8773; Fax: 204/775-0011 – *188 – Gr. K.-6

Winnipeg: St. Emile School, 552 St. Anne's Rd., Winnipeg MB R2M 3G4 – 204/257-3815; Fax: 204/254-8041 – *220 – Gr. K.-8

Winnipeg: St. Gerard's School, 40 Foster St., Winnipeg MB R2L 1V7 – 204/667-4862; Fax: 204/668-7932 – *104 – Gr. K.-6

Winnipeg: St. Ignatius School, 239 Harrow St., Winnipeg MB R3M 2Y3 – 204/475-1386; Fax: 204/475-3961 – *263 – Gr. Pre.-8

Winnipeg: St. John Brebeuf School, 605 Renfrew St., Winnipeg MB R3N 1J8 – 204/489-2115; Fax: 204/489-6097 – *244 – Gr. K.-8

Winnipeg: St. John's-Ravenscourt School, 400 South Dr., Winnipeg MB R3T 3K5 – 204/477-2402; Fax: 204/477-2429 – *683 – Gr. 1-12

Winnipeg: St. Joseph the Worker School, 505 Brewster St., Winnipeg MB R2C 2W6 – 204/222-1832 – *129 – Gr. K.-6

Winnipeg: St. Mary's Academy, 550 Wellington Cres., Winnipeg MB R3M 0C1 – 204/477-0244; Fax: 204/453-2417 – *520 – Gr. 7-12

Winnipeg: St. Maurice School, 1639 Pembina Hwy., Winnipeg MB R3T 2G6 – 204/452-2873; Fax: 204/452-4050 – *303 – Gr. K.-12

Winnipeg: St. Michael's School, 174 Maple St., Winnipeg MB R2W 3L4 – 204/582-4664; Fax: 204/582-4664 – Gr. 1-10

Winnipeg: St. Paul's High School, 2200 Grant Ave., Winnipeg MB R3P 0P8 – 204/031-2300; Fax: 204/831-2340 – *504 – Gr. 9-12

Winnipeg: St. Raphael's Academy, 478 McKenzie St., Winnipeg MB R2W 5B9 – 204/589-0759; Fax: 204/589-0639 – Gr. K.-7

Winnipeg: Southeast College, 1301 Lee Blvd., Winnipeg MB R3T 2P7 – 204/261-3551; Fax: 204/269-7880

Winnipeg: Springs Christian Academy, 261 Youville St., Winnipeg MB R2H 2S7 – 204/235-0863; Fax: 204/235-0390 – *88 – Gr. K.-9

Winnipeg: Talmud Torah, I.L. Peretz School, 427 Matheson Ave., Winnipeg MB R2W 0E1 – 204/586-8366; Fax: 204/586-2652 – *166 – Gr. Pre.-6

Winnipeg: University of Winnipeg Collegiate, #2W04, 515 Portage Ave., Winnipeg MB R3B 2E9 – 204/786-9221; Fax: 204/775-1942 – *458 – Gr. 11-12

Winnipeg: Victorious Faith Centre, 50 Scurfield Rd., Winnipeg MB R3Y 1G4 – 204/488-2487; Fax: 204/489-6040 – Gr. Pre.-12

Winnipeg: Westgate Mennonite Collegiate, 86 West Gate, Winnipeg MB R3C 2E1 – 204/775-7111; Fax: 204/786-1651

Winnipeg Mennonite Elementary School, 250 Bedson St., Winnipeg MB R3K 1R7 – 204/885-1032; Fax: 204/897-4068 – *297 – Gr. K.-6

Winnipeg Montessori Schools Inc., 1525 Willson Pl., Winnipeg MB R3T 4H1 – 204/452-3315; Fax: 204/452-3315 – Gr. Pre.-K

Winnipeg: Zion Christian Academy, 305 Machray Ave., Winnipeg MB R2W 1A3 – 204/582-6541; Fax: 204/586-2039 – Gr. K.-9

# NEW BRUNSWICK

## Department of Advanced Education & Labour

470 York St., PO Box 6000, Fredericton NB E3B 5H1
506/453-3806

Director, Curriculum & Evaluation, Peter Kilburn, 506/453-8226

## Department of Education

PO Box 6000, Fredericton NB E3B 5H1
506/453-3678; Fax: 506/453-3325
URL: http://www.gov.nb.ca/education/index.htm

### CURRICULUM INFORMATION

Curriculum Development, Barry Lydon, 506/453-2155; Email: barryl@gov.nb.ca

Direction des services pédagogiques, Donata Thériault, 506/453-2743; Email: donatat@gov.nb.ca

### CORRESPONDENCE EDUCATION SERVICE

NBCC/CCNB, 1234 Mountain Rd., PO Box 2100, Stn A, Moncton NB E1C 8H9
506/856-2237; Fax: 506/856-2665

**For detailed departmental listings, see Index: "Education, Depts."**

## SCHOOL DISTRICTS

The school district offices hold responsibility for the administration & operation of New Brunswick's schools. Until March 1, 1996, the school districts were accountable to locally elected school boards. As of that date, the school boards in New Brunswick were dissolved & replaced by a network of parental structures established at the school, district & provincial levels. This network will be responsible for advising on, monitoring & providing approval for those matters pertaining to the province's educational direction.

**Boards with an enrollment of more than 10,000 are in bold print.**

District Scolaire #1 – *9,791
533, rue Main, PO Box 398, Shédiac NB E0A 3G0
506/533-3300; Fax: 506/533-3355 – Dir. gén., Lucille Collette; Dir. de l'éducation, Annette Roy

District Scolaire #11 – *5,344
18B, boul Cartier, CP 40, Richibouctou NB E0A 2M0
506/523-7655; Fax: 506/523-7659 – Dir. gén., Lucille Collette; Dir. de l'éducation, Ronald LeVasseur

District Scolaire #3 – *8,236
532, ch Madawaska, Grand-Sault NB E3Y 1A3
506/473-7360; Fax: 506/473-6437 – Dir. de l'éducation, Leo-Paul Charest; Dir. gén., Jocelyne Mallet-Parent

District Scolaire #5 – *4,699
21, rue King, Campbellton NB E3N 1C5
506/789-2255; Fax: 506/789-2269 – Dir. gén., Jocelyne Mallet-Parent; Dir. de l'éducation, Jean-Guy Levesque

District Scolaire #7 – *4,614
970, rue Principale, CP 1000, Beresford NB E0B 1H0
506/547-2771; Fax: 506/547-8814 – Dir. gén., Keith Coughlan; Dir. de l'éducation, Yolande McLaughlin

**District Scolaire #9**
3376, Place du Quai, rue Principale, CP 3668, Tracadie-Sheila NB E1X 1G5
506/394-3400; Fax: 506/394-3455
*10,575
Dir. gén., Keith Coughlan
Dir. de l'éducation, Fernande McLaughlin

School District #10 – *4,730
11 School St., St. Stephen NB E3L 2N4
506/466-7302; Fax: 506/466-7309 – Supt., Vernon Goodfellow; Dir. of Education, Paul Sweeney

School District #12 – *4,783
138 Chapel St., PO Box 40, Woodstock NB E0J 2B0
506/325-4751; Fax: 506/328-6220 – Supt., Vernon Goodfellow; Dir. of Education, Frank Hayes

School District #13 – *4,878
566 East Riverside Dr., PO Box 160, Perth-Andover NB E0J 1V0
506/273-4780; Fax: 506/273-4779 – Supt., Vernon Goodfellow; Dir. of Education, Colleen Spragg

School District #14 – *2,698
464 Montgomery St., PO Box 400, Dalhousie NB E0K 1B0
506/684-7555; Fax: 506/684-7552 – Supt., Robin Roe; Dir. of Education, Donald Thompson

School District #15 – *2,565
270 Douglas Ave., PO Box 1058, Bathurst NB E2A 4H8
506/547-2777; Fax: 506/547-2783 – Supt., Robin Roe; Dir. of Education, Gene Bishop

School District #16 – *7,370
78 Henderson St., Miramichi NB E1N 2R7
506/778-6075; Fax: 506/778-6090 – Supt., Robin Roe; Dir. of Education, Kathy Grebenc

School District #17 – *5,977
2 Civic Ct., PO Box 190, Chipman NB E0E 1C0
506/339-7000; Fax: 506/339-7001 – Supt., Victor Martin; Dir. of Education, Marilyn Ball

**School District #18**
#303, 565 Priestman St., PO Box 10, Fredericton NB E3B 4Y4
506/453-5454; Fax: 506/453-4220
*13,093
Supt., Victor Martin
Dir. of Education, Pam Campbell

**School District #2**
1077 St. George Blvd., Moncton NB E1E 4C9
506/856-3222; Fax: 506/856-3224
*14,331
Supt., Marilyn Adams-Smith
Dir. of Education, William Strugnell

School District #4 – *6,090
1022 Main St., PO Box 1079, Sussex NB E0E 1P0
506/432-2016; Fax: 506/432-2037 – Supt., Marilyn Adams-Smith; Dir. of Education, Greg West

School District #6 – *8,359
70B Hampton Rd., Rothesay NB E2E 5Y2
506/847-6262; Fax: 506/847-6211 – Supt., Dennis Cochrane; Dir. of Education., James Stevenson

**School District #8**
384 Lancaster Ave., Saint John NB E2M 2L5
506/658-5300; Fax: 506/658-5399
*15,143
Supt., Dennis Cochrane
Dir. of Education, Alex Dingwall

## NATIVE SCHOOLS

Big Cove School – *258
RR#1, Site 11, PO Box 6, Rexton NB E0A 2L0
506/523-6880 – Principal, K. Francis

Burnt Church School – *204
RR#2, Lagaceville NB E0C 1K0
506/776-3776 – Principal, Sharon Millar

Eel Ground Federal School – *72
PO Box 265, Newcastle NB E1V 3M3
506/622-4979 – Principal, Peter MacDonald

Eel River Kindergarten – *11
PO Box 1444, Dalhousie NB E0K 1B0
506/684-4533 – Principal, Doreen Gagne

Kingsclear School – *43
RR#6, Fredericton NB E3B 4X7
506/363-3019 – Principal, Tanya Prosser

Oromocto Kindergarten – *13
PO Box 417, Oromocto NB E3V 2G2

Red Bank Federal School – *53
PO Box 30, Red Bank NB E0C 1W0
506/836-7500 – Principal, Mary Jane Ward

St. Mary's Kindergarten – *23
c/o St. Mary's Band Hall, 230 Paul St., Fredericton NB E3A 2V3
506/472-5768 – Principal, H. Paul

Tobique Mah-Sos School – *117
PO Box 840, Perth-Andover NB E0J 1V0
506/273-6815 – Principal, Tim Nicholas

## UNIVERSITIES

### Mount Allison University

Sackville NB E0A 3C0
506/364-2275
URL: http://www.mta.ca/
Chancellor, Harold Purdy Crawford, Q.C., B.A., LL.M., LL.D.

* indicates enrollment figure.

President & Vice-Chancellor, I.D.C. Newbould, B.A., M.A., Ph.D., F.R.H.S.
Chair, Board of Regents, J. James Keith, B.A., M.A.
Vice-President, Academic, W.R. Driedzic, B.Sc., M.Sc., Ph.D.
Vice-President, Administration, John D. Stewart, B.Sc., LL.B.
Asst. Vice-President, Student Service, J. Hollett, B.A., B.Ed.
Dean, Kathryn Eryl Hamer, B.A., M.A., Ph.D.
Dean, Patrick Baker, B.A., Ph.D.
Dean, J.M. Stewart, B.Sc., M.Sc.
Registrar, L.A. Owen, B.A., M.A.

## St. Thomas University

PO Box 4569, Fredericton NB E3B 5G3
506/452-7700; Fax: 506/450-9615
URL: http://www.stthomasu.ca
Chancellor, Most Rev. J. Edward Troy, B.A., B.Ph., Lic. in Phil., Ph.D., LL.D.
President & Vice-Chancellor, Dr. Daniel O'Brien, B.Comm., M.S.W., D.S.W., Email: obrien@stthomasu.ca
Vice-President, Academic, Roger H. Barnsley, B.A., M.A., Ph.D.
Vice-President, Finance & Administration, Lawrence H. Durling, B.B.A., C.A.
Director, Academic Computing, Stephen MOss, B.Sc.
Director, Admissions, Evelyn Sweezey, B.A., B.Ed.
Director, Athletics Office, LeRoy Washburn, B.P.E., B.A., M.Ed.
Director, Development Office, Hon. Noel Kinsella, B.A., B.D., S.T.L., L.Ph., S.T.D., L.Psych.
Director, Student Affairs, Ron Byrne, B.A., LL.B.
Chaplain, Campus Ministry, Rev. Bill Brennan, B.Comm., M.Div.
Comptroller, Financial Services Office, Reginald J. Gallant, B.B.A., C.A.
Registrar, Lawrence A. Batt, B.A., M.A.
Manager, Facilities & Purchasing, Fred Wallace

#### FACULTIES WITH CHAIRS

Arts
Education, Robert W. Lewis, B.A., M.S.W., Ph.D.
Journalism
Social Work, John Coates, B.S., M.Ed., Ed.D.

## Université de Moncton

Moncton NB E1A 3E9
506/858-4000; Fax: 506/858-4379
URL: gopher://gopher.umoncton.ca
Chancelier, Antonine Maillet
Recteur, Jean-Bernard Robichaud, Email: recteur@umoncton.ca
Secrétaire générale, Simone Leblanc-Rainville, Email: secgen@umoncton.ca
Vice-recteur, Administration et ressources humaines, Fernand Landry, Email: landryf@umoncton.ca
Vice-recteur, Enseignement et recherche, Yvon Fontaine, Email: fontaiy@umoncton.ca
Directeur, Développement universitaire, Rhéal Bérubé
Directrice, Education permanente, Colette Landry Martin, Email: martine@umoncton.ca
Directeur, Service des finances, Donald Cormier, Email: cormied@umoncton.ca
Directeur, Services aux étudiants, Gilles Nadeau, Email: nadeauga@umoncton.ca
Bibliothécaire en chef, Pierre Lafrance
Directeur, Services techniques, Normand Dionne
Directeur, Service du personnel, Rhéal Belliveau
Directeur, Service des communications, Paul-Emile Benoit, Email: benoitpe@umoncton.ca
Directeur, Service des anciens et amis, Vincent Bourgeois, Email: bourgev@umoncton.ca

#### FACULTÉS AVEC DOYENS

Administration, George Wybouw
Arts, Zenon Chiasson
Droit, Michel Doucet
Études supérieures et de la recherche, Truong Vo-Van
Sciences, Victorin Mallet
Sciences de l'éducation, Rodrigue Landry
Sciences sociales, Isabelle McKee-Allain

#### ÉCOLES AVEC DIRECTEURS

Education physique et loisir, Hermel Couturier
Génie, Soumaya Yacout
Nutrition et d'études familiales, Lita Villalon
Sciences forestières, Edgar Robichaud
Sciences infirmières, Michèle Trudeau

#### CENTRES UNIVERSITAIRES

Vice-recteur, Saint-Louis-Maillet, Normand Carrier
Vice-recteur, Shippagan, Armand Caron

## University of New Brunswick

PO Box 4400, Stn A, Fredericton NB E3B 5A3
506/453-4666; Fax: 506/453-4599
URL: http://degaulle.hil.unb.ca
Chancellor, F.S. Eaton, O.C., B.A., LL.D.
President, Elizabeth Parr-Johnston, B.A., M.A., Ph.D., Email: epj@unb.ca
Vice-President, Academic, L. Visentin, B.Sc., M.S., Ph.D., Email: visentin@unb.ca
Vice-President, Finance & Administration, J. F. O'Sullivan, B.B.A., LL.D., Email: jos@unb.ca
Vice-President, Research & International Cooperation, J.D. McLaughlin, B.Sc.E., M.Sc.E., Ph.D., Email: rimg@unb.ca
Comptroller, D.V. Murray, B.Comm., C.A., Email: dmurray@unb.ca
University Secretary, S. Strople, B.A., M.A., Email: sstrople@unb.ca
Registrar, Deanne Dennison, B.A., Email: denn@unb.ca
Personnel, J.D. Horn, B.Sc., Email: jdhorn@unb.ca
Dean, Student Affairs & Services, T.A. Austin, B.A., B.Ed., M.Sc.(C.S.), Email: austin@unb.ca
Purchasing Agent, L.M. Spencer, Email: lspencer@unb.ca
Manager, Bookstore, D.G. McConnell, Email: mcconnel@unb.ca

#### FACULTIES WITH DEANS

Administration, F. Simyar, A.A., B.S., M.B.A., M.Acc., D.B.A.
Arts, P.C. Kent, B.A., B.Ed., M.Sc.Econ., Ph.D.
Computer Science, W.D. Wasson, B.Sc.E., S.M., Ph.D.
Education, H. Cowan, B.Comm., M.Ed.
Engineering, W. Faig, Dip.Ing., M.Sc.E., Dr.Ing.
Acting Dean, Forestry & Environmental Management, E.W. Robak, B.Sc.F.E., M.B.A.
Kinesiology, T. Haggerty, B.A., B.P.H.E., M.A., Ph.D.
Law, Anne La Forest, B.A., LL.B., LL.M.
Nursing, Penelope K. Ericson, B.S.N., M.S.N.
Science, I. Unger, B.Sc., M.Sc., Ph.D.

#### SCHOOLS WITH DIRECTORS

Acting Dean, Graduate Studies, J. Sexsmith, B.Sc., M.Sc., Ph.D.
Saint John Campus, PO Box 5050, Saint John NB E2L 4L5 – 506/648-5500; Fax: 506/648-5528 – Vice-President, F.C. Miner

#### AFFILIATED COLLEGES

Maritime Forest Ranger School, RR#10, Fredericton NB E3B 6H6 – 506/458-0199 – Director, Stephen Hoyt, B.Sc.F., M.Sc., M.Sc.F.

## COMMUNITY COLLEGES

#### NEW BRUNSWICK COMMUNITY COLLEGE (BATHURST)/ COLLÈGE COMMUNAUTAIRE DU NOUVEAU-BRUNSWICK(BATHURST)

PO Box 266, Bathurst NB E2A 3Z2
506/547-2145; Fax: 506/547-2741
Principal, Maurice Roy, Email: roymauri@nbnet.nb.ca

#### NEW BRUNSWICK COMMUNITY COLLEGE (CAMPBELLTON)/ COLLÈGE COMMUNAUTAIRE DU NOUVEAU-BRUNSWICK (CAMPBELLTON)

PO Box 309, Campbellton NB E3N 3G7

#### NEW BRUNSWICK COMMUNITY COLLEGE (DIEPPE)/COLLÈGE COMMUNAUTAIRE DU NOUVEAU-BRUNSWICK (DIEPPE)

PO Box 4519, Dieppe NB E1A 6G1
506/856-2200
Principal, M. Richard

#### NEW BRUNSWICK COMMUNITY COLLEGE (EDMUNDSTON)/ COLLÈGE COMMUNAUTAIRE DU NOUVEAU-BRUNSWICK (EDMUNDSTON)

PO Box 70, Edmundston NB E3V 3K7
506/735-2504; Fax: 506/735-1108
Principal, Michel Laroche, Email: ml2504@gov.nb.ca
Registrar, Daniel Plourde, Email: dp2221@gov.nb.ca

#### NEW BRUNSWICK COMMUNITY COLLEGE (MIRAMICHI)/ COLLÈGE COMMUNAUTAIRE DU NOUVEAU-BRUNSWICK (MIRAMICHI)

PO Box 1053, Chatham NB E1N 3W4
506/773-9451
Principal, A. Heckel

#### NEW BRUNSWICK COMMUNITY COLLEGE (MONCTON)/ COLLÈGE COMMUNAUTAIRE DU NOUVEAU BRUNSWICK (MONCTON)

1234 Mountain Rd., Moncton NB E1C 8H9
506/856-2230; Fax: 506/856-3382
Principal, John Lean, Email: JohnLean@gov.nb.ca

#### NEW BRUNSWICK COMMUNITY COLLEGE (SAINT JOHN)/ COLLÈGE COMMUNAUTAIRE DU NOUVEAU-BRUNSWICK (SAINT JOHN)

PO Box 2270, Saint John NB E2L 3V1
506/658-6600; Fax: 506/658-6792
Email: dykemanc@nbccsj.gov.nb.ca; URL: http://www.saintjohn.nbcc.nb.ca
Principal, Cheryl M.G. Robertson

#### NEW BRUNSWICK COMMUNITY COLLEGE (ST. ANDREWS)/ COLLÈGE COMMUNAUTAIRE DU NOUVEAU-BRUNSWICK (ST. ANDREWS)

PO Box 427, St. Andrews NB EOG 2XO
Principal, Gerald Ingersoll
Registrar, Peter Acheson, 506/529-5025; Fax: 506/529-5078; Email: pa5025@gov.nb.ca

## POST-SECONDARY & SPECIALIZED INSTITUTIONS

#### ACADEMY OF LEARNING

#215, 1600 Main St., Moncton NB E1E 1G5
506/855-8973; Fax: 506/855-0929
Computer & business skills training

#### ATLANTIC BUSINESS COLLEGE

130 Carleton St., Fredericton NB E3B 3T4
506/450-1408; Fax: 506/450-8388; Toll Free: 1-800-983-2929
Email: davidmac@abc.nb.ca; URL: http://www.abc.nb.ca
Day school programs, continuing education courses, corporate training

#### COMPUCOLLEGE SCHOOL OF BUSINESS

93 Prince William St., Saint John NB E2L 2B2
506/633-5166; Fax: 506/633-1653; Toll Free: 1-800-663-3761
Business, accounting, computers, legal, medical, travel & tourism programs

**NEW BRUNSWICK COLLEGE OF CRAFT & DESIGN**
15 Carleton St., PO Box 6000, Fredericton NB E3B 5H1
506/453-2305; Fax: 506/457-7352
Director, Janice Gillies

## INDEPENDENT & PRIVATE SCHOOLS

**Schools with enrollment of 50 or more, listed alphabetically by city.**

Fredericton: Devon Park Christian School, 145 Clark St., PO Box 3510, Stn B, Fredericton NB E3A 5J8 – 506/458-9377 – Principal, John Church – *174 – Gr. K.-12
Hartland: Somerville Christian Academy, RR#5, Hartland NB E0J 1N0 – 506/375-4327 – Principal, Angela Walker – *56 – Gr. K.-5
Moncton Wesleyan Academy, 945 St. George Blvd., Moncton NB E1E 2C9 – 506/857-2293 – Principal, Willie Brownlee – *129 – Gr. K.-12
Plaster Rock: Apostolic Christian School, PO Box 28, Plaster Rock NB E0J 1W0 – 506/356-8690 – Principal, Sanford Goodine – *99 – Gr. K.-12
Rothesay: RCS-Netherwood School, College Hill, Rothesay NB E0G 2W0 – 506/847-8224 – Principal, Paul Kitchen – *157 – Gr. 6-12
Rothesay Baptist Christian School, PO Box 4722, Rothesay NB E2E 5X4 – 506/847-7897 – Principal, Dexter Stults – *52 – Gr. K-12

# NEWFOUNDLAND

### Department of Education
PO Box 8700, St. John's NF A1B 4J6
709/729-5097; Fax: 709/729-5896
URL: http://www.gov.nf.ca/edu/startedu.htm

**ADVANCED STUDIES BRANCH**
Director, Institutional and Industrial Training, Barry Roberts, 709/729-2350

**PRIMARY, ELEMENTARY & SECONDARY EDUCATION BRANCH**
Director, Program Development Division, Glen Loveless, 709/729-3004

**For detailed departmental listings, see Index: "Education, Depts."**

## DISTRICT BOARDS
Twenty-seven denominational school boards (16 integrated--Anglican, United Church & Salvation Army--9 Roman Catholic, 1 Penetecostal Assemblies, 1 Seventh Day Adventist) have been reduced to 10 district boards.

Avalon East #10
Atlantic Place, #601, 217 Water St., St. John's NF A1C 6C9
709/758-2372; Fax: 709/758-2386 – Dir. of Education, Brian Shortall
Avalon West #9
PO Box 500, Bay Roberts NF A0A 1G0
709/786-7182; Fax: 709/786-7040 – Dir. of Education, Dr. David Rideout
Baie Verte/Central/Connaigre #5
PO Box 70, Grand Falls-Windsor NF A2A 2J3
709/489-2168; Fax: 709/489-6585 – Dir. of Education, Domino Wilkins
Burin #7
PO Box 4000, Marystown NF A0E 2M0
709/279-2870; Fax: 709/279-2177 – Dir. of Education, Mike Siscoe
Clarenville/Bonavista #8
PO Box 2001, Clarenville NF A0E 1J0
709/466-3401; Fax: 709/466-3987 – Dir. of Education, Wade Sheppard
Labrador #1
PO Box 1810, Stn B, Happy Valley NF A0P 1E0
709/896-4097; Fax: 709/896-9638 – Dir. of Education, Calvin Patey
Lewisporte/Gander #6
3 Bell Place, 3rd Fl., PO Box 416, Gander NF A1B 1W8
709/256-2547; Fax: 709/651-3044 – Dir. of Education, Randell Mercer
Northern Peninsula/Labrador South #2
PO Box 89, Flower's Cove NF A0K 2N0
709/456-2232; Fax: 709/456-2809 – Dir. of Education, Dennis Parsons
Stephenville/Port aux Basques #4
PO Box 5600, Stephenville NF A2N 3P5
709/643-9121; Fax: 709/643-9235 – Dir. of Education, Andrew D. Butt

## UNIVERSITIES

### Memorial University of Newfoundland
PO Box 4200, St. John's NF A1C 5S7
709/737-8000; Fax: 709/737-4569
URL: http://www.mun.ca; gopher://gopher.mun.ca
Official Visitor, The Hon., Dr. A.M. House, Lt. Governor of Newfoundland
Chancellor, J.C. Crosbie, B.A., LL.B., LL.D.
President & Vice-Chancellor, A.W. May, B.Sc.(Hons), M.Sc., Ph.D., D.U., D.Sc.
Vice-President, Academic & Pro Vice-Chancellor, J. Tuinman, B.Ed., M.A., M.O.A., Ph.D., Email: jtuinman@morgan.ucs.mun.ca
Vice-President, Admin. & Finance & Legal Counsel, W.W. Thistle, B.Sc., B.Ed., M.A., LL.B., Email: wthistle@morgan.ucs.mun.ca
Vice-President, Research, K.M.W. Keough, B.Sc., M.Sc., Ph.D., Email: kkeough@kean.ucs.mun.ca
Registrar, G.W. Collins, B.Sc., B.Ed., M.Sc., Email: gcollins@kean.ucs.mun.ca
Comptroller, T. Pound-Curtis, B.Com, C.A., Email: tcurtis@morgan.ucs.mun.ca
University Librarian, R.H. Ellis, B.A., M.L.S.

**FACULTIES WITH DEANS**
Arts, T. Murphy, B.A., M.A., Ph.D.
Business Administration, W. Blake, B.A.(Com.), M.B.A., Ph.D.
Education, T. Piper, B.A., M.A., Ph.D.
Engineering & Applied Science, R. Seshadri, B.E.(Hons.), M.Tech., M.Sc., Ph.D., FCSME
Graduate Studies, G. Kealey, B.A., M.A., Ph.D.
Medicine, H.I. Bowmer, B.Sc., M.D., C.M., F.R.C.P.C.
Science, A. Law, B.A., M.A., Ph.D.
Student Affairs & Services, W.E. Ludlow, B.Sc., B.Ed., M.Ed., Ed.D.

**OTHER DIRECTORS & OFFICERS**
Alumni Affairs & Development, K. Smith, B.A., B.A.(Ed.), M.Ed.
Animal Care Services, L. Husa, M.V.Dr.
Chair, Archaeology Unit, J.A. Tuck, A.B., Ph.D., F.R.S.C.
Art Gallery, P. Grattan, B.A.(Hons.), B.F.A.
Botanical Garden, W. Nicholls, B.Sc., Ph.D.
Budget & Audits, H. Squires, F.C.G.A.
President/CEO, C-CORE, J.A. Whittick, B.Sc.
Cartographic Laboratory, C.H. Wood, B.S., M.S.
Acting Director., Centre for Earth Resources Research, G. Quinlan, B.Sc., Ph.D.
Centre for International Business Studies, B. Winsor, B.A., LL.B., M.B.A.
Centre for Management Development, G. Rowe, B.Comm., M.B.A., Ph.D.
Centre for Offshore & Remote Medicine, H. Manson, M.B., Ch.B., F.F.A.R.C.S., F.R.C.P.C.
Computing & Communications, W. Bussey, B.A.
Continuing Education, D. Whalen, Dip. A.A., B.Voc.Ed., M.B.A.
Counselling Centre, G. Hurley, B.A., M.S., Ph.D.
Facilities Management, G. Bradshaw, B.Eng., M.B.A., P.Eng.
Faculty Relations, J. Strawbridge, B.A., M.A., Ph.D.
Folklore & Language Archive, M.J. Lovelace, B.A., M.A., Ph.D.
General Student Services, W.C. Leonard, B.Sc., B.Ed., M.Ed.
Human Resources, G.A. Hickman, B.A.(Ed.), M.Ed., Ed.D.
Institute of Social & Economic Research, J.A. Tuck, A.B., Ph.D., F.R.S.C.
Acting Director, Labrador Institute of Northern Studies, D. Wilton, B.Sc., M.Sc., Ph.D.
Archivist, Maritime History Archive, H. Wareham, B.A.
Maritime Studies Research Unit, D. Vickers, B.A., Ph.D.
Ocean Engineering Research Centre, N. Bose, B.Sc., Ph.D., C.Eng., P.Eng.
Ocean Sciences Centre, L. Crim, B.A., M.Sc., Ph.D.
Office of Research, B. Cox, B.A.
P.J. Gardiner Institute for Small Business Studies, W.F. King, B.Com., C.A., M.B.A.
School of Music, M. Volk, B.Mus., M.Mus., D.M.
School of Nursing, M. Lamb, B.Sc., N.Ed., M.N.
School of Pharmacy, G.R. Duncan, B.Sc.Phm., M.Sc.Phm., D.Phil.
School of Physical Education & Athletics, W. Redden, B.P.E., M.S.(P.E.), M.Ed. (G.P.S.), Ph.D.
Interim Director, School of Social Work, J. Pennell, A.B., M.S.W., Ph.D..
President & CEO, Seabright Corporation Ltd., D. King, B.Comm., M.B.A., C.A.
Staff Relations, C. Horlick, B.Comm.
Student Development, D. Hardy Cox, B.S.W., M.S.W., Ed.D., R.S.W.
Student Health Service, R. Harpur, M.B., B.Ch., C.C.F.P.
Student Housing & Food Services, B. Johnston, B.A., B.Ed., M.Ed., Ed.D.
Technical Services, R. Sheppard, B.Eng., M.Eng.
Telemedicine Centre, C. Robbins, B.Sc., M.B.A., M.D., C.M., F.R.C.P.C., F.A.C.P.
University Relations, V. Collins, B.A.

**AFFILIATED INSTITUTIONS**
Fisheries & Marine Institute of Memorial University, PO Box 4920, St. John's NF A1C 5R3 – 709/778-0200; Fax: 709/778-0346 – Executive Director, Les O'Reilly, B.A.(Ed.), Dip.Ed., M.Admin.
Queen's College, Prince Philip Dr., St. John's NF A1B 3R6 – 709/753-0116 – Provost, Rev. B. Morgan, B.A., M.Div., M.A.
Sir Wilfred Grenfell College, Memorial University of Newfoundland, University Dr., Corner Brook NF A2H 6P9 – 709/637-6200; Fax: 709/639-8125; Email: kbindon@morgan.ucs.mun.ca – Principal, Dr. Kathryn Bindon

## PROVINCIAL COLLEGE

**PROVINCIAL COLLEGE OF THE NORTH ATLANTIC**
PO Box 5400, Stephenville NF A2N 2Z6
709/643-7701; Fax: 709/643-7808
Dir. of Programs, Pamela Walsh
Registrar, Linda Dunne
Baie-Verte Campus, Baie Verte NF A0K 1B0 – 709/532-8066; Fax: 709/532-4624 – Campus & Area Director, Colin Forward
Bay St. George Campus, PO Box 5400, Stephenville NF A2N 2Z6 – 709/643-7736; Fax: 709/643-5407 – Area Director, Patrick Power
Bonavista Campus, PO Box 670, Bonavista NF A0C 1B0 – 709/468-2610; Fax: 709/468-2004 – Campus & Area Director, Marilyn Coles-Hayley

* indicates enrollment figure.

Burin Campus, PO Box 369, Burin NF A0E 1E0 – 709/891-1253; Fax: 709/891-2256 – Campus & Area Director, Ray Kavanagh

Cabot College - Prince Philip Dr., PO Box 1693, St. John's NF A1C 5P7 – 709/758-7200; Fax: 709/758-7302 – Director, Edna Turpin-Downey

Cabot College - Ridge Rd. Campus, PO Box 1150, St. John's NF A1C 6L8 – 709/758-7007; Fax: 709/758-7126 – Head, Danny Wong

Carbonear Campus, PO Box 60, Carbonear NF A0A 1T0 – 709/596-6139; Fax: 709/596-2688 – Campus & Area Director, Graham Sheppard

Clarenville Campus, PO Box 308, Clarenville NF A0E 1J0 – 709/466-2250; Fax: 709/466-2771 – Campus & Area Director, Steve Quinton

Corner Brook Campus: Corner Brook/St. Anthony District, 141 O'Connell Dr., PO Box 822, Corner Brook NF A2H 6H6 – 709/637-8519; Fax: 709/634-2126 – Area Director, Glen Dicks

Gander Campus, PO Box 395, Gander NF A1V 1W8 – 709/256-4481; Fax: 709/651-3376 – Area Director, Mac Moss

Grand Falls-Windsor Campus, PO Box 413, Grand Falls-Windsor NF A2S 2J8 – 709/489-4317; Fax: 709/489-4180 – Area Director, Cyril Farrell

Happy Valley Campus, PO Box 3013, Happy Valley NF A0P 1E0 – 709/896-3307; Fax: 709/896-3733 – Regional Program Director, Robert Simms

Labrador West Campus, Campbell Dr., Labrador City NF A2V 2Y1 – Principal, Shirley Alport

Northwest River Learning Centre, PO Box 248, North West River NF A0P 1M0 – 709/896-2092; Fax: 709/497-8796 – Principal,

Placentia Campus, PO Box 190, Placentia NF A0B 2Y0 – 709/227-2037; Fax: 709/227-7185 – Campus & Area Director, Gerald O'Reilly

Port-aux-Basques Campus, PO Box 760, Port-aux-Basques NF A0M 1C0 – 709/695-3582; Fax: 709/695-2963 – Area Director, George Anderson

Seal Cove Campus, PO Box 10, Seal Cove NF A0A 3T0 – 709/744-2047; Fax: 709/744-3929 – Campus Manager, Dennis Power

St. Anthony Campus, East St., PO Box 550, St. Anthony NF A0K 4S0 – 709/454-3835; Fax: 709/454-8808 – Area Director, Bill Carpenter

Stephenville Crossing Campus, PO Box 5400, Stephenville NF A0N 2C0 – 709/646-5179; Fax: 709/646-5185 – Area Director, Patrick Power

## POST-SECONDARY & SPECIALIZED INSTITUTIONS

### ACADEMY CANADA CAREER COLLEGE
Fortis Tower, 4 Herald Ave., Corner Brook NF A2H 4B4
709/637-2130; Fax: 709/637-2139; Toll Free: 1-800-561-8000
Email: info@academycanada.com; URL: http://www.academycanada.com

Corner Brook Campus, PO Box 366, Corner Brook NF A2H 6E3 – 709/637-2100; Fax: 709/632-7309

Grand Falls/Windsor Campus, PO Box 128, Grand Falls/Windsor NF A2A 2J4 – 709/489-5977; Fax: 709/489-5181

St. John's Campus, PO Box 8747, St. John's NF A1B 3T2 – 709/739-6767; Fax: 709/739-6797

### ACADEMY OF LEARNING
332 Water St., PO Box 204, St. John's NF A1C 2J5
709/579-7771; Fax: 709/579-7774
Email: ariev@public.compusolt.nf.ca
Computer & business skills training

### ADULT CAREER CENTRES INC.
1062 Topsail Rd., Mount Pearl NF A1C 2C1
709/747-5550; Fax: 709/747-5565

### AQUATIC RESOURCES INC.
PO Box 36, St. Alban's NF A0H 2E0
709/538-3359; Fax: 709/538-3108
Aquaculture training

### ASSOCIATION FOR NEW CANADIANS LANGUAGE SCHOOL
249 Duckworth St., PO Box 2031, Stn C, St. John's NF A1C 5R6
709/726-6848; Fax: 709/754-4407
ESL

### ATLANTIC CONSTRUCTION TRAINING CENTRE
PO Box 236, St. John's NF A1C 5J2
709/726-6264; Fax: 709/726-6255

### AVALON EDUCATIONAL SYSTEMS
65 Whiteway St., St. John's NF A1B 1K5
709/754-3204; Fax: 709/754-3212
Custom designed programs

### AVALON PROFESSIONAL DRIVER TRAINING INSTITUTE
PO Box 174, Upper Island Cove NF A0A 4E0
709/589-2761; Fax: 709/589-2630
Email: apdt@nf.sympatico.ca
Tractor trailer operation, tandem truck, heavy equipment, heavy duty repair

### CANADIAN DIVER TRAINING CENTRE INC.
1 Crosbie Place, St. John's NF A1B 3Y8
709/738-8800; Fax: 709/738-8810

### CAREER ACADEMY
189 Higgin's Line, St. John's NF A1B 4N4
709/753-1123; Fax: 709/753-1142

### CAREERS PLUS
PO Box 1059, Bay Roberts NF A0A 1G0
709/786-3030; Fax: 709/786-9507

### CENTRAC COLLEGE OF BUSINESS, TRADES & TECHNOLOGY
61 Elizabeth Dr., PO Box 473, Gander NF A1V 1W8
709/256-2670; Fax: 709/256-3697
Vice-Principal, Jason Saunders

Creston, PO Box 160, Creston NF A0E 1K0 – 709/279-1999; Fax: 709/279-2004; Toll Free: 1-800-563-1910 – Principal, Darlene Pike

St. John's, 25 Pippy Place, St. John's NF A1B 3V8 – 709/722-9151; Fax: 709/722-9152; Toll Free: 1-800-563-5296 – Principal, Beverley Whalen

### CENTRAL TECHNICAL COLLEGE
Comfort Cove, Newstead NF A0G 3K0
709/244-4400

### CENTRAL TRAINING ACADEMY
15 Main St., PO Box 400, Badger NF A0H 1A0
709/539-5145
Training in commercial transport, heavy equipment operation

### COASTAL COMPUTER ACADEMY
42 Elizabeth Ave., St. John's NF A1A 1W4
709/754-7773; Fax: 709/754-7773

### COMPUCOLLEGE SCHOOL OF BUSINESS
275 Duckworth St., PO Box 6325, St. John's NF A1C 6J9
709/722-8580; Fax: 709/722-8318

### CORONA TRAINING INSTITUTE
3A Earle St., PO Box 819, Grand Falls-Windsor NF A2A 2P7
709/489-7825; Fax: 709/489-5001
Principal, Marilyn Bennett
Manager, Operations, Jacqueline Butler

### INDUSTRIAL TRAINING INSTITUTE
PO Box 28190, St. John's NF A1B 4J8
709/576-9100; Fax: 709/576-1160

### INDUSTRY & ARTS ACADEMY
General Delivery, Great Harbour Deep NF A0K 2Z0
709/843-3291; Fax: 709/843-4103

### KEYIN TECHNICAL COLLEGE
7 Austin St., PO Box 13609, Stn A, St. John's NF A1B 4G1
709/579-1061; Fax: 709/579-6002
Email: shawn@fishtank.keyin.com; URL: http://www.keyin.com
Industry-directed education

### LAWRENCE COLLEGE INC.
120 LeMarchant Rd., St. John's NF A1C 2H2
709/738-1053; Fax: 709/738-3350

### MAGI LEARNING CENTRE
29-31 Rowan St., St. John's NF A1B 2X2
709/754-3328; Fax: 709/754-3250
Email: dgwhite@magi.ns.ca; URL: http://magi.ns.ca

### NEWFOUNDLAND MUSIC ACADEMY
General Delivery, Baie Verte NF A0K 1B0
709/329-3161; Fax: 709/329-3161

### NORPEN TECHNICAL COLLEGE
PO Box 755, Deer Lake NF A0K 2E0
709/635-4474; Fax: 709/635-4473; Toll Free: 1-800-563-1158
Email: norpen@atcon.com
Natural resource-related training

### OPERATING ENGINEERS, EDUCATION & DEVELOPMENT INC.
62 Commonwealth Ave., Mount Pearl NF A1N 1W8
709/229-6464; Fax: 709/229-6469

### PROVINCIAL LEARNING CENTRES
310 LeMarchant Rd., St. John's NF A1E 1R3
709/722-5537; Fax: 709/364-5047

### PROVINCIAL TECHNICAL INSTITUTE
137 Crosbie Rd., PO Box 74, St. John's NF A1E 4N1
709/738-8890; Fax: 709/738-8890

## INDEPENDENT & PRIVATE SCHOOLS

**Schools with enrollment of 50 or more, listed alphabetically by city.**

Churchill Falls: Eric G. Lambert All-Grade School, PO Box 40, Churchill Falls NF A0R 1A0 – 709/925-3371; Fax: 709/925-8306 – Principal, Adrian Clarke – *187 – Gr. K.-12

St. John's: Lakecrest Independent School, 74 The Boulevard, St. John's NF A1A 1K2 – 709/738-1212 – Principal, Francine Frisson-Tuinman – *105 – Gr. K.-8

Whitbourne: Newfoundland-Labrador Youth Centre, PO Box 40, Whitbourne NF A0B 3K0 – 709/729-0944; Fax: 709/759-2611 – Principal, Bill Tucker – *69 – Gr. 7-12

# NORTHWEST TERRITORIES

## Department of Education, Culture & Employment
PO Box 1320, Yellowknife NT X1A 2L9
867/873-7110; Fax: 867/873-0155, 0200, 0109
URL: http://siksik.learnnet.nt.ca

### CULTURE & CAREERS BRANCH
Acting Assistant Deputy Minister, Lesley Allen
Deputy Minister, Mark Cleveland

**EDUCATIONAL DEVELOPMENT BRANCH**
Assistant Deputy Minister, Pauline Gordon

**INCOME SUPPORT REFORM**
Assistant Deputy Minister, Conrad Pilon

**For detailed departmental listings, see Index: "Education, Depts."**

## EDUCATION DISTRICTS

Yellowknife Education District No. 1
PO Box 788, Yellowknife NT X1A 2N6
867/873-5050; Fax: 867/873-5051 – Supt., Dr. Kenneth Woodley
Yellowknife Education District No. 2
PO Box 1830, Yellowknife NT X1A 2P4
867/873-2200; Fax: 867/873-2701 – Supt., Dr. Loretta Foley

## DIVISIONAL EDUCATION COUNCILS

Baffin Divisional Education Council
PO Box 1330, Iqaluit NT X0A 0H0
867/979-5236; Fax: 867/979-4868 – Director, C. McGregor
Beaufort/Delta Divisional Education Council
c/o Bag Service No. 12, Inuvik NT X0E 0T0
867/979-7130; Fax: 867/979-2469 – Director, Vacant
Dehcho Divisional Education Council
PO Box 376, Fort Simpson NT X0E 0N0
867/695-7260; Fax: 867/695-2035 – Director, Nolan Swartzentruber
Dogrib Divisional Education Council
Bag Service #1, Rae Edzo NT X0E 0Y0
867/371-3026; Fax: 867/371-3053 – Director, Gerri-ann Donahue
Keewatin Divisional Education Council
PO Box 90, Baker Lake NT X0C 0A0
867/793-2740; Fax: 867/793-2996 – Director, Curtis Brown
Kitikmeot Divisional Education Council
Coppermine NT X0E 0E0
867/982-7220; Fax: 867/982-3054 – Director, T. Stewart
Sahtu Divisional Education Council
PO Box 64, Norman Wells NT X0E 0V0
867/587-2367; Fax: 867/587-2462 – Director, Michael Campbell
South Slave Divisional Education Council
Fort Smith NT X0E 0P0
867/872-7215; Fax: 867/872-2150 – Director, Dr. Eugene Ewanyshyn

## POST-SECONDARY EDUCATION

**AURORA COLLEGE**
PO Box 1290, Fort Smith NT X0E 0P0
867/872-7009; Fax: 867/872-4730
President, C. Parker
Aurora Campus, PO Box 1008, Inuvik NT X0E 0T0 – 867/979-7878; Fax: 867/979-2850 – Campus Director, Miki O'Kane
Thebacha Campus, PO Box 600, Fort Smith NT X0E 0P0 – 867/872-7520; Fax: 867/872-4511 – Campus Director, R. Holtorf
Yellowknife Campus, #500, 5022 - 49 St., Yellowknife NT X1A 3R7 – 867/920-3030; Fax: 867/873-0333 – Campus Director, Dan Daniels

**NUNAVUT ARCTIC COLLEGE**
PO Box 160, Iqaluit NT X0A 0H0
867/979-4114; Fax: 867/979-4118
President, Greg Welch
Keewatin Campus, PO Bag 002, Rankin Inlet NT X0C 0G0 – 867/645-2529; Fax: 867/645-2387 – Director, M. Shouldice
Kitimeot Campus, PO Bag 200, Cambridge Bay NT X0E 0C0 – 867/983-7234; Fax: 867/983-2404 – Director, C. Isnor
Nunatta Campus, PO Box 600, Iqaluit NT X0A 0H0 – 867/979-4051; Fax: 867/979-7200 – Director, D. Wilman

# NOVA SCOTIA

## Department of Education

Trade Mart, PO Box 578, Halifax NS B3J 2S9
902/424-5168; Fax: 902/424-0519

**CURRICULUM INFORMATION**
Director, French Program Services, Margelaine Holding, 902/424-6646; Fax: 902/424-0613
Director, English Program Services, Bob Leblanc, 902/424-5991; Fax: 902-424-0613

**CORRESPONDENCE STUDIES**
PO Box 1650, Halifax NS B3J 2Z2
902/424-4054

**For detailed departmental listings, see Index: "Education, Depts."**

## REGIONAL SCHOOL BOARDS

Twenty-two district school boards were amalgamated in 1996 into 7 regional school boArds. Enrollment figures shown are for the 1996/97 school year.

**Boards with an enrollment of more than 15,000 are in bold print.**

**Annapolis Valley Regional School Board**
121 Orchard St., PO Box 340, Berwick NS B0P 1E0
902/538-4600; Fax: 902/538-4630; Toll Free: 1-800-850-3887
*18,455
Supt., Dr. James Gunn
Dir., Finance & Operations, Stuart Jamieson
**Cape Breton-Victoria Regional School Board**
275 George St., Sydney NS B1P 1J7
902/564-8293; Fax: 902/564-0123
*24,318
Supt., Dr. Hayes MacNeil
Dir., Finance, Doug Peach
**Chignecto-Central Regional School Board**
60 Lorne St., Truro NS B2N 3K3
902/897-8900; Fax: 902/895-3161
*28,186
Supt., Elmer MacDonald
Finance Officer, Robert Renouf
Conseil scolaire acadien provincial – *4,123
PO Box 360, Meteghan NS B0W 2J0
902/645-3430; Fax: 902/645-3032; Toll Free: 1-888-533-2727 – Supt., Réjean Sirois; Dir., Finance & Operations, Janine Saulnier
**Halifax Regional School Board**
PO Box 1000, Lower Sackville NS B4C 3Z5
902/864-1928; Fax: 902/864-2760
*57,786
Supt., Dr. Don Trider
Dir., Finance, David Gray
**Southwest Regional School Board**
46 Parade St., Yarmouth NS B5A 3A9
902/742-9266; Fax: 902/742-1149
*19,494
Supt., Ann Jones
Dir., Finance & Operations, David Eyre
Strait Regional School Board – *11,658
16 Cemetery Rd., PO Box 300, Port Hastings NS B0E 2T0
902/625-2191; Fax: 902/625-2281 – Supt., Jack Sullivan; Dir., Finance & Operations, John Cameron

## FEDERAL & BAND-OPERATED SCHOOLS

Eskasoni Elementary & Junior High School, 4645 Shore Rd., Eskasoni NS B0A 1J0 – 902/379-2825; Fax: 902/379-2273 – Principal, Philomena Moore
Indian Brook Junior/High School, Shubenacadie Band Council, PO Box 350, Shubenacadie NS B0N 2H0
Mi'Kmaway School, PO Box 536, Chapel Island NS B0E 3B0 – 902/535-2307; Fax: 902/535-3004 – Principal, Charles Boudreau
Muin Si'pu Mi'Kmaq Elementary School, PO Box 210, Bear River NS B0S 1B0 – 902/467-4193; Fax: 902/467-4143
Pictou Landing Elementary School, Box 55, Site 6, Pictou Landing NS B0K 1X0
Wagmatcook School, PO Box 237, Baddeck NS B0E 1B0 – 902/295-3491; Fax: 902/295-1331 – Principal, Josephine Peck
Waycobah School, PO Box 149, Inverness NS B0E 3M0 – 902/756-9000; Fax: 902/756-2171 – Principal, Dave Maston

## SCHOOLS FOR THE VISUALLY/HEARING IMPAIRED

Atlantic Provinces Special Education Authority, 5940 South St., Halifax NS B3H 1S6 – 902/424-7765; Fax: 902/424-5819 – Supt., Deborah Pottie

## UNIVERSITIES

### Acadia University

15 University Ave., Wolfville NS B0P 1X0
902/585-2201; Fax: 902/585-1072
President's Office Fax: 902/585-1077; Library Fax: 902/585-1073
URL: http://www.acadiau.ca; gopher://gopher.acadiau.ca
President, K.K. Ogilvie, B.Sc., Ph.D., D.Sc.
Vice-President, Academic, Allan Tupper, B.A., D.P.A., M.A., Ph.D.
Vice-President, Finance, Harold D. Austin, B.A., R.I.A
Director, Human Resources, Garry Alexa, B.A., C.H.R.P.
Interim Equity Officer, Cindy James
Associate Comptroller & Director, Budgets, Gary Draper, B.B.A., C.A.
Director, Development, Harvey Gilmour, B.A., LL.B.
Director, Student Affairs, Vacant, B.A., M.S.Ed.
Director, Personnel, Robert T. Flecknell, B.Sc.
Registrar, Jane Cayford, B.A., B.Ed.
Director, Office of Public Affairs, Bruce E. Choon, B. Comm., B.Ed.
Executive Director, Associated Alumni, Steve M. Pound, B.Sc., B.Ed., M.Sc., Ph.D.
Manager, Bookstore, Doug Mosher

**FACULTIES WITH DEANS**
Arts, Thomas G. Regan, B.A., M.A., Ph.D.
Acting Dean, Management & Education, William McLeod, B.Sc., M.Sc., D.P.E.
Pure & Applied Science, Michael P. Leiter, B.A., M.A., Ph.D.
Theology, A.D. MacRae, M.A., B.D., D.D.

**SCHOOLS WITH DIRECTORS**
Business Administration, Stephen Ash, B.B.A., LL.B., LL.M.L.
Computer Science, Leslie Oliver, B.Sc., M.Sc., Ph.D.
Education, James H. Fasano, B.Sc., B.Ed., M.Ed., Ph.D.
Acting Director, Engineering, Douglas Seamone, C.A.S., B.Eng., M.Sc., P.Eng.
Acting Director, Music, Gordon J. Callon, B.Mus., M.M.A., D.M.A.
Nutrition & Food Science, E.M. Johnston, B.Sc., M.S., Ph.D.
Recreation & Physical Education, Gary Ness, B.A., M.A., Ph.D.

* indicates enrollment figure.

#### AFFILIATED COLLEGES

Acadia Divinity College, 31 Horton Ave., Wolfville NS B0P 1X0 – 902/542-2285 – Principal, Andrew D. MacRae, M.A., B.D., D.D.

### Dalhousie University

1236 Henry St., Halifax NS B3H 3J5
902/494-2211; Fax: 902/494-2319
URL: http://www2.dal.ca/
Chancellor, Sir Graham Day
Vice-Chancellor & President, Dr. Tom Traves
Chair, Board of Governors, Allan C. Shaw
Vice-President, Academic & Research, Deborah Hobson
Vice-President, Administration & Finance, Bryan Mason
Vice-President, External, Vacant
Vice-President, Student Services, Eric McKee
Registrar, Gudrun Curri

#### FACULTIES WITH DEANS

Arts & Social Sciences, Graham D. Taylor
Dentistry, William MacInnis
Graduate Studies, Peter Ricketts
Health Professions, Lynn McIntyre
Henson College of Public Affairs & Continuing Education, Mary Morrisey
Law, Dawn Russell
Management, Philip J. Rosson
Medicine, John Ruedy
Science, Warwick Kimmins

#### SCHOOLS WITH DIRECTORS

Business Administration, R.E. Klapstein
College of Pharmacy, Frank Chandler
Dental Hygiene, Joanne Clovis
Health Services Administration, Ingrid Sketris
Human Communications Disorders, Walter Green
Library & Information Studies, Dr. B.H. MacDonald
Maritime School of Social Work, Joan Gilroy
Nursing, Joyce Black
Occupational Therapy, Barbara J. O'Shea
Physiotherapy, Lydia Makrides
Public Administration, A.M. Cassin
Recreation, & Physical & Health Education, Larry Maloney
Resource & Environmental Studies, Dr. Ray Côté

#### AFFILIATED COLLEGES

Atlantic School of Theology, 640 Francklyn St., Halifax NS B3H 3B5 – 902/423-6939 – Registrar, Mary Schaefer
University of King's College, Halifax NS B3H 2A1 – 902/422-1271; URL: http://www.ukings.ns.ca – President, Colin J. Starnes

### DalTech

Dalhousie University, 1360 Barrington St., PO Box 1000, Halifax NS B3J 2X4
902/420-7500; Fax: 902/420-7551
URL: http://www.tuns.ca/index.html
NOTE: DalTech was created through an amalgamation between the Technical University of Nova Scotia & Dalhousie University, effective April, 1997.
Chancellor Emeritus, Ruth M. Goldbloom, C.M., D.Hum.L., LL.D.
Principal, Edward Rhodes, B.Sc.Tech., M.Sc.Tech., Ph.D., P.Eng.
Registrar, LaMont Pelletier, B.Sc., B.Ed.
Dean, Students, Ronald C. Gilkie, Ph.D., P.Eng., F.C.S.C.E.
College Administrator, Rick Lowery, C.A.
Librarian, Donna Richardson, B.A., M.L.S.

#### FACULTIES WITH DEANS

Acting Dean, Architecture, Prof. T. Emodi
Engineering, Adam Bell, B.Eng., S.M., M.E., Sc.D., P.Eng.

#### SCHOOLS WITH DIRECTORS

Continuing Education & Conference Centre, Carol Connor
Acting Dean, School of Computer Science, Dr. C.S. Hartzman

### Mount Saint Vincent University

166 Bedford Hwy., Halifax NS B3M 2J6
902/457-6788; Fax: 902/445-3960
URL: http://www.msvu.ca/
President & Vice-Chancellor, Sheila A. Brown, Ph.D.
Chair, Board of Governors, Ruby Blois

### St. Francis Xavier University

PO Box 5000, Antigonish NS B2G 2W5
902/863-3300; Fax: 902/867-5153
URL: http://www.stfx.ca/
President, Sean E. Riley, Ph.D., Email: sriley@stfx.ca
Vice-President, Academic, Hugh Gillis, Ph.D., Email: hgillis@stfx.ca
Vice-President, Administration, J.T. Langley, M.S., C.G.A., Email: tlangley@stfx.ca
Vice-President, University Advancement, Anne Camozzi
Director, Student Services & Registrar, Carson Duncan, Ph.D., Email: cduncan@stfx.ca
Comptroller, J.C. Hagar, B.Comm., C.G.A.
Associate Registrar, Janet Stark, Email: jstark@stfx.ca
Public Relations Officer, Kimberly Dickson, B.Ed., Email: kdickson@stfx.ca
Manager, Procurement Services, Lorris Keizer
Manager, Bookstore, Dave Renny

#### FACULTIES WITH DEANS

Arts, Dr. Ron Johnson, Ph.D.
Science, Ed McAlduff, Ph.D.

#### SCHOOLS WITH DIRECTORS

Coady International Institute, Mary Coyle, B.A., M.A.
Extension Dept., Tom Webb, B.A., M.A.

#### AFFILIATED COLLEGE

Mount Saint Bernard College, 10 Hillcrest St., Antigonish NS B2G 2N5 – 902/867-3859; Fax: 902/867-3866; URL: http://www.stfx.ca/msbresid/ – Principal, Sr. Margaret McDonell, Ph.D.

### Saint Mary's University

923 Robie St., Halifax NS B3H 3C3
902/420-5400; Fax: 902/420-5566
URL: http://www.stmarys.ca
Chancellor, Most Rev. Austin E. Burke, B.A., M.T.L., D.D., D.Lit.
President, Kenneth L. Ozmon, B.A., M.A., Ph.D.
Vice-President, Academic & Research, J.Colin Dodds, B.Sc., M.A., Ph.D.
Vice-President, Administration, G. Noël, B.Eng., P.Eng.
Director, University Advancement, D.P. Keleher, Dip. Eng., B.E.
Director, Continuing Education, J.F. Sharpe, B.Sc., M.A.
Comptroller, R.L. Cochrane, B.Comm., C.G.A.
Registrar, Elizabeth A. Chard, B.A., B.Ed., M.A.
Director, Public Affairs, C.R. Bridges, M.B.A.

#### FACULTIES WITH DEANS

Arts, M.J. Larsen, B.A., M.A., Ph.D.
Commerce, Paul Dixon, Ph.D.
Education, M.J. Larsen, B.A., M.A., Ph.D.
Science, D.H.S. Richardson, B.Sc., M.Sc., M.A., Ph.D.

### Université Sainte Anne

Pointe-de-l'Église NS B0W 1M0
902/769-2114; Fax: 902/769-3120
URL: http://ustanne-59.ustanne.ednet.ns.ca/
President, Harley d'Entremont
Vice-President, Academic, Ian Richmond
Secretary General, Gérald Boudreau
Assistant Registrar, Murielle Comeau
Information Officer, Richard Landry
Manager, Bookstore, Claire Dol
Comptroller, Eric Tufts

### University College of Cape Breton

PO Box 5300, Stn A, Sydney NS B1P 6L2
902/539-5300; Fax: 902/562-6949; Toll Free: 1-888-959-9995
URL: http://www.uccb.ns.ca
President & Vice-Chancellor, Jacquelyn Thayer Scott, Ph.D.
Executive Director, Research & Development, Robert Morgan, Ph.D.
Acting Director, Dept. of Institutional Advancement, Germaine LeMoine, B.A.
Alumni Officer, Deborah MacAuley
Registrar, Graham Sheppard, M.A.
Executive Director, Human Resources & Dean of Student Services, David White
University Librarian, Penelope Marshall, M.L.S.
Director, Human Resources, Gordon MacLean
Manager, Builings & Grounds, Don MacIsaac, P.Eng.
Director, Centre for International Studies, Brian Tennyson, Ph.D.
Curator, Art Gallery, Barry Gabriel, B.F.A., B.A.

#### FACULTIES WITH DEANS

Arts & Letters, Thomas Rendall, Ph.D.
Business, Steve Kavanagh, M.B.A.
Community Studies, Silver Donald Cameron, Ph.D.
Dean (Acting), Extension & Community Affairs, Keith Brown, B.A., M.B.A.
Science & Technology, Stephen Manley, B.S., M.S., Ph.D.

## COMMUNITY COLLEGES

#### NOVA SCOTIA COMMUNITY COLLEGE

Central Office, 5685 Leeds St., Halifax NS B3J 3C4
902/424-4055; Fax: 902/424-4225
President, Jack Buckley
Vice-President, Program Services, Bill Cruden
Vice-President, Extension Services, John Keating
Vice-President, Administrative Services, Robert Shedden
Manager, Human Resources, David McKillop
Coordinator, Communications, Wilma Butts
Annapolis Campus, 295 Commercial St., Middleton NS B0S 1P0 – 902/825-3491; Fax: 902/825-2285 – Principal, Paul LaFleche
Burridge Campus, 372 Pleasant St., Yarmouth NS B5A 2L2 – 902/742-3501; Fax: 902/742-0519 – Principal, Marcel Cottreau
College of Geographic Sciences Campus, RR#1, Lawrencetown NS B0S 1M0 – 902/584-2226; Fax: 902/584-7211 – Principal, Paul LaFleche
Cumberland Campus, 1 Main St., PO Box 550, Springhill NS B0M 1X0 – 902/597-3737; Fax: 902/597-8548
Halifax Campus, 1825 Bell Rd., Halifax NS B3H 2Z4 – 902/424-7999; Fax: 902/424-0553 – Principal, Allister Thorne
I.W. Akerley Campus, 21 Woodlawn Rd., Dartmouth NS B2W 2R7 – 902/434-2020; Fax: 902/462-4320 – Principal, Gerry Mahar
Institute of Technology Campus, 5685 Leeds St., PO Box 2210, Halifax NS B3J 3C4 – 902/424-7529; Fax: 902/424-0534 – Principal, Allister Thorne
Kingstec Campus, Belcher St., PO Box 487, Kentville NS B4N 3X3 – 902/678-7341; Fax: 902/679-1141 – Principal, Janet Kirk
Lunenburg Campus, 75 High St., Bridgewater NS B4V 1V8 – 902/543-4608; Fax: 902/543-0190 – Principal, Tracy Edwards

Marconi Campus, Glace Bay Highway, PO Box 1042, Sydney NS B1P 6J7 – 902/563-2450; Fax: 902/563-0511 – Principal, Mike Kelly

Pictou Campus, 39 Acadia St., PO Box 820, Stellarton NS B0K 1S0 – 902/752-2002; Fax: 902/752-5446 – Principal, Carol Forbes

Shelburne Campus, 1575 Lake Rd., PO Box 760, Shelburne NS B0T 1W0 – 902/875-3091; Fax: 902/875-3797

Strait Area Campus, Reeves St., PO Box 1225, Port Hawkesbury NS B0E 2V0 – 902/625-2380; Fax: 902/625-0193

Truro Campus, 36 Arthur St., Truro NS B2N 1X5 – 902/893-5385; Fax: 902/893-5390 – Principal, Marsha Chase

## POST-SECONDARY & SPECIALIZED INSTITUTIONS

### ATLANTIC BROADCASTING INSTITUTE

#500, 6009 Quinpool Rd., Halifax NS B3K 5J7
902/423-2001; Fax: 902/429-6692
A. Walling

### ATLANTIC HOME BUILDERS TRAINING

53 Leary's Cove Rd., East Dover NS B0J 3L0
902/852-2151; Fax: 902/852-3193
Email: ahbtb@fox.nstn.ca
Industry courses in home builder/renovator management

### C.L. DOUGLAS & ASSOCIATES CENTRE FOR COMPUTER STUDIES

#1008, 2000 Barrington St., Halifax NS B3J 3K1
902/422-2477; Fax: 902/422-0276
Email: cld@istar.ca
Computer software, network management training

### COLLEGE DE L'ACADIE

PO Box 24, Saulnierville NS B0W 2Z0
902/769-0851; Fax: 902/769-0165

### COMPUCOLLEGE SCHOOL OF BUSINESS

1526 Dresden Row, Halifax NS B3J 3K3
902/423-3933; Fax: 902/423-2042
Email: compuhfx@fox.nstn.ns.ca

### GAELIC COLLEGE OF CELTIC ARTS & CRAFTS

PO Box 9, Baddeck NS B0E 1B0
902/295-3411; Fax: 902/295-2912
Executive Director, Sam MacPhee

### THE INSTITUTE FOR EARLY CHILDHOOD EDUCATION & DEVELOPMENTAL SERVICES

60 Lorne St., Truro NS B2N 3K3
902/893-3342; Fax: 902/895-4487
Email: ieceds@istar.ca
Executive Director, Jane M. Norman, Ph.D
Early childhood education, child care personnel, public school program assistants, special education personnel, youth workers training

### MACTECH DISTANCE EDUCATION

PO Box 295, North Sydney NS B2A 3M3
902/794-2205; Fax: 902/794-1414
Distance education

### MARITIME CONSERVATORY OF MUSIC

6199 Chebucto Rd., Halifax NS B3L 1K7
902/423-6995; Fax: 902/423-6029
Director, Jack Brownell

### NOVA SCOTIA AGRICULTURAL COLLEGE

PO Box 550, Truro NS B2N 5E3
902/893-6600; Fax: 902/897-9399
URL: gopher://gopher.nsac.ns.ca
Principal, Dr. H.G. Coffin
Agricultural engineering, pre-veterinary program, technical & technology training, continuing & distance education

### SCOTIA CAREER ACADEMY

503 Sackville Dr., Lower Sackville NS B4C 2S1
902/865-8283; Fax: 902/865-0285
Work related programs

## INDEPENDENT & PRIVATE SCHOOLS

**Schools with enrollment of 50 or more, listed alphabetically by city.**

Cambridge Station: Kings County Christian School, 6185 Hwy. #1, Cambridge Station NS B0P 1G0 – 902/679-6641 – Principal, Barbara C. Billings – *66 – Gr. Pre.-9

Halifax: Armbrae Academy, 1400 Oxford St., Halifax NS B3H 3Y8 – 902/423-7920 – Principal, Eric T. MacKnight – *207 – Gr. Pre.-12

Halifax: Dalhousie Cooperative School, 5846 South St., Bldg. 5, Halifax NS B3H 1S6 – 902/423-9777 – Principal, Molly Hurd – *51 – Gr. Pre.-5

Halifax Grammar School, 5750 Atlantic St., Halifax NS B3H 1G9 – 902/422-6497 – Principal, John A. Messenger – *313 – Gr. Pre.-12

Halifax: Maritime Muslim Academy, 6225 Chebucto Rd., Halifax NS B3L 1K7 – 902/429-9067 – Principal, Iffat S. Akhtar – *89 – Gr. Pre.-10; Islamic studies; Arabic language

Halifax: Sacred Heart School of Halifax, 5820 Spring Garden Rd., Halifax NS B3H 1X8 – 902/423-1358 – Principal, Joan Dormington – *410 – Gr. Pre.-12

Halifax: Shambhala Middle School, 5450 Russell St., Halifax NS B3K 1W9 – 902/454-6100 – Principal, Jane Hester – *50 – Gr. 6-12

Sydney Mines: Northside Christian Academy, 302 Main St., Sydney Mines NS B1V 2M6 – 902/736-6465 – Principal, Pastor Blair Bridle – *82 – Gr. Pre.-12

Timberlea: Halifax Christian Academy, 2020 St. Margaret's Bay Rd., Timberlea NS B3T 1C3 – 902/876-8497 – Principal, Joan Dennis – *248 – Gr. Pre.-12

Truro: Colchester Christian Academy, 15 Elm St., PO Box 393, Truro NS B2N 5C5 – 902/895-6520 – Principal, Colin Murphy – *145 – Gr. Pre.-12

Tusket: Living Waters Christian Academy, PO Box 175, Tusket NS B0W 3M0 – 902/648-2676 – Principal, Mardee Nickerson – *79 – Gr. Pre.-9

Windsor: Kings-Edgehill School, 254 College Rd., Windsor NS B0N 2T0 – 902/798-2278 – Principal, David R. Penaluna – *259 – Gr. 6-12

# ONTARIO

## Ministry of Education & Training

Mowat Block, 90 Bay St., Toronto ON M7A 1L2
416/325-2929; Fax: 416/325-2934; Toll Free: 1-800-387-5514

### ELEMENTARY/SECONDARY OPERATIONS & FRENCH LANGUAGE EDUCATION

Director, French Language Education Policy & Programs, Richard Gauthier, 416/325-2127

### ELEMENTARY/SECONDARY POLICY DIVISION

Director, Policy Branch, Marjorie Mercer, 416/325-2659

### DISTRICT OFFICES

Barrie: 20 Rose St., 2nd Fl., Barrie ON L4M 2T2 – 705/725-7625; 1-800-470-1147 – Manager, Michel Robineau

Greater Toronto: #360, 700 Lawrence Ave. West, 3rd Fl., Toronto ON M6A 1B4 – 416/256-2903; Fax: 416/256-2904 – Director, Richard Admans

Kitchener-Waterloo: 30 Duke St., 9th Fl., Kitchener-Waterloo ON N2H 3W5 – 519/571-6134; Fax: 519/571-6148; 1-800-909-6550 – Manager, Norah Franklin

London: 759 Hyde Park Rd., London ON N6H 3S6 – 519/472-1440; Fax: 519/472-6178 – Manager, Terry Boucher

Metro Toronto: Mowat Block, 900 Bay St., 15th Fl., Toronto ON M7A 1L2 – 416/314-8679; Fax: 416/325-6793 – Manager, Denese Belchetz

North Bay/Sudbury: 447 McKeown Ave., PO Box 3020, North Bay ON P1B 8K7 – 705/474-7210; Fax: 705/494-4075 – Manager, Lise Presseault

Ottawa: 1580 Merivale Rd., 4th Fl., Nepean ON K2G 4B5 – 613/225-9210; Fax: 613/225-2881 – Manager, Maurice Poirier

Thunder Bay: #111, 435 James St. South, PO Box 5000, Thunder Bay ON P7C 5G6 – 807/475-1571; Fax: 807/475-1571 – Manager, Jacqueline Dojack

**For detailed departmental listings, see Index: "Education, Depts."**

## AMALGAMATED DISTRICT SCHOOL BOARDS & SCHOOL AUTHORITIES (IN EFFECT 1998)

The following outlines the planned board amalgamation for the Province of Ontario, which is slated to come into effect January 19, 1998. The current school boards are to be amalgamated into 72 district boards. New district boards are listed below, with the current boards they are replacing. Current school boards follow the list of amalgamated boards (p. 9-28).

### Northern Ontario English-Language Public District School Boards

1: Hearst; Kapuskasing-Smooth Rock Falls; Cochrane, Iroquois Falls/Black River, Matheson; Timmins; Kirkland Lake; Timiskaming
2: Chapleau; Michipicoten; Sault Ste. Marie; Central Algoma; North Shore; Hornepayne
3: Sudbury; Espanola; Manitoulin
4: Nipissing; East Parry Sound; West Parry Sound
5A: Kenora; Red Lake; Dryden
5B: Atikokan; Fort Frances-Rainy River
6A: Lakehead
6B: Beardmore, Geraldton, Longlac; Nipigon-Red Rock; Lake Superior

### Southern Ontario English-Language Public District School Boards

7: Bruce; Grey
8: Huron; Perth
9: Windsor; Essex
10: Kent; Lambton
11: London; Middlesex; Elgin; Oxford
12: North York; Scarborough; Etobicoke; Toronto, York, East York
13: Durham (excluding Clarington)
14: Northumberland & Clarington; Peterborough
15: Victoria; Haliburton; Muskoka
16: York Region
17: Simcoe
18: Wellington; Dufferin
19: Peel
20: Halton
21: Hamilton; Wentworth
22: Lincoln; Niagara South
23: Haldimand; Norfolk; Brant
24: Waterloo
25: Ottawa; Carleton
26: Lanark; Leeds & Grenville; Prescott & Russell; Stormont Dundas & Glengarry
27: Lennox & Addington; Frontenac
28: Renfrew
29: Prince Edward; Hastings

* indicates enrollment figure.

**Northern Ontario English-Language Separate District School Boards**

30A: Hearst; Kapuskasing; Cochrane Iroquois Falls/Black River Matheson; Timmins; Kapuskasing; Kirkland Lake-Timiskaming
30B: Nippissing
31: Sault Ste. Marie; Chapleau; Michipicoten; North Shore
32: Sudbury
33A: Fort Frances-Rainy River; Dryden
33B: Kenora
34A: Geraldton; North of Superior
34B: Lakehead

**Southern Ontario English-Language Separate District School Boards**

35: Bruce-Grey
36: Huron-Perth
37: Windsor; Essex
38: London & Middlesex; Elgin; Oxford
39: Kent; Lambton
40: Metropolitan Separate
41: Peterborough Victoria Northumberland & Clarington
42: York Region
43: Dufferin-Peel
44: Simcoe including District Municipality of Muskoka
45: Durham (excluding Clarington)
46: Halton
47: Hamilton-Wentworth
48: Wellington
49: Waterloo
50: Lincoln; Welland
51: Haldimand-Norfolk; Brant
52: Lanark Leeds & Grenville; Prescott & Russell; Stormont Dundas & Glengarry
53: Ottawa; Carleton
54: Renfrew
55: Hastings-Prince Edward; Frontenac-Lennox & Addington;

**Ontario French-Language Public District School Boards**

56: Kapuskasing-Smooth Rock Falls; Hearst; Cochrane Iroquois Falls/Black River Matheson; Hornepayne; Kirkland Lake; Timiskaming; Timmins; Nipissing; East Parry Sound; West Parry Sound; Muskoka
57: Chapleau; Michipocoten; Sudbury; Sault Ste Marie; Central Algoma; North Shore; Espanola; Manitoulin; Kenora; Red Lake; Dryden; Atikokan; Fort Frances-Rainy River; Nipigon-Red Rock; Lake Superior; Lakehead; Geraldton
58: Bruce; Grey; Huron; Perth; Windsor; Essex; Kent; Lambton; London; Middlesex; Elgin; Oxford, Dufferin; Peel; Halton; Hamilton; Wentworth; Lincoln; Niagara South; Haldimand; Norfolk; Brant; Waterloo; Wellington; North York; Scarborough; Etobicoke; Toronto; Toronto (Conseil); York; East York; Northumberland-Clarington; Peterborough; Victoria; Haliburton; Durham; York Region; Simcoe
59: Ottawa-Carleton; Lanark; Leeds & Grenville; Lennox & Addington; Frontenac; Renfrew; Prescott & Russell; Stormont Dundas & Glengarry; Prince Edward; Hastings

**Ontario French-Language Separate District School Boards**

60A: Timmins; Kirkland Lake-Timiskaming; Hearst; Cochrane Iroquois Falls/Black River Matheson; Kapuskasing
60B: Nipissing
61: Michipicoten; Sault Ste Marie; North Shore; Sudbury; Chapleau
62: Fort Frances-Rainy River; Geraldton; North of Superior; Kenora; Dryden; Lakehead
63: Bruce-Grey; Huron-Perth; Windsor; Essex; London & Middlesex; Elgin; Oxford; Kent; Lambton
64: Halton; Hamilton-Wentworth; Wellington; Waterloo; Lincoln; Welland; Haldimand-Norfolk; Brant; Dufferin-Peel; Metropolitan Separate; Peterborough Victoria Northumberland-Clarington; York Region; Simcoe; Muskoka; Durham
65: Prescott & Russell; Stormont Dundas & Glengarry
66: Ottawa-Carleton; Lanark Leeds & Grenville; Renfrew; Hastings-Prince Edward; Frontenac-Lennox & Addington

**School Authorities (Previously Isolate & Hospital Boards)**

1: Airy and Sabine DSA Board
2: Asquith-Garvey DSA Board
3: Atikokan RCSSB
4: Caramat DSA Board
5: Cardiff-Bicroft Combined RCSSB
6: Collins DSA Board
7: Connell and Ponsford DSA Board
8: Dubreuilville RCSSB
9: Foleyet RCSSB
10: Foleyet DSA Board
11: Gogama DSA Board
12: Gogama RCSSB
13: Hornepayne RCSSB
14: Ignace RCSSB
15: James Bay Lowlands Secondary School Board
16: Kashabowie DSA Board
17: Kilkenny DSA Board
18: Mine Centre DSA Board
19: Missarenda DSA Board
20: Moose Factory Island DSA Board
21: Moosonee RCSSB
22: Moosonee DSA Board
23: Murchison and Lyell DSA Board
24: Nakina DSA Board
25: Northern DSA Board
26: Parry Sound RCSSB
27: Penetanguishene Protestant Separate School Board
28: Red Lake Area Combined RCSSB
29: Sturgeon Lake DSA Board
30: Summer Beaver DSA Board
31: Upsala DSA Board
32: Niagara Peninsula Crippled Children's Treatment Centre
33: Hugh MacMillan Centre
34: Campbell Children's School
35: Waterloo North Children's Centre
36: Essex County Children's Rehabilitation Centre
37: Ottawa Children's Treatment Centre

## PUBLIC SCHOOL BOARDS

**Boards with an enrollment of more than 20,000 are in bold print.**

Atikokan Board of Education – *677
110 Clark St., Atikokan ON P0T 1C0
807/597-6941; Fax: 807/597-6935 – Chair, Judy Eluik; Dir., Wayne McAndrew

Beardmore, Geraldton, Longlac & Area Board of Education – *963
PO Box 909, Geraldton ON P0T 1M0
807/854-1470; Fax: 807/854-1148 – Chair, Stephanie Drajanoff; Dir., Joe Virdiramo

Brant County Board of Education – *16,831
349 Erie Ave., Brantford ON N3T 5V3
519/756-6301; Fax: 519/756-9181 – Chair, Frank Borghoff; Dir., Peter Moffatt

Bruce County Board of Education – *11,430
PO Box 190, Chesley ON N0G 1L0
519/363-2014; Fax: 519/363-3448 – Chair, Jennifer Yenssen; Dir., Paul Martindale

**Carleton Board of Education**
133 Greenbank Rd., Nepean ON K2H 6L3
613/721-1820; Fax: 613/820-6968
*45,003
Chair, Ann MacGregor
Dir., E. Kyle Murray

Central Algoma Board of Education – *2,064
PO Box 10, Richards Landing ON P0R 1J0
705/246-2441; Fax: 705/246-2151 – Chair, Lorraine Aelick; Dir., Melvin L. Baird

Chapleau Board of Education – *459
31 Birch St. East, PO Box 220, Chapleau ON P0M 1K0
705/864-1750; Fax: 705/864-0518 – Secretary, Claire Lavoie; Chair, Earle Freeborn

Cochrane/Iroquois Falls/Black River Matheson Board of Education – *2,051
457 Zealand Ave., PO Box 820, Iroquois Falls ON P0K 1G0
705/232-4015; Fax: 705/232-5450 – Chair, Patricia Toffolo; Dir., Craig Shelswell

Dryden Board of Education – *4,084
Lower Level, 79 Casimir Ave., Dryden ON P8N 2Z6
807/223-5311; Fax: 807/223-4703 – Chair, David Penney; Dir., Murray McFayden

Dufferin County Board of Education – *8,636
40 Amelia St., Orangeville ON L9W 3T8
519/941-6191; Fax: 519/942-2450 – Chair, James McGregor; Dir., Grant Evans

**Durham Board of Education**
400 Taunton Rd. East, Whitby ON L4R 2K6
905/666-5500; Fax: 905/576-1457
*60,692
Chair, Ruth Schedlich
Dir., Grant C. Yeo

East Parry Sound Board of Education – *3,770
24-26 Marie St., PO Box 40, South River ON P0A 1X0
705/386-2387; Fax: 705/386-0670 – Chair, Randy Evers; Dir., Beverley Moore

East York, Board of Education for the Borough of – *16,099
840 Coxwell Ave., Toronto ON M4C 2V3
416/396-2000; Fax: 416/461-7356 – Chair, Gail Nyberg; Dir., Rod Thompson

Elgin County Board of Education – *13,661
400 Sunset Dr., St. Thomas ON N5R 3C8
519/633-2700; Fax: 519/633-1622 – Chair, Karl Buczkowski; Dir., Walter Demra

Espanola Board of Education – *1,756
210 Mead Blvd., PO Box 429, Espanola ON P0P 1C0
705/869-3103; Fax: 705/869-5304 – Chair, Normand Gagne; Dir., Michael Lewis

Essex County Board of Education – *17,571
Essex County Civic & Education Centre, 360 Fairview Ave. West, Essex ON N8M 1Y4
519/776-6421; Fax: 519/776-4457 – Chair, Joan Flood; Dir., Paul de Sadeleer

**Etobicoke, Board of Education for the City of**
1 Civic Centre Court, Etobicoke ON M9C 2B3
416/394-7000; Fax: 416/394-7397
*38,022
Chair, Kathy Haas
Dir., Bill McIntosh

Fort Frances-Rainy River Board of Education – *3,313
522 Second St. East, Fort Frances ON P9A 1N4
807/274-9855; Fax: 807/274-5078 – Chair, Wilma Sletmoen; Dir., John McLeod

**Frontenac County Board of Education**
220 Portsmouth Ave., PO Box 610, Kingston ON K7L 4X4
613/544-6920; Fax: 613/544-6804
*20,150
Chair, Ross Drummond
Dir., Barry C. O'Connor

Grey County Board of Education – *14,518
55 Victoria St., PO Box 100, Markdale ON N0C 1H0
519/986-3410; Fax: 519/986-3691 – Chair, Wally Reif; Dir., Janet Glasspool

Haldimand Board of Education – *7,812
#72, Hwy. 54, PO Box 2000, Cayuga ON N0A 1E0

905/772-3391; Fax: 905/772-3878 – Chair, Arlene Everetts; Dir., Frank J. Kelly
Haliburton County Board of Education – *2,484
PO Box 507, Haliburton ON K0M 1S0
705/457-1980; Fax: 705/457-3040 – Chair, Cheryl Murdoch; Dir., Alexander Saunders
**Halton Board of Education**
2050 Guelph Line, PO Box 5005, Burlington ON L7R 3Z2
905/335-3663; Fax: 905/335-9802
*43,816
Chair, Linda Glover
Dir., Bob Williams
**Hamilton, Board of Education for the City of**
100 Main St. West, PO Box 2558, Hamilton ON L8N 3L1
905/527-5092; Fax: 905/521-2539
*40,868
Chair, Margaret Cunningham
Dir., Merv Matier
Hastings County Board of Education – *18,144
Education Centre, 156 Ann St., Belleville ON K8N 1N9
613/966-1170; Fax: 613/966-0939 – Chair, Ernest Parsons; Dir., Philip Ainsworth
Hearst Board of Education – *346
923 Edward St., PO Box 7000, Hearst ON P0L 1N0
705/372-1459; Fax: 705/362-8093 – Secretary, John Siska; Chair, Ruby Brunet
Hornepayne Board of Education – *232
PO Box 69, Hornepayne ON P0M 1Z0
807/868-2253; Fax: 807/868-2352 – Secretary, Janice Beatty; Chair, Carol Ann Latoski
Huron County Board of Education – *10,257
103 Albert St., Clinton ON N0M 1L0
519/482-3496; Fax: 519/482-7358 – Chair, Allan Carter; Dir., Paul Carroll
Kapuskasing-Smooth Rock Falls & District Board of Education – *783
62 Devonshire Ave., Kapuskasing ON P5N 1C3
705/335-6025; Fax: 705/335-5066 – Chair, Dorothy Enright; Sec., Denis Boyer
Kenora Board of Education – *3,382
100 First Ave. West, Kenora ON P9N 3Z7
807/468-5571; Fax: 807/468-3857 – Chair, Marion Helash; Dir., Patricia Wyder
Kent County Board of Education – *15,384
476 McNaughton Ave. East, PO Box 1000, Chatham ON N7M 5L7
519/354-3770; Fax: 519/354-0662 – Chair, Anne Gilbert; Dir., Wayne Houston
Kirkland Lake Board of Education – *1,824
35 Second St., PO Box 2610, Kirkland Lake ON P2N 3P4
705/567-3271; Fax: 705/568-8503 – Chair, Eileen Miko
Lake Superior Board of Education – *2,478
12 Helmo Dr., PO Bag A, Marathon ON P0T 2E0
807/229-0436; Fax: 807/229-1471 – Chair, Guy Champagne; Dir., Ted Lake
Lakehead Board of Education – *16,694
2135 Sills St., Thunder Bay ON P7E 5T2
807/625-5100; Fax: 807/623-5833 – Chair, Suzan Labine; Dir., Jim McCuaig
Lambton County Board of Education – *18,408
200 Wellington St., PO Box 2019, Sarnia ON N7T 7L2
519/336-1500; Fax: 519/336-0992 – Chair, Ron Orange; Dir., Doug Farrar
Lanark County Board of Education – *10,158
15 Victoria St., Perth ON K7H 2H7
613/267-4210; Fax: 613/267-3860 – Chair, June Timmons; Dir., Gino Giannandrea
Leeds & Grenville County Board of Education – *14,233
25 Central Ave. West, Brockville ON K6V 5X1
613/342-0371; Fax: 613/342-7444 – Chair, Joan Hodge; Dir., David A. Reid
Lennox & Addington County Board of Education – *7,219
264 Camden Rd., PO Box 70, Napanee ON K7R 3M1
613/354-3391; Fax: 613/354-4732 – Chair, John Ibey; Dir., Willis F. Boston
**Lincoln County Board of Education**
191 Carleton St., St. Catharines ON L2R 7P4
905/641-1550; Fax: 905/685-8511
*24,360
Chair, Bill Hodgson
Dir., Willian McLean
**London, Board of Education for the City of**
1250 Dundas St., PO Box 5888, London ON N6A 5L1
519/452-2000; Fax: 519/452-2365
URL: http://www.lbe.edu.on.ca
*47,586
Chair, Heather Wice
Dir., John Laughlin
Manitoulin Board of Education – *1,829
PO Box 489, Little Current ON P0P 1K0
705/368-2860; Fax: 705/368-3811 – Chair, Rob Scott; Dir., Doug M. Hall
**Metropolitan Toronto School Board**
45 York Mills Rd., North York ON M2P 1B6
416/397-2500; Fax: 416/397-2640
Chair, David Moll
Dir., Darrel Skidmore
Michipicoten Board of Education – *845
Winston Rd., PO Box 560, Wawa ON P0S 1K0
705/856-2309; Fax: 705/856-4332 – Chair, Diane Perron; Sec., Frank Springer
Middlesex County Board of Education – *10,657
1980 Hyde Park Rd., London ON N6H 5L9
519/471-3510; Fax: 519/471-1913 – Chair, Donna McImoyle; Dir., Ted D. Anderson
Muskoka Board of Education – *8,553
76 Pine St., Bracebridge ON P1L 1N4
705/645-8704; Fax: 705/645-8452 – Chair, Karen Ellis; Dir., Dusty L.G. Papke
**Niagara South Board of Education**
250 Thorold Rd. West, Welland ON L3C 3W3
905/735-3840; Fax: 905/735-5285
*23,894
Chair, William Ainslie
Dir., William T. Millar
Nipigon-Red Rock Board of Education – *822
Frost St., PO Box 448, Red Rock ON P0T 2P0
807/886-2243; Fax: 807/886-2316 – Chair, Betty P. Chambers; Dir., J.S. Virdiramo
Nipissing Board of Education – *10,328
200 McIntyre St. East, PO Box 3110, North Bay ON P1B 8H1
705/472-8170; Fax: 705/472-9927 – Chair, Kathy Hewitt; Dir., Robert Kennedy
Norfolk Board of Education – *9,664
PO Box 486, Simcoe ON N3Y 4L7
519/428-1880; Fax: 519/428-2484 – Chair, Walter Long; Dir., J.G. Townsend
North Shore Board of Education – *3,684
160 Spruce Ave., Elliot Lake ON P5A 2C5
705/848-3661; Fax: 705/848-9225 – Chair, Robert Whitehead; Dir., Michael J. Lewis
**North York, Board of Education for the City of**
5050 Yonge St., North York ON M2N 5N8
416/395-4661; Fax: 416/225-0297
*66,627
Chair, Gerri Gershon
Dir., Marguerite Jackson
**Northumberland/Clarington Board of Education**
834 D'Arcy St., PO Box 470, Cobourg ON K9A 4L2
905/372-6871; Fax: 905/372-1133
*25,671
Chair, Robert Willsher
Dir., Richard T. Malowney
**Ottawa Board of Education**
330 Gilmour St., Ottawa ON K2P 0P9
613/239-2211; Fax: 613/230-6408
*33,142
Chair, Ted Best
Dir., Carola Lane
Oxford County Board of Education – *15,286
94 Grahman St., PO Box 636, Woodstock ON N4S 7Z8
519/539-4821; Fax: 519/539-1905 – Chair, Graham Hart; Dir., Peter Askey
**Peel Board of Education**
5650 Hurontario St., Mississauga ON L5R 1C6
905/890-1099; Fax: 905/890-1277
*99,461
Chair, Beryl Ford
Dir., Harold M. Brathwaite
Perth County Board of Education – *11,640
210 Water St., Stratford ON N5A 3C5
519/271-0930; Fax: 519/271-2324 – Chair, Wendy Anderson; Dir., A. Paul R. Sherratt
Peterborough County Board of Education – *18,200
150 O'Carroll Ave., PO Box 719, Peterborough ON K9J 7A1
705/743-7431; Fax: 705/743-0341 – Chair, Angela Lloyd; Dir., Len Budden
Prescott & Russell County Board of Education – *4,108
411 Stanley St., Hawkesbury ON K6A 3E8
613/632-0144; Fax: 613/632-0147 – Chair, Colette Brisson-Lacroix; Dir., D.A. Farrow
Prince Edward County Board of Education – *3,434
5 Stanley St. East, PO Box 220, Bloomfield ON K0K 1G0
613/393-3153; Fax: 613/393-2990 – Chair, Sharon Campbell; Dir., Larry L. Langdon
Red Lake Board of Education – *1,232
20 Young St., Red Lake ON P0V 2M0
807/727-2676; Fax: 807/727-3335 – Chair, Richard Smit; Dir., David C. McLeod
Renfrew County Board of Education – *13,565
1270 Pembroke St. West, Pembroke ON K8A 4G4
613/735-0151; Fax: 613/735-6315 – Chair, Lydia Jardine; Dir., Peter W. Hiscott
Sault Ste. Marie Board of Education – *10,983
644 Albert St. East, Sault Ste. Marie ON P6A 2K7
705/945-7111; Fax: 705/942-2540 – Chair, William D. Hall; Dir., R.C. Rosario
**Scarborough, Board of Education for the City of**
Civic Centre, 140 Borough Dr., Scarborough ON M1P 4N6
416/396-7100; Fax: 416/396-4215
*81,696
Chair, Dale Gaye
Dir., Earl Campbell
**Simcoe County Board of Education**
Hwy. 26, Midhurst ON L0L 1X0
705/728-7570; Fax: 705/728-2265
*50,458
Chair, Lynda Murtha
Dir., Terry Lynch
Stormont, Dundas & Glengarry County Board of Education – *13,476
902 Second St. West, Cornwall ON K6H 5S6
613/933-6990; Fax: 613/933-4089 – Chair, Maria Thompson; Dir., J.W. Dilamarter
Sudbury Board of Education – *18,290
Civic Square, West Tower, 5th Fl., 69 Young St., Sudbury ON P3E 3G5
705/674-3171; Fax: 705/647-3167 – Chair, Dr. Doreen Dewar; Dir., Gord Ewin
Timiskaming Board of Education – *3,466
213 Whitewood Ave., PO Box 40, New Liskeard ON P0J 1P0
705/647-7394; Fax: 705/647-9212 – Chair, Juergen Leukert; Dir., Thomas McGrory
Timmins Board of Education – *4,833
153 Third Ave., PO Box 1020, Timmins ON P4N 7H7
705/360-1151; Fax: 705/268-7100 – Chair, George Delich; Dir., John Huggins

* indicates enrollment figure.

**Toronto, Board of Education for the City of**
155 College St., Toronto ON M5T 1P6
416/598-4931; Fax: 416/393-9969
*77,011
Chair, David Moll
Dir., John Davies

Victoria County Board of Education – *11,401
Verulam Rd. South, PO Box 420, Lindsay ON K9V 4S3
705/324-6776; Fax: 705/328-2036 – Chair, Sharon Summers; Dir., Dianne E. Dalton, Ed.D.

**Waterloo County Board of Education**
51 Ardelt Ave., PO Box 68, Kitchener ON N2G 3X5
519/570-0300; Fax: 519/742-1364
*57,205
Chair, Jim G. Wideman
Dir., Patti Haskell

**Wellington County Board of Education**
500 Victoria Rd. North, Guelph ON N1E 6K2
519/822-4420; Fax: 519/822-4487
*25,069
Chair, Jennifer Waterston
Dir., Dr. Martha C. Rogers

Wentworth County Board of Education – *18,438
Memorial Bldg., 357 Wilson St. East, Ancaster ON L9G 4B7
905/523-8621; Fax: 905/648-5583 – Chair, Wallace Bruce; Dir., Allan A. Greenleaf

West Parry Sound Board of Education – *3,188
70 Isabella St., Parry Sound ON P2A 1M6
705/746-9372; Fax: 705/746-7367 – Chair, Sue Woodhouse; Dir., Bradley Burt

Windsor, Board of Education for the City of – *19,892
451 Park St. West, PO Box 210, Windsor ON N9A 6K1
519/255-3200; Fax: 519/255-7053 – Chair, John Bentley; Dir., Mary Jean Gallagher

York, Board of Education for the City of – *18,148
2 Trethewey Dr., Toronto ON M6M 4A8
416/394-2270; Fax: 416/394-3137 – Chair, Sam Wales; Dir., Norman Ahmet

**York Region Board of Education**
60 Wellington St. West, PO Box 40, Aurora ON L4G 3H2
905/969-8131; Fax: 905/727-3984
*77,564
Chair, Bill Crothers
Dir., Bill Hogarth

## COUNTY & DISTRICT COMBINED ROMAN CATHOLIC SEPARATE SCHOOL BOARDS

**Boards with an enrollment of more than 20,000 are in bold print.**

Brant County Roman Catholic Separate School Board – *6,494
322 Fairview Dr., PO Box 217, Brantford ON N3T 5M8
519/756-6369; Fax: 519/756-9913 – Chair, Larry Kings; Dir., Brendan Ryan

Bruce-Grey County Roman Catholic Separate School Board – *4,442
799 - 16 Ave., Hanover ON N4N 3A1
519/364-5820; Fax: 519/364-5882 – Chair, Kenneth Waechter; Dir., Rosemary Kennedy

**Carleton Roman Catholic Separate School Board**
1695 Merivale Rd., Nepean ON K2G 3R4
613/224-2222; Fax: 613/224-5063
*25,090
Chair, June Flynn-Turner
Acting Dir., Philip A. Rocco

Chapleau District Roman Catholic Separate School Board – *390
31 Birch St. East, PO Box 788, Chapleau ON P0M 1K0
705/864-1100; Fax: 705/864-0518 – Secretary, Claire Lavoie; Chair, Keith J. Swanson

Cochrane/Iroquois Falls/Black River Matheson Roman Catholic Separate School Board – *1,525
540, Ste. Hélène St., PO Box 858, Iroquois Falls ON P0K 1G0
705/232-4061; Fax: 705/232-6748 – Chair, Florian Chartier; Dir., Rheal M. Bazinet

Conseil des écoles catholiques de Timmins/Timmins Roman Catholic School Board – *5,827
36 Birch St. South, Timmins ON P4N 2A5
705/267-1421; Fax: 705/267-7247 – Chair, Peter Del Guidice; Dir., Michael Serre

Dryden District Roman Catholic Separate School Board – *785
105 King St., PO Box 781, Dryden ON P8N 2Z4
807/223-4663; Fax: 807/223-4014 – Chair, Frank Bastone; Dir., Paul H. Jackson

**Dufferin-Peel Roman Catholic Separate School Board**
40 Matheson Blvd. West, Mississauga ON L5R 1C5
905/890-1221; Fax: 905/890-7610
*77,521
Chair, James Meany
Dir., Michael Bator

**Durham Region Roman Catholic Separate School Board**
650 Rossland Rd. West, Oshawa ON L1J 7C4
905/576-6150; Fax: 905/576-0953
*26,276
Chair, Tom Oldman
Dir., Grant A. Andrews

Elgin County Roman Catholic Separate School Board – *2,193
21 Parish St., St. Thomas ON N5R 4W7
519/631-8300; Fax: 519/631-1619 – Chair, William Hall; Dir., J.K. Couchman

Essex County Roman Catholic Separate School Board – *15,903
360 Fairview Ave. West, Essex ON N8M 1Y5
519/776-6431; Fax: 519/776-6663 – Chair, Jack Menard; Dir., Brian Bourbean

Fort Frances-Rainy River District Roman Catholic Separate School Board – *713
555 Flinders Ave., Fort Frances ON P9A 3L2
807/274-2931; Fax: 807/274-8792 – Chair, Orielle DeGagne; Dir., Paul Jackson

Frontenac, Lennox & Addington County Roman Catholic Separate School Board – *7,979
84 Stephen St., PO Box 1058, Kingston ON K7L 4Y5
613/544-4927; Fax: 613/544-9616 – Chair, Thomas Foley; Dir., G.T. Cosgrove

Geraldton District Roman Catholic Separate School Board – *569
308 - 4 St. North, PO Box 370, Geraldton ON P0T 1M0
807/854-1421; Fax: 807/854-0446 – Chair, Jack Duhaime; Sec., Guy Legault

Haldimand-Norfolk Roman Catholic Separate School Board – *2,804
55 Park Rd., PO Box 278, Simcoe ON N3Y 4L1
519/426-8370; Fax: 519/426-5333 – Chair, Anthony Bukta; Dir., Denis I. Tschirhart

**Halton Roman Catholic Separate School Board**
802 Drury Lane, PO Box 5308, Burlington ON L7R 3Y2
905/632-6300; Fax: 905/333-4661
*21,757
Chair, Donald Shrenk
Dir., Fred Sweeny

**Hamilton-Wentworth Roman Catholic Separate School Board**
90 Mulberry St., PO Box 2012, Hamilton ON L8N 3R9
905/525-2930; Fax: 905/525-1724
*28,426
Chair, Patrick Daly
Dir., James Daly

Hastings-Prince Edward County Roman Catholic Separate School Board – *5,776
3 Applewood Dr., Belleville ON K8P 4E3
613/966-9210; Fax: 613/966-0204 – Chair, Leona Dombrowsky; Dir., Barbara A. Lynn

Hearst District Roman Catholic Separate School Board – *1,640
923 Edward St., PO Box 1660, Hearst ON P0L 1N0
705/362-4337; Fax: 705/362-8093 – Chair, Rémi Lessard; Dir., Edith Lamontagne

Huron-Perth County Roman Catholic Separate School Board – *4,949
87 Mill St., PO Box 70, Dublin ON N0K 1E0
519/345-2440; Fax: 519/345-2449 – Chair, Michael Miller; Dir., James S. Brown

Kapuskasing District Roman Catholic Separate School Board – *2,705
75 Queen St., Kapuskasing ON P5N 1H5
705/335-6091; Fax: 705/335-8258 – Chair, Louis Veilleux; Dir., André Bordeleau

Kenora District Roman Catholic Separate School Board – *1,272
200 First St. North, Kenora ON P9N 2K4
807/468-9851; Fax: 807/468-8094 – Chair, Paul Landry; Dir., Larry Yaguchi

Kent County Roman Catholic Separate School Board – *7,612
535 Baldoon Rd. North, PO Box 2003, Chatham ON N7M 5L9
519/354-5170; Fax: 519/354-4173 – Chair, Emile Michaud; Dir., Sandy J. Easton

Kirkland Lake-Timiskaming District Roman Catholic Separate School Board – *3,254
21 Armstrong St., PO Bag R, New Liskeard ON P0J 1P0
705/647-7304; Fax: 705/647-8410 – Chair, Roger Larocque; Dir., Paul St-Cyr

Lakehead District Roman Catholic Separate School Board – *9,060
212 Miles St. East, Thunder Bay ON P7C 4Y5
807/625-1555; Fax: 807/623-0431 – Chair, Joleene Kemp; Dir., Kevin Debnam

Lambton County Roman Catholic Separate School Board – *8,025
430 Christina St. South, Sarnia ON N7T 2N8
519/336-6139; Fax: 519/336-5160 – Chair, Daniel Barry; Dir., John F. Ross

Lanark, Leeds & Grenville County Roman Catholic Separate School Board – *6,323
PO Box 427, Smiths Falls ON K7A 4T4
613/283-5007; Fax: 613/283-2782 – Chair, Michel Ringuette; Dir., Frank B. Musca

Lincoln County Roman Catholic Separate School Board – *10,285
80 Grantham Ave., St Catharines ON L2P 3H1
905/682-8354; Fax: 905/682-0012 – Chair, Lorna Constantin; Dir., John Dickhoot

London & Middlesex Roman Catholic Separate School Board – *17,616
165 Elmwood Ave. East, PO Box 5474, London ON N6A 4X5
519/663-2088; Fax: 519/663-9250 – Chair, Paul Whitehead; Dir., Patrick J. Dunne

**Metropolitan Separate School Board**
80 Sheppard Ave. East, Toronto ON M2N 6E8
416/222-8282; Fax: 416/229-5345
*106,169
Chair, Edward McMahon
Dir., Norman Forma

Michipicoten District Roman Catholic Separate School Board – *527
PO Box 560, Wawa ON POS 1KO
705/856-2309; Fax: 705/856-4332 – Chair, Roland Boudreau; Sec., Franklin Springer

Nipissing District Roman Catholic Separate School Board – *8,775
1140 Front St., North Bay ON P1B 6P2
705/472-1520; Fax: 705/472-9398 – Chair, Robert Lucenti; Dir., Brian D. Giroux

North Shore District Roman Catholic Separate School Board – *1,930
8 Woodward Ave., PO Box 460, Blind River ON P0R 1B0
705/356-2223; Fax: 705/356-2563 – Chair, Robert Gallagher

North of Superior District Roman Catholic Separate School Board – *1,028
13 Simcoe Plaza, PO Box 610, Terrace Bay ON POT 2WO
807/825-3209; Fax: 807/825-3885 – Chair, Paul Paradis; Dir., Carole Weir

Ottawa Roman Catholic Separate School Board – *11,274
140 Cumberland St., Ottawa ON K1N 7G9
613/241-5660; Fax: 613/241-2597 – Chair, Jim Kennelly; Dir., W. Dennis Nolan

Oxford County Roman Catholic Separate School Board – *3,044
912 Dundas St., PO Box 97, Woodstock ON N4S 7W5
519/539-4877; Fax: 519/539-1732 – Chair, Lucie Guillemette; Dir., Robert Gutcher

Peterborough-Victoria-Northumberland & Clarington Roman Catholic Separate School Board – *12,730
459 Reid St., Peterborough ON K9H 4G7
705/748-4861; Fax: 705/748-9734 – Chair, James Pilkington; Dir., Donald Folz

Prescott & Russell County Roman Catholic Separate School Board (English Language) – *1,545
1031 Concession St., Russell ON K6A 2E8
613/445-1406; Fax: 613/445-1408 – Chair, Peter Kehoe; Dir., William Crossan

Renfrew County Roman Catholic Separate School Board – *6,269
499 Pembroke St. West, Pembroke ON K8A 5P1
613/735-1031; Fax: 613/735-2649 – Chair, Norma Valiquette; Dir., J.E. Stunt

Sault Ste. Marie District Roman Catholic Separate School Board – *6,855
90 Ontario Ave., Sault Ste. Marie ON P6B 6G7
705/949-5400; Fax: 705/949-4503 – Chair, Jean-Louis Lemieux; Dir., William Struk

Simcoe County Roman Catholic Separate School Board – *18,660
46 Alliance Blvd., Barrie ON L4M 5K3
705/722-3555; Fax: 705/722-6534 – Chair, Gill Robert; Dir., M.J. Obee

Stormont, Dundas & Glengarry County Roman Catholic Separate School Board – *10,050
835 Campbell St., PO Box 130, Cornwall ON K6H 5S8
613/933-1720; Fax: 613/933-5127 – Chair, Michel Pilon; Dir., Roger Davidson

Sudbury District Roman Catholic Separate School Board – *17,243
201 Jogues St., Sudbury ON P3C 5L7
705/673-5621; Fax: 705/673-9160 – Chair, Louie De Longhi; Dir., Léo Lefebvre

**Waterloo Region Roman Catholic Separate School Board**
91 Moore Ave., PO Box 1116, Kitchener ON N2G 4G2
519/578-3660; Fax: 519/578-5291
URL: http://www.watrc.edu.on.ca
*23,787
Chair, Elizabeth. Kreager
Dir., Dr. William A. Brown

Welland County Roman Catholic Separate School Board – *15,053
427 Rice Rd., Welland ON L3C 7C1
905/735-0240; Fax: 905/735-8807 – Chair, Arlene Atherton; Dir., Angelo Di Ianni

Wellington County Roman Catholic Separate School Board – *7,434
75 Woolwich St., PO Box 1298, Guelph ON N1H 6N6
519/821-4600; Fax: 519/824-3088 – Chair, Rocco Furfaro; Dir., John A. Wheatley

Windsor Roman Catholic Separate School Board – *16,475
1485 Janette Ave., Windsor ON N8X 1Z2
519/253-2481; Fax: 519/253-8397 – Chair, Michael Benzinger; Dir., James Molnar

**York Region Roman Catholic Separate School Board**
320 Bloomington Rd. West, Aurora ON L4G 3G8
905/713-2711; Fax: 905/713-1261
*44,050
Chair, Tina Molinari
Dir., F.S. Bobesich

## ROMAN CATHOLIC SEPARATE SCHOOL BOARDS

Atikokan Roman Catholic Separate School Board – *265
120 Marks St., Atikokan ON P0T 1C0
807/597-6748; Fax: 807/597-1209 – Chair, E.A. Morrissette; Sec., Teresa Larson

Cardiff-Bicroft Combined Roman Catholic Separate School Board
c/o Hastings-Prince Edward County R.C.S.S. Board, 3 Applewood Dr., Belleville ON K8P 4E3
613/966-9210; Fax: 613/966-0204 – Chair, Kelly Krick; Sec., B. Casey

Dubreuilville Roman Catholic Separate School Board – *158
1, av du Parc, PO Box 69, Dubreuilville ON P0S 1B0
705/884-2309 – Chair, Nicole Bergeron; Sec., Daniel Martin

Foleyet Roman Catholic Separate School Board – *35
52 Theodore Pl., Timmins ON P4N 7P6
705/267-3521; Fax: 705/899-2682 – Chair, Suzanne Roch; Sec., Lisa Cote

Gogama Roman Catholic Separate School Board – *54
PO Box 70, Gogama ON P0M 1W0
705/894-2775; Fax: 705/894-2866 – Chair, Richard Duguay; Sec., Therese Talbot

Hornepayne Roman Catholic Separate School Board – *85
5 High St., PO Box 430, Hornepayne ON P0M 1Z0
807/868-2010; Fax: 807/868-3026 – Chair, C. MacEachern; Sec., Julie Roy

Ignace Roman Catholic Separate School Board – *44
Hwy. 17, PO Box 930, Ignace ON P0T 1T0
807/934-6426; Fax: 807/934-6282 – Chair, Doris Therrien; Sec., Christiane Leroux

Moosonee Roman Catholic Separate School Board – *140
PO Box 340, Moosonee ON P0L 1Y0
705/336-2605; Fax: 705/336-2881 – Chair, Annie Okimawinew

Parry Sound Roman Catholic Separate School Board – *129
#203, 60 James St., Parry Sound ON P2A 1T5
705/746-6231; Fax: 705/746-7568 – Chair, Peter Cowans; Sec., Constance Peltomaki

Red Lake Area Combined Roman Catholic Separate School Board – *134
48 Discovery Rd., PO Box 888, Red Lake ON P0V 2M0
807/727-3470; Fax: 807/727-3211 – Chair, Teresa Van Dusen; Sec., Nora Kolmel

## SECONDARY SCHOOL BOARDS

James Bay Lowlands Secondary School Board – *285
Keewatin Dr., PO Box 157, Moosonee ON P0L 1Y0
705/336-2903; Fax: 705/336-2170 – Chair, Ivor Jones

## DISTRICT SCHOOL AREA BOARDS (PUBLIC SCHOOLS)

Airy & Sabine District School Area Board – *34
PO Box 190, Whitney ON K0J 2M0
613/637-2019; Fax: 613/637-2019 – Sec., Angela Darragh

Asquith-Garvey District School Area Board – *19
General Delivery, Shining Tree ON P0M 2X0
705/263-2847; Fax: 705/263-2009 – Sec., Sue Evans

Caramat District School Area Board – *30
PO Box 5, Caramat ON P0T 1J0
807/872-2645; Fax: 807/872-2683 – Chair, Armand Giguere

Collins District School Area Board – *12
General Delivery, Collins ON P0V 1M0
807/583-2593; Fax: 807/475-6945 – Chair, Mike Yellowhead

Connell & Ponsford District School Area Board – *98
8 Dickenson Dr., PO Box 280, Pickle Lake ON P0V 3A0
807/928-2952; Fax: 807/928-2144 – Chair, George Seaton

Foleyet District School Area Board – *25
PO Box 100, Foleyet ON P0M 1T0
705/899-2942; Fax: 705/899-2950 – Chair, G. Bromley

Gogama District School Area Board – *16
PO Box 11, Gogama ON P0M 1W0
705/894-2445; Fax: 705/894-2353 – Chair, Donna Cloutier

Kashabowie District School Area Board
Kashabowie ON P0T 1Y0
807/926-2471; Fax: 807/926-2335 – Chair, I. Mayo

Kilkenny District School Area Board – *36
411 Morse St., Thunder Bay ON P7A 1G7
807/683-3949 – Chair, A. Adams

Mine Centre District Area School Board – *93
PO Box 128, Mine Centre ON P0W 1H0
807/599-2836; Fax: 807/599-2815 – Chair, Donald A. Hyatt

Missarenda District School Area Board – *9
PO Box 62, Missanabie ON P0M 2H0
705/234-2820; Fax: 705/234-2567 – Chair, Bill Castagne

Moose Factory Island District School Area Board – *512
PO Box 160, Moose Factory ON P0L 1W0
705/658-4571; Fax: 705/658-4768 – Chair, Randy Kapashesit

Moosonee District School Area Board – *378
PO Box 398, Moosonee ON P0L 1Y0
705/336-2300; Fax: 705/336-2170 – Chair, Jackie Spindloe

Murchison & Lyell District School Area Board – *24
PO Box 39, Madawaska ON K0J 2C0
613/637-5592; Fax: 613/637-2052 – Chair, Jill Bresnahan

Nakina District School Area Board – *94
59 Algoma St., PO Box 330, Nakina ON P0T 2H0
807/329-5257; Fax: 807/329-5207 – Chair, T. Swanson

Northern District School Area Board – *129
PO Box 98, Armstrong ON P0T 1A0
807/583-2010; Fax: 807/583-2614 – Chair, Richard Koski

Slate Falls District School Area Board – *42
405 Isabella St. West, Thunder Bay ON P7E 5E5
807/475-6989; Fax: 807/475-6945 – Chair, Elsie Sakakeesic

Sturgeon Lake District School Area Board
PO Box 660, Ignace ON P0T 1T0
807/934-6932; Fax: 807/475-6945 – Chair, Carol Groves

Summer Beaver District School Area Board – *104
Summer Beaver ON P0T 3B0
807/593-2210; Fax: 807/593-2198 – Chair, Loretta Wabasse

Umfreville District School Area Board
405 Isabella St. West, Thunder Bay ON P7E 5E5
807/475-6989; Fax: 807/475-6945 – Chair, Art Gouriluk

* indicates enrollment figure.

Upsala District School Area Board – *30
General Delivery, Upsala ON P0T 2Y0
807/986-2207; Fax: 807/986-2206 – Chair, Hank Kenuck

## PROTESTANT SEPARATE SCHOOL BOARDS

Penetanguishene Protestant Separate School Board – *235
PO Box 970, Penetanguishene ON L0K 1P0
705/549-6422; Fax: 705/549-2768 – Chair, Lynne Cousens; Sec., Sally J. Baker

## HOSPITALS & TREATMENT CENTRE SCHOOL BOARDS

Campbell Children's School Board of Education, 600 Townline Rd. South, Oshawa ON L1H 7K6 – 905/576-8403; Fax: 905/728-2961 – Chair, K.V. Peacock – *21

Essex County Children's Rehabilitation Centre Board of Education, 3945 Matchette Rd., Windsor ON N9C 4C2 – 519/252-7281; Fax: 519/252-5873 – Chair, Arla Peters – *38

Hugh MacMillan Centre Board of Education, 350 Rumsey Rd., Toronto ON M4G 1R8 – 416/424-3831; Fax: 416/425-6591 – Chair, G. Wilson – *88

Niagara Peninsula Children's Centre Board of Education, 567 Glenridge Ave., PO Box 1454, Fonthill ON L0S 1E0 – 905/688-3550; Fax: 905/688-1055 – Chair, Lee Gage – *79

Ottawa Children's Treatment Centre Board of Education, 395 Smyth Rd., Ottawa ON K1H 8L2 – 613/737-0871; Fax: 613/738-4304 – Dir., Ruth Koch-Schulte – *25

Waterloo North Children's Centre Board of Education, 500 Hallmark Dr., Waterloo ON N2K 3P5 – 519/886-8886; Fax: 519/570-2934 – Chair, Rose Douglas – *57

## FRENCH LANGUAGE SCHOOL BOARDS

Conseil des Écoles Catholiques de Langue Française de la Region d'Ottawa-Carleton/Ottawa-Carleton French Catholic School Board – *14,461
4000 Labelle St., Gloucester ON K1J 1A1
613/746-3025; Fax: 613/746-3081 – Chair, Dominic Giroux; Dir., Pierre Filiatrault

Conseil des écoles françaises de la communauté urbaine de Toronto – *1,839
#207, 1 Concorde Gate, North York ON M3C 3N6
416/391-1264; Fax: 416/391-3892 – Chair, Mohammed Brihm; Dir., Alice Ducharme

Conseil des Écoles Publiques d'Ottawa-Carleton/Ottawa-Carleton Public School Board (French) – *6,840
140 Genest St., Vanier ON K1L 7Y9
613/742-8960; Fax: 613/747-3810 – Prés., Denis Chartrand; Dir., Maurice Proulx

Conseil des écoles separées catholiques de langue française de Prescott-Russell – *10,449
875, rte 17, PO Box 570, L'Orignal ON K0B 1K0
613/675-4691; Fax: 613/675-2921 – Prés., Ronald Lalonde; Dir., Denis Vaillancourt

## CANADIAN FORCES BASE SCHOOL BOARDS

CFB Borden Board of Education, Building E-105, CFB Borden, Borden ON L0M 1C0 – 705/423-2172; Fax: 705/423-2367 – Dir., Martin P. Des Roches – *1,443

CFB Trenton Board of Education, CFB Trenton, Astra ON K0K 1B0 – 613/392-9500; Fax: 613/965-7091 – Chair, L.Col. P.A. Tinsley – *690

## SCHOOLS FOR HEARING OR VISUALLY IMPAIRED STUDENTS

The Ernest C. Drury School – *262
255 Ontario St. South, Milton ON L9T 2M5
905/878-2851 – Sec., R. Dodds; Elem., J. Vanderzand

The Robarts School – *115
1090 Highbury Ave., London ON N5Y 4V9
519/453-4400 – C. Barry

The Sir James Whitney School – *92
350 Dundas St. West, Belleville ON K8P 1B2
613/967-2823 – C. Barnes

The W. Ross Macdonald School – *215
350 Brant Ave., Brantford ON N3T 3J9
519/759-0730 – Sec., D.F. Bethune; Elem., C. Hudson

## DEMONSTRATION SCHOOLS FOR CHALLENGED STUDENTS

The Amethyst School, 1090 Highbury Ave., PO Box 7300, London ON N5Y 4V9 – 519/453-4400 – P. Rouble – *41

Centre Jules-Léger, 1495 Heron Rd, Ottawa ON K1V 6A6 – 613/521-4000 – Roger Frappier – *45

Sagonaska School, 350 Dundas St. West, Belleville ON K8P 1B2 – 613/967-2830 – P.G. Healey – *39

Trillium School, 347 Ontario St. South, Milton ON L9T 3X9 – 905/878-8428 – C. Hodder – *40

## FIRST NATION EDUCATION AUTHORITIES

**Listed by Bands, including federal, provincial & First Nations schools.**

Ahkwesasne Mohawk Board of Education, PO Box 819, Cornwall ON K6H 5T7 – 613/575-2934; Fax: 613/575-2289 – Chair, Angela Barnes – *698 – Elem.; 3 schools

Attawapiskat First Nation Education Authority, General Delivery, Attawapiskat ON P0L 1A0 – 705/997-2114, 2232; Fax: 705/997-2357 – Acting Chair, Steve Hookimaw – *540 – Elem./Sec.

Beausoleil First Nation Education Authority, Cedar Point PO, Christian Island ON L0K 1C0 – 705/247-2051; Fax: 705/247-2239 – Chair, Henry Jackson – *122 – Elem.

Big Grassy River Education Authority, General Delivery, Morson ON P0W 1J0 – 807/488-5916; Fax: 807/488-5345 – Dir., Elizabeth Mitchell – *60 – Elem.

Chippewas of Nawash First Nations Board of Education, RR#5, Wiarton ON N0H 2T0 – 519/534-0882; Fax: 519/534-5138 – Dir., Lewis Debassige – *116 – Elem.; 2 schools

Chippewas of Sarnia Education Committee, 978 Tashmoo Ave., Sarnia ON N7T 7H5 – 519/336-8410; Fax: 519/336-0382 – Chair, Patricia Adams – *16 – Elem.

Chippewas of the Thames First Nation Education Board, RR#1, Muncey ON N0L 1Y0 – 519/289-5555; Fax: 519/289-2351 – Dir., Gina McGahey – *215 – Elem.

Constance Lake Education Authority, General Delivery, Calstock Via Hearst ON P0L 1B0 – 705/463-4101; Fax: 705/463-4124 – Dir., Stella Etherington – *100 – Elem.

Deer Lake Education Authority, General Delivery, Deer Lake ON P0V 1N0 – 807/775-2367; Fax: 807/775-2398 – Chair, Amos Rae – *234 – Elem.

Eabametoong First Nation Education Authority, General Delivery, Fort Hope ON P0T 1L0 – 807/242-1305; Fax: 807/242-1313 – Exec. Asst., Victoria Atlookan – *305 – Elem.

Hishkoonikun Education Authority, PO Box 235, Kashechewan ON P0L 1S0 – 705/275-4538; Fax: 705/275-4515 – Dir., Jonathon Solomon – *400 – Elem.

Kingfisher Lake Education Authority, General Delivery, Kingfisher ON P0V 1Z0 – 807/532-2057; Fax: 807/532-2153 – Dir., Solomon Mamakwa – *100 – Elem.

Marten Falls Education Authority, Ogoki Post via Nakina ON P0T 2L0 – 807/349-2509; Fax: 807/349-2511 – Chair, Mel Baxter – *50 – Elem.

Michikan Education Authority, PO Box 89, Bearskin Lake ON P0V 1E0 – 807/363-1011; Fax: 807/363-2519 – Chair, Greta Mosquito – *131 – Elem.

Migisi Sah Gai Gun Education Authority, PO Box 10, Eagle River ON P0V 1S0 – 807/755-5350; Fax: 807/755-5696 – Chair, Jason Danielson – *46 – Elem.

Mishkeegogamang Education Authority, General Delivery, Mishkeegogamang ON P0V 2H0 – 807/928-2284; Fax: 807/928-2382 – Education Coordinator, Ida Mackuck – *230 – Elem./Sec.; 3 schools

Mundo Peetabeck Education Authority, PO Box 31, Fort Albany ON P0L 1H0 – 705/278-3390; Fax: 705/278-1049 – Administrator, Simon Solomon – *168 – Elem.

Muskrat Dam Education Authority, General Delivery, Muskrat Dam ON P0V 3B0 – 807/471-2650; Fax: 807/471-2649 – Dir., Clara Beardy – *47 – Elem./Sec.

Neskantaga Education Authority, PO Box 105, Lansdowne House ON P0T 1Z0 – 807/479-2570; Fax: 807/479-1138 – Chair, Lillian Moonais – *70 – Elem.

North Caribou Lake First Nation Education Office, PO Box 155, Weagamow Lake ON P0V 2Y0 – 807/469-1222, 1254; Fax: 807/469-1351 – Dir., Saul Williams – *145 – Elem.

North Spirit Lake Education Authority, General Delivery, North Spirit Lake ON P0V 2G0 – Elem.

Obishikokaang Education Authority, General Delivery, Lac Seul ON P0V 2A0 – 807/582-3420; Fax: 807/582-3430 – Chair, Karen Ningewance – *84 – Elem./Sec.

Onyota'a:ka Kalthuny Nihtsla Tehatilihutakwas (OKT) Education Authority, RR#2, Southwold ON N0L 2G0 – 519/652-1580, 1582; Fax: 519/652-3219 – Chair, Tracey Antone – *200 – Elem.

Pic River First Nation Education Authority, General Delivery, Heron Bay ON P0T 1R0 – 807/229-1749; Fax: 807/229-1944 – Dir., Cindy Fisher – *95 – Elem.

Pikangikum Education Authority, General Delivery, Pikangikum ON P0V 2L0 – 807/773-1093; Fax: 807/773-1014 – Chair, Charlie Pascal – *542 – Elem./Sec.

Rocky Bay First Nation Education Authority, 71 Macdonald Ave., Macdiarmid ON P0T 2B0 – 807/885-3265; Fax: 807/885-3266 – Adm., Lyla Onakanakis – *34 – Elem.

Sachigo Lake Education Authority, General Delivery, Sachigo Lake ON P0V 2P0 – 807/595-2577; Fax: 807/595-1134 – Education Coordinator, James Chapman – *110 – Elem./Sec.

Sandy Lake Education Authority, PO Box 8, Sandy Lake ON P0V 1V0 – 807/774-1135; Fax: 807/774-1166 – Dir., Peter Goodman – *540 – Elem./Sec.

Shoal Lake Chief & Council: Education Authority, General Delivery, Kejick ON P0X 1E0 – 807/733-2315; Fax: 807/733-3115 – Chair, Tom Campbell – *60 – Elem.

Sineonokway Education Authority, PO Box 33, Kasabonika ON P0V 1Y0 – 807/535-1117; Fax: 807/535-1152 – Chair, Ida Morris – *200

Six Nations of the Grand River, Indian & Northern Affairs, 188 Mohawk St., PO Box 1960, Brantford ON N3T 5W5 – 519/758-2405; Fax: 519/754-0639 – Financial Services, Darryl Hill – *1,145 – Elem.; 5 schools

Tyendinaga Territory, Indian & Northern Affairs Canada, 188 Mohawk St., PO Box 1960, Brantford ON N3T 5W5 – 519/758-2405; Fax: 519/754-0639 – Financial Services, Darryl Hill – *300 – Elem.

Wabigoon Lake Chief & Council: Education Authority, Site 112, PO Box 24, Dinorwic ON P0V 1P0 – 807/938-6684; Fax: 807/938-1166 – Education Counsellor, Richard McIvor – *24 – Elem.

Walpole Island First Nation Board of Education, RR#3, Wallaceburg ON N8A 4K9 – 519/627-0708; Fax: 519/627-8596 – Chair, Donna Day – *363 – Elem.

Wasaho Education Authority, General Delivery, Fort Severn ON P0V 1W0 – 807/478-2572; Fax: 807/478-1103 – Dir., Matthew Kakekaspan – *102 – Elem.
Weenusk First Nation Education Services, PO Box 2, Peawanuck ON P0L 2H0 – 705/473-2527; Fax: 705/473-2528 – Dir., George Hunter – *57 – Elem.
West Bay Board of Education, PO Box 297, West Bay ON P0P 1G0 – 705/377-4988; Fax: 705/377-5080 – Education Coord., Melvina Corbiere – *170 – Elem.
Whitefish Bay: Northwest Angle Education Authority, General Delivery, Pawitik ON P0X 1L0 – 807/226-5710; Fax: 807/226-1066 – Dir., William Bird – *250 – Elem./Sec.
Wikwemikong Board of Education, PO Box 112, Wikwemikong ON P0P 2J0 – 705/859-3122; Fax: 705/859-3851 – Dir., Grace Fox – *462 – Elem.; 2 schools
Wunnumin Lake Education Authority, General Delivery, Wunnumin Lake ON P0V 2Z0 – 807/442-2559; Fax: 807/442-2627 – Dir., Matthew Angees – *110 – Elem.

## UNIVERSITIES

### Brock University

500 Glenridge Ave., St. Catharines ON L2S 3A1
905/688-5550; Fax: 905/688-2789
URL: http://www.brocku.ca
Chancellor, Robert S.K. Welch
President & Vice-Chancellor, David Atkinson
Vice-President, Academic, Susan M. Clark
Vice-President, Administration, Terrence B. Varcoe
Registrar, Lou Ariano
Secretary to the University, Evelyn Janke
Executive Director, Office of External Relations, Grant Dobson

#### FACULTIES WITH DEANS

Business, Ronald McTavish
Education, Terrance Boak
Humanities, John Sivell
Mathematics & Sciences, William H. Cade
Physical Education, Robert Kerr
Social Sciences, William G. Webster
Acting Dean, Student Affairs, David Siegel

### Carleton University

1125 Colonel By Dr., Ottawa ON K1S 5B6
613/520-7400
URL: http://www.carleton.ca; gopher://gopher.carleton.ca
Chancellor, Arthur Kroeger, B.A., M.A.
President & Vice-Chancellor, Richard J. Van Loon, B.Sc., M.A., Ph.D.
Vice-President, Student & Academic Services, Susan Gottheil, B.A., M.A.
Vice-President, Finance & Administration, J.S. Riordon, M.Eng., D.I.C., Ph.D., P.Eng.
Assoc. Vice-President, Finance & Administration, Duncan Watt, M.B.A., P.Eng.
Asst. Vice-President, International, D.R.F. Taylor, M.A., P.G.C.E., Ph.D.
Vice-President, Academic & University Registrar, John W. ApSimon, B.Sc., Ph.D.
Clerk of Senate, Chong Hon Chan, B.Sc., M.A.Sc., Ph.D.
Secretary, Board of Governors, Donald C. McEown, B.A., Dip. Bus. Admin.
Director, University Services, Katherine Main
Director, Finance, Vacant
Controller, Katherine Downs, C.A.
Director, Carleton International, D.R.F. Taylor, M.A., P.G.C.E., Ph.D.
Director, Public Relations & Information, Patrick O'Brien, B.A., D.P.A.
Director, Development & Alumni Relations, Kim McCuaig, B.A., B.P.H.E.
Bookstore Manager, Joe Gosset, B.A.
Purchasing Manager, Ed Kane
Director, Admissions & Academic Records, Victor J. Chapman, B.A., DPA, M.A.
Director, Physical Plant, Vacant

#### FACULTIES WITH DEANS

Arts, G. Stuart Adam, B.J., M.A., Ph.D.
Engineering, Malcolm J. Bibby, Ph.D., P.Eng.
Graduate Studies & Research, Roger C. Blockley, B.A., M.A., Ph.D.
Science, D.R. Gardiner, B.Sc., Ph.D.
Social Sciences, Tom Wilkinson, B.Sc., Ph.D.

#### SCHOOLS WITH DIRECTORS

Architecture, Benjamin Gianni, B.A., M.Arch.
Biochemistry, Peter Buist, B.Sc., Ph.D., M.C.M.
Business, Vinod Kumar, B.Sc., B.Eng., M.Eng., Ph.D., P.Eng.
Canadian Studies, Pat Armstong, B.A., M.A., Ph.D.
Central/East European & Russian-Area Studies, Carl H. McMillan, M.A., Ph.D.
Computer Science, Evangelos Kranakis, B.Sc., Ph.D.
Continuing Education, Bernadette Landry, B.A.
Industrial Design, Martien Leevw, B.Sc., B.I.D., M.B.A.
Journalism & Communications, Peter Johansen, B.A., M.A.
Public Administration, Frances D. Abele, B.A., M.A., Ph.D.
Social Work, Allan Moscovitch, B.A., M.A.
The Norman Paterson School of International Affairs, M.A. Molot, B.A., M.A., Ph.D.

### Lakehead University

955 Oliver Rd., Thunder Bay ON P7B 5E1
807/343-8110; Fax: 807/343-8023
URL: http://www.lakeheadu.ca; gopher://flash.lakeheadu.ca
Chancellor, L.B. Wilson
President, R.G. Rosehart, 807/343-8200; Email: Bob.Rosehart@Lakeheadu.ca
Vice-President, Academic, J. Whitfield
Registrar, P.A. Paularinne, 807/343-8269; Email: Pentti.Paularinne@Lakeheadu.ca
Chief Librarian,, 807/343-8205
Director, Services, E.G. Walsh
Director, Finance, L. A. Miller
Director, Continuing Education, D. Pakulak
Director, Campus Development, J. Podd
Director, Student Services & Community Relations, J. Himmelman, 807/343-8899; Email: Joy.Himmelman@Lakeheadu.ca
Director, Human Resources, F.W. Bragnalo, 807/343-8757; Email: Bill.Bragnalo@Lakeheadu.ca

#### FACULTIES WITH DEANS

Arts & Sciences, J. Gellert
Business Administration, B. Dadgostar
Education, J.D. Bates
Engineering, G. Locker
Forestry, D. Evler
Research & Graduate Studies, C. Nelson

### Laurentian University of Sudbury/Université Laurentienne de Sudbury

Ramsey Lake Rd., Sudbury ON P3E 2C6
705/675-1151; Fax: 705/675-4812
Email: admissions@nickel.laurentian.ca; URL: http://www.laurentian.ca/
Teaching is in French & English. Certain faculties offer parallel programs in both languages.
President, Ross H. Paul, B.A., M.A., Ph.D.
Vice-President, Academic, Geoffrey Tesson, B.Sc., M.A., Ph.D.
Associate Vice-President, Francophone Affairs, Gratien Allaire, B.A., M.A., L.ès.L., Ph.D.
Director, Services, R. Bertoli
Director, Centre for Continuing Education, D. Mayer, M.Sc.
Executive Director, University Advancement, Joyce Garnett, B.Sc., M.L.S.
Registrar, S. Smith, B.Sc.
Director, Division of Physical Education, Sandy Knox, B.A., M.Sc., Ph.D.
Director, Library, L. Bonin, B.A., M.L.S.
Director, Financial Services, Gerry Labelle, B.Comm., CA

#### FACULTIES WITH DEANS

Humanities, Paul Collili, B.A., M.A., Ph.D.
Professional Schools, J. Mount, B.A., B.L.S., M.B.A., Ph.D.
Science & Engineering, Reid R. Keays, B.Sc., Ph.D.
Social Sciences, Robert Segsworth, B.A., M.A., Ph.D.

#### SCHOOLS WITH DIRECTORS

Commerce, Louis Zanibbi, B.Sc., M.B.A., Ph.D., C.M.A., C.D.P.
Education, Elvine Gignac-Pharand, B.Ed., B.A., M.A., Ph.D.
Graduate Studies, Frank Smith, B.Sc., M.Sc., Ph.D.
Human Movement, Michel Guany, M.Sc., Ph.D.
Nursing, Johanne Pomerleau, B.Sc.N., L.L.M .
Social Work, Jean-Marc Bélanger, B.A., M.S.W., M.A.
Sports Administration, G. Zorbas, B.P.H.E., M.A.
Translators & Interpreters, Ronald Henry, B.A., M.A., B.Ed.

#### AFFILIATED COLLEGES

Algoma University College, Sault Ste. Marie ON P6A 2G4 – President, J. Douglas Lawson, B.A.Sc., M.Sc., Ph.D.
Collège Universitaire de Hearst, Hearst ON P0L 1N0 – Recteur, Raymond Tremblay, B.A., B.Sc., M.A.

#### FEDERATED UNIVERSITIES

Huntington University, Ramsey Lake Rd., Sudbury ON P3E 2C6 – 705/673-4126 – Principal, K.G. MacQueen, B.A., B.D., M.A., Ph.D.
Thorneloe University, Ramsey Lake Rd, Sudbury ON P3E 2C6 – 705/673-1730 – Provost & Vice-Chancellor, Donald Thompson, B.A., M.T.S., Ph.D.
University of Sudbury, Ramsey Lake Rd, Sudbury ON P3E 2C6 – 705/673-5661 – President, Jacques Monet, s.j., B.A., Ph.L., M.A., Ph.D., Th.L.

### McMaster University

1280 Main Street West, Hamilton ON L8S 4L8
905/525-9140; Fax: 905/527-0100
URL: http://www.mcmaster.ca; gopher://gopher.mcmaster.ca
Chair, Board of Governors, D.A.S. Ivison
Chancellor, J.H. Taylor
President & Vice-Chancellor & Chair of Senate, Peter George
Vice-President, Administration, A.L. Darling
Provost & Vice-President, Academic, H. Weingarten
Vice-President, Health Sciences, R. Joffe
Vice-President, Research & International Affairs, G.E. Gerber
Acting Assoc. Vice-President, Academic, F.A. Hall
Executive Director, University Advancement, R. Trull
Secretary, Board of Governors, W.B. Frank
Registrar, G. Granger
Asst. Provost, Student Affairs, M.E. Keyes
Secretary of Senate, J.E. Morris
Manager, Bookstore, R.C. Crawford

#### FACULTIES WITH DEANS

Business, D. Conrath
Engineering, M. Shoukri
Health Sciences, R. Joffe
Humanities, D.P.J.E. Simpson
Science, P. Sutherland
Social Sciences, A.J. Harrison

* indicates enrollment figure.

**SCHOOLS WITH DIRECTORS**
Arts & Science Program, B.M. Ferrier
Continuing Education, Dale Schenk
Geography & Geology, F.L. Hall
Graduate Studies, J.C. Weaver
Social Work, J.M. Macintyre

**AFFILIATED COLLEGE**
McMaster Divinity College, Hamilton ON L8S 4L8 – 905/525-9140, ext.24401 – Principal, W.H. Brackney

## Nipissing University
100 College Dr., North Bay ON P1B 8L7
705/474-3450; Fax: 705/474-1947
Chair, Board of Governors, David Euler
President, David Marshall, Email: davem@admin.unipissing.ca
Vice-President, Murray Green, Email: murrayg@admin.unipissing.ca
Executive Director, University Relations, Al Carfagnini, Email: alc@admin.unipissing.ca
Registrar, Denis Lawrence, Email: denisl@admin.unipissing.ca
Executive Director, Library Services, Brian Nettleford, Email: briann@admin.unipissing.ca
Dean, Arts & Science, Ted Chase, Email: tedc@admin.unipissing.ca
Dean, Education, Laverne Smith, Email: lavernes@admin.unipissing.ca

## Queen's University
99 University Ave., Kingston ON K7L 3N6
613/545-2000; Fax: 613/545-6300
URL: http://info.queensu.ca/
Chancellor, Agnes M. Benidickson, O.C., B.A., LL.D.
Vice-Chancellor & Principal, William C. Leggett, B.A., M.Sc., Ph.D., D.Sc., LL.D., F.R.S.C.
Rector, Peter Gallant, B.Sc.(Hons.), M.Sc.
Vice-Principal, Academic, David H. Turpin, B.Sc., Ph.D.
Vice-Principal, Advancement, Florence M. Campbell, B.A.
Vice-Principal, Health Sciences, Duncan G. Sinclair, D.V.M., V.S., M.S.A., Ph.D.
Vice-Principal, Operations & Finance, John Cowan, B.Sc., M.Sc., Ph.D.
Registrar, Vacant
Secretary of the Senate, University & Board, Alison Morgan, B.Com., M.A.
Director, University Communications, Anji Husain, B.A., M.A.
Secretary of the University Council, Catherine Perkins, B.A.
Dean of Women, Pamela Dickey Young, B.A., M.Div., Ph.D.
Director, Purchasing Services, Mike Stefano
Bookstore Manager, James Patterson

**FACULTIES WITH DEANS**
Applied Science, T.J. Harris, B.Sc., M.Eng., Ph.D., P.Eng.
Arts & Science, Leslie Monkman, B.A., M.A., Ph.D.
Education, Rena Upitis, B.A., LL.B., M.Ed., Ed.D.
Law, Donald Carter, B.A., LL.B., B.C.L.

**SCHOOLS WITH DIRECTORS**
Business, Dr. Margaret Northey, B.A., M.A., Ph.D.
Centre for Canada/Asian Studies, Lorna L. Wright, B.A., M.A., P.G.C.E., M.I.M., Ph.D.
Centre for International Relations, Neil MacFarlane
Centre for Resource Studies, Vacant
English,
Graduate Studies, Ronald J. Anderson, B.Sc., Ph.D., P.Eng.
Industrial Relations Centre, Bryan Downie, B.A., M.B.A., Ph.D.
Institute of Intergovernmental Relations, Doug Brown, B.A., M.A.
Medicine, Duncan G. Sinclair, D.V.M., V.S., M.S.A., Ph.D.
Acting Director, Nursing, Shirley Eastbrook, R.N., Ph.D.
Physical & Health Education, J. Gavin Reid, T.D., D.P.E., M.A., Ph.D.
Rehabilitation Therapy, Malcom Peat, B.P.T., M.Sc., Ph.D.
Principal, Theological College, Hallett E. Llewellyn, B.A., B.D., TH.M., Ph.D.

## Royal Military College of Canada/Collège militaire royal du Canada
PO Box 17000, Stn Forces, Kingston ON K7K 7B4
613/541-6000
URL: http://www.rmc.ca/
Commandant, B.Gen. K.C. Hague, C.D.
Principal & Director of Studies, B.J. Plant, O.M.M., C.D.
Director of Cadets, L.Col. J.J.C. Michaud, C.D.
Director of Administration, L.Col. D.J. Southen, C.D.
Registrar, Dr. M.A. Labbe
Protocol & Information Officer, Lt. A.M. Martin

**FACULTIES WITH DEANS**
Academic Services, D.W. Kirk
Arts, R.G. Haycock
Engineering, A.Y. Chikhari
Graduate Studies, W.F. Furter
Science, A.J. Barrett

## Ryerson Polytechnic University
350 Victoria St., Toronto ON M5B 2K3
416/979-5000; Fax: 416/979-5341
Email: inquire@acs.ryerson.ca; URL: http://www.ryerson.ca/
Chair, Board of Governors, Dale Patterson
Vice-Chair, Dan McIntyre
Chancellor, David Crombie
President & Vice-Chancellor, Claude Lajeunesse
Vice-President, Academic, Dennis Mock
Vice-President, Faculty & Staff Affairs, Michael Dewson
Vice-President, Administration, Linda Grayson
Registrar, Keith Alnwick
Executive Director, University Advancement, Bob Crow
Director, Communications, Ian Marlatt
Acting Manager, Purchasing Dept., Wade Pitman
Manager, Bookstore, Peter Brunner
Secretary of the Board of Governors, Ed Valin

**FACULTIES WITH DEANS**
Applied Arts, Ira Levine
Arts, Errol Aspevig
Business, Stanley Heath
Community Services, Judith Sandys
Continuing Education, Marilynn Booth
Engineering & Applied Science, Derek Northwood

## Trent University
PO Box 4800, Peterborough ON K9J 7B8
705/748-1011; Fax: 705/748-1029
URL: http://www.trentu.ca
Chair, Jalynn Bennett, B.A.
Chancellor, Mary May Simon, C.M., LL.D.
Interim President, David C. Smith, C.M., M.A., Ph.D., LL.D., F.R.S.C.
Acting Vice-President, Administration & University Services, John Earnshaw, B.A., M.A., Ph.D.
Interim Vice-President, Academic, David Morrison
Interim Dean, Arts & Science, Colin Taylor, M.A., Ph.D.
Vice-President, Advancement, Susan Mackle, B.A.
Registrar, Paul Thomson, B.A.
Secretary of the Senate, Dianne Choate, B.A.
Master, Peter Robinson College, George Nader, B.A., Ph.D.
Principal, Catharine Parr Traill College, Heather Avery, M.A.
Master, Champlain College, Stephen Brown, M.A., Ph.D., F.S.A.
Principal, Lady Eaton College, Ken Field, B.Mus.Ed., M.L.S.
Master, Otonabee College, Robert Annett, B.Sc., Ph.D.
Acting Associate Dean & Director, Julian Blackburn College, Jackie Tinson, B.A., M.A.
Director, Financial Services, A.A. van Hoeckel
Manager, Purchasing/Accounts Payable, Lorraine Hayes, B.Sc.
Director, Communications, Kathleen Bain, B.A., B.J.
Director, Athletics, P.S.B. Wilson, B.A.
Bookstore Manager, Ralph Colley, B.A.

## University of Guelph
#158, 50 Stone Rd. East, Guelph ON N1G 2W1
519/824-4120; Fax: 519/824-7962
URL: http://www.uoguelph.ca/
Chancellor, The Honourable Lincoln Alexander
President & Vice-Chancellor, M. Rozanski
Provost & Vice-President, Academic, J.L. Campbell
Assoc. Vice-President & Registrar, Academic, C. Rooke
Vice-President, Development & Public Affairs, J.D. Mabley
Assoc. Vice-President, Student Affairs, B. Sullivan
Vice-President, Research, L.P. Milligan
Vice-President, Finance & Administration, N. Sullivan
Chair, D. Dodds
Director, Development & Alumni Affairs, P. Samson
Acting Director, Communication & Public Affairs, S. Webster
Asst. Vice-President, Finance, J.M. Miles
Director, Office of Open Learning, V. Gray

**FACULTIES WITH DEANS/DIRECTORS**
Arts, C. Stewart
Biological Science, R. Sheath
Family & Consumer Studies, M. Nightingale
Ontario Agricultural College, R.J. McLaughlin
Ontario Veterinary College, A.H. Meek
Physical & Engineering Science, R. McCrindle
Social Science, D. Knight

**SCHOOLS WITH DIRECTORS**
Engineering, L. Otten
Hotel & Food Administration, K.M. Haywood
Landscape Architecture, J. Taylor
Rural Planning & Development, J. FitzGibbon

## University of Ottawa/Université d'Ottawa
PO Box 450, Stn A, Ottawa ON K1N 6N5
613/562-5800; Fax: 613/562-5103
URL: http://www.uottawa.ca; gopher://gopher.uottawa.ca
Chancellor, Huguette Labelle, O.C., B.Sc.N.Ed., B.Ed., M.Ed., Ph.D., D.U., LL.D., D.Sc., D.Hum.L.
Rector & Vice-Chancellor, Marcel Hamelin, B.A., L.ès L., D.ès L., M.S.R.C.
Vice-Rector, Academic, Gilles Patry, B.A.Sc., M.A.Sc., Ph.D.
Vice-Rector, Research, Howard Alper, B.Sc., Ph.D., F.R.S.C.
Asst. Vice-Rector, Teaching, Denis Carrier, M.Sc.Com., Dipl.E.S. (sc.pol.), D.U.
Vice-Rector, Resources, Carole Workman., B.Comm., C.A.
Vice-Rector, University Relations & Development, J.M. Beillard, M.A., Ph.D.
Asst. Vice-Rector, Institutional Research & Planning, Joseph Lloyd-Jones, B.A., M.A., M.B.A., Ph.D.
Secretary, Pierre-Yves Boucher, B.A., LL.B., Dipl.E.S.D.
Asst. Vice-Rector, Alumni & Development, Bonnie Morris

Registrar, Henri Wong, B.Sc., M.Sc., Ph.D.
Chief Librarian, Richard Greene, B.A., B.Bibl., M.L.S.
Director General, Student Affairs, Michel Leduc, B.Adm.
Director, Public Relations & Information Services, Hélène Carty, B.A., M.A.
Legal Counsel, Darryl A. Grandbois, B.A., LL.B.

**FACULTIES WITH DEANS**

Administration, Jean-Louis Malouin, B.Comm., M.Sc., Ph.D.
Arts, David Staines, B.A., M.A., Ph D.
Education, Pierre Calvé, B.Péd., M.S., Ph.D.
Engineering, Vacant
Graduate Studies & Research, Joseph-M. De Koninck, B.A., B.A. (Psy.), M.A. (Psy.), Ph.D.
Health Sciences, Denise Alcock, B.Sc.N., M.A.(Ed.), Ph.D.
Law, Civil Law Section, Louis Perret, LL.L., Dipl.E.S.D.
Law, Common Law Section, Sanda Rodgers, B.A., LL.B., B.C.L., LL.M.
Medicine, Peter Walker, M.D., F.R.C.P.C.
Science, Christian Detellier, L.Sc., D.Sc.
Social Sciences, Caroline Andrew, B.A., M.Sc.Soc., Ph.D.

**AFFILIATED UNIVERSITY**

Saint Paul University, 223 Main St., Ottawa ON K1S 1C4 – 613/236-1393 – Rector, Dale Schlitt, O.M.I., S.T.B., S.T.L., M.A., Ph.D.

## University of Toronto

21 King's College Circle, Toronto ON M5S 3J3
416/978-2011
URL: http://www.utoronto.ca/
Chancellor, The Hon. Henry N.R. Jackman
Chair of the Governing Council, Anthony Comper
President, J. Robert S. Prichard
Vice-President & Provost, Adel S. Sedra
Deputy Provost, Carolyn J. Tuohy
Vice-Provost, Paul W. Gooch
Vice-Provost, Derek McCammond
Vice-Provost, Arnold Aberman
Vice-President, Research & International Relations, Heather Munroe-Blum
Vice-President, Administration & Human Resources, Michael G. Finlayson
Vice-President & Chief Development Officer, Jon S. Dellandrea
Chief Financial Officer, Robert G. White
Comptroller, Anthony Pieterse
Acting University Ombudsperson, Irene Birrell
Associate University Registrar, Admissions & Awards, Karel Swift, 416/978-2190; Fax: 416/978-6089; Email: ask@adm.utoronto.ca
Director, Alumni & Development, Rivi Frankle
Director, Public Affairs, Susan Bloch-Nevitte, 416/978-5947; Fax: 416/978-1632

**FACULTIES WITH DEANS**

Applied Science & Engineering, Michael E. Charles
Architecture & Landscape Architecture, Larry Wayne Richards
Arts & Science, Vacant
Vice-Dean, Arts & Science, Ian Orchard
Assoc. Dean, Arts & Science (Development), Michael Donnelly
Assoc. Dean, Arts & Science (Humanities), Janet Paterson
Assoc. Dean, Arts & Science (Science), Kent Moore
Assoc. Dean, Arts & Science (Social Sciences), Joe Desloges
Dentistry, Barry J. Sessle
Assoc. Dean, Div. 1, Heather J. Jackson
Assoc. Dean, Div. 2, Susan Howson
Assoc. Dean, Div. 3, Don Cormack
Assoc. Dean, Div. 4, G. Harvey Aderson
Education, Michael G. Fullan
Forestry, Rorke Bryan
Graduate Studies, Michael R. Marrus
Vice-Dean, Graduate Studies, Donald E. Moggridge
Information Studies, Lynne Howarth
Law, Ronald J. Daniels
Interim Dean, Management, Paul J. Halpern
Medicine, Arnold Aberman
Assoc. Dean, Medicine (Continuing Education), Dave Davis
Vice-Dean, Medicine (Education), Andrew Baines
Assoc. Dean, Medicine (Postgraduate Medical Education), Murray B. Urowitz
Assoc. Dean, Medicine (Research), Cecil Yip
Assoc. Dean, Medicine (Student Affairs), Miriam Rossi
Assoc. Dean, Medicine (Undergraduate Medical Education), Richard Frecker
Music, David Beach
Nursing, Dorothy Pringle
Pharmacy, Donald G. Perrier
Social Work, Wesley Shera

**SCHOOLS WITH DIRECTORS**

Aerospace Studies, A.A. Haasz
Canadian Institute for Theoretical Astrophysics, J. Richard Bond
Centre for Biomaterials, Robert Pilliar
Centre for Comparative Literature, Peter Nesselroth
Centre for Computer Integrated Engineering, J.D. Gorrie
Centre for Industrial Relations, Frank Reid
Centre for International Studies, Louis W. Pauly
Centre for Management of Technology & Entrepreneurship, Joseph C. Paradi
Centre for Medieval Studies, R. Frank
Centre for Reformation & Renaissance Studies, Konrad Eisenbichler
Centre for Research in Information Studies, Barbara Craig
Centre for Russian & East European Studies, Robert E. Johnson
Centre for South Asian Studies, N.K. Wagle
Centre for Technology & Social Development, W.H. Vanderburg
Acting Director, Centre for Urban & Community Studies, Richard Stren
Centre of Criminology, Clifford D. Shearing
Cinema Studies Program, Cameron Tolton
Continuing Studies, Mary Barrie
David Dunlap Observatory, E.R. Seaquist
Encyclopedia of Ukraine, Danylo H. Struk
Frank Iacobucci Centre for Italian Canadian Studies, Maddalena Kuitunen
Graduate Centre for the Study of Drama, Domenico Pietropaolo
Institute for Environmental Studies, Rodney R. White
Institute for History & Philosophy of Science & Technology, Trevor H. Levere
Institute for Policy Analysis, Frank Mathewson
Institute of Biomedical Engineering, Hans Kunov
Institute of Child Study, Carl Corter
Institute of Medical Science, Mel Silverman
Institute on Human Development, Life Course & Aging, Victor W. Marshall
Interim Director, Joint Centre for Asian Pacific Studies, Bernie Frolic
Joint Program in Transportation, G.N. Steuart
McLuhan Program in Culture & Technology, Derrick de Kerckhove
Museum Studies Program, T. Cuyler Young, Jr.
Peace & Conflict Studies Program, Thomas Homer-Dixon
Pontifical Institute for Medieval Studies, James K. McKonica
Pulp & Paper Centre, D.W. Reeve
School of Continuing Studies, Mary Barrie
School of Physical & Health Education, Bruce Kidd
Toronto School of Theology, Jean-Marc Laporte
Transitional Year Program, Rona Abramovitch

**AFFILIATED COLLEGES**

Emmanuel College, 75 Queen's Park Cres. East, Toronto ON M5S 1K6 – 416/585-4539; Fax: 416/585-4516 (Registrar) – Principal, Robert C. Hutchinson
Knox College, 59 Saint George St., Toronto ON M5S 1A1 – 416/978-4501; Fax: 416/971-2133 – Principal, Rev. Arthur Van Seters
Wycliffe College, Hoskin Ave., Toronto ON M5S 1J6 – 416/979-2870; Fax: 416/979-0471 – Principal Archdeacon, Rev. Michael Pountney

**FEDERATED COLLEGES**

St. Michael's College, 50 Saint Joseph St., Toronto ON M4Y 1J4 – 416/926-1300; Fax: 416/926-7266 (Registrar) – President, Richard M.H. Alway
Trinity College, Hoskin Ave., Toronto ON M5S 1J6 – 416/978-2687; Fax: 416/978-2831 (Registrar) – Provost, W. Thomas Delworth
Victoria College, 73 Queen's Park Cres. East, Toronto ON M5S 1K7 – 416/585-4524; Fax: 416/585-4459 (Registrar) – President, Roseann Runte

**UNIVERSITY COLLEGES**

Erindale College, 3359 Mississauga Rd., Mississauga ON L5L 1C6 – 905/828-5399; Fax: 905/569-4301 (Registrar); URL: http://www.erin.utoronto.ca/ – Principal, Robert H. McNutt
Innis College, 2 Sussex Ave., Toronto ON M5S 1J6 – 416/978-2513; Fax: 416/978-5503 – Principal, John W. Browne
Massey College, 4 Devonshire Pl., Toronto ON M5S 2E1 – 416/978-2895; Fax: 416/978-1759 – Master, John Fraser
New College, 300 Huron, Toronto ON M5S 1A1 – 416/978-2460; Fax: 416/978-0554 – Principal, David Clandfield
Scarborough College, 1265 Military Trail, Scarborough ON M1C 1A4 – 905/287-7080; Fax: 905/287-7525 (Registrar); URL: http://www.scar.utoronto.ca/ – Principal, R. Paul Thompson
University College, 15 King's College Circle, Toronto ON M5S 2V9 – 416/978-3170; Fax: 416/978-6019 (Registrar) – Principal, Lynd W. Forguson
Woodsworth College, 119 Saint George St., Toronto ON M5S 1A1 – 416/978-4444; Fax: 416/978-4088 (Registrar) – Principal, Noah M. Meltz

## University of Waterloo

200 University Ave. West, Waterloo ON N2L 3G1
519/885-1211; Fax: 519/884-8009
URL: http://www.uwaterloo.ca/
Chancellor, M.V. O'Donovan, D.Eng.
Chair, Board of Governors, P.D. Mitchell
President & Vice-Chancellor, J. Downey, O.C., B.A., B.Ed., M.A., Ph.D., D.H.L., D.Litt., LL.D.
Vice-President, Academic & Provost, J.G. Kalbfleisch, B.Sc., M.A., Ph.D.
Vice-President, University Relations, I.H. Lithgow, B.A.
Vice-President, University Research, C.M. Hansson, B.Sc., A.R.S.M., Ph.D., D.I.C., P.Eng.
Associate Provost, Academic & Student Affairs, T.G. Waller, B.S., M.S., Ph.D.
Associate Provost, Human Resources & Student Services, A.C. Scott, B.A.
Associate Provost, General Services & Finance, D. Huber, B.B.A., C.M.A.
University Secretary, L.H.P. Claxton, B.A., B.L.S., M.L.S.
Registrar, K.A. Lavigne, B.A.

**FACULTIES WITH DEANS**

Dean (Interim), Applied Health Sciences, M.T. Sharratt, B.A., M.A., Ph.D.
Arts, B.P. Hendley, B.A., M.A., Ph.D.

Engineering, D.J. Burns, B.Sc., Ph.D., P.Eng., C.Eng.
Environmental Studies, G.R. McBoyle, B.Sc., Ph.D.
Graduate Studies, P.M. Rowe, B.A., M.A., Ph.D.
Mathematics, J.D. Kalbfleisch, B.Sc., M.Math., Ph.D., F.R.S.C.
Science, J.E. Thompson, B.S.A., Ph.D., F.R.S.C.

#### AFFILIATED COLLEGES

Conrad Grebel College, Waterloo ON N2L 3G6 – Principal, J.E. Toews, B.A., M.A., Ph.D.
Renison College, Waterloo ON N2L 3G4 – Principal, G. Cuthbert Brandt, B.A., M.A., Ph.D.
St. Paul's United College, Waterloo ON N2L 3G5 – Principal, H. Mills, B.A., M.A., Ph.D.
University of St. Jerome's College, Waterloo ON N2L 3G3 – President, D.R. Letson, B.A., M.A., Ph.D.

### University of Western Ontario

1151 Richmond St. North, London ON N6A 5B8
519/679-2111
URL: http://www.uwo.ca/
President & Vice-Chancellor, Paul Davenport
Chair, Board of Governors, William Peel
Chancellor, Peter Godsoe
Vice-President, Academic & Provost, Greg Moran
Vice-President, Administration, Peter Mercer
Vice-President, External, Ted Garrard
Vice-President, Research, Bill Bridger
Vice-Provost & Registrar, Roma Harris
Secretary, Board of Governors & Senate, J.K. Van Fleet

#### OTHER DIRECTORS & OFFICERS

Ombudsman, F. Bauer
Public Affairs Officer, J. Noordermeer
Industrial Liaison Officer, Tim Walzak
Alumni Relations & Development, S. Horvath
Communications & Public Affairs, D. Estok
Senior Director, Financial Services, Stu. Finlayson
Executive Director, Foundation Western, Jim Bristow
Senior Director, Housing & Food Services, S. Grindrod
Senior Director, Human Resources, B. Trimble
Senior Director, Information Technology Services, M. Bauer
Institutional Planning & Budgeting, R. Chelladurai
Libraries, C. Quinlan
Occupational Health & Safety, D.G. Barratt
Office of the Registrar, R.J. Tiffin
Part-Time Studies, Vacant
Physical Plant, D.V.B. Riddell
Purchasing, R. Moore
Research Services, Susan Hoddinott
Student Development Centre, G.E. Hutchinson
Student Health Services, T. Macfarlane
University Police, N. Coutu

#### FACULTIES WITH DEANS

Applied Health Sciences, J.D. Cooke
Arts, J.M. Good
Acting Dean, Communication & Open Learning, G. Moran
Dentistry, R.I. Brooke
Education, Allen Pearson
Engineering Science, R.M. Mathur
Graduate Studies, Alan Weedon
Kinesiology, A.W. Taylor
Law, Eileen Gillese
Medicine, R. McMurtry
Music, J. Stokes
Nursing, L. Bramwell
Richard Ivey School of Business, Larry Tapp
Science, Y. Kang
Social Science, Peter Neary

#### SCHOOLS WITH DIRECTORS

Applied Electrostatics Research Centre, I. Inculet
Boundary Layer Wind Tunnel Laboratory, A.G. Davenport
Centre for Activity & Aging, Nancy Ecclestone
Centre for Cognitive Science, Z.W. Pylyshyn
Centre for Health & Well-Being, W. Avison
Centre for Human Nutrition, K.K. Carroll
Centre for Interdisciplinary Studies in Chemical Physics, M. Stillman
Centre for Mass Media Studies, A.M. Osler
Centre for Olympic Studies, B. Barney
Centre for Research & Teaching of Canadian Native Languages, R. Darnell
Centre for Studies in Construction, A.G. Davenport
Centre for Studies in Family Medicine, M. Stewart
Centre for Textual Scholarship, R.J. Shroyer
Centre for Women's Studies & Feminist Research, M. Fleming
Centre for the Study of International Economic Relations, J. Whalley
Centre for the Study of Theory & Criticism, T. Rajan
Chemical Reactor Engineering Centre, I. DeLasa
Geotechnical Research Centre, K. Lo
John P. Robarts Research Institute, M. Poznansky
Museum of London Archaeology, W.D. Finlayson
National Centre for Management Research & Development, K. Hardy
National Tax Centre, B.J. Arnold
Population Studies Centre, R. Fernando
Research Centre in Tribology, W.K. Wan
Surface Science Western, N.S. McIntyre

#### AFFILIATED COLLEGES

Brescia College, 1285 Western Rd., London ON N6G 1H2 – Principal & Dean, Sr. Dolores Kuntz
Huron College, 1349 Western Rd., London ON N6G 1H3 – Principal, D. Bevan
King's College, 266 Epworth Ave., London ON N6A 2M3 – Principal, P. Mueller

### University of Windsor

401 Sunset Ave., Windsor ON N9B 3P4
519/253-3000; Fax: 519/973-7050
URL: http://www.uwindsor.ca/
Chairman of the Board, Donna Miller
Chancellor, Frederic L.R. Jackman
Acting Vice-Chancellor, Gordon W. Wood
President, Ross Paul
Vice-President, Academic, William E. Jones, B.Sc., M.Sc., Ph.D., F.C.I.C.
Vice-President, Administration & Finance, Eric Harbottle, B.A., M.B.A.
Senior Vice-President, Development & Alumni Affairs, Paul V. Cassano, B.A., M.A., Ph.D.
Registrar, F.L. Smith, B.A., M.Ed.
Secretary & General Counsel, D. Charles James, B.A., LL.B.
Director, Human Resources, Jim Butler, B.A., M.A.
Director, Community Relations & Publications, Joan Carter, B.A.
Director, Alumni Affairs, Susan Lester
Director, Physical Plant, Gary A. McMann, B.A.Sc.

#### FACULTIES WITH DEANS

Arts, Sue Martin, B.A., M.A., Ph.D.
Interim Dean, Business Administration, Norman Solomon, B.S., M.A., Ph.D.
Education, Michael Awender, B.A., M.A., M.Ed., Ph.D.
Engineering, Hoda ElMaraghy, B.Eng., M.Eng., Ph.D., P.Eng.
Graduate Studies, Sheila Cameron, R.S.C.N., B.A., M.A. Nurse. Educ., Ed.D., F.A.A.M.R.
Human Kinetics, Michael Salter, B.P.E., M.A., Ph.D.
Law, Juanita Westmoreland-Traoré, B.A., Ll.l.D.es., Doctorate of State, Bar of Québec
Science, Brian Fryer, B.Sc., Ph.D.
Social Science, Kathleen McCrone, B.A., M.A., Ph.D.

#### SCHOOLS WITH DIRECTORS

Computer Science, Richard A. Frost, B.Sc., M.S.E., Ph.D.
Dramatic Art, Diana Mady Kelly, B.A., M.A.
Music, E. Gregory Butler, A.R.C.T., B.M., M.M., D.M.A.
Nursing, Martha E. Horsburgh, Reg.N., Ph.D.
Social Work, James Chacko, B.A, B.S.W., M.S.W., Ph.D
Acting Director, Visual Arts, Iain Baxter, B.Sc., M.Ed., M.F.A., R.C.A.

#### FEDERATED & AFFILIATED INSTITUTIONS

Assumption University, 400 Huron Church Rd., Windsor ON N9B 3P4 – 519/973-7033; Fax: 519/973-7089 – President, Rev. Ulysse Paré, C.S.B., B.A., S.T.L., S.S.L., D.D.
Canterbury College, 172 Patricia Rd., Windsor ON N9B 3B9 – 519/256-6442 – Principal, David T.A. Symons, B.A.Sc., M.A., Ph.D., P.Eng.
Iona College, 208 Sunset Ave., Windsor ON N9B 3A7 – 519/973-7039 – Principal, David Galston, Ph.D.

### Wilfrid Laurier University

75 University Ave. West, Waterloo ON N2L 3C5
519/884-1970; Fax: 519/886-9351
URL: http://www.wlu.ca
President, Robert G. Rosehart, Email: rrosehar@mach2.wlu.ca
Chair of the Board, Jerry Young
Vice-President, Academic, Rowland J. Smith, Email: rsmith@mach2.wlu.ca
Acting Vice-President, Finance & Administration, Robin Armstrong, Email: rarmstro@mach2.wlu.ca
Acting Registrar, Doug Witmer, Email: dwitmer@mach2.wlu.ca
Vice-President, University Advancement, Arthur Stephen, Email: astephen@mach1.wlu.ca
University Bookstore Manager, Shelley Worden, Email: sworden@mach2.wlu.ca
University Librarian, Virginia Gillham, Email: vgillham@mach2.wlu.ca

#### FACULTIES WITH DEANS

Arts & Science, L. Arthur Read
Graduate Studies & Research, Barry D. McPherson
Music, Anne Hall
School of Business & Economics, A. Scott Carson
Social Work, Jannah Hurn Mather
Principal-Dean, Waterloo Lutheran Seminary, Richard Crossman

### York University

4700 Keele St., North York ON M3J 1P3
416/736-2100; Fax: 416/736-5700
URL: http://www.yorku.ca
Chair of the Board, W.A. Dimma, B.A.Sc., M.B.A., D.B.A., P.Eng.
Chancellor, A.R. Haynes, O.C., B.Comm., Hon.D.C.L., Hon.LL.D.
President, L.R. Marsden, B.A., Ph.D., LL.D.
Vice-President, Academic Affairs, H.M. Stevenson, B.A., M.A., Ph.D.
Vice-President, Enrollment & Student Services, D. Hobson, Ph.D.
Vice-President, External Relations, Vacant, B.A.
Vice-President, Administration, P. Clark, B.A., M.A.
Assoc. Vice-President, Academic Information Services, E. Hoffman, B.A., M.A. in L.S.
Assoc. Vice-President, Research & Faculties, M.B. Fenton, B.Sc., M.Sc., Ph.D.
Assoc. Vice-President & Registrar, G. Denzel, B.Sc., M.S., Ph.D.
University Counsel, H.I. Lewis, B.A., M.A., LL.B.
Secretary of the University, M.W. Ransom, B.A.
Asst. Vice-President, Academic Resource Planning, B. Abner, B.A., M.A.

Asst. Vice-President, Student Affairs, C.M. Dusk, B.A., B.Mus., M.Ed.
Asst. Vice-President, Finance & Human Resources, G. Brewer, B.A.Sc., M.B.A.
Asst. Vice-President, Management Information, D. Smith, B.Sc., M.B.A.
Asst. Vice-President, Facilities & Business Operations, P. Struk, B.Mec.Eng., M.A.Sc.
University Librarian, E. Hoffman, B.A., M.A. in L.S.
Chair, Counselling & Development, M. Wilchesky, B.A., M.A., Ph.D.
Director, Hospitality, Food & Beverage Services, N.D. Crandles
Executive Director, Safety & Security, Parking Services, P.A. MacDonald, B.A.
Master Planner, Facilities & Business Operations, M.L. Reimer, MLandArch.
President, York University Development Corporation, R. Hunt, B.Com.

**OTHER DIRECTORS & OFFICERS**

Campaign Director, T. Pursell, B.A.
Academic Staff Relations, P.H. O'Reilly, B.A., LL.B.
Admissions, T.A. Meininger, B.A., M.A., Ph.D.
Alumni Affairs, C. Kennedy, B.A.
Director/Curator, Art Gallery of York University, L. Yarlow, B.A., M.Ed.
Academic Director, Centre for Support of Teaching, S. Mason, B.A., M.A., Ph.D.
Communications, J.M. Rowntree, B.A.
Computer Operations & Telecommunications, Admin. Computing, P. Busby
Computing & Communications Services, S. Spence
Employment Equity, G. Teiman, B.A., M.A., Ph.D.
English Language Institute, M. McNerney, B.A., M.A.
Facilities Development, T. Mohammed, B.Sc., M.Sc., P.Eng.
Facilities Management, K. Irani, B.E., P.Eng.
Facilities Planning, K.M. Brunelle, B.A.
Financial Aid, E.S. Rudyk, B.A.
Information Technology Services, S. Hawkins, B.Sc., M.Sc., M.A., Ph.D.
Innovation York, M.B. Fenton, B.Sc., M.Sc., Ph.D.
Instructional Technology Centre, P. Pow, B.A., M.Ed.
Internal Audit, B. Blackstock, B.A., C.M.A.
Library Computing Services, R. Thompson, B.A.
Occupational Health & Safety, P. Yu, B.Sc.
Office for Persons with Disabilities, K. Swartz, B.A., B.S.W., M.S.W.
Research Administration, N. Swatman, B.A.
Sport & Recreation, P. Murray, B.P.H.E., M.Sc.
Student Affairs, D.L. Glass, B.A., B.Ed., M.E.D.
York International, M.L. Cioni, M.A., Ph.D.
Glendon Campus, 2275 Bayview Ave., Toronto ON M4N 3M6 – 416/487-6710

**FACULTIES WITH DEANS**

Arts, G.B. Fallis, B.A., Ph.D.
Education, S.M. Shapson, B.Sc., M.A., Ph.D.
Environmental Studies, P.A. Victor, B.S.O.S., Ph.D .
Fine Arts, S. Feldman, B.A., Ph.D.
Principal, Glendon College, D. Adam, B.A., B.Ps., M.A., Ph.D.
Graduate Studies, D.R. Leyton-Brown, B.A., M.A., Ph.D.
Joseph E. Atkinson College, L. Visano, B.A., M.A., Ph.D.
Osgoode Hall Law School, M.L. Pilkington, B.A., LL.B., Hon. LL.D.
Pure & Applied Science, R.H. Prince, B.A.Sc., M.Sc., Ph.D.
Schulich School of Business, D. Horvath, B.A., M.B.A., Ph.D.

**SCHOOLS WITH DIRECTORS**

Canadian Centre for German & European Studies, Vacant
Centre for Applied Sustainability, D.V.J. Bell, B.A., A.M., Ph.D.
Centre for Atmospheric Chemistry, G.W. Harris, B.Sc., Ph.D.
Centre for Feminist Research, N. Mandell, B.A., B.Ed., M.A., Ph.D.
Centre for Health Studies, G.D. Feldberg, B.A., M.A., Ph.D.
Centre for International & Security Studies, D.B. Dewitt, B.A., M.A., Ph.D.
Centre for Jewish Studies, M.G. Brown, A.B., A.M., M.H.L., Ph.D.
Centre for Practical Ethics, C.D. MacNiven, B.A., M.A., Ph.D.
Centre for Public Law & Public Policy, P.J. Monahan, B.A., M.A., LL.B., LL.M.
Centre for Refugee Studies, A.F. Bayefsky, B.A., M.A., LL.B., M.Litt.
Centre for Research in Earth & Space Science, G.G. Shepherd, B.Sc., M.Sc., Ph.D., F.R.S.C.
Centre for Research on Latin America & the Caribbean, R. Grinspun, B.A., M.A., Ph.D.
Centre for Research on Work & Society, C. Lipsig-Mummé, B.A., M.A.,Ph.D.
Centre for Vision Research, I.P. Howard, B.Sc., Ph.D.
Centre for the Study of Computers in Education, R.D. Owston, B.Sc., B.Ed., M.Ed., Ph.D.
Centre for the Study of Organized Crime & Corruption, M. Beare, B.A., M.A., M.P.H.L., Ph.D.
Institute for Social Research, J.P. Grayson, B.A., M.A., Ph.D.
Acting Director, Joint Centre for Asia Pacific Studies, B. Frolic, B.A., Ph.D.
La Marsh Centre for Research on Violence & Conflict Resolution, D.J. Pepler, B.A., B.Ed., M.Sc., Ph.D.
Robarts Centre for Canadian Studies, D. Drache, B.A., M.A.

## COLLEGES OF APPLIED ARTS & TECHNOLOGY

**ALGONQUIN COLLEGE**
1385 Woodroffe Ave., Nepean ON K2G 1V8
613/727-4723; Fax: 613/727-7743
Email: gilletr@algonquinc.on.ca; URL: http://www.algonquinc.on.ca/
President, Robert Gillett

**CAMBRIAN COLLEGE OF APPLIED ARTS & TECHNOLOGY**
1400 Barrydowne Rd., Sudbury ON P3A 3V8
705/566-8101; Fax: 705/524-7329
URL: http://www.cambrianc.on.ca/
President, Glenn N. Crombie
Regent Street Campus, 885 Regent St. South, Sudbury ON P3E 4T2

**CANADORE COLLEGE/COLLÈGE CANADORE**
100 College Dr., PO Box 5001, North Bay ON P1B 8K9
705/474-7600; Fax: 705/474-2384
URL: http://www.canadorec.on.ca/
President, Dr. Patricia Groves

**CENTENNIAL COLLEGE**
PO Box 631, Stn A, Scarborough ON M1K 5E9
416/289-5000; Fax: 416/439-7358
URL: http://www.cencol.on.ca
President, Catherine Henderson

**LA CITÉ COLLÉGIALE**
801, promenade de l'Aviation, Ottawa ON K1K 4R3
613/742-2483; Fax: 613/742-2481
Email: admissions@lacitec.onca; URL: http://www.lacitec.on.ca

**COLLÈGE BORÉAL**
21, boul Lasalle, Sudbury ON P3A 6B1
705/560-6673; Fax: 705/675-2370; Toll Free: 1-800-361-6673
URL: http://www.borealc.on.ca

**COLLÈGE DES GRANDS LACS**
76, rue Division, 5e étage, Welland ON L3B 3Z7
905/735-2130; Fax: 905/735-2438; Toll Free: 1-800-590-5227
URL: http://grandslacs.on.ca/

**CONESTOGA COLLEGE**
299 Doon Valley Dr., Kitchener ON N2G 4M4
519/748-5220; Fax: 519/748-3505
URL: http://www.conestogac.on.ca/
President, Dr. John W. Tibbits, Email: jtibbits@cs7.conestogac.on.ca

**CONFEDERATION COLLEGE**
1450 Nakina Dr., PO Box 398, Thunder Bay ON P7C 4W1
807/475-6110; Fax: 807/623-4512
URL: http://www.confederationc.on.ca/
President, Roy Murray

**DURHAM COLLEGE**
2000 Simcoe St. North, PO Box 385, Oshawa ON L1H 7L7
905/721-2000; Fax: 905/721-3115
URL: http://durham.durhamc.on.ca
President, Gary Polonsky

**FANSHAWE COLLEGE**
1460 Oxford St. East, London ON N5V 1W2
519/452-4430; Fax: 519/452-3570
URL: http://www.fanshawec.on.ca/
President, Dr. Howard W. Rundle

**GEORGE BROWN COLLEGE**
PO Box 1015, Stn B, Toronto ON M5T 2T9
416/867-2000; Fax: 416/867-2272; Toll Free: 1-800-265-2002
URL: http://www.gbrownc.on.ca/
President, Frank Sorochinsky

**GEORGIAN COLLEGE**
One Georgian Dr., Barrie ON L4M 3X9
705/728-1968; Fax: 705/722-5123
URL: http://www.georcoll.on.ca
President, Bruce W. Hill
Collingwood Office, 49 Huron St., Collingwood ON L9Y 1L5 – 705/445-2961
Kempenfelt Conference Centre, RR#4, Barrie ON L4M 4S6 – 705/722-8080
Midland Office, 478 Bay St., Midland ON L4R 1K9 – 705/526-3666
Orangeville Office, 5 Armstrong St., Orangeville ON L9W 3H6 – 519/940-0666
Orillia Campus, 825 Memorial Ave., PO Box 2316, Orillia ON L3V 6S2 – 705/325-2740
Owen Sound Campus, 1150 - 8th St. East, PO Box 700, Owen Sound ON N4K 5R4 – 519/376-0840
Parry Sound Office, 26 James St.,Upper Level, Parry Sound ON P2A 1T5 – 705/746-9222
The Georgian Source, 301 Bryne Dr., Barrie ON L4M 4S7 – 705/722-5150
Walkerton Office, #10, 106 Colborne St. North, PO Box 940, Walkerton ON N0G 2V0 – 519/881-2795

**HUMBER COLLEGE**
North Campus/Etobicoke, PO Box 1900, Etobicoke ON M9W 5L7
416/675-6622; Fax: 416/675-1483; Toll Free: 1-800-268-4867
URL: http://www.humberc.on.ca/
President, Robert Gordon
Humber College Sailing Centre, Humber Bay Park West, Lakeshore Blvd., Toronto ON M8V 3A7 – 416/251-7005
Lakeshore Campus, 3199 Lakeshore Blvd. West, Toronto ON M8V 1K8 – 416/252-5571
Student Residences, 203 Humber College Blvd., Etobicoke ON M9W 6V3

**LAMBTON COLLEGE**
Centre for Institutional & International Development, 1457 London Rd., Sarnia ON N7S 6K4
519/542-7751; Fax: 519/542-6667
URL: http://www.lambton.on.ca/
President, Dr. A.T. Easley
Executive Director, Norm Rath
Centre for Advanced Process Technology – 542/542-5033; Fax: 542/542-1017
Riverside Campus – 519/542-7751; Fax: 519/332-6583

**LOYALIST COLLEGE**
PO Box 4200, Belleville ON K8N 5B9
613/969-1913, ext.204; Fax: 613/962-1376
URL: http://www.loyalistc.on.ca/
President, Douglas A.L. Auld

**MOHAWK COLLEGE**
PO Box 2034, Hamilton ON L8N 3T2
905/575-1212; Fax: 905/575-2378
URL: http://www.mohawkc.on.ca/
President, Catherine L. Rellinger
Brantford Campus, 411 Elgin St., Brantford ON N3T 5V2 – 519/ 759-7200
Brantford General Campus, 235 St. Paul Ave., Brantford ON N3R 5Z3 – 519/759-2770
Chedoke Campus, Health Sciences Education Centre, Sanatorium Rd., Hamilton ON L8N 3T2 – 905/575-1515; Fax: 905/575-2378
Fennell Campus, Fennell Ave. & West 5th, Hamilton ON L8N 3T2 – 905/575-1212; Fax: 905/575-2378
Industrial Training Centre, 350 Dosco Dr., Stoney Creek ON L8E 2N5 – 905/662-3700
Stoney Creek Campus, 481 Barton St. East, PO Box 9901, Stoney Creek ON L8G 3Y4 – 905/662-3700
Wentworth Campus, 196 Wentworth St. North, Hamilton ON L8L 5V7 – 905/575-2310

**NIAGARA COLLEGE**
300 Woodlawn Rd., PO Box 1005, Welland ON L3B 5S2
905/735-2211; Fax: 905/735-5671
Email: webmaster@niagarac.on.ca; URL: http://www.niagarac.on.ca/
President, Dan Patterson
Horticultural Centre, Ivan D. Buchanan Hall, 360 Niagara St., St Catharines ON L2M 4W1 – 905/684-4315; Fax: 905/684-3167
Maid of the Mist Centre for Hospitality & Tourism, 5881 Dunn St., Niagara Falls ON L2G 2N9 – 905/374-7454; Fax: 905/374-1116
St Catharines Campus, 59 Welland Vale Rd., St Catharines ON L2R 6V6 – 905/684-4315; Fax: 905/684-3167
Ventures Centre, PO Box 20162, Stn Grantham, St Catharines ON L2M 7W7 – 905/641-2252; Fax: 905/641-2611

**NORTHERN COLLEGE**
Hwy. 101 East, South Porcupine, PO Box 3211, Timmins ON P4N 8R6
705/235-3211; Fax: 705/235-7279
Email: mackierg@northernc.on.ca; URL: http://www.northernc.on.ca/
President, R. Mackie, Fax: 705/235-7277
Haileybury School of Mines Campus, 640 Latchford, Haileybury ON P0J 1K0 – 705/672-3376; Fax: 705/672-2014
James Bay Education Centre Campus, First St., Moosonee ON P0L 1Y0 – 705/336-2913; Fax: 705/336-2393
Kapuskasing Campus, 3 Aurora Ave., Kapuskasing ON P5N 1J6 – 705/335-8504; Fax: 705/335-8343
Kirkland Lake Campus, 140 Government Rd. East, Kirkland Lake ON P2N 3L8 – 705/567-9291; Fax: 705/568-8186

**ST. CLAIR COLLEGE**
2000 Talbot Rd. West, Windsor ON N9A 6S4
519/966-1656; Fax: 519/966-2737; TDD: 519/966-0053
URL: http://www.stclairc.on.ca/
President, J.E. McGee
Thames Campus, 1001 Grand Ave. West, Chatham ON N7M 5W4 – 519/354-9100 – Principal, Patricia McFarlane

**ST. LAWRENCE COLLEGE**
King & Portsmouth, Kingston ON K7L 5A6
613/544-5400; Fax: 613/345-2231; Toll Free: 1-800-463-0752
URL: http://www.stlawrencec.on.ca/
President, Dan Corbett
Brockville Campus, 2288 Parkedale Ave., Brockville ON K6V 5X3 – 613/345-0660; Fax: 613/345-4721 – Principal, J.M. Butt
Cornwall Campus, Windmill Point, Cornwall ON K6H 4Z1 – 613/933-6080; Fax: 613/937-1523 – Principal, A.L. Martin
Kingston Campus, King & Portsmouth, Kingston ON K7L 5A6 – 613/544-5400; Fax: 613/545-3920 – Principal, G. Welch

**THE SAULT COLLEGE**
443, Northern Ave., PO Box 60, Sault Ste. Marie ON P6A 5L3
705/759-6774; Fax: 705/759-1319; Toll Free: 1-800-461-2260
URL: http://www.saultc.on.ca/
President, Gerry McGuire
Chapleau Campus, 34 Birch St., PO Box 787, Chapleau ON P0M 1K0
Elliot Lake Campus, 1 College Place, Elliot Lake ON P5A 3G9
North Algoma Campus, 3 Maple St., PO Box 1490, Wawa ON P0S 1K0
North Shore Campus, PO Box 1238, Blind River ON P0R 1B0

**SENECA COLLEGE**
c/o Newnham Campus, 1750 Finch Ave. East, North York ON M2J 2X5
416/491-5050; Fax: 416/491-3081
URL: http://www.senecac.on.ca/
President, Stephen E. Quinlan
Don Mills Campus, 1380 Don Mills Rd., North York ON M3B 2X2 – 416/491-5050
Dufferin Campus, 1000 Finch Ave. West, North York ON M3J 2V5 – 416/491-5050
Glen Park Campus, 100 Dalemount Ave., North York ON M6B 3C9 – 416/491-5050
Jane Campus, 21 Beverley Hills Dr., North York ON M3L 1A2 – 416/491-5050
King Campus, RR#3, King City ON L0G 1K0 – 905/833-3333
Leslie Campus, 1255 Sheppard Ave. East, North York ON M2K 1E2 – 416/491-5050
Management Development Centre, RR#3, King City ON L0G 1K0 – 905/833-4500
Newmarket Campus, 11775 Yonge St. South, Newmarket ON L3Y 8J4 – 905/898-6199
Richmond Hill Campus, #222, 10720 Yonge St., Richmond Hill ON L4C 3E1 – 905/770-5211
School of Communication Arts, 1124 Finch Ave. West, North York ON M3J 2E2 – 416/491-5050
Sheppard Campus, 43 Sheppard Ave. East, North York ON M2N 2Z8 – 416/491-5050
Vaughan Campus, 3901 Hwy. 7 West, Vaughan ON L4L 6B1 – 905/856-0404
Yorkdale Campus, 2999 Dufferin St., North York ON M6B 3T4 – 416/491-5050

**SHERIDAN COLLEGE**
Trafalgar Road Campus, 1430 Trafalgar Rd., Oakville ON L6H 2L1
905/845-9430; Fax: 905/815-4043
Email: infoSheridan@sheridanc.on.ca; URL: http://www.sheridanc.on.ca
President, Sheldon H. Levy
Davis Campus, McLaughlin Rd., PO Box 7500, Brampton ON L6V 1G6 – 905/459-7533; Fax: 905/874-4345
Skills Training Centre, 407 Iroquois Shore Rd., Oakville ON L6H 1M3 – 905/845-9430; Fax: 905/815-4105

**SIR SANDFORD FLEMING COLLEGE**
Sutherland Campus, Peterborough ON K9J 7B1
705/749-5530; Fax: 705/749-5540
Email: mwideman@flemingc.on.ca; URL: http://www.flemingc.on.ca/
President, Brian L. Desbiens
Lakeshore Campus, 1005 William St., Cobourg ON K9A 5J4 – 905/372-6865; Fax: 905/372-8570 – Facilitator of Campus Operations, Brenda Liston-Hanley
School of Fine Arts, Haliburton Campus, PO Box 339, Haliburton ON K0M 1S0 – 705/457-1680; Fax: 705/457-2255 – Campus Operations Leader, Barbara Bolin
School of Natural Resources, Frost Campus, PO Box 8000, Lindsay ON K9V 5E6 – 705/324-9144; Fax: 705/324-9716 – Academic Team Leader, Jim Madder

## POST-SECONDARY & SPECIALIZED INSTITUTIONS

**ACADEMY OF LEARNING**
Head Office, 100 York Blvd., 4th Fl., Richmond Hill ON L4B 1J8
905/886-8973; Fax: 905/886-8591
Email: academyho_brianr@msn.com
Computer & business skills

**ADVANCED LEARNING INSTITUTE**
219 Burndale, Toronto ON M2N 1T4
416/224-8227
Director of Programs, Ruta Lovett

**ALFRED COLLEGE OF AGRICULTURE & FOOD TECHNOLOGY**
31, rue St-Paul, PO Box 580, Alfred ON K0B 1A0
613/679-2218; Fax: 613/679-2430
Directrice par intérim, Jocelyne Sarault
Agriculture, alimentation et développement international

**ALGONQUIN CAREERS ACADEMY**
1550 Carling Ave., #C, Ottawa ON K1Z 8S8
613/722-7811; Fax: 613/722-4494
Travel & tourism

**AMJ ELECTRONIC COLLEGE**
275 First Ave., Ottawa ON K1S 2G7
613/238-2800; Fax: 613/749-0002
A.M. Jotoff, P.Eng.
Engineering training

**AUTOMOTIVE TRAINING CENTRE**
6095A Yonge St., North York ON M2M 3W2
416/221-3103; Fax: 416/221-3775
URL: http://www.trionline.com/tri/atc
Director, Sam Kasan
Automotive

**BENNS INTERNATIONAL SCHOOLS**
142 Willowdale Ave., North York ON M2N 4Y4
416/223-4003; Fax: 416/223-3419
ESL, floral design, dog & cat grooming, nutrition, reflexology

**CANADA COLLEGE**
583 Annette St., PO Box 293, Stn M, Toronto ON M6S 4T3

416/604-0064; Fax: 416/762-4891; Toll Free: 1-800-387-1940
Correspondence education

**CANADIAN BUSINESS SCHOOL**
Head Office, #1001, 2 Bloor St. West, Toronto ON M4W 3E2
416/925-9929; Fax: 416/925-9220
Email: learn@cbstraining.com
Business, computer, multimedia, programming courses

**CANADIAN CENTRE FOR CREATIVE TECHNOLOGY**
8 Young St. East, Waterloo ON N2J 2L3
519/884-8844; Fax: 519/884-8191
President, Jack Pal
Vice-President, Ron Champion

**CANADIAN CHURCHES' FORUM FOR GLOBAL MINISTRIES**
11 Madison Ave., Toronto ON M5R 2S2
416/924-9351; Fax: 416/924-5356
Email: ccforum@web.apc.org
Coordinator, Outreach & Communication, Robert Faris

**THE CANADIAN COLLEGE OF NATUROPATHIC MEDICINE**
60 Berl Ave., Etobicoke ON M8Y 3C7
416/251-5261; Fax: 416/251-5883
Director, Communications, Audrey Adams-White

**CANADIAN EMERGENCY PREPAREDNESS COLLEGE**
Baskin Dr., PO Box 40, Arnprior ON K7S 3H2
613/623-7931; Fax: 613/563-9095
Email: harry.bloom@epc.pcc.x400.gc.ca
Acting Director, T.A. George

**CANADIAN INSTITUTE OF FINANCIAL PLANNING**
151 Yonge St., 5th Fl., Toronto ON M5C 2W7
416/865-1237; Fax: 416/366-1527; Toll Free: 1-888-865-2437
URL: http://www.mutfunds.com/cifp
Executive Director, John W. Murray

**CANADIAN INSTITUTE FOR ADVANCED RESEARCH**
#701, 179 John St., Toronto ON M5T 1X4
416/971-4255
President & CEO, Dr. J. Stefan Dupré

**CANADIAN INVESTMENT FUNDS COURSE**
c/o Education - The Investment Funds Institute of Canada, 151 Yonge St., 5th Fl., Toronto ON M5C 2W7
416/363-2158; Fax: 416/861-9937; Toll Free: 1-888-865-4342
Email: ific@interlog.com; URL: http://www.mutfunds.com/ific
Québec Branch, #1500, 2000, av McGill College, Montréal PQ H3A 3H3 – 514/985-7025; Fax: 514/985-7000

**CANADIAN JEWELLERS INSTITUTE**
#600, 27 Queen St. East, Toronto ON M5C 2M6
416/368-7616; Fax: 416/368-1986
Assoc. General Manager, Karen Bassels
Coordinator, Shalene Hill

**CANADIAN MEMORIAL CHIROPRACTIC COLLEGE**
1900 Bayview Ave., Toronto ON M4G 3E6
416/482-2340; Fax: 416/482-9745
URL: http://www.cmcc.ca
Chair, Board of Governors, D. Gohn, D.C.
President, J.A. Moss, D.C., M.B.A., Email: president@cmcc.ca
Clinic Director, H. Morrison, D.C.
Registrar, J. Morrison

**CANADIAN POLICE COLLEGE/COLLÈGE CANADIEN DE POLICE**
PO Box 8900, Ottawa ON K1G 3J2
613/998-0785; Fax: 613/990-9738
Management Training Unit, Sgt. John J. Gaudet, B.A.

**CANADIAN SCHOOL OF PRIVATE INVESTIGATION & SECURITY LTD.**
2828 Dufferin St., Toronto ON M6B 3S3
416/785-5701; Fax: 416/785-6064
Private investigation, paralegal, security & law enforcement

**CANADIAN SECURITIES INSTITUTE**
#1550, 121 King St. West, PO Box 113, Toronto ON M5H 3T9
416/364-9130; Fax: 416/359-0486

**THE CAREER ACADEMY**
Ontario Head Office, #1, 520 First St., London ON N5V 3C6
519/451-6440; Fax: 519/451-6663
URL: http://www.careeracademy.com
Computer programming & networking; accounting, secretarial, electronics, travel, Microsoft certification

**CAREER BLAZERS LEARNING CENTRE**
332 Wellington Rd. South, London ON N6C 4P6
519/858-0010; Fax: 519/858-0089

**CAREER BLAZERS LEARNING CENTRE**
295 Wellington St., Bracebridge ON P1L 1P3
705/645-0099; Fax: 705/645-0009
Email: cblazers@muskoka.com; URL: http://www.muskoka.com/busmall/cblazers
Computer software applications

**CAREER CANADA COLLEGE**
Head Office, 385 Yonge St., 3rd Fl., Toronto ON M5B 1S1
416/977-7799; Fax: 416/977-2711
Email: 76533.362@compuserve.com
Health-related programs

**CAREER SCHOOL OF FLORAL DESIGN**
52 Simcoe St. South, Oshawa ON L1H 4G3
905/436-1991; Fax: 905/436-6701
Floristry & business program

**CDI COLLEGE OF BUSINESS & TECHNOLOGY**
Head Office, #1600, 2 Bloor St. West, Toronto ON M4W 3E2
416/964-6707; Fax: 416/964-0520
Computers, accounting & business training

**THE CERTIFIED GENERAL ACCOUNTANTS ASSOCIATION OF ONTARIO**
The Director of Student Services, 240 Eglinton Ave. East, Toronto ON M4P 1K8
416/322-6520; Toll Free: 1-800-668-1454

**CLARKE COLLEGE**
Head Office, #401, 175 Front St., Belleville ON K8N 2Z1
613/966-0904; Fax: 613/966-9526

**CMS TRAINING**
#725, 7305 Woodbine Ave., Markham ON L3R 3V7
905/236-6332; Fax: 905/886-2934
Home study in computer programming

**COLLEGE OF PHYSIOTHERAPISTS**
230 Richmond St. West, 10th Fl., Toronto ON M5V 1V6
416/591-3828; Fax: 416/591-3834; Toll Free: 1-800-583-5885
Email: collegpt@worldchat.com
President, Karen Lee

**COMMERCIAL BUSINESS COLLEGE**
#816, 2161 Yonge St., Toronto ON M4S 3A6
416/480-1546; Fax: 416/480-0772
Banking courses

**COMPLECTIONS INTERNATIONAL - THE MAKE-UP SCHOOL**
85 St. Nicholas St., Toronto ON M4Y 1W8
416/968-6739; Fax: 416/968-7340
Email: nadia@complectionsmake-up.com; URL: http://www.complectionsmake-up.com
Professional make-up artistry training

**COMPUTER COMMUNICATIONS INSTITUTE**
98 Peckham Ave., Willowdale ON M2R 2V5
416/222-3145
Director, Carlos Laredo

**COMPUTER TRAINING CENTRE**
163 - 8th St. East, Owen Sound ON N4K 1K9
519/372-1995; Fax: 519/372-1425

**CONSTELLATION COLLEGE OF HOSPITALITY**
900 Dixon Rd., Etobicoke ON M9W 1J7
416/675-2175; Fax: 416/675-6477
Email: college@regalconstellation.com
Director, Sharon Turner-Brown
Hotel & restaurant operations

**CREATIVE CAREER SYSTEMS INC.**
RR#5, Owen Sound ON N4K 5N7
519/376-7396; Fax: 519/675-6477
Health care aide program

**CREDIT INSTITUTE OF CANADA**
#501, 5090 Explorer Dr., Mississauga ON L4W 3T4
905/629-9805; Fax: 905/629-9809

**DELMAR SCHOOL OF BUSINESS**
#205, 421 Bloor St. East, Toronto ON M4W 3T1
416/927-0784; Fax: 416/927-0714
Email: delmedia@netcom.ca
Business, computer, secretarial, travel & tourism, long-term health care courses

**DIAMOND MANAGEMENT INSTITUTE**
#404, 95 Bayly St. West, Ajax ON L1S 7K8
905/427-1922; Fax: 905/427-2558
Computer, accounting, legal, office administration, entrepreneur programs

**DOMINICAN COLLEGE OF PHILOSOPHY & THEOLOGY**
96 Empress Ave., Ottawa ON K1R 7G3
613/233-5696; Fax: 613/233-6064
Chancellor, Rev. Denis Dion, O.P.
President, Rev. Michel Gourgues, O.P.
Master of Studies/Registrar, Rev. M.-Thérèse Nadeau, C.N.D.
Dean, Faculty of Philosophy, Gabor Csepregi
Dean, Faculty of Theology, Rev. Yvon-D. Gélinas, O.P.
Director, Institute of Pastoral Theology, Rev. J.-Louis Larochelle, O.P.
Sec.-Treas., Jean-Jacques Robillard, O.P.

**DUNDAS VALLEY SCHOOL OF ART**
21 Ogilvie St., Dundas ON L9H 2S1
905/628-6357; Fax: 905/628-1087
Director, T. Hodgson

**DURHAM BUSINESS & COMPUTER COLLEGE**
#305, 2175 Sheppard Ave. East, North York ON M2J 1W8
416/499-0300; Fax: 416/499-4440
Computer programming, graphic design

**ELEGANCE SCHOOLS**
219 Oxford St. West, London ON N6H 1S5
519/434-1181; Fax: 519/434-1182
Esthetics & electrolysis

**ELITE FINANCIAL SERVICES**
#2100, 121 King St. West, Toronto ON M5H 3T9
416/972-6959; Fax: 416/866-8465

**E.L.L. ENGLISH AS A LIVING LANGUAGE PRIVATE SCHOOL**
288 Dupont St., Toronto ON M5R 1V9
416/975-4901; Fax: 416/975-4913
Principal, Susan Hayes

**FRONTIER COLLEGE**
35 Jackes Ave., Toronto ON M4T 1E2
416/923-3591; Fax: 416/323-3522
The Governor General of Canada, Patron
Chair of the Board, Campbell Mackie
President, John Daniel O'Leary

**THE GLENN GOULD PROFESSIONAL SCHOOL OF THE ROYAL CONSERVATORY OF MUSIC**
273 Bloor St. West, Toronto ON M5S 1W2
416/408-2824; Fax: 416/408-3096
Email: rcm@rcmusic.ca; URL: http://www.rcmusic.ca
Dean, Rennie Regehr

**GRAND RIVER POLYTECHNICAL INSTITUTE**
Grand River Territory, Six Nations, PO Box 728, Hagersville ON N0A 1H0
905/768-0448; Fax: 905/768-0424

**GRANTON INSTITUTE OF TECHNOLOGY**
Head Office, 263 Adelaide St. West, Toronto ON M5H 1Y3
416/977-3929; Fax: 416/977-5612
URL: http://www.grantoninstitute.com/
Distance education courses

**HALTON BUSINESS INSTITUTE**
460 Brant St., Burlington ON L7R 4B6
905/637-3415; Fax: 905/637-2843
Administrative & computer programs

**HEALTH CARE VOCATIONAL CENTRES**
Head Office, #9, 1849 Yonge St., Toronto ON M4S 1Y2
416/322-6339; Fax: 416/322-9453
Health care programs

**HERZING CAREER COLLEGE**
#202, 220 Yonge St., Toronto ON M5B 2H1
416/599-6996; Fax: 416/599-0192
Email: hrztoro@io.org
Programming, databases, information systems & business courses

**IGNATIUS COLLEGE**
PO Box 1238, Guelph ON N1H 6N6
519/824-1250; Fax: 519/767-0994
Rector, Rev. Philip Shano, S.J.
Administrator, Rev. Bernard Carroll, S.J.
Treasurer, Wendy Fraser

**THE INSTITUTE OF CHARTERED ACCOUNTANTS OF ONTARIO**
69 Bloor St. East, Toronto ON M4W 1B3
416/962-1841; Fax: 416/962-8900; Toll Free: 1-800-387-0735
Email: exof@icao.on.ca; URL: http://www.icao.on.ca
Chief Executive Officer, David A. Wilson, M.B.A., F.C.A.

**INSTITUTE FOR ADVANCED TECHNOLOGY**
#202, 110 Bloor St. West, Toronto ON M5S 2W7
416/964-8664; Fax: 416/920-6856
Director, Dr. N. Beylerian
Registrar, Lori Trenton
Registrar, Joy Baldwin

**THE INSTITUTE FOR COMPUTER STUDIES**
#402, 155 Gordon Baker Rd., North York ON M2H 3N5
416/499-9522; Fax: 416/499-9386

**INSTITUTE OF TECHNICAL TRADES LTD.**
115 Shorncliffe Rd., Toronto ON M8Z 5K7
416/234-5172; Fax: 416/234-5794
Email: itt@tectrade.com
Welding & CNC machine setup operation

**INTERNATIONAL ACADEMY OF MERCHANDISING & DESIGN LTD.**
31 Wellesley St. East, Toronto ON M4Y 1G7
416/922-3666; Fax: 416/922-7504; Toll Free: 1-800-361-6664
Email: iaod.com; URL: http://www.iaod.com
President, Stephen Bartolini
Vice-President, Larry Gross
Chancellor, Barbara Ann Scott King
Advertising, interior, fashion design; computer graphics, design & animation
Québec Académie at Mart, Place Bonaventure, D-36 Dawson, CP 55, Montréal QC H5A 1A3 – 514/875-9777; Fax: 514/875-9297

**INTERNATIONAL ACADEMY OF NATURAL HEALTH SCIENCES (CANADA)**
380 Forest St., Ottawa ON K2B 8E6
613/820-0318; Fax: 613/828-7107; Toll Free: 1-800-267-8732
URL: http://www.health4all.com
Executive Director, Dorothy Marshall, Ph.D., N.D., C.H.H.P., N.H.C.
Nutrition, herbs, iridology, reflex therapy, shiatsu & stress management

**INTERNATIONAL INSTITUTE OF TRAVEL**
#200, 341 Main St. North, Brampton ON L6X 1N5
905/459-1453; Fax: 905/459-7463
Travel & tourism training

**JOB SKILLS COMPUTER COLLEGE**
45 Oxford St. West, London ON N6H 1R5
519/660-6726
Email: info@jobskills.com; URL: http://www.jobskills.com
Microsoft certified system engineer, certified microsoft office user, desktop application training

**KEMPTVILLE COLLEGE**
University of Guelph, PO Bag 2003, Kemptville ON K0G 1J0
613/258-8336; Fax: 613/258-8384
Director, W.E. Curnoe
Admissions, K. Cavanagh

**K.W. WELDING & FITTING ACADEMY**
Head Office, #9, 440 Phillip St., Waterloo ON N2L 5R9
519/764-3431; Fax: 519/746-8525; Toll Free: 1-800-461-2724
Welding, blueprint reading, layout & fitting courses

**LABORATORY ARTS INSTITUTE**
1333 Neilson Rd., Scarborough ON M1B 4Y9
416/283-8252; Fax: 416/283-3796
Health care related program

**THE LANGUAGE WORKSHOP**
#202, 180 Bloor St. West, Toronto ON M5S 2V6
416/968-1405; Fax: 416/968-6667
Director, Marylou Heenan

**LSC LANGUAGE STUDIES CANADA/METRO TORONTO LANGUAGE SCHOOL**
#300, 20 Eglinton Ave. East, Toronto ON M4P 1A9
416/488-2200; Fax: 416/488-2225
Principal, David S. Diplock

**LUBA MERA SCHOOL OF AESTHETICS, COSMETOLOGY & AROMATHERPY**
515 John St., Burlington ON L7R 2L1
905/681-7882; Fax: 905/648-9705
Aesthetics training

**MEDICAL LABORATORY TECHNOLOGY**
The Canadian Society of Laboratory Technologists, PO Box 2830, Stn LCD1, Hamilton ON L8N 3N8
905/528-8642; Fax: 905/528-4968
Executive Director, E. Valerie Booth

**MEDICAL RADIATION TECHNOLOGY**
c/o Ontario Association of Medical Radiation Technologists, PO Box 1054, Brantford ON N3T 5S7
519/753-6037; Fax: 519/753-6408; Toll Free: 1-800-387-4674

**MHI MATERIALS HANDLING INSTITUTE OF CANADA LTD.**
#4, 100 Westmore Dr., Etobicoke ON M9V 5C3
416/743-4884; Fax: 416/743-2704
Fork lift trucks, overhead crane systems & related equipment operators/instructors training

**MICAN BUSINESS COLLEGE**
1825 Woodward Dr., 2nd Fl., Ottawa ON K2C 0P9
613/224-6211; Fax: 613/224-2739

**NATIONAL COLLEGE**
#705, 1500 Don Mills Rd., North York ON M3B 3K4
416/510-1983; Fax: 416/510-1985
Email: nationalcollege@inforamp.net
Correspondence & computer-based training

**NATIONAL INSTITUTE OF BROADCASTING**
1498 Yonge St., Toronto ON M4T 1Z6
416/922-2793; Fax: 416/922-5470
T. Dickins
Radio & television broadcast training

**NDE INSTITUTE OF CANADA**
135 Fennell Ave. West, Hamilton ON L8N 3T2
905/387-1655; Fax: 905/574-6080
Email: nde@ican.net; URL: http://www.vaxxine.com/ndeinst
Acting Managing Director, Douglas Marshall

**NEW LISKEARD COLLEGE OF AGRICULTURAL TECHNOLOGY**
New Liskeard ON P0J 1P0
705/647-6738; Fax: 705/647-7008
Director, D. Beattie
Administrative Officer, A. Labonte

**NEW SKILLS VOCATIONAL SCHOOLS**
Belleville General Hospital, 265 Dundas St. East, Belleville ON K8N 5A9
613/969-5511; Fax: 613/968-8234
Health care personnel training
London: Meadowpark Nursing Home, 1210 Southdale Rd. East, London ON N6E 1B4 – 519/686-0484; Fax: 519/686-9932
Markham: Green Acres Nursing Home, #303, 135-137 Main St. North, Markham ON L3P 1Y2 – 905/294-5573; Fax: 905/294-1670 – Email: hqpw15a@prodigy.com.ca
Oshawa: Extendicare Nursing Home, 82 Park Rd. North, Oshawa ON L1J 4L1 – 905/579-0011
Peterborough: Marycrest Home for the Aged, 200 St. Luke's Ave., Peterborough ON K9J 1E7 – 705/743-4744; Fax: 705/743-7532
St Catherines: Tufford Nursing Home, 312 Queenston Rd., St Catharines ON L2P 2X4 – 905/682-0503
Windsor: Western Campus, 1453 Prince Rd., Windsor ON N9C 3Z4 – 519/257-5100; Fax: 519/257-5136

**NIAGARA PARKS BOTANICAL GARDENS & SCHOOL OF HORTICULTURE**
PO Box 150, Niagara Falls ON L2E 6T2
905/356-8554; Fax: 905/356-5488

URL: http://www.npbg.org
Director, Deborah Whitehouse

**NOVATECH COMPUTER CAREERS**
857 Norwest Rd., Kingston ON K7P 2N2
613/384-7959; Fax: 613/384-1358

**OMNICOM PROFESSIONAL LANGUAGE SERVICES LTD.**
#1002, 2 Sheppard Ave. East, Willowdale ON M2N 5Y7
416/224-0750; Fax: 416/224-0813

**ONTARIO AGRICULTURAL COLLEGE**
OAC Dean's Office, Univ. of Guelph, 103 Johnstall Hall, Guelph ON N1G 2W1
519/824-4120, ext.6514; Fax: 519/766-1423
Dean, Dr. Rob J. McLaughlin, 519/824-4120, ext.2285; Email: mclaughl@oac.uoguelph.ca
Associate Dean, Cathy MacLean, 519/824-4120, ext.3492; Email: cmaclean@oac.uoguelph.ca
Secretary, Heather Renwick, 519/824-4120, ext.6513; Email: hrenwick@oac.uoguelph.ca

**ONTARIO AGRICULTURAL TRAINING INSTITUTE**
#405, 491 Eglinton Ave. West, Toronto ON M5N 1A8
416/485-3677; Fax: 416/485-5661; Toll Free: 1-800-668-6284
Email: infooati@oati.com

**ONTARIO BIBLE COLLEGE & THEOLOGICAL SEMINARY**
25 Ballyconnor Ct., North York ON M2M 4B3
416/226-6380
Chair, Dr. J. Gordon Freeland
President, Dr. Bruce E. Gordon

**ONTARIO BUSINESS COLLEGE**
Head Office, 54 Victoria Ave., Belleville ON K8N 1Z7
613/962-5308; Fax: 613/962-4421
Legal, medical, business & specialty programs
Barrie, #202, 24 Maple Ave., Barrie ON L4N 7W4 – 705/721-1597; Fax: 705/721-8670
Belleville, 12 Moira St. East, Belleville ON K8P 2R9 – 613/962-9158; Fax: 613/962-7143
Chatham, 59 Adelaide St. South, Chatham ON N7M 4R1 – 519/354-1346; Fax: 519/354-5811
Guelph, #8, 387 Woodlawn Rd. West, Guelph ON N1H 7K9 – 519/767-1328; Fax: 519/767-2601
Kitchener, 59 Frederick St. North, Kitchener ON N2H 2L3 – 519/579-3161; Fax: 519/579-4810
North Bay, 1000 High St., North Bay ON P1B 6S6 – 705/495-1292; Fax: 705/495-0799
Oshawa, #201, 200 John St., Oshawa ON L1J 2B4 – 905/576-9198; Fax: 905/576-3740
Sault Ste. Marie, #300, 473 Queen St. East, Sault Ste. Marie ON P6A 1Z5 – 705/945-9459; Fax: 705/945-0978
Sudbury, 76 Elm St., Sudbury ON P3C 1R8 – 705/673-1190; Fax: 705/673-5364
Thunder Bay, 106 Centennial Sq., Thunder Bay ON P7E 1H3 – 807/623-2120; Fax: 807/623-8975
Windsor, 2970 College Ave., Windsor ON N9C 1S5 – 519/252-3425; Fax: 519/252-2897

**ONTARIO COLLEGE OF ART & DESIGN**
100 McCaul St., Toronto ON M5T 1W1
416/977-6000; Fax: 416/977-0235
Email: ocad.on.ca
Acting President, Peter Caldwell
Vice-President, Administration, Peter Caldwell
Acting Vice-President, Academic, Catherine Wild
Dean, Academic & Student Services, Arthur Wood
Manager, Student Services, Josephine Polera
Dean, Faculty of Art, Katherine Knight
Asst. Dean, Curriculum Planning & Student Advising, B.H. Yael
Asst. Dean, Studio Management, Peter Sramek
Dean, Faculty of Design, Lenore Richards
Asst. Dean, Curriculum Planning & Student Advising, Steve Ouinlan
Asst. Dean, Studio Management, Heather Whitton
Dean, Foundation Studies, Catherine Wild
Director, Library & Audio Visual Services, Jill Patrick
Director, Information Services, Lise Patton
Manager, Academic Computer Centre, Asa Weinstein
OCAD Gallery & Exhibitions Coordinator, Christine Swiderski
Director, Development & Communication Services, Cindy Ball
Manager, Marketing & Publications, Margaret Valois
Manager, Public Relations & Promotions, Jack Kado
Manager, Recruitment & Admissions, Jan Sage
Director, Finance, Peter Fraser

**ONTARIO INSTITUTE FOR STUDIES IN EDUCATION**
252 Bloor St. West, Toronto ON M5S 1V6
416/923-6641; Fax: 416/926-4725
Director, Angela Hildyard, Ph.D., Email: ahildyard@oise.on.ca
Assistant Director, Academic, Malcolm Levin, Ed.D.
Chair, Board of Governors, V. Jane Knox, Ph.D.

**OTTAWA SCHOOL OF ART**
35 George St., Ottawa ON K1N 8W5
613/241-7471; Fax: 613/241-4391
Email: osa@magi.com; URL: http://infoweb.magi.com/~osa/
Executive Director, Jeff Stellick

**PARK COLLEGE**
35 King St. East, 6th Fl., Hamilton ON L8N 4A9
905/528-1108; Fax: 905/528-1105
Business, secretarial, computer training

**PATHFINDER BUSINESS COLLEGE**
#606, 55 Eglinton Ave. East, Toronto ON M4P 1G8
416/485-3737; Fax: 416/485-3900
URL: http://www.pathfindercollege.com
Law clerk, legal assistant, computer programming, virtual reality technology, office administration, travel & tourism programs

**PRIMETECH INSTITUTE**
#280, 255 Consumers Rd., North York ON M2J 1R4
416/756-9989; Fax: 416/756-9926
Email: mail@primetech.com
Computer & technical programs

**RCC SCHOOL OF ELECTRONICS ENGINEERING TECHNOLOGY**
2000 Steeles Ave. West, Concord ON L4K 4N1
905/669-0544; Fax: 905/669-0551
Email: adms@rcc.on.ca; URL: http://www.rcc.on.ca
Computer & electronic engineering technology training

**REDEEMER COLLEGE**
777 Hwy. 53 East, Ancaster ON L9K 1J4
905/648-2131; Fax: 905/648-2134
Email: mvanbev@redeemer.on.ca
President, Justin Cooper, Ph.D.
Chair, Board of Governors, Rev. A. Ben Harsevoort
Vice-President, Academic, M. Elaine Botha, Ph.D.
Vice-President, Advancement, William Van Staalduinen, M.A.
Senior Director, Administration & Finance, Ineke Van Bruinessen, C.G.A.
Associate Dean, Jacob Ellens, Ph.D.
Registrar, Marian Ryks-Szelekovszky, M.Ed.
Community Relations Director, Mark Van Beveren, M.B.A.

**RETS CAREER TRAINING**
#200, 2057 Danforth Ave., Toronto ON M4C 1J8
416/698-5287
Electronics & computer technician, PLC automation control (programmable logic controller)

**RETTER BUSINESS COLLEGE**
120 Eglinton Ave. East, 2nd Fl., Toronto ON M4P 1E2
416/481-7111; Fax: 416/481-5367
Legal, medical, computer programs

**RIDGETOWN COLLEGE - UNIVERSITY OF GUELPH**
Ridgetown ON N0P 2C0
519/674-1500; Fax: 519/674-1515
Director, Gary R. Ablett, B.Sc., M.Sc., Ph.D., Email: gableh@ridgetown@uoguelph.ca
Administrative Officer, J.M. Brooks, Email: jbrooks@ridgetown@uoguelph.ca

**THE ROYAL CONSERVATORY OF MUSIC**
273 Bloor St. West, Toronto ON M5S 1W2
416/408-2825; Fax: 416/408-3096; Email: rcm@rcmusic.ca; URL: http://www.rcmusic.ca

**SA-CO-POL HEALTH CARE TRAINING CENTRE**
760 King St. East, Hamilton ON L8M 1A6
905/577-7707; Fax: 905/577-7738
CPR, first aid courses

**ST. AUGUSTINE'S SEMINARY OF TORONTO**
2661 Kingston Rd., Scarborough ON M1M 1M3
416/261-7207; Fax: 416/261-2529
URL: http://www.canxsys.com/staugust.htm
Rector, Rev. Msgr. John A. Boissonneau, B.A., S.T.B., S.T.L., Th.D.
Dean, Rev. Gordon F. Davies, B.A., S.T.B., S.S.L., S.T.D.

**ST. BASIL'S COLLEGE**
95 St. Joseph St., Toronto ON M5S 2R9
416/925-4368
Rector, J. Leo Walsh, CBS, S.T.L., S.T.D.

**ST. PETER'S SEMINARY**
1040 Waterloo St. North, London ON N6A 3Y1
519/432-1824
Rector & Dean, Theology, Rev. W.T. McGrattan, B.E.Sc., M.Div., S.T.L.
Vice Rector & Dean, Philosophy, Rev. M. Smith, B.A., M.Div., M.A., Ph.D.
Registrar, Rev. J.J. O'Flaherty, B.A., Dip. Catechetics
Spiritual Director, Rev. T.F. O'Connor, M.A., M.T.S., M.Th.
Business Administrator, Frank A. Vita, B.A., B.Comm., M.B.A.
Librarian, Lois Côte, B.A., B.L.S., M.L.S., M.Div.

**SCHOOL OF MAKEUP ART LTD.**
66 Gerrard St. East, Toronto ON M5B 1G3
416/340-1300; Fax: 416/340-1300
Professional make-up training

**SHAW COLLEGE**
365 Bloor St. East, 9th Fl., Toronto ON M4P 1J4
416/920-4380; Fax: 416/920-5838
Email: info@shaw-college.com; URL: http://www.shaw-college.com
Executive Director, M.E. Scarlato
Computer & business applications, legal/medical secretarial, internet, networks, programming

**SHIATSU SCHOOL OF CANADA INC.**
547 College St., Toronto ON M6G 1A9
416/323-1818; Fax: 416/323-1681; Toll Free: 1-800-263-1703
Director, Kaz Kamiya

**THE SOCIETY OF MANAGEMENT ACCOUNTANTS OF ONTARIO**
Assistant Executive Director, Member Programs & Services, #300, 70 University Ave., Toronto ON M5J 2M4
416/977-7741; Fax: 416/977-6079; Toll Free: 1-800-387-2991

* indicates enrollment figure.

**SOFTTRAIN INSTITUTE**
#500, 615 Yonge St., Toronto ON M4Y 1Z5
416/975-0522; Fax: 416/975-8815
Computer courses

**SOUTHWESTERN MEDIX SCHOOL**
1299 Oxford St. East, London ON N5Y 4W5
519/659-4822; Fax: 519/659-2516
Health-related programs

**STERLING BUSINESS ACADEMY**
#101, 200 Queens Ave., London ON N6A 1J3
519/433-3936; Fax: 519/433-5763
Electronic technician exam

**SUCCESS BUSINESS COLLEGE**
#803, 150 Eglinton Ave. East, Toronto ON M4P 1E8
416/487-6493; Fax: 416/487-3818
Computer repairs, legal, medical, dental office, accounting, desktop publishing

**SUTHERLAND CHAN SCHOOL & TEACHING CLINIC**
#400, 330 Dupont St., Toronto ON M5R 1V9
416/924-1107; Fax: 416/924-9413
Massage therapy

**SYMS TRAVEL SCHOOL**
2049A Mount Forest Dr., Burlington ON L7P 1H4
905/335-0125; Fax: 905/335-4880
Travel industry training

**TORONTO ART THERAPY INSTITUTE**
216 St. Clair Ave. West, Toronto ON M4V 1R2
416/924-6221; Fax: 416/924-0156
Director, Academic Program & Internships, Gilda Grossman

**TORONTO BAPTIST SEMINARY & BIBLE COLLEGE**
130 Gerrard St. East, Toronto ON M5A 3T4
416/925-3263; Fax: 416/925-8305
Email: tbs@tbs.edu; URL: http://www.tbs.edu
Principal, A.M. Fountain, B.Sc., M.Div., Ph.D.

**TORONTO INSTITUTE OF PHARMACEUTICAL TECHNOLOGY**
55 Town Centre Ct., Scarborough ON M1P 4X4
416/296-8860; Fax: 416/296-7077
URL: http://www.tipt.com

**TORONTO MONTESSORI INSTITUTE**
8569 Bayview Ave., Richmond Hill ON L4B 3M7
905/889-9201; Fax: 905/886-6516
Co-Director, Nancy Coyle
Co-Director, Jaime Torres

**TORONTO SCHOOL OF BUSINESS - HEAD OFFICE**
Observatory Place, #400, 9555 Yonge St., Richmond Hill ON L4C 9M5
905/883-8520; Fax: 905/883-8589
Email: info@ibschool.com
Business, computers, travel, hospitality & secretarial sciences

**TOWNSHEND COLLEGE OF BUSINESS & COMPUTERS**
#202, 1711 McCowan Rd., Scarborough ON M1S 2Y3
416/297-5627

**TRAVEL TRAINING CAREER CENTRE LTD.**
33 City Centre Dr., Mississauga ON L5B 2N5
905/566-9617
Travel & tourism industry courses
Toronto Campus, #806, 1867 Yonge St., Toronto ON M4S 1Y5 – 416/481-2265

**TREBAS INSTITUTE**
410 Dundas St. East, Toronto ON M5A 2A8
416/966-3066; Fax: 416/966-0030
President, David P. Leonard, 514/845-4141

**VERSAILLES ACADEMY OF MAKE-UP ARTS, ESTHETICS, HAIR**
#5, 1355 Bank St., Ottawa ON K1H 8K7
613/521-4155
Cosmetic, esthetic & hair trades courses

**WESTERVELT COLLEGE**
1060 Wellington Rd., London ON N6E 3W5
519/668-2000; Fax: 519/668-1616
Accounting, law enforcement, travel & technical courses

**WILLIS COLLEGE OF BUSINESS & TECHNOLOGY**
1320 Yonge St., Toronto ON M4T 2W4
416/944-8800; Fax: 416/944-2493
Email: info@willis-training.com; URL: http://www.willis-training.com/
Business & computer training program

## INDEPENDENT & PRIVATE SCHOOLS

**Schools listed alphabetically by city.**

Ajax: Agate Private School, 39 Brookbank Cres., Ajax ON L1S 3R6 – 905/427-1162 – Jerrie Connolly – Elem./Sec.

Ajax: Faithway Baptist Church School, 1964 Salem Rd., Ajax ON L1S 4S7 – 905/686-0951 – L. Allen Homan – *54 – Gr. K./Elem./Sec.

Ajax: Pickering Christian School, 1030 Ravenscroft Rd., Ajax ON L1S 4S7 – 905/427-3120 – Paul Douglas Ogborne – *177 – Elem.

Alliston Community Christian School, PO Box 592, Alliston ON L9R 1V7 – 705/435-4611 – Trevor Tristram – *82 – Gr. K./Elem.

Ancaster: Hamilton District Christian Private School, 92 Gloucester Rd., RR#1, Ancaster ON L9G 3K9 – 905/648-6655 – Jim Vanderkooy – *434 – Sec.

Athens Christian School, PO Box 264, Athens ON K0E 1B0 – 613/924-9500 – Jannie Feenstra – *53 – Elem.

Aurora Montessori School, RR#2, Aurora ON L4G 3G8 – 905/841-0065 – Sharon Kashani – *103 – Elem.

Aurora: St. Andrew's College, 15800 Yonge St. North, Aurora ON L4G 3H7 – 905/727-3178 – Robert P. Bedard – *457 – Sec.

Aylmer: Amish-Mennonite School, RR#4, Aylmer ON N5H 2R3 – 519/773-9225 – D. Eicher – *87 – Gr. K./Elem.

Aylmer: Carlton Christian School, RR#6, Aylmer ON N5H 2R5 – 519/765-1721 – Steven Martin – Elem./Sec. (Amish)

Aylmer: Immanuel Christian School Society, 75 Caverly Rd., Aylmer ON N5H 2P6 – 519/773-8476 – Andrew Vanderploeg – *181 – Gr. K./Elem.

Aylmer: Old Colony Christian School, PO Box 127, Aylmer ON N5H 2R8 – 519/765-1138 – John Dyck – *160 – Elem./Sec.

Bancroft Christian Academy, PO Box 657, Bancroft ON K0L 1C0 – 613/332-3670 – James A. Scheel – *55 – Elem.

Barrie: Heritage Christian Academy, 79 Ardagh Rd., Barrie ON L4M 4S7 – 705/733-0097 – David Bartz – *71 – Gr. K./Elem./Sec.

Barrie: St. Paul's Evangelical Christian School, 50 Anne St. North, Barrie ON L4N 2B6 – 705/728-9026 – Mark Kennedy – Elem.

Barrie: Timothy Christian School, 49 Ferris Lane, Barrie ON L4M 2Y1 – 705/726-6621 – Jane Tjeerdsma – *177 – Gr. K./Elem.

Barwick: Pineview Mennonite School, PO Box 34, Barwick ON P0W 1A0 – 807/487-2443 – Robert Heatwoler – *56 – Elem.

Beamsville: Great Lakes Christian College, 4875 King St., Beamsville ON L0R 1B0 – 905/563-5374 – Brian F. Boden – *100 – Sec.

Belleville: Albert College, 160 Dundas St. West, Belleville ON K8P 1A6 – 613/968-5726; Fax: 613/968-9651; Toll Free: 1-800-952-5237; URL: http://www.telos.ca/quinta/albertc – E. John Rose – *198 – Elem./Sec.

Belleville District Christian School, RR#5, Belleville ON K8N 4Z5 – 613/962-7849 – Peter Shurrock – *109 – Gr. K./Elem.

Belleville: Quinte Christian Private School, 289 Pinnacle St., PO Box 158, Belleville ON K8N 5A2 – 613/968-7870 – Leo Vanarragon – *126 – Elem./Sec.

Bethany: The Bethany Hills School, PO Box 10, Bethany ON L0A 1A0 – 705/277-2866; Fax: 705/277-1279 – Patricia H. Doney – *76 – Elem./Sec.

Big Trout Lake: Aglace Chapman Education Centre, Big Trout Lake ON P0V 1G0 – 807/537-2264 – Cindy Spence – *251 – Gr. K./Elem./Sec.

Bowmanville: Durham Christian High School, RR#1, Bowmanville ON L1C 3K2 – 905/623-5940 – Fred Spoelstra – *113 – Sec.

Bowmanville: Knox Christian School, RR#1, Bowmanville ON L1C 3K2 – 905/623-5871 – W. Helmus – *247 – Gr. K./Elem.

Bracebridge: Cedarbrook Christian School, 541 Cedar Lane, RR#3, Bracebridge ON P1L 1X1 – 705/645-4769 – Pauline Kilduff – *50 – Elem.

Brampton Montessori School, PO Box 488, Brampton ON L6V 2L6 – 905/457-2496 – Alan Shine – *149 – Gr. K./Elem.

Brampton: John Knox Christian School, 82 McLaughlin Rd. South, Brampton ON L6Y 2C7 – 905/822-8131 – Hilda Roukema – *308 – Gr. K./Elem.

Brampton: KRT Christian School, RR#2, Brampton ON L6V 1A1 – 905/846-3771 – Robert J. Boshart – *426 – Gr. K./Elem./Sec.

Brampton: Rowntree Montessori School, 93 Autumn Blvd., Brampton ON L6T 2W1 – 905/793-2196 – Dr. Y.H. Alonso – *137 – Gr. K./Elem.

Brampton: Tall Pines School, 8525 Torbram Rd., Brampton ON L6T 5K4 – 905/458-6770 – Elaine Flett – *183 – Elem.

Brantford: Braemar House School, 948 Colbourne St. East, Brantford ON N3S 3T4 – 519/753-2929 – Neville Bevington – Elem.

Brantford Christian School, 7 Calvin St., Brantford ON N3S 3E4 – 519/752-0433 – Chris Vanderveen – *139 – Gr. K./Elem.

Brantford: Central Baptist Academy, 300 Fairview Dr., Brantford ON N3R 2X6 – 519/448-1445 – Joyce Baker – *215 – Gr. K./Elem.

Brantford: Montessori House of Children, 85 Charlotte St., Brantford ON N3L 3E2 – 519/759-7290 – Perin Alarakhia – *495 – Gr. K./Elem.

Breslau: St. John's-Kilmarnock School, PO Box 179, Breslau ON N0B 1M0 – 519/648-2183 – W.K. Langford – *255 – Elem./Sec.

Breslau: Woodland Christian Private School, RR#1, Breslau ON N0B 1M0 – 519/648-2114 – Gary VanArragon – *162 – Sec.

Brockville Seventh Day Adventist Private School, 100 Perth St., PO Box 794, Brockville ON K6V 5W1 – 613/342-0590 – Sigrid Arnie Robinson – Gr. K./Elem.

Brockville: Grenville Christian College, RR#2, PO Box 610, Brockville ON K6V 5V8 – 613/345-5521 – Robert Y. Phelan – *209 – Gr. K./Elem./Sec.

Burlington: John Calvin Christian School, 607 Dynes Rd., Burlington ON L7N 2V4 – 905/634-8015 – F.C. Ludwig – *330 – Gr. K./Elem.

Burlington: Niagara Montessori Schools, 3132 South Dr., Burlington ON L7N 1H7 – 905/632-2374 – Shirley Gray – *100 – Elem.

Burlington: Park Academy, 1500 Kerns Rd., Burlington ON L4P 3A7 – 905/336-0447 – Bob Euesden – *242 – Gr. K./Elem.

Burlington: Trinity Christian School, 650 Walker's Line, Burlington ON L7N 2E7 – 905/634-3052 – A. Straatsma – *173 – Gr. K./Elem.

Caledonia: Johnsfield Baptist School, PO Box 362, Caledonia ON N0A 1A0 – 519/445-2872 – Duane Wilson – Elem.

Cambridge Christian School, 229 Myers Rd., Cambridge ON N1R 7H3 – 519/623-2261 – Andy Vandorploeg – *198 – Gr. K./Elem.
Cambridge: Temple Baptist Christian Academy, 400 Holiday Inn Dr., Cambridge ON N3T 3C1 – 519/658-9001 – Stephen Limmer – *247 – Gr. K./Elem./Sec.
Campbellville: The Halton Waldorf School, 83 Campbell Rd., PO Box 184, Campbellville ON L0P 1B0 – 905/854-0191 – Janet Myers – *136 – Gr. K./Elem.
Campbellville: Hitherfield Preparatory School, 2439 - 10th Sideroad, Campbellville ON L0P 1B0 – 905/854-0890 – Ann J. Scott – *65 – Elem./Sec.
Carp: Venta Preparatory School, 2013 Old Carp Rd., Carp ON K0A 1L0 – 613/839-2175 – Marilyn C. Mansfield – *52 – Elem./Sec.
Cayuga: Grand River Academy of Christian Education, RR#1, PO Box 1691, Cayuga ON N0A 1E0 – 905/772-5808 – John Elgersma – *133 – Elem./Sec.
Chatham Christian School, 72 Tissiman Ave., Chatham ON N7M 4G5 – 519/352-4041 – Fredric Klooster – *218 – Gr. K./Elem.
Chatham District Christian Secondary School, 90 Park Ave. East, Chatham ON N7M 4G5 – 519/352-4591 – John Van Pelt – *82 – Elem./Sec.
Chatham: Eben-Ezer School, 485 McNaughton Ave. East, Chatham ON N7L 2H2 – 519/354-1142 – W.D. Smid – *92 – Elem.
Claremont: Stouffville Christian School, RR#6, Claremont ON L0H 1E0 – 905/640-3297 – Jessica M. Williams – *129 – Gr. K./Elem./Sec.
Clinton & District Christian School, PO Box 658, Clinton ON N0M 1L0 – 519/482-7851 – Clarence Boss – *227 – Gr. K./Elem.
Cobourg: Northumberland Christian School, RR#5, Cobourg ON K9A 4J8 – 905/372-8766 – Rick Nonnekes – *73 – Gr. K./Elem.
Copetown: Rehoboth Christian School, 198 Inksetter Rd., PO Box 70, Copetown ON L0R 1J0 – 905/627-5977 – Jack Weterink – *288 – Gr. K./Elem./Sec.
Cornwall: Islamic Institute Al-Rasheed, RR#1, Cornwall ON K6H 5R5 – 613/931-2895 – M.M. Alam – *60 – Elem./Sec.
Cottam: Emmanuel Christian Academy, PO Box 220, Cottam ON N0R 1B0 – 519/839-4874 – Velma McCombe – *64 – Gr. K./Elem.
Deep River: The Deep River Science Academy, Mackenzie High School, PO Box 600, Deep River ON K0J 1P0 – 613/584-4541 – Robert G. French – Sec.
Don Mills: Northmount School for Boys, 156 Duncan Mills Rd., Don Mills ON M3B 3N2 – 416/449-8823 – Trevor Pereira – *65 – Elem./Sec.
Downsview: Bnei Akiva Schools, 159 Almore Ave., Downsview ON M3H 2H9 – 416/630-6772 – Dr. N. Smith – *201 – Sec.
Drayton: Calvin Christian School, High St., PO Box 141, Drayton ON N0G 1P0 – 519/638-2935 – J. Ottens – *227 – Gr. K./Elem.
Dresden Private Mennonite School, RR#2, Dresden ON N0P 1M0 – 519/683-6610 – Tina Groening – *61 – Elem.
Dundas: Calvin Christian School, 542 Ofield Rd. North, RR#2, Dundas ON L9H 5E2 – 905/627-1411 – Jack Zondag – *210 – Gr. K./Elem.
Dunnville Christian School, RR#1, Dunnville ON N1A 2W1 – 905/774-5142 – Richard VanEgmond – *185 – Gr. K./Elem.
Etobicoke: Centennial Montessori School, 60 Berl Ave., Etobicoke ON M8Y 3C7 – 416/259-2822 – Susan C. Morand – *167 – Gr. K./Elem.
Etobicoke: International Language Centre Ltd., #300, 5233 Dundas St. West, Etobicoke ON M9B 1A6 – 416/233-3991 – G.M. Banuelos – *1,132 – Sec.
Etobicoke: Kingsley Primary School, 516 The Kingsway, Etobicoke ON M9A 3W6 – 416/233-0150 – U. Morton – *58 – Gr. K./Elem.
Etobicoke: Kingsway College School, 4600 Dundas St. West, Etobicoke ON M9A 1A5 – 416/234-5073 – David R. Richards – *148 – Elem.
Etobicoke: Leonardo Da Vinci Academy of Arts & Sciences, 100 Allanhurst Dr., Etobicoke ON M9A 4K4 – 416/247-6137 – Salavatore Ritacca – *53 – Gr. K./Elem.
Etobicoke: Mississauga Private School, 30 Barrhead Cres., Etobicoke ON M9W 3Z7 – 416/745-1328 – Diane Proctor – *340 – Gr. K./Elem.
Etobicoke: Timothy Christian School, 28 Elmhurst Dr., Etobicoke ON M9W 2J5 – 416/741-5770 – Coby Jonker – *498 – Elem.
Fergus: Emmanuel Christian High School, RR#3, Fergus ON N1M 2W4 – 519/843-3029 – Peter Witten – *91 – Elem./Sec.
Fergus: Maranatha Christian School, RR#3, Fergus ON N1M 2W4 – 519/843-3029 – Peter Witten – *155 – Elem.
Fort Erie: Niagara Christian College, 2619 Niagara Blvd., Fort Erie ON L2A 5M4 – 905/871-6980 – Clare D. Lebold – *139 – Elem./Sec.
Fort Frances: Emmanuel Christian Academy, 308 Butler Ave., Fort Frances ON P9A 2N9 – 807/274-3963 – Fay Edwards – *81 – Elem.
Fort Frances: Lac La Croix High School, PO Box 640, Fort Frances ON P9A 3M9 – 807/485-2446 – Ann Blake – *85 – Elem./Sec.
Fort Frances: Rainy Lake First Nation School, PO Box 297, Fort Frances ON P9A 3M6 – 807/274-2796 – David Lovisa – *128 – Sec.
Fort Hope via Pickle Lake: John C. Yesno School, Fort Hope via Pickle Lake ON P0T 1L0 – 807/242-8421 – James McKernan – Gr. K./Elem./Sec.
Fort Severn: Wasaho First Nation School, Fort Severn ON P0V 1W0 – 807/478-2590 – Anne Marie Levi – *90 – Sec.
Fruitland: John Knox Memorial Christian School, Hwy. 8, PO Box 795, Fruitland ON L0R 1L0 – 905/643-2460 – Julius DeJager – *309 – Gr. K./Elem.
Georgetown District Christian School, Trafalgar Rd., RR#1, Georgetown ON L7G 4S4 – 905/877-4221 – Treena Sybersma – *176 – Gr. K./Elem.
Gloucester: Life Christian Academy, 2214 Innes Rd., Gloucester ON K1B 3K5 – 613/834-6585 – Karen Middleton – *73 – Elem./Sec.
Guelph: Crestwicke Christian Academy, 400 Victoria Rd. North, Guelph ON N1E 5J7 – 519/836-2132 – Neil Paton – *208 – Gr. K./Elem.
Guelph: Elora Road Christian School, 5696 Wellington Rd., RR#5, Guelph ON N1H 6J2 – 519/824-1890 – James Gordon – *51 – Gr. K./Elem.
Hamilton: Calvin Christian School, 547 West 5 St., Hamilton ON L9C 3P7 – 905/388-2645 – Ted Postma – *329 – Gr. K./Elem.
Hamilton: Columbia International College, 1033 Main St. West, Hamilton ON L8S 1B7 – 905/572-7883 – Anna Shkolnik – *240 – Sec.
Hamilton: Guido de Bres Private School, PO Box 20098, RPO Upper James, Hamilton ON L9C 7M5 – 905/574-4011 – J.G. Vandooren – *3059 – Sec.
Hamilton Hebrew Academy Zichron Meir School, 60 Dow Ave., Hamilton ON L8S 2T9 – 905/528-0330 – Rabbi W. Eisenstein – *258 – Elem.
Hamilton: Hillfield - Strathallan College, 299 Fennell Ave. West, Hamilton ON L9C 1G3 – 905/389-1367 – W.S. Boyer – *989 – Gr. K./Elem./Sec.
Hamilton: Southern Ontario College, 35 Brant St., Hamilton ON L8L 4C6 – 905/546-1500 – Martin Harvey – *69 – Sec.
Hamilton: Timothy Canadian Reformed School, PO Box 20007, RPO Upper James, Hamilton ON L9C 7M5 – 905/385-3953 – H.J. Nobel – *171 – Gr. K./Elem.
Hamilton: Yeshiva Beit Yitzchak, 235 Bowman St., Hamilton ON L8S 2T9 – 905/528-5451 – William C. Brown – *77 – Sec.
Hastings: Columbine School for Exceptional Children, RR#2, Hastings ON K0L 1Y0 – 705/696-3295 – Margaret Santon – *50 – Elem./Sec.
Hastings: The Learning Centre, PO Box 312, Hastings ON K8P 5A5 – 613/966-5603 – Michael Maloney – *72 – Elem./Sec.
Hawkesville: Countryside Christian School, PO Box 65, Hawkesville ON N0B 1X0 – 519/699-5793 – Orval D. Zehr – *103 – Gr. K./Elem./Sec.
Hyde Park: Christian Academy of Western Ontario, General Delivery, Hyde Park ON N0M 1Z0 – 519/473-3332 – Philip J. Conley – *245 – Gr. K./Elem./Sec.
Jarvis District Christian School, PO Box 520, Jarvis ON N0A 1J0 – 519/587-4444 – Garry Glashergen – *262 – Gr. K./Elem.
Jordan Station: Heritage Christian School, PO Box 400, Jordan Station ON L0R 1S0 – 905/562-7303 – Joanne Bakker – *468 – Elem./Sec.
Jordan Station: Netherlands Reformed Christian School, 15 St. South, PO Box 69, Jordan Station ON L0R 1S0 – 905/562-4023 – Foppe Vander Zwaag – *93 – Gr. K./Elem.
Kanata: Viewmount Christian Academy, 103 Penfield Dr., Kanata ON K2K 1L9 – 613/599-7992 – Cheryl Kreech – *81 – Elem.
King City: The Country Day School, RR#3, King City ON L0G 1K0 – 905/833-5366 – Paul C. Duckett – *473 – Gr. K./Elem./Sec.
Kingston Christian School, 1212 Woodbine Rd., RR#3, Kingston ON K7L 4V2 – 613/384-9572 – Hugo Marcus – *156 – Gr. K./Elem.
Kingston Learning Centre, 740-742 Arlington Pl., Kingston ON K7M 8H9 – 613/384-6194 – A.S. Stayer – Gr. K./Elem./Sec.
Kingston Montessori School, PO Box 1416, Kingston ON K7L 5C6 – 613/542-7193 – Linda Karshmar – Gr. K./Elem.
Kingsville: Old Colony Christian Academy, 1521 County Rd. 4 West, RR#2, Kingsville ON N9Y 2E5 – 519/733-2891 – Tina Schmitt – *170 – Elem./Sec.
Kitchener: Christ Lutheran School, 146 Trafalgar Ave., Kitchener ON N2A 1Z7 – 519/896-0615 – Richard Orlowski – *181 – Elem.
Kitchener: Laurentian Hills Christian School, 11 Laurentian Dr., Kitchener ON N2E 1C1 – 519/576-6700 – Luke Janssen – *146 – Gr. K./Elem.
Kitchener: Rockway Mennonite Collegiate, 110 Doon Rd., Kitchener ON N2G 3C8 – 519/743-5209 – Dennis Wikerd – *300 – Elem./Sec.
Kitchener: Sunshine Montessori School, 527 Bridgeport St., Kitchener ON N2K 1N6 – 519/744-1423 – Roshima Shamji – *143 – Elem.
Lakefield College School, Lakefield ON K0L 2H0 – 705/652-3324 – David J. Hadden – *281 – Elem./Sec.
Lambeth: Faith Community Christian School, 7 Howard Ave, Lambeth ON N0L 1S2 – 519/668-0015 – Jennifer Charlton – *112 – Gr. K./Elem.
Laurel: Dufferin Area Christian School, Laurel ON L0N 1L0 – 519/941-4368 – N. Mans – *99 – Elem.
Leamington: United Mennonite Educational Institute, 614 Mersea Rd. 6, RR#5, Leamington ON N8H 3V8 – 519/326-7448 – Paul Warkentin – *92 – Sec.
Lindsay: Heritage Christian School, 159 Colborne St. West, Lindsay ON K9V 5Z8 – 705/324-8363 – R.W. Moore – *176 – Gr. K./Elem.
Listowel: Brookside Christian School, RR#4, Listowel ON N4W 3G9 – 519/595-8459 – Clarice Plett – *56 – Gr. K./Elem.
Listowel Christian School, PO Box 151, Listowel ON N4W 3H2 – 519/291-3086 – Peter Van Dyken – *115 – Gr. K./Elem.
Listowel: West Hesson Parochial School, RR#4, Listowel ON N4W 3G9 – 519/595-8644 – Josiah Weber – *56 – Elem.
London: Askin Montessori School, 115 Askin St., London ON N6C 1E7 – 519/433-2671 – Madalaine Milli – *56 – K./Elem.
London: Central Christian School, 602 Queens Ave., London ON N6B 1Y8 – 519/439-0144 – Susan R. Fountain – *72 – Gr. K./Elem.

* indicates enrollment figure.

London Community Hebrew Day School, 247 Epworth Ave., London ON N6A 2M2 – 519/439-8419 – Janet Nish Lapidus – *58 – Gr. K./Elem.

London District Christian School, 24 Braesyde Ave., London ON N5W 1V3 – 519/455-4360 – Henry Kooy – *268 – Sec.

London Parental Christian School, 202 Clarke Rd., London ON N5W 5E4 – 519/455-0360 – Herb Goodhoofd – *212 – Gr. K./Elem.

London Waldorf School, 7 Beaufort St., London ON N6G 1A5 – 519/858-8862 – Merwin Lewis – *118 – Gr. K./Elem.

London: Matthews Hall Private School, 1370 Oxford St. West, London ON N6H 1W2 – 519/471-1506 – Patricia A. Doig – *248 – Gr. K./Elem./Sec.

London: Montessori House of Children, 711 Waterloo St., London ON N6A 3W1 – 519/433-9121 – Sharon Keenan – *495 – Gr. K./Elem.

Lucknow & District Christian School, RR#1, PO Box 550, Lucknow ON N0G 2H0 – 519/528-2016 – Lawrence Uyl – *68 – Gr. K./Elem.

Maple: North York Montessori Learning Centre, 9600 Bathurst St., Maple ON L6A 1R9 – 905/633-2636 – Florence Miller – *133 – Gr. K./Elem.

Markham: Somerset Academy, 7700 Brimley Rd., Markham ON L3R 0E5 – 905/940-8990 – M. Vanloon – *105 – Elem.

Markham: Town Centre Montessori School, 155 Clayton Dr., Markham ON L3R 7P3 – 905/470-1200 – Marie Vanderlugt – *277 – Gr. 3212lem.

Markham: Wishing Well Montessori School, #30, 455 Cochrane Dr., Markham ON L3R 9R4 – 905/498-0331 – Connie Xuereb – *313 – Gr. K./Elem.

Metcalfe: Community Christian School-Metcalfe, PO Box 540, Metcalfe ON K0A 2P0 – 613/821-3669 – M.B. Ripmeester – *53 – Elem.

Millgrove: Covenant Christian School, PO Box 2, Millgrove ON L0R 1V0 – 905/689-3191 – G. Hofsink – *194 – Elem.

Mississauga: Aristotle Greek School, 2146 Waycross Cres., Mississauga ON L5K 1H9 – 905/855-0774 – Chrissanthi Pachiadakisi – *90 – Gr. K./Elem./Sec.

Mississauga: Bronte College of Canada, 2186 Hurontario St., Mississauga ON L5B 1M9 – 905/270-7788 – Ah Sing Chia-Looi – *84 – Sec.

Mississauga: Cedar Grove School, 1884 Lakeshore Rd., Mississauga ON L5J 1J9 – 905/855-0563 – Susan Kendall – *60 – Elem.

Mississauga: The Froebel Kindergarten & School, 1576 Dundas St. West, Mississauga ON L5C 1E5 – 905/277-9371 – Barbara E. Corbett – Elem.

Mississauga: Isna Islamic School, 1525 Sherway Dr., Mississauga ON L4X 1C5 – 905/272-4303 – A.I. Ali – *326 – Gr. K./Elem.

Mississauga: Mentor College, 40 Forest Ave., Mississauga ON L5G 1L1 – 905/271-3393 – Arthur Steinberg – *883 – Gr. K./Elem./Sec.

Mississauga Christian Academy, 2720 Gananoque Dr., Mississauga ON L5N 2R2 – 905/826-4114 – Joy Elliot – *255 – Gr. K./Elem.

Mississauga: Queensway Cathedral Christian School, 1542 Rometown Dr., Mississauga ON L5E 2T9 – 905/255-0141 – D. Broomer – Gr. K./Elem./Sec.

Mississauga: Rotherglen Private School, 3553 South Common Ct., Mississauga ON L5L 2B3 – 905/820-9445 – Marie Lanigan – *376 – Elem.

Mississauga: Sherwood Heights School, 3065 Glen Erin Dr., Mississauga ON L5L 1J3 – 905/569-8999 – Edward Mutlak – *100 – Elem.

Mississauga: Springfield Manor Mississauga, 1444 Dundas Cres., Mississauga ON L5C 1E9 – 905/277-1085 – Winefride Johnson – *123 – Elem.

Mississauga: The Toronto Ability School, 1146 Clarkson Rd. North, Mississauga ON L5T 2W2 – 905/855-3800 – Magvite Wilhans – *52 – Gr. K./Elem.

Mississauga: Tutorial & Educational Assistance in Mississauga (T.E.A.M.), 275 Rudar Rd., Mississauga ON L5A 1S2 – 905/279-7200 – Kenneth B. Philbrook – *184 – Gr. K./Elem./Spec. Ed.

Mobert: Netamisakomik Centre for Education, General Delivery, Mobert ON P0M 2J0 – 807/822-2011 – Angela Voutier – *71 – Elem./Sec.

Mount Forest: Farewell Parochial, RR#5, Mount Forest ON N0G 2L0 – Cheryl Martin – *53 – Elem.

Mount Hope: Grandview Seventh-Day Adventist Academy, 3975 Hwy. #6, Mount Hope ON L0R 1W0 – 905/679-4492 – Garry Proctor – *55 – Elem./Sec.

Nepean: Canadian Montessori Academy, 2 Peter St., Nepean ON K2G 1K2 – 613/727-9427 – Sherie DeMel – *70 – Elem.

Nepean: École Maimonides School, 25 Esquimault Ave., Nepean ON K2H 6Z5 – 613/820-9484 – Rabbi Mordecai Berger – *156 – Gr. K./Elem./Spec. Ed.

Nestleton: Lighthouse Academy, RR#3, Nestleton ON L0B 1L0 – 905/986-5569 – Erika Kiezerbrink – Gr. K./Elem.

Nestor Falls: O-Ne-Ga-Ming School, PO Box 339, Nestor Falls ON P0X 1K0 – 807/484-2510 – M.J. Kelly – *96 – Gr. K./Elem./Sec.

Newmarket: Elizabeth Simcoe Private School, 95 Carlson Dr., Newmarket ON L3Y 3G9 – 905/898-6208 – W.B. Dew – *64 – Elem./Sec.

Newmarket: Holland Marsh District Christian School, RR#2, Newmarket ON L3Y 4V9 – 905/775-3701 – Henry Lise – *322 – Gr. K./Elem.

Newmarket & District Christian Academy, 221 Carlson Dr., PO Box 297, Newmarket ON L3Y 4X1 – 905/895-1119 – David Balik – *207 – Gr. K./Elem.

Newmarket Montessori School, #110, 1100 Stellar Dr., Newmarket ON L3Y 7B7 – 905/895-1921 – S. Soni – Gr. K./Elem.

Newmarket: Pickering College, 16945 Bayview Ave., Newmarket ON L3Y 4X2 – 905/895-1700 – Peter C. Sturrup – *257 – Elem./Sec.

Niagara Falls: Bible Baptist Academy, 9674 Upper's Lane, Niagara Falls ON L2E 6S4 – 905/356-7717 – T. Bruce – *64 – Elem./Sec.

Niagara Community Church School, 9527 McLeod St., RR#2, Niagara Falls ON L2E 6S5 – 905/357-9519 – Chris Halls – *69 – Gr. K./Elem.

Nobleton: Montessori Country School, PO Box 455, Nobleton ON L0G 1N0 – 905/859-4739 – Marianne Perks – *82 – Gr. K./Elem.

North Gower Christian Academy, c/o Pilgrim Holiness Church, PO Box 605, North Gower ON K0A 2T0 – 613/489-2501 – Rev. Lloyd Wolenfeld – Gr. K./Elem./Sec.

North York: ARS Armenian Private School, 45 Hallcrown Pl., North York ON M2J 4Y4 – 416/491-2675 – Markar Saraphanian – *365 – Gr. K./Elem.

North York: Associated Hebrew Schools of Toronto, 252 Finch Ave. West, North York ON M2R 1M9 – 416/223-4845 – S. Rabinowitz – *2,394 – Gr. K./Elem.

North York: Bayview Glen Junior School, 275 Duncan Mill Rd., North York ON M3B 2Y1 – 416/443-1030 – J.T.M. Guest – *419 – Gr. K./Elem./Sec.

North York: Community Hebrew Academy, 200 Wilmington Ave., North York ON M3H 5J8 – 416/636-5984 – Sheldon Friedman – *605 – Sec.

North York: Crawford Adventist Academy, 531 Finch Ave. West, North York ON M2R 3X2 – 416/633-0090 – Vernon Langdon – *470 – Gr. K./Elem./Sec.

North York: The Crescent School, 2365 Bayview Ave., North York ON M2L 1A2 – 416/449-2556 – J. Tansey – *529 – Elem./Sec.; Boys

North York: Crestview Junior Private School, 350 Seneca Hills Dr., PO Box 101, North York ON M2J 4S7 – 416/491-1949 – Leila Esper – *66 – Gr. K./Elem.

North York: Crestwood School, 411 Lawrence Ave. East, North York ON M3C 1N9 – 416/444-5858 – Dalia Eisen – *310 – Elem.

North York: Eitz Chaim Day Schools, 475 Patricia Ave., North York ON M2R 2N1 – 416/225-1187 – Rabbi Jakabovitz – *1,063 – Gr. K./Elem./Sec.

North York: Ellesmere Montessori Private School, 5350 Yonge St., North York ON M2N 5R5 – 416/447-1059 – Jill Weinberger – *110 – Gr. K./Elem.

North York: Hawthorn School for Girls, 230 The Donway West, North York ON M3B 2V8 – 416/444-3054 – Dr. Teresa Tomory – *90 – Elem./Sec.

North York: Holy Cross Armenian School, 61 Curlew Dr., North York ON M3A 2P8 – 416/441-2152 – Diana Hanimyam – *92 – Gr. K./Elem.

North Toronto Christian School, 50 Page Ave., North York ON M2K 2B4 – 416/226-3366 – Stuart W. Cooke – *619 – Gr. K./Elem./Sec.

North York Christian School, 43 Drewry Ave., North York ON M2M 1C9 – 416/222-1675 – Bruce Pike – *58 – Gr. K./Elem.

North York: Or Haemet Sefaradic School, 37 Southborne Ave., North York ON M3H 1A4 – 416/635-9881 – A. Assayag – *189 – Gr. K./Elem.

North York: The Oswald J. Smith Elementary School, 374 Sheppard Ave. East, North York ON M2N 3B6 – 416/222-3341 – Donald J. McNiven – *135 – Gr. K./Elem.

North York: The Paul B. Smith Academy, 374 Sheppard Ave. East, North York ON M2N 3B6 – 416/222-3341 – Donald F. McNiven – *180 – Sec.

North York: She'Arim Hebrew Day School, 100 Elder St., North York ON M3H 5G7 – 416/633-8247 – Elaine Runbinoff – *50 – Elem./Spec. Ed.

North York: Sidney Ledson School Ltd., #107, 220 Duncan Mill Rd., North York ON M3B 3J5 – 416/447-5355 – Sidney Ledson – *89 – Gr. K./Elem.

North York: Willow Wood School, 157 Willowdale Ave., North York ON M2N 4Y7 – 416/222-0631 – Joy Kurtz – *136 – Elem./Sec./Spec. Ed.

North York: Willowdale Christian School, 60 Hilda Ave., North York ON M2M 1V5 – 416/222-1711 – Rick Nonnekes – *170 – Gr. K./Elem.

Norwich: Rehoboth Reformed Private School, PO Box 220, Norwich ON N0J 1P0 – 519/863-2403 – M.C. Vanderspek – *413 – Gr. K./Elem./Sec.

Oakville: Appleby College, 540 Lakeshore Rd. West, Oakville ON L6K 3P1 – 905/845-4681 – Guy S. McLean – *535 – Elem./Sec.

Oakville: Chisholm Educational Centre, 440 Inglehart St., Oakville ON L6J 3J6 – 905/844-3240 – Dr. Howard A. Bernstein – *111 – Elem./Sec.

Oakville: Dearcroft Montessori School, 1167 Lakeshore Rd. East, Oakville ON L6J 1L3 – 905/844-2114 – Barbara Phippen – *163 – Gr. K./Elem.

Oakville: Fern Hill School, 3300 Ninth Line, RR#1, Oakville ON L6J 4Z2 – 905/257-0022 – Wendy Dennick – *367 – Gr. K./Elem./Sec.

Oakville: Glenburnie School, 2035 Upper Middle Rd., Oakville ON L6J 4Z2 – 905/338-6236 – Linda Sweet – *158 – Gr. K./Elem.

Oakville: John Knox Christian School, 2232 Sheridan Garden Dr., Oakville ON L6J 7T1 – 905/822-8131 – Lorna Keith – *228 – Elem.

Oakville: MacLachlan College, 337 Trafalgar Rd., Oakville ON L6J 3Y2 – 905/844-0372 – Audrey Hadfield – *234 – Elem./Sec.

Oakville: The Oakville Christian School, 112 Third Line, Oakville ON L6L 3Z7 – 905/825-1247 – Linda Williams – *211 – Gr. K./Elem.

Oakville: St. Mildred's - Lightbourn School, 1080 Linbrook Rd., Oakville ON L6J 2L1 – 905/845-2386 – Susan Booth – *599 – Gr. K./Elem./Sec; Girls

Orangeville: Hillcrest School, #74A, 90 Lawrence Ave., Orangeville ON L9W 3S4 – 519/942-3251 – Gail P. Hooper – *124 – Gr. K./Elem./Sec.

Orangeville Christian School, RR#5, PO Box 176, Orangeville ON L9W 2Z6 – 519/941-3381 – George Hoytema – *55 – Gr. K./Elem.

Orangeville: Trillium Montessori School of Orangeville, 69 Third St., Orangeville ON L9W 2B7 – 519/942-3550 – Michael Browne – Gr. K./Elem.

Orillia: Bethel Christian Academy, 300 Coldwater Rd. West, Orillia ON L3V 6X5 – 705/326-4561 – Aaron Mossman – *59 – Gr. K./Elem./Sec.

Orillia: Canadian Christian Academy, PO Box 937, Orillia ON L3V 6K8 – 705/327-8975 – Rev. C.K. Fear – *336 – Elem./Sec.

Orillia Christian School, PO Box 862, Orillia ON L3V 6K8 – 705/326-0532 – Scott Bullock – *120 – Gr. K./Elem.

Orleans: Ottawa Islamic School, 1196 Orleans Blvd., Orleans ON K1C 2W1 – 613/727-5066 – Ziggi Lamonthe – *227 – Elem.

Oshawa: College Park School, 1300 King St. East, PO Box 31054, Stn Kingsway, Oshawa ON L1H 8N9 – 905/723-0163 – Marsha Williams – *168 – Gr. K./Elem.

Oshawa: Durham Christian Academy, 900 King St. East, Oshawa ON L1H 1H2 – 905/436-6354 – Michael Broomer – *128 – Gr. K./Elem.

Oshawa: Immanuel Christian School, 849 Rossland Rd. West, Oshawa ON L1H 7K4 – 905/728-9071 – Stan Baker – *133 – Gr. K./Elem.

Oshawa: Kingsway College, 1200 Leland Rd, Oshawa ON L1K 2H4 – 905/433-1144 – Janice Saliba – *206 – Sec.

Ottawa: Ashbury College, 362 Mariposa Ave., Ottawa ON K1M 0T3 – 613/749-5954 – Robert P. Napier – *559 – Elem./Sec.

Ottawa: Bishop Hamilton School, 2199 Regency Terrace, Ottawa ON K2C 1H2 – 613/596-4971 – Elaine Hopkins – *151 – Gr. K./Elem.

Ottawa: École Parsifal, 630 Island Park, Ottawa ON K1Y 0B7 – 613/729-7545 – Celine Treherne – *96 – Gr. K./Elem.

Ottawa: Elmwood School, 261 Buena Vista Rd., Ottawa ON K1M 0V9 – 613/749-6761 – Morag S. Gundy – *355 – Gr. K./Elem./Sec.

Ottawa: Hillel Academy, 881 Broadview Ave., Ottawa ON K2A 2M6 – 613/722-0020 – Mark Weinberg – *452 – Gr. K./Elem./Sec.

Ottawa: Joan of Arc Academy, 130 Keyworth Ave., Ottawa ON K1V 0E6 – 613/728-6364 – Patricia McKelvie – *71 – Gr. K./Elem.; Girls

Ottawa: Lycée Claudel, 1635 Promenade Riverside, Ottawa ON K1G 0E5 – 613/733-8522 – Serge Albinet – *856 – Gr. K./Elem./Sec.

Ottawa Christian School, 2191 Benjamin Ave., Ottawa ON K2A 1P6 – 613/722-5836 – William A. VanDyke – *198 – Gr. K./Elem.

Ottawa Iranian School, 100 Dufferin St., Ottawa ON K1M 2A6 – 613/236-2714 – Shokoh Najmi – *339 – Elem./Sec.

Ottawa Languages Institute Ltd., 1990 Leslie St., Ottawa ON K1H 5M3 – 613/521-3331 – Tin S. Yap – Sec.

Ottawa Montessori Schools, 335 Lindsay St., Ottawa ON K1G 0L6 – 613/521-5185 – Patricia McLaughlin – *339 – Gr. K./Elem.

Ottawa: Parsifal School, 630 Island Park Dr., Ottawa ON K1Y 0B7 – 613/729-7545 – Michèle Auger – *68 – Elem.

Ottawa: Redeemer Christian High School, 2199 Regency Terrace, Ottawa ON K2C 1H1 – 613/721-7142 – Derek R.S. Maggs – *97 – Sec.

Ottawa: Turnbull Learning Centre, 1132 Fisher Ave., Ottawa ON K1Z 6P7 – 613/729-9940 – Wendy Waxman – *97 – Elem./Sec.

Owen Sound Montessori School, 1701 - 3 Ave. East, Owen Sound ON N4K 2M3 – 519/376-9710 – Pamela Vair – *86 – Gr. K./Elem.

Owen Sound: Timothy Christian School, 199 - 4 Ave. West, Owen Sound ON N4K 4V1 – 519/371-9151 – Garth Bierma – *115 – Gr. K./Elem.

Oxford: Springford School with the Bible, PO Box 8, Oxford ON N0G 1X0 – 519/842-7109 – Pastor Lieuwe Schaafsma – *67 – Elem./Sec.

Paris: Grand Valley Adventist Academy, c/o West Dumfries Central School, RR#2, Paris ON N3L 3E2 – 519/759-7290 – Robert Dukeshire – Gr. K./Elem.

Pawitik: Baibombeh Anishinabe School, Pawitik ON P0X 1L0 – 807/226-5698 – Michael Leahy – *304 – Gr. K./Elem./Sec.

Peterborough: Grace Christian Academy, PO Box 2217, Peterborough ON K9J 7Y4 – 705/745-4400 – Gerry Libby – *100 – Gr. K./Elem.

Peterborough: Rhema Christian School, 3195 Parkhill Rd. East, Peterborough ON K9L 1B8 – 705/743-1400 – Ray Hendriks – *196 – Gr. K./Elem.

Pickering: Montessori Learning Centre of Pickering, 401 Kingston Rd., Pickering ON L1V 1A3 – 905/509-1722 – N. Phillips – *157 – Gr. K./Elem.

Picton: Sonrise Christian Academy, 48 Johnson St., Picton ON K0K 2T0 – 613/476-7883 – Matthew J. Bittel – *52 – Elem.

Pikangikum: Eenchokay Birchstick School, General Delivery, Pikangikum ON P0V 2L0 – 807/773-5561 – Lynda Worrod – *84 – Gr. K./Elem./Sec.

Poole: Fair Haven Christian Day School, RR#1, Poole ON N0K 1S0 – 519/595-4568 – Howard Bean – *84 – Gr. K./Elem.

Port Hope: Trinity College School, 190 Ward St., Port Hope ON L1A 3W2 – 905/885-4565 – Roger C. Wright – *405 – Elem./Sec.

Prince Albert: Scugog Christian School, PO Box 3308, Prince Albert ON L9L 1C3 – 905/985-3741 – John Lunshof – *58 – Elem.

Richmond Hill: Academy for Gifted Children, 12 Bond Cres., Richmond Hill ON L4E 3K2 – 905/773-0997 – Barbara Rosenberg – *73 – Elem./Sec.

Richmond Hill: Holy Trinity School, 11300 Bayview Ave., Richmond Hill ON L4C 4X7 – 905/737-1114 – George Rutherford – *555 – Elem./Sec.

Richmond Hill: Lifetime Learning Day School, PO Box 356, Richmond Hill ON L4S 4Y6 – 905/764-2579 – Lynn Howarth – *66 – Elem.

Richmond Hill Montessori & Elementary School, 85 - 16th Ave., Richmond Hill ON L4C 7A6 – 905/882-6000 – Eveline Kopachkov – *199 – Gr. K./Elem.

Richmond Hill: Toronto Montessori Schools, 8569 Bayview Ave., RR#2, Richmond Hill ON L4C 7B5 – 905/789-7828 – P. Glasgow – *689 – Gr. K./Elem.

Rosseau Lake College, PO Box 1967, Rosseau ON P0C 1J0 – 705/732-4351 – Gregory C. Devenish – *99 – Elem./Sec.

Sachigo Lake: Martin McKay Memorial School, General Delivery, Sachigo Lake ON P0V 2P0 – 807/595-2526 – Anna Delaney – *101 – Sec.

St Catharines: Beacon Christian High School, 2 O'Malley Dr., St Catharines ON L2N 6N7 – 905/937-7411 – Ted Harris – *77 – Sec.

St Catharines: Calvary Christian School, 89 Scott St., St Catharines ON L2N 1G8 – 905/935-3854 – Gerda Grubb – *131 – Gr. K./Elem.

St Catharines: Calvin Memorial Christian School, 300 Scott St., St Catharines ON L2N 1J3 – 905/241-1100 – Karen Gerritsma – *255 – Gr. K./Elem.

St Catharines: Garden City Christian Academy, 265 Linwell Rd., St Catharines ON L2N 1S4 – 905/937-6440 – Douglas Osborn – *65 – Gr. K./Elem./Sec.; Boys

St Catharines: Grey Gables Day School, One Dexter St., St Catharines ON L2S 2L4 – 905/685-4577 – Kathleen Miller – *87 – Gr. K./Elem./Sec.

St Catharines: Ridley College, PO Box 3013, St Catharines ON L2R 7C3 – 905/684-8193 – Rupert D. Lane – *576 – Elem./Sec.

St Catharines Montessori Day School, 83 Church St., St Catharines ON L2R 3C7 – 905/684-6110 – Ellen Smith – *53 – Gr. K./Elem.

St Catharines: The Wheatley School of Montessori Education, 154 Martindale Rd., St Catharines ON L2S 2X9 – 905/641-3012 – Eda Varalli – *105 – Elem.

St. Mary's: Brookside Parochial School, RR#4, St. Mary's ON N4X 1C7 – Henry Troyer – Elem.

St. Thomas: Ebenezer Christian School, 77 Fairview Ave., St. Thomas ON N5R 4X7 – 519/633-0690 – Anthony Dekoter – *160 – Elem.

St. Thomas: Faith Christian Academy, 109 Chestnut St., St. Thomas ON N5R 2B1 – 519/633-0943 – Thomas Lancaster – *110 – Gr. K./Elem.

Sandy Lake: Thomas Fiddler Memorial School, Via Favorable Lake Post Office, Sandy Lake ON P0V 1V0 – 807/774-4491 – Sarah Sawanas – Elem./Sec.

Sarnia: Lambton Christian High School, 295 Essex St., Sarnia ON N7T 4S3 – 519/337-9122 – Wayne Drost – *94 – Sec.

Sarnia: New Life School, 867 London Rd., Sarnia ON N7T 4S3 – 519/337-8906 – Elizabeth DeGroot – *53 – Elem.

Sarnia Christian School, 1273 Exmouth St., Sarnia ON N7S 1W9 – 519/383-7750 – P. Weening – *233 – Gr. K./Elem.

Sarnia: Temple Christian Academy, 1410 Quinn Dr., Sarnia ON N7T 7H4 – 519/542-1427 – James D. Loosemore – *74 – Elem.

Scarborough: Agbu Zaroukian School, 30 Progress Crt., Scarborough ON M1G 3T5 – 416/431-2428 – Hasmik Kurdian – *114 – Gr. K./Elem.

Scarborough: Blaisdale Montessori School, 885 Scarborough Golf Club Rd., Scarborough ON M1G 1J6 – 416/289-2273 – Eleanor Wilson – *342 – Gr. K./Elem.

Scarborough: Ellington Montessori School, 2102 Lawrence Ave. East, Scarborough ON M1R 2Z9 – 416/759-8363 – Deborah Renwick – *56 – Elem.

Scarborough: The Hart Academy, #101, 3090 Kingston Rd., Scarborough ON M1M 1P2 – 416/261-0510 – Annette M.P. Dunleavy – Elem.; Special Ed.

Scarborough: Our Lady of Victory Academy, 24 Rowatson Rd., Scarborough ON M1E 1K1 – 416/659-1421 – Penelope Anne Costin – Elem./Sec.

Scarborough Christian Private School, 614 Brimley Rd., Scarborough ON M1J 1B8 – 416/477-4433 – Keith Davies – *489 – Gr. K./Elem./Sec.

Scarborough: Whitefield Christian Jr. Academy, 5810 Finch Ave. East, Scarborough ON M1B 4Y6 – 416/297-1212 – Ruth E. Slade – *175 – Elem.

Sebringville: Stratford District Christian School, 130 Huron Rd., Sebringville ON N0K 1X0 – 519/393-5675 – Edward J. Petrusma – *116 – Gr. K./Elem.

Sharon: The East Gwillimbury Country Day School, RR#1, Sharon ON L0G 1V0 – 905/853-3301 – Mary Pape – Elem.

Simcoe: Bethel Baptist Christian School, PO Box 752, Simcoe ON N3Y 2T2 – 519/426-8421 – Sherrill Booth – *67 – Gr. K./Elem./Sec.

Sioux Lookout: Pelican Falls First Nation High School, PO Box 4127, Sioux Lookout ON P8T 1J9 – 807/737-1110 – Larry Beardy – *141 – Sec.

Sioux Lookout: Washa Distance Education Centre, PO Box 1118, Sioux Lookout ON P8T 1B7 – 807/737-1488 – Norma Kejick – *465 – Sec.

Smithville: John Calvin School of Smithville, Station St., PO Box 280, Smithville ON L0R 2A0 – 905/957-2341 – Judy Kingma – *333 – Gr. K./Elem.

Smithville Covenant Christian School, 6470, RR#14, Smithville ON L0R 2A0 – 905/957-7796 – M. Elzinga – *156 – Elem.

Smithville District Christian High School, 6488 Smithville Rd., Smithville ON L0R 2A0 – 905/957-3255 – M.B. Stroobosscher – *189 – Sec.

Stittsville: Ottawa Waldorf School, 1 Goulbourn Ave., Stittsville ON K2S 1N9 – 613/836-1547 – Millie Johne – *50 – Gr. K./Elem.

Strathroy: John Calvin Christian School, 48 York St., Strathroy ON N7G 2E5 – 519/245-1924 – Henry Wiersema – *178 – Gr. K./Elem.

* indicates enrollment figure.

Strathroy Community Christian School, 48 York St., Strathroy ON N7G 2E5 – 519/245-1924 – Henry Wiersema – *182 – Gr. K./Elem.

Sudbury Christian Day School, 1101 Regent St. South, Sudbury ON P3E 5P8 – 705/523-5550 – T.H. Laakso – *50 – Gr. K./Elem.

Tecumseh: Our Lady of Mercy School, 2078 St. Anne St., Tecumseh ON N8N 1V7 – 519/735-0746 – Donna Hayes – Elem.

Thornhill: Cheder Chabad, 770 Chabad Gate, Thornhill ON L4J 3V9 – 905/764-8721 – Rabbi Chanowitz – *92 – Elem.

Thornhill: The Leo Baeck Day School, 36 Atkinson Ave., Thornhill ON L4J 8C9 – 905/709-3636 – Zita J. Gardner – *501 – Gr. K./Elem.

Thornhill: Ner Israel Yeshiva College, 8950 Bathurst St., Thornhill ON L4J 8A7 – 905/731-1224 – T. Widrich – *145 – Sec.

Thornhill: Netivot Hatorah Day School, 18 Atkinson Ave., Thornhill ON L4J 8C8 – 905/771-1234 – Avrom Schochet – *470 – Gr. K./Elem.

Thornhill: Toronto Waldorf School, 9100 Bathurst St., PO Box 220, Thornhill ON L3T 3N3 – 905/881-1611 – Les Black – *396 – Gr. K./Elem.

Thornton: Thor Secondary Prep School, RR#3, Thornton ON L0L 2P0 – 705/458-9705 – W.H. Madden – *108 – Elem.

Thunder Bay Christian School, RR#2, Stn F, Thunder Bay ON P7C 4V1 – 807/939-1209 – Richard Poortinga – *272 – Gr. K./Elem./Sec.

Timmins: Faith Christian Academy, PO Box 1434, Timmins ON P4N 7N2 – 705/267-5463 – Pastor Gerald Vaillancourt – Elem./Sec.

Timmins Trinity Christian School, 228 Huot St., Timmins ON P4N 7G2 – 705/268-4498 – Ronald Lajeunesse – *50 – Elem.

Toronto: Alan Howard Waldorf School, 250 Madison Ave., Toronto ON M4V 2W6 – 416/962-6447 – Alan Hughes – *129 – Elem.

Toronto: Bais Yaakov Elementary School, 85 Stormont Ave., Toronto ON M5N 2C3 – 416/783-6181 – M. Drebin – *462 – Gr. K./Elem.; Girls

Toronto: Beth Jacob Private School, 410 Lawrence Ave. West, Toronto ON M5M 1C2 – 416/787-4949 – Rabbi A. Stefansky – *302 – Sec.; Girls

Toronto: Bialik Hebrew Day School, 12 Viewmount Ave., Toronto ON M6B 1T3 – 416/783-3346 – Dr. Uri Korin – *793 – Gr. K./Elem.

Toronto: Bishop Strachan School, 298 Lonsdale Rd., Toronto ON M4V 1X2 – 416/483-4325 – Natalie M. Little – *782 – Gr. K./Elem./Sec.

Toronto: Branksome Hall, 10 Elm Ave., Toronto ON M4W 1N4 – 416/920-9741 – Rachel Belash – *814 – Gr. K./Elem./Sec.

Toronto: Cambridge International College of Canada, 35 Ourland Ave., Toronto ON M8Z 4E1 – 416/252-9195 – Irwin Diamond – *145 – Sec.

Toronto: Canadian Heritage School, 110 Eglinton Ave. West, 3rd Fl., Toronto ON M4P 1R3 – 416/322-6010 – Merle Langbord Levine – Elem./Sec.

Toronto: Canadian Outward Bound Wilderness School, #302, 150 Laird Dr., Toronto ON M4G 3Y7 – 416/421-8111 – Philip Blackford – *200 – Sec.

Toronto: Cathedral Christian Academy, 1901 Jane St., PO Box 410, Stn W, Toronto ON M6M 5C1 – 416/241-1100 – Dr. P.D. Melnichuk – *61 – Gr. K./Elem./Sec.

Toronto: Dominion College, 111 Gerrard St. East, Toronto ON M5B 1G8 – 416/348-8708 – Barbara Wehrmann – *63 – Sec.

Toronto: The Great Lakes College of Toronto, 323 Keele St., Toronto ON M6P 2K6 – 416/763-4121 – Sheila Devers – *148 – Sec.

Toronto: Havergal College, 1451 Avenue Rd., Toronto ON M5N 2H9 – 416/483-3519 – Priscilla Winn Barlow – *839 – Gr. K./Elem./Sec.

Toronto: High Park Montessori School, 35 High Park Gdns., Toronto ON M6R 1S8 – 416/763-6097 – Karen L. Fagan – *111 – Gr. K./Elem.

Toronto: Higher Marks Educational Institute, Main Campus, 941 Bathurst St., Toronto ON M5R 3G4 – 416/532-5563 – Ronald E. Blake – *214 – Elem./Sec.; Spec. Ed.

Toronto: Humberside Montessori School, 411 Clendennan Ave, Toronto ON M6P 2X7 – 416/762-8888 – Felix Bednarski – *81 – Elem./Ungraded

Toronto: Imperial College of Toronto, 20 Queen Elizabeth Blvd., Toronto ON M8Z 1L8 – 416/251-4970 – Vojin Stefancic – *369 – Sec.

Toronto: Institute of Child Study, 45 Walmer Rd., Toronto ON M5R 2X2 – 416/978-3454 – Elizabeth Morley – *193 – Elem.

Toronto: Islamic Foundation School, 441 Nugget Ave., Toronto ON M1S 5E1 – 416/321-3776 – *90 – Elem.

Toronto: Lena Brown Seventh Day Adventist School, c/o Knobhill Public School, #201, Seminole Ave., Toronto ON M1J 1M8 – 416/439-2029 – Randolph F. Dixon – Elem.

Toronto: The Mabin School, 50 Poplar Plains Rd., Toronto ON M4V 2M8 – 416/964-9594 – Geraldine Mabin – *151 – Gr. K./Elem.

Toronto: Maria Montessori School, 125 Brentcliffe Rd., Toronto ON M4G 3Y7 – 416/423-9123 – James Brand – *123 – Elem.

Toronto: Metro Toronto Language School, 20 Eglinton Ave. East, Toronto ON M4P 1A9 – 416/488-2200 – D.S. Diplock – *289 – Sec./Ungraded

Toronto: Metropolitan Preparatory Academy, 49 Mobile Dr., Toronto ON M4A 1H5 – 416/285-0870 – Wayne McKelvey – *311 – Elem./Sec.

Toronto: Montcrest School, 4 Montcrest Blvd., Toronto ON M4K 1J7 – 416/469-2008 – Elaine Danson – *165 – Gr. K./Elem.

Toronto: Montessori Learning Centre (Ajax), 22 Delavan Ave., Toronto ON M5P 1T3 – 905/428-3122 – Dorothy Graziani – *73 – Gr. K./Elem.

Toronto: National Ballet School, 105 Maitland St., Toronto ON M4Y 1E4 – 416/964-3780 – Mora I. Oxley – *144 – Elem./Sec.

Toronto: Pathways College, #1801, 1 Yonge St., Toronto ON M5E 1W7 – 416/367-3940 – F. Manson – *66 – Sec.

Toronto: Royal St. George's College, 120 Howland Ave., Toronto ON M5R 3B5 – 416/533-9481 – Hall Hannaford – *400 – Elem./Sec.; Boys

Toronto: St. Clement's School, 21 St. Clement's Ave., Toronto ON M4R 1G8 – 416/483-4835 – Patricia Parisi – *439 – Gr. K./Elem./Sec.; Girls

Toronto: St. Louis Delia Secondary School, 111 Bond St., Toronto ON M5B 1Y2 – 416/979-0301 – Anthony Ho – *73 – Sec.

Toronto: St. Michael's College School, 1515 Bathurst St., Toronto ON M5P 3H4 – 416/653-3180 – Rev. T.F. Mohan – *914 – Sec.; Boys

Toronto: De La Salle College, 131 Farnham Ave., Toronto ON M4V 1H7 – 416/969-8771; Fax: 416/969-9175 – Br. D. Viggiani – Elem./Sec.

Toronto: School of Liberal Arts, #200, 44 Eglinton Ave. West, Toronto ON M4R 1A1 – 416/489-7652 – David L. Ferguson – *85 – Sec.

Toronto: The Sterling Hall School of Toronto, 99 Cartwright Ave., Toronto ON M6A 1V4 – 416/449-3410 – Ian L.F. Robinson – *171 – Elem.; Boys

Toronto: Sunnybrook School, 469 Merton St., Toronto ON M4S 1B4 – 416/487-5308 – Irene Davy – *136 – Gr. K./Elem.

Toronto: Thornton Hall Senior Private School, 241 Poplar Plains Rd., Toronto ON M4V 2N8 – 416/923-3291 – Stuart E. Mackey – *50 – Sec.

Toronto: The Toronto French School, Main Campus, 306 Lawrence Ave. East, Toronto ON M4N 1T7 – 416/484-6533; Fax: 416/488-3090 – Headmaster, Jean Brugniau – *1,144 – Gr. K./Elem./Sec.

Toronto: United Synagogue Day School, 3072 Bayview Ave., Toronto ON M2N 5L3 – 416/781-5658 – Lucy Cohen – *1,388 – Gr. K./Elem./Sec.

Toronto: University of Toronto Schools, 371 Bloor St. West, Toronto ON M5S 2R8 – 416/978-3209 – Stan Pearl – *455 – Elem./Sec.

Toronto: Upper Canada College, 200 Lonsdale Rd., Toronto ON M4V 1W6 – 416/488-1125 – J. Douglas Blakey – *1,050 – Elem./Sec.

Toronto: Weston Montessori School, 40 South Station St., Toronto ON M9N 2B3 – 416/242-3725 – Mark W. Berger – *63 – Elem.

Toronto: Yeshiva Bnei Tzion of Bobov, 44 Champlain Blvd., Toronto ON M3H 2Z1 – 416/633-6332 – David Kessler – *157 – Gr. K./Elem.; Boys

Toronto: Yeshiva Yesodei Hatorah, 77 Glen Rush Blvd., Toronto ON M2N 2T8 – 416/787-1101 – A. Bornstein – *390 – Gr. K./Elem.; Boys

Toronto: Yeshivas Nachalas Zvi, 475 Lawrence Ave. West, Toronto ON M5M 1C6 – 416/782-8912 – J. Rosenfield – *58 – Elem./Sec.

Toronto: York Montessori School, 65 Sheldrake Blvd., Toronto ON M4P 2B1 – 416/483-0541 – Barbara Zeibots – *208 – Gr. K./Elem

Toronto: The York School, 65 Sheldrake Boulevard, Toronto ON M4P 2B1 – 416/483-0541

Toronto Island Montessori School, 18 Wyandot Ave., Toronto Island ON M5J 2M9 – 416/368-1919 – Susan Roy – Gr. K./Elem.

Trenton Christian School, 20 - 4 Ave., Trenton ON K8V 5N3 – 613/392-3600 – I. Witteveen – *208 – Gr. K./Elem.

Unionville: Some Place Special Christian Academy, 100 Lee Ave., Unionville ON M1V 2W6 – 905/513-0011 – Marjorie Serio – *60 – Elem.

Unionville: Trillium Montessori School, 7781 Kennedy Rd., Unionville ON L3R 2C8 – 416/946-1181 – Lily Moon – Elem.

Utterson: Muskoka Christian School, PO Box 150, Utterson ON P0B 1M0 – 705/385-2847 – James C. Atkinson – *91 – Gr. K./Elem.

Vanier: L'Etincelle, 268 Durocher St., Vanier ON K1L 7S6 – 613/733-6919 – Claudette Giguere – Gr. K./Elem.

Vaughan: Children's College Private Elementary School, 7909 Kipling Ave., Vaughan ON L4L 1Z7 – 905/742-0434 – Lynne Taylor – *80 – Gr. K./Elem.

Vaughan: Toronto District Christian High School, 377 Woodbridge Ave., Vaughan ON L4L 2S8 – 905/851-1772 – Ren Siebenga – *294 – Sec.

Wallaceburg Christian School, 693 Albert St., Wallaceburg ON N8A 1Y8 – 519/627-6013 – Peter C . Van Mahen – *94 – Gr. K./Elem.

Wasaga Beach: Silvercrest Christian School, 380 Zoo Park Rd., Wasaga Beach ON L0L 2P0 – 705/429-4303 – Greg Ayrheart – *84 – Gr. K./Elem.

Waterloo: Fellowship Christian School, 306 Erb St. West, Waterloo ON N2L 1W3 – 519/746-0008 – Marilyn Lambert – *55 – Elem.

Waterloo: Kitchener Waterloo Bilingual School, 600 Erb St. West, Waterloo ON N2J 3Z4 – 519/886-6510 – Michel Poinot – *163 – Gr. K./Elem.

Waterloo: Kitchener-Waterloo Montessori School, 194 Allen St. East, Waterloo ON N2J 1K1 – 519/742-1051 – Elizabeth Black – Gr. K./Elem.

Waterloo: St. Judes School, 419 Phillip St., Waterloo ON N2L 3X2 – 519/888-6620 – Frederick Gore – *55 – Elem./Sec./Spec. Ed.

Wellandport: Robert Land Academy, RR#3, Wellandport ON L0R 2J0 – 905/386-6203 – G. Scott Bowman – *86 – Elem./Sec.

Wellandport Christian School, RR#1, Wellandport ON L0R 2J0 – 905/386-6272 – William J. Thies – *283 – Elem.

Wheatley: Old Colony Christian Academy, RR#2, Wheatley ON N0P 2P0 – 519/825-4400 – Henry Klassen – *106 – Elem.

Whitby: Trafalgar Castle School, 401 Reynolds St., Whitby ON L1N 3W9 – 905/668-3358 – George L. Briggs – *144 – Elem./Sec.
Whitby Montessori School, 301 Byron St. South, Whitby ON L1N 4P9 – 905/430-8201 – Rubin Burstyn – *134 – Elem.
White Dog: Wabeseenmoong School, White Dog ON P0X 1P0 – 807/927-2286 – Paul W. Cooke – *251 – Gr. K./Elem./Sec.
Williamsburg: Timothy Christian School, Williamsburg ON K0C 2H0 – 613/535-2687 – Gary Postma – *145 – Gr. K./Elem.
Willowdale: Associated Hebrew Schools of Toronto Junior High Division, 6100 Leslie St., Willowdale ON M2H 3J1 – 416/789-7471 – J.H. Rosenfield – Elem.
Willowdale: People's Christian Academy, 374 Sheppard Ave. East, Willowdale ON M2N 3B6 – 416/222-3341 – Donald F. McNiven – *502 – Elem./Sec.
Windsor: Academie Ste-Cecile Private School, 925 Cousineau Rd., Windsor ON N9G 1V8 – 519/961-1291 – Therese H. Gaddury – *86 – Elem./Sec.
Windsor: Marantha Christian Academy, 939 Northwood St., Windsor ON N9E 2B4 – 519/966-7424 – Peter Baljeu – *90 – Gr. K./Elem.
Windsor: Temple Christian Academy of Windsor, 3005 Temple Dr., Windsor ON N8W 5E5 – 519/945-7077 – Agnita Solomon – *72 – Gr. K./Elem.
Windsor Christian Fellowship Academy, 4490 - 7th Concession, RR#1, Windsor ON N9A 6J3 – 519/972-5977 – Lorraine Collins – *124 – Elem.
Woodbridge: Calvary Christian School, c/o Calvary Baptist Church, 26 Bruce St., Woodbridge ON L4L 1J4 – 905/851-2273 – D.H. Maguire – *72 – Gr. K./Elem.
Woodbridge: Credo Christian School, 8260 Huntington Rd., Woodbridge ON L4L 1A5 – 905/851-1620 – L.P. Maat – *97 – Gr. K./Elem.
Woodbridge: Maple Leaf Montessori School Inc., 8286 Islington Ave., Woodbridge ON L4L 1W8 – 905/856-3359 – Johanna Madeley – *174 – Elem.
Woodstock: John Knox Christian School, 800 Juliana Dr., PO Box 243, Woodstock ON N4S 7W8 – 519/539-1492 – William Barneveld – *249 – Gr. K./Elem.
Woodstock: Kettle Creek Private School, PO Box 167, Woodstock ON N4S 7W8 – 519/539-3473 – Dora Force – *56 – Elem./Sec.
Wunnummin Lake: Lydia Lois Beardy Memorial School, General Delivery, Wunnummin Lake ON P0V 2Z0 – 807/442-2402 – Georgina Nahwegahbo – *126 – Elem./Sec.
Wyoming: John Knox Christian School of Wyoming, PO Box 81, Wyoming ON N0N 1T0 – 519/845-3112 – William Hordyk – *158 – Gr. K./Elem.

### OVERSEAS SCHOOLS

France: Lycée canadien en France, Place du Centenaire, 06230 St.-Jean-Cap-Ferrat France – 011-33-9301-4884; Fax: 011-33-9376-1402 – Principal, Gary O'Meara – *85 – OSSD
Offering the final year or OAC year of high school. Instruction in English. Students are housed locally with French families. Co-educational. Diploma.
Hong Kong: Delia School of Canada, Tai Fung Road, Tai Koo Shing, Quarry Bay Hong Kong – 011-852-884-41654166; Fax: 011-852-886-0813 – Principal, William McGarvie – *852
Hong Kong: S.E.A. Canadian Overseas Sec. School, 166-166A Boundary St., Kowloon Hong Kong – 011-852-336-1116; Fax: 011-852-336-4782 – Principal, Morley Mason – *271
Japan: Columbia International College, #709, Harada Bldg., 2-14-2 Takadanobaga, Shinjuku-ku, Tokyo 169 Japan – 011-81-3-04 2423-3711; Fax: 011-813-03-3204-7404 – Principal, Don McCallum
Malaysia: Sunway College, No. 5 Jalan Kolej, Sengalor Darul Ehsan, 46150 Petaling Jaya Malaysia – 011-603-735-8622; Fax: 011-603-735-8633 – Principal, Rex Sharman – *315
Malaysia: Taylor's College, No. 1, Jalan SS15/8, Subang Jaya New Town Centre, 47500 Petaling Jaya Malaysia – 011-03-734-5211; Fax: 011-03-734-5209 – Principal, Bert Naylor – *503
Romania: A.A.C. Cernavoda School, Centrala Nucleara Cernavoda, Constanta Romania – 011-40-91-239340; Fax: 011-40-1-312-0519
Singapore: Canadian International School, 5 Toh Tuck Rd., Singapore 21659 Singapore – 011-65-467-1732; Fax: 011-65-467-1729 – Principal, Wayne MacInnis – *432
Switzerland: Neuchatel Jr. College, Cret-Taconnet, 4, 2000 Neuchatel Switzerland – 011-41-38-252700; Fax: 011-41-252-38-244259 – Principal, Jim McMurtry – *107

# PRINCE EDWARD ISLAND

## Department of Education

PO Box 2000, Charlottetown PE C1A 7N8
902/368-4600; Fax: 902/368-4663

#### CURRICULUM INFORMATION

Director, French Programs & Services, Tilmon Gallant, 902/368-4671; Fax: 902/368-4622
Director, English Programs & Services, Eldon Rogerson, 902/368-6070; Fax: 902/368-4622

## Office of Higher Education, Training and Adult Learning

PO Box 2000, Charlottetown PE C1A 7N8
902/368-5988; Fax: 902/368-6144
Director, Policy & Programs, Calvin Caiger

**For detailed departmental listings, see Index: "Education, Depts."**

### REGIONAL ADMINISTRATIVE SCHOOL UNITS

There are three regional administrative school boards. The two English boards consist of fifteen elected members; the French school board has nine elected members.

Eastern School District
PO Box 8600, Charlottetown PE C1A 8V7
902/368-6990; Fax: 902/368-6960 – Supt., David McCabe
French Language School Board
Abram's Village, RR#3, Wellington PE C0B 2E0
902/854-2975; Fax: 902/854-2981 – Supt., Gabriel Arsenault
Western School Board
PO Box 312, Slemon Park PE C0B 2A0
902/888-8400; Fax: 902/888-8449 – Supt., Sonia Pritchard; Asst. Supt., Alan Kennedy; Asst. Supt., Jim MacNeill

### BAND-OPERATED INDIAN SCHOOLS

John J. Sark Memorial School, PO Box 124, Lennox Island PE C0B 1P0 – 902/831-2777 – Principal, Sr. Bernice Smith

### UNIVERSITIES

## University of Prince Edward Island

550 University Ave., Charlottetown PE C1A 4P3
902/566-0400; Fax: 902/628-4311
URL: http://www.upei.ca
President & Vice-Chancellor, Elizabeth Epperly, B.A., M.A., Ph.D.
Chancellor, Norman Webster, B.A., M.A.
Chair of the Board, John A. O'Keefe, B.B.A., LL.B.
Registrar, John DeGrace, B.Sc.(Eng.), M.Sc.
Vice-President, Academic Support, John Crossley, B.A., M.A., Ph.D.
Director, Alumni, Development & Public Relations, Sonya Banks, B.A., M.B.A.
Public Afairs Officer, S.L. Copan, B.P.R.
Business Manager, M.S. Stevenson
Purchasing Agent, R.A. Cooke
Manager, Bookstore, E.R. Gallant

#### FACULTIES WITH DEANS

Arts, Philip Smith, B.A., M.A., Ph.D.
Atlantic Veterinary College,
Education, Vianne Timmons, B.A., B.Ed., M.Ed., Ph.D.
School of Business, J. Ronald Collins, B.Sc., M.B.A., Ph.D.
School of Nursing, Margaret F. Munro, R.N., Ph.D.
Science, Winston Pineau, B.Sc., M.Sc.

### POST-SECONDARY SCHOOLS

#### HOLLAND COLLEGE OF APPLIED ARTS AND TECHNOLOGY

Administrative Services, 140 Weymouth St., Charlottetown PE C1A 4Z1
902/566-9510; Fax: 902/566-9509
Email: doiron@reggys.cc.hollandc.pe.ca
President, Alex MacAulay
Atlantic Police Academy, PO Box 156, Slemon Park PE C0A 2A0 – 902/888-6700; Fax: 902/888-6725
Culinary Institute of Canada, 140 Weymouth St., Charlottetown PE C1A 4Z1 – 902/566-9550
Harbourside Centre, 298 Water St., Summerside PE C1N 1B8 – 902/888-6450; Fax: 902/888-6401
Marine Centre, 100 Water St., Summerside PE C1N 1A9 – 902/888-6485; Fax: 902/888-6404
Royalty Centre, 40 Enman Cres., Charlottetown PE C1E 1E6 – 902/566-9330; Fax: 902/566-1955
School of Justice, PO Box 156, Slemon Park PE C0B 2A0 – 902/888-6700; Fax: 902/888-6725
Souris Centre, 120 Main St., Souris PE C0A 2B0 – 902/687-3341; Fax: 902/687-4360
Summerside Centre, 425 Granville St., Summerside PE C1N 3C4 – 902/888-6420; Fax: 902/888-6402
West Prince Centre, PO Box 37, Elmsdale PE C0B 1K0 – 902/853-2200; Fax: 902/853-3586

### INDEPENDENT & PRIVATE SCHOOLS

Charlottetown: Fair Isle Adventist School, 20 Lapthorne Ave., Charlottetown PE C1A 2M3 – 902/894-9301 – Sheila Bergey – Gr. 1-9; Seventh-day Adventist
Charlottetown: Grace Christian School, 50 Kirkdale Rd., Charlottetown PE C1E 1N6 – 902/368-2218 – Principal, Carol Johnston – *132 – Gr. K.-12; Baptist
Charlottetown: Immanuel Christian School, 65 Kirkwood Dr., Charlottetown PE C1A 8C3 – 902/628-6465 – Principal, Allen Bron – *48 – Gr. 1-6

# QUÉBEC

## Ministère de l'Éducation

Direction des communications, 1035, rue De La Chevrotière, 11e étage, Québec QC G1R 5A5
418/643-7095; Fax: 418/646-6561
Email: dircom@meq.gouv.qc.ca; URL: http://www.gouv.qc.ca/francais/minorg/medu/medu_intro.html
Minister, Pauline Marois, 418/644-0664; Fax: 418/646-7551

#### EDUCATION PRÉSCOLAIRE, ENSEIGNEMENT PRIMAIRE & SECONDAIRE

Directeur, Ressources, Roger Vézina, 514/873-7681

#### ENSEIGNEMENT SUPÉRIEUR

Directrice, Affaires éducatives collégiales, Claire Prévost-Fournier, 418/643-6671

* indicates enrollment figure.

**DIRECTION GÉNÉRALE DES RESSOURCES DIDACTIQUES**

Direction Régionale 1: Bas St-Laurent/Gaspésie-Îles-de-la-Madeleine: 376, av de la Cathédrale, Rimouski QC G5L 5K9 – 418/727-3600; Fax: 418/727-3557 – Dir. rég., Michel Doré

Direction Régionale 2: Saguenay-Lac-Saint-Jean: #202, 3750, boul Harvey, Jonquière QC G7X 0L5 – 418/695-7982; Fax: 418/695-7990 – Dir. rég., Claude Pagé

Direction Régionale 3: Québec-Chaudière-Appalaches: 1020, rte de l'Église, 3e étage, Ste-Foy QC G1V 3V9 – 418/644-9716; Fax: 418/643-0972 – Dir. rég., Jeannot Bordeleau

Direction Régionale 4: La Mauricie-Bois-Francs: 100, rue Laviolette, 2e étage, Trois-Rivières QC G9A 5S9 – 819/371-6711; Fax: 819/371-6075 – Dir. rég., Jean-Paul Bournival

Direction Régionale 5: L'Estrie: #3.05, 200, rue Belvédère nord, Sherbrooke QC J1H 4A9 – 820/820-3382; Fax: 820/820-3947 – Dir. gén., Marcel Veillette

Direction Régionale 6.1: Laval-Laurentides-Lanaudière: 300, rue Sicard, 2e étage, Ste-Thérèse-de-Blainville QC J7E 3X5 – 514/430-3611; Fax: 514/430-4005 – Dir. rég., Michel Monfet

Direction Régionale 6.2: La Montérégie: 201, Place Charles-Lemoyne, 6e étage, Longueuil QC J4K 2T5 – 514/928-7438; Fax: 514/928-7451 – Dir. rég., Claude Fortier

Direction Régionale 6.3: Montréal: 600, rue Fullum, 6e étage, Montréal QC H2K 4L1 – 514/873-2050; Fax: 514/873-0620 – Dir. rég., Michel de Celles

Direction Régionale 7: L'Outaouais: 170, rue de l'Hôtel-de-Ville, 4e étage, Hull QC J8X 4C2 – 819/772-3117; Fax: 819/772-3955 – Dir. rég., Denis Dugal

Direction Régionale 8: L'Abitibi-Témiscamingue: #2.02, 180, boul Rideau, Rouyn-Noranda QC J9X 1N9 – 819/797-1766; Fax: 819/797-5074 – Dir. rég., Oliva Carrier

Direction Régionale 9: Côte-Nord: #1812, 625, boul Laflèche, Baie-Comeau QC G5C 1C5 – 418/589-5748; Fax: 418/589-4467 – Dir. rég., Margaret Rioux-Dolan

**For detailed departmental listings, see Index: "Education, Depts."**

## COMMISSIONS SCOLAIRES

The Québec school board networks are denominational. The elementary course usually lasts six years & the secondary course five years. The secondary education is polyvalent in that the students may choose professional options at the same time as general options. In the listings below, (Prot.) indicates Protestant; (RC) indicates Roman Catholic.

Commission des écoles catholiques de Montréal – (RC)
3737, rue Sherbrooke est, Montréal QC H1X 3B3
514/596-6021; Fax: 514/596-7570 – Dir. gén., Yves Archambault; Prés., Michel Pallascio

Commission des écoles catholiques de Québec – (RC)
1460, ch Ste-Foy, Québec QC G1S 2N9
418/682-2041; Fax: 418/682-6058 – Dir. gén., Lise Doyon-Forques; Prés., Lucien Flamand

Commission des écoles catholiques de Verdun – (RC)
1100, 5e av, Verdun QC H4G 2Z7
514/765-7555; Fax: 514/765-7599 – Dir. gén., Guy Dupuis; Prés., Daniel O'Reilly

Commission des écoles protestantes du Grand-Montréal – (Prot.)
6000, av Fielding, Montréal QC H3X 1T4
514/483-7202; Fax: 514/483-7324 – Prés., Allan Butler; Dir. gén., Michael D. George

Commission scolaire Abitibi – (RC)
500, rue Principale, LaSarre QC J9Z 2A2
819/333-5411; Fax: 819/333-3044 – Dir. gén., Robert Caron; Prés., Marguerite Houle

Commission scolaire de l'Amiante – (RC)
650, rue Lapierre, Thetford Mines QC G6G 7P1
418/338-7801; Fax: 418/338-7845 – Dir. gén., Uriel Rouleau

Commission scolaire de l'Argile Bleue – (RC)
480, boul Laurier, Mont-St-Hilaire QC J3H 4R9
514/467-9323; Fax: 514/467-9375 – Prés., Denise Asselin; Dir. gén., Ginette Jacques

Commission scolaire de l'Asbesterie – (RC)
309, rue Chassé, Asbestos QC J1T 2B4
819/879-6907; Fax: 819/879-4350 – Prés., Camille Côté; Dir. gén., Yvon Raymond

Commission scolaire d'Aylmer – (RC)
115, rue Principale, 2e étage, Aylmer QC J9H 3M2
819/685-2520; Fax: 819/685-2525 – Dir. gén., Guy Benoit; Prés., Chantal Leblanc Bélanger

Commission scolaire de Baie-des-Chaleurs – (RC)
151 - 7e rue A, CP 8000, Paspébiac QC G0C 2K0
418/534-3328; Fax: 418/752-5716 – Prés., Pierre Arsenault; Dir. gén., Bertrand Poirier

Commission scolaire Baie-des-Ha Ha – (RC)
3111, rue Monseigneur-Dufour, La Baie QC G7B 4H5
418/544-3307; Fax: 418/544-0257 – Dir. gén., Réjean Simard; Prés., Liz Simard-Gagné

Commission scolaire Baldwin-Cartier – (RC)
10, boul des Sources, Pointe-Claire QC H9S 5K8
514/697-6320; Fax: 514/697-5908 – Dir. gén., France Goulet; Prés., Jacques Mongeau

Commission scolaire de Barraute-Senneterre – (RC)
391, 4e rue ouest, CP 250, Senneterre QC J0Y 2M0
819/737-2382; Fax: 819/237-2039 – Dir. gén., Suzanne Néron; Prés., Paul Veilleux

Commission scolaire Des Basques – (RC)
9, rue Notre-Dame est, CP 1660, Trois-Pistoles QC G0L 4K0
418/851-3341; Fax: 418/851-4968 – Prés., Cécile N. Lamarre; Dir. gén., Denis Leclerc

Commission scolaire de la Beauce-Abénaquis – (RC)
#A, 700, Notre-Dame nord, Ste-Marie QC G6E 2K9
418/387-5960; Fax: 418/387-6885 – Prés., Daniel Fecteau; Dir. gén., Jacques Ouellet

Commission scolaire Beauport – (RC)
643, av du Cénacle, Beauport QC G1E 1B3
418/666-6015; Fax: 418/666-9783 – Prés., Lise C. Harvey; Dir. gén., Diane Provencher

Commission scolaire des Belle-Rivières – (RC)
1900, Place Côté, Québec QC G1N 3Y5
418/688-7818; Fax: 418/688-4071 – Dir. gén., Chantal Dolbec; Prés., Jean Roy

Commission scolaire de Bellechasse – (RC)
189, rue Principale, St-Gervais QC G0R 3C0
418/887-3381; Fax: 418/887-6693 – Dir. gén., Robert Laforest; Prés., Jeannine Morin-Laforesterie

Commission scolaire de Bersimis – (RC)
#16, 5e av, CP 190, Forestville QC G0T 1E0
418/587-2235; Fax: 418/587-6104 – Dir. gén., Guy Lemieux; Prés., Donald Perron

Commission scolaire Berthier-Nord-Joli – (RC)
4671, rue Principale, St-Felix-de-Valois QC J0K 2M0
514/889-5531; Fax: 514/889-8604 – Prés., Bernard Lacasse; Dir. gén., Jacques Laperrière

Commission scolaire de Brossard – (RC)
5885, av Auteuil, Brossard QC J4Z 3P6
514/656-1450; Fax: 514/656-2411 – Prés., Réal Hébert; Dir. gén., Jean-Jacques Maurin

Commission scolaire des Cantons – (RC)
55, rue Court, CP 9000, Granby QC J2G 9H7
514/372-0221; Fax: 514/372-3150 – Dir. gén., Michel Bilodeau; Prés., Viviane Schofield

Commission scolaire Des Cascades-l'Achigan – (RC)
3461, rue Queen, CP 850, Rawdon QC J0K 1S0
514/834-2591; Fax: 514/834-5495 – Prés., Diane Bernard-Riberdy; Dir. gén., Johanne Paradis

Commission scolaire catholique de Sherbrooke – (RC)
2955, boul de l'Université, Sherbrooke QC J1K 2Y3
819/822-5534; Fax: 819/822-5631 – Dir. gén. intérimaire, Jean De Francesco; Prés., Noel Richard

Commission scolaire du Centre de la Mauricie – (RC)
2072, rue Gignac, CP 580, Shawinigan QC G9N 6V7
819/539-6971; Fax: 819/539-7797 – Prés., Normand Lajoie; Dir. gén., Robert Rivard

Commission scolaire de Chapais-Chibougamau – (RC)
596, 4e rue, Chibougamau QC G8P 1S3
418/748-7621; Fax: 418/748-2440 – Dir. gén., Réynald Sylvain; Prés., Clémence Tremblay

Commission scolaire de Charlesbourg – (RC)
7260, boul Cloutier, Charlesbourg QC G1H 3E8
418/622-7800; Fax: 418/622-7809 – Prés., Marguerite Dorion; Dir. gén., Cécile Mélançon

Commission scolaire de Châteauguay – (RC)
184, boul Salaberry nord, Châteauguay QC J6J 4K9
514/691-5028; Fax: 514/698-5100 – Dir. gén., Maurice Brossard; Prés., Marie-Louise Kerneis

Commission scolaire de Châteauguay Valley – (Prot.)
214, rue McLeod, Châteauguay QC J6J 2H4
514/691-1440; Fax: 514/691-0643 – Dir. gén., Keith Fitzpatrick; Prés., Doreen Newell

Commission scolaire de la Chaudière-Etchemin – (RC)
1925, 118e rue, Saint-Georges-de-Beauce QC G5Y 7R7
418/228-5541; Fax: 418/228-5549 – Prés., Marc-Yvon Poulin; Dir. gén., André Roy

Commission scolaire de Chavigny – (RC)
7175, boul Marion, CP 1804, Trois-Rivières-Ouest QC G9A 5M4
819/379-2844; Fax: 819/379-5634 – Prés., Gaétane Martin; Dir. gén., Richard Théoret

Commission scolaire des Chênes – (RC)
211, rue St-Édouard, CP 846, Drummondville QC J2B 6X1
819/478-6700; Fax: 819/478-9166 – Dir. gén., Monique Bertrand Deslauriers; Prés., Gaétan Mercure

Commission scolaire de Chicoutimi – (RC)
36, rue Jacques-Cartier est, Chicoutimi QC G7H 1W2
418/698-5068; Fax: 418/698-5262 – Prés., Jean-Marie Beaulieu; Dir. gén., Ginette Gilbert

Commission scolaire Chomedey de Laval – (RC)
125, boul des Prairies, Laval QC H7N 2T6
514/662-5601; Fax: 514/662-7040 – Prés., André Ferron; Dir. gén., Luc Mauger

Commission scolaire des Chutes-de-la-Chaudière – (RC)
1860, 1re rue, St-Romuald QC G6W 5M6
418/839-0505; Fax: 418/839-0536 – Prés., Anicet A. Gagné; Dir. gén., Bertrand Laroche

Commission scolaire des Chutes-Montmorency – (RC)
2233, av Royale, Beauport QC G1C 1P3
418/821-8988; Fax: 418/821-8862 – Dir. gén., Roger Boudreau; Prés., Jeanne d'Arc Marcoux

Commission scolaire de Coaticook – (RC)
249, rue St-Jean-Baptiste, Coaticook QC J1A 2J4
819/849-7051; Fax: 819/849-0470 – Prés., André Lafaille; Dir. gén., Gérard Ruest

Commission scolaire de la Côte-du-Sud – (RC)
157, rue Saint-Louis, Montmagny QC G5V 4N3
418/248-2016; Fax: 418/248-9797 – Dir. gén., Gaston Caron; Prés., Richard Couillard

Commission scolaire Crie
282, rue Principale, CP 1210, Mistissini QC G0W 1C0
819/923-2764; Fax: 819/923-2072 – Dir. gén., Gordon Blackned; Prés., Luke MacLeod

Commission scolaire Davignon – (RC)
112, rue John, Cowansville QC J2K 1X2
514/263-3087; Fax: 514/263-9583 – Prés., Ghislaine Delisle; Dir. gén. intérimaire, Donald Proteau

Commission scolaire des Découvreurs – (RC)
945, rue Wolfe, Ste-Foy QC G1V 4E2
418/652-2120; Fax: 418/652-2146 – Dir. gén., Sylvain Blanchette; Prés., Claude Gélinas

Commission scolaire dissidente catholique de Greenfield-Park – (RC)
#280, 899, boul Taschereau, Greenfield-Park QC J4V 2J2
514/672-7505; Fax: 514/672-4958 – Dir. gén., Denise Benoît-Lussier; Prés., Gilbert Dionne

Commission scolaire dissidente catholique de Portage-du-Fort – (RC)
CP 10, Portage-du-Fort QC J0X 2T0
819/648-2353; Fax: 819/647-2046 – Dir. gén., Gordon Brennan; Prés., Benedict Tanquay

Commission scolaire dissidente protestante de Baie-Comeau – (Prot.)
39, av Marquette, Baie-Comeau QC G4Z 1K4
418/296-2832; Fax: 418/296-4883 – Dir. gén., Raymond Haché; Prés., Jaan Kull

Commission scolaire dissidente protestante de Laurentienne – (Prot.)
26, rue Napoléon, Ste-Agathe-des-Monts QC J8C 1Z3
819/326-2563; Fax: 819/326-7563 – Prés., William S. Pollock; Dir. gén., Augustino Santini

Commission scolaire dissidente protestante de Rouyn – (Prot.)
218, av Portage, CP 266, Rouyn-Noranda QC J9X 5C3
819/762-2196 – Prés., Walter Charchuk

Commission scolaire District of Bedford – (Prot.)
CP 20, Cowansville QC J2K 3H2
514/266-0944; Fax: 514/266-0954 – Dir. gén., James R. Bissel; Prés., Peter Quilliams

Commission scolaire des Draveurs – (RC)
225, rue Notre-Dame, Gatineau QC J8P 1K3
819/663-9221; Fax: 819/663-6176 – Dir. gén., Jean-Guy Binet; Prés., Christine Émond-Lapointe

Commission scolaire Eastern Townships – (Prot.)
257, rue Queen, CP 5004, Lennoxville QC J1M 2A5
819/821-9570; Fax: 819/821-9586 – Dir. gén., Walter Duszara; Prés., Margaret Paulette

Commission scolaire de l'Eau-Vive – (RC)
790, boul Quinn, Longueuil QC J4H 2N5
514/463-2230; Fax: 514/463-2241 – Dir. gén., André Barrette; Prés., Gabriel Ducharme

Commission scolaire Les Écores – (RC)
#210, 3100, boul de la Concorde est, Laval QC H7E 2B9
514/664-1300; Fax: 514/664-2835 – Prés., Diane Latour-Gadbois; Dir. gén., Denis Roy

Commission scolaire des Falaises – (RC)
102, rue Jacques-Cartier, CP 2003, Gaspé QC G0C 1R0
418/368-3499; Fax: 418/368-6531 – Dir. gén., Carol Paré; Prés., François Tardif

Commission scolaire Fermont – (RC)
130, rue Le Carrefour, CP 190, Fermont QC G0G 1J0
418/287-5491; Fax: 418/287-3576 – Prés., Jocelyn Caron; Dir. gén., Diane Fortin

Commission scolaire Des Frontières – (RC)
474, rue des Étudiants, CP 99, Pohénégamook QC G0L 4J0
418/893-5555; Fax: 418/893-2822 – Prés., Roger Bélanger; Dir. gén., Serge Pelletier

Commission scolaire de Le Gardeur – (RC)
80, rue Jean-Baptiste-Meilleur, Repentigny QC J6A 6C5
514/581-6411; Fax: 514/581-8199 – Dir. gén., Thomas Duzyk; Prés., Claude Giguère

Commission scolaire Gaspésia-Les Îles – (Prot.)
40, rue Mont-Sorel, CP 500, New Carlisle QC G0C 1Z0
418/752-2247; Fax: 418/752-6447 – Prés., Audrey Acteson; Dir. gén., Wade Gifford

Commission scolaire du Goéland – (RC)
50, boul Taschereau, La Prairie QC J5R 4V3
514/444-4484; Fax: 514/659-4195 – Dir. gén., Normand Lapointe; Prés., Jacques Perreault

Commission scolaire du Gouffre – (RC)
50, rue Racine, CP 70, Baie-St-Paul QC G0A 1B0
418/435-2301; Fax: 418/435-2223 – Dir. gén., Gilles E. Bouchard; Prés., Benoit Simard

Commission scolaire de Grandpré – (RC)
100, rue St-Jacques, Louiseville QC J5V 1C2
819/228-2771; Fax: 819/228-8570 – Dir. gén., Gilles A. Lessard; Prés., Michael Marcotte

Commission scolaire de Greater Québec – (Prot.)
2046, ch Saint-Louis, Sillery QC G1T 1P4
418/688-0602; Fax: 418/682-5891 – Prés., Martin Hicks; Dir. gén., William Pennefather

Commission scolaire Harricana – (RC)
341, rue Principale nord, Amos QC J9T 2L8
819/732-6561; Fax: 819/732-1623 – Dir. gén., Jean-Marc Matthieu; Prés., Clément Roy

Commission scolaire du Haut St-Maurice – (RC)
445, rue Lacroix, CP 490, La Tuque QC G9X 3P4
819/523-7582; Fax: 819/676-8025 – Prés., Lise Lapointe; Dir. gén., Gilles Mongrain

Commission scolaire de la Haute Gatineau – (RC)
331, rue du Couvent, Maniwaki QC J9E 1H5
819/449-7866; Fax: 819/449-6083 – Prés., Daniel Moreau; Dir. gén., Louis Pelletier

Commission scolaire de Huntingdon – (RC)
64, rue Châteauguay, Huntingdon QC J0S 1H0
514/264-6191; Fax: 514/264-4536 – Dir. gén., Jean Beauchamp; Prés., Normand Demeule

Commission scolaire d'Iberville – (RC)
600, 4e rue, Iberville QC J2X 3N2
514/347-8556; Fax: 514/347-8388 – Dir. gén., Jean-Pierre Fontaine; Prés., Luc Mercier

Commission scolaire des Îles – (RC)
CP 610, Cap-aux-Meules QC G0B 1B0
418/986-5511; Fax: 418/986-3552 – Dir. gén., Rollande Roy; Prés., Lise Thériault

Commission scolaire Des Îlets – (RC)
80, rue de l'Église, Charlesbourg QC G2N 1C5
418/849-1299; Fax: 418/849-1200 – Prés., André Caron; Dir. gén., Paul-Eugène Roger

Commission scolaire de l'Industrie – (RC)
333, rue Sir-Mathias-Tellier, Joliette QC J6E 6E6
514/755-7000; Fax: 514/755-7290 – Prés., Christian Perron; Dir. gén., Michel Ratelle

Commission scolaire L'Islet-Sud – (RC)
25, rue Principale, St-Pamphile QC G0R 3X0
418/356-3361; Fax: 418/356-2811 – Dir. gén., Thérèse Lachance; Prés., Jacques-Yvan Pelletier

Commission scolaire Jacques-Cartier – (RC)
13, rue Saint-Laurent est, 1er étage, Longueuil QC J4H 4B7
514/670-0730; Fax: 514/670-0250 – Dir. gén., Serge Lefebvre; Prés., Michel Poulin

Commission scolaire Jean-Chapais – (RC)
325, av Chapleau, CP 1000, St-Pascal QC G0L 3Y0
418/492-9970; Fax: 418/492-9792 – Dir. gén., Arthur Bouchard; Prés., Claude Langlois

Commission scolaire de Jean-Rivard – (RC)
1783, av Saint-Édouard, Plessisville QC G6L 2K8
819/362-4400; Fax: 819/362-9157 – Prés., Michel Bernier; Dir. gén., Réal Ouellet

Commission scolaire Jérôme-Le Royer – (RC)
550, 53e av, Montréal QC H1A 2T7
514/642-9520; Fax: 514/642-1590 – Prés., Vincenzo Arciresi; Dir. gén., Micheline Sabourin

Commission scolaire de La Jeune-Lorette – (RC)
184, rue Racine, Loretteville QC G2B 1E3
418/847-8110; Fax: 418/847-8163 – Prés., Lili Paillé; Dir. gén., Jean-Marie Pépin

Commission scolaire de la Jonquière – (RC)
3644, rue St-Jules, CP 1600, Jonquière QC G7X 7X4
418/542-7551; Fax: 418/542-2407 – Dir. gén., André Garon; Prés., Monique Villeneuve

Commission scolaire Kativik
2055, av Oxford, Montréal QC H4A 2X6
514/482-8220; Fax: 514/482-8496 – Dir. gén., Annie Grenier; Prés., George Peters

Commission scolaire de La Pocatière – (RC)
1011, 6e av, CP 940, La Pocatière QC G0R 1Z0
418/856-3690; Fax: 418/856-3232 – Dir. gén., Richard Bernier; Prés., Gaétan Grondin

Commission scolaire du Lac-Mégantic – (RC)
4730, rue Dollard, Lac-Mégantic QC G6B 1G6
819/583-2351; Fax: 819/583-0624 – Prés., Suzanne Durivage; Dir. gén., Colette Roy Laroche

Commission scolaire du Lac Saint-Jean – (RC)
350, boul Champlain sud, Alma QC G8B 5W2
418/669-6000; Fax: 418/669-6016 – Prés., Michel Hudon; Dir. gén., Jean-Claude Lindsay

Commission scolaire Lac-Témiscamingue – (RC)
2, rue Maisonneuve, CP 700, Ville-Marie QC J0Z 3W0
819/629-2472; Fax: 819/629-2791 – Dir. gén., Rémi Barrette; Prés., Doris Roberge

Commission scolaire de Lakeshore – (Prot.)
257, boul Beaconsfield, Beaconsfield QC H9W 4A5
514/697-2480; Fax: 514/697-5919 – Dir. gén., John Killingbeck; Prés., Marcus Tabachnick

Commission scolaire Laure-Conan – (RC)
350, boul de Comporté, CP 5000, La Malbaie QC G5A 1T5
418/665-3905; Fax: 418/665-6805 – Prés., Pierre Asselin; Dir. gén., Gilbert Dumont

Commission scolaire Laurentian – (Prot.)
171, rue Mary, Lachute QC J8H 2C1
514/562-3721; Fax: 514/562-1541 – Prés., Peter Haldimand; Dir. gén., Dominic Martini

Commission scolaire des Laurentides – (RC)
13, rue Saint-Antoine, Ste-Agathe-des-Monts QC J8C 2C3
819/326-0333; Fax: 819/326-2121 – Dir. gén., Gaétan St-Pierre; Prés., Michel Vallières

Commission scolaire Laurenval – (Prot.)
1105, rue Victor-Morin, Laval QC H7G 4B8
514/668-4380; Fax: 514/668-3555 – Dir. gén., Scott Conrod; Prés., Ronald G. Edwards

Commission scolaire de Lévis – (RC)
30, Champagnat ouest, Lévis QC G6V 6P5
418/838-8338; Fax: 418/838-8393 – Prés., Serge Bouchard; Dir. gén., Richard Gagnon

Commission scolaire du Littoral
652, rue Dequen, Sept-Îles QC G4R 2R5
418/962-5558; Fax: 418/968-2942 – Adm., Mederic O'Brien

Commission scolaire du Long Sault – (RC)
189, rue Mary, Lachute QC J8H 2C3
514/562-8841; Fax: 514/562-1905 – Dir. gén., Ghislain Levert; Prés., Jacques Sabourin

Commission scolaire de Lotbinière – (RC)
1159, rue Principale, CP 430, St-Agapit QC G0S 1Z0
418/888-3947; Fax: 418/888-3627 – Dir. gén., Guy Godin; Prés., Alain Lavoie

Commission scolaire Louis-Hémon – (RC)
1950, boul Sacré-Coeur, Dolbeau QC G8L 2R3
418/276-2032; Fax: 418/276-8819 – Dir. gén., Claude Dauphinais; Prés., Rémi Rousseau

Commission scolaire de Malartic – (RC)
340, rue La Sarre, CP 4077, Malartic QC J0Y 1Z0
819/757-3695; Fax: 819/757-6614 – Prés., Ginette McFadden; Dir. gén., Robert Paquin

Commission scolaire de Manicouagan – 6,221 (RC)
771, boul Joliet, Baie-Comeau QC G5C 1P3
418/589-0813; Fax: 418/589-2711 – Dir. gén., Gilles-Maurice Bouchard; Prés., Ginette Côté-Fortin

Commission scolaire des Manoirs – (RC)
775, rue St-Louis, Terrebonne QC J6W 1J7
514/492-3555; Fax: 514/492-3599 – Dir. gén., Jean-Claude Brisson; Prés., Francine Dyon

Commission scolaire de Marieville – (RC)
500, rue Docteur-Poulin, Marieville QC J3M 1R7
514/460-2181; Fax: 514/460-4683 – Prés., Cécile Dubé Marier; Dir. gén., Gilles Roy

Commission scolaire de Matane – (RC)
530, av Saint-Jérôme, Matane QC G4W 3B5

418/566-2502; Fax: 418/562-4805 – Prés., Liane Lebrun-Imbeault; Dir. gén., René Ouellet
Commission scolaire de Memphrémagog – (RC)
449, rue Percy, Magog QC J1X 1B5
819/897-1500; Fax: 819/847-3632 – Dir. gén., Lucien Carrier; Prés., Nellie Vandal
Commission scolaire Miguasha – (RC)
24, rue du Centre Civique, CP 330, Carleton QC G0C 1J0
418/364-3371; Fax: 418/364-7598 – Prés., Roseline Arsenault; Dir. gén., Gérard Thériault
Commission scolaire des Mille-Îles – (RC)
2275, rue Honoré-Mercier, Laval QC H7L 2T1
514/625-6951; Fax: 514/625-2042 – Dir. gén., Jocelyne Darveau; Prés., Lyne Deschamps
Commission scolaire de La Mitis – (RC)
1624, rue Aubin, Mont-Joli QC G5H 2R8
418/775-6000; Fax: 418/775-9192 – Prés., Bernard Côté; Dir. gén., Jean-Marie Thibeault
Commission scolaire des Moissons – (RC)
660, rue Ellice, Beauharnois QC J6N 1Y1
514/429-4671; Fax: 514/429-5046 – Prés., Francine Daigle; Dir. gén., Denis Girard
Commission scolaire Mont-Fort – (RC)
1740, rue Roberval, St-Bruno-de-Montarville QC J3V 3R3
514/441-2919; Fax: 514/441-0838 – Dir. gén., Serge Dubé; Prés., Richard Schiller
Commission scolaire Des Montagnes – (RC)
381, av Principale, Dégelis QC G5T 1L3
418/853-2226; Fax: 418/853-3778 – Dir. gén., Claude Lavoie; Prés., Guilmont Pelletier
Commission scolaire Morilac – (RC)
65, 1re av, Windsor QC J1S 2A4
819/845-2761; Fax: 819/845-2571 – Prés., Manon Beaudry-Roberge; Dir. gén., Susan Tremblay
Commission scolaire de la Moyenne-Côte-Nord – (RC)
1235, rue de la Digue, CP 940, Havre-St-Pierre QC G0G 1P0
418/538-3044; Fax: 418/538-3268 – Prés., Édith Jomphe; Dir. gén., Yves Thériault
Commission scolaire La Neigette – (RC)
435, av Rouleau, Rimouski QC G5L 8V4
418/723-5927; Fax: 418/722-1978 – Dir. gén., Jeanne-Paule Berger; Prés., Raymond Tudeau
Commission scolaire de Normandie – (RC)
581, rue Saint-Paul, CP 10, St-Tite QC G0X 3H0
418/365-5938; Fax: 418/365-3132 – Prés., Martine Duchemin; Dir. gén., Jean Lavoie
Commission scolaire de Normandin – (RC)
1013, rue du Centre Sportif, Normandin QC G8M 4L7
418/274-0000; Fax: 418/274-7183 – Dir. gén., Gaston Plourde; Prés., Marlène Tremblay-Potvin
Commission scolaire du Nouveau-Québec – (RC)
7, rue Petite Allée, CP 190, Matagami QC J0Y 2A0
819/739-4361; Fax: 819/739-4524 – Dir. gén., Bernard Le Régent; Prés., Liliane Pronovost-Gingras
Commission scolaire de Outaouais-Hull – (RC)
225, rue Saint-Rédempteur, Hull QC J8X 2T3
819/771-4548; Fax: 819/771-6964 – Prés., Denise Laferrière; Dir. gén., René Nadeau
Commission scolaire des Patriotes – (RC)
430, boul Arthur-Sauvé, St-Eustache QC J7R 6V6
514/974-7000; Fax: 514/974-7718 – Dir. gén., Pierre Leduc; Prés., Claude St-Jacques
Commission scolaire Pierre-Neveu – (RC)
525, De la Madone, Mont-Laurier QC J9L 1S4
819/623-4310; Fax: 819/623-7979 – Dir. gén., Roger Lapointe; Prés., Gilles Létourneau
Commission scolaire de Pontiac – (RC)
185, rue Principale, CP 520, Fort-Coulonge QC J0X 1V0
819/683-3483; Fax: 819/683-3808 – Dir. gén., Jean-Louis Brizard; Prés., Roland Vallières
Commission scolaire de Port-Cartier – (RC)
12A, rue Boisvert, Port-Cartier QC G5B 1W7
418/766-2912; Fax: 418/766-6034 – Prés., Fatmi Asri; Dir. gén., Richard Banville
Commission scolaire de Portneuf – (RC)
310, rue de l'Église, Donnacona QC G0A 1T0
418/285-2600; Fax: 418/285-2738 – Prés., Alfred Gauthier; Dir. gén., Russel Gilbert
Commission scolaire Prince-Daveluy – (RC)
50, rue Saint-Charles, Princeville QC G6L 4W4
819/364-2074; Fax: 819/364-3508 – Dir. gén., Diane Grandmaitre; Prés., Paulette Rancourt
Commission scolaire protestante de Greater Seven Islands – (Prot.)
530, av Brochu, Sept-Îles QC G4R 2X3
418/968-9804; Fax: 418/962-9601 – Prés., Dave Johnson; Dir. gén., J. Kenneth Robertson
Commission scolaire protestante St-Maurice – (Prot. )
1241, rue Nicolas-Perrot, Trois-Rivières QC G9A 1C2
418/688-8730; Fax: 418/682-5891 – Prés., Raymond MacDonald; Dir. gén., William Pennefather
Commission scolaire Provençal – (RC)
1730, av du Frère-André, St-Césaire QC J0L 1T0
514/469-3112; Fax: 514/469-5239 – Prés., Robert Chicoine; Dir. gén., Denise Renaud
Commission scolaire de Quévillon – (RC)
223, Place Quévillon, CP 70, Lebel-sur-Quévillon QC J0Y 1X0
819/755-4833; Fax: 819/755-4763 – Prés., Robert Picard; Dir. gén., Laurent Therrien
Commission scolaire régionale Eastern Québec – (Prot.)
2046, ch Saint-Louis, Sillery QC G1T 1P4
418/688-0602; Fax: 418/682-5891 – Prés., Peter Marshall; Dir. gén., William Pennefather
Commission scolaire La Riveraine – (RC)
1580, boul Port-Royal, Bécancour QC G0X 2T0
819/233-2757; Fax: 819/233-3300 – Prés., Robert Boucher; Dir. gén., Pâquerette Gagnon
Commission scolaire de Rivière-du-Loup – (RC)
464, rue Lafontaine, CP 910, Rivière-du-Loup QC G5R 3Z5
418/862-8201; Fax: 418/862-0964 – Dir. gén., Marcien Proulx; Prés., André Thériault
Commission scolaire Des Rivières – (RC)
707, rue Saint-Paul nord, Farnham QC J2N 2K4
514/293-5358; Fax: 514/293-2731 – Prés., Jacqueline Lafrance-Tougas; Dir. gén., Jean Rivard
Commission scolaire Roberval – (RC)
828, boul Saint-Joseph, Roberval QC G8H 2L5
418/275-4136; Fax: 418/275-6217 – Prés., Pierrette Fortin; Dir. gén., Julien Guillemette
Commission scolaire de Rocher-Percé – (RC)
348, La Grande Allée est, CP 400, Grande-Rivière QC G0C 1V0
418/385-2231; Fax: 418/385-4446 – Dir. gén. intérimaire, Alain Desmeules; Prés., Jean-Pierre Johnson
Commission scolaire Rouyn-Noranda – (RC)
70, rue des Oblats est, CP 908, Rouyn-Noranda QC J9X 5C9
819/762-8161; Fax: 819/797-5125 – Prés., Denis Bureau; Dir. gén., Yves Charlebois
Commission scolaire de Saguenay – (Prot.)
1770, rue Joule, Jonquière QC G7S 3B1
418/548-0853; Fax: 418/548-9498 – Prés., Judy Francis-Fay; Dir. gén., William Pennefather
Commission scolaire Ste-Croix – (RC)
1100, ch Côte-Vertu, Saint-Laurent QC H4L 4V1
514/748-6991; Fax: 514/748-7529 – Dir. gén., Pierre Grou; Prés., Thérèse LeBrock-Lalonde
Commission scolaire St-Hyacinthe – (RC )
2255, av Sainte-Anne, St-Hyacinthe QC J2S 5H7
514/773-8401; Fax: 514/773-6876 – Prés., Lise Desmarais-Grimard; Dir. gén., Jacques Dupré
Commission scolaire St-Jean-sur-Richelieu – (RC)
210, rue Notre-Dame, St-Jean-sur-Richelieu QC J3B 6N3
514/359-6411; Fax: 514/359-4623 – Dir. gén., Jacques Bédard; Prés., June Galipeau
Commission scolaire St-Jérôme – (RC)
995, rue Labelle, St-Jérôme QC J7Z 5N7
514/436-5040; Fax: 514/436-5277 – Dir. gén., Yves Gaugeon; Prés., Guy Michaud
Commission scolaire de Ste-Thérèse – (RC)
6, rue Tassé, CP 390, Ste-Thérèse QC J7E 4J6
514/433-4601; Fax: 514/433-4626 – Prés., Jeanne d'Arc Duval Paquette; Dir. gén., Jean Poitras
Commission scolaire Samuel-De Champlain – (RC)
41, rue Bellerive, CP 190, Cap-de-la-Madeleine QC G8T 7W2
819/378-6146; Fax: 819/378-5120 – Prés., Yvon Lemire; Dir. gén., André Pelletier
Commission scolaire La Sapinière – (RC)
308, av Palmer, CP 418, East Angus QC J0B 1R0
819/832-4953; Fax: 819/832-4863 – Dir. gén., Jacques Létourneau; Prés., Yvon Turcotte
Commission scolaire du Sault-Saint-Louis – (RC)
8700, boul Champlain, LaSalle QC H8P 3H7
514/365-4600; Fax: 514/595-2083 – Dir. gén., Pierre Beauchamp; Prés., Patrick K. Carroll
Commission scolaire Seigneurie – (RC)
378A, rue Papineau, Papineauville QC J0V 1R0
819/427-6258; Fax: 819/427-8350 – Dir. gén., Marc Anctil; Prés., Jacques Montreuil
Commission scolaire de Sept-Îles – (RC)
30, rue Comeau, Sept-Îles QC G4R 4N2
418/968-9901; Fax: 418/962-7760 – Prés., Gaétan Lavoie; Dir. gén., Richard Roy
Commission scolaire de Sorel – (RC)
41, av de l'Hôtel-Dieu, Sorel QC J3P 1L1
514/746-3990; Fax: 514/746-4474 – Dir. gén., Michel Faust; Prés., Denis Rajotte
Commission scolaire South Shore – (Prot.)
299, boul Wilfrid-Laurier, St-Lambert QC J4R 2V7
514/672-4010; Fax: 514/465-8809 – Dir. gén., David C. D'Aoust; Prés., E.N. Gould
Commission scolaire de Tadoussac – (RC)
184, rue de l'Église, CP 130, Tadoussac QC G0T 2A0
418/235-4489; Fax: 418/235-4674 – Prés., Luciana Hovington; Dir. gén., Irenée Tremblay
Commission scolaire Taillon – (RC)
1890, boul Marie, St-Hubert QC J4T 3R6
514/465-0280; Fax: 514/465-3950 – Dir. gén., Jacquelin Bergeron; Prés., Fernande Leblanc-Sénéchal
Commission scolaire de Témiscouata – (RC)
14, rue Vieux-Chemin, Cabano QC G0L 1E0
418/854-2370; Fax: 418/854-2715 – Dir. gén. intérimaire, Gaston Caron; Prés., Michel Samson
Commission scolaire de Thetford-Mines – (RC)
650, rue Lapierre, Thetford-Mines QC G6G 7P1
418/338-7801; Fax: 418/338-7845 – Dir. gén., Réal Boucher; Prés., Denis Langlois
Commission scolaire de La Tourelle – (RC)
27, ch du Parc, CP 488, Ste-Anne-des-Monts QC G0E 2G0
418/763-2206; Fax: 418/763-5533 – Dir. gén., Yvan Landry; Prés., Michel Thibault
Commission scolaire Tracy – (RC)
1015, rue Saint-Pierre, St-Joseph-de-Sorel QC J3R 1B3
514/743-7991; Fax: 514/743-6907 – Dir. gén., Robert Blanchette; Prés., Jean Cournoyer
Commission scolaire des Trois-Lacs – (RC)
400, av St-Charles, Vaudreuil QC J7V 6B1
514/455-9311; Fax: 514/455-0259 – Dir. gén., Jean-Paul Régis; Prés., Gaëtane Trempe-Koszegi
Commission scolaire de Trois-Rivières – (RC)
1025, Marguerite-Bourgeois, CP 100, Trois-Rivières QC G9A 5E7
819/379-6565; Fax: 819/379-3450 – Dir. gén., Jean Sauvageon; Prés., Pierre Tremblay
Commission scolaire Val-Mauricie – (RC)
800, 6e av, CP 1040, Shawinigan-Sud QC G9P 4E6
819/536-5606; Fax: 819/536-3057 – Dir. gén., Jean-Pierre Hogue; Prés., Jean-Yves Laforest

Commission scolaire de Val d'Or - (RC)
799, boul Forest, Val d'Or QC J9P 2L4
819/825-4220; Fax: 819/825-5305 - Dir. gén., Adrien Boucher; Prés., Gaétan Gilbert

Commission scolaire Valin - (RC)
38, rue Frontenac, CP 2130, Chicoutimi QC
418/549-5381; Fax: 418/549-5880 - Dir. gén., Jean-Marc Dufresne; Prés., Charles Lavoie

Commission scolaire Vallée-de-la-Lièvre - (RC)
582, boul Cité des Jeunes, Buckingham QC J8L 2W2
819/986-8511; Fax: 819/986-9283 - Prés., Martine Bergeron; Dir. gén., Réjean Chalifoux

Commission scolaire Vallée de la Matapédia - (RC)
93, av du Parc, CP 2000, Amqui QC G0J 1B0
418/629-6223; Fax: 418/629-6280 - Prés., Laurent Boudreau; Dir. gén., Laval Morin

Commission scolaire de Valleyfield - (RC)
29, rue Fabre, CP 2000, Salaberry-de-Valleyfield QC J6S 5G3
514/371-1401; Fax: 514/371-4757 - Prés., Jacques Derepentigny; Dir. gén., Michel St-Jacques

Commission scolaire La Vallière - (RC)
1322, boul Sacré-Coeur, CP 7900, St-Félicien QC G8K 2R4
418/679-3620; Fax: 418/679-3887 - Prés., Ghislaine Dallaire; Dir. gén., Roger Guillemette

Commission scolaire de Victoriaville - (RC)
40, boul Bois-Francs nord, CP 40, Victoriaville QC G6P 6S5
819/758-6453; Fax: 819/758-4925 - Dir. gén., Roger Richard; Prés., Henri-Paul Roux

Commission scolaire de Warwick - (RC)
14, rue Hôtel-de-Ville, Warwick QC J0A 1M0
819/358-6801; Fax: 819/358-5668 - Prés., Estelle Luneau; Dir. gén., André Moreau

Commission scolaire Western Québec - (Prot.)
170, rue Principale, Aylmer QC J9H 6K1
819/684-2336; Fax: 819/684-9061 - Prés., Jerry Barber; Dir. gén., Diane Fyfe

Conseil scolaire de l'Île de Montréal
500, boul Crémazie est, Montréal QC H2P 1E7
514/384-1830; Fax: 514/384-2139 - Prés., Jacques Mongeau; Dir. gén., Nicole Ranger

## NATIVE SCHOOLS (FEDERAL)

**Schools with enrollment of 50 or more.**

École fédérale Notre-Dame-du-Nord, CP 428, Notre-Dame-du-Nord QC J0Z 3B0 - 819/723-2533 - *88 - Gr. K./Elem.

École indienne de Lorette, 20, rue de l'Ours, Wendake QC G0A 4V0 - 418/842-3740 - *126 - Gr. K./Elem.

École indienne de Manawan, 150, rue Wapoc, St-Michel-des-Saints QC J0K 1M0 - 819/971-8817 - *452 - Sec.

École indienne de Natashquan, Natashquan QC G0G 2E0 - 418/726-3671 - *219 - Gr. K./Elem./Sec.

École Jimmy Sandy Memorial, Secteur Schefferville, 2046, ch Saint-Louis, Sillery QC G1T 1P4 - 418/688-8730 - *146 - Gr. K./Elem./Sec.

École Johnny-Pilot, 460, rue Évangéline, Sept-Îles QC G4R 2N5 - 418/968-8225 - *175 - Gr. K./Elem.

École Manikanetish, CP 430, Moisie QC G0G 2B0 - 418/927-2250 - *87 - Sec.

École Mikwan, RR#4, Amos QC J9T 3A3 - 819/732-5213

École Olamen, CP 222, La Romaine QC G0G 1M0 - 418/229-2450 - *216 - Gr. K-12

École Pakuaushipu, CP 68, Saint Augustin QC G0G 2R0 - 418/947-2729 - *61 - Gr. K-8

École primaire Nussiem et Kapotakam, 4, rue Pulis, CP 70, Betsiamites QC G0H 1B0 - 418/567-2215 - *317 - Gr. K./Elem.

École primaire de Pointe-Bleue, 403, rue Amishk, Pointe-Bleue QC G0W 2H0 - 418/275-1243 - *226 - Elem.

École secondaire de Pointe-Bleue, 400, rue Amishk, Pointe-Bleue QC G0W 2H0 - 418/275-2473 - *61 - Sec.

École secondaire Uashkaikan, 63, rue Messek, Betsiamites QC G0H 1B0 - 418/567-2271 - *223 - Sec.

École Teuaikan, CP 159, Mingan QC G0G 1V0 - 418/949-2113

École Tshishteshinu, CP 430, Moisie QC G0G 2B0 - 418/927-2956 - *152 - Elem.

École Wejgwapniag, CP 1280, Gesgapegiag QC G0C 1Y0 - 418/759-3422

École de Weymontachie, CP 39, Weymontachie QC G0X 3R0 - 819/666-2226 - *196 - Gr. K./Elem.

Kahnawake Survival School, Nation Mohawk, CP 1978, Kahnawake QC J0L 1B0 - 514/682-8831

Kanatamat Tsitipenitamunu, 224, rue Lorraine, CP 1000, Shefferville QC G0G 2T0 - 418/585-2842 - *170 - Gr. K./Elem./Sec.

Kanesatake Indian School, 681A, Ste-Philomène, RR#1, Oka QC J0N 1E0 - 514/479-8827

Karonhianonhnha School, CP 100, Kahnawake QC J0L 1B0 - 514/638-2970

Kateri School, CP 100, Kahnawake QC J0L 1B0 - 514/632-3350

Kitigan Zibi School, CP 10, Maniwaki QC J9E 3B3 - 819/449-2848

Rapid Lake School, Parc de la Vérendrye, Lac-Rapide QC J0W 2C0 - 819/794-1711

## CANADIAN FORCES BASE SCHOOLS

École Alexander-Wolff, 17, rue Roy, Courcelette QC G0A 1R0 - 418/844-5669 - *415

École Alouette, BFC Bagotville, Édifice 116, La Baie QC G0V 1A0 - 418/693-2352 - *256

École Dollard-des-Ormeaux, 18, rue Ladas, Courcelette QC G0A 1R0 - 418/844-5633 - *282

St. Michael's School, BFC Montréal, Immeuble 101, St-Hubert QC J3Y 5T4 - 514/462-7596 - *196

## SCHOOLS OPERATED BY THE MINISTÈRE DE LA SANTÉ ET DES SERVICES SOCIAUX (Health & Social Services)

Centre d'accueil La Clairière, 950, rue de Louvain est, Montréal QC H2M 2E8 - 514/382-6160

Centre d'accueil l'Escale, 4515, rue de la Colline, Cap-Rouge QC G1Y 3A1 - 418/653-5241 - *50

Centre Marie-Vincent, 840, ch Côte-Vertu, St-Laurent QC H4L 1Y4 - 514/748-7901 - *22

Centre de Rééducation Boscoville, 10950, boul Perras est, Montréal QC H1C 1B3 - 514/648-7426 - *46

Centre Rose-Virginie-Pelletier, 9469, boul Gouin ouest, Pierrefonds QC H8Y 1T2 - 514/685-3200 - *52

## COLLÈGES D'ENSEIGNEMENT GÉNÉRAL ET PROFESSIONNEL (CÉGEP)

Cégep de l'Abitibi-Témiscamingue
425, boul du Collège, CP 1500, Rouyn-Noranda QC J9X 5E5
819/762-0931; Fax: 819/762-3815 - Pierre Falardeau

Cégep Ahuntsic
9155, rue St-Hubert, Montréal QC H2M 1Y8
514/389-5921; Fax: 514/389-4554 - Rock Tremblay

Cégep d'Alma
675, boul Auger ouest, Alma QC G8B 2B7
418/668-2387; Fax: 418/668-3806 - Louisette Perreault

Cégep André-Laurendeau
1111, rue Lapierre, LaSalle QC H8N 2J4
514/364-3320; Fax: 514/364-7130 - Denis Sirois

Cégep de Baie-Comeau
537, boul Blanche, Baie-Comeau QC G5C 2B2
418/589-5707; Fax: 418/589-9842 - Jean-Marc Cliche, Email: jmcliche@cegep-baie-comeau.qc.ca

Cégep Beauce-Appalaches
#1055, 116e rue, St-Georges QC G5Y 3G1
418/228-8896; Fax: 418/228-0562 - Jocelyn Benoît

Cégep de Bois-de-Boulogne
10555, av de Bois-de-Boulogne, Montréal QC H4N 1L4
514/332-3000; Fax: 514/332-5857 - Bernard Lachance

Cégep de Chicoutimi
534, rue Jacques-Cartier est, Chicoutimi QC G7H 1Z6
418/549-9520; Fax: 418/549-1315 - Roger Demeule

Cégep de Drummondville
960, rue St-Georges, Drummondville QC J2C 6A2
819/478-4671; Fax: 819/474-6859; URL: http://www.cdrummond.qc.ca - Paul G. Lemire

Cégep Édouard-Montpetit
945, ch de Chambly, Longueuil QC J4H 3M6
514/679-2630; Fax: 514/679-5570 - Claude Ostiguy

Cégep François-Xavier-Garneau
1660, boul de l'Entente, Québec QC G1S 4S3
418/688-8310; Fax: 418/681-9384 - Jean Asselin

Cégep de la Gaspésie et des Îles
96, rue Jacques-Cartier, CP 590, Gaspé QC G0C 1R0
418/368-2201; Fax: 418/368-7003 - Jules Bourque

Cégep de Granby-Haute-Yamaska
50, rue St-Joseph, Granby QC J2G 9H7
514/372-6614; Fax: 514/372-6565 - Yvan Vaillancourt

Cégep Joliette-De Lanaudière
20, rue St-Charles sud, Joliette QC J6E 4T1
514/759-1661; Fax: 514/759-4468 - Donald Fortin

Cégep de Jonquière
2505, rue St-Hubert, Jonquière QC G7X 7W2
418/547-2191; Fax: 418/547-3359 - Jacques Vézina

Cégep de La Pocatière
140, 4e av, La Pocatière QC G0R 1Z0
418/856-1525; Fax: 418/856-4589 - Michel Toussaint

Cégep de Lévis-Lauzon
205, rue Mgr-Ignace-Bourget, Lévis QC G6V 6Z9
418/833-5110; Fax: 418/833-7323 - Gaétan Poirier

Cégep Lionel-Groulx
100, rue Duquet, Ste-Thérèse QC J7E 3G6
514/430-3120; Fax: 514/971-7883; URL: http://www.clionelgroulx.qc.ca - Francine Senécal

Cégep de Maisonneuve
3800, rue Sherbrooke est, Montréal QC H1X 2A2
514/254-7131; Fax: 514/253-7637 - Guy Lefebvre

Cégep Marie-Victorin
7000, rue Marie-Victorin, Montréal QC H1G 2J6
514/325-0150; Fax: 514/328-3830 - Gilles Lépine

Cégep de Matane
616, av St-Rédempteur, Matane QC G4W 1L1
418/562-1240; Fax: 418/566-2115;
Email: dirgenerale@cgmatane.qc.ca;
URL: http://www.cgmatane.qc.ca - Jean-Pierre Clermont

Cégep Montmorency
475, boul de l'Avenir, Laval QC H7N 5H9
514/975-6100; Fax: 514/975-6116 - Michel Brisson

Cégep de l'Outaouais
333, boul Cité-des-Jeunes, Succ A, Hull QC J8Y 6M5
819/770-4012; Fax: 819/770-8167; URL: http://www.col-outao.qc.ca - Émile Demers

Cégep de la Région de l'Amiante
671, boul Smith sud, Thetford-Mines QC G6G 1N1
418/338-8591; Fax: 418/338-3498 - Vincent Guay

Cégep de Rimouski
60, rue de l'Évêché ouest, Rimouski QC G5L 4H6
418/723-1880; Fax: 418/724-4961 - Alcide Daigneault

Cégep de Rivière-du-Loup
80, rue Frontenac, Rivière-du-Loup QC G5R 1R1
418/862-6903; Fax: 418/862-4959; Toll Free: 1-800-463-8016 - Gilles Bacon

Cégep de Rosemont
6400, 16e av, Montréal QC H1X 2S9
514/376-1620; Fax: 514/376-1440 - Réginald Lavertu

* indicates enrollment figure.

Cégep de St-Félicien
1105, boul Hamel, CP 7300, St-Félicien QC G8K 2R8
418/679-5412; Fax: 418/679-8357 – Ghislain Parent

Cégep de Ste-Foy
2410, ch Ste-Foy, Ste-Foy QC G1V 1T3
418/659-6600; Fax: 418/657-4563 – Denys Larose

Cégep de St-Hyacinthe
3000, rue Boullé, St-Hyacinthe QC J2S 1H9
514/773-6800; Fax: 514/773-09299971; Email: info@cegepsth.qc.ca; URL: http://www.cegepsth.qc.ca – Serge Cloutier

Cégep St-Jean-sur-Richelieu
30, boul du Séminaire, CP 1018, St-Jean-sur-Richelieu QC J3B 7B1
514/347-5301; Fax: 514/358-9350;
Email: communications@cstjean.qc.ca – Gilles Perreault

Cégep de St-Jérôme
455, rue Fournier, St-Jérôme QC J7Z 4V2
514/436-1580; Fax: 514/436-7348 – Jean-Denis Asselin

Cégep de Saint-Laurent
625, av Ste-Croix, Saint-Laurent QC H4L 3X7
514/747-6521; Fax: 514/748-1249 – Claude Boily

Cégep de Sept-Îles
175, rue De La Vérendrye, Sept-Îles QC G4R 5B7
418/962-9848; Fax: 418/962-3852 – Octave Deraps

Cégep de Shawinigan
2263, boul du Collège, CP 610, Shawinigan QC G9N 6V8
819/539-6401; Fax: 819/539-8819 – Francine Bonicalzi

Cégep de Sherbrooke
475, rue du Parc, Sherbrooke QC J1H 5M7
819/564-6350; Fax: 819/564-1579; URL: http://www.collegesherbrooke.qc.ca – Jocelyn Vallée

Cégep de Sorel-Tracy
3000, boul de la Mairie, Tracy QC J3R 5B9
514/742-6651; Fax: 514/742-1878 – Roland Gaudreau

Cégep de Trois-Rivières
3500, rue De Courval, Trois-Rivières QC G8Z 1T2
819/376-1721; Fax: 819/693-4663 – Guy Forgues

Cégep de Valleyfield
169, rue Champlain, Valleyfield QC J6T 1X6
514/373-9441; Fax: 514/377-6035 – Jacques Turgeon

Cégep de Victoriaville
475, rue Notre-Dame est, Victoriaville QC G6P 4B3
819/758-6401; Fax: 819/758-8960 – Réjean Fortin

Cégep du Vieux-Montréal
255, rue Ontario est, Montréal QC H2X 1X6
514/982-3437; Fax: 514/982-3448 – Alain Lallier

Champlain Regional College
1301, boul Portland, CP 5000, Sherbrooke QC J1H 5N1
819/564-3638; Fax: 819/564-3639 – Alex G. Potter

Collège de Limoilou
1300, 8e av, Québec QC G1V 5L5
418/647-6600; Fax: 418/647-6798 – Yvon Beaulieu

Dawson College
3040, rue Sherbrooke ouest, Montréal QC H3Z 1A4
514/931-8731; Fax: 514/931-3567; URL: http://www.dawsoncollege.qc.ca – Patrick Woodsworth

Heritage College
325, boul Cité des Jeunes, CP 1757, Hull QC J8Y 6T3
819/778-2270; Fax: 819/778-7364 – Lawrence Kolesar

John Abbott College
21275, ch Lakeshore, CP 2000, Ste-Anne-de-Bellevue QC H9X 3L9
514/457-6610; Fax: 514/457-4730 – Gerald J. Brown

Vanier College
821, av Ste-Croix, Saint-Laurent QC H4L 3X9
514/744-7500; Fax: 514/744-7952 – Michael Macchiagodena

## UNIVERSITIES

### Bishop's University

PO Box 5000, Lennoxville QC J1M 1Z7
819/822-9600; Fax: 819/822-9661; Toll Free: 1-800-567-2792
Email: sboard@ubishops.ca; URL: http://www.ubishops.ca
Chancellor, Alex K. Paterson, O.C., O.Q., Q.C.
President of Corporation, Ronald E. Lawless
Vice-President of Corporation, J. Ferrabee, B.A.
Registrar, A. Montgomery, B.A.
Chair, Executive Committee, N. Webster, B.A., O.C.L.
Principal, J.M. Hodder, B.A., M.A.
Vice-Principal, Administration, J.-L. Grégoire, C.M.A.
Vice-Principal, Dr. R.D. Cook, B.Sc., Ph.D.
Director, Athletics, T. Allen, B.A.
Director, Graduate School of Education, N. Ferguson, B.A., B.Ed., M.Ed., Ph.D.
Director, Liaison, D. McBride, B.A.
Director, Admissions, J. Wilson, B.A.
Director, Continuing Education, M. Bandrauk, B.A., M.A.
Director, Development, P. McPhail, B.A., M.A.
Director, Alumni & Public Relations, E.B. Stevenson, B.A.
Manager, Bookstore, D. Mimnaugh

#### FACULTIES WITH DEANS

Business Administration, S.D. Barlow, B.Com., M.B.A., C.F.A.
Humanities, R.W.E. Forrest, B.A., M.A., Ph.D.
Natural Sciences, A.P. Dean, B.A., M.M., Ph.D.
Social Sciences, A.F. Johnson, B.A., M.A., Ph.D.
Student Affairs, T. Nowers, B.Sc., M.Ed.

### Concordia University

1455, boul de Maisonneuve ouest, Montréal QC H3G 1M8
514/848-2424; Fax: 514/848-3494
URL: http://www.concordia.ca
Loyola Campus, 7141, rue Sherbrooke ouest, Montréal QC H4B 1R6
Sir George Williams Campus, 1455, boul de Maisonneuve ouest, Montréal QC H3G 1M8
Chancellor, Eric H. Molson
Chair, Board of Governors, Reginald K. Groome, Q.C.
Rector & Vice-Chancellor, Frederick Lowy
Vice-Rector, Services, Charles Emond
Vice-Rector, Academic, Jack Lightstone
Vice-Rector, Institutional Relations, Marcel Danis
University Registrar, Lynne Prendergast
Chief Financial Officer, Larry English
Director, Libraries, Roy Bonin
Interim Director, Public Relations, Laurie Zack, Email: laurie@domingo.concordia.ca

#### FACULTIES WITH DEANS

Arts & Science, Martin Singer
Commerce & Administration, Mohsen Anvari
Engineering & Computer Science, Nabil Esmail
Fine Arts, Christopher Jackson
Graduate Studies & Research, Claude Bedard

### McGill University

845, rue Sherbrooke ouest, Montréal QC H3A 2T5
514/398-4455; Fax: 514/398-4455
URL: http://www.mcgill.ca
Chancellor, Gretta Chambers, O.Q., B.A.
Chair of Board, Richard Pound, O.C., O.Q., Q.C.
Principal & Vice-Chancellor, Bernard J. Shapiro, B.A., M.A.T., Ed.D.
Vice-Principal, Academic, Tak-Hang Chan, B.Sc., M.A., Ph.D., FCIC, FRSC
Vice-Principal, Administration & Finance, Phyllis Heaphy, C.A.
Vice-Principal, Information Systems & Technology, Vacant
Vice-Principal, Research, Pierre R. Bélanger, Ph.D., E.E., S.M., B.Eng.
Secretary General, Victoria Catherine Lees, A.B., M.Phil., Ph.D.
Registrar & Director of Admissions, Mariela Johansen
Director, University Relations Office, Kate Williams, B.A., M.A.

#### FACULTIES WITH DEANS

Agricultural & Environmental Sciences, Buszard Deborah, B.Sc., Ph.D.
Arts, Carman Miller, Ph.D., M.A., B.Ed., B.A.
Director, Centre for Continuing Education, Morty Yalovsky, B.Sc., M.Sc., Ph.D.
Dentistry, James Percy Lund, B.D.S., Ph.D.
Education, A. Edward Wall, B.Ed., M.A., Ph.D.
Engineering, John M. Dealy, B.S., Ch.E., M.F.E., Ph.D.
Graduate Studies & Research, Pierre R. Belanger, Ph.D., E.E., S.M., B.Eng.
Law, Stephen J. Toope, A.B., B.C.L., LL.B., Ph.D.
Management, W.B. Crowston, B.A.Sc., S.M., M.S.C., Ph.D.
Medicine, Abraham Fuks, B.Sc., M.D., C.M.
Music, Richard Lawton, B.Mus., M.Mus.
Religious Studies, B. Barry Levy, B.A., B.R.E., M.A., Ph.D.
Science, Alan G. Shaver, B.Sc., Ph.D.

#### SCHOOLS WITH DIRECTORS

Acting Director, Architecture, David Covo, B.Sc.Arch., M.B.Arch., O.A.Q., M.R.A.I.C.
Communication Sciences & Disorders, Dr. Rachel Mayberry, Ph.D., B.A., M.Sc.
Computer Science, Denis Thérien, B.Sc., M.Sc., Ph.D.
Dietetics & Human Nutrition, Peter Jones, B.Sc., M.Sc., Ph.D.
International Executive Institute, Alistair Duff, B.A., M.A., F.C.A.
Library & Information Studies, J. Andrew Large, B.Sc.A., Ph.D.
Nursing, Laurie Gotlieb, R.N., B.N., M.Sc.(a), Ph.D.
Physical & Occupational Therapy, Sharon Wood-Dauphinee, B.Sc., Dip. Ed., M.S.
Social Work, William Rowe, B.A., M.S.W., D.S.W.
Urban Planning, Jeanne M. Wolfe, B.Sc., M.Sc., M.A.

#### AFFILIATED THEOLOGICAL COLLEGES

The Montréal Diocesan Theological College, 3473, rue University, Montréal QC H3A 2A8 – 514/849-3004, 5997 – Principal, A.C. Capon, M.A., B.D.
The Presbyterian College of Montréal, 3495, rue University, Montréal QC H3A 2A8 – 514/288-5256 – Principal, W.J. Klempa, B.A., M.A., B.D., Ph.D.
The United Theological College of Montréal, 3521, rue University, Montréal QC H3A 2A9 – 514/849-2042 – Principal, Pierre Goldberger, B.A., B.Sc., L.h., D.E.A.

#### INCORPORATED COLLEGES

Macdonald College, 21, 111, ch Bord-du-Lac, Ste-Anne-de-Bellevue QC H9X 1C0 – 514/398-4455 – Vice-Principal, Buszard Deborah, B.Sc., Ph.D.
Royal Victoria College, 3425, rue University, Montréal QC H3A 2A8 – 514/398-6378

### Université Laval

Cité Universitaire, Québec QC G1K 7P4
418/656-2131; Fax: 418/656-2809
URL: http://www.ulaval.ca/index.html
Recteur, François Tavenas, 418/656-2272; Fax: 418/656-7917; Email: rec@rec.ulaval.ca
Vice-recteur à l'admin. et aux finances et vice-recteur exécutif, Jacques Racine, Email: vraf@vraf.ulaval.ca
Vice-recteur adjoint, administration et finances, Jacques Failles, Email: vraf@vraf.ulaval.ca
Vice-recteur, affaires académiques et étudiantes, Claude Godbout, Email: vraae@vraae.ulaval.ca

Vice-rectrice, recherche, Louise Filion, Email: vrr@vrr.ulaval.ca
Vice-recteur, ressources humaines, Jacques Samson, Email: vrrh@vrrh.ulaval.ca
Vice-recteur, développement, Marc-J. Trudel, Email: vrd@vrd.ulaval.ca
Secrétaire général, André-C. Côté, Email: sg@sg.ulaval.ca
Registraire, Vacant, Email: reg@reg.ulaval.ca

#### FACULTÉS AVEC DOYENS

Architecture, aménagement et arts visuels, Takashi Nakajima
Droit, Pierre Lemieux
Études supérieures, Dinh N. Nguyen
Foresterie et géomatique, Claude Godbout
Lettres, Jacques Desautels
Médecine, Louis Larochelle
Médecine dentaire, Diane Lachapelle
Musique, Raymond Ringuette
Pharmacie, Gilles Barbeau
Philosophie, Jean-Marc Narbonne
Sciences de l'administration, Bernard Garnier
Sciences de l'agriculture et de l'alimentation, André Gosselin
Sciences de l'éducation, Jean-Claude Gagnon
Sciences et génie, André Cardinal
Sciences infirmières, Édith Côté
Sciences sociales, Lise Darveau-Fournier
Théologie, René-Michel Roberge

#### ÉCOLES AVEC DIRECTEURS

Actuariat, André Prémont
Architecture, Alexis Ligougne
Arts visuels, André Theberge
Directeur par intérim, Langues vivantes, Jean-Louis Tremblay
Psychologie, Robert Rousseau
Service social, Lise Tessier

### Université de Montréal

CP 6128, Succ Centre-Ville, Montréal QC H3C 3J7
514/343-6111; Fax: 514/343-2098
Email: bisaillo@poste.umontreal.ca; URL: http://www.umontreal.ca
Recteur, René Simard
Vice-recteur, administration, Patrick A. Molinari
Vice-rectrice, enseignement, Irène Cinq-Mars
Vice-rectrice, affaires publiques, vacant
Vice-recteur, recherche & planification, Maurice St-Jacques
Vice-recteur, ressources humaines, Michel Trahan
Secrétaire général, Michel Lespérance
Directeur, finances, André Racette
Registraire, Fernand Boucher

#### FACULTÉS AVEC DOYENS

Aménagement, Michel Gariépy
Arts et sciences, Mireille Mathieu
Directeur, Département d'éducation physique, Claude Alain
Droit, Claude Fabien
Directeur, École d'optométrie, Pierre Simonet
Éducation permanente, Robert Leroux
Études supérieures, Louis Maheu
Médecine, Patrick Vinay
Médecine dentaire, Jean Turgeon
Médecine vétérinaire, Raymond S. Roy
Doyen (par intérim), Musique, M.-Thérèse Lafebvre
Pharmacie, Robert Goyer
Sciences de l'éducation, Gisèle Painchaud
Sciences infirmières, Suzanne Kérouac
Théologie, Jean-Marc Charron

#### AFFILIATED COLLEGES

École des Hautes Études Commerciales, 3000, ch de la Côte-Sainte-Catherine, Montréal QC H3T 2A7 – 514/340-6151; URL: http://www.hec.ca – Directeur, Jean-Marie Toulouse
École Polytechnique, CP 6079, Succ Centre-Ville, Montréal QC H3C 3A7 – 514/340-4724; URL: http://www.polymtl.ca – Directeur, André Bazergui

### Université du Québec

2875, boul Laurier, Ste-Foy, Québec QC G1V 2M3
418/657-3551; Fax: 418/657-2132
Email: bap@uqss.uquebec.ca; URL: http://www.uquebec.ca/
Prés., Pierre Lucier
Vice-président, administration, Michel Leclerc
Vice-présidente, enseignement et recherche, Louise Milot
Secrétaire général, Michel Quimper
Directeur, affaires publiques, Guy Reeves

#### INSTITUTS ET ÉCOLES AFFILIÉS

École Nationale d'Administration publique, 945, av Wolfe, Ste-Foy QC G1V 3J9 – 418/657-2485 – Dir. gén., Pierre De Celles
École de Technologie Supérieure, 1100, rue Notre-Dame ouest, Montréal QC H3C 1K3 – 514/396-8800 – Dir. gén., Robert-L. Papineau
Institut Armand-Frappier, 531, boul des Prairies, Laval QC H7V 1B7 – 514/687-5010 – Directeur General par interim, Alain Soucy
Institut National de la Recherche Scientifique (INRS), 2600, boul Laurier, 6e étage, CP 7500, Ste-Foy QC G1V 4C7 – 418/654-2500; URL: http://www.inrs.uquebec.ca/ – Directeur, Alain Soucy
Télé-Université, 2600, boul Laurier, 7e étage, CP 10700, Ste-Foy QC G1V 4V9 – 418/657-2262; Fax: 418/657-2094; URL: http://www.teluq.uquebec.ca/ – Dir. gén., Anne Marrec
Télé-Université (Montréal), 1001, rue Sherbrooke est, 4e étage, Montréal QC H2X 3M4 – ; Toll Free: 1-800-463-4728

#### UNIVERSITÉS AFFILIÉS

Université du Québec à Chicoutimi, 555, boul de l'Université, Chicoutimi QC G7H 2B1 – 418/545-5011; URL: http://www.uqac.uquebec.ca/ – Recteur, Bernard Angers
Université du Québec à Hull, 283, boul Alexandre-Taché, CP 1250, Succ B, Hull QC J8X 3X7 – 819/595-3900; Toll Free: 1-800-567-1283; URL: http://www.uqah.uquebec.ca/ – Recteur, Francis R. Whyte
Université du Québec à Montréal, CP 8888, Succ Centre-ville, Montréal QC H3C 3P8 – 514/987-3000; URL: http://www.uqam.ca/ – Rectrice, Paule Leduc
Université du Québec à Rimouski, 300, Allée des Ursulines, Rimouski QC G5L 3A1 – 418/723-1986; URL: http://www.uqar.uquebec.ca/ – Recteur, Pierre Couture
Université du Québec à Trois-Rivières, 3351, boul Des Forges, CP 500, Trois-Rivières QC G9A 5H7 – 819/376-5011 – Recteur, Jacques Plamondon
Université du Québec en Abitibi-Témiscamingue, 445, boul de l'Université, Rouyn-Noranda QC J9X 5E4 – 819/762-0971; URL: http://www.uqat.uquebec.ca/ – Recteur, Jules Arsenault

### Université de Sherbrooke

2500, boul de l'Université, Sherbrooke QC J1K 2R1
819/821-7000
Recteur, Pierre Reid
Vice-recteur, Enseignement, Jean-Pierre Kesteman
Vice-recteur, Administration, Daniel Hade
Vice-recteur, Personnel et Étudiants, Jean Comtois
Vice-recteur, Recherche, Jean Nicolas
Secrétaire général, René Turcotte

#### FACULTÉS AVEC DOYENS

Administration, John Ingham
Droit, Jean-Guy Bergeron
École de musique, Normand Wener
Éducation, Mario Laforest
Éducation physique et sportive, Johanne Sarrassin
Lettres et sciences humaines, Normand Wener
Médecine, Michel Baron
Sciences, Jean Goulet
Sciences appliquées, Roger Goulet
Théologie, Éthique et Philosophie, Jean-François Malherbe

#### SERVICES ET BUREAUX

Registraire, Jean-Pierre Bertrand
Directeur, Archives, Guy Cloutier
Directeur intérimaire, Bibliothèques, Michel Beaudoin
Directeur, Centre culturel, Jacques Labrecque
Directeur, Centre sportif, Jean Poirier
Directeur, Communications et soutien institutionnel, Michel Turgeon
Directeur, Coordination, Renald Mercier
Directeur, Équipement, René Alarie
Directeur, Liaison entreprises-Université, Sylvain Desjardins
Directeur, Montérégie, Jean-Louis Martel
Directeur, Personnels, Pierre Lemieux
Directeur, Recherche, Jacques Oliva Bélair
Directrice, Service des finances et de l'approvisionnement, Carole Langlois
Directeur intérimaire, Services aux étudiants, Jean-Pierre Bertrand
Directeur, Services auxiliaires, Jean-Louis Lareau
Directeur, Soutien à l'enseignement, André Normandeau
Directeur, Technologies de l'information, Hermann Théberge

## POST-SECONDARY & SPECIALIZED INSTITUTIONS

#### ACADÉMIE DE L'ENTREPRENEURSHIP QUÉBÉCOIS

#325, 5245, boul Cousineau, St-Hubert QC J3Y 6J8
514/676-5826; Fax: 514/676-2261

#### ACADÉMIE INTERNATIONALE DU DESIGN

Mart D-36, Dawson, Place Bonaventure, CP 55, Montréal QC H5A 1A3
514/875-9777; Fax: 514/875-9297
Managing Director, Larry Gross
President, Doris O'Keefe, Ph.D.

#### ACADÉMIE JULIEN INC.

#300, 2015, rue Drummond, Montréal QC H3G 1W7
514/843-3460; Fax: 514/843-4184
Fashion design & fashion market

#### AEROTAXI - CESPA

6050, rte de l'Aéroport, St-Hubert QC J3Y 8Y9
514/445-4034; Fax: 514/445-2634
Email: aerotaxi@accent.net
Flying school

#### ATELIERS DE DANSE MODERNE DE MONTRÉAL

#201, 372, rue Ste-Catherine ouest, Montréal QC H3B 1A2
514/866-9814
Email: ladml@citenet.net

#### AVIRON QUÉBEC COLLÈGE TECHNIQUE

270, boul Charest est, Québec QC G1K 3H1
418/529-1321; Fax: 418/529-1322

#### COLLÈGE CDI

#400, 3, Place Laval, Laval QC H7N 5N6
514/662-9090; Fax: 514/662-0741

#### COLLÈGE DELTA

#700, 416, boul de Maisonneuve ouest, Montréal QC H3A 1L2
514/849-7725; Fax: 514/849-9034
Computer & computer technology courses

**COLLÈGE D'ELECTRONIQUE DE QUÉBEC**
#105, 710, rue Bouvier, Québec QC G2J 1C2
418/626-8123; Fax: 418/626-7780

**COLLÈGE D'INFORMATIQUE MARSAN**
1001, boul de Maisonneuve est, Montréal QC H2L 4P9
514/525-3030; Fax: 514/525-3314
Email: marsan@accent.net

**COLLEGE INTER DEC**
2120, rue Ste-Catherine ouest, Montréal QC H3H 1M7
514/939-4444; Fax: 514/939-3046
Email: andre.lefebvre@admin.clasalle.cq.ca

**COLLÈGE JEAN-GUY LEBOEUF INC.**
5277, av du Parc, Montréal QC H2V 4G9
514/277-2117; Fax: 514/276-1118
Email: jgleboeuf@collegeleboeuf.qc.ca
Real estate, internet training

**COLLÈGE DE MODE CHÂTELAINE**
1705, ch de Canardière, Ste-Foy QC G1J 2E2
418/660-5242; Fax: 418/660-6268

**COLLÈGE DE PHOTOGRAPHIE MARSAN**
1001, boul de Maisonneuve est, 9e étage, Montréal QC H2L 4P9
514/525-3030; Fax: 514/525-3314

**COLLÈGE SALETTE INC.**
8883, boul St-Laurent, Montréal QC H2N 1M2
514/388-5725; Fax: 514/388-5957
Email: info@collegesalette.qc.ca
Graphic design & computer graphics

**COLLÈGE TECHNIQUE DE MONTRÉAL**
1863, boul René Lévesque ouest, Montréal QC H3H 1R4
514/932-6444; Fax: 514/932-6448
Director, E. Kefalidis

**CONSERVATOIRES DE MUSIQUE**
Conservatoire de musique de Chicoutimi, 202, rue Jacques-Cartier est, Chicoutimi QC G7H 6R8 – 418/698-3505; Fax: 418/698-3521 – Directeur, Jacques Clément
Conservatoire de musique de Hull, 430, boul Alexandre-Taché, Hull QC J9A 1M7 – 819/772-3283; Fax: 819/772-3346 – Directeur, Yvon Pépin
Conservatoire de musique de Montréal, 100, rue Notre-Dame est, Montréal QC H2Y 1C1 – 514/873-5818; Fax: 514/873-4601 – Directeur, Albert Grenier
Conservatoire de musique de Québec, 270, rue St-Amable, Québec QC G1R 5G1 – 418/643-2190; Fax: 418/644-9658 – Directeur, Wilfrand Guillemette
Conservatoire de musique de Rimouski, 22, rue Ste-Marie, CP 1210, Rimouski QC G5L 8M2 – 418/722-3706; Fax: 418/722-3818 – Directrice, Josée Blackburn
Conservatoire de musique de Trois-Rivières, 587, rue Radisson, CP 1146, Trois-Rivières QC G9A 5K8 – 819/371-6748; Fax: 819/371-6955 – Directeur, Pierre Normandin
Conservatoire de musique de Val-d'Or, 88, rue Allard, Val-d'Or QC J9P 2Y1 – 819/825-3585; Fax: 819/825-3297 – Directeur, Yvon Pépin

**ÉCOLE NATIONALE D'AÉROTECHNIQUE**
5555, Place de la Savane, St-Hubert QC J3Y 5K2
514/678-3560; Fax: 514/678-3240

**ÉCOLE NATIONALE DE CIRQUE**
417, rue Berri, Montréal QC H2Y 3E1
514/982-0859; Toll Free: 1-800-267-0859

**ÉCOLE NATIONALE DE L'HUMOUR**
#310, 3575, boul Saint-Laurent, Montréal QC H2X 2T7
514/849-7876; Fax: 514/849-3307

**ÉCOLE DE RADIO ET D'ÉLOCUTION PROMÉDIA**
#700, 1118, rue Ste-Catherine ouest, Montréal QC H3B 1H5
514/861-8951
P. Dufault

**ÉCOLE SUPÉRIEURE DE MUSIQUE**
251, rue St-Jean-Baptiste, Nicolet QC J0G 1E0
819/293-2011
Directeur, Alyne Martin

**ÉCOLE VINCENT D'INDY**
628, ch de la Côte Ste-Catherine, Outremont QC H2V 2C5
514/735-5261; Fax: 514/735-5266
Directrice des études musicales, Jocelyne Desjardins-Melanson

**GREATER MONTRÉAL REAL ESTATE BOARD'S COLLEGE**
600, ch du Golf, Ile des Soeurs QC H3E 1A8
514/762-1862; Fax: 514/762-4975
Real estate market programs

**HERZING INSTITUTE OF MONTRÉAL**
1616, boul René-Lévesque ouest, Montréal QC H3H 1P8
514/935-7494; Fax: 514/933-6182
URL: http://www.herzing.edu
Career training programs

**IAT**
#1400, 2021, rue Union, Montréal QC H3A 2S9
514/285-4520; Fax: 514/285-1254
Registrar, I. Garand

**ICARI INC.**
85, rue St-Paul ouest, 3e étage, Montréal QC H2Y 3V4
514/982-0922; Fax: 514/982-0288

**ICS CANADIAN LTD.**
9001, rue Avon, Montréal QC H4X 2G9
514/482-6951; Fax: 514/482-6868; Toll Free: 1-800-661-9001
URL: http://www.ics-canada.com
At-home training in 50 career fields

**INFORMATIQUE MULTIHEXA**
#220, 2327, boul Versant nord, Ste-Foy QC G1N 4C2
418/681-0082; Fax: 418/681-9207
Data-processing, computer technology & applications, management programs

**INSTITUT CARRIÈRE ET DÉVELOPPEMENT**
#400, 3, Place Laval, Laval QC H7G 3S2
514/662-9090; Fax: 514/662-0741
ICD Longueuil, #101, 1111, rue St-Charles ouest, CP 7, Longueuil QC J4K 5G4 – 514/677-9191
ICD Montréal, #500, 300, Léo-Pariseau, CP 335, Stn Place du Parc, Montréal QC H2W 2N8
IDC Québec, #200, 900, Place d'Youville, Québec QC G1R 3P7 – 418/694-0211

**INSTITUT DEMERS INC.**
#100, 99, Place Charles-Lemoyne, Longueuil QC J4K 4Z1
514/646-4336; Fax: 514/646-2122

**INSTITUT DE FORMATION AUTOCHTONE DU QUÉBEC**
#100, 85A, boul Michel-Laveau, Village-des-Hurons QC G0A 4V0
418/843-6857

**INSTITUT D'INFORMATIQUE DE QUÉBEC**
#385, 1275, ch Ste-Foy, Québec QC G1S 4S5
418/687-5801; Fax: 418/682-8980

**INSTITUT SUPERIEUR D'ELECTRONIQUE**
1500, boul de Maisonneuve est, Montréal QC H2L 2B1
514/527-4147; Fax: 514/527-4140
Email: info@institut.com; URL: http://www.institut.com
Hi-tech electronics, automation, telecom & computer science

**INSTITUT DE TECHNOLOGIE AGRO-ALIMENTAIRE DE LA POCATIÈRE**
401, rue Poirée, La Pocatière QC G0R 1Z0
418/856-1110; Fax: 418/856-1719
Email: scitalp@ogr.gouv.qc.ca

**INSTITUT DE TECHNOLOGIE AGRO-ALIMENTAIRE DE ST-HYACINTHE**
3230, rue Sicotte, PO Box 70, St-Hyacinthe QC J2S 7B3
514/778-6504; Fax: 514/778-6536

**INTERNATIONAL ACADEMY OF DESIGN**
Place Bonaventure, 36, Dawson, Mart D, PO Box 55, Montréal QC H5A 1A3
514/875-9777; Fax: 514/875-9297
Interior/fashion design, fashion merchandising

**THE INTERNATIONAL COLLEGE OF SPIRITUAL & PSYCHIC SCIENCES**
1974, boul de Maisonneuve ouest, CP 1445, Succ H, Montréal QC H3G 2N3
514/937-8359; Fax: 514/937-5380
Dean, Dr. Marilyn Zwaig Rossner, Ph.D.

**MUSITECHNIC EDUCATIONAL SERVICES INC.**
#440, 1717, boul René-Lévesque est, Montréal QC H2L 4T3
514/521-2060; Fax: 514/521-5153; Toll Free: 1-800-824-2060
Email: info@musitechnic.com
Music industry & recording programs

**NATIONAL THEATRE SCHOOL OF CANADA/ÉCOLE NATIONALE DE THÉÂTRE DU CANADA**
5030, rue St-Denis, Montréal QC H2J 2L8
514/842-7954; Fax: 514/842-5661
Director General, Monique Mercure, C.C.
Administrative Director, Simon Brault, c.g.a.
Director, Communications & Development, Rachel Martinez
Director, Design Section, Michael Eagan
Director, English Acting & Playwriting Section, Perry Schneiderman
Director, English Technical Section, Norberts Muncs
Director, French Acting & Playwriting Section, André Brassard
Director, French Technical Section, Pierre Phaneuf

**TREBAS INSTITUTE**
451, rue St-Jean, Montréal QC H2Y 2R5
514/845-4141
President, David P. Leonard

## INDEPENDENT & PRIVATE SCHOOLS

Private schools delivering the official educational program must, according to the Private Education Act, either be declared public interest institutions & recognized for grant purposes or hold a teaching permit. An institution that is recognized for grant purposes is an institution which has not been declared of public interest but which must meet the criteria as defined in the relevant regulations. Public interest institutions & degree granting institutions receive grants as determined annually by the Ministry of Education. The institutions which operate under the Private Schools Act & its regulations receive a teaching permit but are not eligible for grants from the Ministry of Education.

**Schools listed alphabetically by city. Note: "Sec." in Québec is Gr. 7-11**

Ayer's Cliff: Collège Notre-Dame des Servites, 580, Route 141, RR#2, Ayer's Cliff QC J0B 1C0 – 819/

838-4221; Fax: 819/838-4222 – Directeur, Jean-Jacques Marchand – Sec.; Res. & Day

Aylmer: École Montessori de l'Outaouais Inc., 114, rue Principale, Aylmer QC J9H 6L1 – 819/682-3299 – Directrice, Lucie Marchand – Gr. Pre./Elem.

Baie-Comeau: École secondaire Jean-Paul II, 20, av Ramesay, Baie-Comeau QC G4Z 1B2 – 418/296-6212; Fax: 418/296-3654 – Directrice, Suzanne Fortin – Sec.

Baie-d'Urfé: Ecole allemande Alexander Von Humbold inc., 216, ch Victoria, Baie-d'Urfé QC H9X 2H9 – 514/457-2886; Fax: 514/457-2885 – Horst Studte – Gr. Pre./Elem./Sec.; Eng./German

Beauceville: École Jesus-Marie de Beauceville, 670, 9e av de Léry, Beauceville QC G0S 1A0 – 418/774-3709; Fax: 418/774-3775 – Directrice, Paula Bourque – Sec.; Res. & Day

Beauport: École Secondaire François-Bourrin, 50, av des Cascades, Beauport QC G1E 6B3 – 418/661-6978; Fax: 418/661-4778 – Directrice, Sandra Nault – Sec.

Beauport: Pensionnat Saint-Coeur-de-Marie, 30, av des Cascades, Beauport QC G1E 2J8 – 418/663-0605; Fax: 418/661-7543 – Directrice, Jocelyne Thériault – Elem.; Res. & Day

Boisbriand: L'académie des jeunes filles Beth Tziril, 241, av Beth Halevy, Boisbriand QC J7E 4H4 – 514/430-6380; Fax: 514/430-4060 – Directrice, Bracha Udashkin – Elem.

Boucherville: École Les Trois Saisons inc., 80, boul de Mortagne, Boucherville QC J4B 5E4 – 514/641-2000; Fax: 514/641-0927 – Directrice, Monique Mathieu – Elem.

Bromptonville: École Secondaire de Bromptonville, 125, rue du Frère-Théode, Bromptonville QC J0B 1H0 – 819/846-2738; Fax: 819/846-4808 – Directeur, André Choquette – Sec.; Boys; Res. & Day

Brossard: Académie Marie-Laurier, 1555, av Stravinski, Brossard QC J4X 2H5 – 514/923-2787; Fax: 514/923-2291 – Directrice, Monique Bergeron – Gr. K./Elem.; Eng./Fr.

Cap-de-la-Madeleine: Val Marie, 88, ch du Passage, Cap-de-la-Madeleine QC G8T 2M3 – 819/379-8040 – Directrice, Sr Madeleine Lacombe – Gr. Pre./Elem.; Res. & Day

Charlesbourg: Externat St-Jean-Eudes, 650, av Bourg Royal, Charlesbourg QC G2L 1M8 – 418/627-1550; Fax: 418/627-0770 – Directeur, Carol Pelletier – Elem./Sec.

Châteauguay: Collège Héritage de Châteauguay, 270, boul Youville, Châteauguay QC J6J 4R6 – 514/692-5578; Fax: 514/692-5579 – Directeur, Richard Lépine – Elem./Sec.

Chicoutimi: École apostolique de Chicoutimi, 913, rue Jacques-Cartier est, Chicoutimi QC G7H 2A3 – 418/549-3302; Fax: 418/693-8609 – Directrice, Denise Villeneuve – Elem.

Chicoutimi: Lycée du Saguenay Inc., 658, rue Racine est, Chicoutimi QC G7H 1V1 – 418/543-4448; Fax: 418/543-1716 – Directrice, Irenée Beaulieu – Sec.

Chicoutimi: Séminaire de Chicoutimi, 679, rue Chabanel, Chicoutimi QC G7H 1Z7 – 418/549-0190; Fax: 418/549-1524 – Directeur, Marcel Bergeron – Sec.

Coaticook: College Rivier, 343, rue St-Jacques, Coaticook QC J1A 2R2 – 819/849-4833; Fax: 819/849-3621 – Directeur, Mario Asselin – Sec.; Res. & Day

Compton: École primaire des Arbrisseaux, 250, route 147 nord, Compton QC J0B 1L0 – 819/835-9503; Fax: 819/835-9506 – Directeur, Serge Goyette – Elem.; Res. & Day

Côte-St-Luc: Académie Hébraïque Inc., 5700, av Kellert, Côte-St-Luc QC H4W 1T7 – 514/489-5321; Fax: 514/489-8607 – Directrice, Linda Lehrer – Gr. Pre./Elem./Sec.; Eng./Fr.

Côte-St-Luc: École Yechivat or Torah/École Benot Hanna, #7, 7005, rue Kildare, Côte-St-Luc QC H4W 1C1 – 514/488-4449; Fax: 514/738-2972 – Directeur, Daniel Mund – Gr. Pre./Elem.

Dolbeau: Juvénat Saint-Jean (F.I.C.), 200, boul Walberg, Dolbeau QC G8L 2R2 – 418/276-3340; Fax: 418/276-1757 – Jean-Claude Hould – Sec.; Res. & Day

Dollard-des-Ormeaux: Collège de l'Ouest de l'Île Inc., 851, rue Tecumseh, Dollard-des-Ormeaux QC H9B 2L2 – 514/683-4660; Fax: 514/683-1702 – Directeur, Terry D. Davies – Sec.; Eng./Fr.

Dollard-des-Ormeaux: École Chrétienne Emmanuel, 4698, boul Saint-Jean, Dollard-des-Ormeaux QC H9H 4S5 – 514/696-6430; Fax: 514/696-3687 – Directeur, Roderick S. Cornell – Gr. Pre./Elem./Sec.; Eng.

Dollard-des-Ormeaux: École de formation hébraique de la Congrégation Beth Tikvah, 2, prom Hope, Dollard-des-Ormeaux QC H9A 2V5 – 514/684-6270; Fax: 514/684-1998 – Directeur, Rabbin Zev Lanton – Gr. Pre./Elem.; Eng./Fr.

Dorval: Queen of Angels Academy, 100, boul Bouchard, Dorval QC H9S 1A7 – 514/636-0900; Fax: 514/633-8969 – Directrice, Elizabeth Therrien Scanlan – Sec.; Girls; Eng.

Drummondville: Collège St-Bernard, 25, av des Frères, Drummondville QC J2B 6A2 – 819/478-3330; Fax: 819/478-2582 – Directeur, Rolland Dumais – Sec.; Res. & Day

Drummondville: Pensionnat de Drummondville, 235, rue Moisan, Drummondville QC J2C 1W9 – 819/472-4389; Fax: 819/472-3486 – Directrice, Marielle Cliche – Sec.; Girls; Res. & Day

Gatineau: Collège St-Alexandre, 850, av Principale, Gatineau QC J8V 1E7 – 819/561-3812; Fax: 819/561-5205 – Directeur, Hébert Dufour – Sec.

Granby: Collège Mont Sacré-Coeur, 210, rue Denison est, Granby QC J2G 8E3 – 514/372-6882; Fax: 514/372-9219 – Directeur, Frère René Goyette, S.C. – Elem./Sec.

Granby: École Présentation de Marie, 232, rue Principale, Granby QC J2G 2V8 – 514/372-2925; Fax: 514/372-9642 – Directeur, Raynald Jean – Sec.; Girls; Res. & Day

Granby: École Secondaire du Verbe Divin, 1021, rue Cowie, Granby QC J2G 8W8 – 514/378-3469; Fax: 514/378-4566 – Directeur, Pierre Labbé – Sec.

Hull: École secondaire St-Joseph, 174, rue Notre-Dame, Hull QC J8X 3T4 – 819/776-3123; Fax: 819/776-0992 – Directrice, Alice Labrie – Sec.; Girls

Iberville: École secondaire Marcellin-Champagnat, 14, rue Bord-de-l'Eau, Iberville QC J2X 4J3 – 514/347-5343; Fax: 514/347-2423 – Directeur, Jacques Bélisle – Sec.

Joliette: Académie Antoine Manseau, 20, St-Charles-Borromée sud, Joliette QC J6E 3Z9 – 514/753-4271; Fax: 514/753-3661 – Directeur, Gilles Émond – Sec.

Joliette: École les Mélèzes, 393, rue de Lanaudière, Joliette QC J6E 3L9 – 514/752-4433; Fax: 514/752-4337 – Directrice, Renée Champagne – Gr. Pre./Elem.; Girls; Res. & Day

Kirkland: Académie Kuper, 2, rue Aesop, Kirkland QC H9H 4K7 – 514/426-3426; Fax: 514/426-2703 – Directrice, Janet H. Perdue – Gr. K./Elem.; Eng.

Kirkland: Académie Marie-Claire, 18122, boul Elkas, Kirkland QC H9J 3Y4 – 514/697-0001 – Directrice, Marie-Claire Martin – Elem.

La Pocatière: Collège de Ste-Anne-De-la-Pocatière, 100, 4e av, La Pocatière QC G0R 1Z0 – 418/856-3012; Fax: 418/856-5611 – Directeur, Adrien Vaillancourt – Sec.; Res. & Day

La Prairie: Collège Jean-de-la-Mennais, 870, ch de St-Jean, La Prairie QC J5R 2L5 – 514/659-7657; Fax: 514/659-3717 – Directeur, Hervé Lacroix – Sec.

Lachine: Collège Ste-Anne de Lachine, 1250, boul St-Joseph, Lachine QC H8S 2M8 – 514/637-3571; Fax: 514/637-8906 – Directrice, Jeannine Serres, S.S.A. – Sec.

Lafontaine: Académie Lafontaine Inc., 2171, boul Maurice, Lafontaine QC J7Z 5V3 – 514/431-3733; Fax: 514/431-7390 – Directeur, Claude Potvin – Gr. Pre./Elem./Sec.

L'Assomption: Collège de l'Assomption, 270, boul l'Ange-Gardien, L'Assomption QC J5W 1R7 – 514/589-5621; Fax: 514/589-2910 – Directeur, Normand Therrien – Sec.

Laval: Académie Claudel, 4440, boul Samson, Laval QC H7W 2G9 – 514/682-4777; Fax: 514/682-4777 – Directrice, Hélène Boutin-Robeiro – Gr. Pre./Elem.

Laval: Académie Lavalloise, 5290, boul des Laurentides, Laval QC H7K 2J8 – 514/628-1430; Fax: 514/628-1431 – Directeur, David C. Zakaib – Gr. Pre./Elem.

Laval: Collège Laval, 275, rue Laval, Laval QC H7C 1W8 – 514/661-7714; Fax: 514/661-7146 – Directeur, Richard Roy – Sec.

Laval: École Charles Perrault, 1750, boul de la Concorde est, Laval QC H7G 2E7 – 514/975-2233; Fax: 514/975-2248 – Directeur, Jean-Marc Laspeyres – Gr. Pre./Elem./Sec.

Laval: École Démosthène, 3730, boul Lévesque ouest, Laval QC H7V 1E8 – 514/686-8000; Fax: 514/686-2757 – Directeur, Theodore Maniakas – Gr. Pre./Elem.

Laval: École Notre-Dame de Nareg Inc., 2450, rue Rosemère, Laval QC H7E 2J8 – 514/688-4990; Fax: 514/688-4991 – Directeur, Abbé Paul Kazandjian – Gr. Pre./Elem.

Lennoxville: Bishop's College School, PO Box 5001, Lennoxville QC J1M 1Z8 – 819/566-0227; Fax: 819/822-8917 – Director, Nancy J. Layton – Sec.; Eng.; Res. & Day

Léry: École alternative la clé des champs de Léry, 200, boul René-Lévesque, Léry QC J6N 3N6 – 514/699-6802; Fax: 514/699-6802 – Patrick Chaput – Gr. K./Elem./Sec.

Lévis: Collège de Lévis, 9, rue Mgr-Gosselin, Lévis QC G6V 5K1 – 418/833-1249; Fax: 418/833-1974 – Directeur, Denis Delamarre – Sec.

Lévis: Couvent Notre-Dame-de-Toutes-Grâces, 51, rue Déziel, Lévis QC G6V 3T7 – 418/833-7691; Fax: 418/833-1843 – Directrice, Jacqueline Bureau – Sec.; Girls

Lévis: École Marcelle-Mallet, 51, rue Déziel, Lévis QC G6V 3T7 – 418/833-7691; Fax: 418/833-1843 – Directrice, Jacquelin Bureau – Elem./Sec.

Lévis: École Sainte-Famille (Fraternite St-Pie X) Inc., 10425, boul de la Rive-Sud, Lévis QC G6V 7M5 – 418/837-3028; Fax: 418/837-7070 – Directeur, Dominique De Vriendt – Elem./Sec.

Longueuil: Collège Notre-Dame-de-Lourdes, 845, ch Tiffin, Longueuil QC J4P 3G5 – 514/670-4740; Fax: 514/670-2800 – Directrice, Thérèse Messier – Sec.

Longueuil: Dip enr., 905, rue Tiffin, Longueuil QC J4P 3G6 – 514/670-1154; Fax: 514/670-3909 – Directeur, Francis Rodidoux – Sec.

Métabetchouan: Services educatifs du Séminaire Marie-Reine-du-Clergé, 110, rang Caron, Métabetchouan QC G0W 2A0 – 418/349-2816; Fax: 418/349-8055 – Directeur, Serge Tremblay – Sec.; Res. & Day

Mont-St-Hilaire: Collège St-Hilaire Inc., 800, rue Rouillard, Mont-St-Hilaire QC J3G 4S6 – 514/467-7001; Fax: 514/467-9040 – Directeur, André Dufault – Sec.

Montebello: Sedbergh School Association/Association de l'École Sedbergh, 810, Côte Azélie, Montebello QC J0V 1L0 – 819/423-5523; Fax: 819/423-5769 – Directeur, Jérémi I.D. McLean – Elem./Sec.; Eng.; Res. & Day

Montréal: Académie Beth Rivkah pour filles, 5001, rue Vézina, Montréal QC H3W 1C2 – 514/731-3681; Fax: 514/342-4956 – Leib Kramer – Gr. Pre./Elem./Sec.; Girls

Montréal: L'Académie Centennale, 3641, av Prud'homme, Montréal QC H4A 3H6 – 514/486-

5533; Fax: 514/486-1401 – Directeur, Barry S. Stevens – Sec.; Eng.

Montréal: Académie Kells, 6865, boul Maisonneuve ouest, Montréal QC H4B 1T1 – 514/485-8565; Fax: 514/485-8505 – Directrice, Irene Woods – Elem./Sec.; Eng./Fr.; Spec. Ed.

Montréal: Académie Michèle-Provost Inc., 1517, av des Pins ouest, Montréal QC H3G 1B3 – 514/934-0596; Fax: 514/934-2390 – Directrice, Michele Provost – Elem./Sec.; Res. & Day

Montréal: Académie Saint-Louis de France, 4430, rue Bélanger est, Montréal QC H1T 1B3 – 514/725-0340 – Directrice, Catherine Labbé – Gr. Pre./Elem.

Montréal: Académie Solomon Schechter, 5555, ch de la Côte Saint-Luc, Montréal QC H3X 2C9 – 514/485-0866; Fax: 514/485-2267 – Directeur, Shimshon Hamerman – Gr. Pre./Elem.; Eng./Fr.

Montréal: Adventist School of Montreal/École adventiste de Montréal, 2330, West Hill Ave., Montréal QC H4B 2S3 – 514/486-5092 – Directeur, James Duberry – Elem./Sec.

Montréal: Centre François-Michelle, 10095, rue Meunier, Montréal QC H3L 2Z1 – 514/381-4418; Fax: 514/381-2895 – Nicole Rheault – Gr. Pre./Elem./Sec.; Spec. Ed.

Montréal: Centre d'intégration scolaire inc., 2651, boul Crémazie est, Montréal QC H1Z 2H6 – 514/374-8490; Fax: 514/374-3978 – Jean-Marc Rousseau – Elem./Sec.; Spec. Ed.

Montréal: Clinique pédagogique de Montréal, 11015, rue Tolhurst, Montréal QC H3L 3A8 – 514/334-2189; Fax: 514/334-4402 – Lucie Douville – Elem./Sec./Spec. Ed.

Montréal: Collège Ahuntsic, 9155, rue Saint-Hubert, Montréal QC H2M 1Y8 – 514/389-5921; Fax: 514/389-4554

Montréal: Collège Français (1965) Inc., 185, av Fairmount ouest, Montréal QC H2T 2M6 – 514/495-2581; Fax: 514/279-5131 – Directeur, Louis Portal – Gr. Pre./Elem./Sec.; Day & Res.

Montréal: Collège François Primaire inc., 185, av Fairmount ouest, Montréal QC H2T 2M6 – 514/495-2581; Fax: 514/279-5131 – Directeur, Louis Portal – Gr. Pre./Elem.

Montréal: Collège Jean-de-Brebeuf Inc., 3200, ch Côte Ste-Catherine, Montréal QC H3T 1C1 – 514/342-9342; Fax: 514/342-0693 – Directeur, Jean-Claude Gaudet – Sec.; Res. & Day

Montréal: Collège Jean-Eudes, 3535, boul Rosemont, Montréal QC H1X 1K7 – 514/376-5740; Fax: 514/376-4325 – Origéne Voisine – Sec.

Montréal: Collège Marie de France, 4635, ch Queen Mary, Montréal QC H3W 1W3 – 514/737-1177; Fax: 514/737-0789 – Directeur, Jean-Claude Giudicelli – Gr. Pre./Elem./Sec.

Montréal: Collège Mont-Royal, 2165, rue Baldwin, Montréal QC H1L 5A7 – 514/351-7851; Fax: 514/351-3124 – Directeur, Guy Brulé – Sec.

Montréal: Collège Mont St-Louis, 1700, boul Henri-Bourassa est, Montréal QC H2C 1J3 – 514/382-1560; Fax: 514/382-5886 – Directeur, Ralph Smith – Sec.

Montréal: Collège de Montréal, 1931, rue Sherbrooke ouest, Montréal QC H3H 1E3 – 514/933-7397; Fax: 514/933-3225 – Directeur, Jean-Guy Perras – Sec.; Boys

Montréal: Collège Notre-Dame-du-Sacré-Coeur, 3791, ch Reine Marie, Montréal QC H3V 1A8 – 514/739-3371; Fax: 514/739-4833 – Directeur, Charles Edouard Smith – Sec.; Res. & Day

Montréal: Collège Prep International, 7475, rue Sherbrooke ouest, Montréal QC H4B 1S4 – 514/489-7287; Fax: 514/489-7280 – Ursulene-Mora Farmer – Elem./Sec.; Eng.

Montréal: Collège rabbinique du Canada, 6405, av Westbury, Montréal QC H3W 2X5 – 514/735-2201; Fax: 514/739-9723 – Directeur, Rabbin Leib Kramer – Gr. Pre./Elem.; Boys

Montréal: Collège Rachel, 310, rue Rachel est, Montréal QC H2W 1E7 – 514/287-1944; Fax: 514/287-7523 – Directrice, Marie Lachapelle – Sec.

Montréal: Collège Regina Assumpta, 1750, rue Sauriol est, Montréal QC H2C 1X4 – 514/382-4121; Fax: 514/387-7825 – Directrice, Annette Bellavance – Sec.

Montréal: Collège St-Jean-Vianney, 12630, boul Gouin est, Montréal QC H1C 1B9 – 514/648-3821; Fax: 514/648-8401 – Directeur, Roger Bergeron – Sec.

Montréal: Collège Ste-Marcelline, 9155, boul Gouin ouest, Montréal QC H4K 1C3 – 514/334-9651; Fax: 514/334-0210 – Directrice, Sr Orietta Roda – Gr. K./Elem./Sec.

Montréal: Collège Ville-Marie, 2850, rue Sherbrooke est, Montréal QC H2K 1H3 – 514/525-2516; Fax: 514/525-7675 – Directeur, Yves Robillard – Sec.

Montréal: École arménienne Sourp Hagop, 3400, rue Nadon, Montréal QC H4J 1P5 – 514/332-1373; Fax: 514/332-8303 – Directeur, Hagop Boulgarian – Gr. Pre./Elem./Sec.

Montréal: École Augustin Roscelli Inc., 11960, boul de l'Acadie, Montréal QC H3M 2T7 – 514/334-0057; Fax: 514/334-4060 – Directrice, Sr Marie-Germaine Castonguay – Gr. Pre./Elem.

Montréal: École au Jardin Bleu Inc., 1690, rue Sauvé est, Montréal QC H2C 2A8 – 514/388-4949 – Directrice, Nicole Normand – Gr. Pre./Elem.

Montréal: École Marie-Clarac, 3530, boul Gouin est, Montréal QC H1H 1B7 – 514/322-1161; Fax: 514/322-4364 – Directrice, Sr Pierre-Anne Mandato – Gr. Pre./Elem.

Montréal: École Montessori Ville-Marie Inc., 6520, boul Gouin ouest, Montréal QC H4K 1B2 – 514/747-2232 – Directrice, Claudette Debbane – Gr. Pre./Elem.

Montréal: École Orale de Montréal pour les Sourds, 5851, Upper Lachine Rd., Montréal QC H4A 2B7 – 514/488-4946; Fax: 514/488-0802 – Directrice, Agnes H. Phillips – Gr. Pre./Elem.; Spec. Ed.

Montréal: École Pasteur, 12345, av de la Miséricorde, Montréal QC H4J 2E8 – 514/331-0850; Fax: 514/331-2312 – Directeur, Roger Évrard – Gr. Pre./Elem./Sec.

Montréal: École Première Mesifta du Canada, 2325, av Ekers, Montréal QC H3S 1C6 – 514/738-1738; Fax: 514/738-9963 – Directrice, Miriam Landa – Gr. Pre./Elem./Sec.

Montréal: École primaire de l'Institut Garvey/The Garvey Institute Day School, 2515, rue Delisle, Montréal QC H3C 2T1 – 514/933-9013; Fax: 514/934-5398 – Director, June A. Bertley – Gr. Pre./Elem.; Eng.

Montréal: École primaire Socrates, 5757, av Wilderton, Montréal QC H3S 2K8 – 514/738-2421; Fax: 514/340-3586 – Directrice, Nicole St-Germain – Gr. Pre./Elem.

Montréal: École Rudolf Steiner de Montréal, 8205, ch Mackle, Montréal QC H4W 1B1 – 514/481-5686; Fax: 514/481-6935 – Directrice, Francine Laterreur – Gr. Pre./Elem./Sec.

Montréal: École Sacré-Coeur de Montréal, 3635, av Atwater, Montréal QC H3H 1Y4 – 514/937-2845; Fax: 514/937-8214 – Directrice, Mary Burns – Sec.; Girls; Eng.; Res & Day

Montréal: École St-Georges de Montréal Inc., 3100, The Boulevard, Montréal QC H3Y 1R9 – 514/937-9289; Fax: 514/933-3621 – Directeur, James A. Officer – Gr. Pre./Elem./Sec.; Eng.

Montréal: École Saint-Joseph 1985 Inc., 4080, rue De Lorimier, Montréal QC H2K 3X7 – 514/526-8288; Fax: 514/526-5498 – Directrice, Lucille Castonguay – Gr. Pre./Elem.

Montréal: École Sainte-Anne, 6855, 13e av, Montréal QC H1X 2Z3 – 514/725-4179; Fax: 514/725-9962 – Directrice, Monique Cloutier – Gr. Pre./Elem.

Montréal: École secondaire Duval Enr., 9900, av d'Auteuil, Montréal QC H3L 2K1 – 514/382-6070; Fax: 514/382-7207 – Directeur, Jacques Duval – Sec.

Montréal: Ecole secondaire Jeanne-Normandin, 690, boul Crémazie est, Montréal QC H2P 1E9 – 514/381-3945; Fax: 514/381-1695 – Laurent Méthot – Sec.; Girls

Montréal: École secondaire Letendre Inc., 9615, rue Papineau, Montréal QC H2B 1Z6 – 514/389-3513; Fax: 514/385-5545 – Directeur, Renald Larrivée – Sec.

Montréal: École Weston Inc., 5460, rue Connaught, Montréal QC H4V 1X7 – 514/488-9191; Fax: 514/488-9192 – Directeur, James Christopher – Elem./Sec.; Eng.

Montréal: Les Écoles juives populaires et les Écoles Peretz Inc., 5170, Van Horne, Montréal QC H3W 1J6 – 514/731-6456; Fax: 514/731-0343 – Directeur, Edmond Elbaz – Gr. Pre./Elem./Sec.; Eng./Fr.

Montréal: Écoles musulmanes de Montréal, 7445, av Chester, Montréal QC H4V 1M4 – 514/484-8845; Fax: 514/484-3802 – Directeur, Omrane El Gharby – Gr. Pre./Elem./Sec.

Montréal: Éducation Plus, 8396, rue Mayrand, Montréal QC H4P 2C9 – 514/733-9600; Fax: 514/733-3060 – Directeur, James Watts – Sec.

Montréal: Greaves Academy, 2330, av West Hill, Montréal QC H4B 2S3 – 514/486-5092; Fax: 514/486-0515 – James Duberry – Gr. Pre./Elem./Sec.; Eng.

Montréal: Institut Reine-Marie, 9300, boul St-Michel, Montréal QC H1Z 3H1 – 514/382-0484; Fax: 514/858-1401 – Directrice, Johanne Kenyon – Sec.; Girls

Montréal: Lower Canada College, 4090, av Royale, Montréal QC H4A 2M5 – 514/482-9916; Fax: 514/482-0195 – Directeur, Edmond G. Staunton – Gr. Pre./Elem./Sec.; Eng./Fr.

Montréal: Loyola High School, 7272, rue Sherbrooke ouest, Montréal QC H4B 1R6 – 514/486-1101; Fax: 514/486-7266 – Directeur, Eric McLean – Sec.; Boys; Eng.

Montréal: Pensionnat Notre-Dame-des-Anges, 5690, boul Rosemont, Montréal QC H1T 2H2 – 514/254-6447; Fax: 514/254-6261 – Directrice, Sr Réjeanne Paquette – Elem.

Montréal: The Priory School Inc., 3120, The Boulevard, Montréal QC H3Y 1R9 – 514/935-5966; Fax: 514/935-1428 – Directeur, John Marinelli – Gr. Pre./Elem.; Eng.

Montréal: Talmud Torahs Unis de Montréal Inc., 4840, av Saint-Kevin, Montréal QC H3W 1P2 – 514/739-2294; Fax: 514/739-3579 – Directrice, Elaine Cohen – Gr. Pre./Elem./Sec.; Eng./Fr.

Montréal: Trafalgar School for Girls, 3495, rue Simpson, Montréal QC H3G 2J7 – 514/935-2644; Fax: 514/935-2359 – Director, Geoffrey Dowd – Sec.; Girls; Eng.

Montréal: Villa Maria, 4245, boul Décarie, Montréal QC H4A 3K4 – 514/484-4950; Fax: 514/484-4492 – Directeur, Sr Arlita Matte – Sec.; Girls; Eng./Fr.

Montréal: Yeshivah Gedola Merkaz Hatorah, 6155, ch Deacon, Montréal QC H3S 2P4 – 514/735-6611; Fax: 514/343-0083 – Directeur, Rabbin Moshe Glustein – Gr. Pre./Elem./Sec.; Eng./Fr.

Montréal-Nord: Académie Louis-Pasteur, 11280, rue Jules-Dorion, Montréal-Nord QC H1G 4W8 – 514/322-6123; Fax: 514/322-6787 – Directrice, Nicole Daigle – Gr. K./Elem.

Montréal-Nord: Centre académique Fournier, 10339, av Parc-Georges, Montréal-Nord QC H1H 4Y4 – 514/321-2642; Fax: 514/321-0278 – Marie-Claire Fournier – Elem./Sec./Spec. Ed.

Montréal-Nord: Centre de l'enseignement vivant, 4975, rue Amos, Montréal-Nord QC H1G 2X2 – 514/325-8500; Fax: 514/325-2797 – Raymond Girard – Elem./Spec. Ed.

Montréal-Nord: École élémentaire Marie-Soleil inc., 12550, boul Lacordaire, Montréal-Nord QC H1G

4L8 – 514/321-7198 – Directrice, Lise Hade – Gr. K./Elem.

Montréal-Nord: École Michelet Inc., 10550, av Pelletier, Montréal-Nord QC H1H 3R5 – 514/321-9551; Fax: 514/321-9111 – Directrice, Arlette Spandonide – Elem.

Montréal-Nord: École secondaire Marie-Victorin, 10748, boul St-Vital, Montréal-Nord QC H1H 4T3 – 514/322-8111; Fax: 514/322-8112 – Directeur, Gilles Léger – Sec.

Nicolet: Collège Notre-Dame de l'Assomption, 251, rue St-Jean-Baptiste, Nicolet QC J3T 1X9 – 819/293-2011; Fax: 819/293-2099 – Directrice, Pierrette Leclerc – Sec.; Girls; Res. & Day

Outremont: Centre François-Michelle, 5210, rue Durocher, Outremont QC H2V 3Y1 – 514/948-6434; Fax: 514/948-6436 – Nicole Rheault – Gr. K./Elem./Sec./Spec. Ed.

Outremont: Collège Stanislas, 780, boul Dollard, Outremont QC H2V 3G5 – 514/273-9521; Fax: 514/273-3409 – Directeur, Jacques Bourdon – Gr. Pre./Elem./Sec.

Outremont: École Beth Jacob, 1750, av Glendale, Outremont QC H2V 1B3 – 514/739-3614; Fax: 514/739-0172 – Directeur, Rabbin S. Aisenstark – Gr. Pre./Elem./Sec.; Eng./r.; Girls

Outremont: École Buissonnière, centre de formation artistique inc., 215, av de l'Épée, Outremont QC H2V 3T3 – 514/272-4739; Fax: 514/274-3207 – Jacqueline Tremblay – Gr. Pre./Elem.

Outremont: Ecole communautaire Belz, 1495, av Ducharme, Outremont QC H2V 1E8 – 514/271-0611; Fax: 514/271-9329 – Ernest Kisner – Gr. Pre./Elem./Sec.; Fr./Eng.

Outremont: École communautaire Hassidique, 1495, av Ducharme, Outremont QC H2V 1E2 – 514/271-0611; Fax: 514/271-9329 – Directeur, Ernest Kiszner – Gr. K./Elem/.Sec.; Eng./Fr.

Outremont: Écoles communautaires Skver, 1235, av Ducharme, Outremont QC H2V 1E2 – 514/274-8241; Fax: 514/279-3948 – Directeur, Fred Gestetner – Gr. Pre./Elem./Sec.; Eng./Fr.

Outremont: Externat Mont-Jésus-Marie, 1360, boul Mont-Royal, Outremont QC H2V 4P3 – 514/272-1035; Fax: 514/272-5908 – Directrice, Lise Bluteau – Gr. Pre./Elem.

Outremont: Pensionnat du St-Nom-de-Marie, 628, ch Ste-Catherine, Outremont QC H2V 2C5 – 514/735-5261; Fax: 514/735-5266 – Directrice, Sr Rolande Coderre – Sec.; Girls; Res. & Day

Philipsburg: Académie du Domaine, 15, route 133, Philipsburg QC J0J 1N0 – 514/248-7301; Fax: 514/248-7787 – Directrice, Rita Morissette – Elem.

Philipsburg: Pensionnat Saint-Jean-Baptiste, 15, route 133, Philipsburg QC J0J 1N0 – 514/248-7301; Fax: 514/248-7787 – Directrice, Rita Morissette – Elem.; Boys

Pierrefonds: Collège Beaubois, 9509, boul Gouin ouest, Pierrefonds QC H8Y 1T7 – 514/684-7642; Fax: 514/684-3011 – Directeur, Louis Dion – Gr. Pre./Elem./Sec.

Pierrefonds: Collège Charlemagne Inc., 5000, rue Pilon, Pierrefonds QC H9K 1G4 – 514/626-7060; Fax: 514/626-1806 – Directeur, Bernard Laudy – Gr. K./Elem./Sec.

Pierrefonds: École Charles Perrault, 11950, boul Gouin, Pierrefonds QC H8Z 1V6 – 514/684-5043; Fax: 514/975-5048 – Directeur, Denis Faber – Gr. Pre./Elem.

Pointe-aux-Chênes: Séminaire du Sacré-Coeur, 1042, rte 148, Pointe-aux-Chênes QC J0V 1T0 – 819/242-0957; Fax: 819/242 4089 Directeur, Richard Dupuis – Sec.; Res. & Day

Québec: Académie St-Louis (Québec), 1500, rue De La Rive-Boisée, Québec QC G2C 2B3 – 418/845-5121; Fax: 418/845-5244 – Directeur, Jocelyn Lee – Sec.

Quèbec: Collège Marie-Moisan, 640, 8e av, Quèbec QC G1J 3L7 – 418/529-7522; Fax: 418/529-0332 – Directrice, Paule Pouliat – Sec.; Girls; Res. & Day

Québec: Collège Notre-Dame de Bellevue, 1605, ch Ste-Foy, Québec QC G1S 2P2 – 418/681-7781; Fax: 418/681-1244 – Directrice, Sr Lucille Bedard – Sec.; Girls

Québec: Collège St-Charles-Garnier, 1150, boul René-Lévesque ouest, Québec QC G1S 1V7 – 418/681-0107; Fax: 418/681-9631 – Directeur, Henri Marineau – Sec.

Québec: École Saint-Joseph, 1090, boul René-Lévesque ouest, Québec QC G1S 1V5 – 418/527-1072; Fax: 418/527-1512 – Directrice, Sr Claudette Hamel – Elem.

Québec: École des Ursulines de Québec, 4, rue du Parloir, Québec QC G1R 4S7 – 418/692-2612; Fax: 418/692-1240 – Directeur, Remi Boudreau – Elem./Sec.; Girls; Res. & Day

Québec: Externat Saint-Jean-Berchmans, 1160, ch Ste-Foy, Québec QC G1S 2M4 – 418/687-5871; Fax: 418/683-3210 – Directrice, Sr Colette Gagnon – Elem.

Québec: Institut Saint-Joseph Inc., 550, ch Ste-Foy, Québec QC G1S 2J5 – 418/688-0736; Fax: 418/688-0737 – Directeur, Guy Lefrançois – Gr. Pre./Elem.

Québec: Pensionnat Saint-Louis-de-Gonzague, 980, rue Richelieu, Québec QC G1R 1L5 – 418/692-1072; Fax: 418/692-5965 – Directeur, Guy Gauvin – Elem.; Boys

Québec: Le Petit Séminaire de Québec, 6, rue de l'Université, Québec QC G1R 5X8 – 418/694-1020; Fax: 418/694-0803 – Directeur, Louis Bouchard – Sec.

Rawdon: Collège Champagneur, 3713, rue Queen, Rawdon QC J0K 1S0 – 514/834-5401; Fax: 514/834-6500 – Directeur, Raymond Gravel – Sec.; Boys; Res. & Day

Rawdon: École Marie-Anne, 3766, rue Queen, Rawdon QC J0K 1S0 – 514/834-4668; Fax: 514/834-2800 – Directrice, Carole Lalancette – Gr. Pre./Elem.; Res. & Day

Repentigny: Académie François-Labelle, 1227, rue Notre-Dame, Repentigny QC J5Y 3H2 – 514/582-2020; Fax: 514/582-9732 – Jeannine Paradis – Gr. Pre./Elem.

Repentigny: Centre académique Lanaudière, 930, boul L'Assomption, Repentigny QC J6A 5H5 – 514/654-5026 – Directrice, Denise Normandin – Gr. Pre./Elem.

Repentigny: Centre pédagogique Nicolas et Stéphanie inc., 50, rue Thouin, Repentigny QC J6A 4J4 – 514/585-3001; Fax: 514/585-5050 – Diane Harvey Monette – Gr. Pre./Elem./Sec./Spec. Ed.

Rigaud: Collège Bourget, 65, rue St-Pierre, Rigaud QC J0P 1P0 – 514/451-0815; Fax: 514/451-4171 – Directeur, Jean-Marc Saint-Jacques – Elem./Sec.; Res. & Day

Rimouski: École Claire-L'Heureux-Dubé, 77, 2e rue ouest, Rimouski QC G5L 4X3 – 418/724-2511; Fax: 418/724-2524 – Directeur, Marcel Samson – Sec.

Rivière-du-Loup: École secondaire Notre-Dame, 56, rue St-Henri, Rivière-du-Loup QC G5R 3Z5 – 418/862-8257; Fax: 418/862-8495 – Directeur, Fernand Chouinard – Sec.

Rock Forest: Collège du Mont-Ste-Anne, 2100, ch Ste-Catherine, Rock Forest QC J1N 3V5 – 819/823-3003; Fax: 819/569-9636 – Directeur, Andre Bessette – Sec.; Boys; Res. & Day

Rosemère: Externat Sacré-Coeur Rosemère, 535, rue Lefrançois, RR#1, Rosemère QC J7E 4H4 – 514/621-6720; Fax: 514/621-1525 – Directeur, Jacques Lafontaine – Sec.

Ste-Angèle-de-Laval: École secondaire Mont-Bénilde, 1325, av des Pensées, Ste-Angèle-de-Laval QC G0X 2H0 – 819/222-5601; Fax: 819/222-5825 – Directeur, Frère Louis-Paul Lavallée – Sec.; Res. & Day

Ste-Anne-de-Beaupré: Séminaire St-Alphonse, 10026, av Royale, Ste-Anne-de-Beaupré QC G0A 3C0 – 418/827-3744; Fax: 418/827-3745 – Directeur, Mario Doyle – Sec.; Res. & Day

St-Augustin: Collège St-Augustin, 4950, rue Lionel-Groulx, St-Augustin QC G3A 1V2 – 418/872-0954; Fax: 418/872-8249 – Directeur, Charles Fournier – Sec.; Res. & Day

St-Augustin: Séminaire St-François, 4900, rue St-Félix, St-Augustin QC G3A 1X3 – 418/872-0611; Fax: 418/872-5845 – Directeur, Père Jean-Marc Boule – Sec.; Res. & Day

St-Bruno-de-Montarville: Pensionnat des Sacrés-Coeurs, 1575, ch des Vingt, St-Bruno-de-Montarville QC J3V 4P6 – 514/653-3681; Fax: 514/653-0816 – Directeur, Guy Saumure – Gr. Pre./Elem.; Res. & Day

St-Bruno-de-Montarville: Séminaire de la Trés Ste-Trinité, 1475, ch des Vingt, St-Bruno-de-Montarville QC J3V 4P6 – 514/653-2409; Fax: 514/441-4786 – Directeur, Roland Martin – Sec.

Ste-Catherine: Collège Charles-Lemoyne Inc., 3507, boul Marie-Victorin, Ste-Catherine QC J0L 1E0 – 514/638-1282; Fax: 514/638-5975 – Directeur, Jean-Yves Ferland – Sec.

St-Césaire: Collège de St-Césaire, 1390, rue Notre-Dame, St-Césaire QC J0L 1T0 – 514/469-3143; Fax: 514/469-5455 – Directeur, Sylvain Petit – Elem./Sec.; Res. & Day

Ste-Foy: Centre psycho-pédagogique de Québec inc., 1000, av Joli-Bois, Ste-Foy QC G1V 3Z6 – 418/650-1171; Fax: 418/650-1145 – Jean-Marie Guay – Elem./Sec./Spec. Ed.

Ste-Foy: Collège de Champigny, 1400, rte de l'Aéroport, Ste-Foy QC G2G 1G6 – 418/872-0508; Fax: 418/872-6266 – Directeur, Henri Piolain – Sec.

Ste-Foy: Collège Marguerite-d'Youville, 2700, ch des Quatres-Bourgeois, Ste-Foy QC G1V 1X5 – 418/656-9313; Fax: 418/656-9885 – Directrice, Sr Anita Lepage – Sec.; Girls

Ste-Foy: Les écoles prématernelles et maternelles Montessori, 2700, ch des Quatre-Bourgeois, Ste-Foy QC G1V 1X5 – 418/654-1779; Fax: 418/654-1779 – Directeur, Daniel Jutras – Gr. Pre./Elem.

St-Gabriel-de-Valcartier: École secondaire Mont St-Sacrement, 200, boul St-Sacrement, St-Gabriel-de-Valcartier QC G0A 4S0 – 418/844-3771; Fax: 418/844-2517 – Directeur, Jean-Claude Grondin – Sec.

St-Guillaume: Juvénat Saint-Louis-Marie, 96, rue Saint-Jean-Baptiste, St-Guillaume QC J0C 1L0 – 819/396-2076; Fax: 819/396-3331 – Jean-Pierre Vallée – Sec.; Res. & Day

St-Hyacinthe: Collège Antoine-Girouard, 700, rue Girouard est, St-Hyacinthe QC J2S 2Y2 – 514/773-4334; Fax: 514/773-8011 – Directeur, Roger Gauvin – Sec.

St-Hyacinthe: Collège St-Maurice, 630, rue Girouard ouest, St-Hyacinthe QC J2S 2Y3 514/773-7478; Fax: 514/773-1413 – Directeur, Serge Courtemanche – Sec.; Girls; Res. & Day

St-Hyacinthe: Ecole secondaire Saint-Joseph de Saint-Hyacinthe, 2875, av Bourdages nord, St-Hyacinthe QC J2S 5S3 – 514/774-3775; Fax: 514/773-6340 – Michel Lanctot – Sec.; Res. & Day

St-Hyacinthe: La Petite Académie du Boisé Inc., 1090, rue Léon-Pratte, St-Hyacinthe QC J2S 2B6 – 514/771-0644; Fax: 514/771-7242 – Directrice, Sr Estelle Moreau – Gr. Pre./Elem.

St-Jacques: Collège Esther Blondin, 101, rue Ste-Anne, St-Jacques QC J0K 2R0 – 514/839-3672; Fax: 514/839-3951 – Directrice, Claudette Forget – Sec.; Girls; Res. & Day

St-Lambert: Collège Durocher St-Lambert, 857, rue Riverside, St-Lambert QC J4P 1C2 – 514/465-7213; Fax: 514/465-0860 – Directrice, Sr. Jocelyne Latreille – Sec.

St-Laurent: Collège Hillel, 2190, rue Ward, St-Laurent QC H4M 1T7 – 514/744-9707; Fax: 514/744-9747 – Ruth Bensimhon – Gr. Pre./Elem./Sec.

St-Laurent: École Ali Ibn Abi Talib, 275, rue Houde, St-Laurent QC H4N 2J3 – 514/744-0801; Fax: 514/934-3625 – Bilai Jundi – Gr. Pre./Elem./Sec.

Saint-Laurent: École Armen-Québec de l'UGAB, 755, Manoogian, Saint-Laurent QC H4N 1Z5 – 514/744-5636; Fax: 514/744-2785 – Directeur, Dr Archavir Gundjian – Gr. Pre./Elem./Sec.

St-Laurent: École bilingue Notre-Dame de Sion, 1775, boul Décarie, St-Laurent QC H4L 3N5 – 514/747-3895; Fax: 514/747-5492 – Directeur, Shawn O'Donnell – Gr. Pre./Elem.; Eng./Fr.

Saint-Laurent: École Maimonide, 1900, rue Bourdon, Saint-Laurent QC H4M 1V1 – 514/744-5300; Fax: 514/331-4838 – Directeur, Sylvain Abenhaim – Gr. Pre./Elem./Sec.

Saint-Laurent: École Peter Hall, 1455, rue Rochon, Saint-Laurent QC H4L 1W1 – 514/748-6727; Fax: 514/748-5122 – Directeur, Victor P. Elbert – Gr. Pre./Elem./Sec.; Eng./Fr.; Spec. Ed.

St-Laurent: Ecole le Sommet, 1750, rue Deguire, St-Laurent QC H4L 1M7 – 514/744-2867; Fax: 514/744-6410 – Gloria Cherney – Gr. Pre./Elem./Sec./Spec. Ed.; Eng.

Saint-Laurent: École Vanguard Québec Ltée, 1150, rue Deguire, Saint-Laurent QC H4L 1M2 – 514/747-5500; Fax: 514/747-2831 – Directeur, Alain Bougie – Elem./Sec.; Eng./Fr.; Spec. Ed.

St-Léonard: École adventiste de Montréal est, 8885, boul Lacordaire, St-Léonard QC H1K 2B4 – 514/328-2617; Fax: 514/486-0515 – Robert O.A. Samms – Gr. K./Elem.

St-Michel: Collège Dina Bélanger, 1, rue St-Georges, St-Michel QC G0R 3S0 – 418/884-2360; Fax: 418/884-3274 – Directrice, Yvette Rioux – Sec.; Res. & Day

St-Romuald: Juvénat Notre-Dame du Saint-Laurent, 30, rue du Juvénat, St-Romuald QC G6V 6P5 – 418/839-9592; Fax: 418/839-3523 – Omer Tessier – Sec.

Ste-Thérèse: Académie Sainte-Thérèse, 425, rue Blainville est, Ste-Thérèse QC J7E 1N7 – 514/434-1130; Fax: 514/434-0010 – Directeur, Jacques About – Gr. Pre./Elem./Sec.; Res. & Day

Sept-Îles: Institut d'Enseignement de Sept-Îles Inc., 737, rue Gamache, Sept-Îles QC G4R 2J8 – 418/968-9104; Fax: 418/962-8561 – Directeur, Michel Bilodeau – Sec.

Shawinigan: Séminaire Ste-Marie, 5655, boul des Hètres, Shawinigan QC G9N 4V9 – 819/539-5493; Fax: 819/539-1749 – Directeur, Jean Gignac – Sec.

Shawinigan-Sud: Institution secondaire Montfort, 1805, rang St-Mathieu est, Shawinigan-Sud QC G9N 6T5 – 819/536-2544; Fax: 819/536-3609 – Directeur, André Roberge – Sec.

Sherbrooke: Collège Mont Notre-Dame de Sherbrooke inc., 114, rue de la Cathédrale, Sherbrooke QC J1H 4M1 – 819/563-4104; Fax: 819/563-8689 – Directrice, Michelle Drolet – Sec.; Girls

Sherbrooke: Collège du Sacré-Coeur, 155, rue Belvédère nord, Sherbrooke QC J1H 4A7 – 819/569-9457; Fax: 819/820-0636 – Directrice, Micheline Marcotte-Gagnon – Sec.; Girls

Sherbrooke: École Plein-Soleil (Association coopérative), 300, rue Montréal, Sherbrooke QC J1H 1E5 – 819/569-8359; Fax: 819/569-3979 – Directrice, Huguette Larose – Gr. Pre./Elem.

Sherbrooke: Séminaire Salesien, 135, rue Don Bosco nord, Sherbrooke QC J1L 1E5 – 819/566-2222; Fax: 819/566-6969 – Directeur, Pierre Duclos – Sec.

Sherbrooke: Séminaire de Sherbrooke, 195, rue Marquette, CP 790, Sherbrooke QC J1H 1L6 – 819/563-2050; Fax: 819/562-8261 – Directeur, André Nuyt – Sec.

Sillery: Collège Jésus-Marie de Sillery, 2047, ch St-Louis, Sillery QC G1T 1P3 – 418/687-9250; Fax: 418/687-9847 – Directrice, Sr Odile Fortin – Elem./Sec.; Girls; Res. & Day

Sillery: École Montessori de Québec, 1265, av Du Buisson, Sillery QC G1T 2C4 – 418/688-7646; Fax: 418/687-5282 – Directeur, Benoit Dubuc – Gr. Pre./Elem.

Sillery: Séminaire des Pères Maristes, 2315, ch St-Louis, Sillery QC G1T 1R5 – 418/651-4944; Fax: 418/651-6841 – Directeur, Jean-Claude Trotter – Sec.

Stanstead: Pensionnat des Ursulines de Stanstead, 26, rue Dufferin, Stanstead QC J0B 3E0 – 819/876-2795; Fax: 819/876-2797 – Directeur, Benoît Larue – Sec.; Res. & Day

Stanstead College, 4, rue Dufferin, Stanstead QC J0B 3E0 – 819/876-2702; Fax: 819/876-5891 – Directeur, Barry Gallant – Sec.; Eng.; Res. & Day

Terrebonne: École secondaire St-Sacrement, 901, rue St-Louis, Terrebonne QC J6W 1K1 – 514/471-6615; Fax: 514/471-5904 – Directeur, Yves Lemire – Sec.

Trois-Rivières: Collège Marie-de-l'Incarnation, 725, rue Hart, Trois-Rivières QC G9A 5S3 – 819/379-3223; Fax: 819/379-3226 – Directeur, Pierre Papillon – Elem./Sec.; Girls; Res. & Day

Trois-Rivières: Institut secondaire Keranna, 6205, boul des Chenaux, Trois-Rivières QC G9A 5S3 – 819/378-4833; Fax: 819/378-2417 – Directrice, Solange Guimond – Sec.; Girls; Res. & Day

Trois-Rivières: Séminaire St-Joseph de Trois-Rivières, 858, boul Laviolette, Trois-Rivières QC G9A 5S3 – 819/376-4459; Fax: 819/378-0607 – Directeur, Pierre Leclerc – Sec.; Boys; Res. & Day

Val-Morin: Académie Laurentienne (1986) Inc., 1200, 14e av, Val-Morin QC J0T 2R0 – 819/322-2722; Fax: 819/322-3466 – Directeur, Claude Cousineau – Elem./Sec.; Res. & Day

Varennes: Centre éducatif Chante Plume, 104, boul de la Marine, Varennes QC J3X 1Z5 – 514/652-6869; Fax: 514/652-6869 – Colette Cardin – Gr. Pre./Elem.

Varennes: Collège St-Paul, 235, rue Ste-Anne, Varennes QC J3X 1P9 – 514/652-2941; Fax: 514/652-4461 – Directeur, Richard Doyle – Sec.

Victoriaville: Collège d'Arthabaska, 905, boul Bois-Francs sud, Victoriaville QC G6P 5W1 – 819/357-8215; Fax: 819/357-8218 – Directeur, Yvan Turgeon – Sec.; Boys; Res. & Day

Victoriaville: Collège Clarétain, 663, boul Gamache, Victoriaville QC G6P 6R8 – 819/752-4571; Fax: 819/752-4572 – Directeur, Jean-Roch Gagné – Sec.; Boys; Res. & Day

Waterville: Collège François Delaplace, 365, Compton est, Waterville QC J0B 3H0 – 819/837-2882; Fax: 819/837-2916 – Directrice, Sr Jocelyne Boulanger – Sec.; Girls

Westmount: École Akiva, 450, rue Kensington, Westmount QC H3Y 3A2 – 514/939-2430; Fax: 514/939-2432 – Directrice, Frances Levy – Gr. Pre./Elem; Eng./Fr.

Westmount: École ECS Inc./ECS School Inc., 525, av Mount Pleasant, Westmount QC H3Y 3H6 – 514/935-6357; Fax: 514/935-1099 – Directrice, Susyn Bover – Gr. Pre./Elem./Sec.; Girls; Eng.

Westmount: Institut canadien pour le développement neuro-intégratif, 11, av Hillside, Westmount QC H3Z 1V8 – 514/935-1911; Fax: 514/935-9768 – Darlene Berringer – Gr. Pre./Elem./Sec; Spec. Ed.

Westmount: Miss Edgar's & Miss Cramp's School, 525, Mount Pleasant, Westmount QC H3Y 3H6 – 514/935-6357 – Directrice, Susyn Borer – Elem./Sec.

Westmount: Selwyn House Association, 95, ch Côte-St-Antoine, Westmount QC H3Y 2H8 – 514/931-9481; Fax: 514/931-6118 – Directeur, William Mitchell – Gr. Pre./Elem./Sec.; Eng.; Boys

Westmount: The Study, 3233, The Boulevard, Westmount QC H3Y 1S4 – 514/935-9352; Fax: 514/935-1721 – Director, Eve Marshall – Gr. Pre./Elem./Sec.; Eng.; Girls

Westmount: Villa Ste-Marcelline, 815, av Upper Belmont, Westmount QC H3Y 1K5 – 514/488-2528; Fax: 514/488-5384 – Directrice, Sr Mathilde Fantone – Gr. Pre./Elem./Sec.; Girls

# SASKATCHEWAN

## Saskatchewan Education

2220 College Ave., Regina SK S4P 3V7
306/787-2280; Fax: 306/787-7392

### REGIONAL OFFICES IN SASKATCHEWAN

Region One: J. Auburn Bldg., 110 Souris Ave., PO Box 2003, Weyburn SK S4H 2Z9 – 306/848-2431; Fax: 306/848-2455 – Regional Director, Tom Chell

Region Two: 350 Cheadle St. West, Swift Current SK S9H 4G3 – 306/778-8247; Fax: 306/778-8583 – Regional Director, Gary Luke

Region Three: #312, 3085 Albert St., Regina SK S4P 3V7 – 306/787-6075; Fax: 306/787-6139 – Regional Director, Gil Dumelie

Region Four: 122 - 3 Ave. North, 8th Fl., Saskatoon SK S7K 2H6 – 306/933-5028; Fax: 306/933-7469 – Regional Director, Lawrence Chornos

Region Five: 107 Crawford Ave. East, PO Box 6500, Melfort SK S0E 1A0 – 306/752-6166; Fax: 306/752-6168 – Regional Director, Darlene Thompson

Region Six: 1146 - 102 St., North Battleford SK S9A 1E9 – 306/446-7434; Fax: 306/446-7586 – Regional Director, Glenn Wouters

Northern Region: PO Box 5000, La Ronge SK S0J 1L0 – 306/425-4382; Fax: 306/425-4383 – Regional Director, Glenn McKenzie

**For detailed departmental listings, see Index: "Education, Depts."**

### PUBLIC SCHOOL DIVISIONS

Saskatchewan schools are organized as follows: Public School Divisions, Roman Catholic Separate School Divisions, High School Divisions, Comprehensive School Boards.

Under the Education Act, proclaimed 1979, school units & independent school districts became school divisions. All high school districts, with one exception, & all school districts in school units ceased to exist.

The members of school divisions are elected under the Local Government Elections Act for a term of three years on the fourth Wednesday in October. For divisions situated wholly or in part within a town or city, elections are conducted by the town or city clerk. Elections in the other divisions are conducted by a returning officer who is the secretary-treasurer.

The members of comprehensive school boards are not elected, but are appointed from other school boards.

**Divisions with an enrollment of more than 10,000 are in bold print.**

Arcola School Division #72 – *1,595
PO Box 327, Arcola SK S0C 0G0
306/455-2377; Fax: 306/455-2767 – Dir., Thomas E. Chell; Sec.-Treas., Huguette P. Lutz

Battle River School Division #60 – *1,487
5017 - 46th St., PO Box 827, Lloydminster SK S9V 1C2
403/825-2828; Fax: 403/875-7829 – Supt. of Adm., Walter Hardy; Dir., K. Stuart Keys

Battleford School Division #58 – *1,283
122 - 23 St. West, PO Box 460, Battleford SK S0M 0E0
306/937-7702; Fax: 306/937-7721 – Supt. of Adm., Kenneth R. Tebb; Dir., Barry Werth

Biggar School Division #50 – *991
119 Main St., PO Box 310, Biggar SK S0K 0M0
306/948-3348; Fax: 306/948-2005 – Dir., R.B. Arnold; Sec.-Treas., Ray Perzan

Borderland School Division #68 – *1,086
205 Railway Ave., PO Box 89, Rockglen SK S0H 3R0
306/476-2101; Fax: 306/476-2414 – Dir., Ed I. Stelmaschuk; Sec.-Treas., Wilfred Hotsko

Broadview School Division #18 – *1,089
PO Box 130, Broadview SK S0G 0K0
306/696-2566; Fax: 306/696-3267 – Dir., Dexter D. Samida; Sec.-Treas., David Banting

Buffalo Plains School Division #21 – *3,037
3080 Albert St. North, PO Box 1937, Regina SK S4P 3E1
306/949-3366; Fax: 306/543-1771 – Dir., Jim Hopson; Sec.-Treas., Bruce W. Lipinski

Canora School Division #37 – *763
140 - 1 Ave. West, PO Box 869, Canora SK S0A 0L0
306/563-5562; Fax: 306/563-5295 – Dir., Gerry Joynt; Sec.-Treas., Janice Chicilo

Conseils Scolaires Fransaskois
#201, 2222 - 13 Ave., Regina SK S4P 3M7
306/757-7541; Fax: 306/757-2040 – Dir., Florent Bilodeau; Sec. Treas., Gilbert Hautcoeur

Conseils Scolaires Fransaskois
2213 East Hanselman Court, Saskatoon SK S7L 6A8
306/653-8490; Fax: 306/653-8495 – Dir., André Moquin; Sec.-Treas, Lise Garneau

Creighton School Division #111 – *452
325 Main St., PO Box 158, Creighton SK S0P 0A0
306/688-5825; Fax: 306/688-3131; Email: creighto@eagle.wlom.ca – Dir., Don Smith; Sec.-Treas., Virginia R. Hamm

Cupar School Division #28 – *1,184
708 Qu'Appelle Ave., PO Box 250, Cupar SK S0G 0Y0
306/723-4404; Fax: 306/723-4354 – Dir., Wayne Dahlgren; Sec.-Treas., Gary P. Kreklewich

Davidson School Division #31 – *924
PO Box 696, Davidson SK S0G 1A0
306/567-2811, 2812; Fax: 306/567-2878 – Dir., Christine Boyczuk; Sec.-Treas., Jeff D. Alexander

Deer Park School Division #26 – *368
633 Main St., PO Box 1930, Melville SK S0A 2P0
306/728-4426; Fax: 306/728-2351 – Dir., A.A. (Tony) Wihlidal; Sec.-Treas., Gordon Majeran

Eastend School Division #8 – *633
427 Redcoat Dr., PO Box 550, Eastend SK S0N 0T0
306/295-3771; Fax: 306/295-3703 – Dir. (Interim), Lynne Hepfner; Sec.-Treas., Kent Meyer

Estevan Comprehensive High School Board – *886
130 King St., Estevan SK S4A 2T5
306/634-4777; Fax: 306/634-6768 – Dir., Larry E. Steeves; Sec.-Treas., Glen G. Bell

Estevan Rural School Division #62 – *909
130 King St., Estevan SK S4A 2T5
306/634-4741; Fax: 306/634-6768 – Dir., J. Ellery Peters; Sec.-Treas., Glen G. Bell

Estevan School Division #95 – *1,086
130 King St., Estevan SK S4A 2T5
306/634-4777; Fax: 306/634-6768 – Dir., Larry E. Steeves; Sec.-Treas., Glen G. Bell

Eston-Elrose School Division #33 – *994
220 - 4th Ave. East, PO Box 430, Elrose SK S0L 0Z0
306/378-2522; Fax: 306/378-4133 – Dir., James D. Gunningham; Sec.-Treas., Rhonda Saathoff

Grand Coulee School Division #110 – *91
RR#2, Site #200, PO Box 65, Regina SK S4P 2Z2
306/757-2051; Fax: 306/757-1944 – Dir., Helen Horsman; Sec., Judith Vallance

Gravelbourg School Division #109 – *409
Elementary School Bldg., PO Box 748, Gravelbourg SK S0H 1X0
306/648-3229; Fax: 306/684-2269 – Dir., Marion Piche; Sec.-Treas., Ray Perzan

Gray School Division #101 – *13
PO Box 122, Pense SK S0G 3W0
306/345-2261 – Dir., Helen Horsman; Sec.-Treas., Carol Seaberly

Gull Lake School Division #76 – *636
PO Box 30, Gull Lake SK S0N 1A0
306/672-3515; Fax: 306/672-3267 – Supt. of Adm., Robert V. Francis; Dir., Cliff Chutskoff

Herbert School Division #79 – *915
501 Herbert Ave., PO Box 100, Herbert SK S0H 2A0
306/784-2433; Fax: 306/784-3565 – Dir., J. Timothy Peake; Sec.-Treas., Joanne P. Dales

Hudson Bay School Division #52 – *1,148
210 Main St., PO Box 579, Hudson Bay SK S0E 0Y0
306/865-2444, 3163; Fax: 306/865-2128 – Dir., Ron Richardson; Sec.-Treas., Laurie Guderyan

Humboldt High School Division – *246
14th Ave., PO Box 780, Humboldt SK S0K 2A0
306/682-5659; Fax: 306/682-3239 – Dir., Gene Pulak; Sec.-Treas., Fred W. Saliken

Humboldt Rural School Division #47 – *1,329
Hwy. 5 East, PO Box 40, Humboldt SK S0K 2A0
306/682-2558; Fax: 306/682-5154 – Dir., Milton Kerpan; Sec.-Treas., Mona Johns

Humboldt School Division #104 – *559
14th Ave., PO Box 780, Humboldt SK S0K 2A0
306/682-5659; Fax: 306/682-3239 – Dir., Gene Pulak; Sec.-Treas., Fred W. Saliken

Ile a la Crosse School Division #112 – *482
PO Box 89, Ile a la Crosse SK S0M 1C0
306/833-2141; Fax: 306/833-2104 – Dir., William J. Duffee; Sec.-Treas., Deanna Cunningham

Indian Head School Division #19 – *1,798
708 Otterloo St., PO Box 639, Indian Head SK S0G 2K0
306/695-2208; Fax: 306/695-2541 – Dir., Murray W. Sanders; Sec.-Treas., Marlene Pilsner

Kamsack School Division #35 – *800
431 - 3 St., PO Box 339, Kamsack SK S0A 1S0
306/542-2511; Fax: 306/542-2832 – Dir., Wes Prosser; Sec.-Treas., Janet Patterson

Kerrobert School Division #44 – *1,291
PO Box 360, Kerrobert SK S0K 4W0
306/843-2665; Fax: 306/843-2422 – Dir., Ray Johnson; Sec.-Treas., Guy Denton

Kindersley School Division #34 – *1,882
112 - 5 Ave., PO Box 1209, Kindersley SK S0L 1S0
306/463-4657; Fax: 306/463-3077 – Dir., Ken Moore; Sec.-Treas., Dianne Gordon

Kinistino School Division #55 – *812
PO Box 549, Kinistino SK S0J 1H0
306/864-2404; Fax: 306/864-2889 – Dir., Ken Passler; Sec.-Treas., Dennis A. Moniuk

Lanigan School Division #40 – *971
110 Main St., PO Box 100, Lanigan SK S0K 2M0
306/365-2015; Fax: 306/365-2808 – Dir., Richard Buettner; Sec.-Treas., Joan Adams

Last Mountain School Division #29 – *1,300
PO Box 10, Govan SK S0G 1Z0
306/484-2060; Fax: 306/484-2000 – Dir., Ralph Eliasson; Sec.-Treas., Marrion Wolff

Leader School Division #24 – *753
106 - 3rd St. West, PO Box 420, Leader SK S0N 1H0
306/628-3881; Fax: 306/628 4403 – Dir., Ernest Sweeney; Sec.-Treas., Darlene Fitterer

Lloydminster School Division – *1,431 (Sask. only)
5017 - 46 St., Lloydminster SK T9V 1R4
403/875-5541; Fax: 403/875-7829 – Dir., Dr. Donald B. Duncan; Treas., Beverley Henry

Long Lake School Division #30 – *1,145
116 Main St., PO Box 520, Watrous SK S0K 4T0
306/946-3332; Fax: 306/946-3442 – Dir., Ralph Eliasson; Sec.-Treas., Phil J. Benson

Maple Creek School Division #17 – *1,101
217 Marsh St., PO Box 400, Maple Creek SK S0N 1N0
306/662-2424, 2892; Fax: 306/662-3173 – Dir., Ed Bath; Sec.-Treas., Beverley A. Drader

Meadow Lake School Division #66 – *2,596
606 - 5th Ave. West, Meadow Lake SK S9X 1A9
306/236-5614; Fax: 306/236-3922 – Dir., Larry Zemlak; Sec.-Treas., Marilyn Y. Wiklund

Melfort School Division #100 – *1,153
113 Burrows West, PO Box 6000, Melfort SK S0E 1A0
306/752-5741; Fax: 306/752-4347; Email: msd.board@main.nlnet.melfort.sk.ca – Dir., Bob Kroeker; Sec.-Treas., Raymond Kopera

Melville Compehensive School Board – *489
633 Main St., PO Box 1930, Melville SK S0A 2P0
306/728-4426; Fax: 306/728-2351 – Dir., A.A. (Tony) Wihlidal; Sec.-Treas., Gordon Majeran

Melville School Division #108 – *372
633 Main St., PO Box 1930, Melville SK S0A 2P0
306/728-4426; Fax: 306/728-2351 – Dir., A.A. (Tony) Wihlidal; Sec.-Treas., Gordon Majeran

Moose Jaw School Division #1 – *5,079
1075 - 9 Ave. NW, Moose Jaw SK S6H 4J6
306/693-4631; Fax: 306/694-4686 – Dir., Larry T. Booth; Sec.-Treas., James N. Trites

Moosomin School Division #9 – *1,274
1103 Broadway Ave. East, PO Box 700, Moosomin SK S0G 3N0
306/435-3389; Fax: 306/435-2331 – Dir., David B Steele; Sec.-Treas., Laurel St. Onge

Nipawin School Division #61 – *2,197
214 - 1 St. West, PO Box 2044, Nipawin SK S0E 1E0
306/862-4616; Fax: 306/862-9733 – Dir., Gary L. Broker; Sec.-Treas., Len J. Skulmoski

North Battleford School Division #103 – *2,225
#161, 1791 - 110 St., North Battleford SK S9A 3E7
306/445-3827; Fax: 306/445-4332 – Dir., Merv F. Grosse; Sec.-Treas., Jim Gondziola

Northern Lakes School Division #64 – *1,143
116 - First St. East, PO Box 669, Spiritwood SK S0J 2M0
306/883-2424; Fax: 306/883-2415 – Dir., Dennis Tetu; Sec.-Treas., Carol Boechler

Northern Lights School Division #113 – *4,524
Bag Service #6500, La Ronge SK S0J 1L0
306/425-3302; Fax: 306/425-3377 – Dir., Ralph Pilz; Sec.-Treas., Linda Chapman

Outlook School Division #32 – *1,321
305 Saskatchewan Ave. West, PO Box 280, Outlook SK S0L 2N0
306/867-8622; Fax: 306/867-9999 – Dir., Ivan Yackel; Sec.-Treas., Darrel Guy

Oxbow School Division #51 – *1,090
874 Prospect, PO Box 509, Oxbow SK S0C 2B0
306/483-2964; Fax: 306/483-5230 – Dir., Thomas E. Chell; Sec.-Treas., Huguette Lutz

Parkland School Division #63 – *1,654
PO Box 100, Shellbrook SK S0J 2E0
306/747-2611; Fax: 306/747-2618 – Dir., David Thomson; Sec.-Treas., Robert L. Dows

Paynton School Division #102 – *53
123 Railway Ave., PO Box 100, Paynton SK S0M 2J0
306/895-2066; Fax: 306/895-2070 – Dir., Eugene Thera; Sec.-Treas., Garth Merryweather

Pense School Division #98 – *125
PO Box 122, Pense SK S0G 3W0
306/345-2261 – Dir., Helen Horsman; Sec.-Treas., Carol Seaberly

Potashville School Division #80 – *1,725
PO Box 700, Esterhazy SK S0A 0X0
306/745-6641; Fax: 306/745-6549 – Supt. of Adm., Ed M. Boyechko; Dir., Lawrence Chomos

Prairie View School Division #74 – *887
232 Main St., PO Box 60, Milestone SK S0G 3L0
306/436-2160; Fax: 306/436-2128 – Dir., Merv S. Renz; Sec.-Treas., Raymond P. Trew

Prairie West School Division #75 – *988
110 - 11 Ave. NW, Swift Current SK S9H 1B8
306/773-9358; Fax: 306/778-2668 – Dir., Kenneth Ladouceur; Sec.-Treas., Vince Gaudet

Prince Albert Comprehensive High School Board – *1,525
545 - 11 St. East, Prince Albert SK S6V 1B1
306/764-1571; Fax: 306/763-4460 – Dir., Shirley Gange; Sec.-Treas., Dennis A. Moniuk

Prince Albert Rural School Division #56 – *1,801
1308 - 5 Ave. East, Prince Albert SK S6V 2H7

* indicates enrollment figure.

306/764-1511; Fax: 306/763-4072 – Dir., Gordon Rutten; Sec.-Treas., Dave Bridger

Prince Albert School Division #3 – *4,046
545 - 11 St. East, Prince Albert SK S6V 1B1
306/764-1571; Fax: 306/763-4460 – Dir., Shirley Gange; Sec.-Treas., Dennis A. Moniuk

Radville School Division #67 – *487
420 Floren St., PO Box 189, Radville SK S0C 2G0
306/869-2525, 2282; Fax: 306/869-2733 – Dir., Bob Demencuik; Sec.-Treas., Christine Mazenc

Red Coat Trail School Division #69 – *1,122
500 - 1 Ave. East, PO Box 1330, Assiniboia SK S0H 0B0
306/642-3341; Fax: 306/642-3455 – Dir., Edward H. Maksymiw; Sec.-Treas., Arthur J. Warnecke

Regina (East) School Division #77 – *1,035
424 Railway Ave., PO Box 128, Odessa SK S0G 3S0
306/957-2172; Fax: 306/957-2073 – Supt. of Adm., Don L. Pearson; Dir., Wayne Neudorf

**Regina School Division #4**
1600 - 4 Ave., Regina SK S4R 8C8
306/791-8200; Fax: 306/352-2898
*24,169
Dir., Larry Huber
Sec.-Treas., Debra Burnett

Rosetown School Division #43 – *1,411
501 First St. West, PO Box 700, Rosetown SK S0L 2V0
306/882-2677; Fax: 306/882-3366 – Dir., John Ulsifer; Sec.-Treas., Maureen Sample

Saskatchewan Valley School Division #49 – *4,746
121 Klassen St. East, PO Box 809, Warman SK S0K 4S0
306/933-4414; Fax: 306/934-8221 – Dir., Michael James McLeod; Sec.-Treas., Keith R. Kraft

Saskatoon (East) School Division #41 – *1,965
620 Heritage Lane, Saskatoon SK S7H 5P5
306/374-2433; Fax: 306/955-0806 – Dir., Norman Dray; Sec.-Treas., James R. Shields

Saskatoon (West) School Division #42 – *2,604
1359 Fletcher Rd., Saskatoon SK S7M 5H5
306/664-0010; Fax: 306/664-0020 – Dir., Brian Keegan; Sec.-Treas., Ronald W. Walter

**Saskatoon School Division #13**
405 - 3 Ave. South, Saskatoon SK S7K 1M7
306/683-8200; Fax: 306/683-8207
*22,523
Dir., Pat Dickson
Sec.-Treas., Ralph Paquin

Scenic Valley School Division #117 – *1,222
PO Box 100, Neudorf SK S0A 2T0
306/748-2523; Fax: 306/748-2753 – Dir., Lynne Saas; Sec.-Treas., Sharon Bender

Shamrock School Division #38 – *1,233
340 Cameron St., PO Box 130, Foam Lake SK S0A 1A0
306/272-3377; Fax: 306/272-3239 – Dir., Siegrid Schergel; Sec.-Treas., William P. Saban

Shaunavon School Division #71 – *849
499 Centre St., PO Box 10, Shaunavon SK S0N 2M0
306/297-2627; Fax: 306/297-2439 – Dir., Ray J. Dickie; Sec.-Treas., Herb H. Conrad

Swift Current Comprehensive High School Board – *1,153
600 Chaplin St. East, Swift Current SK S9H 1J3
306/778-4600; Fax: 306/773-8011 – Supt. of Adm., Clifford D. Belter; Dir., Bryan Tallon

Swift Current School Division #94 – *1,501
600 Chaplin St. East, Swift Current SK S9H 1J3
306/778-4600; Fax: 306/773-8011 – Supt. of Adm., Clifford D. Belter; Dir., Bryan Tallon

Thunder Creek School Division #78 – *1,235
15 Thatcher Dr. East, PO Box 730, Moose Jaw SK S6H 4P4
306/694-2121; Fax: 306/694-4955 – Dir., Wayne Kiel; Sec.-Treas., Dale S. Clark

Tiger Lily School Division #54 – *1,017
150 McLeod Ave. East, PO Box 550, Melfort SK S0E 1A0
306/752-9391; Fax: 306/752-1933 – Dir., Lynell Pylatiuk; Sec.-Treas., James W. Martin

Timberline School Division #45 – *935
PO Box 869, Canora SK S0L 0A0
306/563-5562; Fax: 306/563-5592 – Dir., Gerry Joynt; Sec.-Treas., Shirley Olson

Tisdale School Division #53 – *1,531
1010 - 102 Ave., PO Box 400, Tisdale SK S0E 1T0
306/873-2674; Fax: 306/873-5222 – Dir., Dwayne Brownridge; Sec.-Treas., Valerie Hvidston

Turtleford School Division #65 – *1,267
318 Railway Ave., PO Box 280, Turtleford SK S0M 2Y0
306/845-2150; Fax: 306/845-3392 – Dir., Robert Lockwood; Sec.-Treas., Gregory C. Gerwing

Wadena School Division #46 – *1,695
245 Main St., PO Box 160, Wadena SK S0A 4J0
306/338-2325, 2167; Fax: 306/338-3527 – Dir., Harvey Bowers; Sec.-Treas., Glen Lazeski

Wakaw School Division #48 – *1,041
200 - 2 St. South, PO Box 280, Wakaw SK S0K 4P0
306/233-4623; Fax: 306/233-4649 – Dir., Harold Mueller; Sec.-Treas., Sandy Gessner

Weyburn Central School Division #73 – *619
21 - 5 St. NE, Weyburn SK S4H 0Y9
306/842-2674; Fax: 306/842-1261 – Dir., Crandall Hrynkiw; Sec.-Treas., Patricia Jones

Weyburn Comprehensive School Board – *566
617 King St. NW, Weyburn SK S4H 2S5
306/842-2811, 2068; Fax: 306/842-2335 – Dir., Ed E. Kolybaba; Sec.-Treas., Gord Young

Weyburn School Division #97 – *1,536
617 King St. NW, Weyburn SK S4H 2S5
306/842-2811, 2068; Fax: 306/842-2335 – Dir., Edward E. Kolybaba; Sec.-Treas., Gord Young

Wilcox School Division #105 – *61
PO Box 280, Wilcox SK S0G 5E0
306/732-4522 – Dir., Leigh Calnek; Sec.-Treas., Pat Maguire

Wilkie School Division #59 – *1,325
206 - 2 St. West, PO Box 360, Wilkie SK S0K 4W0
306/843-2665; Fax: 306/843-2422 – Dir., Ray Johnson; Sec.-Treas., Guy Denton

Wood River School Division #70 – *634
38 - 2 Ave. West, PO Box 280, Lafleche SK S0H 2K0
306/472-5242; Fax: 306/472-3277 – Dir., Sharon Compton

Yorkdale School Division #36 – *1,205
91 Broadway East, Yorkton SK S3N 0L1
306/783-8526; Fax: 306/783-0355 – Dir., Michael J. Clarke; Sec.-Treas., Sandra Wilson

Yorkton Regional High School Board – *874
33 Darlington St. West, Yorkton SK S3N 0E4
306/786-5500; Fax: 306/782-3223 – Dir., Leonard Bode; Sec.-Treas., Florence Halldorson

Yorkton School Division #93 – *2,039
33 Darlington St. West, Yorkton SK S3N 0E4
306/786-5500; Fax: 306/782-3223 – Dir., Leonard Bode; Sec.-Treas., Florence Halldorson

## ROMAN CATHOLIC SEPARATE SCHOOL DIVISIONS

Christ the King Roman Catholic Separate School Division #83 – *121
PO Box 1087, Moose Jaw SK S6H 4P8
306/694-5333; Fax: 306/692-2238 – Dir., Jerry Zimmer; Sec.-Treas., Gerry Gieni

Estevan Roman Catholic Separate School Division #27 – *526
1329 Third St., Estevan SK S4A 0S1
306/634-6711; Fax: 306/634-7023 – Dir., Austin Gerein; Sec.-Treas., Holley Odgers

Humboldt Roman Catholic Separate School Division #15 – *384
809 -10th St., PO Box 2830, Humboldt SK S0K 2A0
306/682-2287; Fax: 306/682-2055 – Dir., Stan Digout; Sec.-Treas., Janet Mueller

Lloydminster Roman Catholic Separate School Division #89 – *695 (Sask. only)
5411 - 50 Ave., Lloydminster SK S9V 0R1
306/825-8911; Fax: 306/825-9855 – Dir., R.V. Mokelky; Sec.-Treas., Tom Schinold

Mankota Our Lady of Fatima Roman Catholic Separate School Division #90 – *34
PO Box 280, Lafleche SK S0H 2K0
306/472-5242; Fax: 306/472-3277 – Dir., Sharon Compton; Sec.-Treas., Ray Perzan

Moose Jaw Roman Catholic Separate School Division #22 – *1,711
502 - 6 Ave. NE, PO Box 1087, Moose Jaw SK S6H 4P8
306/694-5333; Fax: 306/692-2238 – Dir., Jerry Zimmer; Sec.-Treas., Gerry Gieni

North Battleford Roman Catholic Separate School Division #16 – *1,649
9301 - 19 Ave., North Battleford SK S9A 3N5
306/445-6158; Fax: 306/445-3993 – Supt. of Adm., G. Paul Baskey; Dir., Ken J. Loehndorf

Prince Albert Roman Catholic Separate School Division #6 – *2,673
118 - 11 St. East, Prince Albert SK S6V 1A1
306/953-7500; Fax: 306/763-1723 – Dir., Dr. Garry Andrews; Sec.-Treas., Don Orr

**Regina Roman Catholic Separate School Division #81**
2160 Cameron St., Regina SK S4T 2V6
306/791-7200; Fax: 306/347-7699
*11,159
Dir., Gwen Keith
Sec.-Treas., Curt Van Parys

St. Alphonse Roman Catholic Separate School Division #2 – *19
PO Box 71, Viscount SK S0K 4M0
306/944-4446; Fax: 306/944-4446 – Dir., Joe Kammermayer; Sec.-Treas., Mary B. Comeault

St. Gabriel's Roman Catholic Separate School Division #23 – *243
234 - 3 Ave. West, PO Box 1177, Biggar SK S0K 0M0
306/948-3889; Fax: 306/948-5254 – Dir., Ron Arnold; Sec.-Treas., Jean Silvernagle

St. Henry's Roman Catholic Separate School Division #5 – *383
633 Main St., PO Box 1629, Melville SK S0A 2P0
306/728-4426; Fax: 306/728-2351 – Dir., A.A. (Tony) Wihlidal; Sec. -Treas., Gordon Majeran

St. Olivier Roman Catholic Separate School Division, #12 – *149
325 Beckwell Ave., PO Box 579, Radville SK S0C 2G0
306/869-3221; Fax: 306/869-3259 – Dir., Robert Demencuik; Sec.-Treas., Louise Tuchscherer

**St. Paul's Roman Catholic Separate School Division #20**
420 - 22 St. East, Saskatoon SK S7K 1X3
306/668-7000; Fax: 306/668-7085
*14,456
Dir., Ken McDonough
Sec.-Treas., B. Noonan

Spiritwood Roman Catholic Separate School Division #82 – *74
PO Box 353, Spiritwood SK S0J 2M0
306/883-2328 – Dir., Denis Tetu; Sec.-Treas., Gail Ferster

Swift Current Roman Catholic Separate School Division #11 – *381
600 Chaplin St. East, Swift Current SK S9H 1J3
306/778-4666; Fax: 306/773-8011 – Dir., Bryan Tallon; Sec.-Treas., Deborah L. DeMars

Unity Roman Catholic Separate School Division #88 – *222
PO Box 598, Unity SK S0K 4L0
306/228-3118; Fax: 306/228-3598 – Dir., Ken Loehndorf; Sec.-Treas., Dianna Wildeman

Weyburn Roman Catholic Separate School Division #84 – *399
433 - 4 St. NE, Weyburn SK S4H 0Y8
306/842-5256; Fax: 306/842-4544 – Dir., Crandall Hrynkiw; Sec.-Treas., Colleen Court

Wilkie St. George Roman Catholic Separate School Division #85 – *146
9301 - 19th Ave., North Battleford SK S9A 3N5
306/445-6158; Fax: 306/445-3993 – Supt., Paul Baskey; Dir., Ken Loehndorf

Yorkton Roman Catholic Separate School Division #86 – *1,257
259 Circlebrooke Dr., Yorkton SK S3N 2S8
306/783-8787; Fax: 306/783-4992 – Dir., Brian Boechler; Sec.-Treas., Wilfred R. Maier

## NATIVE SCHOOLS

Joe Duquette High School, 919 Broadway Ave., Saskatoon SK S7N 1B8 – 306/668-7490 – *170

## SCHOOLS FOR CHILDREN WITH SOCIAL, EMOTIONAL, BEHAVIOURAL CHALLENGES

Cornwall Alternative School
40 Dixon Cres., Regina SK S4N 1V4
306/522-0044; Fax: 306/359-0720

Radius Community Centre for Education & Employment
#200, 245 - 3rd Ave. South, Saskatoon SK S7K 1M4
306/665-0362

Schaller School
PO Box 570, Pilot Butte SK S0G 3Z0
306/352-1694

## UNIVERSITIES

### The University of Regina

3737 Wascana Pkwy., Regina SK S4S 0A2
306/585-4402; Fax: 306/585-4997
Email: http://www.uregina.ca
Visitor, Lt. Gov. J.E.N. Wiebe
Chairman, Board of Governors, Charles Baldock
Chancellor, Verda L. Petry, B.A., B.Ed., M.Ed.
President & Vice-Chancellor, Donald O. Wells, B.Sc., M.Sc., Ph.D.
Vice-President, Academic, Dianne L. Common, Ph.D., M.Ed., B.Ed., B.A.
Vice-President, Administration, David Barnard, B.Sc., M.Sc., Ph.D.
Assoc. Vice-President, Academic, Robert G. McCulloch, Ph.D., M.Sc., B.S.P.E.
Assoc. Vice-President & Dean, Research & Graduate Studies, Larry R. Symes, B.A., M.S., Ph.D., I.S.P.
Executive Director, University Development, M. Hutchings, B.A., M.B.A.
Registrar & Director, Student Affairs, G. Meehan, B.A., M.Ed.
University Secretary, R. Reid Robinson, B.A., D.Phil.

#### FACULTIES WITH DEANS

Administration, Garnet Garven, B.A., M.B.A., Ph.D. (a.b.d.)
Arts, K. Murray Knuttila, B.A.Hons., M.A., Ph.D.
Education, Michael Tymchak, B.A.Hons., Ph.D.
Engineering, Amit Chakma, M.A.Sc., Ph.D .
Fine Arts, Michael J. Rushton, B.A., M.A., Ph.D.
Physical Activity Studies, Ralph Nilson, B.A., M.Sc., Ph.D.
Science, Keith Denford, B.Sc.Hons., Ph.D.
Social Work, Sharon McKay, B.A., M.S.W.
University Extension, Morris Maduro, A.A., B.A., M.A., Ph.D.

#### SCHOOLS WITH DIRECTORS

Asia Pacific Management Institute, J. Carlson, B.S., M.B.A., Ph.D.
Canadian Plains Research Centre, David A. Gauthier, B.A., M.A., Ph.D.
Centre for Advanced Systems, Michael Wong, B.Sc., M.A., Ph.D.
Communications, Vacant
Conservatory of Music & Dance, John Griffiths, B.Mus.Ed., M.Mus.
Counselling Services, Brian Sveinson, B.A., M.A., Ph.D.
Energy Research Institute, Brian D. Kybett, B.Sc., Ph.D.
Human Justice, Sandra D. Pearce, B.A., M.A., Ph.D.
Institute for Health Studies, R.G. Haennel, Ph.D.
Journalism, Bryan E. Olney, B.A., M.A.
Language Institute, A.N. Lalonde, B.A., M.A., Ph.D.
Mackenzie Art Gallery, Kate Davis, M.A., B.A.
Prairie Justice Research, R. Schriml, B.A., M.S.W.
Regina Water Research Institute, Donald R. Cullimore, B.Sc., Ph.D.
Saskatchewan Instructional Development & Research Unit, C. Krentz, B.A., M.Ed., Ph.D.
Social Administration Research Unit, D. Broad, B.A., M.A., Ph.D.
Social Work, L. Douglas Durst, B.A., M.S.W., Ph.D.
The Development Institute of Saskatchewan, G. Parsons

#### AFFILIATED COLLEGES

Canadian Theological Seminary, 4400 - 4th Ave., Regina SK S4T 0H8 – 306/545-1515 – Acting President, Melvin Sylvester
Gabriel Dumont Institute of Native Studies & Applied Research, 121 Broadway Ave. East, Regina SK S4N 0Z6 – 306/347-4100 – Acting Exec. Director, Robert Devrome

#### FEDERATED COLLEGES

Campion College, c/o University of Regina, Regina SK S4S 0A2 – 306/586-4242; URL: http://www.uregina.ca/calendar/fedcoll/html#camp – President, Joseph G. Schner, S.J., A.B., M.A., M.Div., Ph.D.
Luther College, c/o University of Regina, Regina SK S4S 0A2 – 306/585-5333, 5025 – President, Richard Hordern, B.A., M.Div., S.T.M., M.Phil., Ph.D.
Saskatchewan Indian Federated College, 118 College St. West, Regina SK S4S 0A2 – 306/ 584-8333, 8334; URL: http://www.uregina.ca/calendar/fedcoll.html#sifc – President, Eber Hampton, B.A., Ed.D.

### University of Saskatchewan

105 Admin. Place, Saskatoon SK S7N 5A2
306/966-4343; Fax: 306/966-8670
URL: http://www.usask.ca/
Visitor, The Hon. J.E.N. Wiebe, Lt. Governor of Saskatchewan
Chancellor, Margaret L. McKercher, C.M., B.A.
Chair, Board of Governors, H.E. Wyatt, B.Comm.
President, J.W.G. Ivany, B.Sc., Dip.Ed., M.A., Ph.D.
Vice-President, Academic, M.M. Atkinson, B.A., M.A., Ph.D.
Vice-President, Finance & Administration, A.J. Whitworth, B.Sc., Ph.D., M.B.A., M.Ed., C.Chem., C.M.A.
Assoc. Vice-President, Research, M.E. Corcoran, B.A., M.A., Ph.D.
University Secretary, R.I. MacLean, B.A.
Registrar, K.M. Smith, A.B., M.S., Ph.D.
Controller, L. Kennedy, B. Comm., C.A.
Assoc. Vice-President, Information Technology Services, R.N. Kavanagh, B.E., M.Sc., Ph.D.
Assoc. Vice-President, V. Pezer, B.A., M.A., Ph.D.

#### FACULTIES WITH DEANS

Agriculture, J.W.B. Stewart
Dean (Acting), Arts & Science, C. Thompson
Commerce, V.L. Pearson
Dentistry, R. McDermott
Education, K. Jacknicke
Engineering, F. Berruti
Extension, G. Thompson
Graduate Studies & Research, G. Kachanoski
Law, R.P. MacKinnon
Medicine, D. Popkin
Nursing, Y.M.R. Brown
Pharmacy & Nutrition, T. Hawes
Physical Education, R. Faulkner
Veterinary Medicine, A. Livingston

#### SCHOOLS WITH DIRECTORS

Physical Therapy, E. Harrison, B.P.T., M.Sc., M.C.P.A., Ph.D.

#### AFFILIATED COLLEGES

Central Pentecostal College, 1303 Jackson Ave., Saskatoon SK S7H 2M9 – 306/374-6655 – President, Rev. R. Kadyschuk
College of Emmanuel & St. Chad, 1337 College Dr, Saskatoon SK S7N 0W6 – 306/975-3753 – Principal, Rev. C.W.N. Christensen
Lutheran Theological Seminary, 114 Seminary Cres., Saskatoon SK S7N 0X3 – 306/975-7004; Fax: 306/975-0084 – President, Rev. F. Rohrbough
St. Andrew's College, Saskatoon SK S7N 0W3 – 306/966-8970 – Co-President, Rev. Charlotte Caron
St. Peter's College, PO Box 10, Muenster SK S0K 2Y0 – 306/682-1755 – Co-President, B. Popowich

#### FEDERATED COLLEGES

St. Thomas More College, 1437 College Dr., Saskatoon SK S7N 0W6 – 306/966-8900 – President, J.R. Thompson

## TECHNICAL INSTITUTIONS

#### SASKATCHEWAN INDIAN INSTITUTE OF TECHNOLOGIES

c/o Asimakaniseekan Askiy Reserve, #100, 103A Packham Ave., Saskatoon SK S7N 4K4
306/244-4444; Fax: 306/244-1391
President, Joan Greyeyes
Registrar, Cam Willett

#### SASKATCHEWAN INSTITUTE OF APPLIED SCIENCE & TECHNOLOGY

c/o Secretariat, S.J. Cohen Centre, #401, 119 - 4th Ave. South, Saskatoon SK S7K 5X2
306/933-7331
Communications Officer, Colleen Gallant, Email: gallant@siast.sk.ca
President, Art Knight
Kelsey Institute, PO Box 1520, Saskatoon SK S7K 3R5 – 306/933-6350; Toll Free: 1-800-567-3263
Palliser Institute, PO Box 1420, Moose Jaw SK S6H 4R4 – 306/694-3200; Toll Free: 1-800-667-0055
Wascana Institute, 221 Winnipeg St. North, PO Box 556, Regina SK S4P 3A3 – 306/787-4356; Toll Free: 1-800-667-7730
Woodland Institute, Main Bldg., 1100 - 15 St. East, PO Box 3003, Prince Albert SK S6V 6G1 – 306/953-7000; Toll Free: 1-800-667-9664

## REGIONAL COLLEGES

#### CARLTON TRAIL REGIONAL COLLEGE

623 - 7 St., PO Box 720, Humboldt SK S0K 2A0
306/682-2623; Fax: 306/682-3101
CEO, Dave Kraft

#### CUMBERLAND REGIONAL COLLEGE

501 - 6th St. East, PO Box 2225, Nipawin SK S0E 1E0
306/862-9833; Fax: 306/862-4940
CEO, Steve Rudy

#### CYPRESS HILLS REGIONAL COLLEGE

129 - 2 Ave. NE, Swift Current SK S9H 2C6
306/773-1531; Fax: 306/773-2384
Email: emilr@sympatico.sk.ca

* indicates enrollment figure.

CEO, Emily Rempel
Gravelbourg Learning Centre, 7 Athabasca St., PO Box 652, Gravelbourg SK S0H 1X0 – 306/648-3244; Fax: 306/648-2983
Maple Creek Learning Centre, 110 Jasper St., PO Box 1738, Maple Creek SK S0N 1N0 – 306/662-3829; Fax: 306/662-3849
Shaunavon Learning Centre, #307 - 7 Ave. West, PO Box 1478, Shaunavon SK S0N 2M0 – 306/297-3462; Fax: 306/297-3420

#### NORTH WEST REGIONAL COLLEGE

1381 - 101 St., North Battleford SK S9A 0Z9
306/937-5100; Fax: 306/445-1575
Email: inquiry@nwrc.sk.ca; URL: http://www.nwrc.sk.ca
CEO, Bryan Nylander
Meadow Lake Campus, 607 Centre St., Meadow Lake SK S9X 1E1 – 306/236-5659; Fax: 306/236-6379
Shellbrook Adult Education Centre, PO Box 1026, Shellbrook SK S0J 2E0 – 306/747-3038; Fax: 306/747-2276
Spiritwood Adult Education Centre, PO Box 567, Spiritwood SK S0J 2M0 – 306/883-2341; Fax: 306/883-3002
St. Walburg Adult Education Centre, PO Box 4, St. Walburg SK S0M 2T0 – 306/248-3288; Fax: 306/248-3203
Unity Adult Education Centre, PO Box 1438, Unity SK S0K 4L0 – 306/228-4191; Fax: 306/228-2383

#### NORTHLANDS COLLEGE

PO Box 1000, Air Ronge SK S0J 3G0
306/425-4480; Fax: 306/425-3002
CEO, Bill McLaughlin
Central Region Office, PO Box 509, La Ronge SK S0J 1L0 – 306/425-4353; Fax: 306/425-2696
Eastern Region Office, PO Box 400, Creighton SK S0P 0A0 – 306/688-8838; Fax: 306/688-7710
Western Region Office, PO Box 190, Buffalo Narrows SK S0M 0J0 – 306/235-1765; Fax: 306/235-4346

#### PARKLAND REGIONAL COLLEGE

290 Prince William Dr., PO Box 790, Melville SK S0A 2P0
306/728-4471; Fax: 306/728-2576
CEO, W.J. Rieger

#### PRAIRIE WEST REGIONAL COLLEGE

PO Box 700, Biggar SK S0K 0M0
306/948-3363; Fax: 306/948-2094
CEO, Bruce Probert
Kindersley Office, PO Box 488, Kindersley SK S0L 1S0 – 306/463-6431; Fax: 306/463-1161
Outlook Office, PO Box 1237, Outlook SK S0L 2N0 – 306/867-8857; Fax: 306/867-8722
Rosetown Office, PO Box 610, Rosetown SK S0L 2V0 – 306/882-4236; Fax: 306/882-2262
Warman Office, PO Box 1001, Warman SK S0K 4S0 – 306/242-5377; Fax: 306/242-8662

#### SOUTHEAST REGIONAL COLLEGE

PO Box 2003, Weyburn SK S4H 2Z9
306/848-2501; Fax: 306/848-2517
Email: se.college.12@sk.sympatico.ca
CEO, Arthur Whetstone

### POST-SECONDARY & SPECIALIZED INSTITUTIONS

#### ACADEMY OF LEARNING

226 - 20th St., Saskatoon SK S7K 0A6
306/665-5577; Fax: 306/653-1808
Email: rhumbke@ucomnet.unibase.com
Computer & business skills training

#### BSD TRAINING & RESOURCES LTD.

609 - 25 St. East, Saskatoon SK S4P 0L7
306/244-7504; Fax: 306/978-2230
Skills training for employment, ESL

#### CAREER DEVELOPMENT INSTITUTES LTD.

374 - 3rd Ave. South, Saskatoon SK S7K 1M5
306/244-8585; Fax: 306/244-0788
Computer maintenance; automated office administration

#### CDI COLLEGE OF BUSINESS & TECHNOLOGY

374 - 3rd Ave. South, Saskatoon SK S7K 1M5
306/244-8585; Fax: 306/244-0788
Computer, office, accounting & business programs

#### MCKAY TECH INC.

226 - 20th St. East, Saskatoon SK S7K 0A6
306/652-5352; Fax: 306/653-1808
Medical office/dental assistant, massage therapy, desktop publishing

#### REEVES BUSINESS & CAREER COLLEGE

5012 - 49 St., PO Box 51, Lloydminster SK S9V 0X9
403/875-3308; Fax: 403/875-9209
Secretarial, accounting training

#### SASKATOON ACADEMY OF LEARNING

226 - 20th St. East, Saskatoon SK S7K 0A6
306/665-5577; Fax: 306/653-1808
Secretarial; microcomputer business applications

#### SASKATOON BUSINESS COLLEGE

221 Third Ave. North, Saskatoon SK S7K 2H7
306/244-6333; Fax: 306/652-4888
Business courses

#### UNIVERSAL CAREER COLLEGE

226 - 20th St. East, Saskatoon SK S7K 0A6
306/665-5577, ext.6; Fax: 306/665-1808
Office & business management, travel & tourism

#### WESTERN ACADEMY BROADCASTING COLLEGE LTD.

321 Ave. F South, PO Box 6082, Saskatoon SK S7K 4E5
306/665-1771; Fax: 306/668-1219

#### WESTERN CANADIAN MANAGEMENT INSTITUTE

3300 Second Ave. West, PO Box 2975, Prince Albert SK S6V 7M4
306/763-8558; Fax: 306/953-0910
Hotel/restaurant; small business

### INDEPENDENT & PRIVATE SCHOOLS

**Schools with enrollment of 50 or more, listed alphabetically by city. All day & residential, & co-educational, except as noted.**

Caronport High School, PO Box 73, Caronport SK S0H 0S0 – 306/756-3303 – Principal, Dave Frostad – *273 (Non-Denom.) – Gr. 9-12
Gravelbourg: Collège Mathieu, PO Bag 20, Gravelbourg SK S0H 1X0 – 306/648-3105 – Principal, Bernard Roy – *99 (RC) – Gr. 8-12; French
Outlook: Lutheran Collegiate Bible Institute, Outlook SK S0K 2N0 – 306/867-8971 – Principal, Tony Peter – *142 (Lutheran) – Gr. 10-12; Residential only
Prelate: St. Angela's Academy, PO Box 220, Prelate SK S0N 2B0 – 306/673-2200 – Principal, Jerome Granston – *80 (RC) – Gr. 10-12; Residential; Girls
Prince Albert: Rivier Academy, 1405 - 5 Ave. West, Prince Albert SK S6V 5J1 – 306/764-6289 – Principal, Sr. Mary Woodward – *194 (RC) – Gr. 7-12; Girls
Regina: Harvest City Christian Academy, 40 Sheppard St., Regina SK S4R 3M6 – 306/569-1935 – Principal, Todd Harrison – *104 – Gr. K.-12 (Non-Denom.); Day only
Regina: Luther College High School, 1500 Royal St., Regina SK S4T 5A5 – 306/791-9150 – Principal, Berbel Knoll – *408 (Lutheran) – Gr. 9-12
Regina Christian School, 215 Mikkelson Dr., Regina SK S4P 3W7 – 306/775-0919 – Principal, Rod Rilling – *76 (Non-Denom.) – Gr. K.-8; Day only
Rosthern Junior College, Rosthern SK S0K 3R0 – 306/232-4222 – Principal, Erwin Tiesson – *123 (General Conference Mennonite) – Gr. 10-12
Saskatoon: Christian Centre Academy, 102 Pinehouse Dr., Saskatoon SK S7K 5H7 – 306/242-7141 – Principal, Lou Brunelle – *185 (Non-Denom.) – Gr. K.-12; Day only
Saskatoon: Faith Alive Christian Academy, 637 University Dr., Saskatoon SK S7N 0H8 – 306/652-2230 – Principal, Leslie Semchuk – *67 – Gr. K.-12; (Non-Denom.); Day only
Saskatoon Christian School, 2410 Haultain Ave., Saskatoon SK S7J 1R3 – 306/343-1494 – Principal, Wes Vanstone – *99 (Non-Denom.) – Gr. K.-8; Day only
Wilcox: Athol Murray College of Notre Dame, PO Box 174, Wilcox SK S0G 5E0 – 306/732-2080 – Principal, Dennis Ulmer – *360 (RC) – Gr. 9-12

## YUKON TERRITORY

### Department of Education

PO Box 2703, Whitehorse YT Y1A 2C6
867/667-5141; Fax: 867/393-6254

#### ADVANCED EDUCATION BRANCH

Acting Asst. Deputy Minister, Roland McCaffrey
Director, Training Services, Ken Smith
Student Financial Officer, Carole Theriault
Student Financial Officer, Judy Thrower

#### PUBLIC SCHOOLS BRANCH

Supt. of Schools, Area 3, Carol McCauley
Supt. of Programs, Curriculum, French Programs & Special Programs, Mavis Fisher
Acting Asst. Deputy Minister, Wally Seipp

**For detailed departmental listings, see Index: "Education, Depts."**

The Yukon has 29 public schools (15 in Whitehorse, 14 in other communities) & three private schools. The public schools are administered directly by the Department of Education, although elected officials are gradually assuming more powers under the 1990 Education Act, & may evolve into school boards in the near future.

Curriculum is largely based on that of British Columbia, with flexibility for locally developed courses, particularly from a First Nations perspective (one quarter of the Yukon's 5,800 students are of native ancestry). Seven different native languages are taught in various Yukon schools, as well as French immersion & a French first language school in Whitehorse.

### POST-SECONDARY EDUCATION

#### YUKON COLLEGE

PO Box 2799, Whitehorse YT Y1A 5K4
867/668-8704; Fax: 867/668-8896
URL: http://www.yukoncollege.yk.ca
Chair, Board of Governors, Steve Cardiff
President, Sally Ross

# INDEX TO SELECTED FACULTIES/SCHOOLS

## ADMINISTRATION/MANAGEMENT

Athabasca University
Carleton University
Dalhousie University
McGill University
Université Laval
Université de Montréal
Université de Sherbrooke
The University of Calgary
University of Lethbridge
University of Manitoba
Université de Moncton
University of New Brunswick
University of Northern British Columbia
University of Ottawa/Université d'Ottawa
University of Toronto
The University of Regina

## AGRICULTURE

McGill University
Université Laval
University of Alberta
University of British Columbia
University of Guelph
University of Manitoba
University of Saskatchewan

## ARCHITECTURE

Carleton University
DalTech
McGill University
Technical University of Nova Scotia
Université Laval
University of British Columbia
University of Manitoba
University of Toronto
University of Waterloo

## BUSINESS/COMMERCE

Acadia University
Bishop's University
Brock University
Carleton University
Concordia University
Dalhousie University
École des Hautes Études Commerciales (Université de Montréal)
Lakehead University
Laurentian University of Sudbury/Université Laurentienne de Sudbury
McMaster University
Memorial University of Newfoundland
Queen's University
Ryerson Polytechnic University
Saint Mary's University
Simon Fraser University
Trinity Western University
Wilfrid Laurier University
University of Alberta
University of British Columbia
University of New Brunswick
University of Prince Edward Island
University of Saskatchewan
University of Victoria
University College of Cape Breton
University of Western Ontario
University of Windsor
York University

## COMPUTER SCIENCE/INFORMATION TECHNOLOGY

Acadia University
Athabasca University
Carleton University
Concordia University
McGill University
Memorial University of Newfoundland
Technical University of Nova Scotia
University of New Brunswick
University of Toronto
University of Waterloo
University of Western Ontario
University of Windsor

## DENTISTRY

Dalhousie University
McGill University
Université Laval
Université de Montréal
University of Alberta
University of British Columbia
University of Manitoba
University of Saskatchewan
University of Toronto
University of Western Ontario

## EDUCATION

Acadia University
Brandon University
Brock University
Lakehead University
Laurentian University of Sudbury/Université Laurentienne de Sudbury
McGill University
Memorial University of Newfoundland
Nipissing University
Nova Scotia Teachers College
Queen's University
Saint Mary's University
St. Thomas University
Simon Fraser University
Trent University
Trinity Western University
Université Laval
Université de Moncton
Université de Montréal
Université de Sherbrooke
University of Alberta
University of British Columbia
The University of Calgary
University of Lethbridge
University of Manitoba
University of New Brunswick
University of Ottawa/Université d'Ottawa
University of Prince Edward Island
The University of Regina
University of Saskatchewan
University of Toronto
University of Western Ontario
University of Windsor
University of Victoria
York University

## ENGINEERING

Acadia University
Carleton University
Concordia University
DalTech
Lakehead University
Laurentian University of Sudbury/Université Laurentienne de Sudbury
McGill University
McMaster University
Memorial University of Newfoundland
Royal Military College of Canada
Ryerson Polytechnic University
Simon Fraser University
Technical University of Nova Scotia
Université Laval
Université de Moncton
Université de Sherbrooke
University of Alberta
University of British Columbia
The University of Calgary
University of Guelph
University of Manitoba
University of New Brunswick
University of Ottawa/Université d'Ottawa
The University of Regina
University of Saskatchewan
University of Toronto
University of Victoria
University of Waterloo
University of Western Ontario
University of Windsor

## ENVIRONMENTAL MANAGEMENT/STUDIES

Dalhousie University
McGill University
The University of Calgary
University of New Brunswick
University of Northern British Columbia
University of Toronto
University of Waterloo
York University

## FINE ARTS/VISUAL ARTS

Concordia University
Université Laval
The University of Calgary
University of Lethbridge
University of Manitoba
The University of Regina
University of Victoria
University of Waterloo
University of Windsor
York University

## FORESTRY

Lakehead University
Université Laval
Université de Moncton
University of Alberta
University of British Columbia
University of New Brunswick
University of Toronto

## LAW

Carleton University
Dalhousie University
McGill University
Queen's University
Université Laval
Université de Moncton
Université de Montréal
Université du Québec
Université de Sherbrooke
University of Alberta
University of British Columbia
The University of Calgary
University of Manitoba
University of New Brunswick
University of Ottawa/Université d'Ottawa
University of Saskatchewan
University of Toronto
University of Victoria
University of Western Ontario
University of Windsor
York University

## LIBRARY/INFORMATION SCIENCE

Dalhousie University

# SECTION 10

## LEGAL DIRECTORY



**See ADDENDA at the back of this book for late changes & additional information.**

## COURTS & JUDGES

### FEDERAL

#### SUPREME COURT OF CANADA

Supreme Court Bldg., Wellington St., Ottawa ON K1A 0J1

613/995-4330; Fax: 613/996-3063

The Supreme Court of Canada, first established in 1875 by the *Supreme Court & Exchequer Act*, is now governed by the *Supreme Court Act.*

The Supreme Court sits at Ottawa & exercises general appellate jurisdiction throughout Canada in civil & criminal cases. The judgement of the Court is final & conclusive. The Court is also required to advise on questions referred to it by the Governor in Council. Under section 53 of the *Supreme Court Act*, the constitutionality or interpretation of any federal or provincial law, the powers of Parliament or of the provincial legislatures or of both levels of government, among other matters, may be referred by the Government to the Supreme Court for consideration.

In *civil cases*, appeals may be brought from any final judgement of the highest court of last resort in a province or territory by obtaining leave to do so from that court or from the Supreme Court itself. The Supreme Court will grant permission to appeal if it is of the opinion that a question of public importance is involved, one that transcends the immediate concerns of the parties to the litigation.

In *criminal cases*, the Court will hear appeals as of right concerning indictable offenses where an acquittal has been set aside or where there has been a dissenting judgement on a point of law in a provincial court of appeal. The Supreme Court may, in addition, hear appeals on questions of law concerning both summary convictions & indictable offenses if permission to appeal is first granted by the Court.

There are three sessions of the Court each year, beginning normally on the fourth Tuesday in January, the fourth Tuesday in April & the first Tuesday in October.

The Court consists of a Chief Justice, who is called the Chief Justice of Canada, & eight puisne judges. They are appointed by the Governor in Council & hold office during good behaviour but are removable by the Governor-General on address of the Senate & the House of Commons. They cease to hold office on attaining the age of 75 years.

The Court is responsible for its own administration and budgeting. Its estimates are submitted to Parliament by the Minister of Justice. The Registrar has the rank of Deputy Head and, subject to the direction of the Chief Justice, is responsible for the Registry, the Library, the Supreme Court Reports as well as the general administration of the Court.

***Note:** Gérard La Forest stepped down as Supreme Court Judge in August 1997. Thus, an opening has been created on the nine-member court that, in accordance with long standing convention, will be filled by an appointee from Atlantic Canada.

**Chief Justice of Canada,** The Rt. Hon. Mr. Justice A. Lamer

Puisne Judges Listed Alphabetically (The Hon. Mr./ Madam Justice):

Peter Cory; Charles Gonthier; Frank Iacobucci; Claire L'Heureux-Dubé; John C. Major; Beverley McLachlin; John Sopinka

Registrar, Anne Roland

Executive Legal Officer, James O'Reilly

Deputy Registrar, Louise Meagher

Sr. Legal Counsel, Legal Services, B. Kincaid

Manager, Process Registry, Danielle Beaulieu

Head, Registry & Court Record Services, M.K. Larmour

Chief, Informatics, W. Murray

Director, Reports, Odile Calder

Law Editors, Sally Griffin, Claude Marquis, Archie McDonald

Revisors, R.D. Berberi, C. Després, M. Gendron

Director, Administrative Services, Irene O'Connor

Director, Library & Research Services, Diane Teeple

Director, Corporate Services, Anneliese Villeneuve

#### FEDERAL COURT OF CANADA

Supreme Court of Canada Bldg., Ottawa ON K1A 0H9

613/996-6795; Fax: 613/995-5442

The Federal Court of Canada consists of a Chief Justice, an Associate Chief Justice & not more than 29 other Judges, & has two divisions: the Federal Court of Appeal & the Federal Court (Trial Division).

The Federal Court of Appeal has jurisdiction on appeals from a judgement of the Federal Court (Trial Division) & Tax Court of Canada, a determination on a reference made by federal tribunals, boards or commissions or the Attorney General of Canada & on judicial review in respect of decisions of federal boards, commissions or tribunals listed in section 28 of the *Federal Court Act.*

The Federal Court (Trial Division) has jurisdiction in claims generally by & against the Crown, miscellaneous cases involving the Crown, claims against or concerning Crown officers, agents & servants, relief, including judicial review, against Federal boards, commissions and tribunals, intergovernmental disputes, conflicts with respect to industrial property, including patent, copyright & trade-mark, maritime law, citizenship appeals, aeronautics, inter-provincial works & undertakings, residuary jurisdiction for relief if there is no other Canadian court that has such jurisdiction, & jurisdiction in specific matters conferred by Federal Statutes.

The Court has a Senior Prothonotary, Associate Senior Prothonotary & Prothonotary (Sec. 12 of the Act). Prothonotaries sittings are held in open Court to hear motions at the direction of the Associate Chief Justice (Federal Court Rule 318). A prothonotary has the power to dispose of any interlocutory application, or any action not exceeding a $5,000 claim, assigned to him by direction of the Chief Justice or the Associate Chief Justice (Federal Court Rule 336).

**Chief Justice,** The Hon. Mr. Justice Julius A. Isaac

Assoc. Chief Justice, The Hon. Mr. Justice James A. Jerome, P.C.

Justices (The Hon. Mr./Madam Justice):
Appeal Division: Robert Décary; Alice Desjardins; James K. Hugessen; Gilles Létourneau; Allen M. Linden; Mark R. MacGuigan; Louis Marceau; F. Joseph McDonald; Louis Pratte; Joseph T. Robertson; Arthur J. Stone; Barry L. Strayer
Trial Division: Douglas R. Campbell; Bud Cullen; Pierre Denault; Jean-Eudes Dubé, P.C.; Frederick E. Gibson; L. Marcel Joyal; Allan Lutfy; W. Andrew MacKay; Donna C. McGillis; William P. McKeown; Francis C. Muldoon; Marc Nadon; Marc Noël; Yvon Pinard; Barbara J. Reed; John D. Richard; Marshall E. Rothstein; Paul U.C. Rouleau; Sandra J. Simpson; Max M. Teitelbaum; Danièle Tremblay-Lamer; Howard I. Wetston
Administrator of the Court, Robert Bijan
Judicial Administrator, Trial Division, Monique Major
Sr. Prothonotary, Jacques Lefebvre
Assoc. Sr. Prothonotary, Peter A.K. Giles
Prothonotaries, John A. Hargrave, Richard Morneau

#### LOCAL OFFICES
**(with Regional Director or District Administrator)**

Calgary: 635 - 8 Ave. SW, 3rd Fl., Calgary AB T2P 3M3 – 403/292-5920 – Dan Buell
Charlottetown: Sir Louis Henry Davies Court House, 42 Water St., PO Box 2200, Charlottetown PE C1A 8B9 – 902/892-9900 – E. Dorothy Kitson
Edmonton: Tower 1, 10060 Jasper Ave., 5th Fl., Edmonton AB T5J 3R8 – 403/495-4561 – R. Orrin J. Splane
Fredericton: Westmorland Pl., 82 Westmorland St., Fredericton NB E3B 3L3 – 506/452-3016 – Registry Officer, Willa Doyle
Halifax: #1720, 1801 Hollis St., Halifax NS B3J 3N4 – 902/426-3282 – F. Pilon
Montréal: 30, rue McGill, Montréal QC H2Y 3Z7 – 514/283-4820 – Monique Giroux
Québec: Palais du Justice, #500, 300, boul Jean Lesage, Québec QC G1K 8K6 – 418/648-4920 – Mireille Bonin
Regina: Court House, 2425 Victoria Ave., Regina SK S4P 3V7 – 306/780-5268 – Jan Kernaghan
Saint John: Provincial Bldg., #427, 110 Charlotte St., PO Box 5001, Saint John NB E2L 4Y9 – 506/636-4990 – George S. Thériault
St. John's: Court House, 301 Duckworth St., PO Box 937, St. John's NF A1C 5M3 – 709/772-2884 – Vacant
Saskatoon: Court House, 520 Spadina Cr. East, Saskatoon SK S7K 3G7 – 306/975-4509 – D. Berezowski
Toronto: Canada Life Bldg., 330 University Ave., 7th Fl., Toronto ON M5G 1R7 – 416/973-3356 – Peter Pace
Vancouver: The Pacific Centre, 700 West Georgia St., PO Box 10065, Vancouver BC V7Y 1B6 – 604/666-3232 – C. Stinson
Whitehorse: Andrew A. Phillipsen Law Centre, 2134 - 2 Ave., Whitehorse YT Y1A 5H6 – 403/667-5441; Fax: 403/667-4116 – Linda Adam
Winnipeg: 363 Broadway St., 4th Fl., Winnipeg MB R3C 3N9 – 204/983-2509 – Terry Johnston
Yellowknife: Court House, 4905 - 49th St., Yellowknife NT X1A 2N4 – 403/873-2044 – Lysette Deyelle

#### REGISTRY OF THE COURT
Principal Office, Supreme Court of Canada Building, Ottawa ON K1A 0H9
613/996-6795 (Appeal Division)
613/992-4231 (Trial Division)
Deputy Administrators, Pierre R. Gaudet, Paul F. Scott
Asst. Administrator, Management Services, Robert Misener

### COURT MARTIAL APPEAL COURT OF CANADA
Supreme Court of Canada Bldg., Ottawa ON K1A 0H9
613/996-6795; Fax: 613/952-7226
**Chief Justice,** The Hon. Mr. Justice Barry L. Strayer, 613/995-7886
Puisne Judges (The Hon. Mr./Madam Justice):
Alphonse Barbeau; André G. Biron; John Watson Brooke; Douglas R. Campbell; J.S.G. Bud Cullen, P.C.; Robert Décary; Pierre Denault; Alice Desjardins; J.S. Armand Desroches; Jean-Eudes Dubé, P.C.; Roland Durand; Eugene G. Ewaschuk; Frederick E. Gibson; Walter R.E. Goodfellow; Gordon L.S. Hart; Bonnie M. Helper; Benjamin Hewak; James K. Hugessen; Julius A. Isaac; James A. Jerome, P.C.; L. Marcel Joyal; Louis-Philippe Landry; Gilles Létourneau; Allen M. Linden; Kenneth M. Lysyk; Mark R. MacGuigan, P.C.; W. Andrew MacKay; Edward C. Malone; Louis Marceau; William Roy Matheson; F. Joseph McDonald; Elizabeth C. McFadyen; Donna C. McGillis; William P. McKeown; Perry Meyer; Francis C. Muldoon; Marc Nadon; Marc Noël; Yvon Pinard, P.C.; Lawrence A. Poitras; Joseph H. Potts; Louis Pratte; Barbara J. Reed; John D. Richard; Guy A. Richard; Joseph T. Robertson; Marshall E. Rothstein; Paul Rouleau; Therésè Rosseau-Houle; Melvin E. Shannon; Sandra J. Simpson; Allyre Louis Sirois; Arthur J. Stone; Barry L. Strayer; Max M. Teitelbaum; William J. Trainor; Danièlle Tremblay-Lamer; Jacques Vaillancourt; Joanne B. Veit; Karen M. Weiler; Howard I. Wetston; Mark M. de Weerdt
Administrator of the Court, Robert Bijan, 613/995-6719
Deputy Assistant, Registry of the Court, W. Wendt
Coordinator, Registry of the Court, Greg Smith

#### REGISTRY OF THE COURT
Asst. Administrator, Pierre R. Gaudet
Coordinator, Gregory Smith

### TAX COURT OF CANADA
200 Kent St., Ottawa ON K1A 0M1
613/992-0901; Fax: 613/957-9034

The Tax Court of Canada was established by the *Tax Court of Canada Act*, S.C. 1980-81-82-83, c. 158, which was proclaimed in force on July 18, 1983. It replaced the Tax Review Board, the members of which became Judges. On September 22, 1988, *An Act to amend the Tax Court of Canada Act & other Acts in consequence thereof* (S.C. 1988, c. 61) received Royal Assent.

The Tax Court of Canada has exclusive original jurisdiction to hear & determine references & appeals on matters arising under the *Income Tax Act*, the Canada Pension Plan, the *Old Age Security Act*, the *Petroleum & Gas Revenue Tax Act*, the *Unemployment Insurance Act*, & Part IX of the *Excise Tax Act* for the Goods & Services Tax where references or appeals to the Court are provided in those Acts. The Court also has exclusive original jurisdiction to hear & determine appeals on matters arising under the *Merchant Navy & Civilian War-related Benefits Act* as referred to in section 17 of the *Veterans Appeal Board Act*. The Court also has exclusive original jurisdiction to hear & determine appeals arising under the *Cultural Property Export & Import Act*.

Under the amending legislation, appeals from assessments or reassessments under the *Income Tax Act* follow two procedures: an informal & expeditious procedure where the amount in issue is $12,000 or less, & a general procedure in other cases. Under the informal procedure, paperwork is kept to a minimum &, generally speaking, the rules of evidence are not stringently applied. In cases involving larger amounts, the general procedure is analogous to that in the Federal Court - Trial Division & the rules of evidence are applied in the ordinary way. The practice & procedures in appeals, other than those under the *Income Tax Act*, are governed by other rules, for example, Tax Court of Canada Rules Procedure (*Unemployment Insurance Act*).

The Court, with its principal office in Ottawa, consists of a Chief Judge, an Associate Judge and 20 other Judges, plus four Supernumerary Judges. To ensure the expeditious hearing of appeals, the Chief Judge may, with the approval of the Governor in Council, appoint Deputy Judges. There are currently ten Deputy Judges.
**Chief Judge,** The Hon. Mr. Justice Jean-Claude Couture
Assoc. Chief Judge, The Hon. Mr. Justice Donald H. Christie
Judges (His/Her Hon.):
Pierre Archambault; David W. Beaubier; Ronald D. Bell; Michael J. Bonner; Eric A. Bowie; Donald Bowman; J. Albert Brulé (Supernum.); Pierre R. Dussault; Alban Garon; P. Dean Hamlyn; Lucie Lamarre; Louise Lamarre Proulx; Theodore E. Margeson; Cameron McArthur; Murray A. Mogan; Terrence O'Connor; Gerald J. Rip; Alexander A. Sarchuk; Ronald E. Sobier; Roland St-Onge (Supernum.); Alain Tardif; Delmer E. Taylor (Supernum.); Gordon Teskey; Guy Tremblay (Supernum.)
Registrar of the Court, Raymond P. Guenette

#### LOCAL OFFICES
**(with Regional Director or District Administrator)**

Montréal: #1800, 500, Place d'Armes, 18e étage, Montréal QC H2Y 2W2 – 514/283-9912; Fax: 514/496-1996 – Regional Director, Denis Lussier
Toronto: Sun Life Centre, #902, 200 King St. West, Toronto ON M5H 3T4 – 416/973-9181; Fax: 416-973-5944 – Regional Director, Dorothée McKinlay
Vancouver: Pacific Centre, 700 West Georgia St., 17th Fl., Vancouver BC V7Y 1A1 – 604/666-7987; Fax: 604/666-7967 – Regional Director, Denis Reeve

### PENSION APPEALS BOARD
#327, 381 Kent St., PO Box 8567, Ottawa ON K1G 3H9
613/995-0612; Fax: 613/995-6834
**Chair**, The Hon. Mr. Justice Armand Dureault
Vice-Chair, The Hon. Mr. Justice D.J.A. Rutherford
Registrar, Mina McNamee
Deputy Registrar, René Ducharme

### OFFICE OF THE COMMISSIONER FOR FEDERAL JUDICIAL AFFAIRS
110 O'Connor St., Ottawa ON K1A 1E3
613/992-9175; Fax: 613/995-5615; Email: recep.info@fja-cmf.x400.gc.ca

The Office administers Part I of the *Judges Act*, which provides for the payment of salaries, allowances and annuities to the judges of the Federal Court of Canada, the Tax Court of Canada and all other federally appointed judges of the superior courts of the provinces. It also provides administrative services to the Canadian Judicial Council and is responsible for the preparation of budgetary submissions of the Federal Court of Canada, the Tax Court of Canada and the Canadian Judicial Council. Also included in the services provided by the Office are language training for federally appointed judges, the publication of the Federal Court Reports and the administration of the fifteen Advisory Committees on Judicial Appointments.
**Commissioner**, Guy Y. Goulard, Q.C.
Deputy Commissioner, Denis Guay
Judges Administration Officer, Ginette Beauparlant
Executive Editor, Federal Court Reports, W.J. Rankin
Executive Secretary, Judicial Appointments Secretariat, Andre S. Millar

## ALBERTA

### ALBERTA COURT OF APPEAL
Law Courts Bldg., 1A Sir Winston Churchill Sq., 5th Fl. South, Edmonton AB T5J 0R2
403/422-2416; Fax: 403/427-5507

The Court of Appeal has appellate jurisdiction in all civil & criminal matters.
**Chief Justice,** The Hon. Catherine A. Fraser

Justices of Appeal (The Hon. Mr./Madam Justice):
Ronald L. Berger; Jean E. Coté; Rene P. Foisy; Howard L. Irving; John W. McClung; Ellen I. Picard; Anne H. Russell
Registrar, Lynn E. Varty, 403/422-2415; Fax: 403/422-4127
•Calgary: Court of Appeal, Court of Appeal Bldg., 530 - 7 Ave. SW, Calgary AB T2P 0Y3 – 403/297-7447; Fax: 403/297-5294
Justices of Appeal (The Hon. Mr./Madam Justice):
John D. Bracco (Supernum.); Carole M. Conrad; Mary M.M. Hetherington; Constance D. Hunt; Elizabeth A. McFadyen; Willis O'Leary
Deputy Registrar, Ileen Moore, 403/297-2206; Fax: 403/297-5294

## ALBERTA COURT OF QUEEN'S BENCH

Court House, 611 - 4 St. SW, Calgary AB T2P 1T5
403/297-7223; Fax: 403/297-8617

The Court of Queen's Bench has original jurisdiction in all civil & criminal matters arising in Alberta, unless otherwise indicated by statute.

Surrogate Court has jurisdiction in respect of testamentary matters & all matters arising out of the issue of revocation of grants of probate & administration of estates.

**Chief Justice,** The Hon. Mr. William K. Moore
Justices (The Hon. Mr./Madam Justice):
Suzanne M. Bensler; Robert M. Cairns; Paul S. Chrumka; Roy V. Deyell; Russell A. Dixon (Supernum.); William G.N. Egbert (Supernum.); Gregory R. Forsythe (Supernum.); Robert P. Fraser; Adelle Fruman; Dennis Hart; Gerard C. Hawko; Ernest A. Hutchinson; Colleen Lynn Kenny; M. Earl Lomas (Supernum.); Sal Joseph Lovecchio; Arthur M. Lutz; Donald I. MacLeod; Peter Macdonnell Clark; D. Blair Mason; Ross T.G. McBain (Supernum.); Peter J. McIntyre; Terrence F. McMahon; Donald H. Medhurst (Supernum.); Robert A.F. Montgomery; John S. Moore; Virgil P. Moshansky (Supernum.); Marina S. Paperny; C.S. Phillips; Peter C.G. Power (Supernum.); Hubert S. Prowse (Supernum.); Bonnie L. Rawlins; John D. Rooke; Melvin E. Shannon (Supernum.); Allen B. Sulatycky; William P. Sullivan; Charles G. Virtue (Supernum.); Jack H. Waite (Supernum.); Lloyd David Wilkins
Masters in Chambers:
Keith Roy Laycock
Robert B. Waller, Q.C.
L. Alberstat, 403/297-7385
J.P. Floyd, Q.C., 403/297-7385
•Edmonton: Court of Queen's Bench, Law Courts Bldg., 1A Sir Winston Churchill Sq., Edmonton AB T5J 0R2 – 403/422-2200; Fax: 403/422-9742
Assoc. Chief Justice, The Hon. Mr. Allan H.J. Wachowich
Justices (The Hon. Mr./Madam Justice):
John A. Agrios; Alexander Andrekson (Supernum.); R. Paul Belzil; Myra B. Bielby; Mel Binder; Robert Allan Cawsey (Supernum.); C. Philip Clarke; Alan T. Cooke; Peter T. Costigan; John B. Dea (Supernum.); Joseph Bernard Feehan (Supernum.); Tellex W. Gallant; William J. Girguilis; Cecilia Johnstone; Lionel L. Jones; C. Adele Kent; Donald Lee; Erik Lefsrud; James L. Lewis; Edward P. MacCallum; Richard P. Marceau; Ernest A. Marshall; M.T. Moreau; Alex T. Murray; Eileen M. Nash; Michael B. O'Byrne (Supernum.); Delmar W. Perras; Keith G. Ritter; Sterling M. Sanderman; P. Lawrie Smith; Vernor W.M. Smith (Supernum.); Marguerite J. Trussler; Joanne B. Veit; William E. Wilson
Masters in Chambers:
M.B. Funduk, 403/422-2328
W.J. Quinn, 403/422-2328
W. Breitkreuz, 403/422-2328
•Lethbridge: Court of Queen's Bench, Court House, 320 - 4 St. South, Lethbridge AB T1J 1Z8 – 403/381-5196; Fax: 403/381-5762
Justices (The Hon. Mr./Madam Justice):
W. Vaughan Hembroff; James H. Langston; Lawrence D. MacLean (Supernum.); Clarence G. Yanosik (Supernum.)
•Red Deer: Court of Queen's Bench, Court House, 4909 - 48 Ave., Red Deer AB T4N 3T5 – 403/340-5533; Fax: 403/340-7984
Justices (The Hon. Mr./Madam Justice):
James L. Foster; Jack K. Holmes (Supernum.); John H. MacKenzie

### ADMINISTRATORS/MANAGERS

Red Deer: Court House, 4909 – 48 Ave., Red Deer AB T4N 3T5 – 403/340-5220; Fax: 403/340-7984 – Joe Doyle
Calgary: Court House, 611 - 4 St. SW, Calgary AB T2P 1T5 – 403/297-2395; Fax: 403/297-8617 – Manager, Kevin Hoschka
Drumheller: Court House, 511 - 3 Ave. West, PO Box 759, Drumheller AB T0J 0Y0 – 403/823-1700; Fax: 403/823-6073 – Maureen Gendron
Edmonton: Law Courts Bldg., 1A Sir Winston Churchill Sq., Main Fl. South, Edmonton AB T5J 0R2 – 403/422-2492; Fax: 403/422-9742 – Manager, Wayne Samis
Fort McMurray: Court House, 9700 Franklin Ave., Fort McMurray AB T9H 4W3 – 403/743-7136; Fax: 403/743-7395 – Bev Patterson
Grande Prairie: Court House, 10260 - 99 St., Grande Prairie AB T8V 6J4 – 403/538-5340; Fax: 403/538-5454 – Wendy Smith
Lethbridge: Court House, 320 - 4 St. South, Lethbridge AB T1J 1Z8 – 403/381-5196; Fax: 403/381-5128 – Acting Administrator, Gwen Luchia
Medicine Hat: Law Courts Bldg., 460 - 1 St. SE, Medicine Hat AB T1A 0A8 – 403/529-8710; Fax: 403/529-8607 – Joe Hay
Peace River: Court House, 9905 - 97 Ave., PO Box 900-34, Peace River AB T8S 1T4 – 403/624-6256; Fax: 403/624-6563 – Iris Callioux
Wetaskiwin: Law Courts, 4605 - 51 St., Wetaskiwin AB T9A 1K7 – 403/361-1258; Fax: 403/361-1319 – Bob Mahaffey

## ALBERTA PROVINCIAL COURT

Law Courts Bldg., 1A Sir Winston Churchill Sq., 6th Fl. North, Edmonton AB T5J 0R2
403/427-6330

The Provincial Court has jurisdiction in small claims, family & select criminal matters & is a youth court.

**Chief Provincial Court Judge,** The Hon. Mr. Edward R. Wachowich
•Calgary: Provincial Court (Civil Division), 603 - 6 Ave. SW, Calgary AB T2P 0T3
Judges (The Hon.):
Sandra Hunt McDonald, 403/297-7361; William C. Kerr (Supernum.), 403/297-7749; Ronald H. O'Neil, 403/297-7309; Brian E. Scott (Asst. Chief Judge), 403/297-7233; Douglas J. Tompkins, 403/297-5273
Administrator, Penny Shortridge, 403/297-7217; Fax: 403/297-7374
Sheriff: J.J. Bowlen Bldg., #901, 620 - 7 Ave. SW, Calgary AB T2P 0V8 – 403/297-7120; Fax: 403/297-3953 – Asst. Sheriff, Gordon Fofonoff
•Calgary: Provincial Court (Criminal Division), Provincial Courts Bldg., 323 - 6 Ave. SE, 5th Fl., Calgary AB T2G 4V1 – 403/297-3156
Judges (The Hon.):
Garry G. Cioni; Cheryl L. Daniel; Robert H. Davie; Manfred Delong; Anthony P. Demong; Robert S. Dinkel; Allan A. Fradsham; William N. Gilbert; Sandra A. Hamilton; Kathleen E. Helmer (Supernum.); John D. James; Heather A. Lamoureux; Bernard N. Laven (Supernum.); Francis L. Maloney; Douglas M. McDonald; Thomas B. McMeekin; William R. Pepler; Michael H. Porter; Brian C. Stevenson (Asst. Chief Judge); William Arthur Troughton (Supernum.); Sharon L. Van De Veen
Manager, Criminal & Traffic, David L. Paul, 403/297-3122; Fax: 403/297-3179
•Calgary: Provincial Court (Family & Youth Division), J.J. Bowlen Bldg., 620 - 7 Ave. SW, Calgary AB T2P 0Y8 – 403/297-3474, 3478
Judges (The Hon.):
John S. Brownlee; Edward R.R. Carruthers; Lynn T.L. Cook; Nancy A. Flatters; Karen J. Jordan; Hugh F. Landerkin; N. Peter Leveque; Sharron Prowse-O'Ferrall
Manager, Lorette Olson, 403/297-3470; Fax: 403/297-3461
•Camrose: Provincial Court, Court House, 5210 - 49 Ave., Camrose AB T4V 3Y2 – 403/679-1240
Judges (The Hon.):
Harry D. Gaede
Administrator, Debbie Hollman, 403/679-1240; Fax: 403/679-1253
•Canmore: Provincial Court, Provincial Bldg., 800 Access Rd., Canmore AB T0L 0M0 – 403/678-2355
Judges (The Hon.):
John D. Reilly
Administrator, Cheryl Dubuc, 403/378-2355; Fax: 403/678-4936
•Drumheller: Provincial Court, Court House, 511 - 3 Ave. West, PO Box 759, Drumheller AB T0J 0Y0 – 403/823-1700
Judges (The Hon.):
Gordon W. Clozza
Administrator, Maureen Gendron, 403/823-1700; Fax: 403/823-6073
•Edmonton: Provincial Court (Civil Division), Law Courts Bldg., 1A Sir Winston Churchill Sq., 6th Fl. North, Edmonton AB T5J 0R2 – 403/427-0106
Judges (The Hon.):
Jack Allford, 403/422-4015; Margaret M. Donnelly, 403/422-4012; Ken D. Hope, 403/422-4019; James L. Skitsko, 403/422-4003; Harry F. Wilson (Supernum.), 403/422-4021
Administrator, Donna Farley, 403/422-2510; Fax: 403/427-4348
Sheriff: Law Courts Bldg., 1A Sir Winston Churchill Sq., Main Fl. North, Edmonton AB T5J 0R2 – 403/422-2481; Fax: 403/422-3011 – Sheriff, Dwayne Weatherall
•Edmonton: Provincial Court (Criminal Division), Law Courts Bldg., 1A Sir Winston Churchill Sq., 5th Fl. North, Edmonton AB T5J 0R2 – 403/427-7817
Judges (The Hon.):
Daniel C. Abbott; Paul L. Adilman; P.R. Broda (Supernum.); Peter M. Caffaro (Asst. Chief Judge); H. Ralph Chisholm; Albert G. Chrumka; Pierre-Michael Dubé; Russell L. Dzenick; Sam A. Friedman (Supernum.); Philip G.C. Ketchum; David J. MacNab; Percy C.C. Marshall; William M. Mustard; Ken J. Plomp; Edward R. Saddy; Dean Saks (Supernum.); James C. Spence; Edward D. Stack (Supernum.); Michael Stevens-Guille; David J. Tilley; Leo Wenden; Darlene R. Wong
Manager, Criminal, Ron Babyn, 403/427-7868; Fax: 403/422-9736
Manager, Traffic, Erwin Stoik, 4103/427-4724; Fax: 403/427-5791
•Edmonton: Provincial Court (Family & Youth Division), Law Courts Bldg., 1A Sir Winston Churchill Sq., 6th Fl. North, Edmonton AB T5J 0R2 – 403/427-7805
Judges (The Hon.):
Jonetta G. Bradburn; Donald J. Buchanan; Jack G. Easton; Richard S. Fowler; J. Peter Jorgensen; Walder G.W. White (Asst. Chief Judge); Lawrence S. Witten; Sidney E.W. Wood

•Edmonton: Provincial Court (Rural Division), Law Courts Bldg., 1A Sir Winston Churchill Sq., 6th Fl. North, Edmonton AB T5J 0R2 – 403/427-0110
Judges (The Hon.):
Raymond W. Bradley; Kenneth A. Cush; Norman A.F. Mackie; Lawrence E. Nemirsky; Michael D. Tomyn; Ernest J.M. Walter (Asst. Chief Judge)
•Fort MacLeod: Provincial Court, Court House, 244 Chief Red Crow Blvd., PO Box 1360, Fort MacLeod AB T0L 0Z0 – 403/553-5010; Fax: 403/553-5045
Administrator, Cecilia Baker
•Fort McMurray: Provincial Court, Court House, 9700 Franklin Ave., Fort McMurray AB T9H 4W3 – 403/743-7195
Judges (The Hon.):
Michael Horrocks
Administrator, Bev Patterson, 403/743-7195; Fax: 403/743-7395
•Fort Saskatchewan: Provincial Court, Court House, 10504 - 100 Ave., Fort Saskatchewan AB T8L 3S9 – 403/998-1200
Judges (The Hon.):
Kenneth A. Crush
Administrator, Wendy Komarnisky, 403/998-1200; Fax: 403/998-7222
•Grande Prairie: Provincial Court, Court House, 10260 - 99 St., Grande Prairie AB T8V 6J4 – 403/538-5364; Fax: 403/538-5454
Judges (The Hon.):
J.N. Gary Mitchell; Donald E. Patterson (Asst. Chief Judge)
Administrator, Wendy Smith, 403/538-5360; Fax: 403/538-5454
•High Level: Provincial Court, 10106 - 100 Ave., PO Box 1560, High Level AB T0H 1Z0 – 403/926-3715; Fax: 403/926-4068
Administrator, Shelly Cardinal
•High Prairie: Provincial Court, 4911 - 53 Ave., PO Box 1470, High Prairie AB T0G 1E0 – 403/523-6600
Judges (The Hon.):
Thomas R. Goodson; Roger P. Smith
Administrator, Mae Fjeld, 403/523-6600; Fax: 403/523-6643
•Hinton: Provincial Court, Court House, 237 Jasper St., PO Box 6450, Hinton AB T7V 1X7 – 403/865-8280
Judges (The Hon.):
Donald C. Norheim
Administrator, Karen Hanington, 403/865-8280; Fax: 403/865-8253
•Leduc: Provincial Court, Court House, 4612 - 50 St., Leduc AB T9E 6L1 – 403/986-6911
Judges (The Hon.):
Michael G. Tomyn
Administrator, Ursula Owre, 403/986-6911; Fax: 403/986-0345
•Lethbridge: Provincial Court, Court House, 320 - 4th St. South, Lethbridge AB T1J 1Z8 – 403/381-5275
Judges (The Hon.):
Fred W. Coward; Gerald R. DeBow; Timothy G. Hironaka; Lloyd B. Hogan; Ron A. Jacobson; Jerry N. LeGrandeur; Laurie B. Levine (Supernum.); Eric W. Peterson; James Arthur Wood (Asst. Chief Judge)
Administrator, Gerdy Krogman, 403/381-5223; Fax: 403/381-5763
•Medicine Hat: Provincial Court, Law Courts Bldg., 460 - 1 St. SE, Medicine Hat AB T1A 0A8 – 403/529-8675; Fax: 403/592-2566
Judges (The Hon.):
Dietrich Brand; James P. Wambolt
Administrator, Miles C. Weatherall, 403/529-8644; Fax: 403/529-8606
•Peace River: Provincial Court, Court House, 9905 - 97 Ave., PO Box 900-34, Peace River AB T8S 1T4 – 403/624-6260
Judges (The Hon.):
James R. McIntosh; E. Darrell Riemer
Administrator, Iris Callioux, 403/624-6256; Fax: 403/624-6563
•Red Deer: Provincial Court, Court House, 4909 - 48 Ave., Red Deer AB T4N 3T5 – 403/340-5546
Judges (The Hon.):
Doug L. Crowe (Asst. Chief Judge); N. Patrick Lawrence; David P. MacNaughton; David J. Plosz; Thomas G. Schollie
Administrator, Sandra Mitchell, 403/340-5250; Fax: 403/340-7985
•St. Albert: Provincial Court, Court House, 3 St. Anne St., St. Albert AB T8N 2E8 – 403/458-7300
Judges (The Hon.):
Norman A.F. Mackie; Robert B. Spevakow
Administrator, Sharon Boisvert, 403/458-7300; Fax: 403/460-2963
•St. Paul: Provincial Court, Court House, 4704 - 50 St., PO Box 1900, St. Paul AB T0A 3A0 – 403/645-6324
Judges (The Hon.):
Donald D. Demetrick; Brian H. Fraser; Marshall W. Hopkins (Supernum.); Lawrence E. Nemirsky
Administrator, Patricia Laramee, 403/645-6324; Fax: 403/645-6273
•Sherwood Park: Provincial Court, Court House, 190 Chippewa Rd., Sherwood Park AB T8A 4H5 – 403/464-0114
Judges (The Hon.):
John Maher
Administrator, Wendy Komarnisky, 403/464-0114; Fax: 403/449-1490
•Stony Plain: Provincial Court, Court House, 4711 - 44 Ave., Stony Plain AB T0E 2G0 – 403/963-6205
Judges (The Hon.):
Peter P. Ayotte; Raymond W. Bradley; M. Jeanne Burch; James E. Enright;
Administrator, Maureen McCulloch, 403/963-6205; Fax: 403/963-6402
•Vermilion: Provincial Court, Provincial Bldg., 4701 - 52nd St., Vermilion AB T9X 1J9 – 403/853-8111
Judges (The Hon.):
Ronald L. Tibbitt
Administrator, Craena Coyne, 403/853-8130; Fax: 403/853-8200
•Wetaskiwin: Provincial Court, Law Courts, 4605 - 51 St., Wetaskiwin AB T9A 1K7 – 403/361-1204
Judges (The Hon.):
Norman A. Rolf
Administrator, Susan O'Connor, 403/361-1204; Fax: 403/361-1338

### ALBERTA COURT OPERATIONS

Calgary: Court House, 611 - 4 St. SW, 1st Fl., Calgary AB T2P 1T5 – 403/297-2210; Fax: 403/297-7152 – Director, James McLaughlin
Edmonton: Law Courts Bldg., 1A Sir Winston Churchill Sq., Mezz. Fl., Edmonton AB T5J 0R2 – 403/422-2426, 2428, 2429; Fax: 403/422-9585 – Director, John Bachinski
North (Rural): Court House, 4612 - 50 St., Leduc AB T9E 6L1 – 403/986-6903, 6904; Fax: 403/986-2429 – Director, Ed Towers
Lethbridge, Fort MacLeod, Medicine Hat, Drumheller: Court House, #115, 320 - 4 St. South, Lethbridge AB T1J 1Z8 – 403/381-5450; Fax: 403/381-5762 – District Manager, Clara Finan
South (Rural): Court House, 4909 - 48 Ave., Red Deer AB T4N 3T5 – 403/340-5220; Fax: 403/340-7984 – Director, Owen Lowe

## BRITISH COLUMBIA

### BRITISH COLUMBIA COURT OF APPEAL

Law Courts, 800 Smithe St., Vancouver BC V6Z 2E1
Law Courts, 850 Burdett Ave., Victoria BC V8W 1B4
604/660-2800

An appeal lies to the Court of Appeal from an order of the Supreme Court or an order of a judge of that court & in any matter where jurisdiction is given to it by statute.

**Chief Justice,** The Hon. Allan McEachern
Justices of Appeal (The Hon. Mr./Madam Justice):
T.R. Braidwood; A.B.B. Carrothers; G.S. Cumming; I.T. Donald; William A. Esson; L.S.G. Finch; R.J. Gibbs; D.M.M. Goldie; J.E. Hall; D.B. Hinds; H.A. Hollinrake; C.M. Huddart; J.D. Lambert; A.B. Macfarlane (Victoria); M.V.M. Newbury; P.M. Proudfoot; J.E. Prowse; M.A. Rowles; C.A. Ryan; Mary F. Southin
Registrar, Jennifer Jordan

### BRITISH COLUMBIA SUPREME COURT

Law Courts, 800 Smithe St., Vancouver BC V6Z 2E1
604/660-2800

The Supreme Court is a court of original jurisdiction having jurisdiction in all civil & criminal matters arising in B.C., save & except matters expressly excluded by statute.

**Chief Justice,** The Hon. Bryan Williams
Assoc. Chief Justice, The Hon. P.D. Dohm
Judges (The Hon. Mr./Madam Justice):
M.J. Allan; W.G. Baker; R.J. Bauman; M.E. Boyd; D.I. Brenner; G.D. Burnyeat; H.A. Callaghan; M.I. Catliff; D.L. Clancy; B.I. Cohen; F.W. Cole; Ross Collver; G.R.B. Coultas; V.R. Curtis; J.R. Dillon; I.L. Drost; E.R.A. Edwards; J.L.T. Edwards; G.P. Fraser; K.M. Gill; S.J. Hardinge; R.B. Harvey; A.G. Henderson; R.R. Holmes; S.W. Hood; M.A. Humphries; P.A. Kirkpatrick; M.M. Koenigsberg; R.E. Levine; L.A. Loo; R.T.A. Low; P.D. Lowry; K.M. Lysyk; M.D. Macaulay; B.D. Macdonald; K.C. Mackenzie; Frank Maczko; N. Morrison; W.T. Oppal; R.M.P. Paris; I.H. Pitfield; S.R. Romilly; D.A. Satanove; M.E. Saunders; W.B. Scarth; D.W. Shaw; J.S. Sigurdson; J.A. Sinclair Prowse; B.F. Ralph; H.L. Skipp; K.J. Smith; J.E. Spencer; A.M. Stewart; J.D. Taylor; A.D. Thackray; D.F. Tysoe; D.H. Vickers; T.P. Warren; L.P. Williamson; R.S.K. Wong
District Registrar in Bankruptcy, K. Wellburn
Registrars in Bankruptcy & Masters of the Supreme Court:
Kenneth Doolan, 604/660-0255; Fax: 604/660-2420
Alan Patterson, 604/660-0255; Fax: 604/660-2420
Alan Donaldson, 604/660-2879; Fax: 604/660-2420
Neil Bolton, 604/660-0255; Fax: 604/660-2420
Susan Brandreth-Gibbs, 604/660-2879; Fax: 604/660-2420
Ronald Barber, 604/660-2879; Fax: 604-660-2420
Dennis Tokarek, 604/660-2879; Fax: 604/660-2420

#### OTHER SUPREME COURT LOCATIONS

**with (Registry/County) District Registrars, Registrars in Bankruptcy**

•Chilliwack (Westminster): Supreme Court, Court House, 9391 College St., Chilliwack BC V2P 4L7
Judges (The Hon. Mr./Madam Justice):
W.H. Davies; W.G.E. Grist
Acting Manager, Court Services, Lil Schaufele
•Cranbrook (Kootenay): Supreme Court, Court House, 102 - 11 Ave. South, Cranbrook BC V1C 2P3
Judges (The Hon. Mr./Madam Justice):
T.J. Melnick
Deputy District Registrar, Beth Glassford
•Dawson Creek (Cariboo): Supreme Court, Court House, 1201 - 103 Ave., Dawson Creek BC V1G 4J2
Judges (The Hon. Mr./Madam Justice):
R.D. Wilson
District Registrar, G.W. Schmidt
•Kamloops (Yale): Supreme Court, Court House, 455 Columbia St., Kamloops BC V2C 6K4
Judges (The Hon. Mr./Madam Justice):
R.M.L. Blair; R.B. Hunter; G.W. Lamperson; Robert Robinson
Deputy District Registrar, Vacant

District Registrar, Registrar in Bankruptcy & Master of Supreme Court, Robert Powers, 250/828-4343; Fax: 250/828-4332

•Kelowna (Yale): Supreme Court, Court House, 1355 Water St., Kelowna BC V1Y 9R3 – 250/470-6900

Judges (The Hon. Mr./Madam Justice):

A.J. Beames; N.A. Drossos; C.W. Wilkinson

Registrar in Bankruptcy & Master of the Supreme Court, Michael Bishop, 250/470-6896; Fax: 250/470-6884

District Registrar, Gene C. Watt

•Nanaimo (Vancouver Island): Supreme Court, Court House, 35 Front St., Nanaimo BC V9R 5J1

Judges (The Hon. Mr./Madam Justice):

K.K. Downs; R.M.J. Hutchinson; C.R. Lander; S.J. Shabbits

Registrar in Bankruptcy & Master of the Supreme Court, John W. Horn, 250/741-3846; Fax: 250/741-3845

Deputy District Registrar, B. Murphy

•Nelson (Kootenay): Supreme Court, Court House, 320 Ward St., Nelson BC V1L 1S6

Judges (The Hon. Mr./Madam Justice):

T.M. McEwan

District Registrar, District Registrar in Bankruptcy, Elaine Beaulac

•New Westminster (Vancouver): Supreme Court, Court House, Begbie Sq., New Westminster BC V3M 1C9

Judges (The Hon. Mr./Madam Justice):

H.D. Boyle; T.K. Fisher; I.B. Josephson; S.M. Leggatt; A.W. MacKenzie; R.A. McKinnon; B.M. Preston; J.F. Rowan; T.M. Singh; D.M. Smith; S.S. Stromberg-Stein

Registrars in Bankruptcy & Masters of the Supreme Court, Brian Joyce, Shelley Nitikman, 604/660-8615; Fax: 604/660-2072

•Prince George (Cariboo): Supreme Court, Court House, 250 George St., Prince George BC V2L 5S2

Judges (The Hon. Mr./Madam Justice):

I.C. Meiklem; W.G. Parrett; A.F. Wilson

Registrar in Bankruptcy & Master of the Supreme Court, Eric Chamberlist, 250/614-2776; Fax: 250/614-2791

Deputy District Registrar, Joan Foisy

•Prince Rupert (Prince Rupert): Supreme Court, Court House, 100 Market Pl., Prince Rupert BC V8J 1B8

Judges (The Hon. Mr./Madam Justice):

R.T. Errico

District Registrar, District Registrar in Bankruptcy, J. Jones

•Vernon (Yale): Supreme Court, Court House, 3001 - 27th St., Vernon BC V1T 4W5

Judges (The Hon. Mr./Madam Justice):

K.F. Arkell; B.M. Davies

District Registrar, District Registrar in Bankruptcy, Stan R. Smith

•Victoria (Vancouver Island): Supreme Court, Court House, 850 Burdett Ave., Victoria BC V8W 1B4

Judges (The Hon. Mr./Madam Justice):

J.C. Bouck; J.C. Cowan; J.L. Dorgan; M.L. Drake; R.B. McD. Hutchison; F.A. Melvin; P.J. Millward; D.D. Owen-Flood; G.M. Quijano

Registrar in Bankruptcy & Master of the Supreme Court, William McCallum, 250/387-0095; Fax: 250/356-6806

Registrar in Bankruptcy & Registrar of the Supreme Court of B.C., Elizabeth Dunn, 250/387-0095; Fax: 250/356-6806

Deputy District Registrars, Judy MacFarlane, Michelle Rose

Operations Manager, Vacant

## DISTRICT REGISTRARS

**with (Registry/County) District Registrars; for District Registrars attached to Supreme Court locations, see above**

Ashcroft (Cariboo): PO Box 639, Ashcroft BC V0K 1A0 – 250/453-9174; Fax: 250/453-9049

District Registrar, D.S. McCoy

Campbell River (Vancouver Island): 500 - 13 Ave., Campbell River BC V9W 6P1 – 250/286-7510; Fax: 250/286-7512

District Registrar, Michael Hammell

Courtenay (Vancouver Island): Court House, #100, 420 Cumberland Rd., Courtenay BC V9N 2C4 – 250/334-1115; Fax: 250/334-1191

District Registrar, R. Krayenhoff

Creston (Kootenay): Court House, 224 - 10 Ave. North, PO Box 1790, Creston BC V0B 1G0 – 250/428-3200; Fax: 250/428-3243

District Registrar, Brian J. Gatto

Duncan (Vancouver Island): Court House, 238 Government St., Duncan BC V9L 1A5 – 250/746-1227; Fax: 250/746-1244

District Registrar, Derek D'Altroy

Fernie (Kootenay): Court House, 401 - 4 Ave., Bag 1000, Fernie BC V0B 1M0 – 250/423-4601; Fax: 250/423-6973

District Registrar, Marva Black

Fort Nelson (Cariboo): Bag 1000, Fort Nelson BC V0C 1R0 – 250/774-6990; Fax: 250/774-6904

District Registrar, Shawn Checkley

Fort St. John (Cariboo): Court House, 10600 - 100 St., Fort St. John BC V1J 4L6 – 250/787-3231; Fax: 250/787-3518

District Registrar, Gloria Morton

Golden (Kootenay): 837 Park Dr., PO Box 1500, Golden BC V0A 1H0 – 250/344-7581; Fax: 250/344-7715

District Registrar, Bonnie Carter

Grand Forks (Kootenay): 524 Central Ave., PO Box 1059, Grand Forks BC V0H 1H0 – 250/442-5464; Fax: 250/442-8606

District Registrar, Dave Henly

Kitimat (Prince Rupert): 603 City Centre, Kitimat BC V8C 2N1 – 250/632-4781; Fax: 250/632-4946

District Registrar, Norman Lee

Lillooet (Cariboo): 615 Main St., Bag 700, Lillooet BC V0K 1V0 – 250/256-7445; Fax: 250/256-7458

District Registrar, Cindy Frederick

Merritt (Yale): PO Box 4400, Merritt BC V0K 2B0 – 250/378-9350; Fax: 250/378-1431

District Registrar, Elaine Ohata

100 Mile House (Cariboo): 160 Cedar Ave. South, PO Box 1060, 100 Mile House BC V0K 2E0 – 250/395-5562; Fax: 250/395-5519

District Registrar, Maureen Menzies

Penticton (Yale): Court House, #116, 100 Main St., Penticton BC V2A 5A5 – 250/492-1220; Fax: 250/492-1378

District Registrar, Maureen Corrado

Port Alberni (Vancouver Island): 2999 - 4 Ave., Port Alberni BC V9Y 8A5 – 250/720-2424; Fax: 250/720-2426

District Registrar, Wayne Phalen

Powell River (Vancouver Island): #103, 6953 Alberni St., Powell River BC V8A 2B8 – 604/485-3630; Fax: 604/485-3637

District Registrar, Lowell S. Boran, Jr.

Princeton (Yale): Court House, 151 Vermilion Ave., PO Box 1210, Princeton BC V0X 1W0 – 250/295-3113; Fax: 250/295-7928

District Registrar, Vivian Hedrich

Quesnel (Cariboo): Court House, 350 Barlow Ave., Quesnel BC V2J 2C1 – 250/992-4256; Fax: 250/992-4171

District Registrar, Wayne Hakanson

Richmond (Vancouver): Unified Family Court, 6931 Granville Ave., Richmond BC V7C 4M9 – 604/660-4693; Fax: 604/660-1797

District Registrar, E.D. Kae

Rossland (Kootenay): Court House, 2288 Columbia Ave., PO Box 639, Rossland BC V0G 1Y0 – 250/362-7368; Fax: 250/362-9632

District Registrar, Howard Bondaroff

Salmon Arm (Yale): Court House, 20 Hudson St. NE, Bag 100, Salmon Arm BC V1E 4S4 – 250/832-1610; Fax: 250/832-1749

District Registrar, Gordon Redding

Smithers (Prince Rupert): #40, PO Box 5000, Smithers BC V0J 2N0 – 250/847-7376; Fax: 250/847-7710

District Registrar, J. Caird

Terrace (Prince Rupert): Court House, 3408 Kalum St., Terrace BC V8G 2N6 – 250/638-2111; Fax: 250/638-2116

District Registrar, Irene Blackstone

Vanderhoof (Cariboo): PO Box 1220, Vanderhoof BC V9A 3A0 – 250/567-5763; Fax: 250/567-4158

District Registrar, Gloria Edwards

Williams Lake (Cariboo): Court House, 540 Borland St., Williams Lake BC V2G 1R8 – 250/398-4301; Fax: 250/398-4459

District Registrar, Robert Girvin

## BRITISH COLUMBIA PROVINCIAL COURT

Pacific Centre, #501, 700 West Georgia St., PO Box 10287, Vancouver BC V7Y 1E8

604/660-2864; Fax: 604/660-1108

The Provincial Court has jurisdiction in small claims, family & select criminal matters & is a youth court.

**Chief Judge,** The Hon. Mr. R.W. Metzger

Assoc. Chief Judge, The Hon. E.D. Schmidt

Judges (The Hon.):

P. Collings; N. Friesen; R.C.S. Graham; F.S. Green; J.K. Shaw

•Abbotsford: Provincial Court, 32203 South Fraser Way, Abbotsford BC V2T 1W6 – 604/855-3200; Fax: 604/855-3232

Judges (The Hon.):

M.I. MacAlpine; C.B. MacArthur; C. Gail Maltby, J. Rounthwaite

•Burnaby: Provincial Court, 6263 Deer Lake Ave., Burnaby BC V5G 3Z8 – 604/660-7147; Fax: 604/660-4527

Judges (The Hon.):

W.J. Diebolt; T.J. Gove; D.R. Holmes; K.D. Page; D.M.B. Steinberg; J. Watchuk

•Campbell River: Provincial Court, 500 - 13 Ave., Campbell River BC V9W 6P1 – 250/286-7510; Fax: 250/286-7512

Judges (The Hon.):

P.M. Doherty; B. Saunderson

•Castlegar: Provincial Court, 555 Columbia Ave., Castlegar BC V1N 1G8 – 250/365-8511; Fax: 250/365-8573

Judges (The Hon.):

D.L. Sperry

•Chilliwack: Provincial Court, 9391 College St., Chilliwack BC V2P 4L7 – 604/795-8306; Fax: 604/795-8202

Judges (The Hon.):

B.G. Hoy; W.A. Young

•Courtney: Provincial Court, #211, 420 Cumberland Rd., Courtney BC V9N 5M6 – 250/334-1115; Fax: 250/334-1191

Judges (The Hon.):

C. Lazar

•Cranbrook: Provincial Court, 102 - 11 Ave. South, Cranbrook BC V1C 2P3 – 250/426-1232; Fax: 250/426-1352

Judges (The Hon.):

D.C. Carlgren (Admin. Judge); D.M. Waurynchuk

•Dawson Creek: Provincial Court, 1201 - 103 Ave., Dawson Creek BC V1G 4J2 – 250/784-2278; Fax: 250/784-2339

Judges (The Hon.):

D.M. Levis

•Delta: Provincial Court, 5540 Clarence Taylor Cr., Delta BC V4K 3W3 – 604/940-4350; Fax: 604/940-4364
Judges (The Hon.):
J.R. Lytwyn
•Duncan: Provincial Court, 238 Government St., Duncan BC V9L 1A5 – 250/746-1234; Fax: 250/746-1244
Judges (The Hon.):
Vacant
•Fort St. John: Provincial Court, 10600 - 100 St., Fort St. John BC V1J 4L6 – 250/787-3231; Fax: 250/787-3518
Judges (The Hon.):
C.D. Cleaveley
•Kamloops: Provincial Court, 455 Columbia St., Kamloops BC V2C 6K4 – 250/828-4081; Fax: 250/828-4368
Judges (The Hon.):
W.A. Blair (Admin. Judge); J.P. Gordon; H. Rohrmoser; T.W. Shupe; B. Sundhu
•Kelowna: Provincial Court, 1355 Water St., Kelowna BC V1Y 8M3 – 250/470-6811; Fax: 250/470-6810
Judges (The Hon.):
J.P. Cartwright; B.J. Grannary; W.W. Klinger (Adm. Judge); H.C. Stansfield; B.C. Weddell
•Langley: Provincial Court, 20389 Fraser Hwy., Langley BC V3A 7N2 – 604/530-1164; Fax: 604/533-4853
•Maple Ridge: Provincial Court, 11960 Haney Pl., Maple Ridge BC V2X 6G1 – 604/467-1515; Fax: 604/467-9906
Judges (The Hon.):
S.C. Antifaev
•Nanaimo: Provincial Court, Court House, 35 Front St., Nanaimo BC V9R 5J1 – 250/741-3856; Fax: 250/741-3883
Judges (The Hon.):
S.G. Clark; J.D. Cowling; R.A. Gould; E.L. Iverson (Admin. Judge); J.I.D. Joe
•Nelson: Provincial Court, 320 Ward St., Nelson BC V1L 1S6 – 250/354-6165; Fax: 250/354-6539
Judges (The Hon.):
M.G. Takahashi
•New Westminster: Provincial Court, Law Courts, Begbie Sq., New Westminster BC V3M 1C9 – 604/660-8565; Fax: 604/660-8977
Judges (The Hon.):
L.P. Clare; K.J. Husband
•North Vancouver: Provincial Court, 200 East 23 St., North Vancouver BC V7L 4R4 – 604/983-4059; Fax: 604/983-4034
Judges (The Hon.):
E.M. Burdett (Adm. Judge); D.E. Moss; J.B. Paradis; W.J. Rodgers
•Penticton: Provincial Court, 100 Main St., Penticton BC V2A 5A5 – 250/492-1231; 250/492-1378
Judges (The Hon.):
G.G. Sinclair
•Port Alberni: Provincial Court, 2999 - 4 Ave., Port Alberni BC V9Y 8A5 – 250/720-2424; Fax: 250/720-2426
Judges (The Hon.):
B.R. Klaver
•Port Coquitlam: Provincial Court, 2620 Mary Hill Rd., Unit J, Port Coquitlam BC V3C 3B2 – 604/927-2166; Fax: 604/927-2233
Judges (The Hon.):
M.R. Buller Bennett; A.J. Spence (Admin. Judge); D. Stone; J. Threlfall
•Powell River: Provincial Court, 6953 Alberni St., Powell River BC V8A 2B8 – 604/485-3630; Fax: 604/485-3637
Judges (The Hon.):
S.E. Giroday
•Prince George: Provincial Court, J.D. Wilson Square, 250 George St., Prince George BC V2L 5S2 – 250/614-2770; Fax: 250/614-2790
Judges (The Hon.):
B.L. Dollis (Admin. Judge); P.V. Hogan; R.B. Macfarlane; D.W. Ramsay
•Prince Rupert: Provincial Court, 100 Market Pl., Prince Rupert BC V8J 1B7 – 250/624-7548; Fax: 250/627-7538
Judges (The Hon.):
A.K. Krantz
•Quesnel: Provincial Court, #115, 350 Barlow Ave., Quesnel BC V2J 2C1 – 250/992-4256; Fax: 250/992-4171
Judges (The Hon.):
R.R. Smith
•Richmond: Provincial Court (Criminal Division), 6900 Minoru Blvd., Richmond BC V6Y 1Y1 – 604/660-6900; Fax: 604/660-1797
Judges (The Hon.):
R.D. Fratkin; J.R. Groberman
•Richmond: Provincial Court (Family & Small Claims Division), 6931 Granville Ave., Richmond BC V7C 4M9 – 604/448-2550; Fax: 604/660-1525
Judges (The Hon.):
B.K. Davis
•Rossland: Provincial Court, Court House, PO Box 639, Rossland BC V0G 1Y0 – 250/362-7368; Fax: 250/362-9632
Judges (The Hon.):
R.G. Fabbro
•Salmon Arm: Provincial Court, Court House, PO Box 100, Salmon Arm BC V1E 4S4 – 250/832-1613; Fax: 250/832-1749
Judges (The Hon.):
E.R. Brecknell
•Smithers: Provincial Court, PO Box 5000, Smithers BC V0J 2N0 – 250/847-7379; Fax: 250/847-7710
Judges (The Hon.):
Raymond R. Low
•Squamish: Provincial Court, PO Box 1580, Squamish BC V0N 3G0 – 604/892-5911; Fax: 604/892-2272
Judges (The Hon.):
C.I. Walker
•Surrey: Provincial Court, 14340 - 57th Ave., Surrey BC V3X 1B2 – 604/572-2300; Fax: 604/572-2301
Judges (The Hon.):
T. Alexander; G.J.F. Baker; Norman Collingwood; T.D. Devitt; H. Field; G. Gill; F.E. Howard; P.A. Hyde; R. Lemiski; J.F. Lenaghan; W.G. MacDonald (Admin. Judge); S. MacGregor; R.D.M. Miller; R. Raven; A.E. Rounthwaite; E.D. Scarlett; W.F. Stewart; M.H. Thomas
•Terrace: Provincial Court, #200, 3408 Kalum St., Terrace BC V8G 2N6 – 250/638-2147; Fax: 250/638-2193
Judges (The Hon.):
P.R. Lawrence; E.F. deWalle (Admin. Judge)
•Vancouver: Provincial Court (Criminal Division), 222 Main St., Vancouver BC V6A 1E8 – 604/660-4200, 4300; Fax: 604/660-4322
Judges (The Hon.):
E.A. Arnold; C.L. Bagnall; C.C. Baird-Ellan (Admin. Judge); B.E. Bastin; E.H. Bendrodt; W.G. Craig; E.J. Cronin; J.E. Godfrey; W.J. Kitchen; K.J. Libby; P.L. Maughan; J.L. McCarthy; T.D. McGee; H.J. McGivern; J.K. Scherling; K.A.P.D. Smith; D.I. Smith; C.J. Trueman; H. Weitzel
•Vancouver: Provincial Court (Family & Small Claims Division), 800 Hornby St., PO Box 33, Vancouver BC V6Z 2C5 – 604/660-8377; Fax: 604/660-8405
Judges (The Hon.):
Family Division: Jane Auxier; M. Borowicz; G.D. Gillis; D.R. Pendleton (Adm. Judge); M.E. Rae
Small Claims Division: R.M. Gallagher; D.J. Martinson; M.R. Mondin; M.S. Puhach; R. Tweedale (Adm. Judge); J.F. Werier; H.A. White
•Vernon: Provincial Court, 3001 - 27 St., Vernon BC V1T 4W5 – 250/549-5415; Fax: 250/549-5621
Judges (The Hon.):
D.B. Overend
•Victoria: Provincial Court, Western Communities Court House, 1756 Island Hwy., Victoria BC V9B 1H8 – 250/474-9700; Fax: 250/474-9704
Judges (The Hon.):
A.J. Palmer
•Victoria: Provincial Court (Criminal & Small Claims Division), 850 Burdett Ave., Victoria BC V8W 1B4 – 250/356-1036; Fax: 250/356-6779
Judges (The Hon.):
J.K. Bracken; A.I. Ehrcke; A.E. Filmer; L.J.M. Harvey; R.A. Higinbotham; J.M. Hubbard; J.N. Kay; B.D. MacKenzie; B.M. Neal; L.W. Smith (Admin. Judge)
•Victoria: Provincial Court (Family Division), 1119 Pembroke St., Victoria BC V8V 1X4 – 250/387-1925; Fax: 250/387-8881
Judges (The Hon.):
L.F.E. Chaperon
•West Vancouver: Provincial Court, 1310 Marine Dr., West Vancouver BC V7T 1B5 – 604/660-1232; Fax: 604/775-0311
Judges (The Hon.):
R.D. Grandison
•Williams Lake: Provincial Court, 540 Borland St., Williams Lake BC V2G 1R8 – 250/398-4311; Fax: 250/398-4459
Judges (The Hon.):
J.S. de Villiers; T.C. Smith (Admin. Judge)

## MANITOBA

### MANITOBA COURT OF APPEAL

Law Courts Bldg., 408 York Ave., Winnipeg MB R3C 0P9

The Court of Appeal has appellate jurisdiction in all civil & criminal cases adjudicated by the Court of Queen's Bench & indictable offences adjudicated by the Provincial Court.

**Chief Justice,** The Hon. Mr. R.J. Scott
Justices of Appeal (The Hon. Mr./Madam Justice):
B.M. Helper; C.R. Huband; G.J. Kroft; S.R. Lyon, P.C. (Supernum.); M. Monnin; A.R. Philip (Supernum.); A.K. Twaddle
Registrar, B.T. Cadger, 204/945-2647

### MANITOBA COURT OF QUEEN'S BENCH

Law Courts Bldg., 408 York Ave., Winnipeg MB R3C 0P9

The Court of Queen's Bench is a court of original jurisdiction & has jurisdiction in all civil & criminal cases arising in Manitoba, except matters expressly excluded by statute.

**Chief Justice,** The Hon. Mr. B. Hewak
Assoc. Chief Justice, The Hon. Mr. J.J. Oliphant
Assoc. Chief Justice, The Hon. Mr. G.W.J. Mercier
Judges (The Hon. Mr./Madam Justice): G.J. Barkman (Supernum.); H.C. Beard; A.R. Clearwater; W.M. Darichuk; W.R. DeGraves; A. Dureault (Supernum.); L.A. Duval; T.M. Glowacki; B.M. Hamilton; K.R. Hanssen; A.A. Hirschfield (Supernum.); G.O. Jewers (Supernum.); D.P. Kennedy; B. Keyser; R. Krindle; A. MacInnis; P.S. Morse (Supernum.); N. Nurgitz; P. Schulman; S.I. Schwartz; J.A. Scollin (Supernum.); V. Simonsen; J.G. Smith (Supernum.); F. Steel; W.S. Wright (Supernum.)
Family Division: C.M. Bowman; R. Carr; C.M. Davidson; R.M. Diamond; J.A. Duncan; G.R. Goodman; S. Guertin-Riley; J.A. Mullally; K.F. Stefanson
Administrator, St. Boniface, P. Beaulieu
Master Registrars in Bankruptcy:
M. Goldberg, Q.C.
F.A. Lee

L.W. Ring, Q.C.
C. Sharp
•Brandon: Court of Queen's Bench, 1104 Princess Ave., PO Box 68, Brandon MB R7A 5Y6
Judges (The Hon. Mr./Madam Justice): R. Mykle
Family Division: J.A. Menzies
Master Registrar in Bankruptcy, Errick G. Harrison
•Dauphin: Court of Queen's Bench, 114 River Ave. West, Dauphin MB R7N 0J7
Judges (The Hon. Mr./Madam Justice):
K. Galanchuk
•The Pas: Court of Queen's Bench, 300, East 3 St., PO Box 1259, The Pas MB R9A 1L2
•Portage la Prairie: Court of Queen's Bench, 3 St. SE, Portage la Prairie MB R1N 1M9
•Thompson: Court of Queen's Bench, 59 Elizabeth Dr., Thompson MB R8N 1X9

## MANITOBA PROVINCIAL COURT

Law Courts Bldg., 408 York Ave., Winnipeg MB R3C 0P9

The Provincial Court has jurisdiction in family, youth & select criminal matters.

**Chief Judge,** The Hon. J.M. Webster
Assoc. Chief Judge, The Hon. B.D. Giesbrecht
Assoc. Chief Judge, The Hon. C.M. Sinclair
Assoc. Chief Judge, The Hon. B. Miller
Judges (His/Her Hon.):
F. Aquila; P.L. Ashdown; R.J. Chartier; H. Collerman; A.J. Conner; B.M. Corrin; R.J.B. Cramer; S.V. Devine; I.V. Dubienski (Supernum.); J.J. Enns (Supernum.); M. Garfinkel; L.M. Giesbrecht; J.P. Guy; H.F. Gyles (Supernum.); R.H. Harris; M.W. Howell; R.A. Johnston; E.C. Kimelman (Supernum.); L. Kopstein; T.J. Lismer; G.B. McTavish (Supernum.); R.J. Meyers; S. Minuk; L.R. Mitchell (Supernum.); C.K. Newcombe; W.E. Norton; H.R. Pullen; C.N. Rubin; W.H. Swail
•Brandon: Provincial Court, 1104 Princess Ave., Brandon MB R7A 0P9
Judges (His/Her Hon.):
D.D.S. Coppleman; A. James (Supernum.); K. Tarwid
Sheriff, M. Drosdoski, 204/726-6552
•Dauphin: Provincial Court, 114 River Ave. West, Dauphin MB R7N 0J7
Judges (His/Her Hon.):
K.P. Peters; R.W. Thompson
Sheriff, D. Bertnick, 204/622-2088
•The Pas: Provincial Court, 300 - 3 St. East, The Pas MB R9A 1L2
Judges (His/Her Hon.):
Roger Grégoire; W.R. Martin (Supernum.)
Sheriff, G. Wilson, 204/627-8431
•Portage la Prairie: Provincial Court, 25 Tupper St., Portage la Prairie MB R1N 3K1
Judges (His/Her Hon.):
R.G. Cummings
Sheriff, R. Sim, 204/239-3379
•Thompson: Provincial Court, 59 Elizabeth Dr., Thompson MB R8N 1X4
Judges (His/Her Hon.):
B.G. Colli; J.P. Drapack
Sheriff, Vacant, 204/677-6764

# NEW BRUNSWICK

## NEW BRUNSWICK COURT OF APPEAL

PO Box 6000, Fredericton NB E3B 5H1

The Court of Appeal has appellate jurisdiction in civil & criminal matters.

**Chief Justice,** The Hon. Mr. W.L. Hoyt
Justices of Appeal (The Hon. Mr./Madam Justice):
L.C. Ayles; Michel Bastarache; R.C. Rice; P.A.A. Ryan; W.S. Turnbull
Registrar, A.M. DiGiacinto, Q.C., 506/453-2452
Deputy Registrar, Line Pinet

## NEW BRUNSWICK COURT OF QUEEN'S BENCH

PO Box 6000, Fredericton NB E3B 5H1

The Court of Queen's Bench is a court of original jurisdiction, having jurisdiction in all civil and criminal matters arising in New Brunswick, except those expressly excluded by statute. The Court is comprised of two divisions: Trial and Family.

**Chief Justice,** The Hon. Joseph Z. Daigle
Registrar, Bankruptcy/Divorce & Matrimonial Causes, A.M. DiGiacinto, Q.C., 506/453-2452
Deputy Registrar, Bankruptcy, Line Pinet, 506/453-2452
•Bathurst: Court of Queen's Bench, Court House, 254 St. Patrick St., PO Box 5001, Bathurst NB E2A 3Z9
Judicial District: Gloucester County
Judges (His/Her Hon.):
Family Division: G.W. Boisvert
Trial Division: A. Deschenes; J.R. McIntyre
Regional Manager, R.G. Boudreau
Clerk (Trial Division) & Administrator (Family Division), Donald Arseneau
Sheriff/Coroner, Edgar Aubé
•Campbellton: Court of Queen's Bench, Court House, 157 Water St., PO Box 5001, Campbellton NB E3N 3H5
Judicial District: Restigouche, Parishes of Saint Quentin & Grimmer Counties
Judges (His/Her Hon.):
Trial & Family Division: Gladys J. Young
Clerk (Trial Division) & Administrator (Family Division), Lucien Leblanc
Sheriff/Coroner, Walter Thompson
•Edmundston: Court of Queen's Bench, 121 Church St., PO Box 5001, Edmundston NB E3V 3L3
Judicial District: Madawaska County, Parishes of Drummond & Town of Grand Falls of Victoria County
Judges (His/Her Hon.):
Family Division: J.A. Sirois
Trial Division: J.E. Angers
Clerk, Administrator (Family Division) & Regional Manager, Richard J. Keeley
Sheriff/Coroner, Paul Ringuette
•Fredericton: Court of Queen's Bench, Court House, 423 Queen St., PO Box 6000, Fredericton NB E3B 5H1
Judicial District: York, Sunbury & Queens Counties
Judges (His/Her Hon.):
Family Division: Myrna Athey
Trial Division: M.E.L. Larlee; D.H. Russell
Regional Manager, Beth Nicholas
Sheriff/Coroner, Calvin Pollard
Clerk (Trial Division) & Administrator (Family Division), A. Mehta
•Moncton: Court of Queen's Bench, 770 Main St., PO Box 5001, Moncton NB E1C 8R3
Judicial District: Westmorland, Kent & Albert Counties
Judges (His/Her Hon.):
Family Division: Roger Savoie; David D. Smith
Trial Division: P.S. Creaghan; Paul J.-M. Godin; J. Alfred Landry; R.L. Miller; Guy R. Richard
Regional Manager, David Leger
Clerk (Trial Division) & Administrator (Family Division), Michael Bray
Sheriff/Coroner, Rhéal LeBlanc
•Newcastle: Court of Queen's Bench, Court House, 599 King George Hwy., Newcastle NB E1V 1N6
Judicial District: Northumberland County
Judges (His/Her Hon.):
Trial & Family Division: Thomas Riordon
Deputy Clerk (Trial Division) & Deputy Administrator (Family Division), Matthew Cripps
Sheriff/Coroner, James Muck
•Saint John: Court of Queen's Bench, Court House, 110 Charlotte St., PO Box 5001, Saint John NB E2L 2S3
Judicial District: Saint John, Kings & Charlotte Counties
Judges (His/Her Hon.):
Family Division: Weldon Graser; R.J. Guerette
Trial Division: R.J. Higgins; H.H. McLellan; J.W. Turnbull
Regional Manager, Donna Beaton
Clerk (Trial Division) & Administrator (Family Division), George S. Thériault
Sheriff/Coroner, Joan Collins
•Woodstock: Court of Queen's Bench, Court House, 689 Main St., PO Box 5001, Woodstock NB E0J 2B0
Judicial District: Victoria & Carleton Counties
Judges (His/Her Hon.):
Trial & Faminly Division: Judy L. Clendening
Deputy Clerk (Trial Division) & Deputy Administrator (Family Division), Jean Sewell
Sheriff/Coroner, Gerald Grierson

## NEW BRUNSWICK PROVINCIAL COURT

PO Box 6000, Fredericton NB E3B 5H1
506/453-2935

The provincial Court has jurisdiction in select criminal matters as well as youth matters.

**Chief Judge,** Her Hon. Camille Dumas
•Carleton County: Provincial Court, PO Box 1329, Woodstock NB E0J 2B0
Judges (His/Her Hon.):
Graydon Nicholas
•Charlotte County: Provincial Court, 41 King St., St. Stephen NB E3L 2C1
Judges (His/Her Hon.):
D.E. Rice
•Gloucester County (Bathurst): Provincial Court, PO Box 5001, Bathurst NB E2A 3Z9
Judges (His/Her Hon.):
Frederic Arsenault; Camille Dumas
•Gloucester County (Tracadie): Provincial Court, PO Box 3587, Tracadie NB E1X 1G5
Judges (His/Her Hon.):
Jocelyne Moreau-Bérubé
•Kent County: Provincial Court, PO Box 5001, 73 Main St., Richibucto NB E0A 2M0
Judges (His/Her Hon.):
Joseph C. Michaud
•Kings County: Provincial Court, PO Box 137, Hampton NB E0G 1Z0
Judges (His/Her Hon.):
M.F. Cain
•Madawaska County: Provincial Court, Carrefour Assomption, #235, 121 Church St., PO Box 5001, Edmunston NB E3V 3L3 – 506/739-9803
Judges (His/Her Hon.):
George S. Perusse
•Northumberland County: Provincial Court, 599 King George Hwy., Newcastle NB E1V 1N6
Judges (His/Her Hon.):
Dennis Lordon; Andrew Stymiest
•Restigouche County: Provincial Court, PO Box 5001, Campbellton NB E3N 3H5
Judges (His/Her Hon.):
Pierre Arsenault; Steve Hutchinson
•Saint John County: Provincial Court, 15 Market Sq., 3rd Fl., Saint John NB E2L 1E8
Judges (His/Her Hon.):
Alfred H. Brien; William J. McCarroll; James G. McNamee
•Sunbury-Queens Counties: Provincial Court, PO Box 94, Oromocto NB E2V 2G4
Judges (His/Her Hon.):
G.W.N. Cockburn
•Victoria County: Provincial Court, PO Box 5001, 426 Broadway St., Grand Falls NB E0J 1M0
Judges (His/Her Hon.):
Jacques Desjardins

•Westmorland County: Provincial Court, PO Box 5001, 770 Main St., Moncton NB E1C 8R3
Judges (His/Her Hon.):
Irwin Lampert; Ian P. Mackin; Michael McKee; Sylvio Savoie; Camille Vautour
•York County: Provincial Court, Justice Bldg., PO Box 6000, 423 Queen St., Fredericton NB E3B 5H1
Judges (His/Her Hon.):
Patricia Cumming; J.D. Harper

### NEW BRUNSWICK: PROBATE COURT
PO Box 6000, Fredericton NB E3B 5H1
506/453-2805
The Probate Court has jurisdiction in estate matters.
Clerk, Ashwin Mehta

## NEWFOUNDLAND & LABRADOR

### NEWFOUNDLAND SUPREME COURT: COURT OF APPEAL
Court House, 355 Duckworth St., St. John's NF A1C 1H6
709/729-5147
The Court of Appeal has appellate jurisdiction in criminal and civil matters from decisions of the lower courts and designated administrative boards and tribunals.
**Chief Justice,** The Hon. Mr. James R. Gushue
Justices of Appeal (The Hon. Mr./Madam Justice):
James P. Adams; J.W. Mahoney; William W. Marshall; Arthur S. Mifflin (Supernum.); H.B. Morgan; John J. O'Neill; G.L. Steele

### NEWFOUNDLAND SUPREME COURT: TRIAL DIVISION
Court House, 355 Duckworth St., St. John's NF A1C 1H6
709/729-1059
The Trial Division is a court of original jurisdiction having jurisdiction in all civil and criminal matters arising in Newfoundland, except those excluded by statute. With the exception of the judicial area of St. John's, the Trial Division's original jurisdiction extends to particular family matters.
**Chief Justice,** The Hon. Mr. T.A. Hickman
Judges (His/Her Hon.):
James P. Adams; William G. Adams; F. Aylward; H.H. Cummings (Supernum.); Raymond J. Halley; G. Lang; Nathaniel S. Noel (Supernum.); J. James Puddester; David G. Riche; David L. Russell; Robert Wells
Supreme Court Registrar, Barry R. Sparkes, Q.C.
Sr. Deputy Registrar, Vacant
Sheriff, L.R. Thoms

### NEWFOUNDLAND SUPREME COURT: JUDICIAL CENTRES
Court House, 355 Duckworth St., St. John's NF A1C 1H6
709/729-5147
The Supreme Court has jurisdiction in Bankruptcy.
Registrar in Bankruptcy, Vacant
Asst. Deputy Registrar, Bankruptcy, Louise King
Asst. Deputy Registrar, Bankruptcy, Elaine Burke
•Brigus: Supreme Court, PO Box 100, Brigus NF A0A 1K0
Judges (His/Her Hon.):
Rupert W. Bartlett
•Corner Brook: Supreme Court, PO Box 2006, Corner Brook NF A2H 6J8
Judges (His/Her Hon.):
Denis Roberts (Supernum.); Frederick R. Woolridge
Deputy Registrar, Bankruptcy, Camille Pennell
•Gander: Supreme Court, PO Box 40, Gander NF A1V 2E1
Judges (His/Her Hon.):
Kevin Barry
•Grand Bank: Supreme Court, PO Box 910, Grand Bank NF A0E 1W0
Judges (His/Her Hon.):
G. Easton
•Grand Falls: Supreme Court, Provincial Bldg., Grand Falls NF A2A 1W9
Judges (His/Her Hon.):
Abraham Schwartz
•Happy Valley/Goose Bay: Supreme Court, PO Box 423, Stn B, Happy Valley/Goose Bay NF A0P 1C0
Judges (His/Her Hon.):
Seamus O'Regan

### NEWFOUNDLAND SUPREME COURT: UNIFIED FAMILY COURT
21 Kingsbridge Rd., St. John's NF A1C 3K4
709/753-5873
The Unified Family Court has exclusive jurisdiction for all family matters within the judicial area of metropolitan St. John's.
Judge, Her Hon. Mary E. Noonan
Administrator, Berkley Reynolds

### NEWFOUNDLAND PROVINCIAL COURT
Atlantic Pl., PO Box 5144, St. John's NF A1C 5V5
709/726-7181; Fax: 709/729-2161
The Provincial Court has jurisdiction in select criminal and family (outside the judicial area of St. John's) matters as well as small claims and youth matters.
**Chief Judge,** His Hon. Donald S. Luther
Judges (His/Her Hon.): W.J. Baker; Gregory Brown; O.M. Kennedy; J. LeClair; M.R. Reid; John F. Rorke; Robert T. Smith; J. Woodrow
Traffic Court: Vacant
Youth Court: Robert B. Hyslop
•Bell Island: Provincial Court, Bell Island NF A0A 4H0
•Bonne Bay: Provincial Court, Woody Point NF A0K 1P0
•Channel-Port-aux-Basques: Provincial Court, Channel-Port-aux-Basques NF A0M 1C0
•Clarenville: Provincial Court, Clarenville NF A0E 1J0
Judges (His/Her Hon.):
R.J. Whiffen
•Corner Brook: Provincial Court, Corner Brook NF A2H 6J4
Judges (His/Her Hon.):
James Igloliorte; Richard D. LeBlance; Michael W. Roche
•Gander: Provincial Court, Gander NF A1V 1W7
Judges (His/Her Hon.):
Kymil Howe; D. Peddle
•Goose Bay: Provincial Court, Goose Bay NF A0P 1C0
Judges (His/Her Hon.):
David E. Power
•Grand Bank: Provincial Court, Grand Bank NF A0E 1W0
Judges (His/Her Hon.):
G. Handrigan
•Grand Falls: Provincial Court, Grand Falls NF A2A 1W9
Judges (His/Her Hon.):
R. Fowler; K. Goulding
•Harbour Grace: Provincial Court, Harbour Grace NF A0A 2M0
Judges (His/Her Hon.):
J. Kean
•Placentia: Provincial Court, Placentia NF A0B 2Y0
Judges (His/Her Hon.):
G. Barnable
•Springdale: Provincial Court, Springdale NF A0J 1T0
•Stephenville: Provincial Court, Stephenville NF A2N 3K9
Judges (His/Her Hon.):
B. LeGrow
•Wabush: Provincial Court, Wabush NF A0R 1B0

## NORTHWEST TERRITORIES

### NORTHWEST TERRITORIES COURT OF APPEAL
Court House, PO Box 1320, Yellowknife NT X1A 2L9
403/920-8759
The Court of Appeal has appellate jurisdiction in criminal and civil matters from the Supreme Court and Territorial Court.
**Chief Justice,** The Hon. Mr./Madam C.A. Fraser
Justices of Appeal (The Hon. Mr./Madam Justice):
R.E. Hudson; C. Hunt; W. O'Leary; E. Picard; J.E. Richard; A.H. Russell; J.Z. Vertes; M.M. de Weerdt
Calgary: John D. Bracco; C.M. Conrad; A.M. Harradence; M.M. Hetherington; R.P. Kerans
Edmonton: R.H. Belzil; J.E. Coté; R.P. Foisy; H.L. Irving; S.S. Lieberman; J.W. McClung; E.A. McFadyen; J.J. Stratton
Regina: C.F. Tallis
Whitehorse: H.C.B. Maddison
Registrar, Lysette A. Deyelle

### NORTHWEST TERRITORIES SUPREME COURT
Court House, PO Box 1320, Yellowknife NT X1A 2L9
The Supreme Court is a court of original jurisdiction and has jurisdiction in all civil and criminal matters arising in the Northwest Territories, except those expressly excluded by statute.
Judges (The Hon. Mr./Madam Justice):
J. Edward Richard; J.Z. Vertes; M.M. de Weerdt
Ex-Officio Judges (The Hon. Mr./Madam Justice):
R.E. Hudson; H.C.B. Maddison
Deputy Judges (The Hon. Mr./Madam Justice): B. Hewak
Brigus: R.W. Bartlett
Calgary: John D. Bracco; Paul Chrumka; Carole M. Conrad; Mary M. Hetherington; M. Earl Lomas; Arthur M. Lutz; Peter Power; Charles Virtue
Chilliwack: William H. Davies
Edmonton: Alan T. Cooke; Tellex W. Grant; Howard L. Irving; S.S. Lieberman; E.P. MacCallum; Ernest A. Marshall; Elizabeth McFadyen; T.H. Miller; Ellen I. Picard; Joanne B. Veit; A.H. Wachowich
Halifax: W.J. Grant
Montréal: Jean-Guy Boilard; R.F. Paul; M.L. Rothman
Ottawa: W. Dan Chilcott; J.K. Hugesson
Picton: J.D. O'Flynn
Québec: Paul Trudeau
Regina: C.F. Tallis
Simcoe: J. Pringle
St. John's: Mary E. Noonan
Toronto: D.H. Carruthers; W.D. Griffiths; J.H. Potts; F.K. Roberts
Vancouver: Howard A. Callaghan; Kenneth M. Lysyk; Wallace Oppal; Patricia M. Proudfoot; Randall S.K. Wong
Whitehorse: R.E. Hudson; H.C.B. Madison
Winnipeg: W.R. Degraves; Daniel P. Kennedy
Clerk, Administrator & Registrar, Bankruptcy, Lysette A. Deyelle
Sheriff, Colin McCluskie
Chief Court Reporter, L.A. Young

### NORTHWEST TERRITORIAL COURT
PO Box 550, Yellowknife NT X1A 2M4
403/873-7643
The Territorial Court has jurisdiction in small claims, youth, family and select criminal matters.
**Chief Judge,** The Hon. R.W. Halifax
Judges (His/Her Hon.): R.M. Bourassa; T. Davis
Inuvik: B. Bruser
Iqaluit: B. Browne
Acting Clerk, R.A. Mould

### NORTHWEST TERRITORIES: JUSTICE OF THE PEACE COURT
PO Box 1320, Yellowknife NT X1A 2L9

The Justice of the Peace has jurisdiction in summary conviction matters arising out of territorial statutes and municipal by-laws.

### NORTHWEST TERRITORIES: SMALL CLAIMS COURT

PO Box 1320, Yellowknife NT X1A 2L9

The Small Claims Court has jurisdiction in civil matters not exceeding the amount prescribed by statute.

## NOVA SCOTIA

### NOVA SCOTIA COURT OF APPEAL

The Law Courts Bldg., 1815 Upper Water St., Halifax NS B3J 1S7

The Nova Scotia Court of Appeal has appellate jurisdiction in civil and criminal matters.

**Chief Justice,** The Hon. Mr. Lorne O. Clarke

Justices of Appeal (The Hon. Justice):

Nancy J. Bateman; David R. Chipman; E.J. Flinn; Gerald B. Freeman; J. Doane Hallett; Gordon L.S. Hart (Supernum.); Malachi C. Jones (Supernum.); Kenneth M. Matthews (Supernum.); Ronald N. Pugsley; Elizabeth Roscoe

Registrar, Court of Appeal, Gretchen Pohlkamp, 902/424-9968

### NOVA SCOTIA SUPREME COURT

The Law Courts Bldg., 1815 Upper Water St., Halifax NS B3J 1S7

902/424-4900

The Supreme Court is a court of original jurisdiction having jurisdiction in all civil and criminal matters arising in Nova Scotia, except those matters expressly excluded by statute. The Supreme Court's civil jurisdiction also extends to select family matters.

**Chief Justice,** The Hon. Constance R. Glube

Judges (The Hon. Justice):

N. Robert Anderson; Allan P. Boudreau; Felix A. Cacchione; Hiram J. Carver; John M. Davison; Frank C. Edwards; Walter R.E. Goodfellow; David W. Gruchy; Charles E. Haliburton; Donald M. Hall (Supernum.); M. Jill Hamilton; Suzanne M. Hood; F.B. William Kelly; Joseph Kennedy; A. David MacAdam; Simon J. MacDonald; J. Michael MacDonald; Douglas L. MacLellan; Gerald Moir, Hilroy S. Nathanson; D. Merlin Nunn; K. Peter Richard; Jamie W.S. Saunders; Ted Scanlan; Margaret J. Stewart; Gordon Tidman

Prothonotary, Clerk of the Crown & Registrar in Bankruptcy, Gretchen G. Pohlkamp, 902/424-6905

### NOVA SCOTIA PROVINCIAL COURT

5250 Spring Garden Rd., Halifax NS B3J 1E7

902/424-8718

The Provincial Court has jurisdiction in select criminal matters and acts as a Youth Court for cases involving youths aged 12 to 15 years.

**Assoc. Chief Judge,** The Hon. Jean-Louis Batiot

Judges (The Hon.):

Barbara J. Beach; Patrick H. Curran; John G. MacDougall; Hughes Randall; Michael B. Sherar; Castor H.F. Williams

- Amherst: Provincial Court, PO Box 1148, Amherst NS B4H 4L2 – 902/667-1108
  Judges (The Hon.):
  Ross Archibald; David Cole
- Annapolis Royal: Provincial Court, PO Box 425, Annapolis Royal NS B0S 1A0 – 902/532-5137
  Assoc. Chief Judge (The Hon.):
  Jean-Louis Batiot
- Antigonish: Provincial Court, PO Box 1506, Antigonish NS B2G 2L8 – 902/863-3676
  Judges (The Hon.):
  John D. Embree
- Bridgewater: Provincial Court, 84 Pleasant St., Bridgewater NS B4V 1N1 – 902/543-7143
  Judges (The Hon.):
  Anne Crawford
- Dartmouth: Provincial Court, #200, 277 Pleasant St., Dartmouth NS B2Y 3S2 – 902/424-2390
  Judges (The Hon.):
  R. Brian Gibson; R.B. Kimball; F.K. Potts
- Digby: Provincial Court, PO Box 1089, Digby NS B0V 1A0 – 902/245-4567
  Judges (The Hon.):
  John R. Nichols
- Kentville: Provincial Court, PO Box 457, Kentville NS B4N 3X3 – 902/679-6070
  Judges (The Hon.):
  Claudine MacDonald; J.A. MacLellan
- New Glasgow: Provincial Court, Bridgeview Sq., 115 MacLean St., New Glasgow NS B2H 4M5 – 902/755-5106
  Judges (The Hon.):
  Clyde Macdonald; Robert Stroud
- Port Hawkesbury: Provincial Court, PO Box 190, Port Hawkesbury NS B0E 2V0 – 902/625-2605
  Judges (The Hon.):
  John D. Embree
- Sydney: Provincial Court, Harbour Place, 136 Charlotte St., 2nd Fl., Sydney NS B1P 1C3 – 902/563-3507
  Judges (The Hon.):
  S.D. Campbell; D.L. Matheson; A.P. Ross; Brian D. Williston
- Truro: Provincial Court, 540 Prince St., Truro NS B2N 1G1 – 902/893-5840
  Judges (The Hon.):
  J.G. MacDougall
- Yarmouth: Provincial Court, 403 Main St., Yarmouth NS B5A 1G3 – 902/742-0500
  Judges (The Hon.):
  Robert M.J. Prince

### NOVA SCOTIA: PROBATE COURT

The Probate Court has jurisdiction in respect of estate matters.

Director of Probate (Sydney), Shauna Wilson

- Amherst: Probate Court, PO Box 1148, Amherst NS B4H 4L2 – 902/667-8062
  Registrar, Wm. Fairbanks
- Annapolis Royal: Probate Court, PO Box 129, Annapolis Royal NS B0S 1A0 – 902/532-5582
  Registrar, Lynn Durkee
- Guysborough: Probate Court, PO Box 123, Guysborough NS B0H 1N0 – 902/533-4001
  Registrar, Lorna M. Chisholm
- Halifax: Probate Court, #910, 1660 Hollis St., Halifax NS B3J 1V7 – 902/424-7422
  Registrar, Sharron Grant
- Kentville: Probate Court, 87 Cornwallis St., Kentville NS B4N 2E5 – 902/679-5339
  Registrar, Susan Campbell-Baltzer
- Lunenburg: Probate Court, PO Box 760, Lunenburg NS B0J 2C0 – 902/634-8885
  Deputy Registrar, Claire Feener
- Pictou: Probate Court, PO Box 1199, Pictou NS B0K 1H0 – 902/485-4351
  Acting Registrar, Laura Lannon
- Port Hawkesbury: Probate Court, PO Box 909, Port Hawkesbury NS B0E 2V0 – 902/625-4219
  Deputy Registrar, Karen Gillies
- Sydney: Probate Court, #6, Harbour Place, 136 Charlotte St., Sydney NS B1P 1L3 – 902/563-3545
  Registrar, Shauna Wilson
- Truro: Probate Court, Church St., Truro NS B2N 3Z5 – 902/893-5870
  Deputy Registrar, Carol Babineau
- Yarmouth: Probate Court, Court House, 403 Main St., Yarmouth NS B5A 1G3 – 902/742-5469
  Registrar, Aileen Smith

### NOVA SCOTIA: FAMILY COURT

5151 Terminal Rd., PO Box 7, Halifax NS B3J 2L6

902/424-4632

The Family Court has jurisdiction in family matters and also functions as a Youth Court for cases involving youths aged 12 to 15 years.

**Chief Judge,** His. Hon. Robert Ferguson, 902/424-6824; Fax: 902/424-0395

Director, Family Court Services, Jock Mackinnon, Fax: 902/424-4556

- Amherst: Family Court, PO Box 1148, Amherst NS B4H 4L1 – 902/667-3598; Fax: 902/667-1108
  Judges (His Hon.):
  David Milner
- Annapolis: Family Court, Provincial Bldg., 136 Exhibition St., Kentville NS B4N 4E5 – 902/679-6079; Fax: 902/679-6081
  Judges (His Hon.):
  Robert Levy
- Bridgewater: Family Court, #102, 84 Pleasant St., Bridgewater NS B4V 1N1 – 902/543-4222; Fax: 902/543-0524
  Judges (His Hon.):
  Robert C. Hebb
- Dartmouth: Family Court, 45 Alderney Dr., PO Box 1253, Dartmouth NS B2Y 4B9 – 902/424-4600; Fax: 902/424-0567
  Judges (His/Her Hon.):
  Moira Legere; Robert J. Williams
- Halifax: Family Court, 3380 Devonshire Ave., PO Box 8988, Stn A, Halifax NS B3K 5M6 – 902/424-3990; Fax: 902/424-0562
  Judges (His/Her Hon.):
  Flora I. Buchan; T.T. Daley; William Dyer; Deborah Gass; Corrine E. Sparks
- Kentville: Family Court, 136 Exhibition St., Kentville NS B4N 4E5 – 902/679-6079; Fax: 902/679-6081
  Judges (His Hon.):
  Robert Levy
- New Glasgow: Family Court, PO Box 518, New Glasgow NS B2H 5E7 – 902/755-6520; Fax: 902/755-7176
  Judges (His Hon.):
  Robert J.L. White; James C. Wilson
- Sydney: Family Court, #11, 360 Prince St., Sydney NS B1P 5L1 – 902/563-2200; Fax: 902/563-3666
  Judges (His/Her Hon.):
  J.V. MacDonald; Clare MacLellan; Daryl W. Wilson
- Truro: Family Court, PO Box 1680, Truro NS B2N 5N2 – 902/893-5930; Fax: 902/893-6100
  Judges (His Hon.):
  David R. Hubley
- Yarmouth: Family Court, PO Box 460, Yarmouth NS B5A 4B4 – 902/742-0550; Fax: 902/742-0582
  Assoc. Chief Judge, His Hon. John Comeau

### NOVA SCOTIA: SMALL CLAIMS COURT

5151 Terminal Rd., PO Box 7, Halifax NS B3J 2L6

902/424-7525

The Small Claims Court has jurisdiction in civil claims not exceeding the amount prescribed by statute.

Administrator, Alden Rennie

### NOVA SCOTIA JUSTICE CENTRES

Amherst: 16 Church St., PO Box 1148, Amherst NS B4H 4L2 – 902/667-2256; Fax: 902/667-1108 – District Court Administrator, David Burke

Antigonish: 62 Court St., PO Box 1506, Antigonish NS B2G 2L8 – 902/863-7545; Fax: 902/863-7451 – District Court Administrator, Terry MacDonald

Bridgewater: 80 Pleasant St., PO Box 369, Bridgewater NS B4V 2W9 – 902/543-0588; Fax: 902/543-0639 – District Court Administrator, Margaret Mesiner

Kentville: 87 Cornwallis St., Kentville NS B4N 2E5 – 902/679-4358; Fax: 902/679-6178 – District Court Administrator, Bernie Conrad

New Glasgow: 196 Riverside Pkwy., PO Box 518, New Glasgow NS B2H 5E7 – 902/755-6520; Fax: 755-7176 – District Court Administrator, Jim Hahnen
Port Hawkesbury: PO Box 909, Port Hawkesbury NS B0E 2V0 – 902/625-4218; Fax: 902/625-4220 – District Court Administrator, Terry MacDonald
Sydney: Harbour Place, 136 Charlotte St., 2nd Fl., Sydney NS B1P 1C3 – 902/563-3515; Fax: 902/563-3421 – District Court Administrator, David Muise
Truro: 540 Prince St., Truro NS B2N 1G1 – 902/893-5840; Fax: 902/893-6100 – District Court Administrator, Carmel Standen
Yarmouth:403 Main St., Yarmouth NS B5A 1G3 – 902/742-0500; Fax: 902/742-0678 – District Court Administrator, Lynn Strang

## ONTARIO

### ONTARIO COURT OF APPEAL

Osgoode Hall, 130 Queen St. West, Toronto ON M5H 2N5
416/327-5020; Fax: 416/327-5032

The Court of Appeal is the final court of appeal for Ontario. Appeals from the Court of Appeal may be pursued in the Supreme Court of Canada.

**Chief Justice,** The Hon. Mr. Roy McMurtry
Assoc. Chief Justice, The Hon. Mr. John Wilson Morden
Justices of Appeal (The Hon. Mr./Madam Justice):
Rosalie S. Abella; Louise Arbour; A.M. Austin; John Watson Brooke; James J. Carthy; Marvin Adrian Catzman; Louise Charron; David H. Doherty; George Duncan Finlayson; Stephen T. Goudy; Lloyd William Houlden; Horace Krever; Jean-Marc Labrosse; John I. Laskin; Hilda M. McKinlay; Michael J. Moldar; Coulter Arthur Anthony Osborne; Sydney Lewis Robins; M. Rosenberg; Karen M. Weiler
Registrar, John H. Keamkamp, 416/327-5208

### ONTARIO COURT OF JUSTICE,

All Ontario courts (except the Court of Appeal & the Unified Family Court) form part of the Ontario Court of Justice, which consists of two divisions, the General Division & the Provincial Division. For judicial purposes, Ontario is divided into seven regions.

### GENERAL DIVISION

Osgoode Hall, 130 Queen St. West, Toronto ON M5H 2N5
Fax: 416/326-2224

In addition to its regular trial court functions, the General Division has two branches: the Divisional Court which generally hears appeals from a final order of a Judge of the General Division involving disputes of up to $25,000, & the Small Claims Court which generally hears cases involving claims up to $6,000. The Governor General appoints the Judges to all but the Ontario Court (Provincial Division).

**Chief Justice,** The Hon. Mr. P.J. Lesage
Assoc. Chief Justice, The Hon. Madam H.J. Smith
Registrar in Bankruptcy, J.M. Ferron
Deputy Registrars in Bankruptcy:
G.C. Saunders, H. Garfield, D.H. Sandler, S.D. Cork, H.F.H. Sedgwick, W.R. Donkin, B. Sischy, D.A. Peppiatt, R. Linton, R.B. Peterson, B.T. Clark

•Central East Region: 50 Eagle St. West, 4th Fl., Newmarket ON L3Y 6B1 – 905/853-4810
Justices (The Hon. Mr./Madam Justice):
Barrie: M.P. Eberhard; P.G.M. Hermiston; H.D. Logan; C. Marchand; C. Perkins; P.B. Tobias; T.M. Wood
Bracebridge: S.B. Hogg (Supernum.); R.N. Weekes
Cobourg: H.R. McLean
Lindsay: B.G. MacDougall
Newmarket: R. Boyko; J.A. Goodearle; P.H. Howden; G.R. Klowak; J.R. MacKinnon; D.J. Taliano
Peterborough: S.H. Murphy
Whitby: D.S. Ferguson; J. Jenkins; H.S. Laforme; W.B. Lane; J.R. McIsaac; J.E. Sheppard; A.J. Stong

•Central South Region: 50 Main St. East, Hamilton ON L8N 1E9 – 905/308-7200
Justices (The Hon. Mr./Madam Justice):
Brantford: E.O. Fanjoy (Supernum.); J.C. Kent
Cayuga: T.D. Marshall
Hamilton: T.A. Beckett (Supernum.); N. Borkovich; J.J. Cavarzan; David S. Crane; G. Czutrin; E. Fedak; C.S. Glithero; T. Lofchik; Randolph Mazza; D. Mendes Da Costa; P.W. Perras (Supernum.); P.J. Philp; J.C. Scime; W. Stayshyn; D. Steinberg; J.E. Van Duzer (Supernum.); P.H. Wallace; G. Yates
Kitchener: D.F. Mossop (Supernum.); R.D. Reilly; R.E. Salhany; R.C. Sills; E.F. West (Supernum.)
Simcoe: J.A. Pringle (Supernum.); G.I. Thomson
St Catharines: G.W. Dandie; R.T.P. Gravely (Supernum.); F.J. Kovacs (Supernum.); J.W. Quinn
Welland: J.J. Fleury; M.P. Forestell; E. MacDonald; G.G. Nicholls (Supernum.)

•Central West Region: 7755 Hurontario St., PO Box 8000, Brampton ON L6V 2M7 – 905/452-6623
Justices (The Hon. Mr./Madam Justice):
Brampton: John R. Belleghem; M.L. Caswell; T.M. Dunn; S.C. Hill; Emile Kruzick; K.A. Langdon; A. Donald K. MacKenzie; J.M. Simmons; R.G. Thomas; L.M. Walters; J.B. Webber
Guelph: C. Herold; G.B. Smith
Milton: J.D. Carnwath; J.H. Clarke; W.J. Morrison; C.M. Speyer; R.E. Zelinski
Owen Sound: T.P. O'Connor; R.M. Thompson
Walkerton: J.I. McKay (Supernum.)

•East Region: 161 Elgin St., Ottawa ON K2P 2K1 – 613/239-1400
Justices (The Hon. Mr./Madam Justice):
Belleville: R.G. Byers; B.W. Hurley (Supernum.)
Brockville: P.J. Cosgrove
Cornwall: A.J. Roy
Kingston: M. Dunbar; T.J. Lally; H.K. MacLeod; C. Robertson; L.A. Woods (Supernum.)
L'Orignal: R.J.A. Cusson
Ottawa: J.M. Bell; K.C. Binks; J.B. Chadwick; W.D. Chilcott; J.D. Cunningham; Robert C. Desmarais; C.F. Doyle (Supernum.); J.A. Forget; Roydon Kealey; Colin McKinnon; D.L. McWilliam; P. Mercier; M. Metivier; F.H. Poulin (Supernum.); D.J.A. Rutherford; G.G. Sedgwick; J.G. Sirois; J.P.E.H. Soubliere
Pembroke: E.R. Millette
Perth: G.R. Morin
Picton: J.D. O'Flynn (Supernum.)

•Northeast Region: 155 Elm St. West, Sudbury ON P3C 1V1 – 705/671-5968
Justices (The Hon. Mr./Madam Justice):
Cochrane: R.P. Boissonneault; N.M.J. Karam
Gore Bay: R.G. Trainor (Supernum.)
Haileybury: J.D. Bernstein
North Bay: M.G. Bolan; G.T. Valin
Parry Sound: E. Loukidelis
Sault Ste. Marie: F.R Caputo; C. Bruce Noble; G.I. Pardu; R. Stortini (Supernum.); W. Larry Whalen
Sudbury: M.C. DiSalle; I.M. Gordon; R.J. Huneault; Spyros D. Loukidelis; M.R. Meehan; C.T. Murphy (Supernum.); J.S. Poupore

•Northwest Region: 277 Camelot St., Thunder Bay ON P7A 4B3 – 807/343-2712
Justices (The Hon. Mr./Madam Justice):
Kenora: G.F. Kinsman (Supernum.); E.W. Stach
Thunder Bay: L.C. Kozak; S.R. Kurisko (Supernum.); A. William Maloney; John McCartney; T.A. Platana; J. deP. Wright

•Southwest Region: 80 Dundas St. East, 15th Fl., London ON N6A 2P3 – 519/660-3027; Fax: 519/660-2294
Justices (The Hon. Mr./Madam Justice):
Chatham: E. Browne; J.G. Kerr
Goderich: J.M. Donnelly
London: David Aston; Grant Campbell; R.J. Flinn (Supernum.); B. Thomas Granger; R.J. Haines; Peter B. Hockin; W.A. Jenkins; J.C. Kennedy; G.P. Killeen; Lynne Leitch; M. Marshman; J.F. McCart (Supernum.); D.R. McDermid; H. Vogelsang
Sarnia: John Desotti; W.F. Higgins (Supernum.); K.F. Ross
St. Thomas: J.F. McGarry
Stratford: J.A. Mullen (Supernum.)
Windsor: R. Abbey; J.H. Brockenshire; A.E. Cusinato; R.M.P. Daudlin; J.P. McMahon (Supernum.); L.R. Morin; K.G. Ouellette; C. Zalev (Supernum.); T.G. Zuber (Supernum.)
Woodstock: C.C. Misener (Supernum.)

•Metropolitan Toronto: 361 University Ave., Toronto ON M5G 1T3 – 416/327-5752
Justices (The Hon. Mr./Madam Justice):
G.W. Adams; L.A. Beaulieu; Mary Lou Benotto; R.A. Blair; J.L. Boland (Supernum.); S. Borins; W.J.L. Brennan; D.R. Cameron; Archie G. Campbell; D.H. Carruthers (Supernum.); S. Chapnik; N.D. Coo (Supernum.); M. Corbett; J. Crossland; P.A. Cumming; M.R. Dambrot; G.F. Day; A.P. Dilks; T. Dunnet; N.D. Dyson; G.J. Epstein; E.G. Ewaschuk; J.M. Farley; K.N. Feldman; G.S.P. Ferguson (Supernum.); L.K. Ferrier; W. Festeryga; S.N. Filer; N.E. Garton; P. German (Supernum.); K.M. Gibson (Supernum.); L. Gotlib; S.E. Greer; P.A. Grossi; J.D. Ground; D.J. Haley; J.F. Hamilton; E.P. Hartt (Supernum.); B.C. Hawkins; K.A. Hoilett; D.G. Humphrey (Supernum.); P.G. Jarvis; J.R.R. Jennings; J.C. Kane (Supernum.); H.J. Keenan; F.P. Kiteley; G.D. Lane; S.E. Lang; Joan Lax; S.N. Lederman; C.H. Lissaman; H.R. Locke (Supernum.); W.D. Lyon (Supernum.); J.L. MacFarland; E. Macdonald; J.A.B. Macdonald; J.C. Macpherson; A. Mandel (Supernum.); P.T. Matlow; J.D. McCombs; E.G. McNeely (Supernum.); N.D. McRae; A.M. Molloy; J.W. O'Brien; H.M. O'Connell; J.G.J. O'Driscoll; D.F. O'Leary (Supernum.); V. Paisley; R.R.M. Pitt; J.H. Potts; F.K. Roberts; A.B. Rosenberg (Supernum.); R.C. Rutherford (Supernum.); E. Saunders (Supernum.); R.J. Sharpe; J.D. Sheard (Supernum.); W.P. Somers; J.B.S. Southey (Supernum.); G. Speigel; J.M. Spence; D.R. Steele (Supernum.); R.A.F. Sutherland; E. Then; W.B. Trafford; G.T. Walsh; J.D. Watt; S.P. Webb (Supernum.); B.J. Wein; A.C. Whealy (Supernum.); J.G.M. White; J.C. Wilkins; J. Wilson; W.K. Winkler; W.F. Wren (Supernum.); B. Wright

### PROVINCIAL DIVISION

#2600, 1 Queen St. East, PO Box 91, Toronto ON M5C 2W5

The Provincial Division generally performs functions assigned to it by Acts such as the *Criminal Code of Canada*, the *Provincial Offences Act*, the *Family Law Act*, the *Children's Law Reform Act* & the *Child & Family Services Act* & is a youth court for the purposes of the *Young Offenders Act*. The Lieutenant Governor in Council, on the recommendation of the Attorney General, appoints Provincial Division Judges.

**Chief Justice, Provincial Division,** The Hon. Sidney B. Linden, 416/327-5660

Assoc. Chief Judge, The Hon. Brian W. Lennox, 416/327-6826
Assoc. Chief Judge, The Hon. Marietta L.D. Roberts, 416/327-5616
•Central East Region: 440 Kent St. West, PO Box 4000, Lindsay ON K9V 5P2 – 705/324-1410
Regional Sr. Judge, The Hon. John D.D. Evans
Judges (The Hon.):
Barrie: T.P. Cleary, 705/739-6518; James C. Crawford, 705/739-6518; Roland C. Harris, 705/739-6517; Eric Libman, 705/739-6518; Robert R. Main, 705/739-6517; Gary V. Palmer, 705/739-6517; Bruce E. Payne, 705/739-6517; William Wolski, 705/739-6518
Barrie Per Diem Judges: Donald R. Inch, 705/739-6517; Norman J. Nadeau, 705/739-6517; James T. Robson, 705/739-6517
Bracebridge: Douglas G. Bice, 705/645-2269
Cobourg: John Rhys Morgan, 705/372-3751
Cobourg Per Diem Judge: John D. Bark, 905/372-3751
Lindsay: Karen E. Johnston, 705/324-1414; T.C. Whetung, 705/324-1414
Lindsay Per Diem Judge: George F.W. Inrig, 705/324-1414
Newmarket: Roy E. Bogusky, 905/853-4812; W.W. Bradley, 905/853-4812; M.H. Caney, 905/853-4812; Elizabeth Earle-Renton, 905/853-4812; Stephen E. Foster, 905/853-4802; V.A.R. Lampkin, 905/853-4802; R.A. Minard, 905/853-4802; Terence O'Hara, 905/853-4802; Charles E. Purvis, 905/853-4802; Sherrill M. Rogers, 905/853-4812; David G. Scott, 905/853-4802
Newmarket Per Diem Judge: Hugh E. Zimmerman, 905/853-4802
Orillia: Leonard T. Montgomery, 705/326-2671
Oshawa: Hubert J. Campbell, 905/723-9680; Donald B. Dodds, 905/723-9680; Norman H. Edmondson, 905/723-9680; Donald J. Halikowski, 905/723-9680; P.Z. Magda, 905/436-4900; R.J. Richards, 905/723-9680; M.A. Scott, 905/436-4900; David M. Stone, 905/723-9680; D. Timms, 905/436-4900
Oshawa Per Diem Judge: R.H. Donald (Sr. Judge), 905/436-4900
Peterborough: L.T.G. Collins, 705/876-3846; A.P. Ingram, 705/876-3846; Raymond P.V. Taillon, 905/876-3846
Peterborough Per Diem Judge: Richard B. Batten, 705/876-3846
•Central West Region: 50 Main St. East, 1st Fl., Hamilton ON L8N 1E9 – 905/308-7207
Regional Sr. Judge, The Hon. Anton Zuraw, 905/308-7207
Judges (The Hon.):
Brampton: H.K. Atwood, 905/450-4733; W.B. Blacklock, 905/450-4733; L.M. Budzinski, 905/450-4733; Ian Cowan, 905/450-4733; Bruce Duncan, 905/450-4733; P.W. Dunn, 905/452-6611; Roderick J. Flaherty, 905/450-4733; Peter A.J. Harris, 905/450-4733; Kathryn L. Hawke, 905/450-4733; J.D. Karswick, 905/452-6611; Jane Kerrigan Brownridge, 905/452-6610; Elinore Ready, 905/450-4733; V.T. Rosemay, 905/450-4733; John D. Smith, 905/450-4733; R.E. Stauth, 905/452-6611; J. David Wake, 905/450-4733; G.W. Waldman, 905/450-4733; Brian Weagant, 905/450-4733; Theo Wolder, 905/452-6611
Brantford: P.H. Marjoh Agro, 519/758-3470; Gethin Edward, 519/758-3470; Kenneth G. Lenz, 519/758-3470
Hamilton: Norman Bennett, 905/577-8410; D.S. Cooper, 905/577-8410; Timothy Culver, 905/577-8410; Peter R. Mitchell, 905/577-8410; Morris J. Perozak, 905/577-8410; D. Terry Vyse, 905/577-8410; Robert T. Weseloh, 905/577-8318; Bernd E. Zabel, 905/577-8410
Simcoe: W. Brian Stead, 519/426-1408
St. Catharines: Lesley Balwin; Harry W. Edmondstone; Richard Jennis; Kathleen Ellin McGowan; Wayne D. Morrison; J.W. Scott; Donald J. Wallace – 905/988-6200
Welland: R.L. Budgell (Sr. Judge), 905/734-4164; Marc J. Girard, 905/734-4164; Douglas H. Gowan, 905/734-4164
Milton: F. Stewart Fisher, 905/878-4161; Douglas V. Latimer, 905/878-4161; John E.C. Robinson, 905/637-4125; William S. Sharpe, 905/878-4161; John D. Takach, 905/842-8380
Milton Per Diem Judges: H. Tedford G. Andrews, 905/878-4161; A. James Fuller, 905/878-4161
Orangeville: J.B. Allen, 519/941-5802; William G. Richards, 519/941-5802
•East Region: 161 Elgin St., Ottawa ON K2P 2L1 – 613/239-1521
Regional Sr. Judge, The Hon. P.R. Belanger, 613/239-1521
Judges (The Hon.):
Belleville: S.J. Hunter, 613/962-3468; D.K. Kirkland, 613/968-6759; W.J. Pickett, 613/968-6759
Brockville: Charles D. Anderson, 613/342-5003, ext.46; Rommel G. Masse, 613/342-5003
Cornwall: Johanne Lafrance-Cardinal, 613/933-7500; Gilles Renaud, 613/933-7500
Kingston: E.D. Baker (Sr. Judge), 613/548-6215, ext.6710; Paul H. Meggison, 613/548-6215, ext.6711; K.E. Pedlar, 613/548-6790
Kingston Per Diem Judge: Ross H. Fair, 613/548-6790, ext.322
L'Orignal: J.R. Reginald Levesque, 613/675-4625
Napanee: J. Peter Coulson, 613/354-5450
Ottawa: Jennifer A. Blishen, 613/239-1339; Jean M. Bordeleau, 613/239-1339; J.A. Cousineau, 613/239-1339; David W. Dempsey, 613/239-1339; James A. Fontana, 613/239-1339; H.L. Fraser, 613/239-1339; Maria T. Linhares de Sousa, 613/239-1339; Bruce Edward MacPhee, 613/239-1339; J.P. Michel, 613/239-1339; John D. Nadelle, 613/239-1339; Dianne M. Nicholas, 613/239-1339; Lynn D. Ratushny, 613/239-1339; Bernard T. Ryan, 613/239-1339; A.D. Sheffield, 613/239-1339; Patrick D. White, 613/239-1339; J.P. Wright, 613/239-1339
Pembroke: L.P. Foran, 613/735-6886; C. Russell Merredew, 613/735-6886
Perth: Inger Hansen, 613/267-2021
•Northeast Region: 159 Cedar St., 3rd Fl., Sudbury ON P3C 6A5 – 705/670-7200
Regional Sr. Judge, The Hon. Louise L. Gauthier, 705/670-7200
Judges (The Hon.):
Cochrane: Gerard E. Cloutier, 705/272-4358
Elliot Lake: George Normand Glaude, 705/848-2500
Elliot Lake Per Diem Judge: June Bernard, 705/848-2500
Haileybury: Robert N. Fournier, 705/672-3395
North Bay: L. Duchesneau-McLachlan, 705/495-8308; Jean-Gilles Lebel, 705/495-8315
Parry Sound: Joseph Wilson, 705/746-4237
Parry Sound Per Diem Judge: Lewis S. Geiger, 705/746-4237
Sault Ste. Marie: Wayne W. Cohen; James D. Greco; John Kukurin – 705/945-8000
Sudbury: William F. Fitzgerald, 705/671-5929; Andre L. Guay, 705/670-7250, ext.45; W. Guy Mahaffy, 705/671-5929; Gilles R. Matte, 705/671-5929; Gerald Edward Michel (Sr. Judge), 705/671-5949; R.T. Runciman (Sr. Judge), 705/671-5986
Timmins: W.E. Carr, 705/267-7799; Richard Lajoie, 705/267-7799
•Northwest Region: 1805 East Arthur St., 2nd Fl., Thunder Bay ON P7E 5N7 – 807/625-1625
Regional Sr. Judge, The Hon. Raymond J. Walneck, 807/625-1625
Judges (The Hon.):
Dryden: Peter T. Bishop, 807/223-2348
Kenora: Donald Fraser, 807/468-2882; Judythe Little, 807/468-2884
Thunder Bay: Dianne P. Baig, 807/625-1610; Roderick D. Clarke, 807/625-1610; P.S. Glowacki (Sr. Judge), 807/625-1600; G.R. Kunnas, 807/625-1600; R.B. Lester, 807/625-1610; Frank A. Sargent, 807/625-1610
•West Region: 80 Dundas St. East, 15th Fl., London ON N6A 2P3 – 519/660-2292; Fax: 519/660-2294
Regional Sr. Judge, The Hon. Donald A. Ebbs, 519/660-2292
Judges (The Hon.):
Cambridge: Paddy A. Hardman, 519/621-9220
Chatham: L.G. DeKoning; Lucy Glenn – 519/352-9070
Goderich: R.G.E. Hunter, 519/524-2447
Guelph: Norman Douglas, 519/836-2501; Richard LeDressey, 519/824-0051; Frank Nowak, 519/822-7961
Kitchener: J.E. Allen, 519/741-3366; Donald C. Downie, 519/741-3366; Bruce Frazer, 519/741-3366; Heather L. Katarynych, 519/741-3366; Donald J. MacMillan, 519/741-3366; Colin R. Westman, 519/741-3366; Margaret F. Woolcott, 519/741-3366
Kitchener Per Diem Judge: Gordon H. McConnell (Sr. Judge), 519/741-3366
London: Alan J. Baker (Sr. Judge), 519/660-3014; Walter E. Bell, 519/660-3014; Deborah Kristin Livingstone, 519/660-3014; John L. Menzies, 519/660-3014; Eleanor Schnall, 519/660-3045; J. Douglas R. Walker, 519/660-3014; A.R. Webster, 519/660-3014
London Per Diem Judge: John M. Seneshen, 519/660-3014
Owen Sound: Julia Morneau, 519/376-0285
Owen Sound Per Diem Judge: James F. Laing, 519/376-0185
Sarnia: Deborah J. Austin, 519/336-8830; George Brophy, 519/336-8830; D.F. Kent, 519/337-3474
Sarnia Per Diem Judge: A.L. Eddy, 519/336-8830
St. Thomas: George A. Phillips, 519/633-1230
Stratford: Peter R.W. Isaacs, 519/271-2640; G.A. Pockele, 519/271-9252
Walkerton: R.S. MacKenzie, 519/881-0211
Windsor: Guy F. DeMarco, 519/254-3741; Harry Momotiuk, 519/254-3741; Saul Nosanchuk, 519/254-3741; Douglas W. Phillips, 519/254-6670; Micheline Rawlins, 519/254-3741; S.G. Zaltz, 519/973-6670
Woodstock: Alexander M. Graham, 519/539-6187
•Toronto Region: Old City Hall, 60 Queen St. West, Toronto ON M5H 2M4
Regional Sr. Judge, The Hon. W. Gonet, 416/327-5659
Judges (The Hon.):
Downsview: William P. Bassel, 416/314-4218; Faith M. Finnestad, 416/314-4218; Eric S. Lindsay, 416/314-4218; S.E. Marin, 416/314-4218; Lauren E. Marshall, 416/314-4218; Cathy Mocha, 416/314-4218; C.H. Vaillancourt, 416/314-4218
Downsview Per Diem Judges; C.J. Cannon, 416/314-4218; Arthur K. Meen, 416/314-4218; Harold A. Rice, 416/314-4218
Etobicoke: Harvey P.. Brownstone, 416/327-6300, ext.216; M.L. Cohen, 416/327-6300, ext.215; Ayres Couto, 416/314-3975; Derek T. Hogg, 416/314-3975; M.F. Khoorshed, 416/314-3975; Stanley W. Long, 416/314-3975; Salvatore Merenda, 416/314-3975; M.G. Morten, 416/314-3975; William P. Ross, 416/314-3975
Etobicoke Per Diem Judge: Jack J. Belobradic, 416/314-3975

North York: W.E. MacLatchy, 416/326-3539, ext.221; N. Weisman, 416/326-3539, ext.221; H.D. Wilkins, 416/326-3539, ext.221

North York Per Diem Judge: James P. Felstiner, 416/326-3539, ext.221

Scarborough: D.P. Cole, 416/325-0861; Donna G. Hackett, 416/325-0861; John P. Kerr, 416/325-0861; Marion E. Lane, 416/325-0861; J.P. Nevins, 416/325-0978; Petra E. Newton, 416/325-0861; R.J. Otter, 416/325-0861; Sheila Ray, 416/325-0861; P.A. Sheppard, 416/325-0861; Marvin A. Zuker, 416/325-0978, ext.365

Scarborough Per Diem Judge: C.R. Ball, 416/325-0978, ext.365

Toronto: W. Donald August (Sr. Judge), 416/327-5907; William J.C. Babe, 416/327-5907; D.A. Bean, 416/327-6891; P. Bentley, 416/327-5907; R.G. Bigelow, 416/327-5907; Annemarie Erika Bonkalo, 416/325-8972; Joseph William Bovard, 416/327-5907; Milton A. Cadsby, 416/325-8972; J.F. Casey, 416/327-5907; B. Cavion, 416/327-5907; David Fairgrieve, 416/327-5907; E. Gordon Hachborn, 416/325-8972; Monte H. Harris, 416/327-5907; Mary Jane Hatton, 416/327-6891; M.L. Hogan, 416/327-5907; Walter P. Hryciuk, 416/327-5907; Peter Hryn, 416/327-5907; J.C.M. James, 416/327-6891; Penny Jones, 416/327-6891; Bernard H. Kelly, 416/327-5907; R. Khawly, 416/372-5907; Lynn King, 416/327-6891; Brent Knazan, 416/327-5907; Ian A. MacDonnell, 416/327-5907; D.R. Main, 416/327-6891; Michael E. Martin, 416/327-5907; Maryka Omatsu, 416/325-8972; Edward Francis Ormston, 416/327-5907; Claude H. Paris, 416/327-5907; Paul B. Pickett, 416/325-8972; Hugh D. Porter, 416/325-8972; Paul Henry Reinhardt, 416/327-5907; Harvey M. Salem, 416/327-5907; Charles Scullion (Sr. Judge), 416/325-8972; S. Rebecca Shamai, 416/327-5907; Hugh W. Silverman, 416/327-5907; Geraldine Sparrow, 416/327-5907; Robert Bruce J. Young, 416/327-5907

Toronto Per Diem Judges: James Murphy, 416/325-8972; J.K. Walmsley, 416/327-6891

## COURTS ADMINISTRATION

720 Bay St., Toronto ON M5G 2K1

Asst. Deputy Attorney General, Courts Administration, Heather Cooper, 416/326-2609

Director, Program Development Branch, Linda Leighton, 416/326-4264

Director, Facilities & Special Court Services Branch, Matt Veskimets, 416/326-4033

Asst. Director, Family Support Plan, Vacant, 416/326-4710

### REGIONAL COURT: CENTRAL EAST

Areas served: Durham, Muskoka, Northumberland, Peterborough, Simcoe, Victoria-Haliburton, York Region

•Regional Municipality of Durham: Court House, 605 Rossland Rd. East, PO Box 640, Whitby ON L1N 9G7

Manager, Court Services, Sonia Faryna, 905/430-5810

Enforcement & Process Serving, Barbara Munro, 905/430-5808

Small Claims Court & Local Registrar, Alfred Ruttan, 905/430-5800

Oshawa: 242 King St. East, Oshawa ON L1H 3Z8 – 905/723-5251 – Criminal Matters, Val McGraw

Oshawa: 33 King St., Oshawa ON L1H 1A1 – 905/436-4900 – Small Claims Court & Family Matters, Linda Kurelo

•District Municipality of Muskoka: Court House, 3 Dominion St. North, PO Box 1080, Bracebridge ON P1L 2E6

Local Registrar, Enforcement & Process Serving, Criminal & Family Matters, Cathy Larsen, 705/645-8793

Small Claims Court, Owen McQuillen, 705/645-8793

•Northumberland County, Court House, 860 William St., PO Box 910, Cobourg ON K9A 3A9 – 905/372-3751

Enforcement & Process Serving, Criminal & Family Matters, Jean Wilson, 905/372-3751

•Peterborough County, Court House, 70 Simcoe St., Peterborough ON K9H 7G9

Manager, Court Services, Criminal & Family Matters, Dianne Wylie, 705/755-1860

Peterborough: 300 Water St., Peterborough ON K9J 8M5 – 705/876-3816 – Small Claims Court, Enforcement & Process Serving & Civil Matters, Helen Boyd

•Simcoe County, Court House, 114 Worsley St., Barrie ON L4M 1M1

Manager, Court Services, Joan Scott, 705/739-6577

Enforcement & Process Serving, John Wilson, 705/739-6100

Local Registrar, Small Claims Court & Family Matters, Sue Whalen, 705/739-6144, 6116, 6136

Barrie: Court House, 30 Poyntz St., PO Box 284, Barrie ON L4M 5L4 – 705/739-6500 – Criminal Matters, Eldeen Murphy

Orillia: Cottage C, Memorial Ave., Huronia Regional Centre, PO Box 218, Orillia ON L3V 6J3 – 705/326-5652 – Small Claims Court, Criminal & Family Matters, Joan Scott

•Victoria-Haliburton Counties: Court House, 440 Kent St. West, PO Box 4000, Lindsay ON K9V 5P2 – 705/324-1400

Enforcement & Process Serving, Criminal & Family Matters, Nora MacIsaac

Lindsay: 440 Kent St. West, PO Box 4000, Lindsay ON K9V 5P2 – 705/324-1400 – Manager, Court Services, Nora MacIsaac

Minden: 10 New Castle St., PO Box 270, Minden ON K0M 2K0 – 705/286-6417 – Civil Matters, Nancy Russell

•Regional Municipality of York: Court House, 50 Eagle St. West, Newmarket ON L3Y 6B1 – 905/853-4822

Manager, Court Services, Mary Louise Porcelli

Enforcement & Process Serving, Civil & Family Matters, Mike Terzievski, 905/853-4809

Criminal Matters, Evelyn Thompson, 905/853-4801

Richmond Hill: 855 Major MacKenzie Dr., Richmond Hill ON L4C 4X7 – 905/737-4416 – Small Claims Court, Nicole Cole

### REGIONAL COURT: CENTRAL SOUTH

Areas served: Brant, Haldimand-Norfolk, Hamilton-Wentworth, Niagara (St. Catharines), Niagara (Welland), Waterloo

•Brant County: Court House, 70 Wellington St., Brantford ON N3T 2L9

Manager, Court Services, Cathy Hiuser, 519/752-9069

Enforcement & Process Serving & Civil Matters, Ken Hamilton, 519/752-7828

Brantford: 44 Queen St., Brantford ON N3T 3B2 – 519/758-3460 – Criminal & Family Matters, Ken Hamilton

•Regional Municipality of Haldimand-Norfolk (Cayuga): Court House, 55 Munsee St. North, PO Box 70, Cayuga ON N0A 1E0 – 905/772-3335

Enforcement & Processing Serving & Civil Matters, Sharon Warring

Criminal & Family Matters, Vacant

•Regional Municipality of Haldimand-Norfolk (Simcoe): 530 Queensway West, PO Box 308, Simcoe ON N3Y 4L2 – 519/426-1408

Manager, Court Services, Enforcement & Process Serving & Civil, Criminal & Family Matters, Susan Bridge

•Regional Municipality of Hamilton-Wentworth: Court House, 55 Main St. West, Hamilton ON L8P 1H4

Manager, Court Services, Darlene MacNeil, 905/577-8326

Family Matters, Bernadette Flis, 905/525-1550

Hamilton: 50 Main St. East, Hamilton ON L8N 1E9 – 905/308-7221 – Enforcement & Process Serving, Reno Violin

Local Registrar, Relph Beam-Parker, 905/308-7218

Hamilton: 140 Hunter St., Hamilton ON L8N 4H1 – 905/522-9063 – Small Claims Court, Vacant

Hamilton: 125 Main St. East, Hamilton ON L8N 3Z3 – 905/525-1840 – Criminal Matters, Mary Hudacin

•Regional Municipality of Niagara North (St. Catharines): Court House, 59 Church St., St. Catharines ON L2R 7N8 – 905/988-6200

Manager, Court Services & Criminal Matters, Cathy Hiuser

Enforcement & Process Serving & Family Matters, Ralph Beam-Parker

Bailiff & Small Claims Court, Peter Snyder

Civil Matters, Mary Ellen Hilko

•Regional Municipality of Niagara South (Welland): 3 Cross St., Welland ON L3B 5X6

Criminal Matters & Sheriff, Pam Stringer, 905/732-2493

Family Matters, Connie Novosel, 905/734-7451

Niagara Falls, 4635 Queen St., Niagara Falls ON L2E 2L7

Criminal Matters, Odette Briggs, 905/354-2789

Bailiff & Small Claims Court, Jan Huntington, 905/354-3360

Welland: 102 Main St. East, Welland ON L3B 5R4 – 905/735-0010 – Civil Matters, R. Morin

•Regional Municipality of Waterloo: Court House, 20 Weber St. East, Kitchener ON N2H 1C3

Local Registrar, Enforcement & Process Serving, Larry Ketchmark, 519/741-3203

Cambridge: 89 Main St., Cambridge ON N1R 1W1 – 519/621-9220 – Small Claims Court, Ian Dodgeon

Kitchener: #1000, 200 Frederick St., Kitchener ON N2H 6P1 – 519/741-3396

Manager, Court Services, Bill Hansford

Criminal & Family Matters, Carol Gogos

North Kitchener: #520, 50 Queen St. North, Kitchener ON N2H 6P4 – 519/741-5203 – Small Claims Court, Larry Ketchmark

### REGIONAL COURT: CENTRAL WEST

Areas served: Bruce, Dufferin, Grey, Halton, Peel, Wellington

•Bruce County: Court House, 215 Cayley St., Walkerton ON N0G 2V0

Manager, Court Services, Sheriff, Bailiff & Criminal Matters, Glenna McComb, 519/881-1772

Small Claims Court, David Ellis, 519/881-1772

Local Registrar, Gerald Johnson, 519/881-0211

Family Matters, Nancy Coleman, 519/881-0211

•Dufferin County: Court House, 10 Louisa St., Orangeville ON L9W 3P9

Manager, Court Services, Criminal & Family Matters, Debbie Rogers, 905/941-5802

Local Registrar, Sheriff, Bailiff & Small Claims Court, Thom Collyer, 519/941-9701, 4744

•Grey County: Court House, 595 Ninth Ave. East, Owen Sound ON N4K 3E3

Manager, Court Services, Sharon Vickers, 519/371-2226

Local Registrar & Small Claims Court, Pat Kay, 519/376-3812

Bailiff & Sheriff, Muriel Parkes, 519/376-7535

Owen Sound: 1133 - 2nd Ave. East, Owen Sound ON N4K 2J1 – 519/376-0185 – Enforcement & Process Serving, Criminal & Family Matters, Lynn Kiddle

•Regional Municipality of Halton: Court House, 491 Steeles Ave. East, Milton ON L9T 1Y7 – 905/878-2672
Manager, Court Services, Enforcement & Process Serving, Local Registrar, Family & Criminal Matters, Marion Maslach
Small Claims Court, Fiona MacPherson, 905/878-7281
Burlington: 2021 Plains Rd. East, Burlington ON L7R 4M3 – 905/637-4125 – Small Claims Court, Gloria Owen
Oakville: 1225 Trafalgar Rd., PO Box 84020, Oakville ON L6H 3P1 – 905/842-8380 – Small Claims Court, Clare Patterson
•Regional Municipality of Peel: Court House, 7765 Hurontario St., PO Box 548, Brampton ON L6V 2L1
Manager, Court Services, Lynne Wagner, 905/452-6686
Bailiff & Sheriff, Barbara Turner, 905/452-6600
Brampton: 141 Clarence St., Brampton ON L6W 3E6 – 905/450-4730 – Criminal Matters, Lynne Wagner
Brampton: 7765 Hurontario St., 2nd Fl., PO Box 220, Brampton ON L6V 2L1 – 905/452-6608 – Family Matters, Shan Georgsen
Brampton: 7755 Hurontario St., PO Box 8000, Brampton ON L6V 2M7 – 905/452-6617 – Local Registrar & Small Claims Court, Joyce Lazic
Mississauga: 2301 Haines Rd., Mississauga ON L4Y 1Y5 – 905/275-3080 – Small Claims Court, Joan Zammit
•Wellington County: Court House, 74 Woolwich St., Guelph ON N1H 3T9
Manager, Court Services, Bill Hansford, 519/824-4100
Family & Civil Matters, Norma McDonald, 519/824-4100
Small Claims Court, Bonnie Epoch, 519/824-4169
Guelph: 36 Wyndham St. South, Guelph ON N1G 3T9 – 519/836-2501
Enforcement & Process Serving, Kathleen Cross, 519/824-4430
Criminal Matters, Joanne Riddell, 519/836-2501

**REGIONAL COURT: EAST**

Areas served: Frontenac, Hastings, Lanark, Leeds-Grenville, Lennox-Addington, Ottawa-Carleton, Prescott-Russell, Prince Edward, Renfrew, Stormont-Dundas-Glengarry
•Frontenac County: Court House, 279 Wellington St., Kingston ON K7L 6E1
Manager, Court Services, Vacant, 613/548-6200
Criminal Matters, Arlene Stoness, 613/548-6200
Kingston: Court House, 5 Court St., Kingston ON K7L 2N4 – 613/548-6816
Small Claims Court, Vacant
Local Registrar, Jackie Gumienny
Kingston: 469 Montreal St., Kingston ON K7K 3H9 – 613/548-6789 – Family Matters, Vivianne Carpenter
Sharbot Lake: General Delivery, Sharbot Lake ON K0H 2P0 – 613/279-2537 – Small Claims Court & Bailiff, Donna Ladouceur
•Hastings County: Court House, 235 Pinnacle St., Belleville ON K8N 3A9
Manager, Court Services, Local Registrar, Sheriff & Bailiff, Robert C. Coveney, 613/962-9106, 9694
Small Claims Court, Cyndi Hunt, 613/962-2300
Bancroft: 5 Fairway Blvd., Bancroft ON K0L 1C0 – 613/332-4613 – Small Claims Court, Yvonne Trollope
Belleville: 15 Victoria Ave., Belleville ON K8N 1Z5 – 613/962-3468 – Criminal Matters, Bonnie Gryce
Belleville: #402, Century Pl., PO Box 906, Belleville ON K8N 5B6 – 613/968-6759 – Family Matters, Bonnie Gryce
•Lanark County: Court House, 43 Drummond St. East, Perth ON K7H 1G1 – 613/267-2021
Manager, Court Services, Helen Mick
Local Registrar, Sheriff, Bailiff & Small Claims Court, Vacant
•Leeds & Grenville County: District Court House, PO Box 8, Brockville ON K6V 5T7
Small Claims Court, Jean Jensen, 613/342-2833
Local Registrar & Sheriff, Andrew Gransden, 613/342-2288
Brockville: 75 Water St. West, PO Box 1300, Brockville ON K6V 5Y6 – 613/342-5003 – Criminal & Family Matters, Andrew Gransden
•Lennox & Addington County: 41 Dundas St. West, PO Box 266, Napanee ON K7R 1Z5 – 613/354-3845
Enforcement & Process Serving, Criminal, Family & Civil Matters, Pamela Crockett
Kaladar: Hwy. #7, PO Box 88, Kaladar ON K0H 1Z0 – 613/336-2050 – Small Claims Court & Bailiff, Frances Boomhour
•Regional Municipality of Ottawa-Carleton: Court House, 161 Elgin St., Ottawa ON K2P 2K1
Bailiff, Sheriff, & Criminal Matters, Jackie Henderson, 613/239-1098
Manager, Court Services, Robert St. Clair, 613/239-1490
Local Registrar & Small Claims Court, Joanne Williams, 613/239-1105
Family Matters, Lynda Emerson, 613/239-1034
•Prescott & Russell County: Court House, 59 Court St., L'Orignal ON K0B 1K0 – 613/675-4695
Manager, Court Services, Small Claims Court, Criminal & Family Matters, Liette Giroux
Rockland: 1783 St. Laurent Blvd., PO Box 2, Rockland ON K1K 1C2 – 613/446-5698 – Bailiff, Dennis Houle
•Prince Edward County: Court House, 44 Union St., Picton ON K0K 2T0
Local Registrar & Sheriff, James Bervie, 613/476-6236
Bailiff & Small Claims Court, Donna Stever, 613/476-6236
Criminal & Family Matters, Gloria Stone, 613/476-2606
•Renfrew County: Court House, 297 Pembroke St. East, Pembroke ON K8A 3G2
Local Registrar, Sheriff & Family Matters, Monique Rousseau, 613/732-8581
Small Claims Court, C. Harkins, 613/732-2541
Bailiff, Harry Blackley, 613/732-8581
Pembroke: #415, 417 Pembroke St. West, PO Box 218, Pembroke ON K8A 6X3
Manager, Court Services, Helen Mick, 613/732-8581
Criminal Matters, A.M. Hamilton, 613/735-6886
Renfrew: 315 Raglan St. South, PO Box 386, Renfrew ON K7V 4A6 – 613/432-3193 – Small Claims Court, Joanne O'Gorman
•Stormont, Dundas & Glengarry County: Court House, 340 Pitt St., 4th Fl., PO Box 56, Cornwall ON K6H 5R9 – 613/933-7500
Manager, Court Services, Diane Brunet-Mongeon
Small Claims Court, M. McMartin
Criminal Matters, Lyse Pichie
Family Matters, Diane Plamondon
Local Registrar, Beverly Roy
Enforcement & Process Serving, Anne Senecal
Alexandria: 110 Main St. North, PO Box 699, Alexandria ON K0C 1A0
Criminal Matters, Gabrielle Blais, 613/525-4330
Small Claims Court, J. Wensink, 613/525-1057
Morrisburg: Shopping Mall, Hwy. #2 & #31, Morrisburg ON K0C 1X0 – 613/543-2193 – Small Claims Court & Criminal Matters, Monique LeFebvre

**REGIONAL COURT: NORTHEAST REGION**

Areas served: Algoma, Cochrane, Manitoulin, Nipissing, Parry Sound, Sudbury, Timiskaming
•Algoma District: Court House, 426 Queen St. East, Sault Ste. Marie ON P6A 1Z7
Manager, Court Services, Small Claims Court, Sheriff & Bailiff, Lesley Benderavage, 705/759-9450
Criminal Matters, Anna Callon, 705/759-9466
Local Registrar & Family Matters, Lonnie Ostroski, 705/759-9418
Elliott Lake: Provincial Division: 200 Ontario St., Elliott Lake ON P5A 1Y4 – 705/848-2500 – Small Claims Court, Bailiff, Criminal & Family Matters, Louise Greco
•Cochrane District: Court House, 149 - 4 Ave., PO Box 2069, Cochrane ON P0L 1C0 – 705/272-4256
Manager, Court Services, Paul Langlois
Criminial & Family Matters, Lise Kosloski
Enforcement & Process Serving & Civil Matters, Chris Robin
Iroquois Falls: 885 Centennial St., PO Box 874, Iroquois Falls ON P0K 1G0 – 705/232-7744 – Small Claims Court & Bailiff, Adrien Cyr
Kapuskasing: Ontario Government Bldg., RR#2, Hwy. 11 West, Kapuskasing ON P5N 2X8 – 705/337-1477 – Small Claims Court, Lorese Lauzon
Timmins: #127, 38 Pine St., Timmins ON P4N 6K6 – 705/267-7799
Bailiff, Edward Colbert
Criminal & Family Matters, Theresa Miller
•Manitoulin District: Court House, 27 Phipps St., PO Box 265, Gore Bay ON P0P 1H0
Local Registrar, Sheriff, Bailiff & Small Claims Court, Ron Lane, 705/282-2461
Criminal & Family Matters, Sharon Sloss, 705/282-2531
Little Current: 15 Robinson St., PO Box 358, Little Current ON P0P 1K0 – 705/368-2205 – Small Claims Court, Mary McHarg
•Nipissing District: Court House, 360 Plouffe St., North Bay ON P1B 9L5 – 705/495-8309
Manager, Court Services, Small Claims Court & Criminal Matters, Nestor Prisco
Bailiff, Bob Raycraft
Sturgeon Falls: 229 Main St., PO Box 416, Sturgeon Falls ON P0H 2G0 – 705/753-1090 – Small Claims Court & Bailiff, Marlene Bertrand
•Parry Sound District: Court House, 89 James St., Parry Sound ON P2A 1T7
Manager, Court Services, Nestor Prisco, 705/746-1414
Criminal & Family Matters, Marilyn Helmkay, 705/746-4237
Bailiff, Local Registrar, Sheriff & Small Claims Court, Michael Ryman, 705/746-4251
Burks Falls: PO Box 119, Burks Falls ON P0A 1C0 – 705/382-2571 – Small Claims Court & Bailiff, Vacant
•Sudbury District: Court House, 155 Elm St. West, Sudbury ON P3C 1T9
Manager, Court Services & Criminal Matters, David Lafreniere, 705/671-5923
Local Registrar, Doug Seaton, 705/671-5958
Espanola: #3, 100 Tudhope St., Espanola ON P5E 1S6 – 705/869-4334 – Small Claims Court, Criminal & Family Matters, Linda Fuller
Sudbury: 38 Larch St., Sudbury ON P3E 5M7 – 705/675-4164 – Bailiff, Vacant
Sudbury: 159 Cedar St., 2nd Fl., Sudbury ON P3E 6A5
Small Claims Court, Ruth-Anne Ingram, 705/670-7251
Family Matters, Vacant, 705/670-7250
•Timiskaming District: Court House, 393 Main St., PO Box 609, Haileybury ON P0J 1K0
Local Registrar, Susan Rennie, 705/672-3321
Enforcement & Process Serving & Civil Matters, Carmen MacKewn
Criminal & Family Matters, Nancy Young, 705/672-3395

Englehart: 50 Third St., PO Box 147, Englehart ON P0J 1H0 – 705/544-8177 – Small Claims Court, Patricia Ann Proctor
Kirkland Lake: 4 Kirkland St. West, Kirkland Lake ON P2N 2G2
Small Claims Court, Wendy Lee Rogoza, 705/567-9381
Family Matters, Lina Chartrand-Carriere

**REGIONAL COURT: NORTHWEST REGION**

Areas served: Kenora, Rainy River, Thunder Bay

•Kenora District: Court House, 216 Water St., Kenora ON P9N 1S4 – 807/468-2842
Local Registrar, Sheriff, Bailiff & Small Claims Court, Vacant
Criminal & Family Matters, Susan Newton
Dryden: #127, 479 Government St., PO Box 636, Dryden ON P8N 3B3
Criminal & Family Matters, Adrianne Ridgeway, 807/223-2348
Bailiff & Small Claims Court, Florence Smith, 807/223-2613
Red Lake: Ontario Government Bldg., Howey St., PO Box 1070, Red Lake ON P0V 2M0
Bailiff & Small Claims Court, Judy Jeffrey, 807/727-3310
Criminal & Family Matters, Norma Ewen, 807/727-2376

•Rainy River District: Court House, 333 Church St., Fort Frances ON P9A 1C9 – 807/274-5961
Local Registrar, Sheriff, Bailiff, Small Claims Court, Criminal & Family Matters, John E. Bradley

•Thunder Bay District: Court House, 277 Camelot St., Thunder Bay ON P7A 4B3
Manager, Court Services, Bob Gordon, 807/343-2747
Local Registrar, Sheriff, Bailiff & Small Claims Court, Alvin Franks, 807/343-2728, 2725
Criminal & Family Matters, Bruce McLean, 807/625-1600, 1610
Geraldton: 624 Main St., PO Box 39, Geraldton ON P0T 1M0 – 807/854-1488 – Small Claims Court & Bailiff, Laurette Payeur
Nipigon: 10 Front St., Nipigon ON P0T 2J0 – 807/887-3829 – Small Claims Court & Bailiff, Edna Aubut
Schreiber: 223 Walker Lake Dr., PO Box 248, Schreiber ON P0T 2S0 – 807/824-2543 – Bailiff, Keith Scott

**REGIONAL COURT: SOUTHWEST**

Areas served: Elgin, Essex, Huron, Kent, Lambton, Middlesex, Oxford, Perth

•Elgin County: Justice Bldg., 145 Curtis St., St. Thomas ON N5P 3Z7
Manager, Court Services, Sheriff & Small Claims Court, Gordon Button, 519/631-3530
Local Registrar & Family Matters, Karen Moule, 519/633-1720
Criminal Matters, Anne Patton, 519/633-1230

•Essex County: Court House, 245 Windsor Ave., Windsor ON N9A 1J2
Manager, Court Services, Vacant, 519/973-6604
Local Registrar, Donna Downes, 519/973-6620
Small Claims Court, Marie-Anne Kelly-Lalonde, 519/973-6665
Leamington: #303C, 33 Princess St., Leamington ON N8H 5C5 – 519/326-9854 – Small Claims Court, Pat Mailing
Windsor: Provincial Court, City Hall Sq., PO Box 607, Windsor ON N9A 6N4
Small Claims Court, Marie-Anne Kelly, 519/973-6665
Criminal Matters, Mara Conrad, 519/254-2591
Windsor: Ontario Government Bldg., 250 Windsor Ave., 4th Fl., Windsor ON N9A 6V9
Bailiff & Sheriff, Judy Harris, 519/973-6603
Family Matters, Linda Peltier, 519/973-6669

•Huron County: Court House, 1 Court House Sq., PO Box 400, Goderich ON N7A 1M2
Manager, Court Services, Bailiff, Local Registrar, Sheriff & Small Claims Court, Gord Button, 519/524-7322, 2519
Criminal & Family Matters, Linda McIvor, 519/524-9342

•Kent County: Court House, 21 - 7th St., PO Box 2021, Chatham ON N7M 5L9 – 519/352-9070
Local Registrar, Bailiff, Sheriff, Small Claims Court/Criminal & Family Matters, Shaun Joy

•Lambton County: Court House, 700 North Christina St., PO Box 2587, Sarnia ON N7V 3C2
Manager, Court Services & Small Claims Court, Vacant, 519/337-5314
Local Registrar, Pat Wemple, 519/337-5314
Bailiff, Jim Lowry, 519/337-7964
Sheriff, Kim Policelli, 519/337-8940
Criminal Matters, Marie Burns, 519/336-8830
Family Matters, Carol McKerracher, 519/337-2346

•Middlesex County: Court House, Unit A, 80 Dundas St., Ground Fl., London ON N6A 6A3
Manager, Court Services, Ron Marks, 519/660-3049
Local Registrar, Provincial Division, Criminal & Civil Matters, Connie Holmes, 519/660-3054
Enforcement & Process Serving, Pam Johnson, 519/660-3004
Small Claims Court, Fran Martellotti, 519/660-3000
Strathroy: 52 Frank St., Strathroy ON N7G 2R4 – 519/245-1477 – Small Claims Court & Bailiff, Dean Dolbear

•Oxford County: Court House, 415 Hunter Rd., PO Box 70, Woodstock ON N4S 7W5 – 519/539-6187
Manager, Court Services, Local Registrar, Sheriff, Bailiff, Small Claims Court, Criminal & Family Matters, Virginia Taylor

•Perth County: Administration of Justice Bldg., 100 St. Patrick St., PO Box 1010, Stratford ON N5A 6W4 – 519/271-9252
Manager, Court Services, Virginia Taylor
Criminal & Family Matters, Shirley Creek
Stratford: 17 George St., Stratford ON N5A 1A6 – 519/271-1850 – Small Claims Court, Local Registrar, Sheriff & Bailiff, Don Misener

**REGIONAL COURT: METROPOLITAN TORONTO**

Areas served: Toronto, Metro North (North York), Metro East (Scarborough), Metro West (Etobicoke)

•Etobicoke District: 80 The East Mall, Etobicoke ON M8Z 5X6 – 416/314-3967
Criminal & Family Matters, Kapeel Karandat
Manager, Court Services, Lynn Norris
Toronto: #209, 2265 Keele St., Toronto ON M6M 5B8 – 416/326-6707 – Small Claims Court, Nora Gauer

•York District: 47 Sheppard Ave. East, 3rd Fl., North York ON M2N 5N1
Small Claims Court, Vacant, 416/326-3554
Family Matters, Carmen Carnovale, 416/326-3568
Family Matters, Gemma Castellino, 416/326-3592
Downsview: 1000 Finch Ave. West, North York ON M3J 2V5 – 416/314-4208
Criminal Matters, Rosa Martelli
Scarborough: 1911 Eglinton Ave. East, Scarborough ON M1L 4P4
Manager, Court Services, Sylvia Orgias, 416/325-0357
Sheriff, Vacant, 416/327-6326
Criminal & Family Matters, Micheline Seguin, 416/325-0974
Scarborough: #300, 2130 Lawrence Ave. East, Scarborough ON M1R 5B9 – 416/327-1155 – Small Claims Court. Carol Gottschalk
Toronto: Court House, 361 University Ave., Toronto ON M5G 1T3
Sheriff, Vacant, 416/327-6326
Toronto: Court House, 60 Queen St. West, Toronto ON M5H 2M4
Manager, Court Services, Lou Bartuci, 416/327-5896
Criminal Matters, Felicity Leader, 416/327-5830
Toronto: 311 Jarvis St., Toronto ON M5B 2C4 – 416/963-0677
Manager, Family Court, Hazel Davis
Manager, Family Court, Val Fillippilli
Toronto: 444 Yonge St., 2nd Fl., Toronto ON M5B 2H4 – 416/325-8925 – Small Claims Court & Criminal Matters, Graham Borton
Toronto: #174, 130 Queen St. West, Toronto ON M5H 2N5 – 416/327-5036 – Local Registrar, General Division, Mary Dayton
Toronto: 311 Jarvis St., Toronto ON M5B 2C4 – 416/327-6853 – Family Matters, Jennifer Kerr
Toronto: 439 University Ave., 3rd Fl., Toronto ON M5H 1Y8 – 416/326-2940 – Estates, Joel Persaud
Toronto: #127, 145 Queen St. West, Toronto ON M5H 2N9 – 416/327-6935 – Local Registrar, Marie Singh
Toronto: 393 University Ave., 10th Fl., Toronto ON M5G 1E6 – 416/327-5545 – Manager, Court Services, Pauline Avgeropoulus

## PRINCE EDWARD ISLAND

### PRINCE EDWARD ISLAND SUPREME COURT

Sir Louis Henry Davies Law Courts Bldg., 42 Water St., PO Box 2000, Charlottetown PE C1A 7N8
**Chief Justice,** The Hon. Norman H. Carruthers

### SUPREME COURT: COURT OF APPEAL

Sir Louis Henry Davies Law Courts Bldg., 42 Water St., PO Box 2000, Charlottetown PE C1A 7N8

The Court of Appeal has appellate jurisdiction in criminal and civil matters.

**Chief Justice,** The Hon. Mr. Norman H. Carruthers
Judges (The Hon. Mr./Madam Justice): John McQuaid; Gerard E. Mitchell
Deputy Registrar, Appeal Division, Gloria Panting

### SUPREME COURT: TRIAL DIVISION

Sir Louis Davies Law Courts Bldg., 42 Water St., PO Box 2000, Charlottetown PE C1A 7N8

The Supreme Court is a Court of original jurisdiction and has jurisdiction in all civil (including family, estate and small claims) and criminal matters arising in Prince Edward Island.

**Chief Justice,** The Hon. Mr. Kenneth R. MacDonald
Justices (The Hon. Mr./Madam Justice):
J. Armand Desroches; David Jenkins; Jacquiline Matheson
Registrar, Bankruptcy, George E. MacMillan, 902/368-6025
Deputy Registrar, Estates Section, Gloria Panting
Deputy Registrar, General Section, Marjorie MacDonald
Deputy Registrar, Small Claims Section, Elva Costello
Deputy Registrar, Family Section, Anne Clough

### PRINCE EDWARD ISLAND PROVINCIAL COURT

The Provincial Court has jurisdiction in select criminal matters as well as youth matters.

•Prince County: Provincial Court, Law Courts Bldg., PO Box 2020, Summerside PE C1N 4M1
**Chief Judge,** The Hon. Ralph C. Thompson

•Queens & Kings Counties: Provincial Court, Law Courts Bldg., PO Box 2290, Charlottetown PE C1A 8C1
Judges (The Hon.):
G.L. Fitzgerald; Nancy K. Orr; John R. Douglas

### JUDICIAL OFFICERS

Kings County: Judicial Officers, Court House, Georgetown PE C0A 1L0

Sheriff, Howard Kerwin, 902/652-2215
Deputy Registrar, Shirley Clory, 902/652-8940
Registrar of Deeds, Charlottetown, Kathy Toole, 902/368-4591
Prince County: Judicial Officers, Court House, PO Box 2020, Summerside PE C1N 4M1
Sheriff, Ron Dowline, 902/888-8191
Deputy Registrar, Wayne Lilly, 902/888-8190
Registrar of Deeds, Eileen Gaudet
Queens County: Judicial Officers, Law Courts, PO Box 2000, Charlottetown PE C1A 7N8
Chief Sheriff, Frank Driscoll, 902/368-6055
Prothonotary, G.E. MacMillan
Registrar of Deeds, Kathy Toole, 902/368-4591
Registrar of Supreme Court & Chief Provincial Court Clerk, Dorothy Kitson, 902/368-6005

## QUÉBEC

### QUÉBEC: COUR D'APPEL

The Court of Appeal has appellate jurisdiction in all civil and criminal matters.
Montréal: Cour d'Appel, 1, rue Notre-Dame est, Montréal QC H2Y 1B6
**Juge en chef,** L'Honorable Pierre Michaud
Juges (Les Honorables):
Jean Louis Baudouin; Marc Beauregard; André Brossard; Jacques Chamberland; Marie Deschamps; Morris J. Fish; André Forget; Louise Mailhot; Joseph R. Nuss; Michel Proulx; Michel J. Robert; Melvin L. Rothman (surnum.); Claude Vallerand
•Québec: Cour d'Appel, 300, boul Jean-Lesage, Québec QC G1K 8K6
Juges (Les Honorables):
Roger Chouinard (surnum.); Jacques Deslile; René Dussault; Paul-Arthur Gendreau; Louis Le Bel; Louise Otis; Thérèse Rousseau-Houle; Christine Tourigny

### QUÉBEC: COUR SUPÉRIEURE

300, boul Jean-Lesage, Québec QC G1K 8K6
418/649-3501
The Superior Court has original jurisdiction in all civil and criminal matters arising in Québec, unless otherwise indicated by statute. Judges of the Superior Court have jurisdiction in Bankruptcy.
**Juge en chef,** L'Honorable Lyse Lemieux (Montréal)
Juge en Chef associé, L'Honorable René W. Dionne
Juge en Chef adjoint, Hon. André Deslonchamps (Montréal)
Juges (Les Honorables):
Yves Alain; Jules Allard; Frank Barakett; Jean-Claude Beaulieu; Bruno Bernard; Jacques Blanchard; Danielle Blondin-Gingras; Gérald Boisvert; Armand Carrier; Louis De Blois; Gaston Desjardins; André Desmeules; Jacques Dufour (surnum.); Julie Dutil; André Gervais; Ross Goodwinn; Henri Larue (surnum.); Gérard Lebel; Jean Lemelin; Robert Lesage; René Letarte (surnum.); Édouard Martin; Benoît Morin; Gaétan Pelletier; Jacques Philippon (surnum.); Jean Richard; Claude Rioux (surnum.); Louis Rochette; France Thibault; François Tremblay; André Trottier (surnum.); Paul Vézina, Hubert Walters
Registraire de Faillite, Rm. #1.32, 418/649-3505
•Abitibi:
Juges (Les Honorables):
Laurent Guertin; Ivan St-Julien; Jacques Vien
Registraire de Faillite, 900, 7e rue, Val-d'Or QC J9P 3P8 – 819/825-8571
•Alma: Cour Supérieure, 725, boul Harvey ouest, Alma QC G8B 1P5
Juges (Les Honorables):
Gratien Duchesne
Registraire de Faillite, #31, 418/668-3334
•Amos: Cour Supérieure, 891, rue 3e ouest, Amos QC J9T 2T4
Registraire de Faillite, 418/732-6577
•Arthabaska: Registraire de Faillite, 800, boul Bois-Francs sud, Arthabaska QC G6P 5W5 – 819/357-2054
Registraires, Denis Noël, Nicole Simoneau
•Baie-Comeau: Cour Supérieure, Palais de Justice, 71, rue Mance, Baie-Comeau QC G4C 1N2
Juges (Les Honorables):
Paul A. Corriveau
Registraire de Faillite, 418/296-5534
•Beauce: Registraire de Faillite, 795, av du Palais, CP 820, St-Joseph-de-Beauce QC G0S 2V0 – 418/397-7188
•Beauharnois: Registraire de Faillite, 180, rue Salaberry, Valleyfield QC J6T 2J2 – 514/370-4006
•Bedford:
Juges (Les Honorables):
Paul-Marcel Bellavance; Pierre Boily; Louis-Philippe Galipeau (surnum.); Suzanne Mireault
Registraire de Faillite, 920 rue Principale, Cowansville QC J2K 1K2
•Bonaventure:
Juges (Les Honorables):
Jean-Roch Landry (also New Carlisle)
Registraire de Faillite, 87, rue Principale, CP 517, New Carlisle QC G0C 1Z0 – 418/752-3376
•Chicoutimi: Cour Supérieure, 227, rue Racine est, Chicoutimi QC G7H 1S2 – 418/696-9944
Juges (Les Honorables):
Jacques Babin; J. Roger Bandford; Pierre Bergeron (surnum.); Claude Larouche
Registraire de Faillite, 418/698-3558
•Drummondville: Registraire de Faillite, 1680, boul St-Joseph, Drummondville QC J2C 2G3 – 819/478-2513
•Frontenac: Registraire de Faillite, 693, rue St-Alphonse ouest, CP 579, Thetford Mines QC G6G 3X3 – 418/338-2118
•Gaspé: Registraire de Faillite, Palais de Justice, 124, rte 132, CP 188, Percé QC G0C 2L0 – 418/782-2055
•Granby: Registraire de Faillite, 77, rue Principale, Granby QC J2G 9B3 – 514/263-3520
•Hull: Cour Supérieure, 17, rue Laurier, Hull QC J8X 4C1
Juges (Les Honorables):
Jean R. Dagenais (also Labelle, Pontiac); Orville Frenette (surnum.) (also Labelle, Pontiac); Louis-Philippe Landry (also Labelle, Pontiac); Charles B. Major (surnum.); Jean-Pierre Plouffe; Johanne Trudel (also Labelle, Pontiac)
Registraire de Faillite, #0.210, 819/776-8100, poste 8323
•Iberville: Registraire de Faillite, 109, rue St-Charles, Saint-Jean-sur-Richelieu QC J3B 2C2 – 514/347-3715
•Joliette: Registraire de Faillite, 200, rue St-Marc, Joliette QC J6E 8C2 – 514/753-4807
•Kamouraska: Registraire de Faillite, 33, rue de la Cour, Rivière-du-Loup QC G5R 1J1 – 418/862-3579
•Laval: Cour Supérieure, 2800, boul Saint-Martin ouest, Laval QC H7T 2S9
Juges (Les Honorables):
Jean Filiatreault; Yvan A. Macerola; Paul Trudeau
•Mingan:
Juges (Les Honorables):
Paul A. Corriveau
Registraire de Faillite, 425, boul Laure, Sept-Îles QC G4R 1X6 – 418/962-2154
•Montréal: Cour Supérieure, 1, rue Notre-Dame est, Montréal QC H2Y 1B6 – 514/873-3227
Juges (Les Honorables): Jean Archambault; Guy Arsenault; Georges Audet; Roger Baker; Alphonse Barbeau (surnum.); Marc Beaudoin, François Bélanger; Pierre Béliveau; Nicole Bénard; Claude Benoit (surnum.); Anthime Bergeron (surnum.); Rodolphe Bilodeau; André G. Biron (surnum.); John Bishop; Yvan Bisaillon (surnum.); John Bishop; Jules Blanchet (surnum.); Jean-Guy Boilard; Sylvianne Borenstein; Pierre Boudreault; Paul P. Carrière; Jean-Jude Chabot; Paul Chaput; Vital Cliche (surnum.); Lise Côté; Michel Coté; Jean Crépeau; J.F. Louis Crête; Jean-Jacques Crôteau; Pierre J. Dalphond; Wilbrod Décarie; André Denis; André Deslongchamps (Juge en chef adjoint); Kevin Downs; Roland Durand; Denis Durocher; Nicole Duval-Hesler; Robert T. Flahiff; Bernard Flynn (surnum.); Jean Frappier; John H. Gomery; Benjamin J. Greenberg; Danielle Grenier; Claude Guérin (surnum.); Jean Guibault; Derek A. Guthrie; Irving J. Halperin; Gilles Hébert; René Hurtubise; Pierre Jasmin; Paul Jolin; Claire Barrette Joncas; Pierre Journet; Carole Julien; James T. Kennedy; Marie-Christine Laberge; Maurice E. Lagacé; Claude Larouche; Hélène Lebel; Jean Legault; Jean Louis Leger; Louise Lemelin; Anatole Lesyk (surnum.); Denis Lévesque (surnum.); Diane Marcelin-Laurin; Jean Marquis (surnum.); Fraser J. Martin; Herbert Marx; Israël S. Mass; Yves Mayrand; Victor Melançon; Gilles Mercure; Perry Meyer (surnum.); Nicole Morneau; Jean-Claude Nolin (surnum.); Jean-L. Normand; Luc Parent (surnum.); Réjean F. Paul; Ginette Piché; Pierre Pinard; Pierrette Rayle; Danielle Richer; André Rochon; François Rolland; Gontran Rouleau; Jeannine M. Rousseau; Gérald-J. Ryan (surnum.); Jean-Piere Sénécal; Pierrette Sévigny-McConomy; Lou S. Tannenbaum; Claude Tellier; Pierre Tessier; Daniel H. Tingley; Anne-Marie Trahan; Roland Tremblay; Clement Trudel; Gérard Turmel (surnum.); Jacques Vaillancourt; Jocelyn Verrier; Pierre Viau; Dionysia Zerbisias; Jack J. Zigman
Longueuil: Jean-Guy Dubois; Bernard Gratton (surnum.); Paul Reeves (surnum.)
Registraire de Faillite, #1.195, 514/393-2058
•Richelieu: Registraire de Faillite, 46, rue Charlotte, Sorel QC J3P 6N5 – 514/742-2786
•Rimouski: Cour Supérieure, 183, av de la Cathédrale, CP 800, Rimouski QC G5L 7C9
Juges (Les Honorables):
Gilles Blanchet; Robert Pidgeon
Registraire de Faillite, 418/722-3833
•Roberval: Registraire de Faillite, 750, boul Saint-Joseph, Roberval QC G8H 2L5 – 418/275-3666
•Rouyn: Cour Supérieure, 2, av du Palais, Rouyn QC J9X 2N9
Juges (Les Honorables):
Laurent Guertin (also Témiscamingue); Ivan St-Julien; Jacques Viens
Registraire de Faillite, Rouyn-Noranda & Témiscamingue, 819/764-6709
•St-François:
Juges (Les Honorables):
Paul-Marcel Bellavance; Pierre Boily; Léo Daigle (also Mégantic); Pierre C. Fournier (also Mégantic); Raynald Fréchette; Louis-Philippe Galipeau; Suzanne Mireault; Jean-Louis Peloquin (surnum.); Georges Savoie (surnum.); Thomas Toth (surnum.)
Registraire de Faillite, 375, rue King ouest, Sherbrooke QC J1H 6B9 – 819/822-6902
•St-Hyacinthe: Registraire de Faillite, 1550, rue Dessaules, St-Hyacinthe QC J2S 2S8 – 514/778-6559
•St-Maurice:
Juges (Les Honorables):
Raymond W. Pronovost
Registraire de Faillite, 212, rue 6e, Shawinigan QC G9N 8B6 – 819/536-2571
•Shawinigan: Cour Supérieure, 212, rue 6e, Shawinigan QC G1K 8B6

•Sherbrooke: Cour Supérieure, 375, rue King ouest, Sherbrooke QC J1H 6B9
Juges (Les Honorables):
Suzanne Mireault
•Terrebonne: Registraire de Faillite, 400, rue Laviolette, St-Jerôme QC J7Y 2T6 – 514/431-4412
•Trois-Rivières: Cour Supérieure, 250, rue Laviolette, Trois-Rivières QC G9A 1T9
Juges (Les Honorables):
Yvan Godin; Guy Lebrun (surnum.); Robert Legris; Jacques J. Levesque
Registraire de Faillite, 819/372-4150
•Val-d'Or: Cour Supérieure, 900, rue 7e, Val-d'Or QC J9P 4P8

## QUÉBEC: COUR DU QUÉBEC

The Québec Court has jurisdiction in select civil, criminal and penal matters as well as youth, expropriation, small claims and provincial tax matters.

**Juge en chef,** L'Honorable Louis Morin, Québec (Chambre civile/Civil Division)
**Juge en chef**, L'Honorable Huguette St-Louis, Québec (Chambre civile/Civil Division)
Juge en chef adjoint, L'Honorable Jacques Lachapelle, Montréal (Chambre civile/Civil Division)
Juge en chef adjoint, L'Honorable Bernard Lesage (Chambre civile/Civil Division)
Juge en chef adjoint, L'Honorable Louise Provost, Montréal (Chambre criminelle et pénale/Criminal & Penal Division)
Juge en chef adjoint, L'Honorable Michel Jasmin, Montréal (Chambre de la Jeunesse/Youth Division)
Juge en chef associé, L'Honorable Rémi Bouchard, Québec (Chambre criminelle et pénale/Criminal & Penal Division)
• Québec: 300, boul Jean Lesage, Québec QC G1R 8K6
39, rue St-Louis, Québec QC G1R 3Z2
Juges (Les Honorables):
Chambre Civile: Jean Alarie; Richard Beaulieu; Gilles Bergeron; Lina Bond; Gérald Bossé; Raymond Boucher; André C. Cartier; Pierre Choquette; André Cloutier; Louis-Charles Fournier; Bertrand Gagnon; G. André Gobeil; François Godbout; Anne Laberge; Guy Lambert; Daniel Lavoie; André Marceau; Yvon Mercier; Michael Sheehan; Michel Simard; Michel St-Hilaire; Louis Vézina; Pierre Verdon
39, rue St-Louis, Québec QC G1R 3Z2: Gilles Plante, Paul Yergeau
Chambre Criminelle et Pénale: Michel Babin; Gilles Bergeron; André Bilodeau; Louis Carrier; René De La Sablonnière; Jean-François Dionne; Jean Drouin; Laurent Dubé; Marc Dufour; Jean Dutil; Gilles Garneau; Guy Lambert; Roch Lefrançois; Alain Morand; André Plante; Narcisse Proulx; Pierre-L. Rousseau; Carole St-Cyr
Chambre de la Jeunesse: Andreé Bergeron; Claude C. Boulanger; Louise Galipeault-Moisan; Paule Gaumont; Daniel Lavoie; Lucie Rondeau; André Sirois; Alain Turgeon
•Alma: Cour du Québec, 725, rue Harvey ouest, Alma QC G8B 1P5
Juges (Les Honorables):
Chambre Civile: Maurice Abud
•Amos: Cour du Québec, 891, av 3e ouest, Amos QC J9T 2T4
Juges (Les Honorables):
Chambre Civile, Chambre Criminelle et Pénale: Normand Bonin; Guy Gagnon
•Arthabaska: Cour du Québec, 800, boul Bois-Francs sud, Arthabaska QC G6P 5W5
Juges (Les Honorables):
Chambre Civile: Claude Pinard
•Baie Comeau: Cour du Québec, 71, av Mance, Baie Comeau QC G4Z 1N2
Juges (Les Honorables):
Chambre Civile: Sarto Cloutier
Chambre de la Jeunesse: Claude Tremblay
•Chicoutimi: Cour du Québec, 227, rue Racine est, Chicoutimi QC G7H 1S2
Juges (Les Honorables):
Chambre Civile: Jean-Paul Aubin; Micheline Paradis; Jean Simard; Guy Tremblay; Lucien Tremblay; Jean-Yves Tremblay
Chambre de la Jeunesse: Paul Casgrain; Bernard Gagnon; Micheline Paradis
•Drummondville: Cour du Québec, 1680, boul St-Joseph, Drummondville QC J2C 2G3
Juges (Les Honorables):
Chambre Civile: Gilles Gagnon
• Gaspé: 11, rue de la Cathédrale, CP 1096, G0C 1R0
Juges (Les Honorables):
Chambre Civile, Chambre Criminelle et Pénale; Embert Whittom
•Granby: Cour du Québec, 77, rue Principale, Granby QC J2G 9B3
Juges (Les Honorables):
Chambre Civile: Donald Bissonnette
Chambre Criminelle et Pénale: Pierre Bachand; Donald Bissonnette; Michel Duchesne
Chambre de la Jeunesse: Gilles Therriault
•Hull: Cour du Québec, 17, rue Laurier, Hull QC J8X 4C1
Juges (Les Honorables):
Chambre Civile: Jules Barrière; Bernard Dagenais; Nicole Gibeault; Jean-François Gosselin; Réal Lapointe; Raymond Séguin
Chambre Criminelle et Pénale: Pierre Chevalier; Nicole Gibeault; Jean-François Gosselin; Réal R. Lapointe; Raymond Séguin; Louise Turpin
Chambre de la Jeunesse: Jean-François Gosselin; Réal Lapointe; Michel Séguin; Raymond Séguin; Louise Turpin
•Joliette: Cour du Québec, 200, rue St-Marc, Joliette QC J6E 8C2
Juges (Les Honorables):
Chambre Civile: Monique Sylvestre; Louis Vaillancourt
Chambre Criminelle et Pénale: Lise Gaboury; L. Michel Hétu; François Landry; Maurice Parent; Céline Pelletier; Marc Vanasse
Chambre de la Jeunesse: Lise Gaboury; Paul Grégoire
•Laval: Cour du Québec, #1.03, 2800, boul Saint-Martin ouest, Laval QC H7T 2S9
Juges (Les Honorables):
Chambre Civile: Micheline Sasseville
Chambre Criminelle et Pénale: Michel Duceppe; Micheline Dufour; Claude Melançon
Chambre de la Jeunesse: Normand Lafond; Jacques Lamarche; Claude Melançon
•Longueuil: Cour du Québec, 1111, boul Jacques-Cartier est, Longueuil QC J4M 2J6
Juges (Les Honorables):
Chambre Civile: Jean-Pierre Bourduas; Claude H. Chicoine; Micheline Laliberté; Michel Lassonde
Chambre Criminelle et Pénale: Denis Bouchard; Robert Lafontaine; Yves Lagacé; Ellen Paré; Claude Provost; Gérard Rouleau; Lucien Roy; Richard Therrien
Chambre de la Jeunesse: Mireille Allaire; Claude Crete; Pierre-G. Dorion; Jean-Pierre Saintonge
•Matane: Cour du Québec, 382, av St-Jérôme, Matane QC G4W 3B3
Juges (Les Honorables):
Chambre Civile: Marc Gagnon
•Montmagny: Cour du Québec, 25, rue du Palais, Montmagny QC G5V 1P6
•Montréal: Cour du Québec, 1, rue Notre-Dame est, Montréal QC H2Y 1B6
Chambre de la Jeunesse: 410, rue Bellechasse est, Montréal QC H2S 1X3
Juges (Les Honorables):
Chambre Civile: Armando Aznar; Raol Barbe; René Beaulac; Jacques Biron; Guy Boissonneault; Serge Boisvert; Simon Brossard; Denis Charette; Brigitte Charron; Lucien Dansereau; Antonio De Michèle; Michel Desmarais; Jacques Desormeau; Jean Dionne; Michel Duchesne; Claude-René Dumais; Pierre Durand; François Michel Gagnon; Brigitte Gouin; Luc Grammond; Gilson Lachance; Paule Lafontaine; Jean-Louis Lamoureux; Gérald Locas; Jean-Pierre Lortie; Paul Mailloux; Eliana Marengo; Huguette Marleau; Yvan Mayrand; Yves Morier; Léon Nichols; Michèle Pauzé; Gilles Poirier; Claude Pothier; André Quesnel; Louis Rémillard; André Renaud; Michèle Rivet; René Roy; Bernard Tellier; Gilles Trudel; Claude Vaillancourt; Pierre M. Verdy; Clermont Vermette
Chambre Criminelle et Pénale: John D'Arcy Asselin; Bernard Bilodeau; Jean-Pierre Bonin; Pierre Brassard; Gilles Cadieux; Micheline Corbeil-Laramée; Suzanne Coupal; Rosaire Desbiens; François Doyon; Monique P. Dubreuil; André Duranleau; Jean B. Falardeau; Gérard Girouard; Bernard Grenier; Joël L. Guberman; Maurice Johnson; Claude Joncas; Céline Lacerte-Lamontagne; Lorraine Laporte-Landry; Louis-A. Legault; Jean Longtin; Rolande Matte; Claude Millette; Gilbert Moirier; Yves Morier; Claude Parent; Maximilien Polak; Lucien Roy; Robert Sansfaçon; Jean Sirois; J. Roch St-Germain; Joseph Tarasofsky; Luc Trudel; Roger Vincent
Chambre de la Jeunesse: Gérard Beaudry; Nicole Bernier; Omer Boudreau; Jean-Paul Braun; Barrie H. Brown; Henri Choinière; Oscar D'Amours; Élaine Demers-Nadeau; Ginette Durand-Brault; Françoise Garneau-Fournier; François Godbout; Lucie Godin; Albert Gobeil; Isabelle Lafontaine; Guy Lévesque; Gilles L. Ouellet; Jacques R. Roy; Robert Sacchitelle; André Saint-Cyr; Gaetan Zonato
•Montréal: Cour du Québec (Chambre Civile), 255, boul Crémazie est, Montréal QC H2M 1L5
Juges (Les Honorables):
Chambre Civile: Marc Brière; Robert Burns; Lise Langlois; Louise Ménard; Bernard Prudhomme; Claude Saint-Arnaud
•New Carlisle: Cour du Québec, CP 84, New Carlisle QC G0C 1Z0
Chambre Criminelle et Pénale, Chambre de la Jeunesse: 87, rue Principale, CP 517, New Carlisle QC G0C 1Z0
Juges (Les Honorables):
Chambre Civile: Jean Bécu
Chambre Criminelle et Pénale: Robert Lévesque
Chambre de la Jeunesse: Robert Lévesque
•Percé: Cour du Québec, 124, rte 132, CP 188, Percé QC G0C 2L0
Juges (Les Honorables):
Chambre Civile; Chambre Criminelle et Pénale; Jeunesse: Embert Whittom
•Rimouski: Cour du Québec, 183, rue de la Cathédrale, Rimouski QC G5L 5J1
Chambre Criminelle et Pénale: CP 800, Rimouski QC G5L 7C9
Juges (Les Honorables):
Chambre Civile: Jean-Paul Decoste; Marc Gagnon; Raoul Poirier
Chambre Criminelle et Pénale: Richard Côté; Jean-Paul Decoste
•Rivière-du-Loup: Cour du Québec, 33, rue de la Cour, Rivière-du-Loup QC G5R 1J1
Juges (Les Honorables):
Chambre Civile; Chambre Criminelle et Pénale: Gérald Laforest; Guy Ringuet
Chambre de la Jeunesse: Bertrand Laforest
•Roberval: Cour du Québec, 750, boul St-Joseph, Roberval QC G8H 2L5
Juges (Les Honorables):

Chambre Civile; Chambre Criminelle et Pénale: Rosaire Larouche

•Rouyn-Noranda: Cour du Québec, 2, rue du Palais, Rouyn-Noranda QC J9X 2N9
Juges (Les Honorables):
Chambre Civile: Paul J. Bélanger; Jean-Charles Coutu
Chambre de la Jeunesse: Gilles Gendron

•St-Hyacinthe: Cour du Québec, 1550, rue Dessaules, St-Hyacinthe QC J2S 2S8
Chambre de la Jeunesse: 1150, rue Ste-Anne, St-Hyacinthe QC J2S 5G9
Juges (Les Honorables):
Chambre Civile: Denis Robert
Chambre Criminelle et Pénale: Guy Fortier
Chambre de la Jeunesse: Constant Cordeau

•St-Jean-sur-Richelieu: Cour du Québec, 109, rue St-Charles, St-Jean-sur Richelieu QC J3B 2C2
Juges (Les Honorables):
Chambre Civile: Jacques Rancourt

•St-Jérôme: Cour du Québec, 400, rue Laviolette, St-Jérôme QC J7Y 2T6
Juges (Les Honorables):
Chambre Civile: Denis Charette; Diane Girard; Jean-Claude Paquin; André Soumis
Chambre Criminelle et Pénale: Valmont Beaulieu; Carole Richer
Chambre de la Jeunesse: Jean-Claude Gagnon; Jean La Rue; Marie Lapointe-Prevost; Andrée Ruffo

•St-Joseph-de-Beauce: Cour du Québec, 795, rue du Palais, St-Joseph-de-Beauce QC G0S 2V0
Juges (Les Honorables):
Chambre Civile: Marcel Blais
Chambre Criminelle et Pénale: Hubert Couture

•Sept-Îles: Cour du Québec, 425, boul Laure, Sept-Îles QC G4R 1X6
Juges (Les Honorables):
Chambre Civile: Bernard Lemieux
Chambre Criminelle et Pénale: Gabriel de Pokomandy

•Shawinigan: Cour du Québec, 212, rue 6e, Shawinigan QC G9N 8B6

•Sherbrooke: Cour du Québec, 375, rue King ouest, Sherbrooke QC J1H 6B9
Juges (Les Honorables):
Chambre Civile: Louis-Denis Bouchard; Danielle Côté; Jacques Pagé; Yvon Roberge
Chambre Criminelle et Pénale: Michel Beauchemin; Michel Côté; Danielle Côté; Gérald-E. Desmarais; Gabriel Lassonde
Chambre de la Jeunesse: Lise Dubé; Michel Dubois; Michel Durand

•Sorel: Cour du Québec, 46, rue Charlotte, Sorel QC J3P 6N5
Juges (Les Honorables):
Chambre Criminelle et Pénale: Ronald Dudamaine

•Terrebonne: Cour du Québec
Juges (Les Honorables):
Chambre Criminelle et Pénale: François Beaudoin; Jean R. Beaulieu; Paul Chevallier; Jean La Rue; Hughes St-Germain; Michel Toupin

•Thetford-Mines: Cour du Québec, 693, St-Alphonse ouest, Thetford-Mines QC G6G 3X3
Juges (Les Honorables):
Chambre Civile, James W. Johnson

•Trois-Rivières: Cour du Québec, 250, rue Laviolette, Trois-Rivières QC G9A 1T9
878, rue de Tonnancourt, #1.10, Trois-Rivières QC G9A 4P8
Juges (Les Honorables):
Chambre Civile: Serge Gagnon; Nicole Mallette
Chambre Criminelle et Pénale: René Crochetière; Dominique Slater; Jacques Trudel
Chambre de la Jeunesse: Pierre Houde; Dominique Slater

Val-d'Or: Cour du Québec, 900, rue 7e, Val-d'Or QC J9P 3P8
Juges (Les Honorables):
Chambre Civile: Denis Lavergne; Miville Saint-Pierre
Chambre de la Jeunesse: Normand Bonin; Denyse LeDuc

•Valleyfield: Cour du Québec, 180, rue Salaberry ouest, Valleyfield QC J6T 2J2
Juges (Les Honorables):
Chambre Civile: Raymond Boyer; Pierre Laberge; Michel Mercier; Odette Perron; Marie-Andrée Villeneuve
Chambre Criminelle et Pénale: Michel Mercier; Odette Perron; Marie-Andrée Villeneuve
Chambre de la Jeunesse: Jean Gravel

## COURS MUNICIPALES

The Municipal Courts have jurisdiction in select civil, penal and criminal matters.

**Juge en Chef,** Pierre Lalande

•Acton Vale: Cour municipale, 1025, rue Boulay, Acton Vale QC J0H 1A0
Chefs de la cour: Louise-B Grignon, Alain Boivert

•Alma: Cour municipale, 140, av St-Joseph sud, Alma QC G8B 3R1
Chefs de la cour: Jacques Turcotte, Jean-M. Morency

•Anjou: Cour municipale, 7701, boul Louis-H-Lafontaine, Anjou QC H1K 4B9
Chef de la cour: Richard Chassé

•Asbestos: Cour municipale, 300, boul St-Luc, Asbestos QC J1T 2W2
Chefs de la cour: Roland Lamoureax, Gilles J. Geoffroy

•L'Assomption: Cour municipale, 399, rue Dorval, L'Assomption QC J0K 1G0
Chefs de la cour: Louis Laporte, Gilles Thouin

•D'Autray: Cour municipale, 588, rue Montcalm, D'Autray QC J0K 1A0
Chefs de la cour: Marguerite M. Brochu, Louis Laporte

•Aylmer: Cour municipale, 120, rue Principale, Aylmer QC J9H 3M3
Chefs de la cour: Raymond Séguin, Jacques Sauvé

•Baie-Comeau: Cour municipale
Chefs de la cour: Jean Blouin, Micheline Fournier

•La-Baie: Cour municipale, 200, rue Victoria, La-Baie QC G7B 3M4
Chefs de la cour: Robert Côté, René Lambert

•Barkmère: Cour municipale, RR#1, CP 11, Argenteuil QC J0T 1A0
Chefs de la cour: Gavin Wyllie

•Beaconsfield: Cour municipale, 303, boul Beaconsfield, Beaconsfield QC H9W 4A7
Chefs de la cour: Pierre G. Bouchard, Bernard Lefebvre

•Beauharnois: Cour municipale, 103, rue St-Laurent, Beauharnois QC J6N 1V8
Chefs de la cour: Paul-Émile L'Écuyer, Jean F. Cordeau

•Beaupré: Cour municipale, 216, rue Prévost, Beaupré QC G0A 1E0
Chefs de la cour: Michael E. Hickson

•Bedford: Cour municipale, 14, rue Corriveau, Bedford QC J0J 1A0
Chefs de la cour: Claude Hamann, Alain Boisvert

•Bellechasse: Cour municipale, 100, rue Mgr Bilodeau, St-Lazare QC J0R 3J0
Chefs de la cour: Claude Fortin

•Beloeil: Cour municipale, 777, boul Laurier, Beloeil QC J3G 4S9
Chefs de la cour: Pierre J. Raiche, Luc Alarie

•Blainville: Cour municipale, 1000, rue de la Mairie, Blainville QC J7C 3B5
Chefs de la cour: Robert Diamond, Guy Saulnier

•Boisbriand: Cour municipale, 940, boul Grande-Allée, Boisbriand QC J7G 2J7
Chefs de la cour: Guy Saulnier, André Hotte

•Boucherville: Cour municipale, 500, rue de la Rivière-aux-Pins, Boucherville QC J4B 2Z7
Chefs de la cour: Pierre J. Raiche, Michel Jetté

•Bromptonville: Cour municipale, 133, rue Laval, Bromptonville QC J0B 1H0
Chefs de la cour: Roland Lamoureux, Gerald Lafrance

•Brossard: Cour municipale, 3200, boul Lapinière, Brossard QC J4Z 2B4
Chefs de la cour: Philippe Clément , Claude Céré

•Candiac: Cour municipale, #430, 9, boul Montcalm nord, Candiac QC J5R 3L5
Chefs de la cour: Georges E. Laurin, Jean-Pierre Dépelteau

•Cap-de-la-Madeleine: Cour municipale, 10, rue de l'Hôtel-de-Ville, CP 220, Cap-de-la-Madeleine QC G8T 7W4
Chefs de la cour: Joselyn Crête, Claude Trudel

•Chambly: Cour municipale, 1, Place de la Mairie, Chambly QC J3L 4X1
Chefs de la cour: Pierre J. Raiche, Denis Favreau

•Charlesbourg: Cour municipale, 160, rue 76e est, Charlesbourg QC G1H 7H5
Chef de la cour: Jean-Pierre Gignac

•Charny: Cour municipale, 5333, rue de la Symphonie, Charny QC G6X 3B6
Chef de la cour: Raymond Lavoie

•Château-Richer: Cour municipale, 8006, av Royale, Château-Richer QC G0A 1N0
Chef de la cour: Michel-N. Dugal

•Châteauguay: Cour municipale, 55, boul Maple, Châteauguay QC J6J 3P9
Chefs de la cour: Manon Bourbonnais, Paul-Émile L'Écuyer

•Chibougamau: Cour municipale, 650, rue 3e, Chibougamau QC G8P 1P1
Chefs de la cour: Michel Lapointe, Robert Côté

•Chicoutimi: Cour municipale, 201, rue Racine est, Chicoutimi QC G7H 1S3
Chefs de la cour: Robert Côté, René Lambert

•Coaticook: Cour municipale, 150, rue Child, CP 85, Coaticook QC J1A 2B3
Chefs de la cour: Pierre A. Cloutier, Roland Lamoureux

•Côte St-Luc: Cour municipale, 5801, boul Cavendish, Côte St-Luc QC H4W 3C3
Chefs de la cour: Donald W. Seal, Alfred N. Segall

•Cowansville: Cour municipale, 220, Place Municipale, Cowansville QC J2K 1T4
Chefs de la cour: Claude Hamann, Pierre Raiche

•Deux-Montagnes: Cour municipale, 803, ch Oka, Deux-Montagnes QC J7R 4K1
Chefs de la cour: Robert Diamond, Jacques Lamontagne

•Dolbeau: Cour municipale, 1100, boul Walberg, Dolbeau QC G8L 1G7
Chefs de la cour: Jacquelin Légaré, Robert Côté

•Dollard-des-Ormeaux: Cour municipale, 12001, boul de Salaberry ouest, Dollard-des-Ormeaux QC H9B 2A7
Chefs de la cour: Pierre Mondor, Donald W. Seal

•Donnaconna: Cour municipale, 138, av Pleau, Donnaconna QC G0A 1T0
Chefs de la cour: Jean-R. Côté, Claude Fournier

•Dorval: Cour municipale, 530, boul Bouchard, Dorval QC H9S 1B2
Chefs de la cour: Jean-Pierre Dépelteau, Georges É. Laurin

•Drummondville: Cour municipale, 413, rue Lindsay, Drummondville QC J2B 1G8
Chefs de la cour: Jacques Guertin, Michel Houle

•East Angus: Cour municipale, 146, rue Angus, East Angus QC J0B 1R0
Chefs de la cour: Pierre-A. Cloutier, Gilles J. Geoffroy

•Farnham: Cour municipale, 477, rue de l'Hôtel de Ville, Farnham QC J2N 2H3
Chefs de la cour: Alain Boisvert, Claude Hamann

•Gatineau: Cour municipale, 280, boul Maloney est, Gatineau QC J8P 1C6

Chefs de la cour: François Gravel, Jacques Sauvé
•Granby: Cour municipale, 125, rue Simonds sud, Granby QC J2J 1P7
Chefs de la cour: Hélène Poulin, Pierre Raiche
•Grand'Mère: Cour municipale, 333, av 5e, Grand'Mère QC G9T 2M2
Chefs de la cour: Jean-Marc Champagne, Jean-Louis Sanschagrin
•Greenfield Park: Cour municipale, 158, boul Churchill, Greenfield Park QC J4V 2M3
Chefs de la cour: Denis Boudrias, Jean-Guy Clément
•Hampstead: Cour municipale, 5569 Queen Mary Rd., Hampstead QC H3X 1W5
Chefs de la cour: Donald W. Seal, Alfred N. Segall
•Haut-Saint Laurent: Cour municipale
Chefs de la cour: Manon Bourbonnais, Paul-Émile L'Écuyer
•Hull: Cour municipale, 25, rue Laurier, CP 1970, Hull QC J8X 3Y9
Chefs de la Cour, François Gravel, Jacques Sauvé
•Iberville: Cour municipale, 855, rue 1er, Iberville QC J2X 3C7
Chefs de la cour: Pierre-Armand Tremblay, Denis Boudrias
•Joliette: Cour municipale, 733, rue Richard, Joliette QC J6E 2T8
Chefs de la cour: Marguerite M. Brochu, Louis Laporte
•Jonquière: Cour municipale, 2201, rue De Montfort, CP 278, Jonquière QC G7X 4P6
Chefs de la cour: Jean M. Morency, Jean-Jacques Turcotte
•L'Ancienne-Lorette: Chef de la cour: Gilles Charest
•La Pocatière: Cour municipale, 412, rue 9e, La Pocatière QC G0R 1Z0
Chefs de la cour: Jean Blouin, Louis-Marie Vachon
•Lac Mégantic: Cour municipale, #200, 5527, rue Frontenac, Lac Mégantic QC G6B 1H6
Chefs de la cour: Gabriel Garneau, Jean-Pierre Gignac
•Lachine: Cour municipale, 1800, boul St-Joseph, Lachine QC H8S 2N4
Chefs de la cour: Yves Fournier, Jacques Laurier
•Lachute: Cour municipale, 380, rue Principale, Lachute QC J8H 1Y2
Chefs de la cour: André Hotte, Guy Saulnier
•Lasalle: Cour municipale, 55, av Dupras, Lasalle QC H8R 4A8
Chefs de la cour: Philippe Clément, Denis Laberge
•La Tuque: Cour municipale, 558, rue Commerciale, La Tuque QC G9X 3A9
Chefs de la cour: Jocelyn Crête, Claude Trudel
•Laval: Cour municipale, 55, boul des Laurentides, Pont-Viau QC H7G 2T1
Chefs de la cour: Bernard Caron, Jean-H. Charbonneau
•Lévis: Cour municipale, 225, côte du Passage, Lévis QC G6V 5T4
Chefs de la cour: Gilles Charest, Raymond Lavoie
•Longueuil: Cour municipale, #290, Place Charles-Lemoyne, Longueuil QC J4K 2T4
Chefs de la cour: Richard Alary, Jacques Lamontagne
•Loretteville: Cour municipale, 305, rue Racine, Loretteville QC G2B 1E7
Chefs de la cour: Gilles Charest, Claude Fournier
•Louiseville: Cour municipale, 105, av St-Laurent ouest, Louiseville QC J5V 2L6
Chefs de la cour: Jocelyn Crête, Claude Trudel
•Magog: Cour municipale, 7, rue Principale est, Magog QC J1X 1Y4
Chefs de la cour: Leonard Bergeron, Roland Lamoureux
•Marieville: Cour municipale, 682, rue St-Charles, Marieville QC J0L 1J0
Chefs de la cour: Louis-B. Grignon, Pierre-Armand Tremblay
•Mascouche: Cour municipale
Chefs de la cour: Claude Lemire, Michel Paquin
•Matawinie: Cour municipale
Chef de la cour: Michel Lalande
•Mirabel: Cour municipale, 1411, rue St-Jean, Ste-Monique-deux-Montagnes QC J0N 1R0
Chefs de la cour: André Hotte, Michel Paquin
•Mistassini: Cour municipale, 173, St-Michel, CP 219, Mistassini QC G0W 2C0
Chefs de la cour: Michel J. Lapointe, Jacquelin Légaré
•Mont-Royal: Cour municipale, 90, av Roosevelt, Mont-Royal QC H3R 1Z4
Chefs de la cour: Pierre G. Bouchard, Jérôme C. Smyth
•Mont-St-Hilaire: Cour municipale, 100, rue du Centre-Civique, Mont-St-Hilaire QC J3H 3M8
Chefs de la cour: Luc Alarie, Pierre J. Raiche
•Montcalm: Cour municipale
Chefs de la cour: Marguerite M. Brochu, Louis Laporte
•Montmagny: Cour municipale, 134, rue St-Jean-Baptiste est, Montmagny QC G5V 1K6
Chefs de la cour: Jean Blouin, Louis-Marie Vachon
•Montréal: Cour municipale, 775, rue Gosford, Montréal QC H2Y 3B9
Juge en chef, Raymonde Verreault
Juge en chef adjoint, Jean-Pierre Bessette
Chefs de la Cour: Louise Baribeau, Denis Boisvert, Louise Bourdeau, René Déry, Pierre D. Denault, Antonio Discepola, Gérard Duguay, Pierre Fontaine, Pierre Gaston, Dennis Laliberté, Louis-Jacques Léger, Évasio Massagnini, Jean Massé, Morton S. Minc
•Montréal-Est: Cour municipale, 11370, rue Notre-Dame est, Montréal QC H1B 2W6
Chefs de la cour: Florent Bisson, Jean Hébert
•Montréal-Nord: Cour municipale, 4240, rue Amos, Montréal-Nord QC H1H 1P3
Chefs de la cour: Richard Alary, Jacques Lamontagne
•Montréal-Ouest: Cour municipale, 50, av Westminster sud, Montréal QC H4X 1Y7
Chefs de la cour: Frank Schlesinger, Alfred N. Segall
•Nicolet: Cour municipale, 180, rue Panet, CP 670, Nicolet QC J0G 1E0
Chefs de la cour: Jacques Desaulniers
•Outremont: Cour municipale, 510, av Davaar, Outremont QC H2V 2B9
Chefs de la cour: Georges E. Laurin, Adrien R. Paquette
•Pierrefonds: Cour municipale, 13665, boul Pierrefonds, Pierrefonds QC H9H 4N2
Chefs de la cour: Philippe Clément, Pierre Mondor
•Plessisville: Cour municipale, 1700, rue St-Calixte, Plessisville QC G6L 1R3
Chefs de la cour: Jules Bellavance, Claude Caron
•Pointe-Claire: Cour municipale, 401, St-Jean, Pointe-Claire QC H9R 3J2
Chefs de la cour: Philippe Clément, Pierre Mondor
•La Prairie: Cour municipale, 600, Ste-Elizabeth, La Prairie QC J5R 1V1
Chefs de la cour: Claude Céré, Jean Hébert
•Princeville: Cour municipale, 50, av St-Jacques ouest, CP 370, Princeville QC G0P 1E0
Chef de la cour: Claude Caron
•Québec: Cour municipale, Centrale de Police, 275, rue Gignac, Québec QC G1K 2L3
Juge en chef, Laurent Cossette
Chefs de la cour: J.-Charles Brochu
•Repentigny: Cour municipale, 435, boul d'Iberville, Repentigny QC J6A 2B6
Chefs de la cour: Claude Lemire, Gilles Thouin
•Rimouski: Cour municipale, 205, av de la Cathédrale, CP 710, Rimouski QC G5L 7C7
Chefs de la cour: Jean Blouin, Raymond Lavoie
•Roberval: Cour municipale, 851, boul St-Joseph, Roberval QC G8H 2L6
Chefs de la cour: Michel J. Lapointe, Jacquelin Légaré
•Rosemère: Cour municipale, 100, rue Charbonneau, Rosemère QC J7A 3W1
Chefs de la cour: Guy Saulnier, Robert Diamond
•Roxboro: Cour municipale, 13 Centre Commercial, Roxboro QC H8Y 2N9
Chefs de la cour: Philippe Clément, Ronald J. Montcalm
•Ste-Adele: Cour municipale, 1381, boul Sainte-Adele, Sainte-Adele QC J0R 1L0
Chefs de la cour: J.-H. Denis Gagnon, Michel Lalande
•Ste-Agathe-des-Monts: Cour municipale, 50, St-Joseph, Sainte-Agathe-des-Monts QC J8C 1M9
Chefs de la cour: J.H. Denis Gagnon, Michel Lalande
•Ste-Anne-de-Bellevue: Cour municipale, 109, Ste-Anne, CP 40, Sainte-Anne-de-Bellevue QC H9X 1M2
Chefs de la cour: Jacques Chanimé, Pascal Pillarella
•St-Bruno-de-Montarville: Cour municipale, 1585, boul Montarville, St-Bruno-de-Montarville QC J3V 3T8
Chefs de la cour: Marc Gravel, Guy Houle
•St-Césaire: Cour municipale, 1111, St-Paul, Saint-Césaire QC J0L 1T0
Chefs de la cour: Louis B. Grignon, Pierre-Armand Tremblay
•St-Constant: Cour municipale, 147, rue St-Pierre, Saint-Constant QC J5A 2G2
Chefs de la cour: Yves Fournier, Jacques Laurier
•St-Eustache: Cour municipale, 168, rue Dorion, St-Eustache QC J7R 5S4
Chefs de la cour: Réne Boismenu, Robert Diamond
•St-Félicien: Cour municipale, 1058, boul Sacré-Coeur, CP 7000, St-Félicien QC G8K 2R5
Chefs de la cour: Robert Côté, Michel J. Lapointe
•Ste-Foy: Cour municipale, 1000, rte de l'Eglise, CP 218, Ste-Foy QC G1V 4E1
Chefs de la cour: Jacques Ouellet, Gilles Ouellet
•St-Georges: Cour municipale, 11700, boul Lacroix est, St-Georges QC G5Y 1L3
Chefs de la cour: Gabriel Garneau, Jean-Pierre Gignac
•St-Hubert: Cour municipale, 5900, boul Cousineau, St-Hubert QC J3Y 7K8
Chefs de la cour: Claude Céré, Jean Herbert
•St-Hyacinthe: Cour municipale, 700, av de l'Hôtel de Ville, St-Hyacinthe QC J2S 5B2
Chefs de la cour: Michel Lalande, Louis B. Gringon
•St-Jean-Chrysostome: Cour municipale, 959, rue de l'Hotel de Ville, St-Jean-Chrysostome QC G6Z 2N8
Chefs de la cour: Claude Fortin, Jean-Pierre Gignac
•St-Jean-sur-Richelieu: Cour municipale, 188, rue Jacques Cartier nord, St-Jean-sur-Richelieu QC J3B 7B2
Chefs de la cour: Louis B. Grignon, Pierre-Armand Tremblay
•St-Jérôme: Cour municipale, 280, boul Labelle, St-Jérôme QC J7Z 5L1
Chefs de la cour: René Boismenu, Robert Diamond
•St-Lambert: Cour municipale, 55, Argyle, Saint-Lambert QC J4P 2H3
Chefs de la cour: Marc Gravel, Guy Houle
•St-Laurent: Cour municipale, 777, Laurentien, Saint-Laurent QC H4M 2M7
Chefs de la Cour, Jérôme C. Smyth, Pierre G. Bouchard
•St-Léonard-de-Port-Maurice: Cour municipale, 8400, boul Lacordaire, St-Léonard QC H1R 3B1
Chefs de la cour: Richard Chassé
•St-Luc: Cour municipale, 347, boul St-Luc, Saint-Luc QC J0J 2A0
Chefs de la cour: Denis Boudrias, Pascal Pillarella
•Ste-Marie-de-Beauce-Nord: Cour municipale, 270, rue Marguerite Bourgeois, CP 1750, Ste-Marie-de-Beauce-Nord QC G6E 3C7

Chefs de la cour: Jean-Pierre Gignac, Paul Routhier
•St-Nicolas, St-Rédempteur, Bernières, St-Étienne-de-Lauzon: Cour municipale, 85, rue 19e, St-Rédempteur QC G6K 1C3
Chefs de la cour: Claude Fournier, Jacques Ouellet
•St-Pierre: Cour municipale, 69, av 5e, St-Pierre QC H8R 1P1
Chefs de la cour: Pierre G. Bouchard, Yves Fournier
•St-Raymond: Cour municipale, 375, St-Joseph, St-Raymond QC G0A 4G0
Chefs de la cour: Jean R. Côté, Claude Fournier
•St-Rémi-de-Napierville: Cour municipale, 105, Perras, St-Rémi-de-Napierville QC J0L 2L0
Chefs de la cour: Pierre G. Bouchard, Pascal Pillarella
•Ste-Thérèse: Cour municipale, 6, rue de l'Église, CP 100, Ste-Thérèse QC J7E 4H7
Chefs de la cour: André Hotte, Guy Saulnier
•St-Tite: Cour municipale, 540, rue Notre-Dame, St-Tite QC G0X 3H0
Chefs de la cour: Jean-Marc Champagne, Jean L. Sanschagrain
•Salaberry-de-Valleyfield: Cour municipale, 61, rue Ste-Cécile, Salaberry-de-Valleyfield QC J6T 1L8
Chefs de la cour: Michel Lalande, Paul Lemieux
•Senneville: Cour municipale, 35, rue Senneville, Senneville QC H9X 1B8
Chefs de la cour: Philippe Clément, Pierre Mondor
•Sept-Îles: Cour municipale, 546, rue Dequen, Sept-Îles QC G4R 2R4
Chefs de la cour: Jean Blouin, Guy Pettigrew
•Shawinigan: Cour municipale, 550, av Hôtel de Ville, CP 400, Shawinigan QC G9N 6V3
Chefs de la cour: Jocelyn Crête, Claude Trudel
•Shawinigan-Sud: Cour municipale, 1550, rue 118e, Shawinigan QC G9P 3G8
Chefs de la cour: Jocelyn Crête, Claude Trudel
•Sherbrooke: Cour municipale, 191, rue Palais, Sherbrooke QC J1H 4R1
Chefs de la cour: Pierre A. Cloutier, Roland Lamoureux
•Sillery: Cour municipale, 1445, av Maguire, Sillery QC G1T 1Z2
Chefs de la cour: Jean-Pierre Gignac, René Paquet
•Sorel: Cour municipale, 71, rue Charlotte, CP 368, Sorel QC J3P 7K1
Chefs de la cour: Jacques Guertin, Michel Houle
•Terrebonne: Cour municipale, 775, rue St-Jean Baptiste, Terrebonne QC J6W 1B5
Chefs de la cour: Claude Lemire, Michel Paquin
•Thetford-Mines: Cour municipale, 144, rue Notre-Dame sud, CP 489, Thetford-Mines QC G6G 5T3
Chefs de la cour: Gilles Ouellet, Jacques Ouellet
•Tracy: Cour municipale, 3025, boul de la Mairie, Tracy QC J3R 1C2
Chefs de la cour: Jacques Guertin, Michel Houle
•Trois-Rivières: Cour municipale, 1193, rue Laviolette, CP 969, Trois-Rivières QC G9A 5K2
Chefs de la cour: Jocelyn Crête, Claude Trudel
•Trois-Rivières-Ouest: Cour municipale, 500, côte du Richelieu, Trois-Rivières QC G9A 2Z1
Chefs de la cour: Jocelyn Crête, Claude Trudel
•Val-Bélair: Cour municipale, 1105, av de l'Église nord, Val-Bélair QC G3K 1X5
Chefs de la cour: Claude Fortin, Jean-Pierre Gignac
•Val-d'Or: Cour municipale, 855, av 2e, Val-d'Or QC J9P 4P4
Chef de la cour: Jacques Barbès
•Val-St-François: Cour municipale
Chefs de la cour: J.-Gilles Geoffroy, Léonard Bergeron
•Vaudreuil-Soulanges: Cour municipale
Chefs de la cour: Manon Bourbonnais, Paul-Émile L'Ecuyer
•Verdun: Cour municipale, #104, 4555, av Verdun, Verdun QC H4G 1M4
Chefs de la cour: Denis Boudrias, Jacques Ghanimé
•Victoriaville: Cour municipale, 1, rue Notre-Dame ouest, CP 370, Victoriaville QC G6P 6T2
Chefs de la cour: Jean-Louis Provencher, Gilles Ouellet
•Waterloo: Cour municipale, 417, rue de la Cour, Waterloo QC J0E 2N0
Chefs de la cour: Michel Brun, Alain Boisvert
•Westmount: Cour municipale, 21, rue Stanton, Westmount QC H3Y 3B1
Chefs de la cour: Keith A. Ham, Alfred N. Segall

## REGISTRATEURS

Abitibi: 552, av 1er ouest, CP 160, Amos QC J9T 3A6
Argenteuil: 505, rue Bethanie, CP 337, Lachute QC J8H 3X5
Arthabaska: 800, boul des Bois Francs sud, Arthabaska QC G6P 5W5
L'Assomption: 300, rue Dorval, L'Assomption QC J5W 2Z9
Beauce: 111, rue 107e, Beauceville-est QC G0S 1A0
Beauharnois: 39, rue Richardson, Beauharnois QC J6N 2T4
Bellechasse: 23, av Chanoine-Audet, St-Raphael QC G0R 4C0
Berthier: 180, rue Champlain, CP 299, Berthierville QC J0K 1A0
Bonaventure, Division No. 1: Palais de Justice, CP 250, New Carlisle QC G0C 1Z0
Bonaventure, Division No. 2: 17, rue Lacroix, Carleton QC G0C 1J0
Brôme: 550, ch Knowlton, Lac Brôme QC J0E 1V0
Chambly: 2555, boul Roland Therrien, R.C. 05, Longueuil QC J4M 2J4
Champlain: 211, rue de l'Église, Ste-Genevièeve-de-Batiscan QC G0X 2R0
Charlevoix, Division No. 1: #250, 237, rue St-Etienne, CP 310, La Malbaie QC G5A 1T8
Charlevoix, Division No. 2: #102, 4, Place de l'Église, Baie-St-Paul QC G0A 1B0
Châteauguay: 164, rue St-Joseph, Ste-Martine QC J0S 1V0
Chicoutimi: 227, rue Racine est, Chicoutimi QC G7H 5C5
Coaticook: Hôtel de ville, #04, 150, rue Child, Coaticook QC J1A 2B3
Compton: 89, rue du Parc, CP 459, Cookshire QC J0B 1M0
Deux-Montagnes: #204, 140, rue St-Eustache, St-Eustache QC J7R 2K9
Dorchester: 115, rue Langevin, Ste-Hénédine QC G0S 2R0
Drummond: Palais de Justice, 1680, rue St-Joseph, 2e étage, Drummondville QC J2C 2G3
Frontenac: #219, 5527, rue Frontenac, CP 157, Lac Mégantic QC G6B 2S6
Gaspé: Palais de Justice, CP 128, Percé QC G0C 2L0
Gatineau: #307, 266, rue Notre-Dame, Maniwaki QC J9E 2J8
Hull: #3.120, 170, rue de l'Hôtel de Ville, Hull QC J8X 4C2
Huntington: 25, rue King, Huntington QC J0S 1H0
Îles-de-la-Madeleine: Palais de Justice, CP 97, Hâvre-Aubert QC G0B 1J0
L'Islet: 34, rue Fortin, CP 578, St-Jean-Port-Joli QC G0R 3G0
Joliette: #1.04, 450, rue St-Louis, Joliette QC J6E 2Y9
Kamouraska: 395, rue Chapleau, St-Pascal QC G0L 3Y0
Labelle: 440, boul Albiny-Paquette, Mont-Laurier QC J9L 3G9
Lac St-Jean Est: Palais de Justice, 725, boul Harvey ouest, Alma QC G8B 1P5
Lac St-Jean Ouest: Palais de Justice, 1221, boul St-Dominique, Roberval QC G8H 3B8
Laval: #1.03, 2800, boul St-Martin ouest, Laval QC H7T 2S9
Lévis: 45B, rue Desjardins, Lévis QC G6V 4V3
Lotbinière: 6375, rue Garneau, Ste-Croix QC G0S 2H0
Maskinongé: 649, boul St-Laurent, Louiseville QC J5V 1J1
Matane: 750, rue du Phare ouest, Matane QC G4W 3W8
Matapédia: 27, boul St-Benoît, CP 1508, Amqui QC G0J 1B0
Missisquoi: 4, rue Adhémar Cusson, CP 300, Bedford QC J0J 1A0
Montcalm: 2450, rue Victoria, CP 190, Ste-Julienne QC J0K 2T0
Montmagny: #101, 25, boul Taché ouest, Montmagny QC G5V 2Z9
Montmorency: 7007, av Royal, Château-Richer QC G0A 1N0
Montréal: Palais de Justice, #2.175, 1, rue Notre-Dame est, Montréal QC H2Y 1B6
Nicolet: Palais de Justice, 395, Mgr Couchesne, Nicolet QC J3T 1X6
Papineau: 266, rue Viger, Papineauville QC J0V 1R0
Pontiac: Palais de Justice, CP 310, Campbell's Bay QC J0X 1K0
Portneuf: 185, rte 138, Cap-Santé QC G0A 1L0
La Prairie: 214, rue St-Ignace, La Prairie QC J5R 1E5
Québec: 300, boul Jean-Lesage, R.C. 32, Québec QC G1K 8K6
Richelieu: Maison du Québec, 46, rue Charlotte, Sorel QC J3P 5N8
Richmond: Hôtel de Ville, 745, rue Gouin, Richmond QC J0B 2H0
Rimouski: #04, 337 rue Moreault, Rimouski QC G5L 1P4
Rouville: 500, rue Desjardins, Marieville QC J3M 1N2
Rouyn-Noranda: 2, av du Palais, Rouyn-Noranda QC J9X 2N9
Saguenay: Palais de Justice, 71, av Mance, Baie-Comeau QC G4Z 1N2
Ste-Anne-des-Monts: Palais de Justice, 10, boul Ste-Anne, CP 517, Ste-Anne-des-Monts QC G0E 2G0
St-Hyacinthe: #200, 1150, av Ste-Anne, St-Hyacinthe QC J2S 5G9
St-Jean: 109, rue Saint-Charles, local 1.01, St-Jean QC J3B 2C2
Sept-Îles: 425, boul Laure, Sept-Îles QC G4R 1X6
Shawinigan: Centre Administratif, 212, rue 6e, CP 608, Shawinigan QC G9N 6V6
Shefford: 77, rue Principale, Granby QC J2G 9B3
Sherbrooke: 375, rue King ouest, Sherbrooke QC J1H 6B9
Stanstead: 100, ch Dufferin, CP 240, Stanstead Plain QC J0B 3E0
Témiscamingue: 8, rue St-Gabriel nord, CP 757, Ville-Marie QC J0Z 3W0
Témiscouata: 310, rue Ste-Pierre, Rivière-du-Loup QC G5R 3V3
Terrebonne: #200, 10, rue St-Joseph, St-Jérôme QC J7Z 7G7
Thetford: 865, av l'abbé, Thetford-Mines QC G6G 5S5
Trois-Rivières: Palais de Justice, 878, de Tonnancourt, Trois-Rivières QC G9A 4P8
La Tuque: 290, rue St-Joseph, 2e étage, La Tuque QC G9X 3Z8
Vaudreuil: 640-C, rue Chicoine, Dorion-Vaudreuil QC J7V 8P2
Verchères: #92, 461, boul St-Joseph, Ste-Julie QC J3E 1W8

## PROTONOTAIRES ET SHERIFS

Abitibi: 891, 3e rue ouest, Amos QC J9T 2T4 – 819/732-6577
Alma: #RC31, 725, rue Harvey ouest, Alma QC G8B 1P5 – 418/668-3334
Arthabaska: 800, boul Bois-Franc sud, Victoriaville QC G6P 5W5 – 819/357-2054
Baie Comeau: 71, av Mance, Baie-Comeau QC G4Z 1N2 – 418/296-5534
Beauce: 795, av du Palais, St-Joseph-de-Beauce QC G0S 2V0 – 418/397-7188

Beauharnois: 180, rue Salaberry, Valleyfield QC J6T 2J2 – 514/370-4006

Bedford: 920, rue Principale, Cowansville QC J2K 1K2 77, rue Principale, Granby QC J2G 9B3 – 514/263-3520

Bonaventure: 87, rue Principale, CP 517, New Carlisle QC G0C 1Z0 – 418/752-3376

Charlevoix: 30, ch de la Vallée, La Malbaie QC G5A 1T8 – 418/665-3991

Chicoutimi: 227, rue Racine est, CP 370, Chicoutimi QC G7H 7B4 – 418/696-9944

Drummond: 1680, boul St-Joseph, Drummondville QC J2C 2G3 – 819/478-2513

Frontenac: #1.23, 693, rue St-Alphonse ouest, CP 579, Thetford-Mines QC G6G 3X3 – 418/338-2118

Gaspé: 124, rte 132, CP 188, Percé QC G0C 2L0 – 418/782-2055

Hull: #0.210, 17, rue Laurier, Hull QC J8X 4C1 – 819/776-8100

Iberville: 109, rue St-Charles, St-Jean-sur-Richelieu QC J3B 2C2 – 514/347-3715

Joliette: 200, rue St-Marc, Joliette QC J6E 8C2

Kamouraska: 33, rue de la Cour, Rivière-du-Loup QC G5R 1J1 – 418/862-3579

Labelle: 645, rue de la Madone, Mont-Laurier QC J9L 1T1 – 819/623-9666

Lac Mégantic: #316, 5527, rue Frontenac, Lac Mégantic QC G6B 1H6 – 819/583-1268

Longueuil: 1111, boul Jacques-Cartier est, Longueuil QC J4M 2J6 – 514/646-4009

Mingan: 425, boul Laure, Sept-Îles QC G4R 1X6 – 418/962-2154

Montmagny: 25, rue du Palais, Montmagny QC G5V 1P6 – 418/248-0909

Montréal: 1, rue Notre-Dame est, Montréal QC H2Y 1B6

Pontiac: 27, rue John, Campbell's Bay QC J0X 1K0 – 819/648-5222

Québec: 300, boul Jean-Lesage, Québec QC G1K 8K6 – 418/649-3501

Richelieu: 46, rue Charlotte, Sorel QC J3P 6N5 – 514/742-2786

Rimouski: 183, rue de la Cathédrale, CP 800, Rimouski QC G5L 7C9 – 418/727-3852

Roberval: 750, boul St-Joseph, Roberval QC G8H 2L5 – 418/275-3666

Rouyn-Noranda: 2, av du Palais, Rouyn-Noranda QC J9X 2N9 – 819/764-6709

St-François: 375, rue King ouest, Sherbrooke QC J1H 6B9 – 819/822-6902

St-Hyacinthe: 1550, rue Dessaulles, St-Hyacinthe QC J2S 2S8 – 514/778-6559

St-Maurice: 212 - 6e rue, Shawinigan QC G9N 8B6 – 819/536-2571

Témiscamingue: 8, rue St-Gabriel nord, CP 550, Ville-Marie QC J0Z 3W0 – 819/629-2773

Terrebonne: 400, rue Laviolette, St-Jérôme QC J7Y 2T6 – 514/431-4407

Trois-Rivières: 250, rue Laviolette, Trois-Rivières QC G9A 1T9 – 819/372-4150

## SASKATCHEWAN

### SASKATCHEWAN: COURT OF APPEAL

Court House, 2425 Victoria Ave., Regina SK S4P 3V7

The Court of Appeal has appellate jurisdiction with respect to any judgement, order or decree made by the Court of Queen's Bench and any matter granted to it by statute.

**Chief Justice of Saskatchewan,** The Hon. E.D. Bayda

Justices of Appeal (The Hon. Mr./Madam Justice):

S.J. Cameron; M.A. Gerwing; G.R. Jackson; J.G. Lane; N.W. Sherstobitoff; C.F. Tallis; W.J. Vancise; T.C. Wakeling (Supernum.)

Registrar, M. Herauf

### SASKATCHEWAN COURT OF QUEEN'S BENCH

2425 Victoria Ave., Regina SK S4P 3V7

The Court of Queen's Bench is a court of original jurisdiction having jurisdiction in civil & criminal matters arising in Saskatchewan, except those matters expressly excluded by statute.

**Chief Justice,** The Hon. Mr. D.K. MacPherson

Justices (The Hon. Mr./Madam Justice):

J.R.D. Archambault; G.H.M. Armstrong; R.L. Barclay; C.L. Dawson; E.J. Gunn; D.C. Hunter; L.A. Kyle; K.R.N. MacLeod (Supernum.); E.C. Malone; W.R. Matheson; G.A.F. Maurice; D.E.N. McIntyre; E.A. Scheibel; C.R. Wimmer

Registrar of the Court of Queen's Bench & Provincial Court, J. Kernaghan

Local Registrar, G. Ullman

Sheriff, J. Rhinelander

•Assiniboia: Court of Queen's Bench, Assiniboia SK S0H 0B0
  Deputy Sheriff/Local Registrar & Court Clerk, D. Green

•Battleford: Court of Queen's Bench, Battleford SK S0M 0E0
  The Hon. Mr. Justice, D.K. Kreuger
  Sheriff, Court Clerk & Local Registrar, D.I. Dament

•Estevan: Court of Queen's Bench, Estevan SK S4A 0W5
  The Hon. Mr. Justice, G.N. Allbright
  Deputy Sheriff/Local Registrar & Court Clerk, P. Boxrud

•Humboldt: Court of Queen's Bench, Humboldt SK S0K 2A0
  The Hon. Mr. Justice, P.J. Dielschneider (Supernum.)
  Deputy Sheriff/Local Registrar & Court Clerk, Elaine Lange

•Melfort: Court of Queen's Bench, Melfort SK S0E 1A0
  Deputy Sheriff/Local Registrar & Court Clerk, J. Gabrysh; E. Neigel

•Moose Jaw: Court of Queen's Bench, Moose Jaw SK S6H 4P1
  The Hon. Mr. Justice, R.A. MacLean (Supernum.)
  Deputy Sheriff/Local Registrar & Court Clerk, D. Paquin

•Prince Albert: Court of Queen's Bench, Prince Albert SK S6V 4W7
  Justices (The Hon. Mr./Madam Justice):
  J.D. Milliken; A. Rothery
  Sheriff, Court Clerk & Registrar, David Sinclair

•Saskatoon: Court of Queen's Bench, 520 Spadina Cr. East, Saskatoon SK S7K 2H6
  Justices (The Hon. Mr./Madam Justice):
  G.W. Baynton; P. Blacklock Linn; M.Y. Carter (Supernum.); F.G.W. Dickson (Supernum.); T.L. Geatros (Supernum.); W.F. Gerein; I. Goldenberg; I. Grotsky (Supernum.); P. Hrabinsky; J. Klebuc; R.D. Laing; G.E. Noble (Supernum.); A.L. Sirois (Supernum.); Marian Wedge; D.H. Wright; M.E.R. Wright; Y. Wilkinson
  Local Registrar, D. Berezowsky
  Sheriff, G. Laing

•Swift Current: Court of Queen's Bench, Swift Current SK S9H 0J4
  The Hon. Mr. Justice, I.D. McLellan
  Sheriff, Court Clerk & Local Registrar, R. Peterson

•Weyburn: Court of Queen's Bench, Weyburn SK S4H 0L4
  Sheriff, Court Clerk & Local Registrar, W. Damman

•Wynyard: Court of Queen's Bench, Wynyard SK S0A 4T0
  Deputy Sheriff/Local Registrar & Court Clerk, G. Fewster

•Yorkton: Court of Queen's Bench, Yorkton SK S3N 0C2
  The Hon. Madam Justice, J.L. Pritchard
  Sheriff, Court Clerk & Local Registrar, S. Urbanoski

### SASKATCHEWAN PROVINCIAL COURT

1815 Smith St., Regina SK S4P 3V7

The Provincial Court has jurisdiction in both civil (including small claims and family) and select criminal (including young offender) matters.

**Chief Judge,** The Hon. J.B.J. Nutting

•Estevan: Provincial Court, Court House, 1016 - 4th St., Estevan SK S4A 0W5 – 306/637-4528
  Judges (The Hon.):
  P. Kolenick

•Lloyminster: Provincial Court, 4815 - 50 St., Lloydminster SK S9V 0H8 – 306/825-6420
  Judges (The Hon.):
  K.J. Young

•Meadow Lake: Provincial Court, PO Box 849, Meadow Lake SK S9X 1T7 – 306/236-7575
  Judges (The Hon.):
  J. Nightingale; T.W. White

•Melfort: Provincial Court, PO Box 6500, Melfort SK S0E 1A0 – 306/752-6230
  Judges (The Hon.):
  E.C. Diehl; E.R. Gosselin

•Moose Jaw: Provincial Court, 110 Ominica St. West, Moose Jaw SK S6H 6V2 – 306/694-3612
  Judges (The Hon.):
  G.C. King; D. Orr

•North Battleford: Provincial Court, 1002 - 103 St., North Battleford SK S9A 1K4 – 306/446-7400
  Judges (The Hon.):
  L.P. Deshaye; D. Kaiser; V.H. Meekma

•Prince Albert: Provincial Court, PO Box 3003, Prince Albert SK S6V 6G1 – 306/953-2640
  Judges (The Hon.):
  T.B. Bekolay; S.C. Carter; T.W. Ferris; H.W. Goliath

•Regina: Provincial Court, 1815 Smith St., Regina SK S4P 3V7 – 306/787-5500
  Judges (The Hon.):
  R.H. Allan; K.E. Bellerose; D.E. Fenwick; L.A. Halliday; B.D. Henning; E.A. Lewchuk; J.E. McMurtry; D.I. Morris; G.R. Moxley; L.J. Smith

•La Ronge: Provincial Court, PO Box 500, La Ronge SK S0J 1L0
  Judges (The Hon.):
  C. Fafard; W.K. Tucker

•Saskatoon: Provincial Court, 230 - 20 St. East, Saskatoon SK S7K 2H6
  Judges (The Hon.):
  R.G. Bell; B.P. Carey; R. Finley; B. Goldstein; B.L. Huculak; D.A. Lavoie; J.B.J. Nutting; E. Schmeise; G.T. Seniuk; S.P. Whelan

•Swift Current: Provincial Court, Court House, 121 Lorne St. West, Swift Current SK S9H 0J4 – 306/778-8390
  Judges (The Hon.):
  L.A. Matsalla; G.B. Shaner

•Weyburn: Provincial Court, Court House, 301 Prairie Ave., Weyburn SK S4H 0L4 – 306/848-2357
  Judges (The Hon.):
  W.V. Goliath

•Wynyard: Provincial Court, Court House, PO Box 1449, Wynyard SK S0A 4T0 – 306/554-2155
  Judges (The Hon.):
  D. Ebert

•Yorkton: Provincial Court, Court House, 120 Smith St. East, Yorkton SK S3N 3V3 – 306/786-1400
  Judges (The Hon.):
  K.A. Andrychuk; E.S. Bobowski; R. Rathgeber

## YUKON TERRITORY

### YUKON TERRITORY: COURT OF APPEAL

PO Box 4010, Whitehorse YT Y1A 3S9
403/667-3524; Fax: 403/667-3079

The Court of Appeal has appellate jurisdiction in all civil and criminal matters from decisions by the Territorial Court and Supreme Court.

Justices of Appeal (The Hon. Mr./Madam Justice):
Vancouver: A.B.B. Carrothers; G.S. Cumming; I.T. Donald; William A. Esson; L.S.G. Finch; R. Gibbs; D.B. Gibbs; D.M.M. Goldie; E.E. Hinkson; H.A. Hollinrake; H. Hutcheon; J.D. Lambert; H. Legg; A.B. Macfarlane; A. McEachern; P. Proudfoot; J. Prowse; M.A. Rowles; C.A. Ryan; M.F. Southin; M.R. Taylor; J. Wood
Whitehorse: R.E. Hudson; H.C.B. Maddison
Yellowknife: E. Richard; John C. Vertes
Registrar, Edna Delisle Jackson

### YUKON TERRITORY: SUPREME COURT

PO Box 4010, Whitehorse YT Y1A 3S9
403/667-3524; Fax: 403/667-3079

The Supreme Court is a superior court of record having original jurisdiction in all civil and criminal matters arising in the Yukon, unless excluded by statute.

Judges (The Hon. Mr./Madam Justice):
Whitehorse: Ralph E. Hudson; Harry C.B. Maddison
Ex-Officio Judges (The Hon. Mr./Madam Justice):
Yellowknife: J. Ted Richard; Virginia A. Schuler; John Z. Vertes
Deputy Judges (The Hon. Mr./Madam Justice):
Calgary: Paul S. Chrumka; Carole M. Conrad; Mary M. Hetherington; Roger P. Kerans; Earl Lomas; Arthur M. Lutz; Peter McIntyre; Peter C.G. Power
Edmonton: William J. Girgulis; Edward P. MacCallum; Ernest A. Marshall; Mary Moreau; Allan H. Wachowich
Lethbridge: Clarence G. Yanosik
London: R.J. Haines
Montréal: Perry Meyer; J.E. Marcel Nichols
Nanaimo: Ralph Hutchinson
Québec: Ross Goodwin
Regina: Edward D. Bayda; Calvin F. Tallis
Thunder Bay: Anthony William Maloney
Toronto: Lucien A. Beaulieu; Stephen Borins; Douglas Carruthers; W. David Griffiths; Stanley R. Kuristo
Vancouver: Marion Jean Allan; John C. Bouck; George Peter Fraser; Kenneth M. Lysyk; A. Gordon MacKinnon; Kenneth E. Meredith; Wallace T. Oppal; I. Lee Skipp; David Vickers
Winnipeg: A. Aubrey Hirschfield; Guy J. Kroft
Registrar, Bankruptcy, Edna Delisle-Jackson
Sheriff, Paul Cowan
Deputy Sheriff, R. Taylor
Deputy Sheriff, Gavin Shaw
Deputy Sheriff, J. Tiedman

### YUKON TERRITORY: TERRITORIAL COURT

PO Box 2703, Whitehorse YT Y1A 2C6
403/667-5438; Fax: 403/667-3079

The Territorial Court has jurisdiction in family, youth and select criminal matters.

**Chief Judge,** The Hon. John E. Faulkner
Puisne Judges (The Hon.):
Heino Lilles; Barry D. Stuart
Sr. Court Clerk, Sharon Kerr
Territorial Court Clerks:
Linda Balcaen, Sue Cleaver, Norma Davignon, Edwige Graham, Norm Hamilton, Stella Hearty (Watson Lake), Dorothy Irwin (Dawson City), Sharon Kerr, S.J. McCullough, Sharman Morrison, Arlene Ogden, Iris Warde

## OFFICIAL RECEIVERS

**(UNDER THE BANKRUPTCY & INSOLVENCY ACT)**

Superintendent of Bankruptcy, Marc Mayrand, Industry Canada, 365 Laurier Ave. West, 8th Fl., Ottawa, ON K1A 0C8; 613/941-1000; Fax: 613/941-2862

### Alberta

Industry Canada, Bankruptcy, #725, 9700 Jasper Ave., Edmonton AB T5J 4C3; 403/495-2476, Fax: 403/495-2466
Division No. 1: Edmonton; Red Deer; Wetaskiwin; Camrose (sub-district); Stettler; Peace River; Grande Prairie (sub-district)
Industry Canada, Bankruptcy, Standard Life Tower Bldg., #400, 639 - 5 Ave. SW, Calgary AB T2P; 403/292-567, Fax: 403/292-5188
Division No. 2: Calgary; Medicine Hat; Lethbridge/MacLeod; Drumheller/Hanna

### British Columbia

Industry Canada, Bankruptcy, #900, 300 West Georgia St., Vancouver BC V6B 6E1; 604/666-5007, Fax: 604/666-4610
Division No. 1: Prince Rupert
Division No. 2: Victoria; Nanaimo
Division No. 3: Vancouver ; New Westminster
Division No. 4: Yale; Cariboo
Division No. 5: West Kootenay; East Kootenay
Division No. 6: Parts of Yale and Cariboo; north of 52nd parallel

### Manitoba

Industry Canada, Bankruptcy, 400 St. Mary Ave., 4th Fl., Winnipeg MB R3C 4K5; 204/983-3229, Fax: 204/983-8904

### New Brunswick

Same as Nova Scotia
Division No. 1: Saint John; Queens; Kings; Charlotte
Division No. 2: York; Sunbury; Carleton; Victoria; Madawaska
Division No. 3: Gloucester; Northumberland; Restigouche
Division No. 4: Westmorland; Kent; Albert

### Newfoundland

Same as Nova Scotia

### Northwest Territories

Same as Alta. Div. 1 (Edmonton)

### Nova Scotia

Industry Canada, Bankruptcy Branch, Halifax Insurance Bldg., #900, 5670 Spring Garden Rd., Halifax NS B3J 1H6; 902/426-2900; Fax: 902/426-7275
Division No. 1: Halifax; Hants; Lunenburg; Queens; Annapolis; Kings
Division No. 2: Pictou; Guysborough; Cumberland; Colchester; Antigonish
Division No. 3: Cape Breton; Inverness; Richmond; Victoria
Division No. 4: Digby; Yarmouth; Shelburne

### Ontario

Industry Canada, Bankruptcy, 400 St. Mary Ave., 4th Fl., Winnipeg MB R3C 4K5; 204/983-3229, Fax: 204/983-8904
Division No. 1: Thunder Bay; Rainy River
Industry Canada, Bankruptcy, 25 St. Clair Ave. East, 7th Fl., Toronto ON M4T 1M2; 416/973-6486, Fax: 416/973-7440
Division No. 2: Sudbury; Algoma
Division No. 3: Manitoulin; Simcoe; Muskoka
Division No. 9: York
Division No. 10: Peterborough; Northumberland & Durham; Victoria & Haliburton
Division No. 13: Nipissing
Division No. 14: Parry Sound
Division No. 15: Temiskaming
Division No. 16: Cochrane
Industry Canada, Bankruptcy, The Federal Bldg., #303, 451 Talbot St., London ON N6A 5C9; 519/645-4034, Fax: 519/645-5139
Division No. 4: Dufferin; Grey; Bruce
Division No. 5: Middlesex; Huron; Perth; Oxford; Elgin
Division No. 6: Essex; Lambton; Kent
Division No.8: Waterloo; Wellington
Industry Canada, Bankruptcy, 69 John St. South, 4th Fl., Hamilton ON L8N 2B9; 905/572-2847; Fax: 905/572-4066
Division No. 7: Hamilton-Wentworth; Niagara; Norfolk; Haldimand; Brant; Halton
Division No. 9: Peel
Industry Canada, Bankruptcy, 473 Albert St., Ottawa ON K1A 0E5; 613/995-2994, Fax: 613/996-0949
Division No. 11: Frontenac; Lennox & Addington; Hastings; Prince Edward
Division No. 12: Carleton; Renfrew; Lanark; Russell & Prescott; Stormont, Dundas & Glengarry; Leeds & Grenville

### Prince Edward Island

Same as Nova Scotia

### Québec

Industrie Canada, Direction des Faillites, #800, 5, Place Ville-Marie, Montréal QC H3B 2G2; 514/283-6192, Fax: 514/283-9795
Division No. 1: Montréal; Richelieu; St. Hyacinthe; Beauharnois; Longueuil; Laval
Division No. 8: Joliette
Division No. 18: Terrebonne; Labelle
Division No. 19: Iberville
Industrie Canada, Direction des Faillites, 1040, av Belvedère, 2e étage, Sillery QC G1S 3G3; 418/648-4280, Fax: 418/648-4120
Division No. 2: Québec; Montmagny (Anticosti); La Malbaie
Division No. 3: Rimouski
Division No. 4: Mégantic
Division No. 5: Trois-Rivières; St. Maurice; Shawinigan
Division No. 7: Chicoutimi; Saguenay
Division No. 9: Roberval; Alma
Division No. 10: Kamouraska/Rivière du Loup;
Division No. 11: Gaspé; Bonaventure; New Carlisle; Îles-de-la-Madeleine; Percé
Division No. 13: Beauce
Division No. 14: Îles-de-la-Madeleine
Division No. 15: Arthabaska
Division No. 17: Frontenad
Division No. 22: Hauterive; Mingan; Baie Comeau; Sept Îles
Industrie Canada, Direction des Faillites, #600, 2665, rue King ouest, Sherbrooke QC J1L 1C1; 819/564-5742, Fax: 819/564-5743
Division No. 4: St. François; Lac Mégantic
Division No. 20: Bedford; Granby
Division No. 21: Drummond
Same as Ontario Division No. 11 (Ottawa)
Division No. 6: Hull; Pontiac
Division No. 12: Abitibi
Division No. 16: Rouyn-Noranda-Temiscamingue

### Saskatchewan

Industry Canada, Bankruptcy, #1020, 2002 Victoria Ave., Regina SK S4P 0R7; 306/780-5391, Fax: 780-6947
Division No. 1: Regina
Industry Canada, Bankruptcy, 123 - 2nd Ave. South, 7th Fl., Saskatoon SK S7K 7E6; 306/975-4298, Fax: 306/975-5317

### Yukon Territory

Same as B.C. Div. No. 1 (Vancouver)

# DIRECTORY OF LAW FIRMS

Law firms are listed alphabetically within the Province, City. The reference opposite City is the County or Judicial District.

## ALBERTA

**Airdrie** .......... **Calgary**

R.J. Hashizume, Airdrie Professional Centre, 142 - 1 Ave. NW, PO Box 3700, T4B 2B8 – 403/948-3335 – *1

M. John Wilson, 121E Centre Ave. West, PO Box 3444, T4B 2B7 – 403/948-7302, Fax: 403/948-4347 – *1

**Athabasca** .......... **Edmonton**

Kozina & Gregory, #3, 4907 - 51 St., T9S 1E7 – 403/675-3443, Fax: 403/675-3282 – *2

Paton Croll, 4811 - 50th St., T9S 1C8 – 403/675-5716 – *3

Paul W. Quantz, 4902 - 48 St., T9S 1B8 – 403/675-2534, Fax: 403/675-3161 – *1

**Banff** .......... **Calgary**

Karras, Rathbone, 205 Bear St., PO Box 899, T0L 0C0 – 403/762-2770, Fax: 403/762-5961 – *3

Robert M. Nesbitt, Q.C., PO Box 2129, T0L 0C0 – 403/762-3438, Fax: 403/762-9458 – *2

**Barrhead** .......... **Edmonton**

Driessen & Roy, 5006 - 50 Ave., PO Box 4220, T7N 1A2 – 403/674-2276, Fax: 403/674-4592 – *2

Marvin L. Perry, 5104 - 49A St., PO Box 158, T0G 0E0 – 403/674-2002, Fax: 403/674-4438 – *1

**Bassano** .......... **Medicine Hat**

Ben R. Plumer, PO Box 329, T0J 0B0 – 403/641-4131, Fax: 403/641-4133 – *1

**Beaver Lodge** .......... **Grande Prairie**

Roger Jewitt, PO Box 780, T0H 0C0 – 403/354-2271 – *1

**Blairmore** .......... **Macleod**

Valerie Danielson, PO Box 1620, T0K 0E0 – 403/562-2132, Fax: 403/562-2700 – *1

King & Young, 12305 - 20 Ave., PO Box 450, T0K 0E0 – 403/562-2804 – *2

**Bonnyville** .......... **Edmonton**

Allan Wayne Fraser, Muller Plaza, 4815 - 50 Ave., PO Box 6710, Stn Main, T9N 2H2 – 403/826-3355, Fax: 403/826-6132 – *1

Michel D. Meunier, 5022 - 50 Ave., PO Box 7670, T9N 2H9 – 403/826-3384 – *1

Wood & Wiebe, #101, 5001 - 49 Ave., PO Box 8060, T9N 2J3 – 403/826-5767, Fax: 403/826-4654 – *2

**Bragg Creek** .......... **Calgary**

Judith G. Setrakov, PO Box 336, T0L 0K0 – 403/949-2555, Fax: 403/949-2252 – *1

**Brooks** .......... **Medicine Hat**

Kay, Kay & Riggins, #B, 212 - 3 Ave, PO Box 1227, T0J 0J0 – 403/362-5733 – *3

Lutes & Bell, 103 - 2 Ave West, PO Box 670, T1R 1B6 – 403/362-3447, Fax: 403/362-4379 – *2

**Calgary** .......... **Calgary**

Adel A. Abougoush, 1409 - 18A St. NE, T2E 4W7 – 403/276-8415

Adamson Willoughby & D'Souza, #217, 495 - 36 St. NE, T2A 6K3 – 403/531-9520, Fax: 403/272-6586 – *4

Ahlsten & Company, #320, 521 - 3 Ave. SW, T2P 3T3 – 403/233-7600, Fax: 403/263-2713 – *4

John W. Aikenhead, 124 Westview Dr. SW, T3C 2R9 – 403/242-6699

Anderson & Company, #310, 602 - 11th Ave. SW, T2R 1J8 – 403/543-5177, Fax: 403/543-5175 – *2

Anderson Law Firm, #610, 7015 Macleod Tr. South, T2H 2K6 – 403/253-4597, Fax: 403/253-4599 – *1

Arkell, Damen, #1440, 736 - 6th Ave. SW, T2P 3T7 – 403/531-4151, Fax: 403/531-4153; Email: ar_dam@telusplanet.net – *2

Armstrong Waskiewich Ede, #1520, 734 - 7 Ave. SW, T2P 3P8 – 403/290-1630, Fax: 403/290-1635 – *3

T.J. Bachynski, 112 - 4 Ave. SW, 28th Fl., PO Box 38, T2P 2V5 – 403/269-8690, Fax: 403/269-6213 – *1

Balbi & Company, 1501 MacLeod Tr. SE, T2G 2N6 – 403/269-7300, Fax: 403/265-9790

Verna G. Baldwin, 15 Hillary Cres. SW, T2V 3J3 – 403/255-8739

Ballem MacInnes, First Canadian Centre, #1800, 350 - 7th Ave. SW, T2P 3N9 – 403/292-9800, Fax: 403/233-8979 – *23

Cameron J.G. Bally, #402, 1015 - 4 St. SW, T2R 1J4 – 403/269-1646, Fax: 403/266-5823; Email: morogle@cadvision.com – *1

Deborah L. Barron, Southland Court Building, #231, 10601 Southport Rd. SW, T2W 3M6 – 403/278-3730, Fax: 403/271-8016 – *2

Walter C. Barron, Q.C., First Alberta Pl., 777 - 8 Ave. SW, T2P 3R5 – 403/269-2277, Fax: 403/263-3256 – *1

A.V.M. Beattie, Q.C., 3108 Carleton St. SW, T2T 5Y6 – 403/245-5255, Fax: 403/228-0254 – *1

Beaumont Church, AGT Tower, #2200, 411 - 1 St. SE, T2G 5E7 – 403/264-0000, Fax: 403/264-0478 – *13

Bennett Jones Verchere, Bankers Hall East, #4500, 855 - 2 St. SW, T2P 4K7 – 403/298-3100, Fax: 403/265-7219 – *142

Gary E. Bilyk, #202, 703 - 6 Ave. SW, T2P 0T9 – 403/266-2810, Fax: 403/237-0327 – *1

R. Michael Birnbaum, B.A., LL.B., Rocky Mountain Plaza, #670, 615 Macleod Tr. SE, T2G 4T8 – 403/265-9050, Fax: 403/262-1379; Email: birnbaum@nucleus.com

Bishop & McKenzie, #2230, 700 - 9th Ave. SW, T2P 3V4 – 403/237-5550, Fax: 403/263-3423; Email: bishmc@planet.eon.net – *5

S.L. Blaine, PO Box 1164, T2P 2K9 – 403/246-1733, Fax: 403/249-8398 – *1

Blake, Cassels & Graydon, Bankers Hall East, #3500, 855 - 2nd St. SW, T2P 4J8 – 403/260-9600, Fax: 403/260-9700; Email: jeh@blakes.ca; URL: http://www.blakes.ca – *42

Vivian J. Blochert, 8948 Bayridge Dr. SW, T2V 3M8 – 403/251-3947

Blumell & Hartney, #203, 2411 - 4 St. NW, T2M 2Z8 – 403/282-4544, Fax: 403/284-4503 – *2

Michael J. Bondar, Bankers Hall, #2100, 855 - 2 St., T2P 4J9 – 403/237-4862, Fax: 403/237-4809

Nevine S. Booth, 8 Edgeland Cres. NW, T3A 4C3 – 403/547-0991

James A. Bradford, 2712 - 10 St. SW, T2T 3H2 – 403/245-2694

Britton & Jones, #406, 501 - 18 Ave. SW, T2S 0C7 – 403/229-9333

Brownlee Fryett, Western Tower, #1010, 530 - 8 Ave. SW, T2P 3S8 – 403/232-8300, Fax: 403/232-8408

Bruni Greenan Klym, #1750, 801 - 6th Ave. SW, T2P 3W2 – 403/266-5664, Fax: 403/262-6343 – *4

Bryan & Co., First Canadian Place, #3520, 350 - 7th Ave., T2P 3N9 – 403/269-7220, Fax: 403/269-9304 – *4

David R. Burge, Brentwood Village Mall, #232C, 3630 Morley Trail NW, T2L 1K8 – 403/282-2888 – *1

Burnet, Duckworth & Palmer, First Canadian Centre, #1400, 350 - 7 Ave. SW, T2P 3N9 – 403/260-0100, Fax: 403/260-0332; Email: central@bdplaw.com – *67

Gordon J. Burrell, #401, 1110 Centre St. North, T2E 2R2 – 403/277-3133

Richard A. Cairns, Q.C., #3400, 425 - 1 St. SW, T2P 3L8 – 403/205-3155, Fax: 403/205-3152 – *1

Calgary Legal Guidance, #100, 615 Macleod Trail SE, T2G 4T8 – 403/234-9266, Fax: 403/234-9299 – *3

A.B. Cameron, #850, 10201 Southport Rd. SW, T2W 4X9 – 403/531-2700, Fax: 403/531-2707; Email: camlaw@nucleus.com; URL: http://wwwebster.ab.ca/camlaw – *1

Carscallen Lockwood & Cormie, #1500, 407 - 2 St. SW, T2P 2Y3 – 403/262-3775, Fax: 403/262-2952 – *5

Checkland & Company, #501, 736 - 6 Ave. SW, T2P 5G7 – 403/233-9101, Fax: 403/233-9135 – *2

Malcom P.Y. Chow, #328, 1015 Centre St. North, T2E 2P8 – 403/277-1688, Fax: 403/277-1699

T. Catherine Christopher, #840, 407 - 2 St. SW, T2P 2Y3 – 403/237-8084, Fax: 403/263-6413

S.M. Chumir, #280, 521 - 3 Ave. SW, T2P 3T3 – 403/269-1949 – *1

Clark Dymond McCaffery, Calgary House, #1400, 550 - 6 Ave. SW, T2P 0S2 – 403/265-7070, Fax: 403/232-6750 – *5

Clarke Bonnycastle, #220, 1100 - 8 Ave. SW, T2P 3T9 – 403/237-6300 – *3

Rosemary J. Clarke, 6347 Lynch Cres. SW, T3E 5V1 – 403/240-0008

Code Hunter Wittmann, #1200, 700 - 2 St. SW, T2P 4V5 – 403/298-1000, Fax: 403/263-9193; Email: chw@cadvision.com – *62

John C. Cohen, #210, 2323 - 32 Ave. NE, T2E 6Z3 – 403/250-1582 – *1

Maggie F. Collins, #900, 840 - 7 Ave. SW, T2P 3G2 – 403/269-4222

Cook Duke Cox, #3000, 700 - 9th Ave. SW, T2P 3V4 – 403/298-2400, Fax: 403/262-0007; Email: cdc@ccinet.ab.ca – *19

Timothy J. Corcoran, #505, 777 - 8 Ave. SW, T2P 3R5 – 403/263-6000, Fax: 403/265-1921; Email: tcorcor@telusplanet.com – *1

L.H.A. Creighton, #400, 4600 Crowchild Trail NW, T3B 2C6 – 403/247-1643 – *1

Cummings Verstraten Kugelmass, Deerfoot Ct., Box: 106, 1144 - 29 Ave. NE, T2E 7P1 – 403/250-3570, Fax: 403/291-0389 – *3

Gary A. Daniels, #200, 209 - 19 St. NW, T2N 2H9 – 403/297-0800, Fax: 403/283-7000 – *1

Thomas O. Davis, #300, 840 - 6th Ave. SW, T2P 3E5 – 403/269-5944, Fax: 403/263-5772 – *1

T.M. Dawe, #200, 1409 Edmonton Tr. NE, T2E 3K8 – 403/276-8802

Beverley J.T. Delong, 5120 Carney Rd. NW, T2L 1G2 – 403/282-8260 – *1

Demiantschuk, Milley & Burke, #1130, 1015 - 4th St. SW, T2R 1J4 – 403/252-9937, Fax: 403/263-8529; Email: dsmb@nucleus.com – *5

H.R. Densmore, #800, 603 - 7 Ave. SW, T2P 2T5 – 403/263-0950 – *1

DeVries & Company, #405, 1167 Kensington Cres. NW, T2N 1X7 – 403/299-9177, Fax: 403/299-9172 – *1

J.S. Dhanda, #5, 15 Millrise Blvd. SW, T1Y 2X1 – 403/254-1777, Fax: 403/254-1779

Dixon Law Firm, #1020, 833 - 4 Ave. SW, T2P 3T5 – 403/297-9480, Fax: 403/266-1487 – *3

Docken & Company, #215, 840 - 6th Ave. SW, T2P 3E5 – 403/269-3612, Fax: 403/269-8246; Email: docken@telusplanet.net – *2

Eleanor Doctor, PO Box 72038, RPO Glenmore Landing, T2V 5H9 – 403/640-6242, Fax: 403/640-9911 – *1

M.M. Donlevy-Konkin, 27 Cornwallis Dr. NW, T2K 1T6 – 403/284-0639

Margaret-Ann R. Douglas, #4, 3820 Bow Trail SW, T3C 2E7 – 403/249-1176

Drummond Phillips & Sevalrud, #900, 521 - 3 Ave. SW, T2P 3T3 – 403/221-8700, Fax: 403/264-6654 – *7

Dukeshire Law Office, Provident Professional Bldg., #201, 4616 Valiant Dr. NW, T3A 0X9 – 403/286-7008, Fax: 403/286-7644 – *1

Duncan & Craig, #3250, 700-2nd St. SW, T2P 2W2 – 403/298-2000, Fax: 403/298-2024; Email: duncancraig-cgy@telusplanet.net; URL: http://www.duncanandcraig.com – *4

Duncan, Kelly, #3000, 421 - 7 Ave., T2P 4K9 – 403/543-5500, Fax: 403/543-5505 – *6

Dunphy Calvert, #2100, 777 - 8 Ave. SW, T2P 3R5 – 403/265-7777, Fax: 403/269-8911 – *15

Dworkin & Dworkin, Elveden House, #340, 717 - 7th Ave. SW, T2P 0Z3 – 403/261-3050, Fax: 403/266-5847 – *2

G.M. Eamon, #630, 11012 Macleod Tr. South, T2J 6A5 – 403/271-3221, Fax: 403/271-5909 – *1

Ebbert & Company, 2020 - 10 St. NW, T2M 3M2 – 403/284-1131, Fax: 403/282-1621 – *3

Marc L. Edelson Professional Corporation, #405, 1167 Kensington Cres. NW, T2N 1X7 – 403/777-9940, Fax: 403/777-9944 – *1

Emery Jamieson, #206, 1167 Kensington Cres. NW, T2N 1X7 – 403/543-6010, Fax: 403/270-8080

P. Robert Enns, Westmount Pl., #222, 1100 - 8 Ave. SW, T2P 3T9 – 403/262-6588, Fax: 403/262-6590 – *1

Evans Higa Burgess, #2250, 520 - 5 Ave. SW, T2P 3R7 – 403/294-0015, Fax: 403/294-0017

Faber Gurevitch Bickman, #350, 603 - 7 Ave SW, T2P 2T5 – 403/263-1540, Fax: 403/269-2653 – *9

Felesky Flynn, First Canadian Centre, #3400, 350 - 7 Ave SW, T2P 3N9 – 403/260-3300, Fax: 403/263-9649; Email: felesky@mail.cycor.ca – *13

W.A. Ferguson, #210A, 5403 Crowchild Tr. NW, T3B 4Z1 – 403/288-7601, Fax: 403/228-3689 – *1

Field Atkinson Perraton, First Canadian Centre, #1900, 350 - 7 Ave. SW, T2P 3N9 – 403/260-8500, Fax: 403/264-7084; URL: http://www.fieldlaw.com/ – *33

P.L. Fiess, #825, 603 - 7 Ave. SW, T2P 2T5 – 403/266-0033, Fax: 403/261-4958 – *1

N.A. Flatters, 1307 Klondike Ave. SW, T2V 2L9

G. Lyle Ford, 30 Eagle Ridge Dr. SW, T2V 2V4 – 403/255-5555, Fax: 403/255-5555 – *1

Forsyth & Associates, #100, 1300 - 8 St. SW, T2R 1B2 – 403/244-3829, Fax: 403/229-4063

Foster, Wise & Walden, #750, 839 - 5 Ave. SW, T2P 3C8 – 403/263-6601, Fax: 403/269-6785 – *4

Fric & Lowenstein, Sunridge Professional Centre, #406, 2675 - 36 St. NE, T1Y 6H6 – 403/291-2594, Fax: 403/291-2668 – *3

Gainer & Co., #225, 604 - 1 St. SW, T2N 1M7 – 403/265-9944, Fax: 403/265-9904 – *1

Robert W. Gee, 1725 - 10 Ave. SW, 2nd Fl., T3C 0K1 – 403/245-0640, Fax: 403/244-7955 – *1

German Fong Albus Lam, #418, 715 - 5 Ave. SW, T2P 2X6 – 403/263-7880, Fax: 403/237-7075 – *6

G.J. Godlovitch, #412, 10325 Bonaventure Dr. SE, T2J 5R8 – 403/225-1584 – *1

W.D. Goodfellow, Q.C., #715, 999 - 8th St. SW, T2R 1J5 – 403/228-7102, Fax: 403/228-7199

Gorman, Gorman & Burns, #300, 1333 - 8 St. SW, T2R 1M6 – 403/244-5515, Fax: 403/244-5605 – *2

Mark Avrom Gottlieb, #200, 222 - 16 Ave. NE, T2E 1J8 – 403/282-2516, 230-0712 – *1

Laura Lee Grant, #300, 714 - 1 St. SE, T2G 2G8 – 403/263-5200, Fax: 403/263-4833 – *1

Gregg & Company, Kipling Sq., #300, 611 - 10 Ave. SW, T2R 0B2 – 403/266-3086, Fax: 403/262-6677 – *2

A.F.W. Grenon Professional Corp., #300, 509 - 8th Ave. SW, T2P 1G1 – 403/571-4450, Fax: 403/571-4444 – *1

Grier, Allen, #201, 4616 Valiant Dr. NW, T3A 0X9 – 403/247-2761, Fax: 403/286-0306 – *2

Gruman, Crossfield, #202, 1717 - 10 St. NW, T2M 4S2 – 403/284-4614, Fax: 403/202-1717 – *2

Harrison Guild, #502, 5920 - 1A St., T2H 0G3 – 403/259-5256, Fax: 403/502-5920

Rita J. Guthrie, 3026 Linden Dr., T3E 6C5 – 403/242-9704 – *1

Bryan F. Hagel, 2026 - 33 Ave. SW, T2T 1Z4 – 403/249-5505, Fax: 403/240-0632 – *1

McGuire Hagel, #300, 4515 Bow Trail SW, T3C 2G3 – 403/249-1176, Fax: 403/242-9455 – *1

E.B. Hammelburg, 55 Dalcastle Way NW, T3A 2N4 – 403/286-6239

Hanson & Associates, #101, 3515 - 17 Ave. SE, T2A 0R5 – 403/235-5556, Fax: 403/235-5569 – *1

Hanson & Company, #280, 521 - 3 Ave SW, T2P 3T3 – 403/261-6890, Fax: 403/263-1632; Toll Free: 1-800-523-6162; Email: 73032407@compuserve.com – *2

Harben, Aaron & Rynd, #501, 665 - 8 St. SW, T2P 3K7 – 403/233-7616

Gregory R. Harris, #500, 630 - 4th Ave., T2P 0J9 – 403/266-5035, Fax: 403/265-6368

O.W. Harris, #3, 610 - 8 Ave. SW, T2P 1G5 – 403/266-2261 – *1

L.S. Heald, #200, 634 - 6 Ave. SW, T2P 0S4 – 403/266-2131, Fax: 403/261-6862 – *1

Stephen G. Heinz, #1500, 250 - 6th Ave. SW, T2P 3H7 – 403/531-2781, Fax: 403/264-1262 – *1

Dale Hensley, #230, 1210 - 8 St. SW, T2R 1L3 – 403/229-2938, Fax: 403/229-2977

Norman R. Hess Professional Corporation, 201 - 37 St. NW, T2N 4N6 – 403/299-9161 – *1

Patrick B. Higgerty, #224, 1829 Ranchlands Blvd. NW, T3G 2A7 – 403/241-3153, Fax: 403/241-1108; Email: higgerty@compuserve.com – *1

Higgs & Hooker, #120, 1330 - 15 Ave. SW, T3C 3N7 – 403/245-3493, Fax: 403/229-1547 – *2

C.R. High Wo, #515, 1110 Centre St. NE, T2E 2R2 – 403/276-9877, Fax: 403/277-5733 – *1

Ho MacNeil Jenuth, #680, 140 - 4 Ave. SW, T2P 3N3 – 403/233-2812, Fax: 403/237-8312 – *4

Hoar, Lee & Boers, West Tower, SunLife Plaza, #1220, 144 - 4 Ave. SW, T2P 3N4 – 403/262-4866, Fax: 403/262-4860

Hoffman Dorchik, #600, 5920 MacLeod Trail SW, T2H 0K2 – 403/258-0800, Fax: 403/253-0738 – *4

Howard, Mackie, Canterra Tower, #1000, 400 - 3 Ave. SW, T2P 4H2 – 403/232-9523, Fax: 403/266-1395; Email: postmaster@howardmackie.com; URL: http://howardmackie.com – *62

Louise Huard-Peake, #300, 840 - 6 Ave. SW, T2P 3E5 – 403/239-4666, Fax: 403/239-4356 – *1

M. Ann Hughes, 940 Coachside Cres. SW, T3H 1A5 – 403/560-4579

Ivo Hula, #438, 1421 - 7 Ave. NW, T2M 0Z3 – 403/283-9329

L.D. Hurd, #521, 206 - 7 Ave. SW, T2P 0W7 – 403/262-8280 – *1

H.J. Hurov, #535, 540 - 5 Ave. SW, T2P 0M2 – 403/263-8220 – *1

M.A. Hutchings, #310, 9737 Macleod Tr. South, T2J 0P6 – 403/531-0200

Janet E. Hutchison, #205, 259 Midpark Way SE, T2X 1M2 – 403/256-2249, Fax: 403/256-2440 – *1

Janet E. Hutchison, #205, 259 Midpark Way SE, T2X 1M2 – 403/256-2249, Fax: 403/256-2440

Inglewood Law Office, 1327B - 9 Ave. SW, T2G 0T2 – 403/233-7626, Fax: 403/233-7656 – *1

Michael M. Jamison, 3527 - 18 St. SW, T2T 4T9 – 403/243-8360, Fax: 403/287-1968 – *1

Daniel W.H. Jarvis, 135 Whitefield Dr. NE, T1Y 5X1 – 403/293-2191, Fax: 403/293-5445 – *2

Johnson & Shibley, #116, 8220 Centre St. North, T3K 1J7 – 403/275-3230 – *2

Johnston Robinson Clark, #930, 300 - 5 Ave. SW, T2P 3C4 – 403/261-7600, Fax: 403/269-5866; Email: jrc@netcom.ca – *1

Kenneth C. Johnston, #400, 1201 - 5 St. SW, T2R 0Y6 – 403/262-3122, Fax: 403/266-1847 – *1

G.M. Jumaga, #201, 2411 - 4 St. NW, T2M 2Z8 – 403/284-4587 – *1

Kelly & Kelly, #1640, 700 - 4 Ave. SW, T2P 3J4 – 403/266-6296, Fax: 403/264-2954 – *4

P. Donald Kennedy, Q.C., 59 Cherovan Dr. SW, T2V 2P3 – 403/255-6331, Fax: 403/264-2993

Kenney & Company, #230, 1121 Centre St. North, T2E 7K6 – 403/230-3751, Fax: 403/276-8139 – *3

Robert D. Kerr, #300, 840 - 6 Ave. SW, T2P 3E5 – 403/265-1331, Fax: 403/265-1332; Email: rdkerr@cadvision.com – *1

G.R. Klatt, #400, 7015 Macleod Trail SW, T2H 2K6 – 403/255-3033, Fax: 403/255-0403 – *1

Knibbe McClintock, #900, 441 - 5 Ave. SW, T2P 2V1 – 403/290-1282, Fax: 403/261-5772 – *2

Kutz Hotzel, #316, 1167 Kensington Cres. NW, T2N 1X7 – 403/270-4098 – *2

Laird Armstrong, #770, 340 - 12 Ave. SW, T2R 1L5 – 403/233-0050, Fax: 403/266-1238 – *3

Langlois Legal Centre, 3333 - 23 St. NE, T2E 6V8 – 403/531-9300, Fax: 403/250-8961; Toll Free: 1-800-865-3619 – *1

Linda S. Laratta, 3938 Edenstone Rd. NW, T3A 3Z6 – 403/239-7052, Fax: 403/241-2455

Lee & Kong, #630, 122 - 4 Ave. SW, T2P 0H3 – 403/233-9432, Fax: 403/237-9614 – *2

Dennis A. Lerner, #262A, 1632 - 14 Ave. NW, T2N 1M7 – 403/282-1515, Fax: 403/282-2110 – *1

L.G. Lien, #240, 1100 - 8 Ave SW, T2P 3T9 – 403/234-7787, Fax: 403/232-8885 – *1

Lilburn Ellert, #400, 603 - 7 Ave. SW, T2P 2T5 – 403/269-3315, Fax: 403/269-3329 – *4

Lirenman Peterson, #300, 255 - 17 Ave. SW, T2S 2T8 – 403/245-0111, Fax: 403/245-0115 – *6

Litwiniuk & Company, #205, 4020 - 17 Ave. SE, T2A 0S7 – 403/273-8580, Fax: 403/273-9045 – *2

Lord Russell, #600, 706 - 7 Ave. SW, T2P 0Z1 – 403/262-7722, Fax: 403/262-5991 – *6

Low, Glenn & Card, 3475 - 26 Ave. NE, T1Y 6L4 – 403/291-2532, Fax: 403/291-2534; Email: lgc-law@supernet.ab.ca; URL: http://www.canfind.com/index.html – *4

James A. MacDonald, #710, 304 - 8 Ave. SW, T2P 1C2 – 403/221-9444

Ronald C. MacDonald, 54 Granlea Pl. SW, T3E 4K2 – 403/249-0658

Machida Mack Shewchuk, #304, 1204 Kensington Rd. NW, T2N 3P5 – 403/221-8333, Fax: 403/221-8339 – *3

MacKenzie Welbourn, Mount Royal Pl., #640, 1414 - 8 St. SW, T2R 1J6 – 403/229-9093, Fax: 403/229-1553 – *2

MacKimmie Matthews, Gulf Canada Sq., #700, 401 - 9 Ave. SW, PO Box 2010, T2P 3L5 – 403/232-0611, Fax: 403/232-0888 – *50

Macleod Dixon, Canterra Tower, #3700, 400 - 3 Ave. SW, T2P 4H2 – 403/267-8222, Fax: 403/264-5973; Email: md@lexcom.ab.ca – *97

Major, Caron, #1600, 400 - 3 Ave. SW, T2P 4H2 – 403/262-3000, Fax: 403/237-0111; Email: major.caron@cadvision.com; URL: majorcaron.com – *8

Birjinder P.S. Mangat, #158, 3359 - 27 St. NE, T1Y 5E4 – 403/735-6088, Fax: 403/735-6089; Email: mangatb@cadvision.com

Masuch, Albert & Neale, #C200, 9705 Horton Rd. SW, T2V 2X5 – 403/543-1100, Fax: 403/543-1111; Email: manlaw@telusplanet.net – *2

Martin C. Matheron, #204, 5403 Crowchild Trail NW, T3B 4Z1 – 403/247-2359, Fax: 403/286-4517 – *1

Karen Leigh McBean, 44 Hawksbrow Rd. NW, T3G 2S7 – 403/239-9704 – *1

McCaffery Goss Mudry, #2200, 736 - 6 Ave. SW, T2P 3T7 – 403/260-1400, Fax: 403/260-1444; Email: mgm@cadvision.com – *11

McCarthy Tétrault, #3200, 421 - 7 Ave. SW, T2P 4K9 – 403/260-3500, Fax: 403/260-3501; Email: calgary@mccarthy.ca; URL: http://www.mccarthy.ca – *57

McConnell, MacInnes, Graham, #1160, 10655 Southport Rd. SW, T2W 4Y1 – 403/278-7001, Fax: 403/271-2826 – *5

M.J. McDonald, 1111 - 11 Ave. SW, PO Box 1680, Stn M, T2P 2L7 – 403/253-0000; 245-2024, Fax: 403/244-2135 – *1

McDonald, Plotkins, Anderson & Company, Western Union Bldg., 640 - 8 Ave. SW, 8th Fl., T2P 1G7 – 403/265-9100, Fax: 403/265-7438 – *2

* indicates number of lawyers in law firm.

McGown & Johnson, #245, 1209 - 59 Ave. SE, T2H 2P6 – 403/255-5114, Fax: 403/258-3840 – *3

McGuigan Kitchen & Associates, Western Canada Place, #2210, 705 - 9th Ave. SW, T2P 3V4 – 403/265-7744, Fax: 403/269-4729 – *1

McGuire Hagel, Terry, #300, 4131 Bow Trail SW , Lower Level, T3C 2E9 – 403/249-1176, Fax: 403/242-9455

Neil R. McKay, 5331 LaSalle Cres. NW, PO Box 1284, Stn M, T2P 2L2 – 403/240-1082

Kerry W. McLelland, Crowchild Square, #204, 5403 Crowchild Trail NW, T3B 4Z1 – 403/247-2359, Fax: 403/286-4517 – *1

McLennan Ross, Altius Centre, #1801, 500 - 4th Ave. SW, T2P 2V6 – 403/543-9120, Fax: 403/543-9150; Toll Free: 1-888-543-9120; Email: calgary@mross.com

McLeod & Company, #800, 11012 Macleod Tr. South, T2J 6A5 – 403/278-9411, Fax: 403/271-1769 – *17

McManus Thomson, #2150, 530 - 8 Ave. SW, T2P 3S8 – 403/571-8565, Fax: 403/571-8566 – *5

McNally & Company, #1520, 324 - 8th Ave. SW, T2P 2Z2 – 403/261-1555, Fax: 403/232-8818; Email: mcnally@cadvision.com – *2

Beryl McNeill, #405, 1167 Kensington Cr. NW, T2N 1X7 – 403/299-9179, Fax: 403/299-9172 – *1

McNiven Kelly, SunLife Plaza, West Tower, #1600, 144 - 4th Ave. SW, T2P 3N4 – 403/263-8230, Fax: 403/263-8950 – *10

Anne E. McTavish, 4620 Manilla Rd. SE, T2G 4B7 – 403/255-4400, Fax: 403/252-1581 – *1

Merchant Law Group, #1120, 635 - 8th Ave. SW, T2B 3M3 – 403/250-9777

Millar & Associates, 1124 Kensington Rd. NW, T2N 3P3 – 403/283-1925, Fax: 403/270-8033 – *2

Millard, Johnson & Maxwell, 812A - 16 Ave. SW, T2R 0S9 – 403/228-4317, Fax: 403/228-3391 – *2

Milne, Davis, #850, 933 - 17 Ave. SW, T2T 5R6 – 403/229-3000, Fax: 403/229-3282 – *2

Milner Fenerty, Fifth Ave. Place, 30th Floor, 237 - 4th Ave. SW, T2P 4X7 – 403/268-7000, Fax: 403/268-3100; Email: milfen@milfen.com; URL: http://www.milfen.com – *101

Moore Wittman Phillips, #2700, 801 - 6 Ave. SW, T2P 3W2 – 403/269-2111, Fax: 403/263-5600 – *6

Moreau, Ogle & Hursh, #402, 1015 - 4 St. SW, T2R 1J4 – 403/269-5352, Fax: 403/266-5823 – *3

Scott D. Morgan, #205, 4500 - 16 Ave. NW, T3B 0M6 – 403/286-5056

Johnathan H.B. Moss, #222, 1100 - 8 St. SW, T2P 3T9 – 403/237-6100, Fax: 403/262-6590 – *1

Robert C. Muir, 622 - 5 Ave. SW, 2nd Fl., T2P 0M6 – 403/262-8410

G. Mungan, 1039 Durham Ave. SW, T2T 0P8 – 403/229-4002, Fax: 403/299-7728

J.B. Munholland, #280, 251 Midpark Blvd. SE, T2X 1S3 – 403/254-9266 – *1

Nazarevich & Company, #630, 840 - 6 Ave. SW, T2P 3E5 – 403/261-3030, Fax: 403/266-5350 – *2

D.M. Nielsen, #401, 301 - 14 St. NW, T2N 2A1 – 403/283-1244, Fax: 403/283-8818 – *1

O'Brien Devlin Markey Macleod, #3110, 421 - 7th Ave. SW, T2P 4K9 – 403/265-5616, Fax: 403/264-8146 – *6

Karen M. O'Brien, 1947 - 12 St. SW, T2T 3N3 – 403/245-4745

Ogilvie & Company, Canada Pl., #1600, 407 - 2 St. SW, T2P 2Y3 – 403/237-9050, Fax: 403/262-7896 – *17

Virginia L. Palsgrove, #2100, 520 - 5 Ave. SW, T2P 3R7 – 403/265-6626, Fax: 403/531-4330 – *1

Brenda A. Parker, #540, 840 - 6 Ave. SW, T2P 3E5 – 403/294-6793, Fax: 403/263-5371 – *1

Parlee McLaws, Western Canadian Pl., #3400, 707 - 8th Ave. SW, T2P 1H5 – 403/294-7000, Fax: 403/265-8263; Email: lawyers@parlee.com; URL: http://www.parlee.com – *34

M.H. Patterson, #222, 20 Coachway Rd. SW, T3H 1E6 – 403/240-2573

Kathy I. Pawluk, 115 Forest Cres. SE, T2A 5B1 – 403/272-5642 – *1

Peterson, Shields, Galbraith & Hutchinson, #204, 755 Lake Bonavista Dr. South, T2J 0N3 – 403/271-9710, Fax: 403/271-3942 – *4

M.A. Pettem, 306 - 10 St. NW, T2N 1V8 – 403/230-3777

Phipps Law Office, #303, 8180 MacLeod Trail SE, T2H 6B8 – 403/531-0181, Fax: 403/531-0180 – *1

Jeffrey B. Pike, 3907 - 45 St. SW, T3E 6P2 – 403/240-2435

Pipella, Warren, #600, 404 - 6 Ave. SW, T2P 0R9 – 403/265-8733, Fax: 403/263-3153 – *7

Pomerance & Company, #700, 10655 Southport Rd. SW, T2W 4Y1 – 403/278-5840, Fax: 403/271-6929 – *4

Poole, Laycraft, #1601, 333 - 11th Ave. SW, T2R 1L9 – 403/290-1601, Fax: 403/290-0828; Email: neilfk@telusplanet.net – *5

Lawrence S. Portigal, 6638 Bow Cres. NW, T3B 2B9 – 403/286-6380, Fax: 403/286-1888 – *1

Prodanchuk Dickson, #250, 999 - 8 St. SW, T2R 1J5 – 403/245-4616, Fax: 403/245-4621 – *3

R. Brickard Ratcliffe, #220, 3016 - 19 St. NE, T2E 6Y9 – 403/250-5444, Fax: 403/291-0410 – *1

Reynolds, Mirth, Richards & Farmer, Sunlife Plaza, North Tower, #1790, 140 - 4 Ave. SW, T2P 3N3 – 403/234-9192, Fax: 403/234-9194

Doreen P. Richards, 2220 - 12th St. SW, T2T 3N4 – 403/209-4750, Fax: 403/228-0479; Email: 76604.326@compuserve.com – *1

T.W. Robinson, #930, 300 - 5 Ave. SW, T2P 3C4 – 403/261-7600, Fax: 403/269-5866; Email: 104400.2363@compuserve.com

Rogers & Company, #400, 1010 - 8 Ave. SW, T2P 1J2 – 403/263-6805, Fax: 403/263-6800 – *6

Neil T. Ryan, #200, 703 - 6 Ave. SW, T2P 0T9 – 403/231-2760, Fax: 403/264-6408 – *1

St. Louis & Lomow, #540, 1010 - 1 St. SW, T2R 1K4 – 403/264-2912, Fax: 403/266-2901 – *2

J.P. St. Pierre, 1221A - 11 Ave. SW, T3C 0M5 – 403/229-1129

K.A. Sarjeant, 48 Woodhaven Rd. SW, T2W 5P9 – 403/238-1290

Joann L. Schwager, PO Box 74047, RPO Strathcona, T3H 3B6 – 403/686-7198, Fax: 403/686-3810 – *1

T. Schwartzberg, #201, 602 - 11 Ave. SW, T2R 1J8 – 403/232-1302, Fax: 403/265-1517 – *1

W.J. Shachnowich, 1700 Varsity Estates Dr., NW, T3B 2W9 – 403/269-1313, Fax: 403/247-3127 – *1

Carole A. Shaw, #302, 1550 - 8 St. SW, T2R 1K1 – 403/245-8200 – *1

John R. Shaw, #610, 615 Macleod Tr. SE, T2G 4T8 – 403/294-1414

Shellnutt McKenna Bryant, #405, 603 - 7 Ave. SW, T2P 2T5 – 403/234-8811, Fax: 403/234-7911 – *3

Shennette Leuschner McKay, #600, 700 - 4 Ave. SW, T2P 3J4 – 403/269-8282, Fax: 403/269-8295 – *3

D.J. Simpson, 348 - 14 St. NW, T2N 1Z7 – 403/283-8018

L.F. Sjoman, 2239 - 2 Ave. NW, T2N 0H1 – 403/283-5799

Smith & Smith, #206, 7 Glenbrook Place SW, T3E 6W4 – 403/242-9711 – *2

Smith Lamarsh, #450, 808 - 4 Ave., T2P 3E8 – 403/234-7779, Fax: 403/263-7897; Email: slamarsh@agt.net – *4

W.S. Soboren, 2444 Palisade Dr. SW, T2V 3V3 – 403/281-3741 – *1

Soltysiak & Sparks, #205, 2411 - 4 St. NW, T2M 2Z8 – 403/282-9215, Fax: 403/289-3729 – *2

Spackman & Matt, #375, 1550 - 5 St. SW, T2R 1K3 – 403/229-2429, Fax: 403/228-6415 – *2

Sparrow Law Office, #10, 628 - 12 Ave. SW, T2R 0H6 – 403/234-9722, Fax: 403/237-8748; Email: sparrow@nucleus.com – *1

Spier Harben, #1000, 665 - 8th St. SW, T2P 3K7 – 403/263-5130, Fax: 403/264-9600 – *8

Patricia E. Stark, #600, 706 - 7 Ave. SW, T2P 0Z1 – 403/262-7722, Fax: 403/262-5991 – *1

Kenneth E. Staroszik, #400, 1010 - 8 Ave. SW, T1P 1J2 – *1

Donald V. Steele, 2020 - 10 St. NW, T2M 3M2 – 403/284-2940

Stengl Everard, #406, 1212 - 31 Ave. NE, T2E 7S8 – 403/250-7100, Fax: 403/291-5473 – *3

Stewart & Stewart, #700, 603 - 7 Ave. SW, T2P 2T5 – 403/265-5440, Fax: 403/262-1367 – *3

Stikeman, Elliott, Bankers Hall, #1500, 855 - 2nd St. SW, T2P 4J7 – 403/266-9000, Fax: 403/266-9034 – *17

Story Law Office, #236, 1935 - 32 Ave. NE, T2E 7C8 – 403/250-1918, Fax: 403/250-3287 – *1

Sugimoto & Company, #204, 2635 - 37 Ave. NE, T1Y 5Z6 – 403/291-4650, Fax: 403/291-4099 – *8

Patricia H. Sutherland, 714 Earl Grey Cres. SW, T2S 0N7 – 403/244-1848, Fax: 403/245-5603 – *1

Nancy A. Swanby, #., 5407 Bannerman Dr. NW, T2L 1W1 – 403/289-7723, Fax: 403/282-0478 – *1

Szabo & Company., #500, 1111 - 11 Ave. SW, T2R 0G5 – 403/229-1111, ext. 313, Fax: 403/245-0569; Email: szabo@thelawyers.com; URL: http://www.thelawyers.com – *1

Michael J. Tadman, #10, 628 - 12 Ave. SW, T2R 0H6 – 403/234-9722, Fax: 403/237-8748 – *1

George A. Tapp, 2026 - 33 Ave. SW, T2T 1Z5 – 403/249-5505

C.L. Taylor, Site 11, SS#3, PO Box 16, T3C 3N9 – 403/249-7798

T.N. Taylor, #610, 615 Macleod Tr. SE, T2G 4T8 – 403/269-7561, Fax: 403/232-6535

Taylor, Zinkhofer & Conway, #440, 7220 Fisher St. SE, T2H 2H8 – 403/259-4028, Fax: 403/640-0103

Tharp Sinclair Watson Quigley Taylor, #800, 933 - 17 Ave. SW, T2T 5R6 – 403/245-3666, Fax: 403/245-3777 – *5

H. M. Timmons, 12247 Bonaventure Dr. SE, T1J 3N7 – 403/271-8433 – *1

K.R. Tobler, 68 Signal Hill Circle SW, T3H 2G6 – 403/249-4195

Bruno J. Todesco, #1111, 10 Coachway Rd. NW, T3H 1E5 – 403/242-7757

Tousignant, Young, Whitewater Place, #300, 1717 - 10 St. NW, T2M 4S2 – 403/220-9550, Fax: 403/220-9552 – *7

D.M. Underdahl, 12 Lenton Pl. SW, T3E 5C8 – 403/287-2292 – *1

Vallance & Company, #1400, 550 - 6 Ave. SW, T2P 0S2 – 403/264-3244, Fax: 403/232-6750 – *2

Joseph P.P. Vautour, 594 Strathcona Dr. SW, T3H 1K4 – 403/249-1129

Verenka, Angeline, #1000, 530 - 8 Ave. SW, T2P 3S8 – 403/290-1560, Fax: 403/290-1537 – *1

Viccars & Associates, #820, 665 - 8 St. SW, T2P 2A5 – 403/265-9697, Fax: 403/261-3079 – *3

Lawrence A. Wagar, #1001, 505 - 3 St. SW, T2P 3E6 – 403/266-5414, Fax: 403/266-5439

Walsh Wilkins, #2800, 801 - 6 Ave. SW, T2P 4A3 – 403/267-8400, Fax: 403/264-9400; Toll Free: 1-800-304-3574 – *18

P.M. Ward, #300, 714 - 1st St. SE, T2G 2G8 – 403/263-1158, Fax: 403/262-4869 – *1

Warren Tettensor, 1413 - 2 St. SW, T2R 0W7 – 403/228-7007, Fax: 403/244-1948 – *8

Watts Gottlieb, #8, 5602 - 4 St. NW, T2K 1B2 – 403/275-4881, Fax: 403/274-0367 – *1

William G. Webb, Rocky Mountain Plaza, #610, 615 Macleod Tr. South, T2G 4T8 – 403/294-1414, Fax: 403/263-4784

Brett O. Webber, 2832 - 12 Ave. NW, T2N 1K8 – 403/284-4624

Whitt & Company, #555, 407 - 8th Ave. SW, T2P 1E5 – 403/265-3232, Fax: 403/266-0999; Email: whittmr@biz-law.com – *3

Widdowson MacPhail Webber Harding, #300, 1121 Centre St. North, T2E 7K6 – 403/230-4617, Fax: 403/277-8930 – *5

Wolfman & Company, #300, 116 - 8 Ave. SW, 3rd Fl., T2P 1B3 – 403/263-6710, Fax: 403/266-1896 – *2

Wolfman Ryder, #212A, 805 - 1 St. SW, T2P 7N2 – 403/266-4433 – *2

Laurie I. Wood, #825, 441 - 5 Ave. SW, T2P 2V1 – 403/777-9400, Fax: 403/777-9409 – *1

Madeline J. Wood, #301, 540 - 12 Ave. SW, T2R 0H4 – 403/266-6766, Fax: 403/233-8429

Zenith Hookenson Vogel, #1050, 10201 Southport Rd. SW, T2W 4X9 – 403/259-5041, Fax: 403/253-8036 – *5

Zinner & Sara, #188, 400 - 3rd Ave. SW, T2P 4H2 – 403/269-2425, Fax: 403/233-0392 – *2

**Camrose....................................Wetaskiwin**

Andreassen Olson, #200, 4870 - 51 St., T4V 1S1 – 403/672-3181, Fax: 403/672-0682 – *6

Wilf K. Backhaus, #102, 4909A - 48 St., T4V 1L7 – 403/672-1121, Fax: 403/679-2242; Email: backhaus@wildrose.net; URL: http://wildrose.net/backhaus/strlw1.htm – *1

Farnham Schaffter & Ziebart, 5016 - 52 St., T4V 1V7 – 403/679-0444, Fax: 403/679-0958 – *3

Knaut Johnson Sawle, 4925 - 51 St., PO Box 1630, T4V 1X6 – 403/672-5561, Fax: 403/672-5565 – *3

**Canmore.......................................Calgary**

Robert Elliott, PO Box 2310, T0L 0M0 – 403/678-6078, Fax: 403/678-5173 – *1

Tannis J. Naylor, #202, 820 - 8th Main St., T1W 2B7 – 403/678-5777, Fax: 403/678-5679; Email: naylort@telusplanet.net – *1

Peter Perren, 726 - 10 St., T1W 2A6 – 403/678-6988, Fax: 403/678-5952 – *1

Rencz & McAvity, #2, 714 - 10 St., T1W 2A6 – 403/678-5823, Fax: 403/678-4890 – *2

**Cardston....................................Lethbridge**

T.M. Matkin, 87 - 2 Ave. West, PO Box 1209, T0K 0K0 – 403/653-3391, Fax: 403/653-2786 – *1

Stringam Denecky, PO Box 182, T0K 0K0 – 403/653-3282, Fax: 403/327-1141; Email: lethlaw@telusplanet.net; URL: http://www.dtnm.com.sd – *1

**Chestermere....................................Calgary**

Karl H.H. Trobst, 368 West Chestermere Dr., T1X 1B3 – 403/272-1056, Fax: 403/569-2968 – *1

**Claresholm....................................Lethbridge**

North & Company, 208 - 50 Ave. West, T0L 0T0 – 403/625-4404, Fax: 403/625-4186

Townsend & Malcolm, PO Box 2226, T0L 0T0 – 403/625-3777

**Coaldale....................................Lethbridge**

Leonard D. Fast, 1709 - 20 Ave., PO Box 1360, T1M 1N2 – 403/345-4415, Fax: 403/345-2719

**Cochrane....................................Calgary**

Fercho & Associates, #14, 205 - 1 St. East, T0L 0W1 – 403/932-4477, Fax: 403/932-4084 – *3

Rothecker Law Office, 404 - 1st St. West, PO Box 279, T0L 0W0 – 403/932-3843, Fax: 403/932-3108 – *2

**Cold Lake....................................Edmonton**

Todd & Drake, 4807 - 51 St., PO Box 908, T9M 1P2 – 403/594-7151, Fax: 403/594-2630; Email: ldrake@incentre.net – *2

**Devon....................................Wetaskiwin**

Jackie & Handerek, 14B Athabasca Ave., T0C 1E0 – 403/987-4219

**Didsbury....................................Calgary**

Vernon E. Good, 2012 - 20th St., 2nd Fl., PO Box 1027, T0M 0W0 – 403/335-3347, Fax: 403/335-4775

**Drayton Valley....................................Edmonton**

Paton Croll, 5121 - 51 St., PO Box 6988, T7A 1S3 – 403/542-7677, Fax: 403/542-4889

Prentice & Chow, 5202 - 52nd Ave., PO Box 6777, T7A 1S2 – 403/542-7462, Fax: 403/542-3392; Email: mlchow@ccinet.ab.ca – *3

**Drumheller....................................Drumheller**

Ross, Todd & Company, 98 - 3 Ave. West, PO Box 970, T0J 0Y0 – 403/823-5186, Fax: 403/823-6407 – *5

Schumacher, Gough & Pedersen, 180 Riverside Dr. East, PO Box 2800, T0J 0Y0 – 403/823-2424, Fax: 403/823-6984 – *3

J.L. Sparling, 150 - 3 Ave. West, Lower Level, PO Box 2859, T0J 1Y0 – 403/823-5500, Fax: 403/823-6472

**Edmonton....................................Edmonton**

Abbey Davies Greaves Hunter, MacDonald Place, #200, 9939 Jasper Ave., T5J 2W8 – 403/421-8585, Fax: 403/425-0472 – *5

David R. Abbey, #412, 9707 - 110 St., T5K 2L9 – 403/488-8945, Fax: 403/488-5017; Email: drabbey@oanet.com – *1

Ackroyd, Piasta, Roth & Day, 10665 Jasper Ave., 15th Fl., T5J 3S9 – 403/423-8905, Fax: 403/423-8946 – *17

Jack N. Agrios, Q.C., #2700, 10155 - 102 St., T5J 4G8 – 403/429-1751, Fax: 403/424-5866; Email: cdc@ccinet.ab.ca – *1

Charles R. Allard, 13723 Summit Point, T5N 3S6 – 403/438-2626

Gerard Amerongen, 10236 Connaught Dr. NW, T5N 3J2 – 403/452-7213, Fax: 403/452-7211 – *1

Anderson Carter & Callaghan, #460, 4445 Calgary Trail Southbound NW, T6H 5R7 – 403/438-1787, Fax: 403/437-3089 – *3

Anderson, Dawson, Knisely & Stevens, #300, 9924 - 100 St.., T5K 1C4 – 403/424-9058, Fax: 403/425-0172; Toll Free: 1-800-661-3176 – *5

Andrew, Donahoe & Oake, #300, 10020 - 101A Ave., T5J 3G2 – 403/429-3391, Fax: 403/424-8483; Email: lawyers@albertalaw.com – *9

Anthony-Robinson & Kozyra, River Valley Estates, #101, 10119 - 97A Ave., T5K 2T3 – 403/429-1717, Fax: 403/421-8335 – *3

Ares Kvill, LeMarchand Tower, 11507 - 100 Ave., T5K 2R2 – 403/488-1951, Fax: 403/482-6048 – *4

Donald S. Barber, PO Box 26, T5J 2G9 – 403/453-2386

Barr, Wensel, Nesbitt, Reeson, #1200, 10303 Jasper Ave., T5J 3N6 – 403/421-9900, Fax: 403/421-4151 – *21

Bassie & Zilinski, Wentworth Bldg., #200, 10209 - 97 St., T5J 0L6 – 403/423-2161, Fax: 403/426-1720 – *4

David A. Beckwith, #720, 10150 - 100 St., T5J 0P6 – 403/426-6820, Fax: 403/425-2435 – *1

Bennett Jones Verchere, Canadian Utilities Centre, #1000, 10035 - 105 St. NW, T5J 3T2 – 403/421-8133, Fax: 403/421-7951 – *10

Beresh DePoe Cunningham, MacLean Block, Box: 300, #300, 10110 - 107 St., T5J 1J4 – 403/421-4766, Fax: 403/429-0346 – *8

Marc Berzins, 10426 - 81 Ave., T6E 1X5 – 403/433-4717, Fax: 403/433-6718 – *1

Biamonte Cairo & Shortreed, Midland Walwyn Tower, #1600, 10205 - 101 St., T5J 2Z2 – 403/425-5800, Fax: 403/426-1600 – *13

Bishop & McKenzie, #2500, 10104 - 103 Ave., T5J 1V3 – 403/426-5550, Fax: 403/426-1305; Email: bishmc@planet.eon.net; URL: http://www.tgx.com/bishop-mckenzie – *26

Kerry A. Bjarnason, #100, 10426 - 81 Ave. NW, T6E 1X5 – 403/433-4547, Fax: 403/433-6718 – *1

Eleanor K. Boddy, Q.C., #1120, 10130 - 103 St., T5E 0C1 – 403/429-4520, Fax: 403/429-4591

Peter C. Bowal, #1980, 10123 - 99 St., T5J 3H1 – 403/425-6741

Angus M. Boyd, #405, 10408 - 124 St., T5N 1R5 – 403/488-7477, Fax: 403/488-0965

Braithwaite Boyle, 11816 - 124 St., T5L 0M3 – 403/451-9191, Fax: 403/451-9198; Toll Free: 1-800-661-4902; Email: bba@ccinet.ab.ca; URL: http://www.edmonton.com/web/injurylaw/ – *12

Braul Gaffney, Sun Life Place, #2170, 10123 - 99 St., T5J 3H1 – 403/423-2481, Fax: 403/423-2474 – *8

B.R. Brennand, 15112 - 81 St., T5C 1P5 – 403/473-3184 – *1

Brimacombe, Stroppel & Finlayson, Canada Trust Tower, #747, 10104 - 103 Ave., T5J 0H8 – 403/424-5156, Fax: 403/425-5883 – *5

Broda & Company, #103, 15333 Castle Downs Rd., T5X 3Y7 – 403/456-9330, Fax: 403/456-9339 – *2

Brownlee Fryett, Commerce Place, #2200, 10155 - 102 St., T5J 4G6 – 403/497-4800, Fax: 403/424-3254; Email: brownlee@agt.net – *35

Brumlik Lees, Oxford Tower, Edmonton Centre, #2100, 10235 - 101 St., T5J 3G1 – 403/423-4445, Fax: 403/424-6688 – *3

Bryan & Co., Box: 2600, 10180 - 101 St., T5J 3Y2 – 403/423-5730, Fax: 403/428-6324; Email: bryan-co@telusplanet.net – *33

Bubel Boll & Sorenson, Royal Bank Bldg., #610, 10117 Jasper Ave., T5J 3G2 – 403/421-4040, Fax: 403/421-4146 – *3

J.K.J. Campbell, #208, 4245 - 97 St. NW, T6E 5Y7 – 403/434-8777, Fax: 403/436-6357

Carr & Company, #900, 10020 - 101 Ave. NW, T5J 3G2 – 403/425-5959, Fax: 403/423-4728; Email: mail@carrco.com; URL: http://www.carrco.com – *1

Joseph A. Caruk, #1209, 10104 - 103 Ave., T5J 0H8 – 403/424-7145, Fax: 403/426-2980

Leanne M. Chahley, #1700, 10130 - 103 St. NW, T5J 3N9 – 403/423-3433, Fax: 403/425-6448; Email: 1-800-689-1930; URL: leannec@worldgate.com – *1

Andrew J. Chamberlain, TD Tower, Edmonton Centre, #1103, 10060 Jasper Ave., T5J 2Z1 – 403/423-3661, Fax: 403/426-1293; Email: ajclaw@planet.eon.net – *1

Jack L. Chapman, #4833, 9027 Saskatchewan Dr., T5J 3V4 – 403/439-2639

K.J. Chapman, Esso Tower, Scotia Pl., #901, 10060 Jasper Ave., T5J 3R8 – 403/420-0501, Fax: 403/420-1256; Email: kchapman@v-wave.com – *1

Robert Chappell Law Office, 9360 - 34 Ave., T6E 5X8 – 403/436-8300, Fax: 403/436-7300 – *1

Chomicki Baril, Scotia 2, #2101, 10060 Jasper Ave., T5J 4K1 – 403/423-3441, Fax: 403/420-1763 – *15

R.P. Christensen, 11450 - 124 St., T5M 0K3 – 403/454-0387, Fax: 403/454-0389 – *2

Michael H. Clancy, 9844 - 106 St., T5K 1B8 – 403/424-9014, Fax: 403/424-9023 – *1

Cleall Pahl, Commerce Place, #2500, 10155 - 102 St., T5J 4G8 – 403/425-2500, Fax: 403/425-1222 – *11

Coley, Hennessy & Cassis, #101, 9618 - 42 Ave., T6E 5Y4 – 403/468-2551, Fax: 403/466-8006 – *3

Combe & Kent, #800, 10310 Jasper Ave., T5J 1Y8 – 403/425-4666, Fax: 403/425-9358 – *2

Cook Duke Cox, Commerce Place, #2700, 10155 - 102 St., T5J 4G8 – 403/429-1751, Fax: 403/424-5866; Email: cdc@ccinet.ab.ca – *43

Gary K. Cooper, Q.C., #200, 10020 - 101A Ave., T5J 3G2 – 403/420-6745, Fax: 403/424-8584

Coulter, Kerby & Power, Metropolitan Pl., #2200, 10303 Jasper Ave., T5J 3N6 – 403/423-3331, Fax: 403/420-0049 – *6

Jean K. Coutts, First Edmonton Pl., 10665 Jasper Ave., 15th Fl., T5J 3S9 – 403/423-4357, Fax: 403/423-8946 – *1

Cruikshank Karvellas Law Office, Manulife Place, #3400, 10180 - 101 St., T5J 4W9 – 403/424-3800, Fax: 403/424-1311; Email: cruickar@cklawfirm.com

M.D. Cullen, #403, 10310 - 102 Ave., T5J 2X6 – 403/424-9354 – *1

Cummings Andrews & Mackay, #500, 10150 - 100 St., T5J 0P6 – 403/428-8222, Fax: 403/426-2670 – *10

Brock I. Dagenais, #1405, 10205 - 101 St. NW, T5J 2Z1 – 403/424-8519, Fax: 403/425-0931 – *1

Roger Davies, #442, 10113 - 104 St., T5J 1A1 – 403/421-4040 – *1

* indicates number of lawyers in law firm.

Robert C. Day, Phipps McKinnon Bldg., #950, 10020 - 101A Ave., T5J 3G2 – 403/423-2107
de Villars Jones, Noble Bldg., #300, 8540 - 109 St., T6G 1E6 – 403/433-9000, Fax: 403/433-9780; Email: dpjones@sagecounsel.com – *2
Janet L. Dixon, #301, 9119 - 82 Ave. NW, T6C 0Z4 – 403/469-6699, Fax: 403/469-8700; Email: jdixon@superway.net – *1
Duncan & Craig, Scotia Pl., #2800, 10060 Jasper Ave., T5J 3V9 – 403/428-6036, Fax: 403/428-9683 – *51
D.F. Dunwoodie, 10704 - 108 St. NW, T5H 3A3 – 403/424-3233, Fax: 403/424-2369 – *1
Durocher Simpson, Scotia Place, #801, 10060 Jasper Ave., T5J 3R8 – 403/420-6850, Fax: 403/425-9185; Email: durocher@oanet.com; URL: http://www.tgx.com/durocher – *11
E.L. Eccleston, 235 North Town Mall, T5E 6C1 – 403/478-6635, Fax: 403/476-8587; Email: eccl@planet.eon.net – *1
N.L. (Lori) A. Edlund, 9136 - 141 St. NW, T5R 0L4 – 403/483-5891, Fax: 403/483-5899 – *1
Edney Hattersley & Dolphin, #240, 10123 - 99 St., T5J 3H1 – 403/423-4081, Fax: 403/425-5247; Email: martinh@freenet.edmonton.ab.ca – *3
Edney, Hattersley & Dolphin, #240, 10123 - 99 St., T5J 3H1 – 403/424-7798, Fax: 403/425-5247; Email: martinh@freenet.edmonton.ab.ca – *3
E.A.O. Elford, 50 Westridge Rd., T5T 1B4 – 403/487-3579
Embury, McFayden & Wilson, Centre 104, #502, 5241 Calgary Trail Southbound NW, T6H 5G8 – 403/439-7302, Fax: 403/433-6510 – *1
Emery Jamieson, Oxford Tower, #1700, 10235 - 101 St., T5J 3G1 – 403/426-5220, Fax: 403/420-6277; Email: general@emeryjamieson.com – *29
Environmental Law Centre, #204, 10709 Jasper Ave., T5J 3N3 – 403/424-5099, Fax: 403/424-5133; Toll Free: 1-800-661-4238; Email: elc@web.net; URL: http://www.web.net/~elc – *4
Evans & Co., Weber Centre, #1535, 5555 Calgary Trail South, T6H 5P9 – 403/438-4493, Fax: 403/436-1019; Toll Free: 1-888-326-4529 – *6
Felesky Flynn, Canada Trust Tower, #2600, 10104 - 103 Ave., T5J 0H8 – 403/428-8310, Fax: 403/421-8820; Email: felesky@planet.eon.net – *7
David A. Fennell, Royal Trust Tower, #2302, Edmonton Centre, T5J 2Z2 – 403/423-1619 – *2
Field Atkinson Perraton, Oxford Tower, #2000, 10235 - 101 St., T5J 3G1 – 403/423-3003, Fax: 403/428-9329, 424-7116 – *43
L.R. Flynn, 4731 - 147A St., T6H 5N3
Fuller St. Arnaud & McAllister, #800, 10150 - 100 St., T5J 0P6 – 403/423-2663, Fax: 403/424-4873 – *3
Galbraith Empson, #1800, 10123 - 99 St., T5J 3H1 – 403/424-9558, Fax: 403/424-5852 – *2
Galbraith Law Office, #217, 14925 - 111 Ave., T5M 2P6 – 403/483-6111, Fax: 403/483-6411; Email: glo@connect.ab.ca; URL: http://www.connect.ab.ca/~glo – *1
Dale Gibson Associates, 11018 - 125 St. NW, T5M 0M1 – 403/452-9530, Fax: 403/453-5872; Email: dga@planet.eon.net – *2
R.D. Gillespie, #300, 10209 - 97 St., T5J 0L6 – 403/424-3255, Fax: 403/429-2615
H.S. Gillett, #304, 10209 - 97 St., T5J 0L6 – 403/426-1361, Fax: 403/429-2828
Gledhill Reid, #1950, 10205 - 101 St., T5J 2Z2 – 403/425-3511, Fax: 403/426-5919 – *7
Grace Parrotta-King Professional Corporation, #795, 10020 - 101A Ave., T5J 3G2 – 403/424-2333, Fax: 403/424-3777
Ingolf F. Grape, Campus Tower, #209, 8625 - 112 St., T6G 1K8 – 403/436-8421, Fax: 403/436-8420; Email: grapelaw@oanet.com – *1
Graziano & Associates, 11428 - 100 Ave., T5K 0J4 – 403/482-5846, Fax: 403/482-2191 – *3
Renuka Gupta, 10516 - 31 Ave., T6J 2Y3 – 403/437-1069
Hagen, Feehan & Gilchrist, 8623 - 149 St., T5R 1B2 – 403/486-0207, Fax: 403/483-0848 – *4
Hajduk & Gibbs, Toronto Dominion Centre NW, Edmonton Centre, #2727, T5J 2Z1 – 403/428-4258, Fax: 403/423-3535 – *3
D.L. Hansen, 828 Lee Ridge Rd., T6K 0P8 – 403/426-0734 – *1
Hansma & Associates, 13907 - 127 St., T6V 1A8 – 403/456-3661, Fax: 403/457-9381 – *3
Wayne D. Hatt, #1209, 10104 - 103 Ave., T5J 0H8 – 403/423-3391, Fax: 403/426-2980
Hauptman, Hart, Cherkawsky, #201, 4990 - 92 Ave., T6B 2V4 – 403/465-9191, Fax: 403/469-8889; Email: hhclaw@planet.eon.net – *4
Haymour Keohane, #2031, 10060 Jasper Ave. NW, T5J 3R8 – 403/425-5700, Fax: 403/429-4573 – *3
D.R. Hayward, 4628 - 151 St., T6H 5N8
Hendrickson Gower & Massing, Phipps McKinnon Bldg., #680, 10020 - 101A Ave., T5J 3G2 – 403/421-8816, Fax: 403/424-5864 – *4
Adlynn Miskew Hewitt, Q.C., 7013 - 101 Ave., T6A 0M6 – 403/466-0906 – *1
Leroy N. Hiller, #1209, 10104 - 103 Ave., T5J 0H8 – 403/424-6660, Fax: 403/426-2980 – *2
Harold Hinz, #202, 9644 - 54 Ave. NW, T6E 5V1 – 403/438-4972
Hladun & Company, #100, 10187 - 104 St., T5J 0Z9 – 403/423-1888, Fax: 403/424-0934 – *5
William K. Horwitz, #105, 10423 - 178 St., T5S 1R5 – 403/486-3100, Fax: 403/489-0671 – *1
Hustwick Wetsch Moffat & McCrae, Capital Pl., #200, 9707 - 110 St., T5K 2L9 – 403/482-6555, Fax: 403/482-6613; Email: advocacy@planet.eon.net
George E. Illsley, #202, 15241 Stony Plain Rd., T5P 3Y4 – 403/484-7765 – *1
Ingersoll & Ingersoll, Phipps McKinnon Bldg., #930, 10020 - 101A Ave., T5J 3G2 – 403/422-6207, Fax: 403/424-9955 – *2
Jackson, Arlette, MacIver, #700, 10020 - 101A Ave., T5J 3G2 – 403/424-5146, Fax: 403/426-6566 – *5
Bodil Jelhof Jensen, 10703 - 54 St., T6A 2H7 – 403/469-4241 – *1
Moosa Y. Jiwaji, #1110, 10080 Jasper Ave., T5J 1V9 – 403/448-0467, Fax: 403/448-3962 – *1
James E.B. Johnston, #205, 11523 - 100 Ave., T5K 0J8 – 403/488-0971 – *1
Jomha, Skrobot, #2260, 10123 - 99 St. NW, T5J 3H1 – 403/424-0688, Fax: 403/424-0695; Email: ajomha@planet.con.net – *4
Jones, Bolton, #1528, 10205 - 101 St. NW, T5J 2Z2 – 403/424-3165 – *2
Kalil Haymour, #900, 10665 Jasper Ave., T5J 3S9 – 403/425-5700, Fax: 403/421-8400 – *1
Edward W.S. Kane, #205, 11523 - 100 Ave., T5K 0J8 – 403/488-0971
T.H. Kantor, #740, 10150 - 100 St., T5J 0P6 – 403/423-7786, Fax: 403/426-0101
Saul Katz, #900, 9707 - 110 St., T5K 2L9 – 403/482-7800, Fax: 403/482-7803 – *1
Robert M. Kelcher, Blue Quill Centre, 292 Saddleback Rd., T6J 4R7 – 403/436-0011, Fax: 403/436-7000
Kirwin Kobewka & Stadnyk, 14310 - 111 Ave., T5M 3Z7 – 403/448-7444, Fax: 403/453-3281; Email: kks@oanet.com – *7
Kiss & Davidson, #202, 15241 Stony Plain Rd., T5P 3Y4 – 403/484-7704, Fax: 403/484-1641 – *2
G.M. Kitt, #300, 10036 Jasper Ave., T5J 2W2 – 403/422-6009 – *1
Roy D. Klassen, 10072 Jasper Ave., T5J 1V8 – 403/497-3179, Fax: 403/424-2761 – *1
Knight & Company, 11408 - 103 Ave., T5K 0S4 – 403/488-3333, Fax: 403/482-6200 – *1
Kolthammer, Batchelor & Fedorak, #208, 11062 - 156 St., T5P 4M8 – 403/489-5003, Fax: 403/486-2107; Email: kbf@oanet.com – *4
Methodius Koziak, #300, 9622 - 42 Ave. NW, T6E 5Y4 – 403/466-9191, Fax: 403/463-7557; Email: mkoziak@incentre.net – *1
Oskar H. Kruger & Company, #304, 10209 - 97 St., T5J 0L6 – 403/423-3511, Fax: 403/423-3514; Email: kruganco@oanet.com – *3
H.W. Kuckertz, #202, 8003 - 102 St., T6E 4A2 – 403/432-9308, Fax: 403/439-9950 – *5
P.M.W. Kuehn, #102, 7603 - 104 St., T6E 4C3 – 403/433-2603 – *1
Lavallée, Rackel, #1630, 10250 - 101 St. NW, T5J 3P4 – 403/424-2929, Fax: 403/424-3584; Email: lavrac@planet.eon.net – *4
Gregory C. Lazin Professional Corporation, #203, 10171 Saskatchewan Dr., T6E 4R5 – 403/433-6600, Fax: 403/439-6696
Lennie & Company, #1250, 10180 - 101 St., T5J 3S4 – 403/425-2110, Fax: 403/426-6977; Toll Free: 1-800-583-0788 – *4
C.W. Leviston, 14615 - 91 Ave., T5R 4Y7 – 403/484-7540 – *1
Lim, Parker & Loong, #288, 10704 - 108 St., T5H 3A3 – 403/424-3200, Fax: 403/424-2369
R.V. Lloyd, #1400, 10303 Jasper Ave., T5J 3N6 – 403/421-1818, Fax: 403/429-4453; Email: ogilvie@compusmart.ab.ca – *1
Lucas Bowker & White, Scotia Tower, #1201, 10060 Jasper Ave., T5J 4E5 – 403/426-5330, Fax: 403/428-1066; Toll Free: 1-800-567-7174; Email: lucas@supernet.ab.ca – *29
G.R. Ludwig, #201, 9111 - 39 Ave. NW, T6E 5Y2 – 403/461-5681
Lyons Albert & Cook, Weber Centre, #905, 5555 Calgary Tr. Southbound, T6H 5P9 – 403/437-0743, Fax: 403/438-6695; Email: alalbert@compusmart.ab.ca – *3
Macdonald & Freund, #750, 10665 Jasper Ave., T5J 3S9 – 403/424-7201, Fax: 403/428-7667; Email: gfreund@accessweb.com; bmacdonald@accessweb.com – *1
Mah & Chiu, #1380, 10060 Jasper Ave., T5J 3R8 – 403/428-3888, Fax: 403/425-8383 – *3
Matheson & Company, Matheson Bldg., 10410 - 81 Ave., T6E 1X5 – 403/433-5881, Fax: 403/432-9453; Email: matheson@planet.eon.net – *11
Cheryl J. Matheson, #202, 11714 - 95 St., T5G 1L9 – 403/474-1455, Fax: 403/474-2559 – *1
McBean Becker Cochard Gordon Zwaenepoel & Martin, Park Plaza, #104, 10611 - 98th Ave., T5K 2P7 – 403/425-9777, Fax: 403/425-9779 – *6
McCuaig Desrochers, Bank of Montreal Bldg., #500, 10199 - 101 St., T5J 3Y4 – 403/426-4660, Fax: 403/426-0982; Email: mccuaig@oanet.com; URL: http://www.mccuaig.com – *18
Dennis W. McGechie, #205, 11523 - 100 Ave., T5K 0J8 – 403/488-1974, Fax: 403/488-4783 – *1
McGee Richard, Weber Centre, #1301, 5555 Calgary Trail South, T6H 5P9 – 403/437-2240, Fax: 403/438-5788 – *2
W.N. McKay, #205, 11523 - 100 Ave., T5K 0J8 – 403/488-0971, Fax: 403/482-7417 – *1
McKenna Hewitt, Scotia 2, #701, 10060 Jasper Ave., T5J 3R8 – 403/414-1433, Fax: 403/424-6969 – *2
McLennan Ross, West Chambers, #600, 12220 Stony Plain Rd., PO Box 12040, T5J 3L2 – 403/482-9200, Fax: 403/482-9100, 9101, 9102; Toll Free: 1-800-567-9200; Email: edmonton@mross.com – *42
Ingrid E. Meier, 1108 - 115 St. NW, T6J 6W6 – 403/436-5954, Fax: 403/988-9426; Email: lawyer@v-wave.com – *1
Ian L. Meikle, #304, Kingsway Garden Mall, T5G 3A6 – 403/474-8047 – *1
Ron J. Meleshko, 15412 - 55 St., T5Y 2S4 – 403/414-0298, Fax: 403/414-0298 – *1
Merchant Law Group, 304 Kingsway Garden Mall, T5G 3A6 – *1
Joseph J. Michaels, 1985 Sun Life Place, 10123 - 99 St., T5J 3H1 – 403/424-0354 – *1
Marla S. Miller, 11835 - 102 Ave., T5K 0R6 – 403/482-2888, Fax: 403/482-4600 – *1

Milner Fenerty, Manulife Pl., #2900, 10180 - 101 St., T5J 3V5 – 403/423-7100, Fax: 403/423-7276; Email: milfen@milfen.com; URL: http://www.milfen.com – *53
W. Robert Mitchell, #405, 10408 - 124 St., T5N 1R5 – 403/482-5791, Fax: 403/488-0965 – *1
A.S. Mlonzi, #803, 9725 - 106 St., T5K 1B5 – 403/425-5269
Nick Mosychuk, 1985 Sun Life Place, 10123 - 99 St., T5J 3H1 – 403/424-9364 – *1
Murray, Chilibeck & Horne, #208, 10464 Mayfield Rd., T5P 4P4 – 403/484-2323, Fax: 403/486-4289 – *3
Neuman Thompson, #200, 12220 Stony Plain Rd. NW, T5N 3Y4 – 403/482-7645, Fax: 403/488-0026 – *4
Nicholl & Akers, #200, 10187 - 104 St. NW, T5J 0Z9 – 403/429-2771, Fax: 403/425-1665 – *3
Neil W. Nichols, PO Box 4668, T6E 5G5 – 403/465-0100, Fax: 403/465-1981 – *1
Ian A. Nicholson, #203, 12303 - Jasper Ave., T5N 3K7 – 403/482-1019 – *1
Nickerson, Roberts, Toronto Dominion Tower, Edmonton Centre, #1901, 10205 - 101 St., T5J 2Z1 – 403/428-0041, Fax: 403/425-0272 – *8
Peter G. Northcott, 9902 - 111 St., T5K 1K2 – 403/448-0300, Fax: 403/482-7148 – *2
B.V. Odsen, 11914 - 129 Ave., T5E 0N3 – 403/455-6678, Fax: 403/453-1093 – *1
Ogilvie & Company, Metropolitan Pl., #1400, 10303 Jasper Ave., T5J 3N6 – 403/421-1818, Fax: 403/429-4453; Email: ogilvie@compusmart.ab.ca – *26
Miyako R. Okubo, 7750 Jasper Ave., T5H 3R8 – 403/429-2381 – *1
Russell Olekshy Professional Corp., 10410 - 81 Ave. NW, T6E 1X5 – 403/433-1448, Fax: 403/433-3888; Email: matheson@planet.eon.net – *1
Hermo Toribio Pagtakhan, #1840, 10123 - 99 St., T5J 3H1 – 403/425-6611, Fax: 403/429-4695 – *1
Parlee McLaws, Manulife Pl., #1500, 10180 - 101 St., T5J 4K1 – 403/423-8500, Fax: 403/423-2870; Email: lawyers@parlee.com; URL: http://www.parlee.com – *89
Paton Croll, #1260, 10665 Jasper Ave. NW, T5J 3S9 – 403/424-4042, Fax: 403/428-6936
Pawlowski & Associates, #107, 11831 - 123 St., T5L 0G7 – 403/451-0027 – *2
Peacock & Company, #1850, 10303 Jasper Ave., T5J 3N6 – 403/424-4650, Fax: 403/425-0050; Toll Free: 1-800-520-4529 – *1
G. Perdicaris, #835, 10310 Jasper Ave., T5J 2W4 – 403/423-1097
Keith C. Perkins, #200, 10525 Jasper Ave., T5J 1Z4 – 403/424-3334, Fax: 403/424-4252 – *1
Philp & Collins, 10374 - 172nd St., T5S 1G9 – 403/484-8708, Fax: 403/484-8894 – *2
William R. Picton, 10722 - 113 St., T5H 3H8 – 403/425-8936, Fax: 403/425-8936
Pierzchalski & Company, 11914 - 129 Ave., T5E 0N3 – 403/455-6678, Fax: 403/453-1093 – *3
Polack, Meindersma, Smith & Liddell, Denton Centre, #300, 14925 - 111 Ave., T5M 2P6 – 403/486-0926, Fax: 403/444-1393 – *4
Glen Power, #1110, 10117 Jasper Ave., T5J 1W8 – 403/426-2838, Fax: 403/426-2838 – *1
Alexander Pozniak, #3, 9430 - 118 Ave., T5G 0N6 – 403/474-6314, Fax: 403/479-3732
Pringle, Renouf & Associates, #200, 10237 - 104 St., T5J 4A1 – 403/424-8866, Fax: 403/426-1470 – *5
Proulx & Associates, #201, 9111 - 39 Ave. NW, T6E 5Y2 – 403/462-3663 – *1
Prowse & Chowne, Strathcona Professional Centre, #100, 10328 - 81 Ave., T6E 1X2 – 403/439-7171, Fax: 403/439-0475; Email: prowse@planet.eom.net – *23
M. Naeem Rauf, #220, 9707 - 110 St., T5K 2L9 – 403/453-4399, Fax: 403/488-4783
Michele J. Reeves, #320, 10055 - 106 St., T5J 2Y2 – 403/424-3200
Jerome Reyda, Q.C., 240 Riverside Cres., T5N 3M5 – 403/452-7702 – *1
Reynolds, Mirth, Richards & Farmer, Manulife Pl., #3200, 10180 - 101 St, T5J 3W8 – 403/425-9510, Fax: 403/429-3044; Toll Free: 1-800-661-7673; Email: reynolds@law.ualberta.ca; URL: http://www.ualberta.ca/~law/firms/reynolds/ – *27
G.W. Robertson, #205, 11523 - 100 Ave., T5K 0J8 – 403/488-0971, Fax: 403/482-7417 – *1
Royal, McCrum, Duckett & Glancy, Palomar Bldg., #215, 8204 - 104 St., T6E 4E6 – 403/432-0919, Fax: 403/439-6562 – *4
Orest Rusnak, 454 Rooney Cres., T6R 1C8 – 403/430-7184, Fax: 403/430-1765; Email: orusnak@freenet.edmonton.ab.ca – *1
Russell & Company, #500, 10104 - 103 Ave., T5J 0H8 – 403/420-1004, Fax: 403/426-2582 – *4
R.H. Sawchuk, #403, 10089 Jasper Ave., T5J 0H8 – 403/428-8848
D.L. Schwartz, #430, 10036 Jasper Ave., T5J 2W2 – 403/424-0259 – *1
Scott & Murray, TD Tower, #750, 10205 - 101 St., T5J 2Z2 – 403/423-3271, Fax: 403/428-1963 – *3
Donna V.T. Sekida, 7609 - 152 St., T5R 1K6 – 403/444-0736
Shaw & Tamke, #203, 8657 - 51 Ave. NW, T6E 6A8 – 403/465-9001, Fax: 403/468-2532 – *2
G.P. Shewchuk, #310, 8944 - 182 St. NW, T5T 2E3 – 403/481-1299, Fax: 403/481-1674 – *1
William Shim, Sun Life Place, #2000B, 10123 - 99 St., T5J 3H1 – 403/423-8060, Fax: 403/425-4201
Shoctor Ferguson, #2800, 10060 Jasper Ave., T5J 3V9 – 403/423-2461, Fax: 403/424-5244 – *3
Shtabsky & Tussman, #400, 10235 - 101 St., T5J 3G1 – 403/429-4671, Fax: 403/424-3580; Email: st400@oanet.com; URL: http://www.stlaw.com – *12
Silverman & Shafir, #1104, 10117 Jasper Ave., T5J 1W8 – 403/428-0731, Fax: 403/428-0733 – *2
Smith Gawlinski Parkatti, #1780, 10123 - 99 St., T5J 3H1 – 403/428-6645, Fax: 403/428-6649 – *4
John Stadnyk, 14310 - 111th Ave. NW, T5M 3Z7 – 403/448-7444, Fax: 403/453-3281; Toll Free: 1-800-661-1920; Email: kks@oanet.com – *1
M.P. Stone, #616-21, 10405 Jasper Ave., T5J 3S2 – 403/486-5146, Fax: 403/483-7791; Email: notgilty@freenet.edmonton.ab.ca – *1
Stuffco Olsen, #404, 10216 - 124 St., T5N 4A3 – 403/482-3405, Fax: 403/488-3738 – *7
Tarrabain & Company, Tower One, Scotia Place, #2150, 10060 Jasper Ave., T5J 3R8 – 403/429-1010, Fax: 403/429-0101 – *7
M.E.G. Taylor, 14412 - 63 St., T5A 2B6 – 403/475-9303 – *1
Sylvia O. Tensfeldt, #200, 10525 Jasper Ave., T5J 1Z4 – 403/424-3334, Fax: 403/424-4252 – *1
M.A.T. Terrell, #200, 9707 - 110 St., T5K 2L9 – 403/488-5500
Thom Law Office, Campus Tower, #209, 8625 - 112 St., T6G 1K8 – 403/434-5870, Fax: 403/436-8420; Email: thomlaw@oanet.com – *1
J.A. Thygesen, 9807 - 149 St., T5P 1K5 – 403/451-1316
Tkachuk & Patterson, Energy Sq., #305, 10109 - 106 St., T5J 3L7 – 403/428-1593, Fax: 403/426-6679 – *2
Laurie A. Trahan, #904, CN Tower, 10004 - 104 Ave., T5J 0K1 – 403/424-0070, Fax: 403/424-0640 – *1
Helen S. Tymoczko, 13216 - 79 St. NW, T5C 1J7 – 403/472-1758, Fax: 403/476-4085 – *1
Lee A.I. Tyrrell, 121 Laurier Dr., T5R 5P6
R. Douglas Vigen, 9677 - 45 Ave. NW, T6E 5Z8 – 403/438-2151, Fax: 403/438-2197
Walker, Butler & O'Laughlin, #300, 10209 - 97 St., T5J 0L6 – 403/426-6651
J.M. Walker, Sun Life Place, #575, 10123 - 99 St., T5J 3H1 – 403/426-6651, Fax: 403/424-2369 – *1
Weeks Doherty Schuldhaus, Spencer & Mohan, 1120 One Thornton Ct., T5J 2E7 – 403/426-1382, Fax: 403/426-2094 – *7
Welsh & Company, #888, 4445 Calgary Trail Southbound NW, T6H 5R7 – 403/438-3500, Fax: 403/438-3129 – *1
Uwe Welz, 7904 - 103 St., T6E 6C3 – 403/432-7711, Fax: 403/439-1177 – *1
Wheatley Sadownik, #2000, 10123 - 99 St., T5J 3H1 – 403/423-6671, Fax: 403/420-6327; Email: makuch@compusmart.ab.ca; URL: http://www.wheatleysadownik.com – *4
Whiting, Sachs & Company, #445, 10020 - 101A Ave., T5J 3G2 – 403/424-5577 – *2
William A. Wiese, Noble Bldg., #303, 8540 - 109 St, T6G 1E6 – 403/432-1144, Fax: 403/439-4622 – *1
H.D. Williamson, 8715 Saskatchewan Dr., T6G 2A9 – 403/439-2898 – *1
David R. Willson, 10316 - 121 St., T5N 1K8 – 403/482-6670, Fax: 403/482-2518 – *1
Richard A. Winter, Toronto-Dominion Tower, #2735, Edmonton Centre, T5J 2Z1 – 403/421-8777
Wolff Leia, Tower One, Scotia Place, #500, 10060 Jasper Ave., T5J 3R8 – 403/421-0222, Fax: 403/429-0503 – *2
Craig W. Wood, 10811 - 148 St., T5N 3H4 – 403/454-4433
Laurie I. Wood, #220, 9707 - 110 St., T5K 2L9 – 403/482-3291, Fax: 403/488-4783
Worton & Hunter, #1270, 5555 Calgary Trail, T6H 5P9 – 403/436-8554, Fax: 403/436-8566; Email: main@wortonhunter.com – *3
Ronald J. Young, #780, 10020 - 101A Ave., T5J 3G2 – 403/424-3311 – *1
A.R. Zariwny, #200, 10351 - 82 Ave. NW, T6E 1Z9 – 403/433-5999, Fax: 403/439-6456; Email: zlo@oanet.com – *1

**Edson ........................................ Edmonton**

Robert W. Anderson, 200 - 50 St., PO Box 6748, T7E 1V1 – 403/723-5703, Fax: 403/723-5443 – *1
Dennis C. Calvert, 107 - 50 St., PO Box 6658, T0E 0P0 – 403/723-6047, Fax: 403/723-3602; Email: caldenpo@yellowhead.com – *1
Duane H. Catterall, 5008 - 3 Ave., PO Box 6568, T7E 1T9 – 403/723-5111, 5112, Fax: 403/723-6179 – *1

**Enoch ........................................ Edmonton**

Mandamin & Associates, PO Box 300, T7X 3Y3 – 403/470-5777, Fax: 403/470-3909 – *3

**Fort MacLeod .................................... MacLeod**

J.C. Davis, PO Box 660, T0L 0Z0 – 403/553-3277 – *1
Gaschler & Vallance, 249 Colonel Macleod Blvd., PO Box 757, T0L 0Z0 – 403/553-4484, Fax: 403/553-3444 – *2
North & Company, 324 - 24 St., T0L 0Z0 – 403/553-4998
Welbourn, Maloney, Professional Building, T0L 0Z0 – 403/553-4998

**Fort McMurray ................................ Fort McMurray**

Campbell & Cooper, #212, 9714 Main St., T9H 1T6 – 403/743-5370, Fax: 403/791-0750 – *2
Adam W. Germain (1993) Professional Corp., #212, 9714 Main St., T9H 1T6 – 403/743-0045, Fax: 403/791-0750 – *1
Gorsalitz Law Office, 9912 Manning Ave., T9H 2B9 – 403/791-4115, Fax: 403/743-0040 – *1
Gregory L. Marullo, 243 Berens Place, T9K 2C6 – 403/791-3602, Fax: 403/791-3602
Weeks Doherty Schuldhaus, Spencer & Mohan, #102, 9908 Franklin Ave., T9H 2K5 – 403/791-5505, Fax: 403/743-2428
Wolff Taitinger, #214, 9914 Morrison St., T9H 4A4 – 403/790-9040, Fax: 403/743-1813 – *3

**Fort Saskatchewan ................................ Edmonton**

Jenkins & Jenkins, #200, 9835 - 104 St., T8L 2E5 – 403/998-4200, Fax: 403/998-4370 – *2
Lim, Parker & Loong, 10118 - 99 Ave.., T8L 1X8 – 403/992-1663, Fax: 403/998-1088 – *1
Valens, Fotty & Torok-Both, 10509 - 100 Ave., T8L 1Z5 – 403/998-4841, Fax: 403/998-4821 – *3

* indicates number of lawyers in law firm.

**Grande Cache.................................... Edmonton**

Harry Arnesen, 2502 Pine Plaza, PO Box 385, T0E 0Y0 – 403/827-2458, Fax: 403/827-3734 – *1

**Grande Prairie.............................. Grande Prairie**

Burgess & Gurevitch, 9931 - 106 Ave., T8V 1J4 – 403/539-3710, Fax: 403/532-2788 – *3

Mark E. Enright, #201, 9817 - 101 Ave., T8V 0X6 – 403/538-3520, Fax: 403/538-3523

Kay, Shipley, McVey & Smith, Windsor Ct., #600, 9835 - 101 Ave., T8V 5V4 – 403/532-7771, Fax: 403/532-1158 – *8

Logan Watson & Company, #202, 10027 - 101 Ave., T8V 0X9 – 403/532-0315 – *4

**Grimshaw.................................... Peace River**

G.W.J. Paul, 4905 - 55 Railway Ave., PO Box 829, T0H 1W0 – 403/332-4647, Fax: 403/332-4614 – *1

**Hanna.................................... Hanna**

Kush & Daughter, PO Box 369, T0J 1P0 – 403/854-3361, Fax: 403/854-3985 – *2

**High Prairie.................................... Calgary**

Susan Grattan, Drake Building, PO Box 1680, T0G 1E0 – 403/523-3432 – *1

Harry J. Jong, PO Box 1379, T0G 1E0 – 403/523-4554, Fax: 403/523-5550 – *1

Susan M. Lamothe, 5119 - 48 St., PO Box 1507, T0G 1E0 – 403/523-4944, Fax: 403/523-5055

**High River.................................... Calgary**

W.J. Andresen, PO Box 2080, T0L 1B0 – 403/652-3702 – *1

A. George Dearing, #103, 14 - 2 Ave. SE, T1V 1G4 – 403/652-2771, Fax: 403/652-2699 – *1

**Hinton.................................... Edmonton**

Johnson & McClelland, 213 Pembina Ave., T7V 2B3 – 403/865-2222, Fax: 403/865-8857 – *4

Woods & Robson, 110 Brewster Dr., T7V 1B4 – 403/865-3086, Fax: 403/865-7149 – *4

**Hobbema.................................... Wetaskiwin**

Judith Sayers, PO Box 900, T0C 1N0 – 403/585-3037, Fax: 403/585-2025

Rodney Soonias, #70, c/o Montana Band, T0C 1N0 – 403/585-3998, Fax: 403/585-3264

**Innisfail.................................... Red Deer**

Miller, Lehane & Wild, 5035 - 49 St., PO Box 699, T0M 1A0 – 403/227-3361, Fax: 403/227-2929 – *3

Gary J. Shudra, #201, 4733 - 50 St., PO Box 1625, T0M 1A0 – 403/227-1950

Tulloch & Stretch, 5030 - 50 St., PO Box 6099, T4G 1S7 – 403/227-5591, Fax: 403/227-1230 – *2

**Jasper.................................... Edmonton**

Archibald & Edwards, 100A Connaught St., PO Box 1558, T0E 1E0 – 403/852-4501 – *1

Rodger & Ireland, PO Box 130, T0E 1E0 – 403/852-4905, Fax: 403/852-4440 – *2

**Killam.................................... Vegreville**

Gaede, Fielding, Syed & Smith, 5011 - 50 St., T0B 2L0 – 403/385-3555

**Lac La Biche.................................... Edmonton**

Kozina & Gregory, 10130 Alberta Ave., PO Box 1439, T0A 2C0 – 403/623-4818, Fax: 403/623-2933 – *2

Kozina & Gregory, 10130 Alberta Ave., PO Box 1439, T0A 2C0 – 403/623-4818, Fax: 403/623-2933

Thomas R. Maccagno, 10120 - 101 Ave., PO Box 1270, T0A 2C0 – 403/623-4177, Fax: 403/623-2266

Tarrabain & Company, PO Box 1710, T0A 2C0

**Lacombe.................................... Red Deer**

Roger C. Holteen, 5015 - 50 Ave., PO Box 639, T0C 1S0 – 403/782-6661, Fax: 403/782-2950 – *1

**Leduc.................................... Wetaskiwin**

James K. Arends, #218, 5904B - 50 St., T9E 6J4 – 403/986-1443, Fax: 403/986-1443; Email: jarends@connect.ab.ca – *1

Jackie & Handerek, 4710 - 50 St., T9E 6W2 – 403/986-5081, Fax: 403/986-8807 – *4

E. Kahlke, #101, 5019 - 49 Ave., T9E 6T5 – 403/986-8427, Fax: 403/986-3108 – *1

Zalapski & Pahl, 5304 - 50 St., PO Box 3715, T9E 6M4 – 403/986-8428, Fax: 403/986-2552; Email: zap@tnc.com; URL: http://www.tnc.com/zap/ – *4

**Lethbridge.................................... Lethbridge**

Dimnik & Company, #200, 302 - 10 St. South, T1J 2M6 – 403/320-9800, Fax: 403/320-9124 – *1

Dodic, Toone, Maclean, 416B Stafford Dr. South, T1J 2L2 – 403/329-1330, Fax: 403/329-1311 – *4

D.B. Hepburn, 118A - 8 St. South, T1J 2J3 – 403/320-5350, Fax: 403/328-7217

Terrence J. Huzil, #9, 402 - 5th Ave. South, T1J 0T5 – 403/320-0222, Fax: 403/327-5630 – *1

Ives & Carleton, Lacidem Bldg., #200, 542 - 7 St. South, PO Box 728, T1J 3Z6 – 403/327-3116 – *1

MacLachlan McNab Hembroff, Virco Place, 1003 - 4th Ave. South, T1J 0P7 – 403/381-4966, Fax: 403/329-9300; Email: virco@agt.net; URL: http://www.virco.net – *6

McDonald Harvie MacLennan, #300, 220 - 4 St. South, T1J 4J7 – 403/380-4000, Fax: 403/380-4050 – *3

North & Company, Chancery Ct., #600, 220 - 4 St. South., PO Box 219, Stn Main, T1J 3Y5 – 403/328-7781, Fax: 403/320-8958; Toll Free: 1-800-552-8022 – *13

Ludvik L. Pahulje, #217, 740 - 4 Ave. South, T1J 0N9 – 403/327-6747

Peterson & Purvis, 537 - 7th St. South, PO Box 1165, T1J 4A4 – 403/328-9666, Fax: 403/320-1393 – *6

Pocock & Quan, 449 Mayor Magrath Dr., T1J 3L8 – 403/320-6645, Fax: 403/328-6308 – *2

Pritchard & Stokes, Professional Bldg., #202, 740 - 4 Ave. South, PO Box 127, T1J 3Y3 – 403/328-7728, Fax: 403/328-5589 – *2

Roman Scholdra, PO Box 236, T1J 3Y5 – 403/328-3944 – *1

Shapiro & Company, #200, 427 - 5 St. South., T1J 2B6 – 403/328-9300, Fax: 403/328-9307 – *2

Stringam Denecky, Lethbridge Centre Tower, #900, PO Box 757, T1J 3Z6 – 403/328-5576, Fax: 403/327-1141; Email: lethlaw@telusplanet.net; URL: http://www.dtmn.com/sd – *8

Townsend, Malcolm, Kenwood & Company, #200, 714 - 5 Ave. South, T1J 0V1 – 403/329-0001, Fax: 403/329-0868 – *4

**Lloydminster.................................... Edmonton**

Kindrachuk, Rounce, 5014 - 48 St., T9V 0H8 – 403/875-6600, Fax: 403/875-6601 – *3

Knight Law Office, 5012B - 48th St., PO Box 1500, S9V 1K5 – 403/875-9555, Fax: 403/875-9557; Email: bknight@bordercity.com – *1

**Medicine Hat.................................... Medicine Hat**

Biddell Law Office, 666 - 4 St SE, T1A 0K9 – 403/527-7737, Fax: 403/528-8907 – *1

G.R. Côté, #209, 1899 Dunmore Rd. SE, T1A 1Z8 – 403/529-1888

Gordon, Smith & Company, 378 - 1 St. SE, PO Box 490, T1A 7G2 – 403/527-5506, Fax: 403/527-0577 – *5

Dallas K. Miller, #1, 3295 Dunmore Rd. SE, T1B 3R2 – 403/528-3400, Fax: 403/529-2694 – *1

Francis A. O'Connell, 546 - 2 St. SE, T1A 0C6 – 403/526-0504

Pritchard, Lerner & Co., Professional Bldg., Box: 100, #204, 430 - 6th Ave. SE, T1A 7E8 – 403/527-4411, Fax: 403/527-9806 – *8

D.G. Schindel, #1, 3295 Dunmore Rd. SE, T1B 3R2 – 403/529-5548, Fax: 403/529-2694 – *1

Sihvon Carter Fisher & Berger, 499 - 1st St. SE, T1A 1Z8 – 403/526-2600, Fax: 403/526-3217; Email: scfb@telusplanet.net – *6

**Milk River.................................... Lethbridge**

North & Company, 125 Main St. NW, T0K 1M0 – 403/647-3662

**Morinville.................................... Edmonton**

Allan W. Damer, 10201 - 100 Ave., PO Box 1165, T0G 1P0 – 403/939-2936 – *1

Durocher Simpson, 10201 - 100 Ave., T8R 1P9 – 403/939-2936, Fax: 403/939-2935

**Nanton.................................... Lethbridge/MacLeod**

Roddie & McLellan, 2113 - 20 St., PO Box 100, T0L 1R0 – 403/646-2211, Fax: 403/646-3159 – *2

**Okotoks.................................... Calgary**

E.D. Simper, 84 Elizabeth St., PO Box 1117, T0L 1T0 – 403/938-2101, Fax: 403/938-6020 – *1

**Olds.................................... Calgary**

R. Brent Carlyle, 5001 - 50 Ave., PO Box 3755, T4H 1P5 – 403/556-7762, Fax: 403/556-8859

Alvin F. Ganser, 4834 - 50 St., PO Box 4040, T4H 1P7 – 403/556-8481, Fax: 403/556-3830

**Peace River.................................... Peace River**

Donald W. Freeland, #255, 9913 - 100 Ave., PO Box 6239, T8S 1S2 – 403/624-2944, Fax: 403/624-4225 – *1

Mann & Ambrose, 9902 - 97 Ave., PO Box 2880, T0H 2X0 – 403/624-4860

Mathieu, Hryniuk, Shynkar & Erickson, 10012 - 101 St., PO Box 6210, T8S 1S2 – 403/624-2565, Fax: 403/624-5766 – *6

Simpson, Thietke & Associates, 9910 - 97 Ave., PO Box 6778, T8S 1S5 – 403/624-1122, Fax: 403/624-4443 – *3

**Picture Butte.................................... Lethbridge**

North & Company, 316 Jamieson Ave., T0K 1W0 – 403/732-4436

**Pincher Creek.................................... MacLeod**

Douglas J. Evans, PO Box 2457, T0K 1W0

Jasman & Evans, 985 East Ave., PO Box 2530, T0K 1W0 – 403/627-2877, Fax: 403/627-4495 – *2

W.M.K. McGurk, 345 Canyon Drive, PO Box 1598, T0K 1W0 – 403/627-3862 – *1

North & Company, 765 Main St., T0K 1W0 – 403/627-4688

**Ponoka.................................... Wetaskiwin**

Noble & Kidd, 5024 - 51 Ave., PO Box 4278, T4J 1R7 – 403/783-3325, Fax: 403/783-5080 – *2

**Provost.................................... Vegreville**

Ackroyd, Piasta, Roth & Day, 5101 - 50 St., T0B 3S0

**Red Deer.................................... Red Deer**

Altvater Law Office, #1, 5000 - 51 Ave., T4N 4H8 – 403/342-1336, Fax: 403/341-4688 – *1

A.B. Armstrong, #302, 4820 Gaetz Ave., T4N 4A4 – 403/347-7701 – *1

Norman J. Cavanagh, #308, 4808 Ross St., T4N 1X5 – 403/341-5404

Chapman Riebeek, Professional Bldg., #208, 4808 Ross St., T4N 1X5 – 403/346-6603, Fax: 403/340-1280 – *9

Duhamel Manning Feehan Warrender Glass, 5233 - 49 Ave., 2nd Fl., T4N 6G5 – 403/343-0812, Fax: 403/340-3545 – *8

Fielding & Dixon, 4811 - 48 St., 2nd Fl., T4N 1S6 – 403/343-1160 – *2

Gerig Hamilton Neeland Handel, #501, 4901 - 48 St., T4N 6M4 – 403/343-2444, Fax: 403/343-6522 – *5
Brian E. Grice, #150, 4919 - 59 St., T4N 6C9 – 403/342-2544, Fax: 403/347-9895
J.N. Hawthorne, #306, 4805 - 48 St., T4N 1S6 – 403/343-2121, Fax: 403/342-2550 – *1
M.R. Hetherington, #300, 4808 Ross St., T4N 1S8 – 403/346-4199
Denis R. Huot, 4919 - 48 St., T4N 1S8 – 403/341-5551, Fax: 403/343-7016 – *1
Johnston, Ming, Manning, Royal Bank Bldg., 4943 - 50 St., 3rd & 4th Fl., T4N 1Y1 – 403/346-5591, Fax: 403/346-5599 – *9
Beverly Keeshing, 111 Piper Dr., T4P 1L5 – 403/343-0842, Fax: 403/341-3612
N.W. Lockerby, #202, 4921 - 49 St., T4N 1V2 – 403/343-8660 – *1
Harold Loney, #507, 4808 Ross St., T4N 1X5 – 403/343-0122, Fax: 403/340-1195 – *2
Brian S. MacNairn, Woodward Place, #201, 5008 Ross St., T4N 1Y3 – 403/347-2700, Fax: 403/346-5825 – *1
Pamela S. MacNaughton, 4811 - 48 Ave., PO Box 279, T4N 5E8 – 403/340-1600
P.E.B. MacSween, 4824 - 51 St., T4N 2A5 – 403/342-5595, Fax: 403/341-3130 – *1
McIntosh & Schollie, #206, 4808 Ross St., T4N 1X5 – 403/340-8877, Fax: 403/347-3833 – *2
E.F. Murphy, Q.C., 5008 - 50 St., 2nd Fl., T4N 1Y4 – 403/343-8824
Robert M. Oxman, #3, 4909 - 48 St., 2nd Fl., T4N 1S8 – 403/346-5500, Fax: 403/347-5300 – *1
Siewert Bothwell, Central Block, #204, 5000 - 50 Ave., T4N 6C2 – 403/346-1123, Fax: 403/346-1198 – *2
Sisson Warren Sinclair, First Red Deer Pl., #600, 4911 - 51 St., T4N 6V4 – 403/343-3320, Fax: 403/343-6069; Email: sws@ccinet.ab.ca – *11
Vanden Brink & Elgersma, #500, 4808 Ross St., T4N 1X5 – 403/343-6664, Fax: 403/346-9292; Email: benbrink@agt.net – *2

**Redwater** .......... **Edmonton**
D.L. McCallum, PO Box 396, T0A 2W0 – 403/942-3040, Fax: 403/942-2003; Toll Free: 1-800-390-2257 – *1
Smith Gawlinski Parkatti, 4918 - 49 St., T0A 2W0 – 403/942-3331, Fax: 403/428-6645

**Rocky Mountain House** .......... **Red Deer**
Dunsford & Scott, 4920 - 51 Ave., PO Box 370, T0M 1T0 – 403/845-7112, Fax: 403/845-4670 – *3
Woollard Hopkins & Company, 5133 - 49 St., PO Box 700, T0M 1T0 – 403/845-2545, Fax: 403/845-2285 – *3

**St. Albert** .......... **Edmonton**
William P. Glabb, #400, 22 Sir Winston Churchill Ave., T8N 1B4 – 403/459-2200, Fax: 403/460-8514; Email: 1-888-459-2242 – *1
Goldsman & Ritzen, Grandin Park Tower, #609, 22 Sir Winston Churchill Ave., T8N 1B4 – 403/458-0500, Fax: 403/459-2472 – *4
David A. Haas, Grandin Park Tower, Box: 505, 22 Sir Winston Churchill Sq., T8N 1B4 – 403/459-6914, Fax: 403/459-0875 – *1
Wallace Law Office, #214, 86 McKenney Ave., T8N 2T7 – 403/458-7717, Fax: 403/460-1818 – *2

**St. Paul** .......... **Edmonton**
Langager Law Office, 4705 - 50 Ave., PO Box 2350, T0A 3A0 – 403/645-3366, Fax: 403/645-5185; Email: lelpc@agt.net – *1

**Sherwood Park** .......... **Edmonton**
Gary W. Cable, 395 Estate Dr., T8B 1L9 – 403/417-2000, Fax: 403/417-2200; Email: musiclaw@compusmart.ab.ca – *1
Maureen L. Towns, 78 Highland Way, T8A 2A7 – 403/464-5276

**Slave Lake** .......... **Peace River**
Philip Lokken, 401 - 3 Ave. NE, T0G 2A2 – 403/849-5540, Fax: 403/849-5499 – *1
Larry W. Schimpf, PO Box 818, T0G 2A0 – 403/849-3547 – *1
Catherine M. Twinn, Sawridge Admin. Bldg., 2nd Fl., Caribou Trail, PO Box 1460, T0G 2A0 – 403/849-4319, Fax: 403/849-5099 – *1

**Spruce Grove** .......... **Edmonton**
Hustwick Wetsch Moffat & McCrae, #2, 221 - 1st Ave., T7X 3X2 – 403/962-4200, Fax: 403/962-8071; Email: mentor@planet.eon.net

**Standoff** .......... **Calgary**
Walsh Wilkins, PO Box 270, T0L 1Y0 – 403/737-8050, Fax: 403/264-9400; Toll Free: 1-800-304-3574

**Stettler** .......... **Red Deer**
D.C. Ellis, #1, 5002 - 51 Ave., T0C 2L0 – 403/742-4440
Grant, Hunter & Reesor, 4910 - 51 St., PO Box 430, T0C 2L0 – 403/742-4436, Fax: 403/742-1455 – *3
J.M. Grindley, PO Box 1785, T0C 2L0 – 403/742-4401, Fax: 403/742-1270 – *1
Sloan Landman & Anderson, 4819 - 51 St., PO Box 1630, T0C 2L0 – 403/742-3411, Fax: 403/742-1246 – *3

**Stony Plain** .......... **Edmonton**
Birdsell Grant Gardner, #102, 5300 - 50 St., T7Z 1T8 – 403/963-8181, Fax: 403/963-9618 – *4
Braul Gaffney, PO Box 1624, T0E 2G0 – 403/963-2360 – *1

**Strathmore** .......... **Calgary**
Getz & Associates, 225D Wheatland Trail, PO Box 2370, T1P 1K3 – 403/934-2500, Fax: 403/934-2794 – *2
R.E.J. Jarvis, 325 - 3 St., T1P 1M4 – 403/934-5000, Fax: 403/934-4853 – *2

**Sylvan Lake** .......... **Red Deer**
Chapman Riebeek, 5020 - 50A St., T0M 1Z0 – 403/887-2024, Fax: 403/887-2036
Deborah M. Hanly, PO Box 9113, T4S 1S6 – 403/887-4410, Fax: 403/887-4416; Email: clubmed@msn.com – *1
Shaun C. Langin, #4, 5004 - 46 St., PO Box 29, T4S 1C2 – 403/887-2233, Fax: 403/887-4646

**Taber** .......... **Lethbridge**
Baldry Sugden, 5401 - 50 Ave., T1G 1V2 – 403/223-3585, Fax: 403/223-1732 – *2
E.R. Hirch, 5302 - 48 Ave., PO Box 2107, T0K 2G0 – 403/223-1970, Fax: 403/223-4881
North & Company, 4822 - 53 St., T0K 2G0 – 403/223-4015
Stringam Denecky, 5216 - 48 Ave., PO Box 757, T1J 3Z6 – 403/223-2550, Fax: 403/327-1141

**Three Hills** .......... **Drumheller**
Tainsh Howard, 205 Main St., PO Box 1234, T0M 2A0 – 403/443-2200, Fax: 403/443-2025; Email: tainhow@kneehill.com – *2

**Tofield** .......... **Vegreville**
Braul Gaffney, PO Box 299, T0B 4J0 – 403/662-3143, Fax: 403/662-3423
Nancy A. Buchko, PO Box 549, T0B 4J0 – 403/662-3293, Fax: 403/662-4902

**Turner Valley** .......... **Calgary**
Mootoo & Lambert, #2, 118 Main St., PO Box 501, T0L 2A0 – 403/933-3255, Fax: 403/230-2820 – *1

**Vegreville** .......... **Vegreville**
Duncan & Craig, 4925 - 50 St., PO Box 700, T9C 1R7 – 403/632-2877, Fax: 403/632-2898
M.W. Kawulych, PO Box 989, T0B 4L0 – 403/632-2944 – *1
Kuzyk & Bombak, #301, 5038 - 50 Ave., PO Box 929, T9C 1S1 – 403/632-4552, Fax: 403/632-4553; Email: bombak@agt.net – *2
L.M. Starko, PO Box 1178, T9C 1S3 – 403/632-3551 – *1

**Vermilion** .......... **Vegreville**
Reynolds & Flemke, #11, 5125 - 50 Ave., T9X 1A8 – 403/853-5339, Fax: 403/853-4200 – *2
Wheat Law Office, 5042 - 49 Ave., T9X 1B7 – 403/853-4707, Fax: 403/853-4499 – *2

**Viking** .......... **Vegreville**
J.D. Hunter, PO Box 110, T0B 4N0 – 403/336-3143 – *1

**Vulcan** .......... **Calgary**
Roy W. Elander, 115 - 2 Ave. North, PO Box 479, T0L 2B0 – 403/485-2039, Fax: 403/485-6043 – *1
North & Company, 104 Center St. East, T0L 2B0 – 403/485-2070

**Wainwright** .......... **Vegreville**
Rodnunsky & Marchant, 1032 - 1 Ave., PO Box 1560, T0B 4P0 – 403/842-3396, Fax: 403/842-6104 – *2

**Warner** .......... **Lethbridge**
North & Company, 304 - 2nd St., T0K 2L0 – 403/642-3644

**Westlock** .......... **Edmonton**
W.V. Stilwell, 10030 - 106 St., PO Box 100, T0G 2L0 – 403/349-4448 – *1
Tims & Company, 9531 - 107 St., PO Box 490, T0G 2L0 – 403/349-5366, Fax: 403/349-6510 – *2

**Wetaskiwin** .......... **Wetaskiwin**
Lorne P. Kroetch, 100 Northwood Cres., T9A 3L4
McDonald Street Law Office, 4408 - 51 St., T9A 1K5 – 403/352-0369, Fax: 403/352-0393 – *1
Dennis W. Pike, PO Box 7050, T9A 2Y9 – 403/352-3305
Sirrs Deckert Allen Cymbaluk, 5201 - 51 Ave., PO Box 6060, T9A 2E8 – 403/352-3301, Fax: 403/352-5976; Email: sirrsdec@ccinet.ab.ca – *4
Sockett & Associates, 5118 - 50 Ave., T9A 0S6 – 403/352-6691, Fax: 403/352-0599; Email: ksockett@ccinet.ab.ca – *3

**Winterburn** .......... **Edmonton**
Eileen Powless, PO Box 100, RR#1, Site 2, T0E 2N0 – 403/470-3535, Fax: 403/470-5751
Sharon Venne, Site 2, RR#1, PO Box 100, T0E 2N0 – 403/470-3535, Fax: 403/470-3380

## BRITISH COLUMBIA

**Abbotsford** .......... **Westminster**
Baker Newby, #200, 2955 Gladwin Rd., V2S 6W8 – 604/852-3646, Fax: 604/852-5194; Toll Free: 1-800-533-0990
Fast & Welwood, #305, 2692 Clearbrook Rd., V2T 2Y8 – 604/850-6640, Fax: 604/850-6616; Email: info@faswel.com – *4
L.W. Goddard, #303, 2890 Garden St., V2T 4W7 – 604/853-3535; 856-3537, Fax: 604/853-9033 – *1
Eric J. Janzen, #2, 32056 South Fraser Way, V2T 1V7 – 604/853-6424, Fax: 604/853-9601 – *1
Marcotte Law Office, 2619 Cedar Park Pl., V2T 3S4 – 604/855-6688, Fax: 604/855-6515 – *2
Matsqui-Abbotsford Community Legal Services, #100, 2955 Gladwin Rd., V2T 5T4 – 604/859-2755, Fax: 604/853-3059
W. Wayne Norris, #302, 32555 Simon Ave., V2T 4Y2 – 604/859-6161, Fax: 604/859-0700 – *1
Palmer, Malloch, #1, 33775 Essendene Ave., V2S 2H1 – 604/859-3887, Fax: 604/859-3883 – *4

* indicates number of lawyers in law firm.

Robertson, Downe & Mullally, 33695 South Fraser Way, V2S 2C1 – 604/853-0774; 856-3627 (Vancouver), Fax: 604/852-3829 – *14
Lloyd H. Wilson, 2644 Montrose Ave., V2S 3T6 – 604/853-3355, Fax: 604/853-2644 – *2

**Armstrong .......................................... Yale**

Blakely & Co., 3475 Pleasant Valley Rd., PO Box 357, V0E 1B0 – 250/546-3188, Fax: 250/546-2677; Email: blakely2@junction.net – *1
DuMont & Reif, 3395 Okanagan St., PO Box 549, V0E 1B0 – 250/546-8414, Fax: 250/546-8885 – *4

**Ashcroft .......................................... Yale**

Morelli, Chertkow, 401 Railway Ave., V0K 1A0 – 250/453-2320, Fax: 250/453-2622; Email: mclawyer@mail.netshop.net

**Brentwood Bay .......................... Vancouver Island**

Stevenson Jenko, 7103 West Saanich Rd., PO Box 177, V8M 1R3 – 250/652-5151, Fax: 250/652-9687

**Burnaby .................................. Westminster**

Baily, McLean, Greenbank & Murdoch, #803, 4720 Kingsway, V5H 4N2 – 604/437-6611, Fax: 604/437-3065 – *3
Becker, Mathers, Rogers Dantel Tower, Eaton Centre, #2148, 4710 Kingsway, V5H 4M2 – 604/438-8234, Fax: 604/438-1497 – *8
C.H. Bergen, #200, 5000 Kingsway, V5H 2E4 – 604/430-4244, Fax: 604/430-4210 – *1
W.E. Bergmann, 4550 East Hastings St., V5C 2K4 – 604/298-8211, Fax: 604/298-8216 – *1
Cobbett & Cotton, 4259 East Hastings St., V5C 2J5 – 604/299-6251, Fax: 604/299-6627 – *2
Annabelle Donovan, 4853 East Hastings St., V5C 2L1 – 604/291-8211, Fax: 604/291-2676 – *1
Edwards, Edwards, Edwards & Maskall, #510, 5021 Kingsway, V5H 4A5 – 604/433-2445, Fax: 604/433-8209 – *4
James K. Fraser Law Corporation, #200, 5000 Kingsway, V5H 2E4 – 604/433-0010, Fax: 604/435-0269 – *1
Diane Gradley, #2008, 4330 Kingsway, V5H 4G7 – 604/438-2258, Fax: 604/438-2259 – *1
Hawthorne, Piggott, Emerson & Petronio, #208, 1899 Willingdon Ave., V5C 5T1 – 604/299-8371, Fax: 604/299-1523 – *4
Hean Wylie Peach DeStefanis, #1501, 4330 Kingsway, V5H 4H9 – 604/434-5784, Fax: 604/434-7707 – *10
Hwang, Pollock & Company, #747, 4710 Kingsway, V5H 4M2 – 604/451-0096, Fax: 604/451-0097; Email: mhwang@iiworld.com – *2
Sue M. Kelly, #124A, 4664 Lougheed Hwy., V5C 5T5 – 604/293-4110, Fax: 604/293-1372 – *1
Kerfoot, Cameron & Company, #314, 9600 Cameron St., V3J 7N3 – 604/421-7144, Fax: 604/421-2912; Email: jbt@kercam.com – *9
Philip T. Lau, #402, 3701 East Hastings St., V5C 2H6 – 604/293-1231, Fax: 604/293-1232 – *1
Morag M.J. MacLeod, #1830, 4720 Kingsway, V5H 4N2 – 604/430-8444, Fax: 604/430-1164 – *1
F.T.D. McGovern, #6, 4857 Kingsway, V5H 2C8 – 604/433-0939, Fax: 604/433-9374 – *1
McNamee Law Office, #200, 4603 Kingsway, V5H 4M4 – 604/451-1141, Fax: 604/451-1151; Email: jmcnamee@mcnamee-law.com; URL: http://www.mcnamee-law.com – *1
John W. Motiuk, #201, 6125 Sussex Ave., V5H 4G1 – 604/437-8684, Fax: 604/437-9874 – *1
Ogilvie Law Offices, #201, 3975 North Rd., V3J 1S2 – 604/421-1622, Fax: 604/421-8197 – *1
Pihl & Company, #205, 5481 Kingsway, V5H 2G1 – 604/437-3529, Fax: 604/437-8837 – *2
B.C.E. Russell, 220 - 4411 Hastings East, V5C 2K1 – 604/298-1038, Fax: 604/298-1037 – *1
Saucier & Company, 4750 Kingsway, V5H 2C2 – 604/434-7200, Fax: 604/432-9803 – *2
Smith & Company, #148, 4664 Lougheed Hwy., V5C 5T5 – 604/473-9330, Fax: 604/473-9334 – *3
G. Brian Starr, #315, 5000 Kingsway, V5H 2E4 – 604/435-5588, Fax: 604/430-2912 – *1
Donald M. Tenant, #515, 4710 Kingsway, V5H 4M2 – 604/434-2512, Fax: 604/432-9556 – *1
Audrey H. Vandervelden, #4, 6344 Kingsway, V5E 1C5 – 604/433-8706, Fax: 604/435-5915 – *1
Maureen J. Wesley, 4270 McGill St., V5C 1M9 – 604/298-6555, Fax: 604/298-6555 – *1

**Burns Lake .............................. Prince Rupert**

R.R. Low, 310 Yellowhead, PO Box 389, V0J 1E0 – 250/692-7581, Fax: 250/692-3490 – *1

**Campbell River.......................... Vancouver Island**

John F. Grant & Associates, 964 Island Hwy., V9W 2C5 – 250/287-8855, Fax: 250/286-6227 – *1
McVea, Shook, Wickham & Bishop, 906 Island Hwy., V9W 2C3 – 250/287-8355, Fax: 250/287-8112 – *8
Claire I. Moglove, #201, 909 Island Hwy., V9W 2C2 – 250/286-0050, Fax: 250/286-0052 – *1
B. Ettie O'Connell, 2200 Shetland Rd., V9W 3Y5 – 250/287-3844 – *1
Robin L. Pearson, 799 Eland Dr., V9W 6Y9 – 250/923-6969, Fax: 250/923-1886 – *1
Karen D. Stevan, 798 Marina Blvd., V9W 1X4 – 250/923-1884, Fax: 250/923-3301 – *1
Tees Lloyd Clare & Kiddle, Royal Court Bldg., #200, 1260 Shoppers Row, V9W 2C8 – 250/287-7755, Fax: 250/287-3999; Email: tlck@oberon.ark.com – *8
Thompson, Murdoch & Stein, #201, 400 - 10 Ave., V9W 4E3 – 250/287-9574, Fax: 250/287-4818 – *3

**Castlegar .............................. West Kootenay**

Moran & Company, 1233 - 3rd St., V1N 1Z6 – 250/365-7741, Fax: 250/365-2620 – *3
Polonicoff, Jones & Perehudoff, 1115 - 3 St., V1N 2A1 – 250/365-3343, Fax: 250/365-6307 – *3

**Chilliwack .............................. Westminster**

Baker Newby, 9259 Main St., PO Box 390, V2P 6K2 – 604/792-1376, Fax: 604/792-8711; Toll Free: 1-800-881-3646; Email: info@bakernewby.com; URL: http://www.bakernewby.com – *25
Kaye, Toews & Caldwell, 9202 Young St., PO Box 372, V2P 6J4 – 604/792-1977, Fax: 604/792-7077; Toll Free: 856-8513; Email: ktclawof@uniserve.com – *4
Thome, Jespersen, Hansford, #201, 45820 Wellington Ave., V2P 2C9 – 604/792-9100, Fax: 604/792-1331 – *5

**Clayburn.............................. Westminster**

Bryan J. Haber, 34810 Clayburn Rd, V0X 1E0 – 604/852-8177, Fax: 604/852-1464

**Clearbrook.............................. Westminster**

Linley, Duignan & Company, 2548 Clearbrook Rd, PO Box 2040, V1T 3T8 – 604/859-7134, Fax: 604/859-0843; Email: neill-brown@bc.sympatico.ca – *6

**Cobble Hill .......................... Vancouver Island**

George E. Asp, 896 Chapman, RR#2, V0R 1L0 – 250/748-6315, Fax: 250/748-2812

**Comox .................................. Nanaimo**

Chesterley & Dreyer, 1984 Comox Ave., V9M 3M7 – 250/339-3363, Fax: 250/339-3315 – *4

**Coquitlam.............................. Westminster**

Antifaev & Associates, #221, 3030 Lincoln Ave., V3B 6B4 – 604/464-6822, Fax: 604/464-7335 – *3
David Boulding, #206, 2922 Glen Dr., V3B 2P7 – 604/945-2043, Fax: 604/945-2063 – *1
Burke Tomchenko, #258, 3020 Lincoln Ave., V3B 6B4 – 604/942-1166, Fax: 604/942-2429; Email: btlaw@istar.ca – *5
Feller Drysdale, #211, 1015 Austin Ave., V3K 3N9 – 604/939-8321, Fax: 604/939-7584; URL: http://www.feller_drysdale.com – *8
Goddard & Company, #302, 566 Lougheed Hwy., V3K 3S3 – 604/937-7791, Fax: 604/937-3340 – *1
R. Larry Nixon, #260, 1140 Austin Ave., V3K 3P5 – 604/931-4555, Fax: 604/931-7465 – *1
Spraggs & Company, #202, 1030 Westwood St., V3C 4L4 – 604/464-3333, Fax: 604/464-3335 – *1
Dave R. Way, #302, 566 Lougheed Hwy., V3K 3S3 – 604/937-7791, Fax: 604/937-3340 – *1
Zipp & Company, 820 Henderson Ave., V3K 1P2 – 604/936-7743 – *2

**Courtenay.......................... Vancouver Island**

Gibson Kelly & Ives, 505 - 5 St., V9N 1K2 – 250/334-2416, Fax: 250/334-3198; Email: gkilaw@mars.ark.com – *4
Terrence M.P. Hanlon, PO Box 3352, V9N 5N5 – 250/334-4733, Fax: 250/334-1968 – *1
H. Huibers Law Corporation, 480 - 10th St., V9N 1P6 – 250/334-3108, Fax: 250/334-0621 – *1
C.H.L. Morris, 949 Fitzgerald Ave., V9N 2R6 – 250/338-5311, Fax: 250/338-1818 – *1
Muir, Sinclare, #200, 575 - 10 St., V9N 1P9 – 250/338-6744, Fax: 250/334-3325 – *2
Olstead & Holekamp, 512 - 4th St., V9N 1H2 – 250/338-6747, Fax: 250/338-1833 – *4
Swift Datoo & Company Law Corporation, #201, 467 Cumberland Rd., V9N 2C5 – 250/334-4461, Fax: 250/334-2335; Email: sdc@mars.ark.com – *8

**Cranbrook .............................. Kootenay**

Patrick J. Dearden, #201, 129 - 10th Ave. South, V1C 2N1 – 250/426-7431, Fax: 250/426-3746 – *1
Graham Apps & Company, 122 - 11 Ave. South, V1C 2P2 – 250/426-2277, Fax: 250/426-1903 – *3
Murielle A. Matthews, 801B Baker St., V1C 1A3 – 250/426-0601, Fax: 250/426-4239 – *1
Miles, Daroux & McCormick, 30 - 11th Ave. South, V1C 2P1 – 250/489-3350, Fax: 250/489-2235 – *4
Rella Docking & Paolini, #6, 10 Ave. South, 2nd Fl., V1C 2M8 – 250/426-8981, Fax: 250/426-8987 – *3
Robertson Zimmer Associates, #200, 135 - 10 Ave. South, V1C 2N1 – 250/489-4346, Fax: 250/489-1899 – *2
Steidl, Kambeitz & Bennett, #201, 907 Baker St., V1C 1A4 – 250/426-7211, Fax: 250/426-6100 – *4

**Creston.............................. West Kootenay**

Miller, Dan & Associates, 139 - 10th Ave., PO Box 1429, V0B 1G0 – 250/428-2208, Fax: 250/428-2200 – *1

**Dawson Creek .............................. Cariboo**

Gibb & Syal, #201, 10312 - 12 St., PO Box 510, V1G 4H5 – 250/782-8556, Fax: 250/782-5239 – *3
Mitchell, Schuller & Dellow, #2, 933 - 103 Ave., V1G 2G4 – 250/782-8155, Fax: 250/782-4525 – *4
Plenert Higson, #201, 1136 - 103 Ave., V1G 2G7 – 250/782-9134, Fax: 250/782-9135; Toll Free: 1-888-782-9134 – *4
Valair & Company, 10206 - 10 St., V1G 3T4 – 250/782-3347, Fax: 250/782-3315 – *1

**Delta.............................. Westminster**

Ellard & Company, Tsawwassen Place, #400, 1530 - 56 St., V4L 2A8 – 604/948-1926, Fax: 604/948-1927; Email: rod_ellard@bc.sympatico.ca – *1
Kaminsky & Company, #202, 8435 - 120 St., V4C 6R2 – 604/591-7877, Fax: 604/591-1978 – *5
Kane, Shannon & Weiler, #301, 6935 - 120 St., V4E 2A8 – 604/591-7321, Fax: 604/591-7149 – *11
Lehal & Company, #200, 6905 - 120th St., V4E 2A8 – 604/596-1321, Fax: 604/596-1320 – *3
R.E. Piters, #110, 4977 Trennant St., V4K 2K5 – 604/946-0466, Fax: 604/946-0467 – *2

G.G. Walters, #405, 11861 - 88 Ave., V4C 3C6 – 604/596-3300, Fax: 604/596-9111 – *1

**Denman Island** .......... **Vancouver Island**

Sally Campbell, 1536 Northwest Rd., PO Box 52, V0R 1T0 – 250/335-2505, Fax: 250/335-2221; Email: salal@comox.island.net – *1

**Duncan** .......... **Vancouver Island**

Coleman LaCroix Fraser & Whittome, #201, 58 Station St.., V9L 1M4 – 250/748-1013, Fax: 250/748-2733 – *4

Jean E. Hamilton, #209, 225 Canada Ave., V9L 1T6 – 250/748-5858, Fax: 250/748-6060 – *1

MacCarthy Ridgway, #200, 44 Queens Rd., V9L 2W4 – 250/746-7121, Fax: 250/746-4070 – *7

MacIsaac & Company, Top Floor, 190 Ingram St., V9L 1P1 – 250/746-4422, Fax: 250/746-1811 – *1

McCutcheon & Company, 62 Kenneth St., V9L 1N2 – 250/746-5155, Fax: 250/746-4114 – *1

McDaniel & Tillie, #204, 55 Canada Ave., V9L 1T3 – 250/748-6633, Fax: 250/748-1496 – *2

Sandra McEwan, 5784 Alderlea St., PO Box 482, V9L 3X8 – 250/748-4433

Peter M. Moir, PO Box 951, V9L 3Y2 – 250/746-7114, Fax: 250/746-7115 – *1

Molnar, Desjardins & Associates, Financial Centre, #206, 435 Trunk Rd., V9L 2P5 – 250/748-5253, Fax: 250/746-1511; Email: gmolnar@island.net.ca – *2

Robert Morales, PO Box 356, V9L 3X5 – 250/748-5233

Robert W. Nelford, 3250 Hillwood Rd., V9L 5K6 – 250/746-8555, Fax: 250/748-1957; Email: robertnel@sea-side.net – *1

Richard J.P. Nesbitt, #2, 271 Ingram St., V9L 1P3 – 250/748-1464, Fax: 250/748-4819 – *1

Orchard & Company, 321 St. Julian St., V9L 3S5 – 250/746-5899, Fax: 250/746-7182 – *5

Yvonne Pink, #209, 225 Canada Ave., V9L 1T6 – 250/748-6565, Fax: 250/748-6060 – *1

Taylor & Company, 466 Trans Canada Hwy., V9L 3R6 – 250/748-4444, Fax: 250/748-5920; Toll Free: 1-800-665-5414; Email: info@taylor-co.com; URL: http://www.taylor-co.com/info – *3

Whittome & Whittome, #201, 58 Station St., V9L 1M4 – 250/748-3151 – *2

**Fernie** .......... **Kootenay**

R.W. Bentley, PO Box 2038, V0B 1M0 – 250/423-9241, Fax: 250/423-6440 – *1

**Fort St. James** .......... **Cariboo**

Dene Law Centre, #222, 250 Stuart Dr. East, V0J 1P0 – 250/996-7700, Fax: 250/996-7704; Email: 1-888-221-2175 – *1

**Fort St. John** .......... **Cariboo**

Callison & Company, #201, 10419 - 100 St., V1J 3Z3 – 250/785-8033, Fax: 250/785-4346 – *1

Daley & Earmme, 10740 - 100 St., V1J 3Z6 – 250/785-6961, Fax: 250/785-6967 – *5

Rodney J. Strandberg Law Corp., #320, 9900 - 100 Ave., V1J 5S7 – 250/787-7760, Fax: 250/787-7752 – *1

**Ganges** .......... **Vancouver Island**

McKimm & Lott, Ganges Centre, PO Box 70, V0S 1E0 – 250/537-9951, Fax: 250/537-4341

**Garibaldi Highlands** .......... **Vancouver**

Brian N. Hughes, 38141 - 2nd Ave., PO Box 557, V0N 1T0 – 604/892-5114, Fax: 604/892-5129 – *1

**Gibsons** .......... **Vancouver**

Lynn Chapman, Roberts Creek, 1896 Lower Rd., PO Box 286, V0N 1V0 – 604/886-0382, Fax: 604/886-0366; Email: lynn_chapman@sunshine.net – *1

J. Wayne Rowe, #6, 771 Hwy. 101, PO Box 1880, V0N 1V0 – 604/886-2029, Fax: 604/886-9191 – *1

Leanne L. Turnbull, RR#6, Site 28, Comp. 32, V0N 1V0 – 604/886-7666, Fax: 604/886-7636; Email: lturnbull@sunshine.net – *1

**Golden** .......... **East Kootenay**

Ewan & McKenzie, PO Box 429, V0A 1H0 – 250/344-5258, Fax: 250/344-7374 – *2

**Grand Forks** .......... **West Kootenay**

Ronald C.E. Mellett, PO Box 1870, V0H 1H0 – 250/442-5599, Fax: 250/442-8466 – *1

Somerville & Company, 135 Market Ave., PO Box 1016, V0H 1H0 – 250/442-2105, Fax: 250/442-5262; Email: psomervi@sunshinecable.com; URL: http://www.boundary.bc.ca/Business/PSLC – *1

**Invermere** .......... **East Kootenay**

W.J. MacDonald, PO Box 2400, V0A 1K0 – 250/342-6921, Fax: 250/342-3237 – *1

Randall K. McRoberts, 613 - 12 St., PO Box 1049, V0A 1K0 – 250/342-6975, Fax: 250/342-6299 – *1

**Kamloops** .......... **Yale**

Peter Allik-Petersenn, #205, 141 Victoria St., V2C 1Z5 – 250/828-9545, Fax: 250/828-1297 – *1

P.R. Bianco, 1023 Schubert Dr., V2B 2G6 – 250/376-9911, Fax: 250/372-1514 – *1

Campbell & Associates, #209, 141 Victoria St., V2C 1Z5 – 250/374-9344, Fax: 250/374-1590 – *1

Collins & Co., #101, 1315 Summit Dr., V2C 5R9 – 250/851-0886, Fax: 250/851-2889 – *2

Cundari & Company, #810, 175 - 2 Ave., V2C 5W1 – 250/374-8887, Fax: 250/372-5554; Email: cundari@mail.netshop.net – *1

Elaine Dixon, 683 St. Paul St., V2C 2K2 – 250/828-6662, Fax: 250/828-1156 – *1

Drayton Law Firm, #201, 444 St. Paul St., V2C 2J6 – 250/374-3737, Fax: 250/374-5800 – *3

Fulton & Company, 248 - 2nd Ave., V2C 2C9 – 250/372-5542, Fax: 250/851-2300; Email: fultonco@net-shop.net – *15

J.G. Gnitt, #2, 703 St. Paul St., V2C 2K3 – 250/374-3156 – *1

D.J. Goar, #440, 175 - 2 Ave., V2C 5W1 – 250/374-4627, Fax: 250/374-0035 – *1

Horne Marr Zak, #600, 175 - 2 Ave., V2C 5W1 – 250/372-1221, Fax: 250/372-8339; Email: 1-800-558-1933 – *7

Jensen, Mitchell & Co., Old Firehall #1, #300, 125 - 4 Ave., V2C 3N3 – 250/372-8811, Fax: 250/828-6697 – *4

J. Kurta, #400, 235 First Ave., V2C 3J4 – 250/372-8248, Fax: 250/372-1274 – *1

Mary E. MacGregor, 603 St. Paul St., V2C 2K1 – 250/828-0282, Fax: 250/828-0287 – *1

Mair Jensen Blair, #700, 275 Lansdowne St., V2C 6H6 – 250/374-3161, Fax: 250/374-6992; Toll Free: 1-888-374-3161 – *20

Wade I. Marke, #204, 300 Columbia St., V2C 6L1 – 250/372-1282, Fax: 250/374-1295 – *1

David A. McMillan, #401, 286 St. Paul St., V2C 6G4 – 250/828-0702, Fax: 250/828-0703 – *1

Morelli, Chertkow, #300, 180 Seymour St., V2C 2E3 – 250/374-3344, Fax: 250/374-1144; Toll Free: 1-888-374-3350; Email: mclawyer@mail.netshop.net – *14

B.I. Murphy, 703 St. Paul St., V2C 2K3 – 250/372-1515, Fax: 250/372-1514 – *1

Blair H. Nixon, #203, 153 Seymour St., V2C 2C7 – 250/372-3233, Fax: 250/372-5525 – *2

Craig Nixon Law Corp., #8, 345 Victoria St., V2C 2A3 – 250/374-1555, Fax: 250/374-9992; Toll Free: 1-888-879-9912; Email: onlc@mail.netshop.net – *2

Oien, Church, #212, 220 - 4th Ave., V2C 3N6 – 250/851-8323, Fax: 250/851-8373; Email: halbob@direct.ca – *2

Roger R. Plested, 441 Tranquille Rd., V2B 3G9 – 250/376-1211, Fax: 250/376-1207 – *1

Rogers & Hyslop, 533 Nicola St., V2C 2P9 – 250/374-7179, Fax: 250/374-3818 – *2

Stanford & Bartle, #201, 242 Victoria St., V2C 2A2 – 250/851-8582, Fax: 250/851-8583; Email: michelle.stanford@bc.sympatico.ca – *1

Sheldon B. Tate, 790 Seymour St., V2C 2H3 – 250/372-1899, Fax: 250/372-3090 – *1

Taylor Epp & Dolder, #300, 153 Seymour St., V2C 2C8 – 250/374-3456, Fax: 250/828-6808 – *2

Ley Lynette Tucker, #300, 125 - 4 Ave., V2C 3N3 – 250/314-0133, Fax: 250/314-0166 – *1

**Kelowna** .......... **Yale**

Beairsto & Company, #201, 1940 Kane Rd., V1V 2J9 – 250/762-6111, Fax: 250/762-6480 – *4

Lyndon A. Best, #202, 1636 Pandosy St., V1Y 1P7 – 250/762-2345, Fax: 250/862-5133 – *1

Bishop & Company, #206, 347 Leon Ave., V1Y 8C7 – 250/861-4022, Fax: 250/862-3937 – *4

Burgess & Company, #202, 2365 Gordon Dr., V1W 3C2 – 250/861-5533, Fax: 250/861-4442 – *1

Heather J. Dunlop, 1974 McDougall St., V1Y 1A3 – 250/862-9292

Laura J. Gosset, 232 Caliburn Crt., V1V 1N2 – 250/862-5262, Fax: 250/862-5292 – *1

Martin D. Johnson, #204, 260 Harvey Ave., V1Y 7S5 – 250/868-2848, Fax: 250/868-3080 – *1

Roberta L. Jordan, Landmark Square One, #702, 1726 Dolphin Ave., V1Y 6A8 – 250/862-2909, Fax: 250/862-2906 – *1

Kidston, Helm, Tonsoo, McDougall, #203, 125 Highway 33 East, V1X 2A1 – 250/765-9500, Fax: 250/765-9552 – *3

Kimmitt & Company, #202, 1433 St. Paul St., V1Y 2E4 – 250/763-6441, Fax: 250/763-1633 – *3

Robert Louie, 515 Hwy. 97 South, V1Z 3J2 – 250/769-5666

M. Gail Miller, #904, 1708 Dolphin Ave., V1Y 9S4 – 250/763-6767, Fax: 250/763-0980 – *1

R.G. Phelps, #8, 1638 Pandosy St., V1Y 1P8 – 250/762-2345, Fax: 250/862-5133 – *1

David H. Pihl & Associates, #201, 678 Bernard Ave., V1Y 6P3 – 250/762-5434, Fax: 250/762-5450 – *4

Porter Ramsay, #200, 1465 Ellis St., V1Y 2A3 – 250/763-7646, Fax: 250/762-9960 – *6

Pushor Mitchell, 1665 Ellis St., 3rd Fl., V1Y 2B3 – 250/762-2108, Fax: 250/762-9115; Toll Free: 1-800-558-1155; Email: pmdm@pmdm.com – *22

Salloum Doak, Chancery Place, #200, 537 Leon Ave., V1Y 2A9 – 250/763-4323, Fax: 250/763-4780; Toll Free: 1-800-661-4959; Email: salloum.doak@awinc.com; URL: http://www.awinc.com/salloum – *14

Schlosser, Gunnlaugson & Schlosser, 3017 Tutt St., V1Y 2H4 – 250/763-1393, Fax: 250/862-3779 – *1

Susan Greba Scott, #212, 1511 Sutherland Ave., V1Y 5Y7 – 250/860-8007, Fax: 250/763-8488 – *1

Daniel E. Spelliscy, 1974 McDougall St., V1Y 1A3 – 250/862-9586, Fax: 250/862-9576; Email: spelldan@silk.net – *1

Thiessen, Petraroia, #804, 1708 Dolphin Ave., V1Y 9R9 – 250/861-5332, Fax: 250/861-8772 – *3

Tinker, Kueng & Company, 1573 Ellis St., PO Box 309, V1Y 7N8 – 250/763-7333, Fax: 250/763-5507 – *3

Wageman Bailey, 1674 Bertram St., 2nd Fl., V1Y 9G4 – 250/763-3343, Fax: 250/763-9524 – *8

Marc R.B. Whittemore, #205, 1690 Water St., V1Y 8T8 – 250/868-2202, Fax: 250/868-2270 – *1

**Kimberley** .......... **East Kootenay**

Robert C. Apps, 230 Spokane St., V1A 2E4 – 250/427-2235, Fax: 250/426-5168

Robert Mayne & Company, 104 Deer Park Ave., V1A 2J4 – 250/427-4844, Fax: 250/427-4891 – *2

**Kitimat** .......... **Prince Rupert**

K.P. Douglas, #104, 369 City Centre, V8C 1T6 – 250/632-4727, Fax: 250/632-4885 – *1

* indicates number of lawyers in law firm.

Wozney & Donaldson, 366 City Centre, V8C 1T6 – 250/632-7151, Fax: 250/632-7100 – *2

**Ladysmith ............................... Vancouver Island**

MacIsaac & Company, 19 Gatacre St., PO Box 1589, V0R 2E0 – 250/245-7670, Fax: 250/245-7614 – *1

Robson, O'Connor, 22 High St., PO Box 1890, V0R 2E0 – 250/245-7141, Fax: 250/245-2921; Toll Free: 1-800-641-1311 – *2

**Langley...................................... Westminister**

William J. Alexander Law Corporation, 206 - 20641 Logan Ave., V3A 7R3 – 604/736-0443, Fax: 604/731-7839 – *1

Ash, O'Donnell, Hibbert, 5525 - 208 St., V3A 2K4 – 604/533-4110, 3029, Fax: 604/533-8338; Email: dorothyj@unixg.ubc.ca – *4

Bryenton, Rosberg & Company, #300, 20689 Fraser Hwy., V3A 4G4 – 604/530-7155, Fax: 604/530-8081 – *2

Campbell, Burton & McMullan, #202, 22242 - 48th Ave., V3A 3N5 – 604/533-3821, Fax: 604/533-5521 – *6

K.A. Christofferson, 10162 Allard Cres., V1M 3V7 – 604/888-7641, Fax: 604/888-7217 – *1

Fleming, Olson & Taneda, 4038 - 200B St., V3A 1N9 – 604/533-3411, Fax: 604/533-8749 – *3

Carolyn S. Gulabsingh Law Office, #201, 5755 Glover Rd., V3A 8H4 – 604/534-1686, Fax: 604/534-2382; Email: carolyn@legalmail.com – *1

Lindsay Kenney, #110, 5769 - 201A St., V3A 8H9 – 604/534-5114, Fax: 604/534-5927; Email: info@lindsaykenney.bc.ca; URL: http://www.lindsaykenney.bc.ca

MacCallum McIntyre, 6345 - 197 St., V2Y 1K8 – 604/530-4161, Fax: 604/530-5716 – *6

MacDonald, Boyle & Jeffery, 20450 Fraser Hwy., V3A 4G2 – 604/530-3141, Fax: 604/530-9573 – *3

Meighen & Sissons, #201C, 20651 - 56 Ave., V3A 3Y9 – 604/534-6061, Fax: 604/534-1640 – *3

Milne Selkirk, Bldg. #5, 21183 - 88th Ave., V1M 2G5 – 604/882-5015, Fax: 604/882-5025

Minten Critchley, #221, 20316 - 56 Ave., V3A 3Y7 – 604/530-7187, Fax: 604/530-0237 – *3

Joan E. Mitchell, #108, 19610 - 64th Ave., V2Y 1H3 – 604/533-8811, Fax: 604/533-8244 – *1

Nundal, Cherrington, Easingwood & Kearl, 20570 - 56 Ave., V3A 3Z1 – 604/530-2191, Fax: 604/530-6282 – *4

Joseph M. Prodor, PO Box 3189, Stn A, V3A 4R5 – 604/534-7907, Fax: 604/535-8981 – *1

Severide, Staplin McCallum & Company, 20432 Douglas Cres., PO Box 3400, V3A 4R7 – 604/534-8551, Fax: 604/534-1021 – *5

Sliman, Stander & Company, #105, 6395 - 198 St., V2Y 2E3 – 604/533-2300, Fax: 604/533-2387 – *3

Weber Harvey & Company, #201, 5755 Glover Rd., V3A 8H4 – 604/534-1686, Fax: 604/534-2382 – *1

**Lantzville ........................................ Victoria**

Loy & Rongve, 7186 Lantzville Rd., PO Box 437, V0R 2H0 – 250/390-3157, Fax: 250/390-4857 – *2

**Lions Bay ....................................... Vancouver**

M.A. Roell, 150 Sunset Dr., PO Box 502, V0N 2E0 – 604/921-6972 – *1

**Mackenzie ........................................ Cariboo**

Hope Heinrich, PO Box 209, V0J 2C0 – *1

**Maple Ridge................................. Westminster**

Meighen & Sissons, #9, 20691 Lougheed Hwy., V2X 2P9 – 604/465-4846, Fax: 604/465-5679 – *3

Norquist, Davies, 22299 Dewdney Trunk Rd., V2X 3J1 – 604/467-3477, Fax: 604/467-0018 – *3

Shantz & Associates, 22326 McIntosh Ave., V2X 3C1 – 604/463-8890, Fax: 604/463-6760 – *2

Vernon & Thompson, 22311 - 119 Ave., V2X 2Z2 – 604/463-6281, Fax: 604/463-7497 – *5

**Merritt ............................................. Yale**

Merritt Legal Services, 1964 Quilchena Ave., PO Box 4400, V0K 2B0 – 250/378-6112, Fax: 250/378-4550 – *1

Morelli, Chertkow, 2199 Granite Ave., V0K 2B0 – 250/378-4218, Fax: 250/378-4997; Email: mclawyer@mail.netshop.net

Nicola Valley Native Community Law Office, 1964 Quilchena Ave., PO Box 4400, Stn Main, V1K 1B8 – 250/378-6112, Fax: 250/378-4550; Email: njoe@vbcs.awinc.com – *1

**Mission...................................... Westminster**

Taylor, Tait, Ruley & Company, 33066 First Ave., V1V 1G3 – 604/826-1266, Fax: 604/826-4288 – *4

Walker, Lacusta & Ross, 33137 North Railway Ave., PO Box 3250, V2V 4J4 – 604/826-7104, Fax: 604/826-3229 – *2

Marianne Walters Law Corp., #2, 7101 Horne St., V2V 7A2 – 604/820-1059, Fax: 604/820-1080 – *2

**Nakusp.................................... West Kootenay**

Kenneth R. Watson, PO Box 668, V0G 1R0 – 250/265-3641, Fax: 250/265-3220 – *1

**Nanaimo................................ Vancouver Island**

Allin, Anderson & MacNeil, #505, 495 Dunsmuir St., PO Box 10, V9R 5K4 – 250/753-6435, Fax: 250/753-5285; Email: law@island.net – *6

Bartlett & Company, 225 Vancouver Ave., V9S 4E9 – 250/753-6616, Fax: 250/753-8671 – *2

Bruhaug & Carlson, 669 Terminal Ave. North, V9S 4K1 – 250/753-7582, Fax: 250/753-7583; Toll Free: 1-800-860-8883; Email: brucarl@island.net – *3

Iain A. Currie, 4 Church St., V9R 5H4 – 250/753-0844, Fax: 250/753-0861; Email: icurrie@island.net – *1

Bentley J. Falkenberg, 55 Front St., V9R 5H9 – 250/755-1714, Fax: 250/755-1238 – *1

Hamilton Waterman Law Corp., 70 Prideaux St., V9R 2M5 – 250/755-1783, Fax: 250/754-2349 – *1

Heath, Giovando, Downs & Hansen, #200, 1808 Bowen Rd., V9S 5W4 – 250/753-2202, Fax: 250/753-3949 – *5

A. Peter Hertzberg, 4 Church St., V9R 5H4 – 250/753-0844, Fax: 250/753-0861; Email: phertz@island.net – *1

Hobbs Hargrave, 301 Franklyn St., V9R 2X5 – 250/753-3477, Fax: 250/753-7927 – *3

S.M. Hogan, 515 Campbell St., V9R 3G9 – 250/754-1222 – *1

E. Keith Jones, 207 Milton St., V9R 2K5 – 250/753-4543, Fax: 250/753-8631; Toll Free: 1-800-668-4511 – *1

King, Sutton & Hope, 155 Commercial St., V9R 5G5 – 250/753-6617, Fax: 250/753-6123 – *3

Patricia E. Lebedovich, 151 Skinner St., V9R 5E8 – 250/753-4108, Fax: 250/754-4439 – *1

MacIsaac & Company, #1, 5144 Metral Dr., V9T 2K8 – 250/758-2535, Fax: 250/758-2515 – *1

MacIsaac & Company, 503 Comox Rd., PO Box 455, Stn A, V9R 5L5 – 250/754-1295, Fax: 250/753-7977 – *5

Manning & Kirkhope, #110, 50 Tenth St., V9R 6L1 – 250/753-6766, Fax: 250/753-0080; Email: mannkirk@island.net – *2

Marshall & Lamperson, 41 Chapel St., PO Box 580, V9R 5L5 – 250/716-1667, Fax: 250/753-4032 – *3

A. Ronald McAfee, 486C Franklyn St., PO Box 1106, V9R 6E7 – 250/754-2337, Fax: 250/754-1352 – *1

John B. Morgan, 55 Front St., V9R 5H9 – 250/754-6122 – *1

Patrick A. Penny, 55 Front St., V9R 5H9 – 250/755-7804, Fax: 250/755-7854 – *1

Plazzer & Geselbracht, #3, 4488 Wellington Rd., V9T 2H3 – 250/758-2825, Fax: 250/758-7412

Ramsay Thompson Lampman, 111 Wallace St., V9R 5B2 – 250/754-3321, Fax: 250/754-1148 – *12

Robert N. Stacey Law Corp., 4 Church St., V9R 5H4 – 250/753-0844, Fax: 250/753-0861; Email: bob_s@island.net – *1

Vanstone, Boe & de Turberville, 30 Front St., PO Box 68, V9R 5K4 – 250/754-2362, Fax: 250/754-6304 – *3

Vining, Senini, 30 Front St., PO Box 190, V9R 5K9 – 250/754-1234, Fax: 250/754-8080 – *6

Michael L. Warsh, 151 Skinner St., V9R 5E8 – 250/754-1350, Fax: 250/754-1350

**Nelson ........................................... Kootenay**

Susan Kurtz, #3, 560 Baker St., V1L 4H9 – 250/354-1881, Fax: 250/354-1808 – *1

D.W. Skogstad, PO Box 140, V1L 5P7 – 250/352-7228, Fax: 250/352-5299 – *1

Stacey, Watson & Napora, 405 Baker St., V1L 4M7 – 250/352-3321, Fax: 250/354-4547; Email: tnapora@netidea.com – *2

Suffredine Burch, 466 Josephine St., V1L 1W3 – 250/352-6631, Fax: 250/352-6634 – *3

Susan E. Wallach, #1, 405 Baker St., V1L 4H7 – 250/352-3135, Fax: 250/352-3460 – *1

Eric E. Watson, #1, 405 Baker St., V1L 4M7 – 250/352-3321, Fax: 250/354-4547; Toll Free: 1-800-579-5338; Email: ericw@netidea.com – *1

Wyllie & Okros, #2, 385 Baker St., V1L 4H6 – 250/354-4844, Fax: 250/354-4882 – *2

**New Westminster ............................. Westminster**

Baumgartal & Gould, #370, 550 - 6 St., V3L 3B7 – 604/526-1805, Fax: 604/526-8056 – *2

Gordon J. Bondoreff, #202, 713 Columbia St., V3M 1B2 – 604/526-4491, Fax: 604/526-5979 – *1

Cassady, Insley, Lauener & Burgess, #330, 522 - 7 St., V3M 5T5 – 604/525-3431, Fax: 604/525-5721 – *6

E.M. Doricic, #609, 534 - 6th St., V3L 5K7 – 604/525-8636, Fax: 604/521-1747

Goodwin & Mark, #217, 713 Columbia St., V3M 1B2 – 604/522-9884, Fax: 604/526-8044; Email: gm@goodmark.com – *6

Edel Hass, #202, 713 Columbia St., V3M 1B2 – 604/526-4491, Fax: 604/526-5979 – *1

M.J. Hughes, 815 Massey St., V3L 4S8

Angela S. Kerslake, #200, 555 - 6th St., V3L 5H1 – 604/540-5833, Fax: 604/520-5765 – *1

McQuarrie Hunter, #400, 713 Columbia St., V3M 1B2 – 604/526-1821, Fax: 604/526-4656 – *22

Milne Selkirk, #400, 555 - 6 St., V3L 4Y4 – 604/522-2785, Fax: 604/522-4971; Email: 102760.3401@compuserve.com – *6

Nyack & Persad, #270, 550 - 6 St., V3L 3B7 – 604/521-8808, Fax: 604/521-6166 – *2

Oliver Drabik Carruthers & Chalcraft, 725 Carnarvon St., 2nd Fl., V3M 1E6 – 604/526-4875, Fax: 604/526-1936 – *4

**North Vancouver ................................ Vancouver**

Ardagh Hunter Turner, #300, 1401 Lonsdale Ave., V7M 2H9 – 604/986-4366, Fax: 604/986-9286 – *3

Baldwin & Company, #40, 1199 Lynn Valley Rd., V7J 3H2 – 604/985-8000, Fax: 604/985-5999 – *1

J.Howard Bayntun, International Plaza, Box: 100, 1999 Marine Dr., V7P 3J3 – 604/986-9156, Fax: 604/985-6632 – *1

Susan D. Beattie, 1164 Bracknell Cres., V7R 1V3 – 604/990-9416, Fax: 604/990-9417 – *1

Begin & Company, 117 - 1st St. West, V7M 1B1 – 604/987-5297, Fax: 604/987-6044 – *2

Trevors Bjurman, #205, 1433 Lonsdale Ave., V7M 2H9 – 604/983-3728, Fax: 604/983-0148 – *1

Bradbrooke, Crawford & Green, #600, 171 West Esplanade, V7M 3J9 – 604/980-8571, Fax: 604/980-4019; Email: bcglaw@istar.ca – *9

P.S. Faminow, 743 Roslyn Blvd., V7G 1P4 – 604/929-5141 – *1

Forrest, Gray, Lewis & Gillett, #201, 145 East 15th St., V7L 2P7 – 604/988-5244, Fax: 604/988-0093 – *2

Hobbs & Leigh, 3070 Edgemont Blvd., V7R 2N4

Peter J. Holden, 1617B Mahon Ave., V7M 2S7 – 604/987-4287, Fax: 604/987-4274 – *1

M. Hollander, #320, 145 West 17 St., V7M 1V5 – 604/986-4354, Fax: 604/986-9183 – *1

Jabour, Sudeyko, #300, 147 West 16th St., V7M 1T3 – 604/986-8600, Fax: 604/986-4872 – *3

R.F. Jackson, #200, 132 East 14 St., V7L 2N3 – 604/988-4155, Fax: 604/980-7426 – *1

Robert W. Johnson, #112B, 255 - 1st St. West, V7M 3G8 – 604/984-0305, Fax: 604/984-0304 – *1

E.B. Kroon, #100, 132 East 14 St., V7L 2N3 – 604/980-7021, Fax: 604/980-7428 – *1

Lakes, Straith & Bilinsky, #301, 145 - 15th St. West, V7M 1R9 – 604/984-3646, Fax: 604/984-8573 – *3

Ron Perrick Law Corp., #480, 145 West 17 St., V7M 1V5 – 604/984-9521, Fax: 604/984-9104 – *1

Poyner & Baxter, #408, 145 Chadwick Ct., V7M 3K1 – 604/988-6321, Fax: 604/988-3632 – *3

Reid & Walsoff, #233, 1433 Lonsdale Ave., V7M 2H9 – 604/984-4357, Fax: 604/984-4326 – *2

D.A. Roper, 334 - 15th St. West, V7M 1B5 – 604/986-0488, Fax: 604/984-3463 – *1

K. Gregory Senda, 4723 Mapleridge Dr., V7R 3T6 – 604/990-1360, Fax: 604/983-8473; Email: gsenda@uniserve.com – *1

L. Thomas Symons & Company, Waterfront Place, #19, 119 - 255 West 1st St., V7M 3G8 – 604/985-2750, Fax: 604/985-1056; Email: symons@bc.sympatico.ca – *1

Kenneth N. Taschuk, #5, 3046 Edgemont Blvd., V7R 2N4 – 604/986-3338, Fax: 604/986-1129 – *1

W.D. Yager Personal Law Corporation, 4017 Capilano Park Rd., V7R 4L2 – 604/985-4733, Fax: 604/985-9851 – *1

**Oliver .......... Yale**

Pugh & Frank, PO Box 1800, V0H 1T0 – 250/498-4941, Fax: 250/498-4100 – *1

**100 Mile House .......... Cariboo**

Johann Erickson, PO Box 1690, V0K 2E0 – 250/395-3831, Fax: 250/395-3940 – *1

Messner & Foster, PO Box 819, V0K 2E0 – 250/395-3881, Fax: 250/395-2644 – *2

**Parksville .......... Vancouver Island**

Davis & Avis, #201, 156 Morison Ave., PO Box 1600, V9P 2H5 – 250/248-5731, Fax: 250/248-5730 – *3

John A. Davis, #201, 182 Harrison Ave., V9P 2G5 – 250/248-4148, Fax: 250/248-8240 – *1

J.A. Hossack, 311 McKinnon St., PO Box 1486, V9P 2H7 – 250/248-9241, Fax: 250/248-8375 – *1

**Penticton .......... Yale**

Boyle & Company, #201, 100 Front St., V2A 1H1 – 250/492-6100, Fax: 250/492-4877; Toll Free: 1-800-665-8244 – *11

Gilchrist & Company, #101, 123 Martin St., V2A 7X6 – 250/492-3033, Fax: 250/492-6162 – *3

Kathryn J. Ginther, 409 Ellis St., V2A 4M1 – 250/493-6786, Fax: 250/493-3964; Email: kginther@vip.net – *1

Thomas A. Kampman, 409 Ellis St., V2A 4M1 – 250/493-6786, Fax: 250/493-3964 – *1

Kinsman & Company, #100, 166 Main St., PO Box 40, V2A 6J9 – 250/492-2624, Fax: 250/492-5525 – *8

Robert Wahl, #104, 197 Warren Ave. East, V2A 8N8 – 250/492-5274, Fax: 250/492-7751; Email: rwahl@vip.net – *1

**Pitt Meadows .......... Westminster**

E. John Becker, 19135 Ford Rd., V3Y 2R5 – 604/465-9993, Fax: 604/465-0066; Email: becker@planeteer.com – *1

Thomas Eaton Sprague, #202, 12165 Harris Rd., V3Y 2E9 – 604/465-9993, Fax: 604/465-0066 – *1

**Port Alberni .......... Vancouver Island**

Badovinac, Scoffield & Mosley, 3290 - 3 Ave., V9Y 4E1 – 250/724-1275, Fax: 250/724-7200 – *3

Beckingham, William & Co., 5029 Argyle St., V9Y 1V5 – 250/724-0111, Fax: 250/724-4422; Email: beck@port.island.net – *3

Mary T. Margetis, Site 312, C-44, V9Y 7L7 – 250/724-4907 – *1

Stofer, Smith & Company, 5169 Argyle St., V9Y 1V3 – 250/724-3253, Fax: 250/724-5169 – *3

**Port Coquitlam .......... Westminster**

Baily, McLean, Greenbank & Murdoch, #6215, 2850 Shaughnessy St., V3C 6K5 – 604/941-6215, Fax: 604/941-6207 – *4

Bell Spagnuolo Legal Offices, #560, 2755 Lougheed Hwy., V3B 5Y9 – 604/464-2024, Fax: 604/464-8976; Toll Free: 1-888-873-2829; Email: bs@bellspag.com; URL: http://www.bellspag.com – *6

Michael Z. Galambos Law Corp., #6209, 2850 Shaughnessy St., V3C 6K5 – 604/944-7724, Fax: 604/944-0002 – *5

Garton & Harris, 1542 Prairie Ave., V3B 1T4 – 604/941-9661, Fax: 604/941-5198 – *5

Eugene Lesyk, #1, 2628 Shaughnessy St., V3C 3V1 – 604/941-4055, Fax: 604/941-4002 – *1

Macleod Thorson Darychuk, #310, 2755 Lougheed Hwy., V3B 5Y9 – 604/464-2644, Fax: 604/464-2533 – *4

Smyth & Carter, #330, 2755 Lougheed Hwy., V3B 5Y9 – 604/942-6560, Fax: 604/942-1347 – *2

**Port Hardy .......... Vancouver Island**

Jeffrey Jones & Company, 8755 Granville St., PO Box 1949, V0N 2P0 – 250/949-8533, Fax: 250/949-9255 – *1

Donald L. Mancell, PO Box 1770, V0N 2P0 – 250/949-6777, Fax: 250/949-9091 – *1

Carter N. Nagel, B8785 Gray St., PO Box 1000, V0N 2P0 – 250/949-5111, Fax: 250/949-5156; Email: nagel@trinet.bc.ca – *1

**Port McNeill .......... Vancouver Island**

Elaine Evans, 1705 Campbell Way, PO Box 190, V0N 2R0 – 250/956-4451 – *1

Jones Seaborn & Company, 1488 Beach Dr., PO Box 70, V0N 2R0 – 250/956-3358, Fax: 250/956-4093 – *2

**Port Moody .......... Westminster**

Roderick A. Brown, #6, 86 Moody St., V3H 2P6 – 604/461-2434, Fax: 604/461-9662 – *1

Maryn & Associates, 2613 St. Johns St., V3H 2B5 – 604/936-9600, Fax: 604/936-9800 – *2

**Powell River .......... Vancouver**

J. Garrett-Rempel, 4766 Michigan Ave., V8A 2S9 – 604/485-9898, Fax: 604/485-9850 – *1

Giroday & Company, 4571 Marine Ave., V8A 2K5 – 604/485-2771, Fax: 604/485-2197 – *2

Whyard Villani, 4476 Marine Ave., V8A 2K2 – 604/485-6188, Fax: 604/485-6923 – *3

**Prince George .......... Cariboo**

Anne Baines, #213, 1717 - 3 Ave., V1L 2G7 – 250/564-0001, Fax: 250/562-2100 – *1

Harold J. Bogle, Q.C., Scotiabank Bldg., #515, 1488 - 4 Ave., PO Box 699, Stn A, V2L 4T2 – 250/562-4324, Fax: 250/562-3687

Byl, Dick Law Corp., #900, 550 Victoria St., V2L 2K1 – 250/564-3400, Fax: 250/564-7873; Toll Free: 1-800-835-0088 – *5

Clark Bitzer, #340, 444 Victoria St., V2L 2J7 – 250/614-0330, Fax: 250/614-0331 – *2

J.H. Cluff, #303, 1575 - 5 Ave., V2L 3L9 – 250/563-5339, Fax: 250/563-1567 – *1

John A. Davis, Bank of BC Bldg., #1, 1515 - 2 Ave., V2L 3B8 – 250/564-5544, Fax: 250/562-9427 – *1

Fletcher Repstock, #608, 1488 - 4 Ave., V2L 4Y2 – 250/564-1313, Fax: 250/564-4362 – *2

Gibbs & Company, #205, 715 Victoria St., V2L 2K5 – 250/564-6460, Fax: 250/562-0671 – *2

Heather Sadler Jenkins, #700, 550 Victoria St., PO Box 4500, V2L 2K1 – 250/565-8000, Fax: 250/565-8001 – *14

Hope Heinrich, 1598 - 6 Ave., V2L 5G7 – 250/563-0681, Fax: 250/562-3761; Toll Free: 1-800-663-8230; Email: lawyers@hh.bc.ca – *15

F.A. Howard-Gibbon, #302, 1370 Seventh Ave., V2L 3P1 – 250/562-7261 – *1

Richard B. Krehbiel, 6932 View Pl., V2K 4C6 – 250/962-5843, Fax: 250/962-5843; Email: rkrehbie@pgweb.com – *1

Leverman & Company, #200, 444 Victoria St., V2L 2J7 – 250/564-1212, Fax: 250/563-1879 – *1

R.W. Madill, 1033 - 3rd Ave., V2L 3E3 – 250/562-5000, Fax: 250/562-5105 – *1

Ramsay Nosè Traxler, Scotia Bank Bldg., #614, 1488 - 4 Ave., V2L 4Y2 – 250/563-7741, Fax: 250/563-2953 – *8

Tyo & Clark, 161 Dominion St., V2L 1T2 – 250/564-9777, Fax: 250/564-9779 – *3

Wilson, King & Company, #1000, 299 Victoria St., V2L 5B8 – 250/960-3200, Fax: 250/562-7777 – *13

**Prince Rupert .......... Prince Rupert**

Marina C-K Kan, PO BOX 722, V8J 3S1 – 250/624-6060, Fax: 250/624-6451 – *1

Narbonne Law Office, PO Box 256, V8J 3P6 – 250/624-4899, Fax: 250/624-3046 – *1

Punnett & Johnston, #7, 222 - 3 Ave. West, PO Box 456, V8J 3R2 – 250/624-2106, Fax: 250/627-8805 – *2

Silversides, Wilson & Seidemann, 330 Second Ave. West, PO Box 188, V8J 3P7 – 250/624-2116, Fax: 250/627-7786 – *7

C.J. Trueman, #1, 521 - 2 Ave. West, V8J 1G9 – 250/627-7771 – *1

**Princeton .......... Yale**

Stanley G. Turner, PO Box 568, V0X 1W0 – 250/295-6722, 6972, Fax: 250/295-6722 – *1

**Qualicum Beach .......... Vancouver Island**

Marshall & Lamperson, 710 Memorial Ave., PO Box 879, V9K 1T2 – 250/752-5615, Fax: 250/752-2055 – *3

Walker & Wilson, 707 Primrose St., PO Box 2100, V9K 1T6 – 250/752-6951, Fax: 250/752-6022 – *2

**Quesnel .......... Cariboo**

Chudiak, Schmit & Co., 531 Reid St., V2J 2M8 – 250/992-8341, Fax: 250/992-7349 – *2

Coffey & Bernath, #3, 375 Reid St., V2J 2M5 – 250/992-8317, Fax: 250/992-3224 – *2

**Revelstoke .......... Yale**

S.G. Bernacki, 109 - 2 St. East, PO Box 2699, V0E 2S0 – 250/837-4971 – *1

Christopher H. Johnston, #201, 101 First St. East, PO Box 2639, V0E 2S0 – 250/837-6171, Fax: 250/837-7194 – *1

Bernard Lavallee, PO Box 244, V0E 2S0 – 250/837-5168 – *1

R.A. Lundberg, 119 Campbell Ave., V0E 2S0 – 250/837-5196, Fax: 250/837-4746 – *1

**Richmond .......... Vancouver**

Altman Kahn Zack, #270, 10711 Cambie Rd., V6X 3C9 – 604/270-9571, Fax: 604/270-8282; Email: altman_kahn_zack@akz.com – *14

Ash, O'Donnell, Hibbert, #230, 11180 Voyageur Way, V6X 3N8 – 604/273-9111, Fax: 604/273-1117 – *3

Bacha, Grabowski, #102, 8011 Leslie Rd., V6X 1E4 – 604/273-5536, Fax: 604/270-4714 – *2

* indicates number of lawyers in law firm.

Brodie & Morrice, #250, 5611 Cooney Rd., V6X 3J6 – 604/270-9411, Fax: 604/270-7704 – *4

Campbell Froh May & Rice, #200, 5611 Cooney Rd., V6X 3J6 – 604/273-8481, Fax: 604/273-4729 – *10

V.N. Carvalho, 13811 Gilbert Rd., V7E 2H8 – 604/274-5636, Fax: 604/274-5694 – *1

S.R. Chamberlain, Q.C., #1, 7100 River Rd., V6X 1X5 – 604/244-0646, Fax: 604/244-0617 – *1

Cohen, Buchan, Edwards, #208, 4940 - 3 Rd., V6X 3A5 – 604/273-6411, Fax: 604/273-4512 – *5

Collins & Cullen, #1405, 4380 No. 3 Rd., V6X 3V7 – 604/270-0880, Fax: 604/270-7308 – *1

A. Ted Ewachniuk & Associates, 8331 River Rd., V6X 1Y1 – 604/273-1844, Fax: 604/273-5625 – *4

Fitzsimmons & Scammells, #360, 5951 - 3 Rd., V6X 2E3 – 604/276-8982, Fax: 604/273-2703 – *2

Michael J. Frank, #152, 10551 Shellbridge Way, V6X 2W9 – 604/270-6878, Fax: 604/276-0566 – *1

Friesen & Epp, #220, 8120 Granville Ave., V6Y 1P3 – 604/273-2941, Fax: 604/273-1381 – *4

D.B. Graves, #317, 8055 Anderson Rd., V6Y 1S2 – 604/276-0069 – *1

Bernard Hoodekoff, North Tower, #206, 5811 Cooney Rd., V6X 3M1 – 604/278-8451, Fax: 604/278-8453 – *1

Humphry Paterson, #205, 8171 Park Rd., V6Y 1S9 – 604/278-3031, Fax: 604/278-3021 – *2

Sharen Janeson, 3711 Moncton St., 2nd Fl., V7E 3A5 – 604/272-5171, Fax: 604/275-5578 – *1

Lim & Company, 7871 Westminster Hwy., V6X 1A4 – 604/303-0788, Fax: 604/303-0789 – *2

Conrad A. Margolis, #530, 8100 Granville Ave., PO Box 4, V6Y 3T6 – 604/273-9193, Fax: 604/273-8748 – *1

Mulholland, Webster, #600, 5811 Cooney Rd., V6X 3M1 – 604/273-3741, Fax: 604/273-1265; Toll Free: 1-800-663-4323; Email: mw@unixg.ubc.ca – *7

Phillips Paul, #215, 4800 - 3 Rd., V6X 3A6 – 604/273-5297, Fax: 604/273-1643; Email: phillipspaul@big-foot.com – *3

Pryke Lambert Leathley Russell, North Tower, #500, 5811 Cooney Rd., V6X 3M1 – 604/276-2765, Fax: 604/276-8045 – *17

Scardina & Co., #140, 8351 Alexandra Rd., V6X 3P3 – 604/273-5558, Fax: 604/273-5550 – *1

Arne Silverman, #120, 11181 Vayager Way, V6X 3N9 – 604/270-1430, Fax: 604/270-4588 – *1

John Skapski, 3711 Moncton St., 2nd Fl., V7E 3A5 – 604/274-2526, Fax: 604/275-5578 – *1

David Sky, #270, 10711 Tanbie Rd., V6X 3C9 – 604/273-4315, Fax: 604/270-8282 – *1

Spry Hawkins Micner & Bakonyi, #210, 6411 Buswell St., V6Y 2G5 – 604/273-2977, Fax: 604/273-2908 – *2

Dr. Kenneth Wm. Thornicroft, #206, 5811 Cooney Rd., V6X 3M1 – 604/329-4457, Fax: 604/721-6067; Email: kthornic@business.uvic.ca – *1

James Wingham, #315, 8171 Cook Rd., V6Y 3T8 – 604/273-6448, Fax: 604/273-7442 – *1

Wong & Tsang, #310, 8120 Granville Ave., V6Y 1P3 – 604/279-9023, Fax: 604/279-9025 – *2

**Rossland ................................ West Kootenay**

A.R. Dahlstrom, PO Box 699, V0G 1Y0 – 250/362-5786, Fax: 250/362-7250 – *1

**Salmon Arm ................................ Yale**

H.R. Bartlett, 401 Okanagan Ave., PO Box 910, V1E 4P1 – 250/832-7061, Fax: 250/832-5493 – *1

R. Derek McManus, #303, 370 Lakeshore Dr. NE, PO Box 57, V1E 4N2 – 250/833-4720, Fax: 250/832-4787 – *1

Sivertz, Kiehlbauch & Zachernuk, 316 Hudson Ave. NE, PO Box 190, V1E 4N3 – 250/832-8031, Fax: 250/832-6177 – *3

Verdurmen & Lee, #303, 320 Alexander St., PO Box 826, V1E 4N9 – 250/833-0914, Fax: 250/833-0924 – *2

Garrett N. Wynne, #102, 310 Hudson Ave., PO Box 3009, V1E 4R8 – 250/837-9611, Fax: 250/832-9788 – *1

**Shawnigan Lake ................................ Nanaimo**

Sullivan & Company, 2739 Shawnigan Lake Rd., PO Box 75, V0R 2W0 – 250/743-4468, Fax: 250/743-9147; Email: maureen@island.net – *2

**Sidney ................................ Vancouver Island**

Alice Finall, #304, 9775 - 4th St., V8L 2Z8 – 250/656-6668, Fax: 250/656-9366 – *1

Henley & Walden, #201, 2377 Bevan Ave., V8L 4M9 – 250/656-7231, Fax: 250/656-0937; Toll Free: 1-800-665-5567; Email: henleywalden@pacificcoast.net – *4

Lloyd A. Johnson, 9751 - 5 St., V8L 2X1 – 403/656-0934, Fax: 403/656-9334 – *1

McKimm & Lott, 9830 - 4 St., V8L 2Z3 – 250/656-3961, Fax: 250/655-3329 – *7

**Smithers ................................ Prince Rupert**

Buri, Milne, 3773 - 3 Ave., PO Box 847, V0J 2N0 – 250/847-3241, Fax: 250/847-2659 – *2

G.E. Greene, 3895 Alfred St., PO Box 940, V0J 2N0 – 250/847-4777, Fax: 250/847-4029 – *1

Timothy D. Klaassen, 3868 Broadway Ave., PO Box 2501, V0J 2N0 – 250/847-4222, Fax: 250/847-4282 – *1

Perry & Company, PO Box 790, V0J 2N0 – 250/847-4341, Fax: 250/847-5634 – *4

G. Ronald Toews, PO Box 970, V0J 2N0 – 250/847-2187, Fax: 250/847-2183; Email: grt@mail.net-shop.net – *1

**Sooke ................................ Vancouver Island**

Dinning Hunter & Company, #1, 6631 Sooke Rd., PO Box 91, V0S 1N0 – 250/642-2553, Fax: 250/642-7859

Hallgren & Faulkner, 6595 Sooke Rd., PO Box 939, V0S 1N0 – 250/642-5271, Fax: 250/642-6006; Email: mhallgren@pacificcaoast.net – *2

**Squamish ................................ Vancouver**

Sanguinetti, Braidwood & Company, #201, 1364 Pemberton Ave., V0N 3G0 – 604/892-9311, Fax: 604/892-5239 – *5

V. Donald R. Wilson, #201, 38133 Cleveland Ave., PO Box 1910, V0N 3G0 – 604/892-5284, Fax: 604/892-9725 – *1

**Summerland ................................ Yale**

Bell, Jacoe & Company, 13211 Victoria Rd. North, PO Box 520, V0H 1Z0 – 250/494-6621, Fax: 250/494-8055 – *3

Frances Crowhurst, 13219 North Victoria Rd., PO Box 38, V0H 1Z0 – 250/494-1811, Fax: 250/494-1812; Email: fran-crowhurst@bc.sympatico.ca – *1

Johnston, Johnson & Co., 9921 Main St., PO Box 1530, V0H 1Z0 – 250/494-0442, Fax: 250/494-0402; Toll Free: 1-800-494-0442 – *3

**Surrey ................................ Westminster**

Becker, Mathers, #111, 15225 - 104 Ave., V3R 6Y8 – 604/583-2200, Fax: 604/583-3469 – *5

A. Harvey Blackmore, 7277 King George Hwy., V3W 5A7 – 604/591-2241, Fax: 604/597-0389 – *1

S.A. Bowers, 8893 - 160 St., V4N 2X8 – 604/951-9224, Fax: 604/951-9224; Email: sabowers@axionet.com – *1

James L. Davidson & Company, #403, 16033 - 108 Ave., PO Box 271, V4N 1P2 – 604/951-2990, Fax: 604/951-9368 – *2

Paul E. Del Rossi, 7277 King George Hwy., V3W 5A7 – 604/591-2241, Fax: 604/597-0389 – *1

Kane, Shannon & Weiler, #104, 2055 - 152nd St., V4A 4N7 – 604/535-8770, Fax: 604/535-8771

J. Kelso, 8950 - 152 St., V3R 4E4 – 604/589-1414, Fax: 604/589-2044 – *1

Yair S. Leibovitz, #310, 10524 King George Hwy., V3T 2X2 – 604/951-7511, Fax: 604/585-8525; Email: lawyair@axionet.com – *1

MacMillan, Tucker, Krieger & Mackay, 5690 - 176A St., V3S 4H1 – 604/574-7431, Fax: 604/574-3021 – *5

Maier & Co., #310, 10524 King George Hwy., V3S 2X2 – 604/582-5951, Fax: 604/588-0779 – *1

Manthorpe Law Offices, #102, 15399 - 102A Ave., V3R 7K1 – 604/582-7743, Fax: 604/582-7753 – *2

A.L. McAndrew, #240, 13711 - 72 Ave., V3W 2P2 – 604/591-2288, Fax: 604/591-7366 – *1

McCarthy Tétrault, Station Tower, Gateway, #1300, 13401 - 108th Ave., V3T 5T3 – 604/583-9100, Fax: 604/583-9150; Email: adj@mccarthy.ca; URL: http://www.mccarthy.ca – *2

McEachern Caissie, #302, 15225 - 104 Ave., V3R 6Y8 – 604/586-7200, Fax: 604/583-5870; Email: info@mclaw.bc.ca – *4

Cameron C. McLeod, 16366 Fraser Hwy., V3R 3P5 – 604/583-6318, Fax: 604/589-3583 – *1

McNeney & McNeney, Sunwest Pl., 14888 - 104 Ave., V3R 1M4 – 604/588-7858, Fax: 604/581-7084 – *2

McQuarrie Hunter, #200, 13889 - 104th Ave., V3T 1W8 – 604/581-0461, Fax: 604/581-7110 – *11

Mosher & Treleaven, 13762 - 72 Ave., V3W 2P4 – 604/591-8211, Fax: 604/596-9907 – *2

Murchison Thomson & Clarke, #300, 7380 King George Hwy., V3W 5A5 – 604/590-8855, Fax: 604/597-4512 – *7

Nyack Persad Binpal & Sanghera, #201, 9380 - 120 St., V3V 4B9 – 604/588-9933, Fax: 604/588-2731 – *3

Michael G. Parent, #203, 15225 - 104 Ave., V3R 6Y8 – 604/589-6437, Fax: 604/589-7238 – *1

Peterson Stark, #300, 10366 - 136A St., V3T 5R3 – 604/588-9321, Fax: 604/589-5391 – *1

Richards & Richards, 10325 - 150 St., V3R 4B1 – 604/588-6844, Fax: 604/588-8800 – *3

E.H. Skands, 10246B - 152 St., V3R 6N7 – 604/581-1621, Fax: 604/588-9365 – *1

E.R. Swedahl, #11, 15243 - 91 Ave., V3R 8P8 – 604/581-3232, Fax: 604/589-3741 – *1

Thompson & McConnell, #300, 1676 Martin Dr., V4A 6E7 – 604/531-1421, Fax: 604/531-8402; Toll Free: 1-800-667-1421 – *9

Watchorn & McLellan, 10334 - 152A St., V3R 7P8 – 604/585-4321, Fax: 604/585-8195 – *7

P. Barry Whaites, #200, 5746 - 176A St., V3S 4H2 – 604/574-0770, Fax: 604/574-0107; Email: bwhaites@direct.ca – *1

Worthington, Simm & David, 10430 - 144 St., V3T 4V5 – 604/588-9721, Fax: 604/585-6020 – *5

**Terrace ................................ Prince Rupert**

Crampton, Brown & Arndt, #3, 4623 Park Ave., V8G 1V5 – 250/635-6330, Fax: 250/635-4795 – *3

Brian Christopher Fell, Esq., #301, 4722 Lakelse Ave., V8G 1R6 – 250/635-4944, Fax: 250/635-4968 – *1

Halfyard & Wright, 4730 Lazelle Ave., V8G 1T2 – 250/638-0354, Fax: 250/635-2919 – *2

Cecil C. Pratt, 4509 Lakelse Ave., PO Box 459, V8G 4B5 – 250/638-1161, Fax: 250/638-1162 – *1

Leslie Ann Strike, c/o Deputy Regional Crown Court, #110, 3408 Kalum St., V8G 2N6 – 250/387-3840, Fax: 250/638-3298 – *1

Talstra & Company, #101, 3219 Eby St., V8G 4R3 – 250/638-1137, Fax: 250/638-1306 – *3

Warner Bandstra, #200, 4630 Lazelle Ave., V8G 1S6 – 250/635-2622, Fax: 250/635-4998 – *4

**Trail ................................ West Kootenay**

Adair & Company, 1402 Bay Ave., V1R 4B1 – 250/368-9171, Fax: 250/368-3369 – *1

Jenny Ghilarducci Law Corporation, 1309 Bay Ave., V1R 4A7 – 250/368-6455, Fax: 250/368-6107 – *1

McEwan, Harrison & Co., 1432 Bay Ave., V1R 4B1 – 250/368-8211, Fax: 250/368-9401 – *4

**Vancouver .................................... Vancouver**

Aaron, MacGregor, Gordon & Daykin, #506, 815 Hornby St., V6Z 2E6 – 604/689-7571, Fax: 604/685-8563 – *6

A.S. Alafriz, #401, 1385 West 8 Ave., V6H 3V9 – 604/732-3345, Fax: 604/736-5522 – *1

Alexander, Holburn, Beaudin & Lang, #2700, 700 West Georgia St., PO Box 10057, V7Y 1B8 – 604/688-1351, Fax: 604/669-7642; Email: ahbluser@ahbl.bc.ca – *61

Allan & Lougheed, 1628 - 7 Ave. West, V6J 1S5 – 604/733-2411, Fax: 604/736-6225 – *2

Allard & Company, #600, 815 Hornby St., V6Z 2E6 – 604/689-3885, Fax: 604/687-0814 – *6

Tony D. Allen, #1400, 1166 Alberni St., V6E 3Z3 – 604/682-7794, Fax: 604/669-0869 – *2

Stafford D.R. Alliston, 12 Gaoler's Mews, V6B 4K7 – 604/681-9371, Fax: 604/682-3687 – *1

Alperstein Law Corp., #1800, 1281 West Georgia, V6E 3J7 – 604/689-8741, Fax: 604/682-7643; Email: alc@octf.com – *1

Altridge & Company, #501, 1155 Robson St., V6E 1B5 – 604/688-3557, Fax: 604/688-0535; Email: lawyers@altridge.com – *3

Bruce D. Ames, #1400, 1166 Alberni St., V6E 3Z3 – 604/662-7550, Fax: 604/669-0860 – *1

Paul Andersen, #306, 1530 West 8 Ave., V6J 4R8 – 604/734-8411, Fax: 604/734-8511; Email: andersen_paul@bc.sympatico.ca – *3

Anderson & Galati, #607, 808 Nelson St., Box 12152, V6Z 2H2 – 604/669-2445, Fax: 604/669-4395 – *4

Brian Anderson, #411, 470 Granville St., V6C 1V5 – 604/684-5367 – *1

A. Stewart Andree, Esq., #680, 789 West Pender St., V6C 1H2 – 604/685-8121, Fax: 604/685-8120; Email: alans@e-mo.com – *1

George P. Angelomatis, #601, 134 Abbott St., V6B 2K4 – 604/689-8788, Fax: 604/689-3327 – *1

Armstrong & Company, Scotia Tower, #480, 650 West Georgia St., PO Box 11622, V6B 4N9 – 604/683-7361, Fax: 604/662-3231 – *3

K.T. Au, #201, 124 East Pender St., V6A 1T3 – 604/681-0933 – *1

Aydin & Co., North Office Tower, #530, 650 West 41 Ave., V5Z 2M9 – 604/266-5828, Fax: 604/266-3929 – *1

Baker Newby, #310, 900 Howe St., V6Z 2M4 – 604/684-9713, Fax: 604/684-6401; Email: info@bakernewby.com; URL: http://www.bakernewby.com – *2

Jonathan B. Baker & Associates, 808 Nelson St., V6Z 2H2 – 604/891-0208, Fax: 604/681-3504; Email: jbaker@mail.bc.rogers.wave.ca – *3

Richard D. Ballentyne, #1400, 100 West Pender St., 14th Fl., V6B 1R8 – 604/669-8899, Fax: 604/689-8278 – *1

Banister & Company, #880, 1090 Georgia St. West, V6E 3V7 – 604/662-7276, Fax: 604/662-8782 – *3

Barbeau & Company, #1450, 700 West Georgia St., PO Box 10019, V7Y 1A1 – 604/688-4900, Fax: 604/688-0649; Email: barbeau@msn.com – *2

Gail Barnes, #105, 12 Water St., V6B 1A5 – 604/684-1124, Fax: 604/684-1122 – *1

Barrigar & Moss, #2373, 595 Burrard St., V7X 1J1 – 604/689-9255, Fax: 604/689-9265; URL: http://www.barrmoss.com – *4

David G. Batist, 575 Richard St., 4th Fl., V6B 2Z7 – 604/682-6122, Fax: 604/682-2919 – *1

Beck, Robinson & Company, #700, 686 West Broadway, V5Z 1G1 – 604/874-0204, Fax: 604/874-0820; Email: becklaw@dowco.com – *5

William D.O. Bees, #104, 1128 Hornby St., V6Z 2L4 – 604/669-6990, Fax: 604/669-6944; Email: billbees@compuserve.com – *1

Robert W. Bellows, #401, 1385 West 8 Ave., V6H 3V9 – 604/736-5500, Fax: 604/736-5522 – *1

Bennett, Parkes, #400, 2609 Granville St., V6H 3H3 – 604/734-6838, Fax: 604/738-6789 – *3

Berger & Nelson, #1300, 355 Burrard St., V6C 2G8 – 604/684-1311, Fax: 604/684-6402 – *5

Peter P. Bieg, #606, 1155 Robson St., V6E 1B5 – 604/688-5471, Fax: 604/688-6176 – *1

Bitney & Co., #405, 675 West Hastings St., V6B 1N2 – 604/682-8504, Fax: 604/682-5124 – *1

Blake, Cassels & Graydon, Three Bentall Centre, #2600, 595 Burrard St., PO Box 49314, V7X 1L3 – 604/631-3300, Fax: 604/631-3309; Email: vancouvr@blakes.ca; URL: http://www.blakes.ca – *39

Barbara R. Bluman, 3906 Quesnel Dr., V6L 2X2 – 604/732-6028, Fax: 604/732-5801 – *2

Bolton & Muldoon, 976 Richards St., V6B 3C1 – 604/687-7078, Fax: 604/687-3022 – *7

Boughton Peterson Yang Anderson, Four Bentall Centre, #2500, 1055 Dunsmuir St., PO Box 49290, V7X 1S8 – 604/687-6789, Fax: 604/683-5317; Email: lawyers@bpya.com – *34

Joyce W. Bradley, #202, 3195 Granville St., V6H 3K2 – 604/732-3886, Fax: 604/736-7387 – *1

J.F.C. Bridal, 12 Gaolers Mews, V6B 4K7 – 604/687-4551, Fax: 604/682-3687 – *1

British Columbia International, Commercial Arbitration Centre, #1140, 1090 West Georgia St., PO Box 27, V6E 3V7 – 604/684-2821, Fax: 604/684-2825 – *1

Brown Benson, #1450, 701 West Georgia St., PO Box 10137, V7Y 1C6 – 604/684-7274, Fax: 604/669-9120 – *5

H.K. Brown, #1504, 100 West Pender St., 15th Fl., V6B 1R8 – 604/684-1021, Fax: 604/688-6243 – *1

Brown, McCue, #1650, 999 West Hastings St., V6C 2W2 – 604/684-8411, Fax: 604/687-7430 – *2

Peter W. Brown Law Corp., 2081 - 37 Ave. West, V6M 1N7 – 604/261-0300, Fax: 604/261-0312; Email: hmcgill@unixg.ubc.ca – *3

J.G. Buchanan, #707, 777 West Broadway, V5Z 4J7 – 604/876-0343, Fax: 604/876-9035 – *1

Bull, Housser & Tupper, Royal Centre, #3000, 1055 West Georgia St., PO Box 11130, V6E 3R3 – 604/687-6575, Fax: 604/641-4949; Email: general@bht.com – *98

M.L. Cacchioni, 820 Millbank, V5Z 4A1 – 604/872-0607 – *1

Bradley M. Caldwell, #480, 650 West Georgia, PO Box 11622, V6B 4N9 – 604/689-8894, Fax: 604/662-3231 – *1

E. Anne Cameron, 1199 Hastings St. West, 7th Fl., V6E 3T5 – 604/689-2414, Fax: 604/684-7190 – *1

Camp Church & Associates, Randall Bldg., 555 West Georgia St., 7th Fl., B6B 1Z5 – 604/689-7555, Fax: 604/689-7554; Toll Free: 1-800-689-2322 – *6

Campney & Murphy, #2100, 1111 West Georgia St., PO Box 48800, V7X 1K9 – 604/688-8022, Fax: 604/688-0829; Email: cmlaw@campney.com – *53

J.A. Carr, #1510, 777 Hornby St., V6Z 1S4 – 604/681-4158, Fax: 604/688-9981 – *1

Carr-Harris & Company, CN Bldg., #210, 900 Howe St., V6Z 2M4 – 604/681-2500, Fax: 604/681-2552 – *5

Douglas R. Chalke, #1800, 70 West Georgia St., V7Y 1C6 – 604/683-5096, Fax: 604/980-6469 – *1

Chan Yue & Lee, #212, 475 Main St., V6A 2T7 – 604/687-4576, Fax: 604/683-3258 – *2

Chapman & Company Law Corporation, #204, 5511 West Blvd., V6M 4H3 – 604/266-6294, Fax: 604/266-2352; Email: 104405.3273@compuserve.com – *3

Bernard Charles, 206 - 111 Water St., V6B 1A7 – 604/689-9545, Fax: 604/688-1425

Charlton & Buxton, #520, 601 Broadway West, V5Z 4C2 – 604/871-0371, Fax: 604/871-0372 – *2

Chen & Leung, North Tower, Oakridge Centre, #728, 650 - 41st Ave. West, V5Z 2M9 – 604/264-8331, Fax: 604/264-8387 – *10

Grant Christoff, 6296 Salish Dr., V6N 2C5 – 604/266-6483, Fax: 604/266-6463; Email: grant-christoff@bc.sympatico.ca – *1

Gregory T. Chu, #450, 688 West Hastings St., V6B 1P1 – 604/687-6659, Fax: 604/687-6684; Email: gtchu@direct.ca – *1

Clark, Wilson, Hongkong Bank of Canada Bldg., #800, 885 West Georgia St., V6C 3H1 – 604/687-5700, Fax: 604/687-6314; Email: central@cwilson.com – *49

A.T. Clarke, #960, 777 Hornby St., V6Z 1S4 – 604/683-4493, Fax: 604/683-4416 – *1

Robert C. Claus, 1002 - 777 West Broadway, V5Z 4J7 – 604/873-9098, Fax: 604/361-9600

M.E. Cofman, #2020, 650 West Georgia St., V6B 4N7 – 604/683-9621, Fax: 604/683-5084 – *1

Brian Coleman, 8 Gaolers Mews, V6B 4K7 – 604/683-5821, Fax: 604/683-9354 – *1

Collins & Cullen, #750, 999 West Broadway, V5Z 1K5 – 604/730-2678, Fax: 604/730-2628 – *2

James Comparelli, #704, 510 West Hastings St., V6B 1L8 – 604/683-6888, Fax: 604/688-4497 – *1

Connell Lightbody, Royal Centre, #1900, 1055 West Georgia St., PO Box 11161, V6E 4J2 – 604/684-1181, Fax: 604/641-3916 – *25

Carla Courtenay Law Office, #501, 815 Hornby St., V6Z 2E6 – 604/682-2200, Fax: 604/682-2246 – *1

J. Cove, 923 Denman St., V6G 2L9 – 604/683-6505, Fax: 604/683-2176 – *1

Hartley E. Cramer, #300, 896 Cambie St., V6B 2P6 – 604/684-6301, Fax: 604/684-6303 – *1

F.S. Crestani, #204, 1651 Commercial Drive, V5L 3Y3 – 604/251-1168, Fax: 604/253-7726 – *1

H. Crosby, #201, 5316 Victoria Dr., V5P 3V7 – 604/321-6922, Fax: 604/327-8873 – *2

Dallas, Kinney & Company, 852 Seymour St., V6B 3L6 – 604/681-6171, Fax: 604/683-1000 – *3

A. Kenneth Dangerfield, #2500, 1055 Dunsmere St., PO Box 49290, V7X 1S8 – 604/687-6789, Fax: 604/683-5317 – *1

Danks & Company, #1115, 555 Burrard St., V7X 1S1 – 604/688-3996, Fax: 604/688-5186 – *2

Gail Y. Davidson, #102, 1648 West 7 Ave., V6J 1S4 – 604/736-1175, Fax: 604/736-7402 – *1

Davies & Co., #780, 1333 West Broadway, V6H 4C1 – 604/736-8338, Fax: 604/736-3391 – *2

Davis & Company, Park Pl., #2800, 666 Burrard St., V6C 2Z7 – 604/687-9444, Fax: 604/687-1612; Toll Free: 1-800-665-2343 – *120

Dawson, Wood & Company, #204, 3540 - 41st Ave. West, V6N 3E6 – 604/266-1295, Fax: 604/266-0119; Email: dawson.wood@intouch.bc.ca; URL: http://www.intouch.bc.ca/pub/dawson.wood – *2

A.J. DeMeulemeester, 1976 - 4th Ave. West, V6J 1M5 – 604/731-1388 – *1

Derpak & White, 1933 West Broadway, V6J 1Z3 – 604/736-9791, Fax: 604/736-7197 – *3

J.W. Dobbin, #704, 510 West Hastings St., V6B 1L8 – 604/683-6888, Fax: 604/683-4497 – *1

Hans J.R. Doehring, #100, 1215 Beach Ave., V6E 1V5 – 604/669-3414

Dohn & Jaffer, #268, 3316 Kingsway, V5R 5K7 – 604/438-3369, Fax: 604/438-5578 – *1

M. Dong, 4347 James St., V5V 3H8 – 604/876-5094 – *1

Frank Dorchester, #1800, 999 West Hastings St., V6C 2W2 – 604/683-2784, Fax: 604/683-1375 – *1

Dosanjh & Company, #202, 5887 Victoria Dr., V5P 3W5 – 604/327-6381, Fax: 604/327-2923 – *3

Douglas Symes & Brissenden, One Bentall Centre, Box: 2100, #2100, 505 Burrard St., V7X 1R4 – 604/683-6911, Fax: 604/669-1337; Email: lawyer@ds-b.com – *46

DuMoulin & Boskovich, Pacific Landmark, Box: 52, #1800, 1095 Pender St. West, V6E 2M6 – 604/669-5500, Fax: 604/688-8491 – *11

Kenneth C. Eberhardt, #203, 2609 Westview Dr., V7N 4M2 – 604/983-2818, Fax: 604/980-2624 – *1

Edwards, Kenny & Bray, 1040 West Georgia St., 19th Fl., V6E 4H3 – 604/689-1811, Fax: 604/689-5177; Toll Free: awyer@ekb.com – *26

Norman Einarsson, #306, 1530 West 8 Ave., V6J 4R8 – 604/734-8411, Fax: 604/734-8511 – *1

Ellis, Nauss & Jones, #600, 1665 West Broadway, V6J 1X1 – 604/731-9276, Fax: 604/734-0206 – *3

* indicates number of lawyers in law firm.

Ellis, Roadburg, #200, 853 Richards St., V6B 3B4 – 604/669-7131, Fax: 604/669-7684 – *2

Dick W. Eng Law Corp., #701, 601 Broadway West, V5Z 4C2 – 604/877-0880, Fax: 604/877-0330 – *1

Epstein Wood, #650, 1500 West Georgia St., V6G 3A9 – 604/685-4321, Fax: 604/685-7901 – *10

Evans, Goldstein & Eadie, #1400, 700 West Georgia St., PO Box 10014, V7Y 1A1 – 604/685-5235, Fax: 604/685-9104 – *2

R.J. Falconer, Q.C., #500, 666 Burrard St., V6C 2X8 – 604/683-5674, Fax: 604/683-2780 – *1

Fan & Co., #601, 609 Gore Ave., V6A 2Z8 – 604/683-0471, Fax: 604/638-8748 – *2

Farris, Vaughan, Wills & Murphy, Pacific Centre South, 700 West Georgia St., PO Box 10026, V7Y 1B3 – 604/684-9151, Fax: 604/661-9349; Email: info@farris.com – *55

Fayers & Company, #380, 5740 Cambie St., V5Z 3A6 – 604/325-1246, Fax: 604/325-1261 – *3

Feller Drysdale, Box: 58, #1550, 400 Burrard St., V6C 3A6 – 604/689-2626, Fax: 604/681-5354 – *8

Ferguson Gifford, Park Place, #500, 666 Burrard St., V6C 3H3 – 604/687-3216, Fax: 604/683-2780; Email: 102107.1705@compuserve.com; URL: http://www.fergif.com – *18

K.L.D. Findlay, #1900, 1055 West Georgia, V6E 4J2 – 604/684-1181, Fax: 604/641-3916 – *1

Flader & Phelps, #500, 999 West Broadway, V5Z 1K5 – 604/736-3722 – *2

Flanagan & Assoc., #1400, 1166 Alberni St., V6E 3Z3 – 604/669-0886, Fax: 604/669-0860 – *2

C.C. Fogal, #401, 207 West Hastings St., V6B 1H7 – 604/687-0588, Fax: 604/688-0550 – *1

Robert A. Foran, Oceanic Plaza, #1700, 1066 West Hastings St., PO Box 12546, V6E 3X2 – 604/689-3431, Fax: 604/685-1035 – *1

Fraser & Beatty, Grosvenor Bldg., 1040 West Georgia St., 15th Fl., V6E 4H8 – 604/687-4460, Fax: 604/683-5214; URL: http://www.fraserbeatty.ca – *32

Fraser & Company, #1200, 999 Hastings St. West, V6C 2W2 – 604/669-5244, Fax: 604/669-5791 – *9

Friesen & Epp, #1, 3103 Kingsway, V5R 5J9 – 604/437-4777, Fax: 604/437-1575 – *2

H.G.N. Frith, #509, 198 West Hastings St., V6B 1H2 – 604/681-3811 – *1

George T.H. Fuller, 5261 Dunbar St., V6N 1W1 – 604/261-3199, 3417, Fax: 604/261-3199 – *1

Ganapathi, Ashcroft & Company, #1000, 885 Dunsmuir St., V6C 1N5 – 604/689-9222, Fax: 604/689-4888 – *6

Robert G. Gateman, #202, 1112 Brougton St., V6G 2A8 – 604/687-4911; Email: gateman@unixg.ubc.ca – *1

Gayle D. Gavin, #920, 777 Hornby St., V6Z 1S4 – 604/685-6235, Fax: 604/681-6375 – *1

G.C. Geraghty, #301, 701 West Georgia St., PO Box 10114, V7Y 1C6 – 604/684-8247, Fax: 604/684-8483 – *1

Gibbons Ritchie, #1300, 355 Burrard St., V6C 2G8 – 604/684-0778, Fax: 604/684-0799 – *4

Kenneth Glasner Q.C. Law Corp., #1301, 808 Nelson St., PO Box 12167, V6Z 2H2 – 604/683-4181, Fax: 604/683-0226 – *1

Goldman Mathisen, #1788, 1111 West Georgia, V6E 4M3 – 604/682-6181, Fax: 604/683-5723 – *6

W.C. Gorham, #268, 2025 West 42 Ave., V6M 2B5 – 604/263-1878, Fax: 604/261-8515 – *1

P.D. Gornall, #960, 355 Burrard St., V6C 2G8 – 604/681-7932, Fax: 604/687-7935 – *1

Gounden & Miller, #104, 1260 Hornby St., V6Z 1W2 – 604/684-8877, Fax: 604/684-8844; URL: http://www.discovervancouver/goundenmiller – *1

Gowlings, #2414, 1055 Dunsmuir St., PO Box 49122, V7X 1J1 – 604/683-6498, Fax: 604/683-3558 – *10

Allan Graham, 1316 West 57 Ave., V6P 1S8 – 604/263-5998, Fax: 604/266-9930 – *1

Murray H. Grant, #2020, 650 West Georgia St., PO Box 11547, V6B 4N7 – 604/683-9621, Fax: 604/683-5084 – *1

Greenall & Company, #200, 2443 Kingsway, V5R 5G8 – 604/430-5637, Fax: 604/430-5642 – *2

Charlotte C. Gregory, 2718 Eton St., V5K 1K3 – 604/254-2854, Fax: 604/254-2854; Email: cgregory@istar.ca – *1

Greyell & MacPhail, #1811, 808 Nelson St., V6Z 2H2 – 604/687-4232, Fax: 604/687-4234 – *4

Griffin Law Office, #226, 119 Pender St. West, V6B 1S5 – 604/488-1667, Fax: 604/689-0802 – *1

Grossman & Stanley, #800, 1090 West Georgia St., PO Box 55, V6E 3V7 – 604/683-7454, Fax: 604/683-8602 – *3

Guild, Yule, Sullivan, Yule, Truscott & Slivinski, Three Bentall Centre, #2000, 595 Burrard St., PO Box 49170, V7X 1R7 – 604/688-1221, Fax: 604/688-1315 – *27

W.F. Guinn, 671G Market Hill, V5Z 4B5 – 604/872-6658, Fax: 604/876-3304 – *1

Guy & Company, #510, 190 Alexander St., V6A 1B5 – 604/681-6164, Fax: 604/681-9420 – *2

Hara & Company, #301, 460 Nanaimo St., V5L 4W3 – 604/255-4800, Fax: 604/255-8111 – *3

Harper Grey Easton, 3100 Vancouver Centre, 650 West Georgia St., PO Box 11504, V6B 4P7 – 604/687-0411, Fax: 604/669-9385; Email: hge@hgelaw.com – *4

Harris & Company, #2200, 1111 West Georgia St., V6E 4M3 – 604/684-6633, Fax: 604/684-6632 – *3

James L. Harris Law Corp., #1800, 999 Hastings St. West, V6C 2W2 – 604/682-4466, Fax: 604/682-4467; Email: jharrisllb@aol.com – *1

P.A. Hart, #975, 200 Burrard St., V6C 3L6 – 604/688-6232, Fax: 604/687-7089 – *1

Richard D. Hart, #1311, 808 Nelson St., V6Z 2H2 – 604/608-1222, Fax: 604/488-0124; Toll Free: richhart@unix.ubc.ca – *1

Heenan Blaikie, #600, 1199 West Hastings St., V6E 3T5 – 604/669-0011, Fax: 604/669-5101 – *15

A.G. Helgason, 5559 Alma St.., V6N 1Y2 – 604/263-5009, Fax: 604/263-5013 – *1

John E. Helsing, #204, 1651 Commercial Dr., V5L 3Y3 – 604/253-7731, Fax: 604/253-7726 – *1

Hemsworth, Schmidt, #430, 580 Hornby St., V6C 3B6 – 604/687-4456, Fax: 604/687-0586 – *2

M.B. Hicks, #307, 815 Hornby St., V6Z 2E6 – 604/660-4100, Fax: 604/660-4198 – *1

Christiane B. Hile, 835 Granville St., 2nd Fl., V6Z 1K7 – 604/688-7761, Fax: 604/688-7291; Email: hile@cafe.net – *1

Hobbs & Leigh, #3404, 1055 Dunsmuir St., V7X 1L3 – 604/669-6609, Fax: 604/669-6612; Email: lawyers@hobbsleigh.bc.ca – *4

Hogan & Company, 195 Alexander St., 5th Fl., V6A 1B8 – 604/687-8806, Fax: 604/687-8871 – *1

Holmes, Greenslade, #1440, 1066 Hastings St. West, V6E 3X1 – 604/688-7861, Fax: 604/688-0426; Email: hg@holmesgreenslade.com – *3

Hordo, Ross & Bennett, Nelson Sq., #1801, 808 Nelson St., PO Box 12146, V6Z 2H2 – 604/682-5250, Fax: 604/682-7872 – *8

S. Huberman, 796 Granville St., V6Z 1K1 – 604/654-2262, Fax: 604/682-8879 – *1

Peter J. Hull, 869 West 20 Ave., V5Z 1Y3 – 604/874-1242 – *1

Hutchins, Soroka & Grant, #501, 21 Water St., V6B 1A1 – 604/685-1229, Fax: 604/685-0244 – *6

Hutchinson, Cristall, 796 Granville St., 5th Fl., V6Z 1K1 – 604/654-2250, Fax: 604/682-8879 – *2

L. Hyman, #800, 1200 Burrard St., V6Z 2C7 – 604/685-9277, Fax: 604/681-1576 – *4

Irwin & White, Royal Centre, #2720, 1055 West Georgia St., PO Box 11168, V6E 3R5 – 604/664-3720, Fax: 604/689-2806 – *1

Brian Jackson, #1502, 100 West Pender St., V6B 1R8 – 604/681-7766, Fax: 604/688-6243 – *2

Bridget M. Jacob, #303, 1001 Broadway West, V6H 4B1 – 604/738-1080, Fax: 604/738-1088 – *1

Jarvis & Goulet, #600, 1125 Howe St., V6Z 2K8 – 604/682-0587 – *2

Jeffery & Calder, #601, 815 Hornby St., V6Z 2E6 – 604/669-5534, Fax: 604/669-7563 – *6

A. Jeletzky, 100 West Pender St., V6B 1R8 – 604/687-1037 – *1

Jenkins Marzban Logan, #1414, 808 Nelson St., PO Box 12144, V6Z 2H2 – 604/681-6564, Fax: 604/681-0766 – *6

Azim Jiwa, #904, 808 Nelson St., V6Z 2H2 – 604/689-9357, Fax: 604/689-9367 – *1

Jones McCloy Peterson, 3 Bentall Centre, #1700, 595 Burrard St., 17th Fl., PO Box 49117, V7X 1G4 – 604/682-1851, Fax: 604/682-7329 – *9

D. Jung, 416 Columbia St., V6A 2R8 – 604/682-7151, Fax: 604/669-8042 – *1

R.N. Jussa, #204, 4676 Main St., V5V 3R7 – 604/872-4745, Fax: 604/872-8217 – *1

E.W. Kagna, #612, 825 Granville St., V6Z 1K9 – 604/683-8722, Fax: 604/683-8722 – *1

Kane, Shannon & Weiler, #348, 1275 West 6th Ave., V6H 1A6 – 604/732-4070, Fax: 604/738-7134 – *1

Kaplan & Waddell, #102, 2590 Granville St., V6H 3H1 – 604/736-8021, Fax: 604/736-3845 – *4

Katz & Company, Nelson Square, #1018, 808 Nelson St., PO Box 12135, V6Z 2H2 – 604/669-6226, Fax: 604/669-6752 – *1

Stephen Kelleher, #650, 475 West Georgia St., V6B 4M9 – 604/683-0122, Fax: 604/683-3846 – *1

C. Robert Kennedy, #206, 190 Alexander St., V6A 1B5 – 604/684-3927, Fax: 604/684-3228 – *1

J. Ross Ker, 2021 West 41 Ave., V6M 1Y7 – 604/266-7151, Fax: 604/266-8781 – *1

Kerfoot, Cameron & Company, #300, 5687 Yew St., V6M 3Y2 – 604/263-2565, Fax: 604/263-2737; Email: bbk@kercam.com – *10

Killam, Whitelaw & Twining, #2400, 200 Granville St., V6C 1S4 – 604/682-5466, Fax: 604/682-5217; Email: david_sutherland@kwt.bc.ca – *19

Lawrence A. King, Esq., #930, 777 Hornby St., V6Z 1S4 – 604/688-9921, Fax: 604/688-9981 – *1

William N. King, United Kingdom Bldg., #400, 409 Granville St., V6C 1T2 – 604/682-1245, Fax: 604/682-8417; Email: ewesson@ultranet.ca – *1

Norman C. Kliman, 465 West 26 Ave.., V5Y 2K1 – 604/876-3544, Fax: 604/683-1620 – *1

James R. Klopping, #215, 402 West Pender St., V6B 1T6 – 604/682-8288 – *1

Koffman Birnie & Kalef, 885 West Georgia St., 19th Fl., V6C 3H4 – 604/891-3688, Fax: 604/891-3788 – *4

Kornfeld & Company, #301, 796 Granville St., V6Z 1J8 – 604/689-3838, Fax: 604/689-0526 – *2

E.L. Kornfeld, #1116, 736 Granville St., V6Z 1H7 – 604/688-8241 – *1

Kowarsky & Company, #1050, 1185 West Georgia St., V6E 4E6 – 604/683-6875, Fax: 604/683-2737 – *5

G.R. Kroll, #400, 409 Granville St., V6C 1T2 – 604/682-4704, Fax: 604/682-8417 – *1

Donna L. Kydd, #220, 1501 West Broadway, V6J 4Z6 – 604/732-5031, Fax: 604/732-5071; Email: kyddlaw@portal.ca – *1

Ladner Downs, Waterfront Centre, #1200, 200 Burrard St., PO Box 48600, V7X 1T2 – 604/687-5744, Fax: 604/687-1415; Email: ldmaster@ladner.com; URL: http://www.ladner.com/ladner – *108

Lando & Company, Royal Centre, #2010, 1055 Georgia St. West, PO Box 11140, V6E 3P3 – 604/682-6821, Fax: 604/662-8293 – *6

Lang Michener Lawrence & Shaw, Three Bentall Centre, #2500, 595 Burrard St., PO Box 49200, V7X 1L1 – 604/689-9111, Fax: 604/685-7084 – *46

Lang, Georgialee A. & Associates, #1201, 808 Nelson St., V6Z 2H2 – 604/669-2030, Fax: 604/669-2038 – *3

Langdon, LaCroix & Toews, #1300, 1100 Melville St., V6E 4A6 – 604/681-1188, Fax: 604/681-3019 – *3

Larson Suleman Sohn Boulton., 609 West Hastings St., 6th Fl., PO Box 26, V6B 4W4 – 604/662-7404, Fax: 604/662-7466; URL: http://www.lssb.com – *4

Laughton & Company, #1090, 1090 Georgia St. West, V6E 3V7 – 604/683-6665, Fax: 604/683-6622 – *2

Lauk, La Liberte, #225, 701 West Georgia St., PO Box 10106, V7Y 1C6 – 604/669-8808, Fax: 604/669-2719 – *3

R.E. Lawrence, 1500 West Georgia St., 15th Fl., V6Z 1S4 – 604/681-4171, Fax: 604/681-5103 – *1

Lawson, Lundell, Lawson & McIntosh, Cathedral Place, #1600, 925 West Georgia St., V5C 3L2 – 604/685-3456, Fax: 604/669-1620; Email: genmail@lawsonlundell.com – *79

Laxton & Company, 1285 West Pender St., 10th Fl., V6E 4B1 – 604/682-3871, Fax: 604/682-3704 – *3

Leask, Daniells & Bahen, #201, 111 Water St., V6B 1A7 – 604/683-3206, Fax: 604/662-7511 – *4

LeBlanc & Company, 1826 West Broadway, V6J 1Y9 – 604/731-4628, Fax: 604/731-4620 – *2

Lecovin & Company, #907, 808 Nelson St., PO Box 12157, V6Z 2H2 – 604/687-1721, Fax: 604/687-1799 – *2

Lee & Company, #388, 1190 Hornby St., V6Z 2K5 – 604/687-1212, Fax: 604/669-6868 – *2

Jack L. Lee, 127 East Pender St., 3rd Fl., V6A 1T6 – 604/683-7241 – *1

Legge & Company, #605, 815 Hornby St., V6Z 2E6 – 604/688-8211 – *1

Lesperance Mendes Mancuso, #760, 1050 West Pender St., V6E 3S7 – 604/685-3567, Fax: 604/685-7505 – *4

Lew & Lee, #108, 329 Main St., V6A 2S9 – 604/685-8331, Fax: 604/685-6334 – *3

Chuck Lew, #1010, 207 West Hastings St., V6B 1H7 – 604/688-3601, Fax: 604/688-7866 – *1

H.H. Lew, #600, 210 West Broadway., V5Y 3W2 – 604/879-3151, Fax: 604/879-3707; Email: hhlew@smartt.com – *1

Libby, Moss & Beirne, 157 Alexander St., 3rd Fl., V6A 1B8 – 604/683-4311, Fax: 604/683-4317 – *2

Liddle, Burns, Beechinor & Fitzpatrick, #1210, 400 Burrard St., V6C 3A6 – 604/685-0121, Fax: 604/685-2104 – *9

Lidstone, Young, Anderson, Nelson Sq., #1616, 808 Nelson St., PO Box 12147, V6Z 2H2 – 604/689-7400, Fax: 604/689-3444; Toll Free: 1-800-665-3540 – *16

Lindsay Kenney, 700 West Pender St., 17th Fl., V6C 1G8 – 604/687-1323, Fax: 604/687-2347; Email: info@lindsaykenney.bc.ca; URL: http://www.lindsaykenney.bc.ca – *25

A.L. Lipetz, #201, 2902 West Broadway, V6K 2G8 – 604/733-5611, Fax: 604/738-5611 – *1

P. Litsky, 6330 Fremlin St., V5Z 3X5 – 604/266-7806 – *1

Keith A. Lo, #338, 237 Keefer St., V6A 1X6 – 604/687-4315, Fax: 604/681-2289 – *2

Loh & Company, #708, 650 - 41st Ave. West, V5Z 2M9 – 604/261-1234, Fax: 604/261-1222 – *4

A.D. Long, 375 Southborough Dr., V7S 1M3 – 604/922-8228 – *1

Long, Miller & Co., #400, 409 Granville St., V6C 1T2 – 604/682-1311, Fax: 604/682-8417 – *1

R.H. Long & Co., #102, 4088 Cambie St., V5Z 2Y8 – 604/876-7797, Fax: 604/876-1105 – *1

Lorimer O'Dyer Adelman, #341, 5021 Kingsway, V5H 4A5 – 604/438-7443, Fax: 604/438-7642 – *2

Phillip R. Lundrie, #3, 2597 Hastings St. East, V5K 1Z2 – 604/257-3588, Fax: 604/257-3511 – *1

Macaulay McColl, #600, 840 Howe St., V6Z 2L2 – 604/687-9811, Fax: 604/687-8716; Email: lawyers@macaulay.com; URL: http://www.macaulay.com – *9

Macfarlane, Pearkes, #702, 1055 West Broadway, V6H 1E2 – 604/732-7481, Fax: 604/732-3205 – *2

MacKenzie Fujisawa Brewer Stevenson, #1800, 400 Burrard St., V6C 3A6 – 604/689-3281, Fax: 604/685-6494; Email: mfbs@mindlink.bc.ca – *15

MacKenzie Murdy & McAllister, Four Bentall Centre, 1055 Dunsmuir St., 31st Fl., PO Box 49059, V7X 1C4 – 604/689-5263, Fax: 604/689-9029 – *4

R.H. MacKenzie, #2020, 650 West Georgia St., PO Box 11547, V6B 4N7 – 604/683-9621, Fax: 604/683-5084 – *1

MacKinlay Woodson Diebel, #1170, 1040 West Georgia St., V6E 4H1 – 604/669-1511, Fax: 604/669-1566 – *3

M. Diane MacKinnon, #500, 650 - 41st Ave. West, V5Z 2M9 – 604/263-7891, Fax: 604/266-9046 – *1

MacLeod & Company, #1900, 777 Hornby St., V6Z 1S4 – 604/687-7287, Fax: 604/682-2534; Email: bmacleod@macleodlaw.com – *2

MacLeod Smith, #1240, 701 West Georgia St., V7Y 1A1 – 604/685-2361, Fax: 604/669-3477 – *2

MacQuarrie Hobkirk, #2020, 777 Hornby St., V6Z 1T7 – 604/684-6255, Fax: 604/684-7575 – *5

Michael Mahoney, #716, 402 Pender St. West, V6B 1T6 – 604/689-0770, Fax: 604/689-0403 – *1

Maitland & Company, Standard Life Bldg., #700, 625 Howe St., V6C 2T6 – 604/681-7474, Fax: 604/681-3896; Email: maitco@maitland.com; URL: http://www.maitland.com – *9

Mandell, Pinder, #300, 111 Water St., V6B 1A7 – 604/681-4146, Fax: 604/681-0959 – *6

Leonard F. Maracle, #206, 111 Water St., V6B 1A7 – 604/689-9545

Gerald K. Martin, #308, 650 - 41st Ave. West, V5Z 2M9 – 604/266-1988, Fax: 604/263-0880 – *1

M.V. Mass, #302, 2695 Granville St., V6H 3H4 – 604/736-8741, Fax: 604/736-3241 – *1

Maude, MacKay & Co. Ltd., #304, 1682 - 7th Ave., V6J 4S6 – 604/736-0108, Fax: 604/736-0314

Maxwell, Schuman & Company, 900 Helmcken St., V6Z 1B3 – 604/669-4912, Fax: 604/662-3975 – *6

McAlpine & Associates, The Landing, #250, 375 Water St., V6B 5C6 – 604/685-6272, Fax: 604/685-8434; Email: mcalpine@mindlink.bc.ca

McCarthy Tétrault, Pacific Centre, #1300, 777 Dunsmuir St., PO Box 10424, V7Y 1K2 – 604/643-7100, Fax: 604/643-7900; Email: twb@mccarthy.ca; URL: http://www.mccarthy.ca – *79

Joanne S. McClusky, #300, 744 West Hastings, V6C 1A5 – 604/689-4010, Fax: 604/684-2349 – *1

McCrea & Associates, #102, 1012 Beach Ave., V6E 1T7 – 604/662-8200, Fax: 604/662-8225; Email: mccrea@portal.ca – *3

McCullough O'Connor Irwin, #1100, 888 Dunsmuir St., V6C 3K4 – 604/687-7077, Fax: 604/687-7099; Email: moimail@moisolicitors.com – *7

McEwen Schmitt & Company, #1615, 1055 West Georgia St., 11174, V6E 3R5 – 604/683-1223, Fax: 604/683-2359 – *3

F.G. McGinley, #303, 555 Howe St., V6C 2C2 – 604/687-6916, Fax: 604/687-2933 – *1

McGrady, Askew & Fiorillo, #500, 2695 Granville St., V6H 3H4 – 604/734-4777, Fax: 604/734-1109 – *4

J.E. McInnes, 808 Nelson St., 17th Fl., PO Box 12148, V6Z 2H2 – 604/891-0214, Fax: 604/685-8992 – *1

Ruth E. McIntyre, 1115 - 555 Burrard St., V7X 1S1 – 604/688-5185, Fax: 604/688-5186 – *1

McKenzie & Company, #920, 938 Howe St., V6Z 1N9 – 604/687-7811, Fax: 604/685-4358 – *2

D.J. McKinlay, #2500, 595 Burrard St., V7X 1L1 – 604/691-7477, Fax: 604/689-9111 – *1

McLachlan Brown Anderson, 938 Howe St., 10th Fl., V6Z 1N9 – 604/331-6000, Fax: 604/331-6008 – *10

Harry P. McLaughlin, #1001, 750 West Pender St., V6C 2T8 – 604/682-2771, Fax: 604/682-1183 – *1

McLellan Herbert, #310, 800 Pender St. West, V6C 2V6 – 604/683-5254, Fax: 604/683-5212; Email: lawyers@mclellanherbert.com; URL: http://www.mclellanherbert.com – *2

E.M. McMahon, #215, 1075 West Georgia St., V6E 3C9 – 604/683-6828, Fax: 604/683-8456 – *1

McNeney & McNeney, 970 Richard St., V6G 3C1 – 604/687-1766, Fax: 604/687-0181 – *4

McRae Holmes & King, #1300, 1111 Georgia St. West, V6E 4M3 – 604/681-1310, Fax: 604/681-1307; Email: lawyers@mhklaw.com – *5

McTaggart, Ellis & Company, #1400, 1030 West Georgia St., V6E 2Y3 – 604/682-3131, Fax: 604/682-3353 – *9

Kennith A. Mellquist, 6660 Marine Dr. NW, V6T 1Z4 – 604/221-7676, Fax: 604/221-2330; Email: kmellquist@angio.com – *1

Brian E. Mickelson, 100 West Pender St., 2nd Fl., V6B 1R8 – 604/688-8588, Fax: 604/681-0652 – *1

John L. Mickleson, #302, 1110 Hamilton St., V6B 2S2 – 604/684-0040, Fax: 604/684-0048 – *1

Montpellier McKeen Varabioff Talbot & Giuffre, Three Bentall Centre, #2323, 595 Burrard St., PO Box 49196, V7X 1K8 – 604/662-8082, Fax: 604/891-2700; Email: lawyers@mmtvtg.com – *9

Mortimer & Rose, 1243 Hornby St., V6Z 1W4 – 604/669-0440, Fax: 604/669-0228 – *2

Morton & Company, #1750, 750 West Pender Blvd., V6C 2T8 – 604/681-1194, Fax: 604/681-9652 – *3

Munro & Crawford, 5670 Yew St., V6M 3Y3 – 604/266-7174, Fax: 604/266-7998 – *4

Murphy, Battista, Vancouver Centre, #2020, 650 West Georgia St., PO Box 11547, V6B 4N7 – 604/683-9621, Fax: 604/683-5084 – *5

Murphy, McComb, Witten, #208, 2800 - 1st, V5M 4N9 – 604/255-9018, Fax: 604/255-8588 – *3

Myers, Johnson & Company, 195 Alexander St., 5th Fl., V6A 1B8 – 604/688-8331, Fax: 604/688-8350 – *4

Myers, Johnson, Esson & Doherty, 195 Alexander St., 5th Fl., V6A 1B8 – 604/688-8331, Fax: 604/688-8350 – *4

Nathanson, Schachter & Thompson, #750, 900 Howe St., V6Z 2M4 – 604/662-8840, Fax: 604/684-1598 – *5

B.J. Nelson, #103, 1012 Beach Ave., V6E 1T7 – 604/685-7317, Fax: 604/682-3965 – *1

Kimball R. Nichols, #1050, 1188 West Georgia, V6E 4A2 – 604/682-0541, Fax: 604/682-4428 – *1

Allan S. Nicol, #1800, 999 West Hastings, V6C 2W2 – 604/683-4478, Fax: 604/683-1375 – *1

K.F. Nordlinger, Q.C. & Associates, #109, 1008 Beach Ave., V6E 1T7 – 604/689-5134, Fax: 604/689-5323 – *3

Norton Stewart, #1200, 1055 West Georgia St., PO Box 11104, V6E 3P3 – 604/687-0555, Fax: 604/689-1248 – *5

Karen O'Connor Coulter, 1628 - 7th Ave. West, V6J 1S5 – 604/733-2448, Fax: 604/736-6225; Email: desfried@istar.ca – *1

O'Neill & Company, #1880, 1055 West Georgia St., V6E 3P3 – 604/687-5792, Fax: 604/687-6650 – *6

A. Barry Oland, Vancouver Centre, #2020, 650 West Georgia St., PO Box 11547, V6B 4N7 – 604/683-9621, Fax: 604/669-4556; Email: shiplaw@aboland.com – *2

Oliver & Company, #1920, 777 Hornby St., V6Z 2L1 – 604/681-5232, Fax: 604/681-1331; Email: oco@xl.ca – *4

Orris, Burns, 123 Main St., V6A 2S5 – 604/669-6711, Fax: 604/669-5180 – *5

Osten & Osten, #114, 990 Beach Ave.., V6Z 2N9 – 604/683-9104, Fax: 604/688-0034 – *2

Owen, Bird, Three Bentall Centre, #2900, 595 Burrard St., PO Box 49130, V7X 1J5 – 604/688-0401, Fax: 604/688-2827; Email: owenbird.com – *46

Paine Edmonds, #1100, 510 Burrard St., V6C 3A8 – 604/683-1211, Fax: 604/681-5084; Toll Free: 1-800-669-8599; Email: thargreaves@paine-edmonds.com – *16

Palkowski & Company, #703, 938 Howe St., V6Z 1N9 – 604/331-4422, Fax: 604/331-4466; Email: rjplegal@sfu.ca – *2

R. Pandya, #720, 475 Howe St., V6C 2B3 – 604/685-0507, Fax: 604/685-7249 – *1

Pape & Salter, #460, 220 Cambie St., V6B 2M9 – 604/681-3002, Fax: 604/681-3050 – *4

* indicates number of lawyers in law firm.

Al Paquette, #103, 8584 Granville St., V6P 4Z7 – 604/261-3211, Fax: 604/266-1120 – *1

J. Craig Paterson & Associates, #340, 1090 Homer St., V6B 2W9 – 604/669-7311, Fax: 604/669-2340 – *2

Patterson & Price, #1500, 736 Granville St., V6Z 1G3 – 604/684-5951, Fax: 604/684-2449 – *2

Peterson Stark, #500, 1195 West Broadway, V6H 3X5 – 604/736-9811, Fax: 604/736-2859; Toll Free: 1-800-663-1667 – *16

Pierce Law Group, #850, 475 Georgia St. West, V6B 4M9 – 604/681-4434, Fax: 604/681-9142 – *2

Sandra L. Polinsky, 671D Market Hill, V5Z 4B5 – 604/876-9995, Fax: 604/879-4934 – *1

S.L. Polsky Shamash, #200, 1700 - 75th Ave. West, V6P 6G2 – 604/664-7800, Fax: 604/664-7898 – *1

John E. Potter, 1370 West King Edward, V6H 1Z9 – 604/736-6831, Fax: 604/873-3989 – *1

Poulsen & Co., #1800, 999 West Hastings St., V6C 2W2 – 604/681-0123, Fax: 604/683-1375 – *3

Price Shimizu, #718, 808 Nelson St., PO Box 12159, V6Z 2H2 – 604/685-6426, Fax: 604/685-6412 – *2

William C. Prowse, 2215 Commissioner St., V5L 1B5 – 604/254-5751, Fax: 604/254-0957 – *1

Radelet & Company, #1330, 1075 Georgia St. West, V6E 3C9 – 604/689-0878, Fax: 604/689-1386 – *2

Raibmon & Goulet, #880, 1090 West Georgia St., V6E 3V7 – 604/688-8551, Fax: 604/662-8782 – *2

W.A. Randall, #102, 535 West Georgia St., V6B 1Z6 – 604/685-9411 – *1

Rankin, Bond, 157 Alexander St., V6A 1V8 – 604/682-3621, Fax: 604/682-3919 – *2

Rao, McKercher & Company, #908, 510 Burrard St., V6C 3A8 – 604/664-7474, Fax: 604/664-7477 – *2

Raphanel Cantillon, #102, 853 Richards St., V6B 3B4 – 604/681-5383, Fax: 604/681-6021 – *2

Reid & Company, #1040 1055 Hastings St. West, V6E 2E9 – 604/687-5267, Fax: 604/687-5872; Email: reidvan@istar.ca – *5

Remedios & Company, #1010, 1030 West Georgia St., V6E 2Y3 – 604/688-9337, Fax: 604/688-5590; Toll Free: 1-800-914-0011; Email: ammrlawco@aol.com – *8

Richards Buell Sutton, #300, 1111 Melville St., V6E 4H7 – 604/682-3664, Fax: 604/688-3830; URL: http://www.rbs.com – *28

William D. Riley, #410, 1040 West Georgia St., V6E 4H1 – 604/605-8771, Fax: 604/605-8772; Email: wriley@direct.ca – *1

Rimer & Company, #1220, 808 Nelson St., V6Z 2H2 – 604/684-7330, Fax: 604/684-4589; Email: arimer@rimart.com; URL: http://rimart.com/rimer – *1

Roberts & Griffin, #901, 840 Howe St., V6Z 2L2 – 604/682-9766, Fax: 604/682-6746 – *7

Roberts & Stahl, #500, 220 Cambie St., V6B 2M9 – 604/684-6377, Fax: 604/684-6387 – *3

Robertson & Company, #2350, 1177 Hastings St. West, V6E 2K3 – 604/688-7151, Fax: 604/685-7832; Email: dlr@aurias.com – *1

Daniel J. Rogers, #550, 1199 Pender St. West, V6E 2R1 – 604/681-5600, Fax: 604/681-1475 – *1

Paul E.A. Romeril, #107, 2298 McBain Ave., V6L 3B1 – 604/732-4845, Fax: 604/732-4845 – *1

V. Romilly, 3536 Point Grey Rd., V6R 1A8 – 604/736-7040, Fax: 604/738-5143 – *1

Jeffrey A. Rose, 1243 Hornby St., V6Z 1W4 – 604/688-3288

Rosenberg & Rosenberg, 671D Market Hill, V5Z 4B5 – 604/879-4505, Fax: 604/879-4934 – *3

Rosenbloom & Aldridge, #1300, 355 Burrard St., V6C 2G8 – 604/605-5555, Fax: 604/684-6402; Email: rosenbloom_aldridge@bc.sympatico.ca – *5

J.H. Rosner, #770, 475 West Georgia St., V6B 4M9 – 604/687-6638, Fax: 604/682-2481 – *1

R.D. Ross, 4741 West 2 Ave., V6T 1C1 – 604/228-9701, Fax: 604/228-9055 – *1

K. Roth, #501, 595 Howe St., V6C 2T5 – 604/681-7161, Fax: 604/683-7043 – *1

Howard Rubin Law Corp., #900, 850 Hastings St. West, V6C 1E1 – 604/488-0234, Fax: 604/687-7089 – *1

J.M. Ruckwood, #403, 1720 Balsam St., V6K 3M2 – 604/732-6637 – *1

Rush, Crane, Guenther & Adams, #300, 111 Water St., V6B 1A7 – 604/687-5611, Fax: 604/681-0912 – *4

Russell & DuMoulin, #2100, 1075 West Georgia St., V6E 3G2 – 604/631-3131, Fax: 604/631-3232; Email: rdcounsel@rdcounsel.com; URL: http://rdcounsel.com/rd – *107

Sabatino Moscovich & Aikenhead, #316, 2800 - 1st Ave. East, V5M 4P3 – 604/253-4525, Fax: 604/253-1080 – *5

Morrie Sacks Law Corp., #1050, 1188 Georgia St. West, V6E 4A2 – 604/685-7629, Fax: 604/682-4428; Email: morrie@sackslaw.bc.ca; URL: sackslaw.bc.ca – *1

E.A. Safarik, 2215 Commissioner St., V5L 1A8 – 604/254-5751, Fax: 604/254-0957 – *1

Salley Bowes Harwardt, #1750, 1185 Georgia St. West, V6E 4E6 – 604/688-0788, Fax: 604/688-0778 – *3

Gary M. Salloum, 286 - 21st Ave. West, V5Y 2E5 – 604/872-4939 – *1

Charles A. Sandberg, #108, 2786 - 16 Ave. West, V6K 4M1 – 604/734-7768, Fax: 604/733-1229 – *1

Iqbal Sara, #1, 2535 SW Marine Dr., V6P 6C3 – 604/327-1911 – *1

Henry K. Sarava, 2222 Spruce St., V6H 2P3 – 604/737-1226, Fax: 604/737-1230 – *1

Catherine A. Sas, #501, 134 Abbott St., V6B 2K4 – 604/689-5444, Fax: 604/689-5666; Email: casas@axionet.com – *1

Sauer, Mogan, De Jager & Volkenant, #1600, 1185 Georgia St. West, V6E 4E6 – 604/689-8000, Fax: 604/689-8835 – *4

Alison Sawyer, #601, 207 Hastings St. West, V6B 1H7 – 604/685-0404, Fax: 604/685-0424 – *1

P.N. Scarisbrick, 234 Abbott St., V6B 2K8 – 604/688-0495, Fax: 604/688-0201 – *3

Bernard Schachter, #401, 796 Granville St., V6Z 1J6 – 604/688-1474, Fax: 604/688-5191 – *1

Schiller, Coutts, Weiler & Gibson, Two Bentall Centre, #1485, 555 Burrard St., V7X 1M9 – 604/682-1866, Fax: 604/682-6947; Email: info@scwg.com – *8

Antya Schrack, #101, 5125 Victoria Dr., V5P 3V1 – 604/322-9624, Fax: 604/322-0280 – *1

Schroeder Pidgeion & Company, #1119, 808 Nelson St., PO Box 12168, V6Z 2H2 – 604/888-6737, Fax: 604/888-0271 – *8

D.A. Schwartz, #304, 700 West Pender St., V6C 1G8 – 604/687-0811, Fax: 604/688-9611 – *1

Stanley A. Schwartz, #1800, 701 West Georgia St., PO Box 10142, V7Y 1E9 – 604/681-1077, Fax: 604/682-7643 – *1

Seaton Promislow, Pender Pl., Box: 1202, #1202, 700 West Pender St., V6C 1G8 – 604/688-1466, Fax: 604/688-4157 – *1

A.P. Serka, #707, 777 West Broadway, V5Z 4J7 – 604/876-8761, Fax: 604/876-9035 – *1

Shandro Dixon Edgson, #400, 999 Hastings St. West, V6C 2W2 – 604/689-0400, Fax: 604/685-2009 – *3

Murray H. Shapiro, #702, 686 West Broadway, V5Z 1G1 – 604/879-6777, Fax: 604/874-0820 – *1

Shapray, Cramer & Associates, #670, 999 Canada Place, V6C 3E1 – 604/681-0900, Fax: 604/681-0920 – *4

S.S. Shelton, 2245 Commercial Dr., V5N 4B6 – 604/251-2144, Fax: 604/251-2781 – *1

Shrimpton & Company, 1325 Kingsway, V5V 3E3 – 604/879-2458, Fax: 604/879-4643 – *3

Siddal & Company, #500, 650 - 41st Ave. West, V5Z 2M9 – 604/266-1130, Fax: 604/266-9046 – *5

Sierra Legal Defence Fund, #214, 131 Water St., V6B 4M3 – 604/685-5618, Fax: 604/685-7813; Email: sldf@wimsey.com – *5

Silbernagel & Company, #700, 595 Howe St., V6C 2T5 – 604/687-9621, Fax: 604/687-5960 – *2

Simon, Wener & Adler, #401, 1385 - 8 Ave. West, V6H 3V9 – 604/736-5500, Fax: 604/736-5522 – *4

Singleton Urquhart Scott, #1200, 1125 Howe St., V6Z 2K8 – 604/682-7474, Fax: 604/682-1283; Email: reception@singleton.com; URL: http://www.singleton.com – *19

Sisett & Co., #603, 601 West Broadway, V5Z 4C2 – 604/879-8811, Fax: 604/879-7346 – *4

Skorah, Doyle, Khanna, #1750, 1040 Georgia St. West, V6E 4N6 – 604/602-8500, Fax: 604/608-1660; Email: mskorah@axionet.com – *4

Smart & Biggar, Vancouver Centre, #2200, 650 West Georgia St., PO Box 11560, V6B 4N8 – 604/682-7295, Fax: 604/682-0274; Email: vancouver@smart-biggar.ca – *3

Smart & Williams, #1190, 840 Howe St., V6Z 2L2 – 604/687-6278, Fax: 604/687-6298 – *5

Smith & Hughes, #321, 1525 Robson St., V6G 1C3 – 604/683-4176, Fax: 604/683-2621 – *5

Smith, Hutchison, #410, 355 Burrard St., V6C 2G8 – 604/683-6858

Snarch & Allen, #907, 1030 Georgia St. West, V6E 2Y3 – 604/684-8000, Fax: 604/684-8003 – *3

Sobolewski Anfield, Stock Exchange Twr., Pacific Centre, #1600, 609 Granville St., PO Box 10068, V7Y 1C3 – 604/669-1322, Fax: 604/669-3877 – *6

Soronow & Soronow, 1628 West 7 Ave., V6J 1S5 – 604/733-2411, Fax: 604/736-6225 – *1

Michael P.S. Spearing, #880, 1500 West Georgia St., V6G 2Z6 – 604/681-0699, Fax: 604/682-0713 – *1

Spring Brammall, 2774 Granville St., V6H 3J3 – 604/732-3881, Fax: 604/723-3883 – *1

Bob C. Starkell, #770, 1100 Melville St., V6E 4A6 – 604/681-2157, Fax: 604/684-2627 – *1

Vina A. Starr, #608, 1033 Davie St., V6E 1M7 – 604/683-7383, Fax: 604/683-0272 – *1

Steeves & Company, #300, 111 Water St., V6B 1A7 – 604/687-5611, Fax: 604/681-0912; Email: jsteeves@wimsey.com – *1

D.M.B. Steinberg, #601, 134 Abbott St., V6B 2K4 – 604/689-0051, Fax: 604/689-3327 – *1

Steinberg, Roberts & Lewis, #601, 134 Abbott St., V6B 2K4 – 604/689-0051, Fax: 604/689-3327; Email: reasonabledoubt_srl@bc.sympatico.ca – *2

Stephens & Holman, #300, 1985 Broadway West, V6J 4Y3 – 604/730-4100, Fax: 604/736-2867 – *8

Stewart & Company, Chancery Pl., #903, 865 Hornby St., V6Z 2G3 – 604/688-0033, Fax: 604/685-5238 – *5

Stewart Aulinger & Company, #1200, 805 West Broadway, V5Z 1K1 – 604/879-0291, Fax: 604/874-5551 – *6

Stikeman, Elliott, Park Pl., #1700, 666 Burrard St., V6C 2X8 – 604/631-1300, Fax: 604/681-1825 – *23

Street Morrison Hall, #1701, 1166 Alberni St., V6E 3Z3 – 604/688-7211, Fax: 604/688-4481 – *3

J.M. Sumpton, 10 Gaolers Mews, V6B 4K7 – 604/688-7252 – *1

Swinton & Company, Robson Ct., #1000, 840 Howe St., V6Z 2M1 – 604/687-2242, Fax: 604/643-1200; Toll Free: 1-800-794-6866; Email: svd@swinton.ca; URL: http://www.swinton.ca – *43

Janna L. Sylvest, 896 Commercial Dr., V5L 3Y5 – 604/254-5359, Fax: 604/254-5472 – *1

Ruth Lea Taylor, #1, 2350 Hastings St. East, V5L 1V6 – 604/255-1979, Fax: 604/255-1579 – *1

G.J. Te Hennepe, #203, 4545 West 10 Ave., V6R 4N2 – 604/228-1433, Fax: 604/228-9822 – *1

P.G. Theocharis, #1510, 777 Hornby St., V6Z 1S4 – 604/669-7726, Fax: 604/688-9981 – *1

Richard Thomas, #308, 1080 Mainland St., V6B 2T4 – 604/669-7763, Fax: 604/669-7706 – *1

Thomas, Rondeau, #680, 505 Burrard St., V7X 1M4 – 604/688-6775, Fax: 604/688-6995 – *4

Bonnie L. Thorpe, 6909 Cambie St., V6P 3H1 – 604/325-0663, Fax: 604/325-0020 – *1

Thorsteinssons, Three Bentall Centre, 595 Burrard St., 27th Fl., PO Box 49123, V7X 1J2 – 604/689-1261, Fax: 604/688-4711 – *26

Jennifer Y. Tse, #510, 190 Alexander St., V6A 1B5 – 604/278-2762, Fax: 604/279-0863; Email: jayyytee@intergate.bc.ca – *1
Nelson M. Tsui, #1180, 625 Howe St., V6C 2T6 – 604/688-3831, Fax: 604/688-8377 – *1
Tupper, Jonsson & Yeadon, #1710, 1177 West Hastings St., V6E 2L3 – 604/683-9262, Fax: 604/683-9635 – *9
C.J. Van Twest, #404, 1160 Burrard St., V6Z 2E8 – 604/683-8874, Fax: 604/683-8874 – *1
Varty & Company, Box: 12155, #700, 555 Hastings St. West, V6B 4N5 – 604/684-5356, Fax: 604/443-5001 – *3
Vermette & Co., #230, 200 Granville St., PO Box 40, V6C 1S4 – 604/331-0381, Fax: 604/331-0382; Email: patent@smartt.com – *2
Vertlieb Anderson, 835 Granville St., 2nd Fl., V6Z 1K7 – 604/688-7761, Fax: 604/688-7291 – *4
Vick, McPhee & Liu, #1025, 1185 West Georgia St., V6E 4E6 – 604/682-0926, Fax: 604/688-8615; Email: vml@pro.net – *1
Victory Square Law, #300, 198 West Hastings, V6B 1H2 – 604/684-8421, Fax: 604/684-8427 – *4
Von Dehn & Company, #700, 595 Howe St., V6C 2T5 – 604/688-4541, Fax: 604/687-5960 – *2
T. Wing Wai, #205, 475 Main St., V6A 2T7 – 604/688-2291, Fax: 604/688-8983 – *2
Walden & Company, #307, 736 Granville St., V6Z 1G3 – 604/683-8833, Fax: 604/683-5943 – *2
Walker & Company, #1500, 1030 West Georgia St., V6E 2Y3 – 604/682-8521, Fax: 604/682-8753 – *9
G.B. Walker, #750, 609 West Hastings St., PO Box 14, V6B 4W4 – 604/681-9577 – *1
C.E. Warren, #506, 815 Hornby St., V6Z 2E6 – 604/689-7571, Fax: 604/685-8563 – *1
G.A. Wasko, #D, 1306 Bidwell St., V6C 2L1 – 604/662-3032 – *1
Wasson & Wasson, #222, 470 Granville St., V6C 1V5 – 604/681-2147, Fax: 604/681-5355 – *1
Watson Goepel Maledy, Three Bentall Centre, #3023, 595 Burrard St., PO Box 49096, V7X 1G4 – 604/688-1301, Fax: 604/688-8193; Email: wgm@wgmlaw.com – *21
Watts, Nabata, #570, 999 West Broadway, V5Z 1K5 – 604/734-2766, Fax: 604/731-5274 – *2
R.H. Watts, #740, 475 West Georgia St., V6B 4M9 – 604/682-2671, Fax: 604/682-2348 – *1
K.S. Westlake, #975, 200 Burrard St., V6C 3L6 – 604/687-9831, Fax: 604/687-7089 – *1
Ron J. Wilinofsky, #401, 1385 - 8 Ave. West, V6H 3V9 – 604/736-6818, Fax: 604/736-5522 – *1
Williamson, Walker & Company, #1500, 1030 West Georgia St., V6E 2Y3 – 604/682-8521, Fax: 604/682-8753 – *1
Wilson, Danderfer, Banno & Mitchell, #1450, 1075 West Georgia St., V6E 3C9 – 604/682-0701, Fax: 604/682-7359 – *7
P.J. Wilson, 195 Alexander St., 3rd Fl., V6A 1B8 – 604/684-4751, Fax: 604/684-8319 – *1
Andrew J. Winstanley, #906, 808 Nelson St., V6Z 2H2 – 604/682-2939, Fax: 604/682-2241; Email: ajwinstanley@ultranet.ca – *1
Wirick & Klassen, 6625 Fraser St., 2nd Fl., V5X 3T6 – 604/324-5115, Fax: 604/324-6996 – *2
P.L. Wong, #407, 1541 West Broadway, V6J 1W7 – 604/731-5301, Fax: 604/731-1266 – *1
W.G. Wong, 145 Keefer St., 2nd Fl., V6A 1X3 – 604/685-9361, Fax: 604/684-1299 – *1
A.K. Wooster, 1176 West Georgia St., PO Box 18, V6E 4A2 – 604/684-1204, Fax: 604/682-4428 – *1
Patricia Yaremovich, #610, 207 West Hastings St., V6B 1H7 – 604/688-3469, Fax: 604/688-5706 – *1
D.W.H. Yerxa, #1200, 805 West Broadway, V5Z 1K1 – 604/873-5225, Fax: 604/874-5551 – *1
David L. Youngson, #204, 5701 Granville St., V6M 4J7 – 604/266-6588, Fax: 604/266-6393 – *1
Xiao Zheng, #620, 1040 Georgia St. West, V6E 4H1 – 604/608-0387, Fax: 604/608-0385; Email: zheng@ax-ionet.com – *1

* indicates number of lawyers in law firm.

Deborah Lynn Zutter, 609 West Hastings, PO Box 26, V6B 4W4 – 604/669-2696, Fax: 604/922-8141; Email: dzlawmed@portal.ca – *1

**Vanderhoof ..................................... Cariboo**

Steven F. Peleshok, 2608 Burrard Ave., PO Box 1128, V0J 3A0 – 250/567-9277, Fax: 250/567-2657; Toll Free: spelesho@vhf.nano.bc.ca – *1

**Vernon ............................................ Yale**

Allan, Francis & Pringle, 3010 - 34 St., V1T 5X5 – 250/542-1177, Fax: 250/542-1105 – *5
Robert V. Blakely, #102, 2802 - 30 St., V1T 8G7 – 250/549-1544, Fax: 250/549-4233 – *1
Kenneth R. Crosby, 3309 - 32 Ave.., V1T 2M7 – 250/558-5790, Fax: 250/558-3910 – *1
Davidson & Company, 3205 - 32 Ave., 4th Fl., V1T 2M4 – 250/545-5344, Fax: 250/545-3290 – *7
Alan M. Gaudette, 13004 Kinlock Dr., V1B 1C2 – 250/545-3132, Fax: 250/545-1617
Andrew, Kern, #1, 2906 - 32 St., V1T 5M1 – 250/549-2184, Fax: 250/549-2207
Kidston & Company, #200, 3005 - 30th St., V1T 2M1 – 250/545-0711, Fax: 250/545-4776 – *4
Howard Lawrence, 2903 - 28 St., V1T 4Z5 – 250/549-1555 – *1
Moffat, Ward, 3103 - 28 St., V1T 4Z7 – 250/542-1312, Fax: 250/542-2788; Email: 1-800-371-0181 – *2
Nixon, Wenger & Co., 3201 - 30 Ave., 4th Fl., V1T 2C6 – 250/542-5353, Fax: 250/542-7273; Email: dixon-wegner@bc.sympatico.ca – *15
Sigalet, Maguire & Cole, 2904 - 29th Ave., V1T 1V7 – 250/545-6054, Fax: 250/545-7227; Email: djsiglet@nocdc.bc.ca – *4
Steiner & Company, 3107A - 31 Ave., V1T 2G9 – 250/545-1371, Fax: 250/542-5630 – *1

**Victoria .................................. Vancouver Island**

Acheson & Co., #400, 535 Yates St., V8W 2Z6 – 250/384-6262, Fax: 250/384-5353; Toll Free: 1-800-667-4611; Email: whitley@achesonco.com; URL: http://www.achesonco.com – *4
J. Trevor Alexander, #520, 645 Fort St., V8W 1G2 – 250/360-1777, Fax: 250/360-1778 – *1
Amicus Law Centre, 207 Menzies St., V8V 2G6 – 250/383-5012, Fax: 250/385-1174; Email: amicus@islandnet.com; URL: http://www.islandnet.com/~amicus – *1
Anniko & Hunter, #201, 300 Gorge Rd. West, V9A 1M8 – 250/385-1233, Fax: 250/385-4078; Email: ankohutr@pacificcoast.net – *4
Berge, Sasges & Co., 1190A Fort St., V8V 3K8 – 250/388-9477, Fax: 250/388-9470 – *2
Brooks & Marshall, 736 Broughton St., 2nd Fl., V8W 1E1 – 250/920-0144, Fax: 250/920-0177 – *2
Cardinal, Emberton, Rusk & Carfra, 2789 Jacklin Rd., V9B 3X7 – 250/474-2274, Fax: 250/474-7227; Toll Free: 1-800-733-9633; Email: cardwest@cardlaw.com – *10
R.W. Chard, #421, 645 Fort St., V8W 1G2 – 250/384-9932, Fax: 250/384-9932 – *1
D.H. Christie, 810 Courtney St., V8W 1C4 – 250/385-1022 – *1
Clapp & Company, 1005 Cook St., V8V 3Z6 – 250/388-5266, Fax: 250/388-5663 – *2
Robert C. Claus, 1161 Fort St., V8V 3K9 – 250/361-9600, Fax: 250/361-9181 – *1
Clay & Company, 837 Burdett Ave., PO Box 961, V8W 2S4 – 250/386-2261, Fax: 250/389-1336 – *6
Considine & Lawler, International House, #700, 880 Douglas St., V8W 2B7 – 250/381-7788, Fax: 250/381-1042 – *6
Cook Roberts, 777 Fort St., 4th Fl., V8W 1G9 – 250/385-1411, Fax: 250/413-3300; Email: lawmark@cookroberts.bc.ca – *14
Robert S. Cosburn, #316, 10 Paul Kane Pl., V9A 7J8 – 250/360-1177

Cox, Taylor, Burnes House, 26 Bastion Sq., 3rd Fl., V8W 1H9 – 250/388-4457, Fax: 250/382-4236 – *11
Crease, Harman & Company, #800, 1070 Douglas St., PO Box 997, V8W 2S8 – 250/388-5421, Fax: 250/388-4294 – *14
G.J. Davies, #207, 895 Fort St., V8W 1H7 – 250/380-9978, Fax: 250/479-1512 – *1
Dinning Hunter & Company, #201, 895 Fort St., V8W 1H7 – 250/381-2151, Fax: 250/386-2123; Email: dinco@tnet.net – *8
Jeremy S.G. Donaldson, 824 Fort St., V8W 1H8 – 250/383-5759, Fax: 250/381-7129; Email: marlines@netcom.ca – *1
Frank A.V. Falzon Law Corporation, 520 Comerford St., V9A 6K8 – 250/384-3995, Fax: 250/384-4924 – *1
Robert N. Friedland, #1409, 620 Toronto St., V8V 1P7 – 250/380-2681, Fax: 250/380-2681; Email: ul017@freenet.victoria.bc.ca – *1
Gifford & Company, 1608 Camosun St., V8T 3E6 – 250/385-8080, Fax: 250/385-5999; Email: giffco@bc.sympatico.ca – *3
Peter Golden, #207, 2750 Quadra St., V8T 4E8 – 250/361-3131, Fax: 250/361-9161 – *1
Gordon & Velletta, #302, 852 Fort St., V8W 1H8 – 250/383-9104, Fax: 250/383-1922; Email: gordvell@pinc.com; URL: http://www.vvv.com/~gordvell – *5
Green & Claus, 1161 Fort St., V8V 3K9 – 250/361-9600, Fax: 250/361-9181 – *5
Lenore B. Harlton, #209, 703 Broughton St., V8W 1E2 – 250/382-5161, Fax: 250/383-0611 – *1
Hatter, Thompson & Shumka, #201, 919 Fort St., V8V 3K3 – 250/388-4931, Fax: 250/386-8088 – *4
Heath, Irving & Walton, 3371 Oak St., V8X 1R2 – 250/386-1336, Fax: 250/386-3363 – *3
John A. Hills, #202, 3 Fan Tan Alley, V8W 3G9 – 250/381-6171, Fax: 250/381-3460 – *1
Holmes & Isherwood, 1190 Fort St., V8V 3K8 – 250/383-7157, Fax: 250/383-1535 – *2
Jawl & Bundon, 1007 Fort St., 4th Fl., V8V 3K5 – 250/385-5787, Fax: 250/385-4364 – *6
Johns, Southward, Glazier & Walton, #202, 911 Yates St., PO Box 847, V8W 2R9 – 250/381-7321, Fax: 250/381-1181 – *5
Jones Emery, #1212, 1175 Douglas St., V8W 2E9 – 250/382-7222, Fax: 250/382-5436 – *9
Kardish Ashurst, 409 - 3960 Quadra St., V8X 4A3 – 250/479-9336, Fax: 250/479-6845 – *7
Dennis A. Latham & Associate, #210, 612 View St., V8W 1J5 – 250/388-7575, Fax: 250/388-9642; Email: dennis_latham@pacificcoast.net – *2
Lidstone, Young, Anderson, 501 - 1803 Douglas St., V8T 5C3 – 250/383-2063, Fax: 250/689-3444
Linge Carr & Associates, 520 Comerford St., V9A 6K9 – 250/388-7571, Fax: 250/388-7327
Alice Shun Yee, Lo, #401, 1011 Fort St., V8V 3K5 – 250/380-1423, Fax: 250/380-0920 – *1
S.P. MacCarthy, 1879 Forrester St., V8R 3G7 – 250/387-0483, Fax: 250/387-0527 – *1
MacIsaac & Company, #320, 560 Johnson St., PO Box 933, V8W 2R9 – 250/381-5353, Fax: 250/380-7272; Email: macvic@pinc.com – *9
MacIsaac & Company, 2227 Sooke Rd., V9B 1W8 – 250/474-1940 – *2
MacIsaac & MacIsaac, 734 Goldstream Ave., V9B 2X3 – 250/478-1131, Fax: 250/478-3106 – *4
Maguire & Company, #B, 1609 Fort St., V8R 1H8 – 250/370-0300, Fax: 250/370-0302; Email: magco@islandnet.com; URL: http://www.islandnet.com/~magco – *2
David Main, #209, 703 Broughton St., V8W 1E2 – 250/383-4541, Fax: 250/383-0611 – *1
McConnan, Bion, O'Connor & Peterson, #420, 880 Douglas St., V8W 2B7 – 250/385-1383, Fax: 250/385-2841 – *13
Shari McGlynn, #507, 11 Cooperage Place, V9A 7J9 – 250/380-0311, Fax: 250/386-0227 – *1
McKimm & Lott, 800 Fort St., V8W 1H4 – 250/389-0809, Fax: 250/386-6244

McMicken and Bennett, 303 - 1111 Blanshard St., V8W 2H7 – 250/385-9555, Fax: 250/385-9841 – *2

Robert Moore-Stewart, #616, 620 View St., V8W 1J6 – 250/380-1887, Fax: 250/380-9134; Email: rmoorest@direct.ca – *1

Mullin Demeo Dalsin, #102, 3930 Shelbourne St., V8P 5P6 – 250/477-3327, Fax: 250/477-0980 – *3

David Mulroney & Company, #2A, 1218 Langley St., V8W 1W2 – 250/389-6022, Fax: 250/389-6033; Email: mulroney@islandnet.com – *5

Wilfred E. Oppel, 1672 Hampshire Rd., V8R 5T6 – 250/598-1317, Fax: 250/598-1319 – *1

Pearlman & Lindholm, 736 Broughton St., PO Box 1327, V8W 1E1 – 250/388-4433, Fax: 250/388-5856 – *15

Clark R. Purves, 620 View St., 7th Fl., V8W 1J6 – 250/386-2225, 688-9801, Fax: 250/386-6609 – *1

Quadra Legal Centre, #101, 2750 Quadra St., V8T 4E8 – 250/380-1566, Fax: 250/380-3090 – *3

Randall & Company, #103, 1006 Fort St., V8V 3K4 – 250/382-9282, Fax: 250/382-0366 – *6

Heather Raven, 215 Begbie Bldg., Faculty of Law, University of Victoria, PO Box 2400, V8W 3H7 – 250/721-8185, Fax: 250/721-8149

R. Keith Reed, #535, 645 Fort St., V8W 1G2 – 250/383-3838, Fax: 250/385-4324 – *1

Leandre Rupert-Bailey, PO Box 36056, RPO Esquimalt, V9A 7J5 – 250/360-1665, Fax: 250/381-5661 – *1

Marlene Russo, #110, 1175 Cook St., V8V 4A1 – 250/380-0076, Fax: 250/380-0092 – *1

Sihota & Starkey, 1248 Esquimalt Rd., V9A 3N8 – 250/381-5111, Fax: 250/381-3947 – *1

Victor W. Simeoni, 4051 Ebony Place, V8N 3Z1 – 250/477-3331 – *1

Sidney B. Simons, 620 View St., 7th Fl., V8W 1J6 – 604/688-9801, 386-2225, Fax: 604/386-6609 – *1

Skillings & Company, #B, 777 Blanshard St., V8W 2G9 – 250/388-5136, Fax: 250/388-5195 – *2

Smith, Hutchison, 823 Broughton St., V8W 1E5 – 250/388-6666, Fax: 250/389-0400 – *5

Stevenson, Doell & Company, 999 Fort St., V8V 3K3 – 250/388-7881, Fax: 250/388-7324 – *5

Stevenson, Luchies & Legh, #200, 931 Fort St., V8V 3K3 – 250/381-4040, Fax: 250/388-9406 – *5

Stewart Waddell Raponi & McLean, 1002 Wharf St., V8W 1T4 – 250/385-4311, Fax: 250/385-2012 – *5

Straith & Company, #600, 1070 Douglas St., PO Box 1052, V8W 2C4 – 250/386-1434, Fax: 250/386-1421; Email: straith@bc.sympatico.ca – *5

Christine A. Stretton, #204, 947 Fort St., V8V 3K3 – 250/388-5333, Fax: 250/382-8644 – *1

E.G.L. Tomlinson, #209, 703 Broughton St., V8W 1E2 – 250/383-6432, Fax: 250/383-0611 – *1

Diane E. Tourell, #520, 645 Fort St., V8W 1G2 – 250/384-1443, Fax: 250/360-1778 – *1

Dalmar F. Tracy, #206, 1005 Cook St., V8V 3Z6 – 250/384-5331, Fax: 250/384-5206 – *1

Jill K. Turner, #405, 3258 Alder St., V8X 1P2 – 250/360-0983, Fax: 250/360-0953; Email: jkturner@pinc.coom – *1

Turnham Woodland, 1002 Wharf St., V8W 1T4 – 250/385-1122, Fax: 250/385-6522 – *5

Marlene K. Tyshynski, #110, 826 North Park St., V8W 3B4 – 250/383-6660, Fax: 250/383-1462 – *1

Peter I. Waldmann, #301, 531 Yates St., V8W 1K7 – 250/381-3113, Fax: 250/381-3122; Email: waldmann@vanisle.net – *1

Wilson Marshall, #200, 911 Yates St., V8V 4X3 – 250/385-8741, Fax: 250/385-0433; Email: wilmar@inter-trek.com – *3

Wood & McMillan, #500, 645 Fort St., V8W 1G2 – 604/384-0558, Fax: 604/380-7299 – *2

Woods Adair, #201, 4500 West Saanich Rd., V8Z 3G2 – 250/479-9367, Fax: 250/727-3356 – *2

Woodward & Company, 957 Fort St., V8V 3K3 – 250/383-2356, Fax: 250/380-6560 – *5

Wendy K. Zimmerman, 850 Blanchard St., V8W 2H2 – 250/383-8020, Fax: 250/381-1430; Email: Wendy_Zimmerman@bc.sympatico.com – *1

**West Vancouver** ........ **Vancouver**

Donald E. Brister, #216, 2438 Marine Dr., V7V 1L2 – 604/922-6158 – *1

Christopher B. Chu, #200, 100 Park Royal Shopping Ctr., V7T 1A2 – 604/925-5898, Fax: 604/925-9710 – *1

K.A. Davis, 475 Keith Rd., V7T 1L6 – 604/926-7887 – *1

Rosalind J. Foucault, 1195 Keith Rd., V7T 1M7 – 604/925-1396, Fax: 604/925-3143 – *1

Wm. Randall Fowle, #1003, 100 Park Royal South, V7T 1A2 – 604/922-6310, Fax: 604/922-6302; Email: fowle@axionet.com – *1

Daniel B. Geller, 5349 Monteverdi Place, V7W 2W8 – 604/921-5948 – *1

George Davis & Company, #1100, 100 Park Royal South, V7T 1A2 – 604/922-2151, Fax: 604/925-0457 – *1

Goluboff, Mazzei, #201, 585 - 16th St., PO Box 91700, V7V 3R8 – 604/925-1156, Fax: 604/926-7817 – *4

Gourlay Spencer Slade & Winch, #205, 1455 Bellevue Ave., V7T 1C3 – 604/922-3386, Fax: 604/925-1304 – *5

Christopher H. Hebb, #30, 2231 Folkestone Way, V7S 2Y6 – 604/922-9766 – *1

Alex Irwin Law Corp., 4750 Caulfeild Dr., 2nd Fl., V7W 1G5 – 604/925-4149, Fax: 604/925-4407; Email: airwin@irwinandwhite.com – *1

Myrle L. Lawrence, #300, 235 - 15th St., V7T 2X1 – 604/922-8881, Fax: 604/922-8808 – *1

McCrea & Company, #101, 2221 Folkestone Way, V7S 2Y6 – 604/926-4524, Fax: 604/926-0222 – *1

McLean, Saba, #405, 100 Park Royal South, V7T 1A2 – 604/925-0672, Fax: 604/925-8984 – *2

T.E. Rafael, 475 Keith Rd., V7T 1L6 – 604/926-7887 – *1

A.M. Sweeney, #201, 1590 Bellevue Ave., V7V 1A7 – 604/922-0131, Fax: 604/922-0171 – *1

Dianne M. Tingey, #201, 585 - 16th St., PO Box 91700, V7V 3P3 – 604/925-1156, Fax: 604/926-7817 – *1

Lorne W. Topham, #21, 285 - 17 St., V7V 3S6 – 604/922-9364, Fax: 604/922-9370 – *1

Williams & Ross, 1010 Esquimalt Ave., V7T 1J8 – 604/922-9140, Fax: 604/922-9175 – *2

**Westbank** ........ **Yale**

Bassett & Company, #260, 2300 Carrington Rd., V4T 2N6 – 250/768-5152, Fax: 250/768-3003; Email: lawyers@oklawyers.com; URL: http://www.oklawyers.com – *2

Schauble & Company, #1, 2429 Dobbin Rd., V4T 2L4 – 250/768-1192, Fax: 250/768-1196

**Whistler** ........ **Vancouver**

R.P. Gibbons, PO Box 508, V0N 1B0 – 604/932-2958, Fax: 604/932-2658 – *1

Race & Company, #332, 4370 Lorimer Rd., V0N 1B4 – 604/932-3211; 682-3117(Vancouver), Fax: 604/932-2515 – *6

Ian D. Reith, #14, 4227 Village Stroll, V0N 1B4 – 604/932-6501, Fax: 604/932-5615 – *1

**White Rock** ........ **Westminster**

Cleveland & Doan, 15178 Buena Vista Ave., V4B 1Y3 – 604/536-5002, Fax: 604/536-7002; Email: clevdoan@direct.ca; URL: http://www.meridian-com.com/clevdoan – *3

Kruse, Adams, #305, 1656 Martin Dr., V4A 6E7 – 604/531-5501, Fax: 604/531-6256 – *2

A.D. McRae, #309, 1656 Martin Dr., V6Z 2A9 – 604/538-1511 – *1

Medland & Company, 14582 - 18th Ave., V4A 5V5 – 604/230-8476, Fax: 604/835-4145 – *1

**Williams Lake** ........ **Cariboo**

Michael M. Barbour, #B, 315 Yorston St., V2G 1H1 – 250/398-7045, Fax: 250/398-7710 – *1

Czepil & Co., #201, 220 Oliver St., V2G 1M1 – 250/398-7001, Fax: 250/398-5651 – *1

Oliver, Smith & Co., #106, 235 Oliver St., V1G 1M2 – 250/392-2395, Fax: 250/398-7423 – *2

Thomas A. Rhodes, Q.C., PO Box 4734, V2G 2V7 – 250/392-6856 – *1

Vanderburgh, Scott, Halpin & O'Brian, #5, 123 Borland St., V2G 1R1 – 250/392-7161, Fax: 250/392-7060 – *2

**Winlaw** ........ **Nelson**

Kenyon McGee, PO Box 11, V0G 2J0 – 250/226-7615, Fax: 250/226-7818 – *1

## MANITOBA

**Arborg** ........ **Winnipeg**

Frank Lawrence, General Delivery, R0C 0A0 – 204/376-2333 – *1

**Ashern** ........ **Winnipeg**

D.E., Geisler, PO Box 200, R0C 0E0 – 204/768-2848 – *1

**Birtle** ........ **Russell**

Woody Langford, PO Box 131, R0M 0C0 – 204/842-3930, Fax: 204/842-5159; Email: langford@mts.net – *1

Sims & Company, PO Box 190, R0M 0C0 – 204/842-3355, Fax: 204/842-3446

**Boissevain** ........ **Brandon**

J.A.H. George Law Office, 579 Cook St. South, R0K 0E0 – 204/534-2431, Fax: 204/534-2444 – *2

Michael Waldron, PO Box 235, R0K 0E0 – 204/534-6266, Fax: 204/534-2388 – *1

**Brandon** ........ **Brandon**

Clement, Pearson & Williams, 232 - 10th St.., R7A 4E8 – 204/725-5100, Fax: 204/728-4343 – *2

Terri E. Deller Law Office, 801 Princess Ave., R7A 0P5 – 204/726-0128 – *1

Donald Legal Services, #6, 940 Princess Ave., R7A 0P6 – 204/729-4900, Fax: 204/728-4477; Email: donaldl@docker.com – *2

Hunt, Miller & Combs, 148 - 8 St., R7A 3X1 – 204/727-8491, Fax: 204/727-4350 – *7

G. Fay Lowes, 2044 Currie Blvd., R7A 5Y1 – 204/728-0412, Fax: 204/727-4906 – *1

Meighen, Haddad & Company, 110 - 11 St., R7A 4T4 – 204/727-8461, Fax: 204/726-1948 – *13

Paterson Ross, #1, 1040 Princess Ave., R7A 0P8 – 204/727-2424, Fax: 204/728-4670; Email: 2paterson@techplus.com – *4

Roy Johnston & Company, 363 - 10 St., R7A 5Z7 – 204/727-0761, Fax: 204/726-1339 – *8

Smith Legal, 108 - 18th St., R7A 5A4 – 204/725-1502, Fax: 204/727-8686 – *2

**Carman** ........ **Morden**

Lee & Lee, 5 Centre Ave. West, R0G 0J0 – 204/745-6751, Fax: 204/745-3481 – *2

McKenzie, Mooney & Brown, 71 Main St., R0G 0J0 – 204/745-2028, Fax: 204/745-3513 – *4

**Crystal City** ........ **Morden**

Treble & Company, PO Box 10, R0K 0N0 – 204/873-2427, Fax: 204/873-2656 – *1

**Dauphin** ........ **Dauphin**

Dawson Law Office, 34 - 1 Ave. NW, R7N 1G7 – 204/638-4101, Fax: 204/638-8541 – *1

Johnston & Company, 18 - 3rd Ave. NW, PO Box 551, R7N 2V4 – 204/638-3211, Fax: 204/638-9646 – *4
Parkland Community Law Centre, 19 Memorial Blvd., R7N 2A5 – 204/622-7000, Fax: 204/622-7029; Toll Free: 1-800-810-6977 – *3

**Dugald** .......... **Winnipeg**
A.H. Mackling, Q.C., RR#1, R0E 0K0 – *1

**Elie** .......... **Portage La Prairie**
Miller Miller Pressey, PO Box 36, R0H 0H0 – 204/353-2317

**Fisher Branch** .......... **Winnipeg**
Nathan Golas, PO Box 305, R0C 0Z0 – 204/372-6552, Fax: 204/372-8479 – *1

**Flin Flon** .......... **Flin Flon**
J. Michael D. Bomek, 41 Main St., R8A 1J7 – 204/687-8000, Fax: 204/687-8400 – *1
Ginnell, Bauman & Associates, 47 Main St., PO Box 697, R8A 1N5 – 204/687-3431, 8208, Fax: 204/687-5219, 8051 – *4
McDonald Law Office, #201, 35 Main St., PO Box 880, R8A 1N7 – 204/687-4000, Fax: 204/687-4100 – *1

**Gimli** .......... **Winnipeg**
Tupper & Adams, Lighthouse Mall, R0C 0B0 – 204/642-8192

**Hamiota** .......... **Minnedosa**
McNeill, Poole & Company, PO Box 41, R0M 0T0 – 204/764-2885, Fax: 204/264-2063 – *3

**Headingley** .......... **Winnipeg**
Patricia Grace Ritchie, Q.C., #2, 126 Bridge Rd., PO Box 142, R0H 0J0 – 204/889-1142, Fax: 204/832-5090 – *1

**Holmfield** .......... **Killarney**
Harrison & Harrison, PO Box 26, R0K 1A0 – 204/523-7357 – *1

**Killarney** .......... **Killarney**
Heming & Arraf, 541 Broadway Ave., PO Box 1300, R0K 1G0 – 204/523-4671, Fax: 204/523-8885 – *2
Roy Johnston & Company, PO Box 99, R0K 1G0 – 204/523-4464, Fax: 204/523-5676 – *1

**Lac Du Bonnet** .......... **Beausejour**
W.D. Besel, Hwy. 313, PO Box 566, R0E 1A0 – 204/345-8145 – *1

**Manitou** .......... **Morden**
Selby & Jones, PO Box 279, R0G 1G0 – 204/242-2801, Fax: 204/242-2723 – *2

**Minnedosa** .......... **Minnedosa**
St. John & St. John, PO Box 428, R0J 1E0 – 204/867-2231 – *1
Sims & Company, 76 Main St. South, PO Box 460, R0J 1E0 – 204/867-2717, Fax: 204/867-2434; Email: ajackson@mail.techplus.com – *4

**Morden** .......... **Morden**
Hoeschen & Stewart, 326 Stephen St., PO Box 70, R0G 1J0 – 204/822-4463 – *2
Wiens Gilmour & Co., 278 Stephen St., PO Box 20, R0G 1J0 – 204/822-5466, Fax: 204/822-6984 – *2

**Neepawa** .......... **Minnedosa**
Paterson Ross, 390 Mountain Ave., PO Box 310, R0J 1H0 – 204/476-3311, Fax: 204/476-5430; Email: patersonross@techplus.com – *4
A.J. Platt Lawyer, 244 Hamilton St., R0J 1H0 – 204/476-5053, Fax: 204/476-3789; Email: aplatt@mail.techplus.com

Taylor Law Office, PO Box 309, R0J 1H0 – 204/476-2336, Fax: 204/476-5783 – *1

**Portage La Prairie** .......... **Portage La Prairie**
Greenberg & Greenberg, 231 Saskatchewan Ave. East, PO Box 157, R1N 3B2 – 204/857-6878, Fax: 204/857-3011 – *4
Miller Pressey Selinger, 103 Saskatchewan Ave. East, PO Box 368, R1N 3B7 – 204/857-3436, Fax: 204/857-9238 – *2

**Rivers** .......... **Brandon**
Cram & Juce, 505 - 2 Ave., R0K 1X0 – 204/328-7563

**Roblin** .......... **Dauphin**
Marcel J.J.R. Gregoire, 204 Main St., PO Box 780, R0L 1P0 – 204/937-2117 – *1

**Russell** .......... **Russell**
M.D. Butcher & Associates, 227 Main St. North, PO Box 70, R0J 1W0 – 204/773-2172, Fax: 204/773-3950; Email: mbutcher@mb.sympatico.ca

**St. Boniface** .......... **St. Boniface**
Teffaine Labossière, #201, 185, boul Provencher, CP 36, R2H 3B4 – 204/233-4359, Fax: 204/233-5770 – *3

**Selkirk** .......... **Selkirk**
David L. Moore & Assoc., 407 Main St., R1A 1T9 – 204/482-3921, Fax: 204/482-5564 – *2
Szewczyk Wasel, 244 Manitoba Ave., PO Box 336, R1A 2B3 – 204/482-7425, Fax: 204/482-7409 – *2

**Shoal Lake** .......... **Minnedosa**
Sims & Company, #1, 515 - 4th Ave., PO Box 430, R0J 1Z0 – 204/759-2733, Fax: 204/759-2411

**Snow Lake** .......... **The Pas**
J. Michael D. Bomek, 101 Elm St., R0B 1M0 – 204/358-2039, Fax: 204/687-8400

**Souris** .......... **Brandon**
Forrest & Forrest, 4 Crescent Ave., PO Box 276, R0K 2C0 – 204/483-2171, Fax: 204/483-3389 – *2
M.J. Murray, PO Box 276, R0K 2C0 – 204/483-2171, Fax: 204/483-3389 – *1

**Steinbach** .......... **Winnipeg**
Ruth McNeill, PO Box 21330, RPO Town Square, R0A 2T3 – 204/326-1826, Fax: 204/326-6424 – *1
Plett Goossen & Associates, 336 Main St., PO Box 1960, R0A 2A0 – 204/326-6454, Fax: 204/326-6917 – *5
Smith, Neufeld, Jodoin, PO Box 1267, R0A 2A0 – 204/326-3442, Fax: 204/326-2154; Email: snjlaw@mts.net – *7

**Swan River** .......... **Swan River**
Burnside & Company, 509 Main St. East, PO Box 340, R0L 1Z0 – 204/734-3485, Fax: 204/734-2872 – *3

**The Pas** .......... **The Pas**
D.R. Knight & Associates, 237 Fischer St., PO Box 1769, R9A 0K3 – 204/623-5432, Fax: 204/623-2258 – *3

**Thompson** .......... **Thompson**
Morrison, McDonald, Thompson, #309, 83 Churchill Dr., R8N 0L6 – 204/677-2366, Fax: 204/677-3249 – *4

**Virden** .......... **Virden**
McNeill Poole, Buckingham Bldg., 243 Raglan St. West, PO Box 520, R0M 2C0 – 204/748-1220, Fax: 204/748-3007 – *3

**Winkler** .......... **Morden**
Hoeschen & Stewart, 583 Main St., R6W 4A2 – 204/325-4233, Fax: 204/822-6416

Wiens Gilmour & Co., 564 Mountain Ave., PO Box 1150, R6W 4B2 – 204/325-8807, Fax: 204/325-8352 – *3

**Winnipeg** .......... **Eastern**
Abrams & Tweed, #2, 549 Regent Ave. West, R2C 1R9 – 204/949-3080, Fax: 204/949-3089 – *3
Ram Kishore Agrawal, #207, 83 Sherbrook St., PO Box 218, R3C 2B2 – 204/779-7265, Fax: 204/779-6334 – *1
Aikins, MacAulay & Thorvaldson, Commodity Exchange Tower, 360 Main St., 30th Fl., R3C 4G1 – 204/957-0050, Fax: 204/957-0840; Email: amt@aikins.com; URL: http://www.aikins.com – *78
Stephen D. Alsip, 137 Scott St., R3L 0K9 – 204/475-9420, Fax: 204/453-8522 – *1
F.R. Avanthay, #25, 185, boul Provencher, R2H 0G4 – 204/233-5029 – *1
Baker & Company, Winnipeg Sq., Box: 300, #300, 360 Main St., R3C 3Z3 – 204/957-1700, Fax: 204/942-2325; 947-5995 – *5
Allan P. Baker, #603, 294 Portage Ave., R3C 0B9 – 204/947-0057 – *1
Barber Law Office, 3651 Roblin Blvd., R3R 0E2 – 204/949-3240, Fax: 204/949-3249; Email: jbarber@mb.sympatico.ca – *1
Bernstein & Hirsch, #508, 283 Portage Ave., R3B 2B5 – 204/942-0706, Fax: 204/957-1345 – *2
Booth, Dennehy, Ernst & Kelsch, 387 Broadway Ave., R3C 0V5 – 204/957-1717, Fax: 204/943-6199 – *11
D.E. Bowman, Q.C., 241 Harvard Ave.., R3M 0K1 – 204/477-0484 – *1
Marshall Braunstein, #600, 294 Portage Ave., R3C 0B9 – 204/942-2961 – *1
Shannon M. Breckman, #2710, 83 Garry St., R3C 4J9 – 204/987-2800, Fax: 204/987-2808 – *1
Bradley J. Brooks, 360 Main St., PO Box 27009, R3C 4T3 – 204/992-4700, Fax: 204/992-2462; Toll Free: 1-888-259-4700; Email: bbrooks@mb.sympatico.ca – *1
Brotman & Cramer, #100H, 1485 Portage Ave., R3G 0W4 – 204/942-3168 – *1
Buchwald Asper Gallagher Henteleff, Commodity Exchange Tower, #2500, 360 Main St., R3C 4H6 – 204/956-0560, Fax: 204/957-0227; Email: bagh@escape.ca – *41
Bueti, Baumstark, Kunzman, #206, 897 Corydon Ave., R3M 0W7 – 204/475-3570, Fax: 204/453-0136 – *3
Campbell Marr, 10 Donald St., R3C 1L5 – 204/942-3311, Fax: 204/943-7997 – *10
Champagne Law Office, #217, 375 York Ave., R3C 3J3 – 204/956-1199, Fax: 204/956-5333 – *1
Chapman Goddard Kagan, 1864 Portage Ave., R3J 0H2 – 204/888-7973, Fax: 204/832-3461; Email: 1-800-665-6119 – *8
L. Cholakis, #300, 275 Portage Ave., R3B 2B3 – 204/947-0531, Fax: 204/942-3631 – *1
S. Cohan, #508, 386 Broadway, R3C 3R6 – 204/944-1413, Fax: 204/943-9563 – *1
D'Arcy & Deacon, Royal Trust Bldg., 330 St. Mary Ave., 12th Fl., R3C 4E1 – 204/942-2271, Fax: 204/943-4242; Email: darcy@ilos.net – *29
Deniset & Boily, #200, 202 Provencher Blvd., R2H 0G3 – 204/987-3882, Fax: 204/233-9762 – *3
Derksen & Co., #200, 1135 Henderson Hwy., R2G 1L4 – 204/339-1671, Fax: 204/339-5078 – *2
Dowhan & Dowhan, #1810, 330 Portage Ave., R3C 0C4 – 204/942-4235, Fax: 204/956-4560 – *3
Doyle Riley, #206, 100 Osborne St., R3L 1Y5 – 204/475-4040, Fax: 204/475-8724 – *2
S.J. Drache, Q.C., Bancolare House, 128 Montrose St., R3M 3M6 – 204/488-0665, Fax: 204/956-5262
Duboff Edwards Haight & Schachter, 175 Carlton St., 2nd Fl., R3C 3H9 – 204/942-3361, Fax: 204/943-4498 – *6
Edmond & Associates, #204, 1120 Grant Ave., R3M 2A6 – 204/452-5314, Fax: 204/452-5989 – *6
Neil Enns, #605, 386 Broadway, R3C 3R6 – 204/956-2428, Fax: 204/947-1013 – *1

* indicates number of lawyers in law firm.

Fillmore & Riley, Winnipeg Sq., #1700, 360 Main St., R3C 3Z3 – 204/957-8321, Fax: 204/957-0516 – *4

Flatt Law Office, 242 Dunkirk Dr., R2M 3W9 – 204/253-2253 – *1

Glowacki & Libitka, Lindsay Bldg., #1001, 228 Notre Dame Ave., R3B 1N7 – 204/942-3385, Fax: 204/943-6354 – *2

Stanley Goldberg, #1212, 363 Broadway Ave., R3C 3N9 – 306/942-4160, Fax: 306/942-4301 – *1

Gould Goszer, 175 Carlton St., 2nd Fl., R3C 3H9 – 204/943-0571, Fax: 204/943-4498 – *3

Ronald M. Habing & Associates, 2643 Portage Ave., R3J 0P9 – 204/832-8322, Fax: 204/832-3906 – *2

M.L. Halkewycz, #204, 952 Main St., R2W 3P4 – 204/589-6301, Fax: 204/589-2743 – *1

A.D. Hoffer, #700, 444 St. Mary Ave., R3C 3T1 – 204/947-6801, Fax: 204/947-6800 – *1

A.A. Hoffman, #1212, 363 Broadway Ave., R3C 3N9 – *1

Hogue, Kushnier, 194 Provencher Blvd., R2H 0G3 – 204/237-1231, Fax: 204/233-2689 – *2

Hook & Smith, #201, 3111 Portage Ave., R3K 0W4 – 204/885-4520, Fax: 204/837-9846 – *3

H.A. Huppe, Q.C., 51 St. Anne's Rd., R2M 2Y4 – 204/237-1647 – *1

Inkster, Christie, Hughes, Mackay, #700, 444 St. Mary Ave., R3C 3T1 – 204/947-6801, Fax: 204/947-6800 – *14

Kaufman Cassidy, #508, 386 Main St., R3C 3Z3 – 204/943-7454, Fax: 204/943-9563 – *9

J. Scott Kennedy & Associates, #303, 175 Hargrave St., R3C 3R8 – 204/949-0298, Fax: 204/942-0336 – *2

W.D. Koshowski, #101, 1311 Portage Ave., R3G 0V3 – 204/942-7764 – *1

F. Lawrence, #202, 1382 Henderson Hwy., R2G 1M8 – 204/338-9705 – *1

Victoria E. Lehman Law Offices, 412 Wardlaw Ave., R3L 0L7 – 204/453-6416, Fax: 204/477-1379 – *1

Loewen, Martens & Rempel, 1101 Henderson Hwy., R2G 1L4 – 204/338-9364, Fax: 204/338-8379 – *4

Lofchick, Jones & Associates, 22 Edmonton St.., R3C 1P7 – 204/925-0400, Fax: 204/944-9506 – *7

Allan Ludkiewicz, #204, 150 Henry Ave., PO Box 7000, R3C 4E9 – 204/946-3341, Fax: 204/946-3305 – *1

MacInnes, Burbidge, #500, 177 Lombard Ave., R3B 0W5 – 204/942-5256, Fax: 204/942-5259 – *2

Martens & Associates, 137 Scott St., R3L 0K9 – 204/475-9420, Fax: 204/453-8522 – *1

David Matas, 205 Edmonton St., 2nd Fl., R3C 1R4 – 204/944-1831 – *1

McCreedy, Knight & Associates, 931 Nairn Ave., R2L 0X9 – 204/668-7320, Fax: 204/667-5104 – *3

McJannet Rich, Newport Centre, #1420, 330 Portage Ave., R3C 0C4 – 204/985-8100, Fax: 204/956-0098 – *4

John P. McKinnon, 41 Cambridge St., R3M 3E6 – 204/488-0399 – *1

McRoberts Law Offices, #66K, 1485 Portage Ave., R3G 0W4 – 204/944-7907, Fax: 204/772-1684; Email: mclaw@mb.sympatico.ca – *11

D. Neil McTavish, 1002 Pembina Hwy., R3T 1Z5 – 204/284-3221 – *1

Michaels & Stern, #800, 310 Broadway Ave., R3C 0S6 – 204/989-5500, Fax: 204/947-5845 – *2

James A. Muller, 179 Spence St. NW, 2nd Fl., R3C 1Y5 – *1

Mutchmor, Violago, Overall, Grimes, 390 York Ave., R3C 3S9 – 204/989-1300, Fax: 204/989-1301 – *4

Myers Weinberg Kussin Weinstein Bryk, Cargill Bldg., #724, 240 Graham Ave., R3C 0J7 – 204/942-0501, Fax: 204/956-0625 – *18

R.L. Olesky, #200, 62 Hargrave St., R3C 1N1 – 204/956-0903, Fax: 204/956-4200 – *1

Oliver, Derksen, Arkin, #800, 310 Broadway, R3C 0S6 – 204/947-2007 – *4

Parashin Law Office, 404 McGregor St., R2W 4X5 – 204/582-3558 – *1

Parker, Sarbit, 175 Carlton St., 2nd Fl., R3C 3H9 – 204/944-9682, Fax: 204/943-4498 – *3

Perlov Stewart Lincoln, #1400, One Lombard Place, R3B 3G5 – 204/944-9295, Fax: 204/956-4270 – *7

Pitblado & Hoskin, Commodity Exchange Tower, #1900, 360 Main St., R3C 3Z3 – 204/942-0391, Fax: 204/957-1790; Email: lawyers@pitblado.mb.ca; URL: http://www.mts.net/~lawyers/index.html – *47

A.P. Pittarelli, #803, 213 Notre Dame Ave., R3B 1N3 – 204/942-8886 – *1

Porcher Law Office, #204, 180 Main St., R3C 1A6 – 204/944-0050, Fax: 204/947-5250 – *2

Pullan Guld Kammerloch, #600, 330 Portage Ave., R3C 0C4 – 204/956-0490, Fax: 204/947-3747 – *5

Edward Rice, 70 Arthur St., R3B 1G7 – 204/944-1905, Fax: 204/943-1789 – *1

Robertson & Bond, #807, 294 Portage Ave., R3C 0B9 – 204/943-8439 – *1

James F.C. Rose, 582 Bruce Ave., R3J 0W5 – 204/889-3885, Fax: 204/889-3885; URL: http://www.members.aol.com/rosecruise/wills.htm – *1

Sheldon Rosenstock, 848 Waterloo St., R3N 0T6 – 204/488-4121, Fax: 204/488-1869 – *1

Ross & Associates, 641 St. Mary's Rd., R2M 3M2 – 204/257-0675, Fax: 204/254-7074 – *2

Rutledge & Dyker, #310, 3025 Portage Ave., R3K 2E2 – 204/987-7575, Fax: 204/837-3638 – *2

Savino & Company, 340 Assiniboine Ave., R3C 0Y1 – 204/942-5131, Fax: 204/942-3030; Email: savino@escape.ca – *5

Schulman & Schulman, #808, 444 St. Mary Ave., R3C 3T1 – 204/943-5428, Fax: 204/944-8019 – *1

M.H. Schwartzwald, #912, 363 Broadway Ave., R3C 3N9 – 204/943-2477, Fax: 204/943-2573 – *1

Slusky & Slusky, #1212, 363 Broadway, R3C 3N9 – 204/943-5455, Fax: 204/942-4301 – *2

Remi Smith, #302, 131 Provencher Blvd., R2H 0G2 – 204/958-6851, Fax: 204/958-6855 – *1

Alice Steinbart, #400, 55 Donald St., R3C 1L8 – 204/947-1475 – *1

Swystun Karsevich Windsor, #102, 5 Donald St. South, R3L 2T4 – 204/477-0285, Fax: 204/453-8876 – *6

Tacium, Vincent, Orlikow, 246A St. Anne's Rd., R2M 3A4 – 204/989-4220, Fax: 204/254-7744 – *4

Taylor McCaffrey, 400 St. Mary Ave., 9th Fl., R3C 4K5 – 204/949-1312, Fax: 204/957-0945; Email: taylorm@mbnet.mb.ca – *51

Léo V. Teillet, #302, 131 Provencher Blvd., R2H 0G2 – 204/958-6850, Fax: 204/958-6855 – *1

Thompson Dorfman Sweatman, Toronto-Dominion Centre, #2200, 201 Portage Ave., R3B 3L3 – 204/957-1930, Fax: 204/943-6445; Email: tds@tds.mb.ca – *75

Wolfgang J. Tiegs, 391 McLeod Ave., R2K 0B1 – 204/334-8186, Fax: 204/334-4351 – *1

Michael T. Tracey, 137 Scott St., R3L 0K9 – 204/477-1040, Fax: 204/453-8522 – *1

Tupper & Adams, 200 Portage Ave., 4th Fl., R3C 3X2 – 204/942-0161, Fax: 204/943-2385; Email: fielderj@cycor.ca – *18

W.R. Van Walleghem, #206, 1120 Grant Ave., R3M 2A6 – 204/477-0210, Fax: 204/452-9746 – *2

Walsh, Micay & Company, Richardson Bldg., One Lombard Pl., 10th Fl., R3B 3H1 – 204/942-0081, Fax: 204/957-1261 – *27

E. Waskiw, 441 Perth Ave., R2V 0T9 – 204/334-7372 – *1

Wilder Wilder & Langtry, Richardson Bldg., #1500, 1 Lombard Place, R3B 0X3 – 204/947-1456, Fax: 204/957-1368; Email: wilder@mb.sympatico.ca; URL: http://www.wilderwilder.com – *14

Wolch, Pinx, Tapper, Scurfield, #1000, 330 St. Mary Ave., R3C 3Z5 – 204/949-1700, Fax: 204/947-2593; Email: wolchpts@mts.net – *31

Wolchock & Company, #804, 310 Broadway, R3C 0S6 – 204/925-3500, Fax: 204/925-3509 – *3

Roy A. Yerex, #500, 125 Garry St., R3C 3P2 – 204/947-0438; 947-0455, Fax: 204/943-3247 – *1

Kenneth B. Young, #590, 125 Garry St., R3C 3P2 – 204/944-0133, Fax: 204/943-7094

Zaifman Associates, 191 Lombard Ave., 5th Fl., R3B 0X1 – 204/944-8888, Fax: 204/956-2909; Email: zaifman@escape.ca – *2

Saheel Zaman Law Office, #303, 379 Broadway, R3C 0T9 – 204/943-9922, Fax: 204/943-9517 – *1

Zimmerman & Zimmerman, #101, 207 Donald St., R3C 1M5 – 204/942-6329, Fax: 204/944-8383

Daria Zyla, 1230 Hector Bay West, R3M 3R9 – 204/452-5626 – *1

## NEW BRUNSWICK

**Atholville .................................... Campbellton**

Roger G. Gauvin, 65 Fairview St., E9N 4N3 – 506/753-4545, Fax: 506/753-2006 – *1

**Bathurst .................................... Bathurst**

Chiasson & Roy, PO Box 20010, RPO Plaza, 1212 St. Peter Ave., E2A 4V7 – 506/548-3375, Fax: 506/548-4264 – *2

John Douglas Hazen, 240 King Ave., PO Box 690, E2A 3Z6 – 506/546-9988, Fax: 506/546-3344 – *1

Eliott Y. Levasseur, 470 Murray Ave., E2A 1T5 – 506/546-4488, Fax: 506/546-7445 – *2

Robichaud, Godin, Williamson, Theriault & Johnstone, Keystone Place, 270 Douglas Ave., PO Box 747, E2A 4A5 – 506/548-8821, Fax: 506/548-5297 – *9

Jean-Guy Savoie, #2, 176 Main St., E2A 1A4 – 506/546-3654, Fax: 506/545-6032; Email: jgsavoie@nbnet.nb.ca – *1

Tremblay & Assoc., #206, 275 Main St., E2A 1A9 – 506/548-9801, Fax: 506/548-0559; Email: tremblaw@nbnet.nb.ca – *4

Peter J.C. White, #2, 176 Main St., PO Box 92, E2A 3Z1 – 506/546-9602, Fax: 506/545-6032; Email: pwhite@nbnet.nb.ca – *1

**Bear Island .................................... Fredericton**

Julie A. Abouchar, RR#2, E0H 1P0 – 506/575-1083, Fax: 506/575-1083 – *1

**Beresford .................................... Bathurst**

Eliott Y. Levasseur, 847, rue Principale, PO Box 270, E0B 1H0 – 506/542-2002, Fax: 506/542-1602 – *1

**Bouctouche .................................... Moncton**

Mark Robere, 66 Irving Blvd., PO Box 617, E0A 1G0 – 506/743-2262, Fax: 506/743-9014; Email: roberem@nbnet.nb.ca – *1

**Campbellton .................................... Restigouche**

Terrance H. Delaney, 17 O'Leary St., PO Box 490, E3N 3G9 – 506/753-7618, Fax: 506/759-7315 – *1

Dubé & Dubé, 72 Roseberry St., PO Box 126, E3N 3G1 – 506/753-7641, Fax: 506/753-5428 – *2

John D. Larlee, #703, 157 Water St., PO Box 914, E3N 3H3 – 506/753-5008, Fax: 506/759-7275 – *1

Richard J. Tingley, Q.C., #5, 78 Roseberry St., PO Box 546, E3N 3G9 – 506/753-7743

**Caraquet .................................... Acadie Bathurst**

Bernard Robichaud, 190, rue Blanchard, E1W 1A5 – 506/727-2001 – *1

**Chipman .................................... Fredericton**

Sharon R. Lockwood, 122 Northside Dr., PO Box 58, E0E 1C0 – 506/339-6632, Fax: 506/339-5130 – *1

**Dieppe .................................... Westmorland**

J.E. Michel Bastarache, 341, rue Lavoie, E1A 6P8 – 506/388-2865, Fax: 506/853-5421

**Doaktown................................ Northumberland**

R. Alex Mills, Old River Lodge, RR#2, E0C 1G0 – 506/365-2253, Fax: 506/365-7134 – *1

**Edmundston.................................. Madawaska**

Cyr Ouellette Voyer, 77, rue Rice, E3V 1S8 – 506/735-4791, Fax: 506/735-3942 – *3

Lucie A. LaVigne Q.C., 103, rue St-Francois, E3V 1E5 – 506/739-7369, Fax: 506/735-9017 – *1

McLaughlin Durette McNeil, Edifice du Centre, 176, rue Church, E3V 1K2 – 506/735-8845, Fax: 506/739-5506 – *4

Valcourt, Carrier, 1 Canada Rd., E3V 1T6 – 506/739-0110, Fax: 506/739-0109; Email: tik@atcon.com – *4

**Florenceville .................................. Woodstock**

Crocco, Hunter, Purvis, PO Drawer 240, E0J 1K0 – 506/392-6258, Fax: 506/392-8315 – *2

**Fredericton ........................................ York**

Allen Dixon Bell, #340, 77 Westmorland St., PO Box 1418, Stn A, E3B 5E3 – 506/453-0900, Fax: 506/453-0907 – *8

Ashfield, DeWitt, LeBlanc & Yerxa, 181 Brunswick St., PO Box 1150, E3B 5C2 – 506/458-9600, Fax: 506/450-0758 – *5

Athey, Gregory & Hughes, Rookwood Centre, #200, 206 Rookwood Ave., E3B 2M2 – 506/458-8060, Fax: 506/459-8288 – *4

Atkinson & Atkinson, 108 Queen St., PO Box 700, E3B 5B4 – 506/451-7777, Fax: 506/451-1029 – *5

Buchanan Bell, Frederick Sq., #340, 77 Westmorland St., PO Box 1418, Stn A, E3B 5E3 – 506/453-0900 – *5

Christie & Associates, #301, 500 Beaverbrook Ct., E3B 5X4 – 506/459-2383, Fax: 506/459-0007; Email: christie@nbnet.nb.ca – *1

Clark & Company, 81 Regent St., PO Box 1445, Stn A, E3B 5E3 – 506/457-2797, Fax: 506/451-2113; Email: clarkco@nbnet.nb.ca – *3

Richard B. Cochrane, Q.C., 98 Prospect St. West, E3B 2T8 – 506/452-2844, Fax: 506/452-8225 – *1

Guy Daigle, Services Juridiques, Ministère de la Justice, CP 6000, E3B 5H0 – 506/453-2514, Fax: 506/453-3275; Email: guyd@gov.nb.ca – *1

Mario DiCarlo, 442 Broad St., E3A 5P7 – 506/472-1505, Fax: 506/327-6080 – *1

Eddy, Young, Hoyt & Downs, Barker House, #600, 570 Queen St., PO Box 610, E3B 5A6 – 506/458-8572, Fax: 506/458-9903; Email: eddyb@nbnet.nb.ca – *9

Ronald E. Gaffney, 318 Maple St., E3A 3R4 – 506/458-8124, Fax: 506/458-2652 – *1

Hanson, Hashey, Phoenix Sq., #400, PO Box 310, E3B 4Y9 – 506/453-7771, Fax: 506/453-9600; Email: hanlaw@hansonhashey.nb.ca; URL: http://hansonhashey.nb.ca – *23

John D. Harper, PO Box 155, E3B 4Y9 – 506/458-8290, Fax: 506/450-9391 – *1

J.R. Howie, Q.C., 678 Churchill Row, E3B 1P6 – 506/458-9987 – *1

M. Mck. Hoyt, Q.C., 120 Edinburgh St., E3B 2C9 – 506/454-3136 – *1

Kenny, Jackson & Murray, 228 Brunswick St., PO Box 1572, E3B 5G2 – 506/458-1108, Fax: 506/458-2645; Email: kenny@nbnet.nb.ca – *7

Matthews Oliver Theriault, 255 Main St., E3A 1E1 – 506/458-5959, Fax: 506/460-5934; Email: matolthe@nbnet.nb.ca – *5

McElman & Associates, #210, 65 Regent St., E3B 5B4 – 506/444-8970, Fax: 506/444-8974; Email: mcelman@nbnet.nb.ca – *4

Mockler, Peters, Oley, Rouse & Williams, 839 Aberdeen St., PO Box 547, Stn A., E3B 5A6 – 506/444-6589, Fax: 506/444-6550; Email: mockler@nbnet.nb.ca – *8

J. Shawn O'Toole, 634 Queen St., E3B 1C2 – 506/458-8833, Fax: 506/458-1971 – *1

E. Joanne Oley, 6 Hermitage Ct., E3B 2P2 – 506/455-6599, Fax: 506/455-7009 – *1

Claude J. Pardons, 895 Mitchell, E3B 6E8 – 506/457-0663 – *1

Mark C. Paul-Elias, 352 George St., PO Box 1302, E3B 5C8 – 506/458-1880, Fax: 506/458-9868 – *1

Petrie, Richmond, Goss, #502, 570 Queen St., PO Box 1195, E3B 5C8 – 506/450-8720, Fax: 506/458-1036 – *5

Pink Breen Larkin, #210, 1133 Regent St., E3B 3Z2 – 506/458-1989, Fax: 506/458-1127; Email: pblnb@labour-law.com; URL: http://www.labour-law.com – *2

Ruben & Kingston, 259 Brunswick St., PO Box 1142, E3B 5C2 – 506/458-0000, Fax: 506/451-8766; Email: dflood@nbnet.nb.ca – *4

Michael A.A. Ryan, 57 Carleton St., E3B 3T2 – 506/459-7555, Fax: 506/457-4295 – *1

Smith & Irvine, #103, 212 Queen St., PO Box 487, E3B 4Z9 – 506/453-9919, Fax: 506/453-1882 – *2

Smith, Townsend, Myatt, Toronto-Dominion Tower, #430, 77 Westmorland St., PO Box 38, E3B 4Y2 – 506/452-9900, Fax: 506/452-6726 – *7

Stevenson & Stevenson, 127 George St., PO Box 245, E3B 4Y9 – 506/458-9884, Fax: 506/450-2844 – *2

Wood Melanson Filliter, 61 Carleton St., PO Box 1387, E3B 5E3 – 506/453-0950, Fax: 506/453-0905; Email: wmflegal@nbnet.nb.ca – *3

**Grand Falls.................................. Edmundston**

Duffie, Friel & Deschênes, 346 Chapel St., PO Box 747, E3Z 1C2 – 506/473-2221, Fax: 506/473-3253; Email: friel@sympatico.nb.ca – *3

Godbout, Ouellette, 698 E.H. Daigle Blvd., E3Z 1E7 – 506/473-6272, Fax: 506/473-6065 – *3

Terrance A. McCarthy, PO Box 900, E3Z 1C4 – 506/473-2750, Fax: 506/473-2759 – *1

Pichette, Toner & Murchison, 257 Broadway, PO Box 2050, E3Z 1E3 – 506/473-4776, Fax: 506/473-6493 – *4

Peter Seheult, PO Box 2440, E0J 1M0 – 506/473-2164, Fax: 506/473-5543 – *1

**Hampton ........................................ Kings**

Lutz, Longstaff & Richards, PO Box 500, E0G 1Z0 – 506/832-1500, Fax: 506/832-3848 – *5

Veniot & Company, 600 Main St., E0G 1Z0 – 506/832-3418, Fax: 506/832-3755 – *3

**Kingshurst.................................... Saint John**

John B.M. Baxter, Q.C., 143 Green Rd., E2H 1T2 – *1

**Lameque .................................... Gloucester**

R.A. Noel, 14, rue Principale, PO Box 330, E0B 1V0 – 506/344-2217, Fax: 506/344-5380; Email: ran@nbnet.nb.ca – *2

**Minto ........................................... Queens**

Mario DiCarlo, 255 Main St., E0E 1J0 – 506/327-3312, Fax: 506/327-6080; Email: mdicarlo@nbnet.nb.ca

**Miramichi.................................... Miramichi**

Maynes, Mahoney & Tremblay, 1723 Water St., PO Box 518, E1N 3A8 – 506/778-8336, Fax: 506/778-2103 – *4

**Moncton.................................... Westmorland**

Anderson, McWilliam, LeBlanc & MacDonald, 633 Main St., PO Box 20010, E1C 9M1 – 506/857-2171, Fax: 506/858-0284; Email: amlm@nbnet.nb.ca – *4

Paul J. Arsenault, #202, 814 Main St., E1C 1E6 – 506/858-8400 – *1

Robert N. Charman, 22 Brandon St., #B, E1C 7E6 – 506/854-8656, Fax: 506/854-8684 – *1

H. Reuben Cohen, Q.C., #205, 1111 Main St., E1C 1H3 – 506/857-9510, Fax: 506/858-5462 – *2

Drapeau Robichaud & McNally, 86 Botsford, PO Box 665, E1C 8M7 – 506/857-0360, Fax: 506/859-6038 – *5

Forbes Roth Basque, Heritage Ct., #201, 95 Foundry St., PO Box 480, E1C 8L9 – 506/857-4880, Fax: 506/857-0151 – *7

Fowler & Fowler, #11, 885 Main St., PO Box 721, E1C 8M9 – 506/857-8811, Fax: 506/857-9297 – *3

Gaudet Couturier Maillet Cyr, 132 Weldon St., CP 708, E1C 8M9 – 506/856-8199, Fax: 506/856-8799 – *4

John D. Hughes, 225 Lutz St., PO Box 29072, E1C 9N5 – 506/853-3333

Jones, Beardsworth & Maclean, 63 Church St., E1C 9G1 – 506/853-1131, Fax: 506/853-1139 – *2

LeBlanc Boucher Rodger & Bourque, 740 Main St., E1C 1E6 – 506/858-0110, Fax: 506/858-9497 – *6

Lise Lorrain, PO Box 25117, RPO Mountain Rd., E1C 9M9 – 506/855-6084, Fax: 506/389-3867; Email: llorrain@nbnet.nb.ca – *1

Donald MacLean, PO Box 191, E1C 8K9 – 506/858-9990 – *1

MacPherson Mitchell, 115 Queen St., E1C 1K6 – 506/853-1105, Fax: 506/853-9348 – *3

Gregg McAllister & Assoc., 155 Cornhill St., E1C 6L3 – 506/853-3040, Fax: 506/859-9588 – *2

McGrath Tuck Sutherland, 15 Alma St., PO Box 831, E1C 8N6 – 506/857-0838, Fax: 506/857-9965 – *4

McInnes Cooper & Robertson, Moncton Place, 655 Main St., E1C 8T6 – 506/857-8970, Fax: 506/857-4095; Email: eric.ledrew@mcrlaw.com; URL: http://fox.nstn.ca/~mcrhfx – *3

Murphy Collette Murphy, PO Box 869, E1C 8N6 – 506/856-8560, Fax: 506/856-8579; Email: murco@nbnet.nb.ca; URL: http://www.discribe.ca/marco – *7

Murphy, Murphy & Mollins, 89 Church St., E1C 4Z4 – 506/855-2120, Fax: 506/857-9129 – *3

Patterson Palmer Hunt Murphy, Blue Cross Centre, PO Box 20100, E1C 9M1 – 506/856-9800, Fax: 506/856-8150; Email: pphmmnnb@nbnet.nb.ca – *7

Roy, Yeoman, Savoie, LeBlanc, 86 Church St., E1C 4Z5 – 506/858-9000, Fax: 506/859-0829 – *5

Samuelsen Rideout & Doucet, Blue Cross Postal Outlet, 644 Main St., PO Box 20111, E1C 9M1 – 506/858-9830, Fax: 506/857-0917

Alan D. Schelew, #100, 803 Main St., PO Box 182, E1C 8K9 – 506/857-2272, Fax: 506/857-2276; Email: stottsu@nbnet.nb.ca – *1

Scobie & Marriner, 190 Cameron St., E1C 5Z2 – 506/857-2056, Fax: 506/857-1711 – *2

Stewart & Cooper, 325 Baig Blvd., PO Box 889, E1C 8N8 – 506/857-2110, Fax: 506/858-8402 – *7

Stewart McKelvey Stirling Scales, Blue Cross Centre, #601, 644 Main St., PO Box 20070, E1C 9M1 – 506/853-1970, Fax: 506/858-8454; Email: smss@email.smss.com – *7

Tedford Delehanty Rinzler, #201, 272 George St., PO Box 1083, E1C 8P6 – 506/858-1800, Fax: 506/857-0085; Email: tedford@nb.sympatico.ca – *3

Joseph E. Weir, #205, 111 Main St., E1C 1H3 – 506/857-9510, 857-2162, Fax: 506/858-5462, 857-0450 – *1

**Nasonworth........................................ York**

Karen E. Williamson, 1578 Route 101 Hwy., E3C 2C9 – 506/455-0253, Fax: 506/455-2202 – *1

**Oromocto....................................... Sunbury**

Roach & Morris, #24, 101 Hersey St., PO Box 232, E2V 2G5 – 506/357-3385, Fax: 506/357-5868 – *2

**Perth-Andover................................ Woodstock**

Johnson & Hyslop, PO Box 698, E0J 1V0 – 506/273-6818, Fax: 506/273-6590 – *2

**Petit-Rocher ................................ Gloucester**

Robert M. Boudreau & Assoc., CP 520, E0B 2E0 – 506/783-4246, Fax: 506/783-2354 – *2

* indicates number of lawyers in law firm.

**Petitcodiac** .................................... **Westmorland**

Jones, Beardsworth & Maclean, 2 Kay St., E0A 2H0 – 506/756-3374

**Richibucto** .................................... **Kent**

Michaud, LeBlanc & Co., 103 Main St., PO Box 28, E0A 2M0 – 506/523-4442, Fax: 506/523-4819 – *4

David Plourde & Associates, Rte. 134, Grande-Aldouane, PO Box 490, E0A 2M0 – 506/876-2881, Fax: 506/876-2653; Email: plourded@nbnet.nb.ca – *1

**Riverview** .................................... **Albert**

Wilbur Grew, 706B Coverdale Rd., E1B 3L1 – 506/387-7715, Fax: 506/387-5875 – *4

**Sackville** .................................... **Westmorland**

Meldrum & Meldrum, 7 Bridge St., PO Box 1720, E0A 3C0 – 506/536-3870, Fax: 506/536-2131; Email: meldrumk@nbnet.nb.ca – *3

Ove B. Samuelsen, PO Box 90, E0A 3C0 – 506/536-0511, Fax: 506/536-1169; Email: ovesam@nbnet.nb.ca – *1

**St. Andrews** .................................... **Saint John**

Bartlett & Smart, 159 Water St., E0G 2X0 – 506/529-4000, Fax: 506/529-4777; Email: barsmart@nbnet.nb.ca – *2

Nicholson, Turner, Walker & White, 177 Water St., PO Box 569, E0G 2X0 – 506/529-8831, Fax: 506/529-3066 – *4

**St. George** .................................... **Charlotte**

D'Arcy Leycester, Q.C., Main St., PO Box 367, E0G 2Y0 – 506/755-2810

**Saint John** .................................... **Saint John**

Barry & O'Neil, Royal Bank Bldg., 85 Charlotte St., PO Box 6010, Stn A, E2L 4R5 – 506/633-4226, Fax: 506/633-4206 – *21

Clark, Drummie & Company, 40 Wellington Row, PO Box 6850, Stn A, E2L 4S3 – 506/633-3800, Fax: 506/633-3811; Email: cd@nbnet.nb.ca – *20

Harry G. Colwell, #302, 102 Prince William St., PO Box 7027, Stn A, E2L 4G4 – 506/634-7035, Fax: 506/634-6194 – *1

Allen G. Doyle Law Office, #311, 75 Prince William St., E2L 2B2 – 506/633-4198, Fax: 506/633-0399 – *1

Bruce A. Drost, 300 Union St., 12th Fl., PO Box 5777, E2L 4M3 – 506/632-5110, Fax: 506/658-0517; Email: drost.brucea@jdirving.com – *1

Patricia Gallagher-Jette, 9 Kildare Court, E2H 1C3 – 506/849-2732 – *1

Gilbert, McGloan, Gillis, Mercantile Centre, 55 Union St., PO Box 7174, E2L 4S6 – 506/634-3600, Fax: 506/634-3612; Toll Free: 1-888-246-4529; Email: gmg@nb.sympatico.co – *17

Gorman Nason Ljungstrom, 121 Germain St., PO Box 7286, Stn A, E2L 4S6 – 506/634-8600, Fax: 506/634-8685 – *11

Hanson, Hashey, #1212, 1 Brunswick Sq., E2L 4V1 – 506/652-7771, Fax: 506/632-9600

John M. Henderson, Bank of Canada Bldg., #417, 75 Prince William St., E2L 2B2 – 506/635-5471, Fax: 506/634-1795 – *1

Mary Ann G. Holland, 120 Prince William St., PO Box 7041, Stn Brunswick, E2L 4S4 – 506/652-3774, Fax: 506/847-1564 – *1

Jeffries & Associates, 117 Union St., E2L 1A5 – 506/634-6009, Fax: 506/634-6018; Email: jeffco@nbnet.nb.ca – *2

M.L. McCluskey, 56 Canterbury St., E2L 2C5 – 506/634-0400 – *1

Elizabeth T. McLeod, #5C, 28 King St., PO Box 20045, E2L 5B2 – 506/632-4048, Fax: 506/652-6594 – *1

Mosher Chedore, 57 King St., E2L 1G5 – 506/634-1600, Fax: 506/634-0740 – *7

Northrup Bamford, #311, 75 Prince William St., E2L 2B2 – 506/634-8130, Fax: 506/633-0389; Email: northra@netcity.ca – *2

Riley, John G., Bank of Canada Bldg., #417, 75 Prince William St., E2L 2B2 – 506/634-1188, Fax: 506/634-1795 – *1

Ritchie, Cannell, #200, 120 Prince William St., PO Box 7143, Stn A, E2L 4S5 – 506/632-0006, Fax: 506/632-9015 – *2

Ralph J. Stephen, 135 Douglas Ave., E2K 1E5 – 506/634-7970, Fax: 506/634-7979 – *1

Stewart McKelvey Stirling Scales, Brunswick House, 44 Chipman Hill, 10th Fl., PO Box 7289, Stn A, E2L 4S6 – 506/632-1970, Fax: 506/652-1989; Email: saint-john@email.smss.com; URL: http://www.nstn.ca/smss – *29

Teed & Teed, 127 Prince William St., PO Box 6639, Stn A, E2L 4S1 – 506/634-7320, Fax: 506/634-7423 – *2

Whelly & Whelly, 122 Carleton St., E2L 2Z7 – 506/634-1193, Fax: 506/693-9040 – *5

Patrick R. Wilbur, #417, 75 Prince William St., PO Box 6601, Stn A, E2L 4S1 – 506/632-6001, Fax: 506/633-6031 – *1

David Zed, PO Box 518, E2L 3Z8 – 506/633-1973 – *1

Thomas J. Zed, 15 Market Square, E2L 1E7 – 506/634-0800 – *1

**St. Joseph** .................................... **Westmorland**

Jacques Gauthier, RR#1, CP 440, E0A 2Y0 – 506/758-9002, Fax: 506/758-2400; Email: acadian@nbnet.nb.ca; URL: http://www.legal.info.ca – *1

**St. Quentin** .................................... **Restigouche**

Eliott Y. Levasseur, 366B, rue Canada, CP 198, E0K 1J0 – 506/235-3412, Fax: 506/235-3365

**St. Stephen** .................................... **Charlotte**

G.W.A. Cockburn, #101, 123 Milltown Blvd., PO Box 206, E3L 2X1 – 506/466-6292, Fax: 506/466-3577 – *1

McConkey, Robinson & Cockburn, 196 King St., E3L 2E2 – 506/466-3626, Fax: 506/466-1119; Email: mcconkey@nbnet.nb.ca – *3

Nicholson, Turner, Walker & White, 46 Milltown Blvd., PO Box 218, E3L 1G3 – 506/466-2338, Fax: 506/466-0160; Email: ntwwss@nbnet.nb.ca – *4

**Shippagan** .................................... **Gloucester**

Godin, Lizotte, Robichaud, Guignard, CP 590, E0B 2P0 – 506/336-0400, Fax: 506/336-0409; Email: glrg@nbnet.nb.ca – *4

**Tracadie** .................................... **Gloucester**

Doiron, Lebouthillier, Boudreau, 3674, rue Principale, CP 3010, Succ Bureau, E1X 1G5 – 506/395-0044, Fax: 506/395-0050; Email: dllb@nbnet.nb.ca – *5

## NEWFOUNDLAND

**Bay Roberts** .................................... **St. John's**

Moores, Andrews, PO Box 806, A0A 1G0 – 709/786-7114, Fax: 709/786-6952 – *3

Morrow, Power, Conception Bay Hwy., PO Box 870, A0A 1G0 – 709/786-9207, Fax: 709/786-9507 – *3

**Channel-Port-Aux-Basques** .................... **Burin-St. Georges**

Stagg, Marks & Mills, 174 Caribou Rd., PO Box 640, A0M 1C0 – 709/695-7341, Fax: 709/695-3944 – *3

**Clarenville** .................................... **Trinity North**

Hughes & Brannan Law Offices, #357, 359 Memorial Dr., PO Box 1207, A0E 1J0 – 709/466-3106, Fax: 709/466-3107; Email: hughes.brannan@thezone.net – *2

**Corner Brook** .................................... **Humber**

Monaghan, Seaborn, Marshall, Allen-Westby & Murphy, Box: 815, 17 West St., A2H 6H9 – 709/634-3231, Fax: 709/634-8889 – *6

E.R. Ozon, 62 Park St., PO Box 1166, A2H 6T2 – 709/639-7126 – *1

Poole, Althouse, Clarke, Thompson & Thomas, Western Trust Bldg., #49, 51 Park St., PO Box 812, A2H 6H7 – 709/634-3136, Fax: 709/634-8247, 9815; Email: epoole@pactt.nf.net – *10

Graham C. Watton & Company, 1 Riverside Dr., PO Box 188, A2H 6C7 – 709/634-3132, Fax: 709/634-7229 – *3

**Deer Lake** .................................... **Humber**

Donna E. Andrews Law Office, 45A North Main St., PO Box 518, A0K 2E0 – 709/635-2199, Fax: 709/635-2599 – *1

**Gander** .................................... **Gander-Gr. Falls**

Easton, Facey & Hillier, Polaris Bldg., 61 Elizabeth Dr., PO Box 408, A1V 1W8 – 709/256-4006, Fax: 709/651-2850; Email: gander.law@nf.sympatico.ca – *5

**Grand Falls-Windsor** .................................... **Gander**

Blackmore, Inder, 14 Pinsent Dr., PO Box 731, A2A 2K2 – 709/489-2226, Fax: 709/489-7004 – *3

Gerard G. Griffin, 1A Pinsent Dr., PO Box 220, A2A 2J7 – 709/489-1177, Fax: 709/489-2171 – *1

Michael J. Griffin, 13 High St., PO Box 400, A1A 2J8 – 709/489-7700, Fax: 709/489-2760 – *1

**Labrador City** .................................... **Labrador**

Miller & Hearn, 450 Avalon Dr., PO Box 129, A1V 2K3 – 709/944-3666, Fax: 709/944-5494 – *2

Lyndon Watson Law Office, 201 Humber Ave., PO Box 577, A2V 2L3 – 709/944-2666, Fax: 709/944-2660 – *1

**Manuels** ....................................

Robert R. Regular, Conception Bay South, PO Box 1060, A1W 1N5 – 709/834-2132, Fax: 709/834-3025 – *1

**Mount Pearl** .................................... **St. John's**

Budden, Morris, 44 Bannister St., A1N 1W1 – 709/747-0077, Fax: 709/747-0104 – *2

Heywood, Kennedy, Belbin, 184 Park Avenue, PO Box 250, A1N 2C3 – 709/747-9613, Fax: 709/747-9723 – *8

**Placentia** .................................... **St. John's**

Placentia Legal Services, General Delivery, A0B 2Y0 – 709/227-4000, Fax: 709/227-6080 – *3

**Springdale** .................................... **Gander**

Shawn C.A. Colbourne Law Office, 8 Juniper Rd., PO Box 69, A0J 1T0 – 709/673-3693, Fax: 709/673-3991 – *1

**St. John's** .................................... **St. John's**

Aylward, Chislett, 261 Duckworth St., PO Box 5835, A1C 5X3 – 709/726-6000, Fax: 709/726-1225 – *3

Barry, Smyth, Walsh, 365 Duckworth St., PO Box 5818, A1C 5X3 – 709/754-1666, Fax: 709/754-0106 – *4

Benson, Myles, Atlantic Place, #900, Water St., PO Box 1538, A1C 5N8 – 709/579-2081, Fax: 709/579-2647 – *5

Brian Casey, PO Box 5664, Stn C, A1C 5W8 – 709/738-3700, Fax: 709/738-3701; Email: bcasey@nf.sympatico.ca – *1

Chalker, Green & Rowe, Baine Johnson Centre, 10 Fort William Place, PO Box 5939, Stn C, A1C 5X4 – 709/722-8735, Fax: 709/722-1763 – *20

Ronald A. Cole, #203, 655 Topsail Rd., A1E 2E3 – 709/368-8377, Fax: 709/368-8269 – *2

Crosbie, Ches Barristers, 169 Water St., A1C 1B1 – 709/579-4000, Fax: 709/579-9671; Email: ches.crosbie@

nf.sympatico.ca; URL: http://www.chescrosbie.com – *4

Curtis, Dawe, Royal Trust Bldg., 139 Water St., 11th Fl., PO Box 337, A1C 5J9 – 709/722-5181, Fax: 709/722-7521 – *12

E. Gerard Doucette, PO Box 220, A1C 5J2 – *1

Christopher English, 3 Pine Bud Place, A1B 1N1 – 709/754-4855, Fax: 709/737-2164; Email: cenglis@morgan.ucs.mun.ca – *1

Fraize Law Offices, PO Box 5217, A1C 5W1 – 709/726-7978, Fax: 709/726-8201 – *1

Glube, Jewell, #803, 140 Water St., A1C 6H6 – 709/754-5297, Fax: 709/754-5298; Toll Free: 1-800-399-5297; Email: glube@nf.sympatico.ca – *2

Learmonth, Dunne, Clarke & Simmonds, Fortis Bldg., 139 Water St., PO Box 700, A1C 5L4 – 709/739-8585, Fax: 709/739-8151 – *4

Lewis, Day, TD Pl., #600, 140 Water St., A1C 6H6 – 709/753-2545, Fax: 709/722-2266; Email: lewis.day@nf.sympatico.ca; URL: http://www.lewisday.nf.ca – *2

Martin, Whalen, Hennebury & Stamp, 15 Church Hill, PO Box 5910, A1C 5X4 – 709/754-1400, Fax: 709/754-0915; Email: mwhslaw@nf.sympatico.ca – *12

McGrath, Rose, 18 Argyle St., A1A 1V3 – 709/726-5250, Fax: 709/738-0614 – *2

McInnes Cooper & Robertson, Scotia Centre, #602, 235 Water St., PO Box 547, A1C 5K8 – 709/726-9500, Fax: 709/726-9550; Email: thomas.kendell@mcrlaw.com; URL: http://fax.nstn.ca/~mcrhfx – *6

Noonan, Oakley, PO Box 5303, A1C 5W1 – 709/726-9598, Fax: 709/726-9614; Email: joakley@nf.sympatico.ca – *3

James E. Nurse, Q.C., 70 Portugal Cove Rd., A1B 2M3 – 709/726-7664 – *1

Earle O'Dea, 323 Duckworth St., PO Box 5955, A1C 5X4 – 709/726-3524, Fax: 709/726-9600 – *11

O'Reilly, Noseworthy, Scotia Centre, #401, 235 Water St., A1C 1B6 – 709/726-3321, Fax: 709/726-2992 – *18

Patterson Palmer Hunt Murphy, Scotia Centre, 235 Water St., PO Box 610, A1C 5L3 – 709/726-6124, Fax: 709/722-0483; Toll Free: 1-888-699-7746; Email: pphm@nfld.com – *21

Pike Law Offices, 272 Duckworth St., A1C 1H3 – 709/726-5600 – *1

Simmonds, Kennedy, TD Place, #1001, 140 Water St., A1C 6H6 – 709/739-4141, Fax: 709/739-4145 – *2

Barry R. Sparkes, 29 Carpasian Rd., A1B 2P9 – 709/739-9423, Fax: 709/739-9423 – *1

Stack & Associates, 325 Duckworth St., PO Box 637, A1C 5K8 – 709/753-6066, Fax: 709/753-3608 – *2

Stewart McKelvey Stirling Scales, Cabot Place, 100 New Gower St., PO Box 5038, A1C 5V3 – 709/722-4270, Fax: 709/722-4565; Email: smss@nlnet.nf.ca; URL: http://www.nstn.ca/smss/ – *23

White, Ottenheimer & Baker, Baine Johnson Centre, 10 Fort William Pl., PO Box 5457, A1C 5W4 – 709/722-7584, Fax: 709/722-9210; Email: wob@wob.nf.ca; URL: http://www.wob.nf.ca – *20

Williams, Roebothan, McKay & Marshall, 209 Duckworth St., PO Box 5236, A1C 5W1 – 709/753-5805, Fax: 709/753-5221; Toll Free: 1-800-563-5563 – *12

**Stephenville.................................Stephenville**

William J. Gallant, 87 Gallant St., PO Box 447, A2N 3A3 – 709/643-5688, Fax: 709/643-2906 – *1

Stagg, Marks & Mills, 28 Main St., PO Box 214, A2N 2Z4 – 709/643-5651, Fax: 709/643-5369

**Torbay.................................................**

Torbay Legal Services, PO Box 550, A1K 1E5 – 709/437-5737, Fax: 709/437-6080; Email: duffy.law@nf.sympatico.ca – *3

## NORTHWEST TERRITORIES

**Hay River.................................Western Arctic**

MacDonald & Associates, #5, 6 Courtoreille St., X0E 1G2 – 867/874-6727, Fax: 867/874-6828; Email: maclaw@ssimicro.com; URL: http://www.ssimicro.com/~sevente/flycolor/hayriver/business/macdonald – *2

**Yellowknife.................................Western Arctic**

Bayly Williams, Scotia Centre, #203, 5102 Franklin Ave., X1A 3S8 – 867/920-4542, Fax: 867/873-4790 – *6

Thomas H. Boyd, PO Box 2788, X1A 2N8 – 867/873-8808

Davis & Company, Northwest Tower, #802, 5201 - 50th Ave., X1A 3S9 – 867/873-6455, Fax: 867/873-6456

Peter C. Fuglsang & Associates, 4912 - 49 St., PO Box 2459, X1A 2P8 – 867/920-4344, Fax: 867/873-3386 – *2

Shannon R.W. Gullberg, PO Box 818, X1A 2N6 – 867/873-6370, Fax: 867/873-2758 – *1

Gullberg, Wiest & MacPherson, 4908 - 49 St., PO Box 818, X1A 2N6 – 867/669-5500, Fax: 867/920-2206 – *5

Rick Hardy, #180, 4908 Franklin Ave., X1A 2N6 – 867/873-2451

Keenan Bengts Law Office, 5018 - 47th St., PO Box 262, X1A 2N2 – 867/873-8631, Fax: 867/920-2511; Email: kbengts@internorth.com – *2

Lawson, Lundell, Lawson & McIntosh, #204, 4817 - 49th St., X1A 3S7 – 867/669-9990, Fax: 867/669-9991

Marshall & Company, PO Box 1236, X1A 2N9 – 867/873-4969, Fax: 867/873-6567 – *3

Thomas McCauley, PO Box 386, X1A 2N3 – 867/873-5364

Glennis M. Munro Brydon, PO Box 1441, X1A 2P1 – 867/669-7669, Fax: 867/873-3649 – *1

Jill A. Murray, PO Box 415, X1A 2N3 – 867/920-4144, Fax: 867/920-7985

Peterson, Hudson, Stang & Malakoe, 4902 - 49 St., PO Box 939, X1A 2N7 – 867/873-4456, 6321, Fax: 867/873-6543 – *11

Phillips & Wright, #1100, 4920 - 52 St., X1A 3T1 – 867/873-3335, Fax: 867/873-2773 – *4

Richard Spaulding, PO Box 2517, X1A 2P8 – 867/873-6300, Fax: 867/873-3787 – *1

## NOVA SCOTIA

**Amherst.................................Cumberland**

Archibald, Morley, PO Box 548, B4H 4A1 – 902/667-3856, Fax: 902/667-0104 – *2

Beaton, Blaikie & Farrell, PO Box 295, B4H 3Z2 – 902/667-0515, Fax: 902/667-6161; Email: bbflaw@istar.ca – *3

Creighton Shatford & Drysdale, 14 Electric St., PO Box 398, B4H 3Z5 – 902/667-8490, Fax: 902/667-6081 – *3

Fairbanks Law Office, PO Box 103, B4H 3Y6 – 902/667-7579, Fax: 902/667-0644; Email: william.fairbanks@ns.sympatico.ca – *1

Hicks, LeMoine, 23 La Planche St., PO Box 279, B4H 3G2 – 902/667-7214, Fax: 902/667-5886 – *8

Larry A. McKim, Q.C., 39 Victoria St., B4H 3Z2 – 902/667-2013 – *1

**Annapolis Royal.................................Annapolis**

MacArthur & Associates, PO Box 366, B0S 1A0 – 902/532-2129, Fax: 902/532-5424 – *2

**Antigonish.................................Antigonish**

LeBlanc, MacDonald & Pickup, 133 Church St., B2G 2E3 – 902/863-2120, Fax: 902/863-0030

James C. MacIntosh, 16 Bay St., B2G 2G8 – 902/863-4805, Fax: 902/863-8086 – *1

MacPherson MacNeil Macdonald, 42 West St., B2G 2H5 – 902/863-2925 – *3

**Barrington Passage.................................Shelburne**

Pink Macdonald Harding, PO Box 580, B0W 1G0 – 902/637-2266, Fax: 902/637-3283

**Bedford.................................Halifax**

Blackburn English, Bedford House, Sunnyside Mall, #231, 1595 Bedford Hwy., B4A 3Y4 – 902/835-8544, Fax: 902/835-4310

Lawrence, White & Associates, Sun Tower, #400, 1550 Bedford Hwy., B4A 1E6 – 902/832-0882, Fax: 902/832-0821

Melnick, Doll, Condran, #302, 1160 Bedford Hwy., B4A 1C1 – 902/835-2300, Fax: 902/835-2303; Email: dcmmdc@ns.sympatico.ca – *3

Presse & Mason, #210, 1475 Bedford Hwy., B4A 3Z5 – 902/832-1175, Fax: 902/832-1856 – *2

**Berwick.................................Kings**

Stewart & Turner, 196 Cottage St., PO Box 208, B0P 1E0 – 902/538-3123, Fax: 902/538-7933 – *2

Waterbury Newton, 188 Commercial St., PO Box 475, B0P 1E0 – 902/538-3168, Fax: 902/538-8680

**Bridgetown.................................Annapolis**

D.H. Hatherly, Q.C., PO Box 269, B0S 1C0 – 902/665-4544 – *1

**Bridgewater.................................Lunenburg**

Conrad & Feindel, 70 Dufferin St., B4V 2G3 – 902/543-4655, Fax: 902/543-6853 – *2

Coughlan & Coughlan, 48 Pleasant St., PO Box 169, B4V 2W8 – 902/543-7888, Fax: 902/543-0225; Email: coughlan.law@ns.sympatico.ca – *3

Gordon M. Davidson, 764 King St., B4V 1B4 – 902/453-4556, Fax: 902/453-5293 – *1

Allen C. Fownes, 14 Dufferin St., PO Box 69, B4V 2W6 – 902/543-1421, Fax: 902/543-1359

Milner Morris & Naugler, 344 King St., PO Box 250, B4V 1A9 – 902/543-6661, Fax: 902/543-6639 – *3

Power, Dempsey & Cooper, 84 Dufferin St., B4V 2G3 – 902/543-7815, Fax: 902/543-3196; Email: pdclaw@istar.ca – *4

Theakston, Allen & Peers, 455 King St., B4V 1B2 – 902/543-2437, Fax: 902/543-0243 – *4

**Chester.................................Lunenburg**

David S. Fraser, Q.C., PO Box 4, B0J 1J0 – 902/275-4654, Fax: 902/275-4798 – *1

Hennigar, Wells, Lamey & Baker, 24 Pleasant St., PO Box 310, B0J 1J0 – 902/275-3544, Fax: 902/275-3473 – *5

**Chester Basin.................................Lunenburg**

B.J. Preeper, Q.C., PO Box 99, B0J 1K0 – 902/275-2155, Fax: 902/275-3088 – *1

**Cheticamp.................................Inverness**

Réjean Aucoin, PO Box 328, B0E 1H0 – 902/224-1450, Fax: 902/224-1450; Email: rejean@auracom.com – *1

**Dartmouth.................................Halifax**

Boyne Clarke, PO Box 876, Stn Halifax, B2Y 3Z5 – 902/469-9500, Fax: 902/463-7500; Email: admin@boyneclarke.ns.ca; URL: http://www.boyneclarke.ns.ca – *30

John D. Filliter, Q.C., 56 Lorne Avenue, B2Y 3E7 – 902/466-8424, Fax: 902/463-4168 – *1

David A. Grant, 63 Tacoma Drive, B2W 3E7 – 902/463-6300, Fax: 902/435-7910 – *1

Landry, McGillivray, #300, 33 Ochterloney St., PO Box 1200, B1Y 4B8 – 902/463-8800, Fax: 902/463-0590 – *11

Langille & Associates, #201, 56 Portland St., PO Box 767, B2Y 3Z3 – 902/463-5200, Fax: 902/465-5200 – *3

* indicates number of lawyers in law firm.

Livingstone & Company, 12 Queen St., PO Box 664, B2Y 3Y9 – 902/461-5111, Fax: 902/461-4911 – *4
Pettipas & Richey, PO Box 723, B2Y 3Z3 – 902/465-4481, Fax: 902/463-4319 – *2
Smith Evans, #604, 45 Alderney Dr., PO Box 852, B1Y 3Z5 – 902/463-8100, Fax: 902/465-2581; Email: brevans@fox.nstn.ca – *4
Tippett-Leary Law Firm, #302, 177 Main St., B2X 1S1 – 902/434-1512, Fax: 902/434-1513 – *1
Washington Mahody, #205, 99 Portland St., PO Box 1126, B2Y 4B8 – 902/463-2131, Fax: 902/469-2134; Email: mahody@msn.com – *2
Weldon, Beeler, Mont & Dexter, 19 Portland St., PO Box 465, B1Y 3Y8 – 902/469-2421, Fax: 902/463-4452; Email: ddexter@ns.sympatico.ca – *5
Wolfson, Schelew, Green & Zatzman, Bank of Commerce Bldg., #500, 73 Tacoma Dr., PO Box 2308, B2W 3Y4 – 902/435-7000, Fax: 902/435-4085 – *3

**Enfield ............................................ Hants**

Blackburn English, 287 Hwy. 2, B2T 1C9 – 902/883-2264, Fax: 902/883-8744 – *2

**Glace Bay .................................... Cape Breton**

Crosby, Burke & Macrury, PO Box 86, B1A 5V2 – 902/849-3971, Fax: 902/849-7009 – *3

**Greenwood........................................ Kings**

William J. Dyer, PO Box 1940, B0P 1N0 – 902/765-3301, Fax: 902/765-6493 – *1
Mountaintop Legal Services Ltd., 791 Central Ave., PO Box 403, B0P 1N0 – 902/765-9800, Fax: 902/765-2355 – *2

**Guysborough ................................ Guysborough**

Campbell & MacKeen, 33 Queen St., PO Box 200, B0N 1N0 – 902/533-2644, Fax: 902/533-3526 – *2
LeBlanc, MacDonald & Pickup, PO Box 200, B0H 1N0 – 902/533-2644

**Halifax ........................................... Halifax**

Richard G. Arab, 5162 Duke St., B3J 1N7 – 902/423-5711, Fax: 902/423-1565 – *1
Armsworthy Lynch, 5443 Cogswell St., B3J 1R1 – 902/425-8740, Fax: 902/423-6891 – *4
Blois, Nickerson & Bryson, 1568 Hollis St., PO Box 2147, B3J 3B7 – 902/425-6000, Fax: 902/429-7347; Email: blois@fox.nstn.ca – *17
Buchan, Derrick & Ring, #100, 5525 Artillery Pl., B3J 1J2 – 902/422-7411, Fax: 902/423-3544 – *4
Burchell Hayman Barnes, #1800, 1801 Hollis St., PO Box 36, B3J 2L4 – 902/423-6361, Fax: 902/420-9326; Email: firm@burchell.ns.ca – *14
Burchell, MacDougall, #400, 5121 Sackville St., B3J 1K1 – 902/421-1536, Fax: 902/425-0085; Email: halifax@burmac.ns.ca – *2
R.D. Campbell, #2003, 1470 Summer St., B3H 3A3 – 902/429-5454, Fax: 902/429-5457 – *1
Clare W. Christie's Law Office, 2118 Brunswick St., B3K 2Y8 – 902/422-2297, Fax: 902/422-2162; Email: cclo@fox.nstn.ca – *1
Coady Filliter, #208, 880 Spring Garden Rd., B3H 1Y1 – 902/429-6264, Fax: 902/423-3044 – *5
Cooper & McDonald, Old Auction House, 1669 Granville St., B3J 1X2 – 902/429-2191, Fax: 902/425-3217 – *5
Cox Downie, Purdy's Wharf Tower, Box: 1100, 1959 Upper Water St., PO Box 2380, Stn Central RPO, B3J 3E5 – 902/421-6262, Fax: 902/421-3130; Email: lawyer@coxdownie.ns.ca; URL: http://www.coxdownie.ns.ca – *43
Crowe Dillon Robinson, #2000, 7075 Bayers Rd., B3L 2C1 – 902/453-1732, Fax: 902/454-9948 – *8
Daley, Black & Moreira, PO Box 355, B3J 2N7 – 902/423-7211, Fax: 902/420-1744 – *23
Kevin P. Downie, #1004, 1959 Upper Water St., PO Box 580, Stn Central, B3J 2R7 – 902/425-7233, Fax: 902/425-2252; Email: dow@istar.ca – *1
Flinn Merrick, PO Box 1054, B3J 2X6 – 902/429-4111, Fax: 902/429-8215; Email: fmhfx@fox.nstn.ca – *17
Simon L. Gaum, Q.C., Tower One, Halifax Shopping Centre, #200, 7001 Mumford Rd., B3L 4N9 – 902/423-6391, Fax: 902/455-0974 – *1
Goldberg Thompson, PO Box 306, B3J 2N7 – 902/421-1161, Fax: 902/425-0266 – *8
Green Parish, PO Box 1134, B3J 2X1 – 902/422-3100, Fax: 902/425-2504 – *6
Beatrice A. Havlovic, #308, 5670 Spring Garden Rd., B3J 1H6 – 902/423-8100, Fax: 902/423-6011; Email: lingua@fox.nstn.ca; URL: http://www.linguanet.ns.ca – *1
Jane E. Holmes, PO Box 325, B3J 2N7 – 902/422-8335, Fax: 902/492-0424
Hopkins & Associates Law Office, #105, 276 Bedford Hwy., B3M 2K6 – 902/445-2984, Fax: 902/445-4333 – *1
Huestis Holm, Bank of Commerce Bldg., #708, 1809 Barrington St., B3J 3K8 – 902/429-3400, Fax: 902/422-4713; Email: hh@holm.ns.ca – *14
McInnes Cooper & Robertson, Summit Place, 1601 Lower Water St., PO Box 730, B3J 2V1 – 902/425-6500, Fax: 902/425-6350; Email: mcrhfx@mcrlaw.com; URL: http://fox.nstn.ca/~mcrhfx/ – *51
Patterson Palmer Hunt Murphy, #1600, 5151 George St., PO Box 247, B3J 2N9 – 902/492-2000, Fax: 902/429-5215 – *55
Clyde A. Paul & Associates, 349 Herring Cove Rd., B3R 1V9 – 902/477-2518, Fax: 902/479-1482 – *3
Pink Breen Larkin, 1583 Hollis St., PO Box 160, B3J 2M4 – 902/423-7777, Fax: 902/423-9588; Email: pblns@labour-law.com; URL: http://www.labour-law.com
Pink, Murray, Graham, PO Box 398, B3J 2P8 – 902/492-0550, Fax: 902/492-0570; Email: pmlawcan@criminaldefence.com; URL: http://www.criminaldefence.com – *4
Jack Prince, Q.C., #200, 6265 Quinpool Rd., B3L 1A4 – 902/422-9621, Fax: 902/422-0993 – *1
Scaravelli & Associates, #1750, 1801 Hollis St., B3J 3N4 – 902/429-4104, Fax: 902/423-4009 – *2
Singleton Murphy, Upper Penthouse, 1660 Hollis St., B3J 1V7 – 902/492-7000, Fax: 902/492-4309; Email: singmur@istar.ca – *4
Slone & Munro, #501, 5162 Duke St., B3J 1N7 – 902/492-3310, Fax: 902/492-0013; Email: slonemun@ra.isinet.com – *3
Stewart McKelvey Stirling Scales, Purdy's Wharf Tower One, #900, 1959 Upper Water St., PO Box 997, B3J 2X2 – 902/420-3200, Fax: 902/420-1417; Email: halifax@email.smss.com; URL: http://www.nstn.ca/smss/ – *56
Thomson, Noseworthy, DiCostanzo, 6470 Chebucto Rd., B3L 1L4 – 902/420-2025, Fax: 902/420-2028 – *4
Walker, Dunlop, PO Box 3366, Stn South, B3J 3J1 – 902/423-8121, Fax: 902/429-0621 – *6

**Kentville ........................................ Kings**

Forse, Nathanson, 325 Main St., PO Box 655, B4N 3X7 – 902/678-1616, Fax: 902/678-1615; Toll Free: 1-800-667-3879 – *2
Donald C. Fraser, PO Box 668, B4N 3X9 – 902/678-4006, Fax: 902/678-2999 – *1
Manning & Associates, 27 Cornwallis St., B4N 2E2 – 902/679-1600, Fax: 902/679-5122; Email: vkursell@glint.com – *2
Muttart Tufts Dewolfe & Coyle, 20 Cornwallis St., PO Box 515, B4N 3X3 – 902/678-2157, Fax: 902/678-9455; Email: mtdc_law@mtdc.ns.ca – *6
Taylor, MacLellan & Cochrane, 50 Cornwallis St., B4N 2E4 – 902/678-6156, Fax: 902/678-6010; Email: lawfirm@tmc-law.com – *4
D.E. Thompson-Sheppard, Q.C., Drawer 578, B4N 3X7 – 902/681-6169, Fax: 902/681-1099
Waterbury Newton, 469 Main St., PO Box 98, B4N 3V9 – 902/678-3257, Fax: 902/678-7727 – *17

**Liverpool ........................................ Queens**

Conrad & Feindel, 267 Main St., PO Box 1600, B0T 1K0 – 902/354-5723, Fax: 902/354-2038 – *2
Allen C. Fownes, 333 Main St., PO Box 1739, B0T 1K0 – 902/354-2744, Fax: 902/354-2746; Email: acfownes@atcon.com – *1
Tutty & DiPersio, PO Box 760, B0T 1K0 – 902/354-5756, Fax: 902/354-7395 – *2

**Lower Sackville ................................... Halifax**

Robert W. Newman & Associates, 453 Sackville Dr., B4C 2S1 – 902/864-2722, Fax: 902/864-3164 – *1

**Lunenburg ...................................... Lunenburg**

D.W.T. Brattston, PO Box 1599, B0J 2C0 – 902/634-8474 – *1
Burke & Macdonald, PO Box 549, B0J 2C0 – 902/634-8354, Fax: 902/634-4226 – *2
Walton W.M. Cook, 118 Montague St., PO Box 457, B0J 2C0 – 902/634-8713, Fax: 902/634-8943 – *1

**Mahone Bay ..................................... Lunenburg**

Haysom & Kinley, PO Box 279, B0J 2E0 – 902/624-8337, Fax: 902/624-9401 – *3

**Middleton....................................... Annapolis**

Stephen I. Cole, PO Box 1416, B0S 1P0 – 902/825-6288, Fax: 902/825-4340 – *1
Durland, Gillis, Parker & Richter, 76 Commercial St., B0S 1P0 – 902/825-3415, Fax: 902/825-2522 – *4

**Musquodoboit Harbour ............................. Halifax**

Eastern Shore Law Centre, 1653 Ostrea Lake Rd., PO Box 357, B0J 2L0 – 902/889-3796, Fax: 902/889-3735; Email: mbatalion@aol.com – *1

**New Glasgow...................................... Pictou**

R.A. Balmanoukian, 137 McColl St., B2H 4Z6 – 902/755-3393, Fax: 902/755-6373; Email: blackacre@north.nsis.com – *1
Goodman MacDonald & Patterson, Castlehall, 47 Riverside Dr., PO Box 697, B2H 5G2 – 902/752-5090, Fax: 902/755-3545 – *3
John G. Langley, Q.C., Squire Fraser's Pl., 130 George St., B2H 2K6 – 902/752-1131, Fax: 902/752-7737 – *1
MacIntosh, MacDonnell & MacDonald, 159 George St., PO Box 368, B2H 5E5 – 902/752-8441, Fax: 902/752-7810 – *8
Ian A. MacKay, Q.C., 559 East River Rd., PO Box 926, B2H 5K7 – 902/752-6803 – *1
H. Elizabeth MacKay O'Farrell, 465 Westville Rd., PO Box 1422, B0K 1S0 – 902/752-4227, Fax: 902/755-6218 – *1
J.G. Proudfoot, 260 Westville Rd., B1H 2J5 – 902/752-6220, Fax: 902/755-1763 – *1

**New Minas......................................... Kings**

Waterbury Newton, 1095 Commercial St., B4N 3E3 – 902/678-3257, 1466, Fax: 902/679-1315

**New Waterford.............................. Cape Breton**

Charles Broderick, 3316 Plummer Ave., PO Box 151, B1H 4K4 – 902/862-6471, Fax: 902/862-9513; Email: nstn5702@fox.nstn.ca – *1

**North Sydney ............................... Cape Breton**

Alfred J. Dinaut, PO Box 272, B1A 3M3 – 902/794-7729, Fax: 902/794-7692 – *1
Ryan & Ryan, 208 Commercial St., PO Box 278, B2A 3M3 – 902/794-4784, Fax: 902/794-3042 – *3

**Parrsboro .................................. Cumberland**

Hicks, LeMoine, 4B Spring St., PO Box 267, B0M 1S0 – 902/254-2477, Fax: 902/254-3311

**Pictou ............................................ Pictou**

MacLean & MacDonald, 90 Coleraine St., PO Box 730, B0K 1H0 – 902/485-4347, Fax: 902/485-8887 – *3

K.E.W. Roddam, Q.C., 94 Church St., PO Box 280, B0K 1H0 – 902/485-4385 – *1

**Port Hawkesbury.................................Inverness**

Evans, MacIsaac, MacMillan, PO Box 69, B0E 2V0 – 902/625-0580, Fax: 902/625-2811; Email: emmlaw@avracom.com – *7

**Pubnico.......................................Yarmouth**

d'Entremont & Boudreau, PO Box 118, B0W 2W0 – 902/762-3119, Fax: 902/762-3124; Email: dentandboud@klis.com – *2

**Shelburne.....................................Shelburne**

Pink Macdonald Harding, 30 John St., PO Box 549, B0T 1W0 – 902/875-3611, Fax: 902/875-3414 – *2

**Sherbrooke....................................Shelburne**

Robin W. Archibald, PO Box 176, B0J 3C0 – 902/522-2067; 833-2713, Fax: 902/522-2299 – *1

**Springhill....................................Cumberland**

Hicks, LeMoine, 49 Main St., PO Box 899, B0M 1X0 – 902/597-3725, Fax: 902/597-5880 – *2

**Stellarton....................................Pictou**

Paul Graham, 276 Foord St., B0K 1S0 – 902/755-4522 – *1

Skoke & Company, 286 Foord St., PO Box 850, B0K 1S0 – 902/755-5711, Fax: 902/752-6561 – *3

**Sydney........................................Cape Breton**

Nash Terrance Brogan, 290 George St., B1P 1J6 – 902/539-1390, Fax: 902/564-6722 – *1

Cusack Walsh Law Office, 205 Charlotte St., B1P 1C4 – 902/564-8396, Fax: 902/564-0030 – *2

Dominic P. Goduto, 161 Townsend St., B1P 5E3 – 902/564-9503, Fax: 902/562-0365 – *1

Khattar & Khattar, 378 Charlotte St., PO Box 387, B1P 6H2 – 902/539-9696, Fax: 902/562-7147; Toll Free: 1-800-542-8827; Email: khattar@atcon.com – *5

MacDonald & MacLennan, 295 George St., PO Box 1148, B1P 6J7 – 902/564-4429, Fax: 902/539-2303 – *2

R.G. MacLellan, Q.C., PO Box 854, B1P 6J1 – 902/564-4463, Fax: 902/564-3845 – *1

John W. Morgan, #6, 75 Dodd St., PO Box 195, Stn A, B1P 6H1 – 902/539-2800, Fax: 902/562-2554; Email: johnnie@atcom.com – *1

Parsons, D.L. & Associate, 240 Kings Rd., B1P 1A6 – 902/539-2777, Fax: 902/539-4282 – *3

Sampson McDougall, 642 King's Rd., B1S 1B9 – 902/539-2425, Fax: 902/564-0954 – *8

Stewart McKelvey Stirling Scales, 50 Dorchester St., PO Box 820, B1P 6J1 – 902/539-5135, Fax: 902/539-8256 – *2

**Tatamagouche..................................Colchester**

W.R. Kennedy, PO Box 186, B0K 1V0

**Truro.........................................Colchester**

Burchell, MacDougall, 710 Prince St., PO Box 1128, B2N 5H1 – 902/895-1561, Fax: 902/895-7709 – *20

David F. Curtis Q.C., 559 Prince St., PO Box 458, B2N 1G2 – 902/895-0528, Fax: 902/893-1158 – *1

McLellan, Nichols & Richards, 795 Prince St., PO Box 1064, B2N 5G9 – 902/895-4417, Fax: 902/897-9890 – *1

Patterson Palmer Hunt Murphy, 10 Church St., PO Box 1068, B2N 5B9 – 902/897-2000, Fax: 902/893-3071 – *1

Yuill, Chisholm, #104, 14 Court St., B2N 3H7 – 902/893-0243, Fax: 902/897-0282 – *2

**Upper Tantallon...............................Halifax**

Norma M. Scott, 4 Westwood Blvd., B3Z 1H3 – 902/826-1144, Fax: 902/826-1074 – *1

Smith-Camp & Associates, #203, 5209 St. Margaret's Bay Rd., B3Z 1E3 – 902/826-2193, Fax: 902/826-2193 – *1

**Waverley......................................Halifax**

Conrad & Kelly, PO Box 310, B0N 2S0 – 902/861-1088, Fax: 902/861-4555 – *2

**Windsor.......................................Hants**

Adams & Company, 87 Gerrish St., B0N 2T0 – 902/798-8384, Fax: 902/798-0432 – *2

Lawrence, White & Associates, PO Box 3177, B0N 2T0 – 902/798-5997, Fax: 902/798-8925 – *4

McGrath Alexander & MacKenzie, 99 Water St., PO Box 280, B0N 2T0 – 902/798-5734, Fax: 902/798-5739 – *3

Nelson & Associates, 258 King St., PO Box 2018, B0N 2T0 – 902/798-5797, Fax: 902/798-2332 – *2

**Wolfville.....................................Kings**

Kimball & Brogan, 121 Front St., PO Box 670, B0P 1X0 – 902/542-5757, Fax: 902/542-5759; Email: kimball_brogan.wolfville@ns.sympatico.ca – *3

Lutz & DeMont, 180 Main St., PO Box 1449, B0P 1X0 – 902/542-5701, Fax: 902/542-7230 – *3

**Yarmouth......................................Yarmouth**

Pink Macdonald Harding, 379 Main St., PO Box 398, B5A 4B3 – 902/742-7861, Fax: 902/742-0425 – *9

## ONTARIO

**Acton.........................................Halton**

Braida & Henry, 28 Paisley St., PO Box 1082, L7J 1H4 – 905/824-2242, Fax: 905/824-3049 – *2

MacKenzie & Chapman, 33 Main St. South, L7J 1X3 – 519/853-1330, Fax: 519/853-4645 – *2

**Ajax..........................................Durham**

Daniel J. Balena, 110 Hunt St., L1S 1P5 – 905/683-9601, Fax: 905/683-4610 – *1

Daniel A. Barna, 103 Old Kingston Rd., L1T 3A6 – 905/426-8000, Fax: 905/623-3961 – *1

L.A. Berg, Q.C., 36 Harwood Ave. South, PO Box 228, L1S 3C3 – 905/683-6171, Fax: 905/428-3473 – *1

Walker D. Clark, 20 Church St. North, L1T 2W5 – 905/683-2741, Fax: 905/683-2752 – *1

William E. Foden, 60 Randall Dr., Unit 2, L1S 6L3 – 905/428-8200, Fax: 905/428-8666 – *1

R.J. Fromstein, 15 Harwood Ave. South, L1S 2B9 – 905/683-8900, Fax: 905/683-8534 – *1

Greening & Bucknam, 50 Commercial Ave., L1S 2H5 – 905/683-7037, Fax: 905/683-7627 – *1

J.E. Ort, #1, 30 Hunt St., L1S 3M2 – 905/427-9919, Fax: 905/427-9910 – *1

Parish & Bloodworth, 36 Harwood Ave. South, L1S 2B6 – 905/683-2254, Fax: 905/428-3473 – *2

Polak, McKay & Hawkshaw, 467 Westney South, L1S 6V8 – 905/683-6880, Fax: 905/428-2063 – *4

P.G. Singh, Q.C., 158 Harwood Ave. South, L1S 2H6 – 905/683-1042, Fax: 905/683-7794 – *1

Juanita Wislesky, #101, 144 Old Kingston Rd., L1T 2Z9 – 905/686-1686, Fax: 905/686-8648 – *1

George D. Wright, 543 Kingston Rd. West, PO Box 123, L1S 3C2 – 905/427-7200, Fax: 905/427-2999 – *1

**Alexandria....................................Glengarry**

Jean-Marc Lefebvre, Q.C., 32 Main St. North, PO Box 519, K0C 1A0 – 613/525-1358, Fax: 613/525-3411; Toll Free: lefebvre@alen-net.ca – *2

**Alliston......................................Simcoe**

Gilmore & Gilmore, 458 Victoria St. East, PO Box 250, L9R 1V5 – 705/435-4339, Fax: 705/435-6520; Email: lawyers@blopnex.net – *2

**Almonte.......................................Lanark**

L.G. William Chapman, 77 Little Bridge St., PO Box 362, K0A 1A0 – 613/256-3072, Fax: 613/256-5164; Email: lgwc@istar.ca – *1

Patrick Galway, 359 Ottawa St., K0A 1A0 – 613/256-3480, Fax: 613/256-5895 – *1

Michael W. Swinwood, RR#3, K0A 1A0 – 613/256-5100, Fax: 613/567-3195 – *1

**Amherstburg...................................Essex**

Bondy, Baker, Wolf, 41 Sandwich St. South, N9V 1Z5 – 519/736-2154, Fax: 519/736-2466

**Amherstview...................................Lennox**

William E.M. Vince, 3 Manitou Cres. West, K7N 1S3 – 613/389-6727, Fax: 613/389-6256 – *1

**Angus.........................................Simcoe**

Greenfield Law Office, 189 Mill St., PO Box 600, L0M 1B0 – 705/424-1331, Fax: 705/424-6441 – *1

McLellan Associates, Rainbow Mall, #5, 2 Massey St., L0M 1B0 – 705/424-2219, Fax: 705/424-2766

**Arnprior......................................Renfrew**

Pamela R. LeMay, 64 McGonigal St. West, K7S 1M1 – 613/623-7705, Fax: 613/623-2189 – *1

McLean & Moore, 141 John St. North, PO Box 8, K7S 3H2 – 613/623-3177, Fax: 613/623-9166 – *2

Mulvihill & Murray, 84 John St. North, PO Box 187, K7S 3H4 – 613/623-4246, Fax: 613/623-8547 – *1

**Arthur........................................Wellington**

Smith Janzen & Alaimo, 197 George St., PO Box 220, N0G 1A0 – 519/848-3916, Fax: 519/848-2395 – *3

**Athens........................................Leeds**

Quigley, Ross & Cliffen, 10 Main St. East, PO Box 604, K0E 1B0 – 613/924-2673

**Aurora........................................York Region**

W.H.C. Bailey, 33 Victoria St., PO Box 186, L4G 3H3 – 905/727-9473, Fax: 905/841-8492 – *1

Timothy P. Boland, 14996 Yonge St., L4G 1M6 – 905/841-5717, Fax: 905/841-7128 – *1

Mark W. Kushner, 330 Kennedy St. West, L4G 6L7 – 905/841-1086, Fax: 905/841-7184 – *1

Lonny W. Mark, 15032 Yonge St., L4G 1M4 – 705/727-4285, Fax: 705/727-5569 – *1

McPherson, Shugart, Vrancic & Sorley, 15220 Yonge St., PO Box 338, L4G 3H4 – 905/727-3151, Fax: 905/841-2164 – *4

Kenneth D. Murray, 50 Wellington St. East, L4G 1H5 – 905/841-1850, Fax: 905/841-3659 – *1

Peddle, Boland, 138 Yonge St., L4G 1M6 – *2

Kent F. Pollard, 13 Church St., L4G 1G5 – 905/727-8354, Fax: 905/841-1749 – *1

Smith & Thompson Associates, PO Box 100, L4G 1L9 – 905/727-3127, Fax: 905/727-7096 – *2

Clarke G. Smith, 10 Mosley St., PO Box 100, L4G 1G6 – 905/727-3127, Fax: 905/727-7096 – *1

Steinberg Still & Bruce, 15139 Yonge St., L4G 1M3 – 905/713-1080, Fax: 905/713-1083 – *3

Barry W. Switzer, PO Box 246, L4G 1L8 – 905/727-9488, Fax: 905/841-8647 – *1

Michael L. Young, #160, 34 Berczy St., L4G 1W9 – 905/727-1335 – *1

**Aylmer........................................Elgin**

Doyle & Prendergast, 10 Sydenham St. East, N5H 1L2 – 519/773-3105, Fax: 519/765-1728 – *2

Fordham, Watterworth & Marshall, 34 Talbot St. West, N5H 1J7 – 519/773-3130 – *4

Gloin, Hall & Shields, 139 Talbot St. East, PO Box 8, N5H 2R8 – 519/773-9221, Fax: 519/765-1885 – *5

**Bancroft......................................Hastings**

O. Gregory Anderson, Q.C., 129 Hastings St., PO Box 700, K0L 1C0 – 613/332-3773, Fax: 613/332-5079 – *1

* indicates number of lawyers in law firm.

L.C. Plater, 61 Hastings St. North, PO Box 1150, K0L 1C0 – 613/332-1605, Fax: 613/332-2619 – *1

**Barrie** .......... **Simcoe**

R. Bruce Algie, 84 Worsley St., PO Box 804, L4M 4Y5 – 705/722-3634, Fax: 705/734-1435 – *1

Allison, Nancy Lee, 250 Bradford St., PO Box 308, L4M 4T2 – 705/737-5702, Fax: 705/737-1614 – *1

Peter D. Archibald, 58 Collier St., PO Box 907, L4M 4Y6 – 705/726-4511, Fax: 705/726-0613; Email: pda@bconnex.net – *1

Armstrong Meakings, 111 Toronto St., L4N 1V1 – 705/739-9111, Fax: 705/739-8111 – *2

Debora Batstone, 88 Mulcaster St., L4M 3M5 – 705/722-9615, Fax: 705/722-6920 – *1

Brian Bond, 25 Poyntz St., L4M 3N8 – 705/734-1550, Fax: 705/734-0306

James Bowden, #503, 85 Bayfield St., L4M 3A7 – 705/739-7310, Fax: 705/739-7091 – *1

Susan Brenner, 43 Collier St., L4M 1G5 – 705/734-1801, Fax: 705/734-2047 – *1

Thomas Bryson, 11 Sophia St. West, L4N 1H9 – 705/728-2232, Fax: 705/728-7525 – *1

Burgar, Rowe, 90 Mulcaster St., PO Box 758, L4M 4Y5 – 705/721-3377, 726-6511, Fax: 705/721-4025 – *10

Francis Edward Burns, #101, 89 Dunlop St. East, L4M 5E2 – 705/722-7700, Fax: 705/722-0218 – *1

Stephen R. Canning, 91 Toronto St., L4N 1V1 – 705/739-1264, Fax: 705/739-1265

Carroll, Heyd, 77 Mary St., PO Box 548, L4M 4T7 – 705/722-4400, Fax: 705/722-0704 – *3

Cockburn & Smith, 89 Collier St., PO Box 955, L4M 4Y6 – 705/726-7351, Fax: 705/721-9445 – *2

Cowan & Carter, 107 Collier St., PO Box 722, L4M 4Y5 – 705/728-4521, Fax: 705/728-8744 – *1

Cugelman & Eisen, #201, 28 Owen St., L4M 3G7 – 705/721-1888, Fax: 705/721-7755 – *2

Sam Delmar, 99 Burke St., L4N 7H9 – 705/739-1043, Fax: 705/728-0455

Alfred W.J. Dick, 80 Worsley St., L4M 1L8 – 705/728-9006, Fax: 705/728-9876 – *1

Julianne Ecclestone, #301, 89 Dunlop St. East, L4M 1A7 – 705/725-8050, Fax: 705/722-0189 – *1

Graham, Wilson & Green, 190 Cundles Rd. East, PO Box 987, L4M 5E1 – 705/737-1811, Fax: 705/737-5390; Email: gwg@bconnex.net – *3

Hogben Mayhew Hill, 39 Owen St., PO Box 501, L4M 4T7 – 705/726-3712, Fax: 705/726-3895 – *3

Klaus N. Jacoby, 34 Clapperton St., PO Box 350, L4M 4T5 – 705/726-0238, Fax: 705/726-9197 – *1

Ardel M. Johnston, PO Box 1121, Stn Main, L4M 5E2 – 705/722-8015, Fax: 705/726-3909 – *1

Carolyn L. Jones, 34A Clapperton St., L4M 3G8 – 705/737-0111, Fax: 705/734-0046 – *1

Mark A. Kelly, #200, 17 Poyntz St., L4M 3N6 – 705/739-6955, Fax: 705/739-6956

Kenneth P. Kinnear, 23 Owen St., PO Box 646, L4M 4V1 – 705/726-6497, Fax: 705/722-4749 – *2

Peter Lamprey, 78 Worsley St., L4M 1L8 – 705/722-1114, Fax: 705/722-5484 – *1

Legal Aid, #104, 150 Dunlop St. East, L4M 6H1 – 705/737-3400, Fax: 705/739-0002

K. Joy Levison, 34A Clapperton St., L4M 3E7 – 705/737-5410, Fax: 705/737-5418 – *1

Norman E. Long, #206, 150 Dunlop St. East, L4M 6H1 – 705/737-3960, Fax: 705/722-6734

Gary W. Luhowy, 168 Owen St., PO Box 1063, L4M 5E1 – 705/737-5115, Fax: 705/721-0263; Email: barrie.law@sympatico.ca – *1

Gavin J. May, 88 Mulcaster St., L4M 3M5 – 705/739-9913, Fax: 705/722-6920 – *1

McLellan Associates, 510 Bayfield St., L4M 4S5 – 705/726-7765, Fax: 705/726-8071; Email: mclellan@thelawstore.com; URL: http://www.thelaw-store.com – *2

Peter McPhie, 78 Worsley St., L4M 1L8 – 705/722-1115, Fax: 705/722-5484 – *1

J. Marvin Menzies, #101, 89 Dunlop St. East, PO Box 1175, L4M 5E2 – 705/722-5432, Fax: 705/722-0218 – *1

Miller Pickard, 119 Collier St., L4M 1H5 – 705/734-1181, Fax: 705/722-6387 – *2

Albert Miller, 119 Collier St., PO Box 774, L4M 4Y5 – 705/737-2042, Fax: 705/737-2042 – *1

Wendy Miller, 80 Worsley St., PO Box 1117, L4M 5E2 – 705/737-5192, Fax: 705/734-0276 – *1

Alexander M. Mills, #230, 400 Bayfield St., L4M 5A1 – 705/739-7472, Fax: 705/739-5060 – *1

R. John Mitchell, 40 Clapperton St., PO Box 1, L4M 4S9 – 705/725-8855, Fax: 705/721-0782 – *1

Murray/Ralston, 129B Dunlop St. East, L4M 1A6 – 705/737-3229, Fax: 705/737-5380; Email: ral-mur@bconnex.net – *2

Gerald E. Norman, 99 Bayfield St., PO Box 732, L4M 4Y5 – 705/726-2772, Fax: 705/734-1942 – *1

Oatley, Purser, 151 Ferris Lane, L4M 6C1 – 705/726-9021, Fax: 705/726-2132; Email: oatpur@oatley-purser.com – *12

J.S. Otton, Q.C., #204, 110 Dunlop St. East, L4M 1A5 – 705/728-5822, Fax: 705/728-3179 – *1

Owen, Dickey, 26 Owen St., PO Box 848, L4M 4Y6 – 705/726-1181, Fax: 705/726-1463; Email: odlaw@bconnex.net; URL: http://www.bconnex.net/~odlaw/ – *3

G.W. Paisley, 23 Owen St., L4M 3G7 – 705/737-0688, Fax: 705/722-4749 – *1

Park/Lunn, Barristers & Solicitors, 18 Collier St., L4M 1H4 – 705/739-0929, Fax: 705/725-7977 – *2

Michael E. Reed, 105 Collier St., L4M 1H2 – 705/726-4300, Fax: 705/725-7910; Email: reedlaw@simcoe.net – *1

Catherine Rogers, 115 Collier St., L4M 1H2 – 705/734-2800, Fax: 705/734-2807

Robert C. Rowe, 20 Bowman Ave., L4M 1V3 – 705/737-3119

Charles F. Ruttan, 23 Owen St., PO Box 7, L4M 4Y5 – 705/737-0688, Fax: 705/722-4749 – *1

Service Nichols Macleod, 78 Mary St., PO Box 40, L4M 4S9 – 705/737-2123, Fax: 705/737-2194 – *3

Smith, McLean, 118 Collier St., L4M 1H4 – 705/728-5907, Fax: 705/728-1897 – *3

Helena Song, 58 Mary St., L4N 1T1 – 705/728-0751, Fax: 705/737-5380 – *1

Stewart, Esten, 100 Collier St., L4M 4V3 – 705/728-5591, Fax: 705/728-3566 – *6

Tascona, Alousis, 84 Worsley St., L4M 5E1 – 705/725-1769, Fax: 705/725-1772 – *2

Dennis Tascona, 126 Collier St., L4M 1H4 – 705/734-0440, Fax: 705/734-2324

Eric C. Taves, 86 Worsley, PO Box 295, L4M 4T2 – 705/728-4770, Fax: 705/728-7642 – *1

George Taylor, Q.C., 119 Collier St., L4M 1H5 – 705/722-0221, Fax: 705/722-6387 – *1

W. Michael Temple, Q.C., c/o Ontario Provincial Police Association, 119 Ferris Lane, L4M 2Y1 – 705/728-6161

Judith Turner-MacBeth, 86 Worsley St., PO Box 295, L4M 4T2 – 705/721-5907, Fax: 705/728-7642 – *1

Robin Vogl, #203, 28 Owen St., L4M 3G7 – 705/739-1770

Deborah L. Wall-Armstrong, 631 Yonge St., L4N 4E7 – 705/722-7272, Fax: 705/722-3568 – *1

Webb Graham, #206, 150 Dunlop St., L4M 6H1 – 705/722-8580, Fax: 705/722-6734

David S. White, Q.C., 89 Dunlop St. East, L4M 1A7 – 705/734-0100, Fax: 705/734-1303 – *1

David Wilcox, #206, 150 Dunlop St. East, L4M 6H1 – 705/721-6642, Fax: 705/722-6734 – *1

E.C. Wildman, 11 Sophia St. West, PO Box 1, L4M 4S9 – 705/739-7493, Fax: 705/739-1145 – *1

R.A. Wildman, 80 Worsley St., L4M 1L8 – 705/739-7495, Fax: 705/739-7442 – *1

Charles L. Wilson, Q.C., 25 Berczy St., PO Box 601, L4M 4V1 – 705/726-6581, Fax: 705/739-1420 – *1

Zwicker, Evans & Lewis, #201A, 48 Alliance Blvd., L4M 5K3 – 705/722-6221, Fax: 705/722-4072 – *4

**Barrys Bay** .......... **Renfrew**

Robert B. Howe, PO Box 790, K0J 1B0 – 613/756-2087, Fax: 613/756-5818 – *1

**Beamsville** .......... **Niagara North**

Arthur D. Fleming, 5041 King St., PO Box 694, L0R 1B0 – 905/563-7000, Fax: 905/563-7740

M.G. Vandeyar, Kingsway Plaza, Box: 5041, #7, 5041 King St., L0R 1B0 – 905/563-8818 – *1

**Beaverton** .......... **Durham**

C.C. Calder, PO Box 221, L0K 1A0 – 705/426-7354, Fax: 705/426-9043 – *1

Ivan G. Tomlinson, 402 Simcoe St., PO Box 512, L0K 1A0 – 705/426-7317, Fax: 705/426-5740 – *1

**Belle River** .......... **Essex**

Mousseau, DeLuca, 419 Notre Dame St., N0R 1A0

**Belleville** .......... **Hastings**

M.A. Black, 210 Church St., PO Box 652, K8N 5B3 – 613/969-8346, Fax: 613/968-8985 – *1

Boyle & Keilty, 49 Campbell St., K8N 1S8 – 613/966-2515, Fax: 613/966-2601 – *2

J.B. Corbett, 308 Front St. North, K8P 3C4 – 613/966-6662, Fax: 613/966-0995 – *1

Wendy J. Elliott, 187B Front St. North, K8P 3C1 – 613/966-0394 – *1

Follwell & Follwell, 24 Catharine St., K8P 4Z9 – 613/968-3471, Fax: 613/968-9441 – *1

Raymond Kaufmann, 187B Front St. North, K8P 3C1 – 613/966-7771, Fax: 613/966-6415 – *1

R.R. Ketcheson, #200, 199 Front St., K8N 5H5 – 613/966-1123 – *1

Peter B. McCabe, PO Box 1508, K8N 5J2 – 613/966-0924, Fax: 613/966-5337 – *1

J.C. Miller, 350 Front St., PO Box 22053, K8N 5V7 – 613/966-3483, Fax: 613/962-9050 – *1

Procter, Cameron, 183 Pinnacle St., PO Box 700, K8N 5B3 – 613/962-2584, Fax: 613/962-0968; Email: proctor@connect.reach.net – *4

Reynolds O'Brien Kline Selick, 183 Front St., PO Box 1327, K8N 5J1 – 613/966-3031, Fax: 613/966-2390 – *7

Peter A. Robertson, 350 Front St., K8N 5M5 – 613/969-9611, Fax: 613/969-9775; Toll Free: 1-800-561-6385; Email: probert@connect.reach.net – *1

C. Roderick Rolston, #202, 175 Front St., K8N 2Z1 – 613/962-9154, Fax: 613/962-8109

J. David M. Ross, PO Box 501, K8N 5B2 – 613/966-5355, Fax: 613/966-6915 – *1

Paul Russell, 221 Coleman St., PO Box 1417, K8N 5J1 – 613/962-3433, Fax: 613/962-8978 – *1

Scott & Richardson, 400 Century Place, PO Box 1029, K8N 5B6 – 613/966-4554, Fax: 613/966-5830 – *2

Templeman, Menninga, Kort, Sullivan & Fairbrother, #200, 205 Dundas St. East, PO Box 234, K8N 5A2 – 613/966-2620, Fax: 613/966-2866; Email: tmksf_jm@connect.reach.net – *13

**Blenheim** .......... **Kent**

Lucy C. Glenn, 23 Marlborough St. South, PO Box 1870, N0P 1A0 – 519/676-5451, Fax: 519/676-4911 – *1

Kerr & Wood, 15 George St., PO Box 1150, N0P 1A0 – 519/676-5465, Fax: 519/676-3918 – *2

Carmen D. Titus, 23 Marlborough St. South, PO Box 550, N0P 1A0 – 519/676-7424, Fax: 519/676-4911 – *1

T.R. Warwick, Q.C., 4 Talbot St. West, N0P 1A0 – 519/676-3266, Fax: 519/676-0001 – *1

**Blind River** .......... **Algoma**

Peterson & Peterson, 18 Lawton St., PO Box 1607, P0R 1B0 – 705/356-9877, Fax: 705/356-7498

**Blyth............................................Huron**

John C. Myers, 121 Queen St. South, PO Box 280, N0M 1H0 – 519/523-9148, Fax: 519/523-9148 – *1

**Bolton............................................Peel**

Jean P. Carberry, 210 Bolton Professional Bldg., 30 Martha St., L7E 5V1 – 905/857-2332, Fax: 905/857-2367 – *1

Marilyn Conway Jones, 284 Queen St. South, L7E 4Z5 – 905/951-0504, Fax: 905/951-0074 – *1

Sandra Morra, PO Box 75006, L7E 1H6 – 905/951-2886, Fax: 905/951-2893 – *1

Allan L. Naiman, 69 King St. West, PO Box 822, L7E 5T2 – 905/857-0861, Fax: 905/857-0866

Neiman, Callegari, 18 King St. East, PO Box 550, L7E 1E8 – 905/857-0095, Fax: 905/857-0488 – *3

Palmateer & Muise, 58 King St. West, PO Box 665, L7E 5T5 – 905/857-0847, Fax: 905/857-4410 – *2

Mark E. Penfold, 49 Queen St. North, PO Box 225, L7E 5T2 – 905/857-2835, Fax: 905/857-0091 – *1

Carol E. Struthers, 30 Martha St., L7E 5V1 – 905/951-0503, Fax: 905/951-2929 – *1

**Bowmanville....................................Durham**

Douglas J. Barber, PO Box 339, L1C 3L1 – 905/623-2525, Fax: 905/623-7666 – *1

William Brown, 68 King St. East, L1C 3X2 – 905/623-3305, Fax: 905/623-3287 – *1

Stephen A. Cooper, 36B King St. East, L1C 1N2 – 905/623-5554, Fax: 905/623-3961 – *2

Craig Fromstein, 181 Church St., L1C 1T8 – 905/623-7181, Fax: 905/623-8192 – *1

Hamilton & Mutton, 1 Division St., PO Box 39, L1C 3K8 – 905/623-7744, Fax: 905/623-7759 – *2

Mervyn B. Kelly, 38A King St. East, PO Box 159, L1C 3K9 – 905/623-4444, Fax: 905/623-4712; Email: bkel@istar.ca – *1

Strike, Salmers & Furlong, 38 King St. West, PO Box 7, L1C 3K8 – 905/623-5791, Fax: 905/623-8336 – *3

**Bracebridge....................................Muskoka**

A.R. Black, 50 Ball's Dr., PO Box 1197, P1L 1V3 – 705/645-5251, Fax: 705/645-9193 – *1

Lee, Roche & Kelly, 6 Dominion St., PO Box 990, P1L 1R6 – 705/645-2286, Fax: 705/645-5541 – *3

Brian E. Slocum, 63 Quebec St., P1L 2A4 – 705/645-2900, Fax: 705/645-2549; Email: slocum@muskoka.com – *1

Judith L. Stephenson, 58 Ontario St., P1L 2A6 – 705/645-5251, Fax: 705/645-9193 – *1

Sugg, Fitton & Taylor, 1-5 Chancery Lane, P1L 2A6 – 705/645-5211, Fax: 705/645-8021 – *2

Bruce McLeod Thompson, PO Box 99, P1L 1T5 – 705/646-1000, Fax: 705/645-9193; Email: 1-800-661-8080

Bonnie M. Tulloch, #3, 47 Quebec St., P1L 2A5 – 705/645-9923, Fax: 705/645-1695; Email: tulloch@vianet.on.ca – *1

R.A. Tweedie, 62 Kimberley Ave., P1L 1R8 – 705/645-2221, Fax: 705/645-3943 – *1

**Bradford.........................................Simcoe**

Evans & Evans, 21 Holland St. West, PO Box 190, L3Z 2A8 – 905/775-3381, Fax: 905/775-8835 – *2

Zygmunt J. Fenik, 239 Holland St. West, 3rd Fl., PO Box 100, L3Z 2A7 – 905/775-5313, Fax: 905/775-5462 – *1

W. Roy Gordon, 57 John St. West, PO Box 1660, L3Z 2B9 – 905/775-5301, Fax: 905/775-8152 – *1

Diana S. Riffert, 84 Barrie St., PO Box 1555, L3Z 2B8 – 905/775-5383, Fax: 905/775-6580 – *1

E. Pauline Taylor, 107 Holland St. East, L3Z 2B6 – 905/775-9606, Fax: 905/775-0692 – *1

**Brampton.........................................Peel**

Acri, MacPherson, Fader & Baldock, #200, 134 Queen St. East, L6V 1B2 – 905/459-6160, Fax: 905/459-4606 – *6

Linda B. Alexander, #300, 197 County Court Blvd., L6W 4P6 – 905/450-7757, Fax: 905/455-9190 – *1

Richard A. Allman, 1 Cornwall Rd., L6W 1M8 – 905/454-0397, Fax: 905/454-5072 – *1

Andre Irving, #20, 1 Bartley Bull Pkwy., L6W 3T7 – 905/459-1399, Fax: 905/459-5534

Stephen I. Beck, #230, 2 County Court Blvd., L6W 3W8 – 905/451-9898, Fax: 905/451-9427 – *1

Louise Berman, 14 Nelson St. West., L6X 1B7 – 905/459-8383 – *1

Bowyer, Greenslade & Hall, 6 George St. South, L6Y 1P3 – 416/451-1300, Fax: 416/451-4451 – *5

J. Stephen Braganca, #503, 201 County Court Blvd., L6W 4L2 – 905/450-9111, Fax: 905/450-9640 – *5

Brampton Community Legal Services, 37 George St. North, L6X 1R5 – 905/455-0160, Fax: 905/455-0832 – *2

Edmond O'Donoghue Brown, #100, 205 County Court Blvd., L6W 4R6 – 905/454-4141, Fax: 905/454-4463 – *1

Robert V. Callahan, Q.C., The Mill, #201, 60 Queen St. East, L6V 1A9 – 905/455-7659, Fax: 905/455-7106 – *1

Shawn K. Campbell, #200, 5 Conestoga Dr., L6Z 4N5 – 905/846-4991 – *1

Bonnie Caplan-Stroeder, 480 Main St. North, L6V 1P8 – 905/455-7096, Fax: 905/455-5848 – *1

David Cohen, #116, 44 Peel Centre Dr., L6T 4B5 – 905/792-7000, Fax: 905/792-2036 – *1

Jane A. Connan, 165 Main St. North, L6X 1N1 – 905/454-3070, Fax: 905/454-2964 – *1

Jane A. Connon, 165 Main St. North, L6X 1N1 – 905/454-3070, Fax: 905/454-2964 – *1

Dennis R. Cook, 52 Abelard Ave., L6Y 2K8 – 905/450-0609, Fax: 905/450-5765 – *1

Dale, Streiman & Kurz, 480 Main St. North, L6V 1P8 – 905/455-7300, Fax: 905/455-5848 – *3

Dalzell, Inglis, Waite, 1 Bartley Bull Pkwy., L6W 3T7 – 905/454-2288, Fax: 905/454-2297 – *5

Davis, Webb & Schulze, Brampton Executive Centre, #600, 8 Nelson St. West, L6X 4J2 – 905/451-6714, Fax: 905/454-1876 – *3

Michele L. Desimone, #301, 197 County Court Blvd., L6W 4P6 – 905/453-4253, Fax: 905/459-2826 – *1

Douglas G. Edward, #707, 24 Queen St. East, L6V 1A3 – 905/456-3600, Fax: 905/456-3622; Email: dgedward@netcom.ca – *1

Ron E. Folkes, #1, 14 Nelson St. West, L6X 1B7 – 905/457-2118, Fax: 905/457-3707 – *3

Furlong Collins, 182 Queen St. West, L6W 4P6 – 905/450-9050 – *2

Donald R. Good, #204, 60 Queen St., L6V 2L3 – , Fax: 905/453-1176; Toll Free: 1-800-661-8837

Henderson Law Office, #407, 7700 Hurontario St., L6Y 4M3 – 905/451-7700, Fax: 905/451-6620 – *1

Hendy & Hendy, 280 Main St. North, L6V 1P6 – 905/457-8230, Fax: 905/457-3075 – *2

Hillier & Hillier, 165 Main St. North, L6X 1N1 – 905/453-8636, Fax: 905/453-6267 – *2

Stephen A. Holmes, #201, 60 Queen St. E., L6V 1A9 – 905/796-3030, Fax: 905/796-2157 – *1

Irving, Joseph W., 121 Braidwood Lake Rd., L6Z 4L4 – 905/840-5858, Fax: 905/840-7353 – *1

J.D. Barnett Law Offices, #222, 284 Queen St. E., L6V 1C2 – 905/796-6000, Fax: 905/796-9994 – *6

Ken James & Associates, #210, 1C Conestoga Dr., L6Z 4N5 – 905/846-0000, Fax: 905/846-0001

Paul W. Jeffries, #412, 7700 Hurontario St., L6Y 4M3 – 905/451-1991, Fax: 905/451-7619 – *1

John H. Kalina, #43, 150 Clark Blvd., L6T 4Y8 – 416/410-5482, Fax: 416/410-5482; Email: hjkalina@big-foot.com – *1

Eric M. Kelday, #200, 197 County Court Blvd., L6W 4P6 – 905/459-8281, Fax: 905/459-8284 – *1

Larry Konrad, #200, 2 County Court Blvd., L6W 3W8 – 905/453-9944, Fax: 905/453-1313 – *1

Meyer Korman, 2 Fisherman Dr., Unit 7, L7A 1B5 – 905/840-7108

Laszlo Pandy, 26A Bramsteele Rd., L6W 1B3 – 905/457-0977, Fax: 905/457-8108 – *1

Lawrence, Lawrence, Stevenson, 43 Queen St. West, L6Y 1L9 – 905/451-3040, Fax: 905/451-5058 – *13

D.R. Lent, 38 Queen St. West, L6X 1A1 – 905/457-4215, Fax: 905/457-6454 – *1

Robert S. Leschied, #201, 60 Queen St. East, L6V 1A9 – 905/455-7111, Fax: 905/454-4234 – *1

D.F. Logan Law Office, #103, 45 Bramalea Rd., L6T 2W4 – 905/791-0375, Fax: 905/791-6549 – *1

A. Randall Longfield, 303 Main St. North, L6X 1N5 – 905/452-8622, Fax: 905/452-9761 – *1

Narin N. Malik, 7700 Hurontario St., Unit 311A, L6Y 4M3 – 905/450-9473, Fax: 905/450-9479 – *1

Peter Maloney, 499 Main St. South, L6Z 1N7 – 905/450-0941, Fax: 905/450-1124 – *1

Marcos Associates, 5 Church St. East, L6V 1E8 – 905/451-0002, Fax: 905/451-0003

Holmes A. Matheson, #301, 134 Queen St. East, L6V 1B2 – 905/451-6504, Fax: 905/451-0288 – *1

John W. May, 58 Elizabeth St. N., L6X 1S4 – 905/452-7004, Fax: 905/452-7006 – *1

W.J. McCulligh, #301, 197 County Court Blvd, L6W 4P6 – 905/459-1545, Fax: 905/459-2826 – *1

Robert D. Mcintyre, Q.C., 44 Peel Centre Drive, L6T 4B5 – 905/791-6262, Fax: 905/791-6446; Email: snf@ontlaw.com; URL: http://www.ontlaw.com – *1

Sarah E. Mott-Trille, 268 Main St. N., L6V 1P5 – 905/459-6000, Fax: 905/459-6108 – *1

John P. Mullen, #412, 7700 Hurontario St., L6Y 4M3 – 905/453-7600, Fax: 905/451-7619 – *1

O'Grady, Stephenson, 5A Conestoga Dr., L6Z 4N5 – 905/840-0011, Fax: 905/840-1909 – *2

Offman & Raby, #207, 7956 Torbram Rd., L6T 5A2 – 905/791-3320, Fax: 905/791-3324 – *2

Peel Legal Aid, 200-205 County Court Blvd., L6W 4R6 – 905/453-1723, Fax: 905/453-1743

V.R. Joey Poonai, #2802, 239 Queen St. East, L6W 2B6 – 905/454-3314, Fax: 905/450-8307 – *1

Susan S. Powell, #230, 2 County Court Blvd., L6W 3W8 – 905/455-6677, Fax: 905/455-6724 – *1

Prouse, Dash & Crouch, 50 Queen St. West, L6X 4H3 – 905/451-6610, Fax: 905/451-1549; Email: PDC@ProuseDash.ca – *11

Carol L. Reid, #230, 2 County Court Blvd., L6W 3W8 – 905/451-9539, Fax: 905/451-9427 – *1

Richardson, Schnall & Sanderson, 13 Queen St. East, L6W 2A7 – 905/451-1593 – *1

Peter L.T. Rickards, #209, 341 Main St. North, L6X 1N5 – 905/450-5858, Fax: 905/450-9772 – *1

Kenneth D. Robb, Q.C., #200, 197 County Court Blvd., L6W 4P6 – 905/451-1460, Fax: 905/457-0598 – *1

L.F. Samuel, 21 John St., L6W 1Z1 – 905/453-3500, Fax: 905/454-2270 – *1

Santos Associates, #203, 195 County Court Blvd., L6W 4P7 – 905/452-7733, Fax: 905/452-7665 – *3

Donald M. Seeback, #304, 134 Queen St. E., L6V 1B2 – 905/459-4389, Fax: 905/459-5274 – *1

Simmons, Da Silva & Sinton, #200, 201 County Court Blvd., L6W 4L2 – 905/457-1660, Fax: 905/457-5641 – *11

Mark E. Skursky, #101, 380 Bovaird Dr., L6Z 2S8 – 905/840-0001, Fax: 905/840-0002 – *1

George Paul Smith, 280 Main St. North, L6V 1P6 – 905/457-9791, Fax: 905/457-9798; Email: gpsmith@pathcom.com; URL: http://www.peelbarristers.com – *1

George T. Snowdon, #200, 197 County Court Blvd., L6W 4P6 – 905/457-2340, Fax: 905/457-0598 – *1

Speigel Nichols Fox, #400, 44 Peel Centre Dr., L6T 4B5 – 905/791-6262; Email: snf@ontlaw.com; URL: http://www.ontlaw.com – *6

Brian Starkman, #17, 50 Kennedy Rd. South, L6W 3E7 – 905/456-1053, Fax: 905/456-1206 – *1

Andrea Steiner, 480 Main St. North, L6V 1P8 – 905/455-5441, Fax: 905/455-5848 – *1

* indicates number of lawyers in law firm.

R.C. Stockey, #312, 25 Peel Centre Dr., L6T 3R5 – 905/793-3026, Fax: 905/793-2446 – *1

George Struk, #405, 37 George St. North, L6X 1R5 – 905/453-9591, Fax: 905/453-9722 – *1

Marvin Talsky, #103, 45 Bramalea Rd., L6T 2W4 – 905/791-7171, Fax: 905/793-5094 – *1

Tannahill, Lockhart & Clark, #200, 2 County Court Blvd., L6W 3W8 – 905/453-5770, Fax: 905/453-1313 – *4

Alan Wainwright, #200, 2 County Court Blvd., L6W 3W8 – 905/453-9520, Fax: 905/453-1313 – *1

Cynthia K. Waite, #200, 2 County Court Blvd., L6W 3W8 – 905/450-3800, Fax: 905/450-8376 – *2

Madanjit S. Walia, 860 North Park Dr., L6S 4N5 – 905/459-5117, Fax: 905/459-8418 – *1

Michael J. Walsh, 280 Main St. North, L6V 1P6 – 905/453-4105, Fax: 905/457-3075 – *1

Wanda L. Warren, 400 Queen St. West, L6X 1B3 – 905/840-7034, Fax: 905/840-6395 – *1

Richard J. Weiler, #410, 7700 Hurontario St., L6Y 4M3 – 905/455-3000, Fax: 905/455-3066; Email: agree@compuserve.com – *1

J.T. Wiley, #100, 205 County Court Blvd., L6W 4P3 – 905/454-5600, Fax: 905/454-4463 – *1

Wise, Zeldin, 480 Main St. North, L6V 1P8 – 905/796-9220

Alan M. Zuker, #201, 118 Queen St. West, L6X 1A5 – 905/451-5665, Fax: 905/451-2105 – *1

**Brantford** ........................................ **Brant**

Boddy, Ryerson, 42 Wellington St., PO Box 1265, N3T 5T3 – 519/753-8417, Fax: 519/753-7421 – *6

Donald C. Calder, 40 Nelson St., N3T 2M8 – 519/759-1910, Fax: 519/759-2881 – *1

Cook & Henderson, 105 George St., N3T 5T3 – 519/756-1930 – *2

Gethin Edward, #1417, 82 Charlotte St., N3T 5T7 – 519/756-5217

P.A.R. Giles, 63 Charlotte St., PO Box 216, N3T 5M8 – 519/756-8700, Fax: 519/756-5454 – *1

Hospodar, Davies & Goold, 120 Market St., N3T 5N3 – 519/759-0082, Fax: 519/759-8490 – *3

Lefebvre & Lefebvre, 75 Chatham St., PO Box 488, N3T 5N9 – 519/756-3350, Fax: 519/756-4727 – *5

Ernest W. Painter, 37 Cedarland Dr., N3R 6G8 – 519/756-8330, Fax: 519/756-9275 – *1

Brian T. Pennell, 65 King St., PO Box 1857, N3T 5W4 – 519/752-2555, Fax: 519/752-1648 – *1

Newton Staats, 188 Mohawk St., PO Box 1417, N3T 5T7 – 519/756-5217, Fax: 519/756-4783 – *2

Trepanier, Hagey, Kneale & Wiacek, 63 Charlotte St., PO Box 144, N3T 5M3 – 519/756-5227, Fax: 519/756-5454 – *4

Verity Daboll Gregory & Jones, Holstein Place, 171 Colborne St., PO Box 278, N3T 5M8 – 519/759-4426, Fax: 519/759-1770; Email: brantlaw@worldchat.com – *7

Waterous, Holden, Amey, Hitchon, 20 Wellington St., PO Box 1510, N3T 5V6 – 519/759-6220, Fax: 519/759-8360; Email: whah@worldchat.com – *15

Michael R. White, North Brantford Professional Centre, #103, 525 Park Rd. North, N3R 7K8 – 519/752-9004, Fax: 519/752-0449 – *1

F.B. Wray, RR#8, N3T 5M1 – 519/753-1333 – *1

Wyatt, Purcell, Stillman, Crozier, Karkkainen, 103 Darling St., N3T 2K8 – 519/756-5800, Fax: 519/756-3861 – *4

**Brechin** ........................................ **Simcoe**

Joseph J. McDonald, Box 247, Site 2, Simcoe Rd., Conc. 4, L0K 1B0 – 705/484-0308, Fax: 705/484-0804 – *1

**Bridgenorth** ................................ **Peterborough**

H. Girvin Devitt, Causeway Plaza, Ward St., PO Box 269, K0L 1H0 – 705/292-9235

**Brigden** ........................................ **Lambton**

W.E. Tennyson, 3015 Brigden Rd., PO Box 232, N0N 1B0 – 519/864-1189, Fax: 519/864-1966 – *1

**Brighton** ................................ **Northumberland**

Joseph T. Banbury, 24 Prince Edward St., PO Box 868, K0K 1H0 – 613/475-2421, Fax: 613/475-4087 – *1

Ben A. Ring, 20 Young St., PO Box 1600, K0K 1H0 – 613/475-3444, Fax: 613/475-3447 – *1

Philip S. Staddon, 17 Prince Edward St., PO Box 1360, K0K 1H0 – 613/475-3522, Fax: 613/475-3651 – *1

Thompson & Thompson, 67 Main St., K0K 1H0 – 613/475-1175 – *1

Weaver & Curtis, 25 Main St., PO Box 1660, K0K 1H0 – 613/475-4645, Fax: 613/475-4646 – *1

**Brockville** ........................................ **Leeds**

Bartley & von Cramon, #208, 9 Broad St., K6V 6Z4 – 613/342-3000, Fax: 613/342-0170; Email: voncramon@mulberry.com; URL: http://www.bvc-law.com

Beale, Macintosh, Lewis & Johnston, 2 Court House Ave., PO Box 338, K6V 5V5 – 905/345-5653, Fax: 905/345-6022 – *3

R.W. Flood, 13 Hartley St., PO Box 682, K6V 5V8 – 613/345-0087, Fax: 613/342-5294 – *1

Fraser, Best, 9 Pine St., PO Box 206, K6V 5V2 – 613/345-1435, Fax: 613/345-2007 – *2

David A. Hain, 84 King St. West, PO Box 757, K6V 5W1 – 613/342-5577, Fax: 613/342-1773.; Email: hainlaw@mulberry.com – *1

Hammond Osborne, #207, 9 Broad St., K6V 6Z4 – 613/498-0944, Fax: 613/498-0946; Email: hammond-osborne@cybertap.com – *2

Henderson Johnston Fournier, 61 King St. East, PO Box 217, K6V 5V4 – 613/345-5613, Fax: 613/345-6473 – *5

Jacqueline Regina, 8 Flint St., K6V 3M5 – 613/342-5888, Fax: 613/342-1831; Email: j.regina@msn.com – *1

D.W. Wyatt, 10 Broad St., K6V 4T7 – 613/342-7205, Fax: 613/342-0995 – *1

**Bruce Mines** ........................................ **Algoma**

Peterson & Peterson, 76 Taylor St., PO Box 100, P0R 1C0 – 705/785-3491, Fax: 705/785-3768; Email: la~ryd.peterson@sympatico.ca

**Burk's Falls** ................................ **Parry Sound**

Linda Heyder, 139 Ontario St., PO Box 546, P0A 1C0 – 705/382-3031, Fax: 705/382-2886 – *1

Powell, Cunningham, Kennedy & Grandy, 178 Ontario St., PO Box 460, P0A 1C0

R. Vander Wijst, PO Box 541, P0A 1C0 – 705/382-2746 – *1

**Burlington** ........................................ **Halton**

Patricia E. Anderson, 855 Brant St., L7R 2J6 – 905/333-0903 – *1

Noel R. Bates, 1422A Ontario St., L7S 1G4 – 905/681-1196, Fax: 905/637-0042 – *1

Brechin & Huffman, 3365 Harvester Rd., L7N 3N2 – 905/681-2476, Fax: 905/333-4298 – *2

Bridle & Bridle, 3310 South Service Rd., L7N 3M6 – 905/637-5213, Fax: 905/333-4787 – *2

Cass & Bishop, #31, 3455 Harvester Rd., L7N 3P2 – 905/632-7744, Fax: 905/632-9076 – *3

Cleaver, Crawford, Hunt, O'Driscoll & Fraser, 2019 Caroline St., L7R 3Y2 – 905/634-5581, Fax: 905/634-1563 – *4

Michael J. Darling, 3419 Mainway Dr., L7M 1A9 – 905/332-6696, Fax: 905/332-0021 – *1

Dingle, Charlebois & Swybrous, 2079 Gore St., L7R 1E2 – 905/634-5541; 825-0502, Fax: 905/333-4499 – *2

Dunlop & Associates, 3556 Commerce Ct., L7N 3L7 – 905/681-3311, Fax: 905/681-3635; Email: dunlop@bserv.com – *5

R.B. Easterbrook, #200, 1013 St. Matthew's Ave., L7T 2J3 – 905/333-1633, Fax: 905/333-9684 – *1

Frederick L. Forsyth, 2122 Old Lakeshore Rd., L7R 1A3 – 905/637-5641, Fax: 905/637-5404 – *1

Adam A. Gall, #7A, 355 Plains Rd. E., L7T 4H7 – 905/639-3114, Fax: 905/637-3391 – *1

David Godard, 3540 Commerce Crt, L7N 3L7 – 905/632-2600, Fax: 905/632-2722 – *1

Green Germann, 411 Guelph Line, PO Box 400, L7R 3Y3 – 905/639-1222, Fax: 905/632-6977 – *3

Haber, Haber & Associates, 3370 South Service Rd., L7N 3M6 – 905/639-8894; 825-1953, Fax: 905/639-0459 – *4

John Hicks Law Office, #7, 541 Brant St., L7R 2G6 – 905/681-3131, Fax: 905/333-6688 – *1

Hofbauer Associates, 1455 Lakeshore Rd., L7S 2J1 – 905/634-0040, Fax: 905/634-9119; Email: ideas@capatents.com – *2

J.P. Hourigan, Q.C., 2078 Pine St., L7R 1G2 – 905/637-8291 – *1

Kerr & Hawken, 442 Brant St., L7R 2G4 – 905/632-2822, Fax: 905/333-9594 – *2

Richard R. Kosterski, #111, 2201 Brant St., L7P 3N8 – 905/335-0361, Fax: 905/335-3944 – *1

Paul A. Lafleur, 518 Brant St., L7R 2G7 – 905/632-3842, Fax: 905/632-6821 – *1

Law Line, 1422A Ontario St., L7S 1G4 – , Fax: 905/637-0042

MacIsaac & MacIsaac, #7, 107 Plains Rd. W., L7T 1E8 – 905/333-1246, Fax: 905/333-1248 – *4

Martin Hillyer Bryant, 2122 Lakeshore Rd., L7R 1A3 – 905/637-5641, 847-5277 (Toronto), Fax: 905/637-5404 – *8

McEniry & McEniry, #210, 3310 South Service Rd., L7R 3Y7 – 905/529-1151, Fax: 905/634-9180 – *2

Nancy A. Millar, 7 - 107 Plains Rd. West, L7T 1E8 – 905/333-1246, Fax: 905/333-1248 – *1

Patrick M. Mlot, #204 South, 1455 Lakeshore Rd., L7S 2J1 – 905/634-3677, Fax: 905/681-6510 – *1

Moores & Reynolds, #2, 2021 Plains Rd. E., L7R 4M3 – 905/333-0100, Fax: 905/333-9675 – *2

Michael D. Morgan, #26, 4380 South Service Rd., L7L 5Y6 – 905/681-8747, Fax: 905/681-8769 – *1

Muir & Seed, 468 Elizabeth St., L7R 2M2 – 905/634-8030, Fax: 905/333-4613 – *1

Gloria Nardi-Bell, #256, 2025 Guelph Line, L7P 4X4 – 905/332-8818, Fax: 905/332-8815 – *1

Pichelli & Turingia, 3390 South Service Rd., L7N 3J5 – 905/639-0731, Fax: 905/333-4290 – *2

J. Douglas Redfearn, 442 Brant St., L7R 2G4 – 905/333-5322, Fax: 905/333-9835 – *1

J.C. Savchuk, 1100 Burloak Dr., L7L 6B2 – 905/336-9111 – *1

Simpson & Rich, #12, 460 Brant St., L7R 4B6 – 905/681-1521, 825-0522, Fax: 905/333-5075 – *2

Simpson, Wigle, Sims Square Bldg., #501, 390 Brant St., L7R 4J4 – 905/639-1052, Fax: 905/333-3960; Email: simpwigb@netaccess.on.ca – *7

T.R. Sutherland Q.C., #201, 3190 Harvester Rd., L7N 3T1 – 905/634-5521, Fax: 905/634-5153 – *1

Harold Kim Taylor, 3365 Harvester Rd., Upper Level, L7N 3N2 – 905/681-6400, Fax: 905/681-6510; Toll Free: 1-800-636-7732 – *1

Thatcher & Wands, 501 John St., L7R 2L1 – 905/681-0444, Fax: 905/681-2937 – *2

Elizabeth A. Urban, 3365 Harvester Rd., Upper Level, L7N 3N2 – 905/333-6640, Fax: 905/681-6510 – *1

J.B. Watters, 2031 James St., L7R 1H2 – 905/639-3775, Fax: 905/639-7762 – *1

H.W. Zahoruk, 3077 New St., L7N 1M6 – 905/639-3342, Fax: 905/333-3757 – *1

**Caledon** ........................................ **Peel**

Richard A. Allman, RR#1, L0N 1C0 – 519/940-0415

**Caledon East** ........................................ **Peel**

George W. Jenney, 15891 Airport Rd., PO Box 340, L0N 1E0 – 905/584-9300 – *1

**Caledonia** .................................... **Haldimand**

Arrell, Brown, Osier & Murray, 41 Caithness St. West, N0A 1A0 – 905/765-5414, Fax: 905/765-5144 – *4

Benedict & Ferguson, 322 Argyle St. South, N3W 1K8 – 905/765-4004, Fax: 905/765-3001 – *2

L.S. Humenik, 35 Caithness St. East, PO Box 2112, N3W 2G6 – 905/765-3162, Fax: 905/765-4313 – *1

**Cambridge** .................................... **Waterloo**

D. St.C. Bond, 57 Ainslie St. North, PO Box 22104, N1R 8E3 – 519/623-2311, Fax: 519/623-6957 – *1

G.J. Clement, 43 Cambridge St., N1R 7G7 – 519/621-7779, Fax: 519/621-4301 – *1

Gary Flaxbard, #140, 1315 Bishop St., N1R 6Z2 – 519/623-8340, Fax: 519/623-8720 – *2

B.E. Fogo, 2 Water St. North, PO Box 22022, N1R 8E3 – 519/621-9831, Fax: 519/740-0306 – *1

Goad & Goad, 53 Cambridge St., PO Box 907, N1R 5X9 – 519/623-7660, Fax: 519/623-2594 – *3

Gowlings, 19 Thorne St., N1R 5W1 – 519/621-6910, Fax: 519/621-5028 – *7

Gary E.J. Hauser, 1666 King St. East, N3H 3R7 – 519/653-1521, Fax: 519/650-1466 – *1

Hilborn & Konduros, 39 Queen St. West, PO Box 25008, N3C 4B6 – 519/658-6341, Fax: 519/654-9127 – *2

George R. Ingram, #502, 73 Water St. North, PO Box 22100, N1R 8E3 – 519/621-9000, Fax: 519/621-9009 – *1

Claude Isaacksz, 1434 King St. East, N3H 3R4 – 519/653-0341, Fax: 519/653-9521

Calvin G. Johnson, PO Box 876, N1R 5X9 – 519/623-9160, Fax: 519/740-6023 – *1

David A. Kinder, 546 Grand Ridge Dr., N1S 4Y9 – 519/740-6676, Fax: 519/623-8545 – *1

George E. Loker, 43 Cambridge St., PO Box 1723, Stn Galt, N1R 3R8 – 519/621-4300 – *1

Paul M. Mann, 679 Coronation Blvd., N1R 3G5 – 519/623-0700, Fax: 519/622-4091 – *1

Matlow, Miller, Harris, Thrasher, 39 Dickson St., PO Box 607, N1R 5W1 – 519/621-2430 – *4

Onorato & Zboril & McKnight, 708 Duke St., PO Box 32148, N3H 5M2 – 519/653-3217, Fax: 519/653-3702 – *3

M.G.F. Parrott, 52 George St. North, N1R 5W1 – 519/621-0310, Fax: 519/740-3494 – *1

Pavey, Law, 19 Cambridge St., PO Box 1707, Stn Galt, N1R 7G8 – 519/621-7260, Fax: 519/621-1304; Email: law@paveylaw.com; URL: http://www.paveylaw.com – *7

Pettitt, Schwarz, #403, 73 Water St. North, N1R 7L6 – 519/621-2450, Fax: 519/621-5750; Email: petschlaw@golden.net – *2

Henry R. Shields, 2 Water St. North, N1R 3B1 – 519/622-2150, Fax: 519/623-0997 – *1

Donald A. Thompson, Q.C., 2 Water St. North, PO Box 1297, Stn Galt, N1R 7G6 – 519/621-9850, Fax: 519/621-0820 – *1

David M. Tugender, 1156 King St. East, PO Box 32134, N3H 5M2 – 519/653-1032, Fax: 519/653-0492 – *1

James W. Wiegand, #101, 725 Coronation Blvd., PO Box 1023, Stn Galt, N1R 5Y2 – 519/622-9455, Fax: 519/622-4134 – *1

J. Craig Wilson, 2 Water St. North, PO Box 1297, N1R 7G6 – 519/622-0192 – *1

W.C. Wraight, 15 Main St., PO Box 22103, N1R 8E3 – 519/623-3330, Fax: 519/621-0136 – *1

**Campbellford** .................................... **Northumberland**

William E. Baker, #201, 79 Bridge St. East, K0L 1L0 – 705/653-2011, Fax: 705/653-4205 – *1

Wallace J. Brown, 17 Front St. South, PO Box 1269, K0L 1L0 – 705/653-2041, Fax: 705/653-4063 – *1

J. Wayne C. Buck, 6 Queen St., PO Box 1630, K0L 1L0 – 705/653-4022, Fax: 705/653-2365 – *1

N.R.H. Burgess, 64 Front St., PO Box 1239, K0L 1L0 – 705/653-3400, Fax: 705/653-4811

Paul D.H. Burgess, 64 Front St. North, PO Box 1540, K0L 1L0 – 705/653-5555, Fax: 705/653-5557 – *1

Paul M.G. Smith, Q.C., 32 Pellissier St., PO Box 1057, K0L 1L0 – 705/653-1860, Fax: 705/653-4903 – *1

**Cannington** .................................... **Durham**

Brandon Miller McGrath, 17 Cameron St. West, L0E 1E0 – 705/432-2361, Fax: 705/432-2680 – *1

**Carleton Place** .................................... **Lanark**

Bruun & Bennett, 74 Bridge St., K7C 2V3 – 613/257-1655, Fax: 613/257-8837 – *1

P.D. Courtice, 164 Bridge St., PO Box 29, K7C 3P3 – 613/257-5001, Fax: 613/257-8797 – *1

N. Alan Jones, 92 Bridge St., K7C 2V3 – 613/257-3811, Fax: 613/253-0479 – *1

McNabb, Brooke, 38 Mill St., PO Box 152, K7C 3P4 – 613/257-7620, Fax: 613/257-8830 – *2

**Casselman** .................................... **Russell**

Benoit & Benoit, #203, 708, rue Principale, CP 650, K0A 1M0 – 613/764-3694, Fax: 613/764-3198 – *1

Mireille C. LaViolette, #101, 641, rue Principale, CP 179, K0A 1M0 – 613/764-3747, Fax: 613/764-1000 – *1

**Cayuga** .................................... **Haldimand**

Slimon & Gallagher, 45 Munsee St. North, PO Box 250, N0A 1E0 – 905/772-3369, Fax: 905/772-5113 – *2

Larry P. Thibideau, PO Box 508, N0A 1E0 – 905/772-3513, Fax: 905/772-5918 – *1

**Chapleau** .................................... **Sudbury**

Weaver, Simmons, Pine St., PO Box 329, P0M 1K0 – 705/864-1505

**Chatham** .................................... **Kent**

James E. Allin, 128 Queen St., N7M 2G6 – 519/352-6540, Fax: 519/352-9097 – *1

Archibald & Creed, 237 Wellington St. West, N7M 1J9 – 519/354-2383, Fax: 519/354-3250 – *1

D.H. Asher, 245 St. Clair St., PO Box 1238, N7L 5R9 – 519/351-2116, Fax: 519/351-2318 – *1

L.R. Babcock, 72 Victoria Ave., PO Box 745, Stn Main, N7M 5L1 – 519/354-5600 – *1

Benoit, Van Raay, Spisani & Fuerth, 124 Thames St., PO Box 1087, N7L 2Y8 – 519/352-8580 – *4

William D. Bowsher, 245 St. Clair St., N7L 3J8 – 519/351-5147, Fax: 519/351-2318 – *1

Thomas D. Campbell, Q.C., 75 Thames St., PO Box 522, Stn Main, N7M 5K6 – 519/352-2100, Fax: 519/352-2621 – *1

Carscallen, Reinhart, Mathany, Maslak, 111 1/2 St. Clair St., PO Box 1444, N7M 5W8 – 519/351-2261, Fax: 519/351-2860 – *4

J. Bernard Comiskey, 84 Dover St., PO Box 525, N7M 5K6 – 519/352-1360, Fax: 519/352-7300 – *1

K.E. Hansen, Q.C., 186 Wellington St., PO Box 579, N7M 5K6 – 519/352-2040, Fax: 519/352-9522 – *1

Juba, Elliott, 84 Dover St., PO Box 848, N7M 5L1 – 519/354-9911, Fax: 519/351-7300 – *2

Kee & Robertson, 334 King St. West, PO Box 189, N7M 5K3 – 519/354-1490 – *1

R.A. Kirby, 237 Wellington St. West, N7M 1J9 – 519/351-6849, Fax: 519/354-3250 – *1

D.R. Lachance, 5 - 6 St., PO Box 1293, N7M 5R9 – 519/354-7411, Fax: 519/354-7320 – *1

William P. Magee, 55 Centre St., PO Box 459, N7M 5K5 – 519/352-7950, Fax: 519/352-2699 – *1

R.L. McFalls, 245 St. Clair St., PO Box 1026, N7M 4W3 – 519/351-2777 – *1

McNevin, Gee & O'Connor, 43 William St. North, PO Box 58, N7M 5K1 – 519/352-5450, Fax: 519/352-5452 – *1

Mitchell & Mitchell, #4, 6 St., PO Box 476, Stn Main, N7M 5K5 – 519/351-2200, Fax: 519/354-9862 – *2

William M. Myers Q.C., 186 Wellington St. West, PO Box 579, N7M 5K6 – 519/352-2040, Fax: 519/352-9522 – *1

Paroian, Raphael, Courey, Cohen & Houston, 214 Queen St., PO Box 548, N7M 5K6 – 519/352-0190, Fax: 519/352-0565 – *37

Judith R. Pascoe, #210, 143 Wellington St. West, PO Box 341, N7M 5K4 – 519/354-2844, Fax: 519/354-2255 – *1

E. Carol Peifer, 20 Raleigh St., PO Box 224, N7M 5K3 – 519/351-2424, Fax: 519/351-3611 – *1

Patricia L. Poole, 65 Adelaide St. South, N7M 4R1 – 519/351-3500 – *1

Robert K. Rankin, Q.C., #402, 48 - 5 St., PO Box 341, N7M 5K4 – 519/351-5356, Fax: 519/354-2255 – *1

Rhodes Law Firm, PO Box 1358, N7M 5W8 – 519/352-4700, Fax: 519/352-5616 – *2

Paul D. Watson, 55 Centre St., PO Box 661, N7M 5K8 – 519/351-7721, Fax: 519/351-7726; Email: pwatson@ciaccess.com – *1

**Chelmsford** .................................... **Sudbury**

Gerard E. Guimond, 164 Errington St., PO Box 2225, P0M 1L0 – 705/855-4511, Fax: 705/855-5631

Mailloux & Gray, 128 Errington St., 1347, PO Box 1347, P0M 1L0 – 705/855-9091, Fax: 705/855-4038 – *2

**Chesley** .................................... **Bruce-Grey**

Loucks & Loucks, 84 First Ave. South, PO Box 430, N0G 1L0 – 519/363-3223, Fax: 519/363-2133 – *2

McClelland Law Office, 159 - 1st Ave. South, N0G 1L0 – 519/363-3293, Fax: 519/363-2315 – *1

Ross C. McLean, 27 Main St. South, PO Box 118, N0G 1L0 – 519/363-3190, Fax: 519/363-2213 – *1

**Chesterville** .................................... **Dundas**

Cass, Grenkie, 13 Ralph St., PO Box 700, K0C 1H0 – 613/448-2735, Fax: 613/448-1395 – *3

**Clinton** .................................... **Huron**

Frank A. Cameron, 38 Ontario St., PO Box 148, N0M 1L0 – 519/482-5510, Fax: 519/482-9126 – *1

D. Gerald Hiltz, 52 Huron St., PO Box 1087, N0M 1L0 – 519/482-3414

E. Beecher Menzies, Q.C., 49 Albert St., PO Box 68, N0M 1L0 – 519/482-3475, Fax: 519/482-3779 – *1

**Coboconk** .................................... **Durham**

Tyler P. Higgins, PO Box 219, K0M 1K0 – 705/454-2665, Fax: 705/454-2625 – *1

**Cobourg** .................................... **Northumberland**

Karl G. Bernhardt, #102, 1005 William St., K9A 5J4 – 905/372-8789, Fax: 905/373-0376 – *1

Brent, Steger & Christ, 247 Division St., PO Box 9, K9A 4K2 – 905/372-2217, Fax: 905/372-1783; Email: bsc@eagle.ca – *2

Rodger F. Cooper, 253 Division St., K9A 3P9 – 905/372-8727, Fax: 905/372-0720; Email: cooper@eagle.ca – *1

J Bradley Halls, 203 Durham St., PO Box 664, K9A 4R5 – 905/372-8791, Fax: 905/372-4819 – *1

Ember Leigh Hamilton, 161 Sutherland Cres., K9A 5L6 – 905/373-0589, Fax: 905/373-0928; Email: ember@eagle.ca – *1

William C. Lifeso, 203 Durham St., PO Box 248, K9A 4K8 – 905/372-0119, Fax: 905/372-4819 – *1

Stewart, Mitchell & Macklin, #205, 1005 William St., K9A 5J4 – 905/372-3395, Fax: 905/372-1695 – *4

D.E. Stokes, PO Box 23, K9A 5W4 – 905/372-2791 – *1

John Van Duzer, 177 Queen St., K9A 1N3 – 905/372-8956 – *1

**Cochrane** .................................... **Cochrane**

Boivin & Serré, 174 - 4th Ave., PO Box 1898, P0L 1C0 – 705/272-4346, Fax: 705/272-2991 – *3

Evans, Bragagnolo & Sullivan, 138 Third St., P0L 1C0 – 705/272-5197, Fax: 705/272-4850

* indicates number of lawyers in law firm.

David L. Lanthier, 153 - 3 St., PO Box 2020, P0L 1C0 – 705/272-4205, Fax: 705/272-3467 – *1

**Colborne.................................. Northumberland**

J.A. Carter, 26 King St. East, PO Box 699, K0K 1S0 – 905/355-3322, Fax: 905/355-3104 – *1

**Coldwater....................................... Simcoe**

Raymond J. Morhan, RR#4, L0K 1E0 – 705/835-5752, Fax: 705/835-5742 – *1

Stewart, Esten, GD PO, L0K 1E0 – 705/835-3231 – *3

**Collingwood..................................... Simcoe**

Baulke, Augaitis & Wright, 150 Hurontario St., PO Box 100, L9Y 3Z4 – 705/445-4930, Fax: 705/445-1871 – *3

J.D. Bulmer, Q.C., 137 Hurontario St., PO Box 23, L9Y 3Z4 – 705/445-9244, Fax: 705/444-5741 – *1

Christie Cummings, #302, 115 Hurontario St., PO Box 187, L9Y 3Z4 – 705/444-3650, Fax: 705/444-0024 – *2

Brian Greasley, 33 Ste. Marie St., PO Box 490, L9Y 4B2 – 705/445-9300, Fax: 705/445-2996 – *1

Robert Jacks, Q.C., 31 Simcoe St., PO Box 7, L9Y 1H5 – 705/445-0381, Fax: 705/445-0052 – *1

L.E. Lant, 60 Hume St., PO Box 248, L9Y 3Z5 – 705/445-2886, Fax: 705/444-5837 – *1

Paul Lee & Associates, #3, 207 Hurontario St., L9Y 2M1 – 705/444-0077, Fax: 705/444-9241 – *2

Neathery & Mumford, #4, 450 Hume St., L9Y 1W6 – 705/445-6051, Fax: 705/444-0969 – *2

Shaw, McLellan & Ironside, 10 Schoolhouse Lane, PO Box 280, L9Y 3Z5 – 705/445-1382, Fax: 705/445-7042 – *3

Simcoe Legal Services Clinic, 159 First St., L9Y 1A6 – 705/444-1177, Fax: 705/445-1516

Victor L. Vandergust, 11 Hurontario St., PO Box 39, L9Y 3Z4 – 705/445-4544, Fax: 705/445-4160 – *1

**Concord............................................ York**

Thomas A. Adler, #207, 1600 Steeles Ave. West, L4K 4M2 – 905/660-3637, Fax: 905/660-3863 – *1

Agueci & Calabretta, #312, 1600 Steeles Ave. West, L4K 4M2 – 416/638-8400, Fax: 416/660-7828 – *5

William G. Atwell, 11874 Keele St., PO Box 212, Stn Main, L4K 2S3 – 905/832-8800, Fax: 905/832-3926 – *1

Joseph Baglieri, #312, 1600 Steeles Ave. West, L4K 4M2 – 905/660-1800, Fax: 905/660-7828 – *1

Brian D. Belmont, #222, 1600 Steeles Ave. West, L4K 4M2 – 905/669-6931, Fax: 905/669-7403 – *1

Talal Chehab, #300, 3100 Steeles Ave. West, L4K 3R1 – 905/738-2463, Fax: 905/738-4901

Ralph Ciccia, #300, 3100 Steeles Ave. West, L4K 3R1 – 905/748-4900, Fax: 905/738-4901 – *1

D'Ambrosio Law Office, 3100 Steeles Ave. West, L4K 3R1 – 905/761-7400, Fax: 905/738-1168 – *1

Danson, Recht & Freedman, #15, 3000 Langstaff Rd., L4K 4R7 – 905/660-0818, Fax: 905/660-0891

De Lucia & Associates, #208, 1600 Steeles Ave., L4K 4M2 – 905/660-4500, Fax: 905/660-5580 – *1

Patrick DiMonte, #208, 3100 Steeles Ave. West, L4K 3R1 – 905/738-2101, Fax: 905/738-1168 – *1

Thomas F. Kowal, #300, 3100 Steeles Ave. West, L4K 3R1 – 905/738-5755, Fax: 905/738-4901 – *1

Mark W. Kushner, #231, 1600 Steeles Ave. West, L4K 4M2 – 905/669-7079, Fax: 905/669-7080

Lecce & Marchioni, #300, 3100 Steeles Ave. West, L4K 3R1 – 905/738-5111 – *2

Enzo Salvatori, #203, 2100 Steeles Ave. West, L4K 2V1 – 905/738-1777, Fax: 905/738-2065 – *1

Sherwin H. Shapiro, #309, 3100 Steeles Ave. West, L4K 3R1 – 905/660-4404, Fax: 905/660-4711; Toll Free: 416/410-3736 – *1

Philip Siller, #2000, 128 Adesso Dr., L4K 3C3 – 416/364-7707; Email: phils@ascent.ca – *1

Alan G. Silverstein, #318, 1600 Steeles Ave. West, L4K 4M2 – 905/761-1600, Fax: 905/761-0948 – *1

Simukoff & Waisberg, #220, 1600 Steeles Ave. West, L4K 4M2 – 905/660-6494, Fax: 905/660-6727

S.H. Simukoff, #228, 1600 Steeles Ave. West, L4K 4M2 – 905/660-6494, Fax: 905/660-6722

Warga/Katz Associates, #12A, 207 Edgely Blvd., L4K 4B5 – 905/669-1979, Fax: 905/669-6699 – *2

**Cornwall....................................... Stormont**

Adams, Sherwood, Swabey & Follon, 305 Second St. East, K6H 1Y8 – 613/938-3330, Fax: 613/938-7885 – *7

Bergeron, Filion & McClelland, 103 Sydney St., PO Box 1282, K6H 5V3 – 613/932-2911, Fax: 613/932-2356 – *3

Honor M. Bolger, 120 Sydney St., K6H 3H2 – 613/936-0060, Fax: 613/937-0993 – *1

Garry A. Brunet, 5 - 3rd St. East, K6H 2C6 – 613/938-1826, Fax: 613/938-3310 – *1

Paul E. Burns, 21 Water St. West, 2nd Fl., K6J 1A1 – 613/938-7700, Fax: 613/936-1299 – *1

R.R. Dube, 26 - 9th St. East, K6H 2T8 – 613/938-2857, Fax: 613/938-6784 – *1

Guindon, MacLean, McDonald & Castle, 50 - 2 St. East, K6H 1Y3 – 613/933-3931, Fax: 613/933-6123 – *4

Law Office of Diane M. Lahaie, 28 - 7 St. West, K6J 2X9 – 613/936-8833, Fax: 613/936-6717 – *1

Lamoureux, Gauthier, McDerby & Associates, 1302 - 2 St. West, K6J 1J3 – 613/932-1220, Fax: 613/936-1624 – *2

Leduc, Giovanniello, Bellefeuille, 340 - 2nd St. East, K6H 1Y9 – 613/938-0294, Fax: 613/932-2374 – *3

Paul F. Lemieux, 5 - 3rd St. East, K6H 2C6 – 613/933-8338, Fax: 613/938-3310 – *1

P.J. McDerby, 1302 - 2nd St. West, K6J 1J3 – 613/932-1220, Fax: 613/936-1624; Email: pjmcderby@cnwl.igs.net – *1

McDougall, Dancause, Shields & Airey, 119 Sydney St., PO Box 788, K6H 5T7 – 613/932-3502, Fax: 613/932-9339 – *4

Parisien, Willis, 229 Augustus St., PO Box 127, K6H 5S7 – 613/937-3333, Fax: 613/933-2200 – *2

Ian D. Paul, 702 - 2nd St. East, K6H 2A1 – 613/933-9455, Fax: 613/933-7566 – *1

Stephen B. Renner, 122 Sydney St., K6H 3H2 – 613/933-6540 – *1

Michael R. Salhany, 504 Pitt St., PO Box 912, K6H 5V1 – 613/932-4140 – *1

Donald J. White, 700 Montreal Rd., K6H 1C4 – 613/933-6443, Fax: 613/933-6453

Barrie M. Wilson, 132 - 2nd St. West, K6J 1G5 – 613/938-2224, Fax: 613/938-8005 – *1

**Corunna....................................... Lambton**

Allan Brock, 447 Lyndock St., N0N 1G0 – 519/862-2211, Fax: 519/862-3506 – *1

**Creemore....................................... Simcoe**

Brian Greasley, PO Box 27, L0M 1G0 – 705/466-3336, Fax: 705/445-2269 – *1

**Deep River..................................... Renfrew**

George W. Leconte, 8 Glendale Ave., PO Box 340, K0J 1P0 – 613/584-3154, Fax: 613/584-4877 – *1

Roche & Dakin, 11 Champlain St., PO Box 1240, K0J 1P0 – 613/584-3392, Fax: 613/854-4922 – *2

**Delhi.......................................... Norfolk**

John R. Hanselman, 138 Eagle St., N4B 1S5 – 519/582-0770, Fax: 519/582-1876 – *1

Harrison & Harrison, 148 Eagle St., PO Box 98, N4B 2W8 – 519/582-1900, Fax: 519/582-4978; Email: harrharr@oxford.net – *2

**Deseronto...................................... Hastings**

Elton Brant, RR#1, K0X 1X0 – 613/966-9414

**Dryden......................................... Kenora**

Vermeer & Van Walleghem, PO Box 938, P8N 2Z5 – 807/223-3311, Fax: 807/223-4133 – *2

**Dundas................................ Hamilton-Wentworth**

Hines & Stevens, 161 King St. West, PO Box 8, L9H 1V3 – 905/627-3531, Fax: 905/628-0038 – *2

Johnson, Ramsbottom & Castle, 11 Sydenham St., PO Box 8180, L9H 5G1 – 905/628-2214, Fax: 905/627-5639 – *3

Lee & Lee, PO Box 8587, L9H 5G1 – 905/628-6321, Fax: 905/628-2767; Email: wilklaw@netaccess.on.ca – *1

Leslie T. Paci, 179 King St. West, L9H 1V3 – 905/628-6369 – *1

William J. Wilkins, 63 King St. West, PO Box 8587, L9H 5G1 – 905/628-3611, Fax: 905/628-2767 – *1

**Dunnville...................................... Haldimand**

Chambers, G. Donald, 106 Lock St. East, N1A 1J7 – 905/744-7485, Fax: 905/774-7486 – *1

Hedley & McQuatty, 311 Broad St. East, N1A 1G4 – 905/774-7688, Fax: 905/774-6637 – *2

Timms & McCombs, 129 Queen St., N1A 1H6 – 905/774-9988, Fax: 905/774-7943 – *3

**Dunrobin................................ Ottawa-Carleton**

Leier Law Office, 2837 Maple Ln., RR#1, K0A 1T0 – 613/832-0517 – *1

Alan Pratt, 3550 Torwood Dr., RR#1, K0A 1T0 – 613/832-1261, Fax: 613/832-4978; Email: apratt@hookup.net; URL: http://www.hookup.net/~apratt – *1

**Durham............................................ Grey**

Fallis, Fallis & McMillan, 195 Lambton St. East, PO Box 710, N0G 1R0 – 519/369-2515 – *3

I.C. Johnson, 175 Mill St., PO Box 1070, N0G 1R0 – 519/369-6931, Fax: 519/369-2423; Email: johnslaw@bmts.com – *1

Allen Wilford, RR#1, N0G 1R0 – 519/369-6466, Fax: 519/369-5701 – *1

**Eganville....................................... Renfrew**

H.J. Stewart Lavigueur, PO Box 9, K0J 1T0 – 613/628-2153, Fax: 613/628-2915 – *1

**Elgin............................................ Leeds**

J.T. Monaghan, PO Box 190, K0G 1E0 – 613/359-5108, Fax: 613/359-6105 – *1

Cynthia L. Rotar, 56 Main St., PO Box 238, K0G 1E0 – 613/359-6476, Fax: 613/359-6567 – *1

**Elliot Lake..................................... Algoma**

Aubé, Fabris Associates, 25 Columbia Walk, P5A 1Y6 – 705/848-6993, Fax: 705/848-8621 – *2

André L.J. Berthelot, 13 Elizabeth Walk, PO Box 308, P5A 1Z2 – 705/848-2208, Fax: 705/848-3525 – *1

**Elmira......................................... Waterloo**

Charles R. Davidson, #5, 25 Industrial Dr., N3B 3K3 – 519/669-1539, Fax: 519/669-1530 – *1

D.S. Teahen, 11 Arthur St. North, N3B 1Z4 – 519/669-5300, Fax: 519/669-4412 – *1

Waters & Hastings, 21 Arthur St. South, N3B 2M4 – 519/669-1641, Fax: 519/669-1944 – *2

Weir & Buchler, 11A Arthur St. South, N3B 2M4 – 519/669-1644, Fax: 519/669-3592 – *2

Woods & Clemens, 9 King St., PO Box 216, N3B 2Z6 – 519/669-5101, Fax: 519/669-5618 – *2

Zinszer & Co., 9 Church St. West, N3B 1M2 – 519/669-2200, Fax: 519/669-4349 – *1

**Elmvale......................................... Simcoe**

G.E. French, 10 Queen St. West, PO Box 549, L0L 1P0 – 705/322-3000, Fax: 705/322-0771 – *1

John H. Heacock, 12 Queen St. West, PO Box 419, L0L 1P0 – 705/322-2101, Fax: 705/322-0822 – *1

**Elora....................................... Wellington**

M.P. Hebner, 67 Victoria St., PO Box 640, N0B 1S0 – 519/846-5303, Fax: 519/846-0198 – *1

J.E. Morris, PO Box 338, N0B 1S0 – 519/846-5366, Fax: 519/846-8170 – *1
Gregory A. Oakes, 211 Geddes St., PO Box 248, N0B 1W0 – 519/846-5555, Fax: 519/846-5554 – *1

**Embrun** ................................ **Prescott & Russel**
Beaudet Davidson, 945 Notre Dame, PO Box 220, K0A 1W0 – 613/443-3372 – *1
James D. Campbell, #1, 165 Bay St., K0A 1W1 – 613/443-5683, Fax: 613/443-3285 – *2

**Englehart** ................................ **Temiskaming**
Ramsay, Ramsay, Kemp, Andrew & Maille, P0J 1H0 – 705/544-2223

**Erin** ................................ **Peel**
Kenneth Torrens, 194 Main St., PO Box 325, N0B 1T0 – 519/833-9081, Fax: 519/833-0259 – *1

**Espanola** ................................
Miller, Makj, 78 Centre St., P5E 1S4 – 705/869-5001, Fax: 705/869-5003
Wilkins & Wilkins, #1, 109 Sheppard St., P5E 1A1 – 705/869-4444, Fax: 705/869-5183

**Essex** ................................ **Essex**
Hickey, Brown & McManus, 14 Centre St., N8M 1N9 – 519/776-7349, Fax: 519/776-8161 – *2
W.K. Kendrick, 114 Talbot St. South, N8M 1B2 – 519/253-4431 – *1
Willms & Shier, 115 Talbot St., N8M 2C5 – 519/776-9020, Fax: 519/776-9027; Email: info@willmsshier.com; URL: http://www.willmsshier.com – *2

**Exeter** ................................ **Huron**
Robert J. Deane, Q.C., 417 Main St., PO Box 130, N0M 1S6 – 519/235-0440, Fax: 519/235-3481 – *1
Raymond & McLean, 387 Main St., PO Box 100, N0M 1S6 – 519/235-2234, Fax: 519/235-2671 – *2

**Fenelon Falls** ................................ **Victoria**
David J. Gowanlock, PO Box 607, K0M 1N0 – 705/887-2582, Fax: 705/887-1871 – *1
McQuarrie, Hill, Walden, Chester, McLeod, 57A Lindsay St., PO Box 1136, K0M 1N0 – 705/887-2941, Fax: 705/324-5723
J.R. Webster, 20 Francis St. West, PO Box 103, K0M 1N0 – 705/887-2533 – *1

**Fergus** ................................ **Wellington**
Wilson, Jack & Grant, PO Box 128, N1M 2W7 – 519/843-1960, Fax: 519/843-6888 – *3
Wolfe, Smith & Forster, PO Box 99, N1M 2W7 – 519/843-3650, Fax: 519/843 6907 – *3

**Feversham** ................................ **Grey**
John S. Hood, PO Box 100, N0C 1C0 – 519/922-2259, Fax: 519/922-2805 – *1

**Finch** ................................ **Stormont**
C.A. Martin-Hrycak, PO Box 170, K0C 1K0 – 613/984-2759, Fax: 613/984-2533 – *1

**Fonthill** ................................ **Niagara South**
Jill Anthony, 1450 Pelham St., PO Box 743, L0S 1E0 – 905/892-2621, Fax: 905/892-1022 – *1

**Forest** ................................ **Lambton**
L.M. Crozier, Q.C., 30 King St. West, PO Box 616, N0N 1J0 – 519/786-5221, Fax: 519/786-2135 – *1

**Fort Erie** ................................ **Niagara South**
G.M. Berman, 26 Jarvis St., PO Box 545, L2A 5M6 – 905/871-6699, Fax: 905/871-0442 – *1
David A. Hurren, #4, 1264 Garrison Rd., L2A 6E7 – 905/871-2424, Fax: 905/871-4848 – *1
D.J. Jacobi, 1321 Garrison Rd., PO Box 1028, L2A 5N8 – 905/871-4244, Fax: 905/871-8693 – *1
R.B. Miller, 1222 Garrison Rd., L2A 1P1 – 905/871-4556, Fax: 905/871-5215 – *1
Ruch & Williams, 43 Jarvis St., PO Box 8, L1A 2S3 – 905/871-8711 – *2
J.T. Teal, PO Box 247, L2A 5M9 – 905/871-5796, Fax: 905/871-9151 – *1
Louis Ziff, Q.C., #2, 121 Garrison Rd., L2A 6G6 – 905/871-4466, Fax: 905/871-9255 – *1

**Fort Frances** ................................ **Rainy River**
Clare Allan Brunetta, 420 Victoria Ave., PO Box 656, P9A 3M9 – 807/274-9809, Fax: 807/274-8760; Email: brunetta@fortfrances.lakeheadu.ca – *1
Lawrence A. Eustace, 510 Portage Ave., P9A 2A3 – 807/274-3247, Fax: 807/274-6447 – *1
Ian J. McLennan, 356 Church St., PO Box 254, P9A 3M6 – 807/274-5343, Fax: 807/274-8489 – *1
J. Rod McLeod, Site 206-10, 1455 Idylwyld Dr., P9A 3M3 – 807/274-2832, Fax: 807/274-7968 – *1
Lawrence G. Phillips, 237 Church St., P9A 1C7 – 807/274-8525, Fax: 807/274-5758 – *1
Donald A. Taylor, 504 Armit Ave., P9A 2H7 – 807/274-7811, Fax: 807/274-8485 – *1

**Gananoque** ................................ **Leeds**
Paul D. Beseau, 389 King St. East, K7G 1G6 – 613/382-8841, Fax: 613/382-4295 – *1
Clarke & Wright, 280 King St. East, PO Box 280, K7G 2T8 – 613/382-2112, Fax: 613/382-8107 – *2
Henry J. Knotek, 82 King St. East, K7G 1G1 – 613/382-4567, Fax: 613/382-8586 – *1
Steacy & Delaney, PO Box 70, K7G 2T6 – 613/382-2137, Fax: 613/382-7794 – *2

**Garson** ................................ **Sudbury**
Duane D. Drager, 3547 Falconbridge Hwy., PO Box 190, P3L 1S6 – 705/693-2743, Fax: 705/693-3914 – *1

**Georgetown** ................................ **Halton**
Adele E. Dyrczon, 16 Guelph St., L7G 3Z2 – 905/873-2662, Fax: 905/873-2664 – *1
Jeffrey L. Eason, 116 Guelph St., PO Box 159, L7G 4Y5 – 905/877-6961, Fax: 905/877-9725 – *1
Helson, Kogon, Schaljo, 132 Mill St., L7G 2C6 – 905/877-5206, 454-2889 (Toronto), Fax: 905/877-3948 – *5
W. Glen How & Associates, PO Box 4100, L7G 4Y4 – 905/873-4100, Fax: 905/873-4522; Email: wghow@sprynet.com – *3
R.T. Howitt, Q.C., #301, 83 Mill St., L7G 5E9 – 905/887-5139, Fax: 905/873-4164 – *1
Montogmery T. Hyde, 33 Main St. South, L7G 3G2 – 905/877-0126 – *1
Julian W. Lipkowski, #306, 16 Mountainview Rd. South, L7G 4K1 – 905/873-1648, Fax: 905/873-1576 – *1
William H. Manderson, 2 Guelph St., L7G 3Y9 – 905/873-0121, Fax: 905/873-4114 – *1
O'Connor MacLeod, 134 Main St. South, L7G 3E6 – 905/873-8000, Fax: 905/873-7865
Warren J. Smith, #205, 232A Guelph St., L7G 4B1 – 905/873-6995, Fax: 905/873-6367 – *1
Sopinka & Kort, 145 Mill St., L7G 2C2 – 905/846-2515, Fax: 905/877-0604 – *2
J.T. Walinga, #301, 83 Mill St., L7G 5E9 – 905/873-4144, Fax: 905/873-4164 – *1

**Glencoe** ................................ **Middlesex**
Gary R. Merritt, 213 Main St., PO Box 309, N0L 1M0 – 519/287-3432, Fax: 519/287-2498 – *1
Brian K. Morris, PO Box 428, N0L 1M0 – 519/287-2456, Fax: 519/287-2823; Email: brian-morris@sympatico.ca – *1

**Gloucester** ................................ **Ottawa-Carleton**
Anderson Law Office, 2663 Innes Rd., K1B 3J7 – 613/830-1112, Fax: 613/830-7998 – *2
Bowley, Cuffari, 673 Laverendrye Dr., K1J 7X5 – 613/747-8489, Fax: 613/747-7993
Bunning & Farnand, 2580 Innes Rd., K1B 4N7 – 613/824-0000, Fax: 613/824-9164 – *2
Bruce A. Freeborn, 21 Ryeburn Dr., K1G 3N3 – 613/822-0774, Fax: 613/822-7079 – *1
Mazerolle & Lemay, #202, 1173 Cyrville Rd., K1J 7S6 – 613/746-5700, Fax: 613/746-1783 – *2

**Goderich** ................................ **Huron**
Carey & Ottewell, 50 North St., N7A 2T4 – 519/524-2634, Fax: 519/524-5538 – *2
Mary E. Cull, 164B Court House Sq., PO Box 375, Stn Main, N7A 4C6 – 519/524-1115, Fax: 519/524-1116 – *1
Donnelly & Murphy, 18 The Square, PO Box 38, N7A 3Y7 – 519/524-2154, Fax: 519/524-8550 – *4
Norman B. Pickell, PO Box 430, N7A 4C7 – 519/524-8335, Fax: 519/524-1530 – *1
Prest & Egener, 33 Montreal St., PO Box 218, N7A 3Z2 – 519/524-8368 – *2
Troyan & Fincher, 44 North St., N7A 2T4 – 519/524-2115, Fax: 519/524-4481 – *2

**Gore Bay** ................................ **Manitoulin**
Armstrong & Land, PO Box 90, P0P 1H0 – 705/282-2710, Fax: 705/282-2205 – *2
J.L. Greenspoon, RR#1, P0P 1H0 – 705/282-2485, Fax: 705/282-2485 – *1
James E. Weppler, 65 Meredith St., PO Box 222, P0P 1H0 – 705/282-3354, Fax: 705/282-3211 – *1

**Gorrie** ................................ **Huron**
Crawford, Mill & Davies, General Delivery, N0G 1X0 – 403/335-3528

**Grand Valley** ................................ **Dufferin**
Helen L. Terry, RR#2, L0N 1G0 – 519/928-2316, Fax: 519/928-2316 – *1

**Gravenhurst** ................................ **Muskoka**
Aiken, Christensen & Heath, 195 Muskoka Rd. North, PO Box 70, P1P 1X2 – 705/687-2281, Fax: 705/687-6086 – *2
J.C. Malvern, 190 Hotchkiss St., P1P 1H6 – 705/687-2241, Fax: 705/687-7817 – *1
Stuart, Cruickshank & Beatty, 195 Church St. North, PO Box 1270, P1P 1V4 – 705/687-3441, Fax: 705/687-5405 – *4

**Grimsby** ................................ **Niagara North**
Morris Cree, 18 Elm St., PO Box 69, L3M 4G1 – 905/945-2077, Fax: 905/945-2078 – *1
Paul A. MacLeod, #204, 155 Main St. East, L3M 1P2 – 905/945-9659, Fax: 905/945-0838 – *1
Nicholls & Greenhow, 18 Ontario St., PO Box 187, L3M 4G3 – 905/945-5431, Fax: 905/945-5286 – *2
Sinclair, Murakami & Loney, 55 Main St. West, L3M 1R3 – 905/945-9271, Fax: 905/945-3066 – *3
J.L. Wolfe, 63 Main St. East, L3M 1M7 – 905/945-9231, Fax: 905/945-9166 – *1

**Guelph** ................................ **Wellington**
Abraham Acker, Q.C., 18 Douglas St., PO Box 846, N1H 2S9 – 519/822-5660, Fax: 519/822-0411 – *1
Lynn Archbold, 89 Surrey St. East, N1H 3P7 – 519/763-4748, Fax: 519/824-3443 – *1
Braida & Henry, 28 Paisley St., PO Box 1082, N1H 8N6 – 519/824-2242 – *2
Jane E. Caspers, 89 Surrey St. East, N1H 3P7 – 519/824-0430, Fax: 519/824-3443 – *1
Izaak de Rijcke, 258 Woolwich St., N1H 3W1 – 519/837-2551, Fax: 519/837-0958
Dunbar Goetz Cameron, 32 Douglas St., PO Box 366, N1H 6K5 – 519/822-4260, Fax: 519/822-3370 – *1

* indicates number of lawyers in law firm.

Guy D.E. Farb, 22 Paisley St., N1H 2N6 – 519/763-6644, Fax: 519/763-8091; Email: lawguy@easynet.on.ca – *1

T. Flaherty, 29 Cork St. West, N1H 2W9 – 519/836-5730, Fax: 519/836-8654 – *1

Flesher & Mann, 376 Woolwich St., PO Box 1788, N1H 7A1 – 519/821-6406, Fax: 519/821-6408 – *2

Hungerford, Guthrie & Berry, 59 Woolwich St., PO Box 187, N1H 6J9 – 519/824-2020, Fax: 519/824-2023 – *3

Kearns, McKinnon, 512 Woolwich St., PO Box 930, N1H 6M8 – 519/822-4680, Fax: 519/822-1583 – *11

Maiocco & DiGravio, 230 Speedvale Ave. West, N1H 1C4 – 519/836-2710, Fax: 519/836-7312 – *2

Maxwell & Rinne, 40 Norwich St. East, PO Box 1810, N1H 7A1 – 519/836-2091, Fax: 519/836-1783 – *2

McElderry & Morris, 84 Woolwich St., PO Box 875, N1H 3T9 – 519/822-8150, Fax: 519/822-1921 – *4

Keith R. Millikin, 328 Woolwich St., N1H 3W5 – 519/823-8100, Fax: 519/823-8101 – *1

Moon, Heath, 164 Norfolk St., PO Box 180, Stn Main, N1H 6J9 – 519/824-2540, Fax: 519/763-6785; Toll Free: moonlaw@sentex.net – *6

Richard R. Morrow, 185 Woolwich St., N1H 3V4 – 519/836-4020, Fax: 519/836-1265

Moyer, Malak, Jackman & Rowles, 17 Cork St. West, PO Box 37, N1H 6J6 – 519/824-4883, Fax: 519/821-2910 – *2

Nelson, Watson, 183 Norfolk St., N1H 4K1 – 519/821-9610, Fax: 519/821-8550 – *3

Nicholson & Doney, 137 Norfolk St., PO Box 1505, N1H 6N9 – 519/837-3000, Fax: 519/837-1758 – *2

R.D. Noble, 457 Woolwich St., 2nd Fl., N1H 3X6 – 519/836-7360, Fax: 519/836-7369 – *1

James M. Peluch, 207 Woolwich St., N1H 3V4 – 519/822-3531, Fax: 519/837-3056 – *1

J.A. Runions, Q.C., Canada Trust Bldg., #300, 55 Cork St., PO Box 1117, N1H 6N3 – 519/821-3300, Fax: 519/821-7431 – *1

Judith P. Ryan, RR#2, N1H 6H8 – 519/856-2223, Fax: 519/856-2223

Judith C. Sidlofsky Stoffman, 166 Woolwich St., PO Box 964, N1H 6N1 – 519/822-8511, Fax: 519/821-5421 – *1

J.G. Smart, 115 Woolwich St., N1H 3V1 – 519/836-3000, Fax: 519/836-3578 – *1

David T. Starr, 176 Woolwich St., 2nd Fl., N1H 3V5 – 519/824-9690, Fax: 519/824-7394 – *1

Valeriote & Valeriote, 373 Woolwich St., PO Box 1839, N1H 7A1 – 519/837-0300, Fax: 519/837-1617 – *4

Vorvis, Anderson, Gray, Armstrong & Vorvis, 5 Douglas St., PO Box 184, N1H 6J9 – 519/824-7400, Fax: 519/824-7521 – *5

**Hagersville .................................... Haldimand**

James R. Baxter, 144 Main St. South, PO Box 490, N0A 1H0 – 905/768-3363, Fax: 905/768-1550; Email: jrbaxter@netcom.ca – *1

McCarthy & Fowler, 17 Main St. South, PO Box 879, N0A 1H0 – 905/768-3553, Fax: 905/768-1567 – *2

**Haileybury .................................... Temiskaming**

Robbie D. Gordon, 488 Ferguson Ave., PO Box 490, P0J 1K0 – 705/672-3338, Fax: 705/672-2451 – *2

Katherine A. Scott, 594 Lakeshore Rd., PO Box 1051, P0J 1K0 – 705/672-2937, Fax: 705/672-5744; Email: crowther@ntl.sympatico.ca

Smith, Byck & Grant, 514 Ferguson St. West, PO Box 1240, P0J 1K0 – 705/672-2102, Fax: 705/647-8575; Email: sbgcom@nt.net; URL: http://www.nt.net/sbg/sbg1.html – *2

**Haliburton .................................... Haliburton**

Bishop & Rogers, PO Box 472, K0M 1S0 – 705/457-1440, Fax: 705/457-3042 – *1

R.G. Selbie, PO Box 186, K0M 1S0 – 705/457-2435, Fax: 705/457-3074 – *1

**Hamilton .................................... Hamilton-Wentworth**

Agro, Zaffiro, Parente, Orzel & Baker, 1 James St. South, 4th Fl., PO Box 2069, Stn LCD 1, L8N 3G6 – 905/527-6877, Fax: 905/527-6843 – *21

Joshua M. Bach, #409, 20 Jackson St. West, L8P 1L2 – 905/577-7789, Fax: 905/577-0093 – *1

R.B. Barrs, #204, 640 Upper James St., L9C 2Z2 – 905/387-9212, Fax: 905/387-6109 – *1

T.N. Basciano, 115 Hughson St. North, L8R 1G7 – 905/525-4396 – *1

Alec Z. Beasley, #808, 20 Hughson St. South, L8N 2A1 – 905/527-8348, Fax: 905/527-3863 – *1

Jerome Bergart, #901, 1 King St. West, L8P 1A4 – 905/524-1060 – *1

S.E. Bernstein, 117 Main St. East, L8N 3Z3 – 905/546-1990 – *1

R.A. Blake, #203, 1119 Fennell Ave. East, L8T 1S2 – 905/388-5382, Fax: 905/388-6966 – *1

Borkovich & Ingrassia, 1 Main St. East, L8N 1E7 – 905/522-7442, Fax: 905/522-7191 – *3

Braden & Braden, 123 Ottawa St. North, L8H 3Y9 – 905/547-1987, Fax: 905/549-7899 – *1

Brown, Scarfone, Hawkins, 120 King St. West, L8N 3P9 – 905/523-1333, Fax: 905/523-5878 – *11

Byrne, Martin & Bedford, 166 John St. South, L8N 2C4 – 905/527-3867, Fax: 905/527-3860 – *3

Cain, Gzik & Gardner, 340 Main St. East, L8N 1J1 – 905/528-7933, Fax: 905/528-1326 – *3

Cynthia G. Campling, #1505, 105 Main St. East, L8N 1G6 – 905/523-5570, Fax: 905/522-0988 – *1

Camporese & Associates, #805, 21 King St. West, L8P 4W7 – 905/522-7068, Fax: 905/522-5734 – *3

Paul D.V. Cannon, 19 San Fernando Dr., L9C 2C1 – 905/388-5803 – *1

R.B. Caskie, 101 Hunter St. East, PO Box 934, L8N 3P9 – 905/528-0237, Fax: 905/522-6446 – *1

Philip Castrodale, #1008, 20 Hughson St. South, L8N 2A1 – 905/523-7903, Fax: 905/523-7904 – *1

Robert Charko, 75 Young St., L8N 1V4 – 905/528-5105, Fax: 905/523-5867 – *1

Gary Chertkoff, Q.C., #412, 20 Jackson St. West, L8P 1L2 – 905/522-2439, Fax: 905/522-9198 – *1

Joseph M. Chrolavicius, 124 Young St., L8N 1V6 – 905/522-2704, Fax: 905/529-5112 – *1

L.J. Cohen, Q.C., #407, 20 Hughson St. South, L8N 2A1 – 905/525-0400, Fax: 905/572-1190 – *1

Confente, Garcea, #340, 69 John St. South, L8N 2B9 – 905/529-9999, Fax: 905/529-1160; Email: confente.garcea@freenet.hamilton.on.ca – *2

Cooper & Cooper, Norwich Union Bldg., #700, 4 Hughson St. South, L8N 3Z1 – 905/527-1611, Fax: 905/527-3486 – *1

R.J. Cornale, Norwich Union Bldg., 4 Hughson St. South, 2nd Fl., L8N 3Z1 – 905/521-9989, Fax: 905/572-6509

Emilio D'Ortenzio, 103 John St. South, L8N 2C2 – 905/523-7003, Fax: 905/528-8589 – *1

K.W. Dechert, 66 James St. North., L8R 2K5 – 905/570-0622, Fax: 905/570-0624 – *1

A.F. DeRubeis, 1362 Main St. East, L8K 1B7 – 905/544-1158 – *1

DiCenzo & Associates, #41, 1070 Stone Church Rd. East, L8W 3K8 – 905/574-3300, Fax: 905/574-1766; Email: dca@weblaw.ca

John DiPietro, #201, 72 James St. North, L8R 2K5 – 905/526-0736, Fax: 905/521-2772 – *1

N.V. Dissanayake, 132 Mayfair Cres., L8S 4E8 – 905/525-6629, Fax: 905/522-3920 – *1

James Dodson, #301, 20 King St. East, L8N 1A4 – 905/527-4495 – *1

Dudzic, Barristers & Solicitors, #1014, 105 Main St. East, PO Box 988, Stn A, L8N 3R1 – 905/528-4251, Fax: 905/528-5325 – *3

Brian Duxbury, #1500, 1 King St. West, L8P 1A4 – 905/570-1242, Fax: 905/570-1955 – *1

Marvin D. Dyck, 187 Hughson St. South, L8N 2B6 – 905/526-7395, Fax: 905/523-8875 – *1

Paul H. Ennis, Q.C, #502, 105 Main St. East, L8N 1G6 – 905/525-9335, Fax: 905/525-9988 – *1

Evans, Husband, #901, 20 Hughson St. South, L8N 2A1 – 905/528-0084, Fax: 905/528-7692; Email: euhucra@netaccess.on.ca – *7

John F. Evans Q.C. & Associates, #1201, 1 King St. West, L8P 1A4 – 905/523-5666, Fax: 905/523-8098; Email: jfevans.law@sympatico.ca – *4

Evans, Philp, PO Box 930, Stn A, L8N 3P9 – 905/525-1200, Fax: 905/525-7897; Email: info@evans-philp.on.ca – *15

Raymond L. Fazakas, 942 King St. West, L8S 1K8 – 905/528-8666, Fax: 905/528-8667 – *1

L.A. Ferro, #903, 1 King St. West, L8P 1A4 – 905/522-8702, Fax: 905/522-0841 – *1

Findlay & McCarthy, 66 James St. North, L8R 2K5 – 905/526-8943, Fax: 905/526-8696 – *2

Foreman & Rosenblatt, 425 York Blvd., L8R 3K3 – 905/525-3570, Fax: 905/523-0363 – *2

Stephen M. Frankel, #801, 105 Main St. East, L8N 1G6 – 905/522-3972, Fax: 905/528-2767 – *1

Genesee & Clarke, 143 Main St. East, L8N 1G4 – 905/522-7066, Fax: 905/522-7085 – *4

Colin David Gibson, Q.C., 550 Concession St., L8V 1A9 – 905/522-1163, Fax: 905/574-3299 – *1

Gowlings, #600, 120 King St. West, L8P 4V2 – 905/540-8208, Fax: 905/528-5833 – *5

Guyatt & Gaasenbeek, #201, 131 John St. South, L8N 2C3 – 905/528-8369, Fax: 905/528-9187 – *1

Halford, Findley, 336 Sanatorium Rd., L9C 2A4 – 905/388-0973, Fax: 905/388-2797 – *1

Sidney M. Halpern, 1164 Barton St. East, L8H 2V6 – 905/544-2812, Fax: 905/544-2815 – *1

Harper, Jaskot, #810, 25 Main St. West, L8P 1H1 – 905/522-3517, Fax: 905/522-3555 – *4

Harrington & Harrington, 550 Concession St., L8V 1A9 – 905/383-3331, Fax: 905/574-3299 – *3

Harris & Henderson, 92 King St. East, 12th Fl., L8N 1A8 – 905/528-4242, Fax: 905/528-8808 – *6

Kevin R.L.M. Hope, 57 John St. South, L8N 2B9 – 905/525-3357, Fax: 905/527-4462 – *1

D.E. Horlacher, 75 Young St., PO Box 867, L8N 1V4 – 905/528-5105, Fax: 905/523-5867 – *1

Hovius, John, #425, 135 James St. South, L8P 2Z6 – 905/526-0780, Fax: 905/526-0783 – *1

Hughes, Amys, #1401, One King St. West, L8P 1A4 – 905/577-4050, Fax: 905/577-6301; Email: ajs@h-amys.mhs.compuserve.com

Douglas L.L. Inch, Q.C., 1164 Barton St. East, L8H 2V6 – 905/544-2812, Fax: 905/544-2815 – *1

Inch, Easterbrook & Shaker, 1 King St. West, 15th Fl., L8P 4X8 – 905/525-4481, Fax: 905/525-0031; Email: ies@inchlaw.com – *8

Frank Jaksa, 2134 King St. East, L8K 1W6 – 905/547-1302, Fax: 905/549-7973 – *1

Jaskula, Sherk, Flaherty, Weston & Brock, #302, 135 James St. South, L8P 2Z6 – 905/577-1040, Fax: 905/577-7775; Email: jsfw@netcom.ca – *5

W. Jazvac, 124 Young St., L8N 1V6 – 905/523-0872, Fax: 905/529-5112 – *1

Richard E. Jennis, #901, 1 King St. West, L8P 1A4 – 905/528-7922 – *1

Johnston & Peart, #403, 20 Hughson St. South, L8N 2A1 – 905/527-4521, Fax: 905/527-0447 – *2

H.E. Katz, 2 Ray St. South, L8P 3V2 – 905/522-0040, Fax: 905/522-2981 – *1

Katz, Harvey & Associates, 14 Hess St. South, L8P 3M8 – 905/523-1442, Fax: 905/525-3817 – *5

Michael W. Kelly, #101, 154 Main St. East, L8N 1G9 – 905/546-1920, Fax: 905/546-8471; Email: mikelly@hookup.net; URL: http://www.hookup.net/~mikelly – *1

M.J. Kemeny, 124 MacNab St. South, L8P 3C3 – 905/528-8711, Fax: 905/521-1924 – *1

P.D. Kennedy, #234, 845 Upper James St., L9C 3A3 – 905/389-1351, Fax: 905/389-4241 – *1

Joel B. Kerr, #205, 135 James St. South, L8P 2Z6 – 905/521-1013, Fax: 905/521-9578 – *1

William E. Kosar, #3800, 100 Main St. East, L8N 3W6 – 905/524-0011, Fax: 905/524-1879 – *1

A.V. Kuska, 152 Jackson St. East, L8N 1L3 – 905/523-5920, Fax: 905/529-6051 – *1

Landeg, Spitale, #1004, 20 Hughson St. South, L8N 2A1 – 905/529-7462, 523-1440, Fax: 905/528-6787 – *2

Lazier Hickey Langs O'Neal, 25 Main St. West, 17th Fl., L8P 1H1 – 905/525-3652, Fax: 905/525-6278 – *9

Lees & Lees, #2225, 25 Main St. West, L8P 1H1 – 905/523-7830, Fax: 905/523-4677 – *3

Leggat, Keesmaat & Dixon, LCD 1, #201, 20 Hughson St. South, PO Box 916, L8N 3P6 – 905/527-0202, 529-8403, Fax: 905/527-4948 – *5

Patrick D. Lennon, #101, 100 Main St. East, L8N 3W7 – 905/529-4357, Fax: 905/529-4752

Gary R. Livesey, 75 Young St., L8N 1V4 – 905/523-5850, Fax: 905/523-5867 – *1

Luchak, Lofchik, Sullivan, #101, 46 Jackson St. East, PO Box 91066, Stn Effort Sq., L8N 4G3 – 905/529-1939, Fax: 905/527-3497 – *6

Michael Lypka, #711, 20 Hughson St. South, L8N 2A1 – 905/527-0255 – *1

Mackesy, Smye, Turnbull, Grilli, Jones, Winward & Mahler, 117 Hughson St. South, L8N 1G7 – 905/525-2341, Fax: 905/525-6300 – *7

E.R. Madronich, 1 Charlton Ave. West, L8P 2B8 – 905/523-4191 – *1

W.J.I. Malcolm, 20 Hughson St. South, L8N 2A1 – 905/528-4291, Fax: 905/528-4292 – *1

Martin & Martin, 4 Hughson St. South, L8N 3Z1 – 905/528-5936, Fax: 905/523-4144 – *8

Anthony E. McCusker, #1001, 105 Main St. East, L8N 1G6 – 905/523-0593 – *1

McHugh, Mowat, Whitmore, 337 Queenston Rd., L8K 1H7 – 905/549-4676 – *4

McLaren & McLaren, 1278 Barton St. East, L8H 2W1 – 905/544-5761 – *2

McLelland & Dean, #700, 1 King St. West, L8P 1A4 – 905/522-9261 – *1

Milligan, Gresko, Charuk & Rogers, #330, 110 King St. West, PO Box 57099, L8P 4W9 – 905/522-7700, Fax: 905/522-1502 – *4

Mitchnick & Mitchnick, 1 King St. West, PO Box 907, L8N 3P6 – 905/528-1409, Fax: 905/526-0732 – *2

F. Mohideen, 360 Queenston Rd., L8K 1H9 – 905/545-0442, Fax: 905/545-2645 – *1

John W. Nicholson, 117 Hunter St. East, L8N 1M5 – 905/529-9982 – *1

Nolan, Nolan, McLean & Associates, #700, 1 King St. West, L8P 1A4 – 905/522-9261 – *8

J.Z. Olenski, #203, 1039 Upper James St., L9C 3A6 – 905/387-3922, Fax: 905/387-0291; Email: jolenski@worldchat.com – *1

Leonard H.P. Panek, Effort Sq., #504, 105 Main St. East, L8N 1G6 – 905/527-1119 – *1

George J. Parker, 14 Bold St., L8P 1T2 – 905/523-5636, Fax: 905/523-4910 – *1

Pelech, Otto & Powell, 149 Main St. East, PO Box 91206, L8N 4G4 – 905/522-4696, Fax: 905/528-6608 – *4

Albert K. Perl, #1420, 25 Main St. West, L8P 1H1 – 905/527-5316, Fax: 905/527-0114; Email: alperl@inter-lynx.net – *1

Petrini, Rubenstein & Waxman, 242 James St. South, L8P 3B3 – 905/525-9632, Fax: 905/521-0690 – *3

Leon Price, #610, 135 James St. South, L8P 2Z6 – 905/529-8146 – *1

Geoffrey M. Read, 172 Main St. East, L8N 1G9 – 905/529-2028, Fax: 905/522-6677 – *1

Robinson, McCallum, McKerracher, Graham, #300, 69 John St. South, L8N 2B9 – 905/528-1435, Fax: 905/529-1570 – *1

Rocchi & Rocchi, 120 Hughson St. South, L8N 2B2 – 905/527-1518, Fax: 905/527-7022 – *1

Rosart & Rosart, 36 Hunter St. East, 6th Fl., L8N 3W8 – 905/777-1222, Fax: 905/777-1220 – *1

Ross & McBride, 1 King St. West, 10th Fl., PO Box 907, L8N 3P6 – 905/526-9800, Fax: 905/526-0732 – *20

Ross & Ross, #414, 20 Jackson St. West, L8P 1L2 – 905/522-4657, Fax: 905/527-8550 – *2

Schreiber & Smurlick, 288 Ottawa St. North, L8H 3Z9 – 905/545-1107 – *1

Schreiber, Bordonaro, 126 Jackson St. East, L8N 1L3 – 905/527-4477 – *1

Sharpe, Inglis, Litwiller, #2225, 25 Main St. West, L8P 1H1 – 905/528-5918, Fax: 905/529-5855 – *2

B.B. Shekter, Q.C., 103 John St. South, L8N 2C2 – 905/527-1133 – *1

Simpson & Watson, 950 King St. West, L8S 1K8 – 905/527-1174, Fax: 905/577-0661 – *3

S. Simpson, #407, 20 Hughson St. South, L8N 2A1 – 905/523-7400, Fax: 905/527-1190 – *1

Simpson, Wigle, Commerce Place, #400, 21 King St. West, PO Box 990, L8P 4Y5 – 905/528-8411, Fax: 905/528-9008; Email: simpwigl@netaccess.on.ca; URL: http://www.ads-online.on.ca/ – *21

F.P. Sondola, #1005, 143 James St. South, L8P 3A1 – 905/523-1970, Fax: 905/523-1971 – *1

Spears, Smith & Associates, 44 Hughson St. South, L8N 2A7 – 905/526-0626, Fax: 905/521-1976 – *3

State & Garman, 367 Upper James St., L9B 1K2 – 905/388-8022, Fax: 905/574-1991 – *3

J.J. Steadman, 124 MacNab St. South, L8P 3C3 – 905/529-6400, Fax: 905/521-1924 – *1

Sullivan, Festeryga, Lawlor & Arrell, 39 James St. South, 3rd Fl., L8P 4X6 – 905/528-7963, Fax: 905/527-0077 – *10

Swaye, Gerald A., Q.C., 155 James St. South, L8P 3A4 – 905/524-2861, Fax: 905/524-2313 – *4

Szpiech, Ellis, Skibinski, Shipton, 414 Main St. East, L8N 1J9 – 905/524-2454, 522-8660, Fax: 905/523-1733 – *4

Thoman, Soule, Gage, 46 Jackson St. East, PO Box 187, Stn LCD 1, L8N 3C5 – 905/529-8195, Fax: 905/529-7906 – *9

William J. Tidball, 172 Main St. East, L8N 1G9 – 905/521-8922, Fax: 905/522-6677 – *2

Tkach & Tokiwa, 520 Upper Sherman, L8V 3L8 – 905/383-3545, Fax: 905/574-3020 – *1

Turkstra, Mazza Associates, 15 Bold St., L8P 1T3 – 905/529-3476, Fax: 905/529-3663 – *23

Vance & Vance, Royal Bank Bldg., #212, 32 James St. South, L8P 2Y1 – 905/528-6346, Fax: 905/528-8200 – *1

R.F. Vero, #300, 143 James St. South, L8P 3A1 – 905/523-6363, Fax: 905/523-5130 – *1

Waller & Homer, 241 King St. West, L8P 1A7 – 905/525-6120, Fax: 905/525-6127 – *2

Weisz, Rocchi & Scholes, Effort Trust Bldg., #200, 242 Main St. East, L8N 1H5 – 905/523-1842, Fax: 905/528-9254, 523-4011 – *5

Wellenreiter, A., Q.C., 46 Forest Ave., L8N 1X1 – 905/525-4520 – *2

Terence A. Whelan, Q.C., #403, 393 Rymal Road West, L9B 1V2 – 905/383-6381 – *1

Terry L. Winchie, Q.C., 112 Hughson St. South, L8N 2B2 – 905/525-8911, Fax: 905/529-6688

Yachetti, Lanza & Restivo, #800, 105 Main St. East, PO Box 950, L8N 3P9 – 905/528-7534, Fax: 905/528-5275 – *7

Zimmerman & Associates, #4201, 100 Main St. East, L8N 3W6 – 905/524-0231, Fax: 905/524-2023; Email: lex@zimmerman.on.ca – *8

**Hanover ........ Grey**

Barker & Halpin, 570 - 10 St., N4N 1R7 – 519/364-4720, Fax: 519/364-2407 – *2

Crockford & Duffy, 282 - 10 St., N4N 1P2 – 519/364-1440, Fax: 519/364-6023 – *2

Robert W. Garcia, PO Box 37, N4N 3C3 – 519/364-3643, Fax: 519/364-6594 – *1

Donald R. Neilson, 320 - 10 St., N4N 1P3 – 519/364-3100 – *1

**Harrow ........ Essex**

Karl G. Melinz, 41A Centre St. West, PO Box 880, N0R 1G0 – 519/738-2232, Fax: 519/738-9080; Email: kgmelinz@wincom.net – *1

**Havelock ........ Northumberland**

Wallace J. Brown, 11 George St. West, K0L 1Z0 – 705/778-3381, Fax: 705/778-7722

**Hawkesbury ........ Prescott**

Charbonneau Smith, 300 Main St. West, K6A 2H7 – 613/632-7081, Fax: 613/632-2800; Email: charsmith@hawk.igs.net – *6

Julien & Cormier., 132 Race St., K6A 1V2 – 613/632-0148, Fax: 613/632-1810 – *2

Langlois/Gauthier, 480 McGill St., K6A 1R2 – 613/632-8600, Fax: 613/632-5274 – *2

Woods Parisien Michaud Landry, #200, 115 Main St. East, PO Box 249, K6A 2R9 – 613/632-7015, 8557, Fax: 613/632-3524 – *4

**Hearst ........ Cochrane**

Boivin & Serré, 810 Georges St., PO Box 129, P0L 1N0 – 705/362-8850, Fax: 705/372-1225

Bourgeault, Nadeau, Brunelle, 914 Prince St., P0L 1N0 – 705/362-5922 – *3

**Hillsburgh ........ Wellington**

Robert P. Harper, 115 Main St., PO Box 10, N0B 1Z0 – 519/855-4961, Fax: 519/855-4029 – *1

**Huntsville ........ Muskoka**

James S. Anderson, The East Mall Court, 110 Main St. East, PO Box 1447, P0A 1K0 – 705/789-8823, Fax: 705/789-1272

A.B. Cochran, 110 Main St. East, PO Box 2220, P0A 1K0 – 705/789-5538, Fax: 705/789-1272 – *1

G.A. Smith, #1, 3 Fairy Ave., P1H 1G7 – 705/789-2984 – *1

**Ingersoll ........ Oxford**

Nesbitt Coulter, 183 Thames St. South, PO Box 55, N5C 3K1 – 519/485-5651, Fax: 519/485-6582; Email: em@nesbittlaw.com – *9

Parker, Ross & Blain, 36 King St. East, PO Box 160, N5C 3K5 – 519/485-0300, Fax: 519/485-6588 – *4

**Innisfil ........ Simcoe**

McLellan Associates, 1000 Innisfil Beach Rd., SS#3, PO Box 6500, L0L 2M0 – 705/436-6957, Fax: 705/436-7601

**Iroquois Falls ........ Cochrane**

J. Kenneth Alexander, 328 Main St., PO Box 290, Stn A, P0K 1G0 – 705/232-4309, 6311, Fax: 705/232-5274 – *2

Boivin & Serré, 182 Devonshire, PO Box 399, P0K 1E0 – 705/258-4447, Fax: 705/258-4450

Susan T. McGrath, PO Box 700, P0K 1G0 – 705/232-4055, Fax: 705/232-6301

**Kaladar ........ Lennox & Addington**

Hogle & Doreleyers, PO Box 51, K0H 1Z0 – 613/336-8230, Fax: 613/336-8087

**Kanata ........ Ottawa-Carleton**

Adam & Miller, #400, 300 March Rd., K2K 2E2 – 613/592-6290 – *2

**Kapuskasing ........ Cochrane**

Bourgeault Brunelle Dumais Payeur, 7 Cain Ave., PO Box 446, P5N 1S8 – 705/335-6121, Fax: 705/335-8127 – *4

Bill Matwichuk, Q.C., 4A Drury St., PO Box 220, P5N 1K8 – 705/335-2375, Fax: 705/335-6575 – *1

* indicates number of lawyers in law firm.

**Kemptville .................................... Grenville**

Quist & Humphreys, RR#5, Hwy. 43, K0G 1J0 – 613/258-5711 – *2

R.G. Shaw, 202 Prescott St., PO Box 100, K0G 1J0 – 613/258-5191, Fax: 613/258-5191 – *1

Warren and Jansen, 215 Van Buren St., PO Box 820, K0G 1J0 – 613/258-7462, Fax: 613/258-7761 – *2

**Kenora .................................... Kenora**

Compton, Shewchuk, MacDonell, Ormiston, Richardt & Fregeau, 214 Main St. South, PO Box 1970, P9N 1T2 – 807/468-9828, Fax: 807/468-5504 – *7

David James Elliott, Stone House, 225 Main St. South, P9N 1T3 – 807/468-3355, Fax: 807/468-7858 – *2

Gibson & Wexler, 111 Main St. South, PO Box 2450, P9N 3X8 – 807/468-3061, Fax: 807/468-7940 – *3

Hook, Seller, Zrum & Lundin, Bannister Centre, #204, 301 - 1 Ave. South, P9N 3X8 – 807/468-9831, Fax: 807/468-8384,6505 – *4

**Keswick .................................... York**

Robert Wm. Bailey, 4 The Queensway South, L4P 1Y7 – 905/476-4391, Fax: 905/476-6597 – *1

Joseph O. Dales, Q.C., 314 The Queensway South, L4P 2B7 – 905/476-5135, Fax: 905/476-5415 – *1

Clare C. Green, PO Box 37, L4P 3E1 – 905/476-4271, Fax: 905/476-8977 – *1

R.E. Pollock, 183 The Queensway South, L8P 3T6 – 905/476-0021 – *1

**Kincardine .................................... Bruce**

Diane S. Barker, 329 Durham Market, PO Box 14, N2Z 2Y6 – 519/396-9542, Fax: 519/396-3599 – *1

Mahood & Darcy, 3 Lambton St., N2Z 2Y8 – 519/396-8144, Fax: 519/396-9446 – *1

William S. Mathers, #6, 777 Queen St., N2Z 2Y2 – 519/396-4147, Fax: 519/396-1872 – *1

**King City .................................... York**

John A. Geisler, Q.C., RR#1, L0G 1K0 – 905/727-6326 – *1

**Kingston .................................... Frontenac**

D.J. Atkinson, #201, 105 Wellington St., PO Box 1941, K7L 5J7 – 613/544-4497, Fax: 613/544-3200 – *1

Wm. J.F. Bishop, 338 Montreal St., PO Box 1403, K7L 5C6 – 613/544-0644, Fax: 613/544-2197 – *3

Black & Black, 225 Bagot St., PO Box 607, K7L 4X1 – 613/549-2222, Fax: 613/549-8882 – *1

Black, Lloyd, Caron & Minnema, 249 Brock St., PO Box 247, K7L 4V8 – 613/546-3286, 549-3262, Fax: 613/549-1193; Email: blcm@adan.kingston.net – *3

Caldwell & Moore, 260 Barrie St., K7L 3K7 – 613/545-1860, Fax: 613/545-1862 – *3

Jack W. Chong, 273 King St. East, PO Box 1382, K7L 5C6 – 613/549-1225, Fax: 613/549-3882 – *2

Roy B. Conacher, Q.C., 195 Sydenham St., PO Box 636, K7L 4X1 – 613/544-5660, Fax: 613/546-5369 – *1

Cunningham, Swan, Carty, Little & Bonham, Empire Life Bldg., #500, 259 King St. East, PO Box 460, K7L 4W6 – 613/544-0211, Fax: 613/542-9814; Email: cswaninfo@cswan.com; URL: http://www.cswan.com – *15

Ecclestone O'Connor-Kaiser, 730 Arlington Park Pl., K7M 8H9 – 613/384-0735, Fax: 613/384-0731 – *1

John R. Gale, Gore Bldg., 115 Clarence St., 2nd Fl., K7L 5N6 – 613/546-4283, Fax: 613/546-9861 – *1

John P. Gerretsen Q.C., 195 Sydenham St., PO Box 636, K7L 4X1 – 613/544-5660, Fax: 613/546-5369 – *1

Good & Elliott, 153 Brock St., K7L 1S2 – 613/544-1330, Fax: 613/547-4538 – *2

Headrick & Lord, 770 Bath Rd., K7M 4Y2 – 613/384-4403, Fax: 613/384-7056 – *2

Hickey & Hickey, 93 Clarence St., PO Box 110, K7L 4V6 – 613/548-3191, Fax: 613/548-8195 – *2

Mary Ann Higgs, #206, 275 Ontario St., PO Box 700, K7L 4X1 – 613/548-7399, Fax: 613/548-1862 – *1

N.C. Jackson, City Hall, 216 Ontario St., K7L 2Z3 – 613/546-4291

Jacob Macpherson Menard, 237 Queen St., PO Box 668, K7L 4X1 – 613/544-4780, Fax: 613/544-4286 – *3

Johnston & MacNaughton, 231 Brock St., PO Box 670, K7L 4X1 – 613/547-6790, Fax: 613/547-6815 – *1

Kamin & Letourneau, #303, 863 Princess St., K7L 5N4 – 613/542-7334, Fax: 613/542-7386 – *2

A.L. Mandell, 355 Frontenac St., K7L 3T1 – 613/549-4668 – *1

M.A. McCue, 104 Queen, K7K 1A6 – 613/544-5117, Fax: 613/544-7346 – *1

G.Y. McDiarmid, PO Box 1010, K7L 4X8 – 613/546-3274, Fax: 613/546-1493 – *1

Judith A. Millard, 3 Rideau St., PO Box 1010, K7L 4X8 – 613/546-3274, Fax: 613/546-1493 – *1

A. Laurel Montrose, Macdonald-Cartier Bldg., 49 Place d'Armes, 2nd Fl., K7L 5J3 – 613/548-6305, Fax: 613/548-6650 – *1

Fergus J. (Chip) O'Connor, 104 Johnson St., PO Box 1959, K7L 5J7 – 613/546-5581, Fax: 613/546-5540 – *1

Philip D. Quintin, PO Box 310, K7P 1R7 – 613/549-3000, 384-0830, Fax: 613/384-0831 – *1

Peter J. Radley, Q.C., #208, 303 Bagot St., K7K 5W7 – 613/544-5612, Fax: 613/544-5614 – *1

David G. Rayner, 464 Princess St., K7L 1C2 – 613/549-3400, Fax: 613/549-3142 – *1

Harvey M. Rosen, #303, 863 Princess St., K7L 5N4 – 613/544-1816, Fax: 613/542-7386 – *1

Douglas M. Slack, #1, 817 Blackburn Mews, K7P 2N6 – 613/384-7260, Fax: 613/384-7262; Email: dmslack@istar.ca – *1

A.B. Smith, Q.C., 80 Johnson St., K7L 1X7 – 613/544-6673 – *1

Soloway, Wright, #440, 366 King St. East, K7K 6Y3 – 613/544-7334, Fax: 613/544-6689; Toll Free: 1-800-263-4257 – *1

George N. Speal, Q.C., 74 Brock St., PO Box 81, K7L 4V6 – 613/544-0001, Fax: 613/545-9865 – *1

L.M. Steele, 104 Queen St., K7K 1A6 – 613/544-5117, 5116, Fax: 613/544-7346 – *1

Terence J. Tait, Q.C., 544 Armstrong Rd., K7M 7N8 – 613/544-4770, Fax: 613/544-6266 – *1

Y. Tarnowecky, #5, 633 Norris Ct., K7P 2R9 – 613/384-2354, Fax: 613/384-8904 – *1

Geraldine R. Tepper, 461 Princess St., K7L 1C4 – 613/546-1169, Fax: 613/546-6992 – *1

L.H. Tepper, Q.C., 461 Princess St., K7L 1C4 – 613/546-1168, Fax: 613/546-4162 – *1

Thomson, A.G., 232 Brock St., 2nd Fl., K7L 1S4 – 613/549-5111, Fax: 613/549-4074

I.G. Thorne, PO Box 370, K7L 4W2 – 613/544-1833 – *1

Thomas W. Troughton, 164 Queen St., PO Box 487, K7L 4W5 – 613/546-3277, Fax: 613/546-6825 – *1

Stephen L. Zap, #203, 863 Princess St., K7L 5N4 – 613/542-3688, Fax: 613/542-6793 – *1

**Kingsville .................................... Essex**

Clark, McGregor Sims & O'Neil, 58 Main St. East, N9Y 1A2 – 519/733-8441, Fax: 519/733-6874 – *4

Dunnion & Beneteau, 59 Main St. East, N9Y 1A1 – 519/733-6573 – *2

Karry & Laba, 25 Main St. East, PO Box 9, N9Y 2E8 – 519/733-2372, Fax: 519/733-3110 – *2

Karl G. Melinz, 59 Main St. East, N9Y 1A1 – 519/733-6575, Fax: 519/738-9080; Email: kgmelinz@wincom.net – *1

**Kirkland Lake .................................... Temiskaming**

G. Shorrock, PO Box 490, P2N 3J5 – 705/567-5213, Fax: 705/567-3987 – *1

**Kitchener .................................... Waterloo**

G.C. Amos, 276 Frederick St., N2H 2N4 – 519/576-8480, Fax: 519/579-3042 – *1

Artindale & Partners, #510, 101 Frederick St., PO Box 996, N2G 4E6 – 519/744-3331, Fax: 519/744-5062 – *9

A.D. Barron, #209B, 385 Frederick St., N2H 2P2 – 519/579-5340 – *1

Sidney S. Bergstein, Q.C., 39 Weber St. East, N2H 1C4 – 519/744-3531, Fax: 519/744-2194 – *1

Brock & Brock, 372 Queen St. South, N2G 1W7 – 519/578-8290, Fax: 519/741-0071 – *1

Steven O. Casey & Associates, PO Box 515, Stn C, N2G 4A2 – 519/576-4320, Fax: 519/576-3604 – *3

Chris & Richard, 194 Weber St. East, N2H 1E4 – 519/570-4400, Fax: 519/570-4242 – *3

N.A. Crawford, 1444 King St. East, N2G 2N7 – 519/743-3615, Fax: 519/743-2218 – *1

Fehrenbach Schmidt, Market Sq. Tower, Box: 1112, 22 Frederick St., N2H 6M6 – 519/578-4525, Fax: 519/745-0914 – *3

Lee Fitzpatrick, 276 Frederick St., N2H 2N4 – 519/579-3150 – *1

Flynn & Sorbara, 300 Victoria St. North, N2H 6R9 – 519/576-0460, Fax: 519/576-3234 – *9

Giesbrecht, Griffin, 60 College St., N2H 5A1 – 519/579-4300, Fax: 519/579-8745 – *4

Giffen, Lee, Wagner, Morley & Garbutt, Commerce House, #500, 50 Queen St. North, PO Box 2396, Stn B, N2H 6M3 – 519/578-4150, Fax: 519/578-8740 – *9

Gowlings, #1100, 50 Queen St. North, N2H 6M2 – 519/576-6910, Fax: 519/576-6030 – *23

R.S. Grant, #1003, 55 King St. West, N2G 4W1 – 519/744-3397, Fax: 519/744-6985 – *1

Haalboom & Schafer, #914, 22 Frederick St., N2H 6M6 – 519/579-2920, Fax: 519/576-0471 – *2

Peter B. Hambly, The Prudential Centre Frederick Tower, #911, 101 Frederick St., N2H 6R2 – 519/579-2924, Fax: 519/744-8008 – *2

John A. Harder, PO Box 2368, Stn B, N2H 6R2 – 519/570-1010, Fax: 519/570-2436 – *1

R.J. Hare, 741 King St. West, N2G 1E3 – 519/576-6710, Fax: 519/576-7040 – *1

Sheldon Kosky, 71 Weber St. East, N2H 1C6 – 519/578-1480, Fax: 519/579-2537 – *1

James M. Krakovsky, 51 Francis St. North, N2H 5B4 – 519/570-3700, Fax: 519/570-3399 – *1

Eric M. Kraushaar, 675 Riverbend Dr., N2K 3S3 – 519/743-3911, Fax: 519/742-1841 – *1

Lang & Lang, #101, 678 Belmont Ave. West, N2M 1N6 – 519/578-3330, Fax: 519/578-3337 – *2

Paul W. Lang, Q.C., #201, 684 Belmont Ave. West, N2M 1N6 – 519/571-1440, Fax: 519/571-8555 – *1

R.G.R. Lawrence, Q.C., 194 Weber St. East, N2H 1E4 – 519/742-4443, Fax: 519/570-4242 – *1

Madorin, Snyder, 235 King St. East, PO Box 1234, N2G 4G9 – 519/744-4491, Fax: 519/741-8060 – *13

J.J. Marentette, #810, 50 Queen St. North, N2H 6P4 – 519/743-7530 – *1

Harald A. Mattson, Commerce House, #810, 50 Queen Street North, N2H 6P4 – 519/743-7530

McIntyre, McMurray, 51 Scott St., N2H 2P9 – 519/576-7360, Fax: 519/576-7400 – *2

Morscher & Morscher, #905, 101 Frederick St., N2H 6R2 – 519/749-8100, Fax: 519/749-8141 – *3

J.W.W. Neeb, Q.C., #201, 7 Duke St. West, N2H 6M2 – 519/578-4400, Fax: 519/578-3450 – *3

Olsen, Rotberg & Babcock, 61 Roy St., PO Box 2814, Stn B, N2H 4B4 – 519/576-5070, Fax: 519/576-7451 – *3

Paquette & Travers, #911, 101 Frederick St., N2H 6R2 – 519/744-2281, Fax: 519/744-8008 – *4

Judith E. Phipps, 314 Frederick St., N2H 2N7 – 519/578-9660, Fax: 519/578-9668 – *3

R.C. Potwarka, 18 Irvin St., N2H 1K8 – 519/578-4200 – *1

Roetsch & Schaffer, 284 Frederick St., N2H 2N4 – 519/576-5310, Fax: 519/576-2797 – *2

Daryl W. Schnurr, PO Box 2607, Stn B, N2H 6N2 – 519/578-5650, Fax: 519/576-2030; Toll Free: 1-800-265-2220; Email: schnurr@ibm.net – *1

John D. E. Shannon, 30 Spetz St., N2H 1K1 – 519/743-3654, Fax: 519/578-9521 – *1

Shuh Cline & Grossman, 17 Weber St. West, N2H 3Y9 – 519/578-9010, 961-4078 (Toronto) – *6

Sims Clement Eastman, Market Sq. Tower, #700, 22 Frederick St., PO Box 578, N2G 4A2 – 519/579-3660, Fax: 519/743-2540; Email: scelaw@scelaw.com

Margaret Skowronska-Binek, #911, 101 Frederick St., N2H 6R2 – 519/744-3570, Fax: 519/744-8008 – *1

Smyth, Hobson, #1016, 22 Frederick St., PO Box 1176, N2G 4G1 – 519/578-9400, Fax: 519/578-7482 – *2

Somer, Nanson, PO Box 725, Stn C, N2G 4B6 – 519/579-5700, Fax: 519/741-8259 – *2

Sutherland, Hagarty, Mark & Somerville, 22 Water St. South, N2G 4K4 – 519/745-6801 – *8

Tait, McDonald, 9 Ahrens St. West, N2H 4B6 – 519/576-6500, Fax: 519/744-7811 – *2

Cameron D. Trotter, 27 Roy St., N2H 4B4 – 519/743-4324 – *1

R.M. Van Buskirk, 31 Roy St., PO Box 1786, N2G 4R3 – 519/745-5570 – *1

Villemaire, Levato, 82 Weber St. East, N2H 1C7 – 519/745-5676, Fax: 519/745-9573 – *2

Voll & Santos, 30 Spetz St., N2H 1K1 – 519/578-3400, Fax: 519/578-9521 – *2

Vujic, Dragan, Lawyers, 372 Queen St. South, N2G 1W7 – 519/743-2670 – *1

Walters Gubler, 151 Frederick St., N2H 2M2 – 519/578-8010, Fax: 519/578-9395 – *2

Bernd G. Wolf, 82 Weber St. East, N2H 1C7 – 519/742-6599, Fax: 519/571-9023 – *1

Orlin C. Wood, 155 Frederick St., N2H 2M6 – 519/576-7630, Fax: 519/570-4022 – *1

Jim Ziegler, 3171 King St. East, N2A 1B1 – 519/893-3171 – *1

Zinszer & Company, #201, 871 Victoria St. North, N2B 3S4 – 519/741-3647, Fax: 519/741-3645; Toll Free: 1-888-847-2333 – *2

**Lakefield** .................................... **Peterborough**

G.A. Booth, 34 Bridge St., PO Box 116, K0L 2H0 – 705/652-3378, Fax: 705/652-6823 – *1

T.E. Cole, 8 Bridge St., K0L 2H0 – 705/652-8161, Fax: 705/652-7088; Email: thomas.cole@sympatico.ca – *1

Alex Ramsay, PO Box 1088, K0L 2H0 – 705/652-6000, Fax: 705/652-6966 – *1

**LaSalle** .................................... **Essex**

Ute Wigley-Mueller, 1620 Front Rd., N9J 2B6 – 519/734-1303 – *1

**Leamington** .................................... **Essex**

Pearsall & Marshall, 22 Queens Ave., N8H 3G8 – 519/326-4415, Fax: 519/326-1844 – *3

Reid, Reynolds, Collins & Ricci, 60 Talbot St. West, N8H 1M4 – 519/326-3237 – *4

Sawatzky & Balzer, 5 Russell St., N8H 1T7 – 519/322-2341, Fax: 519/322-2668 – *3

Scaddan & Jakob, 16 Wellington St., N8H 2X4 – 519/326-8638 – *2

Spettigue Spettigue & Cartlidge, 21 Talbot St. East, PO Box 327, N8H 3W3 – 519/326-2687, Fax: 519/326-1344 – *3

**Lindsay** .................................... **Victoria**

R. Dan Cornell, 272 Kent St. West, PO Box 536, K9V 4S5 – 705/324-4312, Fax: 705/324-7525 – *1

J.W. Evans, 219 Kent St., PO Box 427, K9V 4S5 – 705/324-3207, Fax: 705/328-1128 – *1

Frost, Frost & Gorwill, #217, 189 Kent St. West, K9V 5G6 – 705/324-2193, Fax: 705/324-9879 – *1

Glass, Farn & Reynolds, 6 Albert St. North, PO Box 58, K9V 4R8 – 705/324-3577, Fax: 705/324-0060 – *3

Timothy W. Johnston, 40 Lindsay St. South, K9V 2L8 – 705/328-2393, Fax: 705/878-1765 – *1

I.T. McEachern, 18 Cambridge St. North, PO Box 277, K9V 4S1 – *1

McQuarrie, Hill, Walden, Chester, McLeod, 64 Lindsay St. South, PO Box 457, K9V 4S5 – 705/324-6711, Fax: 705/324-5723 – *4

Scott & Scott, #219, 189 Kent St. West, PO Box 660, K9V 4S5 – 705/324-5181, Fax: 705/324-8077 – *2

Staples, Swain & Gunsolus, 10 William St. South, PO Box 455, K9V 4S5 – 705/324-6222, Fax: 705/324-4168 – *3

Warner, Cork & La Mantia, 22 Peel St., PO Box 208, K9V 4S1 – 705/324-6196, Fax: 705/324-7440 – *3

**Listowel** .................................... **Perth**

Benson, Giller, Tarbush & Carter, 140 Barber Ave. South, N4W 3H2 – 519/291-2710, Fax: 519/291-5231 – *3

Robert S. Johns, 218 Main St. West, PO Box 248, N4W 3H4 – 519/291-3420 – *1

Pratt & Pratt, 280 Inkerman St. West, PO Box 10, N4W 3H2 – 519/291-3612, Fax: 519/291-3613 – *1

**Little Current** .................................... **Manitoulin**

Stephen B. Marshall, PO Box 607, P0P 1K0 – 705/368-2424, Fax: 705/368-2967; Email: 1-800-881-1108 – *1

**London** .................................... **Middlesex**

Norman M. Aitken, #207, 795 Wonderland Rd., N6K 3C2 – 519/472-8463, Fax: 519/472-1814 – *1

Karl Arvai, Talbot Centre, #1508, 140 Fullarton St., N6A 5P2 – 519/672-0911, Fax: 519/642-1272 – *2

Daniel S.J. Bangarth, Unit 4A, 490 Wonderland Rd. South, N6K 1L6 – 519/472-2340, Fax: 519/657-8173 – *1

Barnes, S.C., 305 Oxford St. East, N6A 1V3 – 519/439-0558, Fax: 519/439-8938 – *3

Beechie, Madison, Sawchuk & Seabrook, 439 Waterloo St., N6B 2P1 – 519/673-1070, Fax: 519/439-4363 – *4

Behr & Rady, 64 Fullarton St., N6A 1K1 – 519/438-4530, Fax: 519/679-6576 – *2

Belanger, Cassino, Coulston & Gallagher, #153, 759 Hyde Park Rd., N6H 3S2 – 519/472-6310, Fax: 519/657-5189 – *2

G.P. Belch, #1014, 300 Dufferin Ave., PO Box 5035, N6A 4L9 – 519/661-4940, Fax: 519/661-5530; Email: gbelch@city.london.on.ca

Berg, Kennedy, Cleaver, Broad, Talbot Centre, #1900, 140 Fullarton St., N6A 5P2 – 519/679-8000, Fax: 519/679-8042 – *8

Bitz, Szemenyei, Ferguson & MacKenzie, 2479 Main St., PO Box 482, Stn Lambeth, N6P 1R1 – 519/652-1616, Fax: 519/652-1622

Bitz, Szemenyei, Ferguson & MacKenzie, 341 Talbot St., N6A 2R5 – 519/433-8155, Fax: 519/660-4857; Email: bsfm@execulink.com – *7

Brown, Beattie, O'Donovan, City Centre Tower, 380 Wellington St., 16th Fl., N6A 5B5 – 519/679-0400, Fax: 519/679-6350; Email: bboinfo@bbo.on.ca – *14

J.M. Brown, 64 Fullarton St., N6A 1K1 – *1

M.F.J. Burgard, 585 Talbot St. North, N6A 2T2 – 519/679-9900, Fax: 519/679-8546; Email: mburgard@icis.on.ca – *1

Carrier, Robert, 346 Wonderland Rd. South, N6K 1L3 – 519/641-2111, Fax: 519/641-2114 – *2

Chambers & Mueller, 141 Wortley Rd., N6C 3P4 – 519/673-1300, Fax: 519/673-1728 – *3

Rano Channan, 68 Tamarack Cres., N6K 3J7

Chapman & Fowler, 540 Queens Ave., N6B 1Y8 – 519/673-1113, Fax: 519/673-5060 – *2

Chizmar Law Firm, #304, 215 Piccadilly St., N6A 1S2 – 519/672-8440, Fax: 519/679-1994 – *1

Cockburn, Foster, Townsend, Graham & Associates, 551 Waterloo St., N6B 2R1 – 519/672-5272, Fax: 519/672-9313 – *10

Cohen Highley Vogel & Dawson, 1 London Pl., 255 Queens Ave., 11th Fl., N6A 5R8 – 519/672-9330, Fax: 519/672-5960; Email: lawyers@chvd.on.ca; URL: http://www.chvd.on.ca/lawyers – *20

J.A. Tory Colvin, 466 Ridout St. North, N6A 2P7 – 519/433-0500, Fax: 519/434-9279 – *1

Cousins Trudell, 782 Richmond St., N6A 3H5 – 519/438-5185, Fax: 519/438-4687 – *3

Cram & Associates, #514, 200 Queens Ave., N6A 1J3 – 519/673-1670, Fax: 519/439-5011 – *3

Downs, M.P., 489 Talbot St., N6A 2S4 – 519/679-0063 – *2

Kenneth Duggan, #203, 111 Waterloo St., N6B 2M4 – 519/672-5360, Fax: 519/433-6975 – *1

Dyer, Brown, 495 Richmond St., PO Box 818, Stn B, N6A 4Z3 – 519/673-1100, Fax: 519/679-6108 – *16

Eberhard Dobson & Dobbie, 1579 Hyde Park Rd., N6H 5L4 – 519/473-2100, Fax: 519/472-0768 – *5

R.D. Farrington, #201, 255 Dufferin Ave., N6A 5K6 – 519/434-6821 – *1

Filion, Wakely & Thorup, One London Place, #1610, 255 Queens Ave., N6A 5R8 – 519/433-7270, Fax: 519/433-4453; Email: london@filion.on.ca; URL: http://www.filion.on.ca

G.E. Fitzgerald, 308 Wortley Rd., N6C 3R5 – 519/673-0942 – *1

Fulton Rivett Shanfeld, 625 Wellington St., N6A 3R8 – 519/432-6755 – *3

Giffen & Partners, 362 Dufferin Ave., N6B 1Z4 – 519/679-4700, Fax: 519/432-8003 – *2

J.H. Groom, 47 Grand Ave., N6C 1L4 – 519/433-9201 – *1

William B. Hagarty, 517 Dufferin Ave., N6B 2A3 – 519/434-6064 – *1

D.J. Hamilton, RR#5, N6A 4B9 – 519/432-6653, Fax: 519/660-8060 – *1

Hanes, Buchner & Uren, 783 Richmond St., N6A 3H4 – 519/434-7371, Fax: 519/672-5012 – *3

J.G. Harding, 635 Wellington St., N6A 3R8 – 519/439-0641, Fax: 519/439-0643 – *1

Harrison, Elwood, 450 Talbot St., PO Box 3237, N6A 4K3 – 519/679-9660, Fax: 519/667-3362, 663-9341; Email: mail@harrisonelwood.com – *42

Haskett Menear Legate, 100 Fullarton St., N6A 1K1 – 519/672-7370, Fax: 519/663-1165; Email: gtwohey@hml.on.ca – *8

Henry L. Hennick, #908, 383 Richmond St., N6A 3C4 – *1

E.P. Heyninck, 34 Willingdon Ave., N6A 2Y6 – 519/432-4405 – *1

Hicks Morley Hamilton Stewart Storie, #1608, 148 Fullarton St., N6A 5P3 – 519/433-7515, Fax: 519/433-8827

Godfrey Jefferson, 505 Talbot St., N6A 2S6 – 519/438-1727 – *1

Jeffery Associates, 174 King St., PO Box 2095, N6A 4E1 – 519/434-6881, Fax: 519/673-5376 – *9

Lerner & Associates, 80 Dufferin Ave., PO Box 2335, N6A 4G4 – 519/672-4131, 4510, Fax: 519/672-2044; Email: lerner@icis.on.ca; URL: http://www.lerner.ca – *45

V. Libis, #201, 255 Dufferin Ave., N6A 5K6 – 519/434-6821 – *1

Lipson, Frauts, 784 Richmond St., N6A 3H5 – 519/679-3115, Fax: 519/661-0725 – *2

John R. Lisowski, 607 Queens Ave., N6B 1Y9 – 519/679-5000, Fax: 519/673-1717 – *1

J.M. Litterick, 693 Hale St., N5W 1J1 – 519/451-2790 – *1

Little & Jarrett, 412 King St., PO Box 2757, N6A 4H4 – 519/672-8121, Fax: 519/432-0784 – *6

Little, Parker & Ingus, 148 Wortley Rd., N6C 3P5 – 519/672-5415, Fax: 519/672-3906; Email: lpi@sympatico.ca – *2

Little, Reeves, Mahoney & Jarrett, 412 King St., N6B 1S6 – 519/672-8121, Fax: 519/438-9818 – *8

Charles L. Mackenzie, Q.C., #4, 175 Dundas St., N6A 1G4 – 519/672-1772, Fax: 519/672-1880

MacKewn, Winder, Kirwin, 383 Richmond St., PO Box 96, N6A 4V3 – 519/672-2040 – *5

Alfred A. Mamo & Associates, #201, 380 Queens Ave., N6B 1X6 – 519/672-5952, Fax: 519/672-8736 – *3

Edward J. Mann, #605, 137 Dundas St., Stn A, N6A 1E9 – 519/672-8707, Fax: 519/660-4678 – *1

* indicates number of lawyers in law firm.

McCarthy Tétrault, One London Place, #2000, 255 Queens Ave., N6A 5R8 – 519/660-3587, Fax: 519/660-3599; URL: http://www.mccarthy.ca – *21
McGrath, Braiden, 4 Covent Market Pl., N6A 1E2 – 519/672-7410, Fax: 519/645-8516 – *2
McKenzie Nash Bryant, 300 Dundas St., PO Box 3120, Stn B, N6A 4J4 – 519/672-5666, Fax: 519/672-2674; Toll Free: 1-800-261-4844; Email: mnblaw@serix.com; URL: http:///www.mnblawyers.com – *11
McKenzie R.J. McMillan, 607 Queens Ave., PO Box 516, Stn B, N6A 4W8 – 519/672-2116, Fax: 519/679-2020 – *1
McNamara, Pizzale, #38, 267 Dundas St., N6A 1H2 – 519/434-2174, Fax: 519/642-7654 – *2
L.D. Miller, 1333 Brydges St., N5W 2C5 – 519/659-3261 – *1
Mitches & Mitches, 88 York St., Box 98, N6A 1A7 – 519/663-5300, Fax: 519/663-2199 – *1
Murphy & Brown, 311 Dufferin Ave., PO Box 443, N6B 1Z3 – 519/679-8800, Fax: 519/433-7267 – *3
J.M. Neilson, Q.C., 479 Talbot St., N6A 2S4 – 519/672-8470 – *1
Nelligan & Nelligan, #48, 267 Dundas St., N6A 1H2 – 519/438-1709, Fax: 519/672-7455 – *1
James R. O'Donnell, #16, 440 Wellington St., N6A 3P2 – 519/673-0600 – *1
Patton & Associates, #1512, 140 Fullarton St., N6A 5P2 – 519/432-8282, Fax: 519/432-7285 – *2
Norman Peel, Q.C., 466 Ridout St. North, N6A 2P7 – 519/433-2111 – *1
Pensa & Associates, Dufferin Corporate Centre, #1000, 130 Dufferin Ave., PO Box 816, Stn B, N6A 4Z3 – 519/667-4010, Fax: 519/434-9656 – *19
Jeffrey M. Phillips, 11 York St., N6A 1A3 – 519/673-4214, Fax: 519/672-8721 – *1
Robert C. Sheppard, 4 Covent Market Pl., N6A 1E2 – 519/432-3575, Fax: 519/645-8516 – *1
The Law Firm of Siskind, Cromarty, Ivey & Dowler, 680 Waterloo St., PO Box 2520, N6A 3V8 – 519/672-2121, Fax: 519/672-6065; Email: lawyers@siskind.com; URL: http://www.siskind.com – *43
Joseph Sommerfreund, 400 Ridout St. North, N6A 2P4 – 519/438-2708 – *1
Steacy Phillips, 320 Princess Ave., N6B 2A6 – 519/433-6111, Fax: 519/438-9933 – *2
David E. Storry, #226, 1255 Commissioners Rd. West, N6K 3N5 – 519/472-2200 – *1
Thomson Mahoney Elliott Delorey, #200, 145 Wharncliffe Rd., N6J 2K4 – 519/673-1151, Fax: 519/673-3632 – *6
F.E. Troller, 511 Talbot St., N6A 2S5 – 519/672-8335, Fax: 519/672-8972 – *1
Underhill & Joles, 379 Dufferin Ave., N6B 1Z5 – 519/438-1413, 432-4644, Fax: 519/438-3936 – *2
Walker & Wood, 399 Ridout St. North, 3rd Fl., N6A 2P1 – 519/672-3500, Fax: 519/672-2420 – *2
E.M. Walsh, #104, 396 Queens Ave., N6B 1X7 – 519/438-2484, Fax: 519/439-3229 – *1

**Lucknow........................................Bruce**

George J. Brophy, 567 Campbell St., PO Box 610, N0G 2H0 – 519/528-2818, Fax: 519/528-2848 – *1

**Manotick..............................Ottawa-Carleton**

Carolyn R. Green, 5478 West River Dr., K4M 1G7 – 613/692-0748, Fax: 613/692-0871 – *1
Donald P. Hamilton, Q.C., PO Box 510, K4M 1A5 – 613/692-3511, Fax: 613/692-0724 – *1
MacKay & Sanderson, Manotick Mews, PO Box 479, K4M 1A5 – 613/692-2591, Fax: 613/692-6159
Wilson, Prockiw, 5542 Main St., PO Box 429, K4M 1A4 – 613/692-3547, Fax: 613/692-0826 – *2

**Maple....................................York Region**

M.D. Newman, 62 Lancer Dr., L6A 1C9 – 905/832-5602 – *1

**Marathon..................................Thunder Bay**

Filipovic, Brothers & Conway, #4, 65 Peninsula Rd., P0T 2E0 – 807/229-2566, Fax: 807/229-1200 – *1

**Markham..........................................York**

Michael Barmherzig, #550, 11 Allstate Pkwy., L3R 9T8 – 905/477-8855, Fax: 905/477-2488 – *1
Martin Barratt, 201 Whitehall Dr., L3R 9Y3 – 905/475-9738 – *1
Berlin & Azoulay, 101, 16 Esna Park Dr., L3R 5X1 – 905/470-9444, Fax: 905/470-9449
Jay I. Bernholtz, Pilsbury Tower, #505, 675 Cochrane Dr., L3R 0R8 – 905/946-9689, Fax: 416/969-8167
Bongard & Associate, 10 Washington St., PO Box 509, L3P 2R2 – 905/294-7555, Fax: 905/294-8360 – *1
Burstein, Greenglass & Hochman, #200, 7481 Woodbine Ave., L3R 2W1 – 905/475-1266, Fax: 905/475-7851 – *4
Steven J. Carr, #550, 11 Allstate Pkwy., L3R 9T8 – 905/470-9455, Fax: 905/477-2488 – *1
Cattanach Hindson Sutton Van Veldhuizen, 52 Main St. North, L3P 1X5 – 905/294-0666, Fax: 905/294-5688 – *5
Anna Chung, #209, 80 Acadia Ave., L3R 9V1 – 905/940-6802, Fax: 905/970-6804 – *1
Bryan Dale, 123-7225 Woodbine Ave., L3R 1A3 – 905/513-1959, Fax: 905/513-6417 – *1
Ernest Dicker, Q.C., 10 Fairway Heights Cres., L3T 1K2 – 905/889-5556 – *1
Stephen R. Dyment, #500, 7030 Woodbine Ave., L3R 6G2 – 905/474-1718, Fax: 905/474-9309 – *1
M. Fagan, 60 Esna Park Dr., L3R 1E1 – 905/475-1933, Fax: 905/475-1578 – *1
D. Gregory Flude, 180 Renfrew Dr., L3R 8B7 – 905/513-1550 – *1
Fritz Lean, #550, 11 Allstate Pkwy., L3R 9T8 – 905/477-0166, Fax: 905/477-2488
Irving Gleiberman, #208, 50 McIntosh Dr., L3R 9T3 – 905/940-5525, Fax: 905/940-5528
Gordon H. Hall, #550, 11 Allstate Pkwy, L3R 9T8 – 905/940-1581
Robert F. Hopkins, 15 Ambleside Cres., L3R 7T1 – 905/940-1050, Fax: 905/940-1950 – *1
Alexander Jozefacki, 4961 Hwy.#7 East, L3R 1N1 – 905/940-3141 – *1
Kennedy, Dymond, #404, 140 Allstate Pkwy., L3R 5Y8 – 905/470-2077, Fax: 905/470-2075
Patrick Kirby, 65 Ferrier St., 2nd Fl., L3R 3K6 – 905/479-1615, Fax: 905/479-2277 – *1
Gary M. Kuchar, #S550, 11 Allstate Pkwy., L3R 9T8 – 905/513-8822, Fax: 905/477-2488 – *1
Paul Kupferstein, #550, 11 Allstate Pkwy., L3R 9T8 – 905/477-5520, Fax: 905/477-2466 – *1
H.P. Albert Liang, 80 Acadia Ave., L3R 9V1 – 905/513-9022, Fax: 905/513-8657 – *1
Henry Lue, 808-3100 Steeles Ave., L3R 8T3 – 905/513-6528, Fax: 905/513-6526 – *1
Alan J. Luftspring, #219, 7100 Woodbine Ave., L3R 5J2 – 905/479-1200, Fax: 905/479-9769 – *1
Irene L. Matthews, #104, 7225 Woodbine Ave., L3R 1A3 – 905/475-9716, Fax: 905/475-9716 – *1
S.A. McClyment, #220, 60 Columbia Way, L3R 0C9 – 905/513-7560, Fax: 905/513-7563 – *1
Metcalfe, Blainey & Burns, #202, 18 Crown Steel Dr., L3R 9X8 – 905/492-8310, Fax: 905/475-6226 – *5
Midanik, Saul Associates, #550, 11 Allstate Pkwy., L3R 9T8 – 905/477-1721, Fax: 905/477-2488 – *2
Miller Thomson, #600, 60 Columbia Way., L3R 0C9 – 905/415-6700, Fax: 905/415-6777; Email: markham@millerthomson.ca; URL: http://www.millerthomson.ca – *11
Mingay & Vereshchak, 81 Main St. North, L3P 1X7 – 905/294-0550, Fax: 905/294-9141 – *5
G. Arthur Moad, #206, 5762 Hwy. 7, L3P 1A8 – 905/294-6446, Fax: 905/294-4436 – *1
Parker & Zener, #705, 7030 Woodbine Ave., L3R 6G2 – 905/470-6226, Fax: 905/475-4082 – *2
William Popovski, 7725 Birchmount Rd., L3R 9X3 – 905/513-7144, Fax: 905/513-7147 – *1
E.M.D. Read, #110, 1 West Pearce St., L4B 3K3 – 905/882-6666, Fax: 905/882-1082 – *1
Theodore Rotenberg Barristers, #303, 80 Tiverton Crt., L3R 0G4 – 905/479-3331, Fax: 905/479-5017 – *3
Shi Chi Kun, Pacific Mall, #E29, 4300 Steeles Ave. East, L3R 0Y5 – 905/305-1800, Fax: 905/305-9812
Michael A. Siegel, #500, 7030 Woodbine Ave., L3R 6G2 – 905/474-1717, Fax: 905/474-9309 – *1
Paul F. Smith, #202, 5762 Hwy. 7, L3P 1A8 – 905/294-9955, Fax: 905/294-4004 – *1
Solomon & Balinsky, 7507 Kennedy Rd., L3R 0L8 – 905/479-1900, Fax: 905/479-9793 – *3
D.M. Starzynski, Q.C., The 16th Ave. Shopping Centre, 9275 Hwy. 48 North, L6E 1A3 – 905/294-3891, Fax: 905/471-2550 – *1
Still Thompson McGee, 20 Main St. North, L3P 1X2 – 905/472-1072, Fax: 905/472-1077 – *6
Thomas Rod Pelman, 4901 Hwy. 7 East, L3R 1M7 – 905/477-2233, Fax: 905/477-7668 – *1
Deborah L. Wilkins, 107-7225 Woodbine Ave., L3R 1A3 – 905/475-0242, Fax: 905/475-0852 – *1
Wilson, Vukelich, #710, 60 Columbia Way, L3R 0C9 – 905/940-8700 – *7
Jack Zwicker, #306, 7100 Woodbine Ave., L3R 5J7 – 905/470-2544 – *1

**Marmora.....................................Hastings**

A.L. Philpot, 65 Forsyth St., PO Box 430, K0K 2M0 – 613/472-2245, Fax: 613/472-3310 – *1

**Meaford..........................................Grey**

Kopperud, Tamming Law Office, 76 Sykes St. North, N4L 1R2 – 519/538-2044, Fax: 519/538-5323 – *1
Scheifele, Erskine & Renken, 39 Nelson St. West, PO Box 3395, N4L 1A5 – 519/538-2510, Fax: 519/538-1843 – *4

**Midland........................................Simcoe**

Joseph Blake, 366 First St., L4R 3P2 – 705/526-7894 – *1
Chin & Orr, 382 King St., L4R 3M9 – 705/526-5529, Fax: 705/526-3071 – *3
Deacon Taws Friend, 30 Coldwater Rd., PO Box 663, L0K 1E0 – 705/686-3700, Fax: 705/686-3737 – *3
Ferguson & Boeckle, 531 King St., PO Box 306, L4R 4L1 – 705/526-1471, Fax: 705/526-1067; Toll Free: 1-800-563-6348 – *4
Hacker Gignac Rice, 518 Yonge St., L4R 2C5 – 705/526-2231, Fax: 705/526-0313; Email: hack@csolve.net – *7
Heacock & DiTomaso, 361 King St., PO Box 640, L4R 3M7 – 705/526-7886, Fax: 705/526-6872 – *2
James Lunnie, 509 Dominion Ave., PO Box 567, L4R 4L3 – 705/526-6735 – *1
Prost & Associates, 323 Midland Avenue, PO Box 96, L4R 4K6 – 705/526-9328, Fax: 705/526-1209 – *2
Edward F. Symons, 540 Hugel Ave., L4R 1V9 – 705/526-2251, Fax: 705/526-2251 – *1
John Winter & Mark Kowalsky, 362 Midland Ave., L4R 3K7 – 705/526-4560, Fax: 705/528-8499 – *2

**Milton.........................................Halton**

Flannagan & Greenwood, #105, 13 Charles St., L9T 2G5 – 905/878-2804, Fax: 905/878-5610 – *2
Furlong Collins, 64 Ontario St. North, L9T 2T1 – 905/878-8123, Fax: 905/878-2555 – *2
Hedley Grieves, 24 Martin St., L9T 2P9 – 905/878-8843, Fax: 905/876-4891 – *2
Nigel A. Gunding, #203, 15 Martin St., L9T 2R1 – 905/875-4678, Fax: 905/878-3723
Ingrid Hibbard, 539 Moorelands Cres., L9T 4B2 – 905/875-3828, Fax: 905/875-3829 – *1
P.K. McWilliams, Q.C., #203, 15 Martin St., L9T 2R1 – 905/878-4681, Fax: 905/878-3723 – *2
Nichols & Servos, 207 Mary St., L9T 1M1 – 905/878-4149, Fax: 905/878-4984 – *2

D.J. Pressé, #301, 205 Main St. East, L9T 1N7 – 905/876-4721, Fax: 905/878-4282 – *1

**Milverton** .......................................... **Perth**

W. Stirling Kenny Law Office, 11 Main St. North, N0K 1M0 – 519/595-8171

**Minden** .......................................... **Haliburton**

Donald J. Finn, 13 NewCastle St., PO Box 158, K0M 2K0 – 705/286-2611, Fax: 705/286-4460 – *1

**Mississauga** .......................................... **York**

Calvin V. Agard, #111, 93 Dundas St. East, L5A 1W7 – 905/276-6920

David A. Aiken, #330, 1420 Burnhamthorpe Rd. East, L4X 2Z9 – 905/602-5230, Fax: 905/602-0722 – *1

Carol Allen, 6050 Bidwell Trail, L5V 1V6 – 905/826-6799, Fax: 905/826-6799 – *1

David A. Allport, 1646 Dundas St. West, L5C 1E6 – 905/270-2008, Fax: 905/270-2148 – *1

Jeffrey A. Alter, #6, 2145 Dunwin Dr., L5L 4L9 – 905/828-1195, Fax: 905/828-4602 – *1

Mark E. Alter, 7330 Goreway Dr., L4T 4J2 – 905/672-0770 – *1

Anderson, Sinclair, 2170 Torquay Mews, L5N 2M6 – 905/821-8522 – *13

David Arthur & Associates, #6, 2145 Dunwin Dr., L5L 4L9 – 905/828-2300, Fax: 905/828-4602 – *1

Mary E. Atkinson, #227, 92 Lakeshore Rd. East, L5G 4S2 – 905/278-4910, Fax: 905/271-6065 – *1

Robert A. Ault, #6, 25 Watline Ave., L4Z 2Z1 – 905/712-2726, Fax: 905/712-2727 – *1

John R.E. Bacon, Barrister & Solicitor, #15, 1100 Central Pkwy. West, L5C 4E5 – 905/949-4300 – *1

H. Ross R. Bain, Emerald Business Centre, #600, 10 Kingsbridge Garden Circle, L5R 3K6 – 905/568-0000, Fax: 905/568-0080; Email: rbain@primerestaurants.com – *1

Paul Bannon, #360, 33 City Centre Dr.., L5B 2N5 – 905/272-3412 – *2

Barie Benaich, 30 Village Centre Pl., L4Z 1V9 – 905/275-7731, Fax: 905/275-3315

H. Robert Barlow, Q.C., #1600, 90 Burnhamthorpe Rd. West, L5B 3C3 – 905/273-7380, Fax: 905/273-6920 – *1

Barrigar & Moss, #901, 2 Robert Speck Pkwy., L4Z 1H8 – 905/276-2300, Fax: 905/276-7687; Toll Free: 1-800-263-8338; URL: http://www.barr-moss.com – *7

N. Bartels, #102, 2600 Edenhurst Dr., L5A 3Z8 – 905/276-8286 – *1

Bateman & Bowen, #701, 6711 Mississauga Rd. North, L5N 2W3 – 905/567-4440, Fax: 905/821-1572 – *2

Richard T. Bennett, 82 Queen St. South., L5M 1K6 – 905/826-1453, Fax: 905/826-7185 – *2

R.M. Bindoo, ##200, 4265 Sherwoodtowne Blvd., L4Z 1Y5 – 905/803-8255, Fax: 905/803-0843 – *1

Binsky Howard, #6, 2145 Dunwin Dr., L5L 4L9 – 905/828-2247, Fax: 905/828-4607

S.R. Biss, #102, 2600 Edenhurst Dr., L5A 3Z8 – 905/273-3322 – *1

Susan Margaret Black, 42 Peter St. North, L5H 2G8 – 905/274-4738, Fax: 905/274-4948 – *1

Michael J. Bukovac, 1325 Burnhamthorpe Rd. East, L4Y 3V8 – 905/238-1411, Fax: 905/629-9277 – *1

J. Paul Burk, Q.C., #206, 1310 Dundas St. East, L4Y 2L6 – 905/848-1653, Fax: 905/848-5989 – *1

Byrnes, Chan & Associates, #42, 145 Traders Blvd. East, L4Z 3L3 – 905/712-2888, Fax: 905/712-3838

Carey, McCallum, Nimjee & Smith, #100C, 131 Brunel Rd., L4Z 1X3 – 905/568-1900, Fax: 905/568-3854 – *4

J.C. Chapman, 2572 Stanfield Rd., L4Y 1S2 – 905/270-7034, Fax: 905/270-1001 – *1

Chojnacki, Ford, O'Neail, #601, 6733 Mississauga Rd. North, L5N 6J5 – 905/821-3644, Fax: 905/821-8355; Email: rchojnak11@aol.com – *3

R.J. Cornale, 2070 Hadwen Ave., L8K 2C9 – 905/403-1433, Fax: 905/403-1400 – *1

Cousins & Nadler, 30 Village Centre Place, Upper Level, L4Z 1V9 – 905/275-6042, Fax: 905/275-3315 – *3

Douglas M. Davidson, 15 Dundas St. West, L5B 1H2 – 905/279-3330, Fax: 905/279-2735 – *1

Michael J. Day, 93 Queen St. South, L5M 1K7 – 905/826-5670, Fax: 905/826-5673; Email: daylaw@idirect.com – *1

M.G. DeCosimo, 7 Helene St. South, L5G 3A8 – 905/278-7248, Fax: 905/278-7718 – *1

Carmen A. Defacendis, #202, 120 Traders Blvd. East, L4Z 2H7 – 905/712-2655, Fax: 905/712-2654 – *1

Greg Dimitriou, #102, 160 Traders Blvd., L4Z 3K7 – 905/568-9800, Fax: 905/568-9802 – *1

M. DiPaolo, #400, 7050 Weston Rd., L4L 8G7 – 905/850-7575, Fax: 905/850-7050 – *1

P.E. Dubas, #500, 3025 Hurontario St., L5A 2H2 – 905/848-8484, Fax: 905/848-8489 – *1

L. Murray Eades, 7229 Pacific Circle, L5T 1S9 – 905/795-4040, Fax: 905/564-2315

Richard Alan Fellman, #100, 46 Village Centre Pl., L4Z 1V9 – 905/275-2231, Fax: 905/275-8323 – *1

Harold Fink, #200, 19 Dundas St. West, L5B 1H2 – 905/276-1024, Fax: 905/276-4646 – *1

Kim Fullerton, 1347 Crestdale Rd., L5H 1X9 – 905/274-6708 – *1

Hugh H. Galbraith, 2863 Derry Rd. East, L4T 1A6 – 905/671-2462, Fax: 905/671-0859 – *1

Gardner, Cutler, 30 Village Centre Pl., L4Z 1V9 – 905/275-6132, Fax: 905/276-2193

Garvey & Garvey, 972 Clarkson Rd. South, L5J 2V7 – 905/823-4400, Fax: 905/823-5153 – *2

Stanley Gelman, Q.C., #602, 50 Burnhamthorpe Rd. West, L5B 3C2 – 905/270-5110, Fax: 905/220-3002 – *1

Stephen Joel Goldman, #104, 1454 Dundas St. East, L4X 1L4 – 905/281-0119, Fax: 905/281-1013 – *1

Jack E. Harris, Q.C., #300, 4 Robert Speck Pkwy., L4Z 1S1 – 905/275-4673, Fax: 905/275-4680 – *1

K.R. Harris, 1370 Hurontario St., L5G 3H4 – 905/271-4277, Fax: 905/271-8027 – *1

Holmes & Stewart, #6, 2624 Dunwin Dr., L5L 3T5 – 905/607-8879, Fax: 905/607-1074 – *2

Howard & Cook, #300, 34 Village Centre Place, L4Z 1V9 – 905/848-2136, Fax: 905/848-2138; Email: roberthoward@sympatico.ca – *1

James Hoyt, #114, 1801 Lakeshore Rd. West, L5J 1J6 – 905/823-4567, Fax: 905/823-5025

George K. Hutcheson, #105, 3034 Palstan Rd., L4Y 2Z6 – 905/848-3600, Fax: 905/272-1682 – *1

Wm. G. Jeffery, #301, 8 Stavebank Rd. North, L5G 2T4 – 905/278-7271, Fax: 905/278-7514 – *1

Jerry S. Korman & Associates, 46 Village Centre Pl., L4Z 1V9 – 905/270-6660, Fax: 905/270-2665 – *2

Kain & Ball, #240, 1900 Dundas St. West, L5K 1P9 – 905/855-4888, Fax: 905/855-3760; Email: 73617.3151@compuserve.com – *2

Kaiser Reide, #708, 1 City Centre Dr., L5B 1M2 – 905/272-6930, Fax: 905/273-7386

James G. Karas, 930 Lakefront Promenade, L5E 2C4 – 905/274-0900, Fax: 905/274-9640 – *1

Keller Treloar & Sehmi, #301, 25 Watline Ave., L4Z 2Z1 – 905/890-2211, Fax: 905/890-2246 – *3

Kennedy & Associates, 20 Hurontario St., L5G 3G7 – 905/271-1010, Fax: 905/271-8104 – *2

Thomas D. Kerr, 3102 O'Hagan Dr., L5C 2C6 – 905/279-9004, Fax: 905/279-9004 – *1

Keyser Mason Ball, #701, 201 City Centre Dr., L5B 2T4 – 905/276-9111, Fax: 905/276-2298; Email: kmb@kmblaw.com; URL: http://www.kmblaw.com – *25

Killaby, Peter C., 93 Queen St., L1M 1K3 – 905/542-3151 – *3

Korman McNulty, 46 Village Centre Pl., L4Z 1V9 – 905/270-6660, Fax: 905/270-2665 – *2

Michael Krepakevich, 2572 Stanfield Rd., L4Y 1S2 – 905/273-3811, Fax: 905/273-5648 – *1

Frank Laconte, 4311 Village Crater Court, L4Z 1S2 – 905/897-1982, Fax: 905/897-9287 – *1

D. Lafferty, Q.C., 1743 Lakeshore Rd. West, L5J 1J4 – 905/822-3111, Fax: 905/822-8885 – *1

Letman, Forth & Associates, 34 Lakeshore Rd. East, L5G 1C8 – 905/271-0102, Fax: 905/274-0169 – *2

Frank Loconte, #100, 4311 Village Centre Ct., L4Z 1S2 – 905/789-3436, Fax: 905/897-9287 – *1

C.P. Lum, #200, 4265 Sherwoodtowne Blvd., L4Z 1Y5 – 905/949-0799, Fax: 905/949-1749 – *1

Arthur MacColl, #16, 6645 Kitimat Rd., L5N 6J3 – 905/821-3213, Fax: 905/821-2582 – *1

W.E. MacDonald, Q.C., 1370 Hurontario St., L5G 3H4 – 905/271-6223 – *1

MacKay & MacKay, #202, 776A Dundas St. East, L4Y 2B6 – 905/848-3446 – *2

Carol E. MacPherson, 6711 Mississauga Rd. North, L5N 2W3 – 905/5567-9740, Fax: 905/821-1572 – *1

B.R. Madigan, #101, 20 Stavebank Rd., L5G 2T4 – 905/278-7766, Fax: 905/278-4233 – *1

Maguire, Laurel, #6-12, 2145 Dunwin Dr., L5L 1X2 – 905/828-2300 – *1

Malicki & Malicki, 3020 Kirwin Ave., L5A 2K6 – 905/279-6250, Fax: 905/279-3878 – *1

Mangat Manjit Singh, #16, 7033 Delford Way, L5S 1V4 – 905/677-4124, Fax: 905/677-7134

Markowitz & Associates, #401, 10 Kingsbridge Garden Circle, L5R 3K6 – 905/890-1800, Fax: 905/890-8400 – *2

William E. Mathers, #200, 2386 Haines Rd., L4Y 1Y6 – 905/270-8811, Fax: 905/270-2977; Email: wemathers@myna.com – *2

Mazzucco & Boguski, 1090 Dundas St. East, L4Y 2B8 – 905/272-0303 – *3

McClintock, Ingle & O'Connor, Top Floor, 4275 Village Centre Ct.., L4Z 1V3 – 905/896-4370, Fax: 905/896-4926 – *4

Cindy McGoldrick, 3530 Cawthra Rd., L5A 2Y3 – 905/279-0872, Fax: 905/279-1349 – *1

Hugh G. McLean, 1599 Hurontario St., L5G 3H7 – 905/271-1010, Fax: 905/271-1012 – *1

McMillan Binch, #800, 3 Robert Speck Pkwy., L4Z 2G5 – 905/566-2003, Fax: 905/566-2029 – *4

Donald McPherson, 34 Village Centre Pl., L4Z 1V9 – 905/848-7737

David S.H. Mimms, #708, 1 City Centre Dr., L5B 1M2 – 905/276-4211, Fax: 905/273-7386 – *1

Mississauga Community Legal Services, #501A, 130 Dundas St. East, L5A 3V8 – 905/896-2050, Fax: 905/273-4255

David A. Morrison, 67 Lakeshore Rd. East, L5G 1C9 – 905/274-5370, Fax: 905/274-5387 – *5

Ronald F. Mossman, #300, 34 Village Centre Place, L4Z 1V9 – 905/848-4020, Fax: 905/848-4026; Email: mossman@tlx.com – *1

Mussani Law Office, 3701 Price Ct., L5L 4S6 – 905/828-6623, Fax: 905/828-6623

John O'Donnell, #7, 1015 Matheson Blvd. East, L4W 3A4 – 905/625-2522, Fax: 905/625-0614

O.J. Osmak, #2A, 702 Burnhamthorpe Rd. East, L4Y 2X3 – 905/277-0229, Fax: 905/277-4966 – *1

Ovenden & Ovenden, 1 City Centre Dr., L5B 1M2 – 905/270-8544, Fax: 905/273-7386 – *2

Pallett Valo, #1600, 90 Burnhamthorpe Rd. West, L5B 3C3 – 905/273-3300, Fax: 905/273-6920; Toll Free: 1-800-323-3781; Email: debhayes@pallettvalo.com; URL: http://www.pallettvalo.com – *14

Roland Paskar, 1450 Hurontario St., L5G 3H4 – 905/271-3343, Fax: 905/271-3352 – *2

Larry R. Plener, 2564 Confederation Pkwy., L5B 1S2 – 905/897-8611, Fax: 905/897-8807 – *1

Annalisa Pressaco, #606, 6711 Mississauga Rd. North, L5N 2W3 – 905/821-9055, Fax: 905/821-1572 – *1

Pretam K. Prewal, #210A, 7071 Airport Rd., L4T 4J3 – 905/678-0084, Fax: 905/678-1493

David G. Price, 1370 Hurontario St., L5G 3H4 – 905/271-0191 – *1

Peter Quirt, #102, 6850 Mill Creek Dr., L5N 4J9 – 905/858-1366, Fax: 905/858-3622 – *1

* indicates number of lawyers in law firm.

Racioppo Zuber Dionne, Corporate Centre III, #200, 1290 Central Pkwy. West, L5C 4R3 – 905/848-6100, Fax: 905/896-1111; Email: rzlaw@interlog.com – *2
Bonnie Racz, #318, 1 City Centre Dr., L5B 1M2 – 905/949-9555 – *1
Reddington & White, #100, 53 Village Centre Pl., L4Z 1V9 – 905/896-7533, Fax: 905/896-7573 – *2
George Rethy Law Office, 4261 Sherwoodtowne Blvd., L4Z 1Y5 – 905/270-9585
Sheri Richardson, 30 Village Centre Pl., L5A 3R6 – 905/270-4264, Fax: 905/275-3315 – *1
Terry D. Richardson, 18 Mississauga Rd. North, L5H 2H4 – 905/891-0011, Fax: 905/891-1410 – *1
Norman Ronka, 1348 Hurontario St., L4Z 3G1 – 905/271-3636, Fax: 905/271-7779 – *1
G. Martin Rosen, #101, 160 Traders Blvd., L4Z 3K7 – 905/507-4771, Fax: 905/507-0467 – *1
Peter M. Rowland, 872 Whittier Cres., L5H 2X3 – 905/274-4841 – *1
T.D. Salomaa, 2572 Stanfield Rd., L4Y 1S2 – 905/270-7034, Fax: 905/270-1001 – *1
J. Saltzman, #15, 7205 Goreway Dr., L4T 2T9 – 905/671-1178, Fax: 905/671-8030 – *1
Sargeant & Sargeant, #202, 120 Traders Blvd. East, L4Z 2H7 – 905/568-1200, Fax: 905/568-1206 – *2
Susan J. Schell, #59, 6535 Mill Creek Dr., L5N 2M2 – 904/567-7037 – *1
Edgar Schink, 6549B Mississauga Rd., L5N 1A6 – 905/826-8448, Fax: 905/826-2652 – *1
Martin C. Schulz, #510, 2085 Hurontario St., L5A 4G1 – 905/897-2200, Fax: 905/897-1517 – *3
Shadlock, Barycky, Roche, #2300, 4 Robert Speck Pkwy., L4Z 2J1 – 905/270-1900, Fax: 905/270-5750 – *3
Donald N. Shaw, Q.C., 2294 Camilla Road, L5A 2K3 – 905/279-9831 – *1
Shepherd Grenville-Wood, #103, 5710 Timberlea Blvd., L4W 4W1 – 905/629-9035, Fax: 905/629-0264; URL: http://www.sgwmiss.com – *4
Allan Shulman, 2225 Erin Mills Pky., L5K 1T9 – 905/822-3563, Fax: 905/822-6342 – *1
Thomas Simpson, 1721 Lakeshore Rd. West, L5J 1J4 – 905/855-8200, Fax: 905/855-8858 – *1
Suter Law, 100 City Centre Dr., L5B 2G6 – 905/273-6640, Fax: 905/270-7518 – *2
Thompson, MacColl & Stacy, #5, 1020 Matheson Blvd. East, L4W 4J9 – 905/625-5591, Fax: 905/238-3313 – *5
Helen M. Thomson, #3, 205 Matheson Blvd. East, L4Z 3E7 – 905/507-3616, Fax: 905/507-3617 – *1
Barry Trembetzky, 2564 Confederation Pkwy., L5B 1S2 – 905/279-8561 – *1
Turk, Jonah Law Office, #208, 1325 Eglinton Ave. East, L4W 4L9 – 905/625-5883, Fax: 905/625-5885 – *2
Turkstra, Mazza, Reininger Associates, #590, 2 Robert Speck Pkwy., L4Z 1H8 – 905/276-9000, Fax: 905/276-9822 – *1
Marina Ushycky, #316, 6855 Meadowvale Town Circle, L5N 2Y1 – 905/826-6324, Fax: 905/826-3279 – *1
Verbeek & Verbeek, #12, 1020 Matheson Blvd East, L4W 4J9 – 905/602-6000, Fax: 905/602-5000 – *2
Donald P. Warren, #760, 2 Robert Speck Pkwy., L4Z 1H8 – 905/848-2770, Fax: 905/848-2773; Email: dnwarren@greynet.net – *1
Brian M. Watson, #105, 3034 Palston Rd., L4Y 2Z6 – 905/272-0942, Fax: 905/272-1682 – *1
Weir & Foulds, #902, 50 Burnhamthorpe Rd. West, L5B 3C2 – 905/896-1100, Fax: 905/896-0803
Weir Nakon, #710, 1290 Central Pkwy. West, L5C 4R3 – 905/279-7930, Fax: 905/279-3421 – *5
Wheeler & Associates, 10 Front St. North, L5H 2C9 – 905/274-7881, Fax: 905/274-7883 – *2
Willis & Torry, #355, 35 Queen St. South, L5M 1K2 – 905/819-8377 – *2
Annette Wilson, #201, 1515 Matheson Blvd. East, L4W 2P5 – 905/602-1989, Fax: 905/602-6513 – *1
Michael Woods, #209, 5805 Whittle Rd., L4Z 2J1 – 905/568-3810, Fax: 905/568-5816 – *1
Yeoman, Ament Associates, #B, 6549 Mississauga Rd. North, L5N 1A6 – 905/826-6660, Fax: 905/826-2652 – *2

**Mitchell ........ Perth**

William E. Wilson, 89 Ontario Rd., N0K 1N0 – 519/348-8488, Fax: 519/348-4226; Email: scotwill@cyg.net – *1

**Moosonee........ Cochrane**

Keewaytinok Native Legal Services, 40 Revillon Rd. North, PO Box 218, P0L 1Y0 – 705/336-2981, 2982, Fax: 705/336-2577 – *3

**Morrisburg........ Dundas**

Gorrell, Grenkie, Leroy & Rémillard, PO Box 820, K0C 1X0 – 613/543-2922, Fax: 613/543-4228; Email: gglr@mor-net.on.ca – *3
McInnis & MacEwen & Horner, PO Box 733, K0C 1X0 – 613/543-2946, Fax: 613/543-3867 – *2

**Mount Albert........ York**

Wilson, Martin, 19139 Centre St., L0G 1M0 – 905/852-3353 – *3

**Mount Brydges........ Middlesex**

Sylvia A. Loyens, 22 Adelaide St. North, N0L 1W0 – 519/264-9440, Fax: 519/264-2921 – *1

**Mount Forest........ Wellington**

Fallis, Fallis & McMillan, 150 Main St. South, N0G 2L0 – 519/323-2800, Fax: 519/323-4115 – *2
Grant Deverell Lemaich & Barclay, 166 Main St. South, N0G 2L0 – 519/323-1600, Fax: 519/323-3877; Email: gdlb@wcl.on.ca – *4

**Napanee........ Lennox**

G. Graeme G. Dempster, 21 Market Sq., PO Box 310, K7R 3M4 – 613/354-2141, Fax: 613/354-3171 – *1
W.A. & J.M. Grange, PO Box 26, K7R 3L4 – 613/354-3359, Fax: 613/354-6786 – *2
Hogle & Doreleyers, 35 Dundas St. East, PO Box 398, K7R 3P5 – 613/354-3375, Fax: 613/354-5641; Email: 1-800-267-9420 – *2
Frank T. Horn, 22 Meadow Lane, K7R 3R8 – 613/354-6954
Madden, Sirman & Cowle, 3 Bridge St., K7R 3L8 – 613/354-2161, Fax: 613/354-5027 – *3
J.K. Pearce, Q.C., PO Box 308, K7R 3M4 – 613/354-2101, Fax: 613/354-7694 – *1
Smart & Griffin, 130 Centre St. North, PO Box 206, K7R 3M3 – 613/354-9716, Fax: 613/354-3120 – *2

**Nepean........ Ottawa-Carleton**

Chiarelli Cramer Witteveen, 92 Centrepointe Dr., K2G 6B1 – 613/723-9100, Fax: 613/723-9105 – *5
Doraty & Ferris, 28 Northside Rd., K2H 5Z3 – 613/829-7171, Fax: 613/829-0244 – *3
Donald R. Good, Merivale Depot, PO Box 5118, K2C 3H4 – 613/228-9676, Fax: 613/228-7404; Toll Free: 1-800-661-8837 – *1
Noble & Gadient, Toronto-Dominion Bank Bldg., #203, 245 Stafford Rd. West, K2H 9E8 – 613/726-9500, Fax: 613/596-9958 – *2
Stephen A. Ritchie, 92 Centrepointe Dr., K2G 6B1 – 613/723-9100, Fax: 613/723-9105 – *1
Charles Schwartzman, 15 Saddlebrook St., K2G 5N7 – *1
Sterling & Young, 1510 Merivale Rd., K2G 3J6 – 613/224-7786, Fax: 613/224-9150 – *2
Danyl Stotland, #C, 273 Craig Henry Dr., K2G 4C7 – 613/723-7179, Fax: 613/727-0573 – *1
E.W. Tennant, #105, 3740 Richmond Rd., K2H 5B9 – 613/829-5121, Fax: 613/829-9511 – *1
R.A. Vanier, #202, 1370 Clyde Ave., K2G 3H8 – 613/226-3336, Fax: 613/226-8767
Jo-Anne E. Ward, 12 Harrogate Pl., K2H 5L7 – 613/829-2317 – *1

**New Hamburg........ Waterloo**

N.A. Thomas, PO Box 1000, N0B 2G0 – 519/662-1760 – *1

**New Liskeard........ Temiskaming**

Ramsay, Ramsay, Kemp, Andrew & Maille, 22 Armstrong St., PO Box 1540, P0J 1P0 – 705/647-7353, Fax: 705/647-1540 – *4
D. Cragg Ross, Q.C., 18 Paget St. North, PO Box 9, P0J 1P0 – 705/647-6819, Fax: 705/647-9525 – *1
Smith, Byck & Grant, 22 Paget St., PO Box 1210, P0J 1P0 – 705/647-7307, Fax: 705/647-7511; Email: sbglit@nt.net; URL: http://www.nt.net/sbg/sbg1.html

**Newburgh........ Lennox**

Thomas Grant Smyth, PO Box 163, K2K 2S0 – 613/378-6429, Fax: 613/378-6429 – *1

**Newcastle........ York**

Sam L. Cureatz, Q.C., 104 James St., L1B 1C6 – 905/987-3500, Fax: 905/987-3503; Email: dn00123@mail.durham.net – *1
Walters, Dizenbach, Ferguson, 29 King St. East, PO Box 2, L1B 1H3 – 905/987-4735, Fax: 905/987-1061 – *3

**Newmarket........ York**

Boyd Cumming Eady, 130 Main St. S., L3Y 3Y7 – 905/898-6471, Fax: 905/898-5941 – *3
Penelope Bryan, 130 Mulock Dr., Unit 1, L3Y 7C5 – 905/853-4577, Fax: 905/830-1451 – *1
Chisvin Murphy & Lewis, #300, 30 Prospect St., L3Y 3S9 – 905/836-1027, Fax: 905/836-6691 – *3
Christopher & Fysh, 474 Botsford St., L3Y 1T3 – 905/898-7331, Fax: 905/853-9382 – *3
Iain Stewart Cunningham, 227 Eagle St. East, L3Y 1J8 – 905/836-4151, Fax: 905/836-1059 – *1
Joan Cushon, 17705B Leslie St., L3Y 3E3 – 905/898-1673, Fax: 905/898-2477 – *1
Di Cecco, Jones, #200, 496 Davis Dr., L3Y 2P3 – 905/898-1911, Fax: 905/853-9893 – *2
C.E. Dresner, 39 Parkside Dr., L3Y 4R7 – 905/898-6800, Fax: 905/853-7073 – *1
Dunsmuir & Dunsmuir, 17070 Yonge St., PO Box 2003, L3Y 6W4 – 905/895-7741, Fax: 905/895-3337 – *2
Michael Easson, #205, 1091 Gorham St., L3Y 7V1 – 905/853-1746, Fax: 905/853-7603 – *1
J. David Hobson, Q.C., 34 Eagle St. East, L3Y 1J1 – 905/895-6528, Fax: 905/853-1108 – *1
Hunter, Corbett & Losell, 68 Prospect St., L3Y 3T2 – 905/898-1541, Fax: 905/898-5596 – *3
Karnis & Robichaud, 27 Main St. N, L3Y 3Z6 – 905/836-4977, Fax: 905/836-2851 – *2
Neal J. Kearney, #207, 091 Gorham St., L3Y 7V1 – 905/898-3012, Fax: 905/853-9894 – *1
Legal Aid, 50 Eagle St., L3Y 6B1 – 905/888-1575, Fax: 905/898-4932
McChesney Rogers Law Firm, #200, 17360 Yonge St., L3Y 4X7 – 905/895-1007, Fax: 905/895-4064 – *7
D.J. McKee, #213, 16610 Bayview Ave., L3X 1X3 – 905/898-4116, Fax: 905/898-3838 – *1
Peter S. Oliver, #301, 16775 Yonge St.., L3Y 8J4 – 905/836-4946, Fax: 905/836-0364 – *1
Anne L. Roberts, 712 Davis Dr., L3Y 8C3 – 905/895-1090, Fax: 905/895-1090 – *1
Rubin Wintraub, 207 Main St. S., L3Y 3Y9 – 905/898-4440; Toronto Line: 773-6526, Fax: 905/898-3291 – *2
Heather M. Saunders, 17665 Leslie St., L3Y 3E3 – 905/836-5040, Fax: 905/836-0364 – *1
A. Schneider, 291 Davis Dr., L3Y 2N6 – 905/898-1342 – *1
Kimberley Smith, #205, 1091 Gorham St., L3Y 7V1 – 905/853-1746, Fax: 905/853-7603 – *1
Stevens & Stevens, Newmarket Corporate Centre, #302, 1091 Gorham St., L3Y 7V1 – 905/853-2897, Fax: 905/853-7214 – *2

Stiver Vale, 195 Main St., L3Y 4X4 – 905/895-4571, 773-6323, Fax: 905/853-2958 – *8
William D. Turville, Q.C., 34 Eagle St. East, L3Y 1J1 – 905/887-5023, Fax: 905/895-8618 – *1
Wrock & Assoc., 17837 Yonge St., RR#1, L3Y 4V8 – 905/898-5161, Fax: 905/898-1821 – *2

**Niagara Falls ............................... Niagara South**

Broderick, Marinelli, Amadio, Sullivan & Rose, 4625 Ontario Ave., PO Box 897, L2E 3P8 – 905/356-2621, Fax: 905/356-6904 – *8
J.D. Conte, 4624 Ontario Ave., PO Box 928, L2E 6V8 – 905/357-1144, Fax: 905/357-5560 – *1
David A. Crowe, 6617 Drummond Rd., PO Box 58, L2G 4N4 – 905/356-7755, Fax: 905/356-7772 – *1
David P. Czifra, 5146 Victoria Ave., L2E 4E3 – 905/357-6633, Fax: 905/357-6659
Charles A. Galloway, 5146 Victoria Ave., L2E 4E3 – 905/356-2512, Fax: 905/356-2513 – *1
Douglas Goslin, 4780 Portage Rd., L2E 6A8 – 905/357-0500, Fax: 905/357-0501 – *1
Geoffrey G. Hadfield, 4552A Victoria Ave., PO Box 2173, L2E 6Z3 – 905/357-3500, Fax: 905/356-5850 – *1
Kenneth B. Harris, 4444 Drummond Rd., PO Box 206, L2E 6T3 – 905/374-2121, Fax: 905/374-8546 – *1
Hopkins & Kirkham, 4683 Queen St., PO Box 687, L2E 6V5 – 905/357-5820, Fax: 905/357-9686 – *2
Margaret A. Hoy, 4786 Queen St., PO Box 868, L2E 6V6 – 905/354-4414, Fax: 905/354-1272 – *1
Jaluvka & Sauer, 4231 Portage Rd., L2E 6A2 – 905/356-6484 – *2
R.O. Kallio, City Solicitor, City Hall, L2E 6X5 – 905/356-7521, Fax: 905/374-7500; Email: rkallio@city.niagarafalls.on.ca; URL: http://www.niagara.com/city.niagara-falls
S. James Knight, Q.C., 4683 Queen St., L2E 2L9 – 905/356-1524, Fax: 905/357-9686 – *1
Philip C. Lococo, 5079 Victoria Ave., PO Box 958, L2E 6V8 – 905/356-7661, Fax: 905/356-6330 – *1
Joseph A. LoConte, 5146 Victoria Ave., L2E 4E3 – 905/357-5554, Fax: 905/357-6659 – *1
Patricia Lucas, 6268 Colborne St., L2J 1E6 – 905/357-4510, Fax: 905/357-9757 – *1
Martin, Sheppard, Fraser, 4607 Huron St., PO Box 900, L2E 6V7 – 905/354-1611, Fax: 905/354-5540; Toll Free: 1-800-263-2502 – *8
McBurney, Durdan, Henderson & Corbett, 4759 Queen St., PO Box 2148, L2E 6Z2 – 905/356-4511, Fax: 905/356-8938 – *3
D.J. McDonald, 4683 Queen St., L2E 2Z9 – 905/356-1524, Fax: 905/357-9686 – *1
McKay, Heath & Gajer, 4673 Ontario Ave., PO Box 23001, Stn Downtown E, L2E 7J4 – 905/357-0660, Fax: 905/357-5680 – *3
G.F. McNab, Q.C., 6268 Colbourne St., L2J 1E6 – 905/357-4510, Fax: 905/357-9757 – *1
N. Minov, 3879 Portage Rd., L2J 2L2 – 905/356-4420, Fax: 905/356-0333 – *1
Nicoletti & DiPaul, 5001 Victoria Ave., PO Box 2238, L2E 6Z3 – 905/356-5053, Fax: 905/356-9487 – *2
Stephen Paine, 4786 Queen St., PO Box 868, L2E 6V6 – 905/357-3500, Fax: 905/356-3635 – *1
George Radojcic, 4672 Queen St., L2E 2L8 – 905/374-7727, Fax: 905/227-4031 – *1
Andrew Rasuse, 4786 Queen St., PO Box 868, L2E 6V6 – 905/357-3500, Fax: 905/356-3635 – *1
James Rocca, 4056 Dorchester Rd., L2E 6M9 – 905/357-3730, Fax: 905/356-6185 – *1
Ryall, Walker, 4190 Bridge St., PO Box 816, L2E 6V6 – 905/374-3000, Fax: 905/374-6456 – *3
Sharpe, Beresh & Gnys, 4700 St. Clair Ave., L2E 3S8 – 905/357-5555, Fax: 905/357-5760 – *2
Brian N. Sinclair, Q.C., 6617 Drummond Rd., L2G 4N4 – 905/356-7755 – *1
William Slovak, Q.C., 4786 Queen St., PO Box 868, L2E 6V6 – 905/357-3500, Fax: 905/356-3635 – *1
Malcolm A.F. Stockton, 4786 Queen St., PO Box 868, L2E 6V6 – 905/357-3500, Fax: 905/356-3635 – *1
Guy Ungaro, #201, 6225 Huggins St., L2J 1H2 – 905/357-5310, Fax: 905/357-9677; Email: gung@vaxxine.com – *1
George F. Walker, Q.C., 4786 Queen St., PO Box 868, L2E 6V6 – 905/357-3500, Fax: 905/356-3635 – *1
Brian C. Wilcox, 3964 Portage Rd., L2J 2K9 – 905/358-0782, Fax: 905/358-0783; Email: bcwlaw@niagara.com – *1

**Niagara-on-the-Lake ......................... Niagara North**

Richard J.W. Andrews, 431 Mississauga St., PO Box 900, L0S 1J0 – 905/468-3272, Fax: 905/468-5441 – *1
A.C. Dekany, RR#1, L0S 1J0 – 905/262-5521
W.R. King, 431 Mississauga St., PO Box 900, L0S 1J0 – 905/468-3272, Fax: 905/468-5441 – *1
Larry H. Kroeker, 431 Mississauga St., PO Box 1570, L0S 1J0 – 905/646-4447, Fax: 905/468-3898

**Nipigon ..................................... Thunder Bay**

Peter G.F. Young, 64 Front St., P0T 2J0 – 807/887-3204, Fax: 807/345-9886 – *1

**Nobleton .................................... York Region**

Joseph Vroom, PO Box 1037, L0G 1N0 – 905/859-0014, Fax: 905/859-5113 – *1

**Noelville ......................................... Sudbury**

Desmarais, Keenan, 9, rue Notre Dame, P0M 2N0 – 705/898-2245

**North Bay ....................................... Nipissing**

Colvin & Colvin, 577 Main St. West, PO Box 657, P1B 8J7 – 705/476-5161, Fax: 705/476-9902 – *2
Donnelly, Birnie, 116 McIntyre St. West, PO Box 100, P1B 8G8 – 705/497-1900, Fax: 705/497-1700; Email: ellies@sympatico.ca – *5
Lucenti, Rivard & Orlando, 108 Main St. East, PO Box 358, P1B 8H5 – 705/472-9500, Fax: 705/472-4814 – *4
James R. McIntosh, 109 Main St. East, P1B 1A9 – 705/476-2500, Fax: 705/476-9347 – *1
McLachlan Wilcox & DuCharme, 705 Cassells St., P1B 4A3 – 705/476-6333, Fax: 705/476-4397; Email: gducharme@onlink.net – *3
Olah & Olah, 457 Main St. West, PO Box 985, P1B 8K3 – 705/476-1323 – *2
Tafel, Trussler & Eggert, 477 Sherbrooke St., P1B 2C2 – 705/472-4890, Fax: 705/472-9612 – *3
Valin Partners, 140 Main St. West, PO Box 97, P1B 2T5 – 705/474-1220, Fax: 705/474-5630 – *3
Wallace Carr Klein O' Hagan Trenker & Perron, 225 McIntyre St. West, PO Box 37, P1B 8G8 – 705/474-2920, Fax: 705/474-1758 – *6
Douglas D. Woltz, 325 Main St. West, P1B 2T9 – 705/476-1710, Fax: 705/476-8277 – *1
Donald W. Wood, 355 Main St. West, P1B 8H5 – 705/476-1710, Fax: 705/476-8277 – *1

**Oakville .......................................... Halton**

Baggs, Henderson & Brown, 228 Lakeshore Rd., PO Box 249, L6J 5A2 – 905/844-3218, Fax: 905/844-3699 – *1
George A. Benak, 418 North Service Rd. East, L6H 5R2 – 905/845-4004, Fax: 905/845-6917 – *1
David Bereskin, 418 North Service Rd. East, L6H 5R2 – 905/845-6914, Fax: 905/845-6917 – *1
H.D. Brown, #705, 700 Dorval Dr., L6K 3V3 – 905/842-8710 – *1
Roger B. Campbell, #200, 200 Lakeshore Rd. East, L6J 1H6 – 905/849-7000, Fax: 905/849-7145 – *1
Carson Law Office, 2902 South Sheridan Way, 3rd Fl., L6J 7L6 – 950/844-6404, Fax: 950/844-6426 – *1
Stephen B. Collinson, #11, 250 Wyecroft Rd., L6K 3T7 – 905/842-1600, Fax: 905/842-2775 – *1
Coutts, Crane, Ingram, #300, 627 Lyons Lane, L6J 2Y2 – 905/338-0802, Fax: 905/338-3168 – *1
Diane Daly, #4, 132 Allan St., L6J 3N5 – 905/844-5883, Fax: 905/844-9765 – *1
Diab DeCosimo, #A101, 2381 Bristol Cir., L6H 5S9 – 905/829-2900, Fax: 905/829-2903 – *2
J.I.A. Docherty, 1170 Willowbrook Dr., L6L 2J8 – 905/825-2245, Fax: 905/847-9379 – *1
Gordon M. Edwards, #308, 251 North Service Rd. West, L6M 3E7 – 905/844-1604, Fax: 905/844-9592 – *1
William Elias, 301 Church St., L6J 1N9 – 905/842-2070, Fax: 905/842-5334 – *1
J.B. Gardner, 228 Lakeshore Rd. East, PO Box 249, L6J 5A2 – 905/844-3218, Fax: 905/844-3699; Email: gardner@worldchat.com – *1
M. Edward Graham, 420 North Service Rd. East, L6H 5R2 – 905/842-3211, Fax: 905/842-3765 – *1
J.H. Ham, Q.C., 228 Lakeshore Rd. East, PO Box 249, L6J 5A2 – 905/844-3218 – *1
Steven Harrington, 2441 Lakeshore Rd. West, L6L 1H6 – 905/827-8738 – *1
D.K. Haxell, 467 Speers Rd., 2nd Fl., L6K 3S4 – 905/845-0767, Fax: 905/845-7674 – *1
Lorne S. Jackson, #202, 123 Maurice Dr., L6K 2W6 – 905/842-3072, Fax: 905/842-1982; Email: intrepid@idirect.com; URL: http://web.idirect.com/~kid – *1
William B. Kerr, 233 Robinson St., L6J 1G5 – 905/842-8600, Fax: 905/842-4774 – *1
Brian W. King, Q.C., Hopedale Mall, #23, 1515 Rebecca St., L6L 5G8 – 905/827-0808, Fax: 905/827-8380 – *1
LeDressay Van Melle, #101, 700 Kerr St., L6K 3W5 – 905/842-4977, Fax: 905/842-4977 – *2
Lush, Bowker Aird, 261 Lakeshore Rd. East, PO Box 734, L6J 1H9 – 905/844-0381, Fax: 905/849-4540 – *3
Marler & Kyle, 86 Chisholm St., L6K 3H7 – 905/338-2300 – *2
Thomas H. Marshall, Q.C., 296 Randall St., PO Box 955, L6J 5E8 – 905/844-0464, Fax: 905/844-3983 – *1
W. McCrea, #302, 88 Dunn St., L6J 3C7 – 905/844-8881, Fax: 905/844-9970 – *1
David L. McKenzie, #23, 323 Church St.., PO Box 906, L6J 5E8 – 905/842-3421, Fax: 905/842-3422 – *1
McLeod, Horner & Axon, #314, 345 Lakeshore Rd. East, L6J 1J5 – 905/338-2555, Fax: 905/338-2961 – *2
Patricia McNamara, 2227 Wyandotte Dr., L6L 2T4 – 905/847-0356 – *1
Kathryn S. Naumetz, 263 Church St., L6J 1N7 – 905/845-2241, Fax: 905/845-0193 – *1
O'Connor MacLeod, 700 Kerr St., L6K 3W5 – 905/842-8030, Fax: 905/842-2460 – *14
J.G. O'Reilly, 187A Lakeshore Rd. East, L6J 1H5 – 905/845-4111, Fax: 905/845-0011 – *1
John Paladino, #200B, 447 Speers Rd., L6K 3S7 – 905/842-3311, Fax: 905/842-7433 – *1
P. William Perras, Jr., #610, 1275 North Service Rd. West, L6M 3G4 – 905/827-2700, Fax: 905/827-2766 – *1
David J. Pilo, #301, 88 Dunn St., L6J 3C7 – 905/338-2002, Fax: 905/338-3810 – *1
J. Jeffrey Richey, #301, 88 Dunn St., L6J 3C7 – 905/845-5880, Fax: 905/338-3810 – *1
R.M. Rose, 2163 - 6 Line, L6H 3N7 – 905/338-9555 – *1
Ruth A.M. Ross, 226 Randall St., L6J 1P7 – 905/849-8377, Fax: 905/849-8344 – *1
Ryrie, Ford, Kerr, 233 Robinson St., PO Box 100, L6J 4Z5 – 905/842-8600 – *7
Angelo A. Serafini, #202, 447 Speers Rd., L6K 3S7 – 905/842-0300, Fax: 905/842-7433 – *1
Shepherd Grenville-Wood, 1391 Fieldcrest Lane, L6M 2W3 – 905/847-0589
Skrow & Indovina, #208, 243 North Service Rd. West, L6M 3E5 – 905/842-6625, Fax: 905/842-6197 – *1
David B. Smith, #2, 760 Pacific Rd., L6L 6M5 – 905/827-3113 – *1
Randolph I. Smith, 710 Dorval Dr., PO Box 517, L6K 3V7 – 905/849-6700, Fax: 905/849-7145 – *1
Karen A. Thompson, #4, 132 Allan St., L6J 3N5 – 905/338-7941, Fax: 905/844-9765 – *1

* indicates number of lawyers in law firm.

Anthony A. Vale, 420 North Service Rd. East, L6H 5R2 – 905/842-0300, Fax: 905/842-3765 – *1

**Orangeville....................................Dufferin**

Wayne D. Ball, 279 Broadway Ave., L9W 1L2 – 519/942-4492, Fax: 519/942-1530 – *1

Bourque, White, 30 Mill St., L9W 2M3 – 519/941-9440, Fax: 519/941-3803 – *2

William Church, Q.C., 31 First St., L9W 2C8 – 519/941-3782, Fax: 519/941-3837 – *1

Evans, Adams & Adams, 107 Broadway St., L9W 1K2 – 519/941-0810, Fax: 519/941-3333 – *2

Richard J. Harbour, 162 Broadway Ave., L9W 1K3 – 519/942-8555, Fax: 519/942-8583 – *1

Margot L. Hornseth, 12 First Ave., L9W 1H8 – 519/941-2620, Fax: 519/941-6888 – *1

McAlpine & Vroom, #201, 70 First St., L9W 2E5 – 519/941-0218, Fax: 519/941-8057 – *2

Lorna Paradis, 28 Mill St., L9W 2M3 – 519/942-1042 – *1

Parkinson, Parkinson, Pugsley & Maund, 145 Broadway St., L9W 1K2 – 519/941-3627, Fax: 519/941-3444 – *4

Gillian Shute, #18, 28 Mill St., L9W 2M3 – 519/940-0333, Fax: 519/940-0234 – *1

William W. Stutz, 269 Broadway Ave., L9W 1K8 – 519/941-7500, Fax: 519/941-8381 – *1

Tilson & Birchall, 5 Mill St., L9W 2M2 – 519/941-6671, Fax: 519/941-2354 – *2

Wardlaw, Mullin, Carter & Thwaites, 235 Broadway Ave., PO Box 67, L9W 2Z5 – 519/941-1760, Fax: 519/941-3688; Email: wardlaw@beeline.ca; URL: http://www.beeline.ca//wardlaw – *6

L. Anne Welwood, 14 Zina St., L9W 1E1 – 519/941-9710, Fax: 519/941-9244 – *1

**L'Orignal....................................Prescott**

Tolhurst & Miller, 28 Court St., K0B 1K0 – 613/675-4512, Fax: 613/675-1103

**Orillia....................................Simcoe**

Douglas S. Anderson, #B, 190 Memorial Ave., L3V 5X6 – 705/327-1841, Fax: 705/327-3188 – *1

Bourne, Jenkins & Mulligan, 27 Peter St. North, PO Box 368, L3V 6J8 – 705/326-3565, Fax: 705/326-8360 – *3

Crawford, Worling, McKenzie & Donnelly, 40 Coldwater St. East, PO Box 520, L3V 6K4 – 705/325-2753, Fax: 705/325-4913 – *6

Richard Crothers, 674 Atherley Rd., PO Box 205, L3V 6J3 – 705/326-2525 – *1

Michael Drury, 4 Cowan St., L3V 4G2 – 705/ 326-6256 – *1

Aubrey J.F. Ford & Associate, 110 Neywash St., PO Box 788, L3V 6K7 – 705/325-7462, Fax: 705/325-8527 – *2

Allan French, #201, 6 West St. North, PO Box 998, L3V 6K8 – 705/327-6671, Fax: 705/327-9084 – *1

R.M. Haidle, 13 Mississauga St. West, PO Box 2389, L3V 6V7 – 705/325-9524, Fax: 705/325-7079 – *1

W.H. Hamilton, 354 Laclie St., PO Box 2326, L3V 6V7 – 705/325-4556, Fax: 705/325-3108 – *1

W.M. Holdsworth, 63 Coldwater Rd. West, L3V 3L3 – 705/325-4411, Fax: 705/327-3442 – *1

Lisa James, 27 Peter St. North, PO Box 368, L3V 6J8 – 705/325-2762, Fax: 705/326-8360 – *1

Linda D. Lewis, 41 Peter St. North, L3V 4Y9 – 705/329-1957, Fax: 705/329-1574 – *1

Scott Lindsey, 273 Coldwater Rd. West, L3V 3M1 – 705/325-3638, Fax: 705/325-8193 – *1

Winsor MacDonnell, 31 Peter St. North, PO Box 277, L3V 6J6 – 705/326-3431, Fax: 705/325-4699 – *1

Nils Peterson, 66 Matchedash St. South, L3V 4W5 – 705/325-5659, Fax: 705/325-0721 – *1

Russell, Christie, Miller, Koughan, 76 Coldwater St. East, PO Box 158, L3V 6J3 – 705/325-1326, Fax: 705/327-1811 – *6

Ronald W. Sillick, 31 Mississauga St. West, PO Box 428, L3V 6J8 – 705/327-5121, Fax: 705/327-5122 – *1

Simcoe Legal Services Clinic, 71 Colborne St. East, PO Box 275, L3V 6J6 – 705/326-6444, Fax: 705/326-9757

R.G. Sparks, 32 Matchedash St. North, PO Box 2357, L3V 6V7 – 705/325-0082, Fax: 705/327-7537 – *1

Stong, Blackburn, Machon, Bohm & Pond, RR#7, L3V 6H7 – 705/329-2983 – *1

Wilford L.S. Trivett, Q.C., 27 Front St. North, PO Box 157, L3V 6J3 – 705/326-3579, Fax: 705/326-3570 – *1

Brian M. Turnbull, #111, 200 Memorial Ave., L3V 5X6 – 705/327-2110, Fax: 705/327-1952 – *1

Bernard J. Varcoe, PO Box 2195, L3V 6S1 – 705/325-2668 – *1

R. Bruce Waite, 241 West St. North, PO Box 338, L3V 6J6 – 705/327-6655, Fax: 705/325-2081; Email: waitelaw@bconnex.net – *2

Zwicker, Evans & Lewis, 93 Coldwater St. East, PO Box 310, L3V 6J7 – 705/325-6146, Fax: 705/325-0044

**Orleans....................................Ottawa-Carleton**

Beament Green Dust, 2589 St. Joseph Blvd., K1C 1G4 – 613/837-1010, Fax: 613/837-9670; Email: gdust@intranet.ca – *2

Dust Evans Pilon, 2589 St. Joseph Blvd., K1C 1E9 – 613/837-1010, Fax: 613/837-9670 – *3

Marthe Montreuil, #101, 3009 St-Joseph Blvd., K1E 1E1 – 613/837-7408, Fax: 613/837-4204 – *1

**Orono....................................Durham**

W.K. Lycett, Q.C., 5301 Main St., PO Box 87, L0B 1M0 – 905/983-5007, Fax: 905/983-9022 – *1

**Oshawa....................................Durham**

Affleck & Payne, 197 Bond St. East, L1G 1B4 – 905/436-8400, Fax: 905/436-9959 – *2

James Aitchison, Office Galeria, #185, Oshawa Shopping Centre, PO Box 30608, Stn Centre, L1J 8L8 – 905/433-1174, Fax: 905/433-1645 – *1

Alan Berk, #209, 650 King St. East, L1H 1G5 – 905/579-2888, Fax: 905/579-7586 – *1

Aleksandr G. Bolotenko, #303, 17 King St. East, L1H 1A8 – 905/433-1176, Fax: 905/433-0283; Email: abolotenko@speedline.ca – *1

Boychyn & Boychyn, 36 1/2 King St. East, L1H 1B3 – 905/576-2670 – *3

Kay M. Carlson, 106 Stevenson Rd. South, L1J 5M1 – 905/433-0622, Fax: 905/571-7706 – *1

D.H. Creighton, 90 Simcoe St. North, PO Box 2188, L1H 7V4 – 905/579-6561 – *1

Creighton, Victor, Alexander, Hayward & Morison, 235 King St. East, PO Box 26010, Stn 206, L1H 8R4 – 905/723-3446, Fax: 905/432-2323 – *4

Diamond & Fischman, 206 King St. East, PO Box 26008, L1H 8R4 – 905/723-5243, Fax: 905/436-6041 – *3

G.K. Drynan, Q.C., #1001, 33 Richmond St. West, L1G 1A4 – 905/576-9304, Fax: 905/432-2663 – *1

Dutka Partners, 142 Simcoe St. North, L1G 4S7 – 905/571-1411, Fax: 905/436-6098 – *2

Elliott & Hughes, 106 Stevenson Rd. South, L1J 5M1 – 905/571-1774, Fax: 905/571-7706; Toll Free: 686-6416 – *2

Barry L. Evans, 419 King St. West, L1J 2K5 – 905/433-1200, Fax: 905/433-2555 – *1

Farquharson, Adamson, 74 Simcoe St. South, L1H 4G6 – 905/404-1947, Fax: 905/404-9050 – *2

Pasquale Gelsomino, 304 Stevenson Rd. North, L1J 5M9 – 905/571-1916, Fax: 905/571-4254 – *1

Greer, Seiler & Zochodne, 88 Centre St. North, PO Box 917, L1H 7N1 – 905/576-5153, Fax: 905/571-4376 – *3

Higgins, Clark, Cornwall-Taylor, 32 Elgin St. East, L1G 1T1 – 905/434-6411, Fax: 905/571-6114 – *3

Shan K. Jain, Q.C., 215 Simcoe St. North, L1G 4T1 – 905/432-7787, Fax: 905/432-2343 – *1

Kelly, Zuly, Greenway, Bruce, 114 King St. East, PO Box 886, L1H 7N1 – 905/723-2278; 686-5156, Fax: 905/432-2663 – *5

Kitchen, Kitchen, Simeson & McFarlane, 86 Simcoe St. South, PO Box 428, L1H 7L5 – 905/579-5302, Fax: 905/479-6073; Email: mail@kksm.com; URL: http://www.kksm.com – *5

Korb & Billings, 111 Simcoe St. North, 2nd Fl., L1G 4S4 – 905/571-5672, Fax: 905/571-5672 – *2

Koziar, Reczulski, 72 Centre St. North, L1G 4B6 – 905/571-3214, Fax: 905/571-3832 – *2

Myrna L. Lack, 174 Athol St. East, PO Box 1098, Stn B, L1J 5Y9 – 905/579-8866, Fax: 905/579-8913 – *1

K.L. Lancaster, 52 Division St., L1G 5L9 – 905/571-3901, Fax: 905/571-4241 – *1

A.E. Laskowsky, 73 Centre St. South, L1H 4A1 – 905/579-0777, Fax: 905/576-9918 – *1

Legal Aid, 500 King St. West, L1J 2K9 – 905/576-2124, Fax: 905/721-1859

Mack & Kisbee, 146 Simcoe St. North, L1G 4S7 – 905/571-1400, Fax: 905/571-0735 – *3

MacVicar, MacLean, 850 King St. West, L1J 2L5 – 905/404-2233, Fax: 905/404-2234; Email: rjblaise@aol.com – *4

Marks & Marks, 16 Lloyd St., L1H 1X3 – 905/728-5151, Fax: 905/433-4018 – *2

Mazar & Associates, #210, 419 King St. West, L1J 2K5 – 905/571-2558, Fax: 905/571-3548 – *2

McGibbon, Bastedo, Armstrong & Armstrong, National Trust Bldg., 32 Simcoe St. South, PO Box 2396, L1H 7V6 – 905/686-5251, Fax: 905/432-2348 – *3

John N. McKay, 146 Simcoe St. North, L1G 4S7 – 905/571-1400, Fax: 905/571-0735 – *1

McNeely & Kelly, 146 Simcoe St. North, PO Box 735, L1H 7M9 – 905/579-1121, Fax: 905/579-0214 – *2

Kenneth R. McPherson, 85 Bond St. West, L1G 1A6 – 905/434-6555 – *1

Joseph Neal, 142 Simcoe St. North, L1G 4S7 – 905/436-9015, Fax: 905/436-6098 – *1

Josef Neubauer, 106 Stevenson Rd. South, L1J 5M1 – 905/433-1991, Fax: 905/433-7038 – *1

O'Brien, Balka & Elrick, 219 King St. East, L1H 1C5 – 905/427-2908, 576-3402, Fax: 905/576-3915 – *3

Palter, McCarthy, 219 King St. East, L1H 1C5 – 905/576-7501, Fax: 905/576-2909 – *2

Margot Poepjes, 231 King St. East, 2nd Fl., L1H 1C5 – 905/433-4020 – *1

Gregory G. Price, 455 Bond St. East, L1G 1B9 – 905/576-4944, Fax: 905/576-4898 – *1

Reid, Brown & Bell, #202, 200 Bond St. West, L1J 2L7 – 905/571-1301, Fax: 905/576-5022 – *3

Risen, Espey, Scott, Kimball & Olver, Lord Simcoe Place, #1C, 57 Simcoe St. South, PO Box 278, L1H 7L3 – 905/571-3942, Fax: 905/683-4699 – *5

Salmers, Strike & Furlong, 55 William St. East, PO Box 2096, L1H 7V4 – 905/723-1101, Fax: 905/723-1157 – *4

James A. Scott, 1050 Simcoe St. North, L1G 4W5 – 905/571-2001, Fax: 905/571-2002 – *1

Stephen F. Shine, 231 King St. East, L1H 8R4 – 905/571-2559, Fax: 905/579-2846 – *1

Frank H.M. Stolwyk, 25 Brock St. West, PO Box 235, L1G 1R2 – 905/576-8100, Fax: 905/579-6762; Email: franks@4950@aol.com – *1

Ronald L. Swartz, 231 Simcoe St. North, L1G 4T1 – 905/576-3392 – *1

Debra J. Sweetman, 111 Simcoe St. North, L1G 4S4 – 905/404-0386, Fax: 905/404-1202

David B. Thomas, 90 Simcoe St. North, L1G 4S2 – 905/576-5666, Fax: 905/576-5289 – *1

George R. Vella, 231 King St. East, L1H 1C5 – 905/576-0520, Fax: 905/576-0326 – *1

Walters, Dizenbach, Ferguson, Box: 832, 218 Centre St. North, PO Box 2307, L1G 4C5 – 905/579-1066, Fax: 905/579-6811 – *3

J.T. Wilbur, 218 Centre St. North, PO Box 2307, L1H 7V5 – 905/436-0165, Fax: 905/436-0167 – *1

R. Worboy, 153 Simcoe St. North, PO Box 21, L1G 7K8 – 905/723-2288, Fax: 905/576-1355 – *2

**Ottawa .................................... Ottawa-Carleton**

Douglas R. Adams, #400, 100 Sparks St., K1P 5B7 – 613/238-8076, Fax: 613/238-5519 – *1

R.D. Allard, #2, 213 Kent St., K1P 1Z8 – 613/238-2245 – *1

F. James Altimas, PO Box 1168, K1P 5R2 – 613/731-7918, Fax: 613/830-9201 – *1

Janis Apse, #100, 1785 Alta Vista Dr., K1G 3Y6 – 613/738-1713, Fax: 613/738-5056 – *1

Jacqueline Asselin, #110, 261 Cooper St., K2P 0G3 – 613/232-3574 – *1

William T. Badcock, Q.C., 130 Albert St., K1A 0H8 – 613/941-0387, Fax: 613/957-4697 – *1

Gary R. Barnes, #400, 200 Elgin St., K2P 1L5 – 613/225-2529, Fax: 613/225-3930; Email: gbarnes@travel1.travel-net.com – *2

Bayne, Sellar, Boxall, #500, 200 Elgin St., K2P 1L5 – 613/236-0535, Fax: 613/236-6958 – *6

Beaudet Davidson, #1110, 141 Laurier West, K1P 5J3 – 613/234-8497, Fax: 613/236-0989

Bell, Baker, #500, 116 Lisgar St., K2P 0C2 – 613/237-3444, Fax: 613/237-1413 – *12

Bennett Jones Verchere, #1800, 350 Albert St.., PO Box 25, K1R 1A4 – 613/230-4935, Fax: 613/230-3836; Email: george@bjv.ca – *2

Adèle Berthiaume, #200, 440 Laurier Ave. West, K1R 7X6 – 613/782-2248, Fax: 613/521-8561 – *1

Binks, Simpson, 180 Waller St., K1N 9B9 – 613/233-4063, Fax: 613/233-0450 – *3

Peggy J. Blair, 400 Piccadilly Ave., K1Y 0H4 – 403/722-0947 – *1

Blake, Cassels & Graydon, World Exchange Plaza, 45 O'Connor St., 20th Fl., K1P 1A4 – 613/788-2200, Fax: 613/788-2247; Email: ottawa@blakes.ca; URL: http://www.blakes.ca – *11

John E. Bogue, #802, 200 Elgin St., K2P 1L5 – 613/234-4901, Fax: 613/236-8906 – *1

Bosada & Associates, 280 Metcalfe St., 2nd Fl., K2P 1R7 – 613/563-1001, Fax: 613/563-1031 – *1

Bowley, Cuffari, #203, 200 Isabella St., K1S 1V7 – 613/233-9541, Fax: 613/233-9965 – *2

Brennan, Tunney & Emond, #300, 200 Elgin St., K1P 1L5 – 613/232-9441, Fax: 613/232-0448

Bulger, Young, #310, 411 Roosevelt Ave., K2A 3X9 – 613/728-5881, Fax: 613/728-6158 – *4

Burke-Robertson, 70 Gloucester St., K2P 0A2 – 613/233-4195, Fax: 613/235-4430, 233-4195 – *27

Charles, Merovitz & Potechin, #301, 200 Catherine St., K1P 2K9 – 613/563-7544 – *5

Paul-Emile Chiasson, #800, 180 Elgin St., K2P 2K6 – 613/230-8800, Fax: 613/233-6643 – *1

Cogan & Cogan, Bank St. Chambers, 102 Bank St., K1P 5N4 – 613/237-4000, Fax: 613/237-4906 – *4

Conlin & McAlpin, 1678 Bank St., K1V 7Y6 – 613/737-4140, Fax: 613/737-7903 – *3

Counsellor Law Offices, #4000, 210 Gladstone Ave., K1P 0Y6 – 613/237-0505 – *5

Curran Associates, 1125 Baxter Rd., K2C 3R4 – 613/596-2804, Fax: 613/596-2316 – *2

Colombe M. Daigneault, #201, 200 Elgin St., K1P 1L5 – 613/238-4411, Fax: 613/238-4413 – *1

Davis & Company, World Exchange Plaza, #810, 45 O'Connor St., K1P 1A4 – 613/232-7522, Fax: 613/232-7525

Dunlap, Dunlap & McInenly, 1350 Wellington St., K1Y 3C1 – 613/729-0572 – *3

Farber, Segal & Robillard, Westboro Manor, 330 Churchill Ave., K1Z 5B9 – 613/722-9418, Fax: 613/722-5981 – *2

Michael J. Farrell, 34 Hawthorne Ave., K1S 0B1 – 613/238-8006, Fax: 613/230-8855 – *1

Finlayson & Singlehurst, 70 Gloucester St., 4th Fl., K2P 0A2 – 613/232-0227, Fax: 613/232-0542 – *3

Ann L. Flint, #203, 190 Somerset St. West, K2P 0J4 – 613/594-5461 – *1

Forbes, Singer & Smith, 302 Waverley St., K2P 0W3 – 613/238-1424, Fax: 613/238-6741 – *4

Fraser & Beatty, #1200, 180 Elgin St., K2P 2K7 – 613/783-9611, Fax: 613/563-7800; URL: http://www.fraserbeatty.ca – *3

Gibson & Augustine, #1520, 360 Albert St., K1R 7X7 – 613/238-8865, Fax: 613/238-7930 – *4

Goldberg, Shinder, Gardner & Kronick, 280 Slater St., 18th Fl., K1P 1C2 – 613/237-4922, Fax: 613/237-2920; Email: admin@gsgk.com; URL: http://www.gsgk.com – *12

Goldstein & Goldstein, #200, 177 Nepean St., K2P 0B4 – 613/230-9405, Fax: 613/230-2074 – *2

Gowlings, #2600, 160 Elgin St., PO Box 466, Stn D, K1P 1C3 – 613/233-1781, Fax: 613/563-9869; Email: marketing@gowlings.com; URL: http://www.gowlings.com – *111

Ronald G. Guertin, #601, 200 Elgin St., K2P 1L5 – 613/238-5448, Fax: 613/238-4824 – *1

Hale & May, #500, 77 Metcalfe St., K1P 5L6 – 613/230-6524, Fax: 613/237-1156 – *2

John H. Hale, #304, 185 Sommerset St. West, K2P 0J2 – 613/230-0089, Fax: 613/230-2705; Email: fjhale@magi.com

Hall, Ray & Button, #508, 359 Kent St., K2P 0R6 – 613/232-4848, Fax: 613/232-3662 – *2

Hamilton Appotive Callan, 150 Metcalfe St., 11th Fl., K2P 1P1 – 613/238-8400, Fax: 613/238-4085 – *8

James D. Harbic, #700, 200 Elgin St., K2P 1L5 – 613/235-4365, Fax: 613/237-9450 – *1

Hendin, Hendin & Lyon, #726, 50 O'Connor St., K1P 6L2 – 613/563-4804, Fax: 613/563-3878 – *7

Hewitt, Hewitt, Nesbitt, Reid, Fuller Bldg., #604, 75 Albert St., K1P 5E7 – 613/563-0202, Fax: 613/563-0445 – *11

Honey/MacMillan, 146 Richmond Rd., K1Z 6W2 – 613/722-2493, Fax: 613/722-2773; Email: honeymac@ott.hookup.net – *4

Hughes & Young, #600, 225 Metcalfe St., K2P 1P9 – 613/563-1131, Fax: 613/230-8297; Email: hugheslaw@hugheslaw.on.ca; URL: http://www.hugheslaw.on.ca – *3

Ken James & Associates, #906, 75 Albert St., K1P 5E7 – 613/236-2966, Fax: 613/236-8169 – *6

Johnston & Buchan, #1700, 275 Slater St., K1P 5H9 – 613/236-3882, Fax: 613/230-6423; Email: johnbuch@magi.com – *13

Eric A. Johnston, 111 Percy St., K1R 6C5 – 613/560-6025, ext.1215, Fax: 613/560-1383 – *1

Kent & Edgar, 150 Metcalfe St., 18th Fl., K2P 1P1 – 613/236-1995, Fax: 613/236-2485; Email: ipinfo@kent-edgar.com – *4

J.K. Kerr, Q.C., #404, 71 Bank St., K1P 5N2 – 613/232-7902, Fax: 613/232-1805 – *1

Stanley Kershman Law Office, 283 McLeod St., K2P 1A1 – 613/238-1924, Fax: 613/238-4490; Email: info@bankruptlaw.com; URL: http://www.bankruptlaw.com – *1

Kimmel, Victor & Ages, 112 Lisgar St., K2P 0C2 – 613/238-1333, Fax: 613/238-8949; Email: kva@travel-net.com – *8

L. Kos-Rabcewicz-Zubkowski, 214 Roger Road, K1H 5C6 – 613/737-3116; 232-1476, Fax: 613/564-9800 – *1

Lalonde, Chartrand, Colonnier & O'Connor, 214, ch Montreal Rd, K1L 8E3 – 613/745-9446, Fax: 613/745-0800 – *4

Lang Michener, #300, 50 O'Connor St., K1P 6L2 – 613/232-7171, Fax: 613/231-3191 – *25

Laveaux, Franck, #212, 1725 St-Laurent Blvd., K1G 3V4 – 613/523-0307, Fax: 613/521-0164; Email: lavlaw@magi.com; URL: http://www.laveaux.com

Lavery, de Billy, 48 O'Connor St., 20th Fl., K1P 1A4 – 613/594-4936, Fax: 613/594-8783

Lavery, O'Brien, #1600, 50 O'Connor St., K1P 6L2 – 613/238-2229 – *1

Cheryl R. Lean Barrister & Solicitor, #1210, 170 Laurier Ave. West, K1P 5V5 – 613/232-4630, Fax: 613/232-0411; Email: clean@achilles.net – *1

Robert A. Lewis & Associates, #301, 1889 Baseline Rd., K2C 0C7 – 613/226-8815, Fax: 613/226-4930 – *1

Lightstone, Lyon, #420, 875 Carling Ave., K1S 5P1 – 613/729-2460, Fax: 613/729-1710; Email: liteston@fox.nstn.ca

Low, Murchison, #1200, 220 Laurier Ave. West, K1P 5Z9 – 613/236-9442, Fax: 613/236-7942; Email: lawyer@lowmurchison.com – *12

Arthur Lust, #408, 116 Lisgar St., K2P 0C2 – 613/563-7115, Fax: 613/563-3134; Email: lawlust@aol.com – *1

Macdonald, Affleck, #300, 200 Elgin St., K2P 1L5 – 613/236-8712, Fax: 613/232-0363 – *5

Macera & Jarzyna, 81 Metcalfe St., 12th Fl., PO Box 2088, Stn D, K1P 5W3 – 613/238-8173, Fax: 613/235-2508; Email: macjar@ibm.net – *10

J. William MacKinnon, Q.C., 46 Dunvelan Rd., K1K 3L3 – 613/746-6038, Fax: 613/746-6038 – *1

Maclaren, Corlett, #450, 45 O'Connor St., K1P 1A4 – 613/233-1146, Fax: 613/233-7190 – *9

G. Carey MacLellan, #1, 200 Cooper St., K2P 0G1 – 613/232-9364, Fax: 613/230-3551 – *1

Gloria Tongol Malonzo, 41 Second Ave., K1S 2H2 – 613/237-7787, Fax: 613/237-4088 – *1

Howard Mann, 424 Hamilton Ave. South, K1Y 1E3 – 613/729-0621, Fax: 613/729-0306; Email: hmann@ottawa.net – *1

Kay V. Marshall, 1875 Highland Terrace, K1H 5A5 – 613/526-3908, Fax: 613/733-3154 – *1

Marusyk Bourassa Miller & Swain, #1000, 100 Sparks St., PO Box 809, Stn B, K1P 5P9 – 613/567-0762, Fax: 613/563-7671; Email: mbm@mbm-law.com; URL: http://www.mbm-law.com – *8

Leonard Max, Q.C., #201, 357 Preston St., K1S 4M8 – 613/567-5629, Fax: 613/567-5989 – *1

McCann & Giamberardino Law Office, #300, 222 Somerset St. West, K2P 2G3 – 613/236-1410, Fax: 613/563-1367 – *3

McCarthy Tétrault, #1000, 275 Sparks St., K1R 7X9 – 613/238-2000, Fax: 613/563-9386; Email: dcox@mccarthy.ca; URL: http://www.mccarthy.ca – *7

Gordon C. McKechnie, #4000, 210 Gladstone Ave., K2P 0Y6 – 613/237-0505, Fax: 613/238-3258 – *1

John A. McMunagle, 85 Albert St., 9th Fl., K1P 6A4 – 613/235-0337, Fax: 613/237-0071; Toll Free: 1-800-387-3503 – *1

J. Peter McNaughton, #525, 1600 Carling Ave., K1Z 1B2 – 613/722-3660, Fax: 613/722-2140 – *1

McTaggert Blais & Associates, #1000, 100 Sparks St., PO Box 2486, Stn D, K1P 5W6 – 613/232-8389, 237-6430, Fax: 613/563-7671 – *4

T.P. Metrick, Q.C., #1508, 1 Nicholas St., K1N 7B7 – 613/232-1735 – *1

Christopher A. Moore, 70 Gloucester St., 1st Fl., K2P 0A2 – 613/230-9448, Fax: 613/235-4430 – *1

J.C. Moore, #201, 117 Murray St., K1N 5M5 – 613/233-9334, Fax: 613/241-4091 – *1

Jennifer A. Moore, #805, 200 Elgin St., K2P 1L5 – 613/230-2449, Fax: 613/230-2621 – *1

Donald A. Morgan, #505, 200 Elgin St., K2P 1L5 – 613/234-9571 – *1

Anne L. Moxley, #204, 185 Somerset St. West, K2P 0J2 – 613/832-4378, Fax: 613/832-0745 – *1

Nelligan Power, #1900, 66 Slater St., K1P 5H1 – 613/238-8080, Fax: 613/238-2098; Email: cchoquet@nplaw.com – *40

O'Connor, Lavigne & Engel King, #504, 1 Nicholas St., K1N 7B7 – 613/235-4366, Fax: 613/235-0971 – *2

Earle O'Dea, 151 Slater St., K1P 5H3 – 613/238-2327, Fax: 613/236-2672 – *1

W. Gerard O'Dea, #302, 151 Slater St., K1P 5H3 – 613/238-2327, Fax: 613/238-2672 – *1

William O'Halloran, 686 Golden Ave., K2A 2G2 – 613/729-9543 – *1

* indicates number of lawyers in law firm.

O'Reilly, Reid, #805, 200 Elgin St., K2P 1L5 – 613/238-8777, Fax: 613/230-2621 – *2

Ogilvy Renault, #1600, 45 O'Connor St., K1P 1A4 – 613/780-8661, Fax: 613/230-5459; Email: info@ogilvyrenault.com – *16

Osler, Hoskin & Harcourt, #1500, 50 O'Connor St., K1P 6L2 – 613/235-7234, Fax: 613/235-2867; Email: jsomers@osler.com; URL: http://www.osler.com – *35

Joy C. Overtveld, #4, 327 Frank St., K2P 0X7 – 613/238-5858, Fax: 613/238-2610 – *1

Oyen Wiggs Green & Mutala, 81 Metcalfe St., 7th Fl., K1P 6K7 – 613/238-6404, Fax: 613/230-8755 – *4

Paradis, Jones, Horwitz, Bowles Associates, #900, 200 Elgin St., K1P 1L5 – 613/238-5074, Fax: 613/230-3250 – *4

Francis K. Peddle, #406, 116 Lisgar St., K2P 0C2 – 613/232-1740, Fax: 613/232-0407; Email: fpeddle@raynon.com – *1

Perley-Robertson, Panet, Hill & McDougall, #400, 90 Sparks St., K1P 1E2 – 613/238-2022, Fax: 613/238-8775; Toll Free: 1-800-268-8292; Email: lawyers@perlaw.ca; URL: http://www.perlaw.ca – *35

Mindy Pilon, #805, 200 Elgin St., K2P 1L5 – 613/230-2449, Fax: 613/230-2621 – *1

Plaskacz & Associates, #805, 200 Elgin St., K2P 1L5 – 613/230-2449, Fax: 613/230-2621; Email: plaskacz@plaskacz.com; URL: http://www.plaskacz.com – *1

Potvin Law Office, Gillin Bldg., #1000, 141 Laurier Ave. West, K1P 5J3 – 613/236-6628, Fax: 613/234-7529; Email: iplaw@synapse.net – *1

Katrina A. Prystupa, 1276 Wellington St., 2nd Fl., K1Y 3A7 – 613/729-4669, Fax: 613/729-7768 – *1

Helene Bruce Puccini, 247 Fourth Ave., K1S 2L9 – 613/230-6295, Fax: 613/231-2167 – *1

Peter A. Pyper, #300, 100 Sparks St., K1P 5B7 – 613/230-5443, Fax: 613/230 2238 – *1

Quain, Dioguardi, #700, 200 Elgin St., K2P 1L5 – 613/237-2222, Fax: 613/237-9450 – *2

Radnoff, Pearl, Slover, Swedko, Dwoskin, 100 Gloucester St., K2P 0A4 – 613/594-8844, Fax: 613/594-9092 – *9

Raven, Jewitt & Allen, 1600 - 220 Laurier Ave. West, K1P 5Z9 – 613/567-2901, Fax: 613/567-2921 – *7

Walter S. Regan Q.C., 240 Sparks St., PO Box 55095, Stn Sparks St., K1P 1A1 – 613/728-2827 – *1

Larry A. Roine, #203, 1419 Carling Ave., K1Z 7L6 – 613/729-1171, Fax: 613/729-3781 – *1

Heidi N. Ruppert, #4000, 210 Gladstone Ave., K2P 0Y6 – 613/237-0505, Fax: 613/567-3559; Email: heidir@cyberus.ca – *1

Macey Schwartz, #1006, 75 Albert St., K1P 5E7 – 613/236-1872, Fax: 613/236-8639 – *1

Scott & Aylen, 60 Queen St., K1P 5Y7 – 613/237-5160, Fax: 613/230-8842 – *42

Segal, Talarico, Wong & Habib, #200, 2650 Queensview Dr., K2B 8H6 – 613/820-8888, Fax: 613/820-8818 – *5

Seguin, Landriault & Lamoureux, #1110, 141 Laurier Ave. West, K1P 5J3 – 613/236-9141, Fax: 613/236-0989 – *4

M.S. Shaikh, #505, 200 Elgin St., K2P 1L5 – 613/234-9571 – *1

Shapiro, Cohen, Andrews, Finlayson, 112 Kent St., PO Box 3440, Stn D, K1P 6P1 – 613/232-5300, Fax: 613/563-9231; Toll Free: 1-800-563-9390; Email: scaf@idealaw.com – *4

Shepherd Grenville-Wood, 43 Florence St., K2P 0W6 – 613/232-2688, Fax: 613/232-2680 – *2

Smart & Biggar, #900, 55 Metcalfe St., PO Box 2999, Stn D, K1P 5Y6 – 613/232-2486, Fax: 613/232-8440; Email: ottawa@smart-biggar.ca – *19

Smith Lyons, #1700, 45 O'Connor St., K1P 1A4 – 613/230-3988, Fax: 613/230-7085; Email: slottawa@magi.com – *6

J. Mitchell Smith, #410, 47 Clarence St., K1N 9K1 – 613/562-5321, Fax: 613/562-2012; Email: jmslaw@synapse.net – *1

Soloway, Wright, 427 Laurier Ave. West, 9th Fl., K1R 7Y2 – 613/236-0111, Fax: 613/238-8507 – *19

R. Ben Sorensen, Q.C., 1315 Richmond Rd., K1B 8J7 – 613/596-1792, Fax: 613/596-6289 – *1

Jennifer A. Steill, #4000, 210 Gladstone Ave., K2P 0Y6 – 613/237-0505, Fax: 613/237-0510; Email: jstiell@cyberus.ca – *1

Stikeman, Elliott, #914, 50 O'Connor St., K1P 6L2 – 613/234-4555, Fax: 613/230-8877 – *11

Tacit & Traynor, #904, 275 Slater St., K1P 5H9 – 613/230-4097, Fax: 613/230-3981; Email: cstacit@tacitandtraynor.com – *2

Christopher C.C. Tan, #700, 200 Elgin St.., K2P 1L5 – 613/235-2308, Fax: 613/237-9450 – *1

Thom, Malcolm & Associates, #701, 150 The Driveway, K2P 1E7 – 613/594-3469, Fax: 613/594-8985 – *1

Thomas & Davis, #810, 45 O'Connor St., K1P 1A4 – 613/232-7522, Fax: 613/232-7525; Email: ottawa@thomasanddavis.com; URL: http://www.thomasanddavis.com – *4

Thomas & Winship, #303, 251 Bank St., K2P 1X3 – 613/235-6721, Fax: 613/235-6404 – *2

Tierney Stauffer, 175 Holland Ave., 2nd Fl., K1Y 0Y2 – 613/728-8057, Fax: 613/728-9866; Email: tslaw@inforamp.net – *11

Vandor & Company, Aylen-Heney House, 150 Richmond Rd., K1Z 6W2 – 613/798-0078, Fax: 613/798-0277; Email: lav@vandorco.ca; URL: http://www.vandorco.ca – *3

Gilad Vered, 1801 Woodward Dr., K2C 0R3 – 613/226-2000, Fax: 613/225-0391 – *1

Vice & Hunter, 344 Frank St., K2P 0Y1 – 613/232-5773, Fax: 613/232-3509 – *4

Vincent Dagenais Gour Gibson, #600, 325 Dalhousie St., K1N 7G2 – 613/241-2701, Fax: 613/241-2599 – *7

G.D. Warren, #700, 200 Elgin St., K2P 1L5 – 613/236-0852, Fax: 613/237-9450 – *1

Watson, Strachan, Bakaity, #404, 359 Kent St., K2P 0R6 – 613/230-2822, Fax: 613/230-2755; Email: watson@cyberus.ca – *2

Wentzell & Wentzell, #204, 190 Somerset St. West, K2P 0J4 – 613/235-6756 – *2

Williams, McEnery & Davis, 169 Gilmour St., K2P 0N8 – 613/237-0520, Fax: 613/237-3163 – *7

Linda M. Wright, PO Box 8542, Stn T, K1G 3H9 – 613/860-0517, Fax: 613/860-0517; Email: iplaw@ibm.net – *1

Roger C. Young, #22, 635 Richmond Rd., K2A 0G6 – 613/728-4434, Fax: 613/728-4434; Email: ryarbsvc@magi.com – *1

Zinn Hofley, #2000, 150 Metcalfe St., K2P 1P1 – 613/230-3633, Fax: 613/230-7697; Email: labour@zinnhofley.com – *4

**Owen Sound........................................Grey**

Neil J. Arnold, 949 - 2nd Ave. West, 2nd Fl., N4K 4M8 – 519/372-2218, Fax: 519/372-2599 – *1

Herbert E. Boyce, Canada Trust Bldg., #201, 983 - 2 Ave. East, PO Box 968, N4K 6H6 – 519/371-4160, Fax: 519/371-1604 – *1

Chander G. Chaddah, 712 - 2 Ave. East, PO Box 965, N4K 6H6 – 519/376-4343, Fax: 519/376-2547 – *1

P.S. Dykstra, 151 - 8 St. East, PO Box 906, N4K 6H6 – 519/376-4500, Fax: 519/376-7273 – *1

Greenfield & Barrie, 142 - 10 St. West, PO Box 665, N4K 5R4 – *2

Edward P. Horton, Q.C., 1390 - 2 Ave. West, PO Box 787, N4K 5W9 – 519/376-8650, Fax: 519/371-3512 – *2

Kirby, Gordon & Robinson, 930 -1 Ave. West, PO Box 730, N4K 5W9 – 519/376-7450, Fax: 519/376-8288 – *3

Catherine A. Laing, 935 - 2 Ave. West, PO Box 664, N4K 5R4 – 519/371-2202, Fax: 519/376-4683; Email: laing@bmts.com – *1

Lendon & Lovell, 167 - 10 St. West, PO Box 845, N4K 5W9 – 519/376-6700 – *2

Alan E. Marsh, #102, 345 - 8 St. East, PO Box 581, N4K 5R1 – 519/371-8373, Fax: 519/371-8971 – *1

McKerroll & McKerroll, 854 - 1 Ave. West, PO Box 607, N4K 5R4 – 519/376-2050, Fax: 519/371-1256 – *3

Middlebro & Stevens, 1030 - 2 Ave. East, PO Box 100, N4K 5P1 – 519/376-8730, Fax: 519/376-7135 – *4

Murray & Thomson, 912 - 2 Ave. West, PO Box 1060, N4K 6K6 – 519/376-6350, Fax: 519/376-0835; Email: mt@log.on.ca – *4

Scott C. Vining, 249 - 10 St. West, N4K 3R2 – 519/371-6210, Fax: 519/371-6238 – *1

**Paisley........................................Bruce**

Patrick L.J. Kelly, PO Box 190, N0G 2N0 – 519/353-5697 – *1

**Palmerston........................................Wellington**

Fallis, Fallis & McMillan, 233 Main St., N0G 2P0 – 519/343-3527, Fax: 519/343-3528 – *2

Nesbitt Coulter, PO Box 309, N0G 2P0 – 519/343-3796, Fax: 519/539-6832 – *1

**Paris........................................Brant**

Theresa A. McClenaghan, 7 William St. North, N3L 1K7 – 519/442-5571, 5572, Fax: 519/442-5567; Email: tmcclena@web.net – *1

Tarrison & Hunter, 19 William St., N3L 1K9 – 519/442-2287, Fax: 519/442-6421 – *2

**Parry Sound........................................Parry Sound**

Larry W. Douglas, #201, 1 Church St., PO Box 520, P2A 2X5 – 705/746-9471, Fax: 705/746-9606 – *2

David A. Holmes, 2 William St., P2A 1V1 – 705/746-4223, Fax: 705/746-6368 – *1

Lisa M. Lund Barrister & Solicitor, 97 James St., P2A 1T7 – 705/746-4215, Fax: 705/746-5357; Email: llund@zeuter.com – *1

A. Wayne Piddington, #1, 43A James St., P2A 1T6 – 705/746-9365, Fax: 705/746-7159 – *1

Pinckard Wyjad Associates, 43A James St., P2A 1T7 – 705/746-7760, Fax: 705/746-7551

Powell & Powell, 34 Mary St., P2A 1E4 – 705/746-8756, Fax: 705/746-2336 – *2

Powell, Cunningham, Kennedy & Grandy, 88 James St., P2A 1T9 – 705/746-4207, Fax: 705/746-2945 – *4

D. Andrew Thomson, 2 - 7 William St., P2A 1V2 – 705/746-5838, Fax: 705/746-4351 – *1

**Pembroke........................................Renfrew**

Kenneth J. Conroy, 358 Pembroke St. East, PO Box 1266, K8A 6Y6 – 613/735-0645, Fax: 613/732-2603 – *1

B. Lynne Felhaber, 258 Nelson St., K8A 6X9 – 613/735-0666, Fax: 613/732-8825 – *1

Huckabone, Shaw, O'Brien, Radley-Walters & Reimer, 284 Pembroke St. East, PO Box 487, K8A 6X7 – 613/735-2341, Fax: 613/735-0920; Email: hsolawyers@renc.igs.net – *10

Johnson, Fraser, 259 Pembroke St. East, K8A 3J9 – 613/735-0624, Fax: 613/735-0625 – *1

Kelly Kelly & Jones, 1064A Pembroke St. West, K8A 5R4 – 613/735-8226, Fax: 613/735-8474; Email: kkjlawyers@renc.igs.net – *3

Bruce Leach, 256 Nelson St., PO Box 546, K8A 6X7 – 613/735-1013, Fax: 613/732-8825 – *1

M.F.A. Shushack, PO Box 1235, K8A 6Y6 – 613/735-6812, Fax: 613/735-5884 – *1

**Penetanguishene........................................Simcoe**

Deacon Taws Friend, 90 Main St., PO Box 869, L0K 1P0 – 705/549-3131, Fax: 705/549-4682 – *4

Frank N. Grisé, 33 Robert St. West – 705/549-7459, Fax: 705/549-3522 – *1

**Perth** ........................................... **Lanark**

Barker, Willson, Butterworth, James & Scott, 31 Foster St., PO Box 308, K7H 3E4 – 613/267-2800, Fax: 613/267-4852 – *5

O'Donnell, Dulmage, Bond, March & Anderson, 10 Market Square, K7H 1V7 – 613/267-1212, Fax: 613/267-7059 – *4

Rubino & Chaplin, 10A Gore St. West, PO Box 338, K7H 3E4 – 613/267-5227, Fax: 613/267-3951 – *1

K.W. Smith, 27 Foster St., PO Box 157, K7H 3E3 – 613/267-5910, Fax: 613/264-0789 – *1

Woodwark & Stevens, 8 Gore St. West, K7H 2L6 – 613/264-8080, Fax: 613/264-8084 – *3

**Petawawa** ........................................... **Renfrew**

Huckabone, Shaw, O'Brien, Radley-Walters & Reimer, 7 Hilda St., PO Box 148, K8H 2X2 – 613/687-8128, Fax: 613/687-6450 – *10

**Peterborough** ........................................... **Peterborough**

R.W. Beninger, 310 Rubidge St., PO Box 426, K9J 6Z3 – 705/743-0065, Fax: 705/742-8718; Email: lawyer@benlaw.on.ca – *1

Blastorah & Vent, #202, 438 Sheridan St., K9H 3J9 – 705/742-6746, Fax: 705/743-1922 – *2

W. Jelle Bosch, #203, 130 Hunter St. West, PO Box 2364, K9J 7Y8 – 705/741-3630, Fax: 705/741-6339 – *1

William M. Carruthers, 404 Water St., PO Box 1117, K9J 7H4 – 705/743-6471, Fax: 705/743-9306 – *1

Roger Clark, 220 Simcoe St., PO Box 1328, K9J 7H5 – 705/743-9070, Fax: 705/743-7484 – *1

Corkery & Corkery, 164 Hunter St. West, PO Box 331, K9J 6Z3 – 705/742-3869, Fax: 705/742-7311 – *2

G.W. Coros, 394A George St. North, K9H 3R3 – 705/748-4311, Fax: 705/748-3332 – *1

H. Girvin Devitt, 858 Chemong Rd., PO Box 1449, K9J 7H6 – 705/742-5471 – *1

Mary Teresa Devlin, #201, 140 King St., K9J 7Z8 – 705/741-5988, Fax: 705/741-2712 – *1

M.J. Dwyer, 359 Aylmer St. North, PO Box 958, K9J 7A5 – 705/743-4221, Fax: 705/743-2187 – *1

Farquharson Daly, 161 Hunter St. West, K9H 2L1 – 705/742-9241, Fax: 705/741-1601 – *3

J.E. Fitzpatrick, Q.C., 331 Reid St., PO Box 1155, K9J 7H4 – 705/743-9334, Fax: 705/743-7253 – *1

J.M. Guerin, #4, 193 Simcoe St., K9J 7H6 – 705/743-9087, Fax: 705/743-8528 – *1

William F. Hampton, PO Box 1898, K9J 7X7 – 705/876-6900, Fax: 705/876-6922 – *1

A.S. Harries, 308 Park St. North, K9J 3W5 – 705/748-2101, Fax: 705/748-0592 – *1

Howell, Fleming, 415 Water St., PO Box 148, K9J 6Y5 – 705/745-1361, Fax: 705/745-6220; Email: howflem@hflaw.com – *10

Roger A. Howson, PO Box 1077, K9J 7A9 – 705/748-3093 – *1

F.A. Johnston, Q.C., 333 Reid St., PO Box 1899, K9J 7X7 – 705/748-5234 – *1

Rod E. Johnston, 244 Aylmer St. North, PO Box 1718, K9J 7X6 – 705/748-2241, Fax: 705/748-9125 – *1

E.J. Jordan, 359 Aylmer St. North, K9J 7A5 – 705/743-4221, Fax: 705/743-2187 – *1

John E. McGarrity, 438 Sheridan St., PO Box 775, K9J 7A2 – 705/743-1822, Fax: 705/743-4870 – *1

McGillen, Ayotte, PO Box 1718, K9J 7X6 – 705/748-2241, Fax: 705/748-9125 – *2

McMichael, Davidson, 410A Sheridan St., K9H 3J9 – 705/745-0571, Fax: 705/745-0411 – *2

R.J. McVicar, PO Box 456, K9J 6Z6 – 705/748-2211, Fax: 705/748-5592 – *1

Moldaver, McFadden & Moorcroft, 121 George St. North, K9J 7H6 – 705/743-1801, Fax: 705/743-0397 – *3

M.B. Moser, 184 Charlotte St., PO Box 717, K9J 6Z8 – 705/748-5661, Fax: 705/748-4234 – *1

Harry W. Robertson, 191 Hunter St. West, K9H 2L1 – 705/741-3337 – *1

John S. Robertson, Q.C., 191 Hunter St. West, K9H 2L1 – 705/741-2220 – *1

F.G. Steffler, 184 Charlotte St., K9J 7H7 – 705/743-2506, Fax: 705/748-4234 – *1

G.H. Usher, 359 Aylmer St. North, PO Box 327, K9J 6Z3 – 705/743-4221, Fax: 705/743-8692 – *1

Douglas F. Walker, 351 Charlotte St., PO Box 1237, K9J 7H5 – 705/748-3012, Fax: 705/748-2746 – *1

J. Ross Whittington, 359 Aylmer St. North, PO Box 327, K9J 6Z3 – 705/743-4221, Fax: 705/743-8692 – *1

**Petrolia** ........................................... **Lambton**

F. Jordan Edward, PO Box 125, N0N 1R0 – 519/882-0510 – *1

**Pickering** ........................................... **Durham**

Stephen A. Cooper, #703, 1305 Pickering Pkwy., L1V 3P2 – 905/686-6406, Fax: 905/837-7762 – *1

Doyle, Speirs, 345 Kingston Rd., L1V 1A1 – 905/509-4882 – *2

G.W. Edmiston, 1281 Commerce St., L1W 1C7 – 905/839-8270 – *1

Alan Fisher, #1217, 1880 Valley Farm Rd., L1V 6B3 – 905/839-7248 – *1

Harris, Fletcher, Tesluk Associates, PO Box 177, L1V 2R4 – 905/686-7780 – *3

John G. Howes, #702, 1305 Pickering Pkwy., L1V 3P2 – 905/420-8628, Fax: 905/420-8634; Toll Free: 1-800-373-6641; Email: howeslaw@spanit.com – *1

Scott Magder, 1 Evelyn Ave., L1V 1N3 – 905/509-3720, Fax: 905/509-5270 – *1

Ronald A. Rubinoff, 1020 Brock Rd., L1W 3H2 – 905/839-1195, Fax: 905/839-1345 – *1

Henry Silver, 345 Kingston Rd., L1V 1A1 – 905/509-2556, Fax: 905/509-5441 – *1

Harvey Storm, #8B, 1400 Bayly St., L1W 3R2 – 905/839-5121, Fax: 905/420-4062; Toll Free: 1-888-876-5529 – *1

Murray Stroud, 356 Kingston Rd., L1V 1A2 – 905/509-1353, Fax: 905/509-2370 – *2

Cameron J.H. Suggitt, #209, 1550 Kingston Rd., L1V 1C3 – 905/420-4020, Fax: 905/420-4508 – *1

Timothy Vanular, #13, 1450 Kingston Rd., L1V 1C1 – 905/427-4886, Fax: 905/420-0808, (Toronto) 420-1595 – *1

G.R. Wakefield, 1 Evelyn Cres., L1V 1N3 – 905/509-5267, Fax: 905/509-5270 – *2

Walker, Head, Corporate Centre, #506, 1305 Pickering Pkwy., L1V 3P2 – 905/839-4484, Fax: 905/420-1073 – *6

**Picton** ........................................... **Prince Edward**

Campbell & Mathers, 194 Main St., PO Box 1260, K0K 2T0 – 613/476-2366, 2733, Fax: 613/476-6064 – *1

Hurley & Williams, 199 Main St., PO Box 1200, K0K 2T0 – 613/476-3241, Fax: 613/476-5985 – *2

William M. Martin, 316 Main St., PO Box 2060, K0K 2T0 – 613/476-2116, Fax: 613/476-8143 – *1

Walmsley & Walmsley, 340 Main St., PO Box 1500, K0K 2T0 – 613/476-5516 – *1

Jack H. Ward, 51 Mary St., PO Box 530, K0K 2T0 – 613/476-3640, Fax: 613/476-3435 – *1

**Point Edward** ........................................... **Lambton**

Dawson, Carpento & Gallaway, #202, 805 North Christina St., N7V 1X6 – 519/337-2321, Fax: 519/332-6588 – *3

**Port Colborne** ........................................... **Niagara South**

Brendon J. Bulger, 333 Wellington St., L3K 2K4 – 905/835-1445, Fax: 905/834-9085 – *1

F.N. Gibbs, 262 Catherine St., L3K 4K9 – 905/835-5650, Fax: 905/732-1015 – *1

Brian N. Lambie, PO Box 127, L3K 5V8 – 905/835-1141, Fax: 905/835-2185 – *1

Maloney & Maloney, 178 Clarence St., L3K 5V8 – 905/835-5633, Fax: 905/835-8801 – *2

James V. Railton, PO Box 127, L3K 5V8 – 905/835-1141, Fax: 905/835-2185 – *1

Robt. H.H. Reilly, PO Box 127, L3K 5V8 – 905/835-1141, Fax: 905/835-2185 – *1

Brian R. Simpson, PO Box 127, L3K 5V8 – 905/835-1141, Fax: 905/835-2185 – *1

John D. Tuck, 196 West St., PO Box 334, L3K 5W1 – 905/834-4525, Fax: 905/834-3254 – *1

Wilson, Opatovsky, 190 Elm St., PO Box 99, L3K 5V7 – 905/835-1163, Fax: 905/835-2171 – *2

**Port Dover** ........................................... **Norfolk**

A.M. Lee Gaunt, 110 St. Andrew St., PO Box 580, N0A 1N0 – 519/583-1411, Fax: 519/583-1110 – *1

Oswald W. Stahl, 725 Main St., PO Box 610, N0A 1N0 – 519/583-2460, Fax: 519/583-1772 – *1

**Port Elgin** ........................................... **Bruce**

George D. Gruetzner, 667 Goderich St., PO Box 10, N0H 2C0 – 519/832-2482, Fax: 519/389-4617 – *1

John D. King, 700 Goderich St., PO Box 579, N0H 2C0 – 519/832-2075, Fax: 519/389-4030 – *1

Ryder & Planz, 669 Gustavus St., PO Box 209, N0H 2C0 – 519/832-6941, Fax: 519/832-2537 – *1

Sherwood, Wyonch, 482 Goderich St., PO Box 2230, N0H 2C0 – 519/389-3722, Fax: 519/389-3766 – *2

**Port Hope** ........................................... **Northumberland**

Ian W.M. Angus, The Canton Mill, RR#1, L1A 3V5 – 905/753-2500, Fax: 905/753-2180; Email: anguslaw@eagle.ca – *1

Brooks, Harrison, Mann, McCracken & Slessor, 114 Walton St., L1A 1N5 – 905/885-2451, Fax: 905/885-7474 – *5

Roger N. Carr, 50 Walton St., L1A 1N1 – 905/885-8146, Fax: 905/885-7471; Email: carr@eagle.ca

Bruce H. Coleman, 50 Walton St., L1A 1N1 – 905/885-8146, Fax: 905/885-7471 – *1

Wilfred A. Day, 45 Mill St. South, PO Box 65, L1A 3V9 – 905/885-8118, Fax: 905/885-7470; Email: dayphope@eagle.ca – *1

A. Ronald Good, 11 Mill St. North, PO Box 208, L1A 3W3 – 905/885-2428, Fax: 905/885-6060 – *1

Haffey, Sherwood, Hunt, 4 Diane Place, L1A 3Y6 – 905/885-2824, Fax: 905/885-1779

James Thomas Hunt, 4 Diane Pl., L1A 3Y6 – 905/885-2874

Gordon C. Kelly, Q.C., 160 Walton St., PO Box 146, L1A 3W3 – 905/885-8127, Fax: 905/885-8129 – *1

David G.A Purvis, 132 Cavan St., L1A 3B9 – 905/885-7529, Fax: 905/949-5540; Email: dpurvis@flemingc.on.ca

Carene I.C. Smith, 115 Dorset St. West, L1A 1G4 – 905/885-9785, Fax: 905/885-9785

**Port Perry** ........................................... **Durham**

Michael L. Fowler, 175 North St., L9L 1B7 – 905/985-8411, Fax: 905/985-0029 – *1

Siksay & Fraser, 204 Casimir St., L9L 1B7 – 905/985-4141, Fax: 905/985-4598 – *2

George L. Smith, 226 Queen St., PO Box 5243, L9L 1B9 – 905/985-8465, Fax: 905/985-3758 – *1

**Port Stanley** ........................................... **Elgin**

Vedova & Chamberlain, 216 Joseph St., N5L 1C4 – 519/782-4562, Fax: 519/782-4747; Email: vc@web-gate.net – *2

**Portland** ........................................... **Leeds**

Doreen Danner, RR#2, K0G 1V0 – 613/272-2793, Fax: 613/272-3311; Email: danner@rideau.net

**Powassan** ........................................... **Parry Sound**

Robert J. van der Wijst, 496 Main St., PO Box 428, P0H 1Z0 – 705/724-3520, Fax: 705/724-5029 – *1

* indicates number of lawyers in law firm.

**Prescott ........................................ Grenville**

Peter R. Adams, 111 King St. West, PO Box 68, K0E 1T0 – 613/925-2825, Fax: 613/925-2826 – *1

Beaumont & Laushway, 214 King St. West, PO Box 190, K0E 1T0 – *1

Thomas A. Glock, 281 Centre St., PO Box 1630, K0E 1T0 – 613/925-1414, Fax: 613/925-3485

Robert G. Gollinger, RR#2, K0E 1T0 – 613/925-4747

Laushway & Alexander, 214 King St. West, PO Box 190, K0E 1T0 – 613/925-5991, Fax: 613/925-4533 – *2

R.M. Tobin, 257 King St. West, PO Box 760, K0E 1T0 – 613/925-2853, Fax: 613/925-5741 – *1

**Rainy River ........................................ Rainy River**

Emery E. Ruff, 306 - 4th St., PO Box 98, P0W 1L0 – 807/852-3816, Fax: 807/852-3971

**Red Lake ........................................ Kenora**

Glenda R. Bishop, 146 Howey St., PO Box 323, P0V 2M0 – 807/727-3256, Fax: 807/727-3948 – *1

Russel S. Smart, 201 Discovery Rd., PO Box 307, P0V 2M0 – 807/727-3200, Fax: 807/727-1126 – *1

**Renfrew ........................................ Renfrew**

Sharon L. Anderson-Olmstead, 117 Raglan St. South, K7V 1P8 – 613/432-5898, Fax: 613/432-5899

Chown & Crosby, 297 Raglan St. South, K7V 1R6 – 613/432-3669, Fax: 613/432-2874 – *2

Cooke & Dickinson, 191 Plaunt St. South, PO Box 158, Stn Main, K7V 4A3 – 613/432-4825, Fax: 613/432-7053 – *2

Dawe & Edmondstone, 178 Plaunt St. South, PO Box 332, Stn Main, K7V 1M8 – 613/432-4513, Fax: 613/432-5011 – *1

Lawrence E. Gallagher, 33 Renfrew Ave. East, K7V 2W6 – 613/432-8537, Fax: 613/432-8538 – *1

Gwen M. Harvey, 165 Argyle St. South, K7V 1T6 – 613/432-5164; Email: bk516@freenet.carleton.ca

Legris Law Office, 248 Argyle St. South, K7V 1T7 – 613/432-3689, Fax: 613/432-3936; Email: jdlegris@renc.igs.net – *1

McNab, Stewart & Prince, 117 Raglan St. South, PO Box 338, K7V 4A4 – 613/432-5844, Fax: 613/432-7832 – *2

Brian D. Smith, 230 Raglan St. South, PO Box 640, Stn Main, K7V 4E7 – 613/432-8115, Fax: 613/432-7297

N. Jane Wilson, 29 Raglan St. South, PO Box 520, K7V 4B1 – 613/432-4806, Fax: 613/432-2453 – *1

**Richards Landing ........................................ Algoma**

Bradley J. Allison, PO Box 234, P0R 1J0 – 705/246-2901, Fax: 705/246-1058 – *1

**Richmond ........................................ Ottawa-Carleton**

Margaret E. Hill, 11 Cockburn St., PO Box 272, K0A 2Z0 – 613/838-2595, Fax: 613/838-4536

**Richmond Hill ........................................ York**

Ken Anders, 176 Stouffeville Rd., L4E 3P4 – 905/773-1290, Fax: 905/773-1659 – *1

Joseph G. Argier, 70 Leek Cres., L4B 1H1 – 905/882-8666, Fax: 905/882-1082 – *1

Baker & Baker, #202, 9050 Yonge St., L4C 2O2 – 905/882-6363, Fax: 905/882-5585 – *2

Stanley Baker, #404, 100 York Blvd., L4B 1J8 – 905/882-6507, Fax: 905/886-7701

D.E. Buckman, 34 Tomlin Cres., L4C 7T1 – 905/737-4721 – *1

R. Laurent Carrier, 69 Red Oak Dr., L4B 1W2 – 905/889-4400 – *1

James H. Chow, #512, 330 Hwy. 7 East, L4B 3P8 – 905/881-3363, Fax: 905/881-1119

Christie, Saccucci, Matthews, Caskie & Chilco, #202, 9050 Yonge St., L4C 9S6 – 905/882-2211, Fax: 905/882-5585 – *1

Stephen Codas, 9555 Yonge St., L4C 9M5 – 905/883-8212, Fax: 905/737-7691 – *1

Counter & Mitchell, 12800 Yonge St., L4E 3C5 – 905/773-4301, Fax: 905/773-7439 – *2

Deverett Law Offices, Box: 10, #111, 324 Hwy 7 East, L4B 1A6 – 905/882-9308, Fax: 905/882-8609 – *1

Jack Elie, #700, 225 East Beaver Creek Rd., L4B 3P4 – 905/886-9019, Fax: 905/731-5534

S.P. Fienberg, 116 Church St. South, L4C 1W3 – 905/883-5557, Fax: 905/883-4619 – *1

Howard S. Fletcher, #8, 9251 Yonge St., PO Box 200, L4C 9T3 – 416/784-2020, Fax: 416/771-7119

Arnie I. Goldstein, #43, 165 East Beaver Creek Rd., L4B 2N2 – 905/882-2275, Fax: 905/882-6999 – *1

Roger A. Gosbee, #310, 350 Hwy 7 East, L4B 3N2 – 905/882-2559, Fax: 905/882-9573 – *1

Fern E. Grech, 185 Marsi Rd., L4C 9T1 – 905/780-1144, Fax: 905/770-8601

Patrick C. Hengen, 10330 Yonge St., L4C 5N1 – 905/884-9257, Fax: 905/884-9470 – *1

Martin M. Herman, #202, 9350 Yonge St., L4C 5G2 – 905/884-0222, Fax: 905/884-0442 – *1

Herbert Hyman, 62 Crosby Ave., L4C 2R2 – 905/883-9175

Richard M Ittleman, #207, 105 West Beaver Creek Rd., L4B 1C6 – 905/771-9344, Fax: 905/709-9747 – *1

Jorden Kolman, #700, 225 East Beaver Creek Rd., L4B 3P4 – 905/709-1355, Fax: 905/731-5534; Toll Free: 1-800-872-0614

Anthea Koon, #206, 15 Weetheim Ct., L4B 3H7 – 905/889-0698, Fax: 905/889-8390; Email: anthea@accessv.com

Richard Kotarba, 250 Harding Blvd., PO Box 32111, RPO Harding, L4C 9S3 – 905/737-5768, Fax: 905/737-7145; Email: rkotarba@speedware.com

S.E. Krupnik, 103 Windermere Cr., L4C 6Y8 – 905/707-8245, Fax: 905/707-8245

James S.N. Lai, 225 East Beaver Creek Rd., L4B 1M7 – 905/709-9518, Fax: 905/709-9520

Lawlor & LeClaire, Observatory Place Plaza, #408, 9555 Yonge St., L4C 9M5 – 905/884-9133, Fax: 905/884-9507 – *2

G.E. Levine, #205, 10620 Yonge St., L4C 3C8 – 905/709-7404, Fax: 905/883-0406 – *1

Robert C-T Liang, #309, 330 Hwy. 7 East, L4B 3P8 – 905/882-0034, Fax: 905/882-8362

S. Lawrence Liquornik, #421, 9555 Yonge St., L4C 9M5 – 905/883-8193, Fax: 905/737-7691 – *1

Litowitz, Pettle & Shain, #200, 100 Mural St., L4B 1J3 – 905/731-6622, Fax: 905/731-6986 – *4

MacDonald, Sigurdson, #702-703, 15 Wertheim Ct., L3B 3H9 – 905/731-9251, Fax: 905/731-7989 – *3

Nancy E. Macivor, 109 Highland Lane, L4C 3S1 – 905/883-1829, Fax: 905/883-0293

Malach & Fidler, #6, 30 Wertheim Court, L4B 1B9 – 905/889-1667, Fax: 905/889-1139 – *5

Roland N. Mark, #300, 225 East Beaver Creek Rd., L4B 3P4 – 905/709-9518, Fax: 905/709-9520; Email: rnmark@ipoline.com

Martino, Rossi, #301, 1595 - 16th Ave., L4B 3N9 – 905/709-7409, Fax: 905/709-7406 – *2

Peter L. May, 14 Church St. South, PO Box 29, L4C 4X9 – 905/884-1167, Fax: 905/884-5446 – *1

M. Dawn McConnell, #2, 1245 Reid St., L4B 1G4 – 905/881-0333, Fax: 905/881-0343

Louis H. Milrad, 70 Strathearn Ave., L4B 2J5 – 905/737-1385, Fax: 905/508-4482; Email: lou@milradlaw.com

Mitchell, Robinson & Phelan, #208, 15 Wertheim Ct., L4B 3H7 – 905/882-5555, Fax: 905/882-5941 – *1

Paul E. Montgomery, #205, 95 Mural St., L4B 3G2 – 905/881-7765, Fax: 905/881-0348 – *1

Stuart P. Parker, Q.C., #1, 174 West Beavercreek Rd., L4B 1B4 – 905/889-7246, Fax: 905/881-8150 – *1

Cindy M. Pinkus, #20, 155 East Beaver Creek Rd., L4B 2N1 – 905/889-3483, Fax: 905/764-6890

Plaxton & Mann, #100, 10350 Yonge St., L4C 5K9 – 905/884-1115, Fax: 905/884-6722 – *3

Michael Polisuk, 9555 Yonge St., L4C 9M5 – 905/508-8203, Fax: 905/737-7691 – *1

I. Prydatok, #101, 600 Hwy #7 East, L4B 1B2 – 905/882-3118, Fax: 905/882-3124 – *2

Corinne M. Rivers, #104, 13311 Yonge St., L4E 3L6 – 905/773-9911, Fax: 905/773-9927; Email: crivers@interlog.com – *1

Gregory W. Roberts, #404, 100 York Blvd., L4B 1J8 – 905/713-1482, Fax: 905/713-3399; Toll Free: grobe10057@aol.com

Robins, Appleby & Taub, #201, 95 Mural St., L4B 3G2 – 905/731-6622, Fax: 905/731-6986 – *3

Rosenberg, Chadwick, Shankman & Wall, #700, 225 East Beaver Creek Rd., L4B 3P4 – 905/731-7100, Fax: 905/731-5534 – *4

Rumack & Bines, 174 West Beaver Creek Rd., L4B 1B4 – 905/881-5111, Fax: 905/881-8150 – *2

Dennis R. Steinberg, Hillcrest Mall, #200, 9350 Yonge St., L4C 5G2 – 905/884-6353, Fax: 905/884-2655 – *1

Strong, Blackburn, Machon, Bohm, 10350 Yonge St., 4th Fl., L4C 5K9 – 905/884-9242, Fax: 905/884-5445 – *5

Gary Sugar, #700, 225 East Beaver Creek Rd., L4B 3P4 – 905/731-2189, Fax: 905/731-5534

Phil Thompson, #301, 1595 - 16th Ave., L4B 2N9 – 905/881-6505, Fax: 905/881-6731; Email: 102111.3065@compuserve.com

S. Udell, #206, 9350 Yonge St., L4C 5G2 – 905/770-5375, Fax: 905/770-1692 – *1

Verskin, Milton, #700B, 225 East Beaver Creek Rd., L4B 3P4 – 905/731-2189, Fax: 905/731-5534

Joseph Virgilio, #110, 1 West Pearce St., L4B 3K3 – 905/882-8666, Fax: 905/882-1082 – *1

John Vrantsidis, 15 Queensmill Ct., L4B 1N1 – 905/881-7489

Gordon E. Watkin, #200, 9350 Yonge St., L4C 5G2 – 905/884-3778, Fax: 905/884-2655 – *1

Winemaker, Todd, 10023 Yonge St., L4C 1T7 – 905/884-9235, Fax: 905/884-0438; Email: earl_wine@msn.com – *1

Judith M. Wolf, #700, 225 East Beaver Creek Rd., L4B 3P4 – 905/731-3372, Fax: 905/731-5534 – *1

Irene S.L. Yee, 42 Trinity Crescent, L4B 3L7 – 905/886-4277 – *1

T. Raciunas Zenon, 10330 Yonge St., L4C 5N1 – 905/883-8592 – *1

**Ridgetown ........................................ Kent**

Neil J. Campbell, 241 Ridge Rd., PO Box 370, L0S 1N0 – 905/894-4057, Fax: 905/894-1127; Email: quazy_1@forterie.com

McGuire, McFarlane & Thomas, 43 Main St. West, PO Box 519, N0P 2C0 – 519/674-5401, Fax: 519/674-3579; Email: pmcguire@ciaccess.com – *4

Shaw, Nicol, & Little, 64 Main St. East, PO Box 7, N0P 2C0 – 519/674-3372, Fax: 519/674-3352 – *2

Stirling, Faussett, McGuire, McFarlane & Thomas, 43 Main St. West, N0P 2C0 – 519/674-5401, Fax: 519/674-3579 – *4

Watson & Walker, 23 Main St. East, PO Box 549, N0P 2C0 – 519/674-5407, Fax: 519/674-5568 – *1

**Ridgeway ........................................ Niagara South**

Thom W. Arthur, 384 Ridge Rd. North, L0S 1N0 – 905/894-3884, Fax: 905/894-4818 – *1

Peter R. BonEnfant, 241 Ridge Rd., PO Box 239, L0S 1N0 – 905/894-3410, Fax: 905/894-6149 – *1

Community Legal Services of Niagara South Inc., 266 Ridge Rd., PO Box 430, L0S 1N0 – 905/894-4775, Fax: 905/894-6101

Jones, Jamieson & Redekop, 288 Ridge St., L0S 1N0 – 905/894-0220, Fax: 905/894-5356 – *3

**Ripley ........................................ Bruce**

Crawford, Mill & Davies, 38 Queen St., PO Box 100, N0G 2R0 – 519/395-2633, Fax: 519/395-4947 – *3

**Rockland** ........................................ **Prescott**

Michael J. Houle, 2784 Laurier St., PO Box 880, Stn Main, K4K 1L5 – 613/446-6411, Fax: 613/446-4513; Email: mjhoule@istar.ca – *2

**Rockwood** .................................... **Wellington**

Douglas S. Black, 118 Main St. South, PO Box 95, N0B 2K0 – 519/856-4555, Fax: 519/856-4680

**Russell**............................................ **Russell**

Anna E. Sundin, 97 Mill St., PO Box 68, K4R 1C7 – 613/445-0480, Fax: 613/445-3424 – *1

**St. Catharines** ............................. **Niagara North**

Leslie R. Allen, 8 Church St., PO Box 96, L2R 6R4 – 905/685-1701, Fax: 905/685-7651 – *2

O.D. Babij, 195 King St., L2R 3J6 – 905/684-1159, Fax: 905/684-1150 – *1

Bakker, Atamanuk, Taylor & Wenglowski, #201, 60 James St., PO Box 1328, Stn Main, L2R 7J8 – 905/688-1520, Fax: 905/688-6002 – *4

Barr, Giannotti & Leach, 1 Church St., L2R 3B1 – 905/688-6161, Fax: 905/688-6144 – *3

G.L. Black, 55 King St., L2R 6Z1 – 905/641-1551, Fax: 905/641-1830 – *1

W.J. Garry Bracken, 50 Dunvegan Rd., L2P 1H6 – 905/988-9389, Fax: 905/685-1753

Frederick Caplan, 4 Centre St., PO Box 430, Stn Main, L2R 6V9 – 905/688-8811, Fax: 905/688-8933 – *1

J. Ronald Charlebois, 172 James St., PO Box 1626, Stn Main, L2R 7K1 – 905/988-5000, Fax: 905/688-0034 – *1

Chown, Cairns, 80 King St., PO Box 760, L2R 6Y8 – 905/688-4500, Fax: 905/688-0015; Email: lawyers@chown-cairns.com; URL: http://www.chown-cairns.com/northland/cc – *18

Tracy J. Middleton Collini, 234 Vine St., L2M 4T1 – 905/937-9229, Fax: 905/937-9228

Covello, Dennis, 23 Centre St., PO Box 638, L2R 3A8 – 905/688-0066, Fax: 905/688-0477 – *1

Coy, Barch, 46 Ontario St., L2R 5J4 – 905/641-1146, Fax: 905/641-1151 – *2

Crossingham, Brady, Miller, #200, 63 Church St., PO Box 307, L2R 6V2 – 905/641-1621, Fax: 905/685-1461 – *4

Daniel, Wilson, Dominion Bldg., 39 Queen St., PO Box 24022, L2R 7P7 – 905/688-9411, Fax: 905/688-5747 – *17

Luigi W. De Lisio, #16, 261 Martindale Rd., L2W 1A2 – 905/687-4885, Fax: 905/687-3311

Mark F. Dedinsky, 154 James St., L2R 5C5 – 905/688-6275, Fax: 905/682-0264

Michael M. DelGobbo, #304, 110 James St., L2R 7E8 – 905/988-1400, Fax: 905/988-1414

B.W. Doliszny, Q.C., 69 Queen St., L1R 6W8 – 905/682-8321 – *1

Terence J. Donohue, #603, 110 James St., L2R 7E8 – 905/684-8533 – *1

Michael J. Dube, #Lwr., 19 Wellington St., L2R 5P5 – 905/684-8171 – *1

Richard G. Duerinskx, #201, 71 King St., PO Box 1685, L2R 7K1 – 905/688-2889, Fax: 905/688-5772

Forster, Lewandowski & Cords, 82 Lake St., PO Box 1180, Stn Main, L2R 7A7 – 905/688-9110, Fax: 905/688-0901 – *3

Freeman, Frayne & Hummell, 9 Raymond St., L2R 2S9 – 905/684-1147, Fax: 905/684-7147 – *2

Fullerton & Fullerton, 30 Duke St., L2R 5W5 – 905/688-2080, Fax: 905/641-1006 – *2

Graves & Associates, #702, 55 King St., L2R 7K1 – 905/641-2020, Fax: 905/641-0484; Email: graveslaw@niagara.com – *5

Erik Grinbergs, 205 King St., L2R 3J5 – 905/688-9800, Fax: 905/685-8836

B. John Hanna, #604, 55 King St., PO Box 24044, L2R 7P7 – 905/687-9347, Fax: 905/687-3939 – *1

Bernard H. Hawkins, 8 Church St., PO Box 1661, L2R 6R4 – 905/687-9900, Fax: 905/685-7651

Heelis, Williams & Little, 14 Church St., PO Box 1056, L2R 7A3 – 905/687-8200, Fax: 905/684-4844; Email: hwllaw@14churchstreetlawoffice.com; URL: http://www.14churchstlawoffice.com – *6

Donald M. Henderson, Q.C., #16, 261 Martindale Rd., L2W 1A2 – 905/984-4366, Fax: 905/687-3311

Rick J. Hesp, 5 Race St., L2R 3M1 – 905/687-1766, Fax: 905/687-8816

Hetherington & Allen, 8 Church St., PO Box 96, L2R 6R4 – 905/685-1701, Fax: 905/685-7651 – *1

D. Ceri Hugill, #18, 235 Martindale, L2R 6P9 – 905/687-4000, Fax: 905/687-6842 – *1

William A. Huska, Q.C., #3, 8 Church St.., L2R 6R4 – 905/684-1163, Fax: 905/685-7651 – *1

Edward F. Kravcik, 281 Saint Paul St., PO Box 216, L2R 6S4 – 905/984-5822, Fax: 905/685-9102

Charles M. Kray, #206B, 15 King St., PO Box 1473, Stn Main, L2R 7J9 – 905/688-0377, Fax: 905/688-0373 – *1

Lampard, Ellis & Walsh, 51 Queen St., PO Box 338, L2R 6V5 – 905/682-8663, Fax: 905/684-1000 – *4

Lancaster, Mix & Welch, #800, 55 King St., PO Box 790, Stn Main, L2R 6Z1 – 905/641-1551, Fax: 905/641-1830; Email: lmw@lmw.com; URL: http://www.lmw.com – *15

Legal Aid, 110 James St., L2R 7E8 – 905/685-1012, Fax: 905/685-7202

Frank M. Marotta, 21 Duke St., L2R 5W1 – 905/688-5401, Fax: 905/688-6204 – *1

Martens, Lingard, Maddalena, Robinson & Koke, 195 King St., L2R 3J6 – 905/687-6551, Fax: 905/687-6553 – *4

A.J. Mascarin, #303, 15 King St., PO Box 398, Stn Main, L2R 6V9 – 905/684-6567, Fax: 905/684-9669 – *1

Alan McGarvie, 6 Clark St., L2R 5G2 – 905/688-5115, Fax: 905/688-1060 – *1

McKenzie, Lefurgey, 205 King St., L2R 3J5 – 905/685-4321, Fax: 905/685-8836 – *2

Paula McPherson, 51 Hillcrest Ave., L2R 4Y3 – 905/641-0030, Fax: 905/641-0030; Toll Free: 1-888-862-2444; Email: resolve@vaxxine.com

Morgan, Dilts & Toppari, #205, 281 St. Paul St., PO Box 216, Stn Main, L2R 6S4 – 905/685-7391, Fax: 905/685-9102 – *2

Hari S. Nesathurai, #203, 39 Queen St., L2R 5G6 – 905/687-9871, Fax: 905/687-9638

Niagara North Community Legal Assistance, 8 Church St., PO Box 1266, L2R 7A7 – 905/682-6635 – *4

O'Neill & Radford, 154 James St., PO Box 1163, L2R 7A3 – 905/685-1377, Fax: 905/682-0264 – *2

Peter Partington, Q.C., #200, 70 James St., L2R 5C1 – 905/685-6755, Fax: 905/685-4774

Ian G. Pearson, 30 Duke St., L2R 5W5 – 905/688-2080, Fax: 905/641-1006 – *1

Pedwell & Pedwell, 2 Church St., PO Box 24107, L2R 3B2 – 905/688-0710, Fax: 905/688-4100 – *1

Reid, McNaughton, 63 Ontario St., PO Box 577, Stn Main, L2R 6W8 – 905/685-5435, Fax: 905/685-3143; Email: lawyers@reidlaw.com; URL: http://reidlaw.com/lawyers – *7

Repei, Richard, 284 Geneva St., PO Box 785, Stn Main, L2R 6Y3 – 905/646-4437, Fax: 905/646-4173 – *2

Brenda V. Sandulak, 172 James St., PO Box 1626, Stn Main, L2R 7K1 – 905/988-5000, Fax: 905/688-0034

D.S. Shantz, #303, 110 James St., PO Box 1203, Stn Main, L2R 7A7 – 905/688-4650, Fax: 905/984-6314 – *1

David I. Shapiro, #16, 261 Martindale Rd., L2W 1A2 – 905/687-9922, Fax: 905/687-3311

M.J. Shea, #15, 101 King St., L2R 3H6 – 905/688-6561, Fax: 905/688-6562 – *1

Richard D. Sheehy, #3, 141 Church St., L2R 7L7 – 905/682-5267

David N. Sider, 6 Clark St., L2R 5G2 – 905/688-1180, Fax: 905/688-8026

Brian C. Smith, 5 St. Paul Cres., L2R 3P6 – 905/688-9550, Fax: 905/688-9953 – *1

Sullivan, Mahoney, 40 Queen St., PO Box 1360, L2R 6Z2 – 905/688-6655, Fax: 905/688-5814 – *25

A.E. Tessmer, #606, 15 Church St., PO Box 1688, Stn Main, L2R 7K1 – 905/688-9552 – *1

Arno J. Tolonen, 166 James St., L2R 5C5 – 905/688-4636, Fax: 905/688-4637 – *1

George F. Walker, Q.C., 1 Church St., L2R 3B1 – 905/685-3500, Fax: 905/688-6144 – *1

Edgar Warkentin, 4 Lakeside Dr., L2M 1P2 – 905/937-8901, Fax: 905/937-8901; Email: epw@vaxxine.com

Wilson & Wilson, #604, 110 James St., L2R 7E8 – 905/688-1272, Fax: 905/388-0198 – *2

Daniel Wilson, 39 Queen St., PO Box 24022, L2R 7P7 – 905/688-9411, Fax: 905/688-5747

Paul J. Wintemute, 20 Lake St., PO Box 638, Stn Main, L2R 6W8 – 905/687-7044, Fax: 905/687-7085

Donald L. Wolfe, 17 Beecher St., L2R 5S4 – 905/688-4566, Fax: 905/688-9188

Virginia L. Workman, 1 Church St., L2R 3B1 – 905/704-0804, Fax: 905/688-6144

**St. George** ........................................ **Brant**

Howard C. Moore, General Delivery, N0E 1N0 – 519/756-8780, Fax: 519/756-2181 – *1

**St. Isidore de Prescott**............................. **Prescott**

Seguin, Landriault & Lamoureux, St. Catherines St., General Delivery, K0C 2B0 – 613/524-2464, Fax: 613/236-0989

**St. Marys** .......................................... **Perth**

William J. Galloway, 172 Queen St. East, PO Box 897, Stn Main, N4X 1B6 – 519/284-2112, Fax: 519/284-3081

Claire A. Sherwin, 28 Wellington St. South, PO Box 3015, Stn Main, N4X 1A6 – 519/284-0898, Fax: 519/284-0896

Waghorn, Stephens, De Young & Grose, 21 Wellington St. North, PO Box 610, Stn Main, N4X 1B4 – 519/284-3640, Fax: 519/284-1631 – *3

R.J. White, 129 Queen St., PO Box 489, Stn Main, N4X 1B3 – 519/284-2840, Fax: 519/284-4813

**St. Thomas**......................................... **Elgin**

Bruce H. Blake, 16 Metcalfe St., N5R 3J9 – 519/633-5500, Fax: 519/633-5500 – *1

James R. Carrie, 555 Talbot St., PO Box 617, N5P 4B1 – 519/631-8200, Fax: 519/633-9635 – *2

Jerome A. Collins, 36 Hincks St., N5R 3N6 – 519/633-3973, Fax: 519/633-7916

Richard J. Dewsnap, 19 Glanworth Ave., N5R 1E5 – 519/631-6950

William I. Dick, #303, 450 Sunset Dr., N5R 5V1 – 519/631-2140, Fax: 519/637-1182

W.D. Eitel, 59 Metcalfe St., PO Box 550, Stn Main, N5P 3V6 – 519/633-7000, Fax: 519/633-6762 – *1

Fordham, Watterworth & Marshall, 4 Elgin St., N5R 3L6 – 519/631-9090, Fax: 519/633-1371 – *3

Gloin, Hall & Shields, 12 Pearl St., N5P 2N9 – 519/633-3100, Fax: 519/633-9362

William J. Glover, #303, 450 Sunset Dr., N5R 5V1 – 519/633-2300, Fax: 519/637-1182 – *1

J.A. Gundry, 16 Pearl St., PO Box 518, N5P 3V6 – 519/631-9060, Fax: 519/631-7304 – *1

Gunn & Associates, 108 Centre St., PO Box 459, N5P 3V5 – 519/631-0700, Fax: 519/631-1468 – *5

Hennessey, Bowsher, Gibson & Carrie, 108 Centre St., PO Box 548, Stn Main, N5P 3V6 – 519/633-3310, Fax: 519/633-9374 – *5

William O. Herold, Q.C., 130 Centre St., N5R 2Z9 – 519/631-3250, Fax: 519/631-0557 – *1

John E. Hogan, 4 Penhale Ave., N5R 5M9 – 519/633-8573, Fax: 519/633-7235

William W. Johnson, 651 Talbot St., N5P 1C9 – 519/633-3200 – *1

Brian W. Kempster, 48 Stanley St., N5R 3E9 – 519/633-2580, Fax: 519/633-0832; Toll Free: kempster@real.on.ca – *1

* indicates number of lawyers in law firm.

Thomas F. Kierluk, 92 Centre St., 2nd Fl., N5R 2Z5 – 519/637-1162, Fax: 519/637-1911; Email: tkierluk@elgin.net

Michael P. O'Dea, 121 Curtis St., PO Box 20086, N5P 4H4 – 519/637-2400, Fax: 519/637-2402

E.W. Popovich, 24 Curtis St., PO Box 580, Stn Main, N5P 3V6 – 519/631-5600, Fax: 519/631-9789 – *1

T.A. Por, PO Box 190, Stn Main, N5P 3T7 – 519/631-7100 – *1

Mervin L. Riddell, #200, 408 Talbot St., N5P 1B8 – 519/631-3211, Fax: 519/631-8549; Email: riddell@execulink.com – *1

Sanders, Cline, 14 Southwick St., PO Box 70, Stn Main, N5P 3T5 – 519/633-0800, Fax: 519/633-9259 – *3

Brian D. Scott Associates, #200, 408 Talbot St., N5R 1B8 – 519/633-3230, Fax: 519/633-9232 – *1

Allen Skuce, 15 Barrie Blvd., N5P 4B9 – 519/631-7933, Fax: 519/631-2198

Harold E. Stafford, 458 Talbot St., PO Box 575, Stn Main, N5P 3V6 – 519/633-0200, Fax: 519/633-0964 – *1

Robert J. Upsdell, 59 Metcalfe St., PO Box 486, N5R 3K4 – 519/633-7100, Fax: 519/633-6762; Email: upsdell@wwdc.com – *1

Hilary J. Vaughan, 22 Hincks St., N5R 3N6 – 519/631-0909, Fax: 519/613-7682

Arnold B. Walker, 651 Talbot St., PO Box 20022, Stn Centre, N5P 4H4 – 519/633-3273, Fax: 519/633-8585 – *1

**Sarnia.......................................... Lambton**

Carmen Baljeu, C-317 Wellington St., N7T 1H4 – 519/337-2445, Fax: 519/337-1815

Paul R. Beaudet, 251 Exmouth St., PO Box 2162, N7T 7L7 – 519/337-1LAW, 1529, Fax: 519/336-2569 – *1

Terry L. Brandon, #202, 805 Christina St. North, N7V 1X6 – 519/337-4634, Fax: 519/332-6588

Roderick Brown, Q.C., 316 Christina St. North, N7T 5V5 – 519/336-7880, Fax: 519/336-8998 – *1

James J. Carpeneto, 316 Christina St. North, N7T 5V5 – 519/336-6955, Fax: 519/336-5686 – *1

Lyle F. Curran, Q.C., 116 Front St. South, PO Box 698, Stn Main, N7T 7J7 – 519/336-8750, Fax: 519/336-4890 – *1

Dally & Elliott, 500 Exmouth St., N7T 5P4 – 519/336-2253, Fax: 519/336-5870 – *2

W.M. Dawson, Q.C., #201, 805 Christina St. North, N7V 1X6 – 519/337-2321, Fax: 519/337-2466

Francis E. De Sena, 422 East St. North, PO Box 757, N7T 7J7 – 519/336-9999

Joseph M. Donohue, 521 Christina St. North, PO Box 1058, Stn Main, N7T 7K2 – 519/344-7425, Fax: 519/344-1147 – *1

Elliott, Porter, McFadyen & McFadyen, 137 Kendall St., PO Box 1029, Stn Main, N7V 4G6 – 519/336-4600, Fax: 519/336-0400 – *4

J.A. Farina, 425 Christina St. North, N7T 5V8 – 519/337-5468, Fax: 519/337-8939 – *1

Fleck & Daigneault, #102, 704 Mara St., N7V 1X4 – 519/337-5288, Fax: 519/337-5674 – *2

Foreman, Dawson, 1350 L'Héritage Dr., N7S 6H8 – 519/542-7711, 1240, Fax: 519/542-5577 – *6

David Gaviller, Q.C., 316 Christina St. North, PO Box 2047, Stn Main, N7T 7L1 – 519/336-4281, Fax: 519/336-8998 – *1

George, Murray & Shipley, 2 Ferry Dock Hill, PO Box 2196, N7T 7L8 – 519/336-8770, Fax: 519/336-1811 – *9

Gray, Bruce, Kowalyshyn, Cimetta, 1166 London Rd., PO Box 2259, N7T 7L7 – 519/336-9700, Fax: 519/336-3289 – *5

C. Ed Gresham, 805 Christina St. North, PO Box 2107, Stn Main, N7T 7L1 – 519/337-9224, Fax: 519/332-6588

Habel, Jacques, 2121 Huron Shores, N7T 7H6 – 519/869-6324 – *1

David G. Hockin, #406, 265 Front St. North, N7T 7X1 – 519/336-4357, Fax: 519/336-4367

Sterling R. Holmes, #3, 340 Christina St. North, N7T 5V7 – 519/383-7848, Fax: 519/383-7895 – *1

D.J. Kirby, #205, 805 Christina St. North, PO Box 2107, Stn Main, N7T 7L1 – 519/337-3733, Fax: 519/332-6588 – *1

Albert M. Lockyer, D.M.I Professional Bldg., #201, 704 Mara St., Point Edward, N7V 1X4 – 519/337-0181, Fax: 519/337-0906 – *1

Robert McFadden, #104, 560 Exmouth St., N7T 5P5 – 519/344-3683, Fax: 519/337-3995 – *1

J. Douglas McMillin, 103 Mitton St. South, PO Box 921, Stn Main, N7T 7J9 – 519/344-7497, Fax: 519/344-0884

P.E. Melnychuk, 251 Exmouth St., N7T 5M7 – 519/337-3276, Fax: 519/332-0503 – *1

Peter R. Merchant, #108, 805 Christina St. North, Point Edward, N7V 1X6 – 519/332-2550, Fax: 519/332-1587 – *1

Peter E. Peterson, 345 Christina St. North, N7T 5V6 – 519/344-7426

Raymond F. Phillips, 425 Christina St. North, N7T 5V8 – 519/332-0711, Fax: 519/337-8939 – *1

Nancy M. Pringle, 1323 Exmouth St., 2nd Fl., N7S 3Y1 – 519/542-8085, Fax: 519/542-0577

R.E. Rowcliffe, Q.C., 316 Christina St. North, PO Box 187, Stn Main, N7T 7H9 – 519/336-4541, Fax: 519/336-5686 – *1

David J. Stoesser, 291 Exmouth St., PO Box 490, N7T 7J4 – 519/332-2070, Fax: 519/332-5022

Stoner & Gillespie, 1323 Exmouth St., N7S 3Y1 – 519/542-0322, Fax: 519/542-0577 – *2

Peter Westfall, #203, 805 Christina St. North, Point Edward, N7V 1X6 – 519/344-1155, Fax: 519/344-1842; Email: westlaw@ebtech.net – *1

R.A. Whitnall, 345 Christina St. North, N7T 5V6 – 519/336-9460, Fax: 519/336-8366 – *1

John M. Wing, Q.C., 141 Wellington St., N7T 1G4 – 519/336-6191, Fax: 519/344-3532 – *1

Wyrzykowski & Robb, 722 Lite St., PO Box 2200, N7T 7L7 – 519/336-6118, Fax: 519/336-9550; Email: mars@ebtech.net – *3

**Sauble Beach.......................................... Bruce**

Nicoletta C. Jensen, 15 - 2nd Ave. North, N0H 2G0 – 519/422-2122, Fax: 519/422-2563

Ross C. McLean, 202 Main St., N0H 2G0 – 519/422-2888, Fax: 519/422-3309

**Sault Ste. Marie.......................................... Algoma**

Aiello & Pawelek, #102, 123 March St., P6A 2Z5 – 705/946-8590, Fax: 705/946-8589 – *2

Allemano & Fitzgerald, 356 Queen St. East, PO Box 10, P6A 1Z1 – 705/942-0142, Fax: 705/942-7188 – *2

Baxter, Feifel, Walz, Broadbent, 629 Queen St. East, P6A 2A6 – 705/945-8901, Fax: 705/945-9139 – *4

Michael F.W. Bennett, 140 East St., 2nd Fl., PO Box 1257, Stn Main, P6A 6N1 – 519/759-9050, Fax: 519/759-9142

Bisceglia & Associates, #301, 262 Queen St. East, P6A 1Y7 – 705/942-5856, Fax: 705/942-6493 – *3

Aldona V. Bondar, 482 MacDonald Ave., P6B 1H9 – 705/759-6861 – *1

Bortolussi & Palombi, 470 Albert St. East, P6A 2J8 – 705/942-1333, Fax: 705/949-7684 – *2

Frank E. Darou, #202, 616 Queen St. East, P6A 2A4 – 705/254-6491, Fax: 705/949-2454 – *1

Kenneth R. Davies, #8, 477 Queen St. East, P6A 1Z5 – 705/256-7839, Fax: 705/949-8207

DeLorenzi & Gareau, 224 Queen St. East, P6A 1Y8 – 705/949-6467, Fax: 705/942-7972 – *2

David A. Fabbro, #201, 616 Queen St. East, P6A 2A4 – 705/949-3672, Fax: 705/949-2454 – *1

R. Jack Falkins, 176 Wellington St. East, P6A 2L5 – 705/942-2022, Fax: 705/942-2027 – *2

Ferranti & Chorney, 189 East St., P6A 3C8 – 705/949-6200, Fax: 705/949-6208 – *2

Hamilton, Nixon, 67 Elgin St., PO Box 249, P6A 5L8 – 705/759-8498, Fax: 705/759-8781 – *2

Harry & Renaud, 138 Brock St., P6A 3B5 – 705/942-7900, Fax: 705/942-7902 – *2

E.R. Hornstein, 527 Queen St. East, P6A 2A2 – 705/942-8024, Fax: 705/942-9060 – *1

Ian D. Hugill, #505, 421 Bay St., PO Box 457, Stn Tower, P6A 5M1 – 705/949-4504, Fax: 705/949-3904; Email: hugilli@soonet.ca – *1

Kelleher, Laidlaw, Paciocco, Melville, 421 Bay St., 6th Fl., PO Box 819, P6A 5N3 – 705/949-7790, Fax: 705/949-5816 – *3

Henry M. Lang, Q.C., 157 East St., P6A 3C8 – 705/949-3300, Fax: 705/949-3312 – *3

MacDonald, Barsanti, #301, 421 Bay St., P6A 1X3 – 705/946-5830, Fax: 705/946-5835 – *2

Gerald P. Maich, 434 Albert St. East, P6A 2J8 – 705/254-6821, Fax: 705/254-3127 – *1

F.N. Mantello, Q.C., 183 Albert St. East, P6A 2J2 – 705/945-9900, Fax: 705/945-8044 – *1

Anthony P. Marrato, #7, 477 Queen St. East, P6A 1Z5 – 705/945-9110, Fax: 705/945-9195

Eric D. McCooeye, 348 Albert St. East, P6A 2J6 – 705/945-8868, Fax: 705/945-9051 – *2

McLeod, Rossi, 494 Albert St. East, P6A 2K2 – 705/759-0948, Fax: 705/942-6511 – *2

E. Ann McRae, 98 Florwin Dr., P6A 4J2 – 705/256-8010

Orazietti & Kwolek, 128 March St., P6A 2Z3 – 705/256-5601, Fax: 705/945-9427 – *2

Libero C.M. Paci, 479 Albert St. East, P6A 2K1 – 705/254-4311, Fax: 705/254-4704

R.C. Peres, Q.C., #201, 212 Queen St. East, P6A 5X8 – 705/949-9411, Fax: 705/949-3759 – *1

Peterson & Peterson, 626 Wellington St. East, PO Box 1169, P6A 2M5 – 705/942-1011, Fax: 705/942-9543 – *2

Patricia J. Peterson, 524 Albert St. East, P6A 2K4 – 705/942-7672, Fax: 705/942-9162

Helen M. Pierce, 446 Albert St. East, P6A 2J8 – 705/946-4437, Fax: 705/949-0124

Pritchard, Benjamin F., 642 Queen St. East, P6A 2A4 – 705/759-1991, Fax: 705/759-2571 – *1

Provenzano, McMillan, 405 Queen St. East, PO Box 519, Stn Main, P6A 5M6 – 705/949-5411, Fax: 705/949-9899 – *2

Lorna Rudolph, 182 March St., P6A 2Z7 – 705/949-5131, Fax: 705/949-9664 – *1

Sarlo O'Neill, 116 Spring St., P6A 3A1 – 705/949-6901, Fax: 705/949-0618; Email: so-law@soonet.ca; URL: http://www.soonet.ca/sarlo-oneill – *6

William R. Scott, #202, 629A Queen St. East, P6A 2A6 – 705/949-4333, Fax: 705/945-0958 – *1

Carol Shamess, 181 March St., P6A 2Z6 – 705/942-2580, Fax: 705/942-5048 – *1

Skeggs, Paciocco, 169 East St., P6A 3C8 – 705/942-0235, Fax: 705/942-3597 – *1

Roderick W.A. Sonley, #1, 121 Brock St., P6A 3B6 – 705/759-8692, Fax: 705/759-8692; Email: sonleyr@soonet.ca – *1

Jack Squire, 80 March St., PO Box 1196, P6A 5N7 – 705/946-5020, Fax: 705/946-5366 – *1

Walker, Thompson, 421 Bay St., PO Box 428, P6A 5M4 – 705/949-7806, Fax: 705/759-0457 – *2

Willson, Carter, 494 Albert St. East, P6A 2K2 – 705/942-2000, Fax: 705/942-6511 – *2

Wishart & Partners, 390 Bay St., P6A 1X2 – 705/949-6700, Fax: 705/949-2465; Email: wishart@ssm.ca – *6

Roy Youngson, 9 Texas St., PO Box 141, Stn Main, P6A 5L2 – 705/949-7931, Fax: 705/949-7941 – *1

**Schomberg.......................................... York**

Black & Perugini, 233 Main St., L0G 1T0 – 905/939-8515, Fax: 905/939-8279 – *2

Clarke Smith, 250 Main St., L0G 1T0 – 905/939-2344, Fax: 905/727-7096 – *1

**Seaforth ........ Huron**

McConnell, Stewart & Devereaux, 77 Main St. South, PO Box 220, N0K 1W0 – 519/527-0850, Fax: 519/527-2324 – *2

**Shelburne ........ Dufferin**

Ford-Arnold Beverly, 119 Owen Sound St., PO Box 706, L0N 1S0 – 519/925-3737

Courtney H. Foster, RR#4, PO Box 11, L0N 1S8 – 519/925-5854, Fax: 519/925-3159

Shepherd & Osyany, 155 Main St. West, PO Box 760, L0N 1S0 – 519/925-5331, Fax: 519/925-3202; Email: lawyer@headwaters.com – *3

Timmerman & Haskell, 305 Owen Sound St., PO Box 216, L0N 1S0 – 519/925-2608,2260, Fax: 519/925-2268 – *2

**Simcoe ........ Norfolk**

Brimage, Tyrrell, Van Severen & Homeniuk, 21 Norfolk St. North, N3Y 4L1 – 519/426-5840, Fax: 519/426-7515; Email: law@brimage.com; URL: http://www.brimage.com – *7

Cline, Backus & Nightingale, 28 Colborne St. North, PO Box 528, Stn Main, N3Y 4N5 – 519/426-6763, Fax: 519/426-2055 – *5

Cobb & Jones, 2 Talbot St. North, PO Box 548, N3Y 4N5 – 519/428-0170, Fax: 519/428-3105; Email: cobblaw@nornet.on.ca – *6

B.J. Hogan, 81 Norfolk St. South, PO Box 544, N3Y 4N5 – 519/426-8911, Fax: 519/426-8912 – *1

Sheppard, MacIntosh, Lados & Herter, 58 Peel St., PO Box 677, N3Y 4T2 – 519/426-1382, Fax: 519/426-1392 – *4

Smelko Law Office, 25 Norfolk St. North, N3Y 3N6 – 519/426-1711, Fax: 519/426-7863 – *2

Tisdale & Reid, 49 Robinson St., PO Box 69, N3Y 4K8 – 519/426-0503, Fax: 519/426-4364 – *3

**Sioux Lookout ........ Kenora**

Catherine M. Beamish, 50 Queen St., PO Box 1600, P8T 1C3 – 807/737-2809, Fax: 807/737-1211; Email: cbeam@si.lakeheadu.ca – *2

Young & Young, #101, 73 King St., PO Box 38, P0V 2T0 – 807/737-2562, Fax: 807/737-2571 – *2

**Smiths Falls ........ Lanark**

Dixon & Dixon, 40 Main St. West, K7A 4T2 – 613/283-4735 – *3

G.W. Fournier, 35 Daniel St., PO Box 752, K7A 4W6 – 613/283-8818, Fax: 613/283-8951 – *1

Howard & Ryan, 2 Main St. East, PO Box 548, K7A 4T6 – 613/283-6772, Fax: 613/283-8840 – *2

Kirkland, Murphy & Ain, 15 Russell St. East, PO Box 220, K7A 4T1 – 613/283-0515, Fax: 613/283-8557 – *3

Quigley, Ross & Cliffen, 30 Russell St. East, PO Box 804, K7A 4W6 – 613/283-7331, Fax: 613/283-6792 – *4

**Smithville ........ York**

John W. Shipton, 111 Griffin St. North, L0R 2A0 – 905/957-7898, Fax: 905/957-1085 – *1

Van Der Woerd, Faber & Olij, Village Square Mall, Hwy. 20, L0R 2A0 – 905/957-7240, Fax: 905/957-2599 – *2

**South Porcupine ........ Cochrane**

Albert Ristimaki, 69 Harold Ave., PO Box 1060, P0N 1H0 – 705/235-2211, Fax: 705/235-3084 – *1

**Southampton ........ Bruce**

Robert E. Forsyth, Q.C., 243 High St., PO Box 779, N0H 2L0 – 519/797-3223, Fax: 519/797-3192 – *1

**Stayner ........ Simcoe**

Bumstead & Demery, 233 Main St., PO Box 820, L0M 1S0 – 705/428-6000, Fax: 705/428-6427 – *2

**Stirling ........ Hastings**

Alex Winkler, Q.C., 33 Mill St., K0K 3E0 – 613/395-3397, Fax: 613/359-3398 – *1

**Stoney Creek ........ Hamilton-Wentworth**

S.W. Peglar, 286 Barton St. East, L8E 2K6 – 905/662-5404, Fax: 905/664-1977 – *1

Richard P. Startek & Associates, 141 Hwy. 8, L8G 5C1 – 905/662-7727

**Stouffville ........ York**

Button, Armstrong & Ness, 6361 Main St., PO Box 220, L4A 7Z5 – 905/640-3530, Fax: 905/640-7027 – *3

André E. Kozak, 6290 Main St., PO Box 940, L4A 8A1 – 905/640-2211, Fax: 905/640-8161; Email: kozak@accessv.com – *1

H.J. MacLean, 4920 Bethesda Rd., L4A 7X5 – 905/640-0901, Fax: 905/640-9278 – *1

**Stratford ........ Perth**

W.W. Aitchison, 42 Albert St., PO Box 411, N5A 6T3 – 519/273-4822 – *1

Byers, Kenny, Parlee & Thorn, 25 William St., PO Box 722, N5A 6V6 – 519/271-6700, Fax: 519/271-7419 – *3

Michael F. Fair, 24 Downie St., PO Box 844, N5A 6W3 – 519/271-2066, Fax: 519/271-2732 – *1

Gregory & Buechler, 30 Waterloo St. South, N5A 4A6 – 519/271-3520, Fax: 519/271-1490 – *1

Mountain, Mitchell, Hill, Monteith & Ritsma, PO Box 846, N5A 6W3 – 519/271-6770, Fax: 519/271-9261; Email: mmhmr@orc.ca – *5

Neilson, Bell, Skinner, Rogerson & Dunphy, 1 Ontario St., N5A 6T7 – 519/271-7330, Fax: 519/271-1762 – *5

John H. Stratton, Q.C., 313 St. David St., N5A 1E1 – 519/271-7360 – *1

**Strathroy ........ Middlesex**

Robert J. Dack, 16 Front St. East, N7G 1Y4 – 519/245-0370, Fax: 519/245-0523 – *1

Jones, Gibbons & Reis, 39 Front St. West, N7G 1X5 – 519/245-1110, Fax: 519/245-5859 – *3

Quinlan & Somerville, PO Box 28, N7G 3J1 – 519/245-0342, Fax: 519/245-0108 – *2

George E. Sinker, 53 - 55 Front St. West, PO Box 250, N7G 3J2 – 519/245-1144, Fax: 519/245-6090 – *2

Robert G. Waters, 72 Frank St., N7G 2R5 – 519/245-5582, Fax: 519/245-5448 – *1

**Streetsville ........ Peel**

M.C. Foster & Assoc., 151 Queen St. South, L5M 1L1 – 905/826-1177, Fax: 905/826-4926 – *3

Andrew Stabins, 12 Thomas St., PO Box 850, L5M 2C4 – 905/826-3421, Fax: 905/826-5053 – *1

**Stroud ........ Simcoe**

Gibson & Adams, PO Box 100, L0L 2M0 – 705/436-1701, Fax: 705/436-1710 – *3

**Sturgeon Falls ........ Nipissing**

Conrad Proulx, 65 Queen St., P0H 2G0 – 705/753-2780, Fax: 705/753-4753 – *1

**Sudbury ........ Sudbury**

Mike Barnett, 264 Elm St., P3C 1B4 – 705/674-3210, Fax: 705/674-1265 – *1

William G. Beach, 224 Applegrove St., P3C 1N3 – 705/675-5685, Fax: 705/675-6601 – *1

Walter Chmara, #4, 54 Elgin St. South, P3E 3N2 – 705/673-2090 – *1

Conroy, Trebb, Scott, Hurtubise, 164 Elm St. West, P3C 1T7 – 705/674-6441, Fax: 705/673-9567 – *7

De Diana, Eloranta & Longstreet, 219 Pine St., P3C 1X4 – 705/674-4289, Fax: 705/671-1047 – *1

Desmarais, Keenan, Mackey Bldg., Box: 100, 30 Durham St., P3C 5E5 – 705/675-7521, Fax: 705/675-7390 – *10

Dumont, McAndrew, 238 Elm St. West, P3C 1V3 – 705/673-5718, Fax: 705/673-3987 – *2

B. Fredrick Fortier, 139 Pine St., P3C 1X2 – 705/674-8375, Fax: 705/674-6518 – *3

J.M. Fragomeni, 174 Elm St., P3C 1T7 – 705/674-2001, Fax: 705/674-2039

Gatien Braithwaite, 1970 Paris St., P3E 3C8 – 705/523-2222, Fax: 705/523-1048; Email: gatien@counsel.com – *4

Bernard L. Gervais, 111 Durham St., P3E 3M9 – 705/674-4040, Fax: 705/674-4242

Gerard E. Guimond, #300, 96 Larch St., P3E 1C1 – 705/674-5551, Fax: 705/675-2051 – *1

Richard Guy, 143 Applegrove St., P3C 1N2 – 705/673-1101, Fax: 705/673-1134 – *2

Patricia C. Hennessy, 58 Lisgar St., P3E 3L7 – 705/671-2020, Fax: 705/671-0129 – *2

Hinds & Sinclair, 214 Alder St., P3C 4J2 – 705/674-7597, Fax: 705/674-4916 – *2

Ronald N. Horeck, 144 Elm St., P3C 1T7 – 705/674-5398, Fax: 705/674-7632 – *1

Brian N. Howe, 235 Elm St. West, P3C 1T8 – 705/674-8317, Fax: 705/674-2952 – *1

Marc A.J. Huneault, #204, 109 Elm St., P3C 1T4 – 705/674-1866, Fax: 705/674-4490

J.R. Jakabfy, 767 Barrydowne Rd., P3A 3T6 – 705/560-3320, Fax: 705/560-0735 – *1

Elizabeth Kari, 293 Elm St., 2nd Fl., P3C 1V6 – 705/670-2770, Fax: 705/670-9172; Email: ekari@cyber-beach.net

Lacroix, Forest & Del Frate, Place Balmoral, 36 Elgin St., P3C 5B4 – 705/674-1976, Fax: 705/674-6978; Email: office@sudburylaw.com; URL: http://www.sudburylaw.com – *9

Lalande, Keast, Paquette & Renzini, #200, 1188 St. Jerome St., P3A 2V9 – 705/560-2121, Fax: 705/560-8072 – *5

Nelly M. Lanteigne, #164, 166 Elm St., PO Box 849, P3C 1T7 – 705/674-9394, Fax: 705/969-7567 – *1

J. Robert LeBlanc, 139 Pine St., P3C 1X2 – 705/674-8375, Fax: 705/674-9137

C.N.R. MacMillan, 109 Elm St., P3C 1T4 – 705/674-5221, Fax: 705/674-7950 – *1

Mailloux & Gray, 142 Paris St., P3E 3E1 – 705/674-5267, Fax: 705/674-2109 – *2

Robert L. Maranger, 174 Elm St., P3C 1T7 – 705/674-2001, Fax: 705/674-2039

Marcuccio, Buttazzoni, #7, 284 Cedar St., P3B 1M7 – 705/674-4064, Fax: 705/674-0694 – *2

Oliverio E. Massimiliano, 214 Pine St., P3C 1X5 – 705/671-1624, Fax: 705/671-1609

A.J. Reynolds Mastin, #204, 888 Regent St. South, P3E 6C6 – 705/673-2737, Fax: 705/675-1507 – *1

Patricia L. Meehan, 293 Elm St. West, P3C 1V6 – 705/674-2272, Fax: 705/674-5238

Mensour & Mensour, #101, 238 Elm St., P3C 1V3 – 705/673-6787, Fax: 705/673-1418 – *2

Miller, Maki, 176 Elm St., P3C 1T7 – 705/675-7503, Fax: 705/675-8669 – *9

Orendorff Vrbanac, #1, 17 Frood Rd., P3C 4Y9 – 705/673-1200, Fax: 705/673-3050 – *2

Réjean R. Parisé, 111 Durham St., P3E 3M9 – 705/674-4042, Fax: 705/674-4242 – *1

Pharand, Kuyek, 229 Elm St. West, P3C 1T8 – 705/675-1227, Fax: 705/675-5350 – *2

Rolston, Humphrey, Arseneau, Poulson, 125 Durham St., 2nd Fl., P3E 3M9 – 705/674-6491, Fax: 705/674-9457 – *5

Leighton T. Roslyn, #3, 17 Frood Rd., P3C 4Y9 – 705/675-6012, Fax: 705/675-2337; Email: roslynt@isys.ca

Guy W. Roy, #405, 96 Larch St., P3E 1C1 – 705/671-2870, Fax: 705/673-8758

Glenn E.J. Sandberg, #200, 144 Elm St. West, P3C 1T7 – 705/671-9922, Fax: 705/671-2107

J. Herve Sauve, #206, 144 Pine St., P3C 1X3 – 705/670-9011, Fax: 705/674-4358

Steinberg, Fabbro, 54 Elgin St., P3E 3N2 – 705/675-1336, Fax: 705/675-5445 – *2

* indicates number of lawyers in law firm.

Lisa M. Stevens, #300, 96 Larch St., P3E 1C1 – 705/674-2101, Fax: 705/674-7986

Norman G. Stoner, #203, 161 Larch St., P3E 1C4 – 705/675-8307, Fax: 705/675-7245; Email: misty@isys.ca – *1

Sullivan & Horton, 158 Elm St., P3C 1T7 – 705/674-7567, Fax: 705/674-3676 – *2

Stanley J. Thomas, #200, 174 Larch St., P3E 1C6 – 705/674-8306, Fax: 705/674-6789

E.J. Craig Ticalo, #7, 1730 Regent St., P3E 3Z8 – 705/523-0881, Fax: 705/523-1071

Alexander Toffoli, #1, 311 Elm St., P3C 1V6 – 705/675-7990, Fax: 705/675-2107 – *1

Robert C. Topp, #206, 144 Pine St., P3C 1X3 – 705/673-3655, Fax: 705/674-4358

Law Office of Serge F. Treherne, 144 Elm St. West, PO Box 1269, P3C 1T7 – 705/670-9689, Fax: 705/670-9141 – *1

Valin & Innes, 96 Larch St., P3E 1C1 – 705/673-3655, Fax: 705/673-8758 – *1

Vere & Gray, #102, 45 Durham St., P3E 3M2 – 705/675-2454, Fax: 705/675-2820 – *2

Diane A. Violette, 118 Paris St., P3E 3E1 – 705/674-1300, Fax: 705/671-1044

Weaver, Simmons, PO Box 158, P3E 4N5 – 705/674-6421, Fax: 705/674-9948 – *19

Zito Associates, 85 Durham St., P3E 3M5 – 705/674-2134, Fax: 705/674-6085 – *3

Philip M. Zylberberg, 135 Applegrove St., P3C 1N2 – 705/674-2822, Fax: 705/674-2975

**Sundridge.................................... Parry Sound**

Smith & Hardy, 105 Main St. East, PO Box 234, P0A 1Z0 – 705/384-5388, Fax: 705/384-7713 – *2

**Sutton.............................................. York**

Fahey & Reeder, 100 High St., PO Box 487, L0E 1R0 – 905/722-3771, Fax: 905/722-9852 – *2

**Sydenham .................................... Frontenac**

John M. Glassco, PO Box 256, K0H 2T0 – 613/376-3397, Fax: 613/376-6944; Email: glassco@aden.kinston.net

G.Y. McDiarmid, PO Box 81, K0H 2T0 – 613/376-6221, Fax: 613/546-3274 – *1

Trousdale & Trousdale, PO Box 211, K0H 2T0 – 613/546-2231, Fax: 613/546-9001 – *2

**Tavistock ......................................... Oxford**

Shuh Cline & Grossman, 14 Hope St. West, N0B 2R0 – 519/578-9010, Fax: 519/578-1590

**Temagami ...................................... Nipissing**

Smith, Byck & Grant, PO Box 516, P0H 2H0 – 705/672-2102 (Haileybury), Fax: 705/647-8575 – *2

**Terrace Bay .................................. Thunder Bay**

Paul A. Gordon Law Office, Simcoe Plaza, PO Box 940, P0T 2W0 – 807/825-4511 – *1

**Thamesford ....................................... Oxford**

Godfrey Jefferson, 136 Dundas St., N0M 2M0 – 519/438-1727, Fax: 519/673-4966

Nesbitt Coulter, 136 Dundas St., N0M 2M0 – 519/285-3550, Fax: 519/485-6582 – *2

**Thamesville .......................................... Kent**

Thomas G. Chalmers, 7 Victoria St., PO Box 190, N0P 2K0 – 519/692-3842, Fax: 519/692-5455 – *1

**Thedford........................................ Lambton**

Alan M. Gorth, 119 Main St., PO Box 419, N0M 2N0 – 519/296-5959, Fax: 519/296-5609

J. Philip Walden, 2 Victoria St., PO Box 121, N0M 2N0 – 519/296-4951, Fax: 519/296-4497 – *1

**Thornbury........................................ Simcoe**

Kopperud, Tamming Law Office, 34 Bruce St., PO Box 598, N0H 2P0 – 519/599-3308, Fax: 519/599-7399 – *2

R. Michael Martin, 23 Louisa St. West, N0H 2P0 – 519/599-5048

**Thorndale..................................... Middlesex**

Tobin Marcus, West Nissouri Municipal Bldg., 160 King St., N0M 2P0 – 519/461-0660 – *1

P.S. McBirnie, RR#3, N0M 2P0 – 519/462-1300 – *1

**Thornhill........................................... York**

M. Adelson, #216, 2900 Steeles Ave. East, L3T 4X1 – 905/881-8800, Fax: 905/881-7391 – *1

Larry Anklewicz, 27 Carnegie Cres., L3T 5G9 – 905/881-1806, Fax: 905/881-1806 – *1

A.M. Arrigo, Q.C., 48 Guardsman Rd., L3T 6L4 – 905/889-6131 – *1

Auciello Franschman, #580, 8500 Leslie St., L3T 7M8 – 905/882-8080, Fax: 905/882-5483 – *2

Baker & Associates, #404, 100 York Blvd., L4B 1J8 – 905/882-6507, Fax: 905/886-7701

Carol A. Bargman, 7636 Yonge St., L4J 1V9 – 905/881-3116, Fax: 905/881-3199

Beglaubter, Greenberg & Ernst, 7626A Yonge St., L4J 1V9 – 905/886-9535, Fax: 905/886-9540 – *3

Michael Bendel, 40 Glen Cres., L4J 4W6 – 905/889-6162, Fax: 905/889-6580

Peter D. Bouroukis, 15 Wertheim Crt., L4B 3H7 – 905/771-7030, Fax: 905/771-7027 – *1

Edward L. Burlew, 16 John St., L3T 1X8 – 905/882-2422, Fax: 905/882-2431

Chauhan & Associates, #309, 330 Hwy. 7 East, L4B 3P8 – 905/771-1235, Fax: 905/771-1237; Email: 699848@ican.net; URL: http://www.io.org/~chauhan – *1

Alan H. Coles, 46 Simonston Blvd., L3T 4L3 – 905/731-7421, Fax: 905/764-2595; Email: compass@inforamp.net

Michael K. Coyne, 7061 Yonge St., L3T 2A6 – 416/733-0018

Damiani & Associates, #300, 3300 Hwy. 7 West, L4K 4M3 – 905/660-3333, Fax: 905/660-0990 – *5

Alan Direnfeld, #207, 7089 Yonge St., L3T 2A7 – 905/881-2345, Fax: 905/881-8949 – *2

Dymond & Associates, #11, 30 Wertheim Ct., L4B 1B9 – 905/882-2179, Fax: 905/882-6266 – *1

Hercules E. Faga, 137A Langstaff Rd. East, L3T 3M6 – 905/881-2624, Fax: 905/881-0593 – *1

Ronald Filipovich, #173, 7751 Yonge St., L3T 3N3 – 905/737-6809, Fax: 905/737-8363 – *1

Fish & Associates, 7951 Yonge St., L3T 2C4 – 905/881-1500, Fax: 905/881-6535 – *3

Boris G. Freesman, Q.C., 8 Quail Valley Dr., L3T 4R2 – 905/886-5005, Fax: 905/886-5006; Email: freesman@inforamp.net – *1

G.J. Gaglione, #202, 7368 Yonge St., L4J 8H9 – 416/882-0066 – *1

Frances G. Garshowitz, 29 Flamingo Rd., L4J 6Z6 – 905/731-9422, Fax: 905/731-1756

Stephen Z. Goodbaum, 7626A Yonge St., L4J 1V9 – 905/886-9535, Fax: 905/886-9540; Email: lawyer@idirect.com

John R. Grummett, 105 Holsworthy Cres., L3T 4C5 – 905/731-4387, Fax: 905/889-6248

Herman Murray Law Office, 1 Promenade Cir., L4J 4P8 – 905/889-2502

Gerri C. Holder, 75 Dundurn Cres., L4J 6Z3 – 905/764-9732, Fax: 905/626-3069 – *1

Hughes, Etigson, #200, 175 Commerce Valley Dr. West, L3T 7P6 – 905/771-6414, Fax: 905/771-6420; Email: esten@sympatico.ca – *2

Henry K. Hui & Associates, #301, 350 Hwy. 7 East, L4B 3N2 – 905/881-7722, Fax: 905/881-1222 – *3

Iseman & Associate, #216, 2900 Steeles Ave. East, L3T 4X1 – 905/881-8800, Fax: 905/881-7391; Email: siseman@surfen.com – *3

A.L. Jackson, PO Box 81, L3T 3N1 – 905/881-5945, Fax: 905/884-3532 – *1

Barry Klady, #300, 8199 Yonge St., L3T 2C6 – 905/731-6071, Fax: 905/731-4058 – *1

Thomas Ko, #512, 330 Hwy 7 East, L4B 3P8 – 905/881-4842, Fax: 905/881-1119

Kotick & Associates, 60 Commerce Valley Dr. East, L3T 7P9 – 905/882-1200, Fax: 905/882-0086 – *2

Lecker/Gorodensky Associates, #222, 1600 Steeles Ave. West, L4K 4M2 – 905/669-7400, Fax: 905/669-9403 – *3

Leslie Brown, #302, 300 John St., L3T 5W4 – 905/731-5083, Fax: 905/731-4078

Janet MacDougall, #202, 8108 Yonge St., L4J 1W4 – 905/886-4907, Fax: 905/886-8070 – *1

Mandel, Hirsch, #218, 180 Steeles Ave. West, L4J 2L1 – 905/881-3666, Fax: 905/881-9859 – *2

Denise Marchildon, #402, 300 John St., L3T 5W4 – 905/764-1422, Fax: 905/764-9727 – *1

Paul E. Marcus, 105 Tamarack Dr., L3T 4X3 – 416/631-5729, Fax: 416/631-5715

Susan P. Marr, 57 Forest Lane Dr., L4J 3P2 – 905/709-9830

Alvin D. Merman, 7636 Yonge St., L4V 1V9 – 905/709-4533, Fax: 905/881-3199

R.G. Merritt, #205, 7089 Yonge St., L3T 2A7 – 905/889-3430, Fax: 905/889-7290 – *1

S. Ronald Minken & Assoc., #310, 330 Hwy 7 East, L4B 3P8 – 905/771-0025, Fax: 905/771-0805; Email: minken@netcom.ca – *2

Geoffrey L. & Assoc. Ltd., #207, 370 Steeles Ave. West, L4J 6X1 – 905/886-9471, Fax: 905/886-9475 – *1

Dan Moshinsky, 54 Chabad Gate, L4J 2R3 – 905/889-7985

Spiro Nikcolakakos, 102 Wade Gate, L4J 5X4 – 416/410-3132

W.S. Novak, Promenade Mall, #310, 1 Promenade Cir., L4J 4P8 – 905/882-1818, Fax: 905/882-8775 – *1

Rocco Palmieri, #212, 2180 Steeles Ave. West, L4K 2Z5 – 905/669-6232

Tania Perlin, #B10-137, 800 Steeles Ave. West, L4J 7L2 – 416/225-5424, Fax: 416/225-3611

Frank Pizzimenti, #300, 8400 Jane St., L4K 4L8 – 905/660-5253, Fax: 905/738-0528 – *1

D.J. Reeve, 278 Badessa Circle, L4J 6C5 – 905/738-9826, Fax: 905/669-2577 – *1

Riesz, Thomas, #218, 180 Steeles Ave. West, L4J 2L1 – 905/881-5609, Fax: 905/881-9859

Sol Rosenfeld, #11, 30 Wertheim Crt., L4B 1B9 – 905/709-0090, Fax: 905/882-6266

Lloyd Rubinoff, 300 John St., L3T 5W4 – 905/886-3110, Fax: 905/886-0989 – *1

Sheldon Rudolph, 613 York Hill Blvd., L4J 5L3 – 905/886-7988, Fax: 905/886-9388 – *1

Marc E. Schiffer, 83 Breckonwood Cres., L3T 5G8 – 905/881-0056 – *1

Seymour Iseman & Associate, #216, 2900 Steeles Ave. East, L3T 4X1 – 905/881-8800, Fax: 905/881-7391; Email: siseman@surfen.net – *1

Rhonda S. Shousterman, 149 Thornway Ave., L4J 7Z3 – 905/738-2142, Fax: 905/738-2142

Stewart Floyd Sklar, 175 Newport Sq., L4J 7N6 – 905/886-6802, Fax: 905/886-4482 – *1

Robert D. Sloan, 85 Quail Valley Cres., L3T 4P9 – 905/881-4968

Steinberg & Waldman, 7636 Yonge St., L4J 1V9 – 905/881-3116, Fax: 905/881-3199 – *2

Stern & Morganstein, #402, 8199 Yonge St., L3T 2C6 – 905/881-8288, Fax: 905/881-8665; Email: samlaw@interlog.com – *2

L. Stulberg, Thornhill Square, #402, 300 John St., L3T 5W4 – 905/764-1422, Fax: 905/764-9727 – *1

Suter Law, The Promenade Mall, 1 Promenade Circle, L4J 4P8 – 905/886-0529

Charles B. Ticker, Thornhill Corporate Centre, 7626A Yonge St., L4J 1V9 – 905/886-9535, Fax: 905/886-9540

Arthur J. Trebilcock, 56 Sycamore Dr., L3T 5V6 – 905/709-3837, Fax: 905/709-2565; Email: atreb@passport.ca

S.C. Wengle, 22 Vanwood Rd., L3T 2N2 – 905/889-0005, Fax: 905/889-2060
Sheldon Wisener, 7626A Yonge St., L4J 1V9 – 905/886-9535, Fax: 905/886-9540
O.C. Wong, #503, 330 Hwy 7 East, L4B 3P8 – 905/881-2992

**Thorold. . . . . . . . . . . . . . . . . . . . Niagara South**

Brenda A. Glenn, 20 Greenhill Dr., PO Box 519, Stn Thorold, L2V 1W5 – 905/227-5463, Fax: 905/680-2839
Dennis Gross, 9 Pine St. North, L2V 3Z9 – 905/227-8111
Peter J. Jurmain, #103, 15 Albert St., PO Box 235, L2V 2G2 – 905/227-9206, Fax: 905/227-2829
James V. McManamy, 21 1/2 Front St. South, PO Box 235, L2V 3Y9 – 905/227-2731, Fax: 905/227-9206 – *1
S.E. Sherk, 63 Front St. South, PO Box 412, Stn Thorold, L2V 4J6 – 905/227-7581, Fax: 905/227-5352 – *1
John J. Simon, 7 Front St. North, PO Box 505, L2V 4M5 – 905/227-9191, Fax: 905/227-7234 – *1
Young, McNamara, 18 Albert St., PO Box 68, L1V 3Y7 – 905/227-3777, Fax: 905/227-5988 – *2

**Thunder Bay . . . . . . . . . . . . . . . . . . . . Thunder Bay**

Atwood, Shaw, Labine, 501 East Donald St., P7E 6N6 – 807/623-4342, Fax: 807/623-2098 – *3
David J. Auger, 195 Park Ave., P7B 1B9 – 807/345-7466, Fax: 807/345-8450
B. Lee Baig, Q.C., 384 Fort William Rd., P7B 2Z3 – *1
Buset & Partners, 1121 Barton St., P7B 5N3 – 807/623-2500, Fax: 807/622-7808; Email: law@buset.on.ca; URL: http://www.buset.on.ca – *7
Carrel & Partners, 1136 Alloy Dr., PO Box 638, P7C 4W6 – 807/346-3000, Fax: 807/346-3600 – *11
Cheadle Johnson Shanks MacIvor, #2000, 715 Hewitson St., PO Box 429, P7C 4V9 – 807/622-6821, Fax: 807/623-3892 – *7
Christie & Potestio, 263 Park Ave., PO Box 3047, P7B 5G5 – 807/344-6651, Fax: 807/345-1105 – *3
Edwards & Carfagnini, 69 North Court St., PO Box 2237, Stn P, P7B 5E8 – 807/345-0711, Fax: 807/345-3571 – *2
Erickson Larson, 291 South Court St., PO Box 1240, P7C 4X9 – 807/345-1213, Fax: 807/345-2526 – *8
Filipovic, Brothers & Conway, Tomlinson Block, #20, 8A North Cumberland St., P7A 4L1 – 807/343-9090, Fax: 807/345-1397 – *5
Richard Forget, 384 Fort William Rd., P7B 2Z3 – 807/344-7171, Fax: 807/345-3036
Terry L. Gilbart, 217 Van Norman St., P7A 4B6 – 807/345-6538, Fax: 807/345-0337 – *1
Peter Heerema, 142 Algoma St. South, P7B 3B8 – 807/346-4053, Fax: 807/346-8714
Illingworth & Illingworth, #201, 1151 Barton St., P7B 5N3 – 807/623-7222, Fax: 807/622-5297 – *3
Trevor D. Jukes, 1001 William St., P7B 6M1 – 807/344-2244
G.W. Kostyshyn, 123 Brodie St. South, P7E 1B8 – 807/623-5400, Fax: 807/623-6096 – *1
Kovanchak Ferris Ross, 79 Court St. North, PO Box 3197, P7B 5G6 – 807/344-5771, Fax: 807/345-1642 – *3
R.E. Lauder, 217 Van Norman St., P7A 4B6 – 807/345-6538, Fax: 807/345-0337; Email: rlauder@norlink.net; URL: http://www.norlink.net/~rlauder/ – *1
Donald J. Lees, The Chapple Bldg., #312, 101 Syndicate Ave. North, P7C 3V4 – 807/623-5892, Fax: 807/623-1580 – *1
Peter G. Lucas, 10A - 4A Court St. South., P7B 2W4 – 807/345-1996, Fax: 807/344-9136 – *1
Lukinuk & McKenzie, #403, 135 Syndicate Ave. North, PO Box 26, P7C 3V6 – 807/622-6413, Fax: 807/622-6413 – *2
Macgillivray-Poirier & Mullen, 384 Fort William Rd., P7B 2Z3 – 807/344-5847, Fax: 807/345-3036 – *3
Martin Zaitzeff Scrimshaw, 43 North Ct., PO Box 3260, P7B 5G6 – 807/345-3600, Fax: 807/344-8152 – *3
Bruce H. McKillop, 112 Frederica St. East, P7E 3V5 – 807/626-0001, Fax: 807/626-0034
McKitrick, Jones, 17A Cumberland St. South, PO Box 2538, P7B 5G1 – 807/345-1251, Fax: 807/345-0043 – *4
Thomas C. Mitton, The Chapple Bldg., #511, 101 Syndicate Ave. North, PO Box 173, Stn F, P7C 4V8 – 807/623-4320, Fax: 807/622-8038 – *1
A. Michael Montemuro, 106 Bentwood Dr., P7A 7A5 – 807/344-3061
Peter Mrowiec, 395 Fort William Rd., P7B 2Z5 – 807/344-0099, Fax: 807/345-5382; Email: pmrowiec@alumni.lakeheadu.ca
Murray & Courtis, #101, 1151 Barton St., P7B 5N3 – 807/623-7961, Fax: 807/623-4417 – *2
James L. Murray, 501 Donald St. East, P7E 6N6 – 807/622-1222, Fax: 807/623-2098
Petrone Hornak Garofalo Mauro, 76 Algoma St. North, PO Box 3446, P7B 5J9 – 807/344-9191, Fax: 807/345-8391; Toll Free: 1-800-465-3988 – *5
Celina M. Reitberger, 215 Camelot St., P7A 4B2 – 807/345-0563, Fax: 807/344-0830 – *1
Gary J. Schmidt, #5A, 8 Cumberland St. North, P7A 4L1 – 807/345-5225, Fax: 807/345-8400 – *1
Shaffer, Jobbitt, Stead, Halabisky, Karlstedt, Fillmore & Barker, 1020 Victoria Ave. East, PO Box 125, P7C 4V5 – 807/623-4442, Fax: 807/623-8140 – *8
Kenneth R. Tilson, #17, 4 Court St. South, P7B 2W4 – 807/345-1451 – *1
Weiler, Maloney, Nelson, Chapple Bldg., 101 Syndicate Ave. North, 2nd Fl., PO Box 10, P7C 3V5 – 807/623-1111, Fax: 807/623-4947; Email: weiler@air.on.ca – *12
W.C. Wieckowski, 293 Park Ave., P7B 1C4 – 807/345-6566, Fax: 807/345-9982 – *1
Peter G.F. Young, 244 Camelot St., P7A 4B1 – 807/344-0881, Fax: 807/345-9886 – *1

**Tilbury . . . . . . . . . . . . . . . . . . . . Kent**

Thomas C. Odette Jr., Q.C., 13 Queen St. North, N0P 2L0 – 519/682-1644 – *1

**Tillsonburg. . . . . . . . . . . . . . . . . . . . Oxford**

Gibson, Linton, Toth, Campbell & Bennett, 36 Broadway, N4G 3P1 – 519/842-3658, Fax: 519/842-5001 – *4
Groom & Szorenyi, 25 Harvey St., N4G 3J7 – 519/842-4205, Fax: 519/842-4261 – *1
Mandryk & Heeney, 65 Bidwell St., N4G 3T8 – 519/842-4228, Fax: 519/842-7659; Email: mhlaw@oxford.net – *3
Morris, Jenkins & Kee, 19 Ridout St. East, N4G 4H8 – 519/842-9017, Fax: 519/842-3394 – *2
Odorjan, Battin & Slivocka, 35 Bidwell St., PO Box 397, N4G 4H8 – 519/842-9079, Fax: 519/842-6091 – *3

**Timmins. . . . . . . . . . . . . . . . . . . . Cochrane**

J. Kenneth Alexander, 192 - 3 Ave., P4N 1C8 – 705/264-5221, Fax: 705/267-1336 – *2
Sylvano A. Carlesso, Scotia Bank Bldg., #204, 3 Pine St. South, P4N 2J9 – 705/264-1374, Fax: 705/264-1450 – *1
Suzanne Desrosiers, #3, 24 Pine St. South, P4N 2J8 – 705/268-6492, Fax: 705/264-1940 – *1
Peter J. Doucet, #23, 25 Pine St. South, 2nd Fl., P4N 2J9 – 705/267-7600, Fax: 705/267-7550; Email: doucetp@vianet.on.ca
Ellery, Cox, 135 Algonquin Blvd. East, PO Box 1540, P4N 1A6 – 705/360-5879, Fax: 705/264-3297 – *2
Evans, Bragagnolo & Sullivan, #131, 38 Pine St. North, P4N 6K6 – 705/264-1285, Fax: 705/264-7424 – *8
Girones & Associates, 16 Cedar St. South, P4N 2G4 – 705/268-4242, Fax: 705/264-1646 – *9
J.P. Huot, 36 Maple St. South, PO Box 1065, P4N 7H9 – 705/267-6464, Fax: 705/264-3260 – *1
John Kukurin, 30 Spruce St. North, PO Box 1125, P4N 7H9 – 705/267-8441, Fax: 705/267-6811 – *1
Racicot & Bonney, 15 Balsam St. South, P4N 2C7 – 705/264-2385, Fax: 705/268-3949; Email: bonney@nt.net – *5
Robert A. Riopelle, #202, 85 Pine St. South, PO Box 1540, P4N 7W7 – 705/264-9591, Fax: 705/264-1393; Email: riopelle@nt.net – *2

**Toronto . . . . . . . . . . . . . . . . . . . . York**

Aaron & Aaron, #1400, 10 King St. East, M5C 1C3 – 416/364-9366, Fax: 416/364-3818 – *1
C.J. Abbass, #2000, 393 University Ave., M5G 1E6 – 416/593-5599 – *1
G.J. Abols, #101A, 1000 Finch Ave. West, M3J 2V5 – 416/661-1166, Fax: 416/661-7048 – *2
Abraham Duggan, 17 Dundonald St., M4Y 1K3 – 416/921-1700, Fax: 416/921-8936 – *9
Peter Abrahams, #504, 2 Sheppard Ave. East, M2N 5Y7 – 416/250-1313, Fax: 416/250-1303 – *1
G. Chalmers Adams, #100, 1255 Yonge St., M4T 1W6 – 416/929-7232, Fax: 416/929-7225 – *1
Addy & Addy, #210, 1560 Bayview Ave., M4G 3B8 – 416/322-5973 – *1
Bessie Adelman, 98 Roberta Dr., M6A 2J7 – 416/785-6660 – *1
Leo Adler, #3204, 20 Queen St. West, PO Box 40, M5H 3R3 – 416/598-1745, Fax: 416/340-7025 – *1
Advocacy Centre for the Elderly, #701, 2 Carlton St., M5B 1J3 – 416/598-2656, Fax: 416/598-7924
Advocacy Resource Centre for the Handicapped, 255-40 Orchard View Blvd., M4R 1B9 – 416/482-8255, Fax: 416/482-2981; Email: arch@indie.ca; URL: http://www.indie.ca/arch – *5
Advocate Placement Ltd., #902, 1200 Bay St., M5R 2A5 – 416/927-9222, Fax: 416/927-8772; Toll Free: 1-800-461-1275; Email: advolaw@interlog.com – *1
Advocate Placement Ltd., 112 Sorauren Ave., M6R 2E4 – 416/534-7393 – *1
E.M. Agnew, 215 Carlton St., M5A 2K9 – 416/964-0021, Fax: 416/964-0744; Email: yetilaw@istar.ca – *1
R.E. Agnew, 54 Foxbar Rd., M4V 2G6 – 416/935-4007
Joseph Agostino, 321 Bloor St. East, M4W 1H1 – 416/413-3707, Fax: 416/413-3696 – *1
Ahee, McMahon & Meikle, #550, 135 Queen's Plate Dr.., M9W 6V1 – 416/745-2433, Fax: 416/745-6017 – *3
Aiken Associates, Richmond-Adelaide Centre, #410, 120 Adelaide St. West, M5H 1T1 – 416/947-0199, Fax: 416/947-0370 – *1
Melvyn H. Aiken, 878 Wilson Ave., M3K 1E7 – 416/635-7243, Fax: 416/635-7681 – *1
Aird & Berlis, BCE Place, #1800, 181 Bay St., PO Box 754, M5J 2T9 – 416/863-1500, Fax: 416/863-1515; Email: contact@airdberlis.com – *97
Irwin Aisen, 1921 Eglinton Ave. East, M1L 2L6 – 416/285-9988, Fax: 416/285-6801 – *1
Michael V. Akai, #204, 3459 Sheppard Ave. East, M1T 3K5 – 416/292-2565, Fax: 416/292-0473 – *1
Jerome T. Albert, #444, 100 Richmond St. West, M5H 2M9 – 416/368-8480, Fax: 416/368-0950
G.W. Alexandrowicz, 618A Queen St. West, M6J 1E4 – 416/368-5441, Fax: 416/368-5441 – *1
George Alexiou, #203, 785 Carlaw Ave., M4K 3L1 – 416/465-5515, Fax: 416/465-5554 – *1
Demo Aliferis, #200, 717 Pape Ave., M4K 3S9 – 416/778-4498, Fax: 416/463-1216 – *1
Allan & Associate, #2707, 401 Bay St., M5K 2Y4 – 416/363-5431, Fax: 416/363-2506 – *4
Allen and Phelan, #300, 100 Front St. East, M5A 1E1 – 416/865-0295, Fax: 416/865-1241 – *3
Carol Allen, #200, 166 Pearl, M5H 1L3 – 416/351-8600, Fax: 416/351-8331
K. Patricia Alletson, Commerce Court West, #5500, PO Box 85, Stn Commerce Court, M5L 1B9 – 416/869-5600, Fax: 416/947-0866 – *1

* indicates number of lawyers in law firm.

Alpert Law Firm, #900, 1 St. Clair Ave. East, M4T 2V7 – 416/923-0809, Fax: 416/923-1549 – *2
Harriet Altman, 68 Gamier Court, M2M 4C9 – 416/224-5240, Fax: 416/224-0360 – *1
Sheldon L. Altman & Associates, 9 Gloucester St., M4Y 1L8 – 416/929-1313, Fax: 416/972-6885 – *1
Altwerger, Baker, Weinberg, Box: 2450, #2901, 2300 Yonge St., M4P 1E4 – 416/480-1662, Fax: 416/480-0017 – *5
Joseph Amorim, 1310 Dundas St. West, M6J 1Y1 – 416/537-4121, Fax: 416/537-4123 – *4
Amsterdam & Peroff, #1902, 150 York St., M5N 3S5 – 416/367-0076, Fax: 416/367-1334 – *2
Anand, Bragança, Levy & Jebb, #1800, 4950 Yonge St., M2N 6K1
Anderson & Wylde, #2112, 401 Bay St., M5H 2Y4 – 416/363-0338, Fax: 416/868-0332 – *3
Anderson, Burgess, #403, 2333 Dundas St. West, M6R 3A6 – 416/535-1131, Fax: 416/536-3651
Dwight Anderson, #200, 2200 Bloor St. West, M6S 1N4 – 416/769-3522, Fax: 416/763-2522 – *1
Anderson, Sinclair, #209, 3416 Dundas St. West, M6S 2S1 – 416/767-2127 – *1
Edmond Andrade & Associates, 32 Applemore Rd., M1B 1R6 – 416/609-8040, Fax: 416/609-1582 – *1
R. Andreansky, #305, 2161 Yonge St., M4S 3A6 – 416/485-1400, Fax: 416/489-7528 – *1
William Andrews, Q.C., #305, 27 Queen St. East, M5C 2M6 – 416/366-0740, Fax: 416/366-2861 – *1
Andriessen & Associate, #901, 701 Evans Avenue, M9C 1A3 – 416/620-7020, Fax: 416/622-8952; URL: http://ourworld.compuserve.com/homepages/andriessen_and_associates – *2
Raymond Ang, #850, 439 University Ave., M5G 1Y8 – 416/596-7077, Fax: 416/596-7629 – *1
M.J. Angevine, c/o The Law Society of Upper Canada, 130 Queen St. West, M5H 2N6 – 416/947-3301
V. Charles Anipare, 4002 Sheppard Ave. East, M1S 4R5 – 416/609-0540 – *1
R.A. Anisio, #5900, 1 First Canadian Place, PO Box 24, M5X 1K2 – 416/863-0820, Fax: 416/367-3316 – *1
Philip Anisman, #1905, 80 Richmond St. West, M5H 2A4 – 416/363-4200, Fax: 416/363-6200 – *1
Mel Antflyck, 1501 Ellesmere Rd., M1P 4T6 – 416/431-1500, Fax: 416/431-1912 – *1
S.J. Antonette, #213, 455 Spadina Ave., M5S 2G8 – 416/979-2363, Fax: 416/979-0456 – *1
Sandra Antoniani, #780, 439 University Ave., M5G 1Y8 – 416/410-0608, Fax: 416/593-0225 – *1
Sam J. Apelbaum, #202, 4599 Kingston Rd., M1E 2P3 – 416/282-5779 – *1
Dennis Apostolides, 463 Danforth Ave., M4K 1P1 – 416/463-1147, Fax: 416/463-1762 – *1
Cheryl L. Appell, #306, 10 Alcorn Ave., M4V 1E4 – 416/927-0891, Fax: 416/927-0385
Jerry Applebaum, 36 Covington Rd., M6A 1G1 – 416/785-1140 – *1
M.I. Applebaum, Q.C., 4800 Dufferin St., M3H 5S9 – 416/661-9290, Fax: 416/661-6971 – *1
Frank A. Aprile, 2494 Danforth Ave., M4C 1K9 – 416/694-3117 – *1
C.E. Archibald, Q.C., #301, 817 Bloor St. West, M6G 1M1 – 416/534-6369 – *1
Peter D. Archibald, #1501, 393 University Ave., M5G 1E6 – 416/596-0969, Fax: 416/596-0952 – *15
Kenneth Arenson, #1901, 8 King St. East, M5C 1B5 – 416/368-1500, Fax: 416/368-1516 – *1
Argiris & Associates, 693 Pape Ave., M4K 3S6 – 416/466-2184, Fax: 416/466-8707 – *3
Armel, Cohen, Stieber, #800, 55 University Ave., M5J 2K4 – 416/368-1400, Fax: 416/368-0016 – *20
Brian J. Armstrong, 5100 Dundas St. West, M9A 1C2 – 416/232-1358, Fax: 416/234-0259 – *1
Armstrong, Dunne, #1400, 141 Adelaide St. West, M5H 3L5 – 416/868-0180, Fax: 416/863-1814 – *6
D.W. Arn, 380 Bathurst St., M5T 2S6 – 416/364-3658, Fax: 416/368-0379 – *1
Arnold, Falzone & Fyshe, #2210, 439 University Ave., M5G 1Y8 – 416/977-1521, Fax: 416/977-4927 – *4
M.S. Aronoff, 166 Sheppard Ave. East, M2N 3A4 – 416/224-5806, Fax: 416/224-5087 – *1
Judith Arrillaga, #200, 111 Eglinton Ave. East, M4P 1H4 – 416/488-3138, Fax: 416/482-4165 – *1
Harvey Ash, #900, 5799 Yonge St., M2M 3V3 – 416/250-0080, Fax: 416/225-1124; Email: harvie@ash-lawyer.com – *1
Ashbourne & Caskey, 2077 Lawrence Ave. West, PO Box 403, M9N 1H7 – 416/247-6677, Fax: 416/247-3519 – *1
Christopher Ashby, #1200, 8 King St. East, M5C 1B5 – 416/368-4422, Fax: 416/364-1282
Mark E. Atlin, 845 St. Clair Ave. West, M6C 1C3 – 416/658-0885, Fax: 416/653-3891
John Au, #830, 210 Dundas St. West, M5G 2E8 – 416/979-2663, Fax: 416/979-8681 – *1
S.J. AvRuskin, 101 Charles St. East., M4Y 1V2 – 416/922-4147, Fax: 416/920-1554 – *1
Aylesworth, Thompson, Phelan, O'Brien, #3000, South Tower, Royal Bank Plaza, PO Box 15, Stn Royal Bank, M5J 2J1 – 416/865-0101, Fax: 416/865-1398; Email: queries@aylaw.com – *19
J.W. Baerg, #1610, 8 King St. East, M5C 1B5 – 416/366-3705, Fax: 416/366-0157 – *1
Sarah Bagnall, #2000, 390 Bay St., M5H 2Y2 – 416/862-9945, Fax: 416/860-0580 – *1
John H. Bailey, #901, 701 Evans Ave., M9C 1A3 – 416/622-7970, 2725, Fax: 416/622-8952; Email: bailaw@compuserve.com – *1
Karen Bailey, 56 Temperence St., 8th Fl., M5H 3V5 – 416/214-4646, Fax: 416/214-4699 – *1
Paul Bain, Flatiron Bldg., 49 Wellington St. East, 5th Fl., M5C 1C9 – 416/368-4142, Fax: 416/368-1166 – *1
W.N. Bain, #212, 120 Carlton St., M5A 4K2 – 416/924-7647 – *1
Baker & Company, #3300, 130 Adelaide St. West, M4W 1B9 – 416/366-8833, Fax: 416/366-3992; Email: mbaker@bakerlawyers.com – *2
Baker & McKenzie, #2100, 181 Bay St., PO Box 874, M5J 2T3 – 416/865-6941, Fax: 416/863-6275; URL: http://www.bakerinfo.com – *38
Gordon R. Baker, Q.C., Exchange Tower, Box: 426, #1470, 2 First Canadian Place, M5X 1E3 – 416/365-7203, Fax: 416/365-7204; Email: gordbaker@myna.com; URL: http://www.myna.com/~gbaker/ – *1
Baker, Gray, #200, 3875 Keele St., M3J 1N6 – 416/398-1200, Fax: 416/398-8585 – *3
Baker, Ranieri, #403, 164 Eglinton Ave. East, M4P 1G4 – 416/932-1313, Fax: 416/932-1903 – *2
Baker, Schneider, Swartz, #1000, 120 Adelaide St. West, M5H 3V1 – 416/363-2211, Fax: 416/363-0645 – *3
Baksh & Associates, #1204, 347 Bay St., M5H 2R7 – 416/867-1111, Fax: 416/867-2939 – *2
I. Vernon Balaban, Box: 1900, #2200, 181 University Ave., M5K 1B7 – 416/601-6760, Fax: 416/601-1322 – *1
Banks & Starkman, #303, 222 Dixon Rd., M9P 3S5 – 416/243-3394, Fax: 416/243-9692 – *3
T. Gary Bard, 415 Yonge St., 3rd Fl., M5B 2E7 – 416/975-7742, Fax: 416/975-3453 – *1
Anne Barrett, 213 Armour Blvd., M3H 1M6 – 416/638-2990 – *1
Harvey Barron, #202, 2986 Danforth Avenue, M4C 1M6 – 416/691-2666 – *1
J.R. Barrs, #2412, 401 Bay St., M5H 2Y4 – 416/366-6466, Fax: 416/364-2308 – *1
Basman Smith Rose, #1400, 111 Richmond St. West, M5H 2G4 – 416/365-0300, Fax: 416/365-9276 – *8
Bassel & Bassel, 39 Hayden St., M4Y 2P2 – 416/968-1266 – *1
Bassel Sullivan, #2100, 20 Queen St. West, PO Box 61, M5H 3R3 – 416/813-0600, Fax: 416/813-0470 – *5
Robert J. Bassermann, #212, 120 Carlton, M5A 4K2 – 416/323-3741, Fax: 416/922-3939 – *1
Bastedo, Sheldon, McGivney & Peck, #1800, 180 Dundas St. West, M5G 1Z8 – 416/595-5151, Fax: 416/596-7538
Batcher, Wasserman & Associates, #500, 718 Wilson Ave., M3K 1E2 – 416/635-6300, Fax: 416/635-6376 – *4
Beach, Hepburn, #1000, 36 Toronto St., M5C 2C5 – 416/350-3500, Fax: 416/350-3510; Email: lawyers@beachlaw.com – *7
Alexander Beadie, 810 Queen St. East, M4M 1H7 – 416/463-8008, Fax: 416/469-9662 – *1
Beard, Winter, #900, 150 King St. West, M5H 2K4 – 416/593-5555, Fax: 416/593-7760 – *27
Beaudoin & Pepper, #800, 439 University Ave., M5G 1Y8 – 416/598-4775 – *3
Sandra Bebris, #3, 900 Don Mills Rd., M3C 1V8 – 416/510-1324, Fax: 416/441-6898 – *1
D. Casson Bell, Q.C., #811, 44 Victoria St., M5C 1Z2 – 416/363-9011, Fax: 416/363-9012 – *1
Steven Bellissimo, #700, 357 Bay St., M5H 2T7 – 416/362-6437 – *1
Bellmore & Moore, #1600, 393 University Ave., M5G 1E6 – 416/581-1818, Fax: 416/581-1279 – *2
Bennett & Company, #2125, 130 King St. West, M5X 1A6 – 416/363-8688, Fax: 416/363-8083; Email: bennett@ican.net – *3
Bennett Best Burn, #1700, 150 York St., M5H 3S5 – 416/362-3400, Fax: 416/362-2211; Email: bbbsuper@bbburn.com; URL: http://www.bbburn.com – *8
Bennett Jones Verchere, 1 First Canadian Place, #3400, PO Box 130, M5X 1A4 – 416/863-1200, Fax: 416/863-1716 – *26
Benson Percival Brown, #800, 250 Dundas St. West, M5T 2Z6 – 416/977-9777, Fax: 416/977-1241 – *9
Bereskin & Parr, Box: 401, 40 King St. West, M5H 3Y2 – 416/364-7311, Fax: 416/361-1398; Email: dbereskin@bereskinparr.com; URL: http://www.bereskinparr.com – *33
Percy Bergart, 120 Eglinton Ave. East, 5th Fl., M4P 1E2 – 416/482-1311, Fax: 416/483-8017 – *1
Bergstein & Kelly, 113 Davenport Rd., M5R 1H8 – 416/961-3100 – *2
Bradley F. Berns, #2307, 2025 Sheppard Ave. East, M2J 1V7 – 416/490-6456, Fax: 416/490-6439 – *1
Colin M. Berry, 74 - 38 St., M8W 3M3 – 416/251-4698 – *1
David C. Besant, #404, 3601 Victoria Park Ave., M1W 3Y3 – 416/756-4566, Fax: 416/756-3663 – *1
Michael Betcherman, 142 Robert St., M5S 2K3 – 416/924-2143 – *1
Myer Betel, #932, 20 Dundas St. West, Box 77, M5G 2C2 – 416/977-7114, Fax: 416/977-4069 – *1
Bhatia, Minipreet, #405, 3601 Victoria Park Ave., M1W 3Y3 – 416/493-1727, Fax: 416/756-3663
Bigelow, Hendy, #200, 789 Don Mills Rd., M3C 1T5 – 416/429-3110, Fax: 416/429-3057 – *4
R.G. Bigelow, 45 St. Nicholas St., M4Y 1W6 – 416/964-7497, Fax: 416/925-8122 – *1
Mary L. Biggar, #1000, 33 Bloor St. East, M4W 3H1 – 416/961-4100, Fax: 416/961-2531 – *1
Biles & Wratten, #1200, 10 King St. East, M5C 1C3 – 416/368-6178, Fax: 416/368-6170 – *2
Birchall Northey, #400, 144 Front St. West, M5J 2L7 – 416/599-0992, Fax: 416/599-4800 – *2
Birenbaum & Bernstein, #101, 3042 Keele St., M3M 2H5 – 416/633-3720, Fax: 416/633-4546 – *2
Birenbaum, Koffman, Steinberg, #1000, 33 Bloor St. East, M4W 3H1 – 416/961-4100, Fax: 416/961-2531 – *6
Birks, Langdon & Elliott, #2114, 85 Richmond St. West, M5H 1T1 – 416/363-3431, Fax: 416/363-0098 – *2
Irving I. Birnbaum, 108 Combe Ave., M3H 4J9 – 416/633-1870 – *1
Donald H. Bitter, Q.C., 600 Church St., M4Y 2T7 – 416/360-4357 – *1
Black & Cook, #2109, 2 Bloor St. West, M4W 1A1 – 416/924-3311, Fax: 416/925-1711 – *2

Donald D. Black, #101, 5859 Yonge St., M2M 3V6 – 416/225-8806 – *1
Black, Sutherland & Crabbe, #2700, 401 Bay St., PO Box 101, M5H 2Y4 – 416/361-1500, Fax: 416/361-1674; Email: bsclaw@interlog.com – *9
Harry Blaier, #1800, 4950 Yonge St., M2N 6K1 – 416/224-0200, Fax: 416/224-0758 – *1
Blake, Cassels & Graydon, Commerce Court West, 28th Fl., PO Box 25, M5L 1A9 – 416/863-2400, Fax: 416/863-2653, 4250; Email: toronto@blakes.ca; URL: http://www.blakes.ca – *255
Edith M. Blake, #302, 75 The Donway West, M3C 2E9 – 416/445-0310, Fax: 416/445-0316
Blaney, McMurtry, Stapells, Friedman, Cadillac Fairview Tower, #1400, 20 Queen St. West, M5H 3R3 – 416/593-1221, Fax: 416/593-5437; Email: info@blaney.com; URL: http://www.blaney.com – *69
M.E. Blankstein, #100, 133 Berkeley St., M5A 2X1 – 416/363-9024, Fax: 416/363-9291 – *1
Jeffrey A. Blayways, 129 John St., M5V 2E2 – 416/598-3401, Fax: 416/977-3660 – *1
Bliss & Richards-Loghrin, #202, 425 University Ave., M5G 1T6 – 416/506-9600, Fax: 416/506-9970 – *2
Bloom & Lanys, #100, 250 Roehampton Ave., M4P 1R9 – 416/486-9913, Fax: 416/485-6054; Email: blm-inys@tube.com – *1
Deborah M. Bloomberg, 75 Lowther Ave., M5R 1C9 – 416/960-1822, Fax: 416/961-9905 – *1
Joseph L. Bloomenfeld, #2110, 120 Adelaide St. West, M5H 1T1 – 416/363-7315, Fax: 416/363-7697 – *1
Bloor Information & Legal Services, 1072 Dovercourt Rd., M6H 2X8 – 416/531-7376, Fax: 416/531-7580
Bodnaruk & Capone, 720 Spadina Ave., M5S 2T9 – 416/923-7000 – *4
Bogart Robertson & Chu, #1608, 141 Adelaide St. West, M5H 3L5 – 416/601-1991, Fax: 416/601-0006; Email: borobchu@idirect.com – *4
John M. Bolton, 97 Munro Blvd., M2P 1C5 – 416/225-1091 – *1
Robert E. Bombier, 1366 Dundas St. West, M6J 1Y2 – 416/532-1926, Fax: 416/534-2870 – *1
G.H. Bomza, #2303, 180 Dundas St. West, M5G 1Z8 – 416/598-2244 – *1
Richard Borchiver, #900, 119 Spadina Ave., M5V 2L1 – 416/977-2929, Fax: 416/977-0489 – *1
Borden & Elliot, Scotia Plaza, #4400, 40 King St. West, M5H 3Y4 – 416/367-6000, Fax: 416/367-6749; Email: info@borden.com; URL: http://www.borden.com – *219
Harry J. Borenstein, #304, 3335 Yonge St., M4N 2M1 – 416/482-0990, Fax: 416/482-6511 – *1
Howard Borenstein, 9 Gloucester St., M4Y 1L8 – 416/925-1601, Fax: 416/972-6885 – *1
Alex Borman, #601, 130 Bloor St. West, M5S 1N5 – 416/960-5090, Fax: 416/923-1391 – *1
N.H.R. Borski, Q.C., #201, 2256B Bloor St. West, M6S 1N6 – 416/766-2441 – *1
Y.R. Botiuk, Q.C., #212, 2323 Bloor St. West, M6S 4W1 – 416/763-4333 – *1
Botnick & Botnick, #53, 2300 Finch Ave. West, M9M 2Y3 – 416/741-3584, Fax: 416/741-3529 – *4
N. Boutet, 350 Bay St., 9th Fl., M5H 2S6 – 416/363-0650, Fax: 416/367-4098; Email: nboutet@pathcom.com – *1
Eric Bowman, Q.C., LL.M., #116, 2100 Ellesmere Rd., M1H 3B7 – 416/438-9450, Fax: 416/438-9236 – *1
Jerry Boyaner, 100 Adelaide St. West, M5H 1S3 – 416/360-5765, Fax: 416/360-6551 – *1
Mary E.E. Boyce, 69 Elm St., M5G 1H2 – 416/591-7588, Fax: 416/971-9092 – *1
Neil L. Boyko, 878 Wilson Ave., M3K 1E7 – 416/635-1411, Fax: 416/635-7681 – *1
R. Bradburn, #304, 2 Dunbloor Rd., M9A 2E4 – 416/239-8119, Fax: 416/239-6922 – *1
P.G. Bradley, 1051 Tapscott Rd., M1X 1A1 – 416/298-0066, Fax: 416/299-8008 – *1
L.A. Braithwaite, Q.C., C.M., 250 Wincott Dr., M9R 2R5 – 416/249-2288, Fax: 416/249-2280 – *1
David Brannan, 845 Wilson Ave., M3K 1E6 – 416/636-9770 – *1
Brans, Lehun, Baldwin & Champagne, #1700, 120 Adelaide St. West, M5H 1T1 – 416/601-1040, Fax: 416/601-0655
George F. Brant, #405, 120 Carlton St., M5A 4K2 – 416/922-4820, Fax: 416/928-5079; Email: gbrant@ibm.net – *1
Bratty & Partners, Madison Centre, 4950 Yonge St., 20th Fl., M2N 6K1 – 416/226-0660, Fax: 416/226-6395; Email: mourisin@bratty.com; URL: http://www.bratty.com – *17
G.K.C. Braund, Q.C., #204, 3333 Bayview Ave., M2K 1G4 – 416/223-0862 – *1
W. Braverman, 771 St. Clair Ave. West, M6C 1B4 – 416/654-8160 – *1
Brennen Partners, #530, 21 Four Seasons Place, M9B 6J8 – 416/620-9500, Fax: 416/620-1837 – *3
Brent & Paul, #100, 99 Scarsdale Rd., M3B 2R2 – 416/441-2830, Fax: 416/441-4011 – *1
Bresver, Grossman, Scheininger & Davis, #2800, 390 Bay St., M5H 2Y2 – 416/869-0366, Fax: 416/869-0321; Email: bgsdlaw.com – *11
Stephen W. Brett, #1200, 595 Bay St., M5G 2C2 – 416/595-9603 – *1
Domenic C. Brigante, #23, 1170 Sheppard Ave. West, M3K 2A3 – 416/636-6969, Fax: 416/636-6740 – *1
Brigden, George W., Q.C., #602, 425 University Ave., M5G 1T6 – 416/977-3775, Fax: 416/595-0825
Royden Brigham, #800, 75 The Donway West, M3C 2E9 – 416/444-1193, Fax: 416/444-1194 – *1
Peter E. Brodey, Q.C., 298 Avenue Rd., Main Fl., M4V 2H1 – 416/923-1175 – *1
Brodkin, Comba, #1200, 595 Bay St., M5G 2C2 – 416/340-0404, Fax: 416/340-7229 – *3
Michael Brodzky, 69 Elm St., M5G 1H2 – 416/581-8898, Fax: 416/971-9092 – *1
Natalie Bronstein, #1200, 595 Bay St., M5G 2C2 – 416/408-0444, Fax: 416/593-1352 – *1
Brown & Forbes, #2700, 390 Bay St., M5H 2Y2 – 416/366-7927, Fax: 416/363-9602 – *12
Brown & Jones Associates, #104, 5803 Yonge St., M2M 3V5 – 416/223-9126, Fax: 416/223-9343 – *3
Constance M. Brown, Q.C., #1530, 439 University Ave., M5G 1Y8 – 416/598-3388, 3389, Fax: 416/598-2145 – *1
G.P. Brown, 1154 Morningside Ave., M1B 3A4 – 416/283-1200 – *1
Kenneth J. Brown, 45 Mogul Dr., M2H 2M8 – 416/499-8005, Fax: 416/499-8048; Email: kenbrown@better.net – *1
M.H. Brown, 38 Berwick Ave., M5P 1H1 – 416/487-5122, Fax: 416/487-5168 – *1
Peter Brown, 3048 Bloor St. West, M8X 1C4 – 416/234-8682 – *1
Phillip A. Brown, 317 Grace St., M6G 3A7 – 416/538-8328, Fax: 416/533-5174 – *1
Milton J. Brown Q.C. & Associates, Thomson Bldg., 65 Queen St. West, M5H 2M5 – 416/361-1313 – *2
Colin A. Browne, #700, 4 King St. West, M1S 5B3 – 416/864-0246 – *1
Jack Brudner, #203, 2753 Eglinton Ave. East, M1J 2C7 – 416/267-1148, Fax: 416/267-4741 – *1
Arnold Bruner, 167 Danforth Ave., M4K 1N2 – 416/461-0983 – *1
G.J. Bruner, 167 Danforth Ave., M4K 1N2 – 416/461-0983, Fax: 416/462-3347 – *1
Brunner & Lundy, #1800, 401 Bay St., M5H 2Z1 – 416/777-9375, Fax: 416/777-9381 – *2
Anthony G. Bryant, #1700, 150 York St., M5H 3S5 – 416/927-7441, Fax: 416/362-2211; Toll Free: tony-bryant@ilap.com – *1
David G. Bryce, #108, 100 Lombard St., M5C 1M3 – 416/364-9916, Fax: 416/364-7505 – *1
Buckland Werbowyj, #401, 302 The East Mall, M9B 6C7 – 416/233-9461
Frederic Buckland, #401, 302 The East Mall, M9B 6C7 – 416/236-0906, Fax: 416/233-1524 – *1
Elizabeth Slava Budi, 94 Walmer Rd., M5R 2X7 – 416/922-2151, Fax: 416/960-8630 – *1
Victor Bulger, #610, 4211 Yonge St., M2P 2A9 – 416/590-7744, Fax: 416/590-9998
J.J. Burke, #302, 2405 Lakeshore Blvd. West, M8V 1C6 – 416/252-9101, Fax: 416/503-0627 – *1
R.H. Burke, Q.C., #612, 330 Bay St., M5H 2S8 – 416/214-1162, Fax: 416/214-0870 – *1
Harry R. Burkman, One First Canadian Pl., #1410, PO Box 129 Stn First Canadian Place, M5X 1A4 – 416/364-3831, Fax: 416/364-3832 – *1
Burnett & Jacobson, #700, 48 St. Clair Ave. W., M4V 3B6 – 416/922-8710, Fax: 416/964-5840 – *2
Terry Burrell, 317 Grace St., M6G 3A7 – 416/538-0842, Fax: 416/533-5174 – *1
Burt, Burt, Wolfe & Bowman, #202, 2 Adelaide St. West, M5H 1L6 – 416/366-5431, Fax: 416/369-1135 – *2
Bernard Burton, #410, 120 Carlton St., M5A 4K2 – 416/922-1263, Fax: 416/922-1963 – *1
Michael P. Bury, #1001, 65 Queen St. West, M5H 2M5 – 416/363-9966 – *1
Burych, Raimonde, 2200 Lakeshore Blvd. West, M8V 1A4 – 416/252-6550, Fax: 416/252-1843 – *2
Bush, White & Wong, 6 Adelaide St. East, 10th Fl., M5C 1H6 – 416/366-5900, Fax: 416/366-1799; Email: lawyer@canadaimmlaw.com – *6
Bussin & Bussin, #1822, 181 University Ave., M5H 3M7 – 416/364-4925, Fax: 416/868-1818 – *3
Fernandez Buternowsky, 605-10 Saint Mary St., M4Y 1P9 – 416/323-6783, Fax: 416/323-0867 – *1
G.C. Butterill, 92 Hanna Rd., M4G 3N3 – 416/488-5352 – *1
B. Clive Bynoe, Q.C., 480 University Ave., 7th Fl., M5G 1V2 – 416/977-0853, Fax: 416/977-5331 – *1
Byrne, Crosby, #1600, 8 King St. East, M5C 1B5 – 416/364-1616, Fax: 416/363-6455; Email: ccrosby@byrnecrosby.com – *4
Byrne, Johnson & Calzavara, #106, 81 The East Mall, M8Z 5W3 – 416/253-0253, Fax: 416/253-1243 – *3
Frank Calandra, 392 Dundas St. East, M5A 2A5 – 416/944-8544, Fax: 416/944-8085 – *1
Paul Calarco, #780, 439 University Ave., M5G 1Y8 – 416/598-1948 – *1
Ruth L. Cameron, 720 Spadina Ave., M5S 2T9 – 416/929-9562 – *1
Alistair Campbell, #201, 181 Eglinton Ave. East, M4P 1J9 – 416/482-6500, Fax: 416/488-2477 – *1
H.B. Campbell & Associates, #6000, 40 King St. West, M5H 3Z7 – 416/365-1986 – *1
Campbell, Jarvis, McKenzie & Fulton, 372 Bay St., M5H 2W9 – 416/363-6279 – *1
John R. Campbell, Q.C., #107, 8 King St. East, M5C 1B5 – 416/363-5086, Fax: 416/961-0510 – *1
Campione & Vaturi, #400, 1110 Finch Ave. West, M3J 2T2 – 416/665-8133, Fax: 416/665-5752 – *2
G.H. Cancilla, 372 Bay St., 10th Fl., M5H 2W9 – 416/366-9504, Fax: 416/366-9505 – *1
Cannings, John, #400, 145 Adelaide St. West, M5H 3H4 – 416/366-1985, Fax: 416/366-2482 – *4
Ruth Canton, 2489A Bloor St. West, M6S 1R5 – 416/769-5759, Fax: 416/769-3132; Email: cx420@tor-free.net – *1
Rochelle F. Cantor, #204, 100 Lombard St., M5C 1M3 – 416/861-1625, Fax: 416/861-1466 – *1
Capp, Shupak, #1703, 2 St. Clair Ave. West, M4V 1L5 – 416/323-1116, Fax: 416/323-0697 – *4
Stephen L. Cappe, #1704, 55 University Ave., M5J 2H7 – 416/366-7305, Fax: 416/366-3513
Ernest J. Cappellacci, #1400, 65 Queen St. West, M5H 2M5 – 416/203-2988 – *2
Carbonaro, Dakin, Flude & Mikulinski, #1610, 390 Bay St., M5H 2Y2 – 416/368-2500, Fax: 416/368-0909; Email: cdfm@compuserve.com – *7
L.C. Caroe, #1800, 4950 Yonge St., M2N 6K1 – 416/224-0200, Fax: 416/224-0758 – *1
Michael W. Caroline, #5012, 40 King St. West, M5H 3Y2 – 416/366-4300, Fax: 416/366-7076 – *1

* indicates number of lawyers in law firm.

Juan F. Carranza, #317, 1315 Finch Ave. West, M3J 2G6 – 416/633-1065, Fax: 416/633-9782 – *1
John S.H. Carriere, #1810, 65 Queen St. West, PO Box 81, M5H 2M5 – 416/363-5594, Fax: 416/363-8492 – *1
C. Anthony Carroll, 8 King St. East, M5C 1B5 – 416/364-4235, Fax: 416/364-4689 – *1
F.L. Carruthers, #250, 70 University Ave., M5J 2M4 – 416/597-1777, Fax: 416/977-2895 – *1
Carson, Gross & McPherson, #1400, 401 Bay St., M5H 2Y4 – 416/361-0900, Fax: 416/361-3459 – *8
Carter & Wong, #401, 302 Spadina Ave., M5T 2E7 – 416/593-8820, Fax: 416/593-9611 – *2
John R. Casey, Q.C., 119 Underhill Dr., M5G 1V2 – 416/441-1279 – *1
Joy Casey, #1402, 151 Yonge St., M5C 2W7 – 416/368-3847, Fax: 416/366-9808
Caspar Sinnige, 470 King St. East, M5A 1L7 – 416/362-5700, Fax: 416/362-0847 – *1
Cass & Cass, 112 Adelaide St. East, M5C 1K9 – 416/943-4711, Fax: 416/368-2918 – *2
G.M. Cass, #206, 2040 Yonge St., M4S 1Z9 – 416/488-9718, Fax: 416/488-9116 – *1
Marilynne Cass, #210, 335 Bay St., M5H 2R3 – 416/863-9744, Fax: 416/863-9541 – *1
Cass, Miller & Associates, #100, 272 Lawrence Ave. West, M5M 4M1 – 416/787-0641, Fax: 416/787-0645 – *2
Cassels Brock & Blackwell, Scotia Plaza, #2100, 40 King St. West, M5H 3C2 – 416/869-5300, Fax: 416/360-8877; Email: postmaster@casselsbrock.com; URL: http://www.casselsbrock.com/ – *126
Cassels, Mitchell, 497 Eglinton Ave. West, M5N 1A7 – 416/485-9435 – *1
Licio E. Cengarle, 1151 Martin Grove Rd., M9W 4W8 – 416/248-5505, Fax: 416/248-2100 – *1
Oren H. Chaimovitch, #300, 230 Sheppard Ave. West, M2N 1N1 – 416/223-1840
Chaiton & Chaiton, 185 Sheppard Ave. West, M2N 1M9 – 416/222-8888, Fax: 416/222-8402 – *20
Chan & Li, #202, 3640 Victoria Park Ave., M2H 3B2 – 416/498-3333, Fax: 416/498-3340 – *2
Chapin & Chapin, #300, 8 King St. East, M5C 1B5 – 416/867-1799, Fax: 416/366-4892 – *2
Chapnick & Associates, 228 Carlton St., M5A 2L1 – 416/968-2160, Fax: 416/975-9338 – *5
Chappell, Bushell, Stewart, #3310, 20 Queen St. West, M5H 3R3 – 416/351-0005, Fax: 416/351-0002
Gerald J. Charney, Q.C., #200, 70 Bond St., M5B 1X3 – 416/360-8820, Fax: 416/365-7702 – *1
Chatarpaul & Associates, #402, 2065 Finch Ave. West, M3N 2V7 – 416/742-3150, Fax: 416/742-3163 – *2
Max P. Cheng, #1020, 180 Dundas St. West, M5G 1Z8 – 416/598-2998, Fax: 416/598-4374 – *2
Jackson L Chercover, Q.C., #805, 111 Avenue Rd., M5R 3J8 – 416/920-7411, Fax: 416/925-6811 – *2
Chernin & Kirsh, #204, 1497 Yonge St., M4T 1Z2 – 416/925-2444, Fax: 416/925-2446 – *1
M. Chernovsky, 61 Saint Nicholas St., M4Y 1W6 – 416/927-7048, Fax: 416/925-0162 – *1
Adam Ching, #212, 885 Progress Ave., M1H 3G3 – 416/431-4311, Fax: 416/431-5445 – *1
Ronald W. Chisholm, Q.C., #510, 330 University Ave., M5G 1R7 – 416/586-0777, Fax: 416/586-0267 – *2
David Chong, #207, 1370 Don Mills Rd., M3B 3N7 – 416/510-2233, Fax: 416/510-2234 – *1
Christopher E. Chop, North Tower, #716, 175 King St. East, M4W 3R8 – 416/972-0049, Fax: 416/972-0380 – *1
Shirley Chow, #3, 3030 Midland Ave., M1S 5C9 – 416/298-0203, Fax: 416/298-1339 – *1
Robert C. Christie, #1000, 65 Queen St. West, M5H 2M5 – 416/565-3104, Fax: 416/367-3949 – *1
Christie, Saccucci, Matthews, Caskie & Chilco, Confederation Sq., #301, 20 Richmond St. East, M5C 2R9 – 416/367-0680, Fax: 416/367-0429 – *7
B.N. Christoff, 4 Ranleigh Ave., M4N 1W9 – 416/489-5604 – *1
Paul Chumak, 75 Lowther Ave., M5R 1C9 – 416/927-1977, Fax: 416/961-9905 – *1
Andrea Chun, One Corporate Plaza, #700, 2075 Kennedy Rd., M1T 3V3 – 416/754-3060, Fax: 416/754-3321 – *1
Arthur K. Chung, 63 Elm St., M5G 1H2 – 416/977-2700, Fax: 416/977-4359 – *1
G.J. Ciglen, #5, 1474 Bathurst St., M5P 3G9 – 416/656-8400, Fax: 416/656-9823 – *1
Cimetta & Cimetta, #207, 834 Yonge St., M4W 2H1 – 416/921-7470 – *2
Wayne Paul Cipollone, #2330, 130 Adelaide St. West, M5H 3P5 – 416/368-5366, Fax: 416/368-5361 – *3
D.J. Cirone, #206, 2494 Danforth Ave., M4C 1K9 – 416/691-1000, Fax: 416/694-5369 – *1
Arthur H. Clairman, #C, 1966 Yonge St., M4S 1Z4 – 416/481-8658, Fax: 416/481-6055
Clapp & Gibson, 18 Erskine Ave., M4P 1Y2 – 416/484-4827, Fax: 416/484-0821 – *2
J.S. Clarfield, #1106, 45 Bunfield Ave., M4S 2H4 – 416/638-6768 – *1
Deta J. Clark, #201, 5075 Yonge St., M2N 6C6 – 416/733-3135 – *1
S.R. Clark, #1901, 65 Queen St. West, M5H 2M5 – 416/601-1518, Fax: 416/369-0085 – *1
Clarke, Freeman, Miller & Ryan, 1863 Danforth Ave., M4C 1J3 – 416/698-9323, Fax: 416/698-9110 – *3
Bernard Clayman, #1500, 2 St. Clair Ave. East, M4T 2T5 – 416/922-4777, Fax: 416/927-0305 – *1
J.T. Clement, Q.C., #2800, 390 Bay St., M5H 2Y2 – 416/362-1685, Fax: 416/869-0321 – *1
Eric Cliche, #204, 3875 Keele St., M3J 1N6 – 416/398-2290, Fax: 416/398-8358
Peter Clyne, 155 Harbord St., M5S 1H1 – 416/922-0864, Fax: 416/922-6856 – *1
Robert G. Coates, #307, 120 Carlton St., M5A 4K2 – 416/925-6490, Fax: 416/925-4492 – *1
Codina & Pukitis, #1708, 390 Bay St., M5H 2Y2 – 416/361-1404, Fax: 416/361-1390 – *8
Susan Coen, 45 Saint Nicholas St., M4Y 1W6 – 416/925-0004, Fax: 416/925-8122 – *1
Cohen & Associates, #801, 1 St. Clair Ave. East, M4T 2V7 – 416/323-0907, Fax: 416/324-8053; Email: smcohen@interlog.com – *2
B.C. Cohen, #201, 1001 Sandhurst Circle, M1V 1Z6 – 416/293-6000, Fax: 416/293-4027 – *1
Cohen, Goodman, #1500, 439 University Ave., M5G 1Y8 – 416/595-5555, Fax: 416/595-7020 – *2
Harold B. Cohen, Q.C., 10 Foxbar Rd., M4V 2G6 – 416/961-7255 – *1
Howard Cohen, #2412, 401 Bay St., M5H 2Y4 – 416/364-7436, Fax: 416/364-2308 – *1
Kenneth J. Cohen, #200, 65 Queen St. West, M5H 2M5 – 416/363-3351, Fax: 416/363-0252 – *1
M.V. Cohen, #1905, 400 Walmer Rd., M5P 2X7 – 416/927-7891 – *1
Neil Cohen, #115, 2 College St., M5G 1K3 – 416/921-0617, Fax: 416/921-9542 – *1
Victoria Colby, #212, 120 Carlton, M5A 4K2 – 416/323-9660, Fax: 416/924-7166 – *1
V.K. Colebourn, Q.C., #210, 335 Bay St., M5H 2R3 – 416/863-9744, Fax: 416/863-9541 – *1
Allen R. Collins, #1704, 55 University Ave., M5J 2H7 – 416/362-1566, Fax: 416/366-3513 – *1
John Collins, #Penthouse, 121 Richmond St. West, M5H 2K1 – 416/364-9006, Fax: 416/861-0554 – *1
David I. Conn, #1202, 330 Bay St., M5H 2S8 – 416/363-1868, Fax: 416/364-7885 – *1
John R. Connolly, #1202, 390 Bay St., M5H 2Y2 – 416/865-1558, Fax: 416/363-8451 – *1
Nils R. Connor, 69 Elm St., M5G 1H2 – 416/591-2203, Fax: 416/971-9092 – *1
David R. Conway, #601, 130 Bloor St. West, M5S 1N5 – 416/923-4720, Fax: 416/923-1391 – *1
R.H.W. Cook, BCE Place, #4200, 181 Bay St., PO Box 841, M5J 2T3 – 416/368-1041, Fax: 416/865-0896 – *1
Cooper & Cooper, #700, 357 Bay St., M5H 2T7 – 416/362-6459, Fax: 416/363-4130 – *2
Gregory W. Cooper, #1501, 1 Queen St. East., M5C 2W5 – 416/867-1400, Fax: 416/867-1873; Email: gwcooper@rfeasible.com – *2
Harry S. Cooper, #510, 45 Sheppard Ave. East, M1N 5W9 – 416/225-7321, Fax: 416/225-8751 – *1
Kirk J. Cooper, 348 Danforth Ave., M4K 1N8 – 416/778-1200, Fax: 416/778-1291 – *1
Morris Cooper, 99 Yorkville Ave., M5R 3K5 – 416/961-2626, Fax: 416/961-4000 – *1
Cooper, Sandler, West & Skurka, #1900, 439 University Ave., M5G 1Y8 – 416/585-9191, Fax: 416/408-2372 – *3
Stephen E. Cooper, 671 St. Clair Ave. West, M6C 1A8 – 416/651-2641, Fax: 416/651-1295 – *1
Copeland, Campbell, 31 Prince Arthur Ave., M5R 1B2 – 416/964-8126, Fax: 416/960-5456 – *3
Copeland, McKenna, 3638 Lakeshore Blvd. West, M8W 1P1 – 416/252-3351, Fax: 416/252-7519 – *2
J. Copelovici, #707, 40 Sheppard Ave. West, M2N 6K9 – 416/512-2181, Fax: 416/250-6546 – *1
Lori A. Cornwall, #1000, 65 Queen St. West, M5H 2M5 – 416/361-0909, Fax: 416/367-3949 – *1
Willa J. Corse, 78 Shields Ave., M5N 2K4 – 416/488-0257, Fax: 416/488-0591 – *1
F.D. Costa, 1389 Dundas St. West, M6J 1Y4 – 416/534-6357 – *1
Costigan & Costigan, #410, 120 Carlton St., M5A 4K2 – 416/922-8611, Fax: 416/922-1963 – *2
Donald Cosway, #208, 4218 Lawrence Ave. East, M1E 4X9 – 416/281-2502, Fax: 416/281-8957 – *1
D.B. Cousins, #300, 111 Elizabeth St., M5G 1P7 – 416/977-8871 – *1
Coutts, Crane, Ingram, #700, 480 University Ave., M5G 1V2 – 416/977-0956, Fax: 416/977-5331 – *6
Ronald Cowitz, #3, 794 Bathurst St., M5R 3G1 – 416/588-6614, Fax: 416/588-6146 – *1
Cox, Armstrong & Smith, #907, 8 King St. East., M5C 1B5 – 416/861-8695, Fax: 416/861-9074 – *2
Christopher G. Cox, #208, 95 Barber Greene Rd., M3C 3E9 – 416/447-4274, Fax: 416/447-3823 – *1
Peter B. Cozzi, #300, 111 Eglinton Ave. East, M4P 1H4 – 416/440-0046, Fax: 416/440-1682
Crabtree & Ringer, #1600, 8 King St. East, M5C 1B5 – 416/364-4491, Fax: 416/364-0364 – *2
Crawford & Scott, 198 Delaware Ave., M6H 2T3 – 416/531-4229 – *1
T.D. Crawford, #302, 2280A Bloor St. West, M6S 1N9 – 416/760-8118, Fax: 416/760-8175 – *1
F.H. Cremer, #201, 1593 Wilson Ave., M3L 1A5 – 416/244-5575, Fax: 416/247-3844 – *1
Crewe & Marks, #1100, 111 Elizabeth St., M5G 1P7 – 416/506-0423, Fax: 416/506-9173 – *4
Robert C. Cronish, Q.C., #2828, 2 Bloor St. East, M4W 1A8 – 416/961-1088 – *3
L.A. Crosse, #203, 705 Lawrence Ave. West, M6A 1B5 – 416/785-8338, Fax: 416/785-9369 – *1
Paul J. Crowe, #3, 4901A Yonge St.., M2N 5N4 – 416/733-0255, Fax: 416/221-9965 – *1
Crum-Ewing & Poliacik, 56 Sheppard Ave. West, M1N 1M2 – 416/733-9292, Fax: 416/733-9654; Email: poliacik@idirect.com – *2
Sheila Crummey, #300, 100 Front St. East, M5A 1E1 – 416/363-3363, Fax: 416/865-1241 – *1
Patricia A. Cullen, #1704, 55 University Ave., M5J 2H7 – 416/366-7802, Fax: 416/366-3513
G.A.J. Cundari, 1684 Dufferin St., M6H 3M1 – 416/654-9000, Fax: 416/658-7653 – *1
J. Cusmariu, #2, 1272 Dundas St. West, M6J 1X7 – 416/533-1173 – *1
Timothy P. Czajkowski, Plaza 100, #112, 100 Wellesley St. East, M4Y 1H5 – 416/925-9551 – *1
Czuma, Ritter, #502, 481 University Ave., M5G 2E9 – 416/599-5799 – *2
E.L. D'Alimonte, #203, 1111 Albion Rd., M9V 1A9 – 416/741-5373, Fax: 416/740-1154 – *1
D'Andrea, Crupi, 2547 Eglinton Ave. West, M6M 1T2 – 416/656-6500, Fax: 416/656-1420 – *6

Dale & Lessman, Commercial Union Tower, #2000, Toronto-Dominion Centre, PO Box 73, M5K 1E7 – 416/863-1010, Fax: 416/863-1009

H.A. Dale, #412, 120 Carlton St., M5A 4K2 – 416/922-8787, Fax: 416/922-3939 – *1

Daley, Byers, #700, 4 King St. West, M5C 1B6 – 416/864-0246, Fax: 416/864-0192 – *6

Damery & Mamak, 101 Roncesvalles Ave., M6R 2K9 – 416/532-3349 – *2

Timonthy Dang, #910, 65 Queen St. West, M5H 2M5 – 416/368-2851, Fax: 416/360-1056

Daniels & Associates, #601, 4711 Yonge St., M2N 6K8 – 416/226-6602, Fax: 416/226-6388 – *1

Danielson & Fox, #3B, 1911 Eglinton Ave. East, M1L 2L6 – 416/755-3735, Fax: 416/755-3595 – *2

D.A. Danielson, 9 Gloucester St., M4Y 1L8 – 416/972-6966, Fax: 416/972-6885 – *1

Danson, Recht & Freedman, 30 College St., 2nd Fl., M5G 1K2 – 416/929-2200, Fax: 416/929-2192 – *9

Danson, Zucker & Connelly, #500, 70 Bond St., M5B 1X3 – 416/863-9955 – *6

W.G. Danyliw, Q.C., #200, 319 King St. West, M5V 1J5 – 416/591-1588, Fax: 416/977-1282 – *1

Jeffrey Danziger, 969 Gerrard St. East, M4M 1Z4 – 416/778-7062, Fax: 416/778-5442 – *1

David & Co., #1020, 130 Adelaide St. West, M5H 3P5 – 416/366-5900, Fax: 416/366-1799 – *5

David Davies, 2010A Queen St. East, M4L 1J3 – 416/699-5098 – *1

Davies, Ward & Beck, #4400, 1 First Canadian Place, 44th Fl., PO Box 63, M5X 1B1 – 416/863-0900, Fax: 416/863-0871; Email: info@dwb.com; URL: http://www.dwb.com – *102

Davis & Company, #1628, 141 Adelaide St. West, M5H 3L9 – 416/365-6188, Fax: 416/365-7886

Davis & Turk, 1002-347 Bay St., M5H 2R7 – 416/363-1941, Fax: 416/363-4188 – *2

Davis Sullivan, 31 Prince Arthur Ave., M5R 1B2 – 416/921-2500 – *2

Abraham Davis, #804, 55 Eglinton Ave. East, M4P 1G8 – 416/482-1506, Fax: 416/486-8789 – *1

Marie Davison, #102, 327 Eglinton Ave. East, M4P 1L7 – 416/486-9701, Fax: 416/483-1397 – *1

J. David Day, 500 Danforth Ave., M4K 1P6 – 416/461-4888, Fax: 416/461-4296

Day, McDonald, #203, 1941 Weston Rd., M9N 1W8 – 416/247-5327, Fax: 416/247-5328 – *1

Zahava Day, 4901A Yonge St., M2N 5N4 – 416/224-8010, Fax: 416/665-7186; Email: dayzee@wwonline.com – *1

Wayne V.C. De Landro, 1474 Bathurst St., M5P 3G9 – 416/658-6324, Fax: 416/658-0540 – *1

M.B. de Munik, #601, 2161 Yonge St., M4S 3A5 – 416/483-5354, Fax: 416/483-5360 – *1

J.N. De Sommer, #1510, 5140 Yonge St., M2N 6L7 – 416/223-1020, Fax: 416/250-7008

Alp Debreli, 80 Richmond St. West, M5H 2A4 – 416/366-2084

F. Timothy Deeth, #200, 25 Lesmill Rd., M3B 2T3 – 416/443-0080, Fax: 416/443-0279 – *1

Deeth, Williams, Wall, #400, 150 York St., M5H 3S5 – 416/941-9440, Fax: 416/941-9443 – *9

Defensa, Hispana, #204, 2365 Finch Ave. West, M9M 2W8 – 416/742-3351, Fax: 416/742-1693

Christopher DeGeer, #1515, 390 Bay St., M5H 2Y2 – 416/860-7175, Fax: 416/860-1474 – *1

James S. Deitch, #202A, 1415 Bathurst St., M5R 3H8 – 416/539-9803, Fax: 416/535-3065; Email: jdeith@yorku.ca – *1

Robert P. Della Libera, 25 Lesmill Rd., M3B 2T3 – 416/449-4565, Fax: 416/449-2060 – *1

Zorzi DelZotto, #D, 4810 Dufferin St., M3H 5S8 – 416/665-5555, Fax: 416/665-9653 – *14

Jane C. Demaray, 215 Carleton St., M5A 2K9 – 416/975-5167

A.M. Dempsey, Q.C., 533 Queen St. East, M5A 1V1 – 416/364-6755 – *1

David L. Dennis, Q.C., Plaza Tower, Park Plaza Hotel, #300, 4 Avenue Rd., M5R 2E8 – 416/920-8121, Fax: 416/920-5672 – *1

Muneshwar Deopaul, #202, 16 Humber College Blvd., M9V 4E4 – 416/746-7300, Fax: 416/746-3300 – *1

Bonnie E.T. Derby, #201, 14A Hazelton Ave., M5R 2E2 – 416/515-7500, Fax: 416/515-0344 – *1

P.G. Derry, #816, 181 University Ave., M5H 2X7 – 416/868-6483, Fax: 416/364-1697 – *1

Richard G.J. Desrocher, #203, 3425 Dundas St. West, M6S 2S4 – 416/769-5855, Fax: 416/769-9113 – *1

Deverett Law Offices, 250 Sheppard Ave. East, M2N 6M9 – 416/222-5867, Fax: 416/222-7605

Jane H. Devlin, #1017, 111 Richmond St. West, M5H 2G4 – 416/366-3091, Fax: 416/366-0879 – *1

Devry, Smith & Frank, #100, 95 Barber Greene Rd., M3C 3E9 – 416/449-1400, Fax: 416/449-7071; Email: enquiries@devrylaw.on.ca – *8

Dewar & Graham, 4889 Dundas St. West, M9A 1B2 – 416/231-2211, Fax: 416/234-8553 – *2

Iqbal Ismail Dewji, #810, 225 Duncan Mill Rd., M3B 3H9 – 416/449-9600, Fax: 416/449-9348; Email: dewji@myna.com – *1

Philip J. Di Iorio, 821 The Queensway, M8Z 1N6 – 416/253-1223, Fax: 416/253-0186 – *1

Diamond & Diamond, #350, 700 Lawrence Ave. West, M6A 3B4 – 416/256-9490, Fax: 416/256-0100 – *1

Diamond & Tevel, #200, 111 Eglinton Ave. East, M4P 1H4 – 416/482-2666, Fax: 416/482-4165 – *2

DiCecco & Associates, #213, 250 Eglinton Ave. West, M4R 1A7 – 416/484-7470, Fax: 416/484-7471 – *1

DiCenzo & Associates, #200, 212 King St. West, M5H 1K5 – 416/598-2958, Fax: 416/598-3458; Email: dca@weblaw.ca – *2

Irvine P. Dickler, Q.C., #1603, 80 Richmond St. West, M5H 2C2 – 416/364-1656 – *1

Dickson, Sachs, Appell & Beaman, #306, 10 Alcorn Ave., M4V 3A9 – 416/927-0891, Fax: 416/927-0385 – *10

DiGregorio & Associates, 723 Lawrence Ave. West, M6A 1B4 – 416/785-8135, Fax: 416/785-6088 – *2

Dingwall, McLauchlin, #2100, Commercial Union Tower, Toronto-Dominion Centre, PO Box 69, Stn Toronto Dominion, M5K 1E7 – 416/863-1000, Fax: 416/863-1007 – *12

Direnfeld & Nurgitz, #336, 200 Finch Ave. West, M2R 3W4 – 416/226-6060, Fax: 416/226-6900 – *2

H.J. Doan, 18 Wild Briarway, M2J 2L2 – 416/491-2700, Fax: 416/502-9373 – *1

J.J. Doane, 39 Hayden St., 2nd Fl., M4Y 2P2 – 416/968-3454, Fax: 416/968-1211 – *1

T.R. Doidge, Q.C., #404, 170 The Donway West, M3C 2G3 – 416/444-6603, Fax: 416/444-9038 – *1

William B. Donaldson, Q.C., 228 Braymore Blvd., M1B 2G8 – 416/281-2006 – *1

Donnelly & Daigneault, 101 Charles St. East, M4Y 1V2 – 416/920-1553, Fax: 416/920-1554 – *1

Donnelly & Powell, #1509, 180 Dundas St. West, M5G 1Z8 – 416/597-2191 – *2

B.J. Donnelly, #201, 1165A St. Clair Ave. West, M6E 1B2 – 416/653-0311, Fax: 416/653-6653; Email: jbd@netcom.ca; URL: http://www.netcom.ca~jbd.lawtml – *1

John J. Donohue, 75 Lowther Ave., M5R 1C9 – 416/920-0405, Fax: 416/961-9905 – *1

C.H. Dove, #324, 255 Morningside Ave., M1E 3E6 – 416/284-8707, Fax: 416/284-9150 – *1

Downsview Community Legal Services, 520 Wilson Heights Blvd., M3H 2V6 – 416/635-8388, Fax: 416/635-8786

Downtown Legal Services, 84 Queens Park Cres., M5S 2C5 – 416/978-6497, Fax: 416/978-0819; Email: law.dls@utoronto.ca – *1

E.E. Doyle, #1000, 65 Queen St. West, M5H 2M5 – 416/362-4650, Fax: 416/367-3949 – *1

Draimin, Fine Barristers, #300, 30 St. Clair Ave. West, M4V 3A1 – 416/920-4605, Fax: 416/960-0698; Email: draifin@astral.magic.ca – *2

Linda S. Dranoff, #314, 1033 Bay St., M5S 3A5 – 416/925-4500 – *2

Sheldon L. Drebin, Q.C., #1401, 111 Richmond St. West, M5H 2G4 – 416/364-6777, Fax: 416/365-9276 – *1

V.L. Drevnig, Q.C., #1402, 30 St. Clair Ave. West, M4V 3A1 – 416/922-8760, Fax: 416/964-5845; Email: drevnig@interlog.com – *1

J. Blair Drummie, 39 Hayden St., M4Y 2P2 – 416/968-1266, Fax: 416/925-6181 – *1

Todd Ducharme, #2714, 130 Adelaide St. West, M5H 3P5 – 416/868-1825, Fax: 416/868-1990 – *1

Julian O. Dudley, #1000, 65 Queen St. West, M5H 2M5 – 416/867-1442, Fax: 416/367-3949 – *1

P.S. Duffy, Q.C., #305, 180 Dundas St. West, M5G 1Z8 – 416/599-0848 – *1

Mangesh Duggal, #1604, 372 Bay St., M5H 2W9 – 416/363-9421, Fax: 416/363-6950 – *1

Duncan, Fava, Schermbrucker, 56 Temperance St., 8th Fl., M5H 3V5 – 416/861-0313, Fax: 416/214-4699 – *3

John D. Duncan, 160 John St., 4th Fl., M5V 2E5 – 416/593-2513, Fax: 416/593-2514; Email: 699170@ican.net – *1

T.S. Dungey, 46 Fairview Blvd., M4K 1L9 – 416/469-3088 – *1

Hamish Dunlop, 103 Charles St. East, M4Y 1V2 – 416/925-8880 – *1

Brian R. Dunn, 1510-5140 Yonge St., M2N 6L7 – 416/250-5366, Fax: 416/250-0182 – *1

N.L. Durbin, 2530 Jane St., M3L 1S1 – 416/743-2345, Fax: 416/743-0645 – *1

Durno Shea & McMurter, #3, 505 Ellesmere Rd., M1R 4E5 – 416/752-0720, Fax: 416/752-1439 – *3

Reginald J. Dutrizac, #A, 1977 Avenue Rd., M5M 4A3 – 416/483-7409, Fax: 416/483-9782 – *1

Dutton, Brock, MacIntyre & Collier, #1700, 438 University Ave., M5G 2L9 – 416/593-4411, Fax: 416/593-5922 – *16

H.S. Dyment, #910, 390 Bay St., M5H 2Y2 – 416/861-0087 – *1

D.C. Dzwiekowski, 260 Willard Ave., M6S 3R2 – 416/762-7251, Fax: 416/762-7252 – *1

T. Allen Eagleson, 37 Maitland, M4Y 1C8 – 416/924-4116, Fax: 416/924-3005 – *1

East Toronto Community Legal Services, 1320 Gerrard St. East, M4L 3X1 – 416/461-8102, Fax: 416/461-7497 – *4

Bernard L. Eastman, Q.C., 2547 Eglinton Ave. West, M6M 1T2 – 416/656-1420, Fax: 416/766-5957 – *1

Edgar, MacMahon, 2901 Bloor St. West, M8X 1B3 – 416/231-3261 – *2

George Edmonds, Q.C., #2500, 145 King St. West, M5H 3T6 – 416/955-0947, Fax: 416/863-3997 – *1

David V. Eisenkrein, #405, 3601 Victoria Park Ave., M1W 3Y3 – 416/494-4110, Fax: 416/756-3663 – *1

Elgie & Walsh, #502, 145 Adelaide St. West, M5H 3H4 – 416/364-5418, Fax: 416/364-9357 – *1

James Elia, #802, 55 Queen St. East, M5C 1R6 – 416/364-5211 – *1

Elkind, Lipton & Jacobs, #1900, 1 Queen St. East, M5C 2W6 – 416/367-0871, Fax: 416/367-9388; Email: eljtoronto@aol.com – *8

Ellis Clinton, #1005, 5160 Yonge St., M2N 6L9 – 416/250-1300, Fax: 416/250-5097

R.D. Ellwood, 2857 Lakeshore Blvd. West, M6V 1H8 – 416/252-1128, Fax: 416/259-1992 – *1

Anne Empke, Colonia Tower, #1500, 2 St. Clair Ave. East, 15th Fl., M4T 2T5 – 416/923-8748, Fax: 416/927-0305 – *1

Enfield, Adair, Wood & McEwen, #810, 1 Queen St. East, M5C 2W5 – 416/863-1230, Fax: 416/863-1241 – *10

Samuel Eng, #205, 3320 Midland Ave., M1V 5E6 – 416/299-8855, Fax: 416/299-0969

Arnold Epstein, #1, 16 Four Season Pl., M9B 6E5 – 416/621-7070, Fax: 416/620-6535 – *1

Epstein, Cole, #3200, 401 Bay St., PO Box 52, M5H 2Y4 – 416/862-9888, Fax: 416/862-2142 – *11

* indicates number of lawyers in law firm.

Norman Epstein, #417, 45 Sheppard Ave. East, M2N 5W9 – 416/225-5577, Fax: 416/225-2504 – *1
Harry Erlich, #475, 700 Lawrence Ave. West, M6A 3B4 – 416/256-1555, Fax: 416/256-0918 – *1
Thora H. Espinet, 3459 Sheppard Ave. East, M1T 3K5 – 416/321-2631, Fax: 416/292-4508 – *1
John Paul Evans, 926 The East Mall, M9B 6K1 – 416/620-7300, Fax: 416/620-1679 – *1
Sydney Ezrin, 135 Torresdale Ave., M2R 3K2 – 416/739-6568, Fax: 416/739-6584 – *1
Faivish, Jerry, #203, 120 Carlton St., M5A 4K2 – 416/924-1090, Fax: 416/924-5310
Farano, Green, #1100, 22 St. Clair Ave. East, M4T 2Z6 – 416/961-2344, Fax: 416/961-0585; Email: fargreen@fargreen.com; URL: http://www.inforamp.net/~goldfarb/ – *11
Farb, Warren, Bergman, 2313A Bloor St. West, M6S 1P1 – 416/763-4183, Fax: 416/763-1310; Email: farb.warren@sympatico.ca – *3
V. Fargnoli, 1 First Canadian Place, #5900, PO Box 24 Stn First Canadian Place, M5X 1K2 – 416/363-3658, Fax: 416/367-3316 – *1
Joseph S. Farkas, 3089 Bathurst St., M6A 2A4 – 416/784-9550, Fax: 416/784-9552 – *1
Fasken Campbell Godfrey, #3600, 66 Wellington St. West, M5K 1N6 – 416/366-8381, Fax: 416/364-7813; Email: firstname_lastname@fasken.com; URL: http://www.fasken.com/ – *203
Francis X. Fay, Q.C., #301, 215 Victoria St., M5B 1T9 – 416/366-6510 – *1
Ricardo G. Federico, Carlton on the Park, #204, 120 Carlton St., M5A 4K2 – 416/928-1458, Fax: 416/944-8330 – *1
W.B. Fedunchak, #5, 885 Progress Ave., M1H 3G3 – 416/431-1122, Fax: 416/431-1133 – *1
Fefergrad, Dizgun, #2407, 401 Bay St., PO Box 35, M5H 2Y4 – 416/366-7686, Fax: 416/366-0134 – *5
Steven M. Fehrle, 350 Bay St., 9th Fl., M5H 2S6 – 416/777-2077, Fax: 416/367-4098; Email: fehrle@followme.com – *1
R. Eric Feige, #3300, 130 Adelaide St. West, M5H 3P5 – 416/366-8833, Fax: 416/366-3992 – *3
Leonard Feigman, #200, 70 Bond St., M5B 1X3 – 416/363-2233 – *1
Fejer & Associates, #2355, 2 First Canadian Place, M5X 1B1 – 416/364-7710, Fax: 416/364-1828 – *1
Howard J. Feldman, #1100, 372 Bay St., M5H 2W9 – 416/863-9333, Fax: 416/863-6080 – *2
Jodi L. Feldman, #303, 21 St. Clair Ave. East, M4T 1L9 – 416/922-3233, Fax: 416/922-3234
Lawrence T. Feldman, #103, 1000 Finch Ave. West, M3J 2V5 – 416/667-9796, Fax: 416/667-8048 – *1
Stephen Feldman, #415, 4580 Dufferin St., M3H 5Y2 – 416/667-0980, Fax: 416/667-0765 – *1
Avrum Fenson, c/o Legislative Research Service, Queen's Park, M7A 1A9 – 416/325-3675, Fax: 416/325-3696 – *4
Alan Fenster, 258 Wilson Ave., M3H 1S6 – 416/631-6601, Fax: 416/631-6828 – *1
Fernandes, Hearn, Theall, #601, 335 Bay St., M5H 2R3 – 416/362-2600, Fax: 416/203-9444 – *1
Field, Turner, #1000, 439 University Ave., M5G 1Y8 – 416/595-1111, Fax: 416/595-7312 – *3
Gerald Fields, #900, 150 York St., M5H 3S5 – 416/862-8000, Fax: 416/862-8001 – *1
Wm. Fienberg, Q.C., 175 Keewatin Ave., M4P 2A3 – 416/486-5211, Fax: 416/486-0074 – *1
Filion, Wakely & Thorup, #2601, 150 King St. West, M5H 4B6 – 416/408-3221, Fax: 416/408-4814; Email: toronto@filion.on.ca; URL: http://www.filion.on.ca – *21
Fine & Deo, #220, 124 Eglinton Ave. West, M4R 2G8 – 416/489-6600, Fax: 416/489-0036 – *1
Andrew Fine, 2768 Dufferin St., M6B 3R7 – 416/785-9499 – *1
Daniel M. Fine, #506, 4950 Yonge St., M2N 6K1 – 416/733-8815, Fax: 416/733-3758 – *1
Richard Fink, 466 Dupont St.., M5R 1W6 – 416/537-0108, Fax: 416/537-1604; Email: macneill@interlog.com – *2
Finkelstein, Harvey, Q.C., #3, 4901A Yonge St., M2N 5N4 – 416/221-8890, Fax: 416/221-9965 – *1
Fireman & Regan, 181 University Ave., M5H 3M7 – 416/601-1000, Fax: 416/601-9255; Email: mailbox@firemanregan.on.ca – *19
J.Y. Fisch, 394 College St., 2nd Fl., M5T 1S7 – 416/920-6312, Fax: 416/920-1780 – *1
Steven M. Fishbayn, #415, 4580 Dufferin St., M3H 5Y2 – 416/677-0980, Fax: 416/667-0765 – *1
Barry B. Fisher, #2000, 393 University Ave., M5G 1E6 – 416/585-2330, Fax: 416/585-2105 – *1
R.A. Fisher, #300, 95 Barber Greene Rd., M3C 3E9 – 416/449-6890, Fax: 416/449-6482 – *1
Issie Fishman, 5987 Bathurst St., M2R 1Z3 – 416/222-6526, Fax: 416/222-6663 – *1
Donald R. Fiske & Associates, West Tower, Mutual Group Centre, #760, 3300 Bloor St. West, M8X 2X2 – 416/234-2177, Fax: 416/234-9039 – *1
Jean A. Fitzgerald, #3, 123 John St., M5V 2E2 – 416/597-9707, Fax: 416/597-9750; Email: jean@planeteer.com – *1
John Fitzmaurice, 317 Grace St., M6G 3A7 – 416/533-5053, Fax: 416/533-5174 – *1
Richard G. Fitzsimmons, #1510, 5140 Yonge St., M2N 6L7 – 416/224-8044, Fax: 416/250-7008; Email: fitzlaw@sympatico.ca – *1
Flaccavento & Kreger, 2181 Danforth Ave., M4C 1K4 – 416/698-8000, Fax: 416/698-8015 – *2
Flaherty Dow Elliott, #1901, 120 Adelaide St. West, M5H 1T1 – 416/368-0231, Fax: 416/368-9229
Fleischer & Kochberg, 4 Finch Ave. West, M2N 6L1 – 416/223-8102, Fax: 416/225-5992; Email: pkochberg@compuserve.com – *2
Fleming, White, Burgess, Brown, #605, 160 Bloor St. East, M4W 1B9 – 416/961-2868, Fax: 416/961-2964 – *6
Flemingdon Community Legal Services, #350, 10 Gateway Blvd., M3C 3A1 – 416/424-1965, Fax: 416/424-4204
Fleury, Comery, #104, 215 Morrish Rd., M1C 1E9 – 416/282-5754, Fax: 416/282-9906 – *5
A.M. Flisfeder, 785 Carlaw Ave., M4K 3L1 – 416/469-0375, Fax: 416/469-0375 – *1
Ronald Flom, #712, 2345 Yonge St., M4P 2E5 – 416/482-2777, Fax: 416/482-2599 – *1
Floras & Murray, #801, 55 Queen St. West, M5C 1R6 – 416/869-3151, Fax: 416/869-1762 – *3
Fogelman Herschel, #303, 21 St. Clair Ave. East, M4T 1L9 – 416/929-7739, Fax: 416/922-3234
Fogler, Rubinoff, #4400, 77 King St. West, PO Box 95, M5K 1G8 – 416/864-9700, Fax: 416/941-8852 – *46
Peter Folkins, 10 Foxbar Rd., M4V 2G6 – 416/944-0997, Fax: 416/924-9541 – *1
William J. Fong, #305, 155 Marlee Ave., M6B 4B5 – 416/783-3534 – *1
Jamie A. Ford, 372 Bay St., M5H 2W9 – 416/360-1770 – *1
Michael Forrester & Associates, 171 Ravel Rd., M2H 1T1 – 416/495-1411, Fax: 416/495-9128 – *1
Jeffrey M. Fortinsky, #358, 1111 Finch Ave. West, M3J 2E5 – 416/665-5688, Fax: 416/741-1765 – *1
R. Brian Foster Q.C., #218, 111 Richmond St. West, M5H 2G4 – 416/368-3363, Fax: 416/368-4532; Email: bfoster@interlog.com
Barry Fox, 9 Gloucester St., M4Y 1L8 – 416/972-6966, Fax: 416/972-6885 – *1
Walter Fox, #312, 100 Richmond St. West, M5H 3K6 – 416/363-9238, Fax: 416/363-9230 – *1
David A. Fram, #901, 701 Evans Ave., M9C 1A3 – 416/622-2665, Fax: 416/622-8952; Email: dfram@interlog.com – *2
David Franklin, #700, 21 Dundas Sq., M5B 1B8 – 416/365-1971, Fax: 416/365-1824 – *1
Fraser & Beatty, One First Canadian Place, 100 King St. West, PO Box 100, M5X 1B2 – 416/863-4511, Fax: 416/863-4592; Email: webmaster@fraserbeatty.ca; URL: http://www.fraserbeatty.ca – *190
Fraser & Beatty, Madison Centre, #2300, 4950 Yonge St., M2N 6K1 – 416/733-3300, Fax: 416/221-5254; URL: http://www.fraserbeatty.ca – *2
Fraser, Simms and Reid, 1944 Weston Rd., M9N 1W2 – 416/241-0111 – *1
Anne E. Freed, 10 King St. East, 14th Fl., M5C 1C3 – 416/368-7800, Fax: 416/364-3818 – *1
Harvey Freedman, #100, 79 Shuter St., M5B 1B3 – 416/363-1737, Fax: 416/861-9919 – *3
J.P. Freedman, #313, 1415 Lawrence Ave. West, M6L 1A9 – 416/248-6231, Fax: 416/241-0080 – *1
L.S. Freedman, 1577 Bloor St. West, M6P 1A6 – 416/536-1159, Fax: 416/536-3618 – *1
N.J. Freedman, Q.C., #1906, 20 Queen St. West, M5H 3R3 – 416/979-7767, Fax: 416/979-7772
Freeman & Reim, #2310, 4950 Yonge St., M2N 6K1 – 416/733-3400, Fax: 416/733-9810 – *2
C.H. Freeman, 392 Dundas St. East, M5A 2A5 – 416/944-8544, Fax: 416/944-8083 – *1
S.V. Freeman, 111 Bermondsey Rd., M4A 2T7 – 416/288-1919 – *1
Andrew Frei, 181 University Ave., M5H 3M7 – 416/601-6838, Fax: 416/601-9107; Email: afrei@interlog.com – *1
Allan Friedland, #212, 3555 Don Mills Rd., M2H 3N3 – 416/498-1323, Fax: 416/498-8562 – *1
J. Friedman, Q.C., 1 First Canadian Place, #6240, PO Box 169, Stn First Canadian Place, M5X 1C7 – 416/364-5451, Fax: 416/364-9764 – *1
David G. Friend, Q.C., #202, 3459 Sheppard Ave. East, M1T 3K5 – 416/754-0333, Fax: 416/292-0473 – *1
C. Sydney Jr. Frost, Q.C., 50 Bayview Wood, M4N 1R7 – 416/489-5844 – *1
Damien R. Frost, 81 Wellesley St. East, M4Y 1H6 – 416/923-1900, Fax: 416/960-1498 – *1
Harry Frymer, #320, 100 Richmond St. West, M5H 3K6 – 416/869-1073, Fax: 416/869-1840 – *4
Fuerst Fay, 406 King St. East, M5A 1L4 – 416/466-5444, Fax: 416/466-5688
Derrick Fulton, 390 Bay St., M5H 2Y2 – 416/594-3338, Fax: 416/860-1474 – *1
Greta M. Fung, #2320, 2025 Sheppard Ave. East, M2J 1V6 – 416/494-8383 – *1
A.L. Furguiele, #202, 1013 Wilson Ave., M3K 1G1 – 416/630-7900, Fax: 416/630-8671 – *1
Furqan Ahmed Legal Services, 100 McLevin Ave., M1B 2V5 – 416/754-0443, Fax: 416/754-1142
Futerman & Futerman, #1500, 2 St. Clair Ave. East, M4T 2R1 – 416/925-4100, Fax: 416/323-9132 – *5
F.A. Gabriel, #203, 425 University Ave., M5G 1T6 – 416/593-6621, Fax: 416/599-8075 – *1
Gaertner & Math, #400, 144 Front St. West, M5J 2L7 – 416/599-7761, Fax: 416/977-8587 – *4
J. Mark Gahan, #303, 489 College St., M6G 1A5 – 416/927-7253, Fax: 416/972-1992 – *1
Rocco Galati, 372 Bay St., M5H 2W9 – 416/864-1382 – *1
Gary M. Gampel, #203, 345 Wilson Ave., M3H 5W1 – 416/398-0104, Fax: 416/398-0106
F.H. Ganz, Q.C., #2015, 120 Adelaide St. West, M5H 1T1 – 416/364-9212, 364-7717, Fax: 416/364-4813 – *2
Gardiner, Blumberg, #1202, 390 Bay St., M5H 2Y2 – 416/361-1982, Fax: 416/363-8451; Email: info@blumberg-law.com; URL: http://www.blumberg-law.com – *12
Gardiner, Roberts, #3100, 40 King St. West, PO Box 105, M5H 3Y2 – 416/865-6600, Fax: 416/865-6636; Email: colbert@gardiner-roberts.on.ca – *47
John H. Gardner, Q.C., #801, 67 Yonge St., M5E 1J8 – 416/366-7791, Fax: 416/366-7110 – *1
Susan W. Garfin, #1200, 595 Bay St., M5G 2C2 – 416/599-9933, Fax: 416/599-5497
Garfin, Zeidenberg, CenterPoint Mall, Entrance #1, 6400 Yonge St., M2M 3X4 – 416/512-8000, Fax: 416/512-9992 – *4

Garfinkle, Biderman, One Financial Place, #1401, 1 Adelaide St. East, M5C 2V9 – 416/869-1234, Fax: 416/869-0547 – *11

Jacqueline Garrity, 45 Saint Nicholas St., M4Y 1W6 – 416/925-6443, Fax: 416/925-8122 – *1

Garvey, Ferriss, South Tower, Box: 3100, Royal Bank Plaza, PO Box 56, M5J 2J2 – 416/865-0222, Fax: 416/865-0410 – *10

Gass & Associates, #PH, 121 Richmond St. West, M5H 2K1 – 416/365-9878 – *2

Cheryl Gaster, #600, 20 Richmond St. East, M5C 2R9 – 416/360-0463 – *1

Gauthier & Associates, Canada Trust Tower, BCE Place, #4800, 161 Bay St., PO Box 528, M5J 2S1 – 416/868-4848, Fax: 416/868-4840 – *5

Leon Gavendo, Law Chambers, University Centre, #2000, 393 Bay St., M5G 1E6 – *1

L.B. Geffen, #205, 2907 Kennedy Rd., M1V 1S8 – 416/292-6688, Fax: 416/292-6649 – *1

Geller & Minster, 2 Keewatin Ave., M4P 1Z8 – 416/480-2200, Fax: 416/480-2693 – *2

J.W. Gemmell, Q.C., #1605, 8 King St. East, M5C 1B5 – 416/364-4129 – *1

Genest Murray DesBrisay Lamek, #700, 130 Adelaide St. West, M5H 4C1 – 416/368-8600, Fax: 416/360-2625 – *39

Basil L. Georgieff, 3543 St. Clair Ave. East, M1K 1L6 – 416/267-1452, Fax: 416/267-1452 – *1

Seymour E. German, #104, 49 St. Clair Ave. West, M4V 1K6 – 416/920-7800, Fax: 416/920-4580 – *1

Stanley Gershman, 556 Atlas Ave., M6C 3R6 – 416/781-2931 – *1

Lorne Gershuny, 1577 Bloor St. West, M6P 1A6 – 416/539-0989, Fax: 416/536-3618 – *1

A.C. Gerstl, #612, 330 Bay St., M5H 2S8 – 416/214-1165, Fax: 416/214-0870 – *1

J.M.P. Ghalioungui, 1033 Bay St., M5S 3A5 – 416/347-7475 – *1

Stuart Ghan, 1035 McNicoll Ave., M1W 3W6 – 416/502-8845, Fax: 416/497-1999 – *1

Lorne Giacomelli, #204, 40 Eglinton Ave. East, M4P 3A2 – 416/484-9115, Fax: 416/484-0161 – *1

Gilbert & Yallen, 204 Saint George St., 3rd Fl., M5R 2N5 – 416/927-0001, Fax: 416/927-0930 – *2

Jack A. Gilbert, Q.C., #703, 123 Edward St., M5G 1E2 – 416/593-4093, Fax: 416/593-0656 – *1

Gilbert, Wright & Kirby, #1800, 155 University Ave., M5H 3B7 – 416/363-3100, Fax: 416/363-1379 – *7

Gilbertson, Davis, Herceg, Emerson, McCaskill, #1002, 111 Richmond St. West, M5H 2G4 – 416/366-8404, Fax: 416/366-6419 – *8

John D. Gilfillan, Q.C., #1200, 8 King St. East, M5C 1B5 – 416/861-1881, Fax: 416/364-1282 – *1

Leslie M. Giroday, 190 Sixth St., M8V 3A5 – 416/255-1063, Fax: 416/251-8699 – *1

Robert M. Girvan, #1000, 65 Queen St. West, M5H 2M5 – 416/368-4960, Fax: 416/367-3949

Roseanne M Giulietti, 212 King St. West, M5H 1K5 – 416/593-6100, Fax: 416/971-9391 – *1

Glaholt & Associates, #800, 141 Adelaide St. West, M5H 3L5 – 416/368-8280, Fax: 416/368-3467

Glass & Friedland, #2108, 2 Bloor St. West, M4W 3E2 – 416/968-3995, Fax: 416/968-6899 – *3

Alan A. Glass, #415, 4580 Dufferin St., M3H 5Y2 – 416/667-0980, Fax: 416/667-0765 – *1

Donna M. Glassman, #505, 4100 Bathurst St., M3H 3P2 – 416/398-8738, Fax: 416/532-5089 – *1

Jeffrey D. Glatt, 506 Russell Hill Rd., M5P 2S9 – 416/484-7498, Fax: 416/484-8169 – *1

Louis Glatt, 2354 Danforth Ave., M4C 1K7 – 416/422-2107, Fax: 416/422-2606 – *1

Saul I. Glober, #2600, 250 Yonge St., M5B 2M6 – 416/979-2211, Fax: 416/979-1234 – *1

Andrew G.E. Goddard, #PH, 121 Richmond St. West, M5H 2K1 – 416/368-1211

Godfrey & Corcoran, #702, 55 Queen St. East, M5C 1R6 – 416/363-0484, Fax: 416/363-0485 – *1

Alan D. Gold, 29 Tanbark Cr., M3V 1N7 – 416/445-1328 – *1

Peter M. Gold, 39A Hazelton Ave., M5R 2E3 – 416/925-3101, Fax: 416/925-8118 – *1

Golden, Green & Chercover, #200, 101 Yorkville Ave., M5R 1C1 – 416/968-3333, Fax: 416/968-0325 – *8

Sydney L. Goldenberg, #2600, 250 Yonge St., M5B 2M6 – 416/591-6610, Fax: 416/979-1234 – *1

Henry Goldentuler, #220, 1018 Finch Ave. West, M3J 2E1 – 416/663-9309, Fax: 416/650-1782 – *1

H.A. Goldgut, #700, 2 St. Clair Ave. East, M4T 2T5 – 416/968-6400, Fax: 416/968-6985 – *1

Goldhar & Nemoy, #212, 120 Carlton St., M5A 2K1 – 416/928-1488, Fax: 416/924-7166 – *2

H.A. Goldkind, #320, 100 Richmond St. West, M5H 3K6 – 416/366-5280 – *1

Goldman Sloan Nash & Haber, #2100, 181 University Ave., M5H 3M7 – 416/862-8200, Fax: 416/862-9953 – *1

Gordon Goldman, #320, 100 Richmond St. West, M5H 3K6 – 416/367-2388, Fax: 416/869-1840

Jeffrey W. Goldman, #600, 3101 Bathurst St., M6A 2A6 – 416/787-1818, Fax: 416/787-1810 – *1

R.M. Goldman, #2412, 401 Bay St., M5H 2Y4 – 416/860-9900, Fax: 416/364-2308; Email: rmg@counsel2.com – *1

Goldman, Spring, Schwartz & Kichler, #700, 40 Sheppard Ave. West, M2N 6K9 – 416/225-9400, Fax: 416/225-4805 – *7

Cheryl S. Goldsmith, #1314, 181 University Ave., M5H 3M7 – 416/368-5626, Fax: 416/861-0706

Goldstein & Grubner, #212, 3459 Sheppard Ave. East, M1T 3K5 – 416/292-0414, Fax: 416/292-4508 – *2

Goldstein & Rosen, 1648 Victoria Park Ave., M1R 1P7 – 416/757-4156 – *2

H.S. Goldstein, #202, 4889 Yonge St., M1N 5N4 – 416/221-3494, Fax: 416/221-7155 – *1

L.C. Goldstein, #410, 212 King St. West, M5H 1K5 – 416/599-3000, Fax: 416/599-5582 – *1

Thomas Goldstein, #601, 2161 Yonge St., M4S 3A6 – 416/488-2100, Fax: 416/488-2794 – *1

Harry Golish, #403, 2828 Bathurst St., M6B 3A7 – 416/789-2438, Fax: 416/789-2438 – *1

Paul Gollom, #804, 55 Eglinton Ave. East, M4P 1G8 – 416/932-9300, Fax: 416/483-2737; Email: pgollom@sprynet.com – *1

Goodman & Carr, #2300, 200 King St. West, M5H 3W5 – 416/595-2300, Fax: 416/595-0567; Email: mail@goodmancarr.com; URL: http://www.goodmancarr.com – *78

Goodman Phillips & Vineberg, #2400, 250 Yonge St., M5B 2M6 – 416/979-2211, Fax: 416/979-1234 – *123

Henry G. Goodman, #510, 25 Imperial St., M5P 1B9 – 416/488-3303, Fax: 416/488-7085 – *1

I. Goodman, #605, 111 Peter St., M5V 2H1 – 416/598-0246, Fax: 416/598-2815 – *1

Nancy Goodman, #1130, 20 Dundas St. West, Stn 180, M5G 2G8 – 416/977-8045, Fax: 416/591-7333 – *1

Stanley Goodman, Q.C., #1800, 4950 Yonge St., M1N 6K1 – 416/224-0200, Fax: 416/224-0758 – *1

John L.Z. Gora, Penthouse, 481 University Ave., M5G 2E9 – 416/977-6439 – *1

Barbara J. Gordon, #210, 12 Birch Ave., M4V 1C8 – 416/928-0856, Fax: 416/928-0577 – *1

S.L. Gore, 10 Silver Birch Ave., M4E 3K9 – 416/690-2160 – *1

William A. Gorewich, 49 Saint Nicholas St., M4Y 1W6 – 416/927-1109, Fax: 416/924-5443 – *1

Mark Gorlick, 699 Coxwell Ave., M4C 3C1 – 416/778-7788, Fax: 416/778-1876 – *1

J.D. Gorrell, Q.C., 533 Queen St. East, M5A 1V1 – 416/361-1411 – *1

T.G. Gorrie, Q.C., #1100, 27 Queen St. East, M5C 2M6 – 416/368-2928, Fax: 416/368-2955 – *1

Nathan Gotlieb, Madison Centre, #1800, 4950 Yonge St., M2N 6K1 – 416/224-0200, Fax: 416/224-0758 – *1

Gottlieb & Pearson, #1800, 4950 Yonge St., M2N 6K1 – 416/250-1550, Fax: 416/250-7889 – *3

Gottlieb, Connie, #200, 70 Bond St., M5B 1X3 – 416/214-0650, Fax: 416/365-7765

G.L. Gottlieb, Q.C., #309, 600 Bay St., M5G 1M6 – 416/977-3835 – *1

Gottlieb, Hoffman & Kumer, 1214 Lawrence Ave. West, M6A 1E3 – 416/789-0584 – *3

Max A. Gould, #200, 101 Yorkville Ave., M5R 1C1 – 416/964-0290, Fax: 416/964-7102 – *1

Michael J. Gould, #308, 801 York Mills Rd., M3B 1X7 – 416/510-3030, Fax: 416/510-3034 – *1

Gowlings, #4900, Commerce Court West, PO Box 438, Stn Commerce Court, M5L 1J3 – 416/862-7525, Fax: 416/862-7661; URL: http://www.gowlings.com/toronto.htm – *158

Graci & Associates, 350 Bay St., 9th Fl., M5H 2S6 – 416/360-1991, Fax: 416/367-4098 – *1

D.J. Grant, #205, 250 Sheppard Ave. East, M2N 6M9 – 416/225-1161, Fax: 416/225-1243 – *1

Grasset, Fleisher, Toronto-Dominion Bank Tower, #5104, Toronto-Dominion Centre, PO Box 317, Stn TD Centre, M5K 1K2 – 416/214-5651, Fax: 416/214-5655; Email: gflaw@netcom.ca – *4

Jeffrey Gray, #200, 4211 Yonge St., M2P 2A9 – 416/512-1694, Fax: 416/221-8372 – *1

B. Michael Grayson, Q.C., #Penthouse, 121 Richmond St. West, M5H 2K1 – 416/363-1022 – *1

Green & Spiegel, #2200, 121 King St. West, PO Box 114, M5H 3T9 – 416/862-7880, Fax: 416/862-1698 – *8

C. Rodney Green, Q.C., #202, 1053 McNicoll Ave., M1W 3W5 – 416/498-4131, Fax: 416/498-1203 – *9

D.J. Green, 399 Spadina Ave., M5T 2G6 – 416/979-2333, Fax: 416/597-8966 – *1

Elliott Green, Q.C., #1404, 2 Carlton St., M5B 1J3 – 416/977-5575, Fax: 416/977-5576 – *1

Michael S. Green, 1415 Bathurst St., M5R 3H8 – 416/538-2737 – *1

Norman Green, Q.C., 302 Richview Ave., M5P 3G5 – 416/487-7191 – *1

Paul J. Green, #1600, 8 King St. East, M5C 1B5 – 416/860-1723 – *1

Pauline Green, 978 Kingston Rd., M4E 1S9 – 416/699-3826 – *1

Weldon F. Green, Q.C., #1601, 65 Queen St. West, M5H 2M5 – 416/364-4465, Fax: 416/364-3657 – *1

Donald M. Greenbaum, Q.C., 258 Wilson Ave., M3H 1S6 – 416/631-7504, Fax: 416/631-9895 – *1

Greenberg, Jack, #201, 40 Holly St., M4S 3C3 – 416/485-8833, Fax: 416/485-3246 – *3

Morton Greenglass Q.C., Royal Trust Tower, #4400, 77 King St. West, M5K 1G8 – 416/214-1000, Fax: 416/941-8852

Greening & Associate, 1436 Danforth Ave., M4J 1N4 – 416/462-9010, Fax: 416/462-3858 – *2

David B. Greenspan, Q.C., 1201, 131 Bloor St. West, M5S 1S3

Greenspan, Humphrey, #2714, 130 Adelaide St. West, M5H 3P5 – 416/868-1755, Fax: 416/868-1990 – *4

Greenspan, Rosenberg & Buhr, Simpson Tower, #3200, 401 Bay St., M5H 1T7 – 416/366-3961, Fax: 416/366-7994 – *3

Rose Greenstein, #101, 861 College St., M6H 1A1 – 416/533-6044, Fax: 416/532-9845 – *1

E.J. Gresik, 101 Scollard St., M5R 1G4 – 416/924-0781, Fax: 416/960-9650 – *1

John W. Grice, 350 Bay St., 9th Fl., M5H 2S6 – 416/360-4160, Fax: 416/367-4098 – *1

Griffiths & Powell, #523, 524, 1315 Lawrence Ave. East, M3A 3R3 – 416/441-1253, Fax: 416/441-9757 – *3

Saul Grillo, 1463 Wilson Ave., M3M 1J5 – 416/614-6000, Fax: 416/614-6082 – *1

C. Grimanis, 904 Logan Ave., M4K 3E4 – 416/469-1176, Fax: 416/469-4252 – *1

Gerald Gringorten, #424, 100 Richmond St. West, M5H 3K6 – 416/365-7376, Fax: 416/365-1474

Groll & Groll, 112 St. Clair Ave. West, M4V 2Y3 – 416/968-1177, Fax: 416/968-1178 – *2

* indicates number of lawyers in law firm.

Gropper, Greenwood, #500, 4580 Dufferin St., M3H 5Z1 – 416/665-9111, Fax: 416/665-4320; Email: greengro@compuserve.com

James J. Grosberg, #415, 4580 Dufferin St., M3H 5Y2 – 416/667-0980, Fax: 416/667-0765 – *1

Grosman, Grosman & Gale, #1410, 1 Queen St. East, PO Box 61, M5C 2W5 – 416/364-9599, Fax: 416/364-2490; Email: lawyers@grosman.com; URL: http://www.grosman.com – *6

A.H. Gross, #101, 861 College St., M6H 1A1 – 416/533-6044, Fax: 416/532-9845 – *1

Grubner, Krauss, #1540, 5140 Yonge St., M2N 6L7 – 416/222-4446, Fax: 416/222-9788 – *5

Isak Grushka, #7, 1267A St. Clair Ave. West, M6E 1B8 – 416/656-2631, Fax: 416/656-8328 – *1

Guberman, Garson, #1920, 130 Adelaide St. West, M5H 3P5 – 416/363-1234, Fax: 416/363-8760; Email: guberman@passport.ca; URL: http://www.gubermangarson.com – *4

Anand Gucharan, #901, 2 Carlton St., M5B 1J3 – 416/593-5252, Fax: 416/593-4511

Gulycz, Galati, #112, 82 Lombard St., M5C 2S8 – 416/363-7979, Fax: 416/363-7974

J.M. Guoba, 1 St. Clair Ave. East, M4T 2V7 – 416/923-7002, Fax: 416/923-7590 – *1

Albert Gurland, #212, 1210 Sheppard Ave. East, PO Box 41, M2K 1E3 – 416/490-0414, Fax: 416/492-1926 – *1

Gutstein Mandel, #2015, 120 Adelaide St. West, M5H 1T1 – 416/364-7717, Fax: 416/364-4813 – *2

Peter F. Haber, Carlton on the Park, #302, 120 Carlton St., M5A 4K3 – 416/961-0265, Fax: 416/961-1860; Toll Free: 1-888-841-1104; Email: haberllbca@aol.com – *1

L. Hadbavny, #404, 1415 Lawrence Ave. West, M6L 1A9 – 416/247-5357, Fax: 416/247-4307 – *1

Michael P. Haddad, 208 Carlton St., M5A 2L1 – 416/926-8151, Fax: 416/927-9005; Email: mhaddad@istar.ca – *1

Haffey, Sherwood, Hunt, #2330, 120 Adelaide St. West, M5H 3P5 – 416/366-7976, Fax: 416/366-0580; Email: jthunt@eagle.ca – *3

Hahn & Maian, 664 Mount Pleasant Rd., M4S 2N3 – 416/486-9445, Fax: 416/486-1174; Email: johnhahn@idirect.com – *2

K.A. Hahn, #13, 5230 Dundas St. West, M9B 1A8 – 416/231-3353 – *1

Miles M. Halberstadt, Q.C., #412, 120 Carlton St., M5A 4K2 – 416/944-0441, Fax: 416/922-3939 – *1

Sheila K. Halladay, 2126 1/2 Queen St. East, M4E 1E3 – 416/694-5609, Fax: 416/694-4908 – *1

Halman & Halman, #300, 365 Bay St., M5H 2V1 – 416/363-8481, Fax: 416/363-8536 – *2

Munyonzwe Hamalengwa, #900, 2 Sheppard Ave. East, M2N 5Y7 – 416/222-8111, Fax: 416/222-7518

V.W. Hamara, 20 Madison Ave., 2nd Fl., M5R 2S1 – 416/961-5010, Fax: 416/963-8387 – *1

Patricia A. Hamilton, #201, 1969 Weston Rd., PO Box 300, Stn A, M9N 1W8 – 416/235-0105, Fax: 416/235-0750 – *1

Hans & Hans, 10 Foxbar Rd., M4V 2G6 – 416/960-5445, Fax: 416/924-7541 – *2

Haque & Associates, #507, 80 Richmond St. West, M5H 2A4 – 416/366-2337, Fax: 416/366-0936 – *1

Zakaul Haque, #205, 1058A Albion Rd., M9V 1A7 – 416/743-6302, Fax: 416/743-4783 – *1

George M. Harasymowycz, 2311A Bloor St. West, M6S 1P1 – 416/766-2472, Fax: 416/766-3297 – *1

Aaron B. Harnett, 75 Lowther Ave., M5R 1C9 – 416/960-3676, Fax: 416/961-9905 – *1

M.G. Harnum, 1887A Lawrence Ave. East, M1R 2Y3 – 416/752-4994, Fax: 416/752-5640 – *1

Murray P. Harrington, #215, 3447 Kennedy Rd., M1V 3S1 – 416/321-8621, Fax: 416/321-8622 – *1

Harris & Harris, #400, 190 Atwell Dr., M9W 6H8 – 416/798-2722, Fax: 416/798-2715 – *10

Harris & Henderson, #Penthouse, 121 Richmond St. West, M5H 2K1 – 416/862-1661 – *1

David E. Harris, 439 University Ave., M5G 1Y8 – 416/585-9329, Fax: 416/408-2372; Email: delih@in-foramp.net – *1

Gerald Harris, 4122 Bathurst St., M3H 3P2 – 416/638-7277 – *1

W.A. Harrison, #1102, 2 Sheppard Avenue East, M2N 5Y7 – 416/222-7668, Fax: 416/222-9253 – *1

Al Hart, 45 Saint Nicholas St., M4Y 1W6 – 416/925-6443, Fax: 416/925-8122 – *1

Robert S. Hart, Q.C., #1250, 180 Dundas St. West, M5G 1Z8 – 416/593-1161, Fax: 416/977-0717

Paul E. Harte, 119 John St., M5V 2E2 – 416/595-1391, Fax: 416/595-0717; Toll Free: 1-800-966-0339; Email: pharte@litigate.com; URL: http://www.hartelaw.com – *1

S.E. Hartley, 1180 Weston Rd., M6M 4P4 – 416/243-0444 – *1

Ruth Hartman, c/o Workers Compensation Appeals Tribunal, 505 University Ave., M5G 1X4 – 416/531-9714 – *1

Klaus Anton Hartmann, 391 Willowdale Ave., M2N 5A8 – 416/590-0311, Fax: 416/590-0312 – *1

Hartrick & Associates, 116-118 Parliament St., M5A 2Y9 – 416/366-8755, Fax: 416/366-5158 – *5

Jane Harvey Associates, #187, 300 Borough Dr., M1P 4P5 – 416/296-1607, Fax: 416/296-1757 – *1

W.K. Hastings, 60 Sheldrake Blvd., M4P 2B3 – 416/483-5973 – *1

Gabrielle Hauser, 937 Broadview Ave., M4K 2R3 – 416/696-8808, Fax: 416/696-8579 – *1

Frederick Simon Hawa, #1900, 1 Queen St. East, M5C 2W6 – 416/362-2317, Fax: 416/367-9388 – *1

Richard Hayles, 6 Baltic Ave., M4J 1S2 – 416/406-2212, Fax: 416/406-2214 – *1

John J. Hazel, #G-9, 4195 Dundas St. West, M8X 1Y4 – 416/234-1500, Fax: 416/234-9357 – *1

Hazzard & Hore, #1002, 141 Adelaide St. West, M5H 3L5 – 416/868-0074, Fax: 416/868-1468 – *2

Alfred C. Heakes, Q.C., 1920 Weston Rd., M9N 1W4 – 416/249-2237, Fax: 416/249-1200 – *1

David P.V. Healey, 1577 Bloor St. West, M6P 1A6 – 416/532-3036, Fax: 416/536-3618 – *1

Rod Heather, Q.C., #305, 180 Dundas St. West, M5G 1Z8 – 416/979-7416, Fax: 416/599-0847 – *1

Marian D. Hebb, #404, 179 John St., M5T 1X4 – 416/971-6618, Fax: 416/971-4144 – *1

William S. Hechter, #PH, 121 Richmond St. West, M5H 2K1 – 416/364-9517, Fax: 416/364-9391 – *1

Heenan Blaikie, South Tower, Royal Bank Plaza, #2600, PO Box 185, Stn Royal Bank, M5J 2J4 – 416/360-6336, Fax: 416/360-8425; Email: jnoonan@heenan.ca – *5

E.S. Heiber, #200, 70 Bond St., M5B 1X3 – 416/362-2768, Fax: 416/865-5328; Email: esheiber@ican.net – *1

Heifetz, Crozier, Law, #704, 55 University Ave., M5J 2H7 – 416/863-1717, Fax: 416/368-3133 – *4

Heller, Feldman., #902, 130 Adelaide St. West, M5H 3P5 – 416/364-2404, Fax: 416/364-0793 – *4

Heller, Rubel, #208, 111 Richmond St. West, M5H 2G4 – 416/863-9311, Fax: 416/863-9465 – *2

A. Henderson, #1812, 2 Carlton St., M5B 1J3 – 416/977-7700, Fax: 416/977-8570 – *1

Ian S. Hennessey, #108, 100 Lombard St., M5C 1M3 – 416/364-4211, Fax: 416/364-7505 – *1

Harry Herberman, 658 Danforth Ave., M4J 5B9 – 416/461-3171 – *1

Alfred H. Herman & Associates, 1948 Weston Rd., M9N 1W2 – 416/245-2400 – *3

Lawrence L. Herman, #2200, 40 King St. West, M5H 3C2 – 416/488-2696, Fax: 416/488-5752 – *1

W.B. Herman, Q.C., #810, 1 Toronto St., M5C 2V7 – 416/868-0773, Fax: 416/868-6700 – *1

William Hershorn, #104, 964 Albion Rd., M9V 1A7 – 416/741-9494, Fax: 416/741-9479 – *1

Joel Hertz, #200, 111 Eglinton Ave. East, M4P 1H4 – 416/482-8242, Fax: 416/482-4165 – *1

Hicks Morley Hamilton Stewart Storie, TD Bank Tower, 30th Fl., Box 371, TD Centre, M5K 1K8 – 416/362-1011, Fax: 416/362-9680 – *44

J.R. Higgins, #201, 161 St. George St., M5R 2M3 – 416/921-6093 – *1

Enid G. Hildebrand, 39A Hazelton Ave., M5R 2E3 – 416/925-2711, Fax: 416/925-8118 – *1

John L. Hill, 4 Finch Ave. West, M2N 6L1 – 416/226-3221, Fax: 416/226-3222; Email: conlaw@pathcom.com – *1

Hills & Associate, 1168 Warden Ave., M1R 2R1 – 416/752-7078, Fax: 416/752-8769 – *2

D'Arcy Hiltz, #906, 94 Cumberland St., M5R 1A3 – 416/968-6575, Fax: 416/968-3424; Email: hiltzlaw@pathcom.com; URL: http://www.pathcom.com/-hiltzlaw – *1

Sydney Himel, 455 Spadina Ave., M5S 2G8 – 416/979-2155 – *1

Howard P.C. Ho, #405, 120 Carlton St., M5A 4K2 – 416/928-1300, Fax: 416/928-5079 – *1

Rufus Ho, #306, 45 Sheppard Ave. East, M2N 5W9 – 416/590-7737, Fax: 416/590-7738 – *1

J. Gardner Hodder, #2200, 181 University Ave., M5H 3M7 – 416/601-6809, Fax: 416/947-0909 – *1

A. John Hodgins, 603 Evans Ave., M8W 2W3 – 416/251-9390, Fax: 416/251-0449 – *1

Hodgson, Parker, 2346 Danforth Ave., M4C 1K7 – 416/422-2110, Fax: 416/422-0814 – *2

Norman Hoffman, Q.C., #200, 1810 Avenue Rd., M5M 3Z2 – 416/787-1161, Fax: 416/787-3894 – *1

Hoffman, Sillery, Buckstein & Chuback, #200, 1810 Avenue Rd., M5M 3Z2 – 416/787-1161, Fax: 416/787-3894 – *3

Robert Hogan, 21 Lanewood Cres., M1W 1W9 – 416/499-6553, Fax: 416/499-6728 – *1

R.L. Holden, #304, 375 University Ave., M5G 2G1 – 416/979-1446, Fax: 416/979-8669 – *1

J. Todd Holmes, #507, 4100 Yonge St., M2P 2B5 – 416/250-0033, Fax: 416/250-6208 – *1

P. Virginia Holmes, 864 York Mills Rd., M3B 1Y4 – 416/444-7342, Fax: 416/444-2507

Holmested & Sutton, 4 King St. West, M5H 1B3 – 416/364-9317, Fax: 416/364-9118 – *6

Christopher Holoboff, #500, 27 Queen St. East, M5C 2M6 – 416/868-0878, Fax: 416/362-5013 – *1

Judith Holzman Law Offices, 218 Adelaide St. West, 3rd Fl., M5H 1W7 – 416/977-3050, Fax: 416/977-6253 – *1

Shireen E. Hooshangi, 379 Broadview Ave., M4K 2M7 – 416/463-5248, Fax: 416/463-0420 – *1

William B. Horkins, #1900, 439 University Ave., M5G 1Y8 – 416/591-1218, Fax: 416/408-2372; Email: horkins@interlog.com; URL: http://www.interlog.com/~horkins – *1

Brian J. Hornsby, #4068, 3080 Yonge St., M4N 3N1 – 416/482-5853, Fax: 416/322-7097 – *1

Horwitz, Finder, 30 St. Clair Ave. West, M4V 3A1 – 416/961-1177, Fax: 416/961-1251 – *2

Edward J. Houlihan, Belfield Pl., 15 Belfield Rd., M9W 1E8 – 416/243-9501, Fax: 416/243-2990 – *1

Jeffrey A. House, #303, 489 College St., M6G 1A5 – 416/926-9402 – *2

Houser, Henry & Syron, #2000, 145 King St. West, M5H 2B6 – 416/362-3411, Fax: 416/362-3757 – *9

E.N. Hretzay, 945 Wilson Ave., M3K 1E8 – 416/631-5251, Fax: 416/635-9549 – *1

Peter Hryn, Old City Hall, 60 Queen St. West, M5H 2M4 – 416/926-0798 – *1

Hubbard, Favaro, 142 King St. East, M5C 1G7 – 416/366-9558 – *2

Hughes, Amys, Box: 401, #5050, 1 First Canadian Place, M5X 1E3 – 416/367-1608, Fax: 416/367-8821; Email: mail@hughesamys.com; URL: http://www.hughesamys.com – *27

Hughes, Archer, Dorsch, #400, 365 Bay St., M5H 2V1 – 416/868-1300, Fax: 416/861-1147 – *4

Frank T.L. Hughes, 69 Elm St., M5G 1H2 – 416/599-5311 – *1

R.A. Hummel, Q.C., #208, 4218 Lawrence Ave. East, M1E 4X9 – 416/281-2502, Fax: 416/281-8957 – *1
Edward F. Hung, #319, 1033 Bay St., M5S 3A5 – 416/926-8777, Fax: 416/926-1799 – *1
David J. Hunt, #110, 1468 Victoria Park Ave., M4A 2M2 – 416/751-2064, Fax: 416/750-3794 – *1
David V. Hutchinson, 701 Evans Ave., M9C 1A3 – 416/620-0553, Fax: 416/622-8952 – *1
Ken Hutchinson, #300, 48 Kennebec Cres., M9W 2R7 – 416/742-4858 – *1
David L. Hynes, #1206, 150 York St., M5H 3S5 – 416/364-9299, Fax: 416/360-4034 – *1
Iacono Brown, 130 Adelaide St. West, 31st Fl., M5H 3P5 – 416/869-0123, Fax: 416/869-0271 – *13
Nick Iannazzo, #501, 425 University Ave., M5G 1T6 – 416/410-1088, (905) 791-9300, Fax: 416/598-8183, (905) 791-4666; Email: nickiann@sympatico.ca – *1
Iler, Campbell, 160 John St., 2nd Fl., M5V 2E5 – 416/598-0103, Fax: 416/598-3484 – *8
Frederick Innis, #1000, 65 Queen St. West, M5H 2M5 – 416/363-9600, Fax: 416/363-8389 – *2
Sheridan Ippolito, #506, 2 Jane St., M6S 4W3 – 416/763-3399, Fax: 416/763-3443 – *3
Ira E. Book & Associates, 1400 Kingston Rd., M1N 1R3 – 416/698-1157, Fax: 416/698-7680 – *1
Ireland, Nicoll, #1505, 330 Bay St., M5H 2S8 – 416/362-1354, Fax: 416/362-1465 – *2
C.E. Irish, #223, 85 Ellesmere Rd., M1R 4B9 – 416/444-7327, Fax: 416/444-0761 – *1
Alan Irwin, 26 Woburn Ave., M5M 1K6 – 416/322-3142 – *1
Joan M. Irwin, #11, 2300 Lawrence Ave. East, M1P 2R2 – 416/288-9200, Fax: 416/288-1093 – *1
Dr. Richard Isaac, #605, 190 St. George St., M5R 2N4 – 416/968-2808 – *1
Claude Isaacksz, #602, 18 Wynford Dr., M3C 3S2 – 416/444-6006, Fax: 416/449-6969
Philip D. Isbister, #2200, 181 University Ave., M5H 3M7 – 416/601-6797, Fax: 416/363-7875 – *1
Miriam Isenberg, Q.C., 11 Bentworth Ave., M6A 1P1 – 416/785-8787, Fax: 416/785-6266 – *1
Irwin Z. Isenstein, 1202-390 Bay St., M5H 2Y2 – 416/368-2181, Fax: 416/363-8451
Cydney G. Israel, 61 Saint Nicholas St., M4Y 1W6 – 416/962-6188, Fax: 416/925-0162 – *1
J.D. Barnett Law Offices, 1278 St. Clair Ave. West, M6E 1B9 – 416/656-8888, Fax: 416/232-0232
Jackman, Waldman & Associates, 281 Eglinton Ave. East, M4P 1L3 – 416/482-6501, Fax: 416/482-9834 – *4
Carol E.F. Jackson, #300, 8 King St. East, M5C 1B5 – 416/363-3292, Fax: 416/366-4892 – *1
Harvey Jacobson, #222, 3089 Bathurst St., M6A 2A4 – 416/787-0611, Fax: 416/787-4873 – *1
Brandon Jaffe, #424, 100 Richmond St. West, M5H 3K6 – 416/368-2809, Fax: 416/365-1474 – *1
James Jagtoo, #110, 1468 Victoria Park Ave., M4A 2M2 – 416/750-3791, Fax: 416/750-3794 – *1
Michael B. Jameson, Q.C., 101 Chaplin Cres., M5P 1A4 – 416/481-7529, Fax: 416/481-7626 – *1
D.M. Jamieson, #912, 390 Bay St., M5H 2Y2 – 416/366-8742, Fax: 416/366-5182 – *1
Jane Finch Community Legal Services, #409, 1315 Finch Ave. West, M3J 2G6 – 416/398-0677, Fax: 416/398-7172 – *3
Janoscik & Janoscik, 1576 Bloor St. West, M6P 1A4 – 416/537-1266 – *2
Janssen & Associates, 89 Scollard St., M5R 1G4 – 416/929-1103, Fax: 416/929-9610; Email: janssenc@interlog.com – *2
Mary Jarrell, #106, 81 The East Mall, M8Z 5W3 – 416/253-1840, Fax: 416/253-1243 – *1
Johannes Jarvalt, #102, 958 Broadview Ave., M4K 2R6 – 416/463-2737 – *1
Jason, Robert, c/o Fogler Rubinkoff, Royal Trust Tower, Toronto-Dominion Centre, #4400, PO Box 95, M5K 1G8 – 416/941-8828, Fax: 416/941-8852; Email: rrj@foglerubinoff.com
Jeffery, Robertson, Watson & Pendrith, #1812, 2 Carlton St., M5B 1J3 – 416/977-7700, Fax: 416/977-8570 – *2
T. Jegathessan, #201, 2620 Eglinton Ave. East, M1K 2S3 – 416/266-6154, Fax: 416/266-4677 – *1
Robert L. Jenkins, #1200, 20 Toronto St., M5C 2B8 – 416/368-5248, Fax: 416/363-1457 – *1
Jewell, Michael & Obradovich, #700, 390 Bay St., M5H 2Y2 – 416/862-7020, Fax: 416/862-2135 – *3
Larry B. Joffe, 700-55 Town Centre Crt., M1P 4X4 – 416/290-6138, Fax: 416/296-1259 – *1
Stanley Joffe, #312, 2 St. Clair Ave. East, M4T 2T5 – 416/968-6477, Fax: 416/968-6743 – *2
Johnston & Douglas, 2974A Lakeshore Blvd. West, M8V 3B7 – 416/259-4267 – *1
Daphne Johnston, #1130, 20 Dundas St. West, M5G 2G8 – 416/599-9635, Fax: 416/591-7333 – *1
Johnston, Douglas, Senn, 2974A Lakeshore Blvd. West, M8V 1J9 – 416/259-4267 – *1
Kerry W. Johnston, #1110, 36 Toronto St., M5C 2C5 – 416/360-1834, Fax: 416/360-1845 – *1
G.P. Johnstone, #1601, 65 Queen St. West., M5H 2M5 – 416/364-3200, Fax: 416/364-7415 – *1
William R. Johnstone, #1515, 390 Bay St., M5H 2Y2 – 416/860-7150, Fax: 416/860-1474 – *1
Gerald F. Jonas, #1607, 80 Richmond St. West, M5H 2C2 – 416/366-3838, Fax: 416/366-8041 – *1
S. Jonas, #304, 559 College St., M6G 1A9 – 416/961-3474, Fax: 416/961-8094 – *1
Gregory Jones, #300, 111 Elizabeth St., M5G 1P7 – 416/977-3796, Fax: 416/599-8075 – *1
Kevin Jones, 284 Sherbourne St., M5A 2S1 – 416/923-1685 – *1
Jones, Rogers, #1600, 155 University Ave., M5H 3B6 – 416/361-0626, Fax: 416/361-6303; Email: jrlaw@istar.ca – *6
Joseph & O'Donoghue, #1301, 2200 Yonge St., M4S 2B8 – 416/932-0545, Fax: 416/932-0541 – *5
Mary K.E. Joseph, #304, 150 York St., M5H 3S5 – 416/363-8048, Fax: 416/363-8554; Email: mjosephlaw@aol.com – *1
Vesna Josifovski, #604, 130 Bloor St. West, M5S 1N5 – 416/960-0143, Fax: 416/924-2371 – *1
Ron Jourard, #8, 951 Wilson Ave., M3K 2A7 – 416/398-6685, Fax: 416/398-9393; Email: jourard@defencelaw.com; URL: http://www.defencelaw.com – *1
Robert W. Judge, 44 Fairview Blvd., M4K 1L9 – 416/466-7007, Fax: 416/466-7050 – *1
Steven W. Junger, #100, 12 Chiltern Hill Rd., M6C 3B3 – 416/787-7247, Fax: 416/787-3021 – *1
E.A. Jupp, Q.C., #1712, 130 Adelaide St. West, M5H 3P5 – 416/868-0626, Fax: 416/868-0352 – *1
Juriansz & Li, #1709, 5650 Yonge St., M2M 4G3 – 416/226-2342, Fax: 416/222-6874; Email: justice@io.org – *3
Russell G. Juriansz, #1501, 65 Queen St. West, M5H 2M5 – 416/867-7590, Fax: 416/867-7594 – *3
M. Jurjans, #201, 785 Carlaw Ave., M4K 3L1 – 416/466-1101, Fax: 416/466-6335 – *1
Justice for Children & Youth, #405, 720 Spadina Ave., M5S 2T9 – 416/920-1633, Fax: 416/920-5855 – *4
Larry Kagan, #101, 2171 Avenue Rd., M5M 4B4 – 416/485-1193 – *1
Marsha Kagan, #101, 2171 Avenue Rd., M5M 4B4 – 416/485-1195 – *1
R.B. Kallmeyer, #305, 2968 Dundas St. West, M6P 1Y8 – 416/763-2297, Fax: 416/763-2298 – *1
Mohamed M. Kamaluddin, #700, 55 Town Cetnre Ct., M1P 4X4 – 416/267-4884, Fax: 416/296-1259 – *1
Bernard J. Kamin, #401, 111 Eglinton Ave. East, M4P 1H4 – 416/932-1236, Fax: 416/932-1747 – *1
Steven Kaminker, 56 Temperance St., 8th Fl., M5H 3V5 – 416/214-9812, Fax: 416/214-9792 – *1
A. Victor Kanbergs, #101, 5859 Yonge St., M2M 3V6 – 416/225-8806 – *1
Speros Kanellos, 61 Hayden St., M4Y 2P2 – 416/968-1717, Fax: 416/968-7559
C.Y. Kang, #210, 280 Sheppard Ave. East, M2N 3B1 – 416/228-1417, Fax: 416/221-1732 – *1
N.S. Kanji, 61 Alness St., M3J 2H2 – 416/650-0901, Fax: 416/650-0900 – *1
Kapelos & Carlisi, 500 Danforth Ave., M4K 1P6 – 416/465-1145, Fax: 416/465-9560 – *2
Jacob Kaplan, Q.C., 185 Old Yonge St, M2P 1R2 – 416/226-3262 – *1
William Kaplan, #200, 70 Bond St., M5B 1X3 – 416/865-5341, Fax: 416/365-7702; Email: wkaplan@sympatico.ca – *1
Anil K. Kapoor, #210, 20 Adelaide St. East, M5C 2T6 – 416/363-2700, Fax: 416/368-6811; Email: akk@passport.ca – *1
Kappel & Ludlow, #1400, 439 University Ave., M5G 1Y8 – 416/408-4565, Fax: 416/408-4569 – *4
N.H. Karal, Q.C., 17 Joyce Pkwy., M6P 2S7 – 416/787-6101, Fax: 416/787-6102 – *1
Karas & Associates, #410, 212 King St. West, M5H 1K5 – 416/506-1800, Fax: 416/599-5582; Email: karas@karas.ca; URL: http://www.karas.ca – *1
C.N. Karbaliotis, #201, 101 Richmond St. East, M5C 1N9 – 416/364-0388, Fax: 416/364-3756; Email: kartis@techne.com; URL: http://www.techne.com – *1
Joseph H. Kary, 571 Jarvis St., M4Y 2J1 – 416/968-2016, Fax: 416/968-2054 – *1
H.B. Kasman, 500 Danforth Ave., M4K 1P6 – 416/465-7593 – *1
Sheldon L. Kasman & Associates, #201, 1622 Eglinton Ave. West, M6E 2G8 – 416/789-1888, Fax: 416/789-5928 – *2
Garen Kassabian, #340, 49 The Donway West, M3C 2E8 – 416/443-9494, Fax: 416/443-0575 – *1
B.M. Kassirer, Q.C., #1200, 595 Bay St., M5G 2C2 – 416/591-7607 – *1
Kates & Goldkind, #206, 3850 Sheppard Ave. East, M1T 3L4 – 416/291-5587 – *2
Barry M. Kaufman, #201, 2050 Sheppard Ave. East, M2J 5B3 – 416/498-7297, Fax: 416/498-0792 – *1
S.D. Kaufman, 381 Broadview Ave., M4K 2M7 – 416/424-4388 – *1
C.M. Kavanagh, 121 Wineva Ave., M4E 2T1 – 416/410-0486 – *1
J.M. Kavanagh, Q.C., 706 Kennedy Rd., M1K 2B5 – 416/265-3560, Fax: 416/265-1944 – *1
Kavinoky & Cook Foreign Legal Consultants, #455, 207 Queen's Quay West, M5J 1A7 – 416/203-0631, Fax: 416/203-0639 – *4
Robert C. Kay, 31 Adelaide St. East, PO Box 961, Stn Adelaide, M5C 2K3 – 416/362-9999, Fax: 416/362-9999 – *1
Kazman & Associates, #210, 3701 Chesswood Dr., M3J 2P6 – 416/630-9950, Fax: 416/630-9159 – *2
Keel Cottrelle, #920, 36 Toronto St., M5C 2C5 – 416/367-2900, Fax: 416/367-2791; Email: jeasto@keelcottrelle.on.ca – *9
Keith & Kramer, #404, 1200 Bay St., M5R 2A5 – 416/922-4417, Fax: 416/922-9328 – *2
Christina H. Kelk, 94 South Dr., M4W 1R6 – 416/966-1266, Fax: 416/966-2670 – *1
J. Robert Kellermann, #303, 489 College St., M6G 1A5 – 416/926-8034, Fax: 416/972-1992 – *1
Kelly Affleck Greene, One First Canadian Place, #840, PO Box 489, Stn 1st Cdn.Pl, M5X 1E5 – 416/360-2800, Fax: 416/360-5960 – *12
Kelly International Settlement Services Inc., 260 Milan St., M5A 3Z6 – 416/365-1528, Fax: 416/365-1080 – *1
Miriam A. Kelly, #1500, 2 St. Clair Ave. East, M4T 2R1 – 416/926-1602, Fax: 416/926-7532 – *1
Timothy C. Kelly, #405, 11 Church St., M5E 1W1 – 416/941-8952, Fax: 416/366-1799 – *1
F.S. Kelman, #303, 4120 Yonge St., M2P 2B8 – 416/250-6400, Fax: 416/250-6411 – *1
Kevin E. Kemp, #2906, 2045 Lakeshore Blvd West, M8V 2Z6 – 416/251-4428, Fax: 416/251-7590 – *1
Evan Kenley, #601, 2200 Yonge St., M4S 2C6 – 416/932-1148, Fax: 416/932-1108 – *1

* indicates number of lawyers in law firm.

Kennedy Dymond, #200, 4211 Yonge St., M2P 2A9 – 416/733-2807
William I. Kennedy, #500, 370 King St. West, M5V 1J9 – 416/599-1930, Fax: 416/599-1377
Kensington-Bellwoods, #205, 489 College St., M6G 1A5 – 416/924-4244, Fax: 416/924-5904 – *3
M. Kerbel, Q.C., #2412, 401 Bay St., M5H 2Y4 – 416/366-7621, Fax: 416/364-2308 – *1
M.L. Kerbel, #1001, 65 Queen St. West, M5H 2M5 – 416/364-9532 – *1
Kerr & Kerr, #7, 31 Walmer Rd., M5R 2W7 – 416/966-0820, Fax: 416/966-0815; Email: andrew.kerr@sympatico.ca – *1
Carrolyne Kerr, #305, 1033 Bay St., M5S 3A5 – 416/921-4554, Fax: 416/925-2860 – *1
D.W. Kerr, 3 Strathearn Rd., M6C 1R2 – 416/781-7100 – *1
Kerr, Oster & Wolfman, 133 Berkeley St., M5A 2X1 – 416/365-7163, Fax: 416/365-1270 – *3
Helen M. Kersley, #308, 100 Richmond St. West, M5H 3K6 – 416/947-1124, Fax: 416/947-1236 – *1
Kerzner Papazian MacDermid, #500, 121 King St. West, M5H 3T9 – 416/367-4900, Fax: 416/367-8197 – *3
Louis I. Kesten, Q.C., #201, 887 Queen St. East, M4M 1J2 – 416/461-0865, Fax: 416/461-1869 – *3
Kestenberg Siegal Lipkus, 65 Granby St., M5B 1H8 – 416/597-0000, Fax: 416/597-6567 – *7
Kettner, Philp, Gold, Frydman & Rumack, #300, 500 University Ave., M5G 1V7 – 416/598-3277, Fax: 416/340-0884 – *4
El-Farouk Khaki, 81 Pembroke St., M5A 2N9 – 416/925-7227, Fax: 416/925-2450; Email: elfin925@aol.com – *1
Abdul A. Khalifa, #5, 1 Willingdon Blvd., M8X 2H1 – 416/234-0640, Fax: 416/234-9064 – *1
Theodore J. Kielb, Scotia Plaza, 40 King St. West, 41st Fl., M5H 3Y4 – 416/367-1643 – *1
C.W. Kilian, #308, 2401 Eglinton Ave. East, M1K 2M5 – 416/750-4824, Fax: 416/750-4827 – *1
Kimberley, Vaillancourt & Henry, 1937 Gerrard St. East, M4L 2C2 – 416/690-1708, Fax: 416/690-4976 – *1
R.S. Kimel, 444 Adelaide St. West, M5V 1S7 – 416/361-1877, Fax: 416/861-9216 – *1
Blake F. Kinahan, Metro Hall, Stn. 1020, #230, 55 John St., M5V 3C6 – 416/392-4041, Fax: 416/392-4127; Email: blake_f._kinahan@metrodesk.metrotor.on.ca – *1
King & King, #810, 372 Bay St., M5H 2W9 – 416/368-4678, Fax: 416/947-0482 – *1
J. Kingston, #100, 185 Glencairn Ave., M4R 1N3 – 416/322-0612, Fax: 416/322-6488 – *1
Kirby, Lyon, Gatward & Clark, #2405, 1 Dundas St. West, M5G 1Z3 – 416/351-1010, Fax: 416/351-1130 – *4
Terry L. Kirichenko, #1314, 181 University Ave., M5H 3M7 – 416/861-0123 – *1
Fern Kirsch, 5160 Yonge St., PO Box 85, M2N 6L9 – 416/590-7090 – *1
Ernest J. Kirsh, #200, 2901 Bayview Ave., M2K 1E6 – 416/226-4198 – *1
Sheila Kirsh, #816, 181 University Ave., M5H 2X7 – 416/367-1765, Fax: 416/364-1697 – *1
Sheldon E. Kirsh, #306, 27 Queen St. East, M5C 2M6 – 416/360-6411, Fax: 416/360-5738 – *1
Howard Joshua Kirshenbaum, #200, 70 Bond St., M5B 1X3 – 416/865-5339, Fax: 416/777-9255; Email: kirshenbaum@msm.com – *1
Klaiman, Edmonds, #1000, 60 Yonge St., M5E 1H5 – 416/867-9600, Fax: 416/867-9783 – *2
Murray Klein, 12 Highgate Road, M8X 2B2 – 416/231-5476 – *1
A. Klemencic, 332 Brown's Line, M8W 3T6 – 416/251-5281, Fax: 416/251-0029 – *1
Klotz Associates, #700, 347 Bay St., M5H 2R7 – 416/360-4500 – *2
Philip M. Klumak, #1001, 65 Queen St. West, M5H 2M5 – 416/367-2690, Fax: 416/367-4578 – *1
A.W. Klymko, #430, 100 Richmond St. West, M5H 3K6 – 416/366-4583 – *1
Paula Knopf Arbitrations Ltd., 4 Biggar Ave., M6H 2N4 – 416/652-1516, Fax: 416/652-1516 – *1
Linda H. Kolyn, #503, 2 Jane St., M6S 4W3 – 416/604-7677, Fax: 416/762-8494; Email: dadey@pathcom.com; URL: http://www.pathcom.com/~dadey/homepage.htm – *1
Marc Koplowitz Associates, #700, 55 University Ave., M5J 2K4 – 416/368-1100, Fax: 416/368-0016 – *1
Mark B. Koreen, 2424 Bloor St. West, M6S 1P9 – 416/766-2416, Fax: 416/769-5365 – *1
Korman & Company, #203, 121 Richmond St. West, M5H 2K1 – 416/777-2566, Fax: 416/777-0810; Email: korman@globalserve.net – *2
Koroloff & Huckins, #304, 1110 Sheppard Ave. East, M2K 2W2 – 416/229-6226, Fax: 416/229-6517 – *2
Koskie & Minsky, #900, 20 Queen St. West, PO Box 52, M5H 3R3 – 416/977-8353, Fax: 416/977-3316; URL: http://www.koskieminsky.com – *28
R.M. Kostuk, Q.C., 2195 Bloor St. West, M6S 1N2 – 416/766-7666 – *1
Kostyniuk & Associates, 2481A Bloor St. West, M6S 1P8 – 416/762-8238, Fax: 416/762-5042 – *4
Robert Kostyniuk, Q.C., #612, 390 Bay St., M5H 2Y2 – 416/364-4025, Fax: 416/364-4631 – *3
Bernard Kott, Q.C., #1115, 330 Bay St., M5H 2S8 – 416/365-7866 – *1
I. Koziebrocki, #2600, 250 Yonge St., M5B 2M6 – 416/598-2167, Fax: 416/598-3167 – *1
Neil L. Kozloff, #1900, 439 University Ave., M5G 1Y8 – 416/408-1114, Fax: 416/408-2372 – *1
Kozlowski & Company, #401, 5468 Dundas St. W., M9B 6E3 – 416/234-1800, Fax: 416/234-1669 – *4
S.B. Kravetz, #202, 69 Elm St., M5G 1H2 – 416/971-8704, Fax: 416/971-9092 – *1
E.A. Kremer, 845 St. Clair Ave. West, M6C 1C3 – 416/654-4111, Fax: 416/653-3891 – *1
Timothy J. Kreutzer, #1506, 141 Adelaide St. West, M5H 3L5 – 416/364-7292, Fax: 416/864-0175 – *1
J.H. Krieger, 4 Finch Ave. West, M2N 6L1 – 416/223-9577, Fax: 416/225-5992 – *1
Kathleen Kroeger, 2249 Queen St. East, M4E 1G1 – 416/699-8494, Fax: 416/699-8494 – *1
Krol & Krol, #201, 14A Hazelton Ave., M5R 2E2 – 416/964-0138 – *2
Steven Kruck, #211, 2498 Yonge St., M4P 2H8 – 416/484-1607 – *1
Ronald A. Krueger, #1000, 65 Queen St. West, M5H 2M5 – 416/867-1440, Fax: 416/367-3949 – *1
Kennth A. Krupat, #1000, 65 Queen St. West, M5H 2M5 – 416/368-1179, Fax: 416/368-4486; Email: kkrupat@the-wire.com – *1
George J. Kubes, 360 Bloor St. West, M5S 1X1 – 416/926-9298 – *1
E.M. Kudrac, #108, 1415 Lawrence Ave. West, M6L 1A9 – 416/248-0181, Fax: 416/240-1219 – *1
Ernie Kung, #1708, 372 Bay St., M5H 2W9 – 416/777-1722, Fax: 416/777-1624 – *1
Howard Kutner & Associates, 2347 Kennedy Rd., M1T 3T8 – 416/297-4949 – *2
Enn Allan Kuuskne, #1510, 5140 Yonge St., M2N 6L7 – 416/224-2267, Fax: 416/250-7008 – *1
Kvas Miller Everitt, #1502, 77 Bloor St. West, M5S 1M2 – 416/921-6558, Fax: 416/923-0760 – *3
Grace F. Kwan, 571 Jarvis St., M4Y 2J1 – 416/968-2014, Fax: 416/968-2054 – *1
Aaron B. Kwinter, #100, 76 Densley Ave., M6M 2R3 – 416/245-5040, Fax: 416/249-9573 – *1
Wolfgang H. Kyser, #1000, 121 Richmond St. West, M5H 2K1 – 416/863-1053, Fax: 416/861-0191 – *1
Ted Laan, #1508, 330 Bay St., M5H 2S8 – 416/861-1071, Fax: 416/861-1968 – *1
John F. LaBerge, #800, 1243 Islington Ave., M8X 1Y9 – 416/233-4631, Fax: 416/234-0258 – *1
J. Robert Léo, #303, 489 College St., M6G 1A5 – 416/967-9889, Fax: 416/972-1992 – *1
Stephen M. Labow, #700, 357 Bay St., M5H 2T7 – 416/947-1172, Fax: 416/363-4130 – *1
Tony Lacaria, #612, 330 Bay St., M5H 2S8 – 416/214-1390, Fax: 416/214-0870
Lackman, Firestone Law Offices, #401, 357 Bay St., M5H 2T7 – 416/364-0020, Fax: 416/364-0389; Email: lackmanfirestone@shaw.wave.ca; URL: http://www.tor.shaw.wave.ca/~lackman – *2
K.D.L. Lackner, 692 Coxwell Ave., M4C 3B6 – 416/461-8106, Fax: 416/461-8011 – *1
Lafleur Brown, #920, 1 First Canadian Place, PO Box 359, M5X 1E1 – 416/869-0994, Fax: 416/362-5818; Email: lbtor@tor.lafleurbrown.ca – *10
Gregory L. Lafontaine, #1130, 20 Dundas St. West, M5G 2G8 – 416/204-1835, Fax: 416/204-1849 – *2
Laird & Laird, #521, 1315 Lawrence Ave. East, M3A 3R3 – 416/449-0993, Fax: 416/449-9396 – *2
W.W. Laird, Q.C., #1707, 57 Widdicombe Hill Blvd., M9R 1Y4 – 416/245-3114 – *1
Benjamin Laker, Q.C., 121 Westgate Blvd., M3H 1P5 – 416/636-9600, Fax: 416/636-9601 – *1
W.N. Lalka, #208, 5399 Eglinton Ave. West, M9C 5K6 – 416/620-9999, Fax: 416/620-7433 – *1
Christine Lall, #268, 5 Fairview Mall Dr., M2J 2Z1 – 416/498-4688, Fax: 416/498-6201 – *1
D. Wayne Lalonde, #2000, 393 University Ave., M5G 1E6 – 416/585-2868, Fax: 416/593-1352 – *1
Lambert Tweyman & Assoc., #800, 789 Don Mills Rd., M3C 1T5 – 416/467-5555, Fax: 416/467-9906 – *2
Jack S. Lambert, #212, 4211 Yonge St., M2P 2A9 – 416/226-6333, Fax: 416/226-6344 – *1
W.W. Lamberton, Q.C., #101, 1262 Don Mills Rd., M3B 2W7 – 416/445-6800, Fax: 416/445-5468 – *1
Lamont & Lamont, #810, 1 Queen St. East, M5C 2W5 – 416/363-0173, Fax: 416/363-0176 – *2
Garry Lamourie, #1509, 180 Dundas St. West, M5G 1Z8 – 416/597-9828, Fax: 416/597-9808 – *1
Sharon S. Landsman, #2000, 80 Richmond St. West, M5H 2A4 – 416/363-5478, Fax: 416/364-9707 – *1
Landy Marr & Associates, #1000, 2 Sheppard Ave. East, M2N 5Y7 – 416/221-9343, Fax: 416/221-8928 – *2
Lang Michener, BCE Pl., #2500, 181 Bay St., PO Box 747, M5J 2T7 – 416/360-8600, Fax: 416/365-1719; Email: debbies@toronto.langmichener.ca – *85
Aaron Lang, #200, 710 Wilson Ave., M3K 1E2 – 416/398-2210, Fax: 416/398-3317 – *1
C. Robert Langdon, Q.C., 140 Dinnick Cres., M4N 1L8 – 416/483-2887, Fax: 416/484-4306 – *1
Donald J. Lange, #1604, 55 University Ave., PO Box 12, M5J 2H7 – 416/866-2956, Fax: 416/866-7946 – *1
George Lantos, 519A Bloor St. West, M5S 1Y4 – 416/535-4111 – *1
Simonetta A. Lanzi, #900, 1 St. Clair Ave. East, M4T 2V7 – 416/926-8794, Fax: 416/923-1549; Email: sal@inforamp.net – *1
G. Jonathan Lapid, #2200, 4950 Yonge St., M2N 6K1 – 416/222-4324, Fax: 416/222-6223 – *1
P.K. Large, #610, 372 Bay St., M5H 2W9 – 416/867-8669, Fax: 416/867-3079 – *1
Douglas G. Lash, 145 Glengrove Ave., M4R 1P1 – 416/932-2399, Fax: 416/932-9306; Email: dglash@istar.ca – *1
Stephen J. Lautens, #210, 335 Bay St., M5H 2R3 – 416/863-9744, Fax: 416/863-9541; Email: sjl@interlog.com; URL: http://beachnet.org/sjl – *1
Law Offices, #780, 439 University Ave., M5G 1Y8 – 416/593-9300, Fax: 416/593-0225 – *8
Law Society of Upper Canada, 1-130 Queen St. West, M5H 2N5 – 416/947-3300, Fax: 416/947-5967
John V. Lawer, Q.C., #306, 40 St. Clair Ave. East, M4T 1M9 – 416/922-0737, Fax: 416/922-1896 – *1
Daniel Lawson, #1515, 390 Bay St., M5H 2Y2 – 416/594-1234, Fax: 416/860-1474 – *1

Lawson, McGrenere, Wesley, Rose & Clemenhagen, #700, 120 Adelaide St. West, M5H 1T1 – 416/862-8294, Fax: 416/862-2232 – *14

Lax, Smith & Assoc., 348A Queen St. West, 3rd Fl., M5V 2A2 – 416/408-3553, Fax: 416/408-3811 – *2

Laxton, Glass & Swartz, #1000, 80 Richmond St. West, M5H 2B1 – 416/363-2353, Fax: 416/363-7112; Email: laxtonglass.swartz@counsel.com – *7

Sheldon S. Lazarovitz, 31 Westgate Blvd., M3H 1N8 – 416/638-6080, Fax: 416/638-6246; Email: slazar@interlog.com – *1

M.J. Leach, 4 Synnybrae Cres., M6M 4W5 – 416/248-5559, Fax: 416/240-9684 – *1

Timothy Leach, #1300, 100 Adelaide St. West, M5H 1S3 – 416/868-0265, Fax: 416/868-0478 – *1

Christopher K. Leafloor, #603, 347 Bay St., M5H 2R7 – 416/368-8970, Fax: 416/368-8206; Email: leafloor@inforamp.net – *1

Timothy E. Leahy, #408, 5075 Yonge St., M2N 6C6 – 416/226-9889, Fax: 416/226-2882; Email: teleahy@istar.ca

R.N. Lebi, 1331 St. Clair Ave. West, M6E 1C3 – 416/656-6157 – *1

Lee & Associates, #1402, 30 St. Clair Ave. West, M4V 3A1 – 416/922-9220, Fax: 416/964-5845 – *1

John Y.C. Lee, #418, 4002 Sheppard Ave. East, M1S 1S6 – 416/299-8900, Fax: 416/299-8232; Email: johnlee@inforamp.net – *2

Julia Yuen-Nam Lee, #302, 607 Gerrard St. East, M4M 1Y2 – 416/466-6888 – *1

M.Y. Lee, 42 Fulham St., M1S 2A5 – 416/298-4476, Fax: 416/321-1717 – *1

Paul Lee & Associates, 20 Maitland St., M4Y 1C5 – 416/961-2707, Fax: 416/961-5575; Email: pauleee@inforamp.net; URL: http://www.paullee.com – *10

Sunda Lee, #301, 302 Spadina Ave., M5T 2E7 – 416/596-8960, Fax: 416/596-1490 – *1

Legal Aid - Environmental Law, #401, 517 College St., M6G 1A8 – 416/960-2284, Fax: 416/960-9392 – *4

Legge & Legge, 60 St. Clair Ave. East, M4T 1N5 – 416/923-1776 – *5

Anita Leggett, #1300, 100 Adelaide St. West, M5H 1S3 – 416/360-1759, Fax: 416/360-6551 – *1

J.L. Leibel, Q.C., 104 Waterloo Ave., M3H 3Y5 – 416/635-8653 – *1

Jay Leider, #800, 75 Donway West, M3C 2E9 – 416/444-2465, Fax: 416/391-0650 – *1

Janet A. Leiper, #1900, 439 University Ave., M5G 1Y8 – 416/593-5805 – *1

J.C. Lemire, #500, 70 Bond St., M5B 1X3 – 416/363-1097, Fax: 416/863-4896 – *1

Lenczner, Slaght, Royce, Smith & Griffin, #2600, 130 Adelaide St, West, M5H 3P5 – 416/865-9500, Fax: 416/865-9010 – *5

Dennis K. Lenzin, 1724-390 Bay St., M5H 2Y2 – 416/869-3422 – *1

Lerner & Associates, Continental Bank of Canada Bldg., #2400, 130 Adelaide St. West, PO Box 95, M5H 3P5 – 416/867-3076, Fax: 416/867-9192; Email: lerner.toronto@lerner.ca – *28

B.J.B. Letterio, Q.C., #201, 1295A St. Clair Ave. West, M6E 1C2 – 416/652-0780, Fax: 416/652-2723 – *2

Levesque & Taylor, #5030, 3080 Yonge St., M4N 3N1 – 416/322-1458, Fax: 416/322-7493 – *2

Gérard Lévesque, 184 Lake Promenade, M8W 1A8 – 416/253-0129, Fax: 416/253-4737 – *1

Levine Associates, #1400, 10 King St. East, M5C 1C3 – 416/364-2345, Fax: 416/364-3818; Email: slevine@levlaw.com; URL: http://www.interlog.com/~levlaw/ – *3

Lorne Levine, #305, 55 Eglinton Ave. East, M4P 1G3 – 416/483-1251, Fax: 416/483-1257 – *1

Myer S. Levine, #1250, 180 Dundas St. West, M5G 1Z8 – 416/348-0114, Fax: 416/977-0714 – *1

Levine, Sherkin, Boussidan & Linden, #200, 70 Bond St., M5B 1X3 – 416/360-6511, Fax: 416/360-1524 – *4

Yehudah H.J. Levinson, #410, 212 King St. West, M5H 1K5 – 416/591-8484, Fax: 416/599-5582; Email: levinson@pssnet.com – *1

Levinter & Levinter, #2520, 130 Adelaide St. West, M5H 3P5 – 416/863-1930, Fax: 416/361-6168 – *3

Levitan Lawyers, 49 Wellington St. East, 5th Fl., M5B 1C9 – 416/368-4600, Fax: 416/368-1166 – *2

Shirley E. Levitan, #303, 489 College St., M6G 1A5 – 416/927-7263, Fax: 416/972-1992 – *1

Levitt, Beber, Scotia Plaza, 40 King St. West, M5H 3Y4 – 416/367-6630, Fax: 416/367-6631 – *5

Howard Levitt & Associates, #1500, 401 Bay St., M5H 2Y4 – 416/594-3900, Fax: 416/594-2323 – *1

Levitt, Levitt & Lightman, #1, 16 Four Seasons Place, M9B 6E5 – 416/620-0362, Fax: 416/620-5158 – *2

Levitt, Levitt & Lightman, 21 Isabella St., M4Y 1M7 – 416/323-1377, Fax: 416/323-9355; Email: shlevitt@netcom.ca – *1

E.J. Levy, Q.C., #2600, 250 Yonge St., M5B 2M6 – 416/598-2167, Fax: 416/598-3167 – *1

Paul S. Lewin, #405, 3601 Victoria Park Ave., M1W 3Y3 – 416/499-7945, Fax: 416/756-3663

Lewis & Collyer, #401, 160 John St., M5V 2E5 – 416/598-4357, Fax: 416/598-1067 – *2

Eric Lewis & Assoc., 116 Parliament St., M5A 2Y8 – 416/367-1918, Fax: 416/362-1918

Joseph E. Lewis, 327 Eglinton Ave. East, 2nd Fl., M4P 1L7 – 416/486-0084, Fax: 416/486-7363 – *1

Lorne Lichtenstein, #1604, 55 University Ave., M5J 2H7 – 416/947-0550, Fax: 416/866-7946 – *1

Ronald M. Lieberman, 42 Thelma Ave., M4V 1X9 – 416/488-9080 – *1

S.J. Lieberman, #236, 2900 Warden Ave., M1W 2S8 – 416/497-4300 – *1

Lilly, Anderson, Morgan, #900, 330 Bay St., M5H 2S8 – 416/365-6300, Fax: 416/368-7965 – *4

Angela Y. Lin, #412, 90 Eglinton Ave. East, M4P 2Y3 – 416/483-1328, Fax: 416/481-6171 – *1

Lindenberg & Lindenberg, 287 Eglinton Ave. East, M4P 1L3 – 416/484-8177, Fax: 416/322-0807 – *2

C. Lindhout, 16 Northcliffe Blvd., M6H 3H1 – 416/653-3073 – *1

Linett & Karoly, 101 Richmond St. East, M5C 1N9 – 416/366-5100, Fax: 416/366-0250 – *3

Lipman, Zener & Waxman, 1200 Eglinton Ave. West, M6C 2E3 – 416/789-0652 – *7

Murray M. Lipton, #1108, 8 King St. East, M5C 1B5 – 416/364-8283 – *1

Richard Litkowski, #1001, 65 Queen St. West, M5H 2M5 – 416/504-0996 – *1

Charles Litman, 26 Densley Ave., M6M 2R1 – 416/248-2002, Fax: 416/248-2024 – *1

G.E. Litowitz, #5, 2020 Bathurst St., M5P 3L1 – 416/789-7221 – *1

Philip Litowitz, #103, 3845 Bathurst St., M3H 3N2 – 416/398-4655 – *1

C.E. Litwack, 802 St. Clair Ave. West, M6C 1B6 – 416/656-7007, Fax: 416/656-7368 – *1

Nadia Liva, #700, 480 University Ave., M5G 1V2 – 416/598-0106, Fax: 416/977-5331 – *1

Lloyd, Speigel, #810, 111 Richmond St. West, M5H 2H5 – 416/362-2255, Fax: 416/362-7910 – *2

Shirley K.T. Lo, #206, 4002 Sheppard Ave. East, M1S 1S6 – 416/754-8454, Fax: 416/754-7737 – *1

Lisa Loader, #601, 130 Bloor St. West, M5S 1N5 – 416/515-9565, Fax: 416/923-1391; Email: taml@interlog.com – *1

David H. Locke, #1901, 65 Queen St. West, M5H 2M5 – 416/601-1525, Fax: 416/601-0392 – *1

Lockwood & Associates, #2100, 439 University Ave., M5G 1Y8 – 416/598-2323, Fax: 416/598-5581 – *6

Lon Hall Attorneys, #808, 121 Bloor St. East, M4W 3M5 – 416/920-3849, Fax: 416/920-8373; Email: lha_ent_law@compuserve.com; URL: http://ourworld.compuserve.com/homepages/lha_ent_law – *2

Longley & Vickar, #900, 970 Lawrence Ave. West, M6A 3B6 – 416/256-2020 – *2

Loopstra, Nixon & McLeish, Woodbine Place, #600, 135 Queens Plate Dr., M9W 6V7 – 416/746-4710, Fax: 416/746-8319 – *17

Benedict J. Lopes, #111, 215 Morrish Rd., M1C 1E9 – 416/284-2119, Fax: 416/284-4837 – *1

Thomas Lorenz, #307, 500 Danforth Ave., M4K 1P6 – 416/461-1101, Fax: 416/465-9560

Lorenzetti Wolfe, #201, 133 Richmond St. West, M5H 2L5 – 416/366-3064, Fax: 416/366-0208 – *3

S.I. Lovas, #2000, 390 Bay St., M5H 2Y2 – 416/977-7500, Fax: 416/860-0580 – *1

Lowndes & Harrison, Box: 81, #2702, 1 Dundas St. West, M5G 1Z3 – 416/977-8720, Fax: 416/974-9099; Email: lowndes@interlog.com – *3

M. Lubek, #200, 65 Queen St. West, M5H 2M5 – 416/363-6651, Fax: 416/363-0252 – *1

Patricia Lucas, #1509, 180 Dundas St. West, M5G 1Z8 – 416/597-1061, Fax: 416/597-9808 – *1

Olga Luftig, 201-100 Sheppard Ave. W., M2N 1M6 – 416/224-2244, Fax: 416/225-0832 – *1

Patricia M. Lukasewich, 3386 Lakeshore Blvd. West, M8W 1M9 – 416/259-3747, Fax: 416/259-5177 – *1

Francisco B. Luna, #1704, 2 Carlton St., M5B 1J3 – 416/977-3287, Fax: 416/977-1950; Email: fluna@netcom.ca – *1

Karen D. Lundy, #2150, 1 Queen St. East, M5C 2W5 – 416/866-8858, Fax: 416/364-3866 – *1

Earl L. Lutes, #15B, 777 Danforth Ave., M4J 1L2 – 416/463-4411 – *1

Helen Luzius, #1610, 372 Bay St., M5H 2W9 – 416/368-3264, Fax: 416/866-8197 – *1

Michael M. Lynch, Q.C., 99 Charles St. East, M4Y 1V2 – 416/972-9828, Fax: 416/964-0823 – *1

Gordon A. Macartney Q.C., #700, 390 Bay St., M5H 2Y2 – 416/366-7854, Fax: 416/862-2135 – *1

MacBeth & Johnson, #301, 133 Richmond St. West, M5H 2L7 – 416/368-8311, Fax: 416/368-1645 – *4

Bryan A. MacBride, #500, 27 Queen St. East, M5C 2M6 – 416/601-9222, Fax: 416/362-5013 – *1

Peter MacDonald, #500, 70 Bond St., M5B 1X3 – 416/864-1130, Fax: 416/863-4896 – *1

Alison R. Mackay, #203, 425 University Ave., M5G 2G1 – 416/591-7737, Fax: 416/599-8075 – *1

Donald J. MacKay, #5044, 3080 Yonge St., M4N 3N3 – 416/482-6233 – *1

Mackenzie, Magill, Furman, #1000, 65 Queen St. West, M5H 2M5 – 416/367-9100, Fax: 416/367-3949; Email: mmlaw@idirect.com – *2

Judy D. MacLachlan, 70 Bude St., M6C 1X8

Lennox A. MacLean, Q.C., 46 Kingland Cres., M2J 2B7 – 416/496-8985, Fax: 416/496-2445 – *1

T.J. MacLennan, One First Canadian Place, #700, 100 King St. West, PO Box 160, M5X 1C7 – 416/363-8100, Fax: 416/368-7805; Email: tmaclen@idirect.com – *1

Macleod Dixon, BCE Place, #4520, 181 Bay St., PO Box 792, M5J 2T3 – 416/360-8511, Fax: 416/360-8277; Email: 75143.2536@compuserve.com – *1

Doug MacLeod, #701, 123 Edward St., M5G 1E2 – 416/591-1735, Fax: 416/591-9200 – *1

Terence Macli, #1100, 372 Bay St., M5H 2W9 – 416/863-6655, Fax: 416/863-6080 – *1

MacMaster, Poolman & Associates, #840, 100 Sheppard Ave. East, M2N 6N5 – 416/365-0258, Fax: 416/365-1355; Email: macpool@inforamp.net – *1

MacMillan, Rooke & Boeckle, #3005, 401 Bay St., PO Box 96, M5H 2Y4 – 416/360-1194, Fax: 416/360-8469; Toll Free: 1-800-661-7606 – *8

S.G.R. MacMillan, #2110, 120 Adelaide St. West, M5H 1T1 – 416/363-0100; Email: mail@sgrm.com; URL: http://www.sgrm.com – *1

MacTavish, de Lint, Hamersfeld, #200, 196 Adelaide St. West, M5H 1W7 – 416/599-7070, Fax: 416/599-2861; Email: mdlh@inforamp.net; URL: http://www.inforamp.net/~mdlh – *3

Magder & Associates, #420, 90 Eglinton Ave. East, M4P 2Y3 – 416/480-1940, Fax: 416/480-2176 – *3

* indicates number of lawyers in law firm.

Malach & Fidler, #1700, 439 University Ave., M5G 1Y8 – 416/598-1667, Fax: 416/598-5222; Email: mf@netcom.ca – *4

Dan Malamet, 17 Lowther Ave., M5R 1C5 – 416/966-1599, Fax: 416/869-0946 – *1

D.I. Malcolm, 274A Avenue Rd., M4V 2G7 – 416/927-8375, Fax: 416/924-7120 – *1

T.R. Anthony Malcolm, #850, 36 Toronto St., M5C 2C5 – 416/864-1608, Fax: 416/864-1549 – *1

G.A. Maldoff, 55 Medulla Ave., M8Z 5L6 – 416/232-1733, Fax: 416/232-2194 – *1

Anna Mallin, 78 Bideford Ave., M3H 1K4 – 416/638-8897, Fax: 416/633-3010 – *1

Jean MacKinnon Mallory, #700, 2 Bloor St. West, M4W 3R1 – 416/923-3514, Fax: 416/923-2071 – *1

Malo & Pilley, 1067 Bloor St. West, M6H 1M5 – 416/534-7543, Fax: 416/534-7625 – *2

Murray N. Maltz, #203, 3875 Keele St., M3J 1N6 – 416/398-6900, Fax: 416/398-6845 – *1

M.A. Manchee, 31 Clarendon Ave., M4V 1J2 – 416/972-0057, Fax: 416/323-9460 – *1

Mancia & Mancia, #701, 390 Bay St., M5H 2Y2 – 416/363-7422, Fax: 416/363-4975 – *2

Manning & Simone, 174 Avenue Rd., M5R 2J1 – 416/944-8460, Fax: 416/944-8461 – *2

Mantas, Bouwer & Rosen, #1000, 33 Yonge St., M5E 1S9 – 416/777-1400, Fax: 416/777-1999; Email: mbrtor@netcom.ca – *4

Hubert E. Mantha, #216, 215 College St., M5T 1R1 – 416/591-7345, Fax: 416/591-8814 – *1

The Marchant Practice, #1801, One Yonge St., M5E 1W7 – 416/365-1544, Fax: 416/369-0515 – *1

Pierre F. Marchildon, Dundas-Lambton Centre, #308, 4195 Dundas St. West, M8X 1Y4 – 416/236-0686, Fax: 416/236-0650; Email: pfmlaw@idirect.com – *1

Marcos Associates, 1718 Dundas St. West, M6K 1V5 – 416/537-3151, Fax: 416/537-3153 – *2

Harvey Margel, #202, 2365 Finch Ave. West, M9M 2W8 – 416/745-9933, Fax: 416/745-9290 – *1

Marin, Evans, #500, 200 Adelaide St. West, M5H 1W7 – 416/408-2177, Fax: 416/408-1718 – *3

Charles C. Mark, Q.C., #2010, 401 Bay St., PO Box 28, M5H 2Y4 – 416/869-0929, Fax: 416/361-1776 – *1

Robert S.T., #203, 438 University Ave., PO Box 38, M5G 2K8 – 416/977-8383, Fax: 416/977-6968; Email: tmark@ibm.net – *1

Markle, May, Phibbs, Box: 114, 438 University Ave., 21st Fl., M5G 2K8 – 416/593-4385, Fax: 416/593-4478 – *9

Marko, Rose, #Lower, 70 Bond St., M5B 1X3 – 416/867-6196, Fax: 416/867-6199 – *4

H. David Marks, Q.C., #300, 133 Berkeley St., M5A 2X1 – 416/863-1550, Fax: 416/863-9670 – *1

G.A. Marron, Q.C., 99 Charles St. East, M4Y 1V2 – 416/920-1504, Fax: 416/964-0823 – *1

E.E. Marszewski, 13 Maple Ave., M4W 2T5 – 416/927-1820, Fax: 416/967-4549 – *1

Ben Martin, 469 Queen St. East, M5A 1T9 – 416/366-9901, Fax: 416/363-4603 – *1

Calvin Martin, Q.C., 600 Church St., M4Y 2E7 – 416/922-5854, Fax: 416/922-5854; Email: duc14@fox.nstn.ca; URL: http://fox.nstn.ca/~duc14/law.html – *1

David Martin, #402, 20 Adelaide St. East, M5C 2T6 – 416/362-7673, Fax: 416/362-0550 – *1

E.J.S. Martin, Q.C., #215, 555 Burnhamthorpe Rd., M9C 2X3 – 416/622-2224 – *1

J. David Martin, #2200, 181 University Ave., M5H 3M7 – 416/601-0555, Fax: 416/363-7875 – *1

Malcolm Martin, 577 Jarvis St., M4Y 2J3 – 416/961-0501, Fax: 416/961-2749 – *1

R.W. Martin, #1000, 65 Queen St. West, M5H 2M5 – 416/362-3887, Fax: 416/367-3949 – *1

Thomas Martin, #203, 1114A Wilson Ave., M3M 1G7 – 416/636-0056, Fax: 416/636-5908 – *1

Waldo W. Martin, #305, 2401 Eglinton Ave. East, M1K 2M5 – 416/750-0795, Fax: 416/750-0090 – *1

William D. Martin, 1152 Yonge St., M4W 2L9 – 416/968-0322, Fax: 416/968-3725; Email: wdmartin@passport.ca – *1

Martinello & Associates, United Centre, #208, 255 Duncan Mill Rd., M3B 3H9 – 416/510-8866, Fax: 416/449-9977; Email: martinel@sprynet.com – *3

Dawn C. Maruno, 54 Broadleaf Rd., M3B 1C4 – 416/444-9334 – *1

Ray M. Maruschak, 63 Beaver Bend Cres., M9B 5R2 – 416/626-2877, Fax: 416/626-2700 – *1

Ville K. Masalin, #309, 191 Eglinton Ave. East, M4P 1K1 – 416/484-9347, Fax: 416/484-9027 – *1

Dan Marc Mascioli, 467 Roehampton Ave., M4P 1S3 – 416/488-3257 – *1

W.J. Massey, #225, 85 Ellesmere Rd., M1R 4B9 – 416/444-5223, Fax: 416/444-6806 – *1

Masters & Masters, #440, 65 Queen St. West, M5H 2M5 – 416/361-1399, Fax: 416/361-6181 – *2

Gary J. Matalon, 403 St. Clements Ave., M5N 1M2 – 416/481-8596, Fax: 416/481-3789 – *1

Mathews, Dinsdale & Clark, #2500, 1 Queen St. East, M5C 2Z1 – 416/862-8280, Fax: 416/862-8247 – *27

Gaetano P., 1463A Dundas St. West, M6J 1Y7 – 416/530-4488, Fax: 416/530-0485 – *1

David Maubach & Assoc., 810 Queen St. East, M4M 1H7 – 416/469-1115, Fax: 416/469-9662 – *2

J.W. May, #304, 250 Dundas St. West, M5T 2Z5 – 416/593-4385, Fax: 416/593-4478 – *1

D.C. Mayne, 577 Jarvis St., M4Y 2J3 – 416/961-0470, Fax: 416/961-2749 – *1

Joseph M. McBride, 5150 Dundas St. West, M9A 1C3 – 416/231-6555, Fax: 416/231-6630 – *1

McBride, Wallace, Laurent & Cord, 5150 Dundas St. West, M9A 1C3 – 416/231-6555, Fax: 416/231-6630 – *6

McCarthy Tétrault, Toronto-Dominion Bank Tower, #4700, PO Box 48, TD Centre, M5K 1E6 – 416/362-1812, Fax: 416/868-0673; URL: http://www.mccarthy.ca – *186

D.V. McCarthy, #209, 885 Progress Ave., M1H 3G3 – 416/289-9620, Fax: 416/289-1880 – *1

Robert L. McClelland, #313, 2498 Yonge St., M4P 2H8 – 416/481-7360, Fax: 416/481-7360 – *1

S. McClennan, #200, 2200 Bloor St. West, M6S 1N4 – 416/767-5320, Fax: 416/763-2522 – *1

McComb & Associates, Toronto-Dominion Bank Tower, Box: 4411, Toronto-Dominion Centre, PO Box 17, M5K 1A1 – 416/366-1881, Fax: 416/366-0608 – *2

Patrick T. McCool, #110, 964 Albion Rd., M9V 1A7 – 416/740-3684, Fax: 416/740-8495 – *1

K. Wayne McCracken, 90 Sandringham Dr., M3H 1C9 – 416/398-9483 – *1

McDonald & Hayden, #1500, 1 Queen St. East, M5C 2Y3 – 416/364-3100, Fax: 416/601-4100; Email: ddouglas@mchayden.on.ca; URL: http://www.mchayden.on.ca – *17

Peter McGaw & Associates, #1007, 3266 Yonge St., M4N 2P6 – 416/864-1464, Fax: 416/322-4852 – *1

J.G. McGee, 332 Sheppard Ave. East, M2N 3B4 – 416/223-2604, Fax: 416/223-9819 – *1

Robert B. McGee, Q.C., 99 Charles St. East, M4Y 1V2 – 416/925-2232, Fax: 416/964-0823 – *1

McGowan & Associates, #405, 133 Richmond St. West, M5H 2L3 – 416/363-2253, Fax: 416/363-1875 – *3

Bruce McGuire, 2643 Eglinton Ave. West, M6M 1T6 – 416/653-1891 – *1

McIver & McIver, #900, 372 Bay St., M5H 2W9 – 416/864-9000, Fax: 416/864-9190 – *3

McKechnie, Jurgeit & MacKenzie, 655 Dixon Rd., M9W 1J4 – 416/245-5454 – *4

Michael A. McKee, 75 Lowther Ave., M5R 1C9 – 416/928-6611, Fax: 416/961-9905 – *1

D.L. McKelvey, 533 Queen St. East, M5A 1V1 – 416/365-0550 – *1

Lois McKenzie, 75 Lowther Ave., M5R 1C9 – 416/961-8540 – *1

Donald J. McKillop, Q.C., #700, 30 St. Clair Ave. West, M4V 3A1 – 416/483-6969, Fax: 416/975-9766 – *1

McLachlan, Winter, #1500, 123 Edward St., M5G 1E2 – 416/596-7077, Fax: 416/596-7629 – *2

Mary R. Mclaughlin, #1000, 120 Eglinton Ave. East, M4P 1E2 – 416/486-4939 – *1

McLean & Kerr, #2800, 130 Adelaide St. West, M5H 3P5 – 416/364-5371, Fax: 416/366-8571; Email: mail@mcleankerr.com – *23

Gordon W. McLean, #404, 600 Eglinton Ave. East, M4P 1P3 – 416/488-4712, Fax: 416/482-4043 – *1

Mary Keeshan McLean, 30 Banstock Dr., M2K 2H6 – 416/590-9764, Fax: 416/512-1212; Email: mclean.mrjm@sympatico.ca – *1

Reginald M. McLean, #301, 5460 Yonge St., M2N 6K7 – 416/512-1200, Fax: 416/512-1217 – *1

Donald I. McLennan Q.C., #2700, 390 Bay St., M5H 2Y2 – 416/366-7837

McMahon, Raine, #307, 145 Sheppard Ave. East, M1N 3A7 – 416/222-2529, Fax: 416/222-8177 – *2

McMaster, McIntyre & Smyth, 2777 Dundas St. West, M6P 1Y4 – 416/769-4188, Fax: 416/769-4147 – *3

William McMaster, #2408, 180 Dundas St. West, M5G 1Z8 – 416/598-4810, Fax: 416/598-0974 – *1

McMillan Binch, South Tower, #3800, Royal Bank Plaza, M5J 2J7 – 416/865-7000, Fax: 416/865-7048; Toll Free: 1-888-622-4624; URL: http://www.mcbinch.com – *127

Bryan C. McPhadden, #2200, 181 University Ave., M5H 3M7 – 416/601-1020, Fax: 416/601-1721; Email: bmcphadden@mphadden.toronto.on.ca – *1

I.D.C. McPhail, Q.C., 207 Queen St. East, M5A 1S2 – 416/869-3400, Fax: 416/869-0094 – *1

Kenneth McQuaid, 2171 Danforth Ave., M4C 1K3 – 416/690-6939, Fax: 416/690-6941 – *1

McTaggert Blais & Associates, #3300, 20 Queen St. West, CP 33, M5H 3R3 – 416/971-4848, Fax: 416/971-4849 – *6

Faye Mcwatt, 74 Lowther Ave., M5R 1C9 – 416/927-7430, Fax: 416/961-9905 – *1

Meighen Demers, Merrill Lynch Canada Tower, Box: 11, #1100, 200 King St. West, M5H 3T4 – 416/977-8400, Fax: 416/977-5239; URL: http://www.meighendemers.com – *31

Meisels & Associates, #200, 79 Shuter St., M5B 1B3 – 416/363-7700, Fax: 416/861-9919 – *1

Deborah L. Meldazy, 426 Davenport Rd., M4V 1B5 – 416/929-8524, Fax: 416/929-4042 – *1

Menzies, von Bogen, 1071B Bloor St. West, M6H 1M5 – 416/532-2833, Fax: 416/532-6553 – *2

Paul Mergler, #401, 302 The East Mall, M9B 6C7 – 416/232-9589, Fax: 416/232-9201; Email: pabkon@interlog.com – *1

E.H. Merifield, #202, 4889 Yonge St., M2N 5N4 – 416/221-3494, Fax: 416/221-4169 – *1

Edwin Norman Merkur, #4052, 3080 Yonge St., M4N 3N1 – 416/487-3445, Fax: 416/487-9674 – *1

Ephry N. Merkur, Q.C., #Penthouse, 175 Keewatin Ave., M4P 2A3 – 416/486-5211, Fax: 416/486-2254

Clarke A. Merritt, Box: 33, #3300, 20 Queen St. West, M5H 3R3 – 416/971-3306, Fax: 416/971-4849; Email: cmerrittl@aol.com – *1

Ruth E. Mesbur, #210, 335 Bay St., M5H 2R3 – 416/863-9744, Fax: 416/863-9541 – *1

Michela & Gord, #1200, 595 Bay St., M5G 2C2 – 416/972-1137, Fax: 416/966-5053 – *1

David M. Midanik, 470 King St. East, M5A 1L7 – 416/364-1780, Fax: 416/362-0847 – *1

J.S. Midanik, Q.C., 296 Russell Hill Rd, M4V 2T6 – 416/924-1575 – *1

Yaroslav Mikitchook, #210, 204 Richmond St. West, M5V 1V6 – 416/599-2811, Fax: 416/599-2971 – *1

Janet G. Miliaris, #11, 2300 Lawrence Ave. East, M1P 2R2 – 416/288-0887, Fax: 416/288-1093 – *1

J.A. Millard, #109, 964 Albion Rd., M9V 1A7 – 416/742-1233, Fax: 416/742-1237 – *1

Miller & Miller, 1577 Bloor St. West, M6P 1A6 – 416/536-1159, Fax: 416/536-3618 – *2

Miller Thomson, Box: 27, #2500, 20 Queen St. West, M5H 3S1 – 416/595-8500, Fax: 416/595-8695; Email: toronto@millerthomson.ca; URL: http://wwa.millerthomson.ca – *114

Dan Miller, #2200, 121 King St. West, M5H 3T9 – 416/862-2473, Fax: 416/862-1698 – *1

Duncan R. Miller, #1110, 36 Toronto St., M5C 2C5 – 416/362-0234, Fax: 416/860-1845 – *1

G.R. Miller, #402, 43 Eglinton Ave. East, M4P 1A3 – 416/486-7917, Fax: 416/487-4444 – *1

Jonathan Miller, #600, 1120 Finch Ave. West, M3J 3H7 – 416/665-6016, Fax: 416/667-0048 – *1

Mills & Mills, #2500, 145 King St. West, M5H 3T6 – 416/863-0125, Fax: 416/863-3997 – *16

Douglas J. Millstone, #309, 2100 Ellesmere Rd., M1H 3B7 – 416/289-7996, Fax: 416/289-7998 – *1

Minden, Gross, Grafstein & Greenstein, #600, 111 Richmond St. West, M5H 2H5 – 416/362-3711, Fax: 416/864-9223 – *39

Richard R. Minster, #428, 105 Gordon Baker Rd., M2H 3P8 – 416/499-9829, Fax: 416/499-1620 – *1

Allan Mintz, Penthouse, 121 Richmond St. West, M5H 2K1 – 416/864-0330 – *1

Paul Minz, #1, 3520 Pharmacy Ave., M1W 2T8 – 416/499-9350, Fax: 416/499-1463 – *1

Nick Mircheff, #2B, 3030 Midland Ave., M1S 5C9 – 416/321-2885, Fax: 416/321-3345 – *1

Vishnu Misir & Associates, #212, 2357 Finch Ave. West, M9M 2W8 – 416/744-2796, Fax: 416/744-7772 – *5

Miskin Flancman & Frisch, 1286 Kennedy Rd., M1P 2L5 – 416/752-2221, Fax: 416/752-8434 – *2

Mitchell, Bardyn & Zalucky, #200, 3029 Bloor St. West, M8X 1C5 – 416/234-9111, Fax: 416/234-9114 – *10

Heather Mitchell, #306, 10 Alcorn Ave., M4V 1E4 – 416/972-6565, Fax: 416/973-3999 – *1

M.J. Mitchell, Q.C., #1704, 55 University Ave., M5J 2H7 – 416/362-0901, Fax: 416/366-3513 – *1

L.R. Mitz, 185 King St. East, M5A 1J4 – 416/365-7979, Fax: 416/361-0229 – *1

J.W.P. Mo, #207, 834 Yonge St., M4W 2H1 – 416/923-3292, Fax: 416/923-3292 – *1

M.S. Mogil, #610, 4211 Yonge St., M2P 2A9 – 416/590-7999, Fax: 416/590-9998 – *1

Mohan & Mohan, #225, 3300 McNicoll Ave., M1V 5J6 – 416/609-8200, Fax: 416/609-8202 – *2

Alawi K. Mohideen, #207, 2131 Lawrence Ave. East, M1R 5G4 – 416/752-9814, Fax: 416/752-6356 – *2

B. Monaco, #103, 1205 St. Clair Ave. West, M6E 1B5 – 416/651-2299, Fax: 416/651-1954 – *1

Bernard J. Monaghan, 3080 Yonge St., M4N 3N1 – 416/486-9919, Fax: 416/486-1885 – *1

Moore & Costello, #365, 5 Fairview Mall Dr., M1J 2Z1 – 416/493-4148, Fax: 416/493-3979 – *2

John C. Moore, 533 Queen St. East, M5A 1V1 – 416/364-6755 – *1

Robin Morch, #601, 130 Bloor St. West, M5S 1N5 – 416/926-1219, Fax: 416/923-1391

Barbara Morgan, #216, 4195 Dundas St. West, M8X 1Y4 – 416/234-8248, Fax: 416/234-8252 – *1

Morlock & Associates, #500, 1 Richmond St. West, M5H 3W4 – 416/862-0500, Fax: 416/862-9063 – *4

Morris & Morris, #920, 390 Bay St., M5H 2Y2 – 416/366-2277, Fax: 416/366-5988 – *6

Morris Silver Lewis, 1 Yorkdale Rd., M6A 3A1 – 416/781-5222, Fax: 416/781-3110 – *3

D.S. Morris, 129 John St., M5V 2E2 – 416/977-4799, Fax: 416/977-4472 – *1

L.J. Morris, 101 Scollard St., M5R 1G4 – 416/924-0711, Fax: 416/960-9650 – *1

Morris, Rose, Ledgett, Canada Trust Tower, BCE Pl., #2700, 161 Bay St., M5J 2S1 – 416/981-9400, Fax: 416/863-9500 – *61

Steven A. Morris, #306, 500 Danforth Ave., M4K 1P6 – 416/778-9795 – *1

Warren J. Morris, #2200, 181 University Ave., M5H 3M7 – 416/601-6795, Fax: 416/363-7875 – *1

D.A. Morrison, 2773 Lakeshore Blvd. West, M8V 1H4 – 416/251-3364, Fax: 416/251-9331

Stephen Morrison, 112 Adelaide St. East, M5C 1K9 – 416/363-0453, Fax: 416/363-1877 – *1

Mortimer, Clark, Grey & Martin, 153 Glencairn Ave., M4R 1N1 – 416/486-0816, Fax: 416/486-1755

Moses & Associates, #410, 212 King St. West, M5H 1K5 – 416/599-8812, Fax: 416/599-5582 – *1

S.S. Moskowitz, 740 Spadina Ave., M5S 2J2 – 416/961-8864, Fax: 416/961-7654 – *1

Clifford Moss, #336, 200 Finch Ave. West, M2R 3W4 – 416/226-6060, Fax: 416/226-6900 – *1

Mostyn & Mostyn, 845 St. Clair Ave. West, 4th Fl., M6C 1C3 – 416/653-3819, Fax: 416/653-3891 – *5

Anthony Moustacalis, #902, 372 Bay St., M5H 2W9 – 416/363-2656 – *1

Movat, Eccleston., #803, 130 Spadina Ave., M5V 2L4 – 416/504-2722, Fax: 416/504-2686 – *1

Matthew Moyal, 8 Finch Ave. West, M2N 6L1 – 416/733-0330, Fax: 416/250-1818; Email: moyal@idirect.com – *1

Steven Mucha, #300, 50 Richmond St. East, M5C 1N7 – 416/366-5114, Fax: 416/366-1722 – *1

Richard Muir, 420 Nugget Ave., M1S 4A4 – 416/291-1459 – *1

Murrant Brown, 130 Yorkville Ave., M5R 1C2 – 416/975-0821, Fax: 416/975-1531

Murray & Gregory, 160 John St., M5V 2E5 – 416/598-1643, Fax: 416/598-9520 – *2

Muyal, Moses, #601, 2200 Yonge St., M4S 2C6 – 416/932-0786, Fax: 416/932-1108 – *1

Ken H. Nathens, #3, 4901A Yonge St., M2N 5N4 – 416/222-6980, Fax: 416/221-9965 – *1

J. Naumovich, #101, 813 Broadview Ave., M4K 2P8 – 416/466-2119, Fax: 416/466-2581

Neal & Smith, #300, 3443 Finch Ave. East, M1W 2S1 – 416/494-4545 – *3

Neighbourhood Legal Services, 333 Queen St. East, M5A 1S9 – 416/861-0677, Fax: 416/861-1777

Neinstein & Singer, #402, 1183 Finch Ave. West, M3J 2G2 – 416/665-8411, Fax: 416/665-4291 – *2

C. Ann Nelson, #400, 2490 Bloor St. West, M6S 1R4 – 416/760-7076, Fax: 416/760-7338 – *1

Nelson, McNamee, 238 Jane St., M6S 3Z1 – 416/762-7477, Fax: 416/762-0182 – *2

Theodore Nemetz, #801, 1 St. Clair Ave. East, M4T 2V7 – 416/961-6560, Fax: 416/964-2494; Email: nemetz@inforamp.net – *1

Richard Nemis, #1800, 95 Wellington St. West, M2J 2N7 – 416/864-1456, Fax: 416/947-0807 – *1

Neuman & Grant, 508 Bathurst St., M5S 2P9 – 416/961-7400, Fax: 416/921-2949 – *2

R. Geoffrey Newbury, The Exchange Tower, #2125, 130 King St. West, M5X 1A6 – 416/362-4048, Fax: 416/362-4049; Email: newbury@io.org; URL: http://www.io.org/~newbury – *1

Newman Weinstock, #906, 43 Eglinton Ave. East, M4P 2W1 – 416/484-7766, Fax: 416/484-8264 – *1

D.H. Newman, Q.C., 70 Dundas St. East, M5B 1C7 – 416/598-4922 – *1

James L. Newman, #300, 133 Richmond St. West, M5H 2L3 – 416/863-0440, Fax: 416/863-5241 – *1

S.H. Newman, #1201, 44 Charles St. West, M4Y 1R7 – 416/925-8165, Fax: 416/925-8122 – *1

Steve Newman, #305, 343 Wilson Ave., M3H 1T1 – 416/630-8910, Fax: 416/630-8489 – *1

Alexandra Ngan, #306, 1033 Bay St., M5S 3A5 – 416/925-3333, Fax: 416/925-3339 – *1

Peter Ngan, 1911 Kennedy Rd., M1P 2L9 – 416/298-1828, Fax: 416/298-2186 – *1

Cindy Nicholas, 2891 Kingston Rd., M1M 1N3 – 416/266-3080, Fax: 416/264-2330 – *1

A.R. Nicol, 111 Elizabeth St., 3rd Fl., M5G 1P7 – 416/340-9909, Fax: 416/599-8075 – *1

Niebler, Liebeck, Singer & Associates, #2000, 393 University Ave., M5E 1F6 – 416/597-6689, Fax: 416/597-8683 – *3

Howard Nightingale, #411, 1111 Finch Ave. West, M3J 2E5 – 416/663-4423, Fax: 416/663-4424 – *1

Nobbs, Woods & Clark, #250, 70 University Ave., M5J 2M4 – 416/977-1000, Fax: 416/977-2895 – *5

Cinnie Noble, #1505, 330 Bay St., M5H 2S8 – 416/363-8680, Fax: 416/362-1465 – *1

Noik & Associates, #400, 3410 Sheppard Ave. East, M1T 3K4 – 416/754-1020, Fax: 416/754-1784; Email: bern@inforamp.net – *3

C. Randall Nowlan, #1200, 595 Bay St., M5G 2C2 – 416/595-0106, Fax: 416/593-1352 – *1

Nuttall, Rekai, #3204, 20 Queen St. West, M5H 3R3 – 416/598-2311 – *2

O'Connor & Gold, 198 Davenport Road, M5R 1J2 – 416/962-8200, Fax: 416/964-7498 – *3

David F. O'Connor, 75 Lowther Ave., M5R 1C9 – 416/960-1951, Fax: 416/961-9905 – *1

R. Allan O'Donnell, #2200, 181 University Ave., M5H 3M7 – 416/366-0323, Fax: 416/366-3205

O'Donnell, Robertson & Sanfilippo, #2100, 1 Queen St. East, PO Box 100, M5C 2W5 – 416/214-0606, Fax: 416/214-0605 – *2

O'Donohue & O'Donohue, #1600, 390 Bay St., M5H 2Y2 – 416/361-3231, Fax: 416/361-3472 – *4

Kevin J. O'Hara, #424, 100 Richmond St. West, M5H 3K6 – 416/868-1555, Fax: 416/365-1474 – *1

O'Neill, Browning, Pineau, #200, 372 Bay St., M5H 2W9 – 416/868-0544, Fax: 416/868-0724 – *2

O'Reilly, Moll, 300 Main St., M4C 4X5 – 416/690-3324, Fax: 416/690-3330 – *1

Patrick O'Rourke, 75 Lowther Ave., M5R 1C9 – 416/927-7041, Fax: 416/961-9905 – *1

Ogilvie, Ishbel S., 469 Queen St. East, M5A 1T9 – 416/956-4848 – *1

Ogilvy Renault, Royal Trust Tower, TD Centre, #2100, PO Box 141, M5K 1H1 – 416/216-4000, Fax: 416/216-3930; Email: info@ogilvyrenault.com – *22

Okell & Weisman, 352 Bedford Park Ave., M5M 1J8 – 416/787-1105, Fax: 416/787-2130 – *2

Olch, Torgov, Cohen, #1014, 111 Richmond St. West, M5H 2J5 – 416/363-8366, Fax: 416/367-4043 – *2

Oleskiw, Anweiler, #701, 123 Edward St., M5G 1E2 – 416/591-1746, Fax: 416/591-9200; Email: anweiler@inforamp.net – *2

Diane Oleskiw, #701, 123 Edward St., M5G 1E2 – 416/591-1261, Fax: 416/591-9200 – *1

Laura A. Onischuk, 350 Bay St., 9th Fl., M5H 2S6 – 416/869-0751, Fax: 416/367-4098 – *1

Thomas T. Onizuka, Q.C., #201, 425 University Ave., M5G 1T6 – 416/598-2002, Fax: 416/598-8183 – *1

Joanna Opalinski, 131 Silverhill Dr., M9B 3W6 – 416/234-1740, Fax: 416/234-1740 – *1

Orbach, Katzman & Herschorn, 417 Parliament St., M5A 3A1 – 416/967-6777, Fax: 416/967-1506 – *3

M.M. Orkin, Q.C., #1401, 111 Richmond St. West, M5H 2G4 – 416/363-4108, Fax: 416/365-9276 – *1

J.N. Ormston, 739 Bloor St. West, M6G 1L6 – 416/535-3888, Fax: 416/535-3256; Email: rosinor@ister.ca – *1

Orr & Darrah, #700, 4 King St. West, M5H 1B6 – 416/860-0141, Fax: 416/860-0140 – *2

Osak, Osak & Osak, #904, 1000 Finch Ave. West, M3J 2V5 – 416/736-1736, Fax: 416/736-1546 – *3

M.A. Osborne, #201, 100 Sheppard Ave. West, M2N 1M6 – 416/225-1145, Fax: 416/225-0832 – *1

Osler, Hoskin & Harcourt, PO Box 50, One First Canadian Place, M5X 1B8 – 416/362-2111, Fax: 416/862-6666; Email: counsel@osler.com; URL: http://www.osler.com – *209

J.A. Ostrowski, #900, 5075 Yonge St., M2N 6C6 – 416/364-3835, Fax: 416/730-1227 – *1

Anthony Paas, 81 Wellesley St. East, M5A 2Z7 – 416/960-0049, Fax: 416/960-1498 – *1

Pace, Johnson, 5110 Dundas St. West, M9A 1C2 – 416/236-3060, Fax: 416/236-1809 – *4

Page, Hill, #2200, 439 University Ave., M5G 1Y8 – 416/595-9935, Fax: 416/595-1731; Email: adrianhill@sympatico.ca – *7

* indicates number of lawyers in law firm.

Pallo Holdings, #252, 250 Eglinton Ave. West, M4R 1A7 – 416/487-8220, Fax: 416/487-4503 – *1
Susanne I. Palmer, 4 Hillholm Rd., M5P 1M2 – 416/482-2492 – *1
Demetrius Pantazis, 870 Danforth Ave., M4J 1L7 – 416/469-5355, Fax: 416/469-8136 – *1
Papernick & Papernick, #206, 4580 Dufferin St., M3H 5Y2 – 416/665-5660, Fax: 416/665-5662 – *1
Allan Papernick, Q.C., #204, 1711 McCowan Rd., M1S 2Y3 – 416/291-2965, Fax: 416/291-0161 – *1
Ado Park Q.C., #401, 365 Bay St., M5H 2V1 – 416/363-4451, Fax: 416/363-9256 – *1
John Y.S. Park, #203, 53 Spring Garden Ave., M2N 3G1 – 416/512-8755, Fax: 416/512-0074 – *1
Mary Park, #200, 60 St. Clair Ave. East, M4T 1N5 – 416/323-0331, Fax: 416/323-0162 – *1
Parkdale Community Legal Services, 165 Dufferin St., M6K 1Y9 – 416/531-2411 – *1
William J. Parker, Q.C., Penthouse, 121 Richmond St. West, M5H 2K1 – 416/862-8210, Fax: 416/364-9842 – *1
John R. Parkinson, #200, 2401 Eglinton Ave. East, M1K 2M5 – 416/757-8855 – *1
Paroian, Raphael, Courey, Cohen & Houston, #1812, 181 University Ave., M5H 3M7 – 416/594-1812, Fax: 416/594-0868 – *35
Carolyn Parpasniak, 271 Queen St. East, M4E 1G5 – 416/691-9355
Pascale, Zentil, 3800 Steeles Ave. West, M9L 4G9 – 416/746-7420, Fax: 416/746-2100 – *3
Stanley Pasternak, #401, 111 Avenue Rd., M5R 3J8 – 416/961-8144, Fax: 416/961-8730 – *1
Paterson, MacDougall, #2100, 1 Queen St. East, PO Box 100, M5C 2W5 – 416/366-9607, Fax: 416/366-3743; URL: http://www.pmlaw.com – *17
A. Bonwyn Patterson, #204, 345 Wilson Ave., M3H 5W1 – 416/630-2266, Fax: 416/630-6696 – *3
Philip Patterson, #305, 1033 Bay St., M5S 3A5 – 416/968-9188 – *1
Paul & Paul, 39 Hayden St., M4Y 2P2 – 416/968-1777, Fax: 416/968-1211 – *2
J.G. Paul, #5, 1778 Bloor St. West, PO Box 465, M6P 3K4 – 416/767-9919, Fax: 416/767-6272 – *1
Jeffrey Paul, #10, 1278 St. Clair Ave. West, M6E 1B9 – 416/653-3131, Fax: 416/653-6343 – *1
Robert J. Paul, #5, 74 Upper Canada Pl., M2P 2A3 – 416/226-3967 – *1
David A. Payne, #1503, 372 Bay St., M5H 2W9 – 416/863-3901 – *1
Murray E. Payne, 3329 Bloor St. West, M8X 1E7 – 416/232-1242, Fax: 416/231-1280 – *1
Wolfgang J. Pazulla, 16 Four Seasons Pl., M9B 6E5 – 416/622-6669, Fax: 416/622-1440 – *1
Peace, Burns, Halkiw & Manning, Harbord House, 546 Euclid Ave., M6G 2T2 – 416/533-1025, Fax: 416/588-6936 – *3
Roselyn Pecus, #407, 1280 Finch Ave. West, M3J 3K6 – 416/665-6449, Fax: 416/665-7488 – *1
Peikes & Halpert, 35 Howard St., M4X 1J6 – 416/968-7733, Fax: 416/968-7192 – *2
Paul S. Pellman, #2200, 181 University Ave., M5H 3M7 – 416/601-6808, Fax: 416/601-1702 – *1
Penman & Penman, 4168 Dundas St. West, M8X 1X3 – 416/231-5696, Fax: 416/231-5697 – *1
Perks & Hanson, #901, 130 Adelaide St. West, M5H 3P5 – 416/362-3366, Fax: 416/362-3174 – *2
Peters & Kestelman, 245 Coxwell Ave., M4L 3B4 – 416/465-3561, Fax: 416/468-3563 – *1
Mendo Petrovski, 2336 Danforth Ave., M4C 1K7 – 416/423-8455, Fax: 416/423-1581 – *1
V. Walter Petryshyn, 1247 Dundas St. West, M6J 1X6 – 416/534-8431, Fax: 416/531-2455 – *1
Phillips & Phillips, #2200, 181 University Ave., M5H 3M7 – 416/601-6802, Fax: 416/601-9590 – *1
Douglas N. Phillips, 13 Reno Dr., M1K 2V5 – 416/757-3445 – *1
Picov & Kleinberg, #601, 2161 Yonge St., M4S 3A6 – 416/488-2100, Fax: 416/488-2794 – *2
Pikkov, Mart, #108, 100 Lombard St., M5C 1M3 – 416/601-0368
L.A. Piller, #700, 390 Bay St., M5H 2Y2 – 416/862-7020, Fax: 416/862-2135 – *1
Graham F. Pinos, Q.C., #1901, 65 Queen St. West, M5H 2M5 – 416/944-8623, Fax: 416/944-8461 – *1
Piscelli & Faieta, #100, 866 The Queensway, M8Z 1N7 – 416/255-7392, Fax: 416/255-7394 – *2
Jillian M. Pivnick, #410, 350 Lonsdale Rd., M5P 1R6 – 416/484-6306 – *1
Frank Pizzimenti, 370 Bloor St. East, M4W 3M6 – 416/927-9000, Fax: 416/927-9069
Fred A. Platt, #1600, 151 Yonge St., M5C 2W7 – 416/777-1818, Fax: 416/777-1819 – *1
Pledge & Associates, #203, 1013 Wilson Ave., M3K 1G1 – 416/630-8702, Fax: 416/630-8714 – *1
Poch Environmental Lawyer, 236 Old Forest Hill Rd., M6C 2H4 – 416/789-9787, Fax: 416/789-9209 – *1
Pocock & Rogers, #5044, 3080 Yonge St., M4N 3N3 – 416/482-6155 – *2
F. Polla, 1684 Dufferin St., M6H 3M1 – 416/651-2888, Fax: 416/658-7653 – *1
A.S. Pollack, 648 Bedford Park Ave., M5M 1K3 – 416/787-1791 – *1
J.B. Pollock, #304, 3200 Dufferin St., PO Box 8, M6A 2T3 – 416/787-4223, Fax: 416/787-5530 – *1
Eric P. Polten, Guardian of Canada Tower, #2200, 181 University Ave., M5H 3M7 – 416/601-6766, Fax: 416/947-0909; Email: info@poltenhodder.com; URL: http://www.poltenhodder.com/~ph – *1
H.M. Pomerantz, 1035 McNicoll Ave., M1W 3W6 – 416/497-2210, Fax: 416/497-1992 – *1
William Pomerantz, 1035 McNicoll Ave., M1W 3W6 – 416/502-0770
Stephen P. Ponesse, #1600, 111 Richmond St. West, M5H 2G4 – 416/361-3582, Fax: 416/368-7217 – *1
Poole Milligan, #330, 4100 Yonge St., M2P 2B5 – 416/221-4100, Fax: 416/221-6340; Email: info@poolemilligan.com; URL: http://www.poolemilligan.com – *6
Poole, A.F.N., Q.C., 133 Avenue Rd., M5R 2H7 – 416/967-5711, Fax: 416/967-4428; Email: afnpoole@interlog.com; URL: http://web.idirect.com:80/~poole/ – *2
Poon & Ho Law Office, #306, 45 Sheppard Ave. East, M2N 5W9 – 416/590-7737, Fax: 416/590-7738 – *6
Porter Posluns & Harris, #1201, 100 Yonge St., M5C 2W1 – 416/367-0148, Fax: 416/367-4279
Don Poscente, 115 Pembroke St., M5A 2N9 – 416/924-9912, Fax: 416/924-9912 – *1
E.G. Posen, #900, 1 St. Clair Ave. East, M4T 2V7 – 416/962-4180, Fax: 416/923-1549 – *1
Gary Posesorski, #702, 2323 Yonge St., M4P 2C9 – 416/488-5323, Fax: 416/488-3716 – *1
Poss & Halfnight, #200, 1 Queen St. East, M5C 2W5 – 416/361-3200, Fax: 416/361-1405; Email: 71754.1172@compuserve.com – *9
W.G. Posthumus, #1900, 700 Bay St., M5G 1Z6 – 416/598-0747, Fax: 416/971-7656 – *1
Potts, Weisberg & Musil, #202, 586 Eglinton Ave. East, M4P 1P2 – 416/485-7366, Fax: 416/485-7368 – *3
Powell, Michael L., #523, 1315 Lawrence Ave. East, M3A 3R3 – 416/441-6840, Fax: 416/441-0330; Email: powlaw@interlog.com – *3
Powers & Associates, 112 Adelaide St. East, M5C 1K9 – 416/214-2900, Fax: 416/368-2918; Email: powerlaw@inforamp.net – *2
Mark Prager, Barr & Solctr, 2 Sheppard Ave. East, M2N 5Y7 – 416/223-2108, Fax: 416/221-8928
C.G. Preobrazenski, 99 Charles St. East, M4Y 1V2 – 416/964-1717, Fax: 416/964-0823 – *1
Robert Presler, #1230, 65 Queen St. West, M5H 2M5 – 416/364-2000, Fax: 416/364-7027 – *1
Jack J. Press, 394 Old Orchard Grove, M5M 2E9 – 416/783-4256, Fax: 416/783-6528 – *1
Price Grenville, C., Q.C., 1624 Bayview Ave., 2nd Fl., M4G 3B7 – 416/481-6488, Fax: 416/481-5275
Robert G. Price Q.C., #402, 372 Bay St., M5H 3W1 – 416/365-7756, Fax: 416/863-0324
Stephen Price & Associates, #3204, 20 Queen St. West, M5H 3R3 – 416/598-1522, Fax: 416/340-7025 – *1
D.R. Proctor, Q.C., 1921 Eglinton Ave. East, Unit 8A, M1L 2L6 – 416/751-0467, Fax: 416/751-3770 – *1
Prousky & Biback, 2 Toronto St., M5C 2B6 – 416/863-1300, Fax: 416/863-4942 – *3
F.T.M. Pujolas, 2773 Lakeshore Blvd. West, M8V 1H4 – 416/251-3364, Fax: 416/251-9331 – *1
V.E. Purcell, Q.C., 893 O'Connor Dr., M4B 2S7 – 416/757-2801, Fax: 416/757-1130 – *1
Purdon & Ronka, #200, 5415 Dundas St. West, M9B 1B5 – 416/239-4369 – *2
R.G. Pyne, 3329 Bloor St. West, M8X 1E7 – 416/231-3339 – *1
Quirk, McGillicuddy & Sutton, 1661 Dufferin St., M6H 3L9 – 416/652-3543, Fax: 416/652-2730 – *1
Rachlin & Wolfson, #1500, 390 Bay St., M5H 2Y2 – 416/367-0202, Fax: 416/367-1820 – *10
Danuta H. Radomski, #164, 66 Princess St., M5A 2T1 – 416/366-3875, Fax: 416/368-0620 – *1
Louis Radomsky, 10 Otter Cres., M5N 2W2 – 416/364-7764, Fax: 416/787-5059 – *1
Martin N. Rain, #407, 1183 Finch Ave. West, M3J 2G2 – 416/661-4518, Fax: 416/661-2688 – *1
Harvey Ram, #200, 1969 Weston Rd., M9N 1W8 – 416/245-2222, Fax: 416/245-5615 – *1
Adi M. Raman, 1944 Eglinton Ave. West, M6E 2J8 – 416/783-3421, Fax: 416/783-9131 – *1
R. Sam Ramlall, #700, 5799 Yonge St., M2M 3V3 – 416/512-6465, Fax: 416/512-6042 – *1
Brigitte L. Raney, 7 Ansley St., M4R 1X5 – 416/484-6418, Fax: 416/484-6418 – *1
R.P. Rawana, #209, 8130 Sheppard Ave. East, M1B 3W3 – 416/281-8505, Fax: 416/286-4353 – *1
Raymond & Honsberger, Thomson Building, 65 Queen St. West, 17th Fl., M5H 2M5 – 416/366-3726, Fax: 416/367-2502 – *14
Rayson, Kohn Evelyn, #302, 3845 Bathurst St., M3H 3N2 – 416/630-5600, Fax: 416/630-5906
Raza Arif, #207, 2131 Lawrence Ave. East, M1R 5G4 – 416/752-9810, Fax: 416/752-6356
Reble, Ritchie, Green & Ketcheson, #100, 1 Eva Rd., M9C 4Z5 – 416/622-6601, Fax: 416/622-4713 – *6
Redway & Butler, 3080 Yonge St., M4N 3N1 – 416/481-5604 – *2
F. Vincent Regan, Q.C., #1507, 65 Queen St. West, M5H 2M5 – 416/864-9010, Fax: 416/864-9013 – *1
T.S. Reiber, #601, 135 Bay St., M5R 3K4 – 416/927-9841, Fax: 416/975-1531 – *1
Reid, McLean & Scott, 2938 Danforth Ave., M4C 1M5 – 416/591-1131, Fax: 416/699-1958 – *1
William V. Reid, #201, 1114A Wilson Ave., M3M 1G7 – 416/398-5200, Fax: 416/398-9930 – *1
Dorothy J. Reilly, 701 Coxwell Ave., M4C 3C1 – 416/461-7553, Fax: 416/461-2679 – *1
Michael P. Reilly, #201, 1919 Lawrence Ave. East, M1R 2Y6 – 416/757-7773, Fax: 416/757-0771; Email: mreilly@oak.net; URL: http://www.oak.net/reilly – *3
Peter Reiner, #307, 55 Eglinton Avenue East, M4P 1G8 – 416/932-9959, Fax: 416/932-1108 – *1
Reingold & Reingold, #4068, 3080 Yonge St., M4N 3N1 – 416/483-3364, Fax: 416/440-1942 – *1
A.C.J. Reisler, 161 Bridgeland Ave., M6A 1Z1 – 416/781-4002, Fax: 416/781-7797 – *1
Stanley Reisman, 740 Spadina Ave., M5S 2J2 – 416/961-8864, Fax: 416/961-7654 – *1
Moishe Reiter, Q.C., #2030, 130 Adelaide St. West, M5H 3P5 – 416/369-1717, Fax: 416/369-1723 – *1
Rekai & Johnson, #604, 130 Bloor St. West, M5S 1N5 – 416/960-8876 – *4
R.J. Renton, #400, 2 Billingham Rd., M9B 6E1 – 416/237-0294, Fax: 416/232-9291 – *1
Rexdale Community Legal Clinic, #215, 1530 Albion Rd., M9V 1B4 – 416/741-5201, Fax: 416/741-5281

Reznick, Parsons, #2314, 120 Adelaide St. West, M5H 1T1 – 416/863-6026, Fax: 416/863-9334 – *2
Lewis J. Richardson, #2000, 393 University Ave., M5G 1E6 – 416/599-1226, Fax: 416/599-8415 – *1
Riches, McKenzie & Herbert, #2900, 2 Bloor St. East, M4W 3J5 – 416/961-5000 – *6
Richman & Richman, #405, 255 Duncan Mill Rd., M3B 3H9 – 416/510-1575, Fax: 416/510-1580 – *1
D.S. Rickerd, Q.C., 21 Elm Ave., M4W 1M9 – 416/929-5177, Fax: 416/921-8322; Email: drickerd@yorku.ca – *1
Ricketts, Harris, Guardian of Canada Tower, #816, 181 University Ave., M5H 2X7 – 416/364-6211, Fax: 416/364-1697 – *11
Ridout & Maybee, #2400, 1 Queen St. East, M5C 3B1 – 416/868-1482, Fax: 416/362-0823 – *24
Gerald Rifkin, #415, 4580 Dufferin St., M3H 5Y2 – 416/667-0980, Fax: 416/667-0765 – *1
Riley, McGirney, Ryder, Salisbury, #906, 151 Yonge St., M5C 2W7 – 416/364-7611, Fax: 416/364-1636 – *4
Roach, Schwartz & Associates, 688 St. Clair Ave. West, M6C 1B1 – 416/657-1465, Fax: 416/657-1511; Email: charoa@globalserve.net – *6
Robert Adourion, 900 Don Mills Rd., M3C 1W3 – 416/441-4141, Fax: 416/441-6898 – *2
William H. Roberts, #201, 34 Southport St., M6S 3N3 – 416/769-3162, Fax: 416/762-8472 – *1
Robertson & Keith, 2481 Kingston Rd., M1N 1V4 – 416/261-1220, Fax: 416/261-1716 – *1
Paul Robertson, 533 Queen St. East, M5A 1V1 – 416/361-9555, Fax: 416/364-7049 – *1
Robertson, Perrett, Lloyd Manor Rd., PO Box 363, M9B 6H6 – 416/232-4300, Fax: 416/234-6309; Email: robper@netsurf.net – *2
Robins, Appleby & Taub, #2500, 130 Adelaide St. West, PO Box 102, M5H 2M2 – 416/868-1080, Fax: 416/868-0306 – *14
S.M. Robins, #400, 330 Bay St., M5H 2S8 – 416/361-0404, Fax: 416/868-1818 – *1
Robinson Hinkson, #904, 4950 Yonge St., M2N 6K1 – 416/223-7787, Fax: 416/223-7679; Toll Free: 1-800-387-7260 – *4
Mary Grace Robinson, #700, 390 Bay St., M5H 2Y2 – 416/368-7122, Fax: 416/862-2135
Lawlor Rochester, #800, 141 Adelaide St. West, M5H 3L5 – 416/366-2267, Fax: 416/368-3467; Email: lr@glaholt.com; URL: http://www.glaholt.com – *1
R.A. Rodney, Q.C., 85 Scollard St., M5R 1G4 – 416/924-0905 – *1
Roebuck, Garbig, #3200, 401 Bay St., M5H 2Y4 – 416/862-7822, Fax: 416/862-2568 – *4
Rogers & Milne, #1004, 357 Bay St., M5H 2T7 – 416/363-6626, Fax: 416/363-6628; Email: patents@rogersmilne.com
Rogers & Rowland, #2600, 121 King St. West, PO Box 120, M5H 3T9 – 416/364-2333, Fax: 416/864-0271 – *2
Rogers, Campbell, Mickleborough, #1600, 111 Richmond St. West, M5H 2G4 – 416/366-3999, Fax: 416/862-0049 – *4
E.S. Rogers, Commercial Union Tower, #2600, POBox 249, Stn Toronto Dominion, M5K 1J5 – 416/864-2101, Fax: 416/864-2333 – *1
Rogers, Smith, Dick & Thomson, #2606, 2 Bloor St. West, M4W 3E2 – 416/968-7270, Fax: 416/968-6299 – *3
Rohmer & Fenn, #1E, 20 Prince Arthur Ave., M5R 1B1 – 416/921-2299, Fax: 416/921-2999 – *2
Roland & Jacobs, #705, 123 Edward St., M5G 1E2 – 416/593-6601, Fax: 416/593-1045 – *2
Roland Nelson, #704, 130 Spadina Ave., M5V 2L4 – 416/368-2538, Fax: 416/360-6764
William L. Roland, #2900, 390 Bay St., M5H 2Y2
M.B. Romanick, Q.C., #1607, 80 Richmond St. West, M5H 2C2 – 416/362-2585 – *1
Patrick S. Roopchand, #303, 745 Danforth Ave., M4J 1L4 – 416/469-5367, Fax: 416/469-9809 – *1
Rosati, Di Zio, 968 Wilson Ave., 3rd Fl., M3K 1E7 – 416/630-6993, Fax: 416/630-1289 – *2
Rose & Rose, #300, 230 Sheppard Ave. West, M2N 1N1 – 416/590-9990, Fax: 416/590-9991 – *3
Rose, Persiko, Rakowsky, #700, 55 University Ave., M5J 2K4 – 416/868-1908, Fax: 416/868-1708 – *2
A.C. Rosen, #904, 27 Queen St. East, M5C 2M6 – 416/363-1601, Fax: 416/363-5620 – *1
Rosen, Fleming, 370 Bloor St. East, M4W 3M6 – 416/927-9000, Fax: 416/927-9069 – *7
S.L. Rosen, 2933 Dufferin St., M6B 3S7 – 416/789-7133 – *1
Rosenbaum Dickison McKay & Grant, 257 Danforth Ave., M4K 1N2 – 416/466-6264, Fax: 416/466-8465 – *4
Brian Rosenbaum, #102, 1245 Caledonia Rd., M6A 2X6 – 416/785-1157, Fax: 416/787-9709 – *1
Martin Z. Rosenbaum, #1202, 330 Bay St., M5H 2S8 – 416/364-1919, Fax: 416/364-7885 – *1
Rosenberg & Robinson, #702, 205 Richmond St. West, M5V 1V3 – 416/596-1770, Fax: 416/596-2473 – *4
Rosenberg & Smith, #1800, 120 Adelaide St. West, M5H 1S8 – 416/863-1900, Fax: 416/863-1966 – *2
Elliot F. Rosenberg, #201, 4949 Bathurst St., M2R 1Y1 – 416/512-7373, Fax: 416/512-7374 – *1
Hy Rosenberg, 61 Saint Nicholas St., M4Y 1W6 – 416/592-7034, Fax: 416/925-0162 – *1
Irving Rosenberg, 3768 Bathurst St., M3H 3M7 – 416/398-0102, Fax: 416/630-1805 – *1
Rosenblatt Associates, 335 Bay St., 10th Fl., M5H 2R3 – 416/861-9429, Fax: 416/861-1215; Email: rosenb@idirect.com; URL: http://www.immigrate.net – *1
Stanley Rosenfarb, #512, 4002 Sheppard Ave. East, M1S 4R5 – 416/298-8828, Fax: 416/298-7142 – *1
Jonathan M. Rosenthal, #500, 70 Bond St., M5B 1X3 – 416/360-7768, Fax: 416/863-4896 – *1
Stewart Rosenthall, #1402, 151 Yonge St., M5C 2W7 – 416/359-0000, Fax: 416/368-9808 – *1
Michael Ross, 197 Sheppard Ave. West, 1st Fl., M2N 1M9 – 416/730-9399, Fax: 416/730-9476 – *1
R.M. Ross, #700, 390 Bay St., M5H 272 – 416/363-1186, Fax: 416/862-2135 – *1
Ted Ross, 272 Roncesvalles Ave., M6R 2M2 – 416/533-7878 – *1
A.M. Sinclair, #200, 2901 Bayview Ave., M2K 1E6 – 416/226-6508 – *1
Cecil L. Rotenberg, Q.C., United Centre, #808, 255 Duncan Mill Rd., M3B 3H9 – 416/449-8866, Fax: 416/510-9090 – *3
J.S. Rotenberg, 17 Isabella Ave., M4X 1M7 – 416/925-4940, Fax: 416/925-4571 – *1
Robert Rotenberg, 75 Lowther Ave., M5R 1C9 – 416/515-1753, Fax: 416/515-1754 – *1
Rotfleisch & Samulovitch, 350 Bay St., 9th Fl., M5H 2S6 – 416/367-4222, Fax: 416/367-4098; Email: davidr@taxpage.com; URL: http://www.taxpage.com – *1
Frank L. Roth, #500, 70 Bond St., M5B 1X3 – 416/963-8776 – *1
Neal H. Roth, #1420, 439 University Ave., M5G 1Y8 – 416/351-7706, Fax: 416/351-7684 – *1
Rothman & Rothman, #403, 133 Richmond St. West, M5H 2L3 – 416/367-9901, Fax: 416/367-9979 – *2
Allan Rouben, #200, 70 Bond St., M5B 1X3 – 416/360-5444, Fax: 416/365-7765 – *1
Frederick Rowell, Q.C., 99 Charles St. East, M4Y 1V2 – 416/920-9251, Fax: 416/964-0823 – *1
S.J. Ruben, #200, 45 St. Clair Ave. West, M4V 1K6 – 416/922-0511, Fax: 416/967-3945 – *1
D.A. Rubenstein, #305, 3292 Bayview Ave., M2M 4J5 – 416/730-0303, Fax: 416/730-0645 – *1
Benjamin Rubin & Associates, 229 Russell Hill Rd., M4V 2T3 – 416/929-2919 – *1
Janice Rubin, #1200, 595 Bay St., M5G 2C2 – 416/593-4463, Fax: 416/593-4109 – *1
Ruby & Edwardh, 11 Prince Arthur Ave., M5R 1B2 – 416/964-9664, Fax: 416/964-8305 – *7
Victor E. Rudinskas, 27 John St., 2nd Fl., M9N 1J4 – 416/240-0594, Fax: 416/248-6060 – *1
George A. Rudnik, #202, 720 Spadina Ave., M5S 2T9 – 416/927-7788 – *1
Martin K.I. Rumack, #202, 2 St. Clair Ave. East, M4T 2T5 – 416/961-3441, Fax: 416/961-1045 – *1
Brian A. Rumanek, #15, 200 Evans Ave., M8Z 1J7 – 416/252-9115, Fax: 416/253-0494 – *1
R.E. Rusek, 1623 Bloor St. West, 2nd Fl., M6P 1A6 – 416/533-8563, Fax: 416/533-8564 – *1
Rush, G.C., #400, 2970 Lake Shore Blvd. West, M8V 1J7 – 416/251-2291, Fax: 416/251-2292 – *1
Russell Juriansz, 1501-65 Queen St. West, M5H 2M5 – 416/867-7590, Fax: 416/867-7594
C.H. Rutherford, #220, 4580 Dufferin St., M3H 5Y2 – 416/667-1338 – *1
Rebecca Rutherford, #203, 425 University Ave., M5G 1T6 – 416/598-3928, Fax: 416/599-8075 – *1
Judith P. Ryan, #207, 12 Birch Ave., M4V 1C8 – 416/928-1154, Fax: 416/925-6684 – *1
Ryder, Wright, Blair & Doyle, #1812, 438 University Ave., M5G 2K8 – 416/340-9070, Fax: 416/340-9250 – *8
Rye & Partners, #1200, 65 Queen St. West, M5H 2M5 – 416/362-4901, Fax: 416/362-8291 – *5
Lorne Sabsay, 317 Grace St., M6G 3A7 – 416/537-1204, Fax: 416/533-5174 – *1
R.L. Sachter, Q.C., #402, 801 Eglinton Ave. West, M5N 1E3 – 416/787-1165, Fax: 416/787-6532 – *1
Sack Goldblatt Mitchell, #1130, 20 Dundas St. West, PO Box 180, M5G 2G8 – 416/977-6070, Fax: 416/591-7333 – *20
Geraldine Sadoway, #303, 489 College St., M6G 1A5 – 416/926-1447, Fax: 416/972-1992 – *1
H.A. Saffrey, #1704, 55 University Ave., M5J 2H7 – 416/593-8794, Fax: 416/366-3513 – *1
Howard Saginur, #720, 25 Sheppard Ave. West, M2N 6S6 – 416/512-1912, Fax: 416/221-8372 – *1
F.G. Salehmohamed, #105, 747 Don Mills Rd., M3C 1T2 – 416/421-7000 – *1
M. Saltman Arbitrations Ltd., #1017, 111 Richmond St. West, M5H 2G4 – 416/366-3091, Fax: 416/366-0879 – *1
Samac, Darling, #811, 25 Adelaide St. East, M5C 3A1 – 416/363-5195, Fax: 416/363-7485 – *2
Samis, Blouin, Dunn, #1100, 123 Front St. West, PO Box 11, M5J 2M2 – 416/365-0000, Fax: 416/365-9993 – *12
William Samis, 258 Wilson Ave., M3H 1S6 – 416/601-6832, Fax: 416/631-9895 – *1
Paul Sanderson Barrister & Solicitor, 52 St. Patrick St., 2nd Fl., M5T 1V2 – 416/971-6616, Fax: 416/971-4144 – *1
Sandler, Gordon, Saperia & Walman, #702, 1240 Bay St., M5R 2A7 – 416/961-0001, Fax: 416/961-9461 – *4
D.A. Sands, 663 Greenwood Ave., 2nd Fl., M4J 4B4 – 416/463-5982 – *1
S.K. Sanwalka, Q.C., #602, 18 Wynford Dr., M3C 3S2 – 416/449-7755, Fax: 416/449-6969 – *1
Umberto Sapone, 1859A Eglinton Ave., West, M6E 2J3 – 416/789-2689 – *1
Sawers, Liswood, Hickman, Bullivant, Dolan, #2901, 1 Adelaide St. East, M5C 2Z7 – 416/861-0330, Fax: 416/861-9886 – *13
Sax, Isaacs, #802, 111 Richmond St. West, M5H 2G4 – 416/869-0400, Fax: 416/869-3405 – *2
Michael M. Sax, #1700, 22 St. Clair Ave. East, M4T 2S3 – 416/921-5669, Fax: 416/925-5753
Dianne Saxe, 66 Russell Hill Rd., M4V 2T2 – 416/962-5882, Fax: 416/962-8817; Email: dsaxe@envirolaw.com; URL: http://www.envirolaw.com – *1
Scandiffio & Gariepy, 89 Dupont St., M5R 1V4 – 416/928-2066, Fax: 416/925-5528 – *2
P.M. Scandiffio, Q.C., #308, 344 Bloor St. West, M5S 3A7 – 416/515-1660, Fax: 416/515-1526 – *1

* indicates number of lawyers in law firm.

Scarborough Community Legal Services, #9, 695 Markham Rd., M1H 2A5 – 416/438-7182, Fax: 416/438-9869

L.H. Schipper, Q.C., #1010, 22 St. Clair Ave. East, M4T 2S3 – 416/961-5355, Fax: 416/961-7011 – *1

Schmidt Preben, 900-350 Bay St., M5H 2S6 – 416/368-8869, Fax: 416/367-4098

Richard D. Schneider, 49 Saint Nicholas St., M4Y 1W6 – 416/922-6147 – *1

M.M. Schnier, #1500, 2 St. Clair Ave. East, M4T 2T5 – 416/927-0300, Fax: 416/927-0305 – *1

Edmund L. Schofield, #1314, 181 University Ave., M5H 3M7 – 416/868-0824, Fax: 416/861-0706 – *1

P.J. Schrieder, Q.C., 1123 Albion Rd., M9V 1A9 – 416/749-6000, Fax: 416/749-6004; Email: iadvise@ican.net – *1

Jeffrey R. Schroeder, 103 Charles St. East, M4Y 1V2 – 416/944-9465, Fax: 416/925-8882 – *1

Schwartz & Schwartz, #432, 700 Lawrence Ave. West, M6A 1B6 – 416/787-1863, Fax: 416/787-0793 – *2

Cecil Schwartz, #200, 2901 Bayview Ave., M2K 1E6 – 416/250-0083, Fax: 416/226-1162 – *1

Schwartz, De Pasquale, #403, 225 Richmond St. West, M5V 1W2 – 416/596-0477, Fax: 416/596-8784 – *2

Arnold B. Schwisberg, #809, 2001 Sheppard Ave. East, M2J 4Z8 – 416/502-3360, Fax: 416/502-3957; Email: abslegal@total.net – *2

Scott & Aylen, TD Bank Tower, Toronto Dominion Centre, 24th Fl., PO Box 194, M5K 1H6 – 416/368-2400, Fax: 416/363-7246; Email: torinfo@scott-aylen.com – *7

B.M. Scully, 31 Prince Arthur Ave., M5R 1B2 – 416/968-2456, Fax: 416/960-5456 – *1

Peter B. Scully, 31 Prince Arthur Ave., M5R 1B2 – 416/968-2456, Fax: 416/960-5456 – *1

V.M. Seabrook, Q.C., #2200, 181 University Ave., M5H 3M7 – 416/601-6826, Fax: 416/363-7875 – *1

Gary L. Segal, #402, 111 Avenue Rd., M5R 3J8 – 416/967-5400, Fax: 416/967-7877; Email: segalimm@istar.ca – *1

Seligman, Robin, #100, 33 Bloor St. East, M4W 3H1 – 416/967-7878, Fax: 416/967-9069

Erwin S. Seltzer, #101, 2642 Eglinton Ave. East, M1K 2S3 – 416/265-0192, Fax: 416/265-0720 – *1

Seon, Gutstadt, Lash, #1800, 4950 Yonge St., M2N 6K1 – 416/224-0224, Fax: 416/224-0758 – *6

Sera, Harrison & Daniels, #1102, 2 Sheppard Ave. East, M2N 5Y7 – 416/222-7668, Fax: 416/222-9253 – *3

Sereda & Sereda, #500, 365 Evans Ave., M8Z 1K2 – 416/251-8600, Fax: 416/251-5680 – *2

Frederick J. Shanahan, The Thomson Building, #1508, 65 Queen St. West, PO Box 67, M5H 2M5 – 416/362-6449 – *1

Martin A. Shanahan, #1508, 65 Queen St. West, PO Box 67, M5H 2M5 – 416/366-7781, Fax: 416/362-3210 – *1

Shapiro & Associate, #208, 2040 Sheppard Ave. East, M2J 5B3 – 416/494-4899, Fax: 416/494-3024 – *2

Shapiro & Shapiro, #200, 55 St. Clair Ave. West, M4V 2Y7 – 416/960-5853, Fax: 416/960-8265 – *2

P.H. Shapiro, #405, 40 St. Clair Ave. West, M4V 1M2 – 416/323-9744, Fax: 416/323-9744 – *2

David Share Associates, Malvern Town Centre, #31, 31 Tapscott Rd., M1B 4Y7 – 416/754-8822, Fax: 416/754-8915

Chet Sharma, #7, 1658 Victoria Park Ave., M1R 1P7 – 416/285-1550, Fax: 416/285-1698 – *1

Roop N. Sharma, 942 Gerrard St. East, M4M 1Z2 – 416/461-0467, Fax: 416/461-5817 – *1

A.J. Shaul, Q.C., 305 Milner Ave., M1B 3V4 – 416/299-6688, Fax: 416/299-6774 – *1

Joel E. Shaw, #1702, 2200 Yonge St., M4S 2C6 – 416/486-3400 – *1

Victor Shaw, 3416 Dundas St. West, M6S 2S1 – 416/766-3700 – *1

Shearman & Sterling, 199 Bay St., PO Box 247, M5L 1E8 – 416/360-8484, Fax: 416/360-2958

G. James M. Shearn, #4300, 40 King St. West, M5H 3Y4 – 416/367-1325, Fax: 416/367-6749

Brian Shell, 615 Lonsdale Rd., M5P 1R8 – 416/656-6003, Fax: 416/654-8469; Email: bshell@aol.com

Harold Shepherd, #311, 500 Danforth Ave., M4K 1P6 – 416/465-8580, Fax: 416/465-9560

T.M. Sheppard, #1200, 595 Bay St., M5G 2C2 – 416/596-6885, Fax: 416/593-1352 – *1

Irvin H. Sherman, Q.C., #405, 130 Bloor St. West, M5S 1N5 – 416/960-8876, Fax: 416/924-2371; Email: irv.sherman@westonia.com; URL: http://www.home.ican.net/~irv – *1

S.L. Sherman, 2645 Eglinton Ave. East, M1K 2S2 – 416/261-7161, Fax: 416/261-7163 – *1

Sherwin & Associates, #1010, 2 Sheppard Ave. East, M2N 5Y7 – 416/221-8181, Fax: 416/221-8199 – *2

Michelle Sherwood, 317 Grace St., M6G 3A7 – 416/533-3191, Fax: 416/533-5174 – *1

Shibley Righton, The Simpson Tower, #1900, 401 Bay St., PO Box 32, M5H 2Z1 – 416/363-9381, Fax: 416/214-5438 – *25

A. Shields, #1300, 5255 Yonge St., M2N 6P4 – 416/223-8333, Fax: 416/223-3404 – *1

B.S. Shier, 219 Carlton St., M5A 2L2 – 416/923-8997, Fax: 416/923-8380 – *1

Stanley I. Shier, Q.C., #701, 357 Bay St., M5H 2T7 – 416/366-9591, Fax: 416/366-2107 – *1

Ralph Shiff, #605, 1120 Finch Ave. West, M3J 3H7 – 416/665-3003, Fax: 416/665-3004 – *1

Gary Shiffman, #504, 505 Eglinton Ave. West, M5N 1B2 – 416/482-4555 – *1

Charles Shifman, #900, 5799 Yonge St., M2M 3V3 – 416/225-1123, Fax: 416/225-1124 – *1

Albert Shifrin, Q.C., Sterling Tower, #603, 372 Bay St., M5H 2W9 – 416/363-1473 – *1

O.B. Shime, Q.C., #200, 70 Bond St., M5B 1X3 – 416/366-8009 – *1

Shamim Shivji, #305, 489 College St., M6G 1A5 – 416/927-7224, Fax: 416/927-8129 – *1

E.I. Shoihet, #408, 100 Adelaide St. West, M5H 1S3 – 416/863-9594 – *1

M.H. Shore, 61 St. Nicholas St., M4Y 1W6 – 416/925-6416, Fax: 416/925-0162 – *1

Geary B. Shorser, #1130, 20 Dundas St. West, PO Box 180, M5G 2G8 – 416/977-7749 – *1

Gary E. Shortliffe, #832, 150 Bloor St. West, M5S 2X9 – 416/927-7088, Fax: 416/927-7888 – *1

Ian C. Shoub, #415, 4580 Dufferin St., M3H 5Y2 – 416/667-0980, Fax: 416/667-0765 – *1

R.A.L. Shour, #1200, 595 Bay St., M5G 2C2 – 416/977-4492 – *1

J.D. Shulman, #212, 120 Carlton St., M5A 4K2 – 416/961-2934, Fax: 416/924-7166 – *1

A.B. Shusterman, #207, 3320 Midland Ave., M1V 5E6 – 416/291-6176, Fax: 416/291-6047 – *1

Obaid R. Siddiqui, #212, 85 Ellesmere Rd., M1R 4B7 – 416/444-5597, Fax: 416/445-9487 – *1

Sierra Legal Defence Fund, #300, 106 Front St. East, M5A 1E1 – 416/368-7533, Fax: 416/363-2746; Email: sldfto@globalserve.net – *1

F. Scott Sievert, 15 Belfield Rd., M9W 1E8 – 416/243-8756, Fax: 416/243-2990 – *1

Louis D. Silver, Q.C., #2600, 250 Yonge St., M5B 2M6 – *1

Silverberg & Weisberg, 4240 Sheppard Ave. East, M1S 1T5 – 416/291-7701, Fax: 416/291-1766 – *3

Murray D. Silverberg, 1100-5799 Yonge St., M2M 3V3 – 416/226-6006, Fax: 416/225-9846

Silverman & Freed, 700 Bay St., 19th Fl., M5G 1Z6 – 416/979-2335, Fax: 416/597-3828 – *2

Anne M. Silverman, #301, 5075 Yonge St., M2N 6C6 – 416/250-0045, Fax: 416/250-1984 – *1

Sheldon N. Silverman, #638, 121 Richmond St. West, M5H 2K1 – 416/363-6295, Fax: 416/363-3047 – *1

Silverstein & Gelfand, #208, 212 King St. West, M5H 1K5 – 416/595-0655, Fax: 416/595-0799 – *2

Sim, Hughes, Ashton & McKay, 330 University Ave., 6th Fl., M5G 1R7 – 416/595-1155, Fax: 416/595-1163; Email: mailsim@sim-mcburney.com; URL: http://www.simbas.com – *12

Lionel Simbrow, 66 Charles St. East, M4Y 2R3 – 416/964-9292, Fax: 416/928-9484 – *1

Monty M. Simmonds, Q.C., #1000, 2 St. Clair Ave. West, M4V 1L5 – 416/967-6706, Fax: 416/967-9483 – *1

P.C. Simonelis, 1579 Bloor St. West, M6P 1A6 – 416/532-3443 – *1

Michael B. Simrod, #415, 4580 Dufferin St., M3H 5Y2 – 416/667-0980, Fax: 416/667-0765 – *1

Isaac Singer, 2424 Bloor St. West, M6S 1P9 – 416/766-1135, Fax: 416/769-5365 – *1

Singer, Keyfetz, Crackower & Saltzman, 532 Eglinton Ave. East, M4P 1N6 – 416/488-6900, Fax: 416/488-7530 – *2

Singer, Kwinter, Polo Centre, #214, 1033 Bay St., M5S 3A5 – 416/961-2882, Fax: 416/961-6760 – *4

Michael S. Singer, 35A Hazelton Ave., M5R 2E3 – 416/926-1934, Fax: 416/922-2636 – *1

Mimi Singh, 200 Adelaide St. West, 5th Fl., M5H IW7 – 416/593-6259, Fax: 416/921-1398 – *1

Joel Skapinker, #607, 372 Bay St., M5H 2W9 – 416/214-1500, Fax: 416/214-0658; Email: jskapinker@usa.net

S.H. Skolnik, #512, 4002 Sheppard Ave. East, M1S 4R5 – 416/297-7300, Fax: 416/298-7142 – *1

Slansky & Pringle, 601-260 Richmond St. West, M5V 1W5 – 416/596-8192, Fax: 416/596-8449 – *2

Slater & Spiller, 450 Rathburn Rd., M9C 3S6 – 416/622-3233, Fax: 416/622-3302 – *2

Slater, Huston, Wells Associates, 644 Evans Ave., M8W 2W6 – 416/259-4293, Fax: 416/259-1286 – *3

Sloan Barristers & Solicitors, #1020, 121 King St. West, PO Box 27, M5H 3T9 – 416/867-9600, Fax: 416/867-9783 – *2

Barry S. Small, #601, 1235 Bay St., M5R 3K4 – 416/929-4783 – *1

Smart & Biggar, #1500, 438 University Ave., PO Box 39, Stn P, M5S 2S6 – 416/593-5514, Fax: 416/591-1690; Email: toronto@smart-biggar.ca – *11

Andrea Smart, #301, 2490 Bloor St. West, M6S 1R4 – 416/766-9989, Fax: 416/763-6876 – *1

Smith & Hukowich, #400, 2405 Lakeshore Blvd. West, M8V 1C6 – 416/259-7638, Fax: 416/259-7424 – *2

Smith & Zoldhelyi, 2424 Bloor St. West, M6S 1P9 – 416/968-7037 – *2

Smith Lyons, Scotia Plaza, #5800, 40 King St. West, M5H 3Z7 – 416/369-7200, Fax: 416/369-7250; Email: rmconnelly@smithlyons.ca; URL: http://www.smithlyons.ca – *130

B.A. Smith, #601, 2161 Yonge St., M4S 3A6 – 416/483-1331 – *1

Cindy L. Smith, #1509, 180 Dundas St. West, M5G 1Z8 – 416/408-0008, Fax: 416/597-9808

Gary Smith, 101 Scollard St., M5R 1G4 – 416/961-1339, Fax: 416/960-9650 – *1

K.D. Smith, #500, 70 Bond St., M5B 1X3 – 416/361-0232 – *1

Stanley Smither, #B1, 309 Mt. Pleasant Rd., M4T 2C2 – 416/485-7511 – *1

Smookler & Smookler, #1604, 55 University Ave., M5J 2H7 – 416/360-1712, Fax: 416/866-7946 – *2

D.B. Snider, 978 Kingston Rd., M4E 1S9 – 416/699-0424, Fax: 416/699-0285 – *1

Kenneth E. Snider, #309, 2100 Ellesmere Rd., M1H 3B7 – 416/438-4515, Fax: 416/289-7998 – *1

Irving Snitman, 554 Annette St., M6S 2C2 – 416/767-0805, Fax: 416/767-4619 – *1

Louis Sokolov, 31 Prince Arthur Ave., M5R 1B2 – 416/921-7626, Fax: 416/960-5456 – *1

A. Melvin Sokolsky, #605, 505 Consumers Rd., M1J 4V8 – 416/493-3993, Fax: 416/493-2653 – *1

Solish, Fellen, #200, 277 Victoria St., M5B 1W2 – 416/977-7345, Fax: 416/977-8177 – *3

Solmon, Rothbart, Goodman, #1600, 18 King St. East, M5C 1C4 – 416/947-1093, Fax: 416/947-0079 – *8

Victor Solnicki, 53 Hilholm Rd., M5P 1M4 – 416/486-5498, Fax: 416/486-6433 – *1

Solnik & Solnik, 2991 Dundas St. West, M6P 1Z4 – 416/767-7506, Fax: 416/767-4738; Email: tortlaywer@bigfoot.com – *2

Solomon & Solomon, Penthouse, 481 University Ave., 10th Fl., M5G 2E9 – 416/977-7786, Fax: 416/340-0064 – *2

Solomon, Grosberg, #1704, 55 University Ave., M5J 2H7 – 416/366-7828 – *6

Andreas H. Solomos, 1182 Danforth Ave., 2nd Fl., M4J 1M3 – 416/465-9955, Fax: 416/465-8114

Morrey Solway, #1250, 180 Dundas St. West, M5G 1Z8 – 416/599-3960, Fax: 416/977-0717 – *1

Somer & Associates, #300, 365 Bay St., M5H 2V1 – 416/362-1997, Fax: 416/363-8536 – *2

J.J. Somjen, #906, 94 Cumberland St., M5R 1A3 – 416/922-8083, Fax: 416/922-4234 – *1

Sommers & Roth, 268 Avenue Rd., M4V 2G7 – 416/961-1212, Fax: 416/961-2827 – *2

L.S. Sonenberg, 1123 Albion Rd., M9V 1A9 – 416/749-6000, Fax: 416/749-6004 – *1

Sookram & Levine, #710, 43 Eglinton Ave. East, M4P 1A2 – 416/480-9920, Fax: 416/480-9923

Frank Soppelsa, 75 Cuffley Cres. North, M3K 1Y1 – 416/636-9043, Fax: 416/213-5678 – *1

L.B. Sosna, 2627 Eglinton Ave. East, M1K 2S2 – 416/266-2133 – *1

Sosnowski & Mikolajko, #506, 2333 Dundas St. West, M9R 3A6 – 416/538-8493, Fax: 416/538-2274

Sotos, Karvanis, #1250, 180 Dundas St. West, M5G 1Z8 – 416/977-0007, Fax: 416/977-0717; Email: sotos@sotoskarvanis.com; URL: http://www.sotoskarvanis.com – *7

Souraya, Abdu, #307, 5400 Yonge St., M2N 5R5 – 416/222-0243, Fax: 416/222-9304

R.J. Spence, #1200, 595 Bay St., M5G 2C2 – 416/977-4492, Fax: 416/977-4971 – *1

Spencer Romberg Associates, #700, 21 Dundas Square, M5B 1B8 – 416/869-1571, Fax: 416/869-1735 – *3

Steve Speropoulos, 802 St. Clair Ave. West, M6C 1B6 – 416/656-6150, Fax: 416/656-7360 – *1

Larry Spodek, #220, 1018 Finch Ave. W., M3J 2E1 – 416/667-0987, Fax: 416/667-1022 – *1

Harvey Spring, #488, 22 College St., M5G 1K2 – 416/967-0800, Fax: 416/967-2783 – *1

Spurr, Forsythe, #514, 90 Eglinton Ave. East, M4P 2Y3 – 416/483-1242, Fax: 416/483-2903 – *2

C.A. Stafford, 1036 Coxwell Ave., M4C 3G5 – 416/421-3211 – *1

Barry C. Stagg, #8, 1033 Pape Ave., M4K 3W1 – 416/425-7101, Fax: 416/425-0644 – *1

Stainton & Murray, 1624 Bayview Ave., M4G 3B7 – 416/481-1146 – *1

R.J. Stanbrook, #200, 2901 Bayview Ave., M2K 1E6 – 416/490-1611, Fax: 416/490-1751 – *1

Jerome Stanleigh, #302, 120 Carlton St., M5A 4K2 – 416/924-0151, Fax: 416/924-2887; Email: jerome@stanleigh.com; URL: http://www.stanleigh.com – *1

Richard Stanwick, #300, 3443 Finch Ave, East, M1W 2S1 – 416/502-1841, Fax: 416/494-4660 – *1

Brian C. Stark, 198 Davenport Rd., M5R 1J2 – 416/923-8000, Fax: 416/964-7498 – *1

Fred Stasiuk, 250 The East Mall, M9B 3Y8 – 416/236-1487, Fax: 416/236-1518 – *1

R.B. Statton, 52 Hayden St., M4Y 1V8 – 416/922-3200, Fax: 416/922-7377 – *1

James Stefoff, #1505, 80 Richmond St. West, M5H 2A4 – 416/366-7984 – *1

M.M. Steidman, Q.C., #505, 335 Bay St., M5H 2R3 – 416/366-7661, Fax: 416/360-6868 – *1

D.A. Stein, #800, 5075 Yonge St., M2N 5P3 – 416/225-5007 – *1

F.P. Stein, 66 Charles St. East, M4Y 2R3 – 416/928-9390, Fax: 416/928-9484 – *1

Larry C. Stein, #711, 1000 Finch Ave. West, M3J 2V5 – 416/665-3440, Fax: 416/663-5491 – *1

R.B. Steinberg, #1001, 65 Queen St. West, M5H 2M5 – 416/368-8223 – *1

J. Stephens, Q.C., #407, 1280 Finch Ave. West, M3J 3K6 – 416/665-1499, Fax: 416/665-7488 – *1

Peter D. Stephens, #8, 951 Wilson Ave., M3K 2A7 – 416/398-7676, Fax: 416/398-9393 – *1

Stephenson & Stephenson, #313, 1033 Bay St., M5S 3A5 – 416/925-2200, Fax: 416/925-0858 – *2

J.A. Stephenson, Q.C., Box: 91, #5820, First Canadian Place, M5X 1B1 – 416/362-3909, Fax: 416/362-4136 – *1

Michael Sterlin, 55 Town Centre Court, M1P 4X4 – 416/296-7383, Fax: 416/296-1259 – *1

Sterling & Devlin, 2488A Kingston Rd., M1N 1V3 – 416/267-8274, Fax: 416/267-8430 – *1

Stern & Lenzin, #1724, 390 Bay St., M5H 2Y2 – 416/869-3422 – *3

Stewart Roper & Assoc., #906, 95 Wellington St. West, M5J 2N7 – 416/368-7881, Fax: 416/368-0549 – *5

Deborah L. Stewart, #201, 5075 Yonge St., M2N 6C6 – 416/226-9340, Fax: 416/226-5341 – *1

John K.H. Stiff, 257 Coxwell Ave., M4L 3B5 – 416/469-5119, Fax: 416/469-0328

Stikeman, Elliott, #5300, Commerce Court West, PO Box 85, M5L 1B9 – 416/869-5500, Fax: 416/947-0866; Email: info@tor.stikeman.com – *118

Stikeman, Graham & Keeley, Box: 45, #1001, 95 Wellington St. West, M5J 2N7 – 416/367-1930, Fax: 416/365-1813 – *5

Frederick C. Stinson, Q.C., #610, 372 Bay St., M5H 2W9 – 416/867-8669, Fax: 416/867-3079 – *2

Stockwood, Spies & Campbell, #2512, 150 King St. West, M5H 1J9 – 416/593-7200, Fax: 416/593-9345

Stone & Osborne, #201, 100 Sheppard Ave. West, M2N 1M6 – 416/225-1145, Fax: 416/225-0832 – *2

Stone & Wenus, 330 Broadview Ave., M4M 2G9 – 416/469-4125 – *2

Stone & Yack, #608, 1120 Finch Ave. West, M3J 3H7 – 416/663-5656 – *5

Stortini Lee-Whiting, #1907, 80 Richmond St. West, M5H 2C6 – 416/368-1091, Fax: 416/368-7234 – *3

Stortini, Derubeis Galluzzo, #305, 1033 Bay St., M5S 3A5 – 416/925-4000, Fax: 416/925-2860 – *3

Allan Strader, 49 Saint Nicholas St., M4Y 1W6 – 416/924-4488, Fax: 416/924-5443 – *1

David S. Strashin, #702, 55 Eglinton Ave. East, M4P 1G8 – 416/482-8171 – *1

Michael Strathman, 219 Carlton St., M5A 2L2 – 416/923-8997, Fax: 416/923-8380 – *1

James B. Stratton, 60 Glengowan Rd., M4N 1G4 – 416/489-9167, Fax: 416/482-1822 – *1

Earle H. Straus, 15 Purdon Dr., M3H 4W9 – 416/596-3642 – *1

Stringer, Brisbin, Humphrey, #1100, 110 Yonge St., M5C 1T4 – 416/862-1616, Fax: 416/363-7358 – *12

J.F. Stroz, Q.C., 2275 Dundas St. West, M6R 1X6 – 416/536-2131, Fax: 416/536-5451 – *1

J.A.F. Struyk, 1144 Queen St. East, M4M 1L1 – 416/463-1188, Fax: 416/463-9020 – *1

Alan Sugarman, #500, 4002 Sheppard Ave. East, M1S 4R5 – 416/297-7200, Fax: 416/297-7307 – *1

Robert P. Sullivan, 8 King St. East, M5C 1B5 – 416/364-4235, Fax: 416/364-4689 – *1

Summers & Nogueira, #205, 622 College St., M6G 1B4 – 416/531-3030, Fax: 416/531-3069 – *2

Summerville & Riley, #1, 2084 Danforth Ave., M4C 1J9 – 416/423-4412 – *2

Leonard Susman, 6420A Yonge, M2M 3X4 – 416/222-6000

Suter Law, 102 Annette St., M6P 1N6 – 416/760-0529

Ian Sutherland, 568 Annette St., M6S 2C2 – 416/763-0787, Fax: 416/763-0675 – *1

Ralph A. Sutton, #1800, 4950 Yonge St., M1N 6K1 – 416/224-0200, Fax: 416/224-0758 – *1

Swadron Associates, #1100, 30 St. Patrick St., M5T 3A3 – 416/598-3000, Fax: 416/598-3685 – *4

Kenneth P. Swan, #200, 70 Bond St., M5B 1X3 – 416/368-5279, Fax: 416/365-7702

Swanick, Shnier, D'Oliveira, #101, 225 Duncan Mill Rd., M3B 3K9 – 416/510-1888, Fax: 416/510-1945 – *6

Ernie Tadman, 185 Strachan Ave., M6J 2T1 – 416/362-9864, Fax: 416/362-7622 – *1

M.E. Taharally, #23, 1270 Finch Ave. West, M3J 3J7 – 416/661-4301, Fax: 416/661-5447 – *1

J.G. Tait, Q.C., #405, 121 Richmond St. West, M5H 2K1 – 416/364-3117, Fax: 416/364-2178 – *1

Mimi Tang, #229, 40 Dundas St. West, M5G 2C2 – 416/597-8583, Fax: 416/597-3846 – *1

Robert G. Tanner, #1300, 55 Queen St. East, M5C 1R6 – 416/862-7745, Fax: 416/862-7874 – *1

Tanzola & Sorbara, 2950 Keele St., M3M 2H2 – 416/638-0680, Fax: 416/638-9760 – *5

G.E. Tapper, 17 Lynwood Ave., M4V 1K3 – 416/927-7320 – *1

Brian I. Taran, 838 Mount Pleasant Rd., M4P 2L3 – 416/483-7834, Fax: 416/484-1089 – *1

Tatham, Pearson, 5524 Lawrence Ave. East, M1C 3B2 – 416/284-4749, Fax: 416/284-3086 – *2

William Tatsiou, #200, 121 Richmond St. West, M5H 2K1 – 416/362-4318, Fax: 416/362-6003 – *1

Stanley Taube, #1005, 21 St. Clair Ave. East, M4T 1L9 – 416/922-4545 – *1

Brahm M. Taveroff, #1000, 2 Sheppard Ave. East, M2N 5Y7 – 416/221-9343, Fax: 416/221-8928 – *2

Fred Tayar & Associates, #1600, 151 Yonge St., M5C 2W7 – 416/363-1800, Fax: 416/363-3356 – *3

R.R. Taylor, 340 Eglinton Ave. East, M4P 1L8 – 416/489-3030, Fax: 416/322-0524 – *1

Techman & Associates, 8 Finch Ave. West, M2N 6L1 – 416/250-9090 – *1

Teichman S. Blake, 42 Strathearn Blvd., M5P 1T1 – 416/488-0964

Kelly J. Martin, 45 Sheppard Ave. East, M2N 5W9 – 416/733-1771 – *1

Tamara Tenebaum, #3313, 77 King St. West, M5K 1H6 – 416/601-4811, Fax: 416/504-0276 – *1

Teplitsky, Colson, #200, 70 Bond St., M5B 1X3 – 416/365-9320, Fax: 416/365-7702 – *25

B. Tepper, Q.C., 460 College St., M6G 1A1 – 416/961-8228, Fax: 416/961-3628 – *1

Kenneth Tepper, #301, 801 York Mills Rd., M3B 1X7 – 416/445-4502, Fax: 416/445-9060 – *1

Rod B. Thibodeau, #200, 225 Duncan Mills Rd., M3B 3K9 – 416/444-2244, Fax: 416/444-3222 – *2

Stephen Thom, #500, 70 Bond St., M5B 1X3 – 416/364-3371, Fax: 416/364-3376 – *1

Shaun Thompson, 4945A Dundas St. West, M9A 1B6 – 416/233-0399, Fax: 416/233-0399 – *1

W.A.D. Thompson, #102, 175 Shaughnessy Blvd., M2J 1K1 – 416/609-2044 – *1

William H. Thompson, #2825, Commerce Ct. North, PO Box 124, M5L 1E2 – 416/368-0721, Fax: 416/368-0721 – *1

Thomson, Rogers, #3100, 390 Bay St., M5H 1W2 – 416/868-3100, Fax: 416/868-3134 – *35

W.J. Thorne, #9, 290 The West Mall, M9C 1C6 – 416/621-9644, Fax: 416/621-9668 – *1

Ian Thornhill, 902-5255 Yonge St., M2N 6P4 – 416/224-2004, Fax: 416/224-2101 – *1

Thorsteinssons, BCE Place, 161 Bay St., 36th Fl., PO Box 611, M5J 2S1 – 416/864-0829, Fax: 416/864-1106 – *8

Barbara J. Thurston, 201-5075 Yonge St., M2N 6C6 – 416/590-9161, Fax: 416/590-9941 – *1

R.W. Thurston, Q.C., 1425 Bloor St. West, M6P 3L6 – 416/536-4588, Fax: 416/536-9680 – *3

Carmine Tiano, #704, 130 Spadina Ave., M5V 2L4 – 416/360-1985, Fax: 416/360-6764 – *1

Ann Tierney, 470 King St. East, M5A 1L7 – 416/362-5700, Fax: 416/362-0847 – *1

Tikal & Associates, 178 St. George St., M5R 2N2 – 416/968-7070, Fax: 416/968-1876 – *4

Yunus Timol, 815 College St., 1st Fl., M6G 1C9 – 416/531-4388, Fax: 416/940-0074 – *1

* indicates number of lawyers in law firm.

Philip Tinianov, #1000, 65 Queen St. West, M5H 2M5 – 416/363-0866, Fax: 416/367-3949 – *1

Tinkler, Morris, #304, 150 York St., M5H 3S5 – 416/362-2900, Fax: 416/362-6204

M.K. Titherington, 46 Northcliffe Blvd., M6H 3H2 – 416/656-6465 – *1

Tobias & Company, Aetna Tower, #3516, 79 Wellington St. West, PO Box 105, M5K 1G8 – 416/360-4600, Fax: 416/601-1630

Warren W. Tobias, #700, 357 Bay St., M5H 2T7 – 416/947-0911, Fax: 416/363-4130 – *1

Norman W. Tomas, 954A Royal York Rd., M8X 2E5 – 416/233-5567, Fax: 416/233-5567 – *1

Paul V. Tomlinson, 305-180 Dundas St. West, M5G 1Z8 – 416/597-0477, Fax: 416/599-0847 – *1

Toome Holmberg Laar, #1510, 5140 Yonge St., PO Box 10, M2N 6L7 – 416/250-7000, Fax: 416/250-7008 – *4

Dennis M. Topp, #103, 1750 Brimley Rd., M1P 4X7 – 416/291-9161 – *1

Tordoff Thomas, #1610, 8 Godstone Rd., M5J 3C4 – 416/497-8249

Torkin, Manes, Cohen & Arbus, #1500, 151 Yonge St., M5C 2W7 – 416/863-1188, Fax: 416/863-0305; Email: rhalpern@torkinmanes.com – *22

Toronto Legal Aid Office, #204, 375 University Ave., M5G 2G1 – 416/598-0200, Fax: 416/598-0558

Tory Tory DesLauriers & Binnington, #3000, Aetna Tower, Toronto-Dominion Centre, PO Box 270, Stn Toronto Dominion, M5K 1N2 – 416/865-0040, Fax: 416/865-7380 – *193

Wayne Trainer, 388A Browns Line, M8W 3T8 – 416/251-3331 – *1

Traub Moldaver, #400, 7 King St. West, M5H 1B6 – 416/214-6500, Fax: 416/214-7275 – *7

Philip J. Traversy, #100, 272 Lawrence Ave. West, M5M 4M1 – 416/787-0641, Fax: 416/787-4245 – *1

Treloar, Mergler, #401, 302 The East Mall, M9B 6C7 – 416/232-2919, Fax: 416/232-9201 – *3

Paul R. Trethewey, TD Bank Tower, TD Centre, #3400, PO Box 21, M5K 1A1 – 416/868-7537, Fax: 416/868-7538; Email: trethewy@ican.net – *1

Quoc Toan Trinh, 1577 Bloor St. West, M6P 1A6 – 416/533-8987, Fax: 416/536-3618 – *1

K.F. Trotter, 106 Southvale Dr., M4G 1G7 – 416/467-1763

William M. Trudell, #700, 480 University Ave., M5G 1V2 – 416/598-2019, Fax: 416/977-5331 – *1

Alexander Tsang, #228, 40 Dundas St. West, M5G 2C2 – 416/581-0226, Fax: 416/581-0229 – *1

C. Tsantis, 69 Elm St., M5G 1H2 – 416/599-6689, Fax: 416/971-9092 – *1

Tsapralis & Stanoulis, #303, 717 Pape Ave., M4K 3S9 – 416/466-1900, Fax: 416/466-1919 – *4

Tse Kee Sheung, #403, 2347 Kennedy Rd., M1T 3T8 – 416/298-1232, Fax: 416/298-5722

Mary Helen Tso, #1540, 439 University Ave., M5G 1Y8 – 416/598-5545, Fax: 416/598-9834 – *1

M.L. Tucker, 43 Madawaska Ave., M2M 2R1 – 416/221-5122, Fax: 416/226-9737 – *1

Tufman & Associates, 350 Bay St., 9th Fl., M5H 2S6 – 416/360-1689, Fax: 416/367-4098

Tuovi & Yen, #705, 390 Bay St., M5H 2Y2 – 416/956-7755, Fax: 416/956-7754 – *2

Noel W. Turk, 38 Elderwood Dr., M5P 1W7 – 416/968-7848 – *1

Turkstra, Mazza Associates, #1600, 18 King St. East, M5C 1C4 – 416/368-4554, Fax: 416/368-4741

Tytler & Sproule, #1618, 44 Victoria St., M5C 1Y2 – 416/364-3283, Fax: 416/364-3283 – *1

Ulrich & Sherr, #202, 2978 Islington Ave., M9L 2K6 – 416/745-7720, Fax: 416/745-5692 – *2

Richard D. Ulster, 41 Elliotwood Ct., M2L 2P8 – 416/446-1151 – *1

Howard Ungerman, 37 Maitland St., M4Y 1C8 – *1

H.S. Urman, 22 Coreydale Ct., M3H 4T2 – 416/638-8549, Fax: 416/638-8851 – *1

Urquhart, Urquhart, Aiken & Medcof, #439, 1000 University Ave., PO Box 40, M5G 1Y8 – 905/595-1111, Fax: 905/595-7312 – *1

I. Usprech, 21 Dundas Sq., M5B 1B7 – 416/363-0185 – *1

Robert Valentine, #300, 111 Elizabeth St., M5G 1P7 – 416/596-0722 – *1

Simon P. Valleau, #305, 180 Dundas St. West, M5G 1Z8 – 416/593-5511, Fax: 416/599-0847 – *1

Sheldon C. Vanek & Associate, #1610, 8 King St. East, M5C 1B5 – 416/366-1109, Fax: 416/366-0157

George Vano, 528 St. Clair Ave. West, 2nd Floor, M6C 1A2 – 416/653-1148, Fax: 416/653-1148 – *1

Anil Varma, 53 Chicora Ave., M5R 1T7 – 416/921-8880, Fax: 416/921-0440 – *1

Leslie Vasilaros, #1500, 2 St. Clair Ave. East, M4T 2T5 – 416/927-0300, Fax: 416/927-0305 – *1

K.C. Vaughan, #3, 900 Don Mills Rd., M3C 1V8 – 416/441-6313, Fax: 416/441-6898 – *1

Michael B. Vaughan Q.C., #3100, 130 Adelaide St. West, M5H 3P5 – 416/363-9611, Fax: 416/363-9672

Velanoff & Velanoff, 344 Sheppard Ave. East, 2nd Fl., M1N 3B4 – 416/225-3425, Fax: 416/733-3776 – *1

Elana Velensky, #415, 4580 Dufferin St., M3H 5Y2 – 416/789-5373, Fax: 416/667-0763 – *1

Vella & Pratt, #600, 200 Ronson Dr., M9W 5Z9 – 416/244-7706, Fax: 416/244-2288

Peter A. Vesa, Q.C., 1028 Danforth Ave., M4J 1M2 – 416/463-3392 – *1

Vine, Van Houten, #1604, 80 Richmond St. West, M5H 2A4 – 416/863-9341, Fax: 416/863-9342 – *2

Carl Vipavec, 770 Brown's Line, M8W 3W2 – 416/255-7500, Fax: 416/255-6667 – *1

Julia M. Viva, #305, 1256 Yonge St., M4T 1W5 – 416/922-0221, Fax: 416/922-1264 – *1

James D. Vlasis, 99 Charles St. East, M4Y 1V2 – 416/920-3447, Fax: 416/964-0823 – *1

H.J. von Monteton, #8F, 20 Prince Arthur Ave., M5R 1B1 – 416/925-0167 – *1

M.G. Wade, #202, 181 Eglinton Ave. East, M4P 1J9 – 416/487-7181, Fax: 416/487-4199 – *1

Wagman, Sherkin, #200, 756A Queen St. East, M4M 1H4 – 416/465-1102, Fax: 416/465-3941 – *2

Mark Wainberg, 81 Wellesley St. East, M4Y 1H6 – 416/960-0049, Fax: 416/960-1498 – *1

Waldin, de Kenedy, #2150, One Queen St. East, M5C 2W5 – 416/364-6761, Fax: 416/364-3866; Email: waldin@waldin.on.ca – *3

Lorne Waldman, 281 Eglinton Ave. East, M4P 1L3 – 416/482-6501, Fax: 416/489-9618 – *1

David Walfish, Q.C., 156 Danforth Ave., M4K 1N1 – 416/461-3583, Fax: 416/461-7466 – *1

Henry Walfish, 156 Danforth Ave., M4K 1N1 – 416/461-3583 – *1

Bruce E. Walker, #205, 65 Wellesley St. East, M4Y 1G7 – 416/961-7451, Fax: 416/961-5966; Email: bwalker@istar.ca; URL: home.istar.ca/~bwalker/ – *1

Walker, Ellis & Pezzack, Yonge-Richmond Centre, #1302, 151 Yonge St., M5C 2W7 – 416/363-2144, Fax: 416/363-1541 – *3

Trevor Walker, #612, 330 Bay St., M5H 2S8 – 416/214-1162, Fax: 416/214-0870

J.H.G. Wallace, 551 Gerrard St. East, M4M 1X7 – 416/463-6666, Fax: 416/463-8259 – *1

John Walsh, #502, 145 Adelaide St. West, M5H 3H4 – 416/239-1161, Fax: 416/869-5630 – *1

Walsh, McLuskie, Lennox, #935, 525 University Ave., M5G 2L3 – 416/598-8177, Fax: 416/598-5466 – *4

Walton & Kelly, 893 O'Connor Dr., M4B 2S7 – 416/757-2801, Fax: 416/757-1130 – *1

Wanigasekera Gamini, #600, 75 Donway West, M3C 2E9 – 416/449-4294, Fax: 416/449-4369

Wappel Law Office, #200, 500 University Ave., M5G 1V7 – 416/598-1333, Fax: 416/598-5024; Email: wappel@inforamp.com – *3

J.P. Warner, #1600, 372 Bay St., M5H 2W9 – 416/322-3015 – *1

Howard E. Warren, 167 Danforth Ave., M4K 1N2 – 416/461-0983, Fax: 416/462-3347 – *1

Robert D. Warren, #2714, 130 Adelaide St. West, M5H 3P5 – 416/368-5393

Cynthia D. Watson, #705, 130 Spadina Ave., M5V 2L4 – 416/360-1967, Fax: 416/360-6764 – *1

M.O. Watson, 129 John St., M5V 2E2 – 416/977-3879, Fax: 416/977-3660 – *1

Michael J. Waud, 968 Wilson Ave., 3rd Fl., M3K 1E7 – 416/633-4301, Fax: 416/630-1289 – *1

Weatherhead, Weatherhead, #500, 27 Queen St. East, M5C 2M6 – 416/362-1369, Fax: 416/362-5013 – *2

Ian D.A. Webb, 2 First Canadian Place, #2345, PO Box 75, Stn First Canadian Place, M5X 1B1 – 416/777-9583 – *1

Matt Webber, 317 Grace St., M6G 3A7 – 416/533-4086, Fax: 416/533-5174 – *1

John David Webster, Q.C., 290 Lytton Blvd., M5N 1R6 – 416/489-6255, Fax: 416/488-7582 – *1

Michael Edward Webster, #910, 65 Queen St. West, M5H 2M5 – 416/364-6000, Fax: 416/360-1056 – *1

R.L. & J.H. Webster, 2600 Danforth Ave., M4C 1L3 – 416/699-9644, Fax: 416/699-8905 – *2

C.J. Weiler, 207 McCaul St., M5T 1W6 – 416/598-3434, Fax: 416/598-3437 – *1

Robert D. Weiler, Q.C., 2300-439 University Ave., M5G 1Y8 – 416/598-0453 – *1

Allen W. Weinberg, #1002, 347 Bay St., M5H 2R7 – 416/360-8489, Fax: 416/366-3712 – *1

John Weingust, Q.C., 481 University Ave., 10th Fl., M5G 2E9 – 416/977-7786, Fax: 416/340-0064 – *1

F. Sheldon Weinles, 1275 Dundas St. West, M6J 1X8 – 416/535-0915 – *1

Marcie I. Weinman, #305, 5400 Yonge St., M2M 5R5 – 416/229-9242, Fax: 416/229-0278 – *1

Arthur Weinreb, 44 Woodrow Ave.., M4C 5S2 – 416/690-9220 – *1

Ben Weinstein, 340 Rimrock Rd., M3J 3A6 – 416/633-2120, Fax: 416/633-4113 – *1

Gilbert Weinstock, #401, 1850 Victoria Park Ave., M1R 1T1 – 416/759-1354, Fax: 416/759-3256 – *1

Weir & Foulds, 2 First Canadian Place, Exchange Tower, #1600, Box 480, M5X 1J5 – 416/365-1110, Fax: 416/365-1876; Email: firm@weirfoulds.com; URL: http://www.weirfoulds.com – *68

John Weisdorf, Q.C., #810, 65 Queen St. West, M5H 2M5 – 416/861-1000, Fax: 416/363-7558 – *1

M.S. Weisleder, 516 Glencairn Ave., M6B 1Z1 – 416/787-2424 – *1

Stanley J. Weisman, Q.C., 3802 Bloor St. West, M9B 6C2 – 416/236-1141, Fax: 416/237-0458 – *1

A.P. Welman, 1034A Bloor St. West, M6H 1M3 – 416/532-2871, Fax: 416/532-5089 – *1

Weltman, Breatross, #127, 5050 Dufferin St., M3H 5T5 – 416/665-5222, Fax: 416/665-4483 – *2

Irwin Wenus, 27 Acton Ave., M3H 4G6 – 416/633-5830 – *1

West Scarborough Community Legal Services, 6-565 Kennedy Rd., M1K 2B2 – 416/264-4384, Fax: 416/264-2491

R.L. Westell, #200, 303 Eglinton Ave. East, M4P 1L3 – 416/481-3331

Wetstein & Shulman, #204, 3845 Bathurst St., M3H 3N2 – 416/398-1444, Fax: 416/398-1447 – *2

M.J. Wheldrake, Q.C., 2 Alvarado Pl., M3A 3E9 – 416/444-2746

Henry L.E. White, #203, 239 Sheppard Ave. East, M2N 3A8 – 416/224-1757 – *1

Lionel B. White, Q.C., #2314, 120 Adelaide St. West, M5H 1T1 – 416/364-1127, Fax: 416/364-6903 – *1

A.H. Whittaker, #1250, 180 Dundas St. West, M5G 1Z8 – 416/971-9068, Fax: 416/977-0717 – *1

Barry B. Widman, #1515, 123 Edward St., M5G 1E2 – 416/597-0702, Fax: 416/597-1581 – *1

J. Wildgoose, 645 Carlaw Ave., M4K 3K6 – 416/469-4390, Fax: 416/469-0682

Willard & Devitt, 155 Roncesvalles Ave., M6R 2L3 – 416/531-1136, Fax: 416/531-4096 – *1

Sian E. Williams, 92 Gillard Ave., M4J 4N6 – 416/866-8152 – *1
Paul T. Willis, 600 Church St., M4Y 2E7 – 416/926-9806, Fax: 416/926-9737 – *1
Willms & Shier, #900, 4 King St. West, M5H 1B6 – 416/863-0711, Fax: 416/863-1938 – *16
Norman A. Wills, #1707, 8 King St. East, M5C 1B5 – 416/366-8060 – *1
Catherine E. Willson, #346, 67 Mowat Ave., M6K 3E3 – 416/534-9504, Fax: 416/534-9503 – *3
Julie Wilmot, 7 Westlake Crescent, M4C 2X3 – 416/696-7222 – *1
Wilson & Bartlett, #904, 27 Queen St. East, M5C 2M6 – 416/363-1601 – *1
Wilson, Christen, #401, 47 Colborne St., M5E 1P8 – 416/360-6336, Fax: 416/360-7912
David S. Wilson, #810, 111 Richmond St. West, M5H 2H5 – 416/943-1223, Fax: 416/943-1049 – *1
David S. Wilson, 180 Dundas St. West, M5G 1Z8 – 416/979-1223, Fax: 416/972-0717 – *1
Robert Wilson, #221, 2928 Yonge St., M4N 2K1 – 416/489-2576 – *1
T.H. Wilson, #404, 372 Bay St., M5H 2W9 – 416/363-0249 – *1
S.L. Winberg, #400, 44 Eglinton Ave. West, M4R 1A1 – 416/483-3400, Fax: 416/483-3409 – *1
Winch, Gasee & Cohen, #200, 65 Queen St. West, M5H 2M5 – 416/363-3351, Fax: 416/363-0252 – *4
C.F. Winer, Q.C., #201, 270 The Kings Way, M9A 3T7 – 416/233-5524, Fax: 416/233-5526 – *1
Norman Winter, #801, 1 St. Clair Ave. East, M4T 2V7 – 416/964-0325, Fax: 416/964-2494; Email: winlaw@interlog.com – *1
J.K. Winters, Q.C., 118 Holcolm Rd., M2N 2C9 – 416/223-8637 – *1
Wise & Partner, 7 Frost St., M9W 1Y5 – 416/747-1229, Fax: 416/740-2549 – *1
G.R. Wise, 3329 Bloor St. West, M8X 1E7 – 416/231-7399, Fax: 416/231-1280 – *1
Garry J. Wise, #200, 70 Bond St., M5B 1X3 – 416/362-1800, Fax: 416/362-0809 – *1
Roy Wise, #1604, 55 University Ave., PO Box 12, M5J 2H7 – 416/866-4144, Fax: 416/866-7946 – *2
Gary L. Wiseman, #1800, 4950 Yonge St., M2N 6K1 – 416/224-0200, Fax: 416/224-0758; Email: gwiseman@idirect.com – *1
Peter J. Woebbolt, 1554A Bloor St. West, M6P 1A4 – 416/516-4621, Fax: 416/516-1679 – *1
Harold B. Wolfe, #1906, 80 Richmond St. West, M5H 4A7 – 416/863-0333, Fax: 416/863-4968 – *1
N.S. Wolicki, #200, 2200 Bloor St. West, M6S 1N4 – 416/763-3553, Fax: 416/763-2522 – *1
Wilfred Wolman, Q.C., 240 Heath St. West, M5P 3L5 – 416/482-4996 – *1
Mavin Wong, 810 Queen St. East, M4M 1H7 – 416/778-6861, Fax: 416/969-9662 – *1
Wing H. Wong, #202, 4433 Sheppard Ave. East, M1S 1V3 – 416/298-6767, Fax: 416/298-3844 – *1
H.F. Wood, #202, 1900 Eglinton Ave. East, M1L 2L9 – 416/751-4600, Fax: 416/751-3095 – *1
Mary Jane Woods, #3, 1923 Weston Rd., M9N 1W7 – 416/242-5896, Fax: 416/242-9014 – *1
R.L.H. Woolf, 1474 Bathurst St., M5P 3G9 – 416/658-1234, Fax: 416/652-2709 – *1
Woolgar, VanWiechen, #506, 56 The Esplanade, M5E 1A7 – 416/867-1331, 1881, Fax: 416/867-1434; Email: woolvan@inforamp.net – *3
Robert L. Woolner, 782 Broadview Ave., M4K 2P7 – 416/465-7895, Fax: 416/465-3857
Wootten, George A., Q.C., #901, 701 Evans Ave., M9C 1A3 – 416/622-7970, Fax: 416/622-8952 – *1
Nestor Woychyshyn, #301, 2259 Bloor St. West, M6S 1N8 – 416/604-2091; Email: nestorw@interlog.com – *1
K.E. Wright, #1601, 65 Queen St. West, M5H 2M5 – 416/364-1157 – *1
Sara Wunch, #3204, 20 Queen St. West, PO Box 40, M5H 3R3 – 416/595-7001, Fax: 416/340-7025 – *1

S.L. Yale, 42 Strathearn Blvd., M5P 1T1 – 416/488-1297, Fax: 416/488-0622 – *1
Amy Yao, 209-210 Midland Ave., M1V 4W7 – 416/292-3232, Fax: 416/292-2139 – *1
John Yaremko, Q.C., 1 Connable Dr., M5R 1Z7 – 416/921-7158 – *1
Gerald B. Yasskin, #415, 4580 Dufferin St., M3H 5Y2 – 416/667-0980, Fax: 416/667-0765 – *1
Brenda L. Yeates, #1506, 141 Adelaide St. West, M5H 3L5 – 416/777-1114, Fax: 416/864-0174 – *1
K. Dock Yip, 236 Torrens Ave., M4J 2P5 – 416/425-6485 – *1
Yoannou & Petropoulos, #802, 55 Eglinton Ave. East, M4P 1G8 – 416/484-9640, Fax: 416/487-3274 – *2
York Community Services, 1651 Keele St., M6M 3W2 – 416/653-5400, Fax: 416/653-1696
Albert Young, #112, 1801 Eglinton Ave. West, M6E 2H8 – 416/789-4183, Fax: 416/789-4184 – *1
Joseph R. Young, #1808, One Queen St. East, PO Box 88, M5C 2W5 – 416/866-8888, Fax: 416/866-8889 – *1
Younger & Associates, #3400, Toronto Dominion Centre, PO Box 21, Stn T-D, M5K 1A1 – 416/868-7535, Fax: 416/868-7538 – *3
G.R. Youngs, Q.C., #1203, 45 Livingston Rd., M1E 1K8 – 416/265-6901 – *1
Simon Yiu L. Yu, #850, 439 University Ave., M5G 1Y8 – 416/340-8388, Fax: 416/340-8080 – *1
D.R. Zadorozny, #307, 4195 Dundas St. West, M8X 1Y4 – 416/239-2333, Fax: 416/239-1752 – *1
Zaldin & Fine, #1012, 111 Richmond St. West, M5H 2G4 – 416/868-1431, Fax: 416/868-6381 – *4
Zaldin & Zaldin, #1405, 5650 Yonge St., M2M 4G3 – 416/225-3396, Fax: 416/225-3852 – *2
Zammit, Dash & Semple, #601, 130 Bloor St. West, M5S 1N5 – 416/923-2601, Fax: 416/923-1391 – *3
Marisa Zanini, #205, 3875 Keele St., M3J 1N6 – 416/398-9292, Fax: 416/398-8358
C. Zapf, 2424 Bloor St. West, 2nd Fl., M6S 1P9 – 416/766-4208, Fax: 416/769-5365 – *1
E.J. Zaraska, 119 Dunvegan Rd., M4V 2R2 – 416/482-4500, Fax: 416/482-8075 – *1
Daniel Zaretsky, #302, 240 Richmond St. West, M5V 1V6 – 416/599-5254, Fax: 416/599-5330 – *1
Martin R. Zaretsky, #360, 100 Cowdray Crt., M1S 5C8 – 416/754-4404, Fax: 416/754-7280
M. David Zbarsky, 533 Queen St. East, M5A 1V1 – 416/421-6252, Fax: 416/421-7668 – *1
Sidney I. Zelewicz, 1034A Bloor St. West, M6H 1M3 – 416/532-2871, Fax: 416/532-5089 – *1
Zender & Klotz, 1175 Weston Rd., M6M 4P5 – 416/243-2222 – *2
Vincent Zenobio, #415, 4580 Dufferin St., M3H 5Y2 – 416/667-0980, Fax: 416/667-0765 – *1
Zeppieri & Associates, 851 Wilson Ave., M3K 1E6 – 416/631-7800, Fax: 416/631-6170 – *2
David L. Zifkin, 90A Isabella St., 2nd Fl., M4Y 1N4 – 416/927-7720, Fax: 416/964-9348; Email: dzifkin@globalserve.net; URL: http://www.zifkin.com – *1
Ryan Zigler, #404, 3420 Finch Ave. East, M1W 1W9 – 416/499-6553, Fax: 416/499-6728 – *1
Stephen M. Zikman, #802, 130 Spadina Ave., M5V 2L4 – 416/504-2300, Fax: 416/504-2299 – *1
Bram M. Zinman, #1800, 4950 Yonge St., M2N 6K1 – 416/224-0200, Fax: 416/224-0758 – *1
R. Zisman, #307, 120 Carlton St., M5A 4K3 – 416/925-6490, Fax: 416/925-4492 – *1
Morrie Zucker, 637 Lake Shore Blvd. West, M5V 1A8 – 416/591-9300 – *1
Stanley R. Zupan, Q.C., #214, 47 Sheppard Ave. East, M2N 5X5 – 416/223-4014 – *1
Arthur Zutis, #1401, 80 Richmond St. West, M5H 2A4 – 416/366-5946 – *1
Howard G. Zweig, #301, 5460 Yonge St., M2N 6K7 – 416/512-1201, Fax: 416/512-1212 – *1
B.E. Zyla, #200, 3029 Bloor St. West, M8X 1C5 – 416/234-9111, Fax: 416/234-9114 – *1

**Tottenham ........ Simcoe**

Feehely, Gastaldi & Hayes, 5 Mill St. East, PO Box 370, L0G 1W0 – 905/936-4262; 859-0065 (Toronto), Fax: 905/936-5102 – *4
Catherine Rogers, 17 Queen St. South, PO Box 399, L0G 1W0 – 905/936-3793, Fax: 905/936-3793

**Trenton ........ Hastings**

G.W. Bonn, 80 Division St., K8V 5S5 – 613/392-9207, Fax: 613/392-6367 – *3
Davis & Tuckey, 469 Dundas St. West, K8V 3S4 – 613/392-1221 – *1
C. Vincent Graham, 2 King St., PO Box 601, K8V 5R7 – 613/965-6666, Fax: 613/392-0681 – *1
Grant, Donald L., Q.C., 41 Heber St., K8V 1M7 – 613/965-1280, Fax: 613/965-1282; Toll Free: 1-800-387-1280 – *1
Raymond Kaufmann, 257 Dundas St. East, K8V 1M1 – 613/394-3315, Fax: 613/394-6752 – *1
J.S. Robertson, 188 Dundas St. East, K8V 1L6 – 613/392-3659, Fax: 613/392-3521 – *1
Philip S. Staddon, 469 Dundas St. West, K8V 3S4 – 613/394-2228, Fax: 613/475-3651
J.S. Wonnacott, 80 Division St., K8V 5P7 – 613/392-9207, Fax: 613/392-6367 – *1

**Unionville ........ York**

Susan Ambrose, 105 Main St., L3R 2G1 – 905/477-0624, Fax: 905/477-5846; Email: lawgals@the-wire.com – *1
Peter J. Lewarne, 4701 Hwy. 7, L3R 1M7 – 905/477-4381, Fax: 905/477-7601
R. Parnes, 4480 Hwy. 7., L3R 1M3 – 905/477-5151, Fax: 905/477-6778 – *1
W.B. Thomas, Q.C., 4701 Hwy. 7., L3R 1M7 – 905/477-2233, Fax: 905/477-7668 – *1

**Uxbridge ........ Durham**

Bailey & Sedore, PO Box 1030, L4P 1N3 – 905/852-3363, Fax: 905/852-3480 – *2
E.E.P. Iglar, 92 Brock St. West, L9P 1P4 – 905/852-3367, Fax: 905/852-9254 – *1
John M. McKay, 10 Brock St. East, PO Box 519, L9P 1P1 – 905/852-3379; 571-1400, Fax: 905/852-3370 – *1
P.D. Turner, Q.C., #103, 29 Toronto St. South, L9P 1V9 – 905/362-1951, Fax: 905/852-6197; Email: dturner@hookup.net – *2
R.J. Wigdor, 23 Franklin St., L9P 1K3 – 905/852-6402, Fax: 905/852-6496; Email: rwigdor@sprynet.com – *1
Wilson & Martin, 22 Brock St. East, PO Box 1420, L9P 1P1 – 905/852-3353 – *3

**Val Caron ........**

Paquette & Paquette, #203, 2945 Hwy. 69 North, P3N 1N3 – 705/897-7272, Fax: 705/897-7270 – *2

**Vanier ........ Ottawa-Carleton**

Jean Paul Guertin, Chateau Vanier Mall, 158 McArthur Ave., K1L 7E7 – 613/741-7565, Fax: 613/741-7566 – *1

**Vankleek Hill ........ Prescott**

Tolhurst & Miller, 93 Main St., PO Box 730, K0B 1R0 – 613/678-3345, Fax: 613/678-3251 – *2

**Vaughan ........ York**

Bianchi, Presta, #300, 8400 Jane St., L4K 4L8 – 905/738-1078, Fax: 905/738-0528 – *7
Gambin Associates, 3300 Hwy 7 West, 9th Fl., L4K 4M3 – 905/660-6600, Fax: 905/669-5770 – *9
Gardiner, Roberts, Royal Centre, #300, 3300 Hwy. 7, L4K 4M3 – 905/660-3333, Fax: 905/660-0990; Email: gr@gardiner-roberts.on.ca
Piersanti & Company, Royal Centre, #800, 3300 Hwy #7, L4K 4M3 – 905/738-2176, Fax: 905/738-5182; Toll Free: 1-800-531-0708 – *6

* indicates number of lawyers in law firm.

**Walkerton............................................Bruce**

Brian R. Linley, 240 Durham St., PO Box 1448, N0G 2V0 – 519/881-2502, Fax: 519/881-1981 – *1

D.O. McCray, 240 Durham St. East, N0G 2V0 – 519/881-0950, Fax: 519/881-1981 – *1

Joseph A. Reichenbach, 3 Colborne St. North, PO Box 1448, N0G 2V0 – 519/881-4061, Fax: 519/881-2441 – *2

Waechter, Magwood, Van De Vyvere & Thompson, 215 Durham St., N0G 2V0 – 519/881-3230, Fax: 519/881-3595; Email: wmvt@bmts.com – *4

**Wallaceburg............................................Kent**

Burgess & Burgess, 218 Duncan St., N8A 4E3 – *2

Carscallen, Reinhart, Mathany, 619 James St., N8A 4L5 – 519/627-2261, Fax: 519/627-1030 – *4

Hyde, Hyde & McGregor, 233 Creek St., N8A 4L6 – 519/627-2081, Fax: 519/627-1615 – *2

**Wasaga Beach....................................Simcoe**

Maurice Loton, 802 Mosley St., PO Box 500, L0L 2P0 – 705/429-4332, Fax: 705/429-4683 – *1

Carl Mandrish, 310 River Rd. East, L0L 2P0 – 905/847-1780, Fax: 905/847-5054 – *1

Donald F. McKay, #311, RR#3, PO Box 61, L0L 2P0 – 705/429-3280 – *1

**Waterloo.......................................Waterloo**

Amy, Appleby & Brennan, 372 Erb St. West, N2L 1W6 – 519/884-7330, Fax: 519/884-7390; Email: aab_lawoffice@msn.com – *3

John S. Askin, Q.C., 279 Weber St. North, N2J 3H8 – 519/725-7552, Fax: 519/579-1944 – *1

Chris & Volpini, 375 University Ave. East, N2K 3M7 – 519/888-0999, Fax: 519/888-0995 – *3

W. Marlene Fitzpatrick, 421 King St. North, N2J 4E4 – 519/725-9500, Fax: 519/725-2379 – *1

Gehl, Gehl, 421 King St. North, N2J 4E4 – 519/886-8120, Fax: 519/886-8223 – *2

Haney, Haney, Kendall, Melville & Deane, 41 Erb St. East, PO Box 185, N2J 3Z9 – 519/747-1010, Fax: 519/747-9323 – *5

Heimbecker, Richardson & Petker, 295 Weber St. North, PO Box 546, N2J 4B8 – 519/886-1750, Fax: 519/886-8754; Email: hrplaw@easynet.on.ca – *4

Hicks Morley Hamilton Stewart Storie, #290, 100 Regina St. South, N2J 4P9 – 519/746-0411, Fax: 519/747-4829

Hobson, Taylor, Oldfield, Greaves & D'Agostino, 172 King St. South, PO Box 16580, N2J 4T6 – 519/576-7200, Fax: 519/576-0131; Toll Free: 1-800-794-2460; Email: watlaw@wat.hookup.net – *8

Anthony T. Keller, #205, 151 Frobisher Dr., N2V 2C9 – 519/725-2518, Fax: 519/725-2519 – *1

Kominek, Gladstone, Ross, 601 Waterloo Sq., N2J 1P2 – 519/886-1050, Fax: 519/747-9565 – *3

McDowell, Welch, Waterloo City Centre, #290, 100 Regina St. South, N2J 4P9 – 519/747-4504, Fax: 519/747-4829; Email: mcdwelch@ionline.net – *2

McGibbon, Biggs & Boich, #206, 50 Westmount Rd. North, N2L 2R5 – 519/886-5050, Fax: 519/886-1791 – *3

P.M. Miller, 15 Westmount Rd. South, N2L 2K2 – 519/884-1332, Fax: 519/884-1161 – *1

James E. Pitcher, 421 King St. North, N2J 4E4 – 519/725-9444, Fax: 519/725-2379 – *1

Shortt, Hanbidge & Snider, 7 Union St. East, PO Box 550, N2J 4B8 – 519/579-5600, Fax: 519/579-2725 – *4

Sloan, Strype & Feoy, 92 Erb St. East, PO Box 547, N2J 4B8 – 519/886-1590, Fax: 519/886-8545 – *1

Snyder, Dueck & Sauer, #3, 465 Phillip St., N3L 6C7 – 519/884-2620, Fax: 519/884-0254

J.R. Weber, 192 King St. South, N2J 1P9 – 519/742-1004 – *1

White, Jenkins, Duncan & Ostner, 45 Erb St. East, PO Box 457, N2J 4B5 – 519/886-3340 – *12

**Watford.......................................Lambton**

Kilby, Lang, 5274 Nauvoo Rd., N0M 2S0 – 519/876-2742, Fax: 519/876-2073 – *2

**Wawa..........................................Algoma**

Michael Allemano, PO Box 10, P0S 1K0 – 705/856-4970, Fax: 705/856-2713 – *1

Wishart & Partners, 71 Broadway Ave., P0S 1K0 – 705/856-7260

**Welland.................................Niagara South**

George C.M. Banks, 191 Division St., L3B 5P2 – 905/735-1770, Fax: 905/735-7031 – *1

Blackadder Lacavera, 136 East Main St., PO Box 580, L3B 5R3 – 905/735-3620, Fax: 905/735-1577 – *6

Brooks Bielby & Smith, 247 East Main St., PO Box 67, L3B 5N9 – 905/735-5684, Fax: 905/735-3340 – *3

Community Legal Services of Niagara South Inc., 80 King St., L3B 3J2 – 905/735-1559, Fax: 905/732-6133

Flett, Beccario, 190 Division St., PO Box 340, L8B 5P9 – 905/732-4481, Fax: 905/732-2020; Email: flett@fletteccario.com – *6

William V. Frith, #301, 76 Division St., PO Box 757, L3B 5R5 – 905/735-7582, Fax: 905/735-0093 – *1

F.N. Gibbs, Q.C., 59 Empire St., PO Box 414, L3B 5P7 – 905/732-6145, Fax: 905/732-1015 – *1

Gordon & Adams, 800 Niagara St. North, PO Box 820, L3B 5Y5 – 905/735-0181 – *3

Houghton & Sloniowski, 170 Division St., L3B 5R2 – 905/734-4577, Fax: 905/732-3765 – *4

D.G. Humphries, Q.C., 189 Main St. East, PO Box 39, L3B 5N9 – 905/735-8334, Fax: 905/735-4710 – *1

Johnston & Marotta, 189 Main St. East, PO Box 306, L3B 5P7 – 905/734-4517, Fax: 905/734-3987 – *2

Rodney J. Kajan, #102, 60 King St., PO Box 130, L3B 5P2 – 905/732-1352, Fax: 905/732-0531 – *1

Kormos & Evans, 663 King St., L3B 3L5 – *2

LaRose, Taylor & Fazari, 149 Main St. West, PO Box 366, L3B 5P7 – 905/735-2921, Fax: 905/735-4519 – *3

Pylypuk & Associates, 80 King St., PO Box 605, L3B 5R4 – 905/735-2300, Fax: 905/735-9230 – *3

Donald A. Riou, #301, 76 Division St., PO Box 757, L3B 5R5 – 905/735-7582, Fax: 905/735-0093 – *1

Talmage, Stratton, Latinovich & DiFiore, 221 Division St., PO Box 97, L3B 5P2 – 905/732-4477, Fax: 905/732-4718 – *3

**Westport.........................................Leeds**

Barker, Wilson, Butterworth, James & Scott, Church St., PO Box 159, K0G 1X0 – 613/273-3166, Fax: 613/273-3676 – *5

**Wheatley..........................................Kent**

J.H. Eaton, 26 Erie St. South, N0P 2P0 – 519/825-7032, Fax: 519/825-9570; Email: dfeaton@wincom.net, bk258.torfree.net – *1

**Whitby..........................................Durham**

Louis S. Allore, #206, 701 Rossland Dr. East, L1N 8Y9 – 905/666-5111, Fax: 905/666-5181 – *1

Brooks, Whittington, 326 Dundas St. East, L1N 2J1 – 905/430-1755 – *2

Terence Clarke, 101 Dundas St. West, L1N 2M2 – 905/430-8446, Fax: 905/430-3695 – *1

Coath, Livingstone, 128 Byron St. North, PO Box 327, L1N 4M9 – 905/668-3375, Fax: 905/668-7037 – *2

Dixon & Spong, 124 Byron St. North, L1N 4M9 – 905/668-8571, Fax: 905/668-7936 – *3

Flaherty Dow Elliott, 132 Dundas St. West, L1N 2L9 – 905/666-0231, Fax: 905/686-6447 – *2

David J. Franklin, 326 Dundas St. East, L1N 2J1 – 905/668-8651, Fax: 905/668-8373 – *1

D.G. Goodaire, 126 Byron St. North, PO Box 123, L1N 5R7 – 905/668-1842, Fax: 905/668-8576 – *1

Stacy Howell, 1913 Dundas St. East, L1N 2L5 – 905/432-7772, Fax: 905/725-4211

Jenkins & Newman, 126 Byron St. North, L1N 4M9 – 905/666-8588, Fax: 905/666-4873 – *2

Johnston, Morton, Burch & Boland, 201 Byron St. South, L1N 4P7 – 905/666-2252, 686-0306 (Toronto), Fax: 905/430-0878 – *4

M.F. Madill, 610 John St. West, L1N 2V8 – 905/666-8499 – *1

Martial & Martial, 103 Dundas St. West, L1N 2M1 – 905/427-7474, Fax: 905/668-3761 – *1

Murray Miskin, 501 Brock St. South, L1N 4K8 – 905/428-8000, Fax: 905/430-0772 – *1

Edward P. Schein, 107 Kent St., L1N 4Y1 – 905/666-1266, Fax: 905/668-2023 – *1

Schilling, Evans, 330 Bryon St. South, PO Box 267, L1N 5S1 – 905/668-3392, Fax: 905/668-0407 – *2

Schneider, Howard, 107 Kent St., L1N 4Y1 – 905/668-1677, Fax: 905/668-2023 – *1

Robin D. Scott, 306 Dundas St. West, L1N 2M5 – 905/666-2011, Fax: 905/666-2022 – *1

Mark Seetner, Barrister & Solicitor, 1913 Dundas St. East, L1N 2L5 – 905/725-3350, Fax: 905/725-4211 – *1

Shewan, Rapoport, #206, 701 Rossland Rd. East, L1N 8Y9 – 905/668-1712, Fax: 905/430-0772 – *1

Siksay & Fraser, 618 Athol St., L1N 3Z8 – 905/666-4772, Fax: 905/666-3233 – *2

Sims Brady Thomson & Babbs, 117 King St., PO Box 358, L1N 5S4 – 905/668-7704, Fax: 905/668-1268 – *4

R. Les Smith, 413 Dundas St. East, L1N 2J2 – 905/665-8806, Fax: 905/665-8801

Sosna & Shaughnessy, 214 Colborne St. West, L1N 1X2 – 905/686-1286, Fax: 905/668-6999 – *3

B.P. Stelmach, #5, 11 Stanely Ct., L1N 8P9 – 905/430-6611, Fax: 905/430-6828 – *1

Debra J. Sweetman, 340 Byron St. South, L1N 4P8 – 905/666-8166, Fax: 905/666-8163 – *1

**Wiarton............................................Bruce**

H.R. Hendry, 343 William St., N0H 2T0 – 519/534-2610, Fax: 519/534-1372 – *1

Peter Pegg, 847 Berford St., PO Box 569, N0H 2T0 – 519/534-2011, 2012, Fax: 519/534-4494 – *1

**Williamsford......................................Grey**

Harry Landra, Q.C., RR#1, N0H 2V0 – 519/794-3066 – *1

**Winchester......................................Dundas**

David J. Barnhart, 489 Main St., PO Box 730, K0C 2K0 – 613/774-2808, Fax: 613/774-5731 – *1

Robert Lamb, PO Box 850, K0C 2K0 – 613/774-3706 – *1

McInnis, MacEwen & Ault, 522 St. Lawrence St., K0C 2K0 – 613/774-2670, Fax: 613/774-2266 – *2

**Windsor..........................................Essex**

Barat, Farlam, Millson, 510 Westcourt Pl., N9A 6V2 – 519/258-2424, Fax: 519/258-2451 – *6

Bartlet & Richardes, Canada Bldg., #1000, 374 Ouellette Ave., N9A 1A9 – 519/253-7461, Fax: 519/253-2321 – *19

Anita M. Berecz, #300, 33 University Ave. West, N9A 5N8 – 519/258-8306, Fax: 519/258-4184

Bondy, Baker, Wolf, 559 Pelissier St., N9A 4L2 – 519/256-4800, Fax: 519/256-6599 – *5

Bondy, Kuzak, Riggs & Hurst, #400, 1500 Ouellette Ave., N8X 1K7 – 519/258-9494, Fax: 519/258-9985 – *7

Bondy, Riley, Koski, Stewart, Canada Trust Bldg., #310, 176 University Ave. West, N9A 5P1 – 519/258-1641, Fax: 519/258-1725 – *5

Helen M. Carefoot, 397 Moy Ave., N9A 2N1 – 519/252-2761 – *1

K.I. Dodick, Q.C., #711, 176 University Ave. West, N9A 5P1 – 519/252-3432, Fax: 519/252-9789 – *1

Donaldson, Donaldson, Greenaway, Canada Bldg., #904, 374 Ouellette, N9A 1B1 – 519/255-7333, Fax: 519/255-7173 – *8

Fazio Dumont Law Firm, 333 Wyandotte St. East, N9A 3H7 – 519/258-5030, Fax: 519/971-9051 – *5

Julie Fodor, 642 Windermere Rd., N8Y 3E1 – 519/256-8239, Fax: 519/258-5780 – *1
Furlong Chodola Reynolds, #1300, 100 Ouellette Ave., N9A 6T3 – 519/254-6433, Fax: 519/254-7990; Email: furlaw@netcore.ca – *7
Gatti & Associates, #400, 267 Pelissier St., N9A 4K4 – 519/258-1010, Fax: 519/258-0163 – *3
Gignac, Sutts, Westcourt Place, #600, 251 Goyeau St., N9A 6V2 – 519/258-9333, Fax: 519/258-9527 – *21
Michael H. Gordner, 359 Goyeau St., N9A 1G9 – 519/258-0905, Fax: 519/971-0431 – *1
Kamin, Fisher, Burnett & Ziriada, 42 Pitt St. West, N9A 5L4 – 519/252-1123 – *6
Kirwin Partners, 423 Pelissier St., PO Box 1703, N9A 4L2 – 519/255-9840, Fax: 519/255-1413 – *8
Leonard Lyons, 139 University West, N9A 5P4 – 519/258-3492 – *1
MacMillan & Stipic, #1001, 500 Ouellette Ave., N9A 1B3 – 519/258-3201, Fax: 519/258-2665 – *3
MacPhee Law Firm, #1000, 176 University Ave. West, N9A 5P1 – 519/258-8240 – *2
A.R. Mariotti, #500, 267 Pelissier St., N9A 4K4 – 519/258-1931, Fax: 519/973-7575 – *1
McPherson, Prince & Geddes, Canada Bldg., #200, 374 Ouellette Ave., N9A 6S5 – 519/258-6600, Fax: 519/258-9669 – *5
McTague Law Firm, 455 Pelissier St., N9A 6Z9 – 519/255-4300, Fax: 519/255-4384 – *15
McWilliams & McWilliams, 100 Ouellette Ave., PO Box 1449, N9A 6R5 – 519/258-1100, Fax: 519/258-7384 – *1
Samuel A. Mossman, #400, 1500 Ouellette Ave., N8X 1K7 – 519/258-0903, Fax: 519/977-0282 – *1
Mousseau, DeLuca, Canada Trust Bldg., 176 University Ave. West, N9A 5P3 – 519/258-0615, Fax: 519/258-6833 – *7
Louis Mullins, #1, 2825 Lauzon Pkwy., N8T 3H5 – 519/944-7705, Fax: 519/944-6512 – *2
Paul L. Mullins, 691 Ouellette Ave., N9A 4J4 – 519/255-7707, Fax: 519/255-7114 – *1
Ohler, Mingay, 134 University Ave. West, N9A 5N9 – 519/256-5496, Fax: 519/256-1492 – *2
Paroian, Raphael, Courey, Cohen & Houston, 875 Ouellette Ave., PO Box 970, Stn A, N9A 6S7 – 519/258-1166, Fax: 519/258-8361
D.R. Revait, Royal Windsor Terrace, #209, 380 Pelissier, N9A 6W8 – 519/258-7030, Fax: 519/258-2629 – *1
Rivait & Stevens, 185 City Hall Square South, N9A 6W5 – 519/255-1250 – *2
Roberts, Goldstein, DeBiase, Canada Trust Bldg., #900, 176 University Ave. West, N9A 5P1 – 519/253-5242, Fax: 519/253-0218 – *5
Barrie Rubin, 635 Tecumseh Rd. West, N8X 1H4 – 519/258-0650 – *1
Schwartz, Shanfield & Hawrish, 670 Goyeau St., N9A 1H4 – 519/258-3333, Fax: 519/258-1663; Email: shan@mnsi.net – *4
Brian Sherwell, 827 Pillette Rd., N8Y 3B4 – 519/945-1109, Fax: 519/948-0003 – *1
Cynthia A. Thrasher, Canada Trust Bldg., #909, 176 University Ave. West, N9A 5P1 – 519/253-8882 – *1
G.S. Tuck, 528 Victoria Ave., N9A 4M8 – 519/253-3509, Fax: 519/258-1103 – *1
Wilson, Walker, Hochberg, Slopen, #300, 443 Ouellette Ave., PO Box 1390, N9A 6R4 – 519/977-1555, Fax: 519/977-1566 – *17
Floyd Zalev, 2776 Whelpton St., N8Y 1V9 – 519/258-1238 – *1

**Wingham** .......... **Huron**

Crawford, Mill & Davies, 217 Josephine St., PO Box 1028, N0G 2W0 – 519/357-3630 – *2

**Woodbridge** .......... **York**

F. Borgatti, 7135 Islington Ave., 2nd Fl., L4L 1V9 – 905/851-2883, Fax: 905/851-2887 – *1
Borlak & Associates, #300, 140 Woodbridge Ave., L4L 4K9 – 416/324-2610 – *1
Capo, Sgro, Dilena, Hemsworth, Mendicino, #400, 7050 Weston Rd., L4G 8G7 – 905/850-7000, Fax: 905/850-7050 – *8
Lynda L. Ciaschini, #301, 7050 Weston Rd., L4L 8G7 – 905/850-6080, Fax: 905/850-6082; Email: llc@clo.com – *1
Mancini Associates, #505, 7050 Weston Rd., L4L 8G7 – 905/851-7717 – *3
Anthony Maniaci, 4000 Steeles Ave., L4L 4V9 – 905/851-3400, Fax: 905/851-5108 – *1
Joseph Paradiso, #502, 216 Chrislea Rd., L4L 7W3 – 905/781-6171, Fax: 905/850-5616 – *1
Piccin, Bottos, #201, 4370 Steeles Ave. West, L4L 4Y4 – 905/850-0155, Fax: 905/850-0498 – *4
Jan Poot & Maria Pede, 268 Woodbridge Ave., L4L 2T2 – 905/851-1540,1125, Fax: 905/851-1908 – *2
Felix Rocca, #101, 10 Director Ct., L4L 7E8 – 905/851-7747, Fax: 905/851-7834 – *1
Stabile Partners, 3700 Steeles Ave. West, L4L 8K8 – 905/851-6711, Fax: 905/851-5773 – *4
S. Suppa, #103E, 3800 Steeles Ave. West, L4K 4G9 – 905/739-5050, Fax: 905/856-1633 – *1
Turner, Brooks & Diamond, #102, 7000 Pine Valley Dr., L4L 4Y8 – 905/677-3445; 851-7110, Fax: 905/851-4229 – *3
P.M. Valenti, West Bldg., #300, 3800 Steeles Ave., L4L 4G9 – 905/635-9998, Fax: 905/850-9998 – *1

**Woodstock** .......... **Oxford**

Beatty & Associates, 487 Princess St., PO Box 336, N4S 7X6 – 519/537-6629, Fax: 519/539-2459 – *2
J.F. Hutchinson, 395 Dundas St., N4S 1B6 – 519/539-2345 – *1
Kratzmann, Peter H., 48 Vansittart Ave., N4S 6E2 – 519/537-2221, Fax: 519/537-5150; Email: phklaw@oxford.net – *1
Nesbitt Coulter, 432 Simcoe St., PO Box 125, N4S 7W8 – 519/539-1234, Fax: 519/539-6832; Email: chornick@nesbittlaw.com – *9
J.R. Park, 45 Light St., N4S 6G7 – 519/539-5686, Fax: 519/539-8259 – *1
Searle & Lemon, 13 Light St., PO Box 515, N4S 6G7 – 519/537-5554, Fax: 519/537-7532 – *2
D.J.B. Stock, Q.C., 530 Adelaide St., PO Box 337, N4S 7X6 – 519/537-5578, Fax: 519/537-7202 – *1
White, Coad, Kapusta & Oliver, 5 Wellington St. North, PO Box 1059, N4S 8A4 – 519/421-1500, Fax: 519/539-6926; Email: rcoad@execulink.com – *5

## PRINCE EDWARD ISLAND

**Charlottetown** .......... **Queens**

Campbell, Lea, Michael, McConnell & Pigot, 15 Queen St., PO Box 429, C1A 7K7 – 902/566-3400, Fax: 902/566-9266 – *7
Campbell, Stewart, #201, 137 Queen St., PO Box 485, C1A 7L1 – 902/894-5573, Fax: 902/566-9101 – *4
Carr, Stevenson & MacKay, Peake House, 50 Water St., PO Box 522, C1A 7L1 – 902/892-4156, Fax: 902/566-1377; Email: csmlaw@auracom.com; URL: http://www.peinet.pe.ca/csm – *6
Horace B. Carver, Q.C., 104 Kent St., PO Box 2698, C1A 8C3 – 902/892-1224, Fax: 902/368-3311 – *1
Diamond & McKenna, 224 Queen St., PO Box 39, Stn Central, C1A 7K2 – 902/892-1200, Fax: 902/892-4848 – *4
Evans, MacCallum, 126 Richmond St., PO Box 714, Stn Central, C1A 7L3 – 902/628-2025, Fax: 902/628-8661 – *2
Farmer MacLeod MacMillan Fortier, PO Box 2500, C1A 8C2 – 902/368-3003, Fax: 902/566-4265 – *6
John J. Holmes, 138 Richmond St., C1A 1H9 – 902/892-6145 – *1
Donald P. Large, Q.C., PO Box 1265, C1A 7M8 – 902/566-3773, Fax: 902/368-3039 – *1
Ledwell, Larter & Driscoll, #620, 119 Kent St., C1A 1N3 – 902/368-8473, Fax: 902/368-8346; Email: ledwell@auracom.com – *7
MacLeod, MacDougall, Crane & Parkman, 82 Fitzroy St., PO Box 1056, C1A 7M4 – 902/892-3544, Fax: 902/894-7686 – *5
Macnutt & Dumont, 57 Water St., PO Box 965, C1A 7M4 – 902/894-5003, Fax: 902/368-3782 – *2
Matheson & Murray, 106 Kent St., PO Box 875, C1A 7L9 – 902/894-7051, Fax: 902/368-3762 – *4
Philip Mullally Q.C., 51 University Ave., PO Box 2560, C1A 8C2 – 902/892-5452, Fax: 902/892-7013 – *1
Patterson Palmer Hunt Murphy, Landing Place, 20 Great George St., PO Box 486, C1A 7L1 – 902/628-1033, Fax: 902/566-2639; Email: pphmpei@peinet.pe.ca – *15
Reagh & Reagh, 17 West St., C1A 3S3 – 902/892-7667, Fax: 902/368-8629; Email: reagh@isn.net – *2
Sanderson, Howard, 91 Water St., C1A 1A5 – 902/566-9933, Fax: 902/628-9010 – *2
Stewart McKelvey Stirling Scales, 65 Grafton St., PO Box 2140, C1A 8B9 – 902/892-2485, Fax: 902/566-5283 – *18

**Cornwall** ..........

Robert R. MacArthur, PO Box 127, C0A 1H0 – 902/675-2359, Fax: 902/675-4339 – *1

**Montague** .......... **Kings**

Patterson Palmer Hunt Murphy, 35 Main St. North, C0A 1R0 – 902/838-2644, Fax: 902/838-3440

**Mount Stewart** .......... **Cardigan**

M.R. Clark, PO Box 63, C0A 1T0 – 902/676-2954, Fax: 902/676-2954

**Summerside** .......... **Prince**

Diane Campbell, 740 Water St., PO Box 1300, C1N 4K2 – 902/436-2232, Fax: 902/436-0318 – *1
Lyle & McCabe, PO Box 300, C1N 4Y8 – 902/436-4296, Fax: 902/436-4072 – *2
Taylor, McLellan, 37 Central St., C1N 4P6 – 902/436-9211, Fax: 902/436-1514 – *8
Walker & Aylward, 82 Summer St., C1N 3H9 – 902/436-2535, Fax: 902/436-1144 – *3

## QUÉBEC

**Alma** .......... **Alma**

Larouche, Lalancette, Pilote & Bouchard, 723, ch du Pont-Taché nord, G8B 5B7 – 418/662-6475, Fax: 418/662-9239 – *8

**Amos** .......... **Abitibi**

Bigué & Bigué, 91, av 1er ouest, J9T 1T7 – 819/732-8911, Fax: 819/732-1470 – *3
Geoffroy, Matte & Associés, #102, 4, rue Principale, J9T 2K6 – 819/732-1698, Fax: 819/732-7513 – *2

**Aylmer** .......... **Hull**

A.P. Foster, Q.C., 15, rue Port Royal, J9C 1C7 – 819/777-0892

**Baie-Comeau** .......... **Baie-Comeau**

Boivin, Bachir, Wullaert & Tremblay, #6, 283, boul LaSalle, G4Z 1T2 – 418/294-8793, Fax: 418/294-8258 – *4
Carrier, Blouin, Dostie & Associés, #101, 67, Place Lasalle, J4Z 1K2 – 418/296-2251, Fax: 418/296-8454 – *4
Lavoie, Langlois, Tessier, Arnold, 790, rue Bossé, G5C 1L6 – 418/589-5647, Fax: 418/589-9957 – *4

* indicates number of lawyers in law firm.

**Beauport**........................................ **Québec**

J.C. Lord, 637, av du Cenacle, G1E 1B3 – 418/661-7715, Fax: 418/488-7716 – *1

**Bedford**........................................ **Bedford**

François-Lévésque, 14, rue Rivière, CP 540, J0J 1A0 – 514/248-3353 – *1

Paradis, Poulin, 1, rue Rivière, CP 690, J0J 1A0 – 514/248-3355, Fax: 514/248-2491 – *3

**Beloeil**........................................ **St-Hyacinthe**

Bastien, Morand, Blanchette, 201, boul Laurier, J3G 4G8 – 514/467-5849, Fax: 514/467-3152 – *4

Dore, Tourigny, St-Onge, Fiset & Beauchesne, #314, 535, boul Laurier, J3G 5E9 – 514/446-8474, Fax: 514/467-7134 – *5

**Boucherville**........................................ **Longueuil**

Lecompte Deguire, 1019, rue de la Ventrouze, J4B 5V3 – 514/641-0065, Fax: 514/641-3721 – *2

Rocheleau, St-Germain, Labranche, Beaudoin, #201, 650, rue de Montbrun, J4B 5E4 – 514/449-7922, Fax: 514/449-3978 – *2

**Brossard**........................................ **Longueuil**

Lussier, Jean-Pierre, #202, 4, Place du Commerce, J4W 3B3 – 514/671-1925, Fax: 514/671-1915 – *2

**Buckingham**........................................ **Hull**

Bastien, Lalonde, 595, rue Principale, J8L 2H2 – 819/986-3123, Fax: 819/986-1023 – *2

**Chandler**........................................ **Gaspé**

Gilles Gaul, 484, Place Hotel de Ville, CP 757, G0C 1K0 – 418/689-6500, Fax: 418/689-2136 – *1

**Charlesbourg**........................................ **Québec**

Pierre Montreuil, 1050, rue Orléans, G1H 2H2 – 418/621-5032, Fax: 418/621-5092; Email: milady@cmq.qc.ca – *1

**Châteauguay**........................................ **Beauharnois**

Serge Allen, 5, boul Youville, J6J 2P8 – 514/692-6701, Fax: 514/692-7359 – *1

Chevrefils & Montpetit, 264, boul d'Anjou, J6K 1C5 – 514/691-2133, Fax: 514/691-8006 – *2

Stephan, Fuchs, #2, 144, boul St-Jean-Baptiste, J6K 3B2 – 514/691-0304, Fax: 514/691-6054 – *1

Marie-Andree Mallette, 272, boul St-Jean-Baptiste, J6K 3C2 – 514/699-9499, Fax: 514/699-9710 – *1

**Chibougamau**........................................ **Abitibi**

Larouche & Girard, Avocats, #2, 401, 3e rue, G8P 1N6 – 418/748-6468, Fax: 418/748-3313; Email: larouchegirard@compuserve.com – *2

**Chicoutimi**........................................ **Chicoutimi**

Girard, Allard, Beaulieu, #202, 200, rue Racine est, G7H 1S1 – 418/543-0725, Fax: 418/543-1765 – *4

**Cowansville**........................................ **Bedford**

Boisvert, Champoux, #205, 505, rue du Sud, J2K 2X9 – 514/263-0656, Fax: 514/263-8582 – *3

Morin & Beauchesne, 436, rue du Sud, J2K 2X7 – 514/263-5458, Fax: 514/263-7376 – *2

Turner, Monk, 314, rue Principale, J2K 1J5 – 514/263-4077, Fax: 514/263-5260 – *2

**Dorion**........................................ **Montréal**

France Cormier, 3, rue Pierre-Ricard, J7V 8M6 – 514/425-0570, Fax: 514/425-5770 – *1

**Drummondville**........................................ **Drummond**

Hinse, Tousignant, Larivière, 360, rue Marchand, CP 397, J2B 6W3 – 819/477-3424, Fax: 819/477-7728 – *3

Jutras & Associés, 449, rue Hériot, J2B 1B4 – 819/477-6321, Fax: 819/474-5691 – *5

Larose Avocats, 215, rue Lindsay, J2C 1N8 – 819/477-2235, Fax: 819/477-8674 – *2

**Farnham**........................................ **Bedford**

Remi Pageau, 54, boul Normandie Nord, J2N 1W3 – 514/293-6678 – *1

**Gaspé**........................................ **Gaspé**

Luc Houle, 107, rue de la Reine, CP 2255, G0C 1R0 – 418/368-1723, Fax: 418/368-6474 – *1

Joncas & Desbois, CP 1160, G0C 1R0 – 418/368-3358, Fax: 418/368-3432 – *2

Michaud & Coté, 147, rue de la Reine, CP 208, G0C 1R0 – 418/368-2633 – *3

**Gatineau**........................................ **Hull**

Christine Auger, 525, boul Maloney est, J8P 1E8 – 819/669-4022, Fax: 819/669-9627 – *1

Babin, Dupont, Fortin & Dionne, #202, 365, boul Greber, J8T 5R3 – 819/568-0990, Fax: 819/568-4727 – *4

Beaudry, Bertrand, Carrefour des Affaires, #203, 160, boul de l'Hôpital, J8T 8J1 – 819/246-2323, Fax: 819/246-1217

Kehoe, Blais, Major & Parent, #200, 344, boul Maloney est, J8P 7A6 – 819/663-2439, Fax: 819/663-4816 – *5

Lapointe, Cayen, Morel, #200, 370, boul Gréber, J8T 5R6 – 819/568-0663, Fax: 819/568-0226 – *5

Letellier & Associates, #127, 139, boul de l'Hôpital, J8T 8A3 – 819/243-7293, Fax: 819/243-5913

**Gracefield**........................................ **Hull**

Louise Major, 40, rue Principale, J0X 1W0 – 819/463-3489, Fax: 819/463-4603 – *1

**Granby**........................................ **Bedford**

Choinière & Hill, 26, rue Court, J2G 4Y5 – 514/372-7332, Fax: 514/372-1222 – *2

Delorme & Denis, 21, rue Johnson, J2G 6T2 – 514/372-5418, Fax: 514/372-5511 – *2

Grignon, Brun, 18, rue Court, J2G 4Y5 – 514/372-3353, Fax: 514/372-1816

Normandin Brisebois Faucher, 35, rue Dufferin, J1G 4W5 – 514/372-3545, Fax: 514/372-5854 – *4

Viens Nadeau, #1, 22, rue St-Antoine sud, J2G 6W3 – 514/777-1312, Fax: 514/777-8659 – *2

**Grand-Mère**........................................ **St. Maurice**

Goulet & Cote, 570, av 6e, G9T 2H5 – 819/538-1791, Fax: 819/538-3616 – *2

**Grande-Rivière**........................................ **Gaspé**

Guy Gendron, CP 488, G0C 1V0 – 418/385-2333, Fax: 418/385-4418 – *1

**Hull**........................................ **Hull**

Jean-Paul Aubry, #107, 72, rue Laval, J8X 3H3 – 819/771-8645, Fax: 819/778-6534 – *1

Beaudry, Bertrand, Maison du Citoyen, #400, 25, rue Laurier, J8X 4C8 – 819/770-4880, Fax: 819/595-4979, 770-9190 – *15

Bergeron, Gaudreau, 167, rue Notre-Dame, J8X 3T3 – 819/770-7928, Fax: 819/770-1424; Email: vberger@uottawa.ca – *2

Serge Côté, 44, boul Montclair, J8Y 2E6 – 819/776-3101, Fax: 819/776-3954 – *1

Pierre Fontaine, 25, rue Bernier, J8Z 1E7 – 819/771-6578 – *1

André Gingras, #208, 825, boul de la Carrière, J8Y 6T7 – 819/778-2369, Fax: 819/772-4193 – *1

Roger Gosselin, 44, boul Montclair, J8Y 2E6 – 819/776-3101, Fax: 819/776-3954 – *1

Laporte, Angès, 217, boul Gamelin, J8Y 1W5 – 819/772-2521, Fax: 819/772-2492 – *1

Leduc, Bouthillette, 12, rue Ste-Marie, J8Y 2A3 – 819/771-6257, Fax: 819/771-3973 – *6

Letellier & Associates, #500, 15, ch Gamelin, J8Y 1V4 – 819/778-7293, Fax: 819/778-1145 – *13

E. Wayne Lora, 175, rue Champlain, J8X 3R3 – 819/778-6511, Fax: 819/770-5703; Email: wlora@intranet.ca – *1

Clémence Mainguy, 175, rue Champlain, J8X 3R3 – 819/778-6511, Fax: 819/770-5703 – *1

Noël, Berthiaume, 111, rue Champlain, J8X 3R1 – 819/771-7393, Fax: 819/771-5397 – *11

Paquette, Déziel, 17, rue Jeanne-d'Arc, J8Y 2H3 – 819/770-0668, Fax: 819/770-0669 – *2

Pharand, Bélanger, LeBlanc, 166, rue Wellington, J8X 2J4 – 819/771-7781, Fax: 819/771-0608 – *7

Michel Ste-Marie, 175, rue Champlain, J8X 3R3 – 819/777-3864, Fax: 819/777-8378 – *1

Sarrazin, Charlebois, Édifice Themis, 162, rue Wellington, J8X 2J4 – 819/770-4888, Fax: 819/770-0712; Email: sarrazincharlebois@atreide.net – *3

Arnaud Voyer, 6, rue Villeneuve, J8Y 1L2 – 819/771-3712 – *1

**Joliette**........................................ **Joliette**

Ferland & Bélair, 70, Place Bourget sud, J6E 5E8 – 514/759-7412, Fax: 514/759-5366; Email: mbelair@pandora.qc.ca – *4

Gagnon, Chaîné & Associés, 820, rue Notre-Dame, J6E 3J6 – 514/759-6600, Fax: 514/759-5028 – *5

Généreux & Rondeau, 400, rue Baby, J6E 2W1 – 514/752-6655, Fax: 514/752-1098 – *4

Claudette Vincelette, 125, rue Beaudry nord, J6E 6A4 – 514/759-3958, Fax: 514/756-2933 – *1

**Jonquière**........................................ **Québec**

Cain, Lamarre, Wells, #201, 3750, boul du Royaume, G7X 0A4 – 418/695-4580, Fax: 418/547-9590; Email: clw@cybernaute.com – *4

Turcotte, Fortin, Guay, Cantin & Marceau, 2106, rue Ste-Famille, CP 2040, G7X 7X6 – 418/547-2108, Fax: 418/547-9519 – *5

**Kahnawake**........................................ **Bedford**

Mohawk Council of Kahnawake, PO Box 720, J0L 1B0 – 514/638-3011, Fax: 514/638-3663; Email: mcklegal@total.net – *3

**La Malbaie**........................................ **Charlevoix**

Gendron & Moffet, #220, 251, rue Nairn, CP 237, G5A 1T7 – 418/665-6417, Fax: 418/665-6174 – *2

**La Tuque**........................................ **St-Maurice**

Hénaire, Roy, 290, rue St-Joseph, 2e étage, G9X 3Z8 – 819/676-8002, Fax: 819/379-1227

**Lac Beauport**........................................ **Québec**

Robert Bouchard, 208, ch le Tour du Lac, CP 1193, G0A 2C0 – 418/849-9325, Fax: 418/841-3690 – *1

**Lemoyne**........................................ **Longueuil**

Anne Ulrich, #203, 1136, av Victoria, J4R 1R1 – 514/466-3442, Fax: 514/466-3521 – *1

**Lévis**........................................ **Québec**

Gosselin & Associés, #310, 6500, boul de la Rive-Sud, G6V 7M5 – 418/833-4443, Fax: 418/833-6130 – *4

Pelletier, Kronström, Giguère, 6300, boul de la Rive sud, CP 3500, G6V 6P9 – 418/835-8735, Fax: 418/833-6603; Ligne sans frais: 1-800-463-5168; Email: jacques.pelletier@spgdag.ca – *4

**Longueuil**........................................ **Longueuil**

Raymond Allard, 1150, boul Marie-Victorin, J4G 2M4 – 514/442-8600, Fax: 514/463-1043 – *1

Arbour & Cordeau, #403, 2984, boul Taschereau, J4V 2G9 – 514/466-3133, Fax: 514/466-5938 – *2

Bernard, Cimoné, Poupart, Despatis, #200, 101, boul Roland Therrien, J4H 4B9 – 514/670-7900, Fax: 514/670-0673; Email: avocats.bernard.cimone@canis.net – *8

Jacques Boissonnault, 630, ch de Chambly, J4H 3L8 – 514/651-8318, Fax: 514/651-2552 – *1

Dubois & Associés, #116, 70, rue de la Barre, J4K 5J3 – 514/646-2613, Fax: 514/646-4225 – *2
Carole Fallu, 441, boul Ste-Foy, J4J 1X9 – 514/442-4550, Fax: 514/442-2595 – *1
Fortier & Gladu, #104, 45, Place Charles Lemoyne, J4K 5G5 – 514/670-0823, Fax: 514/442-4351; Email: gladu@dsuper.net; URL: http://oracle.dsuper.net/~gladu/fg_com.html – *2
R.E. Fusey, 1115, boul Desaulniers, J4K 1K5 – 514/442-3222, Fax: 514/442-3222 – *1
Lamarre Trépanier Vincent Senc, #200, 370, ch Chambly, J4H 3Z6 – 514/677-9144, Fax: 514/677-3241; Email: lamvin@generation.net – *6
Montgrain, McClure, Marois, Chandonnet, Gibeau, #300, 550, ch Chambly, J4H 3L8 – 514/679-0720, Fax: 514/679-0724 – *7
Periard, Ledoux, 175, ch Chambly, G4H 3L3 – 514/646-2116, Fax: 514/646-3828 – *2
Jean-Pierre Tremblay, 3414, rue Belcourt, J4M 2K9 – 514/448-3751, Fax: 514/677-0982 – *1

**Magog ....................................... St-François**

Chantale Chrétien, 435, rue St-Patrice ouest, J1X 1W8 – 819/868-4228, Fax: 819/868-4005 – *3
André Ladouceur, 515, rue Langlois, J1X 3K5 – 819/847-2127, Fax: 819/847-1842; Email: andouce@archimed.qc.ca – *1

**Maniwaki....................................... Pontiac**

Desjardins & Gauthier, 185, boul Desjardins, J9E 2C9 – 819/449-6075, Fax: 819/449-5679 – *2

**Matagami....................................... Abitibi**

Bigué & Bigué, 177, boul Matagami, J0Y 2A0 – 819/739-4354 – *1

**Matane....................................... Rimouski**

Jean-Pierre Chamberland, #203, 548, av du Phare est, G4W 1A7 – 418/562-1806, Fax: 418/562-7248; Email: chamlire@quebectel.com – *1
Deschenes & Doiron, 352, av St-Jérôrme, G4W 3B1 – 418/562-2097, Fax: 418/562-2926 – *2

**Mont-Laurier....................................... Labelle**

Simard, Morin, Deschênes et Barrette, 445, rue du Pont, J9L 2R8 – 819/623-4259, Fax: 819/623-9628 – *2

**Montmagny....................................... Montmagny**

Réal Garant, 77, av de la Gare, G5V 2T1 – 418/248-0194, Fax: 418/248-0195 – *1
Marcel Guimont, 25, rue du Palais-de-Justice, CP 482, G5V 3S9 – 418/248-1530, Fax: 418/248-4157 – *2

**Montréal....................................... Montréal**

Jacob Aaron, #303, 200, ch Bates, H3S 1A3 – 514/731-7714, Fax: 514/341-1771 – *1
Abbey, Pass, #840, 1310, av Greene, H3Z 2B2 – 514/931-3881, Fax: 514/932-1451 – *1
Allan Adel, #305, 276, rue St-Jacques, H2Y 1N3 – 514/845-4151, Fax: 514/845-0306 – *1
Adessky Poulin, Place Canada Trust, 999, boul de Maisonneuve ouest, 18e étage, H3A 3L4 – 514/288-9797, Fax: 514/288-2697 – *19
Alarie, Legault, Beauchemin, Paquin, Nadon, Jobin & Brisson, 1259, rue Berri, 10e étage, H2L 4C7 – 514/844-6216, Fax: 514/844-8129 – *13
Alepin Gauthier, #601, 3080, boul Le Carrefour, H7T 2K9 – 514/681-3080, 338-3037 (Montréal), Fax: 514/681-1476; Email: alepin@ag.gc.ca; URL: http://www.alepin.com – *9
Allen, Hébert, #200, 7170, boul St-Laurent, H2S 3E2 – 514/274-9393, Fax: 514/274-5614 – *2
Amar, Kugler, Elhadad, #1425, 1, Place Ville-Marie, H3B 2B2 – 514/878-1532, Fax: 514/878-4761 – *5
Amaron, Stead & Viberg, #200, 280, av Dorval, H9S 3H4 – 514/636-4992, Fax: 514/636-8122 – *2
AON Parizeau Inc., 500, boul René-Lévesque ouest, 11e étage, H2Z 1Y4 – 514/871-4500, Fax: 514/871-4411 – *1
Arnault, Thibault, 250, Place d'Youville, 2ième étage, H2Y 2B6 – 514/285-2727, Fax: 514/285-2728 – *2
Aster & Aster, #410, 345, av Victoria, H3Z 2N2 – 514/483-2444, Fax: 514/483-2477 – *2
Axelrod, Price, Brossard, #2314, 1155, boul René-Lévesque ouest, H3B 2K2 – 514/878-9951, Fax: 514/878-3883 – *3
Raymond G. Ayoup, #805, 1255, Carré Phillips, H3B 3G1 – 514/861-9955, Fax: 514/866-4101 – *1
Emile Jean Barakat, #8, 4785, rue St-Kevin, H3W 1N8 – 514/341-6464, Fax: 514/739-8745; Email: meemileb@aol.com – *1
Barkowitz, Strauber, Goldman & Tiger, #300, 4141, rue Sherbrooke ouest, H3Z 1B8 – 514/931-1788, Fax: 514/931-3061 – *4
Baron & Abrams, #450, 5180, ch Queen-Mary, H3W 3E7 – 514/487-7783, Fax: 514/483-2280 – *4
Barron Caron Chartrand Tourangeau, #300, 442, rue St-Gabriel, H2Y 2Z9 – 514/874-2602, Fax: 514/874-2609 – *6
Barsalou Auger, #2420, 1002, rue Sherbrooke ouest, H3A 3L6 – 514/982-3355, Fax: 514/982-2550 – *3
Barza & Lagana, #700, 2015, rue Peel, H3A 1T8 – 514/288-9322, Fax: 514/288-2562 – *5
Robert Beaudet, 5331, rue Bannantyne, H4H 1E8 – 514/769-8527, Fax: 514/769-7466 – *3
Beaudry & Associés, #304, 480, boul St-Laurent, H2Y 3Y7 – 514/282-0727, Fax: 514/282-9363 – *3
Mimi Beaudry, #227, 300, rue du St-Sacrement, H2Y 1X4 – 514/845-5911, Fax: 514/845-4371 – *1
Beaulieu, Semeniuk & Gagnon, #218, 1405, rue Bishop, H3G 2E4 – 514/844-2811, Fax: 514/499-8536 – *3
Beauregard, Ferland, Édifice Canada Trust, 600, boul René-Lévesque ouest, 12e étage, H3B 1N4 – 514/861-1110, Fax: 514/861-1310 – *6
Bélanger & Bélanger, 8136, rue St-Denis, H2P 2G6 – 514/381-7626, Fax: 514/381-0339 – *2
Bélanger, Brunet, #100, 870, boul Décarie, H4L 3L9 – 514/748-6584, Fax: 514/748-7769 – *3
Diane Bélanger, 400, rue St-Gabriel, 4e étage, H2Y 2Z9 – 514/861-7600, Fax: 514/392-7766 – *1
Belanger, Fiore, #300, 685, boul Décarie, H4L 5G4 – 514/744-0825, Fax: 514/744-9861; Email: belafior@interlink.net – *2
Bélanger, Sauvé, #1700, 1, Place Ville Marie, H3B 2C1 – 514/878-3081, Fax: 514/878-3053 – *55
Bell Rudick Edelstein, #3404, 1155, boul René-Lévesque ouest, H3B 3T3 – 514/866-1977, Fax: 514/866-1639 – *5
J.M. Bellaiche, #2280, 800, boul René-Lévesque ouest, H3B 1X9 – 514/954-8888, Fax: 514/954-5077 – *1
Edouard J. Belliardo, #603, 10, rue St-Jacques, H1Y 1L3 – 514/845-6253, Fax: 514/845-8056 – *1
Nicole Benchimol, #1200, 2015, rue Peel, H3A 1T8 – 514/844-1515, Fax: 514/845-4472 – *1
Bennett Jones Verchere, #3900, 1000, rue de La Gauchetière, H3B 4W5 – 514/871-1200, Fax: 514/871-8115 – *9
Robert Benoit, 5325, rue Jean-Talon est, H1S 1L4 – 514/725-9577, Fax: 514/725-8763 – *1
Berger & Winston, #400, 615, boul René-Lévesque ouest, H3B 1P5 – 514/288-4177, Fax: 514/876-1090 – *2
Robert Berger, #500, 4269, rue Ste-Catherine ouest, H3Z 1P7 – 514/931-1883, Fax: 514/931-0040; Email: mgmt@mtl.paradigm-prop.ca – *1
Berkowitz Strauber Tiger, #300, 4141, rue Sherbrooke ouest, H3Z 1B8 – 514/931-1788, Fax: 514/931-3061 – *4
Jean Berthiaume, 1800, rue Sherbrooke est, H2K 1B3 – 514/521-2144, Fax: 514/525-0182 – *1
Bertrand, Deslauriers, 83, rue St-Paul ouest, H2Y 1Z1 – 514/842-8051, Fax: 514/842-8055 – *6
Bertrand, Guerard, 134, av Laurentides, H7G 2T3 – 514/663-0851 – *2
Michael Besner, #500, 1210, rue Sherbrooke ouest, H3A 1H6 – 514/288-5252, Fax: 514/288-7479 – *1
Alexander Biega, Q.C., #705, 276, rue St-Jacques, H2Y 1N3 – 514/842-1126, Fax: 514/842-1290 – *1
Bissonnet, Mercadente & Associés, #202, 5450, rue Jarry est, H1P 1T9 – 514/326-3300, Fax: 514/326-4706 – *7
Elaine Bissonnette, #102, 4139, rue Amiens, H1H 2G3 – 514/323-8770, Fax: 514/323-8700; Email: ebissonnette@sympatico.ca – *1
Harry Blank, #1416, 1255, rue University, H3B 3X1 – 514/866-1125, Fax: 514/866-6898 – *2
Danielle Blier, #402, 266, rue Notre-Dame ouest, H2Y 1T6 – 514/844-8693, Fax: 514/842-6808 – *1
Monique Blondin, #401, 10, rue St-Jacques, H1Y 1L3 – 514/844-2535 – *1
Bloomfield Bellemare, #1720, 1080, Côte du Beaver Hall, H2Z 1S8 – 514/871-9571, Fax: 514/397-0816 – *3
Boivin Guillet, 5083, rue St-Denis, H2J 2L9 – 514/288-5753, Fax: 514/288-6151 – *6
Michele Bolduc, #1608, 1050, Côte du Beaver Hall, H2Z 1S4 – 514/870-8891 – *1
Bouchard & Associés, #1010, 10, rue St-Jacques, H2Y 1L3 – 514/842-2913, Fax: 514/842-5353 – *7
Jean-Pierre Boucher, 1816, rue Sherbrooke est, H2K 1B3 – 514/524-3632 – *2
Boule & Associés, #500, 266, rue Notre-Dame ouest, H2Y 1T6 – 514/284-9681, Fax: 514/284-6606 – *1
Jacques Bourgault, 7575, rue des Ecores, H2E 2W5 – 514/987-3000, Fax: 514/522-8222 – *1
M.L. Anne Boutin, #2220, 7999, boul les Galeries d'Anjou, H1M 1W9 – 514/353-4411, Fax: 514/353-4553 – *1
Boyer, Gariépy, Duplessis, #200, 417, rue St-Nicholas, H2Y 2P4 – 514/287-9585, Fax: 514/844-5243 – *6
Alain Brabant, 8685, rue Sherbrooke est, H1L 1C1 – 514/354-3121, Fax: 514/351-9690 – *1
Sarto Brisebois, 710, rue St-Jacques, H2Y 1L3 – 514/849-9444, Fax: 514/849-0119 – *2
Brisset des Nos, Gravel, Lévesque, Normand, Rioux, #300, 777, rue de la Commune ouest, H3C 1Y1 – 514/875-7975, Fax: 514/875-9433 – *7
Donald R. Brown, 149, Ashley Rd., H9W 1K7
Brunelle, Sirois, Arseneault & Ledoux, #703, 465, rue St-Jean, H1Y 2R6 – 514/844-2802 – *4
Jacques Brunet, 3714, rue Ontario est, H1W 1R9 – 514/524-6638 – *1
Rebecca Butovsky, #328, 300, rue du St-Sacrement, H2Y 1X4 – 514/286-7134 – *1
Byers Casgrain, #3900, 1, Place Ville-Marie, H3B 4M7 – 514/878-8811, Fax: 514/866-2241 – *70
Daniel Caisse, #508, 10, rue St-Jacques, H2Y 1L3 – 514/288-2250, Fax: 514/288-2402 – *1
Diane G. Cameron, #206, 4700, av Bonavista, H3W 2C5 – 514/483-2619, Fax: 514/483-3616; Email: dcameron@autoroute.net – *1
Campbell, Cohen, Seidman, Leveille, 2, Place Alexis-Nihon, #1802, 3500, boul de Maisonneuve ouest, H3Z 3C1 – 514/937-9445, Fax: 514/937-2618; Email: ccsl@cam.org – *6
Andre Carbonneau, 2567, rue Ontario est, H2K 1W6 – 514/524-5080, Fax: 514/524-9602; Email: acarbonn@sprynet.com – *1
J.B. Carisse, #300, 19, rue Le Royer ouest, H2Y 1W4 – 514/843-4569, Fax: 514/843-6612
Carrière, Dame, Paquet, Pinard, Allard, 2356, rue Jean-Talon est, H1E 1V9 – 514/593-1977, Fax: 514/593-4762 – *1
Raymond A. Cartwright, #600, 615, boul René-Lévesque ouest, H3B 1P6 – 514/861-7454, Fax: 514/861-6180 – *1
Jean M. Caumartin, #920, 360, rue St-Jacques, H2Y 1P5 – 514/844-9970, Fax: 514/844-4632 – *1
Cayer, Lapointe, #200, 11903, boul Ste-Gertrude, H1G 5R1 – 514/327-1201, Fax: 514/322-5624 – *3
Cerundolo & Maiorino, 1807, rue Jean-Talon est, H1E 1T4 – 514/376-0335, Fax: 514/376-6334 – *3

* indicates number of lawyers in law firm.

Chaikelson & Spector, #1600, 2000, rue Mansfield, H3A 3A4 – 514/288-2500, Fax: 514/288-7128 – *8
Chait Amyot, #1900, 1, Place Ville Marie, H3B 2C3 – 514/879-1353, Fax: 514/879-1460; Email: info@chait-amyot.ca; URL: http://www.chait-amyot.ca – *27
Chalifoux, Carette & Montpetit, #912, 10, rue St-Jacques, H1Y 1L3 – 514/842-1006, Fax: 514/842-1811 – *11
Champagne & Kouri, #104, 6494, rue Beaubien est, H1M 1A9 – 514/255-1223, Fax: 514/255-0635 – *3
François Chapados, #204, 1010, rue Sherbrooke ouest, H3A 2R7 – 514/844-2234, Fax: 514/844-9330 – *1
Charbonneau & Archambault, 2300, rue Sherbrooke est, H2K 1E5 – 514/527-4561, Fax: 514/522-3364; Email: nathalie_charbonneau@msn.com – *4
Michel, Charbonneau, #201, 4403, rue Beaubien est, H1T 1T2 – 514/725-4773, Fax: 514/725-4828 – *2
Pierre Charbonneau, #1000, 550, rue Sherbrooke ouest, H3A 1B9 – 514/288-9150, Fax: 514/288-9307 – *1
Charness, Charness & Charness, #1100, 440, boul René-Lévesque ouest, H2Z 1V7 – 514/878-1808, Fax: 514/871-1149 – *3
Claude Chauret, #300, 3535, rue St-Charles, H9H 3C4 – 514/697-1421, Fax: 514/426-8677 – *1
Fred Cheftechi, 800, boul René-Lévesque ouest, H3B 1X9 – 514/397-8700, Fax: 514/397-8608 – *2
Marc Chenard, #205, 5174, Côté des Neiges, H3T 1X8 – 514/733-3669, Fax: 514/733-2006 – *1
Maurice Chevalier, #1407, 3555, rue Berri, H1L 4G4 – 514/845-5551 – *1
Choquette Bernstein Rheaume, #200, 5316, av du Parc, H2V 4G7 – 514/270-3192, Fax: 514/270-8876 – *4
Ciampini, Ciampini, Avocats, #205, 8190, boul Newman, H8N LX9 – 514/364-4750, Fax: 514/264-2730 – *2
Mark Anthony Ciarallo, 4838, rue Oka, H9K 1H6 – 514/696-7931, Fax: 514/696-0548 – *1
Clark & LaTraverse, #4200, 1250, boul René-Lévesque ouest, H3B 4W8 – 514/938-1313, Fax: 514/938-3691; Email: litigators@clarklatraverse.com – *6
Coblentz & Coblentz, #1500, 555, boul René-Lévesque ouest, H2Z 1B1 – 514/866-8901, Fax: 514/866-8901 – *2
Paul B. Cohen, #809, 4000, boul de Maisonneuve ouest, H3Z 1J9 – 514/931-3691 – *1
Ralph A. Cohen, #514, 1117, rue Ste-Catharine est, H3B 1H9 – *1
Colby, Monet, Demers, Delage & Crevier, #2900, 1501, av McGill College, H3A 3M8 – 514/284-3663, Fax: 514/284-1961 – *15
A.B. Coleman, #440, 4141, rue Sherbrooke ouest, H3Z 1B8 – 514/935-5030, Fax: 514/935-3559 – *1
Mortimer J. Constantine, #1600, 2000, rue Mansfield, H3A 3A4 – 514/849-8111, Fax: 514/849-8113 – *1
S. Cooperstein, #1051, 400, boul de Maisonneuve ouest, H3A 1L4 – 514/845-1094 – *1
Normand Corbeil, #1021, 50, Place Crémazie ouest, H2P 2T7 – 514/381-1851, Fax: 514/389-1924 – *1
Lulu Cornellier, #3, 1682, boul St-Joseph, H2J 1M9 – 514/598-8179, Fax: 514/598-7787 – *1
Benoit Côté, 376, boul St-Joseph est, H2T 1J6 – 514/287-9796, Fax: 514/843-7471; Email: bencote@total.net – *1
Diane L. Côté, 6977, St. Denis, H2S 2S5 – 514/274-0988, Fax: 514/274-8622 – *1
Crestohl & Associates, #1200, 1, Carré Westmount, H3Z 2P4 – 514/932-7392, Fax: 514/932-0990 – *2
Hyman J. Crystal, #826, 276, rue St-Jacques, H2Y 1N3 – 514/284-1125, Fax: 514/284-2413 – *1
Jacques Cyr, #300, 13001, rue Sherbrooke est, H1A 3W2 – 514/642-2676, Fax: 514/642-1663; Email: jaccyr@rive-nord.net – *1
Allen Dagenais, #110, 1515, boul Chomedey, H7V 3Y7 – 514/686-0500, Fax: 514/337-2733; Email: dagenais@total.net – *13
Johanne Daniel, #900, 666, rue Sherbrooke ouest, H3A 1E7 – 514/499-0101, Fax: 514/281-6699; Email: jdaniel@videotron.ca – *1
Giles Daoust, #304, 4, rue Notre-Dame est, H2Y 1B7 – 514/861-0753, Fax: 514/861-5600 – *1
David & Touchette, #3600, 1155, boul René-Lévesque ouest, H3B 3T9 – 514/871-8174, Fax: 514/871-8052; Email: davidco@masc-web.com; URL: http://www.masc-web.com/dvdtct/ – *2
Davis & Company, Place du Canada, #2250, 11010, rue de la Gauchetiere ouest, H3B 2N2 – 514/392-1991, Fax: 514/392-1999
François de Billy, 1654, rue St-Rose, H2L 2K3 – 514/524-9591, Fax: 514/524-1628; Email: fdebilly@rplus.net – *1
Joanne de Grand'Maison, #1904, 3535, av Papineau, H2K 4J9 – 514/596-3958, Fax: 514/596-0035; Email: plus@jonction.net – *1
De Grandpré, Godin, #2900, 1000, rue de la Gauchetière ouest, H3B 4W5 – 514/878-4311, Fax: 514/878-4333 – *41
Claude de la Madeleine, 3600, boul Henri-Bourassa est, H1H 1J4 – 514/323-2112, Fax: 514/323-2112 – *1
Décary Francescucci & Monty, 3467, rue St-Hubert, H1L 3Z8 – 514/525-2589, Fax: 514/525-2580 – *2
Delvecchio & Bouliane, 5898, av 3e, H1Y 2X1 – 514/376-7569 – *3
Demarais & Hargreaves, #201, 410, boul Henri-Bourassa est, H3L 1C4 – 514/382-8122 – *3
Charles Derome, 5064, av du Parc, H2V 4G1 – 514/271-4700, Fax: 514/271-4708 – *1
Claude Des Marais, 1206, boul St. Joseph, H2J 1L6 – 514/521-0047 – *1
Suzanne Deschamps, 500, Place d'Armes, 12e étage, H2Y 2W2 – 514/872-1624, Fax: 514/872-0036; Email: sudes@ibm.net – *1
Desjardins Ducharme Stein Monast, Tour de la Banque Nationale, #2400, 600, rue de la Gauchetière ouest, H3B 4L8 – 514/878-9411, Fax: 514/878-9092; Ligne sans frais: 1-800-670-0102; Email: avocat@ddsm.ca; URL: http://www.ddsm.ca – *77
Bruno Desjardins, #1502, 2045, rue Stanley, H3A 2V4 – 514/849-3113, Fax: 514/849-2061 – *1
Desjardins, Lapointe, Mousseau, Bélanger, #2185, 600, rue de la Gauchetière ouest, H3B 4L8 – 514/875-5404, Fax: 514/875-5647 – *9
Robert Desjardins, 4515, rue Notre-Dame ouest, H4C 1S3 – 514/766-6285, Fax: 514/932-0412 – *1
Desmarais Picard Garceau Pasquin, 204, Place d'Youville, H2Y 2B4 – 514/845-5171, Fax: 514/845-5578 – *14
Desrosiers, Groulx, Turcotte, #500, 303, rue St-Sulpice, H2Y 3W2 – 514/287-9284, Fax: 514/287-9792 – *3
Jean Desrosiers, 4192, av Girouard, H4A 3C9 – 514/482-7428 – *1
Deveau, Lavoie & Associates, #400, 3131, rue de la Concorde est, H7E 4W4 – 514/664-1515, Fax: 514/664-1438 – *3
Joseph Di Clementi, #224, 759, Victoria Sq., H2Y 2J7 – 514/288-1891, Fax: 514/288-3833 – *1
Donato Di Tullio, 7647, boul Gouin est, H1E 1A7 – 514/648-1048, Fax: 514/648-3288 – *1
Lawrence Diner, #400, 1310, av Greene, H3Z 2B2 – 514/931-3883, Fax: 514/939-1469 – *1
Hrair Djihanian, #300, 320, rue Notre-Dame est, H2Y 1C7 – 514/395-0543, Fax: 514/395-2476 – *1
André R. Dorais Avocats, #1810, 1, Carré Westmount, H3Z 2P9 – 514/938-0808, Fax: 514/938-8888 – *3
Doyon, Nivoix & Goulet, #501, 6455, rue Jean-Talon est, H1S 3E8 – 514/253-3338, Fax: 514/251-0560 – *3
Daniel Drouin, #1802, 666, rue Sherbrooke ouest, H3A 1E7 – 514/287-9050, Fax: 514/897-1592 – *1
Du Mesnil & Lavigne, #1605, 555, boul René-Lévesque ouest, H2Z 1B1 – 514/866-1529, Fax: 514/866-7725 – *2
Dubuc, Marcaix, Trudeau, #2610, 300, rue Léo-Pariseau, CP 963, H1L 1K3 – 514/843-5444 – *3
Laurier Dugas, 4545, av Pierre-de-Coubertin, H1V 3N7 – 514/252-3137, Fax: 514/251-8038 – *1
Duguay, Salois, Dionne, Morneau, Massicotte & Tellier, 425, ch St-Sulpice, H2Y 2V7 – 514/842-9631, Fax: 514/842-1255 – *7
Francine Dumont, 404, rue Saint-Dizier, H2Y 3T3 – 514/288-6060, Fax: 514/288-0630 – *1
Dunton, Rainville, Toupin, Perrault, #4300, 800, Place Victoria, CP 303, H4Z 1H1 – 514/866-6743, Fax: 514/866-8854 – *19
Gilles Dupont, #400, 1594, rue St-Hubert, H2L 3Z2 – 514/526-6621, Fax: 514/524-4341 – *1
Robert Dupuis, 509, rue Lartigue, H7N 3T6 – 514/663-5280, Fax: 514/663-5281 – *1
Jean-Guy Farley, 2544, boul Rosemont, H1Y 1K4 – 514/254-9519 – *1
Emile J. Fattal, #705, 1134, rue Ste-Catherine ouest, H3B 1H4 – 514/861-4545, Fax: 514/874-1639 – *1
Barry Feinstein, #300, 1384, av Greene, H3Z 2B1 – 514/846-4045, Fax: 514/846-4027 – *1
Feldman & Spina, #908, 10, rue St-Jacques, H2Y 1L3 – 514/842-8378, Fax: 514/849-4457 – *1
W.H. Finkelberg, #400, 1155, rue Sherbrooke ouest, H3A 2W1 – 514/284-1186, Fax: 514/849-0527 – *1
C.A. Fitzwilliam, 93, av Easton, H4X 1L3 – 514/484-8722, Fax: 514/485-5719 – *1
I. David Fleming, #523, 1440, Ste. Catherine ouest, H3G 1R8 – 514/866-9988, Fax: 514/861-4116 – *1
Flynn, Rivard & Associés, #444, 2020, rue University, H3A 2A5 – 514/288-7156, Fax: 514/288-2534
Maggie Fortin, 3967, av Verdun, H4G 1L1 – 514/769-4731 – *1
Fournier, Frenette, #1108, 2500, boul Daniel-Johnson, H7T 2P6 – 514/682-7011, Fax: 514/682-0303 – *3
Michel B. Fournier, #204, 4150, boul St-Martin ouest, H7T 1C1 – 514/686-2600, Fax: 514/681-3642 – *1
Yves Fournier & Associés, #301, 8190, boul Newman, H8N 1X9 – 514/364-1912, Fax: 514/364-4270 – *1
Frankel & Frankel, #908, 10, rue St-Jacques, H2Y 1L3 – 514/849-3544, Fax: 514/849-4457 – *2
Franklin & Franklin, Westmount Life Bldg, #545, 4141, rue Sherbrooke ouest, H3Z 1B8 – 514/935-3576, Fax: 514/935-6862; Email: frnklaw@cam.org – *3
Frumkin, Feldman & Glazman, #2270, 1010, de la Gauchetière ouest, H3B 2N2 – 514/861-2812, Fax: 514/861-6062 – *3
Jean-Pierre Gagné, 4797, av Victoria, H3W 2M9 – 514/485-0255, Fax: 514/486-9682 – *1
Gagnon & Oiknine, 1417, rue du Fort, H3H 2C2 – 514/937-3333, Fax: 514/937-5154 – *2
Francine Gagnon, 545A, ch Lakeshore, H9S 2B1 – 514/631-6429, Fax: 514/631-5606 – *1
Richard Gareau, #220, 4400, ch Côte-de-Liesse, H4N 2P7 – 514/344-5614, Fax: 514/344-5613 – *1
Gariepy, Marcoux, Richard, DuBois, #200, 910, rue Sherbrooke ouest, H3A 1G3 – 514/845-3533, Fax: 514/845-9522; Email: gmrd@gmrd.com – *9
Gasco, Lelange, #2100, 1080, Côte du Beaver Hall, H2Z 1S8 – 514/397-0066, Fax: 514/397-0393 – *9
Gauthier, Gregory & Robitaille, #1250, 615, boul René-Lévesque ouest, H3B 1P5 – 514/879-9294, Fax: 514/879-1456 – *5
Ulrich Gautier, #912, 10, rue St-Jacques, H2Y 1L3 – 514/842-1006, Fax: 514/842-1811 – *1
Stanley Gelfand, #306, 189, boul Hymus, H9R 1E9 – 514/695-4542, Fax: 514/695-7975 – *1
Geoffroy Ferron, #503, 1030, rue Cherrier, H2L 1H9 – 514/522-5445, Fax: 514/522-4386 – *2
Gervais & Robert, #1500, 507, Place d'Armes, H2Y 2W8 – 514/288-4241, Fax: 514/843-8104 – *3
Ghanime et Cordeau, 5777, av Verdun, H4H 1L7 – 514/769-9639, Fax: 514/769-5899 – *2
Gingras Ouellet, 4141, av Pierre-de-Coubertin, H1V 3N7 – 514/252-4638, Fax: 514/252-6906 – *3
Mario Girard, #200, 10, rue Notre-Dame est, H2Y 1B7 – 514/861-6794 – *1
Larry Gitman, #2440, 2020, rue University, H3A 2A5 – 514/849-4511, Fax: 514/849-1584 – *1

Glasz, Miedzigorski, 772, rue Sherbrooke ouest, 3e étage, H3A 1G1 – 514/284-9551, Fax: 514/284-3419 – *3

Allan J. Gold, #605, 388, rue St-Jacques ouest, H2Y 1S1 – 514/849-1621, Fax: 514/849-1624 – *1

Gold, Fridhandler, Goldberg, Place du Parc, #2000, 300, rue Leo-Parizeau, CP 994, H1W 2N1 – 514/288-7929, Fax: 514/844-7290 – *4

Goldman & Associates., #400, 1310, av Greene, H3Z 2B2 – 514/931-3883, Fax: 514/939-1469 – *1

Goldstein, Flanz & Fishman, #4100, 1250, boul René-Lévesque ouest, H3B 4W8 – 514/932-4100, Fax: 514/932-4170 – *11

Goldwater & Dubé, #2330, 630, boul René-Lévesque ouest, H3B 1S6 – 514/861-4367, Fax: 514/861-7601 – *3

Albert Gomberg, 5740, av Blossom, H4W 2T3 – 514/488-9778 – *1

Gonzales, Sloan, #306, 10, rue Ontario ouest, H2X 1Y6 – 514/289-9877, Fax: 514/289-9612 – *3

Goodman Phillips & Vineberg, 1501 McGill College Ave., 26th Fl., H3A 3N9 – 514/841-6000, Fax: 514/841-6499; Ligne sans frais: 1-888-841-6400 – *48

R.A. Gordy, #1600, 2000, rue Mansfield, H3A 3A4 – 514/849-8111, Fax: 514/849-8113 – *1

Gottlieb & Pearson, #1600, 2020, rue University, H3A 2A5 – 514/288-1744, Fax: 514/288-6629 – *14

Goulet, St-Pierre & Therrien, 505, Place St-Henri, 2e étage, H4C 2S1 – 514/933-4211, Fax: 514/933-3394 – *1

Gourd & Monette, #5055, 2000, rue Peel, H3A 2R4 – 514/849-0639, Fax: 514/849-2875 – *2

Gravel & Bolduc, 5, Place Ville-Marie, H3B 2X3 – 514/871-1850, Fax: 514/871-1997 – *1

Ura Greenbaum, Boite: 2, 2222, rue René-Lévesque ouest, H3H 1R6 – 514/931-7291, Fax: 514/931-7882 – *3

Elizabeth Greene, #300, 4141, rue Sherbrooke ouest, H3Z 1B8 – 514/932-5868, Fax: 514/931-3061 – *1

Jean-Marc Grenier, #103, 1666, rue Thierry, H8N 2K4 – 514/368-0454 – *2

Grey Casgrain, #2102, 3410, rue Peel, H3A 1W8 – 514/288-6180, Fax: 514/288-8908 – *5

Grondin, Poudrier, Bernier, #710, 425, boul de Maisonneuve ouest, H3A 3G5 – 514/982-0701, Fax: 514/499-9725 – *2

Gross, Pinsky, 2, Place Alexis Nihon, #1000, 3500, boul de Maisonneuve ouest, H3Z 3C1 – 514/934-1333, Fax: 514/933-0810 – *11

Isabelle Grou, #520, 50, Place Crémazie ouest, H2P 2T2 – 514/382-9670, Fax: 514/382-9676 – *3

Gurman, Aumais, #520, 125, rue Chabanel ouest, H2N 1E4 – 514/858-1118, Fax: 514/858-1121 – *4

Guy & Gilbert, #2200, 770, rue Sherbrooke ouest, H3A 1G1 – 514/281-1766, Fax: 514/281-1059, 9948, 5799; Email: courrier@guyetgilbert.qc.ca – *65

Blanka Gyulai, Q.C., 2, av McCulloch, H2V 3L4 – 514/271-6569, Fax: 514/271-6168 – *1

Hadjis & Feng, #707, 1117, rue Ste-Catherine ouest, H3B 1H9 – 514/849-3526, Fax: 514/849-1595 – *3

Martine Hamel, #215, 13301, rue Sherbrooke est, H1A 1C2 – 514/642-4473, Fax: 514/642-8896 – *1

Hamilton, Cooper, Ashkenazy, #401, 4226, boul St-Jean, H9G 1X5 – 514/626-0266, Fax: 514/626-0011 – *3

Linda Hammerschmid, #1290, 1, carré Westmount, H3Z 2P9 – 514/846-1013, Fax: 514/935-6098 – *2

Handelman, Handelman & Schiller, #1610, 1255, rue Université, H3B 3X3 – 514/866-5071, Fax: 514/866-4210; Email: hhslaw@total.net – *3

Hanna, Glace & Sher, #1750, 770, rue Sherbrooke ouest, H3A 1G1 – 514/284-9551, Fax: 514/284-3419 – *4

G.I. Harris, Q.C., 3410, rue Peel, H3A 1W8 – 514/844-3314 – *1

Hart, Saint-Pierre, #2125, 1, Place Ville Marie, H3B 2C6 – 514/866-6883, Fax: 514/866-8323 – *9

Hébert & Bourque, #2405, 500, Place d'Armes, H1Y 2W2 – 514/284-2351, Fax: 514/284-2354 – *3

Hébert Denault, 359, Place Royale, H2Y 2V3 – 514/288-4424, Fax: 514/288-7859 – *19

Heenan Blaikie, #2500, 1250, boul René-Lévesque ouest, H3B 4Y1 – 514/846-1212, Fax: 514/846-3427 – *93

Heller Clarke Blond, 1210, rue Sherbrooke ouest, H3A 1H6 – 514/288-5252, Fax: 514/288-7479 – *13

Jack Hendler, #703, 10, rue St-Jacques, H1Y 1L3 – 514/844-1373 – *1

Hudon, Gendron, Harris, Thomas General Partnership, 630, boul René-Lévesque ouest, H3B 1S6 – 514/871-1398, Fax: 514/871-9987; Email: hght@hght.com – *42

Hussey, Frégeau, 1590, av des Pins ouest, H3G 1B4 – 514/932-1119, Fax: 514/932-5908 – *2

Michel A. Iacono, #2000, 300, av Leo-Pariseau, CP 1141, H2W 2P4 – 514/288-1414, Fax: 514/844-7290 – *1

Iadeluca Morabito & Venneri, #350, 5167, rue Jean-Talon est, H2A 2A9 – 514/727-0332, Fax: 514/727-9315 – *3

Ionata & Lazaris, 615, boul René Lévesque ouest, H3B 1P5 – 514/397-1515, Fax: 514/397-6823 – *2

Izzi & L'Heureux, #307, 700, boul Crémazie ouest, H3N 1A1 – 514/495-1840, Fax: 514/495-2580 – *2

Jallbert, Séguin, Verdon, Caron, Mahoney, 500, Place d'Armes, 21e étage, H2Y 3W9 – 514/872-2993, Fax: 514/872-2828 – *23

Ahmed Jazouli, #22, 5336, ch Queen-Mary, H3X 1T8 – 514/485-6577, Fax: 514/485-6577 – *1

Kalman Samuels, Q.C. & Assoc., 1200, rue du Fort, H3H 2B3 – 514/939-1200, Fax: 514/939-1201 – *4

Harvey S. Kalnitsky, #315, 360, rue St-Jacques, H2Y 1P5 – 514/288-6066, Fax: 514/288-6550 – *2

I.H. Kaufman, #711, 1117, rue Ste-Catherine ouest, H3B 1H1 – 514/282-7401, Fax: 514/282-9209 – *1

Kelada Tremblay Avocats, #5, 8687, rue St-Denis, H2P 2H4 – 514/384-8732, Fax: 514/384-5001 – *2

Kessner, N.S., #1632, 2020, rue University, H3A 2A5 – 514/866-7266, Fax: 514/288-1381 – *2

Kierans & Guay, #440, 606, rue Cathcart, H3B 1K9 – 514/866-3394, Fax: 514/866-3398 – *2

Kliger & Kliger, #808, 1255, Carré Phillips, H3B 3G1 – 514/281-1720, Fax: 514/281-0678 – *2

Lillian Kliger, #550, 4999, rue Ste-Catherine ouest, H3Z 1T3 – 514/481-2180, Fax: 514/481-6707 – *1

Kochenburger Rochefort, #800, 625, boul René Lévesque ouest, H3B 1R2 – 514/874-0491, Fax: 514/874-0489 – *3

H. Kooiman, #705, 276, rue St-Jacques, H2Y 1N3 – 514/288-4900, Fax: 514/842-1290 – *4

Jon Kosorwich, #1006, 7800, boul Gouin ouest, H4K 2K2 – 514/334-3229 – *1

Kravitz & Kravitz, 750, boul Marcel-Laurin, H4M 2M4 – 514/748-2889, Fax: 514/748-5191 – *5

Kugler & Kandestin, #211, 1, Place Ville Marie, H3B 2C6 – 514/878-2861 – *10

Kushnir & Waters, #260, 4950, ch Queen-Mary, H3W 1X3 – 514/340-1807, Fax: 514/340-9945 – *2

J.E. Labelle, 800, Carré Victoria, 17e étage, CP 246, H4Z 1G3 – 514/873-5326, Fax: 514/873-3090 – *1

Lucien Lachapelle, 5971, rue St-Hubert, H1S 2L8 – 514/277-2164, Fax: 514/277-1120 – *1

Lackstone & Turner, 256, rue Devon, H3R 1B9 – 514/731-3544, Fax: 514/737-3770 – *2

Lacoste Langévin, #1400, 2000, rue Mansfield, H3A 3A2 – 514/284-0426, Fax: 514/284-2319 – *4

Laflamme Rousseau, #1100, 801, rue Sherbrooke est, H2L 1K7 – 514/527-3691, Fax: 514/527-3911 – *5

Lafleur Brown, 1, Place Ville Marie, H3B 3P4 – 514/878-9641, Fax: 514/878-1450; Email: lawyers@lafleurbrown.ca; URL: http://www.login.net/lafleurbrown – *44

Gaston Lafleur, #910, 630, rue Sherbrooke ouest, H3A 1E4 – 514/842-6681, Fax: 514/842-7627; URL: http://www.cgcd.com – *1

Gaetan Lagarde, #201, 1554, boul Mont-Royal est, H2J 1Z2 – 514/521-2442, Fax: 514/525-5561 – *1

LaHaye, Moisan, Boucher, Gaudreau, Doray, Richard, Paquette, #202, 28, rue Notre-Dame est, H2Y 1B9 – 514/878-1316, Fax: 514/878-1318 – *7

Lamarche, Pierre, 237A, boul des Prairies, H7N 2T8 – 514/667-9802 – *1

Lambert Cormier, #400, 2550, boul Daniel-Johnson, 7e étage, H7T 2L1 – 514/686-4000, Fax: 514/686-6000; Email: lamcor@lavocat.com – *10

Lamy, Turbide, Lefebvre, #301, 1030, rue Beaubien est, H2S 1T4 – 514/271-1336 – *3

Raymond Landry, #450, 2015, rue Peel, H3A 1T8 – 514/288-9322, Fax: 514/288-2562; Email: rlandry@mlink.net – *1

Langlois Gaudreau, #2600, 1002, rue Sherbrooke ouest, H3A 3L6 – 514/842-9512, Fax: 514/845-6573; Email: langloir@odyssee.net – *39

John P. Lanthier, #127, 1015, Côte du Beaver Hall, H2Z 1S1 – 514/393-8751 – *1

Lapin, Polisuk, Mauer, 1155, boul René-Lévesque ouest, H3B 4S5 – 514/861-8546, Fax: 514/861-1298 – *7

Lapointe Rosenstein, 1250, boul René-Lévesque ouest, H3B 5E9 – 514/925-6300, Fax: 514/925-9001; Email: general@lapros.qc.ca; URL: http://www.lapros.qc.ca – *43

Lapointe, Schachter, Champagne & Talbot, #100, 511, Place d'Armes, H2Y 2W7 – 514/288-8200, Fax: 514/288-6962 – *8

Daniel Latour, #1000, 550, rue Sherbrooke ouest, H3A 1B9 – 514/288-9150, Fax: 514/288-9307 – *1

Laurier, Cêré, 356, 90e av, H8R 2Z7 – 514/363-0220, Fax: 514/363-9495; Email: laurierj@login.net – *3

Francine Lauzé, #610, 8000, boul Lange Lier, H1P 3K2 – 514/329-3560, Fax: 514/852-4505 – *3

Lavery, de Billy, #4000, 1, Place Ville-Marie, H3B 4M4 – 514/871-1522, Fax: 514/871-8977; Email: info@lavery.qc.ca; URL: http://www.laverydebilly.com – *155

Lavery, de Billy, #500, 3080, boul Le Carrefour, H7T 2R5 – 514/978-8100, Fax: 514/978-8111

Lazare & Altschuler, #2812, 1800, av McGill College, H3A 3J6 – 514/288-3341, Fax: 514/288-7634 – *2

Leo Leblanc, 4058, av de Vendôme, H4A 3N1 – 514/842-2002 – *1

Lebovics, Cytrynbaum, Marchessault & Peizler, 4098, rue Ste-Catherine ouest, 2e étage, H3Z 1P2 – 514/866-2995, Fax: 514/861-4359 – *9

Lebrun Papineau, #310, 495, boul St-Martin ouest, H7M 1Y9 – 514/668-4550, Fax: 514/387-5602 – *3

Micheline Lebrun-Sylvestre, #305, 10500, boul de l'Acadie, H4N 2V4 – 514/331-0177 – *1

Lechter & Segal, #1110, 2, Place Alexis-Nihon, H3Z 3C1 – 514/937-2222, Fax: 514/937-8729 – *3

John E. Lechter, #202, 2015, rue Drummond St., H3G 1W7 – 514/845-4287, Fax: 514/845-1803 – *1

Marcel Lefebvre, #210, 1010, rue Ste-Catherine est, H2L 2G3 – 514/842-3466, Fax: 514/842-1044 – *1

Legault Longtin Laurin Haloin, #1800, 630, boul René-Lévesque ouest, H3B 1S6 – 514/879-1124, Fax: 514/397-0370 – *10

Legault, Joly, #315, 390, rue Notre-Dame ouest, H1Y 1T9 – 514/842-8891, Fax: 514/842-6202 – *12

Lemoine & Major, 11553, av Brunet, H1G 5G2 – 514/327-4777 – *2

Levasseur, Fréchette, #202, 2600, boul Saint-Joseph est, H1Y 2A4 – 514/526-0101, Fax: 514/526-5067

Fernand Levesque, #504, 4, rue Notre-Dame est, H2Y 1B8 – 514/861-4719, Fax: 514/861-8467 – *1

Levine, Frishman, #904, 5, place Ville-Marie, H3B 2G2 – 514/398-9549, Fax: 514/398-9792 – *4

Liberman Segall Finkelberg, #650, 4150, rue Ste Catherine ouest, H3Z 2Y5 – 514/937-3976, Fax: 514/397-3415 – *3

Liebman & Associates, #1800, 1, Carré Westmount, H3Z 2P9 – 514/846-0666, Fax: 514/935-2380 – *1

* indicates number of lawyers in law firm.

Judith Lifshitz, #2500, 1250, boul René-Lévesque ouest, H3B 4Y1 – 514/846-2229, Fax: 514/846-3427 – *1

Lightstone, Riback, #900, 615, boul René-Lévesque ouest, H3B 1P5 – 514/861-6373, Fax: 514/861-5218 – *2

Linetsky, Hartman, #200, 1255, Carré Phillips, H3B 3G1 – 514/871-8971, Fax: 514/871-8974 – *3

N. Lord, #210, 1010, rue Ste-Catherine est, H2L 2G3 – 514/842-3466, Fax: 514/842-1044 – *1

Robert Loulou, 7924, rue St-Denis, H2R 2G1 – 514/388-3511, Fax: 514/388-3211 – *1

Michael Ludwick, #1750, 770, rue Sherbrooke ouest, H3A 1G1 – 514/844-4125 – *1

Luterman, Stotland, Davis, #1800, 1, Carré Westmount, H3Z 2P9 – 514/935-7433, Fax: 514/935-2380 – *5

Mackenzie Gervais, #1300, 770, rue Sherbrooke ouest, H3A 1G1 – 514/842-9831, Fax: 514/288-7389; Email: info@macger.qc.ca – *43

T.R. Anthony Malcolm, #2, 3468 , rue Drummond, H3G 1Y4 – 514/849-4134, Fax: 514/849-4137

Mannella & Associés, 3055, boul de l'Assomption, H1N 2H1 – 514/899-5375, Fax: 514/899-0476; Email: mannella@total.net; URL: http://www.mannella.com – *8

Léo René Maranda, 31, rue St-Jacques, H2Y 1K9 – 514/842-6871, Fax: 514/845-3372 – *4

Marchand & Associés, #2000, 300, av Leo-Pariseau, CP 989, H2W 2N1 – 514/844-8631, Fax: 514/844-6691 – *5

Marchand & Kosorwich, #600, 1118, rue Ste-Catherine ouest, H3B 1H5 – 514/866-5061, Fax: 514/866-8741 – *2

Marchand, Magnan, Melançon, Forget, #1640, 600, de la Gauchetière ouest, H3B 4L8 – 514/393-1155, Fax: 514/861-0727 – *21

André Martin, 276, rue St-Jacques, H1Y 1N3 – 514/845-3101 – *1

Martineau, Walker, a/s Fasken Martineau, Stock Exchange Tower, #3400, 800, Place-Victoria, CP 242, H4Z 1E9 – 514/397-7400, Fax: 514/397-7600; Ligne sans frais: 1-800-361-6266; URL: http://www.fasken.com/offices.html – *117

Maynard & Zaor, #1101, 507, Place d'Armes, H2Y 2W8 – 514/288-1101, Fax: 514/499-8548 – *3

McCarthy Tétrault, 1170, rue Peel, H3B 4S8 – 514/397-4100, Fax: 514/875-6246; URL: http://www.mccarthy.ca – *72

McDougall, Caron, #2600, 1000, rue de la Gauchetière ouest, H3B 4W5 – 514/399-1000, Fax: 514/399-1026 – *20

Robert E. McFetridge, #365, 1253, av McGill College, H3B 2Y5 – 514/395-8662, Fax: 514/866-1901 – *1

McGilton & Johnston, 1130, rue Sherbrooke ouest, H3A 2M8 – 514/842-1714, Fax: 514/842-1718 – *3

McMaster Meighen, #900, 1000, rue de la Gauchetière ouest, H3B 4W5 – 514/879-1212, Fax: 514/878-0605 – *51

Melançon, Marceau, Grenier et Sciortino, #300, 1717, boul René-Lévesque est, H2L 4T3 – 514/525-3414, Fax: 514/525-2803 – *12

Ménard & Hurtubise, #500, 266, rue Notre-Dame ouest, H2Y 1T6 – 514/284-0600, Fax: 514/284-6606 – *2

Ménard, Boucher, 3530, rue Jean-Talon ouest, H3R 2G3 – 514/341-3124, Fax: 514/341-4287 – *5

Jean-Pierre Ménard, 5969, rue Hochelaga, H1N 1X3 – 514/253-8044, Fax: 514/253-9404 – *5

Mendelsohn Rosentzveig Shacter, 1000, rue Sherbrooke ouest, 27e étage, H3A 3G4 – 514/987-5000, Fax: 514/987-1213; Email: mrs@mrslaw.com – *43

Jean Mercier, Q.C., #200, 4059, rue Hochelaga, H1W 1K4 – 514/723-0908 – *1

Jean Mignault, 1730, rue Cunard, H7S 2B2 – 514/332-4110, Fax: 514/334-6043; Email: jean.mignault@mks.net – *1

Miller & Khazzam, #2200, 800, boul René-Lévesque ouest, H3B 1X9 – 514/875-8040, Fax: 514/875-8044 – *3

Miller, Adel & Associés, #1210, 507, Place d'Armes, H2Y 2W8 – 514/845-4151, Fax: 514/845-0306 – *3

Moisan Lasalle Payette & Kean, 450, rue Sherbrooke est, H1L 1G8 – 514/844-3077, Fax: 514/844-1018 – *3

Suzanne Moisan-Gerard, ##202, 28, rue Notre-Dame est, H2Y 1B9 – 514/878-1316, Fax: 514/878-1318 – *1

Michele Monast, #1700, 1, Place Ville-Marie, H3B 2C1 – 514/878-3081, Fax: 514/878-3053 – *1

Mondor, Fournier, #2140, 1, Place Ville-Marie, H3B 2C6 – 514/878-1900, Fax: 514/878-3679 – *7

Monette, Barakett, Lévesque, Bourque et Pednault, #2100, 1010, rue de la Gauchetière ouest, H3B 2R8 – 514/878-9381, Fax: 514/878-3957; Email: monbar@cam.org – *20

Morin, Chamberland, #100, 1030, rue Beaubien est, H2S 1H5 – 514/272-1764, Fax: 514/278-1664 – *2

Morris & Morris, #1500, 1, Carré Westmount, H3Z 2P9 – 514/935-6226, Fax: 514/935-2314

Daniel Morris, Q.C., #1600, 2000, rue Mansfield, H3A 3A4 – 514/288-2500, Fax: 514/288-7128 – *3

Morris, Morris & Morris, #1500, 1, Carré Westmount, H3Z 2P9 – 514/935-6226, Fax: 514/935-2314 – *2

I. Myszka, 4781, av Van Horne, H3W 1J1 – 514/737-4069 – *1

Nadeau, Desroches, Seers, 3689, rue St-Hubert, H1L 3Z9 – 514/522-5549, Fax: 514/522-6487 – *6

Nanci, Tommaso, 4755, rue Jarry est, H1R 1X7 – 514/722-3788 – *1

Narvey, Green & Lack, #2270, 800, boul René-Lévesque ouest, H3B 1X9 – 514/871-4992, Fax: 514/871-4995 – *3

Nudleman, Lamontagne & Grenier, La Tour CIBC, #2720, 1155, boul René-Lévesque ouest, H3B 2K8 – 514/866-6674, Fax: 514/866-9822; Email: bnl.legal@top.ca – *7

O'Reilly & Associés, #1007, 1155, rue University, H3B 3A7 – 514/871-8117, Fax: 514/871-9177 – *4

O'Reilly & Grodinsky, CP 1270, Succ B, H3B 3K9 – 514/878-3711 – *1

Ogilvy Renault, #1100, 1981, McGill College Ave., H3A 3C1 – 514/847-4747, Fax: 514/286-5474; Email: info@ogilvyrenault.com – *148

Oligny & Jacques, #1100, 800, boul René-Lévesque ouest, H3B 1X9 – 514/871-2240, Fax: 514/871-8772; Email: oligny@citenet.net – *2

Overland Rosenzveig, #2875, 630, boul René-Lévesque ouest, H3B 1S9 – 514/875-6200, Fax: 514/875-9708 – *3

Papillon HeSert Guilbault, #201, 315, boul René-Lévesque est, H2X 3P3 – 514/844-8804, Fax: 514/844-5927 – *3

Paquette, Perreault, Trudeau & Associés, #900, 200, rue St-Jacques, H2Y 1M1 – 514/842-1864, Fax: 514/842-1868 – *5

Paquin Danis, 55, rue St-James ouest, 6e étage, H2Y 3X2 – 514/842-1884, Fax: 514/842-0605 – *1

Parenteau Archambault, 240, rue St-Jacques, H2Y 1L9 – 514/849-6644, Fax: 514/849-5233 – *5

Parizeau, Richer, #2020, 500, Place d'Armes, H2Y 2W2 – 514/849-6325, Fax: 514/849-9438 – *5

Pateras & Iezzoni, #2314, 500, Place d'Armes, H1Y 2W2 – 514/284-0860, Fax: 514/843-7990 – *6

Denis R. Paul, 4145A, rue St-Denis, H2W 2M7 – 514/287-1884 – *1

Pearl & Associates, 1170, Place du Frère André, 4e étage, H3B 3C6 – 514/861-1170, Fax: 514/861-0850 – *4

Pepin, Létourneau, #2200, 500, Place D'Armes, H2Y 3S3 – 514/284-3553, Fax: 514/284-2173; Email: peplex@odyssee.net – *25

John J. Pepper, Q.C & Associates, #955, 1253, av McGill College, H3B 2Y5 – 514/875-5311, Fax: 514/875-8381 – *6

John J. Pepper, Q.C & Associates, #2500, 1155, boul René-Lévesque ouest, H3B 2K4 – 514/875-5454, Fax: 514/875-8967 – *1

Gregore Perron & Assoc., 84, rue Notre-Dame ouest, H2Y 1S6 – 514/285-6441, Fax: 514/285-8589 – *4

Serge Petit, #3821, 1, Place Ville-Marie, H3B 4M6 – 514/395-0208, Fax: 514/395-0207 – *1

Frederick R. Phillips, 6039, av Verdun, H4H 1M8 – 514/762-0112, Fax: 514/762-0114 – *1

Phillips, Friedman, Kotler, Place du Canada, #900, 1010, rue de la Gauchetière ouest, H3B 2P8 – 514/878-3371, Fax: 514/878-3691, 4676; Email: pfkotler@total.net – *22

André Piché, #101, 6664, rue St-Denis, H2S 2R9 – 514/277-4141, Fax: 514/277-1614 – *2

Pascal Pillarella, #202, 7925, boul Newman, H8N 2N9 – 514/364-3100, Fax: 514/364-1604 – *1

Marcel Plante, 6984, rue St-Denis, H1S 2S4 – 514/272-8217, Fax: 514/272-3823 – *5

Pollack, Machlovitch, Kravitz & Teitelbaum, #2640, 800, boul René-Lévesque ouest, H3B 1Y2 – 514/871-0205, Fax: 514/871-2809 – *6

Pouliot, Caron, Prévost, Bélisle, Galarneau, 300, av Leo-Pariseau, H2W 2N1 – 514/849-3787, Fax: 514/849-8085 – *6

Pouliot, Mercure, 1155, boul René-Lévesque ouest, 31e étage, H3B 3S6 – 514/875-5210, Fax: 514/875-4308 – *40

Poupart & Cournoyer, 3431, rue St-Hubert, H2L 3Z8 – 514/526-0861, Fax: 514/526-9646 – *5

Armand Poupart & Associés, 261, rue St-Jacques, H2Y 1M6 – 514/845-6126, Fax: 514/845-0320 – *2

Claude F. Proulx, #23, 460, rue St-Gabriel, H2Y 2Z9 – 514/395-9521, Fax: 514/392-1566 – *1

Racine, Perrault & Lussier, #407, 7575, rte Transcanadienne, H4T 1V6 – 514/331-8511, Fax: 514/321-0027 – *3

J.L. Ranger, Place Chaumont, 8676, av Chaumont, H1K 1N6 – 514/353-7529 – *1

Jacques Ranger, 5694, av Laurendeau, H4E 3W4 – 514/766-0756, Fax: 514/766-0756 – *1

Sylvain Rheault, #202, 4004, rue Wellington, H4G 1V3 – 514/765-0691 – *1

Alain Richard, #508, 10, rue St-Jacques, H1Y 1L3 – 514/288-2250 – *1

Simon Richter, 455, rue St-Antoine ouest, H1Z 1H9 – 514/866-2981, Fax: 514/866-2983 – *1

Pierre Robert, 2907, boul Pierre-Bernard, H1L 4R2 – 514/355-1214, Fax: 514/355-8657 – *1

Robinson Sheppard Shapiro, Tour Stock Exchange, #4700, 800, Place Victoria, CP 322, H4Z 1H6 – 514/878-2631, Fax: 514/878-1865 – *44

Rousseau, Gaudry, Barette, #2736, 1, Place Ville-Marie, H3B 4G4 – 514/875-8243, Fax: 514/875-8801; Ligne sans frais: 1-888-875-8243 – *4

Isabelle Roy-Egan, 3285, rue Viel, H3M 1H8 – 514/334-4328, Fax: 514/956-9471 – *1

Leonard I. Sabloff & Associates, 6600, rte Trans-Canada, H9R 4S2 – 514/683-1502 – *2

Louise Saint-Amour, #3, 1375, rue Notre-Dame, H8S 2C9 – 514/634-8243, Fax: 514/634-1741 – *1

Normand Saint-Amour, 368, boul Henri-Bourassa est, H3L 1C3 – 514/382-0373, Fax: 514/383-7730 – *3

J.J.J. St. Michael, #660, 4141, rue Sherbrooke ouest, H3Z 1B8 – 514/935-5030, Fax: 514/935-3559 – *1

Johanne St. Pierre, #60, 1395, rue Fleury est, H2C 1R7 – 514/388-8922, Fax: 514/388-3672 – *1

Leo St. Pierre, 7110, av Somerled, H4V 1W1 – 514/488-4191 – *1

Sand & Associates, #1810, 1, Carré Westmount, H3Z 2P9 – 514/938-1056, Fax: 514/935-6098 – *1

Jean Saulnier, 7190, rue St-Denis, H2R 2E2 – 514/273-1525 – *1

Sauvé, Hébert, 1130, boul Cure-Labelle, H7V 3T7 – 514/687-2030 – *2

David I. Schatie, #200, 1255, av Greene, H3Z 2A4 – 514/935-7470, Fax: 514/937-6245 – *1

Schlesinger & Schlesinger, 1, Carré Westmount, 15e étage, H3Z 2P9 – 514/935-6226, Fax: 514/935-2314 – *3
Schnaiberg & Associates, #520, 240, rue St-Jacques, H2Y 1L9 – 514/288-8717, Fax: 514/288-6646 – *1
Irwin Schnaiberg, #812, 1117, rue Ste-Catherine ouest, H3B 1H9 – 514/845-2143, Fax: 514/845-1057 – *1
Bernard K. Schneider, #3, 5365, av Victoria, H2J 2J5 – 514/736-1694, Fax: 514/736-1693 – *1
Schratz, Wong & Melancon, 3614, av du Musée, H3G 2C9 – 514/289-9362 – *3
Norman Schwartz, #805, 1255, Carré Phillips, H3B 3G1 – 514/866-5507, Fax: 514/866-4101 – *1
Sciascia, Fargnoli, Corbeil, Poletto & Associates, #300, 7012, boul St-Laurent, H2S 3E2 – 514/272-0709 – *4
Seal & Associés, #1050, 2015, rue Drummond, H3G 1W7 – 514/842-8861, Fax: 514/288-1708 – *2
Abraham Segal, #1110, 3500, boul de Maisonneuve ouest, H3Z 3C1 – 514/937-2222, Fax: 514/937-8729 – *1
Séguin & Prévost, 2316, rue Sherbrooke est, H2K 1E5 – 514/526-0821, Fax: 514/521-5397 – *4
William P. Shaw, #311, 477, rue St-François-Xavier, H2Y 2T2 – 514/849-4525 – *1
Brian Sher, #1750, 770, rue Sherbrooke ouest, H3A 1G1 – 514/284-9551, Fax: 514/284-3419 – *1
Shriar & Polak, #1500, 1, Carré Westmount, H3Z 2P9 – 514/935-6226, Fax: 514/935-2314 – *2
Silver, Braun et Avocats, #400, 510, boul St. Laurent, H1Y 2Y9 – 514/282-9112, Fax: 514/282-0600 – *8
Roger Simard, #1300, 777, rue Sherbrooke ouest, H3A 1G1 – 514/847-3557, Fax: 514/288-7389 – *1
Henri Simon, #500, 400, rue St-Jacques, H2Y 1S1 – 514/985-0995, Fax: 514/985-0944 – *2
Laizer Sirota, #504, 10, rue St-Jacques, H1Y 1L3 – 514/844-1123, Fax: 514/844-4071 – *1
Smart & Biggar, #3400, 1000, rue de la Gauchetière ouest, H3B 4W5 – 514/954-1500, Fax: 514/954-1396; Email: montreal@smart-biggar.ca – *4
Solomon & Solomon, 300, rue Leo-Pariseau, H1W 2N1 – 514/845-5239 – *2
Spector Seymour, #4, 1236, rue St-Mark, H3H 2E5 – 514/932-6941, Fax: 514/933-4236
Spiegel Sohmer, #1203, 5, Place Ville-Marie, H3B 2G2 – 514/875-2100, Fax: 514/875-8237 – *21
Sproule, Castonguay, Pollack, #2330, 1, Place Ville Marie, H3B 3M5 – 514/879-1737, Fax: 514/879-1733 – *15
A.H. Steckler, 5115, av de Gaspé, H1T 3B7 – 514/273-8891, Fax: 514/273-1576 – *1
Stern & Blumer, 300, av Leo-Pariseau, CP 983, H2W 2N1 – 514/842-1133, Fax: 514/842-3105 – *2
Sternthal Katznelson Montigny, Place du Canada, #1020, 1010, rue de la Gauchetière ouest, H3B 2N2 – 514/878-1011, Fax: 514/878-9195 – *12
Stikeman, Elliott, #3900, 1155, boul René-Lévesque ouest, H3B 3V2 – 514/397-3000, Fax: 514/397-3222; Email: info@mtl.stikeman.com – *110
William Sullivan, #557, 555, boul René-Lévesque ouest, H2Z 1B1 – 514/397-1504, Fax: 514/397-1505 – *1
Hayk Sumbulian, #1610, 1350, rue Sherbrooke ouest, H3G 1J1 – 514/281-1955, Fax: 514/281-1956 – *1
Sweibel, Richter, Usher & Vineberg, 2, Place Alexis-Nihon, H3Z 3C2 – 514/934-3434, Fax: 514/934-3408 – *3
Rosalie Szewczuk, 4420, rue Ste-Catherine ouest, H3Z 1R2 – 514/933-4453, Fax: 514/934-3134 – *1
Charles Takefman, #402, 266, rue Notre-Dame ouest, H2Y 1T6 – 514/842-9662, Fax: 514/842-6808 – *1
Talbot & Clément-Talbot, 4519, rue St-Denis, H2J 2L4 – 514/849-2930, Fax: 514/982-0716 – *2
Tannenbaum & Associates, #100, 203, Place d'Youville, H2Y 2B3 – 514/849-1221, Fax: 514/849-7992 – *6
Tassé, Themens, 2421, rue Allard, H4E 2L3 – 514/769-9654, Fax: 514/769-7363 – *3
Toulch & Assoc., #406, 1117, rue St-Catherine ouest, H3B 1T9 – 514/849-1289, Fax: 514/849-3101 – *3
Toupin & Barrette, 1344, rue Jean-Talon est, H2E 1S1 – 514/278-5400, Fax: 514/278-7584 – *3
Claude Trinque, #1202, 3030, boul Le Carrefour, H2W 2N1 – 514/688-7964, Fax: 514/688-7998 – *1
Trudeau, Provençal, Saint-Pierre & Côte, 7390, rue St-Denis, H2R 2E4 – 514/277-3138, Fax: 514/277-3318 – *4
Trudel, Nadeau, Lesage, Larivière & associés, CP 993, Succ Place du Parc, #2500, 300, av Leo-Pariseau, H2W 2N1 – 514/849-5754, Fax: 514/499-0312; Email: tnll@total.net – *27
Tsimberis, Philpot, Marion, CP 986, Succ Place du Parc, #2201, 300, av Leo-Pariseau, H2W 2N1 – 514/982-0144, Fax: 514/982-0149 – *4
Sergio Tucci, 201, rue St-Zotique est, H2S 1L2 – 514/271-0650, Fax: 514/270-2164 – *1
Turcotte, Nolet, Perras, #300, 1515, boul Chomedey, H7V 3Y7 – 514/681-1400, Fax: 514/681-2099 – *4
Unterberg, Labelle, Lebeau & Associés, #700, 1980, rue Sherbrooke ouest, H3H 1E8 – 514/934-0841, Fax: 514/937-6547 – *7
Vadeboncoeur, Masson & Associates, #905, 276, rue St-Jacques, H2Y 1N3 – 514/286-9100, Fax: 514/286-9453 – *2
Yves Vaillancourt, #912, 10, rue St-Jacques, H2Y 1L3 – 514/842-1006, Fax: 514/842-1811 – *1
Angelo Velentzas, 1255, rue University, H3B 4A3 – 514/861-3742 – *1
Sergio Venneri, #200, 3556, rue Belair, H2A 2A9 – 514/727-0332, Fax: 514/727-9315 – *3
Mark Wener, #2440, 2020, rue University, H3A 2L4 – 514/849-4511, Fax: 514/849-1854 – *1
Wiseman, Hamerman, #2720, 1155, boul René-Lévesque ouest, H3B 2K8 – 514/879-1208, Fax: 514/861-1632 – *2
J.H. Woloshen, 1980, rue Sherbrooke ouest, 11e étage, H3H 1E8 – 514/939-4633, Fax: 514/939-2786 – *1
Yarosky, Daviault, La Haye, Stober & Isaacs, #2536, 800, boul René-Lévesque ouest, H3B 1X9 – 514/878-3505, Fax: 514/861-3065 – *7
Allan Zilbert, #805, 1255, Carré Phillips, H3B 3G1 – 514/866-5507, Fax: 514/866-4101 – *1
Zimmerman & Blitt, #410, 345, av Victoria, H3Z 2N2 – 514/483-2444, Fax: 514/483-2477 – *2

**Québec ........................................ Québec**

Aubut Chabot, #600, 900, boul René-Lévesque est, CP 910, G1R 4T4 – 418/524-5131, Fax: 418/524-1717; Email: aubuchab@microtec.net – *14
Bernatchez, Robitaille & Associés, #310, 400, boul Jean-Lesage, G1K 8W1 – 418/648-0456, Fax: 418/648-9587 – *5
Boutin, Roy, & Associés, #444, 2, rue des Jardins, G1R 4S9 – 418/691-6360, Fax: 418/691-7622 – *9
DeBlois, Gauthier, Samson, #315, 2, Place Québec, G1R 2B5 – 418/529-1784, Fax: 418/529-6077 – *9
Des Rivieres & Vermette, #701, 71, rue St-Pierre, CP 245, Succ B, G1K 7A9 – 418/692-0616, Fax: 418/692-0689 – *10
Desjardins Ducharme Stein Monast, #300, 1150, rue de Claire-Fontaine, G1R 5G4 – 418/529-6531, Fax: 418/523-5391 – *32
Gagné, Letarte, Sirois, Beaudet, #400, 79, boul René-Lévesque est, G1R 5N5 – 418/522-7900, Fax: 418/523-7900 – *18
Grondin, Poudrier, Bernier, #200, 801, ch St-Louis, G1S 1C1 – 418/683-3000, Fax: 418/683-8784; Toll Free: 1-800-463-5172; Email: gpb@videotron.ca – *44
Huot Laflamme Société d'Avocats, #102, 500, Grande Allée est, G1R 2J7 – 418/522-2701, Fax: 418/649-0097; Email: huotlaflamme@sympatico.ca, houtlaflammentl@sympatico.ca – *9
La société d'avocats Garneau, Turgeon, Verdon, 67, rue Ste-Ursule, G1R 4E7 – 418/692-3010, Fax: 418/692-1742 – *7
Labrie & Bellemare, 1247, rue St-Joseph-Vezina, G1T 2L1 – 418/688-4367 – *2
Langlois Gaudreau, Édifice Mérici, #160, 801, ch St-Louis, G1S 1C1 – 418/682-1212, Fax: 418/682-2272 – *19
Lavery, de Billy, #500, 925, ch St-Louis, G9S 1C1 – 418/688-5000, Fax: 418/688-3458
Martineau, Walker, a/s Fasken Martineau, Immeuble le Saint-Patrick, #800, 140, Grande Allée est, G1R 5M8 – 418/640-2000, Fax: 418/647-2455; Ligne sans frais: 1-800-463-2827 – *13
McCarthy Tétrault, Le Complexe St-Amable, #700, 1150, rue de Claire-Fontaine, G1R 5G4 – 418/521-3000, Fax: 418/521-3099; URL: http://www.mccarthy.ca – *10
Gilbert-M. Noreau, 689, Grande Allée est, G1R 2K4 – 418/524-5251, Fax: 418/524-0272 – *1
O'Brien, #420, 500, Grande Allée est, G1R 2J7 – 418/648-1511, Fax: 418/648-9335 – *6
Ogilvy Renault, #520, 500, Grande Allée est, G1R 2J7 – 418/640-5000, Fax: 418/640-1500; Email: info@ogilvyrenault.com – *21
Savard, Nadeau, Kallis & Associates, 838, St-Joachim, G1R 1X1 – 418/648-9771, Fax: 418/648-2778 – *7
Trudel, Nadeau, Lesage, Larivière & associés, #300, 5000, boul des Gradins, G2J 1N3 – 418/623-0610, Fax: 418/622-7000 – *8

**Rimouski ........................................ Rimouski**

Biron, Dolbec & Lacroix, 9, rue Jules-A. Brillant, G5L 1W7 – 418/722-5587, Fax: 418/722-5949 – *3
Casgrain, Blanchet, Gagnon & Desrosiers, Edifice Trust General, #400, 2, boul St-Germain est, CP 580, G5L 7C6 – 418/723-3302, Fax: 418/722-6939 – *5
Marc, Doucet, 205, rue de la Cathédrale, G5L 5G1 – 418/724-3125, Fax: 418/724-3180 – *1
Norman Dumais, 97, St-Germain est, CP 998, G5L 7E1 – 418/723-3179, Fax: 418/723-3195 – *1
Gendreau & Beaulieu, 41, rue de l'Évêché ouest, CP 8, G5L 7C9 – 418/724-4416 – *5

**Rivière-Du-Loup ........................................ Kamouraska**

Dubé Dion, 30, rue de la Cour, CP 787, G5R 3Z5 – 418/862-6301, Fax: 418/862-1083; Email: dubedion@icrdl.net – *4
Francine Giroux, 299, rue LaFontaine, CP 786, G5R 3Z5 – 418/862-1522, Fax: 418/862-4528 – *1
Rioux Bosse Masse & Associés, 12, rue de la Cour, CP 487, G5R 3Z1 – 418/862-3565, Fax: 418/862-4408; Email: rbmm@icrdl.net – *7

**Senneterre ........................................ Abitibi**

Bigué, Bigué, 270A, 3e rue ouest, J0Y 2M0 – 819/737-2305, Fax: 819/737-2902 – *2

**St-Constant ........................................**

Sylvie Savoie, 191, rue St-Pierre, J5A 2G9 – 514/638-4277, Fax: 514/638-4278 – *1

**St-Eustache ........................................ Terrebonne**

Robert Desjardins, 102, av St-Eustache, J7R 2K9 – *1
Saulnier, Leroux & associés, #5070, 430, boul Arthur Sauvé, J7R 6V6 – 514/472-0031, Fax: 514/472-7910 – *4

**St-Georges ........................................ Beauce**

Flynn, Rivard & Associés, #410, 11505, 1re av est, G5Y 7X3 – 418/228-2074, Fax: 418/228-6016 – *2

**St-Hilaire ........................................ St-Hyacinthe**

Edith Des Lauriers, 721, rue P.E. Borduas, J3H 4W7 – 514/446-7055, Fax: 514/446-2497 – *1

**St-Hyacinthe ........................................ Montréal**

Normand Bérubé, #3, 2610, rue Nichols, J2S 2W8 – 514/778-2511, Fax: 514/778-0834 – *1
Brodeur & Boileau, 1700, rue Girouard ouest, J2S 3A1 – 514/773-8566, Fax: 514/778-3749 – *3

* indicates number of lawyers in law firm.

Diane Poirier, 1600, rue Girouard ouest, 3e étage, J2S 2Z8 – 514/773-5176, Fax: 514/773-6788 – *1

Sylvestre & Associés, #236, 1600, rue Girouard ouest, J2S 2Z8 – 514/773-8445, Fax: 514/773-2112 – *5

**St-Jean-sur-Richelieu** .............................. **Iberville**

Bédard, Lord, 188, rue Longueuil, J3B 6P1 – 514/347-8220, Fax: 514/347-3693 – *2

Jacques Cartier, 215, rue Jacques-Cartier nord, J3B 6T3 – 514/346-6817 – *1

Roland Tremblay, Q.C., 220, rue Longueuil, J3B 6P4 – 514/347-5531; 658-4511, Fax: 514/358-9915 – *1

**St-Jérôme** .............................. **Terrebonne**

Boismenu & Racicot, #200, 395, rue Laviolette, J7Y 2P2 – 514/432-4331, Fax: 514/432-4331 – *3

Geraghty, Lapierre & Assoc., #102, 480, rue St-Georges, J7Z 5B3 – 514/436-8022 – *3

Levac & Cotte-Levac, 474, rue Laviolette, J7Y 2T7 – 514/432-3274 – *2

Lord, Lalonde, Gendron & Riendeau, 450, rue Laviolette, J7Y 2T7 – *4

Morin, Perras et La Rue, #200, 30A, rue Legault, J7Z 2B8 – 514/436-8166, Fax: 514/436-6321 – *3

Prévost, Auclair, Fortin & D'Aoust, #400, 55, rue Castonguay, J7Y 2H9 – 514/436-8244, Fax: 514/436-9735 – *17

**St-Joseph-de-Beauce** .............................. **Beauce**

Cliche, Laflamme, Loubier, 109, rue Verreault, CP 160, G0S 2V0 – 418/397-5264, Fax: 418/397-5269; Email: cliclafl@globetrotter.qc.ca – *4

**St-Lambert** .............................. **Longueuil**

Christopher I. Broadbent, 260, av Irvine, J4R 1W9 – 514/671-4347, Fax: 514/671-4347; Email: bshp@musicb.mcgill.ca – *1

Paul Joffe, 360, av Putney, J4P 3B6 – 514/465-3654, Fax: 514/465-5730; Email: p.joffe@sympatico.ca – *1

Edmond D. Pinsonnault, 130, av de Normandie, J4S 1K1 – 514/671-0916 – *1

Luc Racicot, 439, rue Notre-Dame, J4P 2K5 – 514/466-6633, Fax: 514/466-7315 – *1

**St-Romuald** .............................. **Québec**

Huguette Gagnon, 1779, ch du Fleuve, G6W 1Z6 – 418/839-2045, Fax: 418/839-2061 – *1

**Ste-Agathe-Des-Monts** .............................. **Terrebonne**

Paul Gelinas, Q.C., 45, rue St-Antoine, J8C 2C4 – 819/326-4221, Fax: 819/326-6272 – *1

**Ste-Foy** .............................. **Québec**

Brisset des Nos, Gravel, Lévesque, Normand, Rioux, #107, 3350, rue de la Pérade, G1X 2L7 – 418/656-1313, Fax: 418/652-1844 – *5

Brochet, Dussault & Associés, #450, 2795, boul Laurier, G1V 4M7 – 418/657-2424, Fax: 418/657-1793 – *8

Dergerom, Saindon & Trembley, 2750, ch Ste-Foy, G1V 1V6 – 418/651-5901, Fax: 418/651-7467 – *2

Jolin, Fournier, Morisset, Place Iberville Trois, #500, 2960, boul Laurier, G1V 4S1 – 418/651-1900, Fax: 418/651-7410 – *23

Pothier Delisle, #400, 3075, ch des Quatre-Bourgeois, G1W 4X5 – 418/651-9900, Fax: 418/651-5184 – *30

Pouliot L'Ecuyer, Tour des Laurentides, 2525, boul Laurier, 10e étage, G1V 2L2 – 418/658-1080, Fax: 418/658-1414; Email: avocat@droit.com; URL: http://www.droit.com – *21

Tremblay, Bois, Mignault & Lemay, Iberville Un, #200, 1195, av Lavigerie, G1V 4N3 – 418/658-9966, Fax: 418/658-6100; Email: avocats@riq.qc.ca – *27

**Ste-Marie** .............................. **Beauce**

Sylvain, Parent, Gobeil, 225, rue du College, CP 40, G6E 3B4 – 418/387-2727, Fax: 418/387-7070 – *4

**Ste-Thérèse-De-Blainville** .............................. **Terrebonne**

Brazeau, Grégoire, 72, rue Blainville ouest, J7E 1X3 – 514/430-1530, Fax: 514/430-3607 – *3

**Sept-Îles** .............................. **Mingan**

Caron, Coté, Paradis, Bibeau, Desmarais, #72, 690, boul Laure, G4R 4N8 – 418/968-1140 – *7

de Pokomandy, Besnier & Parvu, Dion, 865, boul Laure, G4R 1Y6 – 418/962-9775 – *5

Desrosiers & Ricard, #201, 440, av Brochu, G4R 2W8 – 418/962-7392, Fax: 418/962-6100; Email: desricar@quebectel.com – *2

Gauthier, Nepveu, Leblanc & Brouillette, 1, Place Mingan, G4R 4L8 – *6

**Sherbrooke** .............................. **St-François**

Claude R. Beauchamp, #101, 380, rue King ouest, J1H 1R4 – 819/563-7733, Fax: 819/563-7734 – *1

Pierre Belhumeur, #101, 380, rue King ouest, J1H 1R4 – 819/566-1676, Fax: 819/563-7734 – *1

Gerard G. Boudreau, 2571, boul Portland, J1J 1V6 – 819/562-0848 – *1

Delorme, Bessette, #201, 225, rue King ouest, J1H 1P8 – 819/566-6222, Fax: 819/566-4331 – *14

Demers Bureau Borduas, #400, 455, rue King ouest, J1H 6E9 – 819/569-9056, Fax: 819/569-1259 – *9

Gervais Dube, 144, rue Wellington nord, J1H 5B7 – 819/563-0333, Fax: 819/563-0155 – *1

Grenier, Martel & Company, #110, 337, rue Dufferin, J1H 4M6 – 819/563-0334, Fax: 819/563-5434 – *3

Hackett, Campbell, Bouchard, 80, rue Peel, J1H 4K1 – 819/565-7885, Fax: 819/566-0888; Email: hackett_campbell_bouchard@sympatico.ca – *6

Huard, Théroux & Associés, 191, rue Palais, CP 610, J1H 4R1 – 819/821-5700, Fax: 819/822-6064 – *6

Lamoureux, Roland, 520, rue Bowen, J1G 2E1 – 819/563-0500 – *2

Monty, Coulombe, #200, 234, rue Dufferin, J1H 4M2 – 819/566-4466, Fax: 819/565-2891; Email: montycou@login.net – *24

**Sillery** .............................. **Québec**

Boivin, Hamel, #200, 1330, av Maguire, G1T 1Z3 – 418/681-0693, Fax: 418/681-5121 – *2

Dumas, Gagne, Mercier & Associés, 1965, rue St-Michel, G1S 1J7 – 418/527-9516, Fax: 418/527-3246 – *4

Fortin Dignard Fiset, #200, 1091, ch St-Louis, G1S 1E2 – 418/683-1177, Fax: 418/683-1224 – *3

Hickson, Martin & Blanchard, 1170, ch St-Louis, G1S 1E5 – 418/681-9671, Fax: 418/527-6938; Email: hmb@rtq.qc.ca – *18

**Thetford Mines** .............................. **Frontenac**

Gosselin, Ouellette, Grondin, Houle, 163, rue Pie XI, CP 667, G6G 5V1 – 418/335-9151, Fax: 418/338-4874 – *4

Warren & Ouellet, 108, rue Notre-Dame sud, CP 714, G6G 5V1 – 418/338-3191, Fax: 418/338-5267 – *4

**Trois-Rivières** .............................. **Trois Rivières**

Ayotte, Mallette, Gamache, St-Hilaire & Roy, #603, 1350, rue Royale, G9A 5H5 – 819/379-3766 – *1

Beaumier, Richard, 90, rue des Casernes, CP 365, G9A 5G9 – 819/379-1221, Fax: 819/371-1214; Email: info@beaumier-richard.qc.ca – *8

Biron & Spain, 154, rue Radisson, CP 444, G9A 5G4 – 819/375-4187, Fax: 819/375-7395 – *3

Jacques Desaulniers, 543, boul Laviolette, 2e étage, G9A 1V4 – 819/378-3717, Fax: 819/375-2462 – *1

Godin & Saint-Amant, 190, rue Bonaventure, CP 1474, G9A 5L6 – 819/379-5225, Fax: 819/379-4545 – *3

Heenan Blaikie, #360, 1500, boul Royal, CP 1900, G9A 6E6 – 819/373-7000, Fax: 819/373-0943

Louis Henaire, 983, rue Hart, CP 1745, G9A 5M4 – 819/379-3355, Fax: 819/379-1227 – *2

Pierre Soucy, 5375, rue St-Joseph, G8Z 4M5 – 819/379-0307, Fax: 819/378-9586 – *1

**Val-D'Or** .............................. **Abitibi**

Cliche & Cliche, 1121, rue 6e, CP 460, J9P 4P5 – 819/825-3010, Fax: 819/825-7375 – *10

Claude Cossette, 795, av 3e, J9P 1S8 – 819/825-2787 – *1

Dufresne Ferron St-Julien, 855, av 3e, CP 520, J9P 4P5 – 819/825-4153, Fax: 819/825-9769; Email: avocats@lino.com – *5

St-Julien, Bigué, #202, 855, av 3e, CP 520, J9P 4P5 – 819/825-4153, Fax: 819/825-9769 – *4

Denis Tousignant, 1218, rue 6e, CP 969, J9P 4P8 – *1

**Valleyfield** .............................. **Beauharnois**

Blanchard, Plante, Bourbonnais & Gaulin, 70, rue Nicholson, J6T 4N2 – 514/373-1414, Fax: 514/373-6833 – *8

Lecompte, Drouin & Assoociés, 151, rue Salaberry St., G6T 2H8 – 514/371-6066, Fax: 514/371-5139 – *4

Massé, Gingras, Robert & Toulouse, 145, rue Salaberry, J6T 2H8 – 514/370-3064, Fax: 514/370-3068 – *4

Rancourt, Legault, Boucher & Godbout, 175, rue Salaberry, J6T 2J1 – 514/371-2221, Fax: 514/371-2094; Email: rancourt@rocler.qc.ca; URL: http://www.rocler.qc.ca/rancourt – *9

Vachon, Martin & Besner, 72, rue Montcalm, J6T 2C9 – 514/371-7771, Fax: 514/371-2438; Email: vachon@rocler.qc.ca – *4

**Varennes** .............................. **Richelieu**

Desjardins, Lessard, 1950, boul René Gaultier, J0L 2P0 – 514/652-2957, Fax: 514/652-3484 – *2

**Vaudreuil** .............................. **Beauharnois**

René Boucher, 382, boul Roche, J7V 2M6 – 514/455-3943, Fax: 514/842-3199 – *1

**Victoriaville** .............................. **Arthabaska**

Caron, Dubois & Associes, 268, boul Bois Francs nord, G6P 1G5 – 819/758-8251, Fax: 819/752-4520 – *4

Provencher, Coté & Garneau, 42, boul Carignan, G6P 4Z6 – 819/758-0529 – *3

## SASKATCHEWAN

**Alameda** .............................. **Estevan**

McLellan, Cundall, Bridges & Baumgartner, 115 Fifth St., S0C 0A0 – 306/489-2216, Fax: 306/634-9995

**Assiniboia** .............................. **Assiniboia**

Lewans & Ford, 228 Centre St., PO Box 759, S0H 0B0 – 306/642-4520, Fax: 306/642-5777 – *2

Marlin Law Office, 200 Centre St., PO Box 1088, S0H 0B0 – 306/642-3933, Fax: 306/642-3933 – *1

Mountain & Mountain, 101 - 4 Ave. West, PO Box 459, S0H 0B0 – 306/642-3866, Fax: 306/642-5848; Email: lee.mountain@sk.sympatico.ca – *2

**Biggar** .............................. **Battleford**

Stuart A. Busse Q.C., Credit Union Bldg., 302 Main St., PO Box 669, S0K 0M0 – 306/948-3346, Fax: 306/948-3366 – *2

**Birch Hills** .............................. **Prince Albert**

Mills & Zuk, PO Box 790, S0J 0G0 – 306/922-4700

**Broadview** .............................. **Regina**

Gary G. Moore, PO Box 610, S0G 0K0 – 306/696-2454, Fax: 306/696-3105 – *1

**Brownlee** .............................. **Moose Jaw**

Frederick R.C. Rawlings, PO Box 70, S0H 0M0 – 306/759-2621 – *1

**Canora** .......................................... **Yorkton**

Peet Law Firm, 106 First Ave. East, PO Box 1298, S0A 0L0 – 306/563-5200, Fax: 306/547-5590

**Carlyle** ..........................................

McLellan, Cundall, Bridges & Baumgartner, Falco Place Bldg., 205 Main St., S0C 0R0 – 306/453-2252, Fax: 306/634-9995

**Carnduff** .......................................... **Estevan**

McLellan, Cundall, Bridges & Baumgartner, 102 First St., S0C 0S0 – 306/482-3282, Fax: 306/482-3669

**Davidson** .......................................... **Battleford**

Dellene S. Church, 207 Washington Ave., PO Box 724, S0G 1A0 – 306/567-5554, Fax: 306/567-2831 – *1

**Eastend** .......................................... **Swift Current**

Benison Law Office, 302 Redcoat Dr., S0N 0T0 – 306/295-3250

**Esterhazy** .......................................... **Melville**

MacKenzie Law Office, 500 Maple St., S0A 0X0 – 306/745-3952, 745-6772, Fax: 306/745-6119 – *1

**Estevan** .......................................... **Estevan**

Chicoine Billesberger Grimsrud, 403 - 9th Ave., PO Box 1608, S4A 2L7 – 306/634-5644, Fax: 306/634-8610 – *3

Chicoine Billesberger Grimsrud, 403 - 9th Ave., PO Box 1608, S4A 2L7 – 306/634-5644, Fax: 306/634-8610; Email: chicoine.cbglaw@grill.sk.ca

Ignatiuk Law Offices, PO Box 460, S4A 2A4 – 306/634-6477, Fax: 306/634-8744 – *2

Komarnicki Law Firm, #305, 1133 - 4 St., PO Box 725, S4A 2A6 – 306/634-2616, Fax: 306/634-9881 – *2

McLellan, Cundall, Bridges & Baumgartner, 1138 Third St., PO Box 609, S4A 2A5 – 306/634-2673, Fax: 306/634-9995; Email: mcbb@sk.sympatico.ca – *6

Orlowski Law Office, 1215 - 5th St., S4A 0Z5 – 306/634-3353, Fax: 306/634-7714; Email: orlowski.law@sk.sympatico.ca – *1

**Eston** .......................................... **Swift Current**

Hughes Law Office, PO Box 729, S0L 1A0 – 306/962-4111, Fax: 306/962-3302 – *1

**Foam Lake** .......................................... **Wynyard**

Owen Klebeck, 412 Main St., PO Box 779, S0A 1A0 – 306/272-4330, Fax: 306/272-4330

**Gravelbourg** .......................................... **Gravelbourg**

Guy J. Dauphinais, PO Box 480, S0H 1X0 – 306/648-3325 – *1

Louis E. Stringer, PO Box 927, S0H 1X0 – 306/648-2582, Fax: 306/648-2501 – *1

**Humboldt** .......................................... **Humboldt**

Munkler & Halderman, 607 - 9 St., PO Box 1510, S0K 2A0 – 306/682-2516, Fax: 306/682-5053 – *2

Sutherland, Behiel & Wil, 602 - 9 St., PO Box 878, S0K 2A0 – 306/682-2642, Fax: 306/682-5165; Email: sbw@sk.sympatico.ca – *2

**Indian Head** .......................................... **Regina**

Kenneth J. Karwandy, PO Box 1223, S0G 2K0 – 306/761-6226, Fax: 306/761-6222 – *1

**Kamsack** .......................................... **Yorkton**

Rosowsky & Campbell, 445 - 2 St., S0A 1S0 – 306/542-2646, Fax: 306/542-2510 – *2

**Kelvington** .......................................... **Wynyard**

Bertram, Scrivens, Prior & Stradecki, PO Box 220, S0A 1W0 – 306/327-5111, Fax: 306/327-4765

Peet Law Firm, #5, 201 Main St., S0A 1W0 – 306/327-4343, Fax: 306/547-5590

**Kindersley** .......................................... **Battleford**

Roberts & Company, 115 - 1 Ave. East., PO Box 1510, S0L 1S0 – 306/463-4647, Fax: 306/463-6133 – *2

Sheppard Law Office, 207 Main St., PO Box 1567, S0L 1S0 – 306/463-2035, Fax: 306/463-6270; Email: sheppard.law@sk.sympatico.ca – *1

**Lampman** .......................................... **Estevan**

Chicoine Billesberger Grimsrud, PO Box 40, S0C 1N0 – 306/487-2880, Fax: 306/634-8610

**Langenburg** .......................................... **Yorkton**

Layh Law Office, PO Box 250, S0A 2A0 – 306/743-5520, Fax: 306/743-5568; Toll Free: 1-800-720-5520; Email: layh.law@sk.sympatico.ca – *2

**Lloydminster** .......................................... **Battleford**

Johnston, Bennett, 5105 - 49 St., S9V 0Y6 – 403/875-9105, Fax: 403/875-6748 – *3

Lonsdale Law Office, 5009 - 48 St., PO Box 1248, S9V 1G1 – 403/875-5185, Fax: 403/875-6547; Email: jagman@telusplanet.net – *1

**Maple Creek** .......................................... **Swift Current**

W.R. Orr, PO Box 608, S0N 1N0 – 306/662-2282, Fax: 306/662-2111 – *1

**Meadow Lake** .......................................... **Battleford**

Francis Legal Services, 821 - 9th Ave. West, PO Box 310, S0M 1V0 – 306/236-5540, Fax: 306/236-5571 – *2

**Melfort** .......................................... **Melfort**

Annand Law Office, 208 Main St., PO Box 69, S0E 1A0 – 306/752-2707, Fax: 306/752-4484; Email: mannand@sk.sympatico.ca – *2

Carson & Co., 803 Main St., PO Box 1600, S0E 1A0 – 306/752-5781, Fax: 306/752-4797 – *3

Kapoor Selnes Klimm & Brown, PO Box 2200, S0E 1A0 – 306/752-5777, Fax: 306/752-2712 – *4

Ronald Price-Jones, #3 Highway East, PO Box 129, S0E 1A0 – 306/752-5701, Fax: 306/752-2444 – *1

**Melville** .......................................... **Yorkton**

Schmidt Law Office, 126 - 3 Ave. East, PO Box 160, S0A 2P0 – 306/728-5481, Fax: 306/728-4201 – *1

**Midale** .......................................... **Estevan**

Chicoine Billesberger Grimsrud, S0C 1S0 – 306/458-2277

**Moose Jaw** .......................................... **Moose Jaw**

Murray D. Acton, 330 Main St. North, S6H 3J9 – 306/694-0052, Fax: 306/691-0445 – *1

Chow & MacLowich, 113 High St. West, PO Box 160, S6H 4N8 – 306/693-7536, Fax: 306/693-6444 – *3

Dickinson & Ansell, Hammond Bldg, #414, 310 Main St. North, S6H 3K1 – 306/692-4124, Fax: 306/692-7718 – *2

Grayson & Company, 350 Langdon Cres., PO Box 908, S6H 4P6 – 306/693-6176, Fax: 306/693-1515; Email: grayson@sk.sympatico.ca – *5

Terrance Ocrane Law Office, #106, 12 High St. East, S6H 0B9 – 306/694-4922, Fax: 306/692-6386; Email: terrance.ocrane@sk.sympatico.ca – *1

Whittaker, Craik, Chow & MacLowich, 109 Ominica St. West, PO Box 1178, S6H 4P9 – 306/694-4677, Fax: 306/694-5747 – *4

**Moosomin** .......................................... **Souris/Moose Mtn.**

Olive, Waller, Zinkhan & Waller, 714 Main St., 2nd Fl., S0G 3N0 – 306/435-2131

Osman, Gordon & Co., 626 Carleton St., PO Box 280, S0G 3N0 – 306/435-3851, Fax: 306/435-3962 – *4

**Nipawin** .......................................... **Melfort**

Carson Law Office, PO Box 1983, S0E 1E0 – 306/862-9807, Fax: 306/862-5554 – *1

Eremko & Eremko, PO Box 250, S0E 1E0 – 306/862-4422, Fax: 306/862-4477 – *1

Taylor & Fitzpatrick, PO Box 850, S0E 1E0 – 306/862-3111, Fax: 306/862-2560; Email: taylor.fitz@sk.sympatico.ca – *2

**North Battleford** .......................................... **Battleford**

Cawood Walker Demmans Anderson Baldwin, #201, 1291 - 102 St., PO Box 905, S9A 2Z3 – 306/445-6177, Fax: 306/445-7076 – *6

David Conroy, #101, 1351 - 101 St., S9A 0Z9 – 306/445-3613, Fax: 306/445-9088 – *1

Clifford Holm Law Office, 761A - 106th St., S9A 1V9 – 306/445-7300, Fax: 306/445-4144; Email: c.holm@sk.sympatico.ca – *1

Lojek, Jones & Hudec, 10211 - 12 Ave., PO Box 1179, S9A 3K2 – 306/446-2211, Fax: 306/446-3022 – *5

Maher, Lindgren, Blais & Frank, 1301 - 101 St., PO Box 940, S9A 2Z3 – 306/445-2422, Fax: 306/445-2313 – *7

Wilhelm Migneault Gibbons Greenwood, PO Box 520, S9A 2Y8 – 306/445-4436, 8151, Fax: 306/445-6444 – *5

**Oxbow** ..........................................

McLellan, Cundall, Bridges & Baumgartner, 408 Main St., S0C 2B0 – 306/483-2250, Fax: 306/634-9995

**Porcupine Plain** .......................................... **Melfort**

Kapoor, Selnes, Klimm, Schnell & Brown, McAlister Ave., S0E 1H0 – 306/278-2230

**Preeceville** .......................................... **Yorkton**

Peet Law Firm, 17 First Ave. NW, PO Box 1210, S0A 3B0 – 306/547-3322, Fax: 306/547-5590 – *1

**Prince Albert** .......................................... **Prince Albert**

Balicki Popescul & Forsyth, #200, 110 - 11 St. East, S6V 1A1 – 306/764-2222, Fax: 306/764-2221 – *5

Balon Krishan Melin Law Firm, 1335B - 2nd Ave. West, S6V 5B2 – 306/922-5151, Fax: 306/763-1755 – *3

Cherkewich, Yost & Heffernan, 1005 Central Ave., S6V 4V4 – 306/764-1537, Fax: 306/763-0505 – *5

Delbert M. Dynna, 100A - 10 St. East, S6V 0Y7 – 306/764-6856 – *1

Eggum, Abrametz, Eggum & Bendig, #101, 88 - 13 St. East, S6V 1C6 – 306/763-7441, Fax: 306/764-2882; Email: eggum.abrametz@sk.sympatico.ca – *5

Harradence, Longworth, Logue & Harradence, 1102 - 1 Ave. West, PO Box 2080, S6V 6V4 – 306/764-4244, Fax: 306/764-4949; Toll Free: 1-800-661-6690 – *4

Mills, Wilcox, Zuk, 20 - 12 St. West, S6V 3B3 – 306/922-4700, Fax: 306/922-0633 – *4

Pandila Morin, 15 - 15 St. West, S6V 3P4 – 306/764-2720, Fax: 306/763-8096 – *3

Pandila Morin, Opawikoscikan Reserve #201, PO Box 2890, S6V 7M4 – 306/764-2715, Fax: 306/763-8095

Leo Pinel, 1100 - 1 Ave. East, S6V 2A7 – 306/763-1300, Fax: 306/763-6744 – *1

Sanderson & Karpish, #3, 27 - 11 St. West, PO Box 730, S6V 3A8 – 306/763-8434, Fax: 306/763-1990 – *2

Stephens, Arnot, 2805 - 6th Ave., S6V 6Z6 – 306/764-3456, Fax: 306/922-3772; Email: ed.stephens@sk.sympatico.ca – *2

West, Siwak, 1109 Central Ave., S6V 4V7 – 306/763-7467, Fax: 306/763-7469 – *2

Zatlyn, Holash, 25 - 11 St. East, S6V 0Z8 – 306/922-1444, Fax: 306/922-5848 – *4

**Redvers** .......................................... **Moosomin**

Osman, Gordon & Co., 38 Railways Ave., S0C 2H0 – 306/452-3445

**Regina** .......................................... **Regina**

Balfour Moss, #700, 2103 - 11th Ave., S4P 4G1 – 306/347-8300, Fax: 306/347-8350; Email: balfourmoss.regina@dlcwest.com; URL: http://www.dlcwest.com/~balfourmoss – *17

* indicates number of lawyers in law firm.

Bertram, Scrivens, Prior & Stradecki, #1730, 2002 Victoria Ave., S4P 0R7 – 306/525-2737, Fax: 306/565-3244; Email: bertram.law@sk.sympatico.ca – *4
Cuelenaere, Hunter, Miller, #600, 2500 Victoria Ave., S4R 1A6 – 306/525-6103, Fax: 306/565-8806 – *4
Dahlem, Findlay & von Ledebur, 2100 Smith St., S4P 2P2 – 306/522-3631, Fax: 306/565-2616 – *3
Duchin, Bayda & Kroczynski, 2500 - 13 Ave., S4P 0W2 – 306/359-3131, Fax: 306/359-3372 – *4
Duncan Law Centre, 2360 - 2nd Ave., S4R 1A6 – 306/525-8500, Fax: 306/525-8585 – *1
Gates & Company, 3132 Avonhurst Dr., S4R 3J7 – 306/949-5544, Fax: 306/775-2995 – *8
Gauley & Co., #400, 2201 - 11 Ave., S4P 0J8 – 306/352-1643, Fax: 306/525-8499 – *5
Gerrand Mulatz, Toronto Dominion Bank Bldg., #701, 1914 Hamilton St., S4P 3N6 – 306/525-3561, Fax: 306/781-8150 – *7
Griffin Toews Maddigan & Brabant, 1530 Angus St., S4T 1Z1 – 306/525-6125, Fax: 306/525-5226; Email: griffin.toews@sk.sympatico.ca – *8
Gritzfeld & Associates, #801, 1867 Hamilton St., S4P 2C2 – 306/757-1601, Fax: 306/757-8017 – *2
Cindy M. Haynes Law Office, 4126 Wascana Ridge, S4V 2S1 – 306/789-2242, Fax: 306/789-4950 – *1
Elaine Husk, 2269 Hamilton St., S4P 2E7 – 306/525-8311, Fax: 306/565-2766 – *1
Jaques Law Office, #101, 2515 Victoria Ave., S4P 0T2 – 306/359-3041, Fax: 306/525-4173; Email: jaques.law@dlcwest.com; URL: http://www.dlcwest.com/~jaques.law/ – *1
Kanuka Thuringer, North Canadian Oils Bldg., #1400, 2500 Victoria Ave., S4P 3X2 – 306/525-7200, Fax: 306/359-0590; Email: kanukat@cableregina.com – *25
Kowalishen Law Firm, 1954 Angus St., S4T 1Z6 – 306/525-2385, Fax: 306/525-2386 – *1
Kraus McKay Pederson, #400, 1900 Albert St., S4P 4K8 – 306/761-6200, Fax: 306/761-6222; Email: kmplaw@cableregina.com – *10
M.A. Kuziak, 1872 Angus St., S4T 1Z5 – 306/757-0154 – *1
MacKay & McLean, #124, 2001 Cornwall St., S4P 2K6 – 306/569-1301, Fax: 306/569-8560 – *2
MacLean Keith, Nicol Ct., 2398 Scarth St., S4P 2J7 – 306/757-1611, Fax: 306/757-0712 – *3
MacPherson Leslie & Tyerman, #1500, 1874 Scarth St., S4P 4E9 – 306/347-8000, Fax: 306/352-5250 – *30
Martin & MacLeod, 2114 Robinson St., S4T 2P7 – 306/347-0868, Fax: 306/352-6177 – *4
McDougall, Ready, Royal Bank Bldg., #700, 2010 - 11 Ave., S4P 0J3 – 306/757-1641, Fax: 306/359-0785 – *28
McKercher McKercher & Whitmore, #1000, 1783 Hamilton St., S4P 2B6 – 306/352-7661, Fax: 306/781-7113; Email: mckercher.reg@sk.sympatico.ca – *7
Mellor & Anderson, #1400, 2002 Victoria Ave., S4P 0R7 – 306/789-8868, Fax: 306/789-3366 – *2
Merchant Law Group, Saskatchewan Drive Plaza, #100, 2401 Saskatchewan Dr., S4P 4H8 – 306/359-7777, Fax: 306/522-3299 – *28
Morgan, Khaladkar & Skinner, 2510 - 13 Ave., S4P 0W2 – 306/525-9191, Fax: 306/525-0006 – *4
Murphy & Murphy, #401, 1900 Albert St., S4P 4K8 – 306/757-1656, Fax: 306/347-7931 – *3
Olive, Waller, Zinkhan & Waller, 2255 - 13 Ave., S4P 0V6 – 306/359-1888, Fax: 306/352-0771 – *15
Pedersen, Norman, McLeod & Todd, Bank of Canada Building, #500, 2220 - 12 Ave., PO Box 1037, S4P 3B2 – 306/565-4100, Fax: 306/757-4858; Email: pnmt@sk.sympatico.ca – *14
Phillips & Milen, 2343 Broad St., S4P 1Y9 – 306/569-0811, Fax: 306/565-3434 – *3
Randall, Wellsch & Simaluk, #200, 2425 - 13 Ave., S4P 0W1 – 306/569-1530, Fax: 306/569-0121; Email: ranwel@sk.sympatico.ca – *3
Rath Johnson Hart, #1101, 1867 Hamilton St., S4P 2C2 – 306/757-8571, Fax: 306/757-8017 – *7
Bonnie B. Reid, 39 Quincy Dr., S4S 6L7 – 306/565-8085, Fax: 306/352-5250 – *1
Rendek McCrank, #208, 2208 Scarth St., S4P 2J6 – 306/525-2191, Fax: 306/757-8138 – *7
Robertson Stromberg, #100, 1777 Victoria Ave., S4P 4K5 – 306/569-9000, Fax: 306/757-6443; Email: rs.regina@robertsonstromberg.com; URL: http://www.robertsonstromberg.com – *8
Edwin C. Robinson, 2164 Smith St., S4P 2P2 – 306/569-3322 – *1
Sheppard, Braun & Muma, #204, 3988 Albert St., S4S 3R1 – 306/586-6020, Fax: 306/586-8525 – *3
Tulloch & Tulloch, 310 Gardiner Park Ct., S4V 1R9 – 306/789-0666, Fax: 306/789-1405; Email: tulloch@netlfx.com – *4
Woloshyn Mattison, Saskatchewan Pl., #200, 1870 Albert St., S4P 4B7 – 306/352-9676, Fax: 306/569-8411; Email: rlinka@logicallink.com; URL: http://www.sasklaw.com – *6

**Rocanville .................................... Moosomin**

Osman, Gordon & Co., General Delivery, S0A 3L0 – 306/645-2825

**Rosetown ...................................... Kerrobert**

Aseltine & Turner, 106 Main St., PO Box 158, S0L 2V0 – 306/882-2121, Fax: 306/882-3177 – *1

**Rosthern ....................................... Saskatoon**

Balicki Popescul & Forsyth, 716 Railway Ave., PO Box 779, S0K 3R0 – 306/232-4482, Fax: 306/232-5595 – *1
R.M. Simpson, Q.C., 601 - 1 Ave., S0K 3R0 – 306/232-4331 – *1

**Saskatoon .................................... Saskatoon**

Agnew & Company, 279 - 3 Ave. North, S7K 2H8 – 306/244-7966, Fax: 306/244-8010; Email: agnewco@sk.sympatico.ca – *3
Balfour Moss, #600, 123 - 2nd Ave. South, S7K 7E6 – 306/665-7844, Fax: 306/662-1586; Email: balfourmoss.saskatoon@dlcwest.com; URL: http://www.dlcwest.com/~balfourmoss – *2
Bodnar & Wanhella, 812 Spadina Cres. East, S7K 3H4 – 306/664-3314 – *3
Julian William Bodnar, Concorde Place, #201, 129 Third Ave. South, S7K 2M3 – 306/652-6666, Fax: 306/652-6628 – *1
Rose Boyko, #220, 212 - 10 St. East, S7N 2T6 – 306/665-6816
Brayford - Shapiro, 311 - 21 St. East., S7K 0C1 – 306/244-5656, Fax: 306/244-5644 – *3
Brent & Greenhorn, #216, 3501 - 8 St. East, S7H 5K5 – 306/955-9544, Fax: 306/955-2656; Email: bandg@eagle.wbm.ca; URL: http://broadwaynet.com/~bandglaw – *3
Burlingham Cuelenaere, 1043 - 8 St. East, S7H 0S2 – 306/343-9581, Fax: 306/343-1947 – *4
Morris T. Cherneskey, Q.C., 400 Canada Bldg., S7K 0B3 – 306/244-8551, Fax: 306/244-0205 – *1
Cuelenaere, Hunter, Miller, #510, 128 - 4 Ave. South, S7K 1M8 – 306/653-5000, Fax: 306/652-4171; Email: cuelenaere@getthe.net – *16
Dirk Law Office, #208, 416 - 21st St. East, S7K 0C2 – 306/652-4664, Fax: 306/664-1983 – *1
Donlevy & Company, #500, 402 - 21 St. East, S7K 0C3 – 306/244-8494, Fax: 306/665-7042 – *2
Leila M. Ewing, 1222 Elliott St., S7N 0V6 – 306/652-9610, Fax: 306/652-2187 – *1
Gauley & Co., 701 Broadway Ave., PO Box 638, S7K 3L7 – 306/653-1212, Fax: 306/652-1323; Email: gauleyco@eagle.wbm.ca – *24
Goldstein Jackson Scharfstein Gibbings, #420, 128 - 4th Ave. South, S7K 1M8 – 306/653-2838, Fax: 306/652-4747 – *5
Halyk Dovell, 321 - 6 Ave. North, S7K 2S3 – 306/665-3434, Fax: 306/652-1915 – *5
Haubrich, Borden, Trach, Carlson & Clark, Canada Bldg., #400, 105 - 21 St. East, S7K 0B3 – 306/244-6561, Fax: 306/652-2514; Email: haubrich@sk.sympatico.ca – *5
Henderson Campbell, #202, 135 - 21 St. East, S7K 0B4 – 306/652-1234, Fax: 306/244-6640 – *3
Hnatyshyn Singer Thorstad, #601, 402 - 21 St. East, S7K 0C3 – 306/653-5150, Fax: 306/652-5859 – *14
Linda Jaine, 247 Sylvian Way, S7H 5G1 – 306/374-4952
Jamieson Bains, #801, 119 - 4 Ave. South, S7K 5X2 – 306/653-5410, Fax: 306/652-3031; Email: info@jblawyers.com; URL: http://www.jblawyers.com – *6
Kloppenburg & Kloppenburg, Spadina Towers, #333, 728 Spadina Cres. East, S7K 4H7 – 306/665-7600, Fax: 306/665-7800; Email: juristen@lexsask.com; URL: http://www.lexsask.com – *2
Marusia A. Kobrynsky, #404, 333 - 25th St. East, S7K 0L4 – 306/956-1740, Fax: 306/242-3773 – *1
Koskie & Company, #4, 2175 Airport Dr., S7L 7E1 – 306/242-8478, Fax: 306/653-2120; Email: tkoskie@sk.sympatico.ca; URL: http://www.sk.sympatico.ca/tkoskie – *2
Kraus McKay Pederson, #300, 333 - 3 Ave. North, S7K 2H9 – 306/652-8833, 653-5700, Fax: 306/652-3333 – *7
Leland Kimpinski, #200, 321A - 21st St. East, S7K 0C1 – 306/244-6686, Fax: 306/653-7008 – *5
MacDermid Lamarsh, #905, 201 - 21 St. East, S7K 0B8 – 306/652-9422, Fax: 306/242-1554; Email: macmarsh@macmarsh.com – *10
MacLean Keith, #1210, 410 - 22 St. East, S7K 5T6 – 306/664-9200, Fax: 306/664-1960 – *4
MacPherson Leslie & Tyerman, #1500, 410 - 22nd St. East, S7K 5T6 – 306/975-7100, Fax: 306/975-7145 – *16
Louis E. Martel, 830 - 4 St., S7H 1K4 – 306/652-6830, Fax: 306/652-6830; Email: martel@dlcwest.com – *1
McDougall, Ready, #300, 110 - 21 St. East, S7K 0B6 – 306/653-1641, Fax: 306/665-8511 – *4
McKercher McKercher & Whitmore, 374 - 3rd Ave. South, S7K 1M5 – 306/653-2000, Fax: 306/244-7335; Email: mckerche@eagle.wbm.ca – *32
Merchant Law Group, Canterbury Towers, #501, 224 Fourth Ave. South, S7K 5M5 – 306/653-7777, Fax: 306/975-1983; Toll Free: 1-800-567-7779 – *7
William Nykyforuk, Q.C., #208, 165 - 3 Ave. South, S7K 1L8 – 306/242-1202, Fax: 306/244-4423 – *1
E.C. Partridge, #604, 224 - 4 Ave. South, S7K 5M5 – 306/955-5535, Fax: 306/652-1110 – *1
Pearson, Rask, #102, 294 Venture Cres., S7K 6M1 – 306/242-2500, Fax: 306/242-2538; Email: pearson.rask.law@sk.sympatico.ca – *4
Pillipow & Company, #102, 500 Spadina Cres. East, S7K 4H9 – 306/665-3456, Fax: 306/665-3411; Email: pillipow@aol.com – *5
Michael A. Power, #804, 230 - 22 St. East, S7K 0E9 – 306/242-0072, Fax: 306/242-0071 – *1
Priel, Stevenson, Hood & Thornton, 902 Spadina Cres. East, S7K 3H5 – 306/244-0132, Fax: 306/653-1118 – *10
Quon Ferguson MacKinnon, #704, 224 - 4 Ave. South, S7K 5M5 – 306/665-8828, Fax: 306/665-5519 – *5
Robertson Stromberg, #600, 105 Twenty First St. East, S7K 0B3 – 306/652-7575, Fax: 306/652-2445; Email: rs.stoon@robertsonstromberg.com; URL: http://www.robertsonstromberg.com – *19
Roe Beckie & Olson, #313, 220 - 3 Ave. South, S7K 1M1 – 306/244-9865, Fax: 306/934-6827 – *3
Sandstrom & Scott, #701, 224 - 4 Ave. South, S7K 5M5 – 306/244-0002, Fax: 306/652-2424; Email: sand@sk.sympatico.ca – *3
Schulman, Serne, Boryski & Gall, #604, 224 - 4 Ave. South, S7K 5M5 – 306/933-2233, Fax: 306/652-1110 – *4
Skarsgard Law Office, 1515 Shannon Cres., S7H 2T6 – 306/373-2688, Fax: 306/373-2688 – *1
Sonnenschein Law Office, Lincoln's Inn, 313 - 20th St. East, S7K 0A9 – 306/652-4730, Fax: 306/653-5760 – *2

Leslie G. Tallis, 2410 Irvine Ave., S7J 2A8 – *1

Thair Armitage & Co., Financial Bldg., #405, 230 - 22nd St. East, S7K 0E9 – 306/652-6666, Fax: 306/652-6628; Email: thair.co@sk.sympatico.ca – *1

Thomson & Company, #303, 416 - 21 St. East, S7K 0C2 – 306/652-1620, Fax: 306/664-6732 – *1

Walker, Plaxton & Co., #200, 402 - 21 St. East, S7K 0C3 – 306/653-1500, Fax: 306/664-6659 – *4

Woloshyn Mattison, Scotiabank Bldg., #200, 111 - 2 Ave. South, S7K 1K6 – 306/244-2242, Fax: 306/652-0332 – *9

**Swift Current ................................ Swift Current**

Anderson Nimegeers, 40 Cheadle St. West, PO Box 610, S9H 3W4 – 306/773-2891, Fax: 306/778-3364 – *8

Douglas J. Heinricks, 327 Central Ave. North, PO Box 1327, S9H 3X4 – 306/773-7226, Fax: 306/773-5696 – *2

MacBean Tessem, Box: 550, 151 First Ave. NE, PO Box 550, S9H 3W4 – 306/773-9343, Fax: 306/778-3828 – *7

McLaughlin, Forrester, Heinrichs, #9, 244 - 1 Ave. NE, PO Box 100, S9H 3V5 – 306/773-7205, Fax: 306/773-9715 – *4

**Tisdale ........................................ Melfort**

Annand Nystuen, 1105 Main St., S0E 1T0 – 306/873-2145

Kapoor Selnes Klimm & Brown, PO Box 760, S0E 1T0 – 306/873-4535, Fax: 306/873-3424 – *1

Kapoor, Selnes, Klimm, Schnell & Brown, PO Box 760, S0E 1T0 – 306/873-4535, Fax: 306/873-3424 – *4

**Unity ........................................ Battleford**

Hepting & Piché, 257 - 2 Ave. West, PO Box 600, S0K 4L0 – 306/228-2631, Fax: 306/228-4449 – *3

L. Kenneth Neil, 100 - 1 Ave. West, PO Box 128, S0K 4L0 – 306/228-2693, Fax: 306/228-4465 – *1

**Weyburn ........................................ Weyburn**

Hardy & Thorson, 102 Coteau Ave. NE, S4H 2Z5 – 306/842-2772, Fax: 306/848-3539 – *2

Nimegeers, Schuck, Wormsbecker & Bobbitt, 319 Souris Ave. NE, PO Box 8, S4H 2J8 – 306/842-4654, Fax: 306/842-0522 – *4

**Whitewood ........................................ Moosomin**

Osman, Gordon & Co., 717 Lalonte St., S0G 5C0 – 306/735-4503

**Wilkie ........................................ Battleford**

Lojek, Jones & Hudec, 108 - 2 Ave. East, PO Box 4, S0K 4W0 – 306/843-2661, Fax: 306/446-3022

**Yorkton ........................................ Yorkton**

Stamatinos, Leland, Koskie, Box: 188, 36 - 4 Ave. North, S3N 2V7 – 306/783-8541, Fax: 306/786-7484 – *3

Taylor Yaholnitsky, 4 - 3rd Ave. North, S3N 1B9 – 306/782-5556, Fax: 306/782-5558 – *2

Wrubell & Company, 18 - 1 Ave. North, S3N 1J4 – 306/783-9440, Fax: 306/786-1838 – *2

## YUKON TERRITORY

**Whitehorse ........................................ Whitehorse**

Anton, Campion, Macdonald, Oyler & Buchan, #200, 204 Lambert St., Y1A 3T2 – 867/667-7885, Fax: 867/667-7600 – *9

James Francis Burchill, #13, 501 Alexander St., Y1A 2L9

Robin Roy Dalziel, 6 Lewes Blvd., Y1A 3J2 – 867/668-2888

Davis & Company, #200, 304 Jarvis St., Y1A 2H2 – 867/668-6444, Fax: 867/667-2669; Email: rod_snow@davis.ca; URL: http://www.davis.ca

David Joe, #101, 307 Jarvis St., Y1A 2H3 – 867/668-6681

Brian L. Morris, Horwoods Mall, #202, 100 Main St., Y1A 2A8 – 867/668-3390, Fax: 867/668-6213

O'Brien & Associates, #3, 3089 - 3 Ave., Y1A 5B3 – 867/668-7272, Fax: 867/668-2872 – *2

Willard L. Phelps, Government of Yukon, Legislative Assembly Office, PO Box 2703, Y1A 2C6 – 867/667-5639

Preston, Willis & Lackowicz, 2093 - 2 Ave., Y1A 1B5 – 867/668-5252, Fax: 867/668-5251; Email: yukonlaw@yknet.yk.ca – *11

Eloise P. Spitzer, 67 Walnut Cr., Y1A 5C7

Veale, Kilpatrick, Austring, Fendrick & Fairman, The Drury Building, 3081 - 3 Ave., Y1A 4Z7 – 867/668-4405, Fax: 867/668-3710 – *10

* indicates number of lawyers in law firm.

# INDEX

**EDITOR'S NOTE:**

Wherever possible the listings in this index are arranged alphabetically according to the main word in each entry. Thus the Canadian Bankers Association is listed under "Bankers Assn., Cdn.", and the National Energy Board is listed under "Energy Bd., Ntl.". Government Departments are listed under the name of the Department, and not under the names of provinces. Thus if you are looking for the Ontario Transportation Department, look under "Transportation, Depts.," not under "Ontario".

Listings (such as the International Boundary Commission) are sometimes duplicated, when it was difficult to determine which word a user might consider the main one, or where it was felt that a user would look for an entry under a title that is well-known (such as the National Arts Centre).

See Index Page 72 for commonly used abbreviations.

**Page numbers in bold refer to illustrations found in the colour section.**

**See ADDENDA at the back of this book for late changes & additional information.**

## A

## B

## C

## D

## F

## G

## I

## J

## M

## N

## O

## S

## T

## U

## W

## Y



## Z

## ABBREVIATIONS

Acc. (Accident)
Admin. (Administration)
Admrs. (Administrators)
Adv. (Advancement/Advisory)
Advtg. (Advertising)
Agric./Agricl. (Agriculture/Agricultural)
Alta. (Alberta)
ADM (Assistant Deputy Minister)
Amer. (America/American)
Asst. (Assistant)
Atty-Gen. (Attorney-General)
Auth. (Authority)
Br. (Branch)
B.C. (British Columbia)
Brdcstrs. (Broadcasters)
Broth. (Brotherhood)
Bur. (Bureau)
Cdn. (Canadian); cdn/cdnne (canadien/canadienne)
Cie (Compagnie)
Co./Cos. (Company/Companies)
Commn. (Commission)
Commr. (Commissioner)
Com. (Committee)
Conf. (Conference)
Const. (Construction)
Contrs. (Contractors)
Coord. (Coordinator/Coordination)
Corp./Corps. (Corporation/Corporations)
Dept./Depts. (Department/Departments)
Devel. (Development)
Dir./Dirs. (Director/Directors)
Distrs. (Distributors)
Dist. (District)
Div./Divs. (Division/Divisions)
Educ./Educl. (Education/Educational)
Engrg. (Engineering)
Engrs. (Engineers)
Exec./Execs. (Executive/Executives)
Fed. (Federal)
Fedn./Fedns. (Federation/Federations)
Fdn./Fdns. (Foundation/Foundations)
Fra. (Fraternité)
Gen. (General)
Govt. (Government)
Hist'l (Historical)
Hosp. (Hospital)
Inc. (Incorporated)
Indep. (Independent)
Info. (Information)
Insp. (Inspection)
Ins. (Insurance)
Inst. (Institute)
Intl. (International; intle (internationale)
Ltd. (Limited); ltée (limitée)
Mgmt. (Management)
Mgr./Mgrs. (Manager/Managers)
Man. (Manitoba)
Mfrs./Mfg. (Manufacturers/Manufacturing
Mktg. (Marketing)
Min. (Ministry/Ministre)
Mtge. (Mortgage)
Mun. (Municipal)
Ntl. (National); ntle (nationale)
N.B. (New Brunswick)
Nfld. (Newfoundland)
N. Amer. (North America/North American)
N.W.T (Northwest Territories)
N.S. (Nova Scotia)
Ont. (Ontario)
Org./Orgs. (Organization/Organizations)
P.E.I. (Prince Edward Island)
Prodrs. (Producers)
Profl./Profls. (Professional/Professionals)
Prof. (Professor)
Prov. (Provincial)
Qué. (Québec)
qué. (québécois(e))
Rlwy. (Railway)
Ref. (Reference)
Regl. (Regional)
Regr. (Registrar)
Reg'n (Registration)
Reg'rd (Registered)
Reg./Regs. (Regulation/Regulations)
Rehab. (Rehabilitation)
Rep./Reps. (Representative/Representatives)
Sask. (Saskatchewan)
Sch./Schs. (School/Schools)
Soc./Socs. (Society/Societies or société/sociétés)
Supt. (Superintendent)
Suprv. (Supervisor)
Susp. (Suspension)
Synd. (Syndicat)
Tech. (Technology)
Terrs. (Territories)
Transp. (Transport/Transportation)
Univ. (University/Université)

# ORDER FORM

| QTY. | TITLE | PRICE | TOTAL |
|---|---|---|---|
| | 1. THE REGISTER OF CANADIAN HONOURS | $75.00 | |
| | 2. CANADIAN ALMANAC & DIRECTORY 1998 | $199.00 | |
| | 3. CANADIAN ALMANAC & DIRECTORY 1998 ON CD-ROM | $209.00 | |
| | 4. PAN CARIBBEAN BUSINESS DIRECTORY & HANDBOOK | $299.00 | |
| | 5. ASSOCIATIONS CANADA 1997/98 | $249.50 | |
| | 6. ASSOCIATIONS CANADA 1997/98 ON CD-ROM | $349.50 | |
| | 7. MONEY DAY FINDER 1998 CALENDAR | $24.95 | |
| | 8. MONEY DAY FINDER BASE | $14.95 | |
| | 9. EUROMARKET DAY FINDER 1998 CALENDAR | $39.95 | |
| | 10. EUROMARKET DAY FINDER BASE | $14.95 | |
| | 11. CANADIAN ENVIRONMENTAL DIRECTORY 1997/98 | $249.50 | |
| | 12. CANADIAN ENVIRONMENTAL DIRECTORY 1997/98 ON CD-ROM | $349.50 | |
| | 13. FINANCIAL POST - SURVEY OF INDUSTRIALS | $119.95 | |
| | 14. FINANCIAL POST - SURVEY OF MINES & ENERGY RESOURCES | $119.95 | |
| | 15. FINANCIAL POST - SURVEY OF PREDECESSOR & DEFUNCT COS. | $89.95 | |
| | 16. FINANCIAL POST - CORPORATE SURVEY SET (ALL 3 SURVEY BOOKS) | $299.95 | |

| | |
|---|---|
| SUBTOTAL | |
| SHIPPING ($6.75 PER TITLE) | |
| ADD 7% GST | |
| SUBTOTAL | |
| ONT. BUYERS ADD 8% PST ON ITEMS 3 THROUGH 16 | |
| TOTAL | |

❐ MAILING LISTS

Please call me with more information on mailing lists or send your full information kit. I am particularly interested in ____________________

____________________

____________________

❐ STANDING ORDER PLAN

By indicating a Standing Order you will receive copies of selected books annually on publication and SAVE 5% on all future editions.

## METHOD OF PAYMENT:

❐ CHEQUE/MONEY ORDER

Please find enclosed a cheque payable to Copp Clark Professional in the amount shown as total above.

❐ CREDIT CARD

❐ VISA ❐ AMEX ❐ M/C

CARD # ____________________

EXPIRY DATE ____________________

SIGNATURE ____________________

❐ BILL MY COMPANY

P.O.# if applicable ____________________

## SHIP TO:

NAME ____________________

TITLE/DEPT. ____________________

ORGANIZATION ____________________

ADDRESS ____________________

____________________

CITY ____________________

PROV/POSTAL CODE ____________________

BUSINESS PHONE ____________________

FAX NUMBER ____________________

EMAIL ____________________

ORDER BY PHONE:

**TOLL-FREE 1-800-815-9417, EXT. 1 IN TORONTO: (416) 597-1616, EXT. 1**

FAX THIS FORM TO (416) 597-1617

EMAIL: orders@mail.canadainfo.com

***WHEN ORDERING PLEASE REFER TO NUMBER A244***

**Copp Clark Professional, 200 Adelaide Street West, 3rd Floor, Toronto, Ontario M5H 1W7**

COPP CLARK PROFESSIONAL

# INFORMATION FORM

## CHANGE TO LISTING:

You may find it most convenient to photocopy your existing listing indicating any changes. Fax or mail the form.

PAGE NUMBER ______________________

NAME OF FIRM/ORGANIZATION/GOVERNMENT BODY: ______________________

PLEASE CHANGE OUR LISTING TO REFLECT THE FOLLOWING:

______________________

______________________

______________________

______________________

______________________

______________________

## NEW LISTING:

WE ARE NOT REPRESENTED IN THE DIRECTORY. HERE IS THE INFORMATION ON OUR FIRM/ORGANIZATION/GOVERNMENT BODY:
(Please examine the guidelines in the front of the directory and the entries of similar organizations for an indication of how best to present your data).

______________________

______________________

______________________

______________________

______________________

______________________

______________________

______________________

WE WOULD LIKE TO SEE MORE INFORMATION ON:

______________________

______________________

MAIL INFORMATION TO:

COPP CLARK PROFESSIONAL
200 ADELAIDE STREET WEST
3RD FLOOR
TORONTO, ONTARIO M5H 1W7

EMAIL TO:

ama@mail.canadainfo.com

FAX INFORMATION TO:

THE EDITOR
CANADIAN ALMANAC & DIRECTORY
(416) 597-1617

# ADDENDA

## Section 1

**Page 1-94**

Educational Awards: Under the Canadian Teachers' Federation, the Hillroy Fellowship Program should be known as the Roy C. Hill Awards.

## Section 2

**Page 2-9**

Eric E. Bartlett is now Chairman and CEO of the Certified General Accountants Association of Canada.

**Page 2-24**

Ron M. Jones is now Chairman of the Canadian Automobile Dealers Association.

**Page 2-58**

Duncan Cross is the Executive Director of the Nova Scotia Environmental Industry Association; the association's website is now http://www.nseia.ns.ca.

**Page 2-86**

The Alberta Public Health Association is now located at 3 Wildwood Cres. West, Lethbridge AB T1K 6E1; Tel.: 403/381-3921, Fax: 403/381-4487; the President is Sheilah Sommer.

**Page 2-90**

The Health Care Public Relations Association of Canada is now located at 1318 Wellington St., PO Box 36029, Ottawa ON K1Y 4V3; Tel.: 613/729-2102, Fax: 613/729-7708.

## Section 3

**Page 3-135**

Peter Mesheau becomes the new Conservative MPP in the southeastern New Brunswick riding of Tantramar. The Tory win gives the party seven seats in the legislature, far behind the the Liberals' 46 seat majority. Also in a New Brunswick by-election, Liberal Jim Doyle retains a Liberal hold on the Mirimichi-Bay du Vin riding.

**Page 3-189**

Richard Brown becomes the new opposition Liberal MPP for P.E.I.'s, Charlottetown-King's Square riding, in a November by-election.

**Page 3-199**

Marcel Masse, former Tory cabinet minister, is named Asst. Deputy Minister in Québec's Ministère de la Culture et des communications.

**Page 3-259**

Diane Van Beselaere becomes High Commissioner to Barbados, with concurrent accreditation to Antigua and Barbuda, and St. Vincent and the Grenadines.

**Page 3-262**

Peter F. Walker becomes High Commissioner to the Republic of India, with concurrent accreditation to the Kingdom of Nepal as Ambassador.

## Section 4

**Page 4-42**

Proposed Ontario municipal amalgamations:

Effective January 1, 1999, Essex County will be restructured (pending judicial review).

Effective January 1, 1999, the new town of Bancroft will be created through the amalgamation of the town of Bancroft & the township of Dungannon (under review).

Effective May 1, 1998, the township of Central Manitoulin will be created by the annexation of the townships of Camarvon & Sandfield & unorganized areas (under review).

Effective January 1, 1999, the town of Killarney will be created through the annexation of the township of Rutherford & George Island & unorganized areas (under review).

Effective June 1, 1998, the township of South Algonquin will be created through the annexation of the township of Airy & unorganized areas (order drafted).

Effective January 1, 1999, the town of French River will be created through the annexation of the township of Cosby, Mason & Martland & unorganized areas (under review).

**Page 4-163**

Elected to the Niagara Falls City Council are the following: Mayor, Wayne Thomson; Wayne Campbell; Judy Orr; Kim Craitor; Janice Wing; Pat Cummings; Paisley Janvary; Norm Puttick; Selina Volpatti; Ken Feren; Victor Pietrangelo; Shirley Fisher; Edward Michalczyk.

Elected to the North Bay City Council are the following: Mayor, Jack Burrows; Lynne Bennett; Jay Aspin; Peter Handley; George Maroosis; Wayne Poeta; Jack Smylie; Terry Talentino; Maureen Boldt; Sarah Campbell; Murray Shave.

**Page 4-165**

Elected to the Repentigny City Council are the following: Mayor, Chantal Deschamps; André Cyr; Lucien Goulet; Louise Bélair-Sant; François Beauregard; Jean Langlois; Mario Morais; Fernand Prud'homme; Raymond Hénault; Daniel Labrecque.

**Page 4-168**

Elected to the Sudbury City Council are the following: Mayor, Jim Gordon; Mike Petryna; Ted Callaghan; David Courtemanche; Jim Ilnitski; Gerry McIntaggart; J. Austin Davey; Ricardo de la Riva; Peter Dow; Doug Craig.

**Page 4-170**

Elected to the Waterloo City Council are the following: Mayor, Joan McKinnon; Lynne Woolstencroft; Mike Connolly; Sean Strickland; Scott Jones; Dave Roeder; Bruce Anderson; Bruce Alexander; Brent Needham.

**Page 4-169**

Elected to the Thunder Bay City Council are the following: Mayor, Ken Boshcoff; Lorne Allard; Bert Badanai; Betty Kennedy; Taras Kozyra; Bill Mauro; Ed Metzler; Linda Rydholm; Bill Scollie; Lawrence Timko; Robert Tuchenhagen; Joe Vander Wees; Dick Waddington.

## Section 5

**Page 5-115**

Additional contact information for Paperplate Books in Toronto, Ontario: Fax: 416/651-2960; URL: http://www.perkolator.com; chief officers include Bernard Kelly & Cary Fagan.

**Page 5-141**

Mark Bonokoski is appointed to the postion of Publisher and CEO of the Ottawa Sun.

**Page 5-148**

Address for the Échos du Vieux-Montréal newspaper has changed: 234. rue St-Paul ouest, Montréal QC H2Y 1Z9; 514/844-2133; Fax: 514/844-5858; Email: echo@CAM.ORG. Circulation is 15,000.

**Page 5-175**

Additional contact information for Accident Prevention magazine in Toronto, Ontario: Fax: 416/506-8880; Editor, Scott Williams.

**Page 5-204**

AM Radio Broadcasting Stations:Valley Broadcasters Ltd. of Castlegar, British Columbia, has changed corporate name to Boundary Kootenay Radio. Contact changes include: Toll Free: 1-800-665-1178; Email: BKRNews@Kootenay.net; General Manager, Dennis Gerein.

**Page 5-225**

Additional information on specialty & pay TV services provided by the Specialty & Premium Television Association/Association de la télévision spécialisée et payante, #200, 46 Elgin St., Ottawa ON K1P 5K6; 613/233-8690; Fax: 613/236-9546.

**Page 5-236**

Added to Online Service Providers in Ontario is the following: Weslink Datalink Corporation, 1603 Main St. West, Hamilton ON; Tel: 905/522-4101; Fax: 905/522-2123; Email: info@weslink.ca; URL: http://www.weslink.ca; Manager, Operations, Roger Ternan; Connection Speed: 4.5M; User's Top Speed: 56K

## Section 6

**Page 6-28**

Christine Turgeon is now Directrice at the Musée des Ursulines de Québec.

## Section 9

**Page 9-42**

Added to the list of Independent & Private Schools in Ontario is: Cambridge International College of Canada, 35 Ourland Ave., Toronto ON M8Z 4E1; 416/252-9195; Fax: 416/252-4266. Principal is Irwin Diamond.

## Section 10

**Page 10-1**

Under the Supreme Court of Canada: Michel Bastarache has been appointed to the Supreme Court. John Sopinka died November 24, 1997; the vacancy left by his death will be filled by an appointment from Ontario.